EPISCOPAL CLERICAL DIRECTORY 2011

Revised every two years

Please note: The contents of the biographical entries reported herein have been provided exclusively by the biographees themselves; the publisher therefore cannot vouch for their accuracy.

To purchase additional copies of the *Episcopal Clerical Directory*, please access Church Publishing's website at **www.churchpublishing.org**.

To submit changes to the Directory, write to Editor of Directories, Church Pension Group, 445 Fifth Avenue, New York NY 10016, or send a fax to (212) 592-8279. For security, the signature of the cleric must accompany all submissions.

Church Publishing Incorporated
445 Fifth Avenue
New York, NY 10016
www.churchpublishing.org

Data in this edition is current as of November 10, 2011.

Foreword

The 2011 *Episcopal Clerical Directory* represents further progress toward our goal of providing the Episcopal Church with the most comprehensive data on clergy and institutions possible. Employing the resources of the Church Pension Group's Common Reference Database, this forty-fourth edition of the *ECD* includes biographical information on **18,738** clergy in good standing as of the date indicated on page 2.

Since 2002, the affiliate companies of the Church Pension Group have collaborated on the development of the Common Reference Database, a significant undertaking that enables all of the affiliates of the Pension Group to "read off the same page" about the clergy and institutions and thus to serve them with an even greater degree of efficiency. As with previous editions, we have used the 2011 clergy and institutional update questionnaires as a vehicle for collecting and verifying information that we share among the affiliates, including information that will never be published in any version of the *Episcopal Clerical Directory*. As ever, we count on our clergy and institutions to inform us when incorrect information appears.

With this edition, we have advanced the process of nearly real-time data updating by re-designing the online data collection tools by which institutions and clergy submitted their updated information. For the first time, online updates made by clergy and institutions fed directly into the CPG database. While the launch of the new system certainly was not without its challenges, we are confident that these tools will make it easier for clergy and institutions to make updates whenever the need arises, as the update websites will remain online and available.

The biographical information that appears in the *Directory* has been submitted by each cleric. Clergy who responded to the 2011 clergy information update questionnaire are identified in boldface in the printed. Because we receive updates from clergy and institutions nearly every day, new information submitted after the production deadline for this edition will be available online at the ECDPlus website: **www.ecdplus.org.**

Again in this edition, multiple current positions, including non-parochial ministry-related positions such as health care, school, and military chaplaincies, are shown. All current positions are listed near the beginning of each biography to help the reader discern at a glance each cleric's present ministry. These positions appear with the most recent appointment first. We have also asked clergy to distinguish between their stipendiary service in Episcopal Church institutions and any appointed or voluntary service on church-related bodies such as General Convention commissions, committees, agencies, and boards; diocesan councils; standing committees; or boards of church-related non-profit organizations. This distinction will assist readers in gaining a clearer sense of the breadth of a cleric's ministry.

Clergy who died since the 2009 revised edition of the *Directory* was released, but whose death was reported prior to the date indicated on page 2, have their date of death noted in their biographical entries.

Ordination data and changes in canonical residence are noted by the Recorder of Ordinations after written confirmation from the diocese has been submitted to the Recorder. Biographies of clergy who have transferred into the Episcopal Church from another province of the Anglican Communion, or who have been received from the Roman Catholic Church or another church in full communion with the Episcopal Church, do not include the dates of their ordinations to the diaconate and priesthood, nor the names of the non-Episcopal Church bishops who ordained them; instead, the name of the Episcopal Church bishop who accepted their transfer or received them is listed, along with the date on which that transfer or reception took effect.

As has been the case in each edition of the *Episcopal Clerical Directory* since the late 1990s—and because of our constant concern to protect clergy against identity theft—we no longer publish the cleric's mother's name at birth, as provided on the questionnaire, in the biographical information.

Further, as we began to do with the 2005 edition of the *Directory* and in response to requests from an increasing number of clergy, it is Church Publishing's policy that we no longer publish information on previous marriages, even those that resulted in children. The number of children, if any, from a cleric's previous marriage will continue to be displayed.

Faithfully,
Susan T. Erdey
Editor

To purchase additional copies of the **Episcopal Clerical Directory**, visit Church Publishing's website at **www.churchpublishing.org**.

To submit changes to the **Episcopal Clerical Directory**, write to Editor of Directories, Church Pension Group, 445 Fifth Avenue, New York NY 10016; or send a fax to (212) 592-8279. For security, the signature of the cleric must accompany all submissions.

Abbreviations Used in This Text

AA	Alcoholics Anonymous
AAM	Association of Anglican Musicians
AAMFC	American Association of Marriage and Family Counselors
AAPC	American Association of Pastoral Counselors
AAR	American Academy of Religion
AAUP	American Association of University Professors
AAUW	American Association of University Women
ABA	American Bar Association
ABS	American Bible Society
Acad	Academic, Academy
ACC	Association for Creative Change
Acct	Accountant
Acctg	Accounting
ACLU	American Civil Liberties Union
ACPE	Association for Clinical Pastoral Education
Actg	Acting
ACU	American Church Union
Adj	Adjacent, Adjunct
ADLMC	Association of Diocesan Liturgy and Music Commissions
Admin	Administration, Administrative, Administrator
Admssns	Admissions
Adopt	Adopted
Adv	Advent
Advert	Advertiser, Advertising
Advncd	Advanced
Advoc	Advocate
Advsr	Adviser, Advisor
Advsry	Advisory
AEC	Association of Episcopal Colleges
AEHC	Assembly of Episcopal Hospitals and Chaplains
AF	Air Force
AFB	Air Force Base
Affrs	Affairs
AFP	Anglican Fellowship of Prayer
Afr	Africa, African
Agcy	Agency
AGO	American Guild of Organists
Agt	Agent
Aid	Aidan
AIM	Adventures in Ministry
Alb	Alban
Alco	Alcohol
Alcosm	Alcoholism
Allctns	Allocations
Allnce	Alliance
Alt	Alternate
AltGld	Altar Guild
Alum	Alumna, Alumnae, Alumni, Alumnus
AMA	American Medical Association
Ambr	Ambrose
Amer	America, American
AmL	American Legion
Andr	Andrew
Ang	Angel(s)
Angl	Anglican
Anniv	Anniversary
Annunc	Annunciation
Anth	Anthony
AP	Associated Parishes for Liturgy and Mission
APA	American Psychological Association
Apos	Apostle(s)
Apportnmt	Apportionment
A-RC	Anglican-Roman Catholic Consultation/Dialogue
Archbp	Archbishop
Archd	Archdeacon
Archdnry	Archdeaconry
Archeol	Archaeological, Archaeologist, Archaeology
Archit	Architecture, Architect, Architectural
Archv	Archival, Archives, Archivist
ArmdF	Armed Forces
arts	articles
Ascen	Ascension
ASOR	American School of Oriental Research
Assn	Association
Assoc	Associate(s)
ASSP	All Saints' Sisters of the Poor
Asst	Assistant
Asstg	Assisting
Athan	Athanasius
Atone	Atonement
ATR	Anglican Theological Review
Atty	Attorney
Aug	Augustine
Auth	Author
Aux	Auxiliary
Av	Avenue
A/V	Audiovisual
Awd	Award(ed)
b	born
BACAM	Bishop's Advisory Commission of Aspirants to the Ministry
BACOM	Bishop's Advisory Commission on Ordained Ministry
Bapt	Baptist
Barn	Barnabas
Barth	Bartholomew
Bch	Beach
BCP	The Book of Common Prayer
Bd	Board, Board of
Bdgt	Budget
BEC	Board of Examining Chaplains
Ben	Benedict
Bern	Bernard
BEST	Bishops' Executive Secretaries Together
Beth	Bethesda
Biblic	Biblical
Bk	Book
Bklet	Booklet
Bldg	Building
Blvd	Boulevard
Bon	Boniface
Bp	Bishop

Bro	Brother, Brotherhood
BroSA	Brotherhood of St. Andrew
BSA	Boy Scouts of America
BSG	Brotherhood of St. Gregory
Bus	Business
Busmn	Businessman, Businessmen, Businesswoman, Businesswomen
c	number of children
C-14	Coalition 14
CABp	Council of Advice, House of Bishops
CAC	The Church Agency Corporation
CALC	Clergy and Laity Concerned
Calv	Calvary
CAM	Coalition for the Apostolic Ministry
C&C	Camp and Conference Center(s)
Can	Canada, Canadian
CAP	Civil Air Patrol
Cath	Catholic
Cathd	Cathedral
Cathr	Catherine
Cbnt	Cabinet
CBS	Confraternity of the Blessed Sacrament
Cbury	Canterbury
CCM	College of Church Musicians
CCU	Catholic Clerical Union
CDO	Church Deployment Office(r)
CE	Christian Education
CEEP	Consortium of Endowed Episcopal Parishes
CERN	Christian Education Resources Network
Cert	Certificate, Certified
CFC	The Church Finance Corporation
Ch	Church(es)
Chal Br	Chalice Bearer(s)
Chap	Chapel
Chapl	Chaplain(s), Chaplaincy
Chapt	Chapter
Chars	Charities
Chart	Charter, Chartered
Chas	Charles
Chem	Chemical, Chemist, Chemistry
Chf	Chief
Chld	Child, Children
ChmbrCom	Chamber of Commerce
Chncllr	Chancellor
Chr	Christ, Christian
Chris	Christopher
Chrmstr	Choirmaster
Chrsmtc	Charismatic
Chrsnty	Christianity
Chrys	Chrysostom
CHS	Community of the Holy Spirit
CIC	The Church Insurance Company
Cir	Circle
cl	cum laude
Clem	Clement
Cler	Clergy, Clerical, Clericus
CLIC	The Church Life Insurance Company
Clincl	Clinical
Clnc	Clinic
Cltn	Coalition
Cmdr	Commander
Cmncatn	Communication(s)
Cmnctr	Communicator(s)
Cmnty	Community
Cmpgn	Campaign
Cmsn	Commission
Cmssnr	Commissioner
Cn	Canon(s)
Cncl	Canonical
Cnfrmtn	Confirmation
Cntr	Center, Centre
Cntrl	Central
Cnty	County
Cnvnr	Convener
Cnvnt	Convent
Co	Company
Coadj	Coadjutor
COCU	Consultation on Church Union
CODE	Conference of Diocesan Executives
Coll	College
Collgt	Collegiate
COLM	Committee on Lay Ministry
Com	Committee
COM	Commission on Ministry, Commission on Ordained Ministry
Comf	Comforter
Comm	Communion
Comp	Companion(s), Companionship
Compstn	Compensation
Compsr	Composer
Con	Consecrated
Concep	Conception
Conf	Conference, Confraternity
Confrat	Confraternity
Cong	Congregation
Congr	Congress
Congrl	Congregational, Congregationalist
Const	Constitution, Constitutional
Consult	Consultant, Consultation, Consult
Cont	Continued, Continuing
Contrib	Contributor
Contrllr	Comptroller, Controller
Conv	Convention
Convoc	Convocation, Convocational
Coop	Cooperation, Cooperative
Coordntng	Coordinating
Coordntr	Coordinator
COP	Company of the Paraclete
Corn	Cornelius
Corp	Corporate, Corporation
Coun	Council, Councilor
Counslg	Counseling
Counslr	counselor
Cov	Covenant
CP	Community of the Paraclete
CPA	Certified Public Accountant
CPC	Church Periodical Club
CPE	Clinical Pastoral Education
CPF	The Church Pension Fund
CPF & Affil	The Church Pension Fund and Affiliates
CPG	Church Pension Group
CPI	Church Publishing Incorporated
Cred	Credential(s)
Cres	Crescent

Crisp	Crispin
Crspndg	Corresponding
Crt	Court
Crucif	Crucifixion
CSB	Confraternity of St. Benedict
CSF	Community of St. Francis
CSJ	Community of Servants of Jesus
CSJB	Community of St. John the Baptist
CSM	Community of St. Mary
CSR	Christian Social Relation
CT	Community of the Transfiguration
Cur	Curate
Curric	Curricula, Curricular, Curriculum
Curs	Cursillo
Cuth	Cuthbert
CWM	Council for Women's Ministry
CWU	Church Women United
Cyp	Cyprian

d	daughter of
D	Deacon
DAR	Daughters of the American Revolution
Dav	David
DCE	Director of Christian Education
DD	Doctor of Divinity
(dec)	deceased
Del	Delegate, Delegation
Dep	Deputy
Deploy	Deployment
Dept	Department
Deptl	Departmental
Diac	Diaconal, Diaconate
Dig	Digest
D-in-c	Deacon-in-charge
Dio	Diocese(of)
Dioc	Diocesan
Dir	Director(s), Directress
Disabil	Disabilities, Disability
dist	distinction
Dist	District
Distr	Distributor
(div)	divorced
Div	Divine, Divinity, Division
Dn	Dean
Dnry	Deanery
DOK	Daughters of the King
Dom	Domestic
Dplma	Diploma, Diplomat
Dplymt	Deployment
DRE	Director of Religious Education
DS	Divinity School
DSA	Distinguished Service Award
DSC	Distinguished Service Cross
DSM	Distinguished Service Medal
Dss	Deaconess(es)
Dunst	Dunstan
Dvlp	Develop, Developer
Dvlpmt	Development

E	East
EAAM	Episcopal Asiamerica Ministries
EAM	Episcopal Appalachian Ministries
EBA	Episcopal Booksellers Association
ECA	Episcopal Church Army
ECBF	Episcopal Church Building Fund
Eccl	Ecclesiastical
ECDEC	Episcopal Conference of the Deaf of the Episcopal Church in the USA
ECEC	Executive Council of the Episcopal Church
ECF	Episcopal Church Foundation
ECharF	Episcopal Charismatic Fellowship
ECM	Evangelical and Catholic Mission
ECom	Episcopal Communicators
Econ	Economic, Economics, Economist, Economy
Ecum	Ecumenical, Ecumenism
ECW	Episcopal Church Women
Ed	Editing, Edition, Editor, Editorial
EDEO	Episcopal Diocesan Ecumenical Officers
Edm	Edmund
Educ	Education
Eductr	Educator
Edw	Edward
EEE	Episcopal Engaged Encounter
EFM	Education for Ministry
EGB	Episcopal Guild for the Blind
Elctns	Elections
Elem	Elementary
Elis	Elisabeth
Eliz	Elizabeth
EME	Episcopal Marriage Encounter
Emer	Emeritus
Emm	Emmanuel
Endwmt	Endowment
Engl	England, English
Engr	Engineering, Engineer(s)
Environ	Environment(al)
EPF	Episcopal Peace Fellowship
Epiph	Epiphany
Epis	Episcopal, Episcopalian
ERM	Episcopal Renewal Ministries
ESA	Episcopal Synod of America
ESCRU	Episcopal Society for Cultural and Racial Unity
ESMA	Episcopal Society for Ministry to the Aging
ESMHE	Episcopal Society for Ministry in Higher Education
ESRC	Episcopal Social Relations Conferences
Estrn	Eastern
ETN	Episcopal Training Network
EUC	Episcopal Urban Caucus
Euch	Eucharist
Evaltn	Evaluation
Evang	Evangelical, Evangelism, Evangelist
EvangES	Evangelical Education Society
EWC	Episcopal Women's Caucus
EWHP	Episcopal Women's History Project
Exam	Examiner, Examining
Exch	Exchange
Exec	Executive
Ext	Extension
EYC	Episcopal Youth Commission

FA	Faith Alive
Fac	Faculty, Facilitator
Fam	Family

Fed	Federation, Federated, Federal
Fell	Fellow
Fest	Festival
Fin	Finance, Financial
Fllshp	Fellowship
FMP	Forward Movement Publications
Fndr	Founder
Fndt	Foundation
Form	Former, Formerly
Forw	Forward
Fr	Father
Fran	Francis
Frgn	Foreign
Ft	Fort
Gabr	Gabriel
GAS	Guild of All Souls
GBEC	General Board of Examining Chaplains
GC	General Convention
Gd	Good
Gdnc	Guidance
Geo	George
Geth	Gethsemane
GFS	Girls Friendly Society
Gk	Greek
Gld	Guild
Gnrl	General
Govt	Government
Gr	Grace
Grad	Graduate
Greg	Gregory
Grp	Group
Grtr	Greater
GSA	Girl Scouts of America
GTF	Graduate Theological Foundation
Gvnr	Governor(s)
Gvrng	Governing
H	Holy
HabHum	Habitat for Humanity
Happ	Happening
Hd	Head
Heav	Heavenly
Hebr	Hebrew
HEW	Health, Education, and Welfare
Hisp	Hispanic
Hist	Historian, Historical, History
Hlth	Health
Hm	Home(s)
HOB	House of Bishops
HOD	House of Deputies
Homil	Homiletic(s)
Hmnts	Humanities
hon	honor(s)
Hon	Honorary
Hosp	Hospital, Hospitality
Hq	Headquarters
HR	Human Resources
HS	High School
Hse	House
HSEC	Historical Society of the Episcopal Church
Hsng	Housing
Hstgr	Historiographer
IACCA	International Association of Conference Center Administrators
Ign	Ignatius
Imm	Immanuel
Immac	Immaculate
Incarn	Incarnation
Indep	Independent
Indn	Indian
Indstrl	Industrial
Info	Information
Innoc	Innocents
Ins	Insurance
Inspctn	Inspection
Inspctr	Inspector
Inst	Institute, Institution
Instnl	Institutional
Instr	Instructor
Instrn	Instruction
Int	Interim
Integ	Integrity, Inc.
Interp	Interpretation
Intl	International
Intrnshp	Internship
Intro	Introduction
Intsn	Intercession
Invstmt	Investment
IPC	Interparish Council
Jas	James
JCCMA	Joint Commission on the Church in Metropolitan Areas
JCP	Joint Commission on Peace
Jct	Junction
Jn	John
Jos	Joseph
Journ	Journal(s)
JPIC	Justice, Peace, and the Integrity of Creation
Jr	Junior
Jrnlst	Journalist
JSCN	Joint Standing Committee on Nominations
JSCPBF	Joint Standing Committee on Program, Budget, and Finance
Jub	Jubilee Ministries
Juris	Jurisdiction
Jvnl	Juvenile
Kath	Katherine
KEEP	Kiyosato Education Experiment Project
Lang	Language
Lawr	Lawrence
LayR	Lay Reader
Ldr	Leader
Ldrshp	Leadership
Lectr	Lecturer
Legis	Legislation, Legislator, Legislative

LEM	Lay Eucharistic Minister/Ministry
Lg	Large
Lgr	Larger
Libr	Library, Librarian
Lic	License(d), Licentiate
Lit	Literature
Liturg	Liturgical, liturgics, Liturgist, Liturgy
LivCh	The Living Church
Lk	Luke
LMFT	Licensed Marriage and Family Therapist
LMN	Lay Ministry Network
Ln	Lane
Loc	Local
LocTen	Locum Tenens
Long-R	Long-range
LP	Lay Pastor
Lrng	Learning
Luc	Lucian
Luth	Lutheran
Lv	Leave
m	married
mag	magazine(s)
Magd	Magdalene
Mar	Marriage
Marg	Margaret
Mart	Martin
Matt	Matthew
mcl	magna cum laude
Med	Medical, Medicine
Medtr	Mediator
Mem	Member, Membership
Memi	Memorial
Merc	Merciful
Meth	United Methodist
Metropltn	Metropolitan
Mex	Mexican, Mexico
MFCC	Marriage, Family and Child Counselor
Mfg	Manufacturing
Mgr	Manager
Mgmt	Management
MHA	Mental Health Association
MHE	Ministry in Higher Education
Mich	Michael
Min	Minister, Ministerium
M-in-c	Minister-in-charge
Mk	Mark
Mltry	Military
Mng	Managing
Mnstrl	Ministerial
Mnstrs	Ministries
Mnstry	Ministry
Mntl	Mental
Mo	Mother
Mod	Modern
Monstry	Monastery
MRI	Mutual Responsibility and Interdependence in the Body of Christ
Mrkt	Market
Mssh	Messiah
Mssn	Mission
Mssngr	Messenger
Mssnr	Missioner
Mssy	Missionary
Mstr	Master
Mt	Mount
Mths	Matthias
Mtn	Mountain
Mtyr	Martyr
Mus	Music, Musical, Musician
Mvmt	Movement
NAACP	National Association for the Advancement of Colored People
NAAD	North American Association for the Diaconate
NACA	National Association of Church Administrators
NAECED	National Association of Episcopal Christian Education Directors
NACMB	National Association of Church Business Managers
NAES	National Association of Episcopal Schools
NAMMA	North American Maritime Ministries Association
Narc	Narcotic(s)
NASSAM	National Association for the Self-Supporting Active Ministry
NASW	National Association of Social Workers
Nath	Nathaniel
Nativ	Nativity
Natl	National
NCA	National Cathedral Association
NCCC	National Council of the Churches of Christ in the USA
NCD	National Center for the Diaconate
NCEH	National Conference of Episcopal Historians
NCHM	National Commission for Hispanic Ministries
NE	Northeast, Northeastern
NEA	National Education Association
NEAC	National Episcopal AIDS Coalition
NECAD	National Episcopal Coalition on Alcohol and Drugs
NG	National Guard
Nbrhd	Neighborhood
Nich	Nicholas
Nilt	National Institute of Lay Training
NMHA	National Mental Health Association
NNECA	National Network of Episcopal Clergy Associations
NNLP	National Network of Lay Professionals
No	North
NOEL	National Organization of Episcopalians for Life
Nomin	Nominated, Nominating, Nominations
Non-par	Non-parochial
Non-stip	Non-stipendary
Novc	Novice
Nrsng	Nursing
Nrsry	Nursery
NRTA	National Retired Teacher's Association
NT	New Testament
Nthrn	Northern
Ntwk	Network
NW	Northwest, Northwestern
Nwsltr	Newsletter
Nwspr	Newspaper

OAR	Order of Agape and Reconciliation
OA	Order of the Ascension
OCSA	Oblate Congregation of St. Augustine
Off	Office(r)(s)
Offcl	Official(s)
OGS	Oratory of the Good Shepherd
OHC	Order of the Holy Cross
OHF	Order of the Holy Family
OI	Order of the Incarnation
Oprtns	Operations
Optr	Operator
opt mer	optimum meritum
Ord	Ordained, Ordination, Order(s)
Ordnry	Ordinary
Org	Organist
Org/Choir	Organist/Choir Director
Orgnztn	Organizational, Organization(s)
Orth	Orthodox
OSA	Order of St. Anne
OSB	Order of St. Benedict
OSF	Order of St. Francis
OSH	Order of St. Helena
OSL	Order of St. Luke
OT	Old Testament
OTCG	Order of the Teachers of the Children of God
Ovrs	Overseas

P	Priest
Par	Parish, Parochial
Partnr	Partner(s)
Pat	Patrick
PB	Prayer Book
PBFWR	Presiding Bishop's Fund for World Relief
PBS	Bible and Common Prayer Book Society of the Episcopal Church
PECUSA	Protestant Episcopal Church in the USA
Penit	Penitentiary
PerpD	Perpetual Deacon
Personl	Personnel
Phil	Philip, Phillip
Philos	Philosopher, Philosophical, Philosophy
PHS	Public Health Service
Physcn	Physician
PI	Philippine Islands
P-in-c	Priest-in-charge
P-in-res	Priest-in-residence
Pk	Park
Pkwy	Parkway
Plcy	Policy
Plnng	Planning
Post	Postulancy, Postulant
PPF	Planned Parenthood Federation
Pract	Practice
Prchr	Preacher
Pres	President
Presb	Presbyter, Presbyterian, Presbytery
PBp	Presiding Bishop
Priv	Private
Prlmntrn	Parliamentarian
Prncpl	Principal
Prod	Production
Prof	Professor
Profsnl	Professional
Prog	Program(s), Programmer
Proj	Project
Prom	Promotion
Prot	Protestant
Prov	Province, Provincial
Provsnl	Provisional
Pryr	Prayer
Pstr	Pastor, Pastoral
Psych	Psychiatric, Psychiatrist, Psychiatry, Psychotherapist, Psychotherapy
Psychol	Psychology, Psychologist, Psychological
P-t	Part-time
Ptr	Peter
Pub	Publication(s), Published, Publisher(s), Publishing
Publ	Public, Publicity
Pvrty	Poverty

R	Rector
RACA	Recovered Alcoholic Clergy Association
RC	Roman Catholic
Rcrdng	Recording
Rcreatn	Recreation
Rdr	Reader
Rec	Received, Recipient
Recon	Reconciliation
Redeem	Redeemer
Redemp	Redemption
Reg	Region, Regional
Rehab	Rehabilitation
Rel	Religion(s), Religious
Relatns	Relations, Relationship
Renwl	Renewal
Rep	Representative
Res	Residence, Resident, Residentiary
Reserv	Reservation
Resolutns	Resolutions
Resrch	Research(er)
Resurr	Resurrection
Ret	Retired, Retirement
Revs	Review(s), Revision
Rgnts	Regents
Rgstr	Registrar, Registered
RSCM	Royal School of Church Music
Rt	Right
Rtrdtn	Retardation
Rts	Rights
RurD	Rural Dean
RWF	Rural Workers Fellowship

s	son of
S	Saint
SACEM	Society for Advancement of Continuing Education for Ministry
Sacr	Sacrament, Sacred
Samar	Samaritan
SAMS	South American Missionary Society
Sanat	Sanatorium
Sav	Savior, Saviour
SBL	Society of Biblical Literature

SCAIPWJ	Standing Commission on Anglican and International Peace with Justice
SCCC	Standing Commission on Constitutions and Canons
SCCM	Standing Commission on Church Music
SCCSC	Standing Commission on the Church in Small Communities
SCDFMS	Standing Commission on Domestic and Foreign Missionary Society of PECUSA
SCDME	Standing Commission on Domestic Mission and Evangelism on Ministry
SCER	Standing Commission on Ecumenical Relations
SCF/A	ECEC Standing Committee on Finance/ Administration
Sch	School
SCHAH	Standing Commission on Human Affairs and Health
SCHC	Society of the Companions of the Holy Cross
Schlr	Scholar
Schlrshp	Scholarship
Sci	Science, Scientist, Scientific
SCI	Seamen's Church Institute
scl	summa cum laude
SCLM	Standing Commission on Liturgy and Music
SCMD	Standing Commission on Ministry Development
SCNC	Standing Commission on National Concerns
SCNMCS	Standing Commission on National Mission in Church and Society
SComC	ECEC Standing Committee on Communications
SCP	Standing Committee on Peace
SCSC	Standing Commission on the Structure of the Church
SCSD	Standing Commission on Stewardship and Development
SCWM	Standing Commission on World Mission
SCWMCS	Standing Commission on World Mission in Church and Society
SE	Southeast, Southeastern
Sec	Secretariat
Sectn	Section
Secy	Secretary
Sem	Seminarian, Seminary
Serv	Served, Service(s), Server
Servnt	Servant(s)
sev	several
Sfty	Safety
Shltr	Shelter
SHN	Sisterhood of the Holy Nativity
Shpd	Shepherd
Sis	Sister(s), Sisterhood
SLC	Standing Liturgical Commission
Slsmn	Salesman, Salesmen, Saleswoman, Saleswomen
Sm	Small
So	South
Soc	Social, Society
Sociol	Sociological, Sociologist, Sociology
SocMary	Society of Mary
SocOLW	Society of Our Lady of Walsingham
SOMA	Sharing of Ministries Abroad
SPBCP	Society for the Preservation of the Book of Common Prayer
SPCK	Society for the Promotion of Christian Knowledge
Spec	Special, Specialist, Specialized
Spkng	Speaking
Spnsr	Sponsor
Spprt	Support
Sprg	Spring(s)
Sprt	Spirit
Sprtl	Spiritual
Sprtlty	Spirituality
Sq	Square
Sr	Senior
SS	Saints(')
SSAP	Society of St. Anna the Prophet
SSB	Society of St. Barnabas
SSC	Society of the Holy Cross
SSF	Society of St. Francis
SSJE	Society of St. John the Evangelist
SSM	Society of St. Margaret
SSP	Society of St. Paul
St	State, Street
Sta	Station
Stds	Studies
Stdt	Student
Steph	Stephen
Stff	Staff, Staffing
Sthrn	Southern
Stndg	Standing
Strng	Steering
Strtgy	Strategy
Stwdshp	Stewardship
Suffr	Suffragan
Sum	Summer
Supt	Superintendent
Supvsr	Supervisor
SW	Southwest, Southwestern
Sxlty	Sexuality
Syn	Synod

Tchg	Teaching
Tchr	Teacher
Tech	Technical, Technician, Technological, Technologist, Technology
TEE	Theological Education by Extension: Education for Ministry
T/F	Task Force
Thad	Thaddeus
Theo	Theodore
Theol	Theologian, Theological, Theology
Ther	Therapist, Therapy
Thos	Thomas
Tim	Timothy
Tit	Titus
TMN	Total Ministry Network
Trans	Transferred
Transltr	Translator
Treas	Treasurer
Trien	Triennial
Trin	Trinity
Trng	Training
Trnr	Trainer
Trsfg	Transfiguration
Trst	Trustee(s)
TS	School of Theology, Theological Seminary, Theological School
TSSF	Tertiary of the Society of St. Francis

U	University
UBE	Union of Black Episcopalians
Un	Union
Untd	United
USA	United States of America
US-A	United States Army
USAF	United States Air Force
USAFR	United States Air Force Reserve
US-AR	United States Army Reserve
USCG	United States Coast Guard
USIA	United States Information Agency
USMC	United States Marine Corps
USMCR	United States Marine Corps Reserve
USN	United States Navy
USNR	United States Navy Reserve
USO	United Service Organization
UTO	United Thank Offering

Var	Various
VetA	Veterans Administration
VFW	Veterans of Foreign Wars
Vic	Vicar
Vill	Village
VIM	Venture in Mission
Vinc	Vincent
VISTA	Volunteers in Service to America
Vlly	Valley
Vol	Volunteer(s), Voluntary
VP	Vice President
Vrgn	Virgin
Vstng	Visiting
Vstry	Vestry

w	with
W	West
WBHS	Worker Brothers of the Holy Spirit
WCC	World Council of Churches
Welf	Welfare
Wit	The Witness
Wk	Work
Wlfd	Wilfred
Wm	William
Wmn	Woman, Women('s)
Wrdn	Warden
Wrld	World
Wrshp	Worship
WSHS	Workers Sisters of the Holy Spirit
Wstrn	Western
WTF	Women's Task Force

YA	Young Adult(s)
YP	Young People
YPF	Young People's Fellowship
Yth	Youth

Dioceses and Missionary Districts

Ak	Alaska
Ala	Alabama
Alb	Albany
Ark	Arkansas
At	Atlanta
Az	Arizona
Be	Bethlehem
Cal	California
CFla	Central Florida
CGC	Central Gulf Coast
Chi	Chicago
CNY	Central New York
Colo	Colorado
Colom	Colombia
CPa	Central Pennsylvania
CR	Costa Rica
Ct	Connecticut
Dal	Dallas
Del	Delaware
DomRep	Iglesia Episcopal De Dominicana
DR	Dominican Republic
Eas	Easton
Eau	Eau Claire
EC	East Carolina
ECR	El Camino Real
Ecu	Ecuador
EcuL	Litoral Ecuador
EcuC	Central Ecuador
EMich	Eastern Michigan
EO	Eastern Oregon
EpisSanJ	Episcopal San Joaquin
ES	El Salvador
ETenn	East Tennessee
Eur	Convocation of American Churches in Europe
FdL	Fond du Lac
Fla	Florida
Frgn	Foreign
FtW	Fort Worth
Ga	Georgia
Gua	Guatemala
Hai	Haiti
Haw	Hawaii
HB	Secretary House of Bishops
Hond	Honduras
Ia	Iowa
Ida	Idaho
Ind	Indianapolis
Kan	Kansas
Ky	Kentucky
La	Louisiana
Lex	Lexington
LI	Long Island
Lib	Liberia
Los	Los Angeles
Mass	Massachusetts
Md	Maryland
Me	Maine
Mex	Mexico
MexSE	Southeastern Mexico
Mich	Michigan
Micr	Micronesia
Mil	Milwaukee
Minn	Minnesota
Miss	Mississippi
Mo	Missouri
Mont	Montana
NAM	Navajoland Area Mission
NC	North Carolina
NCal	Northern California
ND	North Dakota
Neb	Nebraska
Nev	Nevada
NH	New Hampshire
NI	Northern Indiana
Nic	Nicaragua
NJ	New Jersey
NMich	Northern Michigan
NonD	Non-Diocesan
Nwk	Newark
NcPh	North Central Philippines
NwPa	Northwestern Pennsylvania
NwT	Northwest Texas
NY	New York
O	Ohio
Okla	Oklahoma
Oki	Okinawa
Oly	Olympia
Ore	Oregon
Pa	Pennsylvania
Pgh	Pittsburgh
PR	Puerto Rico

Q	Quincy
RG	Rio Grande
RI	Rhode Island
Roch	Rochester
RP	Panama
SanD	San Diego
SC	South Carolina
SD	South Dakota
SeFla	Southeast Florida
SJ	San Joaquin
SO	Southern Ohio
SPh	Southern Philippines
Spok	Spokane
Spr	Springfield
SVa	Southern Virginia
SwFla	Southwest Florida
SwVa	Southwestern Virginia
Tai	Taiwan
Tenn	Tennessee
Tex	Texas
U	Utah
USC	Upper South Carolina
Va	Virginia
Ve	Venezuela
VI	Virgin Islands
Vt	Vermont
WA	Washington
WDC	Washington, DC
WK	Western Kansas
WLa	Western Louisiana
WMass	Western Massachusetts
WMich	Western Michigan
WMo	West Missouri
WNC	Western North Carolina
WNY	Western New York
WTenn	West Tennessee
WTex	West Texas
WVa	West Virginia
Wyo	Wyoming

Colleges, Universities, Seminaries

Adel	Adelphi University
Alleg	Allegheny College
Amh	Amherst College
ATC	Anglican Theological College of British Columbia
Berk	Berkeley Divinity School
Bex	Bexley Hall
Bos	Boston University
Bow	Bowdoin College
Bps	Bishop's University, Canada
Br	Brown University
Bryn	Bryn Mawr College
Buc	Bucknell University
Camb	Cambridge University
Carl	Carlton College
CDSP	Church Divinity School of the Pacific
Cit	The Citadel
Col	Columbia University
Colg	Colgate University
Cor	Cornell University
CRDS	Colgate-Rochester Divinity School
CUA	Catholic University of America
CUNY	City University of New York
Dart	Dartmouth College
Duke	Duke University
Dur	Durham University
EDS	Episcopal Divinity School
Emml	Emmanuel College
Ers	Erksine College
ETS	Episcopal Theological School
ETSBH	Episcopal Theological School Claremont Bloy House
ETSC	Episcopal Theological Seminary of the Caribbean
ETSKy	Episcopal Theological Seminary of Kentucky
ETSSw	The Episcopal Theological Seminary of the Southwest
FD	Fairleigh Dickinson University
F&M	Franklin and Marshall College
Ford	Fordham University
Gall	Gallaudet College
Gan	Gannon College
Ge	Gettysburg College
Geo	Georgetown University
Gri	Grinnell College
GTS	General Theological Seminary
GW	George Washington University
Ham	Hamilton College
Harv	Harvard University
Hav	Haverford College
Hob	Hobart College
How	Howard University
Hur	Huron College
IL Wesl	Illinois Wesleyan University
JCU	John Carroll University
JHU	Johns Hopkins University
Ken	Kenyon College
K SU	Kansas State University
L&C	Lewis and Clark College
Laf	Lafayette College
Lawr	Lawrence University
Leh	Lehigh University
Linc	Lincoln University
LIU	Long Island University
LMU	Lincoln Memorial University
Lon	University of London
LSU	Louisiana State University
Man	Manchester University
Mar	Marietta College
Marq	Marquette University
Merc	Mercer University
Mia	Miami University
Mid	Middlebury College
MI SU	Michigan State University
MIT	Massachusetts Institute of Technology
MWC	Mary Washington College
Nash	Nashotah House
NEU	Northeastern University
NWU	Northwestern University
NYTS	New York Theological Seminary
NYU	New York University
Ob	Oberlin College
Occ	Occidental College
OH SU	Ohio State University
OR SU	Oregon State University
Oxf	Oxford University
PDS	Philadelphia Divinity School
Penn	Pennsylvania State University
Pr	Princeton University
PrTS	Princeton Theological Seminary
PSR	Pacific School of Religion
Pur	Purdue University

Rad	Radcliffe College
Rice	Rice Institute
Roa	Roanoke College
Rol	Rollins College
RPI	Rensselaer Polytechnic Institute
Rut	Rutgers - The State University
SATS	St. Andrews Theological Seminary, Philippines
Sea	Seabury Divinity School
SFTS	San Francisco Theological Seminary
S Jn Ca	St. John's College, Canada
Smith	Smith College
SMU	Southern Methodist University
Stan	Stanford University
STUSo	School of Theology, University of the South
SUNY	State University of New York
SWTS	Seabury-Western Theological Seminary
Syr	Syracuse University
Tab	Tabor College
TCU	Texas Christian University
Tem	Temple University
TESM	Trinity Episcopal School for Ministry
Trin	Trinity College
Tufts	Tufts College
Tul	Tulane University
U CA	University of California
U CB	University of California - Berkeley
U Chi	University of Chicago
U Cinc	University of Cincinnati
UCLA	University of California at Los Angeles
U CO	University of Colorado
U Denv	University of Denver
U GA	University of Georgia
U IL	University of Illinois
U MI	University of Michigan
U MN	University of Minnesota
U NC	University of North Carolina
U NoC	University of Northern California
U Pac	University of the Pacific
U Pgh	University of Pittsburgh
Ups	Upsala College
U Rich	University of Richmond
U Roch	University of Rochester
U Sask	University of Saskatchewan
USC	University of Southern California
USMA	United States Military Academy
USMMA	United States Merchant Marine Academy
USNA	United States Naval Academy
U So	University of the South
U Tor	University of Toronto
UTS	Union Theological Seminary
Van	Vanderbilt University
Vas	Vassar College
VMI	Virginia Military Institute
VPI	Virginia Polytechnic Institute
VTS	Virginia Theological Seminary
Wag	Wagner College
WA SU	Washington State University
Wayne	Wayne State University
Wesl	Wesleyan University
Witt	Wittenberg University
W&J	Washington and Jefferson College
W&L	Washington and Lee University
W&M	College of William and Mary
Wms	Williams College
Wood	Woodstock College
WPC	William Paterson College
Wyc	Wycliffe College, Canada
Ya	Yale University
Ya Berk	Berkeley Divinity School at Yale

The Episcopal Clerical Directory 2011 Edition

The name of any biographee not printed in boldface type indicates that no reply to our information update mailing was received prior to the submission deadline.

A

AALAN, Joshua Canon (Pa) 2013 Appletree St, Philadelphia PA 19103 B 4/25/1964 D 12/16/2000 P 7/23/2001 Bp Russell Edward Jacobus. R Ch Of The Incarn Morrisville PA 2003-2009; Cur S Clements Ch Philadelphia PA 2002-2003. joshuacanonaalan@comcast.net

AARON, Stephen Craig (Wyo) 618 Saunders Cir, Evanston WY 82930 B Evanston WY 12/7/1961 s William Aaron & Clara. D 4/2/2003 P 10/29/2003 Bp Bruce Edward Caldwell. m 5/28/1988 Sharlyn April Aaron c 3.

ABBOTT, Barbara Leigh (Pa) 110 Llanfair Rd, Ardmore PA 19003 **The Epis Ch Of The Adv Kennett Sq PA 2010-** B Detroit MI 1/1/1954 D 6/19/2004 P 12/18/2004 Bp Charles Ellsworth Bennison Jr. m 12/29/1988 James Abbott c 4. S Jn's Ch Huntingdon Vlly PA 2007-2009; Assoc R Ch Of The Redeem Bryn Mawr PA 2004-2007. bwabbott@verizon.net

ABBOTT, Gail Eoline (Mil) 743 Milwaukee Rd, Beloit WI 53511 **R S Paul's Epis Ch Beloit WI 2004-** B Cherry Point NC 12/18/1948 AS Miami-Dade Cmnty Coll 1974; BS Florida Intl U 1991; MS U of Miami 1993; MDiv GTS 2003. D 6/21/2003 P 12/20/2003 Bp Leopold Frade. c 2. gailabbott@charter.net

ABBOTT SR, Gary Louis (Ga) Po Box 273, Hawkinsville GA 31036 **S Lk's Epis Hawkinsville GA 2004-** B Millen GA 9/26/1947 s Albert Louis Abbott & Viola Rose. BA Merc 1969; MDiv SW Bapt TS 1972; DMin New Orleans Bapt TS 1978. D 8/3/2002 P 2/10/2003 Bp Henry Irving Louttit. m 7/26/1969 Billie Avalie Uselton. Dio Georgia Savannah GA 2002-2003. abot@cstel.net

ABBOTT, Grant H (Minn) 2163 Carter Ave, Saint Paul MN 55108 B Seattle WA 3/23/1945 s James Wheelock Abbott & Geraldine Ann. BS U of Washington 1968; MDiv PrTS 1971; CAS EDS 1974. D 10/23/1974 P 10/25/1975 Bp Ivol I Curtis. m 7/28/1973 Elaine Elizabeth Tarone c 2. Exec Dir St Paul Area Coun Of Ch S Paul MN 2003-2011; Ecum and Interfaith Off Dio Minnesota Minneapolis MN 1997-2003; GC Dep Dio Minnesota Minneapolis MN 1996-2003; Pres, Cler Assn Dio Minnesota Minneapolis MN 1993-1995; Stndg Com Dio Minnesota Minneapolis MN 1991-1997; Pres, Exam Chapl Dio Minnesota Minneapolis MN 1989-1991; Exam Chapl Dio Minnesota Minneapolis MN 1985-1991; Dioc Coun Dio Minnesota Minneapolis MN 1983-1985; Reg 7 Dn Dio Minnesota Minneapolis MN 1983-1985; R S Matt's Ch St Paul MN 1981-2003; P Assoicate Cathd Ch Of S Mk Minneapolis MN 1980-1981; Int P All SS Ch Northfield MN 1979-1980; P Assoc S Mk's Cathd Seattle WA 1976-1979; Cur S Jas Epis Ch Kent WA 1974-1976. ghabbott@comcast.net

ABBOTT, James Michael (Tex) 305 N 30th St, Waco TX 76710 **Cur S Alb's Epis Ch Waco TX 2010-** B Pasadena CA 3/5/1985 s William Edward Abbott & Christine DiPietro. BA U of Texas 2006; MDiv VTS 2010. D 6/19/2010 P 12/19/2010 Bp C(harles) Andrew Doyle. m 6/12/2010 Margaret Chisholm. abbott.jimmy@gmail.com

ABBOTT, Richard (VI) Po Box 686, Frederiksted VI 00841 B Saint Thomas VI 5/12/1940 s James Alston Abbott & Sarah Eugenie. BA Inter Amer U of Puerto Rico 1960; STB ETSC 1963; MA Col 1968. D 6/15/1963 P 5/23/1964 Bp Cedric Earl Mills. m 2/2/1993 Mary Abbott. S Jn's Ch Christiansted VI 1998-2000; Epis Ch of the H Cross Kingshill VI VI 1978-1987; Vic Epis Ch of the H Cross Kingshill VI VI 1964-1966. vcrabbott@hotmail.com

ABBOTT, Samuel Bassett (Alb) 1 Church St, Cooperstown NY 13326 B East Orange NJ 3/25/1942 s Frederic Everett Abbott & Frances. BA Harv 1963; JD U CA 1969; LLM Ya 1972. D 6/7/1980 Bp Morris Fairchild Arnold P 6/11/1981 Bp John Bowen Coburn. m 7/5/1968 Edith King McKeon c 2. R Chr Ch Cooperstown NY 2004-2009; R Epiph Par Walpole MA 2000-2004; Int Trin Ch Tariffville CT 1999; R Gr Epis Ch New York NY 1992-1998; R S Jas' Epis Ch Cambridge MA 1983-1992; Asst All SS Par Brookline MA 1981-1983; D All SS Par Brookline MA 1980. sabbotte@gmail.com

ABBOTT, S(efton) (WNC) 27 Hildebrand St, Asheville NC 28801 **P-in-c Ch Of S Mths Asheville NC 1999-** B Baltimore MD 9/26/1941 s Sefton Abbott & Jean. BA Duke 1963; BD (MDiv) VTS 1966. D 6/29/1966 P 6/24/1967 Bp Thomas Augustus Fraser Jr. m 8/22/1964 Diane McKay Abbott c 2. R S Martins-In-The-Field Columbia SC 1982-1997; R S Thos Epis Ch Reidsville NC 1978-1982; Dio No Carolina Raleigh NC 1971-1978; Asst S Fran Ch Greensboro NC 1968-1971; M-in-c S Paul's Epis Ch Thomasville NC 1966-1968.

ABBOTT-JONES, Julie (Ak) Sitka Counseling & Prevention Serv, 701 Indian River Rd, Sitka AK 99835 **Sitka Counslg & Prevention Serv Inc Sitka AK 2007-** B St Charles IL 7/30/1953 d Laurel Lloyd Anderson & Elaine Louise. BA Aurora U 1979; MSW U IL 1983; DC Sherman Coll of Chiropractic 2001; MDiv Vancouver TS Vancouver BC CA 2008. D 5/14/2007 Bp Mark William McDonald. c 1. 7julie30@gmail.com

ABDELNOUR, Mark Anthony (USC) St. Simon & St. Jude Epis Church, 1110 Kinley Rd., Irmo SC 29063 B Jacksonville FL 3/14/1955 s Nassif Abdelnour & Elizabeth. BA Engl The U So 1977; MDiv The GTS 2007. D 5/26/2007 P 2/2/2008 Bp Dorsey Felix Henderson. m 9/4/1977 Clarinda Abdelnour c 2. P-in-c Epis Ch Of S Simon And S Jude Irmo SC 2008; S Barth's Ch No Augusta SC 2007-2008. mabdelnour55@gmail.com

ABELEDO-FERNANDEZ, Francisco Benito (Colom) Apartado Aereo 52, Cartagena Colombia B Vigo ES 5/13/1930 s Graciano Abeledo & Manuela. ThD U Of Salamanca Salamanca Es 1955. Rec from Roman Catholic 9/15/1968 Bp David Reed. m 7/16/1966 Irene Ana Fajardo. Dio Colombia Bogota CO 1968-1976; Iglesia Epis En Colombia 1968-1976.

ABELL, Jesse W (WMass) 3 John Street, Westborough MA 01581 **Dio Wstrn Massachusetts Springfield MA 2011-; S Steph's Ch Westborough MA 2011-** B Columbus IN 1/4/1982 s Gary Abell & Donna. BS Indiana Wesl 2004; MPhil U of Cambridge 2005; MDiv TS 2007. D 12/21/2006 P 9/9/2007 Bp Edward Stuart Little II. m 6/12/2010 Allison J Abell. Ecum and Interfaith Off Dio Indianapolis Indianapolis IN 2009-2010; Assoc R S Fran In The Fields Zionsville IN 2007-2010. Contributing Auth, "Interpretative processes [in exegesis]," *Jesus and Psychol*, Darton, Longman, & Todd, 2008; Co-Auth, "Cyberporn use in the context of religiosity," *Journ of Psychol and Theol*, Biola U, 2006. Epis Ch Ntwk for Sci, Tech, and Faith 2007; Epis Ntwk for Animal Welf 2007; Soc of Cath Priests 2008. rector@ststeph.com

ABER, Jack Albert (Q) 96 Walter St, Roslindale MA 02131 B Buffalo NY 8/3/1954 s Richard David Aber & Kathleen Elsie. AA Hilbert Coll Hamburg NY 1974; BS SUNY 1976; MDiv CDSP 1989; MDiv GTS 1991. D 6/1/1993 Bp

Edward Harding MacBurney P 8/30/1994 Bp James Winchester Montgomery. Int Ch Of The Annuniciation Philadelphia PA 2003-2004; S Mk's Ch Philadelphia PA 2001-2002; Asst S Paul's Ch Doylestown PA 1998-2001; Asst S Paul's Par Washington DC 1995-1998. Philadelphia CCU; SocMary; SSC.

ABERNATHEY, James Milton (Tex) 1903 E. Bayshore Dr., Palacios TX 77465 B Atchison KS 8/23/1935 s Hugh Richard Abernathey & Marguerite Evelyn. BS U of Texas 1958; BD Epis TS of The SW 1970. D 6/19/1970 Bp Scott Field Bailey P 5/31/1971 Bp J Milton Richardson. m 9/22/1999 JoAnn Scott c 6. Int S Jn's Epis Ch Sealy TX 2007-2010; Int S Mk's Ch Bay City TX 2005-2006; Int S Fran Epis Ch Victoria TX 2004-2005; Int S Ptr's Epis Ch Rockport TX 2003-2004; R Chr The King Epis Ch Humble TX 1989-2001; Vic S Jn's Epis Ch Silsbee TX 1982-1988; R S Paul's Epis Ch Freeport TX 1974-1982; Vic Chr Ch Matagorda TX 1970-1974; Vic S Jn's Epis Ch Palacios TX 1970-1974. jimaber@peoplepc.com

ABERNATHY, Paul Roberts (WA) 118 3rd Street SE, Washington DC 20003 **R S Mk's Ch Washington DC 1998-** B Saint Louis MO 6/8/1952 s William John Abernathy & Clara Lolita. BA Westminster Coll 1974; MDiv GTS 1977. D 7/30/1977 P 4/15/1978 Bp William Augustus Jones Jr. m 4/3/1988 Pontheolla Mack c 1. R Trin Ch Washington DC 1988-1998; R Calv Ch Charleston SC 1982-1988; R Mssh-S Barth Epis Ch Chicago IL 1979-1982; Cur Calv Ch Columbia MO 1977-1979. ksbpmj@verizon.net

ABERNATHY JR, W Harrison (NY) 50 Bedford Rd, Armonk NY 10504 **Int Sandhills Cluster Hamlet NC 2011-** B Charlotte NC 9/6/1948 s William Harrison Abernathy & Pearl Gray. BA U NC 1970; SMU 1984; MDiv GTS 1986. D 5/31/1986 Bp Richard Frank Grein P 12/6/1986 Bp Robert Campbell Witcher Sr. m 2/16/1974 Penelope Anne Muse c 2. Int Trin Ch Fuquay Varina NC 2010-2011; Stndg Com Dio New York New York City NY 1997-2001; Stndg Com Dio New York New York City NY 1997-2001; Conf Of Deans Dio New York New York City NY 1993-1996; R S Steph's Ch Armonk NY 1989-2008; Cur Trin-St Jn's Ch Hewlett NY 1986-1989. OHC. Phi Beta Kappa U Of Nc Chap Hill NC 1970. whabernathy@gmail.com

ABERNETHY-DEPPE, David Edward (Cal) 19938 Josh Pl, Castro Valley CA 94546 **Epis Sch For Deacons Berkeley CA 2007-; Stwdshp Off Dio California San Francisco CA 2005-** B St Paul Minnesota 6/25/1940 s Edward John Deppe & Earlene Mae. BA Confordia S. Coll Ft Wayne IN 1961; DMin Chr Sem-Seminex 1983; PhD St Louis U 1991; MDiv Concordia Sem St Louis MO 2007. Rec from Evangelical Lutheran Church in America 6/2/2007 Bp Marc Handley Andrus. m 2/2/2004 Jonathan Abernethy c 4. S Jas Ch Fremont CA 2008-2009; Dio California San Francisco CA 2007. daberdep@gmail.com

ABERNETHY-DEPPE, Jonathan (Cal) 1055 Taylor St, San Francisco CA 94108 **Asst S Paul In The Desert Palm Sprg CA 2010-** B Grand Rapids MI 8/26/1947 s Raymond Herbert Abernethy & Rosalie Bush. BMus Pacific Luth U 1969; MDiv Evang Luth TS 1973; MSM Witt 1978. Rec from Evangelical Lutheran Church in America 6/14/2008 Bp Marc Handley Andrus. m 2/2/2004 David Edward David Edward Deppe. Dio California San Francisco CA 2008; Sr Stff Exec Asst Dio California San Francisco CA 2002-2008. jaberdep@gmail.com

ABEYARATNE, Keshini Anoma (Mass) 4 Greenough Cir, Brookline MA 02445 **P Assoc S Paul's Ch Brookline MA 2011-** B London UK 9/15/1955 d Ponniah Yoganathan & Mangayakarasi. BS, RN MI SU 1985; MDiv EDS 2001; Bd Cert Chapl Assn of Profsnl Chapl 2005. D 6/2/2001 Bp Barbara Clementine Harris P 6/8/2002 Bp M(arvil) Thomas Shaw III. m 6/18/1977 Rohan Abeyaratne. Cox Fell Dio Massachusetts Boston MA 2002-2005; Cox Fell The Cathd Ch Of S Paul Boston MA 2002-2005. anoma.abey@gmail.org

ABIDARI, Mehrdad (Cal) Cathedral School for Boys, 1257 Sacramento St, San Francisco CA 94108 **Cathd Sch For Boys San Francisco CA 2005-** B Abadan IR 10/11/1953 s Aziz Abidari & Soraya. BSFS Geo 1975; MDiv GTS 1983. D 6/11/1983 Bp John Thomas Walker P 5/1/1984 Bp William Benjamin Spofford. m 12/28/1976 Jennifer MacPherson. S Matt's Epis Ch San Mateo CA 2001-2005; S Jas Ch Fremont CA 2000-2001; Assoc S Fran Ch Houston TX 1999; R S Geo's Epis Ch Texas City TX 1997-1999; Dir S Bede Epis Ch Houston TX 1990-1995; Cur Gr Ch Charleston SC 1985-1990; Asst S Paul's Epis Ch Summerville SC 1983-1985. Auth, "Var arts & Revs". COM, Multicultural Cmsn. abidari@cathedralschool.net

ABRAHAM, Billie Patterson (Miss) P.O. Box 921, Vicksburg MS 39181 **S Alb's Epis Ch Vicksburg MS 2008-** B Memphis TN 5/22/1947 d William McGehee Patterson & Elizabeth Hughey. BA U of Mississippi 1969; MDiv Wesley TS 2006; Angl Stds The U So (Sewanee) 2007. D 6/2/2007 P 9/21/2008 Bp Duncan Montgomery Gray III. c 3. bilabraham@aol.com

ABRAHAM, John (Az) 9138 North Palm Brook Dr., Tucson AZ 85743 B Newark NJ 4/24/1947 s Maurice Walter John Abraham & F Joan. Dplma Peddie Sch Hightstown NJ 1965; BA Colg Hamilton NY 1969; MDiv VTS 1973. D 5/19/1973 Bp William Henry Mead P 6/1/1974 Bp Thomas Augustus Fraser Jr. c 2. Dio Arizona Phoenix AZ 1995-2011; Assoc S Phil's In The Hills Tucson AZ 1992-1994; R S Chris's Ch River Hills WI 1990-1992; R Ch Of S Matt Tucson AZ 1985-1990; S Ptr's By-The-Lake Ch Montague MI 1985; Gr Ch Grand Rapids MI 1983-1985; S Elis's Epis Ch Memphis TN 1980-1982; R Gr Epis Ch Mt Meigs AL 1977-1980; Asst S Jn's Ch Georgetown Par Washington DC 1974-1977; D S Mary's Epis Ch High Point NC 1973-1974. "Foreward," *I Died Laughing*, Upper Access, Inc., 2001; "The Cler and the Disnefranchised," *Disnefranchised Greif*, Lexington Books, 1989; Auth, "Jest Death Column," *Journ Forum Death Educ*, ADEC, 1985; "Death--The Gift of Life," *Thanatos*, Thanatos, 1982. Certification as Fell in Thanatology Assn for Death Educ & Counslg 2008; Certification as Fell in Thanatology Assn for Death Educ & Counslg 2005; Certification as Thanatologist Assn for Death Educ & Counslg 2003. jlavet@earthlink.net

ABRAHAMSON, Wendy Kay (Ia) St. John's Episcopal Church, 120 First St. NE, Mason City IA 50401 **R S Jn's Ch Mason City IA 2004-** B Saint Paul MN 12/20/1960 d Ellis Abrahamson & Edythe Yvonne. BFA U MN 1988; MFA Pratt Inst 1991; MS Pratt Inst 1993; MDiv VTS 2002. D 6/15/2002 P 12/16/2002 Bp Peter James Lee. m 8/8/2009 Stephen Paul Carroll. Asst Trin Ch Fredericksburg VA 2002-2004. sjrector@rconnect.com

ABRAMS, Mary Elizabeth (Ky) 4100 Southern Pkwy, Louisville KY 40214 B Louisville KY 9/14/1946 d Claude George Montgomery & Esther Belle. BA Estrn KY U 1969; MA Estrn KY U 1973; Doctorate Spalding U 1986. D 4/17/2010 Bp Edwin Funsten Gulick Jr. m 7/1/1983 Jan Abrams c 1. meabrams@bellsouth.net

ABRAMS, Norman Dixon (EpisSanJ) 10120 Arroyo Crest Dr NW, Albuquerque NM 87114 **Vic S Mths Epis Ch Cave Jct OR 1985-** B Canoga Park CA 9/23/1923 s Harold Tedd Abrams & Mary. BA Westmont Coll 1948; MA U of Washington 1960; Cert CDSP 1984. D 6/29/1984 Bp David Rea Cochran P 6/1/1985 Bp Matthew Paul Bigliardi. m 12/21/1956 Doris Elizabeth Abrams. Auth, "Var arts Linguistic Journ". Wycliffe Bible Translators Huntington Bch Ca 1950-1970. Wycliffe Bible Translators Huntington Bch CA 1950.

ABRAMS, Ronald George (EC) 3309 Upton Ct, Wilmington NC 28409 **Trst Epis Ch Cntr New York NY 2006-; R S Jas Par Wilmington NC 1999-** B Hempstead NY 8/6/1957 s Jack Bernard Adams & Rita Gloria. BA LIU 1979; MDiv VTS 1982. D 6/7/1982 P 12/18/1982 Bp Robert Campbell Witcher Sr. m 6/8/1985 Kathleen Ann Flattery c 2. Pres Stndg Comm Epis Ch Cntr New York NY 2002-2004; Dep GC Dio E Carolina Kinston NC 2000-2006; R H Trin Epis Ch Fayetteville NC 1991-1999; R S Ann's Epis Ch Bridgehampton NY 1984-1991; Asst S Mk's Ch Westhampton Bch NY 1982-1984. Auth, *A Look Beyond Our Dio Walls*, 1994; Auth, *One Hundred Years of Nations Hallowed Ground*, 1993. ron@stjamesp.org

ABSHIER, Patsy Ann (Kan) Po Box 1175, Wichita KS 67201 B San Antonio TX 12/18/1934 d Newton Beckwith Chapman & Anna. BS U of Kansas 1957. D 10/6/1999 Bp William Edward Smalley. D S Jn's Ch Wichita KS 2008; D S Jas Ch Wichita KS 1999-2006. Patcabshier@sbcglobal.net

ABSHIRE, Lupton P (Fla) 211 N Monroe St, Tallahassee FL 32301 B Washington DC 9/17/1958 s David Manker Abshire & Carolyn. BS Bos 1981; MDiv Bos 1989; STM GTS 1993; MA California Inst of Integral Stds 2004. D 6/27/1992 P 1/16/1993 Bp Douglas Edwin Theuner. m 10/28/1995 Diane H Abshire c 4. R S Jn's Epis Ch Tallahassee FL 2008-2010; Emm Ch Middleburg VA 2004-2008; Asst Chr Ch Georgetown Washington DC 1992-2001. lupton.abshire@earthlink.net

ABSTEIN II, W(illiam) Robert (Tenn) 9210 Sawyer Brown Rd, Nashville TN 37221 B Jacksonville FL 8/21/1940 s William Russell Abstein & Edith Virginia. BA Florida St U 1962; MDiv STUSo 1965; DMin STUSo 1978. D 6/24/1965 P 3/25/1966 Bp Edward Hamilton West. m 7/1/1966 Roberta Joy Warren c 2. COM Dio Tennessee Nashville TN 1995-1998; R S Geo's Ch Nashville TN 1994-2004; Evang Com Dio Florida Jacksonville FL 1985-1991; R S Jn's Epis Ch Tallahassee FL 1984-1994; R S Jude's Ch Marietta GA 1970-1984; P-in-c S Cyp's Epis Ch Pensacola FL 1965-1967; P-in-c S Monica's Cantonment FL 1965-1967. Auth, "Dating the Last Supper," *S Lk Journ*, 1982. Faithful Alum Awd U So Sewanee TN 1983. wrabstein2@bellsouth.net

ABT, Audra (NC) 2105 W Market St, Greensboro NC 27403 **Asst S Andr's Ch Greensboro NC 2011-; JBduPont Grand Mgr Dio No Carolina Raleigh NC 2010-** B Wooster OH 1/23/1979 d John Joseph Abt & Belicia. BA Ob 2001; no degree SWTS 2007; MDiv Bex 2010. D 6/5/2010 Bp Mark Hollingsworth Jr. aabt@standrewsgreensboro.com

ABUCHAR CURY, Rafael Cury (Colom) Pie de La Popa, Calle 29-D 22-109, Cartagena 00000 Colombia **Iglesia Epis En Colombia 2003-** B Cartagena 11/8/1954 s Enrique Abuchar & Hortencia. Rec from Roman Catholic 11/1/1999. m 1/27/1996 Nicolasa Sierra c 3. padrepiscopalrafael@yahoo.com.es

ACANFORA, Joseph Gerard (Alb) 561 Copes Corners Rd, South New Berlin NY 13843 **R/ Pstr/ P Chr Ch Gilbertsville NY 2007-** B Hoboken NJ 4/25/1959 s Joseph J Acanfora & Pauline. TESM; U of Maryland; Mstr of Arts in Mnstry Nash 2010. D 1/28/2007 Bp Daniel William Herzog P 3/27/2010 Bp William Howard Love. m 7/9/1983 Elizabeth Mattern c 3. acan4a@frontiernet.net

ACCIME, Max (Hai) C/O Lynx Air, PO Box 407139, Fort Lauderdale FL 33340 **Serving Dio Haiti Ft Lauderdale FL 1994-; Dio Haiti Ft Lauderdale FL 1992-** B Port-au-Prince HT 11/25/1964 s Marc Alexis Accime & Andrea.

Haiti TS 1992. D 12/6/1992 Bp Luc Anatole Jacques Garnier P 9/21/1993 Bp Jean Zache Duracin. m 12/15/1994 Anne-Marie Andre c 3. Asst S Mk's Ch Honolulu HI 1992-1994. Soc of S Marg 1989. accimemax@hotmail.com

ACEVEDO, Miriam (NH) 92 Nashua Rd, Pelham NH 03076 **Vic S Chris's Ch Hampstead NH 2000-** B New York NY 12/1/1951 d Tomas Acevedo & Carmen. BFA Pratt Inst 1975; MDiv GTS 1983; DMin EDS 1998. D 6/4/1983 Bp Paul Moore Jr P 6/8/1984 Bp Lyman Cunningham Ogilby. R Chr Ch Hyde Pk MA 1997-2000; Dio Massachusetts Boston MA 1996-2000; Int Ch Of Our Sav Arlington MA 1995-1997; Int S Andr's Ch Framingham MA 1995; S Mary's Epis Ch Philadelphia PA 1987-1994; Asst Chr Ch Philadelphia Philadelphia PA 1983-1987. macevedo2@comcast.net

ACKERMAN, Patricia Elizabeth (NY) 86 Piermont Ave, Nyack NY 10960 **Assoc S Mary's Manhattanville Epis Ch New York NY 2007-; Assoc S Paul's Ch Sprg Vlly NY 2002-** B Hackensack NJ 1/20/1958 d Charles Ackerman & Carolyn. BA New Sch for Soc Resrch 1991; MDiv UTS 1994. D 6/14/1997 P 12/1/1997 Bp Richard Frank Grein. The Fllshp Of Recon Nyack NY 2003; Asst Gr Epis Ch Nyack NY 2000-2002; Dio New York New York City NY 1998-2000; P-in-c Chr Ch Patterson NY 1997-2000; D The Ch of S Clem Alexandria VA 1997. Amer Soc For Grp Psych 1994-2011. Riverkeeper Awd Riverkeeper 2008; Julius T Hansen Memi Awd UTS 1994; Living w Aids Volunteerism Awd People w Aids Cltn 1991. pattiac@mac.com

ACKERMAN, Peter (Va) 101 N. Quaker Ln, Alexandria VA 22304 **R S Chris's Ch Springfield VA 2011-** B 4/22/1962 s Harry Stephen Ackerman & Elinor Donahue. AA Los Angeles Vlly Coll 1983; BA California St U 2004; M.Div VTS 2007. D 5/19/2007 P 12/17/2007 Bp Joseph Jon Bruno. m 9/26/1987 Marie Thompson c 2. Assoc R Imm Ch-On-The-Hill Alexandria VA 2007-2011. peterack@msn.com

ACKERMAN, Thomas Dieden (Mil) 4875 Easy St, Unit # 12, Hartland WI 53029 B Milwaukee WI 6/4/1938 s Lloyd T Ackerman & Dorothy M. BS U of Wisconsin 1961; MSW U CA 1963; MDiv Nash 1973. D 4/28/1973 Bp Donald H V Hallock P 11/3/1973 Bp Charles Thomas Gaskell. Assoc Chr Ch Par La Crosse WI 2004-2007; S Fran Cmnty Serv Inc. Salina KS 1983-1987; R S Ptr's Ch W Allis WI 1975-1983; Cur S Lk's Ch Racine WI 1973-1974. ta_1@sbcglobal.net

ACKERMANN, John Frederick (Oly) 3720 Pennsylvania St, Longview WA 98632 B Centralia WA 3/30/1938 AA Lower Columbia Coll. D 6/29/2003 Bp Sanford Zangwill Kaye Hampton. m 6/23/1962 Sharon Katherine Ackermann c 2. JFACKERMANN@MSN.COM

ACKERSON, Charles Garrett (LI) Po Box 113, Mastic Beach NY 11951 **R All SS Ch Baldwin NY 1987-** B New York NY 1/15/1946 s Charles Ackerson & Viola Louise. BA CUNY- Hunter Coll 1967; MDiv PDS 1970; MS SUNY-Albany 1971; PhD SUNY- Albany 1988; MA SUNY- Stony Brook 1991. D 6/13/1970 P 12/19/1970 Bp Jonathan Goodhue Sherman. Assoc S Mary's Ch Lake Ronkonkoma NY 1986-1987; R S Paul's Ch Patchogue NY 1982-1987; R S Geo's Ch Pennsville NJ 1976-1982; Vic S Tim So Glens Falls NY 1974-1976; Asst S Jn's Epis Ch Troy NY 1970-1972. APA; Amer Psychol Soc; Rel Resrch Assn; Soc for the Sci Study of Rel. Psi Chi. faccga@aol.com

ACKLAND, Lauren Dreeland (Nwk) 6 Madison Ave, Madison NJ 07940 **R Gr Ch Madison NJ 1996-** B Buffalo NY 10/18/1944 d William James Dreeland & Edith Eugenia. BA Rad 1967; MDiv GTS 1984. D 6/9/1984 Bp James Stuart Wetmore P 12/11/1984 Bp Walter Decoster Dennis Jr. m 6/12/1982 George Robert Hayman III. Vic S Alb's Ch Oakland NJ 1987-1996; The GTS New York NY 1987-1996; Cur Ch Of The Ascen New York NY 1984-1987. lackland@gracemadison.org

ACKLEY, Susan M (NH) 28 River St, Ashland NH 03217 B Syracuse NY 10/24/1944 d Benjamin A Ackley & Frances K. BA Manhattanville Coll 1966; MA Col 1973; MA Col 1975; MDiv EDS 1999. D 6/12/1999 P 12/21/1999 Bp Douglas Edwin Theuner. m 6/11/1977 William Cabell c 1. R Ch Of The H Sprt Plymouth NH 2001-2010; Assoc Old No Chr Ch Boston MA 1999-2001. Untd Rel Initiative. ackleysusan@gmail.com

ACOSTA, Juan Maria (SanD) 3552 Hatteras Ave, San Diego CA 92117 B Morelos Sonora MX 3/15/1942 s Juan Acosta & Carmen. BA Instituto de Filosofia Juan Duns Scotto Franciscan Theol Sem 1969; MDiv Instituto Nacional de Estudios Ecclesiasticos Mex City MX 1973; BA S Mary U at San Anonio Texas 1975; Mstr Wk St. Mary's U San Antonio TX 1977; Spec Stds Epis TS of The SW 1978. D 6/5/1978 P 12/19/1978 Bp Scott Field Bailey. c 3. S Mary's/Santa Maria Virgen Imperial Bch CA 2006-2008; S Jn's Ch Indio CA 1999-2009; P-in-c S Matt's Ch Natl City CA 1984-1996; Dio San Diego San Diego CA 1980-2005; Dir of Hisp Mnstry S Matt's Ch Natl City CA 1980-1984; Asst Santa Fe Epis Mssn San Antonio TX 1978-1980. xuanma@aol.com

ACREE, Nancy Pickering (Ga) 207 High Pt, Saint Simons Island GA 31522 B Laurel MS 12/8/1935 d Willis Carl Pickering & Evie. Cert of study TS; TS; TS; TS; BA Eckerd Coll 1997. D 9/18/1994 Bp Robert Gould Tharp P 2/19/2000 Bp Charles Glenn VonRosenberg. Assoc Chr Ch Frederica St Simons Island GA 2002-2010; Asst Ch Of The Ascen Knoxville TN 2000-2001; D Ch Of The Ascen Knoxville TN 1996-1999.

ADAIR, Maryly S (NCal) 19636 Ridge Rd, Red Bluff CA 96080 **S Ptr's Epis Ch Red Bluff CA 2010-** B Berkeley CA 8/4/1946 d David Wellington Samson & Eunice Helen Lyons. BA California St U 1969; MS California St U 1983; MDiv CDSP 2002. D 6/20/2003 P 3/12/2004 Bp Jerry Alban Lamb. m 12/28/1980 Michael F Adair c 2. Dio Nthrn California Sacramento CA 2006-2009; S Ptr's Epis Ch Red Bluff CA 2004-2005; Non-stip D/Assoc. P Trin Cathd Sacramento CA 2003-2004. maryly@mindspring.com

ADAM, A(ndrew) K(eith) M(alcolm) (Chi) University of Glasgow, No 4 The Square, Glasgow G12 8QQ Great Britain (UK) B Boston MA 9/10/1957 s Donald Geikie Adam & Nancy T. BA Bow 1979; MDiv Ya Berk 1986; STM Ya Berk 1987; Schlr Duke 1989; Fllshp ECF 1990; PhD Duke 1991. D 6/7/1986 Bp Alden Moinet Hathaway P 12/6/1986 Bp Robert Bracewell Appleyard. m 6/12/1982 Margaret Anne Bamforth c 3. SWTS Evanston IL 2008; Supervisory Supply P S Lk's Ch Evanston IL 2000; Assoc Prof NT SWTS Evanston IL 1999-2003; Sabbatical Supply P Chr Ch New Brunswick NJ 1999; S Jas Hse Of Pryr Tampa FL 1991-1992; Asst Chr Ch New Haven CT 1986-1987. Auth, *Flesh and Bones: Sermons*, Wipf and Stock, 2001; Auth, "Walk This Way: Difference, Repetition, and the Imitation of Chr," *Interp*, 2001; Auth, *Postmodern Interpretations of the Bible: A Rdr*, Chalice, 2001; Auth, *A Handbook of Postmodern Biblic Interp*, Chalice, 2000; Auth, *A Grammar for NT Gk*, Abingdon Press, 1999; Auth, "Docetism, Kasemann and Christology," *Scottish Journ of Theol*, 1996; Auth, *Making Sense of NT Theol*, Merc Press, 1995; Auth, *What Is Postmodern Biblic Criticism?*, Fortress Press, 1995. Angl Assn of Biblic Scholars; Cath Biblic Assn; SBL; Studiorum Novi Testamentum Societas. Honorable Mention in Biblic Interp Assn of Ch Presses 1996. akm.adam@glasgow.ac.uk

ADAM, Barbara Ann (Kan) 10500 W 140th Ter, Overland Park KS 66221 **D Chr Ch Overland Pk KS 1993-** B Kansas City KS 4/4/1935 d James Martin Mills & Helen Lucille. U of Kansas; BS U Of Dayton 1958. D 3/25/1993 Bp William Edward Smalley. m 12/18/1956 Paul James Adam c 2. adambaba2001@yahoo.com

ADAM, Betty (Tex) 3501 Chevy Chase Dr, Houston TX 77019 B Houston TX 9/29/1939 d George Washington Conrad & Grace. Baylor U 1958; BA U of Texas 1961; MA U CA 1973; MA Rice U 1981; PhD Rice U 1983; MDiv Houston Grad TS 1989; CTh Epis TS of The SW 1990. D 9/2/1990 Bp Anselmo Carral-Solar P 3/1/1991 Bp Maurice Manuel Benitez. m 5/12/1973 William Adam c 2. Cn Chr Ch Cathd Houston TX 1993-2008; S Jn The Div Houston TX 1991-1992. bettycadam@comcast.net

ADAM, John Todd (Neb) 2621 CR 59, Alliance NE 69301 **D S Matt's Ch Allnce NE 1999-** B Hyannis NE 2/27/1944 s George Donald Adam & Marcella. BA Chadron St Coll 1967. D 12/10/1999 Bp James Edward Krotz. m 10/31/1970 Anne Catherine Spearing c 2. NAAD. jtadam44@telecomwest.net

ADAMIK, George F (NC) 221 Union St, Cary NC 27511 **Dioc Trst Dio No Carolina Raleigh NC 2010-; R S Paul's Epis Ch Cary NC 1999-** B Yonkers NY 6/5/1953 s George Francis Adamik & Margaret Mary. BA Cathd Coll of the Immac Concep 1975; MDiv S Jos's Sem Yonkers NY 1979; MS Ford 1985. Rec from Roman Catholic 6/24/1990 as Priest Bp Harold B Robinson. m 11/22/2009 Mary Dougan c 2. Pres of Stndg Com Dio No Carolina Raleigh NC 2010-2011; Stndg Com Dio No Carolina Raleigh NC 2008-2011; Dn of Convoc Dio No Carolina Raleigh NC 2004-2007; Rdr for GOE Retakes Dio New York New York City NY 1997-1998; Co-Chair of Cler Wellness Com Dio New York New York City NY 1996-1999; COM Dio New York New York City NY 1995-1998; Congrl Spprt Plan Com Dio New York New York City NY 1994-1997; Dn of Cler Dio New York New York City NY 1993-1997; Par Crisis Intervention Team Dio New York New York City NY 1992-1999; R S Steph's Ch Pearl River NY 1991-1999. adamik@aol.com

ADAMS, Calvin Charles (Be) Po Box 431, Douglassville PA 19518 B Saint Petersburg FL 8/6/1942 s Charles Chester Adams & Dorothy Helen. BA U of So Florida 1973; MA Jn Hopkins U 1975; MDiv GTS 1983. D 6/17/1983 P 12/17/1983 Bp James Michael Mark Dyer. m 8/23/1973 Pamela M Adams. R S Gabr's Ch Douglassville PA 1987-2008; Asst S Jn's Of Lattingtown Locust Vlly NY 1983-1987. RACA. Hon Cn Pstr Dio Bethlehem 1998. frcalvin@aol.com

ADAMS, Charles Edward (ETenn) 4303 Harbor Dr, Kingsport TN 37664 B Logan WV 9/28/1928 s Raymond Blanford Adams & Sally. AA Marshall U 1951; MS W Virginia U 1959; US Army Chapl Sch 1964; MDiv Epis TS In Kentucky 1965. D 6/9/1965 P 3/1/1966 Bp Wilburn Camrock Campbell. m 11/24/1960 Nancy Jean Robinson. S Mary's Epis Ch Jasper AL 1982-1986; Ch Of The Ascen Montgomery AL 1978-1982; Calv Epis Ch Ashland KY 1977-1978; Min to Aging Dio W Virginia Charleston WV 1966-1968; Cur S Matt's Ch Charleston WV 1966-1968. Natl Assn of Ret Fed Employees 1999; NASW 1958. Commendation Medal Second Infantry Div Second Med Battalion Korea 1952. fr-lee@excite.com

ADAMS JR, Charles G (Ak) 4507 Rosedale St, Juneau AK 99801 B Lewiston ME 7/28/1925 s Charles G Adams & Edith. BA U of Vermont 1951. D 11/7/1973 P 6/1/1974 Bp William J Gordon Jr. m 8/27/1949 Janet Adams.

ADAMS, David Robert (NJ) PO Box 66, Etna NH 03750 B Atlantic City NJ 3/28/1939 s Richard Jones Adams & Grace D. B.A. Ya 1961; B.D. Yale DS 1965; Ph.D. Ya 1979; GTS 1987. D 6/11/1988 P 2/25/1989 Bp George Phelps Mellick Belshaw. m 8/25/1962 Ann Macdonald c 2. Asst The Ch Of S Lk In The Fields New York NY 2000-2009; Prof VTS Alexandria VA 1991-1994; Int Chr Ch New Brunswick NJ 1990-1991; Int Gr-S Paul's Ch Mercerville NJ 1989-1990. DAVID.ADAMS666@GMAIL.COM

ADAMS, Deanna Sue (U) 603 W 2350 S, Perry UT 84302 **D S Mich's Ch Brigham City UT 2008-** B Chattanooga TN 3/1/1942 d William Quentin Duncan & Mamie Dean. Dplma Jn Hopkins Hosp 1963; BS Athens St U 1980; Med Alabama A&M U 1982; BSN Weber St U 1995. D 6/10/2006 Bp Carolyn Tanner Irish. m 5/26/1989 Ivan Adams c 2. dsadams@besstek.net

ADAMS, Edgar George (Pa) 4682 Arrowhead Rd, Richmond VA 23235 **Assoc S Mk's Ch Richmond VA 1998-** B Troy NY 6/12/1931 s John Davry Adams & Ella Frances. Emory U 1949; BS Georgia Inst of Tech 1953; MDiv PDS 1959; Fllshp EDS 1980. D 6/24/1959 Bp Harry Lee Doll P 4/6/1960 Bp Noble C Powell. m 12/31/1994 Rebecca Walker c 3. Dn of Merion Dnry Dio Maryland Baltimore MD 1975-1978; Dn Dio Pennsylvania Philadelphia PA 1975-1978; S Andr's Epis Ch New Kensington PA 1970-1978; Ch Of Our Sav Jenkintown PA 1964-1997; Ch Of S Asaph Bala Cynwyd PA 1964-1997; R Ascen Ch St MD 1960-1964; R Gr Epis Ch Darlington MD 1960-1964; M-in-c Ascen Ch St MD 1959-1960; M-in-c Gr Epis Ch Darlington MD 1959-1960. OHC 1959. egadams007@aol.com

ADAMS, Eloise Ellen (Ct) 495 Laurel Hill Rd Apt 4B, Norwich CT 06360 B Norwich CT 11/7/1947 d Charles Porter Rogers & Eloise Ethal. BS Seattle Pacific Coll 1969. D 12/12/1998 Bp Clarence Nicholas Coleridge. c 3. D S Dav's Ch Gales Ferry CT 1998-2004.

ADAMS JR, Floyd Allen (CFla) 10 Sunny Beach Dr, Ormond Beach FL 32176 B Groton NY 10/16/1920 s Floyd Allen Adams & Josephine Veronica. Cortland Bus Sch Cortland NY 1948; DIT PDS 1964. D 6/13/1964 P 12/19/1964 Bp Robert Lionne DeWitt. m 11/28/1943 Muriel McPherson c 3. H Trin Ch Daytona Bch FL 1986-1988; R S Anne's Ch Crystal River FL 1979-1985; R S Andr's Epis Ch New Kensington PA 1970-1978; R S Mart's Epis Ch Upper Chichester PA 1964-1970.

ADAMS, Frank George (NJ) 107 Devon Dr, Chestertown MD 21620 **P-in-c Chr Ch Worton MD 2011-** B New York NY 11/17/1925 s Hans Christian Adams & Andree. BS Rutgers-The St U 1953; MS Drexel U 1969; Coll of Preachers 1971; AA Nash 1972; MA Villanova U 1978; MBA Monmouth U 1985. D 4/11/1970 P 10/24/1970 Bp Alfred L Banyard. m 9/9/1950 Lisbeth Ann Yates. Assoc Emm Epis Ch Chestertown MD 1993-2003; Vic Trin Ch Riverside NJ 1977-1993; Archit Commision Dio New Jersey Trenton NJ 1976-1993; Cur S Mary's Ch Burlington NJ 1970-1977. SSC 1972. Natl Bus Admin hon Soc Monmouth U 1985; Natl Mechanical Engr hon Soc Rutgers U 1952; Natl Engr hon Soc Rutgers U 1952. fgadams@atlanticbb.net

ADAMS, Gary Jay (ECR) 3002 Hauser Ct, Carson City NV 89701 B Tonopah NV 8/27/1930 s Albert John Adams & Amy Elizabeth. BA U of Nevada at Reno 1951; MDiv CDSP 1964; DMin Claremont TS 1981. D 6/19/1964 P 1/6/1965 Bp William G Wright. m 6/5/1949 Marguerite Goff. R S Mk's Epis Ch Santa Clara CA 1987-1993; S Jn's Epis Ch Marysville CA 1980-1987; Ch Of The Mssh Santa Ana CA 1973-1980; Rur D Dio Los Angeles Los Angeles CA 1969-1973; R S Edm's Par San Marino CA 1966-1969; P-in-c Ch Of The H Innoc San Francisco CA 1965-1966; Vic S Jn's In The Wilderness Ch Glenbrook NV 1964-1965; Vic S Pat's Ch Incline Vill NV 1964-1965. Auth, "The Operation Of Salvation In Par & Person: Soteriological Praxis In Sacramental Context". Alb Inst. Mdiv w dist CDSP Berkeley CA 1964. revgjadams1@aol.com

✠ **ADAMS III, Rt Rev Gladstone Bailey** (CNY) 310 Montgomery St Ste 200, Syracuse NY 13202 **Bp of Cntrl New York Dio Cntrl New York Syracuse NY 2001-** B Baltimore MD 7/26/1952 s Gladstone Bailey Adams & Evelyn Adelle. BS Towson U 1976; MDiv VTS 1980. D 4/26/1980 P 11/8/1980 Bp David Keller Leighton Sr Con 10/27/2001 for CNY. m 8/26/1978 Bonnie Jean Grant c 3. R S Jame's Ch Skaneateles NY 1994-2001; R S Thos Epis Ch Chesapeake VA 1985-1994; Vic S Mk's Ch Groveton NH 1982-1985; R S Paul's Ch Lancaster NH 1982-1985; Cur S Ptr's Epis Ch Ellicott City MD 1980-1982. Cristosal Bd Trst 2001; OHC 1980. Ddiv VTS 2002. bishop@cny.anglican.org

ADAMS, Helen (CFla) 103 Shady Branch Trl, Ormond Beach FL 32174 B Norwalk CT 3/1/1953 d Albert John Kandl & Helen Mary. U Of Cntrl Florida; AS Daytona Bch Cmnty Coll 1975; Inst for Chr Stuides 1997. D 6/6/1998 Bp John Wadsworth Howe. m 11/21/1981 Omar Adams.

ADAMS, James Franklin (WLa) 404 Hiawatha Trl, Pineville LA 71360 **Died 9/11/2009** B Baton Rouge LA 7/19/1922 s James Moore Adams & Ella. BS LSU 1948; MDiv PDS 1956. D 6/30/1956 Bp Iveson Batchelor Noland P 6/24/1957 Bp Girault M Jones. c 1. Louisiana Chapl Assn; Mntl Hlth Cler Assn. sheumais@cox-internet.com

ADAMS, James Harold (Roch) 517 Castle St, Geneva NY 14456 **Lake Delaware Boys Camp Delhi NY 2008-; Stndg Com Dio Rochester Rochester NY 1993-; R S Ptr's Meml Geneva NY 1981-** B Staten Island NY 3/8/1952 s Kenneth H Adams & Gertrude Emma. BA Wag 1975; MDiv Nash 1978. D 6/10/1978 P 1/6/1979 Bp Wilbur Emory Hogg Jr. m 9/21/1974 Suzanne J Adams c 4. D Ne Dist Dio Rochester Rochester NY 1993; Pres Stndg Com Dio Rochester Rochester NY 1991; Stndg Com Dio Rochester Rochester NY 1987-1991; Dep Gc Dio Rochester Rochester NY 1987-1989; COM Dio Rochester Rochester NY 1986-1991; S Paul's Ch Plymouth WI 1982-1986; Chair Yth Commision Dio Rochester Rochester NY 1981-1984; Chair Yth Commision Dio Albany Albany NY 1979-1981; Cur Chr Ch Cooperstown NY 1978-1981. jimandsueadams@gmail.com

✠ **ADAMS JR, Rt Rev James Marshall** (CFla) 428 W Cobblestone Loop, Hernando FL 34442 **Form Bp of Wstrn Kansas Shpd Of The Hills Epis Ch Lecanto FL 2010-** B El Paso TX 6/9/1948 s James Marshall Adams & Mary Kathryn. BS U of Texas at El Paso 1971; MDiv GTS 1979; DD GTS 2003. D 8/6/1979 P 5/1/1980 Bp Richard Mitchell Trelease Jr Con 3/16/2002 for WK. m 8/21/1971 Stacey B Brookman c 1. Bp Dio Wstrn Kansas Hutchinson KS 2002-2010; R Trin Ch Wauwatosa WI 1998-2002; Advsry Bd Dio Milwaukee Milwaukee WI 1998-2001; Instr Sch for Deacons Dio Kansas Topeka KS 1995-1998; R Trin Epis Ch El Dorado KS 1993-1998; R Chr Ch Green Bay WI 1987-1992; Dn Dio Fond du Lac Appleton WI 1982-1986; Vic S Paul's Ch Plymouth WI 1982-1986; Asst R Ch of the H Faith Santa Fe NM 1980-1982; Cur S Mich And All Ang Ch Albuquerque NM 1979-1980. DD GTS 2003. bishopjimsoth@yahoo.com

ADAMS, James Patrick (NC) 120 East Edenton Street, Raleigh NC 27601 **Chr Epis Ch Raleigh NC 2010-** B New London CT 2/1/1965 s Francis Gordon Adams & Carol Ann. MDiv VTS 1997. D 5/31/1997 P 12/5/1997 Bp Douglas Edwin Theuner. m Mary Adams c 6. S Alb's Ch Cape Eliz ME 2001-2010; Asst R S Thos Ch Hanover NH 1997-2000. jamespadams@me.com

ADAMS, James Rowe (WA) 224 Brattle St, Cambridge MA 02138 **Died 9/13/2011** B Lincoln NE 6/30/1934 s Charles Forehand Adams & Grace Gerturde. U of Nebraska 1953; BA GW 1955; STB EDS 1958. D 6/14/1958 P 12/20/1958 Bp Angus Dun. c 3. Auth, *So You Can't Stand Evang?*, Cowley Press, 1994; Auth, *So You Think You're Not Rel?*, Cowley Press, 1989. DSA EDS 2009. jadams@tcpc.org

ADAMS, Jennifer Lin (WMich) 536 College Ave, Holland MI 49423 **R Gr Ch Holland MI 1994-** B Royal Oak MI 11/22/1968 d Marshall Vincent Adams & Linda Ruth. BA Kalamazoo Coll 1990; MDiv CDSP 1994. D 6/11/1994 P 12/17/1994 Bp Edward Lewis Lee Jr.

ADAMS JR, Jesse Roland (La) 6306 Prytania St, New Orleans LA 70118 **Asst Trin Ch New Orleans LA 2004-** B Bruce MS 3/31/1941 s Jesse R Adams & Eulalie. BA U of Mississippi 1963; JD U of Mississippi 1967. D 1/25/2004 P 8/6/2004 Bp Charles Edward Jenkins III. m 1/25/2003 Nancy Blum Adams.

ADAMS JR, John Davry (Va) 16114 Daybreak Ln, Beaverdam VA 23015 B Troy NY 5/6/1928 s John Davry Adams & Ella Frances. BBA Emory U 1950; MDiv VTS 1961. D 7/6/1961 P 6/14/1962 Bp Noble C Powell. m 6/26/1982 Suzanne P Adams c 4. Ch Of Our Sav Montpelier VA 1990-1998; P Ch Of S Jas The Less Ashland VA 1988-1989; Cbury Bk Shop Richmond VA 1985-1998; P Chr Ch Waverly VA 1985-1986; P-in-c Varina Epis Ch Richmond VA 1983-1984; Chair Stewardships Dept Dio Virginia Richmond VA 1970-1977; R S Thos' Ch Richmond VA 1967-1981; Exec Coun Dio Virginia Richmond VA 1965-1967; R Chr Epis Ch Gordonsville VA 1964-1967; Cur S Anne's Par Annapolis MD 1961-1964. adamsatbeechbrook@erols.com

ADAMS, John Stockton (ECR) 24745 Summit Field Road, Carmel CA 93923 B Towaco NJ 2/28/1944 s Ernestus Schenck Adams & Anna D'Oyley. BA U of Virginia 1966; ThB GTS 1969; MA Antioch U 1986; Fllshp PrTS 1986. D 6/4/1969 Bp Leland Stark P 12/14/1969 Bp George E Rath. m 6/25/1983 Tracey Linden c 2. All SS Ch Carmel CA 1995-1999; P-in-c S Barn' Par Pasadena CA 1991-1992; P-in-c S Bede's Epis Ch Los Angeles CA 1989-1990; P-in-c Ch Of The Ascen Tujunga CA 1987-1989; Chapl Harvard-Westlake Sch N Hollywood CA 1979-1986; Chapl Hoosac Sch Hoosick NY 1977-1979; R S Andr's Ch Millinocket ME 1972-1976; Cur Ch Of The Atone Tenafly NJ 1969-1972. johnadams@redshift.com

ADAMS, John Torbet (Alb) 262 Center Rd, Lyndeborough NH 03082 B Muncie IN 6/2/1945 s William Brown Adams & Julia. BS Ashland U 1968; MDiv VTS 1971; Andover Newton TS 1991. D 6/11/1971 P 12/28/1971 Bp John P Craine. S Paul's Ch Salem NY 2000-2003; Chr Ch Coxsackie NY 1993-1995; P-in-c Calv Epis Ch Cairo NY 1989-1997; Gloria Dei Epis Ch Palenville NY 1989-1990; S Jn In-The-Wilderness Copake Falls NY 1987-1988; Ch Of Our Sav Hartville WY 1985; Int Dio Massachusetts Boston MA 1981-1987; S Jas Epis Ch Arlington VT 1975-1979.

ADAMS, Keith Naylor (NwT) 6029 Winners Cir, San Angelo TX 76904 **Died 7/30/2010** B Quantico VA 11/13/1956 s Dwight L Adams & Helen Deane. BA Dickinson Coll 1979; MDiv TESM 1989; Med Oklahoma St U 2003. D 6/16/1989 P 2/15/1990 Bp Charlie Fuller McNutt Jr. c 2. Auth, "Rel In The Untd States Marine Corp"; Auth, "Sexual Harassment In The USN". Bro Of S Andr. revkadams@cox.net

ADAMS, Lesley Margaret (Roch) 630 S Main St, Geneva NY 14456 **Hobart And Wm Smith Colleges Geneva NY 1995-; S Jn's Chap Geneva NY 1995-** B Washington DC 9/4/1958 d James Rowe Adams & Virginia Marie. AB Smith 1980; MDiv Harvard DS 1986. D 6/13/1987 Bp Ronald Hayward Haines P 3/30/1988 Bp William George Burrill. m 8/14/2003 David Newman c 2. S Ptr's Epis Ch Henrietta NY 1988-1989; Bex Columbus OH 1987-1994; S Ptr's Epis Ch Bloomfield NY 1987-1989; S Ptr's Epis Ch Henrietta NY 1987-1988. ladams@hws.edu

ADAMS, Margaret Louise (Tenn) 411 Annex Ave Apt F-1, Nashville TN 37209 B Chillicothe MO 9/2/1949 d Charles Goodrich Adams & Margaret Elizabeth. BD IL Wesl 1971; MS U of Tennessee 1975; MDiv STUSo 1998. D 5/24/1998 P 4/25/1999 Bp Bertram Nelson Herlong. Ch Of Our Sav Gallatin TN 2006-2008; S Geo's Ch Nashville TN 2000-2005; Asst S Phil's Ch Nashville TN 1998-1999.

ADAMS, Marilyn (Los) Po Box 208306, New Haven CT 06520 **Asst S Thos's Ch New Haven CT 1999-** B Oak Park IL 10/12/1943 d William Clark McCord & Wilmah Wanda. BA U IL 1964; PhD Cor 1967; ThM PrTS 1984; ThM PrTS 1985. D 6/20/1987 Bp Oliver Bailey Garver Jr P 12/1/1987 Bp John Mc Gill Krumm. m 6/10/1987 Robert Merrihew Adams. Asst Par Of S Mary In Palms Los Angeles CA 1999-2007; Asst Chr Ch New Haven CT 1997-1999; Asst S Thos's Ch New Haven CT 1994-1997; Asst Chr Ch New Haven CT 1993-1994; Asst Par Of S Mary In Palms Los Angeles CA 1993; Asst S Aug By-The-Sea Par Santa Monica CA 1990-1992; Asst All SS Par Beverly Hills CA 1988-1989; Asst Trin Epis Par Los Angeles CA 1985-1988. Auth, "Horrendous Evils & Goodness Of God," 1999; Auth, "Wm Ockham," 1987. Aar 2000; Amer Philos Assn 1967; Soc For Med & Renaissance Philos 1978; Soc Of Chr Philosophers 1978. Henry Luce Iii Fllshp 2002; Gifford Lectr 1999; Guggenheim Fllshp 1988. marilyn.adams@yale.edu

ADAMS, Mary Lynn (FdL) PO Box 5070, Madison WI 53705 B Milwaukee 11/21/1949 BS U of Wisconsin 1971; BS U of Wisconsin 1987. D 12/3/2005 Bp Russell Edward Jacobus. mary.adams@earthlink.net

ADAMS, Michael Ko (Tex) 209 W 27th St, Austin TX 78705 **R All SS Epis Ch Austin TX 2004-** B Seoul KR 8/23/1963 s William C(lyde) Adams & Gloria G(race). BS LSU 1985; MDiv SWTS 1989. D 6/10/1989 P 12/9/1989 Bp Willis Ryan Henton. m 6/6/1987 Kelley L Lawrence c 3. R S Barn Epis Ch Lafayette LA 1998-2004; R The Epis Ch Of The Epiph New Iberia LA 1993-1998; Asst R Ch Of The Ascen Lafayette LA 1990-1993; D S Jas Epis Ch Shreveport LA 1989. mike@allsaints-austin.org

ADAMS, Patricia Anne (Ak) 3506 Cherokee Dr S, Salem OR 97302 B Lakota IA 1/27/1935 d Herman Andrew Wessels & Mable Velma. RN Methodist-Kahler Sch of Nrsng 1956; U of Washington 1958; BS Oklahoma City U 1978; MDiv SMU 1984; Claremont Coll 1992. D 3/14/1987 P 1/1/1989 Bp Gerald Nicholas McAllister. m 9/27/1958 Ralph Edwin Adams c 3. Asst. P S Mary's Ch Anchorage AK 1995-2000; D-Transitional S Paul's Cathd Oklahoma City OK 1987-1988; Dio Oklahoma Oklahoma City OK 1987; Jubilee Off Dio Oklahoma Oklahoma City OK 1986-1988. cl Perkins TS 1984.

ADAMS, Richard Babcock (Me) PO Box 2052, Ogunquit ME 03907 B Albert Lea MN 11/30/1923 s Harold Beach Adams & Hildred. BA Cntrl Michigan U 1947; BD SWTS 1950. D 3/25/1950 P 10/28/1950 Bp Charles A Clough. Admin Asst to Bp Dio Maine Portland ME 1973-1975; R S Marg's Ch Belfast ME 1971-1973; R Gr Epis Ch Bath ME 1958-1969; R S Paul's Epis Ch On The Green Vergennes VT 1953-1958; P-in-c S Lk's Ch Springfield IL 1951-1953; P-in-c S Steph's Ch Harrisburg IL 1951-1953; Asst The Cathd Ch Of S Paul Springfield IL 1950-1951. radamsog@yahoo.com

ADAMS, Richard Carl (Oly) Po Box 336, Hinesburg VT 05461 B South Bend IN 12/6/1925 s Ralph Edwin Adams & Myrtle Agnes. BS NWU 1947; MDiv SWTS 1952; STM GTS 1958; Fllshp GTS 1961. D 3/10/1952 P 10/5/1952 Bp James R Mallett. Res P S Andr's Ch Northford CT 1971-1976; Asst Chr Ch Ansonia CT 1967-1971; Asst Trin Ch Branford CT 1964-1966; Asst Gr Ch Madison NJ 1962-1964; Tutor/Fell The GTS New York NY 1958-1960; Asst Ch Of The Medtr Bronx NY 1957-1961; Asst Chr Ch Tacoma WA 1956-1957; Tutor/Instr Hellenistic Gk SWTS Evanston IL 1953-1955; Asst The Cathd Ch Of S Jas So Bend IN 1952-1953. Co-Auth, "Through the Years Celebrating...," 2008; Auth, *Meditation and Celebration [CD ROM]*, Quinnipiac Coll, 1999; Auth, *The Sprt of Sport*, Wyndham Hall; Bristol, IN, 1987. Cntr for Theol and Natural Sci; Berkeley, CA 1996; Temple of Understanding 1983. Advsry Bd Temple of Understanding.

ADAMS, Robert Ober (Cal) Po Box 405, Sprague River OR 97639 B San Francisco CA 6/17/1931 s James Douglass Adams & Katharine. BA San Francisco St U 1957; BD CDSP 1960. D 6/26/1960 P 1/14/1961 Bp James Albert Pike. m 5/31/1975 Camilla Elizabeth Hudson. Sprtl Dir Curs Dio California San Francisco CA 1982-1996; Cmsn On Alco Dio California San Francisco CA 1981-1997; Ohlhoff Recovery Prog San Francisco CA 1981-1986; Pres Contra Costa Dnry Dio California San Francisco CA 1977-1978; Gr Ch Martinez CA 1975-1978; Fndr/Vic Ch Of The H Fam Half Moon Bay CA 1971-1975; R S Alb's Ch Los Banos CA 1965-1971; Cur Chr Ch Alameda CA 1962-1965; Vic S Lk's Ch Jolon CA 1960-1962; Vic S Matt's Ch San Ardo CA 1960-1962. Auth, "A Bob Adams Sampler"; Auth, "Call For Mnstry To Cnty Jails". Natl Sheriffs Assn Chapl Div 1991-1994; Pres Klamath Falls, Or Writer'S Gld 1998-2003. Man Of The Year Los Banos Rotary Club 1968. bobandme@cvc.net

ADAMS JR, Thomas Edwin (Mass) PO Box 522, Falmouth MA 02541 **Asst The Ch Of The Adv Boston MA 2005-** B Palm Beach FL 1/1/1944 s Thomas Edwin Adams & Caroline. BA U of Pennsylvania 1966; EDS 1969; Oxf 1972. D 6/28/1969 Bp William Foreman Creighton P 1/1/1970 Bp The Bishop Of Tokyo. m 7/19/2011 Candace Roosevelt. R S Mk's Epis Ch Fall River MA 1997-1999; P-in-c S Mk's Epis Ch Fall River MA 1990-1994; S Barn Ch Falmouth MA 1988; Asst Ch Of The Mssh Woods Hole MA 1979-1981. tea077@aol.com

ADAMS, William (NCal) 7846 Amherst St, Sacramento CA 95832 **P-in-c H Trin Epis Ch Ukiah CA 2011-** B Los Angeles CA 11/3/1952 s James Vinson Adams & Virginia Anita. BA California St U 1981; MDiv CDSP 1985. D 6/16/1985 P 12/18/1985 Bp John Lester Thompson III. m 8/26/1972 Kathlyne Ann Burgan c 2. R Trin Ch Sutter Creek CA 1986-2008; Asst S Mich's Epis Ch Carmichael CA 1985-1986.

ADAMS, William Seth (Oly) 2707 Silver Crest Court, Langley WA 98260 B Fort Smith AR 6/7/1940 s William Seth Adams & Hortense Marie. BS Washington U 1964; BD Bex 1967; MA Pr 1971; PhD Pr 1973. D 6/24/1967 P 1/21/1968 Bp George Leslie Cadigan. m 6/3/1995 Amy Donohue c 2. Int S Jas Ch Austin TX 1998-2001; Prof Epis TS Of The SW Austin TX 1982-2005; Assoc Calv Ch Columbia MO 1973-1975; Assoc All SS Ch Princeton NJ 1969-1973; M-in-c S Paul's Ch Palmyra MO 1967-1969. Auth, "Moving the Furniture: Liturg Theory, Pract and Environmental Theory," Ch Pub, 1999; Auth, "Shaped by Images: One Who Presides," Ch Hymnal, 1995; Co-Ed, "Our Heritage and Common Life," U Press of Amer, 1994. No Amer Acad of Liturg 1977-2009; Societas Liturgica 1980-1991. williamseth1@gmail.com

ADAMS-HARRIS, Anne Jane (Wyo) Po Box 4086, Santa Barbara CA 93140 **D S Mk's Ch Cheyenne WY 2006-** B London UK 8/26/1932 d John Leslie Adams & Doreen Estelle. EFM STUSo. D 10/18/1998 Bp Onell Asiselo Soto. m 3/12/1960 Harry Clark Harris c 1. DOK; Sis Of The H Nativ. haran2@earthlink.net

ADAMS-MASSMANN, Jennifer Helen (Eur) Sebastian-Rinz-Str 22, Frankfurt Germany Germany **Asstg P The Angl/Epis Ch Of Chr The King Frankfurt am Main 60323 DE 2007-** B Norwood MA 12/7/1974 d Clifford John Adams & Rebecca F. BA U NC 1996; MDiv Duke DS 2003. D 5/27/2006 P 5/5/2007 Bp Pierre W Whalon. m 12/29/2004 Alexander Massmann. D The Angl/Epis Ch Of Chr The King Frankfurt am Main 60323 DE 2006-2007. jadamsmassmann@gmail.com

ADAMS-RILEY, Daniel W (Va) 815 E Grace St, Richmond VA 23219 **R S Paul's Ch Richmond VA 2008-** B Columbia SC 3/28/1971 s Weston Adams & Elizabeth Nicholson. BA U So 1993; MDiv VTS 2001. D 6/16/2001 P 5/1/2002 Bp Dorsey Felix Henderson. m 7/7/2001 Gena D Riley c 2. Vic S Jn's Cathd Jacksonville FL 2006-2008; Cler Res Chr Ch Par Pensacola FL 2003-2006; Asst/Cler Res Chr Ch Alexandria VA 2001-2003. wadams-riley@saintjohnscathedral.org

ADAMS-RILEY, Gena D (Fla) 13 N Shields Ave, Richmond VA 23220 B VT 8/19/1971 d Winston Eugene Riley & Mary Young. BS U of Utah 1996; MDiv VTS 2002. D 7/11/2002 P 2/8/2003 Bp Carolyn Tanner Irish. m 7/7/2001 Daniel W Adams-Riley c 1. Cn S Jn's Cathd Jacksonville FL 2006-2008; Assoc for Pstr Care Chr Ch Par Pensacola FL 2003-2006; Ch Of The Ascen Silver Sprg MD 2002-2003. gadamsriley@saintjohnscathedral.org

ADAMS-SHEPHERD, Kathleen Elizabeth (Ct) 64 Main St, Newtown CT 06470 **Com Dio Connecticut Hartford CT 1996-; R Trin Ch Newtown CT 1996-** B Boston MA 2/17/1955 d Raymond Hubert Thorne & Patricia May. BS Bridgewater Coll 1977; MDiv UTS 1981. D 6/5/1982 Bp John Bowen Coburn P 6/25/1983 Bp O'Kelley Whitaker. m 2/28/1981 Richard Allan Adams-Shepherd. R Chr Ch Clayton NY 1987-1996; Stndg Com Dio Cntrl New York Syracuse NY 1987-1996; R St Jn's Ch Clayton NY 1987-1996; Ch Of The Resurr Oswego NY 1982-1987. revkathie@aol.com

ADDIEGO, Jeffrey Clark (Nev) 1429 Bronco Rd, Boulder City NV 89005 **Dn, SE Dnry Dio Nevada Las Vegas NV 2011-; P S Matt's Ch Las Vegas NV 2002-** B San Francisco CA 11/29/1952 BS U Pac 1975. D 5/29/2001 P 2/7/2002 Bp Katharine Jefferts Schori. jaddiego@cox.net

ADDISON, Orlando Joseph (Hond) 3341 Harding St, Hollywood FL 33021 **S Jas-In-The-Hills Epis Ch Hollywood FL 2006-** B Tela HN 10/16/1961 s Charles Emmanuel Addison & Rosa Neoni. BA Universidad De Honduras San Pedro Sula Hn 1988; MDiv VTS 2000. D 5/1/2000 Bp Leopold Frade P 2/24/2001 Bp Wendell Nathaniel Gibbs Jr. m 12/5/1986 Julia Concepcion Bejarano c 2. Cn Cathd Ch Of S Paul Detroit MI 2001-2006; Asst S Jn's Ch Royal Oak MI 2000-2001. froaddison@bellsouth.net

ADE, Daniel Gerard George (Los) 242 E Alvarado St, Pomona CA 91767 **Vice Dn St Johns Pro-Cathd Los Angeles CA 2006-** B New York NY 5/28/1958 s Raymond George Ade & Maureen Anne. BA St. Johns U 1980; MDiv GTS 1992. D 6/13/1992 P 12/12/1992 Bp Richard Frank Grein. m 3/1/1992 Walter

T Killmer. S Paul's Pomona Pomona CA 2003-2006; The Ch Of S Lk In The Fields New York NY 1996-2003; Chapl St Ptr Cmnty Outreach Cntr Inc Dio New York New York City NY 1995-1996; S Ptr's Epis Ch Peekskill NY 1995; Asst S Thos Ch New York NY 1992-1994. revdanade@hotmail.com

ADEBONOJO, Mary (Pa) 50 Bagdad Rd, Durham NH 03824 B Chicago IL 4/3/1936 d Ansel Sumter Bunton & Mildred. BA Rad 1957; MA U CA, Berkeley 1967; PDS 1974; Luth TS 1976. D 4/13/1977 P 4/1/1980 Bp Lyman Cunningham Ogilby. m 2/17/2001 Wayne Douglas Shirley c 3. Assoc Chap Of S Jn The Div Tomkins Cove NY 1997-2002; Assoc Chr Epis Ch Sparkill NY 1997-2002; Assoc S Paul's Ch Sprg Vlly NY 1997-2002; Assoc Trin Epis Ch Garnerville NY 1997-2002; Int P Ch Of S Lk And Epiph Philadelphia PA 1984-1985; Int S Mths Ch Philadelphia PA 1981-1984; Yth Min Dio Pennsylvania Philadelphia PA 1979-1981. Auth, "Free To Choose," Judson Press, 1980. Oblate, Cmnty of St. Jn Bapt. madebon@webtv.net

ADELIA, Laura A (Az) 100 W Roosevelt St, Phoenix AZ 85003 B Chicago IL 4/18/1961 d Michael Addelia & Alice Marie. BAE Arizona St U 1987; MDiv PSR 1999; Cert of Islamic Stds Arizona St U 2007. D 12/11/2010 P 7/2/2011 Bp Kirk Stevan Smith. teachdent@yahoo.com

ADER, Thomas Edmund (At) 3596 Liberty Ln, Marietta GA 30062 B Dayton KY 9/7/1949 s John Edmund Ader & Avenell Francis. U Cinc; BA/BS Mia 1971. D 10/18/1998 Bp Onell Asiselo Soto. m 7/2/1983 Barbara Francis Youmans c 2. The Epis Ch Of S Ptr And S Paul Marietta GA 2006-2009. Bro Of S Andr. tader3596@aol.com

ADESSA, Denise McGovern (Ct) 96 Main St, East Windsor CT 06088 **D S Jn's Ch Pine Meadow CT 2011-** B Hartford CT 11/14/1957 d Carol Ann. BFA U of Connecticut 1982. D 9/10/2011 Bp Laura Ahrens. m 5/9/1992 Richard F Adessa c 1. dadessa@comcast.net

ADINOLFI JR, Jerry Domenick (Kan) 105 Pullins Dr, Coffeyville KS 67337 **R S Paul's Epis Ch Coffeyville KS 1998-** B Brooklyn NY 7/25/1941 s Jerry Domenick Adinolfi & Rose. BS USAF Acad 1963; MS USAF Inst of Tech 1967; Cert GW 1990; MDiv Untd TS Dayton OH 1996; Cert VTS 1996. D 6/29/1996 Bp Herbert Thompson Jr P 4/5/1997 Bp Kenneth Lester Price. c 2. Dn SE Convoc Dio Kansas Topeka KS 2002-2011; Cur S Matt's Ch Westerville OH 1996-1997. Intl Ord of S Lk the Physcn, Chapl 1996. radinolfi2@cox.net

ADKINS, Edna (Ga) Po Box 1601, Tybee Island GA 31328 **D All SS Ch Tybee Island GA 1997-** B Charleston SC 8/27/1933 d Francis Joseph Fishburne & Edna Louise. BS Winthrop U 1955; Med Georgia Sthrn U 1974; EDS U GA 1982. D 1/11/1997 Bp Henry Irving Louttit. m 6/30/1956 Robert Charles c 2. NAAD.

ADKINS, Edward Thomas (Ct) 5954 Plantation Villa Dr N, Macon GA 31210 B Medina NY 1/16/1918 s William Henry Adkins & Bessie. BA Hob 1942; MDiv VTS 1945. D 2/8/1945 Bp Frederick D Goodwin P 9/23/1945 Bp William Scarlett. c 2. Int S Phil's Ch Easthampton MA 1999-2000; Int S Barn And All SS Ch Springfield MA 1993-1994; Int All SS Ch So Hadley MA 1992-1993; Int S Jn's Ch Ashfield MA 1991-1992; Int Ch Of The Atone Westfield MA 1989-1990; Int S Andr's Ch Longmeadow MA 1987-1988; Int Trin Ch Torrington CT 1985-1987; Int Trin Epis Ch Hartford CT 1982-1985; R S Mk's Ch Mystic CT 1973-1982; Dio Connecticut Hartford CT 1973-1978; Dir of Prog Chr Ch Greenwich CT 1966-1973; Dio Missouri S Louis MO 1957-1958; Cur Gr Ch Kirkwood MO 1945-1959. Auth, *Mssn: The Chr's Calling*.

ADKINS JR, Robert Frederick (CNY) 956 Graylea Cir, Elmira NY 14905 **P Emm Ch Elmira NY 2004-** B Detroit MI 5/4/1933 s Robert Frederick Adkins & Mildred Mae. BA U of Massachusetts 1959; MDiv EDS 1963. D 6/22/1963 Bp Anson Phelps Stokes Jr P 5/16/1964 Bp John Melville Burgess. m 12/5/1998 Dagmar Adkins. Vic S Paul's Ch Utica NY 1997-1998; Dist Dn Dio Cntrl New York Syracuse NY 1985-1991; R S Matt's Epis Ch Horseheads NY 1980-1995; R All SS Ch Utica NY 1975-1980; P-in-c S Geo's Epis Ch Chadwicks NY 1971-1975; Cmnty Min Calv Ch Syracuse NY 1970-1971; P-in-c Ch of the Gd Shpd Syracuse NY 1968-1970; R Gr Epis Ch Waterville NY 1966-1970; Cur Epis Ch Of S Thos Taunton MA 1963-1966. Soc Of S Marg. robertdagmar@stny.rr.com

ADLER, John Stuart (SwFla) 9650 Gladiolus Drive, Fort Myers FL 33908 **Vic Iona Hope Epis Ch Ft Myers FL 1998-** B Harvey IL 7/31/1942 s Gordon Carlson Adler & Catherine. BS U IL 1970; JD Chicago-Kent Coll of Law 1973; MDiv SWTS 1989; DMin SWTS 1999. D 6/16/1989 Bp Frank Tracy Griswold III P 12/16/1989 Bp Rogers Sanders Harris. m 8/11/1962 Wanda L Billings c 2. S Monica's Epis Ch Naples FL 1992-1998; Dio SW Florida Sarasota FL 1991; Asst S Bon Ch Sarasota FL 1989-1991. *Rt START: A NOTEBOOK FOR Ch PLANTING (CO-Auth)*, Seabury Resources, 2001; *A LETTER TO CHRIS: THE FIRST SEVEN YEARS OF A NEW PLANT Cong*, Doctoral Dissertation/SWTS, 1999. johnadler@comcast.net

ADNEY, John Gentry (Ia) 525 A Ave Ne, Cedar Rapids IA 52401 B Clinton IA 6/6/1939 s John Robert Adney & Edith Genevieve. D 4/7/2001 Bp Carl Christopher Epting. m 8/3/1957 Patricia Adney c 5. jgadndey@earthlink.net

ADOLPHSON, Donald Richard (Cal) 552 Old Orchard Dr, Danville CA 94526 **D S Paul's Epis Ch Walnut Creek CA 1993-** B Rockford IL 11/9/1930 s Axel Edward Adolphson & Alida Anna. BS Illinois Inst of Tech 1953; MS U IL 1957; Cert California Sch for Deacons 1983. D 6/25/1983 Bp William Edwin Swing. m 8/18/1956 Nancy Ann Adolphson c 3. D S Mths Epis Ch San Ramon CA 1992-1993; D S Mths Epis Ch San Ramon CA 1983-1989. ndadolphson@sbcglobal.net

ADU-ANDOH, Samuel (Pa) 1121 Serrill Ave, Yeadon PA 19050 **Ch Of S Andr And S Monica Philadelphia PA 1999-** B Sefwi Bodi GH 7/11/1948 s Samson A Andoh & Susana. LTh U Of Ghana Legon Gh 1974; DIT TESM 1975; MDiv STUSo 1980; STM STUSo 1981; PhD Pr 1986. Trans from Church of the Province of West Africa 7/13/1999 Bp Charles Ellsworth Bennison Jr. m 4/20/1974 Margaret Nkrumah c 3. Asst S Paul's Ch Doylestown PA 1983-1984. aduandoh@comcast.com

ADWELL, Lynn (Minn) 2505 4th Ave Nw, Austin MN 55912 **Faith Formation Coordntr Chr Ch Austin MN 2005-** B Des Moines IA 8/29/1951 d Dennis M Petty & Beverly. D 6/28/2007 Bp James Louis Jelinek. m 8/10/2007 Jerry M Adwell c 2. ladwell8079@charter.net

ADZIMA, Melissa Lian (NwPa) 4701 Old French Rd, Erie PA 16509 **S Mk's Ch Erie PA 2011-** B Franklin PA 8/3/1986 d Kelly Thomas. BA Gannon U 2008; MDiv VTS 2011. D 12/4/2010 P 6/4/2011 Bp Sean Walter Rowe. m 8/28/2010 Alan Adzima. mbruckart@gmail.com

AFANADOR-KAFURI, Hernan (Ala) 176 Ridgewood Dr., Remlap AL 35133 **Dio Alabama Birmingham AL 2004-** B Dagua CO 9/19/1954 s Primitivo Afanador & Saide. bachellor Sem of Cali Cali CO 1977; Mstr Sem of Manizales Manizales CO 1982; Expert in Eccumenism U of San Buenaventura of Bogota, Colombia 1986; PhD GTF of Indiana 2008. Rec from Roman Catholic 3/21/2002 as Priest Bp John Wadsworth Howe. m 2/22/2001 Patricia Rivero-Diago c 2. H Faith Epis Ch Port S Lucie FL 2004; Ch Of Our Sav Okeechobee FL 2002-2004. hernan_afanador@yahoo.com

AFFER, Licia (Az) 7142 N 14th St, Phoenix AZ 85020 **Assoc All SS Ch Phoenix AZ 2010-** B Milan ITALY 11/15/1969 d Alberto Baldi & Gabriella. Laurea Universita degli Studi, Milan Italy 2001; MDiv GTS 2008. D 10/20/2007 P 5/31/2008 Bp Kirk Stevan Smith. m 9/18/1999 Maurizio Affer c 1. Asst to Cathd Dn Dio Arizona Phoenix AZ 2008-2010. liciaba@gmail.com

AGAR JR, Ralph Wesley (Neb) 2315 Georgetown Pl, Bellevue NE 68123 **Dioc Sfty Off Dio Nebraska Omaha NE 2011-; D S Mart Of Tours Ch Omaha NE 2008-; D S Martha's Epis Ch Papillion NE 2006-; Chair Com on Scouting Dio Nebraska Omaha NE 1995-** B Newton IA 7/4/1950 s Ralph Wesley Agar & Wilma Helen. AA Des Moines Area Cmnty Coll 1970; BS Bellevue U 1998. D 12/23/2006 Bp Joe Goodwin Burnett. m 12/21/1974 Elizabeth Kay Soule c 4. bwagar2315@aol.com

AGBAJE, John Olasoji (SVa) 1 Paddle Ct, Portsmouth VA 23703 **R S Jas Epis Ch Portsmouth VA 2001-** B NG 2/26/1956 s Joseph Ade Agbaje & Esther. Med Inst Of MN MN 1979; BA U MN 1982; MA U MN 1984; MDiv VTS 1995. D 6/28/1995 P 1/1/1996 Bp James Louis Jelinek. m 10/8/1984 Olubunmi O Koleoso c 3. S Edm's Epis Ch Chicago IL 1997-2001; Dio Minnesota Minneapolis MN 1995-1997; S Paul's Ch Brainerd MN 1995. agbajej@aol.com

AGBO, Godwin (Ct) 61 Grove St, Putnam CT 06260 B Udi Nigeria 9/8/1965 s Kenneth Agbo & Felicia. Trans from Church Of Nigeria 7/1/2004 Bp Andrew Donnan Smith. m 11/16/1996 Gladys Ajomiwe c 4. P-in-c S Phil's Epis Ch Putnam CT 2004-2007. gagbo@sbcglobal.net

AGGELER, Harold Griffith (Ida) No address on file. B Ada County ID 3/2/1936 s Harold Griffith & Margaret Burnedet. Idaho Diac. Rec from Roman Catholic 6/1/1998 as Priest Bp John Stuart Thornton. m 7/27/1996 Marilyn Eola Raymer. D S Dav's Epis Ch Caldwell ID 1998-2002.

AGIM, Emeka Ngozi (Tex) 16203 Dryberry Ct, Houston TX 77083 B Kaduna Nigeria 4/19/1963 Trans from Church Of Nigeria 3/8/2005 Bp Don Adger Wimberly. m 4/17/1999 Julia Ngozi Ejiogi c 5. Vic Dio Texas Houston TX 2005-2009. stjosephepis@sbcglobal.net

AGNER, Georgia Ellen (Eau) 17823 57th Ave, Chippewa Falls WI 54729 B Thomasville GA 8/9/1942 d Garland Dean Smith & Ruth Estelle. BD U of Missouri 1965. D 6/9/1991 Bp Roger John White. m 2/4/1967 Hugh Raymond Agner c 2. D S Jn The Div Epis Ch Burlington WI 1991-2004.

AGNEW, Christopher Mack (Va) 12433 Richards Ride, King George VA 22485 **Ecumencial Off Dio Virginia Richmond VA 2009-; Vic S Paul's Epis Ch Montross VA 2002-** B Santa Barbara CA 8/7/1944 s Jack Agnew & Agnes Emma. BA Buc 1967; MA U Of Delaware Newark 1975; PhD U Of Delaware Newark 1980; STM GTS 1991. D 6/8/1991 P 6/13/1992 Bp Cabell Tennis. m 4/25/1998 Elizabeth L Agnew. Assoc Ecum Off Dio Virginia Richmond VA 2002-2009; P-in-c Vauters Ch Champlain VA 2002-2009; P-in-c S Paul's Owens King Geo VA 2000-2002; S Ptr's Ch In The Great Vlly Malvern PA 1997-1999; Int Ch Of The Ascen Norfolk VA 1997; Int S Mich's Ch Litchfield CT 1995-1997; Int All Hallows Ch Wyncote PA 1995; S Mart's Ch Maywood NJ 1995; Assoc All Ang' Ch New York NY 1992-1995; P-in-c S Mk's Ch Teaneck NJ 1992; D S Thos's Par Newark DE 1991-1992; Assoc Ecum Off Epis Ch Cntr New York NY 1989-1994; Dio Delaware Wilmington DE

1989-1991; Rgstr Dio Delaware Wilmington DE 1985-1989. Compiler, "Families of St. Paul's Epis Ch, King Geo Cnty," *Tidewater Virginia Families: A mag of Hist and Genealogy*, 2004; Auth, "Angl Statements on Ecclesiology," *The Riverdale Report*, Forw Mvmt, 1994; Auth, "The Reverend Chas Wharton, Bp Wm White & The Proposed Bk Of Common Pryr," *Angl and Epis Hist*, 1989; Ed, "Var," *The Ecum Bulletin*, The Ecum Off of the Epis Ch, 1989; Auth, "God w Us: Cont Presence," Imm Ch, New Castle, Delaware, 1987; Auth, "An Introductory Hist Of Danville Vt," *Danville Town Report*, Town of Danville, Vermont, 1987; Auth, "The Dio Delaware: A Bicentennial Yearbook," The Dio Deleware, 1985. HSEC 1980; Natl Epis Historians and Archivists 1984; No Amer Acad Of Ecumenists 1990; No Amer Gld Of Change Ringers 1984-1994. drcma@crosslink.net

AGNEW JR, M L (WLa) 113 Whispering Pines Dr, Bullard TX 75757 **P-in-c S Jn The Bapt Ch Tyler TX 2010-** B Meridian MS 2/17/1942 s Martin Luther Agnew & Josephine Floyd. BA U So 1964; MDiv VTS 1967. D 6/24/1967 P 5/23/1968 Bp John M Allin. m 8/28/1965 Patricia Jane Severance c 2. Int S Cyp's Ch Lufkin TX 2008-2009; Mem Bd of Trst The CPG New York NY 1997-2007; S Ann's Ch Kennebunkport ME 1996-1999; Stndg Com on Admin & Fin Epis Ch Cntr New York NY 1994-2000; Dn S Mk's Cathd Shreveport LA 1990-2007; R Chr Epis Ch Tyler TX 1981-1990; R Trin Ch Natchez MS 1975-1981; Cn Pstr S Andr's Cathd Jackson MS 1972-1975; Cur Chr Ch Bay St Louis MS 1968-1970; Vic Ch Of The Nativ Greenwood MS 1967-1968. mla@embarqmail.com

AGUILAR, Norman (Hond) 23 Ave C 21 Calle Col Trejo, #3 Fortesque St Philip, San Pedro Sula SP ZONA8 Honduras **Dio Honduras Miami FL 1998-** B 6/16/1961 m 4/24/1991 Nimia Enriquez Menjivar c 2.

AGUILAR, Richard Joseph (SeFla) 15650 Miami Lakeway N, Miami Lakes FL 33014 **S Margarets Epis Ch Miami Lakes FL 2009-** B San Antonio TX 11/2/1956 s Raphael De La Cruz Aguilar & Fela. BA U So 1979; MDiv Epis TS of The SW 1986. D 6/22/1986 Bp Scott Field Bailey P 1/10/1987 Bp John Herbert MacNaughton. m 12/22/1984 Janet Bonilla c 1. Ch Of The Adv Brownsville TX 2004-2009; Dio Sthrn Ohio Cincinnati OH 2002-2004; R S Andr's Epis Ch Seguin TX 1996-2002; Asst S Mk's Epis Ch San Antonio TX 1993-1996; Asst Ch Of The Adv Brownsville TX 1991-1993; Asst S Paul's Epis Ch Brownsville TX 1991-1993; P-in-c S Paul's Epis Ch Brownsville TX 1988-1990; Int Ch Of The Redeem Eagle Pass TX 1987-1988; Asst Ch Of The Redeem Eagle Pass TX 1986-1987. richardaguilar70@yahoo.com

AGUILAR DE RAMIREZ, Ana Roselia (Hond) Barrio San Martin, 12 C11. 6 y 7 Ave, Puerto Cortes 21105 Honduras **Dio Honduras Miami FL 2006-; Iglesia Epis Hondurena San Pedro Sula 2006-** B Puerto Cortes 9/10/1959 d Enrique Aguilar & Julia. DIT Catolica Romana; Nuestra Senora De La Paz; DIT Programa Diocena Educaion Teologica. D 10/28/2005 Bp Lloyd Emmanuel Allen. m 12/18/1992 Jorge Ramirez Lara c 4. roselia592@yahoo.com

AHLENIUS, Robert Orson (Dal) 2541 Pinebluff Drive, Dallas TX 75228 B Chicago IL 3/17/1938 s William Hilmer Ahlenius & Kathryn Marcella. BA IL Wesl 1960; MDiv Nash 1963; MA NWU 1970. D 6/1/1963 Bp Albert A Chambers P 12/31/1963 Bp Donald H V Hallock. m 8/13/1960 Barbara Ann Barth c 4. S Justin's Canton TX 1997-1998; Long-term Supply S Jas' Epis Ch Kemp TX 1996-2003; R Trin NE Texas Epis Ch Mt Pleasant TX 1992-1995; Area Min, Purchase Area Dio Kentucky Louisville KY 1987-1992; Purchase Area Reg Coun Paducah KY 1987-1992; Dio Kansas Topeka KS 1986-1987; R Gr Ch Chanute KS 1975-1987; R Ch of the H Trin Columbus NE 1970-1975; R Gr Ch Par -Epis Columbus NE 1970-1975; Cur S Mich And All Ang Ch Mssn KS 1966-1969; Mssnr to Deaf Dio Milwaukee Milwaukee WI 1963-1966. LAND 1984-1987; RWF, Inc 1986-2002. bbahlenius38@att.net

AHLVIN, Judith L (ECR) 18325 Crystal Dr, Morgan Hill CA 95037 **Ch Of The H Sprt Campbell CA 2002-** B Santa Monica CA 3/11/1947 d Lloyd E Fondren & Lois F. BA San Jose St U 1984; BA Sch for Deacons 1998. D 6/24/1998 Bp Richard Lester Shimpfky. m 8/23/1969 Bruce R Ahlvin. D S Jn The Div Epis Ch Morgan Hill CA 2002-2003; D S Mk's Epis Ch Santa Clara CA 2000-2002; D Ch Of The H Sprt Campbell CA 1999-2000.

AHN, Matthew Y (Los) 10555 Bel Air Dr, Cherry Valley CA 92223 B Taegu KR 5/27/1936 s Theodore Ahn & Anna. BTh Yonsei U 1964; MA McCormick TS 1970. P 11/1/1975 Bp Robert C Rusack. m 8/22/1967 Grace Hae Kwak. Vic S Nich Korean Mssn Los Angeles CA 1978-1990; St. Nichols Ch Hollywood CA 1977-1989; Dio Los Angeles Los Angeles CA 1975-1976; Vic S Mary's Ch Chicago IL 1971-1976. ahnmatae@aol.com

AHN, Paul C (Chi) 5801 N Pulaski Rd #348, Chicago IL 60646 B 7/11/1938 s Eun D Ahn & Cha H. BD Hankook TS 1965; St. Mich Angl Sem 1967. D 8/4/1967 P 9/8/1967 Bp James Winchester Montgomery. m 11/15/1967 Clara Yoo c 2. Vic S Mary's Ch Chicago IL 1980-1985.

✠ AHRENS, Rt Rev Laura (Ct) 2 Cannondale Dr, Danbury CT 06810 **Bp Suffr of Connecticut Dio Connecticut Hartford CT 2004-** B Wilmington DE 8/9/1962 d Herbert Willis Ahrens & Joan. BA Pr 1984; MDiv Ya Berk 1991; DMin Hartford Sem 2000. D 6/1/1991 Bp David Elliot Johnson P 6/17/1992 Bp Vincent Waydell Warner Con 6/30/2007 for Ct. R S Jas Epis Ch Danbury CT 2000-2007; Assoc R S Lk's Par Darien CT 1995-2000; Assoc R Trin Ch Concord MA 1993-1995; Cur S Ptr's Ch Osterville MA 1991-1993. Soc Of S Jn The Evang. lahrens@ctdiocese.org

AIDNIK, Aileen Marie (NCal) 988 Collier Dr, San Leandro CA 94577 B Red Bluff CA 3/5/1945 d William Clyde Harrison & Lillian Miller. AA Chabot Coll 1974; BD H Name U 1982; BA Sch for Deacons 1990. D 12/5/1992 Bp William Edwin Swing. m 4/4/1964 Joseph C Aidnik. D S Cuth's Epis Ch Oakland CA 1992-2000. NAAD.

AIKEN JR, Charles Duval (Va) 4210 Hanover Ave, Richmond VA 23221 B Richmond VA 6/11/1937 s Charles Duval Aiken & Roberta Mary. BS W&L 1960; BD VTS 1963. D 6/15/1963 P 6/5/1964 Bp Robert Fisher Gibson Jr. m 12/30/1966 Barbara Garnett c 1. S Mk's Ch Richmond VA 1995-2006; P-in-c S Dav's Ch Aylett VA 1966-1975. buckman356@aol.com

AIKEN, Richard L (Ct) P.O. Box 1130, Truro MA 02666 B New York NY 10/11/1929 s Frank Albert Aiken & Margaret. BA Tinity Coll 1953; BD VTS 1956; EdM Harv 1967; DD Tninity Coll 1973. D 6/1/1956 Bp Frederick D Goodwin P 12/1/1956 Bp Harry S Kennedy. c 2. Chapl S Mich's Chap So Kent CT 1976-1981; So Kent Sch So Kent CT 1976-1981; The Choate Sch Wallingford CT 1971-1976; Chapl S Mich's Chap So Kent CT 1970-1971; Assoc Ch Of The H Nativ Honolulu HI 1958-1960. Auth, "The Tchg Of Rel," *Findings*; Auth, "The Tchg Of Rel," *So Kent Quarterly*.

AIKEN JR, Warwick (NC) 700 Riverside Dr, Eden NC 27288 B Memphis TN 5/8/1920 s Warwick Aiken & Jean Elizabeth. BA LSU 1942; ThM Dallas TS 1946; PDS 1950. D 7/27/1950 P 7/27/1951 Bp Duncan Montgomery Gray. m 9/7/1946 Marianne S Sewell c 2. R S Lk's Ch Eden NC 1973-1983; S Mary's Ch Eden NC 1973-1983; R Epis Ch of the Gd Shpd Charleston SC 1970-1973; R Ch Of The Mssh Rockingham NC 1967-1970; Vic S Mary's Ch Eden NC 1958-1967; R S Lk's Ch Eden NC 1955-1967; M-in-c Ch Of The Epiph Tunica MS 1950-1955. Auth, "Var arts," *Greensboro NC News and Record*, 2000; Auth, *Know the Chr*, Rockingham, NC, 1969; Auth, *The Easter Night Bible Class*, Rockingham, NC, 1968. msaiken@netpath-nc.net

AIN, Judith Pattison (ECR) 286 Thompson Rd Unit B, Watsonville CA 95076 B Hollywood CA 6/4/1953 d Robert Arthur Ain & Diantha Pattison. BS Stan 1976; MDiv CDSP 1984. D 6/29/1984 Bp Charles Shannon Mallory. D All SS Epis Ch Watsonville CA 1988-2000; Dio El Camino Real Monterey CA 1985; Assoc Calv Epis Ch Santa Cruz CA 1984-1985. Auth, "Responsive Reading," *A Recon And Healing Serv Between The Victims Of Cler Abuse And The RC Dio Oakland/Roman Cathol*, 2000. EPF, Magd Sacr Ord Of Fools, Snap. Phi Beta Kappa Stan Stanford CA 1976. judithain@stanfordalumni.org

AINSWORTH, Mark J (Pa) 262 Bent Road, Wyncote PA 19095 **R All Hallows Ch Wyncote PA 1999-** B London UK 4/10/1964 s John Dredge Ainsworth & Christine Betty. CTh Oxf 1989; ThM Lon 1992. Trans from Church Of England 8/1/1997 Bp Allen Lyman Bartlett Jr. m 5/18/1991 Claudia Lee. COM Dio Pennsylvania Philadelphia PA 2006-2011; Assoc R Ch Of S Mart-In-The-Fields Philadelphia PA 1996-1999; Asst R Washington Memi Chap Vlly Forge PA 1993-1995. Bp White PB Soc 2003; Soc for the Advancement of Chrsnty in Pennsylvania 2000-2011. MTh w dist Lon London UK 1992. rector@allhallowswyncote.org

AIONA, Darrow Lewis Kanakanui (Haw) Leeward Community College, Pearl City HI 96782 **S Mk's Ch Honolulu HI 1996-** B Honolulu HI 6/21/1935 s John Pa Aiona & Anne Mary. BA U of Hawaii 1957; MA U of Hawaii 1959; Fulbright Fellowow U of Auckland 1960; MDiv CDSP 1963. D 5/17/1963 P 12/1/1963 Bp Harry S Kennedy. m 2/26/1972 Christine Ramona Urban. S Mk's Ch Honolulu HI 1997-2007; Vic Waikiki Chap Honolulu HI 1986-1996; P-in-c S Jn's By The Sea Kaneohe HI 1971-1986; Cur S Aug's Ch New York NY 1966-1967. Auth, "Var arts". Angl Indigenous Ntwk. Bp Hanchett Hon Cn St. Andr's Cathd 2007. kanakanui35@aol.com

AIRD, Isabel May (WVa) 1209 1/2 Williams St, Parkersburg WV 26101 B Osaka JP 4/12/1927 d Hubert Cecil Sarvis & Amy Jean. BA Barnard Coll of Col 1947; MA Syr 1967; BA Med Coll of Virginia 1979. D 6/10/1995 Bp John H(enry) Smith. m 3/1/1953 Alanson Aird c 1. D The Memi Ch Of The Gd Shpd Parkersburg WV 1995-2002. isabelmay@juno.com

AIS, Jean Nesly (Hai) c/o Diocese of Haiti, Boite Postale 1309 Haiti B 9/6/1972 D 1/25/2006 P 2/18/2007 Bp Jean Zache Duracin. m 7/17/2008 Marie Christelle O Ais c 1. jnnesly@yahoo.fr

AITKEN, Ellen Bradshaw (Mass) 258 Olivier Avenue, Westmount QC H3Z 2C5 Canada **Bd Mem Epis Chapl At Harvard & Radcliffe Cambridge MA 2007-; Mem, Bp's Theol Cmsn Dio Montreal Montreal QC 2005-; Mem, Ed Bd, Sewanee Theol Revs The TS at The U So Sewanee TN 1991-** B Riverside CA 2/17/1961 d Hugh George Jeffrey Aitken & Janice Hunter. BA Harv 1982; U of St. Andrews 1983; MDiv STUSo 1986; ThD Harvard DS 1997. D 6/21/1986 P 2/8/1987 Bp Andrew Frederick Wissemann. m 12/9/1990 William R Porter. T/F on the Blessing of H Unions Dio Massachusetts Boston MA 2004-2006; Assoc S Ptr's Ch Springfield MA 1998-2003; T/F of the Diac Dio Massachusetts Boston MA 1997-2005; P Ch Of S Jn The Evang Boston MA 1989-1997; Exam Chapl Dio Wstrn Massachusetts Springfield MA 1988-1994; Co-Chair, Liturg and Mus Cmsn Dio Wstrn Massachusetts Springfield MA 1987-1989; Asst S Paul's Ch Holyoke MA 1986-1989. Auth,

"Relentless Intimacy: The Peculiar Labor of an Angl Biblic Schlr," *ATR*, 2011; Auth, "Relentless Intimacy: The Peculiar Labor of an Angl Biblic Schlr," *ATR*, 2011; Auth, "To Remember the Lord Jesus: Ldrshp and Memory in the NT," *ATR*, 2009; co-Auth, "Rejoicing and Lamenting: Imagining the Unborn in Early Chrsnty Lit," *Imagining the Fetus: Comparative Perspectives*, Oxf Press, 2009; co-Ed, "Bk," *The Bible in the Publ Sq: Reading the Signs of the Times*, Fortress Press, 2008; Auth, "Bk," *Loosening the Roots of Compassion: Meditations for H Week and Eastertide*, Cowley, 2006; Auth, "Tradition in the Mouth of the Hero: Jesus as an Interpreter of Scripture," *Performing the Gospel: Orality, Memory, and Mk*, Fortress Press, 2006; Ed, "Biblic Imagination: Scripture and the Life of FaithEssays in hon of Chris Bryan," *Sewanee Theol Revs*, 2006; Auth, "Wily, Wise, and Worldly: Instrn and the Formation of Character in the Epistle to the Hebrews," *The Changing Face of Judaism, Chrsnty and Other Greco-Roman Rel in Antiquity*, Gutersloher Verlagshaus, 2006; Auth, "The Basileia of Jesus is on the Wood: The Epistle of Barn and the Ideology of Rule," *Conflicted Boundaries in Wisdom and Apocalypticism*, SBL, 2005; Auth, "Bk," *Jesus' Death in Early Chr Memory: The Poetics of the Passion*, Vandenhoeck & Ruprecht, 2004; Auth, "Why a Phoenician? A Proposal for the Hist Occasion for the Heroikos," *Philostratuss Heroikos: Rel, and Cultural Identity in the Third Century C.E.*, SBL, 2004; co-Ed, "Bk," *Philostratus's Heroikos: Rel and Cultural Identity in the Third Century*, Soc of Biblial Lit, 2004; Auth, "The Ordering of Cmnty: NT Perspectives," *ATR*, 2003; Auth, "The Hero in the Epistle to the Hebrews: Jesus as an Ascetic Model," *Early Chr Voices: In Texts, Traditions, and Symbols: Essays in hon of François Bovon*, Brill, 2003; Auth, "The Landscape of Promise in the Apocalypse of Paul," *Walk in the Ways of Wisdom: Essays in hon of Elis Schüssler Fiorenza*, Trin Press Intl , 2003; Auth, "Portraying the Temple in Stone &Text: Arch of Tit & Hebrews," *Sewanee Theol Revs*, 2002; Auth, "The Cult of Achilleus in Philostratuss Heroikos: A Study in the Relation of Cn and Ritual," *Between Magic and Rel: Interdisciplinary Stds in Ancient Mediterranean Rel and Soc*, Rowman & Littlefield, 2001; co-Ed and Transltr, "Bk," *FLAVIUS PHILOSTRATUS: HEROIKOS*, SBL, 2001; Auth, "The Cologne Mani Codex," *Rel in Late Antiquity in Pract (Princeton)*, Pr Press, 2000; Auth, "At the Well of Living Water: Jacob Traditions in Jn 4," *The Interp of Scripture in Early Judaism & Chrsnty*, Sheffield Acad Press, 2000; Auth, "ta dromena kai ta legomena: The Eucharistic Memory of Jesus' Death in 1 Corinthians," *Harvard Theol Revs*, 1998; Co-Ed, "Questions of Mssn: On Being the Ch," *Sewanee Theol Revs*, 1997. Amer Philological Assn 2000-2010; Amer Soc For Gk And Latin Epigraphy 1998; Angl Assn of Biblic Scholars 1992; Assn Internationale d'Épigraphie Grecque et Latine 1998; Can Soc of Biblic Stds 2005; Cath Biblic Assn 2000; No Amer Patristics Soc 2000; SBL 1987. Dubose Awd for Serv STUSo 2006; Pres Angl Assn of Biblic Scholars 2002; ECF Fell ECF 1989; AB scl Harv Cambridge MA 1982; Phi Beta Kappa Harv DS Cambridge MA 1982. ellen.aitken@mcgill.ca

AITON JR, Alexander Anthony (Ia) 633 Agg Ave, Ames IA 50014 **R S Jn's By The Campus Ames IA 1991-** B Newark NJ 12/4/1949 s Alexander Aiton & Marie Whilhemenia. BBA St. Johns U 1972; MDiv GTS 1977; DMin Drew U 1990. D 6/11/1977 P 12/17/1977 Bp George E Rath. m 10/27/1973 Joan Mabee c 3. Cn Planned Giving & Ch Dvlpmt Dio Cntrl Pennsylvania Harrisburg PA 1988-1991; R S Jn's Ch Salem NJ 1984-1988; P-in-c H Trin Ch Pennsauken NJ 1982-1984; R Chr Ch Palmyra NJ 1981-1984; Cur S Geo's-By-The-River Rumson NJ 1977-1981. Hon Cn S Steph Cathd Harrisburg PA 1991. fralaiton@stjohns-ames.org

AJAX, Kesner (Hai) C/O Agape Flights Acc. #2519, 100 Airport Avenue, Venice FL 34285 **Dio Haiti Ft Lauderdale FL 1991-** B Port-au-Prince HT 4/2/1961 s Lanier Ajax & Elodie. BA Cntr Pilote de Formation Profesional Port-au-Prince HT 1986; BA Haiti TS 1989; MA Boston Coll 1997; D.Min U So Sewanee 2008. D 7/22/1990 P 3/14/1991 Bp Luc Anatole Jacques Garnier. m 7/29/1993 Marie Jardine Hyppolite c 1. EPF 1989; Soc S Margareth 1985; Soc of S Jn the Evang 1987. Kesnerajax@yahoo.com

AKER, Edwina Sievers (Mont) 32413 Skidoo Ln, Polson MT 59860 **Int R S Pat's Epis Ch Bigfork MT 2005-** B Albuquerque NM 1/26/1938 d Edwin Ralph Sievers & Dorothy Alice. BA U of Montana 1959. D 10/30/1982 P 11/ 17/1984 Bp David Bell Birney IV. m 10/18/1959 Charles Aker c 2. Int R Chr Epis Ch Kalispell MT 2008-2009; Int R S Andr's Epis Ch Polson MT 2006-2007; Stndg Com Dio Montana Helena MT 1997-2000; R S Andr's Epis Ch Polson MT 1996-2004; Vic Ch Of H Nativ Meridian ID 1992-1993; Vic S Jas Ch Mtn Hm ID 1988-1992; COM Dio Idaho Boise ID 1985-1991; D S Steph's Boise ID 1982-1984. akercne@optimum.net

AKERS III, John Shelley (NC) 3903 Cascade Dr, Greensboro NC 27410 B Lexington KY 11/11/1932 s John Shelley Akers & Ann Elizabeth. BD Epis TS In Kentucky 1962; BA U of Louisville 1962. D 6/9/1962 P 12/13/1962 Bp William R Moody. m 8/8/1964 Sandra Alexander. Sr Cur H Trin Epis Ch Greensboro NC 1984-1997; S Mich And All Ang Ch Dallas TX 1977-1983; R S Ptr's Ch Paris KY 1968-1977; Asst Ch Of The Gd Shpd Lexington KY 1964-1968; Vic S Phil's Ch Harrodsburg KY 1962-1964. AKERSHOME@ MSN.COM

AKIN, Mary Anne (Ala) 100 Potters Wheel Rd, Madison AL 35758 **Assoc Ch Of The Nativ Epis Huntsville AL 2007-** B Nashville TN 9/18/1950 d Earl Mantford Shahan & Mary Dorothy. BA Webster U 1972; MDiv Candler TS Emory U 1975; Cert Amer Assn of Profsnl Chapl 1992. D 9/9/1977 Bp Bennett Jones Sims P 7/27/1978 Bp Furman Stough. m 6/20/1987 Joseph W Akin. Assoc S Steph's Ch Richmond VA 2006-2007; Assoc R Ch Of The H Comf Vienna VA 1999-2002; R Chr Ch Milford DE 1998; Cn Pstr S Jn's Epis Cathd Knoxville TN 1994-1995; R S Jas The Less Madison TN 1986-1987; Pstr TS The TS at The U So Sewanee TN 1985-1986; Assoc S Andrews's Epis Ch Birmingham AL 1982-1984; S Alb's Ch Birmingham AL 1979-1982. Auth, "Listening to the Elder Voices, Chapl Today," *Vol. 18 #1*, 2002; Auth, "Saturday Night," *Wmn Uncommon Prayers*, Morehouse, 2000; Auth, "Mudsong," *Journ of Pstr Care*, 1993. AEHC Natl Secretar 1992; Bd Cert Chapl, Amer Assn of Profsnl. MDiv mcl Emory U 1975; BA cl Webster Coll 1972. makin@nativity-hsv.org

AKIN, Mary Barbara (NwPa) 201 Hillcrest Cir, Grove City PA 16127 B Chicago IL 1/31/1932 d Richard Kirkbride Akin & Margaret Mary. BA S Xavier Coll Chicago IL 1962; MA U Chi 1965; PhD U Chi 1970; Cert SWTS 1978. Rec from Roman Catholic 3/1/1974 Bp Donald James Davis. Vic Ch Of The Epiph Grove City PA 1985-2008; Mem Epis Ch Cntr New York NY 1985-1991; Dep GC Dio NW Pennsylvania Erie PA 1985-1988; D Ch Of The Redeem Hermitage PA 1979-1983. "An Intro to Hist Resrch," Copley Pub Grp, 1991. mbakin@zoominternet.net

AKINA, Eleanore Mayo (Haw) 1237 Mokulua Dr, Kailua HI 96734 B Philadelphia PA 5/11/1921 d Leroy Dimlow Green & Charlotte. BA Swarthmore Coll 1942; MD U of Pennsylvania 1945. D 11/11/1983 Bp Edmond Lee Browning. D Emm Epis Ch Kailua HI 1983-1999. akinae001@hawaii.rr.com

AKINKUGBE, Felix Olagboye (FtW) 2995 Celian Dr, Grand Prairie TX 75052 B Ondo NG 9/16/1944 s Emmanuel Akinkugbe & Simisola. BA Bowie St U 1972; MA U Pgh 1974; Emml Of Theol Ibadan Ng 1993. Trans from Church Of Nigeria 2/6/2001 Bp Jack Leo Iker. m 8/30/1971 Margaret Falana c 3. Dio Ft Worth Ft Worth TX 2000-2006; Vic S Phil The Apos Arlington TX 2000; Cur S Jos's Epis Ch Grand Prairie TX 1999; Asst P S Lk's In The Meadow Epis Ch Ft Worth TX 1998-1999. Auth, "The Living Faith," Ibadan U Press, 1997; Auth, "Living w God In Pryr Fasting And Faith," Ibadan U Press, 1997. Bro Of S Andrews 1999; Full Gospel Busmn Fllshp Intl 1990; Rotary Club Intl 1993. gboyea@sbcglobal.net

AKINS, Keith Edward (Kan) 900 Sw 31st St Apt 219, Topeka KS 66611 **D Dio Kansas Topeka KS 1993-; D Gr Cathd Topeka KS 1993-** B Salina KS 5/14/ 1926 s Murphy Akins & Bertha Beatrice. BS Kansas St Teachers Coll 1950; MA U MI 1957. D 12/11/1993 Bp William Edward Smalley. m 9/3/1948 Reeta DeAun O'Haro c 6. Hall of Fame Awd Kansas St HS Activities Assn. rdoha@ cox.net

AKIYAMA, Diana D (Los) 2745 Glendower Ave, Los Angeles CA 90027 B Wheeler OR 10/24/1958 d Saburo Akiyama & Betty. BS U of Oregon 1981; MDiv CDSP 1988; PhD USC 2001. D 6/19/1988 P 4/1/1989 Bp Rustin Ray Kimsey. m 4/13/1991 Michael L Jackson. All SS Ch Pasadena CA 1997. dakiyama@oxy.edu

AKRIDGE, Alan M (Ga) 108 Worthing Rd, St Simons Island GA 31522 **R S Mk's Ch Brunswick GA 2009-** B Mobile AL 7/21/1967 s David Hawthorn Akridge & Ann Nibbs. MA VTS 1998; MDiv Wake Forest U 2003. D 5/29/ 2004 Bp Robert Hodges Johnson P 12/4/2004 Bp Granville Porter Taylor. m 9/26/1998 Kathleen Harrison Lawson c 2. Assoc R S Alb's Ch Hickory NC 2004-2009. aakridge@saintmarksepiscopal.com

ALAGNA, Frank J (NY) Po Box 1, Rhinecliff NY 12574 **P-in-c Ch Of The H Cross Kingston NY 2011-** B Brooklyn NY 9/8/1945 s Anthony Joseph Alagna & Marie Lucille. MDiv Maryknoll TS 1970; ThM Maryknoll TS 1971; MA U of Connecticut 1977; PhD U of Connecticut 1978. Rec from Roman Catholic 12/19/1982 Bp Paul Moore Jr. m John Meehan c 1. S Andr's Ch Beacon NY 2008-2010; Vic S Marg's Ch Staatsburg NY 1989-2006. fjalagna@gmail.com

ALAN, Stacy Evelyn (Chi) 5540 S Woodlawn Ave, Chicago IL 60637 **Brent Hse (U Of Chicago) Chicago IL 2005-** B Lafayette IN 6/11/1964 d Franklin E Alan & Eliene S. BA Seattle U 1985; MDiv UTS 1992. D 6/13/1998 P 12/ 19/1998 Bp Richard Frank Grein. m 12/11/1993 Ignacio A Salinas c 2. Asst to R S Lk's Par Kalamazoo MI 1999-2004; Ch Of The H Apos New York NY 1992-1998. Alpha Sigma Nu 1983. alansalina@aol.com

ALAVA VILLAREAL, Geronimo Javier (EcuL) Casilla 0901-5250, Guayaquil Ecuador **Litoral Dio Ecuador Guayaquil EQ EC 2004-** B Guayquil ECUADOR 5/11/1968 s Geronimo Alava & Lillian. Litoral Sem Guayaquil Ec 2001. D 7/14/2002 P 10/12/2004 Bp Alfredo Morante-España. m 7/23/1988 Cecilia Garcia c 4.

ALBANESE, Nicholas (Del) 806 Alpha Rd, Wind Gap PA 18091 B Bethlehem PA 5/9/1924 s James V Albanese & Clara. BA U So 1960; LTh STUSo 1963; Cr Spanish Lang Sch 1963. D 8/6/1963 Bp Frederick J Warnecke P 3/3/1964 Bp David Emrys Richards. m 8/7/1965 Angie DeNardo c 2. P-in-c S Mary's Epis Ch Wind Gap PA 1994-2005; Int S Jn's Epis Ch Hamlin PA 1991-1993;

Supply P All SS Epis Ch Delmar DE 1989-1991; R S Phil's Ch Laurel DE 1979-1989; R Trin Epis Ch Carbondale PA 1970-1979; S Jas-S Geo Epis Ch Jermyn PA 1966-1979; Vic Chr Ch Forest City PA 1966-1970. Gd Samar. aana70@gmail.com

ALBANO, Randolph Vicente Nolasco (Haw) St. Paul's Episcopal Church, 229 Queen Emma Square, Honolulu HI 96813 **Stndg Com Dio Hawaii Honolulu HI 2009-; S Pauls Ch Honolulu HI 1999-; Vic S Paul's Epis Ch Honolulu HI 1999-** B Bacarra Ilocos Norte PH 11/26/1955 s Alejo Ver Albano & Florencia Clutarco. AA Trin of Quezon City PH 1975; B. Th. S Andr's TS Manila PH 1980; MDiv S Andr's TS Manila PH 1988. Rec from Philippine Independent Church 6/10/2000 as Priest Bp Richard Sui On Chang. m 1/2/1989 Minina Santiago Javier c 2. Dio Hawaii Honolulu HI 2000-2001. Soc of the Gd Shpd Phillipines 2000. saintpaul@kahala.net

ALBERGATE, Scott P (La) St. Paul's Episcopal Church, 6249 Canal Blvd, New Orleans LA 70124 **R S Paul's Ch New Orleans LA 2009-** B Glen Rock NJ 8/25/1955 s Alfred Albert Albergate & Evelyn Anna. BA Seton Hall U 1977; JD New York Law Sch 1986; MDiv Nash 2000; DMin SWTS 2007. D 12/18/1999 P 6/17/2000 Bp Jack Leo Iker. m 9/15/2001 Katherine Korge. Cn Dio Louisiana Baton Rouge LA 2007-2009; R The Epis Ch Of The Ascen Middletown OH 2006-2007; R S Jn's Ch Gap PA 2003-2005; R S Lk's Ch Eastchester NY 2001-2003; Asst R S Mart In The Fields Ch Keller TX 2000-2001. "Sermon, Dreamers," *Preaching As Prophetic Calling: Sermons That Wk XII*, Morehouse Pub, 2004; Auth, "Var arts," *Living Ch*. The Angl Soc 1998. Polly Bond Awd ECom 2001; MDiv cl Nash Nashotah WI 2000. scottalbergate@gmail.com

ALBERT II, Edwin Edward (SO) 1924 Timberidge Dr., Loveland OH 45140 **S Barn Epis Ch Montgomery OH 2005-** B Bangor ME 4/16/1957 BA S Jos Sem Coll 1981; MDiv Notre Dame Sem 1985; MBA U Cinc 1992. Rec from Roman Catholic 6/3/2001 as Priest Bp Herbert Thompson Jr. m 8/20/1988 Susan Jane Gibson c 3. ted.albert@att.net

ALBERT, Hilario Alejandro (NY) 535 King St, Port Chester NY 10573 **S Ptr's Ch Port Chester NY 2004-; D Ch Of The H Trin New York NY 2003-** B La Romana DO 10/21/1947 s Huntley Albert & Susan. MDiv NYTS; BA/BS R.U.M. Mayaguez PR 1974. D 3/8/2003 P 9/20/2003 Bp Mark Sean Sisk. m 4/1/1995 Sandra Gonzalez c 3. machoh@aol.com

ALBERT III, Jules Gilmore (La) 6249 Canal Blvd, New Orleans LA 70124 **D S Paul's Ch New Orleans LA 2010-** B New Orleans LA 9/16/1953 s Jules G Albert & Nancy H. D 12/4/2010 Bp Morris King Thompson Jr. m 6/5/1976 Margaret Albert c 2. jay@jaymarconstruction.com

ALBINGER JR, William Joseph (Haw) PO Box 411, Lahaina HI 96767 **H Innoc' Epis Ch Lahaina HI 2005-** B 11/27/1945 D 9/13/2003 Bp John Palmer Croneberger P 4/17/2004 Bp Martin Gough Townsend. S Jn's Epis Ch Boonton NJ 2003-2004.

ALBRECHT, John Herman (Mich) 293 Scottsdale Dr, Troy MI 48084 B Detroit MI 2/1/1928 s Herman Fred Albrecht & Esther Marie. BA Amh 1954; MDiv VTS 1959. D 6/13/1959 Bp Robert McConnell Hatch P 5/1/1961 Bp Robert Lionne DeWitt. m 11/7/1986 Christa Tews c 5. Long-Term Supply S Dav's Ch Southfield MI 2007-2008; Asst Chr Ch Detroit MI 2004-2007; Long-Term Supply S Columba Ch Detroit MI 1998-2004; Int Trin Ch S Clair Shores MI 1996-1998; R S Mary's-In-The-Hills Ch Lake Orion MI 1973-1981; R S Jn's Ch Royal Oak MI 1969-1973; R S Kath's Ch Williamston MI 1965-1969; MRI Cmsn Dio Michigan Detroit MI 1964-1965; Asst Min Chr Ch Cranbrook Bloomfield Hills MI 1961-1965; Asst Min Chr Ch Cranbrook Bloomfield Hills MI 1961-1965; Marquis Fllshp Chr Ch Cranbrook Bloomfield Hills MI 1959-1960. Fell Coll of Preachers, Washington, D.C. 1969. jctewsalb@aol.com

ALBRETHSEN, Karen Anne (Nev) 777 Sage St, Elko NV 89801 **P S Paul's Epis Ch Elko NV 2008-** B Jerome ID 6/22/1954 d Holger Albraethsen & Anne Jeanette Winn. BA Adams St Coll 1976; MLIS U CB 1991. D 10/24/2008 P 5/9/2009 Bp Dan Thomas Edwards. m 6/27/1987 Frederick B Lee c 7. kalbrethsen@yahoo.com

ALBRIGHT, John Taylor (WMass) 525 Suffield St, Agawam MA 01001 **Assoc S Mk's Epis Ch E Longmeadow MA 2000-; Southwick Cmnty Epis Ch Southwick MA 1998-** B Norfolk VA 12/17/1957 s John Johnson Albright & Catharine Dudley. S Mary Sem; BA U of Maryland 1979; MDiv Gordon-Conwell TS 1988. D 6/20/1998 P 12/19/1998 Bp Gordon Paul Scruton. m 6/21/1986 Katharine F Fleming c 2. Cur S Mk's Epis Ch E Longmeadow MA 1998-1999. Glor2God@comcast.net

ALBRIGHT, Timothy Scott (Be) 46 S. Laurel St., Hazleton PA 18201 **Cur S Ptr's Epis Ch Hazleton PA 2009-** B Pottstown PA 10/5/1959 s Clarence R Albright & Barbara Y. BS Indstrl Engr Leh 1981; Bp's Sch For Ord Mnstry Dio Bethlehem 2008; Dplma GTS 2009. D 2/2/2009 Bp John Palmer Croneberger P 9/29/2009 Bp Paul Victor Marshall. m 6/18/1983 Sharon Buehler c 2. D S Ptr's Epis Ch Hazleton PA 2009. talbright@ptd.net

ALBURY, Ronald Graham (NJ) 28 Maine Trl, Medford NJ 08055 **Pstr Assoc S Ptr's Ch Medford NJ 2003-** B Cranford NJ 6/12/1930 s Charles Gilbert Albury & Mabelle. BA Ripon Coll Ripon WI 1951; BD SWTS 1954; STM Tem 1958; EdD NYU 1976. D 5/8/1954 Bp Wallace J Gardner P 11/20/1954 Bp Alfred L Banyard. m 5/27/2000 Daryl Van Duzer c 7. Chapl for Ret Cler Dio New Jersey Trenton NJ 1995-2000; R H Cross Epis Ch No Plainfield NJ 1970-1995; R Chr Ch Epis Shrewsbury NJ 1964-1970; R Chr Ch So Amboy NJ 1957-1964; Cur Gr Ch Merchantville NJ 1954-1957. Auth, "arts," *Living Ch*, Vintage Voice, 2006. Cmnty of S Jn the Bapt 1994. Baha'i Race Unity Day Awd 1985; Hon Cn Trin Cathd Trenton NJ 1979. darylalbury@comcast.net

ALCORN, James Krammer (Tex) 906 Sugar Mountain Ct, Sugar Land TX 77478 B Washington DC 1/24/1942 s James Albert Alcorn & Frances. Geo 1962; BS Trin U San Antonio TX 1965; MDiv STUSo 1971. D 6/8/1971 Bp Richard Earl Dicus P 12/19/1971 Bp Harold Cornelius Gosnell. m 10/27/1967 Nancy K Wingert c 2. Dir Pstr Care Cullen Memi Chap Houston TX 1986-2005; Dir Pstr Care St Lk's Epis Hosp Houston TX 1986-2005; R Ch Of The Epiph Houston TX 1982-1986; R Ch Of The Epiph Kingsville TX 1977-1982; S Lk's Epis Ch San Antonio TX 1975-1977; Chapl/Dir Texas Mltry Inst San Antonio TX 1974-1977; Assoc Chr Epis Ch San Antonio TX 1971-1974. Auth, *AIDS: One Life to Give*; Contrib, *Essays on Human Relatns*. jameskalcorn@aol.com

ALDAY, Kristen Nowell (CFla) PO Box 1497, Winter Park FL 32790 **Archd Dio Cntrl Florida Orlando FL 2010-** B Dalton GA 11/17/1962 d David M Nowell & Hazel G. BA Rol 1985; MA Asbury TS 2010. D 12/18/2004 Bp John Wadsworth Howe. m 3/26/1983 Thomas G Alday. D Epis Ch Of The H Sprt Apopka FL 2005-2007. THEREV@INTERLACHEN.NET

ALDER, Steve (U) 3218 Oakcliff Dr, Salt Lake City UT 84124 **Archd Dio Utah Salt Lake City UT 2011-; D S Paul's Ch Salt Lake City UT 2006-** B Albuquerque NM 8/29/1956 s John Jacob Alder & Marilyn Joan. BA Pepperdine U 1977. D 6/10/2006 Bp Carolyn Tanner Irish. m 10/3/2008 Richard John Grennon. Assn for Epis Deacons 2004. aldersteve@mindspring.com

ALDERSON, Frank Carleton (Chi) 1306 Brookside Dr, Rochelle IL 61068 **Died 11/28/2009** B Streator IL 3/2/1917 D 5/30/1946 P 12/1/1946 Bp Wallace E Conkling.

ALDRICH, Dawn Marie (NMich) 1310 Ashmun St, Sault Sainte Marie MI 49783 **D S Jas Ch Of Sault S Marie Sault Ste Marie MI 2006-** B Grand Rapids MI 1/20/1938 d Myron Curtis & Dawn. D 5/28/2006 Bp James Arthur Kelsey. m 7/27/1991 Robert Paul Aldrich c 3. daldrich@eup.k12.mi.us

ALDRICH JR, Kenneth Davis (NJ) 400 4th St., Huntingdon PA 16652 B Philadelphia PA 4/13/1941 s Kenneth Davis Aldrich & Janice Kathryn. U of Paris-Sorbonne FR 1962; BA Trin Hartford CT 1963; MDiv PDS 1966; PrTS 1968; STM PDS 1973; DMin GTF 1997. D 4/23/1966 P 10/29/1966 Bp Alfred L Banyard. m 5/4/1974 Sharon C Aldrich c 3. Dn Monmouth Convoc Dio New Jersey Trenton NJ 1999-2002; Dioc Coun Dio New Jersey Trenton NJ 1989-1993; R Trin Epis Ch Red Bank NJ 1980-2005; Chapt Major Trin Cathd Trenton NJ 1978-1980; R S Lk's Ch Westville NJ 1970-1979; Vic S Jn The Evang Ch Blackwood NJ 1968-1970; Cur H Trin Ch Collingswood NJ 1966-1968. Auth, *Television Dialogue*, WPVI-TV, 1973; Auth, "Serv rendered in Rite I Lang," *The Cranmer Gld*; Auth, "arts," *LivCh*. Mercersburg Soc 1994. trinity@monmouth.com

ALDRICH, Robert Paul (NMich) 1310 Ashmun St, Sault Ste Marie MI 49783 **Mus Dir/Org S Jas Ch Of Sault S Marie Sault Ste Marie MI 1970-** B Sault Ste Marie MI 11/5/1943 s Paul Aldrich & Virginia. BA Cntrl Michigan U 1965; MA Cntrl Michigan U 1967. D 11/28/2005 P 5/28/2006 Bp James Arthur Kelsey. m 7/27/1991 Dawn Marie Aldrich. daldrich@eup.k12.mi.us

ALEXANDER, Bruce Ames (Me) 292 Alexander Rd, Dresden ME 04342 B Rockland ME 8/6/1930 s Leonard Ezekiel Alexander & Nettie Mae. D 5/28/1983 Bp Frederick Barton Wolf P 7/5/1998 Bp Chilton Abbie Richardson Knudsen. m 9/9/1953 Marjorie Moody c 4. St Mths Epis Ch Richmond ME 1995-2005; R's Vic Chr Ch Gardiner ME 1983-2000.

ALEXANDER, Conor Matthew (SVa) 431 Massachusetts Ave, Norfolk VA 23508 **P-in-c S Fran Ch Virginia Bch VA 2010-** B Syracuse NY 12/29/1978 s Larry Alexander & Sandra. BS Cor Ithaca NY 2007; MDiv VTS 2007. D 6/9/2007 Bp Gladstone Bailey Adams III P 12/10/2007 Bp John Clark Buchanan. m 5/20/2006 Samantha Ann Vincent-Alexander. Asst Chr and S Lk's Epis Ch Norfolk VA 2007-2010. conormat@yahoo.com

ALEXANDER, George Moyer (At) 3468 Summerford Ct, Marietta GA 30062 B Louisville KY 12/21/1936 s Jesse W Alexander & Reella O. BA Cntrl St Coll Wilberforce OH 1958; BD Sthrn Bapt TS Louisville KY 1962; MA Col 1971; DMin Pittsburgh TS 1984; MPA Georgia St U 1990. D 10/23/1993 P 1/1/1994 Bp Frank Kellogg Allan. m 5/22/1965 Norma Jean Moody. All SS Epis Ch Atlanta GA 1993-2001. alexander3468@aol.com

ALEXANDER, Gerald G (Fla) 4311 Ortega Forest Dr, Jacksonville FL 32210 **Assoc All SS Epis Ch Jacksonville FL 2008-; Supply Asst Dio Florida Jacksonville FL 1998-** B Jacksonville FL 2/24/1948 s John Thomas Alexander & Claudia Claire. BA Wofford Coll 1970; JD Stetson U 1973; MDiv GTS 1981. D 6/7/1981 Bp Frank Stanley Cerveny P 1/24/1982 Bp Paul Moore Jr. R Ch of S Jude Wantagh NY 1996-1998; Int Trin Epis Ch Roslyn NY 1995-1996; S Paul's Ch Glen Cove NY 1994-1996; Asst S Barth's Ch New

York NY 1993-1995; Asst Ch Of The Gd Shpd New York NY 1989-1992; Vic Calv and St Geo New York NY 1981-1989. galexander@allsaintsjax.org

ALEXANDER, Jane Biggs (WLa) 2015 East Northside Dr., Jackson MS 39211 B Jackson MS 12/4/1939 d Thomas Jones Biggs & Louise Wallis. Tul 1959; CAS Ya Berk 1990; MDiv Yale DS 1990; BD Millsaps Coll 1997. D 5/31/1990 Bp Duncan Montgomery Gray Jr P 1/19/1991 Bp Arthur Edward Walmsley. m 10/15/2007 John Davidson Alexander c 3. Exam Chapl Dio Wstrn Louisiana Alexandria LA 1998-2006; Cn Pstr S Mk's Cathd Shreveport LA 1994-2006; COM Dio Wstrn Louisiana Alexandria LA 1994-1998; Asst S Jas Ch Hartford CT 1991-1993; S Jas's Ch W Hartford CT 1991-1993; Exec Asst to Dn Ya Berk New Haven CT 1990-1991; D S Paul And S Jas New Haven CT 1990-1991. Hicks Prize Ya Berk 1990. jwba39@yahoo.com

ALEXANDER, Jason (Ark) The Episcopal Diocese of Arkansas, P.O. Box 164668, Little Rock AR 72216 **Cn Dio Arkansas Little Rock AR 2009-** B Hot Springs AR 1/11/1978 s Drew Noble Alexander & Twylla. BA Hendrix Coll 2000; MDiv CDSP 2007. D 12/4/2006 Bp Mark Lawrence Mac Donald P 6/7/2007 Bp Marc Handley Andrus. m 7/30/2005 Kathryn Bellm c 3. Cur Trin Cathd Little Rock AR 2007-2009. jloganalexander@gmail.com

ALEXANDER, John David (RI) 974 Pine St, Seekonk MA 02771 **R S Steph's Ch Providence RI 2000-** B Belfast Northern Ireland 4/14/1958 s Harold Rutherford Alexander & Joyce Milicent. BA Jn Hopkins U 1979; MA Jn Hopkins U 1980; MDiv VTS 1992; STM Nash 2004. D 6/13/1992 P 6/5/1993 Bp Allen Lyman Bartlett Jr. m 5/21/1988 Elizabeth Mary Morgan c 2. R Ch Of The Ascen Staten Island NY 1994-2000; Asst S Mary's Ch Wayne PA 1992-1994; Ya Berk New Haven CT 1987-1988. SSC 1994. Phi Beta Kappa JHU Baltimore MD 1979. rector@sstephens.necoxmail.com

✠ ALEXANDER, Rt Rev J(ohn) Neil (At) 2744 Peachtree Rd Nw, Atlanta GA 30305 **Bp Of Atlanta Dio Atlanta Atlanta GA 2001-** B Winston-Salem NC 1/23/1954 s Jasper D Alexander & Jeannette Kelly. BA Moravian TS 1976; MA U of So Carolina 1979; MDiv Luth Theol Sthrn Sem 1980; ThD GTS 1993; DD GTS 2001; DD STUSo 2002. D 6/11/1988 P 11/18/1988 Bp George Phelps Mellick Belshaw Con 7/7/2001 for At. m 1/10/1976 Angela Lynn Tesh c 3. Prof The TS at The U So Sewanee TN 1997-2001; Trin Ch Prof Of Liturg & Preaching The GTS New York NY 1995-1997; Trin Ch Assoc Prof Of Liturg & Preaching The GTS New York NY 1989-1993; Vstng Prof Ya Berk New Haven CT 1987-1988. Auth, "w Ever Joyful Hearts," Ch Pub Inc, 1999; Auth, "Waiting For The Coming," Pstr Press, 1993; Auth, "Time & Cmnty," Pstr Press, 1990; Auth, ",Luther's Reform Of The Daily Off," *Wrshp*, 1983. Acad Of Homil; Liturg Conf; No Amer Acad Of Liturg; Societas Liturgica. Hon Cn Dio Bethlehem 1986. jnalexander@gmail.com

ALEXANDER JR, Joseph Randolph (NY) 1415 Pelhamdale Ave, Pelham NY 10803 **R Par Of Chr The Redeem Pelham NY 2000-** B Marion VA 4/9/1966 s Joseph Randolph Alexander & Mildred Lucille. BA U of Virginia 1988; MDiv GTS 1994. D 6/9/1994 Bp A(rthur) Heath Light P 12/10/1994 Bp Craig Barry Anderson. m 8/22/1998 Patricia Phaneuf c 3. Asst R S Paul's Par Baltimore MD 1997-1999; Cur S Jn's Ch Larchmont NY 1994-1997. Omicron Delta Kappa. Mdiv cl GTS New York NY 1994. rectorchristchurch@hotmail.com

ALEXANDER, Kathryn Bellm (Ark) CHRIST CHURCH, 509 SCOTT ST, LITTLE ROCK AR 72201 **Stndg Com Mem Dio Arkansas Little Rock AR 2011-; Assoc R Chr Epis Ch Little Rock AR 2007-** B Long Beach CA 12/8/1972 d James William Bellm & Claire Frances. PhD candidate Grad Theol Un; BA Mills Coll 1995; MTS Harvard DS 1998. D 6/4/2005 P 12/3/2005 Bp William Edwin Swing. m 7/30/2005 Jason Alexander c 3. Fell ECF 2002. katebalexander@gmail.com

ALEXANDER, Patricia Phaneuf (NY) 1415 Pelhamdale Ave, Pelham NY 10803 **Actg Middle and Upper Sch Chapl S Andr's Epis Sch Potomac MD 2011-** B Boston MA 9/26/1966 d Edgar Alfred Phaneuf & Dorothy May. BA Ya 1988; MA Mid 1994; MDiv VTS 2001. D 3/10/2001 Bp Richard Frank Grein P 9/16/2001 Bp Mark Sean Sisk. m 8/22/1998 Joseph Randolph Alexander c 1. Vic Gr Ch Bronx NY 2004-2011; Asst S Matt's Ch Bedford NY 2001-2005. Mdiv cl VTS Alexandria VA 2001; Ba mcl Ya New Haven CT 1988. revppa@aol.com

ALEXANDER, Sharon Ann (La) 4499 Sharp Rd, Mandeville LA 70471 **P-in-c S Mich's Epis Ch Mandeville LA 2011-** B Edinburg TX 12/17/1959 d Ralph L Alexander & LuAnn. BA U of Texas 1981; MBA U of Texas 1985; JD SMU 1990; MDiv Perkins TS - SMU 2010. D 2/2/2011 P 8/6/2011 Bp Morris King Thompson Jr. SHARONANNALEXANDER@YAHOO.COM

ALEXANDER, Stephen Gray (Lex) 5300 Hamilton Ave Apt 906, Cincinnati OH 45224 B Jacksonville FL 9/25/1940 s George Moyer Alexander & Mary Danto. BA Ken 1962; MDiv VTS 1965. D 6/29/1965 Bp John Vander Horst P 4/18/1966 Bp William Evan Sanders. c 2. S Paul's Ch Newport KY 1981-1996; Dio Lexington Lexington KY 1981-1990; R H Trin Epis Ch Fayetteville NC 1977-1979; Asst S Martins-In-The-Field Columbia SC 1973-1977; R S Lk's Epis Ch Jacksonville FL 1968-1972; P-in-c Ch Of The Redeem Shelbyville TN 1966-1968; D S Ptr's Ch Columbia TN 1965-1966. sgxander@fuse.net

ALEXANDER, William David (Okla) PO Box 846, Pryor OK 74362 B Chicago IL 6/14/1953 s Lulius Alexander & Helen. ThD Carolina U; ThM SWTS; BS Missouri Vlly Coll 1975; MDiv SWTS 1993. D 12/26/1987 Bp Frank Tracy Griswold III P 9/1/1993 Bp Robert Manning Moody. m 11/4/1978 Connie Hill. R S Paul's Ch Claremore OK 1993-2000; D S Jn's Epis Ch Naperville IL 1993.

ALEXANDRE, Hickman (LI) 260 Beaver Dam Road, Brookhaven NY 11719 **Archd of Suffolk Dio Long Island Garden City NY 2011-; P-in-c S Mk's Epis Ch Medford NY 2011-; P-in-c S Jas Ch Brookhaven NY 2002-** B Brooklyn NY 11/23/1973 s Matthieu Alexandre & Marie. BS CUNY 1995; MDiv SWTS 2000. D 6/29/2000 Bp Rodney Rae Michel P 1/20/2001 Bp Orris George Walker Jr. m 7/28/2001 Pierrette Jean-Mary Alexandre c 1. P-in-c S Andr's Ch Mastic Bch NY 2002-2007; Asst R and Chapl S Ptr's by-the-Sea Epis Ch Bay Shore NY 2000-2002. hialex@hotmail.com

ALEXANDRE, Soner (Hai) PO Box 407139, C/O Lynx Air, Fort Lauderdale FL 33340 **Dio Haiti Ft Lauderdale FL 2002-** B 11/5/1970 D.

ALEXIS, Alicia (NC) PO Box 20427, Greensboro NC 27420 B Trinidad WI 2/2/1955 d George Alexis & Cynthia. MS U of Maryland 1986; MA U of Maryland 2003; MDiv Bex 2005. D 6/24/2006 P 3/25/2008 Bp John Leslie Rabb. S Jn's Ch Havre De Gr MD 2008-2009; Ch Of The Redeem Greensboro NC 2008; H Cross Ch St MD 2008; S Phil's Ch Annapolis MD 2006. alexisnursing@msn.com

ALEXIS, Judith (Ct) 5 Rockridge Dr, Norwalk CT 06854 **Dio Connecticut Hartford CT 2009-** B New York NY 2/22/1970 d Jean Baptists Alexis. CUNY; ALA Broward Cmnty Coll 2003; DST Epis TS of The SW 2006. D 7/22/2006 Bp James Hamilton Ottley P 4/13/2007 Bp Mark Hollingsworth Jr. Trin Cathd Cleveland OH 2006-2009. judithalexis@yahoo.com

ALFORD, Billy J (Ga) 3041 Hummingbird Ln, Augusta GA 30906 **S Alb's Epis Ch Augusta GA 1992-** B Sylvester GA 1/18/1953 s M H Alford & Johnnie Mae. BA Albany St U 1976; AA Darton Coll 1976; MDiv VTS 1992. D 6/11/1992 P 3/25/1993 Bp Harry Woolston Shipps. m 8/16/1975 Patricia Ann Randall c 2. STALBANSAUGUSTA@BELLSOUTH.NET

ALFORD JR, H(arold) Bennett (Ala) 680 Calder St, Beaumont TX 77701 B Albertville AL 1/7/1948 s Harold Bennett Alford & Eunice Lee. BS U So 1970; MDiv SWTS 1987. D 6/15/1987 Bp William Hopkins Folwell P 1/4/1988 Bp James Barrow Brown. m 4/1/1972 Lynn Dugan c 1. R Trin Ch Wetumpka AL 2006-2011; S Mk's Ch Beaumont TX 2003-2006; R S Geo's Epis Ch New Orleans LA 1991-2003; Asst To R S Geo's Epis Ch New Orleans LA 1987-1991; S Paul's Ch New Orleans LA 1987-1991. benajr@aol.com

ALFORD, Joseph Stanley Trowbidge (WTenn) PO Box 513, Ripley TN 38063 **Chapl - Cbury Hse Dio Kansas Topeka KS 1989-** B Memphis TN 4/30/1945 s Joseph Foutz Alford & Georgia Arlene. BA SW At Memphis 1967; MA U of Memphis 1974; MDiv GTS 1978. D 1/29/1978 Bp William F Gates Jr P 4/1/1979 Bp William Evan Sanders. m 5/11/1976 Julie Trowbridge c 2. Cnvnr - Commision On Sprtl Dvlpmt Dio Kansas Topeka KS 1992-2005; Cbury At Kansas U Lawr KS 1989-2005; Assoc Calv Ch Memphis TN 1986-1991; Dio E Tennessee Knoxville TN 1985-1986; Cmncatn Off Dio Tennessee Nashville TN 1982-1986; Dio Tennessee Nashville TN 1979-1984; Vic S Fran' Ch Norris TN 1979-1982; D S Jn's Epis Cathd Knoxville TN 1978-1979. ESMHE. Awd For Merit Associated Ch Presses. jalford@covingtone.com

ALFORD, Wiliam (CPa) 302 S Liberty St, Centreville MD 21617 **S Andr's In The Vlly Harrisburg PA 2009-** B Coronado CA 1/7/1949 s William Talor Alford & Frances Seeley. BS Pk Coll Parkville MO 1987; MDiv Epis TS of The SW 1995. D 1/25/1995 P 8/1/1995 Bp Larry Earl Maze. m 3/19/2005 Katherine Gunn Lester. S Jas Ch Lancaster PA 2008; Dio Cntrl Pennsylvania Harrisburg PA 2003-2008; R S Paul's Ch Centreville MD 1999-2003; Dio Arkansas Little Rock AR 1998-1999; Vic S Matt's Epis Ch Benton AR 1997-1999; Cur Intern S Matt's Epis Ch Benton AR 1995-1997. S Andr'S Soc Of The Estrn Shore Of Maryland 2001. walford1809@yahoo.com

ALFORD-BROWN, Vernella (Ct) 689 Bloomfield Ave, Bloomfield CT 06002 **P All SS Epis Ch Meriden CT 2006-** B Camaguey CU 11/5/1926 d Herman Alford & Almena. D 2/17/1987 Bp Arthur Edward Walmsley P 11/21/1987 Bp Clarence Nicholas Coleridge.

ALFRIEND, John Daingerfield (WVa) 224 Muirfield Ct, Charles Town WV 25414 B Weston WV 4/25/1927 s John Shadrach Alfriend & Eliza. BA Hampden-Sydney Coll 1950; BD VTS 1959. D 12/16/1959 Bp David Shepherd Rose P 12/1/1960 Bp George P Gunn. m 2/16/1974 Nancy Deneufville c 4. Nelson Cluster Of Epis Ch Rippon WV 1991-1994; The Nelson Cluster Of Epis Ch Rippon WV 1991-1994; R Zion Epis Ch Chas Town WV 1989-1990; R Ch Of The Epiph Norfolk VA 1978-1987; Dio Sthrn Virginia Norfolk VA 1966; R Gr Ch Yorktown Yorktown VA 1964-1971; Exec Coun Dio Sthrn Virginia Norfolk VA 1963; Dept Of CSR Dio Sthrn Virginia Norfolk VA 1962-1963; P-in-c Chr Ch Boydton VA 1959-1964; P-in-c S Jas Ch Boydton VA 1959-1964; P-in-c S Tim's Epis Ch Clarksville VA 1959-1964. Bd Dir ESMA 1991-1993. jdalfriend@comcast.net

ALGERNON, Marcel Glenford (SwFla) 2055 Woodsong Way, Fountain CO 80817 **Vic S Anselm Epis Ch Lehigh Acres FL 2005-** B New Amsterdam

GY 12/20/1962 s Heyligar Algernon & Miriam. BA U of The W Indies 1986; MA CUNY 1992; Med CUNY 1994. Trans from Church in the Province Of The West Indies 4/20/1993 Bp Orris George Walker Jr. m 6/5/1987 Helen Ann Bend. Off Of Bsh For ArmdF New York NY 1996-2004; Ch Of The H Apos Brooklyn NY 1993-1995; S Andr's Ch Oceanside NY 1993; Supply P S Andr's Ch Oceanside NY 1989-1993; Asst Ch Of S Thos Brooklyn NY 1988-1989.

ALKINS, David Stanley (Oly) P.O. Box 206, Seaview WA 98644 B Bingham ME 4/20/1922 s Maurice Alkins & Barbara. BM New Engl Conservatory of Mus 1942; Grad Dir Ya Berk 1951. D 7/25/1951 P 7/2/1952 Bp Clinton Simon Quin. m 10/30/2008 Joan Mann Graves c 3. Ret Cler S Ben Epis Ch Lacey WA 2000-2008; Dep, GC Dio Spokane Spokane WA 1961-1969; R S Paul's Ch Walla Walla WA 1958-1969; R Chr Ch SEATTLE WA 1955-1958; Rep, Prov Syn Dio Olympia Seattle WA 1955-1958; All SS Epis Ch Hitchcock TX 1953-1955; R Gr Epis Ch Alvin TX 1951-1953. DD Brooks DS, Denver CO 1987.

ALLAGREE, The Rev. Harry R. (NCal) 361 Lincoln Avenue, Cotati CA 94931 **Chapl for Ret Cler & Spouses Dio Nthrn California Sacramento CA 2008-** B Dayton OH 2/27/1937 s Robert Joseph Allagree & Grace Elinor. S Jos's Coll Rensselaer IN 1957; BA U of Dayton 1960; S Chas Sem Carthagena OH 1964. Rec from Roman Catholic 6/2/1982 as Priest Bp John Lester Thompson III. c 2. Dio Nthrn California Sacramento CA 1996-2007; Reg Mssnr H Trin Epis Ch Ukiah CA 1996-2007; Reg Mssnr S Jn's Epis Ch Lakeport CA 1996-2007; R S Jn The Evang Ch Chico CA 1986-1996; Stndg Com Dio Nthrn California Sacramento CA 1984-1994; Vic Gd Shpd Epis Ch Susanville CA 1983-1986; Vic H Sprt Mssn Lake Almanor CA 1983-1986; Asst S Matt's Epis Ch Sacramento CA 1982-1983. Ord of Julian of Norwich, Oblate 1997. Hon Alum CDSP Berkeley CA 1993. coggy37@comcast.net

✠ **ALLAN, Rt Rev Frank Kellogg** (At) 1231 Briarcliff Rd Ne, Atlanta GA 30306 B Hammond IN 5/9/1935 s Bryan Leigh Allan & Julia Grace. BA Emory U 1956; MDiv STUSo 1959; STM STUSo 1970; Fllshp Coll of Preachers 1972; DMin Candler TS Emory U 1977. D 6/16/1959 P 12/1/1959 Bp Randolph R Claiborne Con 2/7/1987 for At. m 6/11/1957 Elizabeth Ansley c 4. Bp of Atlanta Dio Atlanta Atlanta GA 1989-2000; Bp Coadj of Atlanta Dio Atlanta Atlanta GA 1987-1988; R S Anne's Epis Ch Atlanta GA 1977-1987; R S Paul's Ch Macon GA 1968-1977; R S Ptr's Ch Columbia TN 1967-1968; R S Mk's Ch Dalton GA 1959-1967. DD (Hon) STUSo 1988. frankallan@bellsouth.net

ALLARD, Bradley Richard (WMich) 114 Union Ave Ne # 1, Grand Rapids MI 49503 **D H Trin Epis Ch Wyoming MI 2009-** B Muskegon MI 10/25/1949 s Raymond I Allard & Lila M. D 11/19/2005 Bp Robert R Gepert. deacon_brad@hotmail.com

ALLARDYCE, David Bruce (SO) Po Box 40538, Cincinnati OH 45240 B Cincinnati OH 8/6/1935 s Archie Allardyce & Thelma Wanita. BA Ken 1957; MDiv CDSP 1962; OH SU 1974; Cpa 1977; Int Mnstry Prog 1999. D 6/20/1962 P 6/13/1963 Bp Roger W Blanchard. m 11/30/1963 Mary Foster. Locten Chr Ch Xenia OH 2000-2001; Chr Epis Ch Of Springfield Springfield OH 1999-2000; Locten Trin Ch Hamilton OH 1999; Assoc Chr Epis Ch Of Springfield Springfield OH 1985-1990; Locten Chr Epis Ch Of Springfield Springfield OH 1984-1985; Locten Chr Ch Xenia OH 1979-1980; Locten S Matt's Ch Westerville OH 1978-1979; R S Phil's Ch Circleville OH 1967-1976; Vic Trin Ch Bellaire OH 1964-1967; Asst Chr Epis Ch Of Springfield Springfield OH 1962-1964. revdbacpa@fuse.net

ALLEE, Roger G (SeFla) All Saints Episcopal Church, 333 Tarpon Dr., Ft. Lauderdale FL 33301 B Port Jervis NY 4/8/1946 s Hager C Allee & Lillian. Mercer Cnty Cmnty Coll; BS Trenton St Coll 1972; MS Nova U 1981. D 1/26/1996 Bp John Lewis Said P 11/3/2002 Bp Leopold Frade. c 3. P-in-c Ch Of The Intsn Ft Lauderdale FL 2008-2010; Assoc All SS Prot Epis Ch Ft Lauderdale FL 2002-2010; S Benedicts Ch Plantation FL 1998-2002. rga46@comcast.net

ALLEMEIER, James Elmer (Q) 4306 34th Avenue Pl, Moline IL 61265 **Asst All SS Epis Ch Moline IL 2008-** B Perrysburg OH 3/3/1936 s Elmer Carl Allemeier & Myrtle. BA Ohio Wesl 1958; MDiv SWTS 1968. D 6/22/1968 Bp Russell S Hubbard P 12/22/1968 Bp J(ohn) Joseph Meakins Harte. m 7/18/1964 Marguerite Ann Wright. R Chr Ch Peoria IL 1972-2001; Cur S Andr's Ch Downers Grove IL 1970-1972; Chapl All SS Ch Phoenix AZ 1969-1970; Epis Par Of S Mich And All Ang Tucson AZ 1968-1970. MDiv scl SWTS Evanston IL 1968. kalleme310@aol.com

ALLEN, Abraham Claude (Mass) 17 Winthrop St, Marlborough MA 01752 B McRae GA 1/2/1949 s Abe Claude Allen & Lola Mae. BA Shawnee St U 1973; MDiv PrTS 1989; MA EDS 1991. D 6/4/1994 P 12/1/1994 Bp David Elliot Johnson. m 8/30/1981 Frankie Maureen Zimmerman. Trin Ch Concord MA 1996-1998.

ALLEN, Barbara Ann (WA) 6919 Strathmore St Apt C, Bethesda MD 20815 **Vic S Barn' Epis Ch of The Deaf Chevy Chase MD 2002-** B Kilgore TX 8/23/1937 d Robert Leslie Frederick & Carrie Thompson. AA Pasadena City Coll 1957; Pasadena City Coll Sch of Nrsng 1958; BA Geo 1989; MDiv Sthrn Bapt TS Louisville KY 1990; GTS 1999. D 6/24/2000 P 5/13/2001 Bp Charles Ellsworth Bennison Jr. c 2. Dio Washington Washington DC 2002-2009; Asst Calv Ch Conshohocken PA 2001-2002; Dio Pennsylvania Philadelphia PA 2000-2002; D Calv Ch Conshohocken PA 2000-2001. Epis Conf of the Deaf 1993. allen.rev@gmail.com

ALLEN, Charles William (Ind) 4118 Byram Ave, Indianapolis IN 46208 **Dio Indianapolis Indianapolis IN 2004-; Sch For Mnstry Indianapolis IN 2004-** B Fayetteville AR 10/30/1953 BA U of Arkansas. D 6/28/2003 P 2/14/2004 Bp Catherine Elizabeth Maples Waynick. c 2. charlesallen5@yahoo.com

ALLEN, Curtis Tilley (WTenn) 133 Jefferson Sq, Nashville TN 37215 B Durham NC 10/4/1930 s Lyle Kirby Allen & Min. BS U NC 1953; BD Epis TS of The SW 1959. D 9/18/1959 P 3/1/1960 Bp Richard Henry Baker. R Chr Ch Memphis TN 1979-1992; R S Phil's Ch Nashville TN 1971-1979; Vic S Anne's Ch Millington TN 1966-1971; Vic S Mary's Epis Ch Middlesboro KY 1961-1966; Asst R S Mich's Ch Tarboro NC 1960-1961; Vic St Marys Epis Ch Speed NC 1959-1961.

ALLEN SSJE, David Eastman (Mass) 980 Memorial Dr, Cambridge MA 02138 B Spokane WA 12/19/1929 s Clyde David Allen & Harriet Elizabeth. BA WA SU 1952; MDiv CDSP 1958. D 6/17/1958 Bp Edward Makin Cross P 12/21/1958 Bp Spence Burton. S Jn's Chap Cambridge MA 1958-1995. Auth, "Var arts," *Mitsukai, Cowley*, SSJE, 1961. Epis Asiamerica Mnstry 1978; EPF 1965. davida@ssje.org

ALLEN, David Edward (Mass) PO Box 1052, Barnstable MA 02630 B Swampscott MA 12/16/1937 s Edward John Allen & Blanche Alice. BS Bos 1962; MDiv Ya Berk 1965. D 6/26/1965 P 5/31/1966 Bp John Melville Burgess. m 6/27/1965 Ruthanne Gould. R S Mary's Epis Ch Barnstable MA 1979-2002; Commun Ctte Dio Massachusetts Boston MA 1972-1991; R Ch Of Our Sav Middleboro MA 1968-1979; Cur Par Of Chr Ch Andover MA 1965-1968. Auth, "Pstr Care Handbook," *same*, EDS, 1995. allen.anchorage@comcast.net

ALLEN, Diogenes (NJ) 21113 Heather Drive, Princeton Junction NJ 08550 **P All SS Ch Princeton NJ 2002-** B Lexington KY 10/17/1932 s George Allen & Vassiliki. BA U of Kentucky 1954; BA Oxf 1957; BD Yale DS 1959; MA Oxf 1961; MA Ya 1962; Fllshp Rockefeller Fndt 1964; PhD Yale DS 1965; Fllshp Can Coun 1967; Fllshp Assn of Theol SchoolS 1976; Fllshp Cntr for Theol Inquiry 1986; 1992; Fllshp Cntr for Theol Inquiry 1995. D 7/29/2001 P 2/3/2002 Bp David B(ruce) Joslin. m 9/8/1953 Jane Mary Billing Allen c 4. D All SS Ch Princeton NJ 2001-2002. Auth, *Sprtl Theol: the Theol of Yesterday for Help Today*, Cowley, 1997; Auth, *Nature, Sprt, and Cmnty: Issues in the Thought of Simone Weil*, SUNY Albany, 1994; Auth, *Quest: the Search for Meaning through Chr*, Walker & Co., 1990; Auth, *Chr Belief in a Postmodern Wrld: the Full Wealth of Conviction*, Westminster/Knox, 1989; Auth, *Love: Chr Romance, Mar and Friendship*, Cowley, 1987; Auth, *14 books, over 50 arts*. diogenes.allen@ptsem.edu

ALLEN, Donald Frederick (Ct) 34 Ashlar Vlg, Wallingford CT 06492 B New Haven CT 7/18/1926 s Frederick Charles Allen & Mildred Evelyn. Cert U of New Haven 1955; BS U of New Haven 1974. D 6/8/1996 Bp Clarence Nicholas Coleridge. m 11/20/1948 Augusta Hazel Hock c 2. D S Jn's Ch No Haven CT 2002-2009; D S Paul's Epis Ch Shelton CT 1996-2002. Alpha Sigma Lambda; OHC. donald.allen@snet.net

ALLEN, E(arl) Michael (NY) 55 George St, Allendale NJ 07401 **R Ch Of The Epiph Allendale NJ 2007-** B San Francisco CA 9/8/1948 s Earl A Allen & Joyce. BS The Coll of Idaho 1989; MDiv GTS 1991. D 6/8/1991 Bp Earl Nicholas McArthur Jr P 12/20/1991 Bp Harold B Robinson. m 10/1/2004 Penelope Braun c 2. R Chr Ch New Brighton Staten Island NY 1997-2004; Asst The Ch of S Matt And S Tim New York NY 1994-1997; Asst S Mk's Ch Mt Kisco NY 1992-1994; Asst S Thos Ch New York NY 1991-1992. GAS 2000; SocMary 1999. fathermichael@mac.com

ALLEN, Edward Powell (Los) 49 Captains Row, Mashpee MA 02649 B Shanghai CN 1/18/1928 s Arthur Jones Allen & Edith Antoinetta. BA Pomona Coll 1949; BD CDSP 1956. D 6/25/1956 Bp Francis E I Bloy P 2/11/1957 Bp Donald J Campbell. m 6/15/1956 Alice Jean Pierce c 3. Asst S Mary's Epis Ch Barnstable MA 1994-2000; R Epis Ch Of S Andr And S Chas Granada Hills CA 1980-1990; Vic Epis Ch Of S Andr And S Chas Granada Hills CA 1976-1980; Dio Los Angeles Los Angeles CA 1966-1976; Vic S Mich And All Ang Par Corona Del Mar CA 1960-1966; Cur The Par Ch Of S Lk Long Bch CA 1956-1959. evensong@cape.com

ALLEN II, George Curwood (SO) 988 Duxbury Ct, Cincinnati OH 45255 B Parkersburg WV 6/21/1950 s George Curwood Allen & Betty June. BA W Liberty St Coll 1972; MDiv EDS 1977. D 6/8/1977 P 5/20/1978 Bp Robert Poland Atkinson. m 8/26/1972 Judith Lyn Irby c 2. Assoc FMP Cincinnati OH 1999-2009; Dio Newark Newark NJ 1982-1986; R The Ch Of The Annunc Oradell NJ 1980-1999; Dio W Virginia Charleston WV 1979-1980; Assoc R Trin Epis Ch Martinsburg WV 1977-1980. Meritorious Serv Medallion Bp Suffr for Chaplaincies, The Epis Ch 2006; Legion of Merit U S AF 2004. gcajla@prodigy.net

ALLEN, Gordon Richard (NH) 237 Emerys Bridge Rd, South Berwick ME 03908 B Liverpool UK 11/21/1929 s Richard Allen & Katherine. BA S Jn's

Coll Durham GB 1954; DIT S Jn's Coll Durham GB 1955; U of Durham Durham GB 1955; MA S Jn's Coll Durham GB 1958. Trans from Church Of England 5/1/1973 Bp Philip Alan Smith. R S Jn's Ch Portsmouth NH 1975-1995; R The Epis Ch Of S Jn The Bapt Sanbornville NH 1971-1975.

ALLEN, J C Michael (Mo) 165 S Sappington Rd, Saint Louis MO 63122 **Asstg Cler Ch Of The Trsfg Lake S Louis MO 2002-** B Paris FR 10/16/1927 s Jay Cooke Allen & Ruth. BA Harv 1950; U of Paris FR 1951; BD EDS 1957; DD Ya Berk 1976. D 6/17/1957 P 12/21/1957 Bp Horace W B Donegan. m 6/25/1949 Priscilla Ridgely Morison c 3. Dn Chr Ch Cathd S Louis MO 1976-1998; Chair Urban Plcy and Mssn Ctte Dio Missouri S Louis MO 1976-1982; Dn Ya Berk New Haven CT 1971-1976; R S Mk's Ch In The Bowery New York NY 1959-1970; Asst Gr Epis Ch New York NY 1957-1959. Auth, "This Time, This Place," Bobbs-Merrill, 1971; Contrib, *On the Battle Lines*, Morehouse-Barlow, 1964; Contrib, *Mod Cbury Pilgrims*, Morehouse-Gorham, 1956. Micah Awd Amer Jewish Com 1998; BA cl Harv Cambridge MA 1950; Mich Edlin Awd Doorways. jcmallen@sbcglobal.net

ALLEN JR, John Gwin (Ky) 1512 Valley Brook Rd, Louisville KY 40222 **Asst Chapl S Lk's Chap Louisville KY 2009-; P Mssh and H Trin Ch Louisville KY 2005-** B Baton Rouge LA 6/10/1942 s John Gwin Allen & Jonetta Elizabeth. BA LSU 1964; STB Ya Berk 1967. D 7/8/1967 Bp Girault M Jones P 5/1/1968 Bp Iveson Batchelor Noland. m 7/2/1966 Cynthia Miriam Ryone c 2. R S Thos Epis Ch Louisville KY 1992-1999; Asst to Bp Dio Kentucky Louisville KY 1989-1997; Cn For Mnstry Dio Lexington Lexington KY 1987-1989; Dir of Stds Epis TS Lexington KY 1986-1989; Ctte On Mutual Respon/Interdependent Body Of Chr Dio Lexington Lexington KY 1982-1986; Curs Com Dio Lexington Lexington KY 1982-1986; R Emm Epis Ch Winchester KY 1982-1986; Pres Stndg Com Dio Lexington Lexington KY 1980-1982; Dio Lexington Lexington KY 1979-1982; R Ch Of The Cross Columbia SC 1978-1982; Sprtl Dir Curs Dio Louisiana Baton Rouge LA 1976-1978; Vic S Marg's Epis Ch Baton Rouge LA 1974-1978; R S Fran Ch Denham Sprg LA 1969-1977; Asst R S Paul's Ch New Orleans LA 1967-1969. jgafile@aol.com

ALLEN, John M (Oly) 114 20th Ave SE, Olympia WA 98501 **R S Jn's Epis Ch Olympia WA 2010-** B Philadelphia PA 4/15/1945 s John Joseph Allen & Dorothy. BA Rutgers-The St U 1971; MBA U of Pennsylvania 1974; MDiv CDSP 2002. D 6/29/2002 Bp Vincent Waydell Warner P 12/7/2002 Bp William Edwin Swing. m 6/1/1974 Georgene Elizabeth Davis c 2. R S Lk's Epis Ch Vancouver WA 2005-2010; Int All SS Epis Ch Palo Alto CA 2004-2005; Assoc Pstr Gr Cathd San Francisco CA 2002-2003. jatcdsp@aol.com

ALLEN, John Shepley (NH) 229 Shore Dr, Laconia NH 03246 B Glen Ridge NJ 7/3/1938 s Frank Lewis Allen & Margaret Sheply. BA Carleton Coll 1961; BD VTS 1963; MDiv VTS 1965. D 6/12/1965 P 12/1/1965 Bp Leland Stark. m 6/18/1965 Ursula Walch. S Steph's Ch Pittsfield NH 1992-1999; P-in-c Ch Of The Mssh No Woodstock NH 1990-1991; S Jas Epis Ch Laconia NH 1975-1987; R H Trin Epis Ch Hillsdale NJ 1969-1975; Cur S Geo's Epis Ch Maplewood NJ 1965-1969. AAPC. cavecanem@metrocast.net

ALLEN, John T (Mil) 515 Oak St., South Milwaukee WI 53172 **S Mk's Ch So Milwaukee WI 2005-** B Lost Angeles CA 2/26/1945 s M William Allen & Margarette H. AA Fullerton Coll 1964; BA Fullerton Coll 1967; MDiv Wartburg TS 1972; D.Min GTF 1988. Rec from Evangelical Lutheran Church in America 4/27/2005 Bp Steven Andrew Miller. m 10/21/1972 Marilyn Jodell Allen c 3. mallen7@wi.rr.com

ALLEN, Larry Joe (WMo) 3212 S. Jeffrey Cir., Independence MO 64055 **D S Mich's Epis Ch Independence MO 2004-** B Jackson MO 10/24/1942 BD Calv Bible Coll 1965. D 2/7/2004 Bp Barry Robert Howe. m 8/14/1971 Mary Elizabeth Darroch c 3. D S Mich's Epis Ch Independence MO 2004-2006. allenhouse1@prodigy.net

ALLEN, Leland Eugene (Kan) 811 E Wood St, Clearwater KS 67026 **D S Chris's Epis Ch Wichita KS 1998-; D S Andr's Ch Derby KS 1991-** B Hutchinson KS 10/20/1921 s Mary Elizabeth Allen & Flora L. D 10/30/1987 Bp Richard Frank Grein. m 12/17/1966 Roberta Cynthia Perry c 2. D S Jude's Ch Wellington KS 1987-2007.

✠ ALLEN, Rt Rev Lloyd Emmanuel (Hond) PO Box 523900, Miami FL 33152 **Bp Of Honduras Iglesia Epis San Pablo Apostol San Pedro Sula Cortes HN 2001-; Bp of Honduras Dio Honduras Miami FL 1989-** B Tela Atlantida HN 9/25/1956 s Franklyn Eustace Graves & Lusia. MA Epis TS of The SW; MA STUSo; Universidad Autonoma; BA Triunfo De La Cruz 1977. D 1/6/1989 P 1/1/1991 Bp Leopold Frade Con 10/20/2001 for Hond. m 2/26/1983 Rose Martinez. Vic Iglesia Epis Santa Maria de los Angeles Tegucigalpa NY HN 1989-2001. bishopallen43@yahoo.com

ALLEN, Mark Frederick (NCal) 2577 Hepworth Dr, Davis CA 95618 **R Ch Of S Mart Davis CA 2004-** B Prairie City OR 10/30/1951 s Albert Edward Allen & Helen Christine. BS Willamette U 1973; Med Lewis & Clark Coll 1977; CTh Oxf 1985; MDiv CDSP 1986. D 6/11/1986 P 2/14/1987 Bp Robert Louis Ladehoff. m 5/19/1973 Nancy A Tokola c 5. R Ch Of S Nich Paradise CA 1990-2004; Asst S Barth's Ch Beaverton OR 1986-1990. Ord Of S Lk. revd4jc@cal.net

ALLEN, Mary Louise (Oly) 5618 103rd St Ne, Marysville WA 98270 **S Phil Ch Marysville WA 2004-** B Prairie City OR 7/31/1955 d Albert Edward Allen & Helen Christine. BS Willamette U 1977; MDiv CDSP 1986. D 6/10/1986 P 2/2/1987 Bp Robert Louis Ladehoff. R Gr Epis Ch St Geo UT 2000-2004; Dio Utah Salt Lake City UT 1995-2004; Vic Gr Epis Ch St Geo UT 1995-2000; Assoc Ch Of The Gd Shpd Ogden UT 1991-1995; Asst S Steph's Epis Ch Longview WA 1989-1991; Asst R S Jas Epis Ch Tigard OR 1986-1989. Auth, "A Stwdshp Plan," *The Vineyard*, 1989. revmary@comcast.net

ALLEN, Morgan S (Tex) 3201 Windsor Rd, Austin TX 78703 **R The Ch of the Gd Shpd Austin TX 2009-** B Monroe LA 2/18/1975 s Hubert Stephens Allen & Mary Clay. BA LSU 1997; BA LSU 1997; MDiv Epis TS of the SW 2003. D 6/7/2003 P 2/23/2004 Bp D(avid) Bruce Mac Pherson. m 5/16/1998 Susan Melissa Boutte c 2. R S Barn Epis Ch Lafayette LA 2005-2009; Cur S Mths Epis Ch Shreveport LA 2003-2005; 20/30's Mnstry Coordntr S Dav's Ch Austin TX 2000-2003; Lay Asst to the Dn & Cathd Sch Chapl S Mk's Cathd Shreveport LA 1998-2000; Yth Dir Trin Epis Ch Baton Rouge LA 1994-1998. MORGAN@GSAUSTIN.ORG

ALLEN, Patrick Scott (SC) 886 Seafarer Way, Charleston SC 29412 B Lakeland FL 5/15/1968 s James Wellington Allen & Elizabeth. BA Hampden-Sydney Coll 1990; MDiv Cov TS S Louis MO 1996; DAS STUSo 2000. D 7/23/2000 P 1/24/2001 Bp Edward Lloyd Salmon Jr. m 5/3/2003 Ashley Ann Duckett c 1. Ch Of The H Comm Charleston SC 2006-2007; S Jos Of Arimathaea Ch Hendersonville TN 2006-2007; R S Matt's Ch (Ft Motte) S Matthews SC 2000-2003.

ALLEN, Philip Charles (SD) 6045 Lyndale Ave S Apt 213, Minneapolis MN 55419 **Died 3/22/2010** B Pine Ridge SD 3/18/1935 s Martin Bruce Allen & Mollie Marie. BA Black Hill St U 1960; Ya Berk 1961. D 6/20/1964 P 12/21/1964 Bp Conrad Gesner. c 1. revpcallen@yahoo.com

ALLEN, Priscilla Ridgely (Mo) 165 S Sappington Rd, Saint Louis MO 63122 **Asstg Cler Ch Of The Trsfg Lake S Louis MO 2002-** B Paducah KY 9/29/1928 d William George Morison & Charlotte. Rad 1950; U of Paris FR 1951; BA Barnard Coll of Col 1952; MS Washington U 1978; Eden TS 1985. D 6/1/1985 Bp John Bowen Coburn P 6/11/1986 Bp William Augustus Jones Jr. m 6/25/1949 J C Michael Allen c 3. Cn Pstr Chr Ch Cathd S Louis MO 1989-1998; Asst Chr Ch Cathd S Louis MO 1986-1989; D S Barn Ch Florissant MO 1985-1986. jcmallen@worldnet.att.net

ALLEN JR, Radford Bonnie (FtW) 1804 Dakar Rd W, Fort Worth TX 76116 B Lufkin TX 3/15/1925 s Radford Bonnie Allen & Clara Rose. BS Louisiana Tech U 1951; STL Angl TS 1979; U of Durham Durham GB 1981. D 6/25/1978 Bp Robert Elwin Terwilliger P 5/20/1979 Bp A Donald Davies. m 9/6/1950 Lina Lea Lusk c 1. Mssn Com Dio Ft Worth Ft Worth TX 1987-1989; R S Jn's Epis Ch Brownwood TX 1986-1990; Int S Jn's Epis Ch Brownwood TX 1985-1986; Cur All SS' Epis Ch Ft Worth TX 1982-1986; Vic S Mart In The Fields Ch Keller TX 1979-1982; Cur Chr The King Epis Ch Ft Worth TX 1978-1979. CBS 1971; GAS 1971. Chapl of Year CAP, TX Wing 1985. radlina@sbcglobal.net

ALLEN, Robert Edward (Ark) 1101 Glenwood Dr, El Dorado AR 71730 **Dio Arkansas Little Rock AR 2008-** B Stuttgart AR 1/5/1941 s Robert Edward Allen & Margaret Alene. BA Hendrix Coll 1963; BD SMU 1966; STM SMU 1968; MA U of Dallas 1970; Cert U So 1974. D 5/18/1974 Bp Girault M Jones P 9/21/1974 Bp Christoph Keller Jr. c 1. R S Mary's Epis Ch El Dorado AR 1991-2007; Cn Dio W Tennessee Memphis TN 1984-1991; Cn S Mary's Cathd Memphis TN 1984-1991; Liturg Cmsn Dio W Tennessee Memphis TN 1983-1991; R Ch of the H Apos Collierville TN 1981-1984; Vic Ch of the H Apos Collierville TN 1979-1981; Chair Liturg Cmsn Dio Arkansas Little Rock AR 1978-1979; Vic Calv Epis Ch Osceola AR 1974-1979. Ed, *Ch News*, WTenn, 1991; Auth, "H Places," *Liturg Perkins Journ*; Contrib, *S Lukes Journ*. boballen1541@aol.com

ALLEN, Roger D (Ala) St. James Episcopal Church, 347 South Central Avenue, Alexander City AL 35010 **R S Jas' Epis Ch Alexander City AL 2007-** B Thomasville GA 4/21/1954 s Washington Bartley Allen & Mavelene G. ABJ U GA 1976; JD Tul 1980; MDiv TS 2005. D 12/29/2004 P 7/1/2005 Bp Charles Edward Jenkins III. m 5/14/1994 Elisabeth Couret Jumonville Fox. Chapl Chap Of The H Comf New Orleans LA 2005-2007; Chapl Dio Louisiana Baton Rouge LA 2005-2007. stjamesrector@bellsouth.net

ALLEN, Russell Harvey (Ct) 28 Seaward Ln, Harwich MA 02645 **Assoc S Ptr's Ch Osterville MA 2006-** B Hartford CT 10/16/1943 s Samuel Harvey Allen & Lillian Carolyn. BA Bard Coll 1965; MDiv GTS 1968; MA Nthrn Michigan U 1990. D 6/11/1968 Bp Walter H Gray P 5/24/1969 Bp John Henry Esquirol. m 6/1/1968 Louisa M Allen c 2. R Ch Of The H Adv Clinton CT 1999-2006; Pennsylvania Cmsn Harrisburg PA 1991-1998; S Mths Ch Coventry RI 1990-1991; Dio Connecticut Hartford CT 1986-1989; Vic All SS Ch Wolcott CT 1981-1989; Dio Milwaukee Milwaukee WI 1979-1981; Dio W Virginia Charleston WV 1972-1973; Vic Emm Ch Keyser WV 1972-1973; Vic Emm Ch Moorefield WV 1972-1973; Asst S Mary's Epis Ch Manchester CT 1969-1972; Cur S Paul's Epis Ch Willimantic CT 1968-1969. Auth, *Hist: A Revs of New Books*. capecahd@verizon.net

ALLEN, Stephanie Loy (NC) Church of the Nativity, 8849 Ray Road, Raleigh NC 27613 **R Ch Of The Nativ Raleigh NC 2011-** B Asheville NC 7/15/1975 d Daniel Francis Perry & Marcia Gay. BA U So 1997; MDiv The GTS 2008. D 3/15/2008 P 9/20/2008 Bp Mark Sean Sisk. m 8/5/2000 Michael C Allen c 2. Asst Ch Of The Gd Shpd Rocky Mt NC 2008-2011; S Barth's Ch New York NY 1998-2003. stephanieperryallen@gmail.com

ALLEN, Susan Van Leunen (ECR) PO Box 173, King City CA 93930 **S Matt's Ch San Ardo CA 2000-** B Cincinnati OH 4/26/1944 d Paul Van Leunen & Helen Jean. BS Mia 1966; MA CDSP 1988. D 11/26/1996 P 6/24/1997 Bp Richard Lester Shimpfky. c 2. Vic S Mk's Ch KING CITY CA 1998-2004; P-in-c S Matt's Ch San Ardo CA 1997-1998; Asst S Mk's Ch KING CITY CA 1995-1997. "Masters Thesis," Grad Theol Un Libr, Burkeley CA, 1988. revsallen@sbcglobal.net

ALLEN, Thomas Bostwick (WA) 2909 Langholm Pl, Vienna VA 22181 **Died 5/19/2011** B Atlanta GA 1/17/1921 s Thomas Eldredge Allen & Laura Belle. BS Georgia Inst of Tech 1942; BD VTS 1952. D 12/2/1951 Bp Middleton S Barnwell P 6/1/1952 Bp Angus Dun. jfa72714@cs.com

ALLEN, Thomas Wynn (Md) 1960 Moorhill Estate Dr., Sumter SC 29154 **S Mary's Ch Abingdon MD 2011-** B Fort Campbell KY 3/13/1969 s John Edward Allen & Mary Ann Wynn. BA Montreat Coll 1997; M.Div TESM 2003. Rec from Anglican Province of America 8/1/2007 as Priest Bp Edward Lloyd Salmon Jr. m 6/9/2001 Kimberly E Allen. R H Cross Stateburg Stateburg SC 2007-2011. st.marys1928@gmail.com

ALLEN, T Scott (Be) 713 Cherokee St, Bethlehem PA 18015 **GC Dep Dio Bethlehem Bethlehem PA 2010-2013; R S Andr's Epis Ch Allentown PA 2007-; Stndg Com Dio Bethlehem Bethlehem PA 2006-2015** B Heidelburg Germany 12/22/1956 s Billy Frank Allen & Rebecca Rhea. BS W Virginia U 1979; MDiv Ya Berk 1983. D 6/1/1983 P 4/7/1984 Bp Robert Poland Atkinson. GC Dep Dio Bethlehem Bethlehem PA 2008-2010; S Eliz's Ch Schnecksville PA 2001-2006; R S Barth's Ch Pittsboro NC 1995-1999; Assoc R S Matt's Ch Wheeling WV 1985-1989; Int Trin Ch Parkersburg WV 1984-1985; Asst R Trin Ch Parkersburg WV 1983-1984. Auth, "Article," *Wit*, 1981. EPF 1983; EUC 1994; Grad Soc-Ya Berk 1983; Integrity 1999. gamba.guy@verizon.net

ALLEN, Walter Drew (Colo) Po Box 5958, Vail CO 81658 B Hearne TX 4/5/1933 s Drew Ellis Allen & Dorthea Eugenia. D 1/6/2003 P 7/19/2003 Bp William Jerry Winterrowd.

ALLEN, W Frank (Pa) 763 Valley Forge Rd, Wayne PA 19087 **R S Dav's Ch Wayne PA 1997-** B Dallas TX 12/23/1958 s James Allen & Laura. BA Duke 1981; MDiv VTS 1995. D 6/10/1995 Bp Allen Lyman Bartlett Jr P 6/11/1996 Bp A(rthur) Heath Light. m 7/9/1983 Amy Joanne Waldo c 3. COM Dio SW Virginia Roanoke VA 1996-1997; Asst S Jn's Ch Roanoke VA 1995-1997. Auth, *Epis Ch Curric for Jr High*. fallen@stdavidschurch.org

ALLEN, William Quay (Chi) 2435 Fox Dr, Aurora IL 60506 B Memphis TN 2/2/1931 s James Quay Allen & Mary Elizabeth. BS Illinois St U 1955; STB Ya Berk 1958. D 6/1/1958 P 12/1/1958 Bp Gordon V Smith. c 2. R Ch Of Our Sav Elmhurst IL 1984-1999; Assoc Trin Epis Ch Wheaton IL 1964-1965; R Chr Epis Ch Clinton IA 1960-1963; Vic S Mk's Ch Maquoketa IA 1958-1959. Prudential Cmnty Serv Awd 1969.

ALLEN-FAIELLA, Wilifred Sophia Nelly (SeFla) 16745 Southwest 74th Avenue, Miami FL 33157 **R S Steph's Ch Coconut Grove Coconut Grove FL 2001-** B Paris FR 12/24/1951 d George Edmund Morris Allen & Jelisaveta. BA Bryn 1973; MA Schiller Coll Berlin 1974; MDiv VTS 1978. D 6/13/1987 P 3/24/1988 Bp Peter James Lee. m 6/22/1980 Christopher James Faiella c 2. Stndg Com Dio Pennsylvania Philadelphia PA 1997-2001; Dio Pennsylvania Philadelphia PA 1997-2000; Trin Ch Gulph Mills King Of Prussia PA 1991-2002; VTS Alexandria VA 1989-1991; Asst Imm Ch-On-The-Hill Alexandria VA 1987-1991. Finalist Best Sermon Competition 1991; MDiv cl VTS Alexandria VA 1987. revwaf@sseds.org

ALLEN-HERRON, Dawn (Ak) 3886 S Tongass Hwy, Ketchikan AK 99901 **R S Andr's Epis Ch Petersburg AK 2003-** B Corpus Christi TX 4/18/1959 d Charles Allen & Mary. BA Baylor U 1982; MDiv Austin Presb TS 1989. D 9/14/2002 P 3/25/2003 Bp Mark Lawrence Mac Donald. m 5/16/1981 Norman C Herron. dawn@standrewspetersburg.org

ALLEY, Ann Leonard (Spr) 913 W Washington St, Champaign IL 61821 B Fayetteville AR 11/28/1948 D 6/29/2004 Bp Peter Hess Beckwith. m 11/24/1978 Clarence Alley c 4.

ALLEY, Charles Dickson (Va) 1101 Forest Ave, Richmond VA 23229 **R S Matt's Ch Richmond VA 1994-** B Hackensack NJ 4/2/1949 s Charles Dickson Alley & Helen Teresa. BS W&M 1971; MA W&M 1972; PhD Med Coll of Virginia 1977; MDiv VTS 1991. D 5/29/1991 Bp Robert Oran Miller P 1/22/1992 Bp Peter James Lee. m 2/8/1975 Nancye SN Noel c 3. Asst Truro Epis Ch Fairfax VA 1991-1994. "A Tale Of Two Sinners," *LivCh*, 2001. calley_stmatts@verizon.net

ALLEY, Marguerite Cole (SVa) 2107 Wake Forest St, Virginia Beach VA 23451 **Title IV Intake Off Dio Sthrn Virginia Norfolk VA 2011-; Coordntr of Chr Formation Emm Ch Virginia Bch VA 2011-; D Emm Ch Virginia Bch VA 2001-** B Petersburg VA 9/11/1960 d Lofton Holdsworth Alley & Mary Janet. BA Jas Madison U 1982; MA Loyola U 1990; Med W&M 1996. D 6/13/1998 Bp Frank Harris Vest Jr. D Ch Of The Ascen Norfolk VA 1998-2001. Assn of Epis Deacons 1998. MARGUERITESR@GMAIL.COM

ALLEYNE, Edmund Torrence (LI) 972 E 93rd St, Brooklyn NY 11236 **R S Gabr's Ch Brooklyn NY 2007-** B Barbados 5/20/1961 Cert U of The W Indies; BA Codrington Coll 1988. Trans from Church in the Province Of The West Indies 12/19/2002 Bp Orris George Walker Jr. m 12/29/2001 Kay Leann Smith c 3. P-in-c Ch Of The H Apos Brooklyn NY 2003-2006; P-in-c Ch Of The Nativ Brooklyn NY 2003-2006. jseta7@aol.com

ALLICK, Paul DeLain (Minn) 2841 Florida Ave S, St. Louis Park MN 55426 **P-in-c S Geo's Ch St Louis Pk MN 2008-** B Great Falls MT 12/10/1968 s Paul Alexander Allick & Dolores Ann. BA U MN 1993; MDiv SWTS 1996. D 6/7/1996 P 12/7/1996 Bp James Louis Jelinek. Int S Edw The Confessor Wayzata MN 2007-2008; U Epis Cntr Minneapolis MN 2006-2007; U Epis Cntr Minneapolis MN 2005-2006; S Thos Ch Minneapolis MN 2004-2006; Dio Minnesota Minneapolis MN 1999-2003; P-in-c Ch Of The H Apos S Paul MN 1997-1998; Assoc S Chris's Epis Ch Roseville MN 1996-1997. allickpd@aol.com

ALLINDER JR, Samuel Warren (WVa) 14146 Montauk Ln, Fort Myers FL 33919 B Oakdale PA 2/4/1923 s Samuel Warren Allinder & Hilma. W Pennsylvania Horological Inst 1950; LTh Epis TS In Kentucky 1965. D 6/9/1965 P 3/21/1966 Bp Wilburn Camrock Campbell. m 4/26/1944 Rosemary Musico c 2. Int S Steph's Epis Ch Steubenville OH 1994-1996; Int S Paul's Ch Steubenville OH 1991-1993; Vic Ch Of The Gd Shpd Follansbee WV 1967-1971; Vic Olde S Jn's Ch Colliers WV 1967-1971; Chr Ch Wellsburg WV 1965-1989; Vic S Tim's In The Vlly Hurricane WV 1965-1967. mema1924@earthlink.net

ALLING, Fred Augustus (Nwk) 3 Mariners Ln, Marblehead MA 01945 B Newark NJ 5/8/1930 s Frederic Augustus Alling & Helen. BA Pr 1952; STB GTS 1955; MD Col 1961. D 6/11/1955 P 12/17/1955 Bp Benjamin M Washburn. m 12/29/1956 Martha Garrett c 3. Cur Chr Ch Teaneck NJ 1955-1956. "Brief Flights," *Bk*, iUniverse, 2008; "Listening for God w the Third Ear," *Journ of Rel and Hlth*, Journ of Rel and Hlth, 2000.

ALLING JR, Roger (Ct) 8348 Nice Way, Sarasota FL 34238 B Pawtucket RI 12/15/1933 s Roger Alling & Mary. BA Ken 1956; Oxf 1959; BLitt Oxf 1963. D 6/28/1959 Bp The Bishop Of Oxford P 4/25/1960 Bp Dudley S Stark. m 1/30/1982 Dian Jeter Denison c 2. S Fran Acad Inc. Salina KS 1993; Stwdshp and Planned Giving Off Dio Connecticut Hartford CT 1988-1992; R S Mary's Epis Ch Reading PA 1981-1987; R Chr Ch Williamsport PA 1970-1981; Asst Calv and St Geo New York NY 1969; Consult, Stwdshp and Evang Dept Dio Newark Newark NJ 1965-1969; Vic S Andr's Epis Ch Lincoln Pk NJ 1961-1965; P-in-c Gr Ch Amherst MA 1960-1961; Cur Gr Ch Amherst MA 1959-1960. Auth, *Sermons That Wk Volume I - XIV*, Morehouse Pub, 2005; Auth, "Methods of Evang," *ART*. Assoc, Soc of St. Jn the Bapt 1967. DD CDSP 2006. rdalling4@gmail.com

ALLIS SR, A(ndrew) Parker Bateman (SwFla) 1546 Pathway Drive, Carrboro NC 27510 B Mansfield PA 2/27/1938 s Leo Joseph Allis & Evelyn Norton. BS Mansfield U of Pennsylvania 1960; Dplma Naval Chapl Sch 1962; Cert VTS 1963; Dplma Urban Theol Unit Sheffield UK 1978; MA Duquesne U 1983; DMin Pittsburgh TS 1986; MBA GTF 1995; Natl Inst for Int Mnstry Baltimore MD 1996. D 6/15/1963 P 1/15/1964 Bp John T Heistand. m 10/13/1979 Pauline Ann Middleton c 2. Dio SW Florida Sarasota FL 2001; Dioc Cn Pstr Dio SW Florida Sarasota FL 2000-2005; Cler Dvlpmt Com Dio SW Florida Sarasota FL 1997-1999; Crisis Intervention Team Dio SW Florida Sarasota FL 1997-1998; Dio SW Florida Sarasota FL 1996; St Coll of Florida Chapl Bradenton FL 1995-2001; Chair Cler Care Com Dio Rhode Island Providence RI 1990-1993; Founding Memb and Bd of Governers Sch for Mnstry Dio Rhode Island Providence RI 1990-1992; Coordntr Lay Mnstrs Dio Rhode Island Providence RI 1987-1990; R S Jas Epis Ch At Woonsocket Woonsocket RI 1986-1994; Dioc Coun Dio Pittsburgh Monroeville PA 1985-1986; R S Ptr's Ch Pittsburg KS 1979-1986; Chair Cont Educ Dept Dio Pittsburgh Monroeville PA 1979-1983; R S Mk's Ch Johnstown PA 1969-1976; Cn/Pstr Chr Ch Cathd Houston TX 1966-1969; Exec Coun Dio Cntrl Pennsylvania Harrisburg PA 1965-1966; Asst S Jas Ch Lancaster PA 1963-1966. "Passion To Compassion; A Pesonal Account," *Convergence/Compassion: The Quest for a More Just and Loving Wrld*, Distinguished Fellows of the Cntr for Sprtl Life, Ecke, 2007; "Ret Cler: Are We Expecting Too Much," *LivCh*, LivCh Fndt, 2004; "Rock The Boat," *LivCh*, LivCh Fndt, 1996; Auth, "Cler Wellness," *Fellows Journ*, GTF, 1995; Auth, "Care of Cler," *Fellows Yearbook*, GTF, 1995; "Cmnty Coll Chapl Develops Its Own Style," *LivCh*, LivCh Fndt, 1995; Auth, "Seek The Welf of The City," *An Intl Mnstry*, Pittsburgh TS, 1986; Auth, "A Coffee Pot Theol - The Par," *Journ of Urban Theol Unit*, Urban Theol Unit, UK, 1982. Ch & Soc 1986-1990; EUC 1979-1996; GTF 1995; Natl Assn of Epis Int Mnstrs 1997; Urban Theol Unit (Engl) 1978-1995. Distinguished Fell Eckerd Coll 2004; Phi Theta Kappa Manatee Cmnty Coll 1999; Joshua Awd The Lighthouse News 1998; Allen Feinstein Fndt Awd Allen Feinstein Fndt

1994; Outstanding Humanitarian Gvnr of Rhode Island 1994; Intl Man of The Year - Rel 1993 Intl Biographical Cntr, Cambridge, Engl 1993. parkallis@hotmail.com

✠ **ALLISON, Rt Rev C(hristopher) FitzSimons** (SC) 1081 Indigo Ave, Georgetown SC 29440 **Ret Bp of SC Dio So Carolina Charleston SC 1990-** B Columbia SC 3/5/1927 s James Richard Allison & Susan Milliken. BA U So 1949; MDiv VTS 1952; PhD Oxf 1956. D 6/11/1952 P 5/1/1953 Bp John J Gravatt Con 9/25/1980 for SC. m 6/10/1950 Martha Parker c 4. Bp Dio So Carolina Charleston SC 1982-1990; Bp Coadj Dio So Carolina Charleston SC 1980-1982; R Gr Epis Ch New York NY 1975-1980; Prof VTS Alexandria VA 1967-1975; Assoc The TS at The U So Sewanee TN 1956-1967; Asst Trin Cathd Columbia SC 1952-1954. Auth, "Fear, Love & Wrshp," Regent Coll Pub; Auth, "Guilt, Anger & God," Regent Coll Pub; Auth, "The Rise of Moralism," Regent Coll Pub; Auth, "The Cruelty of Heresy," Morehouse. DD VTS 1980; DD U So TS 1978; DD Epis TS in Kentucky 1977.

ALLISON, Judith Anne (SanD) 17007 Matinal Rd, San Diego CA 92127 **Assoc S Barth's Epis Ch Poway CA 2007-** B Canada 9/13/1937 d John Campbell MacKinnon & Rosena Alberta. BS U Tor 1959; MA Roosevelt U 1975; PhD US Intl U 1986; MDiv Ya Berk 2005. D 6/11/2005 P 12/18/2005 Bp James Robert Mathes. c 2. Assoc R S Barth's Epis Ch Poway CA 2007-2009; Pstr Care Assoc The Epis Ch Of S Andr Encinitas CA 2005-2006. jaalison@san.rr.com

ALLISON, Nancy Jean (NC) 3110 Belvin Dr, Raleigh NC 27609 B Allentown PA 9/30/1943 d John Roy Allison & Mildred Dorwart. BA Elmhurst Coll 1965; MDiv UTS 1968; Cert GTS 1987. D 1/6/1988 Bp William Arthur Beckham P 9/14/1988 Bp Rogers Sanders Harris. Asst Ch Of The Nativ Raleigh NC 2010; Assoc Chr Epis Ch Raleigh NC 1994-2009; R All SS Epis Ch Clinton SC 1991-1994; Asst S Mich And All Ang' Columbia SC 1988-1991; D S Chris's Ch Spartanburg SC 1988. allisonnancy@att.net

ALLISON-HATCH, Mary Susan (NCal) 1625 Escalante Ave SW, Albuquerque NM 87104 B St Paul MN 4/20/1948 BA U MN 1970; MA Stan 1990; MDiv CDSP 2003. D 6/28/2003 P 1/3/2004 Bp Richard Lester Shimpfky. m 7/11/1981 Timothy Allison-Hatch. Trin Ch Sonoma CA 2007-2009; S Paul's Ch Oakland CA 2004-2007; S Paul's Day Sch Of Oakland Oakland CA 2004-2007; Pstr Assoc All SS Epis Ch Palo Alto CA 2003-2004. sahcdsp@yahoo.com

ALLMAN, Denny Paul (Miss) 519 Oakwood Dr, Vicksburg MS 39180 B Perry OK 7/29/1932 s Cecil Paul Allman & Billie. U of New Mex 1954; LTh STUSo 1984. D 5/18/1984 P 12/4/1984 Bp Duncan Montgomery Gray Jr. m 4/29/1952 Norma Manatt c 3. Supply All SS Ch Inverness MS 1999-2004; SpirDirCllo Dio Mississippi Jackson MS 1995-1997; R Chr Epis Ch Vicksburg MS 1988-1998; Vic All SS Ch Inverness MS 1984-1988; Vic S Thos Ch Belzoni MS 1984-1988. Auth, "Bk Revs," *Epis Life*, 1999; Auth, "Benediction," *Living Ch*, 1984. Cath Fllshp Epis Ch 1993; Cmnty of S Mary 1985. abbadenny@yahoo.com

ALLMAN, Mary Katherine (SanD) 7946 Calle De La Plata, La Jolla CA 92037 B Monterey CA 1/16/1951 d John C Allman & Elizabeth B. BA SW Texas St U San Marcos 1973; Med SW Texas St U San Marcos 1976; MDiv Epis TS of The SW 1990; DMin EDS 2000. D 6/15/1990 Bp Earl Nicholas McArthur Jr P 12/20/1990 Bp John Herbert MacNaughton. The Bp's Sch La Jolla CA 2000-2011; S Mary's Epis Sch Memphis TN 1992-1998; Asst To The R S Mk's Ch Corpus Christi TX 1990-1992. allperson@aol.com

ALLPORT II, William H (WTex) 2026 Kilakila Dr, Honolulu HI 96817 **R S Helena's Epis Ch Boerne TX 2010-** B Baltimore MD 3/3/1976 s George H Allport & Connie Rosing. BA Dickinson Coll 1998; MDiv VTS 2002. D 6/8/2002 P 2/1/2003 Bp Michael Whittington Creighton. m 7/6/2002 Mary-Carolyn M Morrison c 2. Mem, Dioc Coun Dio Hawaii Honolulu HI 2004-2010; R S Ptr's Ch Honolulu HI 2004-2010; Assoc R S Thos Ch Lancaster PA 2002-2004; Chair, Yth Cmsn Dio Cntrl Pennsylvania Harrisburg PA 1998-2004. revballport@gmail.com

ALLYN, Compton (SO) 900 Adams Crossing #7200, Cincinnati OH 45202 B Dayton OH 6/19/1925 s Stanley Charles Allyn & Helen. BS U of Virginia 1946; MBA Harv 1949; BD EDS 1954; PhD U Cinc 1973. D 5/27/1954 P 12/1/1954 Bp Henry W Hobson. m 9/20/1997 Cecile Stewart Drackett. R Chr Epis Ch Of Springfield Springfield OH 1957-1961; Asst Epis Soc of Chr Ch Cincinnati OH 1954-1957. comptona@aol.com

ALMON JR, Austin Albert (RI) 116 Daggett Ave, Pawtucket RI 02861 B Pawtucket RI 6/4/1943 s Austin Albert Almon & Jeanie Gladys. BS Johnson & Wales U 1976; MBA Wstrn New Engl Coll 1983; Rhode Island Sch For Deacons 1985. D 7/13/1985 Bp George Nelson Hunt III. m 2/10/1968 Jacqueline Louise Tonge c 2. D S Paul's Ch Portsmouth RI 1993-2006; D Gr Ch In Providence Providence RI 1991-1993; Serv St Mich & Gr Ch Rumford RI 1991-1993; D Ch Of The Epiph Providence RI 1990-1991; D Gr Ch In Providence Providence RI 1985-1990; D St Mich & Gr Ch Rumford RI 1985-1990. Fllshp Way Cross.

ALMONO ROQUE, Joel A(ntonio) (Mass) 1524 Summit Ave, Saint Paul MN 55105 **Gr Ch Lawr MA 2006-; Hd Of Evang Dio The Dominican Republic (Iglesia Epis Dominicana) 100 Airport AvVenice FL 1993-; Hd Of Evang Dio The Dominican Republic (Iglesia Epis Dominicana) 100 Airport AvVenice FL 1993-** B San Francisco de Macoris DO 5/26/1959 s Ramon Antonio Almono & Adriana Roque. U Of Santo Domingo Do; Methodist TS 1982; U Third Age Law 1994. D 4/2/1995 P 9/24/1996 Bp Julio Cesar Holguin-Khoury. m 4/3/1993 Susan Charlotte Seaquist c 5. La Mision El Santo Nino Jesus S Paul MN 2004-2006; Dio Minnesota Minneapolis MN 1998-2004; Sub-D La Mision El Santo Nino Jesus S Paul MN 1994-1998. Auth, "Cantos Apocalipticos," *El Nuevo Diario*, 1996; Auth, "Dolor Del Tiempo". joelalmono@hotmail.com

ALMONTE, Salvador (DR) Calle Santiago #114 Gazcue, Santo Domingo Dominican Republic **Dio The Dominican Republic (Iglesia Epis Dominicana) Santo Domingo DO 1995-** B Gaspar Hernandez 6/5/1952 s Salvador Almonte & Gregoria Almonte. Rec from Roman Catholic 7/1/1995 as Priest Bp Julio Cesar Holguin-Khoury. m 8/31/1991 Ana Lidia Toribio.

ALMOS, Richard Wayne (La) 996 Marina Dr, Slidell LA 70458 **D Chr Ch Slidell LA 2005-** B La Crosse WI 1/15/1938 s Willard Lourie Almos & Beatrice Della. D 10/23/2005 Bp Charles Edward Jenkins III. m 6/28/1980 Jean Evelyn Strickland c 2. deacon@christchurchslidell.com

ALMQUIST SSJE, Curtis Gustav (Mass) 980 Memorial Drive, Cambridge MA 02138 **S Jn's Chap Cambridge MA 1987-** B Moline IL 2/1/1952 s Donald Gustav Almquist & Beatrice Lavera. BA Wheaton Coll 1974; MA MI SU 1978; MDiv Nash 1984; DD Ya Berk 2004. D 6/16/1984 Bp Quintin Ebenezer Primo Jr P 12/15/1984 Bp James Winchester Montgomery. Cur S Simons Ch Arlington Heights IL 1984-1987. "The Twelve Days of Christmas," Cowley, 2006; "God's Conditional Love," *I Have Called You Friends*, Cowley, 2006. calmessje.org

ALONGE-COONS, Katherine Grace (Alb) Grace Church, 34 3rd St, Waterford NY 12188 **Gr Ch Waterford NY 2007-** B Hudson NY 10/28/1959 d Charles Gaetaro Alonge & Judith Irene. BA Siena Coll 1980; MS SUNY 1985; MDiv St. Bernards TS and Mnstry Rochester NY 2006. D 6/11/2005 Bp Daniel William Herzog P 1/7/2006 Bp David John Bena. m 6/12/1982 Earl Alfred Coons c 2. D Gr Ch Waterford NY 2005-2006. kcoons@nycap.rr.com

ALONSO MARINA, Jesus Daniel (EcuC) Ava Y Maldonado, Guayaquil Ecuador **P Litoral Dio Ecuador Guayaquil EQ EC 1990-** B Burgos ES 5/7/1948 s Daniel Alonso & Carmen. San Jeronimo Sem Mayor; Inst Espanol De Misiones Extranjeras 1969; Inst Espanol De Misiones Extranjeras 1975. D 12/1/1978 P 7/1/1979 Bp The Bishop Of Colom. m 6/27/1988 Mirian Aguayo Bailon. Litoral Dio Ecuador Guayaquil EQ EC 1991-1996.

ALONZO, Mary (Roch) 541 Linden St, Rochester NY 14620 **D Chr Ch Rochester NY 1992-** B South Orange NJ 6/8/1937 d Joseph Lester Parsons & Mary Louise. Cert U CO; BA Vas 1959; MDiv Bex 1991. D 4/30/1992 Bp William George Burrill. m 12/26/1994 Daniel Arthur Alonzo.

ALONZO MARTINEZ, Gerardo Antonio (Hond) Col. Hato De Enmedico, S2, B26 No. 3820, Tegucigalpa 21105 Honduras **Dio Honduras Miami FL 2006-; Iglesia Epis Hondurena San Pedro Sula 2006-** B 2/18/1965 s Daniel Alonzo & Adela. DIT Programa Diocesana De Ecuc. Teologica 2003. D 10/29/2005 Bp Lloyd Emmanuel Allen. m 12/16/1989 Iris Godoy Odonez c 3. geraepi@yahoo.com

ALSAY, Joseph Caldwell (Okla) 14700 N MAY AVE, OKLAHOMA CITY OK 73134 **R S Aug Of Cbury Oklahoma City OK 2010-** B Chicago IL 5/17/1973 s Glenzia Martin Alsay & Beatrice. Phillips TS; BA Oklahoma Bapt U 1996; MDiv Luth Sch of the Theol@chicago 2004. Rec from Evangelical Lutheran Church in America 1/15/2011 Bp Edward Joseph Konieczny. m 8/6/2005 Cecelia Gray c 4. josephalsay@gmail.com

ALTIZER, Caryl Jean (WTenn) 1830 S 336th St Apt C-202, Federal Way WA 98003 B Huntington WV 2/23/1945 d Emmett Dale Altizer & Susan Margaret. U So; BS Bethel Coll 1967; MA OH SU 1969; MDiv Candler TS Emory U 1984. D 5/22/1984 P 12/18/1984 Bp Furman Stough. The Epis Counslg Cntr Memphis TN 1986-1988; Int S Mich's Epis Ch Birmingham AL 1985-1986; Asst H H Cross Trussville AL 1984-1986. caryl63@q.com

ALTON, Richard (Ct) 8 Armstrong Ln, Riverside CT 06878 **P-in-c S Andr's Ch Stamford CT 2007-** B Manchester CT 6/1/1955 s Richard Charles Alton & Elizabeth Ann. BA Boston Coll 1978; MAR Ya Berk 1980; CAS GTS 1988. D 6/11/1988 Bp Arthur Edward Walmsley P 2/25/1989 Bp Clarence Nicholas Coleridge. m 10/20/1979 Barbara Alton c 1. R S Mk's Ch Philadelphia PA 1997-2007; S Thos Ch New York NY 1994-1997; Trin Epis Ch Southport CT 1990-1994; Cur S Mary's Epis Ch Manchester CT 1988-1990. Ord Of S Jn. ralton@mac.com

ALTOPP, Whitney Lynn (Nwk) 26 Portland Pl # 2, Montclair NJ 07042 **Assoc S Thos' Ch Whitemarsh Ft Washington PA 2007-** B Champaign IL 10/15/1972 d Lawrence Dudley Fink & Deborah J H. BA Greenville Coll 1994; MDiv GTS 2002. D 6/15/2002 P 1/6/2003 Bp Gladstone Bailey Adams III. m 3/21/1992 Michael Paul Altopp c 4. Asst S Jas Ch Upper Montclair NJ 2002-2007; Intern S Mich's Ch New York NY 2000-2001; Yth Dir S Jame's Ch Skaneateles NY 1994-1997. motheraltopp@aol.com

ALVARADO, Luis (PR) No address on file. **Dio Puerto Rico S Just PR 2004-** B 12/28/1959

ALVAREZ-ADORNO, Aida-Luz (PR) P.O. Box 2292, Manatí PR 00674 Puerto Rico **Dio Puerto Rico S Just PR 2007-** B 4/3/1955 d Juan Alvarez Rodriguez & Carmen M. San Pedro Y San Pablo; MA Universidad Cntrl; BA Caribbean U 1980. D 8/27/2006 P 2/11/2007 Bp David Andres Alvarez-Velazquez. c 3. emhvb@yahoo.com

✠ **ALVAREZ-VELAZQUEZ, Rt Rev David Andres** (PR) Diocese of Puerto Rico, PO Box 902, Saint Just PR 00978 **Bp of Puerto Rico Dio Puerto Rico S Just PR 1987-** B Ponce Puerto Rico 8/17/1941 D 5/22/1965 P 11/27/1965 Bp Francisco Reus-Froylan Con 9/20/1987 for PR. m 12/10/1981 Maryleen Mullert. davidal@coqui.net

ALVES, David Alan (NCal) 13840 Tulsa Ct, Magalia CA 95954 **D Ch Of S Nich Paradise CA 1999-** B Dartmouth MA 4/16/1935 s Albert Marshel Alves & Olive Helen. New Bedford Inst of Tech; Sch for Deacons. D 8/31/1980 Bp Charles Shannon Mallory. m 2/17/1963 Marianne Poundstone c 2. D S Edw The Confessor Epis Ch San Jose CA 1991-1999; D Ch Of S Jos Milpitas CA 1982-1991; D S Edw The Confessor Epis Ch San Jose CA 1980-1982. alvesdm@sbcglobal.net

ALVES, Robert (EC) 954 Lake Ave, Greenwich CT 06831 **S Athan Ch Brunswick GA 1995-** B Philadelphia PA 9/7/1958 s James T(homason) Alves & Louella Rice. BA U So 1981; MDiv VTS 1989. D 6/10/1989 Bp John Thomas Walker P 1/13/1990 Bp Ronald Hayward Haines. m 11/26/1983 Polly B Barclay c 2. S Barn Epis Ch Greenwich CT 2004-2010; Dioc Secy Dio No Carolina Raleigh NC 2003-2004; Alt Dep Gc Dio No Carolina Raleigh NC 2003; Dep Gc Dio No Carolina Raleigh NC 2000; Stndg Com Dio No Carolina Raleigh NC 1999-2002; Chair Bp'S Transition Com Dio No Carolina Raleigh NC 1999-2001; Dioc Coun Dio No Carolina Raleigh NC 1996-1999; R All SS Ch Roanoke Rapids NC 1993-2004; Asst S Jn's Epis Ch Fayetteville NC 1989-1993; Liturg Cmsn Dio E Carolina Kinston NC 1989-1992. rector@stjohnsfayetteville.com

ALVEY JR, John Thomas (Ala) 110 W Hawthorne Rd, Birmingham AL 35209 **Cur All SS Epis Ch Birmingham AL 2009-** B Birmingham AL 1/10/1984 s John Thomas Alvey & Herdi. BS U of Alabama 2006; MDiv VTS 2009. D 5/27/2009 P 12/18/2009 Bp Henry Nutt Parsley Jr. m 5/30/2009 Jamie Bryars Jamie Carolyn Bryars. jackalvey@gmail.com

ALWINE, David W (Tex) 1103 N 11th St, Temple TX 76501 **R Chr Epis Ch Temple TX 2000-** B Biloxi MS 8/31/1953 s Wayne Arthur Alwine & Janie Patricia. BA Belhaven Coll 1975; MDiv Reformed TS 1978; MS U of Sthrn Mississippi 1981; STM STUSo 1983. D 12/21/1985 P 1/6/1987 Bp Donis Dean Patterson. m 6/30/1979 Margaret T Taliaferro c 2. R Gr Epis Ch Paris TN 1993-1999; R Ch Of The Ascen (Hagood) Rembert SC 1990-1993; Assc. R S Mich's Epis Ch Charleston SC 1987-1990; Ch Of The Epiph Richardson TX 1985-1987. dalwine@hot.rr.com

AMADIO, Anselm Henry (Chi) Po Box 51, Washington Island WI 54246 **Died 8/1/2010** B Clifton Heights PA 5/8/1927 s Alexander Samuel Amadio & Anna Dorothy. MIT 1946; BA CUA 1949; MA Coll Sant Anselmo Rome It 1956; PhD Oxf 1962; Liturg Inst at Trier 1966; Fllshp Germany 1969; U of Notre Dame 1984. Rec from Roman Catholic 3/21/1976 as Priest Bp James Winchester Montgomery. Auth, "Sprtl Search For Meaning In The Info Age," *Crossroads*, 1994; Auth, "Aristotle: Life And Works," *New Encyclopedia Britannica*, 1990; Auth, "Judiasm, Chrsnty & Islam: Conversions In The Abrahamic Tradition," *No Amer*, Islamic Coll Press, 1990; Auth, "Sprtl Growth As A Personal & Communal Process," *Inst For Sci & Rel*, Univ Chicago Press, 1984; Auth, "Profsnl Ethics In A Pluralistic Soc," 1982; Auth, "The Ch As Sacr," *New Cath Encyclopedia*, 1967; Auth, "Bible And Tech," *New Cath Encyclopedia*, 1967; Auth, "Benedictine Revolution," 1966; Auth, "17th Century Renaissance In Angl Theol," 1962. AAR 1975-1980; Amer Coun U Chapl 1979-1994; Cath Theol Soc 1964-1969; Soc Angl & Luth Theologians 1998. Fullbright Fell U Min Germany 1968; Phi Beta Kappa CUA 1949; Athlete Schlr CUA 1949. aamadio@dcwis.com

AMADIO, Carol Margaret (Chi) Po Box 51, Washington Island WI 54246 B Austin TX 7/30/1945 d William David Iford & Carol Ann. BA U CO 1968; MS Loyola U 1971; JD Loyola U 1975; MDiv McCormick TS 1980; LLM Illinois Inst of Tech 1982; LLM Kent St U 1982. D 6/11/1980 Bp James Winchester Montgomery P 2/24/1981 Bp Quintin Ebenezer Primo Jr. Asst S Simons Ch Arlington Heights IL 2000-2002; Int S Bede's Epis Ch Bensenville IL 1992-1993; Vice-Chncllr Dio Chicago Chicago IL 1989-1997; Int Gr Ch Chicago IL 1989-1991; Int Ch Of S Paul And The Redeem Chicago IL 1988-1989; Asst/P-in-c S Mk's Ch Evanston IL 1982-1988; D Ch Of Our Sav Chicago IL 1980-1982.

AMAYA, Adrian A (CNY) 1612 W Genesee St, Syracuse NY 13219 **S Mk The Evang Syracuse NY 2008-** B Alice TX 7/29/1966 s Alex Luna Amaya & Mary Lou. BA U of Texas 1992; MDiv STUSo 1999. D 6/16/1999 Bp Robert Boyd Hibbs P 1/13/2000 Bp James Edward Folts. m 11/13/1993 Anna Scott c 2. R S Phil's Ch Beeville TX 2002-2008; S Barth's Ch Corpus Christi TX 1999-2002. themayafamily@gmail.com

AMBELANG, John Edward (Eau) 506 Fairway Dr, Sheboygan WI 53081 B Saint Louis MO 4/26/1944 s Charles Drake Ambelang & Audry. BA U of Wisconsin 1966; MDiv Nash 1969. D 3/1/1969 Bp Donald H V Hallock P 9/13/1969 Bp William W Horstick. m 9/11/1965 Karen Krueger. R S Jn's Epis Ch Oxford WI 2002-2010; R S Mary's Epis Ch Tomah WI 2002-2010; R S Fran Ch Menomonee Falls WI 1997-2002; R S Mich's Epis Ch Racine WI 1981-1997; R S Mk's Ch Beaver Dam WI 1976-1981; Vic S Steph's Shell Lake WI 1973-1976; Cur Chr Ch Cathd Eau Claire WI 1972-1973; S Alb's Ch Spooner WI 1969-1976; St Stephens Ch Spooner WI 1969-1976. jambelangwi@gmail.com

AMBLER V, John Jaquelin (SwVa) 507 Sunset Dr, Amherst VA 24521 B Dante VA 11/12/1931 s John Jaquelin Ambler & Cynthia. BA S Johns Coll 1953; MDiv VTS 1959. D 6/12/1959 P 6/1/1960 Bp Frederick D Goodwin. m 8/24/1958 Mirosanda Adjemovitch c 4. Vic S Steph's Ch Romney WV 1963-1969; Asst S Paul's Ch Richmond VA 1959-1963. Auth, "Syllabus For Tchg The Abacus".

AMBLER JR, Michael Nash (Me) 912 Middle St, Bath ME 04530 **R Gr Epis Ch Bath ME 2002-** B New York NY 3/21/1964 BA Pr 1985; JD U MI 1989; MDiv EDS 2000. D 6/3/2000 P 12/16/2000 Bp Chilton Abbie Richardson Knudsen. m 7/13/1985 Deborah Ambler c 3. Dio Maine Portland ME 2000-2002; Asst S Dav's Epis Ch Kennebunk ME 2000-2002. mamblerjr@aol.com

AMBROISE, Rospignac (Hai) Box 1309, Port-Au-Prince Haiti B Mirebabais HT 12/13/1963 s Anne Andree Ambroise. Haiti TS 1992. D 12/6/1992 Bp Luc Anatole Jacques Garnier P 9/1/1993 Bp Jean Zache Duracin. m 12/29/1994 Junie Sagesse. Dio Haiti Ft Lauderdale FL 1992-2006; Asst P Dio Haiti Ft Lauderdale FL 1992-1993. Soc Of S Marg.

AMBROSE, Barbara Lockwood (Va) 236 S Laurel St, Richmond VA 23220 **Transition Com for Bp Suffr Dio Virginia Richmond VA 2011-; D S Andr's Ch Richmond VA 2011-** B Ft Stewart GA 2/4/1957 d Jacob Franklin Lockwood & Sarah Peple. BA Randolp Macon 1979; Chr Ed UTS and Presb Sch of Ed 2003; MSW Virginia Commonwealth U 2003; Graduated Diac Formation Inst 2010. D 2/5/2011 Bp Shannon Sherwood Johnston. m 10/7/1995 John Ambrose. cats4cats@comcast.net

AMBROSE, Colin Moore (Tenn) 116 N. Academy St., Murfreesboro TN 37130 **S Paul's Epis Ch Murfreesboro TN 2009-** B Knoxville TN 7/26/1978 s Paul Seabrook Ambrose & Kathleen Hesse. BA U NC 2000; MDiv Nash 2009. D 10/23/2008 P 5/16/2009 Bp Keith Lynn Ackerman. m 10/7/2001 Trisha Ambrose c 2. colinambrose@gmail.com

AMBROSE, Theodore Grant (EC) 2609 N Glebe Rd # P, Arlington VA 22207 **S Mary's Epis Ch Arlington VA 2011-** B Washington NC 3/24/1979 s Theodore D Ambrose & Bonnie S. BA No Carolina Wesleyan Coll 2001; MDiv VTS 2011. D 6/11/2011 Bp Clifton Daniel III. GRANT.AMBROSE@STMARYSARLINGTON.ORG

AMBROSE, Valerie Twomey (WMich) 6308 Greenway Drive SE, Grand Rapids MI 49546 **P-in-c S Jn's Ch Fremont MI 2011-** B North Hollywood CA 5/27/1947 d Lawrence Arver Twomey & Celine. BA TCU 1967; MRE Wstrn TS 1996. D 4/26/1997 P 1/17/1998 Bp Edward Lewis Lee Jr. c 3. Assoc S Andr's Ch Grand Rapids MI 2007-2010; Int S Mk's Ch Grand Rapids MI 2003-2007; Int Epis Par Of S Jn The Bapt Portland OR 2000-2002; Int S Jas Epis Ch Tigard OR 2000-2001; Int S Tim Ch Richland MI 1999; Assoc S Mart Of Tours Epis Ch Kalamazoo MI 1998-1999. Auth, "Developing a Seasonal Wrshp Template," *Open*, 2001. Associated Parishes Coun 1994-2004; Attending Cler Assn Holland Hosp 1997-1999; Epis Sr Living Serv (Pres.) 2000-2002. Dioc Designee Natl Wmn Hist Proj ECW Dio Wstrn Michigan 1994. valambro@aol.com

AMBURGEY, Cristina Goubaud (Oly) 3213 17th Street Pl Se, Puyallup WA 98374 B Guatamala City GT 9/3/1947 d Antonio Goubaud de Carrera & Frances Elizabeth. BS Arizona St U 1985. D 6/23/2001 Bp Sanford Zangwill Kaye Hampton. m 6/13/1981 Robert M Amburgey c 4. D S Andr's Epis Ch Tacoma WA 2001-2006. NAAD 1996-2006; Sis of S Jos of Peace - Assoc 1995. orthodoggie@earthlink.net

AMEND, Albert Edward (LI) 13821 Willow Bridge Dr, North Fort Myers FL 33903 B Columbus OH 7/1/1930 s Albert Henry Amend & Marie. BA Iona Coll 1957; MA CUNY 1961; Cert Mercer TS 1971. D 6/13/1970 P 6/12/1971 Bp Jonathan Goodhue Sherman. m 6/28/1958 Virginia D Patterson c 2. S Lk's Ch Ft Myers FL 1994-2003; R Epis Ch of The Resurr Williston Pk NY 1976-1992; P-in-c Ch Of S Jn The Bapt Cntr Moriches NY 1972-1976; Dio Long Island Garden City NY 1971-1976; Asst S Paul's Ch Patchogue NY 1970-1971. CCU 1980-1993; Comp & Area Chapl for FL FODC 1993; ESA 1979-1993; SSC 1990. amendnorth@aol.com

AMEND, Russell Jay (WNY) 25 Caspian Ct, Amherst NY 14228 B New York NY 9/24/1933 s Russell Joseph Amend & Marion Virginia. BA Queens Coll, Flushing, Long Island, N.Y. 1955; MDiv Ya Berk 1958. D 4/12/1958 P 10/25/1958 Bp James P De Wolfe. m 6/30/1956 Joan Katherine Valentine c 2. Dioc Coun Dio Wstrn New York Tonawanda NY 1968-1972; R H Apos Epis Ch Tonawanda NY 1966-1998; P-in-c H Apos Epis Ch Tonawanda NY

1965-1966; P-in-c Ch Of The Redeem Niagara Falls NY 1960-1965; Cur Epis Ch of The Resurr Williston Pk NY 1958-1960. Bd Dir: Bible Soc of Wstrn New York 1967-1992. P of the Year Dio Wstrn New York, Bp Dav C. Bowman Buffalo NY 1995. fr.russ5@verizon.net

AMERMAN, Lucy S (Pa) PO Box 57, Buckingham PA 18912 **R Trin Ch Buckingham PA 2006-** B Sewickley PA 12/27/1950 d Lockhart Amerman & Louise Swain. BA Goucher Coll 1972; JD Widener U 1976; MDiv PrTS 2002; Dplma Oxf 2006. D 6/28/2003 Bp David B(ruce) Joslin P 1/5/2004 Bp George Edward Councell. c 2. Asst R S Ptr's Epis Ch Arlington VA 2003-2006. lsla1232004@yahoo.com

AMES, David A (RI) 130 Slater Ave, Providence RI 02906 **P-in-c All SS' Memi Ch Providence RI 2010-** B Glendale OH 9/12/1938 s Malcolm McEwan Ames & Jane Elizabeth. BA Mia 1960; MDiv EDS 1966; DMin EDS 1984; Fell Coll of Preachers 1994; Exec Serv Corps of New Engl 2004; Int Mnstry Prog 2005. D 6/25/1966 P 1/6/1967 Bp Roger W Blanchard. m 1/30/1982 Carol Landau c 2. P-in-c S Mk's Epis Ch Riverside RI 2006-2008; R Gr Ch New Bedford MA 2005; R S Mart's Ch Providence RI 2004-2005; Exec Dir Assoc For Rel & Intellectual Life New Rochelle NY 1989-1993; Chapl Dio Rhode Island Providence RI 1972-2003; Asst Gr Ch In Providence Providence RI 1969-1971; P Ch Of S Edw Columbus OH 1966-1969. Ames, D.A., "A Pstr Perspective on Death and Those Who Survive," *Med and Hlth/Rhode Island*, Rhode Island Med Assn, 2005; Ames, Dav A., "The Role of the Ch in the New Genetics," *A Chr Response to the New Genetics*, Rowman & Littlefiled, 2003; Ames, D.A., "Cultural Ambiguity and Moral Ldrshp," *Plumbline*, Plumbline, 1995. ESMHE 1973-2003. Appreciation for Strategic Plnng Holocaust Educ and Resource Cntr of Rhode Island 2006; Fac Serv Awd Brown Med Sch 2004; DSA PPF of Amer 2003; Years of Serv Awd Br 2000; Cert of Recognition Brown Med Sch 1999; Gilman Angier Awd Planned Parenthood of Rhode Island 1995. daames3@verizon.net

AMES, Richard Kenneth (SeFla) 4917 Ravenswood Dr Apt 1709, San Antonio TX 78227 B Tappan NY 4/25/1935 s Donald Buchanan Ames & Virginia Odell. BS WA SU 1965; MPA Auburn U 1973; MDiv Nash 1983. D 7/28/1982 Bp Edward Mason Turner P 6/1/1983 Bp William Cockburn Russell Sheridan. m 10/5/1956 Dolores Natalie Osgood c 3. S Mk's Ch Palm Bch Gardens FL 1994; R S Jn's Ch Hollywood FL 1986-1994; R S Anne's Epis Ch Warsaw IN 1983-1986. Bro Awd Hollywood Interfaith 1990. abighalo@aol.com

AMMONS JR, Benjamin W (Fla) 325 N Market St, Jacksonville FL 32202 **Cn Dio Florida Jacksonville FL 2011-** B Jacksonville FL 6/9/1980 s Benjamin Wiley Ammons & Janice Kay. BS U of Florida 2002; MDiv VTS 2011. D 12/5/2010 P 6/19/2011 Bp Samuel Johnson Howard. m 12/15/2001 Laura C Chiles. wiley.ammons@gmail.com

AMPAH OSH, Rosina Rhoda Araba (NY) 3042 Eagle Dr, Augusta GA 30906 B Tarkwa GH 12/30/1941 d Samuel Kristus Ampah & Christina Esi. BA Coll of New Rochelle 1990; MDiv NYTS 1993. D 6/12/1993 P 12/11/1993 Bp Richard Frank Grein. Asst S Jn's Ch Hempstead NY 1993-1995; Asst S Jn's Of Lattingtown Locust Vlly NY 1993-1994. Ord of S Helena. Hon Cn Cath Chr King, Cape Coast Ghana 2004. rosinaosh@comcast.net

AMPARO TAPIA, Milton Mauricio (DR) Juan Luis Franco Bido #21, Santo Domingo Dominican Republic **Dio The Dominican Republic (Iglesia Epis Dominicana) Santo Domingo DO 2007-** B Castillo Provincia Duarte 9/4/1966 s Carlos Amparo Garcia & Virginia. MS The London Sch of Econ and Political Sci; BA Intec 1992; BA Instituto Santo Inacio 1998. Rec from Roman Catholic 8/15/1998 Bp Julio Cesar Holguin-Khoury. m 7/2/2005 Kattia Severino. miltonamparo@gmail.com

AMSDEN, Helen (Neb) 9459 Jones Cir, Omaha NE 68114 B Grand Island NE 4/21/1928 d Harold A Prince & Mary. Smith; BA U of Nebraska 1949. D 11/8/1985 Bp James Daniel Warner. m 2/5/1955 Don Bruce Amsden c 3.

AMUZIE, Charles C (WA) 3601 Alabama Ave SE, Washington DC 20020 **R S Tim's Epis Ch Washington DC 2009-** B NG 5/6/1956 s Nathan Obisike Amuzie & Edna Comfort. DMiss Asbury TS; BS U of Nigeria 1982; DIT Imm Coll of Theol Ibadan NG 1986; MDiv Epis TS of The SW 1989; ThM Fuller TS 1992; PhD U of Kentucky 2004. Trans from Church Of Nigeria 11/1/1995 Bp Henry Irving Louttit. m 11/26/1983 Nena Uka c 4. R S Athan Ch Brunswick GA 1995-2008; Vic S Andr's Ch Lexington KY 1992-1995; Yth Min S Lk's Of The Mountains La Crescenta CA 1991-1992; Assoc. P S Jas Ch Austin TX 1986-1989. amuzie42@aol.com

ANCHAN, Israel D (Chi) 298 S. Harrison Ave., Kankakee IL 60901 **R S Paul's Ch Kankakee IL 2009-** B 7/3/1955 s Benony Anchan & Leelavathi. BD Serampore U 1983; STM UTS 2001; ThM Luth TS 2003; DMin Luth TS 2008. Trans from Church of South India 12/15/2008 Bp Jeffrey Dean Lee. m 5/26/1985 Ruth J Ruth Jacqueline Amanna c 2. anchanisrael@hotmail.com

ANDERHEGGEN, George Curtis (Ct) 6 Rosewood Cir, Monroe CT 06468 B Portland OR 2/14/1928 s William Louis Lothar Anderheggen & Josephine Eleanor. BS U of Connecticut 1958; MDiv Ya Berk 1966; PhD Columbia Pacific U 1988. D 6/11/1966 P 3/1/1967 Bp Walter H Gray. m 9/27/1980 Jean Anderheggen c 5. Asst S Jn's Ch Bridgeport CT 1967-1971; Cur S Jn's Ch E Hartford CT 1966-1967. Auth, "A Wish For Your Christmas," *Elem Fun*; Auth, "Willy The Weenie Whiner," *Elem Fun*; Auth, "For Better, For Worse, Struggles," *Pilgrimage*. Amer Assn Of Behavioral Therapists; Amer Assn Of Mar & Fam Therapists; Amer Assn Of Sex Educators, Counselors, & Therapists; Natl Gld Of Hypnotists. Williams Curtis Awd For Rel Natl Gld Of Hypnotists 2002. gcanderheggen@yahoo.com

ANDERS, Florence Kay (RG) Holy Family Episcopal Church, 10 A Bisbee Court, Santa fe NM 87508 **Vic Epis Ch Of The H Fam Santa Fe NM 2008-** B Stockton CA 3/5/1947 d Paul W Houghton & Elizabeth A. BA U of N Colorado 1969; MA U of New Mex 1972; BS U of New Mex 1989; MDiv TESM 2008. D 11/10/2007 P 6/3/2008 Bp William Carl Frey. m 5/9/1998 Peter Anders. kay41h@yahoo.com

ANDERS, Joan M (NJ) 417 Washington St, Toms River NJ 08753 **R Chr Ch Toms River Toms River NJ 2003-** B Lakewood NJ 8/2/1953 d Vincent King Pettit & Virginia Elsa. BA Rutgers-The St U 1975; EFM STUSo 1995; MDiv GTS 1998. D 6/6/1998 Bp David Standish Ball P 12/12/1998 Bp Vincent King Pettit. c 2. S Ptr's Ch Medford NJ 1998-2003; Dio Albany Albany NY 1991-1995. Cnvnt St. Jn Bapt--Assoc 2008; Ord of S Lk 2002. revjanders@aol.com

ANDERSEN, Francis Ian (Cal) 5 Epsom Court, Donvale Victoria VI 3111 Australia B Warwick WA AU 7/28/1925 s Rasmus Ludwig Emil Andersen & Hilda Fanny. BS U Of Queensland Brisbane Qld Au 1947; BA U of Melbourne 1951; MS U of Melbourne 1956; BD Lon 1957; MA Jn Hopkins U 1959; PhD Jn Hopkins U 1960. Trans from Anglican Church Of Australia 9/1/1990 Bp William Edwin Swing. m 12/5/1952 Lois Clarissa Garrett. Prof CDSP Berkeley CA 1963-1972. Auth, "Var Books".

ANDERSEN, Gary Stanley (Cal) 1298 Mcgregor Ave, Petaluma CA 94954 **Died 12/5/2009** B San Francisco CO 9/5/1929 s Robert Christian Andersen. BA Stan 1955; BD VTS 1958. D 6/29/1958 P 5/1/1959 Bp Henry H Shires.

ANDERSEN, John Day (Va) 2702 W Old State Road 34, Lizton IN 46149 **Dioc Sfty Mgr Dio Indianapolis Indianapolis IN 2007-; Dioc Sfty Mgr Dio Indianapolis Indianapolis IN 2007-; Vic Ch Of S Lawr Alexandria Bay NY 2005-** B Auburn NY 5/29/1933 s Robert Julius Andersen & Arlene. BA Hob 1960; MDiv Ya Berk 1963. D 6/11/1963 Bp Walter H Gray P 12/14/1963 Bp John Henry Esquirol. m 1/30/1993 Janet Lewis. Roslyn Managers Corp Richmond VA 1972-1992; Asst S Mk's Ch New Canaan CT 1969-1972. Ed, "ECCC Update," *Epis Camps and Conf Centers*, 1985; Ed, "The Journ," *Intl Assn*, Conf Cntr Admin, 1978. ECCC 1998; IACCA 1972. Washburn Awd for Disting Serv to Conf Ctr Ldrshp IACCA; Fouding Exec and Life Mem Natl Association of Epis Camps and Conf Centers; Staub Awd for Cmnty Serv Thousand Island Pk, New York. ecccdir@aol.com

ANDERSEN, Paul John (Va) PO Box 476, Saluda VA 23149 **R Chr Epis Ch Saluda VA 2006-** B Worcester MA 11/3/1949 s Albert John Andersen & Anna Theresa. BA U of Alabama 1971; MDiv VTS 1977. D 5/26/1977 Bp Furman Stough. m 5/20/1986 Lilith Peklic c 2. Dio Wstrn Massachusetts Springfield MA 2002-2005; R Trin Epis Ch Milford MA 2002-2005; Calv Ch Washington DC 1977. pjaccp@verizon.net

ANDERSEN, Raynor Wade (Ct) 199 Eastgate Dr, Cheshire CT 06410 B New York NY 5/25/1944 s Haakon Jarrel Andersen & Olive. BA Col 1966; STD PDS 1970. D 6/5/1970 P 12/1/1970 Bp Horace W B Donegan. m 8/7/1981 Karla Mary Scholz c 2. Prog/Bdgt Com Dio Connecticut Hartford CT 1994-1998; Hlth/Human Serv Com Dio Connecticut Hartford CT 1983-1988; St Pauls Mssn of the Deaf W Hartford CT 1972-2004; Asst Gr Ch Merchantville NJ 1971-1972; Asst S Ann's Ch For The Deaf New York NY 1970-1971. Cranmer Cup, Victorius Chair 2000-2002; Epis Conf of the Deaf 1972; Oblate, Mulligan Soc 1975; Porter Cup 1996. rayback9@cox.net

ANDERSEN, Richard Belden (Nwk) 275 E Franklin Tpke, Ho Ho Kus NJ 07423 B Bakersfield CA 10/26/1926 s Richard August Andersen & Marion. BA U of Redlands 1950; BD CRDS 1953; GTS 1967; MA FD 1974; MS FD 1974. D 1/8/1967 Bp George E Rath P 5/1/1967 Bp Dudley S Stark. m 9/3/1949 Barbara Joy. Int S Jn's Memi Ch Ramsey NJ 2000-2002; R S Eliz's Ch Ridgewood NJ 1972-1991; Assoc Chr Ch Short Hills NJ 1971-1972; Asst Chr Ch Short Hills NJ 1967-1971.

ANDERSEN, Steven C (U) 75 South 200 East, P.O. Box 3090, Salt Lake City UT 84110 **Chf Fin Off Dio Utah Salt Lake City UT 2009-; Asstg P Ch Of The Resurr Centerville UT 2004-** B Jerome ID 5/15/1956 s Keith Crandall Andersen & LaVerne Shawver. BSBA U of Phoenix 1991. D 6/19/2003 P 2/21/2004 Bp Carolyn Tanner Irish. m 4/4/1977 Annette Olsen c 1. SANDERSEN@EPISCOPAL-UT.ORG

ANDERSON, Albert William (CNY) 12445 Kaywood St Nw, Massillon OH 44647 **Died 7/25/2009** B Watervliet NY 4/5/1922 s Albin F Anderson & Marie F. BA Un Coll Schenectady NY 1947; MDiv VTS 1950; S Geo's Coll Jerusalem IL 1980. D 3/19/1950 P 10/1/1950 Bp Frederick Lehrle Barry. c 3. wifet@aol.com

ANDERSON, Ann Johnston (ND) 2405 W Country Club Dr S, Fargo ND 58103 B Bismarck ND 9/2/1955 d James William Johnston & Joyce Edith. AA No Dakota St U 1977. D 5/10/2002 P 5/9/2003 Bp Andrew Hedtler Fairfield. m

11/24/1984 David Frederick Anderson. D Geth Cathd Fargo ND 2002-2003. annja@cableone.com

ANDERSON, Augusta Anne (WNC) 2 Cedarcliff Road, Asheville NC 28803 **S Jas Ch Black Mtn NC 2010-** B San Rafael CA 1/1/1969 d Richard Charles Rowe & Katherine Whitney. BA Wm Smith 1991; MDiv VTS 1999. D 6/12/1999 Bp Ronald Hayward Haines P 12/11/1999 Bp Robert Hodges Johnson. m 7/21/2001 James Stephen Anderson c 3. S Thos Epis Ch Burnsville NC 2004-2007; Cn The Cathd Of All Souls Asheville NC 1999-2003. aaainnc@yahoo.com

ANDERSON JR, Bert A (Los) 612 Chestnut St, Ashland OR 97520 B Los Angeles CA 2/18/1929 s Bert Axel Anderson & Alma. BA California St U 1956; MDiv CDSP 1959; PhD Sierra U Costa Mesa CA 1988. D 6/22/1959 P 2/1/1960 Bp Francis E I Bloy. m 12/2/1973 Nancy Daniels c 3. Trin Epis Ch Redlands CA 1986-1988; Vic Ch Of The H Sprt Bullhead City AZ 1980-1982; Chair Cmsn On Stwdshp Educ Dio Los Angeles Los Angeles CA 1965-1966; R S Andr's By The Sea Epis Par San Diego CA 1960-1967. Auth, "Mr. Brightside and the Bonfire Nights," *Play*, Self-Pub, 2010; Auth, "BONE: Dying Into Life," *Play*, Self-Pub, 2008; Auth, "Dyspnea During Panic Attacks," *Behavior Modification*, Behavior Modification, 2001; Auth, "Healing Panic Recovery Prog," Self-Pub, 1998. Amer Assnociation Of Psychophysiology And Biofeedback 1985-2001; California Assn Of Fam Therapists 1985-1998; Int Soc For The Advancement Of Respiratory Psychophysiology 1999-2004. berta@bisp.net

ANDERSON, Betsy Neville (Los) 315 Lorraine Blvd, Los Angeles CA 90020 **Assoc The Par Of S Matt Pacific Palisades CA 1997-** B Los Angeles CA 7/31/1948 d James Neville & Jeanne. BA Stan 1970; MDiv Ya Berk 1997. D 6/21/1997 P 1/17/1998 Bp Frederick Houk Borsch. m 6/17/1972 Carl Thomas Anderson c 2. banderson@stmatthews.com

ANDERSON, Bettina (Colo) 822 Fox Hollow Ln, Golden CO 80401 B Seattle WA 9/27/1943 d Frederick G Galer & Vera Louise. BS Colorado St U 1965; MS Colorado St U 1967; PhD Colorado St U 1971; MDiv Pontifical Coll Josephinum 1985. D 6/8/1985 P 12/1/1985 Bp William Grant Black. m 10/4/1973 Wesley D Anderson. R Ch Of S Jn Chrys Golden CO 1995-2000; R S Ptr's Epis Ch Delaware OH 1987-1995; Asst R S Jas Epis Ch Columbus OH 1985-1987; D-in-Trng S Jas Epis Ch Columbus OH 1985.

ANDERSON, Carmen Marie (Kan) 375 Lake Shore Drive, Alma KS 66401 B Wichita KS 8/17/1940 d Harold Lamar Warner & Mildred. BS K SU 1963. D 6/20/1987 Bp Richard Frank Grein. m 5/27/1961 Donald Keith Anderson c 3. Gd Shpd Epis Ch Wichita KS 1990-1992. carmenanderson@embarqmail.com

ANDERSON, Carol Linda (Los) 115 E 87th St Apt 6B, New York NY 10128 B Easton PA 6/18/1945 d William Carlton Anderson & Doris. BA Lycoming Coll 1967; MDiv EDS 1970. D 11/13/1971 P 1/3/1977 Bp Horace W B Donegan. R All SS Par Beverly Hills CA 1989-2010; R All Ang' Ch New York NY 1979-1986; Asst S Jas Ch New York NY 1972-1979; Exec Asst Epis Mssn Soc Epis Ch Cntr New York NY 1971-1972. Auth, *Knowing Jesus in Your Life*, Morehouse Pub, 1993. DDiv w hon Ya Berk New Haven CT 1992. clandersonnyc@gmail.com

ANDERSON, Carolyn Kinsey (Ga) 4221 Blue Heron Ln, Evans GA 30809 B Harvey IL 10/4/1939 Sthrn Illinois U. D 7/10/2002 Bp Henry Irving Louttit. c 3. S Paul's Ch Augusta GA.

ANDERSON JR, C Newell (At) 1884 Rugby Ave, College Park GA 30337 B Columbia SC 11/8/1937 s Claude N Anderson & Kathleen H. BA Georgia Inst of Tech; MDiv STUSo. D 6/24/1972 Bp Milton LeGrand Wood P 4/1/1973 Bp Bennett Jones Sims. m 12/30/1983 Curtissa Smith. P-in-c S Simon's Epis Ch Conyers GA 1999-2003; The Epis Ch Of S Ptr And S Paul Marietta GA 1998-1999; S Cathr's Epis Ch Marietta GA 1997-1998; S Jos's On-The-Mtn Mentone AL 1993; Cur S Jn's Coll Pk GA 1982-1992; Cn Cathd Of S Phil Atlanta GA 1981-1982; Cmncatn Off Dio Atlanta Atlanta GA 1976-1978; Cn Cathd Of S Phil Atlanta GA 1974-1976. Auth, "Dio". canona@bellsouth.net

✠ **ANDERSON, Rt Rev Craig Barry** (SD) PO Box 1595, Eastsound WA 98245 **R (P-t) and Asstg Bp in Olympia Emm Ch Orcas Island Eastsound WA 2007-** B Glendale CA 2/12/1942 s Alvin Leroy Anderson & Glenn Elaine. BA Valparaiso U 1963; MDiv STUSo 1975; MA Van 1981; PhD Van 1986; DD STUSo 1987; Fllshp OH SU 1993; DHL Valparaiso U 1993; Fllshp Uppsala U 1998. D 12/21/1974 Bp William Carl Frey P 6/29/1975 Bp Girault M Jones Con 7/27/1984 for SD. m 8/2/1970 Lizbeth Johnston c 3. Int R and Asstg Bp in Idaho S Thos Epis Ch Sun Vlly ID 2006-2007; Int Bp Dio Vermont Burlington VT 2000-2001; Asst Bp Dio New York New York City NY 1993-1997; Dn, Pres and Prof of Theol The GTS New York NY 1993-1997; Dio So Dakota Sioux Falls SD 1993; Asst Bp Dio Sthrn Ohio Cincinnati OH 1992-1993; Bp Dio So Dakota Sioux Falls SD 1984-1993; P-in-c Chr Ch Alto Decherd TN 1978-1984; Prof Of Pstr Theol The TS at The U So Sewanee TN 1978-1984; Asst Chapl The U So (Sewanee) Sewanee TN 1976-1977; Chapl S Andr's Chap S Andrews TN 1973-1975. Auth, "Two Realms And Their Relationships," *Sci mag*, 1999; Auth, "Fragmentation Of Knowledge," *U Of Tulsa Bell Lecture Series*, 1999; Auth, "Theol Method And Epis Vocation," *ATR*, 1995. Chapl Dok 1991-1994; Cmnty Of S Mary, Assoc 1975; Vstng Bp Ord Of S Helena 1993-1997. Fjellstedt Fell (Post-Doctoral) Uppsala Sweden 1997; Mershon Fell (Post-Doctoral) OH SU 1992; Great Sioux Nation Peace Medal 1991; Gvnr'S Awd For Recon 1991; Woods Ldrshp Awd U So Sewanee TN 1973. landersonster@gmail.com

ANDERSON SR, David Craig (Spr) 2090 Silver Hill Rd, Stone Mountain GA 30087 B Lebanon OR 8/20/1944 s Edwin Jefferson Anderson & Grace Adeline. BA U of Maryland 1967; MDiv VTS 1970; Coll of Preachers 1982; VTS 1997. D 6/27/1970 P 2/14/1971 Bp William Foreman Creighton. m 6/10/1967 Mary Anne Kemp c 3. Hon Cn Cathd Cntr Of S Paul Cong Los Angeles CA 1998-2003; Dn Dnry X Dio Los Angeles Los Angeles CA 1998-2002; Dioc Coun Dio Los Angeles Los Angeles CA 1990-1992; R S Jas' Epis Ch Los Angeles CA 1987-2002; UCI Cbury Bd Dio Los Angeles Los Angeles CA 1987-1989; Dioc Coun Dio So Dakota Sioux Falls SD 1979-1986; R Emm Epis Par Rapid City SD 1978-1987; Exam Chapl Dio Wyoming Casper WY 1976-1978; R S Andr's Ch Basin WY 1973-1978; Trst Dio Montana Helena MT 1971-1973; R S Mary's Ch Malta MT 1971-1973; R S Matt's Ch Glasgow MT 1971-1973; Asst Chr Ch Par Kensington MD 1970-1971. "The Lamb Story," *The Angl Dig*, 2005; Auth, *Intersect (weekly televlsion Prog)*, KEVN-TV Rapid City, SD, 1981; Auth, *Faces of Faith (weekly television Prog)*, KEVN-TV Rapid City, SD, 1979. dcasr@bellsouth.net

ANDERSON, David R (Ct) Saint Luke's Parish, 1864 Post Rd, Darien CT 06820 **R S Lk's Par Darien CT 2003-** B Yankton SD 9/3/1956 s Gerald Wilson Anderson & Aldoris Marie. BA Bob Jones U 1978; MA U Chi 1980; MDiv Ya Berk 1989. D 6/17/1989 Bp Frank Tracy Griswold III P 1/27/1990 Bp Clarence Nicholas Coleridge. m 6/3/1978 Pamela Anderson c 2. R Trin Ch Solebury PA 1992-2003; Assoc R S Lk's Par Darien CT 1989-1992. Auth, "Breakfast Epiphanies," Beacon Press, 2002. david.anderson@saintlukesdarien.org

ANDERSON, David Traynham (Va) 111 Charnwood Rd, Richmond VA 23229 **S Steph's Ch Richmond VA 2003-** B Danville VA 6/16/1954 s Howard Palmer Anderson & Mildred Graham. BA W&L 1976; MDiv Van 1980; PhD UTS Richmond VA 1991. D 6/24/2000 P 2/6/2001 Bp Peter James Lee. m 3/6/1982 Mary Celeste Franko c 3. S Steph's Epis Ch Beckley WV 2003-2011; S Chris's Sch Richmond VA 2000-2003. Auth, "A Bk Revs of A Hist of Ch Schools 1920-1950 by Jn Page Williams," *Virginia Sem Journ*. Who's Who Among Amer Teachers 2000; Armstrong-Jennings Tchr Awd S Chris's Sch Richmond VA 1991; BA cl W&L Lexington VA 1976; Psi Chi (Natl Psychol hon Soc) 1975. danderson@saintstephensrichmond.net

ANDERSON, Devon Elizabeth (Minn) 4712 Washburn Ave S, Minneapolis MN 55410 **Ch Of The Epiph Epis Plymouth MN 2011-; R Trin Ch Excelsior MN 2011-; Dio Minnesota Minneapolis MN 2006-** B Newport Beach CA 10/1/1966 d Glen Anderson & Bonnie. BA U MI 1988; MDiv Harvard DS 1997. D 6/21/1997 P 5/14/1998 Bp R(aymond) Stewart Wood Jr. m 7/11/1998 Michael David McNally c 2. Episcopalians for Global Recon Brandon FL 2009-2011; Assoc S Jn The Bapt Epis Ch Minneapolis MN 2001-2007; Assoc S Clare Of Assisi Epis Ch Ann Arbor MI 1998-2001; Asst Chr Ch Detroit MI 1997-1998. "Herod's Fear," *Sermons That Wk*, 2003; Auth, "Commissioning Ch Sch Teachers," *Awake My Soul: a Liturg Resource for Chld & Adults*, Epis Ch Cntr, 2000; Auth, "Pryr for Stwdshp," *Wmn Uncommon Prayers*, Morehouse Pub, 2000; Auth, "MLK, Jr Remembrance to be linked to Detroit's Hist," *The Record*, 1999; Auth, "Chrsnty Beyond Creeds," *The Record*, 1998. Hopkins Shareholder Harv 1996-1997. devonanderson1@gmail.com

ANDERSON, Douglas Evan (Dal) Po Box 1125, Texarkana TX 75504 **R S Jas Epis Ch Texarkana TX 2004-** B Orillia CA 7/7/1968 s Harry Christopher Anderson & Margaret Alice. BA Trin, Toronto 1991; MDiv Nash 1994. D 6/10/1994 P 12/15/1994 Bp Russell Edward Jacobus. m 6/24/1995 Traci-Lyn A Eldridge. R Chr Ch In Woodbury Woodbury NJ 1997-2004; Cur Ch Of S Mths Dallas TX 1994-1996. Auth, *Var arts*. MDiv cl Nash Nashotah WI 1994; BA cl Trin, U Toronto Toronto Ontario CA 1991. therector@stjamestxk.org

ANDERSON, Douglas Reid (Mont) 408 Westview Dr, Missoula MT 59803 B Moscow ID 9/6/1940 s Carl Swante Anderson & Etheta May. BS U Of Idaho Moscow 1965. D 7/8/1995 Bp Charles Jones III. m 8/26/1961 Judith Kay Finney c 2.

ANDERSON III, Elenor Lucius (Ala) 447 McClung Ave SE, Huntsville AL 35801 **R Ch Of The Nativ Epis Huntsville AL 2003-** B Statesboro GA 7/13/1955 s Elenor Lucius Anderson & Wudie Gay. BA U GA 1977; MBA Georgia St U 1986; MDiv STUSo 1994; DMin STUSo 2006. D 6/4/1994 P 12/10/1994 Bp Frank Kellogg Allan. m 10/17/1981 Tippen H Harvey c 2. R Gr Epis Ch Anderson SC 1999-2003; Cn for Chld Cathd Of S Phil Atlanta GA 1994-1999. "Forming Communities of Recon: The Nativ Cntr for Pilgrimage and Recon," *U So*, U So, 2006. MDiv mcl STUSo Sewanee TN 1994. andy.anderson@nativity-hsv.org

ANDERSON, Elizabeth May (Chi) 141 Main St Unit 323, Racine WI 60046 B Waukegan IL 12/2/1954 d Eric Siegfred Anderson & Madge. BA Lake Forest Coll 1976; MTS Nash 1979; MDiv SWTS 1994. D 6/18/1994 P 12/17/1994 Bp Frank Tracy Griswold III. P-in-c Ch Of The H Fam Lake Villa IL 2003-2009; R Ch Of The Annunc Bridgeview IL 1997-2002; Joliet Dnry rep, Dioc Coun

Dio Chicago Chicago IL 1997-1999; Asst S Lawr Epis Ch Libertyville IL 1994-1997; Waukegan Dnry Del, Suffr Bp Search Com Dio Chicago Chicago IL 1988-1989. Ed-in-Chf, "Let Us Keep the Feast," *Daughters of Sarah*, Daughters of Sarah, Inc., 1996; Ed-in-Chf, "Always Acceptable in Thy Sight," *Daughters of Sarah*, Daughters of Sarah, Inc., 1995; Ed-in-Chf, "The Redemp of Power and Eros," *Daughters of Sarah*, Daughters of Sarah, Inc., 1995; Ed-in-Chf, "On Sprtl Motherhood," *Daughters of Sarah*, Daughters of Sarah, Inc., 1995; Ed-in-Chf, "Contemplative Life and Wrshp," *Daughters of Sarah*, Daughters of Sarah, Inc., 1995. lizele3@att.net

ANDERSON, Eric A (Kan) 2001 Windsor Dr, Newton KS 67114 B Salina KS 4/25/1964 s Donald Colburn Anderson & Edwina. BS California St U 1986; MDiv Wartburg TS 1992; Cert Epis TS of The SW 2004. D 6/26/2004 P 1/26/2005 Bp Dean Elliott Wolfe. R S Matt's Epis Ch Newton KS 2008-2010; Asst Gr Epis Ch Silver Sprg MD 2005-2008. cayusee@hotmail.com

ANDERSON, Evangeline (RI) 34 Stella Dr, North Providence RI 02911 B Baltimore MD 9/20/1947 d Thomas Russell Harrison & Anna George. BA Br 1971; BA Rhode Island Coll 1986; MDiv GTS 1994. D 6/18/1994 P 12/18/1994 Bp George Nelson Hunt III. c 2. R S Alb's Ch No Providence RI 1997-2011; Int Calv Ch Providence RI 1996-1997; Assoc R S Columba's Chap Middletown RI 1995-1996; Asst R S Barn Ch Warwick RI 1994-1995. beckyanderson@juno.com

ANDERSON, Forrest Ewell (USC) 3333 Oakwell Ct Apt 529, San Antonio TX 78218 B Harrison AR 10/7/1939 s Don D Anderson & Louise. BD U of Cntrl Arkansas Conway 1962; MDiv VTS 1977. D 6/11/1977 P 3/16/1978 Bp Christoph Keller Jr. m 8/20/1966 Patrica Louise Bill. Vic S Geo Ch Anderson SC 1990-1994; Vic H Trin Epis Ch In Countryside Clearwater FL 1987-1989; R S Paul's Ch Kilgore TX 1982-1987; R S Jn's Ch Camden AR 1978-1982; Cur S Lk's Ch Hot Sprg AR 1977-1978. feapba@aol.com

ANDERSON, Gene Ray (SwVa) 5631 Warwood Dr, Roanoke VA 24018 **Part Time Supply S Paul's Ch Martinsville VA 2008-; Dioc Transition Off Dio SW Virginia Roanoke VA 1998-** B Independence MO 10/28/1934 s Lewis Pendleton Anderson & Naomi Esther. BS Cntrl Missouri St U 1956; MDiv Epis TS of The SW 1964. D 6/27/1964 P 1/1/1965 Bp Paul Moore Jr. m 3/1/1975 Suzan L Johnson c 3. Int S Mk's Ch Fincastle VA 2007-2008; Int Chr Ch Martinsville VA 2002-2003; Int Chr Ch Martinsville VA 1999-2000; Int Gr Ch Radford VA 1995-1996; Vic Ch Of The Epiph Trumansburg NY 1993-1995; Personl Cmsn Dio Cntrl New York Syracuse NY 1986-1988; R S Jn's Ch Marcellus NY 1978-1993; S Anne's Par Annapolis MD 1977-1978; Vic S Lk's Ch Annapolis MD 1976-1978; R S Mk's Ch Highland MD 1968-1974; Dio Maryland Baltimore MD 1965-1977; R All SS Ch Oakley Av MD 1965-1968; D S Andr's Ch Leonardtown California MD 1964-1965. geneanderson01@verizon.net

ANDERSON, George William (Roch) 1870 Jackson Rd, Penfield NY 14526 **Stwdshp Cmsn Dio Rochester Rochester NY 1983-; Co-Chair/Founding Mem Labor/Rel Cltn Dio Rochester Rochester NY 1981-; Chair Birch Hill Battered Wmn Cntr Dio Rochester Rochester NY 1979-; Urban Strtgy Cmsn Dio Rochester Rochester NY 1979-** B Irondale OH 3/6/1925 s William James Anderson & Virginia Margaret. BA Hiram Coll 1952; BD Bex 1955; MDiv Bex 1976. D 6/18/1955 Bp Nelson Marigold Burroughs P 12/1/1955 Bp Beverley D Tucker. m 8/11/1945 Twila C Cross. Peace/Justice Cmsn Dio Rochester Rochester NY 1981-1984; Chair Webster Yth Serv Dio Rochester Rochester NY 1979-1981; Trst Dio Rochester Rochester NY 1975-1990; Stndg Com Dio Rochester Rochester NY 1972-1975; Dioc Coun Dio Rochester Rochester NY 1972-1974; Trst Dio Rochester Rochester NY 1972-1974; Pres Webster Coun Of Ch Dio Rochester Rochester NY 1964-1965; R Ch Of The Gd Shpd Webster NY 1962-1990; R S Paul's Jeffersonville IN 1958-1962; Chair Dept Of Chr Soc Relatns Dio Nthrn Indiana So Bend IN 1958-1959; Cur S Ptr's Ch Ashtabula OH 1955-1958. Humanitarian Awd Rochester Labor Coun Rochester NY 1988.

ANDERSON, Gordon James (Ind) 2522 E Elm St, New Albany IN 47150 **D S Paul's Epis Ch New Albany IN 1997-** B New Albany IN 4/12/1948 s George W Anderson & Marjorie. Soe Indiana U. D 6/24/1997 Bp Edward Witker Jones. m 6/24/1995 Christy T Chanley. nodrogdeacon@sbcglobal.net

ANDERSON, Hannah Pedersen (WMass) 25 Clydesdale Dr # 1201, Pittsfield MA 01201 **R S Steph's Ch Pittsfield MA 2005-** B Norristown PA 4/15/1953 d Christian Harald Pedersen & Susan Thatcher. BA U of Washington 1976; MDiv STUSo 1994; DMin SWTS 2007. D 6/10/1994 P 6/3/1995 Bp Charlie Fuller McNutt Jr. m 4/20/1996 Robert George Anderson c 2. P-in-c Ch Of The H Comm Mahopac NY 2002-2005; Cn Dio New York New York City NY 2002-2005; Ch Of The H Comm Mahopac NY 2002; R All SS' Epis Ch Briarcliff Manor NY 1999-2002; R Gr Epis Ch Allentown PA 1996-1999; Mt Calv Camp Hill PA 1995-1996; S Andr's Ch Harrisburg PA 1994-1995. CHS 2000-2004. Jonathan Daniels Fllshp Awd EDS Cambridge MA 1993. hannahblessingcup@yahoo.com

ANDERSON, Howard Rae (Los) PO Box 37, Pacific Palisades CA 90272 **The Par Of S Matt Pacific Palisades CA 2008-** B Sioux City IA 1/31/1948 s Carleton W Anderson & Ethel M. BA Hamline U 1970; MA U of Hawaii 1972; PhD U of Hawaii 1976; CTh S Jn's Coll Winnipeg MN CA 1988. D 4/12/1993 Bp Robert Marshall Anderson P 11/28/1993 Bp James Louis Jelinek. m 11/7/2011 Linda Lee Anderson c 3. Wrdn of Cathd Coll Cathd of St Ptr & St Paul Washington DC 2004-2008; R S Paul's Epis Ch Duluth MN 1994-2004; Dio Minnesota Minneapolis MN 1993-1994; GC Dep Dio Minnesota Minneapolis MN 1985-2004; Prog Off Dio No Dakota Fargo ND 1984-1989; Exec Dir Cmsn for Indn Wk Dio Minnesota Minneapolis MN 1982-1988. Auth, *Winter Count: Stories of Native Amer Stwdshp*, Epis Ch Cntr, 1989; Auth, *Recalling, Reliving, Reviewing: Creation Theol in Native Amer & Chr and Jewish Tradition*, NATA Press, 1980; Auth, *The Sprtl Formation of Native Amer Yth*, NATA Press, 1980. Mn Epis Cler Assn 1993; Washington Cler Assn 2004. The Bp Whipple Cross Dio Minnesota 1990. lindaleeanderson@gmail.com

ANDERSON, James Arthur (Mil) 10041 Beckford St, Pickerington OH 43147 B Chicago IL 3/16/1952 s Vernon Melvin Anderson & Elizabeth Jeanne. U IL 1973; BA NE Illinois U 1975; MDiv STUSo 1989. D 6/17/1989 Bp Frank Tracy Griswold III P 12/18/1989 Bp James Barrow Brown. m 10/24/1981 Bernadine Marie DeNardis. R S Jn The Div Epis Ch Burlington WI 1991-1994; Cur S Lk's Ch Baton Rouge LA 1989-1991. Soc For Promoting Chr Knowledge. Janderson6@gmail.com

ANDERSON, James Desmond (WA) 9556 Chantilly Farm Ln, Chestertown MD 21620 B Christiansburg VA 2/9/1933 s Walter Willard Anderson & Sarah Margaret. BA NWU 1955; BD VTS 1961; DD VTS 1997. D 6/24/1961 Bp Charles L Street P 12/1/1961 Bp Donald H V Hallock. m 6/14/1955 Winifred G Guthrie. The Cathd Coll Washington DC 1981-1993; Mssn Dvlpmt Advsry Com Dio Washington Washington DC 1973-1980; Preceptor Consult Intermet Dio Washington Washington DC 1973-1976; Assn For Mnstry Dio Washington Washington DC 1971-1981; Asst To Bp Dio Washington Washington DC 1971-1978; Bd Metropltn Ecum Trng Cntr Dio Washington Washington DC 1971-1976; Bd Atlantic Trng Com Dio Washington Washington DC 1971-1975; Com Dio Washington Washington DC 1970-1980; Dio Washington Washington DC 1967-1981; Dir CE Dio Virginia Richmond VA 1967-1971; Dept Of CE Dio Virginia Richmond VA 1966-1967; P-in-c S Jn's Ch Neosho MO 1965-1967; Dir CE The Epis Ch Of Beth-By-The-Sea Palm Bch FL 1963-1965; Assoc S Matt's Ch Kenosha WI 1961-1963. Auth, "To Come Alive".

ANDERSON, James Russell (WA) 3111 Ritchie Rd, Forestville MD 20747 **Hon Asst S Paul's Par Washington DC 2001-** B Lynchburg VA 10/30/1943 s John R Anderson & Rosalind E. BA U of Maryland 1970; MDiv GTS 1974. D 6/22/1974 Bp William Foreman Creighton P 3/1/1975 Bp John Thomas Walker. S Fran Ch Virginia Bch VA 2003-2010; Ch Of The Epiph Forestville MD 2000-2003; H Redeem Mssn Capitol Heights MD 1993-1999; Int S Mk's Ch Cheyenne WY 1992-1993; Off Of Bsh For ArmdF New York NY 1976-1991; Dio Washington Washington DC 1974-1976; Urban Mssnr S Phil's Epis Ch Laurel MD 1974-1976. JACOBUM10@YAHOO.COM

ANDERSON, Jami Andrea (Wyo) PO Box 847, Pinedale WY 82941 **R Ch Of S Andr's In The Pines Pinedale WY 2010-; R St Jn the Bapt Epis Ch Big Piney WY 2010-** B Havre MT 8/18/1954 d Donald Louis Jensen & Marilyn. BA U of Nthrn Colorado 1977; MEd U of Wyoming 1981; MDiv SWTS 2005. D 6/20/2005 P 12/20/2005 Bp Joe Goodwin Burnett. m 6/11/1976 John Leonard Anderson c 4. R S Eliz's Ch Holdrege NE 2005-2010; R S Pauls Epis Ch Arapahoe NE 2005-2010. revjami@yahoo.com

ANDERSON, Jennie M (Pa) 209 S. 3rd Ave., Royersford PA 19468 **Ch Of The Epiph Royersford PA 2009-** B Boston MA 11/10/1964 d John Timothy Anderson & Elizabeth F. AA Cape Cod Cmnty Coll 1984; BS U of Massachusetts 1987; MDiv Epis TS of the SW 2007. D 6/2/2007 P 1/12/2008 Bp M(arvil) Thomas Shaw III. c 1. jma64@yahoo.com

ANDERSON, Jerry Ray (Los) 339 West Avenue 45, Los Angeles CA 90065 **Gd Samar Hosp Los Angeles CA 2003-** B Herrin IL 3/25/1942 s Everett Ray Anderson & Reva Mae. BA Sthrn Illinois U 1965; STB GTS 1968; CPE Rush Presb-St. Lk's Med Cntr 1973. D 6/8/1968 Bp Albert A Chambers P 12/20/1968 Bp James Winchester Montgomery. Pstr Int S Paul's Pomona Pomona CA 2002-2003; Epis Aids Mnstry Miami FL 1996-2001; Dir/Chapl Epis AIDS Mnstry Trin Cathd Miami FL 1996-2001; Chapl Epis Caring Response to AIDS Dio Washington Washington DC 1987-1995; Int S Monica's Epis Ch Washington DC 1987; Asst S Pat's Ch Washington DC 1981-1986; P-in-c Gr Epis Ch Menominee MI 1973; Asst S Aug's Epis Ch Wilmette IL 1968-1973. janderso@goodsam.org

ANDERSON JR, Jesse Fosset (Pa) 4848 Carrington Cir, Sarasota FL 34243 B New York NY 5/2/1937 s Jesse Fosset Anderson & Elizabeth Anderson. BA Linc 1958; MDiv GTS 1961. D 6/10/1961 Bp Andrew Tsu P 12/16/1961 Bp Joseph Gillespie Armstrong. m 10/12/2002 Constance Drew Lee c 5. R The Afr Epis Ch Of S Thos Philadelphia PA 1991-2001; R S Monica's Ch Hartford CT 1985-1990; S Phil The Evang Washington DC 1979-1985; Exec Coun Dio Washington Washington DC 1969-1972; Urban Mssnr and Assoc S Pat's Ch Washington DC 1966-1973; R Hse Of Pryr Philadelphia PA 1963-1966; Cur Ch Of The Advoc Philadelphia PA 1961-1963. Kappa Alpha Psi 1955; UBE 1978. fatha2@comcast.net

ANDERSON, Joan Wilkinson (ECR) 425 Carmel Ave, Marina CA 93933 B San Francisco CA 4/13/1937 d Harry Horton Wickersham & Gloria Casperson. AA Mt San Antonio Coll 1958; BA San Jose St U 1977; BTS Epis Sch For Deacons 2006. D 2/7/2009 Bp Mary Gray-Reeves. c 2. epiphanydeacon@sbcglobal.net

ANDERSON, Jon R (Los) 663 Douglas Street, Chattanooga TN 37403 **P-in-c Under Spec Circumstances Chr Ch - Epis Chattanooga TN 2011-; Asst S Bede's Epis Ch Santa Fe NM 2007-** B Dallas TX 10/25/1961 s Robert C Anderson & Beverly. BS U of Tennessee 1984; MBA U of Kansas 1986; MDiv CDSP 2002. D 6/2/2002 Bp Chester Lovelle Talton P 12/14/2002 Bp Joseph Jon Bruno. m 1/2/1988 Anne-Drue M Miller c 1. R S Andr's Epis Ch Ojai CA 2005-2007; Cur/Assoc R Ch of the H Faith Santa Fe NM 2002-2005. janderson.smtn@gmail.com

ANDERSON, Judith Kay Finney (Mont) 408 Westview Dr, Missoula MT 59803 B Denver CO 7/23/1940 d Charles Finney & Mildred. BS U Of Idaho Moscow 1963; Mnstry Formation Prog 2000. D 10/14/2000 Bp Charles Jones III. m 8/26/1961 Douglas Reid Anderson c 2.

ANDERSON, Juliana (Mass) 1770 Massachusetts Ave, Cambridge MA 02140 B Pittsburgh PA 3/13/1945 d James Kenneth Collins & Dorothea E. BA Carnegie Mellon U 1967; MDiv EDS 1978. D 6/25/1981 Bp Morris Fairchild Arnold P 5/1/1982 Bp Roger W Blanchard. m 3/22/1969 Will Cline Anderson. S Jn's Ch Barrington RI 2005; Trin Ch Concord MA 2003-2004; S Mk's Ch Foxborough MA 1997-2000; Ch Of S Jn The Evang Boston MA 1995-1996; Chr Ch Hyde Pk MA 1985-1993; Int The Ch Of The Gd Shpd Acton MA 1982-1983; Asst The Ch Of The Gd Shpd Acton MA 1981-1982. revjca@earthlink.net

ANDERSON, Kenneth Edwin (RG) 258 Riverside Dr, El Paso TX 79915 B ND 3/11/1929 s Edwin Anderson. D 7/28/2001 Bp Terence Kelshaw. m 2/4/1951 Jessie Anderson.

ANDERSON, Lawson Moore (Ark) 4400 Arlington Dr, North Little Rock AR 72116 **Cn Pstr Trin Cathd Little Rock AR 1997-** B Helena AR 9/20/1920 s John Lawrence Anderson & Virginia Lambert. BS LSU 1946; LSU 1952; MDiv Epis TS of The SW 1965; Fllshp Epis TS of The SW 1977; DD Epis TS of The SW 1992. D 1/18/1965 P 7/21/1965 Bp Robert Raymond Brown. c 4. R S Lk's Epis Ch No Little Rock AR 1993-1996; Trst Epis TS Of The SW Austin TX 1976-1992; R S Lk's Epis Ch No Little Rock AR 1975-1992; R S Paul's Newport AR 1969-1975; Vic S Thos Ch Springdale AR 1965-1969. DD Epis TS of the SW 1992. lawsonanderson@comcast.net

ANDERSON III, Lenny (Pgh) 2081 Husband Rd, Somerset PA 15501 **D S Fran In The Fields Somerset PA 2010-** B Youngstorm, OH 3/1/1973 s Lennel Vincent Anderson & Deborah Lynn. BA Westminster Coll 1995; MDiv Gordon-Conwell TS 2000; Vrginia TS 2008. D 2/20/2010 P 9/25/2010 Bp James Joseph Shand. m 3/28/2000 Kelly Jennifer Durham. Old Wye Ch Wye Mills MD 2006-2009. ZOOMDADDYA@YAHOO.COM

ANDERSON, Louise Thomas (NC) 901 N Main St, Tarboro NC 27886 **D Ch Of The Gd Shpd Rocky Mt NC 2005-** B Raleigh NC 3/10/1962 d Erwin Bernard Thomas & Anne Love. D 11/9/2005 Bp Michael Bruce Curry. m 6/2/1984 Samuel Anderson c 1. landerson@goodshepherdrmt.org

ANDERSON, Marilyn Lea (Ct) 180 Cross Highway, Redding CT 06896 **Mem of Cathd Chapt Chr Ch Cathd Hartford CT 2008-; Dio Connecticut Hartford CT 2008-; Transition Com chairperson Dio Connecticut Hartford CT 2008-; R Chr Ch Redding Ridge CT 2005-** B Pittsburgh PA 12/9/1953 d John Hopper Conwell & Alice Bertha. BA W&M 1975; MS U IL 1983; Angl St Dplma Ya Berk 1998; MDiv Yale DS 1998; STM GTS 2000. D 6/8/2002 Bp Andrew Donnan Smith P 1/4/2003 Bp James Elliot Curry. m 8/16/1975 Barry Michael Anderson c 2. Mem of Transition Com Dio Connecticut Hartford CT 2007; Mentor, Annand Sprtlty Prog Ya Berk New Haven CT 2006-2007; Asst R S Andr's Ch Madison CT 2002-2005; Par Intern S Jas Epis Ch Danbury CT 2001-2002; Asst For Chr Formation S Paul's Ch Fairfield CT 1998-2001. Designated mcl Yale DS 1998. liturgymom@gmail.com

ANDERSON, Martha Odean (SanD) 1475 Catalina Blvd, San Diego CA 92107 **All Souls' Epis Ch San Diego CA 2011-** B Portsmouth VA 12/30/1956 d Curtis Odean Anderson & Martha Ann M. BA Converse Coll 1978; JD U of San Diego 1981; MDiv The ETS At Claremont 2011. D 4/9/2011 Bp James Robert Mathes. c 2. MARTHA.ANDERSON1230@GMAIL.COM

ANDERSON, Mary Petty (Oly) 10450 NE Yaquina Ave, Bainbridge Island WA 98110 **Assoc Gr Ch Bainbridge Island WA 2008-** B Centreville MS 3/25/1948 d Fred Alvin Anderson & Polly Salmon. BA LSU 1970; MA Mississippi Coll 1991; MDiv Epis TS of The SW 1998. D 6/7/1999 P 12/1/1999 Bp Robert Jefferson Hargrove Jr. c 2. Emm Epis Ch Mercer Island WA 2006; Asst Emm Epis Ch Mercer Island WA 2004-2006; S Pat's Epis Ch W Monroe LA 2000-2001; Int Chr Ch Bastrop LA 2000; Int S Andr's Epis Ch Mer Rouge LA 1999. marypanderson@juno.com

ANDERSON, Mary Sterrett (O) 2581 Norfolk Rd, Cleveland Heights OH 44106 B Dayton OH 6/7/1945 d William Dent Sterrett & Marion Louise. BA Colorado Coll 1967; MDiv EDS 1974. D 11/16/1974 Bp John M Allin P 1/4/1977 Bp John Harris Burt. m 9/8/1973 Philip Alden Anderson c 2. S Thos' Epis Ch Port Clinton OH 2000-2002; Chr Ch Epis Hudson OH 2000-2001; P-in-c S Hubert's Epis Ch Mentor OH 1996-1997; Int Ch Of The Gd Shpd Beachwood OH 1992-1993; Asst S Chris's By-The River Gates Mills OH 1988-1991; Dio Ohio Cleveland OH 1983-2006; Asst Chr Ch Shaker Heights OH 1977-1978. paa@po.cwru.edu

ANDERSON, Michael E (Chi) 1225 Asbury Ave, Evanston IL 60202 B Milwaukee WI 12/31/1948 s Gerald Wilson Anderson & Aldoris Marie. ABS Wheaton Coll 1975; MDiv Nash 1984. D 6/16/1984 Bp Quintin Ebenezer Primo Jr P 12/1/1984 Bp James Winchester Montgomery. m 8/17/1972 Katharine Howard c 3. Ch Of The H Nativ Chicago IL 1986-1998; Ch Of The H Nativ Clarendon Hills IL 1986-1998; Assoc R S Greg's Epis Ch Deerfield IL 1984-1986. Auth, "Chapt," *Evangelicals on the Cbury Trail*, Morehouse Pub, 1989. michael@evanstongroup.com

ANDERSON JR, Otto Harold (Okla) 5901 Canterbury Dr Unit 1, Culver City CA 90230 B Galveston TX 8/30/1924 s Otto Harold Anderson & Angeline Renee. Fllshp Coll of Preachers; BA Phillips U 1948; BD Brite DS 1952. D 10/25/1954 P 4/25/1955 Bp Chilton Powell. Asst S Mk's Par Glendale CA 2003-2011; Asst S Thos The Apos Hollywood Los Angeles CA 1994-2001; Asst The Par Of S Matt Pacific Palisades CA 1984-1994; Dioc Coun Dio Oklahoma Oklahoma City OK 1964-1969; R S Jn's Ch Norman OK 1963-1969; R S Lk's Epis Ch Ada OK 1955-1959; D S Lk's Epis Ch Ada OK 1954-1955.

ANDERSON, Otto Suen (SO) 33 W Dixon Ave, Dayton OH 45419 **D S Paul's Epis Ch Dayton OH 2009-** B Sidney, NY 11/10/1957 s Carl Robert Anderson & Dorothy Helen. BS Clarkson Coll 1979; BS Airforce Inst of Tech 1982; MS Cntrl Michigan 1989. D 6/13/2009 Bp Thomas Edward Breidenthal. m 11/2/2002 Jamie Baker Ferguson c 2. ottoanderson@sbcglobal.net

ANDERSON, Philip Alden (O) 2581 Norfolk Rd, Cleveland Heights OH 44106 **D S Paul's Epis Ch Cleveland Heights OH 1995-** B Cambridge MA 6/11/1948 s Madeleine. BA Harv 1970; MDiv EDS 1973; MD Case Wstrn Reserve U 1978. D 1/10/1976 Bp John Harris Burt. m 9/8/1973 Mary Sterrett c 3. MD alpha omega alpha Med Sch Case Wstrn Reserve U Cleveland OH 1978. paa@case.edu

ANDERSON, Polly Chambers (WLa) 4037 Highway 15, Calhoun LA 71225 B New Orleans LA 10/4/1945 d Fred Alvin Anderson & Marion Francis. BS MSU 1973. D 6/4/2005 Bp D(avid) Bruce Mac Pherson. c 2. S Pat's Epis Ch W Monroe LA 2005-2007. revpolly@hotmail.com

ANDERSON JR, Ralph W (WMass) 114 Lake St, Shrewsbury MA 01545 B Worcester MA 1/22/1937 s Ralph William Anderson & Virginia. BBA Clark U 1959; MA Anna Maria Coll 1994. D 6/20/1981 Bp Alexander Doig Stewart. m 6/5/1965 Marcia K Garrison c 2. D All SS Ch Worcester MA 1989-1992; Asst Trin Epis Ch Shrewsbury MA 1981-1986. The Intl Thos Merton Soc 2004. rwand@townisp.com

ANDERSON, Richard Glover (Ida) 513 Cashmere Rd, Boise ID 83702 **Died 9/27/2009** B Fort Sill OK 11/21/1922 s Richard Emanuel Anderson & Anne White. U CO 1944. D 11/14/1965 Bp Chilton Powell P 6/1/1975 Bp Hanford Langdon King Jr.

ANDERSON, Richard John (NY) 25 Windsor Commons Dr, Kennebunk ME 04043 B Iowa City IA 3/17/1934 s Bernard Anderson & Helene Louise. BA San Diego St U 1958; BD CDSP 1961; STM Dubuque TS 1969. D 6/16/1961 P 12/21/1961 Bp Gordon V Smith. m 4/14/1988 Audrey Flaherty c 3. R S Mk's Ch Mt Kisco NY 1987-1994; ECBF Richmond VA 1986-1987; Epis Ch Cntr New York NY 1975-1986; R S Jn's Gr Ch Buffalo NY 1969-1971; Exec Coun Dio Iowa Des Moines IA 1965-1969; R S Jn's Epis Ch Dubuque IA 1965-1969; Vic S Paul's Ch Durant IA 1961-1965. Auth, *There Shall Be A GC of This Ch.*

ANDERSON, Richard Rupert (EMich) 221 Purdy Dr, Alma MI 48801 B Florence CO 11/6/1924 s Lyman Abbott Anderson & Fleda Isabelle. BA Wayne 1950; MDiv Bex 1953; MDiv Ken 1953; Fllshp Coll of Preachers 1968; Emergency Med Tech 1976; DMin Drew U 1994. D 7/5/1953 P 1/23/1954 Bp Richard S M Emrich. m 6/19/1948 Carolyn Bertha Weigold c 6. Dn Saginaw Vlly Convoc Dio Estrn Michigan Saginaw MI 1992-1995; R S Jn's Epis Ch Alma MI 1954-1991; S Jn's Ch Chesaning MI 1953-1954. rcander@chartermi.net

ANDERSON, Robert Jay (WVa) No address on file. B Bloomington IN 12/19/1953 s Arvin Dale Anderson & Norma June. MDiv EDS 1994. D 6/10/1994 P 6/1/1995 Bp John H(enry) Smith. m 4/25/1980 Diana Lynn Barfield. The Sthrn Cluster Logan WV 1994-1995.

ANDERSON, Robert M(elville) (CFla) 350 Lake Talmadge Rd, Deland FL 32724 B Orlando FL 6/7/1938 s Robert T Anderson & Gertrude J. BA Parsons Coll Fairfield IA 1962; MDiv Nash 1982. D 6/16/1982 P 3/1/1983 Bp William Hopkins Folwell. m 11/11/1989 Rebecca Tatham c 4. R The Ch Of The H Presence Deland FL 1995-2003; R H Trin Epis Ch Bartow FL 1993-1995; Vic S Ptr's Epis Ch Lake Mary FL 1985-1989; Asst H Cross Epis Ch Sanford FL 1982-1984. frander@earthlink.com

ANDERSON, Rosemarie (ECR) 355 Redwood Dr, Boulder Creek CA 95006 B Englewood NJ 6/21/1947 d Roy Gothe Anderson & Miriam Selma. BA Cntrl Coll 1969; MA U of Nebraska 1971; PhD U of Nebraska 1973; MDiv PSR

1983. D 12/6/1986 P 12/5/1987 Bp William Edwin Swing. Calv Epis Ch Santa Cruz CA 1993-1995; Santa Cruz Cbury Fndt Santa Cruz CA 1991-1992; All Souls' Epis Ch San Diego CA 1988-1990. Auth, *Celtic Oracles*, Random Hse, 1998; Auth, *Transpersonal Resrch Methods for Soc Sci*, Sage Pubs, 1998. AAR; APA; Assn for Transpersonal Psychol; Inst of Noetic Sci; Westar Inst. randerson@itp.edu

ANDERSON, Scott Crawford (Colo) 2414 Sunray Ct, Fort Collins CO 80525 **S Jas Epis Ch Wheat Ridge CO 2006-** B Aurora IL 12/28/1954 BA/BS Babson Coll. D 6/14/2003 P 12/13/2003 Bp William Jerry Winterrowd. m 8/20/1988 Jane Lara K Anderson c 2. S Lk's Epis Ch Ft Collins CO 2003-2006. lfj247@q.com

ANDERSON, Scott James (WMich) Saint John'S Episcopal Church, Washington At Kidd, Ionia MI 48846 B Hastings MI 1/28/1951 s Vincent James Anderson & Mary Catherine. BA Aquinas Coll 1974; MDiv Nash 1979. D 5/25/1980 Bp Arthur Anton Vogel P 6/21/1981 Bp Charles Bennison. m 8/16/1974 Lorraine Elaine Luke. Assoc R S Lk's Epis Ch Ft Collins CO 2003-2008; T/F On Wmn In The Ch Dio Wstrn Michigan Kalamazoo MI 1997-1999; S Andr's Ch Tioga PA 1987-2008; S Jn the Apos Epis Ch Ionia MI 1987-2006; Dio W Missouri Kansas City MO 1983-1987; R S Lk's Epis Ch Excelsior Sprg MO 1983-1987; Cur S Phil's Ch Joplin MO 1980-1983. 3rd Ord Of S Ben; Ord Of S Mary; SSC. Phi Alpha Theta.

ANDERSON, Stuart Norman (NCal) 2100 E Washington St Apt 102, Petaluma CA 94954 B Brooklyn NY 10/28/1929 s Carl Albert Anderson & Charlotte Lillian. BA CUNY 1951; MA Stan 1951; BD CDSP 1955. D 6/12/1955 Bp Karl M Block P 12/17/1955 Bp Henry H Shires. m 8/9/1959 LaRayne Eva Oakes. Chr The King Quincy CA 1981-1982; Assoc S Mich's Epis Ch Carmichael CA 1972-1976; R S Jn The Bapt Lodi CA 1964-1970; Assoc R S Ptr's Epis Ch Redwood City CA 1961-1964; Vic S Phil's Ch San Jose CA 1957-1961; Asst Trin Cathd San Jose CA 1955-1957.

ANDERSON JR, Theodore Lester (NJ) 2200 Genesee St, Hamilton NJ 08610 **St Marys Hosp W Palm Bch FL 1992-** B Perth Amboy NJ 1/25/1958 s Theodore Lester Anderson & Loretta Agnes. BA Rutgers-The St U 1980; MDiv Nash 1984. D 6/2/1984 Bp George Phelps Mellick Belshaw P 2/2/1985 Bp Vincent King Pettit. c 1. R S Mths Ch Hamilton NJ 1995-2010; Palm Bch Reg Hosp Palm Sprg FL 1993-2003; H Trin Epis Ch W Palm Bch FL 1987-1993; Cur Ch Of The Gd Shpd Jacksonville FL 1985-1986; Cur S Simeon's By The Sea No Wildwood NJ 1984-1985. theodoreanderson@comcast.net

ANDERSON, Timothy Lee (Neb) P.O. Box 64, Ashland NE 68003 **Cn Epis Tri-Faith Mnstrs Ashland NE 2011-; Fin For Mssn Com Exec Coun Appointees New York NY 2009-2012; Strategic Plnng Com Exec Coun Appointees New York NY 2008-2012; Exec Coun Mem Exec Coun Appointees New York NY 2006-2012** B Kearney NE 3/9/1949 s Joyce Kenneth Anderson & Ardis Mildred. BS U of Nebraska 1981; MDiv Nash 1986. D 2/25/1987 P 9/1/1987 Bp James Daniel Warner. m 3/11/1973 Carla Schnieder c 2. Bp & Trst Dio Nebraska Omaha NE 2004-2011; R S Steph's Ch Grand Island NE 1991-2004; R S Mary's Epis Ch Blair NE 1987-1991; D S Mary's Epis Ch Blair NE 1987. tanderson@episcopaltrifaith.org

ANDERSON III, William (NY) 377 Vanderbilt Beach Rd, Apt 103, Naples FL 34108 B 2/21/1935 BDIV Ya Berk 1960; MBA Cor 1966. D 6/20/1960 P 6/24/1961 Bp J(ohn) Joseph Meakins Harte. Cur S Jn's Ch Ithaca NY 1961-1964; Cur S Mich And All Ang Ch Dallas TX 1960-1961.

ANDERSON, William Alvin (At) 2510 Two Oaks Dr, Charleston SC 29414 B Aiken SC 1/30/1944 s Marcus Eugene Anderson & Thelma Pauline. MA Roosevelt U; BA U GA 1966. D 11/4/1999 Bp Edward Lloyd Salmon Jr. m 11/12/1965 Jane Ellen Everett. S Chris's At-The-Crossroads Epis Perry GA 2003-2008.

ANDERSON, William Clarence (Md) 415 Helmsman Way, Severna Park MD 21146 B Princeton IL 2/2/1941 s Clarence Peter Anderson & Ruth Leona. BS Nthrn Illinois U 1962; MS U IL 1966; Wstrn Washington U 1967; PhD Florida St U 1976; MDiv VTS 2002. D 6/14/1997 Bp Charles Lindsay Longest P 2/2/2003 Bp Peter Hess Beckwith. m 3/20/1971 Jane Farley Alexander c 2. Assoc Epis Ch Of Chr The King Windsor Mill MD 2007-2008; P-in-c S Andr's Ch Pasadena MD 2005-2006; R S Paul's Epis Ch Pekin IL 2003-2005; S Jas Epis Ch Marietta GA 1999-2000; D S Steph's Ch Severn Par Crownsville MD 1999-2000; D S Barth's Ch Baltimore MD 1997-1999. wanders21@verizon.net

ANDERSON-KRENGEL, William Erich (Ct) 191 Margarite Rd, Middletown CT 06457 **P Dio Connecticut Hartford CT 2001-** B Nürnburg DE 9/15/1961 s Walter Franklin Krengel & Carol Louise. D 6/9/2001 Bp Andrew Donnan Smith P 2/16/2002 Bp James Elliot Curry. m 6/9/1984 Sarah Jennings Anderson-Krengel. KAEW1031@SPRINT.BLACKBERRY.NET

ANDERSON-SMITH, Susan (Az) Imago Dei Middle School, PO Box 3056, Tucson AZ 85702 **COM Dio Arizona Phoenix AZ 2010-; Arizona Epis Schools Fndt Dio Arizona Phoenix AZ 2009-; Chapl Imago Dei Middle Sch Tucson AZ 2007-** B Vicksburg MS 9/5/1957 d Bertram Anderson-Smith & Edna Opal. BA U of Mississippi 1979; MDiv EDS 1997. D 6/12/1999 P 4/26/2000 Bp Ronald Hayward Haines. Stndg Com Dio Arizona Phoenix AZ 2006-2007; Epis Fndt for Campus Mnstry Dio Arizona Phoenix AZ 2001-2007; C&C Bd Dio Arizona Phoenix AZ 2001-2005; Assoc S Phil's In The Hills Tucson AZ 2000-2007; Coordntr Dioc Conv Dio Massachusetts Boston MA 1999-2000. Auth, "Accident or Imperative? Rel Pluralism and Epis Schools," *Reasons for Being*, NAES, 2010. Bp Atwood of Arizona Awd EDS 1997; BA cl U of MS Oxford MS 1979. Bellesas@aol.com

ANDONIAN, Kathryn Ann (Pa) 942 Masters Way, Harleysville PA 19438 **Vic Ch Of The H Sprt Harleysville PA 2004-** B Billings MT 6/17/1959 d George Duane Ruff & Phyllis Nadine. BA U CO 1981; MDiv Luth TS at Philadelphia 2002; CAS VTS 2003. D 6/21/2003 P 5/29/2004 Bp Charles Ellsworth Bennison Jr. m 1/5/1985 Marc Hansen Andonian c 1. Philadelphia Cathd Philadelphia PA 2003-2004. revkathy@churchoftheholysprit.us

ANDRES, Anthony Francis (Ind) 795 Elk Mountain Rd, Afton VA 22920 **Vic H Cross Ch Batesville VA 2001-** B Youngstown OH 4/21/1938 s Anton Andres & Frances Elizabeth. BA DePauw U 1960; MDiv VTS 1964; JD Jn Marshall Law Sch 1977. D 6/13/1964 P 12/20/1964 Bp Nelson Marigold Burroughs. m 7/19/1986 Emily A Lewis c 1. P S Chris's Epis Ch Carmel IN 1977-2000; R S Lk's Ch Cleveland OH 1967-1977; Asst Ch Of The Epiph Euclid OH 1964-1967. ealewis@ntelos.net

ANDRES, Justo Rambac (EpisSanJ) 115 E Miner Ave, Stockton CA 95202 **Epis Ch Of S Anne Stockton CA 1998-; Jubilee Off Epis Dio San Joaquin Modesto CA 1992-** B Bacarra PH 11/10/1929 s Ciriaco Andres & Juliana. BTh S Andr's TS Manila Ph 1955; Far Estrn U PI Ph 1962; Garrett Evang TS 1968. Rec 4/1/1955 as Priest Bp The Bishop Of Manila. c 1. H Cross Epis Mssn Stockton CA 1984-1995; Epis Dio San Joaquin Modesto CA 1983; The Par Of Gd Shpd Epis Ch Wailuku HI 1976-1983. Ang Mnstry; Cntrl Mnstrl Assn; Mnstry To Seamen. Citation Gvnr Of Hi. justoandres@comcast.net

ANDREW OSH, Carol (NY) 3042 Eagle Dr, Augusta GA 30906 B Hamilton BM 3/20/1948 d David Clinton Murray & Patricia Zara. BA DePauw U 1969; Ya 1972; GTS 1991; GTS 1993. D 6/12/1993 Bp Richard Frank Grein P 3/18/1994 Bp Craig Barry Anderson. carolandru@comcast.net

ANDREW, John Gerald Barton (NY) 414 E 52nd St Apt 3, New York NY 10022 B Scarborough Yorkshire UK 1/10/1931 s Thomas Barton Andrew & Ena Maud. DD Cuttington U Coll 1976; DD Nash 1980; DD Epis TS In Kentucky 1986; MA Oxf 1995; DD EDS 1996; DD GTS 1996. Trans from Church Of England 11/15/1972 as Priest Bp Horace W B Donegan. P-in-c Gr Epis Ch New York NY 1999-2001; R S Thos Ch New York NY 1972-1996; S Geo's-By-The-River Rumson NJ 1959-1960. Auth, *My Heart Is Ready*, Cowley Pub, 1995; Auth, *The Best of Both Worlds*, Eerdmans, 1991; Auth, *Nothing Cheap & Much That is Cheerful*, Eerdmans, 1988. Venerable Ord of the Hosp of S Jn in Jerusalem 1974. Ord of the British Empire Queen Eliz II London UK 1995; Cn of New York Rt Rev Richard Grein Dio New York 1995; Cross of S Sophia Gk Orth Ch 1967; Cross of S Andr Russian Orth Ch 1965; Six Prchr as Chapl to Archbp of Cbury Cbury Cathd Cbury Engl 1963.

ANDREW SR, Robert Nelson (O) 3800 W 33rd St, Cleveland OH 44109 **Chapl S Barn Ch Bay Vill OH 1999-** B Waterbury CT 10/31/1933 s Walter Scott Andrew & Ruby Louise. Carroll Coll; New Haven St Teachers Coll; U of Connecticut; Ch Army Trng Coll 1959; JCU 1979. D 5/12/1980 P 11/29/1980 Bp John Harris Burt. m 10/17/1959 Eleanor Ann Severson c 4. S Agnes Ch Cleveland OH 1980-2000; Ch Of S Phil The Apos Cleveland OH 1980-1998; Ch Army Captain-in-charge Zion Ch Monroeville OH 1961-1967; Ch Army Captain-in-charge Gr Epis Ch Sandusky OH 1960-1961; Ch Army Captain-in-charge S Paul Epis Ch Conneaut OH 1958-1959. Ch Army Captain 1959; Ord of S Lk Chapl 2001. andrew.robert@sbcglobal.net

ANDREW-MACONAUGHEY, Debra Elaine (SeFla) 111 W Indies Dr, Ramrod Key FL 33042 **S Columba Epis Ch Marathon FL 2007-** B Denison TX 9/25/1957 d Thomas G Andrew & Ruth. BA Tem 1979; MFA NYU 1984; MA VTS 2004. D 1/6/2007 P 6/6/2007 Bp Leopold Frade. m 5/11/2001 Kirk Maconaughey c 2. S Paul's Epis Ch Alexandria VA 1996-2003. downtime@hotmail.com

ANDREWS, Alfred John (Neb) PO Box 141, Sidney NE 69162 **P Chr Ch Sidney NE 2003-** B Townsville 7/20/1930 Moore Theol Coll. Trans from Anglican Church Of Australia 11/7/2003 Bp Joe Goodwin Burnett. m 11/17/1951 Betty May McDonagh c 2. john_bettyandrews@hotmail.com

ANDREWS, Arthur Edward (Ore) 1704 Se 22nd Ave, Portland OR 97214 B Portland OR 3/29/1948 s Edgar Oliver Andrews & Irma Merle. BA Gri 1970; ETSBH 1974; MA Fuller TS 1974; CDSP 1975. D 7/22/1975 P 12/15/1976 Bp Matthew Paul Bigliardi. m 11/22/2003 Sharon S Flegal c 2. Chapl Legacy Gd Samar Hosp Portland OR 1998-2011; Asst S Ptr's by-the-Sea Epis Ch Bay Shore NY 1997-1998; P-in-c Ch Of The Gd Shpd Sandy OR 1994-1996; Asst S Aid's Epis Ch Gresham OR 1984-1988; Chapl St Judes Hm Inc Sandy OR 1983; Vic H Cross Epis Ch Portland OR 1980-1983; Chapl Legacy Gd Samar Hosp Portland OR 1975-1979. AEHC 1988-1992; Assn of Profsnl Chapl 1991-2010. artandrews62@gmail.com

ANDREWS, Betty May (Neb) 1217 10th Ave, Sidney NE 69162 **D Chr Ch Sidney NE 2003-** B Queensland Australia 9/13/1931 Moore Theol Coll; Alcm

London Coll 1949. Trans from Anglican Church Of Australia 11/7/2003 Bp Joe Goodwin Burnett. m 11/17/1951 Alfred John Andrews c 2. john_bettyandrews@hotmail.com

ANDREWS, Carl Machin (Colo) The Diocese of Colorado, 1300 Washington Street, Denver CO 80203 **Cn to the Ordnry Dio Colorado Denver CO 2010-** B Wright-Patterson Air Force Base OH 3/5/1948 s Thomas Joseph Andrews & Kathleen Agnes. BS Colorado St U 1970; MDiv Nash 1977. D 12/21/1976 P 6/1/1977 Bp William Carl Frey. m 10/7/1973 Lynne J Telisak c 2. USAF Chapl Off Of Bsh For ArmdF New York NY 1984-2010; Vic S Mk's Ch Craig CO 1979-1984; Cur S Tim's Epis Ch Centennial CO 1977-1979. Auth, "The Role of the Chapl," *USAF Chapl Pub*, USAF, 2006; Auth, "Var parts of DVDs on Chapl Corp Readiness," *USAF DVD Chapl Corp*, USAF, 2000. Associated Parishes, Tertiary Of The Soc Of S Fran 1977. Mltry Awards USAF 2010. candrews@coloradodiocese.org

ANDREWS JR, David Tallmadge (Del) 732 Nottingham Rd, Wilmington DE 19805 **R Ch of St Andrews & St Matthews Wilmington DE 2010-** B Bronxville NY 10/8/1957 s David Tallmadge Andrews & Kathryn Maude. BA Muskingum Coll 1980; MDiv EDS 1985; MS Marywood U 1996. D 12/15/1990 P 9/11/1991 Bp William George Burrill. m 8/11/1984 Emily Stearns Gibson. R Trin Ch Castine ME 2006-2010; Vic Trin Ch Camden NY 1998-2001; Vic S Paul's Ch Chittenango NY 1997-2006; Vic Ch Of The Gd Shpd Nedrow NY 1992-1994. revdup1@comcast.net

ANDREWS, David Thomas (WA) 500 Merton Woods Way, Millersville MD 21108 **Dioc Ecum Off Dio Washington Washington DC 1996-** B Salem NJ 9/2/1940 s Gilbert Gore Andrews & Mary Wrightson. BA Campbell Coll 1966; PDS 1966. D 4/23/1966 P 10/29/1966 Bp Alfred L Banyard. m 6/11/1966 Kathleen McHale c 2. Pres Stndg Com Dio Washington Washington DC 2000-2002; R H Trin Epis Ch Bowie MD 1974-2006; Stff S Paul's Epis Ch Westfield NJ 1968-1974; Cur H Cross Epis Ch No Plainfield NJ 1966-1968. Assoc OHC; Washington Epis Cler Assn. tomandrews@comcast.net

ANDREWS, Delbert Avery (Colo) 600 E Saguaro Dr Unit 253, Benson AZ 85602 **Died 6/28/2011** B Gunnison CO 5/1/1926 s Herbert Andrews & Helen. Bp TS in the Dio Colorado; Wstrn St Coll of Colorado. D 6/24/1971 P 12/27/1971 Bp Edwin B Thayer. c 5. delpat@theriver.com

ANDREWS, Dianne Peterson (Pa) 1613 California Ave SW #301, Seattle WA 98116 B Sacramento CA 11/19/1955 d Glenn Roy Peterson & Margaret Jane. BS U CA 1978; MDiv Starr King Sch For The Mnstry 1992; CAS CDSP 1994. D 11/9/1996 P 11/9/1997 Bp Michael Whittington Creighton. c 2. Gr Epis Ch Hulmeville PA 2002-2010; Asst to R S Jn's Epis Ch Lancaster PA 1998-2002; Educational Assoc Mt Calv Camp Hill PA 1996-1997. rev.dandrews@hotmail.com

ANDREWS II, George Edward (SeFla) 20 Vine St, Marion MA 02738 B Saginaw MI 12/30/1942 s Edward Napier Andrews & Mary Elizabeth. BA Trin 1966; MDiv VTS 1971. D 6/26/1971 Bp John Melville Burgess P 4/1/1972 Bp Dean T Stevenson. m 6/24/1966 Lillian Coe Taggart.

ANDREWS II, George Strafford (Chi) 102 Starling Ln, Longwood FL 32779 B New York NY 9/11/1929 s George Strafford Andrews & Mary Alora. BA Harv 1952; MBA NWU 1959; MDiv STUSo 1970. D 6/13/1970 Bp James Winchester Montgomery P 12/19/1970 Bp Gerald Francis Burrill. m 6/12/1953 Anne Wescott c 3. Adj Fac SWTS Evanston IL 1984-1989; R S Elis's Ch Glencoe IL 1978-1989; Secy Dioc Conv Dio Chicago Chicago IL 1976-1980; Dioc Coun Dio Chicago Chicago IL 1975-1978; Vic Ch Of The H Apos Wauconda IL 1974-1978; Assoc Gr Epis Ch Hinsdale IL 1970-1974. St. Andrews Soc, Cntrl Fl. Chapt, Chapl 1995. gsand29@aol.com

ANDREWS, John Anthony (NY) PO Box 547, Lima NY 14485 **Supply P Dio Rochester Rochester NY 2006-** B Ottawa Ontario CA 10/22/1942 s Clifford Andrews & Elizabeth Ila. BS SUNY 1964; STM GTS 1967. D 6/3/1967 Bp Allen Webster Brown P 12/9/1967 Bp Charles Bowen Persell Jr. c 4. Int Ch Of The Atone Washington DC 2004-2005; Ch Of The Incarn Upper Marlboro MD 2002; Adj P S Marg's Ch Washington DC 2002; S Mich And All Ang Adelphi MD 2002; Chr Ch Of Ramapo Suffern NY 1980-2002; Vic S Aug Of Cbury Ch Edinboro PA 1977-1980; Vic S Ptr's Ch Waterford PA 1977-1980; S Jos's Ch Port Allegany PA 1973-1977; S Matt's Epis Ch Eldred PA 1973-1977; Cur Chr Ch Of Ramapo Suffern NY 1969-1973; Asst S Andr's Ch Brewster NY 1969-1973. Auth, "Healing," *Sharing mag*. Ord of S Lk 1980. jrutkowski2@rochester.rr.com

ANDREWS, John Joseph (Colo) 5968 S Zenobia Ct, Littleton CO 80123 B Denver CO 2/19/1943 s Douglas Andrews & Helen Josephina. BA U CO 1966; MDiv Nash 1987. D 6/6/1987 P 12/12/1987 Bp William Carl Frey. m 6/5/1965 Carol Robinson c 2. Assoc R Ch Of The Trsfg Evergreen CO 2001-2003; Int S Mart In The Fields Aurora CO 1997-1998; COM Dio Colorado Denver CO 1996-1998; Eccl Crt Dio Colorado Denver CO 1994-1998; Ecum Off Dio Colorado Denver CO 1993-1997; R S Gabr The Archangel Epis Ch Cherry Hills Vill CO 1991-1997; Budet and Fin Com Dio Colorado Denver CO 1988-1992; Dn Mtn Dnry Dio Colorado Denver CO 1988-1991; COM Dio Colorado Denver CO 1988-1990; LARC (Luth Angl RC Dialogue Dio Colorado Denver CO 1988-1990; Vic Epis Ch Of S Jn The Bapt Granby CO 1987-1991; Vic Trin Ch Kremmling CO 1987-1991. revjohnand@msn.com

ANDREWS, Pati Mary (Va) 8217 Roxborough Loop, Gainesville VA 20155 **R S Steph's Ch Catlett VA 2006-** B Washington DC 7/20/1948 d Carl Emory Hirst & Margaret Forsythe. BA Geo Mason U 1994; MDiv VTS 2000. D 6/24/2000 P 2/6/2001 Bp Peter James Lee. m 12/20/1968 Roland Andrews. Vic Ch Of The Gd Shpd Greer SC 2003-2005; Assoc H Innoc Epis Ch Valrico FL 2000-2002. Ord of S Lk 2002; Sursum Corda, Sprtl Dir 2003. patimary@comcast.net

ANDREWS, Robert Forrest (Colo) 30 Hutton Ln, Colorado Springs CO 80906 B DeKalb IL 5/25/1931 s Forrest Walter Andrews & Grace Marie. BS VMI 1953; MDiv Nash 1963. D 6/15/1963 Bp James Winchester Montgomery P 12/21/1963 Bp Joseph Summerville Minnis. m 4/9/1983 Jane Jewell c 3. R S Jas Epis Ch Wheat Ridge CO 1984-1992; P-in-c S Jn's Ch Moorhead MN 1982-1984; R S Steph's Ch Fargo ND 1981-1984; R S Jas Ch Grosse Ile MI 1980-1981; R S Paul's Epis Ch S Jos MI 1968-1980; R All SS Epis Ch Denver CO 1966-1968; Vic Intsn Epis Ch Thornton CO 1963-1966. jbandrews@adelphia.com

ANDREWS, Shirley May (Mass) 2 Palmer St, Barrington RI 02806 B Fall River MA 11/15/1936 d Thomas Scholes & Mary Emma. BA Stratford Coll Danville VA 1970; Med U of Virginia 1974; MDiv GTS 1990. D 6/1/1990 Bp Walter Cameron Righter P 1/19/1991 Bp Charlie Fuller McNutt Jr. m 7/17/1954 Ronald Grant Andrews c 2. R Ch Of The Ascen Fall River MA 2002-2005; Assoc S Jn's Ch Barrington RI 1992-2002; Asst S Jn's Ch Barrington RI 1991-1992; Cur Dio Cntrl Pennsylvania Harrisburg PA 1990-1991; S Andr's Ch St Coll PA 1990-1991.

ANDREWS III, William E (WTenn) St Mary's Cathedral, 692 Poplar Ave, Memphis TN 38105 **S Mary's Cathd Memphis TN 2007-** B Greenville MS 4/18/1967 s William Earl Andrews & Mary Lynn. BBA U of Mississippi 1989; MDiv Epis TS of The SW 1996. D 11/3/1996 P 4/1/1997 Bp James Barrow Brown. m 5/20/2000 Anne F Andrews c 3. S Timothys Epis Ch Southaven MS 2004-2007; Cn S Andr's Cathd Jackson MS 1998-2003; S Jas Epis Ch Baton Rouge LA 1996-1998. aaandrews@bellsouth.net

ANDREWS-WECKERLY, Jennifer Niccole (Del) P.O. Box 3510, Wilmington DE 19807 **Cur Chr Ch Greenville Wilmington DE 2009-** B Atlanta GA 11/19/1976 d Harry Franklin Andrews & Felicia Sue. AB Duke 1999; MDiv VTS 2009. D 6/24/2009 P 1/9/2010 Bp Wayne Parker Wright. m 8/4/2001 Scott J Andrews-Weckerly c 1. jennifer.andrews@alumni.duke.edu

ANDRUS, Archie Leslie (HB) 2701 Bellefontaine St, Houston TX 77025 B 1/18/1935 BA U Of SW Louisiana 1957; STB GTS 1963. D 6/25/1963 Bp Girault M Jones P 5/1/1964 Bp Iveson Batchelor Noland. m 4/15/1966 Diana Lee Cutler. Assoc R S Paul's Epis Ch San Antonio TX 1966-1970; Vic Ch Of The Redeem Oak Ridge LA 1965-1966; Vic S Andr's Epis Ch Mer Rouge LA 1965-1966.

✠ **ANDRUS, Rt Rev Marc Handley** (Cal) 2006 Lyon St, San Francisco CA 94115 **Bp of California Dio California San Francisco CA 2006-** B Oak Ridge TN 10/20/1956 s Francis Haddon Andrus & Mary Frances. BS U of Tennessee 1979; MA Virginia Tech U 1984; MDiv VTS 1987. D 6/20/1987 P 4/1/1988 Bp C(laude) Charles Vache Con 2/7/2002 for Ala. m 9/1/1979 Sheila M Andrus c 1. Bp Suffr Dio Alabama Birmingham AL 2002-2006; R Emm Ch Middleburg VA 1997-2001; Asst Ch Of The Redeem Bryn Mawr PA 1987-1990. bishopmarc@diocal.org

ANEI, Abraham Muong (WMich) 1924 R W Berends Dr Sw Apt 1, Wyoming MI 49519 B Sudan 1/1/1981 s Aivei Lual & Adhet Marou. Koyper Coll Grand Rapids MI; Trin Sem. D 12/9/2006 Bp Robert R Gepert. m 1/1/2003 Uyai Ajak.

ANGELICA, David Michael (Mass) 20 John Hall Cartway, Yarmouth Port MA 02675 B Hartford CT 9/24/1947 s Jospeh Aloysius Angelica & Josephine Mellow. BA Trin Hartford CT 1970; MDiv GTS 1973; PhD NYU 1976; Cert U of Connecticut 1978. D 6/9/1973 P 12/28/1973 Bp Joseph Warren Hutchens. R The Ch Of The H Sprt Orleans MA 1999-2008; Asst S Mary's Epis Ch Barnstable MA 1995-1998; R S Andr's Ch Milford CT 1980-1994; Cur S Andr's Ch Stamford CT 1977-1980; Asst S Lk's Par Darien CT 1974-1976; Assoc Ch Of The Resurr E Elmhurst NY 1973-1974. dmangelica@verizon.net

ANGELL, Debra L (Colo) 13866 W 2nd Ave, Golden CO 80401 **Assoc R S Barn Epis Ch Denver CO 2002-** B Denver CO 2/4/1952 d Wayland Homer Lanning & Elizabeth. BA Colorado Coll 1974; BM U Denv 1981; MDiv Iliff TS 1998. D 6/6/1998 P 12/13/1998 Bp William Jerry Winterrowd. m 6/1/1974 Richard Lee Angell c 3. Asst S Gabr The Archangel Epis Ch Cherry Hills Vill CO 1999-2002; Pstr Asst/Cur Epiph Epis Ch Denver CO 1998. Bm mcl U Denv Denver CO 1981; Ba cl Colorado Coll Colorado Sprg CO 1974. debangell@comcast.net

ANGELL, Michael Richard (SanD) 1525 H St NW, Washington DC 20005 **S Jn's Ch Lafayette Sq Washington DC 2011-** B Denver CO 2/25/1982 s Richard Lee Angell & Debra L. BA U of San Diego 2005; MDiv VTS 2011. D 4/9/2011 P 10/8/2011 Bp James Robert Mathes. Dio San Diego San Diego CA 2006-2008. angellmike@gmail.com

ANGERER JR, Jay (La) 100 Rex Dr, River Ridge LA 70123 **All SS Epis Ch River Ridge LA 2009-** B Hockessin DE 7/29/1970 s John David Angerer & Mary Elayne. MDiv SWTS 2002. D 6/8/2002 P 12/21/2002 Bp Wayne Parker Wright. m 4/19/1997 Lisa Gehley c 2. Epis Campus Min/ Asst S Thos's Par Newark DE 2002-2004. jay.angerer@gmail.com

ANGEVINE, Leo G (NwPa) 1760 Looker Mountain Trl, Rixford PA 16745 B Buffalo NY 3/3/1940 s Wilbur Angevine & Iris. Houghton Coll 1961; S Bonaventure U Alleghany NY 1961; completed Dioc Sch for Mnstry Titusville PA 2005. D 4/30/2005 P 10/30/2005 Bp Robert Deane Rowley Jr. m 3/3/1962 Adeline Angevine c 3. frleo@zoominternet.net

ANGLE, Nancy Scott (Colo) 150 Sipprelle Dr, Battlement Mesa CO 81635 B Houston TX 1/1/1937 d William McCarrell Angle & Ruth Mildred Matthews. BA U CO 1958; MBS U CO 1974. D 11/14/2009 Bp Robert John O'Neill. m 8/10/1974 Marshall Alan Martin c 4. nangle@bresnan.net

ANGULO ZAMORA, Gina Mayra (EcuL) Iglesia Episcopal del Ecuador Diocese Litoral, Amarilis Fuente 603, Guayaquil Ecuador Ecuador **D Litoral Dio Ecuador Guayaquil EQ EC 2008-** B Ricaurte 5/19/1979 d Zenon Campuzano Angulo & Ninfa. D 4/13/2008 Bp Alfredo Morante-España. gina197919@hotmail.com

ANGUS, Caroline Helen (O) 2716 Colchester Rd, Cleveland Heights OH 44106 B Grand Rapids MI 7/16/1936 d Donald A Gezon & Loraine M. SWTS; BA MI SU 1958; MA U MI 1959. D 1/22/1983 P 9/1/1983 Bp John Harris Burt. m 6/25/1960 John Angus c 2. R S Lk's Ch Cleveland OH 1984-1998; Pstr Visitor S Lk's Ch Cleveland OH 1982-1984.

ANGUS, J Lloyd (Ga) 88 Oakwood Dr., Hardeeville SC 29927 B Saint Catherine JM 9/20/1939 s Lorenzo Stanbury Angus & Verena. Educ Dplma Mico U Coll 1963; BD Lon 1969; MA McCormick TS 1973; Cert SWTS 1976; DMin McCormick TS 1980; PhD GTF 1998. D 5/2/1976 P 9/1/1976 Bp Quintin Ebenezer Primo Jr. m 8/30/1967 Rita S Stewart c 3. R S Matt's Ch Savannah GA 1997-2005; R S Phil's Epis Ch Jacksonville FL 1981-1997; Vic Ch Of The H Cross Chicago IL 1976-1980. Auth, "Dynamic Chrsnty: The Impact Of Pan-Afr Immigrants On The Chr Churh In The USA," Auth Hse, 2006; Auth, "Vitalization Process Of An Urban Black Epis Cong". jlangus84@hargray.com

ANKUDOWICH, Stephen (SwFla) 197 Corsica St, Tampa FL 33606 B Northampton MA 9/30/1948 s Kostanty Ankudowich & Mary. BA Trin 1970; MDiv EDS 1974; DMin EDS 1991. D 6/14/1974 P 12/1/1974 Bp Alexander Doig Stewart. m 2/12/1972 Denise Clay c 3. S Anne Of Gr Epis Ch Seminole FL 2004; R S Andr's Epis Ch Tampa FL 1990-2003; R Ch Of The Gd Shpd Wareham MA 1978-1989; Asst R S Mk's Ch New Canaan CT 1976-1978; Dio Wstrn Massachusetts Springfield MA 1974-1976; Asst R S Mich's-On-The-Heights Worcester MA 1974-1976. STEVENANKSTAND@AOL.COM

ANNIS, Charles Michael Patrick (NwPa) 885 High Mountain St, Henderson NV 89015 **Cleric S Tim's Epis Ch Henderson NV 2008-** B Framingham MA 3/1/1939 s Charles Mason Annis & Barbara. BS MIT 1961; BD EDS 1965; Stan 1974. D 6/14/1965 P 12/21/1965 Bp John P Craine. m 8/28/1965 Joyce Blough Roseberger. R S Steph's Ch Fairview PA 1987-2003; R Trin Epis Par Waterloo IA 1974-1987; Vic S Fran In The Fields Zionsville IN 1969-1973; Cur S Paul's Epis Ch Indianapolis IN 1969-1973; P-in-c S Fran In The Fields Zionsville IN 1966-1968; Vic S Ptr's Ch Lebanon IN 1966-1968; Cur Trin Ch Indianapolis IN 1965-1966. jobannis62@aol.com

ANSCHUTZ, Mark Semmes (Dal) Po Box 12385, Dallas TX 75225 B Carthage MO 4/22/1944 s John Raymond Anschutz & Madeleine. BA Drury U 1966; STM Ya Berk 1969; DMin Andover Newton TS 1976. D 5/28/1969 P 1/25/1970 Bp William Foreman Creighton. m 6/25/1970 Margaret Ann Crook c 2. R S Mich And All Ang Ch Dallas TX 1995-2006; R S Jas Ch New York NY 1992-1995; Trst Ya Berk New Haven CT 1983-1987; R Chr Ch Alexandria VA 1977-1992; R S Lk's Ch Worcester MA 1971-1977; Assoc And Coll Chapl S Jn's Ch Northampton MA 1969-1971. Auth, "From the R," Full Crt Press, 2002; Auth, "Grant Them Wisdom". Omecron Delta Kappa 1965. DD STUSo 1997. markanschutz@yahoo.com

ANSCHUTZ, Maryetta Madeleine (Los) P.O. Box 691404, Los Angeles CA 90069 **Hd of Sch The Epis Sch of Los Angeles Los Angeles CA 2010-** B Worcester MA 9/18/1974 d Mark Semmes Anschutz & Margaret. BA U So 1997; MDiv Ya Berk 2001. D 11/17/2001 Bp Peter James Lee P 6/6/2002 Bp James Elliot Curry. Assoc All SS Par Beverly Hills CA 2006-2010; Assoc Dn Ya Berk New Haven CT 2004-2006; Asst Chr And H Trin Ch Westport CT 2001-2004. Contributing Auth, "Sermons," *Feasting on the Word*, Knox, 2010. Monk Preaching Prize Ya Berk New Haven CT 2001. anschutz@es-la.com

ANTHONY, Benjamin Jay (At) 2023 Convent Pl, Nashville TN 37212 B Mansfield OH 7/13/1978 BA Wabash Coll 2000; MDiv Candler TS Emory U 2003. D 6/18/2005 P 7/14/2006 Bp Catherine Elizabeth Maples Waynick. m 4/6/2004 Rebecca Ann Trimm. Dio Atlanta Atlanta GA 2007-2009; Young And YA Coordntr S Lk's Epis Ch Atlanta GA 2005-2007. ben0713@hotmail.com

ANTHONY, Carol Renee (Pa) 627 Kenilworth St, Philadelphia PA 19147 **Ch Of S Lk And Epiph Philadelphia PA 2011-** B Jackson MS 7/13/1957 d Willie Lorell Anthony & Maudie Lee. BS Mississippi U For Wmn 1979; MRE SW Bapt TS 1985; CAS GTS 1995; STM GTS 1996. D 6/22/1996 P 4/5/1997 Bp Alfred Clark Marble Jr. S Ptr's Ch Philadelphia PA 2010-2011; P-in-c Ch Of S Jn The Evang Philadelphia PA 2003-2004; Dio Pennsylvania Philadelphia PA 2001-2004; Chr Ch Philadelphia Philadelphia PA 2000-2003; Epis Cmnty Serv Philadelphia PA 1998-2001; Cur S Andr's Cathd Jackson MS 1996-1998. cranthony@comcast.net

ANTHONY II, Henry F (RI) 727 Hampton Woods Ln SW, Vero Beach FL 32962 B Providence RI 11/13/1933 s Ralph Sayles Anthony & Doris. BA Amh 1956; MDiv STUSo 1987. D 6/27/1987 P 1/1/1988 Bp George Nelson Hunt III. m 6/11/2006 Katherine Harvey. Assoc Ch Of The Gd Shpd Lookout Mtn TN 1992-1994; S Mart's Ch Providence RI 1991-1992; S Ptr's By The Sea Narragansett RI 1989-1991; Assoc R Trin Ch Newport RI 1987-1989. hanthony2@comcast.net

ANTHONY, Joan Marie (Oly) 1549 MW 57th St., Seattle WA 98107 **Cn to the Ordnry Dio Olympia Seattle WA 2003-** B Seattle WA 2/22/1948 d John L Anthony & Anne. BA WA SU 1970; MDiv SWTS 1991; MA Seattle U 1991. D 5/14/1991 P 11/1/1991 Bp Vincent Waydell Warner. m 5/19/2003 Robert Bethea. Vic S Ben Epis Ch Lacey WA 1996-2003; Asst R Epis Ch Of S Fran-In-The-Vlly Green Vlly AZ 1994-1996; Asst R S Jn's Epis Ch Olympia WA 1991-1994. janthony@ecww.org

ANTHONY JR, Joseph Daniel (At) 389 Dorsey Cir Sw, Lilburn GA 30047 B Atlanta GA 10/31/1933 s Joseph Daniel Anthony & Lucy Loeffler. BS USNA 1956; BD VTS 1964. D 6/29/1964 P 9/1/1965 Bp Gray Temple. m 12/27/1957 Betty Carol Kellum c 3. Vic S Barn Ch Trion GA 1983-1985; Asst Par Ch of St. Helena Beaufort SC 1969; P-in-c Chr Ch Denmark SC 1965-1969; P-in-c S Alb's Ch Blackville SC 1965-1969.

ANTHONY, Lloyd Lincoln (LI) 9910 217th Ln, Queens Village NY 11429 **Epis Soc Serv New York NY 2003-; R S Jos's Ch Queens Vill NY 1987-** B BZ 2/16/1950 s Thomas Anthony & Delcy Ann. Belize Teachers Coll 1972; BA Untd Theol Coll of the W Indies 1977; STM NYTS 1983. Trans from Church in the Province Of The West Indies 8/21/1982 Bp Robert Campbell Witcher Sr. m 7/14/1999 Wilma Fletcher c 3. P-in-c Ch Of The H Sprt Brooklyn NY 1983-1984; S Johns Epis Hosp Far Rockaway NY 1981-1986; Assoc Ch Of S Thos Brooklyn NY 1980-1983; Ch Of S Jas The Less Jamaica NY 1978-1979. Cn Dio Wiawso, Ghana 2009. antini_99@yahoo.com

ANTHONY, Robert Williams (RI) 104 Old Stage Rd, Centerville MA 02632 **S Ptr's Ch Osterville MA 2007-** B Port Chester NY 5/18/1940 s Robert Olney Anthony & Gladys Bronwen. BA Amh 1962; STB GTS 1965; MDiv GTS 1972. D 6/19/1965 P 2/1/1966 Bp John S Higgins. m 9/12/1964 Mary Ann Lytle c 2. Fin & Missions Cmsn Dio Rhode Island Providence RI 1994-2006; R Chr Ch Westerly RI 1988-2006; The GTS New York NY 1987-1993; Dept of Soc Serv Dio Wstrn Massachusetts Springfield MA 1980-1983; Dioc Coun Dio Wstrn Massachusetts Springfield MA 1979-1985; R Ch Of The Atone Westfield MA 1976-1988; Dio Wstrn Massachusetts Springfield MA 1976-1988; R Ch of the H Sprt W Haven CT 1968-1976; Cur S Barn Ch Warwick RI 1965-1968. ranthoman@verizon.net

ANTHONY, Thomas Murray (PR) 196 E 19th Ave, VANCOUVER, BC, CANADA 00000 Canada B 9/30/1935

ANTHONY-CHARLES, Ana Graciela (Ve) 49-143 Colinas De Bello Monte, Caracas 1042 Venezuela **Dio Venezuela Colinas De Bello Monte Caracas 10-42-A VE 2004-** B 8/27/1949 D 1/18/1999 P 5/17/2002 Bp Orlando Jesus Guerrero.

ANTOCI, Peter M (WA) Episcopal/Anglican Campus Ministry: UMD, 2116 Memorial Chapel, College Park MD 20742 **Dep to GC Dio Washington Washington DC 2009-2012; Coordntr of Higher Educ Mnstrs Prov III Chester Sprg PA 2009-; Mem of Dioc Coun Dio Washington Washington DC 2005-2012; Vic & Chapl Dio Washington Washington DC 2003-; Adj Cler S Andr's Epis Ch Coll Pk MD 2003-** B New York NY 5/6/1963 s Santo Antoci & Helen. BA GW 1985; MA CUA 1989; PhD CUA 1995; Cert Natl Institutes of Hlth 2000; CAS VTS 2000. D 6/9/2001 Bp Jane Hart Holmes Dixon P 5/26/2002 Bp Allen Lyman Bartlett Jr. m 11/30/2009 Donald Davis. Actg Int All Souls Memi Epis Ch Washington DC 2007; Cur Gr Epis Ch Silver Sprg MD 2001-2004; Chapl Gr Epis Day Sch Silver Sprg MD 2001-2004. Auth, "Serv & Mutuality," 2002; Auth, "An Epis Ecclesiology of Apostolocity, ATR," *Vol. 84 #2*, 2002; Auth, "Scandal and Marginality in the Vitae of H Fools, Chrsnty and Lit," *Vol. 44 # 3-4*, 1996. AAR 1989; HSEC 2010; Ldrshp Washington 1998; Prov III Epis Chapl 2003; Washington Epis Cler Assn 2001. Dioc Coun, Mem 2006-2009 Epis Dio Washington 2006; Trst 1995-1997 Jubilee Hsng, Inc. 1995; Tchg and Resrch Fellowships 1988-1995 Cath U 1988. pmantoci@yahoo.com

ANTOLINI, Holly Lyman (Mass) 11 Quincy St, Arlington MA 02476 **Dn Dio Massachusetts Boston MA 2010-; R S Jas' Epis Ch Cambridge MA 2008-** B Philadelphia PA 11/18/1952 d Richard Wall Lyman & Elizabeth. BA Ya 1974; MDiv CDSP 1991. D 12/8/1990 P 12/9/1991 Bp William Edwin Swing. Alt to GC Dio Virginia Richmond VA 2006-2008; Dn Dio Virginia Richmond VA 2006-2008; Assoc S Paul's Ch Richmond VA 2003-2007; P-in-c S Eliz Of Hungary Portland ME 2002-2003; Int S Ptr's Ch Rockland ME 2002; Stndg

Com Mem Dio Maine Portland ME 1999-2003; Int S Mk's Ch Waterville ME 1999-2001; Dep to GC Dio Maine Portland ME 1996-2003; Prov Rep Epis Prov Of New Engl Dorset VT 1994-1999; Vic S Brendan's Epis Ch Stonington ME 1993-1999; Cur S Ptr's Ch Rockland ME 1992; D S Bede's Epis Ch Menlo Pk CA 1990-1991. Auth, "A Letter to the Nigerian Ch from an Epis P," *Do Justice!: Unofficial Angl Pages*, Dr. Louie Crew, 2005; Auth, "The Da Vinci Code: Vehicle of Gr?," *bellsouthpwp2.net*, 2004; Auth, "Going Loc In Midcoast Maine," *Wit*, 2002; Auth, "Naming Our Demons," *Wit*, 1999; Auth, "Of Pryr And Compost," *Wit*, 1999; Auth, "Mnstry w Teenagers Who are Allergic to Organized Rel," *Progressive Chrsnty.org*, 1998; Auth, "An Environ Stations of the Cross," *Earthministry.org*, 1993. Masters of Div w hon CDSP 1991; BA w hon in Hist Ya 1974. smallvoice@earthlink.net

ANTTONEN, Jennifer (Ida) 288 E Kite Dr, Eagle ID 83616 B Dayton OH 1/2/1949 d Robert Simms Parker & Nancy. BS WA SU 1994; MDiv CDSP 1998. D 6/7/1998 Bp Frank Jeffrey Terry P 12/19/1998 Bp Harry Brown Bainbridge III. m 11/13/1971 John Helmer Anttonen c 2. S Dav's Epis Ch Caldwell ID 2005-2006; Vic Emm Ch Hailey ID 1998-2003. Bp's Outstanding Cong Recognition Dio Idaho Emm Ch Hailey ID 2002; Make a Difference Day $10,000 Natl Awd USA Weekend mag Emm Ch Hailey ID 2002; Friends of Educ Awd Blaine Cnty Educ Assn 2000; BS cl WA SU 1994. jpanttonen@msn.com

APKER, David (Mil) 4400 Deer Park Rd, Oconomowoc WI 53066 B Green Bay WI 12/30/1933 s Merrill Roy Apker & Claudine Veronica. BS U of Wisconsin 1956; MA U of Wisconsin 1972. D 4/7/1984 Bp Charles Thomas Gaskell. m 9/15/1979 Caroline Foth Poh c 2. D S Ptr's Ch No Lake WI 1994-2000; D S Anskar's Epis Ch Hartland WI 1990-1994; D St Mths Epis Ch Waukesha WI 1988-1989; D S Lk's Ch Madison WI 1984-1988. AmL 1998; Cnty Sr Serv Visitor 2001; Mossflower Harbor Residential Facility Chapl 2002; Natl Rifle Assn 1998; Wisconsin Hist Soc 1983; Wisconsin Pro-Life 1991. buccaneer@ameritech.net

APOLDO, Deborah Daum (Ky) PO Box 225, St. Francis In The Fields, Harrods Creek KY 40027 **Assoc for Evang & Discipleship S Fran In The Fields Harrods Creek KY 2003-** B Philadelphia PA 9/4/1955 BS Ithaca Coll 1977; MDiv VTS 2003. D 6/14/2003 Bp Peter James Lee P 12/13/2003 Bp Edwin Funsten Gulick Jr. m 9/18/1982 Charles Frederick Apoldo c 3. The Falls Ch Epis Falls Ch VA 1994-2000. debbiea@stfrancisinthefields.org

APPELBERG, Helen Marie Waller (Tex) 301 University Blvd, Galveston TX 77555 B Blooming Grove TX 9/5/1930 d Charles William Waller & Johnnie Irene. AA Tyler Jr Coll 1949; BA U of No Texas 1951; Med U of Virginia 1955; Med Oklahoma City U 1977; MA Epis TS of The SW 1990; DMin Austin Presb TS 1995. D 6/16/1990 Bp Maurice Manuel Benitez P 1/1/1991 Bp William Elwood Sterling. c 1. St Lk's Epis Hosp Houston TX 1990-2002; S Mart's Epis Ch Houston TX 1990-2001. "Cmnty Of Hope," 14 Module Curric, 1996; "S Lk'S Epis," Hosp Med Cntr Houston Tx. Dok 1986; Ord Of S Ben 1996; Ord Of S Lk 1985; Wrld Cmnty Chr Meditation 1996. helenappelberg@gmail.com

APPLEGATE, Stephen Holmes (SO) 360 E Sharon Rd, Glendale OH 45246 **R S Lk's Ch Granville OH 2003-** B Nashville TN 3/17/1952 s Arthur Homes Applegate & Betty Jane. BA Ham 1974; MDiv GTS 1980. D 5/15/1980 P 11/1/1980 Bp Harold B Robinson. c 1. S Andr's Epis Ch Cincinnati OH 2002-2003; Stndg Com Dio Sthrn Ohio Cincinnati OH 1988; Chr Ch - Glendale Cincinnati OH 1985-1990; Stndg Com Dio Albany Albany NY 1984-1985; BEC Dio Albany Albany NY 1981-1987; S Paul's Cathd Buffalo NY 1981-1985; Sr Cn S Ptr's Ch Albany NY 1981-1985; Asst S Jas' Ch Batavia NY 1980-1981. Auth, "Hist mag Pec". Buffalo Area Metropltn Ministers Soc Of S Jn The Evang. Mdiv cl GTS New York NY 1980. rector_stlukes@windstream.net

APPLEQUIST, Alice Mae (Minn) 16 Winona St Se, Chatfield MN 55923 **P S Matt's Epis Ch Chatfield MN 1997-** B Rochester MN 1/7/1959 d Donald Frank Balcome & Elizabeth Louise. AA Rochester Cmnty Coll 1979; BS Winona St U 1982. D 7/28/1996 P 2/14/1998 Bp James Louis Jelinek. Chatfield Ministral Soc Prayers For Healing 1995. vegag91357@aol.com

APPLETON, Mary Ellen (CFla) 200 Saint Andrews Blvd Apt 1406, Winter Park FL 32792 B Brighton MI 4/24/1939 d Lawrence Bert Appleton & Helen Louise. Wheaton Coll 1960; BS Estrn Michigan U 1964; Med Kent St U 1969. D 10/15/1988 Bp William Hopkins Folwell. D All SS Ch Of Winter Pk Winter Pk FL 1996-2002; D S Sebastian's By The Sea Melbourne Bch FL 1991-1995; D Ch Of Our Sav Palm Bay FL 1988-1991. Chapl Ord Of S Lk.

APPLEYARD, Daniel Scott (Mo) 9 S Bompart Ave, Webster Groves MO 63119 **Emm Epis Ch Webster Groves MO 2009-** B Greenwich CT 7/20/1954 s Katharine Louise. BA Webster U 1976; MDiv Ya Berk 1983. D 6/23/1983 P 3/1/1984 Bp William Augustus Jones Jr. m 11/20/1989 Elizabeth Adler c 2. R Chr Ch Dearborn MI 1993-2009; Cmncatn Com Dio Kansas Topeka KS 1986-1993; R S Lk's Epis Ch Shawnee KS 1986-1993; Cur Gr Ch Kirkwood MO 1983-1986. lizziesapple@aol.com

APPLEYARD, Jonathan Briggs (Me) 26 Montsweag Road, Woolwich ME 04579 **R S Sav's Par Bar Harbor ME 2002-; Dio Maine Portland ME 2000-** B Watertown CT 12/18/1949 s Robert Bracewell Appleyard & Katharine. BA Wms 1972; MDiv GTS 1976. D 5/29/1976 P 1/8/1977 Bp Robert Bracewell Appleyard. m 7/13/1996 Ruth Wiggins c 6. Exec Dir of Yth & Camp Min Dio Massachusetts Boston MA 2000-2002; Camp Dudley Ymca Inc Westport NY 1997-2000; R S Paul's Ch Brunswick ME 1988-1996; Par of Trin Ch New York NY 1984-1988; Trin Educ Fund New York NY 1984-1987; Asst Dn of Stdt Affrs The GTS New York NY 1978-1984; Asst The Ch Of The Redeem Pittsburgh PA 1976-1978. Soc of S Jn the Evang 1975. Cler Renwl Awd Lilly Endwmt Inc. 2008; MDiv w hon GTS New York NY 1976; BA mcl Wms Williamstown MA 1972. jonathanappleyard@gmail.com

APPLEYARD JR, Robert Bracewell (Mass) 2036 Acton Ridge Rd, Acton ME 04001 B New York NY 10/4/1947 s Robert Bracewell Appleyard & Katharine Louise. BA Alleg 1969; MDiv VTS 1972. D 6/10/1972 P 12/9/1972 Bp Robert Bracewell Appleyard. m 8/22/1970 Deborah W Wood c 1. S Barn Ch Falmouth MA 1992-2007; Exam Chapl Dio Massachusetts Boston MA 1987-1993; R S Mich's Ch Milton MA 1977-1992; Asst R Fox Chap Epis Ch Pittsburgh PA 1972-1977. 1920 Club 1977-1992; Massachusetts Cler Assn 1977. revapple@gmail.com

ARAICA, Alvaro (Chi) 4609 Main St, Skokie IL 60076 **Cristo Rey Chicago IL 1996-** B Jinotega NI 7/8/1960 s Ernesto Araica & Maura Villagra. BEd Natl U of Nicaragua 1984; MDiv SWTS 1995. D 10/17/1987 P 7/1/1989 Bp Sturdie Wyman Downs. m 5/10/1982 Marta Aguirre c 3. Dio Chicago Chicago IL 1995-1996; Iglesia Epis Santa Teresa De Avila Chicago IL 1995-1996. epicris@aol.com

ARAMBULO, Arnulfo (NY) 231 City View Ter, Kingston NY 12401 **Hisp Mssnr Chr Ch Poughkeepsie NY 2000-; Dio New York New York City NY 2000-** B CO 9/25/1943 s Sinforoso Arambulo & Agripina. Ph Natl Sem 1971; San Buenaventura U 1975. Rec from Roman Catholic 12/31/1994 Bp Joe Morris Doss. m 11/27/1986 Maria Angel c 2. Ch Of The H Cross Kingston NY 2009; Ch Of The H Cross Kingston NY 2007-2009; Vic/Hisp Mssnr Ch Of The Gd Shpd Newburgh NY 2000; Latina Mssnr Ch Of The H Cross Kingston NY 2000; Gr Epis Ch Eliz NJ 1997-1999. arambulo1@msn.com

ARBOGAST, Stephen Daniel Kirkpatrick (Mass) Grace Church of New York, 802 Broadway, New York NY 10003 **Assoc Gr Epis Ch New York NY 2007-; Chair: Rel, Philos, & Ethics Dept Trin Sch New York NY 2004-** B Dallas TX 12/5/1956 s Edward Francis Arbogast & Barbara Ann. Dplma Ya Berk 2003; MDiv Yale DS 2003; ThM Harvard DS 2005; D.Min. Candidate VTS 2013. D 6/4/2005 P 1/7/2006 Bp M(arvil) Thomas Shaw III. Assoc Par of Trin Ch New York NY 2006-2007. stephen.arbogast@aya.yale.edu

ARBUCKLE, Jacquelyn (Vt) 6608 Route 7, North Ferrisburgh VT 05473 **D S Jn's In The Mountains Stowe VT 2007-** B Lynn MA 11/21/1942 d Eugene Sheperd Fenelon & Margaret Agnes. RN New Engl Bapt Hosp 1963; Med Antioch U New Engl 1983. D 7/30/1991 Bp Daniel Lee Swenson. m 11/7/1964 Allan Rainsbury Arbuckle c 2. D All SS' Epis Ch S Burlington VT 1991-2007. NAAD. jacqallan@aol.com

ARCHER, A(rthur) William (Del) 650 Willow Valley Sq # K-401, Lancaster PA 17602 B Sewickley PA 7/5/1932 s Harry Victor Archer & Hazel Brinthinda. BA Ken 1954; STB Ya Berk 1957; STM STUSo 1966. D 6/29/1957 Bp William S Thomas P 12/21/1957 Bp Austin Pardue. m 9/8/1956 Carolyn Patton c 3. Asst S Jn's Epis Ch Lancaster PA 1994-1995; S Jas Ch Wilmington DE 1980-1994; R S Jas Epis Ch Newport Newport DE 1980-1994; R Trin Ch New Philadelphia OH 1971-1980; Cur S Mk's Epis Ch Toledo OH 1965-1971; R S Paul's Ch Monongahela PA 1960-1964; Asst S Steph's Epis Ch Mckeesport PA 1957-1960.

ARCHER, John Richard (Cal) 80 Harmon St, Hamden CT 06517 B Buffalo NY 2/12/1945 s John Archer & Gertrude. Colg 1964; BA SUNY 1967; Canisius Coll 1970; MDiv GTS 1974; PhD Gnrl Theol Un Berkeley CA 1984. D 5/22/1974 Bp Harold B Robinson P 11/1/1974 Bp George E Rath. R All Souls Par In Berkeley Berkeley CA 1989-1992; Cathd of St Ptr & St Paul Washington DC 1986-1989; Lectr Ch Hist And Liturg CDSP Berkeley CA 1986; Int Ch Of The Resurr Pleasant Hill CA 1984-1986; Lectr Ch Hist And Liturg CDSP Berkeley CA 1981-1983; Fac Dio California San Francisco CA 1980-1986; Vic S Edm's Epis Ch Pacifica CA 1978-1984; R Ch Of The Trsfg Ironwood MI 1975-1978; Cur Gr Ch Nutley NJ 1974-1975. Auth, "The Preaching Of Phil Repindon Bp Of Lincoln". ABELARCHER@COMCAST.NET

ARCHER, Melinda (Az) 26040 N 73rd Dr, Peoria AZ 85383 B Dallas TX 2/11/1946 d Horace Foster Gibson & Irene Horton. BA SMU 1967; MA SMU 1970; MDiv SMU 1991. D 9/11/1999 P 8/26/2000 Bp Julio Cesar Holguin-Khoury. m 7/11/1992 William Clarence Archer c 2. R S Andr's Ch Glendale AZ 2005-2010; S Barn Ch Garland TX 2002-2005; Vic Iglesia Epis San Juan El Bautista Santo Domingo DO 2000-2001; Dio The Dominican Republic (Iglesia Epis Dominicana) Santo Domingo DO 1999-2001. marcher211@aol.com

ARCHER, Michael Duane (Los) 18631 Chapel Ln, Huntington Beach CA 92646 **P-in-c S Wilfrid Of York Epis Ch Huntington Bch CA 2008-** B Oklahoma City OK 11/4/1960 s Ronald Edward Archer & Mary Eva H. D 4/16/2008 P 10/18/2008 Bp Joseph Jon Bruno. c 4. michael1104@sbcglobal.net

ARCHER, Nell B (LI) 199 Carroll St, Brooklyn NY 11231 **S Ann And The H Trin Brooklyn NY 2010-; Cur S Paul's Ch Brooklyn NY 2010-** B Memphis TN 7/29/1961 d Arthur W Archer & Louise Thompson. BA Duke 1983; MDiv The GTS 2009. D 6/22/2009 Bp James Hamilton Ottley P 1/16/2010 Bp Lawrence C Provenzano. c 3. Asst Dio Long Island Garden City NY 2009-2010. nbarcher@gmail.com

ARCHER, Richard B (SC) 1249 Via Ponticello Apt 1, Florence SC 29501 **Int Vic Ch Of The Adv Marion SC 2007-** B Johnson City NY 10/21/1932 s Wilson Post Archer & Viola. BS Drexel U 1961; MDiv TESM 1989. D 6/29/1989 Bp C(hristopher) FitzSimons Allison P 6/1/1990 Bp Edward Lloyd Salmon Jr. m 6/20/1953 Janet Brown c 5. Int H Cross Stateburg Stateburg SC 2000-2007; Int S Paul's Ch Bennettsville SC 1999-2000; Int S Mths Epis Ch Summerton SC 1998-1999; Vic Ch Of The Adv Marion SC 1990-1998; D Ch Of The Adv Marion SC 1989-1990.

ARCHIBALD, David Jost (Del) 32216 Bixler Rd, Selbyville DE 19975 **Dio Delaware Wilmington DE 2002-** B East Orange NJ 3/29/1943 s William David Archibald & Marjorie Viola. Washington and Jefferson U 1963; W Virginia U 1966; BA Thos Edison St Coll 1985; MDiv STUSo 1989. D 7/14/1990 P 1/19/1991 Bp George Lazenby Reynolds Jr. m 6/24/1972 Susan King Archibald. S Martins-In-The-Fields Selbyville DE 2003; R S Mk's Ch Millsboro DE 2002; Chr Epis Ch Tracy City TN 1998-2002; Dio Tennessee Nashville TN 1991-2003; Chr Ch Alto Decherd TN 1990-1994. djarch@mchsi.com

ARCHIE, Andrew John (Mo) 6345 Wydown Blvd, Saint Louis MO 63105 **R S Mich & S Geo Clayton MO 2000-** B Highland Park IL 1/5/1957 s Robert John Archie & Carol May. BA W&L 1979; MDiv VTS 1986. D 6/14/1986 Bp James Winchester Montgomery P 1/1/1987 Bp C(laude) Charles Vache. m 6/25/1983 Margaretta Gallegher c 3. R S Ptr's Epis Ch Purcellville VA 1987-2000; Manakin Epis Ch Midlothian VA 1986-1987; S Lk's Ch Powhatan VA 1986-1987. ajarchie@aol.com

ARCINIEGA, Roberto (Ore) 2065 Se 44th Ave Apt 248, Hillsboro OR 97123 **P-in-c S Mich's/San Miguel Newberg OR 2006-** B Jocotitlan MX 11/1/1956 s Juan Arciniega & Oliva. BA Sem Conculiar De Toluca 1975; BA Inst Superior De Estudies Eclesasticol 1980. Rec from Roman Catholic 5/1/1991 Bp John Lester Thompson III. m 5/26/2006 Kelly Arciniega c 2. Dio El Camino Real Monterey CA 1995; Mssnr Dio Nthrn California Sacramento CA 1991-1995. PBETOA@HOTMAIL.COM

ARD, Eddie Jackson (At) 3880 Glenhurst Dr Se, Smyrna GA 30080 **R S Anne's Epis Ch Atlanta GA 1999-** B Manchester GA 10/23/1956 s Sylvester Hobson Ard & Lovie Christine. BA Presb Coll 1977; MDiv VTS 1983. D 6/11/1983 P 5/6/1984 Bp Charles Judson Child Jr. m 12/20/1986 JoAnn Patrick c 1. R Emm Epis Ch Athens GA 1995-1999; R Gr Ch Anniston AL 1989-1994; Asst R H Innoc Ch Atlanta GA 1983-1989. ejard@saintannes.com

ARD JR, Robert Francis (Mo) 6518 Michigan Ave, St. Louis MO 63111 **S Paul's Ch S Louis MO 2010-** B Bronxville NY 1/3/1972 s Robert Francis Ard & Kathryn Grace. MA, Theol Aquinas Inst of Theol 2002; MDiv Eden TS 2008; STM The TS at The U So 2010. D 5/22/2010 P 12/21/2010 Bp George Wayne Smith. m 9/16/2006 Sharol Ann Warner. roberefrancois@yahoo.com

ARD, Roger Hoyt (At) 104 Sequoia Dr SE, Rome GA 30161 B Manchester GA 4/30/1952 s Sylvester Hobson Ard & Lovie Christine. BA Presb Coll 1973; MDiv Candler TS Emory U 1976; uncompleted PhD Emory U 1982. D 6/14/1980 Bp Bennett Jones Sims P 4/1/1981 Bp Charles Judson Child Jr. m 11/20/2004 Elizabeth Burnett Orr c 2. R S Ptr's Ch Rome GA 2002-2011; Int R Epis Ch Of The H Sprt Cumming GA 1999-2001; Int R S Steph's Ch Milledgeville GA 1999; Int Dn Cathd Of S Phil Atlanta GA 1997-1998; R S Paul's Epis Ch Westfield NJ 1993-1997; Int R S Lk's Epis Ch Atlanta GA 1991-1992; Assoc R S Anne's Epis Ch Atlanta GA 1989-1991; P-in-c S Anne's Epis Ch Atlanta GA 1987-1988; Assoc R S Anne's Epis Ch Atlanta GA 1984-1986; R S Mths Epis Ch Toccoa GA 1980-1984. Consult Ldr, "Involuntary Termination of Cler Within the Epis Ch," *Involuntary Termination of Cler Within the Epis Ch*, ECF, 1996; Auth, "Six Stages of Faith Dvlpmt," *Natl Cath Reporter*, 1979. rogard@comcast.net

ARDLEY, Evan Lloyd (NCal) 435 43rd Ave, #301, San Francisco CA 94121 B Motueka NZ 1/5/1947 s Frank Francis Ardley & Nita Askew. LTh (hons) Chr Ch TS Chr Ch NZ 1969; STh Joint Bd TS Auckland NZ 1975; Lic Trin of Mus London UK 1975; ThM CDSP 1976; DMin Grad Theol Un 1980; PhD GTF 2000. Trans from Anglican Church in Aotearoa, New Zealand and Polynesia 9/1/1976 as Priest Bp Clarence Rupert Haden Jr. m 5/25/1973 Diana Jane Conyers Brown c 2. R Ch Of The Incarn Santa Rosa CA 1988-2000; R St Johns Epis Ch Lafayette IN 1983-1988; Assoc All SS Ch San Diego CA 1980-1983; Vic S Tim's Ch Gridley CA 1976-1979. Auth, "Martyrs of Uganda Hymn," *Ch of Uganda*; Auth, "AIDS Hymn," *Dio Los Angeles*. Assoc of Amer Hospice and Palliative Med 2005; Natl Hospice and Palliative Care Orgnztn 2000. LTh w hon Chr Ch TS Chr Ch NZ 1969; R Hd Mem Awd Outstanding Min to PWAs. eardley727@aol.com

ARDREY-GRAVES, Sara Caroline (WNC) 660 S Main St, Harrisonburg VA 22801 **Emm Ch Harrisonburg VA 2010-; Ch Of The Gd Shpd Raleigh NC 2005-** B Yukon OK 8/14/1980 d Thomas Ardrey & Peggy. BS Appalachian St 2002; MDiv Duke 2005; DAS The TS at The U So 2010. D 5/23/2010 P 1/8/2011 Bp Granville Porter Taylor. m 5/21/2005 Mark W Ardrey-Graves. scardreygraves@gmail.com

ARENTS, Gina (Md) 1511 Long Quarter Ct, Lutherville MD 21093 B New York NY 11/24/1944 d George Arents & Jane. BA Goucher Coll 1975; PhD Jn Hopkins U 1987; MaTh Ecum Inst at St Mary's Sem 2007; M.Div. VTS 2009. D 6/2/2001 Bp Robert Wilkes Ihloff P 12/18/2010 Bp John Leslie Rabb. Asst Chr Ch Columbia MD 2010-2011; D S Ptr's Epis Ch Ellicott City MD 2004-2010; D All SS Epis Ch Reisterstown MD 2001-2004. gina1511@earthlink.net

AREY, Patrick (Md) 249 Wiltshire Lane, Severna Park MD 21146 **Died 7/31/2011** B 7/10/1947 BA W&L 1969; JD W&L 1976. D 6/2/2007 Bp John Leslie Rabb. c 4. parey@abrneu.com

ARGUE, Douglas (SO) 3400 Calumet St, Columbus OH 43214 B Detroit MI 5/25/1966 s Daniel David Argue & Carla June. BA U of Evansville 1988; MSW Indiana U 1992. D 6/14/2008 Bp Thomas Edward Breidenthal. douglasargue@cohhio.org

ARIS-PAUL, Maria Marta (NY) 160 Academy St Apt. 5A, Poughkeepsie NY 12601 B Guatemala City GT 10/5/1933 d Enrique Francisco Aris & Marta Sara. BA Smith 1976; MDiv UTS 1981. D 11/29/1982 Bp Paul Moore Jr P 6/25/1983 Bp Walter Decoster Dennis Jr. m 12/20/1980 Edwin Muller c 7. Pstr Gr Ch White Plains NY 1992-1994; Pstr Mision San Juan Bautista Bronx NY 1988-1991; Exec Dir Instituto Pstr Hispano New York NY 1986-1994; P-in-c S Andr's Epis Ch New Paltz NY 1984-1986. Auth, "Latin Amer and Caribbean Immigrants in the USA: The Invisible and Forgotten," *Revolution of Sprt Ecum Theol in Global Context*, W Erdmansn, 1998; Auth, "A Question: The Ch and the Hisp Cmnty," *ATR*, 1994; Auth, "Lrng Together," *Mnstry Dvlpmt Journ*, 1988. AB cl Smith Northampton MA 1976. mmarispaul002@hvc.rr.com

ARLEDGE JR, Thomas Lafayette (At) 909 Massee Ln, Perry GA 31069 B Chattano GA 10/6/1938 s Thomas Lafayette Arledge & Louise. BS U of Tennessee 1961; MS U of Tennessee 1963; BD STUSo 1970. D 6/28/1970 P 2/1/1971 Bp R(aymond) Stewart Wood Jr. m 10/5/1963 Lora Lee Pearson. P-in-c S Lk's Epis Hawkinsville GA 1996-1998; S Paul's Ch Macon GA 1995; S Steph's Ch Griffin GA 1994-1995; Dio Atlanta Atlanta GA 1970-1994; S Chris's At-The-Crossroads Epis Perry GA 1970-1993; S Mary's Epis Ch Montezuma GA 1970-1993.

ARLIN, Charles Noss (Nwk) 367 Strawtown Rd, New City NY 10956 **Int S Jn's Ch New City NY 2011-** B Cuba NY 5/1/1938 s Aubrey Arlin & Edith Elizabeth. BA Hob 1961; STB GTS 1964. D 6/1/1964 Bp Ned Cole P 6/10/1965 Bp Walter M Higley. m 10/10/1964 Jane M McDonough c 4. Int Ch Of The H Cross Kingston NY 2009-2011; R Ch Of The Gd Shpd Midland Pk NJ 2002-2009; P-in-c All SS Ch Bergenfield NJ 1997-2002; Int Epis Ch On W Kaua'i Eleele HI 1989; Vic H Cross Perth Amboy NJ 1977-1997; Asst S Lk the Evang Roselle NJ 1968-1976; Asst S Jn's Ch New York NY 1966-1968. charlesarlin@aol.com

ARMENTROUT, Katharine Jacobs (At) 202 Griffith Rd, Jasper GA 30143 B Montclair NJ 6/7/1941 d Jay A Jacobs & Phyllis Austin. BA Br 1963; JD U of Maryland 1983. D 6/5/2004 Bp Robert Wilkes Ihloff. m 8/21/1965 Walter Scott Armentrout c 2. godspeedkja@gmail.com

ARMER, Mary Carolyn (WMo) 8170 Halsey St, Lenexa KS 66215 **St Lk's Chap Kansas City MO 2004-** B Phoenix AZ 8/16/1943 d John Henry Armer & Mary Carolyn. MA Arizona St U; BS Nthrn Arizona U 1964; Cert Grand Canyon U 1976; MDiv Epis TS of The SW 1991. Trans 1/1/2004 as Priest Bp Harry Brown Bainbridge III. m 5/27/1967 George W Cox c 1. St Lk's So Chap Overland Pk KS 2004-2010; S Steph's Boise ID 1995; Emm Ch Hailey ID 1994-1995; D/Asst Cathd Ch Of S Mk Salt Lake City UT 1993-1994; Chapl Res Dio Utah Salt Lake City UT 1991-1993. Assn Profsnl Chapl 1995. marycayarmer@yahoo.com

ARMER, Susan Charlee (Oly) 5551 S 300th Pl, Auburn WA 98001 **R S Matthews Auburn WA 2001-** B Phoenix AZ 9/6/1949 d Charles Campbell Armer & Lillian Theresa. BA U of Arizona 1982; MDiv Bex 1988. D 6/2/1988 P 12/8/1988 Bp Joseph Thomas Heistand. m 6/17/1989 Thomas J Sernka c 1. Cn Pstr Cathd Ch Of S Mk Salt Lake City UT 1991-2001; Assoc R Chr Epis Ch Dayton OH 1988-1991. sarmer@comcast.net

ARMINGTON, Shawn Aaron (NJ) 118 Jefferson Rd, Princeton NJ 08540 B Portsmouth NH 7/16/1958 s Allan Armington & Frances. BA Cor 1980; MA Ya Berk 1983; MDiv GTS 1986; ThM PrTS 1994; PhD PrTS 2000. D 6/7/1986 Bp David Standish Ball P 12/21/1986 Bp Vincent King Pettit. m 5/1/1982 Karen Louise Lollo. Vic Trin Ch Rocky Hill NJ 1997-2002; Vic S Jn's Epis Ch Maple Shade NJ 1987-1994; Chr Ch So Amboy NJ 1986-1987. Auth, "Koinonia". SBL. Ba mcl Cornell Ithaca NY 1980; Green Fllshp OT Phd Stds. shawnarmington@yahoo.com

ARMSTEAD, Delaney Wendell (Nev) 2552 Orangeglory Dr, Henderson NV 89052 **D Chr Ch Las Vegas NV 2000-** B Youngstown OH 1/25/1928 s Abram Delaney Armstead & Dorothy Ann. BA Diac Sch For Deacons Menlo

Pk CA 1988. D 12/7/1996 Bp William Edwin Swing. m 8/17/1996 Joann Shirley Roberts. D S Aug's Ch Oakland CA 1996-2000; D S Chris's Ch San Lorenzo CA 1996-2000. Bro Of S Andr; CBS; OHC, Berkeley, Ca 1997. revd631@aol.com

ARMSTRONG, Barbara (NC) 509 Sleepy Valley Rd, Apex NC 27523 B Brooklyn NY 3/21/1939 d Milton Joseph Keegan & Rita Catherine. Geo; BA Meredith Coll 1983; MRE Duke DS 1986. D 10/4/1987 Bp Robert Whitridge Estill. m 1/2/1959 Robert Harding Armstrong c 3. Dir D Formation Dio No Carolina Raleigh NC 2001-2011; D Ch Of The H Fam Chap Hill NC 1991-2008.

ARMSTRONG, Elizabeth (NCal) 2663 Rio Bravo Circle, Sacramento CA 95826 **Asst R Faith Epis Ch Cameron Pk CA 2001-** B Poughkeepsie NY 5/29/1954 d Richard Shumway & Elizabeth. BA California St U 1981; MA California St U 1983; MDiv CDSP 2001. D 6/9/2001 P 1/12/2002 Bp Jerry Alban Lamb. m 6/9/1984 Timothy P Armstrong c 2. earmstrong@prodigy.net

ARMSTRONG, Geoffrey Macgregor (NY) 10 Lanes End, Mervin Village NH 03850 B Detroit MI 8/16/1936 s Charles Armstrong & Beatrice Merle. BA Bow 1958; STB GTS 1961; MA Wstrn Connecticut St U 1972; JD Pace U 1981. D 6/10/1961 P 12/1/1961 Bp Horace W B Donegan. m 6/21/1958 Beverly Lofgren. Cur S Thos Ch Mamaroneck NY 1962-1964; Cur S Paul's Ch Winter Haven FL 1961-1962.

ARMSTRONG, G(lenville) Llewellyn (LI) 3 Martense Ct, Brooklyn NY 11226 B Christ Church BB 7/16/1936 s Wakestone Armstrong & Edna Sylvester. DIT Codrington Coll 1963; BD Lon 1963; Tr Toronto 1967; BA U of The W Indies 1974; MA Col 1975; Med Col 1976; ThD Intl TS 1980; DD Intl TS 1980. Rec 12/1/1963 as Priest Bp The Bishop Of Chichester. R Ch Of Calv And S Cyp Brooklyn NY 1987-2008; R S Geo's Ch Brooklyn NY 1980-1982; Tutor The GTS New York NY 1979-1980; Cur S Geo's Ch Brooklyn NY 1975-1980. Auth, "Educ Mnstry Epis Ch In Inner City". Codrington Coll Alum Assn. gla7@rcn.com

ARMSTRONG, Kenneth Leon (Okla) 901 E Overbrook Ave, Ponca City OK 74601 **R Gr Epis Ch Ponca City OK 1991-** B Okemah OK 1/22/1946 s Jack D Armstrong & Betty. BD St. Edw's U Austin TX 1978; MDiv Epis TS of The SW 1979. D 6/17/1979 P 3/1/1980 Bp Gerald Nicholas McAllister. m 5/21/1972 Ann Johnson c 2. R S Lk's Epis Ch Ada OK 1982-1991; M-in-c S Jas Ch Antlers OK 1979-1982; Vic S Mk's Ch Hugo OK 1979-1982. frken@sbcglobal.net

ARMSTRONG, Linda Joyce (La) 655 Cora Dr, Baton Rouge LA 70815 **S Alb's Chap & Epis U Cntr Baton Rouge LA 2005-** B 8/3/1948 d Robert Leslie Starns & Marie Carpenter. BS LSU 1983. D 10/23/2005 Bp Charles Edward Jenkins III. m 3/31/1978 Joseph Armstrong Lance c 1. ljarmstrong@cox.net

ARMSTRONG, Michael N (Fla) 2349 SW Bascom Norris Dr, Lake City FL 32025 **R S Jas' Epis Ch Lake City FL 2008-** B Athens AL 10/29/1944 d Robert Bruce Armstrong & Mary. BD Jacksonville U 1995; MDiv STUSo 1999. D 6/13/1999 Bp Stephen Hays Jecko P 12/18/1999 Bp Roger John White. Emm Ch Orlando FL 2002; Assoc Gr Ch Madison WI 1999-2001. frmother@bellsouth.net

ARMSTRONG, Phyllis Elaine (SO) 2841 Urwiler Ave, Cincinnati OH 45211 B Cincinnati OH 1/13/1943 d Henry Snowden Berryman & Margaret Lucille. BD U Cinc 1991; Vocational D Sch For Deaconal Mnstry 2005. D 6/4/2005 Bp Herbert Thompson Jr. m 10/13/2001 James M Armstrong c 2. phylmike@fuse.net

ARMSTRONG, Richard Sweet (Mass) 35 Old Fields Way, Castine ME 04421 B Attleboro MA 1/7/1944 s Paul Francis Armstrong & Marian Hunton. BS MIT 1965; MS MIT 1966; BD EDS 1969. D 6/21/1969 Bp Anson Phelps Stokes Jr P 4/1/1970 Bp Donald J Campbell. m 10/21/1967 Patricia Anne Wagner c 2. Cur S Andr's Ch Framingham MA 1969-1970. Auth, *Proj Metran*; Auth, *Underused Ch Property: A Search for Solutions*. richardsarmstrong@gmail.com

ARMSTRONG, Robert Hancock (SVa) 4600 Bruce Rd, Chester VA 23831 B Richmond VA 9/5/1932 s Thomas Christian Armstrong & Julia Bond. BA U of Virginia 1954; BD/MDiv VTS 1963. D 6/21/1963 P 6/1/1964 Bp Robert Fisher Gibson Jr. c 4. Exec Bd Dio Sthrn Virginia Norfolk VA 1993-1996; S Jn's Ch Chester VA 1968-2003; Asst S Jas' Ch Richmond VA 1963-1968. arms32@aol.com

ARMSTRONG, Susan Jean (NCal) 1765 Virginia Way, Arcata CA 95521 **P Assoc (Vol) S Alb's Ch Arcata CA 2006-** B Minneapolis 5/23/1941 d Daniel A Armstrong & Shirley Marian. BA Bryn 1963; PhD Bryn 1976; CAS CDSP 2006. D 6/3/2006 P 12/16/2006 Bp Jerry Alban Lamb. c 4. Sis of the Trsfg (Assoc) 1993. sja3@humboldt.edu

ARMSTRONG, William Henry (WVa) 320 Old Bluefield Rd, Princeton WV 24740 **Vic Ch Of The Heav Rest Princeton WV 2011-** B Pensacola FL 1/30/1946 s William H Armstong. BA Un Coll Barbourville KY 1968; MDiv Duke 1972. D 6/12/1999 Bp John H(enry) Smith P 6/10/2000 Bp C(laude) Charles Vache. m 6/6/1986 Shirley Ann Armstrong c 1.

ARMSTRONG, Zenetta M (Mass) 58 Crawford St Apt 2, Dorchester MA 02121 **R Ch Of The H Sprt Mattapan MA 2000-** B All Saints AG 12/19/1951 d Hubert Aska Armstrong & Enid Beatrice. CUNY; EDS; GW. D 6/11/1988 P 6/1/1989 Bp Don Edward Johnson. Co-R Ch Of The H Sprt Mattapan MA 1992-2000; Assoc Ch Of The H Sprt Mattapan MA 1990-1991; Ch Of The H Sprt Mattapan MA 1988-1990. zenettaarmstrong@aol.com

ARMY, Virginia Wilson (Ct) The Rectory School, Pomfret CT 06258 **P-in-c S Jn's Epis Ch Vernon Rock Vernon CT 2008-; Cler-In-Res Chr Ch Pomfret CT 1992-; Chapl S Andr's Chap Pomfret CT 1991-** B Groton MA 3/17/1957 d Paul Edward Gray & Priscilla Wilson. BA Wesl 1979; MDiv Ya Berk 1982. D 12/18/1992 P 6/1/1993 Bp Arthur Edward Walmsley. m 6/14/1980 Thomas F Army Jr c 3. REVEDVA@GMAIL.COM

ARNASON, Tryggvi Gudmundur (At) 247 Angla Dr Se, Smyrna GA 30082 **R S Alb's Ch Hickory NC 2011-** B Reykdavik IS 12/20/1964 s Arni Jonsson & Bjarney. BA U of W Florida 1992; MDiv Candler TS Emory U 1997. D 7/14/2005 P 2/26/2006 Bp J(ohn) Neil Alexander. m 6/12/2004 Lee Ann Arnason c 2. Asst H Innoc Ch Atlanta GA 2005-2011; H Innoc' Epis Sch Atlanta GA 2005-2007. tarnason@holyinnocents.org

ARNEY, Carol Mary (Haw) 3534 Pakui Street, Honolulu HI 96816 B Bremerton WA 8/7/1945 d Vernon Alfred Arney & Margaret Caroline. BA U of Hawaii 1969; MDiv STUSo 1995. D 6/24/1995 P 2/1/1996 Bp George Nelson Hunt III. R Chr Ch Kealakekua HI 1997-2008; Gd Samar Epis Ch Honolulu HI 1997-2008; Assoc R S Mich And All Ang Ch Lihue HI 1995-1997. arneycm@earthlink.net

ARNHART, James Rhyne (Tenn) 1710 Riverview Dr, Murfreesboro TN 37129 **Supply P Dio Tennessee Nashville TN 1985-** B Ashville NC 1/26/1924 s James William Arnhart & Eula. BS Maryville Coll 1951; MS Washington U 1953; JD Nashville Sch of Law 1971. D 7/25/1979 P 6/1/1980 Bp William Evan Sanders. m 1/1/1952 Bobbye Lynn. Vic S Mk's Ch Antioch TN 1983-1985; Asst S Paul's Epis Ch Murfreesboro TN 1979-1982.

ARNOLD, Beth Kelly (Los) 1231 E. Chapman Ave., Fullerton CA 92831 **R S Andr's Par Fullerton CA 2011-** B Caldwell ID 5/15/1958 d M E Arnold & Helen. BA The Coll of Idaho 1979; MDiv CDSP 1987. D 12/5/1987 P 12/7/1988 Bp William Edwin Swing. Sr Assoc R The Epis Ch Of S Mary The Vrgn San Francisco CA 1999-2011; Ch Of Our Sav Mill Vlly CA 1996-2000; Chr Ch Sausalito CA 1996-1999; Chr Ch Sausalito CA 1993-1994; Asst R S Paul's Epis Ch Burlingame CA 1988-1991. beth@bethkelly.org

ARNOLD, Christopher John (Lex) PO Box 2272, Middlesboro KY 40965 **Stndg Com Dio Lexington Lexington KY 2011-; Cler-in-Charge S Mary's Epis Ch Middlesboro KY 2010-** B Newcastle, UK 3/6/1974 s Geoffrey Arnold & Meredith. BA Univserity of California, Santa Cruz 1995; MDiv CDSP 2008; MA Grad Theol Un 2010. D 6/12/2010 Bp Barry Leigh Beisner P 12/20/2010 Bp Stacy F Sauls. m 12/28/2004 Celeste Williams. GAS 2009; Soc of Cath Priests 2010; SocMary 2009. sursum.corda@gmail.com

ARNOLD, David Wightman (NY) 17 Alder Court, Kingston NY 12401 B White Plains NY 5/19/1927 s Eugene Wightman Arnold & Geraldine. BEd SUNY 1951; MS Ya Berk 1957. D 6/13/1954 P 12/19/1954 Bp Horace W B Donegan. m 8/23/1952 Anneke Ferguson c 4. S Greg's Epis Ch Woodstock NY 1992; S Greg's Epis Ch Woodstock NY 1974-1992; S Greg's Epis Ch Woodstock NY 1968-1974; S Jn's Ch New City NY 1962-1968. Angl Soc 1954; OHC 1952. TABOR1952@aol.com

ARNOLD, Donna J (Alb) 4 Pine Ledge Ter, Gansevoort NY 12831 **Vic Trin Ch Whitehall NY 2008-** B Troy NY 12/27/1946 d Henry Edward Dumas & Elizabeth Ann. BA SUNY 1969; JD Wstrn New Engl Coll 1984; MA St. Bern's Sch of Mnstry & Theol 2004; MA St. Bern's Sch of Mnstry and Theol 2004. D 6/11/2005 Bp Daniel William Herzog P 1/14/2006 Bp David John Bena. m 12/21/1969 Alan Arnold c 2. Asst Chr Epis Ch Ballston Spa NY 2005-2007. Sr. Mem of Law Revs, "Legis-Implied Consent Legis In Drunk Driving Cases: The Case for Repeal," *Wstrn New Engl Law Revs, Vol. 6, Issue 2, 1983*, Wstrn New Engl Coll Sch of Law, 1983. Ret Plaque Saratoga Cnty Bar Assn 2003. aarnold1@nycap.rr.com

ARNOLD, Duane Wade-Hampton (NY) 5815 Lawrence Dr., Indianapolis IN 46226 B Fort Wayne IN 8/5/1953 s Herman Wade-Hampton Arnold & Louise Elizabeth. BA SUNY 1979; MA Concordia TS 1981; Fllshp Dur 1984; STh Lambeth Coll 1984; Dplma U of Cambridge 1984; PhD Dur 1989; Fllshp Coll of Preachers 1992. D 6/27/1987 P 11/1/1987 Bp H Coleman McGehee Jr. m 11/1/1980 Janet Lee Drew. Ecum Cmsn Dio New York New York City NY 1991-1994; Cur S Thos Ch New York NY 1991-1994; Precentor Cathd Ch Of S Paul Detroit MI 1988-1990; Ecum Cmsn Dio Michigan Detroit MI 1987-1991; Epis/Luth Chapl at Wayne Donne Detroit MI 1987-1991. Auth, "Mas Alla de la Fe," Vida, 2004; Auth, "Fieis ate o Fim," Vida, 2003; Auth, "Beyond Belief," Zondervan, 2002; Auth/Ed, "De Doctrina Christiana," U of Notre Dame Press, 1995; Auth, "Praying w Donne & Herbert," SPCK, 1992; Auth, "Prayers Of The Martyrs," Harper Row, 1991; Auth, "Athan Of Alexandria," U. of Notre Dame Press, 1991; Auth, "Fran, A Call to Conversion," Zondervan, 1988; Auth, "In Dire Straits," U. of Detroit, 1987; Auth, "The Way, The

Truth, The Life," Baker, 1982. Chapl Ord Of S Jn Of Jerusalem 1989; Soc Of The Anchor 1994. dwha1863@aol.com

ARNOLD, Kenneth Lloyd (Mass) 1000 SW Vista Ave Apt 1017, Portland OR 97205 B Washington DC 3/29/1944 s Lloyd Cecil Arnold & Violet Henrietta. BA Lynchburg Coll 1966; MA Jn Hopkins U 1967. D 5/16/1998 Bp Richard Frank Grein. m 4/21/2001 Constance Kirk c 2. Ch Pension Fund New York NY 2003-2007; Dir of Cmncatn Dio Massachusetts Boston MA 2001-2003; S Clem's Ch New York NY 1998-2000. Auth, "Night Fishing in Galilee: The Journey Toward Sprtl Wisdom," *Bk*, Cowley Pub, 2002; Auth, "On The Way: Vocation, Awarenes, and Flyfishing," *Bk*, Ch Pub Inc, 2000; Auth, "The Impractical D: A Column," *Diakoneo*, No Amer Assn. for the Diac. No Amer Assn. for the Diac 1998. ken@ken-arnold.com

ARNOLD, Kimball Clark (Az) 3150 Spence Springs Rd, Prescott AZ 86305 **D S Lk's Ch Prescott AZ 2000-** B Chicago IL 3/13/1950 d Donald Wrigley Clark & Helen Kerenhappuch. Nthrn Arizona U 1970. D 10/14/2000 Bp Robert Reed Shahan. m 4/8/1972 Thomas Eads Arnold c 2. ChinoPaulden Mnstrl Assn 2000; NAAD 2000. deaconkimball@cableone.net

ARNOLD, Robert D (WNY) 29 University Park, Fredonia NY 14063 **R Trin Epis Ch Fredonia NY 2006-** B Buffalo NY 10/16/1951 s Dale D Arnold & Lois E. Utica Coll 1971; BA Scarritt Coll 1973; MDiv Candler TS Emory U 1976; Cert SWTS 1992. D 6/7/1992 P 12/1/1992 Bp David Charles Bowman. m 4/18/1982 Patricia I Dahl c 2. Vic Ch Of The H Comm Lakeview NY 2001-2006; P-in-c S Mich's Epis Ch Oakfield NY 1995-2001; R S Jn's Ch Medina NY 1992-2001.

ARNOLD, Robyn Elizabeth (Ala) 2146 Santa Clara Ave Apt 1, Alamed CA 94501 **Dio California San Francisco CA 2008-** B Mt Vernon KY 8/22/1963 d James Arnold & Hilda Faye. BS Cumberland Coll 1986; MS Mississippi St U 1997; PhD U of Alabama at Birmingham 2002; MDiv CDSP 2008. D 5/31/2008 P 12/16/2008 Bp Henry Nutt Parsley Jr. robyna@diocal.org

ARNOLD, Scott A (Ala) 1204 Valridge N, Prattville AL 36066 **R S Mk's Ch Prattville AL 2005-** B Memphis TN 8/30/1960 s David Alton Arnold & Betty Ann. BS Middle Tennessee St U 1982; MDiv STUSo 1987; MS Alabama A&M U 1996. D 7/5/1987 P 2/1/1988 Bp George Lazenby Reynolds Jr. m 9/9/1995 Diane Arnold c 3. All SS Epis Ch Birmingham AL 1997-2000; R S Paul's Epis Ch Corinth MS 1992-1995; Int S Andr's Ch Burke VA 1991-1992; Stff S Ptr's Epis Ch Arlington VA 1989-1991; R The Epis Ch Of The Mssh Pulaski TN 1988-1989; Dio Tennessee Nashville TN 1987-1988; Vic S Matt's Epis Ch McMinnville TN 1987-1988. Auth, "Cler And Divorce," *Alb Inst Action Info*, 1994; Auth, "Paying The Pstr," *The Disciple*, 1990; Auth, "Silent Racism And The Kkk," *Wit*, 1988. APA 1996. frscott@stmarksal.org

ARNOLD, William Bruce (SwFla) 114 Fairway Ct, Greenwood SC 29649 B Owensboro KY 9/1/1931 s Charles Herman Arnold & Martha C. BS U of No Dakota 1954; Med Florida Atlantic U 1966; PhD Florida St U 1969. D 9/30/1974 Bp William Hopkins Folwell. c 3. D S Jn's Epis Ch Clearwater FL 1988-2003; D S Dunst's Epis Ch Largo FL 1974-1988.

ARNOLD JR, William Stevenson Maclaren (Nev) 1855 Baring Blvd Apt 301, Sparks NV 89434 **Asst S Paul's Epis Ch Sparks NV 2003-** B Monterey CA 7/20/1953 s William S M Arnold & Mary Iris. U of Hawaii; U of Nevada at Reno. D 7/7/2002 P 1/25/2003 Bp Katharine Jefferts Schori. m 11/7/1987 Evelyn Gabrielle Pieters. chip@hawsco.com

ARNOLD-BOYD, Annette Ruth (Oly) 12420 SW Tremont St, Portland OR 97225 B Portland OR 9/2/1946 d Charles Arnold & Doris Karoline. BS Wstrn Oregon U 1968; MA Cntrl Washington U 1971; MDiv SWTS 1976. D 9/25/1977 Bp Matthew Paul Bigliardi P 11/20/1978 Bp H Coleman McGehee Jr. m 6/14/1981 Scott W Boyd c 1. S Lk's Epis Ch Vancouver WA 1993-2011; S Steph's Epis Par Portland OR 1985-1986. Chapl CAP - Washington Cnty, OR 1999-2010; Intl Assn of Wmn Ministers 1976. snowball.aab@frontier.com

ARPEE, Stephen T(rowbridge) (WA) 3810 39th St NW Apt A-121, Washington DC 20016 B Evanston IL 3/29/1934 s Edward Arpee & Katherine. BA Coll of Wooster 1957; MDiv GTS 1965. D 6/12/1965 Bp Leland Stark P 9/4/1966 Bp The Bishop Of Iran. m 6/12/1961 Janet Mary Wootton c 2. R Chr Ch S Jn's Par Accokeek MD 2002-2007; P-in-c S Paul's Epis Par Point Of Rocks MD 1997-1999; P-in-c All SS' Epis Ch Chevy Chase MD 1997; P-in-c Ch Without Walls Washington DC 1986-1997; R S Marg's Ch Washington DC 1979-1986. stevearpee@gmail.com

ARQUES, Rafael (PR) Apartado 4211, Vega Baja PR 00694 Puerto Rico B 11/21/1932 s Jose Arques & Rosario. D P. m 5/2/1982 Hilda Margarita Reyes-Rey. Dio Puerto Rico S Just PR 1984-1997.

ARRINGTON, Sandra Clark (Roch) 20 Trumbull Lane, Pittsford NY 14534 B Ticonderoga NY 6/23/1944 d Raymond Chester Clark & Harriet. SUNY 1963; BA SUNY 1966; MDiv St. Bern's Inst Rochester NY 1991; Bex 1992. D 1/29/1994 P 8/6/1994 Bp William George Burrill. c 3. S Thos Epis Ch Rochester NY 2005-2006; S Mk's Epis Ch Le Roy NY 2004-2005; S Lk's Ch Fairport NY 2003-2004; Zion Epis Ch Palmyra NY 2002-2004; Zion Ch Avon NY 2002-2003; S Paul's Ch Rochester NY 1995-2002; Ch Of The Ascen Rochester NY 1994-1995. MDiv w dist S Bern's Inst Rochester NY 1991. sandya@rochester.rr.com

ARROWSMITH-LOWE, Thomas (RG) Episcopal Church of St. John, P.O. Box 449, Alamogordo NM 88310 **R S Jn's Epis Ch Alamogordo NM 2011-** B San Angelo TX 9/2/1948 s James Thomas Lowe & Martha Beatrice. BA U of No Texas 1971; DDS U of Texas 1975; MPH U MN 1980; DBCS TESM 2006. D 10/21/2006 P 5/6/2007 Bp Jeffrey Neil Steenson. c 2. COM Dio The Rio Grande Albuquerque NM 2010-2011; Chair, Bp Search Com Dio The Rio Grande Albuquerque NM 2008-2010. Soc for the Sci Study of Sex 1993; Soc of Ord Scientists 2008. Fell Amer Coll of Epidemiologists 2007; Exemplary Serv Medal US Surgeon Gnrl 1992. fathertom@tularosa.net

ARROYO, Jose Del Carmen (Chi) 25291 W Lehmann Blvd, Lake Villa IL 60046 **Vic Ch Of The H Fam Lake Villa IL 2010-** B Dominican Republic 12/10/1961 s Jose Antonio Arroyo & Juana Dela Cruz. Rec from Roman Catholic 6/27/2009 as Priest Bp Victor Alfonso Scantlebury. m 2/3/2010 Licelot R Arroyo c 1. josecarroyo@yahoo.com

ARROYO, Margarita (WTex) 2112 Tranquilo Trl, Austin TX 78744 B Laredo TX 10/8/1966 d Daniel Eguia & Elisa Margarita. BSW SW Texas St U San Marcos 1989; MS Our Lady Of The Lake U San Antonio TX 1993; MDiv Epis TS of The SW 2000. D 8/31/2000 P 3/14/2001 Bp James Edward Folts. m 6/15/1996 Eric C Arroyo c 1. R Gr Ch Weslaco TX 2002-2004; Asst Ch Of The Gd Shpd Corpus Christi TX 2000-2002. Arroyo@awesomenet.net

ARRUNATEGUI, Herbert (CFla) 2468 Capland Ave, Clermont FL B Panama City PA 4/22/1934 s Joaquin Arrunategui-Sandoval & Aura. Lic U of Panama 1958; STB UTS 1961; ThM Drew U 1972; DMin Drew U 1985. D 5/8/1965 P 11/1/1965 Bp Reginald Heber Gooden. m 12/28/1960 Geny Salazar-Gonzalez. Off Hisp Mnstrs Epis Ch Cntr New York NY 1978-1999; San Jose Epis Ch Eliz NJ 1977; Dio New Jersey Trenton NJ 1974-1999; S Paul's Epis Ch Westfield NJ 1969-1977. Hon Cn El Redentor Cathd Madrid ES 1986. arrunateguiherbert@yahoo.com

ARTRESS, Lauren (Cal) 309 Coleridge St, San Francisco CA 94110 B Cleveland OH 10/10/1945 d Gordon James Artress & Olive Marie. BS OH SU 1967; MA PrTS 1969; AAPC 1978; DMin Andover Newton TS 1986; PhD (Hon) California Inst of Integral Stds 1999. D 6/14/1975 Bp Paul Moore Jr P 11/13/1982 Bp Walter Decoster Dennis Jr. Cn Gr Cathd San Francisco CA 1986-1995; Adj Prof The GTS New York NY 1979-1986. Auth, "The Sacr Path Comp; A Guide to Using the Labyrinth to Heal and Transform," 2006; Auth, "The Labyrinth Seed Kit," Tuttle Pub, 1996; Auth, "Walking A Sacr Path: Rediscovering The Labyrinth As A Sprtl Tool," Riverhead/Putnam Penguin, 1995. AAMFT, Clincl Mem 1979; Dplma AAPC 1978. Hon Cn of Gr Cathd Gr Cathd 2004; Ghandi/King/Ikeda Peace Awd Morehouse Coll 2002; Hon Ph. D California Inst for Integral Stds 1999. lauren@laurenartress.com

ARVEDSON, Peter Fredrick (WNY) 13070 W Bluemound Rd Unit 311, Elm Grove WI 53122 **Died 7/14/2011** B Peoria IL 4/15/1937 s Fredrick St Clair Arvedson & Dorothy Evelyn. BS U IL 1959; PhD U of Wisconsin 1964; STM GTS 1967. D 6/3/1967 P 12/10/1967 Bp Albert A Chambers. c 2. Soc of Ord Scientists 1988. Genesis Awd for Sci and Rel Epis Ch Ntwk for Sci, Tech and Faith 2006. parved@aol.com

ASBURY, Eldridge Eugene (Miss) 742 Mcneece St, Tupelo MS 38804 B Elberton GA 1/10/1929 s James Stewart Asbury & Ruth Aileen. BA U GA; Emory U 1947; MDiv STUSo 1987. D 5/16/1987 P 11/29/1987 Bp Duncan Montgomery Gray Jr. m 11/29/1963 Karen Maria Ellington c 2. All SS' Epis Ch Tupelo MS 1999; Par Of The Medtr-Redeem McComb MS 1994-1999; Epis Ch Of The Incarn W Point MS 1987-1994. mapatup@futuresouth.com

ASBURY, Giles Lee (Los) 844 S Detroit St, Los Angeles CA 90036 B Ronceverte WV 12/14/1947 s Grover Lee Asbury & Margaret Lyn. Hampden-Sydney Coll 1968; BA U So 1969; MDiv CDSP 1973. D 6/23/1973 P 12/1/1974 Bp C Kilmer Myers. m 2/25/1983 Yvonne Lauren Leatherwood. Prov VIII Tagard OR 2004-2006; Cbury Westwood Fndt Los Angeles CA 1995-1999; Dio Los Angeles Los Angeles CA 1981-1995; Int Epis Ch Of The Adv Los Angeles CA 1980-2000. Auth, "To Tell Of Gideon: Storytelling In The Ch"; Auth, "Why The Possum'S Tale Is Bare & Other Sthrn Classics". ESMHE. gilesasbury@gmail.com

ASEL, J(ohn) Kenneth (Wyo) PO Box 1690, Jackson WY 83001 **R Ch Of The Trsfg Jackson WY 2003-; R S Jn's Epis Ch Jackson WY 2003-** B Dallas TX 2/28/1949 s Kenneth H Asel & Evelyn Patricia. BA Van 1970; MDiv SWTS 1973; MRE Notre Dame Sem 1976; DMin GTF 1986. D 4/28/1973 Bp James Winchester Montgomery P 11/1/1973 Bp Iveson Batchelor Noland. m 2/15/1992 Janice D M Morrison c 4. R S Paul's Ch Wilkesboro NC 1992-2003; R Emm Ch Farmville NC 1991-1992; CDO Dio E Carolina Kinston NC 1991; Assoc/Admin S Lk's Epis Ch San Antonio TX 1987-1991; R S Dav's Ch Denton TX 1986-1987; R S Mich's Epis Ch Pineville LA 1979-1986; Educ Consult Dio Louisiana Baton Rouge LA 1976-1979; Asst to Dn Chr Ch Cathd New Orleans LA 1973-1979. Auth, "video," *Verna Dozier Looks Lk*, 1988; Auth, "video," *What Episcopalians Believe*, 1984; Auth, "article," *Making Sense of Things*, 1981. ken@sjecjh.org

ASELTINE, Sara Jane (NCal) 18215 Challenge Cut Off Rd, Forbestown CA 95941 **S Jn's Epis Ch Marysville CA 1990-** B Glendale CA 12/24/1930 d Lloyd Greenville & Jean Murry. CDSP; U CA 1952; BA California St U 1953;

Cert U CA 1964; EFM STUSo 1985; BA Sch for Deacons 1990. D 4/4/1992 Bp Jerry Alban Lamb. m 10/3/1953 Arthur Wylie Aseltine c 4. D S Clare Assisi Challenge Forbestown CA 1992-2005. NoCCA 1992; NAAD 1992; The Cmnty of Hope 2002; Yuba-Feather Chr Mnstrl Assn 1992. awa@lostsierra.net

ASH JR, Evan Arnold (Kan) 1114 E Northview St, Olathe KS 66061 B Saint Louis MO 5/7/1944 s Evan Arnold Ash & Ada M. BA U of Nebraska 1970; MDiv SWTS 1973; MS U of Nebraska 1979; Advncd CPE 1981. D 2/14/1974 Bp Robert Patrick Varley P 4/13/1977 Bp James Daniel Warner. m 2/14/1965 Rosalie Wissler c 2. Vic S Aid's Ch Olathe KS 1996-2001; Trin Ch Arkansas City KS 1994; R S Matt's Epis Ch Newton KS 1992-1993; Legacy Gd Samar Hosp Portland OR 1989-1992; Nebraska Hlth System Omaha NE 1983-1985; R S Mart Of Tours Ch Omaha NE 1977-1980; R S Lk's Ch Plattsmouth NE 1976-1978; Asst Trin Cathd Omaha NE 1975-1976; Asst Ch Of The H Sprt Bellevue NE 1974. Auth, "Promise Of Sorrow," *Caregiver*, 1990. Fllshp Coll Of Chapl 1985-1993; Ord Of S Ben 1971. Highplainspreacher@att.net

ASH, Gerald Arnold (Md) 2206 Endovalley Dr, Cincinnati OH 45244 B Danbury CT 5/2/1941 s George Ash & Kathleen Delancey. BSME Un Coll 1964; BS Un Coll 1964; MDiv GTS 1973. D 6/10/1973 P 6/24/1974 Bp Robert Rae Spears Jr. m 5/2/1987 Cecilia Russell. R Trin Ch Oxford Philadelphia PA 1992-1995; Assoc R S Marg's Ch Annapolis MD 1985-1991; R Ch Of The Gd Samar Amelia OH 1983-1985; R S Jn's Epis Ch Oneida NY 1979-1982; Cn S Paul's Cathd Syracuse NY 1976-1979; Vic Chr Ch Sackets Harbor NY 1973-1976; Cur Trin Epis Ch Watertown NY 1973-1976. Assn of Profsnl Chapl, BCC 2001. gerrycecie@hotmail.com

ASH, Linda D (EMich) 111 S Shiawassee St, Corunna MI 48817 B Owosso MI 4/5/1945 d John A Kretzschmar & Laura E. D 2/23/2008 Bp S(teven) Todd Ousley. m 12/15/1973 Edward H Ash c 2. lash48867@yahoo.com

ASH, Richard Hamilton (Mo) 511 Hazel Pl, Mexico MO 65265 B Toledo OH 3/31/1924 s Lisle E Ash & Mary M. BA Ohio U 1948; STB EDS 1952. D 6/19/1952 P 12/17/1952 Bp Henry W Hobson. m 4/5/1975 Alicia Ann Hadley. Vic S Matt's Epis Ch Mex MO 1975-1989; Vic S Barn Ch Moberly MO 1975-1980; Vic S Alb's Epis Ch Fulton MO 1972-1975; Assoc S Paul's Ch Kansas City MO 1970-1972; Dir Dioc Plnng Com Dio Missouri S Louis MO 1968-1970; R Calv Ch Columbia MO 1959-1965; M-in-c Calv Ch Columbia MO 1955-1959; R S Ptr's Ch Gallipolis OH 1952-1955. annash@midamerica.net

ASHBY, Alice Kay (O) 344 Shepard Rd, Mansfield OH 44907 **S Matt's Ch Ashland OH 2007-** B Winter Haven FL 7/1/1956 d Earl Myers Neel & Alice. BA U of Arkansas 1979; MA Epis TS of The SW 1982; MDiv Lexington TS 1988. D 6/23/1990 P 2/1/1991 Bp Herbert Alcorn Donovan Jr. m 3/22/1981 Joe Lyn Ashby c 1. S Alb's Mssn Muskegon MI 1999-2006; Dio Arkansas Little Rock AR 1996-1999; Vic S Jas Ch Eureka Sprg AR 1996-1999; Exec Coun Dio Arkansas Little Rock AR 1996-1998; Pres Stndg Com Dio Arkansas Little Rock AR 1996-1998; Stndg Com Dio Arkansas Little Rock AR 1995-1998; Gr Ch Siloam Sprg AR 1994-1996; Chapl S Jas Ch Eureka Sprg AR 1991-1995; S Thos Ch Springdale AR 1991-1993. ashbyjlakna@aol.com

ASHBY, Joe Lyn (O) 402 Channel Rd, N Muskegon MI 49445 **Gr Epis Ch Mansfield OH 2006-** B Evansville IN 9/25/1955 s Lindy Ashby & Elizabeth Ann. BA Transylvania U 1976; MDiv Epis TS of The SW 1982. D 6/13/1982 P 6/1/1983 Bp David Reed. m 3/22/1981 Alice Kay Neel c 1. S Paul's Ch Muskegon MI 1999-2006; Exec Coun Dio Wstrn Michigan Kalamazoo MI 1997-2002; Chapl S Fran Ch Madison WI 1992-1999; S Thos Ch Springdale AR 1991-1999; Chair Dio Arkansas Little Rock AR 1990; Day Sch Cmsn Dio Arkansas Little Rock AR 1988-1990; Bd Dir S Fran Ch Madison WI 1988-1990; CE Cmsn Dio Arkansas Little Rock AR 1987-1991; Assoc S Lk's Epis Ch No Little Rock AR 1987-1991; S Raphael's Ch Lexington KY 1985-1987; Ch S Mich The Archangel Lexington KY 1983-1985; D-In-Res Gr Ch Hopkinsville KY 1982-1983. ashbyjlakna@aol.com

ASHBY, Julia (SVa) 4205 Cheswick Ln, Virginia Beach VA 23455 **Sr. Assoc R Estrn Shore Chap Virginia Bch VA 1997-** B Cherry Point NC 12/5/1954 d Nearous Columbus Sizemore & Joan Riggsbee. BA Longwood U 1976; MDiv SWTS 1997. D 6/14/1997 Bp Frank Harris Vest Jr P 1/1/1998 Bp David Conner Bane Jr. m 5/17/1975 Charles Chandler Ashby c 2. jashby@easternshorechapel.org

ASHBY, Lucinda Beth (NCal) 2660 Land Park Dr, Sacramento CA 95818 **Dio Idaho Boise ID 2011-** B Kirkwood MO 9/10/1959 BA Ob 1982; MDiv CDSP 2004. D 1/9/2004 P 7/24/2004 Bp Jerry Alban Lamb. m 7/22/1995 Robert McEvilly c 2. S Matt's Epis Ch Sacramento CA 2005-2011; P Ch Of S Mart Davis CA 2004-2005. lbashby@pacbell.net

ASHBY, Mary-Patricia Neese (Md) 12612 Molesworth Dr, Mount Airy MD 21771 B Brooklyn NY 5/11/1940 d William Gordon Neese & Edith Louise. AA Mt Vernon Jr Coll 1961; BA Amer U 1963; MDiv VTS 1992. D 6/13/1992 P 5/1/1993 Bp A(lbert) Theodore Eastman. m 6/11/1963 John Hall Ashby c 2. R/P in Charge Gr Ch New Mrkt MD 2003-2011; Dio Maryland Baltimore MD 1994-2002; Asst to R S Jn's Ch Mt Washington Baltimore MD 1992-1994. revmom92@comcast.net

ASHCROFT, Andrew Nigel (Eau) 1625 Locust St, Philadelphia PA 19103 B Cape Town South Africa 3/23/1977 s Ernest Ashcroft & Mary Ellen. BA Gordon Coll 1999; Cert Ya Berk 2002; MDiv GTS 2008. D 5/17/2008 P 11/23/2008 Bp Keith Bernard Whitmore. m 5/9/2003 Jennifer L Ashcroft c 1. Cur S Mk's Ch Philadelphia PA 2008-2010. andrew.ashcroft@gmail.com

ASHCROFT, Ernest (Minn) 4015 Sunnyside Road, Edina MN 55424 **R Chr Ch In Woodbury Woodbury NJ 2006-; Chr Ch S Paul MN 2006-** B Saint Helens Lancashire UK 7/17/1945 s Fredrick Ashcroft & Elizabeth. BS U Of Leeds Leeds U.K. 1967; PhD U Of Leeds Leeds U.K. 1970; DIT U of Nottingham 1973. Trans from Church of the Province of Southern Africa 2/1/1983 Bp Robert Marshall Anderson. m 7/9/2005 Elizabeth S Schilling c 4. Int Chr Ch Red Wing MN 2005-2006; R S Steph The Mtyr Ch Minneapolis MN 1992-2004; R Mssh Epis Ch S Paul MN 1983-1992. kritter@visi.com

ASHCROFT, Mary Ellen (Minn) PO Box 1093, Grand Marais MN 55604 **Vic Sprt of the Wilderness Grand Marais MN 2010-** B Salem OR 4/20/1952 d Leslie Edward Nelson & Grace Anna. Cert St. Jn's Coll, Nottingham 1974; BA The Coll of St. Cathr 1987; PhD U MN 1992; Cert U of Cambridge 2000. D 12/20/2001 P 6/20/2002 Bp James Louis Jelinek. c 3. Trin Ch Excelsior MN 2004. Auth, ",Dogspell," Seabury-Ch Pub, 2008; Auth, ",Spirited Wmn," Augsburg Fortress, 2004; Auth, ",The Magd Gospel," Augsburg Fortress, 2002. windcradle@boreal.org

ASHLEY, Danae Michele (Minn) PO Box 336, Hornell NY 14843 **S Edw The Confessor Wayzata MN 2011-** B Spokane WA 10/20/1976 d Alan Michael Ashley & Jamie Joan. BA Whitworth Coll 1998; Gonzaga U, Spokane, Washington 2006; MDiv STUSo 2008. D 6/7/2008 Bp James Edward Waggoner P 12/21/2008 Bp Granville Porter Taylor. m 10/2/2010 Henry Lebedinsky. Tri-Par Mnstry Hornell NY 2011; Assoc R Epis Ch Of S Ptr's By The Lake Denver NC 2008-2010. anglicancelt@hotmail.com

ASHMORE, Christopher Lee (Spr) 17 Forest Park W, Jacksonville IL 62650 **R Trin Ch Jacksonville IL 1998-** B Pittsfield IL 2/2/1950 s Jesse Lee Ashmore & Harriet Elizabeth. Nash; BS U of Maryland 1972; MDiv SW Bapt TS 1976; PrTS 1977; Epis TS of The SW 1978. D 6/19/1978 P 1/7/1979 Bp Scott Field Bailey. m 6/15/1974 Kathryn Louella Paullin c 2. R Ch Of The H Sprt San Antonio TX 1996-1998; Vic Ch Of The H Sprt San Antonio TX 1983-1996; Asst Ch Of Recon San Antonio TX 1980-1983; Cur Ch Of The Adv Brownsville TX 1978-1980. revkash@msn.com

ASHTON, Harroldean (NJ) 681 Village Dr. South #A, North Brunswick NJ 08902 B Atlantic City NJ 8/2/1936 d Odith E Ashton & Henrietta. Trenton St Teachers Coll 1955; BA How 1959; MSW How 1964; CPE 1985; MDiv GTS 1986; STM GTS 1991. D 11/21/1987 P 4/15/1989 Bp George Phelps Mellick Belshaw. Dio New Jersey Trenton NJ 2005-2008; Vic S Alb's Epis Ch New Brunswick NJ 1990-2008; S Barth's Ch New York NY 1987-1990. revdean@verizon.net

ASIS, Debra (Az) 6715 N. Mockingbird Ln., Scottsdale AZ 85253 **S Barn On The Desert Scottsdale AZ 2011-** B East Orange NJ 9/14/1950 d Kenneth Ronald Hoover & Ruth Gladys. BA U of Rhode Island 1976; MA U of Rhode Island 1979; MDiv CDSP 2010. D 6/6/2009 P 12/18/2010 Bp Kirk Stevan Smith. c 1. Asst S Barn On The Desert Scottsdale AZ 2006-2007. debraasis@gmail.com

ASKEW, Angela V (NY) 659 E 17th St, Brooklyn NY 11230 **P-in-c S Ann And The H Trin Brooklyn NY 2003-** B Peterborough UK 11/1/1943 d B Julyan Askew & Peggy May. BA Lon 1966, MDiv EDS 1970, MA UTS 1982. D 5/7/1978 Bp John M Allin P 9/1/1980 Bp John Mc Gill Krumm. Asst Min S Jn's Ch Brooklyn NY 1992-2000; Ch Of The Intsn New York NY 1985-1988; P-in-c S Mary's Manhattanville Epis Ch New York NY 1983-1985; Assoc S Mary's Manhattanville Epis Ch New York NY 1982-1983. Grad Fell ECF 1978. aa659@mindspring.com

ASKEW, Stephen H (ETenn) 814 Episcopal School Way, Knoxville TN 37932 **Cn to the Ordnry/Dioc Deploy Off Dio E Tennessee Knoxville TN 2005-** B Tuscaloosa AL 10/12/1952 s William Arnold Askew & Laura. BS U of Alabama 1974; MEd U of Alabama 1976; MDiv Nash 1982; DMin STUSo 2007. D 6/13/1982 P 12/16/1982 Bp Furman Stough. m 9/25/1999 Patricia Tanzer c 2. Stndg Com Dio E Tennessee Knoxville TN 2003-2005; Asst S Paul's Epis Ch Chattanooga TN 1997-2005; Dio E Tennessee Knoxville TN 1993-1997; R S Thos Epis Ch Knoxville TN 1988-1997; R S Tim's Epis Ch Athens AL 1984-1988; Cur Ch Of The Ascen Montgomery AL 1982-1984. Ord of S Lk. MDiv cl Nash Nashotah WI 1982. askew@etdiocese.net

ASKREN, Robert D. (Fla) 11366 Tacito Creek Dr. South, Jacksonville FL 32223 B Springfield OH 10/1/1941 s Joseph Harvey Askren & Beulah Helen. Certification Assn of Profsnl Chapl; BA U Of Florida 1963; MDiv VTS 1966; PhD Middleham U,Engl 2000; M Ed Stamford Hill U Engl 2004. D 6/29/1966 Bp Henry I Louttit P 12/29/1966 Bp James Loughlin Duncan. m 4/9/1994 Ann Pietrangeli c 2. Int Trin Ch Ft Wayne IN 2004-2006; Int Trin Epis Ch St Aug FL 2002-2004; Assoc R Ch Of Our Sav Jacksonville FL 1996-2002; R S Pat's Ch Ocala FL 1978-1996; R S Agnes Ch Sebring FL 1969-1977; Asst & Headmaster Chr The King Epis Ch Orlando FL 1968-1969. Ed, "Readings In Philos Volumes 1-5," So Florida Cmnty Coll, 1975. Bd Cert Assn Prof Chapl 1995;

Curs Mnstry 1979-2008; EFM Mentor 1998-2002; Kairos Prison Mnstry 1981-1996; OHC Assoc 1984. Dn of Ocala Dnry Dio Cntrl Florida 1996; Trst U So Dio Cntrl Florida 1988; Fndr of Ocala Hospice Marion Cnty Hospice 1982. robert_askren@yahoo.com

ASMAN, Mark Elliott (Los) 1500 State St, Santa Barbara CA 93101 **R Trin Epis Ch Santa Barbara CA 1996-** B Oakland CA 10/28/1950 s Cecil Robert Asman & Mary Anne. BA Willamette U 1972; MDiv GTS 1975. D 6/28/1975 Bp George Richard Millard P 1/11/1976 Bp C Kilmer Myers. Vic Trin Epis Ch Santa Barbara CA 1994-1995; Serv S Thos The Apos Hollywood Los Angeles CA 1992-1994; Serv Ch Of The Adv Of Chr The King San Francisco CA 1984-1990; R S Paul's Epis Ch Oroville CA 1978-1982; Cur Calv Epis Ch Santa Cruz CA 1975-1978. masman@trinitysb.org

ASONYE, Collins Enyindah (Va) 4643 Seminary Rd Apt 203, Alexandria VA 22304 **R Meade Memi Epis Ch Alexandria VA 2008-** B Nigeria 3/21/1961 s Walter Asonye Ogbaegbe & Evelyn Worlu. Dip. Theo/Rel.Studie Trin Un Theogical Coll 1989; BA/MA U Of Port Harcourt 1997; ThM Franciscan U of Steubenville 2000. Trans from Church Of Nigeria 7/24/2003 Bp J Clark Grew II. m 9/29/1984 Peace Asonye c 2. Epis Shared Minist Of Nwohio Sherwood OH 2003-2008; R Gr Ch Defiance OH 2003-2008; Asst S Andr's Epis Ch Toledo OH 2001-2003; Campus Min S Michaels In The Hills Toledo OH 2001-2003. Non. Dn of W Deanary Dio Ohio 2005; Cn Niger Delta Dio 1994. 03prince@comcast.net

ASTARITA, Susan Gallagher (WA) PO Box 816, Del Mar CA 92014 **P Res Cathd Ch Of S Paul San Diego CA 2007-** B Wilmington DE 10/6/1941 d Hugh Francis Gallagher & Alice Pepper. AB Randolph-Macon Wmn's Coll 1963; MA Geo 1973; MDiv ETSBH 1992; STM Ya Berk 1993. D 6/27/1992 P 12/1/1992 Bp Gethin Benwil Hughes. m 5/24/1969 Bruce Astarita c 1. Ch Of The Ascen Silver Sprg MD 2004-2006; Mem, Hisp Mnstrs Com Dio Washington Washington DC 2003-2006; Asst S Geo's Ch Glenn Dale MD 2003-2004; Chr Ch Prince Geo's Par Rockville MD 2000-2003; Mem, Fin Com Dio Washington Washington DC 1998-2000; Mem, Stwdshp Com Dio Washington Washington DC 1996-1998; Dioc Coun Dio Washington Washington DC 1995-1998; Vic/Chapl U Of Maryland Mssn Coll Pk MD 1994-2000; Mem, Angus Dun Com Dio Washington Washington DC 1994-1998; Asst Gr And S Ptr's Epis Ch Hamden CT 1992-1993. astacom@aol.com

ASTLEFORD, Elise Linder (Oly) 2515 NE 80th St, Vancouver WA 98665 B Mansfield OH 1/8/1941 d Albert Louis Linder & Louise Charlotte. BA (hon) Denison U 1963; MRE Andover Newton TS 1965; Westcott Hse Cambridge 1985. D 5/4/1976 Bp Matthew Paul Bigliardi P 9/27/1985 Bp David Rea Cochran. m 2/11/1996 Joseph Fee Astleford c 2. Int S Lk's Epis Ch Gresham OR 2006-2008; Yth Dir S Lk's Epis Ch Vancouver WA 1990-1992; Vic Ch Of The H Sprt Episco Battle Ground WA 1987-2003; Chapl Oregon Epis Sch Portland OR 1985-1987; Asst S Barth's Ch Beaverton OR 1976-1984; Chapl Legacy Gd Samar Hosp Portland OR 1976-1979. Auth, "Sharing," 1988. NNECA 1993. eliseast@gmail.com

ASTON, Geraldine Patricia (Ala) 544 S Forest Dr, Homewood AL 35209 B Newark NJ 9/3/1942 d Lawrence Huxster & Helen. BS Rutgers-The St U 1964; MS U of Alabama 1971. D 10/30/2004 Bp Henry Nutt Parsley Jr.

ATAMIAN, Thomas Michael (Chi) 272 Presidential Ln, Elgin IL 60123 **Asst S Dav's Ch Glenview IL 2010-** B Chicago IL 10/16/1953 s John Ara Atamian & Higo. BA U of So Alabama 1975; MDiv VTS 1979. D 6/9/1979 Bp Quintin Ebenezer Primo Jr P 12/8/1979 Bp James Winchester Montgomery. m 10/14/1978 Marilyn Kendell c 1. R S Hugh Of Lincoln Epis Ch Elgin IL 1992-2010; Assoc S Dav's Ch Glenview IL 1986-1992; R S Mich's Ch Grand Rapids MI 1984-1986; Assoc S Jn's Epis Ch Sharon PA 1981-1984; Cur Ch Of The H Nativ Clarendon Hills IL 1979-1981. tomatamian@gmail.com

ATCHESON, Chuck (Oly) 8529 Caroline Ave N, Seattle WA 98103 B Elmhurst IL 5/19/1938 s Frederick Roberts Atcheson & Annie Gertrude. Dplma Roosevelt HS Seattle WA 1957; BA Stan 1961; MDiv EDS 1964. D 6/29/1964 Bp William F Lewis P 3/1/1965 Bp Ivol I Curtis. m 8/28/1976 Barbara Ann Morris. Int S Clem's Ch Woodlake CA 2002-2003; R All SS Epis Ch Braine-l'Alleud 1420 BE 1991-1998; All SS Rectory Waterloo 1991-1998; R S Barn Ch Arroyo Grande CA 1988-1991; Vic Ch Of The H Cross Redmond WA 1979-1988; Dio Olympia Seattle WA 1976-1979; Cn Pstr S Mk's Cathd Seattle WA 1973-1975; Stwdshp Off Dio Olympia Seattle WA 1970-1977; Vic S Jn's Epis Ch Gig Harbor WA 1968-1973; Vic St Bede Epis Ch Port Orchard WA 1968-1973; Cur Trin Epis Ch Everett WA 1964-1965. Hon Cn Amer Cathd In Paris 1998. catcheson@q.com

ATCITTY, Janice (Ida) Po Box 388, Fort Hall ID 83203 B Pocatello ID 2/25/1955 d Louis Nacke & Charlene. Ft Lewis Coll; Idaho St U. D 1/29/1994 Bp John Stuart Thornton. c 2.

ATEEK, Sari N (WA) 6701 Wisconsin Ave, Chevy Chase MD 20815 **S Jn's Ch Chevy Chase MD 2010-** B Haifa Israel 5/30/1977 s Naim Ateek & Maha. BS Birmingham-Sthrn Coll 2000; MDiv Fuller TS 2006; Cert VTS 2006. D 6/3/2006 P 1/6/2007 Bp Joseph Jon Bruno. m 7/14/2001 Tanory Neel c 3. Assoc S Jas' Par So Pasadena CA 2006-2010. sateek@stjohnsnorwood.org

ATKINS, Hannah E (Tex) Trinity Episcopal Church, 1015 Holman St, Houston TX 77004 **Trin Ch Houston TX 2007-** B Indianapolis IN 5/19/1968 d Henry Lee Atkins & Lucy. BA Rutgers-The St U 1990; MDiv GTS 1996. D 1/27/1996 Bp Joe Morris Doss P 9/6/1996 Bp Martin De Jesus Barahona-Pascacio. m 7/15/2000 Elmer Chavarra c 2. S Jn's Ch Lafayette Sq Washington DC 1999-2007; Dio El Salvador Ambato 18-01-525 Tu EC 1998-1999; Exec Coun Appointees New York NY 1996-1998. Auth, "Dale Color A La Vida," *For Iglesa Epis De El Salvador*; Auth, "Conoce Tu Iglesia," *For Iglesa Epis De El Salvador*. Ord Of S Helena. rector@trinitychurch.net

ATKINS JR, Henry Lee (NJ) 621 Mayflower Rd Apt 204, Claremont CA 91711 B Hickory NC 8/9/1939 s Henry Lee Atkins & Edith. BA Randolph-Macon Coll 1961; MDiv VTS 1964; Oxf 1981; DMin GTF 1992. D 6/13/1964 Bp Robert Fisher Gibson Jr P 6/1/1965 Bp Samuel B Chilton. m 2/20/1965 Lucy Treadwell Davison c 3. Int S Mths' Par Whittier CA 2011; Int S Mich and All Ang Epis Ch Studio City CA 2008-2010; Int S Thos Ch Hanover NH 2003-2007; Epis Chapl The Epis Campus Mnstry at Rutgers New Brunswick NJ 1984-2003; The Wm Alexander Procter Fndt Trenton NJ 1984-2003; Dio No Carolina Raleigh NC 1979-1984; Dir Experimental Mnstrs Cathd of St Ptr & St Paul Washington DC 1976-1979; Exec Chr Soc Relatns Dio Rochester Rochester NY 1972-1976; Asst All SS Ch Indianapolis IN 1965-1969; Cur S Jas' Ch Richmond VA 1964-1965. Auth, "A Ti Juventud (Intro)"; Auth, "arts," *Plumbline*; Auth, "arts," *Sojourners*; Auth, "arts," *Witness*. Epis Ntwk for Econ Justice; EUC; Ord Of S Helena; S Greg Abbey. Hon Cn Ch In Costa Rica 1984. hleeatkins@aol.com

ATKINS, John Merritt (Pa) 749 Durham Rd., Wrightstown PA 18940 **R Ch Of The H Nativ Wrightstown PA 2008-** B Kansas City MO 7/10/1958 s John H Atkins & Barbara Ann. BA Wm Jewell Coll 1981; MDiv PrTS 1985; CAS GTS 1987; MSW Rutgers-The St U 1994. D 6/11/1988 Bp George Phelps Mellick Belshaw P 6/24/1989 Bp Vincent King Pettit. R S Pat's Ch Brunswick OH 2001-2008; Ch Planter Dio Ohio Cleveland OH 1999-2000; Vic All SS Crescentville Philadelphia PA 1994-1999; P-in-c Ch Of The Crucif Philadelphia PA 1993-1994; Vic Ch Of The H Sprt Tuckerton NJ 1989-1992; D S Lk's Epis Ch Atlanta GA 1988-1989. "And All Will Be Well: Planting a New Ch," *Ch Life, Vol. 107, # 1*, The Dio Ohio, 2003; "H and Passionate God," *Race and Pryr*, Morehouse Pub,, 2003; "The Tale of a Ch Planter," *LivCh, Vol. 226, # 12*, LivCh Fndt, 2003. johnatkins1976@gmail.com

ATKINSON, Andy (EC) 321 Pettigrew Dr, Wilmington NC 28412 **D S Jn's Epis Ch Wilmington NC 1988-; D Dio E Carolina Kinston NC 1987-** B Columbia SC 7/17/1947 s Aubrey Law Atkinson & Wyarian. BA/BS E Carolina U 1969. D 2/11/1988 Bp Brice Sidney Sanders. m 5/20/1972 Ada Katherine Beasley c 2.

ATKINSON, Clifford William (SO) 2526 May St, Cincinnati OH 45206 **Died 5/8/2010** B New York NY 5/14/1929 s Carl Walter Atkinson & Edith Gertrude. BA Hob 1949; STB Ya Berk 1952; STM SWTS 1958. D 4/19/1952 Bp James P De Wolfe P 5/29/1953 Bp Shirley Hall Nichols. m 2/12/1999 Kathleen Pohlschneider c 1. Auth, "A Lay Min'S Guide To Bk Of Common Pryr," Morehouse-Barlow; Auth, "Study Guide To Daily Off," Morehouse-Barlow; Auth, "Rites Of Passover Unleavened Bread: A Liturg Study," *ATR*. cliffordwatkinson@gmail.com

ATKINSON, Herschel Robert (At) 509 Rhodes Dr, Elberton GA 30635 B Lebanon OH 11/1/1925 s Ernest Malott & Mary Florence. LTh STUSo 1970. D 6/27/1970 Bp Randolph R Claiborne P 2/27/1971 Bp Milton LeGrand Wood. R S Alb's Ch Elberton GA 1970-1997; R S Andr's Ch Hartwell GA 1970-1997. Hist Soc of TEC 1995. olsmaj@comcast.net

ATKINSON JR, Joel Walter (Be) 321 Wyandotte St, Bethlehem PA 18015 B Ocala FL 5/19/1938 s Joel Walter Atkinson & Helen. BA Florida St U 1961; U Of Florida 1969; MDiv SWTS 1985. D 6/16/1985 Bp Frank Stanley Cerveny P 12/1/1985 Bp Robert Shaw Kerr. m 3/9/1985 Josette B Myers-Atkinson. Cn Cathd Ch Of The Nativ Bethlehem PA 1999-2005; R S Lk's Ch Blackstone VA 1991-1999; R Chr Epis Ch Harlan KY 1989-1991; R S Jn's Ch S Cloud MN 1987-1989; Cur Imm Ch Bellows Falls VT 1985-1987. shadrack38@juno.com

ATKINSON, Kate B (NH) 16 Madison St, Concord NH 03301 **Title IV Conciliator Dio New Hampshire Concord NH 2012-; Mem of Bp Search and Nomin Com Dio New Hampshire Concord NH 2011-; Mem of Cergy Dvlpmt Com Dio New Hampshire Concord NH 2010-; Mem of Dioc Coun Dio New Hampshire Concord NH 2010-; S Paul's Ch Concord NH 2009-** B New Rochelle NY 9/29/1956 d Guy Merkus Cam Bigwood & Jane Gray. BA Smith 1979; CTh U Of Durham 1996. Trans from Church Of England 9/7/2003 Bp Katharine Jefferts Schori. m 4/25/1997 Michael G Atkinson c 1. Int S Andr's Ch Saratoga CA 2007-2009; Mem of Bp's Com Dio Nevada Las Vegas NV 2006-2007; Dioc Fresh Start Fac Dio Nevada Las Vegas NV 2005-2007; Int S Paul's Epis Ch Sparks NV 2005-2007; S Pat's Ch Incline Vill NV 2003-2005. rector@stpaulsconcord.org

ATKINSON, Mark W (Fla) 7801 Lone Star Rd, Jacksonville FL 32211 **R S Andr's Ch Jacksonville FL 2008-** B Kansas City MO 11/16/1952 s Warren Atkinson & Edith. BBA SMU Dallas TX 1978; MBA Jacksonville U 1991;

MDiv STUSo 2006. D 6/4/2006 P 12/10/2006 Bp Samuel Johnson Howard. m 3/14/1986 Dallas S Long c 2. Assoc R Ch Of Our Sav Jacksonville FL 2006-2008. atkinsonm@bellsouth.net

✠ **ATKINSON, Rt Rev Robert Poland** (Va) 9225 Rosewater Lane, Jacksonville FL 32256 B Washington DC 11/16/1927 s William Henry Atkinson & Anna. BA U of Virginia 1950; BD VTS 1953; Fllshp Coll of Preachers 1962; Fllshp Ya Berk 1983. D 6/6/1953 P 2/24/1954 Bp Robert E L Strider Con 5/6/1973 for WVa. m 8/8/1953 Rosemary C Clemence c 3. Asst Bp Dio Virginia Richmond VA 1989-1993; Ret Bp of W Virginia Dio W Virginia Charleston WV 1976-1988; Bp Coadj Dio W Virginia Charleston WV 1973-1976; Dep GC Dio Tennessee Nashville TN 1973; Stndg Com Dio Tennessee Nashville TN 1967-1971; R Calv Ch Memphis TN 1964-1973; Chair BEC Dio W Virginia Charleston WV 1962-1964; R Trin Ch Huntington WV 1958-1964; Dep GC Dio W Virginia Charleston WV 1958-1961; R Chr Ch Fairmont WV 1955-1958; Asst S Matt's Ch Wheeling WV 1953-1955. Hon DD VTS Alexandria VA; Resrch Fllshp Yale DS New Haven. atkinsonsx2@earthlink.net

ATKINSON, William Harold (Vt) 40 Water St, Meredith NH 03253 B Lawrence MA 6/29/1926 s Harold Atkinson & Sarah. BS Springfield Coll 1950; Med Springfield Coll 1960. D 6/11/1964 Bp Walter H Gray P 12/1/1971 Bp Harvey D Butterfield. c 2. S Eliz's Epis Ch Zephyrhills FL 1991-1998; S Mart's Epis Ch Fairlee VT 1972-1984; Asst Calv Ch Enfield CT 1964-1969.

ATLEE, Raymond (Pa) 542 Tawnyberry Ln, Collegeville PA 19426 **Died 9/23/2011** B Columbia PA 8/14/1933 s Raymond Atlee & Pearl. BA Ripon Coll Ripon WI 1955; STB GTS 1958; STM Nash 1968. D 4/9/1958 P 10/15/1958 Bp William Hampton Brady. c 3. "Par Handbook For Environ In The Dio Pennsylvania," 2003. Assn All SS, Sis Of The Poor; OHC. Hon Cn Cathd Of Chr The Sav Philadelphia PA 1993; Nomin For Bp Of Pennsylvania. aratlee@aol.com

ATON JR, James Keyes (Ga) 3321 Wheeler Rd, Augusta GA 30909 **D S Aug Of Cbury Ch Augusta GA 1987-** B Saint Petersburg FL 2/13/1933 s James Keyes Aton & May. U Of Florida 1952; BA Emory U 1954; MD U of Maryland 1958. D 12/13/1987 Bp Harry Woolston Shipps. m 11/21/1946 Margaret Joan Hall c 4.

ATTAS III, Michael (Tex) 2400 Arroyo Rd, Waco TX 76710 **Asst P S Paul's Ch Waco TX 1999-** B Austin TX 3/9/1947 s Michael Attas & Mary Ellen. BA Baylor U 1969; MD U of Texas 1973; MDiv Epis TS of The SW 1999. D 6/20/1998 Bp Claude Edward Payne P 6/29/1999 Bp Leopoldo Jesus Alard. m 8/21/1970 Gail Evonne Treat.

ATTEBURY, Rich Earl (EO) Po Box 123, Lostine OR 97857 **P S Pat's Epis Ch Enterprise OR 1998-** B Pendleton OR 9/9/1942 s Raymond Attebury & Joye. BS U of Oregon 1964; MA U of Oregon 1970; Cert High Desert Chr Coll 1989. D 6/10/1998 P 12/17/1998 Bp Rustin Ray Kimsey. m 8/19/1978 Nancy Lee Garhan. rattebur@eoni.com

ATWELL, John Joseph (Az) 6043 E Ellis St, Mesa AZ 85205 B Shady Side MD 2/13/1917 s William Francis Atwell & Effie Reva. U of Maryland 1948; Washington DC U 1948; VTS 1950. D 6/23/1950 P 5/1/1951 Bp Noble C Powell. c 2. Epis Ch Of The Trsfg Mesa AZ 1976-1988; Vic Chr Ch Florence AZ 1971-1984; Vic Epis Ch Of The Trsfg Mesa AZ 1963-1973; Vic Chr Ch Florence AZ 1957-1963; Vic S Matt's Ch Chandler AZ 1957-1963; R S Matt's Par Oakland MD 1955-1957.

ATWOOD, Mary Hill (Los) 546 Bradford Ct, Claremont CA 91711 B Washington DC 11/21/1944 d Robert Greene Atwood & Lois Creighton. BA Wilson Coll 1966; MDiv CDSP 1980. D 6/28/1980 P 5/31/1981 Bp William Edwin Swing. c 1. Int S Ambr Par Claremont CA 2005-2006; Assoc Ch Of The Incarn San Francisco CA 1999-2002; Int True Sunshine Par San Francisco CA 1998-1999; Int Chr Epis Ch Sei Ko Kai San Francisco CA 1995-1997; Vic Ch Of The Gd Samar San Francisco CA 1983-1985; Vic Iglesia Epis Del Buen Samaritano San Francisco CA 1983-1985; Assoc St Johns Pro-Cathd Los Angeles CA 1980-1983. Int Mnstry Ntwk. rev.mary.atwood@gmail.com

ATWOOD JR, Theodore Oertel (Ga) 6785 El Banquero Pl, San Diego CA 92119 **Assoc H Cross Mssn Carlsbad CA 2010-** B Augusta GA 8/3/1936 s Theodore Oertel Atwood & Frances. BA U GA 1960; MDiv CDSP 1963. D 6/15/1963 P 4/25/1964 Bp Albert R Stuart. m 6/22/1963 Frances Margaret Stillwell c 2. Vic H Cross Mssn Carlsbad CA 2007-2010; Int S Mich's Ch Waynesboro GA 2003-2005; R Chr Ch Augusta GA 1994-2003; Asst S Alb's Epis Ch El Cajon CA 1993-1994; Asst S Dunst's Epis Ch San Diego CA 1989-1993; Chapl Off Of Bsh For ArmdF New York NY 1969-1989; Yth Advsr Dio Georgia Savannah GA 1966-1969; R S Jn's Epis Ch Bainbridge GA 1964-1969; Cur Chr Ch Frederica St Simons Island GA 1963-1964. Legion of Merit USN 1989.

AUBERT, Keri Theresa (Vt) 1700 Le Roy Ave Apt 7, Berkeley CA 94709 **CDSP Berkeley CA 2010-** B 1/29/1962 d Joseph Alibey Aubert & Virginia Theresa Michelli. BS LSU 1984; MS U of Alaska 1990; MDiv CDSP 2006. D 12/18/2005 P 12/2/2006 Bp Thomas C Ely. m 12/6/2009 Jakki Renee Flanagan c 1. Int All SS' Epis Ch S Burlington VT 2008-2009; Dio Vermont Burlington VT 2006. ktaubert@comcast.net

AUBREY, Norman Edward (WMass) 5 College View Hts, South Hadley MA 01075 B Stamford CT 8/10/1927 s Gwilym Oswald Aubrey & Marion. BS Ya 1950; PhD Ya 1954. D 10/9/1982 Bp Alexander Doig Stewart. m 7/3/1965 Barbara Ann Higgins. Soc Of S Jn The Evang.

AUCH, Janice Marie (Dal) 4109 Blue Grass Dr, Flower Mound TX 75028 **S Phil's Epis Ch Frisco TX 2010-** B Cleavand, OH 7/10/1959 d Frederick Geist Auch & Patricia Wolfe. BS Pur 1981; Masters of Div Brite DS TCU 2007. D 12/13/2008 P 5/22/2010 Bp James Monte Stanton. Assoc S Ptr's Ch McKinney TX 2008-2009; S Ptr's Ch McKinney TX 2007-2008. janiceauch@gmail.com

AUCHINCLOSS, R Anne (NY) 250 W 94th St # 4F, New York NY 10025 **D The Ch Of The Epiph New York NY 2010-** B Syracuse NY 9/21/1937 d Anthony Seminara & Julia. BA Syr 1968; D Formation Prog 2002. D 5/18/2002 Bp Mark Sean Sisk. c 2. D Ch Of The Ascen New York NY 2007-2010; D S Jn's Ch New York NY 2002-2007. anneauchin@nyc.rr.com

AUCHINCLOSS, Susan Carpenter (NY) 8 Library Lane, Woodstock NY 12498 **Ecum and Interfaith Cmsn Dio New York New York City NY 2011-** B Monroe MI 5/9/1938 d Malcolm Craig Carpenter & Aileen Catherine. BA Stan 1962; MDiv CDSP 1982. D 6/8/1985 P 6/1/1986 Bp William Edwin Swing. m 9/2/1972 Stuart Auchincloss c 2. R S Jn's Ch New City NY 1996-2004; Ch Of The Gd Shpd Granite Sprg NY 1995-1996; The Melrose Sch Brewster NY 1993-1995; S Paul's Epis Ch Burlingame CA 1985-1988. Auth, "Pulpit Dig". Mdiv w dist CDSP Berkeley CA 1982. simplysusana@verizon.net

AUELUA, Royston Toto'a Stene (NCal) 6963 Riata Dr, Redding CA 96002 **R S Mich's Ch Anderson CA 2001-** B Birmingham UK 8/30/1944 s Toto'a Auelua & Gladys. BA San Jose St Coll. D 6/29/1974 Bp C Kilmer Myers P 5/1/1975 Bp George Richard Millard. m 1/6/1968 Judith Duckles c 1. Dio Nthrn California Sacramento CA 2002-2003; Vic Ch Of The Gd Shpd Orland CA 1999-2003; Gd Shpd Epis Ch Belmont CA 1976-1999. auelua1@charter.net

AUER, Dorothy Kogler (NJ) 320 Glenburney Dr Apt 106, Fayetteville NC 28303 B Syracuse NY 11/25/1933 d Charles Conrad Kogler & Dorothy Elizabeth. BS Syr 1955; MA Syr 1963; Rutgers-The St U 1977. D 6/9/1990 Bp George Phelps Mellick Belshaw P 11/23/1999 Bp Herbert Alcorn Donovan Jr. Asst S Barn Ch Burlington NJ 2001-2005; Mem, Dioc Coun Dio New Jersey Trenton NJ 2001-2004; D in Charge S Mich's Ch Trenton NJ 1995-1997; Supply P Evergreens Chap Moorestown NJ 1992-2004; Mem, Dioc Coun Dio New Jersey Trenton NJ 1992-1995; Bd Mem Evergreens Chap Moorestown NJ 1992-1994; Mem, Epis Election Com Dio New Jersey Trenton NJ 1992-1993. Outstanding Adj Prof Of Engl Bucks Cnty Cmnty Coll 1988. dorothy.auer@comcast.net

AUGUSTIN, Dale Lee (Nev) 422 Red Canvas Pl, Las Vegas NV 89144 **P-in-c Gr In The Desert Epis Ch Las Vegas NV 2007-** B East Saint Louis IL 8/21/1942 s LaVerne Harold Augustin & Eileen Margueite. Nthn Montana Coll 1963; U of Nevada at Las Vegas 1969. D 12/9/1982 P 6/12/1983 Bp Wesley Frensdorff. m 5/15/1965 Maureen Isabelle Parker c 2. Chr Ch Las Vegas NV 2001-2006; P Dio Nevada Las Vegas NV 1982-2000. Lambda Chi Alpha (hon); Sis of Charity. Lambda Chi Alpha. dalea@cox.net

AUGUSTINE, Patrick Parvez (Eau) 427 14th St S, La Crosse WI 54601 **R Chr Ch Par La Crosse WI 2003-** B Gojra Punjab PK 3/17/1950 s Barkat Masih Augustine & Shiela. BA U Of Punjab IN 1972; DIT Lahore TS IN 1976; MDiv Gujrawala TS IN 1982; Cert Coll of Preachers 1993; VTS 1994. Trans from Anglican Church Of Pakistan 4/11/1986 Bp James Winchester Montgomery. m 10/24/1977 Myrna Samuel c 3. S Jn's Epis Ch Waynesboro VA 1996-2003; Asst/Assoc R Ch Of The H Comf Vienna VA 1990-1996; Asst S Greg's Epis Ch Deerfield IL 1987-1988; Asst S Mich's Ch Barrington IL 1984-1986; Mssnr To So Asians S Phil's Epis Palatine IL 1983-1989. Auth, "From Conflict To Road Of Peace- Bleeding In Kashmir And Human Rts Crisis In The Sub-Continent," Aug Desktop Pub, 2000; Auth, "Hear My People'S Cry," Aug Desktop Pub, 1998; Auth, "3 Lessons On The Forgiveness Of Intl Debt," *Lambeth Conf 1998*; Auth, "Var arts," *Var Ch And Secular Periodicals*. Shield For Peace And Recon Wk Prime Min Of Azad, Kashmir 2000. patchristch@centurytel.net

AUGUSTINE, Peter John (Eau) 111 9th St N, La Crosse WI 54601 B 6/9/1952 s Barkat Masih Augustine & Begum Sheila. Trans from Anglican Church Of Pakistan 4/6/2008 Bp Keith Bernard Whitmore. m 8/26/1983 Lily Augustine c 3. peter_augustine46000@yahoo.com

AULENBACH JR, Bil (Haw) The Groves 59, 5200 Irvine Blvd, Irvine CA 92620 B Detroit MI 10/28/1932 s W Hamilton Aulenbach & Pearl. BA Ken 1954; MDiv CDSP 1960; MS U of Hawaii 1972; PhD Glendale U 2007. D 6/11/1960 Bp Oliver J Hart P 12/9/1960 Bp Harry S Kennedy. m 6/17/1961 Anne A Lowry c 3. Pstr Asst S Mary's Par Laguna Bch CA 2000-2003; Dir Prog & Oprtns Dio Hawaii Honolulu HI 1969-1975; Yth Min Ch Of The H Nativ Honolulu HI 1967-1969; Yth Min Ch Of The H Nativ Honolulu HI 1960-1963. Auth, "What's Love Got to w?...Everything Says Jesus," 2008; Auth, "How To Get To Heaven Without Going To Ch," 1997; Auth, "Let Us Pray," 1985. bilaulenbach@yahoo.com

AURAND, Benjamin Kyte (Tex) 5 Cypress Pt, Wimberley TX 78676 B Minneapolis MN 3/30/1941 s Calvin William Aurand & Eleanor. BA Amh 1963; Med Harv 1964; MBA U Chi 1971; MDiv STUSo 1982. D 6/19/1982 Bp Quintin Ebenezer Primo Jr P 2/1/1983 Bp Maurice Manuel Benitez. m 8/24/1965 Nancy Schuetz c 3. Vic Ch Of The Epiph Calvert TX 1988-2004; R S Thos Epis Ch Coll Sta TX 1988-2004; Cur S Matt's Ch Austin TX 1982-1988. baurand@austin.rr.com

AUSTILL, Stephen P (Mass) 12 Mount Vernon St, Saugus MA 01906 B Boston MA 3/14/1929 s William E Austill & Anna. BS Col 1951; MDiv VTS 1954. D 6/19/1954 P 12/1/1954 Bp Norman B Nash. m 2/10/1951 Virginia D Dole. R S Jn's Epis Ch Saugus MA 1960-1969; S Anne's Ch No Billerica MA 1956-1960; Cur Trin Par Melrose MA 1954-1956. STEVEGIN@GIS.NET

AUSTIN, Dorothy A (Nwk) Harvard Yard, Cambridge MA 02138 B Fall River MA 11/5/1943 d Donald Earl Austin & Bessie Corner. BD Andover Newton TS 1969; ThD Harv 1981; MSW Bos 2008. D 11/18/1997 Bp Jack Marston McKelvey P 5/16/1998 Bp John Shelby Spong. m 7/4/2004 Diana Eck. daustin@fas.harvard.edu

AUSTIN, Evette Eliene (Alb) 9 E Main St, Canton NY 13617 **Gr Epis Ch Canton NY 2005-** B Barbados West Indies 10/24/1952 d Jeffrey Wiltshire & Evette. BS Sacr Heart U 2002; MDiv GTS 2005. D 6/11/2005 Bp Andrew Donnan Smith P 1/22/2006 Bp David John Bena. m 7/11/1981 Clarence Austin. jesus141@peoplepc.com

AUSTIN, Henry Whipple (Neb) 4509 Anderson Cir, Papillion NE 68133 B New Brunswick NJ 9/2/1938 D 7/5/2002 Bp James Edward Krotz. m 6/23/1962 Charlotte Small Howard c 4. hwaustin@cox.net

AUSTIN, Jean E (Vt) 7255 The Terraces, Shelburne VT 05482 B Wooster OH 1/24/1947 d Horace Alison Dutton & Martha Ann. BA Coll of Wooster 1968; MDiv EDS 1998. D 5/23/1998 Bp Mary Adelia Rosamond McLeod P 12/19/1998 Bp M(arvil) Thomas Shaw III. m 10/27/2000 Elizabeth Kennedy c 2. Int S Lk's Ch S Albans VT 2007-2008; Int Dio Wstrn Massachusetts Springfield MA 2005-2007; P-in-c S Andr's Ch Readfield ME 2003-2005; Int S Phil's Ch Wiscasset ME 2001-2003; Int S Paul's Epis Ch White River Jct VT 1999-2001; Asst S Ptr's Ch Beverly MA 1998-1999. revjaustin@yahoo.com

AUSTIN, John Brander (La) 520 Evans Ct, 520 Evans Ct, Basalt CO 81621 B Philadelphia PA 9/19/1932 s James Harold Austin & Thelma. BA Tul 1955; MDiv STUSo 1958; Loyola Coll 1961; Med U of New Orleans 1991; Austin Presb TS 1996. D 6/29/1958 Bp Iveson Batchelor Noland P 8/14/1960 Bp Girault M Jones. m 7/19/1974 Margaret Sutton c 2. Int S Jn's Ch Petersburg VA 2002-2003; P-in-c The Fork Ch Doswell VA 1997-2002; Int S Ptr's Epis Ch Uniontown PA 1996-1997; P-in-c S Ptr's Epis Ch Blairsville PA 1995-1996; S Barn' Epis Ch Hartselle AL 1995; Vic S Lk's Ch Cypress Mill TX 1992-1994; Vic S Mich And All Ang Epis Ch Blanco TX 1992-1994; Vic S Matt's Ch Bogalusa LA 1985-1991; S Andr's Paradis Luling LA 1984; P-in-c S Tim's Ch La Place LA 1978-1980; Asst Trin Ch New Orleans LA 1971; P-in-c All SS Epis Ch Ponchatoula LA 1961-1966; Vic S Mths Ch Nashville TN 1958. Auth, "Syllabus In Religous Stds," Coun of Rel Stds, 1973; Auth, "Ways To Understanding," U of New Orleans, 1972; Auth, "Stff Dvlpmt Curric Coordination," U of New Orleans, 1972. revjbrander@yahoo.com

AUSTIN, Margaret Sutton (Colo) 200 Elk Run Dr., Basalt CO 81621 **Vic S Ptr's Ch Basalt CO 2009-** B New Orleans LA 6/8/1946 d Edward Alvin Sutton & Marie Victoria. BA SE Louisiana U 1968; Cert SE Louisiana U 1975; MDiv Epis TS of The SW 1994. D 6/11/1994 P 1/20/1995 Bp James Barrow Brown. m 7/19/1974 John Brander Austin. R S Steph's Ch Lubbock TX 2003-2009; Assoc R S Steph's Ch Richmond VA 1997-2003; Assoc Calv Ch Pittsburgh PA 1995-1997; The TS at The U So Sewanee TN 1994-1995; The U So (Sewanee) Sewanee TN 1994-1995. margaretaus3@aol.com

AUSTIN JR, Vernon Arthur (Pa) 102 Nursery Dr, Plymouth Meeting PA 19462 B Trenton NJ 6/9/1934 s Vernon Arthur Austin & Elizabeth Brown. BA cum lauda Hampden-Sydney Coll 1956; MDiv GTS 1959. D 5/9/1959 Bp Oliver J Hart P 11/14/1959 Bp Andrew Tsu. m 6/6/1964 Judith H Haubens c 2. Alt Dep GC Dio Pennsylvania Philadelphia PA 1982-1989; Dn Vlly Forge Dnry Dio Pennsylvania Philadelphia PA 1977-1980; R S Jn's Ch Norristown PA 1976-1996; R Trin Ch Gloversville NY 1967-1976; Alt Dep GC Dio Albany Albany NY 1964-1976; R Chr Ch Herkimer NY 1964-1967; Cur S Geo's Epis Ch Schenectady NY 1961-1964; Cur Trin Epis Ch Ambler PA 1959-1961. SSC 1984. BA cl Hampden-Sydney Coll Hampden-Sydney VA 1956. vaustin1@verizon.net

AUSTIN, Victor Lee (NY) 1 W 53rd St, New York NY 10019 **Angl-RC Dialogue Co-Chair Dio New York New York City NY 2008-; Theol-in-Res S Thos Ch New York NY 2005-** B Oklahoma City OK 3/29/1956 s Marshall Lee Austin & Dorothy Jeane. BA S Jn's Coll Santa Fe NM 1978; MA U of New Mex 1982; MDiv GTS 1985; PhD Ford 2002. D 6/26/1985 Bp Richard Mitchell Trelease Jr P 2/8/1986 Bp James Stuart Wetmore. m 9/29/1978 Susan L Gavahan c 2. P-in-res H Trin Epis Ch Hollidaysburg PA 2004; Tutor The GTS New York NY 1994; Natl Coun of Ch T/F on Ecclesiology Dom And Frgn Mssy Soc- Epis Ch Cntr New York NY 1993-1998; R Ch Of The Resurr Hopewell Jct NY 1989-2003; Luth-Epis Dialogue Dio New York New York City NY 1989-1995; Cur Zion Epis Ch Wappingers Falls NY 1985-1989. Auth, "Up w Authority: Why We Need Authority to Flourish as Human Beings," Continuum / T & T Clark, 2010; Auth, "P in New York: Ch, St, and Theol," S Thos Ch, 2010; Auth, "Jn Paul II's Ironic Legacy in Political Theol," *Pro Ecclesia*, 2007; Auth, "A P's Journ," Ch Publising, 2001; Auth, "Method In Oliver O'Donovan Desire Of The Nations," *ATR*; Auth, "Ecclesiology Of The Proposed Luth- Epis Concordat Of Agreement," *Mid-Stream*; Auth, "Is There An Angl Method In Theol? Hints From The Lux Mundi Era," *Sewanee Theol Revs*. Angl Soc. victorleeaustin@yahoo.com

AUSTIN, Wilborne Adolphus (Ct) 18 Richard Rd, East Hartford CT 06108 **Vic S Steph's Epis Ch Bloomfield CT 2004-** B BB 9/6/1937 s Norman A Austin & Enid L. Andover Newton TS; Cert Hartford Sem 1986; BD TESM 2002. D 6/12/1993 Bp Arthur Edward Walmsley P 1/22/1994 Bp Clarence Nicholas Coleridge. m 4/17/1965 Mary Shepherd. Asst/Cn Chr Ch Cathd Hartford CT 1994-2004; D S Monica's Ch Hartford CT 1993. Ord Of S Lk. waustin@shet.net

AUSTIN, William Bouldin (CFla) 3508 Lakeshore Dr SW, Smyrna GA 30082 B Abilene TX 8/31/1949 s William Thomas Austin & Johnnie Ellen. BA U So 1971; MDiv SWTS 1975. P 4/4/1976 Bp Anselmo Carral-Solar. m 11/1/1975 Robin S Dahlstrom c 1. Cathd Of S Phil Atlanta GA 1990-1991; R The Epis Ch Of The Redeem Avon Pk FL 1981-1987. Fell Coll Of Chap; OHC. ka4jmq@earthlink.net

AUSTIN, William Paul (WNC) 112 Trotter Pl, Asheville NC 28806 **P Assoc S Mary's Ch Asheville NC 2000-** B Boston MA 10/4/1930 s Mansfield Austin & Grace May. MDiv Ya Berk; BA Trin Hartford CT 1951; Br 1956; Yonsei U 1962; GTS 1966; S Vladimirs 1966; Cidoc Cuernavaca Mx 1971; Cbury Coll 1972; U Of Rome Rome IT 1973; Orth Acad Crete 1983. D 6/20/1959 Bp Anson Phelps Stokes Jr P 2/4/1960 Bp Joseph Summerville Minnis. St Georges Epis Ch Asheville NC 1987-1990; Dio SW Virginia Roanoke VA 1987; Untd Campus Chap St. Louis MO 1986-1987; Hilo Campus Min Dio Hawaii Honolulu HI 1979-1986; Hilo Campus Mnstry Hilo HI 1979-1984; Dio Wstrn No Carolina Asheville NC 1976-1979; Trin Ch Kings Mtn NC 1975-1976; P-in-c S Gabr's Ch Rutherfordton NC 1968-1978; Asst P S Andr's Ch Stamford CT 1966-1968. Auth, "Chr In Prison Today-New Verses For Old Hymns," 2000; Auth, "New Hope". Alcuin Club; Ecumenissts; No Amer Acad; No Amer Acad Of Liturg; Soc Liturgica.

AUTRY, Rosa Maria (Los) 1011 S Verdugo Rd, Glendale CA 91205 **S Paul's Epis Ch Paterson NJ 2010-** B Limon Costa Rica 9/29/1957 MDiv Seminario Biblico Latino Americano 1990; STM GTS 1994. Trans from Iglesia Anglicana de la Region Central de America 7/20/2002 Bp Joseph Jon Bruno. m 5/13/2006 Toney R Autry. Dio Sthrn Ohio Cincinnati OH 2009-2010; Ch Of Our Sav Cincinnati OH 2006-2008; Vic Iglesia Epis De La Magdalena Mssn Glendale CA 2002-2006; Dio Los Angeles Los Angeles CA 2002. rosaautry@earthlink.net

AVALOS, Abdias C (Los) PO Box 16386, Houston TX 77222 **Asst St Johns Pro-Cathd Los Angeles CA 2005-** B San Felipe MX 11/19/1928 s Francisco Avalos & Dolores. Cerritos Coll; Epis TS of The SW; Houston Cmnty Coll; BD Pacific Luth TS; Register LVN; San Jacinto Coll; U of Houston. D 6/23/1985 Bp Gordon Taliaferro Charlton P 7/1/1986 Bp Maurice Manuel Benitez. m 11/12/1972 Essie M Ringo c 5. P-in-c S Barth's Mssn Pico Rivera CA 1991-1995; P-in-c Calv Epis Ch Santa Cruz CA 1988-1991; Vic Mssn De La Santa Cruz Houston TX 1988-1991; Ch Of The Redeem Houston TX 1985-1991; Asst St Johns Pro-Cathd Los Angeles CA 1966-1997. Ministers Against Crime Houston TX 1989-1991. Proud Partnr Awd Clean Houston Clean City Cmsn Houston TX 1990. abd28@sbcgloblal.net

AVCIN, Janet Elaine (CPa) 228 Charles St, Harrisburg PA 17102 B Pittsburgh PA 1/4/1954 d Matthew J Avcin & Janet T. BA S Fran Coll Loretto PA 1986; MDiv Lancaster TS 1989. D 6/14/1991 Bp Charlie Fuller McNutt Jr P 2/1/1996 Bp Michael Whittington Creighton. m 8/20/1988 Mark Randolph Salter. Ch Of The Trsfg Blue Ridge Summit PA 1997; Cathd Ch Of S Steph Harrisburg PA 1992-1997.

AVENI JR, James Vincent (NwT) Po Box 1064, Clarendon TX 79226 B Washington DC 11/30/1952 s James Vincent Aveni & Patricia Jean. AA Amarillo Coll 1976; BS W Texas A&M U 1978; MS Our Lady Of The Lake U San Antonio TX 1980. D 11/13/1999 P 10/20/2001 Bp C(harles) Wallis Ohl. m 4/4/1975 Rhonda Dee Redding. Ministral Allnce. doober@arn.net

AVENT JR, Henry Elbert (SC) 9540 Marlboro Ave, Barnwell SC 29812 **Asst to R S Phil's Ch Charleston SC 2005-** B Columbia SC 3/20/1951 s Henry Elbert Avent & Nancy Lee. BS Clemson U 1973; MDiv TESM 1997. D 6/7/1997 P 12/1/1997 Bp Edward Lloyd Salmon Jr. m 8/7/1976 Gloria Jean Van De Water. Vic Ch Of The H Apos Barnwell SC 1997-2004. Dio Cmsn Archit; SAMS Bd Dir. havent@stphilipschurchsc.org

AVERA, Mark Wayne (SC) PO Box 1043, C/O St Helenas Episcopal Church, Beaufort SC 29901 **Assoc Par Ch of St. Helena Beaufort SC 2003-** B Columbia SC 4/8/1967 s Talcoth Wair Avera & Monta Ethyl. BS Coll of Charleston 1989; ThM Reformed TS 1996; MDiv Nash 2003. D 7/7/2003 P 1/12/

2004 Bp Edward Lloyd Salmon Jr. m 7/27/1991 Joy Melinda Avera c 5. mavera@islc.net

AVERY, Daniel Thomas (SVa) 118 Nina Lane, Williamsburg VA 23188 **Asstg P Bruton Par Williamsburg VA 2002-** B Bainbridge GA 9/26/1948 s Andrew Avery & Alva Lucille. MDiv Sthrn Bapt TS Louisville KY 1974; Ed.D. The W&M 1984. D 6/15/2002 P 1/30/2003 Bp David Conner Bane Jr. m 1/13/1973 Patricia Jo Kinman c 2. Thronateeska1948@yahoo.com

AVERY, Gail (NH) Seafarer's Friend, 77 Broadway, Chelsea MA 02150 **Dioc Coun Mem Dio New Hampshire Concord NH 2011-; Dioc Outreach Cmsn, Ondjiva Angola Sch Proj Com Chair Dio New Hampshire Concord NH 2010-; Cler Dvlpmt Com Dio New Hampshire Concord NH 2009-; Asst S Chris's Ch Hampstead NH 2008-; Prov One Syn Cler Rep Dio New Hampshire Concord NH 2007-; MDG Com Mem Dio New Hampshire Concord NH 2006-** B Boston MA 5/11/1954 d Shailer Avery & Rebecca Farnsworth. BS U of New Hampshire 1976; MDiv EDS 2006. D 8/28/2007 P 6/11/2008 Bp V Gene Robinson. m 12/21/1985 Kirk A Trachy c 4. D S Andr's-In-The-Vlly Tamworth NH 2007-2008. Intl Chr Maritime Assn 2007; No Amer Maritime Mnstry Assn 2007. Excellence in Internation Mssn and Ecum Engagement Boston Theol Inst 2006. gailavery@gmail.com

AVERY III, Gilbert Stiles (Pa) 1141 Spyglass Dr, Eugene OR 97401 B Mason City IA 5/19/1931 s Gilbert Stiles Avery & Susan Spalding. BBA SMU 1952; STM EDS 1955. D 6/23/1955 P 12/23/1955 Bp Everett H Jones. m 12/21/1956 Laura Graves c 2. Epis Cmnty Serv Philadelphia PA 1981-1991; Dep to GC Dio Massachusetts Boston MA 1969-1973; Epis City Mssn Boston MA 1966-1981; R S Jn's S Jas Epis Ch Roxbury MA 1960-1966; Cur S Aug's Ch New York NY 1957-1960; Cur S Mk's Epis Ch San Antonio TX 1955-1957. gilavery@comcast.net

AVERY, Harold Dennison (CNY) 112 Arbordale Pl, Syracuse NY 13219 B Syracuse NY 5/2/1928 s Harold Terry Avery & Anne Patricia. BA Syr 1949; BD EDS 1952. D 6/11/1952 Bp Malcolm E Peabody P 6/21/1953 Bp Dudley S Stark. m 5/25/1985 Jeanne Marie Garrison c 3. Trin Ch Syracuse NY 1970-1984; R S Jn's Ch Canandaigua NY 1959-1970; P-in-c S Jn's Ch Mt Morris NY 1955-1959; Cur S Thos Epis Ch Rochester NY 1953-1955; Cur Trin Epis Ch Watertown NY 1952-1953. averyjeha@yahoo.com

AVERY, James Kelley (Tenn) Po Box 159012, Nashville TN 37215 **Died 3/3/2011** B Alamo TN 1/16/1926 s John Buchanan Avery & Josie Tennessee. Baylor U; SMU; MD U of Tennessee 1948. D 5/22/1980 Bp William F Gates Jr P 5/31/1981 Bp William Evan Sanders. kaverymd@ison.net

AVERY, Joyce Marie (Oly) 1022 Monte Elma Rd, Elma WA 98541 **D S Mk's Epis Ch Montesano WA 1999-** B Aberdeen WA 2/21/1930 d John Raubuch & Jean. 12th No River HS 2047. D 3/15/1999 Bp Sanford Zangwill Kaye Hampton. m 5/3/1980 Lee Arnold Avery. Altar Soc 1970. leejoyce2@hotmail.com

AVERY, Richard Norman (Los) 1026 Goldenrod St, Placentia CA 92870 **Asst The Epis Ch Of The Blessed Sacr Placentia CA 1994-** B Yuma AZ 1/24/1934 s Charles Henry Avery & Lois May. BA San Diego St U 1955; BD SMU 1958; SWTS 1963; California St Polytechnic U 1976. D 9/5/1963 P 3/12/1964 Bp Francis E I Bloy. m 6/21/1953 Marjorie Howe Wygant c 2. S Ambr Par Claremont CA 1989-1994; S Jn's Mssn La Verne CA 1969-1976; Cur Cathd Ch Of S Paul San Diego CA 1963-1966. ESA; SSC.

AVERY, Steven Walter (Ore) PO Box 2617, Florence OR 97439 B Hollywood CA 8/3/1945 s Arthur David Avery & Kathryn Eleanor. AA SW Coll 1968; BA California St U 1970; MA Untd States Intl U 1971; PhD Untd States Intl U 1976; Cert Paths to Serv 1996. D 12/11/1993 Bp Steven Charleston. m 8/8/1971 Margaret Boggs c 2. Dio Oregon Portland OR 2008-2009; S Andr's Epis Ch Florence OR 2008-2009; D S Jas The Fisherman Kodiak AK 1993-2000. avery2617@gmail.com

AVILA, Ricardo (Cal) 14 Cushing Avenue, Dorchester MA 02125 **Asst P S Mary's Epis Ch Dorchester MA 2011-** B Chicago IL 8/1/1966 s Jose Jesus Avila & Maria De la Luz. BA U of Wisconsin 1989; MDiv CDSP 2010. D 6/5/2010 P 12/4/2010 Bp Marc Handley Andrus. m 10/18/2008 William Bonnell. Asst P S Lk's Ch San Francisco CA 2010-2011. ricotime@mac.com

AVILA-NATIVI, Rigoberto (NY) PO Box 3786, Poughkeepsie NY 12603 B Honduras 1/12/1956 s Vergilio Avila & Maria De los Angeles. BA SUNY 2005; MDiv GTS 2006. D 3/11/2006 P 9/23/2006 Bp Mark Sean Sisk. m 4/29/1990 Jacqueline K Reed c 3. Dioc Trng Cntr New York NY 2009. avilareed@yahoo.com

AXBERG, Keith Frederick (EpisSanJ) 8073 N Rowell Ave, Fresno CA 93720 B Seattle WA 8/1/1951 s Oscar Axberg & Eileen. BS WA SU 1974; MDiv Vancouver TS 1984. D 9/13/1984 P 7/13/1985 Bp Leigh Wallace Jr. m 5/12/1979 Barbara J Paul c 2. Ch Of H Fam Fresno CA 2003-2009; R S Paul's Epis Ch Benicia CA 2001-2003; S Mich And All Ang Epis Ch Lincoln Pk MI 1990-2001; Epis Ch Of The Redeem Republic WA 1984-1990; Vic S Jn's Epis Ch Colville WA 1984-1990. Columnist, "THIS OUR Vlly," *Madera Tribune Nwspr*, Madera Tribune, 2009. kfaxberg@gmail.com

AXLEROAD JR, Benjamin (Pa) 4901 Connecticut Ave, NW, Washington DC 20008 **Died 7/16/2011** B Miami FL 11/19/1921 s Benjamin Axleroad & Vera. BA U of Miami 1942; BD VTS 1944; STM GTS 1949; EdM Tem 1973. D 6/22/1944 Bp George W Davenport P 11/1/1945 Bp Athalicio T Pithan. c 2. Auth, *Hosp Vstng: a Guide for Lay Pstr Callers*; Auth, *Notes on the Chapl's Role in Crisis Mnstry*; Auth, *Triumph of Faith & Pryr*. APHA 1965-1987; Coll of Chapl 1965-1987; Profsnl Affiliate Amer Assn of Pstr Counsel 1974-1987. baxl@verizon.net

AYALA-PORFIL, Eugenio (Los) 11551 Arminta St, North Hollywood CA 91605 B 11/10/1941 Trans from La Iglesia Anglicana de Mex 7/8/2002 Bp Joseph Jon Bruno. m 1/3/2004 Vanessa Mildred MacKenzie c 3. Vic H Fam Mssn No Hollywood CA 2002-2005; Dio Mex 1997-2001; Dio Puerto Rico S Just PR 1980-1997; Dio Puerto Rico S Just PR 1968-1979.

AYALA TORRES, Carlos Anibal (EcuC) Bogota S/N Jose Vicente Trujillo, Guayaquil Ecuador B Tumbabiro-Ibarra EC 7/9/1935 s Jukio Cesar Ayala Barahona Fallecido & Rosa Victoria Torres. Coll Tecnico Daniel Geyes Reval; BTh Facultad Limena De Sagraduatea Teologia 1967. P 4/27/1985 Bp Adrian Delio Caceres-Villavicencio. m 9/7/1973 Nancy Carabajo Vera. Litoral Dio Ecuador Guayaquil EQ EC 1986-1994; Iglesia Epis Del Ecuador Ecuador 1985.

AYCOCK, David H (CFla) 759 Phoenix Ln, Oviedo FL 32765 **S Matt's Epis Ch Orlando FL 2003-** B Spartanburg SC 12/7/1937 BA Florida Chr U 2001. D 12/15/2003 Bp John Wadsworth Howe. m 7/3/1963 Jill Ann Aycock c 3. dycock@cfl.rr.com

AYCOCK JR, Marvin B(rady) (NC) 669 N. 6th St., Albemarle NC 28001 B Greenville SC 11/30/1932 s Marvin Brady Aycock & Arminda Elizabeth. Clemson U 1953; BA Furman U 1958; MDiv SE Bapt TS 1962; GTS 1994. D 10/2/1988 Bp Robert Whitridge Estill P 6/1/1995 Bp Robert Carroll Johnson Jr. m 8/15/1959 Sally Rheta Thompson c 3. Vic S Paul's Epis Ch Thomasville NC 2006-2008; Vic S Matt Ch Salisbury NC 2001-2004; Vic S Paul's Ch Salisbury NC 2001-2004; Yadkin Vlly Cluster Salisbury NC 2001-2003; Vic Emm Ch Warrenton NC 1996-2004; Vic All SS Ch Warrenton NC 1996-2001; Warrenton Epis Ch Cluster Warrenton NC 1996-2001; Asst to R S Andr's Epis Ch Charlotte NC 1995-1996; D S Paul's Ch Salisbury NC 1993-1994; D Chr Ch Albemarle NC 1988-1993. marv_sally@yahoo.com

AYER, Kelly Lane (Roch) 10 Park Pl, Avon NY 14414 B Mecklenburg NC 1/30/1973 d Charles H Ayer & Helen S. BS Wingate U 1999; MDiv Van 2004; STM The GTS 2010. D 12/4/2010 Bp Michael Bruce Curry P 7/16/2011 Bp Prince Grenville Singh. kayer@gts.edu

AYERBE, Reynaldo (SwFla) 4012 Penhurst Park, Sarasota FL 34235 **Asst Ch Of The Redeem Sarasota FL 2002-** B CO 10/27/1928 s Julio M Ayerbe & Adeliaida. PhD NYU; BA Vincentian Sem Bogota CO. Trans 2/9/2002 Bp John Bailey Lipscomb. m 8/12/1961 Elin L Ayerbe.

AYERS, John Cameron (Cal) 13601 Saratoga Ave, Saratoga CA 95070 **Chapl S Andr's Sch Saratoga CA 2011-** B Los Angeles CA 10/28/1956 s John Wakeman Ayers & Nancy Ann. BA Loyola Marymount 1978; MA Gonzaga 1981; MDiv Weston TS 1986. Rec from Roman Catholic 7/27/2011 as Priest Bp Marc Handley Andrus. jcamsj@gmail.com

AYERS, Margaret Susan (Miss) St James Episcopal Church, PO Box 494, Port Gibson MS 39150 **S Jas Epis Ch Port Gibson MS 2007-** B Billings, MT 3/2/1958 d David Monroe Ayers & Helen Louise Stieg. BS - Fin Montana St U 1981; MDiv Epis TS - SW 2007. D 6/18/2007 Bp Charles Franklin Brookhart Jr P 2/1/2008 Bp Duncan Montgomery Gray III. ayersma@aol.com

AYERS, Phillip Wallace (Ore) 3232 NE 12th Ave, Portland OR 97212 **Fresh Start Fac Dio Oregon Portland OR 2009-; Assoc S Ptr And Paul Epis Ch Portland OR 2006-** B Newton KS 7/22/1941 s Leo Carlton Ayers & Aloha Lee. BME Wichita St U 1965; MDiv Ya Berk 1970; Cert Ya 1984; Cert Abbott NW Hosp Minneapolis MN 1992. D 6/17/1970 P 12/16/1970 Bp Edward Clark Turner. m 7/31/1965 LaVera Mae Goering c 2. R Ascen Par Portland OR 1999-2004; R Trin Epis Ch Marshall MI 1993-1998; Long Term Supply Ch Of The H Cross Dundas MN 1993; Assoc S Clem's Ch S Paul MN 1991-1993; R S Paul's On-The-Hill Epis Ch St Paul MN 1988-1991; Par Fieldwork Supvsr Ya Berk New Haven CT 1975-1988; R S Jn's Ch No Haven CT 1974-1988; Asst/Mus Dir S Dav's Epis Ch Topeka KS 1972-1974; Cur S Paul's Epis Ch Visalia CA 1971-1972; R Ch Of The Epiph Sedan KS 1970-1971; Vic S Matt's Ch Cedar Vale KS 1970-1971. Compiler, "Plain Prayers for a Vstry," H Cross Monstry, 1995; Auth, "Revs and arts," *The Hstgr*. Iona Cmnty-Assoc 1985; Natl Epis Historians & Archivists 2002; OHC-Assoc 1961. players@hevanet.com

AYERS, Robert Curtis (CNY) 6010 E. Lake Rd., Cazenovia NY 13035 B Roanoke VA 11/20/1927 s Walter Curtis Ayers & Lena Mae. BA Roa 1947; MDiv Luth TS 1950; Fllshp Coll of Preachers 1963; Hoerer U of Munich 1966; PhD Syr 1981. D 9/29/1953 P 4/4/1954 Bp Malcolm E Peabody. m 9/4/1950 Vivian E Harper. R Epis Ch Of SS Ptr And Jn Auburn NY 1991-1998; Vic Epis Ch Of SS Ptr And Jn Auburn NY 1988-1990; Int Emm Ch Norwich NY 1988; Vic Trin Ch Camden NY 1983-1988; P-in-c Emm Ch Adams NY 1954-1958; P-in-c Zion Ch Adams NY 1954-1958; Dio Cntrl New York Syracuse NY 1953-1980. "Der Mann heisst Grannan...," *Festschrift f. Christoph Weber*, Verlag Ptr Lang, 2008; "From Tavern to Temple," Cloudbank

Creations, 2005; "Baroness of the Ripetta," Cloudbank Creations, 2004. Bob6010@aol.com

AYERS, Russell Carlton (Mass) 3737 Seminary Rd, Alexandria VA 22304 B Salisbury MD 9/12/1938 s Roger Morris Ayers & Edna. Moody Bible Inst 1961; BA Gordon Coll 1965; MDiv VTS 1970. D 6/20/1970 P 3/18/1971 Bp John Melville Burgess. m 4/23/1988 Margaret McNaughton. Sthrn Afr Info Access Dio Washington Washington DC 1993-1997; Ch Of The Ascen Silver Sprg MD 1988-1991; Dio Washington Washington DC 1987-1997; Dir Life/Wk Plnng Cntr Dio Washington Washington DC 1987-1993; Team Ldr Nyanga Zimbabwe Mssn Proj Dio Massachusetts Boston MA 1986; Team Ldr Nyanga Zimbabwe Mssn Proj Dio Massachusetts Boston MA 1986; Zimbabwe Com Dio Massachusetts Boston MA 1985-1987; R S Mk's Ch Foxborough MA 1973-1987; Cur S Paul's Ch Newburyport MA 1970-1973. Auth, "Your Next Pastorate," *Starting The Search*, 1990. Angl Afr Internet Info Soc; Comp In Wrld Mssn, Washington Dc; Epis Partnership For Global Mssn 1999-2000; Friends Of Zimbabwe. rcayers1234@gmail.com

AYMERICH, Ramon Ignacio (Mass) 3728 Hunters Run Ln, Matthews NC 28105 **Chr Ch Teaneck NJ 2004-** B Havana CU 7/5/1948 s Ramon R Aymerich & Josefina. BA S Johns Vianney Sem 1971; STB Pontifical Gregorian U Rome It 1974; GTS 1984. Rec from Roman Catholic 11/1/1983 Bp Harold B Robinson. m 1/6/1984 Darlene Joy Rodgers c 2. R S Anne's Ch Lowell MA 2004-2008; R S Jas-In-The-Hills Epis Ch Hollywood FL 1999-2003; R Ch Of The H Comf Miami FL 1987-1998; Hisp Mssn Iglesia De Santa Maria Reading PA 1984-1987; Vic S Mary's Epis Ch Reading PA 1984-1987. Cleric Of Year 1976; Af Humanitarian Serv Awd. fatherramon@aol.com

AYRES, Stephen T (Mass) 193 Salem St, Boston MA 02113 **Dn, Boston Harbor Dnry Dio Massachusetts Boston MA 2006-; Vic Old No Chr Ch Boston MA 1997-; Trst of Donations, Chair SRI Com Dio Massachusetts Boston MA 1992-** B Media PA 12/22/1954 s Russell Ayres & Rebecca. BA Ham 1976; MDiv EDS 1980; MA Tufts U 1988. D 6/11/1980 Bp William Grant Black P 12/14/1980 Bp Arthur Anton Vogel. m 10/26/1996 Lisa Reineman c 1. Stndg Com, Pres 2010-2011 Dio Massachusetts Boston MA 2007-2011; R Emm Epis Ch Wakefield MA 1991-1997; S Jn's Ch Charlestown (Boston) Charlestown MA 1990-1991; Int S Jas Ch Amesbury MA 1985-1986; Assoc S Jas Ch Oneonta NY 1982-1985; Chr Epis Ch Springfield MO 1980-1982. stephentayres@gmail.com

AZAR, Antoinette Joann (SO) 6461 Tylersville Rd, West Chester OH 45069 **Common Mnstry Ch Consult Dio Sthrn Ohio Cincinnati OH 2011-; Mem, Common Mnstry Strng Com Dio Sthrn Ohio Cincinnati OH 2009-; Asst R S Anne Epis Ch W Chester OH 2009-** B Washington DC 8/22/1957 d Anthony Joseph Azar & Eleanor Sue. AB Ohio U 1979; MA Ohio U 1983; MDiv Bex 2009. D 6/13/2009 P 6/19/2010 Bp Thomas Edward Breidenthal. m 7/28/2011 George C Ayres c 2. Assoc, CHS 2004. tj.azar@hotmail.com

AZARIAH, Khushnud Mussarat (Los) 6563 East Ave, Etiwanda CA 91739 **Ch Of Our Sav Par San Gabr CA 2010-** B Pakistan 7/25/1949 d JS Qadir Bakhsh & Florence Qadir. MA (Edu) Punjab Coll 1971; BD Trin Theol Coll 1974; PhD Claremont TS 2005. Trans from Anglican Church Of Pakistan 3/4/2010 Bp Joseph Jon Bruno. m 7/14/1978 Samuel Azariah c 3. kazariah123@gmail.com

B

BAAR, David Josef (Haw) PO Box 427, Kula HI 96790 B San Francisco CA 1/31/1937 s Josef Oliver Baar & Erla March. BA U CA 1959; BD CDSP 1962. D 6/24/1962 P 3/2/1963 Bp James Albert Pike. m 10/20/1979 Geri Aughton c 2. S Jn's Epis Ch Kula HI 1999-2004; Assoc S Jn's Epis Ch Kula HI 1981-1991; Chapl To Bp/Chancery Clerk Dio California San Francisco CA 1965-1967; Cur S Andr's Ch Saratoga CA 1962-1965. Bd w dist CDSP Berkeley CA 1962. david@kula.us

BABB, Trevor Roosevelt (SO) 401 Newfield Ave, Bridgeport CT 06607 B BB 12/2/1955 s Stanley Gilkes Babb & Gladys Elise. Barbados Inst of Mgmt and Productivity 1989; Codrington Coll 1989; BA U of The W Indies 1989. Rec 12/31/1992 Bp Andrew Frederick Wissemann. m 7/30/1983 Marcella Yvette c 2. R S Mk's Ch Bridgeport CT 1994-2005; Dio Wstrn Massachusetts Springfield MA 1993-1994; Int S Mary's Epis Ch Thorndike MA 1992-1994. Chapl Grtr Bridgeport UBE; Cleric Vol Goodwill Industries 1995; Med Detox Unit 96-. Ba w hon U Of The W Indies Kingston JM 1989. tbabb71328@aol.com

BABCOCK, Harold Ross Manly (NH) Old Rossier Farms, 238 Rossier Rd., Montgomery Center VT 05471 B Johnson VT 8/29/1938 s William James Verner Babcock & Geraldine Edith. BA Estrn Nazarene Coll 1960; STB EDS 1965; Harv 1972. D 6/26/1965 Bp John Melville Burgess P 5/1/1966 Bp Frederic Cunningham Lawrence. m 5/31/1985 Carolyn Hesterberg. S Mk's Ch Groveton NH 1975-1981; S Paul's Ch Lancaster NH 1975-1981; R Trin Epis Ch Weymouth MA 1968-1972; Asst R Chr Ch Waltham MA 1965-1968.

BABCOCK, Linda Mae (WMo) Saint Anne'S Church, Lebanon MO 65536 B Nampa ID 9/16/1941 d William Charles Anderson & Ethel Ann. S Thos TS; AA Riverside City Coll 1961; BS California St Polytechnic U 1963. D 10/24/1992 Bp William Jerry Winterrowd. S Steph's Epis Ch Aurora CO 1993; Consult CE S Paul's Epis Ch Lakewood CO 1992.

BABCOCK, Lori Hale (Md) Trinity Cathedral, 314 North St, Easton MD 21601 **R S Jn's Ch Mt Washington Baltimore MD 2009-** B York, PA 5/31/1967 BA Goucher Coll 1989; MDiv The GTS 2007. D 6/2/2007 P 12/12/2007 Bp James Joseph Shand. m 7/11/1987 John Babcock c 4. Trin Cathd Easton MD 2007-2009. loribabcock@verizon.net

BABCOCK, Margaret Anderson (Wyo) 4230 S Oak St, Casper WY 82601 B Waterloo IA 7/14/1953 d Karl Clifton Anderson & Margaret Grace. BA S Olaf Coll 1974; MS Minnesota St U Mankato 1978; MDiv SWTS 1980; DMin SWTS 1998. D 6/14/1980 Bp Walter Cameron Righter P 2/14/1981 Bp Joseph Thomas Heistand. m 6/12/1976 Charles Babcock c 2. Cn for Mnstry and Congrl Dvlpmt Dio Wyoming Casper WY 2006-2010; Cn for Congrl Dvlpmt Dio Idaho Boise ID 2001-2006; R Ch Of S Matt Tucson AZ 1991-2000; Vic S Jn's Ch Williams AZ 1985-1989; Asst S Alb's Epis Ch Tucson AZ 1980-1985. Auth, "New Growth in God's Garden," LeaderResources, 2012; Auth, "Rooted in God," LeaderResources, 1992. margaret.babcock@gmail.com

BABCOCK, Mary Kathleen (Kan) 400 E. Maple St, Independence KS 67301 B Independecne KS 3/22/1944 d Gerald Lee Thomas & Mary Irene. BA Kansas St Coll at Emporia 1965; MPhil U of Kansas 1972; JD U of Kansas 1976; MDiv VTS 2010. D 6/6/2009 P 6/5/2010 Bp Dean Elliott Wolfe. vts_mbabcock@vts.edu

BABCOCK, Ted (CPa) 312 Chestnut Circle, Shippensburg PA 17257 **Cn to the Ordnry Dio Cntrl Pennsylvania Harrisburg PA 2010-** B Bronxville NY 7/14/1950 s Henry Nash Babcock & Mary Warner. BA U MI 1973; MA U of Virginia 1974; MBA Harv 1982; MDiv GTS 2001; ThD GTF/Oxf 2009. D 6/9/2001 P 1/19/2002 Bp Andrew Donnan Smith. m 7/2/1988 Lyn C Babcock c 3. R S Andr's Epis Ch Shippensburg PA 2005-2010; Asst to the R Chr Ch Greenwich CT 2001-2005; Intern S Dav's Ch Bronx NY 1998-2001. fathertedbabcock@yahoo.com

BABENKO-LONGHI, Julie (Chi) 1850 Landre Ct, Burlington WI 53105 **D Dio Chicago Chicago IL 2002-** B 11/14/1954 d James A Phipps & Patricia A. BS Nthrn Illinois U 1978; Sch for Deacons 1997. D 2/7/1998 Bp Herbert Alcorn Donovan Jr. m 5/7/2011 Anthony Peter Longhi c 1. S Paul's Ch McHenry IL 1998-2002.

BABIN, Alexander Raymond (Mich) 69440 Brookhill Dr, Romeo MI 48065 **Int Ch Of The H Cross Novi MI 2008-; Int Mnstry Dio Michigan Detroit MI 2002-** B Detroit MI 4/21/1934 s Anthony Raymond Babin & Margaret. BBA U MI 1957; MBA U MI 1963; Cert Whittaker TS 1974; DMin Ecum TS 1994. D 2/12/1972 Bp Archie H Crowley P 5/4/1974 Bp H Coleman McGehee Jr. m 7/9/1984 Linda Marie Heikkinen c 3. Sprtl Dir Curs Dio Michigan Detroit MI 1990-1993; Dep Gc Dio Michigan Detroit MI 1988-1994; Hod Ctte - Stew & Dev Dio Michigan Detroit MI 1988-1994; Mnstry w The Poor Com Dio Michigan Detroit MI 1987-1991; Exec Coun Dio Michigan Detroit MI 1987-1990; Convoc Dn Dio Michigan Detroit MI 1984-1988; Exec Coun Dio Michigan Detroit MI 1980-1983; Dep Gc Dio Michigan Detroit MI 1979-1996; Dio Michigan Detroit MI 1979; St Paul's Epis Romeo MI 1977-2000; Chair COM Dio Michigan Detroit MI 1976-1978; COM Dio Michigan Detroit MI 1974-1978; Asst S Columba Ch Detroit MI 1972-1976. Auth, "Toward Sprtl Wholeness Sprtlty, Recovery & The Ch (Not Pub," *(Dissertation)*, 2003. OHC Assoc 1994. arbabin@comcast.net

BABIN, Alice Elizabeth Duffy (Md) 65 Verde Valley School Rd Apt C-13, Sedona AZ 86351 B New Orleans LO 4/9/1937 d John Watt Duffy & Alice Elizabeth. AA Stephens Coll 1957; LTh SWTS 1975. D 6/6/1975 Bp James Winchester Montgomery P 3/1/1977 Bp Quintin Ebenezer Primo Jr. R S Geo's Epis Ch Mt Savage MD 1996-1998; S Andr's Priory Sch Honolulu HI 1995-1996; R Chr Ch Kealakekua HI 1980-1986; S Lawr Epis Ch Libertyville IL 1977-1978; Dio Chicago Chicago IL 1975-1976; Cur Gr Epis Ch Freeport IL 1975-1976. mainkaiab@aol.com

BABLER, Emmett John (Minn) 9411 E Parkside Dr, Sun Lakes AZ 85248 B Saint Paul MN 11/11/1948 s John Frederic Babler & Margaret Ann. AA Lakewood 1975; BA Metropltn St U 1976; MA Uop 1989. D 8/28/1976 Bp Philip Frederick McNairy. m 3/9/1968 Joan Burnette Stevens c 3. D S Steph's Ch Sierra Vista AZ 1982-1984; D S Mich's All Ang Ch Monticello MN 1978-1982; Asst Ch Of The H Apos S Paul MN 1977-1978.

BABNIS, Mariann C (WA) 2907 S Columbus St, Arlington VA 22206 B Sharon PA 8/8/1957 BA Clarion U of Pennsylvania 1979; MA Ohio U, Athens, OH 1980; M DIV VTS 2004. D 6/12/2004 P 1/22/2005 Bp John Chane. S Paul's Ch Georgetown DE 2010-2011; S Mary's Epis Ch Pocomoke City MD 2009-2010; H Trin Epis Ch Bowie MD 2005-2008. mbabnis@comcast.net

BABSON, Katharine E (Me) 149 Pennellville Rd, Brunswick ME 04011 **P-in-c St Mths Epis Ch Richmond ME 2010-** B Boston MA 6/8/1950 d Roger Rushmore Earle & Edith. Vas 1970; BA Wms 1972; MDiv VTS 1992; DMin Wesley TS 2009. D 6/13/1992 Bp Robert Poland Atkinson P 12/1/1992 Bp

Peter James Lee. m 8/5/1972 Bradley Ogden Babson c 2. Epis Ch Of S Mary The Vrgn Falmouth ME 2005; S Ptr's Epis Ch Arlington VA 1997-2000; S Geo's Epis Ch Arlington VA 1992. Auth, "The Prov of Myanmar (Burma)," *The Oxford Guide to BCP*, Oxf Press, 2006; Auth, "Preaching and the Film Jesus of Montreal," *The Evang Outlook Vol 29 #4*, EvangES, 1992. EPGM 2001-2011; SCWM 2003-2009. katharine.babson@gmail.com

BACAGAN, Magdaleno K (Los) 225 W Linfield St, Glendora CA 91740 B La Union PH 9/29/1932 s Pedro Bacagan & Benita. Jerusalem St Geo's Sum Sch; ThB S Andr's TS Manila Ph 1958; BA U of The Philippines 1959; VTS 1972; Cbury Sum Sch, Engl 1983; S Geo's Coll, Jerusalem 1985; MDiv S Andr's TS 1987. D 8/10/1958 Bp Lyman Cunningham Ogilby P 8/1/1959 Bp Benito C Cabanban. Ch Of The H Comm Gardena CA 1983-1998; Vic Dio California San Francisco CA 1983-1998; Vic Dio Los Angeles Los Angeles CA 1983-1998; Treas & Mgr, Treas's Off Dio Los Angeles Los Angeles CA 1979-1982; Asst R & P in Charge Ch Of The Atone Washington DC 1972-1978; Assoc Dio Washington Washington DC 1972-1978.

BACHAND-WOOD, Colette (Mass) 16 Highland Ave., Cohasset MA 02025 B New Bedford MA 2/25/1966 d Richard Bachand & Barbara. BS Emerson Coll; MDiv EDS 2008. D 6/7/2008 Bp M(arvil) Thomas Shaw III P 1/10/2009 Bp Roy Frederick Cederholm Jr. m 8/12/1989 Russell Wood c 2. Asst S Steph's Ch Cohasset MA 2008-2009. cwood@ststephenscohasset.org

BACHMANN, Douglas P (Cal) 419 Orchard View Ave, Martinez CA 94553 B New Brunswick NJ 1/15/1949 s Nicholas Jacob Bachmann & Muriel Joyce. BA Amer U 1971; W&M 1972; PDS 1974; MDiv GTS 1975; GTS 1985; MA Jn F. Kennedy U 2001. D 4/26/1975 Bp Albert Wiencke Van Duzer P 1/31/1976 Bp Gray Temple. m 1/3/1976 Dawn Robertson. Assoc R Ch Of The Resurr Pleasant Hill CA 2001-2007; R S Jn's Epis Ch Mankato MN 1995-1997; R Chr Ch Austin MN 1990-1995; Int Chr Ch Red Wing MN 1988-1989; Int Ch Of The H Apos S Paul MN 1987-1988; R S Jas On The Pkwy Minneapolis MN 1985-1986; P S Anne's By The Fields Ankeny IA 1979-1984; Asst R Trin Ch Myrtle Bch SC 1975-1977. doug_bachmann@att.net

BACHSCHMID, Edward Karl (RG) 9024 N Congress St, New Market VA 22844 **D Emm Ch Harrisonburg VA 2006-** B Washington DC 8/18/1940 D 6/19/2004 Bp John Herbert MacNaughton. m 8/22/1964 Judith K Pringle c 2. D S Jas' Epis Ch Mesilla Pk NM 2004-2006. edbachschmid@aol.com

BACIGALUPO, Joseph Andrew (ECR) 1343 Wylie Way, San Jose CA 95130 B Jersey City NJ 6/29/1931 D 9/27/1972 Bp George Richard Millard P 7/1/1981 Bp Charles Shannon Mallory.

BACK, George Henry (Okla) 2520 NW 59 St, Oklahoma City OK 73112 **Dep to GC Dio Oklahoma Oklahoma City OK 2006-** B New York NY 5/3/1942 s George Frederick Back & Grace. BA Bard Coll 1964; STB GTS 1967. D 6/17/1967 P 12/1/1967 Bp Jonathan Goodhue Sherman. m 9/30/1967 Margaret Andrews c 3. Dn S Paul's Cathd Oklahoma City OK 1982-2010; Cn Cathd Ch Of S Lk Orlando FL 1979-1982; R Chr Memi Ch No Brookfield MA 1971-1979; Cur S Jn's Ch Portsmouth NH 1967-1971. Auth, "Christmas Joy: Let Heaven & Nature Sing," *Bk*, Sprt & Intelligence Press, 2007; Bk Revs, "Uncertainty: The Life & Sci of Werner Heisenberg," *CTNS Bulletin*, Cntr for Theol & the Natural Sciences, 1993. Bp's Awd Dio Oklahoma 2006. geoback@mac.com

BACK, Nathaniel (NwT) 602 Meander St, Abilene TX 79602 **Ch Of The Heav Rest Abilene TX 2010-** B Ware MA 7/7/1972 s George Henry Arthur Back & Margaret Andrews. BA U of Oklahoma 1995; MEd U of Oklahoma 1999; MDiv VTS 2002. D 6/29/2002 P 1/11/2003 Bp Robert Manning Moody. m 6/1/2002 Meredith B Bishop c 3. S Paul's Cathd Oklahoma City OK 2002-2010. lback@heavenlyrestabilene.org

BACKLUND, Michael Anders (Cal) 10449 Oak Valley Rd, Angels Camp CA 95222 **Assoc S Paul's Epis Ch Sacramento CA 2005-** B San Bernardino CA 3/13/1951 s James William Backlund & Dorothy Mae. BA U of San Diego 1973; MS U of San Diego 1975; MDiv S Pat's Sem Menlo Pk CA 1979; PhD Palo Alto U 1990. Rec from Roman Catholic 6/1/1981 as Deacon Bp William Arthur Dimmick. m 7/5/2008 Daniel T Brower. Assoc Trin Ch San Francisco CA 1992-2003; Assoc Gr Cathd San Francisco CA 1987-1990; Asst S Phil's Ch San Jose CA 1985-1986; Asst All SS Epis Ch Palo Alto CA 1982-1984; Vic Chr Ch Calumet Laurium MI 1981-1982. Auth, "Faith & AIDS: Life Crisis as a Stimulus to Faith Stage Transition," *Dissertation Abstracts*, 1990. Fell ECF 1984. backlund@scientist.com

BACKSTRAND, Brian E (Mil) 804 E Juneau Ave, Milwaukee WI 53202 **Vic Dio Milwaukee Milwaukee WI 2008-; S Andr's Epis Ch Monroe WI 2008-** B Tacoma WA 3/24/1945 s Samuel Edward Backstrand & Esther Marie. BA Carleton Coll 1967; MDiv No Pk TS 1971; MA U of Wisconsin 1973; DS Seabury Wstrn TS 2008. D 6/26/2008 P 1/3/2009 Bp Steven Andrew Miller. m 6/21/1969 Marilee Backstrand c 3. bcbackstra@aol.com

BACKUS, Brett Paul (ETenn) The Episcopal Church of the Ascension, 800 S. Northshore Drive, Knoxville TN 37919 **Asst to the R Ch Of The Ascen Knoxville TN 2008-** B Knoxville TN 6/26/1981 s Paul Roger Backus & Ann Drucilla. BA U of Tennessee 2004; MDiv VTS 2008. D 5/31/2008 P 1/17/2009 Bp Charles Glenn VonRosenberg. m 7/2/2005 Carla Chavez Torrez c 2. brett@knoxvilleascension.org

BACKUS, Howard G (NC) 600 South Central Avenue, Laurel DE 19956 **R S Phil's Ch Laurel DE 2008-** B Richwood WV 5/6/1947 s Arthur Grose Backus & Marilee Verta. BA W Virginia Wesleyan Coll 1969; Duke DS 1971; MDiv VTS 1973; DMin VTS 1999; CE Cntr for Congrl Hlth 2007. D 6/5/1972 P 2/16/1973 Bp Wilburn Camrock Campbell. m 6/1/1968 Sue Ann Heitz c 3. Int S Thos Epis Ch Reidsville NC 2007-2008; R S Tim's Epis Ch Winston Salem NC 1990-2007; S Steph's Epis Ch Beckley WV 1978-1990; Asst H Trin Par Epis Clemson SC 1975-1978; Vic Ascen Epis Ch Hinton WV 1973-1975. Laurel Mnstrl Assn 2008; YCORE Partnership for Int Mnstry 2007. Doctor Of Mnstry VTS Alexandria VA 1999. revbackus@gmail.com

BACKUS, John Harlow (NY) 300 Hiddendale Rd, Quilcene WA 98376 **Died 9/19/2009** B Wagner SD 7/25/1938 s William Edward Backus & Joyce Margaret. BA Gri 1960; BD CDSP 1965; U of Oxford 1973. D 6/29/1965 P 3/23/1966 Bp Ivol I Curtis. Auth, "Archbp Lang & The Orth," 1973. Sub-Chapl Ord Of S Jn Jerusalem 1990. Archpriest'S Cross Patriarch Of Constantinople 1994; Archpriest'S Cross Patriarch Of Moscow 1993; Grand Cross Of The Great Ch In Constantinople Ecum Patriarch 1975. nevsky40@mac.com

BACKUS, Timothy Warren (CGC) PO Box 12683, Pensacola FL 32591 **Chr Ch Par Pensacola FL 2009-** B Beckley WVA 3/29/1981 s Howard G Backus & Sue Ann. BM Appalachian St U; BS Appalachian St U 2005; MDiv VTS 2009. D 6/13/2009 Bp Michael Bruce Curry P 1/29/2011 Bp Duncan Montgomery Gray III. tbackus22@hotmail.com

BACON JR, J(ames) Edwin (Los) 132 N Euclid Ave, Pasadena CA 91101 **R All SS Ch Pasadena CA 1995-** B Jesup GA 2/14/1948 s James Edwin Bacon & Nancy Ellen. BA Merc 1969; MA Candler TS Emory U 1979. D 6/12/1982 P 5/1/1983 Bp Bennett Jones Sims. m 2/14/1971 Mary Hope Hendricks c 2. Dn S Andr's Cathd Jackson MS 1989-1995; R S Mk's Ch Dalton GA 1984-1989; S Lk's Epis Ch Atlanta GA 1982-1984; Dio Atlanta Atlanta GA 1982-1983. Soc Of S Jn The Evang. Cler Ldrshp Proj 1992. ebacon@allsaints-pas.org

BACON, Lynne Lazier (Neb) 719 Crestridge Rd, Omaha NE 68154 **D All SS Epis Ch Omaha NE 1993-** B Denver CO 4/28/1946 d Harry Austin Lazier & Genevieve Elaine. BA Colorado Coll 1968; MS U of Nebraska 1982. D 9/25/1993 Bp James Edward Krotz. m 8/9/1968 W Meredith Bacon. lynnebacon@cox.net

BADDERS JR, John David (WTex) 11 Saint Lukes Ln, San Antonio TX 78209 **S Lk's Epis Ch San Antonio TX 2010-** B San Antonio TX 12/14/1950 s John David Badders & Ruby Lee. BBA Texas Tech U 1973; MDiv STUSo 1996. D 6/18/1996 Bp Robert Boyd Hibbs P 2/14/1997 Bp James Edward Folts. m 6/4/2011 Christine Welsh c 2. R S Jn's Ch McAllen TX 2000-2010; R S Fran By The Lake Canyon Lake TX 1996-2000. badders1969@gmail.com

BADER-SAYE, Demery Letisha (Be) 334 Knapp Rd, Clarks Summit PA 18411 B Albuquerque NM 5/23/1971 BA U of Nthrn Colorado. D 4/20/2004 P 10/31/2004 Bp Paul Victor Marshall. m 12/22/1996 Scott C Bader-Saye c 4. Dio Bethlehem Bethlehem PA 2004-2009. dbader-saye@diobeth.org

BADGLEY, David Grayum (Nwk) 10130 Douglas Oaks Cir, Apt 101, Tampa FL 33610 B Saint Petersburg FL 1/17/1941 s Charles G Badgley & Florida Rose. AA S Petersburg Jr Coll 1977; BA U of So Florida 1989; MDiv STUSo 1992. D 6/13/1992 P 3/27/1993 Bp Rogers Sanders Harris. m 11/25/1966 Josephine E Firlotte c 2. R S Mary's Ch Haledon NJ 1998-2003; Asst for Yth Mnstry Dio Bethlehem Bethlehem PA 1997-1998; Asst The Epis Ch Of The Medtr Allentown PA 1993-1996; Cur S Steph's Ch New Port Richey FL 1992-1993. dbadgley1@juno.com

BAER, Kenneth Fogle (Nwk) 142 Exeter Ct, Hendersonville NC 28791 **Died 1/24/2011** B Somerset PA 6/22/1917 s Henry W Baer & Evora H. BA Franklin & Marshall Coll 1940; GTS 1965. D 7/11/1964 Bp George E Rath P 5/1/1965 Bp Leland Stark. c 3. kfbaer@bellsouth.net

BAER, Kirsten Herndon (Okla) 4250 W Houston St, Broken Arrow OK 74012 **Cur S Pat's Epis Ch Broken Arrow OK 2011-** B Oklahoma City OK 11/6/1983 d Christopher Michael Herndon & Karen Shotwell. BA U of Oklahoma 2006; MEd U of Oklahoma 2008; MDiv VTS 2011. D 1/22/2011 P 7/23/2011 Bp Edward Joseph Konieczny. m 8/11/2007 Timothy Christopher Baer c 1. kbaer11@gmail.com

BAER, Susan Shellman (Md) 708 5th Ave, Williamsport PA 17701 B Frederick MD 9/22/1946 d Malcolm Baer & Mary Jane. BA Bethany Coll 1968; AA Columbus Coll Mntl Hlth 1977; Med Georgia St U 1981; MDiv VTS 1990. D 6/9/1990 P 5/12/1991 Bp Frank Kellogg Allan. m 5/19/2007 Dennis L Shoemaker. H Cross Ch St MD 2009-2011; S Mary's Ch Williamsport PA 2006-2008; Gleam Williamsport PA 2003-2005; S Andr's Lawrenceville VA 1997-2002; R S Mich And All Ang Knoxville TN 1997-2002; Asst S Andr's Lawrenceville VA 1994-1997; Dio Atlanta Atlanta GA 1991-1993; Assoc S Steph's Ch Milledgeville GA 1991-1993; Asst S Barth's Epis Ch Atlanta GA 1990-1991. shellman2@verizon.net

BAER, Timothy Christopher (Okla) 2623 N Van Dorn St Apt 202, Alexandria VA 22302 **S Jn's Epis Ch Tulsa OK 2011-** B Waterbury CT 5/16/1985 s Henry Clinton Baer & Heather Haniotis. BA U of Oklahoma 2007; MDiv VTS

2011. D 1/22/2011 P 7/23/2011 Bp Edward Joseph Konieczny. m 8/11/2007 Kirsten Herndon c 1. tbaer07@gmail.com

BAER, Walter Jacob (La) 3700 Canal St, New Orleans LA 70119 B Monroe WI 5/30/1954 s Walter Baer & Helen. Columbia TS; U of Karlsruhe DE 1975; BS U of Wisconsin 1979; MDiv Nash 1985. D 3/30/1985 P 10/28/1985 Bp Roger John White. c 2. All SS Epis Ch River Ridge LA 2008-2009; S Mart's Epis Sch Metairie LA 2008-2009; R Gr Ch New Orleans LA 2003-2008; R S Thos' Ch Monroe LA 1996-2003; Dio Wstrn Louisiana Alexandria LA 1990-2003; Cn to the Ordnry Dio Wstrn Louisiana Alexandria LA 1990-1996; Liturg Cmsn Dio Wstrn Louisiana Alexandria LA 1989-1996; Asst S Mk's Cathd Shreveport LA 1985-1990. ADLMC 1989-1996; CODE 1990-1996. MDiv cl Nash Nashotah WI 1985. wbaer85@aol.com

BAETZ III, Bertrand Oliver (Tex) 2128 Barton Hills Dr, Austin TX 78704 **S Mk's Epis Ch Richmond TX 2011-** B San Antonio TX 2/2/1979 s Bertrand Oliver Baetz & Marie Elizabeth Ibarra. BA U of Texas 2001; MDiv Duke DS 2005; Dplma in Theol Stds Epis TS of the SW 2008. D 6/28/2008 P 2/10/2009 Bp Don Adger Wimberly. m 12/22/2007 Sarah Bass Sarah Elizabeth Bass c 1. Cur S Mk's Ch Austin TX 2008-2011. sarahbaetz@gmail.com

BAGAY, Martin John (At) 608 Bay Laurel Cir, Warner Robins GA 31088 **R All SS Ch Warner Robins GA 2007-** B Donora PA 3/4/1950 s Andrew Bagay & Anne. BA Duquesne U 1972; Pittsburgh TS 1974; MDiv EDS 1978; VTS 1986. D 6/3/1978 Bp Robert Bracewell Appleyard P 12/4/1978 Bp John Harris Burt. m 4/13/1991 Katherine Lee Elder c 3. Chr Ch Charlotte NC 2005-2006; R S Mk's Epis Ch Huntersville NC 2002-2005; R S Mary's Ch Sparta NJ 1998-2002; Assoc/Coll Chapl Bruton Par Williamsburg VA 1990-1998; Off Of Bsh For ArmdF New York NY 1987-1990; Assoc Gr Epis Ch Sandusky OH 1982-1984; R Trin Ch New Philadelphia OH 1980-1982; Assoc S Mart's Ch Chagrin Falls OH 1978-1980. bagaym@cbi.mgacoxmail.com

BAGBY, D.Ray (Tex) PO Box 510, Cameron TX 76520 **Vic All SS Ch Cameron TX 2009-** B Richmond VA 11/13/1941 s Thomas Durwood Bagby & Mary D. BS US Mltry Acad 1963; MBA U of So Carolina-Columbia 1981; PhD U of So Carolina-Columbia 1983. D 6/20/2009 Bp C(harles) Andrew Doyle P 1/22/2010 Bp Dena Arnall Harrison. m 7/16/1985 Janet Hall c 1. ray_bagby@sbcglobal.net

BAGBY, John B. (Ala) 3516 Country Club Road, Birmingham, AL 35213 **P-in-c Ch Of The Mssh Heflin AL 2010-** B Birmingham AL 8/27/1949 s Arthur P Bagby & Anna Eleanor. BA U of Alabama 1973; MDiv VTS 1990. D 6/14/1990 P 12/1/1990 Bp Robert Oran Miller. m 8/19/1972 Nancy Hamilton c 2. Int H Comf Ch Gadsden AL 2008-2009; S Mk's Ch Prattville AL 2004-2005; S Mths Epis Ch Tuscaloosa AL 2003-2004; Ch Of The Nativ Epis Huntsville AL 2002-2003; R All SS Epis Ch Birmingham AL 1999-2002; R S Paul's Ch Selma AL 1994-1999; R Gr Ch Cullman AL 1991-1994; Asst St Thos Epis Ch Huntsville AL 1990-1991. bagman8@bellsouth.net

BAGGETT, Edward Allen (Dal) 176 CR 1309, Pittsburg TX 75686 B Fort Worth TX 11/22/1946 s Edward Elisha Baggett & May Rutherford. Cor; BA U of Houston 1970; MDiv TESM 1995. D 11/26/1995 P 6/6/1996 Bp Robert Deane Rowley Jr. m 2/9/1985 Dorothy C Cloughly c 2. S Fran Ch Winnsboro TX 2010; Vic All SS Ch Atlanta TX 2003-2005; P-in-c S Wm Laud Epis Ch Pittsburg TX 2002-2006; R S Jn's Epis Ch Corsicana TX 1998-2002; Asst S Jas Epis Ch Alexandria LA 1996-1998. dottie603blanton@suddenlink.net

BAGGETT, Greenfield Marion (Spok) 103 Colonial Dr, Vicksburg MS 39180 B Vicksburg MS 6/3/1944 s Greenfield Marion Baggett & Frances. Mississippi St U; BA U of Virginia 1966. D 1/4/1997 Bp Alfred Clark Marble Jr P 6/9/2007 Bp James Edward Waggoner. m 2/1/1975 Sandra Claire Wade.

BAGLEY, Robert Chambers (Mil) 4701 Erie St, Racine WI 53402 B Washington DC 6/23/1943 s Francis H Bagley & Betty L. BS U of Maryland 1968; MS Stritch U 1983. D 6/5/2010 Bp Steven Andrew Miller. m 2/14/1993 Judith Frahm c 3. rbagley43@wi.rr.com

BAGUER II, Miguel A (SeFla) 300 Sunrise Dr Apt 1b, Key Biscayne FL 33149 **D S Chris's By-The-Sea Epis Ch Key Biscayne FL 2004-; Trin Cathd Bk and Gift Miami FL 2003-** B Havana Cuba 6/17/1934 s Miguel Baguer & Gertrudis. BA U of Havana Havana CU 1955. D 11/6/2004 Bp Leopold Frade. Trin Cathd Miami FL 2004-2008. kbdeaconmiguel@aol.com

BAGUYOS, Avelino T (Kan) PO Box 40222, Overland Park KS 66204 B Rosario La Union PH 12/5/1938 s Gabriel Galapa Baguyos & Rosenda. U of The Philippines 1964; BTh cl S Andr's TS Manila PH 1965; BA U of The Philippines 1972; MDiv S Andr's TS Manila PH 1973; Full Certification S Lk's Hosp Houston TX 1980. D 10/19/1965 P 4/25/1966 Bp Benito C Cabanban. m 10/5/1967 Erlinda C Castro c 2. R S Chris's Epis Ch Wichita KS 2002-2006; Vic-R S Chris's Epis Ch Wichita KS 1996-2000; LocTens S Chris's Epis Ch Wichita KS 1993-1995; Assoc Chapl/CPE Supvsr St Lk's Chap Kansas City MO 1978-1988; Asst S Barth's Ch Corpus Christi TX 1978; P-in-c Dio Cntrl Philippines 1965-1977. Assn of CPE 1976; Coll of Chapl 1985-1995; Comp Worker Sis of H Sprt 1978-1989. abaguyos@sbcglobal.net

BAGWELL BSG, Robert Randall McDonald (Mass) 81 Seaver St, Stoughton MA 02072 B Greenville SC 7/4/1958 s Robert Alfred Bagwell & Carolyn. BA Furman U 1982; MDiv Duke 1985. D 8/14/1987 Bp William L Stevens P 10/18/1988 Bp William George Burrill. R Trin Epis Ch Stoughton MA 1998-2009; R S Anne Of Gr Epis Ch Seminole FL 1993-1998; Int Gd Samar Epis Ch Clearwater FL 1992-1993; Cur All SS Ch Tarpon Sprg FL 1988-1992; All SS' Epis Ch Chevy Chase MD 1987-1988; Asst H Cross Faith Memi Epis Ch Pawleys Island SC 1987; Asst S Cyp's Epis Ch Georgetown SC 1987. Assn Shrine Of Our Lady Of Walsingham; Bro Of S Greg; Conf Of Blessed Sacr; Ord S Vinc; Soc Of S Jn The Evang, SocMary. naurya@aol.com

BAHLOW, Harold (ETenn) 121 Violet Ln, Bluff City TN 37618 B Windsor Ontario CA 6/24/1935 s Norman Herman Bahlow & Olive Josephine. BA Sacr Heart Sem Detroit MI 1958; STM St. Jn's Prov Sem Plymouth MI 1962; MS Nova U 1983. Rec from Roman Catholic 2/5/1995 Bp Calvin Onderdonk Schofield Jr. m 10/15/1988 Arnetta Massa. S Barth's Ch Bristol TN 2000-2007; P S Columba's Epis Ch Bristol TN 2000-2007; S Mary Magd Ch Fayetteville TN 2000-2007; R S Thos Ch Elizabethton TN 2000-2007; R S Jn's Epis Ch S Johns MI 1998-2000; Sunday Supply P Dio Cntrl Gulf Coast Pensacola FL 1997-1998; Dio E Tennessee Knoxville TN 1995. habah88@cs.com

BAILEY, Anne Cox (Cal) 1944 Tice Valley Blvd., Walnut Creek CA 94595 B Glendale GA 5/21/1953 d Arthur Thomas Cox & Elizabeth Arlene. BA Jn F. Kennedy U 1997; MDiv CDSP 2001. D 6/3/2001 P 12/1/2001 Bp William Edwin Swing. m 8/31/1985 Henry Mayberry Bailey c 1. R S Lk's Ch Walnut Creek CA 2007-2010; Int R S Aug's Ch Oakland CA 2004-2005. "The Great Dance Of Life," *Mod Profiles Of An Ancient Faith*, Dio Of. California, 2001. ponderanew@gmail.com

BAILEY, Audrey Veronica (NY) 777 E 222nd St, Bronx NY 10467 **S Lk's Epis Ch Bronx NY 2010-** B Jamaica 3/13/1957 Dplma in Mnstry Stds The Untd Theol Coll in the W Indies 1993; BA The U of the W Indies 1993. Trans from Church in the Province Of The West Indies 11/10/2010 as Priest Bp Mark Sean Sisk. audrey_bailey@hotmail.com

BAILEY, B(ertram) Cass (Va) 1042 Preston Ave, Charlottesville VA 22903 **Vic Trin Epis Ch Charlottesville VA 2010-** B New York NY 5/1/1960 s James Bailey & Lena. BA Amh 1982; Cert Ya Berk 1995; M.Div Yale DS 1995. D 6/3/1995 Bp Barbara Clementine Harris P 6/9/1996 Bp Alexander Doig Stewart. m 5/6/1995 Patricia V Polgar c 2. R S Chris's Ch Kailua HI 1998-2010; Dio Wstrn Massachusetts Springfield MA 1997-1998; Asst R S Paul And S Jas New Haven CT 1996-1998; Dir Yth Theater Proj Trin Epis Ch Hartford CT 1995-1998. cass@pastor.com

BAILEY, Brian Robert (Cal) PO Box 93703, Pasadena CA 91109 B Bay City MI 11/30/1946 s Robert W Bailey & Miriam M. MDiv CDSP; BA U CA; ThM Fuller TS 1986; PhD Fuller TS 1999. D 6/26/1971 P 1/1/1972 Bp C Kilmer Myers. P Prince Of Peace Epis Ch Woodland Hills CA 2003-2010; S Jude's Epis Par Burbank CA 1986-1990; P-in-c S Barn' Par Pasadena CA 1986; Asst S Jude's Epis Par Burbank CA 1984-1985. Hon Cn The Most Rev M Bernherm Old Cath Cultured 2000. bailey-brian@att.net

BAILEY, Charles James (Lex) No address on file. B 5/2/1926 D 6/14/1956 P 12/27/1956 Bp William R Moody.

BAILEY, David Bruce (SO) 9097 Cascara Dr, West Chester OH 45069 **R S Steph's Epis Ch Cincinnati OH 2003-** B Cincinnati OH 10/4/1951 s Samuel Jett Bailey & Virginia Edith. BS Mia 1973; PhD U of So Carolina 1980; MDiv Untd TS Dayton OH 2001. D 6/24/2000 P 1/6/2001 Bp Herbert Thompson Jr. m 8/16/1986 Mary S Saunders c 2. The Epis Ch Of The Ascen Middletown OH 2000-2002. revdbb@aol.com

✠ **BAILEY, Rt Rev David Earle** (NAM) PO Box 3090, Salt Lake City UT 84110 **Bp of Navajoland Navajoland Area Mssn Farmington NM 2010-** B Canton OH 3/30/1940 s Frank J Bailey & Evelyn G. Glendale Cmnty Coll; DST Epis TS of The SW 1979; MDiv Epis TS of The SW 1991; BA Ottawa U 1991; DMin U Of Creation Sprtlty Oakland CA 2001. D 6/24/1979 P 2/10/1980 Bp Joseph Thomas Heistand Con 8/7/2010 for NAM. m 5/20/1963 Anne Jordan c 3. Cn to Ordnry Dio Utah Salt Lake City UT 2002-2006; GC Dep Dio Utah Salt Lake City UT 2000-2009; Cn Mssnr/Deploy Off Dio Utah Salt Lake City UT 1998-2001; Bp's Dep to C-14 Dio Arizona Phoenix AZ 1989-1993; Chair Native Amer Mnstrs Com Dio Arizona Phoenix AZ 1988-1993; Co-Chair Camp/Conf Cntr Dio Arizona Phoenix AZ 1988-1991; Cmsn On Campus Mnstry Dio Arizona Phoenix AZ 1988-1990; T/F On Human Sxlty Dio Arizona Phoenix AZ 1986-1989; Bp's Dep to C-14 Dio Arizona Phoenix AZ 1986-1988; Chair Action Com Dio Arizona Phoenix AZ 1985-1991; Pres Epis Cmnty Serv Dio Arizona Phoenix AZ 1985-1990; Fin Com Dio Arizona Phoenix AZ 1984-1991; Dio Arizona Phoenix AZ 1984-1985; Exec Coun Dio Arizona Phoenix AZ 1983-1991; Bd Trst Epis Cmnty Serv Dio Arizona Phoenix AZ 1981-1990; Sprtl Dir Curs Dio Arizona Phoenix AZ 1981-1984; S Steph's Ch Phoenix AZ 1979-1998; Dn Jr High Camp Dio Arizona Phoenix AZ 1979-1992; Chair Cmsn On Alcosm & Drug Abuse Dio Arizona Phoenix AZ 1979-1984. dbailey@ec-n.org

BAILEY III, Douglass Moxley (NC) 235 Fairfax Dr, Winston Salem NC 27104 B Clarksburg WV 5/29/1938 BA Wake Forest U. D 6/11/1964 P 12/1/1964 Bp Wilburn Camrock Campbell. Calv Ch Lombard IL 2000-2003; Calv Ch

Memphis TN 1978-2002; S Jn's Par Hagerstown MD 1972-1978. Auth, "Little Scraps Of Wonder"; Auth, "From Ashes To Alleluia". DD VTS. baileydm@wfu.edu

BAILEY, Edwin Pearson (NC) Po Box 2001, Southern Pines NC 28388 B Aldie VA 5/7/1928 s William Otis Bailey & Mary Hardin. BA U of Virginia 1950; MDiv VTS 1955; Fell VTS 1977; Coll of Preachers 1979; Tchr Skills Inst 1982; Sm Ch Ldrshp Conf 1999. D 6/3/1955 Bp Frederick D Goodwin P 6/16/1956 Bp Robert Fisher Gibson Jr. m 3/24/1951 Anne Herrigel c 3. Vic Ch Of The Ascen At Fork Advance NC 1988-2000; Vic Ch Of The Gd Shpd Cooleemee NC 1988-2000; CFS The Sch At Ch Farm Exton PA 1986-1988; S Jn's Ch Winnsboro SC 1984-1986; R S Paul's Epis Ch Smithfield NC 1980-1983; S Fran Epis Ch Great Falls VA 1975-1980; Asst S Jn's Epis Ch McLean VA 1975-1980; Cmsn on Evang Dio Rhode Island Providence RI 1972-1975; R S Geo's Ch Portsmouth RI 1965-1975; Asst Min Chr Ch Greenwich CT 1959-1965; Vic S Barn Epis Ch Greenwich CT 1959-1965; S Jn's Ch W Hartford CT 1956-1959; R S Jn's Ch Warsaw VA 1956-1957. No Carolina Epis Cler Assn 1980-1983; No Carolina Epis Cler Assn 1988. abailey2033@nc.rr.com

BAILEY, Gregory Bruce (Alb) Trinity Episcopal Church, 30 Park St, Gouverneur NY 13642 **D Vic Trin Ch Gouverneur NY 2007-** B Gouverneur NY 9/2/1952 s Bruce Bailey & Verda. D 6/10/2006 Bp Daniel William Herzog. m 3/22/1974 Trudy Jean Fairbanks c 2. Bgregbailey@hotmail.com

BAILEY, Jefferson Moore (Az) PO Box 492, Tucson AZ 85702 **D S Andr's Epis Ch Tucson AZ 2006-** B Schenectady NY 12/4/1944 s Claude Bailey & Martha. BA U of So Carolina 1967. D 10/14/2006 Bp Kirk Stevan Smith. m 5/2/2007 Richard Steen c 1. jbailey@saaf.org

BAILEY, Kermit Marshall (NC) No address on file. **Died 5/28/2010** B Davie County NC 4/13/1936 s Paul Clyde Bailey & Thelma Juanita. BA Guilford Coll 1980; Dioc Of No Carolina Deacons Trng Prog Durham NC 1988. D 10/12/1988 Bp Robert Whitridge Estill. c 2. Ord Of S Lk; Soc Of S Fran; Third Ord Franciscan.

BAILEY, Marjean (NH) 21 Kings Ln, Kennebunkport ME 04046 B Pittsburgh PA 12/13/1929 d Peter Linn & Emily. Cert Perceptual Lrng Consult; Cert Psychosynthesis Ther; BA Alleg 1951; MDiv UTS 1954. D 5/9/1981 P 5/1/1982 Bp H Coleman McGehee Jr. m 5/22/1954 John Amadee Bailey. COM Dio New Hampshire Concord NH 1994-2000; Dioc Coun Dio New Hampshire Concord NH 1989-1993; Vic S Ptr's Epis Ch Londonderry NH 1987-2001; Dio New Hampshire Concord NH 1986-1993; Chair Educ Com Dio New Hampshire Concord NH 1986-1990; Assoc Par Of Chr Ch Andover MA 1982-1986; S Andr's Epis Ch Flint MI 1982; Cur S Andr's Epis Ch Flint MI 1981-1982. Cert Perceptual Lrng Consult; Cert Psychosynthesis Ther. Cert Psychosynthesis Ther. mlb1331@roadrunner.com

BAILEY, Noel Ahlbum (WMass) St. Paul's Church, 113 Main St., Lancaster NH 03584 B Providence RI 12/20/1941 d Sumner Plant Ahlbum & Elizabeth Ann. Rhode Island Sch of Design 1963; MDiv EDS 1986; Cert Ldrshp Acad for New Directions 1995; Berkshire Cmnty Coll 2004; Cler Ldrshp Inst; Appreciative Inquiry 2008; Cler Ldrshp Inst; Mng Change 2008. D 6/11/1988 Bp David Elliot Johnson P 5/26/1989 Bp George Nelson Hunt III. c 2. Int S Paul's Ch Lancaster NH 2008-2011; Int All SS Epis Ch Littleton NH 2007-2008; P-in-c The Chap Of All SS Leominster MA 2005-2007; Mem, Stndg Com Dio Wstrn Massachusetts Springfield MA 2001-2007; R S Geo's Ch Lee MA 1997-2005; Mem, Dioc Coun Dio Albany Albany NY 1993-1997; P-in-c Trin And S Mich's Ch Albany NY 1991-1997; Gvrng Bd Dio Rhode Island Providence RI 1988-1990; Asst S Mich's Ch Bristol RI 1988-1990. FVC 1991. baiey@juno.com

BAILEY, Patricia Ann (RI) 1357 Wampanoag Trl, Apt 130, Riverside RI 02915 B Cleveland OH 3/1/1929 d William Ramsey & Thelma. OH SU; BA Case Wstrn Reserve U 1951; MLS U of Rhode Island 1972. D 6/24/1995 Bp J Clark Grew II. c 2. D S Thos Ch Greenville RI 1999-2001; D Ch Of The Mssh Providence RI 1995-1999. deaconpat2@verizon.net

BAILEY, Paul Calvin (Alb) 320 Henry St, Herkimer NY 13350 **R Chr Ch Herkimer NY 2002-** B Utica NY 6/10/1947 s Edwin Forest Bailey & Nancy. Le Moyne Coll; AOS Cntrl City Bus Inst 1977; BA SUNY 1992; MDiv TESM 1997. D 6/11/1997 P 2/7/1998 Bp David B(ruce) Joslin. m 10/18/1975 Patricia Ann Shandorf c 3. Trin Ch Lowville NY 1999-2002; Trin Memi Ch Binghamton NY 1997-1999. pbailey2@twcny.rr.com

BAILEY, Pauline Rose (Alb) 15 Richards Ave, Oneonta NY 13820 B Oneonta NY 3/11/1955 D 6/12/2004 Bp Daniel William Herzog. c 2.

BAILEY, Paul Milton (La) Po Box 1086, Hammond LA 70404 **R Gr Memi Hammond LA 1999-** B Fort Worth TX 6/21/1954 s George Milton Bailey & Stella Faye. BFA SW U Georgetown TX 1975; MA U of Kansas 1976; U of Texas 1983; MDiv Epis TS of The SW 1985; Cert Shalem Inst of Sprtl Formation Washington DC 1990; Cert Shalem Inst of Sprtl Formation Washington DC 2001. D 6/13/1993 P 12/12/1993 Bp James Barrow Brown. m 9/2/1990 Laura Ragland. R St. Matt's Epis Ch Madison AL 1995-1999; Chr Ch Covington LA 1993-1995. AAPC; Soc of S Jn the Evang, Fllshp 1986; Sprtl Dir Intl . BFA mcl SW U Georgetown TX 1975. frpbailey@gmail.com

BAILEY, Ralph Lomax (Colo) 1303 S Bross Ln, Longmont CO 80501 **R S Steph's Ch Longmont CO 1990-** B Bakersfield CA 3/22/1953 s Ralph William Bailey & Minnie Ruth. BA U CO 1981; MDiv SWTS 1984. D 6/16/1984 Bp William Carl Frey P 12/21/1984 Bp William Harvey Wolfrum. m 5/29/2010 Anne Bailey c 4. Asst Ch Of S Mich The Archangel Colorado Sprg CO 1987-1990; Dioc Counc Dio Colorado Denver CO 1986-1993; Int Epis Ch Of The Trsfg Vail CO 1986-1987; Vic Gr Ch Buena Vista CO 1984-1986; Vic S Geo Epis Mssn Leadville CO 1984-1986. Fell AAPC 1989. 1maxbailey@comcast.net

BAILEY SR, Robert Jerome (RG) 1505 Knudsen Ave, Farmington NM 87401 **Assoc S Jn's Ch Farmington NM 2007-** B Portland OR 2/7/1931 s Clayton Preble Bailey & Naomi Harriett. BD Colegio Franco Espanol 1948; MD Universidad Nacion/Autonoma de Mex 1958; Dplma in Basic Chr Stds Dioc Sch for Mnstry 2005. D 10/21/2006 P 10/21/2007 Bp Jeffrey Neil Steenson. m 7/15/1977 Rhonda Benotti c 3. St Lk's Soc 2002. rjbailey2@msn.com

BAILEY, Sarah (WVa) 401 S Washington St, Berkeley Springs WV 25411 B Pittsburgh PA 11/17/1942 d John Leroy Evrard & Phyllis Margaret. RN S Marg Hosp Sch Of Nrsng Pittsburgh PA 1963; BA Antioch Coll 1989; Untd TS Dayton OH 1992; MDiv SWTS 1993. D 6/26/1993 P 5/14/1994 Bp Herbert Thompson Jr. c 2. R S Mk's Epis Ch Berkeley Sprg WV 2000-2003; Assoc Calv Ch Columbia MO 1995-2000; Chr Epis Ch Dayton OH 1993-1995. Cler Ldrshp Proj Viii; ECW; Natl Epis Aids Cltn; Natl Ntwk Epis Cler Assn. salliebailey@earthlink.net

BAILEY, S(tephanie) Abbott (Va) 423 1/2 S Laurel St., Richmond VA 23220 **R S Andr's Ch Richmond VA 2008-** B Clarksburg, WV 6/28/1969 d Gary Holden Bailey & Martha Anne. BA Eckerd Coll 1992; MPA GW 2000; MDiv Ya Berk 2006. D 6/18/2005 P 12/19/2005 Bp Peter James Lee. Assoc S Steph's Ch Richmond VA 2006-2008; D Par of St Paul's Ch Norwalk Norwalk CT 2005. abbottbailey@comcast.net

BAILEY III, Theodore Harbour (SVa) 133 Leon Dr, Williamsburg VA 23188 B Baltimore MD 12/18/1922 s Theodore Harbour Bailey & Florence Oliphant. BA W&M 1947; MDiv Ya Berk 1958; VTS 1977; DMin UTS Richmond VA 1985. D 6/17/1958 P 12/23/1958 Bp Noble C Powell. m 8/18/1954 Gunda Gabcke c 2. Int Chr Epis Ch Smithfield VA 2000-2002; Int S Jn's Ch Portsmouth VA 1998-1999; Int S Barn Epis Ch Richmond VA 1995-1997; Int S Thos Epis Ch Chesapeake VA 1994-1995; Int S Jn's Ch Hopewell VA 1993; Int Ch Of The Gd Shpd Norfolk VA 1992-1993; Int S Mk's Ch Hampton VA 1991-1992; Int S Anne's Ch Appomattox VA 1990-1991; R S Jn's Epis Ch Tappahannock VA 1975-1988; Asst Cathd Of The Incarn Baltimore MD 1973-1975; R S Jn's Ch Mt Washington Baltimore MD 1966-1973; S Ptr's Epis Ch Ellicott City MD 1958-1966. ASSP. THEODORE.BAILEY@COMCAST.NET

BAILEY, William Edward (Nwk) 3 Northview Dr, Morris Plains NJ 07950 B Detroit MI 9/10/1931 s William Everett Bailey & Mary Alvira. D 6/5/2004 Bp John Palmer Croneberger. m 10/17/1953 Evelyn Oswald c 4. All SS Ch Millington NJ 2004-2010. chapbill@optonline.net

BAILEY FISCHER, Valerie Dianne (Nwk) 283 Herrick Avenue, Teaneck NJ 07666 **R S Mk's Ch Teaneck NJ 2011-** B Philadelphia, PA 9/3/1965 d John W Bailey & Doretha. BA Penn 1988; MDiv UTS 2004; STM Bos 2009. D 6/2/2007 P 1/12/2008 Bp M(arvil) Thomas Shaw III. m 4/1/2000 Robert D Fischer c 1. Asst S Eliz's Ch Sudbury MA 2009-2011; Asst Ch Of The H Sprt Wayland MA 2007-2008. valerie_bailey@brontes.org

BAILLARGEON JR, Henri Albert (SVa) 5057 Cliffony Dr, Virginia Beach VA 23464 B Fall River MA 4/25/1952 s Henri Albert Baillargeon & Theresa Frances. Asn Lake City Cmnty Coll 1978; Florida Sthrn Coll 1988; BA U of So Florida 1991; MDiv VTS 1994. D 6/25/1994 P 1/14/1995 Bp Rogers Sanders Harris. m 4/22/1984 Virginia Suzanne Pabst c 2. R Gd Samar Epis Ch Virginia Bch VA 2000-2007; P S Paul's Ch Vanceboro NC 1998-1999; S Christophers Ch Elizabethtown NC 1994-1996. hgbail@sybercom.net

BAIN, Caroline Margaret (Chi) 939 Harlem #302, Glenview IL 60025 B Evanston IL 10/14/1929 d Robert Charles Lawson & Margaret. BA Mundelein Coll 1977; MA Mundelein Coll 1978; MDiv SWTS 1983. D 6/9/1983 Bp James Winchester Montgomery P 12/18/1983 Bp Quintin Ebenezer Primo Jr. m 9/1/1951 John Bain c 4. Int H Trin Epis Ch Wyoming MI 1994-1996; Int S Greg's Epis Ch Muskegon MI 1993-1994; Int S Paul's Epis Ch Grinnell IA 1992-1993; Int Trin Ch Parkersburg WV 1991-1992; COM Dio NW Pennsylvania Erie PA 1989-1991; Ecum Cmsn Dio NW Pennsylvania Erie PA 1989-1991; Dio NW Pennsylvania Erie PA 1988-1994; Chapl ECW Dio NW Pennsylvania Erie PA 1988-1991; Vic S Aug Of Cbury Ch Edinboro PA 1988-1991; Vic S Ptr's Ch Waterford PA 1988-1991; The Cler Spprt Account Waterford PA 1988-1991; S Paulinus Ch Watseka IL 1985-1988; Cur Trin Ch Highland Pk IL 1983-1985. Fllshp of St. Jn the Evang 2004; Ord of S Helena 1982.

BAIN, Robert Walker (WMass) 1673 Huasna Dr, San Luis Obispo CA 93405 B Framingham MA 7/20/1924 s George Walker Bain & Estelle. Fllshp Coll Of Pathology; MD Bos 1952; Mallory Inst Of Pathology 1968. D 6/23/1962 Bp Walter H Gray P 5/1/1977 Bp Alexander Doig Stewart. m 8/18/1955 Beverly

Jean Wright. Assoc S Matt's Ch Worcester MA 1988-1996; Vic S Andr's Ch No Grafton MA 1986-1988; S Steph's Ch Westborough MA 1970-1986. CBS; Fvc; GAS; OHC 1962. frbain@aol.com

✠ BAINBRIDGE III, Rt Rev Harry Brown (Ida) 173 Louisa Beall Ln, Charles Town WV 25414 **Died 5/27/2010** B Knoxville TN 7/25/1939 s Harry Brown Bainbridge & Grace Bainbridge. BA U So 1961; MDiv TS 1967; DMin TS 1982. D 6/28/1967 Bp William Evan Sanders P 5/1/1968 Bp John Vander Horst Con 6/6/1998 for Ida. c 2. DD U So 1999. bp940@frontiernet.net

BAINES JR, Robert Roy (Dal) 2105 Oakcrest Ct, Denton TX 76210 B San Antonio TX 6/18/1942 s Connie. D 8/31/1972 Bp Harold Cornelius Gosnell P 1/7/1973 Bp Richard Earl Dicus. m 2/5/1972 Gerry Weatherford c 2. Chair Dio Dallas Dallas TX 1991-1992; R S Dav's Ch Denton TX 1988-2005; BEC Dio W Texas San Antonio TX 1986-1988; COM Dio W Texas San Antonio TX 1982-1988; R S Matt's Ch Edinburg TX 1978-1988; Vic Ch Of The H Comf Angleton TX 1975-1978; H Comf Sinton TX 1975-1978; Vic S Chris's By The Sea Portland TX 1975-1978; Liturg Com Dio W Texas San Antonio TX 1973-1984; Assoc/Headmaster S Dav's Epis Ch San Antonio TX 1972-1975. rbaines000@centurytel.net

BAIRD, Gary Clifton (Ark) 617 Tahleguah, Siloan Springs AR 72761 **D Gr Ch Siloam Sprg AR 2000-** B McLeansboro IL 6/16/1950 s James Clifton Baird & Helen Marie. D 10/28/2000 Bp Larry Earl Maze. m 5/27/1972 Sally Ann Smith c 2. baird777@cox.net

BAIRD, Kathryn Jo Anne (Az) 4442 E Bermuda St, Tucson AZ 85712 **Assoc Gr S Paul's Epis Ch Tucson AZ 2011-** B Cedar Rapids IA 11/16/1957 d Robert Baird & Mavis. MS San Diego St U 1987; PhD U of Arizona 2005; MDiv CDSP 2010. D 6/6/2009 P 12/4/2010 Bp Kirk Stevan Smith. ktbaird16@gmail.com

BAIRD, Lynn (Cal) 1026 Springhouse Dr, Ambler PA 19002 B Raleigh NC 7/11/1953 d Charles Joseph Mroczkowski & Zita Elizabeth. AAS Brookdale Cmnty Coll 1985; BS W Chester U of Pennsylvania 1990; MDiv Ch DS of the W 1997. D 11/20/1999 P 6/3/2000 Bp William Edwin Swing. m 11/21/2009 Robert Baird c 1. Pstr Care S Greg Of Nyssa Ch San Francisco CA 1999-2006. lynniebaird@gmail.com

BAIRD, Robert Charlton (SC) 4907 Yadkin Dr, Raleigh NC 27609 B Opelika AL 4/16/1922 s Robert Charlton Baird & Effie Jean. BA Davidson Coll 1943; MDiv VTS 1946; STM U So 1953; Med No Carolina St U 1970. D 2/3/1946 P 10/16/1946 Bp Edwin A Penick. m 12/12/1952 Barbara Lee Spears c 3. Supply P S Chris's Epis Ch Garner NC 1979-1986; Supply P S Mk's Epis Ch Roxboro NC 1978-1979; Stff S Tim's Ch Raleigh NC 1970-1978; R S Paul's Ch Bennettsville SC 1949-1967; P S Barn Ch Dillon SC 1949-1951; P S Thos Epis Ch Sanford NC 1946-1949.

BAIRD, Stephen Earl (Colo) PO Box 1000, Vail CO 81658 B Richmond IN 2/1/1943 s Robert Earl Baird & Dorothy. D 11/20/2010 Bp Robert John O'Neill. m 1/2/1965 Karen Heil c 3. sebscot@aol.com

BAKAL, Pamela (Nwk) 200 Highfield Ln, Nutley NJ 07110 **R Gr Ch Nutley NJ 1997-** B Philadelphia PA 2/16/1951 d Donald G Brownlow & Louise. Bennington Coll 1971; BA CUNY 1973; UTS 1990; MDiv GTS 1992. D 6/13/1992 P 3/1/1993 Bp Orris George Walker Jr. m 2/8/1981 Stuart Bakal c 3. Gr Ch Brooklyn NY 1992-1997. fthrpam@optonline.net

BAKELY, Catherine Mae (SVa) P.O. Box 186, Oak Hall VA 23416 B Baltimore MD 2/4/1939 d Albert Herman Boellner & Ruth Naomi. Dioc Sch for Mnstry 2008. D 11/16/2008 Bp John Clark Buchanan. m 9/23/1961 Ronald Herbert Bakely c 3. boomamae@dmv.com

BAKER, Andrea (NCal) 2620 Capitol Ave, Sacramento CA 95816 **Assoc P Trin Cathd Sacramento CA 2010-** B Ft Belvoir VA 4/8/1962 d Eugene W Allen & Claire R. BS US Mltry Acad 1984; MA U of Hawaii 1996; MDiv CDSP 2010. D 6/12/2010 P 12/18/2010 Bp Barry Leigh Beisner. m 5/24/1984 Brian Neal Baker c 2. S Thos Epis Ch Sun Vlly ID 2000-2006. tvrbaker@comcast.net

BAKER, Anne (Ia) 7815 N 185th Ave, Waddell AZ 85355 **Died 11/10/2010** B San Antonio TX 11/13/1921 d Frederich Hermann Wagner & Margaret. Kansas Wesl; Kansas Wesl; S Louis TS St Louis MO. D 1/6/1977 P 7/30/1977 Bp William Augustus Jones Jr. c 7. Cfec; RWF.

BAKER, Brian Neal (NCal) 1160 Los Molinos Way, Sacramento CA 95864 **Dn Trin Cathd Sacramento CA 2006-** B Del Rio TX 10/14/1961 s George Wayne Baker & Ruth Eugenie. BS USMA At W Point 1983; MDiv VTS 1991; DMin SWTS 1999. D 6/29/1991 P 12/28/1991 Bp Donald Purple Hart. m 5/24/1984 Andrea Allen c 2. R S Thos Epis Ch Sun Vlly ID 1998-2006; Cn Pstr S Mich's Cathd Boise ID 1994-1998; Cur Ch Of The H Nativ Honolulu HI 1991-1994. bnbaker83@gmail.com

BAKER, Brock (Alb) PO Box 1374, Lake Placid NY 12946 **R S Eustace Ch Lake Placid NY 2008-** B New York NY 4/22/1947 s Alfred T Baker & Priscilla Brock. AB Harv 1970; BTh Wycliffe Hall 2008. D 5/31/2008 P 12/13/2008 Bp William Howard Love. m 9/26/1987 Elizabeth H Baker c 2. revbaker@yahoo.com

BAKER, Bruce D'Aubert (Be) St. Alban Episcopal Church, 2848 Saint Albans Drive, Sinking Spring PA 19608 **Assoc P S Alb's Epis Ch Reading PA 2008-** B New Orleans LA 3/17/1941 s William Garrett Baker & Suzanne D'Aubert. BA Baylor U 1963; MA Loyola Marymount U 1975; MAPS Washington Theol Un 1999. Rec from Roman Catholic 6/10/2008 Bp Paul Victor Marshall. m 8/18/2007 Susan Bowers c 5. Auth, "Praying to Hear From You in Your Word," *Share The Word*, Paulist Natl Cath Evangelization Assn, 2004. papabruce8@verizon.net

BAKER JR, Charles Mulford (Ct) PO Box 296, Gales Ferry CT 06335 B Wilmington DE 10/10/1944 s Charles Mulford Baker & Lillian May. BA U of Delaware Newark 1970; MDiv VTS 1987. D 6/11/1987 P 6/12/1988 Bp C(hristopher) FitzSimons Allison. m 4/21/2001 Lee A Nau c 2. R S Dav's Ch Gales Ferry CT 2000-2010; P-in-c S Marys Epis Ch Mt Pleasant SC 1988-2000; Epis Ch of the Gd Shpd Charleston SC 1987-1988.

BAKER, Clarence Dawson (Ark) 692 Poplar Ave, Memphis TN 38105 **R S Lk's Ch Hot Sprg AR 2006-** B San Diego CA 11/22/1945 s Calvin Elwood Baker & Pauline. BD U of Memphis 1988; MS U of Memphis 1990; MDiv VTS 1994. D 6/22/1994 Bp Alex Dockery Dickson P 1/26/1995 Bp James Malone Coleman. m Mary Baker c 4. S Mary's Cathd Memphis TN 1994-2006. Ord Of H Cross. cbbaker@stlukeshs.org

BAKER, Douglas Macintyre (NJ) 246 Quincy Shore Dr Apt 2, Quincy MA 02171 B 2/20/1958 Trans from Anglican Church of Canada 1/31/1994 Bp George Phelps Mellick Belshaw. m 6/20/1987 Joan Mary Burke. Epis Ch Of The Epiph Ventnor City NJ 1994-1996.

BAKER, Edwin Dale (NY) One Hardscrabble Road, PO Box 485, Croton Falls NY 10519 B Oklahoma City OK 5/16/1923 s Edgar Clifton Baker & Jewell Claire. BA Oklahoma City U 1947; Van 1949; MDiv STUSo 1950; Cert Amer Fndt of Rel & Psych 1960; GTS 1960; Cert Fndt Rel Mntl Hlth 1975. D 6/8/1950 P 6/7/1951 Bp Edmund P Dandridge. Int Ch Of The H Trin Pawling NY 2000-2002; S Lk's Ch Somers NY 1989-1991; Asst S Lk's Ch Somers NY 1980-1989. Integrity Inc. Who'S Who In Rel. edalebaker@aol.com

BAKER, Frank Danforth (Mass) 7 Sturtevant St, Waterville ME 04901 B Woburn MA 7/21/1922 s John Eben Baker & May. UTS; AA Bos 1948; BS Bos 1950. D 6/13/1959 P 6/24/1960 Bp Robert McConnell Hatch. c 6. R Emm Ch Boston MA 1966-1987; Emm Ch W Roxbury MA 1966-1987; R S Lk's Ch Hudson MA 1961-1966; Asst S Mich's-On-The-Heights Worcester MA 1959-1961. frankbaker@comcast.net

BAKER, J Jeffrey (O) 160 Keagler Dr, Steubenville OH 43953 **Chr Epis Ch Warren OH 2011-; ECS Chairman Dio Ohio Cleveland OH 2009-; Cmsn on Global and Dom Mssn Dio Ohio Cleveland OH 2008-** B Bloomington IN 1/7/1965 s James Alan Baker & Lyn Wallace. Van 1985; BA Baldwin-Wallace Coll 1988; MDiv Bex 2007. D 6/9/2007 Bp Mark Hollingsworth Jr P 12/15/2007 Bp David Charles Bowman. m 7/14/1990 Kristin M Kristin Dearborn c 2. S Steph's Epis Ch Steubenville OH 2007-2011. bakerspax@aol.com

BAKER, Johanna Michelle (NwPa) 62 Pickering St., Brookville PA 15825 **St Jude's Epis Ch Hermitage PA 2011-** B Brookville PA 3/21/1980 d Dennis Alan Blauser & Nancy. BA Thiel Coll 2003; Dipl. in Angl St Ya Berk 2008; MDiv Yale DS 2008. D 11/1/2008 P 5/30/2009 Bp Sean Walter Rowe. m 1/3/2004 Shawn Baker c 1. D Ch Of The H Trin Brookville PA 2008-2011. johanna@bakerpage.com

BAKER, John Marcus (Va) 8531 Riverside Rd, Alexandria VA 22308 **R S Aid's Ch Alexandria VA 1999-** B San Diego CA 4/2/1953 s Samuel Quentin Baker & Marjorie Elaine. BA U of Memphis 1992; MDiv VTS 1995. D 6/3/1995 P 6/1/1996 Bp James Malone Coleman. m 10/24/1980 Mary F Sanders c 1. Gr - S Lk's Ch Memphis TN 1995-1999. jmbaknmem@aol.com

BAKER JR, John Thurlow (Cal) 2055 Northshore Rd, Bellingham WA 98226 B Kauai HI 3/22/1941 s John Thurlow Baker & Jane. BA Willamette U 1963; MDiv VTS 1966; MS San Francisco St U 1971; EdD Nova U 1980. D 6/29/1966 P 6/1/1967 Bp Clarence Rupert Haden Jr. Assoc S Steph's Ch Gilroy CA 2003-2006; Assoc S Eliz's Epis Ch San Diego CA 1995-2001; Assoc S Jas Ch Fremont CA 1969-1990; Asst S Paul's Epis Ch Burlingame CA 1968-1969; Cur S Jn's Epis Ch Marysville CA 1966-1968. bakerthur@peoplepc.com

BAKER, Josephine Louise (Pa) Po Box 429, Wayne PA 19087 B Oceanville NJ 8/31/1920 d Jacob Redenius & Josephine Hazzard. BA Amer U 1962; MA Amer U 1963; Indstrl Coll of The ArmdF 1964; LHD Tem 1964; MS S Chas Borromeo 1981; MDiv Estrn Bapt TS 1984; DMin ETSBH 1990. D 11/27/1987 Bp Calvin Onderdonk Schofield Jr. m Milton Grafly Baker. D All SS Ch Norristown PA 1993-1997; Comp Dio Com Dio SE Florida Miami FL 1991-1993; D All Souls' Epis Ch Miami Bch FL 1987-1993. Auth, "Mltry Security In Relation To Freedom Of Press"; Auth, "Permanent Diac Serving The Aging In The Dio SE Florida". Dok; Soc Of S Fran. Distinguished Alum Amer U 1969; Legion Of Merit 1967.

BAKER, Joseph Scott (SVa) St. Stephen's Episcopal Church, 372 Hiden Blvd., Newport News VA 23606 **R S Steph's Ch Newport News VA 2005-** B Greensboro NC 10/6/1967 s James Boyd Baker & Carolyn Mann. BS Wstrn Carolina U 1990; MDiv STUSo 2000. D 9/23/2000 P 5/18/2001 Bp Dorsey Felix Henderson. m 1/25/1992 Sheryl W Williams c 1. S Andr's Ch Ayer MA 2002-2005; D Gr Epis Ch Anderson SC 2000-2002. jscottbaker@verizon.net

BAKER, K. Drew (SwVa) 2411 Shiraz Lane, Charleston SC 29414 **Asst S Steph's Epis Ch Charleston SC 2008-** B Falls Church VA 7/24/1965 s K D Baker & Mary D. BS Hampden-Sydney Coll 1986; MD Med Coll of Virginia 1990; MDiv Candler TS Emory U 2001. D 5/31/2003 P 12/13/2003 Bp Robert Hodges Johnson. The Tazewell Cnty Cluster Of Epis Parishes Tazewell VA 2006-2008; S Matt's Epis Ch Spartanburg SC 2004-2006; Gr Ch Morganton NC 2003-2004. kdrewbakermd@aol.com

BAKER, Kim (WA) Washington Episc Sch, 5600 Little Falls Pkwy., Bethesda MD 20816 B Des Moines IA 7/30/1956 d Edward Sylvester Turner & Billye Jean. BA U MI 1978; JD Case Wstrn Reserve U 1983; MDiv Epis TS of The SW 2002. D 6/26/2002 Bp Robert Boyd Hibbs P 2/28/2003 Bp James Edward Folts. m 8/20/1979 Jeffrey Jay Baker c 3. R S Ptr's Ch Westfield NY 2004-2008; S Thos Epis Ch And Sch San Antonio TX 2002-2003.

BAKER, Mark James (At) 238 E 31st St, New York NY 10016 B Alexandria VA 10/31/1947 s Harry James Baker & Jane Guild. BA New Engl Conservatory of Mus 1969; MDiv EDS 1979. D 6/9/1979 Bp John Bowen Coburn P 12/1/1979 Bp Morris Fairchild Arnold. c 2. Int Ch Of The Gd Shpd New York NY 2003-2004; Dio Atlanta Atlanta GA 2003; Vic Ch Of The H Comf Atlanta GA 1995-2003; S Lk's Epis Ch Atlanta GA 1994-1995; S Lk's Epis Ch Atlanta GA 1993-1994; Assoc Gr Ch Lawr MA 1979-1982. mrose@episcopalchurch.org

BAKER, M Clark (Tenn) 780 Laurel Branch Trl, Sewanee TN 37375 **Ch Of The H Comf Monteagle TN 1998-** B Macon GA 4/12/1933 s Emmett H(orne) Baker & Martha. BS U So 1955; LTh GTS 1958. D 6/22/1958 Bp John Vander Horst P 6/25/1959 Bp Theodore N Barth. m 5/29/1982 Rowan Elaine Elrod. Stated Supply S Matt's Epis Ch McMinnville TN 2008-2010; Vic S Bern's Ch Gruetli Laager TN 1995-2002; Vic Ch Of The H Comf Monteagle TN 1995; Stndg Committe Mem Dio Tennessee Nashville TN 1989-1993; Chair of Missions Dio Tennessee Nashville TN 1988-1994; Vic S Bede's Epis Ch Manchester TN 1987-1994; Vic S Andr's Epis Ch New Johnsonville TN 1983-1987; P Gr Ch Sprg Hill TN 1980-1983; P-in-c S Mary Magd Ch Fayetteville TN 1978-1979; P S Phil Ch Bartlett TN 1977-1978; P-in-c Bp Otey Memi Ch Memphis TN 1977; P-in-c Emm Ch Memphis TN 1972-1977; P-in-c S Paul's Ch Mason TN 1970-1971; P-in-c Trin Ch Mason TN 1968-1971; P-in-c Chr Ch Brownsville TN 1967-1968; Cur Chr Ch Memphis TN 1966; R Thankful Memi Ch Chattanooga TN 1963-1966; P-in-c Ch Of The H Comf Monteagle TN 1961-1963; P-in-c S Jas Sewanee TN 1961-1963; P-in-c S Jas Epis Ch Un City TN 1958-1963; P-in-c S Jn's Ch Mart TN 1958-1961. canine2@bellsouth.net

BAKER, Milledge Leonard (CGC) 100 Lynn McGhee Dr, Atmore AL 36502 **P-in-c S Monica's Cantonment FL 2010-** B Walnut Hill FL 3/8/1942 s Marion Baker & Ruby. D 11/23/2008 P 6/20/2009 Bp Philip Menzie Duncan II. m 9/23/1970 Barbara Barbara Sue Sibbach c 1. mlbaker@frontiernet.net

BAKER, Patricia Lucile (Oly) PO Box 369, Snoqualmie WA 98065 **Dioc Rep. Cathd Vstry S Mk's Cathd Seattle WA 2009-; Vic S Clare of Assisi Epis Ch Snoqualmie WA 2004-** B Eugene OR 2/6/1954 d Donn Whyddon Thomas & Mary Alice. BS OR SU 1976; MDiv TS and Mnstry - Seattle U 1999. D 6/28/2003 Bp Vincent Waydell Warner P 1/17/2004 Bp Sanford Zangwill Kaye Hampton. m 7/10/1976 Loren Aquila Baker c 2. D S Steph's Epis Ch Seattle WA 2003-2004. revpattyb@stclareschurch.org

BAKER, Paul Edgar (Alb) 4 St Lukes Pl, Cambridge NY 12816 B Tarrytown NY 4/28/1936 s Francis Leslie Baker & Grace Jeanette. AAS SUNY 1957; BA SUNY 1960; MA SUNY 1961; MDiv GTS 1982. D 6/19/1982 P 12/1/1982 Bp Wilbur Emory Hogg Jr. m Barbara Claire Clapp c 3. R S Lk's Ch Cambridge NY 1982-2006. providencehouse@mindspring.com

BAKER JR, Powell Eugene (Dal) 4443 Sexton Ln, Dallas TX 75229 B Harlingen TX 3/8/1934 s Powell Eugene Baker & Velma. BA SW U Georgetown TX 1956; MDiv Epis TS of The SW 1959; MS U of Texas 1973. Trans from Anglican Church of Canada 5/2/1966 Bp Scott Field Bailey. m 7/16/1976 Dorothy D Nelson c 2. Ch Of Our Merc Sav Kaufman TX 1976; Asst S Lk's Epis Ch Dallas TX 1969-1971; Asst Chr Epis Ch Dallas TX 1965-1969; Vic H Trin Carrizo Sprg TX 1959-1962; Vic S Tim's Ch Cotulla TX 1959-1962. Acad Cert Soc Workers. oldmrgrace@sbcglobal.net

BAKER, Rhonda (Va) Po Box 59, Goochland VA 23063 **R Gr Epis Ch Goochland VA 2001-** B Lynchburg VA 8/31/1950 d Mervyn Wilton Williamson & Rhoda Ruth. BD U IL 1987; MDiv SWTS 1995. D 6/17/1995 P 12/1/1995 Bp Frank Tracy Griswold III. m 6/29/1972 Robert S Baker. Ch Of The H Comm Maywood IL 1996-2001; Assoc One In Chr Ch Prospect Heights IL 1995-1997. Tertiary Of The Soc Of S Fran. mthrrhonda@aol.com

BAKER, Richard Henry (Mo) 3139 Barrett Station Rd, Saint Louis MO 63122 B Detroit MI 7/15/1937 s Henry Kummel Baker & Josephine Elizabeth. BA Carleton Coll 1959; MA U of Missouri 1961; MDiv EDS 1964; PhD S Louis U 1980. D 6/21/1964 P 12/1/1964 Bp George Leslie Cadigan. m 8/5/1961 Sandra Kaye Hem c 3. Ch Of The Gd Shpd S Louis MO 2005-2006; LocTen Ch Of The H Comm U City MO 2001-2002; LocTen S Mart's Ch Ellisville MO 1999-2000; LocTen Ch Of The Trsfg Lake S Louis MO 1995-1996; Cn/Subdean Chr Ch Cathd S Louis MO 1988-1992; LocTen Ch Of The Trsfg Lake S Louis MO 1986-1988; Actg Cn Chr Ch Cathd S Louis MO 1986; LocTen S Steph's Ch Ferguson MO 1985; LocTen S Matt's Epis Ch Warson Warson Woods MO 1984; LocTen S Ptr's Epis Ch St Louis MO 1980-1983; LocTen Ch Of The Gd Shpd S Louis MO 1978-1979; Int S Mich & S Geo Clayton MO 1977-1978; LocTen S Lk's Epis Ch Manchester MO 1975-1977; R S Augustines Ch S Louis MO 1968-1971; Spnsr Yth Grp Chr Ch Cathd S Louis MO 1967-1968; R S Judes Ch Monroe City MO 1964-1967; R S Paul's Ch Palmyra MO 1964-1967. r-h-baker@msn.com

BAKER, Ruth Louise (WMo) 5901 Nw 103rd St, Kansas City MO 64154 **P Assoc Gr Epis Ch Liberty MO 2010-** B Saint Albans NY 10/18/1946 d Claude Clayton Boydston & Ruth Alice. U of Redlands 1965; BA U of Montana 1968; MDiv VTS 1998. D 6/13/1998 P 12/13/1998 Bp John Bailey Lipscomb. m 9/1/1967 James Baker c 2. Chair COM Dio W Missouri Kansas City MO 2008-2009; R Ch Of The Redeem Kansas City MO 2005-2009; R S Matt's Ch St Petersburg FL 1999-2005; Cur S Thos' Epis Ch St Petersburg FL 1998-1999. Ord of S Lk 1993. MDiv cl VTS Alexandria VA 1998. bakerlouise@msn.com

BAKER, Stannard (Vt) 2 Cherry St., Burlington VT 05401 B Manhattan KS 5/3/1946 s Clarence Baker & Hermione Allen. BA Swarthmore Coll 1968; MA Lesley U 1988. D 1/6/2009 Bp Thomas C Ely. m 8/13/2000 Peter Harrigan. sbaker@stpaulscathedralvt.org

BAKER JR, William Allen (Mo) 40 Conwood Ln, Saint Louis MO 63131 B Knoxville TN 11/14/1920 s willia Allen Baker & Lucille Russell. DIT Bex 1962. D 6/3/1962 P 12/1/1962 Bp Roger W Blanchard. m 7/13/1973 Ann Fields. Supply P S Jn's Ch St Louis MO 2001-2004; Int Dio Missouri S Louis MO 1988-1995; Assoc S Mich & S Geo Clayton MO 1978-1988; Epis Hm For Chld St Louis MO 1973-1979; Asst Dir Educ Cntr Dio Missouri S Louis MO 1973-1978; R S Jn's Ch Worthington OH 1967-1973; Assoc S Thos Epis Ch Terrace Pk OH 1962-1967. bake094@worldnet.att.net

BAKER-BORJESON, Susan C (Alb) 119 Crystal Point Rd, Cairo NY 12413 **Dn, Hudson Vlly Dnry Dio Albany Albany NY 2007-; Cmsn on Alco Concerns Dio Massachusetts Boston MA 1992-** B Garden City NY 4/7/1942 d Allan Maynard Woods & Muriel Evelyn. BA Ohio Wesl 1964; Cert U of Paris-Sorbonne FR 1965; MDiv VTS 1979. D 6/25/1979 Bp Robert Marshall Anderson P 1/1/1980 Bp John Brooke Mosley. m 1/9/1988 Ralph William Borjeson c 1. Chr Ch Coxsackie NY 2004-2008; S Ptr's Ch Dartmouth MA 1994-2004; P-in-c S Ptr's Ch Dartmouth MA 1992-1993; Dio Massachusetts Boston MA 1990-2009; Assoc R Ch Of S Jn The Evang Duxbury MA 1989-1991; Int Ch Of S Jn The Evang Duxbury MA 1986-1988; Asst R S Ptr's Ch Glenside PA 1979-1981. DOK 2006.

BAKER-WRIGHT, Michelle Kathryn (Los) 1325 Monterey Rd, South Pasadena CA 91030 **Asst S Jas' Par So Pasadena CA 2011-** B San Jose CA 6/21/1973 d Robert Paul Baker & Charlene Louise. Current PhD Candidate Fuller TS; BMus USC 1995; MDiv Fuller TS 2006. D 6/12/2010 P 1/8/2011 Bp Mary Douglas Glasspool. m 8/30/2003 Mark Wright. mkbakerwright@gmail.com

BAKEY, Joachim Joseph (RG) 3619 Southwood Dr, Easton PA 18045 **Pstr Asst Ch of the H Faith Santa Fe NM 1983-** B Philadelphia PA 1/11/1926 s John Joseph Bakey & Lillian. MRE Loyola U 1970; MS How 1977; DMin Jesuit TS 1981. Rec from Roman Catholic 10/27/1982 as Deacon Bp Richard Mitchell Trelease Jr. m 4/22/1972 Laura Elizabeth Owens.

BAKKER, Cheryl Anne (CFla) 7416 W Seven Rivers Dr, Crystal River FL 34429 **D S Mart's Epis Ch Hudson FL 2002-; D S Anne's Ch Crystal River FL 2001-** B Elyria OH 6/5/1948 d Eric Charles Jones & Marguerite Edna. BS OH SU 1972. D 12/8/2001 Bp John Wadsworth Howe. m 5/25/1984 Bert Bakker. bbakker1@tampabay.rr.com

BAKKER, Greg (EpisSanJ) 41 Station Road, Sholing, Southampton SO19 8FN Great Britain (UK) B Modesto CA 10/10/1966 s Harry Edward Bakker & Donna. AA Modesto Jr Coll 1987; BA California St U 1989; MDiv TESM 1992; Trin Bristol Gb 2000. D 6/6/1992 P 5/30/1993 Bp John-David Mercer Schofield. m 2/17/2001 Jane Judith Campbell c 1. Asst Trin Ch Tariffville CT 1992-1996. sholingvicarage@gmail.com

BAKKUM, Carleton Benjamin (SVa) PO Box 123, Yorktown VA 23690 **R Gr Ch Yorktown Yorktown VA 1989-** B Dalton GA 10/20/1953 s Peter Benjamin Bakkum & Johnnie Elizabeth. BA Eckerd Coll 1976; MDiv PrTS 1982; CAS GTS 1984. D 6/8/1985 P 12/14/1985 Bp John Thomas Walker. m 9/28/1985 Elsa Swift c 3. Asst Trin Ch Upperville VA 1985-1989. cbakkum@gracechurchyorktown.org

BALCOM, John Murray (Mass) 2 Autumn Ln, Amherst MA 01002 B Boston MA 11/16/1918 s Rubric Garfield Balcom & Grace Helena. BA U of Massachusetts 1939; BD EDS 1942; STM Harvard DS 1955. D 6/3/1942 P 12/9/1942 Bp Henry Knox Sherrill. m 6/14/1946 Jeanne Lindsey c 3. R Par Of S Paul Newton Highlands MA 1953-1981; R All SS Ch Chelmsford MA 1948-1953; R S Jn's Epis Ch Holbrook MA 1947; R Epiph Par Walpole MA 1943-1944; Cur Gr Ch Norwood MA 1942-1943. Cler Club of Boston (Pres) 1943-1981. Jlmb46@aol.com

BALDRIDGE SR, Kempton Dunn (Eur) 605 Woodland Drive, Paducah KY 42001 **Chapl for the Ohio River Reg Seamens Ch Inst Income New York NY 2010-** B Cincinnati OH 8/14/1955 s Dickson Bouton Baldridge & Edith. BA Cit 1978; Cert in Angl Stds Ya Berk 1988; MDiv Yale DS 1988. D 6/23/1988 Bp C(hristopher) FitzSimons Allison P 6/1/1989 Bp George Edward Haynsworth. m 9/22/1984 Isabel Curtis c 2. Chair, Cmsn on the Mnstry of the Baptized Convoc of Amer Ch in Europe Paris FR 2004-2010; Cler Dep, GC Convoc of Amer Ch in Europe Paris FR 2003-2009; R All SS Epis Ch Braine-l'Alleud 1420 BE 1999-2010; U Vic S Thos's Par Newark DE 1993-1999; US Navy Chapl Off Of Bsh For ArmdF New York NY 1990-1993; Yth Min S Lk's Epis Ch Hilton Hd SC 1989-1990; Asst R Ch Of The Redeem Orangeburg SC 1988-1989. Auth, "Sir Wm DeLancey: an Amer at Waterloo," *The Hstgr*, HSEC, 2009. Gospel Mus Assn 1994-2001; Intl Critical Incident Stress Fndt 2005. Young Man Of The Year Hilton Hd Island (SC) Jaycees Hilton Hd Island SC 1991. kbaldridge@seamenschurch.org

BALDWIN, Allan (WMass) No address on file. B Whitinsville MA 12/17/1932 s Leonard Baldwin & Ida. AS Becker Jr Coll 1954; BS TCU 1961; MDiv Epis TS of The SW 1965. D 6/24/1965 P 12/26/1965 Bp Robert McConnell Hatch. m 7/9/2009 Bertha Aldonna Kulish. P-in-c S Mary's Epis Ch Thorndike MA 1997-2006; S Mary's Epis Ch Thorndike MA 1996; Cn Dio Wstrn Massachusetts Springfield MA 1987-1996; Chair-Cmsn on Aging Dio Wstrn Massachusetts Springfield MA 1982-1985; Res Cn Chr Ch Cathd Springfield MA 1975-1988; Cmsn on Aging Dio Wstrn Massachusetts Springfield MA 1974-1996; Hosp Chapl Dio Wstrn Massachusetts Springfield MA 1971-1996; S Lk's Ch Springfield MA 1966-1971; Asst Gr Ch Chicopee MA 1966-1968.

BALDWIN, Carissa Elizabeth (Los) 132 N Euclid Ave, Pasadena CA 91101 **All SS Ch Pasadena CA 2010-** B Austin TX 6/7/1972 d Randall H Baldwin & Elizabeth L. BA Wellesley Coll 1994; MDiv ETSS 2007. D 6/23/2007 P 1/26/2008 Bp Don Adger Wimberly. Asst S Steph's Epis Ch Houston TX 2007-2010. cbaldwin@allsaints-pas.org

BALDWIN, Charles Walter (At) P.O. Box 123, Madison GA 30650 **D The Epis Ch Of The Adv Madison GA 1995-** B Atlanta GA 7/29/1944 s Charles Baldwin & Margaret. U GA 1968. D 10/28/1995 Bp Frank Kellogg Allan. m 3/7/1966 Sue Knipfer c 1. charles@baldwinrealtyinc.com

BALDWIN, Frederick Stephen (NJ) 9804 Woodbay Drive, Tampa FL 33626 B Syracuse NY 8/11/1946 s Robert Frederick Baldwin & Elizabeth. BA Geo 1968; MDiv EDS 1976. D 6/16/1976 P 5/4/1977 Bp Ned Cole. m 9/8/2011 Derrick Carr c 1. R S Bern's Ch Bernardsville NJ 1984-2005; Assoc S Jas Ch New York NY 1981-1984; Ch Of The H Trin New York NY 1976-1979; Asst H Trin Epis Ch Inwood New York NY 1976-1979. Chapl for the UN Ch Cntr 1976; Epis Chapl for the Holland Lodge 1979; Ord of S Jn the Bapt 1985; Pres for S Mart's Hse 1984-2006. fsbaldwin@gmail.com

BALDWIN, Gary Lee (CGC) 1204 Jackson Dr, Pulaski TN 38478 **Int Emm Epis Ch Shawnee OK 2011-** B Bucyrus OH 12/16/1949 s Elsworth William Baldwin & Florence Katheryn. BA Sthrn Nazarene U 1972; MA Sthrn Nazarene U 1976; Med Georgia St U 1977; MDiv STUSo 1988. D 6/1/1988 P 12/1/1988 Bp Robert Oran Miller. m 7/30/1989 Kathleen M Baldwin c 2. R S Steph's Ch Brewton AL 2003-2011; R The Epis Ch Of The Mssh Pulaski TN 1991-2003; R S Mary's Epis Ch Childersburg AL 1988-1990. fathergary@murdercreek.com

BALDWIN, Gayle R (Wyo) Po Box 255, Greybull WY 82426 B Orangeburg SC 3/18/1946 d Willie Rae Baldwin & Elizabeth. Marq; Fllshp Marq; BA S Andr's Presb Coll 1969; MA U of No Amer 1972; BS Appalachian St U 1975; MDiv Epis TS of The SW 1979. D 6/30/1979 Bp William Gillette Weinhauer P 1/1/1980 Bp Bob Gordon Jones. S Andr's Ch Basin WY 1998; R S Mary's Epis Ch Dousman WI 1987-1989; Asst Ch Of The H Trin So Bend IN 1986-1987; S Andr's Ch Meeteetse WY 1979-1998. AAR; Cat. GAYLE.BALDWIN@UND.EDU

BALDWIN JR, Harris Edward (Nwk) 83 Ebersohl Cir, Whitehouse Station NJ 08889 **Died 1/15/2010** B Torrington CT 11/17/1918 s Harris Edward Baldwin & Jane Elizabeth. BA S Basil's Coll 1948; MDiv PDS 1951. D 5/19/1951 Bp Oliver J Hart P 11/1/1951 Bp William Blair Roberts. c 1. ruth8@comcast.net

BALDWIN JR, Harry Webster (Va) 1900 Lauderdale Dr Apt E111, Richmond VA 23238 B Goochland VA 9/6/1919 s Harry Webster Baldwin & Bessie Childress. BA U Rich 1945; MDiv VTS 1948. D 6/4/1948 P 6/20/1949 Bp Frederick D Goodwin. m 4/22/1950 Elizabeth King c 1. P-in-c S Jn's Ch Petersburg VA 1997-1999; P-in-c S Mart's Ch Doswell VA 1987-1994; R S Andr's Ch Richmond VA 1952-1982.

BALDWIN, Jerome Maynard (SO) 9477 N Maura Ln., Brown Deer WI 53223 B Seattle WA 10/1/1934 s Maynard Martin Baldwin & Eleanor Hadley. BA Mia 1956; BD Oberlin TS 1963; MS U of Wisconsin 1986. D 3/1/1964 P 12/1/1964 Bp Roger W Blanchard. m 6/24/1967 Johanna Wells Yount. R Our Sav Ch Mechanicsburg OH 1967-1977; Cur Chr Epis Ch Of Springfield Springfield OH 1964-1966. bald53225@cs.com

BALDWIN, John Anson (SVa) 5181 Princess Anne Rd, Virginia Beach VA 23462 **R Emm Ch Virginia Bch VA 1997-** B Washington DC 8/10/1950 s Langford Baldwin & Margaret. BA Ob 1973; MDiv EDS 1978. D 6/17/1978 Bp Alexander Doig Stewart P 12/21/1978 Bp Charles Bennison. m 8/19/1978 Ann Scherm c 2. Congrl Dvlpmt Cmsn Dio Sthrn Virginia Norfolk VA 1999-2011; Dioc Coun Dio Minnesota Minneapolis MN 1995-1997; Stndg Com Dio Minnesota Minneapolis MN 1988-1994; R S Geo's Ch St Louis Pk MN 1987-1997; Dioc Coun Dio Washington Washington DC 1983-1985; R S Jn's Ch Ft Washington MD 1981-1987; Chair Hunger T/F Dio Wstrn Michigan Kalamazoo MI 1980-1981; Cur Gr Ch Grand Rapids MI 1978-1981. Auth, "Geocaching for Chr," *Jamestown Cross*. Soc of the Cinncinnati. episcodad@aol.com

BALDWIN, John Richards (CPa) 1903 Kestrel Ct, Lancaster PA 17603 **D S Thos Ch Lancaster PA 1985-** B Milwaukee WI 11/3/1923 s Schuyler Halsey Baldwin & Alma Dorothy. BA Duke 1948. D 6/15/1985 Bp Charlie Fuller McNutt Jr. m 9/23/1950 Jane Laura Pedersen c 3.

BALDWIN, Judith (Nwk) 119 Main St, Millburn NJ 07041 B Utica NY 8/28/1949 d Mervin M McConnell & Mary Elizabeth. BA Syr 1971; MA U CA 1976; MDiv EDS 1986. D 6/21/1986 Bp O'Kelley Whitaker P 4/1/1987 Bp Douglas Edwin Theuner. m 2/1/1987 Cornelius Tarplee c 1. Hse Of Pryr Epis Ch Newark NJ 2004-2006; S Steph's Ch Millburn NJ 2000-2001; Asst Ch Of The Gd Shpd Nashua NH 1986-1992. revjudyb@aol.com

BALDWIN, Marilyn Elizabeth (Minn) 1387 Park St, White Bear Lake MN 55110 **S Jn In The Wilderness White Bear Lake MN 2006-** B St. Paul MN 6/19/1948 d Martin John Baldwin & Sally Kropelnicki. MS Cardinal Stritch U 1990; CTh SWTS 2006; MDiv Untd TS 2006. D 6/8/2006 P 12/21/2006 Bp James Louis Jelinek. m 7/16/1976 Thomas E Carroll. S Paul's On-The-Hill Epis Ch St Paul MN 2006-2007. baldwinme@aol.com

BALDWIN, Robert Evan (Kan) 1011 Vermont St, Lawrence KS 66044 **Trin Ch Lawr KS 2010-** B Lakeland FL 11/24/1971 s Dennis Van Wey Baldwin & Janice Louise. BA Trin Hartford CT 1993; MDiv Trin Luth Sem 2002. D 10/20/2001 P 6/1/2002 Bp Herbert Thompson Jr. m 1/25/1997 Valerie McCord c 2. P S Jas Ch Piqua OH 2002-2010; S Jn's Ch Worthington OH 1998-2001. rb@trinitylawrence.org

BALDWIN, Victoria Evelyn (Ct) 57 Olive St, New Haven CT 06511 **S Paul And S Jas New Haven CT 2010-** B Glen Cove NY 7/16/1954 d Roland Fred Baldwin & Kathryn Ann. BA Mid 1976; MLS Pratt Inst 1984; MDiv Ya Berk 2005. D 6/12/2010 P 1/8/2011 Bp Ian Theodore Douglas. vicki.baldwin@aya.yale.edu

BALDYGA, Andrea Paula (Be) 201 South Wilbur Ave., Sayre PA 18840 **P-in-c Ch Of The Redeem Sayre PA 2008-** B Boston MA 9/14/1955 d Anthony M Baldyga & Genevieve M. BA Bos 1977; MD Bos 1980; MDiv EDS 1998. D 6/20/1998 Bp J Clark Grew II P 2/27/1999 Bp Arthur Benjamin Williams Jr. Assoc Trin Ch Easton PA 2007-2008; Int S Lk's Ch Phillipsburg NJ 2004-2007; R S Thos Ch Alexandria Pittstown NJ 2001-2004; Epis. Shared Mnstrs Nw Lakewood OH 1998-2001. Auth, "Ethical Dilemmas Postoperative Icu"; Auth, "Hemodialysis Octogenarians". revdocapb@prodigy.net

BALES, Janice (RG) 3112 La Mancha Pl Nw, Albuquerque NM 87104 B Auburn IN 10/27/1943 d Walter Edward Stebing & Virginia Ruth. Dioc Sch for Mnstry; BA Indiana U 1965. D 10/27/1982 Bp Richard Mitchell Trelease Jr. m 8/28/1965 Frederick Bales c 2. S Mich And All Ang Ch Albuquerque NM 2005-2009; The Storehouse Albuquerque NM 1986-1989. janiceb@all-angels.com

BALES, William Oliver (SO) 29405 Blosser Rd, Logan OH 43138 **Nativ Epis Ch Bloomfield Township MI 2002-; S Mk's Ch Seminole OK 2002-; Trin Ch McArthur OH 2002-** B Detroit MI 6/18/1936 s William Richard Bales & Muriel Grace. D 10/28/1995 Bp Herbert Thompson Jr. m 5/17/1958 Kathryn Edith Sheatzley.

BALFE, Martin Kevin (Minn) 315 State St W, Cannon Falls MN 55009 **Ch Of The Mssh Prairie Island Welch MN 2005-** B Faribault MN 10/14/1945 s Kevin Martin Balfe & Evelyn Brigette. D 10/29/2005 Bp James Louis Jelinek. m 9/20/1986 Loretta J Balfe c 7. l.balfe@mchsi.com

BALICKI, John Andrew (Me) 104 Echo Rd, Brunswick ME 04011 **R S Mk's Ch Waterville ME 2011-; Chair, Conv Plnng Com Dio Maine Portland ME 2010-** B Detroit MI 10/9/1949 s Eugene Balicki & Eugenia. BS Wayne 1972; MRP Penn 1976; MDiv CUA 1983. P. m 8/4/1990 Karen Balicki c 2. Assoc R S Alb's Ch Cape Eliz ME 2005-2011. jbalicki@hotmail.com

BALK, Roger Allen (O) 5828 Avenue De L'Esplanade, Montreal QC H2T 3A3 Canada B Toledo OH 7/30/1930 s Earl Theodore Balk & Luella. BA Harv 1952; UTS 1953; U of St. Andrews 1956; PhD Concordia U 1989. D 12/6/1957 Bp Nelson Marigold Burroughs P 6/1/1958 Bp Beverley D Tucker. m 5/22/1953 Patricia Ann Raymond. Mc Gill U 1961-1984; R Harcourt Par Gambier OH 1958-1961. Hon Asst Chr Ch Cathd Montreal Quebec Can.

✠ BALL, Rt Rev David Standish (Alb) 3 Park Hill Dr Apt 5, Albany NY 12204 **Ret Bp of Albany Dio Albany Albany NY 1998-** B Albany NY 6/11/1926 s Percival Ledger Ball & Hazelton. BA Colg 1950; STB GTS 1953; DD GTS 1984. D 6/14/1953 P 12/21/1953 Bp Frederick Lehrle Barry Con 2/20/1984 for Alb. Bp Cathd Of All SS Albany NY 1998; Bp of Albany Dio Albany Albany NY 1984-1998; Dn Cathd Of All SS Albany NY 1960-1984; Cn Precentor

Cathd Of All SS Albany NY 1958-1960; Cn Sacrist Cathd Of All SS Albany NY 1956-1958; Cur Ch Of Beth Saratoga Sprg NY 1953-1956.

BALL, Edwin (CFla) 3740 Pinebrook Cir, Bradenton FL 34209 B Newark NJ 6/2/1914 s Robert Needham Ball & Miriam Wolcott. Pur 1933; AA Lake-Sumter Cmnty Coll 1985; BA U of So Florida 1992. D 2/28/1959 Bp Dudley S Stark. m 1/31/1940 Priscilla Marsten Capen c 3. Asst S Edw The Confessor Mt Dora FL 1976-1979; Asst S Paul's Epis Ch Pittsburgh PA 1975-1976; Asst All SS Ch Millington NJ 1965-1971; Asst S Mk's Ch Basking Ridge NJ 1965-1971; Asst The Ch Of The Sav Denville NJ 1963-1964; Asst All SS Ch Millington NJ 1960-1963; Asst Gr Ch Madison NJ 1959-1960; Asst S Paul's Epis Ch Chatham NJ 1959.

BALL, John Arthur (WA) 46455 Hyatt Ct, Drayden MD 20630 **R S Mary's Chap Ridge St Marys City MD 1994-; R St Marys Par St Marys City MD 1994-** B Ilion NY 4/28/1950 s William Raymond Ball & Anne Ernestine. Cntrl Virginia Cmnty Coll Lynchburg VA 1972; AA GW 1974; BS Geo Mason U 1977; MDiv VTS 1991. D 5/31/1991 P 12/18/1991 Bp A(rthur) Heath Light. m 8/31/1974 Linda Sue Banton c 2. Asst Gr Epis Ch Silver Sprg MD 1991-1994. Auth, "Fest Of Amer Folklife-A Handbook For Teachers," 1978. Alpha Chi Natl Scholastic Soc 1978. jab@ohg.com

BALL, Raymond Carl (Dal) 5421 Victor St, Dallas TX 75214 **Receiving Disabil Ret 2011-** B Lubbock TX 8/25/1952 s Raymond Lawrence Ball & Anita. BS Baylor U 1974; BD Chr Congrl Ministrial Trng 1975; STL Angl TS 1988; DMin Trin Evang Sem 1994. D 6/18/1988 P 6/10/1989 Bp Donis Dean Patterson. m 9/10/1994 Bridget Chase. R All SS Epis Ch Dallas TX 1992-2011; Cur All SS Epis Ch Dallas TX 1988-1992. Auth, "One Lord, One Faith, One Baptism," Berean Bible Coll, 1978; Auth, "Primer In Prot Mysticism," Berean Bible Coll, 1977. Intl Ord Of S Lk the Physcn 1982; Soc of Cath Priests (SCP) 2009; SocMary 1992; Tertiary Of The Soc Of S Fran 1989. none 1988. frrayball@gmail.com

BALLANTINE, Lucia P (NY) 402 Route 22, North Salem NY 10560 **S Jas' Ch No Salem NY 2001-** B Princeton NJ 4/9/1951 d John W Ballantine & Lucia Bradley. BA Kirkland Coll 1973; MDiv Ya Berk 1976. D 6/2/1979 Bp Albert Wiencke Van Duzer P 12/1/1979 Bp George Phelps Mellick Belshaw. m 11/20/2005 Elizabeth B Walden c 1. S Mk's Ch Mt Kisco NY 1999-2000; Assoc S Ptr's Epis Ch Arlington VA 1994-1995; Assoc All SS Epis Par Hoboken NJ 1992-1993; Assoc Ch Of The Incarn New York NY 1987-1992; Assoc The Ch Of S Lk In The Fields New York NY 1979-1987; Chapl S Jas Epis Ch Farmington CT 1976-1978. CHS. peavey7@aol.com

BALLARD, James David (Vt) 139 Sanderson Rd, Milton VT 05468 **D S Lk's Ch S Albans VT 2004-** B Burlington VT 8/14/1953 s Eugene Lloyd Ballard & Elizabeth May. BA Johnson St Coll 1976. D 6/5/2004 Bp Thomas C Ely. m 6/11/1977 Linda Jill Sanderson c 2. jamesbmilton@comcast.net

BALLARD JR, Joseph Howard (Tenn) 216 University Ave, Sewanee TN 37375 **Otey Memi Par Ch Sewanee TN 2008-** B Louisville KY 5/29/1951 s Joseph Howard Ballard & Mary Jane. BS U of Tennessee 1973; MBA U of Tennessee 1980; Fllshp Bossey Ecum Inst 1992; MDiv STUSo 1992. D 6/13/1992 P 1/9/1993 Bp Robert Gould Tharp. m 9/4/1971 Barbara F Freeman c 2. R St Jas Epis Ch at Knoxville Knoxville TN 1996-2008; Coordntr Soc Prog Dio E Tennessee Knoxville TN 1994-2001; Assoc S Lk's Ch Cleveland TN 1992-1996. jhballardjr@aol.com

BALLARD, Kathleen Miller (Nwk) 53 Orchard Rd 2nd Floor, Maplewood NJ 07040 **D Hse Of Pryr Epis Ch Newark NJ 2004-** B Newark NJ 4/22/1925 d Kenneth Smith Miller & Florence Gertrude. BA U CA 1965; MA Seton Hall Universtiy 1975; Cert Newark TS 2005. D 5/21/2005 Bp John Palmer Croneberger. c 2. kathleengrammak@aol.com

BALL-DAMBERG, Sarah (NC) 1014 Monmouth Ave, Durham NC 27701 **St Elizabeths Epis Ch Apex NC 2009-; S Phil's Ch Durham NC 2005-** B Manchester TN 8/10/1963 d Milner Shivers Ball & June Mccoy. BA Mid 1984; MA U MI 1990; MDiv Duke 2005. D 12/17/2005 P 6/24/2006 Bp Michael Bruce Curry. m 11/21/2009 Richard C Damberg c 2. Dio No Carolina Raleigh NC 2006-2008. sballdamberg@gmail.com

BALLENTINE JR, George Young (SVa) 305 Park Blvd N, Venice FL 34285 B Newport News VA 10/6/1929 s George Young Ballentine & Adele Virginia. BA U So 1952; MDiv VTS 1955; MA Oklahoma St U 1970. D 6/24/1955 P 6/30/1956 Bp George P Gunn. m 11/10/1973 Emma Jean Flowers c 2. Dio SW Florida Sarasota FL 1982-1994; Asst S Mk's Epis Ch Venice FL 1979-1981; Dio SW Virginia Roanoke VA 1966-1979; Asst S Andr's Ch Norfolk VA 1964-1966; Assoc All Souls Memi Epis Ch Washington DC 1962-1964; Chr The Redeem Manassas VA 1959-1962; P-in-c S Jn's Ch Centreville VA 1959-1962; Cur Chr and S Lk's Epis Ch Norfolk VA 1956-1959; All SS Ch Richmond VA 1955-1956. BA om U So Sewanee TN 1952.

BALLERT JR, Irving Frank (Alb) 25 Sharon St, Sidney NY 13838 B Cohoes NY 4/10/1926 s Irving Frank Ballert & Elizabeth. BME RPI 1950; BMgtE RPI 1954; MS SUNY 1972. D 6/16/1962 P 12/16/1962 Bp Allen Webster Brown. m 6/19/1949 Dorothy Bridge c 3. Supply P S Tim's Ch Westford NY 2001-2008; Dio Albany Albany NY 1986-1989; Dioc Yth Cmsn Dio Albany Albany NY 1986-1987; Weekend Team Sprtl Advsr - Curs Dio Albany Albany NY 1982-1986; Chair T/Fs Renew Dio Albany Albany NY 1982-1985; Chair., Renwl Evang., Stew. & Lay Mnstrs Dio Albany Albany NY 1982-1985; Consult Par Vancancy Dio Albany Albany NY 1982-1984; Consult Par Vancancy Dio Albany Albany NY 1982-1984; Sprtl Dir - Curs Dio Albany Albany NY 1982-1984; Supply P S Matt's Ch Unadilla NY 1982-1983; Dn-Dnry of the Susquehanna Dio Albany Albany NY 1981-1983; COM Dio Albany Albany NY 1975-1976; Chair Div of Yth Dio Albany Albany NY 1966-1968; R S Paul's Ch Sidney NY 1965-1991; Yth Advsr Troy Dnry Dio Albany Albany NY 1963-1965; Cur S Jn's Epis Ch Troy NY 1962-1965. Franciscan Cmnty of the H Cross 2006. ianddb@frontier.com

BALLING, Valerie L (NJ) 142 Sand Hill Road, Monmouth Junction NJ 08852 **S Barn Epis Ch Monmouth Jct NJ 2011-; Dep to GC Dio New Jersey Trenton NJ 2010-; Dioc Coun Dio New Jersey Trenton NJ 2009-; Bp's Advsry Com on Liturg Dio New Jersey Trenton NJ 2007-; Stndg Cmsn on Cler Compstn Dio New Jersey Trenton NJ 2006-** B Livingston NJ 9/11/1973 d Peter John Balling & Lynn Hazen. BA MI SU 1995; MDiv GTS 2005; Mstr's of Ch Mgmt Villanova U 2011. D 6/11/2005 P 12/17/2005 Bp George Edward Councell. Vic S Steph's Ch Mullica Hill NJ 2005-2011. vballing@comcast.net

BALLINGER, Kathryn Elisabeth (Oly) 9210 Ne 123rd St, Kirkland WA 98034 **D S Thos Ch Medina WA 2004-** B Seattle WA 4/7/1942 d Gunnar Sundin & Hazel. RN Sacr Heart Sch of Nrsng Spokane WA 1966; BSN Gonzaga U 1981; MA Whitworth U 1985; Cert Dio Spokane TS 2000. D 7/22/2000 Bp John Stuart Thornton. m 6/29/1991 Philip Albert Ballinger c 3. D H Trin Epis Ch Spokane WA 2001-2003. kathrynballinger@msn.com

BALLOU, Diedre Schuler (NwT) No address on file. B Lubbock TX 4/27/1961 d Ted Frank Schuler & Shirley. BBA Texas Tech U 1983. D 10/29/2006 Bp C(harles) Wallis Ohl. m 8/31/2002 William David Ballou. dedeballou@calfarley.org

BALMER, Randall (Ct) 91 Minortown Rd, Woodbury CT 06798 **R Chr Epis Ch Middle Haddam CT 2010-** B Chicago IL 10/22/1954 s Clarence Russel Balmer & Nancy Ruth. BA Trin Deerfield IL 1976; MA Trin DS 1981; AM Pr 1982; PhD Pr 1985; MDiv UTS 2001. D 5/20/2006 P 12/7/2006 Bp Jeffrey Neil Steenson. m 1/23/1998 Catharine Louise Randall c 3. R S Jn's Ch Washington CT 2008-2009. Auth, "The Making of Evangelicalism: From Revivalism to Politics and Beyond," Baylor U Press, 2010; Auth, "God in the White Hse: How Faith Shaped the Presidency from Jn F. Kennedy to Geo W. Bush," HarperOne, 2008; Auth, "Thy Kingdom Come: How the Rel Rt Distorts the Faith and Threatens Amer," Basic Books, 2006; Auth, "Growing Pains: Lrng to Love My Fr's Faith," Brazos Press, 2001; Auth, "Blessed Assurance: A Hist of Evangelicalism in Amer," Beacon Press, 1999; Auth, "Grant Us Courage: Travels along the Mainline of Amer Protestantism," Oxf Press, 1996; Auth, "The Presbyterians," Greenwood Press, 1993; Auth, "Mine Eyes Have Seen the Glory: A Journey into the Evang Subculture in Amer," Oxf Press, 1989; Auth, "Perfect Babel of Confusion: Dutch Rel and Engl Culture in the Middle Colonies," Oxf Press, 1989. AAR; Amer Soc of Ch Hist. Doctor of Humane Letters Estrn U 2008. rb281@columbia.edu

BALTUS, D(onald) Barrington (NY) 123 E 15th St # 1504, New York NY 10003 B Columbia SC 3/17/1947 s Donald Frank Baltus & Ida Doris. BA Coll of Charleston 1969; NYU 1973; GTS 1974. D 3/8/1975 Bp Charles Waldo MacLean P 12/1/1975 Bp Jonathan Goodhue Sherman. P-in-c S Andr's Epis Ch Staten Island NY 2000-2006; S Gabr's Ch Brooklyn NY 1999-2000; Hse Chapl Seamens Ch Inst Income New York NY 1996-2000; Assoc Ch Of The Resurr New York NY 1995-1999; Cluster Covenor Dio W Tennessee Memphis TN 1994-1995; Alco And Drugs Com Dio W Tennessee Memphis TN 1994; Coll Wk Com Dio W Tennessee Memphis TN 1989-1995; Chair Aids T/F Dio W Tennessee Memphis TN 1988-1995; T/F On Abortion Dio W Tennessee Memphis TN 1987-1995; A-RC Dio W Tennessee Memphis TN 1983-1995; R The Ch Of The Gd Shpd (Epis) Memphis TN 1983-1995; Epis-Luth Dialogue Dio Long Island Garden City NY 1982-1983; Exec Com Queens Archdeanery Dio Long Island Garden City NY 1980-1983; Missions Dio Long Island Garden City NY 1980-1982; R S Ptr's Ch Rosedale NY 1976-1983; Cur S Andr's Ch Oceanside NY 1975-1976. CBS 1964; Ord Of Julian Of Norwich 1998; SSC 1989. dbb1nyc@yahoo.com

BALTZ, Ann Marie Halpin (Ida) 8947 Springhurst Dr, Boise ID 83704 B New Orleans LA 4/21/1935 d William Joseph Halpin & Evelyn. BS Spalding U 1963. Rec from Roman Catholic 9/1/1991 Bp John Stuart Thornton. m 7/22/1971 Stephen Matthew Baltz. grandmaretired@msn.com

BALTZ, Francis Burkhardt (At) 369 Merrydale Dr SW, Marietta GA 30064 B Irvington NJ 10/20/1944 s Francis Carl Baltz & Hilda Vera. BA Florida St U 1966; MDiv Nash 1969; STM Nash 1979. D 6/29/1969 P 1/4/1970 Bp Albert Ervine Swift. m 6/25/1966 Virginia Lee Beaver c 3. R S Jude's Ch Marietta GA 1985-2007; R S Jn's Epis Ch Of Kissimme Kissimmee FL 1972-1985; Cur S Jas Epis Ch Ormond Bch FL 1969-1972. Auth, "Anges Sanford: A Creative Intercessor," *Unpublished Thesis, Nash*, 1979. frankbaltz@bellsouth.net

BAMBERGER, Michael Andrew (Los) 241 Ramona Ave, Sierra Madre CA 91024 **Dioc Disaster Coordntr, ER&D Dio Los Angeles Los Angeles CA**

2011-; Dn, Dnry V Dio Los Angeles Los Angeles CA 2009-; Co-Chair, Comission on Mnstry Dio Los Angeles Los Angeles CA 2003-; Lead Trnr, Misconduct Prevention Dio Los Angeles Los Angeles CA 2001-; R The Ch Of The Ascen Sierra Madre CA 1985- B Riverside CA 9/20/1955 s Jack Lester Bamberger & Patricia. BA U CA 1977; MDiv Nash 1981. D 6/20/1981 P 12/20/1981 Bp Robert C Rusack. m 8/25/1979 Debra Jean Owen c 2. Vic S Jn The Evang Mssn Needles CA 1981-1985. Hon Cn Cathd Cntr of St. Paul 2004. mab@ascension-sierramadre.com

BAMBRICK, Barbara Ann (SeFla) 1802 Pine St, Perry IA 50220 B Minneapolis MN 8/10/1930 d Chester Laroy Nichols & Dell Sophia. Sch of Mnstry in SE Florida; BA U MN 1952; MS Marywood U 1977. D 7/12/1992 Bp Calvin Onderdonk Schofield Jr. m 5/26/1984 Andrew Bambrick c 3. D S Bern De Clairvaux N Miami Bch FL 1992-1997.

BAMFORD, Marilyn Halverson (Minn) PO Box 3247, Duluth MN 55803 B Marquette MI 11/8/1944 d Lynn Harvey Halverson & Mary Louise. Kalamazoo Coll 1964; BA U MI 1965; D Formation Prog 1989; MS U of Wisconsin 1992. D 7/19/1989 Bp Sanford Zangwill Kaye Hampton. m 12/22/1965 Joel Thomas Bamford c 2. D S Edw's Ch Duluth MN 2002-2006; H Apos Ch Duluth MN 1989-1995. NAAD. joelmari@cpinternet.com

BAMFORTH, Richard Anderson (Me) Po Box 5068, Augusta ME 04332 B Lynn MA 1/7/1930 s Charles Nathaniel Bamforth & Dorothy Allan. BA Bow 1951; MDiv Ya Berk 1958; EdM Bos 1982. D 6/21/1958 Bp Frederic Cunningham Lawrence P 12/20/1958 Bp Arthur C Lichtenberger. m 10/24/1959 Patricia P Pennington c 2. Int S Mk's Ch Augusta ME 1993-1994; R S Mary's Epis Ch Rockport MA 1966-1992; R H Cross Epis Ch Poplar Bluff MO 1960-1966; Cur Gr Ch Kirkwood MO 1958-1960. Ed, "Iron Jaw," Dorrance, 2002. prbamforth@gmail.com

BANAKIS, Kathryn Loretta (Ct) 939 Hinman Ave, Evanston IL 60202 **Cmnty Connector S Lk's Ch Evanston IL 2011-** B Evanston IL 11/18/1980 d Christopher Banakis & Gayle W. BA Yale Coll 2003; MDiv Ya Berk 2009. D 6/11/2011 Bp Laura Ahrens. Beatitudes Soc 2009. kbanakis@gmail.com

BANCROFT III, Francis Sydney (Nwk) Po Box 882, Wellfleet MA 02667 B Nyack NY 8/9/1934 s Francis Sydney Bancroft & Sylvia. BA Wesl 1956; STB GTS 1959. D 5/23/1959 Bp Donald MacAdie P 12/17/1959 Bp Leland Stark. Chapt Trin And S Phil's Cathd Newark NJ 1993-2000; S Jas' Ch Ridgefield NJ 1960-2000; Cur S Ptr's Ch Mtn Lakes NJ 1959-1960. Chapl Emer Lions' Club Dist 16-A 2001; Pioneer Awd Lions' Club NJ 1999; Melvin Jones Awd Intl Lions' Club 1993; Cbury Awd Dio Newark Newark NJ 1981.

BANCROFT, John Galloway (At) 1865 Highway 20 W, Mcdonough GA 30253 **R S Jos's Epis Ch McDonough GA 2000-** B Houston TX 6/3/1948 s John Sidney Bancroft & Myrah. BA Texas A&M U 1970; MDiv VTS 1978. D 6/16/1978 Bp Roger Howard Cilley P 6/7/1979 Bp J Milton Richardson. m 6/25/1983 Mary Strey c 2. R S Mary's Epis Ch Reading PA 1988-2000; Vic Chr Epis Ch Mexia Mexia TX 1978-1988; St Mths Ch Waco TX 1978-1984. patxrev@aol.com

BANCROFT, Stephen Haltom (Mich) 19661 Beverly Rd, Beverly Hills MI 48025 B Kansas City MO 8/7/1946 s John Sidney Bancroft & Myrah. BA Texas A&M U 1969; MDiv VTS 1972. D 6/28/1972 Bp Frederick P Goddard P 6/5/1973 Bp J Milton Richardson. m 12/28/1971 Margaret Kubin c 3. Dn Cathd Ch Of S Paul Detroit MI 1995-2007; R Trin Ch Houston TX 1987-1995; R S Cyp's Ch Lufkin TX 1978-1986; Asst S Jn The Div Houston TX 1975-1978; Asst Chr Ch Nacogdoches TX 1972-1975. shb1871@sbcglobal.net

BANDY, Talmage Gwaltney (NC) 22 Bogie Dr, Whispering Pines NC 28327 **Emm Par Epis Ch And Day Sch Sthrn Pines NC 2000-** B Norfolk VA 10/13/1933 d Talmage Lipscomb Gwaltney & Elizabeth. AA Virginia Intermont Coll 1952. D 6/24/1999 Bp Robert Carroll Johnson Jr. m 11/28/1953 Wilton Claude Bandy c 2. revtally@embarqmail.com

✠ **BANE JR, Rt Rev David Conner** (SVa) 600 Talbot Hall Rd, Norfolk VA 23505 B Morgantown WV 9/11/1942 s David Conner Bane & Barbara. BA Bethany Coll 1964; MBA W Virginia U 1970; MDiv VTS 1985; LHD S Paul's Coll Lawrenceville VA 1998; DD VTS 1998. D 6/5/1985 P 12/7/1985 Bp Robert Poland Atkinson Con 9/6/1997 for SVa. m 2/6/1965 Alice Brogan c 4. Ret Bp of SVa Dio Sthrn Virginia Norfolk VA 1998-2006; Bp Dio Sthrn Virginia Norfolk VA 1997-2006; Bp Coadj Of Sthrn Virginia Dio Sthrn Virginia Norfolk VA 1997-1998; R Chr Epis Ch Dayton OH 1991-1997; Chair Ch Dvlpmt Cmsn Dio New Hampshire Concord NH 1989-1991; Dioc Coun Dio New Hampshire Concord NH 1988-1990; R Par Of S Jas Ch Keene NH 1987-1991; Dnry Convenor Dio New Hampshire Concord NH 1987-1988; R S Jn Wheeling WV 1985-1987. Doctor of Humane Letters St. Paul's Coll 1997; Hon DD VTS 1997. d_banejr@yahoo.com

BANE, Jack Donald (NY) 210 Old North Rd, St Paul's Episcopal Church, Camden DE 19934 B Beaumont TX 12/11/1935 s Jack Samuel Bane & Lois. BA Rice U 1958; STB GTS 1962; Cert Fndt For Rel & Mntl Hlth 1972; MS Iona Coll 1973; ACPE 1979. D 6/22/1962 P 6/1/1963 Bp Frederick P Goddard. P-in-c Ch Of S Nich On The Hudson New Hamburg NY 1998-2003; Chr Epis Ch Tarrytown NY 1998; S Aug's Epis Ch Croton On Hudson NY 1995; Chr Ch Bronxville NY 1994; Trin Epis Ch Ossining NY 1992-1993; Int S Ptr's Epis Ch Peekskill NY 1987-1988; Int S Phil's Ch Garrison NY 1986-1987; S Barn Ch Irvington on Hudson NY 1969-1972; Cur Chr Ch Bronxville NY 1966-1969; Asst S Mk's Ch Beaumont TX 1964-1966; Hon Cn Chr Ch Cathd Houston TX 1962-1964; Vic Chr Ch San Aug TX 1962-1964; Vic S Jn's Epis Ch Cntr TX 1962-1964. Auth, "Death & Mnstry: Pstr Care Of The Dying & The Bereaved"; Auth, "Pstr Psychol & Pulpit Dig". AAPC 1974; Chairman Profsnl Concerns Com Estrn Reg 1988-1992; Clincl Mem ACPE; Diplomate 1979. donaldbane@alumni.rice.edu

BANKS, Cynthia Kay (WNC) 272 Maple Ridge Dr, Boone NC 28607 **R S Lk's Ch Boone NC 2004-** B Louisville KY 3/15/1965 d Stephen Winslow Rauh & Virginia Ruth. BA/BS U of Louisville 1988; MDiv GTS 1994. D 6/25/1994 P 1/6/1995 Bp Edwin Funsten Gulick Jr. m 2/5/2000 James DR Banks c 2. Assoc Chr Ch Cathd Louisville KY 2000-2004; Chr Ch Cathd Louisville KY 1998-1999; Dio Kentucky Louisville KY 1998-1999; Mssn Dvlp S Thos Ch Campbellsville KY 1998-1999; Asst R Chr Epis Ch Bowling Green KY 1994-1998. Auth, "Uncommon Witness: Luth-Epis Mnstrs Bring Concordat To Life," *Journ Of Wmn Mnstrs (Sum)*, 1998. BS/BA Valedictorian U Of Louisville Louisville KY 1988. ckrbanks@gmail.com

BANKS JR, Frederick David (Ky) 2541 Southview Dr, Lexington KY 40503 B Louisville KY 6/26/1945 s Fred D Banks & Patricia Ann. BS U of Louisiana 1968; MDiv UTS 1971; AS U of Louisiana 1973; JD U of Louisiana 1980. D 6/21/1971 P 3/1/1973 Bp Charles Gresham Marmion. m 5/17/1969 Virginia Stone. Chr Ch Cathd Louisville KY 1975-1978; Dir CALC Dio Kentucky Louisville KY 1971-1972. Hon Cn Chr Cathd Louisville Kentucky 1975. n. welsh@insightbb.com

BANKS, Joseph Hilton (EC) 1303 E Caswell St, Kinston NC 28501 **Died 4/28/2011** B Paul's CrossRoads VA 1/3/1912 s William William Banks & Leah Virginia. VTS 1944; BA Virginia Un U 1945. D 6/12/1944 Bp Wiley R Mason P 7/19/1945 Bp Frederick D Goodwin. c 3. jhbankscwebtv.net

BANKS JR, Ralph Alton (SeFla) No address on file. B Savannah GA 3/9/1931 s Ralph Alton Banks & Lucille. BA U So 1954; STB GTS 1959; Med Florida Atlantic U 1979. D 6/16/1957 P 2/1/1958 Bp Albert R Stuart. R S Jn The Apos Ch Belle Glade FL 1995-2000; H Nativ Pahokee FL 1993-2000; Asst Trin Ch Vero Bch FL 1969-1971; Asst S Phil's Ch Coral Gables FL 1966-1969; R S Mich's Ch Mobile AL 1965; Vic S Matt's Epis Ch Fitzgerald GA 1959-1963; Cur S Paul's Ch Augusta GA 1957-1958.

BANKS, Richard Allan (La) 1444 Cabrini Ct, New Orleans LA 70122 B Warren OH 4/4/1951 s Paul Philips Banks & Florence Greenwood. Untd Theol Coll Of The W Indies Kingston Jm; BA U of The W Indies 1993. Trans from Iglesia Anglicana de la Region Central de America 6/6/2003 Bp Charles Edward Jenkins III. m 2/28/1986 Barbara Ann Ellington c 2. H Fam Epis Ch Midland MI 2008-2009; H Fam Epis Ch San Pedro Garza Nuevo Leon 2008-2009; Chap Of The H Comf New Orleans LA 2007-2008; R S Lk's Ch New Orleans LA 2003-2005; Int Trin Ch Arlington VA 2001-2002. rbanks1@cox.net

BANKSTON, Van Alan (Miss) 509 W Pine St, Hattiesburg MS 39401 **Trin Ch Hattiesburg MS 2011-** B Greenwood MS 6/24/1954 s Arthur Waymon Bankston & Mildred Rebecca. BLA Mississippi St U 1976; MAT Mississippi Vlly St U 2004; MDiv The GTS 2011. D 6/4/2011 Bp Duncan Montgomery Gray III. vnbnkstn@aol.com

BANNER, Daniel Lee (Chi) 2431 Bradmoor Dr, Quincy IL 62301 B Bloomington IL 7/7/1928 s Francis Lee Banner & Margaret. BA Millikin U 1950; BD SWTS 1953; MDiv SWTS 1954. D 3/25/1953 P 9/29/1953 Bp Charles A Clough. R S Paul's By The Lake Chicago IL 1970-1992; S Jn's Epis Ch Peoria IL 1959-1970; Cur S Lk's Ch Evanston IL 1956-1959; Vic S Jn's Ch Centralia IL 1953-1956; Vic S Thos Ch Salem IL 1953-1956; Cur S Paul's/Trin Chap Alton IL 1953. SSC 1974.

BANNER, Shelly Ann (CNY) 41 Highmore Dr, Oswego NY 13126 B Oneida NY 11/10/1949 d Harold Willis Banner & Isabel Bresee. Loc Formation Prog By Bexley And Dio Cntrl NY. D 11/19/2005 Bp Gladstone Bailey Adams III. m 8/6/1994 Leon Carapetyan. sabanner@aol.com

BANSE JR, Robert Lee (Va) 221 Orr Rd, Pittsburgh PA 15241 **R Trin Ch Upperville VA 2007-** B Brooklyn NY 4/2/1957 s Robert Lee Banse & Gertrude Anne. Drew U; BA Geo 1980; MDiv VTS 1985. D 5/7/1986 Bp Frederick Warren Putnam P 1/1/1987 Bp Donald Purple Hart. m 12/31/1985 Jane Clark c 2. S Steph's Epis Ch Wilkinsburg PA 2006-2007; R S Paul's Epis Ch Pittsburgh PA 1998-2005; R S Jn's Epis Ch Wilmington NC 1994-1998; Cn Pstr S Mich's Cathd Boise ID 1990-1993; Coun Dio Spokane Spokane WA 1988-1990; P-in-c Ch Of The Resurr (Chap) Roslyn WA 1987-1990; R Gr Ch Ellensburg WA 1987-1990; Pstr Asst S Andr's Cathd Honolulu HI 1986-1987. ROBBANSE@MAC.COM

BAPTISTE-WILLIAMS, Barbara Jeanne (SeFla) 6041 Sw 63rd Ct, Miami FL 33143 B Miami FL 1/8/1941 d Edwin O'Neil Baptiste & Elaine Agatha. BS Tuskegee Inst 1962; MA U of Nthrn Colorado 1974; MDiv VTS 1996. D 11/23/1996 Bp Calvin Onderdonk Schofield Jr P 5/1/1997 Bp John Lewis Said. m 6/29/1974 Clinton Williams c 1. R Ch Of The Trsfg Opa Locka FL 1997-2007. First Black Wmn R Dio SE Florida 1997. ecott24@aol.com

BARBARITO, Melanie Repko (FtW) 5005 Dexter Ave, Fort Worth TX **Par Assoc for Evang & Engagement All SS' Epis Ch Ft Worth TX 2009-** B Battle Creek MI 10/8/1953 d Joseph Stephen Repko & Irene Josephine. SUNY 1974; BS NY St Rgnts Coll 1988; MDiv Bex 1996. D 6/15/1996 Bp William George Burrill P 1/6/1997 Bp Herbert Thompson Jr. c 2. Vic S Fran Epis Ch Eureka MO 2001-2009; Cur The Ch of the Redeem Cincinnati OH 1996-2001. mthbarbarito@asecfw.org

BARBEE JR, William Thomas (Tex) 429 Chickasha Rd Apt N, FORT SILL OK 73503 **Off Of Bsh For ArmdF New York NY 1995-** B Mount Vernon IL 10/4/1958 s William Thomas Barbee & Shirley May. BA Dav Lipscomb Coll Nashville TN 1980; MA Oakland City Coll Grad TS 1986; MDiv Oakland City Coll Grad TS 1987. D 11/1/1994 Bp William Elwood Sterling P 6/1/1995 Bp Claude Edward Payne. m 6/27/1980 Cindy Jean Greer c 2.

BARBER, Barbara Jean (Kan) 5518 Sw 17th Ter, Topeka KS 66604 **D Gr Cathd Topeka KS 1997-** B Plainfield NJ 4/27/1926 d Robert Harold Owen & Edith Selma Katherine. BA Tem 1949; MLS Emporia St U 1995; GTS 1995. D 2/2/1997 Bp William Edward Smalley. m 9/25/1949 Robert Barber. NAAD.

BARBER, Elaine Elizabeth Clyborne (Minn) 4830 Acorn Ridge Rd, Minnetonka MN 55345 B New Praque NM 8/4/1937 d Matthew Albert Rybak & Mary Clara. Marq; BS U MN 1959; Med U MN 1976; Cert SWTS 2003; MDiv Untd TS 2003. D 11/14/1992 Bp Sanford Zangwill Kaye Hampton P 6/12/2003 Bp James Louis Jelinek. m 6/2/1994 Richard Barber. Chapl Dio Minnesota Minneapolis MN 1983-2000. efizdiz3437@hotmail.com

BARBER, Grant Woodward (Mass) 102 Branch St., Scituate MA 02066 **R S Lk's Epis Ch Scituate MA 2005-** B San Francisco CA 7/10/1957 s Robert Dane Barber & Lois Jean. BA Baylor U 1980; MDiv Ya Berk 1987. D 6/13/1987 Bp Arthur Edward Walmsley P 1/1/1988 Bp Jeffery William Rowthorn. m 5/22/1982 Denise Fox c 1. R H Trin Epis Ch Oxford OH 1998-2005; Epis Ch At Yale New Haven CT 1990-1998; Cur S Paul's Epis Ch Willimantic CT 1987-1990. revgrant@comcast.net

BARBER, Grethe Hallberg (Oly) 690 N Shepherd Rd, Washougal WA 98671 B Rochester MN 4/11/1942 d Olav Erik Hallberg & Mildred Virginia. M.A. Marylhurst U 1994; M. Div Ya Berk 2000. D 1/20/2002 Bp Vincent Waydell Warner P 8/24/2002 Bp Sanford Zangwill Kaye Hampton. c 4. Ch Of The Gd Shpd Vancouver WA 2002-2009. Assn of Profsnl Chapl 2001. gretheb@goodshepherdvancouver.org

BARBER, James Frederick (FtW) 3217 Chaparral Ln, Fort Worth TX 76109 **Ecum Off Dio Ft Worth Ft Worth TX 2000-** B Portsmouth VA 8/29/1944 s James Robert Barber & Cora. BA Barton Coll 1966; MDiv Van 1970; DMin Van 1971; USAF 1997; USAF 2003. D 7/6/1975 P 11/8/1975 Bp Robert Bruce Hall. m 8/20/1967 Judith S Barber c 2. Del to GC Dio Ft Worth Ft Worth TX 2009-2011; Pres Stndg Com Dio Ft Worth Ft Worth TX 2009; R Trin Epis Ch Ft Worth TX 1999-2010; Hosp Hlth Ins T/F Dio Wstrn New York Tonawanda NY 1994-1996; R Ch Of The Adv Kenmore NY 1989-1999; Pres Stndg Com Dio Wstrn New York Tonawanda NY 1989-1991; R Chr Ch Lockport NY 1980-1989; R S Mary's Ch Colonial Bch VA 1977-1980; Cur Chr Epis Ch Luray VA 1975-1977. Auth, "Guidelines For Epis/RC Marriages"; Auth, "Operation Desert Storm-Homefront". Operation Desert Storm - Homefront Red Cross; Meritorius Serv Medal (3 Oak Leaf Cluster) Us AF. barberfred@sbcglobal.net

BARBER, James S (Mo) 313 W Hardy St, Saint James MO 65559 **Trin Ch S Jas MO 2007-** B Springfield MO 6/18/1952 s Fred Ross Barber & Aileen R. D 12/20/2006 P 7/7/2007 Bp George Wayne Smith. m 10/5/1986 Glenda Barber. fr.barber@gmail.com

BARBER JR, Vernon H (Eau) 502 County Road Ff, Hudson WI 54016 **Asstg P S Paul's Ch Hudson WI 2009-** B W Palm Beach FL 12/18/1936 s Vernon Hymric Barber & Lois Johnson. BBA Georgia St U; Dplma Gordon Mltry; MA Nash. D 5/30/2009 P 12/12/2009 Bp Russell Edward Jacobus. m 7/3/1997 Leslie Johnson c 2. vbarber@centurytel.net

BARBOUR OHC, Grady Frederic Waddell (Ala) 565 12th Ct, Pleasant Grove AL 35127 B Columbia SC 5/3/1946 s William Jackson Barbour & Gwendolyn. BA U of Miami 1967; MDiv VTS 1973; Full Clincl Supvsr ACPE 1981; Certification Int Pstr - Int Consult 1986; Diplomate Coll of Pstr Supervision and Psych 1992. D 6/7/1973 P 2/1/1974 Bp Wilburn Camrock Campbell. m 7/24/1982 Martha Elise Sanford c 1. R S Mich's Epis Ch Birmingham AL 2004-2009; P-in-c S Jn's Ch Birmingham AL 2001-2004; R So Talladega Cnty Epis Mnstry Sylacacga AL 1995-1997; Int S Mths Epis Ch Tuscaloosa AL 1992-1994; Cn The Cathd Ch Of The Adv Birmingham AL 1986-1988; Baltimore City Hospitals/Fran Scott Key Med Inst Dio Maryland Baltimore MD 1981-1986; Johns Hopkins Med Institutions, Chapl Dio Maryland Baltimore MD 1981-1986; Vic Epis Ch of the Trsfg Buckhannon WV 1973-1979. Auth, "Co-Creators w God," *EARTH Letter*, Earth Mnstry, 2011. Appalacian Inst 1974; ACPE 1986; Coll Pstr Supervision & Psych 1992. Archontes Soc U of Miama 1965. gbarbour@gbarbour.com

BARBOUR, Norman Hugh (Colo) 10760 Zuni Drive, C/o Diana M. Barbour, Westminster CO 80234 B Milwaukee WI 9/30/1924 s Raleigh Widney Barbour & Hazel Olive. BS NWU 1949; MDiv SWTS 1952. D 5/31/1952 P 12/13/1952 Bp Wallace E Conkling. c 3. Hon P Assoc S Jn's Cathd Denver CO 1989-2001; Asst Epiph Epis Ch Denver CO 1968. Auth, "Var arts," *H Cross mag*. Hon P Assoc S Jn's Cathd Denver CO 1989; MDiv cl SWTS Evanston IL 1952; BS cl NWU Evanston IL 1949. normanhbarbour@comcast.net

BARBUTO, Judith Steele (U) 718 Zinnia Way, Sandy UT 84094 B Saint Louis MO 10/19/1950 d Joseph Schall Steele & Virginia Steele. BS U of Utah 1976; JD U of Utah 1981; ETSBH 1996. D 3/25/1998 P 1/23/1999 Bp Carolyn Tanner Irish. m 7/17/2004 Patrick Robert Bruns c 2. Epis Cmnty Serv Inc Salt Lake City UT 1998-2001; All SS Ch Salt Lake City UT 1998; Dio Utah Salt Lake City UT 1994-1998. ACPE; Assn Profsnl Chapl; Delta Soc; Intermountain Ther Animals; Ut Assn Pstr Care. Phi Beta Kappa U Of Utah Salt Lake City UT 1976; Bs mcl U Of Utah Salt Lake City UT 1976. judithbarbuto@hotmail.com

BARCLAY, David Laird (Kan) 10224 Robinson St, Overland Park KS 66212 B Chicago IL 5/30/1929 s Robert Earl Barclay & Esther Mae (Hansen) Barclay Matthews. AA W&M 1951; BA Pk Coll Parkville MO 1953; MDiv EDS 1956; S Geo's Coll Jerusalem IL 1980. D 6/21/1956 P 12/1/1956 Bp Edward Randolph Welles II. R Chr Ch Overland Pk KS 1978-1982; R S Dunst's Epis Ch San Diego CA 1970-1978; R Trin Ch Anderson IN 1961-1970; Cur S Paul's Ch Kansas City MO 1959-1961; Vic All SS Ch W Plains MO 1956-1959; Vic Ch Of The Trsfg Mtn Grove MO 1956-1959. dbarclay1@kc.rr.com

BARDEN III, Albert A (Ct) 254 Father Rasle Rd, Norridgewock ME 04957 B Fort Jackson SC 9/15/1945 s Albert A Barden & Elizabeth Oat. BA Br 1967; MDiv Ya Berk 1970; Cert Ya Berk 1971. D 6/12/1971 Bp Joseph Warren Hutchens P 1/1/1972 Bp Morgan Porteus. m 6/15/1968 Cheryl Ann Coffin c 1. Cur Chr And H Trin Ch Westport CT 1971-1976. Auth, "Finnish Fireplace Construction Manual"; Auth, "Finnish Fireplaces/Heart Of The Hm"; Auth, "Albiecore Construction Manual". mwhco@etel.net

BARDOS, Gordon A (Vt) 9449 N 110th Ave, Sun City AZ 85351 B Gary IN 11/11/1939 s Alex Bardos & Helen Otillia. BA Franklin Coll 1965; Texas Tech U 1967; MDiv SWTS 1982; DMin GTF 1995. D 5/29/1982 P 12/4/1982 Bp Robert Shaw Kerr. c 2. P-in-c Gr Epis Ch Brandon VT 1986-2006; R S Thos' Epis Ch Brandon VT 1986-2006; Vic S Mk's-S Lk's Epis Mssn Castleton VT 1982-1986. Angl Soc 1986; Assoc, SSJE 1995; Associated Parishes 1986; CBS 1969. gabardos@cox.net

BARDUSCH JR, Richard Evans (Mass) PO Box 149, Taunton MA 02780 **R Epis Ch Of S Thos Taunton MA 2010-** B Hampton VA 10/18/1964 s Richard Evans Bardusch & Doris Rose. BA Emory & Henry Coll 1987; MDiv Duke 1992; Cert EDS 1995; DMin Drew U 2006. D 6/5/1995 Bp Robert Carroll Johnson Jr P 4/20/1996 Bp Frank Harris Vest Jr. Assoc R Gr Ch In Providence Providence RI 2006-2009; Ch Of The Mssh Providence RI 2005-2006; Dio Rhode Island Providence RI 2004-2007; Open Door Reg Mnstry Providence RI 2002-2004; R S Ptr's And S Andr's Epis Providence RI 2002-2003; Dir Yth Mnstrs Dio Newark Newark NJ 1997-2002; Cur S Jn's Ch Hampton VA 1996-1997; Gr Ch Yorktown Yorktown VA 1995. "Sneakers," *Sage Advice*, Abingdon Press, 2003; "Mo Cooper," *Sage Advice*, Abingdon Press, 2003; "They Went Thataway," *Sage Advice*, Abingdon Press, 2003; "Keep Paddling," *Sage Advice*, Abingdon Press, 2003. frrich64@aol.com

BARFIELD, DeOla Edwina (Ct) 744 Lakeside Dr, Bridgeport CT 06606 B Winston-Salem NC 9/19/1942 d Edwin Andrew Jones & Mildred DaZelle. BA No Carolina Cntrl U 1964; MS U of Bridgeport 1972; Fairfield U 1987. D 12/9/2000 Bp Andrew Donnan Smith. m 8/13/1983 William Earl Barfield. NAAD (No Amer Assoc. for the Diac) 2000.

BARFIELD, Karen Clay (NC) 501 E Poplar Ave, Carrboro NC 27510 **Vic S Jos's Ch Durham NC 2011-** B Memphis 4/15/1966 d James Nelson Clay & Caroline Church. BA Rice U 1988; MS U of Memphis 1990; MDiv Candler TS Emory U 1994. D 11/22/2003 P 5/29/2004 Bp Don Edward Johnson. m 5/26/1990 Raymond Carlton Barfield c 2. Ch Of The Advoc Carrboro NC 2010-2011; Dio No Carolina Raleigh NC 2009-2010; Int Duke Epis Cntr Durham NC 2009-2010; Assoc R Gr - S Lk's Ch Memphis TN 2007-2008; Cn for Cmnty Mnstrs S Mary's Cathd Memphis TN 2005-2007; Int S Elis's Epis Ch Memphis TN 2003-2005. Theta Phi hon Soc in Rel 1994. kclaybarfield@gmail.com

BARFIELD, William G (WVa) 107 Rockwood Lane, Saint Albans WV 25177 **R S Mk's Epis Ch S Albans WV 2008-** B Jackson MS 3/14/1964 D 6/18/2004 P 2/2/2005 Bp Duncan Montgomery Gray III. m 9/6/2003 Susan A Shroff. Ch Of The Ascen Hattiesburg MS 2004-2008. frbillbarfield@gmail.com

BARFORD, Lee Alton (ECR) 561 Keystone Ave #434, Reno NV 89503 **D Trin Cathd San Jose CA 2005-** B Cheltenham PA 10/14/1961 s Robert Alton Barford & Frances. BA Tem 1982; MS Cor 1985; PhD Cor 1987; BTh Sch for Deacons 2005. D 6/17/2005 Bp Sylvestre Donato Romero. m 1/27/1996 Kirsten A Nelson c 1. lee.barford@trinitysj.org

BARGER, George William (Neb) 508 South 67th, Omaha NE 68106 B Green Valley MO 8/1/1923 s George William Barger & Frieda. BA Butler U 1948; BD Chr TS 1950; MA Chr TS 1952; PhD U of Missouri 1965. D 6/13/1968 P 10/28/1968 Bp Russell T Rauscher. m 12/19/1943 Helen Ross c 4. Asst Trin

Cathd Omaha NE 1980-1995; Chapl S Lk's Chap Omaha NE 1979-1980; Nebraska Hlth System Omaha NE 1978-1979; All SS Epis Ch Omaha NE 1971-1978; Vic S Steph's Ch Grand Island NE 1969-1970; Asst S Andr's Ch Omaha NE 1968-1969. Theta Pi. Phi Beta Kappa Chr TS 1950; Phi Kappa Phi; Theta Phi. gwbarger@msn.com

BARGETZI, David Michael (O) 1417 Larchmont Ave, Lakewood OH 44107 **Urban Mssnr S Lk's Ch Cleveland OH 2000-; S Mk's Ch Cleveland OH 2000-; Epis. Shared Mnstrs Nw Lakewood OH 1999-; Cur S Dunst's: The Epis Ch at Auburn U Auburn AL 1989-** B Endicott NY 3/20/1957 s Robert Edward Bargetzi & Helen Mae. U Of Paris Fr; BA Tul 1979; MDiv Nash 1987. D 5/30/1987 P 12/1/1987 Bp Furman Stough. m 7/17/2003 R Stephen Gracey. S Jn's Ch Cleveland OH 1997-1998; Cbury Chap and Coll Cntr Tuscaloosa AL 1995-1997; Dio Alabama Birmingham AL 1989-1995; Cur Chr Ch Tuscaloosa AL 1987-1989; R S Jn's Ch Cleveland OH 1969-1986. Phi Beta Kappa Tul New Orleans LA 1979.

BARHAM, Michael Preston (Haw) 1515 Wilder Ave, Honolulu HI 96822 **Assoc R The Par Of S Clem Honolulu HI 2008-** B Orlando FL 6/19/1975 s Robert Preston Barham & Janet Claire. BA Millsaps Coll 1999; MDiv Duke 2003; CAS CDSP 2008. D 6/13/2008 P 12/6/2008 Bp Marc Handley Andrus. on.pilgrimage@gmail.com

BARHAM, Patsy Griffin (Tex) St Matthew's Episcopal Church, 214 College Ave, Henderson TX 75654 **P-in-c S Matt's Ch Henderson TX 2007-** B Mesa AZ 11/1/1948 d B V Miller & Bettie Virginia. BA Steph F. Austin St U 1971; MED Steph F. Austin St U 1981; MDiv Iona Sch of Mnstry 2007. D 6/23/2007 Bp Don Adger Wimberly P 1/11/2008 Bp Rayford Baines High Jr. m 8/31/1968 George Stephen Barham c 3. patsybarham@suddenlink.net

BARKER, Ann Biddle (Va) 6231 Kilmer Ct, Falls Church VA 22044 **R S Jn's Epis Ch Arlington VA 2001-** B Charleston WV 3/31/1956 BA U NC 1978; MA Indiana U 1980; MDiv Candler TS Emory U 1996; Cert. TS 1999. D 6/5/1999 Bp Onell Asiselo Soto P 1/29/2000 Bp Herbert Thompson Jr. c 1. Asst R S Pat's Epis Ch Dublin OH 2000-2001; Asst R S Jn's Ch Worthington OH 1999-2000. MDiv mcl Candler TS Atlanta GA 1996; BA w hon U NC/Chap Hill, NC Wilmington NC 1978. stjohnsrector@verizon.net

BARKER, Christie Dalton (NC) 824 Henkel Rd, Statesville NC 28677 B Charlotte NC 11/4/1966 d Jerry Owen Dalton & Judy Ann. BA Arizona St U 2006. D 10/5/2002 Bp Robert Reed Shahan. m 12/31/1994 Jesse Russell Barker. DOK, St. Clare Chapt 2004. christieb@bellsouth.net

BARKER, Christopher Haskins (Pgh) 1062 Old Orchard Dr, Gibsonia PA 15044 B Jacksonville FL 11/21/1943 s Robinson F Barker & Mary H. BA MacMurray Coll 1967; BD VTS 1970; MA Duquesne U 1987; PhD Duquesne U 1995. D 6/6/1970 Bp William S Thomas P 12/19/1970 Bp Robert Bracewell Appleyard. m 8/31/1968 Mary Eleanor Pearce c 2. S Chris's Epis Ch Cranberry Twp PA 1978-1999; R S Lk's Epis Ch Smethport PA 1975-1978; Asst Trin By The Cove Naples FL 1971-1975; Cn Trin Cathd Pittsburgh PA 1970-1971. Auth, "Crosses Or Blessings," *Envoy: Journ Of Formative Reading 13:5*, 1986. Natl Dn'S List. stkitt@zoominternet.net

BARKER, Daniel W (WMass) P.O. Box 92, Block Island RI 02807 **Vic S Ann's-By-The-Sea Block Island RI 2008-** B Painesville OH 10/3/1943 s Kenneth Townsend Barker & Grace Rebecca. BA U of Massachusetts 1971; MDiv Westminster TS 1980. D 9/28/1981 P 3/1/1982 Bp Alexander Doig Stewart. m 12/19/1970 Margaret G Fife c 4. R The Ch Of The H Innoc Henderson NC 2000-2003; S Ptr's Ch Great Falls SC 1997-1999; Chapl York Place Epis Ch Hm For Chld York SC 1996-2000; Dio Cntrl New York Syracuse NY 1993-2008; R S Andr's Ch Vestal NY 1987-1996; R S Thos Epis Ch Auburn MA 1983-1987; Cur/Asst Ch Of The Atone Westfield MA 1981-1983. danielbarker@hotmail.com

BARKER, Gary Joseph (SVa) 111 S Church St, Smithfield VA 23430 **R Chr Epis Ch Smithfield VA 2002-** B Glendale CA 12/17/1956 s Joseph Woodrow Barker & Jeanne Dorothy. BA Tul 1980; MA U of Virginia 1983; MDiv VTS 1990; Cert GTS 1998. D 6/2/1990 Bp Peter James Lee P 2/14/1991 Bp Robert Poland Atkinson. m 7/28/1984 Gail B McGinnis c 4. Vic Gr Ch Stanardsville VA 1994-2002; Asst R Emm Ch Harrisonburg VA 1990-1994. Mdiv cl VTS Alexandria VA 1990. garyjmbarker@verizon.net

BARKER, Herbert James (SanD) 11727 Mesa Verde Dr, Valley Center CA 92082 **Exec Coun Appointees New York NY 2010-** B Marlow GA 8/14/1942 s Lawrence Jackson Barker & Ole May. EdD U of San Diego 1957; BA Berry Coll 1965; MDiv Duke 1968; STM Dubuque TS 1971. D 3/11/1997 P 9/1/1997 Bp Gethin Benwil Hughes. m 12/2/1991 Miyoko Hashimoto. Pstr S Mary's In The Vlly Ch Ramona CA 2008-2010.

BARKER, JoAnn D (Del) 241 Louisiana Circl, Sewanee TN 37375 B LaPorte IN 10/8/1948 d Rudolph Bohmil Dolezal & Helen Therese. AA Ancilla Coll 1969; BS S Fran U Ft Wayne IN 1971; U of Memphis 1992; MDiv TS 1994; DMin SWTS 2006. D 7/9/1994 P 1/14/1995 Bp Larry Earl Maze. m 7/13/1974 Charles Lawrence. Barker c 3. R St Annes Epis Ch Middletown DE 2009-2011; R S Mk's Epis Ch Jonesboro AR 2004-2009; R S Jn's Ch Harrison AR 1996-2004; Cur S Mk's Epis Ch Jonesboro AR 1994-1996. joann.barker@gmail.com

✠ **BARKER, Rt Rev J. Scott** (Neb) 50 South St, Warwick NY 10990 **Bp Dio Nebraska Omaha NE 2011-; R Chr Ch Warwick NY 2002-** B Omaha NE 6/11/1963 s Joseph Barker & Susan. BA Ya 1985; MDiv Ya Berk 1992. D 6/24/1992 P 12/21/1992 Bp James Edward Krotz Con 10/8/2011 for Neb. m 10/1/1988 Anne Elizabeth Latimer c 2. Ch Of The Resurr Omaha NE 1997-2002; Cn Trin Cathd Omaha NE 1992-1997. Auth, "I Want My Ch to Grow," Forw Mvmt, 2007; Auth, "Future of Our Generation in Ch," *Gathering the Next Generation*, Morehouse Pub, 2000; Auth, "A Tale Too Big To Get Your Arms Around," *Sermons That Wk IX*, Morehouse Pub, 2000; Auth, "Easter Terror," *Sermons That Wk VIII*, 1999. Mersick Prize- Exceptional Promise for Pstr Mnstry Ya Berk New Haven CT 1992; Tweedy Prize- Excellence in Preaching Ya Berk New Haven CT 1992. sbarker@episcopal-ne.org

BARKER, Kenneth Lee (CGC) 9409 E 65th St, Tulsa OK 74133 B Shattuck OK 7/6/1952 s Alvin Lee Barker & Anna Ruth. BA Oral Roberts U 1975; MDiv Epis TS of The SW 1978; MA U of No Florida 1990; DMin Reformed TS 2000. D 6/17/1978 Bp Gerald Nicholas McAllister P 6/25/1979 Bp J Milton Richardson. m 7/3/1986 Ellen Knowles Wignall. R Gr Epis Ch Panama City Bch FL 1996-2000; Ch Of Our Sav Jacksonville FL 1992-1996; Vic S Marg's Ch Lawton OK 1980-1984; Asst S Jn The Div Houston TX 1978-1980. Auth, "The Effects Of Ther/Client Value Similarity On"; Auth, "Self-Disclosure In Counslg"; Auth, "Mobilizing Ch Members For Meaningful Mnstry"; Auth, "Orgnztn Culture," *Cmd Revs*. SocMary. klbarker7652@cox.net

BARKER, Lynn Kay (Miss) 29 Melody Ln, Purvis MS 39475 B Staunton VA 6/28/1955 d Nolan Hardison Barker & Helen Elizabeth. BA U of Virginia 1976; MA U NC 1978; PhD U NC 1988; MDiv STUSo 2002. D 5/25/2002 P 12/7/2002 Bp Duncan Montgomery Gray III. All SS Epis Ch Grenada MS 2004-2010; Trin Ch Hattiesburg MS 2002-2004. lynxpad@aol.com

BARKER, Patrick Morgan (Ark) 1521 Mcarthur Dr, Jacksonville AR 72076 **Trin Par Ch Epis Searcy AR 2006-** B Little Rock AR 6/12/1949 s Ernest Milton Barker & Virginia Ellen. BA U of Arkansas 1980; MDiv Epis TS of The SW 1983; PhD ETSBH 1993. D 5/12/1984 P 12/1/1984 Bp Herbert Alcorn Donovan Jr. m 5/12/1979 Neva R Oberste c 3. Dio So Dakota Sioux Falls SD 2004-2006; S Ptr's Par Rialto CA 1998-2004; P-in-c S Mths' Par Whittier CA 1996-1998; S Mk's Epis Sch Upland CA 1996-1997; S Mk's Epis Ch Upland CA 1995-1996; P-in-c S Alb's Epis Ch Yucaipa CA 1990; S Raphaels Ch Chino CA 1988-1990; Vic S Ptr's Ch Conway AR 1984-1989; S Alb's Ch Stuttgart AR 1984-1988. pbarker33@aol.com

BARKER, Paula Suzanne (Chi) 2122 Sheridan Rd, Evanston IL 60201 **S Thos' Ch Garrison Forest Owings Mills MD 2011-** B Ann Arbor MI 1/23/1952 d Joseph Datsko & Doris Mae. BA U MI 1974; MDiv Yale DS 1977; PhD U Chi 1990. D 4/21/1993 Bp Frank Tracy Griswold III P 10/20/1993 Bp William Walter Wiedrich. m 8/18/1974 Charles Barker c 2. SWTS Evanston IL 1993-2010. Auth, "Caritas Pirckheimer: A Female Humanist Confronts the Reformation," *16th Century Journ*, 1995; Auth, "Lord Teach us Pray: Hist & Theol Prespectives on Expanding Liturgal Lang," *How Shall We Pray*, 1994; Auth, "The Motherhood of God in Julian of Norwich's Theol," *The Downside Revs*, 1982. BM w dist U MI Ann Arbor MI 1974. paulabarker@gmail.com

BARKSDALE II, Charles Dudley (SwFla) 712 Sandpiper Ln, Nokomis FL 34275 **Died 2/25/2010** B Charlottesville VA 11/29/1936 s Joshua Hightower Barksdale & Mary Agnes. BA U of Virginia 1958; MDiv SWTS 1961. D 6/11/1961 P 12/1/1961 Bp William R Moody. c 2.

BARLEY, Linda Elizabeth (SwFla) 10922 106th Ave, Largo FL 33778 B Russleville AL 10/28/1948 S Vinc's Sch Of Nrsng Birmingham AL. D 1/18/2003 Bp John Bailey Lipscomb. c 2.

BARLOWE, Michael (Cal) 1055 Taylor Street, San Francisco CA 94108 **Cn Residentary Gr Cathd San Francisco CA 2009-; Cn to the Ordnry Dio California San Francisco CA 2002-** B North Carolina 4/12/1955 s E Lee Barlowe & Pearl Day. BA Harv 1977; MDiv GTS 1983; DMin CDSP 2006. D 6/4/1983 Bp Paul Moore Jr P 12/14/1983 Bp George Phelps Mellick Belshaw. m 7/11/2008 Paul Anthony Burrows. Hon Asst Ch Of The Adv Of Chr The King San Francisco CA 2002-2009; Dn The Cathd Ch Of S Paul Des Moines IA 1991-2002; R Dio Iowa Des Moines IA 1991-2000; R Gr Epis Ch Plainfield NJ 1986-1991; Cur S Paul's Epis Ch Westfield NJ 1983-1986. michael@barlowe.net

BARNABY JR, Alcide (RI) 32 Audubon Ave, Providence RI 02908 B Pawtucket RI 1/31/1944 s Alcide Barnaby & Gladys. BEd Rhode Island Coll 1965; STB Ya Berk 1968. D 6/24/1968 P 3/6/1969 Bp John S Higgins. m 10/25/2011 Daniel Harvey. R S Jas Ch The Par Of N Providence RI 1993-2009; Vic Ch Of The H Sprt Charlestown RI 1972-1981; Asst S Barn Ch Warwick RI 1970-1971; Asst Ch Of The Mssh Providence RI 1968-1969. Integrity; Mercy Of God Cmnty. albarnaby@verizon.net

BARNARD, N. Sandra (ECR) 1267 Black Sage Cir, Nipomo CA 93444 **Assoc S Barn Ch Arroyo Grande CA 1994-** B Whittier CA 5/26/1929 d Thomas Murdock McIntosh Riach & Irene Violet. AA Stephens Coll 1949; BSMT U NC 1951; MDiv Fuller TS 1982. D 12/19/1987 P 6/27/1988 Bp Charles Shannon Mallory. m 8/16/1952 Roger Conant Barnard c 4. Asst S Mk's-In-The-

Vlly Epis Los Olivos CA 1991-1992; Asst S Lk's Ch Atascadero CA 1987-1990. Chapl Ord Of S Lk 1991.

BARNES JR, Bennett Herbert (SwFla) 7 Fiddlehead Fern TRL, Brunswick ME 04011 B Waterbury CT 7/17/1933 s Bennett Herbert Barnes & Mildred Ethel. BA Colg 1955; STB Ya Berk 1958; Fllshp U of Durham Durham GB 1963; STM Ya Berk 1967; EdM Harv 1972; DMin Bos 1993; DD Ya Berk 1994. D 6/11/1958 Bp Walter H Gray P 12/27/1958 Bp John Henry Esquirol. m 7/14/1962 Beth L Dieterly c 2. S Geo's Epis Ch Bradenton FL 2000-2004; Dn Manasota Dnry Dio SW Florida Sarasota FL 1995-1999; All Ang By The Sea Longboat Key FL 1992-1999; Vic S Edw Chap Oklahoma City OK 1963-1976; Vic S Jn's Ch Stamford CT 1958-1961. Cn Pstr Dio SW Florida 2000. bennettbarnes@suscom-maine.net

BARNES, Brian Joseph (Cal) Church Of The Holy Innocents, 455 Fair Oaks St, San Francisco CA 94110 B Philadelphia PA 2/8/1964 s John Barnes & Andrea. BA Sch for Deacons; U of San Francisco; BA U of Texas. D 12/14/2006 Bp Marc Handley Andrus. Ch Of The H Innoc San Francisco CA 2007-2008. brian@holyinsf.org

BARNES, Charles Richard (EO) Po Box 317, Hermiston OR 97838 **D S Jn's Ch Hermiston OR 1996-** B Boise ID 6/28/1947 s Demas Richard Barnes & Arlene Pearl. BTh NW Chr Coll Eugene OR 1971; Cert Oregon Cntr For The Diac Eugene OR 1977; MBA Portland St U 1991. D 3/23/1996 Bp Rustin Ray Kimsey. m 6/14/1970 Robin Lynn Turbyne. NAAD. chuckb@eotnet.net

BARNES, Jeffry Parker (SD) 21285 E Highway 20 Apt 127, Bend OR 97701 B Saint Paul MN 5/27/1941 s Russell George Barnes & Margaret Terhune. BA U MN 1963; MA U MN 1967; Harvard DS 1973; MDiv Nash 1976. D 6/29/1976 P 3/25/1978 Bp Philip Frederick McNairy. m 7/14/1962 Shirley Ann MacMillan c 3. Int Vic Ch Of The H Apos Sioux Falls SD 2008-2010; Cheyenne River Epis Mssn Dio So Dakota Sioux Falls SD 1998-2006; R S Jas Epis Ch Zanesville OH 1989-1998; R S Mart's Epis Ch Fairmont MN 1982-1989; Vic Breck Memi Mssn Naytahwaush MN 1980-1982; Vic S Columba White Earth MN 1980-1982; P in Charge Chr Ch Duluth MN 1977-1980; R S Andr's Ch Le Sueur MN 1977-1980; Dio Minnesota Minneapolis MN 1976-1982. Mdiv cl Nash Nashotah WI 1976; Ba mcl U MN Minneapolis MN 1963. jeffry@bendbroadband.com

BARNES, John David (Ala) P.O. Box 560, 401 N Main Ave, Demopolis AL 36732 **R Trin Ch Demopolis AL 2008-** B Gadsden AL 4/30/1973 s Ruie Andrew Barnes & Rozalind Brooks. BS The U of Alabama 1995; MDiv Epis TS of The SW 2006. D 6/1/2006 P 12/12/2006 Bp Henry Nutt Parsley Jr. m 8/3/1996 Amanda Carroll c 2. Assoc R St Thos Epis Ch Huntsville AL 2006-2008. revjdb@bellsouth.net

BARNES JR, Raymond Whitney (Miss) 412 Washington St, Portsmouth VA 23704 B Syracuse NY 11/24/1922 s Raymond Whitney Barnes & Jeannette Rumrill. BA Wesl 1947; MDiv UTS 1950. D 6/4/1950 P 12/16/1950 Bp Horace W B Donegan. m 4/15/1955 Susan Vance. Supply Cler Dio Sthrn Virginia Norfolk VA 1992-2000; Supply Cler Dio Louisiana Baton Rouge LA 1990-1991; Gr Ch Of W Feliciana S Francisville LA 1984-1985; R S Paul's Ch Woodville MS 1973-1989; Assoc R Trin Ch Natchez MS 1970-1973; R Chr Ch Port Tobacco Paris La Plata MD 1959-1970; Asst R S Andr's Ch Wellesley MA 1950-1951. rwb1122@aol.com

BARNES, Robert Dean (WVa) No address on file. B 8/20/1932 D 6/29/1960 P 1/6/1961 Bp Wilburn Camrock Campbell. m 9/12/1953 Joann Calvert.

BARNES, Robyn M (Mont) 515 N Park Ave, Helena MT 59601 **Ch Of The Nativ/Elkhorn Cluster Helena MT 2010-; Camp P/Off Mgr Dio Montana Helena MT 2008-** B Boxeman MT 5/4/1983 d Kent Barnes & Lynda. BA U of Montana 2005; MDiv The GTS 2008. D 6/1/2008 P 5/31/2009 Bp Charles Franklin Brookhart Jr. Dio Montana Helena MT 2010. theologybird@gmail.com

BARNES, Susan Johnston (Tex) 1403 Alegria Rd, Austin TX 78757 **Assoc R S Matt's Ch Austin TX 2001-** B 9/28/1948 d Charles Wynn Barnes & Marguerite Johnston. BA Rice U 1970; MA NYU 1980; PhD NYU 1986; MDiv Epis TS of the SW 2001. D 6/16/2001 P 6/19/2002 Bp Claude Edward Payne. Co-Auth, "Van Dyck: A complete Catalogue," Ya Press, 2004; Co-Auth, "Anothony Van Dyck," Natl Gallery of Art, 1990; Auth, "The Rothko Chap, An Act of Faith," U of Texas, 1989. susan@stmattsaustin.org

BARNETT, Becca Fleming (Cal) 435 Euclid Ave Apt 1, San Francisco CA 94118 B Parkersburg WV 7/20/1952 d Frederick Haumann Barnett & Ida Watson. PhD California Sch of Profsnl Psychol; BA Alfred U 1978; MS U Roch 1982; MDiv CDSP 1986; MA California Sch of Profsnl Psychol 1991. D 6/3/1989 P 12/1/1990 Bp William Edwin Swing. Serv S Aid's Ch San Francisco CA 2000-2002; Ch Of The H Innoc San Francisco CA 1999-2000; P-in-c S Andr's Epis Ch San Bruno CA 1998-1999; S Ambr Epis Ch Foster City CA 1996-1997; St Johns Epis Ch Ross CA 1995-1996; Assoc S Greg Of Nyssa Ch San Francisco CA 1992-1995; Gr Cathd San Francisco CA 1989-1992; Commision On Mntl Illness Dio California San Francisco CA 1989-1991. Oblate S Ben Camaldolese. bfbarnett@sbcglobal.net

BARNETT JR, Edward Lee (Minn) 5029 Valley View Rd, Edina MN 55436 **Coordntng Com Dio Minnesota Minneapolis MN 1998-; Coordntng Com Dio Minnesota Minneapolis MN 1998-** B AZ 4/13/1924 s Edward Lee Barnett & Gladys. BS NWU 1946; MDiv cum laud SWTS 1959. D 6/20/1959 Bp Gerald Francis Burrill P 12/19/1959 Bp Charles L Street. m 2/2/1980 Diane Wheaton c 6. Adv Ch Farmington MN 2000-2004; S Mich's All Ang Ch Monticello MN 1986-1990; St Michaels All Ang Ch Minneapolis MN 1986-1990; Vic S Barth's Ch Wichita KS 1963-1966; Assoc S Jas Ch Wichita KS 1960-1963; Cur Trin Ch Highland Pk IL 1959. Auth, "Memphis Wmn," *mag's 2000 List of Wmn Who Make a Difference*, 2000. edlbarnett@gmail.com

BARNETT, Edwin Wilson (FtW) 808 Voltamp Dr., Fort Worth TX 76108 **P, Catechist S Chris's Ch And Sch Ft Worth TX 2010-** B Tyler TX 7/6/1954 s Edwin Wilson Barnett & Carolyn. BS Lamar U 1982; MS U of Arkansas 1984; MS SMU 1994; MDiv Nash 1997. D 6/21/1997 P 12/20/1997 Bp Jack Leo Iker. m 5/25/1991 Leigh Ann Wiant c 2. Vic All SS' Epis Ch Ft Worth TX 2009-2010; R S Paul's Ch Doylestown PA 2005-2009; Asst R S Paul's Par Washington DC 1999-2005; Cur S Mk's Ch Arlington TX 1997-1999. homebusiness@me.com

BARNETT JR, James Monroe (Neb) 3401 Poppleton Ave, Omaha NE 68105 B Baton Rouge LA 10/21/1925 s James Mark Barnett & Egeria Overton. BA LSU 1946; MDiv SWTS 1951; DMin STUSo 1979. D 7/15/1951 P 7/25/1952 Bp Girault M Jones. m 8/15/1956 Marian Scofield c 4. COM Dio Nebraska Omaha NE 1983-1986; Exec Coun Dio Nebraska Omaha NE 1976-1990; Bd Trst Dio Nebraska Omaha NE 1976-1985; Chair Liturg Cmsn Dio Nebraska Omaha NE 1969-2005; Dio Nebraska Omaha NE 1969-1992; Exec Coun Dio Nebraska Omaha NE 1969-1970; St Anselms Ch Norfolk NE 1965-1992; R Trin Epis Ch Norfolk NE 1958-1992; Vic S Paul's Epis Ch Lamar CO 1952-1958; Cur Epis Ch Of The Gd Shpd Lake Chas LA 1951-1952. Auth, *The Diac: A Full & Equal Ord, Revised ed.*, Seabury Press, 1981; "Var arts," *Diakoneo*; "Diakonia," *Liturg*. Associated Parishes, Liturg Conf; ADLMC; NAAD. DD SWTS 2004. james.barnett@cox.net

BARNETT, Thomas C (EC) 1219 Forest Hills Dr., Wilmington NC 28403 B Palo Alto CA 7/9/1952 s Charles Francis Barnett & Mildred Edith. BA California St U 1976; MDiv Fuller TS 1979; DMin STUSo 1990; PhD S Louis U 1998. D 3/30/1980 P 4/5/1981 Bp Victor Manuel Rivera. m 8/2/1980 Lynann M Patton c 3. S Jn's Epis Ch Wilmington NC 2008; St Mths Epis Ch Waukesha WI 2005-2008; Int Chr Ch Springfield IL 2002-2005; Off Of Bsh For ArmdF New York NY 2001-2002; Int S Mich & S Geo Clayton MO 1999-2001; Chair Evang Com Dio Missouri S Louis MO 1989-1993; R S Matt's Epis Ch Warson Warson Woods MO 1986-1997; S Andr's Ch Taft CA 1983-1986; Epis Dio San Joaquin Modesto CA 1982; S Paul's Ch Bakersfield CA 1980-1982. Auth, "Who's Afraid of Evang ?: Identifying Pstr Concerns Hindering Evang in the Par," *S Lk Journ Theol*; Contrib, *Selected Sermons*. AAR (AAR); OHC; SBL. lmpb73@aol.com

BARNETT, Webster Gesner (Minn) 9303 Ne Lafayette Ave Apt 3, Bainbridge Island WA 98110 **Died 11/30/2010** B Red Wing MN 11/7/1923 s Joseph Noyes Barnett & Helen Sargent. BA Trin Hartford CT 1948; VTS 1951. D 6/22/1951 Bp Stephen E Keeler P 12/22/1951 Bp Conrad Gesner. c 4. wbarnl6b@msn.com

BARNEY, David Marshall (Mass) 310 Hayward Mill Rd, Concord MA 01742 B Richmond VA 2/11/1940 s Marshall Hobart Barney & Mary. BA U of Virginia 1962; BD STUSo 1965; MLitt U of Cambridge 1975; DMin STUSo 1996. D 6/21/1965 P 6/18/1966 Bp Gray Temple. m 8/29/1964 Beverly G Garrett c 1. R Trin Ch Concord MA 1981-2001; Dep GC Dio Cntrl Gulf Coast Pensacola FL 1979-1982; S Paul's Epis Ch Daphne AL 1972-1981; Int Trin Epis Ch Pinopolis SC 1968; Asst to Dn Cathd Of S Lk And S Paul Charleston SC 1965-1968. revdbarney@aol.com

BARNEY, Roger Alexander (ECR) 19040 Portos Dr, Saratoga CA 95070 **Asst S Andr's Ch Saratoga CA 1998-** B Martinsburg WV 12/26/1939 s James Robinson Barney & Odetta Marie. BA/BS Shpd Coll Shepherdstown WV 1961; Cert Sch for Deacons 1980. D 3/25/1982 P 3/19/1984 Bp Charles Shannon Mallory. m 8/1/1970 Jeannette Keit. Asst S Tim's Epis Ch Mtn View CA 1994-1998; Asst S Andr's Ch Saratoga CA 1982-1994. rogerbarney@comcast.com

BARNHILL JR, James Wallance (SC) P.O. Box 587, Bennettsville SC 29512 **R S Paul's Ch Bennettsville SC 2009-** B Durham NC 10/29/1956 s James Wallace Barnhill & Gladys Greneker. BM The U of So Carolina 1977; MBA The Amer U of Washington,DC 1985; MDiv TESM 2008. D 1/10/2009 P 7/6/2009 Bp Mark Joseph Lawrence. m 12/5/1998 Donna West-Barnhill. james.barnhill@comcast.net

BARNHOUSE, David H (Los) 6844 Penham Pl, Pittsburgh PA 15208 **Pstr Asst Ch Of The Ascen Pittsburgh PA 1993-** B Philadelphia PA 5/17/1929 s Donald Grey Barnhouse & Ruth W. BA Harv 1949; MD Col 1954. D 6/7/1986 P 8/20/1993 Bp Alden Moinet Hathaway. m 5/31/1952 Mary Alice Young. D Ch Of The Ascen Pittsburgh PA 1986-1993. AMA; Amer Urologic Assn. Ba cl Harv Cambridge MA 1949. davidbhous@worldnet.att.net

BARNS, G(eorge) Stewart (Mass) Po Box 381164, Cambridge MA 02238 B Grand Rapids MI 1/3/1945 s George Raymond Barns & Margaret. Bos; BA Trin Hartford CT 1967; BD EDS 1970; ThM Harvard DS 1978. D 6/20/1970 P

B

5/9/1971 Bp John Melville Burgess. Epis Chapl At Harvard & Radcliffe Cambridge MA 1978-2004; The Cathd Ch Of S Paul Boston MA 1976-1978; Ch Of The H Sprt Mattapan MA 1976; Int Ch Of Our Sav Somerset MA 1975-1976; Asst Trin Ch In The City Of Boston Boston MA 1970-1975. Auth, "The Way Of The Cross"; Auth, "The Emerging Spiritulity Of Young Adulthood"; Auth, "Counslg & Referrals When Rel Issues Are Significant Factors". stewart_barns@hotmail.com

BARNUM, Elena (Ct) 112 Bentwood Dr, Stamford CT 06903 B Cambridge MA 11/9/1943 d Edwin Kent Harwich & Sylvia Bagration. Sch of The Museum of Fine Arts 1963; BS Rhode Island Sch Of Design 1965; Cert New York Psychoanalytic Soc and Inst 1989. D 12/7/1991 Bp Arthur Edward Walmsley. m 7/30/1994 Malcolm McGregor Barnum. NAAD.

BARNUM, Malcolm McGregor (Ct) 112 Bentwood Dr, Stamford CT 06903 **Dio Connecticut Hartford CT 2011-** B Detroit MI 1/5/1927 s Richard Fyfe Barnum & Jessie. BA U MI 1949; Pmg Stan 1968; Ord Prog Dio Southwark, London UK 1975; Ord Prog Dio Connecticut 1986. D 12/6/1986 Bp Arthur Edward Walmsley. m 7/30/1994 Elena Harwich c 3. Par of St Paul's Ch Norwalk Norwalk CT 2005-2010; D S Paul's Ch Riverside CT 1998-2007; Archd Dio Connecticut Hartford CT 1991-2005; D Epis Ch of Chr the Healer Stamford CT 1991-1997; D Chr Ch Greenwich CT 1986-1991. Servnt Soc. perfmx@aol.com

BARNWELL, William (La) 1917 Audubon St, New Orleans LA 70118 B Charleston SC 10/12/1938 s William Hazzard Barnwell & Mary Maybank. BA U So 1960; BD VTS 1967; MA Tul 1976. D 6/24/1967 P 6/18/1968 Bp Gray Temple. m 8/17/1976 Corinne Freeman c 3. Chair, Racial Recon Com Dio Louisiana Baton Rouge LA 2008-2011; P Assoc Trin Ch New Orleans LA 2008-2011; Cn Mssnr Cathd of St Ptr & St Paul Washington DC 2005-2008; Dn, Boston Harbor Dnry Dio Massachusetts Boston MA 1997-2002; Assoc R Trin Ch In The City Of Boston Boston MA 1996-2002; Assoc R Trin Ch New Orleans LA 1983-1996; Chapl Ch Of The H Sprt New Orleans LA 1970-1978; Asst R S Martins-In-The-Field Columbia SC 1968-1970; Vic S Paul's Epis Ch Conway SC 1967-1969; Vic The Epis Ch Of The Resurr Surfside Bch SC 1967-1969. Auth, *Reflections: A Thematic Rdr (w Julia P. Thigpen)*, Houghton-Mifflin Co, 1983; Auth, *Writing for a Reason*, 1983; Auth, *Our Story According to S Mk*, HarperOne, 1982; Auth, *The Resourceful Writer*, 1978; Auth, *In Richard's Wrld*, Houghton-Mifflin Co, 1968. Dn, Boston Harbor Dnry 1997-2002; Louisiana Epis Cler Assn 1970-1996; Massachusettes Epis Cler Assn 1996-2002. BD cl VTS Alexandria VA 1967. wbarnwell@trinitynola.com

BAROODY, Roger Anis (NY) 222 Richard Court, Pomona NY 10970 B Beirut LB 9/20/1941 s Anis Antoon Baroody & Agnes. BA U of Virginia 1964; MDiv UTS 1991. D 6/13/1992 P 12/1/1992 Bp Richard Frank Grein. Dio New York New York City NY 1997-2009; Trin Epis Ch Garnerville NY 1997-2009. rbar@rabaroody.net

BARR, David Lee (Fla) 8227 Bateau Rd S, Jacksonville FL 32216 B San Antonio TX 1/25/1942 s Bernice Stone Barr & Doris Jane. BS Texas A&M U 1968; MDiv Epis TS of The SW 1977. D 6/21/1977 P 1/1/1978 Bp Scott Field Bailey. m 6/5/1965 Patsy A Barr. Asst San Jose Epis Ch Jacksonville FL 2004-2005; Asst S Eliz's Epis Ch Jacksonville FL 1999-2003; Chapl, DOK Dio Florida Jacksonville FL 1996-1999; Dir Of Dvlpmt Nash Nashotah WI 1993-1996; Dn of Fac, Hd of Rel Dept Texas Mltry Inst San Antonio TX 1983-1988; Asst S Barth's Ch Corpus Christi TX 1981-1983; R S Paul's Ch Brady TX 1979-1981; Assoc Ch Of Recon San Antonio TX 1977-1979. Dok. davidlbarr@bellsouth.net

BARR, Dixon A (Lex) 308 Clinton Rd, Lexington KY 40502 **Died 10/15/2009** B Gary IN 1/14/1932 s Harold Barr & Matilda. Lexington TS; S Geo's Coll Jerusalem IL; U So; BS Ball St U 1953; MA Col 1959; EdD Col 1965. D 6/5/1994 P 5/1/1996 Bp Don Adger Wimberly. Natl Epis Historians Assn; SHN, SocMary.

BARR, Donna (Lex) 2140 Woodmont Dr, Lexington KY 40502 B Lexington KY 1/30/1947 d James Bailey Faulconer & Anna Ray. BEd U Of Kentucky 1969; CPE U Of Kentucky 1989; EFM STUSo 1991; CPE U Of Kentucky 1991. D 12/21/1994 Bp Don Adger Wimberly. m 6/9/1967 Garland Hale Barr c 1.

BARR, Gillian Rachel (SVa) 2728 6th Ave, San Diego CA 92103 **Epis Chapl, Old Dominion U Cbury Epis Campus Mnstry Norfolk VA 2011-** B Annapolis MD 6/3/1968 d Richard Alfred Barr & Eleanor McAbee. BA W&M 1990; MDiv PrTS 1995; Dplma in Angl Stds VTS 2010. D 9/9/2010 P 4/9/2011 Bp James Robert Mathes. Campus Mssnr, UC San Diego Dio San Diego San Diego CA 2010-2011. Natl Assn for Epis CE Dir 2000. grbarr90@wmalumni.com

BARR, Jane Wallace (Va) 209 Macarthur Rd, Alexandria VA 22305 **Goodwin Hse Baileys Crossroads Falls Ch VA 2011-** B Columbia MS 1/21/1945 d Sardis Gomer Wallace & Ethel. BA Mississippi Coll 1967; MA GW 1975; MDiv VTS 1992. D 6/20/1992 Bp Duncan Montgomery Gray Jr P 3/23/1993 Bp Peter James Lee. m 10/2/1981 Hubert Barry c 1. S Jas Ch Woodstock VT 2010-2011; Int All SS Ch Harrison NY 2008-2009; S Thos Epis Ch McLean VA 2005-2007; Ch Of The H Cross Dunn Loring VA 2004-2005; Gr Ch Stanardsville VA 2003-2004; S Jn's Epis Ch Carlisle PA 2000-2003; Ch Of Our Redeem Aldie VA 1996-2000; Chr Ch Alexandria VA 1993-1995; Asst S Tim's Ch Herndon VA 1992-1993. janewbarr@comcast.net

BARR III, John MacReadie (SC) 16 Swan Lake Dr, Sumter SC 29150 **R Ch Of The H Comf Sumter SC 1995-** B Sewanee TN 4/23/1949 s John Macreadie Barr & Nell. BA U So 1971; VTS 1976. D 6/16/1976 P 6/1/1977 Bp George Moyer Alexander. m 9/2/1972 Laura Ramsey. Chr the King Pawleys Island SC 1991-1995; Assoc All SS Epis Ch Hampton SC 1991-1992; Stndg Com Dio Cntrl Gulf Coast Pensacola FL 1982-1985; Chr Ch Cathd Mobile Mobile AL 1980-1991; Ch Of The Adv Sumner MS 1978-1980; Asst S Thad Epis Ch Aiken SC 1976-1978.

BARR, Norma M (Chi) 3300 W Kinnickinnic River Pkwy, Apt 2, Milwaukee WI 53215 B Dunfermline Scotland 6/20/1941 d Norman Stewart & Noreen. BA (Hons) Trin Theol Coll, Bristol, UK 1999. Trans from Scottish Episcopal Church 7/6/2003 Bp William Dailey Persell. c 2. Gr Ch Pontiac IL 2003-2005. normabarr@gmail.com

BARRAGAN, Juan (Los) 9046 Gallatin Rd., Pico Rivera CA 90660 **Vic S Barth's Mssn Pico Rivera CA 2003-** B Mexico City 3/1/1953 s Hector Barragan & Maria Luisa. Cert Escuela Sup Ventas 1978; CTh ETSBH 1998. D 6/6/1998 P 1/9/1999 Bp Frederick Houk Borsch. m 1/16/1993 Petra Santillana c 3. Vic Epis Chap Of S Fran Los Angeles CA 2001-2002; Asst S Mich's Mssn Anaheim CA 1999-2001; Asst All SS Par Los Angeles CA 1998-1999. juanbarragan@juno.com

BARRAZA, Rene Alfredo (Los) St Athanasius and St Paul's, 840 Echo Park Ave, Los Angeles CA 90026 **Dio Los Angeles Los Angeles CA 2008-** B Olocuilta El Salvador 3/12/1943 s Rosaura. D 7/29/2007 P 2/23/2008 Bp Joseph Jon Bruno. m 8/19/1967 Maria Antonia Lopez c 4. Cong Of S Athan Los Angeles CA 2007. rbarraza@ladioces.org

BARRE, James Lyman (Vt) 1009 Robert E. Lee Drive, Wilmington NC 28412 B Brattleboro VT 7/19/1935 s Ernest Vadnais Barre & Gladys Evelyn. BA U of Vermont 1964; STB GTS 1967. D 6/10/1967 P 12/16/1967 Bp Harvey D Butterfield. m 4/28/1973 Carol Harman c 3. Chapl Cathd Ch Of S Paul Burlington VT 1971-1972; P-in-c Chr Ch Island Pond VT 1969-1970; R S Mk's Epis Ch Newport VT 1967-1970. jamesbarre@msn.com

BARRERA FLORES, Olga I (Hond) IMS SAP Dept 215. PO BOX 523900, Miami FL 33152 Honduras B 4/9/1969 d Domingo H Barrera & Maria Isabel G. D 3/11/2007 P 2/5/2011 Bp Lloyd Emmanuel Allen. c 3. suaroba@yahoo.com

BARRETT, Constance Yvonne (Mil) 3560 N Summit Ave, Shorewood WI 53211 B Pittsburgh PA 5/19/1943 BA U Pgh 1972; MDiv Pittsburgh TS 1975. D 12/12/1981 Bp Robert Bracewell Appleyard P 5/29/1986 Bp Alden Moinet Hathaway. m 1/27/1980 G Richard Meadows. S Chris's Ch River Hills WI 1986-1990; S Paul's Ch Milwaukee WI 1982-1983; Asst Calv Ch Pittsburgh PA 1971-1978.

BARRETT, J (Tex) St Martin's Episcopal Church, 1602 S Fm 116, Copperas Cove TX 76522 **Vic S Mart's Epis Ch Copperas Cove TX 2008-** B Dallas TX 8/13/1949 s Frank S Barrett & Helen Gloria. BS LSU 1971; MD SW Med Sch 1975; Iona Sch for Mnstry 2007. D 6/23/2007 Bp Don Adger Wimberly P 1/12/2008 Bp Dena Arnall Harrison. m 6/22/1974 Margaret B Bushey c 3. D in Charge S Mart's Epis Ch Copperas Cove TX 2007-2008. Auth, "Renal Sodium Wastin," *Salt Wasting Nephropathy*, Texas Med, 1979. jrichbarrett@aol.com

BARRETT, Johanna Elizabeth Langley (Mass) Trinity Church, 124 River Road, Topsfield MA 01983 **R Trin Ch Topsfield MA 2005-** B Utica NY 11/30/1955 d Edwin Blois Barrett & Edith Mae. BA Mt Holyoke Coll 1977; MS Amer U 1984; MDiv VTS 1994. D 6/11/1994 P 12/14/1994 Bp Peter James Lee. Assoc R S Thos Epis Ch Rochester NY 1998-2005; Asst R Chr Ch Corning NY 1995-1998; Asst To Int Ch Of The Resurr Alexandria VA 1994-1995. Auth, "Vstry Resource Guide," 1997. jelbarrett@verizon.net

BARRETT, John Hammond (WTex) 3527 Vancouver Dr, Dallas TX 75229 **Chr Epis Ch San Antonio TX 2005-** B Paris TX 2/13/1960 s Henry Grady Barrett & Joan. BA U So 1982; MA Ford 1991; Med Ford 1996; MDiv TESM 2002. D 6/8/2002 P 3/1/2003 Bp James Monte Stanton. m 5/27/1995 Barbara Crosby Bell c 4. Gd Shpd Epis Sch Dallas TX 2004-2005; Cur S Lk's Epis Ch Dallas TX 2002-2004. johnb@cecsa.org

BARRETT JR, John Henry (CNY) 41 S Woody Hill Rd, Westerly RI 02891 B Westerly RI 2/19/1937 s John Henry Barrett & Mildred. BA U of Rhode Island 1959; MDiv Ya Berk 1963; St Geo's Coll, Jerusalem 1989. D 6/22/1963 P 5/9/1964 Bp John S Higgins. m 8/25/1962 Carol Wells c 3. R All SS Epis Ch Johnson City NY 1996-2002; Dioc Coun Dio Massachusetts Boston MA 1985-1988; R The Ch Of The H Name Swampscott MA 1970-1996; Asst Trin Ch Concord MA 1967-1970; Cur Chr And H Trin Ch Westport CT 1964-1967; Mssnr Cathd Of S Jn Providence RI 1963-1964. Silver Beaver Awd for Serv to Yth BSA 1988. jb.cb1@cox.net

BARRETT, Patricia (Mass) 103 Main St, Falmouth MA 02540 **R S Barn Ch Falmouth MA 2009-** B Brooklyn NY 2/7/1949 d Peter Callan Reynolds & Evelyn Mabel. BA Mt Holyoke Coll 1971; MA Amer Intl Coll 1975; MDiv

EDS 1998. D 6/10/2000 Bp Gordon Paul Scruton P 12/10/2000 Bp Barbara Clementine Harris. m 1/23/1971 William F Barrett c 2. Stndg Com Dio El Camino Real Monterey CA 2007-2009; R Epis Ch Of The Gd Shpd Salinas CA 2004-2009; Int S Lk's Epis Ch Scituate MA 2003-2004; Asst S Paul's Ch In Nantucket Nantucket MA 2000-2002. "Sacr Garden," Morehouse, 2000; "Too Busy To Clean," Storey Pub, 1994. revpat1@mac.com

BARRETT, Rilla Diane (Oly) 670 Rainbow Dr, Sedro-Woolley WA 98284 **P in Charge Ch Of Our Sav Monroe WA 2011-** B Seattle WA 10/5/1947 d Edwin James King. BAEd Wstrn Washington U 1969; MA,Ed Seattle Pacific U 1989; MDiv Vancouver TS BC CA 2009. D 4/17/2009 Bp Gregory Harold Rickel P 11/19/2009 Bp Bavi Rivera. m 6/8/1991 Michael Barrett c 3. Cur Komo Kulshan Cluster Mt Vernon WA 2010-2011. rbarrett@wavecable.com

BARRETT, Robin Carter (EO) 9310 Parakeet Dr, Bonanza OR 97623 B Pasadena CA 2/19/1925 s I Carter Barrett & Elizabeth Trumble. D 8/16/1992 P 7/1/1993 Bp Rustin Ray Kimsey. m 8/16/1952 Marvel Mae Ikenberry Wilson. P S Barn Par Portland OR 1993-2007; D S Barn Par Portland OR 1992.

BARRETT CSL, Sr Bernadette (Nwk) 1 Mt Kemble Ave #212, Morristown NJ 07960 B Lawrence KS 2/10/1946 d Linton Lomas Barrett & Marie Hamilton. BA Albertus Magnus Coll 1970; MA NYU 1972; MDiv GTS 1975; PhD NYU 1986. D 12/15/1975 P 1/10/1977 Bp Paul Moore Jr. Int S Jn's Ch Un City NJ 2008-2011; Int S Jas Ch Upper Montclair NJ 2004-2005; Int Ch Of The Medtr Bronx NY 2003-2004; Int S Andr And H Comm Ch So Orange NJ 2000-2002; R Bergen Epis Area Mnstry Rochelle Pk NJ 1996-2000; Assoc The Ch of S Ign of Antioch New York NY 1992-1996; Asst S Jn's Ch New York NY 1988-1992; Assoc The Ch Of S Lk In The Fields New York NY 1980-1988; Assoc S Mk's Par Berkeley CA 1977-1980; D S Mk's Par Berkeley CA 1975-1977. Auth, "Var arts". Chapl Ord Colonial Lords Of Manors Amer; CBS; Eccl Hist Soc (Britain); Soc Of S Jn The Evang. Mdiv cl GTS New York NY 1975. srbernadetteosb@hotmail.com

BARRETT, S(ylvia) Dawn (Roch) 12 E Genesee St, Wellsville NY 14895 **Mssnr S Phil's Ch Belmont NY 2002-** B Saint John's Newfoundland CA 8/15/1947 d Frederick Mackay Cox & Maisie Ruberta. BA Memi U of Newfoundland 1969; BEd Memi U of Newfoundland 1969; MA Memi U of Newfoundland 1993; MDiv Queen's Theol Coll CA 1996. Trans from Anglican Church of Canada 6/3/2002 Bp Jack Marston McKelvey. m 8/16/1969 Erle Barrett c 3. Dio Rochester Rochester NY 2003-2008; Allegany Cnty Mnstry Belmont NY 2002. "The Role of the Death-Bed Narrative in the Concep Bay Revival of 1768-69," Can Soc of Ch Hist, 1995; "The Wk of God Upon my Soul: The Conversion Narrative and After-Walk Account in the Early Newfoundland Methodist Cmnty," Can Soc of Ch Hist, 1993. acem@eznet.net

BARRETT, Timothy Lewis (Nwk) 10 Crestmont Rd, Montclair NJ 07042 B Dallas TX 3/30/1945 D 6/13/2002 P 12/15/2002 Bp John Palmer Croneberger. m 5/31/1969 Mary Elizabeth DuBose c 1. gracecounseilng@att.net

BARRETT, William Prentiss (FtW) 10129 Lone Eagle Dr, Fort Worth TX 76108 **Asst S Anne's Ch Ft Worth TX 1984-** B Pikeville KY 3/23/1920 s William Walker Barrett & Martha Jane. BA U So 1940; MDiv STUSo 1959; GW 1963; TCU 1969. D 1/10/1943 P 8/6/1943 Bp Henry P A Abbott. c 2. Vic Calv Ch Yates Cntr KS 1979-1983; Vic S Tim's Ch Iola KS 1979-1983; R Trin Ch Scotland Neck NC 1972-1979; R Emm Ch Farmville NC 1969-1972; Assoc Trin Epis Ch Ft Worth TX 1967-1969; R S Paul's Epis Ch Wilmington NC 1965-1967; P-in-c S Thos Ch Beattyville KY 1943-1944; Asst S Paul's Epis Ch Albany NY 1943. Auth, *Epis & Dioc Pub*, 1983.

BARRIE, David Paul (NY) 2109 Broadway # 1241, New York NY 10023 B Toledo OH 2/14/1933 s John Barrie & Rose. BA U of Toledo 1956; MFA CUA 1968; MDiv NYTS 1990. D 6/8/1991 P 12/14/1991 Bp Richard Frank Grein. Amer Soc On Aging; Coll Of Chapl.

BARRINGTON JR, E Tom (Mass) 27 6th Ave, North Chelmsford MA 01863 **R All SS Ch Chelmsford MA 1999-** B Boston MA 9/14/1956 s Evan Tom Barrington & Helene. BA Muhlenberg Coll 1979; MDiv EDS 1988. D 6/11/1988 Bp David Elliot Johnson P 6/17/1989 Bp O'Kelley Whitaker. m 6/7/1980 Linda A Robbins c 2. Vic Ch Of The Gd Shpd Nedrow NY 1994-1999; Vic Emm Ch E Syracuse NY 1992-1999; Cn S Paul's Cathd Syracuse NY 1988-1992. asctom@yahoo.com

BARRIOS, Luis (NY) 295 Saint Anns Ave, Bronx NY 10454 B Rio Piechas PR 1/5/1952 s Esteban Barrios & Maria I. BA Wrld U 1978; PhD Caribbean Cntr for Advncd Stds 1983; MDiv NYTS 1991. D 6/8/1991 P 12/1/1991 Bp Richard Frank Grein. m 7/28/1990 Minerva Mella. S Ann's Ch Of Morrisania Bronx NY 1992-1993; P-in-c S Mary's Manhattanville Epis Ch New York NY 1991-2000; D S Ann's Ch Of Morrisania Bronx NY 1991. Ord Of Ascen.

BARRIOS, Maria Trevino (Dal) 534 W 10th St, Dallas TX 75208 B Mexico 9/21/1957 d Miguel A Trevino & Tomaja. D 11/10/2007 Bp James Monte Stanton. m 1/6/1979 M Armando Barrios c 2.

BARRON JR, Caldwell Alexander (USC) 168 Club Cir, Pawleys Island SC 29585 B Charleston SC 7/27/1945 s Caldwell Alexander Barron & Helen Doar. BA Cit 1967; MDiv STUSo 1970. D 6/29/1970 P 5/9/1971 Bp John Adams Pinckney. m 8/24/1968 Margaret H Handy. Assoc H Cross Faith Memi Epis Ch Pawleys Island SC 2009-2011; Assoc Ch Of The Ascen Knoxville TN 1999-2005; Trin Ch Myrtle Bch SC 1994-1999; S Agnes Epis Ch Franklin NC 1993; Ch Of The Gd Shpd Cashiers NC 1991-1994; R S Mk's Ch Marco Island FL 1984-1991; Dio So Carolina Charleston SC 1982-1984; R Epis Ch of the Gd Shpd Charleston SC 1979-1984; Assoc Gr Epis Ch Anderson SC 1977-1979; P-in-c Calv Ch Pauline SC 1977; R Ch Of The Nativ Un SC 1974-1977; Asst Gr Epis Ch Hinsdale IL 1972-1974; Cur Ch Of The Adv Spartanburg SC 1970-1972. cabjr@sc.rr.com

BARRON, Carol Dunn (SeFla) 3954 SE Fairway E, Stuart FL 34997 **Assoc S Lk's Epis Ch Port Salerno FL 2001-** B Oklahoma City OK 1/4/1948 d Gene Harold Snapp & Dorothy Hope. BS Palm Bch Atlantic U 1973; JD Shepard Broad Cntr For Study of Law Ft Lauderdale FL 1981; MDiv STUSo 2001. D 6/16/2001 P 4/26/2002 Bp Leopold Frade. m 3/22/2005 Richard John Barron. cdbarron1@earthlink.net

BARRON, Scott William (Chi) 1148 N Douglas Ave, Arlington Heights IL 60004 **R S Jn's Epis Ch Mt Prospect IL 2003-** B Chicago Heights IL 3/7/1952 s William Barron & Ann. BA Sthrn Illinois U 1976; MA U Chi 1978; DMin Meadville/Lombard TS 1980. D 6/15/2002 P 12/21/2002 Bp William Dailey Persell. m 9/6/1980 Mary McCarthy c 3. SocMary 2005. saintjohns3@comcast.net

BARROW, Alan Lester (Okla) 5635 E. 71st St., Tulsa OK 74136 **D S Dunst's Ch Tulsa OK 2004-** B Bethesda MD 8/8/1952 s Vernie Barrow & Betty Jean. AA Tulsa Cmnty Coll 1991. D 6/21/2003 Bp Robert Manning Moody. m 5/3/1975 Libby Carlson c 3. Chair Cmsn on Prison Mnstry Dio Oklahoma Oklahoma City OK 2006-2010. abarrow@olp.net

BARROW, Colin Vere (SO) 8592 Roswell Rd Apt.218, Sandy Springs GA 30350 B Saint George BB 10/14/1928 s Clyde Vere Hugo Barrow & Verna Euraline. DIT Codrington Coll 1954; BA Lon 1964; STM NYTS 1979; ThD Intl Bible Inst & TS 1983. Trans from Church in the Province Of The West Indies 10/1/1975 as Priest Bp Paul Moore Jr. m 1/4/1976 Winsome Elaine Fuller c 4. Int S Paul's Epis Ch Greenville OH 2000-2002; Dn W Dayton Dnry Dio Sthrn Ohio Cincinnati OH 1992-1999; R S Marg's Ch Trotwood OH 1985-1999; Vic S Lk's Ch Ft Vlly GA 1980-1985; P-in-c S Lk's Cnvnt Av New York NY 1977-1980; S Mart's Ch New York NY 1975-1980. Bro of S Andr 1975; USPG 1955. winbarr@gmail.com

BARROW, John Condict Hurst (Ind) 8920 Washington Blvd West Dr, Indianapolis IN 46240 B Chicago IL 8/20/1956 s Gordon Hurst Barrow & Josephine Condict. BA Col 1979; MDiv Ya Berk 1984; STM Ya Berk 1985; Sthrn Sem Louisville KY 1989. D 12/18/1985 Bp Gerald Nicholas McAllister P 6/1/1986 Bp Frank Stanley Cerveny. m 3/17/1985 Frances Stallings Hale. S Paul's Epis Ch Gas City IN 1999; S Steph's Elwood IN 1998-1999; Epis Ch Of The Gd Shpd Lake Chas LA 1993-1994; Asst Ch Of The Adv Louisville KY 1989-1993; Asst S Tim's Epis Ch Winston Salem NC 1987-1989; Asst S Jn's Epis Ch Tallahassee FL 1985-1987. jch.barrow@gmail.com

BARROW, John Thomas (EpisSanJ) Po Box 3231, Mammoth Lakes CA 93546 B Wilmington DE 12/10/1940 s Ernest Randolph Barrow & Helen Frances. BS California St U 1989; MDiv TESM 1993. D 7/10/1993 P 3/1/1994 Bp John-David Mercer Schofield. m 3/23/1991 Margaret Aird Howard. S Andr's Ch Taft CA 1996-2000; S Thos Of Cbury Mammoth Lakes CA 1993-1996.

BARROW, Suzanne Hurst (Ky) 600 W Center St, Munfordville KY 42765 **Dio Kentucky Louisville KY 2006-; S Andr's Ch Glasgow KY 2004-** B LaGrange KY 3/21/1949 BA U of Louisiana. D 3/22/2003 P 9/28/2003 Bp Edwin Funsten Gulick Jr. Dio Kentucky Louisville KY 2003. suzanneb@scrtc.com

BARROWCLOUGH, Lisa Shirley (SeFla) St. Mark's Episcopal Church and School, 3395 Burns Road, Palm Beach Gardens FL 33410 **Sch Chapl S Mk's Ch Palm Bch Gardens FL 2006-** B Burlington Ontario CA 7/25/1974 d David Allen Barrowclough & Shirley Edith. BA U of Wstrn Ontario 1996; MDiv Queens Coll 1999; DMin VTS 2009. Trans from Anglican Church of Canada 6/12/2004 Bp John Bailey Lipscomb. Ch Of The Gd Shpd Punta Gorda FL 2004-2006; Gd Shpd Day Sch Punta Gorda FL 2004-2006. pastorlisa@stmarkspbg.org

BARROWS, Jennifer Eve (NY) 1585 Route 9 West, West Park NY 12493 **Dioc Trng Cntr New York NY 2011-; P-in-c Ch Of The Ascen And H Trin Highland NY 2001-** B Vellore IN 1/5/1944 d James Clifford McGilvray & Eva Rachel. BA Hope Coll 1966; MDiv UTS 1992; STM GTS 2001. D 3/10/2001 Bp Richard Frank Grein P 9/16/2001 Bp Mark Sean Sisk. c 2. Dio New York New York City NY 2010; D Ch Of The Ascen And H Trin Highland NY 2000-2001.

BARRUS, Donald Sidney (Fla) 516 Balmora Dr, St Augustine FL 32092 B Springfield MA 10/30/1924 s Donald Sidney Barrus & Agnes Dorothy. BS U of Massachusetts 1949; BD VTS 1955; Med Florida Atlantic U 1971. D 6/11/1952 Bp William A Lawrence P 12/1/1952 Bp Duncan Montgomery Gray. m 9/1/1951 Mary Jaudon c 4. R S Andr's Ch Jacksonville FL 1980-1985; R S Jn's Ch Hollywood FL 1977-1980; Assoc S Greg's Ch Boca Raton FL 1975-1977; Dn Palm Bch Dnry Dio SE Florida Miami FL 1961-1968; H Trin Epis Ch W Palm Bch FL 1960-1968; R S Dav's Epis Ch Lakeland FL

1955-1960; Asst S Jn's Epis Par Waterbury CT 1952-1955. donpop888@aol.com

BARRY, Eugenia (WNC) 11 Lone Pine Rd, Asheville NC 28803 B Washington DC 7/11/1952 d Foster MacKenzie & Eugenia May. BA U of New Hampshire 1975; MALS Dart 1994; MSW U NC 2000; DMin GTF 2006. D 11/23/2002 Bp Robert Hodges Johnson. D Gr Ch Asheville NC 2002-2003. ecmbarry@bellsouth.net

BARRY, Kevin Arnold (LI) Mt De Alvear 1721, Buenos Aires Argentina B New York NY 6/27/1954 s Thomas Bernard Barry & Carmel Joan. BA Ham 1976; JD Van 1981; MDiv Ya Berk 1987. D 10/24/1990 P 4/23/1991 Bp Harold B Robinson. c 2. Int Epis Ch of The Resurr Williston Pk NY 2004-2005; Int S Marg's Ch Plainview NY 2002-2004; Asst All SS Ch Brooklyn NY 2001-2002; Asst The Ch of S Matt And S Tim New York NY 2000-2001; Cmsn On Cn Dio Long Island Garden City NY 1998-2000; R Trin Ch Northport NY 1994-2000; Bd Epis Chars Dio Long Island Garden City NY 1994-1999; Asst Ch Of The H Trin New York NY 1992-1994; Calv and St Geo New York NY 1990-1992; Ch Of The H Comm Mahopac NY 1990-1992. tbw27@hotmail.com

BARRY, Peggy Sue (Ark) 400 Hill St, Forrest City AR 72335 B Yell County AR 11/23/1935 d Sam Opal Bennett & Virginia Sue. BSE U of Cntrl Arkansas 1958; MA Arkansas St U 1993. D 8/17/2010 P 3/11/2011 Bp Larry R Benfield. m 3/10/1959 David Barry c 2. dpbarry1@gmail.com

BARRY-MARQUESS, Richard Livingston (SeFla) 19540 Nw 8th Ave, Miami FL 33169 B Miami FL 11/14/1940 s Albert James Barry & Olive Pauline. BA S Aug's Coll Raleigh NC 1962; Amer U 1963; MDiv VTS 1968; Emory U (Candler Sem) 1974; Fell U of Munich 1978; Oxf 2005. D 6/22/1968 Bp James Loughlin Duncan P 12/22/1968 Bp William Loftin Hargrave. m 8/18/1962 Virla Rolle c 1. R S Agnes Ch Miami FL 1977-2010; Vic Ch Of S Simon The Cyrenian Ft Pierce FL 1968-1977; P-in-c S Monica's Ch Stuart FL 1968-1975. Phi Beta Sigma, AAPC. Invested Hon Cn Trin Cathd, Miami 2000; Invested Hon Cn Afr Orth Ch 1995; DD Virginia Sem 1989.

BARTA, F(rank) Kenneth (ECR) 3635 7th Ave Unit 1A, San Diego CA 92103 B Saint Thomas VI 4/5/1924 s Louis Joseph Barta & Agnes Marie Louise. BA Stan 1950; MDiv CDSP 1953. D 6/22/1953 Bp Francis E I Bloy P 12/22/1953 Bp Albert Ervine Swift. R S Jas' Ch Monterey CA 1978-1984; Bp Of ArmdF-Epis Ch Cntr New York NY 1968-1978; R Trin Par Fillmore CA 1961-1967; Vic Imm Mssn El Monte CA 1958-1961; Vic S Ptr's Ch Jacksonville FL 1956-1958; Asst S Mk's Epis Ch Jacksonville FL 1954-1958; All SS Epis Sch S Thos VI 1953-1954. "De Windt Families of the W Indies," *THE GENEALOGIST*, Pickton Press, 1983. Knight of Justice Sovereign Ord of S Jn of Jersusalem 1966.

BARTA, Heather Marie (EMich) 156 Guanonocque St, Auburn Hills MI 48326 B Lakeside AZ 9/7/1973 MDiv SWTS 2004. D 12/18/2003 P 8/21/2004 Bp Robert R Gepert. m 8/11/2006 Henry Barta. S Paul's Epis Ch Flint MI 2009-2011; Chr Epis Ch Owosso MI 2006-2008; Cbury NW Evanston IL 2004-2006. revbarta@gmail.com

BARTELS, Judith Tallman (Oly) 7322 25th Ave Nw, Seattle WA 98117 **D Dio Olympia Seattle WA 2000-** B Nyack NY 2/15/1936 d Frank Ford Tallman & Eileen. BA Pomona Coll 1957; Oregon Cntr for the Diac 1992; Cert Marylhurst U 1996. D 6/24/1992 Bp Robert Louis Ladehoff. m 8/17/1957 Ronald Earl Bartels c 3. D S Steph's Epis Ch Seattle WA 1997-1999; D S Paul's Ch Seattle WA 1995-1996; D Epis Par Of S Jn The Bapt Portland OR 1992-1994. BA w hon Pomona Coll Claremont CA 1957. judithandronald@msn.com

BARTH, Barbara L (Me) 42 Tailwind Ct Apt 78 D, Auburn ME 04210 **Dio Maine Portland ME 2010-** B Niagara Falls NY 12/4/1957 d Vinton Ross Barth & Alma Marie. BS Niagara U 1980; MA U of Connecticut 1982; MDiv Chr Sem -Seminex/LSTC Chicago IL 1986; Cert Indiv Stds Epis TS of The SW 1998. D 6/20/1998 Bp Claude Edward Payne P 6/23/1999 Bp Leopoldo Jesus Alard. R The Par of S Mich's Auburn ME 2000-2009; Vic S Paul's Epis Ch Woodville TX 1998-1999. Exceptional Serv Awd Galveston Coll 1997; Delta Epsilon Sigma Niagara U 1980; BA mcl Niagara U Niagara NY 1980. barbaralbarth4@gmail.com

BARTHELEMY, Paul Berge (Ore) PO Box 570, Manzanita OR 97130 B Saint Paul MN 1/5/1942 s Carl Rudolph Barthelemy & Juliet. BA U IL 1964; MFA Pr 1967; MDiv Nash 1975. D 6/28/1975 P 5/15/1976 Bp C Kilmer Myers. m 5/22/1980 Mary Kenyon c 2. Dio Oregon Portland OR 2002-2010; Vic S Cathr Of Alexandria Manzanita OR 2002-2010; Assoc Epis Par Of S Jn The Bapt Portland OR 1977-1984; Oregon Epis Sch Portland OR 1977-1984; Asst Chr Epis Ch Los Altos CA 1975-1977. barthelemypaul@gmail.com

BARTHOLOMEW, Gilbert Leinbach (NY) 802 Broadway, New York NY 10003 **Int Ch Of The Ascen Mt Vernon NY 2008-** B Pottstown PA 5/11/1943 s Gilbert Jared Bartholomew & Emma Adams. BA U Pgh 1965; BD Lancaster TS 1968; PhD UTS 1974. D 10/20/2001 P 6/1/2002 Bp Herbert Thompson Jr. m 10/16/1999 Linda M(ilavec) McSparrin c 1. Int The Ch Of The Ascen Rockville Cntr NY 2006-2008; Int Chr Ch Poughkeepsie NY 2005-2006; Dio Sthrn Ohio Cincinnati OH 2001-2005; Indn Hill Ch Cincinnati OH 2001-2005. Co-Auth, "Preaching Verse by Verse," WJK, 2000; Auth, "Pass it on," *Telling and Hearing Stories from Jn*, Untd Ch of Chr, 1992. Ntwk of Biblic Storytellers 1985. aglb43@mac.com

BARTHOLOMEW, Linda M(ilavec) (NY) 802 Broadway, New York NY 10003 **Gr Epis Ch New York NY 2004-** B Pasco WA 10/30/1951 d Donald Richard McSparrin & Roberta. BD U Of Dayton/Marian Coll 1975; MDiv S Fran Sem 1983; DMin McCormick TS 1991; Cert SWTS 1995. D 6/21/1997 P 2/21/1998 Bp Herbert Thompson Jr. m 10/16/1999 Gilbert Leinbach Bartholomew c 1. Epis Soc Of Chr Ch Cincinnati OH 1998-2004; Cn Epis Soc of Chr Ch Cincinnati OH 1998-2000; S Jas Epis Ch Cincinnati OH 1997-1998; Pstr Assoc/Intern S Geo's Epis Ch Dayton OH 1996-1997. Ntwk Of Biblic Storytellers 1990-2000. Honorable Mention, Best Thesis Mccormick TS Chicago IL 1991; Maranatha Awd S Fran Sem 1983. lbartholomew@gracechurchnyc.org

BARTLE, Edward Bartholomew (CFla) 330 Hickory Ave, Orange City FL 32763 **R S Edw The Confessor Mt Dora FL 2009-** B Cass City MI 8/30/1943 s Leonard Bartle & Enola. D 12/18/2004 P 5/30/2009 Bp John Wadsworth Howe. m 12/23/1984 Phyllis Ann Cooper c 5. S Jude's Ch Orange City FL 2009. ebbartle@aol.com

BARTLE, John Dixon (Alb) Po Box E, Richfield Springs NY 13439 **R S Jn's Ch Richfield Sprg NY 1990-** B Bryn Mawr PA 9/14/1945 s Harvey Bartle & Dorothy Lucille. BS U of Pennsylvania 1967; JD Penn St Dickinson Sch of Law 1970; MDiv EDS 1985. D 6/21/1986 Bp Lyman Cunningham Ogilby P 5/1/1987 Bp Allen Lyman Bartlett Jr. c 2. Asst S Mary's Ch Portsmouth RI 1989-1990; Asst S Jn's Ch Barrington RI 1987-1989; Int Ch Of The Advoc Philadelphia PA 1987; Cur Nevil Memi Ch Of S Geo Ardmore PA 1986-1987. ringcross@stny.rr.com

BARTLE, Leonard William (CFla) 3520 Curtis Dr, Apopka FL 32703 **D Epis Ch Of The H Sprt Apopka FL 1979-** B Cass City MI 1/26/1923 s John Earl Bartle & Alice Isobel. D 11/20/1979 Bp William Hopkins Folwell. m 10/8/1982 Mary Heidl c 3.

BARTLE, Phyllis Ann (CFla) 330 Hickory Ave, Orange City FL 32763 **R S Jude's Ch Orange City FL 2006-** B Coldwater MI 9/14/1953 d Harry Cooper & Donna. Valencia Cmnty Coll; BS Rol 1990; MDiv TESM 2006. D 5/27/2006 P 12/10/2006 Bp John Wadsworth Howe. m 12/23/1984 Edward Bartholomew Bartle c 2. phlealess@aol.com

✠ **BARTLETT JR, Rt Rev Allen Lyman** (Pa) 316 South 10 Street, Philadelphia PA 19107 **Ret Bp Dio Pennsylvania Philadelphia PA 1998-** B Birmingham AL 9/22/1929 s Allen Lyman Bartlett & Edith Buell. BA U So 1951; MDiv VTS 1958; DMin VTS 1980. D 7/2/1958 Bp George Mosley Murray P 6/16/1959 Bp Charles C J Carpenter Con 2/15/1986 for Pa. m 12/28/1957 Jerriette L Kohlmeier c 3. Asstg bishiop Dio Washington Washington DC 2001-2004; Dio Pennsylvania Philadelphia PA 1993-1997; Bp Coadj Dio Pennsylvania Philadelphia PA 1986-1987; GC Dep Dio Kentucky Louisville KY 1973-1985; Dn Chr Ch Cathd Louisville KY 1970-1986; GC Dep Dio W Virginia Charleston WV 1964-1967; R Zion Epis Ch Chas Town WV 1961-1970; Vic S Barn Epis Ch Roanoke AL 1958-1961; Vic S Jas' Epis Ch Alexander City AL 1958-1961. Un League of Philadelphia 1995. DD U So 1988; DD VTS 1986; Phi Beta Kappa U So 1950. allen.jerrie@verizon.net

BARTLETT, Anne Kristin (Ore) 281 Talent Ave, Talent OR 97540 B Saint Louis MO 3/5/1946 d Thomas Luverne Croft & Anita Belle. BA Washington U 1967; MA Washington U 1969; MDiv Eden TS 1984; Cert Care and Counslg Cntr of St. Louis 1985; Cert SWTS 1987. D 5/16/1987 P 11/1/1987 Bp William Augustus Jones Jr. m 4/16/1983 William Edward Bartlett c 2. Stndg Com Dio Oregon Portland OR 2005-2009; R Trin Epis Ch Ashland Ashland OR 2001-2010; Assoc Epis Par Of S Jn The Bapt Portland OR 1995-2000; Assoc S Mk's Epis Par Medford OR 1992-1995; P Gr Ch Kirkwood MO 1990-1992; P Ch Of The Adv S Louis MO 1987-1989. "Taking Our Places at the Table," *Sermons that Wk XI*, Morehouse, 2003; "Consider How You Have Fared," *Sermons that Wk VII*, Morehouse, 1998; "But Who Do You Say That I Am?," *Sermons that Wk VI*, Morehouse, 1997. anne@bartlettmail.us

BARTLETT, Arthur Robert (Los) 1742 W 1st St, San Pedro CA 90732 **Died 6/3/2011** B Faversham UK 10/25/1919 s Arthur Percy Bartlett & Mary Elenore. CDSP 1964. D 9/10/1964 P 3/10/1965 Bp Francis E I Bloy. c 3. Assoc OHC 1951. afbartlett@earthlink.net

BARTLETT, Basil A (VI) PO Box 7386, St Thomas VI 00801 B Anguilla B.W.I 11/18/1937 s Oguise Hodge & Hilda Irene. D 6/28/2008 Bp Edward Ambrose Gumbs. m 8/18/1965 Emeline Bartlett c 4. renee560@netzero.com

BARTLETT, Frederick Robert (SanD) 6556 Park Ridge Blvd, San Diego CA 92120 B San Diego CA 8/30/1939 s John Phillip Bartlett & Dorothy J. BA W&M 1962; MDiv CDSP 1965. D 9/16/1965 P 3/12/1966 Bp Francis E I Bloy. m 9/16/1972 Sharon Jean c 2. R S Dunst's Epis Ch San Diego CA 1978-2007; Ch Of The Gd Samar San Diego CA 1976-1978; Asst R S Jas By The Sea La Jolla CA 1970-1974; Asst The Par Of S Matt Pacific Palisades CA 1965-1970. Soc Of S Paul 1971-1998. fredsheri@cox.net

BARTLETT, Harwood (At) 4345 Erskine Rd, Clarkston GA 30021 **All SS Epis Ch Atlanta GA 2007-** B New York NY 4/17/1934 s George Prescott Bartlett & Thelma. BS Georgia Inst of Tech 1956; MDiv VTS 1962. D 6/30/

1962 P 5/1/1963 Bp Randolph R Claiborne. m 5/27/1983 Carol P McNamara c 3. R S Barth's Epis Ch Atlanta GA 1972-1982; Vic S Fran Ch Macon GA 1967-1972; Dio Atlanta Atlanta GA 1966-1982. Auth, "Living By Surprise: A Chr Response to the Environ Crisis," Paulist Press, 2003; Auth, "A Chr Discovers the Environ Crisis," *Journ of the Med Assn of Georgia*, 1999. Ch and City Conf 1982-1994. Individual Achievement in Affordable Hsng Progressive Redevelopment Inc. 2000; Outstanding Personal Mnstry Chr Coun of Metro Atlanta 1988; Ldrshp Atlanta 1975; Young Man of the Year in Rel Atlanta Jaycees 1967. woodybart@gmail.com

BARTLETT, Lois Sherburne (Be) 2716 Tennyson Ave, Sinking Spring PA 19608 B Potsdam NY 6/2/1936 d Frank Wright Sherburne & Dorothy May. BS SUNY 1958; MDiv GTS 1991. D 6/8/1991 P 12/22/1991 Bp James Michael Mark Dyer. m 9/14/1957 Gordon Bartlett c 3. S Geo's Epis Ch Hellertown PA 1998-2001; S Mich's Epis Ch Bethlehem PA 1996-1997; No Par Epis Ch Frackville PA 1993-1996; Dio Bethlehem Bethlehem PA 1991-1992. Gnrl Soc of Mayflower Decendents, Commonwealth of Pennsylvania 2010. lsbartlett@juno.com

BARTLETT, Stephen I(ves) (WMich) St. Marks Episcopal Church, 27 East Chicago Street, Coldwater MI 49036 **R S Mk's Ch Coldwater MI 1999-** B Hartford CT 8/6/1947 s Richard Warren Bartlett & Janice. AB Bow 1969; MDiv SWTS 1981; DMin Ecum TS 1993. D 6/13/1981 Bp H Coleman McGehee Jr P 6/28/1982 Bp Harold B Robinson. m 10/6/1984 Martha Durdan McRoberts. R Ch Of The Mssh Detroit MI 1997-1999; Int S Jn's Ch Royal Oak MI 1996-1997; R S Martha's Ch Detroit MI 1985-1994; Asst S Jas' Ch Batavia NY 1982-1985; Asst S Tim's Ch Detroit MI 1981-1982. OHC, Assoc 1979. sibart3@cbpu.com

BARTLETT, Susan Mansfield (Mo) 906 Mallard Sq, Rolla MO 65401 **D Chr Ch Rolla MO 2005-** B Lexington KY 11/21/1945 d Paul Houston Mansfield & Mildred Croft. D 11/18/2005 Bp George Wayne Smith. c 2. smb@fidnet.com

BARTOLOMEO, Michael Edward (LI) 124 Balaton Ave, Lake Ronkonkoma NY 11779 **R Trin Ch Northport NY 2011-; R Trin Ch Northport NY 2011-; Chair, Bdgt Cmsn Dio Long Island Garden City NY 2003-** B Port Jefferson NY 8/24/1965 s Michael Anthony Bartolomeo & Helen Ruth. BA SUNY 1988; MDiv SWTS 1993. D 6/23/1995 P 3/25/1996 Bp Orris George Walker Jr. m 7/8/2000 Joanne Leung c 1. S Paul's Ch Roosevelt NY 2008-2009; Dioc Coun Dio Long Island Garden City NY 2002-2005; R S Jas Epis Ch S Jas NY 1999-2004; Cur S Mk's Ch Islip NY 1995-1998. Dio Long Island 2003; Dio Long Island 2002; Dio Long Island 2000; Geo Mercer TS,Garden City Ny 1997-2000. frmike@vdot.net

BARTON, Anne Whitlock (Spok) 712 Tumac Drive, Yakima WA 98901 **R S Tim's Epis Ch Yakima WA 2010-** B Minneapolis MN 1/25/1963 d James Ware Barton & Patricia Dell. BA U of New Hampshire 1985; MDiv CDSP 1998. D 9/2/1998 Bp Chilton Abbie Richardson Knudsen P 6/26/1999 Bp Creighton Leland Robertson. R S Paul's Epis Ch Kennewick WA 2005-2010; P Dio Olympia Seattle WA 2004-2005; Vic Gd Samar Epis Ch Sammamish WA 2002-2004; Cur Emm Epis Par Rapid City SD 1998-2002. shebrew48@charter.net

BARTON, Charles D H (Mass) 3602 Stembridge Ct, Wilmington NC 28409 B Wellington NSW AU 1/15/1933 s Denis Hampden Barton & Mary Amy Southey. ThL Moore Theol Coll, Sydney 1962; Bachelor of Div London U 1963; Th. Schol Moore Theol Coll, Sydney 1964; STM Bos 1972; PhD Bos 1982. D 2/24/1964 P 2/24/1965 Bp David Reed. m 8/21/1963 Margaret Evelyn Buchan c 4. Gr Ch Lawr MA 2000; S Paul's Ch Newburyport MA 1994; S Jas Ch Groveland Groveland MA 1970-2002; Asst S Jn's Ch Arlington MA 1968-1970. cdhb2@bellsouth.net

BARTON, Charles Lee (Md) 3101 Monkton Rd, Monkton MD 21111 **R S Jas Ch Monkton MD 2004-** B Honolulu HI 8/5/1953 s Charles Albert Barton & Mary Lee. Catonsville Cmnty Coll; Gri; Jn Hopkins U; MDiv STUSo 1995. D 6/10/1995 Bp Charles Lindsay Longest P 5/18/1996 Bp Robert Wilkes Ihloff. m 5/8/2007 Debra Donnelly c 2. P-in-c S Jas Ch Monkton MD 1998-1999; Cur S Jas Ch Monkton MD 1995-1998. cbarton@saintjames.org

BARTON, Donald Reese (WMo) 1253 South Plaza, Springfield MO 65804 **Died 2/12/2010** B Baltimore MD 8/19/1928 s Winfield Park Bull & Mildred. BA Wichita St U 1951; BD VTS 1967. D 6/11/1967 P 12/13/1967 Bp Edward Clark Turner. DLBARTON1@EARTHLINK.NET

BARTON III, George Lloyd (Va) 625 Lancaster Dr, Irvington VA 22480 B Charlottesville VA 9/9/1917 s George Lloyd Barton & Joan Malachi. BA Ham 1940. D 3/21/1953 Bp George P Gunn P 4/1/1957 Bp William Henry Marmion. Emm Ch Rapidan VA 1974-1984; R S Thos Epis Ch Orange VA 1971-1984; Stndg Com Dio SW Virginia Roanoke VA 1961-1962; Secy Dio SW Virginia Roanoke VA 1959-1962; R S Jn's Ch Bedford VA 1958-1962; Exec Coun Dio SW Virginia Roanoke VA 1958-1960; Asst Bruton Par Williamsburg VA 1953-1955.

BARTON JR, John Clib (Ark) 1024 Stanford Dr Ne, Albuquerque NM 87106 **Pstr S Jn The Bapt Epis Ch Milton DE 2006-** B Fort Smith AR 8/10/1936 s John Clib Barton & Wilma. BA SMU 1958; MDiv SMU 1961. D 1/18/1965 P 7/21/1965 Bp Robert Raymond Brown. m 5/29/1992 Sandra Jan Wayland c 3. Gr Ch Siloam Sprg AR 1999-2003; S Paul's Ch McGehee AR 1993-2000; Mssnr Chapl Ch Of The Gd Shpd Little Rock AR 1993-1999; Dio Arkansas Little Rock AR 1993-1999; Mssnr Chapl Emm Ch Lake Vill AR 870-2652230or8 1993-1999; Mssnr Chapl S Mary's Epis Ch Monticello AR 1993-1999; S Mich's Epis Ch Little Rock AR 1987-1989; Vic S Mk's Ch Hope AR 1983-1991; S Jas Ch Magnolia AR 1981-1985; Vic S Alb's Ch Stuttgart AR 1977-1979; R S Lk's Ch Hot Sprg AR 1969-1975; Vic/R Gr Ch Pine Bluff AR 1965-1969; Vic All SS Epis Ch Russellville AR 1964-1965; Vic Trin Ch Van Buren AR 1964-1965. ACPE 1993. jbarton00@comcast.net

BARTON JR, Lane Wickham (Cal) 12616 Se 11th St, Vancouver WA 98683 B Shelby OH 8/19/1925 s Lane W Barton & Mary. BA Harv 1950; BA/MA Oxf 1958; BD CDSP 1959. D 6/19/1959 P 12/1/1959 Bp Lane W Barton. Vic S Barn Ch San Francisco CA 1959-1965.

BARTON, Nancy Fowler (WMich) 811 Stimson St., Cadillac MI 49601 B Washington DC 7/15/1933 d Robert McSwain Fowler & Betsy Bygate. BA Niagara U 1956; MA U of Kentucky 1972; MDiv Epis TS In Kentucky 1991; DMin STUSo 2002. D 6/12/1988 P 6/24/1995 Bp Don Adger Wimberly. m 6/21/1958 James Bradford Barton c 3. S Mary's Epis Ch Cadillac MI 2000-2005; Ch Of The Ascen Frankfort KY 1998-2000. nancybarton@netonecom.net

BARTON III, William Henderson (Tenn) 328 Bob Stewman Rd, Sewanee TN 37375 **P-in-c Trin Ch Winchester TN 2010-; Dio Tennessee Nashville TN 2009-** B Pensacola FL 8/5/1949 s William H Barton & Barbara Jean. MDiv The TS at The U So 2009. D 6/6/2009 P 12/5/2009 Bp John Crawford Bauerschmidt. m 9/13/1997 Sara D Sara Lynn Dennis c 2. billbarton1@bellsouth.net

BARTUSCH, Robert Frederic (WTenn) 2851 Neeley St # 113, Batesville AR 72501 **D Calv Ch Memphis TN 1969-** B Memphis TN 7/21/1925 s Arno George Bartusch & Olga Mae. BBA Tul 1946. D 9/21/1969 Bp John Vander Horst. m 11/26/1952 Susan Polk O'Brien c 2.

BARTZ, James Perkins (Los) 6343 W 82nd St, Los Angeles CA 90045 **R Thads Santa Monica CA 2006-** B Houston TX 6/12/1970 s Tasso Reed Bartz & Sylvia Bernice. BA U of Texas 1994; MDiv VTS 1999. D 6/19/1999 P 6/23/2000 Bp Claude Edward Payne. m 6/3/1995 Cynthia Polk Nentwich. Assoc All SS Par Beverly Hills CA 2002-2006. jbartz@thads.org

BARWICK III, Frederick Ernest (NC) 111 Manchester Dr, Roxboro NC 27573 **D S Mk's Epis Ch Roxboro NC 2002-** B Charlotte NC 6/4/1936 s Frederick E Barwick & Virginia. BA U NC 1962. D 6/10/2001 Bp Michael Bruce Curry. m 10/24/1992 Frances Lunsford Laws c 3. fredb@embarqmail.com

BARWICK, Mark (Eur) 17 Ave Gustave Latinis, Brussels Belgium 1030 **Cur All SS Epis Ch Braine-l'Alleud 1420 BE 2009-** B Cheverly MD 4/7/1956 s Gerald Clement Barwick & Mary Ellen. BA Washington Coll 1978; MDiv Wesley TS 1989. D 11/1/2009 P 6/5/2010 Bp Pierre W Whalon. c 3. S Jas Ch Charleston SC 1999-2002. mark.barwick@gmail.com

BASCOM, Cathleen (Ia) Cathedral Church of St. Paul, 815 High Street, Des Moines IA 50309 **Dn The Cathd Ch Of S Paul Des Moines IA 2007-** B Denver CO 1/27/1962 d Bruce E Chittenden & Marilyn. BA U of Kansas 1984; MDiv SWTS 1990; MA U of Exeter 1991; DMin 2005. D 6/9/1990 Bp William Edward Smalley P 12/1/1990 Bp Frank Tracy Griswold III. m 11/27/1987 Timothy Bascom c 2. S Steph's Ch Newton IA 2001-2007; Dio Kansas Topeka KS 1993-2001; Chapl S Fran Of Cbury Manhattan KS 1993-2001; Asst R S Greg's Epis Ch Deerfield IL 1990-1993. "Rel Experience in the Chronicles of Narnia," *The Chronicles of Narnia Study Guide*, St. Mk's, 1999; "Campus Mnstry and a Hungry Heart," *Disorganized Rel: the Evangelsim of Yth and YA*, Cowley, 1998. provost@st-pauls-cathedral.com

BASDEN, Michael Paul (SwFla) 495 Galleon Dr, Naples FL 34102 **R Trin By The Cove Naples FL 1999-** B Orlando FL 7/25/1959 s Richard Basden & Lavelle. BA U of Cntrl Florida 1981; MDiv Nash 1985. D 6/15/1985 P 1/6/1986 Bp William Hopkins Folwell. m 8/14/1981 Jill R Richards c 2. R S Anne's Epis Ch Warsaw IN 1987-1999; Cur S Mk's Ch Cocoa FL 1985-1987. mbasden@trinitybytgecove.com

BASILE, Cathleen Anne (WNY) 410 N Main St, Jamestown NY 14701 **D S Lk's Epis Ch Jamestown NY 2005-** B Jamestown NY 5/26/1957 d Norman Leo Cooley & Theresa Katherine. AAS Jamestown Cmnty Coll 1989; BS Ashford U 2009. D 6/19/2005 Bp J Michael Garrison. deaconcathy@gmail.com

BASINGER JR, Elvin David (Ala) 21526 Silver Oaks Circle, Athens AL 35613 B Woodland CA 3/11/1946 s Elvin David Basinger & Verna Georgie. AA Sacramento City Coll 1967; U Of Albuquerque 1977; MDiv STUSo 1996. D 6/13/1996 P 12/14/1996 Bp Henry Irving Louttit. m 6/30/1968 Lynda Gray. R S Tim's Epis Ch Athens AL 2008-2011; Chapl Dio Louisiana Baton Rouge LA 2006-2008; R S Fran Ch Denham Sprg LA 2002-2006; Asst R S Augustines Ch Metairie LA 1999-2002; Vic S Thos Aquinas Mssn Baxley GA 1996-1999; D Gr Ch Waycross GA 1996. davebasinger@aol.com

BASINGER, James A (Ak) 2610 Legacy Dr, Anchorage AK 99516 **R All SS' Epis Ch Anchorage AK 1991-** B Saint Louis MO 7/8/1946 s Charles S Basinger & Mildred. BA Texas A&M U 1968; MDiv VTS 1974. D 6/8/1974 P 5/25/1975 Bp George E Rath. m 11/15/1975 Donna Null c 3. R S Chris's Ch

Sumter SC 1989-1991; R S Fran Ch Macon GA 1985-1989; Asst S Dav's Epis Ch Venetia PA 1982-1985; R Chr Ch Chaptico MD 1978-1982; Asst S Dav's Epis Ch Venetia PA 1976-1978; Asst Ch Of The Ascen Silver Sprg MD 1974-1976. jbasinger@chugach.net

BASKERVILLE-BURROWS, Jennifer Lynn (CNY) 300 Park Ave, Syracuse NY 13204 **Dio Cntrl New York Syracuse NY 2004-; Gr Epis Ch Syracuse NY 2004-; Pstr Assoc All SS' Ch San Francisco CA 2002-** B Staten Island NY 8/12/1966 d Harry Manboy Baskerville & Brenda Carol. BA Smith 1988; MA Cor 1994; MDiv CDSP 1997. D 6/11/1997 P 2/7/1998 Bp David B(ruce) Joslin. m 3/22/2003 Harrison Lynn Burrows. Dir Of Alum/Ae And Ch Relatns CDSP Berkeley CA 2002-2004; Assoc S Ptr's Ch Morristown NJ 1999-2002; Asst R S Paul's Ch Endicott NY 1997-1999. Auth, "To Be Young, Priested And Black: Raising Up The Next Generation Of Black Cler," *Gathering The Next Generation*, Morehouse Pub, 2000. Fllshp Soc Of S Jn The Evang. jlbasker@syr.edu

BASKIN, Cynthia (WA) 10924 Citreon Ct, N Potomac MD 20878 **R S Jas Ch Potomac MD 1999-** B Minneapolis MN 12/3/1946 d Eldar Gerhard Oppen & Georgia May. BA S Olaf Coll 1968; MAT U of St. Thos 1971; MDiv VTS 1995. D 5/24/1995 Bp Stephen Hays Jecko P 12/1/1995 Bp Frank Harris Vest Jr. m 12/1/1949 Robert Marion Baskin. Assoc Ch Of The Redeem Midlothian VA 1995-1999; Prog Dir H Trin Ch Gainesville FL 1981-1992. rector@stjamespotomac.org

BASKIN, Ronald Russell (FtW) 1040 Anston Dr, Roswell GA 30075 B Akron OH 3/1/1928 s Noah Acie Baskin & Mildred Lucille. BA Indiana U NW 1984; MDiv Nash 1989. D 7/19/1988 Bp William Cockburn Russell Sheridan P 6/20/1989 Bp Francis Campbell Gray. m 7/24/1992 Pamela Ann Faison c 5. Asst Ch Of The Annunc Marietta GA 2006-2008; P-in-c S Mary Magd Ch Columbus GA 2003-2005; Asst The Ch Of Our Sav Atlanta GA 2002-2004; Asst S Dav's Ch Roswell GA 1996-2001; R S Simon Of Cyrene Epis Ch Ft Worth TX 1990-1996; Asst S Chris's Ch Crown Point IN 1989-1990. Contrib, "Word From the Pulpit," *La Vita News, Arlington TX*, La Vita Pub, 1992. CCU, 1989-1996; SSC 1991. RoswellRev@aol.com

BASS-CHOATE, Yamily (NY) 4 Gateway Rd, Unit 1-D, Yonkers NY 10703 **Mem Hisp Mnstry New York NY 2005-; Vic San Andres Ch Yonkers NY 2005-** B Bogota CO 1/27/1957 d Antonio Sierra & Ilva Mogollon. MDiv GTS 1999. D 7/31/1999 P 3/4/2000 Bp Alfred Clark Marble Jr. m 11/12/1988 Horace Choate c 2. Cn For Hisp Mnstry Dio Mississippi Jackson MS 2001-2005; Dioc S Andr's Cathd Jackson MS 2001-2005; Dir Of Educ The Epis Ch Of The Medtr Meridian MS 1999-2001. ybchoate@gmail.com

BASSETT, John William (Alb) 301 Otsego St, Ilion NY 13357 **R St Augustines Ch Ilion NY 2010-; Vic All SS Ch Round Lake NY 2002-** B Tyngsborough MA 2/12/1951 s Joseph Francis Bassett & Dorothy Fransis. BS U of Massachusetts 1973; MEd Boston Coll 1980; MDiv Andover Newton TS 1987. D 6/9/2001 P 1/12/2002 Bp Daniel William Herzog. m 5/17/1997 Terry D Tremblay. Int St Augustines Ch Ilion NY 2009-2010; Int S Bon Ch Guilderland NY 2008-2009; Assoc Trin Ch Lansingburgh Troy NY 2007-2008; Int S Mk's Ch Hoosick Falls NY 2005-2007; Cur Chr Epis Ch Ballston Spa NY 2001-2002. Bro of S Andr 2008. frjohnbassett@gmail.com

BASSUENER, Barbara Ann (Va) 20 Third St, Pocomoke City MD 21851 **S Mary's Epis Ch Pocomoke City MD 2010-** B Sheboygan WI 12/31/1946 d Oliver H Bassuener & Helen A. BA The W&M 1968; JD Marshall-Wythe Sch of Law 1971; MDiv VTS 2010. D 6/5/2010 Bp Shannon Sherwood Johnston P 2/5/2011 Bp James Joseph Shand. oliver46@cox.net

BAST, Robert Lee (Eas) 638 Grecken Grn, Peachtree City GA 30269 B Baltimore MD 4/14/1923 s Charles Arthur Bast & Beulah. BA Laf 1944; BD VTS 1947; DD Roa 1974. D 10/26/1946 P 5/1/1947 Bp William McClelland. m 7/2/1955 Frances Jordan c 2. H Trin Ch Churchville MD 1987-1989; Ch Of The H Trin Oxford MD 1986-1989; R S Paul's Epis Ch Jacksonville FL 1982-1986; R S Tim's Ch Fairfield CT 1973-1982; Stndg Com Dio Kansas Topeka KS 1970-1973; BEC Dio Kansas Topeka KS 1966-1973; S Thos The Apos Ch Overland Pk KS 1964-1973; R S Matt's Epis Ch Newton KS 1961-1964; S Jn's Ch Ft Washington MD 1949-1961; Epiph Epis Ch Odenton MD 1947-1948; P-in-c Old Trin Ch Ch Creek MD 1947-1948; P-in-c S Andr's Hurlock MD 1947-1948; P-in-c S Paul's Ch Vienna MD 1947-1948; P-in-c S Steph's Epis Ch E New Mrkt MD 1947-1948.

BASTIAN, Martin James (Tex) 6623 Minola St, Houston TX 77007 B Milwaukee WI 5/14/1963 s James Arthur Bastian & Rita Marie. BA U of Kansas 1986; MDiv VTS 1996. D 6/15/1996 Bp Peter James Lee P 2/1/1997 Bp Claude Edward Payne. S Mart's Epis Ch Houston TX 2006; Epis HS Bellaire TX 2001-2008; Asst S Mart's Epis Ch Houston TX 1996-2000. SAMS. mbastian@stmartinsepiscopal.org

BATARSEH, Peter Bahjat (Tenn) 312 Battle Avenue, Franklin TN 37064 B Adjloun Jordan 11/15/1967 s Bahjat Salem Batarseh & Martha Fakhoury. Elim Bible Inst 1985; STUSo 2005; TESM 2005. D 6/5/2005 P 4/22/2006 Bp Bertram Nelson Herlong. c 3. Ch of the Gd Samar Franklin TN 2008; Dio Tennessee Nashville TN 2005-2007. pb@batarseh.net

BATCHELDER JR, Kelsey (NY) 230 Riverside Dr Apt 6D, New York NY 10025 B 9/17/1932 D 6/20/1959 P 12/21/1959 Bp Hamilton Hyde Kellogg. m 6/26/1965 Marla Shilton.

BATEMAN, David (ETenn) Saint Thaddaeus' Episcopal Church, Box 16305, Chattanooga TN 37416 B Chicago IL 8/9/1954 s Philip Paul Bateman & Roberta Shearer. BA Ken 1976; MDiv Nash 1987. D 6/13/1987 P 4/18/1988 Bp Peter James Lee. m 2/13/2004 Pamela Antoinette Emery c 2. Mt Calv Camp Hill PA 2009-2011; Thankful Memi Ch Chattanooga TN 2008-2009; R S Thaddaeus' Epis Ch Chattanooga TN 1995-2007; Dio Upper So Carolina Columbia SC 1989-1995; Asst H Trin Par Epis Clemson SC 1989-1995; Asst Abingdon Epis Ch White Marsh VA 1987-1989. Auth, "Come & Wrshp: A Chld's Liturg of the Word," Ldr Resources, 2002. dsbate09@yahoo.com

BATES, Allen Layfield (Ark) 1902 W Magnolia St, Rogers AR 72758 B Little Rock AR 4/1/1950 s William Floyd Bates & Viola Ann. BA U of Arkansas 1973; MDiv STUSo 1978. D 6/10/1978 P 6/1/1979 Bp Christoph Keller Jr. m 5/22/1974 Melinda Leah Keck c 2. R S Andr's Ch Rogers AR 1983-2008; Vic S Alb's Ch Stuttgart AR 1980-1983; Int S Steph's Epis Ch Jacksonville AR 1980; Chair CE Dio Arkansas Little Rock AR 1979-1984; S Lk's Epis Ch No Little Rock AR 1979-1980; S Paul's Ch Fayetteville AR 1978-1979. Frederick Denison Maurice Soc.

BATES, Annie Bates (WLa) 905 Dafney Drive, Lafayette LA 70503 **P for Fam & Yth S Barn Epis Ch Lafayette LA 2007-** B New Iberia LA 9/2/1964 d Gordon Brown & Martha. BA LSU 1986; MDiv Epis TS of The SW 2005. D 6/4/2005 P 5/20/2006 Bp D(avid) Bruce Mac Pherson. c 1. Cur Ch Of The Ascen Lafayette LA 2005-2006. annie@stbarnabas.us

BATES, (Charlotte) Chere (Chi) 15136 S. Dillman, Plainfield IL 60544 B Detroit MI 2/5/1944 d Robert Hayes McKnight & Dorothy Gertrude. Alma Coll. D 1/30/1999 Bp Herbert Alcorn Donovan Jr. m 1/23/1971 John Kenneth Bates c 1. D S Edw The Mtyr and Chr Epis Ch Joliet IL 1999-2004. dnchereb@comcast.net

BATES, James Brent (Nwk) 31 Woodland Ave, Summit NJ 07901 **R Gr Ch Newark NJ 2011-** B Garland TX 8/25/1976 s James Leroy Bates & Malda Lyn. BA Harding U 1998; MDiv Abilene Chr U 2001; PhD Drew U 2008; Dipl. in Angl Stds The GTS 2008. D 6/7/2008 Bp George Edward Councell P 12/13/2008 Bp Mark M Beckwith. m 12/18/1999 Jennifer J Thweatt-Bates c 2. Asst Calv Epis Ch Summit NJ 2008-2011. rector@gracechurchinnewark.org

BATES, J Barrington (Nwk) 15 Warren St Unit 117, Jersey City NJ 07302 **Rdr, Gnrl Ord Examination Epis Ch Cntr New York NY 2012-; Bp's Advsry Com on HR Dio Newark Newark NJ 2010-** B Philadelphia PA 9/21/1955 s James Earl Bates & Lauralou Courtney. BA Bos 1979; MDiv CDSP 1997; MA Grad Theol Un 1997; STM GTS 2004; M.Phil. Drew U 2006; Ph.D. Drew U 2009. D 12/5/1998 P 6/5/1999 Bp William Edwin Swing. c 1. R The Ch Of The Annunc Oradell NJ 2007-2011; Cur Ch Of The Ascen New York NY 2002-2007; S Aug's Epis Ch Croton On Hudson NY 2001-2002; The Ch of S Ign of Antioch New York NY 2001-2002; Asst P Ch Of S Mary The Vrgn New York NY 2000-2002; Asst S Mich's Ch New York NY 1999-2000; Asst R S Fran' Epis Ch San Francisco CA 1998-1999. Auth, "Expressing What Christians Believe: Angl Principles for Liturg Revs," *ATR*, 2010; Auth, "Giving What Is Sacr to Dogs? Welcoming All to the Eucharistic Feast," *Journ of Angl Stds*, 2005; Auth, "Reflections on Liturg at Ground Zero," *Journ of Pstr Care and Counslg*, 2005; Auth, "Am I Blue? Some Hist Evidence for Liturg colors," *Studia Liturgica*, 2003; Auth, "The Problem of Cler Misconduct: Preaching Liberation from Bondage to Sin in an Age of Moral Freedom," *Journ for Preachers*, 2002; Auth, "Meetings And Accomplishments," *Preaching Through The Year Of Lk: Sermons That Wk Ix*, 2000. Acad of Homil; AAR; EPF; Hymn Soc of Amer; Integrity; Intl Angl Liturg Consult; No Amer Acad of Liturg; Ord Of H Cross; Screen Actors Gld; Societas Liturgica; Soc of Cath Priests. Who's Who among Students in Amer Universities and Colleges Who's Who 2008. revdocbates@gmail.com

BATES, Margaret Knop (CNY) 5623 Mack Rd, Skaneateles NY 13152 **Chair of Dioc Discernment Team Dio Cntrl New York Syracuse NY 2011-; COM Dio Cntrl New York Syracuse NY 2008-; Assoc R S Jame's Ch Skaneateles NY 2005-** B Binghamton NY 4/18/1943 d Victor R Knop & Katherine. BS SUNY 1964; MDiv Bex 2005. D 11/13/2004 P 9/17/2005 Bp Gladstone Bailey Adams III. m 8/20/1966 C David Bates c 2. Co-Chair of Dioc Discernment Team Dio Cntrl New York Syracuse NY 2008-2011; D Gr Ch Baldwinsville NY 2004.

BATES, Percy Quin (La) 5209 Willowtree Rd, Marrero LA 70072 **S Mk's Epis Ch Harvey LA 2004-** B New Orleans LA 7/7/1944 s Henry Grady Bates & Mildred Foster. D 10/23/2005 Bp Charles Edward Jenkins III. m 2/9/1968 Lauranel Quin Lauranel Seymour c 2. sla46402@allsate.com

BATES, Robert Seaton (Chi) 121 W Macomb St, Belvidere IL 61008 B Colorado Springs CO 11/17/1948 s Ralph William Bates & Margaret. BA U CO 1970; MDiv Nash 1973. D 4/28/1973 P 11/1/1973 Bp Donald H V Hallock. R S Ptr's Epis Ch Sycamore IL 1989-1992; R Chr Ch Streator IL 1983-1989; The Epis Ch Of The H Trin Belvidere IL 1980; R Ch Of The H Comm Lake

Geneva WI 1979-1980; R S Jn The Bapt Portage WI 1975-1979; Cn Precentor All SS' Cathd Milwaukee WI 1973-1975.

BATES, Steven Byron (CGC) 508 S Market St, Scottsboro AL 35768 **R H Nativ Epis Ch Panama City FL 2006-** B Oak Ridge TN 8/7/1957 s John Cecil Bates & Lena Marie. BS U of Alabama 1979; MBA Samford U 1983; MDiv STUSo 2002. D 5/16/2002 P 12/3/2003 Bp Henry Nutt Parsley Jr. m 7/12/1986 Lori Jean Leberte c 2. D S Lk's Ch Scottsboro AL 2002-2005. fr.steve@holy-nativity.org

BATES, Stuart Alan (Tex) 345 Piney Point Rd, Houston TX 77024 **R S Fran Ch Houston TX 2007-** B Saint Louis MO 9/12/1961 s Fred Lay Bates & Anne. BA U of Texas 1984; MA Dallas TS 1991; MDiv Epis TS of The SW 1996. D 6/22/1996 Bp Claude Edward Payne P 1/23/1997 Bp Leopoldo Jesus Alard. c 3. S Mart's Epis Ch Houston TX 2005-2007. sbates@sfch.org

BATES, Thomas Justin (RG) Po Box 53144, Pinos Altos NM 88053 **D Ch Of The Gd Shpd Silver City NM 2001-; BroSA Coordntr Dio The Rio Grande Albuquerque NM 2001-; BroSA Coordntr Dio The Rio Grande Albuquerque NM 2001-** B Wolf Point MT 4/2/1940 s Earl Quay Bates & Helen Elaine. MPS Wstrn Kentucky U 1976; MA Wstrn Kentucky U 1977; Chr Stds TESM 2001. D 7/28/2001 Bp Terence Kelshaw. m 4/21/1962 Jane Spencer Keeton c 2. BroSA 1994. tbates@zianet.com

BATIZ MEJIA, Jose David (Hond) IMS SAP Dept 215, PO BOX 523900, Miami FL 33152 Honduras B Honduras 9/15/1966 s Simeona. Rec from Roman Catholic 3/11/2007 Bp Lloyd Emmanuel Allen. m 12/1/2009 Elizabeth Lopez Santos c 1. iriona66@hotmail.com

BATKIN, Jeffrey Alan (Fla) 395 Winfield Cove Rd, Saluda NC 28773 **Sm Ch Mnstrs Dio Wstrn No Carolina Asheville NC 2010-** B Mount Vernon NY 10/24/1947 s Abraham Batkin & Marilyn. BA Emory U 1969; MDiv STUSo 1972; DMin Luth Theol Sthrn Sem 1990. D 6/24/1972 Bp Milton LeGrand Wood P 4/15/1973 Bp Bennett Jones Sims. m 8/30/1969 Marguerite Dechenaux c 2. Int Ch Of The H Fam Mills River NC 2007-2009; Int R Ch Of The Adv Spartanburg SC 2004-2006; R Trin Epis Ch St Aug FL 1998-2003; Dio Upper So Carolina, Alt Dep GC Dio Upper So Carolina Columbia SC 1994-1997; Dio Upper So Carolina Columbia SC 1992-1993; Dio Upper So Carolina Columbia SC 1991-1993; Dio Upper So Carolina, Curs Coun Dio Upper So Carolina Columbia SC 1991-1992; R Gr Epis Ch Anderson SC 1990-1998; Dio Florida, Dept CE Dio Florida Jacksonville FL 1988-1990; Cn S Jn's Cathd Jacksonville FL 1986-1990; Dio Upper So Carolina Columbia SC 1984-1987; Dio Upper So Carolina, Chair Dept of Constit Dio Upper So Carolina Columbia SC 1981-1985; Vic S Fran of Assisi Chapin SC 1980-1986; Asst Ch Of Our Sav Rock Hill SC 1978-1980; Vic S Chris's Epis Ch Garner NC 1975-1978; Cur S Barth's Epis Ch Atlanta GA 1972-1975. Allin Fllshp The Epis Ch Bossey Switzerland 1988. jabatkin@tds.net

BATSON, Lloyd Samuel (Nwk) 160 W South Orange Ave, South Orange NJ 07079 B 6/25/1960 s Lloyd F Batson & Mavis D. D 5/2/2009 Bp Mark M Beckwith. m 12/26/1988 Donnetta Benn c 3. lbapson@verizon.net

BATSON, Sara Chapman (Pa) 117 Sagewood Dr, Malvern PA 19355 B Clarksville TN 11/1/1941 d William Ren Batson & Evelyn. BD U Of Evansville 1985; MDiv PrTS 1995; Cert GTS 1997. D 10/25/1997 P 4/25/1998 Bp Joe Morris Doss. R Chr Ch Media PA 1998-2007; Assoc Ch Of The Redeem Bryn Mawr PA 1997-1998. Chld'S Crisis Treatment Cntr Of Philadelphia; Cler Advsry Bd-Epis Cmnty Serv; Comp To OGS; Natl Epis Cler Assn Mem; Philadelphia Theol Inst. revscbatson@comcast.net

BATSON III, Stephen Radford (NY) 3721 Wares Ferry Rd Apt 500, Montgomery AL 36109 B Columbia SC 2/18/1943 s Stephen Radford Batson & Orleans Esther. BA U of Virginia 1968; MDiv EDS 1974. D 6/8/1974 P 10/1/1976 Bp Paul Moore Jr. S Mk's Epis Ch Charleston SC 1981-1982; Asst Ch Of S Mary The Vrgn New York NY 1979-1980; Asst The Ch of S Matt And S Tim New York NY 1977-1979; Asst S Steph's Epis Ch Boston MA 1976-1977; Asst The Ch Of The Adv Boston MA 1975-1976; Asst All SS Par Brookline MA 1974-1975. SocMary 2003.

BATTLE, Michael Jesse (NC) 1611 East Millbrook Rd, Raleigh NC 27609 **Sprtl Formation and Curric Epis Ch Cntr New York NY 2011-2013; Six Prchr Cbury Engl Ch Of Engl London 2011-; R Ch Of Our Sav Par San Gabr CA 2008-; Theol Com Epis Ch Cntr New York NY 2000-; Sprtl Fac Credo Inst Inc. Memphis TN 1998-** B New Orleans LA 12/12/1963 s Lorenzo Battle & Sadie Juliet. U of Notre Dame; BA Duke 1986; MDiv PrTS 1989; STM Ya Berk 1990; Cert Sprtl Direction Shalem Inst 1993; PhD Duke 1995. D 2/10/1993 Bp Huntington Williams Jr P 12/12/1995 Bp DM Tutu. m 7/18/1996 Raquel Leslie c 3. Chapl to Lambeth Ch Of Engl London 2008; Provost & Cn Theol Cath Ctr of St Paul Dio Los Angeles Los Angeles CA 2007; Advsry Com to Bonnie Anderson Exec Coun Appointees New York NY 2005-2009; Assoc VTS Alexandria VA 2005-2007; Anglical RC Dialogue Epis Ch Cntr New York NY 2003-2006; R S Ambroses Ch Raleigh NC 2001-2004; Chapl to the HOB Epis Ch Cntr New York NY 2000-2006; Theol Com Epis Ch Cntr New York NY 2000-2006; Asst P Ch Of The H Fam Chap Hill NC 2000-2001; Asst Duke Epis Cntr Durham NC 1999-2004; Asst Prof Of Sprtlty And Moral Theol The TS at The U So Sewanee TN 1995-1999. Auth, "Black Battle, White Knight," Seabury, 2011; Auth, "Ubuntu," Seabury, 2009; Auth, "The Black Ch in Amer: An Afr Amer Sprtlty," Blackwell, 2006; Auth, "Practicing Recon in a Violent Wrld," Morehouse, 2005; Auth, "The Ch Enslaved: A Sprtlty of Racial Recon," Fortress, 2005; Ed, "The Quest for Recon and Liberation," Westminster Jn Knox, 2004; Auth, "Blessed Are the Peacemakers," Merc, 2003; Auth, "The Wisdom Of Desmond Tutu," Westminster Jn Knox, 1998; Auth, "Recon: The Ubuntu Theol Of Desmond Tutu," Pilgrim Press, 1997. michael@michaelbattle.com

BATTS JR, Robert Waverly (SC) 3808C Longley Rd, Abingdon MD 21009 **Assoc S Mary's Ch Abingdon MD 2011-** B Fort Benning GA 7/20/1964 s Robert Batts & Peggy. BS Presb Coll Clinton SC 1986; MDiv TESM 2004. D 1/29/2005 P 6/4/2005 Bp Edward Lloyd Salmon Jr. m 6/27/1987 Georgianne F Batts c 2. Asst Par Ch of St. Helena Beaufort SC 2005-2008. majorbatts@hotmail.com

BAUER, Audrey (NMich) 6837 Lahti Ln, Pellston MI 49769 **D Trsfg Epis Ch Indn River MI 2008-; D Trsfg Epis Ch Indn River MI 2008-** B Toronto ON CA 7/7/1936 d George Silver Thomson & Christina Young. Border Hosp. Coll of Nrsng Scotland; RN Peel Hosp Sch of Nrsng Galashiels GB 1961. D 6/22/1997 Bp Thomas Kreider Ray. m 6/6/1964 George Wayne Bauer c 2. D Ch Of The Gd Shpd S Ignace MI 2008-2011; D S Mk's Ch Crystal Falls MI 1997-2008. audreytbauer@yahoo.com

BAUER, Kathryn Ann (WMo) Po Box 996, Kremmling CO 80459 **Vic Trin Ch Kremmling CO 2000-** B Dodge City KS 7/24/1943 d Ernest Guyton Hudspeth & Wilma Lois. BA 1966; MA 1972; MS 1984. D 11/20/1993 Bp John Clark Buchanan P 6/1/1998 Bp William Jerry Winterrowd. m 3/28/1981 William Eugene Bauerstep. Cleric Trin Ch Kremmling CO 1998-2000; D Dio W Missouri Kansas City MO 1993-1998. NAAD. Psi Chi. bb-kb@worldnet.att.net

BAUER, Ronald Coleman (Los) 27292 Via Callejon Unit B, San Juan Capistrano CA 92675 B Saint Louis MO 9/22/1935 s Herman Gregory Bauer & Charlotte Rose. BA U of Oklahoma 1963; BD Nash 1965. D 6/20/1965 P 12/1/1965 Bp Chilton Powell. m 6/27/1993 Dianne L Pomainville c 2. R S Marg Of Scotland Par San Juan Capistrano CA 1990-1998; R The Epis Par Of S Dav Minnetonka MN 1973-1990; R No Convoc Hannibal MO 1970-1973; Assoc S Paul's Ch Manhattan KS 1969-1970; Assoc Trin Epis Ch Ft Worth TX 1967-1969; Vic S Steph's Ch Guymon OK 1965-1967. rcbauer1@prodigy.net

BAUER, Thomas William (Md) 51 Milburn Cir, Pasadena MD 21122 B Pittsburgh PA 9/5/1936 s Frank Phillips Bauer & Wilhelmina Gunnis. BA Ya 1958; MDiv GTS 1961; STM Yale DS 1965; MA Ya 1965; EdD Harv 1986. D 7/6/1961 Bp Noble C Powell P 6/20/1962 Bp Harry Lee Doll. m 8/26/1961 Ann MacLean Evans c 2. Int S Andr's Ch Pasadena MD 2000-2001; Int All SS Ch So Hadley MA 1999-2000; Dio Wstrn Massachusetts Springfield MA 1999-2000; R S Paul's Ch Petersburg VA 1994-1999; R Westover Epis Ch Chas City VA 1991-1994; Int Chr Ch Chaptico MD 1990-1991; Gr And S Ptr's Ch Baltimore MD 1987-1990; R Par Of S Paul Newton Highlands MA 1983-1987; Int Trin Ch Canton MA 1982-1983; Emm Epis Ch (Piedmont Par) Delaplane VA 1982; Cathd of St Ptr & St Paul Washington DC 1980-1982; Chapl S Alb's Par Washington DC 1980-1982; Ascen Epis Ch Amherst VA 1979-1980; S Mk's Ch Clifford VA 1979-1980; Virginia Epis Sch Lynchburg VA 1977-1980; R Ch Of The Gd Shpd New York NY 1971-1977; Ch Of Chr The King E Meadow NY 1969-1971; Int S Steph's Epis Ch Woodlaw Bronx NY 1967-1969; Vic Gr Ch Bronx NY 1965-1967; P-in-c Bp Seabury Ch Groton CT 1964-1965; Cur S Jn's Ch Washington CT 1962-1964; Cur S Mich And All Ang Ch Baltimore MD 1962; Cur Gr And S Ptr's Ch Baltimore MD 1961-1962. Auth, "Illustrated Bible"; Auth, "Moral Climate & The Cmnty Of Faith". thomaswbauer@verizon.net

BAUERSCHMIDT, Frederick John (LI) 195 Rainbow Ter, Effort PA 18330 **Supply P S Jn's Cathd Jacksonville FL 1997-** B Brooklyn NY 4/13/1924 s Frederick John Bauerschmidt & Ruth Elizabeth. BS SUNY 1951; MS Hofstra U 1955; Cert Mercer TS 1977; EdD SUNY 1977. D 6/17/1978 P 6/1/1979 Bp Robert Campbell Witcher Sr. m 2/12/1949 Ruth Caroline McGown. Int Epis Par Of S Mk And S Jn Jim Thorpe PA 1993-1996; Ch Of The Redeem Merrick NY 1981-1987; Asst S Jas Epis Ch S Jas NY 1980-1981; Assoc S Mk's Epis Ch Medford NY 1979-1980. Auth, "Nys Educ Journ". Bro Of S Andr.

✠ **BAUERSCHMIDT, Rt Rev John Crawford** (Tenn) 50 Vantage Way Ste 107, Nashville TN 37228 **Bp Dio Tennessee Nashville TN 2007-** B Portsmouth VA 9/18/1959 s Alan Donald Bauerschmidt & Conally. BA Ken 1981; MDiv GTS 1984; DPhil Oxf 1996. D 6/9/1984 P 6/1/1985 Bp William Arthur Beckham Con 1/27/2007 for Tenn. m 1/4/1986 Caroline Barnard Pearce c 3. GC Dep Dio Louisiana Baton Rouge LA 2006-2007; Stndg Com Dio Louisiana Baton Rouge LA 2001-2005; R Chr Ch Covington LA 1997-2006; Ecum Off Dio No Carolina Raleigh NC 1994-1997; R Chr Ch Albemarle NC 1992-1997; Cur All SS Ch Worcester MA 1984-1987. Soc Of S Jn The Evang 1985. jcbbishop@episcopaldiocese-tn.org

BAUGHMAN, David Lee (Chi) 804 James Court, Wheaton IL 60189 **D S Mk's Ch Geneva IL 2004-** B Columbus OH 7/25/1939 s Harold Milton Baughman & Florence. AA Morton Coll 1959; BS Illinois St U 1961; MS

B

Illinois Inst of Tech 1966; EdD Nthrn Illinois U 1981. D 2/15/1997 Bp Frank Tracy Griswold III. m 4/13/1963 Marilyn Ann Ostby c 1. Dir, Dioc Sch for Diac Dio Chicago Chicago IL 1998-2001; D Trin Epis Ch Wheaton IL 1997-2004. BroSA 1991-1994. Fell Natl Sci Fndt 1964. baughmandavid@comcast.net

BAUKNIGHT JR, Mack Miller (SwFla) 2440 26th Ave S, Saint Petersburg FL 33712 B Augusta GA 5/24/1951 s Mack Miller Bauknight & Ocie Mae. Paine Coll 1970; Aiken Tech Coll Aiken SC 1975. D 6/25/1994 Bp Rogers Sanders Harris. m Lafaye King c 1.

BAUM, Denis Blaine (CGC) 532 Skyline Drive, N Little Rock AR 72116 **Int Co-R S Jude's Epis Ch Niceville FL 2002-** B Toledo OH 3/5/1937 s James Edward Baum & Freda. BA Bowling Green St U 1959; BD EDS 1963; MA GW 1974. D 6/15/1963 P 12/1/1963 Bp Nelson Marigold Burroughs. m 6/26/1988 Judith W Holloway. H Sprt Epis Ch Gulf Shores AL 1992-1999; R S Thos Ch Greenville AL 1984-1992; Off Of Bsh For ArmdF New York NY 1976-1984; Cur S Jas Ch Painesville OH 1963-1965. 4 Meritorius Serv Medals USAF.

BAUM, George R (O) 16316 Ferndale Rd, Shaker Heights OH 44120 **P-in-c S Pat's Ch Brunswick OH 2009-** B Niagara Falls NY 11/23/1963 s William Walter Baum & Carol Janice. BA Concordia Coll 1990; MDiv The GTS 2009. D 6/13/2009 P 12/19/2009 Bp Mark Hollingsworth Jr. m 9/15/1990 Christin L Wolcott c 2. fathergeorgebaum@gmail.com

BAUM, Nancy Louise (Mich) 411 Walnut St, Green Cove Springs FL 32043 B Guelph ON CA 5/5/1949 d George Baum & Alva. BA U Of Guelph Guelph ON CA 1986; MDiv U of Wstrn Ontario 1993. Trans from Anglican Church of Canada 1/6/1999 Bp R(aymond) Stewart Wood Jr. m 6/22/1996 John Leo Rowland. Dio Michigan Detroit MI 2003; Int S Chris-S Paul Epis Ch Detroit MI 2000-2002; S Andr's Ch Ann Arbor MI 1999-2000; Supply R S Geo's Epis Ch Warren MI 1996-1998; Supply R S Pat's Epis Ch Madison Heights MI 1996-1998. revnbaum@aol.com

BAUMAN, Ward J (Minn) 1111 Upton Ave N, Minneapolis MN 55411 **Dio Minnesota Minneapolis MN 2002-; Dir Hse of Pryr Collegeville MN 2002-** B Los Angeles CA 1/1/1945 s Clifford Hugh Bauman & Joann. BA Biola U 1968; MDiv CDSP 1989. D 6/18/1989 P 12/1/1989 Bp John Lester Thompson III. c 1. Vic S Edm's Epis Ch Pacifica CA 1991-2002; Asst S Lk's Ch San Francisco CA 1989-1991. Auth, "Sacr Food for Soulful Living," Lilja Press, 2010; Co-Auth, "The Luminous Gospels," Praxis Pub, 2008. wardbauman@me.com

BAUMANN, David Michael (Los) 1314 N Angelina Dr, Placentia CA 92870 **R The Epis Ch Of The Blessed Sacr Placentia CA 1978-** B Glendale CA 7/30/1948 s Billy Franklin Baumann & Nancy. BA UCLA 1970; ATC 1972; MDiv Vancouver TS 1973. D 9/15/1973 P 3/16/1974 Bp Robert C Rusack. m 6/6/1971 Sheryl May Cassell c 2. P-in-c S Anselm Of Cbury Par Garden Grove CA 1978; Cur S Anselm Of Cbury Par Garden Grove CA 1975-1977; Cur S Clem's-By-The-Sea Par San Clemente CA 1973-1974. Auth, "Love Stronger Than Death," Lulu, 2006; Auth, "The Starman Saga," Americana Pub, 2004; Auth, "Sprtl Life for the Overbusy," Forw Mvmt Press, 1987. Forw in Faith 1989; Gld of the Living Rosary 1972; SocMary 1980; SSC 1990. dbaumann@pacbell.net

BAUMGARTEN, Betsy Ann (Miss) PO Box 267, Leland MS 38756 B Duluth MN 10/9/1980 d William Baumgarten & Julie. BA St Olaf Coll 2003; MDiv VTS 2008. D 7/26/2007 P 7/8/2008 Bp James Louis Jelinek. m 4/19/2008 Robert William Wetherington. Delta Mssnr Dio Mississippi Jackson MS 2009-2011; Asst S Thos Epis Ch McLean VA 2008-2009; Yth Min S Paul's Epis Ch Duluth MN 2003-2005. betsy.baumgarten@gmail.com

BAUMGARTEN, Jonathan David (Chi) 10 Lathrop Ave, River Forest IL 60305 **Gr Ch Oak Pk IL 2004-** B Praire du Sac WI 8/13/1960 BA St. Jn's Coll Annapolis MD 1982. D 2/7/2004 Bp Victor Alfonso Scantlebury. m 8/14/1982 Marion Tucker Baumgarten c 2.

BAUMGARTEN, William Paul (Mont) 845 2nd Ave E, Kalispell MT 59901 **P-in-c Chr Epis Ch Kalispell MT 2000-** B Seattle WA 6/22/1944 s Otto Charles Baumgarten & Virginia. BA Villanova U 1967; MA Augustinian Coll 1971; MA CUA 1971. Rec from Roman Catholic 12/21/1979 as Priest Bp Robert Munro Wolterstorff. m 6/22/1977 Barbara Baumgarten c 3. Dio Montana Helena MT 2000-2009; S Paul's Epis Ch Santa Paula CA 1989-2000; R S Jn The Div Epis Ch Morgan Hill CA 1983-1989; Asst All SS Ch San Diego CA 1979-1982. bill4baumg@gmail.com

BAUSCHARD, Michael Robert Thomas (NwPa) 5 Cottage Pl, Warren PA 16365 **D Epis Ch Of The Trsfg Mesa AZ 2010-; D S Fran Of Assisi Epis Ch Youngsville PA 2002-** B 9/17/1945 s Robert Harvey Bauschard & Joan Grace. Diac Sch Of Mnstry 1998. D 6/13/1998 Bp Robert Deane Rowley Jr. m 7/17/1993 Christina Ann Guiffre. D Trin Memi Ch Warren PA 1998-2002.

BAUSTIAN, Donald Edward (Ark) 1750 Woodcliff Dr, Camden AR 71701 B Iowa City IA 3/6/1932 s Adolph Baustian & Jennie. BA Augustana Coll 1954; STB GTS 1957. D 6/8/1957 P 12/21/1957 Bp Gordon V Smith. m 6/15/1957 Beverly Ann Kaiser c 3. S Jas Ch Magnolia AR 1994-1997; Vic S Jn's Ch Camden AR 1991-1997; Vic S Mk's Ch Hope AR 1991-1994; Exec Coun Appointees New York NY 1988-1991; Dio Arkansas Little Rock AR 1982-1997; R Chr Epis Ch Little Rock AR 1981-1988; S Jn's Ch Keokuk IA 1967-1981; Dio Louisiana Baton Rouge LA 1962-1981; Vic Ch Of S Thos Algona IA 1957-1964; Vic Trin Ch Emmetsburg IA 1957-1964. wood1750@att.net

BAUTISTA, Simon (WA) 613 Blandford St, Rockville MD 20850 **Latino Mssnr Dio Washington Washington DC 2006-; R Ch Of The Cross Columbia SC 2005-; Dio Washington Washington DC 2005-** B Dominican Republic 3/24/1958 Rec from Roman Catholic 1/10/2004 Bp John Chane. m 3/20/1995 Amarilis D Vargas c 7. Ch Of The Ascen Gaithersburg MD 2004. misionero@verizon.net

BAVARO, Carolyn Margaret (Chi) P.O. Box 30247, Chicago IL 60630 B Chicago IL 1/18/1952 BS Elmhurst Coll 1982; Mdiv SWTS 2003. D 6/21/2003 P 12/20/2003 Bp William Dailey Persell. m 7/29/1975 Louis Rodriguez. R Gr Ch Pontiac IL 2006-2011; Int S Jn's Epis Ch Chicago IL 2005; Int La Iglesia De Nuestra Senora De Las Americas Chicago IL 2004-2006; Cur Ch Of The Adv Chicago IL 2003-2004. camareta@att.net

BAXLEY, Todd Lee (NwT) 1601 S Georgia St, Amarillo TX 79102 B Tucumcari NM 5/15/1965 s Michael W Baxley & Paula L. D 9/11/2009 Bp James Scott Mayer. toddbaxley@aol.com

BAXTER, Barbara (WNY) 16 N Phetteplace St, Falconer NY 14733 **P Assoc S Lk's Epis Ch Jamestown NY 2008-** B Buffalo NY 3/20/1950 d Edward Dows Baxter & Betty Jane. BA Hiram Coll 1972; MMusic TCU 1985; MDiv Bex 1991. D 6/8/1991 P 1/1/1992 Bp David Charles Bowman. Assoc R Calv Epis Ch Williamsville NY 2003-2005; BEC Dio Wstrn New York Tonawanda NY 1994-2009; R St Johns Epis Youngstown NY 1993-2000; P-in-c S Aid's Ch Alden NY 1992-1993; Pstr Assoc S Ptr's Ch Westfield NY 1991-1992; Pstr Assoc Trin Epis Ch Hamburg NY 1991-1992. AAM 1997; Hymn Soc Amer And Can 1984. barbarawbaxter@gmail.com

BAXTER JR, Donald Leslie (NwPa) 300 Hilltop Rd, Erie PA 16509 **Gr Ch Lake City PA 2002-** B Pensicola FL 10/13/1955 D 4/19/2002 P 11/17/2002 Bp Robert Deane Rowley Jr. m 5/13/1978 Susan Rose Paradise c 2. bax4347@aol.com

BAXTER, Lisette Dyer (Vt) 112 Lakewood Pkwy, Burlington VT 05408 **R S Andr's Epis Ch Colchester VT 1996-** B Montreal QC CA 7/16/1946 d Romeo R Baril & Carmelle. BTh McGill U; BA U of Montreal 1967; BS/RN Westminster Coll 1977; MDiv Montreal TS 1992. D 6/1/1977 Bp Otis Charles P 6/24/1992 Bp Daniel Lee Swenson. m 7/28/1979 Larry J Baxter c 2. Trin Ch Shelburne VT 1992-1996; D Cathd Ch Of S Paul Burlington VT 1979-1990; D S Jas Epis Ch Midvale UT 1977-1979. CCN 1981; Soc of S Jn the Evang 1993. revlisette@aol.com

BAXTER SSAP, Nancy Julia (At) 1223 Clifton Rd NE, Atlanta GA 30307 B Atlanta GA 9/10/1945 d Harry Stevens Baxter & Edith Ann. BA Mt Holyoke Coll 1967; MDiv SCL Candler TS Emory U 1981. D 6/13/1981 Bp Charles Judson Child Jr P 5/1/1982 Bp Bennett Jones Sims. c 2. Dio Atlanta Atlanta GA 1982-2007; Chapl Emory Epis Campus Mnstry Atlanta GA 1982-2007; S Barth's Epis Ch Atlanta GA 1982-2007; D Cathd Of S Phil Atlanta GA 1981-1982. Fell Coll of Preachers 1991. nancyjuliabaxter@gmail.com

✠ **BAXTER, Rt Rev Nathan Dwight** (CPa) 115 N Duke St, Lancaster PA 17602 **Bp of Cntrl Pennsylvania Dio Cntrl Pennsylvania Harrisburg PA 1977-** B Coatesville PA 11/16/1948 s Belgium Nathan Baxter & Augusta Ruth. Fllshp Coll of Preachers; Harrisburg Cmnty Coll 1972; MDiv Lancaster TS 1976; DMin Lancaster TS 1984; Grad Theol Un 1985; STD Dickinson Coll 1990; Fllshp Harv 1998. D 6/10/1977 P 12/16/1977 Bp Dean T Stevenson Con 10/21/2006 for CPa. m 5/10/1969 Mary Ellen Baxter c 2. R S Jas Ch Lancaster PA 2003-2006; Dn Cathd of St Ptr & St Paul Washington DC 1992-2003; Assoc Prof EDS Cambridge MA 1990-1992; Lancaster TS Lancaster PA 1986-1990; S Paul's Coll Lawrenceville VA 1984-1986; R S Cyp's Epis Ch Hampton VA 1978-1984; S Jn's Epis Ch Carlisle PA 1977-1978. Auth, "Pub Sermons," *Cases & Essays*. OHC; UBE.

BAXTER, Philip Roland (Va) 612 South Ingraham Avenue, Lakeland FL 33801 **Ret Assoc S Paul's Ch Winter Haven FL 1999-** B Weyauwega WI 7/18/1922 s Perry Milton Baxter & Florence Ellen. BA Carroll Coll 1948; MDiv McCormick TS 1951; GTS 1956; MS U of Wisconsin 1987. D 10/18/1956 Bp Horace W B Donegan P 4/25/1957 Bp Donald H V Hallock. m 7/4/1984 Dorothea F James c 3. Supply P S Dav's Epis Ch Lakeland FL 1995-1996; Assoc All SS Epis Ch Lakeland FL 1990-1994; H Trin Epis Ch Bowie MD 1986-1988; Asst Trin Epis Ch Oshkosh WI 1986-1988; Asst S Jn's Epis Ch McLean VA 1982-1984; S Barn Ch Moberly MO 1967-1969; R H Trin Epis Ch Bowie MD 1958-1968. Auth, "Comments on Counslg," *The Wisconsin Counslr*, 1992. AFP 1965; Fllshp Contemplative Pryr 1961. Phi Mu Alpha; Kappa Sigma Phi. prbaxter@aol.com

BAXTER, William MacNeil (WA) 15 Clifford St Apt 2e, Portland ME 04102 **Chair Bd Faithworks Dio Maine Portland ME 1997-** B Halifax NS CA 10/5/1923 s William John Baxter & Mary Ellen. BA Amh 1945; BD VTS 1951. D 6/20/1951 Bp William Scarlett P 12/23/1951 Bp Arthur C Lichtenberger. m 10/25/1946 Jean Taylor. R Trin Epis Ch Lewiston ME 1988-1998; Lectr Ya

Berk New Haven CT 1963; Pres Epis Cler Assn Dio Washington Washington DC 1961-1964; Lectr VTS Alexandria VA 1958-1966; R S Mk's Ch Washington DC 1954-1966; DCE S Mich & S Geo Clayton MO 1951-1954. Auth, "Rain On The Unjust," *Virginia Sem Journ*, 1993; Auth, "Drama In The Chancel," *Wit*, 1959; Auth, "Commentary On Chr Sxlty," *Journ Of Pstr Care*, 1957. Cosmos Club.

BAXTER JR, William Parker (Fla) 332 Waters Edge Dr S, Ponte Vedra Beach FL 32082 **Died 1/13/2011** B Petersburg VA 4/3/1942 s William Parker Baxter & Pattie Gregg. BA U of Maryland 1965; STB Ya Berk 1968. D 6/29/1968 P 5/31/1969 Bp William Foreman Creighton. c 2. Auth, "arts"; Auth, "Towards a Theol of CE," *Making Sense of Things*. STB cl Berkley DS at Yale New Haven CT 1968; BA cl U of Maryland Coll Pk MD 1965. williampbaxter@gmail.com

BAYACA, Greg G(uerrero) (Los) 3 La Morada Pl, Pomona CA 91766 B Caba La Union Philippines 2/15/1936 S Andr's Epis TS Quezon Ph. Trans from Episcopal Church in the Philippines 1/1/2003 Bp Joseph Jon Bruno. m 7/21/2008 Josefina B Bayaca c 1. Dio Los Angeles Los Angeles CA 2002-2003; S Jn's And H Chld Wilmington CA 1995-2008.

BAYANG, Martin Eugenio (RG) 1406 S Cliff Dr, Gallup NM 87301 B Sagada PH 3/10/1935 s Eugenio Bayang & Agustiona. BA U of The Philippines 1960; BTh S Andr's TS Manila PH 1961; EDS 1965; STM Bos 1966; PhD Bos 1974. D 5/30/1961 P 2/14/1962 Bp Lyman Cunningham Ogilby. m 6/10/1965 Veronica Ag-a Guitelen c 5. All SS Ch Grants NM 1976-2004; Epis Asiamerican Strtgy Epis Ch Cntr New York NY 1974-1975; Asst S Lk's And S Marg's Ch Allston MA 1973-1974. BTh cl S Andr's TS Manila PH 1961. bayang@netzero.net

BAYFIELD, Ralph Wesley (Va) 20902 Adams Mills Pl, Ashburn VA 20147 B Philadelphia PA 4/11/1934 s Ralph Bayfield & Caroline. Penn 1953; BA Wesl 1956; BD/MDiv VTS 1959; STM Luth TS at Gettysburg 1966; Camb 1988; DMin VTS 1997. D 5/9/1959 Bp William P Roberts P 11/24/1959 Bp Nelson Marigold Burroughs. m 8/20/2005 Maeva-Louise Beckwith Hair Maui HI c 2. Int Vic S Peters-In-The-Woods Epis Ch Fairfax Sta VA 2008-2009; R S Thos' Ch Richmond VA 1991-2000; Evang Cmsn Dio Virginia Richmond VA 1986-1999; R S Tim's Ch Herndon VA 1974-1991; Dn Dio Pennsylvania Philadelphia PA 1970-1974; R S Jas Ch Collegeville PA 1968-1974; Assoc Chr Ch Greenville Wilmington DE 1960-1968; Asst S Paul's Epis Ch Cleveland Heights OH 1959-1960. Auth, "Self-Differentiated Ldrshp through Pstr Vision," VTS, 1997; Auth, "Early Evansburg," Nace, 1974; Auth, "Selma Diary," Chr Ch Christians Hundred, 1966. Secy, EvangES 1990. revdocbayfield@verizon.net

BAYLES, Joseph Austin (Kan) 1341 N River Blvd, Wichita KS 67203 B Wichita KS 8/30/1934 s M Ward Bayles & Lura Mae. BS K SU 1956; MDiv Andover Newton TS 1960. D 7/23/1967 P 11/30/1967 Bp William Davidson. m 9/10/1971 Patricia Wittman c 3. R S Barth's Ch Wichita KS 1996-2003; S Jas Ch Wichita KS 1987-1988; Asst S Steph's Ch Wichita KS 1982-1984; Vic Chr Ch Kingman KS 1971-1977; Vic S Anne's Ch McPherson KS 1969-1971; Cur Gr Epis Ch Hutchinson KS 1968-1969. Chapl of the Year Kansas Assn of Chapl 1993; Chapl ofd the Year Kansas Associatioon of Chapl 1993. jbayles1@cox.net

BAYLES, Richard Allen (Oly) Po Box 1115, South Bend WA 98586 **Vic S Ptr's Ch Seaview WA 2008-** B Ottawa KS 5/25/1939 s Milan Ward Bayles & Lura Mae. BA K SU 1961; Andover Newton TS 1963; BD EDS 1971; Cntrl Washington U 1975. D 7/13/1971 P 5/1/1972 Bp John Raymond Wyatt. m 1/7/1983 Sharon Kulish-Bayles c 1. S Matt Ch Castle Rock WA 1995-2002; S Jn's Ch Un Gap WA 1973-1983. Phi Beta Kappa; Phi Beta Kappa. RICKB98685@AOL.COM

BAYNE, Bruce George Cuthbert (Nev) 2875 Idledwild Dr, #108, Reno NV 89505 **P-in-c Chap Of S Jas The Fisherman Wellfleet MA 2009-** B Seattle WA 3/20/1948 s Stephen F Bayne & Lucie. BA Amh 1970; MDiv EDS 1975. D 6/14/1975 Bp Paul Moore Jr P 10/23/1976 Bp Harold Louis Wright. m 6/11/1976 Sarah Collins c 2. R S Lk's Ch San Francisco CA 1993-2008; Dir Of Ch And Alum Relatns EDS Cambridge MA 1989-1993; R Trin Ch Canton MA 1983-1989; Assoc R S Paul's Epis Ch Indianapolis IN 1979-1983; R S Ptr's By-The-Sea Sitka AK 1977-1979; Asst Chr Epis Ch Tarrytown NY 1975-1976. bruce@stlukessf.org

BAYNES, Leopold Cornelius (LI) 2306 98th St, East Elmhurst NY 11369 **R Gr Ch Corona NY 1999-** B Georgetown VC 3/13/1943 s Donald Theophilus Campbelle & Venola Rufina. Codrington Coll 1973; Blanton-Peale Grad Inst 1997. Trans from Church in the Province Of The West Indies 5/5/1999 Bp Orris George Walker Jr. m 9/12/1985 Miranda Sawney c 2. Assoc S Mk's Ch Brooklyn NY 1995-1999; R S Andr's Ch Brooklyn NY 1978-1997.

BAZIN, Jean Jacques Emmanuel Fritz (SeFla) 1 Nw 67th St, Miami FL 33150 **Archd for Immigration & Soc Justice Dio SE Florida Miami FL 2006-** B South Marc HT 6/22/1941 s Antoine K Bazin & Lucienne. BA Coll Of S Pierre Ht 1963. D 12/3/1966 P 6/1/1967 Bp Charles Alfred Voegeli. m 6/4/1983 Pamela H Bazin. Jackson Meml Hosp Miami FL 2002; Dio SE Florida Miami FL 1998-2005; Ch Of S Paul The Apos Miami FL 1981-1992. jfritzbazin@gmail.com

BEACH, Deborah Elizabeth (Alb) 85 Lake Hill Rd, Burnt Hills NY 12027 B Schenectady NY 10/24/1959 d Robert Edward Beach & Marie Elizabeth Tripp. AAS Maria Coll Albany NY 1979; BS Russell Sage Coll 1991. D 5/30/2009 Bp William Howard Love. dbeach21@verizon.net

BEACH, Diana Lee (Nwk) 88 Main Street, Thomaston ME 04861 B Calgary AB CA 9/4/1946 d Hugh Hamilton Beach & Lucille. BA Smith 1968; MDiv Ya Berk 1971; CG Jung Inst 1977; DMin NYTS 1980. D 6/3/1978 P 12/17/1978 Bp Paul Moore Jr. Assoc Chr Ch Short Hills NJ 1996-2000; S Matt's Ch Jersey City NJ 1995-1996; Gr Ch Van Vorst Jersey City NJ 1984; Ch Of The H Innoc W Orange NJ 1980-1983. Auth, "Approaching Merlin's Cave: Ret and Soulwork," 2005; Auth, *In Search of the Goddess*, Ruach, 1992; Auth, *Womansoul Descending: Reflections on Feminine Sprtly*, D.Min. thesis, 1980; Auth, "But the Queen Doesn't Believe in God," 1977; Auth, *Sex Role Stereotyping in Ch Sch Curric*, Jn Knox Press, 1973. Cmnty of St. Jn Bapt, Assoc 2004; Kilin, Dio NY 1981-1999; Schlr's Grp, Dio Newark 1981-1984. Alum Awd Ya Berk New Haven CT 1988; MDiv cl, first in class Ya Berk New Haven CT 1971. dlbeach497@earthlink.net

BEACH, John Tappan (Eur) 39, Route De Malagnou, Geneva 01208 Switzerland **Emm Epis Ch Geneva 1201 CH 2006-** B New Haven CT 11/17/1957 s Prescott Beach & Marjorie Ann. BA McGill U 1980; BTh McGill U 1982; MDiv McGill U 1983. Trans from Anglican Church of Canada 2/1/2006 Bp Pierre W Whalon. m 8/21/1982 Denise Beneteau c 2. Dio Florida Jacksonville FL 1995-2001; Chapl Resurr Chap Tallahassee FL 1995-2001. rector@emmanuelchurch.ch

BEACH, Joseph Lawrence (ETenn) 4768 Edens View Rd, Kingsport TN 37664 B Richmond VA 3/31/1936 s Joseph Elisha Beach & Mary E. BS U of Tennessee 1958; MS U of Tennessee 1960. D 1/27/1985 Bp William Evan Sanders. m 10/14/1961 Emily Faye Yoakum c 3. Serv S Tim's Epis Ch Kingsport TN 1985-1996.

BEACHAM III, Albert Burton (U) 1420 N 3000 W, Vernal UT 84078 B Powell WY 9/20/1938 s Albert Burton Beacham & Thelma Catherine. D 12/26/1985 Bp Otis Charles P 8/1/1987 Bp George Edmonds Bates. m 6/27/1981 Merilyn Madsen. Dio Utah Salt Lake City UT 2003-2004; S Paul's Epis Ch Vernal UT 1987-2003.

BEACHY, William Nicholas (WMo) 431 W 60th Ter, Kansas City MO 64113 B Idaho Falls ID 5/15/1923 s William Johnson Beachy & Gwendolyn Irene. MD LSU 1949; STB Ya Berk 1956. D 6/21/1956 P 12/21/1956 Bp Edward Randolph Welles II. m 6/15/1949 Catherine Ditchburn c 3. Chapl St Lk's Chap Kansas City MO 1960-1986; St Lk's So Chap Overland Pk KS 1960-1986; Vic S Steph's Ch Monett MO 1956-1960. Auth, "My Secret of Healing," *Sharing mag*, OSL the Physcn, 2000. Chapl Worker Sis of the H Sprt 1979; Intl OSL The Physcn 1958. billdad@sbcglobal.net

BEACOM, George Curtis (Ak) 205 W Beaver Ave, Palmer AK 99645 **Died 8/31/2009** B Breckenridge TX 9/17/1923 s Curtis G Beacom & Violet E. Untd States ArmdF Inst 1946; U of Alaska 1967; CDSP 1969. D 10/6/1969 P 5/1/1970 Bp William J Gordon Jr. S Anna And S Simeon Soc.

BEADLE JR, Herbert J (At) 704 Defoors Mill Cir Nw, Atlanta GA 30318 **Died 3/16/2010** B New Haven CT 5/20/1923 s Herbert J Beadle & Geraldine Barbara. BA U of Texas 1947; GTS 1950; 1966. D 6/21/1950 P 1/1/1951 Bp Clinton Simon Quin. c 3. Appalachian People's Serv Orgnztn 1986-1987; Dio Texas Cler Assn. Bd Governers Appalachian People's Serv Orgnztn 1986; Hon Cn S Phil Cathd Atlanta GA 1979.

BEAL, Jennifer D (Los) 1745 Wedgewood Cmn, Concord MA 01742 B Boston MA 8/1/1961 d Thomas Prince Beal & Barbara. BA Ob 1983; MDiv Yale DS 1988. D 6/2/1990 P 6/15/1991 Bp David Elliot Johnson. c 1. Assoc The Ch Of The Ascen Sierra Madre CA 2004-2008; Dioc Coun Mem Dio Los Angeles Los Angeles CA 2001-2002; Int Trin Par Fillmore CA 2000-2002; Ch Of The Ang Pasadena CA 2000; R Emm Ch Braintree MA 1998-1999; Asst S Steph's Ch Cohasset MA 1996-1998; Assoc S Steph's Epis Ch Boston MA 1993-1996; Asst S Paul's Ch Brookline MA 1992-1993; Cox Fell Dio Massachusetts Boston MA 1990-1992. jennifer.beal@mindspring.com

BEAL, M(adeleine) Elizabeth (Me) 35 Beal Rd, Chesterville ME 04938 B San Diego CA 12/24/1959 d William Warner Moss & Madeleine Ann. RN Framingham St Coll 1979; BS U of Maine 1986; Maine Diac Formation Prog 1991. D 4/8/1991 Bp Edward Cole Chalfant. m 6/2/1979 Douglas Foster Beal c 2. D S Lk's Ch Farmington ME 2000-2003; Yth Mssnr Dio Maine Portland ME 1996-1998; D S Matt's Epis Ch Lisbon ME 1993-1995; D S Lk's Ch Farmington ME 1991-1993. NAAD . memb@quixnet.net

BEAL, Stephen Thomas (NCal) 2301 Polk St, Apt 3, San Francisco CA 94109 **P Gr Cathd San Francisco CA 2001-** B Santa Rosa CA 4/30/1948 s Donald Wesley Beal & Patricia Ann. BA U of Arizona 1978; CTh Oxf 1980; MDiv CDSP 1981. D 10/28/1981 P 6/1/1982 Bp John Lester Thompson III. R S Lk's Ch Woodland CA 1989-1995; R Ch Of S Nich Paradise CA 1981-1989. steveb@gracecathedral.org

BEALE, Mary Idella (NH) 45 Derryfield Ct, Manchester NH 03104 B Geneva NY 5/15/1948 d George Walker Beale & Margaret E. BFA Washington U 1970; MDiv Andover Newton TS 1973; Med Bos 1975. D 6/17/1973 P 5/1/1977 Bp William Crittenden. Vic Gr Epis Ch Concord NH 1982-1994; Asst S Geo's Ch Durham NH 1981-1982; S Paul's Sch Concord NH 1977-1980; Trin Memi Ch Warren PA 1973-1974. mlongpond@metrocast.net

BEALE, Norman Victor (Mass) 17 Long Sought For Pond Rd, Westford MA 01886 B Jacksonville FL 6/26/1952 s Warren Wisel Beale & Louise. BA Furman U 1976; MS NYU 1983; MA Fullertheosem/TESM 1996. D 11/22/1995 P 5/1/1996 Bp Keith Lynn Ackerman. m 12/20/1980 Elizabeth Anne Haberer c 2. R S Mk's Ch Westford MA 2003-2008; Asst Gr Epis Ch Orange Pk FL 2001-2003; Angl Frontier Missions Richmond VA 1996-1999. Angl Frontier Mssn; Cerid Resrch Affiliate; Cntrl Asia Fllshp; Himalayan Mnstry Ntwk; Tamang Literacy Proj; Tamang Mnstry Ntwk. rector@st-mark.org

BEALES, Rosemary E (Va) 400 Fontaine St, Alexandria VA 22302 **P Assoc S Paul's Epis Ch Alexandria VA 2008-; Lower Sch Chapl St. Steph's and St. Agnes Sch Alexandria VA 2008-** B Washington DC 2/1/1949 d Charles Melvin Beales & Rosemary Frances. BS U of Maryland 1972; MDiv VTS 2005. D 6/11/2005 Bp Robert Wilkes Ihloff P 12/17/2005 Bp John Leslie Rabb. c 3. Assoc R S Jn's Ch Ellicott City MD 2005-2008. Fac Excellence Awd St. Steph's & St. Agnes Sch 2011. remembrance49@gmail.com

BEAM, Barbara Jean (WMo) 6336 SE Hamilton Rd, Lathrop MO 64465 **P All SS Epis Ch Kansas City MO 2008-** B Kansas City MO 2/6/1941 d Robert Michael Wedow & Jean Condon. BA Avila Coll 1964; Dioc W Missouri Sch For Mnstry 1994; Dioc Sc Trng Prog For Sprtl Dir 1996. D 2/4/1995 P 3/25/1999 Bp John Clark Buchanan. c 2. P-in-c S Jn's Ch Neosho MO 2004-2006; Dioc Coun Dio W Missouri Kansas City MO 2000-2004; Vic S Nich Ch Noel MO 1998-2006; BEC Dio W Missouri Kansas City MO 1995-1998; D S Mary's Epis Ch Kansas City MO 1995-1998. Conf S Greg Abbey. bjbeam@gmail.com

BEAM, Marcia McKay (SeFla) 805 SW 6th Ave, Delray Beach FL 33444 **S Matt's Epis Ch Delray Bch FL 2005-** B Delray Beach FL 2/8/1947 BA S Aug's Coll Raleigh NC 1968; MDiv Bex 2003. D 2/16/2004 P 12/20/2004 Bp Michael Bruce Curry. m 12/31/1970 Vance DeLeon Beam c 2. D Ch Of The H Fam Chap Hill NC 2004.

BEAMER, Charles Wesley (O) 3920 Spokane Ave, Cleveland OH 44109 B Cumberland MD 9/15/1939 s Charles Samuel Beamer & Loretta C. BA Frostburg St U 1969; MDiv PDS 1971. D 6/22/1971 Bp Harry Lee Doll P 4/1/1974 Bp David Keller Leighton Sr. m 1/5/1974 Yvonne Marie Barr. Ch Of The Trsfg Cleveland OH 2000-2004; S Andr's Ch Cleveland OH 1998-2000; Gr Epis Ch Willoughby OH 1988-1995; Par Of The H Apos Mt Airy MD 1982-1988; Vic S Jas Epis Ch Mt Airy MD 1982-1985; All Souls Ch Relay MD 1974-1982; Asst Ch Of The H Cross Cumberland MD 1972-1973. EUC.

BEAN, Kevin D (WMass) All Saints Church, 10 Irving St., Worcester MA 01609 **R All SS Ch Worcester MA 2008-** B Salonika GR 8/21/1954 s Harry Campbell Bean & Marilyn. Ohio Wesl 1974; BD (Hons) U of Edinburgh Scotland UK 1977; ETS, Edinburgh Scotland UK 1978; EDS 1980; Harvard DS 1980. D 12/5/1981 P 6/24/1982 Bp Arthur Edward Walmsley. m 7/14/1978 Megan H Bean c 3. S Barth's Ch New York NY 2005-2008; R Wyman Memi Ch of St Andr Marblehead MA 1997-2005; Trin Epis Old Swedes Ch Swedesboro NJ 1992-1997; Trin Par Wilmington DE 1992-1997; Assoc S Lk's Par Darien CT 1983-1988; Peace Cmsn Dio Connecticut Hartford CT 1982-1985; Cur S Andr's Ch Meriden CT 1981-1983; Coordntr EUC Dio Connecticut Hartford CT 1980-1981. Auth, "arts," *Bulletin of the Atomic Scientists*; Auth, "arts," *Commonweal*; Auth, "arts," *Cross Currents*; Auth, "arts," *Soc Sci Journ*; Auth, "arts," *Sojourners*; Auth, "arts," *The New York Times*. Wm Sloane Coffin / Joan Bates Forsberg Fell Yale DS / Berk 1995. meganbean50@gmail.com

BEAN JR, Theodore William (LI) Cathedral of the Incarnation, 50 Cathedral Avenue, Garden City NY 11530 **Dn Cathd Of The Incarn Garden City NY 2005-** B Decatur IL 2/15/1949 s Theodore William Bean & June Stather. BA U IL 1971; MDiv SWTS 1974; MBA GTF 1991. D 9/7/1974 P 3/1/1975 Bp Donald James Parsons. m 10/7/1989 Karen Theresa Clauson c 3. Archd Dio Long Island Garden City NY 2004-2011; R S Thos Ch Farmingdale NY 2001-2005; Int All SS Ch Bayside NY 1999-2001; Int S Geo's Ch Hempstead NY 1999; Int S Paul's Ch Glen Cove NY 1997-1998; S Ann And The H Trin Brooklyn NY 1997; Int Ch Of The Resurr E Elmhurst NY 1996; Int S Gabr's Ch Hollis NY 1995-1996; R S Paul's Ch Coll Point NY 1990-1992; Chapl Epis Mssn Soc New York NY 1985-1990; Vic S Marg's Ch Plainview NY 1980-1981; R Ch Of The Ascen Greenpoint Brooklyn NY 1976-1979; Cur Trin Epis Ch Peoria IL 1974-1975. Assn Profsnl Chapl 1994-2006. twbean@msn.com

BEAR, Susan Dowler (Miss) 3600 Arlington Loop, Hattiesburg MS 39402 **R Ch Of The Ascen Hattiesburg MS 2004-** B Trenton NJ 4/21/1947 d Thomas Jefferson Dowler & Evelyn Elizabeth. BA Wilson Coll 1969; MEd Auburn U 1980; MDiv TS 1994; DMin TS 2007. D 6/25/1994 P 11/4/1995 Bp James Monte Stanton. m 12/21/1974 John E Bear c 2. R Gr Epis Ch Houston TX 2001-2004; R Chap Of The Cross ROLLING FORK MS 1996-2001; Cur All SS Ch Jackson MS 1995. rfpriest2@aol.com

BEARD, Madeleine Claire (Md) The Episcopal Diocse of MD, 4 E. University PKWY, Baltimore MD 21218 **Del to GC Dio Maryland Baltimore MD 2011-; Jubilee Off Dio Maryland Baltimore MD 2009-** B Cleveland OH 12/3/1947 d Kenneth Jerome Deacon & Johanna Rosina. BA U of Maryland 2006. D 6/10/2006 Bp Robert Wilkes Ihloff. m 12/31/1966 James Lawrence Beard c 3. Dioc Coun Dio Maryland Baltimore MD 2007-2011. beardmcd@verizon.net

BEARDEN, Jane (Mass) 77 Westchester Dr, Haverhill MA 01830 **P-in-c Trin Epis Ch Haverhill MA 2009-** B Winnsboro LA 2/3/1948 d John Nathaniel Bostick & Alice Elizabeth. BS Centenary Coll 1970; MT Memi Hosp Houston TX 1972; MS Mississippi St U 1985; MATS EDS 2006. D 10/6/2001 P 6/3/2006 Bp M(arvil) Thomas Shaw III. c 3. P-in-c Dio Massachusetts Boston MA 2007-2009; The Epis Ch Of The Redeem Biloxi MS 2007-2009; D S Steph's Memi Ch Lynn MA 2001-2006. janebbearden@gmail.com

BEARDSLEY, Herbert Hobman (LI) Po Box 1086, Cutchogue NY 11935 B Flushing NY 7/14/1929 s Herbert Hobman Beardsley & Wilhelmina Argyle. BA Col 1951; ThB PDS 1954; GTS 1966; DD Jn Dewey U Consortium 1988. D 4/24/1954 P 11/13/1954 Bp James P De Wolfe. m 6/25/1955 Carolyn Jones c 4. Int S Mary's Ch Hampton Bays NY 1998-2000; R Ch Of The Adv Westbury NY 1965-1995; Trin Ch Gulph Mills King Of Prussia PA 1957-1965; Cur Ch Of The Adv Westbury NY 1954-1957. Hon DD Jn Dewey U Consortium 1988; Hon Cn Cathd of the Incarn Garden City NY. frbeards@aol.com

BEARL, Dena Stokes (At) P.O. Box 490, Clarkesville GA 30523 **R Gr-Calv Epis Ch Clarkesville GA 2004-** B Jacksonville FL 11/12/1956 d Redmond Frederick Stokes & Frances Dena. BA Florida St U 1980; MDiv VTS 1992. D 6/14/1992 P 12/13/1992 Bp Frank Stanley Cerveny. m 9/15/1979 Robert Anderson Smith c 1. Chr Ch Epis Sch Greenville SC 2000-2003; Chapl/Assoc Chr Ch Greenville SC 2000-2003; Cn S Jn's Cathd Jacksonville FL 1994-2000; Assoc/Chapl S Andr's Ch Jacksonville FL 1992-1994. denabearl@windstream.net

BEASLEY, Battle Alexander (Tenn) 1613 Fatherland St, Nashville TN 37206 **R S Mk's Ch Antioch TN 2001-** B Bolahoon LR 8/29/1952 s William Bodie Rogers Beasley & Marion Kathrine. Georgetown Coll; ba U Of Kentucky 1978; mdiv STUSo 1986. D 6/5/1986 P 6/1/1987 Bp Alex Dockery Dickson. m 9/27/1997 Amy Dawn Harwell c 2. S Ann's Ch Nashville TN 1999-2001; R Ch Of The Redeem Shelbyville TN 1994-1998; Int Chr Ch Memphis TN 1992-1994; Assoc Gr - S Lk's Ch Memphis TN 1989-1992; Dio W Tennessee Memphis TN 1986-1989; Cur S Paul's Ch Memphis TN 1986-1989. Sthrn buddhist sunday Sch Assn all day meeting and 1985; the labyrinth Soc 1998-2001. stmarksrector@bellsouth.net

BEASLEY, Carl H (Eas) 1196, Apt B Firetower Rd, Colora MD 21917 B York PA 10/19/1946 s Carl Huntington Beasley & Frances Sarah. BA Ken 1968; MA VTS 1976; MA Washington Coll 1988; Cert Wilson Coll 1990. D 2/2/1977 P 11/29/1978 Bp Dean T Stevenson. c 1. R S Jn's Ch Marietta PA 1989-1991; R S Mary's Epis Ch Waynesboro PA 1979-1986; Cur The Epis Ch Of S Jn The Bapt York PA 1977-1979. Who's Who Among Amer's Teachers. cbeasley@wna.org

BEASLEY, Elizabeth Parish (Haw) PO Box 300303, Kaaawa HI 96730 **Cn to the Ordnry Dio Hawaii Honolulu HI 2011-** B Norfolk VA 5/14/1958 d Walter Cantrell Parish & Louise. BA Wake Forest U 1979; MDiv Harvard DS 1989; DAS STUSo 1998; STM STUSo 2004. D 6/27/1998 Bp Catherine Elizabeth Maples Waynick P 3/25/1999 Bp Richard Sui On Chang. m 8/17/1996 Donald Kirk Beasley. Cn for Mnstry Dvlpmt Dio Hawaii Honolulu HI 2007-2011; Cmncatn Off Dio Hawaii Honolulu HI 2005-2008; Cmncatn Off Dio Hawaii Honolulu HI 2005-2007; Vic S Jn's By The Sea Kaneohe HI 2005-2007; Int All SS Ch Kapaa HI 2002-2005; COM Dio Hawaii Honolulu HI 2002-2005; Asst Dio Massachusetts Boston MA 2001-2002; COM Dio Hawaii Honolulu HI 2000-2001; Vic S Geo's Epis Ch Honolulu HI 1998-2001. Auth, "An Unclean Sprt," *LivCh*, LivCh, 2008. epbeasley@earthlink.net

BEASLEY, Helen Roberts (SwVa) Po Box 1266, Galax VA 24333 B Knoxville TN 10/28/1944 d Richard Reynolds Beasley & Carrie Mae. BA Hobart and Wm Smith Colleges 1966; MDiv UTS 1990. D 6/11/1993 P 12/21/1993 Bp Richard Frank Grein. c 2. S Jn's Ch Roanoke VA 2006-2007; Trin Epis Ch Rocky Mt VA 1999-2005; S Andr's Epis Ch Hartsdale NY 1996-1999; Wstrn Dutchess Mnstry New Hamburg NY 1995-1996; Assoc Chr Ch Bronxville NY 1994-1996; Assoc Trin S Paul's Epis New Rochelle NY 1993-1996; Dir Proj Hope S Ptr's Epis Ch Peekskill NY 1992-1993. Ord Of S Lk; SCHC. rectorbeasley@comcast.net

BEASLEY, Nicholas Madden (USC) 126 Blyth Avenue, Greenwood SC 29649 **R Ch Of The Resurr Greenwood SC 2007-** B Memphis TN 4/23/1975 s Robert Luther Beasley & Joy Madden. BA U So 1997; MDiv Ya Berk 2000; PhD Van 2006. D 9/23/2000 Bp Dorsey Felix Henderson P 3/25/2001 Bp A(rthur) Heath Light. m 8/17/2002 Elizabeth Irwin Beasley c 2. S Geo's Ch Nashville TN 2003-2006; Asst R Chr Ch Greenville SC 2000-2002. Auth, "Chr Ritual and the Creation of British Slave Societies, 1650-1780," U GA

Press, 2009; Auth, "Dom Rituals: Mar and Baptism in the British Plantation Colonies, 1650-1780," *Angl and Epis Hist*, HSEC, 2007; Auth, "Ritual Time in British Plantation Colonies, 1650-1780," *Ch Hist*, Amer Soc of Ch Hist, 2007; Auth, "Wars of Rel in the Circum-Caribbean: Engl Iconoclasm in Spanish Amer, 1580-1702," *SS and their Cults in the Atlantic Wrld*, U of So Carolina Press, 2006. HSEC 2005. Nelson Burr Prize HSEC 2008; ECF Felllow ECF 2003. nicholas.beasley@gmail.com

BEASLEY, Robert (ETenn) 121 E. Harper Avenue, Maryville TN 37804 B Somerset KY 8/16/1949 s Ray Beasley & Grapel. BA U of Memphis 1971; MDiv SWTS 1974. D 6/26/1974 Bp John Vander Horst P 5/24/1975 Bp William F Gates Jr. m 10/12/1985 Martha Lee Spencer. Int S Andr's Ch Maryville TN 2007-2009; S Phil's Epis Ch Laurel MD 2005; R S Jn's Ch Roanoke VA 2002-2005; R S Phil's Ch Southport NC 1991-2002; Asst R Chr Ch New Bern NC 1988-1991; Asst Ch Of The Ascen Knoxville TN 1980-1984; Asst S Paul's Ch Augusta GA 1979-1980; Vic S Mary Magd Ch Fayetteville TN 1975-1978; D-in-Trng S Geo's Ch Germantown TN 1974-1975. Auth, "The R Painted His Nails," *A Tapestry of Voices*, Knoxville Writers Gld, 2011; Auth, "The Paved Road," *The Storyteller*, 2008; Auth, "What 'Gd News' is Gd," *Witness*, 1990; Auth, "Experiencing the Way of Tea," *Honolulu*, 1987; Auth, "Necessary Number Racket," *Your Ch*, 1984. bobbeasley@charter.net

BEASLEY JR, Thomas Edward (Fla) 6003 Brookridge Rd, Jacksonville FL 32210 B Nashville TN 3/4/1945 s Thomas E Beasley & Martha M. BS Florida St U 1970; VTS 1972; Cert Angl Inst Live Oak FL 2004. D 11/9/2004 P 5/26/2005 Bp Samuel Johnson Howard. m 5/26/1995 Pixianne Carlton Ashby c 2. beesknees@earthlink.net

BEASON, Kenneth G (ECR) 438 N 5th St, Cheney WA 99004 B Columbus OH 12/22/1942 s Carl G Beason & Helen L. BD U of Nebraska 1969; MDiv SWTS 1972. D 6/4/1972 P 12/1/1972 Bp Robert Patrick Varley. m 12/8/2000 Laurel A Beason. R S Jas Ch Paso Robles CA 2000-2007; Cathd Of S Jn The Evang Spokane WA 1996-2000; Off Of Bsh For ArmdF New York NY 1974-1996; Urban Vic Dio Nebraska Omaha NE 1972-1973. Auth, "Pstr Care & USAF Chapl". UBE. k_beason@charter.net

BEATTIE, Richard Edward (Ct) 438 Old Tavern Rd, Orange CT 06477 **Assoc Ch of the H Sprt W Haven CT 2010-** B New Haven CT 6/20/1943 s Edward John Beattie & Ethel Tillie. Bd Cert Chap ACPE & APC - CPE 1996; MAR Sacr Heart U 1996; BSBA U of New Haven 1996. D 12/6/1986 Bp Arthur Edward Walmsley P 1/12/2002 Bp Wilfrido Ramos-Orench. m 6/19/1965 Marilyn Schenk c 3. P-in-c Chr And Epiph Ch E Haven CT 2007-2009; D S Ptr's Epis Ch Milford CT 2001. revddick@optonline.net

BEATTIE, R(ichard) Sherman (Ct) 25 Stuart Dr, Old Greenwich CT 06870 **P-in-c S Andr's Ch Stamford CT 2000-** B Paris FR 5/27/1928 s Ernest Boardman Beattie & Dorothy. BA Trin Hartford CT 1949; MDiv GTS 1952. D 6/17/1952 P 12/19/1952 Bp Walter H Gray. m 6/28/1958 Joan M Beattie. Chr Ch Greenwich CT 1982-1983; Round Hill Cmnty Ch Inc Greenwich CT 1978-1979; R S Paul's Ch Columbus IN 1967-1971; Assoc Ch Of The Heav Rest New York NY 1957-1960; Asst Cathd Ch Of S Paul Burlington VT 1953-1957; Vic Chr Ch Bethany CT 1952-1953; Vic Ch Of The Gd Shpd Orange CT 1952-1953. Phi Delta Kappa.

BEATTY, Anne (Ida) 1908 Humboldt Ave, Davis CA 95616 B Lafayette IN 1/4/1949 d Earl Critton Beatty & Margaret. BA Pomona Coll 1971; MDiv Fuller TS 1985; CDSP 1992. D 1/6/1993 P 7/27/1993 Bp Jerry Alban Lamb. c 2. Dioc Coun Mem Dio Idaho Boise ID 2008-2010; GC Dep Dio Idaho Boise ID 2006; Stndg Comm. Mem Dio Idaho Boise ID 2003-2006; R Trin Epis Ch Pocatello ID 2002-2010; Int Ch Of The Ascen Vallejo CA 2001-2002; Int S Paul's Epis Ch Benicia CA 1999-2001; Dioc Coun Mem Dio Nthrn California Sacramento CA 1995-1998; Asst Ch Of S Mart Davis CA 1993-1999. anbaytee@msn.com

BEATTY, Stephan P (Va) P.O. Box 11, Montpelier VA 23192 B Clarksburg WV 5/31/1955 s Calvin Ray Beatty & Margaret Josephine. BA W Virginia Wesleyan Coll 1977; MS W Virginia U 1979; Grad Sch Of Rel Pk Coll Parkville MO 1988; Rockhurst Jesuit Coll 1988; MDiv Ya Berk 1994. D 9/21/1989 P 6/5/1994 Bp John Clark Buchanan. m 6/29/1985 Angela Marie Beatty c 1. Ch Of Our Sav Montpelier VA 2008-2010; R Chr Ch Somers Point NJ 2000-2007; R Chr Ch Warrensburg MO 1994-2000; D S Mk's Ch New Canaan CT 1992-2000; D S Mary's Epis Ch Kansas City MO 1990-1991; D Trin Ch Independence MO 1989-1990. Auth, "A Statistical Abstract Of W Virginia Reg Vii," Appalachian Reg Plnng Cmsn, 1977. Omicron Delta Kappa. stephanbeatty@embarqmail.com

BEATY, Maureen Kay (Colo) St Mary Magdalene, 4775 Cambridge St, Boulder CO 80301 B Denver CO 5/13/1961 d James Tomlin & Ruth. BS Colorado St U, Ft Collins CO 1984. D 11/17/2007 Bp Robert John O'Neill. c 2. maureen@thebeatys.net

BEAUCHAMP, Robert William (CFla) 409 W Main St, Marion VA 24354 **All SS Epis Ch Norton VA 2008-** B Washington DC 5/7/1962 s Irving Beauchamp & Carol. BA Emory & Henry Coll 1989; MDiv STUSo 1999. D 6/20/1999 P 12/17/1999 Bp Frank Neff Powell. m 5/14/1989 Laura Sherry Hyde c 2. S Andr's Ch Pasadena MD 2002-2005; Asst R Gr Ch Kilmarnock VA 2000-2002; R Chr Epis Ch Marion VA 1999-2000. fishin@rivnet.net

BEAULIEU, Cynthia Rae (Me) 650 Main St, Caribou ME 04736 **D Aroostook Epis Cluster Caribou ME 2008-** B Presque Isle ME 3/26/1949 d Jack Sprague & Capitola. D 8/9/2008 Bp Chilton Abbie Richardson Knudsen. m 11/8/1997 Gerald Beaulieu c 3. cindy@mfx.net

BEAULIEU, Delores Joyce (Minn) Rr 2 Box 246, Bagley MN 56621 B Bagley MN 11/13/1934 d George James Hill & Emily Catherine. D 10/29/2005 Bp James Louis Jelinek. c 2.

BEAULIEU, Joyce Elaine (Chi) 217 E. Hurlbut Ave., Belvidere IL 61008 **Dn, Rockford Dnry Dio Chicago Chicago IL 2011-; R The Epis Ch Of The H Trin Belvidere IL 2008-** B Burlington IA 5/5/1952 d Gail Bowlyow & Betty. ABS IL Wesl 1974; MA U Roch 1976; PhD U MI 1985; MDiv SWTS 2006. D 6/10/2006 P 3/24/2007 Bp Stacy F Sauls. m Mary Lovelock. Epis Ch of Our Sav Richmond KY 2008; Dio Lexington Lexington KY 2007-2008. Natl Epis Hlth Mnstrs Bd Dir 2011; Soc of Comp of the H Cross 1997; Wmn Caucus 2006. Stevenson Awd for Practical Theol Seabury Sem 2006; Wmn Bd Awd to Outstanding Sr Wmn Seabury Wmn Bd 2006. joyce.beaulieu@gmail.com

BEAUMONT, Jerrold Foster (CFla) 8494 Ridgewood Ave Apt 4201, Cape Canaveral FL 32920 B Highland Park MI 1/23/1926 s Francis Wellington Beaumont & Clara Winnifred. Dioc TS; Lawr Tech U; Sacr Heart Sem 1975; ThM Int Mnstry Prog 1985; DD Int Mnstry Prog 1986. D 5/12/1973 Bp Richard S M Emrich P 6/1/1975 Bp H Coleman McGehee Jr. m 6/2/1951 Marjorie Doris Hesman. Vic S Barn' Ch Chelsea MI 1975-2001. Auth, "Success Begins w Me"; Auth, "Reformation-The Ch In Process". Min Assn Faith In Action, Engl Soc Detroit; Ord S Paul. Chapl Of The Year USAF / CAP 1992. bfei@juno.com

BEAUMONT, Katharine Jenetta (Az) 3085 W Brenda Loop, Flagstaff AZ 86001 B 6/26/1943 d Robert Charles Hermon & Netta Elizabeth. BA Whitmon Coll 1965; MA U of Idaho 1968. D 1/26/2008 Bp Kirk Stevan Smith. m 6/18/1966 Randolph Beaumont c 3. jbeaumont5@yahoo.com

BEAUVOIR, Jonas (Hai) c/o Diocese of Haiti, Boite Postale 1309 Haiti **Dio Haiti Ft Lauderdale FL 2008-** B 4/28/1971 s Joseph Beauvoir & Claircile C. D 1/25/2006 P 2/18/2007 Bp Jean Zache Duracin. m 12/29/2007 Luvernia M Mevoicy. jbeauvoir@yahoo.fr

BEAUVOIR, Oge (NY) 76 Avenue Christophe, Port-au-Prince Haiti **Exec Coun Appointees New York NY 2005-; Vol For Mssn New York NY 2004-** B Gros-Morne HT 1/27/1956 s Joseph Beauvoir & Claircine. BTh U of Montreal 1988; Montreal TS 1989; MA U of Montreal 1993. Trans from Anglican Church of Canada 3/31/2000 Bp Richard Frank Grein. m 7/16/1983 Serette Dorvil c 2. Prog Assoc Par of Trin Ch New York NY 1999-2005. Pres Exec Coun Of Franophone Angl Ch 2000. obeauvoir@trinitywallstreet.org

BEAVEN, John Clinton (Me) 5 Lobsterman Way, Phippsburg ME 04562 B New York NY 10/24/1927 s Walter Reginald Beaven & Florence Putnam. BA Col 1949; MA Col 1951; MDiv GTS 1956. D 6/3/1956 Bp Horace W B Donegan P 12/21/1956 Bp Chandler W Sterling. m 5/5/1951 Margaret Beaven c 3. The GTS New York NY 1987-1992; Chair COM Dio Maine Portland ME 1986-1988; Dn Cathd Ch Of S Lk Portland ME 1982-1989; Dioc Coun Dio New York New York City NY 1975-1979; Cathd Of St Jn The Div New York NY 1975-1978; R Gr Ch Millbrook NY 1969-1982; Exec Coun Dio Montana Helena MT 1960-1963; P-in-c Ch Of The Ascen Forsyth MT 1959-1964; R Emm Ch Miles City MT 1959-1964; P-in-c S Paul's Ch Ft Benton MT 1956-1959. Cathd of S Jn the Div,New York NY, Trst 1975-1978; GTS,New York NY, Trst 1987-1992. jcbeaven@gmail.com

BEBB JR, Ernest Leo (U) 6452 South 1650 East, Murray UT 84121 **Asst All SS Ch Salt Lake City UT 1988-** B Scotts Bluff NE 4/10/1932 s Ernest Leo Bebb & Nellie Flo. BS U of Nebraska 1954; MA MI SU 1963. D 1/22/1988 P 11/1/1988 Bp George Edmonds Bates. m 7/11/1959 Jane Sydney Woollam. ejbebb59@comcast.net

BEBBER, Gerald King (Q) 1821 Mcgougan Rd, Fayetteville NC 28303 **Off Of Bsh For ArmdF New York NY 1985-** B Moline IL 3/28/1947 s Donald K Bebber & Ruth I. Command and Gnrl Stff Coll; BA U NC 1971; MDiv VTS 1979; US-A Airborne Sch Ft Benning GA 1986; Advncd Chapl Cert US-A Ft Monmouth NJ 1991; US-A Ft Bragg NC 1993. Trans from Anglican Church of Canada 9/20/1981 Bp Donald James Parsons. m 8/2/1975 Irene Rachel Van Patton c 1. Vic S Jas Epis Ch Lewistown IL 1981-1985. CBS, Archconference Of The H Agony, ESA, Skcm; SSC. Mstr Parachutist Us-Army 1995; The Soldier'S Medal Us-Army. bebbergk@bragg.army.mil

BECHERER, Carl John (Minn) Rec from Roman Catholic 4/1/1975.

BECHTEL, A(lpha) Gillett (Los) Po Box 1361, Gualala CA 95445 **Assoc Shpd by the Sea Epis/Luth Mssn Gualala CA 1987-** B Venice CA 3/23/1921 s Alpha Bechtel & Ruth Alice. BS U CA 1944; MDiv Garrett Evang TS 1947; MA San Diego St Coll 1966; Claremont Coll 1973. D 2/24/1953 P 10/29/1953 Bp Donald J Campbell. m 6/22/1946 Betty Jean Bechtel. S Fran Of Assisi Par San Bernardino CA 1974-1985; The ETS At Claremont Claremont CA 1974-1985; Asst S Ambr Par Claremont CA 1969-1973. Auth, "The Mex Epis Ch," *A Century Of Reform & Revolution*, 1966. gbechtel@mcn.org

BECHTEL, Russell Alphaeus (Pa) 940 Lucaya Ave, Venice FL 34285 **Died 9/30/2009** B Pottstown PA 3/28/1930 s Ira Weldner Bechtel & Margaret Viola. BA Franklin & Marshall Coll 1955; MDiv Harvard DS 1958. D 4/29/1969 Bp John Harris Burt P 5/1/1973 Bp Jonathan Goodhue Sherman. c 3.

BECHTOLD, Bryant Coffin (FtW) 3290 Lackland Rd, Fort Worth TX 76116 B Orlando FL 12/7/1951 s Kenneth Irving Bechtold & Fern Elmira. BD Georgia Inst of Tech 1973; MA Georgia Inst of Tech 1975; PhD U of Utah 1978; MDiv STUSo 1986. D 6/7/1986 P 5/9/1987 Bp William Arthur Beckham. m 5/7/1994 Susan Rosemary Hofeling c 2. Chr The King Epis Ch Ft Worth TX 1997-2006; Vic Ascen S Matt's Ch Price UT 1990-1997; Vic Ch Of The H Trin Price UT 1990-1997; Dio Utah Salt Lake City UT 1990-1997; Asst All SS Epis Ch Enterprise FL 1987-1989; Dio Upper So Carolina Columbia SC 1986-1987; D S Lk's Epis Ch Atlanta GA 1986-1987. frbryant@btinternet.com

BECK, Brien Patrick (FdL) 347 Libal St, De Pere WI 54115 B Milwaukee WI 6/19/1966 s James Arthur Beck & Patricia Jean. D 5/7/2011 Bp Russell Edward Jacobus. m 5/12/1986 Jean Beck c 2. brien_beck@yahoo.com

BECK, Jacob David (WA) 13 Victor Dr, Thurmont MD 21788 B Philadelphia PA 4/28/1933 s Jacob Beck & Anna Marie. BS U of Pennsylvania 1955; MDiv PDS 1958. D 5/10/1958 P 11/29/1958 Bp Oliver J Hart. m 11/24/1962 Carla Wetzsteon c 3. Fin Cmsn Dio Maryland Baltimore MD 1994-1996; Dioc Coun Dio Maryland Baltimore MD 1993-1995; Int Harriet Chap Catoctin Epis Par Thurmont MD 1991-1996; Int S Andr's Ch Pasadena MD 1990-1991; Peace Cmsn Dio Washington Washington DC 1989-1996; Int S Barn Epis Ch Temple Hills MD 1989-1990; Int Gr Ch Elkridge MD 1988-1989; Int S Dunst's McLean VA 1986-1988; Mssy Dvlpmt Advsry Com Dio Washington Washington DC 1985-1988; Int S Phil's Epis Ch Laurel MD 1985-1986; Chr Ch Prince Geo's Par Rockville MD 1981-1985; Cmsn on Angl-RC Relatns Dio Montana Helena MT 1975-1981; Cmsn on the Ch and Soc Dio Montana Helena MT 1975-1981; Eccl Crt Dio Montana Helena MT 1973-1981; Exec Coun Dio Montana Helena MT 1969-1979; S Paul's Ch Ft Benton MT 1965-1981; R S Fran Epis Ch Great Falls MT 1964-1981; Cur Ch Of The H Sprt Missoula MT 1959-1962; Cur Ch Of Our Sav Jenkintown PA 1958-1959. "The Evangel," Ed Dioc Nwspr Dio Montana, 1965. Fllshp of St. Jn, Ret Cler of Assoc. of Dio 1996; Int Ntwk 1982; Natl Epis Cler Assn 1985; Silver Eagles Ret Cler Assn 1985; Washington Epis Cler Assn 1982. Human Rts Awd Educational Assn Great Falls Montana 1976.

BECK, Judith Louise (Pa) 3300 W Penn St, Philadelphia PA 19129 B Cleveland OH 3/13/1942 d Dudley Joseph Taw & Louise Estelle. Keuka Coll 1961; BD U of Pennsylvania 1964; MDiv Luth TS at Gettysburg 1989. D 6/11/1988 P 6/17/1989 Bp Allen Lyman Bartlett Jr. c 3. Assoc R S Ptr's Ch Philadelphia PA 2000-2004; S Ptr's Ch Germantown Philadelphia PA 1992-1999; Asst S Chris's Ch Gladwyne PA 1990-1992; D S Chris's Ch Gladwyne PA 1988-1989. Soc Of S Marg. judithtb@verizon.net

BECK, Sue Ann (Los) St. John The Divine, 183 E. Bay St., Costa Mesa CA 92627 **D S Jn The Div Epis Ch Costa Mesa CA 2009-** B Carroll IA 9/28/1948 d Herbert Aron & Shirley. BS U of Nthrn Colorado 1971; MA Antioch Coll/W 1979; PhD California Grad Inst 1989; MDiv Claremont TS 2005. D 11/15/2007 Bp Chester Lovelle Talton. m 5/8/1982 Robert Beck. SBeckPhD@aol.com

BECK, Tanya (Ind) 5810 Kingsley Dr., Indianapolis IN 46220 **All SS Ch Indianapolis IN 2000-; R Ch Of The H Sprt Sfty Harbor FL 2000-** B Anderson IN 3/5/1932 d Robert J Beck & Margaret S. Chr TS; BA DePauw U 1954; MA Ball St U 1955. D 9/28/1974 Bp John P Craine P 1/8/1976 Bp John Mc Gill Krumm. c 4. Transition P S Mk's Ch Plainfield IN 2008-2010; Int Dn Chr Ch Cathd Indianapolis IN 2005-2008; Int S Matt's Ch Indianapolis IN 2003-2005; Int Gr Ch Muncie IN 2002-2009. Outstanding Wmn In Rel 90; Sagamore Of The Wabash Gvnr'S Awd; Outstanding Alum Awd 90 Depauw U. tanyavonnegutbeck@gmail.com

BECK, Thomas Francis (Ct) 4 Willow Ct, Cromwell CT 06416 B Newark NJ 2/1/1933 s William A Beck & Helen. BA Ups 1955; BD VTS 1963; Med Iona Coll 1976. D 6/8/1963 P 12/1/1963 Bp Dudley S Stark. m 8/12/1960 Marilyn Jean Litten. Gr Ch Stafford Sprg CT 1994-1998; Middlesex Area Cluster Mnstry Higganum CT 1992-1994; Gr Epis Ch Yantic CT 1979-1983; Epis Soc Serv Ansonia CT 1977-1986; R S Jas' Ch New Haven CT 1967-1975; Cur S Jas Ch Upper Montclair NJ 1963-1965. Auth, "Hope When I Despair". AAPC. TOMBECK11@GMAIL.COM

BECKER, Arthur Paul (Minn) 2901 Pearson Pkwy, Brooklyn Park MN 55444 B Stevens Pt WI 9/6/1928 s George Charles Becker & Irene Avina. BA Lawr 1952; MDiv GTS 1956; Coll of Preachers 1960; U of Iowa 1969; MA U of So Dakota 1972. D 6/14/1956 P 12/19/1956 Bp William Hampton Brady. m 8/23/1958 Lois Maxine Becker c 3. Dio Iowa Des Moines IA 1991-1996; Prof Theol Mt St Clare Coll Clinton IA 1990-1999; R S Jn's Ch Clinton IA 1988-1994; Reg Coordntr Prov 6 of ECAEvangelism Dio Iowa Des Moines IA 1983-1989; Archd Individual Accounts Des Moines IA 1974-1988. ACES 1999; APGA 1999; OHC 1953. iacurmudgeon1@comcast.net

BECKER, C S Honey (Haw) PO Box 819, Kailua HI 96734 **D S Andr's Cathd Honolulu HI 2001-** B New Orleans LA 10/19/1946 LSU. D 7/15/2001 Bp Richard Sui On Chang. c 3.

BECKER, Jane (WMass) 44 Mccoy Rd, Jefferson NH 03452 **COM Dio Wstrn Massachusetts Springfield MA 1995-; Ecum Cmsn Dio Wstrn Massachusetts Springfield MA 1987-** B Brooklyn NY 10/7/1929 d Kenneth Avery Barnes & Dorothy. U of New Engl. D 10/9/1982 Bp Alexander Doig Stewart. m 11/3/1951 Roland G Becker c 3. Ecum Off Dio Wstrn Massachusetts Springfield MA 1988-1990; Evang Commision Dio Wstrn Massachusetts Springfield MA 1982-1985. Massachusetts Soc Chr Unity 1986; Soc Of S Jn The Evang 1990.

BECKER, Kim (WA) 13 Cedar Ave, Gaithersburg MD 20877 **P Assoc Ch Of The Ascen Gaithersburg MD 2011-** B Augusta GA 4/1/1965 d Richard J(ulius) Gilley & Geneva. BA U NC 1987; MA U NC 1989; MDiv VTS 2000. D 6/24/2000 Bp Clifton Daniel III P 12/13/2000 Bp Jane Hart Holmes Dixon. c 1. Asst R S Jn's Ch Olney MD 2004-2005; Asst R Chr Ch Par Kensington MD 2000-2003. Auth, "Words Facing E," WordTech Editions, 2011. malinoiskim38@gmail.com

BECKER, Mary Elizabeth (Md) 2076 E County Rd 375 S, Winslow IN 47598 **Ret S Jas Ch Vincennes IN 2010-** B Baltimore MD 8/3/1941 d Adrian Hughes & Mary Elizabeth. BS Towson U 1963; Med Towson U 1982; MA S Mary's Sem & U Ecum Inst 2000. D 6/14/1997 Bp Charles Lindsay Longest. m 8/21/1965 Paul Frederick Becker c 2. D S Andr's Ch Baltimore MD 2002-2007; D S Andr's Epis Ch Glenwood MD 1996-2002. mbinindiana@hughes.net

BECKER, Michael Ray (Pa) 600 E Cathedral Rd Apt WL331, Philadelphia PA 19128 B Chicago IL 7/22/1916 s Ray Becker & Gertrude Frances. Illinois Coll 1937; BA Carroll Coll 1938; MDiv Nash 1941. D 5/16/1940 Bp Benjamin F P Ivins P 6/1/1941 Bp John Chandler White. S Mk's Ch Philadelphia PA 1965-1981.

BECKER, Robert Andrew (Va) 1124 Handlebar Rd, Reston VA 20191 B Long Branch NJ 11/2/1940 s Andrew G Becker & Marjorie L. BA GW 1963; MDiv VTS 1997. D 6/24/2006 P 2/3/2007 Bp Peter James Lee. m 1/25/1964 Carolyn D Becker c 2. Ch Of The Resurr Alexandria VA 2006-2008. rbecker007@comcast.net

BECKER, Stephen David (Va) 13 Braxton Dr, Sterling VA 20165 **Int Emm Epis Ch (Piedmont Par) Delaplane VA 2009-** B Washington DC 12/6/1951 s Francis Marion Becker & Mary Jean. AS Anderson Coll Anderson SC 1973; BTh Amer Chrisitan TS 1976; MDiv TESM 1992. D 7/12/1992 P 4/1/1993 Bp Andrew Hedtler Fairfield. m 9/17/1977 Ellen Joy Weaver c 3. R S Paul's Ch New Orleans LA 2003-2005; R S Geo's Epis Ch Summerville SC 1999-2003; Cn Cathd Ch Of S Ptr St Petersburg FL 1996-1999; Asst Ch Of The Adv Tallahassee FL 1994-1996; D/P Trin Ch Wahpeton ND 1992-1994. sdbecker2@verizon.net

BECKETT JR, Norman James (Los) 3157 E Avenue, #B-4, Lancaster LA 93535 Costa Rica B Medford MA 8/28/1943 s Norman James Beckett & Leontine Louise. BA Trin 1965; STB EDS 1968; PhD California Sch of Profsnl Psychol 1974. D 6/11/1968 Bp Walter H Gray P 3/8/1969 Bp Francis E I Bloy. Vic Epis Ch Of S Andr And S Chas Granada Hills CA 1971-1976; Dio Los Angeles Los Angeles CA 1971-1973; Cur S Thos Of Cbury Par Long Bch CA 1969-1971; Cur S Mich and All Ang Epis Ch Studio City CA 1968-1969. jbeckett@onlineportrait.com

BECKHAM JR, M(aurice) Edwin (At) Emmanuel Episcopal Church, 498 Prince Avenue, Athens GA 30601 **Mem, Cmsn on Global Missions Dio Atlanta Atlanta GA 2011-; Chair, Cmsn on YA Mnstry Dio Atlanta Atlanta GA 2010-; Mem, Cmsn on Liturg Dio Atlanta Atlanta GA 2010-; Assoc R Emm Epis Ch Athens GA 2008-** B Greenville SC 10/28/1968 s Maurice Edwin Beckham & Martha Hunter. BA, mcl Furman U 1990; MDiv Epis TS of the SW 2008. D 12/21/2007 P 6/29/2008 Bp J(ohn) Neil Alexander. m 4/6/1991 Laura McHugh Beckham c 2. The HSEC 2011; The Soc of Cath Priests 2009. edwin.beckham@gmail.com

BECKLES, William Anthony (NY) Po Box 1067, Mount Vernon NY 10551 **S Paul's Ch Mt Vernon OH 1998-** B BB 1/5/1942 s John Kingsley Beckles & Caris Ithene. BA U of The W Indies 1966; MA McMaster U 1967; PhD U Ab 1971; Med U Tor 1977. Trans from Church in the Province Of The West Indies 10/26/1992 Bp John Palmer Croneberger. Gr Ch Corona NY 1997-1998; S Paul's Ch-In-The-Vill Brooklyn NY 1994-1996; S Andr's Ch Newark NJ 1991-1993; Trin Ch Irvington NJ 1991-1993. Amer Assn Chr Counslr, Associated Parishes, Amer Acad Mnstry. wiltonbeck@aol.com

BECKWITH III, John Quintus (SC) 38 Mueller Dr, Charleston SC 29407 B Wilmington NC 8/20/1932 s John Quintus Beckwith & Margaret. BS Coll of Charleston 1955; MDiv VTS 1958. D 6/12/1958 P 5/1/1959 Bp Thomas N Carruthers. m 7/14/1961 Elizabeth George Wiese c 3. Assoc S Mich's Epis Ch Charleston SC 2002-2007; Archd Dio So Carolina Charleston SC 1984-1997; Congrl Dvlpmt Dio So Carolina Charleston SC 1984-1990; Exec Secy Dio So Carolina Charleston SC 1984-1990; Staf Liaison Dept Dio So Carolina Charleston SC 1984-1990; R S Matt's Epis Ch Darlington SC 1976-1984; Dioc Coun

Dio So Carolina Charleston SC 1970-2001; R S Thos Epis Ch No Charleston SC 1966-1976; R S Jn's Epis Ch Marion NC 1962-1966; Asst Trin Cathd Columbia SC 1960-1962. bandj1932@comcast.net

✠ **BECKWITH, Rt Rev Mark M** (Nwk) Episcopal Diocese of Newark, 312 Mulberry St, Newark NJ 07102 **Bp of Newark Dio Newark Newark NJ 2006-** B Milwaukee WI 7/11/1951 s Andrew Beckwith & Heiden E. BA Amh 1973; MDiv Ya Berk 1978; DD Ya Berk 2008; DD GTS 2010. D 6/9/1979 P 2/9/1980 Bp Morgan Porteus Con 1/27/2007 for Nwk. m 5/15/1982 Marilyn C Olson c 2. R All SS Ch Worcester MA 1993-2006; Dio Wstrn Massachusetts Springfield MA 1993-2006; Co-Chair Dioc T/F Dio Newark Newark NJ 1991-1992; R Chr Ch Hackensack NJ 1985-1993; Assoc S Ptr's Ch Morristown NJ 1982-1985; Trin Epis Ch Hartford CT 1981-1982; Asst S Jas Epis Ch Farmington CT 1979-1981. Auth, "From Scarcity To Abundance," Tens, 2001. Fell, SSJE 2001-2011. Bergen Cnty Cmnty Action Prog Serv Awd 1987; Serv Awd Morris Cnty 1985; Ba cl Amh Amherst MA 1973. mbeckwith@dioceseofnewark.org

✠ **BECKWITH, Rt Rev Peter Hess** (Spr) 821 S 2nd St, Springfield IL 62704 B Battle Creek MI 9/8/1939 s Robert Edgar Beckwith & Florence Catheryn. BA Hillsdale Coll 1961; MDiv STUSo 1964; STM Nash 1974; ThD Hillsdale Coll 1988; LHD Nash 1992; DD STUSo 1999. D 6/29/1964 Bp Richard S M Emrich P 1/6/1965 Bp Archie H Crowley Con 2/29/1992 for Spr. m 7/10/1965 Melinda Jo Foulke c 2. Bp Of Springfield Dio Springfield Springfield IL 1992-2010; COM Dio Sthrn Ohio Cincinnati OH 1989-1992; Dio Sthrn Ohio Cincinnati OH 1984-1986; Const And Cn Com Dio Sthrn Ohio Cincinnati OH 1979-1981; R S Jn's Ch Worthington OH 1978-1992; R S Jn's Ch Worthington OH 1978-1992; Cler Compstn Com Dio Sthrn Ohio Cincinnati OH 1978-1981; R S Matt's Epis Ch Saginaw MI 1970-1978; Asst S Paul's Epis Ch Jackson MI 1966-1970; Cur S Jn's Ch Plymouth MI 1964-1966. Auth, "Premarital Counslg: Its Place & Purpose". Assn Cnvnt Trsfg 1982; Assn of Naval Aviation 1984; Assn of the USN 2006; Marine Corps Reserve Assn 1980; Mltry Chapl Assn 1974; Mltry Off Assn of Amer 2006; Naval Reserve Assn 1974; Navy League 1976; Reserve Off Assn 1975; Ret Off Assn 1999; Sons of the Amer Revolution 1958; The AmL 1985. Athletic Hall of Fame Hillsdale Coll 2001; Alumnini Achievement Awd Hillsdale Coll 1984. xbishop@episcopalspringfield.org

BEDDINGFIELD, John (WA) 2745 29th St NW Apt 416, Washington DC 20008 **R All Souls Memi Epis Ch Washington DC 2007-** B Raleigh NC 6/8/1964 s Clarence Richard Beddingfield & Virginia Evelyn. BA U NC 1987; MDiv PrTS 1991; STM GTS 1999. D 3/8/2003 P 9/20/2003 Bp Mark Sean Sisk. Cur Ch Of S Mary The Vrgn New York NY 2003-2007. jbeddingfield@yahoo.com

BEDELL, Bryan Douglas (Roch) 28 Village Trl, Honeoye Falls NY 14472 B Ludington MI 1/10/1943 s Glen Delos Bedell & Gertrude Helena. BA MI SU 1968; MS Rochester Inst Of Tech 1977; MDiv Bex 2007. D 6/30/2007 P 2/21/2008 Bp Jack Marston McKelvey. m 10/26/2003 Marion Overslaugh c 4. P S Ptr's Epis Ch Bloomfield NY 2009; Asst S Geo's Ch Hilton NY 2007-2009; Trin Ch Rochester NY 2007-2009. the.rev.bryan.bedell@frontiernet.net

BEDELL II, George Chester (Fla) 3212 NW 58th Blvd, Gainesville FL 32606 B Jacksonville FL 5/13/1928 s Chester Bedell & Edmonia. BA U So 1950; MDiv VTS 1953; MA U NC 1966; PhD Duke 1969. D 6/29/1953 P 3/25/1954 Bp Frank A Juhan. m 1/22/1983 Elizabeth Reed c 3. Mem, Exec Coun Dio Florida Jacksonville FL 1957-1962; R S Andr's Epis Ch Panama City FL 1956-1962; P-in-c S Barth's Ch High Sprg FL 1953-1956; P-in-c S Jas' Epis Ch Lake City FL 1953-1956. Auth, "Rel in Amer," Macmillan, 1975; Auth, "Kierkegaard & Faulkner: Modalities of Existence," LSU Press, 1972. Florida Hist Soc 1967; Florida and Natl Trusts for Hist Preservation 1960; Mod Lang Assn 1967; Rotary Club 1953. Trst Newberry Libr Chicago 1996; DCL U So TS 1991; Judicial Nomin Com Florida Supreme Crt Tallahassee Florida 1990; Trst Jessie Ball duPont Fund 1985. gbedell@ufl.edu

BEDFORD, Michael John (Mich) 25831 Lexington Dr Unit 1, South Lyon MI 48178 **S Jn's Ch Detroit MI 2001-** B Louisville NY 4/26/1929 s Sanders Shaw Bedford & Muriel Hope. Michigan TS 1980. D 6/26/1976 Bp H Coleman McGehee Jr P 7/24/1982 Bp Henry Irving Mayson. m 6/30/1951 Mary Elizabeth Marshall c 7. S Jn's Ch Detroit MI 1997-2000; S Eliz's Ch Redford MI 1983-1994; D-in-c S Eliz's Ch Redford MI 1981-1982; Asst S Jn's Ch Plymouth MI 1976-1981. SSC 1990. mickybed@aol.com

BEDINGFIELD, John Davis (WLa) 203 Aundria Dr, Lafayette LA 70503 **R S Barn Epis Ch Lafayette LA 2011-; Dn, SE Convoc Dio Texas Houston TX 2009-** B Houston TX 8/9/1956 s Billy Frank Bedingfield & Phyllis Eleanor. BA U of Texas at Dallas 1984; JD U of Texas 1988; MDiv Epis TS of The SW 2005. D 6/11/2005 Bp Don Adger Wimberly P 12/13/2005 Bp Rayford Baines High Jr. m 4/22/1978 Donna J Jarvis c 3. R S Jn's Epis Ch Silsbee TX 2007-2011; Assoc R H Sprt Epis Ch Houston TX 2005-2007. padrejohnb@gmail.com

BEDOYA-BAQUERO, Jaime Enrique (EcuC) 321 Apartado 13-05-335, Manta Ecuador **Died 8/24/2009** B Quito EC 7/16/1926 s Enrique Bedoya Ariza & Victoria Baquero. BA Estudios Superiores. Rec from Roman Catholic 6/1/1973. m Maria Alva Heras Calderon c 4. Third Ord Soc Of S Fran. FLAQUINE@YAHOO.ES

BEDROSIAN, Magar (Ct) 6283 Darien Way, Spring Hill FL 34606 **Assoc S Andr's Epis Ch Sprg Hill FL 1996-** B Milford MA 2/28/1927 s Tanal Bedrosian & Nevart. BA U of Massachusetts 1955; MDiv Ya Berk 1958. D 6/15/1958 Bp Robert McConnell Hatch P 6/20/1958 Bp John Henry Esquirol. m 6/4/1983 Sarah Palmer Roode. R Ch of the H Sprt W Haven CT 1983-1993; Dio Rhode Island Providence RI 1978-1983; S Eliz's Ch Hope Vlly RI 1970-1983; Vic S Thos' Alton Wood River Jct RI 1964-1983; Vic Trin Ch N Scituate RI 1959-1964; Cur S Jn's Ch E Hartford CT 1958-1959. myodarfla@aol.com

BEE, Robert D (Neb) 5109 N Jefferson St, Gladstone MO 64118 B Washington DC 11/22/1938 s Max Culbertson Bee & Florence Agnes. BA Omaha U 1965; MDiv GTS 1968; Cert Assn of Profsnl Chapl 1985. D 6/13/1968 P 12/15/1968 Bp Russell T Rauscher. m 9/3/1966 Diana Mae Parker c 3. Mnstry Dev Asst Dio Nebraska Omaha NE 2001-2008; Assoc Ch Of The H Sprt Bellevue NE 2000-2006; Mgr, Pstr Care Nebraska Hlth System Omaha NE 1979-1999; Chapl S Lk's Chap Omaha NE 1979-1999; R S Mary's Epis Ch Blair NE 1970-1979; Cur All SS Epis Ch Omaha NE 1968-1970. Assembly of Epis Healthcare Chapl Pres 1993-1994; Assn Profsnl Chapl 1985; Bd Cert Chapl 1985. beehiveoma@aol.com

BEEBE, Christine Fair (Ark) P. O. Box 46, Rutherfordton NC 28139 **R S Fran' Epis Ch Rutherfordton NC 2011-** B Memphis TN 10/5/1951 d Burrell Bell Fair & Celia Hughes. MDiv U So TS 2008. D 3/15/2008 P 9/21/2008 Bp Larry R Benfield. m 11/3/1988 Richard A Beebe c 1. Dn of Convoc Dio Arkansas Little Rock AR 2009; Vic All SS Epis Ch Paragould AR 2008-2011. cfairbeebe@gmail.com

BEEBE SR, Fred H (Fla) 124 Peninsular Dr, Crescent City FL 32112 **Vic Ch Of The H Comf Cres City FL 2010-; D Dio Florida Jacksonville FL 2001-** B Newark NJ 3/5/1943 s Donald Deforeest Beebe & Dorothy Julett. AS Brookdale Cmnty Coll 1976. D 10/31/1998 Bp Joe Morris Doss P 10/12/2010 Bp Charles Lovett Keyser. m 6/27/1998 Genevieve Ann Tullo. D Ch Of The H Comf Cres City FL 2000-2010; D All SS Memi Ch Navesink NJ 1998-2000. fredbbplus@aol.com

BEEBE, James Russell (Nev) 205 Mackinaw Ave, Akron OH 44333 **S Pat's Ch Incline Vill NV 2005-** B Neenah WI 4/27/1949 s Robert Lynn Beebe & Mary Sybil. BA Denison U 1971; MA Oklahoma St U 1978; MDiv SE Bapt TS 1982. D 12/5/1992 Bp Brice Sidney Sanders P 6/12/1993 Bp Arthur Benjamin Williams Jr. m 3/22/1969 Deborah Joyce Luckman c 2. Assoc S Paul's Ch Akron OH 1992-2005.

BEEBE, John McRae (WTex) Franklin Park - Sontera, Apt. #4205, San Antonio TX 78258 B Fort Benning GA 3/14/1928 s Lewis Charles Beebe & Dorothy. BS Geo 1955; MDiv Epis TS of The SW 1974. D 5/23/1974 Bp Harold Cornelius Gosnell P 12/1/1974 Bp Richard Earl Dicus. m 8/31/1957 Kate Elizabeth Williams c 3. S Andr's Epis Ch San Antonio TX 1992-2000; R S Paul's Epis Ch San Antonio TX 1980-1992; Gr Ch Cuero TX 1976-1980; Gr Ch Mesquite TX 1976-1980; P-in-c H Comm Epis Ch Yoakum TX 1976-1980; Assoc S Jas Epis Ch Del Rio TX 1974-1976. "Prisoner of the Rising Sun: The Lost Diary of Brig. Gen. Lewis Beebe," Texas A&M U Press, 2006. johnbeebe@mac.com

BEEBE-BOVE, Polly (Vt) 3 Cathedral Sq Apt 2G, Burlington VT 05401 B East Charlotte VT 3/28/1922 d Forrest Walter Carpenter & Mary Ellen. RN Mary Fletcher Hosp, Sch of Nrsng 1943; Cert Dioc Study Prog 1988; BA Trin 1995. D 6/14/1989 Bp Daniel Lee Swenson. c 1. D S Jas Epis Ch Essex Jct VT 1993-1997; D Cathd Ch Of S Paul Burlington VT 1989-1993. NAAD; Ord of S Fran.

BEECHAM, Troy C (At) 3480 E Main St, College Park GA 30337 **R S Jn's Coll Pk GA 2008-** B Houston TX 10/30/1968 Jerusalem U Coll Jerusalem IL 1991; BA Webc Baton Rouge LA 1991; MA Wheaton Coll 1994; STM GTS 2002. D 2/8/2003 P 9/4/2003 Bp Henry Irving Louttit. R Ch Of The Gd Shpd Granite Sprg NY 2005-2008; Int Chr Ch Augusta GA 2003-2004. troybeecham@earthlink.net

BEECHER, Josefina Cameron (Oly) 7134 Steelhead Ln, Burlington WA 98233 **Indo-Hisp Mnstry Com Dio Olympia Seattle WA 1995-2012** B Seattle WA 3/19/1952 d Henry Ward Beecher & Doris Darby. BA Antioch U 1998; MDiv Seattle U Inst For Ecum Stds 2002. D 11/9/2002 Bp Vincent Waydell Warner P 5/30/2003 Bp Martin De Jesus Barahona-Pascacio. m 8/1/2006 Mary McConnaughey c 2. Pres of Stndg Com Dio Olympia Seattle WA 2010-2011; Komo Kulshan Cluster Mt Vernon WA 2008; Bp Suffr Search Com Dio Olympia Seattle WA 2004-2005. beecherj@wavecable.com

BEELEY, Christopher Alfred (Tex) 1527 Sunnymede Ave, South Bend IN 46615 B Houston TX 8/17/1968 s Robert Alfred Beeley & Susan Kay. Fllshp U of Notre Dame; BA W&L 1990; MDiv Ya Berk 1994. D 6/25/1994 Bp Maurice Manuel Benitez P 1/1/1995 Bp Claude Edward Payne. m 4/6/1991 Shannon Betsy Murphy. S Mich And All Ang Ch So Bend IN 1998-1999; Asst S Dav's Ch Austin TX 1994-1996. Fllshp S Alb & S Sergius. Presidential Fllshp U Notre Dame.

BEEM, Charles Lee (Be) 9 Plymouth Pl, Reading PA 19610 B Richland WA 7/1/1947 s Charles C Beem. BS Baker U 1969; MDiv VTS 1972; MA U of Missouri 1976. D 8/12/1972 P 8/11/1973 Bp William Davidson. m 6/2/1973 Jacqueline Beem. Assoc S Alb's Epis Ch Reading PA 1977-2004; Vic S Alb's Epis Ch Fulton MO 1975-1976; Vic Trin Epis Ch Norton KS 1974-1975. Auth, "8 Pub". beemsinpa@comcast.net

BEER, David Frank (Tex) 6810 Thistle Hill Way, Austin TX 78754 **Asstg Cler S Jn's Epis Ch Austin TX 2003-** B Dorking Surrey UK 9/1/1939 s Frank Noel Beer & Eva Kathleen. BA U of Arizona 1963; MA Arizona St U 1965; PhD U of New Mex 1972; MA Epis TS of The SW 1979. D 8/6/1979 Bp Richard Mitchell Trelease Jr P 4/9/1980 Bp Scott Field Bailey. m 9/24/1971 Ruth Elaine Ustby c 1. Asst The Ch of the Gd Shpd Austin TX 1992-2000; Int S Fran By The Lake Canyon Lake TX 1981-1982; Int S Steph's Epis Ch Wimberley TX 1980-1981; Asst Ch Of The Annunc Luling TX 1979-1980. Auth, "Guide To Writing As An Engr. 3rd Ed.," Wiley, 2009; Auth, "Writing & Spkng In The Tech Professions," IEEE, 1992. IEEE 1985-2001. Excellence in Engr Tchg Coll of Engr, U of Texas at Austin 1989; Fulbright Awd 1977. dbeer@mail.utexas.edu

BEERS, Donald William (Nwk) 619 County Road 519, Belvidere NJ 07823 **Died 5/17/2010** B Newark NJ 1/16/1926 s Howard William Beers & Marcella Virginia. BME Cor 1945; MSME Newark Coll of Engr 1951; MDiv GTS 1955; DMin Pittsburgh TS 1984. D 6/12/1954 P 12/1/1954 Bp Benjamin M Washburn. c 4. "ArmdF PB," Ch Hymnal, 1982. Mltry Chapl Assn 1959; Secy 1989-1992. padresbiretta@yahoo.com

BEERS, William Rogers (Chi) 120 1st St, Lodi WI 53555 B Boston MA 12/5/1948 s Roland Frank Beers & Helen Caroline. BA Ge 1967; MDiv EDS 1975; PhD U Chi 1989. D 6/15/1985 Bp Frank Tracy Griswold III P 2/22/1986 Bp Arthur Edward Walmsley. m 10/15/2007 Joann Crowley. Auth, "Fantast and Mourning," *Journ of Pstr Care*, 2006; Auth, *Wmn & Sacrifice*, Wayne Press, 1992; Auth, "Anxiety & Creation in the CPE Context," *Journ of Pstr Care*, 1990; Auth, "The Confessions of Aug," *Amer Imago*, 1988. williambeers@verizon.net

BEERY, Susan (U) 228 S Pitt St, Alexandria VA 22314 **S Ptr's Ch Clearfield UT 2007-** B La Grande OR 7/16/1957 d Charles Theodore Beem & Fern Louise. BS OR SU 1980; MDiv EDS 1984. D 8/11/1984 P 8/13/1985 Bp Rustin Ray Kimsey. m 8/1/1991 John M Beery c 2. Receiving Disabil Ret 2010-2011; Dio Utah Salt Lake City UT 2004-2009; S Paul's Epis Ch Alexandria VA 1998-2001; Asst Ch Of The Epiph San Carlos CA 1995-1996; Epis Mnstry To The Oh St U Columbus OH 1990; S Steph's Epis Ch And U Columbus OH 1986-1989; Asst S Ptr's Ch La Grande OR 1985-1986. susankbb@aol.com

BEERY, William Stocktill (NY) 223 Old Kings Hwy S, Darien CT 06820 B Brooklyn NY 11/27/1947 s Edwin Beery & Evelyn. BA Colg 1969; MDiv Ya Berk 1972; Fllshp Ya Berk 1980; PhD NYU 1983. D 6/17/1972 P 12/23/1972 Bp Jonathan Goodhue Sherman. m 2/28/1981 Ellen Sommers c 4. S Lk's Par Darien CT 2003-2007; Var Parishes - Int and Supply Dio New York New York City NY 1973-1984; Asst S Thos Ch Mamaroneck NY 1972-1973. Auth, *Multi-Occidental Prot Cler: A Test of Hollands Theory*, 1983. Who's Who Among Human Serv Professionals Marquis Who's Who 1983; Who's Who in Amer Marquis Who's Who 1972; Watson Fllshp Ya New Haven CT 1972. william.beery@aya.yale.edu

BEHEN, Ralph Joseph (WMo) 7412 N Brooklyn Ave, Kansas City MO 64118 **Cler Ch Of The Redeem Kansas City MO 2011-; Cler Gr And H Trin Cathd Kansas City MO 2007-** B 11/3/1964 MDiv Epis TS of the SW 2007. D 6/2/2007 P 12/1/2007 Bp Barry Robert Howe. m 8/24/2004 Karen Elizabeth Behen c 2. joe.behen@gmail.com

BEHLING, Daniel Wayne (Az) 3706 E Marble Peak Pl, Tucson AZ 85718 **Died 6/25/2011** B Oshkosh WI 8/2/1931 s Hugo Joseph Behling & Ester Mcguire. D 10/14/2006 Bp Kirk Stevan Smith. c 1. danbehlingphd@aol.com

BEHM, Nancy Anne (FdL) 1703 Doemel St, Oshkosh WI 54901 **D Trin Epis Ch Oshkosh WI 2003-** B Chicago IL 9/22/1949 D 11/29/2003 Bp Russell Edward Jacobus. m 10/28/1967 John William Behm. behmn@uwosh.edu

BEHRENS, Marilyn Jean (ECR) 538 Binscarth Rd, Los Osos CA 93402 **D S Ben's Par Los Osos CA 1997-** B San Francisco CA 10/15/1947 d Silvio Eugene Bisetti & Lorraine Ann. San Francisco St U; AA Coll of San Mateo 1968; BA Sch for Deacons 1997. D 6/20/1997 Bp Richard Lester Shimpfky.

BEIKIRCH, Paula Marie (CFla) 4915 Deter Rd, Lakeland FL 33813 B Olean NY 11/24/1945 d Carlyle Franklin Smith & Marjorie. BS Florida Sthrn Coll 1990; MS U of So Florida 1993. D 12/9/2006 Bp John Wadsworth Howe. c 2. pbeikirch@cs.com

BEILSTEIN, Joan Elizabeth (WA) 400 Hinsdale Ct, Silver Spring MD 20901 **R Ch Of The Ascen Silver Sprg MD 2007-** B Washington DC 12/14/1960 d Frederick B Beilstein & Anna D. BA U of Maryland 1983; MDiv The GTS 1993; DMin VTS 2007. D 6/12/1993 P 1/1/1994 Bp Ronald Hayward Haines. m 12/14/2010 Elizabeth Mary Griffin. Int All Souls Meml Epis Ch Washington DC 2005-2007; R Nativ Epis Ch Temple Hills MD 1999-2005. Ch and Soc Awd The GTS 1993. revjeb@comcast.net

BEIMDIEK, Jill (EC) St. Paul's Episcopal Church, 401 East Fourth St, Greenville NC 27834 **Assoc R S Paul's Epis Ch Greenville NC 2011-** B Portland OR 4/14/1956 BA Whitman Coll 1978; MA Duke 1991; DAS Ya Berk 2004; MDiv Yale DS 2004. D 6/19/2004 Bp Michael Bruce Curry. Assoc R H Trin Epis Ch Fayetteville NC 2007-2011; P-in-c S Steph's Epis Ch Norwood PA 2004-2007. SSM 2003. jbeimdiek@gmail.com

BEISHEIM, Charles Donald (Nwk) 109 Park Pl, Bogota NJ 07603 **Died 2/8/2011** B Irvington NJ 3/31/1927 s Nicholas Beisheim & Marie Agnes. BA Leh 1949; STB Ya Berk 1952. D 6/15/1952 P 12/1/1952 Bp Benjamin M Washburn.

✠ **BEISNER, Rt Rev Barry Leigh** (NCal) Episcopal Diocese Of Northern California, 1318 27th St, Sacramento CA 95816 **Bp of Nthrn California Dio Nthrn California Sacramento CA 2006-** B Dayton OH 6/5/1951 s Max Alfred Beisner & Dolores Grace. BA U CA 1973; MDiv CDSP 1978; STM GTS 1994. D 6/24/1978 Bp William Foreman Creighton P 5/19/1979 Bp Daniel Corrigan Con 9/30/2006 for NCal. m 5/2/1998 L Ann Hallisey c 3. Cn Dio Nthrn California Sacramento CA 2002-2006; R Ch Of S Mart Davis CA 1989-2002; R Ch Of The Incarn San Francisco CA 1983-1989; Dio Nthrn California Sacramento CA 1983-1986; Dio Nthrn California Sacramento CA 1981-1983; Assoc S Mk's Epis Ch Columbus OH 1980-1983; Vic S Paul's Ch Cambria CA 1978-1980; Asst S Steph's Epis Ch San Luis Obispo CA 1978-1979. DD GTS 2007.

BEITZEL, Wallace D (U) 9475 Brookside Ave, Ben Lomond CA 95005 B Olympia WA 9/19/1944 s Stuart Wallace Beitzel & Gordon Margret. BA California St U 1966; MA California St U 1972. D 4/8/1981 P 1/8/1982 Bp Otis Charles. m 9/10/1965 Mary Elizabeth Harter c 2. Asst S Ptr's Ch Clearfield UT 1981-1983. Auth, "Math Applied to Electronics," Prentice Hall, 1980; Auth, "Practical Math for Electronics," The Educ Press, 1970. wbeitzel@prodigy.net

BEIZER, Lance Kurt (ECR) 9 Blackberry Way, P.O. Box 1047, Canaan CT 06018 **Assoc S Jn's Ch Salisbury CT 2009-; Cn-Vic Trin Cathd San Jose CA 2007-; Cn-Vic Trin Cathd San Jose CA 2006-** B Hartford CT 9/8/1938 s Lawrence Sidney Beizer & Victoria Merriam. BA Brandeis U 1960; MA San Jose St U 1967; JD U of San Diego 1975; MDiv CDSP 2005. D 12/18/2004 P 9/10/2005 Bp Sylvestre Donato Romero. m 7/27/2007 Ann Hungerford. Asst Ch Of The H Sprt Campbell CA 2005-2006. OSL (Chapl) 2005. lbeizer@yahoo.com

BEK, Susan Dell (Los) 24901 Orchard Village Rd, Santa Clarita CA 91355 B Van Nuys CA 2/16/1963 d Odell S Hathaway & Marjorie B. BS Pacific Wstrn U 1996; MDiv The ETS At Claremont 2010. D 7/9/2010 P 2/12/2011 Bp Joseph Jon Bruno. m 2/12/1983 Jon Bek c 4. S Steph's Epis Ch Santa Clarita CA 2010. susan_beck@yahoo.com

BELA, Robert Joseph (Mass) 29 Sprague St, Malden MA 02148 B Philadelphia PA 11/3/1939 s Joseph E Bela & Helen C. BA La Salle U 1967; MA Chr TS 1978; MDiv EDS 1980. D 6/24/1980 P 3/1/1981 Bp Edward Witker Jones. m 12/19/1964 Louise Mann c 3. S Helena's Epis Ch Lenox MA 2001-2005; Int Pstr Trin Par Lenox MA 1997-1998; Gr Epis Ch Medford MA 1992-1997; S Paul's Epis Ch Bedford MA 1991-1992; Emm Epis Ch Wakefield MA 1989-1991; All SS Ch Chelmsford MA 1986-1988; Assoc R Chr Ch So Hamilton MA 1984-1986; Int S Jn's Epis Ch Gloucester MA 1983-1984; The Cathd Ch Of S Paul Boston MA 1983; Int S Jas' Epis Ch Cambridge MA 1982-1983; Cur S Paul's Epis Ch Evansville IN 1980-1981. rjbela@hotmail.com

BELASCO, Elizabeth Anne (LI) 612 Forest Ave, Massapequa NY 11758 **D Gr Epis Ch Massapequa NY 2010-** B Jamaica NY 6/12/1930 d William Francis Simendinger & Lucile Winifred. BS CUNY 1950; MA NYU 1952; PhD NYU 1956; CTh Mercer TS 1985; Cert GTS 1996. D 12/21/1984 Bp Robert Campbell Witcher Sr. D S Steph's Ch Port Washington NY 2005-2010; D S Ptr's by-the-Sea Epis Ch Bay Shore NY 2002; D Ch Of The Redeem Astoria NY 2001-2002; Dio Long Island Garden City NY 2000-2002; D Ch Of S Fran Of Assisi Levittown NY 2000-2001; D Epis Ch of The Resurr Williston Pk NY 2000-2001; Dio Long Island Garden City NY 1999-2002; D The Ch Of The Ascen Rockville Cntr NY 1998-2000; Geo Mercer TS Garden City NY 1994-2000; Dioc Coun Dio Long Island Garden City NY 1986-1998. NAAD 1984. Tchr Of The Year The Wheatley Sch 1984. ebelasco@optonline.net

BELCHER, Sandra Alves (Ct) 165 Grassy Hill Rd, Woodbury CT 06798 B Mount Holly NJ 1/26/1948 d Joseph Alves & Mary. BA Mt Holyoke Coll 1969; MA Van 1972; MDiv Ya Berk 1985. D 6/1/1985 P 9/1/1986 Bp John Bowen Coburn. m 5/28/1972 Robert Belcher. S Steph's Ch Ridgefield CT 1987-1994. Assembly of Epis Healthcare Chapl 2001; Assn of Profsnl Chapl 1999.

BELDING SR, David Squire (Chi) 1250 N Dearborn St, Apt 20B, Chicago IL 60610 B Chicago IL 2/12/1932 s Hiram Hurlbert Belding & Rose. BA Wheaton Coll 1954; MDiv Nash 1981. D 5/1/1981 Bp Quintin Ebenezer Primo Jr P 11/1/1981 Bp James Winchester Montgomery. m 5/27/2007 Linda Carol Scotzin c 2. Cur S Ptr's Epis Ch Chicago IL 1981-1986. DSBEL@SBCGLOBAL.NET

BELIVEAU, Harold Edmond (LI) 8 Princeton St, Concord NH 03301 B Concord NH 3/6/1925 s Harold Edmond Beliveau & Ethel Marguerite. BS U of New Hampshire 1951; MDiv Ya Berk 1955; Coll of Preachers 1977. D 6/18/1955 Bp Charles F Hall P 12/21/1955 Bp Shirley Hall Nichols. m 7/5/1982 Edith Kathleen Voigt c 3. R All SS Ch Baldwin NY 1966-1987; R All SS Ch Wichita Falls TX 1963-1966; Vic S Paul's Ch Altus OK 1959-1961; Asst S Lk's Epis Ch Dallas TX 1957-1959; Vic S Aug's Ch Meade KS 1955-1957. B'nai B'rith Merit Awd 1972. revsk@mymailstation.com

BELKNAP, Charles (Los) 1386 Beddis Road, Salt Spring Island BC V8K 2C9 Canada **Asst S Ptr's Par San Pedro CA 2005-** B Pittsburgh PA 3/17/1948 s Charles Belknap & Rosalie Alston. Trin Hartford CT 1971; BA Hampshire Coll 1972; MDiv VTS 1976. D 6/5/1976 Bp George E Rath P 1/14/1977 Bp Robert C Rusack. m 4/19/1997 Sarah Koelling c 2. Assoc S Aid's Epis Ch Malibu CA 2002-2004; Assoc S Cross By-The-Sea Ch Hermosa Bch CA 1995-2002; Int H Trin Alhambra CA 1994-1995; Int S Jn's Mssn La Verne CA 1993-1994; Int S Jos's Par Buena Pk CA 1991-1992; MHA Long Bch CA 1988-2007; S Fran Mssn Norwalk CA 1981-1989; P-in-c H Fam Mssn No Hollywood CA 1980-1984; Assoc St Johns Pro-Cathd Los Angeles CA 1976-1980. thebelknaps@gmail.com

BELKNAP, Sarah (Los) 2066 Empress Ave, South Pasadena CA 91030 B Chicago IL 10/4/1948 d Robert Keith Koelling & Margaret. BA SW at Memphis 1970; MSSW U of Tennessee 1974; MDiv ETSBH 1986. D 6/25/1988 P 1/21/1989 Bp Frederick Houk Borsch. m 4/19/1997 Charles Belknap. R S Ptr's Par San Pedro CA 2003-2009; Assoc Ch Of Our Sav Par San Gabr CA 1999-2003; S Paul's Epis Ch Tustin CA 1996-1999; Asst S Wilfrid Of York Epis Ch Huntington Bch CA 1991-1995; Asst/Int Gr Epis Ch Glendora CA 1988-1991. ESMHE 1991-1996. BA cl SW at Memphis Memphis TN 1970. skbelknap@gmail.com

BELL, Benjamin Franklin (Miss) 4759 Brookwood Pl, Byram MS 39272 B Holyoke MA 10/5/1924 s Jack Morris Bell & Ethel Ann. BS S Louis U 1947; MDiv STUSo 1967. D 6/22/1967 P 5/23/1968 Bp John M Allin. m 5/9/1987 Linda Kay Crippen c 3. All SS Epis Ch Birmingham AL 1990; R Trin Ch Hattiesburg MS 1971-1990; All SS' Epis Ch Tupelo MS 1969-1971; Cur S Paul's Epis Ch Meridian MS 1967-1969. fatherbell1@yahoo.com

BELL JR, Colley Wood (Alb) 108 Elm St., Versailles KY 40383 B New York NY 3/8/1923 s Colley Wood Bell & Marie Frances. BA Pr 1947; MDiv VTS 1955. D 6/18/1955 Bp Angus Dun P 12/1/1955 Bp Benjamin M Washburn. m 6/28/1952 Charline S Stickles c 2. R Ch Of Our Sav New Lebanon NY 1983-1989; St Jn The Bapt Sch Mendham NJ 1981-1983; Assoc The Epis Ch Of Beth-By-The-Sea Palm Bch FL 1980-1981; Marg Hall Sch Versailles KY 1966-1980; Dn Dio New York New York City NY 1960-1965; R S Jn's Ch Cornwall NY 1959-1966. "Is Our Lamp Under A Bushel?," *Educational Register*, Vinc-Curtis, 1973. cubelljr@windstream.net

BELL, David Allen (Ind) 8320 E 10th St, Indianapolis IN 46219 B Anderson IN 7/16/1958 s Donald Edwin Bell & Patricia Annette. BA Indiana U 1983; MDiv STUSo 1988. D 6/24/1988 P 3/17/1989 Bp Edward Witker Jones. m 11/28/1981 Marion Zella Rosene c 3. R S Matt's Ch Indianapolis IN 2000-2003; Asst R S Chris's Ch Pensacola FL 1989-1992; Cur S Alb's Ch Indianapolis IN 1988-1989. zellabell@aol.com

BELL, Emily Susan Richardson (Los) 190 Avenida Aragon, San Clemente CA 92672 **P-in-c Faith Epis Ch Laguna Niguel CA 2002-** B New York NY 1/27/1940 d Wallace B Thomas & Ruthella. Cushing Acad Ashburnham MA 1957; BA New Sch for Soc Resrch 1967. D 12/6/1985 P 6/8/1986 Bp William Benjamin Spofford. m 11/17/1990 Leonard Miller. P-in-c S Mk's Epis Ch Upland CA 2000-2001; Int S Clem's-By-The-Sea Par San Clemente CA 1998-2000; P H Trin Epis Ch Fallon NV 1986-1989. emilysbell@juno.com

BELL, G(erald) Michael (Miss) 418 N King St, Xenia OH 45385 B Jackson MS 2/6/1942 s Gerald Benjamin Bell & Thelma Leigh. BS U of Sthrn Mississippi 1964; MDiv SWTS 1967. D 6/9/1967 P 5/23/1968 Bp John M Allin. m 8/22/1964 Sandra Jean Dunn c 1. Off Of Bsh For ArmdF New York NY 1977-2004; R The Epis Ch Of The Medtr Meridian MS 1973-1977; Asst R Gr - S Lk's Ch Memphis TN 1972-1973; Vic Ch Of The Ascen Hattiesburg MS 1971-1972; Vic Gr Ch Carrollton MS 1968-1971; Vic S Mary's Ch Lexington MS 1968-1971; Cur Ch Of The Nativ Greenwood MS 1967-1968. g_michaelbell@sbcglobal.net

BELL JR, Hugh Bell (Tex) 919 S John Redditt Dr, Lufkin TX 75904 B Tampa FL 12/3/1941 s Hugh Oliver Bell & Frances. BA U of Mississippi 1965; MDiv STUSo 1977. D 6/24/1977 Bp Robert Elwin Terwilliger P 1/10/1978 Bp A Donald Davies. m 8/25/1968 Florence G Green. Int R S Mk's Ch Palm Bch Gardens FL 2004-2005; R S Cyp's Ch Lufkin TX 1998-2004; Asst R S Simon's On The Sound Ft Walton Bch FL 1989-1998; Vic S Fran Ch Edmond OK 1984-1989; R S Lk's Ch Chickasha OK 1979-1984; Vic S Mich And All Ang Ch Lindsay OK 1979-1982; Cur S Jn's Epis Ch Corsicana TX 1977-1979. Ord Of S Lk 1985. hobell@yahoo.com

BELL, Jocelyn (ETenn) 643 Westview Rd, Chattanooga TN 37415 B Salisbury MD 3/1/1941 d Henry James Jones & Rosemary. BA Mt Holyoke Coll 1963; MA Yale DS 1965; MDiv SWTS 1993. D 6/19/1993 Bp R(aymond) Stewart Wood Jr P 4/20/1994 Bp William Walter Wiedrich. c 2. R Chr Ch - Epis Chattanooga TN 1999-2010; Vic Trin Epis Ch Kirksville MO 1994-1999; CE Coordntr S Chris's Epis Ch Oak Pk IL 1993-1994; S Alb's Ch Simsbury CT 1968-1969; S Jas Epis Ch Farmington CT 1966-1968; S Jn's Ch W Hartford CT 1965-1966. EPF 2002; EUC 2002. BA mcl Mt Holyoke Coll So Hadley MA 1963. jocelyn_bell@comcast.net

BELL, John Michael (WMich) 406 2nd St, Manistee MI 49660 **R H Trin Epis Ch Manistee MI 2009-** B Murphysboro IL 3/2/1945 s Howard Middleton Bell & Virginia Fay. BA/MA Sthrn Illinois U 1971; MDiv EDS 2003. D 6/19/2005 P 12/17/2005 Bp Edwin Max Leidel Jr. m 11/17/1990 Helen Reid c 1. Calv Epis Ch Hillman MI 2005-2009; R Gr Epis Ch Lachine MI 2004-2009. jmbell@earthlink.net

BELL JR, John Robinson (Oly) 2454 E Palm Canyon Dr # 4d, Palm Springs CA 92264 **Int P S Anth Of The Desert Desert Hot Sprg CA 2003-** B Monroe GA 11/3/1932 s John Robinson Bell & Clara. BA Emory U 1954; MDiv STUSo 1960. D 6/22/1960 P 12/22/1960 Bp Randolph R Claiborne. S Jn's Epis Ch Snohomish WA 1989-1996; All SS Ch Seattle WA 1988; Int S Mk's Cathd Seattle WA 1986-1988; R S Ptr's Ch Jacksonville FL 1964-1986; Vic S Paul's Epis Ch Newnan GA 1960-1964. Auth, "The H Sprt Among Episcopalians"; Contrib, "The Journey". ACC. jbell84450@aol.com

BELL, Karl Edwin (Eur) Po Box 171, Fifty Lakes MN 56448 B Saint Paul MN 2/3/1933 s Clifford Paul Bell & Louise Apollonia. BA U MN 1956; MDiv SWTS 1961; Ya 1965; Oxf 1971. D 6/24/1961 Bp Hamilton Hyde Kellogg P 6/1/1962 Bp Philip Frederick McNairy. P-in-c Chr Ch Clermont-Ferrand France Clermont-Ferrand FR 2002-2004; R Ch of S Aug of Cbury 65189 Wiesbaden DE 1992-1993; Stndg Com Dio Eau Claire Eau Claire WI 1990-1991; Epis Asiamerican Mnstry Dio Eau Claire Eau Claire WI 1989-1990; R Chr Ch Par La Crosse WI 1979-1992; R Chr Ch Albert Lea MN 1976-1979; Vic S Paul's Ch Naples FL 1967-1970; Asst Trin By The Cove Naples FL 1967-1968; Asst Min The Epis Cathd Of Our Merc Sav Faribault MN 1961-1965. Auth, "What Price Man?". mitchelllake@yahoo.com

BELL, (Mary) Cynthia (Mass) 402 Nasketucket Way, Fairhaven MA 02719 **P-in-c S Jas' Ch No Salem NY 1997-** B Flushing NY 12/3/1932 d Edward Patrick Ward & Mary Messenger. Cert Endicott Coll Pride's Crossing MA 1952; BA Coll of New Rochelle 1976; MA GTS 1991; CAS GTS 1995. Rec from Roman Catholic 4/2/1977 Bp Harold Louis Wright. m 12/30/1952 Stanley Parsons Bell c 2. Assoc P S Jn's Ch Larchmont NY 1995-1997. revmcbell@comcast.net

BELL, Michael S (Kan) c/o Episcopal Diocese of Kansas, 835 SW Polk St, Topeka KS 66612 **Mem, Nomin and Elctns Com Dio Kansas Topeka KS 2011-; Mem, Bp's Cmsn for Campus Mnstry Dio Kansas Topeka KS 2010-** B TX 12/7/1969 s Martin T B & Shurley A. EdM Harvard Grad Sch of Educ 1996; MTS Harvard DS 1997; n/a ETS at Claremont 2009. D 6/12/2010 Bp Mary Douglas Glasspool P 1/8/2011 Bp Dean Elliott Wolfe. Co-Chair, Coordntng Team for Consecrations of new Bishops Suffr Dio Los Angeles Los Angeles CA 2010; Sem in-Res S Aug By-The-Sea Par Santa Monica CA 2009-2010. Thos Cranmer Schlrshp ETS at Claremont 2009. agape2day@msbell.com

BELL, Patrick William (Spok) 501 E Wallace Ave, Coeur D Alene ID 83814 **R S Lk's Ch Coeur D Alene ID 2002-** B Spokane WA 1/1/1952 s William Lloyd Bell & Beverly Jean. BA Whitworth U 1974; MA Fuller TS 1977; CTh Epis TS of The SW 1989; SWTS 1999. D 6/12/1989 Bp Leigh Wallace Jr P 12/15/1989 Bp Rustin Ray Kimsey. m 3/16/2002 TinaMarie Bell c 3. Deploy Off Dio Estrn Oregon The Dalles OR 1996-2001; Secy Of Dioc Conv Dio Estrn Oregon The Dalles OR 1996-2000; Dioc Coun Dio Estrn Oregon The Dalles OR 1992-2000; R S Matt's Epis Ch Ontario OR 1989-2001; Chair Of Stwdshp Dept Dio Spokane Spokane WA 1986-1988. Dom Mssy Partnership 1994-2003; RWF 1989-1992. frpbell@frontier.com

BELL OSB, Roger Craig (Pgh) 56500 Abbey Rd, Three Rivers MI 49093 B Otwell IN 6/20/1928 s William Franklin Bell & Edna. BA Indiana U 1949; MDiv Nash 1960. D 12/22/1956 Bp Donald H V Hallock P 6/29/1957 Bp William W Horstick. R The Ch Of The Adv Jeannette PA 1963-1971; R Chr Ch Chippewa Falls WI 1958-1963; Vic S Simeon's Ch Stanley WI 1958-1963. jbell@net-link.net

BELL, Susan Endicott (WLa) 403 East Flournoy Lucas Road, 04/01/0158, Shreveport LA 71115 **Serv Coordntr Ch Of The H Cross Shreveport LA 2002-** B New Haven CT 2/23/1932 d Reverand William Godsell Wright & Marian. BA U of Texas 1954; Med U of Louisiana 1982; CTh Epis TS of The SW 2001. D 6/23/2001 P 1/5/2002 Bp Robert Jefferson Hargrove Jr. c 3.

BELL JR, William R (Md) 2901 Boston St Apt 601, Baltimore MD 21224 **Asst S Anne's Par Annapolis MD 2011-** B Durham NC 4/27/1952 s William Reed Bell & Nell. BA Rice U 1974; MD Duke 1978; Res Duke U Med Cntr 1982; MDiv Ya Berk 2007. D 6/2/2007 P 5/10/2008 Bp Philip Menzie Duncan II. m 5/11/1975 Katherine Dressner c 3. Epis Chapl to Johns Hopkins Hospitals Dio Maryland Baltimore MD 2009-2011; Cur H Nativ Epis Ch Panama City FL 2007-2009. Assn of Profsnl Chapl 2010. Bd Cert Chapl BCI 2011; Bd Cert Chapl Bd Certifying Chapl, Inc 2011. revwrbell@gmail.com

BELL, Winston Alonzo (LI) 2263 Sedgemont Dr, Winston Salem NC 27103 B Winchester KY 3/24/1930 s Edward Child Bell & Margaret Lee. BA Fisk U 1951; MA U MI 1955; EdD U MI 1963; STB GTS 1964. D 6/20/1964 P 12/21/1964 Bp James P De Wolfe. R Ch Of S Jas The Less Jamaica NY 1967-1974; Cur S Aug's Ch New York NY 1964-1966.

BELLAIMEY, John Edward (Minn) 4233 Linden Hills Blvd, Minneapolis MN 55410 B Detroit MI 9/20/1955 s Henry Edward Bellaimey & Mary Ellen. BA Harv 1976; MDiv Harvard DS 1989. D 6/24/1989 Bp H Coleman McGehee Jr P 1/9/1990 Bp Robert Marshall Anderson. m 10/13/1984 Lynnell Margaret Mickelsen. Auth, "Wrld Rel: A Journey For Teachers & Their Students," Naes, 1992; Auth, "The Wheel Of The Year"; Auth, "The Five Senses & H Objects". john.bellaimey@breckschool.org

BELLAIS, William Frank (WMo) 440 Dickinson St, Chillicothe MO 64601 B Colon PA 8/28/1934 s Charles Earl Bellais & Dorothy Anna. BA New Mex St U. 1960; MA New Mex St U. 1980; Cert Prchr Lewis Sch Of Mnstry 1983; EdD New Mex St U. 1988. D 11/14/1983 Bp Richard Mitchell Trelease Jr P 6/22/1991 Bp John Clark Buchanan. m 10/22/1960 Eleanoar Ann Beauchamp c 2. Gr Epis Ch Chillicothe MO 1993-2009; Chr Ch Epis Boonville MO 1992; Dio W Missouri Kansas City MO 1991; Vic S Mary's Ch Fayette MO 1990-1992; D S Andr's Epis Ch Las Cruces NM 1983-1988. Auth, "An Owl Among the Ruins," Vantage Press, 2008. Phi Delta Kappa 1982; Phi Kappa Phi 1980. Bronze Star Medal U.S. Army 1969. drbellais@yahoo.com

BELLIS, Elaine (Chi) 1747 E 93rd St, Chicago IL 60617 **Mssh-S Barth Epis Ch Chicago IL 2004-** B East Grand Rapids MI 5/21/1943 d George Eugene Bellis & Heneritta Rickie. D 1/30/1999 Bp Herbert Alcorn Donovan Jr. c 1. elainebellis@sbcglobal.net

BELLISS, Richard Guy (Los) 25454 Via Heraldo, Santa Clarita CA 91355 B Pittsfield MA 9/13/1932 s Francis Cyril Belliss & Vaughan. BA Whittier Coll 1953; BD/ M Div CDSP 1956. D 6/25/1956 P 2/19/1957 Bp Francis E I Bloy. m 8/27/1954 Joan Arlene Floyd c 2. Asst S Steph's Epis Ch Santa Clarita CA 1994; R All SS Epis Ch Riverside CA 1969-1994; R S Anselm Of Cbury Par Garden Grove CA 1958-1969; Cur S Cross By-The-Sea Ch Hermosa Bch CA 1956-1958. r.belliss@sbcglobal.net

BELLNER, Elisabeth Ann (CFla) 1056 Saddleback Ridge Rd, Apopka FL 32703 B 6/20/1945 AS Valencia Cmnty Coll 1985; AA Valencia Cmnty Coll 1993. D 12/10/2005 Bp John Wadsworth Howe. m 12/14/1991 Joseph Ann Bellner c 2. bbellner@aol.com

BELLOWS, Carol Hartley (WMass) 119 Day Rd-Fawncrest Meadows, Lyman ME 04002 B Plainfield NJ 4/2/1934 d John Henry Hartley & Jessie Ivamy. U of Massachusetts 1953; BS Westfield St Coll 1971; Hartford Sem 1980; Dio Wstrn Mass. 1982. D 10/9/1982 Bp Alexander Doig Stewart. m 6/6/1953 Richard S Bellows c 4. Cmsn on Wrld Mssn Dio Wstrn Massachusetts Springfield MA 1992-1998; D S Paul's Epis Ch Stockbridge MA 1988-1991; D S Paul's Ch Kinderhook NY 1986-1988; D Ch Of The Atone Westfield MA 1982-1986; T/F on Mt. Kilimanjaro Mssn Dio Wstrn Massachusetts Springfield MA 1982-1986. Auth, "Benjamin Monkey," *(Books for Middle Age Students)*, Authorhouse, 2010; Auth, "The Whack of The Closing Stanchions-Far From Papa's Hill in Vietnam 1967," *(For All Ages)*, Authorhouse, 2010; Auth, "Icabog Bear and Icey," *(Books for Young Chld)*, Authorhouse, 2009; Auth, "Fall - A Performance of Peace," *Kittery to the Kennebunks*, Pilot Press, 1999. AFP 1982-1986. Wk in Elem Educ Outstanding Teachers of Amer 1972. rbellows@roadrunner.com

BELLOWS, Richard Sears (WMass) 60 Western Ave, Westfield MA 01085 B 5/31/1959 s Carol Hartley. D 6/13/1992 Bp David Standish Ball P 12/19/1992 Bp Orris George Walker Jr. c 2. Chemung Vlly Cluster Elmira NY 1994-1998; S Ptr's by-the-Sea Epis Ch Bay Shore NY 1992-1994. Tertiary Of The Soc Of S Fran 1997. rickbellows@yahoo.com

BELLOWS, Scott P (Md) Saint Davids Church, 4700 Roland Ave, Baltimore MD 21210 **Coun Mem, Prov III Dio Maryland Baltimore MD 2011-2014; Deputation Chair, 77th GC Dio Maryland Baltimore MD 2011-2014; Co-Chair, Capital Cmpgn for the Bp Claggett Cntr Dio Maryland Baltimore MD 2011-2012; GC Dep Dio Maryland Baltimore MD 2008-; R S Dav's Ch Baltimore MD 2008-** B Tupper Lake NY 1/4/1960 s G Ross Bellows & Eva E. BA Ob 1987; MBA SUNY-Binghamton 1992; MDiv GTS 1996. D 6/1/1996 P 12/7/1996 Bp Richard Frank Grein. Stndg Com (Pres, 2007-2010) Dio Maryland Baltimore MD 2006-2010; Pres, Washington Cnty Reg Coun Dio Maryland Baltimore MD 2006-2007; Dep Alt, 76th GC Dio Maryland Baltimore MD 2005-2008; Chair, Dioc Conv Liturg Plnng Team Dio Maryland Baltimore MD 2005-2007; GC Dep - Alt Dio Maryland Baltimore MD 2005-2007; Mem, Dioc Coun Dio Maryland Baltimore MD 2003-2004; R S Jn's Par Hagerstown MD 2001-2008; Pres, Frederick Reg Coun Dio Maryland Baltimore MD 1999-2000; Assoc All SS Ch Frederick MD 1998-2001; Chair, Dioc Conv Plnng Team Dio Maryland Baltimore MD 1998-1999; Mem, Bp Suffr Search Com Dio Maryland Baltimore MD 1997-1998; Asst All SS Ch Frederick MD 1996-1998. s.bellows@stdavidsbalt.com

BELL-WOLSKI, Dedra Ann (Ind) 86208 Fieldstone Dr, Yulee FL 32097 **Off Of Bsh For ArmdF New York NY 1992-** B Joliet IL 1/1/1958 d Robert Daniel Bell & Donna Rae. BA Florida Sthrn Coll 1980; MDiv GTS 1983. D 6/11/1984 Bp Calvin Onderdonk Schofield Jr P 1/18/1985 Bp John Shelby Spong. m 7/26/1997 Vince Wolski c 2. Cn Chr Ch Cathd Indianapolis IN 1987-1988; Int Trin Cathd Miami FL 1986-1987; S Paul's Epis Ch Paterson NJ 1984-1985. navychaps@earthlink.net

BELMONT JR, John C (NJ) 300 S Main St, Pennington NJ 08534 **R S Matt's Ch Pennington NJ 1976-** B Trenton NJ 10/11/1946 s John Charles Belmont & Hannah. BA Rider Coll 1968; MDiv PDS 1971; STM NYTS 1982. D 4/24/1971 P 10/1/1971 Bp Alfred L Banyard. m 12/4/1971 Sandra Yelenies c 2. Chair Of COM Dio New Jersey Trenton NJ 1999-2003; Dioc Fndt Dio New Jersey Trenton NJ 1988-1991; Stndg Com Dio New Jersey Trenton NJ 1984-1988; Chair Of Loan Com Dio New Jersey Trenton NJ 1983-1987; Dioc Fndt Dio New Jersey Trenton NJ 1982-1984; Cathd Chapt Trin Cathd Trenton NJ 1981-1983; Asst S Lk's Ch Gladstone NJ 1973-1976; R Ch Of S Andr The Apos Camden NJ 1971-1973.

BELMONTES, Mervyn Lancelot (LI) 812 Nebraska Ave, Bay Shore NY 11706 B 11/2/1939 s Leo Belmontes & Eastlyl. Codrington Coll 1974; Queens Coll 1979; Lehman Coll 1984. Rec 5/1/1975 as Priest Bp The Bishop Of Trinidad. m 8/9/1975 Carol Patricia Spencer c 3. Chair-Com of Miscellaneous Bus Dio Long Island Garden City NY 2001-2006; Chair-Dept of Bdgt Dio Long Island Garden City NY 2001-2003; R S Gabr's Ch Brooklyn NY 2000-2006; Dioc Coun Dio Long Island Garden City NY 1997-2006; Cmsn on Mnstrs Dio Long Island Garden City NY 1995-2001; R S Steph's Epis Ch Jamaica NY 1992-2000; Vic Ch Of The Mssh Cntrl Islip NY 1984-1992; Asst S Lk's Epis Ch Bronx NY 1980-1984. mervynl@prodigy.net

BELMORE, Constance (Nev) 719 Luminoso St, Las Vegas NV 89138 **Assoc Ch Of The H Cross Decatur GA 1988-** B Charlotte NC 12/15/1955 d Thomas Clinton Stroupe & Patricia Ada Lancaster. BA U NC 1978; MDiv GTS 1983. D 6/25/1983 Bp Brice Sidney Sanders P 4/1/1984 Bp William Moultrie Moore Jr. m 8/22/1981 Kent Belmore c 2. Mssn P S Anna's Ch Atmore AL 2005-2007; Cn for Cmnty Mnstrs Dio Atlanta Atlanta GA 1994-2004; Dio Atlanta Atlanta GA 1989-2004; Assoc Dir Of Cmnty Mnstrs Dio Atlanta Atlanta GA 1989-1994; Chapl Gr Ch Charleston SC 1983-1988. Wmn Of The Year So Carolina Bus And Profsnl Wmn 1986. conniedee@cox.net

BELMORE JR, Kent (Nev) 719 Luminoso St, Las Vegas NV 89138 B Macon GA 8/23/1952 s Kent Belmore & Frances. BA U NC 1974; MDiv GTS 1982. D 6/7/1982 Bp Robert Campbell Witcher Sr P 12/1/1982 Bp William Gillette Weinhauer. m 8/22/1981 Constance Stroupe c 2. R Chr Ch Las Vegas NV 2007-2011; R All SS Epis Ch Mobile AL 2004-2007; Dio Atlanta Atlanta GA 1995; Dio Atlanta Atlanta GA 1994; Dio Atlanta Atlanta GA 1993-1994; R Ch Of The H Cross Decatur GA 1988-2004; Ch Of The H Comm Charleston SC 1985-1988; Cur Gr Ch Charleston SC 1983-1985; Cur S Ptr's by-the-Sea Epis Ch Bay Shore NY 1982-1983. Cumberland Soc. buckbelmore@cox.net

BELNAP, Ron(ald) Victor (U) 8952 Golden Field Way, Sandy UT 84094 **Asst All SS Ch Salt Lake City UT 2005-** B Salt Lake City UT 1/6/1932 s Orsen Victor Belnap & Mary Myrtle. BS U of Utah 1960; MSW U of Utah 1962; MDiv CDSP 1992. D 6/2/1991 P 12/5/1991 Bp George Edmonds Bates. m 5/24/1974 Nancy Smith c 3. P-in-c S Jude's Ch Cedar City UT 1992-1997; Dio Utah Salt Lake City UT 1991-1997. therealgitor@gmail.com

BELSER, Richard Irvine Heyward (SC) 71 Broad Street, Charleston SC 29401 B Fort Bragg NC 4/8/1942 s Irvine Furman Belser & Gladys. BA W&L 1964; MDiv VTS 1969. D 6/29/1969 P 4/5/1970 Bp John Adams Pinckney. m 7/11/1992 Anne Holcomb. R S Mich's Epis Ch Charleston SC 1986-2008; Dep GC Dio So Carolina Charleston SC 1980-2006; Stndg Com Dio So Carolina Charleston SC 1980-1998; S Jn's Epis Par Johns Island SC 1974-1985; Asst S Jn's Epis Ch Columbia SC 1973-1974; Vic S Paul's Epis Ch Ft Mill SC 1969-1973. rbelser@stmichaelschurch.net

✠ **BELSHAW, Rt Rev George Phelps Mellick** (NJ) 15 Boudinot St, Princeton NJ 08540 **Ret Bp of New Jersey Dio New Jersey Trenton NJ 1995-; Dio New Jersey Trenton NJ 1988-** B Plainfield NJ 7/14/1928 s Harold Belshaw & Edith. STB GTS 1954; STM GTS 1959; Fllshp Coll of Preachers 1968. D 6/19/1954 Bp Norman B Nash P 12/18/1954 Bp Harry S Kennedy Con 2/3/1975 for NJ. m 6/12/1954 Elizabeth Wheeler c 3. Actg Dn & Pres The GTS New York NY 1997-1998; Dio New Jersey Trenton NJ 1993-1996; PBp's Coun of Advice Epis Ch Cntr New York NY 1993-1996; Chair, Bd Trst The GTS New York NY 1992-2000; Bp Dio New Jersey Trenton NJ 1983-1994; Bp Suffr Dio New Jersey Trenton NJ 1975-1982; R S Geo's-By-The-River Rumson NJ 1965-1975; R Chr Ch Dover DE 1959-1965; Vic S Matt's Epis Ch Waimanalo HI 1954-1957. "The Rel of the Incarn," *ATR*, 1994; "The issue of Chr Sprtlty," *ATR*, 1967; *Lent w Wm Temple*, Morehouse Barlow, 1966; *Lent w Evelyn Underhill*, Morehouse Barlow, 1964; "Theol Definition and Explanation," *ATR*, 1963. DD U So 1994; DD GTS 1975; Fell Coll of Preachers 1968; Fell GTS New York NY 1957. gpmbelshaw@aol.com

BELSKY, Emil Eugene (U) 1195 Angelita Ct, Salt Lake City UT 84106 **R S Paul's Ch Salt Lake City UT 2006-** B Omaha NE 2/12/1948 s Emil Elvin Belsky & Louise. BA U of St. Thos 1970; MA S Thos Sem Denver CO 1974. Rec from Roman Catholic 4/7/1993 Bp James Edward Krotz. m 6/29/1990

Cynthia Dirgo c 2. Dioc Coun Dio Utah Salt Lake City UT 2007-2010; Asst to R All SS Epis Ch Omaha NE 1993-2006. Assoc, OHC 1996. sarum99@msn.com

BELT, Michel (Ct) 119 Huntington St, New London CT 06320 **R S Jas Ch New London CT 2002-** B Wichita KS 11/26/1948 s Harold Belt & Alice. BME Wichita St U 1970; MBA U of Miami 1983; MDiv EDS 1997. D 5/31/1997 Bp Jack Marston McKelvey P 12/6/1997 Bp John Shelby Spong. Vic S Greg's Epis Ch Parsippany NJ 1997-2002. OHC, Assoc. mbelt@att.net

BELTON, Allan Edgar (O) 128 Kings Creek Rd., Irmo SC 29063 B Akron OH 1/24/1941 s Edgar Gray Belton & Freda. BA U Of Akron 1963; BD Bex 1966; MA Cleveland St U 1971. D 6/12/1966 P 12/18/1966 Bp Nelson Marigold Burroughs. m 2/12/2000 Ruth Anne McGavack Clary c 2. Int S Jn's Epis Ch Cuyahoga Falls OH 2004-2006; Chr Ch Epis Hudson OH 2001-2004; R Chr Ch Albemarle NC 1999-2001; Int S Martins-In-The-Field Columbia SC 1998-1999; Gr Epis Ch Willoughby OH 1995-1996; New Life Epis Ch Uniontown OH 1993-1998; Chr Epis Ch Kent OH 1992-1995; S Paul's Epis Ch Of E Cleveland Cleveland OH 1990-1992; Int Dio Ohio Cleveland OH 1987-1998; Ch Of The Incarn Cleveland OH 1987-1990; Vic S Tim's Ch Macedonia OH 1976-1979; Cur Chr Ch Epis Hudson OH 1968-1970; Cur S Andr Epis Ch Mentor OH 1966-1968. Bdiv cl Bex Gambier OH 1966. padreab@bellsouth.net

BELTON, Colin Charles (Alb) 18 Trinity Pl., Plattsburgh NY 12901 **R Trin Ch Plattsburgh NY 2008-** B 12/12/1950 s John Francis Belton & Margaret Irene. Trans from Anglican Church of Canada 6/15/2009 Bp William Howard Love. m 7/29/1989 Penelope A Tucker c 2. cpbltn@gmail.com

BELZER, John Alfred (Okla) 13 Lake Ln, Shawnee OK 74804 B Washington DC 5/7/1944 s John Elwood Belzer & Clara Irene. BA Oklahoma St U 1967; M.Ed. U of Cntrl Oklahoma 1974; PhD U of Oklahoma 1988. D 6/18/2005 Bp Robert Manning Moody. m 2/27/1990 Alma Lee Belzer c 2. jabelzer@allegiance.tv

BEMIS, Harlan Arnold (WNC) 30 Hidden Meadow Dr, Candler NC 28715 **Assoc S Andr's Epis Ch Canton NC 2006-** B Providence RI 5/28/1939 s Harlan George Bemis & Margaret Luella. BS Worcester Polytechnic Inst 1959; GTS 1962; CG Jung Inst 1968. D 11/12/1972 Bp Paul Moore Jr P 6/3/1973 Bp Roger W Blanchard. m 12/23/1998 Joan M Saviano. Vic Ch of the Ascen Merrill WI 1999-2005; P S Aelred Cluster Merrill WI 1999-2005; Vic S Barn Epis Ch Tomahawk WI 1999-2005; Vic St Ambr Epis Ch Antigo WI 1999-2005; Int Dio Estrn Michigan Saginaw MI 1998-1999; Int Thumb Epis Area Mnstry Deford MI 1997-1999; Int S Mk's Ch Warren RI 1995-1997; Int Ch Of The Mssh Foster RI 1989-1995; Int Galilee Mssn To Fisherman Narragansett RI 1984-1986; Int Dio Rhode Island Providence RI 1983-1997; Int Emm Epis Ch Cumberland RI 1983-1984; Int Epis Sr Communities Walnut Creek CA 1979; Int Epis Seamens Serv San Francisco CA 1977-1981; Int S Cyp's Ch San Francisco CA 1976-1977; Asst P S Jn's Ch New York NY 1974-1991; Int Dio California San Francisco CA 1973-1980. h.bemis@charter.net

BENAVIDES, Laurie Pauline (RG) 140 Hazeltine Drive, Georgetown TX 78628 B San Antonio TX 12/5/1954 d Richard Walker & LeMoyne Lynn. BS SW Texas St 1976; MEd SW Texas St 1980. D 10/29/2006 Bp C(harles) Wallis Ohl. m 12/18/1983 Roy Benavides c 3. NAAD 2007; The OSL the Physcn 2008; The Ord of the DOK 1996. lpbenavides@gmail.com

BENBROOK, James Gordon (WLa) 403 Holly St, Vidalia LA 71373 **R Ch Of The Redeem Ruston LA 2009-** B Herber Springs AR 8/20/1948 s Maurice Gordon Benbrook & Bonnie Anita. AA Essex Coll Essex MD 1972; BS Towson U 1976; MDiv STUSo 2005. D 6/4/2005 P 9/2/2006 Bp D(avid) Bruce Mac Pherson. m 8/3/2005 Rebecca June Benbrook c 3. D The Epis Ch Of The Gd Shpd Vidalia LA 2005-2008. benbrookjg@suddenlink.net

BENCKEN, Cathi (Ia) 211 Walnut St., Muscatine IA 52761 **R Trin Ch Muscatine IA 2008-** B Harlan IA 9/24/1951 d Robert Carl Head & Phyllis Maude. BSN U of Iowa Coll of Nrsng 1973; MDiv Bex 2007. D 4/13/2007 P 12/8/2007 Bp J Michael Garrison. m 12/27/1997 Charles Bencken c 5. Assoc S Paul's Epis Ch Lewiston NY 2007-2008. revcathib@machlink.com

BENCKEN, Charles (WNY) 2461 Longhurst Ct., Muscatine IA 52761 B Chico CA 6/19/1938 s George Leon Bencken & Anna Maria. M.A.; Ed.D U of San Francisco; BA S Jos's Minor Sem Mtn View CA 1958; /DD S Pat's Coll/ Major Sem, Menlo Pk, CA 1964; MA TS U Of San Francisco 1969; EDS U of Iowa 1972; JD U Pac, McGeorge Sch of Law 1989. Rec from Roman Catholic 5/16/1999 as Priest Bp Stewart Clark Zabriskie. m 12/27/1997 Cathi Head c 5. Int S Thos' Epis Ch Sioux City IA 2008-2009; R Chr Ch Albion NY 2005; Vic Ch Of The Epiph Niagara Falls NY 2001-2004; Vic Ch Of The Redeem Niagara Falls NY 2001-2004; R S Ptr's Ch Niagara Falls NY 2001-2004; Dio Nevada Las Vegas NV 1999-2001. frchasfb@aol.com

BENDALL, R Douglas (Nwk) 26 Howard Court, Newark NJ 07103 B Baltimore MD 5/9/1939 s Robert Richard Bendall & Lillian May. BA S Johns 1961; M.Div. Epis TS of The SW 1968; Grad study U CA/Berkeley 1971; Grad study U of Tubingen, Germany 1972; Ph.D. Grad Theol Un 1977. D 7/25/1968 Bp Everett H Jones P 1/26/1969 Bp Harold Cornelius Gosnell. m 6/9/2001 Vera M Bendall c 2. Vic S Andr's Ch Newark NJ 1995-2005; Vic H Sprt Mssn Lake Almanor CA 1987-1994; Asst S Paul's Epis Ch San Antonio TX 1968-1969. *The Naturalization of Whitehead's God*, Dissertation Abstracts Ann Arbor Mich., 1977. AAR 1975; SBL 1977. rdbendall@aol.com

BENDER, David R (NY) 104 Fairview Avenue, Poughkeepsie NY 12601 **D S Jas Ch Hyde Pk NY 1999-** B Long Branch NJ 7/20/1947 D 12/11/1982 Bp Addison Hosea. m 12/6/1969 Carol Anne Lynn.

BENDER, Frederick Tuttle (Ct) 203 Wilbon Rd. Apt. 607, Fuquay Varina NC 27526 B Newark NJ 4/6/1923 s Lester Frederick Bender & Lois Elizabeth. Summit Sch of Mus 1943; Rutgers-The St U 1956; GTS 1958; Oxf 1978; Coll of Preachers 1979. D 6/14/1958 Bp Benjamin M Washburn P 12/21/1958 Bp Frederick J Warnecke. c 4. Assoc S Lk's Par Darien CT 1988-1992; Dn of Mid-Fairfield Deanry Dio Connecticut Hartford CT 1983-1988; R S Steph's Ch Ridgefield CT 1981-1988; Assoc S Lk's Par Darien CT 1972-1981; Stndg Com Dio Bethlehem Bethlehem PA 1967-1968; Dept of Missions Dio Bethlehem Bethlehem PA 1966-1969; R Gr Epis Ch Allentown PA 1964-1969; R S Jn's Epis Ch Palmerton PA 1960-1964; Asst Cathd Ch Of The Nativ Bethlehem PA 1958-1960. Auth, *Serv of Affirmation When Parents are Separating*. fbender2@nc.rr.com

BENDER, Jane Arrington (Be) 557 W 3rd St Apt K, Bethlehem PA 18015 **P-in-c All SS Epis Ch Lehighton PA 2006-** B Greenville SC 5/12/1951 d John White Arrington & Jane. BA Furman U 1973; MDiv Moravian TS 1997; DAS GTS 1998. D 9/19/1998 P 5/29/1999 Bp Paul Victor Marshall. c 1. S Anne's Epis Ch Trexlertown PA 2001-2005; Int Cathd Ch Of The Nativ Bethlehem PA 1999-2000; D S Anne's Epis Ch Trexlertown PA 1998-1999. Soc For Promoting Chr Knowledge, EPF. Mdiv cl Moravian TS Bethlehem PA 1997. jane.a.bender@gmail.com

BENDER, John Charles (Tenn) Our Saviour Episcopal Church, 704 Hartsville Pike, Gallatin TN 37066 B Marietta OH 6/13/1949 s Samuel Vaughn Bender & Caroline Weaver. BA Marshsall U 1971; DAS U So TS 2007. D 2/23/2008 P 12/20/2008 Bp John Crawford Bauerschmidt. m 7/23/1974 Lynda G Bender c 4. P-in-c Ch Of Our Sav Gallatin TN 2008; D Dio Tennessee Nashville TN 2008. friar-tuck@comcast.net

BENDER, William Dexter (Ala) 402 S Scott St, Scottsboro AL 35768 **R S Lk's Ch Scottsboro AL 2009-** B Gainesville FL 9/26/1946 s William Madison Bender & Leona. BA Shpd Coll Shepherdstown WV 1969; MDiv VTS 1994. D 6/25/1994 P 1/6/1995 Bp Rogers Sanders Harris. m 4/30/1977 Heidi Chiappini c 6. Int St Thos Epis Ch Huntsville AL 2008-2009; Int Ch Of The Gd Shpd Lookout Mtn TN 2006-2008; Assoc R Chr Ch Bradenton FL 2000-2006; R S Chris's Ch TAMPA FL 1996-2000; Asst S Andr's Epis Ch Tampa FL 1994-1996. fatherdex@aol.com

BENDER-BRECK, Barbara (Cal) 3226 Adeline St, Oakland CA 94608 B Dallas TX 5/6/1949 d Robert James McGill & Eleanor. BA Notre Dame Coll 1971; JD U of San Francisco 1975; MDiv CDSP 1993. D 6/4/1993 P 6/1/1994 Bp William Edwin Swing. c 2. S Barth's Ch Beaverton OR 2009-2011; Int S Lk's Ch San Francisco CA 2008-2009; S Anne's Ch Fremont CA 2006-2007; Ch Of The H Trin Richmond CA 2004-2005; Ch Of Our Sav Mill Vlly CA 2003-2004; S Mich And All Ang Concord CA 2002-2003; Assoc Gr Cathd San Francisco CA 1999-2002; Ch Of The Redeem San Rafael CA 1996-1999; S Paul's Epis Ch San Rafael CA 1994-1996. Tertiary Of The Soc Of S Fran. revb3@yahoo.com

BENEDICT, Richard Alan Davis (NJ) 1625 SE 10th Ave Apt 602, Fort Lauderdale FL 33316 B Toledo OH 4/20/1948 s Edward Hastings Benedict & Adell Alice. BA U of Toledo 1973; MA U of Toledo 1974; MDiv SWTS 1977. D 6/25/1977 Bp John Harris Burt P 1/28/1978 Bp David Keller Leighton Sr. Dio New Jersey Trenton NJ 1986-1987; R Chr Ch Bordentown NJ 1985-2008; Dio Maryland Baltimore MD 1981-1983; Asst to R All SS Ch Frederick MD 1977-1984. CCU. radbenedict@comcast.net

BENES, Sandra S (Mich) 122 White Lake Dr, Brooklyn MI 49230 B Adrian MI 9/30/1943 d Michael Mark Dunny & Martha Helen. Siena Heights Coll; U of Toledo; Whitaker TS. D 7/2/1980 Bp William J Gordon Jr P 5/22/1984 Bp H Coleman McGehee Jr. m 8/25/1962 E Michael Benes c 4. Dn of Lyster Area Coun Dio Michigan Detroit MI 1994-1997; Dn of SW Convoc Dio Michigan Detroit MI 1988-1990; R S Mich And All Ang Onsted MI 1982 2005. sbenes@comcast.net

BENESH, Jimi Brown (NCal) 334 D St, Redwood City CA 94063 **D S Ptr's Epis Ch Redwood City CA 2002-** B FJ 3/10/1944 s Lewis Brown Benesh & Esita. D 12/7/2002 P 12/6/2003 Bp William Edwin Swing. m 12/7/1964 Violet Koi.

✠ **BENFIELD, Rt Rev Larry R** (Ark) Episcopal Diocese Of Arkansas, 310 W 17th St, Little Rock AR 72206 **Bp of Arkansas Dio Arkansas Little Rock AR 2007-** B Johnson City TN 7/28/1955 s Clyde R Benfield & Madge Lena. BS U of Tennessee 1977; MBA U of Pennsylvania 1979; MDiv VTS 1990. D 6/16/1990 Bp Maurice Manuel Benitez P 1/31/1991 Bp Anselmo Carral-Solar Con 1/6/2007 for Ark. R Chr Epis Ch Little Rock AR 2001-2006; Cn Admin Dio Arkansas Little Rock AR 1998-2000; Int S Lk's Ch Hot Sprg AR 1996-1997; S Mk's Epis Ch Little Rock AR 1992-1996; Chapl of the Epis Stdt

Cntr Dio Texas Houston TX 1990-1992. DD VTS 2008; DD U So 2007. larrybenfield@mac.com

BENHAM, David D (Ark) 2701 Old Greenwood Rd, Fort Smith AR 72903 B Fayetteville AR 1/27/1942 s Hoyt Benham & Ida T. BSEd U of Arkansas 1965; MRE SW Bapt Theol 1969; MDiv Golden Gate Bapt TS 1985. D 10/16/2010 P 5/7/2011 Bp Larry R Benfield. m 6/15/1962 Jessie A Evans c 3. S Andr's Ch Rogers AR 2011. adbenham@gmail.com

✠ **BENHASE, Rt Rev Scott Anson** (Ga) 611 E Bay St, Savannah GA 31401 **Bp of Georgia Dio Georgia Savannah GA 2010-** B Lancaster OH 6/4/1957 s Carl Kenneth Benhase & Annaree. BA DePauw U 1979; MDiv VTS 1983; MS Cleveland St U 1990. D 6/23/1983 P 3/17/1984 Bp Edward Witker Jones Con 1/23/2010 for Ga. m 5/12/1984 Kelly J Jones c 3. S Alb's Par Washington DC 2006-2009; R S Phil's Ch Durham NC 1995-2006; Vic Trin Epis Ch Charlottesville VA 1990-1995; S Paul's Epis Ch Of E Cleveland Cleveland OH 1986-1990; R S Paul's Epis Ch Cleveland Heights OH 1986-1990; Cur Trin Ch Indianapolis IN 1983-1986. OA 1988. scott_benhase@juno.com

✠ **BENITEZ, Rt Rev Maurice Manuel** (Tex) 6103 Mountain Villa Cv, Austin TX 78731 **Ret Bp Of Texas Dio Texas Houston TX 1995-** B Washington DC 1/23/1928 s Enrique M Benitez & Blossom. BS USMA At W Point 1949; BD STUSo 1958; DD STUSo 1973. D 6/20/1958 P 3/1/1959 Bp Edward Hamilton West Con 9/13/1980 for Tex. m 12/18/1949 Joanne Dossett. Bp Dio Texas Houston TX 1980-1995; Chair Bd Trst Epis TS Of The SW Austin TX 1980-1995; R S Jn The Div Houston TX 1974-1980; Exec Bd, Ch Stwdshp Dept Dio Texas Houston TX 1974-1979; Regent The TS at The U So Sewanee TN 1973-1979; Dep Gc Dio W Texas San Antonio TX 1970-1973; R Chr Epis Ch San Antonio TX 1968-1974; R Ch Of The Gd Shpd Silver City NM 1962-1968; R Gr Epis Ch Of Ocala Ocala FL 1962-1968; P-in-c S Jas' Epis Ch Lake City FL 1958-1961. Ch Pension Fund, New York Ny 1988-1995; Epis HS, Houston Tx 1983-1985; Epis TS Of The SW, Austin Tx 1980-1995; S Lk'S Epis Hosp, Houston Tx 1980-1995; STUSo, Sewanee Tn 1973-1979; STUSo, Sewanee Tn 1969-1969. Caring Sprt Awd Inst Of Rel 1994. bentex747@aol.com

BENITEZ, Wilfredo (Los) 1105 E Oak St, Anaheim CA 92805 B Bronx NY 3/27/1956 s Julio Benitez & Angelina. BA Universidad Interamericana De Puerto Rico Mercedita PR 1979; Med Bank St Coll of Educ 1982; MDiv GTS 1991. D 6/8/1991 P 12/1/1991 Bp Richard Frank Grein. S Anselm Of Cbury Par Garden Grove CA 2008; S Clem's-By-The-Sea Par San Clemente CA 1993; Asst For Latino Mnstrs Chr Ch Poughkeepsie NY 1991-1993.

BENJAMIN, Judith Benjamin (Cal) 1400 Loma Drive, Ojai CA 93023 B Salem MA 4/27/1948 d Richard Watson Benjamin & Lois Elizabeth. BS U CA 1971; BA Sch for Deacons 2000. D 6/2/2001 Bp William Edwin Swing. m 1/22/1989 Ian Hall c 2. S Bede's Epis Ch Menlo Pk CA 2001-2010. heyjude.benjamin@gmail.com

BENJAMIN, Roy Allen (Mass) 7 Carriage Way, Danvers MA 01923 B Brighton MA 10/19/1935 s James Benjamin & Eleanor Louise. BA Tufts U 1958; BD Bex 1963; MA Tufts U 1963. D 6/23/1963 P 5/23/1964 Bp Anson Phelps Stokes Jr. m 6/28/1958 Sally Richmond. S Fran Epis Ch Great Falls VA 2001-2003; Int Pohick Epis Ch Lorton VA 1999-2001; Int Trin Ch Portland CT 1998-1999; Int Trin Ch Shelburne VT 1997-1998; Chr Ch So Hamilton MA 1994-1997; R Trin Ch Randolph MA 1966-1994; Cur S Mk's Ch Foxborough MA 1963-1966. benjamin@pohiale.org

BENKO, Andrew Grayson (FtW) 908 Rutherford St, Shreveport LA 71104 B Metairie LA 3/1/1980 s Ronald Barry Benko & Dean Kent. BA Coll of Santa Fe 2002; MDiv SWTS 2005. D 12/29/2004 Bp Charles Edward Jenkins III P 6/29/2006 Bp George Wayne Smith. m 9/17/2003 Hope Tinsley c 1. Dio Wstrn Louisiana Alexandria LA 2010-2011; S Mk's Cathd Shreveport LA 2009-2011; Dio Missouri S Louis MO 2007-2009. brother.benko@gmail.com

BENKO, Hope Tinsley (FtW) 9700 Saints Cir, Fort Worth TX 76108 **All SS' Epis Sch Of Ft Worth Ft Worth TX 2011-** B Alexandria LA 8/4/1981 d Richard Kenneth Tinsley & Mary D. BS Stephens Coll 2003; MDiv SWTS 2006. D 12/21/2005 P 6/29/2006 Bp George Wayne Smith. m 9/17/2003 Andrew Grayson Benko c 2. S Mk's Cathd Shreveport LA 2009-2011; Emm Epis Ch Webster Groves MO 2006-2009. hope@stmarkscathedral.net

BENNER, Stephen Thomas (Ind) 106 W. Charlestown Ave., Jeffersonville IN 47130 B Streator IL 5/9/1968 s Lawrence Benner & Evelyn. Johann-Wolfgang-Goethe Universität, Frankfurt am Main, Germa; BA Illinois St U Normal IL 1990; MA The OH SU Columbus OH 1993; Rheinische-Friedrich Wilhelms Universitat Bonn Germany 1996; PhD The OH SU Columbus OH 2000; MDiv Bex 2007; Indiana Wesl, Marion, IN 2012. D 6/23/2007 Bp Catherine Elizabeth Maples Waynick P 2/2/2008 Bp Kenneth Lester Price. m 5/31/1988 David K Worley. Confrater, Ord of S Ben (St. Greg' Abbey, Three R 1987. frstevebenner@gmail.com

BENNET, Richard Wilson (FdL) 7220 Newell Road, Hazelhurst WI 54531 B San Francisco CA 10/28/1928 s Richard Wilson Bennet & Helen Victoria. BA Colg 1951; Med U of Vermont 1968; PhD U CO 1971; MDiv Nash 1988. D 3/19/1991 P 9/19/1991 Bp Charles Jones III. m 2/4/1996 Joellen Abbott. Ret Dio Fond du Lac Appleton WI 1997; R Ch Of S Jn The Bapt Wausau WI 1994-1997; Dio Montana Helena MT 1993-1994; Ch Of The Trsfg Billings MT 1992-1993. jandrbennet@verizon.net

BENNETT III, Arthur Lasure (WVa) 16 Ashwood Dr, Vienna WV 26105 B Clarksburg WV 2/15/1943 s Arthur Luman Bennett & Betty Lou. BA W Virginia Wesleyan Coll 1966; MDiv Bex 1969; ThD Columbia Pacific U 1988. D 6/11/1969 P 12/1/1969 Bp Wilburn Camrock Campbell. m 8/20/1966 Linda Bennett c 2. Archd for the No Dio W Virginia Charleston WV 1994-2002; R The Memi Ch Of The Gd Shpd Parkersburg WV 1984-2009; Archd for Prog and Educ Dio W Virginia Charleston WV 1976-1980; R St Christophers Epis Ch Charleston WV 1973-1984; R S Paul's Ch Wheeling WV 1970-1973; Cur S Steph's Epis Ch Beckley WV 1969-1970. ARTBENNETT3@JUNO.COM

BENNETT JR, Bertram George (NY) 384 E 160th St, Bronx NY 10451 **S Dav's Ch Bronx NY 1997-** B New York NY 9/23/1951 s Bertram George Bennett & Marjorie Irene. BA Shaw U 1973; MDiv GTS 1977. D 6/11/1977 Bp Paul Moore Jr P 6/1/1978 Bp James Stuart Wetmore. m 4/12/1982 Ledda Del Rosario Pritchard c 3. Cur The Ch of S Matt And S Tim New York NY 1979-1980; S Marg's Ch Bronx NY 1977-1979.

BENNETT, Betsy Blake (Neb) 325 W. 11th St., Hastings NE 68901 **Exec Cmsn Mem Dio Nebraska Omaha NE 2011-; D S Steph's Ch Grand Island NE 2007-** B Akron OH 5/22/1951 BA Earlham Coll 1973; MA OH SU 1975. D 6/21/2004 Bp Joe Goodwin Burnett. m 3/22/1975 Gary Lee Bennett c 2. D S Mk's Epis Pro-Cathd Hastings NE 2004-2007. deaconbetsy@windstream.net

BENNETT, Bill (Tex) 3711 Hidden Holw, Austin TX 78731 B Birmingham AL 5/1/1945 s Clyde Frederick Bennett & Mildred. BS Portland St U 1975; MDiv CDSP 1982; DD Epis TS of The SW 1997. D 6/27/1992 P 2/1/1993 Bp Maurice Manuel Benitez. m 11/1/1969 Molly Shehane c 1. Dio Texas Houston TX 1997-2007; R S Mk's Ch Austin TX 1996-2007; Provost Epis TS Of The SW Austin TX 1992-1996; VP CDSP Berkeley CA 1976-1982. Ch Hist Soc Of The Dio Texas 1997. wmbennett@austin.rr.com

BENNETT, Christine Aikens (Me) 30 Turtle Cove Rd, Raymond ME 04071 B Cambridge MA 9/1/1946 d Keith Robert Aikens & Catherine. U of Maine; U of Sthrn Maine. D 10/17/1998 Bp Chilton Abbie Richardson Knudsen. m 6/7/1969 Lawrence Bennett c 3. D S Ann's Epis Ch Windham Windham ME 1998-2007.

BENNETT, Debra Q (LI) 36 Cathedral Ave, Garden City NY 11530 B New York, NY 2/10/1958 d Gerald Lawrence Bennett & Clara F. BA Wag 1980; MDiv Bex 2009. D 6/22/2009 Bp James Hamilton Ottley P 1/16/2010 Bp Lawrence C Provenzano. REVNDDEB@GMAIL.COM

BENNETT, Denise Harper (Roch) 2882 Country Road 13, Clifton Springs NY 14432 **R S Jn's Ch Clifton Sprg NY 2007-** B New Rochelle NY 1/7/1946 d James Harper & Barbara Lindesay. BA Cedar Crest Coll 1968; CSD GTS 1998; MDiv Drew U 2003. D 6/7/2003 P 12/6/2003 Bp John Palmer Croneberger. m 11/16/1968 Thomas Mason Bennett c 2. Assoc R Dir of Mnstry Dvlpmt S Mk's Ch Teaneck NJ 2004-2007; Asst Ch Of The Redeem Morristown NJ 2003-2004. denniebennett@att.net

BENNETT, E Gene (Miss) 981 S Church St, Brookhaven MS 39601 B Chattanooga TN 2/19/1941 s Ernest Franklin Bennett & Sarah Ruth. BS U So 1963; MDiv STUSo 1967; DDiv Van 1970. D 7/2/1967 Bp William F Gates Jr P 4/1/1968 Bp John Vander Horst. m 11/27/1986 Carole Petro c 1. R Ch Of The Redeem Brookhaven MS 2001-2009; Int Trin Ch Hattiesburg MS 2000-2001; R S Geo's Par La Can CA 1991-1994; R S Barn On The Desert Scottsdale AZ 1988-1991; R S Lk's Ch Brandon MS 1974-1988; Vic Ch Of Our Sav Gallatin TN 1968-1971; D Ch Of The Ascen Knoxville TN 1967-1968; S Jas Ch Jackson MS 1871-1973. Auth, "S Lk Journ Of Theol"; Auth, "Dance Of The Pilgrim"; Auth, "The Secular Chr"; Auth, "Image Of Man In Mod Lit". AAMFT 1971. gbenn7@earthlink.net

BENNETT, Ernest L (CFla) Diocese of Central Florida, 1017 E Robinson St, Orlando FL 32801 **Cn to the Ordnry Dio Cntrl Florida Orlando FL 1993-** B Norfolk VA 3/17/1943 s Ernest Dorian Bennett & Edith Pearl. BA U of Florida 1965; MDiv VTS 1968. D 6/24/1968 Bp Henry I Louttit P 12/28/1968 Bp James Loughlin Duncan. m 5/25/1968 Roslyn Bruder c 2. R S Andr's Epis Ch Ft Pierce FL 1985-1993; R S Andr's Epis Ch Sprg Hill FL 1971-1985; Asst Trin By The Cove Naples FL 1968-1971. epdiocenfl@aol.com

BENNETT JR, Franklin Pierce (EMich) 1051 Virginia Ave, Marysville MI 48040 B Syracuse NY 9/5/1935 s Franklin Pierce Bennett & Florence Concordia. BA Harv 1957; Intrnshp Emory U 1960; BD EDS 1961; Fllshp Seatlantic / Rockefeller U 1973; Fllshp Dio Missouri 1990; Fell PrTS 1990. D 6/29/1961 Bp Richard S M Emrich P 2/1/1962 Bp Archie H Crowley. m 2/5/1983 Marsha Ann Nelson c 1. Asst Gr Epis Ch Port Huron MI 2001-2006; Supply P Dio Estrn Michigan Saginaw MI 1998-2006; Long-term Supply P S Jn's Epis Ch Dryden MI 1997; P-in-c Gr Ch Detroit MI 1992-1995; R S Paul's Epis Ch Grand Forks ND 1988-1990; R S Paul's Epis Ch St. Clair MI 1969-1988; Assoc Chr Ch Grosse Pointe Grosse Pointe Farms MI 1963-1969; Asst Chr Ch Dearborn MI 1961-1963. Allin Fllshp Dio Missouri 1990; Par Mnstry Fllshp Sealantic /Rockefeller 1973; Danforth Sem Intrnshp Danforth Fndt 1959. franklinbennett@sbcglobal.net

BENNETT, Gail Louise (NJ) 803 Prospect Ave, Spring Lake NJ 07762 **D Trin Ch Asbury Pk NJ 2004-; D/Asst S Jas Ch Bradley Bch NJ 1985-** B 9/10/1938 d Frank Fitzerald & Norma. D 4/13/1985 Bp George Phelps Mellick Belshaw. c 2.

BENNETT, Gerald L (SwFla) 5134 Wedge Ct E, Bradenton FL 34203 B Detroit MI 5/4/1934 s William Lloyd Bennett & Hattie. BS Wayne 1962; Med Wayne 1965; EdD Estrn Michigan U 1971; TS Harvard DS 1985. D 7/9/1977 Bp William J Gordon Jr P 10/4/1985 Bp Henry Irving Mayson. c 1. Assoc Ch of the Nativ Sarasota FL 1996-2001; R S Geo's Epis Ch Bradenton FL 1990-1995; Int Ch Of The H Sprt Osprey FL 1989-1990; Int S Barth's Ch St Petersburg FL 1988; Asst Vic Ch Of The H Cross Novi MI 1979-1988; Asst Vic S Anne's Epis Ch Walled Lake MI 1979-1988. nonobucko@verizon.net

BENNETT, Jack Marion (ETenn) 234 E Kathy Ln, Freeport FL 32439 B Winston-Salem NC 7/14/1929 s Clyde Marion Bennett & Mildred. BA U So 1950; MDiv VTS 1954; STM STUSo 1963. D 6/26/1954 P 7/1/1955 Bp Richard Henry Baker. m 7/31/1982 Phyllis Barlow Hetrick. R S Tim's Ch Signal Mtn TN 1968-1979; Chair Of Dept Of Chr Soc Relatns Dio Wstrn No Carolina Asheville NC 1966-1968; R S Jas Epis Ch Hendersonville NC 1961-1968; Asst Ch Of The Adv Spartanburg SC 1958-1961; P-in-c S Jn's Ch Battleboro NC 1957-1958.

BENNETT, JoAnne (Ore) 6310 Stoneridge Mall Rd, Pleasanton CA 94588 **R S Geo's Epis Ch Roseburg OR 2009-** B New York NY 9/28/1955 d David Gray Bennett & Joan E. BA U CA 1978; MDiv CDSP 2001. D 12/1/2001 P 6/1/2002 Bp William Edwin Swing. Vic S Chris's Ch San Lorenzo CA 2001-2008. joannebntt@aol.com

BENNETT, Kyle Vernon (SwFla) St. Mark's Episcopal Church, 1101 N. Collier Blvd, Marco Island FL 34145 **R S Mk's Ch Marco Island FL 2005-** B Sandusky OH 7/19/1963 s Michael John Bennett & Kristen Kesinger. MA U of Mississippi; BA U So 1985; MDiv Epis TS of The SW 1994; DMin TS 2009. D 6/4/1994 P 4/2/1995 Bp Alfred Clark Marble Jr. m 3/15/1986 Dody Louise Hall c 2. Assoc St Thos Epis Ch Huntsville AL 2003-2005; R S Patricks Epis Ch Long Bch MS 1997-2003; S Ptr's Ch Oxford MS 1996-1997; Dio Mississippi Jackson MS 1994-1995; Yth Min S Thos Epis Ch Diamondhead MS 1987-1989. Sprt of Marco Island winner Rotary 2007. kyle@stmarksmarco.org

BENNETT, Marionette Elvena (Colo) 15625 E Atlantic Cir, Aurora CO 80013 **D S Steph's Epis Ch Aurora CO 1996-** B Charleston SC 3/23/1949 d John Henry Bennett & Rosena Edith. BS Paine Coll 1970. D 11/2/1996 Bp William Jerry Winterrowd. NAAD.

BENNETT, Patricia Houston (O) Po Box 218, Gates Mills OH 44040 B Cleveland OH 11/26/1946 d Egon Claude Powell & Barbara Houston. Skidmore Coll 1967; Ursuline Coll 1993. D 11/8/1996 Bp J Clark Grew II. m 1/30/2008 Peter Todd Vanderveen. D Ch Of The Trsfg Cleveland OH 1996-2000.

BENNETT, Pattiann Benner (Mont) 200 Terning Dr W, Eureka MT 59917 **S Mich And All Ang Eureka MT 2002-** B Skowhegan ME 8/25/1951 d Roy Maynard Benner & JoAnne Elizabeth. Mnstry Formation Prog 2000. D 10/9/2001 P 9/20/2002 Bp Charles Lovett Keyser. m 6/30/1979 Bruce Roberts Bennett.

BENNETT, Philip Wesley (Ala) Po Box 839, Eutaw AL 35462 **Died 12/12/2010** B Franklin NC 10/2/1951 s William Cecil Bennett & Laverne. BA So-Estrn Coll 1973; MDiv Candler TS Emory U 1976. D 6/20/1981 P 11/1/1981 Bp William Gillette Weinhauer. c 2. PBNT35462@GMAIL.COM

BENNETT, Phillip C (Pa) 2001 Hamilton St Apt 303, Philadelphia PA 19130 **Asstg P Ch Of S Mart-In-The-Fields Philadelphia PA 2008-; Fresh Start Stff Dio Pennsylvania Philadelphia PA 2006-; Dir of Sprtl Formation, Sch for the Diac Dio Pennsylvania Philadelphia PA 1990-** B Pasadena CA 6/17/1952 s Charles G Bennett & May Adele. BA Beloit Coll 1975; MDiv SWTS 1979; STM UTS 1992; PhD Un U 1994. D 6/9/1979 Bp Quintin Ebenezer Primo Jr P 6/13/1980 Bp James Winchester Montgomery. m 8/20/2004 Joseph G Schaller. Asstg P S Ptr's Ch Philadelphia PA 1992-2000; Dir of Sprtl Formation, Sch for the Diac Dio Pennsylvania Philadelphia PA 1990-1995; P-in-c S Ptr's Ch Germantown Philadelphia PA 1990-1993; Chair, Sprtl Growth Com Dio Pennsylvania Philadelphia PA 1984-1988; Assoc S Mk's Ch Philadelphia PA 1982-1990; Dioc Coun Dio Chicago Chicago IL 1980-1982; Assoc S Mk's Epis Ch Glen Ellyn IL 1980-1982; Asst to the Bp Dio Colorado Denver CO 1979-1980. Auth, "Let Yourself Be Loved," Paulist Press, 1997. AAPC 1989; APA 1990; Shalem Inst Sprtl Direction Assoc 1994. Phi Beta Kappa Beloit Coll 1975. drpbennett@aol.com

BENNETT, Rachel Marybelle (ECR) 201 Glenwood Cir Apt 19e, Monterey CA 93940 **Decaon La Iglesia De San Pablo Seaside CA 1999-** B Carmel CA 8/1/1954 d Norman L Bennett & Mary Rachel. AA Monterey Peninsula Coll 1974; BA Sonoma St U Rohnert Pk 1976; Cert Sonoma St U Rohnert Pk 1977; BA Sch for Deacons 1996. D 12/2/1996 Bp Richard Lester Shimpfky. NAAD.

BENNETT, R Dudley (Nwk) 16 Warwick Way, Jackson NJ 08527 B Grand Rapids MI 11/22/1928 s Roscoe Dudley Bennett & Laura Ann. BA Calvin Coll 1950; Army Gnrl Sch 1953; STB Ya Berk 1956; Inst of Advance Pstr Stds 1962; Coll of Preachers 1963; Rutgers U 1968. D 6/23/1956 Bp Dudley B McNeil P 1/16/1957 Bp Archie H Crowley. m 5/24/2007 Marcia Hagen c 3. Ch Of The Trsfg Towaco NJ 1976-1977; P-in-c S Andr's Epis Ch New Paltz NY 1959-1963; Vic S Paul's Ch Greenville MI 1956-1959. Auth, "Const Of Planet Earth," Authorhouse, 2011; Auth, "Rebirthing The Amer Dream," Authorhouse, 2009; Auth, "Pedagogy of Silence," Authorhouse, 2008; Auth, "Successful Team Bldg," Amacom, 1980; Auth, "Transactional Analysis And The Mgr," Amacom, 1976. Amer Natl Trng 1970-2010. Humanitarian Awd Municipal Cnty City Of Newark Newark NJ 1990. dudley.bennett@juno.com

BENNETT, Richard (Spr) 1200 E College Ave, Normal IL 61761 B Evanston IL 8/26/1926 s Samuel William Rosey & Dorothy Marie. BA Carroll Coll 1950; MA NWU 1956; MDiv Nash 1965. D 6/12/1965 Bp James Winchester Montgomery P 12/18/1965 Bp Gerald Francis Burrill. m 5/11/1946 Alice Lindbom c 5. Asst Ch Of The Annunc Holmes Bch FL 1991-2008; Dn of the Estrn Dnry Dio Springfield Springfield IL 1988-1989; Vic S Alb's Epis Ch Olney IL 1987-1990; Vic S Mary's Ch Robinson IL 1987-1990; Stndg Com Dio Springfield Springfield IL 1980-1983; Dn of the NE Dnry Dio Springfield Springfield IL 1977-1979; S Matt's Epis Ch Bloomington IL 1974-1987. Phi Alpha Theta Carroll Coll 1949. sonar44@yahoo.com

BENNETT, Robert Avon (Mass) Po Box 380367, Cambridge MA 02238 B Baltimore MD 1/11/1933 s Robert Avon Bennett & Irene Julia. BA Ken 1954; Fllshp U of Copenhagen Copenhagen DK 1954; STB GTS 1958; Jn Hopkins U 1963; STM GTS 1966; PhD Harv 1974. D 6/17/1958 P 2/21/1959 Bp Harry Lee Doll. m 8/15/1982 Marceline Malica Donaldson c 2. Int S Barth's Ch Cambridge MA 1986-1988; Int S Cyp's Ch Roxbury MA 1976-1978; EDS Cambridge MA 1968-1993; Asst S Anne's In The Fields Epis Ch Lincoln MA 1965-1968; Tutor The GTS New York NY 1963-1965; Asst S Jas' Epis Ch Baltimore MD 1958-1963. Auth, "The Bk of Zephaniah," *The New Interpreter's Bible Volume VII*, Abingdon Press, 1996; Auth, "Afr," *Oxford Comp to the Bible*, Oxford Press, 1993; Auth, "Black Experience and the Bible," *Afr Amer Rel Stds*, Duke Press, 1989; Auth, "Zephaniah," *The Books of the Bible Volume I*, Scribner's, 1989; Auth, "The Power of Lang in Wrshp," *Theol Today*, 1987; Auth, *An Inclusive Lang Lectionary: Readings For Year C/ Year B/ Year A*, Westminster, 1985; Auth, "Black Episcopalians and the Dio Massachusetts," *The Epis Dio Massachusetts*, Epis Dio Massachusetts, 1984; Auth, "Howard Thurman and the Bible," *God and Human Freedom: A Festschrift in hon of Howard Thurman*, Friends Untd Press, 1983; Auth, "Episcopalians," *Encyclopedia of Black Amer*, McGraw Hill, 1981; Auth, *The Bible for Today's Ch*, Seabury Press, 1979; Auth, "Symposium on Biblic Criticism," *Theol Today*, 1977; Auth, *God's Wk of Liberation: A Journey Through the OT w the Liberation Heroes of Israel*, Morehouse-Barlow, 1976; Auth, "Biblic Theol and Black Theol," *Journ of the Interdenominational Theol*, 1976; Auth, "Freedom Motifs in Psalm 14:53," *Bulletin of the Amer Schools of Oriental Resrch*, 1975; Auth, "Black Episcopalians: A Hist From the Colonial Period to the Present," *The Hist mag of the Prot Epis Ch*, 1974; Auth, "Afr and the Biblic Period," *Harvard Theol Revs*, 1971. Fulbright Awd Danish Govt Copenhagen Denmark 1954; AB mcl Ken Gambier OH 1954; Phi Beta Kappa Ken Gambier OH 1953. BETTINA-NETWORK@COMCAST.NET

BENNETT, Sarah (Tex) 7002 Rusty Fig Dr, Austin TX 78750 B Shreveport LA 4/26/1963 d Edgar Galloway & Julia Conger. BA U Of Houston 1996; MDiv Epis TS of The SW 1998. D 6/20/1998 Bp Claude Edward Payne P 6/29/1999 Bp Leopoldo Jesus Alard. m 1/12/1985 Gregg P Bennett c 2. Vic S Mart's Epis Ch Copperas Cove TX 2002-2004; S Paul's Ch Waco TX 1998-2002. sgbennett@austin.rr.com

BENNETT, Susan Parker (At) 141 Proctors Hall Rd Apt 2, Sewanee TN 37375 B Orangeburg SC 2/23/1952 d Marion Walker Parker & Mattie Edmonds. BA U NC 1974; MDiv The TS at The U So 2011. D 12/18/2010 Bp J(ohn) Neil Alexander. c 3. susanbennett@hotmail.com

BENNETT, Thaddeus Albert (Vt) 17 Lane Dr, Newfane VT 05345 **Consult ECF Inc New York NY 2011-; NDNV Coordntr The ECF New York NY 2010-** B New York NY 9/3/1952 s Earl Donald Bennett & Betty. BA Dart 1976; MDiv GTS 1980. D 6/14/1980 P 1/24/1981 Bp Morgan Porteus. m 5/28/2004 George T Connell. Cn Dio Vermont Burlington VT 2001-2010; R S Mary's In The Mountains Wilmington VT 2001-2010; Cn Dio Los Angeles Los Angeles CA 1995-2001; Int S Mk's Par Altadena CA 1994-1995; Int S Mk's Par Berkeley CA 1992-1993; Exec Dir of AIDS Mnstrs Dio Connecticut Hartford CT 1987-1992; P Ch Of The Gd Shpd Hartford CT 1980-1987. Auth, *Fresh Start: A Resource for Cong and Cler in Transition*, DFMS, 2000; Auth, *Being Chr in Age of AIDS*, DFMS, 1995; Auth, *Epis Guide To TAP (Teens for AIDS Prevention)*, DFMS, 1994; Auth, *The Poor Pay More: Food Shopping in Hartford*, 1986. thadinvt@svcable.net

BENNETT, Thomas Edward (EMich) 337 Orchard St, Standish MI 48658 B Gateshead UK 12/21/1917 s Thomas Bennett & Mary Louise. STh Montreal TS 1943; MA Estrn Michigan U 1969. Trans from Anglican Church of Canada 12/1/1953 as Priest Bp Richard S M Emrich. m 2/21/1988 Jacqueline L LaBrosse c 3. S Jn's Epis Ch Midland MI 1977-1985; S Paul's Epis Ch Gladwin MI 1971-1977; R S Paul's Epis Ch Port Huron MI 1956-1969; Asst S Jn's

Epis Ch Midland MI 1953-1956. "God Had Other Plans," Bay-Arenac Intermediate Sch Dist, 2004; "An Autobiography". jbennett6848@charter.net

BENNETT, Virginia Lee (Spr) 1404 Gettysburg Lndg, Saint Charles MO 63303 **Dep to GC Dio Springfield Springfield IL 2003-; R S Andr's Epis Ch Edwardsville IL 1996-** B Des Moines IA 5/4/1946 d Clifton Elvin Keller & Dorothy Sue. DC Cleveland Chiropractic Coll 1972; AA Missouri Bapt Med Cntr, Sch of Nrsng 1981; Eden TS 1986; MA/MDiv Aquinas Inst of Theol 1988; DMin SWTS 1993. D 6/4/1989 P 1/25/1990 Bp William Augustus Jones Jr. c 2. Co-Chair Of BEC Dio Springfield Springfield IL 1997-2002; R S Mich And All Ang Ch Mssn KS 1994-1995; R All SS Ch Florence SC 1993-1994; Int S Fran Epis Ch Eureka MO 1992-1993; Assoc S Mich & S Geo Clayton MO 1990-1992; Cur Ch Of The Gd Shpd S Louis MO 1989-1990; Cur S Mich & S Geo Clayton MO 1989-1990. Auth, "(3 Homilies) Homilies For The Chr People," 1989. Ma/Mdiv w hon Aquinas Inst Of Theol 1988. ginnybennett@charter.net

BENNETT, Vivian Rose (Be) Rr 3 Box 14b, Meshoppen PA 18630 B Mount Ephraim NJ 5/1/1937 d Hugh McMillan Kerr & Alice Ethel Bertha. BA Glassboro St U 1964; Cert Widener U 1977; Cert Trng & Formation for Deacons Dio Pennsylvania 1992. D 2/20/1993 Bp Franklin Delton Turner P 3/25/2001 Bp Paul Victor Marshall. m 3/30/1957 Normand Joseph Bennett c 3. S Ptr's Epis Ch Tunkhannock PA 2009; Prince Of Peace Epis Ch Dallas PA 2002-2005; S Ptr's Epis Ch Tunkhannock PA 1998-2002; Chr Ch Media PA 1995-1998; Ch Of S Jn The Evang Philadelphia PA 1990-1993. NAAD 1990-2001. vrbennett@switchol.com

BENNETT JR, William Doub (NC) Po Box 28024, Raleigh NC 27611 **Assoc R Ch Of The Gd Shpd Raleigh NC 1999-** B Greenville NC 3/29/1955 s William Doub Bennett & Ruby. BA E Carolina U 1978; MDiv STUSo 1994. D 6/24/1994 Bp Huntington Williams Jr P 12/1/1994 Bp Harry Woolston Shipps. m 9/8/2001 Jessica Nicole Whaley Kozma. Vic Trin Ch Cochran GA 1996-1999; Vic Chr Epis Ch Cordele GA 1994-1999; S Matt's Epis Ch Fitzgerald GA 1994. Alb Inst; Associated Parishes; Cath Fllshp Of The Epis Ch; Liturg Conf. assoc2@ggs.nasmail.net

✠ **BENNISON JR, Rt Rev Charles Ellsworth** (Pa) 240 S 4th St, Philadelphia PA 19106 **Bp of Pennsylvania Dio Pennsylvania Philadelphia PA 1997-** B Minneapolis MN 11/30/1943 s Charles Bennison & Marjorie. BA Lawr 1965; SWTS SWTS 1966; BD Harvard DS 1968; ThM Harvard DS 1970; MA Claremont TS 1977; Fllshp Coll of Preachers 1979; STM UTS 1992; DD EDS 1997. D 9/13/1968 P 7/13/1969 Bp Charles Bennison Con 2/22/1997 for Pa. m 6/17/1967 Joan Kathryn Reahard c 2. Dir of Congrl Stds EDS Cambridge MA 1992-1997; R S Lk's Epis Ch Atlanta GA 1988-1992; Fndr/P-in-c S Clare Of Assisi Rancho Cucamonga CA 1986-1988; R S Mk's Epis Ch Upland CA 1971-1988. Auth, *In Praise of Congregations*, Cowley Press, 1999; Auth, "arts & Revs," *ATR*. cebennison@verizon.net

BENO, Brian Martin (FdL) 17 Yorkshire Dr, Fond du Lac WI 54935 **Dn S Paul's Cathd Fond du Lac WI 2008-** B Milwaukee WI 4/9/1949 s Emil Victor Beno & Hedwig Martha. BA St. Fran Sem Coll Milwaukee WI 1971; MDiv St. Fran Sem Milwaukee WI 1976; CAS SWTS 2001. Rec from Roman Catholic 3/22/2005 Bp Russell Edward Jacobus. m 2/6/2005 Theresa L Hansen. R S Mk's Ch Waupaca WI 2005-2008. brianbeno@charter.net

BENSHOFF, Bruce L (Mass) 30 Peirce St, Middleboro MA 02346 **Asst S Jn's Ch Sandwich MA 2004-; co-Mssnr Bristol Cluster Taunton MA 2003-; Dioc Counsel Dio Massachusetts Boston MA 1984-** B Ravenna OH 4/6/1943 s Robert Benshoff & Eleanor Sue. BA Kent St U 1966; MDiv Andover Newton TS 1971. D 6/26/1971 Bp John Harris Burt P 6/8/1972 Bp Charles F Hall. m 4/12/1965 Joanne R Romano c 2. R Ch Of Our Sav Middleboro MA 1981-2003; Ecum Cmsn Dio Wstrn Massachusetts Springfield MA 1977-1981; Vic S Dav's Ch Feeding Hills MA 1975-1981; Asst R S Alb's Epis Ch Annandale VA 1974-1975; Cur S Jn's Ch Portsmouth NH 1971-1974. Hon Citizen Awd Town Of Agawam. wolf5011@verizon.net

BENSON, David Howard (Mo) 6309 Burnham Cir Apt 323, Inver Grove Heights MN 55076 B New Haven CT 7/15/1928 s John Leonard Benson & Lillie Marie. Augustana Coll 1948; U Tor 1950; BA U MN 1952; MDiv SWTS 1957. D 6/24/1957 P 2/8/1958 Bp Hamilton Hyde Kellogg. m 9/15/1950 Betty Alwin c 3. Asst-Non stipendary Emm Epis Ch Webster Groves MO 1982-2003; Chair of the Epis City Mssn Dio Missouri S Louis MO 1976-1980; Long-R Plnng Com Dio Missouri S Louis MO 1972-1975; S Ptr's Epis Ch St Louis MO 1965-1981; Assoc S Jn The Evang S Paul MN 1961-1965; CE Dept Dio Minnesota Minneapolis MN 1958-1963; Vic Ch Of The Gd Samar Sauk Cntr MN 1957-1961; Vic S Steph's Epis Ch Paynesville MN 1957-1961. Auth, "A Field Study of End User Computing," *MIS Quarterly*, 1983. MDiv mcl SWTS Evanston IL 1957; BA mcl U MN Minneapolis MN 1952. dhb-bab@comcast.net

BENSON, E(llen) Heather (CNY) 60 Elm St, Ilion NY 13357 **Trin Epis Ch Canastota NY 2004-; Trin Epis Ch Canastota NY 2004-** B Camp LeJeune NC 2/11/1944 d Alexander Ross Benson & Claire Ellen. BA Washington Coll 1965; MDiv EDS 1976; ThM U Tor 1987. D 6/12/1976 P 4/25/1978 Bp Lyman Cunningham Ogilby. S Geo's Ch Utica NY 2000-2003; S Paul's Ch Utica NY 1999-2004; Vic S Mk's Ch Clark Mills NY 1995-1998; S Geo's Ch Utica NY 1990-1999; Epis Mnstry Whitesboro NY 1990-1998; S Ptr's Ch Oriskany NY 1990-1998; Paris Cluster Chadwicks NY 1988-1989; Trin Ch Lowville NY 1986-1987; Int R Trin Ch Lowville NY 1985-1986; Vic Ch Of The H Comm Lakeview NY 1983-1984; Trin Epis Ch Hamburg NY 1983-1984. SBL. MDiv w dist EDS Cambridge MA 1976. hthrbenson@aol.com

BENSON, George Andrew (Neb) 8800 Holdrege St, Lincoln NE 68505 B Cincinnati OH 1/3/1952 s George A Benson & Ann Caroline. BA S Louis U 1973; MDiv GTS 1976; STM UTS 1977; MBA W Texas A&M U 1982. D 8/22/1976 Bp William Augustus Jones Jr P 2/20/1977 Bp George Leslie Cadigan. m 12/29/1974 Katherine Klamon c 1. S Dav Of Wales Epis Ch Lincoln NE 2006-2011; New Life Epis Cluster Seward NE 2003-2005; S Mk's Epis Ch Aberdeen SD 1998-2003; Cmsn On Recon Dio So Dakota Sioux Falls SD 1996-2003; Pres Of Stndg Com Dio So Dakota Sioux Falls SD 1996-2003; Dio So Dakota Sioux Falls SD 1995-1998; S Matt's Epis Ch Rapid City SD 1994; S Steph's Ch Blytheville AR 1994; Vic S Steph's Ch Blytheville AR 1986-1994; Calv Epis Ch Osceola AR 1983-1994; Cmsn On Mssn And Mnstry Dio NW Texas Lubbock TX 1980-1983; Dio NW Texas Lubbock TX 1979-1983; Instr In Bible Dept Dio NW Texas Lubbock TX 1979-1982; Vic Epis Ch Of S Geo Canyon TX 1979-1982; Asst S Nich' Epis Ch Midland TX 1978-1979; Cur The Ch Of The Epiph New York NY 1976-1978. Auth, "Will The Byte From The Apple Be More Than We Can Swallow?"; Auth, "Computing & Ethics: Where To Next?". Outstanding Young Men Of Amer. gabinne@inebraska.com

BENSON, H William (NY) 1 Tongore Kill Rd, Olivebridge NY 12461 B Mount Vernon NY 7/22/1939 s Harold Benson & Jean. BA CUNY 1961; STB GTS 1965; MLS Pratt Inst 1971. D 6/12/1965 P 12/1/1968 Bp Horace W B Donegan. Assoc Ch Of The Ascen New York NY 1967-1976; Cur S Ptr's Epis Ch Peekskill NY 1965-1967.

BENSON, J(ohn) Bradley (Roch) 110 Robie St, Bath NY 14810 **Dep, GC Dio Rochester Rochester NY 2010-; Dist Dn Dio Rochester Rochester NY 2008-; Stndg Com Dio Rochester Rochester NY 2008-; Vic Ch Of The Gd Shpd Savona NY 2005-; R S Thos' Ch Bath NY 2005-** B 7/10/1953 s Gilbert Eugene Benson & Gwendolyn Billie. BA U of Wyoming 1975; MFA Syr 1981; MDiv Bex 2001. D 6/1/2002 P 3/1/2003 Bp Jack Marston McKelvey. m Carl Johengen. Pres, Stndg Com Dio Rochester Rochester NY 2009-2010; Co-chair Transition Com Dio Rochester Rochester NY 2008-2009; Cur The Ch Of The Epiph Rochester NY 2002-2005. bradbenson28@hotmail.com

BENSON, Kathleen (Del) 4830 Kennett Pike Apt 2537, Wilmington DE 19807 **P-in-c Imm Ch Highlands Wilmington DE 2004-** B ChattanoogaTN 5/29/1929 d Henry Bond & Kathleen James. VTS; BA Van 1951; Med U of Delaware Newark 1972; MDiv Lancaster TS 1985. D 6/15/1985 Bp William Hawley Clark P 4/1/1986 Bp Quintin Ebenezer Primo Jr. m 4/24/2004 Robert Benson c 3. Int S Lk's Epis Ch Seaford DE 1994-1995; Stndg Com Dio Delaware Wilmington DE 1992-1996; Dio Delaware Wilmington DE 1986-1988; Assoc S Jas Epis Ch Newport Newport DE 1986-1988; Vic S Nich' Epis Ch Newark DE 1985-1993. Delaware Epis Cleric Assoc, EWC.

BENSON, Ricky Lynn (Tex) 1616 Driftwood Ln, Galveston TX 77551 B San Diego CA 11/11/1948 s Jack L Benson & Bette Jane. BA U of the Incarnate Word 1976; MDiv STUSo 1983. D 6/29/1983 Bp Stanley Fillmore Hauser P 1/6/1984 Bp Scott Field Bailey. m 5/6/2006 Susan Wilson c 4. S Mk's Epis Ch Richmond TX 2003-2009; St Lk's Epis Hosp Houston TX 2002-2003; R Gr Ch Galveston TX 1990-2002; Assoc R S Steph's Ch Beaumont TX 1988-1990; Dio W Texas San Antonio TX 1985-1988; Vic H Comm Epis Ch Yoakum TX 1983-1984; Vic S Jas Ch Hallettsville TX 1983-1984. abbaruah@sbcglobal.net

BENSON, Thomas E (Me) 21 Boyd St. Apt. 1406, Bangor ME 04401 **D S Jn's Ch Bangor ME 1978-** B Winthrop MA 11/30/1924 s John Thomas Benson & Beatrice. D 6/3/1978 Bp Frederick Barton Wolf. m 6/5/1948 Marteile Butler c 2. alohamaine@aol.com

BENSON, Virginia Hilary (Los) 1432 Engracia Ave, Torrance CA 90501 **S Andr's Par Torrance CA 2007-** B Orange CA 10/31/1951 d James Milton Benson & Lillian Abigail. BS U CA 1974; MS California St U 1979; ETSBH 1991; MDiv Ya Berk 1993. D 6/12/1993 Bp Chester Lovelle Talton P 1/15/1994 Bp Frederick Houk Borsch. Asst S Anselm Of Cbury Par Garden Grove CA 2005-2007; Asst S Wilfrid Of York Epis Ch Huntington Bch CA 2004-2005; P-in-c S Andr's Epis Ch Irvine CA 2000-2004; Int Chr Ch Par Redondo Bch CA 1999-2000; Assoc R S Cross By-The-Sea Ch Hermosa Bch CA 1994-1999; The Par Ch Of S Lk Long Bch CA 1993-1994. vhbparsonage@netscape.net

BENTER JR, Harry William (SwFla) 812 Augusta Dr, Sun City Center FL 33573 **Asst S Jn The Div Epis Ch Sun City Cntr FL 2006-** B Duluth MN 9/27/1935 s Harry Wiiliam Benter & Leona Breneman. BS Bradley U 1961; MS GW 1971; MDiv EDS 1989. D 6/10/1989 P 1/13/1990 Bp Edward Cole Chalfant. m 1/17/2004 Jacqualine H Hodous c 4. Asst R St Johns Epis Ch Tampa FL 2000-2002; Asst S Jn The Div Epis Ch Sun City Cntr FL

1996-2000; Assoc Trin-St Jn's Ch Hewlett NY 1989-1996. hwbenter@gmail.com

BENTLEY JR, John R (Tex) 15410 Misty Forest Ct., Houston TX 77068 **P Assoc for Pstr Care S Mart's Epis Ch Houston TX 2008-** B Houston TX 12/9/1942 s John Richard Bentley & Elizabeth L. U So 1966; BA U of No Texas 1972; MDiv VTS 1975. D 6/16/1975 Bp Scott Field Bailey P 6/15/1976 Bp John E Hines. m 12/11/1982 Pamela Bentley c 3. Dir of Pstr Care S Mart's Epis Ch Houston TX 2004-2008; R S Dunst's Epis Ch Houston TX 1984-2004; Dn of the Cntrl Convoc Dio Texas Houston TX 1980-1984; R S Ptr's Epis Ch Brenham TX 1977-1984; Asst S Mart's Epis Ch Houston TX 1975-1977. jrbentley42@gmail.com

BENTLEY, Susan Emmons (SwVa) 4515 Delray St Nw, Roanoke VA 24012 **R S Jas Ch Roanoke VA 2000-** B Chicago IL 8/5/1953 d Olin Neill Emmons & Mary. BA Hollins U 1975; MDiv SWTS 1990. D 6/25/1990 P 4/10/1991 Bp A(rthur) Heath Light. m 8/10/1985 Michael L Bentley c 3. P-in-c Gr Ch Radford VA 1999-2000; P-in-c S Thos Epis Christiansburg VA 1998-1999; P-in-c S Ptr's Epis Ch Callaway VA 1997-1998; Assoc S Lk's Ch Evanston IL 1991-1996; D Gr Ch Radford VA 1990-1991. DOK 2002. seb@rev.net

BENTLEY-SHELTON, Elizabeth Michael (Wyo) 2511 Coffeen Ave, Sheridan WY 82801 **D S Ptr's Epis Ch Sheridan WY 2003-** B Long Beach CA 3/3/1935 d James Stuby Bentley & Fanny Beatrice. BA Carleton Coll 1957. D 10/8/2003 Bp Bruce Edward Caldwell. m 5/26/1959 Richard Lee Shelton c 3.

BENVENUTI, Anne Cecilia (Chi) 4945 S Dorchester Ave, Chicago IL 60615 B Fullerton CA 6/21/1953 d Benjamin Benvenuti & Corinne. PhD U CA Los Angeles 1992. D 4/26/2009 Bp Jeffrey Dean Lee P 11/22/2009 Bp Victor Alfonso Scantlebury. m 6/22/2008 Elizabeth Jayne Louise Davenport. Ch Of S Paul And The Redeem Chicago IL 2010. anne.benvenuti@gmail.com

BENZ, Charles Frederick (NC) 4118 Pin Oak Dr, Durham NC 27707 B Chicago IL 5/5/1948 s Ralph A Benz & Charlotte M. BA U of Arizona 1971; BA Trin Bristol Gb 1976; MDiv CDSP 1978. D 9/7/1978 Bp Robert Bracewell Appleyard P 7/1/1979 Bp Robert Hume Cochrane. c 1. P-in-c S Alb's Ch Littleton NC 1993-2001; Dio San Diego San Diego CA 1987-1988; Asst Emm Epis Ch Mercer Island WA 1978-1981. Aafrc 1980; Nahd 1996; Npga 1987; Nsfre 1988; Sopgrt. Cert Planned Giving Exec 1988; Cert Fund Raising Exec 1987. chazbenz@mindspring.com

BERARD, Jeffrey Jerome (Mil) 1622 Quincy Ave, Racine WI 53405 B Racine WI 4/13/1956 s Francis Jerome Berard & Vera Maude. Cert Nash 1990. D 4/13/1991 Bp Roger John White. m 5/31/1986 Lynda Kay Klaus c 2. D S Mich's Epis Ch Racine WI 1991-2002; Chapl S Lk's Hosp Racine WI 1989-2001.

BERBERICH, Gloria Carroll (Va) 673 Evergreen Ave, Charlottesville VA 22902 B Fredericksburg VA 4/28/1928 d Carroll Prince Kennedy & Eula Pauline. BS Geo Mason U 1973; MDiv VTS 1976. D 5/22/1976 Bp John Alfred Baden P 5/21/1977 Bp Robert Bruce Hall. m 12/15/1951 John Valentine Berberich. Asst Chr Epis Ch Charlottesville VA 1985-2000; Vic S Lk's Simeon Charlottesville VA 1982-2000. gkberb@comcast.net

BERCKMAN, Edward Milton (Ga) 2517 Buena Vista Cir, Valdosta GA 31602 **Died 11/28/2009** B Changchow CN 2/7/1931 s James Hart Hoadley Berckman & Margaret Ruth. BA Wofford Coll 1952; BD Harvard DS 1958; MA U Chi 1966; PhD U Chi 1972. D 6/21/1958 Bp Frederic Cunningham Lawrence P 6/24/1959 Bp George Mosley Murray. c 3. Auth, "On Enemies and Enmities," *LivCh*, 1989; Auth, "Living Thankfully," *Forw*, 1988; Auth, "Tanya Beck: P, Psychol, Counslr," *Journ of Wmn Mnstrs*, 1984; Auth, "Urban Mnstry w a Human Face," *Wit*, 1982; Auth, "Heroes and Antiheroes in Chld's Television," *Chr Century*, 1979; Auth, "The Medium of Wrshp and its Message," *LivCh*, 1977. ECom 1979-1988. Polly Bond Awd ECom 1983. kberckman@valdosta.edu

BERCOVICI, Hillary Rea (NY) 8 Sound Shore Dr Ste 130, Greenwich CT 06830 **Sr Fell Trin Inst Greenwich CT 2004-** B New York NY 2/18/1954 s Ralph U Bercovici & Genevieve. BA Trin 1977; MDiv TESM 1983; PhD Un Grad Sch Cincinnati OH 1986. D 6/2/1984 P 12/18/1984 Bp Alden Moinet Hathaway. m 6/16/1979 Priscilla Williams Willams c 2. R S Mary's Ch Of Scarborough Scarborough NY 1989-2004; R S Mary's Epis Ch Pocomoke City MD 1986-1989; Asst Ch Of The Sav Ambridge PA 1984-1985. hbercovici@optonline.net

BERDAHL, Peder Grant (Ind) 4810 Crystal River Ct, Indianapolis IN 46240 B Fresno CA 2/19/1943 s Arthur Berdahl & Mildred. BA S Olaf Coll 1965; MDiv SWTS 1973. D 6/17/1973 P 12/16/1973 Bp Edward Clark Turner. m 1/28/1981 Betty Berdahl c 2. Cn Dio Indianapolis Indianapolis IN 2005-2008; Dn of the SE Deanry Dio Indianapolis Indianapolis IN 1994-1998; R S Paul's Ch Columbus IN 1988-2005; Pres of Stndg Com Dio Kansas Topeka KS 1984-1987; R S Andr's Ch Derby KS 1983-1988; Vic S Lk's Ch Wamego KS 1980-1983; Vic S Mk's Ch Blue Rapids KS 1980-1983; Assoc S Mk's Epis Ch Glen Ellyn IL 1975-1979; Vic Calv Ch Yates Cntr KS 1973-1975; Vic S Tim's Ch Iola KS 1973-1975. berdahl@mindspring.com

BERENDS, April L (Mil) St. Mark's Episcopal Church, 2618 N. Hackett Ave., Milwaukee WI 53211 **Mem, Stndg Com Dio Milwaukee Milwaukee WI 2010-2014; Mem, COM Dio Milwaukee Milwaukee WI 2009-2012; S Mk's Ch Milwaukee WI 2008-** B 11/13/1976 DAS Ya Berk; MDiv Yale DS 2002. D 12/22/2004 Bp James Hamilton Ottley P 7/22/2005 Bp Leopold Frade. m 6/8/2002 Michael Andrew Bunting c 1. Cathd of St Ptr & St Paul Washington DC 2005-2008.

BEREY, Edward Joseph (Cal) 42 Charles St Apt 122, Cotati CA 94931 **Died 12/24/2010** B New York NY 5/14/1930 s Joseph Berey & Irene. BA Guilford Coll 1951; MDiv GTS 1956. D 6/3/1956 P 12/1/1956 Bp Horace W B Donegan. c 4. "Elderberey (weekly column)," *The Cmnty Voice.com*, 2005.

BERG, Dustin David (O) Saint Mark's Church, 515 48th St NW, Canton OH 44709 **P-in-c S Mk's Ch Canton OH 2011-** B Bemidji MN 6/2/1980 s Palmer Eugne Berg & Constance Lynn. BA Concordia Coll 2002; Dplma Ya Berk 2007; MDiv Yale DS 2007. D 12/11/2006 P 6/29/2007 Bp Michael Gene Smith. m 1/30/2010 Heather Louise Hill. Supply Ch Of S Thos Berea OH 2010; Supply Gr Epis Ch Willoughby OH 2009-2010; Campus Chapl S Aid's Epis Ch Boulder CO 2007-2009. ddberg02@yahoo.com

BERG, James Christopher (Mich) 642 Woodcreek Dr, Waterford MI 48327 B Brooklyn NY 6/9/1948 s James Thomas Berg & Margaret Mary. BA Knox Coll 1970; MDiv GTS 1975; DMin GTF 1998; MA U of Detroit 2004. D 6/5/1976 Bp Jonathan Goodhue Sherman P 12/7/1976 Bp William Arthur Dimmick. m 5/24/1980 Elizabeth Eaton c 1. Dn of Oakland Convoc Dio Michigan Detroit MI 1990-1994; R S Andr's Ch Waterford MI 1987-2008; Emm Ch Detroit MI 1980-1985; Vic Chr Ch Calumet Laurium MI 1976-1980. Outstanding Adj Fac for 2007 Oakland Cmnty Coll 2007; Allen S Whitney Educ Awd U MI 1985; Phi Beta Kappa Knox Coll 1970. jcberg5301@comcast.net

BERGE JR, William Clark (Oly) 310 North K, Tacoma WA 98403 B 2/25/1958 s William Clark Berge & Eleanor Marian. BA Whitman Coll 1980; MDiv GTS 1984. D 6/30/1984 Bp Robert Hume Cochrane P 9/1/1985 Bp The Bishop Of Polynesia. Chr Ch Tacoma WA 1985-1989; Asst Ch Of S Mary The Vrgn New York NY 1984-1985. clarkssf@aol.com

BERGEN, Franklyn Joseph (Az) 4076 N Hidden Cove Pl, Tucson AZ 85749 B Waterbury CT 12/18/1935 s Franklyn Joseph Bergen & Doris Blanche. Fairfield U 1955; BA Boston Coll 1959; MA Boston Coll 1960; MDiv Weston Jesuit TS 1967; MA U CA 1970. Rec from Roman Catholic 12/8/1994 as Priest Bp Chester Lovelle Talton. m 9/2/1989 Patricia Ann Chase. All SS Epis Ch Las Vegas NV 2002-2004; Int Ch Of The H Apos Hilo HI 2000-2001; Assoc Ch Of The Apos Oro Vlly AZ 1999-2005; Int S Steph's Ch Sierra Vista AZ 1998-1999; Assoc Gr S Paul's Epis Ch Tucson AZ 1995-1998; Asst S Mk's Par Altadena CA 1994-1995. fjbergen@comcast.net

BERGER, Fred (Ia) 25111 Valley Drive, Pleasant Valley IA 52767 **D Trin Cathd Davenport IA 1996-** B Davenport IA 3/26/1934 s Fred Berger & Alice. JD U of Iowa 1957. D 11/16/1996 Bp Carl Christopher Epting. m 12/19/1956 Shirley Ann Vollmer.

BERGER, Jere Schindel (Alb) Montvert Road #1125, Middletown Springs VT 05757 **Supply P All SS Ch No Granville NY 1995-** B Philadelphia PA 9/17/1931 s Carl Oho Berger & Mary Hausman. BA Ob 1953; MDiv EDS 1956; STM UTS 1965; MFA Carnegie Mellon U 1969; PhD Carnegie Mellon U 1973. D 6/30/1956 Bp Joseph Gillespie Armstrong P 1/19/1957 Bp Oliver J Hart. m 8/28/1954 Josephine N Berger c 5. S Paul's Ch Salem NY 1989-1996; Trin Ch Rutland VT 1987; P-in-c S Thos' Epis Ch Brandon VT 1986-1987; P-in-c Zion Ch Manchester Cntr VT 1985-1986; Vic S Tim's Ch McKees Rocks PA 1967-1969; P-in-c Trin Ch Swarthmore PA 1966-1967; Assoc Gr Ch Amherst MA 1959-1964; Vic Ch Of The H Sprt Plymouth NH 1957-1959; Cur S Ptr's Ch Glenside PA 1956-1957. Auth, "The Wheelbarrow (play produced at Martinique Theatre, NY," *NY)*, 1968; Auth, "selected poems," *The Massachusetts Revs*, 1964; Auth, "selected poems," *The U of Massachusetts Literary mag*, 1962. Dorset Players 1996; Green Mtn Gld 1976-1990; Middletown Sprg Hist Soc 1986; Vermont Symphony Orchestra Chorus 1997. Danforth Fllshp Danforth Fndt 1965; Hon Mention Jennie Tane Awd for poetry 1964.

BERGER, Martha Branson (Mil) 1616 Martha Washington Dr, Wauwatosa WI 53213 **Int S Fran Ch Menomonee Falls WI 2011-** B Beatrice NE 6/9/1953 d Vernon Lee Branson & Jessie Marie. BA U of Kansas 1975; BSN U of Kansas 1977; MA U of Kansas 1983; MDiv Nash 1996. D 5/18/1996 P 11/23/1996 Bp Roger John White. m 7/16/1983 William Langston Berger c 2. Int S Lk's Ch Racine WI 2006-2009; P-in-c S Anskar's Epis Ch Hartland WI 2004-2006; Int S Dav Of Wales Ch New Berlin WI 2002-2003; Int S Mart's Ch Brown Deer WI 2001-2002; Int S Jas Ch W Bend WI 1999-2001; Int S Jn In The Wilderness Elkhorn WI 1998-1999; Int S Thos Of Cbury Ch Greendale WI 1997-1998. martha.branson.berger@gmail.com

BERGERON, Mary Lee (ETenn) 6823 Sheffield Dr, Knoxville TN 37909 **P Assoc Ch Of The Ascen Knoxville TN 2008-** B Huntsville TX 7/5/1940 d Lawrence Dixon Clepper & Verna Mae. BS Louisiana Coll 1963; MS Case Wstrn Reserve U 1965; TS 2004. D 6/28/1998 Bp Robert Gould Tharp P 6/12/2004 Bp Charles Glenn VonRosenberg. m 9/7/1968 Paul H Bergeron c 3. Cn S Jn's Epis Cathd Knoxville TN 2004-2007; D S Jn's Epis Cathd Knoxville TN 1999-2004. Ord of S Lk. mlbergeron@stjohnscathedral.org

B

BERGESEN, David E(chols) (Colo) 8231 N Wheatfield Dr, Tucson AZ 85741 **Assoc Chr The King Ch Tucson AZ 1994-** B Coronado CA 8/12/1928 s Alf Ole Ruh Bergesen & Virginia Chloe. Dart; BA W&M 1954; BD VTS 1958; Spanish Lang Sch San Jose Cr 1962; STM GTS 1968. D 6/13/1958 Bp Frederick D Goodwin P 6/13/1959 Bp Robert Fisher Gibson Jr. m 10/22/1971 Victoria Ann Connelly c 2. Exec Coun Appointees New York NY 1987-1993; R S Tim's Epis Ch Centennial CO 1979-1987; Dio Colorado Denver CO 1974-1979; Dir Of Theol Educ Dio Colorado Denver CO 1974-1978; Grad Stdt The GTS New York NY 1967-1968; Asst Truro Epis Ch Fairfax VA 1958-1960. Auth, "Able on the Way!," Xlibris, 2007; Auth, "Back in battery," Xlibris, 2007; Auth, "Murder Crosses The Equator," Recovery Cmncatn, 1998; Auth, "Manual Del Libro De Oracion Comun," Iseta, 1993; Auth, "Manual Del Pstr," Iglesia Epis Del Ecuador, 1992; Auth, "Manual De Liturgia," Iseta, 1990; Auth, "Manual De Teologia," Iseta, 1989. dandvbergesen@yahoo.com

BERGH JR, P A (Ida) 180 kings court, mountain home ID 83647 B Watertown SD 5/9/1934 s Palmer A Bergh & Bertina. BS So Dakota St Coll 1957. D 1/29/1994 P 10/1/1994 Bp John Stuart Thornton. m 8/5/1955 Roberta J Hunter c 4. Cn S Jas Ch Mtn Hm ID 1994-2006. pabobergh@msn.com

BERGIE, Patricia (Wyo) Po Box 903, Fort Washakie WY 82514 **D Our Fr's Hse Ft Washakie WY 1996-** B WY 10/6/1946 d Enos Enos & Barbara. Cert Cntrl Bus Coll 1965. D 7/21/1996 Bp Bob Gordon Jones. m 8/27/1969 Frank Bergie c 1.

BERGIN, Joseph Alphonsus (CNY) 1612 W Genesee St, Syracuse NY 13204 **R Chr Epis Ch Jordan NY 2010-** B Dublin IE 7/29/1935 s Patrick Christopher Bergin & Mary. Cert Dominican Hse Of Stds 1961; BA U Coll Cork Cork Ie 1964. Rec from Roman Catholic 10/15/1991 as Priest Bp William L Stevens. m 6/9/1990 Loreen Madeline Hedlund. S Mk The Evang Syracuse NY 1996-2007. jam6358822@aol.com

BERGMANN, J(ohn) Stephen (O) 577 Wetherby Terrace Dr, Ballwin MO 63021 **Asst S Ptr's Epis Ch St Louis MO 2006-; Trst Bex Columbus OH 2002-** B Saint Louis MO 1/31/1942 s John Henry Bergmann & Dorthea Louise. U of Indianapolis and Chr Theol Seminar; BA Drury U 1964; BD Bex 1968. D 6/22/1968 Bp George Leslie Cadigan P 12/22/1968 Bp Roger W Blanchard. m 2/24/1990 Nancy Ellen Vandeveter c 2. Int S Matt's Par Of Jamestown Jamestown RI 2004-2006; Int S Mary's Ch Portsmouth RI 2003-2004; Int S Chris's By-The River Gates Mills OH 2001-2003; R S Paul's Epis Ch Medina OH 1995-2001; Dioc Coun Dio W Missouri Kansas City MO 1992-1995; R Calv Epis Ch Sedalia MO 1991-1995; Dn of Cntrl Dnry Dio W Missouri Kansas City MO 1991-1995; S Jn's Ch Washington IN 1991; Int P S Jn's Ch Washington IN 1990; R S Tim's Ch Indianapolis IN 1986-1990; Stndg Com Dio Missouri S Louis MO 1977-1986; R Chr Ch Cape Girardeau MO 1970-1986; Cur S Alb's Epis Ch Of Bexley Columbus OH 1968-1970. Bex, Rochester NY 2002; Dioc Camp Bd, Dio W Missouri 1991-1995. jsb42@charter.net

BERGMANN, William Carl (WMass) 85 E Main St, Ayer MA 01432 **BEC Dio Wstrn Massachusetts Springfield MA 2002-; P-in-c The Chap Of All SS Leominster MA 2002-; Ch Of The Gd Shpd Clinton MA 1994-** B Syracuse NY 11/28/1952 s Donald Eugene Bergmann & Isabel. BS Loyola U 1974; MDiv Nash 1979; MA Sem Of The Immac Concep Huntington NY 1991; ThD Bos 2001. D 6/9/1979 Bp Quintin Ebenezer Primo Jr P 12/8/1979 Bp James Winchester Montgomery. m 10/10/1998 Maria M Galvin c 5. Assoc S Mich's-On-The-Heights Worcester MA 2000-2002; Int Chr Ch Fitchburg MA 1999-2000; Dio Wstrn Massachusetts Springfield MA 1994-2003; Int S Mk's Ch Leominster MA 1994-1996; R Trin Ch Northport NY 1988-1992; Cmsn On Higher Educ Dio Chicago Chicago IL 1983-1988; R S Ann's Ch Woodstock IL 1982-1988; Cur S Paul's Ch Dekalb IL 1979-1982. AAR, SBL 1993-2000; Napts 1994; Soc Of S Jn The Evang 1977. Mdiv cl Nash Nashotah WI 1979. wmbergmann@aol.com

BERGMANS, Susan Estelle (Cal) 16401 San Pablo Ave Spc 137, San Pablo CA 94806 B Berkeley CA 6/18/1944 d Hubert Francis Bergmans & Lois Dorothy. RN Highland Sch Of Nrsng Oakland CA 1967; MDiv CDSP 1975. D 6/28/1975 Bp George Richard Millard P 1/5/1977 Bp C Kilmer Myers. The Parsonage San Francisco CA 1991-1992; Int The Epis Ch Of The Gd Shpd Berkeley CA 1984-1985; Asst The Epis Ch Of The Gd Shpd Berkeley CA 1979-1983; Dep Vic S Clare's Epis Ch Pleasanton CA 1976-1977; Assoc S Anselm's Epis Ch Lafayette CA 1975-1976. Integrity. churchseb@aol.com

BERGNER, Mario Joseph (Spr) 149 Asbury St, South Hamilton MA 01982 B Thet Ford Mines QC CA 11/29/1958 s Richard Karl Bergner & Jinette Madieline. BFA U of Wisconsin 1985; MDiv TESM 1995. D 2/15/2001 P 2/17/2001 Bp Keith Lynn Ackerman. m 5/11/1996 Nancy Ruth Pearce c 5. Assoc R Chr Ch So Hamilton MA 2006-2009; D S Andr's Ch Peoria IL 2001-2006. "Setting Love In Ord," *Bk*, Baker Bk Hse, 1995. mario@redeemedlives.org

BERGSTROM, Carl Edwin (Mass) 2914-109 Street, #1211, Edmonton AB T6J 7E8 Canada B Medford MA 12/1/1929 s Carl Edwin Bergstrom & Ellen Sigrid. BA Butler U 1952; MDiv VTS 1958. D 5/31/1958 Bp William A Lawrence P 12/16/1958 Bp Robert McConnell Hatch. m 9/17/1988 Patricia Marjorie Lyons c 7. Supply P S Lk's Epis Ch Malden MA 1994-1997; Vic Gr Ch Oxford MA 1963-1964; Vic S Thos Epis Ch Auburn MA 1959-1964. pcbergstrom@shaw.ca

BERGSTROM, Fiona M (NC) 113 W Nash St, Southport NC 28461 B Letchworth Hertfordshire UK 12/1/1942 d Robert Gillepsie Richardson & Nan Wallace. BA Trenton St Coll 1992; MDiv Duke 1995; CAS STUSo 1995. D 3/28/1987 Bp Roger John White P 12/21/1995 Bp Robert Carroll Johnson Jr. m 6/9/1965 Lars Anders Bergstrom c 2. Vic S Cyp's Ch Oxford NC 2000-2006; R S Steph's Ch Oxford NC 2000-2006; The Epis Ch of Oxford Oxford NC 2000-2006; Asst R All SS' Epis Ch Concord NC 1996-2000; S Mk's Epis Ch Raleigh NC 1995-1996; Admin for COM Dio New Jersey Trenton NJ 1989-1991; D S Matt's Ch Pennington NJ 1988-1992; D S Ptr's Ch W Allis WI 1987-1988. EWC 1990-2006; Ord of S Lk 1998-2000. larsfiona@ec.rr.com

BERITELA, Gerard Frederick (CNY) 360 S Collingwood Ave, Syracuse NY 13206 **Liturg & Mus Cmsn Mem Dio Cntrl New York Syracuse NY 2007-; Ch Of The Sav Syracuse NY 2002-; Emm Ch E Syracuse NY 2002-** B Rochester NY 12/7/1954 s Frederick Francis Beritela & Clara V. BA St. Jn Fisher Coll 1977; MDiv Nash 1983; MA Syr 2001; Ph.D Syr 2009. D 7/22/1983 Bp William Harvey Wolfrum P 1/28/1984 Bp Addison Hosea. Mnstry Grant Com Dio Cntrl New York Syracuse NY 2004-2008; Jubilee Grant Com, Chair Dio Cntrl New York Syracuse NY 2001-2004; Assoc S Paul's Cathd Syracuse NY 2000-2001; Prog Com, Chair Dio Cntrl New York Syracuse NY 1999-2003; Gr Ch Mex NY 1994-2000; Int Emm Ch Adams NY 1993-1994; Int Zion Ch Adams NY 1993-1994; Int S Matt's Epis Ch Liverpool NY 1992-1993; Supply Dio Montana Helena MT 1988-1991; Vic S Paul's Ch Hamilton MT 1988; S Steph's Epis Ch Stevensville MT 1988; Majestic Mountains Mnstry Sheridan MT 1986-1988; Int S Steph's Epis Ch Aurora CO 1985-1986; Asst Calv Epis Ch Ashland KY 1983-1985. Auth, "Supergirls and Mild-Mannered Men: Gender Trouble in Metropolis," *The Amazing Transforming Superhero! Essays on the Revs of Characters in Comic Books, Film and Television.*, McFarland, 2007. Ba scl S Jn Fisher Coll Rochester NY 1977. gfberitela@aol.com

BERK, Dennis Bryan Alban (Be) 27 Grace Avenue, Schuylkill Haven PA 17972 B Akron OH 6/22/1965 s Clarence Clayton Berk & Olga Jane. BA Wheaton Coll 1986; MDiv U Tor 1990; DMin Lancaster TS 1998. Trans from Anglican Church of Canada 11/1/1995 Bp James Michael Mark Dyer. c 1. Int R Gr Epis Ch Kingston PA 2008-2009; Int Chr Memi Epis Ch Danville PA 2007-2008; S Andr's Epis Ch Lewisburg PA 2006-2007; Exec Coun Appointees New York NY 2003-2006; R S Alb's Epis Ch Reading PA 1996-2001; Hon. Assoc. S Mary's Epis Ch Reading PA 1994-1996. Auth, "Martyrs, SS and Sinners," Morris Pub, 2009; Auth, "Sprtl Sightseeing," Morris Pub, 2007; Auth, "Zambian Journ," Morris Pub, 2007; Auth, "Embracing Inclusion," Morris Pub, 1999; Auth, "Comprehensiveness in Anglicanism," UMI Press, 1998. Fraternity of Friends of St. Albans Abbey 2007. dberk@mirfield.org.uk

BERKAW JR, B Frederic (SC) St Pauls Episcopal Church, 111 Waring St, Summerville SC 29483 **D S Paul's Epis Ch Summerville SC 2007-** B Roanoke VA 10/9/1943 s Bergen Frederic Berkaw & Susanne Ellett. Va Poly Inst & St U 1965; BS Charleston Sthrn U 1968; MA Cetnral Michigan U Mt Pleasant MI 1978. D 9/8/2007 Bp Edward Lloyd Salmon Jr. m 10/24/1970 Mary G Groseclose. fredb@stpaulssummerville.org

BERKOWE, Kathleen Hawkins (Ct) 628 Main St, Stamford CT 06901 **Asst to the R S Jn's Ch Stamford CT 2010-** B Milwaukee WI 12/21/1951 d Robert Owen Hawkins. AB Harv 1973; JD Bos Sch of Law 1976; MDiv The GTS 2010. D 3/13/2010 P 9/25/2010 Bp Mark Sean Sisk. c 2. kberkowe@stjohns-stamford.org

BERKTOLD, Penny (Ore) 170 Brookside Dr, Eugene OR 97405 B Birmingham Warwickshire UK 2/8/1935 d John Redvers Webley & Clara. BS Minnesota St U Moorehead 1979; STB Universite de Leuven Leuven Belgium 1981. D 12/27/1982 Bp Matthew Paul Bigliardi. m 7/20/1974 Theodore Anthony Berktold c 3. Dn - Cntr for the Diac Dio Oregon Portland OR 1985-2008; Asst to the Par S Mary's Epis Ch Eugene OR 1983-2000. ESMA 1988-2004; NAAD 1982-2009. berktolds@earthlink.net

BERKTOLD, Theodore Anthony (Ore) 170 Brookside Dr, Eugene OR 97405 B Lake City MN 2/21/1946 s Engelbert John Berktold & Margaret Eleanor. BA S Mary's U MN 1967; BD EDS 1971; STM UTS 1972. D 6/30/1971 P 6/7/1972 Bp Philip Frederick McNairy. m 7/20/1974 Penny Webley c 3. R S Mary's Epis Ch Eugene OR 1982-2009; R S Jn's Ch Moorhead MN 1974-1979; Vic S Lk's Ch Detroit Lakes MN 1974-1979; Dio Minnesota Minneapolis MN 1972-1979. ESMHE, 1982-2009; Ord of S Lk 1982-2009. berktolds@earthlink.net

BERLENBACH, Betty Lorraine (Vt) 1961 Plains Rd., Perkinsville VT 05151 B Huntington NY 3/7/1944 d Joseph Charles Buehl & Elizabeth Marie. BA SUNY, Harper Coll 1966; MDiv PrTS 1983. D 6/11/1988 Bp George Phelps Mellick Belshaw P 4/15/1989 Bp Vincent King Pettit. m 8/27/1966 John Berlenbach c 2. Geth Ch Proctorsville VT 1995-2004; The Epis Ch Of The H Comm Fair Haven NJ 1990-1995; Gr Ch Pemberton NJ 1988-1989; Asst S

Dav's Ch Cranbury NJ 1982-1987. Auth, "Sharing Our Vision & Story," *Designs For CE*.

BERLENBACH, Kirk Thomas (Pa) 5720 Ridge Ave, Philadelphia PA 19128 **Com on Fin and Property, Chair Dio Pennsylvania Philadelphia PA 2010-; Dep to GC, C1 Dio Pennsylvania Philadelphia PA 2010-; Fin Revs Com Dio Pennsylvania Philadelphia PA 2010-; R S Tim's Ch Roxborough Philadelphia PA 2003-** B Philadelphia PA 1/26/1969 s Thomas Lake Berlenbach & Prudence. BA Ham 1991; MDiv PrTS 1994; MSW Rutgers-The St U 1995. D 5/9/1998 P 1/19/1999 Bp Joe Morris Doss. m 12/12/1992 Rebekah Arianntzi Sassi c 2. Dep to GC, C1 Dio Pennsylvania Philadelphia PA 2010; Prog Bdgt Com, Chair Dio Pennsylvania Philadelphia PA 2008-2010; Dioc Coun Dio Pennsylvania Philadelphia PA 2004-2010; Asst S Alb's Ch Newtown Sq PA 1999-2003. fatherkirk@comcast.net

BERLENBACH, Thomas Lake (NJ) 428 Jasper St, Camden NJ 08104 B Allentown PA 8/2/1940 s John Berlenbach & Virginia Irene. BA Penn 1963; MDiv PDS 1966; MA Glassboro St U 1983. D 6/16/1966 Bp Jonathan Goodhue Sherman P 12/17/1966 Bp Albert Ervine Swift. m 2/7/1992 Anna Maria. R Trin Epis Ch Vineland NJ 1992-1999; Asst Ch Of Our Sav Camden NJ 1986-1992; Asst Gr Ch In Haddonfield Haddonfield NJ 1976-1986; R Chr Ch Collingswood NJ 1968-1976; Cur S Anne's Ch Abington PA 1966-1968. Ord Of S Lk, AEHC.

BERLIN II, George Albert (Colo) 3155 Kendall St, Wheat Ridge CO 80214 **R Ch Of S Phil And S Jas Denver CO 2000-** B Denver CO 4/4/1948 s George A Berlin & Avis M. BA U of Nthrn Colorado 1970; LTh Epis TS In Kentucky 1973. Trans from Anglican Church of Canada 1/15/1979 Bp William Carl Frey. m 6/3/2000 Sarah Aline Butler c 3. Chr Epis Ch Denver CO 1987-1990; All SS' Epis Sch Vicksburg MS 1986-1987; Epis Ch Of S Jn The Bapt Breckenridge CO 1984-1986; Cur Epiph Epis Ch Denver CO 1976-1977. gberlinsab@aol.com

BERLIN, Sarah Aline (Colo) 3155 Kendall St, Wheat Ridge CO 80214 **S Jos's Ch Lakewood CO 2007-** B Denver CO 12/29/1948 d Leon Butler & Hester Ann. BA Coll of the Rockies 1973; MA Regis 1987. D 7/26/1987 Bp Paul Victor Marshall P 5/25/1994 Bp William Jerry Winterrowd. m 6/3/2000 George Albert Berlin c 2. Ch Of S Phil And S Jas Denver CO 2006; R Ch Of S Jn Chrys Golden CO 2002-2005; S Jn's Cathd Denver CO 1990-2002. Auth, "Contemplative Compassion," *Renovare*, Renovare, 2009; Auth, "Lectio Divina as a Tool For Discernment," *Sewanee Theol Revs*, Sewanee Theol Revs, 2000; Auth, "Caring Mnstry: A Contemplative Approach to Pstr Care," *Continuum*, Continuum, 1999; Auth, "Pstr Care & Centering Pryr," *Sewanee Theol Revs*, Sewanee Theol Revs, 1996. AIDS Interfaith Ntwk 1990-1994.

BERMAN, Elizabeth Sievert (Mass) 6 Heritage Dr, Lexington MA 02420 **Cn for Congregations Dio Massachusetts Boston MA 2011-** B Huron SD 4/23/1964 d Richard Edward Sievert & Ruth Fuller. BA Harv 1986; M. Ed. Harv 1992; MDiv EDS 1998. D 6/2/2001 Bp Barbara Clementine Harris P 6/8/2002 Bp M(arvil) Thomas Shaw III. m 8/18/1991 Mark Elliot Berman c 2. P-in-c Ch Of The Adv Medfield MA 2008-2011; Int Emm Epis Ch Wakefield MA 2006-2008; Asst S Eliz's Ch Sudbury MA 2001-2003. lberman@diomass.org

BERMUDEZ, Maria De Los Angeles (PR) Condominio Sagrado Corazon, Calle 1 Apt 711, Ponce PR 00716 Puerto Rico B 2/13/1930 D 5/13/1984 P 10/24/1984 Bp Francisco Reus-Froylan. Dio Puerto Rico S Just PR 1984-1993.

BERNACCHI, Jacqueline A (SD) 3600 25th St S, Fargo ND 58104 **Trin Epis Ch Watertown SD 2011-** B 10/1/1951 D 2/9/2001 P 2/9/2001 Bp Andrew Hedtler Fairfield. m 9/8/1991 Leslie P Bunker. Dio No Dakota Fargo ND 2001-2009; R All SS Ch Minot ND 2001-2007. JBERNACC@MIDCO.NET

BERNACKI, James Bernard (NC) P.O. Box 657, Albemarle NC 28002 **R Chr Ch Albemarle NC 2003-** B Buffalo NY 12/21/1950 s John B Bernacki & Lottie M. BA Canisius Coll 1975; EdM SUNY 1977; MDiv Chr The King Sem 1987; Cert SWTS 1990; DMin SWTS 2002. Rec from Roman Catholic 6/29/1990 Bp David Charles Bowman. m 9/9/1988 Sandra L Pulvino c 2. Gr Ch Ravenswood WV 1997-2003; S Jn's Ripley WV 1997-2000; R Chr Ch Point Pleasant WV 1994-2003; S Matt's Ch Buffalo NY 1991-1994. jbernacki@windstream.net

BERNAL, Jose J (Dal) 635 N Story Rd, Irving TX 75061 **R S Mary's Epis Ch And Sch Irving TX 2008-** B MX 10/28/1961 s Ernesto Bernal Mendoza & Florentina Cruz. MDiv Sem Jos/Guadalupe Mex Mx 1989; MA F.S.T. (Gtu) Berkeley CA 1995; CAS CDSP 2003. D 6/5/2004 P 6/4/2005 Bp William Edwin Swing. m 5/22/1993 Rosario Hernandez c 3. S Lk's Epis Ch Dallas TX 2007-2008; Dio California San Francisco CA 2005-2007. BERNALJJ@HOTMAIL.COM

BERNARD, Michael Allen (Kan) 305 Old Colony Ct, North Newton KS 67117 **Asst S Matt's Epis Ch Newton KS 2003-** B Winslow AZ 2/3/1945 s Bennett Owen Bernard & Emma Sue. D 11/8/1981 P 5/1/1982 Bp Richard Mitchell Trelease Jr. m 6/1/1968 Patricia Annette Austin. michaelbernard@cox.net

BERNARDEZ JR, Teogenes Kalaw (Nev) 832 N Eastern Ave, Las Vegas NV 89101 B Philippines 9/29/1969 s Teogenes Bernardez & Catherine S. Trans from Episcopal Church in the Philippines 7/3/2008 Bp Dan Thomas Edwards. m 11/20/2004 Clarice Kawi c 3. R S Lk's Epis Ch Las Vegas NV 2009. pammatik@yahoo.com

BERNARDI, Frank Alan (EpisSanJ) 1815 S Teddy St, Visalia CA 93277 B Merced CA 3/3/1970 BA California St U. D 8/18/2001 P 5/24/2003 Bp John-David Mercer Schofield. m 12/29/1995 Anne Elizabeth Douglas c 3.

BERNHARD, Margaret (Ore) 1180 NW Country Ct, Corvallis OR 97330 **Cmsn on Litugy and Mus Dio Oregon Portland OR 2011-; Dioc Coun Dio Oregon Portland OR 2011-; COM- Ord Dio Oregon Portland OR 2008-; D The Epis Ch Of The Gd Samar Corvallis OR 2006-; Comm. of CE and Life-long Dormation Dio Oregon Portland OR 1995-** B Orange NJ 5/5/1942 d William Thomas Maguire & Lorraine Kline. BA Cor 1964; M.ED W&M 1982. D 7/10/1990 Bp Robert Louis Ladehoff. m 6/27/1964 Robert Bernhard c 2. Chapl Dio Oregon Portland OR 2006-2008; D The Epis Ch Of The Gd Samar Corvallis OR 2002-2006; D The Epis Ch Of The Gd Samar Corvallis OR 1990-2002. CHS 1994. First Place on Sermon Competition Epis Evang Fndt,Inc. 1994; First Place in Sermon Competition Epis Evang Fndt,Inc. 1994. pegber@aol.com

BERNIER, Daniel L (Mass) PO Box 719, Wareham MA 02571 **R Ch Of The Gd Shpd Wareham MA 2010-** B Sanford ME 7/7/1963 s Ronald Ferdinand Bernier & Rachel. BA Wadhams Hall Sem Coll 1989; MDiv S Mary's Sem Baltimore MD 1993. Rec from Roman Catholic 4/9/2005 Bp V Gene Robinson. m 6/1/2001 Leslie A Bernier c 1. Vic Chr Ch Portsmouth NH 2005-2010. dan.bernier@goodshepherdwareham.org

BERRY JR, Barton Douglass (CPa) 256 Briar Ln, Chambersburg PA 17201 **Died 10/14/2011** B Atlanta GA 3/8/1941 s Barton Douglass Berry & Grace. BA Washington Coll 1963; MDiv PDS 1966. D 6/11/1966 P 3/8/1967 Bp Robert Lionne DeWitt. c 2. jberry@innernet.net

BERRY, Beverly DeWitt (Pa) 212 W Lancaster Ave, Paoli PA 19301 **Cler Assoc Ch Of The Gd Samar Paoli PA 2006-** B Cadillac MI 9/13/1951 d Wilfred DeWitt & Ella. BS Florida St U 1972; JD Florida St U 1985; MDiv TESM 2006. D 6/4/2006 P 12/10/2006 Bp Samuel Johnson Howard. m 8/21/1971 Michael Linden Berry. beverly@good-samaritan.org

BERRY JR, Charles Herbert (WTex) 317 Sidney Baker St S Ste 400 Pmb 230, Kerrville TX 78028 B Rochester MN 7/31/1927 s Charles Herbert Berry & Edith Lucille. BA Macalester Coll 1951; MDiv Bex 1954; S Geo's Coll Jerusalem IL 1977. D 2/21/1954 Bp Stephen E Keeler P 8/8/1954 Bp Hamilton Hyde Kellogg. m 12/27/1950 Zona Berry c 2. Dn of Cntrl Convoc Dio W Texas San Antonio TX 1983-1986; R S Steph's Epis Ch San Antonio TX 1971-1991; Prov Del Dio W Texas San Antonio TX 1971-1981; Asst S Lk's Epis Ch San Antonio TX 1965-1971; Asst R S Barn On The Desert Scottsdale AZ 1964-1965; Dio Olympia Seattle WA 1961-1964; Vic S Lk's Ch Sequim WA 1959-1964; S Paul's Epis Ch Port Townsend WA 1959-1964; Bp's Coun Dio Minnesota Minneapolis MN 1958-1959; R Chr Epis Ch Grand Rapids MN 1955-1959; S Paul's Epis Ch Duluth MN 1955-1959. czberry@cebridge.net

BERRY, Donald LeRoy (CNY) 49 University Ave, Hamilton NY 13346 **Supply The Ch Of The Epiph Sherburne NY 2007-** B Goshen IN 9/3/1925 s William Thomas Berry & Florence A. BA Goshen Coll 1947; BD U Chi 1950; STM Yale DS 1954; PhD Ya 1959. D 5/30/1971 P 4/13/1972 Bp Ned Cole. m 6/1/1957 Wanda Jean Warren c 2. Int S Paul's Ch Chittenango NY 2006-2007; Int S Thos Ch Hamilton NY 1998-2000; Int S Mk's Epis Ch Chenango Bridge NY 1993-1994; R S Geo's Epis Ch Chadwicks NY 1977-1990. Auth, "H Words and H Ord: As Dying Behold We Live," U Press of Amer, 2009; Auth, *Through a Glass Darkly: The Ambiguity of the Chr Tradition*, U Press of Amer, 2006; Auth, *Traveller's Advsry (Poems)*, Mellen Press, 1990; Auth, *Mutuality: The Vision of Mart Buber*, SUNY Press, 1985. dberry@colgate.edu

BERRY JR, Graham Pete (Chi) 1021 S Orange Grove Blvd, Unit 107, Pasadena CA 91105 **Asst S Mk's Par Altadena CA 2005-** B Riverside CA 11/5/1944 s Graham Gardner Berry & Cynthia. BS K SU 1979; MS K SU 1980; MDiv SWTS 1983. D 6/10/1983 Bp Arthur Anton Vogel P 1/1/1985 Bp James Winchester Montgomery. m 11/28/1987 Virginia Ann Braun c 2. S Bon Ch Tinley Pk IL 1992-1997; P-in-c Gr Epis Ch New Lenox IL 1991-1992; Ch of the H Name Dolton IL 1987-1991; Trin Epis Ch Lansing IL 1987-1991; Chr Ch Waukegan IL 1985-1987; D Ch Of The H Apos Wauconda IL 1983-1984. PeteBerry@earthlink.net

BERRY, John Emerson (NMich) 53245 State Highway M26, Lake Linden MI 49945 B Parkersburg WVA 1/27/1954 s Myron Garland Berry & Betty Marie. BA Ripon Coll 1976; Juris Doctor Thos M. Cooley Law Sch 1981. D 8/17/2005 P 2/26/2006 Bp James Arthur Kelsey. m 8/19/1978 Scarlet Berry c 4. jeberry@pasty.com

BERRY, Mary Helen (Miss) **S Matt's Epis Ch Kosciusko MS 2002-** D 6/13/1999 Bp Stephen Hays Jecko P 3/4/2000 Bp Alfred Clark Marble Jr.

BERRY JR, Max Bright (Okla) 2717 NW 24th St, Oklahoma City OK 73107 B Muskogee OK 3/26/1937 s Max Bright Berry & Juanita Alma. BS U of Oklahoma 1964; MDiv SWTS 1966; DMin Phillips U 1979. D 6/21/1969 P 12/14/1969 Bp Chilton Powell. m 11/3/1962 Carole Anne Haggard c 4. R Gr Ch Muskogee OK 1990-2004; Assoc R All Souls Epis Ch Oklahoma City OK 1988-1990; Vic S Edw Chap Oklahoma City OK 1982-1988; R S Dav's Ch

Oklahoma City OK 1981-1983; Assoc R S Dunst's Ch Tulsa OK 1980; Vic S Edw Chap Oklahoma City OK 1976-1980; R S Lk's Ch Chickasha OK 1972-1976; R Gd Shpd Epis Ch Sapulpa OK 1969-1972. Auth, *The Determination & Validation of Rel Experience in Two Mod Renwl Movements*. Bp's Awd the Rt Reverend Robert Moody,Dio Oklahoma 2004.

BERRYMAN II, Jerome Woods (Colo) 2353 Rice Blvd, Houston TX 77005 B Ashland KS 6/4/1937 s Jerome Charles Berryman & Marjorie Louise. BA U of Kansas 1959; MDiv PrTS 1962; JD U of Tulsa 1969; DMin PrTS 1996. D 7/28/1985 Bp Maurice Manuel Benitez P 12/10/1985 Bp Gordon Taliaferro Charlton. m 6/3/1961 Dorothea Grace Schoonyoung. H Sprt Epis Ch Houston TX 1994-1995; Chr Ch Cathd Houston TX 1985-1994. Auth, "Tchg Godly Play The Sunday Morning Handbook," Abingdon Press, 1995; Auth, "Godly Play," *An Imaginative Approach To Rel Educ*, Augsburg Press, 1995; Auth, "Young Chld & Wrshp," Westminster Jn Knox, 1989; Auth, "Life Maps: The Journey Of Human Faith," Word Press, 1978. ABA (Fam Law); Amer Montessori Soc; Assn Of Professors & Researchers In Rel Educ; Intl Seminar For Rel Educ & Values. jerome.berryman@godlyplay.org

BERSIN, Ruth Hargrave (Ct) 4 Holmes Rd, Boxford MA 01921 **Assoc Trin Ch Topsfield MA 2011-; Refugee Immigration Mnstry Malden MA 1998-** B LaPorte IN 9/16/1939 d Jacob Harold Hargrave & Rowena. BS Indiana U 1962; MA CRDS 1965; MDiv Ya Berk 1982; DMin GTF 1994; Ph.D. GTF 2008. D 6/11/1983 Bp Arthur Edward Walmsley P 5/2/1984 Bp Clarence Nicholas Coleridge. m 7/25/1976 Richard Lewis Bersin c 2. Assoc Gr Ch Lawr MA 1996-1999; Phoenix Cmnty Serv Burke VA 1995-1997; Ecum Cmsn Dio Washington Washington DC 1995-1996; Ch Of The Gd Shpd Burke VA 1994; Interfaith Conf Of Metropltn Wash Dc Washington DC 1992-1993; Tell 1989-1992; Ascen Ch New Haven CT 1989; Ecum Cmsn Dio Connecticut Hartford CT 1984-2005; Epis Soc Serv Ansonia CT 1983-1989. Auth, *Healing Traumatic Memories: A Sprtl Journey (Libr for the 21st Century)*, Peterson, Rodney, Eerdmans, 2002; Auth, *Basic Reading Skills*, 1983; Auth, *Let's Begin*, 1974; Auth, *Engl Through Folk Songs*, 1973. AAWW; AAPC 1992-2007; AEHC 1994-2003; Assn Fundraising Profsnl 1987-2003; IATSC 1994-2003; ISTSS 1995-1998; NSFRF. Humanitarian Awd Boston Theol Inst 2007. ruth.bersin@verizon.net

BERTOLOZZI, Michael Alan (Nev) 3625 Marlborough Ave, Las Vegas NV 89110 B Valdosta GA 9/10/1953 s Kenneth Alan Bertolozzi & Florence Ann. D 9/29/2000 Bp George Nelson Hunt III. m 12/1/1974 C Belinda Griffin. MICHEAL107@COX.NET

BERTRAND, Michael Elmore (WTex) 2310 N Stewart Rd, Mission TX 78574 **Vic St Ptr & St Paul Ch Mssn TX 2011-** B Homestead AFB FL 10/5/1977 s Richard Sherman Elmore & Charlene. BA U So 2000; MDiv Nash 2005. D 12/29/2004 P 8/7/2005 Bp Charles Edward Jenkins III. m 8/20/2005 Lydia Bertrand c 2. Dioc Coun Dio Wstrn Louisiana Alexandria LA 2009-2011; Com on Mus and Liturg Dio Wstrn Louisiana Alexandria LA 2009-2011; Cur S Jas Epis Ch Alexandria LA 2008-2011; Vic S Eliz's Mssn Collins MS 2006-2008; Vic S Steph's Ch Columbia MS 2006-2008; Cur S Paul's Ch New Orleans LA 2005. elmore21@msn.com

BESCHTA, Gerald Thomas (WNC) 175 Mimosa Way, Hendersonville NC 28739 **COM Dio Wstrn No Carolina Asheville NC 2007-** B Los Angeles CA 11/29/1940 s George John Beschla & Edith Mae. BS USC 1963. D 11/23/2002 Bp Robert Hodges Johnson. m 5/2/1987 Joyce Marie Pierce c 2. jerjoy@wildblue.net

BESCHTA, Joyce Marie (WNC) 65 Mimosa Way, Hendersonville NC 28739 **D Ch Of S Jn In The Wilderness Flat Rock NC 2006-** B Roanoke VA 7/18/1945 d Edgar Ross Pierce & Cora Emaline. - GW; BS MWC 1978. D 1/28/2006 Bp Granville Porter Taylor. m 5/2/1987 Gerald Thomas Beschta c 4. jerjoy@wildblue.net

BESENBRUCH, Peter Ray (Haw) 1679 California Ave, Wahiawa HI 96786 **Supply Cler S Matt's Epis Ch Waimanalo HI 2008-** B New York NY 2/1/1952 s Max Ludwig Besenbruch & Elizabeth Ann. BA Carleton Coll 1979; MDiv SWTS 1982; U of Hawaii 1987. D 6/24/1982 P 1/1/1983 Bp Robert Marshall Anderson. m 6/10/1979 Valarie Lynn Naughton. H Cross Kahuku HI 2001-2003; S Lk's Epis Ch Honolulu HI 2001; S Nich Epis Ch Kapolei HI 1999-2000; S Geo's Epis Ch Honolulu HI 1997-1998; S Steph's Ch Wahiawa HI 1990-1993; Ch Of The Epiph Honolulu HI 1986; P-in-c S Steph's Ch Wahiawa HI 1985-1990; Cur S Greg's Epis Ch Deerfield IL 1982-1984.

BESHEARS, Earl D (SwFla) 13050 Tigers Eye Dr, Venice FL 34292 **Assoc S Mk's Epis Ch Venice FL 2010-** B portsmouth, va 7/12/1946 s Howard Beshears & Lela Grace. BS No Carolina St U 1972; MS No Carolina St U 1974; MDiv VTS 2001. D 5/19/2001 Bp Martin Gough Townsend P 11/17/2001 Bp Charles Lindsay Longest. m 1/13/1968 Lydia J Beshears c 1. R S Paul's Ch Georgetown DE 2002-2010; Chr Ch St Michaels MD 2001-2002; Ch Of The Resurr Alexandria VA 1999-2001. jbeshears45@gmail.com

BESHEER, Kimbrough Allan (Oly) 600 1st Ave Ste 632, Seattle WA 98104 B Kansas City MO 8/15/1951 s Norman O Besheer & Patricia A. BA U of Missouri 1978; MDiv EDS 1981; Dplma Analytical Psychol CG Jung Inst 1991. D 6/20/1981 P 5/16/1982 Bp George Nelson Hunt III. c 2. Int Ch Of The H Sprt Vashon WA 2009-2010; Int S Fran Epis Ch Mill Creek WA 1997-1999; P-in-c Gr Ch Duvall WA 1996-1997; Int S Columba's Epis Ch And Chilren's Sch Kent WA 1995-1996; Emm Epis Ch Mercer Island WA 1994-1995; P-in-c S Geo Epis Ch Maple Vlly WA 1994-1995; Assoc S Steph's Epis Ch Longview WA 1983-1986; Asst S Aug's Ch Kingston RI 1981-1983. Intl Assn for Analytical Psychol 1991. kbesheer@jungseattle.com

BESIER, Bettine Elisabeth (RI) 30 Scotch Cap Rd, Quaker Hill CT 06375 **Vic S Thos' Alton Wood River Jct RI 1997-** B Denver CO 10/1/1957 d Rudolph Frederick Besier & Ruth Elinor. BS U of Connecticut 1979; MA SUNY 1981; MDiv Ya Berk 1988. D 6/10/1989 Bp Arthur Edward Walmsley P 12/15/1989 Bp Clarence Nicholas Coleridge. m 6/7/1986 James Albert Nuttall c 4. DRE Calv Ch Stonington CT 1995-1996; DRE S Jn's Epis Ch Niantic CT 1993-1995; Cur S Mk's Ch Mystic CT 1989-1993. jnuttall8@hotmail.com

BESS, Sandra S (RG) 8009 David Blvd #2310, North Richland Hills TX 76182 B Albuquerque NM 4/1/1943 d Earnest Murrell Bess & Barbara Frances. ABS Ft Hays St U 1969; MDiv CDSP 1977. D 9/23/1977 P 5/18/1978 Bp Richard Mitchell Trelease Jr. Assoc S Mich And All Ang Ch Albuquerque NM 1999-2006; Vic Epis Ch Of The Epiph Socorro NM 1988-1992; Stndg Com Dio The Rio Grande Albuquerque NM 1981-1983; Trans Pecos Reg Epis Mnstry Alpine TX 1979-1984; Dio The Rio Grande Albuquerque NM 1977-1978. Auth, "Grieving During the Holidays," *Crossroads of Life*, Natl Hospice Mgmt, 1998; Auth, "Hospice & You," *People of God*, Archdiocese of Santa Fe, 1997; Auth, "Coping w the Holidays," *People of God*, Archdiocese of Santa Fe, 1997. swsss@thuntek.net

BESS JR, Walter (Cal) 118 Tamalpais Rd, Fairfax CA 94930 B Dade County FL 1/30/1948 s Walter B Bess & Edna. BA New Coll of California 1974; MDiv Nash 1981. D 6/19/1982 P 12/1/1983 Bp William Edwin Swing. m 9/26/1982 Rebecca A Bess. Asst S Columba's Ch Inverness CA 1983-1987; Cur S Lk's Of The Mountains La Crescenta CA 1982-1983. walterbess@earthlink.net

BESSE, Alden (Mass) 86 Weaver Ln # 4069, Vineyard Haven MA 02568 B Syracuse NY 7/11/1924 s Arthur Lyman Besse & Eleanor. BA Harv 1948; MDiv VTS 1951. D 6/8/1951 Bp Frederick D Goodwin P 12/11/1951 Bp Noble C Powell. m 10/12/1957 Barbara Ham c 3. Gr Ch Vineyard Haven MA 1990-2003; Dn of Estrn and Sthrn Worcester Deaneries Dio Wstrn Massachusetts Springfield MA 1985-1988; R Trin Epis Ch Whitinsville MA 1980-1990; Dio Wstrn Massachusetts Springfield MA 1980-1989; Dn of Estrn Bay Deanry Dio Rhode Island Providence RI 1978-1980; Chair of Com on Extra-Dioc Missions Dio Rhode Island Providence RI 1975-1980; R St Mich & Gr Ch Rumford RI 1963-1980; Cathd Ch Of S Steph Harrisburg PA 1960-1990; R S Lk's Epis Ch Altoona PA 1957-1963; M-in-c S Lk's Ch Annapolis MD 1951-1957; Cur S Anne's Par Annapolis MD 1951-1956. Auth, "Gd News for You," *Forw Day by Day*, FMP. FWC 1969. Hon Cn of St. Steph's Cathd Epis Dio Cntrl Pennsylvania 1960.

BESSLER, Jeffrey Lee (Ind) 24 S 21st Street, Richmond IN 47374 **S Jas Ch Piqua OH 2011-** B Milwaukee WI 3/18/1950 BA Luther Coll. D 6/29/2002 P 7/13/2003 Bp Catherine Elizabeth Maples Waynick. m 1/14/1987 Alan Barry Cramer. Chr Ch Cathd Indianapolis IN 2006-2007; S Ptr's Ch Lebanon IN 2003-2006. BESSLERCRAMER@EARTHLINK.NET

BESSON JR, Michael Wallace (Tex) 9610 Roarks Psge, Missouri City TX 77459 **St. Lukes Hlth System Bd Dio Texas Houston TX 2010-; Stndg Com Dio Texas Houston TX 2010-; Vic St. Cathr Of Sienna Missouri City TX 2010-** B Beaumont TX 5/23/1965 s Michael Besson & Carol. BS Lamar U 1990; MDiv STUSo 2004. D 6/12/2004 Bp Don Adger Wimberly P 12/15/2004 Bp Rayford Baines High Jr. m 10/26/1991 Eleanor A Besson c 1. R S Jn's Ch La Porte TX 2006-2010; Asst. To R Ch Of The Gd Shpd Tomball TX 2004-2006. Urban T. Holmes Excellence In Preaching U So 2004. fathermike23@gmail.com

BEST, Stephen Warren (Oly) 17421 Ne 139th Pl, Redmond WA 98052 **P/Assoc For Couples And Fam Life S Thos Ch Medina WA 2002-** B Seattle WA 11/30/1957 s Irvin Warren Best & Patricia Ann. BA U of Washington 1980; MDiv PrTS 1984; MS Seattle Pacific U 1987. D 6/28/1997 P 1/13/2007 Bp Vincent Waydell Warner. m 10/28/1989 Mary Janine Adams c 1. D Ch Of The H Cross Redmond WA 1997-2001. Tertiary Of The Soc Of S Fran. stevewbest@aol.com

BETANCES, Ramon Antonio (At) 925 Whitlock Ave Apt 1308, Marietta GA 30064 **Dio Atlanta Atlanta GA 2007-; S Jude's Ch Marietta GA 2006-** B Dominican Republic 6/8/1961 s Antonio Betances & Andreita. St Thos Santo Domingo. Rec from Roman Catholic 12/3/2006 Bp J(ohn) Neil Alexander. m 11/15/2003 Gregoria Gregoria Cedano c 2. BETANCESCEDENO@HOTMAIL.COM

BETE, Vincent Songaben (Ia) 204 E. 5th St., Ottumwa IA 52501 **Vic Trin Ch Ottumwa IA 2009-** B Baguio City Philippines 12/30/1970 s Robert Bete & Francisca. Trans from Episcopal Church in the Philippines 6/18/2007 Bp Alan Scarfe. m 6/9/1995 Isabelle Bete c 3. vincentsbete@yahoo.com

BETENBAUGH, Helen R (CGC) 1025 Elm Dr, Providence Village TX 76227 B 2/10/1943 B.M. Westminster Choir Coll 1964; M.M. Peabody Conservatory of Mus 1967; M.Div. Perkins TS, SMU 1993; 1st, 2nd Degrees Usui Reiki 1996; D.Min. Perkins TS, SMU 1997; 3rd Degree Usui Reiki 1998; Lic Labyrinth Fac Veriditas 2000. D 6/29/1996 P 6/17/1997 Bp James Monte Stanton. m 6/5/1965 Gordon Murray Betenbaugh c 2. Receiving Disabil Ret 2006-2008; R S Lk's Ch Marianna FL 2004-2006; R S Alb's Epis Ch Wichita KS 1999-2003; Assoc Epis Ch Of The Ascen Dallas TX 1998-1999; Cur Ch Of The Gd Shpd Dallas TX 1996-1997; DCE The Epis Ch Of The Trsfg Dallas TX 1990-1996. Auth, "Journeys In Bldg The Ch Of Today," *Ruach*, EWC, 2001; Auth, "Disabil: A Lived Theolgy," *Theol Today*, PrTS, 2000; Co-Auth, "Prayers of Truth and Transformation," *Ch Mus Workshop*, Abingdon Press, 1998; Co-Auth, "Disabling The Lie: Prayers Of Truth And Transformation," *Human Disabil & The Serv Of God*, Abingdon Press, 1997; Auth, "ADA and the Ch: The Moral Case," *A Look Back: The Birth of the Americans w Disabil Act*, The Haworth Press, 1996; Auth, "ADA and the Ch: The Moral Case," *Journ of Rel in Disabil & Rehab*, Haworth Pstr Press, 1996; Auth, "The Ch and Disabil: A Trin of Issues," *Disabil Stds Quarterly*, Brandeis Univ. Press, 1995; Auth, "Not Frederick," *Re-Imagining*, Re-Imagining Cmnty, 1995; Auth, "A Vessel Full Of Hist," *Re-Membering & Re-Imagining*, Re-Imagining Cmnty, 1995; Auth, "Disabil In The Wrld Of The Hebr Scriptures," *Catechist*, Ptr Li, Inc., 1994; Ed, "Prog Bk (232 pgs)," *Natl Conv Guide 1994*, AGO, 1994; Auth, "Transforming The M.D.eity," *A Journ Of Wmn Mnstrs*, ECUSA, 1993; Auth, "A Letter from Leah," *A Letter from Leah*, EWC, Dio Dallas, 1992; Auth, "22 arts 1968-1988," *Var Ch Mus Journ & AGO*, Var, 1968. AGO 1962; AGO 1963-2008; AAM 1991; EWC 1991; Integrity 1996; Mensa 1979; No Amer Acad Of Liturg 1999; The Labyrinth Soc 1999. Who's Who Madison 2006; Biographee Internatiional Who's Who of Bus & Profsnl Wmn 2005; Who's Who in the Wrld 2004; Biographee Dictionary of Intl Biography 2004; Wmn of the Year Intl Biographical Cntr 2004; Who's Who in Amer 2003; Who's Who in Mus Intl Who's Who in Mus 2003; Biographee Intl Who's Who of Bus and Profsnl Wmn 2000; Who's Who of Amer Wmn 1997; Soc Ethics B'Nai B'rith 1993; Graduation Awd in Soc Ethics B'Nai B'rith, Dallas at Perkins, SMU 1993; Wm DeJernett Homil Perkins, SMU 1993; W. D. Jernett Awd in Homil Perkins, SMU 1993; Who's Who in Mus Intl Who's Who in Mus 1992; Handicapped Profsnl Wmn of the Year Pilot Club & Sears 1988. hbwheels@aol.com

BETHANCOURT JR, A(rthur) (Los) 1145 W Valencia Mesa Dr, Fullerton CA 92833 **R Emm Par Fullerton CA 1995-** B Phoenix AZ 9/19/1952 s Arthur Robert Bethancourt & Martha Adele. USAF Acad Colorado Sprg CO 1971; BA Arizona St U 1974; MDiv CDSP 1978. D 12/2/1978 P 2/9/1980 Bp John Lester Thompson III. m 8/9/1973 Cynthia Hofmann c 2. Assoc Emm Par Fullerton CA 1983-1994; Assoc St Johns Epis Ch Petaluma CA 1980-1983; S Jn The Evang Ch Chico CA 1979-1980. Auth, "Let the Chld Come," *Mus for Chld's Chap*, Barking Dog Productions, 2001; Auth, "He is the Light," *Praise and Wrshp*, Homecourt Productions, 1993; Auth, "Mr. Noah's Fabulous Floating Zoo," *Chld's Mus*, Homecourt Productions, 1990; Auth, "Emm: God w Us," *Rite II Eucharistic Mus*, Homecourt Productions, 1990. rbethancou@aol.com

BETHEA, Mary Marjorie (Los) 31641 La Novia Ave, San Juan Capistrano CA 92675 **S Marg Of Scotland Par San Juan Capistrano CA 2010-; S Marg's Epis Sch San Juan Capo CA 2010-** B Charleston SC 4/17/1982 d James F Bethea & Linda N. BA Pepperdine U Malibu 2004; MDiv Fuller TS 2009; NCC Fuller TS 2010. D 6/12/2010 P 1/8/2011 Bp Mary Douglas Glasspool. mmbethea07@gmail.com

BETHEA, Robert (Oly) 1549 NW 57th St., Seattle WA 98107 B Augusta GA 5/3/1940 s Robert Little Bethea & Anne Olivia. BA Presb Coll Clinton SC 1982; MDiv SWTS 1982. D 8/3/1982 P 8/1/1983 Bp Robert Hume Cochrane. m 5/19/2003 Joan Marie Anthony c 4. Receiving Disabil Ret 2003-2005; Ch Of The Resurr Bellevue WA 1996-2003; P-in-c S Fran Epis Ch Mill Creek WA 1984-1996; Asst S Mich And All Ang Ch Issaquah WA 1982-1984. robertbethea@mac.com

BETHELL, T(albot) James (Tex) 290 Fall Creek Dr., Oceanside OR 97134 B Redlands CA 2/21/1942 s James Talbot Bethell & Elizabeth Hatfield. BA U of Redlands 1964; BD CDSP 1967; DD CDSP 2000. D 6/21/1967 P 4/5/1968 Bp George Henry Quarterman. m 10/14/1967 Anne Maxwell Wingate-Saul. Int Ch Of The Gd Shpd Vancouver WA 2006-2008; Int S Mich And All Ang Ch Lihue HI 2004-2006; R S Dav's Ch Austin TX 1981-2002; R S Dav's Epis Ch Topeka KS 1974-1981; Cur S Jn's Epis Ch Odessa TX 1967-1970; Vic S Mths Ch Lubbock TX 1967-1970. Associated Parishes 1974-1990; Downtown Epis Cler Of The New So 1991-2002; Urban-Surban Cler Conferance 1997-2002. jabethell@embarqmail.com

BETIT, John David (LI) 5 Pleasant St, Sutton MA 01590 **Dio Long Island Garden City NY 2010-** B Pittsfield MA 12/1/1967 Rec from Roman Catholic 8/11/2002 Bp Gordon Paul Scruton. c 3. S Jn's Epis Ch Sutton MA 2002-2010. dileedaly@gmail.com

BETTACCHI, Karen Elizabeth (Mass) 6 Garfield St, Lexington MA 02421 B Washington DC 4/16/1943 d Howard Clinton Zahniser & Alice Bernita. BA Greenville Coll 1965; MS Loyola Coll 1977; MDiv EDS 1992. D 5/30/1992 P 5/30/1993 Bp David Elliot Johnson. m 4/4/1970 Robert John Bettacchi c 2. S Mich's Epis Ch Holliston MA 2004; R S Lk's And S Marg's Ch Allston MA 1996-2001; Asst R The Ch Of Our Redeem Lexington MA 1993-1996; D S Mary's Epis Ch Dorchester MA 1992-1993. Massachusetts Epis Cleric Assn 1997. kzbettacc@verizon.net

BETTINGER, Robert Louis (Cal) 3940 Park Blvd Apt 911, San Diego CA 92103 B Springfield MA 8/17/1928 s Jesse Samuel Bettinger & Florence May. BA Hob 1952; Ya Berk 1955; MS Sthrn Connecticut St U 1970; PhD Saybrook U San Francisco CA 1975. D 6/11/1955 Bp William A Lawrence P 12/21/1955 Bp Henry Hean Daniels. c 4. Int S Paul's Epis Ch Salinas CA 1988; P Ch Of S Jn The Bapt Aptos CA 1984-1987; P S Mths Epis Ch San Ramon CA 1982-1984; P S Barth's Epis Ch Livermore CA 1982; Asstg P S Aid's Ch San Francisco CA 1975-1982; P S Andr's Ch Madison WI 1962-1965; Cur Chr Ch Westerly RI 1961-1962; R H Trin Epis Ch Sulphur LA 1957-1959; P in charge Geth Ch Manhattan MT 1956-1957. robertbettinger@yahoo.com

BETTMANN, John Charles (Spr) 10 Indian Ridge Rd., Asheville NC 28803 **S Mary's Ch Asheville NC 2011-** B Alton IL 1/1/1945 s Erwin Henry Bettmann & Mary Louise. BA Elmhurst Coll 1967; MDiv SWTS 1970. D 6/13/1970 Bp James Winchester Montgomery P 12/16/1970 Bp Allen Webster Brown. m 5/7/1976 Vibeke Bentzen c 2. R S Paul's Epis Ch Carlinville IL 2003-2010; Vic S Ptr's Ch Carlinville IL 2003-2010; S Annes Epis Ch Caseyville IL 2000-2003; Chr Ch Collinsville IL 1997-1999; Ch Of The H Cross Fairview Heights IL 1994-1999; Int S Augustines Ch S Louis MO 1993-1994; Int S Tim's Epis Ch Creve Coeur MO 1991-1992; Assoc S Lk's Epis Ch Manchester MO 1990-1991; Vic S Jn's Ch Centralia IL 1973-1974; Cur Chr Ch Cooperstown NY 1970-1973. Alb Inst 1998-2000; Conf Ord of S Ben 1995; P Assoc., Soc. of Our Lady of Walsingham 2004; SocMary 1992. MDiv scl SWTS Evanston IL 1970; BA scl Elmhurst Coll Elmhurst IL 1967. jcbveb1@gmail.com

BETTS III, A(lbert) Raymond (SO) 5810 Mccray Ct, Cincinnati OH 45224 B Cincinnati OH 8/2/1925 s Albert Raymond Betts & Lucille. BA Ya 1948; EDS 1955; MA U Cinc 1972. D 6/15/1955 P 12/1/1955 Bp Henry W Hobson. m 5/11/1985 Mary McClain c 3. S Andr's Epis Ch Elyria OH 1988; The Par Of Gd Shpd Epis Ch Wailuku HI 1987-1988; S Andr's Ch Dayton OH 1986-1987; S Alb Epis Ch Cleveland Heights OH 1985-1986; Chr Ch - Glendale Cincinnati OH 1984-1985; S Lk's Epis Ch Idaho Falls ID 1983-1984; R Gr Ch Cincinnati OH 1966-1983; R S Paul's Ch Chillicothe OH 1960-1966; R Chr Ch Xenia OH 1955-1960. mary.mclain55@gmail.com

BETTS, Ian Randolph (NY) 222 E 35th St Apt 3-K, New York NY 10016 **D Ch Of The Trsfg New York NY 2010-; Assoc Account Spec, Med Trust The CPG New York NY 2007-; Commisson on Mnstry Dio New York New York City NY 2002-** B Brockville ON CA 7/28/1960 s John LeRoi Betts & Annie Laura. NY D Formation Prog 1998; B.S. Concordia Coll, Bronxville NY 2008. D 5/16/1998 Bp Richard Frank Grein. D Cathd Of St Jn The Div New York NY 2002-2010; Commisson on Mnstry Dio New York New York City NY 2002-2007; D Ch Of The Gd Shpd New York NY 1998-2002. ibetts@erols.com

BETTS, Robert Hamilton (Pa) 7706 Gate Rd, Wyndmoor PA 19038 B Kansas City MO 1/9/1938 s Lindley Henley Betts & Alice Marion. PrTS; BA U of Missouri 1960; MDiv EDS 1965; PrTS 1973; MA Washington U 1977; MSW Washington U 1980. D 6/19/1965 P 1/12/1966 Bp George Leslie Cadigan. m 7/12/1975 Susan Kirchen c 4. Int All SS Ch Norristown PA 2009-2010; Exec Dir Epis Cmnty Serv Dio Pennsylvania Philadelphia PA 1991-2003; Int S Jn's Ch No Haven CT 1988-1989; Int Gr Ch Old Saybrook CT 1987-1988; Exec Dir Epis Soc Serv Dio Connecticut Hartford CT 1980-1987; S Matt's Epis Ch Warson Warson Woods MO 1977-1979; Asst S Tim's Epis Ch Creve Coeur MO 1975-1977; Vic S Barn Ch Moberly MO 1974-1975; R Trin Ch St Chas MO 1968-1974; Cur Gr Ch Salem MA 1966-1968; Cur S Mich & S Geo Clayton MO 1965-1966. Epis Cmnty Serv, USA 2000; Urban Cacsus 1980-1999. robertbettsnj@comcast.net

BETZ, Madelyn Louise (NH) 150 Goss Road, Enfield NH 03748 B Portland ME 1/26/1954 d Ernest Henry Waterhouse & Virginia Louise. BMus Gordon Coll 1976; MMus Boston Conservatory 1979; MDiv EDS 2008. D 6/23/2008 P 1/21/2009 Bp V Gene Robinson. c 2. Cur S Thos Ch Hanover NH 2008-2011; Par Admin All SS Ch Peterborough NH 1990-2007. betz.madelyn@gmail.com

BETZ, Nancy Elizabeth (CNY) 412 Hugunin St, Clayton NY 13624 **Int Chr Epis Ch Brandy Sta VA 2011-** B Amsterdam NY 10/8/1944 d James Ellis Clizbe & Sylvia Louise. AAS Big Bend Cmnty Coll 1976; BS SUNY 1987; MDiv Bex 1994. D 6/18/1994 Bp William George Burrill P 12/21/1994 Bp Arthur Benjamin Williams Jr. c 3. R Chr Ch Clayton NY 1997-2010; R St Jn's Ch Clayton NY 1997-2010; R S Paul's Epis Ch Put-In-Bay OH 1994-1997. motherbetz@verizon.net

BEUKMAN, Christian Arnold (Mass) 12 Quincy Ave, Quincy MA 02169 **D Chr Ch Quincy MA 2009-** B 3/9/1956 s Cornelis Beukman & Adriana. MDIV Harvard DS 1983; DMIN Andover Newton 1996. D 6/6/2009 Bp

M(arvil) Thomas Shaw III. m 10/17/1982 Lucy Joan Sollogub c 2. cbeukman@post.harvard.edu

BEVAN JR, Charles Albert (Ct) The Towers 24 Park Place, PH24-B, Hartford CT 06106 **P-in-c S Andr's Ch Milford CT 2009-; Monthly Assoc Chr Ch Cathd Hartford CT 1985-** B Camden NJ 12/12/1944 s Charles Albert Bevan & Dorothy Pape. MDiv PDS 1970; ThM PrTS 1974; Fllshp VTS 1976; Fllshp Ya Berk 1985; DMin GTF 1986; Harvard DS 1993. D 4/11/1970 P 10/24/1970 Bp Alfred L Banyard. m 10/14/1972 Virginia F Bevan c 1. Vic Chr Ch Waterbury CT 2004-2009; Int R Gr Epis Ch Hartford CT 2002-2004; Ecum Commision Dio Connecticut Hartford CT 2000-2004; Int R S Paul's Ch Southington CT 2000-2002; P-in-c S Jn The Evang Yalesville CT 1999-2000; Dn, Litchfield Dnry Dio Connecticut Hartford CT 1990-1996; Ecum Cmsn Dio Connecticut Hartford CT 1985-1996; Cathd Chapt Dio Connecticut Hartford CT 1985-1989; Exec Commitee Dio Connecticut Hartford CT 1980-1981; R S Jn's Ch Salisbury CT 1979-1996; Dn, Second Convoc Dio Sthrn Virginia Norfolk VA 1977-1979; Exec Coun Dio Sthrn Virginia Norfolk VA 1977-1979; COM Dio Sthrn Virginia Norfolk VA 1975-1979; Asst R Galilee Epis Ch Virginia Bch VA 1974-1979; Assoc R Chr Ch Glen Ridge NJ 1972-1974; Cur Gr Epis Ch Plainfield NJ 1970-1972. Alpha Delta Phi Fraternity 1994; Engl Spkng Un 1985; Harvard Club Of Boston 1996; Litchfield Cnty U Club 1979-1996; Ord Of Hosp Of S Jn Of Jerusalem 1984. Who'S Who In Rel 1987; Who'S Who In Amer 1985. cab2@snet.net

BEVANS, Bruce Sinclair (SVa) 3030-2a Stony Lake Drive, Richmond VA 23235 **Trin Ch Moundsville WV 2011-; P-in-c S Jn's Ch Petersburg VA 2007-** B Cambridge MA 7/21/1953 s William Joseph Bevans & Natalie Pearl. BA Geo Mason U 1989; MDiv VTS 1996; Cert. Chesterfield Cnty Police Acad, VA 2006. D 6/15/1996 P 1/17/1997 Bp Peter James Lee. m 12/18/1999 Marjorie Salling Bell c 3. S Jn's Ch Hopewell VA 2003-2007; Manakin Epis Ch Midlothian VA 2000-2003; R Calv Ch Bath Par Dinwiddie VA 1998-2000; Asst S Andr's Ch Burke VA 1996-1998. Meritorious Serv Medal Us AF 1993; Outstanding Achievement In Philos Geo Mason U Fairfax VA 1989; Ba w dist Geo Mason U Fairfax VA 1989. lomens5125@aol.com

BEVANS, Marjorie Salling (WVa) 903 Charles St, Parkersburg WV 26101 **R The Memi Ch Of The Gd Shpd Parkersburg WV 2010-** B Nassawadox VA 10/22/1960 d Everett Thomas Bell & Ruthann Salling. BA U of Virginia 1987; MDiv Nash 2000. D 6/3/2000 P 1/28/2001 Bp Donald Purple Hart. m 12/18/1999 Bruce Sinclair Bevans. S Andr's Lawrenceville VA 2010; Dn Dio Sthrn Virginia Norfolk VA 2006-2009; Int S Paul's Ch Petersburg VA 2005-2009; Exec Bd Dio Sthrn Virginia Norfolk VA 2005-2008; Int S Mk's Ch Richmond VA 2004-2005; Asst S Mich's Ch Bon Air VA 2001-2004; Merchants Hope Epis Ch Prince Geo Hopewell VA 2000-2001; Asst R S Jn's Ch Chester VA 2000-2001. romans5125@aol.com

BEVENS, Myrna Eloise (Colo) 46 N Albion St, Colorado Springs CO 80911 B Colorado Springs CO 2/22/1942 d Edger G Bevens & Evelyn M. S Thos Sem; TESM; BA Wstrn St Coll of Colorado 1964; MDiv Chr Gospel Intl 1971. D 10/18/1985 P 6/13/1990 Bp William Harvey Wolfrum. S Andr's Ch Manitou Sprg CO 1989-2007; Dio Colorado Denver CO 1987-2007; Ch Of Our Sav Colorado Sprg CO 1986-1988.

BEVERIDGE, Robert Hanna (CNY) 1416 34th Ave, Seattle WA 98122 B Richmond VA 7/11/1932 s George Bruce Beveridge & Charlotte Margaret. St. Lawr Canton NY; Whitworth U; BA Emory U 1956; MDiv CDSP 1969. D 7/3/1969 Bp Edward McNair P 2/5/1970 Bp Clarence Rupert Haden Jr. m 8/29/1959 Alberta Anne Whittle c 4. R Trin Epis Ch Fayetteville NY 1987-1994; Assoc S Geo's Epis Ch Arlington VA 1982-1987; S Barth's Ch Beaverton OR 1980-1981; R S Mk's Epis Ch Moscow ID 1971-1980; Cur Trin Cathd Sacramento CA 1969-1971. EPF 1993; EUC 1983; Fllshp of Recon 1997; Natl Ntwk of Epis Cler Assn 1971. rbbeve@yahoo.com

BEVERIDGE, Robin Lorraine (NY) 143 N Putt Corners Rd, New Paltz NY 12561 **D The Epis Ch Of Chr The King Stone Ridge NY 2009-** B Washington DC 2/26/1956 BFA SUNY New Paltz 1978; AAS Dutchess Cmnty Coll 1984. D 5/14/2005 Bp Mark Sean Sisk. m 7/9/1988 William Beveridge c 3. D S Jn's Ch Cornwall NY 2005-2008. beveridge@saintly.com

BEYER, Jeanie Tillotson (Fla) 2872 N. Hannon Hill Dr., Tallahassee FL 32309 **Archd Dio Florida Jacksonville FL 2010-; D Gr Mssn Ch Tallahassee FL 2008-** B Kansas City MO 5/29/1948 d John Edward Tillotson & Shirley Bobel. BA U of Missouri 1971; W Missouri Sch of Mnstry 1977; MA S Paul TS 2002. D 2/14/1998 Bp John Clark Buchanan. m 1/15/1972 Philip Beyer c 2. D All SS Epis Ch Kansas City MO 1998-2001. Assn of Profsnl Chapl 2006; COM 2000-2006; Dioc Yth Coun 2002-2004; Haitian Epis Lrng Proj 1995-2006; NAAD, Gd Samariatn Ca. Reach4god@aol.com

BEZILLA, Gregory (NJ) 39 Ross Stevenson Cir, Princeton NJ 08540 **Com on Lifelong Chr Formation Dio New Jersey Trenton NJ 2009-; Com on the Priesthood Dio New Jersey Trenton NJ 2008-; Chapl The Epis Campus Mnstry at Rutgers New Brunswick NJ 2004-** B Chitose JP 10/8/1962 s Robert Bezilla & Elaine Beatrice. BA Jn Hopkins U 1984; MA Col 1985; MA Col 1989; MDiv Candler TS Emory U 1998. D 6/2/2001 P 1/19/2002 Bp David B(ruce) Joslin. m 8/6/1994 Jacqueline E Lapsiey c 2. Epis Ch Cntr New York NY 2011; Cur S Geo's-By-The-River Rumson NJ 2001-2004. gbezilla@mac.com

BEZY, Bernard Anthony (Lex) 1407 Gemstone Blvd, Hanahan SC 29410 **Off Of Bsh For ArmdF New York NY 1998-** B New Albany IN 4/1/1959 s Gustave Joseph Bezy & Esther Ruth. BS Indiana U 1983; MDiv Asbury TS 1990. D 12/30/1995 P 6/1/1997 Bp Don Adger Wimberly. m 8/2/1986 Jennifer Lynn Bigler c 3. Asst to R Ch Of The Resurr Jessamine City Nicholasville KY 1996-2000; Ch Of The Ascen Frankfort KY 1996. bezyfam@earthlink.net

BIANCHI, Mary Elizabeth (Nev) 1674 Harper Drive, Carson City NV 89701 **D S Barth's Ch Ely NV 2000-** B Bradley FL 5/21/1932 d Benjamin Mitchell Fortner & Retha L. RN Orange Memi Sch Of Nrsng Orlando FL 1953. D 4/2/2000 Bp John Stuart Thornton. m 9/29/1956 Valentino A Bianchi c 3. bettybianchi@gmail.com

BIBENS, Robert Lee (Okla) 4642 E 57th Pl, Tulsa OK 74135 **Trin Ch Tulsa OK 2003-; All SS Chap Tulsa OK 1993-; Holland Hall Sch Tulsa OK 1993-** B Kansas City MO 12/26/1956 s Robert Frank Bibens & Evelyn Joyce. BS U of Oklahoma 1978; MA Cntrl St U 1982. D 6/27/1987 Bp Gerald Nicholas McAllister. m 6/1/1985 Susan Eleanor Safley c 3. Trin Ch Tulsa OK 1990-1993. Auth, "Yth Mnstry: Simplified (audio)," Indep, 1986; Contributing Auth, "Passion For Tchg". Bbibens@yahoo.com

BICE, Michael Kenneth (Chi) 1244 N Astor St, Chicago IL 60610 **Asst Epis Ch Of The Atone Chicago IL 2011-** B 11/9/1938 M.D. U of Sydney 1963; M.Div GTS 1967. D 5/20/1967 Bp Harvey D Butterfield P 12/16/1967 Bp Horace W B Donegan. Asst Bp Anderson Hse Chicago IL 1975-1977. Fulbright Schlr USA 1964. MKBICE@AOL.COM

BICKERTON, (Frances) Catherine (NJ) 164 Buttonwood Dr, Fair Haven NJ 07704 **Assoc Chr Ch Middletown NJ 1984-** B Philadelphia PA 2/21/1949 d Robert Matthew Baur & (Frances) Louise. BA Vas 1971; MDiv Pittsburgh TS 1974; DMin Drew U 2006. D 1/18/1975 Bp Robert Bracewell Appleyard P 2/5/1977 Bp Lyman Cunningham Ogilby. m 8/31/1974 Michael W Bickerton c 3. Assoc Chr Ch Middletown NJ 1984-1986; Asst S Mary's Epis Ch Ardmore PA 1979-1984; S Elis's Ch Philadelphia PA 1977-1979; Asst S Mary's Epis Ch Ardmore PA 1975-1977; S Mk Pittsburgh PA 1975. "Theodicy and CPE: Exploring the Problem of Suffering through the Stories of Holocaust Survivors," ProQuest, 2006. ACPE, Inc., Decatur, GA 1982; Assn of Profsnl Chapl 1993. DMin w dist Drew U 2006; MDiv mcl Pittsburgh TS Pittsburgh PA 1974. cbickerton@sbhcs.com

BICKFORD, Wayne Elva (HB) 8212 Kelsey Whiteface Rd, Cotton MN 55724 B Grand Rapids MI 3/18/1941 s HP Bickford & Jenny. MDiv. D 6/29/1973 P 4/1/1974 Bp Philip Frederick McNairy. m 1/28/1961 Sandra Linder. R S Tim's Epis Ch Henderson NV 1979-1981; R S Jn's Ch Eveleth MN 1975-1979; R S Paul's Ch Virginia MN 1975-1979; Dio Minnesota Minneapolis MN 1973-1975.

BICKING, David Darlington (WVa) 813 Bowling Green Rd, Front Royal VA 22630 B West Chester PA 6/4/1942 s Frank Kirk Bicking & Kathryn. BS Penn 1965; MDiv VTS 1975. D 5/24/1975 Bp Robert Poland Atkinson P 12/1/1975 Bp Wilburn Camrock Campbell. m Sara Louise Bird. P-in-c Mt Zion Epis Ch Hedgesville WV 1990-2003; Vic S Phil's Ch Chas Town WV 1979-1988; Asst R S Jn's Epis Ch Charleston WV 1977-1979; R S Lk's Ch Wheeling WV 1975-1977. golf813@embarqmail.com

BICKLEY, Robert James (Mich) Oakwood Common, 16351 Rotunda Dr #311, Grosse Pointe Park MI 48120 **Asst S Andr's Ch Ann Arbor MI 2008-** B Wyandotte MI 12/13/1928 s Joseph Bickley & Maude. BA U MI 1950; BD EDS 1954; MS Wayne 1980. D 7/10/1954 P 1/1/1955 Bp Richard S M Emrich. c 3. All SS Ch Detroit MI 1991-1993; S Columba Ch Detroit MI 1962-1981; R All SS Ch Brooklyn MI 1957-1960; Asst Calv and St Geo New York NY 1957-1959; Vic S Geo's Ch Milford MI 1952-1957. som1056@aol.com

BIDDLE, Blair Charles (Alb) Po Box 1029, Plattsburgh NY 12901 **D S Paul's Ch Plattsburgh NY 1998-** B Philadelphia PA 10/9/1943 s C Ralph Biddle & Eva Catherine. AAS USAF Cmnty Coll; BS SUNY 2001. D 11/18/1995 Bp David Standish Ball. m 10/19/1982 Joella Claire LaFountaine. D Trin Ch Plattsburgh NY 1995-1998. Diakoneo. bcbiddle@aol.com

BIDDLE III, Craig (Va) 364 Friar Trl, Annapolis MD 21401 B Philadelphia PA 9/27/1931 s Craig Biddle & Alice Jones. BA Wms 1953; BD VTS 1964; ThM PrTS 1970. D 6/13/1964 P 12/1/1964 Bp Leland Stark. m 4/3/2006 Jane Grissmer c 7. Int Ch Of The Resurr Alexandria VA 1993-1996; Int Trin Ch Upperville VA 1991-1993; S Columba's Ch Washington DC 1987-1995; Impact Inc- Epis Ch Cntr New York NY 1984-1987; Impact-Washington Washington DC 1984-1987; R S Paul's Ch Richmond VA 1977-1983; R Trin Ch On The Green New Haven CT 1970-1977; R The Ch Of The Annunc Oradell NJ 1966-1970; Cur S Ptr's Ch Morristown NJ 1964-1966. Auth, *Contrib Var Books & mag.* cbiddleiii@aol.com

BIDWELL, Mary Almy (NH) 1145 Jerusalem Rd, Bristol VT 05443 **R Jerusalem Gathering Bristol VT 1994-** B Bronxville NY 7/12/1943 d John Bidwell & Anne. BA Hollins U 1965; MDiv EDS 1969. D 6/29/1972 Bp Charles F Hall P 1/18/1977 Bp Philip Alan Smith. S Paul's Epis Ch Wells VT 1994-2000. mbidwell@gmaut.net

BIDWELL-WAITE, Davidson (Cal) 3900 Alameda De Las Pulgas, San Mateo CA 94403 **D Trsfg Epis Ch San Mateo CA 2007-** B Santa Ana CA 9/12/1948 s David Mc Cormack & Dorothy Smith. BA U CA 1970; MPA U CA 1972; JD Armstrong Colloge Sch of Law 1980; Diac Stds The Sch for Deacons 2006. D 12/1/2007 Bp Marc Handley Andrus. davidsonbidwell@comcast.net

BIEGA, Richard A (Ark) 199 Barcelona Rd, Hot Springs Village AR 71909 **R H Trin Epis Ch Hot Sprg Vill AR 2007-** B Perth Amboy NJ 1/18/1947 s Andrew Walter Biega & Helen Magdalena. BA S Mary Orchard Lake 1968; MDiv SS Cyril & Methodius Sem 1977; Wake Forest U 1982; Cert Epis TS of The SW 1989. Rec from Roman Catholic 4/29/1989 Bp John Herbert MacNaughton. m 11/24/1986 Elizabeth B Brewer c 5. Dio Upper So Carolina Columbia SC 2006-2007; S Mich And All Ang' Columbia SC 2004-2006; R All SS Ch Cayce SC 1996-2004; Dio Upper So Carolina Columbia SC 1991-1996; S Eliz's Epis Ch Buda TX 1990-1991; R Emm Epis Ch Lockhart TX 1989-1991. holytrin@suddenlink.net

BIEGLER, James Cameron (Dal) 11202 Prairie View Ct, Westchester IL 60154 **S Paul's Par Riverside IL 2010-** B Elmhurst IL 9/18/1950 s John Charles Biegler & Jeannette Mae. BA U Chi 1972; MDiv Nash 1975. D 6/14/1975 Bp Quintin Ebenezer Primo Jr P 1/1/1976 Bp James Winchester Montgomery. m 8/7/2004 Linda Biegler. R The Epis Ch Of The H Nativ Plano TX 1994-2003; Dio Cntrl Florida Orlando FL 1988-1991; R S Paul's Epis Ch New Smyrna Bch FL 1983-1994; Vic S Pat's Epis Ch W Monroe LA 1979-1983; Cur S Jas Epis Ch Alexandria LA 1977-1979; Cur The Ch Of S Uriel The Archangel Sea Girt NJ 1976-1977. padrejb@comcast.net

BIELSKI, Diane Irene (Colo) P O Box 1558, Fraser CO 80442 **D Epis Ch Of S Jn The Bapt Granby CO 2008-** B Passaic NJ 10/18/1953 D 11/6/1999 Bp William Jerry Winterrowd. m Daniel Bielski. sheepdeacon@juno.com

BIERHAUS JR, Edward Gibson (Ct) St Pauls Towers, 100 Bay Pl Apt 1216, Oakland CA 94610 **P Assoc S Mary's Ch Asheville NC 2000-** B Vincennes IN 4/6/1932 s Edward Gibson Bierhaus & Martha. BA U So 1954; MDiv GTS 1957; DFA Ya 1969; Oxf 1970. D 6/21/1957 Bp Richard Ainslie Kirchhoffer P 12/21/1957 Bp Robert McConnell Hatch. c 3. P-in-c S Jn's Ch Guilford CT 1965-1969; Asst Trin Ch Branford CT 1959-1964; Cur S Thos's Ch New Haven CT 1957-1959. Auth, "Afr," *Cadillac Cicatrix*; Auth, "Style," *Laurel Leaves*; Auth, *No Wrld of its own: Look Back in Anger 20 Years Later*, Mod Drama; Auth, "The Lion's Prey (play)," *Sthrn Appalachian Repertory Threatre*; Auth, "Pax Vaticana," *Sthrn Hmnts Revs*; Auth, *Strangers in a Room: A Delicate Balance Revisited*, Mod Drama; Auth, "Fever of Life," *The Abegweit Revs*, Marathon Plays; Auth, "Mindset (play)," *Warren Wilson Coll Theatre*. Dramatist's Gld; EPF. jbierhs@warren-wilson.edu

BIEVER, Robert Ray (Oly) 3310 N Bennett St, Tacoma WA 98407 **Vic All SS Ch Tacoma WA 1992-** B Fargo ND 2/26/1952 s Milo Jack Biever & Dorothy Annabelle. BA Minnesota St U Moorehead 1974; MDiv Nash 1979. D 6/24/1979 Bp George Theodore Masuda P 3/24/1980 Bp Emerson Paul Haynes. S Jn's Epis Ch Olympia WA 1986-1987; S Chris's Epis Ch Olympia WA 1984-1992; Asst Chr Ch Tacoma WA 1984-1985; Cur S Hilary's Ch Ft Myers FL 1979-1981. robert_biever@hotmail.com

BIFFLE, Robin Lee (Spok) 111 S. Jefferson St., Moscow ID 83843 **R S Mk's Epis Ch Moscow ID 2008-** B Pueblo CO 10/14/1951 d Robert Park Biffle & Mary Elizabeth. BA Whitman Coll 1974; MDiv The U So (Sewanee) 2008. D 6/1/2008 Bp Charles Franklin Brookhart Jr P 12/13/2008 Bp James Edward Waggoner. c 1. rector@moscow.com

BIGELOW, Thomas Seymour (Oly) Box 20489, Seattle WA 98102 **Assoc S Clem's Epis Ch Seattle WA 2007-** B Milwaukee WI 5/9/1933 s Chester Schley Bigelow & Marion Elizabeth. BS USC 1955; MDiv CDSP 1963. D 6/23/1963 P 5/16/1964 Bp C J Kinsolving III. R S Lk's Epis Ch Renton WA 1994-2004; Assoc S Lk's Epis Ch Seattle WA 1968-1970; Vic S Steph's Ch Lubbock TX 1966-1968; Vic S Mk's Epis Ch Pecos TX 1964-1966; Vic S Steph's Epis Ch Ft Stockton TX 1964-1966; Cur Pro Cathd Epis Ch Of S Clem El Paso TX 1963-1964. OSH 1994; OHC 1994. ThomasSBigelow@aol.com

BIGFORD, Jack N(orman) (Oly) 520 Scenic Way, Kent WA 98030 B Seattle WA 12/7/1922 s Everett Merit Bigford & Esther Barbara. MS U of Massachusetts; Bp Huston TS 1968. D 10/5/1968 Bp Ivol I Curtis. D /Asst S Jas Epis Ch Kent WA 1968-1987.

BIGGADIKE, Maylin Teresa (Nwk) 398 Shelbourne Ter, Ridgewood NJ 07450 **Assoc S Eliz's Ch Ridgewood NJ 2000-** B 1/12/1948 d Emilio Cheuy & Graciela. BA U of Massachusetts 1974; MA Boston Coll 1976; MA GTS 1994; MA GTS 1994; PhD UTS 2006. D 5/30/1998 P 10/30/1999 Bp John Shelby Spong. m 8/16/1970 Ernest Ralph Biggadike c 3. D's Asst All SS' Epis Ch Glen Rock NJ 1998-2000. "A Chr Soc Ethical Response to Pvrty," *Econ Dvlpmt Through the Eyes of Poor Wmn in Developing Countries*, 2006. maylin.biggadike@gmail.com

BIGGERS, Helen Hammond (Spok) 4803 W Shawnee Ave, Spokane WA 99208 B Ventura CA 9/4/1928 d Stephen Reginald Hammond & Hattie Wilhelmina. AA Huntington Memi Sch of Nrsng 1950. D 12/21/2002 Bp James Edward Waggoner. m 12/16/1949 Walter David Biggers c 5. stdavids1@qwest.net

BIGGERS, Jackson Cunningham (Miss) 10100 Hillview Dr Apt 537, Pensacola FL 32514 B Corinth MS 5/16/1937 s Neal Brooks Biggers & Sarah Eleanor. BA U of Mississippi 1960; BD STUSo 1963; DD STUSo 2000. D 6/24/1963 Bp John M Allin P 4/1/1964 Bp Duncan Montgomery Gray. Dio Mississippi Jackson MS 1995-1997; R The Epis Ch Of The Redeem Biloxi MS 1977-1995; Ch in the Prov Of The W Indies New York NY 1975-1977; Chapl To The PBp Epis Ch Cntr New York NY 1974-1975; R S Steph's Epis Ch Indianola MS 1971-1972; Cur The Epis Ch Of The Redeem Biloxi MS 1970-1971; Cur S Jas Ch Jackson MS 1963-1965. Cmnty Of S Mary (Assoc); SSC. Bp Emer Dioc Syn, No Malawi 2002; Hon Cn Likoma Cathd Dio Lake Malawi Cntrl Afr 1983. jckbggrs@aol.com

BIGGS, Carolyn Kirk (CFla) 6071 Sabal Hammock Cir, Port Orange FL 32128 B Kansas City KS 11/1/1957 d William Robert Hildreth Kirk & Juanita LaVerne. U of Cntrl Florida 1999; SWTS 2002. D 6/8/2002 P 12/7/2002 Bp John Wadsworth Howe. m 5/10/2005 David Lee Biggs c 2. S Matt's Ch St Petersburg FL 2006-2010; Asst R Gr Epis Ch Inc Port Orange FL 2002-2006. ckbiggs57@earthlink.net

BIGGS, John Winston (WMo) 2632 S Wallis Smith Blvd, Springfield MO 65804 B Danville IL 12/17/1937 s Harold Edward Biggs & Alwilda Mae. BA U of Missouri, Kansas City 1959; MDiv Nash 1962. D 4/24/1962 P 11/8/1962 Bp Edward Randolph Welles II. m 8/18/1962 Marcia C Clock c 3. Dio Fond du Lac Appleton WI 1996-1999; R S Aug's Epis Ch Rhinelander WI 1988-2001; Dioc Coun Dio W Missouri Kansas City MO 1984-1986; R S Jas' Ch Springfield MO 1983-1988; Gr Ch Carthage MO 1978-1983; R S Lk's Ch Ft Madison IA 1973-1978; R The Epis Ch Of The H Trin Belvidere IL 1968-1973; S Jn's Epis Ch Oxford WI 1964-1968; Vic S Mary's Epis Ch Tomah WI 1964-1968. Fllshp of St. Jn; Life Mem Conf Of The Bless Sacr. Bp'S Cross Dio Fond Du Lac 2001; Bp'S Shield Dio W Missouri 1985; Eagle Scout BSA. jwbmo@sbcglobal.net

BIGHAM JR, Jesse Yonge (Ct) 412 Main St, Terryville CT 06786 B Houston TX 3/17/1932 s Jesse Yonge Bigham & Opal Mae. BA U of Texas 1955; STB Ya Berk 1967. D 6/15/1967 Bp William Paul Barnds P 12/21/1967 Bp Theodore H McCrea. c 2. P-in-c S Jas' Epis Ch Winsted CT 2000; S Paul's Epis Ch Jackson MI 1999-2000; Int S Jn's Ch Salisbury CT 1997-1998; Int S Lk's Ch Ft Madison IA 1996-1997; Int Chr Ch Florence AZ 1995-1996; Int S Mich's Ch Coolidge AZ 1995-1996; R S Chris's Ch Sun City AZ 1988-1994; R Chr Ch Easton CT 1974-1980; R Trin Epis Ch Bristol CT 1970-1974; Assoc Chr And H Trin Ch Westport CT 1968-1970; Cur S Paul's Epis Ch Dallas TX 1967-1968. Bro Way Cross; OHC.

BIGLEY, Mark Charles (ETenn) 792 Keith Salem Rd., Ringgold GA 30736 **P-in-c S Alb's Epis Ch Hixson TN 2011-** B Toledo OH 5/26/1951 s Charles Junior Bigley & Yvonne. BA Bowling Green St U 1973; MDiv VTS 1977; MA Ashland TS 1983; MSW Wayne 2005. D 6/25/1977 Bp John Harris Burt P 2/1/1978 Bp Scott Field Bailey. m 3/17/2006 Kathleen J McGinnis c 2. P-in-c S Paul's Ch Oregon OH 2006-2009; Int All SS Epis Ch Toledo OH 2004-2006; Asst S Alb's Epis Ch Arlington TX 1998-2001; R S Raphael Epis Ch Colorado Sprg CO 1995-1998; Assoc Trin Ch Victoria TX 1993-1995; Vic Calv Ch Menard TX 1992-1993; Vic Trin Ch Jct TX 1992-1993; R Trin Ch Lander WY 1990-1992; Assoc R Ch Of Recon San Antonio TX 1983-1990; R S Thos' Epis Ch Port Clinton OH 1979-1983; Asst S Barth's Ch Corpus Christi TX 1977-1979. Chapl, "Death: The Crumbling Of Our Assumptive Words And Sprtl Growth," *In Intouch Ohio Hospice And Palliative Care Orgnztn*, In Intouch Ohio Hospice And Palliative Care Orgnztn, 2003. Confrater S Greg Abbey. bigleymc@gmail.com

BILBY, Gary Eugene (NwT) 1501 S Grinnell St, Perryton TX 79070 B 1/5/1939 s Carl Bilby & Shirley. D 10/29/1999 Bp C(harles) Wallis Ohl.

BILLER, Larry Ray (NI) 9064 E Koher Rd S, Syracuse IN 46567 **P-in-c S Jas' Epis Ch Goshen IN 2008-; D All SS Ch Syracuse IN 2006-** B Goshen IN 10/17/1942 s Lowell Biller & Bette. D 6/9/2006 Bp Edward Stuart Little II. m 8/24/1963 Gertrude Biller c 3. lbillerallsts@maplanet.net

BILLINGS, Stephen Robb (Pa) 225 S 3rd St, Philadelphia PA 19106 B Coral Gables FL 6/20/1941 s Elliot Allen Billings & Priscilla. Cert Mar Coun Of Philadelphia; BA Ya 1963; MDiv EDS 1966. D 6/25/1966 Bp Anson Phelps Stokes Jr P 5/6/1967 Bp John Melville Burgess. m 4/13/1991 Barbara Morrison c 2. Assoc S Mary's Epis Ch Ardmore PA 1994-2003; Dir Of Ch And Cmnty Serv Dio Pennsylvania Philadelphia PA 1993-2006; Epis Cmnty Serv Philadelphia PA 1993-2006; R H Apos And Medtr Philadelphia PA 1975-1993; Asst S Mary's Epis Ch Ardmore PA 1969-1973; Cur Ch Of The Mssh Lower Gwynedd PA 1966-1969. Clincl Mem Of The Amer Assn For Marrigae & Fam Ther; EUC. srobbbil@aol.com

BILLINGSLEA, Wendy Ward (Fla) 400 San Juan Dr, Ponte Vedra Beach FL 32082 **Chr Epis Ch Ponte Vedra Bch FL 2009-** B Corpus Christi TX 3/2/1955 d John Joseph Ward & Joy. BA Wells Coll 1978; MDiv Epis TS of The SW 1996. D 6/8/1996 Bp R(aymond) Stewart Wood Jr P 1/18/1997 Bp Calvin Onderdonk Schofield Jr. m 5/26/1979 Arthur C Billingslea c 3. R S Andr's Ch

Greensboro NC 2001-2009; Asst S Thos Epis Par Coral Gables FL 1996-2001. wbillingslea@standrewsgreensboro.com

BILLINGSLEY, Michael (Mass) Saint Paul's Episcopal Church, 61 Wood St., Hopkinton MA 01748 **P-in-res S Paul's Epis Ch Hopkinton MA 2005-** B Holyoke MA 1/4/1947 s George Leroy Billingsley & Georgia Lee. BS USCG Acad New London CT 1969; MS Pur 1977; MDiv VTS 1992. D 6/6/1992 P 12/12/1992 Bp Frank Kellogg Allan. m 6/7/1969 Judith S Seavey c 2. R S Teresa Acworth GA 1996-2005; Asst S Cathr's Epis Ch Marietta GA 1992-1996. Bro Of S Andr. MNJBILLINGSLEY@COMCAST.NET

BILLINGTON, James Hadley (Cal) 1 S El Camino Real, San Mateo CA 94401 B Philadelphia PA 7/29/1961 s James Billington & Marjorie. BA Harv 1983; MBA Harv 1987; MDiv EDS 1996. D 6/24/1996 P 2/1/1997 Bp Edward Witker Jones. m 8/29/1992 Julia Ann Silverman c 2. S Matt's Epis Ch San Mateo CA 1999-2006; S Matt's Ch Bedford NY 1996-1999.

BILLMAN, Daniel Robert (Ind) 8165 Gwinnett Pl., Indianapolis IN 46250 **Affilliate All SS Ch Indianapolis IN 2007-; P-in-c S Mths Ch Rushville IN 1987-** B Indianapolis IN 5/2/1936 s Vernon Robert Billman & Lena Irene. BS U Cinc 1959. D 6/24/1986 P 5/1/1987 Bp Edward Witker Jones. m 2/21/1959 Muriel Jane Bowermaster. dbjby@yahoo.com

BILLMAN, Sharon Lynn (Kan) 1738 24000 Rd, Parsons KS 67357 B Erie KS 10/14/1946 d Edward Milton Bowman & Irene Loucille. AA Labette Cmnty Coll 1986; BA Pittsburg St U 1989; MS Pittsburg St U 1989; Kansas Sch of Mnstry 2001. D 12/21/2002 P 6/22/2003 Bp William Edward Smalley. m 6/4/1966 David Ralph Billman c 1. D S Jn's Ch Parsons KS 2002-2003. vicar@stjohnsparsons.org

BILLOW JR, William Pierce (WA) PO Box 242, Barboursville VA 22923 **Trst Prot Epis Cathd Fndt Washington DC 2011-** B Elgin IL 2/28/1953 s William Pierce Billow & Nancy Jean. BA U of Washington 1976; MDiv VTS 1979. D 6/9/1979 Bp Quintin Ebenezer Primo Jr P 12/1/1979 Bp James Winchester Montgomery. Cathd of St Ptr & St Paul Washington DC 1985-2010; Asst R S Columba's Ch Washington DC 1981-1985; Cur S Mk's Barrington Hills IL 1979-1981. Wm P Billow Chair in Chapl St Albans Sch 2010; Wm Pierce Billow Chair in Chapl St Albans Sch 2010; Wm Pierce Billow Jr Chair in Chapl St Albans Sch 2010. WILLIAMJR@ME.COM

BILLUPS, Beatrice (Md) 1514 Gordon Cove Dr, Annapolis MD 21403 B Jacksonville FL 9/9/1940 d Charles Bowen Moore & Beatrice Bellinger. Villanova U 1989; MDiv GTS 1992. D 6/13/1992 P 5/1/1993 Bp Allen Lyman Bartlett Jr. m 11/30/1963 Frederick Harding Billups. S Andr The Fisherman Epis Mayo MD 1997-1998; Dioc Com Dio Easton Easton MD 1994-1999; Chr Ch Par Kent Island Stevensville MD 1992-1997.

BILSBURY, Stephen Robert (Okla) St. Philip's Episcopal Church, 516 McLish St, Ardmore OK 73401 **Bp's Chair Ardmore Vill Ardmore OK 2010-; Bp's Chair & Hd Mstr Search Oak Hall Epis Sch Ardmore OK 2010-; Chapl & Rel Educ Tchr Oak Hall Epis Sch Ardmore OK 2010-; R St Phil's Epis Ch Ardmore OK 2010-** B Wright Patterson AFB OH 8/19/1965 s Stephen James Bilsbury & Barbara Joy. BS OH SU 1989; MDiv Bex 2006. D 5/14/2005 Bp Herbert Thompson Jr P 6/24/2006 Bp Kenneth Lester Price. m 10/14/1989 Kimberly A Wachhaus c 3. Wrld Mssn Coun Dio W Texas San Antonio TX 2009-2010; Asst Ch Of The Gd Shpd Corpus Christi TX 2008-2010; Wrld Mssn Coun Dio W Texas San Antonio TX 2008-2010; Chapl & Rel Educ Tchr S Jas Epis Sch Of Corpus Christi Inc. Corpus Christi TX 2008-2010; Evang Com Dio Sthrn Ohio Cincinnati OH 2006-2008; P-in-c S Mary Magd Ch Maineville OH 2006-2008; D Ch Of The Epiph Urbana OH 2006; D S Geo's Epis Ch Dayton OH 2005-2006. steve@bilsbury.us

BIMBI, James (Del) 4828 Hogan Dr, Wilmington DE 19808 **Stndg Com Dio Delaware Wilmington DE 2010-; R S Jas Ch Wilmington DE 2002-** B Newark NJ 5/22/1951 s Louis John Bimbi & Alice Louise. Monmouth Coll 1971; MDiv Nash 1992. D 6/20/1992 P 12/19/1992 Bp William Jerry Winterrowd. m 1/16/1999 Cythia Ann Klipfel c 5. Chair, COM Dio Delaware Wilmington DE 2004-2011; Dioc Coun Dio Delaware Wilmington DE 2003-2004; Vice Chair, COM Dio Colorado Denver CO 2000-2002; R Ch Of S Ptr The Apos Pueblo CO 1994-2002; Cmsn on HIV/AIDS Dio Colorado Denver CO 1994-1996; Congrl Discernment Com Dio Colorado Denver CO 1993-1994; Asst R Trin Ch Greeley CO 1992-1994. jamesbimbi@verizon.net

BINDER, Donald Drew (Va) 9301 Richmond Hwy, Lorton VA 22079 **R Pohick Epis Ch Lorton VA 2001-** B Allentown PA 4/2/1962 s Donald Dean Binder & Joy Eileen. BS Penn 1984; S Geo's Coll Jerusalem IL 1988; MDiv VTS 1989; Fllshp ECF 1997; PhD SMU 1997; Fllshp VTS 1997. D 6/12/1989 P 12/16/1989 Bp Calvin Onderdonk Schofield Jr. m 7/6/1985 Christine T Trevorrow c 3. Prof Dio Dallas Dallas TX 1998-2001; Asst P S Jn's Epis Ch Dallas TX 1994-2001; Prof Dio SE Florida Miami FL 1990-1993; Asst Dn of No Dade Dnry Dio SE Florida Miami FL 1990-1992; Asst to Dn Trin Cathd Miami FL 1989-1993. Co-Auth, "The Ancient Synagogue from Its Origins to 200 CE," Brill, 2008; Auth, "The Origins of the Synagogue: An Evaltn," *The Ancient Synagogue*, Coniectanea Biblica, 2003; Auth, *Into The Temple Courts*, SBL, 1999. Assn of Angl Biblic Scholars 1995. ECF Fell ECF 1996; Bell-Woolfall Fllshp VTS Alexandria VA 1994; MDiv cl VTS Alexandria VA 1989. dbinder@pohick.org

BINDER, Thomas Francis (Mil) 1190 Aspen Ct, Grafton WI 53024 **D Chr Ch Whitefish Bay WI 2001-** B Milwaukee WI 4/4/1938 s Frank Binder & Elizabeth. D 1/20/2001 Bp Roger John White. m 7/9/1988 Christine Ann Vajoa Fluegel. tfbinder@sbcglobal.net

BINFORD, John Edward (Tex) 909 Texas St Unit 1314, Houston TX 77002 **Int S Lk The Evang Houston TX 2008-** B Houston TX 5/5/1937 s Thomas John Binford & Mildren Elizabeth. BS U Of Houston 1959; Med U Of Houston 1964; MDiv Epis TS of The SW 1972. D 6/28/1972 Bp Scott Field Bailey P 6/1/1973 Bp J Milton Richardson. m 6/10/1957 Clara Bing Binford. R St Andrews Epis Ch Houston TX 1978-1999; R S Barth's Ch Hempstead TX 1976-1978; Asst S Chris's Ch Houston TX 1974-1976; Asst S Dav's Ch Austin TX 1972-1974. cabinford@comcast.net

BINGHAM, John Pratt (NCal) 9851 Horn Road, Suite 180, Sacramento CA 95827 **Consult Dio Nthrn California Sacramento CA 2009-** B Los Angeles CA 11/26/1945 s Edwin S Bingham & Anne. BA Willamette U 1967; MDiv VTS 1971; MA Antioch Coll 1979; CG Jung Inst 1980. D 9/11/1971 P 3/18/1972 Bp Francis E I Bloy. m 7/23/1989 Barbara Lynn Bingham c 3. R S Lk's Par Monrovia CA 1975-1978; Asst Cathd Ch Of S Paul San Diego CA 1971-1975. Auth, "God and Dreams," Resource Pub, 2010; Auth, "Inner Treasure," *Reflections on Teachings of Jesus*, Dove Pub, 1989. binghamcounseling@hotmail.com

BINGHAM, Patricia M (Cal) 1 Key Capri 713 East, Treasure Island FL 33706 B Ottawa KS 1/27/1941 d John Burnell Pierson & Dorothy Marie. BA U of Kansas 1963; MDiv CDSP 1985; Appalachian Sch of Law 2001. D 6/8/1985 P 6/7/1986 Bp William Edwin Swing. m 12/21/1961 David A Bingham c 2. Asst P S Lk's Epis Ch Merritt Island FL 1992-1993; Assoc R S Jas Ch Oakland CA 1989-1991; Vic S Lk's Ch Detroit Lakes MN 1986-1989; Cur S Steph's Epis Ch Orinda CA 1985-1986; Org And Chrmstr S Jas Ch Oakland CA 1979-1980. Auth, "Pstr Pat'S Sprtl Perspectives," *The Treasure Island Reporter*, 1993. Spanish Campo Schlrshp Prov 8/Dio Ca 1990; Provencial Del: Prov VI Dio Minnesota 1988; Preaching Schlrshp Knights Templar Soc 1984. revpatb@aol.com

BINGHAM, Sally (Cal) 7 Laurel St, San Francisco CA 94118 **Environ Mnstry Gr Cathd San Francisco CA 1999-; Chair Cmsn for the Environ Dio California San Francisco CA 1993-** B San Francisco CA 3/5/1941 d Lafayette Chace Grover & Esther. BA U of San Francisco 1989; MDiv CDSP 1994. D 6/7/1997 P 12/6/1997 Bp William Edwin Swing. c 3. Environ Mnstry S Lk's Ch San Francisco CA 1997-1999. Auth, "Love God Heal Earth," *Bk*, St. Lynn's Press, 2008; Auth, "Comm w Life," *essay, H Ground*, Sierra Club, 2008; Auth, "Epis Power & Light," *Earth Light mag*, 2002; Auth, "Almighty Power," *Time*, 2001; Auth, "Epis Power & Light," *Yes mag (Winter Ed)*, 2000. Hon Doctorate U of So, Sewanee 2008; Climate Protection Awd US Environ Protection Agcy 2007; Energy Globe Awd Energiesparverband Austria 2002; Green Power Ldrshp Awd Dept Of Energy / Cntr For Resource Solutions 2001; Cert Of hon: Sacr Gift To The Planet Wrld Wildlife Fund / Allnce For Rel & Conservation Kathmandu Nepal 2000; Ba mcl U Of San Francisco San Francisco CA 1989. sally@theregenerationproject.org

BIPPUS JR, William Lloyd (FdL) 917 Church St, Marinette WI 54143 **R S Paul's Ch Marinette WI 1986-** B Hartford CT 6/24/1948 s William Lloyd Bippus & Shirley. BA Br 1971; MA Trin Hartford 1981; MDiv SWTS 1984. D 6/16/1984 Bp William Jackson Cox P 3/30/1985 Bp Gerald Nicholas McAllister. Cur S Mich's Epis Ch Norman OK 1984-1986. SHN, Conf of the Blessed S. stpaulsmarinette@centurytel.net

BIRCH, Lucene Kirkland (Fla) 2012 E Dellview Dr, Tallahassee FL 32303 **Ch Of The H Comf Tallahassee FL 1998-** B Webb AL 4/27/1926 d Arthur Lee Kirkland & Rossie Lee. BA Florida St U 1955; MA Emory U 1958. D 9/13/1998 Bp Stephen Hays Jecko. m 11/21/1992 Donald Birch. lucene@earthlink.com

BIRCHER, Victor Malcolm (Miss) 102 Edie St, Columbia MS 39429 B Salem MO 6/8/1938 s Victor Hugo Bircher & Ruth Margarette. BA Cntrl Methodist U 1960; LTh STUSo 1963. D 6/15/1963 Bp George Leslie Cadigan P 12/16/1963 Bp Charles Gresham Marmion. c 2. Vic S Steph's Ch Columbia MS 1980-1997; S Alb's Epis Ch Vicksburg MS 1970-1980; R S Matt's Ch Covington TN 1968-1970; Vic S Paul's Epis Ch Corinth MS 1965-1968; Cur Gr Ch Paducah KY 1963-1965.

BIRD, David John (ECR) 81 North 2 Street, San Jose CA 95113 **Dn Trin Cathd San Jose CA 2003-** B Dorridge Warwickshire UK 12/16/1946 s John Dawson Bird & Winifred. BA S Dav's Coll Lampeter GB 1970; STM GTS 1974; PhD Duquesne U 1987. Trans from Church Of England 9/1/1978 as Priest Bp Alexander Doig Stewart. m 6/9/1979 Diane Elizabeth Curren c 2. R Gr Ch Washington DC 1989-2003; Cn Theol Dio Pittsburgh Monroeville PA 1988-1989; R S Andr's Epis Ch New Kensington PA 1979-1989; Vic Chr Ch Rochdale MA 1978-1979; Assoc Chr And S Steph's Ch New York NY 1977-1978. Auth, *Serving Unity*, EDEO-NADEO, 2000; Auth, *Toward a Gd Chr Death*, Morehouse, 1999; Auth, *Assisted Suicide and Euthanasia*,

Morehouse, 1997; Auth, *Before You Need Them*, Forw Mvmt, 1995; Auth, *Receiving the Vision*, Liturg Press, 1995. Rotary 1979-1987. david3933@aol.com

BIRD, Edith Simonton (Ark) 28 Prospect Ave, Eureka Springs AR 72632 B Bethesda MD 4/7/1961 d John Adams Bird & Mary Alice. BA Harv 1983; Cert Epis TS of The SW 1989; MDiv Weston Jesuit TS 1989. D 6/17/1989 P 5/1/1990 Bp Robert Manning Moody. m 3/7/2009 Graham Ernest Robinson. Int S Andr's Ch Rogers AR 2009-2010; S Jas Ch Eureka Sprg AR 2000-2008; S Mart's U Cntr Fayetteville AR 2000-2002; S Paul's Ch Fayetteville AR 1999; P-in-c S Mart's Ch Pryor OK 1998; Vic S Aid's Epis Ch Tulsa OK 1991-1993; Dio Oklahoma Oklahoma City OK 1989-1993; Cur And Hosp Chapl S Dunst's Ch Tulsa OK 1989-1991. Auth, "Our Disregard For The Earth Is Killing Us," *Epis Life*, 2002; Auth, "Setting Thos Merton On Fire," *Epis New Yorker*, 2000; Auth, "On Either Side Of Forgiveness," *Sojourners*, 1999. edie.bird@att.net

BIRD, Frederick Lee (WVa) 1009 S Henry Ave, Elkins WV 26241 **The No Cntrl Cluster Elkins WV 2003-; Stff Epis Ch of the Trsfg Buckhannon WV 1999-; Stff Gr Epis Ch Elkins WV 1999-; Stff S Mths Grafton WV 1999-** B Montgomery WV 11/9/1946 s Wilford Bird & Wava. BA Inst Of Tech W Virginia U Morgantown WV 1969; MS U of Tennessee 1973. D 6/13/1998 P 6/12/1999 Bp John H(enry) Smith. m 10/23/1993 Donetta Elizabeth Hulver c 3. NASW, Acsw.

BIRD, Henry Lonsdale (Me) 330 Bethel Point Rd, Harpswell ME 04079 B Wilmington DE 5/29/1927 s Samuel Bancroft Bird & H Lonsdale. BA Pr 1950; BD EDS 1956; MDiv EDS 1968. D 6/16/1956 Bp John Brooke Mosley P 12/16/1956 Bp Frederic Cunningham Lawrence. m 6/14/1955 Hildegarde B Brewster c 5. Downeast Epis Cluster Swans Island ME 1987-1989; S Fran By The Sea Blue Hill ME 1987-1989; Epis Ch Of The Epiph Socorro NM 1979-1986; Vic S Paul's Epis Ch Truth or Consequences NM 1979-1985; Dio The Rio Grande Albuquerque NM 1976-1987; Vic Navajoland Area Mssn Farmington NM 1976-1979; All SS Farmington NM 1973-1979; Asst P Navajoland Area Mssn Farmington NM 1972-1974; Assoc S Paul's Ch Brunswick ME 1966-1968; Gr Ch Vineyard Haven MA 1959-1966; M-in-c S Paul's Epis Ch Bedford MA 1956-1959. "Tentmaking Mnstry," *CE Findings*. BEC, Epis Ch 1988-1994; Third Ord, Soc of S Fran 1956. Chairman, COM Dio Rio Grande 1980; Soc of the Sigma (elected by the Princeton Chapt) Sci Resrch Soc 1950. h-hbird@suscom-maine.net

BIRD JR, John Edwin (NJ) 304 S Girard St, Woodbury NJ 08096 B Pittsburgh PA 8/27/1940 s John Edwin Bird & Esther Linda. BA Monmouth U 1966; MDiv PDS 1969; DMin VTS 1993. D 4/19/1969 P 10/25/1969 Bp Alfred L Banyard. m 5/20/1961 Mary Beth Kiel c 1. The Ch Of S Uriel The Archangel Sea Girt NJ 1988-1999; R Ch Of The Gd Shpd Jacksonville FL 1983-1988; R Ch Of S Lk And Epiph Philadelphia PA 1975-1983; Cur Chr Ch In Woodbury Woodbury NJ 1969-1975. Mdiv w hon PDS Philadelphia PA 1969; Ba cl Monmouth U W Long Branch NJ 1966. jebmbb@comcast.net

BIRD, Julie Childs (SC) Po Box 128, Clinton WA 98236 **D S Augustines In-The-Woods Epis Par Freeland WA 2004-** B Baltimore MD 9/16/1936 MDiv Harvard DS 1997. D 9/14/2002 Bp Edward Lloyd Salmon Jr. m 5/22/1998 Edward Dennis Bird. D Gr Ch Charleston SC 2002-2004. birdchildsnw@whidbey.com

BIRD, Michael Andrew (NY) 7 Library Ln, Bronxville NY 10708 **R Chr Ch Bronxville NY 2004-** B Philadelphia PA 10/11/1967 s John Edwin Bird & Mary Beth. BA Swarthmore Coll 1989; MDiv GTS 1997. D 5/3/1997 Bp Joe Morris Doss P 11/1/1997 Bp Herbert Alcorn Donovan Jr. m 7/22/1989 Catherine Murray c 2. S Mk's Ch New Canaan CT 1997-2004. mbird1@me.com

BIRD, Patricia A (Del) 28582 Gazebo Way Unit 85, Millsboro DE 19966 B Baltimore MD 3/16/1942 d Clifford Bird & Lena Louise. BA Philadelphia Mus Acad 1964; MDiv Bex 1977; MA Mundelein Coll 1983. D 6/4/1977 P 4/1/1978 Bp Harold B Robinson. Trin Par Wilmington DE 2006-2008; Int S Paul's Par Kent Chestertown MD 2005-2006; Int S Ptr's Ch Lewes DE 2004-2005; Int St Annes Epis Ch Middletown DE 2002-2003; Int S Christophers Epis Ch Oxford PA 2000-2002; P-in-res S Jn's Ch Bala Cynwyd PA 1997-2000; Assoc to R S Ptr's Ch Phoenixville PA 1993-1996; S Matt's Ch Evanston IL 1983-1985; Vic S Jn's Ch Wilson NY 1978-1982; Asst S Paul's Cathd Buffalo NY 1977-1978. Auth, *Pavane-Faure*; Auth, *Prelude on Picardy*; Auth, *Today's Par*. pbird3@aol.com

BIRD, Peter (FdL) 315 E. Jefferson St., Waupun WI 53963 **H Trin Epis Ch Waupun WI 2000-** B Kansas City MO 6/20/1943 s Robert Adam Bird & Nellie Flora. BA Ripon Coll Ripon WI 1966; JD SMU 1972; MDiv Nash 1977. D 6/18/2000 P 12/21/2000 Bp Russell Edward Jacobus. m 6/3/2000 Lila Lee Roberts c 2. prb-htw@sbcglobal.net

BIRD, Robert Dale (Mich) 824 W Maple Ave, Adrian MI 49221 **D Chr Ch Adrian MI 2011-** B Ridgeway MI 9/8/1935 s Walter James Bird & Jennie. Whitaker TS. D 9/10/1987 Bp H Coleman McGehee Jr. m 5/11/1957 Eunice Jane Haracourt c 3. NAAD.

BIRD, Van Samuel (Pa) 2430 W Lehigh Ave, Philadelphia PA 19132 B Waycross GA 9/6/1924 BA Ft Vlly St U 1948; MDiv SWTS 1951; S Aug's Coll Cbury Gb 1958; MA Tem 1969; PhD Tem 1976. D 5/26/1951 P 11/1/1951 Bp Wallace E Conkling. m 6/29/1946 Eva Ruth Brown. S Simon The Cyrenian Ch Philadelphia PA 1984-1990; Dio Pennsylvania Philadelphia PA 1975-1984; Vic S Barth's Ch Philadelphia PA 1968-1975; Vic S Andr's Ch Charlotte Amalie VI VI 1964-1966; Vic H Trin Epis Ch Baltimore MD 1953-1964; Cur The Afr Epis Ch Of S Thos Philadelphia PA 1951-1953.

BIRD, Virginia Lee (SD) Po Box 9412, Rapid City SD 57709 **D S Andr's Epis Ch Rapid City SD 1987-** B Holloman Air Force Base NM 6/13/1950 d Walter Harned Bird & Virginia Lee. California St Polytechnic U 1970; BS Loma Linda U 1972; MA TCU 1982. D 9/14/1987 Bp Craig Barry Anderson. Chapl Dio So Dakota Sioux Falls SD 2007-2009. Recognition of Diac Mnstry in the tradition of St. Stephe NAAD (NAAD) 2007. vbird@rap.midco.net

BIRDSALL, James Andrew (Ct) PO Box 2252, Orleans MA 02653 B Toledo OH 10/17/1932 s Russell Evans Birdsall & Beatrice. Adel 1954; MDiv Ya Berk 1957; Fllshp Harv 1986. D 4/27/1957 Bp James P De Wolfe P 11/23/1957 Bp Jonathan Goodhue Sherman. m 8/25/1956 Marcia A Arnold c 4. R Chr Ch Pomfret CT 1973-1994; Vic S Ptr's Ch So Windsor CT 1962-1972; Vic Gr Ch Broad Brook CT 1961-1965; Cur All SS Ch Great Neck NY 1957-1961. Rotary Racine Awd For Cmnty Serv Connecticut 1994; Lions Club Man of the Year So Windsor 1970; BA mcl Adel Garden City NY 1954. omabrdsl@aol.com

BIRDSALL, John Burton (Eas) 419a Evans St Apt 2, Williamsville NY 14221 **Assoc S Paul's Epis Ch Harris Hill Williamsville NY 1994-** B Highland Park MI 9/7/1925 s Otis Burdette Birdsall & Dorothy Ruth. BA Ken 1949; LTh GTS 1952; STB GTS 1960. D 6/9/1952 P 2/12/1953 Bp Lauriston L Scaife. c 2. R S Steph's Ch Earleville MD 1981-1988; Hon Cn S Paul's Cathd Buffalo NY 1979-1989; R S Ptr's Epis Ch Eggertsville NY 1967-1980; Asst Calv Epis Ch Williamsville NY 1962-1967; Cur The Epis Ch Of The Gd Shpd Buffalo NY 1952-1954. Epis Curs 1982. jackandninab@mailstation.com

BIRDSEY, Robert Bruce (EC) 215 Ann St, Beaufort NC 28516 B Macon GA 11/6/1947 s Herbert Ford Birdsey & Cynthia. BA Van 1970; MDiv Candler TS Emory U 1977. D 6/11/1977 P 3/9/1978 Bp Bennett Jones Sims. m 1/30/1971 Brenda Hicks c 2. Chr Epis Ch Luray VA 2009-2010; Ch Of The H Comf Richmond VA 2006-2008; S Jas' Epis Ch Dexter MI 2004-2006; S Ptr's By-The-Sea Swansboro NC 2004; R S Paul's Ch Beaufort NC 2001-2003; Assoc S Phil's Ch Brevard NC 1998-2001; R The Epis Ch Of The Medtr Allentown PA 1986-1998; Dioc Nwspr Atlanta GA 1981-1986; R Epis Ch Of The H Sprt Cumming GA 1981-1986; S Jude's Ch Marietta GA 1978-1981; Dio Atlanta Atlanta GA 1977-1978. bb07768@gmail.com

BIRDWELL, Harland Bryan (RG) 266 Elm Cove Cir, Abilene TX 79605 B Snyder TX 11/1/1928 s James Henry Birdwell & Ethel Louise. Texas Tech U 1949; MDiv Epis TS In Kentucky 1965; BA U of Kentucky 1965. D 5/29/1965 Bp William R Moody P 12/1/1965 Bp George Henry Quarterman. c 2. Pstr Asst Ch Of The Heav Rest Abilene TX 2000-2006; Int S Steph's Ch Sweetwater TX 1998-2000; Cn to the Ordnry Dio The Rio Grande Albuquerque NM 1989-1993; R S Andr's Ch Roswell NM 1980-1989; R The Epis Ch Of S Mary The Vrgn Big Sprg TX 1968-1980; Vic All SS Ch Colorado City TX 1965-1968; Vic S Steph's Ch Sweetwater TX 1965-1968. Auth, *Those Crazy Episcopalians Dio NW Texas*, 1970. Phi Beta Kappa The U of Kentucky Lexington KY 1965. birdwellshbb@sbcglobal.net

BIRKBY, Charles H (CNY) 79 Ripplebrook Lane, Minoa NY 13116 **Ret Dio Cntrl New York Syracuse NY 2004-; ArmdF Mnstry Coordntr Dio Cntrl New York Syracuse NY 2001-** B Washington DC 1/15/1942 s Fred Charles Birkby & Estella Kathryn. BA Auburn U 1964; PDS 1966; Coll of Preachers 1980; SUNY 1988. D 4/20/1968 P 10/26/1968 Bp Alfred L Banyard. m 8/17/1968 Dorothy Frances Lutz c 3. R Emm Ch E Syracuse NY 1981-1986; P Assoc Trin Cathd Trenton NJ 1981; Assoc R S Ptr's Ch Medford NJ 1978-1980; Vic The Ch Of The Gd Shpd Berlin NJ 1973-1978; Mem Yth Cmsn Dio New Jersey Trenton NJ 1968-1981; Sem in Charge/Vic Ch Of The H Sprt Tuckerton NJ 1966-1973. Auth, ""Invisible Prisoners,"" *Living Ch.* GAS 1981. frcharliesr@netscape.net

BIRKENHEAD, Harold G (Mass) 667 Washington Ave, Portland ME 04103 **Ch Of The H Nativ So Weymouth MA 2006-** B Boston MA 9/9/1948 s William James Birkenhead & Mary. AA Massasoit Cmnty Coll 1986; BS Bridgewater Coll 1988; MDiv VTS 1992. D 5/30/1992 P 5/15/1993 Bp David Elliot Johnson. m 3/23/2006 Charlene Birkenhead c 4. S Ptr's Ch Portland ME 1995-2006; Asst to R Epis Ch Of S Thos Taunton MA 1992-1995. Auth, "God Is w Us In Our Pain & Suffering," Dow Pub, 1997. hbirkenhed@aol.com

BIRNBAUM, Rachelle Eskenaizi (Va) 3421 Franconia Rd, Alexandria VA 22310 **R All SS Ch Alexandria VA 1998-** B Bronx NY 8/26/1948 d Leo Birnbaum & Sarina. BA Drew U 1972; MDiv Ya Berk 1977. D 12/21/1977 P 11/1/1978 Bp Paul Moore Jr. Assoc Mssnr S Marg's Epis Ch Little Rock AR 1995-1998; Assoc Trin Ch In The City Of Boston Boston MA 1990-1994; CDSP Berkeley CA 1984-1990; Chr And S Steph's Ch New York NY 1981-1984; Epis Ch Cntr New York NY 1981-1984; Asst Par Of The Epiph Winchester MA 1980-1981; Chr And S Steph's Ch New York NY 1979-1980; Chapl Dio New York New York City NY 1977-1980; Diocn Msnry & Ch

Extntn Socty New York NY 1977-1980; Dpt Of Missions Ny Income New York NY 1977-1980. revreb111@aol.com

BIRNEY, Edith Hazard (Me) 11 Perkins St, Topsham ME 04086 B Louisville KY 1/25/1947 d Charles Ware Blake Hazard & Edith Bruce. Hollins U 1967; Katharine Gibbs Sch 1967; BA Bow 1985. D 6/12/1999 Bp Chilton Abbie Richardson Knudsen. m 11/27/2004 James Gillespie Birney c 4. S Paul's Ch Brunswick ME 2001-2002. Auth, *Singing for Your Supper*, Algonquin, 1996; Auth, *Rising to the Occasion*, Algonquin, 1993. ehazard@blazenetme.net

BIRNEY III, James Gillespie (Me) 1110 North Rd, North Yarmouth ME 04097 B Hanover NH 3/10/1950 s James Gillespie Birney & Marion Elizabeth. BA Wms 1972; MDiv VTS 1979. D 7/14/1979 P 2/6/1980 Bp Harold B Robinson. m 11/27/2004 Edith Hazard Birney c 2. S Barth's Epis Ch Yarmouth ME 1983-1989; S Paul's Sch Concord NH 1980-1983. EPF. jbirney@bowdoin.edu

BIRNEY, James Gillespie (WNY) Wellington, 1361 E Boot Rd #114, West Chester PA 19380 B Washington DC 3/26/1924 s Dion Scott Birney & Sarah Booth. BA Dart 1950; MDiv VTS 1953. Rec 10/7/1966 Bp Angus Dun. m 3/21/1992 Barbara S Sullivan c 5. Assoc S Ptr's Ch In The Great Vlly Malvern PA 2002-2006; Shattuck-S Mary's Sch Faribault MN 1976-1982; R Ch Of The Adv Kenmore NY 1972-1976; Admin Asst To Bp Dio Wstrn New York Tonawanda NY 1969-1972; Asst To Bp Dio Delaware Wilmington DE 1962-1969; Exec Coun Dio Delaware Wilmington DE 1960-1963; Stndg Com Dio Delaware Wilmington DE 1960-1963; R S Lk's Epis Ch Seaford DE 1955-1962; Asst S Alb's Par Washington DC 1953-1955. Auth, "An Outline Of Chr Faith," *Dio Delaware*, 1960. jasgb1142@aol.com

BIRTCH, John Edward McKay (SwFla) 1001 Carpenters Way Apt H108, Lakeland FL 33809 **Asst P All SS Epis Ch Lakeland FL 1999-** B Woodstock Ontario Canada 6/12/1929 s John Mckay Birtch & Evelyn Mary. BA U of Wstrn Ontario 1951; LTh Hur 1952; DIT S Aug's Coll Cbury Gb 1955; BD Hur 1961; DMin VTS 2001. Rec 8/1/1971 as Priest Bp The Bishop Of Huron. m 8/19/1953 Patricia Joanne Milburn. R Calv Ch Indn Rocks Bch FL 1978-1994; R S Barth's Ch St Petersburg FL 1971-1978; Cn Trin Cathd Miami FL 1971. "Pryr Workshop 101 Proj Thesis," Virginia Sem, 2001. AFP, Trst; Ord Of S Lk, Bro Of S Andr. Hon Cn Trin Cathd Miami 1971; R Emer Calv Epis Indn Rocks Bch Fl. jojohnpolk@netscape.com

BISHOP, Barbara Elaine (Chi) 827 Canterbury Dr, Crystal Lake IL 60014 **D Pstr Assisant S Mary Epis Ch Crystal Lake IL 1991-** B DeKalb IL 6/26/1942 d Charles Warner Mosher & Ruth. BA Alderson-Broaddus Coll 1964; MRE Nthrn Bapt TS 1966; Cert Dio Chicago Sch for Deacons 1991. D 12/7/1991 Bp Frank Tracy Griswold III. m 9/16/1967 Robert Bishop. Admin COM Dio Chicago Chicago IL 1999-2009. Contrib, "Many Servnt," *Many Servnt: An Intro to Deacons*, Cowley, 2004. Bd Mem NAAD 1999-2011; Dio Chicago Deacons' Coun 1992-2002; No Amer Assn for Diac 1990; Pres NAAD 2007-2009; Vice Pres/Pres Elect NAAD 2005-2007. bbishop@mc.net

BISHOP, Christopher M (Pa) 400 King of Prussia Rd, Wayne PA 19087 **Liturg Plnng Cmsn Dio Pennsylvania Philadelphia PA 2011-; P-in-c S Mart's Ch Radnor PA 2011-** B Cincinnati OH 9/19/1960 s John Wesley Bishop & Joann. BA St Lawr Canton NY 1983; MFA Col Nyc 1988; MDiv Luth TS Philadelphia PA 2007. D 6/9/2007 Bp Charles Ellsworth Bennison Jr P 12/15/2007 Bp Franklin Delton Turner. Chapl All SS Epis Day Sch Hoboken NJ 2007-2009; P All SS Epis Par Hoboken NJ 2007-2008. cmbishop919@yahoo.com

BISHOP, Edwin (Ore) 130 Gables Way, Kitty Hawk NC 27949 B Seattle WA 2/24/1930 s Edwin Nmn Bishop & Velma Marie. BA U of Washington 1952; STB GTS 1955; Med Virginia Commonwealth U 1977; MA Presb Sch of CE Richmond VA 1978. D 6/29/1955 P 2/6/1956 Bp Stephen F Bayne Jr. m 8/11/1956 Joan Gail Avery c 3. Int All SS' Ch Sthrn Shores NC 2002-2003; Int Hickory Neck Ch Toano VA 2000-2001; Int Ch Of The Gd Shpd Raleigh NC 1994-1995; Int All SS' Epis Ch Ft Worth TX 1992-1994; Int S Jn's Par Hagerstown MD 1991-1992; Int Pac Cure Par Cartersville VA 1989-1990; Int Chr And Gr Ch Petersburg VA 1988-1989; Int H Innoc' Epis Ch Lahaina HI 1987-1988; Int Ch Of The Creator Mechanicsville VA 1987; Int Ch Of The H Comf Richmond VA 1986-1987; Int S Andr's Ch Richmond VA 1985; Int S Cyp's Epis Ch Hampton VA 1984-1985; Intrim Spec Dio Sthrn Virginia Norfolk VA 1984; Int S Mich's Ch Colonial Heights VA 1982-1983; Int S Andr's Ch Norfolk VA 1982; Int Gr Epis Ch Goochland VA 1981; Int Emm Ch At Brook Hill Richmond VA 1979; Int S Mths Epis Ch Midlothian VA 1978-1979; Int Spec Dio No Carolina Raleigh NC 1977-1995; Int Spec Dio Virginia Richmond VA 1977-1995; Int S Paul's Ch Petersburg VA 1977-1978; Chapl S Marg's Sch Tappahannock VA 1972-1976; R All SS Ch Hillsboro OR 1960-1966; Yth Mnstrs Dio Nevada Las Vegas NV 1958-1960; Vic S Mk's Ch Tonopah NV 1958-1960; Dept of Missions Dio Olympia Seattle WA 1957-1958; Vic S Anne's Epis Ch Washougal WA 1955-1958; Cur S Lk's Epis Ch Vancouver WA 1955-1957. Auth, *Occasional Mnstrs*, U.S. Navy, 1984; Auth, *Love in Deed.* Int Mnstry Ntwk 1980; Mltry & Hospitaler Ord S Jn Jerusalem 1986; OHC 1947. frtbish@aol.com

BISHOP JR, Harold Ellsworth (Md) Box 128, Cottage 505-B, Quincy PA 17247 **Assoc S Mary's Epis Ch Waynesboro PA 1994-** B Cumberland MD 8/1/1928 s Harold Ellsworth Bishop & Minnie Gertrude. BS W Virginia U 1950; MS Frostburg St U 1971. D 6/2/1982 P 6/1/1983 Bp Robert Poland Atkinson. m 1/19/1951 Norma Virginia Crump. R S Geo's Epis Ch Mt Savage MD 1986-1994; Cur Emm Ch Keyser WV 1982-1984; Cur Emm Ch Moorefield WV 1982-1984.

BISHOP, John Jacob (Mass) 206 Linden Ponds Way Unit 135, Hingham MA 02043 B Dayton KY 5/31/1924 s Nelson Devon Bishop & Marie Anna. BA U Cinc 1948; MA U MI 1949; MDiv EDS 1952. D 6/11/1952 Bp Henry W Hobson P 12/14/1952 Bp Raymond A Heron. m 6/25/1955 Elizabeth R Reynolds c 4. Int Ch Of The Mssh Woods Hole MA 2001-2002; Int The Ch Of S Mary Of The Harbor Provincetown MA 1997-1998; Int S Paul's Ch Dedham MA 1992-1994; Int S Barn Ch Falmouth MA 1991-1992; Stndg Com Dio Massachusetts Boston MA 1984-1988; Co-Chair of COM Dio Massachusetts Boston MA 1972-1978; R Par Of The Epiph Winchester MA 1966-1989; Homil Instr EDS Cambridge MA 1964-1974; R S Jn's Epis Ch Westwood MA 1956-1966. Bp Arnold Awd - Epis City Mssn Dio Massachusetts 1991.

BISHOP, Nila Ruth (WMo) 1433 NW R D Mize Rd, Blue Springs MO 64015 B Linn Co. MO 6/11/1944 d Ora Wesley Irick & Emma Ruth Maxwell. Non-degree Prog Geo Herbert Inst of Pstr Stds. D 6/4/2011 Bp Martin Scott Field. c 2. nila.bishop@comcast.net

BISSELL-THOMPSON, Geraldine Vina (Alb) 11 E Main St, Lebanon VA 24266 B Eugene OR 10/31/1942 d Clare Marquart Bissell & Vina Daisy. BA U of Oregon 1969; MA U of Oregon 1970; PhD U of Oregon 1974; LTh McGill U 1985. D 6/8/1985 P 10/26/1986 Bp O'Kelley Whitaker. m 2/2/1963 Howard Thompson c 5. Gr Epis Ch Canton NY 1999-2004; S Barn Ch Warwick RI 1997-1999; P-in-c Trin Chap Morley Canton NY 1988-2002; Trin Ch Lowville NY 1988-1997; P Emm Ch E Syracuse NY 1986-1988; D Chr Ch Morristown NY 1985-1986. tnhow1@juno.com

BITSBERGER, Donald Edward (Va) 4970 Sentinel Dr Apt 505, Bethesda MD 20816 B Fort Wayne IN 5/4/1928 s William Frank Bitsberger & Nellie May. BA Ya 1950; BDiv EDS 1953. D 6/13/1953 P 5/1/1954 Bp William A Lawrence. m 12/30/1997 Carol D Hendricks. Asst Ch Of Our Sav Silver Sprg MD 1998-2004; Chr Ch Alexandria VA 1990-1991; Epis EvangES Arlington VA 1987-1993; Chair EDS Cambridge MA 1984-1985; EDS Cambridge MA 1978-1980; R Ch Of The Redeem Chestnut Hill MA 1968-1987. Auth, *Forw Day By Day*, 1985. BDiv cl Epis TS Cambridge MA 1953; Polly Bond Awd for Excellence, Theol Reflection; Yale Medal DSA Ya New Haven CT. donbits@verizon.net

BITTNER, Merrill (Me) 118 Lone Pine Rd, Newry ME 04261 B Pasadena CA 9/17/1946 d John Merrill Bittner & Ethel Lewis. BA Lake Erie Coll 1969; MDiv Bex 1972; MS U of Sthrn Maine 1996. D 1/6/1973 Bp Robert Rae Spears Jr P 7/29/1974 Bp Daniel Corrigan. S Barn Ch Rumford ME 2001-2006; Dio Rochester Rochester NY 1973-1976; Assoc Ch Of The Gd Shpd Webster NY 1973-1975. mbittner@megalink.net

BLACK, Cynthia Louise (Nwk) 4900 Nathan Ln N, Plymouth MN 55442 **R Ch Of The Redeem Morristown NJ 2011-; Exec Coun Com on the Status of Wmn Epis Ch Cntr New York NY 2006-2012** B Newton MA 3/18/1959 d William Spence Black & Barbara Ann. BA Wm Smith 1981; MDiv CDSP 1985; D.D. CDSP 2006. D 7/6/1985 Bp William George Burrill P 1/18/1986 Bp John Shelby Spong. m 9/2/2011 Rebecca Walker. Int Ch Of The Epiph Epis Plymouth MN 2010-2011; Advsr, WCC Del Epis Ch Cntr New York NY 2006; Exec Coun Epis Ch Cntr New York NY 2000-2006; Dn Cathd Par Of Chr The King Portage MI 1991-2010; Int S Ptr's Ch Essex Fells NJ 1990-1991; Assoc S Ptr's Ch Essex Fells NJ 1985-1990. Dir and Producer, "Voices of Witness Afr," 2009; Auth, "Var arts," *Ruach*. Polly Bond Awd ECom 2010; Lifetime Mem EWC 2000. revclb@gmail.com

BLACK, David Paul (WA) 3601 Edelmar Ter, Silver Spring MD 20906 B Hopkins MN 12/9/1920 s Robert H Black & Carol P. VTS; BS USAF Inst of Tech MS 1952. D 6/17/1972 P 2/1/1973 Bp William Foreman Creighton. m 12/4/1943 Opal E Smith c 3. P S Mary Magd Ch Silver Sprg MD 1991-1999; Ch Of Our Sav Silver Sprg MD 1985-1986; Asst Nativ Epis Ch Temple Hills MD 1978-1982; Nativ Epis Ch Temple Hills MD 1973-1977.

BLACK, G(eorge) Donald (At) 215 N Edenfield Ridge Dr, Rome GA 30161 B Swainsboro GA 4/29/1935 s George Alton Black & Runelle. BA U Rich 1962; MDiv STUSo 1963; Fllshp STUSo 1972; DMin STUSo 1990; The Cbury Course, Cbury Cathd 1996. D 6/27/1963 Bp David Shepherd Rose P 6/11/1964 Bp George P Gunn. m 6/29/1963 Suzanne D DuPuy c 2. Vic S Jas Ch Cedartown GA 2002-2009; R S Ptr's Ch Rome GA 1986-2000; R Chr Ch Blacksburg VA 1978-1986; R S Mths Epis Ch Midlothian VA 1968-1978; R S Geo's Ch Pungoteague Accomac VA 1965-1968; R S Jas' Ch Accomac VA 1965-1968; Cur Ch Of The Ascen Norfolk VA 1963-1965. Contrib, "Walking w Wounded Feet," *Simul Iustus et Pecctor*, The TS, Sewanee, 2003; Auth, "Lord of All Hopefulness," *St. Lk's Journ*, The TS, Sewanee, 1982. The DuBose Awd for Serv The TS, Sewanee 2005. gdb035@gmail.com

BLACK, **Katharine C** (Mass) 13 Louisburg Sq, Boston MA 02108 **Ch Of S Jn The Evang Boston MA 2006-** B Boston MA 1/1/1945 d Mandel E Cohen & Winifred Hamlen. BA Rad 1962; PhD CUA 1985; MDiv EDS 1986. D 6/11/1988 P 5/1/1989 Bp Don Edward Johnson. m 6/15/1967 Peter Black. Chr Ch Needham MA 2002; Trin Par Melrose MA 1999-2001; S Eliz's Ch Sudbury MA 1997-1998; S Mk's Ch Westford MA 1995-1996; S Paul's Ch In Nantucket Nantucket MA 1992-1993; Par Of The Epiph Winchester MA 1990-1991; Asst Par Of The Epiph Winchester MA 1989-1990; S Mich's Ch Marblehead MA 1989-1990; Cur S Mich's Ch Marblehead MA 1987-1988. KATHARINECBLACK@GMAIL.COM

BLACK JR, Milton England (WTex) 1704 N 10th St, Longview TX 75601 **Ch Of The Gd Shpd Corpus Christi TX 2008-** B Houston TX 11/8/1962 s Milton England Black & Bess. BA U of Texas 1986; MBA U of Texas 1994; MDiv VTS 2000. D 6/17/2000 Bp Claude Edward Payne P 6/29/2001 Bp Don Adger Wimberly. m 10/7/1989 Elizabeth H Head c 2. Dio W Texas San Antonio TX 2007-2008; S Jn's Epis Ch Sonora TX 2004-2007; R Trin Ch Longview TX 2002-2003; D Trin Ch Longview TX 2000-2001. mblack@cotgs.org

BLACK, Rebecca Lynn (Mass) 128 Village St, Millis MA 02054 **Epiph Par Walpole MA 2011-** B Millington TN 1/30/1960 d William Gilbert Black & Marcia Yvonne. Marist Coll; BA Estrn Connecticut St U 1984; MDiv EDS 2000. D 5/22/2000 Bp M(arvil) Thomas Shaw III P 5/23/2001 Bp Barbara Clementine Harris. c 1. R S Paul's Ch Boston MA 2005-2010; Asst S Andr's Ch Framingham MA 2000-2004. revrebec@aol.com

BLACK, Robert E. (Ct) 21Jerimoth Dr., Bradford CT 06405 B Lima OH 1/23/1922 s Hezekiah Porter Black & Dessie Mae. BA Wayne 1946; MA U MN 1948; Schlr 1956; MDiv Bex 1959; STM NYTS 1969. D 6/15/1957 P 12/1/1957 Bp Arthur C Lichtenberger. m 11/30/1984 Patricia Dondero c 1. Vic S Jn The Evang Yalesville CT 1966-1972; R Ch Of The Gd Shpd Houlton ME 1959-1966; Vic S Matt's Epis Ch Warson Warson Woods MO 1957-1959. Auth, "Var arts". Soc Of S Jn The Evang 1962-1967. Firestone Schlr 1955.

BLACK JR, Robert William (NC) 3506 Lawndale Drive, Greensboro NC 27408 **Asst R S Fran Ch Greensboro NC 2010-** B Hollywood FL 1/20/1984 s Robert W Black & Patricia Ann. BA Wake Forest U 2006; MDiv VTS 2009. D 6/13/2009 Bp Michael Bruce Curry P 1/16/2010 Bp John Chane. m 5/27/2008 Tyler B Chapman. Asst R S Jn's Ch Lafayette Sq Washington DC 2009-2010. robertwblack@gmail.com

BLACK, Ruth Buck (Miss) 1704 Poplar Blvd, Jackson MS 39202 B Nashville TN 10/4/1939 d John Carl Wallace & Ruth Craven. BA Belhaven Coll 1960; Fllshp Harv 1971; Fllshp Harv 1971; PhD Harv 1979; CPE Jackson St U 1981; EFM STUSo 1985. D 5/31/1986 P 2/1/1987 Bp Duncan Montgomery Gray Jr. m 6/6/1970 Dewitt Carlisle Black c 1. Cur S Phil's Ch Jackson MS 1986-1988. Auth, "Scraps From An Organic Quilt"; Auth, "The Gospel Imperative In The Midst Of Aids". Comp H Cross Soc, ACPE. Ndea Fell & Harvard Schlr Harv 1968.

BLACK, Sheryl Leonard (Spr) 12806 Mallard Dr., Whittington IL 62897 **P-in-c S Jas Epis Ch Marion IL 2011-; COM, Cler Mem Dio Springfield Springfield IL 2009-; Mem at Lg, ECW Dio Springfield Springfield IL 2008-** B Farmington NM 7/2/1959 d John Rodney Leonard & Audrey Ann. BS Greenville Coll 2004; MDiv TESM 2008. D 2/2/2008 P 11/1/2008 Bp Peter Hess Beckwith. m 11/2/1985 Larry William Black c 1. Chair, Dept. Soc Concerns Dio Springfield Springfield IL 2008-2011; Hale Dnry Team Mnstry Springfield IL 2008-2011; Asst S Jas Epis Ch McLeansboro IL 2007-2011. be_loved_1@msn.com

BLACK, Timothy Horace (At) 4393 Garmon Rd NW, Atlanta GA 30327 **Asst H Innoc Ch Atlanta GA 2010-; H Innoc' Epis Sch Atlanta GA 2010-** B Marietta GA 9/20/1966 s Reuben Black & Marjorie Joyce. BA Furman U 1988; MDiv Candler TS Emory U 2010. D 12/19/2009 Bp J(ohn) Neil Alexander. m 10/12/1991 Patricia Babuka c 3. timblack@gmail.com

BLACK, Vicki Kay (Me) 73 Bristol Rd, Damariscotta ME 04543 **D S Andr's Ch Newcastle ME 2006-** B Cordell OK 6/22/1961 d William Gober Black & Nancy Carolyn. BA SMU 1983; MDiv Nash 1987. D 3/28/1987 Bp Roger John White. D S Dav's Epis Mssn Pepperell MA 1992-2002; S Mk's Ch Milwaukee WI 1990-1991; COM Dio Milwaukee Milwaukee WI 1988-1991; Dio Milwaukee Milwaukee WI 1987-1989; Admin Of Catechumenate Dio Milwaukee Milwaukee WI 1987-1988; D Trin Ch Wauwatosa WI 1987-1988. "Welcome To BCP," Morehouse Pub, 2005; "And A Little Chld Shall Lead Them," Atr, 2004; "Welcome To The Ch Year," Morehouse Pub, 2004. NAAD. Phi Beta Kappa SMU Dallas TX 1983. vickiblack@earthlink.net

BLACK, Vincent (O) 2230 Euclid Ave, Cleveland OH 44115 **Cn for Chr Formation Dio Ohio Cleveland OH 2009-** B Cleveland OH 11/10/1969 s Dennis Black & Eleanor. BA JCU 1992; MDIV Bex 2009. D 6/13/2009 P 4/10/2010 Bp Mark Hollingsworth Jr. vincentblack@ameritech.net

✠ **BLACK, Rt Rev William Grant** (SO) 4101 W Iles Ave Apt 2213, Springfield IL 62711 **Ret Bp of Sthrn Ohio Dio Sthrn Ohio Cincinnati OH 1992-** B Muncie IN 4/17/1920 s Joseph Charles Black & Verna Dell. BA Greenville Coll 1941; MA U IL 1953; BD U Chi 1955; DD Ken 1980; LHD Ohio U 1992; LHD Hebr Un Coll 1993. D 10/8/1961 P 4/18/1962 Bp Roger W Blanchard Con 11/8/1979 for SO. m 5/15/2000 Frances Mathewson. Bp Dio Sthrn Ohio Cincinnati OH 1980-1992; Bp of Sthrn Ohio Dio Sthrn Ohio Cincinnati OH 1980-1992; Bp Coadj Dio Sthrn Ohio Cincinnati OH 1979-1980; R Ch Of Our Sav Cincinnati OH 1973-1979; R Ch Of The Gd Shpd Athens OH 1962-1973. Alum of the Year DS, U Chi Chicago IL 1972; Man of the Year Ohio SE Reg Commision 1971; Hon Cn Coventry Cathd in Engl 1968.

BLACKBURN, Elliot Hillman (Spr) 603 South Grant, Mason City IA 50401 B Springfield MA 7/2/1936 s George Victor Blackburn & Vera Adeline. BA Drew U 1958; MDiv Ya Berk 1962. D 6/16/1962 P 12/21/1962 Bp Robert McConnell Hatch. m 6/6/1959 Helen C Christianson c 3. R S Geo's Ch Belleville IL 1984-2000; R S Jn's Ch Mason City IA 1970-1984; Cur Ch Of The Atone Westfield MA 1962-1965. Hon Cn Cathd Ch of St. Paul, Springfield, IL 2002. ehblackburn@att.net

BLACKBURN, Gerald Jackson (EC) 815 2nd Ave, New York NY 10017 **Epis Ch Cntr New York NY 2001-; Dir Of Mltry Mnstrs Epis Ch Cntr New York NY 2001-** B West Point GA 12/18/1944 s Marvin Lafayette Blackburn & Lila Palestine. BA Samford U 1968; MDiv Sthrn Sem Louisville KY 1973; VTS 1998. D 9/30/1994 P 9/1/1995 Bp Brice Sidney Sanders. m 6/1/1968 Marilyn McGraw c 2. Off Of Bsh For ArmdF New York NY 1994-2001; D-In-Trng S Ptr's By-The-Sea Swansboro NC 1994-1995. gblackburn@episcopalchurch.org

BLACKBURN, James Clark (Md) 105 Tunbridge Rd, Baltimore MD 21212 B Cleveland OH 2/17/1934 s Paul Vincent Blackburn & Sylvia Mabel. BA Amh 1956; BD VTS 1959; MA U of Pennsylvania 1969. D 5/31/1959 Bp Joseph Gillespie Armstrong P 12/19/1959 Bp Oliver J Hart. m 6/14/1986 Judith Stewart c 3. Int All Hallows Par So River Davidsonville MD 1996-1999; Int Epis Ch Of Chr The King Windsor Mill MD 1995-1996; Int Chr Ch St Michaels MD 1994-1995; Int All SS Epis Par Sunderland MD 1992-1993; Int S Geo's Ch Perryman MD 1990-1992; Int S Jn's Ch Georgetown Par Washington DC 1989-1990; Int Dio Maryland Baltimore MD 1988-1989; Int S Mich And All Ang Ch Baltimore MD 1987-1988; Int S Marg's Ch Washington DC 1985-1987; Assoc The Ch Of The Redeem Baltimore MD 1981-1985; Archd for Prog Dio Newark Newark NJ 1978-1981; Glascow Ecum Mnstry Middletown DE 1976-1978; Coordntr Recon Prog Dio Pennsylvania Philadelphia PA 1970-1973; Assoc S Mart's Ch Radnor PA 1967-1970; St Pauls Epis Ch Oaks PA 1963-1967; Archd Dio Wstrn Kansas Hutchinson KS 1962-1963; Cur S Paul's Ch Philadelphia PA 1959-1962. "Ed," *Var arts*, Leaven NNECA, 1976; *Var arts*, Leaven NNECA, 1963. Phi Beta Kappa Amh Amherst MA 1956; BA mcl Amh Amherst MA 1956. james@speedfish.com

BLACKBURN, Terence Gene (NJ) 230 Melrose Terrace, Linden NJ 07036 **R St Jn the Bapt Epis Ch Linden NJ 2001-** B Warren OH 1/8/1946 s Harry Blackburn & Leonna. BA MI SU 1967; AMLS U MI 1968; MDiv GTS 1988. D 6/11/1988 P 12/11/1988 Bp Paul Moore Jr. R S Lk the Evang Roselle NJ 1992-2007; Cur Par Of Chr The Redeem Pelham NY 1988-1992. Auth, "Send Us Now Into the Wrld," *Liturg*, 1987. ter2413@msn.com

BLACKERBY JR, William S (Ala) 4307 Clairmont Ave S, Birmingham AL 35222 **Chapl Dio Alabama Birmingham AL 1993-** B Birmingham AL 1/27/1953 s William Spruiell Blackerby & Annie Lois. BA Birmingham-Sthrn Coll 1975; MA U of Alabama 1984; MDiv SWTS 1987. D 6/6/1987 P 12/1/1987 Bp Furman Stough. m 7/30/1983 Margaret Anne Thiele c 2. S Jn's Ch Birmingham AL 1996-1999; Int P-in-c S Jn's Ch Birmingham AL 1994-1995; Cur S Mary's-On-The-Highlands Epis Ch Birmingham AL 1988-1993; Cur S Mich's Ch Barrington IL 1987-1988. wsb4307@bellsouth.net

BLACKETT, Margaret (LI) 201 Drexel Ave, Westbury NY 11590 B Barbados West Indies 11/30/1952 D 11/21/2003 Bp Orris George Walker Jr. c 1. PEGGY317@VERIZON.NET

BLACKLOCK JR, Charles William (Alb) 2040 Helderberg Ave, Schenectady NY 12306 B New York NY 11/8/1927 s Charles William Blacklock & Barbara. BA SUNY 1965; MDiv PDS 1968. D 6/1/1968 Bp Charles Bowen Persell Jr P 12/7/1968 Bp Allen Webster Brown. m 4/27/1991 Gail J Homer. P-in-c Chr Ch Greenville NY 2002-2003; P-in-c Trin Ch Rensselaerville Rensselaerville NY 2002-2003; P-in-c S Lk's Ch Chatham NY 2000-2002; Supply S Andr's Ch Scotia NY 1999 2000; P-in-c Ch Of The H Sprt Schenevus NY 1991-1998; P-in-c S Tim's Ch Westford NY 1991-1998; P-in-c Chr Ch Greenville NY 1989-1991; P-in-c Trin Ch Rensselaerville Rensselaerville NY 1989-1991; Zion Ch Morris NY 1988; P-in-c Chr Ch Gilbertsville NY 1987-1989; R S Paul's Ch Schenectady NY 1971-1987; R Ch Of The Nativ Star Lake NY 1968-1971.

BLACKLOCK, Martha Grace (NJ) POBox 2973, Silver City NM 88062 **Asst Ch Of The Gd Shpd Silver City NM 2011-** B Saint Louis MO 5/1/1940 d Carl Conrad Gobdel & Maurine. BA Baldwin-Wallace Coll 1962; MFA U of Montana 1971; MDiv GTS 1976; DMin EDS 1996. D 6/5/1976 Bp George E Rath P 1/18/1977 Bp John Shelby Spong. m 7/15/2010 Twana Sparks. Vic S Mary's Ch Keyport NJ 1999-2004; Vic S Mk's Epis Ch Keansburg NJ 1999-2001; Vic S Clem's Ch New York NY 1980-1984; P Newark Epis Coop For Min & Miss Newark NJ 1979-1980; P No Porch Wmn & Infants Centers

Newark NJ 1979-1980; R S Barn Ch Newark NJ 1978-1980; Archd Dio Newark Newark NJ 1977-1978; Archd Voice Dioc Paper Newark NJ 1977-1978; Bp and Resource Cntr Newark NJ 1977. hayranur@gmail.com

BLACKMON, A(ndrew) Thomas (La) 120 S New Hampshire St, Covington LA 70433 **R Chr Ch Covington LA 2008-; Trst The CPG New York NY 2006-** B Jacksonville FL 4/8/1947 s Warren L Blackmon & Della Mae. Davidson Coll 1966; BA U Of Florida 1969; MDiv EDS 1975. D 5/18/1975 P 3/1/1976 Bp James Loughlin Duncan. m 2/1/1992 Margaret Steele c 2. Cur Ch Of The Incarn Dallas TX 1999-2008; Sr Assoc S Mich And All Ang Ch Dallas TX 1984-1999; Assoc S Alb's Par Washington DC 1977-1984; Asst H Trin Epis Ch W Palm Bch FL 1975-1977. Auth, "A Matter Of Faith"; Auth, "Leaven". Cornerstone Proj Ch 1988-1996; Cornerstone Proj City Conf 1981-1986; EvangES 1980-1990; NAECED 1997; Natl Ntwk Of Epis Cler 1979. tblackmon@christchurchcovington.com

BLACKSTOCK, Ross H(olcomb) (Colo) 31045 L Rd, Hotchkiss CO 81419 B Gunnison CO 4/27/1925 s Joseph Ross Blackstock & Ruth. BS U CO 1950; MDiv STUSo 1976. D 3/19/1977 P 10/29/1977 Bp Otis Charles. m 6/13/1953 Virginia Harriet Arnott. Vic S Jn's Epis Ch Ouray CO 1992-1994; Dio Colorado Denver CO 1988-1991; Ch Of The Nativ Grand Jct CO 1987; Vic S Mich's Paonia CO 1980-1992; S Jas' Epis Ch Alexander City AL 1979-1980; S Paul's Epis Ch Vernal UT 1977-1979; Vic S Tim's Epis Ch Rangely CO 1977-1978. vb@tds.net

BLACKWELL JR, Charles David (Wyo) 744 E 22nd St, Casper WY 82601 B Los Alamos NM 3/29/1947 s Charles D Blackwell & Marjorie Loreen. BS Utah St U 1972; Med Utah St U 1974; MDiv SWTS 1990. D 5/25/1990 P 1/1/1991 Bp Bob Gordon Jones. m 9/13/1969 Claudia Blanche Cluff. Ch Of S Andr's In The Pines Pinedale WY 1993-1995; R S Steph's Ch Casper WY 1990-1993. Ord Of S Lk 1990. cdb744@hotmail.com

BLACKWELL, Norma Lee (WA) 10754 Main St Apt 202, Fairfax VA 22030 B Metropolis IL 5/15/1942 d Phinis Norman Blackwell & Minnie Lee. BA Sthrn Illinois U 1964; MA Sthrn Illinois U 1966; MDiv VTS 1982. D 6/12/1982 P 1/1/1983 Bp John Thomas Walker. Dio Washington Washington DC 1991-1994; Asst R Calv Ch Washington DC 1988-1991; Asst S Andr's Ch Burke VA 1985-1987; Cathd of St Ptr & St Paul Washington DC 1982-1984. Ord Of S Lk.

BLACKWELL, Robert Hunter (Ala) 305 Arnold Street, Cullman AL 35055 **R Gr Ch Cullman AL 2007-** B Decatur AL 3/3/1956 s Paul Blackwell & Sarah Elizabeth. BA Auburn U 1978; MDiv Nash 1984. D 5/29/1984 P 12/18/1984 Bp Furman Stough. m 5/13/1978 Mary Katherine Loyd c 2. Exec Coun Appointees New York NY 2005-2006; R S Ptr's Epis Ch Talladega AL 1988-2005; R S Jos's On-The-Mtn Mentone AL 1984-1988. gracecullman@aol.com

BLACKWOOD, Deb (NC) 14103 Wilford Ct, Charlotte NC 28277 **Coord Pstr Care Ch Of The H Comf Charlotte NC 2009-** B Charleston WV 5/19/1943 d Edward James Mills & Betty Berry. BA W Virginia U 1965; MA W Virginia U 1967; PhD Ohio U 1974; non-degree Duke DS 2009. D 6/12/1999 Bp John Bailey Lipscomb. m 11/2/1963 Allen Blackwood c 1. Dir of Cmncatn/Tech S Jn's Epis Ch Charlotte NC 2009-2010; Chapl, Tech Catalyst Trin Epis Sch Charlotte NC 2005-2009; Dio SW Florida Sarasota FL 2001-2004. debblackwood@gmail.com

BLADON, Doyle Gene (Az) 310 W Union Ave, Monticello AR 71655 B Clearfield IA 7/17/1926 s Vernon A Bladon & Vera M. BA U of Iowa 1956; DDS U of Iowa 1959. D 3/1/1977 Bp Joseph Thomas Heistand. m 5/24/1952 Helen Troy Martin c 2.

BLAGG, James Raymond (Okla) 117 Sandpiper Cir, Durant OK 74701 **R S Jn's Ch Durant OK 1988-** B Brownwood TX 2/17/1953 s Richard Raymond Blagg & Rosemary. BA Angelo St U 1974; MDiv TCU 1977; U So 1979; M Behavioral Stds SE Oklahoma St U 1995. D 6/16/1979 P 6/1/1980 Bp Willis Ryan Henton. m 8/21/1976 Caroline Kinloch Terrell c 2. Assoc R Ch Of The Heav Rest Abilene TX 1987-1988; Vic S Jas Ch Monahans TX 1980-1987; Vic S Ptr's Ch Kermit TX 1980-1985; Cur The Epis Ch Of S Mary The Vrgn Big Sprg TX 1979-1980. revjames@blagg.com

BLAIES-DIAMOND, Sarah (Eau) 201 Fairview Rd, Mooresville NC 28117 **Chr Ch Cleveland NC 2011-** B New Hampshire 5/21/1961 d Donald Blaies & Joan. BS Carroll Coll U; MDiv The GTS 2009. D 2/19/2009 Bp Keith Bernard Whitmore P 1/16/2011 Bp Michael Bruce Curry. m 9/3/2005 Daryl Edward Diamond c 3. Asst P S Pat's Mssn Mooresville NC 2010-2011. momjbe@aol.com

BLAIN, Judd Huntley (ND) 230 Stillwater Rd, Deerfield MA 01342 **Adj Min Trin Ch Shelburne Falls MA 2002-** B Los Angeles CA 7/29/1935 s John Huntley Blain & Eleanor Alvina. BA Harv 1957; MDiv VTS 1960; U of New Mex 1966. D 6/30/1960 P 5/24/1961 Bp Richard R Emery. m 9/27/1958 Beatrice Young c 4. M-in-c S Jas Ch Ft Yates ND 1961-1965; M-in-c S Lk's Ch Ft Yates ND 1961-1965; Cur S Geo's Epis Ch Bismarck ND 1960-1961. judbeaty@comcast.net

BLAINE, Carol (Tex) 307 Palm Dr, Marlin TX 76661 B Houston TX 10/22/1940 d Thomas D McGown & Charlotte. BA U of Texas 1963; MDiv Epis TS of The SW 2002. D 6/22/2002 Bp Claude Edward Payne P 7/19/2003 Bp Don Adger Wimberly. c 3. R Gr Epis Ch Houston TX 2005-2011; P-in-c S Jn's Epis Ch Marlin TX 2002-2005. revblaine@yahoo.com

BLAINE-WALLACE, William Edwards (Me) 161 Wood Street, Lewiston ME 04240 B Salisbury NC 5/22/1951 s William McKinley Wallace & Lucy. BA Lenoir-Rhyne Coll 1975; MDiv Luth Theol Sthrn Sem 1980; PhD Caholic Univerity of Brabant, the Netherlands 2009. D 9/26/1992 P 4/1/1993 Bp Don Edward Johnson. m 7/7/2001 Victoria Blaine c 3. Ch Of Our Sav Arlington MA 2005-2006; R Emm Ch Boston MA 1993-2005. Auth of Chapt in Bk, "The Politics of Tears," *Inustice and the Care of Souls*, Fortress, 2009; Auth, "Water In The Wastelands," Cowley, 2003. wblainew@bates.edu

BLAIR, Alexander (Cal) 1801 Marin Ave, Berkeley CA 94707 B Greensboro NC 3/6/1925 s Alexander Blair & Dorothy. BS Georgia Inst of Tech 1946; MA Harv 1950; MDiv CDSP 1957; Fllshp CDSP 1982; PhD Grad Theol Un 1984. D 8/25/1957 P 12/1/1958 Bp C J Kinsolving III. m 6/30/1956 Joan Frances MacDonald. Assoc All Souls Par In Berkeley Berkeley CA 1993; Dioc Coun Dio California San Francisco CA 1991-1993; S Alb's Epis Ch Brentwood CA 1988-1993; Ch Of The Nativ San Rafael CA 1986; Instr in Sch for Deacons Dio California San Francisco CA 1982-2006; CDSP Berkeley CA 1980-1982; Assoc All Souls Par In Berkeley Berkeley CA 1978-1987; COM Dio The Rio Grande Albuquerque NM 1975-1977; The Cbury Cntr Albuquerque NM 1971-1978; Chair Cbury Cntr NMSU Dio The Rio Grande Albuquerque NM 1971-1977; Dioc Coun Dio The Rio Grande Albuquerque NM 1969-1971; R S Jn's Epis Ch Alamogordo NM 1964-1970; Asst San Juan Mssn Farmington NM 1957-1958. JOAN@THEBLAIR.NET

BLAIR, Ernest Hunter (Az) 4 Sw Pepper Tree Ln, Topeka KS 66611 B Topeka KS 7/18/1917 s Hunter Blair & Flossie Arlene. D 10/30/1955 Bp Goodrich R Fenner. m 7/26/1942 Dorothe Arlene Willett c 1. D/Asst S Dav's Epis Ch Topeka KS 1955-1980.

BLAIR, John Kenneth (Mo) 137 E Lockwood Ave Apt 1g, Saint Louis MO 63119 **Asst Chr Ch Cathd S Louis MO 2001-** B 4/24/1972 s John B Blair & Charmaine Estelle. MDiv Eden TS; BA U of Missouri 1994. Chapl St Lk's Chap Kansas City MO 2000-2002. taranatha@hotmail.com

BLAIR, Paige Michele (SanD) PO Box 336, Del Mar CA 92014 **DOK, co-Chapl Dio San Diego San Diego CA 2010-; Strategic Plnng Com, co-chair Dio San Diego San Diego CA 2010-; R S Ptr's Epis Ch Del Mar CA 2009-** B March Air Force Base CA 6/16/1970 d Michael Irwin Blair & Letitia Ann. BA Bos 1992; MDiv Bos 1995; CAGS EDS 1996. D 5/1/1996 P 2/1/1997 Bp Donald Purple Hart. m 8/26/2000 Gene T Fox. Strategic Plnng Com Exec Coun Appointees New York NY 2009-2010; GC Dep Dio Maine Portland ME 2005-2009; Com on H Ord, co-chair Dio Maine Portland ME 2002-2009; GC Alt Dio Maine Portland ME 2002-2005; Com on H Ord, Mem Dio Maine Portland ME 2001-2002; R S Geo's Epis Ch York Harbor ME 2000-2009; Mus and Liturg Com Dio Massachusetts Boston MA 1999-2000; Cler Compstn Com Dio Massachusetts Boston MA 1998-2000; Micah Proj Bd Dir Dio Massachusetts Boston MA 1998-2000; Assoc R S Jn's Ch Beverly Farms MA 1997-2000; Coll Wk Com Dio Massachusetts Boston MA 1996-2000; Boston Univ Epis Chap Brookline MA 1996-1997; D S Lk's And S Marg's Ch Allston MA 1996-1997; D and Chapl to the ARK Proj S Andr's Ch Edgartown MA 1996. Contrib, "U2charist," *Ancient Faith Future Mssn: Fresh Expressions in the Sacramental Tradition*, Cbury Press and Ch Pub, Inc, 2009; Auth, "Finding God in a Single's Bar & Other Watering Holes," *ABF Bulletin*, 1993. Phi Beta Kappa Bos Boston MA 1992; BA scl Bos Boston MA 1992. pblair1@earthlink.net

BLAIR, Rebecca H (RI) 3 Beverly Drive, Plainville MA 02762 **R S Andr's Ch New Bedford MA 2003-** B New Delhi IN 11/3/1958 d Henry Parkman Homans & Martha Louise. BA Pomona Coll 1984; MDiv Harvard DS 1986. D 6/11/1988 Bp David Elliot Johnson P 6/1/1989 Bp Brice Sidney Sanders. m 7/25/1987 James Arthur Blair c 3. R Emm Epis Ch Cumberland RI 1995-2003; Asst All SS Ch Worcester MA 1994-1995; Int S Lk's Ch Worcester MA 1993-1994; Int S Jas' Epis Ch Alexandria VA 1993; Asst Trin Ch Manassas VA 1990-1992; Asst Emm Ch Farmville NC 1988-1989; Asst S Steph's Ch Goldsboro NC 1988-1989. rhbstandrewsnb@verizon.net

BLAIR, Ruth Lincoln (Chi) 1464 N Morse St, Wheaton IL 60187 B Hingham MA 3/29/1927 d Augustus Hudson Lincoln & Ruth Mary. U of New Mex 1957. D 12/26/1987 Bp Frank Tracy Griswold III. m 9/1/1957 Billy Windell Blair c 2. D Trin Epis Ch Wheaton IL 1987-2008. deaconbl@worldnet.att.net

BLAIR JR, Thom Williamson (Va) Po Box 1059, Kilmarnock VA 22482 B Key West FL 6/30/1944 s Thom Williamson Blair. BA Davison 1966; BD VTS 1970; PhD Duke 1977. D 6/25/1970 Bp Thomas Augustus Fraser Jr P 11/1/1973 Bp James Winchester Montgomery. m 6/6/1969 Mary Louisa Hamilton. S Steph's Ch Richmond VA 1994-2005; Gr Ch Kilmarnock VA 1984-1994; S Matt's Epis Ch Warson Warson Woods MO 1979-1984; Asst S Steph's Ch Richmond VA 1977-1979; Cur S Mk's Barrington Hills IL 1974-1977. TWBLAIR@MECKCOM.NET

BLAIR-LOY, Mary Frances (SanD) 747 W University Ave, San Diego CA 92103 B El Paso TX 11/12/1962 d Alexander Blair & Joan Frances. BA U Chi

1983; MDiv Harvard DS 1987; PhD U Chi 1997. D 12/6/1987 P 12/1/1988 Bp William Edwin Swing. m 9/8/1990 John David Blair-Loy. Dio San Diego San Diego CA 2004-2006; Asst To R S Fran Of Assisi Ch Novato CA 1987-1990. Auth, "Amer Sociol Revs"; Auth, "Amer Journ Sociol".

BLAKE, Sandra Jean (Colo) 645 Kittredge St, Aurora CO 80011 B Phillips County KS 8/18/1943 d Dean Caswell & Dorothy. BFA U CO 1964; MDiv Iliff TS 2004. D 6/11/2005 P 12/17/2005 Bp Robert John O'Neill. m 1/29/1965 Peter Blake c 2. S Tim's Epis Ch Centennial CO 2008-2011; Part Time Assoc S Steph's Epis Ch Aurora CO 2005-2007. Auth, "Disguised as a Poem," *ATR*, 2002. sandyat6@comcast.net

BLAKE, Sidney Spivey (NY) 204 W 134th St, New York NY 10030 **D S Phil's Ch New York NY 2009-** B Mount Vernon NY 1/27/1940 s Joseph Henry Blake & Lylace Michael. BA Hunter Coll - CUNY 1972. D 5/2/2009 Bp Mark Sean Sisk. m 7/5/1986 Philip Spivey. lenoxguy@nyc.rr.com

BLAKE JR, Thomas William (Ind) 4401 W Pondview Ct, Muncie IN 47304 **R Gr Ch Muncie IN 2004-** B Wilmington NC 4/12/1972 s Thomas William Blake & Permelia. BA Duke 1994; MDiv VTS 2000. D 6/24/2000 Bp Clifton Daniel III P 6/8/2001 Bp Robert Wilkes Ihloff. Asst to R Middleham & S Ptr's Par Lusby MD 2001-2004; Asst To R S Mk's Ch Highland MD 2000-2001. t.blake.april12@comcast.net

BLAKELOCK, Douglas Paul (Alb) 295 Main St, Unadilla NY 13849 B Rotterdam NY 11/29/1928 s Douglas Albert Blakelock & Harriet Ann. AAS Paul Smith's Coll 1951; U of Maine 1953. D 1/12/2002 Bp David John Bena. m 9/19/1953 Sally Ann Lyons c 5. D Zion Ch Morris NY 2005-2010; D S Matt's Ch Unadilla NY 2002-2005.

BLAKELY, W(ayne) A(llen) (Kan) PO Box 20742, Louisville KY 40250 B Lyons KS 11/5/1930 s Ansel M Blakely & Ella Mae. BA Ashbury Coll 1953; BD Candler TS Emory U 1957; MA Emory U 1958; PhD Emory U 1964. D 8/24/1989 Bp John Forsythe Ashby P 2/1/1990 Bp William Edward Smalley. m 11/20/1995 Gloria Perry Webb c 2. Barren River Area Coun Russellville KY 1996-1997; Chr Ch Columbia MD 1993-1997; P-in-c S Andr's Ch Glasgow KY 1993-1997; Gr Epis Ch Winfield KS 1992-1994; R Epis Ch Of The Redeem Oklahoma City OK 1990-1992; S Barth's Ch Wichita KS 1990; Asst S Jas Ch Wichita KS 1990. wabla@att.net

BLAKEMORE, Barbara Keller (Va) 8499 Anderson Ct, Mechanicsville VA 23116 B Roanoke VA 4/28/1938 d Peyton Randolph Keller & Mary Lee. BA Randolph-Macon Wmn's Coll 1960; MDiv VTS 1990. D 5/26/1990 Bp C(laude) Charles Vache P 2/23/1991 Bp Frank Harris Vest Jr. m 7/23/1960 William A Blakemore. R S Paul's Ch Hanover VA 1996-2003; S Thos Epis Ch Chesapeake VA 1990-1996. bkb2007@comcast.net

BLAKLEY, Raymond Leonard (WTenn) 761 Spaulding Dr, Roseville CA 95678 B Christchurch NZ 5/14/1926 s Vernon Blakley & Edith Maude. MS New Zealand U Nz 1947; PhD New Zealand U Nz 1951; Dsc The Australian Natl U 1965. Trans from Anglican Church Of Australia 5/1/1972 Bp Walter Cameron Righter. m 5/12/1949 Beryl Blakley c 1. Asst P S Hilary's Ch Ft Myers FL 1999-2001. rayb1926@aol.com

BLAKSLEE, John Charles (NI) 418 Dogwood Ln, Lowell IN 46356 **P-in-c S Steph's Epis Ch Hobart IN 1997-** B Canton IL 8/30/1934 s Claude Calvin Blakslee & Barbara. BS U IL 1959; JD U IL 1962; MDiv Nash 1972. D 6/19/1971 Bp Gerald Francis Burrill P 12/18/1971 Bp James Winchester Montgomery. m 4/17/1982 Helen Elizabeth Clifton c 4. Dir Of Dioc Fndt Dio Nthrn Indiana So Bend IN 1998-2000; Dir Of Dioc Fndt Dio Nthrn Indiana So Bend IN 1991-1996; Pres Of Stndg Com Dio Nthrn Indiana So Bend IN 1988-1990; S Paul's Epis Ch Munster IN 1975-1996; Vic S Tim's Ch Griffith IN 1975-1977; R S Paul's Ch Milwaukee WI 1972-1975; Dvlpmt Off Nash Nashotah WI 1970-1975. Auth, "arts Legal Ethics," *Journ Of The ABA*, ABA, 1966; Auth, "The H Euch From A Biblic Perspective," Self Pub through donors; Auth, "Brf Journey Through The Word-Romans," Bible Reading Fllshp. friartuck3@juno.com

BLANCH, Paul Frederick (Alb) 30 N Ferry St, Schenectady NY 12305 **The Reverend S Geo's Epis Ch Schenectady NY 2009-** B Durham England 3/4/1956 s Frederick Blanch & Doreen. Cert in Theol Chichester Theol Coll 1986; BA (Hons) Dur 1997. Trans from Church Of England 10/16/2009 as Priest Bp William Howard Love. m 3/8/1997 Margaret Ryder c 2. P Assoc of the H Hse of Our Lady of Walsingham 1986. PPSTFRANCIS@GOOGLEMAIL.COM

BLANCHARD, Louise Browner (Va) St. Stephen's Episcopal Church, 6000 Grove Avenue, Richmond VA 23226 **Assoc R S Steph's Ch Richmond VA 2007-** B Charlottesville VA 11/22/1957 BA U of Virginia 1979; JD W&L 1985; MDiv UTS-PSCE 2007; VTS 2007. D 6/16/2007 P 12/18/2007 Bp Peter James Lee. m 11/30/1985 Charles A Blanchard c 4. Dir Of Childrens Mnstrs S Steph's Ch Richmond VA 2002-2004. wblanchard@saintstephensrichmond.net

BLANCHARD, Louise Sharon (Colo) 6774 Tabor St, Arvada CO 80004 **Dio Colorado Denver CO 2001-** B Boulder CO 7/6/1949 d E George Patterson & Gloria S. BS Colorado St U 1971; MDiv Iliff TS 1989; Cert S Thos Sem 1991. D 6/15/1991 P 12/7/1991 Bp William Jerry Winterrowd. m 8/22/1971 Frank T Blanchard c 2. The Ch Of Chr The King (Epis) Arvada CO 1996-2005; Assoc R S Lk's Epis Ch Ft Collins CO 1995-1996; Exec Coun Dio Colorado Denver CO 1992-1995; S Ambr Epis Ch Boulder CO 1991-1996. Auth, *Living The Gd News Adult Curric*, 1991. loutedb@earthlink.net

BLANCHARD, Mary Margaret (ETenn) 100 Steven Ln., Harriman TN 37748 B Chattanooga TN 12/19/1949 d Ettore Storto & Edna Annabelle. BA Kennesaw St U 1985; MDiv TS Univ of the So 1991. D 6/8/1991 Bp Frank Kellogg Allan P 12/21/1991 Bp Robert Oran Miller. S Lk's Ch Boone NC 2002; S Jas Epis Ch of Greeneville Greeneville TN 2000-2002; Vic S Mk's Ch Copperhill TN 1995-2000; Dio E Tennessee Knoxville TN 1995-1999; Assoc S Eliz's Epis Ch Knoxville TN 1993-1994; Cur S Paul's Ch Selma AL 1991-1993. Cath Fllshp Of Epis Ch. Outstanding Alum Kennesaw Coll 1992. revpeg@hotmail.com

BLANCHARD, Sudie Mixter (Me) 25 Southside Rd, York ME 03909 **D S Geo's Epis Ch York Harbor ME 2006-** B Boston MA 7/3/1947 d James Mixter & Phebe. BA Vas 1970; MLS U MI 1972. D 6/24/2006 Bp Chilton Abbie Richardson Knudsen. m 4/14/1973 Peter Blanchard c 2. Assn of Profsnl Chapl 2011; NAAD 2004. sblanchard@stgeorgesyorkharbor.org

BLANCHETT, David Harvey (Ak) 1100 Pullman Dr, Wasilla AK 99654 B Vallejo CA 12/31/1945 s Powertan Blanchett & Sarajane Anita. BA U of Alaska 1975; Cert A.M.E.Z. AK Conf Theol Anchorage AK 1982. D 6/6/2004 P 12/7/2004 Bp Mark Lawrence Mac Donald. m 8/7/1982 Martha Nanugak Charlie c 7. Dio Alaska Fairbanks AK 2008-2009. FATHERBLANCHETT@GMAIL.COM

BLANCK, Charles Kenneth (WNC) 977 Collins Rd, Sparta NC 28675 B Rockford IL 6/29/1931 s Edward Henry Blanck & Ione Edith. BA Duke 1952; BD Epis TS of The SW 1964; STM Luth Theol Sthrn Sem 1970. D 6/27/1964 P 6/29/1965 Bp John Adams Pinckney. m 3/6/2003 Margaret Collins Barlow c 3. Vic/R S Lk's Ch Boone NC 1975-1996; R/D-in-Res S Tim's Ch Columbia SC 1964-1966; Chr Ch Greenville SC 1960-1975. BLANCKPAGE2@GMAIL.COM

BLANCO-MONTERROSO, Leonel (Okla) 5500 S Western Ave., Oklahoma City OK 73109 **Dio Oklahoma Oklahoma City OK 2004-; Mssnr Santa Maria Virgen Epis Oklahoma City OK 2004-** B 12/19/1945 s Julio Valerio Blanco & Adela. Escuela de Bellas Artes; Instituto Teologico Epis. D 11/12/1974 P 11/1/1975 Bp Anselmo Carral-Solar. m 5/14/1977 Clara De Blanco. Dio Honduras Miami FL 1988-2003; Dio Guatemala Guatemala City 1974-1988. leonelb60@cox.net

BLAND, John D (Minn) 1431 Cherry Hill Rd, Mendota Heights MN 55118 B Jersey City NJ 3/29/1923 s Percival Millard Bland & Mildred Eugenia. Drew U; BS U MN 1949. D 6/24/1968 Bp Hamilton Hyde Kellogg. m 6/30/1945 Betty Lois Burley c 3. Asst Mssh Epis Ch S Paul MN 1978-1986; Asst S Mary's Ch St Paul MN 1968-1978. Epis Conf of the Deaf of the Epis Ch in the. BLLAND010@UMN.EDU

BLAND SR, Thomas James (NC) 4608 Pine Cove Rd, Greensboro NC 27410 B Philadelphia PA 6/5/1942 NYU. D 1/18/1997 Bp J(ames) Gary Gloster. m 7/9/1995 Leslie Rasmussen Boyd. Dir Of Food Pantry S Andr's Ch Greensboro NC 1997-1998; D S Matt's Epis Ch Kernersville NC 2004.

BLASDELL, Machrina Loris (Cal) 804 Cottonwood Dr., Lansing KS 66043 B Phoenix AZ 3/17/1953 d James Arden Blasdell & Machrina Pauline. BA Colorado St U 1975; MA Arizona St U 1980; MDiv CDSP 1984. D 5/31/1984 Bp Joseph Thomas Heistand P 6/1/1985 Bp William Edwin Swing. m 8/20/1983 Michael Gregory Munro c 2. Affiliated S Paul's Ch Leavenworth KS 2000-2004; Asst S Jas' Epis Ch Warrenton VA 1986-1987; Ch Of The Gd Shpd Burke VA 1985-1987; Asst Trin Par Menlo Pk CA 1984-1985. Tertiary Of The Soc Of S Fran 1979-2006. hannahlump@aol.com

BLATZ, Nils (LI) 79 Zophar Mills Road, Wading River NY 11792 **Int Ch Of The Redeem Mattituck NY 2002-** B Oceanside NY 8/12/1940 s I(rving) Hanson Blatz & Elizabeth Joyce. BA Bow 1962; STB GTS 1965. D 6/19/1965 P 12/21/1965 Bp Jonathan Goodhue Sherman. m 8/25/1962 Leslie D Dickenson c 4. R Gr Ch Brooklyn NY 1994-2002; Dio Long Island Garden City NY 1982-2002; Chair of COM Dio Long Island Garden City NY 1977-1979; Chair of Chr Fndt Dio Long Island Garden City NY 1973-1980; R Trin Epis Ch Roslyn NY 1972-1994; COM Dio Long Island Garden City NY 1972-1979; Dio Long Island Garden City NY 1966-1967; Cur Trin Epis Ch Roslyn NY 1965-1967. OHC - Assoc 1970-1994. enilsb@gmail.com

BLAUSER, Dennis Alan (NwPa) 215 Dermond Rd, Hermitage PA 16148 B Oil City PA 10/12/1947 s Norman Wesley Blauser & Mary Grace. BA Thiel Coll 1974; MDiv SWTS 1979. D 6/16/1979 P 12/21/1979 Bp Donald James Davis. m 12/18/1965 Nancy Irvine c 5. Trin Ch Hermitage PA 2004-2010; Archd Dio NW Pennsylvania Erie PA 1991-2004; R Ch Of The Redeem Hermitage PA 1984-1991; Chr Ch Punxsutawney PA 1979-1984; Vic Ch Of The H Trin Brookville PA 1979-1984. frdenny@earthlink.net

BLAUVELT II, Charles Joseph (NH) 162 Sagamore St., Manchester NH 03104 B Morristown NJ 4/12/1952 s Charles Joseph Blauvelt & Margel Louise. BA Susquahanna U 1974; MDiv GTS 1983. D 6/10/1983 P 12/17/1983 Bp Charlie Fuller McNutt Jr. m 6/20/1987 Darcy Elizabeth O'Hara c 2. R Gr Ch Manchester NH 2002-2010; R S Tim's Ch Roxborough Philadelphia PA

1993-2002; R S Mary's Epis Par Northfield VT 1988-1993; S Paul's Epis Ch Harrisburg PA 1983-1988. frcjb@comcast.net

BLAUVELT, Jeremy David (USC) 125 Church Ave, Pass Christian MS 39571 **S Jn's Epis Ch Congaree Hopkins SC 2010-** B 9/8/1976 s James Andrew Blauvelt & Joyce Evelyn. Liberal Stds Iowa St U 2000; MDiv TESM 2005. D 2/17/2008 Bp Robert William Duncan P 8/17/2008 Bp Duncan Montgomery Gray III. m 12/29/2004 Jessica L Blauvelt c 1. Trin Ch Epis Pass Chr MS 2008-2010. tesmlion@yahoo.com

BLAVIER JR, Donald Charles (WTex) 404 Salisbury Ln, Victoria TX 77904 B Chester PA 11/28/1933 s Donald Charles Blavier & Marguerite Anna. BFA U of Houston 1954; Epis TS of The SW 1961; MA U of Houston at Victoria Victoria TX 1990; PhD Texas Tech U 1993. D 6/2/1961 P 5/1/1962 Bp Frederick P Goddard. m 8/4/1974 Betsy Benton. P-in-c S Lk's Epis Ch Levelland TX 1990-1993; Gr Ch Falfurrias TX 1988-1990; S Jas Epis Ch Hebbronville TX 1988-1990; Gr Ch Port Lavaca TX 1988; R Trin Ch Victoria TX 1974-1988; R Chr Epis Ch Temple TX 1966-1970; R All SS Epis Ch San Benito TX 1964-1966; Vic S Andr's Ch Port Isabel TX 1964-1966; R Chr Ch Jefferson TX 1963-1964; M-in-c Chr Ch Jefferson TX 1961-1962. Auth, "Internalized Shame and Perceptions of Marital Equity, Intimacy," *Amer Journ of Marital Ther*, 1993. AAMFT. dblavier@sbcglobal.net

BLAYER, Brian David (LI) 15117 14 Rd, Whitestone NY 11357 **P-in-c Gr Epis Ch Whitestone NY 2010-** B New York NY 11/20/1970 s Norman Blayer & Christine. BA Queens Coll 1992; MDiv GTS 2006. D 4/25/2006 P 10/28/2006 Bp Orris George Walker Jr. m 7/12/1998 Susan D Lorenzo c 1. Asst S Ann's Ch Sayville NY 2008-2010; Cur S Anselm's Ch Shoreham NY 2006-2008; P-in-c S Mk's Epis Ch Medford NY 2006-2008. revblayer@gmail.com

BLEDSOE, Faith Elizabeth (WTex) 3042 Eagle Drive, Augusta, GA GA 30906 **R S Fran Epis Ch Victoria TX 2005-** B Chickasha OK 12/3/1960 d Charles Norris Bledsoe & Katherine Elizabeth. BS K SU 1983; MA K SU 1985; MDiv Epis TS of The SW 2002. D 6/18/2002 Bp Robert Louis Ladehoff P 2/28/2003 Bp James Edward Folts. Assoc R All SS Epis Ch Corpus Christi TX 2002-2005. stfrancisfeb@sbcglobal.net

BLEDSOE, Sharon C (SVa) 116 Victorian Lane, Jupiter FL 33458 B Saskatoon SK CA 12/20/1945 d Charles Vernon Calloway & Aline Ruth. BA U Sask 1967; MA Pur 1972; MDiv GTS 1997. D 6/14/1997 Bp Frank Harris Vest Jr P 4/18/1998 Bp Rodney Rae Michel. m 7/11/1997 Richard L Cosnotti c 2. Cur S Jn's Ch Cold Sprg Harbor NY 1997-2001. Auth, "Mary Magdalen: The Lost Diary," Fair Havens Press, Inc., 2011. Cmdr Ord of S Jn of Jerusalem 2010; Sub-Chapl Ord Of S Jn Of Jerusalem 1998; BA cl U Sask Saskatchewan CA 1967. gk2me@aol.com

BLEND, Jennifer (Colo) 4775 Cambridge St, Boulder CO 80301 **Asst P S Mary Magd Ch Boulder CO 1994-** B Paterson NJ 6/5/1943 d William Tilden Davis & Elizabeth. BTh The Coll of Emm and St. Chad 1993. Trans from Anglican Church of Canada 2/1/1996 Bp William Jerry Winterrowd. m 12/5/1983 Carroll Clarence Blend. Auth, "Dream Kitchen," *Kitchen Talk*. SBL. jenniferblend@hotmail.com

BLESSING, Kamila Abrahamova (Pgh) Po Box 817, Mars PA 16046 **P-in-c S Barn Ch Brackenridge PA 2011-; P-in-c S Barn Ch Brackenridge PA 2011-** B Pittsburgh PA 12/12/1948 d Karel Louis Novak & Lillian Mary. BS Carnegie Mellon U 1971; MS U Pgh 1976; PhD U Pgh 1977; PhD Duke 1996. D 10/15/1983 P 5/16/1984 Bp Alden Moinet Hathaway. S Paul's Epis Ch Pittsburgh PA 2005-2006; Int S Lk's Epis Ch Montclair NJ 2004; S Mary's Ch Sparta NJ 2002-2004; Int Emm Epis Ch Webster Groves MO 2001-2002; Chr Bd Pub St Louis MO 2000-2001; Ch Of The Adv Enfield NC 1996-1998; S Jn's Ch Battleboro NC 1996-1998; P-in-c Chr Ch Rocky Mt NC 1993-1998; Int S Paul's Epis Ch Kittanning PA 1989-1990; Vic S Ptr's Epis Ch Brentwood Pittsburgh PA 1986-1990; Dio Cntrl New York Syracuse NY 1986; S Jas' Ch Clinton NY 1985-1986; R St Andrews Epis Ch Rome NY 1985-1986; Pstr Min Ch Of The Ascen Pittsburgh PA 1983-1985. Auth, "Speak Ye First the Kingdom: A Mainline Pstr's Journey into Abundance," *(Bk)*, Ecum Stwdshp Fndt, 2011; Auth, "Families of the Bible: A New Perspective," *(Bk)*, Praeger, 2010; Auth, "Murray Bowen'S Fam Systems Theory As Bible Hermeneutic Using The Fam Of The Prodigal, Lk 15:11-32," *Journ Of Psychol And Chrsnty*, 2000; Auth, "It Was a Miracle: Stories of Ordnry People and Extraordinary Healing," *(Bk)*, Augsburg Fortress, 1999; Auth, "Many Journ arts on systems theory as hermeneutic; and healing.," 1990. CHS 1981; Int Mnstry Ntwk 2002; Ord Of S Lk 1987; SBL 1990. kamila@zoominternet.net

BLESSING, Mary Elizabeth Brunner (ECR) 5271 Scotts Valley Dr, Scotts Valley CA 95066 **Bd Trst Dio El Camino Real Monterey CA 2010-; Vic S Phil The Apos Scotts Vlly CA 2006-; Chair T/F Plcy Protect Chld Dio El Camino Real Monterey CA 2005-** B Oakland CA 3/28/1954 d John Richard Brunner & Ruth. NA Ob 1972; BA Mills Coll 1976; MDiv CDSP 1992. D 6/1/1996 P 6/7/1997 Bp William Edwin Swing. m 4/2/1977 James Edward Blessing c 2. Dioc Coun, Chair, Bdgt Com Dio El Camino Real Monterey CA 2001-2003; Assoc R Ch Of S Jude The Apos Cupertino CA 2000-2006; Asst S Tim's Epis Ch Mtn View CA 1998-2000; S Mich And All Ang Concord CA 1996-1997; Coordntr Gr Cathd San Francisco CA 1992-1994. Chair, Dioc Bdgt Com 2001-2002; Chair, ECR Peace and Justice Cmsn 2004-2006; Dept of Missions 2008; ECR Dioc Coun 2000-2002; El Camino Cler Orgnztn, Bd Mem 1994; NNECA 1994. pastor.stphilips.sv@gmail.com

BLESSING, Robert Alan (SanD) 12539 Sundance Ave, San Diego CA 92129 **P S Andr's Ch La Mesa CA 2006-** B Eugene OR 6/5/1958 s William J Blessing & Norma J. Fuller TS; BA U of Washington 1980; MDiv CDSP 1984. Trans 1/15/2004 Bp Don Adger Wimberly. m 12/12/1987 Anne Christine Cary c 2. Spec Mobilization Spprt Plan Washington DC 2010-2011; Assoc P Ch Of The Gd Samar San Diego CA 2003-2006; Pension Fund Mltry New York NY 2002-2003; S Mich And All Ang' Epis Ch Longview TX 2000-2002; Off Of Bsh For ArmdF New York NY 1994-2000; Gr Epis Ch Kent WA 1992-1994; Emm Ch Seattle WA 1992-1993; Asst S Lk's Epis Ch Seattle WA 1985-1986. rbless@aol.com

BLEWETT, Heather Back (Ky) 744 Sherwood Dr, Bowling Green KY 42103 **Chr Epis Ch Bowling Green KY 2011-** B Portsmouth NH 8/8/1969 d George Henry Back & Margaret Elizabeth. BA U of Oklahoma 1990; MDiv VTS 1996. D 6/29/1996 P 12/21/1996 Bp Robert Manning Moody. m 5/31/1997 Michael Blewett c 2. S Mich & S Geo Clayton MO 2001-2008; Assoc R All SS Epis Ch Austin TX 1999-2001; Assoc The Epis Ch Of S Thos The Apos Dallas TX 1997-2002; S Thos The Apos Epis Ch Houston TX 1997-1999; Dio Oklahoma Oklahoma City OK 1996-1997; Cur Gr Ch Muskogee OK 1996-1997. hbblewett@gmail.com

BLEWETT, Michael (Ky) 1215 State St, Bowling Green KY 42101 **R Chr Epis Ch Bowling Green KY 2008-** B Lansing MI 4/2/1966 s John Elwyn Burton Blewett & Helen. BA Westminster Choir Coll of Rider U 1988; U MI 1989; MDiv VTS 1997. D 6/22/1997 Bp Robert Deane Rowley Jr P 5/1/1998 Bp Claude Edward Payne. m 5/31/1997 Heather Back c 2. Assoc R S Mich & S Geo Clayton MO 2001-2008; Vic S Paul's Epis Ch Pflugerville TX 1999-2001; Asst R S Jn The Div Houston TX 1997-1999. michael@cecbg.com

BLICK, Warren Scott (Tex) 1042 Orchard Hill St, Houston TX 77077 B Joplin MO 12/5/1952 s Sherman Harold Blick & Elizabeth Margaret. BA Phillips U 1974; MDiv STUSo 1977; DMin GTF 1986. D 6/18/1977 Bp Gerald Nicholas McAllister P 1/1/1978 Bp Frederick Warren Putnam. m 7/26/1997 Kathleen M Blick c 2. H Sprt Epis Ch Houston TX 2002-2004; Cn Dio Texas Houston TX 2000-2002; Int S Jas Epis Ch Houston TX 1999-2000; Emm Ch Houston TX 1998-1999; St Lk's Epis Hosp Houston TX 1994-1995; Assoc Trin Ch Houston TX 1994-1995; R S Chris's Ch Houston TX 1990-1994; R S Paul's Epis Ch Orange TX 1985-1990; Asst S Mk's Cathd Shreveport LA 1982-1985; Vic Leonidas Polk Memi Epis Mssn Leesville LA 1979-1982; R Trin Epis Ch Deridder LA 1979-1982; Int Epis Ch Of The Resurr Oklahoma City OK 1979; Cur S Paul's Cathd Oklahoma City OK 1977-1979. Auth, "Fellows Yearbook 86," Gtf, 1989. wskmblick@sbcglobal.net

BLINDENBACHER, Kenneth Reihmann (Pa) No address on file. **Died 12/14/2009** B Camden NJ 4/6/1948 s Kenneth Feydt Blindenbacher & Dorothy. BA U of So Carolina 1971; MDiv VTS 1977. D 6/4/1977 P 12/1/1977 Bp Albert Wiencke Van Duzer. Pstr Counslg Fndt. Affiliate Amer Psychol Assn.

BLINMAN, Clifford Louis (Ore) 2092 E. Bighorn Mountain Dr, Oro Valley AZ 85755 **Vol Assoc S Phil's In The Hills Tucson AZ 2000-** B Sacramento CA 3/5/1936 s Foster Samuel Blinman & Edna Rosetta. Penn 1969; Cert CDSP 1981; BA Sch for Deacons 1985. D 9/18/1978 Bp C Kilmer Myers P 7/22/1981 Bp William Edwin Swing. m 2/27/2010 Mary Blinman c 3. R Trin Epis Ch Ashland Ashland OR 1993-1999; S Anne's Ch Fremont CA 1988-1993; S Tim's Ch Danville CA 1987-1988; Asst S Paul's Epis Ch Walnut Creek CA 1978-1988. frcliff@aol.com

BLISS, John Derek Clegg (Cal) 4 Edgewater Hillside, Westport CT 06880 B Wisbech Cambridgeshire UK 7/13/1940 s Clarence Clegg Bliss & Cicely Mary. Salisbury TS Gb; U Of Durham Durham Gb. Trans from Church Of England 2/17/1981 Bp Victor Manuel Rivera. Asst S Steph's Ch Coconut Grove Coconut Grove FL 2001; R H Trin Epis Ch Madera CA 1980-1989. Human Outreach Agnecy, Hayward Ca 1992-1996. jb106600@aol.com

BLISS, Robert Francis (Tex) 2103 N Beal St, Belton TX 76513 **D in Charge S Lk's Epis Ch Belton TX 2011-** B Houston TX 12/22/1948 s Cecil Lee Bliss & Mary Louise. BS Texas A & M U 1976; Iona Sch for Mnstry 2010. D 6/19/2010 Bp C(harles) Andrew Doyle P 1/8/2011 Bp Dena Arnall Harrison. m 11/17/1989 Melanie Hoag c 3. bob@theblissranch.com

BLISS, Vernon Powell (CNY) 86 E Taylor Hill Rd, Montague MA 01351 B Cincinnati OH 5/24/1934 s Vernon Woodward & Hilma Clara. BA Ken 1957; MDiv GTS 1960; PhD Un Inst 1975. D 6/29/1960 P 1/1/1961 Bp Roger W Blanchard. m 10/15/2005 Sarah Grant c 2. Mssy S Geo's Epis Ch Chadwicks NY 1961-1967; Cur Ch Of The Adv Cincinnati OH 1960-1961. reweave@mapinternet.com

BLIZZARD, Charles Fortunate-Eagle (Okla) 1301 Andover Ct, Oklahoma City OK 73120 **Casady Sch Oklahoma City OK 2006-; Vic/Chapl S Edw Chap Oklahoma City OK 2006-** B Alpine TX 4/21/1981 s Franklin Blizzard & Susan. BS Sul Ross St U 2003; MDiv TESM 2006. D 5/20/2006 Bp Jeffrey

Neil Steenson P 7/14/2007 Bp Robert Manning Moody. m 7/2/2004 Nicolette Fortunate-Eagle Martinez. charlesblizzard@netscape.net

BLOCH, Elizabeth Appling (Oly) St. Paul's Episcopal Church, P.O. Box 753, Port Townsend WA 98368 **R S Paul's Epis Ch Port Townsend WA 2006-** B San Mateo CA 11/2/1945 d Richard Huff Appling & Kathleen Elizabeth. BA Occ 1967; MA Stan 1970; MDiv CDSP 1995. D 6/3/1995 P 6/1/1996 Bp William Edwin Swing. m 10/31/1980 Michael Edward Bloch. Dio Olympia Seattle WA 2004; Dioc Coun Mem/Pres Dio California San Francisco CA 1998-2002; Dioc Stwdshp Cmsn Dio California San Francisco CA 1996-2002; S Tim's Ch Danville CA 1995-2002. eab@cablespeed.com

BLOCK, Lee Sampson (Kan) Po Box 371, Leavenworth KS 66048 **Died 3/9/ 2010** B Del Rio TX 8/25/1934 s Edwin Hart Block & Lois Em. BA U of Texas 1956; GD STUSo 1961. D 7/25/1961 Bp Everett H Jones P 2/24/1962 Bp Richard Earl Dicus.

BLODGETT, Jeremy (Cal) 9 Quail Ct, San Rafael CA 94903 B Minneapolis MN 4/27/1931 s Robert Oliver Blodget & Helen. BA U MN 1956; MDiv CDSP 1995. D 12/2/1995 P 12/1/1996 Bp William Edwin Swing. m 8/20/1994 Eleanor Sue Blodgett. Ch Of The Redeem San Rafael CA 1999-2003; Ch Of The Nativ San Rafael CA 1998-1999; Ch Of The Incarn Santa Rosa CA 1995-1997.

BLOEMKER, Emily J (Mo) 732 Orange St, New Haven CT 06511 **Trin Par New York NY 2011-; Trin Par New York NY 2011-** B Indianapolis IN 10/ 31/1982 d Edward Bloemkes & Penny Jo. BA Washington U in S Louis 2004; MDiv Ya Berk 2009. D 12/15/2008 P 6/27/2009 Bp George Wayne Smith. S Tim's Epis Ch Creve Coeur MO 2009-2011. emily.jo.scott@gmail.com

BLOIS, Bruce Douglas (Ia) 438 Laurelwood Ln, Naples IA 34112 B Attleboro MA 1/17/1942 s William Henry Blois & Mary Elizabeth (Kay). BA Ken 1964; MDiv GTS 1967. D 6/24/1967 P 6/8/1968 Bp Anson Phelps Stokes Jr. m 10/ 23/1976 Theresa D (Giovino) Blois. R S Jn's Ch Keokuk IA 2002-2007; Int S Paul's Epis Ch Hopkinton MA 2000-2002; Asst R Gr Ch No Attleborough MA 1999-2000; Asst R S Paul's Ch Natick MA 1968-1970; S Jn's Ch Keokuk IA 1967-1969; Walnut Hill Sch Natick MA 1967-1969; Cur S Mk's Ch Foxborough MA 1967-1968. bdblois@yahoo.com

BLOOM, Barry Moffett (Mass) 3030 Union St, Emeryville CA 94608 B Newton MA 11/10/1937 s Galen A Bloom & Elizabeth. BA Wesl 1960; BD CDSP 1963. D 6/23/1963 Bp James Albert Pike P 5/1/1964 Bp George Richard Millard. m 9/5/1958 Judith Evelyn Marsh c 3.

BLOOM, Carl Richard (Spr) 1989 East Gleneagle Drive, Chandler AZ 85249 B Chicago IL 1/18/1928 s Carl Ewald Bloom & Helga Jone. BA Augustana Coll 1951; BD SWTS 1954; MDiv SWTS 1971. D 1/9/1954 P 7/17/1954 Bp Charles L Street. m 9/3/1949 Valerie May Swanson c 5. Asst S Mk's Epis Ch Mesa AZ 1998-2007; Dio Springfield Springfield IL 1988-1995; Lead P - Team Mnstry S Jas Epis Ch Marion IL 1988-1995; Lead P - Team Mnstry S Mk's Ch W Frankfort IL 1988-1995; Lead P - Team Mnstry S Steph's Ch Harrisburg IL 1988-1995; R Calv Ch Lombard IL 1968-1977; Exec Coun Dio Chicago Chicago IL 1965-1968; R The Epis Ch Of The H Trin Belvidere IL 1960-1968; Vic Chr The King Epis Ch Huntington IN 1956-1960; Chapl to Shimer Coll Dio Chicago Chicago IL 1954-1956; P-in-c Gr Epis Ch Galena IL 1954-1956. Chapl Ord of S Lk 1972; OHC 1956. carlbloom@q.com

BLOOMER, Nancy H (NY) 4 Grant St, Essex Junction VT 05452 B Binghamton NY 6/13/1939 d Ronald Dudley Bloomer & Ruth Royce. BA SUNY 1969; MA SUNY 1970; PhD SUNY 1976; MDiv GTS 1986. D 6/13/1987 Bp Paul Moore Jr P 12/18/1987 Bp Daniel Lee Swenson. c 2. Chair of Environ Mnstry Team Dio Vermont Burlington VT 2002-2005; S Paul's And Trin Par Tivoli NY 1995-1998; Int Zion Ch Manchester Cntr VT 1994-1995; Int S Mary's Epis Par Northfield VT 1993-1994; Assoc S Jn's In The Mountains Stowe VT 1991-1992; S Ann's Ch Sheldon VT 1990-1991; Dioc Coun Dio Vermont Burlington VT 1989-1995; S Matt's Ch Enosburg Falls VT 1987-1990. "Var arts," *The Living Pulpit*, 2007; Auth, "Greed," *The Living Pulpit*, 2003; Auth, "Preaching to Heal thePreaching to Heal the Earth," *The Living Pulpit*, 2000; Auth, "Sabbath Time," *The Living Pulpit*, 1998. Ord of S Helena, Assoc; OHC, Assoc. nbloomer@comcast.net

BLOSSOM JR, John Dickson (Q) 125 Sw Jefferson Ave, Peoria IL 61602 **Cn for Strategic Plnng Dio Quincy Peoria IL 2005-; Cn S Paul's Cathd Peoria IL 1992-** B Peuria IL 11/9/1940 s John Dickson Blossom & Jane Mangas. U CO 1962; MBA GTF 1995. D 6/6/1973 Bp Francis W Lickfield P 6/1/1974 Bp Donald James Parsons. m 5/15/1987 Linda Byrne c 2. Cn Dio Quincy Peoria IL 1998-2002; P-in-c All SS Ch Quincy IL 1987-1992; Asst P S Andr's Ch Peoria IL 1986-1987. Mem of Amer Soc of Pension Actuaries 1971. Outstanding Young Man of 1974 Jr ChmbrCom City of Peoria 1974; Mem Amer Soc Pension Actuaries. johnb@oldsailorshome.com

BLOTTNER, William Eugene (Chi) 510 First Ave, Farmville VA 23901 B Richmond VA 8/9/1929 s Herman Eugene Blottner & Gwynn Dole. BS VPI 1951; MDiv VTS 1956; MA Cleveland St U 1980; DMin GTF 1994. D 6/1/ 1956 P 7/13/1957 Bp Frederick D Goodwin. c 3. Int Ch Of The Gd Shpd Bath Par Mc Kenney VA 1997-1998; Chapl Johns Meml Epis Ch Farmville VA 1996-2007; Int Dio Sthrn Virginia Norfolk VA 1996-2004; Int S Andr's Lawrenceville VA 1996-1997; Int S Anne's Ch Appomattox VA 1995-1996; Vic S Fran Epis Ch Chicago IL 1989-1994; Int Ch Of The Redeem Lorain OH 1988-1989; Int S Andr Epis Ch Mentor OH 1986-1988; Int S Ptr's Ch Akron OH 1985-1986; Int All SS Ch Parma OH 1984-1985; Int S Paul Epis Ch Norwalk OH 1982-1983; Int S Paul's Epis Ch Of E Cleveland Cleveland OH 1981-1982; St Stephens Ch Vermilion OH 1977-1979; Int S Andr's Ch Cleveland OH 1968-1969; P-in-c S Agnes Ch Cleveland OH 1967-1970; Asst S Mich's Ch Bon Air VA 1960-1966; Asst S Tim's Ch Catonsville MD 1958-1960; M-in-c Epis Ch Of Leeds Par Markham VA 1956-1957. Sociol Hon Soc Alpha Kappa Delta 1978. bnblottner@kinex.net

BLOW, John Wright (Fla) 579 Homewood Dr, Auburn AL 36830 **Died 7/19/ 2010** B Miami FL 3/26/1928 s Augustus Sanders Blow & Ruby Margaret. BA U Of Florida 1955; MDiv STUSo 1963; MSW U of Alabama 1972. D 6/29/ 1963 P 2/1/1964 Bp George Mosley Murray. c 6. johnblow@att.net

BLOXSOM, Barbara Kessel (Kan) 2319 Sw Brookhaven Ln, Topeka KS 66614 B Evanston IL 5/1/1941 d Werner Hans Kessel & Betty. BA Chatham Coll 1963; Cert Washburn U 1964; MDiv Epis TS of The SW 1988. D 3/26/ 1990 P 10/13/1990 Bp R(aymond) Stewart Wood Jr. c 3. R Ch Of The Epiph Sedan KS 1997-2008; R S Matt's Ch Cedar Vale KS 1997-2008; R Ch Of The H Fam Mills River NC 1993-1997; Asst S Jn's Epis Ch Troy NY 1990-1993. Phi Beta Kappa Chatham Coll 1963. bbloxsom@sbcglobal.net

BLUBAUGH, Susan Jo (NI) 4805 Locksley Dr E, Rensselaer IN 47978 B Elkhart IN 11/13/1953 d Frederick Theodore Endress & Barbara Rose. BS Ball St U 1976; MA Ball St U 1980; CTS SWTS 1991; Cert Pur 1999. D 12/20/ 1991 P 7/8/1992 Bp Francis Campbell Gray. m 6/26/1976 Robert Daniel Blubaugh c 3. P S Mary's Fllshp Monticello IN 1994-2007; P S Ptr's Ch Rensselaer IN 1992-2009. sjblubaugh@gmail.com

BLUE, Eddie Michael (Md) Church Of The Holy Trinity, 2300 W. Lafayette Ave., Baltimore MD 21216 **R Ch Of The H Trin Baltimore MD 1984-** B Indianapolis IN 5/15/1950 s Houston Blue & Johnnie. BA Indiana U 1972; MDiv Bex 1979. D 5/31/1979 Bp Edward Witker Jones P 6/24/1980 Bp Lyman Cunningham Ogilby. m 5/8/1982 Lucy Ryan c 3. Dep Gc Dio Maryland Baltimore MD 1994-2009; Dio Pennsylvania Philadelphia PA 1979-1982; Asst S Mary Epis Ch Chester PA 1979-1981. Auth, "Living in Hope," *Sermons That Wk*, Ch Pub, 2001. Maryland Clerics Assn. eddie_blue@verizon.net

BLUE, Gordon Kenneth (Ak) 2902 Sawmill Creek Rd, Sitka AK 99835 **Sitka Counslg & Prevention Serv Inc Sitka AK 2007-; Asst S Ptr's By-The-Sea Sitka AK 2005-** B Seattle WA 10/23/1951 s Harold Blue & Virginia. MDiv Vancouver TS 2006. D 11/1/2004 P 4/9/2005 Bp Mark Lawrence Mac Donald. m 7/11/1998 Sarah Lynn Klosterman c 3. gblue@scpsak.org

BLUE, Susan Neff (WA) 270 El Diente Dr., Durango CO 81301 B Kalamazoo MI 3/2/1942 d Richard Francis Neff & Wilma Homan. Duke 1962; BS NYU 1965; MDiv GTS 1986; ThM New Brunswick TS 1989. D 6/14/1986 P 1/17/ 1987 Bp George Phelps Mellick Belshaw. c 2. Anti-racism Com Dio Washington Washington DC 2007-2010; R S Marg's Ch Washington DC 1997-2010; R Trin Ch Matawan NJ 1991-1997; Cur S Lk's Epis Ch Metuchen NJ 1986-1991. sblue832@gmail.com

BLUME, Andrew Charles (NY) 160 West 95th Street, Apt. 8B, New York NY 10025 **Com on Campus Mnstry Dio New York New York City NY 2010-; COM Dio New York New York City NY 2009-; Com on Deacons Dio New York New York City NY 2009-; R The Ch of S Ign of Antioch New York NY 2007-** B Bethesda MD 2/1/1967 s Ralph Stuart Blume & Nancy Ann. BA Trin Hartford CT 1989; PhD Harv 1995; MDiv EDS 2005. D 6/4/2005 Bp M(arvil) Thomas Shaw III P 1/7/2006 Bp Roy Frederick Cederholm Jr. m 10/ 3/1993 Jacalyn Ruth Blume c 1. COM Dio New York New York City NY 2009-2010; Angl-RC Dialogue in New York Dio New York New York City NY 2008-2010; Ecum Cmsn Dio New York New York City NY 2008-2010; Asst The Ch Of The Adv Boston MA 2006-2007; Asst S Andr's Ch Framingham MA 2005-2006; Com on Liturg and Mus Dio Massachusetts Boston MA 2004-2007. "Numerous arts in Acad Journ". rector@saintignatiusnyc.org

BLUMER, Gary R (Be) Po Box 623, Portland PA 18351 B Minneapolis MN 8/6/1935 s Charles Blumer & Erna. BA U MN 1957; MDiv Nash 1960; STM GTS 1979. D 2/4/1960 Bp Albert Ervine Swift P 8/1/1960 Bp William W Horstick. Int S Jn's Ch Norristown PA 1994-1996; S Jn's Epis Ch Hamlin PA 1994-1996; Trin Epis Ch Williamsport PA 1994-1996; Chr Ch Forest City PA 1992-1993; Int Trin Epis Ch Carbondale PA 1992-1993; Par Of The H Fam Pen Argyl PA 1991-1992; Int S Jos's Ch Pen Argyl PA 1990-1992; Int Chr Ch Media PA 1989-1990; S Mary's Ch Keyport NJ 1987-1988; Asst Chr Ch New Brunswick NJ 1980-1986; R Chr Ch Chippewa Falls WI 1967-1975; R S Simeon's Ch Stanley WI 1967-1975; Vic S Marg's Pk Falls WI 1962-1967; Cur Chr Ch Par La Crosse WI 1960-1962.

BLUNDELL, Gayle (Gay) A(nn) (ECR) 2100 Emmons Rd, Cambria CA 93428 **D S Lk's Ch Atascadero CA 1998-** B Saint Louis MO 2/26/1936 d Gale Loren Swango & Clara Dell. BA Syr 1957; MA Fuller TS 1989. D 6/22/1999 Bp Richard Lester Shimpfky. m 10/19/1957 William Edward Blundell. Dir S Geo's Par La Can CA 1978-1983.

BLUNDELL, James Henry (Oly) 1316 Evergreen Park Dr Sw Apt 2, Olympia WA 98502 B Corpus Christi TX 9/7/1931 s Solon Anderson Blundell & Mary Evelyn. BBA U of Texas 1956; BD CDSP 1959. D 6/22/1959 Bp James Parker Clements P 6/1/1960 Bp Frederick P Goddard. m 6/14/1956 Meredith Ann Blundell. S Jn's Epis Ch Olympia WA 1975-1991; R Gr Ch Ellensburg WA 1970-1975; Vic Ch Of The Nativ San Rafael CA 1962-1967; Vic S Jn's Epis Ch Carthage TX 1959-1962.

BLUNT JR, Howard Elton (NY) 184 16th St, Brooklyn NY 11215 **Assoc S Ptr's Ch Bronx NY 2003-; Assoc Trin Ch Of Morrisania Bronx NY 2003-** B Providence RI 6/27/1941 s Howard Elton Blunt & L'Marie. BA Leh 1964; STB GTS 1967; Dio New York New York NY 1999. D 6/17/1967 P 3/1/1968 Bp John S Higgins. c 2. New York Spec Account New York NY 1994-2001; Epis Mssn Soc New York NY 1987-1989; Epis Mssn Soc New York NY 1987-1989; The GTS New York NY 1986-1987; P-in-c S Phil's Ch New York NY 1985; Asst Ch Of S Simon The Cyrenian New Rochelle NY 1982-1985; Dpt Of Missions Ny Income New York NY 1976-2000; Diocn Msnry & Ch Extntn Socty New York NY 1976-1993; S Lk's-Roosevelt Hosp Cntr New York NY 1973-2001; Asst S Aug's Ch New York NY 1969-1973; Cur S Mart's Ch Providence RI 1967-1969. Cler, Manhattan No Bd S Margeret Cntr; Epis Black Caucus New York. hebluntjr@gmail.com

BOARD, John C (Mont) 2704 Gold Rush Ave, Helena MT 59601 **Cathd Ch Of The Nativ Bethlehem PA 2005-** B Onarga IL 5/18/1936 s Victor Lee Board & Georgia Pearl. BA Ball St Teachers Coll 1958; MA U of Wyoming 1964; MLS U of Oregon 1972; Montana Mnstry Formation Prog 2005. D 9/18/2005 Bp Charles Franklin Brookhart Jr. m 6/15/1965 Mait Birgitt Erickson c 2. "Great Teachers Are Not Solo Performers," *Educ Week*, Educ Week, 1992; "A Spec Relatns: Our Teachers and How We Learned (B00K)," *A Spec Relatns: Our Teachers and How We Learned(Bk)*, Pushcart Press, 1991; "Passion is the shared trait among great teachers," *The Middletown Press*, The Middletown Press (Connecticut), 1991; "Jeannette Rankin: The Lady from Montana," *Montana, The mag of Wstrn Hist*, Montana Hist Soc, 1967. jcboard@bresnan.net

BOARD III, J(ohn) Paul (O) 313 E Wayne St, Maumee OH 43537 **R S Paul's Ch Maumee OH 1997-** B Wertzburg DE 10/16/1964 s John Paul Board & Ruth Frances. BA U So 1989; MDiv VTS 1995; DMin SWTS 2007. D 6/24/1995 Bp R(aymond) Stewart Wood Jr P 2/12/1996 Bp J Clark Grew II. m 7/17/1993 Lori Ann King c 3. Asst R Chr Epis Ch Warren OH 1995-1997. paul@stpaulsmaumee.org

BOASE, David John (Spr) 4902 Blu Fountain Dr, Godfrey IL 62035 **R S Paul's/Trin Chap Alton IL 2004-** B Millom UK 7/4/1949 s Donald Usher Boase & Jean. BA U Of Durham UK 1971; PGCE Oxf UK 1973; CTh Ripon Coll Cuddesdon 1973. Trans from Church Of England 11/1/2004 Bp Peter Hess Beckwith. c 2. david.boase@dunelm.org.uk

BOATRIGHT, William Emanuel (NY) 1901 N. DuPont Highway, New Castle DE 19720 B Avon Park FL 1/31/1953 s Manuel Boatright & Thelma. BA Stetson U 1977; Chandler TS 1979; MDiv Andover Newton TS 1982; Cert: Angl Stds Nash 1986; STM GTS 1989. D 10/19/1987 Bp Henry Boyd Hucles III P 12/1/1988 Bp Orris George Walker Jr. m 4/17/2003 Kahlil Boatright c 1. Asst Cathd Ch Of S Jn Wilmington DE 2003-2006; Int Chr Ch-Epis Port Jefferson NY 2000; Chapl St Marys Cnvnt Greenwich NY 1999-2000; P-in-c S Jas Epis Ch Fordham Bronx NY 1998-2000; Int S Andr's Ch New York NY 1997-1998; Chapl Dio Atlanta Atlanta GA 1991-1996; Asst S Mk's Ch Brooklyn NY 1990-1998; Asst Dio Long Island Garden City NY 1987-1989. wboatwright2011@gmail.com

BOATRIGHT-SPENCER, Angela (NY) 425 Lee Avenue, Wadesboro NC 28170 **Permanent Supply Chap Of Chr The King Charlotte NC 2010-** B Newark NJ 2/8/1951 d John Louis Robinson & Laura Louise. BA Cor 1973; MS Col 1975; MDiv UTS 1988; Dplma GTS 1991; CNA I So Piedmont Comm. Coll 2008. D 6/15/1991 Bp Orris George Walker Jr P 1/25/1992 Bp Frank Kellogg Allan. m 6/30/2007 Richard Lewis Spencer c 3. Longterm Supply Ch Of The Mssh Rockingham NC 2008; Vic S Paul's Ch Sprg Vlly NY 2002-2007; Assoc Trin Epis Ch Garnerville NY 2002-2007; Asst S Mary's Manhattanville Epis Ch New York NY 1997-2001; Chapl St. Mary's Cntr Inc. New York NY 1996-2001; Vic S Tim's Decatur GA 1994-1996; P-in-c S Steph's Ch Griffin GA 1991-1994. Auth, "Recon, Redemp & Gr," *Wisdom Found (edited by Lindsay Hardin Freeman)*, Forw Mvmt, 2010; Co-Auth, "The Heir," XLibris, 2008; Auth, "Spec Delivery , Thanksgiving Pryr," *Race and Pryr (edited by M. Boyd and C.Talton)*, Morehouse, 2003; Auth, "In The Time Of Trouble," Ldr Resources, 2002. Ord Of S Helena 1982-1984. Wmn of dist Awd Alpha Phi Alpha 2007; Cert of Merit NY St Senate 2006; Cert of Merit NY St Assembly 2005; DSA Rockland Cnty Legislature 2004; Humanitarian Awd NAACP 2003. angelaspirittalk@aol.com

BOBBITT, Kathleen Morrisette (SVa) 1005 Windsor Rd, Virginia Beach VA 23451 **Int S Thos Epis Ch Chesapeake VA 2011-** B Norfolk VA 9/22/1942 d William Gordon Morrisette & Myra Virginius. BS U of Maryland, European Div, Heidelberg, Germa 1988; MDiv VTS 1993. D 6/5/1993 Bp Jack Marston McKelvey P 1/15/1994 Bp John Shelby Spong. m 12/16/1967 Joseph Rosser Bobbitt c 3. Int S Geo's Epis Ch Newport News VA 2010; Estrn Shore Chap Virginia Bch VA 2008; Galilee Epis Ch Virginia Bch VA 2008; Dn Dio Sthrn Virginia Norfolk VA 2006-2010; Goodwin Hse Incorporated Alexandria VA 2000-2005; Assoc R For Pstr Care S Jn's Epis Ch McLean VA 1995-2000; Cur Trin Ch Arlington VA 1993-1995. Assn Of Friends Of The Warterloo Com 1996; Colonial Dames 2002; Jr League 1972-1987. revbobbitt@gmail.com

BOBO, Melinda (Wyo) P.O. Box 1177, Dubois WY 82513 **Mnstry Dvlp Dio Wyoming Casper WY 2010-** B Washington DC 1/18/1964 d Charles Ezell Bobo & Annie Ruth. BA Pur 1984; MA Pur 1986; PhD (ABD) U of Wyoming 1998; MDiv SWTS 2001. D 6/20/2001 P 12/20/2001 Bp Bruce Edward Caldwell. Vic S Mk's Ch Craig CO 2004-2005; Asst R S Mart's By The Lake Epis Minnetonka Bch MN 2001-2004. revbobo.wy@gmail.com

BOCCHINO, James Robert (RI) 589 Smithfield Rd, North Providence RI 02904 **Int Chr Ch Westerly RI 2010-** B Pawtucket RI 4/24/1950 s John Bocchino & Josephine. BS Wag 1972; MDiv EDS 1984. D 6/23/1984 P 3/2/1985 Bp George Nelson Hunt III. m 11/30/2002 Barbara Elizabeth Fox. Int S Jn's Ch Barrington RI 2008-2010; R All SS' Memi Ch Providence RI 1987-2008; Asst S Mary's Ch Portsmouth RI 1984-1987. jim.boc@verizon.net

BOCK, Susan Kay (Mich) 529 E Kirby St, Detroit MI 48202 **Gr Ch Mt Clemens MI 2010-; R S Gabr's Epis Ch Eastpointe MI 2001-** B Pontiac MI 12/10/1948 d William Thomas Barr & Patricia Ann. Sch of Nrsng Henry Ford U Hosp 1970; Epis TS of The SW 1984. D 6/30/1984 Bp Henry Irving Mayson P 10/1/1985 Bp H Coleman McGehee Jr. m 1/6/2008 James Brown c 2. Cn S Andr's Cathd Jackson MS 1998-2001; R S Aid's Ch Ann Arbor MI 1997-1998; S Clare Of Assisi Epis Ch Ann Arbor MI 1989-1997; Asst P S Mich's Ch Grosse Pointe Woods MI 1986-1989; Asst P S Dav's Ch Southfield MI 1985-1988. Auth, "Liturg for the Whole Ch: Multigenerational Resources for Wrshp," Ch Pub, 2008. therealgirlpriest@yahoo.com

BOCKUS, Ian Lawrence (Me) 496 N Searsport Rd, Prospect ME 04981 **Cn Cathd Ch Of S Lk Portland ME 1997-** B Cowansville QC CA 4/13/1933 s Elton Earl Bockus & Carrie Marion Margaret. BA Bps 1954; BD McGill U 1957; LTh Montreal Dioc Coll 1957. Trans from Anglican Church of Canada 7/1/1961 Bp Oliver L Loring. m 9/3/2011 Brian MacFarland c 2. R S Pat's Ch Brewer ME 1984-1998; S Paul's Epis Ch Vermillion SD 1982-1984; R S Jas Ch Trenton Yardville NJ 1970-1982; Asst Chr Ch Par Kensington MD 1964-1966; R S Lk's Ch Caribou ME 1961-1964. Hon Cn S Lk's Cathd Portland ME 1997. ibockus13@gmail.com

BODIE, Park McDermit (NY) 235 W 56th St Apt 11m, New York NY 10019 B South Charleston WV 4/11/1950 s George Wilbur Bodie & Jean Johnson. BA W Virginia St U 1981; MDiv STUSo 1986. D 6/29/1986 P 4/21/1987 Bp William Evan Sanders. m 11/20/1981 Suzanne Woody c 2. Supply P Chr Ch Garden City NY 2009-2011; Int S Barn Ch Irvington on Hudson NY 2008-2009; Int S Eliz's Ch Eliz NJ 2007-2008; Consult Trin Par New York NY 2006; Precentor S Thos Ch New York NY 1997-2005; Vic S Columba's Epis Ch Bristol TN 1988-1997; Bp's Coun Dio E Tennessee Knoxville TN 1988-1992; Cler Spprt and Dvlpmt Com Dio E Tennessee Knoxville TN 1988-1992; Cur S Tim's Ch Signal Mtn TN 1986-1988. pmb202@aol.com

BOELTER, Sarah (Cal) 41485 S. I-94 Service Drive, Belleville MI 48111 B Detroit MI 7/14/1947 d Albert Edward Allen & Lilah Mary. BA Cntrl Michigan U 1969; MLS Estrn Michigan U 1986; MDiv Ecum TS 1995; MDiv SWTS 1995. D 6/24/1995 P 4/1/1996 Bp R(aymond) Stewart Wood Jr. m 6/21/1969 Richard Boelter c 2. Assoc R S Paul's Epis Ch Burlingame CA 2007-2011; R S Raphael's Ch Lexington KY 2002-2007; Assoc R Trin Ch Belleville MI 1995-2002. Blue Ribbon Awd. revsally2@yahoo.com

BOESCHENSTEIN, Kathryn C (Colo) PO Box 208, Westcliffe CO 81252 **Vic S Lk's Ch Westcliffe CO 2007-** B Brooklyn NY 7/19/1944 BA CUNY 1966; MA Hunter Coll 1973; MDiv. GTS 2003. D 6/14/2003 Bp William Jerry Winterrowd P 12/20/2003 Bp Robert John O'Neill. c 2. R S Andr's Epis Ch Polson MT 2005-2007; S Gabr The Archangel Epis Ch Cherry Hills Vill CO 2003-2005. kathylilbe@yahoo.com

BOESSER, Mark Alan (Ak) 17585 Point Lena Loop Rd, Juneau AK 99801 B Winston-Salem NC 5/19/1926 s Christian Mark Boesser & Sara Wilhelmina. BS U of Texas 1946; BD VTS 1951; DMin Andover Newton TS 1974. D 6/2/1951 P 5/1/1952 Bp Edwin A Penick. m 12/22/1948 Mildred Post. P-in-c/R S Dav's Ch Wasilla AK 1977-1991; Dio Alaska Fairbanks AK 1973-1991; R The Ch Of The H Trin Juneau AK 1959-1973; P-in-c S Chris's Ch League City TX 1955-1959; M-in-c Galloway Memi Chap Elkin NC 1951-1955; M-in-c Trin Ch Mt Airy NC 1951-1955. Soc Of S Simeon & S Anna. mboesser@gci.net

BOEVE, Phillip Dale (Spr) 303 Merchants Avenue, Fort Atkinson WI 53538 **S Barn Ch Havana IL 2010-** B Holland MI 12/3/1953 s Dale Roger Boeve & Patricia Ann. BA No Cntrl Michigan Petoskey MI 1977; BA Hope Coll 1981; MDiv VTS 1984. D 7/25/1984 Bp Charles Ellsworth Bennison Jr P 6/1/1985 Bp Howard Samuel Meeks. c 4. R S Peters Epis Ch Ft Atkinson WI 1993-2009; R S Mary's Epis Ch Cadillac MI 1986-1993; Cur S Thos Epis Ch

Battle Creek MI 1984-1986. ERM; Epis Untd; EvangES, Associated Parishes. boevephillip@hotmail.com

BOGAL-ALLBRITTEN, Rose (Ky) 1504 Kirkwood Dr, Murray KY 42071 B Chicago IL 3/4/1951 d Edward Henry Bogal & Mary Valentina. BA Loyola U 1972; MS Loyola U 1974; PhD Loyola U 1977. D 5/2/2004 Bp Edwin Funsten Gulick Jr. m 3/6/1982 William Allbritten c 1. Assn for Epis Deacons 2003. rose.bogal@att.net

BOGAN III, Leslie Eugene (CGC) 1336 Greenvista Ln, Gulf Breeze FL 32563 B Houston TX 3/15/1936 s Leslie Eugene Bogan & Margarita. BA Van 1958; BD Epis TS of The SW 1961; STM Epis TS of The SW 1964. D 7/18/1961 Bp Everett H Jones P 2/6/1962 Bp Richard Earl Dicus. m 3/3/1982 Eleana McKinley c 3. Asst to R S Fran Of Assisi Gulf Breeze FL 1993-2002; Asst The Epis Ch Of The Medtr Allentown PA 1965-1967; R Ch Of The H Sprt Graham TX 1963-1965; Vic Gr Ch Llano TX 1961-1963. Auth, "(Var Columns) 1967-1970," *Bethlehem Globe Times*; Auth, "News Stories 1970-1976," *Pensacola News Journ*. bogans4@gmail.com

BOGARDUS JR, James Furnas (Los) 25921 Oak St Unit 206, Lomita CA 90717 B Plymouth MA 10/6/1925 s James Furnas Bogardus & Catharine Clampitt. BS U of Pennsylvania 1949; BD CDSP 1959. D 6/29/1959 Bp Stephen F Bayne Jr P 5/21/1960 Bp William F Lewis. Asst S Andr's Par Torrance CA 1983-2000; Asst Chr Ch Par Redondo Bch CA 1974-1983; Asst Trin Ch Cliffside Pk NJ 1972-1973; Cur Chr Ch Par Redondo Bch CA 1966-1971; Cur Ch Of The H Innoc Corte Madera CA 1961-1965; Asst S Paul's Ch Seattle WA 1959-1960. kimobog@aol.com

BOGART, John Lawrence (NCal) 227 Baker St, Benicia CA 94510 B Torrance CA 8/18/1929 s Wayne Ayers Bogart & Merle. BA USC 1951; STB Ya Berk 1954; ThM CDSP 1969; ThD Grad Theol Un 1973. D 6/2/1954 Bp Francis E I Bloy P 2/1/1955 Bp Donald J Campbell. m 8/15/1953 Mary Louise Rapoza c 2. Hon Cn Dio Nthrn California Sacramento CA 1984-1990; S Patricks Ch Kenwood CA 1979-1990; CDSP Berkeley CA 1974-1980; R H Trin Epis Ch Ukiah CA 1965-1972; R Gr Ch S Helena CA 1958-1965; Vic The Epis Ch Of S Andr Encinitas CA 1955-1958; Cur All SS Ch San Diego CA 1954-1955.

BOGDANICH, George R (Ct) 1722 S Carson Ave Apt 905, Tulsa OK 74119 **Died 6/8/2011** B GR 2/21/1923 s Amabile Charles Joseph Bogdanich & Maria. U of Athens Athens GR 1939; BA U of Tulsa 1952; ThB PDS 1955; U of Pennsylvania 1956; Fllshp Coll of Preachers 1959; MA Ya 1961. Rec from Roman Catholic 4/2/1950 Bp Thomas Casady. c 3. Coll Prchr Washington Cathd 1959. Dplma & Silver Medal Mnstry of Frgn Affrs France 1938.

BOGDON, Judith Lynn (Mich) 8874 Northern Ave, Plymouth MI 48170 **Trin Ch S Clair Shores MI 2008-** B Ypsilanti MI 12/25/1954 AA Schoolcraft Cmnty Livonia MI 1997; BS Estrn Michigan U Ypsilanti MI 1999; DMin SWTS 2005. D 7/2/2005 P 2/8/2006 Bp Wendell Nathaniel Gibbs Jr. c 2. Trin Ch S Clair Shores MI 2007-2008; Cur Ch Of The Incarn Pittsfield Twp Ann Arbor MI 2005-2007. jlbgdn@excite.com

BOGEL, Marianne (Oly) 11844 Bandera Rd #148, HELOTES TX 78023 B Oklahoma City OK 8/18/1945 d Amos Graves Bogel & Erile Louise. RN Barnes Hosp Sch Of Nrsng 1966; GTS 1976. D 6/4/1976 P 1/1/1977 Bp Furman Stough. S Hilda's - S Pat's Epis Ch Edmonds WA 1982-1987; Ch Of The Mssh Dexter ME 1979-1980. Soc Of S Marg.

BOGERT-WINKLER, Hilary Megan (Ky) 14 Boltwood Ave., Amherst MA 01002 **Dio Wstrn Massachusetts Springfield MA 2009-** B Louisville KY 2/5/1983 d Christopher Michael Bogert & Ronnah Lynn. BA Wstrn Kentucky U 2005; MTS Harvard DS 2007; Ya Berk 2009. D 6/19/2009 P 1/16/2010 Bp Edwin Funsten Gulick Jr. m 7/25/2009 Richard Winkler. hbw@gracechurchamherst.org

BOGGS, Timothy A (Me) 2023 Hillyers Place Nw, Washington DC 20009 **S Albans Sch Washington DC 2007-** B Wisconsin 6/23/1950 s Russell Ralph Boggs & Valarie. Geo; BA U Of Wisconsin Madison WI; MDiv The GTS 2007. D 6/9/2007 P 1/19/2008 Bp John Chane. Cathd of St Ptr & St Paul Washington DC 2010; Asst S Alb's Par Washington DC 2007-2010. timothyboggs@aol.com

BOGHETICH, Barbara Ann (Hond) IMC-SAP 564, PO Box 52-3900, Miami FL 33152 B Milwaukee WS 8/27/1937 d Erwin Charles Ford & Dorothy Ann Kramer. none Epis TS of the SW; BBA Adel 1960; MDiv Houston Grad TS 1996. D 10/28/2005 P 1/12/2008 Bp Lloyd Emmanuel Allen. c 1. SAMS Ambridge PA 2005-2009; SAMS Ambridge PA 1997-2005. bboghetich@yahoo.com

BOHLER JR, Lewis Penrose (Los) PO Box 16216, Augusta GA 30919 **Chr Ch Augusta GA 2002-** B Augusta GA 11/28/1927 s Lewis Penrose Bohler & Margie Alice. BA W Virginia St U 1951; MDiv Ob 1954; MDiv Bex 1955. D 6/18/1955 P 6/23/1956 Bp Nelson Marigold Burroughs. c 2. S Mary's Ch Augusta GA 1996-1999; R Epis Ch Of The Adv Los Angeles CA 1961-1996; M-in-c S Aug's Epis Ch Youngstown OH 1955-1961. Auth, "The Mt Vernon Plan".

BOHNER, Charles Russell (Del) 1309 Grinnell Rd # N33, Wilmington DE 19803 B Wilmington DE 11/25/1965 s Charles Henry Bohner & Mary Jean. BA U Of Delaware Newark 1989; MDiv SWTS 2003. D 1/18/2003 P 10/16/2003 Bp Wayne Parker Wright. m 11/6/2004 Diane Bohner c 2. Chr Ch Greenville Wilmington DE 2003-2008; Asst S Barn Ch Wilmington DE 2003-2008. russbohner@me.com

BOHYER, Robert Donald (Neb) Po Box 205, Carter MT 59420 B Bloomington IL 5/8/1930 s Jacob Donald Bohyer & Lela Elizabeth. DC U of Natl Healing Arts 1951; ATC 1966; Great Falls Coll 1975. D 3/18/1966 P 5/25/1967 Bp Chandler W Sterling. m 12/24/1950 Jean E Hook c 6. R S Matt's Ch Allnce NE 1991-1996; Dio So Dakota Sioux Falls SD 1984-1991; R S Jas Ch Lewistown MT 1966-1984. Auth, *Montana Evang*.

BOIVIN, Barbara Ann (Nev) 250 Big Horn Dr, Boulder City NV 89005 **D S Chris's Epis Ch Boulder City NV 2005-** B Harrisburg IL 9/13/1937 d Hiram William Tate & Geneva. D 10/15/2005 Bp Katharine Jefferts Schori. m 3/23/2000 Jean Roland Boivin c 3. N.A.A.D. 2006. ronbarb@cox.net

BOJARSKI, Mitchell T (Ky) 1215 State St, Bowling Green KY 42101 **S Thos Ch Campbellsville KY 2010-** B Buffalo NY 6/30/1978 s Alan Bojarski & Martha Ann. BA Roberts Wesleyan Coll 2000; MDiv VTS 2008. D 5/24/2008 Bp Peter James Lee P 1/11/2009 Bp Edwin Funsten Gulick Jr. m 4/21/2001 Beth Frary c 1. Assoc R Chr Epis Ch Bowling Green KY 2008-2010. Rosary Soc 2005. fr.mitch.bojarski@gmail.com

BOLAND, Geoffrey Allan (CFla) 1861 Peninsular Dr, Haines City FL 33844 B Jamaica NY 2/11/1946 s Arthur Francis Boland & Shirley Elizabeth. BA SUNY 1969; MDiv Nash 1974. D 12/22/1973 Bp Allen Webster Brown P 11/30/1974 Bp Charles Bowen Persell Jr. m 8/30/1969 Alayne Noyes c 1. S Mk's Epis Ch Haines City FL CA 1999-2007; Environ Cmsn Dio Wstrn New York Tonawanda NY 1991-1999; Dn Of Cattaraugus Dnry Dio Wstrn New York Tonawanda NY 1989-1999; Dioc Coun Dio Wstrn New York Tonawanda NY 1989-1992; R S Mary's Ch Salamanca NY 1981-1999; Yth Conf Stff Dio Wstrn New York Tonawanda NY 1981-1995; CE Cmsn Dio Wstrn New York Tonawanda NY 1981-1990; Dioc Coun Dio Wstrn New York Tonawanda NY 1981-1984; Chr Ch Coxsackie NY 1980-1981; Trin Ch Coxsackie NY 1976-1981; Dio Albany Albany NY 1976-1979; Cur S Jas Ch Oneonta NY 1974-1976. geoffreyboland@mindspring.com

BOLDINE, Charles Stanley (RG) 6009 Costa Brava Ave NW, Albuquerque NM 87114 B Ely MN 10/18/1950 s Stanley Joseph Boldine & Justine Pauline. Spec Educ UTEP; AA Vermillion St Jr Coll 1971; BS St. Cloud St U 1973; MDiv SWTS 1987. D 8/5/1987 Bp Richard Mitchell Trelease Jr P 4/1/1988 Bp William Davidson. m 2/25/2006 Mary Smith c 3. R Ch Of The H Cross Edgewood NM 1998-2006; Int H Sprt Epis Ch El Paso TX 1995-1996; R S Lk's Epis Ch Anth NM 1989-1993; Pstr S Mary's Ch Lovington NM 1987-1989. chaz_bo_50@q.com

BOLI, Judith Davis (EMich) 4444 State St Apt F-318, Saginaw MI 48603 **R S Paul's Epis Ch Saginaw MI 1999-** B Detroit MI 4/5/1938 d Calvin Davis & Elma Dora. BS Wayne 1959; Cert Whitaker TS 1978; MA MI SU 1984. D 6/29/1976 Bp H Coleman McGehee Jr P 1/1/1978 Bp Henry Irving Mayson. m 7/1/1966 William Wilkins Boli c 2. S Paul's Epis Ch Saginaw MI 1995-1996; Assoc S Paul's Epis Ch Saginaw MI 1976-1993. Phi Kappa Phi. jboli@charter.net

BOLI, William Wilkins (EMich) 4444 State St Apt F-215, Saginaw MI 48603 B Pittsburgh PA 3/13/1927 s Robert F Boli & Jane A. BA Buc 1950; Pittsburgh TS 1956; VTS 1978. D 6/29/1957 Bp Austin Pardue P 12/21/1957 Bp William S Thomas. m 7/1/1966 Judith Davis c 4. P-in-c S Paul's Epis Ch Corunna MI 1996-2003; S Jn's Ch Chesaning MI 1993-1996; R Calv Memi Epis Ch Saginaw MI 1991-1993; R S Paul's Epis Ch Saginaw MI 1966-1993; S Geo/S Mths Ch Chicago IL 1960-1966. EPF 1995. wwboli@charter.net

BOLIN, William Eugene (Md) 244 Braeburn Cir, Walkersville MD 21793 B Baltimore MD 7/2/1940 s Carroll Eugene Bolin & Helen Gertrude. BA U of Washington 1965; MDiv UTS 1984; DAS VTS 1992. D 11/14/1992 Bp Ronald Hayward Haines P 5/1/1993 Bp Jane Hart Holmes Dixon. m 8/16/1998 Marianna Busching c 1. The Gathering: A Fam Of Faith Epis Ch Buckeystown MD 2004-2006; Dio Maryland Baltimore MD 1997-2003; Ch Planter Dio Maryland Baltimore MD 1994-2006; P-in-c S Anne's Ch Damascus MD 1993-1997; Dio Washington Washington DC 1992-1993. Auth, "Chr Witness On Campus," Broadman Press; Auth, "Growing Up Caring," McGraw-Hill. SBL, EPF, Nat. frb7240@aol.com

BOLLE, Stephen M (NY) 1 Chipping Ct, Greenville SC 29607 **Int Dn Trin Cathd Columbia SC 2010-** B Oconomowoc WI 9/23/1940 s Victor Emil Hans Bolle & Lucille Elizabeth. BA Mia 1963; STB Ya Berk 1967; S Geo's Coll Jerusalem IL 1988. D 4/1/1967 P 10/28/1967 Bp Donald H V Hallock. m 7/27/1974 Margaret Ann Muncie c 2. P-in-c Ch Of The Adv Spartanburg SC 2008-2010; Int R Chr Ch Greenville SC 2008; Int R S Mk's Ch Mt Kisco NY 2007-2008; Assoc S Mich's Ch New York NY 2000-2007; Cn to the Dn Epis Soc of Chr Ch Cincinnati OH 1995-2000; Int R S Thos Epis Ch Terrace Pk OH 1990-1995; Asst S Barn Epis Ch Greenwich CT 1989-1990; R S Lk's Ch Katonah NY 1972-1989; Asst S Mk's Ch Islip NY 1967-1972. Epis Cmnty Serv, Dio Sthrn Ohio 1996-2000. smgvb@earthlink.net

BOLLE, Winnie Mckenzie Hoilette (SeFla) 6055 Verde Trl S Apt H316, Boca Raton FL 33433 **Asst Chap Of S Andr Boca Raton FL 1997-** B JM 8/17/

1924 d Luther Josiah Hoilett & Rosa Dottie. BS Lon 1959; MA U CA 1968; MDiv CDSP 1969. P 6/5/1982 Bp Calvin Onderdonk Schofield Jr. Dio SE Florida Miami FL 1982-1991; Assoc Trin Cathd Miami FL 1980-1997. Fell Coll Of Chapl. Hon Cn Trin Cathd Miami FL 1996. bollevandw@aol.com

BOLLES, Hebert Winslow (RI) 45 De Arruda Ter, Portsmouth RI 02871 **Asst S Columba's Chap Middletown RI 1998-** B New York NY 9/30/1924 s Norman Taylor Bolles & Mary Winslow. BA Br 1945; MA Br 1948; MDiv GTS 1951. D 3/27/1951 P 10/4/1951 Bp Granville G Bennett. m 6/4/1955 Elizabeth Sands Elliot c 4. Vic S Andr's By The Sea Little Compton RI 1989-1994; S Lk's Epis Ch E Greenwich RI 1986-1987; S Paul's Ch Portsmouth RI 1985-1986; Off Of Bsh For ArmdF New York NY 1962-1969; Cn Chr Ch Cathd Indianapolis IN 1957-1962; R Ch Of The Ascen Wakefield RI 1953-1957; Cur S Steph's Ch Providence RI 1951-1952. Assoc of SHN 1953; Gld of the Ascen 1957-1977. hwbolles@cox.net

BOLLES-BEAVEN, Anne Elizabeth (Nwk) 32 Yale St, Maplewood NJ 07040 **Assoc S Andr And H Comm Ch So Orange NJ 2004-; Bd Trst No Porch Wmn & Infants Centers Newark NJ 2000-** B Indianapolis IN 4/10/1959 d Hebert Winslow Bolles & Elizabeth Sands. BA Barnard Coll of Col 1981; MDiv GTS 1988. D 10/22/1988 P 3/3/1990 Bp George Nelson Hunt III. m 1/2/1982 Paul William Bolles-Beaven. Tchr S Jn's Epis Ch Montclair NJ 2010; Sabbatical P S Geo's Epis Ch Maplewood NJ 2009; Int S Ptr's Ch Essex Fells NJ 2002-2004; CE Cmsn Dio Newark Newark NJ 2001-2003; Int S Mk's Ch W Orange NJ 2000-2002; Int Ch Of The H Sprt Verona NJ 1999-2000; Assoc S Geo's Epis Ch Maplewood NJ 1994-1998; Asst S Ann And The H Trin Brooklyn NY 1989-1993. Auth, "Monthly Column," *Rhode Island Epis News*, 1997; Auth, "Books In Revs," *Epis Life*, 1994; Auth, "Naming Wmn Priests Reveals Dilemma About God," *Epis Life*, 1992; Auth, "The Eye Of The Needle (Poem)," *LivCh*, 1988. COM, Dio Newark 2006; No Porch Bd 2001; Wmn Cmsn, Dio Newark 2000-2005. Wmn of Influence Brooklyn YWCA 1990. bollesbeaven@aol.com

BOLLINGER II, David Glenn (CNY) 6429 Montrose Turnpike, Owego NY 13827 B Mount Vernon OH 9/27/1954 s Charles Earl Bollinger & Frances Wright. Eisenhower Coll Rit 1979; MDiv EDS 1983; Oxf 1991; Oxf 1998; SUNY 2003. D 6/11/1983 Bp Ned Cole P 5/9/1984 Bp O'Kelley Whitaker. m 8/13/1977 Kelly Ann Adair c 1. Dio Cntrl New York Syracuse NY 2005; COM Dio Cntrl New York Syracuse NY 1990-1993; R S Paul's Ch Owego NY 1986-2005; Asst S Mary's Epis Ch Barnstable MA 1984-1986; Asst S Lk's Ch Gladstone NJ 1983-1984. Consortium Endowed Epis Parishes; Fllshp Of The Soc Of S Jn The Evang. dbollinger@stny.rr.com

BOLT, Michelle Warriner (ETenn) Tyson House, 824 Melrose Place, Knoxville TN 37919 **Tyson Hse Stdt Fndt Knoxville TN 2006-** B Atlanta GA 5/9/1975 d John Warriner & Joan. BA U of Tennessee 1997; MA Harvard DS 2000; MDiv SWTS 2006. D 5/27/2006 P 9/29/2007 Bp Charles Glenn VonRosenberg. m 5/26/2001 Patrick McClure Bolt c 1. Dio E Tennessee Knoxville TN 2007-2009; Asst S Paul's Epis Ch Burlingame CA 2006-2007. mwbolt@gmail.com

BOLTON, Carolyn Marie (Cal) 1125 Brush St, Oakland CA 94607 **D S Paul's Ch Oakland CA 2011-** B Oakland CA 8/3/1948 d Adam Robert & Nathalie. AA Laney Jr Coll 2003; BA Sch for Deacons 2005. D 12/3/2005 Bp William Edwin Swing. m 4/26/1980 Howard Bolton c 3. NAAD 2010; Soroptimist Intl of Oakland 1994; St. Mary's Cntr Bd - Oakland 2005; UBE 2000. cbolton730@aol.com

BOLTON, John Donald (At) 2833 Flat Shoals Rd, Decatur GA 30034 B Cullercoats Northumberland UK 1/7/1940 s John Dixon Bolton & Dorothy Christina. Profsnl Counslg Lic St Of Georgia; Profsnl Counslg Lic St Of Virginia; U So 1964; TS Of Edinburgh Gb 1965; MS Virginia Commonwealth U 1980. Rec 7/1/1973 as Priest Bp Kenneth Moir Carey. m 7/5/2002 Linda A Sparks c 4. The Ch Of Our Sav Atlanta GA 2006-2010; R Ch of the Resurr Sautee Nacoochee GA 2002-2006; S Anth's Epis Ch Winder GA 2001-2002; Int Chr Epis Ch Kennesaw GA 2000-2001; S Tim's Decatur GA 1997-2000; Epis Ch Of The H Fam Jasper GA 1990-1991; S Tim's Epis Ch Calhoun GA 1990-1991; Int The Epis Ch Of S Ptr And S Paul Marietta GA 1989-1990; Gr Epis Ch Goochland VA 1982-1983; Ch Of The Gd Shpd Richmond VA 1975-1979; Asst Chr And Gr Ch Petersburg VA 1973-1975. revjbolton@webtv.net

BOMAN, Ruth Kay (Okla) 424 E St Nw, Miami OK 74354 B Wichita KS 9/22/1953 d William Boman & Alice. BA Oklahoma St U 1975; MS Pittsburg St U 1980. D 6/22/1996 Bp Robert Manning Moody.

BOMAN, Samuel Ratliff (Neb) 262 Parkside Ln, Lincoln NE 68521 B Pierceville KS 7/17/1927 s Samuel Nelson Boman & Artemecia Swango. BA SW Coll Winfield KS 1948; SWTS 1950. D 11/7/1950 P 9/21/1951 Bp Goodrich R Fenner. m 6/2/1947 Mary Ann Reighley c 4. Ch Of The H Trin Lincoln NE 1993-1995; S Dav Of Wales Epis Ch Lincoln NE 1976-1990; Ch Of Our Sav No Platte NE 1960-1976; R Chr Ch Epis Beatrice NE 1954-1959; P-in-c S Mk's Ch Blue Rapids KS 1952-1953; P-in-c S Paul's Ch Marysville KS 1952-1953; Asst S Lk's Ch Wamego KS 1950-1951; Asst S Paul's Ch Manhattan KS 1950-1951. bomanlincoln4@aol.com

BOMBARD, Thom H (Alb) 20 Lincoln Ave, Glens Falls NY 12801 B Glens Falls NY 3/3/1950 s Victor Howard Bombard & Shirley. D 6/10/2006 Bp Daniel William Herzog. m 7/3/1971 Deborah S Kelly c 5. dbombard@nycap.rr.com

BONADIE, LeRoy Rowland (Md) 609 Wellington Ln, Cumberland ND 21502 B St Vincent, West Indies 5/15/1939 s Vincent Bonadie & Muriel. D 10/21/2000 Bp David B(ruce) Joslin P 1/6/2007 Bp John Leslie Rabb. m 10/9/1994 Barbara Barbara English c 4. lrowb@verizon.net

BOND, Barbara Lynn (O) 455 Santa Clara St Nw, Canton OH 44709 **R S Paul's Ch Canton OH 2006-** B Washington DC 5/14/1945 d Francis John Davis & Althea. BA Carleton Coll 1967; MA Steph F. Austin St U 1974; MFA Hochschule der Kunste Berlin DE 1979; MDiv SWTS 1993; DMin SWTS 2005. D 1/6/1996 P 7/29/1996 Bp John Stuart Thornton. m 4/20/2002 Norman Van Cleve. R S Paul's Ch Lock Haven PA 2000-2006; Vic Ch Of H Nativ Meridian ID 1996-2000. Assn Profsnl Chapl 1998-2009. revblbond@msn.com

BOND, Eric Burns (Pa) 2122 Washington Ln, Huntingdon Valley PA 19006 **P-in-c Ch Of Our Sav Jenkintown PA 2011-; S Jn's Ch Huntingdon Vlly PA 2009-** B Des Plaines IL 6/25/1976 s David Bond & Catherine. BA Penn St Coll PA 1998; MA U Chi Chicago IL 2002; MDiv EDS 2006. D 6/10/2006 P 12/16/2006 Bp Charles Ellsworth Bennison Jr. m 6/26/1999 Carolyn Burns Bond c 3. CFS The Sch At Ch Farm Exton PA 2006-2009. ebond@gocfs.net

BOND, Jeremy William (CPa) 676 N 12th Street Unit 25, Grover Beach CA 93433 **Ret P S Barn Ch Arroyo Grande CA 2004-** B Detroit MI 7/9/1938 s Julian Maddocks Bond & Eleanor Lulie. BA Ken 1959; MDiv GTS 1962. D 6/9/1962 P 12/22/1962 Bp Horace W B Donegan. m 9/29/1962 Kathleen Bartlett c 3. Cn Cathd Ch Of S Steph Harrisburg PA 1993-2003; Vic S Mk's Epis Ch Northumberland PA 1989-2003; R S Matt's Epis Ch Sunbury PA 1979-2003; R S Paul's Epis Ch Harrisburg PA 1968-1979; Cn Cathd Ch Of S Steph Harrisburg PA 1964-1968; Asst Min Cathd Of St Jn The Div New York NY 1962-1964. Ord of Ascen 1992. Hon Cn Cathd Ch of St. Steph, Harrisburg, PA 1993. kajog@charter.net

BOND, L(eonard) Wayne (Oly) 5810 Fleming St Unit 66, Everett WA 98203 B Elmhurst IL 11/19/1930 s Leland Francis Bond & Cleo Vesta. BA Florida Sthrn Coll 1953; MDiv Garrett Evang TS 1956; BA U of Oregon 1968; BS Cntrl Washington U 1981. D 12/12/1961 P 6/21/1962 Bp Russell S Hubbard. m 8/17/1951 Marie Jean Tilley. Asst Trin Epis Ch Everett WA 1977-1997; Ch Of Our Sav Monroe WA 1976-1977; Serv S Phil Ch Marysville WA 1973-1974; Serv S Jn's Epis Ch Snohomish WA 1969-1972; DCE S Thos' Epis Ch Eugene OR 1968-1969; Vic S Chris's Ch Port Orford OR 1962-1966; Vic S Jn-By-The-Sea Epis Ch Bandon OR 1962-1966.

BOND, Marvin Monroe (WTex) 213 Stephanie Dr, Kerrville TX 78028 B Mexia TX 3/26/1919 s David Lee Bond & Ruby. Texas Tech U 1938; Arizona St U 1940; Lamar U 1955; Epis TS of The SW 1958. D 6/12/1958 Bp Richard Earl Dicus P 12/1/1958 Bp Everett H Jones. m 11/26/1986 Michael Nichols. R S Peters Epis Sch Kerrville TX 1967-1987; S Ptr's Epis Ch Kerrville TX 1967-1987; R H Trin Epis Ch Port Neches TX 1964-1967; R S Thos Ch Wharton TX 1960-1964; Vic Gr Ch Llano TX 1958-1960.

BOND, Michael David (Chi) 10550 Knickerbocker Ct, Saint John IN 46373 **Pstr Assoc Brent Hse (U Of Chicago) Chicago IL 2011-; Bldg and Prod Mgr Dio Chicago Chicago IL 2000-** B Bryn Mawr PA 9/16/1948 s Richard Doremus Bond & Olivia. D 2/5/2000 Bp William Dailey Persell. m 8/11/1990 Mary Jean Bond c 2. D Chr The King Ch Lansing IL 2000-2007. aBSG 2000; aOHC 2001. deaconmikebond@comcast.net

BOND, Michele (Eas) 19524 Meadowbrook Rd, Hagerstown MD 21742 B Baltimore MD 3/31/1944 d Edward Bomze & Audrey Laverne. BA Pepperdine U 1966; MDiv VTS 1989. D 6/17/1989 Bp A(lbert) Theodore Eastman P 5/7/1990 Bp Charles Lindsay Longest. m 6/29/1969 Ronald Bond c 3. R S Paul's Ch Trappe MD 2007-2009; Dir of Fam Mnstrs Trin Evang Luth Ch Hagerstown MD 2002-2007; Dir of Fam Mnstrs Cathd Of The Incarn Baltimore MD 1996-2000; Assoc S Jas Ch Monkton MD 1989-1995. mommabond@gmail.com

BOND, Thomas Dudley (SanD) 3405 Mount Carol Dr, San Diego CA 92111 **Assoc S Jas By The Sea La Jolla CA 2003-; P, Assoc for Pstr Care S Ptr's Epis Ch Del Mar CA 2003-** B San Antonio TX 1/16/1930 s Thomas Andrew Bond & Zora Gladys. Sul Ross St Coll 1949; BA U of Texas 1951; MDiv CDSP 1961. D 7/7/1961 Bp Everett H Jones P 1/7/1962 Bp Richard Earl Dicus. m 8/15/1971 Arlene Joan Bond c 2. S Ptr's Epis Ch Del Mar CA 1991-2002; Off Of Bsh For ArmdF New York NY 1966-1991; Vic Santa Fe Epis Mssn San Antonio TX 1961-1962. tdaj007@earthlink.net

BOND JR, Walter Douglas (Mass) 10 Dana St Apt 212, Cambridge MA 02138 B Evanston IL 8/16/1944 s Walter Edwin Douglas Bond & Mary Ann. BA Cor 1967; MDiv EDS 1972; CSS Harv 1993. D 6/9/1973 Bp Paul Moore Jr P 6/10/1975 Bp Ned Cole. Asst All SS Par Brookline MA 1983-1984; R S Geo's Ch Maynard MA 1977-2004; Int Chr Ch Medway MA 1976-1977; Assoc Chr Ch Waltham MA 1974-1976. Soc of King Chas the Mtyr. bond@post.harvard.edu

BONDURANT, Stephen Bryce (SO) 785 Ludlow Ave, Cincinnati OH 45220 B Saint Louis MO 1/27/1945 s Bryce Harold Bondurant & Helen May. BA

Drury U 1967; Med S Louis U 1970; MDiv Eden TS 1972; U of Edinburgh GB 1974; EdD U Cinc 1977. D 12/22/1985 P 5/1/1986 Bp Don Adger Wimberly. m 5/17/1980 Rachelle Marie Bondurant. Gr Ch Cincinnati OH 2003-2006; Int Gr Ch Cincinnati OH 1996-1997; R S Alb's Ch Indianapolis IN 1994-1995; S Mary's Epis Ch Hillsboro OH 1992-1993; Asst to R S Andr's Ch Ft Thos KY 1986-1990. Auth, "This Monday Morning I Have a Confession," *Monday Morning mag*, 1978; Auth, *Collection of Poems*, Catacomb Poets, 1973. AAR; APA 1978; Assn CT 1995; No Amer Paul Tillich Soc 1990. Phi Delta Kappa U Cinc Cincinnati OH 1977. gechurch@aol.com

BONE, Patrick Joseph (ETenn) Po Box 129, Church Hill TN 37642 B San Antonio TX 5/25/1942 s Patrick Emmet Bone & Anne Marie. Med Assumption Sem 1970; D.Min. VTS 2006. Rec from Roman Catholic 5/11/2003 Bp Charles Glenn VonRosenberg. m 6/1/1992 Ina Katherine Sifferd. "Aliens Of Transylvania Cnty," Silver Dagger Mysteries, 2002; "Amelungeon Winter," Silver Dagger Mysteries, 2001; "Blood Mary: The Mystery Of Amanda'S Magic Mirror," The Overmountain Press, 1999. kayandpatbone@aol.com

BONEBRAKE, Aletha Green (EO) 2347 Campbell St, Baker City OR 97814 **Vic S Steph's Baker City OR 2010-** B Seattle WA 3/30/1941 d Philip Green & Charlotte C. AA GW 1961; BA U of Wisconsin 1982; MLS U of Wisconsin 1983; GOE Dio Estrn Oregon Sup. Prog 2006. D 11/22/2006 Bp William O Gregg P 12/13/2007 Bp James Edward Waggoner. c 3. alethaboneb@msn.com

BONELL, John W. (NH) 3 Bodfish Av, Wareham MA 02571 B Pasadena CA 4/26/1951 s William Henry Bonell & Blanche. BA U CA 1976; MDiv CDSP 1980. D 6/20/1981 Bp Robert C Rusack P 1/1/1982 Bp Arthur Anton Vogel. m 2/9/2002 Nancy Finigan c 2. P-in-c S Ptr's Ch On The Canal Buzzards Bay MA 2005-2007; S Andr's Ch Methuen MA 2002-2003; Int S Sav's Epis Ch Old Greenwich CT 2000-2002; R Ch Of The Trsfg Derry NH 1990-2000; Asst R, Coll Chapl All SS Epis Ch Atlanta GA 1985-1990; Chapl Of Par Day Sch S Paul's Ch Kansas City MO 1981-1985. ESMHE 1983-1989. personjohn@comcast.net

BONES JR, William Lyle (Mich) 3865 Lincoln Rd, Bloomfield Hills MI 48301 **D S Jas Epis Ch Birmingham MI 1994-** B Detroit MI 3/13/1928 s William Lyle Bones & Charlotte Brooks. BS Pur 1952; Whitaker TS 1994. D 6/11/1994 Bp R(aymond) Stewart Wood Jr. m 10/26/1966 Martha Katherine Bones.

BONEY, Lois (NC) 110 Rockfish Court Cir, Wallace NC 28466 B Brownsville TN 12/5/1959 d Samuel Ashford Boney & Marcia Lois. BA Maryville Coll 1981; MA U of Tennessee 1984; MDiv VTS 1988. D 6/18/1988 P 4/1/1989 Bp Brice Sidney Sanders. m 6/3/1989 Kenneth Earl Bradshaw c 2. Ch Of The Nativ Raleigh NC 2009-2010; S Chris's Epis Ch Garner NC 2008-2010; Care Inc Smithfield NC 1996-2003; Assoc H Innoc Ch Atlanta GA 1990-1993; Vic Ch Of The Epiph Crestview FL 1989-1990; D S Jn's Epis Cathd Knoxville TN 1988-1989.

BONEY, Samuel Ashford (Miss) 10100 Hillview Dr. Apt 433, Pensacola FL 32514 B Athens GA 10/19/1927 s Sam Means Boney & Kathryn. BA U So 1955; MDiv STUSo 1958. D 6/22/1958 Bp Theodore N Barth P 3/14/1959 Bp John Vander Horst. m 8/6/1955 Marcia Lois Kline c 3. Cn Pstr S Andr's Cathd Jackson MS 1984-1991; Asst S Paul's Epis Ch Chattanooga TN 1981-1984; R S Mary's Epis Ch Dyersburg TN 1960-1980; P-in-c Chr Ch Brownsville TN 1958-1960; P-in-c Imm Ch Ripley TN 1958-1960. mkboney@cox.net

BONILLA-TIZALEMA, Henry Danilo (EcuC) Calle Hernando Sarmiento, N 39-54 Y Portete, Ecuador Ecuador **Ecuador New York NY 2009-; Iglesia Epis Del Ecuador Ecuador 2009-** B 5/8/1983 D 5/30/2009 P 10/2/2010 Bp Luis Fernando Ruiz Restrepo. m 12/19/2009 Lourdes Rocio Carrasco-Cruz.

BONNER, Bruce Hughes (Tex) 2200 Avenue E, Bay City TX 77414 **Chr Epis Ch Cedar Pk TX 2005-; Chr Epis Ch Cedar Pk TX 1999-** B Corpus Christi TX 8/29/1957 s Robert Hughes Bonner & Donna. BS Pk Coll 1993; MDiv Epis TS of The SW 1999. D 6/19/1999 P 6/22/2000 Bp Claude Edward Payne. m 8/26/1989 Kathryn Jernigan c 2. R S Mk's Ch Bay City TX 2002-2005; Ch Of The Epiph Houston TX 1999-2002. revbruce@christ-episcopal.com

BONNER, George Llewellyn (LI) 783 E 35th St, Brooklyn NY 11210 **S Alb's Ch Brooklyn NY 1987-** B BZ 12/15/1947 s Wilfred Gerald Bonner & Lessie Eleanor. DIT Codrington Coll 1977; BA U of The W Indies 1977; MS CUNY 1990. Rec 2/1/1987 as Priest Bp Robert Campbell Witcher Sr. m 8/26/2000 Marjorie Bonner c 2. gbonner138@aol.com

BONNER III, John Hare (EC) Holy Trinity Episcopal Church, 207 S Church St, Hertford NC 27944 **R H Trin Epis Ch Hertford NC 2006-** B Lumberton NC 12/5/1947 s John Hare Bonner & Henrietta. BS U of Tennessee 1976; MDiv VTS 1987. D 6/28/1987 P 5/1/1988 Bp William Evan Sanders. m 6/5/1971 Deborah Seward Bonner c 3. S Jas' Epis Ch Alexander City AL 2003-2006; R Chr Ch Epis So Pittsburg TN 1988-2003; D-In-Trng Ch Of The Ascen Knoxville TN 1987-1988. Mem Cranmer Cup And Porter Cup - Us Team Of 8 Epis Cler Ecusa ECUSA vs Engl Scotland Wales 2000. rector@holytrinityhertford.org

BONNER-STEWART, Ann Pinckney (EC) c/o St. Paul's Episcopal Church, 401 East Fourth Street, Greenville NC 27858 **Chapl S Mary's Chap Sch Raleigh NC 2009-; S Mary's Sch Raleigh NC 2009-** B Greenville SC 4/26/1979 d William Pinckney Bonner & Myra Huffstetter. ABS Duke 2001; MDiv Ya Berk 2006. D 6/3/2006 Bp M(arvil) Thomas Shaw III P 12/9/2006 Bp Clifton Daniel III. m 7/19/2003 Jeffrey Franklin Stewart c 1. Assoc R S Paul's Epis Ch Greenville NC 2006-2009. R. Lansing Hicks Prize Ya Berk 2006; Thos Philips Memi Reward Ya Berk 2006; Eleanor Lee McGee Prize Ya Berk 2004. abstewart@sms.edu

BONNEY, Isaac Kojo Nyame (Pa) 250 E Wynnewood Rd Apt E13, Wynnewood PA 19096 **The Afr Epis Ch Of S Thos Philadelphia PA 2005-** B Adjabeng Accra Ghana 4/18/1977 s Frank Bonney & Elizabeth. BA Wabash Coll 2000; MDiv Candler TS Emory U 2004. Trans from Church of the Province of West Africa 8/31/2006 as Priest Bp Charles Ellsworth Bennison Jr. m 10/31/2011 Doreen D Bonney. fr.ibonney@verizon.net

BONNINGTON, Robert Lester (NwT) 2820 Goddard Pl, Midland TX 79705 **S Ptr's Ch Kermit TX 1998-** B Brooklyn NY 8/26/1932 s Lester Bonnington & Ethel Lillian. PhD U of Iowa 1968; MDiv Epis TS of The SW 1982. D 6/6/1982 P 1/6/1983 Bp Sam Byron Hulsey. m 7/21/1972 H Joanne Bonnington. R S Paul's Epis Ch Sikeston MO 1992-1995; The Epis Ch Of S Mary The Vrgn Big Sprg TX 1982-1992. Auth, "Mod Bus: A Systems Approach". robonn@aol.com

BONNYMAN, Anne Berry (Mass) Trinity Church, 206 Clarendon Street, Boston MI 02116 **R Trin Ch In The City Of Boston Boston MA 2006-** B Knoxville TN 9/2/1949 d Gordon Bonnyman & Isabel. BA U of Tennessee 1971; MA Villanova U 1976; MDiv VTS 1982. D 6/30/1982 Bp William F Gates Jr P 5/12/1983 Bp William Evan Sanders. c 3. R Trin Par Wilmington DE 1995-2006; Int Ch Of The Ascen Knoxville TN 1994-1995; Ch Of The Gd Samar Knoxville TN 1988-1994; Vic S Eliz's Epis Ch Knoxville TN 1985-1988; Dio E Tennessee Knoxville TN 1985-1987; Asst Ch Of The Ascen Knoxville TN 1982-1984. abbonnyman@gmail.com

BONOAN, Raynald Sales (SwFla) 18612 Chemille Dr, Lutz FL 33558 **Ch Of The H Sprt Sfty Harbor FL 2001-** B Bacarra I Locos Norte PH 12/16/1954 s Emerson Acosta Bonoan & Alicia. AA Trin U of Asia, Phil. 1975; Bth S Andr's TS Ph 1979; MDiv S Andr's TS Ph 1989. Rec from Philippine Independent Church 6/13/1998 Bp John Bailey Lipscomb. m 3/31/1979 Unidad Reyes c 3. Dio SW Florida Sarasota FL 1999-2001; Cn S Andr's Epis Ch Tampa FL 1999-2001; Vic S Lk's Ch Land O Lakes FL 1998-1999; St Lukes Ch Ellenton FL 1998. Auth, "Gentle Yoke, Light Burden Pstr'S Corner," *The Laker*, 1994; Auth, "To Believe Is To Know Pstr'S Corner," *The Laker*, 1994. frbonoan@juno.com

BONSEY, Steven Charles (Mass) 138 Tremont St, Boston MA 02111 **Cn The Cathd Ch Of S Paul Boston MA 2005-** B Molokai HI 5/24/1956 s W(illiam) Edwin Bonsey & Kathryn. AB Harvard Coll 1978; MDiv Ya Berk 1984; STM Ya Berk 1987. D 12/7/1986 P 11/1/1987 Bp Christoph Keller Jr. m 8/28/1982 Elisabeth Wilson Keller c 4. Int Ch Of The Redeem Chestnut Hill MA 2003-2004; P-in-c Chr Ch Somerville MA 2000-2003; Chapl Epis Chapl At Tufts Medford MA 2000-2003; R The Par Of S Clem Honolulu HI 1995-2000; Int S Jas' Epis Ch Cambridge MA 1992-1993; Chapl Gr Epis Ch Medford MA 1991-1995; Assoc S Paul's Memi Charlottesville VA 1987-1990. ",A Reluctant Giver's Guide to the Pract of Stwdshp," Dio Massachusetts, 2006; "A Shy Person's Guide To The Pract Of Evang," Dio Massachusetts, 2004. ESMHE 1988-1996; Fllshp of S Jn 1998. sbonsey@diomass.org

BONSEY, W(illiam) Edwin (Haw) 401 SAnta Clara Av e Apt 309, Oakland CA 94610 B Greeley CO 5/26/1929 s William Edwin Bonsey & Hannah Elisabeth. BA Ob 1951; MDiv CDSP 1954. D 6/19/1954 Bp Henry H Shires P 12/17/1954 Bp Harry S Kennedy. m 6/17/1952 Kathryn Brownell c 4. Camp Mokule'Ia Waialua HI 1988-1992; R Ch Of The H Apos Hilo HI 1974-1988; R S Eliz's Ch Honolulu HI 1963-1974; Vic S Steph's Ch Wahiawa HI 1957-1963; Vic Gr Ch Hoolehua HI 1954-1957. ekbonsey@netscape.com

BONSTEEL, Susan (NY) 94 Clifton Ave, Kingston NY 12401 **Mid-Hudson D for Jail and Prison Mnstry S Jn's Epis Ch Kingston NY 2008-** B Staten Island NY 9/8/1948 d Joseph Martin Layh & Marilyn Rose. BS Keuka Coll 1970. D 5/16/1998 Bp Richard Frank Grein. m 7/25/1970 Roger Edward Bonsteel c 2. D S Paul's Ch Poughkeepsie NY 2007-2008; D The Epis Ch Of Chr The King Stone Ridge NY 2003-2007; D S Jn's Epis Ch Kingston NY 1998-2003. NAAD. bonsteel@aol.com

BONTING, Sjoerd L (Cal) Specreyse 12, Goor 7471 TH Netherlands B Amsterdam NL 10/6/1924 s Sjoerd Lieuwe Bonting & Johanna H. BS U of Amsterdam Amsterdam NL 1944; MS U of Amsterdam Amsterdam NL 1950; PhD U of Amsterdam Amsterdam NL 1952; Intermediate degree Univ. of London, GBIntermediate degree 1975. D 6/29/1963 P 2/14/1964 Bp William Foreman Creighton. m 2/27/1987 Erica Schotman c 3. S Mk's Epis Ch Palo Alto CA 1990-1993; S Thos Epis Ch Sunnyvale CA 1987-1989; Cur S Lk's Ch Trin Par Beth MD 1963-1965. "Creation and Double Chaos," Fortress Press, Minneapolis, 2005; "Chaos Theol, a revised creation Theol," Novalis, Ottawa, Can, 2002; "Tussen geloof en ongeloof," *Between Belief and Unbelief*, Meinema, Zoetermeer, NL, 2000; "Mens, chaos, verzoening," *Man, Chaos, Recon*, Kok, Kampen, NL, 1998; Auth, "Schepping en evolutie," *Creation & Evolution*, Kok, Kampen, NL, 1996. Comp OGS 1957; Soc of Ord Scientists 1987. Citation for Wk in Netherlands Archbp of Cbury 1985; Team

Achievement Awd, Spacelab-1 Mssn European Space Agcy 1984; Hon. Lic in Theol St. Mk's Inst of Theol, London 1975; Arthur S. Flemming Awd Jun. Chamber of Comm., Washington DC 1964; First Prize, Enzymology of Leukocytes Karger Fndt, Basel, Switzerland 1964; Fight for Sight Citation, 2 Nat. Coun to Combat Blindness 1962; Fight for Sight Citation, 1 Nat. Coun to Combat Blindness 1961. s.l.bonting@wxs.nl

BONWITT, Martha (WA) 14303 Old Marlboro Pike, Upper Marlboro MD 20772 **R Trin Ch Upper Marlboro MD 2000-** B Kearny NJ 12/16/1950 d George King Torrance & Elinore Mulford. BA Montclair St U 1991; MDiv UTS 1996. D 6/1/1996 Bp John Shelby Spong P 12/7/1996 Bp Jack Marston McKelvey. m 3/17/1996 William Bonwitt c 1. P-in-c S Andr's So Fallsburg Woodbourne NY 1997-2000; P-in-c S Jas Ch Callicoon NY 1997-2000; Gr Ch Nutley NJ 1997. Interfaith Outreach Untd 1997-2000. marthajes@verizon.net

BOODT, Mary Ione (Ind) 100 Oakview Dr, Mooresville IN 46158 B Kokomo IN 12/9/1938 d Malcolm Keith Benham & Mary Elizabeth. BA Marian Coll 1971; MS Pur 1973; PhD Indiana U 1979; MA SWTS 1992; Cert SWTS 1993. D 6/24/1993 P 2/26/1994 Bp Edward Witker Jones. Vic S Mary's Epis Ch Martinsville IN 1997-2003; Int S Jn's Epis Ch Crawfordsville IN 1995-1997; S Mk's Ch Plainfield IN 1995; Assoc R S Mk's Ch Plainfield IN 1994-1995; Pstr Asst S Lk's Ch Evanston IL 1993-1994. OHC. ioneboodt@sbcglobal.net

BOOHER, David Lewis (SVa) 724 West H St., Elizabethton TN 37643 B Wheeling WV 1/27/1946 s Samuel Wilson Booher & Helen. BA U of Mississippi 1969; MDiv STUSo 1975. D 5/28/1975 P 5/4/1976 Bp Duncan Montgomery Gray Jr. m 12/21/1968 Leslie Williams c 3. Int S Mary's Epis Ch Middlesboro KY 2008-2009; R Emm Ch Halifax VA 2000-2007; R S Jn's Epis Ch Halifax VA 2000-2007; S Steph's Epis Ch New Harmony IN 1990-2000; R S Alb's Epis Ch Vicksburg MS 1983-1990; Vic All SS Ch Inverness MS 1978-1983; Vic S Thos Ch Belzoni MS 1978-1983; S Paul's Ch Columbus MS 1975-1978. Assoc, Cmnty of S Mary 1994; Oblate, OSB, Archabbey of St. Meinrad 1997. branselm@gmail.com

BOOK, Robert TM (At) 170 Trinity Ave SW, Atlanta GA 30303 B Detroit MI 9/26/1949 s Robert V Book & Mina Rose. BA Hillsdale Coll 1972; BEd Dalhousie U 1977; MDiv Waterloo Luth Sem 1989. D 3/28/2008 Bp J(ohn) Neil Alexander P 10/15/2008 Bp Keith Bernard Whitmore. m 7/28/1973 Holly M Book c 3. The Ch of the Common Ground Atlanta GA 2009-2011. beavcanuck@gmail.com

BOOKER JR, James Howard (Az) 700 E Georgia Ave, Deland FL 32724 **Non-par Dio Cntrl Florida Orlando FL 2011-** B Beaumont TX 12/9/1957 s James Howard Booker & Eleanor Nance. PhD (cand) U Of Exeter Exeter Engl; Cert in Comercial Diving Ocean Corp 1983; GME (MDiv eqv) Edinburgh Theol Coll Edinburgh Scotland 1989; MMinTheol (DMin eqv) Sheffield U Sheffield Engl 2002; BTh (2nd Class hon) Aberdeen U Aberdeen Scotland 2003. Trans from Scottish Episcopal Church 2/14/2006 Bp Kirk Stevan Smith. m 5/29/2003 Chrissie Herbert c 2. Vic S Thos Of The Vlly Epis Clarkdale AZ 2005-2010; Supply S Thos Of The Vlly Epis Clarkdale AZ 2004; Dio Truro, Cornwall Ch Of Engl London 2000-2003; Peterhead Scottish Epis Ch Edinburgh 1992-2000; Peterhead Scottish Epis Ch Edinburgh 1990-1992; Longside, Old Deer & Strichen (w Peterhead) Scottish Epis Ch Edinburgh 1989-1990. Thesis, "Escape to Zoar," *2002*, Sheffield U Press, 2002. Profsnl Assn of Dive Instructors 2002. 2nd Class hon U of Aberdeen, Scotland 2003. jimbooker@cfl.rr.com

BOOKER, Vaughan P L (WA) 5537 Holmes Run Pkwy, Alexandria VA 22304 B Philadelphia PA 9/17/1942 s Lorenzo S Booker & Mary E. Age Northampton Cnty Cmnty Coll 1975; BA Villanova U 1978; MDiv VTS 1992. D 3/1/1975 Bp Lyman Cunningham Ogilby P 6/1/1992 Bp George Phelps Mellick Belshaw. m 6/30/1979 Portia McClellan c 2. Dio Washington Washington DC 2006-2007; Calv Ch Washington DC 2003-2006; Dio Sthrn Ohio Cincinnati OH 1998-2000; R Meade Memi Epis Ch Alexandria VA 1993-1998; D S Alb's Epis Ch New Brunswick NJ 1984-1989; Epis Cmnty Serv Philadelphia PA 1975-1979. Alpha Sigma Lambda 1977; Natl Hon Soc.

BOOMGAARD, Michelle C (SO) 1734 Mountain View Dr., Monroeville PA 15146 **D S Ptr's Epis Ch Brentwood Pittsburgh PA 2011-** B Wilkinsburg PA 6/4/1971 d Dirk J Boomgaard & Catharine. BA Brandeis U 1992; PhD Cath U 2002; MDiv Berk 2011. D 6/29/2011 Bp Thomas Edward Breidenthal. m.boomgaard@att.net

BOONE, Arthur Robinson (Vt) 1616 Harmon St, Berkeley CA 94703 B Yonkers NY 3/17/1938 s Frank Fall Boone & Gladys. BA Pr 1960; MA Br 1962; BD UTS 1965. D 6/12/1965 P 12/21/1965 Bp Horace W B Donegan. c 4. Int S Aug's Ch Oakland CA 2005-2006; Int S Aug's Ch Oakland CA 1995-1996; Int S Aug's Ch Oakland CA 1982-1983; Serv Dio Vermont Burlington VT 1971-1972; Asst Trin Ch Rutland VT 1968-1971; Cur Ch Of The Trsfg Cranston RI 1967-1968; Asst Ch Of The Mssh Providence RI 1965-1967. "Intro to Recycling," *Total Recycling Assoc*, 2006; Auth, "Eeo Trng Resources," 1982; Auth, "Investigating Charges Of Employment Discrimination," 1980. Hitchcock Prize In Ch Hist UTS New York NY 1965. arboone3@yahoo.com

BOONE, Connie Louise (EO) 42893 Pocahontas Rd, Baker City OR 97814 **D S Steph's Baker City OR 2002-** B Hardin MT 1/5/1945 d Hugh Franklin Hamilton & Lena Mae. D 1/6/2002 Bp William O Gregg. m 5/7/1966 Douglas Roy Boone c 2. Cert Alco and Drug Counslr ACCBO 1996. cboone@q.com

BOONE JR, Robert Augustus (WNC) 900b Centre Park Dr, Asheville NC 28805 B Birmingham AL 2/8/1946 s Robert Augustus Boone & Rosemond. BS U of Mobile 1968; MA U of So Alabama 1972; MDiv STUSo 1980. D 6/14/1980 Bp George Mosley Murray P 5/1/1981 Bp Charles Farmer Duvall. m 10/29/2006 Sharon Carleton Boone c 2. Cn Dio Wstrn No Carolina Asheville NC 2005-2009; R Ch Of The Ascen Hickory NC 1999-2005; R S Jas Epis Ch Greenville SC 1988-1999; S Chris's Ch Pensacola FL 1980-1988. Auth, "Receiving Chld Into the Cong," *The Rel Educ of Preschool*, Sheed and Ward, 1989. swannaboone@charter.net

BOOTH, Errol Kent (WA) 2811 Deep Landing Rd, Huntingtown MD 20639 B JM 5/14/1945 s Azariah Constantine Booth & Viola J. MDiv VTS 1984. D 6/9/1984 P 1/5/1985 Bp John Thomas Walker. m 1/3/1970 Olga Haynes c 3. Chr Epis Ch Clinton MD 2001-2009; Ch Of Our Sav Washington DC 1999-2001; P-in-c S Phil's Chap Baden Brandywine MD 1990-1999; R S Agnes And S Paul's Ch E Orange NJ 1986-1989; Int S Phil The Evang Washington DC 1985-1986; Cur S Geo's Ch Washington DC 1984-1985. kobooth@gmail.com

BOOTH, F(rancisca) Cora (Roch) 130 Durland Ave, Watkins Glen NY 14891 B New York NY 4/17/1950 d Alfred Morris Ehrenclou & Francisca. BA Bos 1972; Cert Dominican Coll 1973; Bex 1996. D 5/27/1989 Bp David Standish Ball P 6/11/1996 Bp Mary Adelia Rosamond McLeod. m 8/20/1988 Mark Booth c 1. S Jn's Epis Ch Watkins Glen NY 1997-2008; S Paul's Ch Montour Falls NY 1997-2008; S Jas' Epis Ch Watkins Glen NY 1996-2005; D Dio Vermont Burlington VT 1992-1996; D S Jn's Ch Essex NY 1989-1992. anniesmith7@yahoo.com

BOOTH, James Alexander (ECR) 48 Miramoute Rd., Carmel Valley CA 93924 **Archd All SS Ch Carmel CA 2007-; Dio El Camino Real Monterey CA 1993-** B Fort Smith AK 10/6/1950 s Kenneth Loring Booth & Miriam. BS U of So Carolina 1972; BA Sch for Deacons 1992. D 6/6/1992 Bp Richard Lester Shimpfky. m 12/16/2000 Bridget Booth c 2. Archd Ch of S Mary's by the Sea Pacific Grove CA 1995-2000. NAAD. james@montereyins.com

BOOTH, James Thomas (EpisSanJ) 313 Marc Avenue, Stockton CA 95207 **Asst S Mk's Epis Ch French Camp CA 1995-** B Needles CA 9/24/1921 s James Thomas Booth & Henrietta Ernestine. BA S Jn's TS Camarillo CA 1942; S Jn's TS Camarillo CA 1946; JCD The Ponitifical Lateran U 1952; LLD U of San Diego 1966. Rec from Roman Catholic 4/1/1973 Bp Victor Manuel Rivera. m 4/2/1989 Stephanie Titus c 2. R S Jn's Epis Ch Stockton CA 1974-1988; Cn Pstr S Jas Epis Cathd Fresno CA 1971-1974. Auth, "Fr Luis Jayme," *California's 1st Mtyr*; Auth, *CE Problems in the St of California*; Auth, *Mssn San de Alcala*.

BOOTH, Stephen P (WMass) Rr#1 45 Nauss Dr, Chester NS B0J1J0 Canada **Epis Ch Of The Epiph Ventnor City NJ 2003-; R Trin Par Lenox MA 2003-** B 9/22/1943 Trans from Anglican Church of Canada 12/14/2004 Bp Gordon Paul Scruton. m 10/5/1984 Gillian Booth. canon_stephen_paul_booth@hotmail.com

BOOTY, John Everitt (NH) 612 Mt Israel Rd, Center Sandwich NH 03227 B Detroit MI 5/2/1925 s George Thomas Booty & Caroline Alma. DD STUSo; DD VTS; BA Wayne 1952; BD VTS 1953; MA Pr 1957; PhD Pr 1960; Fllshp Folger Shakespeare Libr Washington DC 1964; Fllshp Natl Endwmt for the Hmnts 1979; Fllshp Natl Endwmt for the Hmnts 1982. D 7/5/1953 Bp Richard S M Emrich P 1/30/1954 Bp Russell S Hubbard. m 6/10/1950 Catherine Louise Smith c 4. The TS at The U So Sewanee TN 1982-1990; Prof EDS Cambridge MA 1967-1982; Asst VTS Alexandria VA 1958-1967; Cur Chr Ch Dearborn MI 1953-1955. "Reflections On The Theol of Richard Hooker," The U So Press, 1998; "The Chr We Know," Cowley Pub, 1987; "Meditating on Four Quartets," Cowley Pub, 1983; "Jn Jewel As Apologist of the Ch of Engl," S.P.C.K., 1963. HSEC 1958. DD Hon U So Sewanee TN 1996; DD Hon VTS Alexandria VA 1991.

BOOZER, Alcena Elaine (Ore) 5256 NE 48th Ave, Portland OR 97218 B Portland OR 3/19/1938 d Lawrence Edward Caldwell & Marcelene. BS OR SU 1970; MS Portland St U 1974; Cert CDSP 1984. D 8/24/1979 Bp Matthew Paul Bigliardi P 6/29/1984 Bp David Rea Cochran. c 2. Dio Oregon Portland OR 2000-2010; R S Phil The D Epis Ch Portland OR 2000-2010; P-in-c S Phil The D Epis Ch Portland OR 1998-2000; Par Asst S Phil The D Epis Ch Portland OR 1979-1984. alcena1@comcast.net

BORAH, Timothy Glenn (SO) 65 E Hollister St, Cincinnati OH 45219 B Fairfield IL 2/7/1963 s Ivan Borah & Linda. BA Estrn Illinois U 1990; BS Sthrn Illinois U 1995; Angl Acad 2007. D 6/23/2007 Bp Kenneth Lester Price. m 9/2/1995 Rebecca S Sutherland c 2. GAS 2009. borahtg@yahoo.com

BORDADOR, Noel Estrella (NY) 512 E 12th St Apt 11, New York NY 10009 B 9/3/1964 D 3/10/2001 Bp Richard Frank Grein P 9/16/2001 Bp Mark Sean Sisk. St. Mary's Cntr Inc. New York NY 2002.

BORDELON, Joseph Ardell (WLa) 5704 Monroe Hwy, Ball LA 71405 **Vic H Comf Ch Ball LA 1992-; Vic Trin Epis Ch Ball LA 1992-** B Pineville LA 6/23/1933 s Pierre Morris Bordelon & Mary. D 9/16/1989 Bp Willis Ryan Henton P 9/11/1993 Bp Robert Jefferson Hargrove Jr. m 3/8/1954 Grace Leona Johnson c 5. Int S Tim's Ch Alexandria LA 1997-1998; P-in-c Chap of the H Fam Pollock LA 1993-1996; Hardtner C&C Pollock LA 1992-1997. No Amer Assn Of Diac 1989-1993; Rfw 1980. jaborde@bellsouth.net

BORDEN, Robert Bruce (Vt) Po Box 425, Rochester VT 05767 B Boston MA 4/19/1933 s Milton L Borden & Elizabeth. BA Ya 1954; MA Bos 1974. D 10/22/2000 Bp Mary Adelia Rosamond McLeod P 7/14/2001 Bp Thomas C Ely. m 7/21/1967 Florine S Batte. D Chr Ch Bethel VT 2000-2001.

BORDERS, Calvin Leroy (Oly) 602 24th Ave, Longview WA 98632 B Rushville NE 11/7/1931 BA Nebraska Wesl 1954; LLB U of Washington 1959. D 2/28/2004 Bp Sanford Zangwill Kaye Hampton P 11/13/2004 Bp Vincent Waydell Warner. m Donna Carter. ledonna-kelso@prodigy.net

BORDERS, John Ollie (Lex) Church of the Ascension, 311 Washington St, Frankfort KY 40601 **D Ch Of The Ascen Frankfort KY 2006-** B Lebanon KY 8/11/1932 s Cleaver William Borders & Mary Agnes. Rec from Roman Catholic 7/16/2006 Bp Stacy F Sauls. m 11/24/2000 Roberta Borders c 4. jbord@aldephia.net

BORDIN, Richard F (CFla) 832 Summeroaks Rd, Winter Garden FL 34787 **H Cross Ch Winter Haven FL 2008-** B Reno NV 2/10/1947 s Willard H Bordin & Rosaline. BA U of No Florida 1975; DMin Drew U 1990; Angl Stds Sewanee 2006. D 5/27/2006 P 12/23/2006 Bp John Wadsworth Howe. m 12/31/1999 Shannon M Hungate c 2. Ch Of The Mssh Winter Garden FL 2006-2008. preachit@aol.com

BORDNER, Kenneth Edward (Roch) 410 Wellington Ave., Rochester NY 14619 B Canton OH 5/2/1941 s Edward Robert Bordner & Evelyn Lemoine. BA Pr 1963; MA U of Massachusetts 1965; MFA U of Massachusetts 1966; MDiv VTS 1996. D 6/8/1996 Bp William Jerry Winterrowd P 1/1/1997 Bp Peter James Lee. m 7/13/1963 Elizabeth Bruce Bordner c 3. R S Steph's Ch Rochester NY 1999-2007; S Anne's Epis Ch Reston VA 1996-1999. kbordner@rochester.rr.com

BORG, Manuel (Chi) 1072 Ridge Ave, Elk Grove Village IL 60007 **P-in-c S Nich w the H Innoc Ch Elk Grove Vill IL 2011-** B Detroit MI 9/15/1958 s Charles Borg & Martha. Rec from Roman Catholic 7/29/2009 as Priest Bp Jeffrey Dean Lee. vanborg@sbcglobal.net

BORG, Marianne (Ore) 1133 Nw 11th Ave Apt 403, Portland OR 97209 **Trin Epis Cathd Portland OR 1993-** B Dhahran SA 1/8/1951 d Ralph Wells & Margaret. U of Oregon; BA OR SU 1986; MDiv CDSP 1991. D 6/11/1991 P 12/11/1991 Bp Robert Louis Ladehoff. m 8/24/1985 Marcus J Borg c 2. Asst S Barth's Ch Beaverton OR 1991-1993. MARIANNEWBORG@COMCAST.NET

BORGESON, Josephine (NCal) 458 Occidental Cir, Santa Rosa CA 95401 **D Trin Ch Sonoma CA 2011-** B Duxbury MA 8/15/1946 d John Alvin Borgeson & Harriet. BA Rad 1968; MDiv CDSP 1974. D 6/22/1974 Bp Wesley Frensdorff. Mnstry Dvlp Dio Nthrn California Sacramento CA 2007-2010; D S Barn' Epis Ch Los Angeles CA 1991-2000; CE Mssnr Dio Los Angeles Los Angeles CA 1990-1995; Mnstry Dvlpmt Dio Nevada Las Vegas NV 1975-1989. Auth, "Reshaping Mnstry," *Reshaping Mnstry*, Jethro Pub, 1990. DD CDSP 2008; MDiv w hon CDSP Berkeley CA 1974; AB cl Rad Cambridge MA 1968. phinaborgeson@gmail.com

BORGMAN, Dean Wylie (Mass) 5 Heritage Dr, Rockport MA 01966 **Asstg Chr Ch So Hamilton MA 1997-** B Bridgeport CT 10/28/1928 s Arnold Christian Borgman & Winifred. BA Wheaton Coll 1950; MA Fairfield U 1954; CAGS NEU 1975. D 6/7/1980 Bp Morris Fairchild Arnold P 6/1/1981 Bp John Bowen Coburn. m 12/28/1973 Gail Renee Powers. Assoc Chr Ch So Hamilton MA 1982-1992. Auth, "Hear My Story: Understanding the Cries of Troubled Yth," Hendrickson Pub, 2003; Auth, "When Kumbaya Is Not Enough: a Practical Theol for Yth Mnstry," Hendrickson Pub. Assn of Yth Ministy Educators 1998; Intl Assn for the Study of Yth Mnstry 1995. Distinguished Serv & Achievement Assn of Yth Mnstry Educators 2006. dborgman@gcts.edu

BORMES, Richard Joseph (Minn) 4350 Brookside Ct Apt 117, Edina MN 55436 **P H Trin Epis Ch Elk River MN 2006-** B Saint Paul MN 7/31/1937 s Louis Anton Bormes & Ruth Katherine. S Thos Coll St Paul MN 1957; AMS U MN 1959; MDiv SWTS 1989. D 6/22/1989 Bp Robert Marshall Anderson P 12/16/1989 Bp Frank Tracy Griswold III. c 3. S Jn's Ch S Cloud MN 2004-2006; Dio Minnesota Minneapolis MN 1999-2003; Cn to the Ordnry Dio Missouri S Louis MO 1993-1999; Vic S Matt's Epis Ch Mex MO 1990-1993; Assoc S Chas Ch S Chas IL 1989-1990. Bd, S Andr Fndt; Cathd Mssn Soc; Epis Cmnty Serv.

BOROM, James Robinson (HB) Po Box 26, Eutawville SC 29048 B Atlanta GA 4/30/1938 s James Hill Borom & Margery. Oglethorpe U 1962; LTh STUSo 1965. D 6/26/1965 P 3/1/1966 Bp Randolph R Claiborne. m 1/26/1980 Harriet E Borom. S Mary's Epis Ch High Point NC 1974-1976; Asst to R Chr Ch Greenville SC 1972-1974; R Ch Of The Gd Shpd Greer SC 1970-1972; Assoc R Ch Of Our Sav Rock Hill SC 1967-1970; Vic S Chris's At-The-Crossroads Epis Perry GA 1965-1967; Vic S Mary's Epis Ch Montezuma GA 1965-1967.

BORREGO, John Edward (Okla) 422 E Noble Ave, Guthrie OK 73044 **R Trin Ch Guthrie OK 2007-** B Bogota CO 12/20/1951 s Edward Candelario Borrego & Mary Annette. BA Ya 1973; MDiv VTS 1978; U of Oklahoma 1994. D 6/17/1978 Bp Gerald Nicholas McAllister P 6/1/1979 Bp Thomas Augustus Fraser Jr. m 6/17/1977 L(aurel) Lynn Griffith c 1. Epis Ch Of The Resurr Oklahoma City OK 1997-1999; S Andr's Epis Ch Lawton OK 1987-1993; S Andr's Epis Ch Charlotte NC 1980-1987; S Fran Ch Greensboro NC 1978-1980. Auth, "Angl & Epis Hist". johnborrego@gmail.com

BORREGO, L(aurel) Lynn (Okla) 422 E Noble Ave, Guthrie OK 73044 **Vic S Mk's Ch Seminole OK 2002-; Vic S Paul's Epis Ch Holdenville OK 1999-; P-in-c S Paul's Ch Clinton OK 1997-** B San Francisco CA 4/3/1951 d Reese Philip Griffith & Rosalind Linnea. AA W Vlly Cmnty Coll 1972; BA San Jose St U 1974; MDiv VTS 1978. D 6/13/1992 P 12/12/1992 Bp Robert Manning Moody. m 6/17/1977 John Edward Borrego c 2. Part Time/ Int Vic S Aug Of Cbury Oklahoma City OK 2008-2010; S Mk's Ch Seminole OK 1999; Dio Oklahoma Oklahoma City OK 1997-2007; Cur S Mary's Ch Edmond OK 1993-1995. lynnborrego@gmail.com

BORRETT, Craige Norton (SC) 5005 Chapel Rd, Yonges Island SC 29449 **R Chr/St Paul's Epis Par Yonges Island SC 1992-** B El Paso TX 10/2/1954 s George Ross O Borrett & Jacqueline. BBA U of Texas 1977; MDiv VTS 1990. D 6/30/1990 Bp Terence Kelshaw P 8/6/1991 Bp Edward Lloyd Salmon Jr. m 11/6/1982 Nancy Borrett. Asst Ch Of The H Comm Charleston SC 1990-1992. CNBORRETT@EARTHLINK.NET

✠ BORSCH, Rt Rev Frederick Houk (Los) 2930 Corda Ln, Los Angeles CA 90049 **Ret Bp Of Los Angeles Dio Los Angeles Los Angeles CA 2002-** B Chicago IL 9/13/1935 s Reuben August Borsch & Pearl Irene. BA Pr 1957; BA Oxf 1959; STB GTS 1960; PhD U of Birmingham 1966; DD SWTS 1978; STD CDSP 1981; STD Ya Berk 1985; DD GTS 1988. D 6/18/1960 Bp Gerald Francis Burrill P 12/17/1960 Bp Charles L Street Con 6/18/1988 for Los. m 6/25/1960 Barbara Edgeley Sampson. Int CDSP Berkeley CA 2001-2003; Bp Of Los Angeles Dio Los Angeles Los Angeles CA 1988-2002; Pr Princeton NJ 1981-1988; Pres CDSP Berkeley CA 1972-1980; Prof The GTS New York NY 1971-1972; Asst Prof Of NT SWTS Evanston IL 1966-1969; Cur Gr Ch Oak Pk IL 1960-1963. Auth, "The Lessons Of The Ch Year: A Guide For Lay Readers And Congregations," Seabury Press/Trin Int'L, 2009; Auth, "Day by Day," *Loving the Lord More Dearly*, Morehouse/Ch Pub, 2009; Auth, "The Sprt Searches Everything," *Keeping Life's Questions*, Cowley, 2005; Auth, "The Magic Word," *Stirrings and Stories of Faith and Mnstry*, Cathd Cntr Press, 2001; Auth, "Outrage And Hope: A Bp'S Reflections In Times Of Change And Challenge," Trin Press Intl , 1996; Auth, "Chr Discipleship And Sxlty," Forw Mvmt Press, 1993; Auth, "The Bible'S Authority In Today'S Ch," Trin Press Intl , 1993; Auth, "Many Things In Parables: Extravagant Stories Of New Cmnty," Fortress Press, 1988; Auth, "Jesus: The Human Life Of God," Forw Mvmt Press, 1987; Auth, "Anglicanism And The Bible," Morehouse-Barlow, 1984; Auth, "Power In Weakness: New Hearing For Gospel Stories Of Healing And Discipleship," Fortress Press, 1983; Auth, "Coming Together In The Sprt," Forw Mvmt Press, 1980; Auth, "God'S Parable," Scm/Westminster, 1976; Auth, "Introducing The Lessons Of The Ch Year: A Guide For Lay Readers And Congregations," Seabury Press/Trin Int'L, 1976; Auth, "The Chr And Gnostic s Man," Scm Press, 1970; Auth, "The s Man In Myth And Hist," Scm/Westminster, 1967. AAR 1966; Soc Of Arts, Rel And Contemporary Culture 1986; SBL 1966; Studiorum Novi Testamenti Societas 1964. Humanitarian Awd Natl Conf For Cmnty And Justice 2000; Stb cl GTS New York NY 1960; Ab w First Class Honours Oxf Oxford UK 1959; Phi Beta Kappa Pr Princeton NJ 1957; Ab scl Pr Princeton NJ 1957; Keasby Schlr The Keasby Fndt 1957. fuborsch@earthlink.net

BORSCH, Kathleen Ann (NwT) 1718 43rd St, Lubbock TX 79412 B 8/2/1955 d Harry McGuire & Barbara. D Formation Prog Dio NW Texas; California St U 1974; Lvn Certification So Plains Coll 1986. D 10/29/2006 Bp C(harles) Wallis Ohl. c 3. kathleen.borsch@ttuhsc.edu

BORZUMATO, Judith Alice (NY) 500 State Rte 299 Apt 24C, Highland NY 12528 **D The Epis Ch Of Chr The King Stone Ridge NY 1992-** B Woonsocket RI 3/1/1936 d Frederic Patrick Dowling & Sibyl. Emerson Coll 1955; AAS Ulster Cnty Cmnty Coll 1980. D 5/30/1992 Bp Richard Frank Grein. m 6/15/1957 Lawrence Paul Borzumato c 1. OHC 1978. lborz@aol.com

BOSBYSHELL, William Allen (SwFla) 106 21st Ave Ne, Saint Petersburg FL 33704 B Philadelphia PA 10/15/1933 s John Herman Bosbyshell & Lilla G. BA Swarthmore Coll 1955; STB GTS 1958; Med U of Florida 1967; PhD U of Florida 1970. D 5/11/1958 Bp William P Roberts P 11/29/1958 Bp Oliver J Hart. m 5/31/1958 Caroline Thomas c 3. Cn Cathd Ch Of S Ptr St Petersburg FL 1990-1998; Asst S Jn's Epis Ch Clearwater FL 1977-1990; Dir of Samar Cntr Dio SW Florida Sarasota FL 1976-1990; Asst Ch Of The Ascen Clearwater FL 1972-1976; The Samar Cntr Clearwater FL 1970-1990; LocTen S Barth's Ch High Sprg FL 1967-1969; R S Jn's Ch Melbourne FL 1962-1966; Cathd Ch Of S Lk Orlando FL 1959-1962; Cur Gr Epiph Ch Philadelphia PA

1958-1959. AAPC, Fell 1972; Mem, APA 1972; Mem, Assn for Psychol Type 1972-1999. wbosbyshell@tampabay.rr.com

BOSLER, Sarah Mather (Be) 1188 Ben Franklin Hwy E, Douglassville PA 19518 B Baltimore MD 5/30/1948 d Frank Watkins Mather & Caroline Thornbury. BA Buc 1970. D 9/29/2007 Bp Paul Victor Marshall. m 7/19/1969 Thomas Bosler c 3. smbosler@dejazzd.com

BOSLEY, Dennis Vaughn (NwT) 502 Locust St., Sweetwater TX 79556 **Vic All SS Ch Colorado City TX 1999-; Vic S Steph's Ch Sweetwater TX 1999-** B Seattle WA 6/24/1949 s George Vaughn Bosley & Mary Louise. BA Willamette U 1971; MDiv CDSP 1985. D 6/22/1985 P 12/21/1985 Bp Charles Brinkley Morton. m 8/17/1968 Jacqueline Bosley c 3. R S Mart's Ch Moses Lake WA 1994-1999; Vic S Paul's Ch Cheney WA 1986-1994; S Tim Med Lake WA 1986-1994; Asst/Chapl All SS Ch San Diego CA 1985-1986. GAS 2002. episcopalchurch@sbcglobal.net

BOSMAN, John Adrian (Tex) 1126 Thornton Rd, Houston TX 77018 **R Emer Hope Epis Ch Houston TX 1990-** B Maplewood NJ 10/3/1920 s William Marinus Bosman & Johanna Elizabeth. BS U of Pennsylvania 1942; MDiv UTS 1949; VTS 1950. D 6/4/1950 Bp Charles K Gilbert P 12/1/1950 Bp Austin Pardue. m 6/10/1950 Elsie Sebastian. Vic Ch Of The Incarn Houston TX 1961-1985; R Hope Epis Ch Houston TX 1956-1985. lisa.bosman@sbcglobal.net

BOSS, Bruce William (Ind) 7300 Lantern Rd, Indianapolis IN 46256 **Dep to GC Dio Indianapolis Indianapolis IN 2009-; Stndg Com Dio Indianapolis Indianapolis IN 2009-; R Ch Of The Nativ Indianapolis IN 2002-** B Louisville KY 4/19/1949 s Edward Ferdinand Boss & Mary Ann. BA U Of Kentucky 1971; MDiv VTS 1974; DMin SWTS 2003. D 6/1/1974 P 12/6/1974 Bp Addison Hosea. m 5/24/1970 Virginia Sue Cooper. Dep to GC Dio Indianapolis Indianapolis IN 2007-2010; Dn, No Cntrl Dnry Dio Indianapolis Indianapolis IN 2005-2009; Dep to GC Dio Indianapolis Indianapolis IN 2004-2007; COM Dio Indianapolis Indianapolis IN 2003-2009; COM Dio Kentucky Louisville KY 1995-2001; Exam Chapl Dio Kentucky Louisville KY 1995-2001; Trst & Coun Dio Kentucky Louisville KY 1994-1997; R Ch Of The Adv Louisville KY 1993-2002; Dep to GC Dio Lexington Lexington KY 1989-1992; Vic Ch Of The Resurr Jessamine City Nicholasville KY 1986-1992; Dep to GC Dio Lexington Lexington KY 1986-1989; Exec Coun Dio Lexington Lexington KY 1986-1989; Eccl Crt Dio Lexington Lexington KY 1985-1986; Dep to GC Dio Lexington Lexington KY 1983-1986; Stndg Com Dio Lexington Lexington KY 1982-1985; Exec Coun Dio Lexington Lexington KY 1979-1981; Compaion Relatns Cmsn Dio Lexington Lexington KY 1978-1991; Vic St Gabriels Ch Lexington KY 1977-1985; Vic S Jas Epis Ch Prestonsburg KY 1974-1977. Phi Beta Kappa U Of Kentucky Lexington KY 1971; Phi Beta Kappa. bwmboss@sbcglobal.net

BOSS, Michael Cleare (Fla) 3727 Tully Ct, Jacksonville FL 32207 B Jacksonville FL 10/13/1938 s Aldrich Whitfield Boss & Louise. BA U So 1960; MDiv STUSo 1966. D 6/21/1966 P 3/31/1967 Bp Edward Hamilton West. m 12/20/1960 Nancy Laurie Davis. R S Paul's Epis Ch Jacksonville FL 1987-1991; R Epis Ch of the Gd Shpd Charleston SC 1975-1987; R Trin Epis Ch St Aug FL 1971-1975; Asst S Chris's Ch Pensacola FL 1966-1971. bossmc@comcast.com

BOSSART, Lee Mark (Nev) 4201 W Washington Ave, Las Vegas NV 89107 **Died 9/28/2009** B Batavia NY 9/6/1930 s Mark L Bossart & Helen L. SUNY 1950; BS RPI 1958; MS U of New Mex 1968; MDiv SWTS 1975. D 8/6/1975 P 3/26/1976 Bp Richard Mitchell Trelease Jr.

BOSSIERE, Jacques Paul (NY) 1 Garrett Pl Apt 6b, Bronxville NY 10708 **Chr Ch Bronxville NY 1996-** B 5/29/1919 s Paul Ferdinand Bossiere & Claire Jeanne. LPH/LTH CUA 1945; Dl Ya 1966. Rec from Roman Catholic 5/1/1959 Bp Horace W B Donegan. m 7/20/1974 Carrie Lee Martin. French Ch Of S Esprit New York NY 1988-1991; Cn Theol The Amer Cathd of the H Trin Paris 75008 FR 1985-1988; S Mk's Ch Fincastle VA 1980-1985; S Lk's Ch Hot Sprg VA 1978-1979. Auth, "The Experience Of Pryr," Schott, 1999; Auth, "Mort Et Liberte Critique Et Creation," *Morals & Meditation*, 1970; Auth, "Recent Problems In Dioc Cler," 1948. Chairman Wrrr 2000; Pres, French War Veterans For The St Of New York 1988. Dl mcl Ya New Haven CT 1966. drbossiere@gmail.com

BOSS WOLLNER, Ernesto (Colom) Cra 86 # 46-38 Apto 202, Medellin ANTIOQUIA Colombia B Bogota Colombia 6/11/1951 s Arno Joaquin Boss & Eva. Centro De Estudios Teologicas. D 10/14/2006 Bp Francisco Jose Duque-Gomez. m 6/16/1976 Luz Elena Agudelo Hoxos c 2. eboxx616@yahoo.com

BOST, Emily Catherine (Ark) 532 E Spring St, Fayetteville AR 72701 B 4/18/1942 d Rockie Angelo Paladino & Marise. RN St Vinc Sch Of Nrsng 1969. D 12/16/2006 Bp Larry Earl Maze. m 7/2/1976 James Bost c 3. emily@stpaulsfay.org

BOSTIAN, Nathan Louis (WTex) 20955 W Tejas Trl, San Antonio TX 78257 **Texas Mltry Inst San Antonio TX 2010-; Campus Mnstry Dio Dallas Dallas TX 2008-** B North Little Rock AR 1/14/1974 s Rondall Jay Bostian & Peggy Lynn. BA Texas A & M U 1996; MDiv SMU - Perkins TS 2008. D 12/13/2008 P 11/21/2009 Bp James Monte Stanton. m 1/9/1999 Kimberly Kristen Kimberly Lyle c 2. Dir of Coll & YA S Mich And All Ang Ch Dallas TX 2009-2010; Campus Mnstrs Dio Dallas Dallas TX 2000-2008. kimbostian@gmail.com

BOSTON, James Terrell (Ore) 518 NE Dean Dr, Grants Pass OR 97526 **P-in-c S Mths Epis Ch Cave Jct OR 2000-; Chair: Yth Ctte, Fin Dept, Bdgt Revs, Comp Dio Ctte Dio Oregon Portland OR 1980-** B Patuxent River MD 8/29/1947 s Leadore Glen Boston & Mary Jane. BA Amer U 1968; MDiv CDSP 1976; Cert Oxf 1977; Ldrshp Acad for New Directions 1986; DMin VTS 2002. D 11/30/1976 Bp The Bishop Of Oxford P 1/24/1978 Bp Matthew Paul Bigliardi. m 11/12/1995 Pamela Evans. Dioc Coun, Chair Mssn Ctte Dio Oregon Portland OR 2006-2009; Dioc Coun, Chair Agenda Ctte Dio Oregon Portland OR 1992-1995; Convoc Dn, Jubilee Off Dio Oregon Portland OR 1990-2001; R S Lk's Ch Grants Pass OR 1987-2009; Pres of Stndg Ctte Dio Oregon Portland OR 1987-1990; Gen Conv Dep (2) , 1st Alt (3), Alt (3) Dio Oregon Portland OR 1982-2011; Vic S Jas Ch Lincoln City OR 1980-1986; Vic Ch Of Chr The King On The Santiam Stayton OR 1978-1980; Trst Oregon Epis Sch Portland OR 1978-1980; Assoc S Paul's Epis Ch Salem OR 1978-1980. Ord of H Cross 1976. jtboston@cdsnet.net

BOSWELL JR, Frederick Philip (Colo) 9200 W 10th Ave, Lakewood CO 80215 B Saint Louis MO 10/17/1944 s Frederick Philip Boswell & Caroline. BA Laf 1967; BD VTS 1970. D 6/13/1970 Bp George Leslie Cadigan P 12/1/1970 Bp Christoph Keller Jr. m 6/14/1969 Barbara Carol Braund c 2. R S Paul's Epis Ch Lakewood CO 1997-2006; Int Chr Ch Cn City CO 1996-1997; Int Gd Shpd Epis Ch Centennial CO 1995-1996; S Jas Ch Upper Montclair NJ 1986-1993; R S Steph's Ch Fairview PA 1981-1986; Trin Ch Hannibal MO 1978-1981; River Parishes Reg Mnstry Hannibal MO 1974-1977; P-in-c Calv Epis Ch Osceola AR 1971-1974; P-in-c S Steph's Ch Blytheville AR 1971-1974; DCE Chr Epis Ch Little Rock AR 1970-1971. Bp'S Outstanding Serv Awd 1992. fpboswell@hughes.net

BOSWELL, Kathryn Mary (Alb) 21 Cherry St., Potsdam NY 13676 **R S Phil's Ch Norwood NY 2010-** B Springfield, MA 8/20/1956 d John O'Connor & Francine Marie. BA SUNY Potsdam 2006; MA Nash 2010. D 6/5/2010 Bp William Howard Love. m 6/2/1973 Carroll Boswell c 10. boswellandco@yahoo.com

BOTH, M Blair (EC) 305 S 5th Ave, Wilmington NC 28401 B Roanoke VA 12/17/1943 d Richard John Both & Blair. BA Sweet Briar Coll 1965; MDiv TESM 1987. D 7/22/1987 Bp Robert Whitridge Estill P 9/24/1988 Bp Frank Harris Vest Jr. Ch Of The Servnt Wilmington NC 2006-2008; Assoc Ch Of The H Comm Memphis TN 2003-2004; S Tim's Ch Wilson NC 2000-2002; R S Mart's Epis Ch Charlotte NC 1995-1998; Chair of Stwdshp Cmsn Dio No Carolina Raleigh NC 1991-1995; Asst S Mich's Ch Raleigh NC 1987-1995. bboth@ec.rr.com

BOTT, Harold Ray (At) 3750 Peachtree Rd NE Apt 905, Atlanta GA 30319 B Shreveport LA 8/25/1928 s Whewell Edward Bott & Clara L. BS Louisiana Polytechnic Inst 1950; STB Ya Berk 1954. D 6/2/1954 Bp Girault M Jones P 5/1/1955 Bp Iveson Batchelor Noland. c 2. R S Jn's Coll Pk GA 1965-1990; Vic S Mich And All Ang Lake Chas LA 1954-1958. hrbot@canterburycourt.org

BOUCHER, Edward Charles (RI) 341 Seaview Ave, Swansea MA 02777 B Central Falls RI 9/11/1945 s Reginald Henry Boucher & Pauline Marie. BA Providence Coll 1967; MA U of Virginia 1968; MDiv Ya Berk 1978. D 6/17/1978 P 12/20/1978 Bp Frederick Hesley Belden. m 6/2/1989 Janice Rainone c 3. P-in-c Ch Of The Gd Shpd Pawtucket RI 2004-2009; Int All SS Ch Whitman MA 2002-2003; R Chr Ch Swansea MA 1981-2003; Cur Ch Of The Trsfg Cranston RI 1978-1981.

BOUCHER, John Paul (SVa) 12020 Smoketree Dr, Richmond VA 23236 **R S Mths Epis Ch Midlothian VA 2000-** B Detroit MI 7/9/1948 s Joseph Louis Boucher & Zay. BA CUA 1970; MDiv Candler TS Emory U 1976; DMin STUSo 1988. D 6/12/1976 P 6/3/1977 Bp Bennett Jones Sims. m 6/6/1973 Laura Scott Sims c 2. Cn to the Ordnry Dio Easton Easton MD 1998-2000; R S Thos Epis Ch Columbus GA 1996-1997; Dio Michigan Detroit MI 1994-1995; Gr Epis Ch Port Huron MI 1988-1995; S Phil's Ch Nashville TN 1983-1988; Assoc Chr Ch Cathd Nashville TN 1981-1983; R S Marg's Ch Carrollton GA 1977-1981; Asst S Pat's Epis Ch Atlanta GA 1976-1977. Auth, "Stress on the Episcopate," *Living Ch*, 2000; Auth, "Does a Call End?," *Living Ch*, 1988; Auth, *Ret as a Rite of Passage*, 1988; Auth, "Re-ing Cler Need a Rite of Passage," *Episcopate*, 1985. HSEC 1993-1996. boucherls@aol.com

BOULTER, Matthew Rutherford (Tex) 118 S. Bois d'Arc, Tyler TX 77702 **Asst Chr Epis Ch Tyler TX 2010-** B Lubbock TX 9/19/1972 s Eldon Beau Boulter & Rosemary Rutherford. BBA/BA The U of Texas at Austin 1996; MDiv Westminster TS 2000; Dplma in Angl Stds Epis TS of the SW 2009. D 11/22/2009 Bp C(harles) Andrew Doyle P 5/25/2010 Bp Dena Arnall Harrison. m 8/30/1997 Bouquet Souksomboun c 2. Asst S Richard's Of Round Rock Round Rock TX 2009-2010. MATTBOULTER@GMAIL.COM

BOULTER, Richard Ottmuller (Mich) 11575 Belleville Rd, Belleville MI 48111 B Louisville Twp NY 8/27/1939 s Thomas William Boulter & Jennie

Ottmuller. Cert The Whitaker TS; BS Trenton St Tchr Coll 1969. D 6/13/2009 Bp Wendell Nathaniel Gibbs Jr. m 2/3/1962 Judith M Moore c 3. richard_boulter@comeast.net

BOULTER, Robert James (WA) St. Columba's Episcopal Church, 4201 Albemarle St NW, Washington DC 20016 **Assoc S Columba's Ch Washington DC 2008-** B Watertown NY 6/9/1963 s John Louis Boulter & Elizabeth Harnett. BM Ithaca Coll 1985; Angl Cert Ya Berk 2006; MDvi Yale DS 2006. D 6/10/2006 P 12/16/2006 Bp Andrew Donnan Smith. m 9/19/1987 Sally G Boulter c 2. Assoc Cathd of St Ptr & St Paul Washington DC 2006-2008. rev. rob.boulter@gmail.com

BOULTON, David Watson (Ct) 84 Broadway, New Haven CT 06511 B Spencer MA 12/8/1928 s Howard Carpenter Boulton & Ellen. BA Bow 1948; MA Ya 1949; STB GTS 1962. D 6/20/1962 P 12/1/1962 Bp Robert McConnell Hatch. Chr Ch New Haven CT 1971-1983; R S Jn's Ch Athol MA 1967-1971; Vic S Mary's Epis Ch Thorndike MA 1964-1967; Cur Gr Ch Amherst MA 1962-1964.

BOURDEAU, Mary Ellen (Md) 2 Saint Peters Pl, Lonaconing MD 21539 B Allentown PA 10/3/1940 d Arthur Leibensperger & Ellen. BE,BA Syr 1962. D 9/7/2008 Bp John Leslie Rabb. c 3. me_bourdeau@yahoo.com

BOURGEAULT OSB, Cynthia Warren (Colo) 77 Meadowood Dr, Aspen CO 81611 **Aspen Chap Aspen CO 2004-; Chr Epis Ch Aspen CO 2004-** B Philadelphia PA 3/13/1947 d Warren Keen Simmons & Mary. BA OH SU 1967; PhD U of Pennsylvania 1972; EDS 1975. D 12/19/1975 P 8/1/1979 Bp Lyman Cunningham Ogilby. c 2. Asst Chr Epis Ch Aspen CO 1994-1998; Downeast Epis Cluster Swans Island ME 1990-1992; Asst Nevil Memi Ch Of S Geo Ardmore PA 1978-1980. "The Wisdom Jesus," Shambhala, 2008; "Chanting the Psalms," Shambhala, 2006; Auth, "Centering Pryr and Inner Awakening," Cowley, 2004; "The Wisdom Way of Knowing," Wiley, 2003; Auth, "Mystical Hope," Cowley, 2001; Auth, "Love is Stronger than Death," Bell Tower Praxis, 1998; Ed, "Intimacy w God," 1993; Ed/Co-Auth, "Medieval Mus Drama," Oxf Press, 1980. Oblate Ord Of S Ben. treaven@earthlink.net

BOURHILL, John William (NY) 26 Huron Rd, Yonkers NY 10710 B Bronxville NY 3/6/1935 s James Bourhill & Elenor Catherine. D 5/19/2001 Bp Richard Frank Grein. m 6/2/2002 Susan Summitt-Bourhill c 2.

BOURLAKAS, Mark Allen (Ky) 421 S 2nd St, Louisville KY 40202 **Dn Chr Ch Cathd Louisville KY 2007-** B Vincennes IN 4/7/1963 s Luke Bourlakas & Judy Jo. BA U So 1985; MDiv SWTS 1997. D 5/24/1997 P 12/6/1997 Bp Robert Gould Tharp. m 5/6/1989 Martha Elizabeth Johnson c 3. R S Alb's Ch Davidson NC 2003-2007; R S Fran of Assisi Chapin SC 2000-2003; Asst Chr Ch Greenville SC 1998-2000; Cur S Lk's Ch Cleveland TN 1997-1998. mark@christchurchlouky.org

BOURNE-RAISWELL, Margaret Lafayette (ECR) 20025 Glen Brae Dr, Saratoga CA 95070 B Fresno CA 8/6/1950 d Robert Lafayette Bourne & Margaret Roberta. BA U Pac 1972; MS California St U 1975; MDiv CDSP 1991. D 5/29/1991 P 6/3/1992 Bp Richard Lester Shimpfky. m 5/29/1976 Dwight Goodwin. S Andrews Epis Ch Port Angeles WA 2007-2008; Ch Of The H Sprt Campbell CA 1999-2001; Assoc S Andr's Ch Saratoga CA 1993-1999; Chair Of Cmsn For Deaf And Hearing-Impaired Dio El Camino Real Monterey CA 1991-1993; D Ch Of S Jude The Apos Cupertino CA 1991-1992. Bd Managers Ymca 1991; Chair Dio Cmsn For The Deaf & Hearing Impaired 1991-1993; Dio Cmsn On Stwdshp 1999.

BOURQUE, Mary Elizabeth (Me) 20 Union St., Hallowell ME 04347 B Camden ME 8/10/1943 d Clarence Herbert Thomas & Elvira Berry Stevenson. BS U of Maine, Orono 1965; BS U of Maine, Farmington 1997. D 6/20/2009 Bp Stephen Taylor Lane. m 10/15/1966 Peter Bourque c 3. mary.bourque61@gmail.com

BOUSFIELD, Nigel J (FdL) 1432 Foxfire Ct, Waupaca WI 54981 **S Mk's Ch Waupaca WI 2008-** B Kent UK 5/30/1957 s Maurice Jay Bousfield & Enid Christine. AA Scottsdale Cmnty Coll 2000; MDiv Nash 2003. D 12/14/2002 P 6/29/2003 Bp Keith Lynn Ackerman. Chr Ch Babylon NY 2006-2008; S Jn's Ch Huntington NY 2003-2006. nigel.b@prodigy.net

BOUTAN, Marc Robert (SC) 29 Rue Capitaine Crespel, Brussels Belgium B Watertown SD 1/8/1953 s Pierre Jean Boutan & Marilyn. BA U of Iowa 1974; MDiv Fuller TS 1990; DAS VTS 1991. D 8/22/1991 Bp Edward Cole Chalfant P 3/14/1992 Bp Edward Lloyd Salmon Jr. m 10/1/1977 Patricia M Hartman c 2. Asst S Andr's Ch Mt Pleasant SC 2006-2007; Assoc S Phil's Ch Charleston SC 2001-2006; Assoc S Jas Ch Charleston SC 1999-2000; Asst H Trin Brussels 1996-1999; Asst S Andr's Ch Mt Pleasant SC 1991-1996. mboutan@gmail.com

BOUTCHER, Ann Louise (SC) 710 Main St, Conway SC 29526 B Reading PA 12/28/1938 d Robert James Schmehl & Dorothy. BSED Tem 1971; MSN U of Pennsylvania 1981. D 9/11/2010 Bp Mark Joseph Lawrence. m 2/27/1960 Donald C Boutcher c 2. annboutcher@yahoo.com

BOW, (Chien-kwang) Peter (Tai) 398 Chestnut Street, Union NC 07083 **Died 6/5/2010** B Shanghai CN 11/13/1929 s Yang-chia Bow & Chiu-ling. BD Orient TS 1977; ThM Orient TS 1979; MA Trin TS 1982. D 8/24/1985 Bp Pui-Yeung Cheung. Gideon Intl .

BOWDEN, George Edward (Mo) 624 Saffron Ct, Myrtle Beach SC 29579 B Paterson NJ 4/21/1943 s George Smith Bowden & Jean Roberta. BA Leh 1965; MDiv GTS 1969. D 6/14/1969 P 12/13/1969 Bp Dudley S Stark. m 5/27/1967 Helen Frances LaPointe c 2. Dioc Coun Dio Missouri S Louis MO 2005-2007; R H Cross Epis Ch Poplar Bluff MO 1999-2009; Int S Andr's Ch Dayton OH 1998-1999; Cler Cont Educ Com Dio Sthrn Ohio Cincinnati OH 1994-1996; R S Andr's Epis Ch Washington Crt Hse OH 1990-1998; R All SS Epis Ch Lakewood NJ 1975-1990; R St Jn the Bapt Epis Ch Linden NJ 1971-1975; Cur S Ptr's Epis Ch Livingston NJ 1969-1971. gbowden3@sc.rr.com

BOWDEN JR, John T (SC) 3982 Creekmoor Dr, Orangeburg SC 29118 B Great Falls SC 3/30/1938 s John T Bowden & Ruth B. BS So Carolina St U 1960. D 1/17/2008 Bp Edward Lloyd Salmon Jr P 8/9/2008 Bp Mark Joseph Lawrence. tedruth1@sc.rr.com

BOWDEN JR, Talmadge Arton (Ga) 3409 Wheeler Rd, Augusta GA 30909 **The Ch Of The Gd Shpd Augusta GA 2002-** B Coral Gables FL 8/16/1940 D 9/18/2001 P 3/21/2002 Bp Henry Irving Louttit. m 12/11/1993 Cecilia Murphy c 2. putterdog60@hotmail.com

BOWDEN, Teresa Thomas (Haw) 2573 California Ave, Wahiawa HI 96786 **Asst S Steph's Ch Wahiawa HI 2005-** B Jacksonville FL 10/19/1936 BS U GA 1977; MDiv Epis TS of The SW 2001. D 6/17/2001 P 4/14/2002 Bp Richard Sui On Chang. m 2/28/1959 William Eugene Bowden c 2. Assoc S Tim's Ch Aiea HI 2002-2004. alohayouall@earthlink.net

BOWDISH, Lynn Eastman (Cal) 172 Northgate Ave, Daly City CA 94015 **Assoc H Chld At S Mart Epis Ch Daly City CA 2010-; Dio California San Francisco CA 2000-** B Eureka CA 5/15/1937 d Philip Chester Eastman & Hally Foster. BA U Pac 1959; MDiv CDSP 1978; DMin VTS 1991. D 6/24/1978 Bp William Foreman Creighton P 6/16/1979 Bp George West Barrett. c 2. Vic S Eliz's Epis Ch So San Francisco CA 1981-2009; S Andr's Epis Ch San Bruno CA 1980-1981. Tertiary Of The Soc Of S Fran. Grant Rec Lilly Fndt 2000. vicarlynn@aol.com

BOWEN, Anthony DeLisle (LI) 180 Kane St, Brooklyn NY 11231 **D Chr Ch Cobble Hill Brooklyn NY 2009-** B 3/7/1948 s Harcourt Ince & Ena Augusta. Cert The Geo Mercer TS; Assoc Borough of Manhattan Cmnty Coll 1978. D 6/1/2009 Bp Richard Lester Shimpfky. c 1. TONYBO@VERIZON.NET

BOWEN, Carol (Cal) 2401 Carlmont Dr Apt 14, Belmont CA 94002 B Columbus OH 12/20/1946 d Charles Joseph Staley & Florence Josephine. BA New Coll of California 1988; MA Coll of Notre Dame 1994; BA Sch for Deacons 1997. D 12/5/1998 Bp William Edwin Swing. m 3/2/1984 Mike Bowen. S Mk's Epis Ch Palo Alto CA 2000-2004. Amer Art Ther Assn; Caamft; D Coun Dio Ca; NAAD. cb4healing@comcast.net

BOWEN, Elizabeth Anne (Mo) Trinity Episcopal Church, 318 S Duchesne Dr, Saint Charles MO 63301 **D Trin Ch St Chas MO 2007-** B Kingston Jamaica 2/25/1939 d Arthur Braine Walcott & Hyacinth Lucille. Epis Sch of Mnstry 2007. D 10/23/2007 Bp George Wayne Smith. m 8/24/1962 David Bowen c 3. DBowen472@email.com

BOWEN, George Harry (Nwk) 308 River Oaks Dr, Rutherford NJ 07070 **Cn Trin And S Phil's Cathd Newark NJ 1993-** B East Rutherford NJ 5/1/1932 s Charles Sargent Bowen & Mary. BA Trin Hartford CT 1954; GTS 1957. D 6/15/1957 P 12/21/1957 Bp Benjamin M Washburn. Gr Ch Newark NJ 1976-1994; Pres of Hackensack Convoc Dio Newark Newark NJ 1972-1974; R Trin Ch Cliffside Pk NJ 1961-1974; Cur Gr Ch Newark NJ 1957-1961. Hon Cn, Trin and S Phil's Cathd Newark NJ 1993. canonbowen@aol.com

BOWEN, Paul (Tex) 324 Sherwood Ave, Staunton VA 24401 B Mobile AL 5/14/1944 s Paul Richard Bowen & Helen. BA Cit 1965; MDiv VTS 1968. D 6/11/1968 P 12/18/1968 Bp Wilburn Camrock Campbell. m 11/28/1969 Martha Kennon Radspinner c 2. S Steph's Epis Sch Austin TX 2002-2007; York Sch Monterey CA 1994-2002; St. Steph's and St. Agnes Sch Alexandria VA 1991-1994; Dio Virginia Richmond VA 1986-1988; CFS The Sch At Ch Farm Exton PA 1979-1982; Cathd of St Ptr & St Paul Washington DC 1973-1991; Asst S Matt's Ch Wheeling WV 1968-1970. Auth, "Opportunities for Mnstry in Epis Schools," *NAES Reasons for Being*, 1997; Auth, "Challenge," *The Cathd Age*, 1986. Outstanding Tchr Washingtonian mag. proger.bowen@gmail.com

BOWEN, Pauline Mason (WNY) 138 Castle Hill Rd, East Aurora NY 14052 **BEC Dio Wstrn New York Tonawanda NY 2011-; D S Mths Epis Ch E Aurora NY 2001-; Dioc Coordntr, EFM Dio Wstrn New York Tonawanda NY 1988-** B State College PA 2/7/1936 d David D Mason & Leda E. AAS Trocaire Coll 1973; BS Medaille Coll 1988; MA Chr The King Sem 1991; MDiv Chr The King Sem 1999. D 6/11/1988 Bp David Charles Bowman. m 5/14/1955 Charles Daniel Bowen c 3. BEC Dio Wstrn New York Tonawanda NY 2000-2003; Diac Formation Dio Wstrn New York Tonawanda NY 1994-1996; Educ Cmsn Dio Wstrn New York Tonawanda NY 1988-1991. Auth, "Prog," *Letting Go*, 1992; Auth, "Prog," *Journeying Hm*, 1991; Auth, *arts & Poetry*. Ord of S Lk 1981-1989. hon - Scripture Chr the King Sem 1999. smceadeacon@verizon.net

BOWEN, Peter Scott (Me) 20 Sky Harbor Dr, Biddeford ME 04005 **D Chr Ch Biddeford ME 2006-** B Hartford CT 5/26/1944 s Harvey Moser Bowen & Anita LeCompte. BA St. Mich's Coll 1967; MBA Nasson Coll 1986; MDiv Bangor TS 2006. D 6/24/2006 Bp Chilton Abbie Richardson Knudsen. m 11/23/2002 Shirley Williams c 2. pbowen@maine.rr.com

BOWEN, Shirley Williams (Me) 20 Sky Harbor Dr, Biddeford ME 04005 **R Chr Ch Biddeford ME 2007-; Campus Mssnr Dio Maine Portland ME 2005-; Mssnr for Campus Mnstry/Epis Chapl @ USM Dio Maine Portland ME 2005-** B Marietta OH 1/29/1959 d Merrill Britt Williams & Kathleen Virginia. BA in Educ Glenville St Coll 1981; MA in Educ W Virginia U 1985; M.Div. EDS 2004. D 6/11/2005 P 12/10/2005 Bp Chilton Abbie Richardson Knudsen. m 11/23/2002 Peter Scott Bowen. shirleybowen@maine.rr.com

BOWER, Jeffrey L (Ind) 4160 Broadway St, Indianapolis IN 46205 **S Jn's Ch Speedway IN 2007-** B Greensburg IN 9/23/1961 s Ora Franklin Bower & Frances. BA Wabash Coll 1983; MA Chr TS 1997; MDiv Chr TS 1999; CTh SWTS 2004. D 6/24/2006 P 2/10/2007 Bp Catherine Elizabeth Maples Waynick. c 2. Assn of Profsnl Chapl 2003. Presidential Schlr Chr TS 1998. rectorsj@sbcglobal.net

BOWER, John A(llen) (SO) 466 Grandin Avenue, Springdale OH 45246 B Parkersburg WV 10/3/1937 s Jack Gibson Bower & Joanne. U IL - Chicago 1958; BA Nthrn Illinois U 1960; MDiv Nash 1963. D 6/15/1963 Bp James Winchester Montgomery P 12/21/1963 Bp Gerald Francis Burrill. m 8/10/1963 Louise Annette Emenheiser c 3. Int S Mary's Ch Waynesville OH 2000-2001; Ch Pension Fund Com Dio W Virginia Charleston WV 1996-1998; R Zion Epis Ch Chas Town WV 1991-1998; Evang and Renwl Cmsn Dio Sthrn Ohio Cincinnati OH 1986-1987; Dioc Coun Dio Sthrn Ohio Cincinnati OH 1984-1986; R Chr Epis Ch Ottawa IL 1971-1979; Cur Chr Ch Waukegan IL 1963-1965. CT Assoc 1980. jab103@fuse.net

BOWER, Richard Allen (CNY) 681 N Hill Cross Rd, Ludlow VT 05149 B Santa Ana CA 5/30/1940 s Gerald C Bower & Mary M. BA USC 1965; MDiv Fuller TS 1968; ThM PrTS 1969; Cert PDS 1970; Fllshp EDS 1990. D 4/11/1970 P 10/24/1970 Bp Alfred L Banyard. m 8/8/1964 Stephanie D Bower c 3. Dear and R S Paul's Cathd Syracuse NY 1991-2000; Int Chr Ch Ridgewood NJ 1990-1991; EDS Cambridge MA 1989-1990; Rep of Panama Exec Coun Appointees New York NY 1986-1990; Assoc R Trin Ch Princeton NJ 1979-1986; R Ch Of S Mary's By The Sea Point Pleasant Bch NJ 1973-1979; Cur S Lk's Epis Ch Metuchen NJ 1970-1973. Auth, "Cuentos Panamenos," *Cuentos Panamenos:Stories of Struggle & Faith in Rural Panama*, Friendship Press, 1993; Auth, "Liturg as Lang," *Chld in the Euch*, Epis Ch Cntr, 1990; Auth, "Par Priesthood: Expectations and Reality," *ATR*, 1984; Auth, "Unity, Constancy & Peace: Liturg & Simplicity, Liturg & Simplicity," *Seabury Press NYC*, 1984; Auth, "Daring to Learn," *Making Sense of Things*, Seabury, 1981; Auth, "Meaning of Epituchano in Epistles of S Ign of Antoich, Vigiliae Christianae Vol. 28," *Vigiliae Christianae*, No Holland Publ. Co, Amsterdam, 1974. OHC 1970; Pstr Min, L'Arche Zone USA 1995; l'Arche Intl 1994. Elected Dn Emer St Paul's Cathd, Syracuse NY 2000; Cert of Recognition for Wk in Human Rts St Assembly, NY St 1999. rabvt@tds.net

BOWER, Roger Andrew (NI) 505 Bullseye Lake Rd, Valparaiso IN 46383 **R S Andr's Epis Ch Valparaiso IN 2010-** B Concord MA 5/8/1961 s Leroy Charles Bower & Roberta Marie. BA U of St. Thos 1985; MDiv U of St. Thos 1989. Rec from Roman Catholic 10/24/2000 as Priest Bp Daniel William Herzog. m 2/14/1996 Barbara Douglas Graham c 2. Dio Colorado Denver CO 2009; R H Apos Epis Ch Englewood CO 2008-2009; Vic Ch Of The H Sprt Cherry Hills Vill CO 2004-2007; Assoc S Marg's Epis Ch Palm Desert CA 2003; R S Lk's Ch Mechanicville NY 2000-2003. rbower@standrewsvalpo.org

BOWERFIND, Ellis Tucker (Va) 8727 Bluedale St, Alexandria VA 22308 **R S Lk's Ch Alexandria VA 2003-** B Cleveland OH 9/16/1958 s Edgar Sihler Bowerfind & Maria. BA S Johns Coll 1984; MDiv Ya Berk 1991; MA Ursuline Coll 1999. Trans 10/9/2003 Bp M(arvil) Thomas Shaw III. m 10/3/1992 Delea Free c 4. Assoc R S Mary's Epis Ch Barnstable MA 1999-2003; Assoc R S Paul's Epis Ch Cleveland Heights OH 1991-1999. rector@saintlukeschurch.net

BOWERS, Albert Wayne (Alb) 17 Woodbridge Ave, Sewaren NJ 07077 B Macon GA 4/8/1942 s Louie Mack Bowers & Mattie Mae. BA Estrn Nazarene Coll 1976; MDiv GTS 1986. D 6/14/1986 Bp William Gillette Weinhauer P 12/20/1986 Bp Vincent King Pettit. c 1. Zion Ch Hudson Falls NY 2000-2009; Cn Mssnr S Mk's-S Lk's Epis Mssn Castleton VT 1998-2000; Vic S Lk And All SS' Ch Un NJ 1991-1998; S Jn's Ch Sewaren NJ 1991-1997; Cur Trin Ch Woodbridge NJ 1986-1991. Auth, "A Cognitive Model Of Original Sin Arise & Shine". albert.w.bowers@gmail.com

BOWERS, David Douglas (SwFla) 513 Nassau St S, Venice FL 34285 B Thomasville GA 9/9/1963 s George Franklin Bowers & Elizabeth Ann Caley. BA U So 1985; MDiv Nash 1989. D 5/14/1989 P 4/1/1990 Bp Harry Woolston Shipps. c 1. S Mk's Epis Ch Venice FL 1991-1995; The Ch Of The Gd Shpd Augusta GA 1990-1991; Trin Ch Statesboro GA 1989-1990.

BOWERS, Eugene Vincent (CNY) Box 2 (Capron Road), Woodgate NY 13494 **Died 12/30/2009** B Buffalo NY 11/14/1921 s Roy Thomas Bowers & Margaret. BS SUNY 1949; MS SUNY 1952; EdD U Roch 1972. D 6/21/1986 P 5/1/1987 Bp O'Kelley Whitaker. c 2.

BOWERS, George Franklin (Ga) Po Box 2408, Darien GA 31305 B Berwick Nova Scotia 12/12/1935 D 2/3/2001 P 11/26/2002 Bp Henry Irving Louttit. m 10/5/1985 Patrcia Bowers c 1. halcion@surfsouth.com

BOWERS, J(ohn) E(dward) (SO) 1276 Coonpath Rd Nw, Lancaster OH 43130 B Cincinnati OH 4/2/1936 s Harry Edward Bowers & Mary Eldora. BA Ken 1958; MDiv Bex 1965. D 6/26/1965 P 1/1/1966 Bp Roger W Blanchard. m 6/21/1986 Nancy Bowers. Int S Pat's Epis Ch Dublin OH 2002-2003; E Cntrl Ohio Area Mnstry Cambridge OH 1997-1998; S Jn's Epis Ch Cambridge OH 1979-1996; P-in-c S Phil's Ch Cincinnati OH 1974-1979; P-in-c H Sprt Epis Ch Cincinnati OH 1967-1970; Cur S Jas Epis Ch Cincinnati OH 1965-1966. nancytaggart@gmail.com

BOWERS, Marvin Nelson (NCal) 202 Tucker St, Healdsburg CA 95448 B Sapulpa OK 11/11/1944 s Marvin Henry Bowers & Cecil Ann. BA U CA 1966; MDiv/STB GTS 1969. D 7/1/1969 Bp Edward McNair P 1/31/1970 Bp Clarence Rupert Haden Jr. m 6/25/1966 Bonnie Agnes Bowers c 5. RurD Dio Nthrn California Sacramento CA 1995-1999; RurD Dio Nthrn California Sacramento CA 1976-1981; S Paul's Ch Healdsburg CA 1972-2006; Vic S Lk's Mssn Calistoga CA 1969-1972. frmarvinbowers@gmail.com

BOWERS, Terry L. (Chi) 2042 Bronson St., Fort Collins CO 80526 B Rockford IL 4/24/1953 d Bernard Burdette Barnes & B Dawn. BS Colorado St U 1975; MDIV SWTS 2003. D 1/31/2007 Bp Victor Alfonso Scantlebury P 9/11/2007 Bp William Dailey Persell. m 7/8/2009 Sharon Hamman c 3. terrybowers24@gmail.com

BOWERS, Thomas Dix (NY) 304 Lord Granville Dr, Morehead City NC 28557 B Norfolk VA 2/2/1928 s George Hubert Bowers & Nellie. BS VMI 1949; BA U So 1953; MDiv VTS 1956; DD Nash 1983; DD VTS 1983; DD TS 1984. D 6/13/1956 Bp William A Brown P 6/17/1957 Bp George P Gunn. m 12/26/2003 Palmer Ulmer c 4. Int S Dav's Ch Austin TX 2002-2003; Int S Jn's Ch Lafayette Sq Washington DC 1993-1994; R S Barth's Ch New York NY 1978-1993; R S Lk's Epis Ch Atlanta GA 1971-1978; R S Pat's Ch Washington DC 1961-1971; Assoc S Alb's Par Washington DC 1959-1961; R S Geo's Ch Pungoteague Accomac VA 1956-1959; R S Jas' Ch Accomac VA 1956-1959. Auth, "Come To The Table," *Come to the Table*. DEACONS 1973-1993; The Club 1979-1993. Tom Bowers's Day Atlanta 1978 Mayor Maynard Jackson Atlanta GA 1978; Human Relatns Awd Mart Luther King Cntr Soc Change 1977. pubowers@yahoo.com

BOWERSOX, Ned Ford (WTex) 8607 Tomah Dr, Austin TX 78717 **Int S Mk's Ch San Marcos TX 2011-; S Helena's Epis Ch Boerne TX 2000-** B Midland MI 12/9/1942 s Ford Bowersox & Mildred Leona. AA Florida St U 1965; BS Florida St U 1969; MDiv VTS 1973. D 5/18/1973 P 12/5/1973 Bp William Hopkins Folwell. m 6/22/1968 Phyllis Anne Potsko c 2. R Ch Of The Gd Shpd Corpus Christi TX 1995-2007; R S Jn's Ch Melbourne FL 1979-1994; S Chris's Ch Orlando FL 1976-1979; Vic Ch Of The New Cov Winter Sprg FL 1975-1979; Dio Cntrl Florida Orlando FL 1975-1976; Asst Gr Epis Ch Of Ocala Ocala FL 1973-1975. soxs04@aol.com

BOWERSOX, Sally Ann (Colo) 367 Peerless St, Louisville CO 80027 **Adj Cler S Ambr Epis Ch Boulder CO 2005-; Exec Dir St Ben Hlth and Healing Mnstry Louisville CO 2005-** B Lakewood OH 2/3/1954 d Robert O Bowersox & Beatrice. AS Lansing Cmnty Coll 1975; MA Naropa U 1987; MDiv Iliff TS 2002; CSD Vincentian Cntr for Sprtlty at Wk Denver CO 2005. D 6/8/2002 P 12/21/2002 Bp William Jerry Winterrowd. c 1. Asst P Our Merc Sav Epis Ch Denver CO 2002-2005. ECW 2002; EPPN 2006; Natl Jubilee Mnstry 2005; Publ Plcy Advsry Bd, Dio Colorado 2008; Sprtl Dir Intl 2005. sallyosb7@comcast.net

BOWES, Bruce Orin (NY) 254 Bloomer Rd, Lagrangeville NY 12540 B Mount Vernon NY 7/27/1941 s Nelson Dowd Bowes & Naomi Arlene. BA Washington and Jefferson U 1964; MDiv Nash 1967. D 6/3/1967 P 12/1/1967 Bp Horace W B Donegan. m 6/29/1968 Adele Evelyn Bowes. Ch Of The Resurr Hopewell Jct NY 1974-1988; Asst R Gr Epis Ch Nyack NY 1967-1969. bobowes3@gmail.com

BOWHAY, Christopher Andrew (Tex) 5019 Grape Street, Houston TX 77096 **Dn, W Harris Cnty Convoc Dio Texas Houston TX 2009-; Rectory S Thos Ch Houston TX 2006-** B Santa Ana CA 8/17/1968 Bachelor's (w hon) U CA at Berkeley 1991; BST St. Jos of Arimathea Angl Theol Coll 1992; Mstr's Stan 2000. D 6/12/2004 P 1/6/2005 Bp Don Adger Wimberly. m 10/4/1997 Sally S Brooks c 1. Dir, Fam, Yth, and Outreach Mnstrs S Mart's Epis Ch Houston TX 2004-2006. rectorste@stes.org

BOWLIN BSG, Howard B (ETenn) 348 Deer Run Dr, Maryville TN 37803 **P-in-c S Thos Epis Ch Knoxville TN 2010-** B East Saint Louis IL 8/31/1946 s Howard Kenneth Bowlin & Helen Gertrude. BA U IL 1972; U CO 1973; MDiv VTS 1992. D 6/13/1992 P 1/16/1993 Bp Ronald Hayward Haines. m 5/15/1976 Gail Anne Gifford c 1. Int S Fran Of Assisi Epis Ch Ooltewah TN 2008-2009; R S Matt's Epis Ch Bloomington IL 1998-2007; R Chr Ch

Lockport NY 1993-1998; Asst R S Alb's Epis Ch Annandale VA 1992-1993. BSG 2000. mira180aa@hughes.net

BOWLING, Jack Denver (WMich) 3383 Yonge Ave, Sarasota FL 34235 B Huntington WV 1/7/1929 s Oakley Denver Bowling & Mae. BA Van 1951; MDiv EDS 1954; MS U of Sthrn Maine 1969; S Fran Coll Ft. Wayne IN 1971; Oxf 1983; Indiana U 1985; U Coll London London GB 1988. D 6/12/1954 Bp Frank W Sterrett P 4/25/1955 Bp Theodore N Barth. m 12/12/1953 Louise Fuller Foster c 3. Ch Of The Redeem Sarasota FL 1994-2011; Assoc St Jn's Epis Ch of Sturgis Sturgis MI 1969-1990; Cur The Ch Of The Adv Boston MA 1956-1961. Dn S Mich. Conf Young Chmn, W. Hartford, CT 1960; NECCU, Sec/Treas 1957-1961. na

BOWMAN, Andrea C (Spok) 104 E 17th Ave, Ellensburg WA 98926 B Everett WA 6/30/1946 D 8/20/2000 Bp John Stuart Thornton P 6/2/2001 Bp James Edward Waggoner. Ch Of The Resurr (Chap) Roslyn WA 2009-2011; Ch Of The Resurr (Chap) Roslyn WA 2008. BOWMANA@FAIRPOINT.NET

✠ **BOWMAN, Rt Rev David Charles** (WNY) 3289 Grenway Rd, Shaker Heights OH 44122 **Asst Dio Ohio Cleveland OH 2005-; Ret Bp of Wstrn NY Dio Ohio Cleveland OH 2005-** B Oil City PA 11/15/1932 s Robert Charles Bowman & Ella. BA Ohio U 1955; MDiv VTS 1960. D 6/14/1960 Bp Beverley D Tucker P 12/14/1960 Bp Nelson Marigold Burroughs Con 9/14/1986 for WNY. m 6/30/1962 Nancy Lou Betts c 3. Asst Bp Dio Cntrl New York Syracuse NY 2000-2001; Int Dn Trin Cathd Cleveland OH 2000-2001; Bp of Wstrn New York Dio Wstrn New York Tonawanda NY 1987-2000; Bp of Wstrn New York Dio Wstrn New York Tonawanda NY 1987-1999; Bp Coadj of Wstrn New York Dio Wstrn New York Tonawanda NY 1986-1987; R Trin Ch Toledo OH 1980-1986; Pres of Stndg Com Dio Ohio Cleveland OH 1976-1980; Pres of the Stndg Com Dio Ohio Cleveland OH 1975-1980; R S Jas Ch Painesville OH 1973-1980; Vic S Andr's Ch No Grafton MA 1963-1966; Asst Ch Of The Epiph Cleveland OH 1960-1963; Asst Ch Of The Epiph Euclid OH 1960-1963. DD VTS 1987. dcbowman@wowway.com

BOWMAN JR, Locke E (NC) 807 Davis St. Unit 905, Evanston IL 60201 **Dio No Carolina Raleigh NC 1996-** B Clinton MO 1/12/1927 s Locke E Bowman & Naomi. BA Wm Jewell Coll 1948; MDiv McCormick TS 1951; LHD Schiller U Eur 1972. D 9/11/1983 P 2/15/1984 Bp Joseph Thomas Heistand. c 1. VTS Alexandria VA 1986-1995; Prof VTS Alexandria VA 1983-1985. Ed, "Benedictine Reflections," St Paul'S Monstry, 1997; Auth, "Tchg For Chr Hearts," *Souls & Minds*, HarperCollins, 1990; Auth, "Tchg Today: The Ch's First Mnstry," Westminster Press, 1980. Oblate Ord Of S Ben 1982. Citation for Achievement Wm Jewell Coll 1968. lebowman.bowman@gmail.com

BOWMAN, Marlin Leonard (LI) Po Box 926, San Andreas CA 95249 **Died 2/7/2010** B Santa Barbara CA 5/30/1930 s Leonard Leon Bowman & Christina Ruth. BA U of San Francisco 1953; MDiv CDSP 1958. Trans 2/21/1959 Bp James Albert Pike. Angl Soc 1990. Man of the Year Awd JFK Airport 1985; Who's Who in Rel 1984; Who's Who in Rel 1980; Who's Who in Rel 1977; Fndr, Awards Bp Wright Air Industry; Civic Awd of the Year Awd BSA Queens NY; Fndr Senator Wm Reynolds Civic Awards; Fndr Shrine of S Jas of Jerusalem.

BOWMAN, Sallie Wirt (Ore) 6251 SW 55th Dr, Portland OR 97221 **P-in-c Legacy Gd Samar Hosp Portland OR 2011-; Assoc S Mich And All Ang Ch Portland OR 2003-** B Richmond VA 4/25/1957 d Charles Luther Bowman & Sallie Edwards. BA W&M 1979; MDiv CDSP 2003. D 4/30/2003 Bp Robert Louis Ladehoff P 11/15/2003 Bp Johncy Itty. c 1. sbowman@lhs.org

BOWMAN, Susan Blount (Alb) 65 E Highland Dr, Apt 1, Albany NY 12203 B Richmond VA 2/6/1947 d Howard Lewis Blount & Belle Ray. BA W&M 1969; MDiv STUSo 1984. D 2/23/1985 P 1/25/1986 Bp C(laude) Charles Vache. c 1. Vic S Mk's Ch Hoosick Falls NY 2001-2005; Pres Of Stndg Com Dio Albany Albany NY 1995-1996; S Mich's Albany NY 1991-2001; Vic All SS Ch So Hill VA 1987-1991. sbb2ladyfr@roadrunner.com

BOWRON, Joshua Dan (At) 1623 Carmel Rd, Charlotte NC 28226 **S Jn's Epis Ch Charlotte NC 2011-** B Detroit MI 12/15/1975 s Brian Lee Bowron & Sue Ellen. BA Merc 2000; MDiv The TS at The U So 2011. D 12/18/2010 P 6/18/2011 Bp J(ohn) Neil Alexander. m 3/16/2002 Brittany S Stewart c 2. joshbowron@gmail.com

BOWYER, Charles Lester (NwT) 5806 Emory St, Lubbock TX 79416 B Richwood WV 6/3/1939 s Charles Cicero Bowyer & Delores Irene. BA Berea Coll 1961; MDiv Epis TS In Kentucky 1964; DMin GTF 1991; PhD La Salle U 1995. D 5/30/1964 Bp William R Moody P 5/8/1965 Bp George Henry Quarterman. Assoc S Paul's On The Plains Epis Ch Lubbock TX 1975-1984; Vic S Jn's Ch Lamesa TX 1966-1975; Cur The Epis Ch Of S Mary The Vrgn Big Sprg TX 1964-1966. c.bowyer@suddenlink.net

BOYD, Billie Rufe (FtW) 105 Lakeway Dr, Fort Worth TX 76126 **Died 3/3/2011** B Sulphur Springs TX 3/25/1923 s Mack Boyd & Sybil Rufe. LTh Epis TS In Kentucky 1970. D 6/15/1970 Bp William Paul Barnds P 12/20/1970 Bp Theodore H McCrea. c 2. OHC. brboyd@aol.com

BOYD, Catherine Tyndall (Tex) 4720 Eagle Feather Dr, Austin TX 78735 **Trin Epis Sch Of Austin W Lake Hills TX 2007-** B Columbia MO 4/25/1958 d Brent Vincent Tyndall & Constance Flanigan. BA U of Missouri 1980; Lexington TS 2003; MDiv Epis TS of The SW 2006. D 6/24/2006 P 1/13/2007 Bp Don Adger Wimberly. m 5/9/1981 David Allen Boyd c 2. S Jn's Epis Ch Austin TX 2006-2007. ECom 1987-1992; Fllshp of SSJE 1997. cboyd@austintrinity.org

BOYD, David Allen (Tex) 4720 Eagle Feather Dr, Austin TX 78735 **S Dav's Ch Austin TX 2003-** B Janesville WI 4/15/1955 s Ronald Oliver Boyd & Sidney Lewis. BS Sthrn Illinois U 1977; MDiv Nash 1984. D 4/7/1984 P 10/27/1984 Bp Charles Thomas Gaskell. m 5/9/1981 Catherine Tyndall c 2. Mem, Stndg Com Dio Texas Houston TX 2007-2010; Mem, Exec Coun Dio Lexington Lexington KY 1998-2000; R Ch S Mich The Archangel Lexington KY 1996-2003; S Andr's Ch Milwaukee WI 1990-1996; Urban Mssnr S Jn Ch/Mision San Juan Milwaukee WI 1990-1994; Mem, Stndg Com Dio Milwaukee Milwaukee WI 1989-1994; R S Jn The Div Epis Ch Burlington WI 1986-1990; Asst Gr Ch Madison WI 1984-1986. Cler Ldrshp Proj 1992-1995; Fllshp of SSJE 2000. dboydfly@gmail.com

BOYD, Iain Peyton (SC) 10 Laurel St Apt 5, Conway SC 29526 **Assoc R Trin Ch Myrtle Bch SC 2008-** B Charlotte NC 10/14/1981 s Kenneth Boyd & Patrice. BA Cit 2003; MDiv Nash 2006. D 7/1/2006 P 1/8/2007 Bp Edward Lloyd Salmon Jr. m 6/17/2006 Michelle Boyd. Asst R S Paul's Epis Ch Conway SC 2006-2008. boydmonster@yahoo.com

BOYD, James R (WTenn) 6367 Shadowood Ln, Memphis TN 38119 B Providence RI 3/22/1947 s John William Boyd & Lucile MaryAnn. BA Van 1969; MDiv Intermet Sem 1977. D 12/17/1976 P 6/25/1977 Bp William Hopkins Folwell. m 11/28/1970 Martha Milford c 3. Pres Bridges Inc Memphis TN 1995-2011; R S Paul's Epis Ch Salem OR 1990-1995; R H Trin Epis Ch Fayetteville NC 1984-1990; Cn Evang Dio W Tennessee Memphis TN 1983-1984; Exec Dir Epis Metropltn Mnstry Of Memphis Memphis TN 1980-1982; Cn Cathd Ch Of S Lk Orlando FL 1977-1980; Asst Min S Mk's Ch Washington DC 1976-1977. jboyd54321@aol.com

BOYD, Jeffrey Howard (Mass) 57 Bethany Woods Rd, Bethany CT 06524 B Morristown NJ 11/13/1943 s Francis Orsemus Boyd & Ruth Elizabeth. BA Br 1965; BD Harvard DS 1968; MD Case Wstrn Reserve U 1976; MA Ya 1981. D 6/22/1968 Bp Anson Phelps Stokes Jr P 1/1/1969 Bp John Melville Burgess. m 6/29/1968 Patricia Ann Boyd. "Being Sick Well: Joyful Living Despite Chronic Illness," Baker Books, 2005. jeffrey.boyd@sbcglobal.net

BOYD, Julia Woolfolk (NC) Po Box 6124, Charlotte NC 28207 B Bloominton IN 4/9/1969 d William Douglas Boyd & Margaret. BA Davidson Coll 1991; MDiv Yale DS 1995. D 10/9/1999 Bp J(ames) Gary Gloster P 10/28/2000 Bp Michael Bruce Curry. S Paul's Epis Ch Winston Salem NC 2005-2008; Asst Chr Ch Charlotte NC 1999-2005; S Ptr's Epis Ch Charlotte NC 1996-1998. boydj@christchurch-clt.org

BOYD, Lawrence Robert (Neb) 2325 S 24th St, Lincoln NE 68502 B Kansas City KS 1/1/1941 s Robert Andrew Boyd & Helen Margaret. BA Wichita St U 1965; BD SWTS 1968. D 6/1/1968 P 12/18/1968 Bp Edward Clark Turner. m 11/21/1993 Andrea D Boyd c 4. R S Matt's Ch Lincoln NE 1999-2006; R S Ptr's Ch Litchfield Pk AZ 1993-1999; R Gr Epis Ch Lake Havasu City AZ 1990-1993; Dn Chr Ch Cathd Eau Claire WI 1983-1987; R Gr Epis Ch Ponca City OK 1978-1982; R St Johns Epis Ch Wisconsin Rapids WI 1973-1978; Asst Trin Epis Ch Oshkosh WI 1971-1973; Cur S Dav's Epis Ch Topeka KS 1968-1971. grampsretired@gmail.com

BOYD, Malcolm (Los) PO Box 5121654, Los Angeles CA 90051 **P/Writer in Res Cathd Cntr Of S Paul Cong Los Angeles CA 1996-** B Buffalo NY 6/8/1923 s Melville Boyd & Beatrice. BA U of Arizona 1944; BD CDSP 1954; STM UTS 1956. D 6/21/1954 P 12/21/1955 Bp Francis E I Bloy. Dio Los Angeles Los Angeles CA 1989-1995; S Aug By-The-Sea Par Santa Monica CA 1987-1995; Dio Los Angeles Los Angeles CA 1984-1987; Interracial Mnstry Team Ch Of The Atone Washington DC 1965-1970; Dio Los Angeles Los Angeles CA 1964-1970; Gr Ch Detroit MI 1964-1965. "Are You Running w Me, Jesus?," *Fortieth Anniv Ed*, Cowley, 2006; "In Times Like These...How We Pray," *Co-edited w J. Jon Bruno*, Seabury, 2005. Unitas Awd UTS Col 2005; DD CDSP 1995; Chr & Jews Awd to Understanding Untd Amer Hebr Congr 1980. malcolmboyd@ladiocese.org

BOYD, Norman Herriman (Los) Po Box 6044, San Pedro CA 90734 B San Diego CA 6/29/1926 s Charles Harriman Boyd & Dorothy Evelyn. BA U CA 1951; MDiv CDSP 1956; S Aug's Coll Cbury Gb 1966. D 12/23/1955 P 6/1/1956 Bp Karl M Block. Asst S Ptr's Par San Pedro CA 1991-1998; Asst S Ambr Par Claremont CA 1972-1974; Asst The Ch Of The Ascen Sierra Madre CA 1968-1970; Asst S Martha's Epis Ch W Covina CA 1966-1967; Assoc S Edm's Par San Marino CA 1963-1966; Asst S Mk's Epis Ch Palo Alto CA 1958-1961; Vic S Lk's Ch Jolon CA 1956-1958; Vic S Matt's Ch San Ardo CA 1956-1958. nhboyd1@juno.com

BOYD JR, Robert Johnston (Va) 1600 Westbrook Ave Apt 425, Richmond VA 23227 **Died 9/20/2010** B Philadelphia PA 10/13/1930 s Robert Johnston Boyd & Margaret Louise. BS Davidson Coll 1952; BD UTS 1956; STM STUSo 1967; Fllshp Coll of Preachers 1976; Fllshp STUSo 1980. D 6/22/1957 P 12/21/1957 Bp Angus Dun. c 2. Res Fellowow Stuso Sewanee TN 1980; Fellowow Coll Of Preachers Washington DC 1976.

B

BOYD, Sally Ann (Wyo) 436 Sundance Circle, Wright WY 82732 **Cn S Fran On The Prairie Ch Wright WY 1998-** B Brighton CO 9/24/1951 d Theodore Arthur Abrams & Ella Fern. BA Wstrn St Coll of Colorado 1977. D 4/14/1998 P 5/19/1999 Bp Bruce Edward Caldwell. m 2/25/1979 Timothy Jo Boyd.

BOYD, Samuel Lee (Tex) Po Box 1884, Chandler TX 75758 B Tyler TX 12/4/1946 s Robert Ira Boyd & Margaret Marita. AA Tyler Jr Coll 1967; BBA Baylor U 1970; MDiv STUSo 1999. D 6/22/2002 Bp Claude Edward Payne. m 6/3/1967 Jan Jordan Johnson. S Phil's Epis Ch Palestine TX 2004-2009; Vic Trin Ch Jacksonville TX 1999-2004. sljjboyd@embarqmail.com

BOYD, Sandra (Colo) 8251 E Phillips Pl, Englewood CO 80112 **BEC Dio Colorado Denver CO 1995-** B Council Bluffs IA 12/29/1938 d Floyd Earl Hughes & Jane Elizabeth. BA Colorado Coll 1961; MA U MN 1966; MDiv EDS 1978. D 6/17/1978 Bp William J Gordon Jr P 4/21/1979 Bp H Coleman McGehee Jr. c 2. Alum/ae Exec Coun EDS Cambridge MA 2006-2010; Int S Barn Epis Ch Denver CO 2006-2007; Ch Of The Trsfg Evergreen CO 2006; Int S Gabr The Archangel Epis Ch Cherry Hills Vill CO 2004-2005; The Ch Of Chr The King (Epis) Arvada CO 2003; Int S Raphael Epis Ch Colorado Sprg CO 1998-2000; Ecum Off Dio Colorado Denver CO 1997-2009; Int S Paul's Epis Ch Lakewood CO 1997; BEC Dio Colorado Denver CO 1995-2009; Int Ch Of S Jn Chrys Golden CO 1994-2002; The Ch Of The Ascen Denver CO 1994; Asst Gd Shpd Epis Ch Centennial CO 1992-1993; Int S Jn's Ch Charlestown (Boston) Charlestown MA 1983-1984; Assoc Chr Ch Cambridge Cambridge MA 1981-1986. Auth, "Epis Wmn: Gender," *Sprtlty & Commitment*, 1992; Auth, "Wmn In Amer Rel Hist: A Bibliography & Guide To Sources," 1985; Auth, "Cultivating Our Roots: Guide To Womens Hist For Ch Wmn"; Auth, "Wmn P In The 80'S:An Autobiographical Essay". Colorado Coun of Ch 1997-2008; Colorado Coun of Ch, Pres 2006-2008. Whitely Awd For Excellence In Sociol 1996. revsandy@earthlink.net

BOYD, Virginia Ann (Md) 10901 Farrier Rd, Frederick MD 21701 **R S Jn's Par Hagerstown MD 2009-** B Shreveport LA 11/15/1944 d Fletcher Willard Lewis & Bess Juanita. PhD LSU 1971; MAT S Mary's Baltimore MD 2003; Cert EDS 2004. D 7/29/2004 Bp John Leslie Rabb P 2/20/2005 Bp Robert Wilkes Ihloff. c 1. R S Paul's Epis Ch Mt Airy MD 2005-2010; Asst R S Jn's Par Hagerstown MD 2004-2005. Ann Boyd and M. Najati, "Hlth Care in a Democracy," *Eubios Journ of Asian and Intl Bioethics*, 19:98-103, 2009; Ann Boyd, "Moral Theol and Ethics Meet at the Bedside of the Dying," *Moral Theol*, U Press of the So, 2009; L Gravey and A Boyd, "Global Hlth Concerns and Publ Hlth for the Common Gd," *Eubios Journ of Asian and Intl Bioethics*, 18:40-45, 2008; Ann Boyd, "HIV/AIDS Exposes Gender Injustice," *Eubios Journ of Asian and Intl Bioethics*, 0149-04-01, 2007; Ann Boyd, "HIV/AIDS Exposes Gender Injustice," *Eubios Journ of Asian and Intl Bioethics*, 17:144-149, 2007; A.L. Boyd, "Anagogy of Autonomy," *Eubios Journ of Asian and Internatinoal Bioethics*, 0119-03-01, 2000; A.L. Boyd, "Anagogy of Autonomy," *Eubios Journ of Asian and Internatinoal Bioethics*, 10:113-119, 2000. Amer Soc of Microbiology 1971; Intl AIDS Soc 1990; Intl Assn for Educ in Ethics 2010; Phi Kappa Phi 1971; Sigma Xi 1971. Grad Sch Outstanding Tchr Awd Hood Coll 2007; Jas Arthur Muller Prize in Hist EDS 2004; Deans Awd for Ethics and Moral Theol Ecum Inst of Theol 2003; Wm Fenn Lectr Unit5ed Bd CE 1996; Amer Acad of Microbiology Fell ASM 1994; Tchg excellence Awd Hood Coll 1991. boyd@hood.edu

BOYD, William Marvin (Fla) 2361 Gayland Rd, Jacksonville FL 32218 B Memphis TN 7/29/1948 s Roger Wiley Boyd & Ruby. BA U of Sthrn Colorado 1981; MDiv Nash 1986. D 6/14/1986 P 12/1/1986 Bp William Carl Frey. m 9/6/1968 Deborah Christine Boyd c 1. S Eliz's Epis Ch Jacksonville FL 1998-1999; S Jas' Epis Ch Lake City FL 1995-1998; S Anne's Epis Sch Denver CO 1989-1991; Dio Colorado Denver CO 1987-1993; Gr Ch Buena Vista CO 1986-1987.

BOYD, William Orgill (At) 210 E Robert Toombs Ave, Washington GA 30673 B Brownsville TN 10/19/1924 s Graham Stanley Boyd & Florence. BA U So 1949; VTS 1952. D 6/24/1952 Bp Edmund P Dandridge P 6/23/1953 Bp Theodore N Barth. m 9/26/1953 Betty Boyd c 2. Vic Ch Of The Medtr Washington GA 1972-1990; Vic Ch Of The Redeem Greensboro GA 1972-1983; Vic S Jas Ch Cedartown GA 1966-1972; P-in-c All SS' Epis Ch Morristown TN 1953-1966; Asst Trin Ch Clarksville TN 1952-1953.

BOYD-ELLIS, Sue (WNY) No address on file. B Jamestown NY 12/10/1945 d Frederick Ingolls Boyd & Helen Eugenia. BA SUNY 1985. D 6/13/1987 Bp Harold B Robinson. D Trin Epis Ch Hamburg NY 1997-2003.

BOYER, Donald Ernest (Vt) RR1 Box 360, Woodstock VT 05091 B Worcester MA 3/6/1934 s Ernest Arthur Boyer & Wilhelmina Anne. BA U So 1955; STB Ya Berk 1958. D 6/11/1958 Bp Robert McConnell Hatch P 12/1/1958 Bp Vedder Van Dyck. m 1/29/1981 Marcia H Martin c 2. S Jas Ch Woodstock VT 1982-1999; Cathd Ch Of S Paul Burlington VT 1971-1982; Cn To Ordnry Dio Vermont Burlington VT 1971-1973; Cur Cathd Ch Of S Paul Burlington VT 1958-1962.

BOYER JR, Ernest Leroy (ECR) PO Box 360832, Milpitas CA 95036 **Ch Of S Jos Milpitas CA 2010-** B Orlando FL 6/21/1951 s Ernest Leroy Boyer & Kathryn G. BA Earlham Coll 1973; MLS SUNY Albany 1976; MDiv Harvard DS 1984; ThD Harvard DS 2002; Cert. of Angl Stds CDSP 2008. D 6/6/2009 P 12/12/2009 Bp Mary Gray-Reeves. m 5/26/2002 Sondra Allphin c 3. D S Lk's Ch Los Gatos CA 2009. boyer.ernest@gmail.com

BOYER, Geoffrey Thomas (Mich) 124 Charles Road, Rochester MI 48307 **R S Phil's Epis Ch Rochester MI 2003-** B Youngstown OH 5/18/1947 s Thomas Blackmore Boyer & Martha. BA Florida St U 1969; MA Florida St U 1971; MDiv SWTS 1990; DMin SWTS 2003. D 6/30/1990 Bp John Wadsworth Howe P 6/11/1991 Bp John H(enry) Smith. m 6/19/1971 Susan H Hawkins c 1. COM Dio Michigan Detroit MI 2004-2009; Ldrshp Trng Prog Dio Michigan Detroit MI 2004-2007; Ldrshp Prog for Par Musicians Dio Michigan Detroit MI 2003-2006; Eccl Crt Dio Michigan Detroit MI 2002-2005; Dioc Coun & Exec Com Dio Michigan Detroit MI 2001-2002; Cathd Chapt & Exec Com Dio Michigan Detroit MI 1997-2000; RurD, Capital Area Coun Dio Michigan Detroit MI 1997-2000; R S Mich's Epis Ch Lansing MI 1996-2003; Dioc Evang Com Dio W Virginia Charleston WV 1995-1996; Dioc Cmncatn Com Dio W Virginia Charleston WV 1994-1996; Dn, Dioc Study Prog Dio W Virginia Charleston WV 1993-1996; Vic S Mths Grafton WV 1993-1996; Vic S Barn Bridgeport WV 1992-1996; Dir, Creative Arts Camp for Yth Dio W Virginia Charleston WV 1992-1993; Cmsn on Liturg and Mus Dio W Virginia Charleston WV 1991-1996; Cur Trin Ch Huntington WV 1990-1992. Auth: Congrl Thesis, "Mnstry in the Marketplace," *Unpublished*, SWTS, 2003. H Cross Assoc 1985. Red Ribbon for Theol Reflection Lois Leonard Ch Nwsltr Contest 2005; Blue Ribbon for Theol Reflection Lois Leonard Ch Nwsltr Contest 2001; Red Ribbon for Theol Reflection Lois Leonard Ch Nwsltr Contest 2000; Dramatic Awd SWTS 1990. gboyer47@att.net

BOYER, John Paul (WNY) 3951 Seneca St, West Seneca NY 14224 **Vic S Paul's Epis Ch Stafford NY 2007-** B Niagara Falls NY 6/29/1942 s George Krauser Boyer & Ethal Marie. BA Cntr Coll 1964; MDiv EDS 1967; BA Oxf 1969; MA Oxf 1973. D 6/17/1967 Bp Lauriston L Scaife P 1/1/1968 Bp Stephen F Bayne Jr. Bex Columbus OH 2001-2005; R S Dav's Epis Ch W Seneca NY 1988-2004; S Jn's Ch Wilson NY 1983-1988; Dio Sthrn Ohio Cincinnati OH 1983; R H Trin Ch Cincinnati OH 1978-1982; Asst Ch Of S Mary The Vrgn New York NY 1969-1978.

BOYER, Marcia H (Vt) PO Box 494, Woodstock VT 05091 B Boston MA 2/24/1950 d Stuart Thompson Martin & Margaret Dorothy. BA Kirkland Coll 1972; MDiv EDS 1977; JD Vermont Law Sch 1988. D 6/11/1977 P 1/1/1978 Bp Robert Shaw Kerr. m 1/29/1981 Donald Ernest Boyer. Ch Of The Gd Shpd Barre VT 1984; Asst R S Jas Ch Woodstock VT 1982-1988; Cathd Ch Of S Paul Burlington VT 1977-1982. Jd cl Vermont Law Sch So Royalton VT 1988.

BOYER, William James (CFla) 126 E Palmetto Ave, Howey in the Hills FL 34737 B Rochester MN 5/13/1946 s Charles Lorimer Boyer & Margaret Giles. AA St Petersburg Jr Coll 1966; BS Florida St U 1968; MDiv Candler TS,Emory U 1972. D 12/12/2009 P 6/26/2010 Bp John Wadsworth Howe. m 6/5/1982 Nancy West Boney c 2. howey126@hotmail.com

BOYLE, George Anne (Oly) PO Box 3811, Lacey WA 98509 **S Ben Epis Ch Lacey WA 2005-** B Point Pleasant NJ 4/21/1969 d Gordon G Boyle & Joyce Suzanne. BA Coll of S Eliz 1991; MDiv SWTS 2002. D 5/18/2002 Bp Roger John White P 1/25/2003 Bp Vincent Waydell Warner. m 7/1/2005 Elizabeth A McDonnell c 2. Assoc for Yth and YA S Thos Ch Medina WA 2002-2005. "I Remember A Different Story," *The Olympian*, The Olympian Nwspr, Olympia WA, 2007; "The Devil Is In The Details," *The Olympian*, The Olympian Nwspr, Olympia WA, 2007. laceyvicar@yahoo.com

BOYLE, Patton Lindsay (Spok) 1342 Bartlett Ave, Wenatchee WA 98801 B Charlottesville VA 3/3/1943 s Eldridge Roger Boyle & Sarah Lindsay. BA U of Virginia 1965; MDiv VTS 1970; CPE Inst of Rel and Human Dvlpmt 1973; CPE Georgia Mntl Hlth Inst 1977. D 6/20/1970 Bp Philip Alan Smith P 5/1/1971 Bp Addison Hosea. c 2. P-in-c S Lk's Epis Ch Wenatchee WA 2005-2009; Vic S Jn's By The Sea Kaneohe HI 2003-2005; P-in-c S Ptr's Ch Honolulu HI 2001-2003; Int S Ambr Epis Ch Boulder CO 1999-2001; Pstr Counslr Pastorial Counslg Cntr Corvallis OR 1993-1995; R Chr Ch Biddeford ME 1988-1993; Int Chr Ch Gardiner ME 1987-1988; Int Ch Of The Epiph Danville VA 1986-1987; Vic Emm Ch Lake Vill AR 870-2652230or8 1975-1976; Vic S Clem's Ch Arkansas City AR 1975-1976; Asst S Paul's Epis Ch Meridian MS 1973-1974; Int Calv Ch Golden CO 1971-1972; Part time Asst Chr Ch Cathd Lexington KY 1970-1971. Auth, "Screaming Hawk Returns," Sta Hill Press, 1997; Auth, "Screaming Hawk," Sta Hill Press, 1994. AAPC 1983-1998. pattonboyle@msn.com

BOYLE, Peter (Alb) 10 Lindbergh Ave, Rensselaer NY 12144 **R Ch Of The Redeem Rensselaer NY 1999-** B Somerville NJ 12/25/1943 s William Edward Boyle & Jane. BA Leh 1966; MA Rutgers-The St U 1969; Cert GTS 1972. D 6/10/1972 Bp Leland Stark P 3/17/1973 Bp George E Rath. m 4/19/1969 Jeanne Evelyn Baumuller. Supply H Cross Perth Amboy NJ 1996-1999; Vic Ch Of Our Sav Secaucus NJ 1974-1976.

BOYNTON, Caroline Cochran (NY) 12 W 96th St Apt 17c, New York NY 10025 B 5/18/1947 D 5/19/2001 Bp Richard Frank Grein.

BOYNTON, Dana Fredrick (Mass) 3639 Cactus St., Myrtle Beach SC 29577 B Wareham MA 6/2/1943 s Ralph Boynton & Natalie Yvonne. BA Bridgewater Coll 1968; MDiv Andover Newton TS 1991. D 6/1/1991 Bp David Elliot Johnson P 5/15/1992 Bp David Bell Birney IV. m 4/11/1964 Marsha Beard c 2. R Epis Ch Of S Thos Taunton MA 2002-2008; All SS Ch Whitman MA 1994-2002; Ch Of The H Sprt Mattapan MA 1991-1994. revdb@aol.com

BOZARTH, Alla Renee (Minn) 43222 SE Tapp Rd, Sandy OR 97055 B Portland OR 5/15/1947 d Rene Malcolm Bozarth & Alvina. BSS NWU 1971; MA NWU 1972; PhD NWU 1974; Cert Gestalt Trng Cntr of San Diego 1978. D 9/8/1971 Bp James Walmsley Frederic Carman P 7/29/1974 Bp Daniel Corrigan. Auth, *This Mortal Mar: Poems of Love, Lament and Praise*, iUniverse ,, 2003; Auth, *Womanpriest: A Personal Odyssey*, Wisdom Hse, 2002; Auth, *Accidental Wisdom*, iUniverse,, 2000; Auth, *Life is Goodbye/Life is Hello: Grieving Well through All Kinds of Loss*, Hazelden, rev. ed., 1993; Auth, *Wisdom & Wonderment*, Sheed and Ward,, 1993. allabearheart@yahoo.com

BOZZUTI-JONES, Mark Francisco (Mass) 74 Trinity Place, New York NY 10006 **Trin Par New York NY 2007-** B Kingston Jamaica 1/15/1966 MDIv Jesuit TS Berkeley 1997. Rec from Roman Catholic 5/31/2003 as Priest Bp M(arvil) Thomas Shaw III. m 10/2/1999 Kathleen Mary Bozzuti-Jones c 1. S Barth's Ch New York NY 2005-2007; Assoc R Chr Ch Cambridge Cambridge MA 2003-2005. Auth, "Informed by Faith," *Educ Bk*, Cowley, 2006; Auth, "Womb of Adv," *Adv Meditation*, Cowley, 2005; Auth, "The Mitre Fits Fine: Bp Harris," *Biography*, Cowley, 2005; Auth, "Jesus the Word," *Childrens Bk*, Augsburg, 2005; Auth, "God Created," *Childrens Bk*, Augsburg, 2003; Auth, "Never Said a Mumbalin Word," *Lenten Meditation*, Augsburg, 2002. mbozzuti-jones@trinitywallstreet.org

BRACE, William Shannon (SeFla) 4600 Middleton Park Cir E Apt C-237, Jacksonville FL 32224 B Homestead PA 9/22/1916 s Rodney Brace & Mary Elizabeth. BA Hob 1938; GTS 1941; MS Nova U 1975. D 5/31/1941 Bp Frank W Sterrett P 2/12/1942 Bp John J Gravatt. m 6/10/1942 Amelia Hildebrand c 1. Stndg Com Dio SE Florida Miami FL 1973-1975; Dep GC Dio SE Florida Miami FL 1970-1973; Exec Coun Dio SE Florida Miami FL 1969-1982; Dio SE Florida Miami FL 1969-1972; Dio SE Florida Miami FL 1964-1968; R All SS Prot Epis Ch Ft Lauderdale FL 1962-1981; Hon Cn Cathd Ch Of S Lk Orlando FL 1961-1969; R St Johns Epis Ch Tampa FL 1957-1962; Dioc Secy Dio Georgia Savannah GA 1952-1957; R Gr Ch Waycross GA 1948-1957; P-in-c Ch Of The Ridge Trenton SC 1943-1948; Our Sav Epis Ch Trenton SC 1943-1948; P-in-c Trin Ch Edgefield SC 1943-1948; Exec Coun Dio Upper So Carolina Columbia SC 1943-1944; Cur Trin Cathd Columbia SC 1941-1943. Hon Cn Trin Cathd, Miami Miami 1969; Hon Cn S Lk's Cathd, Orlando Orlando 1961.

BRACKETT, Thomas L (WNC) 13 Kent Pl, Asheville NC 28804 **Epis Ch Cntr New York NY 2008-; Epis Ch Cntr New York NY 2008-** B Norfolk VA 8/7/1960 s Burton Merrick Brackett & Helga Johanna Magdalena. BA Vermont Coll Of Norwich U 1997; MDiv Bangor TS 2001. D 6/23/2001 Bp Chilton Abbie Richardson Knudsen P 12/23/2001 Bp Gethin Benwil Hughes. m 11/7/1987 Cheri A Leonard c 1. St Georges Epis Ch Asheville NC 2004-2008; Ch Of The Mssh Murphy NC 2003-2004; Brevard Epis Mssn Brevard NC 2003; Assoc S Jas By The Sea La Jolla CA 2001-2002. tbrackett@bellsouth.net

BRADA, Netha Nadine (Ia) 345 Lincoln Ave, Iowa Falls IA 50126 B Rockwell IA 9/22/1937 d Elmer Edwin Juhl & Irene Mae. Educ for Minist Sewanee TS 1991. D 8/23/1997 P 6/20/1998 Bp Carl Christopher Epting. m 6/15/1957 Ronald George Brada c 3. P S Matt's-By-The-Bridge Epis Ch Iowa Falls IA 1998-2007. nethanbrada@gmail.com

BRADBURY, John Saferian (Ind) No address on file. B 5/27/1928 D 6/14/1965 Bp John P Craine P 3/3/1965 Bp James Winchester Montgomery.

BRADBURY, Stephanie (Mass) 390 Main St, North Andover MA 01845 **R S Paul's Epis Ch No Andover MA 2007-** B Boston MA 9/21/1963 d Richard Conant Chase & Eva-Maria. BA U of Virginia 1985; MDiv Ya Berk 1995. D 6/15/1996 P 2/15/1997 Bp Robert Wilkes Ihloff. m 4/24/2010 William John Bradbury c 2. Exec Coun Appointees New York NY 2005-2007; Resolutns Com Chair Dio Maryland Baltimore MD 2003-2004; COM Mem Dio Maryland Baltimore MD 2001-2004; R All SS Epis Par Sunderland MD 1999-2004; Evang Com Mem Dio Maryland Baltimore MD 1998-2001; The Ch Of The Redeem Baltimore MD 1996-1999. whitestole@gmail.com

BRADBURY, William John (Mass) 133 School Street, New Bedford MA 02740 **R Gr Ch New Bedford MA 2006-** B Portchester NY 10/12/1951 s John Sholars Bradbury & Polly. BA U GA 1973; MDiv VTS 1978. D 6/10/1978 Bp Charles Judson Child Jr P 5/24/1979 Bp Bennett Jones Sims. m 4/24/2010 Stephanie Chase c 4. R S Ptr's Epis Ch Washington NC 1985-2005; Assoc R S Paul's Ch Augusta GA 1982-1985; Vic S Andr's In-The-Pines Epis Ch Peachtree City GA 1979-1982. MDiv cl VTS Alexandria VA 1978; AB scl U GA Athens GA 1973. massdawg@gmail.com

BRADEN, Anita Luise (Mil) N26 W24150 River Park Drive, Milwaukee WI 53072 **Vic/Urban Mssnr S Andr's Ch Milwaukee WI 2001-** B New York NY 11/9/1957 d Ernest Giddens & Marion R. Trin Evang DS Deerfield IL; BA Lakeland Coll 1993; BA Milwaukee Theol Inst 1998. D 2/4/2001 P 8/4/2001 Bp Roger John White. m 8/19/2001 Warren R Braden c 2. S Fran Ch Menomonee Falls WI 2004-2010; Dio Milwaukee Milwaukee WI 2001-2004. anitabraden@yahoo.com

BRADEN, Deborah Susan (Ala) 1910 12th Ave. S., Birmingham AL 35243 **Died 9/25/2010** B Anniston AL 5/5/1953 d Rudolph L Braden & Ada J. BS Jacksonville St U 1974; MS Jacksonville St U 1977; JD Cumberland Sch of Law 1983; MDiv STUSo 2004. D 5/25/2004 P 12/2/2004 Bp Henry Nutt Parsley Jr. m 7/9/2009 Robert Steven Norton. deb@stmarysoth.org

BRADFORD, Kathleen Diane (Cal) 1713 Daisy Way, Antioch CA 94509 **D S Alb's Epis Ch Brentwood CA 1999-** B Oakland CA 11/12/1952 d Roderic Douglas Ross & Marian. AA Diablo Vlly Coll 1972; BA Sch for Deacons 1998. D 6/5/1999 Bp William Edwin Swing. m 4/28/1977 Ricky Eugene Bradford. NAAD.

BRADFORD, Lawrence James (Colo) 4131 E 26th Ave, Denver CO 80207 **S Phil In-The-Field Sedalia CO 2010-; Epis Ch Of S Ptr And S Mary Denver CO 2008-** B Oklahoma City OK 1/2/1942 s Lawrence James Bradford & Bonnie Blanche. BA S Mary Of The Plains Dodge City KS 1964; Med Wichita St U 1969; PhD U CO 1979; MDiv Iliff TS 2001. D 6/9/2001 P 12/23/2001 Bp William Jerry Winterrowd. m 7/23/1994 Ann Haywood Marsden c 2. S Barn Of The Vlly Cortez CO 2009-2010; Ch Of S Phil And S Jas Denver CO 2009; H Trin Epis Ch Wyoming MI 2005-2007; R Ch Of The H Redeem Denver CO 2001-2003. lbradford59@gmail.com

BRADFORD, Richard Sterling (Mass) 10 Saint Theresa Ave, West Roxbury MA 02132 B Chicago IL 2/8/1945 s Charles Lobdell Bradford & Margaret Ann. BA W&L 1967; STB GTS 1970. D 6/13/1970 Bp James Winchester Montgomery P 12/1/1970 Bp Gerald Francis Burrill. m 9/7/1968 Judith Dawn Loyer c 1. The Par Of All SS Ashmont-Dorches Dorchester MA 1991-1996; R S Jas' Epis Ch Goshen IN 1986-1991; R S Tim Ch Richland MI 1974-1986; Cur S Mich's Ch Barrington IL 1970-1974. SSC, ESA,CBS, GAS, SocMary, CCU.

BRADLEY, Gary Joseph (Los) Immanuel Mission, 4366 Santa Anita Ave., El Monte CA 91731 **Imm Mssn El Monte CA 2010-** B Seattle WA 12/4/1947 s Francis Samuel Bradley & Marion Dorothea. BA S Johns Sem Coll 1970; MA S Jn Major Sem 1973; ISEE Mex City Sem 1974; DAS ETSBH 1988. Rec from Roman Catholic 2/26/1988 as Deacon Bp Oliver Bailey Garver Jr. m 8/23/1980 Margaret Elizabeth Bowerman c 4. Ch Of Our Sav Par San Gabr CA 1998-2010; All SS Ch Pasadena CA 1989-1998. Auth, "Par: Sacr of Presence," *Par Educ Booklets*, Franciscan Cmncatn, 1983. garyandpeg@aol.com

BRADLEY, James (Ct) 16 Church St, Waterbury CT 06702 B Welch WV 4/17/1947 s Virgil Hoyt Bradley & Marian Cleo. BA W Virginia U 1969; MA Harvard DS 1971; MDiv VTS 1975; DMin Hartford Sem 1998. D 5/24/1975 Bp Wilburn Camrock Campbell P 5/15/1976 Bp Robert Poland Atkinson. m 9/5/1970 Bernadine Bradley c 2. R S Jn's Epis Par Waterbury CT 1989-2010; R S Paul And S Jas New Haven CT 1980-1985; Vic S Jas Ch Charleston WV 1975-1980. Auth, *Gathering the Body Scattered*, 1998. padrejgb@aol.com

BRADLEY, Margaret Elizabeth (Los) 619 W Roses Rd, San Gabriel CA 91775 **Ch Of Our Sav Par San Gabr CA 2009-** B Mesa AZ 9/11/1952 d Lloyd Bowerman & Marlene. Arizona St U; BS Nthrn Arizona U 1978; MDiv ETSBH 2003. D 12/18/2005 P 9/8/2007 Bp Joseph Jon Bruno. m 8/23/1980 Gary Joseph Bradley c 4. S Jas' Par So Pasadena CA 2006-2009. garyandpeg@prodigy.net

BRADLEY, Martha Jean (Spr) 3621 Troon DR, Springfield IL 62712 **D The Cathd Ch Of S Paul Springfield IL 1987-** B Carbondale IL 10/27/1930 d Don Bell Bradley & Bertha Estelle. BA NWU 1952; Med Sthrn Illinois U 1965; Coc 1989. D 11/1/1987 Bp Donald Maynard Hultstrand. Auth, "Living Ch". Epis Chapl Coll Chapl. bradley8858@att.net

BRADLEY, Matthew Bryant (Ky) St. John's Episcopal Church, 1620 Main St, Murray KY 42071 **P-in-c S Jn's Ch Murray KY 2008-** B Louisville KY 5/14/1983 s James Michael Bradley & Judy Katherine. BSE Tul 2005; MDiv VTS 2008. D 12/21/2007 P 6/21/2008 Bp Edwin Funsten Gulick Jr. mbradleytu@gmail.com

BRADLEY, Michael Lee (NH) 15 Park Court, Durham NH 03824 **R S Geo's Ch Durham NH 1997-** B Taunton MA 12/15/1956 s Robert Lee Bradley & Janet Ellen. BA U of Sthrn Maine 1979; MDiv Harvard DS 1990. Trans from Anglican Church of Canada 4/1/1997 as Priest Bp Douglas Edwin Theuner. m 8/24/1979 Becky Lynn Bailey c 1. BA mcl U of Sthrn Maine Portland ME 1979. rectorstg@comcast.net

BRADLEY, M Mantelle (NJ) 318 Elton Ln, Galloway NJ 08205 **R Ch Of S Mk And All SS Absecon Galloway NJ 2008-** B Newport News VA 6/7/1968 d William E Bradley & Martha. BA W&M 1990; MDiv GTS 1996. D 5/25/1996 Bp Frank Harris Vest Jr P 12/7/1996 Bp Joe Morris Doss. c 2. Vic H Sprt Bellmawr NJ 1998-2008; Vic S Lk's Ch Westville NJ 1998-2008; Timber Creek Epis Area Mnstry Gloucester City NJ 1998-2005; Trin Ch Moorestown NJ 1996-1998. revmmb@comcast.net

BRADLEY, Nancy Bown (CFla) 427 Timberlake Dr, Melbourne FL 32940 B Brooklyn NY 5/17/1923 d Carlton Fellows Bown & Harriet Adele. BA SUNY 1974. D 12/10/1984 Bp William Hopkins Folwell. m 4/29/1945 Francis M

Bradley c 3. D Hope Epis Ch Melbourne FL 1990-1994; Ch Of Our Sav Palm Bay FL 1990. Ord of S Lk the Physcn. bradleyfm@aol.com

BRADLEY, Patrick John (WNY) 505 Riverdale Ave, Lewiston NY 14092 **D S Ptr's Ch Niagara Falls NY 2001-** B Niagara Falls NY 4/27/1954 s Melvin Jackson Bradley & Dorothy Evelyn. BA SUNY 1976. D 5/6/2000 Bp J Michael Garrison. m 11/13/1982 Linda Ann Hamilton. bradleypj@gmail.com

BRADLEY, Raymond Earle (Ind) 13039 Venito Trl, Fishers IN 46037 B Buffalo NY 6/15/1940 s Earle Bradley & Helen. BA SUNY 1963; Bangor TS 1966; TS 1970; BA SUNY 1972; MS LIU 1984. D 6/22/1969 Bp Charles Waldo MacLean P 12/22/1969 Bp Lauriston L Scaife. m 8/21/1964 Franka Helen Welbourn c 2. R Trin Ch Anderson IN 2000-2004; Assoc Chr Ch Cathd Indianapolis IN 1996-2000; Off Of Bsh For ArmdF New York NY 1975-1996; R S Alb's Ch Danielson CT 1972-1975; R Trin Ch Warsaw NY 1970-1972; Cur H Trin Epis Ch Hicksville NY 1969-1970. AUSA 1976; H Cross Monstry 1969; Mltry Chapl Assn. raybradley@comcast.net

BRADNER, Lawrence Hitchcock (RI) 67 Slater Ave, Apt 9, Providence RI 02906 **Assoc S Mart's Ch Providence RI 2006-** B Providence RI 5/13/1934 s Leicester Bradner & Harriet. BA Ya 1956; MAT Br 1960; STB GTS 1964; Cert Assn of Mntl Hlth Clerics 1981. D 6/20/1964 P 2/12/1966 Bp John S Higgins. m 1/2/1965 Marcia May Bradner c 3. Ch Of The Ascen Cranston RI 1990-1991; Calv Ch Providence RI 1984-1985; S Matt's Par Of Jamestown Jamestown RI 1982-1983; Ch Of The Resurr Warwick RI 1980; Ch Of The Redeem Providence RI 1978; Dio Rhode Island Providence RI 1976-1998; Stff The Epis Ch Of S Andr And S Phil Coventry RI 1975-1977; P-in-c Epiph Ch 1971-1975; Cur S Paul's Ch Pawtucket RI 1964-1965. Auth, *Following the Trail of the Old Narragansett Ch*, 1990; Auth, "The Plum Bch Light: Birth," *Life & Death of a Lighthouse*, LH Bradner Pub, 1989; Auth, *The Med Cntr & Publ Hlth Care in Rhode Island*. Cert Assn Mntl Hlth Cleric 1980; Felloship of St. Jn 1970. lhbradner@cox.net

BRADSEN, Kate (Az) 340 S 3rd Ave, Tucson AZ 85701 **Vic S Andr's Epis Ch Tucson AZ 2011-** B Evanston IL 10/26/1978 d William Steven Bradley & Kathryn Mann. BA NWU 2000; MDiv EDS 2005. D 12/18/2004 P 7/2/2005 Bp Alan Scarfe. m 8/9/2007 Carol S Bradsen. Imago Dei Middle Sch Tucson AZ 2008-2011; Asst Gr S Paul's Epis Ch Tucson AZ 2005-2007; Epis Chapl At Harvard & Radcliffe Cambridge MA 2005. fatherkate@gmail.com

BRADSHAW, Charles Robbins (Me) Church of Our Father, PO Box 186, Hulls Cove ME 04644 **Sprtl Dir, Maine Curs Dio Maine Portland ME 2006-; R Ch Of Our Fr Hulls Cove ME 1999-** B Lake Forest IL 7/20/1951 s Charles Baker Bradshaw & Sarah. BA Harv 1973; MDiv TESM 1992; DMin TESM 2011. D 6/13/1992 Bp Arthur Edward Walmsley P 12/16/1992 Bp John Clark Buchanan. m 4/22/1984 Elizabeth Will c 2. Exam Chapl Dio NW Pennsylvania Erie PA 1996-1999; R Emm Epis Ch Emporium PA 1994-1999; R S Agnes' Epis Ch S Marys PA 1994-1999; Asst Chr Epis Ch S Jos MO 1992-1994. Anglicans for Life 2006; BroSA 1989; Maine Epis Curs 2000. cbbradshaw@myfairpoint.net

BRADSHAW, C(ouncil) Foy (NC) 905 Saint Andrew St, Tarboro NC 27886 **Vic Ch Of The Sav Jackson NC 2002-** B Lenoir NC 4/30/1938 s Julius Foy Bradshaw & Virginia. BS U NC 1961; MPA E Carolina U 1987; Cert Dio NC Deacons' Trng Prog Durham NC 1989. D 6/17/1989 Bp Robert Whitridge Estill P 12/16/2001 Bp Michael Bruce Curry. m 9/24/1960 Velma Rene Bradshaw c 3. D Calv Ch Tarboro NC 1995-2001; D S Mich's Ch Tarboro NC 1993-1995; D Trin Ch Scotland Neck NC 1992-1993; D Ch Of The Epiph Rocky Mt NC 1991-1992; D Calv Ch Tarboro NC 1989-1991; Calv Ch Tarboro NC 1000. cfoyb@aol.com

BRADSHAW, Paul F (NI) University of Notre Dame, 1 Suffolk Street, London SW1Y 4HG Great Britain (UK) **Hon Cn Dio Nthrn Indiana So Bend IN 1990-** B Preston Lancashire UK 8/9/1945 s Reginald Samuel Bradshaw & Marian. BA U of Cambridge 1966; MA U of Cambridge 1970; PhD London U GB 1971; DD Oxf 1994. Trans from Church Of England 1/1/1990 Bp Francis Campbell Gray. m 12/5/1970 Rowenna Mary Street. Cn Dio Nthrn Indiana So Bend IN 1990. Auth, *Early Chr Wrshp*, SPCK, 1996; Auth, *The Search for Origins of Chr Wrshp*, SPCK/OUP, 1992; Auth, *Ord Rites of the Ancient Ch of E and W*, Pueblo, 1990; Auth, *Daily Pryr in the Early Ch*, SPCK/OUP, 1981; Auth, *The Angl Ordinal*, SPCK, 1971. DD GTS 2005; Hon Cn Dio NI 1990. bradshaw.1@nd.edu

BRADY, Amanda B Mandy (At) PO Box 15007, Atlanta GA 30333 **Chapl to Emory U Dio Atlanta Atlanta GA 2010-** B Lewes DE 12/31/1965 d James H R Brady & Amanda. BS W&M 1989; MDiv GTS 1997. D 6/7/1997 Bp Robert Wilkes Ihloff P 12/13/1997 Bp Frank Kellogg Allan. Int S Mk's Ch Evanston IL 2008-2010; Int S Paul's Epis Ch Newnan GA 2007-2008; P-in-c Emm Epis Ch Athens GA 1999-2007; Asst R S Mich And All Ang Ch Stone Mtn GA 1997-1999. mothermandy@emory.edu

BRADY, Christian Mark (CPa) 18 Hampton Ct, State College PA 16803 **D S Andr's Ch St Coll PA 2007-** B Houston TX 9/9/1968 s Charles D Brady & Martha Ann. BA Cor 1992; MA Wheaton Coll 1994; MS Oxf 1999; PhD Oxf 2000; Locally Formed 2002. D 12/21/2005 Bp Charles Edward Jenkins III P 10/20/2007 Bp Nathan Dwight Baxter. m 8/14/1993 Elizabeth Warma Brady c 2. cbrady@targoman.org

BRADY, Jane Tanaskovic (NJ) 45 Elizabeth St, Pemberton NJ 08068 **R Gr Ch Pemberton NJ 2007-** B Englewood NJ 6/7/1950 d John Tanaskovic & Mary J. BA U of Pennsylvania 1976; MDiv PrTS 1999; ThM PrTS 2001. D 12/13/2005 P 7/8/2006 Bp George Edward Councell. Ch of S Jn on the Mtn Bernardsville NJ 2006-2007. jane_brady@alumni.upenn.edu

BRADY, Susan Jane (Colo) No address on file. **D Ch Of The H Comf Broomfield CO 1985-** B Salt Lake City UT 10/8/1944 d Archibald Alexander Sproul & Margaret Lulu. BA U of Nthrn Colorado 1966. D 8/21/1985 Bp William Carl Frey. NAAD.

BRADY JR, Thomas Joseph (Chi) 5733 North Sheridan Road #16-C, Chicago IL 60660 B Chicago IL 3/6/1936 s Thomas Joseph Brady & Maxine. BA U IL 1958; STB GTS 1961. D 6/24/1961 Bp Charles L Street P 12/23/1961 Bp Gerald Francis Burrill. R S Clem's Ch Harvey IL 1964-1994; Cur Epis Ch Of The Atone Chicago IL 1961-1963. tbrady3578@aol.com

BRADY II, William Donald (CFla) 9870 W Fort Island Trl, Crystal River FL 34429 **S Marg's Ch Inverness FL 2007-** B Erie PA 5/28/1943 s William Brady & Elizabeth. AA Belhaven Coll 2007; Inst for Chr Stuides 2007. D 6/2/2007 Bp John Wadsworth Howe. m 7/2/1964 Wanda Brady c 2. Sexton S Anne's Ch Crystal River FL 2007-2008. skipwanda@gmail.com

BRAINARD, Mary-Lloyd (Ct) 3A Gold St, Stonington CT 06378 B Hartford CT 5/28/1936 d William Edmund Carey & Kathryn Margaret. BA Connecticut Coll 1995. D 12/12/1998 Bp Andrew Donnan Smith. c 3. D Calv Ch Stonington CT 1998-2005. NAAD. mlbrainard@snet.net

BRAINE, Beverly (Md) 2132 Corbett Rd., Monkton MD 21111 B Atlanta GA 1/9/1946 d Elmer Lee Barfield & Barbara Jane. BA Georgia St U 1969; MS Indiana U 1974; MDiv STUSo 1981; Med Towson U 1995. D 6/9/1981 P 1/1/1982 Bp William Gillette Weinhauer. c 4. Imm Epis Ch Glencoe MD 2002-2005; The Ch Of The Redeem Baltimore MD 1999-2002; S Dav's Ch Baltimore MD 1995-1996; Trin Ch Towson MD 1986-1993; Stuart Hall Staunton VA 1981-1986. bev46bud43@gmail.com

BRAKE, Mary Wood (Va) No address on file. B Fort Benning GA 12/13/1950 d Ralph Wilson Brake & Phyllis Elizabeth. U NC 1972; BA Amer U 1974; MDiv VTS 1978; U Of Basel Basel Ch 1983. D 8/18/1978 Bp John Alfred Baden P 3/1/1980 Bp David Henry Lewis Jr. Asst S Paul's Ch Ivy VA 1988-2002; Asst Emm Epis Ch Geneva 1201 CH 1978-1980. EvangES.

BRAKE JR, William Howard (EC) 104 Rockfish Ln, Duck NC 27949 B Rocky Mount NC 2/2/1941 s William Howard Brake & Minnie. BA U NC 1963; MDiv VTS 1966; Ldrshp Acad for New Directions 1977. D 6/29/1966 P 1/6/1967 Bp Thomas H Wright. m 11/3/1990 Jeannie Beatrice Hudspeth c 2. Assoc S Andr's By The Sea Nags Hd NC 2000-2006; R Pohick Epis Ch Lorton VA 1983-1999. Co-Ed, *Cmnty Action-A Drug Prog*; Auth, *Restoration & Rebirth of Little Fork Ch*. Bro of S Andr 1975. Jas T. Houghteling Awd BroSA 2006; Legion of Merit Awd BroSA 1999. billbrake@charter.net

BRAKEMAN, Lyn G (Mass) 203 Pemberton St Unit #, Cambridge MA 02140 **EFM Co-Coordntr Dio Massachusetts Boston MA 2009-** B New York NY 8/7/1938 d McDonald Gillespie & Margaret. BA Smith 1960; MA Col 1962; MDiv Yale DS 1982. D 6/13/1987 P 3/25/1988 Bp Arthur Edward Walmsley. m 11/23/1986 Richard John Simeone c 4. Assoc S Jn's Epis Ch Gloucester MA 1997-2010; Assoc S Alb's Ch Simsbury CT 1991-1997; Int H Trin Epis Ch Enfield CT 1990-1991; Asst Calv Ch Enfield CT 1987-1990. Auth, "Pray As You Are," *Presence*, SpiritualDirectors Intl , 2008; Auth, "The God Between Us: A Sprtlty of Relationships," Innisfree Press / Augsburg Fortress, 2001; Auth, "Sprtl Lemons, Biblic Wmn, Irreverant Laughter and Righteous Rage," Innisfree/Augsburg Books, 1997. Fell AAPC 1992; Rel Sis of Mercy 1996. lgb3888@earthlink.net

BRALL, Catherine Mary (Pgh) 321 Parkside Ave, Pittsburgh PA 15228 **Provost Trin Cathd Pittsburgh PA 2004-** B Evergreen Park IL 6/17/1958 d Donald Brall & Carol Anne. BS U IL 1981; MEM NWU 1988; MDiv TESM 1995; D.Min. Fuller TS 2010. D 6/17/1995 Bp Frank Tracy Griswold III P 12/17/1995 Bp Alden Moinet Hathaway. Stndg Com Pres Dio Pittsburgh Monroeville PA 2006; Stndg Com Dio Pittsburgh Monroeville PA 2003-2006; Dioc Coun, Presisent Dio Pittsburgh Monroeville PA 2000-2001; Cong Dvlp Dio Pittsburgh Monroeville PA 1999-2003; Cong Dvlp Dio Pittsburgh Monroeville PA 1999-2003; R Ch Of The Adv Pittsburgh PA 1995-2003. Dissertation, "Using the Rule of Ben to Form and Equip Cler for Epis Par Mnstry," Fuller TS, 2010. brall@trinitycathedralpgh.org

BRAMAN, Bruce Owen (Los) 417 Gough #326, San Francisco CA 94102 B Detroit MI 2/22/1942 s Robert Mann Braman & Lois Kathleen. BA Wayne 1964; Fuller TS 1966; STB EDS 1968. D 9/7/1968 P 3/1/1969 Bp Francis E I Bloy. S Paul's Epis Ch Elko NV 1978-1983; Asst S Thos Of Cbury Par Long Bch CA 1977-1978; Assoc R The Par Ch Of S Lk Long Bch CA 1975-1977; Asst The Par Of S Matt Pacific Palisades CA 1974-1975; Asst R S Paul's Epis Ch Tustin CA 1972-1974; Vic Ch Of The H Comm Gardena CA 1969-1972; Cur All SS Epis Ch Riverside CA 1968-1969. Auth, "Ti Einai Theologia". bob22scribe@yahoo.com

BRAMBILA, Gerardo Brambila (Los) 483 W. 80Th. Avenue, Denver CO 80221 **Stndg Com Mem Dio Colorado Denver CO 2011-; R Our Merc Sav Epis Ch Denver CO 2010-** B Oaxaca Oaxaca Mexico 1/7/1958 Ae Unam/ Nunez Pragosa Mex City Mx 1980; CTh Epis TS of The SW 2001. D 6/2/2001 P 1/12/2002 Bp Joseph Jon Bruno. m 2/3/2010 Viviana Elena Brambila c 5. Vic H Fam Mssn No Hollywood CA 2005-2009; P-in-c S Marg's Epis Ch So Gate CA 2004-2005; Assoc S Fran' Par Palos Verdes Estates CA 2001-2004. gerardobrambila@hotmail.com

BRAMBLE, Peter Wilkin Duke (LI) 1417 Union St, Brooklyn NY 11213 **R S Mk's Ch Brooklyn NY 1997-** B Harris MS 7/27/1945 s Charles William Bramble & Margaret Gertrude. Lic Codrington Coll 1970; MA Ya 1972; STM Ya Berk 1974; PhD U of Connecticut 1976. Trans from Church in the Province Of The West Indies 8/1/1977 Bp David Keller Leighton Sr. m 12/28/1972 Jocelyn Cheryl Nanton. Ch Of S Kath Of Alexandria Baltimore MD 1977-1997; Asst P Ch Of The H Trin Middletown CT 1973-1976. pwdbramble@juno.com

BRAMLETT, Bruce Richard (ECR) 5 Pine Tree Ct, San Rafael CA 94090 B Middletown CT 9/9/1948 s James Bramlett & Olive Marie. Fllshp CDSP; Fllshp Grad Theol Un; BA Cntrl 1970; MDiv EDS 1976. D 6/18/1977 P 2/1/1978 Bp Alexander Doig Stewart. c 2. R S Paul's Epis Ch San Rafael CA 1995-2003; S Mths Epis Ch San Ramon CA 1994-1995; S Jn The Bapt Lodi CA 1986-1988; S Mk's Ch Teaneck NJ 1979-1985; Assoc S Ptr's Ch Essex Fells NJ 1979; S Jn's Ch Williamstown MA 1977-1978. Auth, "Israel, Land & St In Tchg Jewish-Chr Relatns," *Shofar mag*, 1988. Soc Of S Jn The Evang, Epis Peace Fellowshi. Graebe Awd; Bogert Tchg Fell CDSP; Newhall Tchg Fell Grad Theol Un; Mart Luther King Awd Marin Cnty Human Rts Cmsn. brucebramlett@sbcglobal.net

BRAMLETT, Robert Gordon (Mil) 419 E Court St, Janesville WI 53545 B Detroit MI 10/6/1941 s Kenneth R Bramlett & Jane. BA NEU 1971; MDiv SWTS 1974; DMin McCormick TS 1985. D 6/8/1974 Bp Quintin Ebenezer Primo Jr P 12/14/1974 Bp James Winchester Montgomery. m 8/22/1970 Linda J Field c 1. R Trin Ch Janesville WI 1991-2004; R S Andr's Epis Ch Valparaiso IN 1985-1990; Ch Of The Annunc Bridgeview IL 1979-1985; Vic S Anselm Epis Ch Lehigh Acres FL 1975-1979; Cur S Mary's Ch Pk Ridge IL 1974-1975. OHC. frrgb@charter.net

BRANCHE, Ronald Clifford (VI) PO Box 28, Main Street, Tortola British Virgin Islands **Reverend S Geo Mtyr Ch Tortola VG 2002-** B Trinidad 8/18/ 1946 BA U of The W Indies. Trans from Church in the Province Of The West Indies 5/10/2002 Bp Theodore Athelbert Daniels. m 11/26/1972 Heather Sharon Theresa Nicholas c 1. S Geo Sch Tortola 2002-2004. stgeorgeschurch@surfbvi.com

BRANDENBURG, John Paul (SO) 56482 Boyd Avenue, Bridgeport OH 43912 **Mem, Dioc Coun Dio Sthrn Ohio Cincinnati OH 2010-; P-in-c E Cntrl Ohio Area Mnstry Cambridge OH 2006-** B Louisville KY 2/5/1946 s John Paul Brandenburg & Betty Mary. BA Franciscan U of Steubenville 1967; S Jn Vianney Sem 1971; Wheeling Jesuit U 2006. Rec from Roman Catholic 3/8/1992 as Deacon Bp William Grant Black. m 10/2/1971 Marian Kay Brandenburg c 1. D E Cntrl Ohio Area Mnstry Cambridge OH 2003-2005; D Ch Of Our Sav Cincinnati OH 1991-2003. Angl Acad, Cincinnati OH 1991; EUC 1990-1994; Living Stones 2003-2007. john_brandenburg@comcast.net

BRANDENBURG, Nancy Lee (SO) Saint John'S Church, Worthington OH 43085 B Sioux City IA 11/2/1938 d Lester Howard Hamman & Letty Emma. MS OH SU; BD Capital U 1982; Angl Acad 1994. D 11/11/1994 Bp Herbert Thompson Jr. m 8/28/1976 David Brandenburg c 4. NAAD Curs. nancyb1102@aol.com

BRANDON, Bonnie Patricia (Los) 604 S Dickel St, Anaheim CA 92805 B Anaheim CA 7/7/1961 d Richard Ellison Brandon & Lorraine Idabell. AA Fullerton Coll 1986; BA Chapman U Orage CA 2002; MDiv ETSBH 2007. D 6/9/ 2007 P 1/12/2008 Bp Joseph Jon Bruno. Assoc S Andr's Epis Ch Irvine CA 2007-2009; S Clem's-By-The-Sea Par San Clemente CA 2002-2007. bonniebrandon@adelphia.net

BRANDON, Karen Dale (RG) 226 Jupiter Dr, White Sands Missile Range NM 88002 B Granite City IL 9/21/1948 MDiv SW Bapt TS 1973; DMin SW Bapt TS 1984; MS The U of Virginia 2005. D 11/23/2002 P 6/21/2003 Bp Terence Kelshaw. bogsnake2@mac.com

BRANDON II, Miles Raymond (Tex) 1501 W 30th St, Austin TX 78703 **All SS Epis Ch Austin TX 2002-** B Houston TX 12/3/1973 s Nathan Ray Brandon & Ellen Gordon. BA U of Texas 1998; MDiv VTS 2002. D 6/22/2002 Bp Claude Edward Payne P 5/17/2003 Bp Don Adger Wimberly. m 11/3/2007 Ashley Brandon c 1. Yth Min S Mart's Epis Ch Houston TX 1996-1999. mbrandon@stjuliansaustin.org

BRANDT JR, George Walter (NY) 225 W 99th St, New York NY 10025 **R S Mich's Ch New York NY 1994-** B New York NY 11/30/1943 s George Walter Brandt & Lillian Bertha. BA Franklin & Marshall Coll 1965; JD Boston Coll 1968; EDS 1976; MDiv Nash 1978; Cert Col 1995. D 6/3/1978 Bp Paul Moore Jr P 12/17/1978 Bp James Winchester Montgomery. Dir Emmaus Hse Epis Ch Atlanta GA 1991-1994; Cn For Wrshp And Cmnty Outreach Cathd Of S Phil Atlanta GA 1988-1994; All Souls Ch New York NY 1988; P-in-c All Souls Ch New York NY 1987-1988; Exec Coun Appointees New York NY 1983-1988; Ch Of The Ascen Buffalo NY 1982-1983; Urban Mssnr Dio Wstrn New York Tonawanda NY 1982-1983; Vic S Marg's Ch Chicago IL 1978-1982. Assoc Soc Of S Jn The Evang; EUC; UBE. Cn Prov Ch Of Cntrl Afr 1995. gwbrandt16@gmail.com

BRANDT, Robert George (LI) 25 Rocky Hill Road, Mt. Sinai NY 11766 B New York NY 7/26/1938 s George Wilma Brandt & Edith Virginia. Cert Hofstra U 1963; BA Hofstra U 1963; MA U of Vermont 1966; MA St U of NY at Stony Brook 1968; MALS St U of NY at Stony Brook 1970; (PhD) ABD St. Jn's U 1973; Cert St. Jn's U 1973; Cert in Theol Stds Mercer TS 1976; Cert Yashiva U 1982; Fllshp Natl Endwmt for the Hmnts 1983; Fllshp Fulbright Fndt 1988; Fllshp Natl Endwmt for the Hmnts 1993; Fllshp Milton V Brown Fndt 1995. D 6/5/1976 P 12/18/1976 Bp Jonathan Goodhue Sherman. m 6/1/ 1963 Phyllis Joan Schaaf. Vic Chr Ch-Epis Port Jefferson NY 2002-2010; Supply P Dio Long Island Garden City NY 2000-2001; P-in-c S Mk's Epis Ch Medford NY 1995-2000; Asst S Mk's Epis Ch Medford NY 1986-1995; Asst Chr Ch-Epis Port Jefferson NY 1983-1986; Asst S Jn's Ch Huntington NY 1981-1983; Asst S Ann's Ch Sayville NY 1976-1981. Auth, "Jn Ruskin & The Gld Of S Geo"; Auth, "Indn Art As A Reflection Of The Indn Wrld View"; Auth, "The Icon," *A Window Into The Byzantine Mind.* Ord Of S Lk, ERM; Tertiary Of The Soc Of S Fran. Fndt Fell Milton V Brown 1995; Fell Natl Endwmnt For Hmnts 1993; Fulbright Fellowow To India 1988; Fell Natl Endwmnt For Hmnts 1987. rgbrandt38@yahoo.com

BRANNOCK-WANTER, Christina Combs (Lex) PO Box 27, Paris KY 40362 **S Ptr's Ch Paris KY 2010-** B Johnson City TN 10/12/1956 d Kent Combs Brannock & Beatrice Anna. BFA E Tennessee St U 1977; MA Emory U 1983; MDiv GTS 1983. D 6/15/1986 P 5/1/1987 Bp William Evan Sanders. m 7/14/ 2001 Henry Paul Wanter c 2. S Paul's Ch Windsor VT 2010; R S Jas Ch Woodstock VT 2000-2009; Ch Of The Gd Samar Knoxville TN 1999-2000; Chair of Anglo-Cath Strng Com Dio E Tennessee Knoxville TN 1994-1995; R Thankful Memi Ch Chattanooga TN 1992-1998; Anglo-Cath Strng Com Dio E Tennessee Knoxville TN 1992-1994; Dept of Yth Dio E Tennessee Knoxville TN 1987-1992; Vic S Mk's Ch Copperhill TN 1987-1992; D Gr Ch Chattanooga TN 1986-1987. cbrannockwanter@gmail.com

BRANNOCK-WANTER JR, Henry Paul (Vt) 257 Us Route 5, Hartland VT 05048 **R S Lk's Ch Chester VT 2002-** B Niagara Falls NY 5/15/1949 s Henry Paul Wanter & Vera Arlene. Van; BS Un 1972; MDiv GTS 1984. D 7/1/1984 P 4/1/1985 Bp William Evan Sanders. m 7/14/2001 Christina Combs Brannock c 1. R S Raphael's Epis Ch Crossville TN 1995-2001; Dio E Tennessee Knoxville TN 1985-1994; Vic S Raphael's Epis Ch Crossville TN 1985-1994; D-In-Trng Gr Ch Chattanooga TN 1984-1985. hpwant@gmail.com

BRANNON, Kenneth Hoffman (Ida) St. Thomas Episcopal Church, PO Box 1070, Sun Valley ID 83353 **Chair, Deputation to GC 2012 Dio Idaho Boise ID 2010-; Secy, Stndg Com Dio Idaho Boise ID 2008-; R S Thos Epis Ch Sun Vlly ID 2007-** B Fort Collins CO 8/23/1968 s Richard Bland Brannon & Judith Hoffman. BA Wheaton Coll 1990; MA NYU 1997; MDiv VTS 2003. D 3/8/2003 P 9/20/2003 Bp Mark Sean Sisk. m 3/18/1995 Rachel Miller c 2. Assoc R S Barn Ch Irvington on Hudson NY 2003-2007; Sem S Alb's Par Washington DC 2002-2003; CE Dir Ch Of The H Trin New York NY 1996-2000. Co-Auth, "Superheroes, monsters, and babies," *The Arts in Psych*, Elsevier Sci, 2002. Soc for the Increase of the Mnstry 2001. Graduated cl VTS 2003; Merit Schlrshp VTS 2000. millerbrannon@cox.net

BRANNON, Stephen Nave (NCal) 19275 Robinson Rd, Sonoma CA 95476 B Metropolis IL 4/20/1944 s William Andrew Brannon & Mary Hester. Sthrn Illinois U 1964; BA U IL 1966; STB GTS 1969; JD U of San Francisco 1981. D 5/24/1969 P 12/1/1969 Bp Albert A Chambers. m 1/30/1965 Barbara F Brannon c 1. R Trin Ch Sonoma CA 1995-2005; Stndg Com Dio Nthrn California Sacramento CA 1991-1994; Dio Nthrn California Sacramento CA 1989-2000; Chapl Berkeley Cbury Fndt Berkeley CA 1988-1995; Vic S Edm's Epis Ch Pacifica CA 1984-1988; Int Trsfg Epis Ch San Mateo CA 1984; Assoc Ch Of The Adv Of Chr The King San Francisco CA 1981-1984; Assoc Trin Ch San Francisco CA 1977-1981; Vic S Andr's Ch Peoria IL 1975-1977; Int S Matt's Epis Ch Bloomington IL 1973-1974; Vic S Thos Ch Salem IL 1969-1972; Dio Nthrn California Sacramento CA 1000. Cmnty Of S Mary; OHC. snbrannon@aol.com

BRANSCOMB JR, Wm (Ala) 532 W Ariel Ave, Foley AL 36535 B Dayton OH 9/22/1925 s William Maurice Branscomb & Ada Loiza. BA Otterbein Coll 1960; BD VTS 1963; MDiv VTS 1964. D 6/15/1963 Bp Robert Fisher Gibson Jr P 6/1/1964 Bp Samuel B Chilton. m 5/28/1949 Berta Branscomb c 3. Vic Imm Ch Bay Minette AL 2006-2007; R Gr Ch Birmingham AL 1988-1997; R Ch Of The H Comm Charleston SC 1984-1987; R S Andrews's Epis Ch Birmingham AL 1971-1984; Asst S Paul's Epis Ch Alexandria VA 1968-1971; Asst Min Chr Epis Ch Charlottesville VA 1965-1968; R Gr Ch Bremo Bluff VA 1963-1965. Awd Cmnty Kitchen 2006; Golden Rule Awd 1997; Bro Brian Awd 1982.

BRANSCOMBE, Mike (SwFla) 1010 Charles St, Clearwater FL 33755 **Assoc R Ch Of The Ascen Clearwater FL 2003-** B Birmingham UK 2/23/1965 BA U of Durham GB 1995; DMin TESM 2008. Trans from Church Of England 6/14/2003 as Priest Bp John Bailey Lipscomb. m 8/27/1988 Margaret Valerie Booker c 1. COM (Chair) Dio SW Florida Sarasota FL 2007-2011; Asst R S Alfred's Epis Ch Palm Harbor FL 2001-2003. mikeb@churchofascension.org

BRANSCOME III, Dexter Arno (Miss) 1 Oakleigh Pl, Jackson MS 39211 **S Phil's Ch Jackson MS 2003-** B Greenwood MS 6/8/1937 BA U of Mississippi 1959; MA U of Alabama 1975. D 1/4/2003 Bp Alfred Clark Marble Jr. c 4. dexbran@jam.rr.com

BRANSON III, John (Ct) 65 Myrtle Ave, Westport CT 06880 **R Chr And H Trin Ch Westport CT 1991-** B Concord NH 5/28/1948 s John H Branson & Virginia. BA Coll of Wooster 1971; MDiv Ya Berk 1974. D 6/5/1974 Bp Philip Alan Smith P 3/1/1975 Bp Morgan Porteus. m 6/23/1973 Judyth Branson c 1. R S Paul's Epis Ch Chatham NJ 1980-1991; Trin Epis Ch Hartford CT 1974-1980. jbranson@chtwestport.org

BRANSTETTER, Kent Alan (At) 3332 James Harbor Way, Lawrenceville GA 30044 **R S Edw's Epis Ch Lawrenceville GA 1996-** B Boone IA 12/4/1950 s Robert Deane Branstetter & Geraldine I. BA Oral Roberts U 1976; MA Point Loma Coll 1982; MDiv Ya Berk 1985; MA Drew U 1989. D 6/22/1985 P 12/1/1985 Bp Charles Brinkley Morton. m 8/24/1991 Rebecca Jean Adams c 2. P-in-c Ch Of The Atone Fair Lawn NJ 1991-1996; Int S Andr's Epis Ch Lincoln Pk NJ 1990-1991; Int S Mk's Ch W Orange NJ 1989-1990; Cur S Barth's Epis Ch Poway CA 1985-1987. kbranstetter@stedwardsonline.org

BRANT, George Henry (Nwk) 601 Park St Apt 11-D, Bordentown NJ 08505 B Stanton Bridge UK 10/1/1921 s William John Brant & Mary Elizabeth. ATCM U Tor 1937; LTh Emml Saskatoon Sask. 1945; BA U Sask 1945; BD Emml Saskatoon Sask. 1947. Trans from Anglican Church of Canada 10/1/1950 Bp Charles Bernard Barfoot. m 5/15/1966 Josephine Joan Calvacca c 3. S Jas' Epis Ch Hackettstown NJ 1969-1986; Assoc Gr Ch Madison NJ 1964-1966; P-in-c S Jn's Ch Dover NJ 1950-1952. bordharry@aol.com

BRANTINGHAM, Nancy Marie (Minn) 3185 County Road 6, Long Lake MN 55356 **Assoc R S Steph The Mtyr Ch Minneapolis MN 2009-** B Minneapolis MN 1/13/1954 d Robert John Provo & Sue Rita. BA U MN 1981; MA The Coll of St. Cathr 2002; Cert SWTS 2004. D 6/15/2005 P 12/15/2005 Bp James Louis Jelinek. m 4/6/1974 Henry Baldwin Baldwin Brantingham c 2. Assoc R Trin Ch Excelsior MN 2005-2009. nancy.brantingham@gmail.com

BRATHWAITE, Christopher Ethelbert (CFla) 1709 N John Young Pkwy, Kissimmee FL 34741 B Barbados 9/1/1947 s Whitley Dacosta & Louise. MTS Asbury TS 2008. D 9/7/2008 P 5/30/2009 Bp John Wadsworth Howe. m 9/26/1986 Genevieve Kelly c 2. chris.brat@hotmail.com

BRATHWAITE, Percy Alphonso (NY) 17 Granada Cres Apt 6, White Plains NY 10603 **Gr Ch (W Farms) Bronx NY 2002-; Vic S Martha's Ch Bronx NY 2002-** B BB 11/19/1940 s Percy Brathwaite & Octavia. MDiv Ya Berk 1989. D 7/8/1989 Bp Clarence Nicholas Coleridge P 1/1/1990 Bp Walter Decoster Dennis Jr. m 11/17/1990 Delores Scott Whittle. Vic Calv and St Geo New York NY 1996-2002; S Andr's Ch New York NY 1993-1995; Gr Ch White Plains NY 1991-1993. Epis Black Caucus. DEEPERCY@AOL.COM

BRAUN, Elise (Vt) Wood Road, Box 1033, Stowe VT 05672 B New Britain CT 10/7/1932 d Samuel Seymour Holmes & Julia. U of Miami; BA U NC 1954; Cert Dioc Study Prog for Lay People Middlebury VT 1991. D 10/2/1991 Bp Daniel Lee Swenson. m 4/24/1970 Robert Thompson Braun c 1. D S Jn's In The Mountains Stowe VT 1991-1999.

BRAUN, James Richard (Mil) 3810 Sherrie Ln, Racine WI 53405 **R S Matt's Ch Kenosha WI 1985-** B Racine WI 5/24/1949 s Jerome J Braun & Dorothy J. BS U of Wisconsin 1971; MDiv Nash 1974. D 4/19/1974 P 11/1/1974 Bp Charles Thomas Gaskell. m 8/14/1976 Karen Killingstad c 2. R S Matt's Ch Kenosha WI 1985-2011; Cur S Matt's Ch Kenosha WI 1975-1984; Asst Gr Ch Madison WI 1974-1975. jrbraun@gmail.com

BRAUZA, Ellen Lederer (WNY) 4210 Gunnville Road, Clarence NY 14031 **Vic St Johns Epis Youngstown NY 2005-** B Buffalo NY 10/9/1950 d Erwin August Lederer & Norma Lillian. BA Valparaiso U 1972; MA Chr The King Sem 1986; MDiv Bex 2000. D 1/20/2001 P 8/19/2001 Bp J Michael Garrison. m 11/12/1977 Walter Brauza c 2. Co-Vic Ch Of The Ascen Buffalo NY 2004-2005; Asst S Paul's Epis Ch Harris Hill Williamsville NY 2001-2003; Adj Instr Bex Columbus OH 2000-2003. Buffalo CHS 2005; SCHC 2002-2011. godmom1@gmail.com

BRAWLEY, Anna (Ala) 65 E Huron St, Chicago IL 60611 **R S Barth's Epis Ch Florence AL 2010-** B Greenwood SC 7/3/1965 d Robert Lawson Brawley & Jane Amelia Patrick. AB Erskine Coll 1987; MDiv Ya Berk 1992; STM Ya Berk 1994; PhD Van 1999; Cert. in Angl Stds SWTS 2008. D 6/6/2009 P 6/15/2010 Bp Jeffrey Dean Lee. anna_brawley@hotmail.com

BRAWLEY, Joan Biddles (CFla) 631 W Lake Elbert Dr, Winter Haven FL 33881 **Assoc The Epis Ch Of The Gd Shpd Lake Wales FL 2007-** B Portsmouth VA 5/18/1951 d Frank Langley Kirby & Lucy Joan. BA Mary Baldwin Coll Stanton VA 1973; MDiv Asbury TS 2007. D 6/2/2007 Bp John Wadsworth Howe. m 7/19/1975 Marion Porter Brawley c 4. jkbrawley@hotmail.com

BRAXTON JR, Louis (Nwk) 480 Warwick Ave, Teaneck NJ 07666 B Paris TN 6/5/1956 s Louis Braxton & Shirley Junita. MS No Dakota St U; SWTS; BA Concordia Coll 1978; MA EDS 1984. D 1/6/1985 Bp Harold Anthony Hopkins Jr P 9/1/1985 Bp Walter Decoster Dennis Jr. Chr Ch Teaneck NJ 1986-1993; Chr's Ch Rye NY 1985-1986; Cur Chr Ch Teaneck NJ 1984-1986; Asst Geth Cathd Fargo ND 1981-1982.

BRAY, Doris S (Be) 443 Franklin Ave, Palmerton PA 18071 **Cn Pstr Dio Bethlehem Bethlehem PA 1996-** B Palmerton PA 11/21/1929 d Walter Thomas Steinmetz & Laura Amelia. Cert Moravian TS 1980. D 9/21/1978 P 6/2/1979 Bp Lloyd Edward Gressle. m 7/12/1952 Marvin Walter Bray c 3. Chair of Renwl and Evang Com Dio Bethlehem Bethlehem PA 1994-1998; Assoc All SS Epis Ch Lehighton PA 1989-1999; Assoc S Jn's Epis Ch Palmerton PA 1989-1999; Stwdshp Consult Dio Bethlehem Bethlehem PA 1988-1994; Renwl and Evang Com Dio Bethlehem Bethlehem PA 1985-1994; Sprtl Dir for Curs Dio Bethlehem Bethlehem PA 1985-1986; COM Dio Bethlehem Bethlehem PA 1980-1986; Search Consult Dio Bethlehem Bethlehem PA 1978-1999; Asst All SS Epis Ch Lehighton PA 1978-1988; Asst S Jn's Epis Ch Palmerton PA 1978-1988. SCHC 1993. Cn Pstr Dio Bethlehem 1996. revdoris@ptd.net

BRAY, Norman H. (CGC) 4362 Lafayette St, Mariana FL 32446 **R S Lk's Ch Marianna FL 2007-** B El Paso TX 9/2/1951 s James Lee Bray & Mary Jean. BS U Of Mobile Mobile AL 2004; MDiv GTS 2007. D 6/2/2007 P 5/3/2008 Bp Philip Menzie Duncan II. m 1/26/1970 Eileen M Bray c 2. norbray@yahoo.com

BRDLIK, Christopher M F (Nwk) 914 Ridge Rd, Newton NJ 07860 B Hinsdale IL 9/7/1951 s Mel F Brdlik & Dolores. AB Ham 1973; MDiv VTS 1977; Fllshp Coll of Preachers 1988. D 6/12/1977 Bp Frank Stanley Cerveny P 1/6/1978 Bp Jackson Earle Gilliam. m 6/18/1977 Debra Cleveland c 3. R Calv Epis Ch Summit NJ 1995-2010; VTS Alexandria VA 1991-1995; R S Jn's Epis Ch Waynesboro VA 1984-1995; R S Andr's Ch Clifton Forge VA 1981-1984; Cur Ch Of The Incarn Great Falls MT 1977-1981. Auth, *arts & Revs*. chrisbrdlik@gmail.com

BREAKEY, Pamela Jean (WMich) 54581 California Rd, Dowagiac MI 49047 B Berkeley CA 3/26/1946 d Loyd Warner Breakey & Bethea Betty Emily. BA MI SU 1969; MA MI SU 1973; MDiv SWTS 1996. D 6/8/1996 P 2/26/1997 Bp Edward Lewis Lee Jr. m 1/2/2002 Michael Heidenreich c 3. Assoc R S Barn Epis Ch Portage MI 2003-2004; R S Paul's Epis Ch Dowagiac MI 2000-2003; Assoc R Chr Epis Ch No Hills Pittsburgh PA 1997-2000. Contributing ABC Patient, "The Quiet War: Profiles of Wmn Facing Advncd Breast Cancer," *Documentary Film*, Affinity Films, 2006. scarletdahlia@frontier.com

BRECHNER, Eric Lonell (NJ) Po Box 126, Gibbsboro NJ 08026 **Ch Of S Jn-In-The-Wilderness Gibbsboro NJ 1996-** B Los Angeles CA 1/12/1955 s Verne Lonell Brechner & Virginia Marguerite. BA W&M 1977; MDiv GTS 1982; STM GTS 1990. D 6/19/1982 P 2/5/1983 Bp Robert C Rusack. Asst S Jas Ch New York NY 1988-1989; S Jas Epis Ch S Jas NY 1988-1989; S Jn The Evang Mssn Needles CA 1986-1988; Cur The Epis Ch Of The Blessed Sacr Placentia CA 1982-1985. ebrechner@sprynet.com

BRECHT, Laura Berger (SanD) 3425 Santa Saba Rd, Borrego Springs CA 92004 **R S Barn Ch Borrego Sprg CA 2010-** B Cincinnati OH 10/23/1949 d Carl G Berger & Martha L. BA U CO 1971; MCP Harv 1976; MDiv The TS at The U So 2008. D 6/14/2008 P 1/24/2009 Bp John Leslie Rabb. m 8/27/1977 Lyle A Brecht c 2. Epis Campus Min Dio Maryland Baltimore MD 2002-2005. laura.brecht@gmail.com

BRECKENRIDGE, Elaine Howlett (Spok) 31 W 37th Ave, Spokane WA 99203 **R S Dav's Ch Spokane WA 2004-** B Henderson NV 6/11/1957 d Gail Edward Howlett & Phyllis Mina. BA Westminster Coll 1980; MDiv EDS 1987. D 4/25/1987 Bp George Edmonds Bates P 3/25/1988 Bp Allen Lyman Bartlett Jr. m 5/12/1990 Frank G Breckenridge c 2. Assoc Gr Ch Tucson AZ 1998-2004; Vic S Jn's Epis Ch Logan UT 1994-1998; Dio Utah Salt Lake City UT 1993-1998; Int Ch Of The Resurr Centerville UT 1993-1994; Dio Kentucky Louisville KY 1992; Asst S Thos Epis Ch And Sch San Antonio TX 1991-1992; Asst Trin Ch Swarthmore PA 1989-1991; Cur S Dav's Ch Wayne PA 1987-1989. mother_elaine@comcast.net

BRECKENRIDGE, Ella Huff (Miss) 1825 Albert Street, Alexandria LA 71301 B Orlando FL 1/27/1941 d Marshall Edward Huff & Aileen L. MS Florida St U 1981; M Ed U of No Florida 1985; MDiv Epis TS of The SW 2002. D 6/15/2002 Bp Robert Jefferson Hargrove Jr P 5/29/2003 Bp D(avid) Bruce Mac Pherson. c 1. Chr Ch Corning NY 2009-2011; S Thad Epis Ch Aiken SC 2006-2009; Ch Of The Nativ Greenwood MS 2005-2006; Dio Alabama Birmingham AL 2005; Trin Epis Ch Florence AL 2003-2005; Cur S Mich's Epis Ch Pineville LA 2003; S Tim's Ch Alexandria LA 2002. ehbreck@aol.com

BRECKENRIDGE, William Allen (Az) 2721 N Dos Hombres Rd, Tucson AZ 85715 B New Orleans LA 4/7/1952 s Sidney Taylor Breckenridge & Francis Thelma. AA Jones Cnty Jr Coll Ellisville MS 1972; BA Mississippi St U 1975; MDiv STUSo 1978. D 5/21/1978 P 6/1/1979 Bp Duncan Montgomery Gray Jr. m 8/18/1973 Donna Durham. R Ch Of S Matt Tucson AZ 2001-2009; Dio

Arizona Phoenix AZ 1992-2001; Dio Sthrn Virginia Norfolk VA 1981-1992; Vic S Fran Of Assisi Ch Philadelphia MS 1978-1981; Vic S Matt's Epis Ch Kosciusko MS 1978-1981. ESMHE.

BRECKINRIDGE IV, Alexander Negus (Oly) 8398 NE 12th St, Medina WA 98039 **S Thos Ch Medina WA 2009-** B Beckley WV 12/7/1951 s Alexander Negus Breckinridge & Beverly. BA U NC 1974; JD Tul 1979; MDiv Epis TS of The SW 1998. D 5/30/1998 Bp Charles Edward Jenkins III P 6/24/1999 Bp Claude Edward Payne. m 5/28/1977 Jeanne Ledoux Provosky c 3. S Andrews Epis Sch Austin TX 2005-2009; R S Alb's Epis Ch Austin Manchaca TX 1999-2005; Assoc S Mich's Ch Austin TX 1998-1999. lbreckinridge@gmail.com

BREDLAU, Mary Theresa (Nev) 8520 W Hammer Ln, Las Vegas NV 89149 **Dn Dio Nevada Las Vegas NV 2011-; Dn Dio Nevada Las Vegas NV 2010-; P Gr In The Desert Epis Ch Las Vegas NV 2008-** B Milbank SD 7/2/1945 d Jerome Anthony Loehrer & Avelline Adelaide. AA Corbett Jr Coll Crookston MN 1966; BA Our Lady Of The Lake U San Antonio TX 1970; Cert Corpus Christi Cntr Phoenix AZ 1988; Dplma Creighton U 1988; MA S Mary U Winona MN 1991; Sprtl Dir Redemptorist Renwl Cntr, Tucson, AZ 2005; CT Assoc Death Ed & Counslg 2006. D 2/14/1995 P 9/17/1995 Bp Stewart Clark Zabriskie. c 2. P Chr Ch Las Vegas NV 2001-2008; Int All SS Epis Ch Las Vegas NV 1999-2000; Dio Nevada Las Vegas NV 1990-1996. Auth, "Grief Guides," self: copyrighted. AssemblyEpHealthcareChaplaincy 1995; Assn Of Profsnl Chapl 1991; Benedictine Oblate 1982; Interfaith Coun Nccj 1990-1996. revmaryb@cox.net

BREEDEN, James Pleasant (Mass) 29 Rope Ferry Rd # 3755, Hanover NH 03755 B Minneapolis MN 10/14/1934 s Pleasant George Breeden & Florence Beatrice. BA Dart 1956; Cert Grad Sch Ecum Stds 1959; MDiv UTS 1960; EdD Harv 1972. D 6/1/1961 P 12/1/1961 Bp Anson Phelps Stokes Jr. Bp'S Vic On Civil Rts Dio Massachusetts Boston MA 1963-1965; Cn The Cathd Ch Of S Paul Boston MA 1963-1965; Cur S Jn's S Jas Epis Ch Roxbury MA 1961-1963. Cmsn On Ch And Race / Massachusetts Coun Of Ch 1967-1969. Man Of The Year Boston Jr ChmbrCom 1964; Roxbury Proj Awd 73; Alper Awd Ma Clu 78.

BREEDLOVE, William L (Kan) 6630 Nall Ave, Mission KS 66202 **Assoc S Mich And All Ang Ch Mssn KS 2009-** B 8/23/1962 s Harry Breedlove & Linde. BS U of Sout Carolina 1984; MA U of So Carolina 1986; PhD The Florida St U 1993; MDiv Nash 2009. D 5/28/2009 Bp Mark Joseph Lawrence P 12/8/2009 Bp Dean Elliott Wolfe. m 6/19/1993 Susan P Morgan c 2. bill@stmaa.com

BREEDLOVE II, William Otis (NJ) 10 Winthrop Road, Somerset NJ 08873 B Indianapolis IN 1/15/1941 s William Otis Breedlove & Bessie. BA Butler U 1963; BD U Chi 1966; MS U IL 1968; CSD GTS 1991; DAS GTS 1991. D 6/8/1991 P 1/11/1992 Bp George Phelps Mellick Belshaw. m 8/17/1968 Elizabeth Ann Breedlove. S Andr's Ch Trenton NJ 2001-2003; Int S Andr's Ch Mt Holly NJ 1997-1999; Vic Trin Epis Old Swedes Ch Swedesboro NJ 1991-1995. Third Ord, SSF 1988. wbreedloveii@verizon.net

BREESE, Mary Schrom (WMo) 2533 Francis St, Saint Joseph MO 64501 B Kansas City MO 12/27/1946 d Stanley James Schrom & Helen. BA Bryn 1969; MA U of Iowa 1973; Lon 1977; MDiv Nash 1981. D 5/24/1982 P 11/1/1982 Bp Richard Frank Grein. m 6/5/1988 Sidney Samuel Breese. P-in-c S Lk's Epis Ch Excelsior Sprg MO 1995-2002; Assoc For Pstr Care Gr And H Trin Cathd Kansas City MO 1993-1995; R Gr Epis Ch Ottawa KS 1990-1993; R S Mk's Epis Ch Wadsworth OH 1988-1990; Vic Epis Ch Of S Geo Canyon TX 1984-1988; Chapl Dio NW Texas Lubbock TX 1983; Cn To The Ordnry Dio Kansas Topeka KS 1982-1983. Auth, "Mod Liturg". Epis TS Of The SW, Austin Tx 1990-1993. Mdiv cl Nash Nashotah WI 1981. momary1400@aol.com

BREESE, Sidney Samuel (WMo) 2533 Francis St, Saint Joseph MO 64501 B Schenectady NY 1/23/1942 s Samuel Sidney Breese & Ruth Avery Page. Resurr CA 1965; BA U of Waterloo 1965; MDiv VTS 1969; Washington Urban Trng Prog 1969; IAPS 1974; Ldrshp Acad for New Directions 1980; Shoresh Study Tour IL 1996. D 6/11/1969 P 6/1/1970 Bp Ned Cole. m 6/5/1988 Mary Schrom c 2. R Chr Epis Ch S Jos MO 1998-2007; P-in-c S Mary's Ch Savannah MO 1997-1998; Yth Dir Dio Kansas Topeka KS 1993-1996; R S Ald's Ch Olathe KS 1990-1995; R Ch Of S Jas The Apos Clovis NM 1985-1987; R S Andr's Epis Ch Las Cruces NM 1981-1985; P-in-c Centralia Effingham Salem Bradenton FL 1980-1981; P-in-c S Jn's Ch Centralia IL 1978-1980; P-in-c S Thos Ch Salem IL 1978-1980; R S Jude's Epis Ch Fenton MI 1975-1978; Asst Chr Ch Detroit MI 1973-1975; R Trin Epis Ch W Branch MI 1971-1973; Cur Emm Ch Norwich NY 1969-1971. Auth, *Chr Looks at Drugs*. ssbreese@aol.com

BREHE, Stephen Louis (Mont) 912 Stuart St., Helena MT 59601 B Springfield IL 3/8/1947 s Melvin Louis Brehe & Mildred. BA Mar 1969; MA U of Missouri 1972; MDiv SWTS 1979; DMin GTF 1986. D 9/5/1979 Bp James Winchester Montgomery P 3/24/1980 Bp Quintin Ebenezer Primo Jr. m 6/9/1969 Jacqueline Ellert c 2. S Ptr's Par Helena MT 1991-2010; R S Paul's Ch Minneapolis MN 1986-1991; Ch of the H Sprt Belmont MI 1980-1986; Cur S Mary's Ch Pk Ridge IL 1979-1980. sbrehe912@gmaill.com

✠ **BREIDENTHAL, Rt Rev Thomas Edward** (SO) Diocese Of Southern Ohio, 412 Sycamore St, Cincinnati OH 45202 **Bp of Sthrn Ohio Dio Sthrn Ohio Cincinnati OH 2007-** B Jersey City NJ 3/3/1951 s Leslie Breidenthal & Ruth. BA Portland St U 1974; MA U of Victoria 1977; MDiv CDSP 1981; D Phil Oxf 1991. D 6/28/1981 P 6/12/1982 Bp Matthew Paul Bigliardi Con 4/28/2007 for SO. m 7/7/1984 Margaret Ann Garner c 2. Asstg P Ch Of S Mary The Vrgn New York NY 1999-2001; Prof of Chr Ethics and Moral Theol The GTS New York NY 1992-2001; R Trin Epis Ch Ashland Ashland OR 1989-1992; Sr Chapl Harvard-Westlake Sch N Hollywood CA 1986-1988; Stdt ECF Inc New York NY 1983-1984; Asst to the R S Mich And All Ang Ch Portland OR 1981-1983. Auth, "Sacr Unions," *Sacr Unions*, Cowley, 2006; Auth, "Neighbor-Christology: Reconstructing Chrsnty Before Supersessionism," *Cross Currents*, 1999; Auth, "The Politics of Incarn," *Mod Theol*, 1998; Auth, "Chr Households: The Sanctification of Nearness," *Chr Households: The Sanctification of nearness*, Cowley, 1997; Auth, "Sanctifying Nearness," *Our Selves, Our Souls & Bodies*, Cowley, 1996. Fell ECF 1983. tbreidenthal@diosohio.org

BREINER, Bert Fredrick (NY) 401 W 24th St, New York NY 10011 B Burlington VT 7/20/1948 s Roy Breiner & Margeret Helen. BD Geo 1970; STM GTS 1973; PhD U Of Birmingham Birmingham Gb 1988. D 6/16/1973 Bp Jonathan Goodhue Sherman P 12/1/1973 Bp Robert Lionne DeWitt. Hon Assoc Chr And S Steph's Ch New York NY 2002-2004; Gr Ch Sch New York New York NY 2001-2004; Assoc Gr Epis Ch New York NY 2000-2004; Assoc Chr And S Steph's Ch New York NY 1994-2000; Epis Ch Cntr New York NY 1993-2000; Exec Coun Appointees New York NY 1976-1993; Ch Of S Mart-In-The-Fields Philadelphia PA 1973-1976. Auth, "0pus Dei"; Auth, "European Judaism"; Auth, "Nwsltr Cntr For Study Of Islam & Chr-Muslim Relatns".

BRELSFORD, Diane (Oly) 507 5th Ave W, Seattle WA 98119 B Dallas TX 2/22/1930 d Hubard Taylor Bowyer & Virginia. BA U Denv 1966; MA U Denv 1969; MDiv CDSP 1986. D 6/28/1986 Bp Gayle Elizabeth Harris P 6/6/1987 Bp William Edwin Swing. Assoc Ch Of The Ascen Seattle WA 1993-2004; Asst The Epis Ch Of The Gd Shpd Berkeley CA 1986-1988. Assn Cmnty Of S Mary; ECW; EPF; Recovery Mnstrs. Epis Peace Fellowowship. dianebrelsford@comcast.net

BRENEMEN, Betty Jo (CGC) 200 Partin Dr N, Niceville FL 32578 B Oklahoma City OK 5/3/1942 d Jack Joseph Brenemen & Gladys Dale. MS U of Florida 1964; MS U of W Florida 1971; MA U of W Florida 1999; D Sch 2010. D 2/10/2011 Bp Philip Menzie Duncan II. c 1. bettyjobrenemen@cox.net

BRENMARK-FRENCH, Regina Kay (Chi) 2105 Cumberland St, Rockford IL 61103 **D S Chad Epis Ch Loves Pk IL 2001-** B Chicago IL 8/17/1941 d Edward Brenmark & Catherine. BA Roosevelt U 1996. D 2/3/2001 Bp William Dailey Persell. m 6/7/1998 Chellis F French.

BRENNEIS, Michael Joseph (Va) 2309 N Kentucky St, Arlington VA 22205 **P-in-c S Mary's Epis Ch Arlington VA 2004-** B New York NY 2/9/1955 BA SW Bapt Coll Bolivar MO 1978; MA Spalding Coll 1982; MDiv Sthrn Bapt TS Louisville KY 1983; PhD Geo Mason U 2000; DAS VTS 2003. D 1/14/2004 Bp Peter James Lee P 7/24/2004 Bp David Colin Jones. m Jeanne Elaine Maguire c 2. mjbrenn@patriot.net

BRENNOM, Kesha Mai (Los) 144 S C St, Oxnard CA 93030 B 3/22/1974 d Howard Rae Anderson & Linda Lee. BA U MI 1996; MDiv VTS 2009. D 12/20/2008 P 6/21/2009 Bp Alan Scarfe. m 5/13/2000 Wade J Brennom c 1. P-in-c All SS Epis Ch Oxnard CA 2009-2011; Dio Iowa Des Moines IA 2000-2005. kbrennom@gmail.com

BRENTLEY, David J (SO) 804 Clearfield Ln, Cincinnati OH 45240 B Pittsburgh PA 1/10/1936 s Roy Brentley & Viola. BA Duquesne U 1961. D 10/28/1995 Bp Herbert Thompson Jr. c 1. vidatt@juno.com

BRENTNALL, Burden (Oly) 9086 Chickadee Way, Blaine WA 98230 **D Dio Los Angeles Los Angeles CA 1992-** B La Jolla CA 8/18/1930 s Samuel Robert Brentnall & Natalie. BS USMA at W Point 1953; MS U MI 1958; MS U MI 1958; PhD Stan 1963. D 6/27/1992 Bp Chester Lovelle Talton. c 3. D Chr Epis Ch Blaine WA 2000-2010. brentnalls@earthlink.net

BRENY, Judith Mary (WNY) 745 Ashland Ave, Buffalo NY 14222 **Vic Ephphatha Epis Ch Of The Deaf Eggertsville NY 2003-** B Dumont NJ 6/16/1943 d Charles John Breny & Mary Agnes. MS SUNY 1993; MDiv GTS 2003. D 6/4/2003 P 12/13/2003 Bp J Michael Garrison. c 3. Dio Wstrn New York Tonawanda NY 2004-2009. jbreny@gmail.com

BRERETON, Thomas F (Colo) 2741 Freedom Heights, Colorado Springs CO 80904 B Rochester NY 3/31/1927 s Frederick Raymond Brereton & Charlotte. BA W Virginia Wesleyan Coll 1951; MDiv Garrett Evang TS 1954; Command and Gnrl Stff Coll 1975. D 12/17/1958 P 6/21/1959 Bp Frederick Lehrle Barry. m 1/19/2011 Gloria Brereton c 3. Ret - Asstg S Raphael Epis Ch Colorado Sprg CO 1989-2010; R S Mary's Ch Morganton NC 1983-1987; R S Jn's Ch Richfield Sprg NY 1972-1983; Cur S Jn's Epis Ch Troy NY 1958-1960.

Bronze Star Medal US-A; Meritorious Serv Medal US-A; Army Commendation Medal US-A. w2tjo@msn.com

BRESCIANI, Eduardo Roberto (Los) 9037 Park St, Bellflower CA 90706 **R S Marg's Epis Ch So Gate CA 2005-** B 2/22/1951 s Eduardo Bresciani & Maria Raquel. Pacific Luth TS; Pontifical Cath U of Chile; U of Chile. D 6/27/1992 Bp Chester Lovelle Talton. Assoc S Paul's Pomona Pomona CA 2003-2005; D S Phil's Par Los Angeles CA 1992-1994.

BRESNAHAN, Paul Bisson (Mass) 2 Fairfield St, Salem MA 01970 **P-in-c S Ptr's Ch Salem MA 2007-** B Somerville MA 9/9/1945 s Paul Bisson Bresnahan & Pauline Fern. Glendon Coll Toronto ON CA; BA York U 1967; MDiv EDS 1972. D 6/24/1972 P 12/16/1972 Bp John Melville Burgess. m 10/13/1979 Cynthia Ann Saltalamacchia c 3. R S Mk's Epis Ch S Albans WV 1995-2006; R S Andr's Ch Methuen MA 1991-1995; H Cross Faith Memi Epis Ch Pawleys Island SC 1991; Dio Ohio Cleveland OH 1988-1989; R Ch Of The Epiph Euclid OH 1983-1990; R Chr Ch Hyde Pk MA 1975-1983; P-in-c S Lk's Epis Ch Malden MA 1972-1975; Cur Chr Ch Quincy MA 1972-1974. Auth, "Everything You Need to Know About Sex in Ord to Get to Heaven," Xlibris, 2005; Auth, "Growing Ordnry Ch"; Auth, "User Friendly Evang," Forw Mvmt. Man of the Year City of S Albans, W Virginia 2006; Mountaineer of the Year Gvnr of W Virginia 2006. paulbresnahan@gmail.com

BRETSCHER, Robert George (SwFla) 240 Hancock Ln, Athens GA 30605 B New York NY 10/13/1933 s George Bretscher & Christine. BA Wesl 1956; BD VTS 1963; MA U of So Florida 1971; PhD U GA 1974. D 6/11/1963 Bp Duncan Montgomery Gray P 1/1/1964 Bp Joseph Warren Hutchens. m 9/2/1961 Ann Devore Bretscher c 3. R S Mary's Ch Dade City FL 1967-1969; Asst Ch Of The Ascen Clearwater FL 1965-1967; Cur S Paul's Ch Wallingford CT 1963-1965. Eaa. babret@negia.net

BRETTMANN, William Sims (EC) 557 Fearnington Post, Pittsboro NC 27312 B Junction City KS 6/1/1936 s James W Brettmann & Jean. BA Oxf 1961; BA U So 1962; MA Oxf 1965; STM Yale DS 1965; Fllshp Coolidge Resrch Collegium 1990. D 8/24/1962 P 6/1/1963 Bp Charles C J Carpenter. m 9/14/1963 Lelia Gordon Brettmann c 2. R S Steph's Ch Goldsboro NC 1993-1999; Asst to Bp Dio No Carolina Raleigh NC 1991-1993; Dir/Secy Dio No Carolina Raleigh NC 1985-1993; R Trin Ch Columbus OH 1978-1984; Chair of COM Dio Florida Jacksonville FL 1974-1975; R Gr Epis Ch Orange Pk FL 1970-1978; Cn Chr Ch Cathd Louisville KY 1966-1969; Cur Trin Epis Ch Mobile AL 1962-1964. Fellowowship Coolidge Resrch Colloguim 1990; Fell Coolidge Resrch Colloqium 90; Life Mem Citation Ohio Pastors Convoc. wbrettmann@nc.rr.com

BRETZ, Donald Walter Andrew (WVa) 5 Hattaras Ct, Bordentown NJ 08505 **Off Of Bsh For ArmdF New York NY 1998-** B Portsmouth OH 2/21/1957 s Donald Walter Bretz & Jean. BS U Cinc 1979; MA Webster U 1984; MDiv Epis TS of The SW 1988. D 5/25/1988 Bp John Herbert MacNaughton P 12/1/1988 Bp Earl Nicholas McArthur Jr. m 3/31/1979 Darla Fay Bretz. The Memi Ch Of The Gd Shpd Parkersburg WV 1994-1998; R Chr Ch Wellsburg WV 1991-1994; Asst R Ch Of The Gd Shpd Corpus Christi TX 1988-1991; S Jas Epis Sch Of Corpus Christi Inc. Corpus Christi TX 1988-1991. CBS, GAS, Soc Of S Fran. donald_bretz@hotmail.com

BREUER, David R (ECR) 20 University Ave, Los Gatos CA 95030 **R S Lk's Ch Los Gatos CA 1993-** B San Mateo CA 9/24/1946 s Arthur R Breuer & Ethel Marie. AA San Mateo Coll 1965; BA Golden Gate U 1969; MBA Golden Gate U 1972; MDiv Nash 1975. D 6/28/1975 Bp C Kilmer Myers P 12/1/1975 Bp J(ohn) Joseph Meakins Harte. R Chr Ch Sausalito CA 1979-1993; Asst Epis Par Of S Mich And All Ang Tucson AZ 1975-1979. Soc Of S Jn The Evang. drbreuer@aol.com

BREWER, Anne (NY) No address on file. B Kansas City MO 3/16/1949 d Chester Leland Brewer & Martha Helen. BA Br 1971; MDiv EDS 1979; MD U of Vermont 1979. D 5/22/1979 P 5/1/1980 Bp Robert Shaw Kerr. m 9/4/1976 James August Kowalski. Asst Ch Of The Gd Shpd Hartford CT 1982-1993; Asst Trin Ch Newtown CT 1980-1982.

BREWER, Floyd William (SwFla) 601 S Manhattan Ave, Tampa FL 33609 B Chatanooga TN 9/10/1931 s Floyd William Brewer & Ruth Naomi. BA/BS U Of Florida 1958; MDiv STUSo 1996. D 6/15/1996 Bp Rogers Sanders Harris P 1/24/1997 Bp John Bailey Lipscomb. m 2/5/1989 Anne Blake Brewer. S Cecilia's Ch Tampa FL 1999-2000; Vic S Chad's Ch Tampa FL 1997-1999; D S Alfred's Epis Ch Palm Harbor FL 1996-1997.

BREWER, Gregory Orrin (NY) 209 East 16th St., 61 Gramercy Park North, New York NY 10010 **Calv and St Geo New York NY 2009-** B Richmond VA 7/6/1951 s Robert Orrin Brewer & Olivia. BA Lynchburg Coll 1973; MDiv VTS 1976. D 6/5/1976 Bp William Henry Marmion P 1/6/1977 Bp William Hopkins Folwell. m 9/11/1981 Laura Lee Brewer c 6. R Ch Of The Gd Samar Paoli PA 1997-2008; TESM Ambridge PA 1992-1996; R Ch Of The New Cov Winter Sprg FL 1977-1992; Cur All SS Ch Of Winter Pk Winter Pk FL 1976-1977. Auth, "Journey Through The Word". greg.brewer@calstg.org

BREWER, Johnny Lyvon (CGC) 7810 Navarre Pkwy, Navarre FL 32566 B Monroe LA 11/18/1957 s Bernisc Lyvon Brewer & Ira Ira. AAS Lamar U. D 2/10/2011 Bp Philip Menzie Duncan II. m 12/31/1992 Antoinette Louise Antoinette Louise Coward Gamble c 2. brotherjohn@mchsi.com

BREWER JR, Luther Gordon (ETenn) 584 Lebanon Rd, Kingsport TN 37663 **EAM Knoxville TN 2010-** B Lumberton NC 8/26/1960 s Luther G Brewer & Mary George. BA Mars Hill Coll 1983; MEd E Tennessee St U 2001. D 12/5/2009 Bp Charles Glenn VonRosenberg. m 1/22/1994 Mary C Carlock c 1. lgordonbrewer@gmail.com

BREWER, Richard Elliott (Okla) 6606 E 99th Pl, Tulsa OK 74133 **Chr Epis Ch Tulsa OK 2005-** B Raton NM 2/16/1945 s Paul Eli Brewer & Helen. BA U So 1967; MDiv GTS 1970. D 6/20/1970 P 12/1/1970 Bp Chilton Powell. m 5/30/1970 Deanna Basarab c 1. Dio Oklahoma Oklahoma City OK 2005-2011; Oaces Inst Oklahoma City OK 1981-1991; Vic S Aid's Epis Ch Tulsa OK 1977-1981; S Andr's Ch Stillwater OK 1971-1976; Cur S Dunst's Ch Tulsa OK 1970-1972. Auth, "Common Lessons & Parallel Guides For Efm"; Auth, "Practically Chr:"; Auth, "A Prog For Practical Chr," *Active Reflection & Pryr*; Auth, "Venture: Exploring Ideas & Images Of Chr F," *Venture: Exploring Ideas & Images Of Chr Faith*. rick_brewer@msn.com

BREWER III, Richard Frederick (LI) Prestwick Farm, 2260 County Route 12, Whitehall NY 12887 **Stndg Com Dio Long Island Garden City NY 2008-** B Johnson City TN 1/10/1947 s Richard Frederick Brewer & Anne Rorer. BA Van 1968; MHA Duke 1973; MDiv GTS 1981. D 9/14/1981 Bp Paul Moore Jr P 3/25/1982 Bp Walter Decoster Dennis Jr. c 2. Int Deploy Off Dio Long Island Garden City NY 2010; Dep to GC Dio Long Island Garden City NY 2004-2006; Stndg Com Dio Long Island Garden City NY 1994-2002; Chapt Mem Cathd Of The Incarn Garden City NY 1993-1999; R The Ch Of S Lk and S Matt Brooklyn NY 1986-2010; Cur Trin-St Jn's Ch Hewlett NY 1982-1986; The GTS New York NY 1982; The GTS New York NY 1981-1982. Hon Cn Cathd of the Incarn 2010; Trst of the Year Untd Hosp Fund of New York 2001. rfbrewer3@aol.com

BREWER, Todd Hamilton (ND) 4048 Brownsville Rd, Pittsburgh PA 15227 B Orlando FL 8/19/1984 s Gregory Orrin Brewer & Laura Lee. BA Laf 2006; MDiv TESM 2009. D 11/12/2009 P 6/2/2010 Bp Michael Gene Smith. m 6/3/2006 Kelly Hough. Int S Ptr's Epis Ch Brentwood Pittsburgh PA 2010. brewer.todd@gmail.com

BREWER, Virginia Gale (SeFla) Po Box 427, Monteagle TN 37356 B Troy NY 7/2/1959 d Howard Bradley Ganther & Angela. STUSo; BS Florida Atlantic U 1986; BA Florida Atlantic U 1991; Dioc SE Florida Sch For Chr Stds FL 1998. D 9/11/1998 Bp Calvin Onderdonk Schofield Jr. m 8/5/1989 James William Brewer. D S Jos's Epis Ch Boynton Bch FL 1998-2000. jimandgigi@worldnet.att.net

BREWIN-WILSON, Debra M (WA) 14300 Saint Thomas Church Rd, Upper Marlboro MD 20772 **R Ch Of The Incarn Upper Marlboro MD 2009-; R S Thos Par Croom Upper Marlboro MD 2009-** B Woodbury NJ 9/14/1959 d Walter Lawrence Brewin & Florence. BD U of Pennsylvania 1980; MS Seton Hall U 1983; Cert U of S Andr's 1999; MDiv VTS 2006. D 6/3/2006 P 12/16/2006 Bp George Edward Councell. m 12/20/1980 Bradford Scott Wilson c 2. P-in-c All SS Epis Ch Lakewood NJ 2007-2009; D Trin Epis Ch Cranford NJ 2006. dbwharpy@aol.com

BREWSTER, John Gurdon (CNY) 376 Shaffer Rd, Newfield NY 14867 **Vic Ch Of The Epiph Trumansburg NY 2003-** B New York NY 4/11/1937 s Carroll Harwood Brewster & Blandina. Gestalt Ther Inst; BA Hav 1959; The Art Stdt League 1962; BD UTS 1962; STM UTS 1970. D 6/10/1962 P 12/1/1964 Bp Horace W B Donegan. m 6/16/1962 Martha Anne Klippert c 4. Epis Ch At Cornell Ithaca NY 1996-1999; Dio Cntrl New York Syracuse NY 1965-1996. "No Turning Back," *My Sum w Daddy King*, Orbis Pub, 2007. gurdonbrewster@gmail.com

BREWSTER, John Pierce (At) 1064 Can Tex Dr, Sewanee TN 37375 B Atlanta GA 4/24/1939 s Maurice Ray Brewster & Dorothy. BS Georgia Inst of Tech 1962; MDiv VTS 1977. D 6/11/1977 Bp Bennett Jones Sims P 3/1/1978 Bp Charles Judson Child Jr. m 10/9/2010 Emily Herman. Ch Of The Atone Sandy Sprg GA 1985-2001; R Calv Epis Ch Cleveland MS 1980-1985; R Gr Ch Rosedale MS 1980-1985; S Jas Epis Ch Marietta GA 1977-1980. sewanee99@gmail.com

BREWSTER JR, William (O) 7 Bond Rd, Kittery Point ME 03905 B Hartford CT 1/11/1934 s Elizabeth. BA U of Texas 1955; MDiv CDSP 1960; MA U Chi 1966; Fllshp Coll of Preachers 1981. D 6/29/1960 Bp Richard S M Emrich P 1/1/1961 Bp Stephen F Bayne Jr. m 6/17/1966 Arlene Blank Brewster c 3. Dn of Youngstown Dnry Dio Ohio Cleveland OH 1995-1999; Stndg Com Dio Ohio Cleveland OH 1987-1991; Com on Ch and Soc Dio Ohio Cleveland OH 1980-1986; R S Jn's Ch Youngstown OH 1979-1999; Assoc Chr Ch Cranbrook Bloomfield Hills MI 1972-1979. Auth, *Ch Life*, 1984; Auth, *Texts of Synoptic Sources*. Acad Par Cleric, Epis Soc for Mnstry in Hig. wmbrew34@comcast.net

BREYER, Chloe Anne (WA) 601 West 11th Street, Apartment 3e, New York NY 10025 B Boston MA 10/23/1969 d Stephen Breyer & Joanna. BA Harv 1992; MDiv GTS 2000. D 6/10/2000 Bp Ronald Hayward Haines P 5/24/2001

Bp Jane Hart Holmes Dixon. m 8/16/1997 Greg Scholl c 1. Cathd Of St Jn The Div New York NY 2000-2003. Ba mcl Harv Cambridge MA 1992.

BREYFOGLE, Elizabeth Elain (Dal) 511 Foote St., McKinney TX 75069 **D S Ptr's Ch McKinney TX 2007-** B Bay Shore NY 11/11/1949 d Clifford Emerson Schoone & Elizabeth Harriette. BSN U of Tennessee 1971. D 11/10/2007 Bp James Monte Stanton. c 3. bbreyfogle@stpetersmckinney.com

BREZNAU, Jack Charles (EMich) PO Box 1882, Caseville MI 48725 B Detroit MI 1/23/1927 D 7/1/2001 P 12/29/2001 Bp Edwin Max Leidel Jr. m 9/8/1951 Nancy Ann Breznau c 2. naja154@yahoo.com

BREZNAU, Nancy Ann (EMich) PO Box 1882, Caseville MI 48725 B Weehauken NJ 3/5/1931 D 7/1/2001 P 12/29/2001 Bp Edwin Max Leidel Jr. m 9/8/1951 Jack Charles Breznau c 3. naja154@yahoo.com

BRICE, Geoffrey Lloyd (Roch) 224 Alexander St, Rochester NY 14607 B New York NY 2/13/1930 s James Edward Brice & Frances Marion. BA U of Virginia 1953; EDS 1956. D 6/21/1956 P 2/1/1957 Bp Dudley S Stark. m 6/15/1963 Paula Joanne Crerar c 1. The Genessee Hosp Rochester NY 1979-1994; S Paul's Ch S Louis MO 1970-1979; Assoc R S Jn's Ch Royal Oak MI 1963-1970; Vic Gr Ch Scottsville NY 1959-1962; Vic S Andr's Epis Ch Caledonia NY 1959-1962; Cur Trin Meml Ch Binghamton NY 1956-1959.

BRIDGE, Melvin Alden (FtW) 729 Carette Dr, Fort Worth TX 76108 **Chapl All SS' Epis Sch Of Ft Worth Ft Worth TX 1996-** B Vallejo CA 11/19/1950 s Lawrence Arden Bridge & Nellie Grace. BS Florida St U 1972; MS Florida St U 1973; Reformed TS 1979; MDiv Columbia TS 1982; CAS SWTS 1987. D 6/29/1987 P 11/11/1987 Bp William Hopkins Folwell. m 12/31/1982 Ruth Bridge c 2. R Ch Of The Trsfg Bat Cave NC 1993-1996; Assoc R S Mk's Ch Cocoa FL 1991-1992; Assoc R S Mk's Ch Cocoa FL 1987-1990. swagmanfw@sbcglobal.net

BRIDGE, Michael James (WK) 117 S McCall St, Pittsburg PA 17101 B Pittsburgh PA 3/3/1978 s Charles Edward Bridge & Loretta Jean. BA U Pgh 2000; MDiv TESM 2004. D 6/12/2004 Bp Robert William Duncan P 12/18/2004 Bp James Marshall Adams Jr. m 7/31/2004 Bonnie F Bridge c 3. R/Vic S Jn's Ch Ulysses KS 2004-2010. kanyon40@comcast.net

BRIDGE, Peter James (NJ) 1509 Esther Ln, Yardley PA 19067 **Assoc P Trin Cathd Trenton NJ 2002-** B Johannesburg ZA 7/7/1942 s Basil Joseph Bridge & Kathleen. BA U of So Afr Pretoria ZA 1972; MSW Rutgers-The St U 1975; DMin Lancaster TS 1984. Rec from Roman Catholic 6/21/2002 as Priest Bp David B(ruce) Joslin. m 8/27/1977 Jane Anderson c 4. Co-Auth, "Pstr Correspondence," *Dictionary of Pstr Care and Counslg*, Abingdon, 1990; Auth, "Documentation of Psych Supervision," *Psych in Priv Pract*, Haworth Press, 1990; Auth, "A Record Form for Psych Supervision," *Innovations in Clincl Pract*, Profsnl Resource Exch, 1988. Samar Sprt Awd Samar Counslg Cntr/ Philadelphia 2008. pbridge777@comcast.net

BRIDGERS, Anne (Pa) 2475 St. Peters Rd., Malvern PA 19355 **R S Ptr's Ch In The Great Vlly Malvern PA 2008-** B Montgomery AL 10/27/1951 d Eulon Fred Horne & Elizabeth. U of Montevallo 1971; BS U of Alabama 1974; MDiv VTS 1998. D 5/30/1998 P 1/25/1999 Bp Charles Farmer Duvall. m 8/20/1981 John Dixon Bridgers c 4. Chr Epis Ch Ponte Vedra Bch FL 2006-2008; S Jn's Cathd Jacksonville FL 2001-2006; Trin Epis Ch Mobile AL 1998-2001. rector@stpetersgv.org

BRIDGES, Melva Gayle (Okla) 12719 S Couts Dr, Mustang OK 73064 **D Epis Ch Of The Resurr Oklahoma City OK 1988-** B Hobart OK 12/10/1935 d Melvin Ratleff Embree & Bessie Mae. MA Cntrl St U. D 6/20/1984 Bp Gerald Nicholas McAllister. m 6/14/1953 John Wesley Vernon Bridges. Cleric S Jas Epis Ch Oklahoma City OK 1984-1988. Auth, "Trng Fac As Developmental Gdnc Facilitators"; Auth, "Dealing w Isolation In The Classroom Bldg The Affective Triangle: Parents," *Teachers & Kids*.

BRIDGES, Nancy (Okla) 408 Ridge Rd, Edmond OK 73034 **D S Mary's Ch Edmond OK 2001-** B Litchfield CT 4/16/1944 d Norton R Kilbourn & Helen. U Of Cntrl Oklahoma; BS OH SU 1967. D 6/16/2001 Bp Robert Manning Moody. m 7/6/1968 Timothy Robert Bridges.

BRIDGES, Penelope Maud (Va) 1239 Wild Hawthorn Way, Reston VA 20194 **R S Fran Epis Ch Great Falls VA 2003-** B Belfast IE 4/13/1958 d Gibbon Fitzgibbon & Alice Joan. BA U of Cambridge 1979; MDiv Ya Berk 1997. D 6/21/1997 P 2/2/1998 Bp Douglas Edwin Theuner. m 4/9/1983 Stephen Bridges c 2. Asst R Gr Epis Ch Alexandria VA 1997-2003. revpbridges@gmail.com

BRIDGFORD, Peter W (WNY) 18 Harbour Pointe Cmn, Buffalo NY 14202 B Indianapolis IN 1/17/1934 s Oral William Bridgford & Agnes. BA NWU 1956; MDiv CDSP 1968. D 6/28/1968 P 1/11/1969 Bp Lauriston L Scaife. m 7/2/1960 Belmore Kobler Hicks c 1. R S Jn's Gr Ch Buffalo NY 1974-2000; Vic Ch Of The H Comm Lakeview NY 1970-1974; Cur S Lk's Epis Ch Jamestown NY 1968-1970. petebridgford@aol.com

BRIDGFORD, Richard Oliver (SVa) 707 Steiner Way, Norfolk VA 23502 **R Ch Of The Epiph Norfolk VA 1993-** B Chicago IL 11/12/1941 s Archie Paul Bridgford & Helen. BA Old Dominion U 1965; MDIV STUSo 1968. D 6/22/1968 P 6/2/1969 Bp George P Gunn. Dn - Convoc III Dio Sthrn Virginia Norfolk VA 2005-2011; Int Ch Of H Apos Virginia Bch VA 1990-1993; Int Ch Of The Epiph Norfolk VA 1988-1989; Int S Jas Epis Ch Portsmouth VA 1985-1986; Int S Thos Epis Ch Chesapeake VA 1983-1985; Int S Mk's Ch Hampton VA 1982-1983; Int S Steph's Ch Norfolk VA 1981-1982; Int S Jn's Ch Suffolk VA 1979-1980; Int S Aid's Ch Virginia Bch VA 1978-1979; Norfolk Urban Outreach Mnstry Norfolk VA 1975-1978; Asst to R Ch Of The Gd Shpd Norfolk VA 1968-1974. DuBose Awd for Serv STUSo 2005. bridgford@earthlink.net

BRIDGFORTH, David Elgin (USC) 900 Calhoun St, Columbia SC 29201 B Wilmington DE 6/22/1943 s David Thomas Bridgforth & Grace Elma. BA Newberry Coll 1965; MDiv VTS 1969. D 6/29/1969 P 6/25/1970 Bp John Adams Pinckney. m 8/8/1970 Sandra Ann Jacobs. R S Tim's Ch Columbia SC 1987-2006; Dio Upper So Carolina Columbia SC 1987-1989; Chair BEC Dio Upper So Carolina Columbia SC 1986; Chair Ch Pension Fund Com Dio Upper So Carolina Columbia SC 1984-1985; Bp'S Coun Dio Upper So Carolina Columbia SC 1979-1981; Dept Of Missions Dio Upper So Carolina Columbia SC 1977-1979; Dn S Steph's Ch S Steph SC 1977-1979; S Matt's Epis Ch Spartanburg SC 1972-1987; Vic Ch Of The Adv Spartanburg SC 1972-1976; Vic Ch Of The Ascen Seneca SC 1970-1972. Auth, "Cats & Birds & Blessings Of God". Dio Upper So Carolina 1987-1989.

BRIELAND, Donald M (HB) 5742 5th Ave, Pittsburgh PA 15232 **Died 9/30/2011** B Pencer MN 1/15/1924 s Martin Lars Brieland & Gene Pauline. BA Carleton Coll 1943; MA NWU 1945; SWTS 1945; PhD U MN 1949. D 9/6/1945 Bp Stephen E Keeler P 1/15/1948 Bp Elwood L Haines. c 2. Sigma Xi 1945. Phi Beta Kappa 1943.

BRIGGS, Barbara K (Ct) 126 Lakewood Cir N, Manchester CT 06040 **P-in-c S Alb's Ch Simsbury CT 2011-; BEC Dio Connecticut Hartford CT 2008-** B Boston MA 5/2/1961 d Gilbert King & Katharine. ABS Smith 1983; Lic in Theol Universite Catholique De Lyon 1996. D 6/2/2007 Bp Gordon Paul Scruton P 12/15/2007 Bp Andrew Donnan Smith. m 9/1/2002 Paul R Briggs c 1. Bp's Convoc for Pryr Dio Connecticut Hartford CT 2008-2010; BEC Dio Connecticut Hartford CT 2008-2010; Asst R Trin Epis Ch Hartford CT 2007-2011; Dio Wstrn Massachusetts Springfield MA 2000-2006. bakbriggs@yahoo.com

BRIGGS, Lyn Zill (U) 661 Redondo Ave, Salt Lake City UT 84105 **Dioc Coun, Exec Com Dio Utah Salt Lake City UT 2010-; EFM Coordntr Dio Utah Salt Lake City UT 2007-** B Sioux City IA 10/21/1955 d Marcus Tietje Zill & Marilyn Ruth. Concordia Coll 1974; BA U of Nebraska 1977; Epis TS at Claremont 2004; MDiv CDSP 2006. D 6/10/2006 P 1/20/2007 Bp Carolyn Tanner Irish. m 5/21/1977 Nathan H Briggs c 2. Assoc S Paul's Ch Salt Lake City UT 2006-2009; Par Adm All SS Ch Salt Lake City UT 1989-2004. lynzbriggs@gmail.com

BRIGGS, Michael Eugene (Ark) 531 W College Ave, Jonesboro AR 72401 **S Mk's Epis Ch Jonesboro AR 2011-** B West Memphis AR 4/21/1964 s Jerry Glen Briggs & Clarice Olivia. AA Shelby St Cmnty Coll 2001; BS Chr Brothers U 2002; MDiv Memphis TS 2009. D 3/11/2011 P 9/25/2011 Bp Larry R Benfield. m 6/26/2010 Timothy White. mebriggs64@gmail.com

BRIGGS II, Paul R (Ct) 14 Melody Ln, East Longmeadow MA 01028 **Dn Hartford Dnry Manchester CT 2011-; Bd Dir Seabury Ret Cmnty Bloomfield CT 2008-** B Hartland ME 3/9/1954 s Paul Revere Briggs & Ida Ethel. BA Mt Allison U 1976; MDiv GTS 1981. D 6/18/1981 Bp Frederick Barton Wolf P 12/18/1981 Bp Philip Alan Smith. m 9/1/2002 Barbara K King c 4. P-in-c S Mary's Epis Ch Manchester CT 2008-2011; R S Mk's Epis Ch E Longmeadow MA 1986-2008; Asst S Dav's Ch Austin TX 1983-1986; Int Par Of S Jas Ch Keene NH 1981-1983. gregnyssa@gmail.com

BRIGHAM, Peter Bent (CFla) 8128 Gondola Dr, Orlando FL 32809 **D S Mary Of The Ang Epis Ch Orlando FL 1972-** B White Plains NY 11/8/1929 s Malcolm Murray Brigham & Maryland. Stetson U; BA Rol 1967. D 1/17/1972 Bp William Hopkins Folwell. m 1/20/1951 Ann R Brigham c 4. Auth, "Tech arts". Bro Of S Andr. deeque@bellsouth.net

BRIGHAM, Richard Daniel (At) 208 Edgewater Way, Peachtree City GA 30269 B Kansas City MO 5/22/1940 s Richard Stewart Brigham & Mary Louise. BA U of Missouri 1962; MA U of Missouri 1967; BD EDS 1968. D 6/14/1968 Bp Robert Rae Spears Jr P 2/1/1969 Bp Edward Randolph Welles II. m 8/29/1964 Vivian Ruth Preston. R S Andr's In The Pines Epis Ch Peachtree City GA 1983-2006; All SS Ch W Plains MO 1976-1983; Vic All SS Ch W Plains MO 1974-1975; R Gr And H Trin Cathd Kansas City MO 1972-1974; P-in-c Gr Epis Ch Chillicothe MO 1968-1972; P-in-c S Phil's Ch Trenton MO 1968-1972. Fllshp S Alb & S Sergius.

BRIGHT, Carl Connell (CGC) 198 Beardsley Court, Muscle Shoals AL 35661 B Montgomery AL 7/16/1938 s Henry Clay Bright & Asa. BS U of Alabama 1960; MDiv STUSo 1976. D 5/31/1976 P 12/17/1976 Bp Furman Stough. m 8/12/1960 Caroline Mushat Marbury c 3. Int Assoc R St Thos Epis Ch Huntsville AL 2008-2009; Int S Mary's Epis Ch Jasper AL 2007-2008; Int Chr Epis Ch Albertville AL 2004-2005; Dio Cntrl Gulf Coast Pensacola FL 1999-2003; Cmncatn Com Dio Cntrl Gulf Coast Pensacola FL 1999-2001; Stndg Com Dio Cntrl Gulf Coast Pensacola FL 1995-1998; R Chr The King Epis Ch Santa Rosa Bch FL 1991-2003; Missions Cmsn Dio Cntrl Gulf Coast Pensacola FL

B

1989-1992; R Gr Ch Anniston AL 1988-1989; Dept Of CE Dio So Carolina Charleston SC 1986-1988; Dioc Coun Dio So Carolina Charleston SC 1985-1988; R S Jn's Ch Florence SC 1984-1988; Dioc Coun Dio Alabama Birmingham AL 1982-1984; Chair - Dept Of Camp Mcdowell Dio Alabama Birmingham AL 1981-1984; R Gr Ch Sheffield AL 1978-1984; Cur Ch Of The Ascen Montgomery AL 1976-1978. ccbright@comcast.net

BRIGHT SR, Dee Wellington (WMass) 511 South Cabin Lake Drive, San Antonio TX 78244 **S Ptr's Ch Springfield MA 2003-** B River Cess LR 1/13/1961 s William Samuel Bright & Yansawon. BA Cuttington U Coll 1986; MA Epis TS of The SW 1999. Trans from Church of the Province of West Africa 6/1/1999 Bp James Edward Folts. m 11/7/1987 Monyue Odell c 3. R S Phil's Ch San Antonio TX 1999-2003. afi83@earthlink.net

BRIGHT, John Adams (Cal) 812 Southwest Saint Clair Ave. Apt 1, Portland OR 97209 B Portland OR 9/1/1927 s George Adams Bright & Helen. BA Pr 1949; MDiv CDSP 1956. D 6/29/1956 P 1/8/1957 Bp Benjamin D Dagwell. m 4/6/1975 Sandra Bright c 3. Int The Par Of S Clem Honolulu HI 1990-1991; R S Fran' Epis Ch San Francisco CA 1983-1989; Dn S Andr's Cathd Honolulu HI 1978-1983; R Chr Ch Par Lake Oswego OR 1965-1978; R Trin Ch Bend OR 1962-1965; Vic S Andr's Ch Portland OR 1957-1960; Asst S Mk's Epis Par Medford OR 1956-1957. Auth, *Carry A Story*. MDiv w hon CDSP Berkeley CA 1956. sandrajbr@live.com

BRIGHT, Patrick Edmund (Okla) 11901 Maple Hollow Ct, Oklahoma City OK 73120 **Assoc R All Souls Epis Ch Oklahoma City OK 1995-** B Ottawa 10/13/1953 s John Eric Bright & Mona. BA U of King's Coll Halifax NS CA 1977; MDiv U Tor 1980. Trans from Anglican Church of Canada 4/1/1995 Bp Robert Manning Moody. m 6/20/1981 Rhea Nadine Skerrett c 5. Assoc R S Jn's Ch Savannah GA 1984-1989. PB Soc of Can. pebright1@cox.net

BRIGHT, Wheigar Jefferson (NC) PO Box 858, Yanceyville NC 27379 **S Lk's Epis Ch Yanceyville NC 2010-** B Liberia 4/22/1958 s John Jellico Bright & Julia Victoria. BA Cuttington U Coll 1986; MDiv Nash 1991. Trans from Church of the Province of West Africa 7/19/2010 Bp Michael Bruce Curry. m 1/14/1995 Frances Kolison c 2. brightwheigar@yahoo.com

BRIGHTMAN, Dorothy Louise (RI) 17 N Country Club Dr, Warwick RI 02888 **D S Lk's Epis Ch E Greenwich RI 2006-** B Providence RI 7/13/1935 d Lester Chandler Brightman & Marion Ruth. BS Tufts U 1957; MA U of Connecticut 1964; EdD U NC 1979; MS Simmons Coll 1986; Var Rhode-Island Sch for Mnstrs 1997. D 5/25/2006 Bp Geralyn Wolf. dlbrightman@aol.com

BRIGHTMAN SR, Edward Scipio (WA) 4106 Beachcraft Ct, Temple Hills MD 20748 **Died 6/30/2010** B Charleston SC 1/26/1914 s Peter Jackson Brightman & Katie. BA CUNY 1950; BD VTS 1957; MA Creighton U 1969; MS Creighton U 1972; ThM Duke 1977; DMin Duke 1984; DMin Wesley TS 1984. D 4/19/1952 P 4/1/1953 Bp James P De Wolfe. c 2. OHC.

BRILL, Steven G (Oly) St Luke's Episcopal Church, PO Box 1294, Elma WA 98541 **P S Lk's Epis Ch Elma WA 1999-** B Salt Lake City UT 1/15/1957 s Paul Gerhart Brill & Geraldine. AA S Jn 1975; BA Bethany Coll 1979. D 3/15/1999 Bp Sanford Zangwill Kaye Hampton P 9/29/1999 Bp Vincent Waydell Warner. m 5/30/1992 Elizabeth C Murphy. goodnatured@earthlink.net

BRINDLEY, Thomas (Cal) 704 Sutro Ave, Novato CA 94947 B Port Arthur TX 3/28/1952 s Melvin L Brindley & Geraldine. Texas A&M U 1971; BS Lamar U 1975; MDiv VTS 1978. D 6/21/1978 Bp Roger Howard Cilley P 6/1/1979 Bp J Milton Richardson. m 9/14/1991 Lorna Joan Brindley c 3. R S Columba's Ch Inverness CA 1994-2010; R S Cuth's Epis Ch Houston TX 1981-1994; S Lk's Ch Livingston TX 1978-1980; Vic S Paul's Epis Ch Woodville TX 1978-1980. tnlbrindley@gmail.com

BRINKMAN, Charles Reed (Pa) 6838 Woodland Avenue AL B Pittsburgh PA 2/15/1947 s Albert Morrison Brinkman & Anna Margaret. BS Indiana U of Pennsylvania 1973; MDiv EDS 1977; DMin STUSo 2004. D 9/11/1977 Bp Robert Bracewell Appleyard P 3/18/1978 Bp William Hawley Clark. m 9/7/1975 Paula Joy Hansen c 2. R S Jas (Old Swedes) Ch of Kingsessing Philadelphia PA 1981-2007; Vic Chr Ch Delaware City DE 1977-1981; Cur Imm Ch On The Green New Castle DE 1977-1981. crbrink07@verizon.net

BRINKMANN, Mark Ransom (SC) All Saints Episcopal Church, 3001 Meeting St, Hilton Head Island SC 29926 **Assoc All SS Ch Hilton Hd Island SC 2007-** B Cincinnati OH 2/22/1956 s James Herbert Brinkmann & Martha Carolyn. BA U of Iowa 1980; MDiv SWTS 1985. D 6/14/1986 P 1/17/1987 Bp James Winchester Montgomery. m 8/20/1988 Kendell Leann Cudworth c 3. R S Jas Epis Ch Midvale UT 1999-2007; R S Andr's Ch Chelan WA 1993-1999; Assoc S Mths' Par Whittier CA 1986-1993. ADLMC, Associated Parishes. saintsassociate@hargray.com

BRINKMOELLER, Leonard Joseph (WMich) 312 Maple Street, Paw Paw MI 49079 B Cincinnati OH 8/9/1942 s Leonard Joseph Brinkmoeller & Marie Antoinette. Ford; BA S Chas Sem Carthagena OH 1965; MA U Of Dayton 1968. Rec from Roman Catholic 11/1/1983 as Priest Bp William Cockburn Russell Sheridan. m 5/2/1980 Marla Rae Archer. R Trin Epis Ch Marshall MI 2000-2008; R H Trin Epis Ch Manistee MI 1993-2000; R S Steph's Epis Ch Hobart IN 1984-1993. ellbee1942@gmail.com

BRINSON, Katherine Herrington (Ga) 4227 Columbia Rd, Martinez Branch GA 30907 **Gr Ch Waycross GA 2011-** B Millen GA 7/25/1952 d Edwin F Herrington & Anne J. BS Georgia Sthrn U 1975; MA Georgia Sthrn U 1978; EDS Georgia Sthrn U 1982; Cert In Angl Stds STUSo 2007. D 2/3/2007 P 9/8/2007 Bp Henry Irving Louttit. Epis Ch Of S Mary Magd Louisville GA 2010-2011; S Mich's Ch Waynesboro GA 2008-2010; D Ch Of Our Sav Martinez GA 2007. kitbrinson187@msn.com

BRION, Theresa Markley (Md) Episcopal Diocese of Maryland, 4 E University Parkway, Baltimore MD 21218 **Vic Ch Of The H Cross Cumberland MD 2012-; Vic S Geo's Epis Ch Mt Savage MD 2012-; Bishops' Dep for Wstrn Maryland Dio Maryland Baltimore MD 2010-; Cmsn on Mnstrs Dio Maryland Baltimore MD 2010-** B Elizabethtown KY 9/11/1958 d Robert Steele Markley & Augusta Cook. BS Longwood U 1980; JD W&L 1985; Cert Florida Inst of Tech 1997; MDiv EDS 2009. D 2/13/2010 Bp Frank Neff Powell P 10/2/2010 Bp John Leslie Rabb. m 5/26/2001 Denis Joly Brion. tbrion@ymail.com

BRIONES, Miguel Angel (Chi) 5101 W Devon Ave, Chicago IL 60646 B Atlixco Puebla Mexico 3/4/1966 s Leonardo Briones & Lidia. D 8/31/2011 Bp Jeffrey Dean Lee. m 3/4/1995 Norma Catalina Cid c 2. S Mk's Epis Ch Glen Ellyn IL 1998-2011. miguelabriones@yahoo.com

BRISBANE, Paul Owen (Colo) 513 N. Union City Rd., Coldwater MI 49036 **Supply P Dio Wstrn Michigan Kalamazoo MI 2001-; Supply P Dio Wstrn Michigan Kalamazoo MI 2001-** B Kalamazoo MI 9/29/1936 s William Clements Brisbane & Viola May. BA Wstrn Michigan U 1958; MDiv CDSP 1962. D 6/21/1962 Bp Charles Bennison P 5/23/1963 Bp Conrad Gesner. m 7/9/1983 Judith Elaine Meyers c 4. R S Jas' Epis Ch Meeker CO 1991-2001; Dn NW Epis Reg Mnstry Goodland KS 1989-1990; Dep, GC Dio Wstrn Kansas Hutchinson KS 1988; Dioc Coun Dio Wstrn Kansas Hutchinson KS 1987-1991; Vic Ascen-On-The-Prairie Epis Ch Colby KS 1985-1991; R S Paul's Epis Ch Goodland KS 1985-1991; Dioc Coun Dio Wstrn New York Tonawanda NY 1976; Vic Ch Of The H Comm Lakeview NY 1975-1977; Dioc Coun Dio Kansas Topeka KS 1972-1975; Pres, Stndg Com Dio Kansas Topeka KS 1972-1975; Dn, SE Convoc Dio Kansas Topeka KS 1969-1975; Vic Ch Of The Ascen Neodesha KS 1968-1975; R Ch Of The Epiph Independence KS 1968-1975; Dn, W Convoc Dio Milwaukee Milwaukee WI 1965-1968; R Trin Epis Ch Mineral Point WI 1965-1968; Vic Trin Epis Ch Platteville WI 1964-1968; Vic Emm Ch Lancaster WI 1964-1965; Vic H Trin Epis Ch Prairie Du Chien WI 1964-1965; Chapl Of Rosebud Boarding Sch Rosebud Epis Mssn Mssn SD 1963-1964; Cur S Paul's Ch Brookings SD 1962-1963. RWF 1964-2000. pobris@cbpu.com

BRISBIN, James Andrew (Alb) 2647 Brookview Rd., Castleton NY 12033 B Rotterdam New York 4/17/1961 s Phillip Brisbin & Julie. D 5/10/2008 Bp William Howard Love. m 8/18/1984 Laurie Ann Trahan c 4. whenbrokenglassfloats@gmail.com

BRISON, William Stanly (Ct) 2 Scott Ave, Bury BL9 9RS Great Britain (UK) B West Chester PA 11/20/1929 s William P Brison & Marion. BS Alfred U 1951; Westcott Hse Theol Coll Cambridge 1955; MDiv Ya Berk 1957; STM Ya Berk 1971. D 5/29/1957 Bp William A Lawrence P 12/1/1957 Bp Robert McConnell Hatch. m 6/16/1951 Marguerite Brison c 4. R Emm Epis Ch Stamford CT 1969-1972; Vic Chr Ch Bethany CT 1957-1959. "A Tale of Two Visits to Chechnya," Self-Pub, 2005. CMS 1992. Hon Cn Manchester Cathd 1982.

BRISSON JR, James L (Az) 4033 Alvord Dr, Fort Irwin CA 92310 B St Paul MN 12/2/1959 s James L Brisson & Helen J. AA City Colleges of Chicago 1985; BS U of Maryland 1987; MDiv Trin Evang DS 1990; MA Trin Evang DS 1990. D 6/6/2009 P 12/9/2009 Bp Kirk Stevan Smith. m 9/19/1981 Tina C Anderson c 4. james.brisson@us.army.mil

BRISTOL, Joan Esther (Ore) 2529 Bel Abbes Ave, Medford OR 97504 **D S Lk's Ch Grants Pass OR 1988-** B Grants Pass OR 8/24/1945 d Fayette Ingalls Bristol & Esther Desire. BA OR SU 1967; BS OR SU 1969; MS U of Oregon 1982. D 6/29/1988 Bp Robert Louis Ladehoff. NAAD.

BRISTOL, Wallace Edward (Oly) 9115 Fortuna Dr, Rm. 105, Mercer Island WA 98040 **Died 6/7/2010** B Seattle WA 9/18/1921 s Halsey Ames Bristol & Eveline Elsie. CDSP 1964. D 6/29/1964 Bp William F Lewis P 3/27/1965 Bp Ivol I Curtis. c 3.

BRITCHER, Sharon Ann (CFla) 1010 Pennsylvania Ave, Fort Pierce FL 34950 **D S Andr's Epis Ch Ft Pierce FL 1999-** B Daytona Beach FL 10/29/1946 d Clyde Alston Rush & Majorie. D 6/19/1999 Bp John Wadsworth Howe. m 9/16/1975 Edward Stanley Britcher c 1. D S Andr's Epis Ch Ft Pierce FL 1999-2003. esbrit@bellsouth.net

BRITNELL, Offie Wayne (Ak) 18609 S. Lowrie Loop, Eagle River AK 99577 B Hackleburg AL 1/2/1943 s Offie Leaborn Britnell & Constance. Auburn U; U of Alaska; U of Maryland; EFM STUSo 1989; Dio Alaska 1997. D 6/20/1998 Bp Mark Lawrence Mac Donald P 8/7/1999 Bp Cabell Tennis. m 12/16/1967 Gussie Mae Buckner c 3. P/R S Christophers Ch Anchorage AK 2001-2008. frwayneb@aol.com

BRITO, Antonio Peguero (At) 1015 Old Roswell Rd, Roswell GA 30076 **Hisp Vic S Dav's Ch Roswell GA 2011-** B Dominican Republic 6/12/1959 s

Antonio Brito & Ramona. Santo Tomas de Aquino 1987. Rec from Roman Catholic 2/2/2011 Bp J(ohn) Neil Alexander. m 6/14/2003 Roxanna Jacqueline Brito c 2. abrito@stdavidchurch.org

BRITO, Napoleon Ramon (DR) Box 764, Santo Domingo Dominican Republic **Dio The Dominican Republic (Iglesia Epis Dominicana) Santo Domingo DO 1993-** B Salcedo 7/17/1944 s Jose Brito Hinojosa & Maria. Theol Lic St. Thos De Aquino Sem 1972; Instituto De Catequesis 1977; LMFT San Pietro In Latere U 1985. Rec from Roman Catholic 12/1/1993 as Priest Bp Julio Cesar Holguin-Khoury. m 8/19/1990 Nelly Mercedes Martinez c 2. napoleonbrito@hotmail.com

BRITT, Diane (NY) 15 Settlers Hill Rd., Brewster NY 10509 **R S Lk's Ch Katonah NY 2005-** B Greenville TX 6/29/1952 d Patrick Henry Britt & Teni. BS Texas A&M U 1975; BS Texas A&M U 1977; MDiv VTS 2002. D 6/22/2002 P 3/9/2003 Bp Michael Bruce Curry. Asst Ch Of The Gd Shpd Rocky Mt NC 2002-2005. tdianebritt@aol.com

BRITT, Lawrence Albert (WNC) 236 Camelot Dr, Morganton NC 28655 **Advsr The TS at The U So Sewanee TN 1991-** B Montgomery AL 8/15/1938 s Albert Cronin Britt & Mary Glenn. BA Huntingdon Coll 1960; MDiv STUSo 1986. D 8/9/1986 Bp Quintin Ebenezer Primo Jr P 2/28/1987 Bp William Gillette Weinhauer. m 5/22/1976 Martha Lee Mires c 4. R S Mary's Ch Morganton NC 1998-2006; R All Faith Epis Ch Charlotte Hall MD 1993-1998; S Andr Ch Mt Holly NC 1986-1993. Cmnty of S Mary 1987. Distinguished Flying Cross USAF 1965. lbritt@compascable.net

BRITT, Marc Lawrence (WA) 9805 Livingston Rd, Fort Washington MD 20744 **R S Jn's Ch Ft Washington MD 1999-** B Hampton VA 9/27/1950 s Cecil Alfred Britt & Katherine Carol. BA U of Maryland 1973; MA W Virginia U 1976; RPI 1979; MDiv EDS 1990. D 6/9/1990 Bp Ronald Hayward Haines P 12/16/1990 Bp Otis Charles. R Ch Of The Redeem Lorain OH 1996-1999; R All SS Ch Oakley Av MD 1990-1996. Auth, "Bk Revs: By Way Of The Heat The Word Is Very Near You"; Auth, "Epis Life". Cath Fllshp Epis Ch.

BRITT, Sarah Eugenia (Swiss) (At) 253 Lake Somerset Dr Nw, Marietta GA 30064 B Birmingham AL 2/23/1940 d Harold Henry Larsen & Sadie. EFM; U Of Florida; U of Alabama. D 10/18/1998 Bp Onell Asiselo Soto. m 2/25/1961 Pope Patterson Britt.

BRITT, Stephen (Fla) San Jose Episcopal, 7423 San Jose Blvd., Jacksonville FL 32217 **R San Jose Epis Ch Jacksonville FL 2006-** B Fort Wayne IN 11/18/1969 s Larry Gene Smellie & Susan Joy. BA Erskine Coll 1991; MA U of So Carolina 1993; MDiv STUSo 1996. D 6/15/1996 Bp Rogers Sanders Harris P 2/9/1997 Bp John Bailey Lipscomb. m 12/17/1994 Carol Lee Jarvis c 1. Assoc The Ch Of The Gd Shpd Augusta GA 1999-2006; Asst H Innoc Epis Ch Valrico FL 1996-1999. Auth, "Encouragement, Hope, And Relatns," *From The Mtn*, 2000; Auth, "All In A Days Wk For God," *Living Ch*, 2000; Auth, "Young Cler Discuss New Ways To Share Faith," *Living Ch*, 1999; Auth, "The Prophet Of Adv," *Sewanee Theol Revs*, 1998. frbritt@sanjoseepiscopal.com

BRITTON, John Clay (Chi) 680 Madrona Ave S, Salem OR 97302 B Bellefonte PA 3/9/1956 s Joseph Henry Britton & Jean. BA Ham 1978; MDiv Ya Berk 1981; Willamette U 1988. D 6/12/1981 Bp Dean T Stevenson P 1/1/1982 Bp Charlie Fuller McNutt Jr. m 10/18/1981 Sara Ruth Britton. Cur S Mk's Barrington Hills IL 1982-1986; Int Cathd Ch Of S Steph Harrisburg PA 1981-1982. Auth, "Soc Sci Revs"; Auth, "Population Rel Ideology," *& Economical Efficency A Case Study Of The*. j-britton525@hotmail.com

BRITTON, Joseph Harp (Cal) 409 Prospect St, New Haven CT 06511 **Bd Mem The Friends Of Cbury Cathd In The Untd States Washington DC 2011-; Pres and Dn Ya Berk New Haven CT 2003-** B Fort Collins CO 3/11/1960 s Charles Cooper Britton & Maxine. AB Harv 1982; MDiv GTS 1989; ThD Institut Catholique De Paris 2002. D 6/8/1989 Bp William Carl Frey P 12/9/1989 Bp Richard Frank Grein. m 7/17/1982 Karla Marie Britton c 1. Cmsn on the Mnstry of the Baptized Convoc of Amer Ch in Europe Paris FR 1997-2011; R All Souls Par In Berkeley Berkeley CA 1993-1996; Kellogg Fell Epis Chapl At Harvard & Radcliffe Cambridge MA 1991-1993; Asst R S Paul's Ch Dedham MA 1991-1993; Assoc R S Mich's Ch New York NY 1989-1991. Auth, "The Berkeley Rite," *The Serious Bus of Wrshp*, T & T Clark, 2010; Ed, "Toward a Theol of Ldrshp," *ATR*, 2009; Auth, "The Breadth of Orthodoxy: On Phillips Brooks," *One Lord, One Faith, One Baptism*, Eerdmans, 2006; Auth, "The Evangelicity of the Episcopate," *ATR*, 2003; Auth, "Piety & Moral Conciousness," *ATR*, 1999; Auth, "Dispersed Authority," *Sewanee Theol Revs/Angl and Epis Hist*, 1999. Assoc Ed, ATR 2004-2009; Soc of S Jn the Evang 1992. DD GTS 2004; Fell ECF 1998; Fell Scaife Anderson 1997. joseph.britton@yale.edu

BRITTON SR, Judith A (NMich) 365 Kirkpatrick Ln, Gwinn MI 49841 B Escanaba MI 5/17/1938 d Oren K King & Katherine Susan. AD Nthrn Michigan U; Dio Nthrn Michigan 2001. D 7/1/2001 Bp James Arthur Kelsey. m 9/7/1957 Robert Britton c 3. Archd H Innoc Epis Ch Marquette MI 2001. Soc of the Comp of the H Cross 2004. rbritton@nmu.edu

BRITTON JR, Richard Carlisle (Tenn) 419 Woodland St., Nashville TN 37206 **R S Ann's Ch Nashville TN 2008-** B Pittsburgh PA 6/13/1951 s Richard C Britton & Mildred S. BA U Pgh 1975; MDiv GTS 1978. D 5/24/1978 Bp Robert Bracewell Appleyard P 5/5/1979 Bp William Carl Frey. m 7/20/1985 Donna Felicien c 2. S Lk's Epis Ch Atlanta GA 1999-2008; Cn Trin Cathd Columbia SC 1996-1999; R Ch Of The Incarn Atlanta GA 1990-1996; Vic S Anselm's Epis Ch Nashville TN 1980-1989; Ch Of The H Redeem Denver CO 1978-1980. rick@stannsnashville.org

BRITTON, Wayne Eugene (At) 175 Woodberry Ct, Athens GA 30605 B LaGrange GA 8/13/1930 s Wayne Prather Britton & Ruth. BA U GA 1954; MDiv VTS 1968. D 6/29/1968 Bp R(aymond) Stewart Wood Jr P 4/1/1969 Bp Randolph R Claiborne. m 6/29/1995 Nicola J Wolstenholme c 2. Assoc Emm Epis Ch Athens GA 2000-2001; S Greg The Great Athens GA 1986-1995; Ch Of The Resurr Coll Pk GA 1979-1986; R Ch of the Resurr Sautee Nacoochee GA 1979-1986; Dio Atlanta Atlanta GA 1979; Vic S Clem's Epis Ch Canton GA 1977-1979; P-in-c Chr Epis Ch Kennesaw GA 1977-1978; R S Marg's Ch Carrollton GA 1970-1977; Asst Cathd Of S Phil Atlanta GA 1968-1970. nicolgen@negia.net

BRO, Andrew Harmon (Chi) Po Box 111, Mount Carroll IL 61053 B Chicago IL 12/17/1930 s Albin Carl Bro & Margueritte. BA Denison U 1956; SWTS 1957; BD U Chi 1957; MA U of Iowa 1970. D 6/15/1957 Bp Charles L Street P 12/21/1957 Bp Gerald Francis Burrill. m 7/28/1956 Adalu Bro c 2. Gr Ch Boone IA 1997-1999; Cur S Aug's Epis Ch Wilmette IL 1957-1959. andybro@jcwifi.com

BROACH, Merrill Kilburn (Kan) 3401 Plymouth Pl, New Orleans LA 70131 **Vic Mt Olivet Epis Ch New Orleans LA 1998-** B Tulsa OK 7/24/1926 s Roland M Broach & Anna. LTh STUSo 1972. D 7/1/1972 Bp Chilton Powell P 12/1/1972 Bp Frederick Warren Putnam. m 1/30/1947 Virginia Louise Barnes. P-in-c S Matt's Ch Bogalusa LA 1992-1996; R S Paul's Epis Ch Clay Cntr KS 1978-1991; Gr Ch Henryetta OK 1978; Assoc S Ptr's Ch Tulsa OK 1976-1978; Cur Gr Ch Muskogee OK 1972-1973. Bro Of S Andr. dbroach@cox.net

BROAD, Thomas Michael (WNY) 19 N Washington St, Randolph NY 14772 **Dioc Coun Dio Wstrn New York Tonawanda NY 2011-; Title IV Disciplinary Bd, Pres Dio Wstrn New York Tonawanda NY 2011-; COM Dio Wstrn New York Tonawanda NY 2010-; Fresh Start, Fac Dio Wstrn New York Tonawanda NY 2010-; R Gr Ch Randolph NY 2008-** B Buffalo NY 12/27/1954 s Thomas Broad & Mabel Agnes. BS RPI 2007; MDiv GTS 2008. D 9/2/2007 P 9/13/2008 Bp J Michael Garrison. m 7/9/1977 Susan L LeViness. thomas.broad@gmail.com

BROADFOOT III, Walter Marion (Ala) 315 Clanton Ave, Montgomery AL 36104 **Assoc R Ch Of The Ascen Montgomery AL 2008-** B Memphis TN 1/20/1962 s Walter Marion Broadfoot & Anne. BS Mississippi St U 1984; MDiv STUSo 2008. D 5/14/2008 P 12/16/2008 Bp Henry Nutt Parsley Jr. m 11/18/2009 Rebecca S Soldan c 2. Grad Ldrshp Montgomery 2011. cbroadfoot@coascension.org

BROADHEAD, Alan John (ND) 517 3rd Ave Se, Jamestown ND 58401 B Birmingham UK 6/14/1938 s Wilfred Harold Broadhead & Hilda Mary. MD Lon 1962; Ripon Coll Cuddesdon 1966. Trans 11/1/1981 Bp Arthur Edward Walmsley. m 12/18/1965 Mary Patricia Broadhead. Assoc S Jn's Epis Ch Dickinson ND 1997-2005; Ch Of The Adv Devils Lake ND 1995-1997; Dio No Dakota Fargo ND 1992-2004; S Thos Ch Ft Totten ND 1992-1995; SS Mary And Mk Epis Ch Oakes ND 1991; Vic Zion Epis Ch No Branford CT 1982-1990. broadheadp@aol.com

BROADLEY, Rodger Charles (Pa) 336 S Camac St, Philadelphia PA 19107 **Cur Ch Of S Lk And Epiph Philadelphia PA 1980-** B Philadelphia PA 11/2/1951 s Harry Charles Broadley & June Mary. BA Mid 1973; MDiv EDS 1978. D 6/17/1978 P 5/1/1979 Bp Lyman Cunningham Ogilby. Cur Ch Of The Redeem Bryn Mawr PA 1978-1980. rodgercb@aol.com

BROCATO, Christian F (Mass) St. Peter's Episcopal Church, 838 Mass Ave., Cambridge MA 02139 **All SS Ch Stoneham MA 2009-** B Helena AR 11/27/1950 s Sam Francis Brocato & Jeannine King. MFA U MN 1978; PhD U MN 1986; MA Aquinas Inst of Theol St. Louis MO 1989. Rec from Roman Catholic 1/12/2008 Bp M(arvil) Thomas Shaw III. m 12/31/2004 Jeffrey John Hickey. christian.brocato@att.net

BROCHARD, Philip Thomas (Cal) 2729 Kinney Dr, Walnut Creek CA 94595 **R All Souls Par In Berkeley Berkeley CA 2008-** B San Francisco, CA 9/20/1974 BA U CA. D 6/7/2003 P 12/6/2003 Bp William Edwin Swing. m 1/6/2001 Sarah Oneto c 2. Assoc R S Paul's Epis Ch Walnut Creek CA 2003-2008. rector@allsoulsparish.org

BROCK, Charles Fuller (Va) 4801 Ravensworth Rd, Annandale VA 22003 **Assoc R S Barn Ch Annandale VA 2007-** B Boston MA 7/31/1960 s Kenneth Summer Brock & Anne. BA Hav 1983; MDiv VTS 2007. D 6/30/2007 P 1/18/2008 Bp Bavi Rivera. m 11/22/2003 Heidi B Biggs c 1. charles.brock@yahoo.com

BROCK, James William (ECR) 1262 Truchard Ln, Lincoln CA 95648 **S Dunst's Epis Ch Carmel Vlly CA 1992-** B Denver CO 7/20/1930 s Herbert

Perks Brock & Mary Francis. BA U CO 1952; MDiv CDSP 1955. D 6/29/1955 P 1/25/1956 Bp Joseph Summerville Minnis. m 8/16/1952 Virginia LaShell c 4. R S Dunst's Epis Ch Carmel Vlly CA 1962-1990; Alcosm Coun Dio El Camino Real Monterey CA 1962-1966; Pres of Cler Dio Colorado Denver CO 1958-1962; Cur S Lk's Ch Denver CO 1957-1962; Asst Trin Ch Greeley CO 1955-1957. jimandgin@sbcglobal.net

BROCK, Laurie M (Lex) 2029 Bellefont Dr, Lexington KY 40503 **Bp Nomin Com Dio Lexington Lexington KY 2011-; Bdgt Com Dio Lexington Lexington KY 2011-; Disciplinary Com Dio Lexington Lexington KY 2011-; R Ch S Mich The Archangel Lexington KY 2010-** B Fayette AL 10/24/1968 d Thomas Leon Brock & Linda Joyce. BS U of Sthrn Mississippi 1991; JD U of Alabama 1995; MDiv GTS 2002. D 6/1/2002 P 5/31/2003 Bp Philip Menzie Duncan II. Assoc S Jas Epis Ch Baton Rouge LA 2007-2010; Cur Trin Epis Ch Mobile AL 2002-2007; Chapl Dio Cntrl Gulf Coast Pensacola FL 2002. Auth, "This Should Be Interesting," *Ruach*, EWC, 2011; Auth, "Christmas Fruitcakes," *Ecumininet*, Ecumininet.com, 2009; Auth, "A Hm of Her Own," *Fidelia's Sis*, Young Cler Wmn, 2008; Auth, "Sex, Affrs, and the Absence of Ch," *Fidelia's Sis*, Young Cler Wmn, 2008; Auth, "Alpha Females at the Altar," *In Search of a Feminist Faith*, Pilgrim Press, 2005; Auth, "The Fifteenth Psalm," *The Adelphean*, The Adelphean, 2004; Auth, "Sacraments," *The Angl Digets*, The Angl Dig, 2004. lmbrock10@aol.com

BROCK, Velma Elaine Wooten (WA) 233 Cambridge St, Syracuse NY 13210 B Washington DC 4/20/1937 d James Abraham Wooten & Martha. MS Fed City Coll 1973; AS Washington Tech Inst 1975; MDiv Wesley TS 1993. D 6/11/1994 P 4/1/1995 Bp Ronald Hayward Haines. S Phil's Chap Baden Brandywine MD 2004-2007; Dio Washington Washington DC 2000-2003; Vic/Chapl U Of Maryland Mssn Coll Pk MD 2000; U Meth Ch Syracuse NY 1994-2000; Prog Asst Cathd of St Ptr & St Paul Washington DC 1993-1994. Intl Rel Coun Cny; UBE. bwb420@yahoo.com

BROCK, William Marshall (Ga) 230 Pinecrest Dr Apt 25, Fayetteville NC 28305 **S Mich And All Ang Savannah GA 1999-** B Spartanburg SC 11/1/1957 s Ralph Leonard Brock & Angeline. BA Clemson U 1979; MDiv VTS 1986. D 10/4/1986 P 5/1/1987 Bp William Arthur Beckham. m 10/15/1988 MaryAnne B Brock. Assoc R S Jn's Epis Ch Fayetteville NC 1993-1999; Asst R S Jas Par Wilmington NC 1990-1993; Ch Of The Nativ Un SC 1987-1990; D Ch Of The Resurr Greenwood SC 1986-1987.

BROCKILL, Raymond (Mass) 7 Joseph St, Andover MA 01810 B Sterling IL 11/28/1940 s Victor Brockill & Pearl. BA Hob 1981; MS Syr 1983; Cert EDS 1985. D 9/6/1986 P 7/1/1987 Bp William George Burrill. m 6/17/1979 Jennifer B S Reiley. Asst Trin Epis Ch Haverhill MA 1998-2000.

BROCKMAN, Bennett A(lbert) (Ct) 362 Lake St, Vernon CT 06066 **P-in-c Gr Ch Stafford Sprg CT 2010-** B Greer SC 10/14/1942 s Albert Hoy Brockman & Lois Faye. BA Furman U 1964; MA Van 1966; PhD Van 1970. D 6/13/1987 P 3/9/1988 Bp Arthur Edward Walmsley. m 6/12/1965 Linda Leigh Brockman c 2. Dioc Exec Com Dio Connecticut Hartford CT 2002-2008; Exam Chapl Chair Dio Connecticut Hartford CT 1997-1999; Ch Missions Pub Co Bd Dio Connecticut Hartford CT 1994-1998; R S Paul's Ch Fairfield CT 1993-2008; Exam Chapl Mem Dio Connecticut Hartford CT 1993-1999; Cur S Mich's Ch Litchfield CT 1987-1993. brockben@aol.com

BROCKMAN, John Martin (Ind) 82 E. Colony Acres Dr., Brazil IN 47834 B Batesville IN 6/26/1934 s Martin A Brockman & Margaret. BS Xavier U 1957; Med Xavier U 1977; CAS EDS 1999. Rec from Roman Catholic 12/11/1999 Bp Douglas Edwin Theuner. m 8/29/1998 Sylvia Ann Brockman. S Mk's Ch Plainfield IN 2005-2006; Int S Jn's Epis Ch Crawfordsville IN 2004-2005; S Mk's Epis Ch Perryville MD 2000-2004. brockmanjs@aol.com

BROCKMANN, R John (Mass) 150 Chapel St, Norwood MA 02062 **Min Prov Third Av Cmnty Churc Columbus OH 2011-; R Gr Ch Norwood MA 2010-** B New York NY 5/25/1951 s Robert J Brockmann & Marilyn Leone. BA Geo 1973; MA U Chi 1974; DA U MI 1981. D 6/14/1997 P 12/13/1997 Bp Cabell Tennis. m 8/28/1993 Sarah Long c 2. Chr Ch Delaware City DE 2005-2009. Auth, "Commodore Robert F. Stockton (1792-1867)," Cambria Press, 2009; Auth, "Twisted Rails/Sinking Ships: Rhetoric of 19th Century Accident Investigations," Baywood Pub, 2004; Auth, "Exploding Steamboats, Senate Debates, and Tech Reports," Baywood Pub, 2002; Auth, "From Millwrights to Shipwright to the 21st Century," Hampton Press, 1998; "Writing Better Computer Documentation for Users: From Paper to Hypertext," Jn Wiley & Sons, 1990; "Ethics and Tech Cmncatn," Soc for Tech Cmncatn, 1989; "The Writer's Pocket Almanack," Info Books, 1988; "The Case Method in Tech Cmncatn: Theory and Models," Assn of Teachers of Tech Writing, 1985; "New Essays in Sci and Tech Cmncatn," Baywood Pub, 1983. Third Ord Soc of S Fran 1993. jbrockma@udel.edu

BROCKMANN, Sarah (Mass) 92 Main St # 277, Warwick MD 21912 **R Trin Epis Ch Rockland MA 2009-** B Worcester MA 3/10/1964 d Richard Rice Long & Virginia Helen. BS Bos 1986; MDiv Harvard DS 1994. D 5/11/2000 P 2/2/2002 Bp Wayne Parker Wright. m 8/28/1993 R John Brockmann c 2. Asst and Epis Campus Min S Thos's Par Newark DE 2007-2009; Yth Dir Dio Delaware Wilmington DE 2006; Asst Imm Ch Highlands Wilmington DE 2001-2006; Yth Dir Ch of St Andrews & St Matthews Wilmington DE 2000. imabiah@yahoo.com

BROCKMEIER, Alan Lee (RG) 8516 N Prince St, Clovis NM 88101 **Asst Ch Of S Jas The Apos Clovis NM 2005-** B Freeport IL 7/7/1948 s Lowell Lee Brockmeier & Barbara Jean. AS Estrn New Mex U 1987; BS Estrn New Mex U 2001; Grad Dplma TESM 2003. D 6/21/2003 P 7/11/2004 Bp Terence Kelshaw. m 7/8/1994 Suzanne Brockmeier c 1. Bro of S Andr 2007; Ord of S Lk 2007. spcaptain@plateautel.net

BRODERICK, Janet (Nwk) 268 2nd St, Jersey City NJ 07302 **R S Ptr's Ch Morristown NJ 2009-** B New York NY 9/7/1955 d James Broderick & Patricia. BA U MI 1977; MDiv GTS 1990. D 6/9/1990 P 12/15/1990 Bp Richard Frank Grein. m 11/1/2006 Joseph Michael Kraft c 2. Gr Ch Van Vorst Jersey City NJ 2001-2009; Vic Gr Epis Ch New York NY 1998-2001; All SS' Epis Ch Briarcliff Manor NY 1994-1997; The Ch Of The Epiph New York NY 1990-1994; Sem S Jas Ch New York NY 1990-1991. janetbroderick@gmail.com

BRODERICK, Lynn Remmel (Roch) 149 Genesee St, Geneva NY 14456 B Rochester NY 2/24/1937 d Norman Arthur Remmel & Lillian H. BS SUNY 1958. D 3/29/2008 Bp Jack Marston McKelvey. m 6/21/1958 Edward Broderick c 2. lrbroderick@yahoo.com

BRODERICK, Rosemarie (NJ) P.O. Box 326, Navesink NJ 07752 B Belefonte PA 9/12/1962 d John Joseph Broderick & Diane Kay. BS Trin and U 2001; DCW Dio New Jersey Sch for Deacons 2009. D 5/16/2009 Bp Sylvestre Donato Romero. c 2. rosemarie.broderick@verizon.net

BRODERICK Y GUERRA, Cecily Patricia (LI) 3495 Hawthorne Dr N, Wantagh NY 11793 **Epis Hlth Serv Bethpage NY 2008-; VP of Pstr Care S Jos's Epis Chap Far Rockaway NY 2007-** B Mountain Home ID 6/15/1960 d Cecil Balfour Broderick & Mercedes Milagros. Supvsr Cert CPE; DMin SFTS; Cert Oxf 1982; BA Trin Hartford CT 1982; MDiv Ya Berk 1987. D 6/13/1987 P 1/10/1988 Bp Paul Moore Jr. c 1. P-in-c S Phil's Ch New York NY 2002-2006; R S Jn's Ch Hempstead NY 1992-2002; Cn Cathd Of St Jn The Div New York NY 1990-1991; Cur S Phil's Ch New York NY 1988-1990; Asst S Martha's Ch Bronx NY 1987-1988. Auth, ",Inheriting Our Mo's Gardens," Fortress; Auth, ",Wmn Voices & Visions of the Ch," WCC; Auth, ",St. Jn's First 100 Years: Story as a Resource for Ch Life," San Francisco Theol Semianry (dissertation). Black Caucus; UBE. Mercer Preaching Awd Ya Berk New Haven CT. broderickguerra@verizon.net

BRODIE, Robert Earle (Spr) 2609 Kipling Dr, Springfield IL 62711 **Dn The Cathd Ch Of S Paul Springfield IL 2006-** B Miami FL 12/7/1946 s Earle Wilder Brodie & June Virginia. BA U of Miami 1970; MDiv STUSo 1978; MA U of Miami 1980; DMin Bethany TS 1985; MEd UTC 1985; CAS S Mich's 1990; Coll of Preachers 1991; PsyD Sthrn 1999; MA Amer Mltry U 2011; DMin STUSo 2012. D 6/4/1978 P 12/1/1978 Bp James Loughlin Duncan. m 4/16/1983 Linda Mcbrayer. Cn for Mnstry Dio Tennessee Nashville TN 1996-2006; Cn To Ordnry Dio E Tennessee Knoxville TN 1994-1996; R S Paul's Ch Athens TN 1987-1993; R Chr Ch Epis So Pittsburg TN 1980-1987; Cur S Phil's Ch Coral Gables FL 1978-1980. Auth, "The Use Of Rel Lang In Suicide Attempts," *Journ of Crisis Intervention*, Sthrn Mississippi Press, 1985; Auth, "A Discussion Of Ethical Implications Of The Plcy Of Detente In View Of The Siviet Definitn Of Detente," *White Paper for U.S. Congr*, The Wackenhut Security Study Cntr, 1974. Acad Of Par Cleric Amer Mnstry Assn 1985; Amer Acad Of Homil 1987; AAR 2010; Assn of Form Intelligence Off 2003; CODE 1986-2006; Int Mnstry Ntwk 1997; Intl Conf Police Chap 1983; No Amer Dn's Assn 2006. Hon Cn The Cathd od St Paul, TEC Dio Quincy 2009; Iron Arrow Hon Soc U Miami 1969. deanbrodiesp@comcast.net

BRODY, Mary Ann (Roch) 267 Penhurst Rd, Rochester NY 14610 **P-in-c S Steph's Ch Rochester NY 2007-; U Roch Med Cntr - Strong Memi Hosp Rochester NY 2006-** B Shelby NC 11/24/1959 d William Harvey Brody & Carolyn Rheta. BA Pur 1983; MA Wake Forest U 1985; Med Leh 1988; MDiv Bex 2004. D 6/5/2004 P 5/27/2006 Bp Jack Marston McKelvey. m 2/24/2011 Nancy Ramsay c 1. Asst S Lk And S Simon Cyrene Rochester NY 2006-2009. ststephenspastor@frontiernet.net

BROESLER, Robert Joseph (Del) 220 N Star Rd, Newark DE 19711 **R S Barn Ch Wilmington DE 2001-** B Mineola NY 10/10/1955 s Joseph Walter Broesler & Patricia Ann. BS SUNY 1980; MDiv STUSo 1985; MA Antioch U New Engl 2000. D 5/20/1985 P 12/1/1985 Bp Robert Campbell Witcher Sr. m 4/6/2009 Karen Ann Schwarz c 3. R S Andr's Ch Meriden CT 1991-2001; Cn Cathd Of The Incarn Garden City NY 1986-1991; Cur S Mary's Ch Lake Ronkonkoma NY 1985-1986; Epis Cmnty Serv Long Island 1927 Garden City NY 1980-1982. frbob2000@yahoo.com

BROGAN, Betty Jean (Mich) 17665 E Kirkwood Dr, Clinton Township MI 48038 **D S Gabr's Epis Ch Eastpointe MI 2002-** B Marietta OH 11/1/1927 d Cornelius R Brogan & Mae G. BA Duke 1948; MA U Of Detroit 1964; EdD Wayne 1978. D 6/15/2002 Bp Wendell Nathaniel Gibbs Jr. Dioc Tithes and Offerings Com Dio Michigan Detroit MI 2007-2009; Dioc Nomin Com Dio Michigan Detroit MI 2005-2007; Dioc Coun Dio Michigan Detroit MI 2005-2006; Bd Dir Whitaker TS Dio Michigan Detroit MI 2004-2009; Dioc

CESA Com Dio Michigan Detroit MI 2004-2008; Bd Dir St. Anne's Mead Dio Michigan Detroit MI 2004-2007. bbrogan1@comcast.net

BROGAN, Margaret (Cal) 1432 Eastshore Dr, Alameda CA 94501 B Cleveland OH 9/11/1949 d James Michael Brogan & Margaret Helen. BA Guilford Coll 1971; California St U 1974; MDiv CDSP 1993. D 6/8/1994 P 6/1/1995 Bp William Edwin Swing. m 6/15/2003 Wendell Kawahara c 3. S Andr's Sch Saratoga CA 2006-2011; Cur S Clare's Epis Ch Pleasanton CA 1994-2005. Outstanding Cler Awd Natl Allnce For Mntl Illness 2002. revmeg@comcast.net

BROKAW, Ronald Gene (CFla) 1106 Dorchester St, Orlando FL 32803 B Kirksville MO 1/12/1930 s Edward C Brokaw & Minnie V. BA U of Missouri 1953; MDiv CDSP 1957; MS Kansas St Teachers Coll 1966. D 6/22/1957 Bp Edward Clark Turner P 12/21/1957 Bp Goodrich R Fenner. m 11/23/1959 Jeanne (McBee) Mc Bee. Int S Ptr's Epis Ch Lake Mary FL 1989-1990; Trin Preparatory Sch Of Florida Winter Pk FL 1968-1989; R S Andr's Epis Ch Emporia KS 1959-1968; Asst S Jas Ch Wichita KS 1957-1959. Associated Parishes. rbrokaw@cfl.rr.com

BROME, Henderson LeVere (Mass) 51 Sumner St, Milton MA 02186 **R S Cyp's Ch Roxbury MA 1979-** B BB 2/12/1942 s Leon Brome & Constance. MDiv Ya Berk 1973; PhD Col 1978. Rec 1/1/1980 Bp The Bishop Of Chichester. m 10/3/1986 Deborah Ridley c 2. S Cyp's Ch Roxbury MA 1980-2009. hbrome@aol.com

BROMILEY, Hugh Philip (CFla) 1250 Paige Pl, The Villages FL 32159 **R S Geo Epis Ch The Villages FL 2007-** B Aldershot UK 8/29/1953 s Norman Philip Bromiley & Katherine Judith. Tchr Certification Alexander Tchg Cntr 1980; B.Th Trin Theol Coll, Bristol UK 1989; M.Th Westminster Coll, Oxford UK 1999. Trans from Church Of England 7/3/1989 Bp Charles Shannon Mallory. m 12/8/1984 Khara M Allen. R Trin Epis Ch Redlands CA 2003-2005; R S Thos Ch Savannah GA 1998-2003; R S Jas' Ch Monterey CA 1993-1997; R S Lk's Ch Auburn CA 1991-1993; Cur All SS Ch Carmel CA 1989-1991. Auth, "In Search of a Miracle," *In Search of a Miracle*, iuniverse, 2001. Chapl and Speaker Ord Of S Lk 1991. frhugh@stgeorge-episcopal.net

BRONDSTED, Linda Cole Judd (CFla) 1880 Taylor Ave, Winter Park FL 32789 B New Britain CT 8/4/1944 d Harlan Cole Judd & Mary. Newton Hosp Sch of Nrsng 1965; BD Indiana U 1985; Inst for Chr Stds 1985. D 3/10/1986 Bp William Hopkins Folwell. c 1. D Cathd Ch Of S Lk Orlando FL 1994-2002; Archd Dio Cntrl Florida Orlando FL 1993-2010; All SS Ch Of Winter Pk Winter Pk FL 1990-1994. NAAD 1992. Steph Mnstry Awd NAAD 2001. lindabron@aol.com

BRONK JR, Harold R (Mass) 27 Curtis Road, Milton MA 02186 B New York NY 3/4/1928 s Harold R Bronk & Anna Marie. BA Hofstra U 1951; MDiv Ya Berk 1954; cand/dr.theol U of Tuebingen 1967; Cert U of Massachusetts 1992. D 6/2/1954 Bp Charles F Hall P 12/4/1954 Bp Oliver J Hart. m 12/10/1988 Joyce C Caggiano c 6. Int S Eustace Ch Lake Placid NY 2004-2005; P-in-c Gr Ch Detroit MI 2004; Bd Dinner Prog Ch Of S Jn The Evang Boston MA 2002-2003; Int Belmont Chap at S Mk's Sch Southborough MA 1999-2000; S Jas Ch Amesbury MA 1998-2000; Int S Mk's Ch Southborough MA 1997-1998; R Ch of the Ascen Munich 81545 DE 1994-1996; Int S Andr's Ch Framingham MA 1992-1993; Liturg Cmsn Dio Massachusetts Boston MA 1986-2000; P-in-c S Dav's Epis Ch Cambria Heights NY 1957-1959; R The Ch Of S Mary Of The Harbor Provincetown MA 1956-1957. Auth, "Das Streben Nach Glueck," *Beitraege zur Situation....*, Rombach, Freiburg, Germany, 1981; Auth, "Bleiben Unsere Kinder Sitzen?," *Beitraege zur Situation....*, Rombach, Freiburg, Germany, 1980; Auth, "Infermiere-Didattiche," *Rapporto del seminario....*, Ministero sanitaria, Milano, Italia, 1976. Soc of Cath Priests 2011. haroldrbronk@me.com

BRONOS, Sarah L. (CFla) 7718 White Ash Street, Orlando FL 32819 **Ch Of The Gd Shpd Maitland FL 2009-** B Doncaster Yorkshire U.K. 6/12/1952 d George Albert Richmond & Alma Nall. Dip. d'Etudes Franc. Inst Francais Du Royaume 1973; M.Div., cl Nash 2007. D 6/2/2007 P 12/29/2007 Bp John Wadsworth Howe. m 10/6/1979 Patiste Bronos c 2. Writer, "A Journey Through the Bible (Nahum-Malachi)," *The Journey*, Bible Reading Fllshp, 2009. sbronos@yahoo.com

BRONSON, David Louis (NY) 414 Cottekill Rd, Stone Ridge NY 12484 B Jackson MI 7/2/1929 s Glenn Potter Bronson & Yetchen Helene. BA U MI 1953; STM Ya Berk 1956. D 6/20/1956 Bp Richard S M Emrich P 7/6/1957 Bp Charles L Street. R Ch Of The H Cross Kingston NY 1963-1989; Cur S Paul's Ch Fairfield CT 1961-1963; Cur Chr Ch Waukegan IL 1956-1957.

BROOK, Robert Charles (Mich) 6112 W Longview Dr, East Lansing MI 48823 B Canada 6/4/1937 s Charles E Brook & Jean. BA MI SU 1959; BD Bex 1963; MA MI SU 1964; EdD MI SU 1968. D 6/29/1963 Bp Archie H Crowley P 1/20/1964 Bp Robert Lionne DeWitt. m 9/5/1959 Suzanne Brook c 3. Trin Epis Ch Grand Ledge MI 1998-1999; Cbury on the Lake Waterford MI 1997-2002; Vic S Aug Of Cbury Mason MI 1969-1970; Vic S Aug Of Cbury Mason MI 1963-1966. rcbsbb@mac.com

BROOK JR, William Varina (SO) 131 Page Ct, Delaware OH 43015 B New Bedford MA 3/21/1936 s William Varina Brook & Mildred Evelyn. BA Marshall U 1958; Bex 1961; MA Methodist TS In Ohio 1994. D 6/11/1961 P 4/24/1963 Bp Wilburn Camrock Campbell. m 8/14/1965 Margaret May Brook c 1. AIDS T/F Dio Sthrn Ohio Cincinnati OH 1987-1991; Stwdshp Com Dio Sthrn Ohio Cincinnati OH 1986-1989; Inst on Racism Dio Sthrn Ohio Cincinnati OH 1984-1991; Bd Managers Dio Sthrn Ohio Cincinnati OH 1980-1991; Ecum Com Dio Sthrn Ohio Cincinnati OH 1980-1985; R S Paul's Ch Chillicothe OH 1979-1991; Vic Ch Of The Gd Shpd Bluemont VA 1970-1979; R Gr Ch Berryville VA 1970-1979; Vic S Mary's Memi Berryville VA 1970-1979; S Jn's Ch Harpers Ferry WV 1968-1970; Vic Gr Epis Ch Middleway WV 1966-1970; Vic S Phil's Ch Chas Town WV 1966-1968; Dept of Chr Soc Relatns Dio W Virginia Charleston WV 1965-1967; Exec Coun Dio W Virginia Charleston WV 1964-1966; R Ascen Epis Ch Hinton WV 1963-1966; Cur S Lk's Epis Ch Welch WV 1961-1963. Omicron Delta Kappa. hierus@aol.com

BROOKE-DAVIDSON, Jennifer (WTex) 6000 Fm 3237 Unit A, Wimberley TX 78676 **Dir of Chr Ed S Steph's Epis Ch Wimberley TX 2009-** B Corpus Christi TX 6/29/1960 d John Charles Brooke & Sherry Sigler. AB Ya 1982; JD U of Texas Sch of Law 1985; MAGL Fuller TS 2009. D 6/8/2009 P 12/16/2009 Bp Gary Richard Lillibridge. m 8/17/1985 Charles Carrick Brooke-Davidson c 2. JENNIFERB@STSTEVE.ORG

BROOKFIELD, Christopher Morgan (Va) 1870 Field Rd, Charlottesville VA 22903 B Rye NY 6/12/1936 s William Lord Brookfield & Louise. BA Pr 1958; MA Col 1963; BD UTS 1968. D 12/19/1976 P 12/10/1977 Bp Robert Bruce Hall. m 6/8/1963 Lynne Brookfield c 2. Assoc S Mary's Ch Richmond VA 1996-2008; Co-Dir and Fac, Inst. for Sch Mnstry VTS Alexandria VA 1988-1994. Co-Auth, *Rel & Educ*, NAIS, 1972; Co-Auth, *Yth in Crisis*, Seabury Press, 1966; Ed/Co-Auth, *Take Off Your Shoes & Walk*, Devin-Adair, 1961. NAES 1976-1984. BD cl UTS New York NY 1968.

✠ **BROOKHART JR, Rt Rev Charles Franklin** (Mont) 515 N Park Ave, PO Box 2020, Helena MT 59601 **Bp of Montana Dio Montana Helena MT 2003-** B Parkersburg WV 8/30/1948 s Charles Franklin Brookhart & JoAnn. BA Witt 1970; Van 1971; MDiv Luth TS 1974; DMin Untd TS 1984. D 6/1/1988 P 10/22/1988 Bp Robert Poland Atkinson Con 9/27/2003 for Mont. m 6/15/1974 Susan Jane Moyer c 2. R The Lawrencefield Chap Par Wheeling WV 1988-2003. Ed and Contrib, "Make Us One w Chr," TEC and Meth Ch, 2006. Anamchara Fllshp 2008. cfbmt@qwestoffice.net

BROOKMAN, Cathleen Anne (Chi) 29 West 410 Emerald Green Drive, Warrenville IL 60555 **S Jn's Epis Ch Naperville IL 2000-** B Lakewod OH 11/12/1943 d Kenneth Robinson & Anne. MS Geo 1985; MS Wms 1985. D 2/5/2000 Bp William Dailey Persell. Cathleenbrookman@sbcglobal.net

BROOKS, Ashton Jacinto (VI) C/O All Saints Church, 5A5 Mandahl Peak - PO Box 1148, St. Thomas Virgin Islands (U.S.) **Dn Cathd Ch of All SS St Thos VI VI 1998-** B 9/11/1942 s Eduardo Brooks & Maria Louisa. Santo Domingo Autonoma U Santo Domingo Do 1963; BA Inter Amer U of Puerto Rico 1966; STB ETSC 1969; Cert EDS 1979; STM GTS 1989; DD CDSP 1993. D 5/25/1969 P 11/1/1969 Bp Paul Axtell Kellogg. m 4/24/1969 Margaret Brooks. The Coun of Theo Edu in Latin Amer & the Car Santo Domingo 2009-2011; Cn In Res Cathd Of St Jn The Div New York NY 1993-1998; Novena Provincia Iglesia Epis 1988-1993; R Iglesia Epis San Andres Santo Domingo DO 1972-1979; Dio The Dominican Republic (Iglesia Epis Dominicana) Santo Domingo DO 1969-1988. Auth, "Eclesiologia: Presencia Anglicana En La Reg Cntrl De Amer". DD CDSP 1993. ajbrooks23@yahoo.com

BROOKS, Donald Edgar (WTenn) 1436 Forest Drive, Union City TN 38261 **S Jas Epis Ch Un City TN 2004-** B Alvin TX 8/2/1946 s Weldon Franklin Brooks & Edna Mae. BA Austin Peay St U 1969; Med U of Memphis 1975; MA U of Memphis 1982; U So 1987. D 11/29/1981 Bp William F Gates Jr P 12/1/1982 Bp William Evan Sanders. Chr Ch Brownsville TN 1987-2004; Vic Imm Ch Ripley TN 1987-2004; Vic Imm Epis Ch La Grange TN 1987-1992; Vic S Thos Ch Somerville TN 1987-1992; Asst S Jas Bolivar TN 1981-1986. Auth, "A Hist Of Temple Adas Israel Brownsville Tn w Symbology Of The Windows". Spck/Usa. bdonbrooks@cs.com

BROOKS, Ethelridge Albert (Hond) Aptd 28, La Ceiba Atlantida 31101 Honduras **P-in-c Iglesia Epis Santisima Trinidad La Ceiba At HN 1976-** B Tola Atlantida HN 1/1/1941 s Albert Ernest Gordon Brooks & Mary Ann. MA Universidad Nacional Autonoma De Mex Mx 1971, Cert Inst Theologico Epis 1973; Cert Epis TS of The SW 1976. D 6/26/1971 Bp William Carl Frey P 8/24/1977 Bp Anselmo Carral-Solar. m 1/10/1973 Maria del Carmen Morales de Brooks. Dio Honduras Miami FL 1972-2010. ealbrooks2008@yahoo.com

BROOKS, James Buckingham (Ida) Po Box 36, Letha ID 83636 **D S Mich's Cathd Boise ID 1987-** B Boise ID 10/30/1938 s Orville Perry Brooks & Frances Elizabeth. Boise St U; E Oregon U; The Coll of Idaho. D 3/28/1987 Bp David Bell Birney IV. m 1/24/1960 Susan Jane Brooks c 2. Auth, "Treasurers Of Imagination," *The Intl Libr Of Poetry*, 2000; Auth, "Heart Sounds". Love Awd (Ldr Of Excellence) Idaho Hosp Assoc 1999; Dsa For Publ Serv. hocdu@yahoo.com

BROOKS, Kimberly (CPa) 248 Seneca St., Harrisburg PA 17110 **S Paul's Epis Ch Harrisburg PA 2007-** B Harrisburg PA 10/21/1956 s Jesse Russell Brooks & Rebecca Ann. BS Lancaster Bible Coll; MDiv Lancaster TS 2005; VTS

Alexandria VA 2007. D 6/9/2007 P 2/9/2008 Bp Nathan Dwight Baxter. m 7/16/2006 Shelley Baker Shelley Baker c 4. kimbrk4@aol.com

BROOKS, Porter Harrison (Va) 9797 Kedge Ct, Vienna VA 22181 B Chicago IL 7/5/1926 s Hugh Moore Woods & Lucy Elizabeth. BA McMurry U 1948; MDiv VTS 1951; US-A Chapl Sch 1962; Command and Gnrl Stff Coll 1964; Command and Gnrl Stff Coll 1966. D 1/3/1951 P 7/4/1951 Bp George Henry Quarterman. m 8/21/1954 Norma Margaret Brooks c 3. Assoc S Jn's Epis Ch McLean VA 1987-1992; Int S Alb's Epis Ch Annandale VA 1986-1987; Int Trin Ch Arlington VA 1985-1986; Int S Mary's Epis Ch Arlington VA 1983-1985; Emm Epis Ch (Piedmont Par) Delaplane VA 1982; Off Of Bsh For ArmdF New York NY 1955-1969; R S Matt's Ch Pampa TX 1953-1955. Auth, "Cross, Crook, and Candle: Story of Rel at Ft Myer," *Virginia*, 1974.

BROOKS, Richard Smith (WK) 1333 Crescent Ln, Concordia KS 66901 B Glasco KS 6/9/1924 s Earl Richardson Brooks & Leona Caroline. AA SUNY 1973; BS Cameron U 1976. D 11/21/1997 P 10/30/1998 Bp Vernon Edward Strickland. m 2/12/1944 Alve May Lee c 2. P-in-c Ch Of The Epiph Concordia KS 1998-2005. Who'S Who In Amer Universities 1976; Phi Kappa Phi 1974. frbrooks@nckcn.com

BROOKS JR, Robert Brudon (NY) 4 Quail Ridge Rd, Hyde Park NY 12538 B Allentown PA 5/15/1936 s Robert Brudon Brooks & Elizabeth. BA Alleg 1958. D 6/4/1994 Bp Richard Frank Grein. m 9/15/1973 A Jayne Brooks c 2. D Ch Of The Mssh Rhinebeck NY 1994-2008. deacon36@roadrunner.com

BROOKS, Robert Johnson (Ct) 19 Ellise Rd, Storrs Mansfield CT 06268 **Chair and Mem, Dioc Litergy and Mus Cmsn Dio Connecticut Hartford CT 2001-; Mem, Dioc Soc Concerns and Witness Dio Connecticut Hartford CT 2001-; Cn to the Bp for Intl Affrs Dio El Salvador Ambato 18-01-525 Tu EC 1997-** B Austin TX 3/25/1947 s Robert Max Brooks & Marietta. BA St. Edw's U Austin TX 1970; MDiv CDSP 1973; MA U of Notre Dame 1980. D 6/25/1973 Bp Scott Field Bailey P 6/22/1974 Bp J Milton Richardson. R S Paul's Epis Ch Willimantic CT 2001-2004; Bp's Mssn Strtgy Advsry Grp Dio Washington Washington DC 1994-1999; Dir of Govt Relatns Washington D.C Epis Ch Cntr New York NY 1988-1998; Mem, SLC Epis Ch Cntr New York NY 1985-1988; S Thos' Par Washington DC 1984-2000; S Thos Ch Houston TX 1981-1982; All SS Ch Baytown TX 1973-1983; Dio Texas Houston TX 1973-1983. Contrib, "The Baptismal Mystery & Catechumenate," Ch Pub Inc, 1988. Coun of AP 1981; EUC 2006; Intl Consult of Angl Liturgists 1985; Most Venerable Ord of S Jn of Jerusalem 1998; No Amer Acad of Liturg 1981; OHC 1973; Societas Liturgica 1982; The Consult Strng Com 2004. Rossiter Lectr Bex/Rochester, NY 1991. canbrooks@hotmail.com

BROOKS, Robert Thomas (RI) 285 West Main, Little Compton RI 02837 **Assoc P S Andr's By The Sea Little Compton RI 2011-** B Washington DC 12/16/1946 s William Francis Brooks & Katherine. AB Harv 1968; MBA Harv 1973; MDiv EDS 1995. D 6/10/1995 Bp Allen Lyman Bartlett Jr P 12/19/1995 Bp J Clark Grew II. m 12/28/1968 Rhea Brooks c 2. Int R S Andr's By The Sea Little Compton RI 2009-2010; R Gr Ch In Providence Providence RI 2000-2009; R Chr Epis Ch Kent OH 1995-2000. Auth, "Conjugating The Verb To Be," *Preaching Through The Year of Lk*, Morehouse Pub, 2000. Fllshp of S Jn the Evang 1995. revbobbrooks@aol.com

BROOKS, Theodora Nmade (NY) 750 Kelly St, Bronx NY 10455 **S Marg's Ch Bronx NY 1997-** B Grassfield LR 2/2/1963 d John Theodore Wea Brooks & Ida Kedo. U Liberia LR; BA Cuttington U Coll 1987; MDiv VTS 1992; STM GTS 2000. Trans 12/9/1996 Bp Walter Decoster Dennis Jr. m 6/22/2002 Paul Erik Block c 2. tnbrooks@optonline.net

BROOKS, Thomas Gerald (NY) 35 Cambridge Ct, Highland NY 12528 B Seattle WA 6/4/1939 s Thomas James Brooks & Winnifred May. BA U of Washington 1962; MDiv GTS 1965. D 9/11/1965 P 3/28/1966 Bp Ivol I Curtis. c 2. Chr Ch Marlboro NY 2004-2011; Cur S Paul's Epis Ch Bremerton WA 1965-1967. brookstg@optonline.net

BROOKS, William Earl (SeFla) 1750 E Oakland Park Blvd, Oakland Park TX 33334 **Assoc Palmer Memi Ch Houston TX 2011-** B Houston TX 6/9/1951 s James Marvin Brooks & Hazel. BFA U of Houston 1976; MA U of Houston 1978; MDiv VTS 1981. D 6/18/1981 P 3/1/1982 Bp Maurice Manuel Benitez. m 10/18/1986 Suzanne Lee c 2. S Mk's Epis Sch Ft Lauderdale FL 2006-2011; S Paul's Ch New Orleans LA 2004-2006; Assoc Epis HS Bellaire TX 1993-2004; Asst S Fran Ch Houston TX 1981-1993. dubbrooks@gmail.com

BROOME, John Tol (NC) 3009 Round Hill Rd, Greensboro NC 27408 B Orlando FL 12/9/1931 s Lafayette Ericson Broome & Lillie Brown. BA U So 1954; MDiv VTS 1958. D 8/20/1958 P 3/14/1959 Bp Thomas H Wright. m 7/11/1959 Mary Hines Nicholson c 3. R H Trin Epis Ch Greensboro NC 1972-1994; Asst S Andr's Epis Ch Coll Pk MD 1965-1968; R S Paul's Ch Beaufort NC 1962-1965; R Emm Ch Farmville NC 1960-1962; P-in-c S Jas Epis Ch Belhaven NC 1958-1960. Auth, "Yth arts," *'64 EYC Notebook*. jbroome@triad.rr.com

BROOME JR, William Bridges (Chi) 504 E Earle Street, Landrum SC 29356 **P-in-c Santa Teresa de Avila Chicago IL 2000-; Dio Chicago Chicago IL 1985-** B Spartanburg SC 1/12/1950 s William Bridges Broome & Grace. BA Newberry Coll 1972; MEd U of So Carolina 1974; MDiv SWTS 1979; CPE Alexian Brothers 1980; Masters H Apos Sem 2005. D 6/27/1979 Bp George Moyer Alexander P 5/1/1980 Bp James Winchester Montgomery. R The Annunc Of Our Lady Gurnee IL 1998-1999; P in Charge Santa Teresa de Avila Chicago IL 1997; R S Raphael The Archangel Oak Lawn IL 1989-1997; Vic S Chad Epis Ch Loves Pk IL 1985-1989; Asst P S Alb's Ch Chicago IL 1979-1981. Missionaries of the H Apos 2003. bbbroome@yahoo.com

BROOMELL, Ann Johnson (Ct) 78 Olive St Apt 412, New Haven CT 06511 **Transitional P-in-c S Paul's Ch Brunswick ME 2011-** B New Rochelle NY 10/3/1946 d John Paul Broomell & Ethel Irene. Buc 1966; BA Cedar Crest Coll 1968; MDiv EDS 1994; DMin SWTS 2003. D 6/3/1995 Bp Barbara Clementine Harris P 4/26/1996 Bp M(arvil) Thomas Shaw III. c 2. Int R S Barn Epis Ch Greenwich CT 2010-2011; Int R S Paul's Ch Fairfield CT 2010; Assoc Wrshp/Formation Chr Epis Ch Ponte Vedra Bch FL 2007-2009; Fin Com Dio Easton Easton MD 2003-2007; Cathd Dn Trin Cathd Easton MD 2003-2007; R Ch Of S Asaph Bala Cynwyd PA 1999-2003; Dioc Coun Dio Massachusetts Boston MA 1996-1998; D/P-in-c S Paul's Epis Ch Bedford MA 1995-1998; D Ch Of The Gd Shpd Waban MA 1995. No Amer Com, St. Geo's Coll, Jerusa 2007; Soc of Cath Priests 2009. abroomell@aol.com

BROSEND II, William Frank (Ky) 335 Tennessee Ave., Sewanee TN 37383 **Assoc. Prof. of Homil The TS at The U So Sewanee TN 2006-** B Cincinnati OH 3/10/1954 s William F Brosend & Lucille. BA Denison U 1976; MDiv Van 1979; PhD U Chi 1993. D 6/4/2005 P 12/10/2005 Bp Edwin Funsten Gulick Jr. m 3/10/1984 Christine Green c 1. D Chr Ch Cathd Louisville KY 2005-2006. Ed, "Feasting on the Gospels," WJKP, 2012; Auth, "The Preaching of Jesus," WJKP, 2010; co-Auth, "Feasts of Jesus and the H Fam," *Commentary on Feasts, Fasts and H Days*, Fortress Press, 2007; Auth, "The Parables," *Conversations w Scripture*, Morehouse Pub, 2005; co-Auth, "Adv and Christmas," *New Proclamation Lectionary Commentary Year B*, Fortress Press, 2005. Acad of Homil 2003; Angl Assn of Biblic Scholars 2002; SBL 1992. Phi Beta Kappa Denison U 1976. wbrosend@sewanee.edu

BROTHERTON, Curt Paul (CFla) 692 Linville Falls Dr, West Melbourne FL 32904 **D H Trin Epis Ch Melbourne FL 1997-** B CT 8/12/1930 s Earl Wayne Brotherton & Margaret. BS U of Bridgeport 1952; CLU Amer Coll of Life Underwriters 1967; Inst for Chr Stuides 1996. D 6/28/1997 Bp John Wadsworth Howe. m 8/2/1997 Barbara Ann Brotherton. cpb@digital.net

BROTHERTON, Elizabeth Ann (Tex) P.O. Box 368, Manchaca TX 78652 **Dio Texas Houston TX 2011-; St Lk's Epis Hosp Houston TX 2010-** B IL 9/30/1946 d LeRoy T Carter & Helen M. BA Cntrl Methodist Coll 1968; RN Missouri Bapt Hosp Sch of Nrsng S Louis MO 1986; MDiv Epis TS of the SW 2008. D 5/31/2008 P 12/13/2008 Bp Robert LeRoy Fitzpatrick. m 3/1/1968 Thomas J Brotherton c 2. Assoc R S Alb's Epis Ch Austin Manchaca TX 2008-2009. revannbrotherton@gmail.com

BROUCHT, Mary Louise (CPa) 126 N. Water St., Lancaster PA 17603 B Lancaster PA 1/13/1935 d Joseph Leroy Grassel & Frances Elizabeth. Lancaster TS. D 6/16/1983 Bp Charlie Fuller McNutt Jr. c 2. S Jas Ch Lancaster PA 1989-1997. NANNYLOU@HOLEINTHEWALLPUPPETS.COM

BROUGHTON, Jacalyn Irene (Eau) E4357 451st Ave, Menomonie WI 54751 B Lubbock TX 1/24/1955 d Jack Russell Kelly & Bernadine Irene. D 5/4/2008 Bp Mark Lawrence Mac Donald. m 12/14/1979 William Broughton c 4. jacalyn.broughton@gmail.com

BROUGHTON, William (SanD) 1830 Avenida Del Mundo Unit 712, Coronado CA 92118 B New Bedford MA 8/29/1929 s Harry Broughton & Anne. BA Wheaton Coll 1955; MA Wheaton Coll 1956; BD SWTS 1958; SFTS 1981; UTS 1981; USN 1982. D 9/27/1958 Bp Charles L Street P 4/1/1959 Bp Gerald Francis Burrill. Stff Par of Trin Ch New York NY 1978-1981; Off Of Bsh For ArmdF New York NY 1968-1969; Asst R Chr Ch Winnetka IL 1966-1968; Cur Chr Ch Winnetka IL 1958-1960. Ascalon Excavation Soc, Ecum Fraternity Of Jerusalem; Helenic Inst For Preservation Of Ancient Ships. Presidental Meritorious Serv Awd Jewish/Chr/Muslim Trialogue; Hon Cn S Paul Cathd San Diego.

BROUILLETTE, Paul Thomas (Chi) 2148 Plainfield Dr, Des Plaines IL 60018 B Chicago IL 4/12/1944 s Lordeen V Brouillette & Dorothy. BA Div Word Coll 1967; Grad Study DePaul U 1968; MDiv Cath Theol Un 1971; Grad Study DePaul U 1980. Rec from Roman Catholic 12/19/1976 as Priest Bp James Winchester Montgomery. m 10/7/1972 Judith Ann Dwyer c 2. Asstg P S Mary's Ch Pk Ridge IL 1979-1980; Asst S Mart's Ch Des Plaines IL 1977-2004. NASSAM 1976. paultentmaker@cs.com

BROWDER III, James Wilbur (SVa) Po Box 133, Courtland VA 23837 **S Lk's Ch Courtland VA 1982-** B Richmond VA 9/30/1943 s James Wilbur Browder & Alice Mae. BA Wake Forest U 1965; Med U of Virginia 1969; MDiv VTS 1981. D 6/24/1982 P 3/1/1983 Bp C(laude) Charles Vache. Vic S Paul's Epis Ch Surry VA 1982-1986.

BROWER, Anne Clayton (SVa) 1016 Baldwin Ave, Norfolk VA 23507 B Plainfield NJ 5/7/1938 d Charles H Brower & Elizabeth. BA Smith 1960; MD Coll of Physicians and Surgeons 1964. D 6/9/2001 Bp David Conner Bane Jr P 12/15/2001 Bp O'Kelley Whitaker. m 9/29/2001 Glenn Allen Scott c 2. Old

Donation Ch Virginia Bch VA 2001-2002. "I Am Not Ready to Die Just Yet: Healing Stories," R. Brent Whittington, 2005; "Arthritis in Black and White," Sanders, 1988; "65+ med Journ artcls / Bk chptrs". SOVAC 2004; TCPC 2006. annecbrower@att.net

BROWER, David Angus (WMich) 7895 Adams St, Zeeland MI 49464 **Int Ch Of The H Cross Kentwood MI 2009-** B Zeeand MI 9/25/1942 s Angus J Brower & Emma V. BD Grand Rapids Bapt Sem 1964; MA Wstrn Michigan U 1966; MDiv EDS 1979; DMin GTF 2001. D 6/16/1979 P 4/12/1980 Bp H Coleman McGehee Jr. m 7/11/1964 Clara Elizabeth Brower c 1. Int P-in-c S Lk's Par Kalamazoo MI 2011; S Greg's Epis Ch Muskegon MI 2005-2008; Gr Ch Lockport NY 2000-2005; R S Jas Ch Piqua OH 1997-2000; R S Mk's Ch Sidney OH 1997-2000; R S Paul's Epis Ch Greenville OH 1997-2000; R Gr Epis Ch Southgate MI 1982-1996; Asst All SS Epis Ch Pontiac MI 1979-1982. stgregorys@verizon.net

BROWER, Gary Robert (Colo) 2050 E Evans Ave Ste 29, Denver CO 80208 B Portland OR 8/29/1955 s Robert Wilbur Brower & Selma Regina. BA NW Chr Coll 1978; BS U of Oregon 1978; MDiv CDSP 1981; PhD Duke 1996. D 4/5/1992 Bp Huntington Williams Jr P 4/19/1993 Bp Robert Whitridge Estill. m 7/3/1982 Susan Lynn Bailey c 2. Berkeley Cbury Fndt Berkeley CA 1996-2007; Dio No Carolina Raleigh NC 1994-1996; Assoc S Tit Epis Ch Durham NC 1992-1994. Auth, "The Monks' Carols," The Fac Club, UC Berkeley, 2005; Auth, "Cato of Clermont-Ferraud: A Case of Charcter Assassination in Greg's Hist of the Franks?," *Medieval Perspectives*, 1991. Distinguished Ldrshp Awd YA and Higher Educ Mnstrs 2007; MDiv w dist CDSP Berkeley CA 1981. gary.brower@du.edu

BROWER, George C (Ct) 503A Heritage Village, Southbury CT 06488 **P-in-c Imm S Jas Par Derby CT 2005-** B Port Chester NY 8/11/1930 s George Nehemiah Brower & Florence Mary. U of Bridgeport 1950; Iona Coll 1955; Concordia Coll 1960; LTh STUSo 1963; MDiv STUSo 1970. D 6/11/1963 P 12/21/1963 Bp Horace W B Donegan. m 12/30/1983 Evelyn F Brower c 4. P-in-c Chr Ch Oxford CT 1998-2004; P-in-c S Jn's Ch Sandy Hook CT 1995-1997; P-in-c Chr Ch Bethlehem CT 1995-1996; Asst Litchfield Hills Reg Mnstry Bridgewater CT 1993-1995; R S Tim's Epis Ch Kingsport TN 1966-1970; Cur Chr Ch Of Ramapo Suffern NY 1963-1964. H Cross 1962. Paul Harris Fellowship 1991; Paul Harris Fellowship 1989; Geo Shettle Awd Publ Spkng 1963; Who's Who in the So 1963. revgcb@gmail.com

BROWER, Katherine Moore (WMich) 1416 Pontiac Rd Se, Grand Rapids MI 49506 B East Liverpool OH 4/6/1947 d Robert James Moore & Katherine Louise. BA Albion Coll 1969. D 5/7/1994 Bp Edward Lewis Lee Jr. m 6/20/1970 Robert Brower c 3. D S Andr's Ch Grand Rapids MI 2009-2010; D Gr Ch Grand Rapids MI 1994-2008. NAAD. browerkatherine@yahoo.com

BROWN JR, Allen Webster (Va) 3625 SE 17th Pl, Cape Coral FL 33904 **Epis Ch Cntr New York NY 1997-** B Cooperstown NY 4/24/1931 s Allen Webster Brown & Helen Ruth. BS USNA 1955; Untd States Naval Postgraduate Sch 1963; STB PDS 1966; Command and Gnrl Stff Coll 1975; DMin Trin TS 1981. D 3/20/1966 P 9/24/1966 Bp Allen Webster Brown. m 3/26/1989 Mary Turon Llewellyn c 2. Consult For Congrl Dvlpmt Epis Ch Cntr New York NY 1989-1996; S Hilary's Ch Ft Myers FL 1981-1987; COM Dio Virginia Richmond VA 1980-1984; Exec Asst To Bp Of Virginia Dio Virginia Richmond VA 1980-1984; R S Andr's Epis Ch Palmetto Bay FL 1979-1980; Dio Virginia Richmond VA 1976-1984; Off Of Bsh For ArmdF New York NY 1967-1976; Cur S Jn The Evang Ch Lansdowne PA 1966-1967. Auth, "Mssn Fulfilling: Story Rural & Sm Cmnty Workk Of Epis Ch 20th Century," Morehouse Pub, 1997; Auth, "Congrl Hlth Mnstry: Challenge & Opportunity," Ch Pub Inc, 1997; Auth, "arts Theol & Mltry Pub"; Auth, "Models Of Ecum," Atr; Ed, "AltGld," Morehouse-Barlow. AFP, Conf Of Dioc Exec. abrown5217@aol.com

BROWN, Ashmun Norris (CGC) 3516 Rossmere Rd, Port Charlotte FL 33953 **Asst S Dav's Epis Ch Englewood FL 2008-** B Yakima WA 6/9/1930 s Nathaniel Usher Brown & Marie. JD Bos 1958; LLM U MI 1959; DMin GTF 1989. D 10/18/1984 Bp William Hopkins Folwell P 9/1/1991 Bp John Wadsworth Howe. m 5/25/1981 Rita Lucille Brown. P-in-c S Agatha's Epis Ch Defuniak Sprg FL 1999; S Fran Of Assisi Ch Bushnell FL 1994-1999. Auth, "Co As Tentative As Flight".

BROWN, Barton (NJ) **Int Gr Epis Ch Rutherford NJ 2010-** D 6/11/1960 P 12/17/1960 Bp Horace W B Donegan.

BROWN, Bernard Owen (Chi) 5417 S Blackstone Ave, Chicago IL 60615 B Brooklyn NY 5/24/1930 s C Maxwell Brown & Dorothy. Duke 1950; BD U Chi 1955; MA U Chi 1965; PhD U Chi 1973. D 6/13/1970 Bp James Winchester Montgomery P 12/1/1970 Bp Gerald Francis Burrill. m 6/13/1951 Carol Jean Smith. Auth, "W Side Orgnztn & Ideology Of Deviance"; Auth, "Seasons Of His Mercy". bbrown@midway.uchicago.edu

BROWN, Charles Homer (Okla) 1416 Stoneridge Pl, Ardmore OK 73401 B Paris TX 3/24/1927 s Charles Homer Brown & Mamie Elizabeth. BA TCU 1948; BD Ya Berk 1952; U So 1966; U of Oklahoma 1971. D 9/9/1961 P 5/1/1962 Bp John E Hines. m 8/28/1949 Bettye Dukeminier Crawford. S Ptr's Ch Coalgate OK 1992-1993; Ardmore Vill Ardmore OK 1988-1994; S Mk's Par Altadena CA 1981-1994; R Ch Of The Adv Houston TX 1966-1971; Assoc S Mk's Ch Houston TX 1962-1966. charleshbrown@cableone.net

BROWN, Christopher Aubrey (Alb) 437 Old Potsdam Parishville Road, Potsdam NY 13676 **R Trin Ch Potsdam NY 2000-** B Zurich CH 3/6/1955 s William Henry Brown & Anne. BA Amh 1977; MDiv GTS 1985; PhD UTS 2001. D 6/1/1985 P 6/20/1986 Bp John Bowen Coburn. m 6/24/1989 Starr Marie Brown c 2. Int Par Of Chr The Redeem Pelham NY 1998-2000; Int S Jn's Epis Ch Kingston NY 1997-1998; Gr Epis Ch New York NY 1988-1997; Cur Par Of Chr The Redeem Pelham NY 1985-1987. Auth, "Real Presence," *Angl Dig*, 1999; Auth, "Can Buddhism Save? Finding Resonance in Incomensurability," *Cross Currents*, 1999; Auth, "More than Affirmation: The Incarn as Judgement and Gr," *The Rule of Faith: Scripture*, Morehouse Pub, 1988. revcab@slic.com

BROWN, Clifford Ross (Mass) 351 Pearl St # 1, Cambridge MA 02139 **Bd Mem Epis City Mssn Boston MA 2008-; R Chr Ch Quincy MA 2005-** B Cambridge MA 10/17/1955 s Herbert Elliott Brown & Muriel. BS Estrn U 1981; Cert Afr Stds Bp Tucker Theol Coll 1991; MDiv Andover Newton TS 1992. D 6/15/2002 P 5/31/2003 Bp M(arvil) Thomas Shaw III. Asst S Steph's Memi Ch Lynn MA 2002-2005; Theol Stdt Angl Stds Vol For Mssn New York NY 1989-1990. cbrown@christchurchquincy.org

BROWN, Colin (Los) 1024 Beverly Way, Altadena CA 91001 B Bradford Yorkshire UK 2/26/1932 s Robert Brown & Maud Mary. BA U of Liverpool 1953; BD Tyndale Hall Bristol/Lon GB 1958; MA U of Nottingham 1961; PhD Tyndale Hall Bristol/Lon GB 1970; DD U of Nottingham 1994. Trans from Church Of England 1/4/1981 Bp Robert C Rusack. c 3. Assoc R S Mk's Par Altadena CA 1981-2007. Auth, "Chrsnty & Wstrn Thought," *vol1 From the Ancient Wrld to the Age of Enlightenment*, InterVarsity Press, 1990; Auth, *Hist & Faith*, InterVarsity Press, 1987; Auth, "European," *Jesus in ProtestantThought 1778-1860*, Labyrinth, 1985; Auth, "Report," *That You May Believe*, Paternoster Press, 1985; Auth, "Report," *Miracles & the Critical Mind*, Eerdmans, 1984; Auth, *The New Intl Dictionary of NT Theol (3 volumes)*, Paternoster Press, 1978; Auth, "Hist," *Criticism & Faith (French translation)*, InterVarsity Press, 1976; Auth, *Philos & the Chr Faith*, InterVarsity Press, 1969; Auth, *Karl Barth & the Chr Message*, InterVarsity Press, 1967. AAR 1982; SBL 1982. Hensley Henson Lectures U of Oxford Oxford UK 1993; Awd for Excellence C Davis Weyerhaeuser 1988; Gold Medallion Evang Bk Pub Assoc 1985. colbrn@fuller.edu

BROWN, Craig Howard (WK) 3710 Summer Ln, Hays KS 67601 **Chair - COM Dio Wstrn Kansas Hutchinson KS 2007-** B Melbourne FL 1/1/1967 BS U Of Florida 1990; Med U Of Florida 1997; MDiv TESM 2004. D 5/30/2004 Bp Samuel Johnson Howard P 12/4/2004 Bp James Marshall Adams Jr. m 7/29/2000 Elizabeth Christie Shad c 2. D S Mich's Ch Hays KS 2004-2009. bravos4059@aol.com

BROWN, Daniel Aaron (NC) 936 Cannock St, Grovetown GA 30813 B Savannah GA 11/29/1947 s Henry Jesse Brown & Mildred. BA Armstrong Atlantic St Coll 1974; MDiv STUSo 1996. D 6/8/1996 Bp Don Adger Wimberly P 12/15/1996 Bp J(ames) Gary Gloster. m 7/27/1985 Donna Brown c 1. P-in-c All Souls Ch Wadesboro NC 1996-2005; R Calv Ch Wadesboro NC 1996-2005. dbrown936ga@bellsouth.net

BROWN, Daniel Barnes (At) Po Box 490, Clarkesville GA 30523 **Dio Atlanta Atlanta GA 2003-** B Harlan KY 11/13/1953 s Thomas Rhoades Brown & Dora. BA Furman U 1976; MDiv STUSo 1993. D 6/12/1993 Bp William Arthur Beckham P 1/21/1994 Bp Harry Woolston Shipps. m 11/24/1989 Cynthia Leigh Carson c 2. S Julian's Epis Ch Douglasville GA 2001-2003; R Gr-Calv Epis Ch Clarkesville GA 1998-2001; Asst The Ch Of The Gd Shpd Augusta GA 1993-1998. frdann@me.com

BROWN, David Churchman (WNC) 500 Christ School Rd, Arden NC 28704 **Chapl Chr Sch Arden NC 1995-** B Marianna FL 10/18/1953 s David Samuel Brown & Anne. BA Davidson Coll 1975; MA U of Virginia 1977; MDiv VTS 1992. D 6/6/1992 Bp A(rthur) Heath Light. c 2. Assoc R S Jn's Ch Roanoke VA 1992-1995. kirkbr@aol.com

BROWN, David Crane (NY) 125 Prospect Ave Apt 9G, Hackensack NJ 07601 B Englewood NJ 12/25/1947 s Percival Chapel Brown & Katherine Elizabeth. BA CUNY- Hunter Coll 1969; MDiv The PDS 1972. D 6/3/1972 P 12/9/1972 Bp Paul Moore Jr. Dir of Pstr Care Morningside Hse Nrsng Hm Bronx NY 1994-2008; R Ch Of S Mary The Vrgn Ridgefield Pk NJ 1982-1994; Assoc S Matt's Ch Bedford NY 1974-1982; Cur Ch Of The Mssh Rhinebeck NY 1972-1974. Auth, "S Fran of Assisi," *The Journ for Better Living*. davidc.brown@worldnet.att.net

BROWN, David Frederick (Cal) 12 Caversham House, Caversham Street, London SW3 4AE Great Britain (UK) **Died 8/24/2010** B Richmond VA 5/27/1938 s Paul Jean Brown & Rhoda. BA U Il 1960; MDiv SWTS 1967. D 6/17/1967 Bp James Winchester Montgomery P 12/1/1967 Bp Gerald Francis Burrill. Auth, "Var Books & arts". Ch Fllshp For Psychical & Sprtl Stds; Coll Hlth Care Chapl. DaveyChelsea@aol.com

BROWN, David Wooster (Ct) 729 W Beach Rd, Charlestown RI 02813 B Waterbury CT 8/23/1926 s Harold Wooster Brown & Ruth Eliza. BA Ya 1948;

MDiv Ya Berk 1959; Ldrshp Acad for New Directions 1975. D 6/11/1959 Bp Walter H Gray P 12/5/1959 Bp John Henry Esquirol. m 7/19/1952 Carole Bower c 6. Dio Connecticut Hartford CT 1989; Middlesex Area Cluster Mnstry Higganum CT 1981-1989; Grtr Hartford Reg Mnstry Dio Connecticut Hartford CT 1980-1989; R Chr Ch Montpelier VT 1966-1980; Ch Of The Resurr Norwich CT 1963-1965. Auth, "Var arts & Revs". OHC 1961. The Berkeley Awd The Ya Berk 1985. brownest@riconnect

BROWN, Deborah Eleanor (Minn) 1297 Wilderness Curv, Eagan MN 55123 B Carmel CA 1/20/1940 d Charles Edward French & Lois Eleanor. BA Occ 1961; MDiv Epis TS of The SW 1989. D 6/22/1989 Bp Robert Marshall Anderson P 5/1/1990 Bp Anselmo Carral-Solar. m 7/6/1963 Ronald Earl Brown c 2. S Clem's Ch S Paul MN 2005-2006; S Lk's Ch Minneapolis MN 2000-2001; Int S Lk's Ch Minneapolis MN 1999-2000; Int S Jn The Evang S Paul MN 1998-1999; Dio Minnesota Minneapolis MN 1995-2008; S Chris's Epis Ch Roseville MN 1993-1998; P Gr Epis Ch Georgetown TX 1989-1992. Minnesota Epis Cler Assn. debronmn@aol.com

BROWN OJN, Deborah Renee (Roch) 250 Meigs St. Apt 408, Rochester NY 14607 **Asst Trin Ch Geneva NY 2011-** B Charlotte NC 3/30/1966 d Robert Brown & Dorothy. BM Eastman Sch of Mus 1989; MME Winthrop U 1998; MDiv Duke DS 2006; Cert. of Theol Stds SWTS 2008. D 6/6/2009 P 12/7/2009 Bp Prince Grenville Singh. m 6/2/2007 Shannon Hickey. Presiding Yth Mssnr Dio Rochester Rochester NY 2010-2011; D Tri-Par Mnstry Hornell NY 2009. Writer of one Pryr, "Anthology of Prayers," *Lifting Wmn Voices: Prayers to Change the Wrld*, Morehouse Pub, 2009. The Janet Skogen Stff Appreciation Awd SWTS 2008; Seabury-Wstrn Prize SWTS 2008. dbrown192@rochester.rr.com

BROWN, Dennis Roy Alfred (CGC) 306 Grant St, Chickasaw AL 36611 **Vic S Thos Ch Citronelle AL 2008-** B 4/15/1948 s Charles Henry Brown & Frances Rosyna. S Johns Au 1979; MDiv STUSo 1983. D 7/15/1983 P 5/1/1984 Bp Charles Farmer Duvall. Wilmer Hall Mobile AL 2005-2008; Dio Cntrl Gulf Coast Pensacola FL 1996-1998; P-in-c S Mich's Ch Mobile AL 1989-2008; R S Jas Ch Eufaula AL 1985-1989; Cur S Jas Ch Fairhope AL 1983-1985. REV. DBROWN@GMAIL.COM

BROWN JR, Dewey Everrett (SwFla) 37637 Magnolia Ave, Dade City FL 33523 **COM Dio SW Florida Sarasota FL 2010-; P S Mary's Ch Dade City FL 2009-** B Fort Knox KY 9/2/1956 s Dewey Everrett Brown & Dolores Nina. BBA MI SU 1979; Cebs U of Pennsylvania 1992; MDiv VTS 2001. D 6/9/2001 Bp David Conner Bane Jr P 12/18/2001 Bp Clifton Daniel III. m 4/22/1981 Deborah Elizabeth Bennett c 3. Chair, Dioc Conv Nomin Com Dio Newark Newark NJ 2007-2009; Eccl Crt Dio Newark Newark NJ 2007-2009; Dioc Working Grp on Evang Dio Newark Newark NJ 2006-2009; Dist 9 Rep to Conv Dio Newark Newark NJ 2006-2009; Dioc Bp's Nomin Commitee for Dio Newark Dio Newark Newark NJ 2005-2007; Dioc Revs Com Dio Newark Newark NJ 2004-2007; P S Lk's Epis Ch Haworth NJ 2003-2009; Bp's Personl Com Dio E Carolina Kinston NC 2001-2003; Dioc Exec Coun Dio E Carolina Kinston NC 2001-2003; P S Jn's Epis Ch Wilmington NC 2001-2003. frdewey@stmdc.com

BROWN, Don (La) 224 Pecan Ave, New Roads LA 70760 B Elsberry MO 11/10/1942 s Ralph Waldo Brown & Florence Aletha. BS U of Missouri 1964; MDiv Nash 1981. D 1/3/1981 P 7/25/1981 Bp Donald James Parsons. m 1/4/1997 Geraldine Brown c 2. P-in-c S Mary's Ch New Roads LA 2006-2009; R S Paul's/H Trin New Roads LA 2006-2009; R S Jn's Epis Ch Decatur IL 2001-2006; All SS Epis Ch Russellville AR 1996-2001; R S Fran Ch Denham Sprg LA 1990-1996; Vic Ch Of The Redeem Oak Ridge LA 1984-1990; R S Andr's Epis Ch Mer Rouge LA 1984-1990; Dio W Missouri Kansas City MO 1981-1984; Vic S Oswald In The Field Skidmore MO 1981-1984; Vic S Paul's Ch Maryville MO 1981-1984. frdonbrown@gmail.com

BROWN, Donald Franklin (RG) 205 2nd Ave Ne, Jamestown ND 58401 B Lubbock TX 5/5/1937 BBA Texas Tech U 1966; MDiv TESM 1989. D 6/8/1996 P 12/20/1996 Bp John-David Mercer Schofield. m 4/6/1986 Diane Adele Brown. Gr Epis Ch Jamestown ND 2002-2004; Dio No Dakota Fargo ND 2002-2003; Assoc R/Pstr Care S Lk's Epis Ch Hilton Hd SC 2000-2002; D-On-Stff S Paul's Ch Bakersfield CA 1996-1997. Auth, "Islam: Friend Or Foe," *LivCh 8/11/1996*. Phi Delta Theta.

BROWN, Donald Gary (Cal) 2821 Claremont Blvd, Berkeley CA 94705 **non-stipendiary P Assoc All Souls Par In Berkeley Berkeley CA 2005-** B Eureka CA 7/23/1946 s Donald Franklin Brown & Ilene Anita. BA Willamette U 1968; STB EDS 1971; DMin CDSP 1998. D 6/22/1971 P 1/22/1972 Bp James Walmsley Frederic Carman. m 7/5/1975 Carol A Brown c 2. Dio Nthrn California Sacramento CA 1993-2005; Chair Of COM Dio Nthrn California Sacramento CA 1989-1992; Dn Trin Cathd Sacramento CA 1987-2005; Dio Nthrn California Sacramento CA 1987-1992; Stndg Com Dio Nthrn California Sacramento CA 1987-1991; Chair Of COM Dio Olympia Seattle WA 1984-1987; Evaltn Com Dio Olympia Seattle WA 1981-1984; Dioc Coun Dio Olympia Seattle WA 1979-1980; R S Steph's Epis Ch Longview WA 1977-1987; Assoc Chr Ch Par Lake Oswego OR 1973-1977; Dept Of CE Dio Oregon Portland OR 1971-1975; Assoc S Paul's Epis Ch Salem OR 1971-1973. EvangES. DD CDSP 2005. carolanne.brown@gmail.com

BROWN, Donna Hvistendahl (WA) 8815 Courtyard Way, Knoxville TN 37931 B Worthington MN 10/31/1946 d Dale Eli Hvistendahl & Charlotte Ann. BA Hur 1968; MDiv VTS 1993. D 6/24/1993 Bp Craig Barry Anderson P 1/6/1994 Bp George Clinton Harris. m 5/21/1994 Kenneth E Brown c 3. R S Mk's Ch Fairland Silver Sprg MD 2000-2011; Assoc R Chr Epis Ch Warren OH 1998-2000; Asst S Lk's Par Kalamazoo MI 1995-1998; Assoc Chr Epis Ch Lead SD 1994-1995; Assoc S Jn's Ch Deadwood SD 1994-1995; Dio So Dakota Sioux Falls SD 1993-1995; Cur Calv Cathd Sioux Falls SD 1993-1994. dospadres@aol.com

BROWN, Donn H(aswell) (At) 217 Booth St Apt 119, Gaithersburg MD 20878 B Albany CA 12/2/1932 s Howard Stewart Brown & Ethel E. U of Hawaii 1952; Arizona St U 1958; CDSP 1969; BD CDSP 1975. D 6/10/1969 Bp Edwin Lani Hanchett P 12/14/1969 Bp Edmond Lee Browning. m 10/22/1955 Pauline Ione Tuvell c 3. P-in-c S Jn's Epis Ch Franklin NC 1998-2006; R S Jas Epis Ch Clayton GA 1992-1996; P Ch Of The H Cross Decatur GA 1990-1992; Vic Dio Hawaii Honolulu HI 1985-1990; Counslr For Jn Howard Assn Dio Hawaii Honolulu HI 1983-1985; Vic S Matt's Epis Ch Waimanalo HI 1981-1983; Dio Hawaii Honolulu HI 1979-1980; P S Ptr's Ch Honolulu HI 1976-1985; Asst Secy/Secy Dio Hawaii Honolulu HI 1973-1980; R S Nich Epis Ch Kapolei HI 1973-1976; Dio Hawaii Honolulu HI 1973-1975. Ed, "Adv In The Hm"; Auth, "The Euch As Preparation For Mssn"; Auth, "Bible Study Aids". panddbrown@verizon.net

BROWN, Dorothy Lynne (At) 53 Woodlawn Dr, Toccoa GA 30577 B Pittsburgh PA 1/11/1947 d Howard Roscoe Brown & Mildred Marie. BS Indiana U of Pennsylvania 1968; MS Buc 1971; MA U of Virginia 1979; MDiv STUSo 1986. D 12/9/1986 Bp Peter James Lee P 6/29/1987 Bp Charles Jones III. R S Mths Epis Ch Toccoa GA 2003-2009; R S Thos a Becket Epis Ch Morgantown WV 1992-2003; Vic Ch Of The Incarn Greg SD 1989-1992; RurD Rosebud Reg Dio So Dakota Sioux Falls SD 1989-1992; R Trin Epis Ch Winner SD 1989-1992; Asst S Jas Ch Bozeman MT 1987-1989. dlbrown2@windstream.net

BROWN, Dwight Larcom (Va) Po Box 678, Berryville VA 22611 **R Gr Ch Berryville VA 1984-; Vic S Mary's Meml Berryville VA 1984-** B Bridgeport CT 2/12/1954 s Ralph Adams Brown & Joy. BA Trin Hartford CT 1976; MDiv VTS 1981. D 5/30/1981 P 12/18/1981 Bp Alexander Doig Stewart. m 7/11/1981 Catherine Elizabeth Brown c 2. VTS Alexandria VA 1989-1992; Dn, Reg XIV Dio Virginia Richmond VA 1987-1991; Asst Min Trin Ch Arlington VA 1981-1984. Phi Beta Kappa. browndlbceb@yahoo.com

BROWN, Elly (WA) 5006-B Barbour Dr, Alexandria VA 22304 **Vic Chr Ch Palmyra NJ 2011-** B Pittsburgh PA 6/14/1950 d Clifford Henry Sparks & Arlene Elizabeth. BA Seton Hill U Greensburg PA 1972; MA CUA 1977; MDiv VTS 1984; DMin Wesley TS 1991. D 6/23/1984 Bp Peter James Lee P 6/1/1985 Bp David Henry Lewis Jr. m 10/6/1990 Hugh Eldridge Brown. R Old Fields Chap Hughesville MD 1999-2008; R Trin Epis Par Hughesville MD 1999-2007; All SS Ch Richmond VA 1990-1993; Assoc R S Lk's Ch Alexandria VA 1984-1989. ellysb@aol.com

BROWN, Enrique Ricardo (WA) 5248 Colorado Ave Nw, Washington DC 20011 **Int S Matt's Epis Ch Hyattsville MD 2011-** B Ancon PA 6/3/1944 s Sherman Ralph Brown & Una Lendora. U Of Panama PA; BA New Sch U 1971; MDiv Ya Berk 1974. D 12/14/1974 Bp James Stuart Wetmore P 6/28/1975 Bp Harold Louis Wright. m 6/15/1974 Irene Viola Jackson. Int S Mk's Ch Jackson Heights NY 2006-2010; P-in-c S Paul's Rock Creek Washington DC 2002-2006; Int S Jas' Epis Ch Baltimore MD 2000-2002; Assoc Ch Of The Ascen Gaithersburg MD 2000; Dio Washington Washington DC 1995-1999; Latino/Hisp Mssnr Mssn San Juan Washington DC 1995-1999; Int Hisp Mnstry New York NY 1993-1995; Archd Diocn Msnry & Ch Extntn Socty New York NY 1985-1992; Archd Dpt Of Missions Ny Income New York NY 1985-1992; Latino/Hisp Mssnr Dio Connecticut Hartford CT 1977-1985; Asst S Lk's/S Paul's Ch Bridgeport CT 1975-1977. Auth, "Renwl Of The Ch In The City". ENRIQUERB@AOL.COM

BROWN III, Ervin Adams (Eas) 2212 E Baltimore St, Baltimore MD 21231 **R Chr Ch St Michaels MD 1996-** B Birmingham AL 8/27/1937 s Ervin Adams Brown & Anilee. BA U of Alabama 1958; MPA Indiana U 1961; MDiv VTS 1965. D 6/22/1965 P 6/7/1966 Bp Harry Lee Doll. m 6/4/1960 (Marion) Letetia Holloway c 3. Int Dn Cathd Of The Incarn Baltimore MD 2008-2009; Chair of COM Dio Easton Easton MD 1998-2002; Chr Ch St Michaels MD 1995-2002; Stndg Com Dio Michigan Detroit MI 1994-1995; Exec Coun Dio Michigan Detroit MI 1988-1995; R Chr Ch Detroit MI 1981-1995; Stndg Com Dio SW Virginia Roanoke VA 1976-1979; R S Paul's Epis Ch Lynchburg VA 1973-1981; COM Dio SW Virginia Roanoke VA 1973-1976; R S Jn's Ch Reisterstown MD 1967-1973. baltimoreerv@aol.com

BROWN, Freda Marie Stewart (Dal) 602 N. Old Orchard Ln., PO Box 292365, Lewisville TX 75077 **P Ch Of The Annunc Lewisville TX 2009-** B Greenville MS 10/31/1956 d Leon S Stewart & Marie A. BS Xavier U of LA 1979; MTS SMU 2002; MAR Epis TS Of The SW 2009. D 6/6/2009 Bp James

Monte Stanton P 3/25/2010 Bp Paul Emil Lambert. m 5/24/1981 Charles E Brown c 1. fsbrwn@sbcglobal.net

BROWN, Frederick Ransom (Vt) 346 Gladys Avenue, Long Beach CA 90814 B Springfield VT 4/26/1941 s Milton Boyd Brown & Emmy Lou. BA Ya 1963; BD CDSP 1966; MSW Smith 1974. D 6/29/1966 P 1/1/1967 Bp Harvey D Butterfield. Asst Cathd Ch Of S Paul Burlington VT 1966-1968.

BROWN JR, F Wilson (SwVa) 715 Sunset Drive, Bedford VA 24523 **R S Jn's Ch Bedford VA 2008-** B Richmond VA 12/14/1961 s Francis Wilson Brown & Leslie. BA W&M 1984; MDiv VTS 1991. D 6/15/1991 Bp C(laude) Charles Vache P 1/1/1992 Bp William George Burrill. m 7/11/1992 Kara S Wagner c 3. R H Sacr Pembroke Pines FL 2004-2008; R S Mk's Epis Ch Le Roy NY 1994-2004; Asst S Paul's Ch Rochester NY 1991-1994. wbrownstjohns@verizon.net

BROWN III, George Willcox (Dal) 409 Prospect St, New Haven CT 06511 **R Ch Of The H Cross Dallas TX 2007-; Epis Ch At Yale New Haven CT 2005-** B 3/31/1979 BA U So 2001; MDiv Yale DS 2005. D 2/5/2005 P 7/9/2005 Bp Henry Irving Louttit. Ch Of S Mths Dallas TX 2006. gwbrown@gmail.com

BROWN, Ginny (Colo) 706 E. 3rd Avenue, Durango CO 81301 B Highland Park MI 7/14/1940 d John Palmer Wood & Madeline Schurr. BS NWU 1962; MS U Denv 1991. D 4/26/2003 Bp William Jerry Winterrowd. m 11/1/1980 Donald R Brown c 2. ginnyindgo@yahoo.com

BROWN, Gregory Bryan Francis (WMich) 1020 E Mitchell St, Petoskey MI 49770 **R Emm Ch Petoskey MI 2005-** B 11/6/1965 s David E Brown & Marilyn Lillian. BS MI SU 1989; MDiv GTS 2001. D 6/2/2001 P 12/8/2001 Bp Edward Lewis Lee Jr. m 6/24/1995 Catherine R Nickerson c 3. R Trin Epis Ch Grand Ledge MI 2001-2005; Dio Wstrn Michigan Kalamazoo MI 1995-1997. revgregbrown@gmail.com

BROWN III, Henry William (CFla) Po Box 1420, Homosassa Springs FL 34447 **D S Anne's Ch Crystal River FL 1988-** B Dunedin FL 3/17/1953 s Henry William Brown & Juanita. Marion Mltry Inst 1972; BA U So 1975. D 11/17/1988 Bp William Hopkins Folwell. m 6/11/1976 Virginia Diane Brown c 2.

BROWN JR, H (Horace) Frederick (WTex) 309 S Someday Dr, Boerne TX 78006 B Austin TX 6/17/1938 s Horace Frederick Brown & Naomi. BA U So 1960; JD S Mary U San Antonio TX 1970; MDiv Houston Grad TS 1992; CAS CDSP 1996. D 6/22/1996 Bp Claude Edward Payne P 1/18/1997 Bp William Elwood Sterling. m 5/2/1964 (Dorothy) Sue Parker. S Eliz's Epis Ch Buda TX 2005-2008; Asst S Helena's Epis Ch Boerne TX 2000-2005; Dio Nthrn California Sacramento CA 2000; Asst to R H Trin Ch NEVADA CITY CA 1997-1999; D Chr Ch Jefferson TX 1996-1997; D Trin Ch Marshall TX 1996-1997. hfbjr@boernenet.com

BROWN III, Hugh Eldridge (NJ) 16 All Saints Rd, Princeton NJ 08540 **R All SS Ch Princeton NJ 2007-** B Roanoke VA 7/7/1959 s Hugh Eldridge Brown & Josephine. BA W&M 1981; MA U of Virginia 1985; MDiv VTS 1988; DMin Wesley TS 1999. D 6/24/1988 P 9/1/1989 Bp A(rthur) Heath Light. m 10/6/1990 Elly Sparks. S Thos Par Croom Upper Marlboro MD 2003-2007; S Phil's Chap Baden Brandywine MD 1999-2003; S Jn's Ch Lafayette Sq Washington DC 1997-1999; R Chr Epis Ch Kent OH 1993-1995; Asst Chr Epis Ch Charlottesville VA 1990-1993; Co-Chapl R E Lee Memi Ch (Epis) Lexington VA 1988-1990. Auth, "Vts Sem Journ". ESMHE; Iaf-Win/Apt. hughandelly@aol.com

BROWN, Ian Frederick (Mich) 26 Tower Dr., Saline MI 48176 B Cape Town ZA 7/2/1932 s Frederick Richard Brown & Dorothy. BD U Chi 1958; MS Wayne 1971. D 7/17/1966 Bp Archie H Crowley P 11/1/1966 Bp C Kilmer Myers. m 6/10/2000 Susan Davis c 3. S Jn's Ch Clinton MI 2000-2004; Vic All SS Epis Ch Marysville MI 1966-1969. revs_2@netzero.com

✠ **BROWN, Rt Rev James Barrow** (La) 2136 Octavia St, New Orleans LA 70115 **Ret Bp Of Louisiana Dio Louisiana Baton Rouge LA 1998-** B El Dorado AR 9/26/1932 s John Alexander Brown & Ella May. BS LSU 1954; BD Austin Presb TS 1957; Goettingen U DE 1960; Fllshp PrTS 1963; GTS 1965; DD STUSo 1976; Tubingen U Tubingen DE 1984. D 6/22/1965 Bp Girault M Jones P 12/15/1965 Bp Iveson Batchelor Noland Con 4/24/1976 for La. m Mary J Strausser. Asst Dio Texas Houston TX 2000-2002; Int Trin Ch Galveston TX 1998-2000, Bp Dio Louisiana Baton Rouge LA 1976-1998; Archd Dio Louisiana Baton Rouge LA 1971-1976; Cur S Andr's Epis Ch New Orleans LA 1968-1971; BEC Dio Louisiana Baton Rouge LA 1967-1976; Cur Gr Epis Ch Monroe LA 1966-1968; Cur S Geo's Ch Bossier City LA 1965-1966. DD U So 1976. jbx98@aol.com

BROWN, James Louis (O) No address on file. B Kansas City KS 4/7/1945 s Louis Brown & Margaret Louise. BD Emporia St U 1967; MA Emporia St U 1968; PhD K SU 1975. D 6/4/1982 Bp Richard Frank Grein. m 8/9/1970 Neea Beth Brown c 2. D S Mich And All Ang Ch Mssn KS 1982-2001. Auth, "Origins Of Black Engl," 1979; Auth, "Tchg Engl In Cmnty Coll," *Ar Engl Bulletin*, 1979. jbrown777@kc.rr.com

BROWN, James Thompson (Cal) 6225 Vine Hill School Rd, Sebastopol CA 95472 B Salt Lake City UT 3/16/1927 s Harold Ross Brown & Norinne. BA Ya 1950; STB GTS 1960. D 5/20/1960 P 11/1/1960 Bp Richard S Watson. The Cathd Ch Of The Adv Birmingham AL 1985-1998; Ch Of The Ascen Knoxville TN 1977-1985; R The Epis Ch Of S Jn The Evang San Francisco CA 1977-1983; Dio Tennessee Nashville TN 1969-1972; R E Lee Memi Ch (Epis) Lexington VA 1963-1969; All SS Epis Ch Norton VA 1960-1963; Asst To Dn Cathd Ch Of S Mk Salt Lake City UT 1960-1963. jt6225@aol.com

BROWN JR, James Williamson (SVa) 508 Lynn Shores Dr, Virginia Beach VA 23452 **Died 11/13/2010** B 2/23/1929 c 2.

BROWN, Janet Easson (CPa) 140 N Beaver St, York PA 17401 B Braintree MA 12/24/1951 d Alexander Bruce Brown & Barbara Robinson. Vocational Diac Formation Dio Cntrl PA Sch of Chr Stds; Mstr of Soc Wk Virginia Commonwealth U; BA Dickinson Coll 1973. D 10/31/2010 Bp Nathan Dwight Baxter. m 12/3/1983 Roy Drinkwater c 1. jeassonb@ptd.net

BROWN, Janet Kelly (Vt) Po Box 351, Jericho VT 05465 **P-in-Partnership Gr Ch Sheldon VT 2008-** B Flushing NY 8/1/1942 d Thomas J Kelly & Janet K. BA Swarthmore Coll 1964; MA Wesl 1965; MA Antioch U New Engl 1987. D 6/2/1974 Bp Harvey D Butterfield P 1/6/1977 Bp Robert Shaw Kerr. m 8/21/1965 John R B Brown c 2. P-in-c Ch Of The Gd Shpd Barre VT 1998-2001; Int Trin Epis Ch Poultney VT 1996-1998; H Trin Epis Ch Swanton VT 1988-1991; Trin Milton VT 1979-1982; S Ann's Ch Sheldon VT 1978-1979; Int S Matt's Ch Enosburg Falls VT 1978-1979; S Jas Epis Ch Essex Jct VT 1974-1979. janetkbrown88@comcast.net

BROWN, Jennifer Clarke (NC) 2212 Tyson Street, Raleigh NC 27612 **Chr Epis Ch Raleigh NC 2009-** B New York NY 3/21/1961 d Robert Leslie Clarke & Lynn. BA Pr 1983; JD Duke 1988; MDiv Andover Newton TS 1996. D 9/8/1996 P 3/8/1997 Bp M(arvil) Thomas Shaw III. m 11/24/2007 Davin Brown c 2. Asst S Tim's Epis Ch Cincinnati OH 1999-2004; Asst S Anne's In The Fields Epis Ch Lincoln MA 1998-1999; Asst S Jn's Ch Beverly Farms MA 1996-1998. jclarkebrown@yahoo.com

BROWN, Jennifer Elaine (NY) 1558 Unionport Rd Apt 7E, Bronx NY 10462 **Chr Ch Bronxville NY 2009-** B 3/23/1954 d Fetzgerald Brown & Barbara. Psychol Utica Coll 1992; MSW Yeshiva U 1992; MDiv The GTS 2009. D 3/7/2009 P 9/12/2009 Bp Mark Sean Sisk. m 7/8/1995 James L Lanier c 3. jebrown321@aol.com

BROWN JR, John Ashmore (USC) 9 Sweet Branch Ct, Columbia SC 29212 B Gaffney SC 1/27/1948 s John Ashmore Brown & Bobbie Helen. BA Wofford Coll 1970; Med U of So Carolina 1972; MDiv VTS 1986. D 6/7/1986 P 5/1/1987 Bp William Arthur Beckham. m 6/21/1969 Pamela Hammett c 1. S Lk's Ch Newberry SC 1986-1989. OHC.

BROWN, John Clive (Ore) 431-A Red Blanket Rd, Prospect OR 97536 **Vic Ch Of The Gd Shpd Prospect OR 1997-** B Riverside CA 12/9/1933 s John Adams Brown & Pauline Lucille. U CA; U CA. D 7/30/1996 P 2/26/1997 Bp Robert Louis Ladehoff. m 10/10/1973 Esther Gertrude Knight. jackbrow@ix.netcom.com

BROWN, John Daniel (Dal) 7610 Rockingham Rd, Prospect KY 40059 **H Trin Epis Ch Garland TX 2007-** B Torrence CA 12/1/1952 BS USNA. D 6/14/2003 Bp Peter James Lee P 12/13/2003 Bp Edwin Funsten Gulick Jr. m 3/6/1976 Evelyn Louise Colman c 2. Assoc S Fran In The Fields Harrods Creek KY 2003-2007. jdecbrown@aol.com

BROWN, John Pairman (Cal) 1630 Arch St, Berkeley CA 94709 **Died 4/5/2010** B Hanover NH 5/16/1923 s Bancroft Huntington Brown & Eleanor. BA Dart 1944; Fllshp Harv 1949; STB GTS 1956; ThD UTS 1958. D 6/3/1952 Bp Charles F Hall P 3/1/1953 Bp Benjamin M Washburn. c 4. Auth, *Israel & Hellas - 3 volumes*, 1995; Auth, *Numerous arts & Books*. SBL. demily@mindspring.com

BROWN, John Thompson (Ala) 4157 Winston Way, Birmingham AL 35213 B Nashville TN 12/7/1933 s John Thompson Brown & Vera Louise. BA Georgia Inst of Tech 1956; MDiv VTS 1960. D 6/24/1960 P 6/1/1961 Bp Charles Gresham Marmion. m 9/5/1959 Ann R Robinson c 2. Admin The Cathd Ch Of The Adv Birmingham AL 1985-1998; Ch Of The Ascen Knoxville TN 1980-1985; Assoc R E Lee Memi Ch (Epis) Lexington VA 1963-1969; Vic All SS Epis Ch Norton VA 1960-1963. Auth, "Healing, Some Sci & Theolical Considerations, Sewanee Theol Revs," *Michaelmas*, 1998; Auth, "On-The-Job Profsnl Growth For Par Cler," *Assn Of Mntl Hlth Cler*; Auth, "Bowen Theory & Pstr Care," *Assn Of Mntl Hlth Cler*. Amhc. jbrown36@bham.rr.com

BROWN, Keith Burton (EpisSanJ) 1776 S Homsy Ave, Fresno CA 93727 B Los Angeles CA 4/5/1945 s Delbert Frederick Brown & Elizabeth. BA USC 1967; MBA U of Utah 1975; MDiv CDSP 1982. D 1/16/1983 P 12/9/1984 Bp Charles Shannon Mallory. m 6/7/1986 Linda Ann Brown. Proj Consult Ch Pension Fund New York NY 2002-2011; Cn Mssnr Epis Dio San Joaquin Modesto CA 1995-2002; Epis Dio San Joaquin Modesto CA 1995-1999; Vic Our Lady of Guadalupe Fresno CA 1986-1994; Cur S Dunst's Epis Ch Carmel Vlly CA 1983-1984. Auth, "On The Road Again," *Mng Evang And Stwdshp For The Kingdom*, Ch Pub, 2001; Auth, "Numerous arts Dio Nwspr". kbbrown4545@msn.com

BROWN, Kenneth E (WA) 12621 Old Columbia Pike, Silver Spring MD 20904 B Evanston IL 9/20/1945 s Seth Edwin Brown & Lydia Joy. BA U of So Dakota 1967; STB GTS 1970. D 6/13/1970 Bp James Winchester

Montgomery P 12/19/1970 Bp Gerald Francis Burrill. m 5/21/1994 Donna Hvistendahl c 2. Assoc S Mk's Ch Fairland Silver Sprg MD 2003-2011; Int S Lk's Ch Brighton Brookeville MD 2000-2002; P-in-c S Andr's Ch Akron OH 1998-2000; P-in-c S Alb's Mssn Muskegon MI 1997-1998; R Chr Epis Ch Lead SD 1989-1995; R S Jn's Ch Deadwood SD 1989-1995; R S Marg's Ch Hazel Pk MI 1985-1989; Trin Ch Three Rivers MI 1973-1985. dospadres@aol.com

BROWN, Kevin S (NC) Church of the Holy Comforter, 2701 Park Rd, Charlotte NC 28209 **R Ch Of The H Comf Charlotte NC 2010-; GC Cler Dep Dio W Tennessee Memphis TN 2008-** B Asheville NC 12/3/1968 s Rober Brown & Rudi. BS Duke Durham NC 1991; MBA U Of W Florida Pensacola FL 1996; MDiv GTS 2007. D 6/2/2007 P 12/15/2007 Bp Don Edward Johnson. m 8/7/1993 Caroline C Brown c 2. R Gr Epis Ch Paris TN 2007-2010. kevinb@holycomfortercharlotte.org

BROWN, Lawrence Edward (Oly) 10901-176th Circle Ne, Apt#3513, Redmond WA 98052 B Bixby OK 3/25/1924 s Marion Lee & Ollie Dell. BA U of Washington 1950; LLB U of Washington 1952. D 3/2/1996 Bp Vincent Waydell Warner P 11/1/1996 Bp Sanford Zangwill Kaye Hampton. m 12/16/1950 Airy Elizabeth Dye. P S Lk's Epis Ch Elma WA 1996-2002.

BROWN, Lawrence Mitchell (Los) 2095 Stoneman St, Simi Valley CA 93065 **R Trin Par Fillmore CA 2010-** B Greenwood MS 9/14/1951 s Alvin Lauren Brown & Mary Estelle. BA Rhodes Coll 1973; BS Rhodes Coll 1975; Cert ETSBH 1996; MDiv Claremont TS 1997. D 6/1/1996 Bp Frederick Houk Borsch P 1/18/1997 Bp Chester Lovelle Talton. m 7/11/1975 Nancy Edwards c 3. P Asstg S Stephens Epis Ch Valencia CA 2005-2010; P Asstg Ch Of The Epiph Oak Pk CA 2001-2005; P Asstg S Aug By-The-Sea Par Santa Monica CA 1999-2000; P Asstg S Patricks Ch And Day Sch Thousand Oaks CA 1997-1998. OHC 1992; Soc of Cath Priests 2010. lmb3065@pacbell.net

BROWN, Lila Byrd (Fla) 2358 Riverside Ave. #704, Jacksonville FL 32204 B Jacksonville FL 9/25/1948 d Connor Alexander Brown & Claude. BA Queens Coll 1971; MDiv VTS 1996. D 5/26/1996 P 12/8/1996 Bp Stephen Hays Jecko. Cn Dio Florida Jacksonville FL 2002-2004; Int S Mk's Epis Ch Jacksonville FL 1999-2002; Assc R S Jn's Epis Ch Tallahassee FL 1996-1998. saintbyrd@aol.com

BROWN, Lydia Huttar (Minn) 10 Buffalo Rd, North Oaks MN 55127 **R S Anne's Epis Ch Sunfish Lake MN 2004-** B Chicago IL 1/20/1954 d Charles Adolph Huttar & Joy Anne. BA Hope Coll 1977; MA U MI 1978; MDiv Untd TS of the Twin Cities 2001; CTh SWTS 2002. D 12/20/2001 P 6/20/2002 Bp James Louis Jelinek. m 9/3/1977 Mark Leslie Brown c 4. Co-Chair, Cmsn on Liturg and Mus Dio Minnesota Minneapolis MN 2007-2010; Chair, Cler Cont Educ Com Dio Minnesota Minneapolis MN 2006-2008; Dn Reg 7 Dio Minnesota Minneapolis MN 2005-2009; Asst to the R Chr Ch S Paul MN 2002-2004; D S Jn In The Wilderness White Bear Lake MN 2002. lydiabrown10@msn.com

BROWN, Lyle L (Ia) 605 Avenue E, Fort Madison IA 52627 **The Reverend S Lk's Ch Ft Madison IA 2010-; The Reverend S Lk's Ch Ft Madison IA 2009-** B Davenport IA 1/26/1937 s Leslie E Brown & Edna Dann. BA U of Iowa 1959; MA U Denv 1963. D 10/25/2009 Bp Alan Scarfe. m 8/26/1967 Gwen Zeitler c 2. lbgb1008@mchsi.com

BROWN, Margaretta Yount (Oly) 114 20th Ave SE, Olympia WA 98501 **Died 5/30/2010** B Williamsport PA 9/23/1925 d Paul Yount & Margaretta H. D 12/2/1989 Bp Arthur Edward Walmsley. c 4. mybrev@aol.com

BROWN, Marilynn M(arie) (Ore) 23834 SE 248th St, Maple Valley WA 98038 B Cheyenne WY 5/27/1933 d Clarence Ralph Ferguson & Adah Eleanor. BS USC 1956; U of Washington 1976; MDiv GTS 1991. D 12/14/1986 Bp Donald Purple Hart P 6/9/1991 Bp Allen Lyman Bartlett Jr. m 9/2/1976 Robert Eugene Brown c 5. Asst S Mich And All Ang Ch Portland OR 2004-2005; Sunset Convoc Dn Dio Oregon Portland OR 2002-2004; Stndg Com Dio Oregon Portland OR 2001-2004; R S Fran Of Assisi Epis Wilsonville OR 1997-2003; Racism Cmsn Dio Oregon Portland OR 1994-1996; Dioc Coun Dio Oregon Portland OR 1993-1999; Assoc S Fran Of Assisi Epis Wilsonville OR 1992-1996; Asst Chr Ch And S Mich's Philadelphia PA 1991; D Chr Ch And S Mich's Philadelphia PA 1989-1991; D S Ptr's Ch Glenside PA 1987-1988; D S Chris's Ch Kailua HI 1986-1987. mmbrown76@comcast.net

BROWN, Marion Mackey (SwFla) 208 Ne Monroe Cir N Apt 103-C, Saint Petersburg FL 33702 **D S Giles Ch Pinellas Pk FL 1992-** B Pittsburgh PA 8/7/1935 d Thomas Algeo Brown & Marion Paige. Eckerd Coll; GTS; S Petersburg Jr Coll; Rider Coll 1959. D 6/13/1992 Bp Barbara Clementine Harris. m 9/26/1959 Harry Thomas Brown c 3. D Cathd Ch Of S Ptr St Petersburg FL 1992-1994.

BROWN SSJE, Mark (Mass) 980 Memorial Dr, Cambridge MA 02138 B Peoria IL 9/9/1949 s Jesse Raymond Brown & Naomi Jane. BA U IL 1971; MA U IL 1976; MDiv SWTS 1994. D 5/7/1994 P 3/1/1995 Bp Peter Hess Beckwith. R Ch Of S Jn The Bapt Mt Carmel IL 1995-1997; Dioc Coun Dio Springfield Springfield IL 1995-1997; D S Mk's Ch Hoosick Falls NY 1994-1995. mark@ssje.org

BROWN, Mary K (Va) 228 Pitt St, Alexandria VA 22314 B Kittanning PA 3/5/1959 d Glenn A Brown & Lois V. BSW U Pgh 1981; MSW Case Wstrn Reserve U 1983; MDiv The Prot Epis TS 2008. D 5/24/2008 P 12/14/2008 Bp Peter James Lee. m 6/18/1994 Mark Eugene Boyer c 2. S Dav's Ch Ashburn VA 2008-2009; Asst S Paul's Epis Ch Alexandria VA 2008-2009. mkbrownboyer@yahoo.com

BROWN, Melvin Ray (Oly) 1115 5th St, Anacortes WA 98221 **Died 9/10/2009** B Bucklin KS 10/22/1921 s Jennings Bryan Brown & Opal Lucile. MDiv CDSP 1957; BA U of Kansas 1957. D 6/26/1960 P 6/22/1961 Bp James Albert Pike. c 2.

BROWN, Nancy (Los) 2095 Stoneman St, Simi Valley CA 93065 **R S Paul's Par Lancaster CA 2005-** B Dyersburg TN 10/8/1947 d Harry Ircell Edwards & Opal Eulail. D 6/25/2000 Bp Chester Lovelle Talton P 1/6/2001 Bp Frederick Houk Borsch. m 7/11/1975 Lawrence Mitchell Brown. Int S Patricks Ch And Day Sch Thousand Oaks CA 2000-2005.

BROWN, Nancy Elisabeth (Okla) 401 S. Olympia Avenue, Tulsa OK 74127 B Flint MI 10/20/1953 d Herbert Gladstone Nabb & Doris Evelyn. Oral Roberts U 1973. D 6/24/2000 Bp Robert Manning Moody. Asst S Jn's Epis Ch Tulsa OK 2001-2005. naturalnancybrown@gmail.com

BROWN, Percival George (LI) 926 Dana Ave, Valley Stream NY 11580 B Miami FL 2/23/1949 s Percy Gustave Brown & Carmetta Louise. BA U Of Florida 1969; MDiv VTS 1972. D 7/9/1972 P 6/29/1973 Bp James Loughlin Duncan. m 4/9/1991 Roslyn Ann Ferguson c 2. R Gr Ch Jamaica NY 1989-2005; Assoc Trin Educ Fund New York NY 1981-1988; Liturg Off Par of Trin Ch New York NY 1980-1989; Vic S Phil's Ch Pompano Bch FL 1977-1980; R Ch Of S Chris Ft Lauderdale FL 1972-1980. Outstanding Young Men Amer 1976. padreperc@verizon.net

BROWN, Ralph Douglas (Ind) Po Box 1596, Old Fort NC 28762 B New York NY 12/22/1934 s Ralph Alfred Brown & Dorothy Helen. BA Br 1956; MDiv STUSo 1984. D 2/16/1985 P 9/18/1985 Bp Craig Barry Anderson. m 5/11/1958 Ruth Evelyn Heaman c 2. Stwdshp Com Dio Indianapolis Indianapolis IN 1989-2000; R S Paul's Ch Richmond IN 1988-2000; Chr Ch Chamberlain SD 1985-1988; Vic H Comf Ch Lower Brule SD 1984-1988. ruthevelyn21@frontier.com

BROWN, Raymond Dutson (Mont) 6162 Lazy Man Gulch, Helena MT 59601 B Philadelphia PA 2/3/1933 s Allen Webster Brown & Helen Ruth. BA Br 1959; MDiv PDS 1962. D 6/16/1962 P 12/23/1962 Bp Allen Webster Brown. m 2/10/1978 Joyce F Foor c 5. Int S Ptr's Par Helena MT 2011; R Trin Ch Ennis MT 1997-2000; Int Ch Of The Incarn Great Falls MT 1995-1996; Stndg Com Dio Montana Helena MT 1993-1996; Int S Jn's Ch Butte MT 1986-1987; Int S Fran Epis Ch Great Falls MT 1984-1986; Chair of Ch and Soc Cmsn Dio Montana Helena MT 1983-1986; EDEO Dio Montana Helena MT 1974-1975; S Ptr's Par Helena MT 1966-1975; Asst S Matt's Ch Columbia Falls MT 1963-1966; Asst S Mich And All Ang Eureka MT 1963-1966; Cur S Paul's Ch Schenectady NY 1962-1963. ray003@aol.com

BROWN, Raymond Francis (EC) 205 Bedell Pl, Fayetteville NC 28314 **R H Trin Epis Ch Fayetteville NC 2001-** B Danville KY 11/5/1945 s Francis Read Brown & Lu. BA Cntr Coll 1968; JD Duke 1974; MDiv Ya Berk 1986. D 6/24/1986 P 4/27/1987 Bp David Reed. m 5/31/1969 Judith Ann Muller c 2. R Ch Of The H Trin Georgetown KY 1988-2001; Asst R S Mk's Epis Ch Louisville KY 1986-1988. Archibald Prize Ya Berk New Haven CT 1986; Daggett Prize Ya Berk New Haven CT 1986; Mdiv mcl Ya Berk New Haven CT 1986; Julia Archibald Prize & Oliver E Daggett Prize Yale 1986; Jd w dist Law Sch, Duke Durham NC 1974; Ba mcl Cntr Coll Danville KY 1968. browntown@nc.rr.com

BROWN, Rebecca Susan (Colo) 18 Spring St, Mansfield MA 02048 **P-in-c The Ch Of Chr The King (Epis) Arvada CO 2011-; R S Mk's Ch Foxborough MA 2001-** B Kingston NY 8/20/1950 d Donald E Brown & Betty Jane. Kalamazoo Coll 1969; Kalamazoo Coll 1973; BS Carnegie Mellon U 1981; Pittsburgh TS 1991; MDiv GTS 1992. D 6/6/1992 P 12/8/1992 Bp Alden Moinet Hathaway. m 8/21/1971 Andrew L Reitz c 3. Assoc R All SS Ch Worcester MA 1995-2001; Dio Wstrn Massachusetts Springfield MA 1995-2001; Int The Ch Of The Redeem Pittsburgh PA 1994; Dio Pittsburgh Monroeville PA 1993-1994; Trin Cathd Pittsburgh PA 1992-1994. rebsubrown@aol.com

BROWN, Reed Haller (Vt) 49 Brewer Pkwy, South Burlington VT 05403 B Cooperstown NY 7/28/1935 s Allen Webster Brown & Helen Ruth. BA Trin Hartford CT 1960; MDiv GTS 1963; PhD U of Vermont 1975. D 6/10/1963 Bp Allen Webster Brown P 12/21/1963 Bp Harvey D Butterfield. m 8/20/1960 Gail Beverly Clark c 2. R S Paul's Epis Ch On The Green Vergennes VT 1997-2002; P-in-c Inter Par Coun Of Churchs Enosburg Falls VT 1995-1996; Cn Pstr Gr Ch Sheldon VT 1994-1996; Cn Pstr S Ann's Ch Sheldon VT 1994-1996; Cn Pstr S Matt's Ch Enosburg Falls VT 1994-1996; Consulting Psychol Rock Point Sch Burlington VT 1974-1980; Consulting Psychol Dio Vermont Burlington VT 1973-1979; Vic All SS' Epis Ch S Burlington VT 1964-1969; Asst Cathd Ch Of S Paul Burlington VT 1963-1965. rbrown3@myfairpoint.net

BROWN III, Richard Baxter (Mass) 9 Massasoit St, Medway MA 02053 **Supply, metro SW area Dio Massachusetts Boston MA 2000-** B Arlington MA 9/19/1930 s Richard Baxter Brown & Harriette Bradley. BS NEU 1954; MDiv EDS 1988. D 6/2/1990 P 5/25/1991 Bp David Elliot Johnson. m 4/8/1991 Marilyn Jeanne Leggee c 6. Com On Admssns Of Parishes And Missions Dio Massachusetts Boston MA 1995-1999; P-in-c S Mart's Epis Ch New Bedford MA 1993-1999; Assoc R S Mk's Epis Ch Riverside RI 1990-1993. Interfaith Allnce 1991; Ma Epis Cler Assn 1990. Bs cl NEU Boston MA 1954. rbbrown3@verizon.net

BROWN III, Richard Julius (ETenn) 1431 Armiger Lane, Knoxville TN 37932 B Charleston SC 5/23/1937 s Richard Julius Brown & Helen Ruby. BA Furman U 1960; BD SE Bapt TS, Wake Forest, NC 1965; ThM SE Bapt TS, Wake Forest, NC 1967; MA Appalachian St U 1976; PhD U NC at Greensboro 1981. D 2/6/1994 P 10/1/1994 Bp Robert Oran Miller. m 5/28/1972 Geneva Leek Brown c 1. Int S Eliz's Epis Ch Knoxville TN 2009-2010; Cn S Jn's Epis Cathd Knoxville TN 2001-2005; Int Gr Epis Ch Mt Meigs AL 2000-2001; Assoc Ch Of The H Comf Montgomery AL 2000; P Epis Ch Of The Epiph Montgomery AL 1996-1997; P-in-c S Mk's Ch Prattville AL 1995-1996; P-in-c Trin Epis Ch Clanton AL 1994-1995. RJBROWN@MINDSPRING.COM

BROWN, Robert Eugene (Ore) 23834 SE 248th St, Maple Valley WA 98038 B Berkeley CA 11/12/1937 s Russell Eugene Brown & Thelma Lavinia. BA California St U at Long Bch 1960; MDiv CDSP 1966; Cert Pstr Inst of Washington WA 1972; Cert Samar Counslg Cntr 1991. D 3/5/1966 Bp George Richard Millard P 9/7/1966 Bp Harry S Kennedy. m 9/2/1976 Marilynn M(arie) Ferguson c 3. Exec Asst to Bp Dio Oregon Portland OR 1996-1999; Chair of COM Dio Oregon Portland OR 1994-1996; R S Fran Of Assisi Epis Wilsonville OR 1992-1996; COM Dio Pennsylvania Philadelphia PA 1988-1990; R S Ptr's Ch Glenside PA 1987-1992; Stndg Committe, Chair Dio Hawaii Honolulu HI 1980-1983; R S Chris's Ch Kailua HI 1979-1987; R S Mich And All Ang Ch Issaquah WA 1973-1979; Cn to the Ordnry Dio Olympia Seattle WA 1972-1973; Assoc Ch Of The Epiph Seattle WA 1967-1972; Vic Chr Ch Kealakekua HI 1966-1967. bobbrown76@comcast.net

BROWN, Robert Henry (Pa) 117 Pine Lake Dr, Whispering Pines NC 28327 **Vic S Mary Magd Ch W End NC 2007-** B Philadelphia PA 12/10/1930 s Henry Brown & Elizabeth Almira. BA La Salle U 1968; MDiv Luth TS at Philadelphia 1996. D 6/1/1996 P 6/7/1997 Bp Allen Lyman Bartlett Jr. m 11/9/1957 Jean Walker Colesberry. R S Faith Ch Havertown PA 1998-2003.

BROWN, Robert Hirschmann (Los) 1 Church Rd, Thousand Oaks CA 91362 B Pasadena CA 3/5/1951 s Frank Harshman Brown & Evelyn Lee. BA USC 1974; MDiv Nash 1987. D 6/13/1987 P 12/1/1987 Bp Charles Brinkley Morton. m 6/4/1983 Elizabeth Lee Vassall c 1. Cur S Patricks Ch And Day Sch Thousand Oaks CA 1994-2000; R Trin Par Fillmore CA 1990-1993; Cur S Jn The Evang Ch Elkhart IN 1988-1990; Cur S Barth's Epis Ch Poway CA 1987-1988. Auth, "some more psalms," *poems*, self Pub, 2009; Auth, "An Elegant Grief," *novel*, self Pub, 2008; Auth, "After Ado," *stage play*, self Pub, 2007. Fllshp of the SSP 1990. TOBROWN3@VERIZON.NET

BROWN, Robert James Crawford (FdL) 778 Hillside Ter, Ripon WI 54971 **Cn S Paul's Cathd Fond du Lac WI 1993-** B Chambersburg PA 9/8/1932 s John Edgar Brown & Sybilla. BA Ripon Coll Ripon WI 1954; BD Nash 1957. D 12/1/1956 P 6/2/1957 Bp Donald H V Hallock. S Ptr's Ch (S Mary's Chap) Ripon WI 1966-1997; Cur S Mk's Ch Milwaukee WI 1959-1966; Instr of NT Gk Nash Nashotah WI 1959-1960; Vic Gr Epis Ch Galena IL 1958-1959; Vic Trin Epis Ch Platteville WI 1957-1959. CBS; Forw in Faith No Amer; GAS; SHN. Hon Cn S Paul's Cathd Fond du Lac WI 1993. canonrb@vbe.com

BROWN, Robert Lee (USC) 531 Old Iron Works Rd, Spartanburg SC 29302 **R S Matt's Epis Ch Spartanburg SC 2003-** B Greer SC 10/28/1960 s John Brown & Bobbie Simmons. BA U of So Carolina 1984; MDiv STUSo 1995. D 6/10/1995 P 5/18/1996 Bp Dorsey Felix Henderson. m 4/23/1988 Sandra Dean McGee c 2. Assoc R Ch Of The Adv Spartanburg SC 1996-2003; D S Fran of Assisi Chapin SC 1995-1996. ROBSC@CHARTER.NET

BROWN, Rodney K (Eas) 32659 Seaview Loop, Millsboro DE 19966 B Richmond VA 1/14/1945 s Theron Towner Brown & Sarah Katherine. BA Westminster Choir Coll of Rider U 1969; MDiv VTS 1974. D 6/7/1975 P 6/1/1976 Bp John Harris Burt. m 6/1/1968 Gretchen Diane Brown c 2. R Ch Of The H Trin Oxford MD 1990-2009; St Steph Sch Alexandria VA 1988-1990; The Ch Of The Epiph Oak Hill VA 1987-1988; Epis HS Alexandria VA 1981-1987; Truro Epis Ch Fairfax VA 1976-1986. rod.brown@mchsi.com

BROWN, Royce Walter (Wyo) Central Wyoming Hospice, 319 S Wilson, Casper WY 82601 B Scottsbluff NE 5/25/1942 s Walter Jacob Brown & Pauline Mae. AS Scottsbluff Jr Coll 1962; BA U of Nebraska-Kearney 1964; MDiv PDS 1967. D 6/20/1967 P 12/21/1967 Bp Russell T Rauscher. m 6/4/1966 Sandra Helen Cremen c 3. R S Mk's Epis Ch Casper WY 1986-2004; Eccl Crt Dio Wyoming Casper WY 1986-2000; Stwdshp Com Dio Wstrn Kansas Hutchinson KS 1981-1985; R S Andr's Epis Ch Liberal KS 1980-1986; Exec Coun Dio Nebraska Omaha NE 1976-1980; Vic S Geo's Ch Sidney NE 1973-1980; Vic S Paul's Ch Ogallala NE 1973-1980; Vic S Pauls Epis Ch Arapahoe NE 1969-1973; D Calv Ch Hyannis NE 1967-1969; D S Jos's Ch Mullen NE 1967-1969. Bro of S Andr 1987-2006; Intl Ord of S Lk 1987; Reg VI Dir 2000-2006. r.brown3423@bresnan.net

BROWN, Roy F (Mass) 1731 Beacon St Apt 19, Brookline MA 02445 **Died 8/10/2009** B Coventry UK 3/6/1937 s Sidney George Brown & May. Coventry Coll of Arts and Tech 1955; Florissant Vlly Cmnty Coll 1963; MDiv Ya Berk 1971. D 6/12/1971 P 12/1/1971 Bp George Leslie Cadigan. c 2. Integrity 1976. royfbrown@aya.yale.edu

BROWN, Ruth Ellen (EO) 3277 N.W. 10th St., Redmond OR 97756 B Colorado Springs CO 3/12/1937 d Lewis Stephen Grandy & Lucile. BA U GA 1957. D 7/11/2007 Bp Johncy Itty. m 4/7/2005 Richard Brown c 2. raregbrown@yahoo.com

BROWN, Sally Sims (Colo) 2500 Locust Street, Denver CO 80207 **Ret Dio Colorado Denver CO 2009-** B Portland OR 4/5/1936 d Darwin Merrill Sims & Doris Lee. BA U CO 1958; Iliff TS 1978. D 7/19/1987 Bp William Carl Frey. c 4. Stndg Com Dio Colorado Denver CO 2003-2009; Diac Coun Dio Colorado Denver CO 2001-2009; D S Andr's Ch Denver CO 1996-2009; BEC Dio Colorado Denver CO 1993-1996; D S Thos Epis Ch Denver CO 1992-1995. EPF 1992; NAAD 1990. Diac Mnstry-Tradition of St. Steph No Amer Assoc.for Diac 1999. skb4536@aol.com

BROWN, Scott Jeffrey (WTex) 1300 Wiltshire Ave, San Antonio TX 78209 **R S Alb's Ch Harlingen TX 2007-** B Houston TX 5/10/1975 s James Ray Brown & JoAnne. BS Victoria Coll U Of Houston Victoria TX 1999; MDiv STUSo 2002. D 6/20/2002 Bp Robert Boyd Hibbs P 2/28/2003 Bp James Edward Folts. m 7/2/2004 Kimberly Ann Saunders c 2. Chapl Texas Mltry Inst San Antonio TX 2004-2007; Asst S Dav's Epis Ch San Antonio TX 2002-2004. Auth, "Just Where Does God Live?," WinePress, 2009. sbrown@stalbansharlingen.org

BROWN, Thomas James (Mass) 70 Church St., Winchester MA 01890 **Trst Ch Pension Fund New York NY 2009-; R Par Of The Epiph Winchester MA 2009-** B Bruce Crossing MI 9/28/1970 s Dennis George Brown & Suzanne Louise. BS Wstrn Michigan U 1992; CFS The OH SU 1993; MDiv CDSP 1997. D 6/28/1997 P 1/17/1998 Bp Edward Lewis Lee Jr. m 6/28/2003 Thomas Nordboe Mousin. R S Mich's Epis Ch Brattleboro VT 2000-2009; CDSP Berkeley CA 1997-2000; Assoc The Epis Ch Of S Jn The Evang San Francisco CA 1997-1999. Soc of S Jn the Evang 1994. tbrown@3crowns.org

BROWN RC, Virginia Dabney (WMo) Rivendell Motherhouse, 365 E. 372nd Rd., Dunnegan MO 65640 **P-in-c S Mk's Epis Ch Kimberling City MO 2008-** B Savannah GA 2/27/1948 d William Minor Dabney & Jeanne. BS MI SU 1969; MDiv SWTS 1974; MA New Mex St U. 1981; doctoral U of New Mex 1984. D 9/10/1974 P 1/28/1977 Bp Richard Mitchell Trelease Jr. c 3. R Shpd Of The Hills Branson MO 2007-2010; Assoc R Chr Epis Ch Springfield MO 2000-2004; Assoc Recyot Gr - S Lk's Ch Memphis TN 1993-2000; R S Thos A Becket Ch Roswell NM 1988-1993; Prof Dio The Rio Grande Albuquerque NM 1980-1988; Vic S Chad's Epis Ch Albuquerque NM 1976-1979. "Bringing the Story to Life," *Benedictines*, 2006. mothervirginiadb@gmail.com

BROWN JR, Walter Raymond (Ark) 12415 Cantrell Rd, Little Rock AR 72223 **S Mich's Epis Ch Little Rock AR 2011-** B Wilmington NC 6/17/1954 s Walter Raymond Brown & Betty May Todd. BA Pacific Chr Coll 1976; MDiv Phillips TS 1984. D 5/31/2011 Bp Larry R Benfield. m 8/17/1979 Royce Bales c 2. brownray72@yahoo.com

BROWN, Wanda Gaye (NC) 308 W Main St, Elkin NC 28621 **Vic Galloway Memi Chap Elkin NC 2010-** B Elkin NC 7/20/1943 d Dennis Clemont Brown & Mary Adams. BA Salem Coll Winston-Salem NC 1965; MDiv DS, Van 1969. D 6/7/2008 P 12/14/2008 Bp William Carl Frey. c 1. Asst H Trin Epis Ch - Mssn Raton NM 2008-2009. peacewgb@yadtel.net

BROWN, William Garland (Lex) 311 Washington St, Frankfort KY 40601 **Asstg P Ch Of The Ascen Frankfort KY 2008-** B Lexington KY 2/20/1939 s Jo Brown & Mary Margaret. BA S Paul Sem 1959; MA Mt S Mary Sem 1964; Ph.D U of St. Thos, Rome Italy 1969. Rec from Roman Catholic 12/8/2003 Bp Stacy F Sauls. m 6/29/1996 Linda Snelling. Ch Of The Ascen Frankfort KY 2006-2007. bbrown@midway.edu

BROWN III, William Hill (Va) 5103 Harlan Cir, Richmond VA 23226 B Washington DC 6/25/1937 s William Hill Brown & Charlotte Tiffany. AB Pr 1959; GTS 1960; BA Oxf 1962; MA Oxf 1966. D 11/24/1962 Bp Samuel B Chilton P 11/24/1963 Bp Robert Fisher Gibson Jr. m 2/13/1965 Margaret K Kennedy c 2. Dio Virginia Richmond VA 1975-1982; Gr & H Trin Epis Ch Richmond VA 1962-2001. Ch Schools of the Dio Virginia 1975-1982; S Cathr's Sch, Richmond, VA 1978-1990; Westminster-Cbury Hse, Richmond Va 1982-1986. farhills45@aol.com

BROWN, William Stewart (Ida) 5605 Lynwood Pl., Boise ID 83706 **S Andr's Epis Ch McCall ID 2004-** B San Francisco CA 1/21/1948 s William S Brown & Blanche Elizabeth. BA OR SU 1971; MDiv CDSP 1976. D 6/26/1976 Bp C Kilmer Myers P 1/6/1978 Bp John F Conlin. m 10/26/2010 Laurel Crookston c 2. Dir Paradise Point Camp Dio Idaho Boise ID 1999-2004; Cn S Mich's Cathd Boise ID 1983-1989. wsbrownrev@gmail.com

B

BROWN, Willis Donald (Ky) 2402 Glenview Ave, Louisville KY 40222 B Fort Worth TX 10/7/1930 s Willis Kyle Brown & Claire Elaine. BBA Texas Tech U 1953; MDiv VTS 1980. D 2/18/1984 P 12/17/1988 Bp David Reed. m 7/31/1983 Patricia Lou Knadler Brown. S Jn's Ch Louisville KY 1994-1999. donpatbrown@bellsouth.net

BROWN DOUGLAS, Kelly Delaine (WA) 12519 Hawks Nest Ln, Germantown MD 20876 B Dayton OH 2/28/1957 d William Lewis Brown & Mary Elizabeth. BS Denison U 1979; MDiv UTS 1982. D 10/9/1982 Bp William Grant Black P 9/1/1983 Bp Walter Decoster Dennis Jr. Ch Of The Intsn New York NY 1982-1986.

BROWNE, Bliss (Chi) 910 W Castlewood Ter, Chicago IL 60640 B Atlanta GA 8/15/1950 d Emory Williams & Janet. Saguaro Seminar In Civic Engagement Kennedy Sch of Harv; Smith 1969; BA Ya 1971; Fllshp Rockefeller Fndt 1972; MDiv Harvard DS 1974; MBA NWU 1978; Fllshp Kellogg Fndt 1991. D 6/23/1974 Bp James Winchester Montgomery P 8/6/1977 Bp Quintin Ebenezer Primo Jr. m 2/20/1977 Howell Browne. Asst Cathd Of S Jas Chicago IL 1987-1995; Asst Trin Ch Chicago IL 1978-1987; Serv Ch Of Our Sav Chicago IL 1976-1977; Cur S Paul And S Jas New Haven CT 1974-1976. Imagine Chicago 1992. Natl Ldrshp Fell Kellogg Fndt 1988; Fell Rockefeller Fndt 1971; Mercedes Mentor Awd Chicago IL; Saguaro Seminar In Civic Engagement Harvard Kennely Sch. bliss@imaginechicago.org

BROWNE, Gayle (SO) 212 Tulane Ave, Oak Ridge TN 37830 **Vic S Andr's Epis Ch Washington Crt Hse OH 2008-** B Bunkie LA 2/26/1950 d Hubert Jacob Hansen & Marilyn Lucille. BS LSU 1971; MA U So 1992. D 2/2/1986 P 12/1/1990 Bp William Evan Sanders. c 3. S Lk's Ch Knoxville TN 2002-2008; Ch Of The Resurr Loudon TN 1999-2001; S Steph's Epis Ch Oak Ridge TN 1991-1999; Dio E Tennessee Knoxville TN 1990-1991; D S Jn's Epis Cathd Knoxville TN 1986-1989. ghbrowne@msn.com

BROWNE III, Joseph M (EC) 200 NC Highway 33 W, Chocowinity NC 27817 **Chair of Liturg Cmsn Dio E Carolina Kinston NC 2009-; Chair of Deputation to GC Dio E Carolina Kinston NC 2008-; Mem, Conv Com Dio E Carolina Kinston NC 2008-; Archd Dio E Carolina Kinston NC 2006-; R Trin Epis Ch Chocowinity NC 2004-** B Greenville NC 5/13/1977 s Joseph Browne & Virginia. BA U NC 1999; MA U NC 2001; MDiv VTS 2004. D 6/19/2004 P 2/24/2005 Bp Clifton Daniel III. Mem of Exec Coun Dio E Carolina Kinston NC 2005-2008; Mem, Bd Trin Cntr Dio E Carolina Kinston NC 2005-2008. jmbrowne3@hotmail.com

BROWNE, Joy Elizabeth (Ky) 922 Milford Ln, Louisville KY 40207 B Berkeley CA 10/21/1949 d Leon Richard Browne & Maxine Louise. BA U of Washington 1971; MA U Chi 1976; MDiv CRDS 1989; PhD Emory U 1995. D 6/2/1990 Bp Charles Shannon Mallory P 1/1/1992 Bp Richard Lester Shimpfky. Dio Long Island Garden City NY 2005; S Jn's Ch Hempstead NY 2004-2005; S Thos's Par Newark DE 2001-2002; Vic S Geo's Epis Ch Louisville KY 1997-2000; Dio Kentucky Louisville KY 1997-1999; Asst S Mart In The Fields Ch Atlanta GA 1993-1994. Auth, "Itc Journ". AAR; Black Wmn In Ch & Soc; SBL. crossandcup@aol.com

BROWNE, Robert T (Tex) 2210 Potomac Dr Unit 2, Houston TX 77057 **Died 9/19/2009** B Waco TX 8/19/1926 s Theron Humphries Browne & Ludie Caroline. BA SMU 1949; MDiv SMU 1952; Nash 1974; DMin STUSo 1978. D 10/20/1963 P 5/1/1964 Bp John E Hines. c 3. Auth, *Epis BSA Ch Supplement*; Auth, *Return To Hepu; Lambeth 88- The Call*; Auth, *Witnesses To the Sprt*. bbrowne@pdg.net

BROWNE, Samuel Jonathan (SeFla) 426 Cypress Dr, Lake Park FL 33403 B Key West FL 10/30/1929 s John H Brown & Ruth Eloise. BA S Aug's Coll Raleigh NC 1956; Nash 1959. D 7/4/1959 Bp Henry I Louttit P 1/16/1960 Bp William Francis Moses. m 6/25/1960 Lottie Christine Major c 2. S Patricks Ch W Palm Bch FL 1964-1994; P-in-c Ch Of S Jn Lake Worth FL 1964-1988; Incharge S Aug's Epis Ch St Petersburg FL 1959-1964.

BROWNELL, Leona Weiss (Del) 4830 Kennett Pike #3504, Wilmington DE 19807 B Waterloo IA 10/24/1923 d Leonard Johann Michael Weiss & Anna Barbara Catherine. BA U of Nthrn Iowa 1944; MS U of Wisconsin 1948; PhD U of Delaware Newark 1967; PDS 1974; MDiv Luth TS at Gettysburg 1976. D 6/25/1977 P 2/11/1979 Bp John Harris Burt. m 10/25/1952 Robert M Brownell c 2. Supply Dio Delaware Wilmington DE 1991-1994; Supply P Dio No Carolina Raleigh NC 1987-1988; D-in-Res S Jas Ch Painesville OH 1977-1979. Auth, *Var Books-Biology*. Coll Chapl, ACPE, 1990. BA w high hon U of Nthrn Iowa Cedar Falls IA 1944. lw_brnl@yahoo.com

BROWNING JR, Bob (NY) 108 Overlook Rd, Poughkeepsie NY 12603 **P-in-c Gr Epis Ch Rutherford NJ 2011-; Vic S Andr's Ch Poughkeepsie NY 2006-** B Jersey City NJ 8/18/1946 s Robert Franklin Browning & Margaret Adeline. BA New Jersey City U 1974; MA WPC 1978; MDiv Prot TS 2006. D 3/11/2006 P 9/23/2006 Bp Mark Sean Sisk. c 1. Dio New York New York City NY 2007-2008. robert_browning4@msn.com

BROWNING II, Charles Alex (SeFla) 211 Trinity Pl, West Palm Beach FL 33401 **H Trin Epis Ch W Palm Bch FL 2011-** B Memphis TN 10/3/1982 s Richard E Rome & Dorothy Eugene. BA Palm Bch Atlantic U 2007; MDiv VTS 2011. D 12/21/2010 Bp Leopold Frade. m 5/21/2011 Cainna Beth Jirilowic. c.a.browningii@gmail.com

✠ BROWNING, Most Rev Edmond Lee (EO) 5164 Imai Rd, Hood River OR 97031 B Corpus Christi TX 3/11/1929 s Edmond Lucian Browning & Mae Lee. DD CDSP; BA U So 1952; BD STUSo 1954; Japanese Lang Sch 1965; DD Epis TS of The SW 1970. D 7/2/1954 P 5/1/1955 Bp Everett H Jones Con 1/5/1968 for Oki. m 9/10/1953 Patricia Alline Sparks c 5. Epis Ch Cntr New York NY 1986-1997; Exec & Secy Off New York NY 1986-1989; Bp Dio Hawaii Honolulu HI 1976-1985; Bp Convoc of Amer Ch in Europe Paris FR 1971-1974; R Ch Of The Redeem Eagle Pass TX 1956-1959; Asst Ch Of The Gd Shpd Corpus Christi TX 1954-1956. Auth, *A Year of Days*; Auth, *Essay*; Auth, *No Outcast*. DD U So Sew 1970; Hon Degree CDSP; Hon Degree EDS; Hon Degree GTS New York City NY; Hon Degree SW; Hon Degree VTS Alexandria VA. edbrowning@gorge.net

BROWNING, Peter Sparks (Los) 13909 Crow Rd, Apple Valley CA 92307 **Vic S Andr's Epis Ch Irvine CA 2004-** B Okinawa JP 7/10/1960 s Edmond Lee Browning & Patricia Alline. BA Whitworth U 1983; MDiv GTS 1991. D 6/15/1991 P 1/1/1992 Bp Frederick Houk Borsch. m 6/19/1988 Melissa Louise Browning c 1. R S Tim's Epis Ch Apple Vlly CA 1996-2003; S Jas' Par So Pasadena CA 1991-1996. peter@standrewsivine.org

BROWNING JR, robert guy (SwFla) 7038 West Brandywine Circle, Fort Myers FL 33919 B Philadelphia PA 7/29/1930 s Robert Guy Shipton Browning & Sara Ellen. BA Ge 1960; BD/MDiv Nash 1963; U of Pennsylvania Wharton 2048. D 6/8/1963 P 12/14/1963 Bp Joseph Gillespie Armstrong. m 9/7/1957 Alva Barbara Miller c 5. Dio SW Florida Sarasota FL 1965-1996; R S Hilary's Ch Ft Myers FL 1965-1996; Vic S Hilary's Ch Ft Myers FL 1965-1968; R S Steph's Ch Philadelphia PA 1963-1965. Angl-RC Ecclectic Relation 1965-1996. Angl-Roman Catholicc Eccl Cmsn on Religio 1965. rgbrowning@yahoo.com

BROWNING, Trace (U) Rowland Hall St Marks School, 720 Guardsman Way, Salt Lake City UT 84108 **Chapl Rowland Hall/S Mk's Sch Salt Lake Cty UT 2005-** B Ogden UT 5/20/1961 s Merlin Browning & Lois. BA Weber St U 1990; MDiv Bex 1995. D 6/17/1995 Bp George Edmonds Bates P 12/10/1995 Bp William George Burrill. m 9/4/1981 Karen Kikuno Wood c 5. R S Pauls Epis Ch The Dalles OR 2000-2005; Asst S Jn's Ch Portsmouth NH 1997-2000; Bex Columbus OH 1996-1997; Assoc S Ptr's Epis Ch Henrietta NY 1996-1997; R Calv/St Andr's Par Rochester NY 1995-1996. MDiv w dist Bex Rochester NY 1995; BA mcl Weber St U Ogden UT 1990. tracebrowning@rowlandhall.org

BROWNLEE, Annette Geoffrian (Colo) 410 W 18th St, Pueblo CO 81003 **Wycliffe Coll 2008-** B Washington DC 8/20/1955 d Donald Henry Brownlee & Antoine. BA U of Iowa 1977; MS U IL 1978; MA U of Iowa 1983; MDiv GTS 1987. D 6/13/1987 Bp Walter Cameron Righter P 5/21/1988 Bp James Russell Moodey. m 1/24/1987 Ephraim Louis Radner c 2. Assoc Ch Of The Ascen Pueblo CO 1998-2007; Emm Epis Ch Stamford CT 1989-1997; Asst S Paul's Epis Ch Cleveland Heights OH 1988-1989. "Not on the Same Page," *The Angl Vol. 32(2)*, 2003; Auth, "The Dark Night of Hope," *Journ of Rel & Aging*; "The Lectionary Commentary," *Theol Exegesis for Texts*. annettebrownlee113@msn.com

BROWNLEE, Hugh Richard (SO) 14741 Shannon Ct, Burton OH 44021 **Died 9/4/2011** B Cleveland OH 11/24/1927 s Ivan Stitt Brownlee & Mabel Jane. BS Baldwin-Wallace Coll 1950; BD Ken 1961; Case Wstrn Reserve U 1969; Gestalt Inst 1976. D 6/10/1961 P 12/10/1961 Bp Nelson Marigold Burroughs.

BROWNMILLER, David Clark (Ore) 16379 Nw Charlais St, Beaverton OR 97006 **Int All SS Ch Hillsboro OR 2008-** B Shawnee OK 4/21/1945 s William Harry Miller & Charlene Louise. BA U of Oklahoma 1969; JD U Denv 1972; MDiv SWTS 1994. D 6/11/1994 P 12/3/1994 Bp William Jerry Winterrowd. m 3/29/1986 Gail Marie Brown c 2. Dio Oregon Portland OR 2008-2009; S Gabr Ch Portland OR 1999-2004; Vic S Eliz's Epis Ch Brighton CO 1994-1998. stgabe@teleport.com

BROWN-NOLAN, Virginia (WA) 12613 Meadowood Dr, Silver Spring MD 20904 **S Mk's Ch Fairland Silver Sprg MD 2011-** B Brooklyn NY 3/5/1948 d Dillard Houston Brown & Sarah Virginia. BA Lake Forest Coll 1970; MS U IL 1974; MDiv CDSP 1986. D 6/29/1986 Bp Frederick Warren Putnam P 3/1/1987 Bp Donald Purple Hart. m 8/29/1992 Nathaniel Nolan c 4. R S Lk's Ch Washington DC 1999-2011; Coordntr Dio Michigan Detroit MI 1995-1999; Vic Ch Of The H Comm Maywood IL 1988-1994; Asst Ch Of Our Sav Mill Vlly CA 1986-1988. vbnolan48@yahoo.com

BROWNRIDGE, Walter B.A. (O) The Cathedral Church of St. Andrew, 229 Queen Emma Square, Honolulu HI 96813 **Stndg Cmsn on Const & Cn Mem Exec Coun Appointees New York NY 2011-2015; Dn S Andr's Cathd Honolulu HI 2011-** B Toledo OH 10/2/1956 s Walter Wilson Brownridge & Eunice Elizabeth. BA JCU 1978; MA U of San Diego 1985; JD Geo 1987; MDiv GTS 2000. D 6/24/2000 Bp J Clark Grew II P 6/9/2001 Bp Arthur Benjamin Williams Jr. m 12/18/1982 Christina Marie Nader c 2. Assoc Dn The TS at The U So Sewanee TN 2006-2011; Appointed Mssy -Cathd Cn The Cathd Ch of St. Geo the Mtyr, Cape Town So Afr (ACSA) Exec Coun Appointees

New York NY 2003-2006; Assoc R Chr Ch Shaker Heights OH 2000-2003. Auth, "'We'Ve Come This Far By Faith, Reflections On Anglo-Catholicism," *Fllshp Papers*, 1994. Affirming Catholicism No Amer 1997; EUC 2002; NAACP 1994; Potomac Cltn 2004; UBE 1997; Urban League 1979-1984. Seymour Preaching Prize For Extemp Preaching GTS 2000; Preaching Excellence Prog Fell 2000 Preaching Excellence Prog 2000; Who'S Who Among Amer Law Students Who's Who 1987; One Of The Outstanding Young Men Of Amer OYMA 1985. dean@thecathedralofstandrew.org

BROYLES, Elizabeth Ruth (NY) 37 Chipmunk Hollow Rd, Kerhonkson NY 12446 B Moenchweiller DE 1/6/1961 d Jerome Michael Broyles & Ruth Anne. BA Rutgers-The St U 1982; MDiv UTS 1992; Cert in Sprtl Direction The Haden Inst 2011. D 6/11/1994 P 12/1/1994 Bp Richard Frank Grein. P-in-c Ch Of The H Trin Pawling NY 1998-2002; Asst Gr Ch White Plains NY 1994-1998. ERBROYLES@GMAIL.COM

BRUBAKER GARRISON, Tasha (Ore) 418 Stonewood Dr, Eugene OR 97405 B Bakersfield CA 7/24/1971 d David Alan Brubaker & Linda Vache'. BA Stan 1993; HSC London Sch of Econ 1995; M. Div. GTS 2003. D 6/28/2003 Bp Vincent Waydell Warner P 1/3/2004 Bp Francis Campbell Gray. m 10/21/2006 Blaine G Garrison c 1. R Ch Of The Resurr Eugene OR 2008-2011; Asst Chr Ascen Ch Richmond VA 2003-2007; Chr Ch Glen Allen VA 2003-2007. "September 13 2001," Epis Dio Pittsburgh, 2002. btgarrison@hotmail.com

BRUCE, David Allison (Me) Brigham'S Cove Road, Box 243 HCR 63, West Bath ME 04530 B 5/19/1948 s Donald Allison Bruce & Madelyn Vanessa. AA Nthrn Essex Cmnty Coll 1968; BA U of Massachusetts 1971; BD U Of Edinburgh Edinburgh Gb 1977. Trans from Anglican Church of Canada 8/25/1983 Bp Frederick Barton Wolf. All Soul's Epis Ch 2003-2006; Assoc Gr Memi Portland OR 1986-2008; Off Of Bsh For ArmdF New York NY 1984-1986.

✠ **BRUCE, Rt Rev Diane M Jardine** (Los) 5 W Trenton, Irvine CA 92620 **Bp Suffr of Los Angeles Dio Los Angeles Los Angeles CA 2010-** B Pequannock NJ 6/22/1956 d Donald Wesley Jardine & Mary Alice. BA U CA at Berkeley 1979; MDiv ETSBH 1997; DMin SWTS 2010. D 6/7/1997 Bp Robert Marshall Anderson P 1/17/1998 Bp Frederick Houk Borsch Con 5/15/2010 for Los. m 11/8/2011 Gregory S Bruce c 2. R S Clem's-By-The-Sea Par San Clemente CA 2000-2010; Assoc R Ch Of The Mssh Santa Ana CA 1997-2000. revdjb@gmail.com

BRUCE, Jane (NC) 1186 Fearrington Post, Pittsboro NC 27312 B Fordyce AR 10/17/1941 d Imon Elba Bruce & Catherine Louise. BA Mt Holyoke Coll 1963; MA U of Arkansas 1964; MDiv GTS 1987. D 6/13/1987 Bp Ronald Hayward Haines P 6/18/1988 Bp Frank Harris Vest Jr. Vic S Dav's Epis Ch Laurinburg NC 1990-2002; Asst Ch Of The Gd Shpd Rocky Mt NC 1987-1990. OHC. cjbruce@earthlink.net

BRUCE, John Allen (Ore) 4909 Mulholland Dr, Lake Oswego OR 97035 B Kansas City MO 9/17/1934 s Basil Frederick Bruce & Thelma May. BA Wesl 1956; MDiv GTS 1959; PhD U MN 1972. D 6/20/1959 Bp Angus Dun P 12/1/1959 Bp Horace W B Donegan. m 7/22/1989 Judith Bruce. Vic Ch Of The Resurr San Antonio TX 1967-1968; Assoc Chr Ch Charlotte NC 1962-1964; R Ch Of The Div Love Montrose NY 1961-1962; Cur S Barn Ch Irvington on Hudson NY 1959-1961. Cosmos Club. Who'sWho. jaandjebruce@yahoo.com

BRUCE, Todd (WMo) 4952 Bell St, Kansas City MO 64112 **Assoc R S Paul's Ch Kansas City MO 2007-** B Snellville, GA 8/19/1981 s J R Bruce & V Dillard. AB U GA 2002; MDiv VTS 2007. D 12/21/2006 Bp J(ohn) Neil Alexander P. tbruce@stpaulskcmo.org

BRUCE, Tracy Ann (Md) 5814 19th St N, Arlington VA 22205 **S Jn's Ch Reisterstown MD 2006-** B Cincinnati OH 4/22/1952 d Dean Collins Bruce & Faye. BS U Of Kentucky 1974; MDiv GTS 1991. Trans 7/7/2004 Bp J(ohn) Neil Alexander. m 8/13/1966 Stephen Rintoul Davenport c 3. Assoc S Mary's Epis Ch Arlington VA 2002-2006; Asst S Lk's Epis Ch Atlanta GA 1993-1994; Asst The Ch Of Ascen And H Trin Cincinnati OH 1991-1993. Cramer Middler Acad Awd UTS New York NY 1990; Flinchbaugh Ot/Hebr Awd UTS New York NY 1989; Sullivan Medallion U Of Kentucky Lexington KY 1974. tracy.bruce@stjohnsglyndon.org

BRUCKART, Robert Monroe (CFla) 2327 Saint Andrews Cir, Melbourne FL 32901 B Columbus OH 11/11/1951 s William Lee Bruckart & Jessie Hocker. Mntl Hlth Counslr Lic St Of Florida; BA Westminster Coll 1973; MDiv SWTS 1979; MA Webster U 1998. D 6/9/1979 P 12/7/1979 Bp Robert Bracewell Appleyard. m 9/10/1977 Deborah Elizabeth Bruckart c 2. Assoc For Pstr Care H Trin Epis Ch Melbourne FL 1995-1998; Epis Ch Cntr New York NY 1993-1995; Assoc R H Trin Epis Ch Melbourne FL 1984-1994; Vic S Jn's Epis Ch Donora PA 1979-1984; S Paul's Ch Monongahela PA 1979-1984. Lic Mntl Hlth Counslr St Of Florida. deborahbruckart@gmail.com

BRUDVIG, Dale Keith (EC) 163 Bull Bay Dr, Harrells NC 28444 **Died 7/28/2010** B Huron SD 7/24/1935 s Carl Oscar Brudvig & Viles Marie. BS U CA 1957; MA Command and Gnrl Stff Coll 1966; US-A War Coll 1976; MDiv VTS 1990. D 6/2/1990 Bp Peter James Lee P 12/13/1990 Bp Robert Poland Atkinson. Curs 1984. Paul Harris Fell Rotary 2006. daleandnancy@intrstar.net

BRUGGER, Stephanie Black (SO) 335 Lincoln Ave, Troy OH 45373 B 6/5/1958 d William Black & Ruth. AD Edison St 1984. D 10/20/2001 Bp Herbert Thompson Jr. c 3. blackbrugger@earthlink.net

BRUMBAUGH, Charles Fredrick (SO) 72 Reily Rd, Cincinnati OH 45215 **Assoc The Ch of the Redeem Cincinnati OH 2002-** B Greenville OH 1/28/1956 s Philip Dickes Brumbaugh & Nancy. BS Mia 1978; MDiv VTS 1986. D 6/14/1986 P 1/10/1987 Bp William Grant Black. m 10/18/2003 Anne Keely Dormire c 2. Dir of Marketing FMP Cincinnati OH 2001-2002; R The Ch Of Ascen And H Trin Cincinnati OH 1994-2001; Assoc S Paul's Epis Ch Pittsburgh PA 1991-1993; R Chr Ch Cape Girardeau MO 1988-1991; Asst Calv Ch Cincinnati OH 1986-1988. cfbrumbagh@gmail.com

BRUMBAUGH, George William (Ark) 1000 Pavilions Circle, Traverse City MI 49684 B Sioux Falls SD 12/27/1925 s Morris M Brumbaugh & Cara A. BA Morningside Coll 1950; MA MI SU 1951; PhD U MN 1966. D 6/29/1963 Bp Hamilton Hyde Kellogg P 3/2/1964 Bp Philip Frederick McNairy. R S Tim Ch Richland MI 1965-1975; Vic S Barth's Epis Ch Bemidji MN 1963-1965.

BRUMBY III, James Remley (Fla) 67 Connie Dr, Crawfordville FL 32327 **Died 1/16/2010** B Marietta GA 4/24/1921 s James Remley Brumby & Martha Louise. U of Florida 1942; BA U So 1948; MDiv STUSo 1951. D 7/22/1951 P 2/24/1952 Bp Henry I Louttit. *I Am a Part of All That I Have Met*, Personal Histories, 2000. Actg Dir Ch Relatns U of So 1984; Dep GC 1969; Hon Cn S Lk Cathd Orlando Fla 1966; Trst U So Sewanee TN 1963.

BRUNEAU, Betsy (NCal) 66 E. Commercial St., Willits CA 95490 B Rockville Center NY 3/19/1944 d Russell Raymond Yost & Isabelle Landrum. BA Stan 1965. D 4/28/2005 P 11/26/2005 Bp Jerry Alban Lamb. m 9/5/1983 William Bruneau c 2. stfranciswillits@hotmail.com

BRUNELLE, Denis Charles (LI) PO Box 2733, East Hampton NY 11937 **R S Lk's Ch E Hampton NY 2009-** B Manchester NH 10/27/1951 s Ferdinand Charles Brunelle & Muriel Violet. BA Allentown Coll Allentown PA 1974; MDiv Cath Theol Un 1977; MA Cath Theol Un 1978; MA San Diego St U 1988; U IL 1988. Rec from Roman Catholic 5/26/1992 as Priest Bp Peter Hess Beckwith. Geo Mercer TS Garden City NY 2006-2009; R S Ptr's by-the-Sea Epis Ch Bay Shore NY 1998-2006; R The Par Ch Of S Lk Long Bch CA 1995-1998; R S Ptr's Ch Huntington WV 1992-1994. Auth, *Preaching the Ch Year*, 1986. Phi Kappa Phi. dcbrune@aol.com

BRUNETT, Harry Edgar (Md) 9855 S Iris Ct, Littleton CO 80127 B Baltimore MD 1/18/1936 s Harry Edgar Brunett & Minnie Amelia. BA W&L 1958; MA Bos 1959; BD EDS 1962; MBA Loyola U 1982; DMin SWTS 1998. D 6/26/1962 Bp Harry Lee Doll P 4/1/1963 Bp Noble C Powell. m 9/2/1961 Joan Marilyn Forsell c 3. R S Andr's Epis Ch Glenwood MD 1998-2003; Asst S Jn's Ch Ellicott City MD 1992-1997; Cur Ch Of S Marks On The Hill Pikesville MD 1962-1963. Auth, "Seeking the Sprt," *How to Create a Cmnty of Seekers*, Morehouse Pub, 2006; Auth, *Seeker Mnstry for Next Generation*, Seabury-Wstrn. Commision On Anti-Racism 2004; ESMA Bd; Mssn Strtgy Grp 1996. hbrunett@gmail.com

BRUNNER, Arthur F (Pa) Po Box 1190, N Cape May NJ 08204 B Providence RI 2/21/1932 s Arthur Frederick Brunner & Esther Francesca. Br 1950; US-A 1952; BS Tem 1957; MDiv PDS 1960. D 5/14/1960 Bp Joseph Gillespie Armstrong P 11/1/1960 Bp Oliver J Hart. m 11/22/1952 Joan F Lafferty. Calv Ch Glen Riddle PA 1970-1997. Auth, *Don't Pk the Ark*. Human Rts Awd City of Philadelphia Philadelphia PA 1968. SINTAX_08204@yahoo.com

BRUNO, Jean M (DR) Box 1309, Port-Au-Prince Haiti B Croix des Bouquets HT 7/27/1945 s Merove Bruno & Antoinette. MDiv ETSC 1971. D 11/21/1971 P 6/1/1972 Bp Luc Anatole Jacques Garnier. m 3/29/1973 Marise Bruno. Dio The Dominican Republic (Iglesia Epis Dominicana) Santo Domingo DO 1999-2007; Dio Haiti Ft Lauderdale FL 1971-1998.

✠ **BRUNO, Rt Rev Joseph Jon** (Los) 3505 Grayburn Rd., Pasadena CA 91107 **Bp Dio Los Angeles Los Angeles CA 2002-; Bp Dio Los Angeles Los Angeles CA 2000-** B Los Angeles CA 11/17/1946 s Joseph John Bruno & Dorothy Annette. BA California St U 1973; MDiv VTS 1977. D 6/18/1977 P 1/14/1978 Bp Robert C Rusack Con 4/29/2000 for Los. m 12/30/1984 Mary Woodrich. Cathd Cntr Of S Paul Cong Los Angeles CA 1993-1999; Mssnr For Stwdshp And Dvlpmt Dio Los Angeles Los Angeles CA 1990-1993; Dio Los Angeles Los Angeles CA 1988-1993, Cong Of S Athan Los Angeles CA 1986-1999; R Cathd Cntr Of S Paul Cong Los Angeles CA 1986-1992; Assoc S Paul's Pomona Pomona CA 1983-1986; Vic S Matt's Epis Ch Eugene OR 1980-1983; Assoc S Mary's Epis Ch Eugene OR 1979-1980; S Patricks Ch And Day Sch Thousand Oaks CA 1977-1979. EWC; EvangES; Ord Of S Lk. jonbruno@ladiocese.org

BRUNO, Suzanne Lee (NC) 9528 Spurwig Ct, Charlotte NC 28278 **D S Marg's Epis Ch Waxhaw NC 2010-** B Los Angeles CA 8/1/1944 d Allen Theodore Lee & Ada Charlotte. BA Occ 1966; Tchg Cert Occ 1967; Cert Inst for Chr Stds 1994. D 12/18/1993 Bp John Wadsworth Howe. m 9/24/1966 Paul Michael Bruno c 2. D S Jn's Epis Ch Charlotte NC 2009-2010; Bd, Cbury Retreat Ctr Dio Cntrl Florida Orlando FL 2006-2008; D Epis Ch Of The Resurr Longwood FL 1993-2008. Assoc, Ord Of S Helena 1994; NAAD 1994-1999. sbrunorev@aol.com

BRUNS, Thomas Charles (Mo) 222 Montwood, Seguin TX 78155 **Emm Epis Ch Lockhart TX 2001-** B El Paso TX 7/15/1938 s Joseph Louis Bruns & Florence Julia. BS U of Texas 1961; BD VTS 1964. D 7/15/1964 Bp Everett H Jones P 2/1/1965 Bp Richard Earl Dicus. m 9/24/1983 Martha Guerrero c 1. Int S Phil's Ch Beeville TX 1998; R H Cross Epis Ch Poplar Bluff MO 1985-1998; Trin Mssn Pearsall TX 1978-1979; P-in-c All SS Epis Ch Pleasanton TX 1966-1985; P-in-c S Tim's Ch Cotulla TX 1966-1974; Vic Gr Ch Llano TX 1964-1966. tcbruns@satx.rr.com

BRUNSON, Catherine E (NJ) 124 Harrow Dr, Somerset NJ 08873 B New Brunswick NJ 9/15/1949 Rutgers-The St U; AAS Mcc 1969. D 11/21/2002 Bp David B(ruce) Joslin. c 2. S Alb's Epis Ch New Brunswick NJ 2002-2009. catherine.brunson@aonhroutsourcing.com

BRUSCO, Kathleen (Minn) 112 Crestridge Dr, Burnsville MN 55337 B Saint Paul MN 10/9/1970 d Richard Kyle & Jane. BA S Olaf Coll 1992; MDiv SWTS 1999. D 6/11/1999 Bp Calvin Onderdonk Schofield Jr P 12/17/1999 Bp James Louis Jelinek. m 1/14/1995 Paul Joseph Brusco. Assoc Ch Of The Nativ Burnsville MN 1999-2003; Dio Minnesota Minneapolis MN 1999-2003.

BRUSSO, Leonard George (SeFla) 1225 Knollcrest Ct, Venice FL 34285 B New York NY 7/28/1934 s Leonard Jacob Brusso & Ida May. BA Adel 1957; MDiv GTS 1960. D 4/23/1960 P 10/29/1960 Bp James P De Wolfe. m 10/16/1976 Wendy Jean Squire. Pres of Stndg Com Dio SE Florida Miami FL 1995-1996; Chair of Assessment Appeals Com Dio SE Florida Miami FL 1993-1998; Stndg Com Dio SE Florida Miami FL 1993-1995; Com on Cn Dio SE Florida Miami FL 1992-1996; Cathd Chapt Dio SE Florida Miami FL 1989-1991; Chair of Agenda Com Dio SE Florida Miami FL 1989-1990; Exec Bd Dio SE Florida Miami FL 1988-1990; Chair of COM Dio SE Florida Miami FL 1982-1985; R S Andr's Epis Ch Palmetto Bay FL 1981-1998; Dio SE Florida Miami FL 1981-1985; COM Dio SE Florida Miami FL 1981-1982; R S Paul's Ch Glen Cove NY 1968-1981; COM Dio Long Island Garden City NY 1966-1978; R Ch of S Jude Wantagh NY 1963-1968; Cur Epis Ch of The Resurr Williston Pk NY 1960-1963. lenwen1@msn.com

BRUST, John Costello (SwFla) 1201 Yellowstone Dr, Naples FL 34110 B Medina NY 9/21/1920 s Philip Brust & Mary. BS SUNY 1943. D 6/30/1990 Bp Rogers Sanders Harris. m 7/2/1949 Elsie Ruth Brust c 3. D S Mary's Epis Ch Bonita Sprg FL 1990-2001. NAAD.

BRUTTELL, Susan Margaret (SeFla) 706 Glenwood Ln, Plantation FL 33317 B Milford CT 2/6/1949 d Harold Raymond Lund & Margaret. Nova U Davie FL 1993; MDiv Ya Berk 2005. D 11/15/2006 P 5/26/2007 Bp Leopold Frade. m 6/14/1969 Thomas Allen Bruttell c 4. sbruttell@aol.com

BRUTTELL, Thomas Allen (SeFla) 706 Glenwood Ln, Plantation FL 33317 **Dio SE Florida Miami FL 2007-; Archd for Deploy Dio SE Florida Miami FL 2006-** B Fort Lauderdale FL 5/19/1949 D 6/21/2003 P 12/21/2003 Bp Leopold Frade. m 6/14/1969 Susan Margaret Bruttell. S Chris's By-The-Sea Epis Ch Key Biscayne FL 2006-2007; H Trin Epis Ch W Palm Bch FL 2003-2006. tbruttell@aol.com

BRUTUS, Joseph Mathieu (Hai) Box 1309, Port-Au-Prince Haiti **Dio Haiti Ft Lauderdale FL 1977-** B Leogane HT 9/6/1947 s Dumonvert Brutus & Milosia. BA Coll S Pierre 1971; Utcwi 1976; Cntr D'Etudes Theol 1977. D 9/18/1977 P 5/1/1978 Bp Luc Anatole Jacques Garnier. m 4/17/1980 Marie Victoria Brutus.

BRYAN, Christopher (Tenn) The School of Theology, The University of the South, 335 Tennessee Ave, Sewanee TN 37398 B London UK 1/24/1935 s William Joseph Bryan & Amy. BA Oxf 1957; MA Oxf 1959; PhD U of Exeter 1983. Trans from Church Of England 11/1/1983 Bp William Evan Sanders. m 7/1/1972 Wendy Elizabeth Bryan. C K Ben Prof of NT The TS at The U So Sewanee TN 1983-2007. Auth, "The Resurr of the Mssh," Oxf Press, 2011; Auth, "Render to Caesar," Oxf Press, 2005; Auth, "A Preface to Romans," Oxf Press, 2004; Auth, "And God Spoke: The Authority of the Bible for the Ch Today," Cowley Pub, 2002; Auth, "A Preface to Mk," Oxf Press, 1997; Auth, "Numerous arts, Revs, etc.". Cath Biblic Assn 1983; SBL 1983. Schlrshp and Resrch Awd Assn of Theol Shcools 1989; Glanfield Exhibitioner Wadham Coll, Oxford 1958; Woodward Schlr Wadham Coll, Oxford 1954. cbryan@sewanee.edu

BRYAN, Elizabeth Persis (SD) 130 Talavera Pkwy Apt 734, San Antonio TX 78232 B Escanba MI 6/15/1945 d Robert Frederick Branch & Carol Elizabeth. Calvin Coll 1965; Hope Coll 1967; BA NW Coll 1968; MDiv VTS 1989. D 7/23/1990 P 6/11/1991 Bp Craig Barry Anderson. m 11/3/1972 Richard Bryan. Ch Of The H Sprt San Antonio TX 2001-2002; S Jn's Ch Gap PA 1999-2001; S Jas Epis Ch Belle Fourche SD 1994-1997; S Thos Epis Ch Sturgis SD 1994-1997; Asst The Ch Of The Epiph Oak Hill VA 1991-1992; Gr Epis Ch Alexandria VA 1990-1991. Peo Educational Soc. 9bryan@supernet.com

BRYAN, Joan Carr (Fla) PO Box 1584, Ponte Vedra Beach FL 32004 B Evanston IL 5/7/1944 d Charles William Carr & Anne Virginia. BA U of Florida 1966; MDiv TS 1990. D 6/10/1990 P 12/9/1990 Bp Frank Stanley Cerveny. m 7/23/1966 Patrick Bryan c 2. COM, Chair Dio Florida Jacksonville FL 2003-2007; Stndg Com, Pres Dio Florida Jacksonville FL 1995-1997; Assoc Chr Epis Ch Ponte Vedra Bch FL 1990-2006. Cmnty of S Mary 1990. joancb@bellsouth.net

BRYAN, Jonathan (Va) 7815 Midday Ln, Alexandria VA 22306 **P Assoc S Aid's Ch Alexandria VA 2001-** B Richmond VA 12/22/1934 s Corbin Braxton Bryan & Alice. BA U of Virginia 1957; MA GW 1967; PhD Amer U 1972; VTS 1982. D 6/9/1982 Bp David Henry Lewis Jr P 5/1/1983 Bp Charles F Hall. m 12/28/1961 Judith Drayton Mayers c 3. R Ch Of The H Cross Dunn Loring VA 1983-1999; Asst S Dunst's McLean VA 1983-1985; Asst Ch Of The Resurr Alexandria VA 1982-1983. Auth, "The Whole Biblic Narrative: A Holistic Reading," Wordclay Pub, 2011; Auth, "Questings: A Parable," iUniverse Pub, 2009; Auth, "Nonetheless, God Retrieves Us," iUniverse Pub, 2006; Auth, "CrossRoads: Musings on a Fr-Son Pilgrimage," Trafford Pub, 2003; Auth, "Life of Love, Love of Life," Trafford Pub, 2002. jonathanbryan@cox.net

BRYAN, Nancy Ann (Cal) 2111 Hyde St # 404, San Francisco CA 94109 **D The Epis Ch Of S Mary The Vrgn San Francisco CA 2009-; D Ch Of The Incarn San Francisco CA 2005-** B St Paul MN 4/8/1938 d Burt Charles Henry & Harriet Rebecca. U CA 1960; BA Sch for Deacons 2005. D 12/3/2005 Bp William Edwin Swing. m 7/8/1961 Richard Bryan c 3. nhbsf@hotmail.com

BRYAN, Peggy Lynn (ECR) 532 Center St, Santa Cruz CA 95060 **Stndg Com Mem Dio El Camino Real Monterey CA 2011-; Outreach Assoc S Andr's Ch Saratoga CA 2010-** B Santa Cruz CA 6/26/1951 d Raymond Arthur Bryan & Edith Jane. BA USC 1973; MS USC 1975; MDiv CDSP 2007. D 12/5/2009 P 6/25/2010 Bp Mary Gray-Reeves. c 2. peg06262@yahoo.com

BRYAN, Walter Lee (WNC) PO Box 1356, Columbus NC 28722 **Ch Of The Gd Shpd Tryon NC 2004-** B Rutherfordton NC 10/5/1939 s James Fisher Bryan & Eula M. No Carolina Agricultural & Tech St U 1960; U NC 1972; Epis TS In Kentucky 1976; Loyola Coll 1988. Trans 1/12/2004 Bp William Dailey Persell. m 3/8/1961 Carolyn Bryan c 2. Gr Ch Pontiac IL 1991-2002; Ch Of S Thos Chicago IL 1986-1990; Lawr Hall Sch Chicago IL 1986; Dio Chicago Chicago IL 1985; R Mssh-S Barth Epis Ch Chicago IL 1982-1984; R S Lk's Ch New Orleans LA 1981-1982; R S Phil's Ch Buffalo NY 1979-1981; Asst S Andr's Ch Lexington KY 1976-1979. wlbryan@alltel.net

BRYANT, Bronson Howell (Miss) 5408 Vinings Lake View, SW, Mableton GA 30126 B Ocala FL 12/4/1931 s Bronson Worthington Bryant & Martha Esther. BA U Of Florida 1953; STB Harvard DS 1958. D 12/7/1958 P 6/24/1959 Bp Edward Hamilton West. m 9/8/1956 Mildred Elizabeth Hall. R Trin Ch Epis Pass Chr MS 1985-1996; P-in-c Epis Ch Of The Epiph Leeds AL 1981-1985; Chapl S Martins-In-The-Pines Ret Comm Birmingham AL 1978-1985; Asst The Cathd Ch Of The Adv Birmingham AL 1973-1979; R Gr Ch Sheffield AL 1965-1973; Asst S Paul's By-The-Sea Epis Ch Jacksonville Bch FL 1961-1965; P-in-c S Mary's Epis Ch Green Cove Sprg FL 1959-1961; Asst Chr Ch Par Pensacola FL 1958-1959. bronson@bellsouth.net

BRYANT, Julie (Los) The Parish of Saint Matthew, 1031 Bienveneda Avenue, Pacific Palisades CA 90272 **Ch Of The Trsfg Arcadia CA 2009-; The Par Of S Matt Pacific Palisades CA 2009-** B Houston TX 3/15/1960 d Douglas Herbert Bryant & Mary Pauline. BA U CA 1982; MDiv STC 1996. D 6/8/1996 P 12/8/1996 Bp Gethin Benwil Hughes. c 2. Area Dir of Epis Cmnty Serv Dio San Diego San Diego CA 1997-1999; Epis Cmnty Serv San Diego CA 1997-1999; All SS Epis Ch Riverside CA 1997. jdbtransfiguration@gmail.com

BRYANT, Katherine Seavey (Va) 14 Cornwall St NW, Leesburg VA 20176 **Asst S Jas' Epis Ch Leesburg VA 2006-** B Washington DC 7/27/1951 d Hollis Mackay Seavey & Anne Munger. BA JHU 1973; MA NYU 1976; Dipl Ang Stud Ya Berk 2006; MDiv Ya 2006. D 3/11/2006 P 9/23/2006 Bp Mark Sean Sisk. Soc of St. Marg 2007. kate@stjamesleesburg.org

BRYANT, Laura Annette (At) 2456 Tanglewood Rd, Decatur GA 30033 **Assoc R S Bede's Ch Atlanta GA 1996-** B Boston MA 6/1/1958 d Dudley Stimpson Bryant & Judith Ann. BA Duke 1980; MDiv Candler TS Emory U 1987. D 11/5/1989 P 5/1/1990 Bp Frank Kellogg Allan. m 7/30/1983 John Thomas Hutton c 1. Asst P Ch Of The Epiph Atlanta GA 1989-1996.

BRYANT JR, Napoleon (SO) 3527 Skyview Ln, Cincinnati OH 45213 B Cincinnati OH 2/22/1929 s Napoleon Bryant & Katie. BS U Cinc 1959; MA Indiana U 1968; EdD Indiana U 1970. D 2/24/1985 Bp William Grant Black. m 7/15/1950 Ernestine C Bryant c 4. "Afr Amer Men: Soon Gone!," *Journ of Afr Amer Men*, Vol. 4, Issue 4, Sprg, 2000; "Sci Any Time," Harcourt Brace, 1996. NAAD 1985; UBE 1983. Hon Fell of STAN Sci Teachers Assn of Nigeria 2001; Distinguished Serv to Sci Educ Natl Sci Teachers Assn 1992; Hon Life Mem Assn of Sci Teachers of Jamaica 1981. ernanap@aol.com

BRYANT, Peter F (Roch) 4160 Back River Rd, Scio NY 14880 **Vol S Andr's Ch Friendship NY 2004-** B Gowanda NY 10/5/1952 D 12/8/2001 P 10/26/2002 Bp Jack Marston McKelvey. m 3/19/1977 Nancy Bryant c 2.

BRYANT, Richard Gordon (Md) 678 Dave Ct, Covington KY 41015 B Covington KY 5/17/1946 s Gordon Thomas Bryant & Mildred Elizabeth. MDiv Epis TS In Kentucky; BA U Of Kentucky. D 6/22/1972 P 12/23/1972 Bp Addison Hosea. Ch Of The Adv Baltimore MD 1989-2000; R S Lk's Ch Baltimore MD

1978-1983; Asst S Geo's Epis Ch Schenectady NY 1974-1978; Cur Calv Epis Ch Ashland KY 1972-1974. CBS; SocMary.

BRYANT, Robert Harrison (Ore) 6300 Sw Nicol Rd, Portland OR 97223 **Cn Theol Dio Oregon Portland OR 2011-; R Epis Par Of S Jn The Bapt Portland OR 2002-** B Richmond VA 1/2/1957 s Francis Epes Bryant & Catherine. BA Coll of Wm & Mary 1979; MDiv Nash 1988. D 6/4/1988 P 6/3/1989 Bp William Edwin Swing. R Ch Of Our Sav Mill Vlly CA 1990-2002; Asst Ch Of S Jn The Bapt Aptos CA 1988-1990. bryantr@oes.edu

BRYANT, Todd Alan (Tex) 5826 Doliver Dr, Houston TX 77057 **Ch Of The Ascen Houston TX 2011-** B Tulsa OK 12/26/1970 s Harlin Bryant & Rosemary. BS Oklahoma U Norman OK 1994; MDiv Epis TS of the SW 2006. D 6/26/2006 Bp Don Adger Wimberly P 1/12/2007 Bp Dena Arnall Harrison. m 4/28/2002 Kimberly Bryant c 3. Palmer Memi Ch Houston TX 2008-2011; Assoc R S Chris's Ch League City TX 2006-2008. todd.alan.bryant@gmail.com

BRYANT, William Reid (WLa) 715 Lewisville Rd, Minden LA 71055 B Minneapolis MN 3/11/1938 s Frank Leytze Bryant & Virginia. BA LSU 1964; MBA U Of Dallas 1975; STL Angl TS 1988. D 6/18/1988 P 6/7/1989 Bp Donis Dean Patterson. m 9/17/1966 Judith Bayliss c 2. Pres of Stndg Com Dio Wstrn Louisiana Alexandria LA 2008-2009; GC First Alt Dio Wstrn Louisiana Alexandria LA 2006-2009; P-in-c S Jas Epis Ch Shreveport LA 2005-2010; GC Dep Dio Wstrn Louisiana Alexandria LA 2003-2006; S Alb's Epis Ch Monroe LA 2003-2004; P-in-c The Epis Ch Of The Gd Shpd Vidalia LA 2003; Cn Dio Wstrn Louisiana Alexandria LA 2002-2003; Dio Wstrn Louisiana Alexandria LA 2001-2003; S Jn's Epis Ch Minden LA 1995-2001; COM Dio Wstrn Louisiana Alexandria LA 1995-1999; Asst The Epis Ch Of The Trsfg Dallas TX 1988-1995. rectory@shreve.net

BRYCE, Christopher David Francis (USC) 54 Highway 20, Abbeville SC 29620 B Adrian MI 7/25/1948 s David George Bryce & Elsie Alberta. BA Saginaw Vlly St U 1972; MDiv Epis TS In Kentucky 1976. D 3/19/1976 P 12/1/1976 Bp Addison Hosea. m 5/12/2000 Susan David Francis Walker. Trin Ch Abbeville SC 1998-2001; S Ptr's Ch Plant City FL 1990-1994; Int S Dav's Epis Ch Englewood FL 1990; Int S Nath Ch No Port FL 1989-1990; Dio SW Florida Sarasota FL 1982; S Jn's Epis Ch St Jas City FL 1980-1989; Assoc S Jn's Epis Ch Clearwater FL 1980-1982; S Steph's Epis Ch Covington KY 1978-1979; Vic S Alb's Ch Morehead KY 1976-1978. Outstanding Young Men Amer Awd 1985. cdfbryce@gmail.com

BUB, Sally Letchworth (Wyo) 30 Diversion Dam Rd, Kinnear WY 82516 **Dio Wyoming Casper WY 2010-; Ch Of The H Nativ Kinnear WY 2002-; R S Helen's Epis Ch Laramie WY 2000-** B Princeton NJ 5/11/1942 d James Whedbee Mullen & Elizabeth Scudder. BA Smith 1964; MDiv GTS 1993. D 8/24/1993 P 2/25/1994 Bp Bob Gordon Jones. m 6/19/1993 Richard Joseph Bub c 2. St Jn Luth Ch Riverton WY 2002-2005; S Thos Ch Dubois WY 1997-2000; Vic St Jn the Bapt Epis Ch Big Piney WY 1993-1996. Educ for Minitstry 1998-2007. sbub@wyoming.com

BUCCO, Dennis M (RI) 58 Arrowhead Ln, West Greenwich RI 02817 **R S Lk's Ch Pawtucket RI 2009-** B Warwick RI 12/25/1967 s Harry Bucco & Genevieve. Bos; BS Johnson & Wales U 1991; MDiv GTS 2007. D 6/13/2007 P 2/2/2008 Bp Geralyn Wolf. m 3/17/1996 Madeline M McHenry c 2. S Lk's Epis Ch E Greenwich RI 2007-2009. frdennis@cox.net

BUCHAN III, Thomas Nicholson (CFla) 2385 Rice Creek Ct, Oviedo FL 32765 B Rahway NJ 3/24/1972 d Thomas Nicholson Buchan & Marilyn Louise. Wheaton Coll; MPhil Drew U 1999; PhD Drew U 2003. D 5/30/2009 P 12/1/2009 Bp John Wadsworth Howe. m 12/18/1993 Margaret Michelle Skaff c 4. thomas.buchan@asburyseminary.org

BUCHANAN, Andrew (SVa) 3928 Pacific Ave, Virginia Beach VA 23451 **R Galilee Epis Ch Virginia Bch VA 2009-** B Bishop CA 1/9/1970 s James Douglas Buchanan & Claudia Anne. BA U So 1992; MDiv TESM 1997; STM Yale DS 2003. D 6/14/1997 P 12/15/1997 Bp John-David Mercer Schofield. m 6/28/1997 Dana Buchanan c 4. R S Paul's Ch Brookfield CT 2003-2009; Asst Trin Ch Tariffville CT 1997-2003. andrewbuchanan@aya.yale.edu

BUCHANAN, Furman Lee (USC) 910 Hudson Road, Greenville SC 29615 **S Ptr's Epis Ch Greenville SC 2010-** B Barnwell SC 7/30/1966 s Furman Buchanan & Rosanne F. BA Wofford Coll 1989; MDiv STUSo 2006. D 6/24/2006 P 1/20/2007 Bp Dorsey Felix Henderson. m 7/28/1990 Kim D Davis c 3. Asst S Martins-In-The-Field Columbia SC 2006-2010. buchananf@charter.net

BUCHANAN, Hollis Herbert (SC) 122 E Magnolia Ave, Howey In The Hills FL 34737 **Cn Cathd Of S Lk And S Paul Charleston SC 1993-** B Tampa FL 9/16/1927 s Herbert Charles Buchanan & Lena Anne. BA U of Florida 1950; MDiv SWTS 1953. D 6/21/1953 Bp Martin J Bram P 1/25/1954 Bp Henry I Louttit. c 3. S Jas Epis Ch Leesburg FL 1992-1993; Vic S Mths Epis Ch Summerton SC 1984-1992; Asst All SS Ch Florence SC 1979-1984; Asst Trin Ch Vero Bch FL 1978-1979; R S Richard's Ch Winter Pk FL 1960-1978; Trin Cathd Miami FL 1953-1957. Hon Cn S Lk & S Paul Cathd, Charleston, SC Charleston SC 1993. hhbcanon@embarqmail.com

BUCHANAN, H Ray (CGC) 2201 Pine Needle Dr E, Mobile AL 36609 **R The Ch Of The Redeem MOBILE AL 2006-** B Waverly TN 12/16/1955 s Herman Davis Buchanan & Hilda Louise. AA Mart Methodist Coll 1976; BS Tennessee Tech U 1978; MDiv Duke DS 1981; MA Vermont Coll Of Norwich U 1994. D 11/4/1984 Bp William Evan Sanders P 10/6/1985 Bp Edward Witker Jones. m 4/1/2005 Nancy Jacobson c 1. P in Charge/Vic S Lk's Ch SPRINGFIELD TN 1996-2006; Assoc Trin Ch Clarksville TN 1986-1996. buchananr55@gmail.com

✠ **BUCHANAN, Rt Rev John Clark** (WMo) 1171 Parkway Dr, Mount Pleasant SC 29464 **Provsnl Bp Dio Quincy Peoria IL 2009-** B Laurens County SC 5/6/1933 s Dock Jones Buchanan & Ella Virginia. BA U of So Carolina 1958; JD U of So Carolina 1960; MDiv GTS 1969; DMin McCormick TS 1975; DD GTS 1989. D 6/25/1969 P 1/24/1970 Bp Gray Temple Con 2/25/1989 for WMo. m 11/28/1964 Peggy Annelle Brown c 2. Int Bp Dio Sthrn Virginia Norfolk VA 2006-2008; Asstg Bp Dio Texas Houston TX 2004-2006; Bp-in-Res S Mich's Epis Ch Charleston SC 2000-2004; Bp, W Missouri Dio W Missouri Kansas City MO 1989-1999; R S Andr's Ch Mt Pleasant SC 1975-1989; R S Matt's Epis Ch Darlington SC 1971-1975; Vic S Barn Ch Dillon SC 1969-1971. DD GTS New York NY 1989. bpjcb@bellsouth.net

BUCHANAN, Margaret Grace (WNC) 827 Montreat Rd, Black Mountain NC 28711 **D Trin Epis Ch Asheville NC 2002-** B Rochester NY 9/8/1947 d Charles William Durrant & Ruth Elizabeth. Asheville-Buncombe Tech Cmnty Coll 1979. D 12/9/1995 Bp Robert Hodges Johnson. m 11/29/1985 John Haywood Buchanan c 3. D S Jas Ch Black Mtn NC 2000-2002.

BUCHANAN, Susan Jill (NH) PO Box 1135, Glen NH 03838 **Convoc Cnvnr Dio New Hampshire Concord NH 2011-; GC Dep Dio New Hampshire Concord NH 2004-; R Chr Ch No Conway NH 2002-; P-in-c Ch of theTransfiguration N Conway NH 2002-** B Orlando FL 10/14/1957 d Harry Richard Buchanan & Charlotte Mae. BA Wheaton Coll 1985; MDiv VTS 1994. D 11/8/1994 Bp Frank Clayton Matthews P 5/14/1995 Bp Peter James Lee. m 10/16/2004 Richard A Smith c 2. Dioc Coun Dio New Hampshire Concord NH 2006-2009; Re-imagining Com Dio New Hampshire Concord NH 2003-2004; COM Dio New Hampshire Concord NH 2002-2009; UTO Grant Com Dio Virginia Richmond VA 1996-2002; Mid-Atlantic Par Trng Prog Bd Dir Dio Virginia Richmond VA 1996-2000; Assoc R Chr Epis Ch Winchester VA 1994-2002. Polly Bond Awd of Excellence for Theol Reflection ECom 2007. sjbuchanan@gmail.com

BUCHHOLZ, Paige Randolph (ETenn) 1211 Oakdale Trl, Knoxville TN 37914 B Alexandria VA 3/27/1948 d Donald Murray Buchholz & Margaret Isabel. BA U NC 1969; MDiv VTS 1988. D 6/11/1988 P 3/1/1989 Bp John Thomas Walker. Dio E Tennessee Knoxville TN 2007-2008; Assoc S Eliz's Epis Ch Knoxville TN 2001-2007; Vic S Lk's Ch Knoxville TN 1991-2008; Cleric S Steph's Epis Ch Charleston SC 1989-1991; Dio E Tennessee Knoxville TN 1988-2000. paigebuchholz@yahoo.com

BUCK, David E (NC) 616 Watson St., Davidson NC 28036 **R S Alb's Ch Davidson NC 2007-** B Birmingham AL 5/22/1949 s David Edgar Buck & Doris P. ABS Davidson Coll 1971; MDiv New Orleans Bapt TS 1977; ThM PrTS 1984; DMin Candler TS Emory U 1996; GTS 2003. D 2/16/2004 P 10/24/2004 Bp Michael Bruce Curry. m 11/24/2009 Andrea Baker c 5. Assoc Ch Of The Nativ Raleigh NC 2004-2007. davidbuck49@earthlink.net

BUCK, Elizabeth (EC) 744 Lakeside Dr Se, Bolivia NC 28422 B Columbia SC 7/17/1927 d Eugene H Salmon & Elizabeth. BA U of So Carolina 1946; MA Appalachian St U 1969. D 5/2/1990 Bp Brice Sidney Sanders. m 11/9/1945 Robertson Williams Buck c 4. D S Jas The Fisherman Epis Ch Shallotte NC 1990-2000. Dok.

BUCK, Leonard Frank (HB) No address on file. B Scranton PA 8/12/1940 s Leonard Frank Butkiewicz & Janet Frances. BA Penn 1962; MA Penn 1963; STB PDS 1967. D 6/17/1967 Bp Frederick J Warnecke P 5/31/1968 Bp Donald J Campbell. m 12/28/1966 Margaret Guyer Porter Moore.

BUCK, Martha (ECR) 651 Sinex Ave Apt L115, Pacific Grove CA 93950 **D S Jas' Ch Monterey CA 2001-** B Orange NJ 3/27/1935 d Carl Buck & Adelaide. BS Skidmore Coll 1956; BA Sch for Deacons 1997. D 12/6/1997 Bp William Edwin Swing. D S Mk's Par Berkeley CA 1997-2001. Contrib, "Initial Resrch on Pay Equity," *Bargaining for Pay Equity*, Natl Com on Pay Equity, 1990. mbccg@aol.com

BUCK, Robert Allen (Colo) 3070 Indiana St, Golden CO 80401 B Pasadena CA 7/18/1932 s Robert Russell Buck & Faith Edna. BS U CA 1957; MDiv CDSP 1968. D 7/1/1968 P 2/12/1969 Bp C J Kinsolving III. m 8/20/1955 Mary Ogden Stuart c 3. Pres Of Epis Fndt Dio Colorado Denver CO 1983-1985; R S Paul's Epis Ch Lakewood CO 1981-1997; Vic/R Epis Ch Of The Gd Shpd San Angelo TX 1972-1981; Vic S Mary's Ch Lovington NM 1968-1972. m-r-buck1955@msn.com

BUCK-GLENN, Judith (Pa) 1031 N Lawrence St, Philadelphia PA 19123 **Assoc Chr Ch Epis Ridley Pk PA 2002-** B London ON CA 8/28/1947 d Conrad Charles Leroy Buck & Joan. Penn; U of Wisconsin; BA U of Massachusetts 1973; MDiv Estrn Bapt TS 1991; MA Tem 1995. D 6/19/1999 P 5/20/2000 Bp Charles Ellsworth Bennison Jr. m 10/14/1989 Gary Scott Glenn. Dio Pennsylvania Philadelphia PA 1999-2001; Cur S Anne's Ch Abington PA 1999-2001. Auth, "Homilies," *Homily Serv*, 1996; Auth, "The Legend Of The

B

Donkey'S Cross"; Auth, "One Room Sunday Sch". Hist Soc Of Pennsylvania. buckglenn@earthlink.net

BUCKINGHAM, Carole Sylmay (Wyo) PO Box 12, Kaycee WY 82639 B 8/28/1957 d Roy House & Pauline M. D 8/22/2008 P 3/7/2009 Bp Bruce Edward Caldwell. m 10/13/1979 Ord Allen Buckingham c 6. onediamondbar@rtconnect.net

BUCKINGHAM, Karen Burnquist (Wyo) 608 6th St, Rawlins WY 82301 **P Ch Of S Thos Rawlins WY 2010-** B Taft CA 3/26/1937 d Charles Robert Burnquist & Virginia Beryl. AA Pasadena City Coll 1959. D 5/21/2009 P 1/30/2010 Bp Bruce Edward Caldwell. m 12/27/1964 Harold Buckingham c 3. hbuckingham@bresnan.net

BUCKLEY, Herbert Wilkinson (U) 1964 Colorado Gulch Dr, Helena MT 59601 B Brooklyn NY 3/31/1927 s Herbert W Buckley & Phoebe G. BS Newark St Teachers Coll NJ 1950. D 12/21/1971 P 7/1/1975 Bp Jackson Earle Gilliam. m 7/27/1952 Charlee H Buckley. Dio Utah Salt Lake City UT 1992; Vic S Mich's Ch Brigham City UT 1989-1992; Supply P Dio Montana Helena MT 1985-1989; Int Ch Of The Incarn Great Falls MT 1985; P-in-c S Jn's Ch/Elkhorn Cluster Townsend MT 1982-1984; Supply P Dio Montana Helena MT 1981-1982; Vic S Jn's Ch Williams AZ 1979-1980; Mssy All SS Epis Ch Whitefish MT 1976-1978; Flathead Epis Fllshp Kalispell MT 1976-1978; Mssy S Matt's Ch Columbia Falls MT 1976-1978; Assoc S Ptr's Par Helena MT 1971-1976.

BUCKWALTER, Georgine (Ky) 2511 Cottonwood Dr, Louisville KY 40242 **S Lk's Chap Louisville KY 1998-** B Pt Pleasant NJ 3/14/1947 d Leonard George Lomell & Charlotte. U So; BA Westminster Choir Coll of Rider U 1969; MDiv Sthrn Bapt TS Louisville KY 1990. D 5/8/1989 Bp David Reed P 1/1/1995 Bp Edwin Funsten Gulick Jr. c 2. H Trin Ch Brandenburg KY 1996-1998; Presb Hm & Serv Of Ky Inc Louisville KY 1993-1998. Auth, "Handbook Of Themes For Preaching"; Auth, "Weavings: Sprtlty".

BUCKWALTER, Paul William (Az) 927 N 10th Ave, Tucson AZ 85705 B Orange NJ 10/9/1934 s Paul Bernard Buckwalter & Julia Katherine. BA Ya 1956; MA Ya 1960; MDiv EDS 1963; MCP U Cinc 1972. D 6/22/1963 Bp Robert McConnell Hatch P 12/18/1963 Bp Roger W Blanchard. m 5/7/1994 Casey Cason c 4. Exec Assoc S Phil's In The Hills Tucson AZ 1984-1996. "Bldg Power: Finding and Developing Leaders in Arizona Congregations," *Soc Plcy Sprg v.33 #3*, 2003; Auth, "Drums Along the Penobscot," *Cincinatti Horizons*, 1981. Oblate Ord of S Ben 1990. buckokc@earthlink.net

BUDD, Dorothy Reid (Dal) 3707 Crescent Ave, Dallas TX 75205 **D Ch Of The Incarn Dallas TX 2006-** B Charlottesville VA 3/9/1954 d Rust Reid & Jeanne. BA Colorado Coll 1980; JD Ut Law Sch 1983; MDiv Perkins TS 2006. D 12/2/2006 Bp James Monte Stanton. m 5/3/1985 Russell Budd c 2. dbudd@airmail.net

BUDD, Richard Wade (SVa) 120 Cypress Crk, Williamsburg VA 23188 B Henderson MD 8/24/1934 s Bryan William Budd & Dorothea Marie. BA Bowling Green St U 1956; MA U of Iowa 1962; PhD U of Iowa 1964. D 4/13/1985 Bp George Phelps Mellick Belshaw. m 8/28/1955 Claudia Lynn Wolff c 3. R Chr The King Epis Ch Tabb VA 2006-2009; R Ch Of The Gd Shpd Richmond VA 2002-2006; D Hickory Neck Ch Toano VA 1998-2000; D H Trin Ch So River NJ 1993-1996. Auth/Ed, "Approaches To Human Cmncatn"; Auth/Ed, "Beyond Media"; Auth, "Content Analysis". Who'S Who In Amer. rwbudd@msn.com

BUDDE, Mariann Edgar (Minn) 4612 Colfax Ave S, Minneapolis MN 55419 **Dio Washington Washington DC 2011-; S Jn The Bapt Epis Ch Minneapolis MN 1993-** B Summit NJ 12/10/1959 d William Budde & Ann. MA U Roch 1982; MDiv VTS 1988. D 5/28/1988 Bp John Shelby Spong P 3/4/1989 Bp James Russell Moodey. m 5/24/1986 Paul Edward Budde. Trin Ch Toledo OH 1988-1993. mariannbudde@gmail.com

BUDHU, Esar (Nwk) 206 Renshaw Ave, East Orange NJ 07017 **S Agnes And S Paul's Ch E Orange NJ 1987-** B Georgetown GY 10/2/1947 s Raikmoon Budhu & Ishmatie. Lic Codrington Coll 1975; BA Codrington Coll 1981. Trans from Church in the Province Of The West Indies 3/15/1987 Bp John Shelby Spong. m 6/26/1976 Jessica Forde c 2. esar6786716@aol.com

BUDNEY, Karen Vickers (CNY) 18 Cross St., Dover MA 02030 **Pstr Assoc S Andr's Ch Wellesley MA 2007-** B Philadelphia PA 7/26/1946 d Raymond Vickers & Helen Keys. BS W Chester St Coll 1968; MDiv Harvard DS 1991. D 6/1/1991 Bp David Elliot Johnson P 5/9/1992 Bp Barbara Clementine Harris. m 6/15/1968 Albert Joseph Budney c 2. S Dav's Ch De Witt NY 2002; Cn Pstr S Paul's Cathd Syracuse NY 1999-2002; Asst S Paul's Cathd Syracuse NY 1997-1998; Asst S Paul's Ch Kansas City MO 1994-1995; Chapl for Epis Day Sch S Paul's Epis Day Sch Kansas City MO 1994-1995; Int R Chr Ch Warrensburg MO 1993-1994; Cathd Chapt Dio Massachusetts Boston MA 1992-1993; Int Assoc R The Ch Of Our Redeem Lexington MA 1992-1993; D S Jn's Ch Newtonville MA 1991-1992. Harvard DS Alum/Ae Coun 2000-2006; Harvard DS Dn's Coun 2006; Newton Wellesley Hosp Prot Chapl Coun 2009; Samar Cntr Bd Dir 1998-2006. revkar7@comcast.net

BUECHELE, Thomas J (Haw) PO Box 220, Kapaau HI 96755 B Davenport IA 10/5/1942 s Carl W Buechele & Dorothy K. BA St Ambr U Davenport IA 1964; M.Th. Mt S Bern Sem Dubuque IA 1968. Rec from Roman Catholic 9/25/2002 as Priest Bp Robert Reed Shahan. m 1/23/1993 Jean Buechele. Vic S Aug's Epis Chap Kapaau HI 2005-2010; Dio Arizona Phoenix AZ 2004-2005; S Jn's Epis Ch Bisbee AZ 2002-2003. tombuechele@mac.com

BUECHNER, Deborah Ann (CFla) 1078 Coastal Cir, Ocoee FL 34761 **Epis Ch Of The Ascen Orlando FL 2005-** B Clemons MI 11/27/1951 d John Martens & Betty. AA Valencia Cmnty Coll 2000. D 12/10/2005 Bp John Wadsworth Howe. m 7/27/1991 William Buechner c 2. wbuechner@cfl.rr.com

BUECHNER, Frederick Alvin (Ga) PO Box 2626, Thomasville GA 31799 **R All SS Epis Ch Thomasville GA 1988-** B Saint Louis MO 3/9/1952 s Alvin Wendell Buechner & Elinor Elisabeth. BA U of Virginia 1974; MDiv VTS 1980. D 4/28/1980 P 1/27/1981 Bp (George) Paul Reeves. m 12/27/1975 Kathy Louise Buechner. R Chr Epis Ch Dublin GA 1986-1988; Dn Of Dublin Convoc Dio Georgia Savannah GA 1985-1986; Assoc S Jn's Ch Savannah GA 1981-1986; Asst Chr Ch Frederica St Simons Island GA 1980-1981. fabuechner@aol.com

BUEHLER, Lynnsay Anne (At) 147 Shadowmoor Dr, Decatur GA 30030 **Dir, The Julian of Norwich Ctr. S Bede's Ch Atlanta GA 1998-** B Abington PA 5/24/1956 d Martin Howard Buehler & Patricia Anne. BA Duke 1978; MDiv cl Candler TS Emory U 1982. D 6/10/1989 P 5/25/1990 Bp Frank Kellogg Allan. m 7/28/1981 Robert Burwell Townes c 1. Pstr Counslr/Sprtl Dir S Barth's Epis Ch Atlanta GA 1994-1998; Sprtl Formation Com Dio Atlanta Atlanta GA 1991-1998; Assoc R Ch Of The Atone Sandy Sprg GA 1989-1993. AAPC 1992; EFM Mentor 1988; Green Bough Hse Of Pryr Assoc 1998; Sprtl Dir Intl 1991. MDiv cl Candler TS, Emory U 1982. buehlertownes@aol.com

BUEHRENS, Gwen (Mass) 57 Dedham Ave., Apt #201, Needham MA 02492 **Assoc S Mary's Ch Newton Lower Falls MA 2005-** B Chicago IL 9/6/1943 d Malcolm Paradis Langdoc & Mignonne. BA U CA 1968; MA Ya 1972. D 6/24/1972 Bp C Kilmer Myers P 11/30/1985 Bp Donis Dean Patterson. m 6/21/1972 John Buehrens. S Andr's Ch Wellesley MA 1994-2003; Assoc S Andr's Ch Wellesley MA 1993-2003; Assoc S Paul's Ch Dedham MA 1993-1994; Assoc Chr And S Steph's Ch New York NY 1989-1993; Epis Ch Cntr New York NY 1989-1991; Asst Ch Of The H Trin New York NY 1987-1989; The Epis Ch Of The Trsfg Dallas TX 1985-1986; Asst Ch Of The Epiph Richardson TX 1981-1983; Asst S Mich And All Ang Knoxville TN 1979-1981. gbuehrens@comcast.net

BUELL, Susan Davies (NwPa) 75 Perry St. 2A, New York City NY 10014 B Upper Darby PA 7/6/1939 d Frank James Davies & Mary Georgiana Jane. BA Ladycliff Coll 1968; MLS U of Texas 1974; MDiv Epis TS of The SW 1978; Cert Institut Catholique De Paris 1991; Cert Natl Archv 2003. D 9/23/1977 P 5/1/1978 Bp Richard Mitchell Trelease Jr. m 6/21/1959 William Collins Buell c 3. Chr Epis Ch Meadville PA 1992-2004; All SS Ch Pasadena CA 1987-1990; Asst to R S Fran Ch Houston TX 1982-1987; Chapl To Epis Sch Pro Cathd Epis Ch Of S Clem El Paso TX 1980-1981; Dio The Rio Grande Albuquerque NM 1977-1982. Auth, "Our Lady Of Guadalupe: A Feminine Mythology In The New Wrld," Susan Davies Buell, 1984. Doc. Honoris Causa ETSSW 1994. sjdb72@gmail.com

BUELOW, Peggy Butterbaugh (SVa) 23397 Owen Farm Road, Carrollton VA 23314 **R S Mk's Ch Hampton VA 1992-** B Pensacola FL 11/2/1947 d John Otto Butterbaugh & Georgia Christine. BS U of W Florida 1969; MA U of W Florida 1979; MDiv VTS 1986. D 5/24/1986 P 4/1/1987 Bp C(laude) Charles Vache. m 6/1/1980 John Peter Buelow c 3. Chapl Off Of Bsh For ArmdF New York NY 1989-1992; Asst R All SS' Epis Ch Virginia Bch VA 1986-1989. sun.dance@verizon.net

BUENO BUENO, Francisco Javier (Colom) No address on file. B 9/27/1968 s Bernardino Bueno & Ana Sofia. D 5/15/1994 Bp Bernardo Merino-Botero. Iglesia Epis En Colombia 1995-1999.

BUENTING, Julie Ann (Chi) 3857 N Kostner Ave, Chicago IL 60641 B Brockport NY 7/12/1960 d John Warren Buenting & Mary Ann Borst. BSN SUNY Brockport 1981; MS SUNY Buffalo 1986; DNS SUNY Buffalo 1990; MA St. Bern's Inst Rochester NY 1997; MDiv SWTS 2009. D 6/6/2009 P 12/5/2009 Bp Jeffrey Dean Lee. jbuenting@hotmail.com

BUENZ JR, John Frederick (ECR) 22115 Dean Ct, Cupertino CA 95014 **Assoc Chr Epis Ch Los Altos CA 1997-** B San Antonio TX 7/27/1932 s John F Buenz & Harriett Elaine. BS U of Texas 1955; MDiv CDSP 1965. D 6/20/1965 Bp James Albert Pike P 12/28/1965 Bp George Richard Millard. m 11/27/1975 Marilyn A Mueller. Int The Epis Ch In Almaden San Jose CA 2004-2005; Int Ch of S Mary's by the Sea Pacific Grove CA 1999-2000; Vstng Chapl CDSP Berkeley CA 1996-1997; Chair of Futures Com Dio Spokane Spokane WA 1993-1996; Bp Search Com Dio Spokane Spokane WA 1989-1990; Dn Cathd Of S Jn The Evang Spokane WA 1986-1996; Chair of Strng Com for Formation Dio El Camino Real Monterey CA 1979; Stndg Com Dio California San Francisco CA 1974-1979; R Ch Of S Jude The Apos Cupertino CA 1973-1986; Asst S Mk's Epis Ch Santa Clara CA 1965-1967. DD CDSP 1996. jbuenz0835@att.net

BUERKEL HUNN, Michael Carter (NC) 412 N East St, Raleigh NC 27604 **Cn to the Ordnry Dio No Carolina Raleigh NC 2006-** B Palo Alto CA 10/27/

1970 s Bruce Douglas Hunn & Thera Joyce. BA Mid 1994; MA U of Cambridge 1996; Cert SWTS 1997. D 5/17/1997 P 11/22/1997 Bp Mary Adelia Rosamond McLeod. m 7/27/2009 Meg Buerkel c 2. S Alb's Ch Davidson NC 2004-2006; Ch Of The H Comf Kenilworth IL 2001-2004; Kent Sch Kent CT 1997-2001; Chapl S Jos's Chap at the Kent Sch Kent CT 1997-2000. mhunn@episdionc.org

BUFFONE, Gregory James (Tex) 4203 University Blvd, Houston TX 77005 B Steubenville OH 5/17/1948 s Harry Joseph Buffone & M'Elise. MS U of So Florida 1973; PhD U NC 1975; Iona Sch for Mnstry 2007. D 9/17/2007 Bp Don Adger Wimberly. m 5/23/1970 Janet Louise Buffone c 2. gbuffone@sjd.org

BUGLER, Derek Leslie (Me) 51 Raymond Road, Brunswick ME 04011 **Cn Cathd Ch Of S Lk Portland ME 1988-** B Dorchester UK 4/27/1925 s Arthur Thomas Bugler & Nora. GTS 1964. D 6/13/1964 Bp Oliver L Loring P 12/19/1964 Bp Joseph Warren Hutchens. m 5/26/1948 Honor Elizabeth Day c 2. R S Paul's Ch Ft Fairfield ME 1987-1990; Gr Epis Ch Bath ME 1970-1989; Vic S Paul's Ch Plainfield CT 1964-1966. FVC. Hon Cn Cathd of S Lk Portland ME 1988. derek@bugler.com

BUHRER, Richard Albert (Oly) 2021 15th Ave S Apt 1, Seattle WA 98144 **D St Ptr's Epis Par Seattle WA 2010-** B Pasco WA 5/9/1948 s Albert Buhrer & Betty. BA Gonzaga U 1970; MDiv Loyola U 1978. Rec from Roman Catholic 6/28/2002 Bp Vincent Waydell Warner. D S Paul's Ch Seattle WA 2003-2009. richard.buhrer@mac.com

BUICE, Bonnie Carl (At) 115 Maplewood Ave Sw, Milledgeville GA 31061 B East Point GA 5/20/1932 s Bonnie Carl Buice & Elizabeth Ramsey. BA Merc 1954; JD Merc 1957; MA U of Notre Dame 1975. D 6/26/1965 Bp Randolph R Claiborne P 9/1/1975 Bp Bennett Jones Sims. m 2/18/1984 Hulane Evans c 4. S Jas Ch Macon GA 1992-2004; S Steph's Ch Milledgeville GA 1990-1991; R S Fran Ch Macon GA 1979-1984; Cur H Trin Par Decatur GA 1975-1979; D, Asst Gr Epis Ch Gainesville GA 1965-1974. caelbuice@windstream.net

BUICE, Samuel Walton (Ga) 3 Westridge Rd, Savannah GA 31411 **S Ptr's Epis Ch Savannah GA 2002-** B Atlanta GA 6/2/1959 s Bonnie Carl Buice & Elizabeth Patterson. BA La Cen Coll 1982; MDiv VTS 1991. D 6/8/1991 P 1/26/1992 Bp Frank Kellogg Allan. m 5/24/1982 Margaret Ann Bennett c 4. R S Mths Epis Ch Toccoa GA 1994-2001; Vic Epis Ch Of The H Fam Jasper GA 1991-1994; Vic S Tim's Epis Ch Calhoun GA 1991-1994. sambuice@bellsouth.net

BUICE, William Ramsey (Hond) 10100 Hillview Dr #4A, Pensacola FL 33251 B Atlanta GA 12/23/1926 s Bonnie Carl Buice & Elizabeth Ramsey. BS U GA 1948; MS USAFIT 1962; MBA GW 1963; MDiv STUSo 1977; DMin Van 1985. D 10/27/1977 P 9/1/1978 Bp David Reed. m 2/3/1982 Lillian Ruth Stilwell c 4. Vic S Patricks Epis Ch Long Bch MS 1980-1985; Vic S Jn's Ch Morganfield KY 1977-1980. Cmnty of S Mary-Assoc 1975. Purple Heart U.S.A.F. 1968; Air Medal U.S.A.F. 1968; Distinguished Flying Cross U.S.A.F. 1968. buice@cox.net

BUIE, Delinda (Ky) 2341 Strathmoor Blvd, Louisville KY 40205 B Evansville IN 4/7/1951 d Eldee Stephens & Margaret Joy. U of Louisiana; AA Alice Lloyd Coll 1971; BA Spalding Coll 1973; U Of Edinburgh Gb 1974; MLS U Of Kentucky 1975; Louisville Presb TS 1983. D 8/6/1987 Bp David Reed. m 9/15/1973 Gregory Lea Buie c 3.

BUISSON, Pierre-Henry (Md) 4 Clos Bardon Lagrange, Cadillac 33410 France **Asst R St Martins-In-The-Field Ch Severna Pk MD 2010-** B France 4/5/1959 s Jacques Paul Buisson & Josette. BD Lycee Sv Etupery S Dizier FR 1978; SGeneral TS Poitiers Poitiers FR 1986; MDiv GTS 1990. Rec from Roman Catholic 1/31/2004 as Priest Bp Pierre W Whalon. m 6/21/1997 Sophie Rodriguez c 3. buissonph@gmail.com

BUITRAGO-VALENCIA, Roberto Anibal (Colom) Carrera 15 No. 26-19, Armenia, Quindio Colombia **Iglesia Epis En Colombia 2008-** B 8/14/1943 s Luis Benjamin H Buitrago & Teresita Valencia. Licenciatura en Teologia Pontificia Universidad 1992. D 3/24/2007 P 2/20/2010 Bp Francisco Jose Duque-Gomez. c 6. roabuival@hotmail.com

BUKER, Karen Elaine (Mil) 3380 S Jeffers Dr, New Berlin WI 53146 **D S Ptr's Ch W Allis WI 1995-** B Milwaukee WI 4/21/1947 d Kenneth Truman Larson & Isabel Elsie. (Attended) U of Wisconsin - Oshkosh. D 6/3/1995 Bp Roger John White. m 12/14/1968 Lee Arthur Buker c 2. Photographer, "Var photographs and arts," *The Cov (Nwspr)*, Dio Milwaukee. Bp's Shield Awd Bp Steven Miller-Dio Milwaukee 2010. karen4u2001@hotmail.com

BULL, Julian Patrick (Los) 5049 Gloria Ave, Encino CA 91436 **Campbell Hall Vlly Vill CA 2004-** B Albuquerque NM 11/27/1959 s Malcolm Stirling Bull & Audrey Vivien. ABS Dart 1982; MA Boston Coll 1988; MDiv VTS 2007. D 2/28/2004 P 9/29/2007 Bp Joseph Jon Bruno. m 6/26/1993 Katherine Des Jardins c 2. NAES 1995. bullj@campbellhall.org

BULL, Terry Wayne (WNY) 125 Curtis Pkwy, Buffalo NY 14223 **R Ch Of The Adv Kenmore NY 2001-** B Wichita KS 8/27/1954 s Harold Horace Bull & Kathryn Hilda. BA California St U 1984; MDiv SWTS 1996. D 6/8/1996 P 12/20/1996 Bp Gethin Benwil Hughes. m 12/31/1976 Karen Diana Overmier c 2. Epis Sr Mnstrs Dio Washington Washington DC 2000-2001; R Chr Ch Durham Par Nanjemoy MD 1996-2001. twbull@adelphia.net

BULLARD, Carol Ann (Neb) 1603 17th St, Mitchell NE 69357 **Ch Of The H Apos Mitchell NE 2004-** B 7/3/1948 D 9/12/1999 Bp Charles Jones III P 11/7/2001 Bp Charles Glenn VonRosenberg. S Tim's Ch Scottsbluff NE 2004-2006; Dio E Tennessee Knoxville TN 2001-2004; R S Matt's Ch Dayton TN 2001-2004. bullardca@gmail.com

BULLARD, Jill Staton (NC) 403 E Main St, Durham NC 27701 B Winston Salem NC 1/29/1948 d W Reid Staton & Muriel Q. D 6/14/2008 Bp Michael Bruce Curry. c 3. jillfoodshuttle.org

BULLARD, Lynn Huston (Ala) 8020 Whitesburg Dr S, Huntsville AL 35802 B Sylacauga AL 6/24/1952 d Jack Huston & Nona. BS U of Alabama 1975. D 10/30/2004 Bp Henry Nutt Parsley Jr. m 12/8/1984 William Thomas Bullard c 2. lynn.bullard@compassbank.com

BULLION, James Regis (Ga) 512 Flamingo Ln., Albany GA 31707 B Homestead PA 10/30/1940 s Francis Regis Bullion & Gertrude. BA Duquesne U 1981; MA Duquesne U 1982; DMin STUSo 2003. D 6/17/1982 P 1/21/1983 Bp (George) Paul Reeves. m 1/13/1984 Mary White Glennan. R S Patricks Ch Albany GA 1993-2008; Vic S Barn Epis Ch Valdosta GA 1989-1993; S Paul's Ch Augusta GA 1985-1988; Ch Of The H Sprt Dawson GA 1983-1985; H Trin Epis Ch Blakely GA 1983-1985; D Intern S Alb's Epis Ch Augusta GA 1982-1983. jimbullion@aol.com

BULLION, Jim (Chi) 1093 Poplar Ct, Lake Zurich IL 60047 B Detroit MI 10/10/1935 s Marvin Bullion & Helen. BA Sacr Heart Sem 1957; STB St. Jn Sem 1961; MA U of Detroit 1963. Rec from Roman Catholic 11/4/1995 Bp Frank Tracy Griswold III. m 3/22/1974 Sharon K Lagos c 2. Asst S Mich's Ch Barrington IL 1998-2006; Ch Of The H Apos Wauconda IL 1997-2005. jsgold1@att.net

BULLITT-JONAS, Margaret (Mass) 83 Bancroft Rd, Northampton MA 01060 **Assoc Gr Ch Amherst MA 2004-** B Cambridge MA 10/24/1951 d John Marshall Bullitt & Sarah Cowles. BA Stan 1974; PhD Harv 1984; MDiv EDS 1988; Cert Shalem Inst for Sprtl Formation Washington DC 1988. D 6/11/1988 Bp David Elliot Johnson P 6/17/1989 Bp Barbara Clementine Harris. m 10/25/1986 Robert A Jonas c 1. Lectr in Pstr Theol EDS Cambridge MA 1996-2005; Assoc R All SS Par Brookline MA 1996-2004; Asst R Gr Ch Newton MA 1992-1996; Assoc Emm Ch Boston MA 1991-1992; Cur Par Of Chr Ch Andover MA 1988-1991. Auth, "Made for Goodness (Bk Revs)," *Presence*, Sprtl Dir Intl , 2010; Auth, "Running to the Empty Tomb (sermon)," *Cowley*, SSJE, 2008; Auth, "The Majesty of Your Loving (Bk Revs)," *Presence*, Sprtl Dir Intl , 2008; Auth, "Conversion to Eco-Justice," *EARTH AND WORD: MEDITATIONS ON ECOLOGY, CREATION, NATURE, AND JUSTICE*, Continuum, 2007; Auth, "When Heaven Happens," *HEAVEN*, Seabury, 2007; Auth, "Missionaries to the Planet (Bk Revs)," *Sojourners*, 2007; Auth, "Marg Bullitt-Jonas (interview)," *FEEDING THE FAME*, Hazelden, 2006; Auth, "Open Your Hand: The Pract of Generosity," *Shalem News*, 2006; Auth, "The Art of Sponsorship," *Steps*, 2005; Auth, "Coming to Sense," *Epis Times*, 2003; Auth, "Chr'S PASSION, OUR PASSIONS," Cowley, 2002; Auth, "H HUNGER," Knopf; Vintage Paperback, 2000; Auth, "Faith at Our Fingertips (Sermon)," *Sermons That Wk IX*, Morehouse Pub, 2000; Auth, "From Kitchen Stool To Meditation Cushion," *Sprtlty and Hlth*, 1999; Auth, "Feeling & Pain & Pryr," *Revs for Rel*, 1995; Auth, "Doubting as Step Toward Sprtl Growth"," *Human Develpment*, 1994; Auth, "Even at the Grave We Make Song," *Revs for Rel*, 1994; Auth, "Sprtl Direction for Adult Chld of Alcoholics," *Human Dvlpmt*, 1991. EPF 1991. Distinguished Alum/ae Awd EDS 2008; Sprtlty & Justice Awd All SS Par, Brookline, MA 2004; Legacy Awd Boston Wmn Cmnctr 2003; Lehman Fell Harv Cambridge MA 1977; BA w dist Stan Stanford CA 1974. margaretbj@aol.com

BULLMAN, Anthony Horsley (O) 510 Jamie Dr, Selah WA 98942 **Died 9/12/2010** B Soham Cambridge UK 1/10/1931 s Fredrick Cecil Bullman & Susan May. DIT The Coll of Emm and St. Chad 1966. Trans from Anglican Church of Canada. c 2. ANTHONYBULLMAN@YAHOO.COM

BULLOCK, A(rlan) Richard (Ore) 22346 Se Hoffmeister Rd, Damascus OR 97089 **Assoc S Mich And All Ang Ch Portland OR 2002-** B Shenandoah IA 5/9/1937 s Arlan Fletcher Bullock & Helen Doris. BA U of Cntrl Missouri 1960; MDiv Ya Berk 1963; DMin Eden TS 1972; St. Louis U 1974; Coll of Preachers-Fell 1978. D 6/29/1963 Bp Gordon V Smith P 12/28/1963 Bp Russell T Rauscher. m 8/6/1960 Ruthanne Kruse c 3. Mem - Mutual Mnstry Revs Com ECF Inc New York NY 2001-2004; Dio Oregon Portland OR 2000-2001; Proj Dir - Election of a Bp Natl Ntwk Of Epis Cler Assn Lynnwood WA 1997-1999; Dn Of Metro-E Convoc And Cler Dio Oregon Portland OR 1988-1992; R S Lk's Epis Ch Gresham OR 1987-2000; Mssnr For Congrl Dvlpmt Dio Los Angeles Los Angeles CA 1985-1986; R S Paul's Epis Ch Tustin CA 1982-1985; Alum Coun Ya Berk New Haven CT 1982-1984; R S Fran Epis Ch San Jose CA 1975-1981; Assoc S Mich & S Geo Clayton MO 1970-1974; P-in-c Calv Epis Ch Sioux City IA 1963-1968. Auth, "Cler Renwl: The Alb Guide To Sabbatical Plnng," Alb Inst, 1999; Auth, "Proj Mgr: The Raising Up Of Epis Ldrshp," *Manual*, Off Of Pstr Dvlpmt - HOB, 1997; Auth,

"Mutual Mnstry Revs For Cler & Cong," Cornerstone Proj, 1994; Auth, "Sabbatical Plnng For Cler & Cong," The Alb Inst, 1987; Auth, "Do You Know The Way To Jan Jose: One Pstr'S Search For A Job," The Alb Inst, 1975. Assn Of Pstr Counselors 1974-1995; Natl Ntwk of Epis Cler Assn 1974. Appreciation For Serv Girl Scouts of Oregon and SW Washington Columbia River 1992. cmymtn@comcast.net

BULLOCK, Debra K (Chi) St. Mark's Episcopal Church, 1509 Ridge Avenue, Evanston IL 60201 **R S Mk's Ch Evanston IL 2011-** B Wausau WI 9/22/1969 d Robert Bullock & Brenda. BA Luther Coll 1992; MTS Bos 1994; MDiv SWTS 2006. D 6/3/2006 P 12/16/2006 Bp William Dailey Persell. m 10/15/2007 Andrea M Nowack. Vic S Barn By The Bay Villas NJ 2007-2011; Asst. to R S Mary's Epis Ch Stone Harbor NJ 2007-2011; Cur Ch Of The Trsfg Palos Pk IL 2006-2007. "Bk Revs: Mo of Pearl, by Melinda Haynes," *The BookReporter.com*, http://www.bookreporter.com/Revs/0671774670.asp, 1997. rector@stmarksevanston.org

BULLOCK, Jeffrey L (Los) 83 Eucalyptus Lane, Santa Barbara CA 93108 **R All SS-By-The-Sea Par Santa Barbara CA 2002-** B Chicago IL 10/26/1949 s Lester Bullock & Lura. BA Morningside Coll 1971; MDiv CDSP 1980; DMin CDSP 1999. D 6/28/1980 P 6/29/1981 Bp William Edwin Swing. m 11/24/2000 Nancy Lowe c 4. R S Barn On The Desert Scottsdale AZ 1998-2002; Pres of Cler Assn Dio Oregon Portland OR 1994-1995; Chr Ch Par Lake Oswego OR 1991-1998; Chair of Stndg Com Dio Wstrn Kansas Hutchinson KS 1987-1992; Gr Epis Ch Hutchinson KS 1986-1991; S Steph The Mtyr Ch Minneapolis MN 1984-1986; R Emm Epis Ch Alexandria MN 1982-1984; Assoc S Jn's Epis Ch Oakland CA 1980-1981. Auth, *CTI papers*, Cntr of Theol Inquiry; Auth, *Theol & Bk Revs*, Alb Inst and Theol Today; Auth, *Theol Today and Wrshp*, Princeton Sem and Liturg Press. Los Angeles Cler Assn; NECCA; Natl Rel Ldrshp Fndt; PACT. Pstr Theol Cntr of Theol Inquiry, Princeton Sem 2000; Doctor of Divnity Alberston Coll 1999; Lilly Ldrshp Lilly Fndt 1997. j.bullock@mac.com

BULLOCK, Kenneth R (Pa) 980 Clover Ct, Blue Bell PA 19422 B Rugby ND 12/9/1944 s Ralph Franklin Bullock & Anna Elizabeth. BM U CO 1968; BD SWTS 1970; MSW U of Wisconsin 1984. D 6/22/1970 Bp George Theodore Masuda P 12/19/1970 Bp Gerald Francis Burrill. m 2/4/1967 Norma K Rice c 2. P-in-c S Dunstans Ch Blue Bell PA 2007-2011; Int Gr Epiph Ch Philadelphia PA 2005-2007; P-in-c S Aidans Ch Cheltenham PA 2001-2005; P S Ptr's Ch No Lake WI 1990-1991; R S Alb's Ch Sussex WI 1976-1982; Vic S Barth's Ch Pewaukee WI 1976-1979; P Epis Ch Of S Jn The Bapt Breckenridge CO 1975-1976; Epis Ch Of The Trsfg Vail CO 1974-1975; P S Geo Epis Mssn Leadville CO 1974-1975; Cur The Ch Of Chr The King (Epis) Arvada CO 1973-1974; Cur S Tim's Epis Ch Centennial CO 1972-1973; Cur Gr Epis Ch Hinsdale IL 1970-1971. padreken@verizon.net

BULLOCK, Michael Anderson (USC) 1040 Brentwood Dr, Columbia SC 29206 **P-in-c Gr Epis Ch And Kindergarten Camden SC 2011-** B Schenectady NY 7/10/1950 s Raymond Powell Bullock & Gladys Madelin. BA U NC 1972; MDiv Ya Berk 1976. D 4/26/1978 Bp Joseph Warren Hutchens P 1/26/1979 Bp Morgan Porteus. m 6/16/1979 Beverly Jean Lyman c 3. Cn to the Ordnry Dio Upper So Carolina Columbia SC 2008-2011; R S Martins-In-The-Field Columbia SC 1999-2008; R Chr Ch Manlius NY 1986-1999; Assoc S Paul's Ch Dedham MA 1981-1986; Kent Sch Kent CT 1978-1981. mab1040@gmail.com

BULSON, William Lawrence (Minn) 13000 Saint Davids Rd, Minnetonka MN 55305 **Assoc The Epis Par Of S Dav Minnetonka MN 2009-** B Marion OH 1/22/1965 s Leo Lawrence Bulson & Jessie Vernell. Udostoverenie Pushkin Inst., Moscow, USSR 1986; BA U Of Kentucky 1988; MA OH SU 1990; MDiv VTS 1996. D 6/29/1996 Bp Herbert Thompson Jr. m 5/1/1993 Katherine Twyford Lewis c 1. Vic Ch Of The H Apos S Paul MN 2004-2009; Asst Geth Ch Minneapolis MN 2000-2001; Cn Cathd Ch Of S Mk Minneapolis MN 1998-1999; Vic E Cntrl Ohio Area Mnstry Cambridge OH 1996-1998. Oblate, Ord of Julian of Norwich 2009. WILLIAMLBULSON@AOL.COM

BUMILLER, William Norton (SO) 320 Lonsdale Ave, Dayton OH 45419 B Cincinnati OH 9/4/1931 s Theodore Max Bumiller & Elizabeth Isabelle. BS U Cinc 1953; MDiv CDSP 1958; U So 1960. D 6/10/1958 P 12/17/1958 Bp Henry W Hobson. m 5/31/1954 Nancy A Bumiller c 3. S Jas Ch Piqua OH 1995-1996; Int S Mk's Ch Sidney OH 1995-1996; Int Trin Ch Hamilton OH 1993-1994; Int S Chris's Ch Fairborn OH 1991-1993; S Geo's Epis Ch Dayton OH 1976-1990; Assoc S Paul's Epis Ch Dayton OH 1963-1976; R Trin Epis Ch London OH 1958-1963.

BUMP, Anne Glass (Mich) 1708 Jamestown Place, Pittsburgh PA 15235 B East Cleveland OH 10/11/1948 d Elwood Gray Glass & Flora Wood. BA Ohio Wesl 1970; MDiv Pittsburgh TS 1999. D 12/18/1999 Bp Arthur Benjamin Williams Jr P 6/26/2000 Bp J Clark Grew II. c 2. R Gr Ch Mt Clemens MI 2004-2010; R Chr Epis Ch Geneva OH 1999-2004; R S Paul Epis Ch Conneaut OH 1999-2002. bump252@comcast.net

BUNCH, Wilton H. (Ala) Po Box 292252, Birmingham AL 35229 **Assoc H Apos Ch Birmingham AL 2001-** B Walla Walla WA 1/12/1935 s Walter Hamilton Bunch & Winnifred May. BA Walla Walla Coll 1956; MD Loma Linda U 1960; PhD U MN 1967; MBA U Chi 1983; MDiv CDSP 1998. D 6/7/1997 P 12/13/1997 Bp William Jerry Winterrowd. m 11/27/1983 Victoria Mae Duonch c 3. Assoc S Alb's Epis Ch St Pete Bch FL 1998-2001; Assoc Epis Ch Of S Jn The Bapt Granby CO 1997-1998. Auth, "Ethics of Direct to Consumer Advert," *Spineline*, 2009; Auth, "On the Ethics of Reducing Pain to a Number," *Loyola Orthopaedic Journ*, 2007; Auth, "Courts should seek justice, not revenge," *The Birmingham Tribune*, 2007; Auth, "Conflict-of-Interest: The Need for Rules," *Spineline*, 2006; Auth, "Capital Punishment: A Hoax and Delusion," *Birmingham News*, 2005; Auth, "The Ethics of Indep Med Examiners," *Journ of the Amer Acad of Disabil Evaluating Physicians*, 2005; Auth, "Cloning is not Concep: But that doesn't make it Rt," *Chr Ethics Today*, 2002; Auth, "Revs: Natural and Div Law: Reclaiming the Tradition for Chr Ethics by Jean Porter," *ATR*, 2001; Auth, "Revs: Who Are We? By Jean Elstham," *ATR*, 2001; Auth, "A Theol Inclusive Of The Experience Of Disabil, Journ Of Rel," *Disabil And Hlth*, 2001; Auth, "The Ethics Of Gene Ther," *Clincl Orthapedics & Related Resrch*, 2000; Auth, "The Virtuous Orthapedist Has Fewer Malpractice Suits," *Corr*, 2000; Auth, "Moral Decisions Regarding Innovation: The Case Method," *Corr*, 2000; Auth, "Informed Consent," *Corr*, 2000; Auth, "Moral Resoning, Professionalism And Tchg Of Ethics To Orthapedic Surgeons," *Corr*, 2000. vmdwhb@aol.com

BUNDAY, Roger Jack (Mil) 1121 N Waverly Pl Apt 1102, Milwaukee WI 53202 **Died 2/26/2011** B Northfield MN 8/23/1919 s Leslie Wallace Bunday & Glenis Elizabeth. BA Carleton Coll 1942; MDiv SWTS 1945; MA U of Wisconsin 1968; PhD U of Wisconsin 1974. D 4/21/1945 P 12/21/1945 Bp Stephen E Keeler. Irish-Amer Cultural Inst. Phi Beta Kappa Carleton Coll Northfield MN 1942; BA scl Carleton Coll Northfield MN 1942.

BUNDER, Peter Joseph (Ind) 610 Meridian St, West Lafayette IN 47906 **Dio Indianapolis Indianapolis IN 2009-** B Rochester NY 8/1/1951 s Peter Bunder & Sophia. BA St. Jn Fisher Coll 1973; MDiv U Tor/St. Mich's 1977; Bex 1982. Rec from Roman Catholic 5/23/1982 as Priest Bp Robert Rae Spears Jr. m 6/26/1982 Kathleen Lynn Bunder c 2. Pres Stndg Com Dio Indianapolis Indianapolis IN 2006-2007; Chapl Chap Of The Gd Shpd W Lafayette IN 1985-2009; R E Lee Memi Ch (Epis) Lexington VA 1982-1985; Transition Prog Dio Rochester Rochester NY 1981-1982. W Lafayette City Coun Dist #2 2011; W Lafayette City Coun Dist #2 2007. peter@goodshep.org

BUNDROCK, Bonnie Rae (WNY) Po Box 66, Gasport NY 14067 B Lockport NY 12/29/1956 d Raymond John Bundrock & Joyce Marilyn. AA Niagara Cc Sanborn NY 1977; BS SUNY 1998. D 9/14/2001 Bp J Michael Garrison. D Chr Ch Lockport NY 2001-2008. boopwitt@yahoo.com

BUNKE, Jeff L (SO) 6292 Stonyford Ct, West Chester OH 45069 **COM Dio Sthrn Ohio Cincinnati OH 2008-; R S Anne Epis Ch W Chester OH 2007-** B Defiance OH 7/31/1954 s Walter George Henry Bunke & Margaret Elizabeth. BA Valparaiso U 1976; MDiv SWTS 1981. D 6/27/1981 P 1/24/1982 Bp John Harris Burt. m 10/23/1976 Kay A Stites c 3. R Gr Epis Ch Inc Port Orange FL 1992-2007; R S Jn's Epis Ch Cuyahoga Falls OH 1985-1992; Asst Min S Paul's Ch Maumee OH 1981-1985. ComT 1987. bunkehouse@cinci.rr.com

BUNN III, George Strother (SwVa) 518 Beech Forest Rd, Bristol TN 37620 B Pulaski VA 9/4/1932 s George S Bunn & Winifred. SWTS; BS Florida St U 1954; U So 1957. D 7/13/1957 P 11/1/1959 Bp William Henry Marmion. m 3/31/1959 Barbara Marie Bunn c 2. Emm Epis Ch Bristol VA 1975-1998; Vic S Thos Epis Christiansburg VA 1957-1962. georgeiii@chartertn.net

BUNSY, Martin (EpisSanJ) 1327 N Del Mar Ave, Fresno CA 93728 **Asst S Mart Of Tours Epis Ch Fresno CA 2005-** B Vientrane Laos 11/21/1951 s Outhai Bunsy & May. Dongdok U Laos 1968; Bible Trng Sch Ft Worth TX 1984; Fresno City Coll Fresno CA 1991. D 9/10/2004 P 4/23/2005 Bp John-David Mercer Schofield. c 2. laomission@yahoo.com

BUNTAINE, Raymond Earl (NJ) 106 Palmwood Ave, Cherry Hill NJ 08003 B Kalamazoo MI 3/1/1920 s Ralph Russell Buntaine & Elva Leora. Wstrn Michigan U 1939; BA U MI 1942; MA U MI 1946; GTS 1963. D 8/18/1956 P 2/23/1957 Bp Alfred L Banyard. m 10/23/1976 Virginia Buntaine. R S Jn The Evang Ch New Brunswick NJ 1959-1970; Vic S Geo's Epis Ch Helmetta NJ 1956-1957.

BUNTING, Michael Andrew (Mil) 2211 E Kenwood Blvd, Milwaukee WI 53211 **R Epis Ch Of The Resurr Mukwonago WI 2009-** B Fayetteville NC 5/21/1975 s Michael Linwood Bunting & Glyn Lorraine. BA Wms 1997; MDiv Ya Berk 2002. D 12/6/2002 Bp Leopold Frade P 9/6/2003 Bp Dorsey Felix Henderson. m 6/8/2002 April L Berends. S Columba's Ch Washington DC 2005-2008; Cur/Chapl S Steph's Ch Coconut Grove Coconut Grove FL 2002-2005. drewbunting@gmail.com

BUNYAN, Frederick Satyanandam (Colo) 1749 Stove Prairie Cir, Loveland CO 80538 **Chairman Colorado Epis Fndt Denver CO 2012-** B Jammalmadugu IN 1/21/1945 s Alfred Bunyan & Shantha Jessica. BA Andhra Chr Coll 1967; BD Bp's Theol Coll, Calcutta 1970; STM SMU 1972. Trans from Church of South India 6/1/1977 Bp William Carl Frey. m 7/15/1974 Ann Sotherden c 3. R All SS Ch Loveland CO 1982-2010; Asst Ch Of Our Sav Colorado Sprg CO 1978-1982; Asst The Ch Of The Ascen Denver CO 1977-1978;

Asst Ch Of The Resurr Austin TX 1975-1977. Colorado Epis Fndt 2002; Colorado Link, Co-Workers of Mo Teresa 1982; Loveland Police Chapl 1982; Loveland Rotary Club - Pres 1991-1992. Bp's Cross Dio Colorado 2000. sathiandann@gmail.com

BUOTE-GREIG, Eletha A (RI) Po Box 192, North Scituate RI 02857 **R S Jas Epis Ch At Woonsocket Woonsocket RI 2004-** B Providence RI 5/6/1942 d James Albert Buote & Elsie Jane. BA U of Rhode Island 1982; MDiv EDS 1986. D 6/21/1986 P 12/23/1986 Bp George Nelson Hunt III. m 10/2/1967 William Buote-Greig. R S Jn's/S Steph's Ch Fall River MA 1995-2004; R S Steph's Ch Fall River MA 1992-1998; Assoc S Lk's Epis Ch E Greenwich RI 1987-1991; Chapl Dio Massachusetts Boston MA 1986-2000. Comp of the H Cross. ebgwbg8@aol.com

BUQUOR, Anthony Francis (Mass) 1357 Old Marlboro Rd, Concord MA 01742 **R Trin Ch Concord MA 2003-** B San Antonio TX 3/11/1946 s Anthony Alexander Buquor & Mildred Carmen. BA So Dakota St U 1968; MS Troy St U-Troy AL 1976; MDiv SWTS 1996. D 4/10/1996 P 11/11/1996 Bp Creighton Leland Robertson. m 1/18/1970 Louann Buquor c 2. Cn to the Ordnry Dio So Dakota Sioux Falls SD 1999-2003; R Chr Epis Ch Yankton SD 1996-1999. buquor@trinityconcord.org

BURBANK, Kristina Dawn (Ore) 34820 Henshaw Dr, Brownsville OR 97327 **Reverend D S Jas Ch Lincoln City OR 2004-** B Spokane WA 7/22/1949 d Donald Burbank & B Evelyn. BA Ft Wright Coll Of H Names 1976; BA Marylhurst U 1988. D 9/18/2004 Bp Johncy Itty. deaconkristina@hotmail.com

BURCH, Charles Francis (Mil) W356 N5928 Meadow Court, Oconomowoc WI 53066 **D Zion Epis Ch Oconomowoc WI 1998-** B Jersey City NJ 12/2/1941 s Joseph Leonard Burch & Hazel Catherine. BS FD 1974. D 5/9/1998 Bp Roger John White. m 4/12/1969 Mary Ann Burch c 3. Phi Omega Epsilon FD 1972. cfrancisburch@aol.com

BURCH, Suzanne (ETenn) 4111 Albemarle Ave, Chattanooga TN 37411 B Oak Ridge TN 9/7/1947 d Robert Abel Burch & Ruth Louise. BS U of Tennessee 1992. D 12/15/2001 Bp Charles Glenn VonRosenberg. D S Mart Of Tours Epis Ch Chattanooga TN 2002-2011; D Gr Ch Chattanooga TN 2001-2002. suzburch@epbfi.com

BURCHARD, Russell Church (SwVa) 51 Mayapple Gln, Dawsonville GA 30534 B Jacksonville NC 1/11/1944 s Roswell B Burchard & Thelma C. BA Amer U 1968; MPA GW 1973; MDiv VTS 1979. D 5/27/1979 P 12/1/1979 Bp Alexander Doig Stewart. m 11/23/1968 Sharon Fitzgerald c 2. R Chr Ch Martinsville VA 2000-2002; Assoc Galilee Epis Ch Virginia Bch VA 1994-2000; R Chr Ch Par Epis Watertown CT 1987-1994; R Gr Ch Broad Brook CT 1982-1987; S Steph's Ch Pittsfield MA 1982; Dio Wstrn Massachusetts Springfield MA 1979-1982; Asst S Steph's Ch Pittsfield MA 1979-1982. Auth, "The Sprtl Gifts Workbook," St Andr's Mnstrs. cherinruss@windstream.net

BURCHILL, George Stuart (SwFla) 2611 Bayshore Blvd, Tampa FL 33629 B Newcastle New Brunswick CA 12/5/1927 s Henry Sterling Burchill & Blanche Margaret. BA Dalhousie U 1949; LTh U Of King's Coll Halifax Ns CA 1952; BD U Of King's Coll Halifax Ns CA 1961. Trans from Anglican Church of Canada 10/1/1954 Bp Henry I Louttit. m 2/7/1952 Elizabeth Anne Ellis c 4. St Johns Epis Ch Tampa FL 1954-1992. Auth, "arts Liturg Classics," *Var Subjects*.

BURDEKIN, Edwina Amelia (Colo) 4566 Winewood Village Dr, Colorado Springs CO 80917 B Twillingate NF CA 7/11/1932 d Edwin Josiah Colbourne & Annie May. D Formation Prog; A.D.N Pikes Peak Cmnty Coll 1986. D 11/2/1996 Bp William Jerry Winterrowd. c 5. BEC Dio Colorado Denver CO 1997-2002; D Ch Of S Mich The Archangel Colorado Sprg CO 1996-2003. NAAD 1996. eaburdekin@pcisys.net

BURDEN, Richard James (Lex) 2323 Lexington Rd, Richmond KY 40475 **Chair, Nomin Com for the 7th Bp of the Dio Dio Lexington Lexington KY 2011-; Chair, Coll Wk Cmsn Dio Lexington Lexington KY 2010-; P-in-c Epis Ch of Our Sav Richmond KY 2009-** B Loveland CO 7/14/1964 s Roy Miles Burden & Mary Ellen Elizabeth. BA Colorado St U 1986; MA U CO@Denver 1996; PhD U Chi 2006; MDiv CDSP 2009. D 6/6/2009 Bp Sergio Carranza-Gomez P 12/21/2009 Bp Stacy F Sauls. m 8/15/1999 Monica Turk c 2. rjburden@uchicago.edu

BURDEN, William Robertson (Chi) PO Box 273, Orangeville IL 61060 **Asst Cathd Ch Of S Ptr St Petersburg FL 2010-** B Rockford IL 11/13/1943 s William Frederick Burden & Marjory Currier. BA Bos 1965; MDiv GTS 1968; MA Loyola U 1978. D 6/15/1968 Bp James Winchester Montgomery P 12/21/1968 Bp Gerald Francis Burrill. m 9/28/1997 Irene Meros c 2. R Trin Epis Ch Aurora IL 1975-2005; R All SS Epis Ch Chicago IL 1970-1975; Cur Chr Ch Winnetka IL 1968-1970. Auth, "High Rises For Low & Middle Income Families," *Challenge*, HUD. nancytruesdale@gmail.com

BURDESHAW, Charles Abbott (Tenn) 139 Brighton Close, Nashville TN 37205 **D S Ann's Ch Nashville TN 1990-** B Chattanooga TN 5/24/1940 s James Ralph Burdeshaw & Cornelia. Emory U 1960; U of Tennessee 1961; DDS U of Tennessee 1965; U of Missouri 1968; Epis TS In Kentucky 1990. D 10/28/1989 Bp George Lazenby Reynolds Jr. m 3/18/1964 Rosemary Dean Burdeshaw c 1. cabddspc@aol.com

BURDETT, Audrey (At) 3223 Rilman Rd Nw, Atlanta GA 30327 B Flushing NY 12/7/1922 d Walter Birdsall Brown & Ottilie. BA Georgia St U 1984; MDiv Candler TS Emory U 1988. D 6/11/1988 P 10/12/1988 Bp Charles Judson Child Jr. m 5/25/1945 Lucien Briscoe Burdett. D Cathd Of S Phil Atlanta GA 1988-1995. Auth, "Personal Plnng Guide". DOK.

BURDETTE, Christina Lynn (SO) 7041 Cable Rd, Cable OH 43009 B Huntington WV 3/6/1962 d Dempsy Fry & Lena Ruth. AA Columbus St Cmnty Coll Columbus OH 1983; Cert Epis Dio Sthrn Ohio 1994. D 11/11/1994 Bp Herbert Thompson Jr. m 6/12/1982 Jack White Burdette.

BURDICK II, Edward Noyes (SO) 2437 Swans Rd Ne, Newark OH 43055 B Westerly RI 12/15/1923 s Harry Russell Burdick & Prudence. BS Ya 1948; BD/MDiv UTS 1953. D 6/13/1953 P 1/23/1954 Bp William A Lawrence. m 12/19/1959 Nancy Griffith Neill. R S Lk's Ch Granville OH 1960-1989; Cur S Jn's Ch Northampton MA 1953-1957.

BURDICK III, Henry Carlyle (Ct) 152 Wharf Landing Dr Unit A, Edenton NC 27932 B New London CT 1/26/1943 s Henry Carlyle Burdick & Eleanor Louise. BA U of Connecticut 1970; MEd. Antioch U 1982; MDiv Ya Berk 1985. D 6/8/1985 P 12/1/1985 Bp Arthur Edward Walmsley. m 8/5/1967 Kathrine Lillian Burdick. R S Dav's Ch Gales Ferry CT 1988-1999; Trin Ch Branford CT 1985-2009; Wmns Seamens Frd Soc Of Ct New Haven CT 1985-1999. Wmn Seamen's Friend Soc Of Connecticut, New Haven Ct 1983-2001. hcburdick@gmail.com

BURG, Michael John (FdL) 2515 Lakeshore Dr, Sheboygan WI 53081 **D All SS Elkhart Lake Sheboygan WI 1989-** B Lena WI 6/28/1944 s Norbert Joeseph Burg & Marion. BS U of Wisconsin 1971; Diac Sch Dio Fond du Lac 1990. D 9/12/1990 Bp William L Stevens. m 7/21/1962 Valerie Jean Burg c 3. D Gr Epis Ch Sheboygan WI 1990-2006. vmburg@yahoo.com

BURGDORF, David H (Los) 36270 Avenida De Las Montanas, Cathedral City CA 92234 B Auburn NY 12/7/1944 s Kenneth Dunham Burgdorf & Winona. BA SUNY, Buffalo 1966; MDiv GTS 1969; MA U of St. Thos, MN 1989. D 6/21/1969 P 12/22/1969 Bp Lauriston L Scaife. Vic S Jos Of Arimathea Mssn Yucca Vlly CA 1997-1999; Vic Ch of the H Name Dolton IL 1975-1978; Cur Emm Epis Ch Rockford IL 1971-1975; Cn S Paul's Cathd Buffalo NY 1969-1971. SSF 1978-1986; Third Ord, SSF 1991. dewi1944@aol.com

BURGER, Charles Sherman (Ida) 198 Rainbow Dr # 9863, Livingston TX 77399 B Saint Louis MO 5/29/1938 s Joseph Eagleton Burger & Eleanor Dorothea. BA Trin Hartford CT 1960; BD CDSP 1966. D 3/5/1966 Bp George Richard Millard P 9/4/1966 Bp Harry S Kennedy. m 1/17/1984 Leah Diane Hambleton. S Thos Epis Ch Sun Vlly ID 1985-1997; S Paul's Epis Ch Elko NV 1983-1985; H Innoc' Epis Ch Lahaina HI 1973-1983; Vic S Mich And All Ang Ch Lihue HI 1966-1968. rareburgers@earthlink.net

BURGER, Douglas Clyde (RI) 214 Oakley Rd, Woonsocket RI 02895 B New Haven CT 4/10/1938 s William James Burger & Alice Katherine. Coll of Wooster 1959; BA DePauw U 1960; MA Indiana U 1963; BD SWTS 1966. D 6/11/1966 Bp John P Craine P 12/1/1966 Bp William R Moody. m 7/2/1959 Elizabeth Hay Kelly c 2. Assoc S Steph's Ch Providence RI 1993-2002; Vic S Phil's Ch Harrodsburg KY 1966-1967. Auth, "A Complete Bibliography Of The Schlrshp On The Life & Works Of S Jn Chrysostem".

BURGER, Robert Franz (Wyo) Po Box 579, Estes Park CO 80517 **Asst S Barth's Ch Estes Pk CO 2001-** B Saint Louis MO 4/5/1929 s Joseph Eagleton Burger & Eleanor Dorothea. Pasadena City Coll; BA USC 1950; BD CDSP 1953. D 6/22/1953 P 2/1/1954 Bp Francis E I Bloy. R All SS Epis Ch Torrington WY 1986-1989; S Chris's Ch Trona CA 1978-1986; Epis Dio San Joaquin Modesto CA 1975-1976; Vic Trin Memi Epis Ch Lone Pine CA 1975-1976; Vic S Anne's Epis Ch Washougal WA 1974-1975; Vic S Jn's Epis Ch So Bend WA 1969-1974; Vic S Paul's Epis Ch Port Townsend WA 1964-1969; Cur S Paul Epis Ch Bellingham WA 1962-1963; Vic Ch Of S Jn The Div Springfield OR 1956-1962; Cur S Mk's Epis Par Medford OR 1955-1956; Vic Chr The Gd Shpd Par Los Angeles CA 1954-1955; Cur S Jas Par Los Angeles CA 1953-1955.

BURGER, Timothy Hinton (Nwk) 11 Berkeley Pl, Glen Rock NJ 07452 **All SS' Epis Ch Glen Rock NJ 2010-** B Athens GA 10/24/1978 s Raymond Burger & Mary. BA U GA 2002; MDiv GTS 2005. D 12/21/2004 P 6/16/2005 Bp J(ohn) Neil Alexander. m 2/9/2010 Gregory C Lisby c 2. St Mich & Gr Ch Rumford RI 2007-2010; Ch Of The Epiph Providence RI 2007-2009; S Mary's Epis Ch Ardmore PA 2005-2007. timothyhburger@gmail.comcom

BURGESS, B(arbara) Candis (NC) Po Box 1547, Clemmons NC 27012 **Vic S Mart's-In-The-Fields Mayfield KY 2000-; Vic S Paul's Ch Hickman KY 2000-** B Jacksonville FL 9/23/1958 d Willard Francis Burgess & Marian Pauline. BA U So 1981; MDiv STUSo 1996. D 6/15/1996 Bp Rogers Sanders Harris P 2/22/1997 Bp John Bailey Lipscomb. S Paul's Ch Salisbury NC 2009-2010; S Clem's Epis Ch Clemmons NC 2005-2009; Vic S Ptr's of the Lakes Gilbertsville KY 2000-2006; Parc Area Vic Dio Kentucky Louisville KY 2000-2005; Vic Trin Epis Ch Fulton KY 2000-2005; Dio Nthrn Michigan Marquette MI 2000; R S Jas Ch Of Sault S Marie Sault Ste Marie MI

B

1998-2000; Asst to R S Andr's Epis Ch Sprg Hill FL 1996-1998. revcburgess@gmail.com

BURGESS, Brian Kendall (NJ) 62 Delaware St, Woodbury NJ 08096 **Trst The U So (Sewanee) Sewanee TN 2011-; Dioc Coun Mem Dio New Jersey Trenton NJ 2009-; R Chr Ch In Woodbury Woodbury NJ 2005-; Dio Louisiana Baton Rouge LA 2001-** B Tampa FL 11/6/1960 s Willard Francis Burgess & Marian Pauline. BS Ball St U 1983; MDiv (w hon) STUSo 1999. D 6/12/1999 P 12/18/1999 Bp John Bailey Lipscomb. m 4/9/1985 Denise Lee Swing c 2. Convoc Dn Dio New Jersey Trenton NJ 2006-2010; Stndg Cmsn on Cler Compstn Dio New Jersey Trenton NJ 2006-2009; Assoc P/Chapl of Par Day Sch S Lk's Ch Baton Rouge LA 2001-2005; Dio SW Florida Sarasota FL 1999-2001; R S Jn's Epis Ch Brooksville FL 1999-2001. SSC 2005. frburgess@christchurch.woodburynj.org

BURGESS, Carol Jean (NC) 721 7 Lks N, Seven Lakes NC 27376 **D S Mary Magd Ch W End NC 1999-** B Duluth MN 1/29/1939 d Stuart Dixon Anderson & Audrey Leone. BS Hamline U 1961; Med U of Wisconsin 1982; Reg II Dioc Minn 1987. D 10/25/1987 Bp Robert Marshall Anderson. m 6/23/1962 Timothy John Burgess c 2. D Emm Par Epis Ch And Day Sch Sthrn Pines NC 1998-1999; D S Edw's Ch Duluth MN 1987-1998. tcburgess@embarqmail.com

BURGESS, Judith Fleming (RG) Hc 65 Box 271, PO Box 477, Alto NM 88312 **R Epis Ch In Lincoln Cnty Ruidoso NM 2010-** B Rotan TX 4/24/1950 d Albert Alvin Fleming & Erin. BA U of Texas 1972; MA U of Washington 1975; MA Col 1979; MDiv VTS 1984. D 6/23/1984 Bp Peter James Lee P 4/13/1985 Bp Clarence Nicholas Coleridge. m 10/13/1990 Seth B Burgess. Vic Big Bend Epis Mssn Alpine TX 1996-2010; R Gr Epis Ch Goochland VA 1989-1993; Cur S Geo's Ch Fredericksburg VA 1986-1989; Cur S Mich's Ch Naugatuck CT 1984-1986. judithfburgess@gmail.com

BURGESS, Vicki Tucker (Tenn) 4016 Brush Hill Rd, Nashville TN 37216 **Chair, GC Deputation Dio Tennessee Nashville TN 2011-2014; Pres, Stndg Com Dio Tennessee Nashville TN 2011-2012; Mem, Stndg Com Dio Tennessee Nashville TN 2009-2012; R S Phil's Ch Nashville TN 2007-** B Winter Haven FL 11/30/1954 d Arthur Sherman Tucker & Carol Ann. BS U of Tennessee 1976; MDiv STUSo 2003. D 6/22/2003 P 4/18/2004 Bp Bertram Nelson Herlong. m 7/26/1975 John Thomas Burgess c 3. Chair, GC Deputation Dio Tennessee Nashville TN 2008-2011; Mem, Episcopate search Com Dio Tennessee Nashville TN 2005-2006; Ch Of The Gd Shpd Brentwood TN 2004-2007. vicki@stphilipsnashville.org

BURGESS, Walter F (Eas) 105 Gay St, Denton MD 21629 **R Chr Ch Denton MD 2007-** B Baltimore MD 5/20/1948 s Franklin Smith Burgess & Helen May. BS Towson U 1982; MDiv GTS 1993. D 6/12/1993 Bp A(lbert) Theodore Eastman P 6/1/1994 Bp Charles Lindsay Longest. Ch Of S Paul The Apos Baltimore MD 2003-2005; P-in-c S Lk's Ch Baltimore MD 1997-2002; Cur/Asst Gr And S Ptr's Ch Baltimore MD 1993-1997. wallydpriest_1999@yahoo.com

BURGOS, Joe A (Tex) 305 Sunset Drive, North Manchester IN 46962 B Merida Yucatan MX 9/15/1937 s Alejandro Burgos-Grajales & Isabel. AA Warren Wilson Coll 1958; BA Maryville Coll 1960; BD McCormick TS 1964; MA Prairie View A&M U 1984. D 6/13/1993 P 3/24/1994 Bp Maurice Manuel Benitez. m 8/25/1962 Janice Mary Burgos c 3. Supply P S Alb's Ch Houston TX 1995-1996; Ch Of The Redeem Houston TX 1993-1996. joejanburgos@frontier.net

BURGOYNE, Douglas G (Va) 11757 Triple Notch Ter, Richmond VA 23233 B Orange NJ 7/24/1930 s Robert Wilson Burgoyne & Marion Campbell. BA Wms 1952; MDiv EDS 1958. D 5/31/1958 Bp William A Lawrence P 12/1/1958 Bp Lane W Barton. m 12/27/1952 Joanna Cutter Turner c 5. Int Ch Of S Jas The Less Ashland VA 2005-2007; P-in-c S Mart's Epis Ch Henrico VA 2001-2004; R All SS Ch Richmond VA 1992-2000; Stndg Com Dio Sthrn Virginia Norfolk VA 1989-1991; R S Andr's Epis Ch Newport News VA 1975-1991; R S Jn's Ch Williamstown MA 1964-1975; R S Matt's Epis Ch Ontario OR 1958-1964. Auth, "arts Ch mag". Hon Cn Cntrl Tanganyika 1969. dougburgoyne@verizon.net

BURHANS III, Charles F (CFla) 1104 Hartbourne Ln, Ormond Beach FL 32174 **R Gr Epis Ch Inc Port Orange FL 2008-** B Lakeland FL 9/30/1951 BA Stetson U 1975; MDiv TESM 2005. D 5/28/2005 P 12/8/2005 Bp John Wadsworth Howe. m 5/5/1985 Carolyn Anderson c 1. Asst S Jas Epis Ch Ormond Bch FL 2005-2008. rector@egracepo.org

BURHOE, Alden Read (Mass) 54 Grant Ave, Somerset MA 02726 **Asst S Mk's Ch Marco Island FL 2002-** B Providence RI 12/15/1931 s Paul Edward Burhoe & Ruth Laura. BA Br 1953; BD EDS 1956. D 6/23/1956 P 3/23/1957 Bp John S Higgins. m 6/6/1953 Audrey Janet Brothers c 2. Vic and R Ch Of Our Sav Somerset MA 1958-1994; Cur S Mart's Ch Providence RI 1956-1958.

BURK, John Harry (EpisSanJ) 599 Colton St, Monterey CA 93940 B Binghamton NY 1/30/1940 s Donald John Burk & Ruth Ida. BS Un Coll Schenectady NY 1960; MDiv SWTS 1966; MLS San Jose St 1992. D 6/11/1966 Bp James Winchester Montgomery P 12/1/1966 Bp Gerald Francis Burrill. m 9/5/1962 Anne Petersen c 2. S Mk's Epis Ch French Camp CA 1985-1990; Epis Dio San Joaquin Modesto CA 1982-1985; Ch Of The Resurr Clovis Clovis CA 1982-1984; R S Jn's Ch Mt Morris NY 1976-1982; Weber - Davis Hsng Corp Layton UT 1975-1976; Vic S Ptr's Ch Clearfield UT 1969-1976; Cur Emm Epis Ch Rockford IL 1966-1969. Phi Sigma Kappa 1956. Bp Anderson Schlr 1966; Alpha Phi Omega 1956. johnhb11@att.net

BURK, William H (Va) 7159 Mechanicsville Tpke, Mechanicsville VA 23111 **R Ch Of The Creator Mechanicsville VA 1998-** B Washington DC 4/16/1962 s Paul William Burk & Mildred Elizabeth. BA/BS California St U 1990; MDiv VTS 1996. D 10/12/1996 P 4/1/1997 Bp Frank Clayton Matthews. m 6/1/1996 Jennifer Louise Bacon c 5. Asst R Gr Ch Kilmarnock VA 1996-1998. frbillburk@comcast.net

BURKARDT, Jay Peter (NC) Canterbury Episcopal Day School, 5400 Old Lake Jeanette Rd, Greensboro NC 27455 B Rochester NY 7/10/1978 s Peter Burkardt & Judith. BA Mt Un Coll 2001; MDiv Epis TS of The SW 2004. D 6/5/2004 P 4/20/2005 Bp Jack Marston McKelvey. m 5/21/2005 Leslie Sue Burkardt. Cbury Sch Greensboro NC 2007-2010; Cur Ch Of The Gd Shpd Corpus Christi TX 2004-2007. jaypeter_muc@hotmail.com

BURKARDT, Leslie Sue (NC) 2105 W. Market St., Greensboro NC 27403 **S Andr's Epis Ch Charlotte NC 2010-** B Muncie IN 9/10/1975 d John Brown & Dana. MDiv Epis TS of The SW 2006. D 7/3/2006 Bp Barry Robert Howe P 1/12/2007 Bp Gary Richard Lillibridge. m 5/21/2005 Jay Peter Burkardt c 1. S Andr's Ch Greensboro NC 2008-2010; Assoc R All SS Epis Ch Corpus Christi TX 2007; S Andr's Ch Kansas City MO 2000-2003; DCE S Andr's Epis Ch Corpus Christi TX 2000-2003. rector@standrewscharlottenc.org

BURKE, Anne B (RI) 66 Elm St Apt 1, Westerly RI 02891 **D Ch Of The Ascen Cranston RI 2010-** B 7/24/1950 d John S Burke & Stan O. AA Pine Manor Coll 1970. D 9/12/2009 Bp Geralyn Wolf. c 2.

BURKE, Celine Ann (WMich) 1033 NW Stannium Rd, Bend OR 97701 B Covington KY 2/12/1946 d John Edward Austing & Hilda Louise. BS Dominican Coll 1968; MS U of Wisconsin 1973; MDiv VTS 1985. D 6/22/1985 Bp Peter James Lee P 1/26/1986 Bp John Shelby Spong. m 4/9/1988 Richard M Burke c 1. Stwdshp Com Dio Wstrn Michigan Kalamazoo MI 2003-2008; R H Trin Epis Ch Manistee MI 2001-2008; R S Jn's Ch Clinton IA 1995-2001; Com On Episcopate Dio Maryland Baltimore MD 1991-1994; R H Trin Ch Churchville MD 1988-1995; Asst S Ptr's Ch Morristown NJ 1985-1987. Sprtl Dir Intl 2006. celine@bendbroadband.com

BURKE, Cyril Casper (Ct) 26 Hoskins Rd, Bloomfield CT 06002 B Cambridge MA 11/3/1926 s Casper Rawle Burke & Paulina Estelle. St. Aug Coll CA 1946; Mercer TS 1964; DMin Hartford Sem 1982. D 6/20/1964 P 12/21/1964 Bp James P De Wolfe. m 12/27/1947 Avis Eaves. P-in-c S Mart's Ch Hartford CT 1999-2002; Int S Andr's Ch New Haven CT 1994-1998; Int S Ptr's Ch Springfield MA 1992-1993; S Aug's Coll Raleigh NC 1984-1991; S Monica's Ch Hartford CT 1966-1984; Cur S Geo's Ch Brooklyn NY 1964-1965. Auth, "Predominantly Black Middle Class Congregations Attempts To Min To Its Cmnty"; Auth, "Cmnty". ESMHE; Rel & The Intellectual Life.

BURKE, Geneva Frances (Mich) 21514 Deguindre, #202, Warren MI 48091 B Lake City FL 6/26/1933 d James Dewitt Talmadge Combs & Nancy Arabelle. Cert EDS; BS Lewis Coll of Bus 1971. D 7/11/1981 Bp Quintin Ebenezer Primo Jr. D Emm Ch Detroit MI 1981-1991.

BURKE, Harry Taylor (SwFla) No address on file. **Died 4/8/2011** B Bowling Green KY 11/13/1909 s Ransom Marion Burke & Callie Belle. ThM VTS 1934; BS U CA 1947; MS Bos 1954; Harv 1955. D 6/22/1934 Bp Charles E Woodcock P 12/21/1934 Bp William T Capers. Hon Cn All SS Cathd Bontoc Place.

BURKE, Joseph Daniel (RI) 111 Pottersville Road, Little Compton RI 02837 B Mineola NY 8/30/1931 s Joseph D Burke & Lillian G. BA Ohio Wesl 1953; BD ETS 1961; Fllshp Coll of Preachers 1981. D 6/29/1961 Bp Richard S M Emrich P 2/18/1962 Bp Archie H Crowley. m 1/2/1965 Cynthia Jane Cummings c 3. Vic S Andr's By The Sea Little Compton RI 1997-2000; Dio Rhode Island Providence RI 1989-1996; R S Mart's Ch Providence RI 1978-1996; Chapl Med Ctr Of Ann Arbor Ann Arbor MI 1971-1976; Asst S Andr's Ch Ann Arbor MI 1961-1963. Auth, *arts Var Pub*. Abrahamic Accord, Providence RI 1986-2004. jburke288@aol.com

BURKE, Michael Edward (Ak) 3221 Amber Bay Loop, Anchorage AK 99515 **R S Mary's Ch Anchorage AK 2000-** B Glens Falls NY 11/30/1962 s Robert Joseph Burke & Magery Grace. Cor 1984; BS U of Alaska 1990; MDiv CRDS 1995. D 8/12/1995 P 6/1/1996 Bp Steven Charleston. m 8/19/1989 Nancy Irene Burke c 2. Dio Rochester Rochester NY 1998-2000; R S Geo's Ch Hilton NY 1997-2000; Assoc S Lk And S Simon Cyrene Rochester NY 1995-1997. MDiv w dist Colgate-Rochester Div Sch Rochester NY 1995. michael@godsview.org

BURKE, Norman Charles (Az) Hc 1 Box 630, Strawberry AZ 85544 **P-in-c S Geo's Epis Ch Holbrook AZ 2011-; Vic S Paul's Epis Ch Winslow AZ 2006-** B Chicago IL 3/27/1934 s Benjamin Norman Burke & Phyllis. BA Ripon Coll Ripon WI 1956; MDiv Nash 1960. D 6/18/1960 Bp Gerald Francis Burrill P 12/1/1960 Bp Charles L Street. m 6/25/1960 Arlene Ford c 4. Vic S Paul's Ch Payson AZ 1996-2006; S Jn The Bapt Epis Ch Glendale AZ

1979-1996; Int S Aug's Epis Ch Tempe AZ 1977-1978; Dio Arizona Phoenix AZ 1976-1978; Vic S Bede's Epis Ch Bensenville IL 1967-1976; Vic Ch Of The Gd Shpd Momence IL 1961-1967; Asst S Paul's Ch Kankakee IL 1961-1967; Cur Chr Ch Waukegan IL 1960-1961. Cn Dio Arizona 2005. ncbapb@yahoo.com

BURKE, Richard Early (Mass) 91 Shadow Lake Rd., Salem NH 03079 B Baltimore MD 2/5/1946 s Edmund Potts Burke & Margaret. U CA 1965; BA Ia Wesleyan U Coll Mt Pleasant 1967; BD EDS 1970. D 7/1/1970 Bp Jose Guadalupe Saucedo P 5/1/1971 Bp John Melville Burgess. Cur Gr Ch Lawr MA 1970-1972. mail2burke@aol.com

BURKE, Robert Thomas (NwPa) Grace Episcopal Church, 10121 Hall Ave, Lake City PA 16423 B Union City PA 7/18/1953 s Thomas R Burke & Doris L. D 12/11/2004 P 6/12/2005 Bp Robert Deane Rowley Jr. m 8/4/1957 Wendy Davis Burke c 2. ipeto@msn.com

BURKE, Sean D (Ia) 201 Hollihan St, Decorah IA 52101 **P-in-c S Jas Epis Ch Independence IA 2008-** B Rahway NJ 9/30/1972 s William Burke & Lorraine. BA Concordia Coll 1994; MDiv Luth TS at Philadelphia 1998; PhD Grad Theol Un/CDSP 2009. D 6/3/2006 Bp William Edwin Swing P 12/2/2006 Bp Marc Handley Andrus. seandburke@aol.com

BURKE, Terry Celeste (Az) 3043 N Conestoga Ave, Tucson AZ 85749 B New York NY 1/6/1945 d Robert Juliando & Laura. BA Hofstra U 1966; MA U of Phoenix 2002. D 10/9/2004 Bp Robert Reed Shahan. m 8/8/1980 Leigh Richmond Burke. lburke21@cox.net

BURKERT, Alfred Paul (Mil) 7707 N Brookline Dr Apt 326, Madison WI 53719 B Bronx NY 7/3/1929 s Alfred Jacob Burkert & Olive Lillian. BA Ups 1953; LTh Nash 1956; MDiv Nash 1972. D 12/22/1956 P 6/22/1957 Bp James P De Wolfe. m 9/29/1956 Irene Gladys Schanbacher c 2. Supply S Andr's Epis Ch Monroe WI 1997-1998; S Jn Ch/Mision San Juan Milwaukee WI 1986-1995; S Johns Communities INC Milwaukee WI 1986-1995; Bd Gvnr Cliff Sprg/Camp Richland Dio W Missouri Kansas City MO 1981-1984; Dio W Missouri Kansas City MO 1980-1986; Vic S Geo Epis Ch Camdenton MO 1980-1986; Vic Trin Epis Ch Lebanon MO 1980-1986; R Chr Ch Chippewa Falls WI 1975-1980; Exec Coun Dio Eau Claire Eau Claire WI 1975-1980; Vic S Simeon's Ch Stanley WI 1975-1980; P-in-c Emm Epis Ch Of Sheepshead Bay Brooklyn NY 1958-1961; Cur S Ann And The H Trin Brooklyn NY 1957-1958.

BURKETT, William Vernard (SwFla) 2902 Weset San Rafael Street, Tampa FL 33629 **R S Barth's Ch St Petersburg FL 2005-** B Huntsville AL 9/5/1960 s Vernard Manning Burkett. BA Birmingham-Sthrn Coll 1982; MDiv SMU 1985; MS U of Alabama 1988; STUSo 2002. D 4/6/2002 Bp Duncan Montgomery Gray III P 1/4/2003 Bp John Bailey Lipscomb. m 12/21/1991 Patricia A Roman c 2. Cur S Thos' Epis Ch St Petersburg FL 2002-2004. rector.st.barts@verizon.net

BURKHART, John Delmas (Lex) 701 E Engineer St, Corbin KY 40701 B Barnesville OH 8/2/1933 s Vernon Wilfred Burkhart & Leota Lucille. BA St. Chas 1956; The Athenaeum of Ohio 1960; MA OH SU 1969; PhD OH SU 1972. Rec from Roman Catholic 6/1/1973 as Priest Bp Addison Hosea. m 8/3/1996 Milly Alice Hubbard c 4. P-in-c S Jn's Ch Corbin KY 1994-2001; P-in-c Chr Epis Ch Harlan KY 1992-1996; Vic Chr Ch Cathd Louisville KY 1991-1994; Vic S Phil's Ch Harrodsburg KY 1983-1991. stjohns2@bellsouth.net

BURKS, Bill Edward (WTenn) 98 Jim Dedmon Rd., Dyer TN 38330 **P-in-c S Thos The Apos Humboldt TN 2004-** B Lawrenceburg TN 6/30/1939 s Royce Edward Burks & Willa. BS Austin Peay St U 1960; MDiv STUSo 1971. D 7/5/1971 Bp William Evan Sanders P 5/1/1972 Bp John Vander Horst. m 12/21/1969 Janice Ann Walker c 1. R Gr Ch Oak Pk IL 1989-1993; R S Mary's Epis Ch Middlesboro KY 1977-1989; D S Ptr's Ch Chattanooga TN 1971-1972. billburks19@gmail.com

BURLEIGH, Judith Cushing (Me) PO Box 8, Presque Isle ME 04769 **D Aroostook Epis Cluster Caribou ME 2007-; D S Jn's Ch Presque Isle ME 2007-** B Presque Isle ME 3/24/1934 d Parker Prescott Burleigh & Mamie Washburn. BA Wellesley Coll 1956; MEd Harv 1957; PhD U of Connecticut 1966. D 8/4/2007 Bp Chilton Abbie Richardson Knudsen. jcushlei@mfx.net

BURLEY, Aloysius Englebert John Timothy (Minn) 615 W Tanglewood Dr, Arlington Heights IL 60004 B Ada MN 12/10/1928 s Andrew Englebert Burley & Philomene Ann Catherine. BA; BA. Rec from Roman Catholic 12/1/1973. m 5/15/1965 Gisela E Burley.

BURLEY III, Clarence Augustus (ECR) 651 Broadway, Gilroy CA 95020 **S Steph's Ch Gilroy CA 2007-** B Evanston IL 12/15/1947 s Clarence Augustus Burley & Shirley. BA Claremont Coll 1970; MDiv CDSP 1977. D 6/25/1977 Bp C Kilmer Myers P 11/1/1978 Bp Hanford Langdon King Jr. c 2. S Paul's Epis Ch Salinas CA 2006-2007; S Barn Ch Arroyo Grande CA 2005-2006; S Clare's Epis Ch Pleasanton CA 2004; S Lk's Ch Bakersfield CA 1990-2001; Int S Mich's Epis Par Ridgecrest CA 1990; S Mk's Epis Ch Idaho Falls ID 1988-1989; Dio Idaho Boise ID 1986-1989; Int S Jas Ch Burley ID 1986-1989; Int St Matthews Epis Ch Rupert ID 1986-1989; Int S Jn's Ch Powell WY 1981-1982; Int S Alb's Ch Worland WY 1980-1981; S Andr's Ch Basin WY 1979-1980; Assoc Ch Of The Ascen Twin Falls ID 1978-1979; Asst S Mich's Cathd Boise ID 1977-1978. revcab@aol.com

BURLEY, John David (SC) 440 Whilden St., Mt Pleasant SC 29464 **S Andr's Ch Mt Pleasant SC 2003-** B Columbia SC 6/21/1953 s Charles Carroll Burley & Margaret. BS Coll of Charleston 1977; MDiv TESM 1980. D 6/6/1980 Bp Gray Temple P 12/5/1980 Bp C(hristopher) FitzSimons Allison. m 1/3/1976 Margaret Gayle Burley c 3. Galilee Epis Ch Virginia Bch VA 1993-2003; Asst The Falls Ch Epis Falls Ch VA 1982-1993; P S Barn Ch Dillon SC 1980-1982. john@samp.cc

BURLINGTON, R(obert) Craig (RI) 19 Hillcrest Dr, North Kingstown RI 02852 B Elizabeth NJ 3/1/1944 s Walter Bernard Burlington & Dorothy. BA Rutgers-The St U 1966; STB GTS 1969; STM NYTS 1975; DMin NYTS 1980; Fllshp GTS 1985. D 6/14/1969 Bp Leland Stark P 12/19/1969 Bp George E Rath. m 7/1/1967 Adelene Burlington. Dio Rhode Island Providence RI 2000-2003; Chair Stwdshp Cmsn Dio Rhode Island Providence RI 1994-1998; R S Lk's Epis Ch E Greenwich RI 1992-2010; Interfaith Holocaust Com Dio Newark Newark NJ 1980-1992; R S Geo's Epis Ch Maplewood NJ 1975-1992; Dept of Chr Soc Responsibility Dio Rhode Island Providence RI 1975-1981; CE Com Dio Newark Newark NJ 1973-1978; Assoc S Geo's Epis Ch Maplewood NJ 1969-1974. Epis Chars 2002-2004. craigdor@cox.net

BURMEISTER, Melissa Lynne (Mil) 5556 E. Colonial Oaks Dr., Monticello IN 47960 B Elmhurst IL 8/14/1962 d Marvin Dean Girtz & Veronica Ann. BS N Ill U Dekalb 1984; MDiv SWTS 1999. D 12/2/1999 Bp William Dailey Persell P 7/1/2000 Bp James Barrow Brown. m 8/17/1985 Douglas W Burmeister c 1. S Mk's Epis Ch Harvey LA 2004-2005; Zion Epis Ch Oconomowoc WI 2003; S Jn In The Wilderness Elkhorn WI 2001-2003; S Paul's Ch New Orleans LA 1999-2001. mgburmeister@comcast.net

BURNARD, Karen (SO) 25 E Walnut St, Oxford OH 45056 **R H Trin Epis Ch Oxford OH 2006-** B Columbus OH 5/2/1950 d George James Kartsimas & Katharine. BA OH SU 1972; MS U IL 1977; SWTS 1990; MDiv Trin Luth Sem 1992. D 6/22/1991 Bp William Grant Black P 6/1/1992 Bp Herbert Thompson Jr. m 6/25/1982 Robert Burnard c 1. Vic S Andr's Ch Pickerington OH 1995-2006; Trin Ch Columbus OH 1991-1995. htrector@gmail.com

✠ **BURNETT, Rt Rev Joe Goodwin** (Neb) 4 E University Pkwy, Baltimore MD 21218 **Asst Bp of Maryland Dio Maryland Baltimore MD 2011-** B Jackson MS 5/15/1948 s Marshall Emmett Burnett & Mary Julia. BA Millsaps Coll 1970; MDiv SMU 1974; DMin SMU 1985. D 6/1/1974 Bp John M Allin P 5/15/1975 Bp Duncan Montgomery Gray Jr Con 9/13/2003 for Neb. m 4/27/1996 Marty Wheeler c 3. Bp Dio Nebraska Omaha NE 2003-2011; Prof The TS at The U So Sewanee TN 1999-2003; R Trin Ch Hattiesburg MS 1991-1999; R S Ptr's By The Sea Gulfport MS 1984-1991; Vic Ch Of The Creator Clinton MS 1980-1983; Asst S Jas Ch Jackson MS 1976-1980; Cur S Jn's Epis Ch Pascagoula MS 1974-1976. Auth, "Reconsidering a Bold Proposal: Reflections, Questions, and Concerns Regarding a Theol of Cnfrmtn," *ATR*, ATR, 2006; Auth, "The Marvelous Memory Of God: Pstr And Personal Reflections On Preaching Lk," *Sewanee Theol Revs*, Sewanee Theol Revs, 2001; Auth, "Always And Everywhere: BCP 1979 & The Promise Of Liturg Evang," *w Ever Joyful Hearts*, Ch Pub Inc, 1999. ATR Bd 2005; Epis Ch Bd Archv 2006. DD GTS Jackson MS 2005. jburnett@episcopalmaryland.org

BURNETT, Joseph Goodwin (Miss) 543 Beulah Rd NE, Vienna VA 22180 **Asst R Ch Of The H Comf Vienna VA 2009-** B Jackson MS 1/23/1981 s Joe Goodwin Burnett & Barbara Wynn. BA U of Sthrn Mississippi 2006; MDiv VTS 2009. D 5/30/2009 Bp Joe Goodwin Burnett P 12/6/2009 Bp Shannon Sherwood Johnston. Dir of Yth & YA Mnstrs Trin Ch Hattiesburg MS 2003-2006. jburnett@holycomforter.com

BURNETT, Richard Alvin (SO) 125 E Broad St, Columbus OH 43215 **Dn Dio Sthrn Ohio Cincinnati OH 2000-; Dn Columbus Dnry Dio Sthrn Ohio Cincinnati OH 2000-; R Trin Ch Columbus OH 1997-** B New York NY 1/28/1957 s A W Burnett & Mary Elizabeth. BA Dickinson Coll 1978; MDiv Ya Berk 1983. D 6/11/1983 Bp John Thomas Walker P 12/17/1983 Bp James Stuart Wetmore. m 7/30/1988 Katharine Ward Burnett. Geo Mercer TS Garden City NY 1995-1997; Dioc Coun Dio Long Island Garden City NY 1991-1997; Econ Justice Com Dio Long Island Garden City NY 1990-1997; R S Jas Epis Ch S Jas NY 1990-1997; Chair Dio New York New York City NY 1987-1990; S Barth's Ch In The Highland White Plains NY 1983-1990. Auth, "The Quest For Common Lrng," Carnegie Fndt, 1981. r-burnett@trinitycolumbus.org

BURNETT, William Melbourne (Oly) 3175 Saratoga Rd, Langley WA 98260 B Seattle WA 5/5/1936 s Melbourne E Burnett & Marian C. BA U of Washington 1958; MDiv CDSP 1961. D 6/29/1961 P 6/16/1962 Bp William F Lewis. Stndg COM Dio Olympia Seattle WA 1982-1985; Dio Olympia Seattle WA 1978-1992; S Augustines In-The-Woods Epis Par Freeland WA 1969-1998; Vic S Jn's Ch Kirkland WA 1964-1968; Cur Ch Of The Ascen Seattle WA 1961-1964. Auth, "R Emer," 2001; Auth, "Strike So In Address To Read". wburnett@whidbez.com

BURNETTE, William Marc (Ala) 1930 Fairfax Dr, Florence AL 35630 B Atlanta GA 12/10/1967 s William Carlton Burnette & Suzanne. BA U of Alabama 1990; MFA U of Alabama 1994; MDiv GTS 1999. D 5/24/1999 P

11/1/1999 Bp Henry Nutt Parsley Jr. m 11/25/1995 Jennifer Roth c 2. R S Andrews's Epis Ch Birmingham AL 2001-2009; Trin Epis Ch Florence AL 1999-2001. canterburymarc@gmail.com

BURNHAM, Frederic Bradford (NY) 326 Dawnbrook Drive, Flat Rock NC 28731 B Cambridge MA 7/21/1938 s Bradford Hinckley Burnham & Anna. AB Harv 1960; MDIV EDS 1963; Cert U of Cambridge 1964; PhD Jn Hopkins U 1970; DD Hob 1985. D 6/12/1965 Bp Charles Bowen Persell Jr P 9/17/1967 Bp Allen Webster Brown. m 3/17/1991 Regan Church O'Connell c 2. Par of Trin Ch New York NY 1984-2003; Trin Educ Fund New York NY 1984-1994; R Memi Ch Of All Ang Twilight Pk NY 1977-1989; Asst Chr Ch Detroit MI 1976-1978. Auth, "Links: Establishing Communities Of Dialogueon Campuses," *Educational As Transformation*, Lang, 2000; Auth, "Chaos: A New Theol," *Mundi Medicina*, 1992; Auth, "Horizons In Biblic Theol," *Maker Of Heaven & Earth: A Perspective Of Contemporary Sci*, 1990; Ed, "Postmodern Theol: Chr Faith In A Pluralist Wrld," Harper, 1989; Ed, "Love: The Fndt Of Hope," Harper, 1988; Auth, "The Bible & Contemporary Sci," *Rel & Intellectual Life*. AAR; Soc For Values In Higher Educ. fbburnham21@gmail.com

BURNHAM, Karen Lee (Colo) 2029 Pine St, Pueblo CO 81004 B Cortland NY 3/27/1947 d Carl Malcolm Burnham & Alice. BA Wheaton Coll 1969. D 11/11/2000 Bp William Jerry Winterrowd. D S Andr's Ch Manitou Sprg CO 2000-2006. No Amer Assn on the Diac (NAAD) 2000-2008. kburnham2000@yahoo.com

BURNS, A(nn) Lyn (Colo) PO Box 635, La Veta CO 81055 **Mem of Stndg Com Dio Colorado Denver CO 2011-; P-in-c Par Ch Of S Chas The Mtyr Ft Morgan CO 2011-** B Pretoria South Africa 2/12/1950 d Herbert Bernard Horrell & Evelyn Jessie Welsh Schultz. BA U of Witwatersrand 1972; M. Div VTS 2006. D 6/10/2006 P 12/18/2006 Bp Robert John O'Neill. c 2. Vic S Ben Epis Ch La Veta CO 2007-2010. lyn@in2l.com

BURNS, Deborah Stanbrough (Kan) 3021 Steven Dr, Lawrence KS 66049 B St Louis MO 2/28/1952 d Raymond Arthur Stansbrough & Ruth Evelyn. BD U of Kansas 1998. D 12/22/2001 Bp William Edward Smalley. m 5/31/1975 Garth Burns c 1. deboreil@aol.com

BURNS, Duncan Adam (NY) 209 Albany Ave, Kingston NY 12401 **R S Jn's Epis Ch Kingston NY 2005-** B Bay Shore NY 8/27/1957 Econ Colg 1979; M-Div SWTS 2003. D 6/28/2003 Bp Alan Scarfe P 7/1/2004 Bp DM Tutu. m 7/17/1982 Barbara McCartney c 3. Chr Ch Alexandria VA 2003-2005. dbu626@yahoo.com

BURNS, Jacquelyn Mae (SO) St John's Episcopal Church, 700 High St, Worthington OH 43085 B Indianapolis IN 12/5/1947 d Jack Llewellyn & Dolores Mae. D 6/23/2007 Bp Kenneth Lester Price. c 4. jaslan@columbus.rr.com

BURNS, James Karl (SC) 1306 Grove Park Dr, Charleson SC 29414 **All SS Ch Florence SC 2011-** B Atlanta GA 1/29/1961 s Samuel Mitchell Burns & Cynthia. BS U of So Dakota; MDiv Nash 2007. D 6/6/2007 P 12/2/2007 Bp Edward Lloyd Salmon Jr. m 8/7/1982 Susan Burns c 2. Cur Old S Andr's Par Ch Charleston SC 2007-2009; Porter-Gaud Sch Charleston SC 2007-2009. susanandkarl@comcast.net

BURNS, James Lee (NY) 111 Hunt Road, Hillsdale NY 12529 **R Ch Of The Heav Rest New York NY 1996-** B Indianapolis IN 6/10/1946 s David Vawter Burns & Jessie. BA Mia 1968; MS U of Idaho Moscow 1972; MDiv STUSo 1982. D 6/27/1982 Bp William F Gates Jr P 1/5/1983 Bp William Evan Sanders. m 5/7/1976 Nancy Diane VanderNaald c 2. Dn Chr Ch Cathd Lexington KY 1988-1996; R S Thos Epis Ch Knoxville TN 1987-1988; Vic S Thos Epis Ch Knoxville TN 1982-1987. Auth, *The Bible and Episcopalians*, Forw Mvmt. jlbged@gmail.com

BURNS, Jerome Wilson (SO) 6130 Gioffre Woods Ln, Columbus OH 43232 **R S Phil's Ch Columbus OH 2002-** B Jackson MS 11/29/1944 s Emmitt Burns & Clara. BA Jackson St U 1966; JD Sthrn U Baton Rouge LA 1975; MDiv VTS 1978. D 6/22/1978 P 5/1/1979 Bp Duncan Montgomery Gray Jr. m 6/5/1976 Carol Byrd c 1. Ch Of The H Cross Pittsburgh PA 1993-2002; R S Steph's Ch Petersburg VA 1986-1993; Asst S Jas Epis Ch Houston TX 1983-1986; Vic Ch Of The Resurr Houston TX 1982-1983; S Mary's Ch Vicksburg MS 1978-1982. jburn35121@aol.com

BURNS JR, Jervis Oliver (Miss) 204 Donnybrook Dr, Carriere MS 39426 B New Orleans LA 10/18/1942 s Jervis Oliver Burns & Mary Lou. BA Tul 1964; MDiv SWTS 1968; Command and Gnrl Stff Coll 1995. D 6/25/1968 Bp Girault M Jones P 5/1/1969 Bp Iveson Batchelor Noland. m 8/1/1964 Susan Barrow Dunlap c 2. S Fran Cmnty Serv Inc. Salina KS 2002-2004; Hon Cn Dio Louisiana Baton Rouge LA 1997-2004; Epis Black Belt Mnstry Demopolis AL 1996-2001; S Mich's (Faunsdale) Faunsdale AL 1996-2001; S Mich's Ch Faunsdale AL 1996-2001; R Trin Ch Demopolis AL 1996-2001; S Wilfrid's Ch Marion AL 1996-1997; Dio Louisiana Baton Rouge LA 1993-1996; S Paul's Ch Greensboro AL 1984-1993; R S Matt's Epis Ch Houma LA 1975-1985; Vic Leonidas Polk Memi Epis Mssn Leesville LA 1971-1975; R Trin Epis Ch Deridder LA 1971-1975; Int S Ptr's By The Sea Gulfport MS 1969-1971; D S Paul's Ch Winnfield LA 1968-1969; Cur Trin Epis Ch Natchitoches LA 1968-1969. CODE 1985-1996. jervisb@bellsouth.net

BURNS, Leonetta Faye (Me) 52 Dondero Rd, Chelsea ME 04330 **Com on Indn Relatns, Chair Dio Maine Portland ME 2010-; D S Giles Ch Jefferson ME 2004-** B Augusta ME 9/2/1945 d Warren William Winter & Evelyn Louise. AA U of Maine 1981. D 6/19/2004 Bp Chilton Abbie Richardson Knudsen. m 6/3/1967 Robert Scottie Burns c 3. lwbdidache@aol.com

BURNS JR, Richard Joseph (Fla) 408 N Manila Ave, Perry FL 32347 **Died 4/18/2011** B Saint Louis MO 9/21/1934 s Richard Joseph Burns & Evelyn Lelia. BA U of Missouri 1956; STB EDS 1959. D 6/13/1959 P 12/21/1959 Bp George Leslie Cadigan. Auth, "arts," *Grassroots*. padre@fairpoint.net

BURNS, Thomas Dale (NwT) 3402 W Ohio Ave, Midland TX 79703 **D S Nich' Epis Ch Midland TX 2009-** B Huron SD 8/11/1948 D 10/27/2002 Bp C(harles) Wallis Ohl. m 12/9/1988 Gwendolyn Rae Beeler. D Ch Of The H Trin Midland TX 2002-2009. tburns@apex2000.net

BURR, John Terry (Roch) 594 Stearns Rd, Churchville NY 14428 **D S Lk And S Simon Cyrene Rochester NY 1969-** B Springfield OH 3/27/1932 s Irving Wingate Burr & Priscilla. BA Gri; PhD Pur. D 4/30/1968 Bp George West Barrett. m 4/24/1993 Antoinette Marie Bradford c 2. Asst S Lk's Ch Brockport NY 1968-1973. Auth, "Var Sci Papers". johnburr@frontiernet.net

BURR, Whitney Haight (Mass) 175 Shane Dr, Chatham MA 02633 B New York NY 12/13/1943 s Vernon Cobb Burr & Elizabeth. BS Bos 1967; MDiv Ya Berk 1971. D 6/5/1971 P 12/18/1971 Bp Horace W B Donegan. m 4/12/1969 Leslie Ellen Meyer c 2. Dioc Coun Dio Massachusetts Boston MA 1990-1995; Stndg Com Dio Massachusetts Boston MA 1988-2002; R S Chris's Ch Chatham MA 1982-2001; Consult Dio Massachusetts Boston MA 1979-2009; R Trin Epis Ch Wrentham MA 1977-1981; Asst S Mary's Epis Ch Barnstable MA 1973-1977; Vic S Paul's Ch Westbrook CT 1971-1973. wlburr@verizon.net

✠ **BURRILL, Rt Rev William George** (Az) 10776 E Caribbean Ln, Scottsdale AZ 85255 **All SS Ch Phoenix AZ 2000-; Asstg Bp of Arizona Dio Arizona Phoenix AZ 2000-** B New York NY 4/17/1934 s Gerald Francis Burrill & Elna Jean. BA U So 1955; STB GTS 1959; DD GTS 1985. D 6/20/1959 P 12/1/1959 Bp Charles L Street Con 4/26/1984 for Roch. c 4. Trst The GTS New York NY 1986-1999; Bp Dio Rochester Rochester NY 1984-1999; Archd Dio Nthrn California Sacramento CA 1981-1984; Dio Nthrn California Sacramento CA 1978-1984; COM Dio Nthrn California Sacramento CA 1971-1983; Stndg Com Dio Nthrn California Sacramento CA 1969-1980; Dn Sacramento Dnry Dio Nthrn California Sacramento CA 1966-1967; Ch Of S Mart Davis CA 1962-1982; Cur S Jn The Evang Ch Elkhart IN 1959-1962. Auth, *Var arts in Rel Journ*. kburrill@earthlink.net

BURRIS, Richard R (Okla) 900 Schulze Dr., Norman OK 73071 B Sheridan WY 5/4/1948 s Ralph Wesley Burris & Julia Brooks. BS Linfield Coll 1970; MDiv Nash 1987. D 5/30/1987 Bp Charles Jones III P 12/19/1987 Bp James Daniel Warner. m 5/18/1970 Carmelita Maxine Bare c 2. Contrllr Dio Oklahoma Oklahoma City OK 2004-2009; Chair Liturg Cmsn Dio Oklahoma Oklahoma City OK 1996-2001; R S Mich's Epis Ch Norman OK 1992-2004; R Ch Of The H Apos Mitchell NE 1987-1992. rrburris@swbell.net

BURROUGHS, Joseph Parker (Md) 7236 Gaither Rd, Sykesville MD 21784 B Wadesboro NC 6/3/1933 s Robert Clyde Burroughs & Margaret Grace. BA Davidson Coll 1955; STB EDS 1958. D 6/29/1958 Bp Edwin A Penick P 6/24/1959 Bp Richard Henry Baker. R S Barn Epis Ch Sykesville MD 1978-1998; R St Martins Ch Triangle VA 1967-1978; Asst S Paul's Ch Richmond VA 1961-1967; R S Andr's By The Sea Nags Hd NC 1960-1961.

BURROWS JR, Henry Cragin (NY) Clam Harbour, Rr 1, Lake Charlotte B0J 1Y0 Canada **Died 11/28/2010** B Newton MA 8/2/1923 s Henry Cragin Burrows & Cecile Courtney. BA Ob 1949; Schlr Gr 1951; Harv 1953. D 7/4/1959 Bp James P De Wolfe P 1/1/1960 Bp Charles Alfred Voegeli. Auth, "Messe Haitienne".

BURROWS, Judith Dawson (WNY) 4289 Harris Hill Rd, Williamsville NY 14221 B Syracuse NY 4/28/1940 d Charles Chester Dawson & (Mary) Jean. BA U Roch 1962; MDiv EDS 1965; MA U Cinc 1974. D 6/4/1977 P 4/8/1978 Bp Harold B Robinson. c 2. R S Paul's Epis Ch Harris Hill Williamsville NY 1986-2006; R S Mart In The Fields Grand Island NY 1981-1986; P-in-c S Mart In The Fields Grand Island NY 1977-1980. SCHC 1977. Phi Beta Kappa U Roch Rochester NY 1962; Ab w High hon U Roch Rochester NY 1962. jburrows@saviorpc.com

BURROWS, Paul Anthony (Cal) 162 Hickory St, San Francisco CA 94102 **R Ch Of The Adv Of Chr The King San Francisco CA 2001-** B Harpenden Hertfordshire UK 5/8/1955 s Reginald Harry Burrows & Vera Winifred. BA U of Nottingham 1977; Oxf 1979; STM GTS 1988. Trans from Church Of England 6/20/1986 Bp George Phelps Mellick Belshaw. m 7/11/2008 Michael Barlowe. R S Mk's Epis Ch Des Moines IA 1996-2001; Cn The Cathd Ch Of S Paul Des Moines IA 1996-2001; R S Barn Epis Ch Temple Hills MD 1990-1995; Vic S Lk And All SS' Ch Un NJ 1985-1990. CBS 1984; Oblate Ord of S Ben 1980. paulanthonyburrows@gmail.com

BURROWS III, William Russell (NwPa) 1972 Countess Ct, Naples FL 34110 **Died 2/10/2011** B Schenectady NY 1/23/1931 s William Russell Burrows &

Alice Earl. BA Wms 1953. D 11/29/1992 P 12/4/1993 Bp Robert Deane Rowley Jr. c 1. wwrrbb33@aol.com

BURSON, Grace Pritchard (NH) 106 Lowell St, Manchester NH 03101 **Ch Of The H Sprt Plymouth NH 2011-; Cur Gr Ch Manchester NH 2008-** B New Haven CT 12/8/1978 d Arnold Jan Pritchard & Gretchen Wolff. BA Wms 2000; MDiv Ya Berk 2004. D 6/14/2008 Bp Andrew Donnan Smith P 1/17/2009 Bp V Gene Robinson. m 6/22/2002 Joshua R Burson c 2. holyspiritrector@gmail.com

BURT III, Augustus Moody (WA) 4010 Fearrington Post, Pittsboro NC 27312 B Greensboro NC 7/25/1935 s Augustus Moody Burt & Ruby. BA W&L 1956; MDiv VTS 1959. D 9/27/1959 P 4/1/1960 Bp Richard Henry Baker. m 6/14/1980 Catharine Louise Wilson c 1. R S Andr's Epis Ch Coll Pk MD 1973-1997; Assoc Min S Geo's Epis Ch Arlington VA 1969-1973; R The Epis Ch Of Gd Shpd Asheboro NC 1964-1969; Cur Chr Epis Ch Raleigh NC 1961-1964; P-in-c Chr Ch Walnut Cove NC 1959-1961; P-in-c Ch Of The Mssh Mayodan NC 1959-1961. catharineburt@gmail.com

BURT, Donald Vernon (Colo) 2425 Colorado Ave, Boulder CO 80302 B Cleveland OH 9/10/1943 s Harry Donald Burt & Valley Virginia. D 11/14/2009 Bp Robert John O'Neill. m 1/15/1982 Barbara Canobell c 2. dburt@probita.com

BURT, William R (Md) 114 N Union Ave, Havre de Grace MD 21078 **R S Jn's Ch Havre De Gr MD 2010-** B Newark, NJ 2/17/1952 s William R Burt & Jemima Joan. BSc CUNY 1996; MDiv U of Trin 2007. Trans from Anglican Church of Canada 6/16/2010 as Priest Bp John Leslie Rabb. revpipes@gmail.com

BURTENSHAW, Noel C (At) 2813 Greenhouse Pkwy, Alpharetta GA 30022 **R S Aid's Epis Ch Milton GA 1994-** B Dublin IE 12/12/1936 s Frederick Burtenshaw & Christina. BA All Hallows Coll 1960; MDiv All Hallows Coll 1962. Rec from Roman Catholic 12/1/1993 as Priest Bp Frank Kellogg Allan. c 1. S Aid's Epis Ch Milton GA 1995-2003; S Dav's Ch Roswell GA 1994. rectornoel@comcast.net

BURTON, Anthony John (Dal) 3966 McKinney Ave, Dallas TX 75204 **R Ch Of The Incarn Dallas TX 2008-** B 8/11/1959 s Peter Michael Burton & Rachel Wood. BA Trin 1983; Grad Wk U of King's Coll Halifax NS CA 1985; BA U of Oxford 1987; MA U of Oxford 1992. Trans from Anglican Church of Canada 10/10/2008 Bp James Monte Stanton. m 4/8/1989 Anna Kristine Erickson c 2. aburton@incarnation.org

BURTON, Bob (Az) 9502 W. Hutton Drive, Sun City AZ 85351 **R All SS Of The Desert Epis Ch Sun City AZ 2009-** B Eugene OR 4/17/1949 s Harry Robert Burton & Phyllis A. BA Albion Coll 1971; MDiv CDSP 1974. D 6/15/1974 P 4/20/1975 Bp Robert C Rusack. m 12/8/1998 Anne Marie Macmurdo c 2. R S Paul's Epis Ch Salem OR 2005-2009; S Lk The Physcn Miami FL 1999-2005; S Jn's Epis Ch Sonora TX 1998-1999; S Mk The Evang Ft Lauderdale FL 1998-1999; S Jas Epis Ch Baton Rouge LA 1991-1998; S Jas Epis Ch Ft McKavett TX 1991-1998; S Aug's Ch Ft Smith AR 1987-1991; S Jn's Epis Ch Ft Smith AR 1984-1991; R S Marg's Epis Ch Palm Desert CA 1978-1983; Asst Chr Ch Coronado CA 1976-1978; Assoc S Edm's Par San Marino CA 1974-1976. bbrtn@cs.com

BURTON, Cassandra (WA) Christ Episcopal Church, 8710 Old Branch Ave., Clinton MD 20735 **R Chr Epis Ch Clinton MD 2010-** B East Oarange NJ 1/31/1945 d William Rolos Mateo & Gwendolyn Rogers. BA U Of Baltimore Baltimore MD 1979; MDiv VTS 2007. D 6/16/2007 Bp Peter James Lee P 12/18/2007 Bp Shannon Sherwood Johnston. m 6/2/1979 Malachi Burton c 3. Asst S Lk's Ch Washington DC 2007-2009. revcassandra@comcast.net

BURTON, Frank Alan (NY) 309 Bennett'S Farm Road, Ridgefield NJ 06877 B Montreal PQ CA 7/25/1929 s Arthur John Burton & Gladys Eva. LMFT Nj; BA Sir Geo Wms Montreal Qc CA 1951; MDiv McGill U 1956; Amer Fndt of Rel & Psych 1965; Cert Int Mnstry Prog 1977; Cgp Grp Psych 1994. Trans from Anglican Church of Canada 3/8/1966 Bp Horace W B Donegan. m 9/19/1998 Theodora Burton. Chr Ch Patterson NY 2000-2002; Int S Jas' Ch Goshen NY 1999-2000; Int S Alb's Epis Ch Staten Island NY 1997-1999; P-in-c Chr Ch New Brighton Staten Island NY 1996-1997; Gr Epis Ch Plainfield NJ 1982; Supvsr Pstr Care Par of Trin Ch New York NY 1962-1969. Agpa, Conf Fac 1996; Amer Assn Of Monotone Therapists, Supvsr 1978; AAPC 1973; Amer Grp Psych Assn, Clinician 1993; Cntr For Advancement Grp Ther, Fndr 1984. fbcgpmft@aol.com

BURTON, Jack C(alvin) (SO) Norton Orchard Rd, PO Box 5195, Edgartown MA 02539 **Ch Pension Fund Benefici New York NY 2005-** B Saint Louis MO 4/29/1936 s Henry Imkamp Burton & Lorine Pearl. BS Washington U 1959; MDiv EDS 1963. D 6/15/1963 P 12/22/1963 Bp Roger W Blanchard. c 3. R S Jn's Epis Ch Cambridge OH 1968-1972; Asst S Mk's Epis Ch Columbus OH 1965-1968; Asst S Tim's Epis Ch Cincinnati OH 1963-1965. Auth, "Article," *Chld's Commision*, Comm/Living Ch, 1970. jackcburton@verizon.net

BURTON, James Michael (SC) 126 Taylor Cir, Goose Creek SC 29445 B Greenville SC 1/25/1939 s T Edgar Burton & Mary Lou. BA S Mary Coll Leavenworth KS 1961; MA CUA 1965. Rec from Roman Catholic 1/1/1995 as Priest Bp Edward Lloyd Salmon Jr. m 6/23/1984 Patricia Fosberry c 1. Vic Ch Of The H Fam Moncks Corner SC 1996-2002; Dio So Carolina Charleston SC 1995-2002; S Steph's Ch S Steph SC 1995-1996.

BURTON, JOHN DRYDEN (Ark) 807 COUNTY ROAD 102, EUREKA SPRINGS AR 72632 **Asst S Jas Ch Eureka Sprg AR 2007-** B Waco TX 1/20/1942 s William Dryden Burton & Frances Elizabeth. BS Texas A&M U Coll Sta TX 1963; MS Baylor U 1968; Truett TS 2000. D 12/10/2006 Bp Larry Earl Maze P 8/12/2007 Bp Larry R Benfield. m 12/24/1992 Gloria Belcher c 3. frjohndb@gmail.com

BURTON, John L (Ct) 100 Mullen Hill Rd, Windham CT 06280 **Vic S Paul's Ch Windham CT 2006-** B Chicago IL 5/13/1956 BA Bard Coll 1978; DAS Ya Berk 2004; MDiv Ya Berk 2004. D 6/12/2004 Bp Andrew Donnan Smith P 12/18/2004 Bp James Elliot Curry. m 5/15/1999 Kaice Burton c 2. Cur S Mary's Epis Ch Manchester CT 2004-2006. windham.vicar@yahoo.com

BURTON, John Peter (Chi) 4839 W Howard, Skokie IL 60076 **S Richard's Ch Chicago IL 2004-** B Vienna Austria 8/29/1922 s Alfred Burton & Elfriede. SWTS 1985. D 5/23/1970 Bp Gerald Francis Burrill P 7/1/1985 Bp James Winchester Montgomery. m 5/2/1950 Leonora Gordon c 2. Asst H Trin Ch Skokie IL 1970-1993. S Geo Medal.

BURTON, Kenneth William Fowler (Colo) 472 Crystal Hills Blvd, Manitou Springs CO 80829 B Manchester UK 1/19/1928 s Harold Fowler Burton & Sarah. BA U of Cambridge 1948; MA U of Cambridge 1952. D 7/14/1974 Bp Edwin B Thayer P 11/1/1974 Bp William Carl Frey. m 8/4/1950 Mary Bailey. Chr Ch Cn City CO 1992; Gr And S Steph's Epis Ch Colorado Sprg CO 1988-1992; Ch Of Our Sav Colorado Sprg CO 1987-1988.

BURTON, Perry Cooper (Ky) PO Box 397, Flat Rock NC 28731 **Died 5/8/2010** B Nashville TN 10/30/1928 s Spickard Perry Burton & Lucia Denny. BA U So 1950; MDiv VTS 1954. D 6/22/1954 P 12/1/1954 Bp Chilton Powell. c 4. pcburton@webtv.net

BURTON-EDWARDS, Grace (Ind) 3243 N Meridian St, Indianapolis IN 46208 **Cnvnr Global Missions Cmsn Dio Indianapolis Indianapolis IN 2011-; Alt Dep GC Dio Indianapolis Indianapolis IN 2010-2012; Assoc R and Sch Chaplian Trin Ch Indianapolis IN 2007-** B Raleigh NC 3/27/1967 d Robert Henry Burton & Lydia Jane. BA Mississippi Coll 1989; MDiv Chr TS 1993; DMin SWTS 2005. D 1/28/2007 P 11/18/2007 Bp Catherine Elizabeth Maples Waynick. m 1/6/1991 Taylor Edwards c 2. St. Richard's Sch Chapl Trin Ch Indianapolis IN 2005-2007; DCE S Matt's Ch Indianapolis IN 2004-2007. Auth, "The Screen of Common Pryr: Using Visual Media Tech in Epis Liturg," *Seabury DMin thesis*, Seabury-Wstrn, 2005; Writer/Ed, "Bookmarks Yth Curric," *Bookmarks*, Judson Press, 2000; Writer, "Intersection Yth Curric," *Intersection*, Smyth and Helwys, 1993. Pstr Fllshp Wabash Coll 2010. gburtonedwards@juno.com

BURTS, Ann Horton (Md) 1070 Foxcroft Run, Annapolis MD 21401 **Int S Lk's Ch Annapolis MD 2011-** B Chicago IL 8/10/1944 d James Everett Horton & Honora. BA Duke 1966; MA Duke 1968; MDiv Duke 1993; CAS GTS 1994. D 5/11/1994 Bp Robert Whitridge Estill P 5/1/1995 Bp Charles Lindsay Longest. m 5/28/1967 Richard Burts c 2. Int S Johns Epis Ch Wake Forest NC 2009-2010; S Jn's Ch Mt Washington Baltimore MD 2008-2009; S Dav's Ch Baltimore MD 2008; Int All Hallows Par So River Davidsonville MD 2006-2007; Pstr Assoc S Anne's Par Annapolis MD 1994-2006. Soc of S Marg. annburts@earthlink.net

BURWELL, John Beckett (SC) 24 Edgewater Aly, Isle Of Palms SC 29451 **Ch Of The H Cross Sullivans Island SC 1987-** B Dunn NC 9/6/1951 s Edward Langworthy Burwell & Ruth. BA U of So Carolina 1973; MDiv TESM 1984. D 6/14/1984 P 5/1/1985 Bp C(hristopher) FitzSimons Allison. m 9/18/1976 Sylvia Marie Fender. Assoc R Ch Of The Redeem Orangeburg SC 1984-1987.

BUSCH, Edward L (SanD) 11650 Calle Paracho, San Diego CA 92128 **Asst S Tim's Ch San Diego CA 2009-** B Chicago IL 8/16/1930 s Morris Ralph Busch & Rose. BS U IL 1951; MD U IL 1955; 1980 Angl TS (Dallas, TX) 1980. D 6/20/1981 P 6/1/1982 Bp A Donald Davies. m 2/26/1994 Babs Marie Meairs c 3. Vic S Columba's Epis Ch Santee CA 2001-2008; Asst Epis Ch Of The Redeem Irving TX 1997-2000; Asst Ch Of The Gd Shpd Cedar Hill TX 1995-1997; R S Chris's Ch And Sch Ft Worth TX 1987-1992; Cur Ch Of The H Apos Aledo TX 1983-1987; Cur S Chris's Ch And Sch Ft Worth TX 1981-1983. edwbus@hotmail.com

BUSCH, Glenn Edward (NC) 3024 Cardinal Pl, Lynchburg VA 24503 B Kissimmee FL 11/14/1945 s Russell Walter Busch & Sarah Jane. BA Penn 1967; MDiv VTS 1971; DMin UTS 1974. D 5/22/1971 P 12/11/1971 Bp Robert Bracewell Appleyard. m 6/13/1970 Kathleen Gayle Cooney c 2. S Mary's Epis Ch High Point NC 2000-2007; Pres Stndg Com Dio No Carolina Raleigh NC 1990-1991; Dn - Greensboro Convoc Dio No Carolina Raleigh NC 1986-1988; Dioc Coun Dio No Carolina Raleigh NC 1984-1986; R S Jn's Ch Bedford VA 1975-1981; Asst S Steph's Ch Richmond VA 1971-1975. Auth, "101 Things You Didn't Know About Judas," Adams Media, 2007; Auth, "Portraits of the Div Presence," *Portraits of the Div Presence*, St. Mary's Ch Press, 2007; Auth, "Of Doves and Serpents," *Epis Life*, Dom and Frgn Mssy Soc, 2005; Auth, "Filling our Empty Nets: Encouraging," St. Mary's Ch Press, 1999; Auth, "Talking to the Devil," *PreachingThrough the Year of Mk*, Morehouse, 1999;

Auth, "Look into my Eyes," *Lectionary Homil*, Lectionary Homil, 1997; Auth, "Somthing to Cling to," *The Communicant*, Dio No Carolina, 1997; Auth, "A Tale of Two Tables," *Sermons That Wk V*, Forw Mvmt, 1995; Auth, "Filling Our Empty Nets," *Sermons That Wk III*, Forw Mvmt, 1993. AAPC 1981-2008. Sermon Competition Epis Evang Fndt 1995; Sermon Competition Epis Evang Fndt 1993; S Geo Epis Awd 1987. glenn.busch@gmail.com

BUSCH, Richard Alan (Los) 4125 36th St S, Arlington VA 22206 B New York NY 10/27/1932 s Richard Busch & Helen. BA W&L 1954; BD Ya 1959; Ripon Hall Theol Coll 1960; PhD Claremont TS 1975. D 9/14/1959 Bp Theodore N Barth P 6/3/1960 Bp John Vander Horst. m 3/4/1972 Lewise Langston c 2. Prof VTS Alexandria VA 1976-1999; Asst H Faith Par Inglewood CA 1970-1974; R S Paul's Epis Ch Tustin CA 1967-1970; Asst All SS Par Beverly Hills CA 1962-1967; Asst Gr Ch Chattanooga TN 1960-1962. dickbusch@comcast.net

BUSH JR, Arnold Arlington (CGC) 1109 Bristol Way, Birmingham AL 35242 **Coordntr for Evang/Congrl Dvlpmt Prov IV 2007-** B Laurel MS 2/25/1937 s Arnold A Bush & Lillian Larue. BA Millsaps Coll 1959; MDiv STUSo 1962; VTS 1976. D 6/29/1962 P 5/22/1963 Bp Duncan Montgomery Gray. m 6/3/1960 (Margaret) Zoe Harvey c 5. Chair Ch Growth Cmsn Dio Cntrl Gulf Coast Pensacola FL 1997-2000; R S Jude's Epis Ch Niceville FL 1995-2002; Assoc R Chr Epis Ch San Antonio TX 1990-1995; Vic S Ptr's By The Lake Brandon MS 1981-1990; Dio Georgia Savannah GA 1975-1983; R S Anne's Ch Tifton GA 1972-1981; Vic S Eliz's Epis Ch Jacksonville FL 1968-1972; Vic S Fran Of Assisi Gulf Breeze FL 1964-1968; Vic Dio Mississippi Jackson MS 1962-1990; Vic Ch Of The Redeem Brookhaven MS 1962-1964. Auth, "Faith Growing," FA Org. FA 1970. Liberty Bell Awd Tift Cnty Bar Tift Cnty 1980. revaab@earthlink.net

BUSH, Emilie Chaudron (Los) St. Paul's, PO Box 726, Barstow CA 92312 **Vic S Paul's Mssn Barstow CA 2001-** B Hawkinsville GA 4/16/1952 d Fred Ervin Howard & Rietta Winn. ETSBH; BA Tul 1974; MDiv Claremont TS 2001. D 6/9/2001 P 1/12/2002 Bp Frederick Houk Borsch. m 6/15/1974 John Lincoln Bush c 2. lilibush@gmail.com

BUSH, Frederick Judson (Miss) 5108 39th St W, Bradenton FL 34210 B Weiser ID 3/21/1917 s Homer Ellis Bush & Sada Elvira. BA Millsaps Coll 1939; BD STUSo 1950. D 12/27/1949 P 7/25/1950 Bp Duncan Montgomery Gray. m 11/25/1989 Margaret Ruth Taylor c 1. CDO Dio Mississippi Jackson MS 1971-1984; Cn to the Ordnry Dio Mississippi Jackson MS 1967-1984; Archd Dio Mississippi Jackson MS 1965-1967; R S Phil's Ch Jackson MS 1962-1965; Secy Dio Mississippi Jackson MS 1958-1985; Dep GC Dio Mississippi Jackson MS 1958-1982; R S Jas Ch Jackson MS 1954-1962; R Chap Of The Cross ROLLING FORK MS 1950-1954; P-in-c S Paul's Ch Hollandale MS 1950-1954. Auth, *A Hist of the Epis Ch in Dio Mississippi*, 1992; Ed, *Mnstry & Compstn*, 1975. Chairman of CODE C.O.D.E. 1973. fjbush@verizon.net

BUSH, Jack Keith (Ala) 7700 Seawall Blvd Apt 1202, Galveston TX 77551 **Died 12/21/2009** B Winter Park FL 12/17/1922 s Isaac M Bush & Annie. GD STUSo; BA U Denv. D 10/6/1960 Bp George Mosley Murray P 7/1/1961 Bp Charles C J Carpenter.

BUSH, Katherine McQuiston (WTenn) 718 Charles Place, Memphis TN 38112 **Chapl S Mary's Epis Sch Memphis TN 2010-** B Memphis TN 1/31/1975 BA Rhodes Coll 1997; MDiv VTS 2003. D 6/28/2003 P 1/10/2004 Bp Don Edward Johnson. m 11/7/1998 Stephen C Bush c 2. Assoc R Ch Of The H Comm Memphis TN 2005-2010; Cn S Mary's Cathd Memphis TN 2003-2005. Contrib, "Homiletical Essays," *Feasting on the Word, Year C, Vol 3*, Westminster Jn Knox Press, 2010. Harris Awd VTS 2003. katherinembush@gmail.com

BUSH, Patricia (SanD) 4642 Utah Street #1, San Diego CA 92116 B National City CA 1/8/1943 d Alvin Charles Bush & Audrey. BA San Diego St U 1964; MDiv Claremont TS 1983. D 11/18/1983 P 6/16/1984 Bp Charles Brinkley Morton. c 2. Vic S Eliz's Epis Ch San Diego CA 1991-1999; Dir Sch for Lay Mnstry Dio San Diego San Diego CA 1988-1990; Asst S Barth's Epis Ch Poway CA 1987-1990; Cur The Epis Ch Of S Andr Encinitas CA 1984-1986. SBL 1987-2009. pattbush43@sbcglobal.net

BUSHEE, Grant Sartori (Cal) 1225 Rosefield Way, Menlo Park CA 94025 **D S Ptr's Epis Ch Redwood City CA 2002-** B Los Angeles CA 7/25/1945 s Grant Roy Bushee & Joan Elizabeth. BS U CA 1968; MBA Stan 1974; BD Sch for Deacons 2002. D 6/1/2002 Bp William Edwin Swing. m 9/28/1968 Jean Marie Goncalves c 1. sbushee@walt.com

BUSHEY JR, Howard Wallace (La) 8833 Goodwood Blvd, Baton Rouge LA 70806 B Temple TX 3/21/1943 s Howard Wallace Bushey & Margaret Elizabeth. BA LSU 1966; MA Webster U 1980; JD LSU 1992; MA STUSo 2000. D 12/29/1999 P 8/6/2000 Bp Charles Edward Jenkins III. m 9/16/1995 Carolyn Sue Phelps c 2. Dio Louisiana Baton Rouge LA 2010-2011; Epis Ch Of The H Sprt In Baton Rouge Baton Rouge LA 2008-2010; S Marg's Epis Ch Baton Rouge LA 2008; S Lk's Ch Baton Rouge LA 2005-2008; S Paul's/H Trin New Roads LA 2005; Mssnr Dio Louisiana Baton Rouge LA 2000-2010; R S Steph's Ch Innis LA 2000-2004; Mssnr S Mary's Ch New Roads LA 1999-2000. La Bar Assn. hbushey@att.net

BUSHNELL, Peter Emerson (Ct) Holy Trinity Church, 383 Hazard Ave., Enfield CT 06082 **H Trin Epis Ch Enfield CT 2007-** B Winsted CT 5/1/1948 s Waldo Emerson Bushnell & Helen Ruth. BA Gordon Coll 1970; MDiv PDS 1973. D 6/8/1974 P 2/24/1975 Bp Joseph Warren Hutchens. m 5/19/1973 Kathryn P Potter c 4. Exec Coun Dio Connecticut Hartford CT 2000-2006; Sr Mssnr Calv Ch Enfield CT 1993-2008; Sr Mssnr Gr Ch Broad Brook CT 1993-2008; Sr Mssnr S Andr's Epis Ch Enfield CT 1993-2008; No Cntrl Reg Mnstry Enfield CT 1993-2007; R All SS Epis Ch Meriden CT 1977-1992; Dio Connecticut Hartford CT 1977-1980; Cur Chr Ch Ansonia CT 1974-1977. pbushn8849@aol.com

BUSHONG JR, Edward S (SVa) 2806 E. Marshall St., Richmond VA 23223 B Hagerstown MD 5/12/1944 s Edward Stuart Bushong & Rachel Ann. BA U of Maryland 1966; MDiv Ya Berk 1970; MA Antioch U 1978; PhD Un Inst & U Cincinnati OH 1990. D 6/23/1970 Bp Harry Lee Doll P 3/20/1971 Bp David Keller Leighton Sr. m 8/8/1981 Martha Louise Menser. R S Jn's Ch Hopewell VA 1995-2002; R S Anne's Ch Appomattox VA 1991-1995; S Andr's-On-The-Mt Harpers Ferry WV 1988-1991; R All SS Ch Collingdale PA 1985-1988; S Andrews Sch Of Delaware Inc Middletown DE 1983-1985; Cn Mssnr Cathd Ch Of S Jn Wilmington DE 1981-1983; Dio Delaware Wilmington DE 1979-1981; Washington Co Mssn Hagerstown MD 1975-1977; Dio Maryland Baltimore MD 1970-1973. esbushongjr@gmail.com

BUSLER, George Warren (LI) P. O. Box 55, Westhampton Beach NY 11978 **Asst Ch Of The Redeem Sarasota FL 2000-** B Philadelphia PA 9/12/1938 s George Warren Busler & Kathryn. BA Ursinus Coll 1960; STB PDS 1963; Fllshp ECF 1964; STM UTS 1964; Fllshp Coll of Preachers 1973; Cert VTS 1983; DD Cumberland U 1999; Fllshp Rotary Intl 1999. D 6/8/1963 P 12/14/1963 Bp Joseph Gillespie Armstrong. m 6/23/1962 Joy Kline c 2. Prof Geo Mercer TS Garden City NY 1994-1999; Exec Com,Chairman of Med Stff Committe Dio Long Island Garden City NY 1971-1999; R S Mk's Ch Westhampton Bch NY 1966-1999. Auth, "Abortion:Theol & Expediency," 1975; Auth, "Theol & Jurisprudence," 1966; Auth, "Legal Philos of Justice Holmes," 1964. DD Degree Cumberland U 1999; Paul Harris Fell Rotary Intl 1999; STM mcl UTS New York NY 1964; STB cl PDS Philadelphia PA 1963. jkbusler@comcast.net

BUSSE, Mary Ruth (Fla) 3580 Pine St, Jacksonville FL 32205 B Saint Louis MO 9/19/1943 d George Anthony Utter & Arline Ruth. Duke 1996; Oxf 1999; VTS 1999. D 6/11/2000 P 12/10/2000 Bp Stephen Hays Jecko. c 2. Assoc Ch Of Our Sav Jacksonville FL 2008; Assoc R The Epis Ch Of S Ptr And S Paul Marietta GA 2001-2005; Int S Jn's Cathd Jacksonville FL 2000-2001. busse.mary@comcast.net

BUSTARD-BURNSIDE, Carol (Md) 1106 Woodheights Ave, Baltimore MD 21211 B Memphis TN 11/2/1955 d Wade Walker Burnside & Sarah. BA U of Arkansas 1979; MDiv EDS 1992. D 6/6/1992 Bp Jack Marston McKelvey P 12/12/1992 Bp John Shelby Spong. m Barbara Bustard-Burnside. Ch Of The Ascen Baltimore MD 2006-2010; S Alb's Epis Ch Glen Burnie MD 2004-2005; R S Mary's Epis Ch Woodlawn Baltimore MD 1999-2003; S Mk's Ch W Orange NJ 1994-1999; Assoc R S Jas Ch Upper Montclair NJ 1992-1993. Newark Cler Assn. shinyredtruck@msn.com

BUSTRIN, Robert C (Az) 118 Lafayette Ave, Brooklyn NY 11217 **Vic S Mary's Epis Ch Phoenix AZ 2010-** B Phoenix AZ 7/13/1953 s James Harold Bustrin & Mary Louise. BA Arizona St U 1975; MDiv SWTS 1979. D 6/10/1979 Bp J(ohn) Joseph Meakins Harte P 1/1/1980 Bp Charles Bennison. Asst P S Mich's Ch New York NY 1986-2000; Asst H Trin Ch Gainesville FL 1982-1984; Cur S Lk's Par Kalamazoo MI 1979-1982. Soc Of S Jn The Evang. CRAIGPLUS@MAC.COM

BUTCHER, Geoffrey (Ky) 607 5th Ave W, Springfield TN 37172 **P-in-c Trin Ch Russellville KY 2010-** B Orange NJ 4/18/1941 s Harold Butcher & Elizabeth. RSCM; BA Hob 1961; MDiv GTS 1965; MA New Mex Highlands U 1970; DMin McCormick TS 1979. D 5/7/1965 P 4/2/1966 Bp C J Kinsolving III. c 2. Cn Chr Ch Cathd Nashville TN 1997-2010; Assoc for Pstr Care Chr Ch Cathd Nashville TN 1992-1997; Cn S Jn's Cathd Albuquerque NM 1968-1992; Vic H Trin Epis Ch - Mssn Raton NM 1966-1968; P-in-c S Paul's/Peace Ch Las Vegas NM 1966-1968; Cur S Andr's Epis Ch Las Cruces NM 1965-1966. revgbutcher@gmail.com

BUTCHER, Gerald Alfred (Okla) 1720 W Carolina Ave, Chickasha OK 73018 **D S Lk's Ch Chickasha OK 2002-** B Ponca City OK 10/10/1955 s Clarence Amanual Butcher & Reva Catherine. BS Oklahoma St U 1977. D 6/22/2002 Bp Robert Manning Moody. m 8/13/1977 Debra Ann Stotts.

BUTCHER, James Thaddeus (Mil) 135 Rockwell St, Oconomowoc WI 53066 B Chippewa Falls WI 10/3/1954 s James William Butcher & Lorraine Elanora. BA U of Montana 1976; MDiv Nash 1980. D 6/29/1980 P 1/1/1981 Bp Jackson Earle Gilliam. m 8/21/1976 Lori Melnarik c 1. Zion Epis Ch Oconomowoc WI 2003-2010; R S Jn's Ch Butte MT 1987-2003; S Pat's Epis Ch Bigfork MT 1981-1987; Dio Montana Helena MT 1980. NOEL. TLBUTCHER@MSN.COM

BUTCHER, John Beverley (Cal) 228 Hedge Road, Menlo Park CA 94025 **Died 6/18/2011** B New York NY 11/3/1936 s Harold Butcher & Elizabeth. BA Harv

1957; MDiv Ya Berk 1960. D 6/13/1960 Bp Walter H Gray P 12/11/1960 Bp Arthur Kinsolving. c 1. Auth, "An Uncommon Lectionary," Polebridge Press, 2002; Auth, "Telling The Untold Stories," Trin Press Intl , 2000; Auth, "The Tao of Jesus," Harper San Francisco, 1994. Assoc Fell Jesus Seminar 1998; Fell Can Coll for Chinese Stds 1986. jbbnow@earthlink.net

BUTCHER, Kenneth P F (Colo) 3306 Morris Ave, Pueblo CO 81008 **D Ch Of The Ascen Pueblo CO 1992-** B Snodland Kent UK 11/3/1937 s Cecil Frederick Butcher & Bessie Ella. BA U Of Southampton Southhampton Gb 1960; U Of Reading Gb 1961; MA U of Nthrn Colorado 1971. D 10/24/1992 Bp William Jerry Winterrowd. m 8/11/1962 Barbara Rosemary Griffin c 1. Tchg Fac For Diac Formation Dio Colorado Denver CO 1996-2002. Auth, "Performance Pract Of 16th Century Part Bk," *Amer Choral Dir'S Journ*, 1985; Auth, "Contrib Ch Hymnal Series V," Ch Hymnal Corp., 1980. NAAD 1990. Hall Of Fame Colorado Mus Educators Assn 1999.

BUTEHORN SR, Robert Frank (Md) 5222 David Greene Rd, Cambridge MD 21613 B Baltimore MD 6/10/1930 s Frank Thomas Butehorn & Idabel E. BA U of Maryland 1952; BD STUSo 1955. D 7/8/1955 P 5/15/1956 Bp Noble C Powell. m 4/26/1975 Elinor T Bartsch. S Mary's Epis Ch Woodlawn Baltimore MD 1984-1997; R S Mk's Ch Highland MD 1959-1965; Cur Trin Ch Glen Arm MD 1955-1959.

BUTERBAUGH, Matthew L (NJ) Church of St. John the Evangelist, 189 George St., New Brunswick NJ 08901 **R S Jn The Evang Ch New Brunswick NJ 2009-** B 4/24/1980 s James Loyal Buterbaugh & Charlotte Marie. BA Oklahoma St U 2003; MDiv SWTS 2007. D 6/9/2007 P 1/7/2008 Bp Dean Elliott Wolfe. m 1/9/2010 Kristen Wold. S Dav's Epis Ch Topeka KS 2007-2009. stjohnrector@gmail.com

BUTIN, John Murray (Ga) 303 Cannon Ct, St Simons Island GA 31522 B Wichita KS 4/1/1964 s James Walker Butin & Betty Belle. BA U of Kansas 1986; MDiv Candler TS Emory U 1994; LLD Emory U 1994. D 8/3/2002 P 2/17/2003 Bp Henry Irving Louttit. m 12/26/1981 Mary Margaret McGeachy c 3. S Mk's Ch Brunswick GA 2002-2004. jmbutin@toslaw.com

BUTLER III, Andrew Garland (Nwk) 59 Montclair Ave, Montclair NJ 07042 **S Jn's Epis Ch Montclair NJ 2010-** B Richmond VA 1/31/1967 s Andrew Garland Butler & Phyllis Bowery. MA Presb Sch CE Richmond VA 1999; MDiv PrTS 2001; Cert of Wk VTS 2008. D 5/24/2008 Bp Peter James Lee P 12/6/2008 Bp Edward Lewis Lee Jr. c 3. Assoc R Ch Of The Redeem Bryn Mawr PA 2008-2010; Mus Min S Thos' Ch Richmond VA 2002-2007. agbmawr67@gmail.com

BUTLER, Barbara Thayer (Minn) 2324 Branch St, Duluth MN 55812 B Duluth MN 12/28/1932 d Jorice Edward Brown & Verna. U MN 1951; BA Carleton Coll 1954. D 10/25/1987 Bp Robert Marshall Anderson. m 10/6/1956 John Tyler Butler c 4. Deacons' Coun Dio Minnesota Minneapolis MN 1989-1992; Dir of Acolytes S Paul's Epis Ch Duluth MN 1987-2001.

BUTLER, C(harles) Roger (CNY) 28205 Nc 73 Hwy, Albemarle NC 28001 B Huntington WV 1/4/1932 s Charles Everett Butler & Genevieve Wallace. BA Marshall U 1953; MDiv VTS 1956. D 6/11/1956 P 6/1/1957 Bp Wilburn Camrock Campbell. m 12/19/1981 Joyce Griffith c 3. P Assoc All SS' Epis Ch Concord NC 2001-2011; R S Paul's Ch Watertown NY 1989-1994; Pres of Dioc Coun Dio Pittsburgh Monroeville PA 1986-1988; Vic Ch Of The H Innoc Leechburg PA 1980-1989; Int Chr Ch New Brighton PA 1979-1980; Vic S Mary Epis Ch Red Bank Templeton PA 1963-1989; R S Paul's Epis Ch Kittanning PA 1963-1975; Assoc R Ch Of The Ascen Pittsburgh PA 1960-1963; Vic S Ann's Ch New Martinsville WV 1956-1960. rogerandjoyce@carolina.rr.com

BUTLER, Clarence Elliot (Roch) Rector, Trinity Church, Geneva NY 14456 B Shelby MS 1/30/1941 s Robert Butler & Addie Lee. BA Washington U 1963; MA U of Kansas 1965; STB EDS 1967; PhD Washington U 1973. D 6/24/1967 P 6/1/1968 Bp George Leslie Cadigan. c 2. EDS Cambridge MA 2010-2011; R Trin Ch Geneva NY 2006-2009; Int Trin Ch Geneva NY 1993-1995; Asst to R Trin Ch Geneva NY 1979-1992; Serv Ch Of The Ascen S Louis MO 1968-1970; Dio Missouri S Louis MO 1968-1969; S Mk's Ch S Louis MO 1968. Auth, "Heinz Meyer Die Zahlenallegorese im Mittelalter," *German Quarterly*, 1977; Auth, *Rel Stds Revs*. butler@hws.edu

BUTLER, Guy Harry (Tex) 10019 Beaverdam Creek Rd, Berlin MD 21811 B Reading PA 12/9/1933 s Bruce Butler & Elizabeth. BA Franklin & Marshall Coll 1956; MDiv PDS 1959; Coll of Preachers 1963; Coll of Preachers 1966; Coll of Preachers 1977. D 6/27/1959 Bp Earl M Honaman P 1/9/1960 Bp John T Heistand. m 2/11/1961 Joanna Gehar Van Horn. Trin Ch Jacksonville TX 1993-1996; Trin Ch Natchez MS 1993-1996; Dio NW Pennsylvania Erie PA 1987-1993; Tri-Dioc Stwdshp Com 1987-1992; R Chr Epis Ch Meadville PA 1978-1987; Vic S Mary's Ch Erie PA 1976-1978; Vic S Jos's Epis Ch Grand Prairie TX 1965-1976; Vic S Alb's Epis Ch Salisbury MD 1961-1965; Cur Cathd Ch Of S Steph Harrisburg PA 1959-1961.

BUTLER III, Hardie Taylor (SVa) 1518 Woodland Ct, Farmville VA 23901 **D Johns Meml Epis Ch Farmville VA 2011-** B Atlanta GA 9/1/1938 s Hardie Taylor Butler & Juanita. Merc 1961; U of Tennessee 1964. D 6/18/2011 Bp Herman Hollerith IV. c 1. htbutler@yahoo.com

BUTLER, Josh (O) 471 Crosby St, Akron OH 44302 B Youngstown OH 3/10/1949 s Joseph Green Butler & Dorothy Dennison. D 11/12/2010 Bp Mark Hollingsworth Jr. m 2/10/2006 Denise Rinn c 3. joshbutler@aol.com

BUTLER, Keith Wayne (WVa) 150 Caldwell Dr, White Sulphur Springs WV 24986 **Died 8/16/2010** B Martinsburg WV 3/20/1952 s Richard Wayne Butler & Phyllis Virginia. BA Shpd Coll Shepherdstown WV 1999; MDiv STUSo 2001. D 9/21/2000 Bp C(laude) Charles Vache P 6/1/2001 Bp William Michie Klusmeyer. revkb52@gmail.com

BUTLER, Marilyn M (Ida) 4251 N 1800 E, Buhl ID 83316 **P Trin Ch Buhl ID 1994-** B Twin Falls ID 11/20/1940 d Pete George Tesar & Mildred Mae. BS Colorado St U 1961; MS Colorado St U 1966. D 1/29/1994 P 8/1/1994 Bp John Stuart Thornton. m 9/9/1959 Calvin Charles Butler. cbutler@magiclink.com

BUTLER, Mark Hilliard (NC) 225 Arbutus Ln, Hendersonville NC 28739 B Poughkeepsie NY 5/23/1945 s Frank Marechal Butler & Alice Mae. BA U of So Florida 1969; MDiv 1976; 1977. Trans 8/11/2003 Bp James Edward Waggoner. m 8/12/1991 Margaret Whittle c 2. Chr Ch Babylon NY 2003-2005; Dio Spokane Spokane WA 2000-2005; Dioc Coun Dio Spokane Spokane WA 2000-2003; R Epis Ch of the Nativ Lewiston ID 2000-2003; Stndg Com Dio Oregon Portland OR 1996-2000; COM w Gays And Lesbians Dio Oregon Portland OR 1994-2000; R Gr Epis Ch Astoria OR 1994-2000; Chair Cler Fam Com Dio Upper So Carolina Columbia SC 1993-1994; Cmsn Stwdshp And Dvlpmt Dio Upper So Carolina Columbia SC 1992-1994; R Ch Of The Incarn Gaffney SC 1991-1994; Cler Fam Com Dio Upper So Carolina Columbia SC 1991-1993; Vic S Davids Ch Brunswick GA 1988-1991; Vic S Mk's Ch Brunswick GA 1988-1991; S Mk's Epis Ch Woodbine GA 1988-1991; Int S Paul's Epis Ch Jacksonville FL 1985-1987. Auth/Ed, "Employee Assistance Prog Supervisory Trng Manual," 1985. markbutler@aol.com

BUTLER, Pauline Felton (CFla) 815 E Graves Ave, Orange City FL 32763 B Norfolk VA 10/12/1944 d George E Kneiple & Muriel L. AS Dayton Bch Cmnty Collge 1991; AS Dayton Bch Cmnty Collge 1992; AA Dayton Bch Cmnty Collge 1994; BA U of Cntrl Florida 1995. D 12/12/2009 Bp John Wadsworth Howe. m 6/20/2009 Gary Butler c 2. pfelton@pd18.net

BUTLER, Robert Mitchell (Me) 35821 Pradera Dr, Zephyrhills FL 33541 **Asst S Eliz's Epis Ch Zephyrhills FL 1992-** B Philadelphia PA 5/24/1925 s Freeman Prescot Butler & Bertha Marian. BA U of Maine 1951; GTS 1965. D 12/18/1965 P 12/17/1966 Bp Oliver L Loring. c 2. R Ch Of The Gd Shpd Houlton ME 1975-1989; Vic S Giles Ch Jefferson ME 1972-1975; Const and Cn Dio Maine Portland ME 1970-1975; Dir Dioc Conf Cntr Dio Maine Portland ME 1970-1975; Prog Coordntr Dio Maine Portland ME 1970-1975; Bp's Stff Dio Maine Portland ME 1970-1972; Cur Chr Ch Gardiner ME 1965-1967; Stff Dioc Conf Cntr Dio Maine Portland ME 1963-1967. frbobb@aol.com

BUTLER, Susan J (ETenn) 20 Belvoir Ave, Chattanooga TN 37411 **P-in-c Gr Ch Chattanooga TN 2010-** B Scranton PA 2/9/1954 d Edwin James Butler & Mildred Ann. BA Franklin & Marshall Coll 1976; MDiv Drew U 1997. D 5/31/1997 Bp Jack Marston McKelvey P 12/13/1997 Bp John Shelby Spong. m 12/5/2008 Robert Dayton Mitchell c 2. S Ptr's Ch Mtn Lakes NJ 2007-2009; Ch Of The Epiph Allendale NJ 2007; Chr Ch Newton NJ 2002-2003; Asst Trin Ch Solebury PA 1999-2002; Cur S Ptr's Ch Morristown NJ 1997-1998. susanjbutler@att.net

BUTLER, Tony Eugene (Cal) Po Box 4380, Sparks NV 89432 B Muskegon MI 8/10/1947 s Alfred H Butler & Joanne M. BA Unr 1969; MDiv CDSP 1973. D 6/6/1973 P 5/1/1974 Bp Wesley Frensdorff. m 6/5/1976 Linda Jones c 1. S Geo's Epis Ch Antioch CA 1981-1983; Ch Of Coventry Cross Minden NV 1975-1981; Cur Trin Epis Ch Reno NV 1973-1975. Auth, "Var arts". tbutler@comcast.net

BUTLER-NIXON, Grahame Gordon (USC) 314 Granby Xing, Cayce SC 29033 B Sydney NSW AU 6/16/1932 s Herbert Gordon Butler-Nixon & Joyce Kathleen. LLB U of Adelaide AU 1955; ThL S Jn's Theol Coll NSW AU 1959; MDiv GTS 1964; Fllshp GTS 1966; U of Pennsylvania 1968. Trans from Anglican Church Of Australia 5/1/1969 as Priest Bp Jonathan Goodhue Sherman. Eccl Crt Dio Upper So Carolina Columbia SC 1991-1998; Gr Epis Ch And Kindergarten Camden SC 1986-1997; R Trin Epis Ch Asheville NC 1978-1983; S Barn And All SS Ch Springfield MA 1977-1978; Gr Ch Dalton MA 1977; Stndg Com Dio Newark Newark NJ 1975-1977; R Gr Ch Newark NJ 1971-1977; Assoc S Jn's Of Lattingtown Locust Vlly NY 1968-1971; Fell & Tutor The GTS New York NY 1964-1966. butnix@aol.com

BUTT, J(ohn) Reginald (Oly) 700 216th Pl NE, Sammamish WA 98074 **Died 1/29/2010** B Heart's Content,,CA 4/14/1921 s Arthur James Butt & Emma Mildred. MDiv PDS 1951. D 4/21/1951 Bp Jonathan Goodhue Sherman P 11/8/1951 Bp Henry Hean Daniels. c 1. jrbutt7@aol.com

BUTTERBAUGH, Anna Marie (CGC) 401 Live Oak Ave, Pensacola FL 32507 **Par Admin and Vstry Clerk S Jn's Ch Pensacola FL 2010-** B Monticello FL 7/18/1957 d Charles V Favre & Margaret G. BA U of W Florida 1979; MTS Sprg Hill Coll 2002; MDiv Epis TS Of The SW 2010. D 12/19/2009 P 1/22/2011 Bp Philip Menzie Duncan II. m 6/25/1977 Timothy R Butterbaugh. tb17003@aol.com

BUTTERFIELD JR, Asa Van Wormer (ECR) Apartado Postal 5-124, Guaralajara, Jalisco, Guadalajara Jalisco 45042 Mexico B Cincinnati OH 3/20/1928 s Asa V Butterfield & Willa Dorothy. BFA Amer U Mex DF 1963; MDiv CDSP 1966; MA Amer U Mex DF 1971; PhD U Of Guanajuato 1978. D 6/19/1966 Bp James Albert Pike P 3/4/1967 Bp Angus Dun. c 4. Vic Santa Maria Virgen Epis Oklahoma City OK 1992-1994; Hisp Mssnr Dio Oklahoma Oklahoma City OK 1992-1993; Hispanicmissioner Dio El Camino Real Monterey CA 1983-1988; Dio El Camino Real Monterey CA 1982-1987; Exec Coun Appointees New York NY 1980-1982; Asst All SS Ch Portland OR 1979-1980; Asst The Epis Ch Of S Mary The Vrgn San Francisco CA 1978-1979; Vic Iglesia Epis Del Buen Samaritano San Francisco CA 1968-1971; Vic The Epis Ch Of S Jn The Evang San Francisco CA 1968-1971. Auth, "Visualization Pryr"; Auth, "Well-Being Exercises"; Auth, "Cross Cultural Evang". Ord Of S Lk 1966; OHC 1965. asavb@yahoo.com

BUTTERFIELD-PRESLER, Jane (Vt) 2534 Hill West Rd., Montgomery VT 05471 **P-in-Partnership S Matt's Ch Enosburg Falls VT 2011-; Epis Ch Cntr New York NY 2000-** B Plymouth MA 6/5/1950 d Charles Perry Butterfield & Virginia Lee. Bard Coll 1969; BS/CAS Bos 1972; MDiv EDS 1989. D 6/3/1989 Bp David Elliot Johnson P 6/10/1990 Bp David Bell Birney IV. m 4/6/1974 Titus Leonard Presler c 4. Gr Ch White Plains NY 2006-2010; S Jn's Ch Staten Island NY 2006; Epis Ch Cntr New York NY 1999-2005; P-in-c S Aug And S Mart Ch Boston MA 1996-1999; All SS Ch Stoneham MA 1995-1996; Co-R S Ptr's Epis Ch Cambridge MA 1991-1995; Assoc R S Paul's Ch Dedham MA 1989-1991. "Windows on Mssn (DVD)," DFMS; "The Scripture of Their Lives," Morehouse Pub. Twenty Club. Hon Cn St. Jn's Cathd in the Dio Peshawar, Ch of Pale. janebutterfieldpresler@gmail.com

BUTTERWORTH, Gary Wayne (SVa) 484 Mountain Rd., Halifax VA 24558 **Curs Sec Spiritial Dir Dio Sthrn Virginia Norfolk VA 2010-; Exec Bd Dio Sthrn Virginia Norfolk VA 2010-; Chair, Liturg Cmsn Dio Sthrn Virginia Norfolk VA 2009-; R S Jn's Epis Ch Halifax VA 2008-; R Trin Epis Ch So Boston VA 2008-** B Marion OH 1/18/1956 s Wayne Russell & Mary Louetta. BS Excelsior Coll 1996; MMAS Command and Gnrl Stff Coll 2001; MBA Touro U Intl 2004; MDiv U So TS 2008. D 2/1/2008 P 8/1/2008 Bp John Clark Buchanan. m 10/4/1983 Christina Christina Marie Slaney c 2. gary.butterworth@gmail.com

BUTTS, Roger Paul (Md) 2206 Pheasant Run Dr, Finksburg MD 21048 B Baltimore MD 5/17/1936 s Roger Ernest Butts & Alice Olivia. BA McDaniel Coll 1959; MDiv Wesley TS 1962; VTS 1965. D 6/22/1965 P 6/1/1966 Bp Harry Lee Doll. m 6/25/1960 Lois Elizabeth Martin c 2. Emm Ch Baltimore MD 1994-1998; S Paul's Par Kent Chestertown MD 1993-1994; Ch Hosp Corp Baltimore MD 1985-1993; S Paul's Epis Ch Mt Airy MD 1981-1985; Ch Of-Ascen & Prince-Peace Baltimore MD 1965-1981; Cur Ch Of The Ascen Baltimore MD 1965-1968. hophead@adelphia.net

BUTTS, Stephen Jack (Tex) 314 N Henderson Blvd, Kilgore TX 75662 B Placerville CA 12/7/1948 s Jack Chester Butts & Anna Loreen. AA Sierra Coll Rocklin CA 1973; BA Chapman U 1992; MDiv CDSP 1995. D 5/31/1995 Bp Jerry Alban Lamb P 12/1/1995 Bp Claude Edward Payne. m 7/6/1985 Eva Costa c 2. R S Paul's Ch Kilgore TX 1995-2010. OHC 1993. frstephen2@msn.com

BUXO, David Carlyle (Mich) 14510 E 7 Mile Rd, Detroit MI 48205 B Levara GD 12/16/1939 s Ivan Pope-Buxo & Beryl Agnes. BA Lon 1967; MDiv GTS 1981. Trans from Church in the Province Of The West Indies 9/1/1993 Bp R(aymond) Stewart Wood Jr. m 2/14/1987 Jennifer Williams. S Mk's Ch Detroit MI 1995-1996; R S Tim's Ch Detroit MI 1993-1994. dbuxo@aol.com

BUXTON JR, Eugene Harvey (Tex) 514 Belleair Pl, Clearwater FL 33756 B Akron OH 1/29/1931 s Eugene Harvey Buxton & Vesta Martha. BA Coll of Wooster 1952; BD Bex 1955. D 6/18/1955 Bp Nelson Marigold Burroughs P 1/6/1956 Bp Harry S Kennedy. Extended Supply P Dio Ohio Cleveland OH 1992-1996; Int Dio Texas Houston TX 1990; S Aug's Epis Ch Galveston TX 1985-1989; R Trin Ch Connersville IN 1964-1973; Vic S Jn's Epis Ch Sparta WI 1958-1964; Int S Mary's Epis Ch Honolulu HI 1956-1957. ehbuxton@yahoo.com

BUXTON-SMITH, Sarah Wallace (WNY) 100 Beard Ave, Buffalo NY 14214 **Trst Dio Wstrn New York Tonawanda NY 2010-; R S Andr's Ch Buffalo NY 2002-** B Summit NJ 10/23/1949 d Horace Childs Buxton & Ann. BA VPI & St U 1971; MFA U NC 1977; Washington Theol Un 1986; DAS Ya Berk 1994; MDiv Yale DS 1994. D 6/11/1994 Bp Peter James Lee P 3/25/1995 Bp Clarence Nicholas Coleridge. m 6/25/1994 Stephen John Stanyon Smith. Dioc Coun Dio Wstrn New York Tonawanda NY 2005-2009; Stndg Com Dio Wstrn New York Tonawanda NY 1999-2005; Assoc Trin Epis Ch Buffalo NY 1999-2001; Int Chr Ch New Haven CT 1994-1998. Producer, "Walking Into Difference," *Interfaith Wmn at the Millennium*, Avocado Productions, 2002; Auth, "Fr Lady," *Magnificent: Celebrating Wmn Priests*, Buckfriars Press, 2000. Affirming Angl Catholicism 1996; Cmnty Of The Cross Of Nails 1985; Compass Rose Soc 1995; Fllshp Of S Jn 2002; OHC 1992-2002. Preaching Awd Ya Berk New Haven CT 1994. swbuxton@aol.com

BUZZARD, Henry Lewis (NY) 71 Wayne Ave, White Plains NY 10606 **P S Ann's Ch For The Deaf New York NY 1997-** B Normal IL 6/7/1923 s Robert Guy Buzzard & Alice Irene. Estrn Illinois U 1945; BA Wabash Coll 1946; MA Clark U 1949; MLS U IL 1951. D 9/26/1996 Bp William Edwin Swing P 6/28/1997 Bp E(gbert) Don Taylor. m 6/9/1956 Juliet Dickinson Barnett. Auth, "Thos Gallaudet: Apos To The Deaf," 1989. Empire St Assn Of The Deaf; Epis Conf Of The Deaf; New York City City Assn Of The Deaf. noemail@noemail.noemail

BWECHWA, Oswald (Mil) 3400 E Debbie Drive, Oak Creek WI 53154 **P-in-c S Mart's Ch Brown Deer WI 2008-** B Muleba TZ 7/20/1958 s Damian Protas Kabumgo & Magdalen. BA Miltown Pk Inst 1985; BS Marq 1990; MDiv Hekima Coll 1993; ThM Berkeley Jesuit TS 1998; DAS VTS 1999; MSW U of Wisconsin 2003. Rec from Roman Catholic 6/1/1999 as Deacon Bp Roger John White. m 5/29/1999 Rosemarie Nhonoli c 1. R S Nich Epis Ch Racine WI 1999-2000. obwechwa@sbcglobal.net

BYE, Michael (NC) P.O. Box 942, wadesboro NC 28170 **R Calv Ch Wadesboro NC 2005-** B Harrisburg PA 1/21/1947 s Theodore Woolings Bye & Grace. BS Campbell U 1968; VTS 1970; MDiv Ya Berk 1971. D 6/26/1971 Bp Robert Fisher Gibson Jr P 5/1/1972 Bp Robert Bruce Hall. m 11/23/2009 Judy B Brittingham. S Clem's Epis Ch Clemmons NC 2003-2005; Dio No Carolina Raleigh NC 2003; Vic Chap Of Chr The King Charlotte NC 1999-2003; S Paul's Ch Georgetown DE 1991-1999; Vic S Andr The Fisherman Epis Mayo MD 1981-1988; Vic St Jas Epis Ch Muncy PA 1977-1982; R S Jas Ch Muncy PA 1977-1981; Asst Ch Of The Gd Shpd Burke VA 1975-1977; S Ptr's Epis Ch Arlington VA 1973-1975; S Jas' Ch Richmond VA 1971-1973. frmikebye@yahoo.com

BYE, Tommy Frank (FtW) 1201 Overhill St, Bedford TX 76022 **S Lk's Ch Cypress Mill TX 2000-** B Abilene TX 7/6/1945 s Jessey Columbus Bye & Mollya. Choir Coll Of The SW 1969; AA El Centro Dallas TX 1971; U Of Dallas 1990; MDiv Nash 1994. D 12/27/1993 Bp Clarence Cullam Pope Jr P 7/1/1994 Bp Jack Leo Iker. m 4/11/1980 Connie Jean Appleton c 1. R S Lk's In The Meadow Epis Ch Ft Worth TX 1997-2007; S Vinc's Cathd Bedford TX 1994-1997. byetommy@yahoo.com

BYER, Martha Russell (WMo) 3907 Ivanhoe Blvd, Columbia MO 65203 B Little Rock AR 9/24/1940 d Wesley Holmes Russell & Martha Louise. BS Texas Wmn's U-Denton 1964. D 2/2/2002 Bp Barry Robert Howe. c 3. mbyer@tranquility.net

BYERS, Mark Harrison (Ct) 38 Grove St, Thomaston CT 06787 **R S Ptr's-Trin Ch Thomaston CT 2011-** B Philippines 12/18/1965 s Clarence Richard Byers & Sara Lynn. BA Hav 1995; MDiv Ya Berk 1998. D 6/9/2001 Bp Andrew Donnan Smith P 12/15/2001 Bp Wilfrido Ramos-Orench. m 7/20/2002 Jessica Byers c 3. Ch of the Apos La Quinta CA 2009-2011; Cur S Jn's Epis Ch Essex CT 2001-2004. frmarkbyers@yahoo.com

BYERS, William (WMass) 35 Nedwied Rd, Tolland CT 06084 **Non-par P S Jn's Epis Ch Vernon Rock Vernon CT 1980-** B Boston MA 1/27/1936 s Douglas Swain Byers & Dorothy. BA Colby Coll 1961; MDiv Bex 1966. D 6/22/1966 P 12/13/1966 Bp Robert McConnell Hatch. m 11/25/1978 Susan Kinsloe c 2. Asst Min All SS Ch Worcester MA 1966-1971. Auth, "Sculpting Wood: Contemporary Tools & Techniques," Davis Pub, 1986; Auth, "Pollen & Archeology At Wetherill Mesa". Chapl Ord Of S Lk. wbyers1@comcast.net

BYRD, Frederick Colclough (USC) 1115 Marion St, Columbia SC 29201 B Augusta GA 9/21/1942 s Frederick Percival Byrd & Addie. BS Clemson U 1964; MDiv VTS 1968. D 6/23/1968 P 5/1/1969 Bp John Adams Pinckney. Archd Dio Upper So Carolina Columbia SC 1979-2003; Vic S Lk's Ch Newberry SC 1969-1979; Asst S Jas Epis Ch Greenville SC 1968-1969. Soc Of First Families Of So Carolina; So Carolina Huguenot Soc. Who'S Who In Amer Colleges And Universities; Personalitites Of The So; Outstanding Young Men In Amer. frebyr@aol.com

BYRD, Janice Lovinggood (NwT) 430 Dallas St, Big Spring TX 79720 **D The Epis Ch Of S Mary The Vrgn Big Sprg TX 2002-** B Breckenridge TX 3/29/1932 d Thurman Lovinggood & Dorothy Louise. BS Texas Wmn's U-Denton 1954. D 10/27/2002 Bp C(harles) Wallis Ohl. c 2.

BYRD, Jeffrey Yona (CGC) 403 W College St, Troy AL 36081 **D-In-Trng S Mk's Epis Ch Troy AL 2005-; S Mich's Ch Mt Pleasant IA 2005-** B Knoxville TN 2/17/1962 s Frank Malloy Gibson & Joyce June. BS Austin Peay St U 1992; MS Austin Peay St U 1994; MDiv Epis TS of The SW 2005. D 6/4/2005 P 5/6/2006 Bp Philip Menzie Duncan II. m 1/9/1988 Elizabeth A Ensor c 2. frbyrd62@gmail.com

BYRD JR, Ralph Milledge (La) 4533 Neyrey Dr, Metairie LA 70002 **S Mk's Epis Ch Harvey LA 2007-; Ch Pension Fund Benefici New York NY 2005-; R S Augustines Ch Metairie LA 1989-** B Charleston SC 5/28/1938 s Ralph Milledge Byrd & Elise Macmurphy. BA Cit 1960; MDiv VTS 1963; DMin STUSo 1987. D 6/17/1963 P 6/1/1964 Bp Gray Temple. m 6/24/1972 Elizabeth Ravenel Boykin c 2. S Augustines Ch Metairie LA 1990-2005; Dn of Students All SS' Epis Ch Tupelo MS 1987-1989; All SS' Epis Sch Vicksburg MS 1987-1989; S Mart's Epis Sch Metairie LA 1981-1987; Dio No Carolina Raleigh NC 1978-1981; Asst Chr Ch Epis Savannah GA 1974-1977; Asst

R S Phil's Ch Charleston SC 1971-1974; Asst R Chr Ch Par Pensacola FL 1966-1968; R S Matt's Ch (Ft Motte) S Matthews SC 1964-1966; R The Ch Of The Epiph Eutawville SC 1964-1966; Asst S Andr's Ch Mt Pleasant SC 1963-1964. ralphb1776@cox.net

BYRD, Ronald (Mich) 1514 Columbine Dr, East Lansing MI 48823 **S Kath's Ch Williamston MI 2009-** B Detroit MI 2/7/1960 s Robert L Byrd & Elizabeth J. AA Northwood U 1980; BBA Northwood U 1982; MDiv VTS 2007. D 12/16/2006 P 9/15/2007 Bp Wendell Nathaniel Gibbs Jr. m 11/28/2003 Jennifer Byrd c 7. S Paul's Epis Ch Lansing MI 2007-2009. roneagle6@comcast.net

BYRER, Johnine Vaughn (NJ) 6 Juniper Dr, Whitehouse Station NJ 08889 **D Ch Of The H Sprt Lebanon NJ 2002-** B Ann Arbor MI 11/19/1946 d John Rutherford Vaughn & Laura. BS Estrn Michigan U 1968; MA Estrn Michigan U 1971. D 9/21/2002 Bp David B(ruce) Joslin. m 10/7/1972 Donald V Byrer c 4. NAAD 2002. S Steph Awd NAAD 2007.

BYRNE, Anne Spottswood Chamblin (Md) 126 E. Liberty St., Oakland MD 21550 **Assoc Cler S Matt's Par Oakland MD 2008-** B Portsmouth VA 7/13/1961 d John Drummond Chamblin & Anne Gardner. Cont Educ Garrett Cmnty Coll; MMP Wstrn Maryland Coll 2008. D 7/5/2008 P 6/27/2009 Bp John Leslie Rabb. m 5/18/1985 William Hamilton Byrne c 3. ascb617@msn.com

BYRNE, Laurence Goodwin (Ct) 21433 40th Ave., Bayside NY 11361 **All SS Ch Bayside NY 2006-** B Wilmington DE 11/29/1962 s Richard Carroll Byrne & Beatrice Carolyn. BA U of Delaware Newark 1985; MDiv VTS 1994. D 6/25/1994 P 12/9/1995 Bp Cabell Tennis. m 5/18/1996 Susan R Byrne c 1. Ch Of The Resurr Kew Gardens NY 2006-2007; S Paul's Ch Riverside CT 2002-2004; Chr Ch Easton CT 1999-2002; Cur S Paul's Ch Fairfield CT 1994-1999. lgbyrne1129@aol.com

BYRUM, Emory Etheridge (Nwk) Trinity Episcopal Church, 6587 Upper York Rd. PO Box 377, Solebury PA 18963 **Int Trin Ch Solebury PA 2009-** B Portsmouth VA 8/17/1933 s Daniel Joseph Byrum & Grace Thelma. Chowan Coll Murfreesboro NC 1955; BA Carson-Newman Coll 1959; MDiv SE Bapt TS 1962; DMin UTS Virginia 1981. D 3/5/1994 Bp Jack Marston McKelvey P 9/17/1994 Bp John Shelby Spong. c 3. S Mary's Ch Belvidere NJ 1994-2005. Cbury Schlr/P of the Year Dio Newark Conv 2000. emoryb@earthlink.net

BYRUM, Philip Robert (NC) 4005 Heritage Dr W, Wilson NC 27893 **Vic S Mk's Ch Wilson NC 1991-** B Durham NC 7/24/1941 s Robert Mauney Byrum & Ada Margaret. BA Greensboro Coll 1963; BD EDS 1966. D 6/29/1966 P 6/24/1967 Bp Thomas Augustus Fraser Jr. c 2. R S Tim's Ch Wilson NC 1991-2000; Dio No Carolina Raleigh NC 1991-1993; Stndg Com Dio No Carolina Raleigh NC 1983-1985; S Mary Magd Ch W End NC 1982-1983; R Chr Ch Albemarle NC 1969-1991; Liturg Cmsn Dio No Carolina Raleigh NC 1969-1981; M-in-c S Mich's Ch Tarboro NC 1966-1969; M-in-c St Marys Epis Ch Speed NC 1966-1969. pbyrum@myglnc.com

BYRUM, Rick Yervant (Los) 28648 Greenwood Pl, Castaic CA 91384 **The Epis Hm Communities Pasadena CA 2008-** B Pasadena CA 11/8/1955 s Richard Leon Byrum & June Margaret. BA Div Word Coll Epworth IA 1979; MDiv Cath Theol Un 1990. D 6/19/1999 P 1/8/2000 Bp Frederick Houk Borsch. m 2/25/1989 Anita Elliott. Ch Of The H Trin and S Ben Alhambra CA 2005-2008; S Jas Par Los Angeles CA 2001-2005. frybyrum@sbcglobal.net

C

CABALLERO, Daniel (Mil) 4305 Rolla Ln, Madison WI 53711 B Mercedes TX 10/21/1935 s Arcadio Caballero & Josephine. BA Sherwood Conservatory of Mus Chicago IL 1958; MA New Mex Highlands U 1965; MDiv Nash 1986. D 5/9/1986 P 1/10/1987 Bp Roger John White. m 6/25/1966 Gretchen Lentz c 4. Mssnr - Hisp Mnstry Off Epis Ch Cntr New York NY 1999-2005; Int S Mk's Ch Beaver Dam WI 1995-1998; Int S Lk's Ch Madison WI 1994-1995; Hisp Mnstry-P-in-c Mision San Miguel Madison WI 1990-1999; Chapl Epis City Msn Of Madison Inc Madison WI 1988-1999; Dio Milwaukee Milwaukee WI 1988-1998; P S Barn Richland Cntr WI 1986-1988; D Dio Milwaukee Milwaukee WI 1986. Hisp. Mins. Mssnr - Ed, "Las fiestas menores y los días de ayuno - 2003," *Lesser Feasts & Fasts - 2003 (1st Spanish Ed)*, ECC Hisp. Mnstry Off, 2005. Phi Kappa Phi 1965. Cn Reformed Epis Ch of Spain, Madrid, Spain 2002. daddydan13@sbcglobal.net

CABANA, Denise Elizabeth (WA) 6 Leslie Dr, Indian Head MD 20640 **S Jas' Ch Indn Hd MD 2006-** B Northampton MA 1/26/1961 d Norman Harvey Cabana & Jean Elizabeth. BA No Adams St Coll 1983; MA U of Maine 1985; MDiv VTS 2002. D 6/8/2002 Bp Andrew Donnan Smith P 1/25/2003 Bp Wilfrido Ramos-Orench. m 5/7/1994 Charles D Scott. Assoc R Trin Ch Branford CT 2002-2006. d.cabana@attbi.com

CABRERA, Amador Fredy (Hond) IMS SAP Dept 215. PO Box 523900, Miami FL 22152 Honduras B Tegucigalpa, Honduras 4/28/1963 s Fredy Cabrera Amador. D 3/11/2007 Bp Lloyd Emmanuel Allen. m 12/10/1995 Doris Estela Rubio Ercobar c 3. fredyllamoda@yahoo.es

CABRERO-OLIVER, Juan M (LI) 443 Maren St, West Hempstead NY 11552 B , 6/21/1948 s Juan Manuel Cabrero & Awilda. BA Ford 1970; MFA U of New Mex 1977; MDiv CDSP 1988. D 6/4/1988 P 12/1/1989 Bp William Edwin Swing. The GTS New York NY 2002-2008; Dio Long Island Garden City NY 2000-2006; Assoc Gd Shpd Epis Chap Garden City NY 1998-2002; Dio New Jersey Trenton NJ 1996-1997; Epis Sch For Deacons Berkeley CA 1994-1995; Trin Cathd San Jose CA 1994; The Epis Ch Of S Jn The Evang San Francisco CA 1993-1994; Asst S Mk's Epis Ch Palo Alto CA 1988-1990. Auth, "Liturg Stds Iii"; Auth, "Liturg Stds Ii". OHC. Fte Dissertation Fllshp 1995. tzeuezt@gmail.com

CABUSH, David Walter (Nwk) 2 Pond Hill Rd # 7960, Morristown NJ 07960 **Ch Of The Trsfg Towaco NJ 2009-; S Andr's Epis Ch Lincoln Pk NJ 2009-** B Racine WI 1/31/1942 s Walter James Cabush & Gladys. BA San Diego St U 1964; MS San Diego St U 1968; PhD MI SU 1971; Cert Washington Sch of Psych 1990; MDiv PrTS 1994; ThM PrTS 1995; GTS 2002. D 9/20/2003 P 3/27/2004 Bp John Palmer Croneberger. m 6/9/1990 Diane Lynn Gabrielsen c 3. S Jn's Memi Ch Ramsey NJ 2005-2009; Assoc S Ptr's Ch Morristown NJ 2003-2005. drscabush@aol.com

CACOPERDO, Peter A(nthony) (RG) PO Box 1747, Elephant Butte NM 87935 B Brooklyn NY 10/7/1941 s Anthony Cacoperdo & Lucille Rose. AA Nassau Cmnty Coll 1974; Cert. Mercer TS 1977; Lic TS 1977; BA SUNY 2000. D 3/22/1980 P 10/18/1981 Bp Robert Campbell Witcher Sr. m 12/8/1962 Margaret Rose Richards c 3. Int S Lk's Epis Ch Anth NM 2010-2011; P-in-c Chr Ch Hillsboro NM 2003-2008; Vic S Paul's Epis Ch Truth or Consequences NM 2003-2008; Dept Of Missions Dio Long Island Garden City NY 1997-1999; R H Trin Epis Ch Hicksville NY 1994-2002; Int S Bon Epis Ch Lindenhurst NY 1992-1994; Assoc S Bon Epis Ch Lindenhurst NY 1981-1992. frpeterc@valornet.com

CADARET, John Michael (Va) 8411 Freestone Ave, Richmond VA 23229 **Gr & H Trin Epis Ch Richmond VA 2006-** B Richmond VA 7/22/1967 s Albert Joseph Cadaret & Sharon Judy. LTh VTS 2003. D 6/14/2003 P 12/20/2003 Bp Peter James Lee. m 11/20/1993 Cari Ann Taylor c 2. Varina Epis Ch Richmond VA 2006-2009; P-in-c All SS Epis Ch Jacksonville FL 2006; P-in-c All SS Epis Ch Jacksonville FL 2006; All SS Epis Ch Jacksonville FL 2004-2006; Trin Ch Upperville VA 2003-2004. michaelcadaret@verizon.net

CADDELL, Christopher Len (WTex) 1417 E Austin Ave, Harlingen TX 78550 **S Alb's Ch Harlingen TX 2010-** B Odessa TX 9/23/1976 s Len Macon Caddell & Patricia Ann. BS Texas A&M U 1999; MDiv The TS at The U So 2010. D 6/8/2010 Bp Gary Richard Lillibridge P 12/19/2010 Bp David Mitchell Reed. m 1/8/2000 Bryn S Skelton c 2. clcaddell@gmail.com

CADENA, Enrique (Az) 2801 N 31st Street, Phoenix AZ 85008 **Vic Dio Arizona Phoenix AZ 2008-; Vic Iglesia Epis De San Pablo Phoenix AZ 2008-** B Mexico City Mexico 5/20/1952 MA Colgate DS 1989. Rec from Roman Catholic 10/4/2003 Bp J Michael Garrison. c 2. Chr Ch Albion NY 2005-2008; R S Paul's Ch Holley NY 2004-2008. "A Quest For Freedom," Olde Ridge Bk Pub, 1999. cadenaenr@aol.com

CADIGAN, C(harles) Richard (Mo) 1625 Masters Drive, DeSoto TX 75115 B Northampton MA 3/20/1937 s Charles Howard Cadigan & Elizabeth. BA Wesl 1959; MDiv EDS 1962. D 6/20/1962 Bp Robert McConnell Hatch P 12/15/1962 Bp George Leslie Cadigan. m 3/21/1981 Linda Renasco c 4. Tchr,Dn of Students,Headmaster Wooster Sch Danbury CT 1970-1979; Assoc Emm Epis Ch Webster Groves MO 1966-1967; Asst Emm Epis Ch Webster Groves MO 1962-1965. crcadigan@sbcglobal.net

CADWALLADER, Douglas Stephen (Tex) PO Box 35303, Houston TX 77235 B Orlando FL 2/1/1944 s Harold Lee Cadwallader & Lenora. BA LSU 1966; BS LSU 1972; MDiv VTS 1977; MA LSU 1994. D 5/18/1979 Bp J Milton Richardson P 11/1/1979 Bp Roger Howard Cilley. Asst S Thos Ch Houston TX 1996-2010; R S Steph's Ch Liberty TX 1986-1989; Asst Trin Ch Houston TX 1981-1986; Chapl St Lk's Epis Hosp Houston TX 1981; Vic Chr Ch Matagorda TX 1979-1981; Vic S Jn's Epis Ch Palacios TX 1979-1981. DouglasSCadwallader@HOTMAIL.COM

CADWELL, Matthew P (Mass) 94 Newbury Ave #309, North Quincy MA 02171 **R Emm Epis Ch Wakefield MA 2008-** B Minneapolis MN 11/3/1972 s Peter William Cadwell & Mary Ann. U Tor; BA Gustavus Adolphus Coll 1995; MDiv EDS 1999. D 6/12/2004 Bp M(arvil) Thomas Shaw III P 1/8/2005 Bp Gayle Elizabeth Harris. Ch Of S Jn The Evang Boston MA 1999-2001. "A Hist of EDS," Trst of EDS, 2000. Eileen and Geo Carey Awd in Angl Stds Angl Dio Toronto 2005; Doctoral Fllshp Trin, U Tor 2003; Bp Atwood of Arizona Awd in Ch Hist EDS 1999; Geo Hall Prize for Schlrshp in Rel Gustavus Adolphus Coll 1995; Phi Beta Kappa Gustavus Adolphus Coll 1995. mathew.cadwell@comcast.net

CADY III, Mark Stone (Dal) 650 Copper Creek Circle, Alpharetta GA 30004 B Warren PA 12/21/1943 s Mark Stone Cady & Marion. BAS NWU 1965; MDiv SWTS 1968. D 6/22/1968 Bp John Raymond Wyatt P 12/1/1968 Bp Jackson Earle Gilliam. m 12/19/1964 Diana Robinson c 1. P S Thos The Apos Ch Overland Pk KS 1976-1984; R S Barn Ch Garland TX 1974-1976; Ch Of Our Lady Of Gr Dallas TX 1973-1974; S Mk's Ch Evanston IL 1972-1973;

Cur S Mk's Epis Ch Glen Ellyn IL 1969-1972; D Calv Epis Ch Red Lodge MT 1968; D Our Sav Epis Joliet MT 1968.

CAFFERATA, Gail Lee (NCal) 4794 Hillsboro Cir, Santa Rosa CA 95405 **P-in-c H Fam Epis Ch Rohnert Pk CA 2003-** B Brooklyn NY 3/20/1945 d Herbert Erickson & Ruth. BA SUNY 1966; MA SUNY 1969; PhD U Chi 1974; MDiv EDS 1997. D 6/7/1997 Bp M(arvil) Thomas Shaw III P 4/14/2002 Bp Jerry Alban Lamb. m 6/10/1967 Robert L Cafferata c 2. Ch Of The Incarn Santa Rosa CA 2010-2011; Dio Nthrn California Sacramento CA 2004-2005; Asst Ch Of The Incarn Santa Rosa CA 2002-2003; Assoc Ch Of The Gd Shpd Watertown MA 1999-2000; Asst S Ptr's Ch Weston MA 1998-1999; D All SS Par Brookline MA 1997-1998. gailcafferata@mac.com

CAFFREY, David Leslie (Los) PO Box 514, Joshua Tree CA 92252 **Trin Epis Ch Redlands CA 2005-; R S Jos Of Arimathea Mssn Yucca Vlly CA 1999-** B Tuscon AZ 8/28/1947 s Howard Caffrey & Violet. AA California Cmnty Coll; BA California St U; MDiv EDS 1974; STM GTS 2007. D 6/15/1974 P 1/4/1975 Bp Robert C Rusack. m 5/31/2008 Louisa Parker c 1. R S Fran Of Assisi Par San Bernardino CA 1986-1999; R S Alb's Ch Worland WY 1981-1985; Vic S Jn The Evang Mssn Needles CA 1974-1981; Reg Vic Dio Los Angeles Los Angeles CA 1974-1975. "The Daily Off in the Ch Today," Unpublished MS, 2007; Auth, *Songs of the Desert*, 1983. CREDO Fac Mem 2006; Desert Journeys 1986; Friends of St. Ben 2003; OHC 1978. Cn of Cathd Dio Los Angeles 2006. desertfather@earthlink.net

CAGE JR, Stewart Bernard (La) 8932 Fox Run Ave, Baton Rouge LA 70808 **P-in-c S Aug's Ch Baton Rouge LA 2007-; P-in-c S Mich's Ch Baton Rouge LA 2004-** B Baton Rouge LA 5/10/1943 s Stewart Bernard Cage & Eleanor Gertrude. D 9/29/2000 P 11/14/2001 Bp Charles Edward Jenkins III. m 3/3/1991 Diane Thomas. s2dcage@bellsouth.net

CAGGIANO, Diane Ruth (Ct) 11 Overvale Rd, Wolcott CT 06716 **D S Jn's Epis Ch Bristol CT 2011-** B Waterbury CT 12/31/1944 d Frederick Elliott Harrison & Ruth Elizabeth. BA Cntrl Connecticut St U 1990. D 9/17/2005 Bp Andrew Donnan Smith. m 6/4/1966 Robert Caggiano c 2. D S Andr's Ch Meriden CT 2005-2011. dcaggiano@att.net

CAGGIANO, Joyce C (Mass) 27 Curtis Rd., Milton MA 02186 **Acctg Mgr, Epis City Mssn Dio Massachusetts Boston MA 2008-; P-in-c S Paul's Ch Peabody MA 2007-** B Bethpage NY 12/24/1949 d Armand Caggiano & Renee. BA U of Massachusetts 1982; MDiv Yale DS 1985; Fllshp Harv 1996; PhD Un Inst & U Cincinnati OH 2000. D 6/4/1986 Bp John Bowen Coburn P 6/20/1987 Bp David Elliot Johnson. m 12/10/1988 Harold R Bronk c 2. Epis City Mssn Boston MA 2008-2010; Ch Of Our Sav Arlington MA 2006-2007; Exec Dir, Epis Cmnty Serv Dio Michigan Detroit MI 2002-2004; Chr Ch Grosse Pointe Grosse Pointe Farms MI 2002; Crossroads Of Michigan Mnstrs Detroit MI 2000-2002; Cathd Ch Of S Paul Detroit MI 2000; S Paul's Ch Newburyport MA 1996-2000; R Gr Ch Everett MA 1988-1992; The Cathd Ch Of S Paul Boston MA 1986-1989. Auth, "No God, No Mstr," *Rel Socialism*, 2001; Auth, "Who Will Be The Teachers?," *Ch Eductr*, 1979. Epis Cmnty Serv Of Amer, Treas 2002-2004; Treas EWC Mass Chapt; Treasurerurer 1999-2000; Treas Phillips Brooks Cler 1998-2000; VP Merrimack Vlly Proj 1998-2000. Merrill Fell Harvard DS 1996. revjchristine@gmail.com

CAGUIAT, Carlos J (Mich) 20 Oakwood Road, Saranac Lake NY 12983 B New York NY 1/23/1937 s Carlos Carmelo Caguiat & Carmen. BA CUNY 1958; MDiv GTS 1965; MPA NYU 1976. D 6/12/1965 P 12/18/1965 Bp Horace W B Donegan. m 8/29/1958 Julianna Skomsky c 3. P-in-c Ch Of The Gd Shpd Elizabethtown NY 1994-1996; Assoc The Ch of St Lk The Beloved Physcn Saranac Lake NY 1992-2009; S Fran Cmnty Serv Inc. Salina KS 1990-2002; S Annes Ch Dewitt MI 1987-1990; R Ch Of The Gd Shpd Wakefield Bronx NY 1976-1981; Exec Dir, Proj for Human Cmnty Dio New York New York City NY 1971-1973; Cur, St. Chris's Chap Trin Par New York NY 1965-1967. SSJE Assoc 2003. Commendation Medal U.S. Army 1962. carjul@roadrunner.com

CAGUIAT, Julianna (Alb) 20 Oakwood Road, Saranac Lake NY 12983 **D Asst The Ch of St Lk The Beloved Physcn Saranac Lake NY 1997-** B New York NY 4/24/1940 d William Skomsky & Evelyn. BS CUNY 1975. D 12/20/1997 Bp David Standish Ball. m 8/29/1958 Carlos J Caguiat c 3. SSJE Assoc 2003. carjul@roadrunner.com

CAHILL, Patricia Ann Bytnar (ETenn) 317 Windy Hollow Dr, Chattanooga TN 37421 B Pittsburgh PA 1/27/1944 d Leonard John Bytnar & Josephine Agnes. BA Seton Hill Coll Greensburg PA 1965; PhD U of Tennessee 1969; MDiv VTS 1998. D 6/13/1998 P 1/25/1999 Bp Robert Gould Tharp. m 11/29/1997 Edward Eugene Cahill c 2. R Thankful Memi Ch Chattanooga TN 2000-2007; Dio E Tennessee Knoxville TN 1999; S Fran Of Assisi Epis Ch Ooltewah TN 1998-1999. patedcahill@aol.com

CAHOON, Vernon John (NC) 428 Pee Dee Ave, Albemarle NC 28001 B Fall River MA 9/16/1957 s Vernon J Cahoon & Constance F. BA U of Massachusetts 1979; JD NEU 1986. D 6/19/2010 Bp Michael Bruce Curry. m 2/27/1987 Lori Lori McCall Earls c 5. vjcahoon@windstream.net

CAIMANO, Catherine Anne (NC) 201 Saint Albans Dr, Raleigh NC 27609 **Cn for Reg Mnstry Dio No Carolina Raleigh NC 2011-** B Saint Louis MO 10/17/1966 d Nicholas Anthony Caimano & Barbara Ann. BS Geo 1989; MDiv GTS 1999. D 6/19/1999 Bp J(ames) Gary Gloster P 1/22/2000 Bp Robert Carroll Johnson Jr. m 12/31/2004 Christopher Clayton Chapman. Chair, BEC Dio Kansas Topeka KS 2008-2011; Fac, Kansas Sch of Mnstry Dio Kansas Topeka KS 2008-2011; R S Jn's Ch Wichita KS 2007-2011; Assoc R S Phil's Ch Durham NC 2001-2007; Cur Ch Of The H Trin New York NY 1999-2001. Auth, "Many Signs And Wonders: A Travel Guide For You," Dom & Frgn Mssy Soc, 2000; Auth, "Epis Ch Q & A'S," Fmp, 1999. Mdiv Wth hon GTS New York NY 1999. frcathie@me.com

CAIN, Donavan Gerald (Lex) St Peter's Episcopal Church, PO Box 27, Paris KY 40362 **S Mk's Epis Ch Jacksonville FL 2010-** B Corbin KY 6/14/1974 s Billy Gerald Cain & Debra Cain. BS Un Coll 1997; MA Appalachian St U 2001; MDiv GTS 2007. D 6/9/2007 P 12/21/2007 Bp Stacy F Sauls. m 8/3/1996 Cynthia R Reynolds c 2. Dep-GC Dio Lexington Lexington KY 2008-2009; R S Ptr's Ch Paris KY 2007-2010; Lay Coll Chapl Dio Lexington Lexington KY 2003-2004. The SocMary 2008. rector@stpetersparis.org

CAIN JR, Everett Harrison (Tex) 7705 Merrybrook Circle, Austin TX 78731 B Humble TX 6/1/1936 s Everett Harrison Cain & Doris Lee. BS Lamar U 1960; BD Austin Presb TS 1963. D 11/23/1966 Bp Everett H Jones P 3/1/1967 Bp Richard Earl Dicus. m 9/2/1955 Marilyn Branch c 1. The Ch of the Gd Shpd Austin TX 1986-1999; R Trin Ch Houston TX 1978-1986; R S Alb's Epis Ch Waco TX 1974-1978; Asst S Jn The Div Houston TX 1970-1974; R Trin Epis Ch Pharr TX 1969-1970; Cur S Lk's Epis Ch San Antonio TX 1966-1969. ehc@austin.rr.com

CAIN, George Robert (SwFla) 1813 Echo Pond Pl, Wesley Chapel FL 33543 B Boston MA 4/28/1938 s Carroll Marston Cain & Mildred Hayes. BA Mid 1960; MDiv EDS 1964; ThM PrTS 1975. D 6/20/1964 Bp Anson Phelps Stokes Jr P 1/10/1965 Bp Lauriston L Scaife. m 12/17/1966 Polly Ellen Keech c 2. Vic Gr Ch Tampa FL 2000-2004; Dioc Stff Dio SW Florida Sarasota FL 1997-2000; Chair Coll Wk Com Dio SW Florida Sarasota FL 1988-1993; Int S Paul's Ch Natick MA 1987; St Albans Sch Cathd of St Ptr & St Paul Washington DC 1979-1985; Pstr Assoc S Dunst's Ch Tulsa OK 1974-1979; Chapl Holland Hall Sch Tulsa OK 1973-1979. OHC, Assoc 1975-2005. canongrc@aol.com

CAIRES, Joy MarieLouise (O) 12671 Woodside Drive, Chesterland OH 44026 B Kahului Maui HI 8/18/1978 d Gordon Caires & Sallie Mae. BA Smith 2000; MDiv EDS 2006. D 6/3/2006 P 1/9/2007 Bp Mark Hollingsworth Jr. m 9/4/2004 Lona Caires. Ch Of Our Sav Akron OH 2008-2011; Luth Chapl Serv Cleveland OH 2006-2008. joy.caires@uhhospitals.org

CALAFAT, Karen Anne (Los) 2647 Mayflower Ave, Arcadia CA 91006 B Texas 12/16/1964 D 6/19/2004 P 1/22/2005 Bp Joseph Jon Bruno. m 10/2/1993 Philip Paul Calafat c 2. The Reverend S Jas' Par So Pasadena CA 2004-2006; Hillsides Educ Cntr Pasadena CA 2004; Chapl Hillsides Hm For Chld Pasadena CA 1999-2004. kcalafat@att.net

CALCOTE, A(lan) Dean (Tex) 5615 Duff St, Beaumont TX 77706 **Chair Dioc Schools Cmsn Dio Texas Houston TX 1977-** B Shreveport LA 7/25/1933 s Aucie Daniel Calcote & Patty Lewis. BA Tul 1955; MDiv GTS 1958; STM GTS 1963. D 6/21/1958 Bp Iveson Batchelor Noland P 5/8/1959 Bp Girault M Jones. c 2. Asst S Mk's Ch Beaumont TX 1974-1998; Dio Louisiana Baton Rouge LA 1969-1974; The GTS New York NY 1962-1963; S Paul's Ch New Orleans LA 1958-1963; The GTS New York NY 1958-1961. Auth, "The Proposed PB of 1785," *Hist mag of the Prot Epis Ch, Vol XLVI*, 1977. Citation for Outstanding Serv to Epis Schools SW Assn of Epis Schools 2007; Citation for Outstanding Serv to Epis Schools NAES 1998; STB cl GTS New York NY 1958; Phi Beta Kappa Tul New Orleans LA 1955. dcalcote@gt.rr.com

CALDBECK, Elaine S (SO) 2709 McGee Ave., Middletown OH 45044 **The Epis Ch Of The Ascen Middletown OH 2009-** B Des Moines IA 1/5/1957 d Jim Caldbeck & Velma Irene. BS Iowa St U 1980; MS U MN 1987; MDiv SWTS 1995; MA Garrett Evang TS 1996; PhD NWU 2000. D 6/19/2004 P 12/18/2004 Bp William Dailey Persell. Dio Chicago Chicago IL 2006-2008; S Matt's Ch Evanston IL 2005-2006. "The Poetry of Pauli Murray: Afr Amer Civil Rts Lawyer and P," Ruether Fortress Press, 2002. ecaldbeck@gmail.com

CALDWELL, Brenda Ann (Wyo) 1167 Hidalgo Dr, Laramie WY 82072 B Tampa FL 11/8/1948 d George Monroe Doyle & Lillian Cornelius. AA S Petersburg Cmnty Coll 1968; BA U of So Florida 1996. D 12/30/1999 Bp Bruce Edward Caldwell. m 12/13/1971 Bruce Edward Caldwell c 2. Cathd Hm For Chld Laramie WY 2003-2007; Dio Wyoming Casper WY 1999-2002.

✠ CALDWELL, Rt Rev Bruce Edward (Wyo) 104 S 4th St, Laramie WY 82070 B Painesville OH 7/8/1947 s Robert M Caldwell & Lois. BA U of So Florida 1973; MDiv GTS 1978; DD GTS 1998. D 6/22/1978 P 3/1/1979 Bp Emerson Paul Haynes Con 9/26/1997 for Wyo. m 12/13/1971 Brenda Ann Doyle c 1. Bp Of Wyoming Dio Wyoming Casper WY 1997-2010; R S Geo's Epis Ch Bismarck ND 1991-1997; Dio Alaska Fairbanks AK 1989-1991; R S Steph's Ch Ft Yukon AK 1989-1991; R S Jas Hse Of Pryr Tampa FL 1984-1989; S Thos Epis Christiansburg VA 1979-1980; Asst St Johns Epis Ch Tampa FL 1978-1984. bruce@wydiocese.org

CALDWELL, Charles Francis (Spr) 45 Heritage Way, Naples FL 34110 B DeLand FL 5/5/1935 s Charles Barrett Caldwell & Adelaide Letitia. BA U of Florida 1957; BD SWTS 1961; STM STUSo 1970; PhD U of Notre Dame 1978. D 7/2/1961 Bp Henry I Louttit P 1/6/1962 Bp James Loughlin Duncan. m 5/26/1956 Eleanor Marguerite Trump c 4. Asst Prof Nash Nashotah WI 1985-1995; Vic S Jn's Ch Centralia IL 1982-1985; Vic S Thos Ch Salem IL 1982-1985; Supply P Dio Nthrn Indiana So Bend IN 1974-1978; Vic Gloria Dei Epis Ch Cocoa FL 1969-1974; Asst S Barn Ch Deland FL 1966-1968; Asst S Andr's Epis Ch Tampa FL 1961-1964. Auth, *Hd & Glory*, Preservation Press, 1996. Phi Beta Kappa; Phi Kappa Phi; SSC, SocMary, Soc King Chas M. Phi Beta Kappa U of Florida Gainesville FL 1957.

CALDWELL, Edward Frederick (Alb) 100 Farmington Dr, Camillus NY 13031 B Rochester NY 5/1/1926 s Francis Kerison Caldwell & Winifred Margaret. BA U Roch 1949; STB GTS 1959; STM GTS 1989. D 6/8/1952 P 12/1/1952 Bp Dudley S Stark. c 4. S Paul's Ch Bloomville NY 1986-1991; S Ptr's Ch Hobart NY 1982-1983; R Chr Ch Walton NY 1975-1991; R Trin Ch Gouverneur NY 1967-1975; Vic S Hilda's - S Pat's Epis Ch Edmonds WA 1964-1967; Assoc S Lk's Epis Ch Seattle WA 1963-1964; P-in-c S Jas Ch Sedro-Woolley WA 1958-1963; Cur S Paul's Epis Ch Indianapolis IN 1956-1958; P-in-c S Paul's Ch Angelica NY 1952-1956; P-in-c S Phil's Ch Belmont NY 1952-1956. Auth, "Chr Affirmations," 1996. Assoc, OHC 1980; Ch Cmncatn Ntwk. e.caldwel@twcny.rr.com

CALDWELL, Gary Edward (VI) Po Box 121, Mount Pleasant IA 52641 B Mount Pleasant IA 5/4/1931 s Edward Paschal Caldwell & Ida Macil. BA Iowa Wesleyan Coll 1953; STB GTS 1960. D 6/11/1960 P 12/16/1960 Bp Gordon V Smith. Asst S Paul's Epis/Angl Ch Frederiksted VI VI 1978-1982; Asst S Jn's Ch Christiansted VI 1962-1968; Vic S Jas Epis Ch Independence IA 1960-1962. GAS. Ba scl Iowa Wesleyan Coll Mt Pleasant IA 1953.

CALDWELL, George M (Va) 501 Slaters Ln Apt 521, Alexandria VA 22314 B Dublin IE 5/9/1951 s Robert W Caldwell & Martha. BA Cor 1973; MA U CA 1974; MDiv VTS 1998. D 6/13/1998 P 4/15/1999 Bp Peter James Lee. Assoc S Paul's Epis Ch Alexandria VA 1998-2006.

CALDWELL, James Hardy (Chi) 1307nW Logan St, Freeport IL 61032 B Chicago IL 4/8/1936 s W Wendell Caldwell & Josephine H. BA Cor 1958; BD VTS 1964. D 6/26/1964 Bp Philip Frederick McNairy P 3/1/1965 Bp Donald H V Hallock. c 1. Dio Hawaii Honolulu HI 2009-2010; Asst S Fran' Par Palos Verdes Estates CA 2007-2009; Gr Epis Ch New Lenox IL 2005-2006; Int Chr Ch Joliet IL 1998-2004; Asst S Giles' Ch Northbrook IL 1984-1998. jameshcaldwell@yahoo.com

CALDWELL, Michael Lee (FtW) 3401 Bellaire Dr S, Fort Worth TX 76109 **Dnry Rep to Exec Coun Dio Ft Worth Ft Worth TX 2010-; Trst The U So (Sewanee) Sewanee TN 2010-; Cur Trin Epis Ch Ft Worth TX 2009-** B Abilene TX 7/6/1967 s James E Caldwell & Ruby N. BS Trin U 1989; MBA Schiller Intl U 1992; MDiv The U So (Sewanee) 2009. D 12/20/2008 P 8/8/2009 Bp C(harles) Wallis Ohl. m 9/21/2002 Dawn Marie Bangart. mcaldwellt09@yahoo.com

CALDWELL JR, Ralph Martin (Va) 3915 Hope Valley Rd, Durham NC 27707 B Spartanburg SC 8/5/1928 s Ralph Martin Caldwell & Ruth. BA Davidson Coll 1948; BD Duke 1951; GTS 1952; MA Col 1956; UTS 1956. D 6/18/1952 P 12/19/1952 Bp Edwin A Penick. m 6/12/1982 Elizabeth S Shinnick c 2. Asst S Tim's Ch Raleigh NC 2002-2008; Int Dio No Carolina Raleigh NC 1993-2002; Int Dio Texas Houston TX 1982-1993; S Jas' Ch Richmond VA 1979-1982; P-in-c Gr Ch Madison NJ 1977-1979; R Emm Par Epis Ch And Day Sch Sthrn Pines NC 1956-1976; Assoc Chr's Ch Rye NY 1954-1956. Auth, *Lift Up Your Hearts*, Morehouse-Gorham, 1956; Auth, *Marcion & His Influence*, Col, 1956. kimartin@mindspring.com

CALDWELL, Samuel Hawks (Nev) 2256 Meadowbrook Ln, Carson City NV 89701 **Died 1/30/2011** B Cambridge MA 7/3/1929 s Samuel Hawks Caldwell & Elva Alice. BFA Ohio U 1956; BD Bex 1966; MDiv Bex 1973. D 6/11/1966 P 1/25/1967 Bp Nelson Marigold Burroughs. c 2. Auth, *Cnfrmtn Manual*, Self-Pub for sev parishes; Auth, "Jackopalians," *Photo Series*, Dioc Nwspr. sndcaldwell@sbcglobal.net

CALDWELL, Stephen Russell (RG) 9632 Allande Rd. NE, Albuquerque NM 87109 B Springfield OH 8/30/1938 s Russell Warder Caldwell & Cora Catherine. BA OH SU 1960; MDiv GTS 1969. D 6/7/1969 P 12/10/1969 Bp Horace W B Donegan. m 12/30/1972 Barbara Jean Sybrandt c 3. R S Chad's Epis Ch Albuquerque NM 1989-2003; R S Agnes Ch Sebring FL 1978-1988; Assoc All SS Epis Ch Lakeland FL 1973-1978; Cur/Headmaster S Paul's Ch Winter Haven FL 1969-1973. srcabq@comcast.net

CALDWELL, Wallace Franklin (Mo) Po Box 277, Fremont MI 49412 B Saint Louis MO 4/8/1947 s Robert W Caldwell & Martha P. BA Cor 1970; MDiv Bex 1974. D 7/10/1974 P 6/1/1976 Bp Ned Cole. Trin Epis Ch Kirksville MO 2001-2009; S Jn's Ch Fremont MI 1999-2001; All SS Epis Ch Whitefish MT 1997-1998; P-in-c Ch Of The Gd Shpd Forrest City AR 1994-1996; Ch of the Redeem Addison NY 1989-1990; S Paul's Ch Montour Falls NY 1987-1994; P-in-c S Mk's Ch Candor NY 1982-1986; Trin Ch Lowville NY 1978-1980; P-in-c Ch Of The Epiph Trumansburg NY 1976-1978. Phi Beta Kappa. wallacecaldwell@cableone.net

CALDWELL III, Withers Waller (Chi) 400 Ravine Ave, Lake Bluff IL 60044 **Died 10/7/2011** B Knoxville TN 7/10/1963 s Withers Waller Caldwell & Constance Ann. BA Trin U San Antonio TX 1986; MDiv SWTS 1991. D 6/22/1991 Bp Donis Dean Patterson P 7/1/1992 Bp William Walter Wiedrich.

CALER, Joshua Morgan (Va) 900 Broadway, Nashville TN 37203 **Cur Chr Ch Cathd Nashville TN 2011-** B Sewickley PA 6/16/1982 s Jerry Rae Caler & Laura Kim. BA Grove City Coll 2004; M.Div Duke DS 2011. D 6/4/2011 Bp Shannon Sherwood Johnston. m 7/24/2004 Mary E Caler. jcaler@christcathedral.org

CALEY BOWERS, Elizabeth Ann Caley (Fla) 9252 San Jose Blvd. Apt. 3703, Jacksonville FL 32257 B Kingsport TN 3/4/1937 d Arthur Douglas Caley & Helen. BA Katharine Gibbs Sch 1957. D 7/7/1993 Bp Harry Woolston Shipps. c 3. D S Paul's By-The-Sea Epis Ch Jacksonville Bch FL 2002-2005; D Dio Georgia Savannah GA 1993-2000; D S Thos Epis Ch Thomasville GA 1993-2000. abowers954@comcast.net

CALHOUN III, Bill (WTex) 355 Marina Dr, Port Aransas TX 78373 B Camden NJ 2/28/1933 s William Brown Calhoun & Evelyn Mae. Leh 1952; Rutgers-The St U 1953; Rutgers-The St U 1959; STh Epis TS of The SW 1982. D 6/17/1982 Bp Scott Field Bailey P 1/1/1983 Bp Stanley Fillmore Hauser. m 11/29/1958 Judith Barbara Schmieler. Int Trin-By-The-Sea Port Aransas TX 1998-2001; S Helena's Epis Ch Boerne TX 1985-1998; Assoc S Lk's Epis Ch San Antonio TX 1982-1984. HSEC. c-chip@walipapa.com

CALHOUN, Dolores Moore (CPa) Po Box 32, Jersey Mills PA 17739 B Williamsport PA 10/27/1941 d Amos A Moore & Susan. BS Lock Haven U 1963; Denai St 1973; Cert Pennsylvania Diac Sch 1985; CPE Hershey Med Cntr 1987. D 6/10/1988 Bp Charlie Fuller McNutt Jr P 10/6/2007 Bp Nathan Dwight Baxter. m 7/17/1964 Larry David Calhoun c 1. D S Mk's Epis Ch Lewistown PA 1992-1993. deemc41@yahoo.com

CALHOUN, Janis Leigh (Ore) 16530 Nottingham Dr, Gladstone OR 97027 **D S Steph's Ch Newport OR 2002-** B Everett WA 2/17/1941 d Carl W Calhoun & Genevieve E. BS Portland St U 1963; MS Portland St U 1966. D 12/27/1990 Bp Robert Louis Ladehoff. c 3.

CALHOUN JR, Joseph (Cal) William (ETenn) 9420 States View Dr, Knoxville TN 37922 **R Ch Of The Gd Samar Knoxville TN 2005-** B Omaha NE 8/29/1963 s Joseph William Calhoun & JoAnne Prindle. Rice U 1983; BS U of Sthrn Mississippi 1986; MDiv Epis TS of The SW 2002. D 6/1/2002 P 12/28/2002 Bp Duncan Montgomery Gray III. m 9/22/1990 Anna Webb c 2. Cur Ch Of The Nativ Greenwood MS 2002-2005. calcalhoun@knology.net

CALHOUN, Nancy Ellen (Del) 31 Dresner Cir, Boothwyn PA 19061 B Hartford WI 1/12/1947 d Allen Ross Calhoun & Ann Elizabeth. BA U of Wisconsin 1971; MDiv SWTS 1981; DMin Chicago TS 1992. D 6/2/1983 Bp James Winchester Montgomery P 12/13/1986 Bp Frank Tracy Griswold III. Assoc The Ch Of The Ascen Claymont DE 2007-2009; S Dav's Epis Ch Wilmington DE 2002; Dio Delaware Wilmington DE 1998; Brandywine Epis Parishes Wilmington DE 1996-1997; R Calv Epis Ch Hillcrest Wilmington DE 1996-1997; S Gabr The Archangel Ch Vernon Hills IL 1992-1995; Pstr Assoc S Aug's Epis Ch Wilmette IL 1984-1991. rosievi olet@att.net

CALHOUN, Ora Albert (WK) 26627 Midland Rd, Bay Village OH 44140 B Aurora OH 1/12/1941 s Charles Adams Calhoun & Winifred Maude. Cleveland St U; LTh VTS 1972. D 6/17/1972 P 5/12/1973 Bp John Harris Burt. m 8/31/1963 Mary Lou Henwood c 3. LocTen S Phil's Epis Ch Topeka KS 1994-1995; S Fran Cmnty Serv Inc. Salina KS 1991-2004; S Lk's Epis Ch Niles OH 1987-1989; Vic S Matt's Ch Ashland OH 1973-1980; Asst S Lk's Ch Cleveland OH 1972-1973. ocalhoun1@me.com

CALHOUN, Royce (WTex) 103 Bluff Vista, Boerne TX 78006 **Vic S Mich And All Ang Epis Ch Blanco TX 1994-** B Kaufman TX 11/5/1938 s Grover W Calhoun & Sarah Susan. BS E Texas Bapt Coll 1961; MDiv SW Bapt TS 1965; ThM SW Bapt TS 1968; Th.D SW Bapt TS 1972; Ph.D. SW Bapt TS 1975. D 3/3/1993 Bp Earl Nicholas McArthur Jr P 12/20/1993 Bp John Herbert MacNaughton. m 7/6/1985 Angeline Harrington. Vic S Lk's Ch Cypress Mill TX 1994-2006; Asst St Fran Epis Ch San Antonio TX 1993-1994. Amer Assn for Mar and Fam Ther 1976; AAPC 1974; Soc for the Advancement of Sexual Hlth 2007. Kemper Awd Webster U 2009; Appreciation of Serv Awd Keystone Sch 1999; Outstanding Contribution Awd SW Reg, AAPC, 1999. roycecalhn@aol.com

CALHOUN-BRYANT, Julie Elizabeth (CNY) Po Box 91, Camillus NY 13031 **S Alb's Ch Syracuse NY 2006-** B Albany NY 4/23/1961 d Francis Taylor Bryant & Dagmar Marketa. AAS Corning Cmnty Coll 1980; BA Wm Smith 1982; MDiv Ya Berk 1988. D 6/18/1988 P 6/17/1989 Bp O'Kelley Whitaker. m 5/17/1986 Brian Russell Calhoun-Bryant. S Jn's Ch Marcellus NY 2002-2006; R S Lk's Epis Ch Camillus NY 1995-2002; Asst S Paul's Ch Endicott NY 1991-1995; Int Dio Cntrl New York Syracuse NY 1989-1991; D S Paul And S Jas New Haven CT 1988-1989. Ba mcl Wm Smith Geneva NY 1982. jcbslc@aol.com

C

CALKINS, Linda (WA) 10617 Eastwood Ave, Silver Spring MD 20901 **R S Barth's Ch Laytonsville MD 2010-** B Long Island NY 4/18/1955 d Willis Duane Calkins & Jeanne Francis. MA Washington Theol Un 1999; MS Loyola Coll 2000; MDiv VTS 2001. D 6/9/2001 Bp Jane Hart Holmes Dixon P 1/19/2002 Bp Allen Lyman Bartlett Jr. c 2. Int S Jn's In The Mountains Stowe VT 2008-2009; P-in-c S Lk's Ch Washington DC 2007-2008; Asst R S Jn's Ch Olney MD 2001-2004. lindacalkins@me.com

CALKINS, Matthew H(amilton)) (Ct) 4670 Congress St, Fairfield CT 06824 **S Tim's Ch Fairfield CT 2001-** B Los Angeles CA 9/10/1955 s Richard Halister Calkins & Marylou. BA Mid 1977; MDiv UTS 1998. D 6/13/1998 P 12/19/1998 Bp Richard Frank Grein. m 6/23/1984 Mary Anne Bulakowski c 1. Chr And H Trin Ch Westport CT 1998-2001. Ba w hon Mid Middlebury VT 1977. calkins@sttimschurch.org

CALLAGHAN, Alice Dale (Los) 307 E 7th St, Los Angeles CA 90014 **Las Familias Del Pueblo Los Angeles CA 1994-** B Calgary AB CA 6/2/1947 d Henry Robert Callaghan & Olga. D 6/20/1981 P 1/1/1982 Bp Robert C Rusack.

CALLAGHAN, Carol Lee (Eas) 308 Elm Ave, Easton MD 21601 **Chr Ch S Ptr's Par Easton MD 2008-** B Baltimore MD 9/9/1946 d James Allen Cox & Marilynn Jeanette. BA U of Charleston 1975; MA MD Consortium of Grad Wk Rockville MD 1983. D 7/23/2005 Bp James Joseph Shand. m 7/8/1989 Kevin Thomas Callaghan c 1. carol@christchurcheaston.org

CALLAHAM, Arthur A (Tex) 203 Crown Colony Dr, Lufkin TX 75901 **R S Cyp's Ch Lufkin TX 2009-** B Arlington Heights IL 12/23/1975 s Arnold Arthur Callaham & Ruth Anne. BS Virginia Tech 1997; MS Virginia Tech 2000; MDiv U Chi 2006. D 6/24/2006 P 1/27/2007 Bp John Leslie Rabb. m 6/14/2003 Erica L Moore c 1. acallaham@gmail.com

CALLAHAN, Gary Edward (ETenn) Po Box 21275, Chattanooga TN 37424 B New York NY 10/15/1943 s Frederick William Callahan & Catherine. BA Col 1964; STB GTS 1969; DMin STUSo 1982. D 6/7/1969 P 12/1/1969 Bp Horace W B Donegan. m 12/27/1969 Barbara Rathjen c 2. R S Mart Of Tours Epis Ch Chattanooga TN 1998-2008; R S Dav's Ch Southfield MI 1977-1998; Vic Ch of the H Sprt Belmont MI 1974-1977; Asst S Lk's Par Kalamazoo MI 1969-1974. Auth, "Together In Life & Death".

CALLAHAN, Griffin Clay (WVa) 1621 College Ave, Bluefield WV 24701 **Dio W Virginia Charleston WV 2000-** B Bluefield WV 10/31/1919 s Griffin Elwood Callahan & Marion Arnott. BA W&M 1941; MDiv VTS 1943. D 9/27/1943 P 5/1/1944 Bp Robert E L Strider. m 5/19/1984 Mary Elizabeth Burton c 5. Pstr Asst S Steph's Epis Ch Beckley WV 1986-1990; Vic All Souls' Epis Ch Daniels WV 1980-1992; Asst Ascen Epis Ch Hinton WV 1977-1980; Asst S Andr's Ch Mullens WV 1977-1980; Worker P Dio W Virginia Charleston WV 1975-1985; Assoc All Souls' Epis Ch Daniels WV 1975-1977; Dn Of Ohio Vlly Convoc Dio W Virginia Charleston WV 1962-1974; R Trin Ch Parkersburg WV 1960-1974; Assoc Calv Ch Pittsburgh PA 1955-1960; R S Ptr's Ch Huntington WV 1949-1955; Dn Of New River Convoc Dio W Virginia Charleston WV 1947-1949; M-in-c All SS Ch Un WV 1943-1944. Auth, "How Come?," Clinch Vlly, 2000; Auth, "Kairos Moments Remembered".

CALLARD, Tom Adams (Los) All Saints Parish, 5619 Monte Vista St., Los Angeles CA 90042 **R All SS Par Los Angeles CA 2007-** B Burlington VT 1/24/1967 BA U of Massachusetts. D 1/10/2004 P 9/10/2004 Bp M(arvil) Thomas Shaw III. m 7/27/2003 Sagrario C Callard c 2. Vic S Lk's/San Lucas Epis Ch Chelsea MA 2004-2007. t.collard@comcast.net

CALLAWAY, James Gaines (NY) 404 Riverside Dr, New York NY 10025 **Secy Gnrl The AEC New York NY 2011-** B Kansas City MO 4/16/1944 s James Gaines Callaway & Martha-Hall. BA U So 1966; MDiv GTS 1969; DD U So 2008. D 11/28/1970 Bp Edward Randolph Welles II P 7/1/1971 Bp Paul Moore Jr. m 5/20/1972 Mary Howard c 2. Dep for Faith Formation and Dvlpmt and Angl Partnerships Trin Par New York NY 1980-2011; R The Ch Of The Annunc Oradell NJ 1975-1980; Asst S Paul's Ch Englewood NJ 1973-1975; Asst S Mary's Manhattanville Epis Ch New York NY 1970-1973. Auth, "How Is a Preschool Evacuated?," *Trin News*, 2001; Auth, *Sprtly of Endwmt*, 1994; Auth, *Endwmt: Friend or Foe*, 1987. Soc of S Marg, Dir Cmnty of the H Spiri. Hon Cn Dio Cape Coast, Ghana 2009; Chairman Emer Psychotheapy Spiritualty Inst 2008; Prov Cn Ch of the Prov of Sthrn Afr 2004. jcallaway@trinitywallstreet.org

CALLAWAY, Richard Henry (At) 6513 Blue Creek Ct, Douglasville GA 30135 **Cn To The Ordnry Dio Atlanta Atlanta GA 2001-** B Bluefield WV 9/19/1946 s Murray Richard Callaway & Ellen Gregory. BA VPI 1969; MDiv GTS 1984; Cert SWTS 2003. D 6/23/1984 Bp Peter James Lee P 6/29/1985 Bp Robert Whitridge Estill. m 12/7/1991 C Wynn Rainey c 2. Pres Of Stndg Com Dio Atlanta Atlanta GA 1998-2000; R S Julian's Epis Ch Douglasville GA 1991-2001; Vic Ch Of The Nativ Raleigh NC 1987-1991; Vic S Mich's Ch Raleigh NC 1987-1991; Asst To R Ch Of The Gd Shpd Rocky Mt NC 1984-1987. rcallaway@episcopalatlanta.org

CALLENDER, Francis Charles (EpisSanJ) 1060 Cottage Ave, Manteca CA 95336 B Limerick IR 10/18/1948 s Francis Edmund Callender & Alberta Patricia. BA Trin-Dublin Ie 1970; Trin-Dublin Ie 1971; MA Trin-Dublin Ie 1973; GOE Ireland Theol Coll Ie 1979. Trans from Church of Ireland 1/1/1989 Bp John-David Mercer Schofield. m 3/17/1976 Susan Elizabeth Anderson c 2. S Mary's Ch Manteca CA 1989-1990. Trin Theol Soc, Chr Un, ERM, SOMA, Arm, SAMS.

CALLENDER, Randy Kyle (Pa) 2645 E Venango St, Philadelphia PA 19134 **The Reverend Gr Ch And The Incarn Philadelphia PA 2010-** B Philadelphia, PA 1/22/1983 s Sereta. BA Cheyney U 2007; MDiv Epsicopal DS 2010. D 6/5/2010 Bp Edward Lewis Lee Jr P 1/22/2011 Bp Charles Ellsworth Bennison Jr. randycallender@yahoo.com

CALLOWAY, N(ancy) (WNC) 1119 Old Fort Sugar Hill Rd, Old Fort NC 28762 B Morgantown NC 11/29/1950 d James Calloway & Mildred. BA Mars Hill Coll 1973; MDiv Duke 1978. D 11/23/2002 Bp Robert Hodges Johnson. lcalloway1@charter.net

CALVERT, Cara J (SO) 1129 Franklin St, Hamilton OH 45013 **Serv Dio Sthrn Ohio Cincinnati OH 1989-** B Poplar Plains KY 7/24/1923 s Erastus Dean Calvert & Carrie Inez. Denison U 1943; Lic Epis TS In Kentucky 1989. D 3/14/1989 Bp Herbert Thompson Jr. c 5. Associated Parishes; NAAD. dcnjay@aol.com

CALVERT, George Morris (SanD) 3990 Bonita Rd, Bonita CA 91902 **R Ch Of The Gd Shpd Bonita CA 1998-** B San Diego CA 2/19/1956 s Lowell Morris Calvert & Maxine Frances. BA U CA 1979; MDiv VTS 1986; DMin Fuller TS 1997. D 6/14/1986 P 2/21/1987 Bp Charles Brinkley Morton. m 8/6/1988 Nancy Lyn Vyvjala c 2. Dioc Coun Dio San Diego San Diego CA 2007-2010; Dioc Coun Dio San Diego San Diego CA 2000-2003; Dio San Diego San Diego CA 1998-1999; Exec Coun Dio Colorado Denver CO 1995-1998; S Paul's Epis Ch Lamar CO 1993-1998; Dio Colorado Denver CO 1990-1993; Cur S Patricks Ch And Day Sch Thousand Oaks CA 1988-1990; Asst S Fran' Par Palos Verdes Estates CA 1986-1988. calvert@calalum.org

CALVO, Gustavo Alberto (Alb) 7882 York Rd, Rd Ext, Pavilion NY 14525 B Havanna Cuba 5/22/1962 AAS Orange Cnty Cmnty Coll 1990; BSW SUNY 2002; MA St. Bern's Inst Rochester NY 2005. D 6/11/2005 P 12/10/2005 Bp Daniel William Herzog. m 1/3/1998 Noel Smith c 1. S Jn The Evang Columbiaville NY 2007-2010; Reverend S Mk's Ch Malone NY 2005-2007; S Steph's Ch Delmar NY 2002. calvo_gus@yahoo.com

CALVO PEREZ, Antonis de Jesus (Colom) C165 No. 36 A-30, Bogota Colombia **Iglesia Epis En Colombia 2005-** B Turbana Bolivar 3/29/1963 s Humberto Calvo & Ana Maria. Universidad Javeriana; Filosofia + Pstr Instituto Pstr Y Filosofia Cepaf 1999. D P. antonisdej@hotmail.com

CAMACHO-OSORIO, Nabor (Ve) Calle Vakairles, Edificio Sagrado Corozan, San Felis, Estado Bolivar 6301 Venezuela **Dio Venezuela Colinas De Bello Monte Caracas 10-42-A VE 2004-** B 7/12/1952 D 12/19/1992 P 6/29/1993 Bp Onell Asiselo Soto. c 1.

CAMERON, David Albert (SD) 1607 Pevans Pkwy, Rapid City SD 57701 B El Paso TX 8/13/1947 s David Molloy Cameron & Ruth Ann. BA U So 1969; MA Oxf 1973; MDiv SWTS 1974. D 9/10/1974 Bp Richard Mitchell Trelease Jr P 3/14/1975 Bp Jackson Earle Gilliam. m 6/26/2004 Constance Nelson Lane c 4. Dioc Coun Dio So Dakota Sioux Falls SD 1998-2004; Gen. Conv Dep Dio So Dakota Sioux Falls SD 1991-2003; Black Hills Dnry Dio So Dakota Sioux Falls SD 1990-1998; Stndg Com, Pres Dio So Dakota Sioux Falls SD 1989-1996; EFM Mentor Dio So Dakota Sioux Falls SD 1987-2006; R Emm Epis Par Rapid City SD 1987-2006; R S Andr's Epis Ch New Orleans LA 1982-1987; EFM Mentor Dio Louisiana Baton Rouge LA 1981-1987; Epis Cmnty Serv, Bd. of Dir. Dio Louisiana Baton Rouge LA 1981-1987; LA. Epis Cler Assn, Bd., Pres. Dio Louisiana Baton Rouge LA 1980-1987; Chair, Dept. of CE Dio Louisiana Baton Rouge LA 1978-1987; Exec Bd Dio Louisiana Baton Rouge LA 1978-1987; R S Fran Ch Denham Sprg LA 1977-1982; Cur S Lk's Ch Billings MT 1974-1977; Yth Dir Dio Montana Helena MT 1974-1976; Yth Dir, Stndg Com Dio Montana Helena MT 1974-1976. Epis Cler Assn 1977-1987. revdac08@gmail.com

CAMERON, Jacqueline Rene (Chi) 513 W Aldine Ave Apt 2h, Chicago IL 60657 **Bp Anderson Hse Chicago IL 2005-** B San Gabriel CA 10/20/1962 BA Wheaton Coll 1984; MA King's Coll - Lon 1994; MD NWU Med Sch 1994; MDiv GTS 2004. D 6/19/2004 P 12/18/2004 Bp William Dailey Persell. Epis Ch Of The Atone Chicago IL 2008-2010; S Matt's Ch Evanston IL 2004-2005. Auth, "Minding God/Minding Pain: Chr Theol Reflection On Recent Advances In Pain Resrch," Zygon Vol.40 No. 1, 2005. jrcameron@earthlink.net

CAMERON, Krista Ann (Roch) 3345 Edgemere Dr, Rochester NY 14612 **S Lk's Ch Brockport NY 2008-** B Indianapolis IN 10/18/1955 d Robert Christ Cameron & Dolores Ann. BA Ball St U 1978; MA Ball St U 1989; MDiv SWTS 1995. D 6/23/1995 Bp Edward Witker Jones P 6/15/1996 Bp John H(enry) Smith. Gr Ch Lyons NY 2007-2008; Gr Ch Lyons NY 2006-2007; R S Geo's Ch Hilton NY 2002-2006; Int Ch Of The Nativ Indianapolis IN 2000-2001; S Paul's Ch Richmond IN 2000; Boys Hm Covington VA 1999; Int Yth Mnstry Coordntr Dio SW Virginia Roanoke VA 1998-1999; Supply P Chr Ch Pearisburg VA 1997-1999; Cur S Jn's Ch Huntington WV 1995-1996. revkrista@juno.com

CAMERON, Meigan Cameron (Chi) 4140 N Lavergne Ave, Chicago IL 60641 B Washington,DC 8/2/1957 d James Burris & Margaret. BA U CA 1980; BS U of Idaho Moscow 1990; MDiv SWTS 1999. D 6/26/1999 Bp R(aymond) Stewart Wood Jr P 11/1/2001 Bp Victor Alfonso Scantlebury. c 2. Vic Ch Of The Epiph Chicago IL 2004-2010; Assoc Gr Ch Oak Pk IL 2001-2004; S Chrys's Ch Chicago IL 1999-2000. Catechesis Gd Shpd. meigancameron@hotmail.com

CAMERON JR, Robert Speir (CFla) 1200 W International Speedway Blvd, Daytona Beach FL 32114 B Albany NY 9/22/1932 s Robert Speir Cameron & Ruth. BD U of So Carolina 1955; MS U Of Florida 1967; EdD Nova U 1979. D 6/15/1975 Bp William Hopkins Folwell. m 12/20/1955 Joyce Metts. D S Jas Epis Ch Ormond Bch FL 1975-1978. Ees, NAAD.

CAMMACK, David Walker (Md) 7200 3rd Ave, Sykesville MD 21784 **Assoc Emm Ch Baltimore MD 1995-** B Huntington WV 6/14/1925 s Howard Haworth Cammack & Sara Burd. BS USNA 1947; MA U of Delaware Newark 1953; MDiv VTS 1955; U of Virginia 1959; Jn Hopkins U 1974; DD McKendree Sch of Rel Baltimore MD 1997. D 6/3/1955 P 1/6/1956 Bp Frederick D Goodwin. m 12/21/1974 Shirley Deane. Emm Ch Baltimore MD 1992; R Trin Ch Waterloo Elkridge MD 1983-1992; R S Mary's Epis Ch Woodlawn Baltimore MD 1976-1983; R Ch Of The Gd Shpd Bluemont VA 1963-1970; R Gr Ch Berryville VA 1963-1970; R S Mary's Memi Berryville VA 1963-1970; Assoc S Paul's Memi Charlottesville VA 1955-1963. Citizens for Global Solutions 2047; Soc for Values in Higher Educ 2001; Untd Rel Initiative (for Wrld peace) 1999. Eclectic Cler Soc Baltimore, MD Baltimore MD 1972; Raven Soc U VA U VA 1958.

CAMP IV, E(dmond) Weyman (SC) 8934 Sandy Creek Rd, Edisto Island SC 29438 **R Trin Ch Edisto Island SC 1991-** B Charleston SC 12/16/1961 s Edmond Weyman Camp & Helen Oeland. AA Emory-at-U of Oxford Oxford GB 1981; BBA Emory U 1983; MDiv TESM 1990. D 6/4/1990 P 6/19/1991 Bp Edward Lloyd Salmon Jr. m 4/4/1994 Melissa Thurber. Dioc Coun Dio So Carolina Charleston SC 1993-1996. creekcamps@aol.com

CAMPBELL, Alene L (Los) 144 S C St, Oxnard CA 93030 B Farmington NM 5/26/1971 d Ivan Leslie Campbell & Emma Bernyce. BA Coll Ozarks Point Lookout MO 1993; MA Boston Coll 2006; MDiv CDSP 2009. D 1/31/2009 P 1/28/2010 Bp Edward Joseph Konieczny. S Jn's Par San Bernardino CA 2009-2011. alc_kairos@juno.com

CAMPBELL, Anne (Oly) 3438 161st Pl Se Apt 51, Bellevue WA 98008 B 4/19/1939 d Frank Ellis Campbell & Myrtle. BA NWU 1965; MA NWU 1967; MA SWTS 1978. D 11/18/1978 P 5/1/1979 Bp Otis Charles. c 3. Dio Utah Salt Lake City UT 1988-1989; St Marks Hosp Salt Lake City UT 1981-1984; S Jas Epis Ch Midvale UT 1979-1981; S Ptr's Ch Clearfield UT 1979.

CAMPBELL, Benjamin Pfohl (Va) Richmond Hill, 2209 E Grace St, Richmond VA 23223 **Pstr Dir Richmond Hill Richmond VA 1988-; P-in-res S Paul's Ch Richmond VA 1979-** B Washington DC 2/2/1941 s Edmund Douglas Campbell & Elizabeth. BA Wms 1961; MA Oxf 1964; MA (Oxon) Oxf 1964; MDiv VTS 1966; Grad Sch Pecos Benedictine Abbey 1987. D 11/1/1966 Bp Robert Bruce Hall P 6/15/1967 Bp Robert Fisher Gibson Jr. m 8/12/1989 Ann Elizabeth Hopkins c 2. Int Ch Of The Creator Mechanicsville VA 1987-1988; Urban Mssnr S Paul's Ch Richmond VA 1979-1982; Cmncatn Dir Dio Virginia Richmond VA 1970-1978; Vic S Mary's Whitechapel Epis Lancaster VA 1966-1970; Vic Trin Epis Ch Lancaster VA 1966-1970. Auth, "Richmond's Unhealed Hist," Brandylane, 2011; Auth, "No Alien Power," Forw, 1985; Ed, "The Virginia Churchman," *The Virginia Churchman*, Dio Virginia, 1978. DD VTS 2010; Mdiv mcl VTS Alexandria VA 1966; Ba mcl Wms Williamstown MA 1961; Rhodes Schlr Rhodes Schlrshp Trust 1960. bcampbell@richmondhillva.org

CAMPBELL, Bruce Alan (Mich) 160 Walnut St, Wyandotte MI 48192 **P Assoc S Jn's Ch Plymouth MI 2010-** B Highland Park MI 12/1/1945 s Edwin Trenner Campbell & Margaret Adele. Wheaton Coll 1965; BA Wayne 1967; MDiv GTS 1971. D 6/29/1971 Bp Richard S M Emrich P 1/1/1972 Bp Archie H Crowley. m 7/6/1968 Sarah Gerig. R S Steph's Ch Wyandotte MI 1988-2010; Assoc R Chr Ch Dearborn MI 1982-1988; P-in-c S Mich And All Ang Onsted MI 1976-1981; Assoc Chapl Cbury Hse Ann Arbor MI 1973-1975. frbruce@wyan.org

CAMPBELL, Catherine Mary (Va) 3420 Flint Hill Place, Woodbridge VA 22192 **Dio Virginia Richmond VA 2005-; Vic La Mision Hispana El Divino Salvador Sacramento CA 1995-** B Mexico City MX 12/6/1956 d David Alexander Campbell & Edith. BA U of So Florida 1977; MDiv VTS 1988. D 9/27/1990 Bp Robert Poland Atkinson P 4/27/1991 Bp Peter James Lee. Vic S Jas Epis Mssn Lincoln CA 1999-2005; Hisp Mssnr Dio Nthrn California Sacramento CA 1995-2005; Assoc Trin Par Wilmington DE 1993-1995; Ch of the Incarn Mineral VA 1990-1993. revcat@earthlink.net

CAMPBELL, Claude Alan (Mo) 2831 N Prospect Ave, Milwaukee WI 53211 B San Antonio TX 5/7/1927 s Claude Amos Campbell & Kate. Fllshp Coll of Preachers; BS U of Texas 1950; BD VTS 1964. D 7/8/1964 Bp Everett H Jones P 1/1/1965 Bp Richard Earl Dicus. m 6/19/1997 Linda Ann Crick c 2. Assoc Ch Of The Incarn Dallas TX 1970-1974; Vic S Matt's Ch Edinburg TX 1964-1968; Asst S Jn's Ch McAllen TX 1964-1966. ACPE.

CAMPBELL, Dana L(ou) (Ct) 58 Greenwood St, East Hartford CT 06118 **Ch Of The Gd Shpd Hartford CT 2009-** B Tulsa OK 2/22/1948 d Colin Clyde Campbell & Helen Kimball. BA Kalamazoo Coll 1970; MDiv Ya Berk 1996. D 6/14/1997 Bp Clarence Nicholas Coleridge P 2/14/1998 Bp Andrew Donnan Smith. Grtr Hartford Reg Mnstry E Hartford CT 1999-2009; Asst S Andr's Ch Meriden CT 1997-1999. mother-dana@juno.com

CAMPBELL, Dennis Gail (Ark) 1501 32nd Ave S, Seattle WA 98144 **P-in-c S Clem's Epis Ch Seattle WA 2010-** B Michigan City IN 1/4/1956 s Dolan Campbell & Juanita. U Of Florida 1979; BSE Arkansas St U 1983; MA Arkansas St U 1985; MDiv Memphis TS 1990; DMin STUSo 1999. D 6/23/1990 P 12/28/1990 Bp Herbert Alcorn Donovan Jr. c 6. Cn Dio Arkansas Little Rock AR 2001-2009; Cn S Marg's Epis Ch Little Rock AR 2000-2009; Vic S Jas Sewanee TN 1995-2001; Fac Dir Of Congrl Mnstry The TS at The U So Sewanee TN 1994-2002; Vic S Matt's Epis Ch Benton AR 1990-1994. Auth, "Developing Congregations As Lrng Communities:Tools To Shape Your Future," The Alb Inst, 2000; Auth, "Lrng Orgnztn Theory Applied To Congrl Dvlpmt," 1999. Ch Dvlpmt Inst Nationalntrainers Ntwk; Saccem; Soc Of Angl And Luth Theologians. Mdiv mcl Memphis TS Memphis TN 1990. dgc777@gmail.com

CAMPBELL, Ernest Francis (Spok) 825 Wauna Vista Dr, Walla Walla WA 99362 **R Emer S Paul's Ch Walla Walla WA 1991-** B Evanston IL 8/17/1927 s Ernest Francis Campbell & Celia. BS NWU 1950; LTh SWTS 1953. D 6/6/1953 P 12/12/1953 Bp Charles L Street. m 2/4/1956 Margaret R Carruthers c 4. R S Paul's Ch Walla Walla WA 1969-1990; Dn The Epis Cathd Of Our Merc Sav Faribault MN 1967-1969; Assoc S Geo's Ch St Louis Pk MN 1960-1967; Asst S Jn The Evang S Paul MN 1956-1960; Cur S Mk's Ch Evanston IL 1953-1955.

CAMPBELL, Ernestina (NCal) 1617 32nd Ave, Sacramento CA 95822 **D Trin Cathd Sacramento CA 1993-** B Long Beach CA 9/27/1947 d Isauro Corona Rodriguez & Elisa. BA U CA 1969; MA California St U 1981; Cert Dio Of Nthrn California Sch For Deacons At Berkeley 1985. D 2/23/1991 Bp John Lester Thompson III. m 11/27/1971 Brian Lorne Campbell. D S Lk's Ch Woodland CA 1991-1993. NAAD.

CAMPBELL III, George Latimer (NJ) 257 4th St, South Amboy NJ 08879 **R Chr Ch So Amboy NJ 1998-** B Ithaca NY 3/24/1950 s George Latimer Campbell & Jean Marie. BA Sir Geo Wms Montreal Qc CA 1976. Trans from Anglican Church of Canada 2/14/1983 Bp Henry D Robinson. m 1/27/1973 Marcia Veronica Mary Tetley c 3. Litchfield Hills Reg Mnstry Bridgewater CT 1991-1995; S Mk's Ch Bridgewater CT 1989-1991; R Ch Of The H Trin Pawling NY 1986-1989; Estrn Dutchess Min Coun Pawling NY 1985-1988; R S Paul's Epis Ch Angola NY 1983-1986; S Alb's Ch Silver Creek NY 1983-1985. glc3@optonline.net

CAMPBELL, James Donald (La) 525 N Laurel St, Amite LA 70422 B Mountain View AR 6/1/1925 s James Thurman Campbell & Ruth May. BS Hendrix Coll 1948. D 12/1/1996 P 6/1/1997 Bp James Barrow Brown. m 11/2/1954 Margaret Antoinette Cain. D Ch Of The Incarn Amite LA 1996-1997.

CAMPBELL, Janet Bragg (Oly) 1556 NE 148th St, Shoreline WA 98155 **Liturg and Arts Cmsn Dio Olympia Seattle WA 2011-; Cn for Liturg Dio Olympia Seattle WA 2010-; Cmsn for Ch Archit Dio Olympia Seattle WA 2010-** B Waukegan IL 9/24/1944 d John Kendal Bragg & Mary. BA Vas 1966; MDiv GTS 1988. D 6/6/1988 Bp Robert Campbell Witcher Sr P 2/18/1989 Bp Orris George Walker Jr. m 7/9/2009 Roger Charles Campbell c 1. Int R S Steph's Epis Ch Seattle WA 2007-2010; Dir Of Liturg And The Arts S Mk's Cathd Seattle WA 2001-2007; Cn For Liturg Cathd Of S Jas Chicago IL 1993-2000; Dioc Liturg Dio Chicago Chicago IL 1993-2000; Assoc Vic S Ptr's Ch New York NY 1988-1992. Auth, "Through The Window Of The Ordnry: Experiences Of H Week," Ch Pub Grp, 2002. revjanetcampbell@gmail.com

CAMPBELL, Jean C (NY) 42 Timberline Dr, Poughkeepsie NY 12603 **R Trin Ch Fishkill NY 2005-** B Buffalo NY 3/22/1946 d Donald Alexander Campbell & Clara Anna. BS SUNY 1967; MA U of Notre Dame 1981; DD SWTS 1994. D 8/11/1989 P 2/24/1990 Bp Richard Frank Grein. Assoc Zion Epis Ch Wappingers Falls NY 2000-2004; P S Mk's Epis Ch Chelsea NY 1998-2004; Adult Chr Formation Ch Of The H Apos New York NY 1982-1984; Chr Formation Calv and St Geo New York NY 1978-1981. Auth, "Var arts". Coun Of Associated Parishes 1984; No Amer Acad Of Liturg 1982; Ord Of S Helena - Life Professed 1974-2010. DD Seabury Wstrn TS 1993. jccampbell@verizon.net

CAMPBELL, Karen Ann (WMass) 58 Hildreth St, Westford MA 01886 B Bakersfield CA 4/24/1948 d Edwin Paul Veverka & Jean Lewis. BA California St U 1970; MDiv EDS 1991. D 1/8/2000 Bp Mary Adelia Rosamond McLeod P 10/28/2000 Bp Gordon Paul Scruton. m 7/12/1969 Graham Ross Campbell c 3. Ch Of The Gd Shpd Fitchburg MA 2000-2010. Ba cl California St U Long Bch CA 1970. gardener58@verizon.net

CAMPBELL, Kathryn S. (Ia) 106 3rd Ave, Charles City IA 50616 **Theol Consult Dio Iowa Des Moines IA 2006-; Vic Ch Of The Sav Clermont IA 1999-** B Santa Barbara CA 10/7/1942 d Joseph Gary Campbell & Margaret Elizabeth. U of Aberdeen Aberdeen GB 1964; PhD U IL 1973; U of Iowa 1978; CPE S Lk's Hosp Cedar Rapids IA 1984; CPE Cherokee Mntl Hlth Inst Cherokee IA 1985; CAS SWTS 1986; DMin CDSP 2003; No Iowa Cmnty Coll 2011. D 6/11/1986 P 12/12/1986 Bp Walter Cameron Righter. Mnstry Dvlpmt Consult Dio Iowa Des Moines IA 2004-2007; S Jn's Ch Mason City IA 2001; Supply S Andr's Epis Ch Waverly IA 2000-2002; Chair NE Dnry Dio Iowa Des Moines IA 1995-1997; Vic Gr Epis Ch Chas City IA 1992-2005; Supply Ch Of The Sav Clermont IA 1992-1999; Mssnr Dio Iowa Des Moines IA 1991-1992; Cnvnr of Theol Reflection Grp Dio Iowa Des Moines IA 1990-1991; Vic S Andr's Epis Ch Waverly IA 1987-1990; Mssn Cmsn Dio Iowa Des Moines IA 1986-1989; Int Vic Gr Epis Ch Chas City IA 1986-1987; Int S Andr's Epis Ch Waverly IA 1986-1987. Auth, "Undinna thaettir: Structure in the Gisla Saga," *Neophilologys*, 1985; Auth, "Medieval and Mod and the Allegory of Rhetoric," *Allegorica*, 1979; Auth, "Y Gymraeg yn Iowa," *Tudalen y Dysgwyr*, Y Cymro, 1978; Auth, "Iowerth Ddu and Gwilym Pue," *Fourteenth Century Mystics Quarterly*, 1977. AAR 1986; Assn for Amer Indn Affrs 1988-2007; Assn of Iowa Cistercians 1997; Interfaith Allnce, Iowa 1998; Rural Mnstrs Ntwk 2000. Finalist, Iowa Bus Plan Competition Pappajohn Corp 2011. ccpiskie@rconnect.com

CAMPBELL, Kenneth Stuart Bradstreet (WMass) 5 Peace Lane, Box 306, South Orleans MA 02653 B Hyannis MA 6/19/1941 s Douglas Leslie Campbell & Gwendolyn. BS Boston St Coll 1963; MA Brigham Young U 1965; M.Div. EDS 1969. D 6/21/1969 P 5/26/1970 Bp John Melville Burgess. m 8/26/1967 Ruth Ellen Williams c 3. Int Chr Ch Epis Harwich Port MA 2007-2008; R Epis Ch Of The Epiph Wilbraham MA 1981-2005; Pres. Stndg Comm. Dio Wstrn Massachusetts Springfield MA 1981-2004; R S Anne's Ch No Billerica MA 1972-1981; Cur The Ch Of The H Sprt Orleans MA 1969-1972; P-in-c Chap Of S Jas The Fisherman Wellfleet MA 1969-1971. EPF 1975; OHC 1982-2004. ksbcampbell@verizon.net

CAMPBELL, Leslie R (SD) Po Box 722, Mobridge SD 57601 B Sisseton SD 8/10/1938 s Adelord Matthias Campbell & Alice Marie. Flandreau Indn Sch. D 1/25/1975 P 6/1/1976 Bp Walter H Jones. m 1/1/1995 Patricia Mavis Blacksmith c 2. S Jas Epis Ch Mobridge SD 1995-1996; Dio Minnesota Minneapolis MN 1984-1987; Dio So Dakota Sioux Falls SD 1976-2004.

CAMPBELL, Linda McConnell (ECR) 2065 Yosemite St., Seaside CA 93955 **R Epis Ch Of The Gd Shpd Salinas CA 2009-** B Fresno CA 3/17/1955 d Willis James McConnell & Janet Ann. BA U CA 1979; MA PSR 1998; CAS CDSP 2002. D 8/10/2002 P 3/1/2003 Bp Jerry Alban Lamb. m 4/29/1995 Jerry L Campbell c 3. Int S Alb's Ch Albany CA 2006-2009; Asst St Johns Epis Ch Ross CA 2004-2006; Asst Ch Of The Incarn Santa Rosa CA 2002-2004. linda@poetpriest.com

CAMPBELL, Lynn Marie (Mass) 1132 Highland Ave, Needham MA 02494 **Cur Chr Ch Needham MA 2011-** B Reading PA 12/16/1975 d Roger Dennis Campbell & Christine Marie. BA Coll of the H Cross 1998; MDiv Weston Jesuit TS 2003; Post Grad Dplma VTS 2010. D 6/25/2011 Bp M(arvil) Thomas Shaw III. lynn@ccneedham.org

CAMPBELL, Martin John (CFla) 1240 Lake Dora Dr, Tavares FL 32778 B London UK 1/17/1932 s William Archibald Campbell & Marianne Alsie. LLB Lon 1965; MDiv STUSo 1967; JD Florida St U 1975. D 6/12/1967 Bp James Loughlin Duncan P 12/13/1967 Bp Henry I Louttit. m 12/5/1995 Pamela C Worley c 3. Asst S Edw The Confessor Mt Dora FL 1995-2001; Vice-Chncllr Dio Cntrl Florida Orlando FL 1989-1999; Vic S Fran Of Assisi Ch Bushnell FL 1978-1994; Com on Const and Cn Dio Cntrl Florida Orlando FL 1973-1976; Vic S Fran Of Assisi Epis Ch Lake Placid FL 1971-1976; P-in-c S Fran Of Assisi Epis Ch Lake Placid FL 1970-1971; Vic S Mary's Epis Ch Palmetto FL 1969-1970; Vic H Faith Epis Ch Port S Lucie FL 1967-1969. Auth, "Another Side of Laud". engtchrpam@aol.com

CAMPBELL, Mary Maxine Lockwood (Ind) 5011 Bobwhite Ln Apt A, Indianapolis IN 46254 **Died 11/6/2010** B Chicago IL 7/2/1929 d Max Millard Raab & Margaret Mae. BA Cbury Coll 1951; MS Butler U 1956; MDiv STUSo 1980. D 6/24/1980 P 1/1/1981 Bp Edward Witker Jones. c 3. Cmnty Of S Mary.

CAMPBELL, Maurice Bernard (EpisSanJ) 1151 Park View Ct, Sheridan WY 82801 **D S Paul's Ch Bakersfield CA 1992-** B Sheriden WY 1/29/1930 s Earl T Campbell & Cecilia M. BS U of Wyoming 1959. D 5/15/1972 Bp C Kilmer Myers. m 12/28/1957 Carola J Rowland c 2. trombomo@aol.com

CAMPBELL, Peter Nelson (Chi) 519 Franklin Ave, River Forest IL 60305 B Atlanta GA 3/4/1948 s Nelson Campbell & Mary Priscilla. BS Trin Hartford CT 1970; MS Georgia St U 1975; MDiv SWTS 1986. D 6/14/1986 Bp James Winchester Montgomery P 12/1/1986 Bp Frank Tracy Griswold III. Extended Supply P The Epis Ch Of The H Trin Belvidere IL 2007-2008; S Ign Of Antioch Ch Antioch IL 2006-2007; Extended Supply P Chr Ch River Forest IL 2004-2006; R H Trin Ch Skokie IL 1992-2004. padrepnc@juno.com

CAMPBELL II, Ralph Marion (LI) 9825 Georgetown St. N.E., Louisville OH 44641 B Radford VA 4/15/1947 s Ralph Marion Campbell & Virginia Blanche. BA Ohio U 1969; MDiv GTS 1973; Coll of Preachers 1983. D 12/22/1974 Bp Hal Raymond Gross P 11/30/1975 Bp Matthew Paul Bigliardi. c 2. Regular Sunday Supply S Andr's Ch Yaphank NY 2010-2011; R S Ann's Ch Sayville NY 2006-2010; Mem, Philos Com, Gd Samar Epis Hosp Dio Oregon Portland OR 1998-1999; Stndg Com Dio Oregon Portland OR 1997-2000; Stndg Com Dio Oregon Portland OR 1991-1994; R S Tim's Epis Ch Salem OR 1980-2005; Vic S Tim's Epis Ch Salem OR 1978-1979; Assoc S Barth's Ch Beaverton OR 1977-1978; Asst, Yth Min Epis Par Of S Jn The Bapt Portland OR 1974-1977. Cmnty H Sprt. Citizen Awd Marion Cnty City of Salem; Citizen Awd Drug & Alco Plannig Com. frrick2006@yahoo.com

CAMPBELL, Robert Dean (Spok) 915 Golden Street, PO Box 186, Oroville WA 98844 B Alamosa CO 4/19/1936 s Edwin Wayne Campbell & Eva Belle. BA Colorado St U 1963; MDiv Nash 1966; Cert Int Mnstry Prog 1996. D 6/6/1966 Bp William Hampton Brady P 12/21/1966 Bp Richard S Watson. c 3. Reg Mssnr S Anne's Ch Omak WA 1998-2002; Trin Ch Oroville WA 1998-2002; Dio Spokane Spokane WA 1995-2001; Trin Ch Oroville WA 1990-1995; D S Chris's Ch Bluff UT 1966-1967. rcampbel@nvinet.com

CAMPBELL JR, Ross Walton (Mich) 899 Greenhills Dr, Ann Arbor MI 48105 B Detroit MI 2/14/1923 s Ross Walton Campbell & Ernestine Augusta. BS USMA at W Point 1945; JD U MI 1955; Cert Whitaker TS 1982. D 6/13/1981 Bp H Coleman McGehee Jr P 4/13/1987 Bp William J Gordon Jr. m 6/26/1983 Beverly Jean Taylor c 2. D S Clare Of Assisi Epis Ch Ann Arbor MI 1981-1987. Auth, "Chld Custody," *Judges Journ*, 1978; Auth, "The Atty in Jvnl Crt," *Michigan St Bar Journ*, 1965. Soc of S Paul the Tentmaker 1981-1983.

CAMPBELL, Scott Duncan (Colo) PO Box 1961, Monument CO 80132 **R S Mths Epis Ch Monument CO 2001-** B Denver CO 7/4/1965 s Malcolm Campbell & Mary Alice. BA U CO 1990; MDiv GTS 1997. D 6/7/1997 P 12/20/1997 Bp William Jerry Winterrowd. m 7/1/2006 Heather Lisowski c 3. Assoc S Matt's Ch Grand Jct CO 1997-2001. padrescott@gmail.com

CAMPBELL, Solomon Sebastian (SeFla) P.O. Box 50222, Nassau Bahamas B Arthurs Town Cat Island BS 9/7/1956 s Sebastian Arthur Campbell & Almeda Sheila. DIT Codrington Coll 1980; BA U of The W Indies 1980; MA PrTS 1988. Trans from Church in the Province Of The West Indies 3/21/1986 Bp Calvin Onderdonk Schofield Jr. m 4/7/1980 Agatha Maria Antionette Wells c 1. S Matt's Epis Ch Delray Bch FL 1987-1988. ssebastiancampbell@hotmail.com

CAMPBELL, Thomas Wellman (SD) 234 W. Kansas Street, Spearfish SD 57783 B Deadwood SD 3/24/1939 s John Thomas Campbell & Ruberta Mae. BA Augustana Coll 1962; MDiv GTS 1965; So Dakota St U 1975. D 6/11/1965 P 12/1/1965 Bp Conrad Gesner. R S Thos Epis Ch Sturgis SD 1998-2001; S Fran Cmnty Serv Inc. Salina KS 1994-1998; S Mich's Epis Day Sch Carmichael CA 1991-1994; Int S Steph's Ch Norfolk VA 1987-1989; Norfolk Acad Norfolk VA 1986-1991; S Edw's Sch Vero Bch FL 1984-1986; Shattuck-S Mary's Sch Faribault MN 1982-1984; R Ch Of The Gd Shpd Sioux Falls SD 1981-1982; Locumtenens Gr Epis Ch Jamestown ND 1977-1980; P-in-c Gr Epis Ch Madison SD 1973-1976; R Chr Epis Ch Tarrytown NY 1969-1971; R Ch Of All Ang Spearfish SD 1966-1969; Cur Calv Cathd Sioux Falls SD 1965-1966. Nais, Cris; NAES. fathertomcampbell@gmail.com

CAMPBELL, William Edward (Spok) 3020 W Prentice Ave Apt J, Littleton CO 80123 **Asst S Mich And All Ang' Ch Denver CO 2004-** B Lincoln NE 3/16/1932 s Henry William Campbell & Beatrice Jane. BA Occ 1954; MDiv CDSP 1957. D 6/24/1957 P 3/6/1958 Bp Francis E I Bloy. m 6/21/1985 Anne D Campbell. Bp Search Com Dio Spokane Spokane WA 2011; R Emm Ch Kellogg ID 1993-2004; R H Trin Epis Ch Wallace ID 1993-2004; Int Dio Colorado Denver CO 1987-1993; Asst Ch Of S Phil And S Jas Denver CO 1986-1987; Int, Supply and Vic All SS Of The Mtn Epis Chap Crested Butte CO 1984-1993; Asst H Apos Epis Ch Englewood CO 1984-1985; Dio Utah Salt Lake City UT 1984; Stndg Com S Fran Ch Moab UT 1981-1984; Dept Of Missions Dio Dallas Dallas TX 1976-1980; R H Trin Epis Ch Garland TX 1974-1980; Vic S Chris's By The Sea Portland TX 1969-1974; Vic S Barn Epis Ch Fredericksburg TX 1968-1969; Vic S Bon Ch Comfort TX 1968-1969; R S Paul's Epis Ch Tustin CA 1960-1967; Asst S Jas Par Los Angeles CA 1957-1960. Ord Of S Lk 2007. fthrbill2004@comcast.net

CAMPBELL-DIXON OHC, Robert A (NY) 455 W 148th St, New York NY 10031 B Corn Island NI 10/5/1934 s Frank Campbell & Susan. Inst Angl De Nicaragua Ni; S Barbara Cmnty Coll. Trans from Church in the Province Of The West Indies 11/22/1982. Cur S Ptr's Ch Bronx NY 1986-2004; Dio Nicaragua Managua 1982-1986.

CAMPO, JoAnne Crocitto (NY) 101 N Central Ave, Hartsdale NY 10530 **S Lk's Ch Eastchester NY 2010-** B Mt Pleasant NY 8/1/1946 d Pasquale J Crocitto & Evelyn Rose Zucca. AAS/RN Dutchess Cmnty Coll 1989; SS Concordia Coll 2005; MDiv The GTS 2009. D 3/7/2009 P 9/12/2009 Bp Mark Sean Sisk. m 8/8/1998 Joseph John Campo c 3. jocampo10@aol.com

CAMPO, Joseph John (NY) 98 Stewart Ave, Eastchester NY 10709 **P-in-c S Andr's Epis Ch Hartsdale NY 2006-** B New Rochelle NY 1/24/1950 s Anthony Campo & Theresa. BA Cathd Coll Douglaston NY 1971; MA

Gregorian U 1975; JCL S Paul U Ottawa On CA 1984; Dplma in Angl Stds GTS 2003. Rec from Roman Catholic 6/28/2003 Bp Mark Sean Sisk. m 8/8/1998 JoAnne Crocitto Campo. Assoc P Gr Ch White Plains NY 2003-2006. jocampo10@aol.com

CANADY III, Hoyt Paul (EC) Christ Church, P.O. Box 1246, New Bern NC 28563 **COM Dio E Carolina Kinston NC 2011-; Disciplinary Bd (Title IV) Dio E Carolina Kinston NC 2011-; Assoc Chr Ch New Bern NC 2009-** B Knoxville TN 2/21/1976 s Hoyt Paul Canady & Marilyn Loyd. BA Middle Tennessee St U 1998; VTS 2009; MDiv Wesley TS 2009. D 8/22/2009 P 4/19/2010 Bp John Chane. m 7/19/2003 Emily Gowdy c 1. Dep for Yth Mnstry Dio Washington Washington DC 2002-2009; Yth Min S Jn's Ch Ellicott City MD 2002; Dioc Yth Coun Dio W Tennessee Memphis TN 2000-2002; Epis Yth Event Design Team Epis Ch Cntr New York NY 2000-2002; Yth Min S Geo's Ch Germantown TN 1998-2002; Prov IV Yth Event Prov IV 1998-2001. paulcanady@christchurchnewbern.com

CANAN, David A (Pa) 708 S Bethlehem Pike, Ambler PA 19002 **R Trin Epis Ch Ambler PA 1999-** B Ravenna OH 8/6/1953 s Ellsworth Canan & Julia. BS Kent St U 1976; MDiv TESM 1990. D 6/2/1990 P 1/25/1991 Bp Alden Moinet Hathaway. m 6/30/1984 Anne Louise Zaynor c 2. Ch of the Gd Shpd Rahway NJ 1994-1999; Assoc S Thos' Ch Whitemarsh Ft Washington PA 1990-1994; Prog Coordntr for Yth Dept Dio Pittsburgh Monroeville PA 1987-1990. rector@trinityambler.com

CANAVAN, Mary A (Ct) 1969 Main St, Stratford CT 06615 **Int Chr Ch Stratford CT 2010-** B Pawtucket RI 6/1/1963 d Robert Joseph Canavan & Sarah Elizabeth. BS Bryant U 1985; MDiv GTS 1999. D 5/26/1999 Bp Robert Louis Ladehoff P 12/11/1999 Bp Roger John White. c 2. R S Andr's Ch Madison CT 2009-2010; Vic Calv Ch Providence RI 2002-2009; Asst P S Paul's Ch No Kingstown RI 2000-2002; Chr Ch Whitefish Bay WI 1999. Oregon Soc of CPA's 1991. scl Bryant U 1985; Natl hon Soc Bryant U 1985. mcanavan99@aol.com

CANDLER, Samuel Glenn (At) 2744 Peachtree Rd Nw, Atlanta GA 30305 **Dn Cathd Of S Phil Atlanta GA 1998-** B Panama City FL 8/12/1956 s Samuel Ozburn Candler & Beth. BA Occ 1978; MDiv Ya Berk 1982. D 6/12/1982 P 5/11/1983 Bp Bennett Jones Sims. m 5/25/1980 Barbara Mayo c 3. Stndg Com Dio Upper So Carolina Columbia SC 1995-1998; Ya Berk New Haven CT 1994-1998; Dn Trin Cathd Columbia SC 1993-1998; Epis Ch Of The H Sprt Cumming GA 1988-1993; S Paul's Epis Ch Summerville SC 1985-1987; Cathd Of S Phil Atlanta GA 1984-1991; Com On Liturg And Mus Dio Atlanta Atlanta GA 1984-1991; S Jude's Ch Marietta GA 1982-1985. Auth, "Var arts," 2003. Associated Parishes; Assn Of Dioc Liturg & Mus Comm; Ccs; NNECA. Mdiv mcl Ya Berk New Haven CT 1982; Phi Beta Kappa Occ Los Angeles CA 1978; Ba cl Occ Los Angeles CA 1978. scandler@stphilipscathedral.org

CANELA CANELA, Ramon Antonio (DR) Ms Digna Valdez, Box 764, Dominican Republic Dominican Republic **Dio The Dominican Republic (Iglesia Epis Dominicana) Santo Domingo DO 2008-** B 6/30/1969 s Basilio Canela & Melania Martina. Rec from Roman Catholic 10/2/2008 Bp Julio Cesar Holguin-Khoury. m 12/20/2002 Ana Espinal c 3.

CANGIALOSI, Grace Louise (Va) 2209 E Grace St, Richmond VA 23223 B Salina KS 8/14/1943 d John Frederick Saefke & Grace Louise. BA U MI 1964; MA U of Maryland 1977; MDiv VTS 1989. D 6/10/1989 Bp Peter James Lee P 2/1/1990 Bp Robert Poland Atkinson. c 2. S Geo's Ch Stanley VA 1991-2000; Asst to R The Ch of S Clem Alexandria VA 1989-1990. Auth, "A Kairos Winter". Advoc Of The Year Page Cnty 1993.

CANHAM, Elizabeth Jean (WNC) 51 Laurel Ln, Black Mountain NC 28711 **Calv Epis Ch Fletcher NC 2004-** B Hatfield Herts UK 8/20/1939 d Robert William Canham & Marjorie. BD (Hons) Lon 1972; M Th. Lon 1978; STM GTS 1983; DMin GTF 1990. Trans from Church Of England 12/1/1980 as Deacon Bp John Shelby Spong. Stillpoint Mnstrs Arden NC 1994-2002; P Gr Ch Asheville NC 1994-1998; Dio Wstrn No Carolina Asheville NC 1992-1999; P The Sav Epis Ch Newland NC 1991-1993; S Barth's Ch New York NY 1983-1985; Asst S Dav's Ch Kinnelon NJ 1981-1982. Auth, *A Table of Delight*, Upper Room, 2005; Auth, *Heart Whispers*, Upper Room, 1999; Auth, *Pilgrimage to Priesthood*, SPCK, 1993; Auth, *Journaling w Jeremiah*, Paulist Press, 1992; Auth, *Praying By the Bible*, Cowley, 1987. elizabethcanham@aol.com

CANION, Gary Yates (Tex) 5435 Whispering Creek Way, Houston TX 77017 B Seadrift TX 8/10/1937 s Leslie Bailey Canion & Mae Jean. BA Rice U 1959; BD Epis TS of The SW 1962; STM SWTS 1968; Cert Texas Inst of Rel 1969; Cert SW Paralegal Inst 1981. D 6/18/1962 Bp John E Hines P 8/21/1963 Bp Frederick P Goddard. c 4. Chapl S Mk's Pstr Care Cntr Salt Lake City UT 1972-1976; St Marks Hosp Salt Lake City UT 1972-1976; Cn Sacristan Trin Cathd Trenton NJ 1965-1967; Vic S Jn's Epis Ch Carthage TX 1962-1964.

CANNELL, John Edward (WTex) 11107 Wurzbach Rd Ste 401, San Antonio TX 78230 B Scottsbluff NE 8/6/1952 s John Lee Cannell & Maxine Vivian. BA U Denv 1975; MA U of Nebraska 1977; MDiv Nash 1980; PhD U of Nebraska 1986. D 5/31/1980 P 12/1/1980 Bp James Daniel Warner. m 5/20/1978 Judith Lynne Hanse. Int S Helena's Epis Ch Boerne TX 1998-1999; Int Trin Ch San Antonio TX 1992-1993; Asst St Fran Epis Ch San Antonio TX 1983-1991; Ch Of The H Trin Lincoln NE 1980-1981. Phi Beta Kappa U Denv Denver CO 1975; Pi Gamma Mu U Denv 1974.

CANNING, Michael Jacob (Ida) 2333 W Duck Alley Rd, Eagle ID 83616 B St. John's Newfoundland 5/25/1954 BA Memi U of Newfoundland. Rec 3/25/2003 Bp J Clark Grew II Trans from Anglican Church of Canada 3/25/2003. m 8/25/1982 Clarissa A Canning c 3. Ch Of H Nativ Meridian ID 2009-2011; R S Paul's Ch Bellevue OH 2002-2004. mjbcanning@gmail.com

CANNON JR, Alberry Charles (USC) 51 Roper Rd, Flat Rock NC 28731 B Greenville SC 5/12/1936 s Alberry Charles Cannon & Mary. BA Cit 1957; MDiv STUSo 1963. D 6/22/1963 Bp Robert E Gribbin P 5/1/1964 Bp John Adams Pinckney. m 6/15/1957 Nancy Sterling c 4. Asst Ch Of S Jn In The Wilderness Flat Rock NC 2000-2005; Int Trin Ch Abbeville SC 1997-1998; R S Andr's Epis Ch Greenville SC 1991-1996; Calv Ch Pauline SC 1986-1991; S Thos Epis Par Coral Gables FL 1976-1985; S Mk's Ch Cocoa FL 1973-1976; Campus Min Dio So Carolina Charleston SC 1970-1973. Auth, *The Maxwells of Greenville*, 1989; Auth, *Centennial History of the Cotillion Club of Greenville So Carolina*, 1988. S Andr's Soc of Upper SC. accannon@mchsi.com

CANNON, Carl Thomas (La) 1550 El Camino Real, Suite 628, The Villages FL 32159 B Orlando FL 9/5/1939 s Edwin E Cannon & Jane G. BA U Of Cntrl Florida 1970; MDiv SWTS 1973. D 6/9/1973 P 12/21/1973 Bp William Hopkins Folwell. c 3. S Lk's Ch Baton Rouge LA 1996-1999; R All SS Epis Ch Memphis TN 1987-1996; R The Epis Ch Of The Mssh Pulaski TN 1982-1987; Assoc S Vinc's Epis Ch St Petersburg FL 1981-1982; Vic H Fam Ch Orlando FL 1975-1980; Cur H Cross Epis Ch Sanford FL 1973-1975. SSC. carlcannon9619@gmail.com

CANNON III, Charles (SeFla) 87500 Overseas Highway, Islamorada FL 33036 **R S Jas The Fisherman Islamorada FL 2011-** B Greenville SC 6/14/1958 s Alberry Charles Cannon & Nancy Estelle. BA U of Florida 1982; MS Barry U 1985; Cert Dio SE Florida TS FL 1998; MA TS 2011. D 9/11/1998 Bp John Lewis Said P 6/19/2011 Bp Leopold Frade. m 12/29/1984 Lauren Donelan c 2. D S Christophers Ch Haverhill FL 1998-2004. Cmnty of Blessed Sacr 1975; GAS 1975; Soc of Cath Priests 2011; SocMary 1975. chascan58@gmail.com

CANNON, Charles Wilcken (Haw) 291 Shady Glen Ave., Point Roberts WA 98281 B Glendale CA 3/17/1935 s Charles Wilcken Cannon & Irene. BS California Maritime Acad 1956; MDiv CDSP 1968; Ripon Coll Cuddesdon Oxford Gb 1968. D 8/23/1968 Bp James Albert Pike P 3/8/1969 Bp George Richard Millard. m 8/24/1984 Shirley Loraine Green. R H Innoc' Epis Ch Lahaina HI 1994-2001; Vic S Andr's Ch Ben Lomond CA 1970-1974; Asst Trin Cathd San Jose CA 1968-1970. ccannons@whidbey.com

CANNON, Daniel M (EMich) 2582 Midland Rd, Saginaw MI 48603 **R S Jn's Epis Ch Saginaw MI 2011-; P(D)-In-Charge Chr Epis Ch E Tawas MI 2007-** B Detroit MI 2/25/1981 s Richard Allen Cannon & Nancy Ruth. BA U MI 2003; MDiv Nash 2007. D 1/21/2007 P 8/25/2007 Bp S(teven) Todd Ousley. m 8/6/2005 Christine Christine Szalkowski c 1. therevcannon@gmail.com

CANNON, David Lawrence (Ct) #93 Route 2-A Pouquetanuck, Preston CT 06365 B Buffalo NY 5/18/1937 s Raymond Theodore Cannon & Marian Laura. BS Springfield 1961; STB Ya Berk 1964; MDiv Ya Berk 1964. D 6/11/1964 Bp Duncan Montgomery Gray P 12/1/1964 Bp Joseph Warren Hutchens. m 12/28/1957 Ann-etta Newmarker. S Jas Ch Preston CT 1970-1999; Cur Chr Epis Ch Norwich CT 1964-1965. dcannon1959@comcast.net

CANNON, John Dyson (NY) 138 Jewett St FL 1, Providence RI 02908 B 1/1/1934 s Douglas H P Cannon & Emily. AB Harvard Coll 1956; MDiv UTS 1959. D 6/11/1959 P 12/1/1959 Bp Horace W B Donegan. c 4. Int Vic and Chapl to the U S Aug's Ch Kingston RI 1997-1998; Supply & Int Mnstry Dio Maine Portland ME 1995-1997; Supply & Int Mnstry Dio New Hampshire Concord NH 1995-1997; Mstr of Rel Stds and Chapl S Paul's Sch Concord NH 1985-1995; R S Jn's Ch New York NY 1975-1985; Asst to the Bp Dio New York New York City NY 1973-1975; Asst to the Bp Dio New York New York City NY 1972-1975; Asst to the R S Thos Ch New York NY 1959-1963. jdcannon@cox.net

CANNON, Justin Russell (Cal) 1055 Taylor St, San Francisco CA 94108 **D S Clem's Ch Berkeley CA 2011-; Prog Mgr Epis Chars San Francisco CA 2009-** B Detroit MI 7/9/1984 s Richard Allen Cannon & Nancy Ruth. BA Earlham Coll 2006; MDiv CDSP 2009. D 6/4/2011 Bp Marc Handley Andrus. Ed, "Homosexuality in the Orth Ch," CreateSpace, 2011; Auth, "The Bible, Chrsnty, & Homosexuality," CreateSpace, 2008; Ed, "Sanctified: An Anthology of Poetry by LGBT Christians," CreateSpace, 2008. Soc of S Fran (Assoc) 2009. Top 25 Leading Men of 2007 INTop 25 Leading Men of 2007, HonoSTINCT mag 2007. toseekjustice@gmail.com

CANNON, Thomas Kimball (Chi) 141 S Taylor Ave, Oak Park IL 60302 B Oak Park IL 5/5/1934 s Joseph William Cannon & Mary. BS Nthrn Illinois U 1960; LTh Nash 1964. D 6/11/1966 Bp James Winchester Montgomery P 12/1/1966 Bp Gerald Francis Burrill. m 6/8/1963 Kathleen Marie Kirby c 2. S Andr's Ch Chicago IL 2000-2006; St Leonards Hse Chicago IL 1978-1982; Dio Chicago

Chicago IL 1973-1977; Cur Trin Epis Ch Wheaton IL 1966-1968. Amer Correctional Chapl Assn.

C

CANO, George Luciano (EpisSanJ) 3605 Shady Valley Ct, Modesto CA 95355 B San Mateo CA 2/28/1937 s Francis Cano & Frances. Mennonite Brethren Biblic Sem; San Joaquin Schools For Mnstry; TESM. D 12/13/2003 Bp John-David Mercer Schofield. m 11/2/1968 Jeanne Cano c 5. D Chr The King Ch Riverbank CA 2003-2004; Ch Of The Gd Shpd Tomball TX 2003-2004. geewizme@yahoo.com

CANON, Cham (Ark) 3535 Kirby Rd Apt G319, Memphis TN 38115 B Memphis TN 11/25/1921 s Willie House Canon & Laura. BS Rhodes Coll 1947; MS Indiana U 1949; MDiv St Lk's Sch. of Theol Univ. of the So 1959; Fllshp Coll of Preachers 1972. D 6/27/1959 Bp John Vander Horst P 2/22/1960 Bp Theodore N Barth. m 2/14/1998 Hazel Canon c 4. Vic S Steph's Epis Ch Jacksonville AR 1983-1986; Vic All SS Epis Ch Paragould AR 1979-1983; S Bernards Ch Okolona MS 1977-1979; R All SS' Epis Ch Tupelo MS 1973-1979; Asst S Mary's Cathd Memphis TN 1966-1973; R S Paul's Epis Ch Murfreesboro TN 1963-1966; P-in-c S Paul's Epis Ch Murfreesboro TN 1961-1962; Asst S Steph's Epis Ch Oak Ridge TN 1959-1961.

CANTELLA, Frances French (Los) 30015 Buchanan Way, Castaic CA 91384 **R S Barn' Epis Ch Los Angeles CA 2010-** B Los Angeles CA 9/16/1947 d William French & Frances. BS Woodbury U 1997. D 11/14/2004 Bp Joseph Jon Bruno P 5/15/2005 Bp Chester Lovelle Talton. m 4/26/2003 Vincent Cantella c 1. frances.cantella@nbcuni.com

CANTER, Matthew A (SC) PO Box 127, Carlsbad CA 92018 **Cur S Michaels By-The-Sea Ch Carlsbad CA 2011-** B Zanesville OH 3/3/2011 s Robert Charles Canter & Kathy Marie. BSS Ohio U 2008; MDiv Nash 2011. D 6/4/2011 Bp Mark Joseph Lawrence. m 12/9/2006 Ashley Danielle Pursley c 2. frmatthew@stmichaelsbythesea.org

CANTERBURY, Marion Lucille (RG) 5304 Rincon Rd Nw, Albuquerque NM 87105 B Fort Worth TX 5/3/1927 d Claude Edward Canterbury & Emma Lucille. BA New Mex St U. 1976; MDiv CDSP 1979. D 8/6/1979 P 6/1/1980 Bp Richard Mitchell Trelease Jr. Int Chr Epis Ch Douglas WY 1997-2002; Int S Geo's Ch Lusk WY 1997-2002; Int S Jn The Bapt Ch Glendo WY 1997-2002; S Andr's Epis Ch Las Cruces NM 1989-1990; Nat'L Religeous Partnership New York NY 1985-1988; Dio The Rio Grande Albuquerque NM 1979-1985. harmeyer1234@msn.com

CANTOR, Este Gardner (Cal) 1105 High Ct, Berkeley CA 94708 **P-in-c Ch Of The H Trin Richmond CA 2010-; Vic The Epis Ch Of The Gd Shpd Berkeley CA 2010-; Chapl An Epis Mnstry to Convalescent Hospitals (Aemch) Alameda CA 2006-** B Sandusky MI 6/28/1950 Corcoran Sch Of Art Washington DC 1975; BA Antioch San Francisco CA 1977; MDiv CDSP 2005. D 6/4/2005 P 12/3/2005 Bp William Edwin Swing. m 10/14/1989 Matt Geoffrey Cantor c 2. Assoc R for Chld's and Yth Mnstrs Ch Of Our Sav Mill Vlly CA 2006-2009; Peace, Justice and Integrity of Creation Com Dio California San Francisco CA 2006-2007; Assoc P All Souls Par In Berkeley Berkeley CA 2005-2006. estegcantor@gmail.com

CANTRELL, Darla (Nev) PO Box 181, Austin NV 89310 B Reno NV 4/23/1954 d Chas Britton Winrod & Shirley Adele. D 10/24/2008 P 4/26/2009 Bp Dan Thomas Edwards. m Mitchell D Cantrell c 2. stgeooge8931@yahoo.com

CANTRELL, Laura Quattlebaum (USC) 3317 Cannon St, Columbia SC 29205 **Trin Cathd Columbia SC 2006-** B Charleston SC 5/22/1949 d Paul Quattlebaum & Margaret. BA Converse Coll 1971; MLS U of So Carolina 1973; MDiv Bex 1992. D 6/13/1992 Bp Edward Lloyd Salmon Jr P 1/30/1993 Bp William George Burrill. c 2. R All SS Epis Ch Clinton SC 2000-2006; S Phil's Epis Ch Greenville SC 1999; Trin Ch Abbeville SC 1998; S Paul's Epis Ch Stafford NY 1994-1996; Serv S Mk's And S Jn's Epis Ch Rochester NY 1992-1993. cantrell@trinitysc.org

CANTRELL JR, William C (FtW) 3425 Fairway Lane, Durham NC 27712 B Fort Worth TX 6/29/1956 s William Clyde Cantrell & Patricia. BA Texas A&M U 1982; MDiv Nash 1989. D 12/28/1988 P 12/5/1989 Bp Clarence Cullam Pope Jr. m 8/22/1987 Catherine S Cantrell c 1. Navy Chapl Spec Mobilization Spprt Plan Washington DC 2001-2002; Pres/CEO S Judes Ranch Boulder City NV 1999-2001; R S Jn's Chap Monterey CA 1997-1999; R Ch Of The H Cross St Petersburg FL 1993-1995; R The Epis Ch Of The H Nativ Plano TX 1990-1993; Cur S Chris's Ch And Sch Ft Worth TX 1989-1990. SSC 1990. frcantrell@gmail.com

CAPELLARO, John (Los) 13900 Marquesas Way, Apt 5104, Marina del Rey CA 90292 B Philadelphia PA 2/1/1951 s Leon James Capellaro & Jane Theresa. Penn 1971; MDiv STUSo 1995. D 6/3/1995 P 12/9/1995 Bp Richard Frank Grein. m 1/16/1971 Bernadette Carmella Verderese c 2. Dio Los Angeles Los Angeles CA 2007-2008; S Mich and All Ang Epis Ch Studio City CA 2004-2007; S Paul's Ch Norfolk VA 1998-2005; Asst Trin Ch Solebury PA 1995-1998. "Searching the Heart of God," Green Tree Press, 2003. cap@primebeachrealty.com

CAPITELLI, Stephen Richard (Mil) St John in the Wilderness, 13 S Church St, Elkhorn WI 53121 **P-in-c S Jn In The Wilderness Elkhorn WI 2007-** B Peoria IL 2/25/1954 s Richard E Capitelli & Mary Louise B. BS U.S.N.Y 1990; MDiv Nash 2007. D 12/11/2006 P 2/5/2007 Bp Keith Lynn Ackerman. m 9/1/2001 Cathy Cathy Fravell c 3. wilderchurch@elknet.net

CAPON, Robert Farrar (LI) 37 Brander Parkway, Box 3023, Shelter Island Heights NY 11965 B New York NY 10/26/1925 s Frederick William Capon & Maybelle Fletcher. BA Col 1946; MA Col 1947; BD SWTS 1949; STD SWTS 1966. D 3/25/1949 P 11/19/1949 Bp James P De Wolfe. m 8/3/1977 Valerie Carole Thomas c 4. S Lk's Ch E Hampton NY 1985-1996; Dio Long Island Garden City NY 1957-1977; P Chr Ch-Epis Port Jefferson NY 1949-1977; P All Souls Ch Stony Brook NY 1949-1958. Auth, "The Fingerprint of God: Tracking the Div Suspect Through a Hist of Images," Eerdmans, 2003; Auth, "Genesis: the Movie," Eerdmans, 2003; "The Supper of the Lamb: A Culinary Reflection," Mod Libr, 2002; "Kingdom, Gr, Judgment: Paradox, Outrage, and Vindication in the Parables of Jesus," Eerdmans, 2002; Auth, "The Foolishness of Preaching: Proclaiming the Gospel Against the Wisdom of the Wrld," Eerdmans, 1998; Auth, "Between Noon & Three: Romance, Law & the Outrage of Gr," Eerdmans, 1997. OHC.

CAPPEL, Jerry Jay (Ky) 5719 Prince William St, Louisville KY 40207 **S Matt's Epis Ch Louisville KY 2009-** B North Platte NE 7/20/1956 s Clarence Arvine Cappel & Velda. BA Lubbock Chr U 1979; MDiv Harding Grad Sch Memphis TN 1983; PhD Sthrn Bapt TS Louisville KY 1994. D 6/4/2005 P 12/10/2005 Bp Edwin Funsten Gulick Jr. m 6/24/2001 Jean Gail Hawxhurst c 2. D Resurr Ch Louisville KY 2005-2009. jjcappel@hotmail.com

CAPPER, Steve (Tex) 4405 McKinney St, Houston TX 77023 B Columbus OH 8/28/1953 s Robert Sherman Capper & Barbara Joan. BS Texas A&M U 1974; MDiv Epis TS of The SW 1980. D 8/6/1980 P 4/1/1981 Bp Richard Mitchell Trelease Jr. m 7/20/1974 Karen Lynne Cates c 3. R Ch Of The Redeem Houston TX 1994-2003; R S Jn's Ch Speedway IN 1987-1994; Asst Pro Cathd Epis Ch Of S Clem El Paso TX 1980-1987. "The Marks of a Mentor," *The Mentoring Handbook*, Afr Mnstry Resources, 2005. ERM 1982-1993; SOMA 1994-2003. steve@missionhouston.org

CAPPERS, Linda Frances (Me) 30 Hemlock Dr, Saco ME 04072 B Brockton MA 10/17/1946 d Girdham Henry Durkee & Lillian. BA Wm Smith 1968; Rhode Island Sch for Deacons 1995. D 6/24/1995 Bp J Clark Grew II. m 8/31/1968 Stephen Roger Cappers. D Chr Ch In Lonsdale Lincoln RI 2000-2006; D S Paul's Ch Pawtucket RI 1996-2000; D S Mart's Ch Pawtucket RI 1995-1996. Fell S Jn; NAAD; SCHC. Phi Beta Kappa Wm Smith Geneva NY 1968. deaconlfc@aol.com

CAPWELL, Kim F (Del) 2400 W 17th St, Wilmington DE 19806 **R Imm Ch Highlands Wilmington DE 2008-** B Paterson NJ 8/19/1953 s Milton A Capwell & Betty. AAS Bergen Cmnty Coll 1980; BA/BS WPC 1984; MDiv VTS 1988. D 5/28/1988 P 12/3/1988 Bp John Shelby Spong. m 8/13/1977 Sharon L Anderson c 3. R S Ptr's Ch Mt Arlington NJ 1992-2008; R All SS' Epis Ch Glen Rock NJ 1990-1992; R Trin Ch Irvington NJ 1988-1990. kfcapwell@verizon.net

CARABIN, Robert Jerome (WTex) 210 Lavaca St, San Antonio TX 78210 **Asstg prist S Paul's Epis Ch San Antonio TX 2006-** B San Antonio TX 5/8/1935 s Robert Jerome Carabin & Evelyn Inge-Marie. BA Immac Concep Sem 1960; BD Immac Concep Sem 1964; BA St. Mary's U San Antonio TX 1966; Med Our Lady of the Lake U San Antonio TX 1971; EdD Texas A&M U 1981. Rec from Roman Catholic 1/1/1977 as Priest Bp Scott Field Bailey. m 12/27/1974 Joan Anne Cook. Asstg P Chr Epis Ch San Antonio TX 2001-2005; Chr Epis Ch San Antonio TX 1996-2000; Vic S Matt's Epis Ch Kenedy TX 1994-1995; S Mk's Epis Ch San Antonio TX 1992-1994; Asst S Fran Epis Ch Victoria TX 1988-1992; R Gr Ch Port Lavaca TX 1986-1988; Vic All SS Epis Ch Pleasanton TX 1986; Vic S Mths Devine TX 1983-1986; Vic S Tim's Ch Cotulla TX 1983-1986; Asst S Andr's Epis Ch San Antonio TX 1979-1982; Asst St Fran Epis Ch San Antonio TX 1977-1979. Auth, "So Common a Name," *LivCh*, 1996; Auth, "Pryr Cats," *LivCh*, 1996. jcarabin@sbcglobal.net

CARADINE, Billie Charles (Ala) Po Box 787, Asotin WA 99402 B Flat Creek AL 12/3/1928 s Thomas Edward Caradine & Cladys. BA Birmingham-Sthrn Coll 1957; MDiv STUSo 1966. D 6/16/1966 P 4/29/1967 Bp George Mosley Murray. m 8/15/1992 Francine Mennet. Int Epis Ch of the Nativ Lewiston ID 1998-2000; Exec For Mssn Plnng Epis Ch Cntr New York NY 1988-1995; Exec Coun Appointees New York NY 1987-1988; Cn Ordnry Dio Alabama Birmingham AL 1984-1987; Dio Alabama Birmingham AL 1974-1988; S Mich's Epis Ch Birmingham AL 1974-1984; Vic S Mich's Ch Ozark AL 1967-1971; Vic Ch Of The Epiph Enterprise AL 1966-1971. Auth, "Alabama Plan". bcaradine@cableone.net

CARBERRY, Timothy Oliver (SO) 49 Dipper Cove Rd, Orrs Island ME 04066 B Warwick NY 2/12/1944 s Oliver Douglas Carberry & Louise Sarah. BA Hob 1966; MDiv GTS 1969. D 6/11/1969 Bp John Henry Esquirol P 12/13/1969 Bp Joseph Warren Hutchens. c 2. R S Alb's Epis Ch Of Bexley Columbus OH 1982-2002; Chr Ch Oxford CT 1970-1982; Vic S Ptr's Epis Ch Oxford CT 1970-1972; Cur S Mary's Epis Ch Manchester CT 1969-1970. Auth, "They Were Spoken Here (Bklet Sermons)". toc1944@gmail.com

CARCEL-MARTINEZ, Antonio (Hond) Apdo 52, Camino Rio Mar, Puerto Cortes Honduras **Vic Iglesia Epis San Fernando-Rey Omoa Co HN 1993-; Vic Mision Epis Bola Laguna Puerto Cortes HN 1993-** B Los Duques Reguena ES 5/10/1943 s Dionisio Pardo Pardo & Amparo Gonzales. Lic U Of Barcelona Barcelona Es; U of Madrid. Rec from Roman Catholic 1/1/1995 as Priest Bp Leopold Frade. m 5/11/1990 Maria Gladis Argentina Vasquez c 1. Dio Honduras Miami FL 1995-2011. ANTONIOCARCEL@YAHOO.ES

CARD, June (Los) 24102 Avenida Corona, Dana Point CA 92629 B 2/27/1931 d Charley Jo Coffey & Ruby Gladys. ETSBH 2006. D 12/2/2006 Bp Chester Lovelle Talton. m 11/6/1967 Jack Card c 6. sjcard@sbcglobal.net

CARDEN, Larry Edward (Tenn) University Of The South, Spo, Sewanee TN 37375 **The TS at The U So Sewanee TN 1982-** B New York NY 11/18/1944 s Paul Edward Carden & Wynona Alice. BA DePauw U 1967; BD Yale DS 1970; PhD Van 1980. D 2/21/1977 Bp William Evan Sanders P 3/1/1978 Bp William F Gates Jr. m 8/28/1971 Barbara Ellen Fittz. Chr Ch Cathd Nashville TN 1981; P Chr Ch Cathd Nashville TN 1977-1980. Auth, "Theol," 1988; Auth, "Waiting Sprtl Transformation & The Absence Of God," *S Lk Journ.*

CAREY, Amos Clark (Cal) 650 Pegasus Ln, Foster City CA 94404 B Philadelphia PA 10/18/1926 s Amos Howe Carey & Florence Edith. BS U IL 1949; MA U IL 1950; MDiv CDSP 1954. D 7/2/1954 P 1/6/1955 Bp William Crittenden. c 2. Pstr Assoc Gd Shpd Epis Ch Belmont CA 1990-2000; Pstr Assoc S Ambr Epis Ch Foster City CA 1983-1990; Asst H Nativ Par Los Angeles CA 1975-1983; R S Geo's Epis Ch Texas City TX 1960-1966; Secy Dio NW Pennsylvania Erie PA 1957-1960; Vic S Mary's Ch Erie PA 1954-1960. Auth, "Pioneer burial sites in Sacramento Cnty California," *A Grave Marker Primer*, 1998; Auth, "Nineteenth century cemeteries, San Mateo Cnty, California," *Some Engl Gravestone Inscriptions*, 1997; Auth, "Hist of Pestilence & Faith Inscriptions in Var Caribbean Islands," *Dio Erie (NW Pennsylvania): 1910-1969*. padrecarey@sbcglobal.net

CAREY, Brenton Henderson (SanD) 4432 Benhurst Ave, San Diego CA 92122 B Cleveland OH 8/18/1953 s Frank Leo Carey & Phyllis Henderson. BA OH SU 1976; MDiv CDSP 1993. D 6/7/1997 Bp William Edwin Swing P 12/6/1997 Bp Douglas Edwin Theuner. m 4/12/1997 Elizabeth Hickok Hardy c 4. R S Dav's Epis Ch San Diego CA 2001-2010; Assoc R S Jn's Ch Lynchburg VA 1998-2001; Cur Chr Ch Exeter NH 1997-1998. brenrev@earthlink.net

CAREY, Grant S (NCal) 2701 Capitol Ave Apt 302, Sacramento CA 95816 **Cn Res Trin Cathd Sacramento CA 2006-** B Oakland CA 11/11/1925 s Grant Spray Carey & Mildred Belle. BA California St U 1951; MA California St U 1952; MDiv CDSP 1957. D 6/29/1957 Bp Archie W N Porter P 1/18/1958 Bp Clarence Rupert Haden Jr. Trin Cathd Sacramento CA 1983-1990; Vic S Jn's Epis Ch Lakeport CA 1957-1961. DD CDSP 2007. Gcarey@trinitycathedral.org

CAREY, Peter Michael (Va) 5602 Cary Street Rd, Richmond VA 23226 **Emm Epis Ch Greenwood VA 2009-; S Cathr's Sch Richmond VA 2009-** B Middlebury VT 6/20/1969 s Jason Carey & Carolyn. BA Bates Coll Lewiston ME 1991; Med GW Washington DC 1995; MDiv VTS 2007. D 6/9/2007 Bp Charles Ellsworth Bennison Jr P 12/18/2007 Bp Peter James Lee. m 6/30/2001 Lisa Plog c 2. revpetercarey@gmail.com

CAREY, Peter R (NY) 150 9th Ave Apt 1, New York NY 10011 **Asstg P Ch Of The H Apos New York NY 1998-** B New York NY 12/14/1938 s Peter Carey & Kathleen. BA Providence Coll 1962; MA S Steph Coll 1964; STL Dominican Hse Of Stds 1967; MA Aquinas Inst of Theol 1970. Rec from Roman Catholic 6/1/1990 Bp Harold B Robinson. m 10/6/2007 David Michael Natoli. Vic S Steph's Epis Ch Woodlaw Bronx NY 1998-2000; S Steph's Epis Ch Woodlaw Bronx NY 1991-1996. prcarey@earthlink.net

CAREY SSF, Tom (LI) 2449 Sichel St., Los Angeles CA 90031 **Ch Of The Epiph Los Angeles CA 2010-** B Santa Monica CA 4/9/1951 s Harry Carey & Marilyn. Actors' and Dir' Lab 1975; BA Col 1998; MDiv CDSP 2002. D 5/27/2002 Bp Jerry Alban Lamb P 2/28/2003 Bp Orris George Walker Jr. P-in-c S Pat's Ch Deer Pk NY 2005-2010; Cur Ch Of The Redeem Astoria NY 2002-2004; Yth Dir All SS Ch Richmond Hill NY 1989-1999. Auth, "Sm Crimes," Blazevox Books, 2011; Auth, "Desire: Poems 1989-1999," Painted Leaf Press, 1997. tomascarey@hotmail.com

CARGILL, David Cyrus (RI) 39 Cherry Rd, Cranston RI 02905 **Died 7/9/2011** B Newport VT 5/10/1930 s Ulsford Eugene Cargill & Margaret Leona. BA Bos 1952; MDiv Bex 1955. D 6/18/1955 P 6/1/1956 Bp Charles F Hall. c 1. dcyrusc@cox.net

CARHARTT, Forrest Andrew (Colo) 4737 Mckinley Dr, Boulder CO 80303 **Dio Colorado Denver CO 1997-; Asst P S Jn's Epis Ch Boulder CO 1997-** B Denver CO 9/28/1923 s Forrest Milton Carhartt & Helen. BS USMA at W Point 1945; MDiv Pittsburgh TS 1954; DMin McCormick TS 1985; CAS Iliff TS 1997. D 6/7/1997 P 12/28/1997 Bp William Jerry Winterrowd. m 10/12/1946 Virginia Whipple c 5. Auth, *These Days*, Presby Ch (USA), 1982; Auth, *These Days*, Presby Ch (USA), 1976; Auth, *These Days*, Presby Ch (USA), 1974. Assn of Graduates USMA W Point 1945. office@stjohns-boulder.org

CARL, Elizabeth (WA) 1414 Montague St NW, Washington DC 20011 B Houston TX 5/28/1947 d Emory T Carl & Margaret M. BA Occ 1969; GW 1972; MLS CUA 1976; MDiv UTS 1990. D 6/9/1990 P 6/5/1991 Bp Ronald Hayward Haines. Int R S Thos' Par Washington DC 2003-2004; Int R S Phil's Epis Ch Laurel MD 2000-2001; Assoc. Fac The Cathd Coll Washington DC 1995-2007; Mem of COM Dio Washington Washington DC 1994-2000; Mem, Comm On Mnstry Dio Washington Washington DC 1994-2000; Int Assoc The Ch Of The Epiph Washington DC 1993-1994; Asst The Ch Of The Epiph Washington DC 1991-1992; D S Mary Magd Ch Silver Sprg MD 1991; D S Mary Magd Ch Silver Sprg MD 1990-1991. Auth, "Going Fishing," *The Bk Of Wmn Sermons*, Riverhead Books, 1999; Auth, "Bk Revs," *Chrsnty & Crisis*, 1991. EWC 1980; Integrity 1978; Washington DC Epis Cler Assoc. 1990. Maxwell Fell. for Excellence In Pstr Mnstry UTS NY NY 1990; Hudnut Preaching Prize UTS NY NY 1989. friendofjonah@aol.com

CARLETTA, David Mark (Mich) 26 W 84th St, New York NY 10024 **Asst. to the R The Ch of S Matt And S Tim New York NY 2010-** B Rochester, NY 9/2/1967 s Paul Charles Carletta & Mary Ann. PhD MI SU 2009; MDiv The GTS 2010. D 5/29/2010 P 12/3/2010 Bp Wendell Nathaniel Gibbs Jr. m 8/12/2006 Susanne Karin Eineigel. dmcarletta@hotmail.com

CARLIN, Christine (EC) 810 Fisher St Apt 4, Morehead City NC 28557 B Ridgewood NJ 8/10/1952 d John Herbert Carlin & Clare. BA Jas Madison U 1975; MA Kent St U 1977; MDiv VTS 1991. D 6/15/1991 Bp Ronald Hayward Haines P 2/1/1992 Bp David Reed. Assoc R S Tim's Epis Ch Greenville NC 2000-2005; S Fran Ch Greensboro NC 1998-2001; R Gr Ch Newton MA 1996-1998; Assoc S Fran In The Fields Harrods Creek KY 1991-1996. CCARLINJUST42DAY@AOL.COM

CARLIN II, William B (Okla) 3508 Robert Drive, Duncan OK 73533 B Jackson MS 7/14/1950 s William B Carlin & Betty C. BS U of Sthrn Mississippi 1972; MDiv STUSo 1996; DMin SWTS 2008. D 6/22/1996 P 12/21/1996 Bp Alfred Clark Marble Jr. c 1. R S Andr's Epis Ch Lawton OK 2002-2010; R S Alb's Epis Ch Vicksburg MS 1998-2002; Vic S Mary's Ch Lexington MS 1996-1998; Vic S Matt's Epis Ch Kosciusko MS 1996-1998. wcarlin2@aol.com

CARLING, Paul Joseph (Ct) Saint Paul's Episcopal Church, 661 Old Post Road, Fairfield CT 06824 **Assoc R S Paul's Ch Fairfield CT 2011-** B New York NY 11/2/1945 s James Andrew Carling & Mary Amelia. BA U of Pennsylvania 1971; MS U of Pennsylvania 1973; PhD U of Pennsylvania 1977; MDiv EDS 2002. D 6/16/2002 P 12/21/2002 Bp Thomas C Ely. m 6/17/1995 Cherise Ann Rowan c 2. Assoc R S Lk's Par Darien CT 2004-2011; Assoc R S Mich's Epis Ch Brattleboro VT 2002-2004; Dir Bp Booth Conf Cntr Burlington VT 2002. Auth, "Multiple Bk Chapters - arts In Psychol Journ," 1998; Auth, "Coming Hm," Guilford Press, 1995. Fllshp Of The Soc Of S Jn The Evang 2000. Excellence In Liturg Reading Massachusetts Bible Soc 2001. paul.carling@att.net

CARLISLE, Charles Richard (Dal) 5100 Ross Ave, Dallas TX 75206 **R S Barn Ch Garland TX 2005-** B Fort Worth TX 11/26/1940 s Thurston Clyde Carlisle & Ruby. Angl TS; Fuller TS; VMI; BA U of Arizona 1962; MA U of Arizona 1966; PhD U of Arizona 1971. D 6/26/1982 P 3/12/1983 Bp A Donald Davies. m 12/23/1975 Susan Ann Hill c 4. S Lk's Epis Ch Dallas TX 2004-2005; Int Ch Of The Epiph Richardson TX 2002-2004; P-in-c Ch Of Our Sav Dallas TX 1992-2000; Asst R S Mk's Ch San Marcos TX 1987-1989; Hisp & U Mssnr S Mk's Ch San Marcos TX 1982-1984. Auth, "Voices En Claroscuro," El Lector, 1987; Auth, "Tesserae Latitudes," El Lector, 1984; Auth, "El Impermeable De Harpo Marx," Siglo Xxi, 1982; Auth, "Ecos Del Viento," *Silencios Del Mar*, Playor, 1977. Angl Soc Of No Amer; Soc Of King Chas The Mtyr. buckshotb24@aol.com

CARLISLE, Christopher Arthur Elliott (WMass) 758 N Pleasant St, Amherst MA 01002 **Chapl Dio Wstrn Massachusetts Springfield MA 1983-** B Windsor ON CA 4/15/1953 s Arthur Elliott Carlisle & Elizabeth. BA Col 1975; MA Harvard DS 1978; MDiv Ya Berk 1982. D 9/26/1981 P 3/26/1982 Bp Alexander Doig Stewart. m 6/7/2008 Nathalie Lavoie c 4. S Andr's Ch Longmeadow MA 1982-1983. Auth, "The Real Meaning Of The Reformation (Humor)," *The Wittenburg Door*, 1990; Auth, "The Christmas Chld," 1984; Auth, "In Memoriam," 1983. ESMHE. carlisle@comcol.umass.edu

CARLISLE, Dorothy(Dutch) Mae (Spok) 2348 Harris Ave, Richland WA 99354 **D All SS Ch Richland WA 1999-** B Washington DC 2/9/1925 d Robert Milton Gillett & Margaret Ann. Sawyers Bus Coll U of New Hampshire. D 8/14/1999 Bp Cabell Tennis. m 7/7/1946 Charles Stuart Carlisle. deacon. dutch@verizon.net

CARLISLE, Michael Emerson (Lex) 85 Mikell Ln, Sewanee TN 37375 B Lexington KY 8/7/1947 s Ralph Emerson Carlisle & Thelma. K SU 1967; BA U of Mississippi 1971; MDiv STUSo 1975. D 5/28/1975 P 6/21/1976 Bp Duncan Montgomery Gray Jr. m 12/31/1996 Doris Bentley c 1. S Ptr's Ch Paris KY 1995-2005; Dio Atlanta Atlanta GA 1989-1995; Liturg Cmsn Dio Atlanta Atlanta GA 1984-1988; R Ch Of The Ascen Cartersville GA 1982-1988; Assoc H Sprt Epis Ch Houston TX 1979-1982; Vic S Mary's Ch Enterprise MS

1975-1979; Cur S Paul's Epis Ch Meridian MS 1975-1979; Vic Trin Ch Newton MS 1975-1979. corkycarlisle@bellsouth.net

CARLISTO, John Bradley (EC) 121 Radley Ln, Beaufort NC 28516 **R S Paul's Ch Beaufort NC 2004-; Dio Alabama Birmingham AL 2002-** B Jacksonville NC 4/29/1954 s John Charles Carlisto & Thelma Roberta. BS Natl U 1983; MDiv STUSo 1986. D 5/23/1986 Bp Furman Stough P 12/11/1986 Bp Robert Oran Miller. m 4/16/1977 Janice Marie Skotte c 3. Evang Cmsn Dio E Carolina Kinston NC 2009-2010; Fin Com Dio E Carolina Kinston NC 2005-2008; Hisp Mnstry Cmsn Dio Alabama Birmingham AL 2000-2002; Evang Dept Dio Alabama Birmingham AL 1989-1991; R Chr Epis Ch Albertville AL 1988-2004; Cur S Jn's Ch Decatur AL 1986-1988. Citizen of the Year Chamber of Commerece Albertvile AL 1997; scl Natl U San Diego CA Sewanee TN 1983. john.carlisto@gmail.com

CARLO, Joseph William (Mo) 621 Coquina Ct, Shell Point Retirement Community, Fort Myers FL 33908 B Cincinnati OH 6/22/1924 s Angelo Carlo & Anna. BA Baylor U 1950; MDiv Amer Bapt Sem of The W 1956. D 9/14/1960 P 3/15/1961 Bp George Leslie Cadigan. Chr Ch Rolla MO 1960-1990.

CARLOZZI, Carl Gillman (Az) 10801 East Happy Valley Road, Lot #53, Scottsdale AZ 85255 B Canton OH 6/28/1940 s Carl M Carlozzi & Barbara H. BA Ken 1962; MDiv EDS 1965; DMin Luther Rice TS 1977. D 6/29/1965 Bp Nelson Marigold Burroughs P 2/12/1966 Bp Plinio L Simoes. m 11/8/1985 Muriel S McClellan c 4. Cn Trin Cathd Phoenix AZ 1992; Cathd Chapt Dio Arizona Phoenix AZ 1989-1992; Cathd Chapt Dio Arizona Phoenix AZ 1989-1992; COM Dio Arizona Phoenix AZ 1981-1984; R All SS Ch Phoenix AZ 1980-2002; R S Chris's Ch Chatham MA 1969-1980; Asst S Jas Ch Upper Montclair NJ 1967-1968; Cur S Paul's Ch Maumee OH 1965-1967. Auth, "Death & Contemporary Man"; Auth, "Through Life's Window"; Auth, "Pocket Parables"; Auth, "Episcopalians & the Bible"; Auth, "The Epis Way"; Auth, "The New Epis Way"; Auth, "Prayers for Pstr & People"; Auth, "Promises & Prayers for Healing". Hon Kachina Awd for Volunteerism 1999; Hon Cn Trin Cathd Phoenix AZ 1992. fathercarl@aol.com

CARLSEN, Gail Melin (Az) 3756 E Marble Peak Pl, Tucson AZ 85718 B Glen Ridge NJ 12/22/1944 d Carl Axel Peter Carlsen & Mildred Helen. BA Wellesley Coll 1966; BFA U of Arizona 1976; MDiv Ya Berk 1991. D 6/8/1991 P 12/29/1991 Bp Joseph Thomas Heistand. m 7/9/2009 John Knox Freeman. Assoc S Phil's In The Hills Tucson AZ 2004-2009; S Mk's Ch New Canaan CT 1996-2002; S Phil's In The Hills Tucson AZ 1993-1995; Asst To Dn Ya Berk New Haven CT 1991-1992. GMCARLSEN@COMCAST.NET

CARLSEN, Stephen Earl (Ind) 55 Monument Cir Ste 600, Indianapolis IN 46204 **Dn And R Chr Ch Cathd Indianapolis IN 2007-** B Des Moines IA 9/14/1965 s Charles Joseph Carlsen & Sherrian Lee. PrTS; BA Wheaton Coll 1988; MDiv U Chi 1994. D 6/15/1996 P 1/17/1997 Bp Frank Tracy Griswold III. c 2. Sub-Dn and Cn S Jn's Cathd Denver CO 2003-2007; R Harcourt Par Gambier OH 1998-2003; Cur Chr Ch Winnetka IL 1996-1998. Auth, "A Message So Gd As To Border On Folly," *Preaching Through The Year Of Mk: Sermons That Wk Viii*, Morehouse Pub, 1999. stephen.carlsen@gmail.com

CARLSEN, Vause Smith (EMich) 745 E Main St, Flushing MI 48433 B Gallipolis OH 12/25/1932 d John Griffith Smith & Veta Lee. BA Marshall U 1954; MA Ohio U 1955. D 2/11/2006 Bp Edwin Max Leidel Jr. m 9/2/1955 Paul Carlsen c 3. vcarlsen@comcast.net

CARLSON, Carol Emma (NwPa) Po Box 328, Mount Jewett PA 16740 **Int Ch Of The H Cross No E PA 2003-** B Bradford PA 8/2/1945 d Carl Edvin Carlson & Vivian Muriel Bernadette. BA Rad 1967; MDiv EDS 1980; SUNY 1992. D 6/17/2000 P 12/17/2000 Bp Robert Deane Rowley Jr. c 2. S Mary's Ch Erie PA 2006-2007; Int Chr Ch Coudersport PA 2000-2002; D Gr Epis Ch Ridgway PA 2000. Soc Of S Fran 1973. carolc@pennswoods.net

CARLSON, Constance Jo (Oly) St Andrew's Episc Church, 111 NE 80th St, Seattle WA 98115 **P Assoc for Pstr Care S Andr's Ch Seattle WA 2009-** B Seattle WA 12/8/1944 d Ronald M Canedy & Muriel E. BA Seattle Pacific U 2002; MDiv CDSP 2007. D 1/26/2008 Bp Gregory Harold Rickel. m 1/29/1965 Lawrence Carlson c 3. cojo21@aol.com

CARLSON, Cynthia Everest (NJ) 11520 SE Sunnyside Road #407, Clackamas OR 97015 B Ridgewood NJ 6/25/1942 d Guy Neil Everest & Roberta Elizabeth. BD Pine Manor Coll 1962; BS Col 1965; MS Rutgers-The St U 1991; MDiv GTS 1997. D 5/3/1997 Bp Joe Morris Doss P 6/26/1999 Bp George Phelps Mellick Belshaw. m 8/10/1996 Robert John Carlson. Assoc Gr Epis Ch Plainfield NJ 1997-2000. SSJS 1997. carlsoncynthia@comcast.net

CARLSON, David John (Mich) 28217 Edward Ave, Madison Heights MI 48071 B Detroit MI 8/19/1946 s David Axel Carlson & Phyllis Jane. BS Wayne 1969; MA U MI 1972; Whitaker TS 1986. D 2/2/1991 Bp R(aymond) Stewart Wood Jr. m 12/29/1967 Kay Frances Lajiness c 2. D S Pat's Epis Ch Madison Heights MI 2011; D S Lk's Ch Ferndale MI 1997-2008; D S Marg's Ch Hazel Pk MI 1997-2007; D S Andr's Ch Clawson MI 1991-1996. Auth, "The Diac Trng Cntr of the Dio Michigan," *Diakoneo*, 2000. NAAD 1991. impreachin@wowway.com

CARLSON, David Lee (NY) 84 Seward Ave, Port Jervis NY 12771 **Vic Gr Epis Ch Port Jervis NY 2008-** B Rockville Centre NY 12/24/1958 s Edwin Albert Carlson & Gwendolyn Audrey. BA Ham 1981; Cert The London Acad of Mus and Dramatic Art 1982; MDiv GTS 1992. D 3/25/1992 Bp Leigh Wallace Jr P 9/1/1992 Bp Walter Decoster Dennis Jr. m 10/16/2009 Timothy Smith. R Ch Of The Gd Shpd New York NY 2005-2008; R S Aug's Epis Ch Croton On Hudson NY 1996-2005; Cur Ch Of S Mary The Vrgn New York NY 1992-1996. Ord Of S Jn Of Jerusalem 1996; OHC 1994. davidleecarlson3@aol.com

CARLSON, Geraldine Beatrice (WMich) 1287 La Chaumiere Drive # 5, Petoskey MI 46770 B Philadelphia PA 10/7/1923 d Melville Gerard Ramsey & Geraldine Zelda. EFM STUSo 1996. D 7/7/1996 Bp Edward Lewis Lee Jr. m 8/14/1948 Howard Carlson c 1. D Emm Ch Petoskey MI 1996-2004.

CARLSON, Katherine Ann (Mich) 907 Southlawn Ave, East Lansing MI 48823 **R All SS Ch E Lansing MI 2007-** B Indianapolis IN 3/6/1959 d Harry Hull Carlson & Katherine Elizabeth. MI SU 1978; BS U Of Florida 1980; MDiv VTS 2000. D 6/10/2000 Bp Ronald Hayward Haines P 12/16/2000 Bp Jane Hart Holmes Dixon. m 6/14/1980 Wendell Dana Lynch c 2. Assoc Ch Of The Ascen Gaithersburg MD 2000-2007. Auth, "Working Dogs:Tales From The K9-5 Wrld," Discovery Books/ Random Hse, 2000; Auth, "Bringing Up Baby: Wild Animal Families," Crown Pub, 1998; Auth, "The Leopard Son," Mcgraw Hill, 1996. Mem Washington Epis Cler Assn 2000; SBL 1998-2000. Read Prchr/Schlr Awd Madison Av Presb Ch New York NY 2000; Mdiv cl VTS Alexandria VA 2000. pastorkitcarlson@gmail.com

CARLSON, Kelly B (Mo) Saint Peter's Episcopal Church, 110 N Warson Rd, Saint Louis MO 63124 **Bd Dir, Epis City Mssn Dio Missouri S Louis MO 2011-; Dioc BEC Dio Missouri S Louis MO 2011-; Assoc R S Ptr's Epis Ch St Louis MO 2011-** B Hannibal MO 11/4/1964 d Rodney Lee Carlson & Carol Ann. BA Westminster Coll Fulton MO 1987; JD Ya 1990; MA Marylhurst U 2003; MDiv CDSP 2008. D 6/7/2008 Bp Johncy Itty. Asst to the R S Ptr's Epis Ch St Louis MO 2008-2011. kcarlson@stpetersepiscopal.org

CARLSON, Philip Lawrence (Az) 7147 N 78th St, Scottsdale AZ 85258 **Assoc S Barn On The Desert Scottsdale AZ 2002-** B Moline IL 6/2/1939 s Lawrence John Carlson & Ruth Elizabeth. BS IL Wesl 1961; MDiv Garrett Evang TS 1965. D 10/27/2001 P 6/8/2002 Bp Robert Reed Shahan. m 9/10/1983 Bonnie Louise Parchen c 2. pcarlson@saintbarnabas.org

CARLSON, Robert Bryant (Ore) 15242 Sw Millikan Way Apt 517, Beaverton OR 97006 B Springfield OR 9/22/1974 s John Joseph Carlson & Donna Lee. D 6/24/2000 Bp Vincent Waydell Warner P 1/7/2001 Bp Robert Louis Ladehoff. Asst S Barth's Ch Beaverton OR 2000-2008; S Barth's Ch Beaverton OR 2000.

CARLSON, Robert John (Spok) 25 State Rd 13 Apt C2, St Johns FL 32259 B Waltham MA 2/24/1929 s John Albert Philip Carlson & Natalie. BA Tufts U 1950; MDiv VTS 1956; Costa Rica 1962; Mex 1969; HRT TX 1974; Ldrshp Acad for New Directions 1986; S Geo's Coll Jerusalem IL 1986. D 6/23/1956 Bp Norman B Nash P 12/23/1956 Bp Anson Phelps Stokes Jr. Assoc Ch Of The H Redeem Lake Worth FL 2003-2004; R Ch Of Our Sav Pasco WA 1988-1993; Hisp Mssnr Dio Spokane Spokane WA 1988-1993; Vic S Matt's Ch Prosser WA 1988-1993; Exec Coun Appointees New York NY 1961-1988; R S Mk's Ch Dorchester MA 1956-1960. Soc of S Jn the Evang 1963-1997; Third Ord Soc of S Fran 1998.

CARLSON, Robert Warren (Pa) 1001 Cresthaven Dr, Silver Spring MD 20903 B Brooklyn NY 7/5/1928 s Arthur Muritz Carlson & Ruth Alva. BA Drew U 1950; MDiv Drew U 1953; DMin Wesley TS 1974. D 6/9/1956 P 12/22/1956 Bp Angus Dun. m 6/3/1951 Elisabeth Cabarga c 3. Cn for Cler Deploy Dio Washington Washington DC 2002-2003; Int Gr Ch Elkridge MD 1999-2000; Int Chr Ch And S Mich's Philadelphia PA 1998-1999; Int S Mk's Ch Philadelphia PA 1995-1996; Cler Deploy and Ord Process Dio Pennsylvania Philadelphia PA 1987-1993; S Mk's Ch Evanston IL 1984; Prof SWTS Evanston IL 1976-1987; R Nativ Epis Ch Temple Hills MD 1959-1976; Asst S Matt's Epis Ch Hyattsville MD 1955-1959. Auth, "The Ch as Setting for Older Adult Mnstry," *Older Adult Mnstry*, Hayworth, 2005; Auth, "Aging & the Growth of Wisdom," *Affirmative Aging*, Moorehouse, 1994; Auth, "Epis Seminaries & Aging," *Journ Rel & Aging*. Bd ESMA 1997-2000; Bd Natl Coun on the Aging 2000-2002; Chair Natl Interfaith Coaltion Aging 2000-2002; Espiscopal Sr Mnstrs, VP 2006. bob_carlson@ecunet.org

CARLSON, Sara Sessions (Oly) 17320 97th Pl Sw Apt 603, Vashon WA 98070 B Seattle WA 9/10/1943 d Edward Stackpole Shelton & Florence Calista. LSU 1963; Dioc Sch Of Mnstry And Theol Seattle WA 2004. D 6/26/2005 Bp Vincent Waydell Warner. c 1. D Ch Of The H Sprt Vashon WA 2006-2010. deacon@holyspiritvashon.org

CARLSON, Walter Donald (Nwk) 6 Otis Pl, Verona NJ 07044 B Glen Ridge NJ 2/3/1934 s Robert Hilding Carlson & Anna Louise. BA Rutgers-The St U 1958; MDiv GTS 1967. D 6/10/1967 P 12/21/1967 Bp Leland Stark. m 7/18/1964 Marlene Joyce Varga. R Ch Of The Atone Fair Lawn NJ 1977-1991; Dept Of Missions Dio Newark Newark NJ 1977-1990; R S Mary's Ch Belvidere NJ 1974-1977; R Trin Ch Bayonne NJ 1971-1974; Asst S Steph's Ch Pittsfield MA 1968-1971; Cur Chr Ch Pompton Lakes NJ 1967-1968. carlson973@aol.com

CARLSON, Wayne Harold (Chi) 2881 Huntington Blvd., Apt 138, 2881 Huntington Blvd. Apt 138, Fresno CA 93721 B Fremont NE 5/16/1944 s Harold Gunnard Carlson & Verla Elaine. BS U of Nebraska 1965; MDiv SWTS 1971; DMin SWTS 1999. D 6/18/1971 Bp Robert Patrick Varley P 12/20/1971 Bp Russell T Rauscher. m 6/10/1967 Diane Marie Krull c 2. R Ch Of The H Fam Pk Forest IL 1994-2011; R S Lk's Epis Ch Manchester MO 1977-1994; R Chr Ch Cntrl City NE 1971-1977; Vic S Johns Ch Albion NE 1971-1977. carlsonw621@aol.com

CARLSON, William August (Chi) 515 Woodrow St, Rockford IL 61101 B Belvidere IL 7/6/1934 AA Chicago Jr Coll Chicago IL. D 2/6/2000 Bp William Dailey Persell. D S Chad Epis Ch Loves Pk IL 2000-2008.

CARLSON, William Douglas (At) 114 Grady Ridge Dr, Ashville NC 28806 **D St Georges Epis Ch Asheville NC 2008-** B Minneapolis MN 4/27/1931 s Carl William Carlson & Gladys. BBA U MN; EFM STUSo 1981. D 1/25/1983 Bp William Gillette Weinhauer. m 3/19/1955 Helen Ann Zilliox. S Pat's Epis Ch Atlanta GA 1994-2003; D Ch Of The Mssh Murphy NC 1983-1992; D in Charge S Fran Of Assisi Cherokee NC 1983-1988. carlson2@mindspring.com

CARLTON-JONES, Anne Helen (SwFla) 15608 Fiddlesticks Blvd, Fort Myers FL 33912 B Birmingham England 6/21/1934 D 6/13/1998 Bp John Bailey Lipscomb. m 10/3/1955 Dennis Carlton-Jones c 2.

CARLYON, Robert David (Be) P.O.Box 262, Orwigsburg PA 17961 B Hazleton PA 6/14/1937 s Robert Carlyon & Dorothy. BA Lycoming Coll 1959; MDiv PrTS 1963; Cert VTS 1965; DMin Untd TS 1981. D 6/26/1965 Bp Earl M Honaman P 1/1/1966 Bp Walter M Higley. m 1/20/1986 Christine Carlyon. P-in-c Calv Ch Tamaqua PA 1978-1980; R S Jas Ch Schuylkill Haven PA 1971-1997; R S Jas Ch Muncy PA 1968-1971; Cur Trin Memi Ch Binghamton NY 1965-1968. Auth, "Hlth Care & The Ch," Dayton Untd Sem, 1981. carlyonr@usa.net

CARMAN, Charles Churchill (RG) 94 Winterhaven Drive, Nellysford VA 22958 B Denver CO 8/3/1932 s James Walmsley Frederic Carman & Phyllis. BS Lewis & Clark Coll 1957; MDiv CDSP 1960. D 6/22/1960 P 1/4/1961 Bp James Walmsley Frederic Carman. m 11/23/1985 Mary Ann Thorpe c 2. Int S Jas Epis Ch Taos NM 1992-1994; Int S Jn's Epis Ch Alamogordo NM 1991-1992; Ch Of The Ascen High Rolls NM 1991; Int S Mart's Epis Ch Henrico VA 1989-1990; Brandon Epis Ch Disputanta VA 1988-1989; Epis Ch Of S Paul And S Andr Kenbridge VA 1987; Gibson Memi Crewe VA 1987; S Andr's Ch VICTORIA VA 1987; Hickory Neck Ch Toano VA 1985-1986; Calv Ch Bath Par Dinwiddie VA 1985; Int Dio Sthrn Virginia Norfolk VA 1984-1989; Johns Memi Epis Ch Farmville VA 1984-1985; Int S Andr's Ch Richmond VA 1982-1983; S Thos' Ch Richmond VA 1981-1982; Vic Gr Epis Ch Lake Havasu City AZ 1977-1981; Cur Epis Par Of S Mich And All Ang Tucson AZ 1975-1977; Vic S Paul's Epis Ch Modesto CA 1973-1975; Vic S Dunstans Epis Ch Modesto CA 1970-1973; Vic S Jn The Bapt Epis Clarendon TX 1960-1964; Vic S Mich And All Ang Ch Shamrock TX 1960-1964. chickmaryann@hotmail.com

CARMICHAEL, Anna Roope (EO) 400 11th St, PO Box 25, Hood River OR 97031 **R The Par Of S Mk The Evang Hood River OR 2010-** B NC 5/20/1975 d Michael Wayne Roope & Donna Brauer. BA Barton Coll 1997; MS Longwood Coll 1998; MTS Vanguard U 2005; MDiv CDSP 2008. D 6/7/2008 P 1/10/2009 Bp Joseph Jon Bruno. m 7/19/2008 Matthew D Carmichael. Chapl S Marg Of Scotland Par San Juan Capistrano CA 2008-2010. DOK 2005. revannacarmichael@gmail.com

CARMICHAEL, (Mary) Jean (Oly) 1600 Marshall Cir Unit 328, Dupont WA 98327 B Los Angeles CA 5/12/1931 d James Robert Carmichael & Esther Sugar. AA U CA 1952; BS San Diego St U 1955; Diac TS 1989; Cert Sprtl Dir Formation 1994. D 6/18/1991 Bp Vincent Waydell Warner. Asstg D S Andr's Epis Ch Tacoma WA 1998-2002; D Chr Ch Tacoma WA 1995-1997; D S Andr's Epis Ch Tacoma WA 1991-1994. Assn for Epis Deacons 1986. deaconmjc@comcast.net

CARMICHAEL, Standrod Tucker (SwVa) 3755 Peachtree Rd NE, Atlanta GA 30319 **Died 8/7/2011** B Bowling Green KY 7/27/1924 s Henry St George Tucker Carmichael & Lelle. BA W&L 1947; STM EDS 1953; MA Mid 1974. D 6/20/1953 Bp Charles Clingman P 12/23/1953 Bp Charles F Hall. c 8. Auth, *Mus For The Liturg, A Jazz Mass*, 1961.

CARMIENCKE JR, Bayard Collier (LI) 1145 Walnut Ave, Bohemia NY 11716 B Brooklyn NY 5/26/1933 s Bayard Collier Carmiencke & Frances Catherine Ellison. BA Hofstra U 1959; MDiv PDS 1962; Med St. Johns U 1971; Fllshp Coll of Preachers 1976; 1992; 1997; Cert 1997. D 4/28/1962 P 12/21/1962 Bp James P De Wolfe. Asst S Mary's Ch Lake Ronkonkoma NY 1995-1997; S Lukes Ch Bohemia NY 1980-1995; Ch Of The Redeem Merrick NY 1980; S Thos' Epis Ch Bellerose Vill NY 1968-1980; R S Jas Epis Ch Westernport MD 1964-1966; Asst Gr And S Ptr's Ch Baltimore MD 1962-1964. allimar@optonline.net

CARMINE, Barbara Evelyn (SwFla) 1700 3rd Ave W #S-130, Bradenton FL 34205 **Died 3/1/2010** B Medford MA 1/8/1925 d Dean Carmine & Elsie Carolyn. BA Ottawa U 1979. D 6/14/1986 Bp Emerson Paul Haynes. DOK; NAAD; Ord of S Lk; Worker Sis of the H Sprt. barbara.carmine@verizon.net

CARMODY, Alison Cutter (Ala) 6 Montrose Cir, Birmingham AL 35213 **S Steph's Epis Ch Birmingham AL 2005-** B Wilmington NC 8/12/1945 d Edward Parker Cutter & Marjorie. BS U of Tennessee 1967; MA Austin Peay St U 1970; MDiv VTS 2000. D 6/3/2000 P 12/5/2000 Bp Henry Nutt Parsley Jr. m 12/27/1968 Richard Patrick Carmody c 1. Assoc R All SS Epis Ch Birmingham AL 2003-2005; Asst All SS Epis Ch Birmingham AL 2000-2002. acarmody@bellsouth.net

CARMONA, Paul Bernard (SanD) 4658 El Cerrito Dr, San Diego CA 92115 **Assoc R S Mk's Ch San Diego CA 2003-** B Los Angeles CA 9/11/1947 D 6/8/2002 P 12/21/2002 Bp Gethin Benwil Hughes. m 9/26/1980 Marie-Therese Henckens.

CARNAHAN, Patricia King (Pgh) 4201 Saltsburg Rd, Murrysville PA 15668 B Boston MA 1/6/1949 d Robert Francis King & Marion. BA Chatham Coll 1970; BS U Pgh 1978; MDiv Pittsburgh TS 1980; DMin GTF 1991. D 6/13/1981 P 12/20/1981 Bp Robert Bracewell Appleyard. m 11/30/1974 Byron Lee Carnaham. S Brendan's Epis Ch Sewickley PA 1988-1997; Dio Pittsburgh Monroeville PA 1983-1985; Chair Dio Pittsburgh Monroeville PA 1983-1985; Chr Epis Ch No Hills Pittsburgh PA 1982-1987; Dio Pittsburgh Monroeville PA 1981-1982. Soc Of S Marg. CLOUDPATH@VERIZON.NET

CARNES, Ralph Lee (Chi) 4507 Dayton Blvd, Chattanooga TN 37415 B Tallapoosa GA 5/28/1931 s Randal Julian Carnes & Letitia. BA Emory U 1959; MA Emory U 1960; PhD Emory U 1965; Cert SWTS 1986; Fllshp Coll Chapl 1989. D 6/1/1987 Bp James Winchester Montgomery P 12/1/1987 Bp Frank Tracy Griswold III. m 4/28/1967 Valerie Folts Bohanan. Auth, "The Road To Damascus"; Auth, "Dictionary Of Intl Bios". Apha. 74667.2723@compuserve.com

CARNES, Valerie Folts (Mil) 4507 Dayton Blvd, Chattanooga TN 37415 **S Ptr's Ch Chattanooga TN 2005-** B Chattanooga TN 11/19/1940 d Ross W Bohanan & Valerie. MA Emory U 1963; PhD Emory U 1967; MA Loyola U 1989; MDiv SWTS 1994; CAS SWTS 1995. D 8/26/1995 Bp Roger John White P 6/1/1996 Bp Robert Gould Tharp. m 4/28/1967 Ralph Lee Carnes. Asst Gr Ch Chattanooga TN 1999-2005.

CARNEY, Joseph Patrick (Oly) 529 Whiskey Hill Rd, Lopez Island WA 98261 B Vancouver BC CA 12/23/1929 s Robert Charles Carney & Nora Agnes. Ord to Priesthood Sem of Chr the King, Can 1957; MMin Seattle U, TS & Mnstry 1986. Trans from Anglican Church of Canada 10/16/1967 as Priest Bp Ivol I Curtis. m 11/29/1965 Tanya Dournovo. Vic Gr Ch Lopez Island WA 1997-2000; Vic St Bede Epis Ch Port Orchard WA 1989-1995; R S Chas Angl Par Poulsbo WA 1980-1989. FA 1970-1995. jtcarney@centurytel.net

CARNEY, Michael Rex (Colo) 1401 E Dry Creek Rd, Centennial CO 80122 **R S Tim's Epis Ch Centennial CO 2006-** B Osage IA 9/1/1952 s Clarence Stanley Carney & Jacquelyn. BA U MN 1978; MDiv CDSP 1998. D 6/6/1998 P 12/5/1998 Bp William Edwin Swing. m 4/10/1982 Marsha Smith Heron c 2. Vic S Geo's Epis Ch Antioch CA 2000-2006; Asst S Steph's Par Belvedere CA 1998-2000. Auth, "Liturg Mus in the Postmodern Age," *The Hymn*, 1999; Auth, "Sacagawea's Story," *Many Voices: True Tales from Amer's Past*, Natl Story Telling Press, 1995. michaelcarney1@msn.com

CARNEY, Paul Martin (Alb) 146 N First St, Troy NY 12180 B Troy NY 11/9/1955 s Paul W Carney & Julia D. AAS Hudson Vlly Cmnty Coll 1975. D 5/30/2009 Bp William Howard Love. m 5/1/1976 Marilyn E Carney c 2. hamn2uzr@aol.com

CARNEY, Susan Roberta (RI) 9924 Pointe Aux Chenes Road, Ocean Springs MS 39564 **Off Of Bsh For ArmdF New York NY 1984-** B Ankara TR 8/27/1952 d Richard A Carney & Bernice. BS SW Missouri St U 1975; MDiv PrTS 1978; CPE Bethany Coll 1979; GTS 1979; STM Ya Berk 1984. D 6/7/1980 P 12/1/1980 Bp Albert Wiencke Van Duzer. Int S Jn's Ch Guilford CT 1983-1984; Assoc S Lk's Ch Ewing NJ 1982-1983.

CAROLIN, Philip Leonard (Nev) 5271 Alfalfa St, Las Vegas NV 89120 **Died 3/20/2010** B Chicago IL 10/23/1938 s Phillip Leonard Carolin & Shirley Ann. Lake Forest Coll; S Jos Franciscan Sem; Untd States Frgn Serv Inst. D 2/24/1996 P 8/28/1996 Bp Stewart Clark Zabriskie. carolynp@worldnet.att.net

CARON, Donald Raymond (At) 116 Forte Dr Nw, Milledgeville GA 31061 **R S Steph's Ch Milledgeville GA 2005-** B Norwich CT 2/17/1949 s Raymond Caron & Beatrice. BA Providence Coll 1971; MA Providence Coll 1979; MDiv Weston Jesuit TS 1984. Rec from Roman Catholic 11/21/2005 Bp J(ohn) Neil Alexander. m 1/31/1998 Melanie Weber. doncaron1@windstream.net

CARON II, Joseph Auridas (Alb) 271 Stevenson Rd, Greenwich NY 12834 B Bay Shore NY 10/7/1936 s Joseph A Caron & Mary Ann. BA Barrington Coll 1968; MDiv Ya Berk 1971; DMin Drew U 1993. D 6/9/1973 P 12/15/1973 Bp Paul Moore Jr. c 5. S Paul's Epis Ch Greenwich NY 1993-1994; Ch Of The H Cross Troy NY 1986-1991; R S Paul's Epis Ch Greenwich NY 1976-1983. Alum Achievement Stony Brook Sch 1983. cambridgecaron@aol.com

CARPENTER, Allen Douglas (Alb) 62 S. Swan St., Albany NY 12210 **Cathd Of All SS Albany NY 2008-** B Oneonta NY 1/10/1947 s Orson M Carpenter & Ingehorg N. BA Bard Coll 1969. D 5/10/2008 Bp William Howard Love. adasst@nyca.rr.com

CARPENTER, Catherine (Minn) 1289 Hartford Ave, Saint Paul MN 55116 B Evanston IL 8/5/1958 d Eugene Frederick Carpenter & Helen MacKay. BA St Cathr U 2007; MDiv The GTS 2012. D 6/30/2011 Bp Brian N Prior. m 8/25/2001 Jonathan David Holmer. cathy_jon@msn.com

CARPENTER, Charles Monroe (Ind) 91 Smiths Rd, Mitchell IN 47446 **R S Jn's Epis Ch Bedford IN 2003-** B La Grange KY 11/25/1948 s Joseph Hardin Carpenter & Elizabeth. BS Indiana St U 1970; MDiv Epis TS of The SW 2000. D 6/23/2000 P 2/11/2001 Bp Catherine Elizabeth Maples Waynick. Dio Indianapolis Indianapolis IN 2000-2003; S Lk's Epis Ch Cannelton IN 2000-2002. father_charlie@yahoo.com

CARPENTER, Douglas Morrison (Ala) 3037 Overton Rd, Birmingham AL 35223 **Chapl to Ret Dio Alabama Birmingham AL 2006-** B Savannah GA 5/22/1933 s Charles C J Carpenter & Alexandra. BA Pr 1955; MDiv VTS 1960; Fell Coll of Preachers 1971. D 6/24/1960 Bp Charles C J Carpenter P 3/15/1961 Bp George Mosley Murray. m 8/30/1989 Ann Piper c 4. R S Steph's Epis Ch Birmingham AL 1973-2005; R S Paul's Epis Ch Lynchburg VA 1969-1973; Dio Coun,Dept Fin,Stdg Com,Comp Dio Com,Dep GC,BEC Dio Alabama Birmingham AL 1965-2000; R S Steph's Epis Ch Huntsville AL 1963-1969; R S Mary's Epis Ch Andalusia AL 1960-1963; R S Steph's Ch Brewton AL 1960-1963. Auth, "Terrifying Tales and Inspiring Stories," *Terrifying Tales and Inspiring Stories*, Self Pub, 2008; Auth, "The Story of St. Steph's," *The Story of St. Steph's*, Self Pub, 2006; Auth, "A Casserole for a Horse," *A Casserole for a Horse*, Mercy Seat Press, 2005. DSA Epis Conf of Deaf 1995. carpenter.doug7436@att.net

CARPENTER, Francis Newton (Chi) 337 Ridge Rd, Barrington Hills IL 60010 B Port Chester, NY 9/18/1947 s Francis Newton & Patricia. BA U of So Carolina 1970. D 2/6/2010 Bp Jeffrey Dean Lee. m 1/18/1986 Joan May Shemmer c 1. rncarpenter3@aol.com

CARPENTER, George Harrison (Oly) Po Box 343, Medina WA 98039 B Colusa CA 4/1/1934 s Leslie Herman Carpenter & Elizabeth Ann. BA U CA Chico 1958; ThM CDSP 1961; MA U of Washington 1978. D 6/15/1961 P 12/21/1961 Bp Clarence Rupert Haden Jr. m 4/20/1967 Patricia Ann Schmitz. Asstg P S Thos Ch Medina WA 1977-1980; Asst S Jn's Epis Ch Snohomish WA 1965-1968; Vic S Mich's Ch Anderson CA 1961-1964. gcarpenter3600@gmail.com

CARPENTER, James Anderson (NY) 26 Owens Rd, C/O Brandon Wilde, Evans GA 30809 B Kings Mountain NC 2/4/1928 s Clarence Edward Carpenter & Elizabeth Jane. BA Wofford Coll 1948; BD Duke 1951; GTS 1952; Schlr U Of S Andrews Fife Gb 1957; PhD U of Cambridge 1959; LHD Hebr Un New York NY 1993. D 6/18/1952 P 2/11/1953 Bp Edwin A Penick. m 2/12/1954 Mary Louise Dunbar c 1. Asst Prof/Sub-Dn The GTS New York NY 1963-1993; Vic S Tim's Ch Alexandria LA 1959-1963; R S Barth's Ch Pittsboro NC 1952-1953. Ed, "Jews & Chr In Dialogue"; Auth, "Gore," *A Study In Liberal Cath Thought*; Auth, "Nature & Gr," *Toward An Integral Perspective*. Amer Theol Soc. marvone@aol.com

CARPENTER, John Paul (Pa) 3937 Netherfield Rd, Philadelphia PA 19129 B Saint Paul MN 9/29/1936 s Edwin Gilbert Carpenter & Helen. BA U MN 1959; BD Nash 1962; JD Tem 1971. D 6/29/1962 Bp Hamilton Hyde Kellogg P 5/1/1963 Bp Daniel Corrigan. m 8/27/1958 Pamela VanDusen. Cn Gr Cathd Topeka KS 1964-1966.

CARPENTER, Judith (Mass) 192 N. Main Street, Rockland ME 04841 B Somerville MA 10/7/1942 d Richard Smith Perry & Ruth Constance. BA cl U MN 1963; MDiv Andover Newton TS 1981; DMin EDS 1995. D 5/30/1981 Bp John Bowen Coburn P 6/9/1982 Bp George E Rath. m 6/5/1965 John Brooks Carpenter c 4. Auth, "Voices:Wmn of Color," *Indep Sch mag*, 1991. Phi Beta Kappa U MN Minneapolis MN 1963. jpcarpenter@myfairpoint.net

CARPENTER, Leslie Scott (Ind) 6050 N. Meridian St., Indianapolis IN 46208 **Asst R S Paul's Epis Ch Indianapolis IN 2008-** B Austin TX 5/3/1979 s Scott Sutherland Carpenter & Eva Jean Brown. BA The W&M, Williamsburg, VA 2002; MDiv SWTS 2008. D 6/28/2008 Bp Bavi Rivera. m 6/18/2005 Kristin RS Sanders c 1. lcarpenter@stpaulsindy.org

CARPENTER II, Marion George (NI) Saint Annes, 424 W Market St, Warsaw IN 46580 **D S Anne's Epis Ch Warsaw IN 2007-** B Goshen IN 1/27/1954 s Marion G Carpenter & Delores. D 11/16/2007 Bp Edward Stuart Little II. m 7/10/1976 DeBra Ann Carpenter c 2. wcmgc@hotmail.com

CARPENTER, (Mary) Elizabeth (WA) 12097 Stansbury Dr, Monrovia MD 21770 B Mobile AL 12/22/1940 d Darius Inge Carpenter & Mary Lee. BA Duke 1963; MS U of Texas at Dallas 1984; MDiv Harvard DS 1991. D 6/22/1991 Bp Donis Dean Patterson P 7/22/1992 Bp Barbara Clementine Harris. c 1. R S Anne's Ch Damascus MD 1999-2011; Asst S Jn's Epis Ch Gloucester MA 1994-1995; Vic S Eliz's Ch Wilmington MA 1992-1994; Pstr Asst Trin Ch Concord MA 1992-1993; Int S Jn's Epis Ch Westwood MA 1991-1992. Washington Epis Cler Assn. revelizabethcarpenter@yahoo.com

CARPENTER, Morton Eugene (EC) 1603 E Walnut St, Goldsboro NC 27530 **R S Steph's Ch Goldsboro NC 2001-** B Repton AL 11/29/1948 s Morton Free Carpenter & Sallie Lou. BS Auburn U 1971; MDiv STUSo 1986. D 7/12/1986 P 5/9/1987 Bp Charles Farmer Duvall. m 10/9/1976 Judy Lee Wade c 1. R S Lk's Ch Marianna FL 1991-2001; Vic Ch Of The H Cross No E PA 1988-1991; Cur Trin Epis Ch Mobile AL 1986-1988. mecarpenter1@gmail.com

CARPENTER, Nicholas (Los) 15757 Saint Timothy Rd, Apple Valley CA 92307 **D S Tim's Epis Ch Apple Vlly CA 2010-** B Dallas TX 1/7/1947 s Robert James Carpenter & Lottie Pearl. Cert ETS at Claremont 2010. D 2/13/2010 Bp Chester Lovelle Talton. nicholas2two@gmail.com

CARPENTER, Ralph Schenck (Lex) 355 S Broadway Apt 301, Lexington KY 40508 B Montclair NJ 12/29/1925 s Louis Schenck Carpenter & Gertrude Patricia. BA Pr 1949; BD PrTS 1952; STM UTS 1961; DD Epis TS In Kentucky 1983. D 9/20/1965 P 1/21/1966 Bp William R Moody. m 5/22/1976 Gail P Vollrath c 2. Auth, "Gd Grief," *Your Hlth After 60*. AAPC 1968; ACPE 1953. qvcarpenter@insightbb.com

CARPENTER, Stephen Morris (NCal) 1020 Westview Dr, Napa CA 94558 **R S Mary's Epis Ch Napa CA 1983-** B Santa Monica CA 11/2/1951 s Austin Derwent Carpenter & Margaret Mae. BMu Estrn New Mex U Portales NM 1974; MDiv SWTS 1979. D 5/12/1979 P 11/30/1979 Bp John Lester Thompson III. m 8/26/1974 Frances R Malinowski. P Trin Cathd Sacramento CA 1979-1983. canonstephen79@yahoo.com

CARPENTER, Susan M (RI) PO Box 505, Greenville RI 02828 **Bd Dir - The Epis Conf Cntr Dio Rhode Island Providence RI 2010-; Cmsn on Congrl Dvlpmt Dio Rhode Island Providence RI 2010-; P-in-c S Thos Ch Greenville RI 2010-** B Providence RI 12/2/1953 d Donald Parker Morrison & Shirly Davy. BS Rhode Island Coll 1975; MEd Rhode Island Coll 1983; MDiv The GTS 2008. D 6/14/2008 Bp Geralyn Wolf. m 11/24/2009 Brian E Carpenter c 2. Assoc R S Jn's Ch Barrington RI 2008-2010. cherryval@aol.com

CARR, Burgess (At) 2833 Flat Shoals Rd, Decatur GA 30034 B Crozierville LR 7/8/1935 s James H Carr & Cerue. BS Cuttington U Coll 1958; BD Cuttington U Coll 1961; ThM Harvard DS 1967; DCL S Aug's Coll Raleigh NC 1982; DD GTS 1987. D 8/13/1961 Bp George Clinton Harris P 5/1/1962 Bp William A Brown. m 9/1/1962 Francesca Verdier. P S Tim's Decatur GA 2001-2004; Epis Ch Cntr New York NY 1987-1994; Assoc Prof Ya Berk New Haven CT 1982-1987; P S Andr's Ch New Haven CT 1982-1987; Ya New Haven CT 1982-1983; The Cathd Ch Of S Paul Boston MA 1980-1981; P S Mk's Ch Dorchester MA 1979-1981. Auth, "Afr'S Moral Imperetives: Liberation, Identity, Humanness, Mit Press, Cambridge," *Ma*, 1978; Auth, "The Relation Of Un To Mssn," *Midstream*, 1975; Auth, "Confessing Jesus Chr In Afr Today," *The Future Of The Mssy Enterprise*, 1975. Bp'S Recognition: 40 Years Of Mnstry Dio Georgia 2002; The Bp'S Awd Dio Connecticut 1980; Hon Citizen Of Alexandria Egypt 1977; Ord Of The Star Of Afr Liberia Afr 1976; Humane Ord Of Afr Redemp Liberia Afr 1972; Ord Of The Two Niles Sudan Afr 1972. burgesscarr@bellsouth.net

CARR, Clifford Bradley (Be) 526 11th Avenue, Bethlehem PA 18018 B Newport RI 6/28/1939 s Oliver Bradley Carr & Gladys. BA Leh 1961; MDiv GTS 1964. D 6/20/1964 P 3/27/1965 Bp John S Higgins. Ecum Off Dio Bethlehem Bethlehem PA 1994-1999; R Trin Ch Easton PA 1993-2000; Cn Dio Bethlehem Bethlehem PA 1987; Chair of Liturg Cmsn Dio Bethlehem Bethlehem PA 1980-1998; Trin Epis Ch Pottsville PA 1980-1993; Par Of The H Fam Pen Argyl PA 1974-1980; Vic S Jos's Ch Pen Argyl PA 1974-1980; R No Par Epis Ch Frackville PA 1968-1974; Asst S Mk's Ch Warwick RI 1966-1967; Cur S Lk's Epis Ch E Greenwich RI 1964-1966. AAM 1985-2005. Hon Cn Dio Bethlehem 1987. FACC4@AOL.COM

CARR, Dale Robert (Ore) 5223 NE Everett St, Portland OR 97213 **Assoc P S Steph's Epis Par Portland OR 2005-** B Melford OR 4/12/1957 s Robert Merrill Carr & Karen Dale. BS OR SU 1979; MBA Monterey Inst of Intl Stds 1989; MDiv GTS 2001. D 6/16/2001 Bp William O Gregg P 1/27/2002 Bp Pierre W Whalon. Cur Ch of the Ascen Munich 81545 DE 2001-2004. Assembly of Epis Healthcare Chapl 2005; Assn of Profsnl Chapl 2007. DALECARR@ORST.EDU

CARR, John Joseph (WNY) 56 Mckinley Ave, Kenmore NY 14217 B Akron OH 11/15/1937 s Owen Carr & Mary Catherine. Maryknoll TS; Wadhams Hall Sem Coll; BA S Jn's TS 1961; STL S Jn's TS 1965. Trans from Anglican Church of Canada 9/26/1984 Bp Harold B Robinson. m 3/7/1969 Gloria Ann Grey c 4. S Mary's Epis Ch Gowanda NY 1984-1985.

CARR, Michael Gordon (SanD) 651 Eucalyptus Ave, Vista CA 92084 **All SS Ch Vista CA 2007-** B Fayetteville NC 9/12/1956 s Peter Gordon Carr & Margaret. BA TCU 1979; MDiv Nash 1982. D 6/26/1982 Bp A Donald Davies P 7/20/1983 Bp Charles Brinkley Morton. m 8/31/1980 Kelly Elizabeth Johnson c 1. R S Andrews Epis Ch Port Angeles WA 1994-2007; R S Swithin Forks Forks WA 1994; Vic S Richard's Epis Ch Lake Arrowhead CA 1989-1994; R S Bede's Epis Ch Los Angeles CA 1986-1989; Asst Ch Of Our Sav Par San Gabr CA 1985-1986; Asst S Jn's Epis Ch Chula Vista CA 1983-1985; Cur S Anne's Ch Ft Worth TX 1982-1983. mkcarr@cox.net

CARR, Michael Leo (Mich) 9132 Pine Valley Dr, Grand Blanc MI 48439 **Co-R Chr The King Epis Ch Taylor MI 1998-; Co-R S Lk's Epis Ch Allen Pk MI 1998-; Ord Translated from RC Cathd Ch Of S Paul Detroit MI 1994-; Serv Dio Michigan Detroit MI 1994-** B Indianapolis IN 11/11/1940 s

John Carr & Bridget. BA S Mary Sem 1963; Mstr (EQIV) S Maur's Sem 1967; MDiv Immac Concep Sem 1982; Bd Cert Chapl Natl Assn of VetA Chapl 1991; DMin GTF 1992; PhD GTF 1996. Rec from Roman Catholic 10/1/1994 as Priest Bp R(aymond) Stewart Wood Jr. m 12/19/1990 Karen Christine Cooley. Co-R Dream Cluster Taylor MI 1998-2011. Auth, *Psychol Importance of the Sprtl in Recovery Process ofVietnam PTSD Veterans*, Wyndham Hall Press of Indiana, 1998; Ed, *Fells Yearbook*, Wyndham Hall Press, 1992; Auth, *A Unique Journey*. ACPE; ACC; Fed Fire Chapl - Fed of Fire Chapl; Fell GTF; Michigan St Fireman's Assn; Mltry Chapl Assn; Natl Assn of VA Chapl-Bd Cert. Secy's Awd for Excellence in Chapl Secy of Veterans' Affrs Washington DC 2002. mlc.carr@yahoo.com

CARR, Spencer David (Colo) 4661 Wilson Dr, Broomfield CO 80023 **Asst S Mary Magd Ch Boulder CO 2011-** B San Diego CA 10/15/1944 s Albert Richard Carr & Shirley Elaine. BA Occ 1966; PhD U MI 1970; MDiv SWTS 2000. D 6/10/2000 P 12/16/2000 Bp William Jerry Winterrowd. m 6/8/1997 Karla J Johnson. R Epis Ch Of S Jn The Bapt Granby CO 2001-2011; Cur S Mary Magd Ch Boulder CO 2000-2001. SPENCERCARR711@GMAIL.COM

CARR, Virginia Rose (WNY) 12 Elm St, Westfield NY 14787 B Queens New York 3/3/1955 d Robert Martin & Rose Marie. MA S Bonaventure U 2003; Cert Angl Stds Nash 2009. D 7/2/2010 Bp J Michael Garrison. m 6/27/1992 Owen C Carr c 3. SAMS Ambridge PA 1994-1998. virginiacarr@windstream.net

✠ **CARR, Rt Rev William Franklin** (USC) 4249 Cedar Grove Rd, Murfreesboro TN 37127 B Alexandria VA 1/21/1938 s Franklin Lee Carr & Virginia Lorraine. VTS; BS E Tennessee St U 1961; MDiv VTS 1970. D 6/11/1970 P 2/1/1971 Bp Wilburn Camrock Campbell Con 6/1/1985 for WVa. m 3/19/1960 Lena Mae Herman c 4. Asst Bp Of Upper So Carolina Dio Upper So Carolina Columbia SC 1990-1994; Bp Suffr Dio W Virginia Charleston WV 1985-1990; Asst to Bp Dio W Virginia Charleston WV 1981-1985; Chair Dept Of Mssn And Mnstry Dio W Virginia Charleston WV 1978-1980; Dn Of SW Convoc Dio W Virginia Charleston WV 1976-1980; R S Jn's Ch Huntington WV 1975-1981; Vic S Barn Bridgeport WV 1972-1975; Vic Olde S Jn's Ch Colliers WV 1970-1972. DD VTS 1980. lmc.carr@gmail.com

✠ CARRANZA-GOMEZ, Rt Rev Sergio (Los) PO Box 512164, Los Angeles CA 90051 B Mexico City MX 8/18/1941 s Faustino Carranza-Valencia & Belina. BA Universidad Nacional Autonoma De Mex 1958; BA Universidad Nacional Autonoma De Mex 1964; MDiv VTS 1967. D 5/20/1967 Bp William Foreman Creighton P 12/8/1967 Bp Jose Guadalupe Saucedo Con 8/20/1989 for Mex. Dio Los Angeles Los Angeles CA 2003-2010; Dio Mex 2001-2002; Iglesia Epis Mexicana 1988-1989; Dio Wstrn Mex Zapopan Jalisco CP 45150 1967-1984. OHC, Jn 23 Ecum Assn. DD VTS 1990. sergiocarranza@ladiocese.org

CARREKER, Michael Lyons (Ga) 1 West Macon Street, Savannah GA 31401 B Atlanta GA 11/19/1954 s James William Carreker & Mary. Gordon-Conwell TS; BA U GA 1976; DIT Oxf 1978; MA Dalhousie U 1983; Cert S Lk Sem 1988; PhD Dalhousie U 1993. D 9/14/1988 P 9/20/1989 Bp Harry Woolston Shipps. m 7/30/1977 Frances Lynne Allen c 2. R S Jn's Ch Savannah GA 1999-2006; Assoc S Jn's Ch Savannah GA 1989-1990; Chr Ch Frederica St Simons Island GA 1989; D Chr Ch Frederica St Simons Island GA 1988-1989; Dio Georgia Savannah GA 1988-1989. Isaac Walton Killam Schlr Dalhousie U; Gk Tchg Fell Gorgon-Conwell TS. michaelcarreker@gmail.com

CARRENO-GAMBOA, Bladimir Francisco (Ve) 49-143 Colinas De Bello Monte, Caracas 1042 Venezuela **Dio Venezuela Colinas De Bello Monte Caracas 10-42-A VE 2004-** B 10/8/1958 D 12/16/1992 P 6/20/1993 Bp Onell Asiselo Soto.

CARRICK, Judith Trautman (LI) 4 Kenny St, Hauppauge NY 11788 **S Thos Of Cbury Ch Smithtown NY 2008-** B Flushing NY 10/15/1935 d Henry Trautman & Estelle. BA Tufts U 1957; MS Adel 1979; Cert Mercer TS 1994. D 6/23/1995 Bp Orris George Walker Jr. m 5/2/1959 Edward Bird Carrick c 2. D S Anselm's Ch Shoreham NY 2002-2005; D S Jn's Ch Hempstead NY 2001-2002; D S Mk's Ch Islip NY 1999-2000; D S Ptr's by-the-Sea Epis Ch Bay Shore NY 1995-1998. Preached Ord/Consec R Michel, Suffr Long Island Garden City NY 1997. revjudy95@aol.com

CARRIERE, Anne Stone (Ark) 31 Stonecrest Ct, Mountain Home AR 72653 B Memphis TN 2/4/1943 d Coe Stone & Elizabeth. BA Van 1964; MDiv Memphis TS 1981. D 7/12/1981 Bp William F Gates Jr P 6/27/1982 Bp William Evan Sanders. m 7/10/1965 John G Carriere c 2. S Andr's Ch Mtn Hm AR 1998-2003; Ch of the H Apos Collierville TN 1990-1997; Gr - S Lk's Ch Memphis TN 1983-1990. jacarriere@suddenlink.net

CARRINGTON, James Henry (ECR) 1743 Southwood Dr, San Luis Obispo CA 93401 B 1/28/1935 D 6/22/1959 P 2/16/1960 Bp Francis E I Bloy. m 7/30/1992 Rosemarie Carrington. S Steph's Epis Ch San Luis Obispo CA 1995-1996.

CARR-JONES, Philip Bohdan (NJ) 3 Haytown Rd, Lebanon NJ 08833 **R Ch Of The H Sprt Lebanon NJ 1987-** B Plainfield NJ 11/6/1957 s William Howry Jones & Mary. BA Juniata Coll 1980; MDiv EDS 1984. D 6/2/1984 P 3/1/1985 Bp George Phelps Mellick Belshaw. m 8/29/1982 Janmarie Carr-Jones c 3. Cur S Ptr's Ch Perth Amboy NJ 1984-1987. "A Survey Of Leahets," Aplm, 2004. Soc Cappodocian Fathers (Patristics). carr-jones@att.net

CARROLL, Charles Moisan (Me) PO Box 195, Brunswick ME 04011 B Anesburg MA 8/1/1940 s Marcus C Carroll & Geraldine Moisan. AB Pr 1962; MA Bangor TS 2011. D 6/25/2011 Bp Stephen Taylor Lane. m 5/17/1981 Ann Ann Adden Kuhn c 4. chickcarroll76@hotmail.com

CARROLL, Christian (Nwk) 173 Oakland Rd, Maplewood NJ 07040 B Brooklyn NY 8/22/1950 s Vincent Gubitosi & Ann Carroll. MA New Sch For Soc Resrch NY NY 1979; MS Hunter Coll Sch Of Soc Wk NY NY 1988; MDiv Drew U 2005. D 6/2/2007 P 12/8/2007 Bp Mark M Beckwith. m 7/10/2004 Christine West. ccarroll500@comcast.net

CARROLL, Diana Elizabeth (O) The Church of the Holy Trinity, 1904 Walnut Street, Philadelphia PA 19103 **Asst to the R The Ch Of The H Trin Rittenhouse Philadelphia PA 2008-** B Barrington IL 12/29/1981 d Peter F Carroll & Catherine B. AB Ken 2004; MDiv Ya Berk 2008. D 6/7/2008 Bp David Charles Bowman. the.rev.diana@gmail.com

CARROLL, Diane Phyllis (Va) 10360 Rectory Ln, King George VA 22485 **R Hanover w Brunswick Par - S Jn King Geo VA 2006-** B Brooklyn NY 5/4/1948 d Lewis Gruschow & Anita. BA S Leo Coll 1999; MDiv VTS 2003. D 6/14/2003 P 12/6/2003 Bp Carol Joy Gallagher. m 7/4/1974 Matthew Carroll c 3. S Aid's Ch Virginia Bch VA 2003-2005. carrollvts@hotmail.com

CARROLL, Douglas James (Roch) 3387 County Route 6, Cohocton NY 14826 B Princeton NJ 3/7/1933 s Richard Anthony Carroll & Ida Margaret. BA Washington and Jefferson U 1960; BD EDS 1963. D 6/15/1963 Bp William S Thomas P 12/1/1963 Bp Austin Pardue. m 8/27/1954 Donna Ellis Louderback. Allegany Cnty Epis Mnstry Belfast NY 1981-1992; Epis Tri-Par Mnstry Dansville NY 1969-1979; R Chr Epis Ch Hornell NY 1969-1975; R Chr Epis Ch Indiana PA 1963-1969; P-in-c S Ptr's Epis Ch Blairsville PA 1963-1969. dcarroll@infoblvd.net

CARROLL, James Earle (SanD) 3750 Amaryllis Dr, San Diego CA 92106 **Assoc All Souls' Epis Ch San Diego CA 2002-** B Tucson AZ 6/2/1929 s Glen Lee Carroll & Margaret Christiana. BA U of Puget Sound 1951; BD SWTS 1954. D 6/29/1954 P 6/29/1955 Bp Stephen F Bayne Jr. m 11/1/1958 Lanita Laneane Maddux c 3. Cathd Ch Of S Paul San Diego CA 1978-1994; Dn Cathd Of S Jas Chicago IL 1972-1978; R Trin Epis Ch Reno NV 1966-1972; R All SS Par Los Angeles CA 1959-1966; Assoc S Mk's Par Van Nuys CA 1956-1959; Vic Chr Epis Ch Anacortes WA 1954-1956. Auth, "Eucharistic Sacrifice: An Angl Consideration," Amer Ch Quarterly, 1961; Auth, "Fllshp Papers"; Auth, "PB Cn and Pstr Choices"; Auth, "Legitimate heirs 0f the Cath Mvmt"; Auth, "Bloy Hse Paper"; Auth, "Sxlty and Chr". Affirming Angl Catholicism 1994. DD SWTS Evanston IL 1981. jecarroll@aol.com

CARROLL, Jerry Don (Okla) 1701 Drury Ln, Oklahoma City OK 73116 B Stratford OK 5/6/1941 s John B Carroll & Lois M. MS U of Oklahoma 1968; MDiv TESM 1984. D 6/16/1984 Bp William Jackson Cox P 3/1/1985 Bp Gerald Nicholas McAllister. c 2. Asst S Paul's Cathd Oklahoma City OK 1988-1996; Vic S Jas Epis Ch Oklahoma City OK 1987-1988; Vic S Mk's Epis Ch Weatherford OK 1984-1987; Vic S Paul's Ch Clinton OK 1984-1987.

CARROLL, Kevin Charles (Mil) 3309 N Knoll Terrace, Wauwatosa WI 53222 **Dn All SS' Cathd Milwaukee WI 2010-** B Janesville WI 5/15/1960 BS U of Wisconsin 1984; MDiv Nash 2003. D 3/25/2003 Bp Chilton Abbie Richardson Knudsen P 11/1/2003 Bp Steven Andrew Miller. m 9/2/1995 Jane Vinopal c 2. P-in-c S Jas Ch W Bend WI 2006-2010; Asst S Mk's Ch Milwaukee WI 2003-2006. janekevincarroll@gmail.com

CARROLL III, R. William (SO) 206 E State St, Athens OH 45701 **R Ch Of The Gd Shpd Athens OH 2006-** B Glendale CA 10/8/1969 A.B. Harv 1992; M.Div. U Chi 1996; Cert TS 2002; Ph.D. U Chi 2005. D 12/14/2002 P 1/28/2004 Bp Dorsey Felix Henderson. m 8/14/1993 Tracey Fiore Carroll c 2. The TS at The U So Sewanee TN 2004-2006; Dir Of Chr Formation S Fran of Assisi Chapin SC 2003. gsrector@gmail.com

CARROLL, Steven E (NJ) 76 Market Street, Salem NJ 08079 **Com on Nomin Dio New Jersey Trenton NJ 2011-; Com on Priesthood Dio New Jersey Trenton NJ 2010-; Dn of Woodbury Convoc Dio New Jersey Trenton NJ 2010-; P-in-c S Jn's Ch Salem NJ 2009-** B Detroit MI 9/23/1949 s Edward James Carroll & Helen Ruth. BA Wayne 1976; MDiv U Tor 1979. D 6/16/1979 Bp H Coleman McGehee Jr P 5/1/1980 Bp Henry Irving Mayson. R Trin Ch Newark OH 2005-2009; S Phil And S Steph Epis Ch Detroit MI 2004-2005; S Jas Ch Grosse Ile MI 2001-2003; P-in-c S Jn The Bapt Epis Ch Glendale AZ 1998-2001; S Steph's Ch Sierra Vista AZ 1992-1998; Vic S Jn's Epis Ch Bisbee AZ 1989-1993; Dio Arizona Phoenix AZ 1989-1991; Vic Ch Of The H Sprt Bullhead City AZ 1988-1989; Int Trin Epis Ch Pocatello ID 1987-1988; R S Jn's Ch Howell MI 1980-1986; Asst All SS Epis Ch Marysville MI 1979-1980; Asst Gr Epis Ch Port Huron MI 1979-1980. fathersteve@comcast.net

CARROLL, Tracey Fiore (SO) 335 Tennessee Ave, Sewanee TN 37383 **S Paul's Ch Chillicothe OH 2010-** B New Milford CT 6/7/1964 d Carmine Frank Fiore & Nellie. BA Natl U 1993; MDiv SWTS 1997. D 6/14/1997 P 12/

1/1997 Bp Gethin Benwil Hughes. m 8/14/1993 R. William Carroll III. H Trin Par Epis Clemson SC 1998-2001. tcarroll@innova.net

CARROLL, Vincent John (SwVa) 2518 2nd St, Richlands VA 24641 B Tillson NY 9/2/1943 s Vincent Carroll & Virginia. BA Niagara U 1965; JD Ford Law 1968; MPA U of Indiana 1978. D 5/27/2006 P 12/9/2006 Bp Frank Neff Powell. m 12/11/1982 Marilyn B Carroll c 3. vjc_10@yahoo.com

CARROON, Robert Girard (Ct) 24 Park Pl, Apt 22A, Hartford CT 06106 **Cn Chr Ch Cathd Hartford CT 2000-; Dio Connecticut Hartford CT 1988-; Hstgr Dio Connecticut Hartford CT 1988-; Assoc Gr Epis Ch Hartford CT 1988-** B Kansas City MO 5/24/1937 s Matthew Arnold Carroon & Agnes Girardeau. BA Indiana St U 1959; MDiv Nash 1962; MA U of Wisconsin 1970; DLitt U of Sussex 1977. D 4/28/1962 P 10/20/1962 Bp Donald H V Hallock. Secy Bd Archv of ECUSA Epis Ch Cntr New York NY 1997-2009; Litchfield Hills Reg Mnstry Bridgewater CT 1991-1993; Archv/Hstgr Dio Connecticut Hartford CT 1985-2004; Dio Connecticut Hartford CT 1984-2004; Archv Dio Connecticut Hartford CT 1984-2004; Asst S Jas Epis Ch Milwaukee WI 1977-1981; Asst Trin Ch Wauwatosa WI 1974-1976; Asst S Lk's Ch Racine WI 1969-1974; Archv/Hstgr Dio Milwaukee Milwaukee WI 1968-1981; Dn All SS' Cathd Milwaukee WI 1964-1968; Cur S Lk's Ch Racine WI 1962-1964. Auth, *Provost Marshal of Charleston*, Between the Lakes Grp, 2007; Auth, *Un Blue: The Hist of the Mltry Ord of the Loyal Legion of the US*, White Mane Pub Co, 2000; Auth, *From Freeman's Ford to Bentonville*, White Mane Pub Co, 1998; Auth, *A New Heart and A New Sprt*, Morehouse-Barlow, 1988; Auth, *Broadswords & Bayonets*, Soc of Colonial Wars, 1984. Coufraternity of the Blessed Sacr 1962; GAS 1961; NOEL 1970. Ven. Ord of St. Jn HM Eliz II of Great Britain 2003; Ord of S Mich Grand Duke Vladimir of Russia 1992. jcaroon@aol.com

CARRUBBA, Amity Lynn (Chi) 1000 Preston Ave. #2, Elgin IL 60120 **Epis Serv Corps Chicago IL 2011-; Assoc Ch Of The Redeem Elgin IL 2008-; S Mary's Ch Pk Ridge IL 2008-** B Syracuse NY 7/25/1975 BS U IL; MDiv EDS 2006. D 6/3/2006 P 12/16/2006 Bp William Dailey Persell. Cur S Mary's Ch Pk Ridge IL 2006-2007. amitycarrubba@gmail.com

CARSKADDEN, Ralph Richard (Oly) 3026 17th Avenue South, Seattle WA 98144 **Died 9/13/2011** B Seattle WA 6/25/1940 s Thomas Franklin Carskadden & Evelyn Gertrude. BA Witt 1962; STB Ya Berk 1965; BFA U of Washington 1990. D 8/10/1967 P 3/23/1968 Bp Ivol I Curtis. Pro Christo et Ecclesia Bp of Olympia 2008. scottiepa@juno.com

CARSKADON, Garrett Harvey (Md) 32 Main St, Westernport MD 21562 B Keysen WV 11/29/1949 s Garrett Parsons Carskadon & Elva Ellen. BS Frostburg St U 1971; M Ed Frostburg St U 1977. D 12/21/2007 Bp John Leslie Rabb P 6/29/2008 Bp Katharine Jefferts Schori. gcarskadon@frontiernet.net

CARSNER, Robert Joseph (EO) 1014 Laughlin St, The Dalles OR 97058 B The Dalles OR 9/20/1940 s James Warden Carsner & Dorothy Verna. BS U of Oregon 1963; MS Portland St U 1971. D 9/29/1999 Bp Rustin Ray Kimsey. carsner@gorge.net

CARSON, Boyd Rodney (SwFla) 1875 Massachusetts Ave Ne, Saint Petersburg FL 33703 **S Bede's Ch St Petersburg FL 1983-** B Lafollette TN 11/15/1946 s Boyd Albert Carson & Ireland. BS Cumberland U 1968; BS Epis TS In Kentucky 1978. D 5/15/1978 P 12/17/1978 Bp Addison Hosea. Assoc Cathd Ch Of S Ptr St Petersburg FL 1980-1982; S Paul's Sch Clearwater FL 1978-1980. OHC. boydabbu@aol.com

CARSON, Julie Ann (Mass) 500 Brook St, Framingham MA 01701 **R S Andr's Ch Framingham MA 2007-** B Newton MA 11/29/1973 d Domenic Francis Cannistraro & Dorothy Ann. BA Keene St Coll 1995; MDiv Andover Newton TS 2000. D 6/7/2003 P 6/5/2004 Bp M(arvil) Thomas Shaw III. m 6/28/2003 Phillip Thomason Carson c 2. Asst R for Fam Mnstry S Andr's Ch Wellesley MA 2003-2007; S Andr's Ch Wellesley MA 2000-2003. julie@philandjulie.com

CARSON, Mary (O) 14523 Lake Ave, Lakewood OH 44107 **Int R Ch Of The Redeem Lorain OH 2010-; GC Dep Dio Ohio Cleveland OH 2006-** B Hillsboro OH 10/18/1964 d John Gregg Carson & Jean Hopkins. BA Ken 1986; MA Bex 1989; MDiv Bex 1992. D 6/13/1992 P 12/29/1992 Bp William George Burrill. Assoc Exec Dir and Int Exec Dir Luth Chapl Serv Cleveland OH 2007-2011; GC Dep Dio Ohio Cleveland OH 2006-2007; Asst Gr Epis Ch Sandusky OH 1996-1999; Asst S Chris's Ch Gladwyne PA 1994-1996; Cur Trin Ch Newport RI 1992-1994. Phi Beta Kappa Ken Gambier OH 1985. mcarson1018@gmail.com

CARSON, Rebecca Jayne (CGC) 1707 Government St, Mobile AL 36604 B Bessemer AL 9/17/1950 d Arthur James Salter & Lena Drucilla. BS U of Sthrn Alabama 1983; MS U of Sthrn Alabama 1992. D 2/10/2011 Bp Philip Menzie Duncan II. jaynecarson@bellsouth.net

CARSON, Stephen Wilson (WTex) 11 Saint Lukes Ln, San Antonio TX 78209 **Cur S Lk's Epis Ch San Antonio TX 2010-** B Dallas TX 1/5/1975 s James W Carson & Kenny D. BA U of Texas at San Antonio; MDiv The TS at The U So 2010. D 6/9/2010 Bp Gary Richard Lillibridge P 12/10/2010 Bp David Mitchell Reed. m 1/11/2003 Julie L Dobyns c 2. stephenc@stlukes-sa.net

CARSON JR, Thomas Hill (USC) 209 S Woodgreen Way, Greenville SC 29615 B Wilkinsburg PA 7/20/1926 s Thomas Hill Carson & Edith. BA U of New Mex 1950; BD STUSo 1954; Fllshp Coll of Preachers 1960; DD STUSo 1979. D 6/3/1954 P 12/15/1954 Bp Theodore N Barth. m 6/8/1948 Mary Jane Sutherland. Exec For Stwdshp Epis Ch Cntr New York NY 1979-1989; Vol In Mssn Cbnt Dio Upper So Carolina Columbia SC 1976-1979; Dep Gc Dio Upper So Carolina Columbia SC 1969-1976; Chair Mssn Dept Dio Upper So Carolina Columbia SC 1969-1970; Chair Mssn Dept Dio Upper So Carolina Columbia SC 1969-1970; Fin Com Dio Upper So Carolina Columbia SC 1969-1970; Bp'S Coun Dio Upper So Carolina Columbia SC 1968-1971; Del Prov Iv Syn Dio Upper So Carolina Columbia SC 1968-1970; Stndg Com Dio Upper So Carolina Columbia SC 1966-1971; R Chr Ch Greenville SC 1964-1979; R S Ptr's Ch Chattanooga TN 1957-1964; Bp'S Coun Dio Tennessee Nashville TN 1955-1957; P-in-c S Jas Epis Ch of Greeneville Greeneville TN 1954-1957. Auth, "Stwdshp," *The Main Wk Of The Ch*.

CARTAGENA MEJIA DE AREUALO, Maria Consuelo (Hond) San Angel B-26, C4202, Tegucigalpa C Honduras **Dio Honduras Miami FL 1998-** B Juanita Dpto Lewpina 11/10/1944 d Belizario Cartagena. Programa De Educ. Teologica; Universidad Biblica Latinoamericana. D 4/15/1998 P 1/1/2000 Bp Leopold Frade. c 5. consuelocartagena@hotmail.com

CARTER, Bente (Cal) 60 Pinehurst Way, San Francisco CA 94127 B Horsens DK 2/2/1950 d Gunnar Rasmussen & Alyss. U CA; BA U CA 1972; MDiv CDSP 1992. D 12/5/1992 P 12/1/1993 Bp William Edwin Swing. m 8/28/1971 James Carter c 3. R S Fran' Epis Ch San Francisco CA 1999-2009; Asst Trin Par Menlo Pk CA 1995-1999; Asst R S Lk's Ch San Francisco CA 1993-1995. bente.carter@gmail.com

CARTER III, Charles Alexander (Pa) 8018 Navajo St, Philadelphia PA 19118 B Nashville TN 4/10/1937 s Charles Alexander Carter & Madrienne Rose. BA Van 1958; BD EDS 1963. D 7/15/1963 Bp William Evan Sanders P 5/1/1964 Bp John Vander Horst. m 6/19/1993 Sarah Stevens. The Ch Of The Trin Coatesville PA 2000-2011; S Ptr's Ch Phoenixville PA 1997; Dio Pennsylvania Philadelphia PA 1996-1998; S Paul's Ch Philadelphia PA 1984-1995; Cn-in-Res Cathd Of St Jn The Div New York NY 1978-1984; Urban Mssnr Dio W Tennessee Memphis TN 1975-1978; Memphis Urban Mnstry Memphis TN 1975-1978; Vic S Mary's Ch Jacksonville FL 1969-1975; Asst Chr Ch Cathd Nashville TN 1965-1969.

CARTER, Charles Elton (Cal) 3172 Oak Brook Ln, Eustis FL 32736 B Panama City PA 11/18/1929 s Charles Chifford Carter & Alexandra Louise. MDiv Ya Berk 1959; ThM CDSP 1969. D 6/27/1958 P 7/11/1959 Bp Charles Francis Boynton. m 11/26/1960 Sonia Paulina Chipsen c 4. Chair of Dioc Dept Dio California San Francisco CA 1986-1992; R S Aug's Ch Oakland CA 1983-1994; Trst Dio Michigan Detroit MI 1978-1981; Trin Ch Detroit MI 1977-1983; St Pauls Ch 1973-1977; Dio Panama 1958-1977. Detroit City Coun, Hon 1983. ccarter848@comcast.net

CARTER, David Morgan (Ct) 521 Pomfret Street (Box 21), Pomfret CT 06258 **R Chr Ch Pomfret CT 1996-** B New York NY 3/15/1953 s David William Carter & Patricia. BA Clark U 1976; MDiv UTS 1980; MA Col 1981. D 6/14/1986 P 7/25/1987 Bp Arthur Edward Walmsley. m 8/8/1981 Christine L'Abbe Amiot c 2. Cur S Jn's Ch Portsmouth NH 1988-1996. dmorganc@snet.net

CARTER, Davis Blake (WTex) Po Box 707, Aberdeen MS 39730 B Luling TX 5/22/1925 s John Sidney Carter & Lucille Willia. BA U of Texas 1947; BD STUSo 1953. D 6/11/1953 P 12/1/1953 Bp Everett H Jones. m 7/18/1945 Mary E Busch c 2. Asst Min Cathd of St Ptr & St Paul Washington DC 1954-1964; P-in-c Gr Ch Llano TX 1953-1954; P-in-c S Lk's Epis Ch San Saba TX 1953-1954; R S Paul's Ch Brady TX 1953-1954.

CARTER JR, Frederick LeRoy (U) 472 Gordon Cir, Tooele UT 84074 B Roanoke VA 9/28/1935 s Frederick Leroy Carter & Mildred Lois. BA Bridgewater Coll 1958; MS VPI 1960. D 3/19/1979 P 9/1/1980 Bp Otis Charles. m 12/27/1958 Nancy Marie Crockett. Dio Utah Salt Lake City UT 1996-2002; Presb S Barn EpiscopalChurch Tooele UT 1980-2003. flcarterjr@msn.com

CARTER, Grayson Leigh (RG) 1602 Palmcroft Dr Sw, Phoenix AZ 85007 B San Diego CA 3/25/1953 s James Charles Carter & Iona Mary. BS USC 1976; MA Fuller TS 1984; PhD Oxf 1990; Oxf 1990. Trans from Church Of England 12/27/1996 Bp Brice Sidney Sanders. m 9/10/1988 Catherine Louise Randall c 3. Int Trin Ch Lumberton NC 2002; Asst H Trin Epis Ch Fayetteville NC 1996-2000. Auth, "Angl Evangelicals. Protestent Secession from the via media, c.1800-1850," Wipf and Stock, 2012; Auth, "Miscellaneous arts," *The Oxford Dictionary of Natl Biography*, 2003; Auth, "Angl Evangelicals. Protestent Secession from the via media, c.1800-1850," Oxf Press, 2000; Auth, "Miscellaneous arts," *Rel in Geschichte und Gegenwart*, 2000; Auth, "Jn Henry Newman and Henry Bulteel," *The Angl Cath*, 2000; Auth, "The Case of the Revd Jas Shore," *Journ of Eccl Hist*, 1996; Auth, "Miscellaneous arts," *The Blackwell Encyclopedia of Evang Biography*, 1995. gcarter@fuller.edu

CARTER, Halcott Richardson (Oly) 141 Advent St, Spartanburg SC 29302 **Ch Of The Adv Spartanburg SC 2011-** B Everett WA 2/17/1984 s Donald

Carter & Marla. BA The U of Puget Sound 2006; MDiv The TS at The U So 2011. D 2/15/2011 Bp Gregory Harold Rickel. cartehr0@sewanee.edu

CARTER, James Currie Mackechnie (Va) 4413 W Franklin St, Richmond VA 23221 B Norfolk VA 8/26/1948 s Worral Reed Carter & Margaret Mae. Bachelors VPI 1971; MDiv Epis TS of The SW 1980; Masters Virginia Commonwealth U 2004. D 6/8/1980 P 6/1/1981 Bp C(laude) Charles Vache. m 1/1/2000 Sandra Carter. S Dav's Ch Aylett VA 1996-1997; S Asaph's Par Ch Bowling Green VA 1989-1992; S Ptr's Port Royal Port Royal VA 1989-1990; S Dav's Ch Aylett VA 1987-1989; Asst All SS Ch Richmond VA 1982-1987; Vic S Lk's Ch Courtland VA 1980-1982; Vic S Paul's Epis Ch Surry VA 1980-1982.

CARTER, James Lee (SwFla) 9925 Ulmerton Rd Lot 40, Largo FL 33771 **D S Dunst's Epis Ch Largo FL 2010-** B Fortville IN 8/1/1930 s John Wallace Carter & Fern. Carroll Coll. D 10/4/1982 Bp Edward Witker Jones. m 9/1/1950 Delores Anne Fair. Calv Ch Indn Rocks Bch FL 1990-1994; Asst to R Trin Ch Anderson IN 1982-1988. rev.jim2@verizon.net

CARTER JR, James Robert (Ga) 601 Washington Ave, Savannah GA 31405 **Cn S Paul's Ch Savannah GA 2002-** B Selma AL 8/5/1938 s James Robert Carter & Laura Gertrude. BA U So 1960; MDiv Candler TS Emory U 1968; MA Emory U 1968; CPE Emory U 1969; PhD Emory U 1977. D 2/24/1977 P 11/1/1977 Bp (George) Paul Reeves. m 1/26/1985 Jan McEachern. Cn S Paul's Ch Savannah GA 2002; Cn To Ordnry Dio Georgia Savannah GA 1988-2002; Vic Trin Ch Statesboro GA 1985-1988; S Barn Epis Ch Valdosta GA 1983-1985; S Jas Epis Ch Quitman GA 1980-1984; Cur Chr Ch Valdosta GA 1977-1982. Auth, "Gascon Archive Materials In A British Museum Manuscript". Ord Of S Helena, Assoc. bobjanc@aol.com

CARTER, John F (Ct) Po Box 391, Salisbury CT 06068 **R S Jn's Ch Salisbury CT 1998-** B New York NY 2/4/1944 s Lewis Franklin Carter & Gertrude. BA Ya 1967; MDiv VTS 1984. D 6/1/1985 Bp John Bowen Coburn P 6/14/1986 Bp Don Edward Johnson. m 8/31/1974 Deborah Carter c 3. All SS Ch Highland Pk NJ 1998; R Chr Ch Norwalk CT 1992-1998; Asst R S Phil's Ch Brevard NC 1986-1992. Auth,Mus, *Carry The Dream*, 1983. deborahscarter@yahoo.com

CARTER, Linda Susan (Mich) 425 Everett Dr., Lansing MI 48915 **P-in-c S Jn's Ch Howell MI 2010-** B Columbus OH 11/18/1950 d Edward Herman Carter & Jane Joseph. BA MI SU 1984; JD Wayne 1988; MA Wayne 1991; MDiv The GTS 2009. D 12/20/2008 Bp Wendell Nathaniel Gibbs Jr. c 1. sucarter@msu.edu

CARTER III, Philander Lothrop (WMich) 1296 Siena Way, Boulder CO 80301 B Ann Arbor MI 5/7/1947 s Collins Lothrop Carter & Mary. BA Stan 1974; MA Amer Grad Sch of Intl Mgmt Glendal 1980; MDiv TESM 1989. D 6/12/1989 Bp John Wadsworth Howe P 12/1/1989 Bp Peter James Lee. m 8/16/1975 Gretchen Carter c 3. Chr Epis Ch Charlevoix MI 1989-1998. Bro Of S Andr.

CARTER, Robert Douglas (Fla) Berkeley Prepatory School, 4811 Kelly Road, Tampa FL 33615 **Berkeley Preparatory Sch Tampa FL 2000-** B Tampa FL 9/8/1951 s A Robert Carter & Claire. BA Millsaps Coll 1973; MDiv VTS 1976. D 6/25/1981 Bp Duncan Montgomery Gray Jr P 5/29/1982 Bp The Bishop Of Tokyo. m 9/30/1992 Susan E Roine. Chr Ch 1995-2000; R All Ang Ch Miami Sprg FL 1991-1995; Assoc S Dav's Epis Ch Englewood FL 1988-1991; Vic Ch Of The Ascen Brooksville MS 1986-1988; Chapl Ch Of The Resurr Starkville MS 1986-1988. Auth, "Epis Identity Amidst Rel Pluralism: How One Sch Traveled Back to Its Roots," *Ntwk*, NAES. cartedou@berkeleyprep.org

CARTER, Stanley Edward (ETenn) 1930 Chelsea Jo Ln., Sevierville TN 37876 B Charleston WV 6/4/1944 s Garnett L C Carter & Sara Ruby. BA U Of Kentucky 1970; MA U Of Kentucky 1976; MDiv Epis TS In Kentucky 1982. D 6/5/1982 Bp Charles Gresham Marmion P 12/1/1982 Bp Addison Hosea. m 11/9/2002 Linda E Jurgens. Trin Epis Ch Gatlinburg TN 1993-1999; Vic Ch of the Nativ Sarasota FL 1985-1993; Vic S Lk's Ch Newberry SC 1983-1985. SSC. scmtnman@bellsouth.net

CARTER, Thomas Brooke (Md) 105 Dunkirk Rd, Baltimore MD 21212 **R The Ch Of The Nativ Cedarcroft Baltimore MD 2000-** B Baltimore MD 10/19/1946 s Harry Gilmore Carter & Edith. W Georgia Coll; LTh VTS 1992. D 12/12/1992 P 6/1/1993 Bp William Arthur Beckham. m 9/18/1971 Patricia Boring c 3. S Mths Ch Rock Hill SC 1998-2000; Dio Upper So Carolina Columbia SC 1996-1997; P-in-c Ch Of The Ascen Hickory NC 1995-1996; Asst R Ch Of The Ascen Hickory NC 1993-1994; Asst R Gr Epis Ch Anderson SC 1992-1993. tom-b-carter@comcast.net

CARTER, Wayne Ervin (WLa) 396 Country Club Circle, Minden LA 71055 **R S Jn's Epis Ch Minden LA 2002-** B Portland ME 1/26/1940 s Thomas Charles Carter & Florence Whitney. BS Gorham St Teachers Coll Gorham ME 1965; MA U of Maine 1967; PhD U of So Carolina 1974; LST Angl TS 1983. D 6/11/1983 Bp Robert Elwin Terwilliger P 5/22/1984 Bp Donis Dean Patterson. c 1. Dio Wstrn Louisiana Alexandria LA 2004-2005; R Trin Epis Ch Pharr TX 1996-2002; R S Paul's Epis Ch Dallas TX 1985-1996; P-in-c Dept Of Missions Dallas TX 1985; Cur S Chris's Ch Dallas TX 1983-1984. Auth, *Evaltn of CE*, Profsnl paper given, 1981; Auth, *A Taxonomy of Educational Evaltn*, (PhD dissertation), 1974. CHS 1983; Dallas Ward (Chapl) 1986-1996. wecpadre@aol.com

CARTER, Willard Swann (Ga) 610 Bradwell St, Hinesville GA 31313 B MT 11/6/1943 BD U of Wyoming 1966; MBA Wright St U 1970; MDiv Epis TS of The SW 2004. D 2/7/2004 P 8/14/2004 Bp Henry Irving Louttit. m 6/11/1966 Judy Carter c 3. Ch Of Our Sav Martinez GA 2009-2011; R S Phil's Ch Hinesville Hinesville GA 2004-2009. fr.will@gmail.com

CARTER, Wilson Rosser (NC) 447 Hom-a-gen Lane, Providence NC 27315 B Winston-Salem NC 7/3/1940 s Edward Wilson Carter & Margaret. BA Wake Forest U 1962; MDiv VTS 1968; UTS 1985. D 6/29/1968 P 6/28/1969 Bp Thomas Augustus Fraser Jr. m 12/17/1966 Janie L Wall. Int S Ambroses Ch Raleigh NC 1999-2000; H Trin Epis Ch Greensboro NC 1998-1999; R Gr Epis Ch Lexington NC 1971-1995; Asst Ch Of The H Comf Charlotte NC 1968-1971. wrcarter@mebtel.net

CARTER-EDMANDS, Lynn (SO) 3984 Wynding Dr, Columbus OH 43214 **COM (CoM) Dio Sthrn Ohio Cincinnati OH 2011-; Chapl for Ord Process Dio Sthrn Ohio Cincinnati OH 2010-; Cmsn on Congrl Life (CoCL) Dio Sthrn Ohio Cincinnati OH 2007-; R S Jas Epis Ch Columbus OH 2006-** B Modesto CA 8/24/1953 d Robert Ditson Carter & Nancy Pearl. BA California St U 1987; MDiv GTS 1990. D 10/31/1992 P 6/3/1993 Bp William George Burrill. m 5/2/1981 Frank A Edmands. Ecum Off Dio Sthrn Ohio Cincinnati OH 2008-2011; Bp's Coun of Advice, chair Dio Cntrl Pennsylvania Harrisburg PA 2004-2006; COM (CoM) Dio Cntrl Pennsylvania Harrisburg PA 2000-2006; Stndg Com Dio Cntrl Pennsylvania Harrisburg PA 1998-2000; R S Andr's Epis Ch Lewisburg PA 1997-2006; Cmsn on Liturg and Mus Dio Cntrl Pennsylvania Harrisburg PA 1997-2001; Sch Min Ch Of The H Trin Pawling NY 1994-1997; Sch Min Trin-Pawling Sch Pawling NY 1994-1996; Int Dio Rochester Rochester NY 1993-1994; Asst Ch Of The Gd Shpd Webster NY 1992-1993. Soc of Cath Priests 2010. cartered@sbcglobal.net

CARTIER, Fred Claire (NY) 222 Starbarrack Rd, Red Hook NY 12571 B Morristown NJ 6/16/1940 s Harold Augusta Cartier & Antoine. BA Moravian Coll 1965; STB PDS 1968. D 4/20/1968 P 10/26/1968 Bp Alfred L Banyard. m 6/22/1968 Rosalie Ann Yarosh c 2. Chr Ch Red Hook NY 1976-2005; Asst R S Geo's Ch Hempstead NY 1975-1976; Cur Gr Ch Merchantville NJ 1968-1970. fred@theservices.org

CARTWRIGHT, Gary Earle (SwFla) 2202 Wildwood Hollow Dr, Valrico FL 33594 **Dep For Diac Mnstrs Dio SW Florida Sarasota FL 2000-** B New Bedford MA 6/27/1938 s Earle Edward Cartwright & Dorothy Mae. NE Inst Of Indstrl Tech Boston MA 1957. D 6/14/1997 Bp Barbara Clementine Harris. m 4/11/1959 Simone Marie Martin. Dio SW Florida Sarasota FL 2001-2003; D H Innoc Epis Ch Valrico FL 1997-2000. gary@oga.com

CARTWRIGHT JR, Howard Mott (Los) 15997 Molino Dr, Victorville CA 92395 **Dioc Yth Cmsn Dio Los Angeles Los Angeles CA 1980-** B Detroit MI 6/5/1930 s Howard Mott Cartwright & Ola Bessie. BA California St U 1964; Cert ETSBH 1968; MDiv CDSP 1969. D 9/13/1969 P 3/21/1970 Bp Francis E I Bloy. m 8/21/1986 Mary Alice Cartwright. Asstg P Trin Epis Ch Orange CA 1988-2003; Vic S Mich Ch Alturas CA 1983-1984; P-in-c S Mary's Ch Winnemucca NV 1977-1978; Vic S Jn The Div Epis Ch Costa Mesa CA 1972-1976; Dioc Camping Cmsn Dio Los Angeles Los Angeles CA 1972-1974; Vic Ch Of The H Sprt Bullhead City AZ 1971-1972; Vic S Jn The Evang Mssn Needles CA 1971-1972; Vic S Phil's Preaching Sta Parker AZ 1971-1972; Cur S Andr's Par Fullerton CA 1969-1971. Bro Of S Andr 2001; Westar Inst 1999. hmott@verizon.com

CARTWRIGHT, Thomas Lisson (Ore) 1720 Ten Oaks Ln, Woodburn OR 97071 B Lubbock TX 7/15/1935 s Thomas Fry Cartwright & Teresa Ellen. BA Duke 1957; STB GTS 1961. D 6/20/1961 Bp Charles A Mason P 12/1/1961 Bp J(ohn) Joseph Meakins Harte. m 4/4/1970 Jocelyn Stewart. Vic S Mary's Ch Woodburn OR 1993-2000; Dio Oregon Portland OR 1992-2000; S Ptr's Epis Ch Red Bluff CA 1992; Int S Ptr's Epis Ch Red Bluff CA 1991; R S Mk's Ch Yreka CA 1966-1990; Cur S Lk's Ch Denison TX 1964-1965; Cur S Matt's Cathd Dallas TX 1961-1964. Who'S Who In Rel. dagdfr@aol.com

CARTY, Shawn (Ida) PO Box 117, Bellevue ID 83313 **R Emm Ch Hailey ID 2005-** B La Grange IL 3/26/1970 s John Pitman Carty & Elaine Mary. BA Seattle Pacific U 1992; MDiv Drew U 1996. D 6/26/2004 Bp Vincent Waydell Warner P 4/1/2005 Bp Bavi Rivera. m 6/27/1992 Jeanne A Smith c 1. cartysj@msn.com

CARUSO, Frank (Mass) 112 Spring St, Hopkinton MA 01748 B Salem MA 12/20/1950 D Formation Prog; BS U of Massachusetts 1981; MS Suffolk U 1984; EdD Bos 1989; Massachusetts Diac Formation Prog 2006. D 6/3/2006 Bp M(arvil) Thomas Shaw III. m 7/18/1999 Sheila Reindl c 2. fscaruso50@comcast.net

CARUSO, Kevin Garrett (Chi) 647 Dundee Ave, Barrington IL 60010 **Cur S Mich's Ch Barrington IL 2011-** B Hartford CT 6/12/1981 s Daniel Joseph Caruso & Betty Moore. BA U Chi 2003; MDiv Ya Berk 2011. D 6/5/2010 P 6/28/2011 Bp Jeffrey Dean Lee. m 10/9/2004 Kathryn Franklin c 1. Yth Dir Ch Of Our Sav Chicago IL 2004-2008. kcaruso@stmichaelsbarrington.org

CARUTHERS, Mary C (Ark) PO Box 367, Newport AR 72112 **S Paul's Newport AR 2010-** B Memphis TN 2/8/1948 D 12/21/2001 P 7/19/2003 Bp Larry Earl Maze. m 12/31/1976 Laird D Caruthers c 3. Dio Arkansas Little Rock AR 2009-2010; Chr Epis Ch Little Rock AR 2003-2005. marycraigcaruthers@yahoo.com

CARVER, Barbara (Spok) 1904 Browning Way, Sandpoint ID 83864 B Huntington IN 10/29/1948 d Richard Lamar Schenkel & Mary Ellen. Indiana U 1970; BA/BS U of Maryland 1981; Natl-Louis U 1994; Gonzaga U 2005. D 9/28/1994 Bp Francis Campbell Gray. m 6/4/1977 John Phillip Carver. COM Dio Spokane Spokane WA 2002-2008; D H Sprt Epis Ch Sandpoint ID 1999-2009; D S Mary's Bonners Ferry Bonners Ferry ID 1999-2003; D H Fam Ch Angola IN 1994-1998. The Ord Of The DOK 1994. jpbcarver@frontier.com

CARVER, John Phillip (Spok) 1904 Browning Way, Sandpoint ID 83864 **Stndg Com, VP Dio Spokane Spokane WA 2006-** B Spokane WA 11/26/1947 s Harold Phillip Carver & Marguerite Louise. BA U of Washington 1970; MDiv SWTS 1994. D 12/4/1993 Bp John Stuart Thornton P 7/1/1994 Bp Francis Campbell Gray. m 6/4/1977 Barbara Schenkel. Stndg Com, VP Dio Spokane Spokane WA 2006-2008; Vic H Sprt Epis Ch Sandpoint ID 1999-2009; Dioc Coun, Mem Dio Spokane Spokane WA 1999-2005; Vic S Mary's Bonners Ferry Bonners Ferry ID 1999-2003; Dioc Coun, Mem Dio Nthrn Indiana So Bend IN 1995-1997; R H Fam Ch Angola IN 1994-1998. jpbcarver@frontier.com

CARVER, Larry Alfred (WK) 18 E 28th Ave, Hutchinson KS 67502 B Detroit MI 10/17/1944 s Roger Alfred Carver & Mary Elizabeth. AA Schoolcraft Coll, Livonia MI 1966; BA Oakland U, Rochester, MI 1968; MDiv VTS 1972; CLU & ChFC The Amer Coll 1985; MI SU 1992; MS Emporia St U 2007. D 6/29/1972 Bp Richard S M Emrich P 3/10/1973 Bp H Coleman McGehee Jr. m 4/29/1999 Joyce A Carver c 1. Vic Chr Ch Kingman KS 1995-2008; Dio Wstrn Kansas Hutchinson KS 1995-2008; Vic All SS Ch Pratt KS 1995-2001; Vic S Mk's Ch Pratt KS 1995-2001; Vic Gr Ch Anth KS 1995-1999; R Chr Enrichment Cntr Flint MI 1976-1978; R S Paul's Epis Ch Brighton MI 1974-1976; Asst Gr Ch Mt Clemens MI 1972-1973. Auth, "The Vic's View," *syndicated weekly Nwspr column in Kansas*, 1997. lcarver44@gmail.com

CARVER, Lynne (Ia) St. Peter's Episcopal Church, 2400 Middle Rd., Bettendorf IA 52722 **R S Ptr's Ch Bettendorf IA 1999-** B Radford VA 8/17/1951 d James Carroll Tyson & Ann Gywnolyn. BS Pur 1973; MA U of No Dakota 1975; PhD U of No Dakota 1978; MDiv SWTS 1992. D 5/31/1992 Bp Thomas Kreider Ray P 12/19/1992 Bp Frank Tracy Griswold III. m 9/1/1978 Richard G Carver c 1. Stndg Com Pres Dio Iowa Des Moines IA 2008-2009; Stndg Com Pres Dio Iowa Des Moines IA 2004-2005; Assoc S Lawr Epis Ch Libertyville IL 1997-1999; Int The Annunc Of Our Lady Gurnee IL 1996-1997; Advoc Hlth Care Oak Brook IL 1992-1999; Assoc Ch Of Our Sav Chicago IL 1992-1993. revdrltc@aol.com

CARVER, Robert Cody (Oly) 1511 N Orchard St, Tacoma WA 98406 B Phoenix AZ 6/23/1946 s William Pharoah Carver & Eileen. BA California St U 1968; MDiv CDSP 1971; ADN Pierce Coll 2008. D 9/11/1971 Bp Francis E I Bloy P 3/1/1972 Bp Philip Frederick McNairy. m 6/16/1968 Kristin Elizabeth Ritter. Primary Mssnr All SS Epis Ch Williamsport PA 2002-2004; Gleam Williamsport PA 2002-2004; Ch Of Our Sav Montoursville PA 2000-2004; S Lk's Ch Tacoma WA 1994-1999; R S Simons Ch Miami FL 1985-1994; R S Andr's Epis Ch Aberdeen WA 1978-1985; Vic Emm Epis Ch Alexandria MN 1975-1978; R Ch Of The Gd Samar Sauk Cntr MN 1975-1977; Asst S Helen's Ch Wadena MN 1974-1978; Asst S Steph The Mtyr Ch Minneapolis MN 1972-1974; Vic S Mary's Ch Ely MN 1971-1972; Vic S Steph Hoyt Lakes MN 1971-1972. Auth, *The Creator's Wrld*. bc013@live.com

CARVER, Sarah Frances (EMich) 3113 Gibson Street, Midland MI 48640 **R H Fam Epis Ch Midland MI 2010-; COM Dio Estrn Michigan Saginaw MI 2008-** B Petoskey MI 1/19/1978 d Carlos William Fossati & Edwardine Frances. BS Alma Coll 2000; MDiv GTS 2007. D 6/23/2007 P 2/9/2008 Bp S(teven) Todd Ousley. m 1/9/2010 Peter carver. COM Dio Estrn Michigan Saginaw MI 2008-2010. sffoss@yahoo.com

CASE, Clarice J (Miss) 104 Heritage Dr, Kosciusko MS 39090 **D S Matt's Epis Ch Kosciusko MS 1997-** B Kosciusko MS 5/2/1932 d John D Stuckey & Beatrice Rema. Mississippi Sch for Diac 1997. D 1/4/1997 Bp Alfred Clark Marble Jr. c 3. D S Mary's Ch Lexington MS 1997-2001; Admin Asst Dio New York New York City NY 1970-1974. Assoc of H Cross 1970; Kosciusko/Williamsville (MS) Mnstrl Assn 1990; NAAD 1997.

CASE, Doris May (Mich) 10242 Joslin Lake Rd, Gregory MI 48137 B Ann Arbor MI 6/6/1935 d John Christian Schmid & Virginia May. D 12/10/2005 Bp Wendell Nathaniel Gibbs Jr. m 4/8/1961 Leon Folsome Case c 1. dmcase8607@aol.com

CASE, Jaime J (Oly) 426 E Fourth Plain Blvd, Vancouver WA 98663 **R S Lk's Epis Ch Vancouver WA 2011-** B Kaufman TX 12/30/1957 s Norman De Lyria Case & Thelma Louise. BA Coe Coll 1980; MDiv Epis TS of The SW 1994. D 6/25/1994 Bp James Monte Stanton P 1/9/1995 Bp Maurice Manuel Benitez. m 12/20/1980 Amy Diane Peterson c 3. Dio Texas Houston TX 2005-2011; The Cntr For Hisp Mnstrs Austin TX 2003-2005; San Francisco De Asisi Austin TX 2000-2003. "Jugar Junto a Dios (Mng Ed, Spanish of Godly Play) Vols 1-4," Living the Gd News, 2007; "La Serie del Descubrimiento (The Discovery Series, Ed, Spanish Ed)," The Epis Dio Texas, 2005; "Preparacion de Niños para la Santa Eucaristia (Comunmente Llamado Primera Comunión)," Cntr for Hisp Mnstrs, 2004. CODE 2005; Chapl, BroSA's 2003-2004; UBE (Assoc) 2005. napudno@gmail.com

CASE, Margaret Timothy (RG) 14 Pinon Ridge Dr, Placitas NM 87043 **Asst S Chad's Epis Ch Albuquerque NM 2010-; Epis Ch Of The H Fam Santa Fe NM 2006-** B Columbus OH 10/20/1949 BA U NC 1971; M. Div Nash 2005. D 7/30/2005 Bp Terence Kelshaw P 6/4/2006 Bp Jeffrey Neil Steenson. S Jn's Cathd Albuquerque NM 2008-2009; COM Dio The Rio Grande Albuquerque NM 2006-2008. mcase505@comcast.net

CASEY, Dayle Alan (Colo) 3795 McKay Road, Colorado Springs CO 80906 B Dallas TX 9/27/1937 s Lester William Casey & Wanda. BA TCU 1959; MA Duke 1960; MA Brandeis U 1962; MDiv Nash 1977. D 4/16/1977 P 10/24/1977 Bp Charles Thomas Gaskell. m 6/6/1959 Judith Ann Rominger c 2. R Ch Of Our Sav Colorado Sprg CO 1986-2009; Vic S Mary's Epis Ch Dousman WI 1977-1986. Auth, "The Rts Of Americas". Mdiv cl Nash Nashotah WI 1977; Ba cl TCU Ft Worth TX 1959. daylecasey@mindspring.com

CASEY, Stephen Charles (CPa) 429 Camp Meeting Rd, Landisville PA 17538 **Asst Ecum Affrs Off Dio Cntrl Pennsylvania Harrisburg PA 2008-; R S Edw's Epis Ch Lancaster PA 1998-; Dio Cntrl Pennsylvania Harrisburg PA 1995-** B Hull UK 11/9/1946 s James Henry Casey & Hilda. BA Ge 1991; MDiv VTS 1995. D 6/9/1995 Bp Charlie Fuller McNutt Jr P 3/16/1996 Bp Michael Whittington Creighton. m 8/13/1983 Rayelenn Sparks c 2. VP Cler Assn Dio Cntrl Pennsylvania Harrisburg PA 2000-2002; Chair Dept Of Congrl Dvlpmt Dio Cntrl Pennsylvania Harrisburg PA 1998-2005; S Paul's Ch Lock Haven PA 1995-1998. Hon Cn St. Steph's Cathd, Harrisburg, PA Dio Cntrl Pennsylvania 2008; Phi Beta Kappa Ge Gettysburg PA 1991; Ba mcl Ge Gettysburg PA 1991. vicarsteds@aol.com

CASEY-MARTUS, Sandra (WTex) All Saints By the Sea, Santa Barbara CA 93108 **Assoc All SS-By-The-Sea Par Santa Barbara CA 2011-** B New Rochelle NY 7/1/1948 d Charles Nicholas Martus & Patricia Ann. BA Springfield Coll Springfield MA 1970; MEd Springfield Coll Springfield MA 1971; MTS Oblate TS 1983; CITS Epis TS of The SW 1993. D 6/16/1996 P 12/7/1996 Bp John Stuart Thornton. c 2. R All SS Epis Ch Corpus Christi TX 2009-2011; Assoc All SS Epis Ch Austin TX 2005-2009; Vic Dio Idaho Boise ID 2005; Epis TS Of The SW Austin TX 1998; Vic S Fran Of The Tetons Alta WY 1996-2005. Auth, "Simplicity Silence Pryr," *Teton ValleyTop to Bottom (Winter)*, 2001; Contributing Auth, "Centering Pryr and Priestly Formation," *Centering Pryr in Daily Life and Mnstry*, Continuum Press Inc., 1998; Auth, "Centering Pryr & Priestly Formation," *Sewanee Theol Revs*, U So, 1997; Auth, "Concordance to the Lessons," Ex-Libris; Auth, "The Lessons: How to Understand Sprtl Principles, Sprtl Acativities and Rising Emotions," Wheatmark; Auth, "The Best Kept Secret," Wheatmark. 2005 Hal Brook Perry Awd Epis Sem of the SW 2005. sandy@asbts.org

CASHMAN, Patricia (Pa) 8201 Frankford Ave, Philadelphia PA 19136 **Ch Of The Ascen Rochester NY 2011-** B SD 5/16/1953 d Henry Robert Coffey & Verden. BD Widener U 1983; MS Neumann Coll Aston PA 1987; MDiv Luth TS at Gettysburg 1995. D 7/29/1995 Bp Allen Lyman Bartlett Jr P 9/28/1996 Bp Franklin Delton Turner. m 5/18/1974 Paul Cashman c 3. R Emm Ch Philadelphia PA 1999-2003; Int S Faith Ch Havertown PA 1997-1998. patcashman2010@gmail.com

CASILLAS, Laina Wood (Cal) 4942 Thunderhead Ct, El Sobrante CA 94803 **D S Mich And All Ang Concord CA 1996-** B CA 12/22/1954 d Harrell Wood & Eleanor Raine. BA Sch for Deacons 1990. D 12/7/1996 Bp William Edwin Swing. m 10/27/1973 Frank J Casillas. blessings@laina.us

CASKEY, Anna H (Mass) Po Box 6026, Lincoln MA 01773 **Died 1/29/2011** B 1/13/1925 MDiv EDS; BS Rad. D 6/1/1985 Bp John Bowen Coburn P 5/16/1986 Bp Roger W Blanchard. ahcaskey@aol.com

CASKEY, Charles C (Chi) 24410 Reserve Ct Apt 103, Bonita Springs FL 34134 **R Chr Epis Ch S Jos MO 2011-; S Lk's Ch Evanston IL 2004-** B Mooresville NC 7/22/1946 s Clinton Barnett Caskey & Olive Virginia. No Carolina St U 1967; BA Wake Forest U 1968; GW 1971; MDiv VTS 1975; Indiana U 1993. D 5/22/1975 Bp Robert Bruce Hall P 12/28/1975 Bp Frederick Hesley Belden. m 5/22/1971 Elizabeth Thayer Lee c 2. S Andr's Par Fullerton CA 2010-2011; Int S Chris's Ch River Hills WI 2008-2009; S Thos Epis Ch Battle Creek MI 2007-2008; R Chr Ch Waukegan IL 2006-2007; S Elis's Ch Glencoe IL 2004-2005; Int S Lk's Ch Evanston IL 2000-2004; S Jn The Div Epis Ch Burlington WI 1999-2000; H Cross Epis Ch Wisconsin Dells WI 1999; S Andr's Ch Milwaukee WI 1997-1999; Trin Epis Ch Bloomington IN 1987-1993; R S Paul's Ch Marquette MI 1981-1987; R Ch Of The Gd Shpd Pawtucket RI 1979-1981; S Cathr's Sch Richmond VA 1978-1979; Asst Min Gr Ch In Providence Providence RI 1975-1978. EPF, ESMHE, Cleric & Laity Concerned; Witness For Peace. charlesccaskey@aol.com

CASON JR, Charles Edward (FdL) 1805 Arlington Dr, Oshkosh WI 54904 **Cn S Paul's Cathd Fond du Lac WI 2006-** B Vidalia GA 11/16/1937 s Charles Edward Cason & Sarah Lou. BS Georgia Sthrn U 1960; MDiv SWTS 1963; Coll of Preachers 1971. D 6/22/1963 P 4/25/1964 Bp Albert R Stuart. m 7/20/1963 Joan Prescott Brain. R Trin Epis Ch Oshkosh WI 1977-1997; R Zion Epis Ch Oconomowoc WI 1974-1977; R Gr Epis Ch Menomonie WI 1967-1974; P-in-c H Trin Epis Ch Blakely GA 1967-1974; Vic S Fran Ch Camilla GA 1964-1967; S Jas Epis Ch Quitman GA 1963-1966. CBS. Royal Ord Of Scotland 1998. ccason2@hotmail.com

CASPARIAN, Peter Frasius (LI) 65 East Main St, Oyster Bay NY 11771 **R Chr Ch Oyster Bay NY 2004-** B New York NY 1/17/1951 s George Armen Casparian & Patricia. BA Rhodes Coll 1971; MDiv STUSo 1974; MA U of Missouri 1980; DMin STUSo 1988. D 6/29/1974 P 2/1/1975 Bp David Reed. m 4/16/1977 Marguerite West c 2. R S Jas Epis Ch Firenze IA IT 1995-2004; R Ch S Mich The Archangel Lexington KY 1986-1995; Chapl Cbury At Kansas U Lawr KS 1979-1986; Chapl S Marks Sch Of Texas Dallas TX 1978-1979; Asst S Andr's Ch Kansas City MO 1974-1977. Photographer, "The PBp Visits Armenia," *Episcipal Life*, 2005. Consortium of Endowed Parishes 2004; EPF 1979; ESMHE 1979-1993. peter_casparian@yahoo.com

CASSELL JR, John Summerfield (Md) 708 Milford Mill Rd, Baltimore MD 21208 **Vic S Tim's Ch Walkersville MD 2008-** B Baltimore MD 12/31/1938 s John Summerfield Cassell & Beulah Mae. BS Loyola Coll 1961; MDiv PDS 1965. D 6/22/1965 P 6/23/1966 Bp Harry Lee Doll. m 7/29/1977 Carol Ann Lusby Cassell c 1. Vic S Tim's Ch Walkersville MD 1992-2008; Int Ch Of The Redemp Baltimore MD 1990-1991; Int Ch Of The H Cov Baltimore MD 1987-1988; Int Ch Of The Redemp Baltimore MD 1985-1986; Vic H Cross Ch Baltimore MD 1967-1975; Asst to the Vic H Cross Ch Baltimore MD 1965-1967. Maryland Epis Cler Assn 2010.

CASSELL, Jonnie Lee (Mo) Po Box 778, Grandview MO 64030 B Boise MS 3/29/1943 d John Nmw Chew & Virginia. BA Mt Mercy Coll 1982; MDiv Epis TS of The SW 1996. D 5/17/1997 P 11/22/1997 Bp Robert Deane Rowley Jr. R S Andr's Ch S Louis MO 1998-2001; Stff Cathd Of S Paul Erie PA 1997-1998; Dio NW Pennsylvania Erie PA 1997. Auth, "Build Yourself A Future"; Auth, "Ms Lady"; Auth, "A Trip". Outstanding Performance,Outstanding Conciliatory Efforts/Results Untd States Dept Hud 1988; Mart Luther King Jr Awd, Outstanding Citizen Loc P3 Meat Cutters & Butchers Of Amer Cedar Rapids IA; Pi Sigma Alpha Awd Mt Mercy Coll; Wmn Of Worth Awd Older Wmn League. femaleblackrev7@peoplepc.com

CASSELL JR, Warren Michael (SeFla) 2718 Sw 6th St, Boynton Beach FL 33435 B Philadelphia PA 4/21/1934 s Warren Michael Cassell & Ann Louise. BS Colg 1954; U of Birmingham Birmingham GB 1954; ThM PDS 1957; MA Tem 1969. D 6/1/1957 Bp Oliver J Hart P 6/15/1958 Bp Russell S Hubbard. m 7/6/1991 Sharon Donnelley c 5. Dn of So Palm Dnry Dio SE Florida Miami FL 1995-1998; R S Jos's Epis Ch Boynton Bch FL 1985-2000; Dn of Niagara Dnry Dio Wstrn New York Tonawanda NY 1978-1985; R S Ptr's Ch Niagara Falls NY 1971-1985; Assoc Ch Of Our Sav Jenkintown PA 1963-1966; R Ch Of Our Merc Sav Penns Grove NJ 1959-1963; Vic Chr Epis Ch Zillah WA 1957-1959. Tertiary of the Soc of S Fran 1959. ThM w hon PDS Philadelphia PA 1957. cassellsd@aol.com

CASSEUS, Frantz Joseph (SeFla) 7835 Jean Vincent, Montreal QC H1E 3C4 Canada **Eglise Du Bon Pasteur Miami FL 2003-; P-in-c Dio SE Florida Miami FL 2001-** B Arcahaie HAITI 8/15/1947 s Andre Casseus & Anacile. MA U of Montreal 1978; BA Montreal TS 1981; Licence Séminaire de Théologie, Haiti 1990; Ph.D. Col 1993. D 6/23/1991 P 1/1/1992 Bp Luc Anatole Jacques Garnier. m 1/27/1975 Yvrose Pierre-Charles c 3. Auth, "Depression & Culture Counslg For Low Socioeconmic Patient"; Auth, "Chld Abused Sexually"; Auth, "Jvnl Delinquency In Haiti". fcasseus@yahoo.com

CASSINI, Mary Ellen Dakin (SeFla) 2805 Duncan Dr Apt C, Boca Raton FL 33434 **S Mk The Evang Ft Lauderdale FL 2011-** B Miami FL 12/27/1956 d Thelus Dakin & Betty. DMin Barry U Miami FL; BA Barry U Miami FL 1977; MA Barry U Miami FL 1984; Cert The Prot Epis TS 2005. D 11/7/2006 Bp Leopold Frade P 5/12/2007 Bp Calvin Onderdonk Schofield Jr. m 1/6/1978 Charles Jean-Marie Cassini c 2. maryellen.cassini@gmail.com

CASSON, Lloyd Stuart (Del) 732 Nottingham Rd, Wilmington DE 19805 **Cn Mssnr Ch of St Andrews & St Matthews Wilmington DE 1976-** B Dover DE 2/17/1935 s Clarence R Casson & Nancy J. BA U Of Delaware Newark 1961; MDiv VTS 1964. D 6/23/1964 P 6/5/1965 Bp John Brooke Mosley. m 6/11/1983 Janet Neville Shirley Latchman c 2. Ch of St Andrews & St Matthews Wilmington DE 1997-2007; Epis Ch Cntr New York NY 1995-1997; Cathd Of St Jn The Div New York NY 1985-1988; Cathd of St Ptr & St Paul Washington DC 1976-1985; R Ch of St Andrews & St Matthews Wilmington DE 1969-1972; Actg R Ch of St Andrews & St Matthews Wilmington DE 1967-1968; Asst Ch of St Andrews & St Matthews Wilmington DE 1964-1967. EUC. canonbhai@comcast.net

CASTANO, Peter George (Colo) 330 Corona St, Denver CO 80218 **Died 5/17/2011** B Brockton MA 10/26/1918 s Joseph Castano & Maria. Wentworth Inst of Tech 1939; NEU 1943; LST Epis TS In Kentucky 1966. D 5/29/1965 P 5/1/1966 Bp William R Moody. c 5. Ord Of S Lk.

CASTELLAN, Megan Laura (Az) 114 W Roosevelt S, Phoenix AZ 85003 **Chapl Dio Arizona Phoenix AZ 2009-; Chapl Epis Cbury Fllshp - Northen Arizona U Flagstaff AZ 2009-** B Newport News VA 7/12/1983 d Stephen Castellan & Barbara. BA W&M 2005; MDiv The GTS 2008. D 2/1/2008 P 8/1/2008 Bp John Clark Buchanan. Cur Estrn Shore Chap Virginia Bch VA 2008-2009. mcastellan@mac.com

CASTELLON, Paul Frank (NJ) 115 Kensington Ave, Trenton NJ 08618 B Havana Cuba 4/28/1936 s Francisco Castellon & Maria Agustina. BS U Of Florida 1957; MS U CA 1971; Sch for Deacons 2007. D 6/9/2007 Bp George Edward Councell. m 8/20/1977 Patricia McGhee c 3. fcastellon@comcast.net

CASTILLO, Guillermo Antonio (Ark) 406 W Central Ave, Bentonville AR 72712 **Assoc All SS Ch Bentonville AR 2011-** B Santa Ana El Salvador 3/26/1975 s Bernardino de Jesus Castillo & Rosa Lidia. Teology and Phylosopy San Jose dela Montana 2001. Rec from Roman Catholic 3/11/2011 Bp Larry R Benfield. m 6/9/2008 Araceli Herrera c 3. GUILLERMOC20@HOTMAIL.COM

CASTILLO, Sandra Ann (Chi) 4238 S Mozart St Fl 2, Chicago IL 60632 **Vic S Jn's Epis Ch Sparta WI 2011-** B Chicago IL 8/5/1948 BA U IL. D 6/19/2004 P 12/18/2004 Bp William Dailey Persell. c 4. St Jn's Epis Ch of Sturgis Sturgis MI 2010-2011; La Iglesia De Nuestra Senora De Las Americas Chicago IL 2006-2010; Ch Of The Adv Chicago IL 2006-2009; Cur S Ptr's Epis Ch Chicago IL 2004-2006. sca652@yahoo.com

CASTLE JR, Robert Wilkinson (NY) Po Box 5, Derby VT 05829 B Jersey City NJ 8/21/1929 s Robert Wilkinson Castle & Fredrica. MS Ya; BA St. Lawr Canton NY 1952; STB Ya Berk 1955. D 6/11/1955 P 12/1/1955 Bp Benjamin M Washburn. m 12/24/1987 Katherine Betsch. S Mary's Manhattanville Epis Ch New York NY 1986-1999; Brookhaven Hm For Boys Chelsea VT 1982-1985; R Chr Ch Island Pond VT 1979-1982; R S Mk's Epis Ch Newport VT 1974-1982; Vic S Andr's Epis Ch Lincoln Pk NJ 1955-1960. Auth, "Prayers From The Burned-Out City". bobandkatecastle@surfglobal.net

CASTLEBERRY, Howard Glen (Tex) 300 N Main St, Temple TX 76501 **R Chr Ch Nacogdoches TX 2011-** B Hutchinson KS 2/17/1961 BA The U of Houston 2004; MDiv The TS at The U So 2009. D 6/20/2009 Bp C(harles) Andrew Doyle P 1/9/2010 Bp Dena Arnall Harrison. m 5/21/1994 Joanne Wilson Castleberry c 4. Cur Chr Epis Ch Temple TX 2009-2011. fr.castleberry@att.net

CASTLES, Charles William (Ga) 1552 Pangborn Station Dr, Decatur GA 30033 B St. Petersburg FL 10/29/1933 s David W Castles & Catherine S. BA Florida Sthrn Coll 1959; BD Columbia TS 1963; MDiv Columbia TS 1971. D 2/26/2005 Bp J(ohn) Neil Alexander. m 2/12/1965 Janice Louise Sapp. castlesj@mindspring.com

CASTO, David Cameron (Pgh) 9 Cliff Rd. Apt. B2, Woodland Park NJ 07424 **Asstg P S Jas Ch Upper Montclair NJ 1990-** B Wadsworth OH 12/29/1931 s Cameron Bland Casto & Mabelle Blanche. BA Ohio Wesl 1953; BD U Chi 1957. D 5/30/1958 P 12/6/1958 Bp Nelson Marigold Burroughs. m 7/23/2000 Doranne O'Hara c 3. Cn Res S Steph's Ch Jersey City NJ 1992-1993; St Stephens Ch Newark NJ 1992-1993; All SS Ch Bergenfield NJ 1991-1992; Cn Res Ch Of The H Innoc W Orange NJ 1990; S Jas Ch Upper Montclair NJ 1988-1989; Ch Of The Epiph Allendale NJ 1984; S Steph's Ch Millburn NJ 1983-1984; Trin Epis Ch Kearny NJ 1982-1983; S Andr's Ch Harrington Pk NJ 1980-1982; Ch Of The H Comm Norwood NJ 1979; Ch Of The Trsfg Towaco NJ 1978; Int P Dio Newark Newark NJ 1974-1990; Dio Newark Newark NJ 1974-1984. davdor181@aol.com

CASTO, R Richard (CFla) Po Box 2068, Dunnellon FL 34430 **Int Chr Ch S Marys GA 2007-** B Buckhannon WV 4/25/1926 s Ralph Clyde Casto & Bess. W Virginia Wesleyan Coll. D 6/3/1981 P 6/1/1982 Bp Robert Poland Atkinson. m 6/18/1971 Constance Ada Friday. H Faith Epis Ch Dunnellon FL 1987-1997; R Chr Ch Point Pleasant WV 1984-1987; D S Mths Grafton WV 1981-1984. castorich@tds.net

CASTRO, Reinel (CFla) 155 Clark St, Enterprise FL 32725 **R All SS Epis Ch Enterprise FL 2000-** B CO 6/20/1967 s Jose L Castro & Maria G. Sem Mayor De Tunja CO; U of Tampa 1994, BA S Jn Vianney Coll Sem 1995; MA S Vinc De Paul Regular Sem Boynton Bch FL 1995. Rec from Roman Catholic 5/29/1987 as Priest Bp John Wadsworth Howe. m 10/31/1997 Jennifer James Castro-Smith c 1. P-in-c Ch Of Our Sav Okeechobee FL 1998-2000. fatherrei@cfl.rr.com

CASWELL, Robert Weston (SC) 140 Kenzgar Dr, Myrtle Beach SC 29588 B Buffalo NY 3/21/1963 s Fred Weston Caswell & Sandra. BA Duke 1986; MDiv Gordon-Conwell TS 1991; STM Ya Berk 1992. D 7/25/1992 P 5/15/1993 Bp Herbert Thompson Jr. m 8/13/1989 Alice Patterson Harper c 3. The Epis Ch Of The Resurr Surfside Bch SC 1998-2007; Assoc S Lk's Epis Ch Hilton Hd SC 1994-1998; Assoc Chr Ch - Glendale Cincinnati OH 1992-1994. bcaswell63@gmail.com

CATALANO, Patricia (ECR) 300 C St NE, Washington DC 20002 **Assoc Epiph Luth & Epis Ch Marina CA 2008-** B Bogota Colombia 5/14/1953

Mstr of Div CDSP 2005. D 4/30/2005 Bp Sylvestre Donato Romero P 2/28/2006 Bp George Richard Millard. c 1. Assoc All SS Ch Carmel CA 2006-2008; S Bede's Epis Ch Menlo Pk CA 2005-2006; Dio El Camino Real Monterey CA 2005. patricia@catalano.net

CATANIA, Jason Alexander (Md) 816 N Eutaw St, Baltimore MD 21201 **R Mt Calv Ch Baltimore MD 2006-** B Livingston NJ 9/8/1971 s Vito Catania & Marjolie. BA U of Notre Dame 1993; MA Washington U 1995; MDiv CUA 1999; STM Nash 2000. D 5/27/2000 Bp Keith Lynn Ackerman P 12/21/2000 Bp Daniel William Herzog. S Jas Ch Delhi NY 2001-2006; Cur S Geo's Epis Ch Schenectady NY 2000-2001. CBS; GAS; Soc Of King Chas The Mtyr; SocMary; SSC (SSC). STM cl Nash Nashotah WI 2000. rector@mountcalvary.com

CATCHING, Louis Allen (WK) Po Box 897, Millbrae CA 94030 **Died 9/21/2011** B Cincinnati OH 2/18/1933 s Louis Mills Catching & Jessie Virginia. San Andres Sem Mex City Df Mx; BA U of Virginia 1959; MFA Inst Allende 1968. D 3/20/1982 P 11/1/1982 Bp Jose Guadalupe Saucedo.

CATCHINGS, Robert Mitchell (WA) 1100 GA Highway 39, Donalsonville GA 39845 B 5/7/1941 D 6/23/1973 Bp Milton LeGrand Wood P 12/23/1973 Bp Bennett Jones Sims. m 6/16/1996 Joy L Catchings c 1. Dio Washington Washington DC 1980-1988.

CATHERS, Robert Earl (SwFla) 2291 Hebron Rd, Hendersonville NC 28739 B Wellington KS 7/10/1939 s Robert Roy Cathers & Winfred Dilena. PhD Texas Tech U 1966; MDiv STUSo 1983. D 6/17/1977 P 12/1/1977 Bp Edward Clark Turner. m 11/27/1981 Kimberly Freshwater c 3. All Souls Epis Ch No Ft Myers FL 1987-1989; R Trin Ch Mt Airy NC 1983-1987; Assoc S Andr's Ch Derby KS 1981-1982; Vic S Andr's Ch Derby KS 1978-1979.

CATINELLA, Gayle Louise (O) 16507 S Red Rock Dr, Strongsville OH 44136 **R Ch Of S Thos Berea OH 2004-** B Chicago IL 7/14/1962 d David Catinella & Dorothy. BA Loyola U 1984; MS U IL 1989; MA Creighton U 2001. D 12/13/2001 P 6/29/2002 Bp James Edward Krotz. m 4/8/1989 Daniel James McGuire c 6. Asst S Matt's Ch Lincoln NE 2002-2004; Cur S Jas' Epis Ch Fremont NE 2001-2002.

CATIR JR, Norman Joseph (FtW) 31 John St, Providence RI 02906 B Bangor ME 11/2/1932 s Norman Joseph Catir & Ruth Harriet. BA Trin Hartford CT 1955; MDiv Ya Berk 1958; MA Trin Hartford CT 1962. D 6/11/1958 P 12/22/1958 Bp Horace W B Donegan. m 6/6/1964 Zulette Goodrich Masson. Chair Liturg Cmsn Dio New York New York City NY 1973-1979; R Ch Of The Trsfg New York NY 1971-1998; R S Andr's Ch Stamford CT 1964-1971; Cur S Steph's Ch Providence RI 1961-1964; Cur S Paul's Ch Wallingford CT 1958-1961. Contrib, "towards a Living Liturg," *Towards A Living Liturg*, 1970; Auth, "St. Steph's Ch in Providence," *S Steph's Ch in Providence*, 1964. Amer Friends of the Angl Cntr in Rome 1991; CCU 1961; Engl Spkng Un 1965; Hope Club 2000. zulette.catir@verizon.net

CATLIN, Herbert Harold (EMich) 1845 Mackie Rd, Cookeville TN 38506 B Ogdensburg NY 10/14/1933 s Herbert Harold Catlin & Mary Grennon. BA Maryville Coll 1955; BD Epis TS of The SW 1958. D 6/23/1958 Bp Theodore N Barth P 3/8/1959 Bp John Vander Horst. m 6/18/1955 Elizabeth Gilmer c 2. R Trin Epis Ch Bay City MI 1973-1994; R Calv Memi Epis Ch Saginaw MI 1964-1973; Cur S Jn's Ch Ogdensburg NY 1962-1964; Vic S Mich's Epis Ch And U Cookeville TN 1958-1962. harebhctn@cookeville.com

CATO, Phillip Carlyle (WA) 8617 Hidden Hill Ln, Potomac MD 20854 **P-in-c S Mary's Epis Ch Foggy Bottom Washington DC 2002-** B Charlotte NC 11/1/1934 s Thornwell Hilliard Cato & Edna Dale. BA Duke 1956; STB EDS 1959; Duke 1965; STUSo 1965; PhD Emory U 1977; DD S Paul's Coll Lawrenceville VA 1980. D 6/25/1959 P 1/2/1960 Bp Richard Henry Baker. m 7/7/1984 Sarah Hatcher Maier. P-in-c All SS' Epis Ch Chevy Chase MD 1997-2001; P S Jas' Epis Ch Warrenton VA 1992-1997; P S Chris's Ch New Carrollton MD 1990-1992; Pagan Intl Washington DC 1987-1988; Cmsn On Minnistry Dio Washington Washington DC 1985-1988; S Fran Ch Potomac MD 1982-1986; S Andr's Ch Harrington Pk NJ 1982; Stndg Com Dio Newark Newark NJ 1981-1982; Gr Epis Ch Rutherford NJ 1981-1982; Dep Gc Dio Newark Newark NJ 1979-1982; Chair COM Dio Newark Newark NJ 1977-1982; R Ch Of The H Comm Norwood NJ 1973-1981; Asst R S Ptr's Ch Morristown NJ 1973-1981; Asst All SS Epis Ch Atlanta GA 1968-1973; Chapl Ch Of The H Comf Charlotte NC 1960-1963; Vic S Jas Ch Mooresville NC 1959-1960. Auth, "Cler Need Coaches , Too," *Leaven*, 2003; Auth, "Beyond Sex: A Broader Look At Cler Ethics," *Leaven: The Journ Of The Natl Ntwk Of Epis Cler*, 2002. ESMHE; Navy Chapl Fndt 2000; Sacem 2003. phillipcato@yahoo.com

CATON, Lisa Elfers (NJ) 23 E Welling Ave, Pennington NJ 08534 **Coll of NJ Chapl Dio New Jersey Trenton NJ 2008-** B Camden NJ 11/27/1954 d Robert Allen Elfers & Lisa Gail. BA NYU 1978; MPA NYU 1988; MDiv GTS 2007. D 6/9/2007 P 1/20/2008 Bp George Edward Councell. m 10/1/1983 Philip Caton c 3. CE Dir All SS Ch Princeton NJ 2007-2009. lisaecaton@aol.com

CATRON, Antoinette (U) 1710 Foothill Dr, Salt Lake City UT 84108 B Camden NJ 2/21/1940 d Angelo Ranoldo & Domenica. Cert Utah Mnstry Formation Prog; BA Hood Coll 1961; MA Mid 1962. D 6/11/2011 Bp Scott Byron Hayashi. anitacatron@gmail.com

CAUCUTT, Mary Allison (Wyo) 820 River View Dr, Cody WY 82414 **Chr Ch Cody WY 2006-** B Lansing MI 5/12/1966 d Gregory Lee Caucutt & Amy Mead. BA Trin U San Antonio TX 1988; MDiv EDS 1992. Trans 12/1/2003 Bp Bruce Edward Caldwell. m 1/6/2001 Casey Owen Horton c 1. S Jn's Ch Newtonville MA 2003-2006; Vic Ch Of S Andr's In The Pines Pinedale WY 1996-2003; R S Hubert The Hunter Bonduran Jackson WY 1996-2003; S Mich & S Geo Clayton MO 1994-1996. mcaucutt@wyoming.com

CAUDLE, Stephen (WLa) 208 E Hayes Ave, Morton TX 79346 B 8/22/1951 BA Austin Coll; MDiv Nash; MA U of Texas. D 6/25/1978 P 5/25/1979 Bp Robert Elwin Terwilliger. m 7/11/1980 Gaylan Frances Carr. S Geo's Ch Bossier City LA 1989-1991; Chr Ch Epis Beatrice NE 1985-1989; Dio Ft Worth Ft Worth TX 1980-1985; All SS' Epis Ch Ft Worth TX 1978-1980.

CAUGHEY, Robert Grover (Cal) 721 E 16th Ave, San Mateo CA 94402 **D S Matt's Epis Ch San Mateo CA 1999-** B Salt Lake City UT 12/17/1926 s J Robert Caughey & Marian. BS Eng(Math) U MI 1949; Profsnl Engr 1955. D 11/26/1973 Bp C Kilmer Myers. m Nancy A Caughey. S Ptr's Epis Ch Redwood City CA 1990-2000; Pstr to Deacons (Dio) S Paul's Epis Ch Burlingame CA 1984-1990; D Trsfg Epis Ch San Mateo CA 1973-1984.

CAULFIELD, Dorothee Renee (NY) 25 Gordon Ave, Briarcliff Manor NY 10510 **D All SS' Epis Ch Briarcliff Manor NY 2006-; D S Mary's Ch Of Scarborough Scarborough NY 2006-; D S Pauls On The Hill Epis Ch Ossining NY 2006-; D Trin Epis Ch Ossining NY 2006-** B Hicksville NY 4/8/1957 d Francis Rene Bourquin & Carol Louise. D 5/6/2006 Bp Mark Sean Sisk. m 5/5/1984 Frederick C Caulfield c 3. Chr's Ch Rye NY 2001-2006. drcmom@gmail.com

CAULKINS, Rodney LeRoy (SVa) 267 Jefferson Dr, Palmyra VA 22963 B Williamsport PA 8/27/1934 s Frank Arthur Caulkins & Elsie Jane. BA Penn 1956; BD VTS 1966; MDiv VTS 1970. D 6/18/1966 P 3/1/1967 Bp Frederick J Warnecke. m 4/2/1955 Janyce Belle Crossley c 4. P-in-c S Lk's Simeon Charlottesville VA 2000-2007; P S Jn's Ch Hampton VA 1980-1999; P S Marg's Ch Woodbridge VA 1969-1980; Vic S Barn Ch Kutztown PA 1966-1969. ashisland1@embarqmail.com

CAVALERI, Eva Maria Kopp (Minn) 1000 Shumway Ave, Faribault MN 55021 **Chapl Shattuck-S Mary's Sch Faribault MN 2009-** B Port Huron MI 1/19/1973 d Clemens Kopp & Marjorie. BA Albion Coll 1994; MDiv EDS 2004. D 6/10/2004 Bp James Louis Jelinek P 1/22/2005 Bp Joseph Jon Bruno. m 6/12/2004 Jorma Cavaleri c 2. Assoc R Trin Epis Ch Santa Barbara CA 2006-2009; Stff Assoc Ch Of Our Sav Par San Gabr CA 2004-2006. Awd For Excellence In The Liturg Reading Of The Scriptures The Massachusetts Bible Soc 2003. eva.koppcavaleri@gmail.com

CAVALIERE, Denise B(ourgeois) (NJ) 15 Paper Mill Rd., Cherry Hill NJ 08003 **D S Jas Ch Trenton Yardville NJ 2000-** B Fitchburg MA 7/21/1949 d Henry J Bourgeois & Agnes Alice. BA St. Johns U, New York 1971. D 10/21/2000 Bp David B(ruce) Joslin. m 9/27/1975 Louis Cavaliere c 2. dcav721@comcast.net

CAVANAGH, David Nathan (NCal) 2901 Owens Ct, Fairfield CA 94534 **P Assoc Gr Epis Ch Fairfield CA 2008-** B Colfax WA 4/26/1943 s Nathan David Cavanagh & Marjorie Dora. BA WA SU 1966; MDiv Candler TS Emory U 1971. D 6/22/1977 P 7/2/1978 Bp Clarence Rupert Haden Jr. P-in-c S Andr's In The Highlands Mssn Antelope CA 2004-2006; Int S Jn's Epis Ch Marysville CA 2002-2003; Int Gr Epis Ch Fairfield CA 2000-2002; Assoc R Gr Epis Ch Fairfield CA 1990-2000; V.A. Hosp. Martinez CA Trin Cathd Sacramento CA 1977-1980. AEHC; ACPE.

CAVANAUGH, Sean Harris (Va) 1795 Johnson Ferry Rd, Marietta GA 30062 **St. Steph's and St. Agnes Sch Alexandria VA 2004-** B Chattanooga TN 3/9/1969 s Deborah Rae. BA E Carolina U 1991; MDiv VTS 1996. D 7/14/1996 Bp Brice Sidney Sanders P 1/1/1997 Bp Clifton Daniel III. m 6/19/1993 Jennifer Marie Clemons c 2. Assoc R The Epis Ch Of S Ptr And S Paul Marietta GA 1999-2004; Asst S Andr's On The Sound Ch Wilmington NC 1996-1999. thecavs@comcast.net

CAVANAUGH, William Jeffrey (Dal) 421 Custer Road, Richardson TX 75080 **R Ch Of The Epiph Richardson TX 2004-** B New Brunswick NJ 6/1/1954 s Vincent J Cavanaugh & Ruth E. BS Drexel U 1976; MDiv GTS 1981. D 6/20/1981 Bp Lyman Cunningham Ogilby P 1/25/1982 Bp Scott Field Bailey. m 7/16/1983 Melissa Morris c 2. S Paul's Epis Ch Salem OR 2004; Dio Oregon Portland OR 2002-2003; R S Barth's Ch Corpus Christi TX 1990-1996; S Marg's Epis Ch San Antonio TX 1984-1989; Asst S Mk's Epis Ch San Antonio TX 1981-1984. "The Wink Wink factor," LivCh, 2004. frbill@epiphany-richardson.org

CAVANNA, Robert Charles (Minn) 6910 43rd Ave Se, Saint Cloud MN 56304 **P Ch Of Our Sav Little Falls MN 2002-; P Ch Of The Gd Samar Sauk Cntr MN 2002-; P S Steph's Epis Ch Paynesville MN 2002-** B New York NY 11/5/1943 s Charles Cavanna & Margaret Eleanor. BA Pace U 1966; MA U of New Mex 1968; EdD U of Wyoming 1977. D 4/6/2002 Bp Frederick Warren

Putnam P 10/6/2002 Bp Daniel Lee Swenson. m 8/4/1973 Regina Clipper c 2. rcavanna@resourcetraining.com

CAVE, Daniel Eugene (RG) 97 Arizona Sunset Rd Ne, Rio Rancho NM 87124 **Asst S Fran Ch Rio Rancho NM 2007-** B Rantoul IL 5/29/1955 s Norman Edward Cave & Beverly. MDiv Trin Ambridge 2007. D 10/21/2006 Bp Jeffrey Neil Steenson. m 7/7/1979 Jane Kay Vanourney c 2. Dioc Yth Dir Dio The Rio Grande Albuquerque NM 2007-2010. danielecave1955@gmail.com

CAVE JR, George Harold (SwFla) 6306 S Macdill Ave Apt 710, Tampa FL 33611 **Asst S Mary's Par Tampa FL 2008-** B Newton MA 2/22/1927 s George Harold Cave & Charlotte Elizabeth. FCC Rad/Telgraph Lic Untd States Maritime Serv Radio Sch 1945; BA U So 1956; STB Ya Berk 1959; STM STUSo 1964. D 6/20/1959 Bp Anson Phelps Stokes Jr P 12/21/1959 Bp Henry I Louttit. m 4/10/2005 Constance Ann Hatges c 4. St Johns Epis Ch Tampa FL 1985-1992; Vic S Columba Epis Ch Marathon FL 1962-1964; Vic Ch Of Our Sav Okeechobee FL 1959-1962. AAR 1972-1992; ESMHE 1972-1992. w4kdx@aol.com

CAVE, Jeffrey Paull (At) 3550 Wyoming St, Kansas City MO 64111 B Delano CA 2/22/1940 s Howard Layman Cave & Julia Ann. BA Harv 1961; STB GTS 1965; Fllshp EDS 1978. D 9/16/1965 P 3/1/1966 Bp Francis E I Bloy. m Matthew L Hess c 3. R S Mary's Epis Ch Kansas City MO 2003-2005; Vic S Mary's Epis Ch Montezuma GA 1996-2003; S Lk's Ch Ft Vlly GA 1995-2003; Assoc R All SS Ch Carmel CA 1985-1988; Mt Holyoke Coll So Hadley MA 1981-1984; Cn Precentor Cathd of St Ptr & St Paul Washington DC 1972-1977; Cur The Ch Of The Epiph New York NY 1970-1972; Pstr Ch Of The Ang Pasadena CA 1967-1970; Cur S Paul's Epis Ch Tustin CA 1965-1967. Auth, "To Stand In The Cross". Associated Parishes. JEFFREYCAVE@HOTMAIL.COM

CAVENDISH, John Claude (Lex) 240 Cedar Cliff Rd, Waco KY 40385 B Cleveland OH 11/30/1927 s Charle Arthur Francis Cavendish & Helene Anna. BA Jn Hopkins U 1952; BD CDSP 1961; DD Epis TS In Kentucky 1970; DMin Lexington TS 1980; Oxf 1986; MA Lexington TS 1996. D 6/10/1961 P 12/1/1961 Bp James P De Wolfe. Walnut Hill Epis Ch Lexington KY 1978-1979; R S Hubert's Ch Lexington KY 1973-1975; Epis TS Lexington KY 1971-1980; Cur Trin Ch San Francisco CA 1961-1962.

CAVIN, Barbara (Mich) Saint Paul's Episcopal Church, 711 S Saginaw St, Flint MI 48502 **P-in-c S Paul's Epis Ch Flint MI 2011-** B Minneapolis MN 12/23/1949 d William Brooks Cavin & Dorothy Jane. BS Colby Coll 1972; MDiv EDS 1980. D 8/18/1980 Bp Robert Marshall Anderson P 4/1/1981 Bp William J Gordon Jr. S Jn's Ch Plymouth MI 2010; R Ch Of The H Sprt Livonia MI 2002-2009; Vic H Faith Ch Saline MI 1988-2002; H Faith Ch Saline MI 1988-2002; S Andr's Ch Ann Arbor MI 1984-1988; S Aid's Ch Ann Arbor MI 1981. SCHC. rectoratstpauls@ameritech.net

CAWTHORNE, John Harry (Md) 12B Ridge Rd, Greenbelt MD 20770 B Edgewood MD 9/22/1944 s David M Cawthorne & Lorraine A. BA U of Maryland 1970; MDiv EDS 1977. D 6/25/1977 Bp William Foreman Creighton P 3/28/1978 Bp John Thomas Walker. m 7/1/1995 Bonnie Cawthorne c 3. Vic All SS Ch Annapolis Jct MD 2000-2001; Int S Jn's Ch Havre De Gr MD 1998-1999; Assoc All SS Ch Frederick MD 1988; R Gr Ch New Mrkt MD 1986-1988; R S Geo's Epis Ch Mt Savage MD 1981-1985; Chr Epis Ch Clinton MD 1981; Int R Chr Epis Ch Clinton MD 1980-1981; Asst S Jn's Ch Wichita KS 1979; Vic Chr Ch Wm And Mary Newburg MD 1977-1978. Cler Assn of Maryland; NAACP Fund. NAL Awd for Creating Nonprint Media Multiple Replicating Hold USDA 1997. johncawthhorne@google.com

CAWTHORNE, Walter Wallace (SwFla) 6136 26th Ave N, Saint Petersburg FL 33710 **Died 6/1/2010** B Warrenton NC 8/1/1924 s John Cawthorne & Rebecca. BA U So 1950; BD STUSo 1951. D 6/13/1951 P 6/21/1952 Bp John J Gravatt. c 5. WCAWTHOR1@TAMPABAY.RR.COM

CAYLESS, F(rank) Anthony (LI) 108 Woodbridge Ln, Chapel Hill NC 27514 B Leicester UK 1/6/1933 s Frank Sidney Cayless & Hilda Avice. BA S Dav's Coll Lampeter 1953; LTh St. Dav's Coll Lampeter Wales 1955; Dplma UWI - BIMAP 1972; MA Adel 1987; DMin GTF 1995; Cert Linwood Sprtl Dir Trng 2003. Trans from Church in the Province Of The West Indies 2/1/1984 as Priest Bp Robert Campbell Witcher Sr. m 12/27/1956 Suzette Lily Couldrick c 1. Int S Andr's Epis Ch New Paltz NY 2002-2006; S Thos Ch Farmingdale NY 2000-2001; Geo Mercer TS Garden City NY 1994-2000; Cathd Of The Incarn Garden City NY 1991-2000; St Pauls Sch Garden City NY 1984-1991; Cathd Schools Garden City NY 1984-1988. Auth, "Gk for Groups," *Gk for Groups*, 1995; Auth, "Hist of St. Geo Glebe," *Journ BMHS Vol XXXVIII # 2*, Barbados Museum and Hist Soc, 1988; Auth, "S Geo Glebe," *Barbados-An Ethnographic Study*, U.M.I. Ann Arbor MI, 1987; Draft and Edit, "Mssn and Evang," *ACC-3 Report*, London, 1976. Ord of H Cross 2000. Bp Burgess Fllshp St. Dav's Coll 1953; Evan Jones Gk Prize St. Dav's Coll Lampeter 1953; Van Mildert Schlr St. Dav's Coll Lampeter 1951. fcayless@nc.rr.com

CAZDEN, Jan Steward (Cal) 479 Vienna St, San Francisco CA 94112 B Dallas TX 3/11/1948 d Thomas Brooks Steward & Ima Jean. BTS Sch for Deacons 1991; MA U of San Francisco 2000. D 12/7/1991 Bp William Edwin Swing. m 6/25/1978 Burton Cazden c 1. California Pacific Med Cntr San Francisco CA 2007-2011; D Trin Ch San Francisco CA 2007-2009; Dio California San Francisco CA 2004-2007; D S Greg Of Nyssa Ch San Francisco CA 2000-2006; Ch Of The H Innoc San Francisco CA 1998; S Lukes Hosp San Francisco CA 1997-2004; Epis Sch For Deacons Berkeley CA 1996-1997; Asst Trsfg Epis Ch San Mateo CA 1994-1996; D S Fran Of Assisi Ch Novato CA 1991-1994; St Johns Epis Ch Ross CA 1991-1992. NAAD 1991; Oblate Ord of S Ben 1990. jscazden@gmail.com

CEBIK, Ronald J (Ct) 59 Heritage Vlg, A, Southbury CT 06488 **S Jn's Epis Par Waterbury CT 2002-** B Bridgeport CT 3/12/1936 s James S Cebik & Ella Ethel. BA U of Bridgeport 1958; BD Andover Newton TS 1962; EdD Oklahoma St U 1985. D 1/26/1997 Bp Andrew Donnan Smith. m 10/10/1970 Christine Ruth Cebik c 2. rjcebik@snet.net

CEDERBERG, Todd Lee (Pa) 214 SE Ashley Oaks Way, Stuart FL 34997 **R S Mary's Epis Ch Stuart FL 2011-** B Bay City MI 12/23/1958 s Ernest Herman Cederberg & Eleanor Amy. BA Wheaton Coll 1981; MDiv VTS 1986; D Min. Fuller TS 2005; Ch FC Amer Coll 2006. D 6/8/1986 Bp William J Gordon Jr P 12/1/1986 Bp H Coleman McGehee Jr. m 6/17/1982 Darla Jean Martin c 4. Assoc Ch Of The Gd Samar Paoli PA 1997-2011; Asst S Barth's Ch Bristol TN 1993-1997; Vic Nativ Cmnty Epis Ch Holly MI 1986-1993. frtodd@stmarys-stuart.org

✠ CEDERHOLM JR, Rt Rev Roy Frederick (Mass) 499 Webster St, Needham MA 02494 **Bp Suffr of Massachusetts Dio Massachusetts Boston MA 2001-** B Brockton MA 7/1/1944 s Roy F Cederholm & Roberta. BA Bos 1966; MDiv Bex 1971. D 6/26/1971 P 5/20/1972 Bp John Melville Burgess Con 3/24/2001 for Mass. m 5/20/1966 Ruth Ann Lyon c 2. R Chr Ch Needham MA 1989-2001; R S Paul's Epis Ch White River Jct VT 1976-1989; S Steph's Ch Cohasset MA 1975-1976. DD Bex 2001. budc@diomass.org

CELL, John Albert (FdL) 825 N Webster Ave, Green Bay WI 54302 B Philadelphia PA 1/1/1943 s John Abram Cell & Clara Olive. BS Tem 1970; MDiv ETS in Kentucky 1978. D 5/28/1978 Bp William R Moody P 12/16/1978 Bp Charles Bennison. RurD Green Bay Dnry Dio Fond du Lac Appleton WI 2004-2007; R The Blessed Sacr Ch Green Bay WI 1982-2010; Cur S Paul's Ch Muskegon MI 1978-1982. CBS 1989; Interfaith Seafarers Mnstry 1983; P Assoc. Of Our Lady Of Walsingham 1997; P Assoc. Of The Sis Of The H Nativ 1983; SSC 1998. frjac78@yahoo.com

CELLA, Richard Louis (Colo) 15501 E 112th Ave Unit 38a, Commerce City CO 80022 **D S Steph's Epis Ch Aurora CO 1991-** B Baltimore MD 5/6/1933 s Emil Cella & Susann Josephine. BS U of Oklahoma 1968. D 2/3/1991 Bp William Harvey Wolfrum. m 6/14/1987 Mary Ann Bliss c 5. D Dio Colorado Denver CO 1991-2009. Bro of S Andr 1970; No Amer Assn Diac 1991. deacondickmary@comcast.net

CEMBALISTY INNES, Susan Eve (Be) 108 Fern Way, Clarks Summit PA 18411 B Springfield MA 4/26/1950 d Richard John Robert Cembalisty & Charlotte Dorothy. BA Mt Holyoke Coll 1972; U of S Andrews GB 1977; MDiv TESM 1984; U of S Andrews GB 2002. D 6/2/1984 P 1/2/1985 Bp Alden Moinet Hathaway. c 1. S Lk's Ch Scranton PA 2005; Ch Of The Epiph Glenburn Clarks Summit PA 2002-2005; R The Ch Of The Ascen Claymont DE 1996-1999; Dio Delaware Wilmington DE 1995-1996; R Trin Ch Boothwyn PA 1986-1990. Auth, "Soc Concerns in Calvin's Geneva," Pickwick Press, Allison Pk,PA, 1992. Commendation for Congrl Dvlpmt & Ch Growth Dio Delaware 2000. secinnes@hotmail.com

CENDESE, William Ivan (U) 521 9th Ave, Salt Lake City UT 84103 **R S Fran Ch Moab UT 2007-; Cn Cathd Ch Of S Mk Salt Lake City UT 1993-** B 3/8/1936 s James Cendese & Angela. BA CUA 1961; Med Utah St U 1973; PhD U of Utah 1980. Rec from Roman Catholic 8/6/1989 as Priest Bp George Edmonds Bates. m 7/1/1978 Jan Worsley c 2. Dio Utah Salt Lake City UT 1995-2003; Cn to the Ordnry Dio Utah Salt Lake City UT 1995-2002; Cathd Ch Of S Mk Salt Lake City UT 1990-1991. weilland@attbi.com

CENTER, Robert J (NI) 2924 Loma Portal Way, Michigan City IN 46360 **Died 6/26/2010** B Metropolis IL 4/28/1924 s James Perry Center & Reba Helen. BA Indiana St U 1949; MDiv SWTS 1953; STM SWTS 1962. D 3/25/1953 P 9/29/1953 Bp Charles A Clough. Auth, "Our Heritage," Peterson Press, 1973; Auth, "Orientals Have A Hm In Chicago," *Advance mag*; Auth, "The Flowering Of The Catechetical Sch Of Alexandria," *Amer Ch Quarterly*; Auth, "Clay Feet & Barren Souls," *Taylor U mag*. Mdiv cl SWTS Evanston IL 1953.

CERRATO III, John A (WMass) 73 Federal Street, Greenfield MA 01301 **Dn of the Franklin-Hampshire Dnry Dio Wstrn Massachusetts Springfield MA 2011-; Bement Waterfield Educational Grants Dio Wstrn Massachusetts Springfield MA 2010-; S Jas' Ch Greenfield MA 2008-** B West Chester PA 9/19/1955 s John Anthony Cerrato & Blanche Elizabeth. BA W Chester U 1978; MDiv Gordon-Conwell TS 1983; ThM Harvard DS 1985; DPhil Oxf 1997. Trans from Church Of England 2/2/1993 Bp Cabell Tennis. m 8/26/2010 Mary E Cerrato. Ch Archit Com Dio New Jersey Trenton NJ 2007-2008; P-in-c S Bern's Ch Bernardsville NJ 2005-2008; Bd Missions Dio New Jersey Trenton NJ 2004-2007; S Thos Ch Alexandria Pittstown NJ 2004-2005; P-in-c Chr Ch Three Bridges NJ 2003-2004; Int S Paul's Epis Ch

Bound Brook NJ 2001-2002; Chr Ch Greensburg PA 1995-1996; Coordntr of The Epiph Partnership Dio Pittsburgh Monroeville PA 1995-1996; P-in-c The Ch Of The Adv Jeannette PA 1995-1996; P-in-c All Souls Ch No Versailles PA 1994-1995; Yth Com Dio Delaware Wilmington DE 1989-1991; Yth Dir S Thos's Par Newark DE 1989-1991. Auth, "Hippolytus," *Oxford Dictionary of Late Antiquity*, Oxf Press, 2013; Auth, "Revs of Aragione and Norelli, Des Eveques," *Journ of Eccl Hist*, Camb Press, 2012; Auth, "Hippolytus and Cyril of Jerusalem on the Antichrist," *Apocalyptic Thought in Early Chrsnty*, Baker Acad, 2009; Auth, "Hippolytus," *Dictionary of Major Biblic Interpreters*, IVPAcademic, 2007; Auth, "Origen's Encounter w Hippolytus," *Studia Patristica 43*, Peeters Intl , 2005; Auth, "The Assn of the Name Hippolytus w a Ch Ord, now known as The Apostolic Tradition," *St. Vladimir's Theol Quarterly*, St. Vladimir's Sem, 2004; Auth, "Hippolytus Between E and W," *Oxford Theol Monographs*, Oxf Press, 2002; Auth, "Martha And Mary In The Commentaries Of Hippolytus," *Studia Patristica 34*, Peeters Intl , 2002; Auth, "Revs of Allen Brent, Hippolytus and the Roman Ch," *Journ of Early Chr Stds*, The JHU Press, 1996; Auth, "Hippolytus On The Song Of Songs & The New Prophecy," *Studia Patristica 31*, Peeters Intl , 1996. AAR 1994-1998; No Amer Patristic Soc 1994. MDiv mcl Gordon-Conwell TS So Hamilton MA 1983; Phi Alpha Chi hon Soc Gordon-Conwell TS 1983; BA cl W Chester U W Chester PA 1978. cerrato.ja@gmail.com

CERTAIN, Robert Glenn (At) 1795 Johnson Ferry Rd, Marietta GA 30062 **R The Epis Ch Of S Ptr And S Paul Marietta GA 2007-** B Savannah GA 12/4/1947 s Glenn Nelson Certain & Myrtle. BA Emory U 1969; MDiv STUSo 1976; DMin STUSo 1990. D 7/27/1975 P 4/28/1976 Bp Harold Cornelius Gosnell. m 5/25/1972 Robbie Lee Wade c 2. Pres, Stndg Com Dio San Diego San Diego CA 2005-2007; Dioc Coun Dio Arizona Phoenix AZ 1999-2000; R S Marg's Epis Ch Palm Desert CA 1998-2007; Assoc Pstr S Barn On The Desert Scottsdale AZ 1995-1998; R S Alb's Ch Harlingen TX 1990-1994; R Ch of the H Apos Collierville TN 1985-1989; R Trin Ch Yazoo City MS 1978-1985; Asst S Peters Epis Sch Kerrville TX 1977-1978; Off Of Bsh For ArmdF New York NY 1975-1977; Asst Chr Ch Epis So Pittsburg TN 1974-1976. "Sprtl Quest," ETC Pub, 2007; "Salvation Through Chr Alone: Not a Question for Debate," *LivCh mag*, 2006; "Unchained Eagle: From Prisoner of War to Prisoner of Chr," ETC Pub, 2003; "Quite by Accident," *LivCh mag*, 2001; Auth, "Charcoal 1 Delta: The Story of the First B-52 Crewmember to be captured in Vietnam," *Air & Space mag*, Smithsonian, 2000; "Trin Ch: A Sesquicentennial Hist of the Epis Ch in Yazoo Cnty, Mississippi," Kenroe Printing, 1984; Auth, "In the Light of His Mercy," *ATR*, Seabury-Wstrn Sem, 1982. eagle@unchainedeagle.com

✠ CERVENY, Rt Rev Frank Stanley (Fla) 3711 Ortega Blvd, Jacksonville FL 32210 B Ludlow MA 6/4/1933 s Frank Charles Cerveny & Julia Victoria. DD Epis TS In Kentucky; STD Trin Hartford CT; BA Trin Hartford CT 1955; MDiv GTS 1958; DD GTS 1976; DD STUSo 1976; DD Trin Hartford CT 1977; STD Epis TS In Kentucky 1979. D 6/11/1958 Bp William A Lawrence P 12/17/1958 Bp Henry I Louttit Con 5/23/1974 for Fla. m 11/1/1961 Emmy Thomas Pettway. Ch Pension Fund New York NY 1993-1997; Exec VP/Mgr The CPG New York NY 1993-1997; Dio Florida Jacksonville FL 1974-1992; Trst The TS at The U So Sewanee TN 1974-1992; Trst The GTS New York NY 1974-1982; Bp Coadj Dio Florida Jacksonville FL 1974-1975; Dn S Jn's Cathd Jacksonville FL 1972-1974; R S Jn's Epis Cathd Knoxville TN 1969-1972; R S Lk's Epis Ch Jackson TN 1963-1969; Stff Par of Trin Ch New York NY 1961-1963; Asst Ch Of The Resurr Biscayne Pk FL 1958-1961. Advsry Com Chair - Cntr For Chr Sprtlty 1975-1979; Amer Friends Of Jerusalem; Bible And Common PB Soc 1992; Bible Reading Fllshp 1982-1986; Bd - AFP 1979-1988; Bro Of S Andr, Natl Bd; Caribbean Cov Com 1992-1992; Chair, Amer Del, Partnr In Mssn To Cuba 1984-1984; Chair, Strategic Plnng For Theol Educ 1983-1986; Com Of 200; Compass Rose Soc 1996-1999; Environ Stwdshp Team 1992-1996; Eub; Interfaith Coun On Christians And Jews; Irenaeus, Bd; Metropltn Coun; Urban Cltn Of Bishops; Vice Chair, Angl Coun On No Amer And The Caribbean 1980-1985. bishopfsc@aol.com

CESAR, Gerard David (Hai) Box 1309, Port-Au-Prince Haiti **Dio Haiti Ft Lauderdale FL 1991-** B HT 3/1/1965 s Adam Cesar & Carmicile. Law Sch 1988; BA H Trin Sem 1991. D 9/15/1991 P 4/1/1992 Bp Luc Anatole Jacques Garnier. m 6/3/1993 Kyria Evangeline Heraux. Soc Of S Marg.

CESARETTI, Charles Antony (NJ) Po Box 408, New Milford PA 18834 B Trenton NJ 1/2/1941 s Charles Angelo Cesaretti & Angelina Rita. BA Rutgers-The St U 1962; MDiv PDS 1965; ThM PrTS 1975. D 5/1/1965 P 11/6/1965 Bp Alfred L Banyard. Exec Dir Trin Par New York NY 1998-2001; S Lk's Ch Gladstone NJ 1996-1997; Trin Cathd Trenton NJ 1996; Int S Lk's Ch Gladstone NJ 1995-1996; Ch Of S Mary The Vrgn Ridgefield Pk NJ 1994-1995; Int S Matt's Ch Paramus NJ 1993-1995; Trin Par New York NY 1991-1994; Int Chr Ch Short Hills NJ 1989-1990; Dep Of Angl Relatns Epis Ch Cntr New York NY 1985-1990; Stff Off For Hunger Epis Ch Cntr New York NY 1976-1979; Cur S Paul's Epis Ch Westfield NJ 1971-1974; R St Jn the Bapt Epis Ch Linden NJ 1967-1971; Asst Gr Epis Ch Plainfield NJ 1965-1966. Auth, "To Care Enough"; Auth, "The Prometheus Question"; Auth, "Let The Earth Bless The Lord"; Auth, "Rumors Of War". charles.cesaretti@yahoo.com

CEYNAR, Marlene (Minn) 1811 Southbrook Ln, Wadena MN 56482 B Park Rapids MN 5/12/1947 d Lloyd Hruby & Marian Mae. BS U MN 1969; MS Bemidji St U 1978. D 10/25/1987 Bp Robert Marshall Anderson. m 1/1/1977 Paul Julian Ceynar c 1. D S Helen's Ch Wadena MN 1987-2008.

CHABOT, Bruce Guy (Tex) 5919 Wild Horse Run, College Station TX 77845 B Pomona CA 11/9/1962 s Wilfred R Chabot & Belia. AA Del Mar Coll 1982; BA U Of Dallas Irving 1984; MDiv Pontifical Coll Josephinum 1988; MA Texas A&M U 1996; PhD Texas A&M U 2003. Rec from Roman Catholic 1/16/2002 as Priest Bp James Barrow Brown. m 6/8/2002 Nancy Griffin Stebbins c 4. S Paul's Ch Navasota TX 2003-2010; S Thos Epis Ch Coll Sta TX 2002-2003. Auth, "Majerista Theol: Xicana Writers Claim Liberation," *Chrsnty And Lit*, Baylor U, 2001; Auth, "Salve Deus Rex Judaeorum," Intl Literary Symposium (London, Uk), 2000; Auth, "Beginning In A Dark Room," *Scottish Rite Journ*, 1995; Auth, "Reading The Tapestry," *Revs Of Cmncatn*. Ancient Free And Accepted Masons 1992; BSA 1972. Past Mstr Sul Ross Lodge 2003; Outstanding Stdt - Frgn Lang Del Mar Coll 1982; Hall Of Fame Del Mar Coll 1982; Hall Of Fame Incarnate Wrld Acad 1982; Outstanding Stdt - Engl Dept Del Mar Coll. bruce.chabot@tamu.edu

CHACE, Alston R (WMass) 144 Pine Bluff Rd, Brewster MA 02631 B Fall River MA 2/22/1932 s Frank Clinton Chace & Alice Leach. BS Tufts U 1954; CPE Boston St Hosp 1956; PostGrad Stds Harv 1956; MDiv/STM EDS 1957; PostGrad Stds Duke 1962; PostGrad Stds U of Edinburgh New Coll Edinburgh GB 1965; USAF 1972; MS Troy St U-Troy AL 1973. D 6/8/1957 P 1/4/1958 Bp William A Lawrence. m 6/11/1955 Beverly Anne Morse c 3. Supply P Dio Massachusetts Boston MA 1997; Dio Wstrn Massachusetts Springfield MA 1990-1997; R S Paul's Epis Ch Gardner MA 1990-1997; Off Of Bsh For ArmdF New York NY 1961-1990; Asst Chr Ch Fitchburg MA 1958-1961; Cur All SS' Epis Ch Belmont MA 1957-1958. Auth, *Mar Enrichment Model Bldg Prog Gdnc for AF Chapl*, Air U, Maxwell AFB, 1973; Auth, *The AF Acad Cadet Attrition Rate*, AF Chapl's Sch, 1968; Auth, *Amer's Commitment to Freedom*, Freedoms; Auth, *Human Goals - Fndt of our Heritage*, Freedoms Fndt; Auth, *My Responsibilities in Keeping my Country Free*, Freedoms Fndt; Auth, *Spec Occasion Pryr for AF Chapl*, AF Chapl; Auth, *What is an Amer?*, Freedoms Fndt. Bro of S Andr; Life Mem Mltry Chapl Assn of Amer 1973. Epis Bp nomination, ArmdF ArmdF Epis Ch 1989; Distinguished Eagle Scout Awd (Eagle Scout 1947) Trans Atlantic Boy Scout Coun, Europe Europe 1987; Geo Washington hon Medal Freedom Fndt Writing Awd Vlly Forge PA 1977; Geo Washington hon Medal Freedom Fndt Writing Awd Vlly Forge PA 1976; Geo Washington hon Medal Freedom Fndt Writing Awd Vlly Forge PA 1971; Geo Washington hon Medal Freedoms Fndt Writing Awd Vlly Forge PA 1971; Mltry hon Epis Mltry Chapl. ARCBAC@CAPECOD.NET

CHACE, Elizabeth Marian Maxwell (EMich) PO Box 109, 5313 Trails End, Frederic MI 49733 B Hartford CT 9/2/1947 d William Clifford Maxwell & June Elizabeth. BA Simmons Coll 1970; Cert SUNY 1984; MDiv EDS 2002. D 3/9/2003 P 10/25/2003 Bp Edwin Max Leidel Jr. m 11/10/2009 Brian D Chace c 3. Eccl Trial Crt Dio Estrn Michigan Saginaw MI 2008-2011; COM Dio Estrn Michigan Saginaw MI 2003-2006; P-in-c S Barth's Epis Ch Mio MI 2003-2005; P-in-c S Fran Epis Ch Grayling MI 2003-2005; D-in-c S Barth's Epis Ch Mio MI 2003; D-in-c S Fran Epis Ch Grayling MI 2003. EWC 2000. elizabeth@chace.net

CHACE, Laura Lambert (SO) 2145 Blue Bell DR, Cincinnati OH 45224 **Died 5/1/2011** B Cincinnati OH 1/17/1937 d Allan Mason Chace & Adaline McCrea. BA U Cinc 1959; MLS U MI 1961; Epis Dio Sthrn Ohio 1998. D 10/24/1998 Bp Herbert Thompson Jr. llchace@one.net

CHACON, Frank Joe (NCal) 35355 County Road 31, Davis CA 95616 **D S Lk's Ch Woodland CA 2004-** B Sacramento CA 8/15/1947 D 9/17/2004 Bp Jerry Alban Lamb. m 8/15/1990 Susan Orsborn. chacon@onemain.com

CHADWICK, Leslie Elizabeth (Va) 11290 Spyglass Cove Lane, Reston VA 20191 **Assoc R S Tim's Ch Herndon VA 2006-** B Valdosta GA 3/10/1971 d John Turner Hiers & Phyllis Ann. BA U So 1993; MA U of Virginia 1995; MDiv VTS 2004. D 2/7/2004 P 8/18/2004 Bp Henry Irving Louttit. m 12/31/2001 George Albert Chadwick c 1. Chr Ch Alexandria VA 2004-2006. "In Sure and Certain Hope," *Congregations*, The Alb Inst, 2006. The Chas and Janet Harris Awd VTS 2004; The Fund for Theol Educ Mnstry Fllshp Fund for Theol Educ 2001; The Howard D. King and Ruth King Mitchell Merit Schlrshp for VTS 2001. george.chadwick@verizon.net

CHADWICK, Loring William (CFla) 11440 SW 84th Avenue Rd, Ocala FL 34481 **Asstg P, Org Ch Of The Adv Dunnellon FL 1999-** B Providence RI 9/22/1932 s William Henry Chadwick & Laura Jane. BA Br 1954; MDiv EDS 1957; Med Rhode Island Coll 1975. D 6/15/1957 P 2/23/1958 Bp John S Higgins. m 7/4/1957 Muriel E Bolas c 1. Asst Chr Ch In Lonsdale Lincoln RI 1992-1999; Assoc & Dir of Mus Emm Epis Ch Cumberland RI 1990-1992; Assoc St Mich & Gr Ch Rumford RI 1988-1990; P-in-c Gr Ch In Providence Providence RI 1983-1988; Chair Ch Mus Cmsn Dio Rhode Island Providence RI 1975-1979; Org/Choir Emm Epis Ch Cumberland RI 1968-1983; Cn Pstr

Cathd Of S Jn Providence RI 1966-1967; Asst Trin Ch Newport RI 1961-1966; Dio Rhode Island Providence RI 1960-1963; Asst All SS' Meml Ch Providence RI 1959-1961; Vic S Thos' Alton Wood River Jct RI 1957-1959. Auth, *Mass of the Incarn*; Auth, *Mass of the Sprt*; Auth, *Song of Mary*. revlchad@aol.com

CHADWICK, Thora L (Vt) 267 Hildred Dr, Burlington VT 05401 **P-in-c, Borders Reg Mnstry S Lk's Ch Alburgh VT 2005-** B Greenfield MA 10/31/1937 d Robert Chambers Libbey & Thelma Louise. BA Wilson Coll 1959; MLS Rutgers-The St U 1967; MDiv GTS 1981. D 6/6/1981 Bp Albert Wiencke Van Duzer P 12/12/1981 Bp George Phelps Mellick Belshaw. c 1. Int S Matt's Ch Enosburg Falls VT 2002-2005; R S Mk's Epis Ch Newport VT 1995-1999; Mssnr Ohio Vlly Cluster S Ann's Ch New Martinsville WV 1991-1994; Mssnr Ohio Vlly Cluster S Paul's Ch Sistersville WV 1991-1994; Dir of Stds, Vocational Diac Prog Dio New Jersey Trenton NJ 1987-1990; Assoc Chr Ch Middletown NJ 1985-1990; Vic Ch Of S Clem Of Rome Belford NJ 1984-1991; Int All SS Ch Bay Hd NJ 1983-1984; Cur Ch Of S Mary's By The Sea Point Pleasant Bch NJ 1981-1983; CE Dir S Bern's Ch Bernardsville NJ 1976-1978; CE Coordntr S Lk's Epis Ch Metuchen NJ 1974-1976. Auth, *Var arts - Sermons - Curric*. tlchadwick@comcast.net

CHAFFEE, Adna Romanza (Ga) 302 E General Stewart Way, Hinesville GA 31313 B 7/8/1939 D 2/15/2008 Bp Henry Irving Louttit.

CHAFFEE, Barbara B (EC) 10618 Peppermill Dr, Raleigh NC 27614 B Sheboygan WI 12/6/1938 d John J Boersma & Beatrice Alice. BA Wheaton Coll at Norton 1960; MDiv SWTS 1990. D 2/23/1990 Bp Thomas Kreider Ray P 12/15/1990 Bp Frank Tracy Griswold III. c 2. Assoc R Chr Epis Ch Raleigh NC 2000-2008; Stndg Com Dio E Carolina Kinston NC 2000; COM Dio E Carolina Kinston NC 1998-2000; Dio E Carolina Kinston NC 1998; Congrl Dvlpmt Dio E Carolina Kinston NC 1996-2000; Sprtl Life Com Dio E Carolina Kinston NC 1995-2000; Camp Trin Com Dio E Carolina Kinston NC 1994-1996; S Thos' Ch Windsor NC 1993-2000; Asst Dio E Carolina Kinston NC 1990-1993; S Aug's Epis Ch Wilmette IL 1990-1993. SCHC. revbarb@aol.com

CHALARON, Janice Belle Melbourne (At) 1136 Forrest Blvd., Decatur GA 30030 **R S Bede's Ch Atlanta GA 2004-** B 5/25/1953 d Roy Malcolm Melbourne & Viginia. BA U NC 1975; MS U NC 1982; MDiv Duke 1987; STM STUSo 1997. D 5/26/1990 Bp Huntington Williams Jr P 5/1/1991 Bp Robert Whitridge Estill. m 6/3/1984 Pierre Rivalier Chalaron c 3. R S Andr's Ch Rocky Mt NC 1996-2004; Ch Of The H Comf Burlington NC 1990-1996. Cmnty Of S Mary 1990. jchalaron@stbedes.org

✠ CHALFANT, Rt Rev Edward Cole (Me) PO Box 2056, Ponte Vedra Beach FL 32004 **Ret Bp of Maine Chr Epis Ch Ponte Vedra Bch FL 2001-; Ret Bp Dio Maine Portland ME 1996-** B Pittsburgh PA 8/14/1937 s Edward Trimble Chalfant & Helen Louise. BA Wesl 1960; MDiv VTS 1963; DD VTS 1985. D 6/12/1963 Bp William Loftin Hargrave P 12/18/1963 Bp Henry I Louttit Con 9/21/1984 for Me. m 8/29/1959 Marydee Wimbish c 2. Dio Maine Portland ME 1984-1996; Bp Coadj Dio Maine Portland ME 1984-1986; R S Mk's Epis Ch Columbus OH 1972-1984; Vic S Jn's Epis Ch Clearwater FL 1967-1972; Asst Ch Of The Ascen Clearwater FL 1963-1967. Hon DD VTS Alexandria VA 1985. ecchalfant@aol.com

CHALFANT-WALKER, Nancy Oliver (Pgh) 33 Thorn St, Sewickley PA 15143 **Chair, Bp Search Transition Com Dio Pittsburgh Monroeville PA 2010-; S Steph's Epis Ch Wilkinsburg PA 2007-; Cmsn on Racism Dio Pittsburgh Monroeville PA 2004-** B Pittsburgh PA 10/14/1950 BA Chatham Coll 1973; MBA Bos 1979; MDiv Pittsburgh TS 2002. D 6/14/2003 P 1/6/2004 Bp Robert William Duncan. m 7/8/1978 John Walker c 3. Chair, Stndg Com Dio Pittsburgh Monroeville PA 2010; S Paul's Epis Ch Pittsburgh PA 2006-2007; S Mart's Epis Ch Monroeville PA 2004-2006. NANOJON@GMAIL.COM

CHALK, David Paul (WTex) 651 Pecan St, Canyon Lake TX 78133 **R S Fran By The Lake Canyon Lake TX 2010-** B Kansas City MO 11/14/1958 s Paul Marion Chalk & Marie Chalk. DMin Pittsburgh TS; BA Whitman Coll 1982; MDiv Bex 1990. D 6/9/1990 Bp William Harvey Wolfrum P 3/9/1991 Bp William Carl Frey. m 5/14/1983 Julie Raymond c 2. R S Jas Epis Ch Del Rio TX 2000-2010; R Ch Of The Gd Shpd Beachwood OH 1993-2000; Asst to R S Ptr's Epis Ch Lakewood OH 1990-1993. dpchalk@gmail.com

CHALK, Michael Dulaney (WTex) 315 E Pecan St, San Antonio TX 78205 **S Mk's Epis Ch San Antonio TX 2003-** B Houston TX 12/23/1947 s Dulaney Joe Chalk & Thelma. BA U of No Texas 1970; MS VTS 1973. D 6/24/1973 Bp Richard Earl Dicus P 1/1/1974 Bp Harold Cornelius Gosnell. m 8/15/1970 Paula Catherine Walker c 1. R S Jas The Apos Epis Ch Conroe TX 1983-1994; S Andr's Epis Ch Seguin TX 1976-1983; S Mk's Epis Ch San Antonio TX 1973-1976. mchalk@stmarks-sa.org

CHALKER, Gae Marguerite (Az) 400 S. Old Litchfield Rd., Litchfield Park AZ 85340 **R S Ptr's Ch Litchfield Pk AZ 2000-** B Burbank CA 3/20/1954 d Howard Merle Davidson & Gretchen. BA U of Nevada at Las Vegas 1994; MDiv CDSP 1998. D 11/30/1997 P 5/30/1998 Bp Stewart Clark Zabriskie. c 1. Chr Ch Las Vegas NV 1998-2000. gdchalker@gmail.com

CHALMERS, Glenn Burr (NY) 296 9th Ave, New York NY 10001 **R/Exec Dir Ch Of The H Apos New York NY 2009-** B Paterson NJ 1/3/1954 s Andrew Burr Chalmers & Joyce Irene. BA Hope Coll 1976; MDiv PrTS 1980; Cert SWTS 1981; MS Rutgers-The St U 1982. D 6/5/1982 Bp Albert Wiencke Van Duzer P 1/1/1983 Bp George Phelps Mellick Belshaw. c 3. Ch Of The Epiph Chicago IL 2002-2003; Cathd Shltr Chicago IL 1997-2009; R Gr Ch Lawr MA 1990-1997; Epis City Mssn Boston MA 1988-1990; Vic Gr Epis Ch Eliz NJ 1982-1987. Auth, "The Chr Mnstry"; Auth, "City Issues". Comp Ord Of Ascen. phippsburg1@yahoo.com

CHALMERS, Jon David (USC) 10 N. Church St., Greenville SC 29601 **Assoc for Missions and Outreach Chr Ch Greenville SC 2009-** B Pittsburgh PA 12/12/1971 s Fred Joseph Gaskin & Margaret. BA U of Alabama 1994; EdM Harv 1998; Dplma Ya Berk 2007; MDiv Yale DS 2007. D 6/3/2007 P 12/11/2007 Bp Henry Nutt Parsley Jr. m 6/11/2004 Margaret P Poll c 2. Cbury Chap and Coll Cntr Tuscaloosa AL 2007-2009. jchalmers@ccgsc.org

CHAMBERLAIN, Carol Moore (Pa) 8272 Thomson Rd, Elkins Park PA 19027 B Princeton NJ 11/17/1946 d Frank Leslie Moore & Lucille. BS Syr 1968; MDiv EDS 1975. D 6/14/1975 P 1/15/1977 Bp Lyman Cunningham Ogilby. m 6/12/1976 Barry Chamberlain c 2. R S Aidans Ch Cheltenham PA 1982-2001; Int Ch Of S Jn The Evang Philadelphia PA 1981; Dio Pennsylvania Philadelphia PA 1977-1978; S Nathanaels Ch Philadelphia PA 1975-1977. mothercarolee@yahoo.com

CHAMBERLAIN, David Morrow (EC) 6000 River Rd Apt 404, Columbus GA 31904 B Chattanooga TN 10/10/1946 s Augustus Wright Chamberlain & Myrle Delano. BA U of Chattanooga 1968; MDiv VTS 1971. D 7/4/1971 Bp John Vander Horst P 1/30/1972 Bp William Evan Sanders. m 1/8/1972 Patricia Ann Magill c 2. Dio E Carolina Kinston NC 1997-2001; Sprtl Advsr for Curs Dio E Carolina Kinston NC 1990-1994; Dio E Carolina Kinston NC 1988-1992; R S Jn's Epis Ch Fayetteville NC 1987-2002; Cathd Of S Phil Atlanta GA 1980-1987; S Dav's Epis Ch Topeka KS 1978-1980; R S Jn's Epis Ch Arlington VA 1976-1980; Supvsr VTS Alexandria VA 1973-1980; Asst S Andr's Epis Ch Arlington VA 1973-1976; Asst Calv Ch Memphis TN 1972-1973; P S Jn's Epis Ch Johnson City TN 1971-1972. Auth, "The Bible in Capsule Form," 1955. Who's Who in Rel 1985. davepat431@yahoo.com

CHAMBERLAIN, Donald Fred (WMass) 340 Burncoat St, Worcester MA 01606 **Cn Dio Wstrn Massachusetts Springfield MA 1993-; Hon Cn Dio Wstrn Massachusetts Springfield MA 1993-** B Springfield MA 8/3/1933 s Walter Roy Chamberlain & Ruby. BA Amer Intl Coll 1964; GTS 1967. D 6/22/1967 P 12/1/1967 Bp Robert McConnell Hatch. m 8/1/2005 Sylvia Roseen c 4. R S Mich's-On-The-Heights Worcester MA 1973-1995; P-in-c S Mart's Ch Pittsfield MA 1971-1973; Cur S Steph's Ch Pittsfield MA 1967-1968. Auth, "The Attitudes Of White Police Off Toward Negro Offenders"; Auth, "Transitional Par In A Sm City". Phi Beta Kappa Amer Intl Springfield MA 1964; Hon Cn 93 Dio Wmass. dandschamb@aol.com

CHAMBERLAIN-HARRIS, Naomi Redman (Cal) 4467 Crestwood Cir, Concord CA 94521 B Oakland CA 4/17/1940 d Howard Kenneth South & Jean Redman. BA Sch for Deacons 2009. D 12/5/2009 Bp Marc Handley Andrus. m 6/9/2007 Paul Richard Harris c 3. orchids@astound.net

CHAMBERLIN, Marjory (CNY) 135 Colonial Dr, New Hartford NY 13413 **Pstr Assoc S Steph's Ch New Hartford NY 1986-** B Ridgewood NJ 10/29/1927 d Irvin Halsey Beach & Jennie V. BA Wm Smith 1949. D 6/21/1986 P 5/25/1987 Bp O'Kelley Whitaker. m 10/6/1947 John S Chamberlin. Soc Of S Marg 1980. mbcnjsc@juno.com

CHAMBERS, Joe Martin (Miss) 25018 Butterwick Dr, Spring TX 77389 B El Dorado AR 4/6/1937 s Joe C Chambers & Jessie Lee. BA Centenary Coll 1960; STB PDS 1966. D 9/20/1966 Bp Girault M Jones P 5/20/1967 Bp Iveson Batchelor Noland. m 12/19/1982 Carol Springer c 3. P-t H Comf Epis Ch Sprg TX 2006-2009; P-t P-in-c S Jas Epis Ch Port Gibson MS 2004-2006; R S Lk's Ch Brandon MS 1999-2003; R S Paul's Epis Ch Picayune MS 1988-1999; P-in-c S Jas Epis Ch Port Gibson MS 1981-1988; R S Steph's Epis Ch Hurst TX 1980-1981; St Stephens Ch Hurst TX 1980-1981; S Mths' Epis Ch Athens TX 1980; S Paul's Epis Ch Greenville TX 1979; R Ch Of The Gd Shpd Terrell TX 1972-1978; P-in-c S Jn's Ch Oakdale LA 1971-1972; R Calv Ch Bunkie LA 1969-1972; D Ch Of The Redeem Oak Ridge LA 1966-1967; D S Andr's Epis Ch Mer Rouge LA 1966-1967. ACPE, Icpc. jmchambers@myway.com

CHAMBERS, Joseph Michael Cortright (Mo) 3906 Tropical Ln, Columbia MO 65202 **Dio Missouri S Louis MO 2006-** B Springfield MO 11/15/1978 s Alfred Joseph Jewson & Dayna. BS S Louis U S Louis MO; MDiv GTS 2006. D 12/21/2005 P 6/29/2006 Bp George Wayne Smith. m 9/23/2005 Amy Ethel Marie Chambers Cortright c 1. therevjoechambers@gmail.com

CHAMBERS, Rex (Colo) PO Box 8017, Breckenridge CO 80424 **R S Alb's Ch Windsor CO 2008-** B 4/19/1944 s Charles Chambers & Phyllis. BA Sacramento St U 1971; MMIN Iliff TS 2007. D 1/22/2000 P 8/5/2000 Bp William Jerry Winterrowd. m 8/28/1970 Dana Cherie Lane c 2. St Fran Ch-Dillon Dillon CO 2004-2006; P Epis Ch Of S Jn The Bapt Breckenridge CO 2000-2006. chambers_dana@yahoo.com

CHAMBERS, Richard Graeff Mark (CFla) 91 Church St, Seymour CT 06483 B Middletown CT 3/19/1941 s Julian Graeff Chambers & Velma Katherine. BA U of Miami 1963; STB GTS 1967. D 6/13/1967 Bp Walter H Gray P 3/1/1968 Bp Joseph Warren Hutchens. m 10/19/1985 Jane Trollinger c 1. R Trin Ch Seymour CT 1989-2007; R Trin Ch Hampton NH 1982-1985; All SS Ch Of Winter Pk Winter Pk FL 1979-1982; R Trin Ch Brooklyn CT 1969-1979; Cur S Steph's Ch Ridgefield CT 1967-1969. frchambers@aol.com

CHAMBERS, Stanford Hardin (NY) 2749 Northaven Rd Apt 3046, Dallas TX 75229 B Louisville KY 11/1/1934 s Loyal Bruce Chambers & Mary Louise. BA U So 1956; MDiv GTS 1959. D 6/20/1959 P 12/1/1959 Bp Charles A Mason. Ch Of The Epiph Dallas TX 2000-2005; S Marg's Ch Bronx NY 1977-1991; Dpt Of Missions Ny Income New York NY 1975-1977; Diocn Msnry & Ch Extntn Socty New York NY 1975-1976; Asst Cathd Of St Jn The Div New York NY 1967-1968; Assoc S Jn's Ch New York NY 1966-1975; Asst S Ptr's Ch Spotswood NJ 1964-1966; Cur Gr Ch Muskogee OK 1963-1964; Vic S Laurence Epis Ch Grapevine TX 1960-1962; Vic The Epis Ch Of The H Nativ Plano TX 1960-1962; Cur Ch Of The Gd Shpd Dallas TX 1960-1961. ephiany2415@cs.com

CHAMBLISS, Rebecca Arrington (Mass) 7 Eldridge Rd, Jamaica Plain MA 02130 **Exec Dir of Life Together: Diomass Intern Prog Dio Massachusetts Boston MA 2008-** B Winston-Salem NC 8/1/1966 BA U Rich 1988; MDiv Harvard DS 1999. D 6/7/2003 P 6/5/2004 Bp M(arvil) Thomas Shaw III. Assoc Wyman Memi Ch of St Andr Marblehead MA 2003-2008. racbliss@gmail.com

CHAMPION, Peter O (Cal) 703 Mariposa Avenue, Rodeo CA 94572 **Cert Anti-Racism Trnr Dio California San Francisco CA 2010-; R S Jn's Epis Ch Clayton CA 2008-** B New York NY 7/5/1952 s Jean Rene Champion & Hertha. BA Br 1974; Cert Los Angeles Trade Tech Coll 1976; MDiv SWTS 1989. D 6/29/1989 Bp Robert Hume Cochrane P 1/6/1990 Bp David Charles Bowman. m 6/23/1973 Susan Manley c 2. S Alb's Epis Ch Brentwood CA 2007-2008; P-in-c/Vic Emm Epis Ch Kailua HI 2001-2006; COM Dio Estrn Oregon The Dalles OR 1993-1999; Mentor P S Barn Ch Bonanza OR 1992-2001; Co-R S Paul's Ch Klamath Falls OR 1992-2001; Asst S Jas' Ch Batavia NY 1989-1992; Asst S Paul's Epis Ch Stafford NY 1989-1992. Anglimergent 2008; Bread for the Wrld 1990; EPF 1989. Whipple Schlr SWTS Evanston IL 1989; Preaching Excellence Conf Epis Evang Fndt 1988; Anderson Schlr SWTS Evanston IL 1988; Phi Beta Kappa Br Providence RI 1974. peterchamp@hotmail.com

CHAMPION, Susan Manley (Cal) 703 Mariposa Ave., Rodeo CA 94572 **Vic Chr The Lord Epis Ch Pinole CA 2006-** B Houston TX 12/23/1953 d John Shelton Manley & Phyllis Reynolds. BA Br 1974; Cert Pacific Luth U 1980; SWTS 1989; MDiv Bex 1991. D 11/14/1991 P 5/14/1992 Bp David Charles Bowman. m 6/23/1973 Peter O Champion c 2. S Andr's Priory Sch Honolulu HI 2001-2006; Co-R S Paul's Ch Klamath Falls OR 1992-2001; S Barn Akron NY 1992. ACPE 1990-2000. Allin Fllshp Bex Rochester NY 1990; NT Awd SWTS Evanston IL 1986; Hebr Awd SWTS Evanston IL 1986; Phi Beta Kappa Br Providence RI 1974; Freshman French Awd Br 1971. susanchamp@hotmail.com

CHAMPION-GARTHE, Maurice Vinck (Mont) 155 Colter Loop, Helena MT 59602 B Mount Vernon OH 12/15/1944 s Carl Murdella Champion & Marie. BA Ashland U 1966; MDiv Bex 1969. D 6/14/1969 P 5/7/1970 Bp John Harris Burt. m 7/22/1989 Marybeth Gaddell c 3. Cn Dio Montana Helena MT 2005-2010; R Trin Ch Ennis MT 2002-2005; New Life Epis Cluster Seward NE 2001-2002; S Dav Of Wales Epis Ch Lincoln NE 1991-2000; Dio W Missouri Kansas City MO 1990-1991; Gr Epis Ch Liberty MO 1988-1990; S Lk's Epis Ch Excelsior Sprg MO 1988; R Ch Of The Redeem Kansas City MO 1981-1988; R Gr Ch Galion OH 1976-1981; S Paul Epis Ch Conneaut OH 1971-1976; Cur S Matt's Epis Ch Toledo OH 1969-1971. Oblate of S Ben 1999-2008. mcg@imt.net

CHAMPLIN, Jeffrey Fletcher (Ark) 2701 Old Greenwood Rd, Fort Smith AR 72903 **R S Barth's Epis Ch Ft Smith AR 1998-** B Providence RI 4/26/1956 s Arthur Doyle Champlin & Julia Jane. BA Wesl 1978; MDiv Ya Berk 1983; Ldrshp Acad for New Directions 1986. D 6/8/1985 Bp Arthur Edward Walmsley P 12/1/1985 Bp William Bradford Hastings. m 8/22/1981 Anne Elizabeth Kelly c 3. S Andr's Epis Ch Liberal KS 1991-1998; Middlesex Area Cluster Mnstry Higganum CT 1985-1991. jchamplin@stbartsfs.org

CHAN, Charles Yang-Ling Ping-Fai (Colo) Po Box 662, Mukwonago WI 53149 **P-in-c Dio So Dakota Sioux Falls SD 2005-** B HK 1/26/1955 s Dick-Kwong Chan & Woon-Fong. Marq; BA U Denv 1978; MDiv Nash 1981. D 4/29/1981 Bp William Harvey Wolfrum P 10/1/1981 Bp William Carl Frey. m 4/23/2010 Ewa Ming Lui Chan. P-in-c Epis Ch Of Our Sav New York NY 2003-2005; Epis Ch Of The Resurr Mukwonago WI 1997-2003; S Ptr's Ch Honolulu HI 1988; S Ptr's Epis Ch Chicago IL 1983-1987; Assoc S Jas Epis Ch Milwaukee WI 1982-1983; Assoc S Jn Ch/Mision San Juan Milwaukee WI 1982-1983; P-in-c Epis Ch Of Our Sav New York NY 1981-1982. Ban Zung Ci; Zhu An Ji #1:. moelai@hotmail.com

CHAN, Henry Albert (LI) 3410 Silver Stream Way NW, Kennesaw GA 30144 B Demerara GY 1/7/1946 s Clarence Kenneth Chan & Ruby Verna. BS SUNY 1978; MBA Dowling Coll 1980; DPA Nova SE U 1981; Cert of Grad Mercer TS 1982; DMin STUSo 1987; STM GTS 1992; PhD GTF 1994; PsyD GTF 2005. D 12/21/1982 Bp Robert Campbell Witcher Sr P 12/10/1983 Bp Henry Boyd Hucles III. m 4/26/1969 Jean Flora Langdon c 3. Co-Chair Racial Justice Com Dio Long Island Garden City NY 1995-1996; R S Ptr's Ch Rosedale NY 1988-2008; Dio Long Island Garden City NY 1987; Mem Cler Conf Plnng Com Dio Long Island Garden City NY 1985-1986; Cur Ch Of The Trsfg Freeport NY 1983-1987. Auth, "The Humanity of Mediators: From A Study of the Major Concepts of Viktor E. Frankl," Wyndham Hall Press, Lima, Ohio, 2007; Auth, "The Medtr As Human Being: From A Study of the Major Concepts of Sigmund Freud, Carl Jung, Erik Erikson and Abraham Maslow," Wyndham Hall Press, Lima, Ohio, 2005; Auth, "A Primary Mssn--The Sermon Is A Vital & Important Part of the Liturg," *Living Ch*, 1985; Auth, "Par Computer--An Aid in Many Aspects of the Ch's Wk," *Living Ch*, 1983. APA 2005; Amer Soc for Publ Admin 2008; C.G. Jung Fndt 1998-2007; NYS Dispute Resolution Assn 2002; Viktor Frankl Inst of Logotherapy 2007. Mem of the Year Awd Assn of Chinese Professionals 2010; Mem of the Year Awd Assn of Chinese Professionals, Atlanta, GA 2010; Serv and Humanitarian Awd Guyana Missions/Consulate/Tri-St Allnce 2002; A Point of Light for All Americans US Congr, Hse of Representatives 2001; Who's Who in Amer Marquis 2000; Who's Who in the E Marquis 1999. caribbeanhombre@aol.com

CHANCE, Robin Leea (Wyo) 2602 Deming Blvd, Cheyenne WY 82001 **R S Chris's Ch Cheyenne WY 2002-** B New York NY 5/24/1951 d Robert Gurnee Hewitt & Barbara Ann. BA Wstrn St Coll of Colorado 1973; MDiv SWTS 1995. D 6/22/1995 Bp Bob Gordon Jones P 1/5/1996 Bp William Harvey Wolfrum. m 8/17/1974 Kenneth Leroy Chance c 3. Chapl Cbury Hse Laramie WY 1995-2002; Dio Wyoming Casper WY 1995-2002; Cur S Matt's Epis Cathd Laramie WY 1995-1999. DOK 1996. rector@stchrischeyenne.org

CHANDLER, Archie Lee (SC) 103 Woodland Dr, Darlington SC 29532 **D S Matt's Epis Ch Darlington SC 2000-** B Orangeburg SC 12/16/1922 s William Eugene Chandler & Ella Rowe. Cit; U of So Carolina 1947; BA GW 1950. D 9/4/1999 Bp Edward Lloyd Salmon Jr. m 12/30/1945 Martha Nell Wilkins.

CHANDLER, Belinda (Chi) 3025 Walters Ave, Northbrook IL 60062 **Assoc S Giles' Ch Northbrook IL 2010-** B Geneva NY 4/6/1953 d Hamond Leroy Chandler & Marjorie Joan. BA Methodist Coll 1978; MDiv SWTS 1998. D 9/1/2010 P 3/1/2011 Bp Jeffrey Dean Lee. m 12/27/1997 Henry Austin c 3. P-in-c S Giles' Ch Northbrook IL 2011. bchan46@earthlink.net

CHANDLER, Gail Stearns (Me) St. David's Episcopal Church, 138 York St, Kennebunk ME 04043 B New York NY 6/13/1947 d George Franklin Waldron & Phyllis Stearns. BA U of New Hampshire 1969; MA S Jos Coll 1983. D 6/28/2008 Bp Chilton Abbie Richardson Knudsen. c 2. gchandler2@roadrunner.com

CHANDLER, John Herrick (Los) 2286 Vasanta Way, Los Angeles CA 90068 B San Francisco CA 8/7/1928 s Ralph W Chandler & Gwen. BA U CA 1952; BD U Chi 1958; PhD U Chi 1963. D 6/22/1959 P 2/1/1960 Bp Francis E I Bloy.

CHANDLER, June (NC) 2 Rock Cottage Ct # 2d, Durham NC 27707 **Died 1/5/2010** B Firebaugh CA 1/22/1924 d Carl Leonard Thompson & Sylvia. Epis TS of The SW; GTS; San Jose St U. D 4/7/1986 P 1/1/1987 Bp Charles Farmer Duvall. Auth, "S Simon'S Lectionary Notes". Ord Of S Helena.

CHANDLER, Nan Elizabeth (EC) 301 Bretonshire Rd, Wilmington NC 28405 **Chapl for Ret Cler & Spouses Dio E Carolina Kinston NC 2008-; R All Souls Ch NW Leland NC 1995-; R All Soul's Ch Leland NC 1995-** B Charleston WV 10/8/1943 d Obadiah Chandler & Jeannette. BS U of Kentucky 1966; MHA Xavier U 1978; MSW CUA 1980; MDiv VTS 1985. D 6/5/1985 P 12/14/1985 Bp Robert Poland Atkinson. Assoc S Mk's Ch Westhampton Bch NY 1990-1993; Asst Cleric Gr Ch Cincinnati OH 1988-1990; R S Paul's Ch Wheeling WV 1985-1987. revchandler@bellsouth.net

CHANDLER, Paul Gordon (Spok) PO Box 360, Winfield IL 60190 **Exec Coun Appointees New York NY 2003-** B Dayton OH 4/1/1964 s Wilfred Ray Chandler & Nancy Jean. Adv Cert of French Allnce Francaise De Paris, Fr 1986; B.A. Wheaton Coll 1986; C of E Ord Chichester Theol Coll 1993. Trans from The Episcopal Church in Jerusalem and the Middle East 2/1/2003 Bp James Edward Waggoner. m 1/27/1990 Lynne E Chandler c 2. "Songs in Waiting: Reflections on the Middle Estrn Songs Surrounding Chr's Birth," Morehouse Pub (Ch Pub), 2009; "Pilgrims of Chr on the Muslim Road: Exploring a New Path Between Two Faiths," Cowley Pub (Rowman & Littlefield), 2007; "God'S Global Mosaic: What We Can Learn From Christians Around the Wrld," Intervarsity Press (IVP), 2000; "Div Mosaic," S.P.C.K. / Triangle, 1997. leschandlers@cs.com

CHANDLER JR, Richard Anthony (Alb) 224 Main St, Hudson Falls NY 12839 **R Zion Ch Hudson Falls NY 2009-** B Schenectady NY 9/24/1968 s Richard Anthony Chandler & Carolyn Brown. BA SUNY Potsdam 1992; MS Sage Grad Sch 1995. D 5/31/2008 P 12/7/2008 Bp William Howard Love. m 7/2/1994 Kelly W Evans-Chandler c 3. laughtersmiles1@nycap.rr.com

CHANDLER, Susan Esco (Mass) 195 Patmos Rd., Sawyer's Island, Rowley MA 01969 **P-in-c S Jas Ch Amesbury MA 2006-** B Oklahoma City OK 5/22/1952 d Joe Walter Esco & Martha Sue. BA U of Oklahoma 1974; MDiv GTS 2001. D 7/28/2001 Bp Terence Kelshaw P 6/28/2002 Bp M(arvil) Thomas Shaw III. m 5/19/2001 Alfred D Chandler c 2. S Jn's Ch Beverly Farms MA 2001-2006. sechandler@verizon.net

CHANDLER-WARD, Constance (Mass) 16 School St., Tenants Harbor ME 04860 B Cambridge MA 10/26/1935 d Edgar Hugh Storer Chandler & Ruth Speare. BA U Of Dublin, Dublin, Ireland 1957; MA U Of Dublin, Dublin, Ireland 1959; MDiv Yale DS 1961. D 11/15/1975 P 2/13/1977 Bp Robert Bruce Hall. m 6/3/1961 David Ward c 2. Assoc Gr Ch In Providence Providence RI 1980-1981; COM Dio Virginia Richmond VA 1978-1979; Asst S Paul's Memi Charlottesville VA 1977-1979. conniechandler@lycos.com

CHANDY, Kuruvilla Kulangana (NJ) 1115 New Pear St, Vineland NJ 08360 **S Andr's Ch Mt Holly NJ 2006-** B Kerala IN 3/13/1967 d Kulangana Kuruvilla Chandy & Saramma Iype. BS Rutgers-The St U 1991; MDiv GTS 1995. Trans 4/1/1998 Bp John Shelby Spong. m 1/22/1994 Simi Varghese c 3. Trin Epis Ch Vineland NJ 2001-2006; Chr Ch Ridgewood NJ 1999-2001; All SS Epis Par Hoboken NJ 1998-1999. schandy91@gmail.com

✠ CHANE, Rt Rev John (WA) Episcopal Diocese of Washington, Mount Saint Alban, Washington DC 20016 **Bp of Washington Dio Washington Washington DC 2002-** B Washington DC 5/13/1944 s Daniel Thurston Chane & Vivienne Norma. BA Bos 1969; MDiv Ya Berk 1972. D 6/24/1972 Bp John Melville Burgess P 1/6/1973 Bp George E Rath Con 6/1/2002 for WA. m 1/21/1967 Karen Albright c 2. Dn Cathd Ch Of S Paul San Diego CA 1996-2002; Percept Strng Com Dio San Diego San Diego CA 1996-2002; T/F on Educ Dio Massachusetts Boston MA 1994-1996; Cn 21 Consult Dio Massachusetts Boston MA 1993-1996; Par Consult Dio Massachusetts Boston MA 1992-1996; Long-R Plnng Com Dio Massachusetts Boston MA 1990-1996; Chair of Gdnc and Pstr Care of Post and Candidates Dio Massachusetts Boston MA 1989-1996; COM Dio Massachusetts Boston MA 1989-1996; Mssn Prog and Plnng Com Dio Massachusetts Boston MA 1989-1996; T/F on Hunger Dio Massachusetts Boston MA 1988-1996; R S Mk's Ch Southborough MA 1987-1996; Dioc Coun Dio NW Pennsylvania Erie PA 1976-1977; Cn Cathd Of S Paul Erie PA 1975-1987; Cur S Paul's Ch Montvale NJ 1972-1974. Auth, "And Even Grtr Things Than This You Will See," *Angl Dig*; Auth, "The MA Miracle, Mnstry in the 90's," *Epis Life*; Auth, "An Easter Vision of the Moral Life's Loaves & Stones," *Epis Life*; Auth, "Moral Relativism & Sport Crisis of the 90's," *IOA-IOC-Journ*; Auth, *New Directions in Athlete Chapl & Counslg*; Auth, *Perspective on Olympic Chapl*; Auth, "Wmn Conscience & Priesthood," *USOA-Wit*. Bishops Working for a Just Wrld 2004; Bd Ecum Coun San Diego 1997-2002; Cntr for Urban Mnstry 1996-2002; Curs 2000; EPF 1969; EWC 1978; No Amer Dn Conf 1996-2002; Soc of S Jn the Evang 1994; Soc of S Paul in the Desert 1996; TEC Natl Concerns Comm. 2002; VP, Ecum Coun San Diego 1997-2002. Inter-Faith Bridge Builder EDS, Cambridge DD 2008; Pres Medal G.W. U VTS DD 2003; Schlrshp Bk Prize Ya Berk DD New Haven CT 1972. jchane@edow.org

CHANEY, Myrna Faye (Mont) 14 September Dr, Missoula MT 59802 **D Ch Of The H Sprt Missoula MT 1999-** B Boise ID 4/6/1940 d Nelson Leo Eyerly & Glenva Viola. BA U of Montana 1962; MA Stan 1963. D 12/5/1999 Bp Charles Jones III. m 6/15/1963 Robert Bruce Chaney.

CHANG, Hsin-Fen (Los) 15694 Tetley St, Hacienda Heights CA 91745 **Dio Los Angeles Los Angeles CA 2011-** B Taiwan 3/5/1965 d Wen-chang Chang & Li-cheng. BA Tunghai U 1987; MA U of Wisconsin-Madison 1990; PhD U Tor 2007; MDiv Logos Evang Sem 2010. D 6/11/2011 Bp Diane M Jardine Bruce. hsinfenchang@hotmail.com

CHANG, Lennon Yuan-Rung (Tai) Wen-Hua 3rd Road, 4th Place #75, Pei-Tan Taiwan B Taipei 4/2/1955 s Feng-Ji Chang & Ging-Mei. BA Fu-Jen Cath U 1980; MA Fu-Jen Cath U 1983; Dplma Trin Theol Cntr 1994; Phd Tamkang U 1998. D 12/21/1995 Bp John Chih-Tsung Chien P. m 10/18/1980 Spring Fen-Jen Wei c 2. iechang@mail.sju.edu.tw

CHANG, Ling-Ling (Tai) 280 Fu-Hsing South Road, Sec 2, Taipei Taiwan B Chang-Hua TW 1/5/1962 d Yin-Chin Chang & Li-Hsia. BA Chung Yuan U Chung-Li Tw 1983; MA Fu-Jen Cath U 1998. D 10/28/2000 Bp John Chih-Tsung Chien.

CHANG, Mark Chung-Moon (Nwk) 11 Foakes Drive, Ajax LIT 3K5 Canada B 11/27/1930 s Byung-kul Chang & Soon-Hwa. Methodist Theol Coll 1959; BA Song-Sil U Seoul Kr 1962; S Mich's TS 1964; ThM Yonsei U 1969; STM GTS 1970; PhD Pacific Wstrn U Los Angeles 1986. Trans from Anglican Church of Canada 10/1/1987 Bp John Shelby Spong. m 1/10/1957 Esther Haing-Im Pak. S Ptr's Korean Ch No Bergen NJ 1998; S Peters Ch Bogota NJ 1987-1989. Auth, "b Of A Wmn"; Auth, "Space-Time Talk".

✠ **CHANG, Rt Rev Richard Sui On** (Haw) 1760 S. Beretania Street, Apt. 11C, Honolulu HI 96826 **Ret Bp of Hawaii Dio Hawaii Honolulu HI 2007-** B Honolulu HI 11/30/1941 s Dick Chang & Flora Yuk Ten. BA Trin Hartford CT 1963; MDiv CDSP 1966; U of Hawaii 1970. D 3/5/1966 Bp George Richard Millard P 9/4/1966 Bp Harry S Kennedy Con 1/4/1997 for Haw. m 8/10/1969 Delia Morrish c 2. Dio Hawaii Honolulu HI 1997; Asst to PBp Epis Ch Cntr New York NY 1991-1996; Exec Off Dio Hawaii Honolulu HI 1979-1985; Chair HI E Dio Hawaii Honolulu HI 1976-1977; Vic Chr Memi Ch Kilauea HI 1974-1978; COM Dio Hawaii Honolulu HI 1974-1978; R All SS Ch Kapaa HI 1970-1978; Archd Dio Hawaii Honolulu HI 1970-1974; Dioc Coun Dio Hawaii Honolulu HI 1970-1971; Bp's Cbnt Dio Hawaii Honolulu HI 1968-1970; Asst Ch Of The H Nativ Honolulu HI 1966-1970. CODE 1979-1986; LAND 1976-1986. DD CDSP 1997; AB cl Trin Hartford CT 1963; Pi Gamma Mu Trin Hartford CT 1963. rsochang@episcopalhawaii.org

CHANGO, Georgianna (NwPa) Rr 6 Box 324, Punxsutawney PA 15767 **D Ch Of Our Sav DuBois PA 1991-** B Punxsutawney PA 8/6/1940 d John Lellock & Thelma Ruth. D 11/1/1991 Bp Robert Deane Rowley Jr. m 9/28/1956 Anthony Reynold Chango c 2.

CHANNON, Ethel Marie (Dal) 2304 County Ave, Texarkana AR 71854 B East St. Louis IL 5/5/1951 d Charles Andrew Channon & Bernice Snyder. BA Sthrn Illinois U Edwardsville IL 1973; BA Sthrn Illinois U Edwardsville IL 1973; Mnstry Cathd Cntr for Mnstry Formation Dallas TX 2006. D 12/5/2006 Bp James Monte Stanton. emchan@aol.com

CHAPLIN, George Manton (RI) 1201 Capella South, Goat Island, Newport RI 02840 B Newport RI 3/11/1923 s Arthur Wilfred Chaplin & Florence Ella. Aeronautical U Chicago IL 1943; Barrington Coll 1967; EDS 1967; Providence Coll 1967; Salve Regina Coll/Univ 1968. D 3/8/1969 P 12/20/1969 Bp John S Higgins. c 4. Int The Ch Of The H Cross Middletown RI 1999-2000; Supply Dio Rhode Island Providence RI 1993-1998; Int The Ch Of The H Cross Middletown RI 1992-1993; Dio Rhode Island Providence RI 1978-1980; R S Mk's Ch Warren RI 1969-1989. gmchapinri@verizon.net

CHAPMAN, Alton James (SwFla) 12905 Forest Hills Dr, Tampa FL 33612 B Negaunee MI 3/12/1940 s Ellsworth Richard Chapman & Estelle Marie. BA U of So Florida 1967; VTS 1970. D 6/29/1970 P 11/1/1971 Bp William Loftin Hargrave. m 4/24/1971 Elizabeth Ewan Higginbotham c 3. R S Clem Epis Ch Tampa FL 1998-2005; Gr Ch Cedar Rapids IA 1988-1998; Vic S Lk's Ch Land O Lakes FL 1976-1987; St Lukes Ch Ellenton FL 1976-1986; R S Jas Hse Of Pryr Tampa FL 1970-1976. DOK-Chapl. alnbets@verizon.net

CHAPMAN JR, Chuck (Ark) 525 N Madison Ave, El Dorado AR 71730 **R S Mary's Epis Ch El Dorado AR 2009-; Cur S Mary's Epis Ch El Dorado AR 1997-** B Memphis TN 12/23/1955 s Charles Taylor Chapman & Betty Jane. BA Un U Jackson TN 1976; MDiv Sthrn Bapt TS Louisville KY 1979; CTh Epis TS of The SW 1986. D 5/28/1986 P 5/26/1987 Bp Alex Dockery Dickson. Int R S Mary's Epis Ch El Dorado AR 2008; R S Mk's Epis Ch Plainview TX 1992-1997; St Andrews Sch Of Amarillo Amarillo TX 1991-1992; R Gr Epis Ch Winfield KS 1990-1991; Gr-S Lk's Epis Sch Memphis TN 1986-1990; Asst to R Gr - S Lk's Ch Memphis TN 1980-1990. Auth, "The Message Of The Bk Of Revelation," Liturg Press, 1995; Auth, "Lyrics Of Easter Hymn," GIA, 1983; Auth, "Lyrics Of H Gifts," GIA, 1983. Oblate Of St. Ben Of Subiaco Abbey 1996. Silver Beaver BSA 2009; Cross of St. Geo BSA 2007. chaschap@yahoo.com

CHAPMAN, Donald Earl (USC) 249 Heathwood Dr, Spartanburg SC 29307 **Died 3/22/2011** B Syracuse NY 10/25/1919 s Glen Maurice Chapman & Frances Mabel. BA Hob 1949; MA Col 1950; DMin STUSo 1984. D 7/8/1955 Bp John Vander Horst P 2/1/1956 Bp Theodore N Barth. c 2. Auth, "Acad Goals," *H Cross mag*, 1965. Phi Beta Kappa Hob Geneva NY 1949.

CHAPMAN SSF, Edward Carter (Md) 16 Washington St, Cumberland MD 21502 **R Emm Ch Cumberland MD 1985-** B New Rochelle NY 1/24/1948 s George Memory Chapman & Elizabeth. BA W&L 1970; MDiv EDS 1973. D 6/9/1973 Bp Paul Moore Jr P 1/25/1974 Bp (George) Paul Reeves. c 1. R Chr Epis Ch Marion VA 1978-1985; Int Chr Ch Frederica St Simons Island GA 1978; Cur Chr Ch Frederica St Simons Island GA 1973-1978. Auth, "O Prosper Thou Thy Handiwork," Printers Inc, 2003. The SSF 2008. emmanuel@ang-md.org

CHAPMAN, George Memory (Mass) 41 Garth Road, West Roxbury MA 02132 B Greensboro NC 1/8/1942 s George Memory Chapman & Elizabeth. AB W&L 1963; BD EDS 1968. D 6/8/1968 P 12/21/1968 Bp Horace W B Donegan. m 6/26/1965 Margaret Rand c 3. R S Paul's Ch Brookline MA 1978-2007; Yth Mnstry Coordntr Prov II 1974-2011; Sr Cn S Paul's Cathd Buffalo NY 1972-1978; P-in-c Imm Ch Highlands Wilmington DE 1968-1970. "Will I?," *Sermons that Wk X*, Morehouse, 2001; Auth, "Revelation at the Teller Windows," *Sermons that Wk IX*, Morehouse, 2000; Auth, "Jesus is Lord," *Pulpit Dig*, 1970. Fell - SSJE 1988. gmcpadre@gmail.com

CHAPMAN, Hugh William (Fla) 13 Bb Misgunsi, St. Thomas 802 Virgin Islands (U.S.) **S Phil's Epis Ch Jacksonville FL 2007-** B Guyana South America 2/28/1954 Trans 7/1/2001 Bp Theodore Athelbert Daniels. m 6/12/1980 Paula G Chapman c 3. P Dio Vrgn Islands St Thos VI VI 2001-2005. hugh_chappy50@yahoo.com

CHAPMAN, Jerry Wayne (Dal) 11201 Pickfair Dr, Austin TX 78750 **Asstg S Matt's Ch Austin TX 2000-** B Dallas TX 12/26/1943 s Wayne Leon Chapman & Archie Maye. BS U of Texas 1970; TS 1980. D 6/28/1980 Bp A Donald Davies P 5/1/1981 Bp Robert Elwin Terwilliger. c 2. Asst S Matt's Ch

Austin TX 1987-1989; Asst S Geo's Ch Austin TX 1981-1987; Asst S Jn's Epis Ch Austin TX 1980-1981. jwchap@yahoo.com

CHAPMAN, Justin Paul (Minn) 3006 Avalon Cove Ct NW, Rochester MN 55901 **P-in-c S Ptr's Epis Ch Kasson MN 2008-** B Minneapolis MN 4/20/1979 s Dann Chapman & Linda. BS U MN 2001; MDiv CDSP 2008. D 7/26/2007 P 7/8/2008 Bp James Louis Jelinek. m 10/20/2007 Katie Virginia Brandt. Cur S Lk's Epis Ch Rochester MN 2008-2011. justinpchapman@gmail.com

CHAPMAN, Michael (Alb) 22 Bergen St, Brentwood NY 11717 B Miami Beach FL 6/27/1951 s Lipscomb Lykes Chapman & Mary. BA Florida Atlantic U 1972; MDiv Nash 1990. P 12/1/1990 Bp Orris George Walker Jr. m 4/17/1982 Linda Upton Murphy c 2. Vic Chr Ch Brentwood NY 1990-1999. thwmac@juno.com

CHAPMAN, Phillip (Neb) 322 S 15th St, Plattsmouth NE 68048 **D S Lk's Ch Plattsmouth NE 2003-** B Franklinville NY 7/15/1943 BA Bellevue U. D 1/6/2003 Bp James Edward Krotz P 11/11/2009 Bp Joe Goodwin Burnett. m 7/15/1963 Diana Rogerson c 2. phil358@hotmail.com

CHAPMAN, Tansy (Mass) PO Box 832, Mendocino CA 95460 **Assoc S Mich And All Ang Ch Ft Bragg CA 2006-** B 12/29/1937 d Conrad Frederick Rogenhagen & Gillian Mary. BA U of Leicester 1959; Oxf 1960; MS London Inst Gb 1961; MDiv EDS 1982. D 6/5/1982 Bp John Bowen Coburn P 5/1/1983 Bp Roger W Blanchard. m 4/3/1965 Paul H Chapman c 3. Assoc Trin Ch Topsfield MA 1997-2002; S Eliz's Ch Wilmington MA 1988-1992; S Mk's Epis Ch Burlington MA 1982-1987; Vic S Eliz's Ch Wilmington MA 1982-1983. Fell Soc Of S Jn The Evang; S Anne Cnvnt Arlington Ma. tansyr@comcast.net

CHAPPELEAR III, Albert Simpson (SO) 3203 L Pavia Blvd, Venice FL 34292 B Cambridge OH 6/4/1931 s Albert Simpson Chappelear & Alice Margaret. BA Ken 1953; MDiv Bex 1956. D 10/21/1956 P 5/1/1957 Bp Henry W Hobson. m 7/23/1964 Virginia West Hunt c 1. Supply P Dio Sthrn Ohio Cincinnati OH 1995-2002; Asst S Mk's Epis Ch Venice FL 1966-1968; R Our Sav Ch Mechanicsburg OH 1960-1966; S Ptr's Ch Gallipolis OH 1956-1960. Hugenot Soc 1982. Merit Awd Salvation Army 1969. LENWEN1@MSN.COM

CHAPPELL, Annette Mary (Md) 1437 Towson St, Baltimore MD 21230 **Mem, Liturg and Mus Com Dio Maryland Baltimore MD 2006-; R Ch Of The Redemp Baltimore MD 2003-; Mem, Compstn and Benefits Com Dio Maryland Baltimore MD 2003-** B Washington DC 10/31/1939 d Joseph John Chappell & Annette Brown. MA U of Maryland, Coll Pk 1964; PhD U of Maryland, Coll Pk 1970; MDiv GTS 2003. D 6/14/2003 P 12/13/2003 Bp Robert Wilkes Ihloff. Mem, Liturg and Mus Com Dio Maryland Baltimore MD 2006-2011. Soc of Cath Priests 2009. achappell@towson.edu

CHAPPELL, Veronica Donohue (CPa) 1118 State Route 973 E, Cogan Station PA 17728 **R Trin Ch Jersey Shore PA 2006-** B Philadelphia PA 3/30/1954 d Mark Ignatius Donohue & Clare Delores. BA Tem 1987; M. Div. Luth TS at Gettysburg 2009. D 6/9/2000 Bp Michael Whittington Creighton P 10/6/2007 Bp Nathan Dwight Baxter. m 10/7/1977 Daniel Elwood Chappell c 1. Yoke Min S Mk's Epis Ch Northumberland PA 2003-2004; Yoke Min S Matt's Epis Ch Sunbury PA 2003-2004; D Trin Epis Ch Williamsport PA 2000-2002. chappellthreads1@verizon.net

CHAPPELLE, Laurinda (Nev) 1230 Riverberry Dr, Reno NV 89509 **R St Cathr of Siena Reno NV 2009-** B Englewood NJ 3/1/1947 d James Chubb & Margaret. BA Stetson U 1968; MEd. U Of Florida 1969. D 1/31/2006 P 7/31/2006 Bp Katharine Jefferts Schori. P-in-c Dio Nevada Las Vegas NV 2007-2008. peach@gbis.com

CHAR, Zachariah (WMich) 4232 Alpinehorn Dr Nw, Comstock Pk MI 49321 **Gr Ch Grand Rapids MI 2007-** B 1/1/1982 s Mayen K Char & Akon. AA Grand Rapids Cmnty Coll Grand Rapids MI; Kuyper Grand Rapids MI 2009. D 12/9/2006 Bp Robert R Gepert P 6/16/2007 Bp Robert Alexander Gepert Jr. m 12/9/2004 Tabitha Nyawut Char c 1. zachar1982@yahoo.com

CHARD JR, Arthur Cameron (WVa) 1206 Maple Lane, Anchorage KY 40223 **Assoc S Lk's Ch Anchorage KY 2002-** B Brainerd MN 2/19/1933 s Arthur Cameron Chard & Kathleen. BS Minnesota St U Moorehead 1956; MDiv Epis TS In Kentucky 1967. D 5/27/1967 P 12/1/1967 Bp William R Moody. m 6/1/1968 Judy Sams c 1. R All SS Ch Charleston WV 1981-1995; P-in-c S Pat Ch Somerset KY 1968-1981; Cur S Jn's Ch Versailles KY 1967-1968. j2achard@insightbb.com

CHARLES, D Maurice (Chi) 5439 S Cornell Ave Apt 2, Chicago IL 60615 **Asst Epis Ch Of The Atone Chicago IL 2008-** B Cleveland OH 2/1/1963 s Henry Charles & Jeanie Mae. BA cl Case Wstrn Reserve U 1987; MDiv U Chi 1990; CAS CDSP 1995; PhD (Candidate) U Chi 2012. D 12/7/1996 P 6/7/1997 Bp William Edwin Swing. c 1. Bd Mem The Ch Hm At Montgomery Place Chicago IL 2008-2010; Search Com/Bd Mem Brent Hse (U Of Chicago) Chicago IL 2003-2007; P-in-c Ch Of S Thos Chicago IL 2003-2004. OHC 1995. imago@uchicago.edu

CHARLES, Jean-Elie (Hai) Box 1309, Port-Au-Prince Haiti B Gros-Morne HT 4/19/1941 s Murat Charles & Celie-Anne. Coll Of S Pierre Ht 1965; Sem Epis Del Caribe PR 1969. D 12/14/1969 Bp John Brooke Mosley P 12/20/1970 Bp Paul Axtell Kellogg. m 1/30/1971 Anne Marie Jamine Pierre-Charles. Dio Haiti Ft Lauderdale FL 1969-2006.

CHARLES, Kathleen Jane (Eau) 1010 Cass St, La Crosse WI 54601 **R S Mary's Epis Ch Tomah WI 2010-; D Chr Ch Par La Crosse WI 2001-** B Chippewa Falls WI 12/30/1949 d George E Nasseth & Elizabeth J. Epis Acad D Sch Menomonie WI 2002; BA Viterbo U 2002; MDiv Untd TS 2005; MDiv SWTS 2008. D 6/9/2001 P 5/19/2007 Bp Keith Bernard Whitmore. m 5/8/1971 Nicholas Robert Charles c 2. D S Jn's Epis Ch Sparta WI 2002-2004. revkjc49@centurytel.net

CHARLES, Leonel (SeFla) Box 1309, Port-Au-Prince Haiti **Ch Of S Chris Ft Lauderdale FL 2002-** B Cap Haitien HT 2/9/1965 s Dieubonne Jacques Philippe Charles & Romaine. Ceteeh 1989. D 7/30/1989 P 2/1/1990 Bp Luc Anatole Jacques Garnier. Dio Haiti Ft Lauderdale FL 1989-1995.

✠ CHARLES, Rt Rev Otis (U) 584 Castro Street, #379, San Francisco CA 94114 B Norristown PA 4/24/1926 s Jacob Otis Charles & Elizabeth Frances. BA Trin Hartford CT 1948; STB GTS 1951; STM GTS 1959; DD GTS 1983; DD EDS 1993. D 3/31/1951 Bp Wallace J Gardner P 10/7/1951 Bp Alfred L Banyard Con 9/12/1971 for U. m 4/24/2004 Felipe Paris c 4. Int Dio California San Francisco CA 1998-1999; The Epis Ch Of S Jn The Evang San Francisco CA 1993; Dn/Pres EDS Cambridge MA 1985-1993; Bp Navajoland Area Mssn Farmington NM 1976-1978; Epis Media Cntr Inc Atlanta GA 1972-1978; Bp of Utah Dio Utah Salt Lake City UT 1971-1986; Dio Utah Salt Lake City UT 1971-1985; R S Jn's Ch Washington CT 1959-1968; P-in-c S Andr's Ch Beacon NY 1953-1959; Cur S Jn's Ch Eliz NJ 1951-1953. Ed, *Millenium 3*, 1999; Auth, "Breaking the Silence," *Out in the Wk Place*, Allyson Pub, 1995. Annual Integrity Awd Integrity, Inc 1980; Hon DD EDS Cambridge MA; Hon DD GTS New York NY. otis@otischarles.com

CHARLES, Randolph (WA) 1331 19th Rd S, Arlington VA 22202 **R The Ch Of The Epiph Washington DC 1994-** B Florence SC 2/17/1947 s Randolph Cassells Charles & Harriet Breeden. BA U So 1969; MDiv GTS 1976. D 1/24/1976 P 8/6/1976 Bp Gray Temple. m 5/17/2008 Joanne F Charles c 3. BEC Dio Sthrn Virginia Norfolk VA 1989-1994; COM Dio Sthrn Virginia Norfolk VA 1989-1994; Ldrshp Trng Prog Dio Sthrn Virginia Norfolk VA 1988-1994; R S Paul's Ch Newport News VA 1983-1994; Gr Ch Charleston SC 1978-1983; P-in-c H Cross Faith Memi Epis Ch Pawleys Island SC 1976-1978; Asst Chr the King Pawleys Island SC 1976-1977. rcc1331@comcast.net

CHARLES, Winston Breeden (NC) 114 East Drewry Lane, Raleigh NC 27609 B Bennettsville SC 11/5/1948 s Randolph Cassells Charles & Harriet Winston. BA U So 1970; MDiv cl VTS 1974; MA UTS 1989; Ph.D. UTS 1995. D 6/8/1974 P 12/14/1974 Bp Gray Temple. m 12/20/1970 Judy H Hunter c 1. R Chr Epis Ch Raleigh NC 1993-2008; Assoc S Jas Ch New York NY 1991-1993; P-in-c S Andr's Epis Ch Staten Island NY 1990-1991; R S Geo's Epis Ch Summerville SC 1979-1985; Cur S Paul's Epis Ch Summerville SC 1977-1978; Asst Min Gr Ch Charleston SC 1976-1977; Vic Epis Ch Of The H Trin Ridgeland SC 1974-1976; Vic The Ch Of The Cross Bluffton SC 1974-1976. "Remembrance as a Dynamic of Faith in the Theol of Mart Luther [dissertation]," 2005. wjcharles@nc.rr.com

✠ CHARLESTON, Rt Rev Steven (Okla) 2702 Silvertree Dr, Oklahoma City OK 73120 **Ret Bp of Alaska S Paul's Cathd Oklahoma City OK 2010-; Asst Bp Dio California San Francisco CA 2009-; Ret Bp of Alaska EDS Cambridge MA 2008-** B Duncan OK 2/15/1949 s Gilbert Mike Charleston & Billie Louise. BA Trin Hartford CT 1971; MDiv EDS 1976; DD Trin Hartford CT 1992; DD Albany Law Sch 1993. D 8/10/1982 Bp William Charles Wantland P 3/1/1983 Bp Everett H Jones Con 3/23/1991 for Ak. m 7/28/1978 Susan Flora Shettles c 1. Dio California San Francisco CA 2008-2010; Pres/Dn EDS Cambridge MA 2000-2008; Dio Connecticut Hartford CT 1998-1999; Trin Chap Hartford CT 1996; Dio Alaska Fairbanks AK 1990-1996; Luther NW Theo Sem S Paul MN 1984-1990; Dakota Ldrshp Prog Mobridge SD 1983-1984. Auth, "Reflection On A Revival: The Native Amer Alt"; Auth, "Respecting The Cir : Sharing In Wrshp w Native Americans"; Auth, "OT Of Native Amer". chata-1@msn.com

✠ **CHARLTON, Rt Rev Gordon Taliaferro** (Tex) 132 Lancaster Dr Apt 310, Irvington VA 22480 **Ret Bp Suffr Of Texas Dio Texas Houston TX 1989-** B San Antonio TX 9/29/1923 s Gordon Taliaferro Charlton & Enid Lynn. BA U of Texas 1944; MDiv VTS 1949. D 7/5/1949 Bp Everett H Jones P 1/6/1950 Bp Clinton Simon Quin Con 8/28/1982 for Tex. c 3. Bp Suffr Dio Texas Houston TX 1982-1988; Dn Epis TS Of The SW Austin TX 1973-1982; Asst VTS Alexandria VA 1967-1973; R Ch of St Andrews & St Matthews Wilmington DE 1963-1967; R S Matt's Epis Ch Fairbanks AK 1951-1954; Asst S Jas Epis Ch Houston TX 1949-1951. LHD Epis TS of the SW 1990; DD STUSo 1988; DD VTS 1974. gordon@kaballero.com

CHASE JR, Benjamin Otis (Vt) 95 Worcester Village Rd, Worcester VT 05682 B Boston MA 4/21/1939 s Benjamin Otis Chase & Dorothy Olivia. BA Norwich U 1962; BD CDSP 1965. D 6/26/1965 Bp John Melville Burgess P 5/1/1966 Bp Henry Knox Sherrill. m 8/14/1965 Alberta Bea Voss. Exec Coun Appointees New York NY 1988-1999; R Chr Ch Montpelier VT 1982-1988;

Vic S Mk's-S Lk's Epis Mssn Castleton VT 1978-1981; Vic Gr Ch Sheldon VT 1973-1978; R H Trin Epis Ch Swanton VT 1973-1978; Vic S Jn's Ch Swanton VT 1973-1978; Vic S Lk's Ch Alburgh VT 1973-1978; Vic S Paul's Ch Canaan VT 1967-1970; Vic S Steph's Epis Mssn Colebrook NH 1967-1970; Cur Gr Ch Manchester NH 1965-1967. barchase@together.net

CHASE, Christopher Gray (SanD) 10885 Caminito Cuesta, San Diego CA 92131 **Ch Of The Gd Samar San Diego CA 2006-** B Boston MA 12/17/1960 s Harry Gray Chase & Norma Sue. BA U of Nottingham 1984; MA Bos 1991; Cert EDS 1996. D 9/8/1996 P 5/18/1997 Bp M(arvil) Thomas Shaw III. m 10/2/1993 Rebecca Ann Manning c 2. Dio E Tennessee Knoxville TN 2002-2006; S Fran' Ch Norris TN 1998-2002; Asst to R S Anne's In The Fields Epis Ch Lincoln MA 1996-1998. revcgchase@hotmail.com

CHASE IV, Edwin Theodore (Ted) (LI) 432 Lakeville Road, The Church of St. Philip and St. James, Lake Success NY 11042 **P-in-c S Phil And S Jas Ch New Hyde Pk NY 2011-; for Hisp Mnstrs The Ch Of S Lk and S Matt Brooklyn NY 1993-** B Philadelphia PA 7/30/1947 s Edwin Theodore Chase & Lois. BA Laf 1969; MDiv GTS 1973. D 6/23/1973 Bp Robert Lionne DeWitt P 12/22/1973 Bp Adrian Delio Caceres-Villavicencio. c 2. for Hisp Mnstry S Geo's Par Flushing NY 1990-2010; R Ch Of Calv And S Cyp Brooklyn NY 1979-1984; Cur Chr Ch and H Fam Brooklyn NY 1975-1979. Transltr, "El Libro de Oración Común," Ch Pub, 1989. tchaseiv@aol.com

CHASE JR, John Garvey (Tex) P.O. Box 103, Crockett TX 75835 **Vic All SS Epis Ch Crockett TX 2009-** B Concord MA 4/30/1947 s John Garvey Chase & June Eilene. BA Coll of the H Cross 1969; Cert Iona Sch for Mnstry 2008. D 6/28/2008 Bp Don Adger Wimberly P 1/17/2009 Bp Rayford Baines High Jr. m 7/9/1980 Rosalie Cooper. Vic All SS Epis Ch Crockett TX 2008-2009. jgchase@valornet.com

CHASE, Peter (WMass) 355 Blackstone Blvd Apt 104, Providence RI 02906 **Cn Chr Ch Cathd Springfield MA 1980-** B Boston MA 1/22/1921 s Helen Grace. BA Br 1948; STB GTS 1951; DAS St. Augustines Coll Cbury UK 1955. D 3/27/1951 P 10/6/1951 Bp Granville G Bennett. m 6/19/1954 Virginia Hunter Zimmerman c 3. Sum Org S Andr's By The Sea Little Compton RI 1986-1997; Dio Wstrn Massachusetts Springfield MA 1973-1986; R S Jas' Ch Greenfield MA 1973-1986; Vic S Andr's Ch Turners Falls MA 1973-1984; Asst Min Cathd Of St Jn The Div New York NY 1960-1961; Cur Trin Ch Newport RI 1951-1953. Angl Soc; AAM; Fllshp of the Way of the Cross (FVC). Cn Chr Cathd Wstrn MA Springfield MA 1980. malabar@prodigy.net

CHASE, Peter Gray Otis (Mass) 258 Concord St, Newton MA 02462 B Frankfurt NY 1/14/1947 s Benjamin Otis Chase & Dorothy. BA Bishops U 1971; MDiv CDSP 1980. D 3/25/1982 P 2/1/1983 Bp Charles Shannon Mallory. m 1/29/1977 Abbie Gowdy c 2. R S Mary's Ch Newton Lower Falls MA 1992-2009; Bountiful Cmnty Ch Bountiful UT 1983-1992; S Andr's Ch Saratoga CA 1982-1983. pgoc555@aol.com

CHASE JR, Randall (Mass) P O Box 924, Barnstable MA 02630 B Sanford FL 12/12/1946 s Randall Chase & Julia. BS Florida St U 1968; MDiv VTS 1972; DMin Bos 1980. D 6/1/1972 P 12/13/1972 Bp William Hopkins Folwell. c 2. Actg Pres & Dn of Admin EDS Cambridge MA 2006-2010; Cn Dio Rhode Island Providence RI 1997-2003; R S Eliz's Ch Sudbury MA 1991-1997; Int Par Of The Epiph Winchester MA 1990-1991; Dio Massachusetts Boston MA 1989-1990; EDS Cambridge MA 1984-1989; R Chap Of S Andr Boca Raton FL 1980-1984; R Epis Ch Of The H Fam Miami Gardens FL 1979-1980; Chapl Sarasota Dnry Chapl Sarasota FL 1974-1978; Asst R S Dav's Epis Ch Lakeland FL 1972-1974. ECom; ESMHE; Ord Of S Anne; Soc Of S Jn The Evang. ranchase@comcast.net

CHASSE, Richard P (Nwk) 176 Palisade Ave, Jersey City NJ 07306 B Hartford CT 11/14/1941 s Eudore Chasse & Rita. AA Lasalette Jr Coll 1961; BA Lasalette Major Sem 1964; MA Assumption Coll 1972. Rec from Roman Catholic 11/1/1975 as Priest Bp Robert Bruce Hall. m 9/15/1973 Donna Jean Chasse c 1. Chr Hosp Jersey City NJ 1979-1999. Auth, "Cancer Trends"; Auth, "Leukemia & The Fam". rpchasse@gmail.com

CHASSEY JR, George Irwin (USC) 9b Exum Dr, West Columbia SC 29169 B Bridgewater MA 9/12/1921 s George Irwin Chassey & Merriel. U of Paris FR 1945; BA Stetson U 1951; MA Stetson U 1955; STUSo 1959. D 9/12/1959 P 9/29/1960 Bp Clarence Alfred Cole. m 1/14/1943 Mary Hildreth c 3. Dep GC Dio Upper So Carolina Columbia SC 1985-1988; Cn Admin Dio Upper So Carolina Columbia SC 1983-1989; Cn Mssnr for Stwdshp and Dvlpmt Dio Los Angeles Los Angeles CA 1980-1983; Dio Upper So Carolina Columbia SC 1976-1979; Cn to Bp Dio So Carolina Charleston SC 1969-1980; R H Trin Epis Ch Charleston SC 1963-1969; R Ch Of The H Apos Barnwell SC 1961-1963; Asst S Martins-In-The-Field Columbia SC 1959-1961. gchassey@aol.com

CHASTAIN, Gordon Lee (Ind) 3941 N Delaware St, Indianapolis IN 46205 B Indianapolis IN 1/22/1938 s Charles A Chastain & Thelma R. BA DePauw U 1959; STB Ya Berk 1962. D 6/17/1962 P 12/16/1962 Bp John P Craine. m 10/18/2011 Thomas Honderich c 3. Dep GC Dio Indianapolis Indianapolis IN 2000-2003; R All SS Ch Indianapolis IN 1994-2001; The Damien Cntr Indianapolis IN 1990-1994; Cur S Paul's Epis Ch Indianapolis IN 1969-1978; Stndg Com Dio Indianapolis Indianapolis IN 1968-1969; R S Andr's Epis Ch Greencastle IN 1966-1968; Cur S Chris's Epis Ch Carmel IN 1962-1966; Vic S Ptr's Ch Lebanon IN 1962-1966. Bd NEAC 1995-2003; Chair, Bd Natl Epis Hlth Mnstrs 2006. GLCTEH@MSN.COM

CHATHAM, Charles Erwin (Az) 500 S Jackson St, Wickenburg AZ 85390 B Fort Worth TX 3/18/1942 s Charles L Chatham & Martha Virginia. Sam Houston St U 1961; BS Baylor U 1964; MDiv Epis TS of the SW 1970. D 6/18/1970 Bp Frederick P Goddard P 6/24/1971 Bp J Milton Richardson. m 6/23/1961 Melynda Ann Ricketts c 3. R S Alb's Epis Ch Wickenburg AZ 2000-2005; R Gr Ch Morganton NC 1992-2000; R S Mk's Epis Ch Abilene TX 1982-1991; Vic S Steph's Epis Ch Jacksonville AR 1980-1982; Vic All SS Farmington NM 1980; Assoc S Mk's Epis Ch Little Rock AR 1976-1980; Vic Trin Ch Jacksonville TX 1975-1976; P-in-c St Jas Ch Mcgregor TX 1971-1974; R S Lk's Epis Ch Belton TX 1970-1973. Alumi Assn, Epis TS of the Southw 1970; CHS 1978; Ord of S Ben 1985. cmchatham1@msn.com

CHATTIN, Lloyd Gage (NJ) 13 Perdicaris Pl, Trenton NJ 08618 **Died 10/12/2010** B Philadelphia PA 8/16/1925 s Haney Lloyd Chattin & Alice Violet. BA Rutgers-The St U 1950; ThB PDS 1953; ThM PDS 1957. D 4/25/1953 Bp Alfred L Banyard P 10/1/1953 Bp Wallace J Gardner. c 4. Pres Angl Soc. Hon Vp Sci Philadelphia PA.

CHATTIN, Mark Haney (NJ) 839 Haddon Ave., Collingswood NJ 08108 **GC--Alt Dep Dio New Jersey Trenton NJ 2008-; Dn--Camden Convcation Dio New Jersey Trenton NJ 2007-; R H Trin Ch Collingswood NJ 1998-** B Philadelphia PA 4/19/1953 s Lloyd Gage Chattin & Mary Louise. BA Glassboro St U 1975; MDiv SWTS 1978. D 6/3/1978 P 12/16/1978 Bp Albert Wiencke Van Duzer. m 6/15/1974 Theresa H Chattin c 3. GC--Alt Dep Dio New Jersey Trenton NJ 2008; Stndg Com Dio New Jersey Trenton NJ 2005-2008; Vic S Fran Ch Dunellen NJ 1980-1998; Vic St Andrews Ch Plainfield NJ 1978-1980; Cur H Cross Epis Ch No Plainfield NJ 1978-1979. OHC, Angl Soc. revmhc@verizon.net

CHAVEZ, Karen Sue (Los) 3160 Graceland Way, Corona CA 92882 B Pheonix AZ 5/22/1948 d William Kleinz & Eula. MDiv ETS At Claremont CA; BS U Of Souther California Los Angeles CA 1982. D 12/2/2006 Bp Joseph Jon Bruno. m 7/3/1994 Louis Chavez c 3. loucuz@sbcglobal.net

CHAVEZ, Velma (Wyo) 29 Shipton Lane, Fort Washakie WY 82514 **D Shoshone Epis Mssn Ft Washakie WY 1999-** B Fort Washakie WY 5/5/1930 d Wallace Saint Clair & Winnie. D 8/28/2001 Bp Bruce Edward Caldwell.

CHAVEZ-CHACON, Rafael (Hond) C/O Igelsia Episcopal, PO Box 523900, Miami FL 33152 **Dio Honduras Miami FL 1998-** B 2/17/1941 m 8/13/1993 Eufemia Lopez De Chavez.

CHAVEZ FRANCO, Juan Eloy (EcuL) Iglesia Episcopal del Ecuador-Diocesis Litoral, Amarilis Fuente 603, Guayaquil Ecuador Ecuador **D Litoral Dio Ecuador Guayaquil EQ EC 2008-** B Montecristi 6/24/1960 s Fernando Chavez Ronda & Angela Franco. D 4/13/2008 Bp Alfredo Morante-España. m 8/15/2007 Rosario U Serrano Castro c 3.

CHECO, Antonio (LI) 2510 30th Rd Apt 2L, Astoria NY 11102 **D S Mk's Ch Jackson Heights NY 2007-** B Dominican Republic 5/6/1952 s Ramon Checo & Dolores. MDiv GTS; ScD Docmm 1981; MS Ford 1991. D 1/18/2007 P 4/25/2008 Bp Orris George Walker Jr. acheco@nyc.rr.com

CHEE, David Tsu Hian (Los) 700 Devils Drop Ct, El Sobrante CA 94803 B Singapore 5/19/1948 s Siew Kee Chee & Swee. BA Natl Taiwan U 1971; MA Natl Taiwan U 1973; Taipei Theol Coll Tw 1974; CDSP 1980; DMin PSR 1983. D 8/24/1975 P 6/11/1977 Bp James T M Pong. m 1/25/1975 Amy Bih Chee c 3. R S Gabr's Par Monterey Pk CA 1999-2005; Dio Los Angeles Los Angeles CA 1998-1999; Chr Epis Ch Los Altos CA 1995-1998; Chinese Mssnr Dio California San Francisco CA 1993-1998; Dio California San Francisco CA 1993-1994. Auth, "Epistemology Of Tao"; Auth, "Turning To God In Taiwan: A Study Of Conversion". Hsutze8@hotmail.com

CHEEK, Alison Mary (Mass) Po Box 356, Tenants Harbor ME 04860 B Adelaide South Australia AU 4/11/1927 d Hedley Noel Western & Dora Annie. BA U Of Adelaide Au 1947; MDiv VTS 1969; DMin EDS 1990. D 1/29/1972 Bp Robert Bruce Hall P 7/29/1974 Bp Edward Randolph Welles II. m 5/8/1948 Bruce M Cheek. Fac; Dir Stds In Feminist Liberation Theol EDS Cambridge MA 1989-1995; Assoc Trin Meml Ch Philadelphia PA 1980-1982; Asst Ch Of S Steph And The Incarn Washington DC 1975-1979; Asst D S Alb's Epis Ch Annandale VA 1972-1974; Asst Chr Ch Alexandria VA 1969-1971. Auth, "Journ Of Pstr Psych"; Auth, "Time"; Auth, "Shifting The Paradigm: Feminist Bible Study," *Searching Scripture: Feminist Intro*. CHS, EWHP; Greenfire Retreat Cntr For Wmn. Paradigm Shift Awd - Courage, Faith/Change Gndr Priesthood 1999; Scarlett Awd - Courag'S Contrib'N To Life Of Ch 1994; Cover Article Time mag 1976; Mnstry To Wmn 1975. acheek@midcoast.com

CHEESMAN JR, Benbow Palmer (Mil) 2501 S 60th St, Milwaukee WI 53219 B Charlottesville VA 12/17/1942 s Benbow Palmer Cheesman & Lucile. Mia 1963; BA Morris Harvey Coll 1964; M.Div. GTS 1967; JD U of Wisconsin 1986. D 6/12/1967 P 12/20/1967 Bp Wilburn Camrock Campbell. m 5/17/1969 Gail Evernden. Eccl Crt Dio Milwaukee Milwaukee WI 2005-2011; S

C

Paul's Epis Ch Beloit WI 2003; Cur S Mk's Ch Milwaukee WI 1973-1975; Asst Gr Ch Madison WI 1971-1973; S Chad's Ch Sun Prairie WI 1971-1973; Dio W Virginia Charleston WV 1967-1971; Vic S Jas Ch Charleston WV 1967-1971. Auth, "Plain Lang Legal Guide To Helping Elderly Clients," *Plain Lang Legal Guide*, Cntr for Publ Representation, 1985. Cmnty Of S Mary 1971. BENBOWCHEESMAN@HOTMAIL.COM

CHEN, Charles Chin-Ti (Tai) 23 Wu-Chuan West Road, 403, Taichung Taiwan B Matou TW 12/10/1935 s Lau-Kuai Chen & Li. MDiv Tainan Theol Coll Taipei Tw 1969; DMin STUSo 1993. D 6/29/1969 Bp James Chang L Wong P 6/1/1970 Bp Charles P Gilson. m 1/8/1959 Mary Jo Chang. Auth, "Morning Star"; Auth, "Resurr & Eternal Life"; Auth, "Introducing Chrsnty Tp Non-Chr In Tai". CHARLESCTCHEN@YAHOO.COM

CHEN, Luke H H (Tai) No 67 Lane 314 Ming Shen Rd, Shin Hua County, Tainan Hsien 71246 Taiwan B Taiwan 11/21/1940 s Tin-lu Chen & Chin. BPHARM Kaohsiung Med U 1965; MDiv Tainan TS Tw 1983. D 7/25/1979 Bp James T M Pong P 7/1/1983 Bp Pui-Yeung Cheung. m 5/20/1967 Su-yuan Lin c 3. Paul2000@ms7.hinet.net

CHEN, Samuel Ta-Tung (Tai) 7 Lane 105, South Hangchow R, Taipei Taiwan B 6/11/1924 s Sung-lu Chen & Pei-lan. Oxf; BD Tainan Theol Coll Tw 1964. D 9/19/1962 Bp Harry S Kennedy P 9/1/1963 Bp Charles P Gilson. m 11/1/1965 Hsiow-hwa Chen c 3. Auth, "Hist Of 1st 20 Years Of Tai Epis Ch".

CHENEY III, A(rthur) Milton (WMass) 38 Barnes Ln, West Greenwich RI 02817 B Worcester MA 10/5/1936 s Arthur Milton Cheney & Helen. BA Hob 1958; LTh Ya Berk 1961; MA Providence Coll 1996. D 6/20/1961 P 12/23/1961 Bp Robert McConnell Hatch. m 4/19/1986 Lois B Obrien c 3. Dio Wstrn Massachusetts Springfield MA 1996-2003; R S Jn's Ch Athol MA 1996-2003; R S Mary's Ch Warwick RI 1975-1996; Asst Chr Ch Fitchburg MA 1967-1975; Vic S Jn's Ch Millville MA 1961-1967. GAS 2011; NOEL 1975; New Engl CCU 1961-2010. mcheney2@cox.net

CHENEY, Barbara June (Ct) 90 Rogers Rd, Hamden CT 06517 B Fort Lauderdale FL 3/17/1943 d Robert Kollock Thomas & June Marie. BA Connecticut Coll 1963; MDiv VTS 1980; DMin SWTS 2000. D 6/2/1980 Bp Frederick Barton Wolf P 12/27/1980 Bp H Coleman McGehee Jr. m 9/26/1981 Knight Dexter Cheney c 2. Bd Pres VTS Alexandria VA 1998-1999; Stndg Com Dio Connecticut Hartford CT 1997-2002; R S Paul And S Jas New Haven CT 1993-2010; Dio Michigan Detroit MI 1992-1993; S Gabr's Epis Ch Eastpointe MI 1985-1993; Long Range Plnng Com Dio Michigan Detroit MI 1985-1986; Bd Exam Liturgists Dio Michigan Detroit MI 1981-1988; Asst S Jn's Ch Royal Oak MI 1980-1985. Auth, "H Baptism: A Rite for the Reconstituting of Sacr Commun,OPEN," AP, 2003. Ecam Dio Michigan 1989-1990; Soc of Comp of the H Cross 2001. Hon Cn Chr Ch Cathd Hartford CT 2010; Hon Cn Chr Ch Cathd Hartford CT 2010. bjtcheney@snet.net

CHENEY SR, Bruce David (Miss) 8320 Highway 178, Olive Branch MS 38654 **Vic H Cross Epis Ch Olive Branch MS 2006-** B Manchester NH 6/17/1960 s George Cheney & Claire. BS New Sch U 1986; MPS Loyola U 2000; MDiv VTS 2006. D 6/24/2006 P 2/7/2007 Bp Peter James Lee. m 2/17/1979 Nancy S Cheney c 2. holycrossrev@yahoo.com

CHENEY, Knight Dexter (Ct) 90 Rogers Rd, Hamden CT 06517 B Cleveland OH 10/5/1941 s Thomas Langdon Cheney & Anne. BBA Nichols Coll 1964; MBA U of Oregon 1969; MDiv EDS 1980. D 6/14/1980 Bp David Henry Lewis Jr P 1/1/1981 Bp H Coleman McGehee Jr. m 9/26/1981 Barbara June Thomas. Dio Connecticut Hartford CT 2006; Ch Of S Jn By The Sea W Haven W Haven CT 2005-2006; Ch of the H Sprt W Haven CT 2005-2006; All SS' Epis Ch E Hartford CT 2002-2008; Grtr Hartford Reg Mnstry E Hartford CT 2002-2004; S Mk's Chap Storrs CT 2001-2002; Int S Mich's Ch Naugatuck CT 2000-2001; S Geo's Ch Middlebury CT 1998-2000; Middlesex Area Cluster Mnstry Higganum CT 1998; St Gabr's Ch E Berlin CT 1997; Interfaith Coop Mnstrs New Haven CT 1994-1996; All SS Ch Ivoryton CT 1993-1995; Admin Dio Michigan Detroit MI 1985-1993; S Columba Ch Detroit MI 1980-1985. Auth, *Checkpoint*. Testimonial Resolution & Sprt of Detroit Awd Detroit City Coun. kdcheney@snet.net

CHENEY, Michael Robert (Mass) 117 Forest St, Malden MA 02148 B New Haven CT 4/11/1960 s Milton Cheney & Leanne. BA Hob 1982; MDiv GTS 1992. D 6/13/1992 P 12/19/1992 Bp Andrew Frederick Wissemann. m 5/1/1999 Dana L Neptune. R S Paul's Ch Malden MA 1996-2000; Assoc Ch Of The Nativ Northborough MA 1992-1996; Dio Wstrn Massachusetts Springfield MA 1992-1996; Chair Yth Com Dio Wstrn Massachusetts Springfield MA 1984-1986; Ecum Yth Min Trin Epis Ch Ware MA 1983-1985. Fllshp Of The Way Of The Cross. stpaulsparish@aol.com

CHENEY, Peter Gunn (Az) 6800 E Pico Del Monte, Tucson AZ 85750 **Chapl S Ann's Ch Kennebunkport ME 2002-** B Worcester MA 9/17/1947 s Francis Xavier Cheney & Winona Ann. BA Transylvania U 1969; MDiv VTS 1975; DD STUSo 2003. D 6/11/1975 P 3/25/1976 Bp Lloyd Edward Gressle. Natl Assoc Of Epis Schools- Epis Ch New York NY 1998-2007; Assoc S Phil's In The Hills Tucson AZ 1993-1998; Int S Andr's Epis Ch Hopkinton NH 1984-1987; S Paul's Sch Concord NH 1983-1992; R S Geo's Epis Ch Hellertown PA 1977-1983; Asst Ch Of The Gd Shpd And S Jn Milford PA 1975-1977; Asst Gr Epis Ch Port Jervis NY 1975-1977. Auth, "Three Truths of the Sprtl Life," *NAES Pamphlet*, 2002; Auth, "Schools and Parents: Partnr in Lrng and Dvlpmt," *NAES Pamphlet*, 2000; Auth, "Gd Schools," *Ntwk*, 2000; Auth, "The Epis Sch Trst as Ambassador," *Ntwk*, 2000; Auth, "Ldrshp," *Educational Directions*, 1999. Amer Associations of Pstr Counselors, Clincl Mem 1982. pgcheney@aol.com

CHENEY II, Reynolds Smith (WTenn) 60 Eastland Dr, Memphis TN 38111 **Cn Chapl to Cler Families and Ret Cler Dio W Tennessee Memphis TN 2007-** B Jackson MS 7/19/1936 s Reynolds Smith Cheney & Winifred. BA Millsaps Coll 1957; U of Pennsylvania 1960; BD EDS 1961. D 6/16/1961 Bp Duncan Montgomery Gray P 12/1/1961 Bp John M Allin. m 11/26/1999 Stephanie Cheney c 3. S Mary's Cathd Memphis TN 2002; Ch Of The H Comm Memphis TN 1981-2002; R S Jas Ch Greenville MS 1968-1981; Vic Ch Of The Redeem Greenville MS 1968-1971; R S Jn's Ch Aberdeen MS 1963-1968; D Gr Ch Carrollton MS 1961-1963; D S Mary's Ch Lexington MS 1961-1963; D S Matt's Epis Ch Kosciusko MS 1961-1963. scheney@episwtn.org

CHENG, Ching-Shan (Tai) 40 Ta Tung Rd, Wu Feng, Taichung County 852 Taiwan **Dio Taiwan Taipei TW TW 2007-** B Tainan Taiwan 2/5/1953 s Kao Cheng & Bi-Yun. MDiv Tainan Theol Coll And Sem; BA Taiwan Normal U. D 3/31/2007 P 3/29/2008 Bp Jung-Hsin Lai. m 12/19/1977 Kuo-Li Chi c 2.

CHENOWETH JR, Russell M (NJ) 410 Crest Rd, Oreland PA 19075 B Saint Louis MO 8/7/1935 s Russell M Chenoweth & Evelyn. BA Rutgers-The St U 1957; STB PDS 1963; MLS Rutgers-The St U 1965. D 4/27/1963 P 11/1/1963 Bp Alfred L Banyard. m 6/6/1964 Nancy P Coates c 1. Asst Gr Epis Ch Plainfield NJ 1963-1964. Auth, "Shadow Walkers".

CHERBONNEAU, Allen Robert (Ala) 4367 East River Road, Box 282, Mentone AL 35984 B Springfield MA 7/26/1944 s Vincent E Cherbonneau & Rita A. BA U of Massachusetts 1967; MDiv TESM 1995. D 11/22/1995 P 5/1/1996 Bp Keith Lynn Ackerman. m 6/23/1973 Jan Cynthia Barket. R S Jos's On-The-Mtn Mentone AL 1996-2000. revallen@peop.tdsnet.com

CHERBONNIER, Edmond La Beaume (Mo) 843 Prospect Ave, Hartford CT 06105 B Saint Louis MO 2/11/1918 s Edward Goodwin Cherbonnier & Adelaide Alice. BA Harv 1939; BD UTS 1947; BA U of Cambridge 1948; PhD Col 1951; DD U of Vermont 1959. D 5/28/1947 Bp William Scarlett. m 10/14/1943 Phyllis White c 1. D Dio Connecticut Hartford CT 1947-1990; D Dio New York New York City NY 1947-1990. Auth, "Hardness Of Heart".

CHERISME, Charles Mitilien (Hai) 472 Beech St, Roslindale MA 02131 **Assoc Ch Of The H Sprt Mattapan MA 1989-** B 5/8/1936 s Mertilus Cherisme & Derina. Coll Of S Pierre Ht 1962; ETSC 1966. D 12/4/1965 P 6/1/1966 Bp Charles Alfred Voegeli. m 12/7/1967 Marie J Dubuisson c 4. Dio Haiti Ft Lauderdale FL 1965-1990. Ord Of S Marg 1968. CHARLESSENIOR2005@YAHOO.COM

CHERISOL, Burnet (Hai) Chemin Des Dalles #76, Port-Au-Prince BP 365 Haiti B 12/30/1952 s Cherisol Bolivar & Gericia. BA Sem Of Our Lady; U Javeriana CO. Rec from Roman Catholic 5/1/1994 as Priest Bp Jean Zache Duracin. m 8/26/1993 Marie Yolene Marseille. Dio Haiti Ft Lauderdale FL 1993-1996. bcherisol@hotmail.com

CHERRY, Charles Shuler (Minn) 734 7th St S, Breckenridge MN 56520 B Durham NC 7/13/1934 s Albert Ludwig Cherry & Tommie Cleo. BA Wake Forest U 1956; STB GTS 1967; MA Spalding Coll 1973; MA No Dakota St U 1993. D 10/14/1967 P 11/1/1968 Bp Charles Gresham Marmion. m 5/29/1993 Shirley Hunkins c 2. S Jn's Ch Moorhead MN 1995-1998; P-in-c S Jn's Ch Moorhead MN 1991-1995; R Trin Ch Wahpeton ND 1985-1988; R S Jas' Epis Ch Fergus Falls MN 1985-1987; R St Georges Epis Ch Asheville NC 1979-1985; Vic S Mart's-In-The-Fields Mayfield KY 1978-1979; Vic S Ptr's of the Lakes Gilbertsville KY 1978-1979; R Ch Of Our Merc Sav Louisville KY 1972-1977.

CHERRY, Jacqueline A (Cal) 1076 De Haro St, San Francisco CA 94107 **D Beekeeper The Epis Ch Of S Jn The Evang San Francisco CA 2009-** B San Diego CA 2/21/1961 d William Robert Cherry & Mary Jane. BA U CA Santa Cruz 1983; RN San Francisco St U 2000; BA Epis Sch for Deacons, Berkeley 2008. D 6/6/2009 Bp Marc Handley Andrus. m 10/23/2008 Elizabeth Freeman c 1. jaccherry@yahoo.com

CHERRY, Mary Jane (Ky) 425 S 2nd St Ste 200, Louisville KY 40202 **Cmncatn Dir Dio Kentucky Louisville KY 2010-** B Louisville KY 9/22/1951 d Lee Allen Busroe & Mary Norine. BA U of Kentucky 1978; MA U of Louisville 1996. D 4/17/2010 Bp Edwin Funsten Gulick Jr. m 8/12/1978 Stephen Cherry. Dio Kentucky Louisville KY 2005-2010. maryjane@episcopalky.org

CHERRY, Timothy B (Dal) 56 Cedar Ln, Osterville MA 02655 **R Ch Of The Apos Coppell TX 2009-** B Portsmouth VA 12/4/1965 s Aaron T Cherry & Kay. BS USNA 1988; MDiv VTS 1997. D 6/14/1997 Bp Peter James Lee P 3/13/1998 Bp Frank Clayton Matthews. m 11/25/1989 Jennifer L Cherry c 3. Ch Of The H Cross Paris TX 2007-2009; R S Ptr's Ch Osterville MA 2000-2007; Cur Chr Ch St Michaels MD 1997-2000. Mdiv cl VTS Alexandria VA 1997. revtcherry@juno.com

CHESHIRE, G(rady) Patterson (WNC) 1131 S Edgemont Ave, Gastonia NC 28054 B Charlotte NC 9/22/1950 s John Allyn Cheshire & Phyllis. BA Erskine

Coll 1972. D 12/21/1996 Bp Robert Hodges Johnson. m 10/13/1984 Kathy Ann Bailey. D All SS' Epis Ch Gastonia NC 1996-2005. baileycheshire@aol.com

CHESS, Jean Dawson (Pgh) 1012 Murrayhill Ave, Pittsburgh PA 15217 **Archd Dio Pittsburgh Monroeville PA 2009-; D St Andrews Epis Ch Pittsburgh PA 2001-** B Pittsburgh PA 8/4/1958 d James Chess & Nolly. BS Denison U 1980; MS Carnegie Mellon U 1988. D 6/10/2000 Bp Robert William Duncan. D Calv Ch Pittsburgh PA 2000-2002. deacon@standrewspgh.org

CHESTERMAN JR, Thomas Charles (DR) 2418 Hidden Valley Dr, Santa Rosa CA 95404 B San Francisco CA 8/14/1931 s Charles T Chesterman & Helen. ABS Harv 1953; AB Harv 1953; MDiv EDS 1956; PhD Toledo E. P. ES 1978. D 7/1/1956 P 1/26/1957 Bp Karl M Block. c 3. Exec Coun Appointees New York NY 1989-1992; R Iglesia Epis Epifania Santo Domingo Di DO 1989-1992; Assoc Trin Epis Ch Reno NV 1981-1989; Chapl S Jn's Mltry Sch Salina KS 1978-1979; R Ch Of The Gd Shpd Silver City NM 1975-1977; Int S Cyp's Ch San Francisco CA 1975; Vic S Chris's Ch San Lorenzo CA 1966-1975; Mssn Vic True Sunshine Par San Francisco CA 1960-1966; R S Barn Ch Arroyo Grande CA 1959-1960; Vic S Edm's Epis Ch Pacifica CA 1956-1959. Auth, "Records of Fest Celebration," *(Translation)*, La Hermandad Mozarabica, 1977. NNECA 1966-1975; Wstrn Par Trng Prog Supvsr 1963-1973. Vic Emer True Sunshine Ch, San Francisco 2005. taslsc@smic.net

CHEVES, Henry Middleton (SC) 635 Foredeck Lane, Edisto Island SC 29438 B La Jolla CA 12/18/1944 s Henry Charles Cheves & Chilton. BS U of So Carolina 1967; MBA Cit 1976; MDiv STUSo 1992. D 5/30/1992 P 11/30/1992 Bp John Clark Buchanan. m 7/27/1984 Susan Bussey c 4. Assoc R Trin Ch Edisto Island SC 2003-2009; R S Paul's Ch Bennettsville SC 2000-2003; Vic S Paul's Epis Ch Lees Summit MO 1996-2000; Vic Trin Epis Ch Lebanon MO 1992-1996. frhmc@aol.com

CHICHESTER IV, Helon Lewis (Cal) PO Box 524, Tahoma CA 96142 B Macon GA 10/29/1929 s Helon Lewis Chichester & Jeanette. BS U GA 1951; BD CDSP 1962; MA U CA 1968; PhD U CA 1975. D 6/30/1962 P 7/25/1963 Bp Randolph R Claiborne. m 7/23/1993 Sara Maria Kristina Hauge c 4. S Pat's Epis Ch Oakland CA 1983-1984; S Anne's Ch Fremont CA 1982; S Cuth's Epis Ch Oakland CA 1981; Serv S Jn's Epis Ch Oakland CA 1978-1981; LocTen All Souls Par In Berkeley Berkeley CA 1969-1970; Instr CDSP Berkeley CA 1966-1970; Asst All SS Par Beverly Hills CA 1965-1966; D S Jas Ch Cedartown GA 1962-1963. Auth, *Study Guides*. chichesterherelon@hotmail

✠ CHIEN, Rt Rev John Chih-Tsung (Tai) 70-1 Goubei Village, Dalin Township, Chiayi County 62245 Taiwan B Chiayi TW 3/23/1940 s Ching-Mu Chien & Yu-Li. BA Tunghai U TW 1963; BD Tainan TS TW 1967; STM VTS 1974; Selly Oak Coll Birmingham GB 1985; EDS 2002. D 5/21/1967 P 11/1/1967 Bp James Chang L Wong Con 3/25/1988 for Tai. m 3/29/1967 Hui-Nu Chiu c 3. "Ten Years' Memoir," Taiwan Epis Ch; "Dimensions of Chr Living," Taiwan Epis Ch. Distinguished Alum Chia-yi Sr HS 1999; Hon Doctorate VTS 1998. jhnchien@yahoo.com.tw

CHILD, Kendrick H (Mass) Po Box 2085, New London NH 03257 B Brockton MA 5/4/1943 s Ralph Warren Child & Lois. BA Bates Coll 1965; BD Yale DS 1965; DMin Bos 1990. D 6/21/1969 Bp Anson Phelps Stokes Jr P 12/21/1969 Bp Frederick Barton Wolf. m 8/23/1987 Pamela Thompson c 2. S Aug's Ch Lawr MA 2005-2006; Assoc The Cathd Ch Of S Paul Boston MA 1993-1996; Asst S Paul's Ch Malden MA 1989-1993; Ch Of The Trsfg Derry NH 1982-1987; R S Matt's Epis Ch Lisbon ME 1970-1982; Cur Trin Epis Ch Portland ME 1969-1970. Auth, "Don't Be Afraid To Say A Gd Word for Jesus," *Sem Dvlpmt News*, 1997; Auth, "One Among Many: Sem Dvlpmt in a U Setting," *Sem Dvlpmt News*, 1992.

CHILDERS, Robert T J (ETenn) Church of the Good Shepherd, P.O. Box 145, Lookout Mountain TN 37350 **R Ch Of The Gd Shpd Lookout Mtn TN 2008-; COM Dio Alabama Birmingham AL 2002-** B Selma AL 10/14/1954 s Benjamin Meek Miller Childers & Hallie Milhous. BA Van 1978; JD U of Alabama 1981; MDiv GTS 1991. D 6/18/1991 P 12/21/1991 Bp Robert Oran Miller. m 10/28/1981 Teresa Kahlmus c 2. R Gr Ch Anniston AL 1995-2008; Dioc Coun Dio Alabama Birmingham AL 1995-1998; R S Jos's On-The-Mtn Mentone AL 1993-1995; Cur Chr Ch Tuscaloosa AL 1991-1993. robert@goodshepherdlookout.com

CHILDRESS JR, John Robinson (Ark) 10702 Crestdale Ln, Little Rock AR 72212 **Epis Collgt Sch Little Rock AR 2004-** B Canton MS 12/7/1952 s John Robinson Childress & Virginia Duvall. BS Mississippi St U 1974; MDiv SWTS 1989. D 6/3/1989 P 12/21/1989 Bp Duncan Montgomery Gray Jr. m 8/11/1978 Pamela DeGraw c 2. R S Paul's Newport AR 1996-2004; R S Paul's Ch Abbeville LA 1995-1996; Vic S Fran Of Assisi Ch Philadelphia MS 1989-1995; Vic S Matt's Epis Ch Kosciusko MS 1989-1995. nptepis@ipa.net

CHILDS, Henry Clarence (Okla) No address on file. **Died 7/16/2010** B Tulsa OK 8/2/1926 s Vernon Stanton Childs & Flavia. U Denv 1948; BA Oklahoma City U 1968; MDiv/STB GTS 1970. D 2/4/1968 P 10/1/1968 Bp Chilton Powell. c 2. Hon Cn Amer Cathd Paris France.

CHILES, Robert Lee (USC) The Reverend Robert L Chiles, 303 Brook Hollow Drive, Columbia SC 29223 **Assoc Chr Ch Greenville SC 2011-; COM Dio Upper So Carolina Columbia SC 2008-; Sch for Mnstry Com Dio Upper So Carolina Columbia SC 2003-** B Greenville SC 4/7/1952 s Jack Moore Chiles & Margaret Lee. BA Furman U 1974; MDiv SWTS 1990. D 6/9/1990 P 5/16/1991 Bp William Arthur Beckham. m 5/3/1975 Christine Rose Zimmerman c 2. R S Dav's Epis Ch Columbia SC 1996-2011; COM Dio Nthrn Indiana So Bend IN 1993-1995; S Jn The Evang Ch Elkhart IN 1991-1996; Asst S Barth's Ch No Augusta SC 1990-1991. BA cl Furman U Greenville SC 1974. frchiles@aol.com

CHILLINGTON, Joseph Henry (Ind) 215 N 7th Street, Terre Haute IN 47807 **Stndg Com Dio Indianapolis Indianapolis IN 2008-; Invstmt & Fin Com Dio Indianapolis Indianapolis IN 2001-; R S Steph's Ch Terre Haute IN 1993-** B Whittier CA 12/12/1947 s Joseph Henry Chillington & Edwardine. BA Occ 1970; DIC Imperial Coll London GB 1972; MS Lon 1972; MDiv VTS 1984. D 6/9/1984 P 1/6/1985 Bp Arthur Edward Walmsley. m 6/4/1983 Robin Eatherly c 1. Const & Cn Dio Indianapolis Indianapolis IN 2000-2011; COM Dio Indianapolis Indianapolis IN 1998-2001; COM Dio Indianapolis Indianapolis IN 1993-1996; Int All SS Epis Ch Meriden CT 1993; Int S Jn's Epis Ch Essex CT 1992-1993; Evang Com Dio Connecticut Hartford CT 1989-1991; St Gabr's Ch E Berlin CT 1984-1991; Cur Gr Ch Newington CT 1984-1986. jchillin@ma.rr.com

CHILTON, Bruce (NY) Bard College, Annandale-on-Hudson NY 12504 **Bard Coll Annandale On Hudson NY 2008-; R Ch Of S Jn The Evang Red Hook NY 1987-** B Roslyn NY 9/27/1949 s Bruce David Chilton & Virginia Marie. BA Bard Coll 1971; MDiv GTS 1974; PhD Camb 1976. Trans from Church Of England 6/29/1975 Bp WILLIAN F Wall Jr. m 7/3/1982 Odile Sevault Chilton c 2. Auth, *Rabbi Jesus*, Doubleday, 2000; Auth, *Galilean Rabbi & His Bible*; Auth, *Jesus & the Ethics of the Kingdom*; Auth, *Jesus' Pryr & Jesus' Euch*; Auth, *Profiles of A Rabbi*; Auth, *Pure Kingdom: Jesus' Vision of God*; Auth, *Targumic Approaches to the Gospels*; Auth, *The Isaiah Targum*. Inst for Biblic Resrch; Inst of Advncd Theol; SBL; Studiorum Novi Testamenti Societas. chilton@bard.edu

CHILTON, Frank Eugene (Fla) 107 Golf Course Ln, Crescent City FL 32112 B Dayton OH 8/12/1925 s Alfred Henry Chilton & Lestie. D 5/28/1997 P 12/1/1997 Bp Stephen Hays Jecko. m 10/14/1950 Martha Lucille Brown. Asst S Mk's Ch Palatka FL 2000-2002; Vic Emm Ch Welaka FL 1997-2000. revfrank@gbso.net

CHILTON, Mary Habel (Alb) 3 Woods Edge Ln, West Sand Lake NY 12196 B Newport News VA 8/22/1941 d John Woodrow Habel & Margaret Hudgins. BA Utica Coll 1975; MA SUNY 1977; EdD Syr 1991; MDiv GTS 1995. D 2/25/1995 Bp David B(ruce) Joslin P 12/1/1997 Bp Robert William Duncan. m 7/1/1962 R Hunter Chilton. Cn to the Ordnry Dio Albany Albany NY 1999-2002; S Andr's Ch Scotia NY 1999-2000; Supply P Dio Pittsburgh Monroeville PA 1998-1999; Int TESM Ambridge PA 1997-1998; Asst Trin Epis Ch Beaver PA 1995-1997. Auth, *Our Mssy God: Perspectives in Wrld Missions*, Trin Epis Sem, 1997. mchilton@nycap.rr.com

CHILTON, William Parish (Eas) 214 Wye Ave, Easton MD 21601 B Birmingham AL 9/8/1939 s John Irby Chilton & Virginia. BA Ya 1961; BD VTS 1966. D 6/18/1966 Bp Charles C J Carpenter P 6/10/1967 Bp George Mosley Murray. m 6/5/1965 Kathleen Boissevain c 2. Dio Easton Easton MD 1981-1994; R S Lukes Ch Ch Hill MD 1979-2005; Dio Alabama Birmingham AL 1977; Grtr Birmingham Mnstrs Birmingham AL 1975-1979; Nicaragua-El Salvador New York NY 1975-1977; S Jas' Ch Livingston AL 1968-1970; Assoc Cbury Chap and Coll Cntr Tuscaloosa AL 1966-1970. Hon Cn, Trin Cathd Dio Easton 2005. chiltonk@verizon.net

CHIN, Mary Louise (LI) Po Box 650397, Fresh Meadows NY 11365 B Jamaica NY 11/9/1946 d John Francis Grecky & Eleanor Mary. Cert Mercer TS 1986; MS Adams St Coll 1992; Advncd Inst for Analytic Psych Jamaica NY 1997. D 12/15/1986 Bp Robert Campbell Witcher Sr. m 9/10/1972 Philip Chin. Asst S Ptr's by-the-Sea Epis Ch Bay Shore NY 1999-2001; Asst S Marg's Ch Plainview NY 1986-1994; S Johns Epis Hosp Far Rockaway NY 1986-1991.

CHINERY, Edwin Thomas (NJ) 165 Essex Ave Apt 102, Metuchen NJ 08840 **Gr Epis Ch Plainfield NJ 2010-; S Mk's Epis Ch Keansburg NJ 2010-** B Plainfield NJ 7/9/1957 s Edwin Thomas Chinery & Helen Gloria. BA Thos Edison St Coll 2007; MDiv The GTS 2010. D 11/14/2009 P 6/19/2010 Bp George Edward Councell. edwinchinery@yahoo.com

CHING, Winston Wyman (Cal) 754 E 6th St Apt 6B, New York NY 10009 **Assoc Ch Of The Gd Shpd New York NY 1993-** B Honolulu HI 6/23/1943 s Carl Lin Kau Ching & Ellen Kam Chin. BA U of Hawaii 1965; MDiv CDSP 1968; PSR 1973; DD CDSP 1991; NYTS 1996. D 5/10/1968 Bp Edwin Lani Hanchett P 12/21/1968 Bp Harry S Kennedy. Int Ch Of The Gd Shpd New York NY 2008-2009; Dir, Congrl Mnstrs Epis Ch Cntr New York NY 1994-2001; Pstr Consult Epis Ch Of Our Sav New York NY 1993-2003; Asiamerica Mnstry Off Epis Ch Cntr New York NY 1974-2002; Bp's Rep for Amer Indn Wk Dio California San Francisco CA 1971-1973; Vic The Epis Ch

Of S Jn The Evang San Francisco CA 1970-1974. DD CDSP Berkeley CA 1991. wching.ny@netzero.net

CHINLUND, Stephen James (NY) 445 W 19th St, New York NY 10011 B New York NY 12/23/1933 s Edwin F Chinlund & Helen Alice. BA Harv 1955; BD UTS 1958. D 6/14/1958 P 12/8/1958 Bp Benjamin M Washburn. m 12/24/1966 Caroline Cross c 3. Epis Soc Serv New York NY 1988-2004; R Trin Epis Ch Southport CT 1982-1988; Cur H Trin Epis Ch Inwood New York NY 1963-1966; Cur S Aug's Ch New York NY 1960-1963; Cur Gr Epis Ch New York NY 1958-1960. Auth, "Lrng by Going Inside," *Rel and Mntl Hlth*, 2003; Auth, *A Way to Measure Success in Rehab of Drug Addicts*; Auth, *Alt Pursuits for Amer's 3rd Century*; Auth, *Healing & Hell: The Contradiction*. stephenchinlund@yahoo.com

CHIPPS, Kathleen Dawn (Va) 9000 Belvoir Woods Pkwy Apt 208, Fort Belvoir VA 22060 **P-in-c S Marg's Ch Woodbridge VA 2007-** B Mansfield OH 6/20/1945 d Norman Clarance Madore & Mary Clara. BA GW 1968; MDiv VTS 1984; Cert Virginia Tech U 1994; Int Basic Trng 2000. D 7/25/1984 Bp Robert Bruce Hall P 10/26/1985 Bp Peter James Lee. m 1/5/2010 James Chipps. Int Chr Epis Ch Gordonsville VA 2003-2004; Int S Steph's Epis Ch Culpeper VA 2000-2001; Int Little Fork Epis Ch Rixeyville VA 1999-2000; Dio Washington Washington DC 1997-1998; Int S Barn' Epis Ch of The Deaf Chevy Chase MD 1997-1998; Assoc S Dav's Ch Ashburn VA 1995-1998; Trin Epis Ch Washington VA 1994; S Lk's Ch Remington VA 1992-1993; H Trin Mnstry Of The Deaf Richmond VA 1986-1992; Mssnr For The Deaf Olivet Epis Ch Franconia VA 1986-1992; DRE S Jn's Ch Chevy Chase MD 1984-1985. Auth, "A Litany Of Wholeness". kchipps@verizon.net

CHIRINOS-HERNANDEZ, Jose A (Hond) No address on file. **Dio Honduras Miami FL 2001-** B 9/2/1961

CHISHAM, Anne (SanD) 47568 Hawley Boulevard, San Diego CA 92116 B San Diego CA 8/12/1934 d John Richard Beardsley & Florence. ETSBH; BA Mills Coll 1955. D 12/19/1992 Bp Gethin Benwil Hughes. c 2. D All Souls' Epis Ch San Diego CA 1994-2007; Serv S Tim's Ch San Diego CA 1993-1994.

CHISHOLM, Alan Laird (NY) 209 S Broadway, Nyack NY 10960 B Washington DC 1/6/1937 s Robert Kerr Chisholm & Margaret Sale. BA Amh 1958; Drew U 1960; MDiv GTS 1961; Cert Blanton-Peale Grad Inst 1973; Cert Natl Assn for the Advancement of Psychoanalysis 1995. D 6/10/1961 Bp Horace W B Donegan P 12/14/1961 Bp Francis E I Bloy. m 2/3/1962 Linda Carol Armstrong c 3. Hon Assoc Gr Epis Ch Nyack NY 1981-2002; Supply Chr Ch Of Ramapo Suffern NY 1979-1980; Vic All SS Epis Ch Vlly Cottage NY 1970-1976; Diocn Msnry & Ch Extntn Socty New York NY 1970-1976; Dpt Of Missions Ny Income New York NY 1970-1976; R S Jn's Ch So Salem NY 1965-1970; Cur Chr Ch Bronxville NY 1962-1965; Cur S Jas Par Los Angeles CA 1961-1962. Cert Psychoanalyst NAAP 1995; Clincl Mem AAMFT 1975-2007; Diplomate AAPC 1973. alchisholm@verizon.net

CHITTENDEN, Nils Philip (NC) 200 W Morgan St Ste 300, Raleigh NC 27601 **Chapl, Epis Cntr at Duke Dio No Carolina Raleigh NC 2010-; Mssnr for YA Dio No Carolina Raleigh NC 2010-** B Folkestone England 4/15/1969 s John Chittenden & Kirsten. BA St Chad's Coll, U of Durham, UK 1991; CTM Westcott Hse, U of Cambridge, UK 1995; MA Northumbria U, Newcastle-upon-Tyne, UK 1999. Trans from Church Of England 3/28/2011 Bp Michael Bruce Curry. m 7/9/2010 Kelly D Skaggs. NILS. CHITTENDEN@DUKE.EDU

CHO, Francis Soonhwan (NJ) 16 Rodak Cir, Edison NJ 08817 **H Cross Perth Amboy NJ 1999-** B 11/18/1939 s Byung Ork Cho & Myung. Presb TS; S Mich's Angl Sem. D 4/1/1970 P 7/1/1970 Bp The Bishop Of Seoul. m 7/17/1972 Beatrice Yanniga Rim. Port Chapl Seamens Ch Inst Income New York NY 1985-2005. fathercho@aol.com

CHOATE JR, Horace (NY) 429 Violet Dr, Madison MS 39110 **The Ch Of S Jos Of Arimathea White Plains NY 2010-** B Macon GA 9/10/1950 s Horace Choate & Sally. BA U of Mississippi 1973; MDiv GTS 1998. D 7/2/1998 P 1/31/1999 Bp Alfred Clark Marble Jr. m 11/12/1988 Yamily Sierra c 2. R Zion Epis Ch Wappingers Falls NY 2005-2010; Assoc S Columb's Ch Ridgeland MS 2001-2005; Vic/P-in-c S Mary's Ch Lexington MS 1999-2001; Vic/P-in-c S Matt's Epis Ch Kosciusko MS 1999-2001; Ch Of S Mary The Vrgn New York NY 1998-1999; Media Spec Epis Ch Cntr New York NY 1998-1999. rectoratzion@verizon.net

CHOI, Beryl (WNY) 51 Virginia Pl, Buffalo NY 14202 **The Fork Ch Doswell VA 2003-** B 4/29/1926 d Alfred Turner & Nellie. BA S Chris's Coll Gb 1947; Wm Temple 1950; STh Lon 1952. D 10/19/1973 P 1/1/1977 Bp Robert Bracewell Appleyard. c 3. Asst P Trin Epis Ch Buffalo NY 1996-1998; Int Trin Epis Ch Fredonia NY 1995-1996; Int The Epis Ch Of The Gd Shpd Buffalo NY 1994-1995; Calv Epis Ch Williamsville NY 1986-1994; P Eductr The Par Ch Of S Lk Long Bch CA 1984-1986; Asst Min Calv Ch Pittsburgh PA 1976-1983; Ch Of The Ascen Pittsburgh PA 1974-1976. Wmn Of The Year In Rel Awd U Pgh Pittsburgh PA 1978; Archbp Of C'Bury Cmsn As Tchr Of Theol. berylchoi@msn.com

CHOI, Stephen Young Sai (NY) 5 77th St # 7047, North Bergen NJ 07047 B 5/23/1945 s In Boong Choi & Boo. BA U Of Korea Kr 1970; MA S Mich's Angl Sem 1974. Trans 7/1/1991 Bp Walter Decoster Dennis Jr. m 10/26/1974 Young Hee. Vic S Jn's Korean-Amer Ch New York NY 1992-1996. Auth, "Korea U Engl Nwspr".

✠ CHOI, Rt Rev William Chul-Hi (Los) 8105 232nd St Se, Woodinville WA 98072 B Um Song KR 4/26/1930 s Basil Kun Choi & Busilla. BA S Mich Seoul Kr 1954; ThL S Fran Coll Brisbane Au 1962; MA Rikkyo U Tokyo Jp 1972; Concordia TS 1974; CDSP 1984. Trans from Anglican Church Of Korea 12/10/1988 Bp Frederick Houk Borsch Con 1/1/1974 for Anglican Church Of Korea. m 7/16/1980 Catherine Misao Kagami. Dio Olympia Seattle WA 1991-2002; Sup Ch Of The H Apos Bellevue WA 1991-2000. Auth, "Future Of Martime Mssn In The Far Estrn Perspective," Intl Assn For Study Of Martime Missions., 2002; Auth, "Bridges Toward Effective Multicultural Mnstry, Pontifical Coun For The Pstr Care," *Rome In People On The Move.*, Vatican City, 1999; Auth, "A Survey Of Chr Growth," Korea Chr Pub., 1996; Auth, "Buddhism And It'S Influence In Korea," Intl Chr Martime Assn Paper, 1989.

CHOLAS, Gus (Colo) 339 Kapii Place, Hilo HI 96720 B Scofield UT 1/31/1924 s Steve Cholas & Genevieve Elizabeth. DVM Colorado St U 1952; MA U MN 1962; Cert Nash 1979. D 4/25/1981 Bp William Harvey Wolfrum P 4/1/1983 Bp William Carl Frey. S Lk's Epis Ch Ft Collins CO 1984-1994; D S Lk's Epis Ch Ft Collins CO 1981-1983. cscholas@hawaii.rr.com

CHOLLET, Mari (Mo) 232 South Woods Mill Rd., Chesterfield MO 63017 **S Lk's Hosp Chesterfield MO 2006-** B Curitiba Brazil 10/2/1971 d Jose Joaquim & Teresa. MDiv Equivalent Luth Fac of Theol - FLT (Brazil) 1993; Post Grad Study No Brazil Bapt TS 1996; Clincl Psychol Tuiuti U (Brazil) 2000; Supervisory CPE 2004. D 12/20/2006 P 6/29/2007 Bp George Wayne Smith. m 1/20/1996 Sidnei Chollet c 2. mari.chollet@stlukes-stl.com

CHORNYAK, Christopher John (Me) 3 Spring House Ln, Ellsworth ME 04605 **R S Dunst's Ch Ellsworth ME 1994-** B Boulder CO 7/28/1951 s John Chornyak & Dorothy May. BA U of Massachusetts 1973; MDiv Nash 1977. D 11/1/1977 P 12/1/1978 Bp Alexander Doig Stewart. m 11/26/1977 Joyce Ann Trepanier c 3. Int Chr Epis Ch Eastport ME 1988-1989; R S Anne's Ch Calais ME 1982-1994; Vic St Lukes Ch Woodland ME 1982-1987; S Paul's Ch Milwaukee WI 1980-1982; Cur Gr Ch Amherst MA 1977-1979. BA cl U of Massachusetts, Amherst Amherst MA 1973. cjchornyak@myfairpoint.net

CHOYCE, George (ETenn) 27 Cool Springs Rd, Signal Mountain TN 37377 **S Tim's Ch Signal Mtn TN 2002-** B 9/17/1963 Georgia Sthrn U; BA Georgia St U 1985; MDiv VTS 1992. D 6/20/1992 Bp John Wadsworth Howe P 1/30/1993 Bp Charles Farmer Duvall. m 8/3/1985 Anne Statham Choyce c 4. Gr Ch Newington CT 1997-2002; Calv Ch Pittsburgh PA 1994-1997; S Andr's Epis Ch Panama City FL 1992-1994; Trin Ch Vero Bch FL 1987-1989. gchoyce@sttimsignal.com

CHRISMAN JR, John Aubrey (RI) 7118 Treymore Ct, Sarasota FL 34243 **P in Res S Bon Ch Sarasota FL 2004-** B Charlotte NC 10/18/1933 s John Aubrey Chrisman & Alice White. No Carolina St U 1952; BS USNA 1958; Westcott Hse Cambridge,UK 1988. Trans from Church Of England 5/1/1991 Bp George Nelson Hunt III. m 9/19/1959 Donna Lee Rouse c 3. Assoc Emm Ch Newport RI 2002-2005; R S Geo's Ch Portsmouth RI 1991-2001. Fed of Fire Chapl 1993-2001. Fatherjack@comcast.net

CHRISMAN, Robert Edwin (Oly) 1214 184th Pl, Long Beach WA 98631 B Lindsay CA 12/21/1944 s Edwin Merrill Chrisman & Garnet May. BA Marylhurst U 1983; MDiv CDSP 1985. D 7/3/1985 P 1/1/1986 Bp Rustin Ray Kimsey. m 8/5/2005 Mary Etta Ewing c 4. Chr Ch Tacoma WA 2008-2010; Dio Oregon Portland OR 2005-2007; Int S Lk's Epis Ch Vancouver WA 2004-2005; S Jn's Ch Hermiston OR 2003-2004; R The Par Of S Mk The Evang Hood River OR 1996-2002; R S Jas Epis Ch Laconia NH 1989-1993; Vic Epis Ch Of The Trsfg Sis OR 1985-1989. bob@xman-wa.com

CHRISNER, Marlen Ronald (At) 2320 Nw 53rd Avenue Rd, Ocala FL 34482 B Jackson MI 1/19/1936 s Marlen Chrisner & Rosa. BS Wayne 1970; MDiv Ya Berk 1973. D 6/30/1973 P 10/31/1974 Bp H Coleman McGehee Jr. m 8/23/1958 Marcella A Shano c 3. R Gd Shpd Epis Ch Austell GA 1999-2000; H Innoc Ch Atlanta GA 1994-2001; H Innoc' Epis Sch Atlanta GA 1994-2001; R S Paul's Ch Sharpsburg MD 1993-1994; S Jas Sch St Jas MD 1991-1994; Jacksonville Epis HS Jacksonville FL 1985-1991; Asst P S Paul's Epis Ch Jacksonville FL 1985-1991; Queen Anne Sch Upper Marlboro MD 1976-1985; S Dunst's Epis Ch Davison MI 1973-1976. ronchrisner@gmail.com

CHRISTENSEN, Bonniejean (ND) 4001 Beneva Rd Apt 334, Sarasota FL 34233 B Los Angeles CA 7/19/1931 d Robert Earl McGuire & Elsa Jeanne. Fllshp Ndea; MA Claremont TS 1953; BA USC 1953; PhD USC 1969. D 6/26/1978 Bp George Theodore Masuda. m Francis Christensen c 3. D/Asst S Wlfd's Epis Ch Sarasota FL 1985-1988. Auth, "New Rhetoric"; Auth, "The Christensen Method". ESMHE. Phi Beta Kappa USC Los Angeles CA 1953; Phi Kappa Phi; Doctoral Fell Ndea.

CHRISTENSEN, Kris Cay (Spok) PO Box 8508, Spokane WA 99203 B Santa Rosa CA 10/3/1966 d Chris K Christensen & Arlene S. BA Estrn Washington U 1984; MFA Estrn Washington U 1999. D 6/26/2011 Bp James Edward

Waggoner. m 6/17/1988 Anthony Mark Macias c 1. KRIS@TRINITYSPOKANE.ORG

CHRISTENSEN, Roberta Joan (Mont) 32316 Skidoo Ln, Polson MT 59860 **Died 7/29/2011** B Great Falls MT 10/23/1925 d John Robert Engelking & Margery Leora. BA U of Montana 1947; BA Montana St U 1987. D 5/22/1999 Bp Charles Jones III. c 2. D S Andr's Epis Ch Polson MT 1999-2005. jchrist@cyberport.net

CHRISTIAN, Carol Jean (SO) No address on file. B Cincinnati OH 10/12/1950 Cert Sch for Deacons 2004. D 6/12/2004 Bp George Richard Millard. seajean@yahoo.com

CHRISTIAN, Charles Ellis (Ind) 3627 E Crystal Valley Dr, Vincennes IN 47591 B Gadsden AL 9/18/1953 s Ellis Christian & Charlotte Rosalie. AS Gadsden St Jr Coll 1973; BS Lacrosse U 2004. D 6/24/1994 Bp Edward Witker Jones. m 2/23/1974 Mary Elizabeth Dugger c 4. deacon_cio@avenuebroadband.com

CHRISTIAN, David Victor (WTenn) 8282 Macon Rd, Cordova TN 38018 B Northampton MA 6/29/1948 s Jack Gordon Christian & Zipporah Francis. NR Duke 1979; MMS Nova SE U 2005. D 6/26/2010 Bp Don Edward Johnson. m 9/1/1972 Marilee Nordfors c 2. david.christian@mac.com

CHRISTIAN, Earl Rix (SVa) 25 Tripp Ter, Hampton VA 23666 B New York NY 1/26/1944 s Ernest Christian & Mary. Cert Germain Sch Of Photography New York NY 1979; AAS CUNY 2000. D 4/26/1997 Bp Richard Frank Grein. m 8/26/1981 Claire Evans c 1. D Emm Epis Ch Hampton VA 2002-2004.

CHRISTIAN JR, Frank Stanaland (Ga) 212 W Pine St, Fitzgerald GA 31750 **P-in-c S Matt's Epis Ch Fitzgerald GA 2011-** B Valdosta GA 10/4/1948 s Frank S Christian & Carolyn Bowen. Dplma U of Freiburg 1969; BA Stetson U 1970; MDiv Sthrn Bapt TS Louisville KY 1973; PhD Sthrn Bapt TS Louisville KY 1977. D 2/7/2009 P 8/29/2009 Bp Henry Irving Louttit. m 8/7/1971 Charlotte Rostron Christian c 3. fstanc@bellsouth.net

CHRISTIAN, Julia Wadsworth (SanD) 78482 Bent Canyon Court, Bermuda Dunes CA 92203 B Washington DC 4/6/1945 d James Alfred Wadsworth & Julia Reynolds Vaughan. Smith 1965; BS Hofstra U 1967; MDiv VTS 1994. D 6/11/1994 P 1/14/1995 Bp Gethin Benwil Hughes. m 8/3/1968 Alvern Dale Christian c 1. Int S Barn Ch Borrego Sprg CA 2008-2009; Assoc S Jas By The Sea La Jolla CA 2002-2007; Vic S Fran Of Assisi Epis Ch Simi Vlly CA 1996-2002; Asst S Marg's Epis Ch Palm Desert CA 1994-1996. jwchris@earthlink.net

CHRISTIANSON, Regina Lee (Vt) 3164 Nebraska Valley Rd, Stowe VT 05672 B Panama Canal Zone 10/21/1948 d Charles S Christianson & Dorothy. BA Excelsior Coll; MDiv EDS 2006. D 11/29/2006 Bp Thomas C Ely. m 6/20/1987 Stephen Whiteley. S Ptr's Mssn Lyndonville VT 2009-2010; D S Mary's Epis Par Northfield VT 2007. revgina@pshift.com

CHRISTIANSSEN, Paul Jerome (NCal) 1362 Lafayette Rd., Apt. S, Claremont CA 91711 B Chicago IL 6/9/1939 s Einar Christianssen & Ida Rosella. BA Wheaton Coll 1961; BD/MDiv UTS 1964; STM GTS 1965; U of Texas 1970; Claremont Coll 1995. D 6/6/1964 P 12/19/1964 Bp Horace W B Donegan. m 10/15/1966 Sarah Louise Christianssen c 2. S Steph's Epis Ch Colusa CA 1981-1994; S Mich's Epis Ch Carmichael CA 1976-1981; Dio Nthrn California Sacramento CA 1971-1976; Chapl All SS Epis Ch Austin TX 1968-1970; Cur Ch Of The Ascen New York NY 1965-1968; Cur All SS Ch Bayside NY 1964-1965. oliverivanboris@aol.com

CHRISTIE, (Bob) (Oly) 6350 Portal Way Unit 72, Ferndale WA 98248 B Olympia WA 8/13/1936 s Elmer Burton Chistie & Margaret Barbara. U of Washington 1964; Everett Jr Coll 1965; BA Seattle Pacific Coll 1967; MDiv CDSP 1970. D 8/6/1970 P 6/29/1971 Bp Ivol I Curtis. m 9/28/1957 Marjorie Ann Reinhardt c 3. Asst S Paul Epis Ch Bellingham WA 1998-2003; S Geo's Ch Seattle WA 1990-1998; Dep GC Dio Olympia Seattle WA 1988-2003; COM Dio Olympia Seattle WA 1987-1993; Stndg Com Dio Olympia Seattle WA 1983-1986; Vic All SS' Epis Ch Vancouver WA 1979-1990; S Mk's Epis Ch Montesano WA 1972-1979; Cur S Jas Epis Ch Kent WA 1970-1972. Chapl COP 1992-1995. eitsirhc@comcast.net

CHRISTMAN, Angela Gale Russell (EC) 311 Patleigh Rd, Catonsville MD 21228 B Corpus Christi TX 1/24/1958 d Eugene Benjamin Russell & Mary Carolyn. BA U of Virginia 1979; MDiv VTS 1986; PhD U of Virginia 1995. D 5/21/1986 P 3/1/1988 Bp Brice Sidney Sanders. m 6/21/1986 Thomas Jackson Christmas. VTS Alexandria VA 1989-1992. I should be removed from the c, "my Dio is aware of my resignation.". No Amer Patristics Soc, Soc Of Biblic Literatu. Pres Fell U Va Charlottesville 1987; Fell 90-93 Ecf.

CHRISTOFFERSEN, Timothy Robert (Cal) 234 Via Bonita, Alamo CA 94507 B Los Angeles CA 3/25/1942 s Daniel Woodrow Christoffersen & Betty Louise. BA Stan 1964; MDiv UTS 1967. D 6/2/2001 P 12/1/2001 Bp William Edwin Swing. m 7/24/1965 Susan Griffiths Gray c 1. S Anselm's Epis Ch Lafayette CA 2001-2002. Phi Beta Kappa Stan Stanford CA 1964. tim@timchristoffersen.com

CHRISTOFFERSON, Jean Milligan (WNC) 114 Exeter Ct, Hendersonville NC 28791 B Pittsburgh PA 10/10/1934 d Elmer B Milligan & Jean J. D 9/17/1983 Bp Donald James Davis P 10/27/1996 Bp Edward Lewis Lee Jr. m 8/6/1955 James Christofferson. Gr Ch Holland MI 1990-1994; D Ch Of The Epiph Grove City PA 1983-1987. Conf of the CHS 1978.

CHRISTOPHER JR, Charles Harry (EO) 61157 Princeton Loop, Bend OR 97702 B Denver CO 4/26/1946 s Charles Harry Christopher & Margaret Ann. BA U CO 1968; MDiv SWTS 1971; DMin CDSP 2000. D 12/27/1970 P 6/1/1971 Bp Edwin B Thayer. m 8/19/1967 Patricia McLaughry Port c 2. Transition Consult S Alb's Epis Ch Redmond OR 2008-2010; Transition P Trin Ch Bend OR 2006-2008; Transition Consult S Fran Of Assisi Epis Wilsonville OR 2005-2006; Transition Consult S Paul's Epis Ch Salem OR 2004-2005; S Mk's Epis Par Medford OR 1999-2001; R All SS Ch Richland WA 1991-1999; Dio Colorado Denver CO 1990-2002; R S Barn Ch Glenwood Sprg CO 1987-1991; Eccl Cmsn Dio Colorado Denver CO 1982-1986; R Calv Ch Golden CO 1980-1987; R Ch Of The Gd Samar Gunnison CO 1973-1980; Vic S Jas Ch Lake City CO 1973-1980; S Mich And All Ang' Ch Denver CO 1964-1969; Dio Colorado Denver CO 1964-1968; S Andr's Ch Manitou Sprg CO 1962-1964. friarchuck@gmail.com

CHRISTOPHER, Mary (Ia) 2110 Summit St, Sioux City IA 51104 **S Mich's Ch Mt Pleasant IA 2010-** B New York NY 8/22/1950 AA Brookdale Cmnty Coll 1987; BA Monmouth U 1990; MDiv GTS 1995. D 5/21/1995 Bp Joe Morris Doss P 1/1/1996 Bp Craig Barry Anderson. c 2. R S Thos' Epis Ch Sioux City IA 1997-2005; Asst Chr Ch Epis Shrewsbury NJ 1995-1997. revmarychristopher@yahoo.com

CHRISTOPHER, Melanie (Colo) 371 Upham St, Lakewood CO 80226 **D S Jos's Ch Lakewood CO 2011-; D S Jos's Ch Lakewood CO 2008-; D Dio Colorado Denver CO 2000-** B Santiago CU 8/23/1937 d Jesus Chicoy & Melania. BA FD 1977. D 12/18/1999 Bp Robert Hodges Johnson. m 10/11/1979 Leonard Henry Christopher c 3. D Epis Ch Of S Ptr And S Mary Denver CO 2005-2008; D Ch Of S Phil And S Jas Denver CO 2000-2005. Auth, "Wake Up Call!," *Colorado Epis*, Dio Colorado, 2000; Auth, "Servnt Mnstry," *Highland Epis*, Dio WNC, 1999. Dio WNC Hisp Ministers Com 1995-2000; Dio Colorado Hisp Minstry Com 2002; Dio Colorado Mssn Strtgy Com 2006. Vol of the Year St of NC Hlth Dept. 1998. mellenchris@comcast.net

CHRISTOPHERSON, Paul Conrad (Minn) Wildlife Run, New Vernon NJ 07976 B Minneapolis MN 2/8/1946 s Paul Christopherson & Edna Marie. BA Wms 1968; MDiv EDS 1971; MBA Col 1974. D 6/29/1971 P 4/1/1972 Bp Horace W B Donegan. m 7/3/1971 Elizabeth Jean Good. Asst S Thos Ch New York NY 1971-1973.

CHRYSTAL, Susan (Nwk) 129 Hillcrest Ave., Summit NJ 07901 B Shaker Hgts OH 1/17/1958 d Robert W Pfaff & Susanne. BA Ya 1980; MBA U Chi 1984; MDiv UTS 1990; Cert. Blanton-Peale Grad Inst 2003. D 6/2/1990 Bp John Shelby Spong P 12/1/1990 Bp Walter Cameron Righter. m 11/24/1984 John Chrystal c 1. Cur S Paul's Epis Ch Morris Plains NJ 1992-1995; Cur S Eliz's Ch Ridgewood NJ 1990-1991. spchrystal81615@aol.com

CHUBB JR, Donald Allen (Kan) 1011 SW Cambridge Ave, Topeka KS 66604 **D Gr Cathd Topeka KS 1976-** B Topeka KS 12/14/1946 s Donald Allen Chubb & Elisabeth. BS U of Kansas 1968. D 9/26/1976 Bp Edward Clark Turner. m 9/2/1967 Janet Anderson c 1. donchubb@cjnetworks.com

CHUBB, Janet Anne (Kan) 1329 Grand Ave, Parsons KS 67357 B Davenport IA 8/7/1955 d TE Lindemann & Gertrude. BA Pittsburg St U 1980. D 1/25/1997 P 8/9/1997 Bp William Edward Smalley. m 7/5/1975 Gary Alan Chubb c 2. P Calv Ch Yates Cntr KS 1997-2004; P Gr Ch Chanute KS 1997-2004; P S Jn's Ch Parsons KS 1997-2004; P S Tim's Ch Iola KS 1997-2004. janchubb@sbcglobal.net

CHUBOFF, Esther Lois (Ct) 83 E Main St, Clinton CT 06413 **S Paul's Ch Windham CT 1986-** B North Bergen NJ 1/28/1932 d Peter Kyril Chuboff & Lydia Johanna. BS Rutgers-The St U 1952; CRDS 1986. D 6/21/1986 P 6/29/1987 Bp O'Kelley Whitaker. Int Chr Ch Sharon CT 2000-2002; Ch of the H Sprt W Haven CT 2000; Ch Of The Gd Shpd Shelton CT 1999-2000; Ch Of The H Adv Clinton CT 1998-1999; Trin Ch Boonville NY 1988-1992; D S Mk The Evang Syracuse NY 1986-1987. arrabon@aol.com

CHUMBLEY, Kenneth Lawrence (WMo) 601 E Walnut St, Springfield MO 65806 **R Chr Epis Ch Springfield MO 1995-** B Louisville KY 8/10/1953 s Gilbert Hurt Chumbley & Anine. B.A. w hon U of Louisville 1976; M.Div. GTS 1986; Cert Coll of Preachers 2000; Cont Stds Oxf 2002; M.A. (anticipated) Missouri St U 2012. D 6/24/1986 P 3/1/1987 Bp David Reed. m 8/14/1976 Penny Gordon c 1. R All SS Epis Ch Johnson City NY 1989-1994; Asst. R Chr Epis Ch Bowling Green KY 1986-1989. Auth, *Sojourners*; Auth, *The Chr Century*; Auth, *The Chr Source Bk (3 Chapters)*; Auth, *The Other Side*; Auth, "monthly Rel/ethics column," *The Springfield (MO) News Ldr*. Soc of S Marg 1991. qdisgood@sbcglobal.net

CHUN, Franklin Seu Hook (Haw) 1163 Lunaanela St, Kailua HI 96734 **Chapl to Ret Cler & Spouses /Partnr, and Surviving Spouses Dio Hawaii Honolulu HI 2009-; Ret Cler & Spouses/Partnr and Surviving Spouses Dio Hawaii Honolulu HI 2009-** B Honolulu HI 8/13/1942 s Ahee Quan Yit Chun & Margaret Kam Yuk. BA U of Hawaii 1965; MDiv CDSP 1968. D 5/10/1968 Bp Edwin Lani Hanchett P 12/8/1968 Bp Harry S Kennedy. m 6/19/1966 Norma F Fung c 3. R Ch Of The Epiph Honolulu HI 2003-2008; COM

Dio Hawaii Honolulu HI 2001-2005; Chapl S Alb's Chap Honolulu HI 1996-2002; Cn S Andr's Cathd Honolulu HI 1992-1996; Chapl S Andr's Priory Sch Honolulu HI 1981-1992; R S Ptr's Ch Honolulu HI 1973-1981; Assoc S Ptr's Ch Honolulu HI 1968-1970. Co-Transltr, *Da Jesus Bk (Hawaii Pidgin NT)*, Wycliffe, 2000. Chinese Chr Assn 1968. Hon Cn S Andr Cathd Honolulu HI 1996; HS Tchr of the Year S Andr Priory 1991. revfchun@hawaii.rr.com

CHURCH, Susan Campbell (Ore) Po Box 1014, Newport OR 97365 **Vic S Lk's Ch Waldport OR 1989-; Vic S Steph's Ch Newport OR 1989-** B Oregon City OR 9/9/1953 d McGregor Lenoir Church & Linda. BA U of Oregon 1977; MDiv CDSP 1985. D 6/22/1985 Bp Matthew Paul Bigliardi P 5/30/1986 Bp Robert Louis Ladehoff. Asst The Epis Ch Of The Gd Samar Corvallis OR 1985-1989. CHS. stmavis@peak.org

CHURCH, Susan Jean (NMich) Christ Church, 3906 5th St, Calumet MI 49913 B Detroit MI 12/8/1946 d George Edward Staughton & Mary Leone. Detroit Coll Of Bus Dearborn MI; Ferris St Coll Big Rapids MI; Mutual Mnstry Calumet MI. D 11/28/2006 Bp James Arthur Kelsey P 9/18/2007 Bp Thomas Kreider Ray. m 6/23/1989 Alan Jeffrey Church c 4. schurch@pasty.net

CHURCHILL, Gregg Hardison (Los) Po Box 1082, Lompoc CA 93438 B Los Angeles CA 11/26/1935 s Edwin Perry Churchill & Coralynn. BS Colorado St U 1957; BD Fuller TS 1964; ThD Claremont TS 1972. D 3/12/1966 P 9/1/1966 Bp Francis E I Bloy. m 10/3/1992 Patricia Kiphut. S Steph's Epis Ch Santa Clarita CA 1991; S Mary's Par Lompoc CA 1990-2001; Cur S Mk's Par Downey CA 1966-1968.

CHURCHMAN, Jean (Nina) Wood (Colo) 4820 E Vassar Ln, Denver CO 80222 **P-in-c S Laurence's Epis Mssn Conifer CO 2009-** B The Hague Holland NL 2/2/1952 d Michael Steel Bright Churchman & Jean Virginia. BA U of Pennsylvania 1974; MS Pur 1978; MDiv Ya Berk 1995. D 6/8/1996 P 1/18/1997 Bp William Jerry Winterrowd. m 9/6/1986 Leo Martin Eisel c 2. S Paul's Epis Ch Ft Collins CO 2008; Supply S Paul's Epis Ch Ft Collins CO 2007-2008; Assoc R S Tim's Epis Ch Centennial CO 2001-2007; R Epis Ch Of S Ptr And S Mary Denver CO 1999-2001; Asst R Gd Shpd Epis Ch Centennial CO 1996-1999. ninachuchu@q.com

CHURCHMAN, Michael Arthur (Neb) 25002 Hackberry Rd, Council Bluffs IA 51503 B Council Bluffs IA 6/14/1928 s Henry Clarence Churchman & Teresa Marie. BA S Paul Sem 1950; MA Creighton U 1955. Rec from Roman Catholic 1/1/1981 as Deacon Bp James Daniel Warner. Assoc R S Andr's Ch Omaha NE 1991-2003; Vic S Pauls Epis Ch Arapahoe NE 1984-1990; S Ptr's In The Vlly Lexington NE 1982-1990; Vic S Christophers Ch Cozad NE 1981-1990. NLDSRATTY@YAHOO.COM

CIANNELLA, Domenic Kenneth (LI) 320 Great River Rd, PO Box 586, Great River NY 11739 **P-in-c Emm Epis Ch Great River NY 2004-; Chr Ch Babylon NY 2002-** B Far Rockaway NY 3/23/1921 s Vito Ciannella & Adeline Cecelia. BA U So 1943; MDiv STUSo 1945. D 12/24/1944 P 7/1/1945 Bp James P De Wolfe. m 11/27/1945 Annette Ciannella c 5. Camp DeWolfe Bd Managers Dio Long Island Garden City NY 2006-2011; Dioc Coun Dio Long Island Garden City NY 2006-2011; Int S Fran Epis Ch Springboro OH 2001-2002; Int Calv Ch Cincinnati OH 1998-2000; Int H Trin Epis Ch Oxford OH 1997-1998; Int Trin Ch Columbus OH 1995-1997; Int R Chr Ch Babylon NY 1994-1995; Int S Jn's Ch Huntington NY 1993-1994; GC Dep Dio Long Island Garden City NY 1982-1991; Eccl Crt Dio Long Island Garden City NY 1967-1991; R H Trin Epis Ch Hicksville NY 1959-1992; Prof of Pstr Theol, Theory & Pract of Mnstry Geo Mercer TS Garden City NY 1958-1993; R S Paul's Ch Patchogue NY 1951-1959; P-in-c S Mary's Ch Lake Ronkonkoma NY 1947-1951; P-in-c Ch Of The Mssh Cntrl Islip NY 1945-1951; P-in-c S Mk's Epis Ch Medford NY 1945-1947. Dubose Awd for Serv The Schoo of Theol 2005; Hon Cn Cathd Incarn Garden City New York 1989. emmanuelgr@verizon.net

CIANNELLA, J(oseph) Domenic Kennith (Mass) 13 Park Dr, West Springfield MA 01089 B Mineola NY 9/7/1946 s Domenic Kenneth Ciannella & Annette. BA LIU 1973; MDiv SWTS 1998. D 6/20/1998 P 1/16/1999 Bp Herbert Thompson Jr. m 9/12/1998 Elizabeth Tilley c 2. R Ch Of The Gd Shpd W Springfield MA 2002-2006; R S Phil's Ch Circleville OH 1999-2002; Cur S Matt's Ch Westerville OH 1998-1999. therevdomenic@comcast.net

CICCARELLI, Sharon Lynn (Mass) 13 Turner Ter, Newton MA 02460 B Boston MA 11/3/1955 d Eugene Charles Ciccarelli & Margaret Eunice. BA Ya 1977; MDiv Epis TS of The SW 1993. D 6/5/1993 P 6/11/1994 Bp David Elliot Johnson. c 2. Assoc Trin Ch Newton Cntr MA 1998-2004; D Chr Ch Cambridge Cambridge MA 1993-1994.

CICORA, Julie Anne (Roch) 556 Forest Lawn Dr, Webster NY 14580 **Dio Rochester Rochester NY 2009-** B Laconia NH 1/29/1958 d Kenneth Lee Herrick & Betty Jean. AA Colby-Sawyer Coll 1977; BA Wellesley Coll 1979; MDiv Bex 1999. D 6/5/1999 Bp William George Burrill P 5/27/2000 Bp Jack Marston McKelvey. m 10/8/1994 F Scott Cicora c 5. R S Ptr's Epis Ch Henrietta NY 2006-2009; S Jn's Ch Canandaigua NY 2003-2006; Assoc S Lk's Ch Fairport NY 1999-2003. julie@rochesterepiscopalciocese.com

CIESEL, Barbara (Bitsey) Bitney (SD) 126 N Park St Ne, Wagner SD 57380 **All SS Epis Ch Greg SD 2000-; S Phil the D Ch Wagner SD 2000-; Woniya Wakan/Ch Of The H Sprt Wagner SD 2000-** B Ann Arbor MI 8/18/1939 d Dewey Hobson Bitney & Barbara. BS MI SU 1963; MS MI SU 1965; MA Mt Marty Coll Yankton SD 2006. D 6/12/2000 Bp Creighton Leland Robertson. m 8/24/1968 Conrad Henry Ciesel. Sis of the H Nativ - Assoc 1973.

CIESEL, Conrad Henry (SD) Po Box 216, Lake City SD 57247 B Buffalo NY 12/26/1941 s Henry Stanislaus Ciesel & Irene Amelia. BA SUNY 1968; ETSBH 1975; MDiv GTS 1977. D 6/18/1977 P 1/1/1978 Bp Robert C Rusack. m 8/24/1968 Barbara (Bitsey) Bitney c 1. Dio So Dakota Sioux Falls SD 1994-2007; Vic Chr The King Quincy CA 1988-1994; S Richard's Epis Ch Lake Arrowhead CA 1982-1988; Vic S Columba's Epis Mssn Big Bear Lake CA 1977-1988; Vic S Alb's Epis Ch Yucaipa CA 1977-1980. Auth, "Measurement Of Kidney Parenchyma P02 & Pc02 During In Vitro," Perfusion; Auth, "Direct Measurement Of Renal Cortical Oxygen & Carbon Dioxide," Pressures; Auth, "Induced Seizures As Ther Of Experimental Strokes In Dogs". Ord Of S Lk, SHN.

CIHAK, Susan Elizabeth (Az) 12990 E Shea Blvd, Scottsdale AZ 85259 **D S Anth On The Desert Scottsdale AZ 2009-** B La Jolla CA 6/25/1970 d George Garfield Buckley & Doris Elizabeth. BS U of Arizona 1995. D 1/24/2009 Bp Kirk Stevan Smith. m 10/25/1997 Stephen Cihak c 2. cheehawk@qwest.net

CILLEY, Norman H (CFla) 23 E Hampton Dr, Auburndale FL 33823 **D Dio Cntrl Florida Orlando FL 1993-** B North Danville VT 4/6/1932 s H Norman Cilley & Florance G. D 12/3/1988 Bp Arthur Edward Walmsley. m 2/14/1954 Mona Nadine Stewart. D Dio Connecticut Hartford CT 1988-1993.

CIMIJOTTI, Jerry Anthony (SD) 2822 S Division St, Spokane WA 99203 B Mason City IA 9/11/1964 s Raymond Lenord Cimijotti & Rosemary. TESM 1999. D 6/10/2000 Bp Robert William Duncan P 12/10/2000 Bp Edwin Max Leidel Jr. m 8/27/1999 Courtney Kathryn Thimsen c 3. R S Mary's Epis Ch Mitchell SD 2002-2005; D S Jn's Epis Ch Midland MI 2000-2001. cimijotti2@msn.com

CIRIELLO, Mary Anne (Ct) 3768 Anslow Drive, Leland NC 28451 B New York NY 8/8/1950 d Albert Milton Grafmueller & Gertrude. BA Bennington Coll 1973; BS U of Massachusetts 1976; MDiv TESM 1982. D 6/9/1984 Bp Arthur Edward Walmsley P 1/1/1985 Bp William Bradford Hastings. m 6/27/1992 John Louis Ciriello. R Gr Ch Broad Brook CT 1988-1991; Asst to R S Jas's Ch W Hartford CT 1984-1988; Intern Chr Ch Cathd Hartford CT 1982-1984.

CIRILLO, James Hawthorne (Va) Po Box 847, Buckingham PA 18912 **R Gr Ch Casanova VA 2004-** B Alexandria VA 11/18/1953 s John Richard Cirillo & Ada Lavonia. BA Emory & Henry Coll 1976; MDiv TESM 1983; VTS 1983. D 8/16/1983 Bp David Henry Lewis Jr P 3/15/1984 Bp Walter H Jones. m 7/7/1979 Dale Hilgartner c 3. R Trin Ch Buckingham PA 1996-2003; Assoc Ch Of The Gd Samar Paoli PA 1988-1996; Asst S Lk's Epis Ch Hilton Hd SC 1985-1988; Cur Emm Epis Par Rapid City SD 1983-1985; Pstr Intern Truro Epis Ch Fairfax VA 1981-1982. Bd Mem Widows & Orphans Corp. revjhc@aol.com

CIRVES, Judith Melanie (Mil) No address on file. **D S Lk's Ch Madison WI 2000-** B Milwaukee WI 10/29/1940 d John Mckeen Pendleton & Pearl Charlotte. U of Wisconsin. D 9/10/1988 Bp Roger John White. D Ch Of The Gd Shpd Sun Prairie WI 1988-1990.

CISNEROS, Hilario (Nev) 832 N Eastern Ave, Las Vegas NV 89101 **Discilinary Cmsn Dio Nevada Las Vegas NV 2011-; R S Lk's Epis Ch Las Vegas NV 2009-** B Michoacan Mexico 8/21/1957 s Luis Cisneros & Maria Moreno. Degree in TH Salesian Sch of TH, Guadalajara MX 1992. Rec from Roman Catholic 11/1/2009 Bp Dan Thomas Edwards. m 3/9/2006 Ruth A Flores Torres. Las Vegas Vlly Interfaith S Com 2009. hcisne7@yahoo.com

CIVALIER, Gordon Richard (NJ) 1823 Kimball Ave, Willow Grove PA 19090 B Camden NJ 7/26/1947 s Gordon Civalier & Anna Marie. BA Morningside Coll 1969; MDiv PDS 1972. D 4/22/1972 P 10/28/1972 Bp Alfred L Banyard. H Sprt Bellmawr NJ 1997-2007; S Lk's Ch Westville NJ 1997-2007; Timber Creek Epis Area Mnstry Gloucester City NJ 1997-2005; Ch Of The Ascen Gloucester City NJ 1980-1996; Cur Chr Ch Middletown NJ 1972-1974. Bd Mem & Secy for the Cmnty Plnng & Advocacy 1989-2002. Vol of the Year Sthrn NJ AIDS Cltn 1989. rcivalier1@verizon.net

CLABUESCH, Ward Henry (Mich) 3176 Topview Ct, Rochester Hills MI 48309 B Bad Axe MI 6/1/1927 s Ernst G Clabuesch & Bertha. BA MI SU 1950; STB GTS 1953. D 6/27/1953 Bp Richard S M Emrich P 12/1/1953 Bp Russell S Hubbard. c 2. Asst All SS Epis Ch Pontiac MI 1991-1992; Chr Ch Dearborn MI 1971-1991; R S Lk's Epis Ch Allen Pk MI 1961-1971; R S Paul's Epis Ch Corunna MI 1955-1961; Cur All SS Epis Ch Pontiac MI 1953-1955. rev1@flash.net

CLADER, Linda Lee (NCal) 2451 Ridge Rd, Berkeley CA 94709 **Prof Homil Dn of Acad Affrs CDSP Berkeley CA 1991-** B Evanston IL 2/11/1946 d Carl Walter Clader & Geraldine Virginia. BA Carleton Coll 1968; MA Harv 1970; PhD Harv 1973; MDiv CDSP 1988. D 6/23/1988 P 1/25/1989 Bp Robert Marshall Anderson. m 4/6/1991 Robert N Ristad. Adv Ch Farmington MN 1989-1990. Co-Auth, "The Formation of a Eucharistic Prchr," *Preaching at the Double Feast, ed. Monshau*, Liturg Press, 2006; Auth, "Voicing the Vision:

Imagination and Prophetic Preaching," Morehouse, 2003; Auth, "Preaching the Liturg Narrative: The easter Vigil and the Lang of Myth," *Wrshp*, 1998; Co-Auth, "At the Wedding of Peleus & Thetis: Trans of Catullus 64," Black Oak, 1981; Auth, "Helen: Evolution from Div to Heroic in Gk Epic Tradition," E.J. Brill, 1976. Phi Beta Kappa 1968. lclader@aol.com

CLAGGETT III, Thomas West (Md) 1123C Jefferson Pike, Knoxville MD 21758 **D Gr Ch Brunswick MD 2011-; D S Paul's Epis Par Point Of Rocks MD 2011-** B Baltimore MD 2/20/1938 s Thomas West Claggett & Blanche Joyce. BS Jn Hopkins U 1966; MA St. Mary's Sem & U 1974. D 5/12/1979 Bp David Keller Leighton Sr. m 6/11/1960 Lucy Margaret Simmons c 2. D All SS Ch Frederick MD 1979-2011. barleywood1793@gmail.com

CLANCEY, William (ECR) 802 Windridge Cir, San Marcos CA 92078 **Died 1/26/2011** B Cincinnati OH 6/17/1926 s William Power Clancey & Marian. BA U CA Berkeley 1948; MA U CA Berkeley 1950; JD U CA Berkeley 1957; MDiv CDSP 1964. D 6/21/1964 Bp James Albert Pike P 6/2/1965 Bp George Richard Millard. c 4. ComT 1960; OHC 1975. wpc0302@sbcglobal.net

CLAPP JR, Schuyler L (EMich) 1102 W Front St, Traverse City MI 49684 B Oceanside NY 4/22/1931 s Schuyler Lamb Clapp & Florence Dunbar. BA Yankton Coll 1952; STM SWTS 1955; MS Wayne 1968. D 6/23/1955 Bp Archie H Crowley P 12/1/1955 Bp Conrad Gesner. m 1/10/1988 Pauline Esther Saunders c 5. Dio Michigan Detroit MI 1992-1994; R S Andr's Epis Ch Gaylord MI 1987-1997; LocTen S Jas Epis Ch Belle Fourche SD 1981-1987; Dio Michigan Detroit MI 1965-1968; R Calv Memi Epis Ch Saginaw MI 1960-1964; Cur All SS Ch Detroit MI 1959-1960; Vic Chr Epis Ch Gettysburg SD 1955-1959. Auth, *Video: Sons of Single-Parent Mothers*, 1991. peteclapp@att.net

CLARK, Adelaide Sampselle (NY) 45 Miami Dr. Unit B, Monroe OH 45050 B Logan WV 8/11/1944 d John Shephard Sampselle & Josephine. Witt 1963; BS OH SU 1965; Untd TS 1986; MDiv GTS 1988. D 6/18/1988 P 12/18/1988 Bp William Grant Black. m 8/28/1965 Larry Edward Clark c 2. The Ch Of S Jos Of Arimathea White Plains NY 1997-2009; Dio Indianapolis Indianapolis IN 1991-1996; Vic S Lk's Epis Ch Shelbyville IN 1990-1996; D S Lk's Ch Marietta OH 1988-1989. addieclark@yahoo.com

CLARK, Alan R (Minn) 8827 Ironwood Ave S, Cottage Grove MN 55016 B Minneapolis MN 10/30/1931 s Lowell Homer Clark & Eleanor Florence. Luther TS; SWTS 1955; BA U MN 1955; BD NW Semnorthwestern Sem Minneapolis MN 1958. D 6/11/1958 P 12/22/1958 Bp Hamilton Hyde Kellogg. m 6/4/1955 Elinore Clark. P-in-c S Mths Ch St Paul Pk MN 1998-2002; Assoc S Mths Ch Coventry RI 1994-1998; Cur S Jas On The Pkwy Minneapolis MN 1963-1964; R Ascen Ch St Paul MN 1960-1963; Vic S Columba White Earth MN 1958-1960. "Apos To The Indians," *LivCh*, 1959. clarkalan@aol.com

CLARK, Albert Lee (Md) 1111 N Ocean Blvd # 404, Box 15697, Surfside Beach SC 29587 B Sunbury PA 2/3/1934 s Anthony Lee Clark & Ruth Esther. AB Dickinson Coll 1955; MDiv VTS 1958; DMin Candidate Lancaster TS 1973. D 6/16/1958 P 12/16/1958 Bp John T Heistand. m 2/7/1976 Mary M S Smith c 3. Pstr Assoc The Epis Ch Of The Resurr Surfside Bch SC 1999-2001; R S Andr's Ch Baltimore MD 1983-1997; Stndg Com Dio Cntrl Pennsylvania Harrisburg PA 1972-1975; R S Thos Ch Lancaster PA 1966-1974; Pres/Secy/Treas Potomac Cler Dio Virginia Richmond VA 1963-1965; Assoc S Geo's Epis Ch Arlington VA 1961-1966; Vic S Andr's Ch Tioga PA 1958-1961. marynal2@verizon.net

CLARK, Anthony P (CFla) 108 Ludlow Dr, Longwood FL 32779 **Dn Cathd Ch Of S Lk Orlando FL 2006-** B Springfield MA 4/2/1961 s John Charles Clark & Patricia Levia. BA Stetson U 1983; MDiv VTS 1992; Dplma US Army Command and Gnrl Stff Coll 2009. D 6/14/1992 Bp Frank Stanley Cerveny P 12/16/1992 Bp John Wadsworth Howe. m 6/17/1989 Laurie Boss c 2. Ch Of The H Sprt Apopka FL 2003; Pension Fund Mltry New York NY 2003; Epis Ch Of The H Sprt Apopka FL 1999-2006; Epis Ch Of S Mary Belleview FL 1994-1999; All SS Ch Of Winter Pk Winter Pk FL 1992-1994. Auth, "Commentary on Jas," *The Journey: God's Word for Daily Living*, The Bible Reading Fllshp, 2007; Auth, "Commentary on 1 and 2 Tim," *The Journey: God's Word for Daily Living*, The Bible Reading Fllshp, 2000; Auth, "Commentary on Philippians and Colossians," *The Journey: God's Word for Daily Living*, The Bible Reading Fllshp, 1998; Auth, "Commentary on Ephesians," *The Journey: God's Word for Daily Living*, The Bible Reading Fllshp, 1997; Auth, "Commentary on Matt 8-17," *The Journey: God's Word for Daily Living*, The Bible Reading Fllshp, 1995. Abbey of S Greg 1995. Min of the Year Stetson U 1996. deanclark@stlukescathedral.org

CLARK, Beatryce Arlene (NCal) 581 Ridgewood Dr, Vacaville CA 95688 **Archd Dio Nthrn California Sacramento CA 2010-; D Epis Ch Of The Epiph Vacaville CA 2004-** B Newark NJ 5/8/1935 d Edward Barwell & Margaret Elizabeth. BBA Ups 1957; BTA Sch for Deacons 2004. D 7/4/2004 Bp Jerry Alban Lamb. m 8/15/1981 Philip Clark c 3. cookie.clark@sbcglobal.net

CLARK, Bradford Duff (Mass) Po Box 25, Arlington VT 05250 **R Ascen Memi Ch Ipswich MA 2006-** B Providence RI 7/14/1960 s Donald Judson Clark & Ruth. BA Hob 1982; MA U Chi 1985; Cert SWTS 1989. D 8/19/1989 P 3/22/1990 Bp Edward Cole Chalfant. m 5/25/1992 Caron Marie Nardi. S Jas Epis Ch Arlington VT 1994-2006; Confederation For N.W. Area Mnstry Swanton VT 1992-1994; R Dio Vermont Burlington VT 1992-1994; Asst S Alb's Ch Cape Eliz ME 1989-1991. rectoramc@verizon.net

CLARK, Carole Sue (Okla) Hc 67 Box 82, Indianola OK 74442 **D Dio Oklahoma Oklahoma City OK 1998-; D Trin Ch Eufaula OK 1998-** B Cushing OK 10/5/1946 BA Oklahoma St U. D 5/30/1998 Bp Robert Manning Moody. m 2/6/1970 Bill Clark c 2.

CLARK, C(aroline) Robbins (Cal) 36 Larkhay Road, Hucclecote Gloucester AE GL3 3NS Great Britain (UK) B Washington DC 8/19/1945 d Alonzo Webster Clark & Elizabeth Caroline. BA Mt Holyoke Coll 1967; BS Col 1970; MS U CA 1975; Cert Oxf 1980; MDiv CDSP 1981. D 6/27/1981 P 5/29/1982 Bp William Edwin Swing. R S Mk's Par Berkeley CA 1993-2010; R S Bede's Epis Ch Santa Fe NM 1985-1993; Cur S Mk's Epis Ch Upland CA 1981-1984. revrobbin@gmail.com

CLARK, Carol Ruth (NMich) 10401 V.05 Rd, Rapid River MI 49878 B Dayton OH 6/27/1930 d Bailey Wright & Jessie A. RN Miami Vlly Hosp Sch Dayton OH 1951. D 9/30/1990 P 4/14/1991 Bp Thomas Kreider Ray. m 8/24/1951 Donald Eugene Clark. Ord Of S Lk. caclark@uplogon.com

CLARK, Cathy A (NMich) P.O. Box 601, Ishpeming MI 49849 B Ishpeming MI 3/5/1960 d John Perkins Clark & Sally Janet. BS Nthrn Michigan U 2006. D 11/4/2007 Bp Rustin Ray Kimsey. catsatthesummit@charter.net

CLARK, Charles Halsey (NH) 5 Timber Ln Apt 228, Exeter NH 03833 B New York NY 12/2/1926 s Alfred Marling Clark & Martha. BA Ya 1948; BD VTS 1952; MA Ya 1956; STD Ya Berk 1982; LHD Mid 1991. D 6/8/1952 P 12/22/1952 Bp Horace W B Donegan. m 5/15/1953 Priscilla Hannah. P-in-c Ch Of S Jn The Evang Dunbarton NH 1999-2011; R S Paul's Sch Concord NH 1982-1992; Dn Ya Berk New Haven CT 1977-1982; Asst Gr And S Ptr's Epis Ch Hamden CT 1952-1953. Fndt For Theol Educ In SE Asia; Soc For Values In Higher Educ ; Untd Bd For Chr Higher Educ In Asia. granitekelly@gmail.com

CLARK, Cheryl Lynn (Ark) 1106 Deer Run N, Pine Bluff AR 71603 **R Gr Ch Pine Bluff AR 2002-** B Saint Louis MO 1/20/1950 d Terry Allen Clark & Dorothy Jean. BA W&M 1972; MA U of York 1975; EdD Bos 1982; MDiv VTS 2002. D 12/22/2001 P 6/22/2002 Bp Larry Earl Maze. clarkark@cablelynx.com

CLARK, Constance Lee (Va) PO Box 183, Earlysville VA 22936 **Vic Buck Mtn Epis Ch Earlysville VA 2008-** B Alexandria VA 12/14/1954 d Harry Harmon Clark & Edna Louise Gorham. BA U Chi 1976; MA St. Steph's Coll 2008. D 9/23/2005 P 4/1/2006 Bp Bruce Edward Caldwell. m 5/20/1978 Guy A Lushin. "Faith," Salt Lake Tribune, 2006; "The Faith Factor: Proof of the Healing Power of Pryr," Viking Penguin, 1998; "H Meeting Ground," Shalem Inst, 1993; "In the Line of Duty," Potomac Pub, 1988. revclc@gmail.com

CLARK, D(arrah) Corbet (Oly) 11520 Sw Timberline Dr, Beaverton OR 97008 **Dio Oregon Portland OR 2011-; Chapl Oregon Epis Sch Portland OR 2011-; Assoc Gr Memi Portland OR 1998-** B Seattle WA 3/4/1951 s Irving Marshall Clark & Anne Trumbull. BA Harv 1972; MA Ya 1974; Coll of the Resurr Mirfield Gb 1976; MDiv GTS 1977; DMin VTS 2011. D 7/26/1977 P 6/29/1978 Bp Robert Hume Cochrane. m 8/7/1976 Myra Florence Waite c 2. Assoc S Jas Epis Ch Tigard OR 1989-1998; Chr Ch Tacoma WA 1980-1984; Int Dio Olympia Seattle WA 1979; Cur Ch Of The Ascen Seattle WA 1977-1979. Auth, "Amer Wines Of The NW," Wm Morrow, 1989; Auth, "The Frugal Gourmet Cooks w Wine," Wm Morrow, 1986. Phi Beta Kappa 1972. dcorbetc@gmail.com

CLARK, David Lang (Haw) 38 New Province Rd, Sunapee NH 03782 **Died 2/4/2011** B Medford MA 3/20/1932 s Herbert Randolph Clark & Ethel Miriam. BA Ya 1954; MDiv EDS 1957; ThD Harvard DS 1967. D 6/22/1957 P 12/1/1957 Bp Anson Phelps Stokes Jr. c 5. Auth, "Vasari's Temptation of St. Jerome," *Stds in Iconography 10*, 1984; Auth, "Optics for Preachers: the De oculo morali of Ptr of Limoges," *Michigan Acad Papers*, 1982; Auth, "Fillipinno Lippi's St. Bern," *Stds in Iconography 8*, 1982; Auth, *Jacques Ellul: Interpretive Essays*, Univ. Illinois Press, 1981. langd32@msn.com

CLARK, David Norman (Md) 12265 Boyd Rd, Clear Spring MD 21722 **S Anne's Epis Ch Smithsburg MD 2002-** B Lewisburg PA 4/21/1949 s Vance Norman Clark & Elva Madelynn. BA McDaniel Coll 1971; MDiv VTS 1976. D 5/22/1976 P 12/4/1976 Bp David Keller Leighton Sr. m 6/10/2000 Colleen Barbot c 4. S Andr's Ch Clear Sprg MD 2001-2007; Dio Cntrl Pennsylvania Harrisburg PA 1980-1981; R S Mary's Ch Williamsport PA 1978-1980; Asst S Ptr's Epis Ch Ellicott City MD 1976-1977. clark12265@myactv.net

CLARK, Diana (Nwk) 59 Montclair Ave, Montclair NJ 07042 **Stndg Com Dio Newark Newark NJ 1988-** B Bridgeport CT 3/5/1945 d Harrison Trask Doyle & Carolyn May. BA Ge 1967; MDiv Drew U 1987. D 5/28/1988 P 12/18/1988 Bp John Shelby Spong. m 7/15/1967 Charles P Clark c 2. S Jn's Epis Ch Montclair NJ 1991-2010; Assoc R S Geo's Epis Ch Maplewood NJ 1988-1991; Ethics Com Dio Newark Newark NJ 1986-1997; Com Dio Newark Newark NJ 1983-1984. dianadoyleclark@yahoo.com

CLARK, Diane Catherine (WA) 13 Eleanor Avenue, Saint Albans, Hertfordshire AL35TA Great Britain (UK) B Attleboro MA 2/15/1954 d Paul Vincent

FitzGerald & Blanche Mae. BA U of Rhode Island 1976; MDiv GTS 1986. D 6/21/1986 P 2/28/1987 Bp George Nelson Hunt III. m 7/31/1982 Charles Graham Clark. P-in-c S Pat's Ch Washington DC 1994-1995; Supply P Dio Washington Washington DC 1993-1994; All SS' Epis Ch Chevy Chase MD 1989-1992; Cur S Mich's Ch New York NY 1986-1989. Auth, *QUEST*, 1989; Auth, *The Angl*, 1989. Cmsn Liturg & Mus Dio Washington DC 1990-1992. mo.clark@btinternet.com

CLARK, Douglas Burns (SeFla) 116 Prospect Park W # 2r, Brooklyn NY 11215 **Hon Assoc S Mary's Manhattanville Epis Ch New York NY 1987-** B Los Angeles CA 1/24/1948 s Martin Burns Clark & Beverly Jean. AAPC; BA Amh 1970; MDiv GTS 1973; Cert Blanton-Peale Grad Inst 1976; Cert Blanton-Peale Grad Inst 1977. D 6/9/1973 Bp Paul Moore Jr P 5/1/1974 Bp Harold Louis Wright. m 9/5/1970 Eleanor Preston. Assoc S Mary's Ch Brooklyn NY 1988-2008; Asst S Mary's Manhattanville Epis Ch New York NY 1973-1975. Auth, "Cler As Systems Analyst (The Guide To Pstr Counslg And Care)," Psychosocial Press, 2000; Auth, "Aspects Narcissistic Revenge Elicited In Grp Psych". Aamft. Tchg Fell Inst Of Rel & Hlth 1976; Fell Agpa; Fell Egps. theclarkgroup2003@yahoo.com

CLARK, Frances M (NJ) 201 Penbryn Rd, Berlin NJ 08009 **D The Ch Of The Gd Shpd Berlin NJ 2008-; D S Ptr's Ch Medford NJ 2002-** B Philadelphia PA 3/15/1949 D 9/21/2002 Bp David B(ruce) Joslin.

CLARK, Frank Herbert (Az) 7810 W Columbine Dr, Peoria AZ 85381 **P-in-c S Jn The Bapt Epis Ch Glendale AZ 2010-; Congrl Consult Dio Arizona Phoenix AZ 2008-; S Jn The Bapt Epis Ch Glendale AZ 1971-** B Pontiac MI 11/24/1941 s Harold Reynolds Clark & Dorothy Adaline. BS MI SU 1964; MDiv Nash 1971. D 3/5/1971 P 9/11/1971 Bp Donald H V Hallock. m 7/30/1966 Carolyn Christiansen c 2. P-t Assoc P All SS Ch Phoenix AZ 2008-2009; R All SS Of The Desert Epis Ch Sun City AZ 1997-2008; Pres of the Stndg Com Dio No Dakota Fargo ND 1988-1996; Liturg Off Dio No Dakota Fargo ND 1986-1997; Dn Geth Cathd Fargo ND 1986-1997; Secy of the Stndg Com Dio So Dakota Sioux Falls SD 1978-1985; Liturg Off Dio So Dakota Sioux Falls SD 1976-1986; R Trin Epis Ch Pierre SD 1976-1985; Rep Untd Mnstrs in Higher Educ - Wisconsin Dio Milwaukee Milwaukee WI 1971-1976; Vic Trin Epis Ch Mineral Point WI 1971-1976; Vic Trin Epis Ch Platteville WI 1971-1976. Auth, "Out Of The Ashes," *Faith & Form*, Interfaith Forum on Rel, Art & Archetecture, 1995. Hon Cn Dio Arizona/Trin Cathd, Phoenix 2007; Silver Beaver BSA 1994; St Geo Awd The Epis Ch 1985. fhclark@cox.net

CLARK, Holland Ball (SC) 63 Club Course Dr, Hilton Head SC 29928 **Died 6/11/2010** B Savannah GA 10/18/1926 s Reuben Grove Clark & Katherine. BA Ya 1950; BD VTS 1954; STM STUSo 1967. D 6/27/1954 Bp Middleton S Barnwell P 3/30/1955 Bp Albert R Stuart.

CLARK, Jane Alice (Chi) 1608 W Plymouth Dr, Arlington Heights IL 60004 **R S Andr Ch Grayslake IL 2006-** B Joliet IL 3/15/1953 d Francis Edward Haley & Sarah Louise. BSN IL Wesl 1975; MSN CUA 1981; MDiv SWTS 2005; DMin GTF 2010. D 6/18/2005 P 12/17/2005 Bp William Dailey Persell. m 6/11/1977 Michael Alice Clark c 2. janeaclark@comcast.net

CLARK II, Jim B. (Az) 6715 N Mockingbird Lane, Paradise Valley AZ 85253 **R S Barn On The Desert Scottsdale AZ 2004-** B Oklahoma City OK 2/13/1951 s Jack Loyd Clark & Anne. BA Oral Roberts U 1985; M. Div. Fuller TS 1991. D 6/15/1991 P 1/11/1992 Bp Frederick Houk Borsch. m 12/8/1978 Betsy Holland c 4. Assoc Ch Of Our Sav Par San Gabr CA 1991-2004. jclark@saintbarnabas.org

CLARK, Joan Bonnell (CFla) 5066 S Austin Pt, Homosassa FL 34446 **D Shpd Of The Hills Epis Ch Lecanto FL 1996-** B Highland NY 10/1/1931 d Walter Truman Bonnell & Viola Dorcas. BA U IL 1954; MS U IL 1967; Cert STUSo 2002. D 2/3/1996 Bp Frank Tracy Griswold III. m 7/4/1991 Sherman Clark c 4. Auth, *Glimpses of God & Seasonal Chr Poems*, First Books Libr, 2003. Amer Benedictine Acad 1998-2005; Benedictine Secular Cn 1998; NAAD 1996; Ord Julian of Norwich 1995. Beta Phi Mu Intl Libr hon Soc 1967; Zeta Phi Eta Natl Speech hon Soc 1954. jclark3@mindspring.com

CLARK, John Leland (SO) #1712 - 8888 Riverside Dr E, Windsor ON N8S 1H2 Canada B Saint Louis MO 8/17/1933 s John Leland Clark & Marian. BA Ken 1955; BD EDS 1958; MCP U Cinc 1967; PhD U Cinc 1970. D 6/20/1958 Bp Frederic Cunningham Lawrence P 12/7/1958 Bp Henry W Hobson. m 3/7/2007 Janet Finlay c 3. Asst Calv Ch Cincinnati OH 1960-1964; Asst S Jn's Ch Worthington OH 1958-1960. jclark@jet2.net

CLARK SR, Johnny (John) Warren (WLa) 321 Horseshoe Drive, Crowley LA 70526 **Assoc P S Barn Epis Ch Lafayette LA 2011-; P-in Charge S Lk's Ch Jennings LA 2011-; Dn of Convoc Dio Wstrn Louisiana Alexandria LA 2007-** B Roswell NM 5/22/1947 s Jim Clark & Madeline E. BS New Mex St U. 1971; MDiv Epis TS of The SW 2000. D 6/3/2000 P 12/9/2000 Bp Robert Jefferson Hargrove Jr. m 11/18/1977 Phyllis King c 3. Int P S Barn Epis Ch Lafayette LA 2009-2011; Assoc P S Barn Epis Ch Lafayette LA 2008-2009; Pres of Stndg Com Dio Wstrn Louisiana Alexandria LA 2007-2009; Mem of Stndg Com Dio Wstrn Louisiana Alexandria LA 2006-2009; Hd of Anti-Racism Com Dio Wstrn Louisiana Alexandria LA 2004-2009; Mem of Dioc Coun Dio Wstrn Louisiana Alexandria LA 2003-2006; R Trin Ch Crowley LA 2000-2009; Mem of COM Dio Wstrn Louisiana Alexandria LA 2000-2003. jclark2@prodigy.net

CLARK, Joseph Madison (WA) 402 Grove Ave, po box 1098, Washington Grove MD 20880 B Wichita KS 4/11/1940 s Howard Charles Clark & Vera May. BA NWU 1963; MDiv VTS 1966; U of Maryland 1970; STM GTS 1993. D 6/11/1966 Bp Edward Clark Turner P 3/1/1967 Bp Hamilton Hyde Kellogg. c 3. R Ch Of The Ascen Gaithersburg MD 1991-2006; Trin Ch Torrington CT 1986-1991; R S Alb's Epis Ch Salisbury MD 1977-1986; Cur S Jn The Evang S Paul MN 1966-1967. woodherb@gmail.com

CLARK, Judith Freeman (Mass) 10 Ida Rd., Worcester MA 01604 **R S Jn's Epis Ch Westwood MA 2006-** B Southbridge MA 6/22/1949 d Milton George Freeman & Lillian Elizabeth. BA U of Massachusetts 1978; MA U of Massachusetts 1984; MDiv Bos 1999. D 5/29/1999 P 11/30/1999 Bp Douglas Edwin Theuner. m 5/12/1984 Robin Ervin Clark c 2. Vic Gr Epis Ch Concord NH 2001-2005; Int P Ch Of The H Sprt Plymouth NH 2000-2001; Asst to the R S Andr's Ch New London NH 1999-2000. Auth, "Encyclopedia Of Chld Abuse," *2nd Ed.*, Facts On File, Inc., 2000; Auth, "Awesome Facts To Blow Your Mind," Price Stern Sloan, Inc., 1993; Auth, "Amer'S Gilded Age," Facts On File, Inc., 1992; Auth, "Disciplines 1989 - 2002," Upper Room Pub, 1989; Auth, "Almanac Of Amer Wmn Of The 20th Century," Prentice Hall Press, 1987; Auth, "From Colony To Commonwealth: and Illustrated Hist of Massachusetts," Windsor Books, 1987; Auth, "I Remember," *Yankee mag*, 1985. judithclark49@gmail.com

CLARK, Katherine Hampton (Los) 3969 Bucklin Pl, Thousand Oaks CA 91360 B San Francisco CA 2/25/1939 d Robert Roy Hampton & Jane. BA Mills Coll 1961; Cert ETSBH 1986; MA ETSBH 1987. D 6/20/1987 P 5/14/1988 Bp Oliver Bailey Garver Jr. c 2. Assoc Prince Of Peace Epis Ch Woodland Hills CA 1997-2004; Assoc R Prince Of Peace Epis Ch Woodland Hills CA 1988-1995; Asst S Patricks Ch And Day Sch Thousand Oaks CA 1987-1988; Asst Trin Par Fillmore CA 1987. DOK 1992. shnugzkhc@msn.com

CLARK, Margaret Ann Peckham (LI) 1579 Northern Boulevard, Roslyn NY 11576 **Vice Chncllr Dio Long Island Garden City NY 2006-; R Trin Epis Ch Roslyn NY 2003-** B Binghamton NY 9/27/1967 d Eugene E Peckham & Judith. BA CUNY 1992; JD New York Law Sch 1995; MDiv GTS 2001. D 5/26/2001 Bp Andrew Hedtler Fairfield P 1/26/2002 Bp Mark Sean Sisk. m 12/19/1999 Winifred Harold Clark c 1. COM Mem Dio Long Island Garden City NY 2004-2006; Asst R All Ang' Ch New York NY 2001-2003; Com on Cn Mem Dio No Dakota Fargo ND 1998-2002. trinityrector@optonline.net

CLARK, Marlene Mae (Mich) Tiziano 52190, Col Real Vallarta, Zapopan 44630 Mexico B Manistique MI 11/18/1933 d Walter Ernest Hickson & Rhea Lucia. U of New Mex 1957; MDiv SWTS 1989. D 6/24/1989 Bp James Malone Coleman P 4/1/1990 Bp R(aymond) Stewart Wood Jr. m 7/8/1967 Robert Lee Clark. S Jn's Ch Chesaning MI 1993-1994; S Andr's Epis Ch Flint MI 1989-1993; Par Admin S Paul's Epis Ch Corunna MI 1973-1982. rev89mmc@hotmail.com

CLARK, Martha K (WA) 600 M St SW, Washington DC 20024 **S Aug's Epis Ch Washington DC 2005-** B New Haven CT 3/14/1957 d Charles Halsey Clark & Priscilla. BA Harv 1982; MDiv Duke 1992. D 2/14/1993 Bp Huntington Williams Jr P 2/1/1994 Bp Robert Whitridge Estill. m 11/27/1983 Neil Guthrie Boothby c 3. S Marg's Ch Washington DC 1999-2001; Asst Emm Epis Ch Geneva 1201 CH 1997-2000; Vic S Andrews Ch Durham NC 1993-1995; Dio No Carolina Raleigh NC 1993. Auth, "Sthrn Exposure". marthakclark@yahoo.com

CLARK, Philip C (Minn) 128 Canterbury Cir, Le Sueur MN 56058 B Syracuse NY 1/8/1933 s Henry John Clark & Catherine Rose. BS Syr 1954; MS Syr 1958. D 11/21/1993 P 6/18/1994 Bp Sanford Zangwill Kaye Hampton. m 5/2/1957 Shirley A Welsh. Loc P Dio Minnesota Minneapolis MN 1994-2002. phil@mnic.net

CLARK, Ralph (EC) 801 Bobby Jones Drive, Fayetteville NC 28312 B Latrobe PA 7/14/1965 s Harry James Clark & Gretchen Emily. BA Cit 1987; MDiv STUSo 2001; MA Webster U 2011. D 6/16/2001 P 11/25/2003 Bp Clifton Daniel III. c 2. R H Trin Epis Ch Hertford NC 2001-2005. revroc@gmail.com

CLARK JR, Richard Johnston (Fla) 1623 7th St, New Orleans LA 70115 **Ch Of The Incarn Gainesville FL 2011-; S Mich's Ch Gainesville FL 2011-** B Rantoul IL 4/10/1970 s Richard J Clark & Helen Christine. BA LSU 1992; MBA Nimbas 2001; MDiv Wycliffe Coll 2009. D 12/27/2008 P 6/27/2009 Bp Charles Edward Jenkins III. m 12/31/2004 Cinda L Clark. Mssnr Dio Louisiana Baton Rouge LA 2009-2011. rev.richard.clark@gmail.com

CLARK, Richard Neece (WMich) 3601 Trail Lake Dr, Fort Worth TX 76109 **Pstr Care S Andr's Ft Worth TX 2001-** B Kingsville TX 7/25/1944 s Ralph Neil Clark & Willie Boult. BMus SMU 1966; MDiv Nash 1969. D 6/18/1969 P 12/22/1969 Bp Charles A Mason. m 10/21/2011 Kimberly P Pulley c 1. R Trin Ch Three Rivers MI 1986-1999; S Andr's Ch Mtn Hm AR 1985-1986; Vic S Jas Ch Eureka Sprg AR 1977-1984; Asst Trin Cathd Little Rock AR

1971-1977; Cur S Alb's Epis Ch Arlington TX 1969-1971. Abbey of S Greg - Oblate 1983. rnclarktx@gmail.com

CLARK, Richard Tilton (Mass) 16 Timothy St, Fairhaven MA 02719 B Portsmouth NH 12/1/1934 s Bradley Marston Clark & Helen Francis. BA U of New Hampshire 1956; MDiv Andover Newton TS 1961. D 11/13/1963 Bp Dudley S Stark P 3/1/1964 Bp Charles F Hall. m 5/20/1983 Dianne Bergeron. Supplement Accounts Boston MA 1972-1977; Vic Ch Of The Gd Shpd Fairhaven MA 1967-1982; Cur S Mart's Epis Ch New Bedford MA 1965-1967; Cur Ch Of The Gd Shpd Nashua NH 1963-1965.

CLARK, Robert Edgar (Alb) 10 Benmost Bur Ln, Lake George NY 12845 **Died 11/3/2010** B Batavia NY 5/29/1930 s Charles Edward Clark & Emily Constance. BS Bowling Green St U 1958; STB PDS 1961; ThM Rochester Cntr for Theol Stds 1972. D 6/23/1961 P 4/1/1962 Bp Lauriston L Scaife. c 4. Commandant's Awd USNA 1989. yreclark@aol.com

CLARK, Susan McCarter (EMich) 3340 Whiting Ave Apt 12, Stevens Point WI 54481 B Madison WI 5/4/1934 d John Carroll McCarter & Jean. Nash; VTS; BA Whitman Coll 1956. D 5/10/1980 Bp Charles Thomas Gaskell P 5/28/1987 Bp Roger John White. c 2. R S Paul's Epis Ch St. Clair MI 1992-2001; Sr Assoc Chr Ch Whitefish Bay WI 1988-1992; Asst to R Chr Ch Whitefish Bay WI 1983-1987; Adj Fac Nash Nashotah WI 1981-1991; DRE Chr Ch Whitefish Bay WI 1971-1983. smclark2911@gmail.com

CLARK, Taylor Brooks (Ore) 211 W Center St, Silverton OR 97381 B Joplin MO 3/14/1950 s Richard J Clark & Gladys E. BS Portland St U 2005; MSW Portland St U 2007. D 9/16/2000 Bp Richard Sui On Chang. c 2. taylorbclark@comcast.net

CLARK, Vance Norman (CPa) 925 S. Lincoln Ave., Apt. G, Tyrone PA 16686 B Canton OH 5/14/1926 s Harold Nelson Clark & Loretta Katherine. BA Dickinson Coll 1947; STM Wesley TS 1950; U So 1956. D 6/16/1957 P 2/1/1958 Bp Albert R Stuart. c 3. P-in-c Ch Of The H Trin Houtzdale PA 1992-1997; Int H Trin Epis Ch Hollidaysburg PA 1989-1990; S Lk's Epis Ch Altoona PA 1980-1982; Dio Cntrl Pennsylvania Harrisburg PA 1978-1984; R Trin Epis Ch Tyrone PA 1972-1986; P-in-c S Jn's Epis Ch Huntingdon PA 1972-1976; R S Anne's Ch Tifton GA 1958-1962; Cur S Mk's Ch Brunswick GA 1957-1958. Meritorious Achievement Medal 1978; Bronze Star 1968. vvancepa1066@aol.com

CLARK, Vanessa Elaine (O) 131 N State St, Painesville OH 44077 **S Jas Ch Painesville OH 2009-** B Lexington KY 9/3/1973 d Kenneth Black & Vivian. BA U CO 1995; MDiv Bex 2007. D 12/2/2006 P 6/16/2007 Bp Kenneth Lester Price. m 2/23/2002 Mark D Clark c 3. P-in-c S Paul's Epis Ch Greenville OH 2007-2009; S Jn's Ch Worthington OH 2001-2004. rev.vanessa@hotmail.com

CLARK JR, Walter Daniel (WTex) 532 Zion Church Rd, Maurertown VA 22644 B New York NY 12/18/1939 s Walter Daniel Clark & Jane. BA U of Virginia 1961; MDiv VTS 1967. D 6/13/1967 Bp Walter H Gray P 12/1/1967 Bp Joseph Warren Hutchens. m 6/3/1967 Sarah Anne Wolfe Locke c 2. Int Chr Epis Ch Luray VA 2002-2003; Chr Epis Ch Luray VA 2000; Int Emm Ch Staunton VA 1998-1999; Int S Paul's Ch Sharpsburg MD 1997-1998; P-in-c Ch Of Our Sav Aransas Pass TX 1978-1982; R S Ptr's Epis Ch Rockport TX 1975-1996; Assoc H Sprt Epis Ch Houston TX 1972-1975; P-in-c S Jn's Epis Ch Silsbee TX 1971-1972; Vic S Ptr's Epis Ch Oxford CT 1967-1969. wclark@shentel.net

CLARK, William Whittier (Alb) Po Box 56, Medusa NY 12120 B Albany NY 5/30/1949 s Richard Bierce Clark & Jane. AAS Paul Smith's Coll 1969; BS Syr 1978. D 5/14/1994 Bp David Standish Ball. m 6/15/1974 Kathleen Loraine O'Keefe c 2.

CLARKE, Barbara Jean (Me) 11 Daisey Ln, Brewer ME 04412 B Ellsworth ME 2/10/1941 d John Clarke & Vivian Force. BA U of Maine 1963; MS U of Maine 1965; PhD Tul 1974; Cert EDS 1995; MDiv Wesley TS 1996. D 6/17/1995 Bp Jane Hart Holmes Dixon P 5/9/1996 Bp Ronald Hayward Haines. S Pat's Ch Brewer ME 2008; S Aug's Epis Ch Washington DC 2004-2005; P-in-c S Lk's Ch Trin Par Beth MD 2001-2003; Int S Matt's Epis Ch Hyattsville MD 1999-2001; S Marg's Ch Washington DC 1996-1997; Ch Of The Ascen Gaithersburg MD 1995-1996. Auth, "Healing Power of Anger," *Through Eyes of Wmn:Insights in Pstr Care*, 1996. bjclarke208@roadrunner.com

CLARKE, Bonnie Jeanne Smith (EC) 122 Doris Dr, Goldsboro NC 27534 **Disciplinary Bd Dio E Carolina Kinston NC 2011-; Ch Of The H Innoc Seven Sprg NC 2008-; Anti-Racism Cmsn Dio E Carolina Kinston NC 2007-; R S Aug's Epis Ch Kinston NC 1991-** B Washington DC 8/10/1957 d John Kirkland Smith & Edith. BA Converse Coll 1979; MDiv Ya Berk 1983. D 6/11/1983 P 5/1/1984 Bp William Arthur Beckham. m 6/19/1982 Frederick W Clarke c 2. Liturg Cmsn Dio E Carolina Kinston NC 2007-2011; Dn, Trin Dnry Dio E Carolina Kinston NC 1997-1999; Exec Coun Dio E Carolina Kinston NC 1995-2003; Chair, COM Dio E Carolina Kinston NC 1992-1995; Dioc Coun Dio So Carolina Charleston SC 1987-1989; Vic Ch Of The H Comm Allendale SC 1984-1989; Ch Of The Heav Rest Estill SC 1983-1989; All SS Epis Ch Hampton SC 1983-1986. Career Achievement Awd 86 Converse Coll 1986; Outstndng Yng Wmn Amer 1984. staugkinston@embarqmail.com

CLARKE, Charles Ray (Wyo) 796 Garner Dr, Lander WY 82520 **Cn 9 P Dio Wyoming Casper WY 2002-** B Hebron NE 3/2/1943 s Darrell Wayne Clarke & Margaret Francis. BS U of Wyoming 1971; EFM STUSo 1990. D 1/24/1993 Bp Bob Gordon Jones P 11/30/2002 Bp Bruce Edward Caldwell. m 8/29/1969 Cheryl Ann Caufman. NAAD. cclarke@rmisp.com

C

CLARKE JR, Daniel Lee (SC) 94 Willow Oak Cir, Charleston SC 29418 **Cur Ch Of The H Comm Charleston SC 1999-** B Sumter SC 8/24/1955 s Daniel Lee Clarke & Una Annette. BA Belmont Abbey Coll 1976; MA Cit 1980; MDiv Nash 1999. D 6/17/1999 P 12/19/1999 Bp Edward Lloyd Salmon Jr. Assn Our Lady Of Walsingham; CBS, GAS, SocMary; Living Rosary Our Lady Of S Dominic Soc King Chas Mtyr. FATHERDANIEL@HOTMAIL.COM

CLARKE, Debra (NJ) 187 Aster Ct, Whitehouse Station NJ 08889 **D S Thos Ch Alexandria Pittstown NJ 2009-; Dir of Yth Mnstry Dio New Jersey Trenton NJ 2005-** B Plainfield NJ 1/11/1959 D 9/21/2002 Bp David B(ruce) Joslin. m 9/5/1981 Stephen Clarke c 2. debraclarke@comcast.net

CLARKE, Gervaise Angelo Morales (Nwk) 34 Orane Ave, Meadowbrook Mews Kingston 19 Jamaica **Cathd Chapt Dio Newark Newark NJ 2004-; Const & Cn Com Dio Newark Newark NJ 2004-; Dioc Coun Dio Newark Newark NJ 2004-** B Kingston JM 7/7/1940 s Vincent Morrison Clarke & Maude Gwendolyn. LTh Untd Theol Coll Of The W Indies Kingston Jm 1968; BA U of The W Indies 1974; ThM PrTS 1981; PhD Thornewood U Amsterdam Nl 2001. Trans 2/1/1987 Bp The Bishop Of Jamaica. m 7/13/1968 Joan F Binger c 2. Cathd Chapt Dio Newark Newark NJ 1989-1992; Cn Ch Of The Epiph Orange NJ 1987-2007. "Intl & Jamaican Track And Field," *Track And Field Jamaica (Quarterly)*, 1998. Fell Of The Royal Geographical Soc 1983; Lions Club Of Kingston 1969-1984; Rotary Club Of Orange 1987. Paul Harris Fell In Rotary Rotary Club Of Orange 2000; Off Of The Ord Of dist (O.D) Govt Of Jamaica 1998; Hon Cn Dio Belize 1984. calabar52@hotmail.com

CLARKE, James Alexander (At) 601 Alston Lane, Cornelia GA 30531 B Atlanta GA 8/15/1937 s James Thomas Clarke & Mildred (Alexander) Clarke Clarke. BBA Georgia St U 1960; MDiv STUSo 1967. D 6/24/1967 Bp Randolph R Claiborne P 6/29/1968 Bp Milton LeGrand Wood. m 10/3/1992 N Carolyn Tuck c 4. P-in-c St Mary's Atlanta GA 1983-1999; Asst To Bp For Spec Ministires Dio Atlanta Atlanta GA 1973-1980; Vic S Cathr's Epis Ch Marietta GA 1967-1973; Asst S Jas Epis Ch Marietta GA 1967-1970. 2jaclarke@windstream.net

CLARKE, James Munro (Alb) Po Box 405, Downsville NY 13755 B Newport RI 9/28/1951 s David Clarke & Claudia. BA Muskingum Coll 1974; MDiv Yale DS 1978. D 6/17/1978 P 12/17/1978 Bp Frederick Hesley Belden. m 12/6/1997 J Gwendolyn Clarke c 3. S Mary's Ch Downsville NY 2001-2002; All SS Epis Ch Kansas City MO 1999-2001; Prov Syn Dio Albany Albany NY 1998-1999; Dioc Coun Dio Albany Albany NY 1996-1999; Co-Chr Yth Mnstry Metropltn Dnry Dio Albany Albany NY 1990-1991; R S Andr's Ch Scotia NY 1988-1999; Chair Yth Com Dio Albany Albany NY 1988-1992; Assoc R All SS Ch Tarpon Sprg FL 1987-1988; Ce Com Dio SW Florida Sarasota FL 1987-1988; Yth Com Dio SW Florida Sarasota FL 1985-1988; Asst R All SS Ch Tarpon Sprg FL 1984-1986; Cmsn Chr Formation Dio Cntrl Florida Orlando FL 1982-1984; Epis Sch Assn Dio Cntrl Florida Orlando FL 1981-1984; S Edw's Sch Vero Bch FL 1981-1984; Epis HS Alexandria VA 1978-1981.

CLARKE, Janet Vollert (SeFla) 33406 Fairway Rd, Leesburg FL 34788 **D S Thos Epis Ch Eustis FL 1996-** B New York NY 2/1/1931 d Rudolph Vollert & Ada Darrell. Rutgers-The St U 1953; Barry U 1984; Cert Diac Sch Mnstry Miami FL 1988; AA Miami-Dade Cmnty Coll 1988. D 6/4/1988 Bp Calvin Onderdonk Schofield Jr. m 4/22/1979 Ronald Clarke c 5. D S Andr's Epis Ch Palmetto Bay FL 1988-1996. NAAD 1989. McKnight Schlrshp Acad Excellence MDCC. jclarke993@aol.com

CLARKE, John David (NY) 790 11th Ave Apt 29a, New York NY 10019 B Providence RI 5/16/1939 s Kenneth Parker Clarke & Ruth Helen. AA Bos 1960; BS U of Arizona 1969. D 5/19/2001 Bp Richard Frank Grein. m 5/28/1978 Maria Antonia Velez c 2. S Barth's Ch New York NY 2007-2009; S Barth's Ch New York NY 2001-2007. clarke@stbarts.org

CLARKE, John Robert (Mass) 52 Waltham St, Boston MA 02118 **P-in-c S Paul's Ch Malden MA 2004-** B Boston MA 5/14/1948 s Buell Maclean Clarke & Anne. BA Wheaton Coll 1970; MDiv Weston Jesuit TS 1997. D 6/6/1998 P 5/29/1999 Bp M(arvil) Thomas Shaw III. m 9/29/2007 William James Theisen. Par Of The Mssh Auburndale MA 2001-2004; Int Ascen Memi Ch Ipswich MA 1999-2000; Asst S Steph's Epis Ch Boston MA 1998-1999. Affirming Cath; Alpha Sigma Nu; Human Rts Cmpgn Fund; MECA; Rel Cltn for the Freedom to Marry. revjohn.clarke@comcast.net

CLARKE, Julian Maurice (VI) 123 Circle Dr, Saint Simons Island GA 31522 B Tortola VI 6/19/1938 s Cardigan Clarke & Elsa Eudora. Cert ETSC 1969; Advncd CPE 1973; MDiv ETSC 1974; Fell VTS 1988; VTS 1990. D 6/27/1969 P 1/1/1970 Bp Cedric Earl Mills. m 12/27/1961 Esther Alicia Pickering c 2. Cur S Paul's Epis Ch Orangeburg SC 1999; R S Geo Mtyr Ch Tortola VG 1993-1999; R S Athan Ch Brunswick GA 1990-1993; R S Andr's Ch Charlotte Amalie VI VI 1979-1990; Cn to Bp of VI Dio Vrgn Islands St Thos VI VI

1976-1984; Vic S Andr's Ch Charlotte Amalie VI VI 1975-1978; Vic Ch of the H Sprt St Thos VI VI 1974-1987; Cur Cathd Ch of All SS St Thos VI VI 1969-1972. Auth, "The Test," *Ten Who Tithe*, The Epis Ch Cntr, 1980; Auth, "Culture and Sprtl Aspects of Aging," *Procedings of the First Caribbean Inst on Gerontology*, Coll of the Vrgn Islands, 1979. Cn Cathdral Ch of All SS 2006; Off of the British Empire Eliz II, Queen of Engl 1999; League of British Vrgn ISlands Awd League of British Vrgn Islands 1998; Legis Awd for Dedicated Serv to People of VI 1990; Soc Worker of Achievement NASW VI Chapt 1987. jmc38@aol.com

CLARKE, Kenneth Gregory (SO) 3090 Montego Ln. Apt. 1, Maineville OH 45039 B Chicago IL 7/10/1929 s Arthur Marshall Clarke & Leta Grace. BA Denison U 1952. D 6/13/2009 Bp Thomas Edward Breidenthal. c 1. kclarke1@cinci.rr.com

CLARKE, Richard Kent (WMass) 162 Laurelwood Dr, Hopedale MA 01747 B Springfield MA 8/8/1935 s Louis Campbell Clarke & Hazel Gertrude. BA Wesl 1957; UTS 1958; BD EDS 1960. D 6/28/1960 Bp Robert McConnell Hatch P 12/29/1960 Bp William J Gordon Jr. m 6/12/1965 Katherine W Wood. Int S Andr's Ch No Grafton MA 1996-1997; Bement/Waterfield Grants Com Dio Wstrn Massachusetts Springfield MA 1985-2010; Natl Bd EME Dio Wstrn Massachusetts Springfield MA 1984-1986; R The Chap Of All SS Leominster MA 1981-1996; Assoc Chr Ch Fitchburg MA 1979-1981; Bd Mgr Dio Wstrn Massachusetts Springfield MA 1972-1979; R Trin Epis Ch Whitinsville MA 1970-1979. Ord Lectio Divina. RKCLARKE35@GMAIL.COM

CLARKE, Robert Burton (Chi) 524 Sheridan Sq Apt 3, Evanston IL 60202 B Chicago IL 9/10/1952 s Thomas Howard Clarke & Thelma Irene. BA Luther Coll 1982; MDiv SWTS 1982; DMin Chicago TS 1995. D 6/11/1983 Bp Quintin Ebenezer Primo Jr P 12/1/1983 Bp James Winchester Montgomery. m 7/8/2010 Laurel Austin c 1. Gr Epis Ch Sheboygan WI 2010-2011; S Dav's Ch Glenview IL 2008-2010; The Cathd Ch Of S Paul Springfield IL 2004-2006; S Paul's Cathd Fond du Lac WI 2001-2003; Int Chr Ch River Forest IL 2000-2001; P-in-c Ch Of S Ben Bolingbrook IL 1986-1987; P-in-c S Bride's Epis Ch Oregon IL 1985-1986; Asst S Aug's Epis Ch Wilmette IL 1984-2000. rdrbclarke@aol.com

CLARKE, Sheelagh (Nwk) 119 Main St, Millburn NJ 07041 **R S Steph's Ch Millburn NJ 2011-** B Aylesbury UK 4/21/1956 d Anthony Harris & Joan Elizabeth. BEd U of Reading Reading GB 1977; MA Open U Milton Keynes GB 1990; MDiv GTS 2005. D 6/11/2005 P 1/14/2006 Bp George Edward Councell. m 6/19/2003 Michael Christopher Clarke c 1. Int S Barn Epis Ch Monmouth Jct NJ 2009-2011; Asst S Paul's Epis Ch Westfield NJ 2007-2009; Asst S Lk's Ch Gladstone NJ 2005-2007. sheelaghclarke@hotmail.com

CLARKE, Thomas George (Los) 1549 E Lobo Way, Palm Springs CA 92264 **Trst VTS Alexandria VA 2001-; Hon Cn Dio Los Angeles Los Angeles CA 1993-** B Los Angeles CA 7/31/1945 s Thomas W Clarke & Majory Rider. BA U of Redlands 1967; MDiv VTS 1970. D 9/13/1970 Bp Francis E I Bloy P 3/1/1971 Bp Victor Manuel Rivera. Pres Natl Assoc Of Epis Schools- Epis Ch New York NY 1990-1992; Trst Natl Assoc Of Epis Schools- Epis Ch New York NY 1987-2003; Campbell Hall Vlly Vill CA 1971-2004; Asst The Ch Of The Epiph Washington DC 1970-1971. Distinguished Alum Awd Campbell Hall/Argyll Acad Alum Assn 2008; The Jn Verdery Awd Nat. Assoc. of Epis Schools 2008. clarketg@earthlink.net

CLARKE, Thomas McTyghe (Md) 2523 Lear Ct, Murfreesboro TN 37129 B Washington DC 11/7/1923 s Charles Joseph Clarke & Marjorie. AA GW 1947; BA GW 1948; MDiv VTS 1967. D 6/24/1967 P 6/1/1968 Bp William Foreman Creighton. m 7/10/1948 Margaret Louise McCoy. D Chr Ch Wm And Mary Newburg MD 1967-1968. Auth, "A Plan & Proposal For An Alco Sfty Proj For The Grtr Baltimore Prod Analysis".

CLARKE JR, Walter Malcolm (ECR) 285 Laureles Grade, Salinas CA 93908 **Died 10/9/2009** B Oakland CA 4/14/1913 s Walter Malcolm Clarke & Emma Minola. BA Berea Coll 1941; BD Yale DS 1944; MA U CA 1958. D 6/10/1950 P 12/1/1950 Bp Sumner Walters.

CLARKSON, Frederick C (NC) 4401 Statesville Blvd., Salisbury NC 28147 **Vic Ch Of The Gd Shpd Cooleemee NC 2008-; Dio No Carolina Raleigh NC 2008-** B Bogota Colombia 11/1/1970 s Frederick Findlayson Clarkson & Gwinneth Ann. MA U of St Andrews 1993; MDiv The Prot Epis TS 2008. D 5/24/2008 Bp Peter James Lee P 11/29/2008 Bp William O Gregg. fclarkson@yadtel.net

CLARKSON, Julie Cuthbertson (NC) 1420 Sterling Rd, Charlotte NC 28209 B Charlotte NC 6/6/1929 d William Reynolds Cuthbertson & Julia Hagood. BA Agnes Scott Coll 1951; MDiv Duke 1984; Cert GTS 1987. D 8/30/1987 Bp Frank Harris Vest Jr P 9/1/1988 Bp Robert Whitridge Estill. c 3. S Ptr's Epis Ch Charlotte NC 1996-1998; Gr Epis Ch Lexington NC 1993-1995; S Chris's Epis Ch High Point NC 1987-1992. jclarkson@carolina.rr.com

CLARKSON, Michael Livingston (SC) 4416 Betsy Kerrison PKWY, Johns Island SC 29455 **R Ch Of Our Sav Johns Island SC 2008-** B Bremerhaven Germany 3/16/1948 s Richard Livingston Clarkson & Patricia Sutherland. BA U CA Santa Barbara 1970; JD Loyola U Law Sch 1973; Cert. Theol. Oxf 1989. Trans from The Episcopal Church in Jerusalem and the Middle East 1/30/2007 Bp Edward Lloyd Salmon Jr. m 8/23/1969 Linda Clarkson c 2. Assoc R The Ch Of The Cross Bluffton SC 2007-2008. mikec@gulf-net.org

CLARKSON, Ted Hamby (Ga) Po Drawer 929, Darien GA 31305 **R S Andr's Ch Darien GA 2006-** B Augusta GA 2/18/1958 s Allen Clarkson & Mary. BS Wofford Coll 1979; JD U GA 1982; MDiv U So 2006. D 2/4/2006 P 8/9/2006 Bp Henry Irving Louttit. m 6/28/1980 Allison H Clarkson c 3. clarkth9@sewanee.edu

CLARKSON IV, William (WA) 1424 W Paces Ferry Rd Nw, Atlanta GA 30327 **Cler Assoc All SS Epis Ch Atlanta GA 2002-** B Corsicana TX 2/17/1947 s William Clarkson & Mary. BA Duke 1970; MDiv GTS 1973; DMin SMU 1982. D 6/11/1973 P 12/1/1973 Bp A Donald Davies. m 5/27/1972 Lucile McKee c 2. Asst Chr Ch Georgetown Washington DC 1981-1983; Cur S Mich And All Ang Ch Dallas TX 1978-1981; S Marks Sch Of Texas Dallas TX 1975-1978; Cur S Alb's Epis Ch Arlington TX 1973-1975. billclarkson@westminster.net

CLARY, S(idney) Grayson (NC) 1179 Ivy Hill Drive, Mendota Heights MN 55118 B Disputanta VA 10/16/1921 s Thomas Fenner Clary & Evelyn Clark. BA W&M 1943; MDiv VTS 1949. D 6/10/1949 Bp William A Brown P 6/10/1950 Bp George P Gunn. m 8/3/1946 Jean Beazley. Alum Bd VTS Alexandria VA 1980-1983; Stndg Com Dio Minnesota Minneapolis MN 1971-1977; R S Jn The Evang S Paul MN 1964-1986; Dio So Carolina Charleston SC 1959-1986; R S Phil's Ch Charleston SC 1957-1964; R Calv Ch Tarboro NC 1951-1957; Emm Ch Callaville FREEMAN VA 1949-1951; R S Andr's Lawrenceville VA 1949-1951; P-in-c Trin / S Mk's Alberta VA 1949-1951. DD SWTS 1983. clary002@umn.edu

CLASPER, Paul (Los) 721 Harrison Ave., Claremont CA 91711 **Asst S Ambr Par Claremont CA 1992-** B Spencerville OH 1/9/1923 s John Clasper & Anna. BA Taylor U Upland IN 1944; BD Sthrn Bapt TS Louisville KY 1947; STM UTS 1950; PhD UTS 1952. Trans from Hong Kong Anglican Church 12/14/1975 Bp Richard Henry Baker. m 7/9/2009 Mary Fitzpatrick c 2. Theol-in-res Dio California San Francisco CA 1987-1991. Auth, "Yogi," *Commissar & Mind-Thrid Wrld*; Auth, *Estrn Paths & Chr Way*; Auth, *New Life in Chr*. Unitas Distingushed Alum Awd Un Theologoical Sem, NY 2007.

CLAUSEN, Kathryn Pearce (SO) 3623 Sellers Drive, Millersport OH 43046 **P-in-c Trin Ch Newark OH 2010-** B Dayton OH 6/17/1941 d George Call Pearce & Katherine Louise. BA OH SU 1962; MD OH SU 1966; MS OH SU 1968; MTS Trin Luth Sem 2001. D 10/28/2000 P 6/23/2001 Bp Herbert Thompson Jr. m 6/13/1964 William Clausen c 2. P-in-c S Jas Epis Ch Zanesville OH 2006-2009; Int Trin Epis Ch London OH 2005-2006; Bex Columbus OH 2003-2006; P-in-c Trin Ch Newark OH 2001-2006. Auth, "Numerous Med arts In," *Numerous Med arts In Var Pub*. Sprt of Wmn Awd OH SU Med Ctr 1999; Tchg Awards x 4 OH SU Med 1986; Alum Achievement Awd OH SU Med 1986; Prof of Year OH SU Med 1976; AOA hon Med Soc OH SU 1966; Med awards Var 1961. kpclausen@me.com

CLAUSEN, Ruth Lucille (Mich) 100 N. College Row Apt. 165, Brevard NC 28712 B Mansfield OH 3/18/1930 d Ray Davis Schaaf & Florence Marie. Baldwin-Wallace Coll 1949; BS OH SU 1952; MSW U MI 1969; CDSP 1988. D 6/25/1988 Bp Henry Irving Mayson P 1/28/1989 Bp H Coleman McGehee Jr. c 1. Trin Ch Detroit MI 1992-1997; S Mich's Ch Grosse Pointe Woods MI 1991-1992; R S Geo's Epis Ch Warren MI 1988-1992. rclausen2@mac.com

CLAVIER, Anthony FM (NI) 708 Harrison St, La Porte IN 46350 **Exam Chapl Dio Nthrn Indiana So Bend IN 2009-; of Wstrn Dnry Dio Nthrn Indiana So Bend IN 2008-; S Paul's Epis Ch La Porte IN 2008-** B Worsbrough Dale UK 4/19/1940 s Forbes Moreton Clavier & Ethel. Bern Gilpin Soc Durham Gb 1960; Inst Of Theol London Gb 1964; BD Geneva TS 1974; STD Geneva TS 1975; Nash 1994. Trans 2/15/2004 Bp Creighton Leland Robertson. m 12/22/1995 Patricia c Belt c 3. Int S Thos a Becket Epis Ch Morgantown WV 2005-2008; Amer Ch In Europe 2004-2005; Dn Convoc of Amer Ch in Europe Paris FR 2004-2005; Exec Coun Appointees New York NY 2004; Dn Dio Arkansas Little Rock AR 2001-2004; Dio So Dakota Sioux Falls SD 2001-2004; R Trin Epis Ch Watertown SD 2001-2004; Trin Ch Pine Bluff AR 1999-2001. patclavier@gmail.com

CLAWSON, Donald Richard (SeFla) 1605 Paseo Del Lago Ln, Vero Beach FL 32967 B Pittsburgh PA 4/17/1933 s Richard N Clawson & Hannah Margaret. BA U Pgh 1955; MDiv GTS 1958. D 6/14/1958 Bp William S Thomas P 12/21/1958 Bp Austin Pardue. m 1/3/1988 Stacey Hanna c 3. Chair - Duncan Conf Cntr Bd Dir Dio SE Florida Miami FL 1984-1987; R S Paul's Ch Delray Bch FL 1977-1998; R S Jn's Ch Hollywood FL 1975-1976; R Dio Cntrl Gulf Coast Pensacola FL 1970-1975; R S Paul's Ch Mobile AL 1970-1975; R Gr Epis Ch Orange Pk FL 1963-1970; DeptCE Dio Pittsburgh Monroeville PA 1959-1963; P-in-c S Phil's Ch Coraopolis PA 1958-1963. Hon HLD El Shaddai Sem Toledo 1996. donaldclaw@aol.com

CLAWSON, Jeffrey David (Los) 3 Bayview Ave., Belvedere CA 94920 B Garden Grove CA 7/21/1959 s David Warren Clawson & Suzanne. BA California St U 1984; MS California St U 1986; MDiv CDSP 2008. D 6/7/2008 P 1/10/2009 Bp Joseph Jon Bruno. All SS Par Los Angeles CA 2009-2010; Assoc R S Steph's Par Belvedere CA 2008-2009. jeffreyclawson@aol.com

CLAXTON, Constance Colvin (Minn) 101 N 5th St, Marshall MN 56258 B Tulsa OK 10/31/1940 d Richard Asby Colvin & Muzetta Nadine. BA S Cathr 1981; MDiv SWTS 1985. D 6/24/1985 P 1/1/1986 Bp Robert Marshall Anderson. m 1/2/1989 Roger Claxton c 3. S Lk's Epis Ch Hastings MN 2004-2010; R S Jas Ch Marshall MN 1995-2002; R Emm Epis Ch Alexandria MN 1989-1994; Asst Chr Ch S Paul MN 1986-1989; P-in-c S Mary's Basswood Grove Hastings MN 1985-1989. CONNIECLAXTON@COMCAST.NET

CLAXTON, Leonard Cuthbert (Minn) RR #2, Box 207, Truman MN 56088 **Supply S Andr's Epis Ch Waterville MN 1996-** B Superior WI 4/1/1923 s Cuthbert Anderson Claxton & Mary Hannah. Minnesota St U Mankato 1959; U MN 1962; U of No Dakota 1970. D 2/24/1966 P 9/1/1966 Bp Russell T Rauscher. m 4/24/1948 Shirley Gamble. S Andr's Ch Le Sueur MN 1985-1989; S Andr's Epis Ch Waterville MN 1985-1989; S Steph's Epis Ch Stevensville MT 1982-1985; Exec Counsel Dio Montana Helena MT 1981-1985; Chair Dio Montana Helena MT 1979-1985; Vic S Paul's Ch Hamilton MT 1974-1985; Bd Trst Dio Montana Helena MT 1974-1981; Cur S Lk's Ch Billings MT 1971-1974; Chair Dio Montana Helena MT 1970-1975; Vic S Thos Ch Hardin MT 1970-1971; Vic Ch Of The Gd Shpd Helena MT 1969-1971; Vic S Alb's Epis Ch Laurel MT 1969-1971; Vic S Ptr And S Jas Ch Grafton ND 1966-1969. Ord Of S Lk. shirlen@bevcomm.net

CLAY, Frederick Guion (Mass) 38 Brook Rd, Sharon MA 02067 B 1/8/1929 D 6/8/1956 P 2/25/1957 Bp Frederick J Warnecke.

CLAY, Thomas Davies (WA) 15003 Reserve Rd, Accokeek MD 20607 B Huntington WV 5/23/1938 s Earl Taft Clay & Mary. BA Marshall U 1960; MDiv Epis TS In Kentucky 1963. D 6/1/1963 P 12/1/1963 Bp William R Moody. m 4/5/1997 Kathleen Jenkins O'Day c 2. P-in-c Chr Ch Wm And Mary Newburg MD 1998-2002; S Andr's Ch Leonardtown California MD 1994-1998; R Calv Epis Ch Front Royal VA 1978-1994; R S Mk's Epis Ch Lagrange GA 1969-1978; Asst S Ptr's Epis Ch Washington NC 1966-1969. thomasclay@verizon.net

CLAYTON JR, Paul Bauchman (NY) 4 Townsend Farm Rd, Lagrangeville NY 12540 B Port Arthur TX 6/17/1939 s Paul Bauchman Clayton & Bernice Joy. BA U of Texas 1961; STB GTS 1964; STM GTS 1968; MA UTS 1975; PhD UTS 1985. D 6/18/1964 P 12/18/1964 Bp Theodore H McCrea. m 6/1/1988 Sharon Hoffman Chant c 2. Adj Prof of Patristics The GTS New York NY 1992; R S Andr's Ch Poughkeepsie NY 1971-2005; The GTS New York NY 1966-1971; Asst Zion Zion Epis Ch Wappingers Falls NY 1966-1971; Vic Ch Of The H Apos Aledo TX 1964-1966; Cur All SS' Epis Ch Ft Worth TX 1964-1965. Auth, "The Christology of Theo Cyrus: Antiochene Christology," *From the Coun of Ephesus (431) to the Coun of Chalcedon (451)*, Oxf Press, 2007; Auth, "arts," *Encyclopedia Amer*, 1972. Alcuin Club 1964-2005; Amer Soc Ch Hist 1964; Angl Soc 1964; HSEC 1964; No Amer Acad Ecumenists 1987; Oxford Intl Conf of Patristic Stds 1971; Soc of Angl and Luth Theologians 1988. Fell ECF 1971; Phi Beta Kappa U of Texas 1961. pbclayton@aol.com

CLAYTON, Sharon Hoffman Chant (NY) 4 Townsend Farm Rd, Lagrangeville NY 12540 **S Paul's And Trin Par Tivoli NY 2007-** B New York NY 10/9/1946 d Bernard Hoffman & Geraldine Dorothea. Premier Degree de la langue francaise U of Paris FR 1967; BA w hon CUNY 1968; MDiv GTS 1986. D 6/7/1986 Bp Paul Moore Jr P 12/1/1986 Bp Walter Decoster Dennis Jr. m 6/1/1988 Paul Bauchman Clayton. Gr Ch Millbrook NY 1999-2000; Cur S Andr's Ch Poughkeepsie NY 1989-2005; Asst Chr's Ch Rye NY 1986-1988. Auth, *Joining the Conversation*. shclayton1988@aol.com

CLAYTON, Timothy Wayne (Alb) 392 Walnut Hill Rd, North Yarmouth ME B Charlotte NC 10/11/1966 s Beverly Clayton & Judy. BA U NC 1988; MDiv Gordon-Conwell TS 1999. D 9/1/2005 P 3/4/2006 Bp David John Bena. m 5/29/1993 Cheryl Krusen c 3. S Jn's Epis Ch Charlotte NC 2007-2009. timclayton@mac.com

CLAYTOR, Susan Quarles (CPa) 310 Elm Avenue, Hershey PA 17033 **All SS' Epis Ch Hershey PA 2009-** B Atlanta GA 7/29/1961 d Willie Raymond Quarles & Ethel Loretta. BA U of No Florida 2001; MDiv VTS 2004. D 5/30/2004 P 12/5/2004 Bp Samuel Johnson Howard. m 8/4/1979 Francis Parr Claytor c 6. S Jas' Epis Ch Lake City FL 2007-2008; Trin Epis Ch St Aug FL 2004-2007; Ch Of Our Sav Jacksonville FL 1991-2001. claytor79@gmail.com

CLEAVER-BARTHOLOMEW, Dena Marcel (CNY) 4566 Stoneledge Ln, Manlius NY 13104 **Chair, Cler Cont Educ Team Dio Cntrl New York Syracuse NY 2011-; COM Dio Cntrl New York Syracuse NY 2011-; R Chr Ch Manlius NY 2010-** B Chinon FR 11/8/1960 d Bruce Hayes Cleaver & Jeanene. BA Tem 1983; MDiv Ya Berk 1988; ThM Candler TS Emory U 1994. D 6/10/1988 P 7/6/1989 Bp Charlie Fuller McNutt Jr. m 8/22/1987 David Gordon Bartholomew c 2. Dioc Coun Dio Ohio Cleveland OH 2007-2010; Congrl Dvlpmt Cmsn Dio Ohio Cleveland OH 2006-2010; Assoc R S Paul's Ch Akron OH 2006-2010; Assoc R New Life Epis Ch Uniontown OH 2005-2006; Assoc R S Jas' Epis Ch Dexter MI 2000-2005; P Ch Of The Epiph Atlanta GA 1993-1995; Assoc R H Trin Par Decatur GA 1991-1993; Assoc R S Ptr's Par San Pedro CA 1989-1991; D S Lk's Epis Ch Atlanta GA 1988-1989. denac-b@sbcglobal.net

CLEAVES JR, George Lucius (EMich) 9020 South Saginaw Road, Grand Blanc MI 48439 **R S Christophers Epis Ch Grand Blanc MI 1992-** B Needham MA 10/18/1942 s George Lucius Cleaves & Marie Bernice. BA/BS Bentley Coll 1976; MDiv EDS 1984. D 6/3/1989 Bp David Elliot Johnson P 6/14/1990 Bp Robert Rae Spears Jr. Assoc S Jas Ch New York NY 1990-1992. gcleaves810@aol.com

CLECKLER, Michael Howard (Ala) 1513 Edinburgh Way, Birmingham AL 35243 B Birmingham AL 8/21/1947 s Robert Marion Cleckler & Kathleen Edith. BA Samford U 1969; JD Cumberland Sch of Law 1972; MDiv Epis TS of The SW 1989. D 6/7/1989 P 12/1/1989 Bp Robert Oran Miller. c 3. St. Matt's Epis Ch Madison AL 1992-1994; Dio Alabama Birmingham AL 1991-1992; Chr Ch Tuscaloosa AL 1989-1991. mcleckler@realtysouth.com

CLEGHORN, Charlotte Dudley (WNC) 1811 Meadowbrook Ter, Hendersonville NC 28791 B Ocala FL 2/3/1949 d Edward Cleghorn & Bettie. AA Bennett Coll 1969; BA Bos 1971; MRE Gordon-Conwell TS 1975; MDiv VTS 1986. Trans 1/21/2004 Bp Joseph Jon Bruno. The Cathd Of All Souls Asheville NC 2005-2010; Int Ch Of The H Fam Mills River NC 2004-2005; Int S Jas Epis Ch Hendersonville NC 2002-2004; Assoc P S Geo's Epis Ch Laguna Hills CA 1998-2001; Dio Los Angeles Los Angeles CA 1997-1998; R S Ann's Epis Ch Windham Windham ME 1989-1996; Asst S Paul's Epis Ch Cleveland Heights OH 1986-1989. cdcleghorn@gmail.com

CLEGHORN, Maxine Janetta (NY) 4401 Matilda Ave, Bronx NY 10470 B Jamaica 4/16/1963 d Noel Lloyd Cleghorn & Urdella. MDiv NYTS; BA Untd TS. Trans from Church in the Province Of The West Indies 3/2/2010 Bp Mark Sean Sisk. Asst Ch Of The Gd Shpd Wakefield Bronx NY 2010. clegmax@aol.com

CLELAND, Carol Elaine (Cal) 1550 Portola Avenue, Palo Alto CA 94306 B Malden MA 12/14/1940 d Robert John Nolte & Della. BS Bos 1965; MA FD 1979; MDiv CDSP 1991; MA U of San Francisco 2003; Candidate Psychoanalytic Inst of Nthrn California 2009. D 12/7/1991 P 12/5/1992 Bp William Edwin Swing. m 9/4/1965 Alan Stuart Cleland. S Anne's Ch Fremont CA 1994-2006; Int Ch Of The Epiph San Carlos CA 1993-1994; Asst S Lk's Ch San Francisco CA 1991-1993. cacleland@aol.com

CLEMENT, Betty Cannon (Dal) 4120 Jasmine St, Paris TX 75462 **D Ch Of The H Cross Paris TX 2001-** B Paris TX 2/18/1937 d Bill Ellis Cannon & Bessie Maud. Lm Angl TS 2001. D 12/19/2001 Bp James Monte Stanton. m 6/2/1957 Wayne Clement c 2. bclement1@cox-internet.com

CLEMENT, James Marshall (Q) 1434 N West St Apt 15, Galesburg IL 61401 **S Jn's Epis Ch Kewanee IL 2010-** B Charleston SC 8/21/1967 s Samuel M Clement & Anne R. BA Coll of Charleston 2001; MA Coll of Charleston, Grad Sch 2005; BA (Hons) Coll of the Resurr, Mirfield 2006; MDiv Nash 2007. D 12/8/2007 P 6/14/2008 Bp Keith Lynn Ackerman. Credo Inst Inc. Memphis TN 2010; Gr Epis Ch Galesburg IL 2007-2008. rector@stjohnil.org

CLEMENTS, C(harles) Christopher (USC) 1523 Delmar St, West Columbia SC 29169 **Asstg P S Mary's Ch Columbia SC 2002-** B Cleveland TN 11/28/1939 s Charles Groner Clements & Mary Arthur. BS U of Tennessee 1961; STB GTS 1964. D 6/29/1964 Bp John Vander Horst P 5/22/1965 Bp William Evan Sanders. m 7/2/1964 Julia Ann Bush. S Steph's Epis Ch Ridgeway SC 1989-2001; S Jn's Ch Winnsboro SC 1987-1988; S Jn's Epis Ch Johnson City TN 1975-1986; R S Johns Ch Old Hickory TN 1966-1968; Cur S Lk's Epis Ch Jackson TN 1965-1966. ccclements@aol.com

CLEMENTS, Elaine Gant (La) St Andrew's Episcopal Church, 1101 S Carrollton Ave, New Orleans LA 70118 B Ft Worth TX 4/3/1950 d Roy F Gant & Helen G. BA No Texas U 1972. D 12/1/2007 Bp Charles Edward Jenkins III. m 11/27/1977 John Clements c 2. egclements@aol.com

CLEMENTS, Robert (Ct) Po Box 809, Litchfield CT 06759 **R Chr Ch Roxbury CT 2009-** B Xenia OH 10/23/1956 s Carl Emery Clements & Mary Margaret. BA Thiel Coll 1978; MDiv GTS 1985; DMin PrTS 2000. D 6/15/1985 Bp James Russell Moodey P 9/15/1986 Bp Donald James Davis. m 6/24/1989 Jennings Matheson. R Trin Ch Lakeville CT 2006-2009; Int S Paul's Epis Ch Shelton CT 2005-2006; Transition Consult S Mart's Ch Providence RI 2004; Int Trin Epis Ch Hartford CT 2002-2004; Int S Jas's Ch W Hartford CT 2001-2002; Int Chr Ch Roxbury CT 1999-2001; Pstr Assoc S Paul's Epis Ch Bantam CT 1998-1999; Int Trin Ch Lakeville CT 1998-1999; Transition Consult Dio Wstrn Massachusetts Springfield MA 1998; Int S Paul's Epis Sum Chap Otis MA 1997-1998; Int S Geo's Ch Lee MA 1996-1997; Chapl Hoosac Sch Hoosick NY 1988-1993; P-in-c All SS Ch Hoosick NY 1988-1990; Vic S Aug Of Cbury Ch Edinboro PA 1986-1988; Vic S Ptr's Ch Waterford PA 1986-1988. Auth, *Ten Ways From Sunday: Raising a Faithful Teenager*, Eschaton, 2003; Auth, *Stdt Perceptions of Indep Sch Chapl Prog*, Princeton, 2000. rclements@snet.net

CLEMMENS, Jacob Stephen (Okla) 718 P St. S.W., Ardmore OK 73401 **Died 10/1/2009** B Claremore,OK 12/18/1940 s Stephen Leonard Clemmens & Lucille Sarah. AA NE A OK 1960; BA Oklahoma 1962; BD Sthrn Bapt TS Louisville KY 1966; Med NE St U 1971; CTh Epis TS of The SW 1989. D 6/17/1989 P 2/1/1990 Bp Robert Manning Moody. c 2. jslaclem@cableone.net

C

CLEMMONS, Geraldine Dobbs (Alb) 105 23rd St., Troy NY 12180 **D in charge S Jn's Ch Cohoes NY 2009-** B Memphis TN 4/27/1943 d James Edward Dobbs & Marguerite C. MA Memphis St U 1982; BS Med U of So Carolina 1995; MDiv TESM 2008. D 5/31/2008 P 11/8/2009 Bp William Howard Love. m 10/9/1982 Byard Q Clemmons c 3. gerryattrinity@yahoo.com

CLEMONS, D David (NCal) 8148 Emerson Ave, Yucca Valley CA 92284 B Oklahoma City OK 11/2/1937 s William Duffie Clemons & Lelah Lockard. BA U of Oklahoma 1959; BD SWTS 1963; CDSP 1974; Cert CPE 1978; Untd States-Army Chapl Sch 1982; Command and Gnrl Stff Coll 1983; DMin SWTS 2001. D 6/11/1963 P 12/16/1963 Bp Chilton Powell. m 12/29/1979 Kathryn Lee Mahlum c 2. Gr Epis Ch Wheatland CA 2002; R S Lk's Ch Auburn CA 1994-2002; Trin Epis Ch Pocatello ID 1988-1993; Asst S Paul's Epis Ch Ventura CA 1983-1988; S Dunst's Epis Ch San Diego CA 1982-1983; Assoc S Marg's Epis Ch Palm Desert CA 1980-1982; P-in-c H Trin Epis Ch Elk River MN 1977-1978. "Dining w Jesus Then & Now," *The Commensality of Jesus Chr and Congrgational Dvlpmt:*, doctoral thesis on file at Seabury Wstrn/NW U., 2001; "Last Supper Soliloquies". RACA 1975. Meritorious Serv Medal 90 Dept of the Army 1991; Commendation Medal 88 US-A 1988; Jas Mills Fllshp Dio Okla 1973. dkclem@verizon.net

CLEMONS JR, E(arlie) Roland (NJ) 132 S Adelaide Ave Apt 1b, Highland Park NJ 08904 **S Aug's Ch Camden NJ 2006-** B Austin TX 10/9/1946 s Earlie Clemons & Velma Rae. BS Texas Sthrn U 1969; MDiv Epis TS of The SW 1982. D 10/22/1987 Bp Maurice Manuel Benitez P 2/27/1988 Bp Gordon Taliaferro Charlton. m 7/7/1967 Catherine E Dabney-Clemons c 3. S Wilfrid's Ch Camden NJ 2009-2011; All SS Ch Highland Pk NJ 2004-2006; S Phil's Ch New York NY 1998-2003; Exec Bd Dio Texas Houston TX 1994-1997; Chair Csmn Black Mnstry Dio Texas Houston TX 1991-1998; S Fran Of Assisi Epis Prairie View TX 1990-1998; Epis Black Mnstry Cmsn Dio Texas Houston TX 1989-2000; Dio Texas Houston TX 1987-1998; Vic S Jas Ch Austin TX 1987-1990. Distinguished Awd Black Cultural Workshop 1986. eclem456@aol.com

CLENDENIN, Evan Graham (NwPa) 545 West 2nd Street, Erie PA 16507 **Cathd Of S Paul Erie PA 2011-** B Meadville PA 7/11/1980 s John Campbell Clendenin & Dona Graham. BA Reed Coll 2002; Pittsburgh TS 2008; MDiv VTS 2011. D 12/4/2010 P 9/25/2011 Bp Sean Walter Rowe. m 8/8/2009 Amy L Seese-Bieda. evanc@mithaca.com

CLENDINEN JR, James H. (Ga) 818 Miracle Ln, Vidalia GA 30474 **R The Epis Ch Of The Annunc Vidalia GA 2009-** B Rockledge FL 9/29/1955 s James Henderson Clendinen & Mary Emma. AA Brevard Cmnty Coll 1974; BA Florida St U 1976; MS Florida St U 1978; MA Candler TS Emory U 1980; Emory U 1983; CAS Nash 1990. D 6/17/1990 P 12/21/1990 Bp Harry Woolston Shipps. m 1/14/1978 Anne Powers c 3. R S Jn's Epis Ch Bainbridge GA 2003-2009; P-in-c S Thos Aquinas Mssn Baxley GA 1999-2002; R S Paul's Epis Ch Jesup GA 1994-2002; Vic S Eliz's Epis Ch Richmond Hill GA 1992-1994; R S Phil's Ch Hinesville Hinesville GA 1990-1994. Phi Beta Kappa Alpha Chapt, Florida St U 1976. jclendinen@gmail.com

CLERKIN OJN, Shawn Jeffrey (NwPa) 662 Silliman Ave, Erie PA 16510 **S Mary's Ch Erie PA 2009-** B Ridgway PA 9/15/1963 s Charles Edward Clerkin & Violet Mae. BA Gannon U 1986; MFA Virginia Commonwealth U 1989; MDiv Bex 2008. D 12/12/2004 P 6/26/2005 Bp Robert Deane Rowley Jr. m 6/15/1985 Almitra Clemente Clerkin c 1. Dioc Coun Dio NW Pennsylvania Erie PA 2008-2011; Cathd Of S Paul Erie PA 2007-2009. clerkin001@gannon.edu

CLEVELAND JR, Cromwell Cook (La) 3010 Windermere Rd, Lexington KY 40502 B Newport News VA 12/6/1948 s Cromwell Cook Cleveland & Gene Rickey. BA Cntr Coll 1971; MDiv GTS 1975. D 5/18/1975 Bp Addison Hosea P 12/6/1975 Bp William Augustus Jones Jr. Ch Of The Ascen Frankfort KY 2001; Vic S Jn's Ch Kenner LA 1993-2000; Vic S Andr's Ch Lexington KY 1989-2000; S Andr's Paradis Luling LA 1989-2000; Int S Andr's Epis Ch New Orleans LA 1987-1988; Asst R S Mich & S Geo Clayton MO 1975-1977. AAPC; Apha; ACPE; Fell Coll Chapl; La Cleric Assn. Amer Rel Freedom Fell Geo Mason U 1992. frcromwell@aol.com

CLEVELAND, Jennifer B (Oly) 125 SW Eckman St, McMinnville OR 97128 **Chapl Oregon Epis Sch Portland OR 2009-** B Seattle WA 4/19/1961 d Richard Cleveland & Nancy. BA Smith 1983; MDiv PSR 1991; CAS CDSP 1993. D 11/12/1993 P 7/11/1994 Bp Vincent Waydell Warner. m 6/25/1988 Stewart Rule Stout c 2. Assoc Trin Epis Cathd Portland OR 2001-2008; Assoc S Barth's Ch Beaverton OR 2000-2008; Assoc S Lk's Ch Evanston IL 1997-2000; S Tim's Epis Ch Yakima WA 1995. clevelandj@oes.edu

CLEVELAND, Thomas Grover (Mass) 1519 Cleveland Hill Rd, Tamworth NH 03886 B Baltimore MD 10/18/1927 s Richard Folsom Cleveland & Ellen Douglas. BA Pr 1949; BD VTS 1954. D 6/5/1954 Bp Robert Fisher Gibson Jr P 12/1/1954 Bp William J Gordon Jr. m 7/6/1996 Ruth Elaine Cleveland c 4. The Milton Acad Milton MA 1965-1997; P-in-c S Jas Ch Tanana AK 1961-1965; P-in-c S Barth's Ch Palmer AK 1960-1961; S Jn The Evang Taunton MA 1958-1960. TOMCLEVE@NCIA.NET

CLEVELEY, Susan Cleveley (Spok) 111 S. Jefferson St., Moscow ID 83843 B Honolulu HI 7/16/1964 d David Edward Oliver & Phyllis Eleanor. BFA U of Idaho Moscow 1987. D 6/7/2008 P 12/13/2008 Bp James Edward Waggoner. m 11/27/1986 Charles Brian Cleveley c 1. s.clev@verizon.net

CLEVENGER, Mark R (LI) PO Box 606, Shoreham NY 11786 **Dioc Revs Com, Mem Dio Long Island Garden City NY 2011-; Prov Crt of Revs, Mem Prov II 2011-; R S Anselm's Ch Shoreham NY 2008-; Katrina Mssnr Ecusa / Mssn Personl New York NY 2007-** B Fort Wayne IN 11/25/1960 s Elmer Robert Clevenger & Iris Ivy. BA U MI 1983; MDiv Ya Berk 1986; JD U of Kansas 1989. D 5/16/1986 Bp William Cockburn Russell Sheridan P 1/10/1987 Bp Richard Frank Grein. m 3/26/2001 Beth A Benson. Eccl Crt, Mem Dio Long Island Garden City NY 2009-2010; Dio Upper So Carolina Columbia SC 2005-2007; Bp's Dep for Stwdshp Dio Long Island Garden City NY 2002-2004; Const and Cn Com, Mem Dio Long Island Garden City NY 2002-2004; Dioc Stwdshp Com, Chair Dio Long Island Garden City NY 2002-2004; Exec Dir Epis Chars Dio Long Island Garden City NY 2002-2004; Dio Mssn Dev Dio Chicago Chicago IL 2000-2002; Bd Dir, Mem Hse of Pryr Collegeville MN 1998-2000; Joint Plnng Cmsn Epis/Luth Concordat Dio Minnesota Minneapolis MN 1998-1999; Cn Mssn Strat Dio Minnesota Minneapolis MN 1996-2000; Vic Ch Of The Nativ Burnsville MN 1996-1998; Dioc Coun, Mem Dio Kansas Topeka KS 1993-1994; Dioc Trst Mem Dio Kansas Topeka KS 1992-1996; S Marg's Ch Lawr KS 1991-1996; Apportnmt Com, Chair Dio Kansas Topeka KS 1988-1992; Alt Dep to GC Dio Kansas Topeka KS 1988; Trin Ch Lawr KS 1987-1988; Co-Chapl Cbury At Kansas U Lawr KS 1986-1991; Dio Kansas Topeka KS 1986-1989. Auth, "Seasons of Stwdshp Series," *The Dominion*, Dio Long Island, 2002; Ed/Auth, "Pstr's Tool Box Series," *Mssn Matters*, Dio Chicago, 2001; Ed/Auth, "Congrl Dvlpmt - Ch Coach Series," *The Great Cmsn*, Dio Minnesota, 2000; Creator, "Gratitude Mangament". padre.clevenger@gmail.com

CLIFF, F(rank) Graham (Be) 15 Bede Circle, Honesdale PA 18431 **P-in-c S Jas-S Geo Epis Ch Jermyn PA 2009-** B Melton Mowbray UK 3/17/1938 s Frank Cecil Cliff & Florence May. Cert S Paul Tchr Coll GB 1960; Chilton TS 1966; DIT Lon 1966. Trans from Church Of England 6/1/1972 Bp J Milton Richardson. m 6/9/1990 Mary-Jo Romberger c 5. R Chr Ch Honesdale PA 1994-2005; R Gr Epis Ch Honesdale PA 1994-2005; R Ch Of The Adv Pittsburgh PA 1987-1994; St Philips Mssn Pittsburgh PA 1987; Dio Pittsburgh Monroeville PA 1986; Dn - Middle Convoc Dio Easton Easton MD 1983-1984; Vice-Pres - Dioc Coun Dio Easton Easton MD 1981-1984; R Chr Ch Denton MD 1978-1985; Dio Easton Easton MD 1978-1983; Asst to the Bp Dio Easton Easton MD 1978-1982; Asst S Jas Ch Potomac MD 1974-1978; S Alb's Epis Ch Waco TX 1972-1978; Asst S Thos Ch Houston TX 1971-1972. cliffam@ptd.net

CLIFFORD III, George Minott (NC) **Assoc Ch Of The Nativ Raleigh NC 2011-** D 8/3/1992 P 2/1/1993 Bp Charles Lovett Keyser.

CLIFT, Jean Dalby (Colo) 2130 E Columbia Pl, Denver CO 80210 **Assoc S Jn's Cathd Denver CO 1988-** B Naples TX 2/21/1930 d Roy Warren Dalby & Willie Mae. BA U of Texas 1950; JD U of Texas 1952; CG Jung Inst 1966; MA U Denv 1972; PhD U Denv 1978. D 6/11/1988 P 12/13/1988 Bp William Carl Frey. m 1/23/1954 Wallace B Clift c 3. Auth, "The Myster of Love and The Path of Pryr," Amazon.com, 2008; Auth, "Where Would You Be Now?," *Journeys*, AAPC, 2006; Co-Auth, "The Archetypd of Pilgrimage: Outer Journey w Inner Meaning," Paulist Press, 1996; Auth, "Core Images of the Self," Crossroad, 1992; Co-Auth, "The Hero Journey in Dreams," Crossroad, 1988; Auth, "Theory & Pract in Clincl Supervision in Pstr Counslg," *Jnl of Supervision and Trng*, 1988; Auth, "An Excerpt from Responses to Ord Questions," *Jnl of Wmn & Rel*, 1988; Auth, "Pstr Mnstry: A Macedonian Plea," *Jml of Wmn Mnstrs*, 1985; Co-Auth, "Symbols of Transformation in Dreams," Crossroad, 1984; Auth, "15 poems," *LivCh*, 1967. AAPC 1982; Pres,AAPC 1994-1996. Cn Pstr Emer Bp of Colorado 2002. wclift@du.edu

CLIFT, Joe Walter (Ga) 343 Gander Rd, Dawson GA 39842 B Chattanooga TN 9/12/1940 s Walter Davis Clift & Ray. BA Bethel Coll 1962; MDiv Van 1965; DMin STUSo 1989. D 3/18/1989 P 9/17/1989 Bp Harry Woolston Shipps. m 7/11/1964 Sandra Bates c 2. Ch Of The H Sprt Dawson GA 1995; R The Epis Ch Of S Jn And S Mk Albany GA 1993-2007; Vic Chr Epis Ch Cordele GA 1989-1993; D S Paul's Ch Albany GA 1989. Amer Assn of Mar and Fam Therapists 1996; Amer Soc of Clincl Hypnosis 1998. jsclift711@windstream.net

CLIFT JR, Wallace B (Colo) 2130 E Columbia Pl, Denver CO 80210 B Robert Lee TX 3/27/1926 s Wallace Bruce Clift & Ruth. BA U of Texas 1949; JD Harv 1952; MDiv CDSP 1960; CG Jung Inst 1966; MA U Chi 1967; PhD U Chi 1970; DD CDSP 2003. D 6/24/1960 P 5/26/1961 Bp John E Hines. m 1/23/1954 Jean Dalby c 3. S Jn's Cathd Denver CO 1992-2002; Ch Of The Resurr Houston TX 1960-1964. Auth, *The Archetype of Pilgrimage: Outer Action w Inner Meaning*, Paulist Press, 1996; Auth, *Journey into Love*, Crossroad, 1990; Auth, *The Hero Journey in Dreams*, Crossroad, 1988; "Four arts," *Encyclopedia of Rel*, Macmillan, 1987; Auth, *Symbols of Transformation in Dreams*, Crossroad, 1984; Auth, *Jung & Chrsnty: Challenge of Recon*,

Crossroad, 1982. AAPC, Amer Acad o 1982. D.D., honorus causa CDSP 2003; Study Grant - 6 year Farish Fndt 1964. wclift@du.edu

CLIFTON JR, Ellis Edward (Mich) St. Clement'S Episcopal Church, 4300 Harrison Road, Inkster MI 48141 **R S Clem's Epis Ch Inkster MI 2007-** B Detroit MI 1/15/1953 s Ellis Edward Clifton & Marie. BS Cntrl St U 1974; OH SU 1975; MDiv TESM 1991. D 6/6/1992 P 8/1/1993 Bp Alden Moinet Hathaway. m 7/26/1975 Wanda Agee. Ch Of The Resurr Ecorse MI 2004-2006; P-in-c S Mary's Epis Ch Dorchester MA 2000-2004; Assoc S Mich's Ch Milton MA 1998-2000; S Andr's Epis Ch Cincinnati OH 1998; Vic Ch Of S Mich And All Ang Cincinnati OH 1995-1997; Int Ch Of The H Innoc Leechburg PA 1994-1995; Cur Ch Of The H Cross Pittsburgh PA 1993-1994. Bro S Andr 1988; Mercy Of God Cmnty Assoc 1999; UBE 1994. cplus04@aol.com

CLIFTON, Steve (CFla) 3137 Denham Ct, Orlando FL 32825 **Bd Trst The U So (Sewanee) Sewanee TN 2011-; R Chr The King Epis Ch Orlando FL 2003-** B Savannah GA 8/23/1960 s Gay Max Clifton & Joan. BMusEd Troy St U Troy AL 1981; MDiv Nash 1984; DMin STUSo 2000. D 5/16/1984 Bp (George) Paul Reeves P 5/10/1985 Bp Harry Woolston Shipps. m 6/14/2003 Sonia Tutan c 2. Overseeing Pstr S Barn Epis Ch Valdosta GA 2001-2003; R S Geo's Epis Ch Bradenton FL 1996-2000; Assoc S Thos Ch Savannah GA 1993-1996; Dioc Coun Dio Georgia Savannah GA 1989-1992; Vic S Jn's Epis Ch Bainbridge GA 1985-1993; Cur S Aug Of Cbury Ch Augusta GA 1984-1985. stevec60@gmail.com

CLINE JR, Allen David (Lex) 8537 E Us Highway 60, Rush KY 41168 **Died 8/26/2011** B Pikeville KY 6/16/1933 s Allen D Cline & Marie. BS USNA 1956; BS U Of Kentucky 1961. D 5/29/1965 Bp William R Moody. c 2. Scovell Soc. Gamma Sigma Delta Ord Of Merit; Eta Kappa Nu; Tau Beta Pi.

CLINEHENS JR, Harold O (EpisSanJ) 1055 S. Lower Sacramento Road, Lodi CA 95242 **Dioc Coun Epis Dio San Joaquin Modesto CA 2010-; R S Jn The Bapt Lodi CA 2009-** B Fayetteville AR 7/28/1947 s Harold Oscar Clinehens & Virginia Anne. USMA At W Point 1966; BS U of Arkansas 1971; MDiv CDSP 1979. D 6/9/1979 P 2/23/1980 Bp Christoph Keller Jr. m 1/6/2007 Beverley C Clinehens c 2. Int Gr S Paul's Epis Ch Tucson AZ 2008-2009; Int S Anth On The Desert Scottsdale AZ 2007-2008; Dio Los Angeles Los Angeles CA 2000-2009; S Wilfrid Of York Epis Ch Huntington Bch CA 1999-2007; Stndg Com Dio Nthrn California Sacramento CA 1997-1999; R S Paul's Epis Ch Benicia CA 1991-1999; R S Paul's On The Plains Epis Ch Lubbock TX 1985-1991; Stndg Com Dio NW Texas Lubbock TX 1985-1988; Assoc S Andr's Epis Ch Amarillo TX 1982-1985; Dioc Coun Dio Arkansas Little Rock AR 1981-1982; Vic Calv Epis Ch Osceola AR 1980-1982; Dio Arkansas Little Rock AR 1979-1980; Cur S Jn's Ch Harrison AR 1979-1980. Auth, "Sermons That Wk IV". Prize Winning Sermon Epis Evang Fndt 1994. harcli@aol.com

CLINGENPEEL, Ronald Harvey (Mo) 1210 Locust St, Saint Louis MO 63103 B Chadron NE 3/21/1953 s Harvey Henry Clingenpeel & Luella Pearl. BS Ed. U of Nebraska 1975; MDiv GTS 1978; Montana St U 1982; U So 1986. D 6/3/1978 P 12/21/1978 Bp James Daniel Warner. m 11/28/1992 Linda Clingenpeel c 4. Dn Chr Ch Cathd S Louis MO 2002-2008; Cn Ordnry Dio Louisiana Baton Rouge LA 1998-2002; Dio Louisiana Baton Rouge LA 1996-2002; Chapl Ch Of The H Sprt New Orleans LA 1987-1998; Dio Kansas Topeka KS 1983-1987; K SU Manhattan KS 1982; S Jas Ch Bozeman MT 1980-1982; Asst Trin Cathd Omaha NE 1978-1979. Contributing Auth, "Disorganized Rel," Cowley Press, 1998; Ed/Contrbuting Auth, "In the Great Hall," Plumbline/ESMHE, 1993. ESMHE 1978; NAAD 2000. rhclingenpeel@yahoo.com

CLIVER, Stanley Cameron (Wyo) Po Box 176, Sundance WY 82729 B Saint Louis MO 8/28/1924 s Benjamin Brown Cliver & Elsie Caroline. Eden TS 1963. D 6/15/1963 P 3/1/1964 Bp George Leslie Cadigan. m 12/24/1943 Marceline Blankenship. Ch Of The Gd Shpd Sundance WY 1971-1980; St Johns Ch 1971-1980; Cur S Jn's Ch St Louis MO 1963-1965.

CLODFELTER, Jonathan Norwood (Pa) 4442 Frankford Ave, Philadelphia PA 19124 **R S Mk's Ch Philadelphia PA 2002-** B Saint Louis MO 9/30/1954 s Robert Lee Clodfelter & Jean. BS SUNY 1993; MDiv VTS 1999. D 12/17/1999 Bp Peter James Lee P 6/25/2000 Bp J(ames) Gary Gloster. m 8/31/1985 Alice Maria Sales Gilson c 4. Thompson Chld's Hm Charlotte NC 1999-2002. jonclodfelter@gmail.com

CLOSE, David Wyman (Ore) 7990 Headlands Way, Clinton WA 98236 B Seattle,WA 3/24/1947 s Donald Wyman Close & Ruth Mary. BS U of Washington 1969; MDiv CDSP 1973; DMin VTS 1997. D 7/17/1973 P 7/6/1974 Bp Ivol I Curtis. m 2/24/1979 Wendy Boyd c 3. R S Mk's Epis Par Medford OR 1987-2004; S Jas Ch Sedro-Woolley WA 1979-1987; Asst S Steph's Epis Ch Seattle WA 1973-1979. frclose@aol.com

CLOSE, Leroy Springs (RI) 316 W Main Rd, Little Compton RI 02837 B Charlotte NC 6/22/1950 s Hugh Close & Anne Springs. BA Tul 1972. D 5/20/2000 Bp Richard Frank Grein. m 8/14/1971 Lucy Garrett Hart c 3. D S Geo And San Jorge Cntrl Falls RI 2008-2011; D S Andr's By The Sea Little Compton RI 2005-2008; D S Mk's Ch Mt Kisco NY 2000-2004. buckclose@gmail.com

CLOSE, Patrick Raymond (NJ) Grace Episcopal Church, 19 Kings Hwy E, Haddonfield NJ 08033 **Curs Sprtl Dir Dio New Jersey Trenton NJ 2007-; Cbury Way-Bp Dep Dio Newark Newark NJ 2000-; R Gr Ch In Haddonfield Haddonfield NJ 1997-** B Elmira NY 3/8/1952 s Julion Raymond Close & Myrtie Laura. BA U of Maryland 1974; MDiv VTS 1984; DMin Drew U 1994. D 6/23/1984 P 6/8/1985 Bp Peter James Lee. m 1/4/1975 Diane Elaine Daniel c 2. Cmsn on Stwdshp Dio New Jersey Trenton NJ 2010-2011; COM Dio New Jersey Trenton NJ 2003-2009; Com Dio New Jersey Trenton NJ 1998-2000; Coun Dio Newark Newark NJ 1995-1997; R S Ptr's Ch Mtn Lakes NJ 1991-1997; R S Jn's Epis Ch Montclair NJ 1986-1991; Pres-Epis Cmnty Servs Dio Newark Newark NJ 1986-1989; Assoc S Tim's Ch Herndon VA 1984-1986. Assoc P, Convenor of St. Jn Bapt 1991-2009; Chapl, Haddonfield Fire Dept 2006; Chapl, Hospice-Vstng Nurses Assn 1995-1996; Chapl, Nj Assn Of Deaf 1991-1997; Pres, Haddonfield Coun Of Ch 1999-2000. Haddonfield Haddonfield Human Rts Cmsn 2006; Herndon Times Citizen Year Herndon Times Citizen Year 1984. drprclose@aol.com

CLOSE ERSKINE, Christine Elaine (EO) 60960 Creekstone Loop, Bend OR 97702 **R Trin Ch Bend OR 2008-** B Seattle WA 11/28/1956 d Donald Wyman Close & Ruth Mary. BS U of Puget Sound 1979; MBA U of Washington 1987; MDiv Ya Berk 1994. D 1/4/1994 P 7/9/1994 Bp Vincent Waydell Warner. m 6/8/1996 John (Jack) Arthur Erskine c 3. Assoc P Ch Of The Gd Shpd Vancouver WA 1994-2008. jerskine15@aol.com

CLOUD, Vernon Luther (SD) 13696 448th Ave, Waubay SD 57273 B Sisseton SD 9/28/1942 s Iver Vernnie Cloud & Gertrude Victoria. Assoc Sthrn St Coll 1967; Assoc Nthrn St Coll 1969. D 9/10/2011 Bp John Thomas Tarrant. m 6/7/1964 Sharon Lee Cloud c 3. vlcloud@itctel.com

CLOUGHEN JR, Charles Edward (Md) PO Box 313-, Hunt Valley MD 21030 **Dir of Planned Giving, Stwdshp and Dvlpmt,Dio Maryland Dio Maryland Baltimore MD 2009-** B Teaneck NJ 1/1/1942 s Charles Edward Cloughen & Anna Edwina. BA Hob 1964; STB Ya Berk 1969; Cert Hartford Sem 1990. D 6/14/1969 Bp Leland Stark P 12/22/1969 Bp Charles P Gilson. m 5/5/1984 Judith Elizabeth Huntress c 2. R S Thos Epis Ch Towson MD 1990-2008; R S Andr's Ch Pasadena MD 1986-1990; Int Spec Dio Dallas Dallas TX 1985-1986; Int S Mary's Epis Ch Manchester CT 1984-1985; Asst S Jn's Epis Par Waterbury CT 1982-1984; R S Matt's Par Of Jamestown Jamestown RI 1973-1982; Asst S Mart's Ch Providence RI 1969-1973. Auth, "Sixty-Second Stwdshp Serv," Liturg Press, 2000; Auth, "One Minute Stwdshp Sermons," Morehouse, 1997. Ord of St Jn 2005; Pres, Amer Friends of the Epis Dio Jerusal 2004-2007. Distinguished P Awd Dio Maryland 2006; Resrch Fell Ya New Haven CT 1983. ccloughen@episcopalmaryland.org

CLOWERS, Grantland Hugh (Kan) 2007 Miller Dr, Lawrence KS 66046 B Joplin MO 8/31/1956 s Ted M Clowers & Alline V. BA U of Missouri 1978; MDiv GTS 1983. D 10/18/1983 P 5/1/1984 Bp Richard Frank Grein. S Andr's Ch Ft Scott KS 1997-1998; S Lk's Epis Ch Shawnee KS 1993-1994; Asst Trin Ch Lawr KS 1986-1992; Calv Ch Yates Cntr KS 1983-1986; S Tim's Ch Iola KS 1983-1986. grantclowers@yahoo.com

CLUETT JR, Richard (Be) 119 W. Johnston St., Allentown PA 18103 **Cathd Ch Of The Nativ Bethlehem PA 1970-** B New York NY 6/5/1942 s Richard Ide Cluett & Jane Cluett. BA Hob 1965; Ya Berk 1967; MDiv VTS 1970. D 6/27/1970 Bp William Foreman Creighton P 2/13/1971 Bp John Thomas Walker. m 4/12/1969 Patricia K Knight c 3. Archd Dio Bethlehem Bethlehem PA 1984-2004; R S Marg's Ch Emmaus PA 1978-1984; Dio Rochester Rochester NY 1975-1976; Assoc Chr Ch Corning NY 1972-1978; Asst S Lk's Ch Trin Par Beth MD 1970-1972. rick@cluett.org

COAN, Barbara Frances Smith (Haw) 1311 Nahele Pl, Kapaa HI 96746 **D S Mich And All Ang Ch Lihue HI 1996-** B Hackensack NJ 9/8/1923 d Frank Jay Smith & Marie. Art Students League of New York; Bos; Maine Diac Formation Prog; Queensland U. D 7/19/1993 Bp Edward Cole Chalfant. m 9/4/1948 Edward Morel Coan. Chair Bd Dio Maine Portland ME 1999-2000; Dio Cnvnr Dio Maine Portland ME 1995-1996; D S Dunst's Ch Ellsworth ME 1995-1996; D Ch Of Our Fr Hulls Cove ME 1993-1996; Prov I Rep Untd Thenk Off Dio Maine Portland ME 1985-1991. Fllshp Soc Of S Jn The Evang; NAAD. One-Person Art Shows Intl. barbcoan@gmail.com

COATS, Christopher Vincent (CGC) Wharf Marina Slip #38, Orange Beach AL 36561 **R H Sprt Epis Ch Gulf Shores AL 2006-** B Coral Gables FL 7/25/1950 s Hall Piere Coats & Clotilda. BA U of W Florida 1983; MDiv VTS 1987. D 6/27/1987 P 2/14/1988 Bp Charles Farmer Duvall. m 4/3/1971 Barbara A Blackburn c 2. R S Geo's Ch Belleville IL 2002-2006; R S Steph's Ch Brewton AL 1994-2002; Vic S Jn's Ch Pensacola FL 1987-1994. Alabama NG Chapl; US Army Reserve Chapl. hsfrchris@gmail.com

COATS, John Rhodes (Cal) 15814 Champion Forest Dr, Spring TX 77379 B Pasadena TX 7/25/1946 s W R Coats & Doris Ann. BA Steph F. Austin St Coll 1969; MDiv VTS 1973. D 6/21/1973 Bp Scott Field Bailey P 6/1/1974 Bp J Milton Richardson. m 10/12/1968 Pamela Faye Coats. S Anne's Ch Fremont CA 1978-1981; Assoc H Sprt Epis Ch Houston TX 1975-1978; Asst Chr Epis Ch Tyler TX 1973-1975. Auth, "Journ Of Acad Of Par Cler". OHC. JOHNRCOATS@GMAIL.COM

COATS, William Russell (Nwk) 19 Elmwood Ave., Ho Ho Kus NJ 07423 B New Rochelle NY 10/22/1936 s Guy Harold Coats & Marjorie Frances. BA U CA, Los Angeles 1959; STB GTS 1964. D 8/23/1964 Bp Daniel Corrigan P 6/1/1965 Bp David Shepherd Rose. m 5/24/2005 Deborah K Coats c 2. Int S Paul's Epis Ch Chatham NJ 2010-2011; Int Ch Of The Epiph Orange NJ 2008; Int Ch Of The H Comm Norwood NJ 2006-2007; Int S Jn's Ch Un City NJ 2002; R S Clem's Ch Hawthorne NJ 1988-2002; Int Trin Ch Glen Arm MD 1987-1988; Int Ch Of The Redeem Morristown NJ 1986-1987; R The Ch Of The Redeem Pittsburgh PA 1978-1986; Assoc Min S Cyp's Epis Ch Hampton VA 1964-1965. Auth, "God In Publ". ESMHE 1968-1978. wrcoats@optonline.net

COBB, Christina Rich (Mo) 1212 Ringo St, Mexico MO 65265 **R S Matt's Epis Ch Mex MO 2006-** B Unionville MO 5/11/1971 d James Rich & Frances. BS U of Missouri 1993; Cntrl Bapt TS 1996; MS U of Missouri 1996; Epis Sch for Mnstry 2006. D 5/31/2006 P 12/9/2006 Bp George Wayne Smith. m 8/10/2002 Michael William Cobb c 2. christinacobb511@yahoo.com

COBB, David (Ct) 84 Broadway, New Haven CT 06511 **Chr Ch New Haven CT 2002-** B Mobile AL 11/14/1955 s Hiram Cleopas Cobb & Gladys Inez. BA U of Alabama 1978; MDiv SWTS 1983. D 6/2/1983 P 12/1/1983 Bp Furman Stough. m 11/21/1982 Ruth Sheridan c 3. R S Paul's Par Baltimore MD 1996-2002; R S Chris's Epis Ch Oak Pk IL 1987-1996; Cur Ch Of Our Sav Chicago IL 1984-1987; Cur S Paul's Ch Selma AL 1983-1984. Pres Swts Alum Assn. dacobb@aol.com

COBB JR, Harold James (SVa) 1931 Paddock Rd, Norfolk VA 23518 **R Gr Ch Norfolk VA 1995-** B Burlington NC 6/10/1958 s Harold James Cobb & Armadia Bernice. Morehouse Coll 1979; BA U NC 1982; MDiv VTS 1990. D 11/15/1990 Bp Robert Whitridge Estill P 11/1/1991 Bp Huntington Williams Jr. m 6/29/1991 Sheliah Jeffries c 1. R S Steph's Epis Ch Winston Salem NC 1990-1995. Auth, "Black Seminars In The Epis Ch". UBE, Black Epis Seminarians. Who'S Who In Black Amer. frdrcobb@cox.net

COBB, John Pierpont (SO) 36 Ledge Rd, Gloucester MA 01930 B Chicago IL 9/25/1923 s Evelyn P Cobb & Daphne. BA Harv 1948; BD CDSP 1961. D 6/25/1961 Bp James Albert Pike P 2/1/1962 Bp Roger W Blanchard. S Mk's Epis Ch Dayton OH 1969-1995; Asst Epis Soc of Chr Ch Cincinnati OH 1961-1963.

COBB, Lewis Milner (Va) 56 Bertrand Pl, Lancaster VA 22503 **Died 2/21/2011** B Los Angeles CA 4/15/1923 s Donald Kemp Cobb & Georgia. M VTS 1969. D 6/24/1969 Bp David Shepherd Rose P 6/29/1970 Bp George P Gunn. c 4. lousrcobb@kaballero.com

COBB, Matthew Mickey (Kan) 1915 Montgomery Dr, Manhattan KS 66502 **S Lk's Ch Wamego KS 2008-; R/Campus Min S Fran Of Cbury Manhattan KS 2001-** B Statesboro GA 10/19/1968 s Marvin Mickey Cobb & Linda Rose. BA Rockhurst U 1993; MDiv Epis TS of The SW 1996; MA Creighton U 2001. D 6/8/1996 P 1/18/1999 Bp John Clark Buchanan. m 8/3/1991 Erica Olson-Cobb c 2. Dio Kansas Topeka KS 2001-2005; Dio Iowa Des Moines IA 1999-2001; Asst/Campus Min S Jn's By The Campus Ames IA 1999-2001; Dio W Missouri Kansas City MO 1998; Trans D S Jn's Ch Kansas City MO 1997-1999; Chapl - Cbury Hse Dio Kansas Topeka KS 1997-1998; Dio W Missouri Kansas City MO 1997; Trans D S Andr's Ch Kansas City MO 1996-1997; St Lk's So Chap Overland Pk KS 1996-1997; Dio W Missouri Kansas City MO 1996. frmatt66503@hotmail.com

COBB, Melissa Louise (Ore) 4987 Nomore St N, Keizer OR 97303 **D S Tim's Epis Ch Salem OR 2001-** B San Francisco CA 9/5/1962 d Giles Sheldon Green & Celine Lydia. D 1/31/1998 Bp John Stuart Thornton. m 5/5/1984 John Howard Cobb. D The Epis Ch Of The Prince Of Peace Salem OR 1998-2000.

COBB, Terry Robert (USC) Po Box 882, Lexington SC 29071 **Died 8/10/2011** B Memphis TN 10/12/1935 s Jesse Eaton Cobb & Mildred Taylor. BBA U of Memphis 1962; MDiv STUSo 1972. D 6/27/1972 Bp William F Gates Jr P 10/1/1973 Bp John Vander Horst. Ord Of S Vinc, Ord Of S Lk. COBBTC@GMAIL.COM

COBB-ANDERSON, Vienna (Va) 1138 West Ave, Richmond VA 23220 B Richmond VA 7/8/1935 d Robert Edward Anderson & Vienna Amanda Louisa. Schlr London Acad of Mus & Dramatic Arts; AAS Briarcliff Coll 1955; Shakespeare Inst Stratford-on-Avon gb 1957; Yale Sch of Drama 1958; The London Acad of Mus and Dramatic Art 1959; BFA Richmond Profsnl Inst 1964; MFA Ya 1967; Spec Mnstry Prog Washington DC 1977; DMin PrTS 1986; DMin PrTS 1986; LHD Lynchburg Coll 1988. D 6/25/1977 Bp William Foreman Creighton P 2/26/1978 Bp John Thomas Walker. S Paul's Ch Richmond VA 1996-2001; R S Marg's Ch Washington DC 1987-1996; S Marg's Ch Woodbridge VA 1987-1996; Adj Prof VTS Alexandria VA 1978-1996; Assoc S Alb's Par Washington DC 1977-1984. Auth, "H Faces, H Places," *H Faces, H Places*, Dimenti Milestone Pub, 2008; Auth, "Prayers of Our Hearts," *Prayers of Our Hearts*, Crossroad Continuum, 2001; Auth, "Celebrations of Life," *Celebrations of Life*, Morehouse Barlow; Auth, "Create & Celebrate," *Create & Celebrate*, Morehouse Barlow; Auth, "The People & P Make Euch," *The People & P Make Euch*, U Micro Films. Associated Parishes 1968. L.H.D. 1988; Fulbright Schlr 1957. wieniii@me.com

COBBS IV, Richard Hooker (SwFla) 1808 Main St., Greensboro AL 36744 **Died 10/7/2011** B Gadsden AL 3/18/1935 s Richard Hooker Cobbs & Elizabeth Dorn. BA Auburn U 1957; MDiv Epis TS of The SW 1969. D 6/28/1969 P 2/22/1970 Bp George Mosley Murray. c 2. Cmnty Cross of Nails. cardrec@bellsouth.net

COBDEN JR, Edward Alexander Morrison (Mich) Po Box 295, South Egremont MA 01258 B Larchmont NY 12/21/1935 s Edward Alexander Morrison Cobden & Clementine. BA Wms 1957; MDiv EDS 1960; MA Assumption Coll 1974; DMin VTS 1983. D 6/25/1960 P 2/11/1961 Bp Robert McConnell Hatch. c 2. R Chr Ch Grosse Pointe Grosse Pointe Farms MI 1982-1997; Assoc Chr Ch Greenwich CT 1979-1982; R H Trin Epis Ch Southbridge MA 1967-1979; Cur All SS Ch Worcester MA 1960-1963.

COBDEN III, Edward Alexander Morrison (NY) 374 Sarles St, Bedford Corners NY 10549 B Worcester MA 7/19/1960 s Edward Alexander Morrison Cobden & Evelyn. BA Wms 1982; MDiv VTS 1988. D 6/6/1988 Bp Robert Campbell Witcher Sr P 1/1/1990 Bp William Bradford Hastings. m 8/13/1983 Cynthia Ann Graves. All Ang' Ch New York NY 1994-1997; S Barth's Ch In The Highland White Plains NY 1992-1994; Assoc S Lk's Par Darien CT 1988-1989.

COBLE JR, John Reifsnyder (Be) 1929 Pelham Rd, Bethlehem PA 18018 B Lebanon PA 11/19/1933 s John Reifsnyder Coble & Pauline Sarah. BS Rider Coll 1960; MDiv PDS 1963. D 6/15/1963 P 3/10/1964 Bp Frederick J Warnecke. m 8/26/1961 Patricia Ann Seaman c 1. R Trin Ch Bethlehem PA 1984-1997; Dio Bethlehem Bethlehem PA 1976-1984; Cn Ordnry Dio Bethlehem Bethlehem PA 1976-1984; Vic S Geo's Epis Ch Hellertown PA 1970-1976; R S Jas Ch Schuylkill Haven PA 1968-1970; D Chr Ch Frackville Frackville PA 1963-1968; D S Jas Ch Schuylkill Haven PA 1963-1964. jrcoble735@enter.net

COBLE, Robert Henry (Pa) 535 Haws Ave, Norristown PA 19401 B Lebanon PA 2/20/1944 s John R Coble & Pauline S. BA Salem Coll Salem WV 1967; MDiv PDS 1970. D 6/27/1970 P 5/1/1971 Bp Frederick J Warnecke. m 7/28/1979 Barbara Conlin c 1. R All SS Ch Norristown PA 1978-2009; R S Steph's Epis Ch Norwood PA 1972-1978; Asst Trin Ch Easton PA 1970-1972. revrobertcoble@yahoo.com

COBURN, Ann Struthers (Mass) 2451 Ridge Rd, Berkeley CA 94709 **Dir of Alum/ae and Ch Relatns CDSP Berkeley CA 2005-** B Portchester NY 2/19/1949 d William Wood Struthers & Lilly Ferrell. BA Georgian Crt Coll 1972; MDiv CDSP 1977; DMin Georgian Crt U 2009. D 6/11/1977 Bp Paul Moore Jr P 12/17/1977 Bp John Bowen Coburn. c 2. Int Gr Ch New Bedford MA 2003-2005; R S Mart's Ch Providence RI 1998-2003; R S Jas Epis Ch Danbury CT 1982-1998; Cn Chr Ch Cathd Hartford CT 1979-1981; Asst S Jas Epis Ch Danbury CT 1977-1979. revanncoburn@yahoo.com

✠ COBURN, Rt Rev John Bowen (Mass) 82 Essex Ct, Bedford MA 01730 **Died 8/8/2009** B Danbury CT 9/27/1914 s Aaron Cutler Coburn & Eugenia Bowen. BA Pr 1936; BD UTS 1942; DD Amh 1955; DST Ya Berk 1958; DD Pr 1960; DD Harv 1964; DD Hur 1964; DST Hob 1965; DST GTS 1968; DCL Ken 1968; DST EDS 1969; DD Buc 1970; DD Mid 1970; DCL U Of Kent Cbury Gb 1978; DD Trin 1980; DST Ham 1982; DD Wms 1982. D 1/18/1943 P 7/1/1943 Bp Benjamin M Washburn Con 10/2/1976 for Mass. c 4. Auth, "Hope Of Glory"; Auth, "Chr'S Life: Our Life"; Auth, "Feeding Fire".

COBURN, Michael (RI) 55 Linden Road, Barrington RI 02806 **P-in-c Ch Of The Ascen Cranston RI 2010-** B Northampton MA 11/7/1949 s John Bowen Coburn & Ruth. BA Pr 1972; MDiv CDSP 1977. D 6/11/1977 Bp Paul Moore Jr P 12/17/1977 Bp John Bowen Coburn. m 3/4/2005 Carol Lewis c 3. P-in-c All SS' Memi Ch Providence RI 2009-2010; S Mart's Ch Providence RI 1998-2002; R S Jas Epis Ch Danbury CT 1982-1998; Cn Chr Ch Cathd Hartford CT 1979-1981; Asst S Jas Epis Ch Danbury CT 1977-1979. mikecoburn77@hotmail.com

COCHRAN, A(ndrew) Royston (RI) 57 Grande Ville Ct Suite 1110, Wakefield RI 02879 B Providence RI 8/29/1920 s John M Cochran & Jessie K. BA Hob 1942; BD VTS 1944; MA Br 1954; MS Bos 1968. D 5/18/1944 P 11/30/1944 Bp James D Perry. R S Paul's Ch Natick MA 1955-1965; DeptCE Dio Massachusetts Boston MA 1953-1955; DeptCE Dio Rhode Island Providence RI 1948-1951; Asst Trin Ch Newport RI 1945-1948; Asst Chr Ch Cambridge Cambridge MA 1944-1945. Auth, "An Hist Sketch of Trin Ch Newport". arcochran@cox.net

COCHRAN, Carlotta B (SVa) 713 Seagrass Reach, Chesapeake VA 23320 **Asstg Cler Old Donation Ch Virginia Bch VA 2011-; Pres of Alum/ae Assn VTS Alexandria VA 1994-** B Norfolk VA 11/14/1957 d Charles Edward Bell & Carlotta. BS Mia 1982; MDiv VTS 1993. D 6/5/1993 Bp O'Kelley Whitaker P 1/25/1994 Bp Frank Harris Vest Jr. m 3/25/1978 Thomas Hale Cochran c 2. Assoc for Pstr Care S Dav's Ch Wayne PA 2009-2010; Int Gd Samar Epis Ch Virginia Bch VA 2008-2009; Asstg Cler Old Donation Ch Virginia Bch VA 2007-2008; R Time Certain S Paul's Epis Ch Suffolk VA 2004-2006; Exec Dir AFP Orlando FL 2002-2003; Assoc Chr and S Lk's Epis

Ch Norfolk VA 1999-2002; Pres of Alum/ae Assn VTS Alexandria VA 1994-1995; Assoc S Jn's Ch Roanoke VA 1993-1999; AAEC VTS Alexandria VA 1993-1995. Auth, "Pstr Pract Seeking Understanding," 1995. AFP - Exec Dir 2002-2004. cochran.carlotta@gmail.com

COCHRAN, Elizabeth Jane (Oly) St Matthew's Episcopal Church, 412 Pioneer Ave, Castle Rock WA 98611 **R S Matt Ch Castle Rock WA 2004-** B Hiawatha KS 7/27/1937 d Virgil Evans & Helen. BS Kansas St Teachers Coll 1959. D 2/28/2004 Bp Sanford Zangwill Kaye Hampton P 11/13/2004 Bp Vincent Waydell Warner. m 6/1/1959 Jere Cochran c 4. janie@toledotel.com

COCHRAN, Paul Coleman (Be) 110 Richfields Ave, Georgetown KY 40324 B Detroit,MI 12/14/1941 s Maurice William Cochran & Ellanna. BA St. Jn's Coll MD 1963; STB GTS 1970; ThD GTS 1976; ABD GTS 1982. D 6/14/1970 Bp Harold Cornelius Gosnell P 12/1/1970 Bp Richard Earl Dicus. m 9/21/1966 Efthymia Papademetriou-Papatzikou. S Ptr's Epis Ch Hazleton PA 2002-2003; Dio Long Island Garden City NY 2000-2001; Ch of S Jude Wantagh NY 1999-2000; Int S Geo's Ch Hempstead NY 1998-1999; P-in-c S Aug's Epis Ch Croton On Hudson NY 1994; Int All Ang' Ch New York NY 1987-1988; R Holyrood Ch New York NY 1980-1987; Ch Of The H Apos New York NY 1976-1977; The GTS New York NY 1972-1976; Vic Ch Of The H Cross San Antonio TX 1970-1972. Fell Ecf 1978. lillymcallister141@hotmail.com

✠ COCHRANE, Rt Rev Robert Hume (Oly) 5906 NE 60th St, Seattle WA 98115 **Died 5/7/2010** B Charleston SC 7/9/1924 s William Arthur Cochrane & Raven Toomer. BA CUNY 1948; STB GTS 1951. D 3/31/1951 Bp James P De Wolfe P 11/3/1951 Bp Sumner Walters Con 1/25/1976 for Oly. c 2. DD GTS New York NY 1976. bobterry51@gmail.com

COCKBILL, Douglas J (Chi) 428 King St, Wenatchee WA 98801 Great Britain (UK) B Joliet IL 2/19/1953 s William Thomas Cockbill & Margaret Jane. BA U Chi 1975; MDiv GTS 1978. D 6/17/1978 Bp Quintin Ebenezer Primo Jr P 10/1/1979 Bp Edward Clark Turner. m 1/20/1979 Veronica Louise Blatch c 2. S Lk's Epis Ch Wenatchee WA 2010; Asst Epis Ch Of The Atone Chicago IL 1989-1990. Auth, "Update Of The Mvmt For The Reform Of Infant Baptism," 1996. dcockbill22@yahoo.com

COCKE, Reagan Winter (Tex) 2450 River Oaks Blvd, Houston TX 77019 **Assoc R S Jn The Div Houston TX 2002-** B San Antonio TX 9/5/1962 s Bartlett Cocke & Winifred Ellynn. BA U of Pennsylvania 1985; MArch U of Pennsylvania 1988; DOM Oxf 1999. D 8/23/2000 Bp James Edward Folts. m 6/21/1986 Stephanie H Hetos c 2. Asst Ch Of The Adv Brownsville TX 2000-2002. rcocke@sjd.org

COCKRAM-ASHLEY, Louis (RG) 465 E Lisa Dr, Chaparral NM 88081 **Died 9/12/2010** B 6/21/1936 s Alfred William Anthony Ashley & Norah Winifred. MDiv TESM 1988. D 6/7/1986 P 12/1/1986 Bp Alden Moinet Hathaway.

COCKRELL, Ernest William (ECR) 1538 Koch Ln, San Jose CA 95125 B Port Arthur TX 8/15/1938 s Herman William Cockrell & LaVerne Graham. BA Oklahoma City U 1960; STM Harvard DS 1963; Cert EDS 1964. D 6/20/1964 P 1/9/1965 Bp Anson Phelps Stokes Jr. m 8/24/1963 Jill S Shirk c 2. The Stndg Com Dio El Camino Real Monterey CA 2000-2004; R S Andr's Ch Saratoga CA 1992-2007; Chair Dio Mass Ltrgc Cmsn Dio Massachusetts Boston MA 1986-1990; R S Gabr's Epis Ch Marion MA 1967-1992; Cur Ch Of The Redeem Chestnut Hill MA 1964-1967. Auth/Compsr, "The Heav Host"; Auth, "Samson'S Shadow"; Auth, "Sama (Listening) Voices Of Palestinians/Israeli Peacemakers". The Bp's Cross Dio El Camino Real 2005. james.n.maleta@wellsfargo.com

COCKRELL, John Grafton (SC) Rr 4 Box 538, Bluefield WV 24701 B Ophelia VA 11/3/1937 s Dandridge Addison Cockrell & Retha Zenephine. BA Randolph-Macon Coll 1959; MDiv Duke 1962; ThM Duke 1963; CAS EDS 1965. D 6/29/1965 P 6/29/1966 Bp Thomas Augustus Fraser Jr. c 3. R S Steph's Epis Ch No Myrtle Bch SC 1997-2001; Ch Of The Cross Columbia SC 1992; So Carolina Epis Min To The Aging Columbia SC 1987-1991; R Ch Of Our Sav Rock Hill SC 1973-1987; Assoc Chr Ch Charlotte NC 1969-1972; Vic S Mk's Epis Ch Raleigh NC 1967-1969; Vic Ch Of The Ascen At Fork Advance NC 1965-1967; Vic Ch Of The Gd Shpd Cooleemee NC 1965-1967. Pi Delta Epsilon R.M. Coll 1958. jgcockrell@citilink.net

COCKRELL, Richard (USC) 2104 E North Ave, Anderson SC 29625 B Madison WI 7/12/1925 s Frank P Cockrell & Grace W. Newberry Coll,Newberry,SC 1944; Tul,New orleans, LA 1945; BA U of Wisconsin 1949; MA MI SU 1953; MDiv CDSP 1957; STM Yale DS 1974. D 6/30/1957 Bp Richard S M Emrich P 1/1/1958 Bp Archie H Crowley. m 7/7/1990 Betty M Milford c 4. Asst-Ret Chr Ch Greenville SC 1991-1995; Int Gr Epis Ch Anderson SC 1989-1990; Int S Jn's Epis Ch Troy NY 1987-1988; Asst Chr Ch Ridgewood NJ 1986; Int Trin Ch Paterson NJ 1985; Int R Ch Of The Epiph Newport NH 1983-1984; Int S Andr's Ch Manchester NH 1983-1984; Dio New Hampshire Concord NH 1982-1984; Asst Calv Epis Ch Williamsville NY 1982-1983; Ch Of The Epiph Newport NH 1982-1983; Tchr Sch Rel Dio Vermont Burlington VT 1979-1981; Cmnty Serv Dio Vermont Burlington VT 1974-1981; Ecum Coun Peace T/F Dio Vermont Burlington VT 1974-1981; S Jas Ch Woodstock VT 1974-1981; S Jas's Ch W Hartford CT 1974-1981; Mus & Liturg y Com Dio Connecticut Hartford CT 1971-1974; Trin Ch On The Green New Haven CT 1971-1973; Ch Of The Gd Shpd Hartford CT 1967-1970; Asst S Andr's Ch Ann Arbor MI 1959-1966; Dept CSR Dio Michigan Detroit MI 1958-1965; Cur Chr Ch Grosse Pointe Grosse Pointe Farms MI 1958-1959; Vic S Barn' Ch Chelsea MI 1957-1958. Auth-Coordntr, "An Amer Renaissance," *7 Videos: Healing our Professions*, Anderson U,And. SC, 2005; Auth, "Mnstry Proposal for NJ Dio," *Study of the Ch of Atlantic City,NJ*, DioceseNJ, 1987. Anderson TS for Lay Persons, Anderson, SC 1989; Cntr for Progressive Chrsnty 1998; Inst of Servnt Ldrshp 1995; Untd Rel Initiative-URI 1999. Citation of Faithful Serv Downtown Coop Mnstry,New Haven, CT 1974; Citation of Faithful Serv Sage Advocates-Trin Ch.New haven, CT 1974; Citation of Faithful Serv Cntr city Ch, Hartford, CT 1971. ricardocee@aol.com

CODE, David Arthur (NJ) 1 Dyke Rd, Setauket NY 11733 B Redvers Canada 5/29/1965 s Arthur Warren Code & Alice Gertrude. PrTS; BA Ya 1987; MDiv GTS 2002. D 6/22/2002 Bp David B(ruce) Joslin P 1/11/2003 Bp James Elliot Curry. m 4/26/1997 Karen Bysiewicz c 2. Caroline Ch Of Brookhaven Setauket NY 2004-2005; Asst S Steph's Ch Ridgefield CT 2002-2003. davidacode@gmail.com

CODY, Daphne Ceil (Chi) 380 Hawthorn Ave, Glencoe IL 60022 **S Elis's Ch Glencoe IL 2005-** B Parkersburg WV 12/1/1966 d Cecil Charles Daugherty & Constance. BA Coll of Wooster 1989; MS NWU 1991; MDiv SWTS 1996. D 6/15/1996 Bp Frank Tracy Griswold III P 5/1/1998 Bp Herbert Alcorn Donovan Jr. m 8/10/1991 Jason Andrew Cody c 2. Assoc S Mary's Ch Pk Ridge IL 1999-2004. cody@steglencoe.org

COE III, Frank S (WVa) 74 Rhodes Court, Harpers Ferry WV 25425 **P Assoc Trin Ch Shepherdstown WV 2010-** B East Orange NJ 10/11/1937 s Frank Seymour Coe & Hazel. BS VPI 1960; U of Houston 1964. D 6/13/1998 P 6/12/1999 Bp John H(enry) Smith. m 8/20/1960 Wilma Cassell c 2. Int Mt Zion Epis Ch Hedgesville WV 2009-2010; Int S Mk's Epis Ch Berkeley Sprg WV 2009-2010; P Assoc Trin Ch Shepherdstown WV 2006-2009; Int S Mk's Epis Ch Berkeley Sprg WV 2003-2006; Exec Dir Peterkin C&C Dio W Virginia Charleston WV 1997-2003. frankcoe@frontiernet.net

COE, Wayland Newton (Tex) 5934 Rutherglenn Dr, Houston TX 77096 B Austin TX 10/5/1960 s Gordon Earl Coe & JoeAnn Williams. Drury U 1981; BBA U of Texas 1983; MDiv TESM 1990. D 6/16/1990 Bp Maurice Manuel Benitez P 1/30/1991 Bp William Elwood Sterling. m 6/23/1984 Janet Lynn Gay c 2. S Thos Ch Houston TX 1993-2005; Asst to R Chr Ch Nacogdoches TX 1990-1993; Dio Texas Houston TX 1990. PB Soc of the USA 1993. retiredcoe@gmail.com

COENEN, Susan Ann (FdL) 304 W Smith Ave, Oshkosh WI 54901 **D Trin Epis Ch Oshkosh WI 2005-** B Oshkosh WI 3/16/1949 d Robert Louis Laurent & Annabelle Lorraine. D 8/27/2005 Bp Russell Edward Jacobus. scoenen2@new.rr.com

COERPER, Milo George (Md) 7315 Brookville Rd, Chevy Chase MD 20815 **Cathd Chapl Cathd of St Ptr & St Paul Washington DC 1986-** B Milwaukee WI 5/8/1925 s Milo Wilson Coerper & Rose Catherine. BS USNA 1946; LLB U MI 1954; MA Geo 1957; PhD Geo 1960; ST STUSo 1980. D 7/5/1978 Bp William Jackson Cox P 5/6/1979 Bp David Keller Leighton Sr. m 4/11/1953 Lois Yvonne Hicks c 3. R S Andr's Ch Clear Sprg MD 1979-1985. Auth, "A Deeper Dimension," *Experience*, ABA, 1995. Actg Chair Cbury Cathd Trust in Amer 1991-1991; Advsry Bd, Camaldolese Benedictines 1991-2001; Advsry Coun, Shalem Inst for Sprtl Formation 2000; Bd Dir, Shalem Inst for Sprtl Formation 1980-2000; Bd Dir, The Jn Main Inst, Ltd 1991-1999; Bd Dir, Treas, the Evelyn Underhill Assn 1991-2010; Bd Dir, Wrld Cmnty for Chr Mediation 1997-1999; Fllshp of Contemplative Pryr 1975; Mem, Coun, Friends of Cbury Cathd in US 1999-2005; Mem, Living Ch Fndt 1989-2004; Oblate Camaldolese Benedictines 1995; Oblate S Anselm Benedictine Abbey 1989; Off Most Venerable Ord of the Hosp of S Jn Jeru 1989-2010; Pres Natl Assn for the Self-Supporting Active M 1981-1983; Trst, Friends of Cbury Cathd in US 2005-2010; V-Chair Cbury Cathd Trust in Amer 1981-1997. Patron Wrld Cmnty for Chr Meditation 1999; Patron Friends of S Ben 1997. wmcoerp@verizon.net

COERPER, Rebecca Blackshear (CNY) 111 Waring St, Summerville SC 29483 **R S Jame's Ch Skaneateles NY 2010-** B New Rochelle NY 3/2/1956 d David Singleton Blackshear & Marion Speers. BA Coll of Wooster 1978; MDiv TS 2003. D 5/29/2003 P 11/29/2003 Bp Edward Lloyd Salmon Jr. m 7/1/1978 Milo Wilson Coerper c 2. Assoc R S Paul's Epis Ch Summerville SC 2003-2010. beckycoerper@gmail.com

COFFEY, Bridget Eileen (Lex) 5 School House Ln, North East MD 21901 **Chr Epis Ch Winchester VA 2011-** B Greenville NC 11/2/1979 d John Edward Coffey & Marlene Ann. BS Chris Newport U 2003; MDiv The GTS 2009. D 6/13/2009 Bp James Joseph Shand P 12/21/2009 Bp Stacy F Sauls. Chr Ch Cathd Lexington KY 2009-2010; S Aug's Chap Lexington KY 2009-2010. bcoffey@ccclex.org

COFFEY, E Allen (Va) 10231 Fenholloway Dr, Mechanicsville VA 23116 B New York NY 9/13/1947 s Edward Coffey & Rosa. BA Randolph-Macon Coll 1969; MDiv VTS 1973; DMin UTS Richmond VA 1986. D 5/26/1973 P 5/11/

1974 Bp Robert Bruce Hall. m 4/27/2002 Deborah Waters c 1. Buck Mtn Epis Ch Earlysville VA 2007; S Paul's Epis Ch Miller's Tavern VA 2007; Abingdon Epis Ch White Marsh VA 2002-2007; Stndg Comm Dio Virginia Richmond VA 1996-1999; R Emm Ch At Brook Hill Richmond VA 1991-2002; Assoc R S Jas' Ch Richmond VA 1988-1991; P-in-c S Dav's Ch Aylett VA 1981-1982; Conv Plnng Com Dio Virginia Richmond VA 1980-1982; Rgstr Dio Virginia Richmond VA 1979-2001; Exec Bd Dio Virginia Richmond VA 1978-1981; Mssns Com Dio Virginia Richmond VA 1978-1981; R S Ptr's Par Ch New Kent VA 1973-1988. Auth, *A Hist of the Dio Virginia & Its Bishops*; Auth, *S Ptr's Par 1679-1979: 300 Years*; Auth, *Some Thoughts on Chr Stwdshp*; Auth, *Video- (videotape tour) S Ptr's Par Ch 1701*. EvangES 1974-1998. eallencoffey@attbi.com

COFFEY, Gary Keith (WNC) 23 Forest Knoll Dr, Weaverville NC 28787 **R Gr Ch Asheville NC 2001-** B Shelby NC 4/30/1953 s James Clarence Coffey & Hannah Uzella. BA U NC 1977; MDiv TESM 1983. D 6/25/1983 P 5/23/1984 Bp William Gillette Weinhauer. m 8/11/1973 Astrid Zwetsloot c 2. R Chr Ch Cedar Rapids IA 1997-2001; Asst Trin Ch Myrtle Bch SC 1983-1987. gracerevcoffey@bellsouth.net

COFFEY, J(anet) Paris (Chi) 240 S. Marion St., 1N, Oak Park IL 60302 **R S Chris's Epis Ch Oak Pk IL 1998-** B Lynchburg VA 12/15/1950 d William Samuel Hooten & Margaret Christine. BA U of Missouri 1973; MA Eden TS 1988. D 5/18/1995 P 5/29/1996 Bp Hays H. Rockwell. m 10/11/1975 Robert Michael Coffey c 2. Assoc S Tim's Epis Ch Creve Coeur MO 1995-1997. Cathd Chapt 1995-1997; Cathd Shltr Bd 2005; Dioc Coun 2003-2005; SSJE Sprtl Dir Trng 1986-1987; Sprtl Dir Intl 1988-1995. jpcoffey240@comcast.net

COFFEY JR, Jonathan Bachman (Fla) 4903 Robert D Gordon Rd, Jacksonville FL 32210 **S Mk's Epis Ch Jacksonville FL 2006-** B Chattanooga TN 2/17/1950 s Jonathan Bachman Coffey & Mary Elizabeth. DMin S Vladimir Orth Sem Yonkers NY; BA Goddard Coll 1972; MDiv SWTS 1977; STM GTS 1984. D 6/22/1977 Bp William Hopkins Folwell P 12/21/1977 Bp Charles Bennison. m 7/6/1974 Julie Allen Gibson c 2. R S Anth On The Desert Scottsdale AZ 1998-2006; R Ch Of S Jas The Less Scarsdale NY 1992-1998; R S Paul's Ch Fayetteville AR 1989-1991; R S Richard's Ch Winter Pk FL 1983-1989; R S Alb's Epis Ch Auburndale FL 1980-1983; Asst Gr Epis Ch Traverse City MI 1977-1980; Vic S Christophers Ch Northport MI 1977-1980; Vic S Paul's Epis Ch Elk Rapids MI 1977-1980; Grand Traverse City Area Mssn Traverse City MI 1977-1979. Auth, "9/11: A Wakeup Call to the Ch," *Living Ch*, 2002; "Var arts," *Living Ch*. OHC- Assoiate 2004. Whipple Schlr SWTS Evanston IL. jbcjr50@msn.com

COFFEY, Jonathan Bachman (SeFla) 1701 SW Capri St Apt 262, Palm City FL 34990 **Screen & Nomntns Com Elctns Bp Dio SE Florida Miami FL 1978-; Dept Ecum Rela Dio SE Florida Miami FL 1963-** B Chattanooga TN 9/26/1921 s Charles Shelby Coffey & Mary Margaret. BA U of Chattanooga 1943; MDiv CDSP 1955. D 7/8/1955 Bp John Vander Horst P 1/25/1956 Bp Theodore N Barth. m 12/27/1946 Mary Corey c 4. Asstng P S Mary's Epis Ch Stuart FL 1994-2006; Exec Bd Dio SE Florida Miami FL 1982-1985; R All SS Epis Ch Jensen Bch FL 1978-1986; R All Souls' Epis Ch Miami Bch FL 1965-1978; Vic All Ang Ch Miami Sprg FL 1957-1960; D Chr Ch Epis So Pittsburg TN 1955-1956. coffcoff@bellsouth.net

COFFEY, Kevin Patrick Joseph (Nwk) 2-06 31st St, Fair Lawn NJ 07410 **R Ch Of The Atone Fair Lawn NJ 2000-** B Lackawanna NY 6/8/1954 s William Joseph Coffey & Frances Helen. BS Quinnipiac U 1982; Ya Berk 1983; MDiv GTS 1988. D 6/4/1988 Bp Harry Woolston Shipps P 3/11/1989 Bp Charles Lee Burgreen. m 8/4/1977 Kathy Ann Propst c 2. Wmn Cmsn Dio Newark Newark NJ 1997-2005; Cathd Chapt Trin And S Phil's Cathd Newark NJ 1997-2001; Co Mssnr Bergen Epis Area Mnstry Rochelle Pk NJ 1996-2000; Ch Of The Atone Fair Lawn NJ 1996-2000; Ch of the Ascen Munich 81545 DE 1996-2000; S Mart's Ch Maywood NJ 1996-2000; S Ptr's Ch Newark NJ 1996-2000; Assoc R The Angl/Epis Ch Of Chr The King Frankfurt am Main 60323 DE 1992-1996; Pstr Ch Of The Gd Shpd Newburgh NY 1989-1992; Hudson Vlly Mnstrs New Windsor NY 1989-1992; Assoc S Phil's Ch Garrison NY 1988-1989. Soc of Cath Priests 2009. kpjcoffey@gmail.com

COFFEY, Margaret Louise (NJ) 541 Harding Rd, Little Silver NJ 07739 B Youngstown OH 7/10/1934 d John Howard Hall & Mary Louise. BA Wellesley Coll 1956; MDiv GTS 1983. D 6/4/1983 Bp George Phelps Mellick Belshaw P 12/10/1983 Bp John Harris Burt. m 6/25/1955 Gerald Dillon Coffey c 3. S Geo's Epis Ch Helmetta NJ 2000; S Andr The Apos Highland Highlands NJ 1990-2000; Assoc S Thos Epis Ch Red Bank NJ 1986-1990; Chr Ch Sheridan MT 1985-1986; Int The Epis Ch Of The H Comm Fair Haven NJ 1985-1986; Asst Chr Ch Middletown NJ 1983-1984. hallcoffey@aol.com

COFFIN, Lewis Edward (CNY) PO Box 141, Newfield NY 14867 B Lake Forest IL 5/15/1924 s Fletcher Barker Coffin & Frances Josephine. BA Hav 1945; STB NYTS 1949; MDiv Ya Berk 1952. D 11/1/1952 P 11/1/1953 Bp Charles F Hall. c 5. Vic S Mk's Ch Candor NY 1991-2003; S Jn's Ch Ithaca NY 1987-1990; St Johns Epis Ch Berkshire NY 1976-1990; R Ch Of The Epiph Trumansburg NY 1973-1976; R S Mich's and All Ang' Ch Fairview MT 1967-1973; R S Ptr's Epis Ch Williston ND 1967-1973; R H Trin Epis Ch Luverne MN 1964-1967; R S Paul's Ch Pipestone MN 1964-1967; Assoc Trin Ch Toledo OH 1960-1964; Vic All SS Epis Ch Wolfeboro NH 1952-1960.

COFFIN, Peter R (NH) 35 Woodbury St, Keene NH 03431 B Salem MA s Lloyd Coffin & Martha. BA Bos 1982; MDiv SWTS 1988. D 6/11/1988 P 5/6/1989 Bp David Elliot Johnson. m 12/31/1994 Tania Coffin c 2. R Par Of S Jas Ch Keene NH 2000-2007; R S Paul's Ch Lancaster NH 1994-2000; Cn Res Cathd Ch Of S Steph Harrisburg PA 1990-1994; Cur Ch Of The H Cross Tryon NC 1988-1990. Soc Of S Jn The Evang 1988. eli1dog@mac.com

COGAN, Timothy Bernard (NJ) 38 The Blvd/RFD659, Edgartown MA 02539 **Asst The Epis Ch Of Beth-By-The-Sea Palm Bch FL 2004-; Cn Trin Cathd Trenton NJ 1982-** B Boston MA 2/24/1935 s Bernard Sheridan Cogan & Mary Constance. AB Harv 1956; MDiv VTS 1959; DD VTS 2004. D 6/10/1959 P 5/30/1963 Bp Anson Phelps Stokes Jr. m 5/20/1967 Ruth Mitchell c 2. Asst S Paul's Epis Ch No Andover MA 1988-2002; Int S Andr's Ch Edgartown MA 1987; Sch Min Brooks Sch Chap No Andover MA 1985-2002; Sch Min Brooks Sch No Andover MA 1985-2002; Chapl The Wm Alexander Procter Fndt Trenton NJ 1972-1985; Asst Gr Epis Ch New York NY 1966-1969; Cur S Phil's Ch New York NY 1965-1966; Min Ch Of The Gd Shpd Fairhaven MA 1960-1961; Asst S Andr's Ch New Bedford MA 1960-1961; Cur S Jn's Ch Beverly Farms MA 1959-1960. Auth, "Let all the Peoples Praise Him," *Let all the Peoples Praise Him*; Auth, "The Ch Boarding Sch," *The Ch Boarding Sch*; Auth, "The Story & the Meal," *The Story & the Meal*; Auth, "Worshiping on the Margin," *Worshiping on the Margin*. Sr Mem/Assoc Kings Coll, Camb 2004; DD VTS 2004. timothycogan45@hotmail.com

COGGI, Lynne Marie Madeleine (NY) 3206 Cripple Creek St Apt 39b, San Antonio TX 78209 **Supply P Dio W Texas San Antonio TX 2007-** B New York NY 10/16/1933 d Herbert James Donald & Hilda Rebecca Violet. BA CUNY 1963; CUNY 1965; MDiv UTS 1985. D 10/25/1985 Bp Walter Decoster Dennis Jr P 12/7/1988 Bp Edmond Lee Browning. c 2. Supply P Dio W Texas San Antonio TX 1999-2002; Int S Phil's Ch San Antonio TX 1998-1999; Supply P Dio W Texas San Antonio TX 1995-1998; Supply P Dio Long Island Garden City NY 1992-1995; P-in-c S Steph's Epis Ch Jamaica NY 1990-1992; AIDS Consult Epis Ch Cntr New York NY 1985-1988; Cur S Ptr's Ch Bronx NY 1985-1986. Auth, "A Time for Caring," Epis Ch Cntr, 1985.

COGGIN, Bruce Wayne (FtW) 3700 Ellsmere Ct, Fort Worth TX 76103 B Lafayette LA 5/2/1941 s Ross Wayne Coggin & Martha Jane. BA U of Texas 1962; MA Col 1964; MDiv SWTS 1966; PhD U of Texas 1982. D 6/15/1966 Bp Charles A Mason P 12/21/1966 Bp Theodore H McCrea. c 3. All SS' Epis Ch Ft Worth TX 1990; Gd Shpd Granbury TX 1989; R S Tim's Ch Ft Worth TX 1987-1989; Ch Of The H Comf Cleburne TX 1979-1987; Asst All SS Epis Ch Austin TX 1974-1977; R S Ptr's Ch McKinney TX 1969-1974; Vic S Mary's Ch Hamilton TX 1966-1969; Vic S Matt's Ch Comanche TX 1966-1969. The Philadelphia Soc 1978. Phi Beta Kappa U of Texas 1962. brucecoggin@charter.net

COGILL, Richard Leonard (Minn) 1200 Nicollet Ave Apt 502, Minneapolis MN 55403 B Capetown ZA 1/27/1966 s Henry Alec Cogill & Veronica Gwendoline. BA Gustavus Adolphus Coll 1994; MDiv Luther TS 1997; STM GTS 2002. D 6/15/2002 P 12/17/2002 Bp James Louis Jelinek. Dio Minnesota Minneapolis MN 2002-2003; Cur Trin Ch Excelsior MN 2002-2003.

COGSDALE, Michael H (WNC) 845 Cherokee Place, Lenoir NC 28645 **Dep Genral Conv Dio Wstrn No Carolina Asheville NC 2009-; R S Jas Epis Ch Lenoir NC 2005-** B Norfolk VA 6/8/1956 s Alvin Bland Cogsdale & Charlotte Anne. BS Appalachian St U 1979; MDiv VTS 1987. D 5/15/1987 P 12/19/1987 Bp William Gillette Weinhauer. m 7/18/1987 Elizabeth Graham Gartman c 2. Dioc Coun Dio Wstrn No Carolina Asheville NC 2005-2007; R Ch Of The Epiph Newton NC 2001-2005; COM Dio E Carolina Kinston NC 1998-2000; Com Mnstry Dio Wstrn No Carolina Asheville NC 1998-2000; Com Mnstry Dio Wstrn No Carolina Asheville NC 1998-2000; R Gr Epis Ch Plymouth NC 1998-2000; P S Paul's Ch Vanceboro NC 1997-1998; Int Gr Epis Ch Plymouth NC 1995-1996; Asst Bp For Yth Mnstry Dio Wstrn No Carolina Asheville NC 1992-1994; Valle Crucis Conf Cntr Banner Elk NC 1990-1995; The Patterson Sch Lenoir NC 1988-1990; Cur Gr Ch Morganton NC 1987-1988. rector@saintjamesepiscopal.org

COGSWELL, Colby Adams (Cal) 131 Fairfield Place, Moraga CA 94556 **Died 11/11/2009** B Hartford CT 11/30/1917 s Eliot Sanborn Cogswell & Ruth. BA Dart 1939; BD CDSP 1963. D 6/23/1963 P 4/1/1964 Bp James Albert Pike. c 2. WILLCOGSWELL@GMAIL.COM

COHEE, William Patrick (Az) 114 W Roosevelt St, Phoenix AZ 85003 B Phoenix AZ 9/4/1955 s William Pinkney Cohee & Patricia Jean. D 1/26/2008 Bp Kirk Stevan Smith. bcohee@cox.net

COHEN, Georgia Shoberg (NJ) Po Box 5, Blawenburg NJ 08504 B Cleveland OH 6/21/1946 d Raymond Victor Shoberg & Elaine Coates. BA U MI 1967; Amls U MI 1968; MDiv VTS 1976; PhD PrTS 1987. D 6/26/1976 P 3/9/1977 Bp H Coleman McGehee Jr. m 6/4/1988 Larry Louis Cohen. Ch Of The Annunc Lawnside NJ 2002-2005; S Ptr's Ch Medford NJ 1993-1997; Dio Michigan Detroit MI 1987-1989; Com Dio Virginia Richmond VA 1980-1981;

Asst Imm Ch-On-The-Hill Alexandria VA 1977-1980; VTS Alexandria VA 1976-1981. Atla.

COHOON, Frank Nelson (Kan) 44 Sw Pepper Tree Ln, Topeka KS 66611 B Oklahoma City OK 9/12/1925 s Cecil Culver Cohoon & Sally Estelle. Phillips U 1945; BA TCU 1947; STB GTS 1954. D 6/22/1954 P 12/21/1954 Bp Chilton Powell. m 3/1/1992 Mary Curry c 3. Planned Giving Off Dio Kansas Topeka KS 1992-2000; Exec Off Dio Kansas Topeka KS 1987-1992; Dvlpmt Off Dio Kansas Topeka KS 1985-1993; Archd Mssn Dio Kansas Topeka KS 1978-1992; CDO Dio Kansas Topeka KS 1978-1987; Chair Cmsn Strtgy & Cong Dvlpmt Dio Kansas Topeka KS 1978-1987; Dio Kansas Topeka KS 1976-1992; Vic Calv Ch Yates Cntr KS 1976-1978; Vic S Tim's Ch Iola KS 1976-1978; R S Dav's Epis Ch Topeka KS 1966-1974; Chair Liturg Cmsn Dio Kansas Topeka KS 1965-1970; COM Dio Kansas Topeka KS 1961-1987; R Ch Of The Cov Jct City KS 1961-1965; Vic S Chris's Ch Midwest City OK 1956-1961; R Chr Memi Epis Ch El Reno OK 1954-1956; Admin Asst. to the Dn S Paul's Cathd Oklahoma City OK 1947-1951. Angl Soc; Associated Parishes; RWF. fncohoon@cox.net

COHOON, Richard Allison (CPa) 500 E Guardlock Dr, Lock Haven PA 17745 B Worcester MA 7/28/1929 s Charles Allison Cohoon & Barbara. Fllshp Coll of Preachers; BA Coll of Wooster 1951; BD EDS 1954. D 6/24/1954 P 12/1/1954 Bp Dudley S Stark. m 5/17/1952 Diana Rees Storch c 2. R S Paul's Ch Lock Haven PA 1985-1994; Chr Ch Stroudsburg PA 1985; Vic S Anne's Epis Ch Trexlertown PA 1971-1975; Assoc The Epis Ch Of The Medtr Allentown PA 1967-1975; R S Jn's Ch Sodus NY 1959-1967; R Chr Ch Sodus Point NY 1959-1962; R Gr Ch Lyons NY 1954-1959. AAMFC 1974. masmida@diocesecpa.org

COIL, John Albert (WMo) 7917 Lamar Ave, Prairie Village KS 66208 **Vic S Lk's Epis Ch Excelsior Sprg MO 2002-** B Kendallville IN 6/3/1951 s John Athol Coil & Virginia. STUSo; Valparaiso U 1970; BA Phillips U 1973; MDiv STUSo 1977. D 6/18/1977 P 1/8/1978 Bp Gerald Nicholas McAllister. m 8/12/1973 Janette Lucas c 3. COM Dio W Missouri Kansas City MO 2000-2006; Epis Ch Of The H Sprt Kansas City KS 1996-2001; Int S Aug's Ch Kansas City MO 1993-1994; Admin R S Andr's Ch Kansas City MO 1986-1991; Dn, Reg 4 Dio Oklahoma Oklahoma City OK 1979-1986; Vic S Jn's Epis Ch Woodward OK 1979-1986; S Steph's Alva Alva OK 1978-1981; S Paul's Cathd Oklahoma City OK 1977-1978. Auth, "Yes, But How Do I Become a Nonanxious Presence?," *Congregations*, The Alb Inst; Auth, "Effective Del Skills Promote Vital Congregations," *Congregations*, The Alb Inst. Ord of S Ben. johnacoil@jacanda.com

COIL, Paul Douglas (At) 4141 Wash Lee Ct Sw, Lilburn GA 30047 **R The Ch Of S Matt Snellville GA 1992-** B Washington DC 4/23/1945 s Everett Johnston Coil & Mary. BA Salem Coll Salem WV 1970; MDiv Ya Berk 1973. D 6/23/1973 Bp William Foreman Creighton P 2/22/1975 Bp Wilburn Camrock Campbell. m 7/24/1971 Carolyn Hendrix c 2. R H Trin Epis Ch Bartow FL 1981-1992; Vic Chr Memi Ch Williamstown WV 1974-1981; Asst S Pat's Ch Washington DC 1973-1974. Auth, "Two Curric Guides for CE". OHC 1972. revpdc@bellsouth.net

COKE III, Henry Cornick (Dal) 5433 N Dentwood Dr, Dallas TX 75220 B New Haven CT 9/6/1928 s Henry Cornick Coke & Ethel Randall. BA Ya 1950; MDiv GTS 1954; STM SMU 1971. D 6/16/1954 Bp Harry Tunis Moore P 12/1/1954 Bp Charles A Mason. m 6/26/1954 Anne Schoellkopf. S Mich And All Ang Ch Dallas TX 1961-1980; Vic S Mich's U Mssn Island Isla Vista CA 1958-1961. Auth, "Why Baptize Babies?". hcokeiii@aol.com

COKE, Paul T (Tex) 9426 Peabody Ct, Boca Raton FL 33496 B Long Beach CA 4/15/1933 s Paul Edward Coke & Beatrice Ethel. BA Pomona Coll 1954; BA Oxf 1958; STB GTS 1959; MA Oxf 1962; ThD GTS 1971. D 6/22/1959 P 2/16/1960 Bp Francis E I Bloy. m 4/30/1960 Ethel Beard. Epis TS Of The SW Austin TX 1974-1998; Cur S Jas Par Los Angeles CA 1959-1960. Auth, *Mtn & Wilderness: Pryr & Wrshp in the Biblic Wrld & Early Ch*. Fell Royal Soc of Arts London Engl.

COLANGELO, Preston Hart (Ala) 1663 Bradford Ln, Bessemer AL 35022 **D Dio Alabama Birmingham AL 2004-** B Lockport NY 2/1/1951 s Anthony Robert Colangelo & Carolyn Louise. AAS SUNY 1980. D 10/30/2004 Bp Henry Nutt Parsley Jr. m 8/25/1972 Denise Emminger c 2. Acolyte Fr, Vstry; Chris. Edu. Dir;SLEM St Mk Epis Ch No Tonawanda NY 1976-1996. Delta Soc 2005; Natl Italian Amer Fed 2009. deacon_bench@bellsouth.net

COLBERT, Paul A (EpisSanJ) 45694 Windmill Rd, Coarsegold CA 93614 **Vic St Nich Epis Ch Atwater CA 2010-; Vic H Trin Epis Ch Madera CA 2009-; Vic St Raphael Epis Ch Oakhurst CA 2009-; Mssnr for Madera/MerceCounties Epis Dio San Joaquin Modesto CA 2008-; Vic S Raphaels Ch Chino CA 2008-** B Louisville KY 7/28/1954 s George P Colbert & Jean P. BS No Carolina St U 1978; MS U NC 1985. D 10/11/2002 P 4/26/2003 Bp Katharine Jefferts Schori. Asst Chr Ch Las Vegas NV 2006-2008; Pres, Dioc Revs Com Dio Nevada Las Vegas NV 2004-2008; P S Lk's Epis Ch Las Vegas NV 2003-2008. Cmnty of Solitude 2010. pcolbert@peacenet.org

COLBOURNE, Albert St George (Cal) 892 Marina Dr, Napa CA 94559 B Baie Verte NF Canada 8/25/1915 s Alfred Francis Colbourne & Bertha Jane. BEd Seattle U 1955; BD Nash 1958; MS California St U 1972; MDiv Nash 1974. D 11/30/1945 P 8/24/1946 Bp Benjamin F P Ivins. Assoc S Lk's Mssn Calistoga CA 1995-2000; Assoc S Mary's Epis Ch Napa CA 1990-1995; Asst Trsfg Epis Ch San Mateo CA 1986-1989; Ch Of The Ascen Vallejo CA 1978-1989; P-in-c Gr Epis Ch Fairfield CA 1967-1968; R Ch Of The Ascen Vallejo CA 1955-1967; R S Clem's Epis Ch Seattle WA 1950-1955; R Gr Ch Cedar Rapids IA 1947-1950; Emm Ch Lancaster WI 1945-1950. Sprtl Dir Intl 1985.

COLBURN, Suzanne Funk (Me) Po Box 185, Boothbay Harbor ME 04538 B New York NY 7/23/1946 d Merton Thompson Funk & Edna. BA Bow 1987; MA Harvard DS 1990; MDiv EDS 1996. D 6/7/1997 P 6/1/1998 Bp M(arvil) Thomas Shaw III. c 2. S Jn's Ch Beverly Farms MA 2009-2011; Int S Columba's Epis Ch Boothbay Harbor ME 2007-2009; Dio Maine Portland ME 2004-2009; Chr Ch Biddeford ME 2004-2006; Dn Dio Massachusetts Boston MA 2002-2004; Emm Ch Boston MA 1998-2003; D S Ptr's Epis Ch Cambridge MA 1997-1998. SBL; Soc Of S Jn The Evang. sfcolburn@gmail.com

COLBY, Christopher Gage (Miss) PO Box 459, Pass Christian MS 39571 **R Trin Ch Epis Pass Chr MS 1997-** B Great Lakes Naval Trng Sta IL 9/25/1952 s Gage Colby & Sylvia Lorraine. BS Iowa St U 1974; MDiv SWTS 1977. D 6/24/1977 P 4/4/1978 Bp Philip Frederick McNairy. m 5/26/1990 Deborah Ellis c 2. S Mk's Epis Ch Harvey LA 1986-1997; S Lk's Ch Baton Rouge LA 1984-1985; Dio Ft Worth Ft Worth TX 1984; The Epis Ch Of S Ptr And S Paul Arlington TX 1983; Dio Dallas Dallas TX 1981-1982; Cur S Geo's Epis Ch Dallas TX 1979-1981; Assoc R Pro Cathd Epis Ch Of S Clem El Paso TX 1977-1979. frcheese@aol.com

COLBY, Richard Everett (Me) 3702 Haven Pines Dr, Kingwood TX 77345 B Bath ME 6/3/1937 s Earl Blanchard Colby & Madeline Palmer. BA Indiana U 1959; STB Ya Berk 1962; Spanish Stds CostaRica 1965; Cntr Intercultural Formation Mex 1966. D 6/2/1962 P 12/6/1962 Bp Oliver L Loring. m 8/14/1965 Janet Meredith Russell c 3. Assoc R S Matt's Epis Ch Lisbon ME 1990-1995; R Ch Of The Epiph Pittsburgh PA 1984-1990; Vic S Steph The Mtyr Epis Ch E Waterboro ME 1980-1984; Assoc Trin Epis Ch Portland ME 1978-1979; Assoc Trin Epis Ch Portland ME 1971-1975. Auth, "Sm Ch Are Beautiful". chilecolbys@hotmail.com

COLE, Allan Hunter (USC) 1680 Shady Ln, Columbia SC 29206 **S Paul's Epis Ch Lakewood CO 2007-** B Atlanta GA 8/26/1966 s Willis Hunter Cole & Betty Marie. BA U NC 1996; MDiv STUSo 2000. D 12/16/2000 Bp Charles Glenn VonRosenberg. c 3. Heathwood Hall Epis Sch Columbia SC 2003-2005; D S Andr's Ch Maryville TN 2000-2003. ALLAN.COLE@HOTMAIL.COM

COLE, Anson Dean (O) 565 S Cleveland Massillon Rd, Akron OH 44333 B Kansas City MO 1/31/1931 s Anson Dean Cole & Helen Elizabeth. BS U of Kansas 1952; U CO 1957; MDiv Nash 1960. D 6/21/1960 P 12/1/1960 Bp Joseph Summerville Minnis. m 6/11/1960 Gail Cannon. Assoc R S Lk's Epis Ch Akron OH 1987-1997; S Andr's Epis Ch Toledo OH 1987; Assoc R S Paul's Ch Maumee OH 1986; Ch Of The Mssh Detroit MI 1971-1978; Colorado St U Ft Collins CO 1970-1971; Cur S Andr's Ch Denver CO 1970-1971; R S Barn Of The Vlly Cortez CO 1963-1970; Vic Epis Ch Of S Jn The Bapt Granby CO 1960-1963; Vic Trin Ch Kremmling CO 1960-1963. fatherdeancole@yahoo.com

COLE, Brian Lee (WNC) 10 Briar Br, Black Mountain NC 28711 **Dn The Cathd Of All Souls Asheville NC 2005-; Assoc The Cathd Of All Souls Asheville NC 2002-** B Hayti MO 12/7/1967 s Bruce John Cole & Betty Sue. BS Murray St U 1989; MDiv Sthrn Bapt TS Louisville KY 1992. D 6/8/2002 P 12/7/2002 Bp Robert Hodges Johnson. m 9/5/1998 Susan P Weatherford c 1. Affirming Catholicism 2002; Assoc Of The OHC 2002. brian@allsoulscathedral.org

COLE JR, C Alfred (CFla) 125 Larkwood Dr, Sanford FL 32771 B Charlotte NC 7/3/1942 s Clarence Alfred Cole & Catharine Tate. BS U of So Carolina 1965; CPA - 1967; MDiv VTS 1984; VTS 1992. D 6/8/1985 P 5/10/1986 Bp William Arthur Beckham. m 2/1/1969 Mary M Brunson c 2. R H Cross Epis Ch Sanford FL 1993-2004; Exec Asst to Bp Dio Albany Albany NY 1992-1993; Dioc Coun (Ex officio) Dio So Carolina Charleston SC 1989-1992; Reg Dn Dio So Carolina Charleston SC 1988-1992; Trst Dio So Carolina Charleston SC 1988-1992; R The Ch Of The Epiph Eutawville SC 1987-1992; Trst Dio So Carolina Charleston SC 1987-1991; Asst to the R S Fran Ch Greenville SC 1985-1987; Asst to the R Epis Ch Of The Redeem Greenville SC 1984-1985.

COLE JR, Cecil T (Mass) 2210 E Tudor Rd, Anchorage AK 99507 **Assoc S Mary's Ch Anchorage AK 2009-** B New York NY 10/27/1968 s Cecil T Cole & Jean Audrey. BA Mid 1990; MTS Harvard DS 1993; PhD Bos 2007. D 6/4/2005 Bp M(arvil) Thomas Shaw III P 1/7/2006 Bp Roy Frederick Cederholm Jr. m 11/7/2006 Lucia Moss. Int Chr Ch Par Plymouth MA 2008-2009; Cur Chr Ch Par Plymouth MA 2005-2008. tedcolejr@gmail.com

COLE, Christopher Owen (WTex) 5909 Walzem Rd, San Antonio TX 78218 **R Ch Of The Resurr San Antonio TX 2008-** B Philadelphia PA 3/3/1966 s Raymond Elden Cole & Cornelia Fay. BA U of Kansas 1988; MDiv SWTS 1998. D 6/20/1998 Bp Chilton Abbie Richardson Knudsen P 1/18/1999 Bp Robert Louis Ladehoff. m 10/19/1991 Laura G Laura Jeanne Goltz c 2. R All

SS Ch Hillsboro OR 2001-2008; S Paul's Epis Ch Salem OR 1998-2001. chris.cole6@gmail.com

COLE, Dennis C (Oly) 3917 Ne 44th St, Vancouver WA 98661 **Assoc S Lk's Epis Ch Vancouver WA 1998-** B Portland OR 4/21/1946 s Howard Curtis Cole & Ruth Eva. BA Willamette U 1968; MDiv Yale DS 1971; Tubingen U Tubingen DE 1972. D 6/20/1998 P 12/1/1998 Bp Vincent Waydell Warner. m 6/1/1968 Susan Joyce Cole c 3. dancingletters@comcast.com

COLE, Donald Dean (Ida) 2704 Applegrove Cir, El Dorado Hills CA 95762 B Okanogan WA 5/14/1931 s Earl Lewis Cole & Mary Flora. BA U of Washington 1957; MDiv Nash 1960. D 6/13/1960 P 12/1/1960 Bp William W Horstick. m 7/1/1966 Shirley Beyritz. Emm Epis Ch Grass Vlly CA 1999-2006; Dn S Mich's Cathd Boise ID 1989-1997; S Paul's Epis Ch Visalia CA 1973-1989; R All SS Epis Ch Las Vegas NV 1969-1973; Asst Trin Epis Ch Reno NV 1966-1969; Asst S Jas Epis Ch Milwaukee WI 1964-1966; Vic S Mary's Epis Ch Tomah WI 1960-1964. bunlet@theunion.net

COLE, Elaine Agnes (SwFla) 330 Forest Wood Ct, Spring Hill FL 34609 **D S Mart's Epis Ch Hudson FL 2005-** B Central Falls RI 2/19/1950 d William James Greer & Elmira Antoinette. D 6/26/1993 Bp George Nelson Hunt III. m 11/15/1969 Raymond L Cole c 2.

COLE, Elise Beckwith (Mich) 109 W Washington Ave Unit 16, Jackson MI 49201 B Yonkers NY 11/18/1937 d Wendall Parker Beckwith & Anna Elise. AS Jackson Jr Coll Jackson MS 1957; BS U MI 1960; Cert Whitaker TS 1997. D 3/11/2000 Bp R(aymond) Stewart Wood Jr. m 8/29/1959 Robert Flint Cole c 2. D S Paul's Epis Ch Jackson MI 2000-2009. ebcole2000@aol.com

COLE, Ethan (WNY) 5083 Thompson Rd, Clarence NY 14031 **Calv Epis Ch Williamsville NY 2007-** B Dunkirk NY 10/22/1979 BA Hob. D 12/20/2003 P 11/6/2004 Bp J Michael Garrison. All Souls Memi Epis Ch Washington DC 2006-2007; Cn S Paul's Cathd Buffalo NY 2004-2006. ethan.cole@stpaulscathedral.org

COLE, Frantz (Hai) Box 1309, Port-Au-Prince Haiti **Dio Haiti Ft Lauderdale FL 1987-** B 12/12/1958 s Roger Cole & Genevieve. U 2 Yrs; Sem 1986. D 2/8/1987 P 11/1/1987 Bp Luc Anatole Jacques Garnier. Soc Of S Marg.

COLE JR, H(oward) Milton (Pa) 2001 S. 40th Court, West Des Moines IA 50265 B Newport News VA 5/21/1944 s Howard Milton Cole & Susie. W&M; BS Virginia Commonwealth U 1970; MA U Of The Dist Of Columbia 1975; MDiv GTS 1982; Cert Cuernavaca Lang Inst Mex Mx 1992; Lang Inst Of Mex Mx 1992. D 6/29/1983 P 5/31/1984 Bp C(laude) Charles Vache. m 1/6/1999 Mary Duvall Cole c 3. Dio Pennsylvania Philadelphia PA 1998; S Paul's Ch Elkins Pk PA 1994-1998; Int S Andr's By The Sea Nags Hd NC 1992-1994; Exec Coun Appointees New York NY 1989-1992; Cur Trin Ch Portsmouth VA 1983-1989. Auth, "Resolution Of Commendation Ecec 92". Peacemaker Among Us Pacem In Terris Delaware 1999; Resolutn Of Commendation Ecec 1992; Gd Samar Awd Cath Fam Serv Dio Richmond 1987. misterdubose@aol.com

COLE, Judith Poteet (WNC) 8015 Island View Ct, Denver NC 28037 **D Epis Ch Of S Ptr's By The Lake Denver NC 1996-** B South Charleston WV 4/8/1940 d Russell Lee Poteet & Virginia Crawford. BS Morris Harvey Coll 1962; MS Marshall U 1968. D 12/21/1996 Bp Robert Hodges Johnson. m 7/24/1959 David Ray Cole c 2. Sis of the Trsfg 1993. jpoteetcole@charter.net

COLE, Marguerite June (Nev) 5268 Jodilyn Ct Apt 150, Las Vegas NV 89103 **D Gr In The Desert Epis Ch Las Vegas NV 2008-** B Washington PA 6/3/1936 d Gustav A Schweinebraten & Margaret Mary. BS W Virginia U 1958; EFM STUSo 1980; Cert Prchr Lewis Sch of Mnstry 1982. D 4/29/1985 Bp Richard Mitchell Trelease Jr. m 2/9/1973 John Wyatt Cole c 4. D Chr Ch Las Vegas NV 2000-2007. mcole448@gmail.com

COLE, Mary Duvall (Ia) 2001 S. 40th Court, West Des Moines IA 50265 **R S Tim's Epis Ch W Des Moines IA 2004-** B Saint Louis MO 5/7/1959 d Harmann Duvall & Vilma. BA Columbia Coll 1981; MDiv Epis TS of The SW 1996. D 6/3/1997 Bp James Monte Stanton P 1/17/1998 Bp Robert William Duncan. m 1/6/1999 H(oward) Milton Cole c 3. Com Dio Delaware Wilmington DE 1999-2004; Asst Chr Ch Greenville Wilmington DE 1997-2004. Corp Individual Awd Aids Delaware 2002; Citizenship Awd City Of Wilmington 2002; Peacemaker Among Us Pacem In Terris 2001. maryduvall@msn.com

COLE, Michael George (SC) 1202 Stonegate Way, Crozet VA 22932 **H Cross Faith Memi Epis Ch Pawleys Island SC 2002-** B Sudbury Suffolk UK 4/26/1935 s Bertie William Cole & Elsie Mabel. LTh Lichfield Theol Coll 1960; DMin Wesley TS 1989. Trans from Church Of England 12/1/1982 Bp John Thomas Walker. m 8/2/1962 Valerie Hart c 4. R S Jn's Epis Ch Halifax VA 1994-1998; R The Memi Ch Of The Prince Of Peace Gettysburg PA 1990-1994; Chr Ch Chaptico MD 1983-1990. UN Peace Keeping Medal Untd Nations 1976; Can Decoration Can ArmdF 1974. nzgrcr6@comcast.net

COLE JR, Raymond Elden (WTex) 3614 Hunters Dove, San Antonio TX 78230 B Newburyport MA 7/14/1938 s Raymond Elden Cole & Emily Katherine. BA Leh 1960; MDiv GTS 1963. D 6/8/1963 P 12/1/1963 Bp Joseph Gillespie Armstrong. m 8/31/1963 Cornelia Cox. R S Geo Ch San Antonio TX 1996-2004; R S Mk's Epis Ch Glen Ellyn IL 1979-1996; Asst R Ch Of The Gd Samar Paoli PA 1973-1979; Vic Ch Of The Epiph Royersford PA 1966-1973. raycole@flash.net

COLE, Roy Allen (NY) 1333 Bay St, Staten Island NY 10305 **R S Jn's Ch Staten Island NY 2008-** B San Diego CA 7/19/1956 s Roy Adelbert Cole & Alice Mae. BA Warner Pacific Coll 1984; MA U of Nevada at Reno 1995; GTS 2003; STM GTS 2004; DMin SFTS 2007. D 8/6/2003 Bp E(gbert) Don Taylor P 7/26/2004 Bp Catherine Scimeca Roskam. P in Charge S Mk's Epis Ch Yonkers NY 2004-2008; P-in-c S Paul's Ch Yonkers NY 2004-2008. frcole@me.com

COLE III, Roy W (USC) 184 Clifton Ave, Spartanburg SC 29302 B El Paso TX 7/9/1939 s Roy W Cole & Nancy. BS USMA at W Point 1962; MDiv EDS 1974; MA Rhode Island Coll 1983. D 6/15/1974 P 12/1/1974 Bp Frederick Hesley Belden. m 6/9/2000 Barbara Cole c 3. Ch Of The Adv Spartanburg SC 2007-2009; S Marg's Epis Ch Boiling Sprg SC 2003-2004; Int S Matt's Ch Charleston WV 2000-2003; Int S Steph's Epis Ch And U Columbus OH 1999-2000; Int S Thos Epis Ch Towson MD 1998-1999; Int H Trin Ch Churchville MD 1995-1997; Int S Geo's Ch Perryman MD 1992-1995; P-in-c S Lk's Epis Ch Las Vegas NV 1989-1991; R Emm Ch Newport RI 1976-1985; Asst S Jas Epis Ch At Woonsocket Woonsocket RI 1974-1976. Fell 85 Coll of Preachers 1985; Adams Prize for Preaching Epis TS 1974. rwcempower@aol.com

COLE, Suzanne Louise (Alb) 41 Gardiner Pl, Walton NY 13856 **R Chr Ch Walton NY 2002-** B Northport NY 6/19/1957 d Richard Chouinard & Barbara Grace. BS SUNY 1979; MA Theol St Bern's Inst Rochester NY 2003. D 6/2/2002 Bp David John Bena P 12/8/2002 Bp Daniel William Herzog. m 10/20/1979 Jack Richard Cole c 3. revscole@yahoo.com

COLEGROVE, Jerome 'Kip' (O) 551 Rockwell Street, Kent OH 44240 **Dn of Cntrl E Mssn Area Dio Ohio Cleveland OH 2010-; P-in-c Ch Of Our Sav Salem OH 2009-; P-in-c Trin Ch Allnce OH 2009-** B Fort Lewis WA 2/21/1948 s Alpha Willis Colegrove & Mary Ellen. BS Geo 1972; MDiv SWTS 1977; MA U of Virginia 1989; CSD The Open Door Inc Charlottesville VA 1991. D 4/28/1996 P 12/11/1996 Bp Martin Gough Townsend. m 8/14/1982 Julie Blake Fisher. Int R S Jas Ch Painesville OH 2007-2009; R S Mary's Ch Nebraska City NE 1999-2006; R S Mk's Epis Ch Perryville MD 1996-1999. colegrovek@yahoo.com

COLEMAN, Bernice (LI) 10206 Farmers Blvd, Hollis NY 11423 B Claremont Saint Ann JM 7/31/1935 d George Williams & Susan Caroline. Cert Coll Of Arts Sci & Tech 1978; Cert Merc TS 1989. D 6/17/1989 P 6/1/1990 Bp Orris George Walker Jr. Epis Hlth Serv Bethpage NY 1992-2007; Dir Pstr S Jn's Epis Chap Brooklyn NY 1992-1997; Cur All SS' Epis Ch Long Island City NY 1990-1992; Asst All SS' Epis Ch Long Island City NY 1989-1990. AEHC; Black Caucus; Bd Cert Mem Coll Chapl; UBE. bcoleman@ehs.org

COLEMAN, Betty Ellen Gibson (SO) 4325 Skylark Dr, Englewood OH 45322 B Dayton OH 11/21/1943 d Isaac Steve Gibson & Ellen. BS Wilberforce U 2000; MDiv Bex 2005. D 1/23/1993 P 6/25/2005 Bp Herbert Thompson Jr. c 4. Epis Soc Of Chr Ch Cincinnati OH 2005-2007; S Andr's Ch Dayton OH 1993-2007. bcoleman@cccath.org

COLEMAN, Brian Ray (WMich) 252 Chestnut St, Battle Creek MI 49017 **R S Thos Epis Ch Battle Creek MI 2008-** B Fort Worth TX 12/14/1971 s Ray Coleman & Rebecca Jane. U So 1991; Fullerton Coll 1992; BA California St U 1994; MDiv SWTS 1998. D 6/13/1998 Bp Chester Lovelle Talton P 1/9/1999 Bp Frederick Houk Borsch. Assoc R S Jas Par Los Angeles CA 1998-2000. Soc of Cath Priests 2005. fatherbrian@mac.com

COLEMAN, Carolyn A (Tenn) Holy Cross Episcopal Church, 1140 Cason Land, Murfreesboro TN 37128 **Vic Ch of the H Cross Murfreesboro TN 2011-; Contingent Fac The TS at The U So Sewanee TN 2011-** B Nashville TN 3/24/1970 d Robert Finley Coleman & Rodalyn Napier. BA U of Tennessee 1992; MA Mia 1994; MDiv Bos TS 2007. D 6/12/2007 P 12/15/2007 Bp Chilton Abbie Richardson Knudsen. m 7/12/1997 Joe H Bandy c 2. Cn Cathd Ch Of S Lk Portland ME 2007-2010; Yth Dir Dio Maine Portland ME 2007-2010; Par Admin S Alb's Ch Cape Eliz ME 1998-2004. ccoleman70@gmail.com

COLEMAN JR, Dale D (Spr) 105 E. D St., Belleville IL 62220 **Dn Dio Springfield Springfield IL 2011-; R S Geo's Ch Belleville IL 2010-** B Hillsdale MI 3/24/1954 s Dale Duane Coleman & Eva Rebecca. BA U of Wisconsin 1976; MDiv Nash 1980. D 3/22/1980 P 9/27/1980 Bp Charles Thomas Gaskell. m 8/7/2010 M Joan Wood c 3. P-in-c S Geo's Ch Belleville IL 2007-2010; Dn Dio The Rio Grande Albuquerque NM 1997-2007; R Ch of the H Faith Santa Fe NM 1996-2007; Dn Dio Wstrn Louisiana Alexandria LA 1992-1996; R S Mths Epis Ch Shreveport LA 1990-1996; R S Thos Of Cbury Ch Greendale WI 1983-1990; Assoc Gr Ch Madison WI 1980-1983. Auth, "Taking Conversion Seriously," *LivCh*, 1994; Auth, "The Angl Sprt," Cowley, 1991; Auth, "Our Great Angl Heritage," St. Geo's Ch; Auth, "Easter w St. Pat," St. Geo's Ch; Auth, "Journey in Faith," St. Geo's Ch. Chapl Ord of St. Jn of Jerusalem 2002; Adj Prof of Ch Hist TESM 2000; Adj Prof of Wrshp TESM 2000; Hon Cn Dio The Rio Grande 1998. frdale@sbcglobal.net

COLEMAN, Edwin Cabaniss (Tenn) 4715 Harding Pike, Nashville TN 37205 B Jackson MS 8/24/1929 s John Stuart Coleman & Edna Lee. BA LSU 1950; MDiv STUSo 1953. D 6/25/1953 Bp Iveson Batchelor Noland P 5/1/1954 Bp Girault M Jones. m 11/26/1954 Mary Alexandra Parker. Assoc R S Geo's Ch Nashville TN 1985-1995; Chair Com Dio So Carolina Charleston SC 1970-1980; Exec Bd Dio So Carolina Charleston SC 1967-1984; Chair Deptce Dio So Carolina Charleston SC 1967-1970; Bec Dio So Carolina Charleston SC 1966-1980; Bec Dio So Carolina Charleston SC 1966-1980; R S Mich's Epis Ch Charleston SC 1965-1985; R S Jn's Coll Pk GA 1958-1965; P-in-c S Phil's Boyce LA 1954-1958; Cur Calv Ch Bunkie LA 1953-1954. eccoledadoo@aol.com

COLEMAN JR, Fred George (NY) 2048 Lorena Ave., Akron OH 44313 **Ch Pension Fund Benefici New York NY 2005-** B Bronx NY 9/22/1936 s Fred George Coleman & Marion Cecilia. BD Stevens Inst Of Tech 1957; MDiv GTS 1964. D 6/6/1964 P 12/1/1964 Bp Horace W B Donegan. m 7/8/2009 Susan Louis Meyer. Asst S Andr's Ch Akron OH 1977-1981; Asst S Paul's Ch Akron OH 1973-1977; Vic S Jn The Evang Ch Napoleon OH 1971-1973; Asst S Paul's Ch Akron OH 1970-1971; Asst S Andr's Ch Akron OH 1968-1970; Cur S Ptr's Ch Freehold NJ 1967-1968; Cur Chr Ch Schenectady NY 1966-1967; Cur S Andr's Ch Baltimore MD 1965-1966; Cur S Geo's Par Flushing NY 1964-1965. fcole1@msn.com

COLEMAN, Henry Douglas (NY) 39 W Lewis Ave, Pearl River NY 10965 B 8/27/1936 s Henry Rogers Coleman & Gladys Laura. BA Trin 1958; STB GTS 1961. D 6/10/1961 P 12/1/1961 Bp Horace W B Donegan. m Marilyn Jamieson. Gr Ch Bronx NY 1980-2004; St Pauls Ch New Rochelle NY 1966-1987; Cur S Jn's Ch Getty Sq Yonkers NY 1961-1966. jamiesonm@teaminfocus.com

✠ COLEMAN, Rt Rev James Malone (WTenn) 3052 Tyrone Dr, Baton Rouge LA 70808 **Ret Bp of WTenn Dio W Tennessee Memphis TN 2001-** B Memphis TN 8/26/1929 s Fredrick Lee Coleman & Dorris White. BS U of Tennessee 1953; MDiv STUSo 1956; DMin Wake Forest U 1975; DD STUSo 1994. D 7/3/1956 Bp John Vander Horst P 5/5/1957 Bp Theodore N Barth Con 11/13/1993 for WTenn. m 3/30/2005 Emily Douglass Stewart. Bp of WTenn Dio W Tennessee Memphis TN 1994-2001; Bp of WTenn Dio W Tennessee Memphis TN 1994-2001; Bp Coadj of WTenn Dio W Tennessee Memphis TN 1993-1994; R S Jn's Epis Ch Memphis TN 1989-1993; Trst The TS at The U So Sewanee TN 1986-1989; Dep GC Dio W Tennessee Memphis TN 1979-1988; R S Jas Epis Ch Baton Rouge LA 1975-1989; R Chr Ch Martinsville VA 1972-1975; Pres Alum Assn The TS at The U So Sewanee TN 1969-1971; COM Dio Tennessee Nashville TN 1968-1972; R S Jn's Epis Ch Johnson City TN 1966-1972; R Ch Of The Gd Shpd Knoxville TN 1962-1966; P-in-c Ch Of Our Sav Gallatin TN 1957-1960; P-in-c The Ch Of The Epiph Lebanon TN 1957-1960. james.coleman8@gte.net

COLEMAN, James Patrick (CFla) 4820 Lake Gibson Park Rd, Lakeland FL 33809 B Chicago IL 8/22/1932 s John Francis Coleman & Sarah Ann. BA S Mary-Lake TS/Loyola U 1955; MA S Mary-Lake Theol/Loyola 1959. Rec from Roman Catholic 3/1/1984 as Deacon Bp William Hopkins Folwell. m 10/26/1975 Beth M Hogan. S Ptr's Epis Ch Charlotte NC 2000; S Dav's Epis Ch Lakeland FL 1984-1998. Auth, "The Sacr Of Recon". Profsnl Softball Wrld Champions Chicago 1951. JIMANBETHCOLEMAN@YAHOO.COM

COLEMAN, John Charles (Ala) 315 Clanton Ave, Montgomery AL 36104 **R Ch Of The Ascen Montgomery AL 2007-; Par of St Monica & St Jas Washington DC 2005-** B Hutchinson KS 7/11/1968 s James Francis Coleman & Janice Kay. BA U of Alabama 1991; JD U of Alabama 1994; MDiv GTS 2005. D 6/4/2005 P 5/20/2006 Bp Philip Menzie Duncan II. m 8/29/1998 Mary J Coleman c 3. S Mary's Epis Ch Andalusia AL 2005-2007. johnccoleman@mac.com

COLEMAN, Karen (Mass) 59 Fayerweather St # 2138, Cambridge MA 02138 **S Jas Epis Ch Teele Sq Somerville MA 2010-** B Detroit MI 9/9/1957 BA U MI. D 2/14/2004 P 9/11/2004 Bp John Palmer Croneberger. m 12/2/2006 James F Reamer. Trin Ch Randolph MA 2007-2010; Chr Ch Needham MA 2004-2007; Epis City Mssn Boston MA 2004.

COLEMAN, Kenneth Robb (Ct) 14 Hulls Highway, Southport CT 06890 **Died 1/25/2011** B New Haven CT 11/16/1926 s Huber Kenneth Coleman & Ada Irene. BA Ya 1947; MDiv Yale DS 1953. D 6/13/1953 P 12/1/1953 Bp Angus Dun. c 3. KRCR585@WEBTV.NET

COLEMAN, Kim Latice (Va) 2601 Park Center Dr Apt C201, Alexandria VA 22302 **Exec Bd Mem Dio Virginia Richmond VA 2008-2012; Trin Ch Arlington VA 2002-** B Hampton VA 5/7/1958 d Warren Barrington Coleman & Carole Jayne. BA Penn 1980; MDiv VTS 2001. D 6/23/2001 P 12/29/2001 Bp Peter James Lee. S Geo's Epis Ch Arlington VA 2001-2002. trydstohn@aol.com

COLEMAN, M Joan (Spr) 601 Garden Blvd, Belleville IL 62220 B Santa Fe NM 8/13/1960 d H Joe Wood & Mary Huss. TESM. D 5/10/2002 Bp Terence Kelshaw. m 8/7/2010 Dale D Coleman c 2. D S Barth's Ch Granite City IL 2010-2011; D S Thos Epis Ch Glen Carbon IL 2010-2011; D/Par Admin Ch of the H Faith Santa Fe NM 2002-2007; Par Admin Ch of the H Faith Santa Fe NM 1994-2002. mjoan1960@yahoo.com

COLENBACK, Patricia Riley (Mass) 4001 N Main St Apt 517, Fall River MA 02720 B Englewood NJ 12/10/1931 d Harry Winslow Riley & Margarithe Dorthea. Smith 1951; BA U CO 1953; MA Ya 1966; MDiv EDS 1991. D 6/22/1991 P 2/29/1992 Bp George Nelson Hunt III. c 4. Int S Ptr's Epis Ch Hebron CT 1996-1997; Vic S Andr's Epis Ch Colchester VT 1993-1996; Vic S Jas Ch Mtn Hm ID 1992-1993. Int Mnstry Ntwk 1995-1997; Safe Ch Ntwk; Taskforce Mem 2001. percol@attbi.com

✠ **COLERIDGE, Rt Rev Clarence Nicholas** (Ct) 29 Indian Rd, Trumbull CT 06611 B Georgetown 11/27/1930 s Charles Coleridge & Ina. BA Howard 1954; MDiv Drew U 1960; GTS 1961; Amer Fndt of Rel & Psych 1966; MS U of Connecticut 1973; DMin Andover Newton TS 1977; STD Ya Berk 1984; DD GTS 1984. D 1/27/1961 P 1/1/1962 Bp Leland Stark Con 10/23/1981 for Ct. m 9/8/1962 Euna Idris Volda Jervis c 2. Asst Dio Pennsylvania Philadelphia PA 1999-2000; Exec Coun Dio Connecticut Hartford CT 1981-2000; Epis Soc Serv Ansonia CT 1974-1981; R S Mk's Ch Bridgeport CT 1966-1981; Cur S Geo's Ch Brooklyn NY 1962-1966. DD Berkeley TS; DD GTS; DD Trin.

COLES, Clifford Carleton (NC) 3927 Napa Valley Dr, Raleigh NC 27612 **S Aug's Coll Raleigh NC 2004-** B Brooklyn NY 12/14/1928 s Walter Edward Coles & Clara. BA Shaw U 1952; MS Col 1961; EdD No Carolina St U 1982. D 7/18/1992 Bp Huntington Williams Jr P 7/11/1993 Bp Robert Whitridge Estill. m 11/21/1981 Marsha Coles. Ch Of The Redeem Greensboro NC 2000; R S Steph's Epis Ch Winston Salem NC 1996-2000; Dio No Carolina Raleigh NC 1995-1996; Vic Ch Of The Epiph Rocky Mt NC 1993-1996. Auth, "Princeville Centennial," 1985; Auth, "Persistence In Engr: Selected Variables And Participation In Acad Spprt Prog (Doctoral Dissertation)," 1983; Auth, "Perception Of Ncsu By Upward Bound Students," 1979; Auth, "A Study Of Accessibility Of Ncsu To The Handicapped," 1979; Auth, "Soc Welf Attitudes Among Selected Ldrshp In Montclaire, Nj," 1961. Rockefeller Intrnshp In Higher Educ 1975; Fllshp Natl Prog For Educational Ldrshp 1971; Fllshp Nation Urban League 1959.

COLES, Constance Carolyn (NY) 1047 Amsterdam Ave, Synod House, New York NY 10025 **Cn for Mnstry Dio New York New York City NY 2001-; Trst Cathd Of St Jn The Div New York NY 1994-** B Brooklyn NY 4/13/1945 d Robert Reed Coles & Edna May. BA Wells Coll 1967; MRE UTS 1970; MDiv UTS 1978. D 6/3/1978 P 1/14/1979 Bp Paul Moore Jr. m 12/21/1968 William B McKeown c 2. Stndng Com Dio New York New York City NY 1996-2000; R All SS Ch Harrison NY 1986-2001; Asst The Ch Of The Epiph New York NY 1978-1986. Wider Quaker Fllshp 1980. ccc@cherubim.net

COLETON, John Mortimer (Kan) 7224 Village Dr, Prairie Village KS 66208 B Troy NY 4/25/1924 s John Mortimer Coleton & Anna Theresa. SUNY 1948. D 12/13/1968 Bp Edward Clark Turner. c 4. D S Thos The Apos Ch Overland Pk KS 1996-1997; D S Lk's Epis Ch Shawnee KS 1978-1984. jmcoleton@msn.com

COLLAMORE JR, (Harry) Bacon (Ct) 899 Turtle Ct, Naples FL 34108 **D Dio Connecticut Hartford CT 1988-** B Hartford CT 6/25/1928 s Harry Bacon Collamore & Dorothy Huston. BA Pr 1950. D 12/3/1988 Bp Arthur Edward Walmsley. m 6/23/1951 Elizabeth Caldwell Jones c 3. Bp'S Awd For Ch And Cmnty Dio Connecticut 1998. bcollamore@aol.com

COLLEGE, Philip Anthony (SO) 5691 Great Hall Ct, Columbus OH 43231 **R S Jn's Ch Worthington OH 2007-** B Biloxi MS 8/16/1953 s Conrad G College & Alice M. BS Morehead St U 1975; BA U Of Kentucky 1978; MS Cntrl Michigan U 1987; MDiv GTS 1994. D 6/17/1994 P 5/1/1995 Bp Herbert Thompson Jr. c 2. Int S Mk's Epis Ch Columbus OH 2006-2007; Int S Jas Epis Ch Columbus OH 2004-2005; R S Jas Epis Ch Zanesville OH 1999-2002; Supply Dio Sthrn Ohio Cincinnati OH 1997-1999; Asst S Alb's Epis Ch Of Bexley Columbus OH 1994-1997. stjohnsrector@ameritech.net

COLLER, Patricia Marie (WMass) 445 Fifth Avenue, New York NY 10016 **Exec VP, Chf Eccl Off The CPG New York NY 2000-** B Philadelphia PA 8/16/1951 d Harry Gray McClaren & Margaret Eve. BS Kutztown U of Pennsylvania 1987; MDiv Ya Berk 1991. D 9/14/1991 Bp Cabell Tennis P 9/29/1992 Bp Andrew Frederick Wissemann. m 8/8/2009 Frank E Wismer c 3. Cn to the Ordnry Dio Wstrn Massachusetts Springfield MA 1995-2000; Assoc R S Jn's Ch Northampton MA 1994-1995; Cur S Jn's Ch Northampton MA 1991-1994. pcoller@cpg.org

COLLEY-TOOTHAKER, Samuel Scott (SVa) 437 Hawthorne Drive, Danville VA 24541 **R Ch Of The Epiph Danville VA 2007-** B Portland ME 5/3/1960 s Clifford Toothaker & Erna. BA Vermont Coll Of Norwich U 2003; MDiv EDS 2004. D 4/3/2005 P 10/27/2005 Bp Chilton Abbie Richardson Knudsen. m 10/13/1984 Linda Louise Colley c 2. S Andr's Epis Ch Newport News VA 2005-2007. FATHERSAM@EPIPHANYDANVILLE.ORG

COLLIER, Caitlin Finley (SD) 206 Linden Ave, Vermillion SD 57069 **D S Paul's Epis Ch Vermillion SD 2005-** B Kansas City KS 1/21/1956 d Barron Bevis Collier & Patricia Raymond. MDiv Vancouver TS; BA U of So Dakota

1980; JD U of So Dakota 1987. D 11/1/2005 Bp Creighton Leland Robertson. m 4/23/1988 Ronald L Moyer c 2. caitcollier@hotmail.com

COLLIER, Catherine Hudson (Ala) 605 Lurleen B Wallace Blvd N, Tuscaloosa AL 35401 **Assoc Chr Ch Tuscaloosa AL 2009-** B Jacksonville NC 10/16/1954 d Willard Dale Hudson & Patricia Barnes. BS Troy St U-Montgomery AL 1980; MS Troy St U-Montgomery AL 1981; EdS Troy St U-Montgomery AL 1982; PhD U of Alabama 1992; MDiv The U So (Sewanee) 2009. D 5/20/2009 P 12/18/2009 Bp Henry Nutt Parsley Jr. m 12/10/1988 Samuel D Collier c 4. ccollier@christchurch1828.org

COLLIER, Daniel R (NH) 155 Salem Rd, Billerica MA 01821 **25 Hrs/Week S Andr's Ch Manchester NH 2007-** B Lynn MA 9/24/1959 s Raymond Collier & Claire. Cert EDS; MA Weston TS Cambridge MA 1991; PhD NEU Boston MA 2003. D 6/4/2002 P 1/7/2006 Bp M(arvil) Thomas Shaw III. m 7/30/2004 W Michael Hamilton. D S Paul's Epis Ch Bedford MA 2005-2007. daniel.collier@comcast.net

COLLIER, Mary Anne (NwT) 1605 W Pecan Ave, Midland TX 79705 B Pittsburgh PA 9/30/1959 d Delwood Lee & Mary. BA SW Texas St U San Marcos 1982; MA Lon 1989. D 10/31/2004 Bp C(harles) Wallis Ohl. m 7/9/1983 Patrick Collier c 2.

COLLIN, Winifred Nohmer (Roch) 2696 Clover St, Pittsford NY 14534 **R Chr Ch Pittsford NY 1999-** B New York NY 7/14/1944 d Fritz Heinrich Noehmer & Martha Emma. D 6/22/1988 P 1/1/1989 Bp William George Burrill. m 6/3/1967 Dwight R Collin c 2. R The Ch Of The Epiph Rochester NY 1995-1998; S Paul's Ch Rochester NY 1990-1995. winifredcollin@gmail.com

COLLINS, Aaron Paul (Ky) 6630 Orchard Club Pl, Louisville KY 40291 **R S Alb's Epis Ch Fern Creek Louisville KY 2006-** B Arakonam INDIA 2/24/1954 s Abraham Aaron & Mary. B.Sc. U of Madras 1979; BD Un Biblic Sem/Serampore U, Pune, Maharas 1993; M.Th Untd Theol Coll/Serampore U, Bangalore, 1997. Trans from Church of North India 7/26/2004 as Priest Bp Stacy F Sauls. m 11/12/1982 Anita Collins c 3. P-in-c S Andr's Ch Lexington KY 2004-2006; Asst To The R Ch Of The Ascen Frankfort KY 2002-2004; Int S Raphael's Ch Lexington KY 2002. Biblic Lit Soc 2006. apcollins@bellsouth.net

COLLINS, Charles Blake (WTex) 431 Richmond Pl Ne, Albuquerque NM 87106 B Silver City NM 4/19/1953 s Charles Walter Collins & Nancy Ann. TESM; BA U of Texas 1976; MDiv Epis TS of The SW 1980. D 8/6/1981 P 5/3/1982 Bp Richard Mitchell Trelease Jr. m 7/9/1979 Ellen McMahon c 4. R Chr Epis Ch San Antonio TX 2001-2010; R S Mk's On The Mesa Epis Ch Albuquerque NM 1990-2001; R H Fam Ch Orlando FL 1985-1990; Asst R Trin Ch Vero Bch FL 1983-1985; S Fran On The Hill El Paso TX 1982-1983; Dio The Rio Grande Albuquerque NM 1981-1982. Auth, "Separated By Love"; Auth, "A R Should Learn To Wk w The Vstry"; Auth, "No Hope For Sick Paradigm," *Living Ch*; Auth, "Helen W & The Three Legged Stool," *Mssn & Mnstry*; Auth, "Sin," *Not Promiscuous Genes*. chuckc.sa@gmail.com

COLLINS, David Browning (At) 132 Hearthstone Dr, Woodstock GA 30189 B Hot Sprgs AR 12/18/1922 s Charles Collins & Agnes Elizabeth. BA U So 1943; BD STUSo 1948; S Aug's Coll Cbury GB 1961; STM STUSo 1962. D 6/16/1948 P 3/11/1949 Bp Richard B Mitchell. m 10/14/1945 Maryon Virginia Moise c 4. Cathd Of S Phil Atlanta GA 1966-1985; Coll Wk Cmsn Dio Tennessee Nashville TN 1957-1959; Chapl and Assoc Prof of Rel The TS at The U So Sewanee TN 1953-1966; P-in-c Ch Of The H Cross W Memphis AR 1949-1953; D-in-c S Andr's Ch Marianna AR 1948-1949. Auth, *Memoirs: There is Lad Here*, Privately Pub see Amazon.com. DD U So 1974. davidbrev@bellsouth.net

COLLINS, David William (SeFla) 2548 Centergate Dr Apt 304, Miramar FL 33025 **Ch Of The Intsn Ft Lauderdale FL 2011-** B Abington PA 6/11/1963 s John Nelson Collins & Evelyn McCandless. BA Gordon Coll 1981; MDiv Ya Berk 2003. D 12/10/2008 Bp Leopold Frade. H Sacr Pembroke Pines FL 2010; S Lk's Epis Ch Port Salerno FL 2009. DAVE@DAVECOLLINS.NET

COLLINS, Diana Garvin (Vt) 535 Woodbury Rd, Springfield VT 05156 B Rahway NJ 8/6/1943 d Lester Garvin & Barbara Waldron. Vermont Dio Study Prog VT; A.D.N Vermont Coll 1963; BD Vermont Coll 1985. D 6/15/1993 Bp Daniel Lee Swenson. m 8/10/1963 Christian Collins c 3. D S Paul's Epis Ch White River Jct VT 1993-2002.

COLLINS, E Selden (NMich) 1628 W Town Line Rd, Pickford MI 49774 **R S Jas Ch Of Sault S Marie Sault Ste Marie MI 2006-** B 12/19/1946 d Gilbert Cowan & Nancye. D 11/28/2005 P 5/28/2006 Bp James Arthur Kelsey. c 1. mahlon@lighthouse.net

COLLINS, Gary David (Los) 2720 Colt Rd, Rancho Palos Verdes CA 90275 B Oakland CA 10/5/1952 s Ronald George Collins & Lola Edith. BA San Francisco St U 1974; MDiv CDSP 1977. D 6/25/1977 Bp C Kilmer Myers P 6/7/1978 Bp CE Crowther. m 7/28/1984 Heather Kaye Shawhan c 1. S Ptr's Par San Pedro CA 1988-1992; S Paul's Epis Ch Walnut Creek CA 1988; S Anne's Ch Fremont CA 1982-1987; S Paul's Epis Ch San Rafael CA 1980-1982; S Andr's Ch Saratoga CA 1977-1980.

COLLINS, Gerald Shelton (Md) Emmanuel Episcopal Church, 811 Cathedral St, Baltimore MD 21201 **Int Emm Ch Baltimore MD 2010-** B Baltimore MD 1/29/1949 s William Shelton Collins & Evelyn Hilda. BS Morgan St U 1976; MPS NYTS 1994; MDiv UTS 1996; CTh Oxf 2001. D 6/1/1996 P 12/7/1996 Bp Richard Frank Grein. R Ch Of S Mary The Vrgn Baltimore MD 2005-2010; Int S Chris's Ch Fairborn OH 2005; R S Andr's Epis Ch Cincinnati OH 2003-2005; R S Jn's Epis Ch Springfield Gardens NY 1998-2003; Assoc R S Aug's Ch New York NY 1996-1998. Auth, "Absalom Jones Sermon," *Wrshp That Works*, 2003; Auth, "A Witness For The Lamb Of God," *Wrshp That Works*, 2002; Auth, "Finding A Way Out Of The Wifinding A Way Out Of The Wilderness," *Wrshp That Works*, 2002. Bd Dir New Fed Theater Ny 1996-1998; Bro Of S Andr; Chair, Dept Of Bdgt 1999-2003; COM 2008; Curs #56 Dio Li 2002; Dioc Coun Li 1999; Epis Black Caucus Dio Ny 1996-1998; EUC 2009; Geo Freeman Bragg Fell 1996-1998; Liturg and Wrshp 2005-2008; Prog and Bdgt 2008; UBE 1996. jaycoll1906@comcast.net

COLLINS, Guy J(ames) D(ouglas) (NH) 9 W Wheelock St, Hanover NH 03755 **S Thos Ch Hanover NH 2007-** B Runnymede England 6/24/1974 M.Theol U of St. Andrews 1996; PhD U of Cambridge 2000. Trans from Church Of England 10/30/2003 Bp Charles Ellsworth Bennison Jr. m 11/29/2002 Kristin A Bornholdt c 2. R S Jn's Ch Huntingdon Vlly PA 2003-2007; Serv S Thos Ch Hanover NH 2000-2003. "Defending Derrida: A Response To Milbank And Pickstock," Scottish Journ Of Theol T Clark, 2001; "Questioning Theol: Affirming Culture," Theol Spck, 2001; "Thinking The Impossible: Derrida And The Div," Lit And Theol Oxf Press, 2000. guy.collins@dartmouth.edu

COLLINS JR, Harry Nuttall (NJ) 8 Mallard Dr., Lewes DE 19958 B Camden NJ 7/27/1932 s Edith Mae. BS Glassboro St U 1958; MA Glassboro St U 1965. D 4/20/1968 P 10/26/1968 Bp Alfred L Banyard. m 3/29/1954 Joan Beuchamp c 3. Vic S Steph's Ch Mullica Hill NJ 1968-2004. collinsgrmp@wmconnect.com

COLLINS, James Edward (ECR) 615 Santa Paula Dr, Salinas CA 93901 B Pittsburgh PA 5/8/1949 s Kenneth Collins & Dorothea. BA Gordon Coll 1971; MDiv Gordon-Conwell TS 1974; DMin Gordon-Conwell TS 1985. Trans from Anglican Church of Canada 3/1/2007 Bp Sylvestre Donato Romero. c 6. "One Man's Mile," *Gnrl Store Pub Hse, Renfrew, Ontario*, 2004. jcol211009@gmail.com

COLLINS, Jean Griffin (Mont) 325 University Ave, Missoula MT 59801 B Denver CO 7/29/1956 d John Griffin Collins & Virginia Murray. BA U of Montana 1980; MDiv VTS 1983. D 8/25/1983 P 1/31/1985 Bp Jackson Earle Gilliam. c 2. S Paul's Ch Hamilton MT 1997-2003; R S Steph's Epis Ch Stevensville MT 1994-2009; Ch Of The H Sprt Missoula MT 1994-1996; Dio Montana Helena MT 1991-2003; Int Trin Ch Moorestown NJ 1991; R S Paul's Ch Chittenango NY 1986-1990; Asst Gr Ch Utica NY 1985-1986; Geriatric Min Trin Ch Upper Marlboro MD 1984-1985. jgcollins@montana.com

COLLINS III, John Milton (SanD) 701 Kettner Blvd Unit 94, San Diego CA 92101 B Washington DC 10/7/1933 s John Milton Collins & Josephine Wilson. BA U of Maryland 1959; BD EDS 1962; MDiv EDS 1972. D 6/16/1962 P 12/22/1962 Bp William Foreman Creighton. m 2/20/1999 Janet Elizabeth Kopf c 4. S Anne's Epis Ch Oceanside CA 1995; Int R S Anne's Epis Ch Oceanside CA 1994-1995; Ch Of The Gd Samar San Diego CA 1992-1995; Asst to R S Barth's Epis Ch Poway CA 1990-1999; Chapl U. S. Navy Off Of Bsh For ArmdF New York NY 1963-1990; P-in-c S Andr's Ch Leonardtown California MD 1962-1963; P-in-c The Ch Of The Ascen Lexington Pk MD 1962-1963. SSP 1975. Geo Washington Hon Medal Freedoms Fndt. padrejmc@cox.net

COLLINS, Judith Tindall (RI) 84 Benefit St # 3, Providence RI 02904 **D Ch Of The Redeem Providence RI 2005-** B Somerville MA 5/8/1940 d Frederick Tindall & Esther Hayward. BA Guilford Coll 1962. D 6/20/1992 Bp George Nelson Hunt III. c 3. D Trin Ch Cranston RI 2000-2005; D Ch Of The Ascen Cranston RI 1996-2000; D S Geo's Ch Portsmouth RI 1995-1996; D S Barn Ch Warwick RI 1992-1995. jtcol@aol.com

COLLINS, Loretta Lehman (CPa) 21 S Main St, Lewistown PA 17044 **D S Mk's Epis Ch Lewistown PA 2010-** B Lancaster PA 9/20/1952 d Lester Mark Lehman & Elva Groff. BA Estrn Mennorite U 1975; MA CUA 1978. D 10/31/2010 Bp Nathan Dwight Baxter. m 7/8/1989 Patrick Anthony Collins. lelcollins@comcast.net

COLLINS, Lynn Arnetha (LI) 21 Eldridge Ave, Hempstead NY 11550 **R S Jn's Ch Hempstead NY 2005-** B New York NY 12/4/1953 d James Edward Lassiter & Elsie Elenor. AA Queensborough Cmnty Coll 1974; BA CUNY 1976; MDiv NYTS 1989; DMin NYTS 2000; Post Grad- Ldrshp Harvard DS 2002. D 7/9/1990 Bp Richard Frank Grein P 3/2/1991 Bp Arthur Benjamin Williams Jr. c 1. R St Johns Pro-Cathd Los Angeles CA 2003-2005; P-in-c S Steph's Epis Ch Jamaica NY 2003; Nat'l Off Epis Ch Cntr New York NY 1995-2002; R S Paul's Epis Ch Of E Cleveland Cleveland OH 1992-1995; Urban Missions Dio Ohio Cleveland OH 1990-1992. laclmc@aol.com

COLLINS, M A (SanD) 3847 Balsamina Dr, Bonita CA 91902 **R S Mk's Ch San Diego CA 1998-** B San Diego CA 9/26/1952 s Arthur Collins & Mary Lou. BA Point Loma Coll 1977; MA Fuller TS 1978; MA Point Loma Coll 1978; PhD Fuller TS 1986. D 11/22/1986 P 6/22/1987 Bp Charles Brinkley Morton. m 8/15/1992 Constance Elizabeth Lawthers. S Barth's Epis Ch Poway

CA 1996-1997; Dio San Diego San Diego CA 1995; S Mary's In The Vlly Ch Ramona CA 1995; Luth Ch Of The Incarn Poway CA 1991-1992; Min Ce Cathd Ch Of S Paul San Diego CA 1987-1990. Auth, "God & Evil In The Process Thought Of An Whitehead". Comp Bsp; Soc Of S Paul. stmarksoffice@prodigy.net

COLLINS, Mark R (NY) 88 Saint Nicholas Avenue, New York NY 10026 **Asst Chr And S Steph's Ch New York NY 2008-** B Memphis TN 10/7/1959 s Vernon Lowell Collins & Peggy Robbins. BA City Coll of New York 1997; MDiv GTS 2008. D 3/15/2008 P 9/20/2008 Bp Mark Sean Sisk. m Denton Stargel. Epis Response to AIDS 2008. father.mark.collins@gmail.com

COLLINS, Patrick Anthony (CPa) 640 N 67th St, Harrisburg PA 17111 **Congrl Dvlpmt Cmsn Dio Cntrl Pennsylvania Harrisburg PA 2011-; Convenor, Altoona Convoc Dio Cntrl Pennsylvania Harrisburg PA 2010-; Coun of Trst Dio Cntrl Pennsylvania Harrisburg PA 2010-; Stndg Com Dio Cntrl Pennsylvania Harrisburg PA 2010-; Instr, Sch of Chr Stds Dio Cntrl Pennsylvania Harrisburg PA 2009-; R S Jn's Epis Ch Huntingdon PA 2009-; Chair, Chld's Cmsn Dio Cntrl Pennsylvania Harrisburg PA 2007-; Dir, BASIC camping Prog Dio Cntrl Pennsylvania Harrisburg PA 2006-; Partnr in Mssn Cmsn Dio Cntrl Pennsylvania Harrisburg PA 2006-** B Washington DC 8/31/1965 s Robert Steven Collins & Andrea Jean. AA Ferrum Coll 1985; BS Ferrum Coll 1988; MDiv GTS 2006. D 6/3/2006 Bp Michael Whittington Creighton P 12/13/2006 Bp Nathan Dwight Baxter. m 7/8/1989 Loretta Lehman Collins. Cur Cathd Ch Of S Steph Harrisburg PA 2006-2009. cakcirtap@gmail.com

COLLINS, Paul Michael (Oly) 2269 E Howe St, Seattle WA 98112 **R Trin Par Seattle WA 1998-** B Colfax WA 3/17/1947 s Robert D Collins & Elsie L. MDiv CDSP 1972. D 8/26/1972 Bp Ivol I Curtis P 5/1/1981 Bp Robert Hume Cochrane. m 5/15/1981 Kathy Deviny. Vic S Hilda's - S Pat's Epis Ch Edmonds WA 1988-1998; S Andr's Ch Seattle WA 1984-1988; S Geo's Ch Seattle WA 1982-1983; S Dunst-The Highlands Shoreline WA 1972. N0VEMBER@MSN.COM

COLLINS, Stanley Penrose (EpisSanJ) 1401 Locke Rd, Modesto CA 95355 B Philadelphia PA 3/27/1935 s Berry Penrose Collins & Lillian. BA Tem 1959; MDiv Epis TS of The SW 1983. D 6/22/1983 P 1/30/1984 Bp Gordon Taliaferro Charlton. m 6/17/1967 Carole Schweizer c 6. Vic S Mk's Epis Ch French Camp CA 2004-2007; Int Vic S Mary's Ch Manteca CA 2002-2004; Int R Chr The King Ch Riverbank CA 2002; Dn, Yosemite Dnry Epis Dio San Joaquin Modesto CA 1996-2002; Dioc Coun Epis Dio San Joaquin Modesto CA 1995-2001; R S Paul's Epis Ch Modesto CA 1994-2002; Dioc Invstmt Trust Epis Dio San Joaquin Modesto CA 1994-1995; Vic St Lukes Ch Katy TX 1989-1994; Chairman of Bd S Vincents Hse Galveston TX 1986-1989; Chair, Bldg Com S Vincents Hse Galveston TX 1985-1986; R Gr Ch Galveston TX 1984-1989; CE Plcy Bd Dio Texas Houston TX 1983-1986; Asst to R Ch Of The Gd Shpd Friendswood TX 1983-1984. "Motivational Messages on Faith & Renwl," *Dear Par Fam*, 2003; "Column on Sprtl Direction," *Texas Epis Churchmen*, 1986; "Var arts," *The Angl Dig*, 1986. Chapl Ord of S Lk 1985; OHC 1983. carostanc@sbcglobal.net

COLLINS, Victoria Lundberg (CFla) 688 Ebony St, Melbourne FL 32935 B Orlando FL 8/28/1940 d Henric Victor Lundberg & Edna Bragg. BS Richmond Profsnl Inst; NO SWTS 1975; Cert In Sem Stds Inst For Chr Stds/Sch Of Diac Stds 1995. D 3/23/1996 Bp John Wadsworth Howe. c 1. D H Trin Epis Ch Melbourne FL 2005-2011; D Epis Ch Of The H Apos Satellite Bch FL 1996-2005. perrywcollins@bellsouth.net

COLLINS JR, William Andrew Jr (Okla) 509 Nw 169th St, Edmond OK 73003 B Corpus Christi TX 8/21/1930 s William Andrew Collins & Ona Mae. LSU 1951; CDSP 1966. D 12/23/1971 P 7/1/1972 Bp Edwin Lani Hanchett. m 7/9/1949 Frances Jones c 2. Cleric S Andr's Ch Breckenridge TX 1995-1996; S Mich's Epis Ch Norman OK 1991-1992; S Aug Of Cbury Oklahoma City OK 1989-1991; Vic All Souls Epis Ch Oklahoma City OK 1981-1988; S Nich Epis Ch Kapolei HI 1977-1978; Vic Emm Epis Ch Kailua HI 1972-1977; D S Andr's Cathd Honolulu HI 1971-1972.

COLLINS, William Gerard (Ga) 209 Maple St, Saint Simons Island GA 31522 **S Thos Ch Savannah GA 2009-** B IE 10/29/1945 s Michael Collins & Sara Grace. MA S Patricks Coll 1971; MA Merc 1994. Rec from Roman Catholic 6/1/1996 Bp Henry Irving Louttit. m 11/20/1994 Mary Sheehan Brennan. Assoc/Chapl S Paul's Ch Savannah GA 2009-2010; R S Mk's Ch Brunswick GA 2003-2008; Assoc S Mk's Ch Brunswick GA 1996-2002. liamgcollins@bellsouth.net

COLLIS, Geoffrey (NJ) 32 Lafayette St, Rumson NJ 07760 B Red Bank NJ 3/28/1950 s Harry John Collis & Margaret Elsie. BS Rider U 1972; MDiv GTS 1976. D 6/5/1976 P 12/18/1976 Bp Albert Wiencke Van Duzer. Int Epis Ch Of The Epiph Ventnor City NJ 2006-2007; S Dav's Ch Cranbury NJ 2005; Int Trin Epis Ch Cranford NJ 2003-2004; Vic S Ptr's At The Light Epis Barnegat Light NJ 2001-2002; Int Chr Ch Somers Point NJ 1999-2000; S Jas Ch Long Branch NJ 1981-1999; Asst Chr Ch Toms River Toms River NJ 1976-1981. nghtyvicar@aol.com

COLLIS, Shannon J (Los) 502 W Avenue K, Lancaster CA 93534 **S Hilary's Epis Ch Hesperia CA 2009-; Assoc S Paul's Par Lancaster CA 2008-** B San Diego CA 11/28/1956 d John Joseph Collis & Shirley Naatz. BA San Diego St U 1986; MA San Diego St U 1992; MDiv CDSP 2008. D 6/7/2008 P 1/10/2009 Bp Joseph Jon Bruno. shannon_collis@roadrunner.com

COLLUM, David Joseph (Alb) 62 South Swan St., Albany NY 12210 **Dn Cathd Of All SS Albany NY 2010-** B Southampton NY 6/25/1958 BS USMMA 1980; MBA RPI 1992; MA St. Bernards TS And Mnstry Rochester NY 2005; Dplma TESM 2007. D 6/12/2004 P 12/18/2004 Bp Daniel William Herzog. m 5/2/1992 Elizabeth J Page c 2. R S Jn's Ch Delhi NY 2005-2010; R S Ptr's Ch Hobart NY 2005-2010; Asst Chr Epis Ch Ballston Spa NY 2004-2005. deancollum@gmail.com

COLMORE III, C(harles) Blayney (SanD) Po Box 516, Jacksonville VT 05342 B Orange NJ 8/27/1940 s Charles Blayney Colmore & Margaret Luisa. BA U of Pennsylvania 1963; MDiv EDS 1966. D 6/25/1966 Bp Anson Phelps Stokes Jr P 12/5/1966 Bp Nelson Marigold Burroughs. m 12/26/1979 Lacey J Jennings c 3. Pres/Stndg Com Dio San Diego San Diego CA 1992-1993; Chair Dio San Diego San Diego CA 1988-1991; R S Jas By The Sea La Jolla CA 1987-1996; R S Paul's Ch Dedham MA 1973-1987; St. Jn's, Lafayette Sq, Washington, D.C. S Jn's Ch Lafayette Sq Washington DC 1969-1973; Cur S Paul's Ch Akron OH 1966-1969. Auth, "Meander: Wooing Ms. Maudie," *Novel*, Xlibris, 2010; Auth, "God Knows; It's Not About Us," *Novel*, Xlibris, 2004; Auth, "In The Zone; Notes on Wondering Coast To Coast," *Fiction/Non-fiction Collection*, Xlibris, 2000; Auth, "Notes From Zone 4 & 10," *Zone Notes*, Internet, 1995; Auth, "arts," *Epis Ch TimesVarious Pub*, 1966. blayneyc@earthlink.net

COLON TORRES, Lydia (PR) PO Box 902, Saint Just PR 00978 Puerto Rico B Adjuntas PR 3/24/1942 d Antonio Colon Martine & Angelica. AA Hostos Cmnty Coll 1974; BA Universidad Catolica 1980; MA Universidad Catolica 1986. D 11/22/2009 Bp David Andres Alvarez-Velazquez. m 11/21/2004 Daniel Guadalupe Mendoza c 2. lydiac42@yahoo.com

COLTON, Elizabeth Wentworth (Pa) 2645 E Venango St, Philadelphia PA 19134 **R Gr Ch And The Incarn Philadelphia PA 2004-** B Albany NY 8/23/1951 d James Byers Colton & Ruth. BA Elmira Coll 1973; MA H Names U 1978; Cert Pennsylvania Diac Sch 1992; MTS EDS 2004. D 9/19/1992 Bp W Mutebi P 5/29/2004 Bp Charles Ellsworth Bennison Jr. D/Par Admin Ch Of The H Sprt Harleysville PA 2000-2002; D Philadelphia Cathd Philadelphia PA 1998-2000; Dio Pennsylvania Philadelphia PA 1995-1998; D S Mary's Ch Hamilton Vill Philadelphia PA 1992-1994. graceincarnation@verizon.net

COLVIN, Jeremi Ann (Mass) 160 Rock St, Fall River MA 02720 **Asst R for Mssn in Homeless Mnstry Ch of the H Sprt Fall River MA 2011-** B Mineola NY 3/17/1958 d Donald D Colvin & Jeannette. BA SUNY New Paltz 1980; MDiv EDS 2009. D 6/5/2010 Bp Gayle Elizabeth Harris P 1/8/2011 Bp M(arvil) Thomas Shaw III. c 1. revjacolvin@yahoo.com

COLVIN, Myra Angeline (Mich) 226 Spring Lake Dr, Chelsea MI 48118 B Lima Ohio 2/5/1921 d Samuel Shephard & Myrtle. D 12/10/2005 Bp Wendell Nathaniel Gibbs Jr. c 4. myra.colvin@earthlink.net

COLWELL, Charles Richard (NY) 172 Ivy St, Oyster Bay NY 11771 **Bp Coadjudacator Transition Team, Chair Dio New York New York City NY 1998-** B Ellsworth ME 11/1/1937 s George Albert Colwell & Dorothy Rebecca. BA U of Maine 1960; MDiv GTS 1963; NYTS 1967; Postgraduate Cntr for Mntl Hlth 1967; DMin Drew U 1977. D 6/8/1963 Bp Oliver L Loring P 12/21/1963 Bp Horace W B Donegan. m 8/29/1964 Judith Hubbard c 3. Reg II Advsry Bd Dio New York New York City NY 2002-2003; Mem of the Eccl Crt Dio New York New York City NY 2000-2003; Mem of Congrl Spprt Reveiw Ctte Dio New York New York City NY 1999-2000; Mem Evang Ctte Dio New York New York City NY 1989-1992; Stndg Com-Pres Dio New York New York City NY 1984-1988; Cler Compstn Ctte, chair Dio New York New York City NY 1975-1976; R S Barn Ch Irvington on Hudson NY 1972-2008; Assoc Ch Of The H Trin New York NY 1967-1972; Cur S Marg's Ch Bronx NY 1963-1966. Auth, "Collision of Worlds: A P's Life," 2008; Producer, "An Island in Time," *Video*, 2002; Auth, "Will the Dust Praise You?," *Video*, 1989; Auth, "The Power of Touch," *Video*, 1988; Auth, "arts," *Living Ch, The Epis New Yorker*; Auth, "arts," *Personal Journey, Guideposts mag*. The Cntr for Jewish-Chr-Muslim Understanding, Fndr a 2002-2009; The Holocaust and Human Rts Cmsn Advsry Bd 2006-2008. Excellence in Pstr Care Ord of S Jn the Theol, Bp of New York 1998. chascolwell@gmail.com

COLWELL II, Kirby Price (O) 14721 S Woodland Rd, Shaker Heights OH 44120 **S Paul's Epis Ch Cleveland Heights OH 2002-** B Amarillo TX 9/8/1949 s Kirby Price Colwell & Olga Willa. W Texas A&M U; TESM 1997. D 2/21/1998 Bp Terence Kelshaw. m 12/24/1984 Gail Gatewood. Sons of the Amer Revolution 1995. kpcolwell@ameritech.net

COMBS, Leslie David (NY) Po Box 366, Millbrook NY 12545 B KC City MO 4/17/1948 s Josef Truxton & Lois Margaret. MDiv SWTS; U of Missouri 1967; BA U of Kansas 1970. D 4/25/1976 Bp Quintin Ebenezer Primo Jr P 11/1/1976 Bp James Winchester Montgomery. m 5/15/1976 Barbara Mansfield. R

Gr Ch Millbrook NY 1983-1986; R Ch Of The Ascen Buffalo NY 1978-1983; Cur S Ptr's Epis Ch Chicago IL 1976-1978. Leslie.combs@lhh.com

COMBS, William (At) 2100 Hilton Ave, Columbus GA 31906 **S Gabr's Epis Ch Oakwood GA 2007-** B 2/18/1961 D 6/7/2003 P 1/18/2004 Bp J(ohn) Neil Alexander. m 7/17/2003 Jennifer W Combs c 2. S Thos Epis Ch Columbus GA 2003-2007. billcombs@bellsouth.net

COMEAU, Molly Stata (Vt) 70 Poor Farm Rd, Alburg VT 05440 B Burlington VT 5/13/1948 d Cyrus Alquire Stata & June. BS Trin Burlington VT 1983. D 5/29/1982 P 5/12/1983 Bp Robert Shaw Kerr. m 5/6/1967 Joseph Kerry Vaughn Comeau c 3. P-in-c S Jas Epis Ch Essex Jct VT 2000-2003; Cn Ordnry Dio Vermont Burlington VT 1994-2000; Bp Booth Conf Cntr Burlington VT 1993-1994; R S Jas Epis Ch Arlington VT 1990-1993; Assoc S Jn's In The Mountains Stowe VT 1989; H Trin Epis Ch Swanton VT 1985-1989. OHC. mscomeau@ix.netcom.com

COMEAUX, Andrew Anthony (WLa) 3602 Gilbert Dr, Shreveport LA 71104 B Plaquemine LA 8/27/1948 s Wilmot Jude Comeaux & Aline Mary. BA S Jos Sem Coll 1970; MDiv Notre Dame Sem 1974; MS Tul 1998. Rec from Roman Catholic 2/1/1999 as Priest Bp Charles Edward Jenkins III. m 7/13/1996 Eydie Marie Gunter c 6. S Mk's Cathd Shreveport LA 2002-2009; R S Jas Epis Ch Shreveport LA 2000-2002; R Ch Of The H Comm Plaquemine LA 1999-2000. recacom@bellsouth.net

COMEGYS JR, David Pierson (Dal) 25721 Weston Dr, Laguna Niguel CA 92677 B Shreveport LA 3/5/1932 s David Pierson Comegys & Harriet. BA W&L 1954; Epis TS of The SW 1957; MDiv CDSP 1966. D 6/24/1957 Bp Iveson Batchelor Noland P 5/8/1958 Bp Girault M Jones. m 11/3/1960 Elizabeth Miller Hemphill c 3. R S Lk's Epis Ch San Antonio TX 1975-1981; R Trin Epis Ch Ft Worth TX 1972-1975; Asst S Mich And All Ang Ch Dallas TX 1966-1972; R S Geo's Ch Bossier City LA 1963-1966; Assoc S Paul's Epis Ch Shreveport LA 1960-1963; Cur Epis Ch Of The Gd Shpd Lake Chas LA 1957-1960. Auth, "Collar," *Collar*, Auth Hse, 2005. davidcomegys@cox.net

COMER, Fletcher (Ala) 898 Running Brook Dr, Prattville AL 36066 B Memphis TN 12/7/1946 s John Fletcher Comer & Bettie B. STUSo 1966; BS Auburn U 1968; MBA Auburn U 1969; MDiv STUSo 1975. D 6/1/1975 P 12/1/1975 Bp Furman Stough. m 3/15/1969 Judith Walton c 2. S Lk's Ch Scottsboro AL 2006; Epis Black Belt Mnstry Demopolis AL 1998-2005; R S Wilfrid's Ch Marion AL 1998-1999; S Mk's Ch Prattville AL 1985-1996; The Cathd Ch Of The Adv Birmingham AL 1979-1985; S Andr's Epis Ch Sylacauga AL 1975-1979; R S Mary's Epis Ch Childersburg AL 1975-1979. Co-Fndr Noah, Outreach Mnstry & Par Spprt. Algernon Sydney Sullivan Awd 1968; Who'S Who So & Sw 90.

COMER, Harold Leroy (WMich) 1231 Fran Dr, Frankfort MI 49635 **R S Phil's Ch Beulah MI 1998-** B Goshen IN 5/1/1949 s Harold E Comer & Evelyn L. LTh Nash 1983. D 5/13/1983 P 11/30/1983 Bp William Cockburn Russell Sheridan. m 6/21/1985 Molly A Hoke c 1. R S Alb's Epis Ch Ft Wayne IN 1986-1998; Cur Trin Ch Ft Wayne IN 1983-1986. skip-molly@att.net

COMER, Judith Walton (Ala) 2813 Godfrey Ave NE, Fort Payne AL 35967 **Chair of Hisp Cmsn Dio Alabama Birmingham AL 2011-; P-in-c S Phil's Ch Ft Payne AL 2008-** B 4/23/1947 d James Lamar Walton & Margaret Josephine. BS Auburn U 1969; MA Auburn U 1971; MDiv STUSo 2008. D 5/17/2008 Bp Henry Nutt Parsley Jr P 12/16/2008 Bp John McKee Sloan. m 3/15/1969 Fletcher Comer c 4. Freeman Awd for Merit TS, Sewanee 2006. stphilipsrector@boonlink.net

COMER, Kathleen Susan (La) 4105 Division St, Metairie LA 70002 B New Orleans LA 9/16/1947 d Sidney Comer & Margaret. BA SE Louisiana U 1970; Cert Sch for Mnstry Dio Louisiana 2002. D 2/23/2002 Bp Charles Edward Jenkins III. D S Mart's Epis Ch Metairie LA 2002-2009. kcomer3@cox.net

COMER, Susanne Darnell (Tex) 1941 Webberville Rd, Austin TX 78721 **S Mk's Ch Austin TX 2011-** B Quito Ecuador 8/8/1959 d James Millen Darnell & Susanne Benson. BA Rice U 1981; MDiv Columbia TS 1984; ThM Harvard DS 1990; MSW Simmons Coll 1996; Dplma of Angl Stds Epis TS Of The SW 2010. D 6/19/2010 Bp C(harles) Andrew Doyle. m 8/17/1996 Robert Scott Comer c 2. Asst R S Jas Ch Austin TX 2010-2011. yarn1@austin.rr.com

COMFORT, Alexander Freeman (WNC) 105 Sunny Ln, Mars Hill NC 28754 B Cleveland OH 9/14/1948 s William Rayburn Comfort & Anne Barwick. BA U So 1970; MA Duke 1971; MDiv STUSo 1978. D 6/17/1978 Bp Hunley Agee Elebash P 1/13/1979 Bp Gray Temple. m Ann Pietrangeli c 1. Trin Ch Spruce Pine NC 2009-2010; Mt Olivet Epis Ch New Orleans LA 1989-1995; R S Lk's Epis Ch Jackson TN 1983-1986; Asst Trin Ch New Orleans LA 1980-1983; Asst Par Ch of St. Helena Beaufort SC 1978-1980. Auth, "Temptation At Geth," *Ch Eductr*, 1986. Outstanding Fund Raising Exec Assn of Fundraising Professionals New Orleans 1995. alexcfaia@citcom.net

COMFORT, Clifford Alexander (SwFla) 194 Coconut Dr., Fort Myers Beach FL 33931 **Cleric S Jn's Epis Ch St Jas City FL 1989-** B Newburgh NY 8/20/1918 s Harvey Harrison Comfort & Grace Amelia. BA U of Miami 1959; MDiv Nash 1972. D 11/26/1955 Bp Martin J Bram P 7/1/1962 Bp James Loughlin Duncan. m 8/23/1997 Anna Lee P Walton c 3. S Raphael's Ch Ft Myers Bch FL 1962-1980; Asst Emm Epis Ch Rockford IL 1961-1962. Soc Of S Jn The Evang 1972. D.D. Nashota Hse 2001.

COMINOS, Peter (EMich) P. O. Box 30, 301 East Westover St., East Tawas MI 48730 B Salinas CA 8/25/1940 s Mitchell Nicholas Cominos & Argero. Hartnell Coll; Cert USALS 1961; BA Golden Gate U 1987; MDiv CDSP 1990. D 2/21/1986 Bp Charles Shannon Mallory P 6/1/1990 Bp John-David Mercer Schofield. m 8/3/1973 Patricia Ann Morrison. R Trin Epis Ch Bay City MI 1996-2006; R S Paul's Ch Altus OK 1993-1996; Ch Of The Resurr Clovis Clovis CA 1990-1993; D Epis Ch Of The Gd Shpd Salinas CA 1986-1987. OHC 1978. fpc10@chartermi.net

COMMINS, Gary Lee (Los) 1114 Opal St Apt D, Redondo Beach CA 90277 **R The Par Ch Of S Lk Long Bch CA 2001-** B Los Angeles CA 2/12/1952 s Richard Commins & Marcia Fay. BA U CA 1974; MDiv CDSP 1980. D 6/21/1980 P 12/21/1980 Bp Robert C Rusack. c 1. R H Faith Par Inglewood CA 1990-2001; Vic S Mich's U Mssn Island Isla Vista CA 1983-1990; Asst S Geo's Epis Ch Laguna Hills CA 1980-1983. Auth, "Is Suffering Redemptive?," *Hist and Theol Reflection of Mart Luther King, Jr.*, Sewanee Theol Revs, 2008; Auth, "Becoming Bridges," *The Sprt and Pract of Diversity*, Cowley, 2007; Auth, "Thos Merton's Three Epiphanies," *Theol Today*, 1999; Auth, "Death & The Circus: The Theol Of Wm Stringfellow," *ATR*, Atr, 1997; Auth, "Harlem And Eschaton, Robert Slocum'S:Prophet Of Justice," *Prophet Of Life*, Ch Pub Inc, 1997; Auth, "Sprtl People/Radical Lives," *Internationl Scholars Press*, 1996; Auth, "Woody Allen's Theol Imagination," *Theol Today*, 1987. Cn The Rt. Rev. J. Jon Bruno 2010; Hon DD CDSP 2001. commins@stlukeslb.org

CONANT, Louise R (Mass) 24 Bowdoin St, Cambridge MA 02138 B Cincinnati OH 10/2/1937 d Hugh McDiarmid Ritchey & Mary Corinne. BA Smith 1959; MA Ya 1960; MDiv EDS 1984. D 6/1/1985 Bp John Bowen Coburn P 5/1/1986 Bp David Elliot Johnson. m 6/27/1964 Loring Conant c 2. Assoc R Chr Ch Cambridge Cambridge MA 1988-1999; S Paul's Ch Brookline MA 1985-1988. MECA 1985.

CONATY, Peter Michael (Tex) 404 Buena Vista Ln, West Columbia TX 77486 **R S Mary's Ch W Columbia TX 1999-** B New York NY 4/4/1948 s Peter Joseph Conaty & Anna Theresa. AA S Ptr's Coll Baltimore MD 1968; BA S Paul Washington DC 1971; Washington Theol Un 1974; CTh Epis TS of The SW 1987. Rec from Roman Catholic 5/1/1987 as Priest Bp Gordon Taliaferro Charlton. m 11/24/1994 Susan Melinda Johnson c 1. Vic S Jn's Epis Ch Sealy TX 1990-1999; Asst S Mk's Ch Houston TX 1987-1990. "Yo-Yo Inspires VBS," *Faith @ Wk*, Faith At Wk, Inc, 2004. Chapl Comp H Cross 1990. pmcsmc2@centurylink.net

CONAWAY, Arthur Clarence (Lex) 1403 Providence Rd, Richmond KY 40475 **Supply S Alb's Ch Morehead KY 2008-; Supply S Thos Ch Beattyville KY 2008-** B Kent OH 8/8/1927 s Charles Nicholas Conaway & Clara Louise. AA U of Baltimore 1960; BA U of Baltimore 1965; MDiv Epis TS In Kentucky 1969; U of Kentucky 1971. D 12/15/1968 P 5/15/1969 Bp William R Moody. m 4/6/1946 Martha Agnes Smith c 2. Supply S Mk's Ch Hazard KY 1995-1996; Asst Chr Ch Columbia MD 1980-1995; Asst S Pat Ch Somerset KY 1976-1979; D S Jas Epis Ch Prestonsburg KY 1968-1969. Life Mem Bro of S Andr 1994.

CONDIT, Mary Garidel (Cristina) (WNC) 5155 Western Ave, Morganton NC 28655 **Died 4/23/2010** B Orange NJ 8/17/1949 d Albert Nelson Condit & Margaret Halsey. Lynchburg Coll 1969; BS SUNY 1970; MS OR SU 1976; PhD U NC 1982; MDiv Epis TS of The SW 1991. D 6/9/1991 P 3/1/1992 Bp Robert Hodges Johnson. Chapl Dok 1992-1997. spiritcc@compascable.net

CONDON, Joshua T (NY) 98 Steward Ave, Eastchester NY 10709 **S Steph's Ch Armonk NY 2009-** B Louisville, KY 3/3/1978 BA U GA 2000; MDiv VTS 2003. D 6/7/2003 P 1/4/2004 Bp J(ohn) Neil Alexander. m 12/4/2007 Sarah Condon c 1. S Lk's Ch Eastchester NY 2008-2009; Asst Gr Epis Ch Gainesville GA 2003-2006. jcondon.ststephens@gmail.com

CONGDON, William Hopper (Ct) SEC OF THE HOUSE OF BISHOPS 00000 Canada B 3/1/1934 D 6/13/1961 Bp Walter H Gray P 3/24/1962 Bp Joseph Warren Hutchens.

CONGER, George Arthur Munger (CFla) Po Box 97, Vero Beach FL 32961 B Camp Lejeune NC 6/27/1962 s Oliver Carrington Conger & Cynthia. Oxf; BA Duke 1984; MBA Duke 1985; MDiv Yale DS 1995. D 9/20/1997 P 5/21/1998 Bp Robert William Duncan. m 6/8/1985 Susan Baxter c 2. R S Eliz's Epis Ch Sebastian FL 2000-2002. Bd Cert Chapl Assn of Profsnl Chapl 2008; Resrch Fell Yale DS New Haven CT 1999; Hon Cn S Mathews Cathd, Dallas TX Dallas TX 1998. george.conger@aya.yale.edu

CONGER, George Mallett (NY) 9 Angel Rd, New Paltz NY 12561 B New York NY 3/1/1934 s Frederic P M Conger & Elizabeth. BA Harv 1956; MDiv GTS 1959; Med Boston Coll 1974. D 6/13/1959 P 12/1/1960 Bp Horace W B Donegan. m 9/23/1973 Jane O'Hare c 1. Ch Of The Gd Shpd New York NY 1983-1986; Assoc Ch Of The Gd Shpd Wakefield Bronx NY 1982-1986; Team Monticello NY 1982; S Jn's Memi Ch Ellenville NY 1977-1981; Hoosac Sch Hoosick NY 1975-1977; Asst R S Geo's Epis Ch Newburgh NY

1969-1973; Asst The Ch Of The Adv Boston MA 1962-1964; Asst S Ptr's Ch New York NY 1960-1962. Auth, "Chelsea Revs".

CONGER, John Peyton (Cal) 851 Regal Rd, Berkeley CA 94708 B 3/3/1935 D 10/28/1961 Bp Anson Phelps Stokes Jr P 11/6/1965 Bp Alfred L Banyard. johncongerphd@gmail.com

CONIGLIO, Robert Freeman (SVa) 21313 Metompkin View Lane, Parksley VA 23421 B Nashville TN 6/4/1950 s John G Coniglio & Carmen Sylvia. BA Emory & Henry Coll 1972; PA Cert Med U of So Carolina 1980; Cert Dio Sthrn Virginia: Sch for Mnstry Formation 2010; Cert VTS 2010. D 6/12/2010 P 12/18/2010 Bp Herman Hollerith IV. m 8/14/1976 Joanne Coniglio c 3. D Assoc Emm Ch Cape Chas VA 2010-2011. robertconiglio@mac.com

CONKLIN, Andrea Caruso (Tex) 1819 Heights Blvd, Houston TX 77008 **D St Andrews Epis Ch Houston TX 2010-** B Englewood NJ 10/2/1950 d Andrew Caruso & Elizabeth. BA Roa 1972; Iona Sch for Mnstry 2010. D 6/19/2010 Bp C(harles) Andrew Doyle. m 10/25/1986 George Conklin c 1. andreasacc@aol.com

CONKLIN, Caroline Elizabeth (Mont) 13231 15th Ave N.E., Seattle WA 98125 B Tucson AZ 9/18/1935 d Warren Aldrich Roberts & Blanche Elizabeth. BA Rad 1957; MA U of Montana 1971. D 6/24/1991 Bp Charles Jones III. m 8/23/1958 William Conklin c 4. D Ch Of The Incarn Great Falls MT 1991-2006. Auth, *MEDITATIONS FOR AltGld MEMBERS*, Morehouse Pub, 2000. cconklin@bresnan.net

CONKLIN, Daniel G (Oly) Neue Jakob Strasse 1, Berlin 10179 Germany B Phoenixville PA 9/27/1943 s Henry Clayton Conklin & Evelyn Ruth. BA Penn 1965; MDiv PDS 1968; Tubingen U Tubingen DE 1973. D 6/8/1968 P 12/21/1968 Bp Robert Lionne DeWitt. Shpd for Pstr Care S Mk's Cathd Seattle WA 2009-2010; Assoc R Ch Of The Epiph Seattle WA 1997-2008; Docent for OT - TS Dio Olympia Seattle WA 1996-2009; Pstr German Untd Ch Of Chr Seattle WA 1994-1997; Cur S Paul's Ch Philadelphia PA 1968-1970. Auth, "Jesus and ET," *Bangalore Theol Journ*, Bangalore TS, 2007; Auth, "The Virtues," *Forw Series*, Forw Mvmt, 2002; Transltr, "Icons - The Facination & the Reality," *Bk*, Riverside, 1998; Contrib, "Var Sermons in German," *Homiletische Monatshefte*, Vanderhoek und Ruprecht, 1978. danielgconkln@gmail.com

CONKLIN, Edward Wilbur (NC) 980 N May St Apt 7, Southern Pines NC 28387 B Jamaica NY 2/3/1922 s Leonard Erle Conklin & Bessie Pearsal. BS USNA 1944; BD VTS 1949; Fllshp Coll of Preachers 1965; Fllshp VTS 1982. D 6/19/1949 P 1/1/1950 Bp Benjamin M Washburn. m 9/12/1953 Lila M Crocheron c 2. R Trin Ch Athens PA 1980-1985; Dio Bethlehem Bethlehem PA 1970-1980; R Resurr Ch Louisville KY 1953-1967; Asst Trin And S Phil's Cathd Newark NJ 1949-1953. Auth, "Thirsting on That Hewn Tree," *Fleet St Poet*, 1984; Auth, "The Hewn Tree," *Seabury in Memoriam*, 1983. First Hlth MRH Outstanding Vol 2004; Outstanding Moore Cnty Vol Serv Awd 2002.

CONKLING JR, Allan Alden (WTex) PO Box 314, Bandera TX 78003 **S Chris's Ch Bandera TX 2011-** B Temple TX 8/29/1952 s Allan Alden Conkling & Alice. BA SW Texas St U San Marcos 1974; MA S Mary's U San Antonio TX 1978; MDiv STUSo 1985. D 6/18/1985 Bp Stanley Fillmore Hauser P 1/1/1986 Bp Scott Field Bailey. m 1/8/2000 Kelly Schneider c 5. Emm Epis Ch San Angelo TX 2005-2011; Assoc R S Thos Epis Ch And Sch San Antonio TX 1998-2004; Ch Of The Epiph Kingsville TX 1996-1998; S Fran By The Lake Canyon Lake TX 1993-1996; R Chr Ch Epis Laredo TX 1988-1993; Asst R Ch Of The Gd Shpd Corpus Christi TX 1985-1988. aac829@aol.com

CONKLING, Kelly Schneider (NwT) 198 Doe Creek Rd, Bandera TX 78003 **Asst Ch Of The H Sprt San Antonio TX 2011-; P Dio NW Texas Lubbock TX 2010-** B Beeville TX 4/5/1955 d Joseph Robert Schneider & Virgina Davis. BFA Sam Houston St U 1977; Cert SW Texas St U San Marcos 1984; MS Texas A&M U 1991; MDiv Epis TS of The SW 1997. D 6/26/1997 Bp Robert Boyd Hibbs P 12/1/1997 Bp C(harles) Wallis Ohl. m 1/8/2000 Allan Alden Conkling c 2. Calv Luth Ch San Angelo TX 2009; The Epis Ch Of S Mary The Vrgn Big Sprg TX 2007-2008; Emm Epis Ch San Angelo TX 2005-2006; S Chris's By The Sea Portland TX 2004; Asst S Andr's Epis Ch San Antonio TX 2000-2003; Ch Of The Heav Rest Abilene TX 1997-1999; S Mk's Epis Ch Abilene TX 1997. Auth, "Pryr of the Heart," Moorehouse Pub, 2006. ksconkling@aol.com

CONLEY, Alan Bryan (WTex) P.O. Box 350, 231 Cave Springs Dr. W., Hunt TX 78024 B Pampa TX 1/4/1934 s Elmer Mitchell Conley & Fern Marie. BA Texas Tech U 1956; MDiv VTS 1959. D 6/22/1959 P 4/1/1960 Bp George Henry Quarterman. m 8/26/1956 Corinne Hamill c 3. R S Peters Epis Sch Kerrville TX 1988-2001; S Ptr's Epis Ch Kerrville TX 1988-2001; Asst R/Headmaster Ch Of The Gd Shpd Corpus Christi TX 1975-1988; Cur S Andr's Epis Ch Amarillo TX 1964-1975; Vic All SS Ch Colorado City TX 1959-1964. conley@hctc.net

CONLEY, Joan Frances (Nwk) 169 Fairmount Rd, Ridgewood NJ 07450 **Cler Asst S Eliz's Ch Ridgewood NJ 2010-** B Brockton MA 2/10/1964 d John F Conley & Marian E. BA U of Notre Dame 1986; MDiv Drew TS 2010. D 6/5/2010 P 12/11/2010 Bp Mark M Beckwith. c 2. conley7of7@hotmail.com

CONLEY, Kris (Me) 17 Littlefield Dr, Kennebunk ME 04043 B Buffalo NY 1/8/1947 BSW U of Sthrn Maine 1992. D 6/24/2006 Bp Chilton Abbie Richardson Knudsen. m 1/28/1969 Greg Conley c 2. krisconley17@yahoo.com

CONLEY, Nancy Ida (Haw) 47-775 Ahilama Rd, Kaneohe HI 96744 B Detroit MI 9/3/1936 d Ernest Eminger & Edna. Sch for Deacons; Cert Healing Touch 2001; Cert Sprtl Direction Course (Mercy Cntr) 2003. D 8/16/1991 Bp Donald Purple Hart. c 4. D S Geo's Epis Ch Honolulu HI 1991-2003. Healing Touch Mnstry Practitioner, Sprtl Dir, 3rd Or 2006; NAAD, Fllshp of the. spirlife@lava.net

CONLEY, Patricia Ann (Chi) 1993 Yasgur Dr, Woodstock IL 60098 **R S Ann's Ch Woodstock IL 2005-** B Modesto CA 8/10/1951 d Charles Conley & Ruth Irene. BA Regis U Denver CO 1997; MDiv SWTS 2000. D 6/15/2002 P 12/21/2002 Bp William Dailey Persell. m Roma Karon Simons. Dir of Par Hlth Mnstrs S Matt's Ch Evanston IL 2002-2005. Suma cl Regis U. pconley100@gmail.com

CONLEY, Thomas Herbert (At) 2215 Cheshire Bridge Road NE, Atlanta GA 30324 B Jacksonville FL 1/24/1937 s Thomas Herbert Conley & Mary Elizabeth. BA Furman U; MDiv Sthrn Bapt TS Louisville KY 1962; ThM Sthrn Bapt TS Louisville KY 1964. D 6/10/1995 Bp Frank Kellogg Allan P 12/16/1995 Bp Onell Asiselo Soto. m 8/16/1959 Helen Elizabeth Bishop. Cathd Of S Phil Atlanta GA 1999-2002; Ch Of The Annunc Marietta GA 1996-1999; S Bede's Ch Atlanta GA 1995-1996. Auth, "The Common Cup," Trafford Press, 2005; Auth, "Wrshp & The Diakonic Task," Hm Mssn Bd, 1982; Auth, "Pstr Care For Personal Growth," Judson Press, 1977; Auth, "Two In Pulpit-Sermons In Dialogue," Word, 1973.

CONN JR, Doyt LaDean (Oly) 1805 38th Ave, Seattle WA 98122 **R Ch Of The Epiph Seattle WA 2008-** B Rochester MN 1/13/1967 BS NWU 1989; MBA Case Wstrn Reserve U 1997; MDiv VTS 2003. D 6/14/2003 P 12/30/2003 Bp J Clark Grew II. m 7/23/1994 Kristin Leigh Phillips c 2. Assoc R For Pstr Care All SS Par Beverly Hills CA 2003-2008. dconn@epiphanyseattle.org

CONN, John Hardeman (Mass) 4 Alton Court, Brookline MA 02446 B Norfolk VA 4/26/1935 s John Hardeman Conn & Virginia. BA Lander U 1966; MDiv EDS 1969. D 6/21/1969 Bp Anson Phelps Stokes Jr P 5/1/1971 Bp John Melville Burgess. c 2. Int Emm Ch Braintree MA 1996-1998; Int Trin Ch Bridgewater MA 1995; Int S Eliz's Ch Sudbury MA 1984-1986; Int Dio Massachusetts Boston MA 1976-1999; R S Paul's Epis Ch Hopkinton MA 1971-1973; Cur Trin Par Melrose MA 1969-1971. jconnh@yahoo.com

CONN, Judy Ann (Minn) 10027 Pillsbury Ave S, Minneapolis MN 55420 **D S Nich Ch Richfield MN 2005-** B Minneapolis MN 4/2/1940 d Donald McDonald & Mary Jane. U MN. D 1/5/1989 Bp Robert Marshall Anderson. m 6/10/1978 Jerry Allan Conn c 4. S Alb's Epis Ch Edina MN 1990; Epis Ch Cntr New York NY 1989-1992.

CONN, Rodney Carl (Be) 108 N. 5th St., Allentown PA 18102 **Chapl Dio Bethlehem Bethlehem PA 2008-; D Gr Epis Ch Allentown PA 2008-** B Willoughby OH 5/18/1962 s Carl Lewis Conn & Patricia Ann. BS U of Akron 1986. D 2/2/2008 Bp Paul Victor Marshall. m 7/18/1999 Sarabel Ryan Conn. rcconn@rcn.com

CONNELL, George Patterson (Ky) 11 Saint Lukes Ln, San Antonio TX 78209 **R Trin Epis Ch Owensboro KY 1998-** B Belle Glade FL 3/10/1952 s Hueston Eugene Connell & Betty Jean. BA Shorter Coll 1974; MDiv Epis TS of The SW 1981. D 6/24/1981 Bp Wesley Frensdorff P 1/1/1982 Bp Scott Field Bailey. m 8/5/1977 Diana Holman c 2. S Lk's Epis Ch San Antonio TX 1995-1998; S Andr's Epis Ch Seguin TX 1989-1995; Gr Ch Cuero TX 1984-1989; Asst Trin Ch Victoria TX 1981-1984. georgeconnell@bellsouth.net

CONNELL, John Baade (Haw) 95-1050 Makaikai St. Apt. 17M, Mililani HI 96789 B Waukegan IL 7/23/1930 s John Davis Connell & Phillis Baade. BA U of Hawaii 1959; MDiv CDSP 1985. D 7/18/1985 Bp Edmond Lee Browning P 5/1/1986 Bp Frederick Warren Putnam. m 12/17/1960 Carol Booth c 3. Int Vic S Aug's Epis Chap Kapaau HI 1998-2001; S Alb's Chap Honolulu HI 1987-1988; Vic S Nich Epis Ch Kapolei HI 1985-1998. Hawaii Epis Cler Assn. 1985; Int Mnstry Ntwk, 1995. jbccbc@hawaii.rr.com

CONNELL, Susan (Okla) 210 3rd Ave NW, Miami OK 74354 **R All SS Epis Ch Miami OK 2006-** B Traverse City MI 5/5/1949 d Chester Cox Green & Garie Hutton. BA Bethany Coll 1971; Gordon-Conwell TS 1973; MDiv EDS 1976; LPN Middlesex Vocational HS 1977. D 6/18/1977 Bp Alexander Doig Stewart P 12/8/1990 Bp Walter Decoster Dennis Jr. c 2. R Ch Of The Gd Samar Gunnison CO 2003-2006; Int Epis Ch Of S Mk The Evang No Bellmore NY 2000-2003; Vic Trin Epis Ch Stratford NJ 1998-1999; Assoc S Raphael The Archangel Brick NJ 1990-1998; D S Mk's Ch Hammonton NJ 1979-1983; Chapl The Epis Campus Mnstry at Rutgers New Brunswick NJ 1977-1978. Sis of S Greg 1989-2007. First Superior, Sis of S Greg Sis of S Greg 1999. susan.cnnll@gmail.com

CONNELLY III, Albert Pinckney (CFla) 16 Hawks Lndg, Weaverville NC 28787 B Orlando FL 8/15/1940 s Albert Pinckney Connelly & Frances Rachael. BSA U of Florida 1962; STB Ya Berk 1965; ThM Duke DS 1977; MBA

Florida Inst of Tech 1984. D 6/29/1965 Bp James Loughlin Duncan P 12/29/1965 Bp Henry I Louttit. m 8/17/1963 Lillian Judith Brown c 2. Off Of Bsh For ArmdF New York NY 1968-1979; Cur S Thos' Epis Ch St Petersburg FL 1966-1968; Vic Ch Of Our Sav Palm Bay FL 1965-1966. bert_connelly@yahoo.com

CONNELLY, Charles Evans (SwFla) 2401 Bayshore Blvd., Apt. 505, Tampa FL 33629 **COM Dio SW Florida Sarasota FL 2011-; Dioc Hlth Plan/Lay Pension Plan T/F Dio SW Florida Sarasota FL 2011-; Asst Treas The GTS New York NY 2011-; Cler Advsry Com on Men's Mnstrs Dio SW Florida Sarasota FL 2007-; Dioc Schools Com Dio SW Florida Sarasota FL 2007-; Assoc R and Chapl to the Sch St Johns Epis Ch Tampa FL 2007-** B Toledo OH 10/19/1948 s Jack Lane Connelly & Elizabeth Wall. BS U NC 1970; MBA Col 1972; MDiv GTS 2007. D 6/2/2007 P 12/9/2007 Bp Dabney Tyler Smith. Eccl Trial Crt Dio SW Florida Sarasota FL 2008-2011. ceconnelly@yahoo.com

CONNELLY, Constance R (NC) 1950 S Wendover Rd, Charlotte NC 28211 **S Simon's On The Sound Ft Walton Bch FL 2011-** B Morganton NC 5/12/1944 d Bejamin Sandford Roper & Isbel. BA Converse Coll 1967; MDiv GTS 2001. D P 7/10/2002 Bp Michael Bruce Curry. m 12/23/1965 Charles Wearn Connelly c 2. Chr Epis Ch Raleigh NC 2009-2010; Chr Ch Greenwich CT 2005-2009; S Mart's Epis Ch Charlotte NC 2003-2004; Dio No Carolina Raleigh NC 2001-2003. cerconnelly@yahoo.com

CONNELLY, John Vaillancourt (Chi) 2327 Birchwood Ave, Wilmette IL 60091 **Cn for the Bp's Endwmt Fund Dio Chicago Chicago IL 2011-; Asst S Lk's Ch Evanston IL 1996-** B Syracuse NY 9/24/1958 s William Lawrence Connelly & Shirley. BA Wheaton Coll 1981; MA U of Rhode Island 1983; MDiv Yale DS 1986. D 6/21/1986 P 12/1/1986 Bp George Nelson Hunt III. m 8/27/1983 Mary Farley c 3. S Ann's Epis Ch Old Lyme CT 1992-1994; Assoc R S Andr's Ch Downers Grove IL 1989-1992; Asst R S Mart's Ch Providence RI 1986-1989. vaillacourt1958@aol.com

CONNELLY JR, Walter Joseph (Mass) 231 Bowdoin St, Winthrop MA 02151 **R S Jn's Ch Winthrop MA 2011-** B Boston MA 8/19/1965 A.B. Geo 1990; M.Div. Weston Jesuit TS 1996. D 6/7/2003 P 6/5/2004 Bp M(arvil) Thomas Shaw III. P-in-c S Jn's Ch Winthrop MA 2008-2011; extended supply S Matt And The Redeem Epis Ch So Boston MA 2004-2008; Asst Bristol Cluster Taunton MA 2004. wconnelly1@aol.com

CONNER, Georgene Davis (SwFla) Po Box 1581, Saint Petersburg FL 33731 B Tampa FL 10/18/1944 d Thomas Hartley Davis & Marian Searle. U Of Detroit; U of Mississippi; MDiv EDS 1991. D 6/21/1991 Bp Henry Irving Mayson P 2/1/1992 Bp R(aymond) Stewart Wood Jr. c 2. Cler Cathd Ch Of S Ptr St Petersburg FL 1999-2009; S Mich's Ch New York NY 1995-1999; S Paul's Rock Creek Washington DC 1991-1995. Bp Pk Matsumoto Prize; Frederick Mcghee Adams Prize In Homil. gigipriest@prodigy.net

CONNER, Lu-Anne (Me) 140 The Kings Hwy, Newcastle ME 04553 **R S Andr's Ch Newcastle ME 2010-** B Boston MA 11/18/1962 d Malcolm Alexander Conner & Luella Joan. BA Connecticut Coll 1984; MDiv UTS 2001. D 6/23/2001 P 2/2/2002 Bp Chilton Abbie Richardson Knudsen. m 7/16/2004 Kathryn A McCormick. Assoc S Eliz's Ch Ridgewood NJ 2001-2010. kamlac2@aol.com

CONNER, Martha Hathcock (Az) 11102 W. Kolina Lane, Sun City AZ 85351 **S Chris's Ch Sun City AZ 2008-** B Spokane WA 11/13/1957 d Edgar Wayne Hathcock & Eula Evelyn. BS Troy St U-Dothan AL 1978; MS U of Sthrn Mississippi 1985; MDiv VTS 2000; DMin VTS 2006. D 6/3/2000 P 2/24/2001 Bp Charles Farmer Duvall. m 6/11/1977 Michael J Conner c 2. So Carolina Epis Hm At Still Hopes W Columbia SC 2007-2008; Ch Of The Epiph Danville VA 2006-2007; Asst. R S Thad Epis Ch Aiken SC 2004-2006; R S Mk's Epis Ch Troy AL 2002-2004; Asst R S Jude's Epis Ch Niceville FL 2000-2002. revmarty@gmail.com

CONNER, Ronald Parks (RI) 4430 Grant Rd Nw, Washington DC 20016 **Died 1/30/2011** B Washington DC 6/15/1945 s Francis Willard Conner & Vivian Johnstone. BA U So 1967; STB GTS 1970; STM GTS 1971; ThM PrTS 1980; DMin Drew U 1982; ThD Bos 2003. D 6/27/1970 Bp William Foreman Creighton P 12/27/1970 Bp Jonathan Goodhue Sherman. Auth, "arts," *Cathd Age*; Ed, *Prayers for Eastertide*.

CONNER, Sarah A (Mass) 4 Ernest Rd # 3, Arlington MA 02474 **Int S Mich's Ch Milton MA 2010-** B Boston MA 11/18/1962 d Malcolm Alexander Conner & Luella Joan. BA Connecticut Coll 1984; MDiv Harvard DS 1988. D 6/5/1996 P 5/17/1997 Bp M(arvil) Thomas Shaw III. Int S Ptr's Ch On The Canal Buzzards Bay MA 2007-2010; Int S Dunstans Epis Ch Dover MA 2005-2007; P-in-c Chr Ch Quincy MA 2002-2005; Asst All SS Par Brookline MA 1996-2002. sconner77@comcast.net

CONNERS, John H (EC) 75 Stone Ridge Way Apt 3F, Fairfield CT 06824 B Menominee MI 5/1/1950 s Harold James Conners & Luella Rose. BM U MI 1973; MDiv GTS 1990. D 12/30/1989 P 7/18/1990 Bp William L Stevens. c 1. Vic S Mich's Ch Trenton NJ 2000-2004; Assoc Ch Of S Mary The Vrgn New York NY 1996; Int Trin Ch Lawrenceburg IN 1994; Int S Thos' Ch Windsor NC 1991-1993; D Ch Of S Mary The Vrgn New York NY 1990. john@johnconners.net

CONNOLLY, Emma French (WTenn) 480 S. Greer St., Memphis TN 38111 **D S Jn's Epis Ch Memphis TN 2007-** B Hattiesburg MS 10/19/1949 Millsaps Coll; U of Sthrn Mississippi. D 1/15/2005 Bp Duncan Montgomery Gray III. m 12/11/1999 Robert P Connolly c 4. S Andr's Cathd Jackson MS 2005-2007. emma@stjohnsmemphis.org

CONNOR, Alice Elizabeth (SO) 5735 Lester Rd, Cincinnati OH 45213 **Gd Shpd Luthern Ch Cincinnati OH 2009-** B Portland OR 6/20/1977 d Thomas Harvey Van Brunt & Nancye Eileen. BA Transylvania U 1999; MDiv Bex 2005. D 5/22/2004 P 6/25/2005 Bp Herbert Thompson Jr. m 9/11/1999 Leighton Lewis Connor c 1. The Ch of the Redeem Cincinnati OH 2004-2009. alice@redeemer-cincy.org

CONNORS, Barbara Mae (Ct) 35350 E Division Rd, Saint Helens OR 97051 **D S Paul's Epis Ch Salem OR 1999-; D Chr Ch S Helens OR 1996-** B Portland OR 9/1/1936 d John Henry Sayles & Ethel Florence. RN Emm Hosp Sch Nrsng 1959; BA New Engl Coll 1985; MA Andover Newton TS 1988. D 12/29/1996 Bp Robert Louis Ladehoff. m 12/7/1963 David Loring Connors.

CONRAD JR, James Wallace (Az) 11653 N. Desert Holly Drive, Oro Valley AZ 85737 B Phoenix AZ 3/15/1948 s James Wallace Conrad & Anna Parsons. BA Humboldt St U 1970; MDiv CDSP 1973; DMin Jesuit TS 1979. D 7/14/1973 P 2/1/1974 Bp Victor Manuel Rivera. m 9/12/1981 Donna K Downing-Conrad c 4. Ch Of The Apos Oro Vlly AZ 1993-2005; Dio Arizona Phoenix AZ 1991-1992; R S Alb's Epis Ch Tucson AZ 1987-1991; Ch Of Coventry Cross Minden NV 1981-1987; Vic S Alb's Ch Los Banos CA 1973-1979; Epis Dio San Joaquin Modesto CA 1973-1977. conradfreedom@gmail.com

CONRAD, John William (Los) All Saints Episcopal Church, 3847 Terracina Dr, Riverside CA 92506 **R All SS Epis Ch Riverside CA 2006-** B Victorville CA 2/27/1952 s Lloyd Ray Conrad & Eva Talitha. BA Thos Edison St Coll 1993; MDiv CDSP 1996; DMin CDSP 2005. D 6/8/1996 Bp Robert Marshall Anderson P 1/18/1997 Bp Frederick Houk Borsch. m 8/23/2009 Shannon Marie Murphy c 2. Int Ch Of The Gd Samar San Diego CA 2005-2006; R S Alb's Epis Ch El Cajon CA 1999-2005; S Mk's Par Glendale CA 1996-1999. Auth, "Var arts," *Sermons That Wk*; Auth, *Var arts*. frconrad@gmail.com

CONRAD, Matthew McMillan (ECR) 5318 Palma Ave., Atascadero CA 93422 **R S Lk's Ch Atascadero CA 1984-** B Exeter CA 6/25/1954 s James Wallace Conrad & Anna Parsons. BA Humboldt St U 1976; MDiv CDSP 1980. D 8/2/1980 P 7/18/1981 Bp Victor Manuel Rivera. m 9/3/1977 Diana Marcellus c 3. Cur S Mk's Epis Ch Santa Clara CA 1982-1983; Cur Epis Ch Of S Anne Stockton CA 1980-1982. mdrad@sbcglobal.net

CONRADO VARELA, Victor Hugo (Chi) 6230 N Kenmore Ave, Chicago IL 60660 **S Mk's Epis Ch Glen Ellyn IL 2011-; S Simons Ch Arlington Heights IL 2011-** B Colombia 2/26/1975 s Victor M Conrado & Carmen A. BA Jesuit TS. Rec from Roman Catholic 7/6/2011 Bp Jeffrey Dean Lee. m 10/11/2008 Lucia E Cuevas c 1. vichuconva@gmail.com

CONRADS, Alexandra Kennan (Los) **Vic S Martha's Epis Ch W Covina CA 2004-** D 6/23/2001 P 12/29/2001 Bp Peter James Lee.

CONRADS, Nancy Alice (Chi) 4801 Spring Creek Rd, Rockford IL 61114 B Rockford IL 8/26/1941 d Paul Edward Conrads & Beatrice Helen. BA Lawr 1963; MSW U IL 1969. D 2/7/2009 Bp Jeffrey Dean Lee. nac29@aol.com

CONRADT, James Robert (FdL) W1693 Echo Valley Rd, Kaukauna WI 54130 **Dn, Green Bay Dnry Dio Fond du Lac Appleton WI 2010-; Exec Coun Dio Fond du Lac Appleton WI 2010-; Stndg Com Dio Fond du Lac Appleton WI 2006-; S Paul's Ch Suamico WI 2002-** B Lessor WI 2/19/1937 s Elmer Arthur Conradt & Irene Mary. W&M; U of Wisconsin. D 9/6/1996 P 10/4/2001 Bp Russell Edward Jacobus. m 12/24/1983 Nancy F Hager c 2. D S Paul's Ch Suamico WI 2000-2001; D S Anne's Ch De Pere WI 1996-2000. fatherjimc1@aol.com

CONROY, Mary E (Mass) 1121 Andalusia, Coral Gables FL 33134 **P-in-c S Phil's Ch Coral Gables FL 2009-** B Pittsfield MA 5/17/1963 d Edward Nicholas Conroy & Anne. BS Marymount Coll 1985; MS Ford 1988; MDiv SWTS 1996; D. Min. SWTS 2009. D 6/8/1996 Bp Robert Reed Shahan P 6/7/1997 Bp Claude Edward Payne. Int Ch Of The Ascen Pueblo CO 2008-2009; Assoc R Trin Ch In The City Of Boston Boston MA 1999-2008; Asst Palmer Memi Ch Houston TX 1997-1999; Chapl Chr Ch Greenville SC 1996-1997; D Chr Ch Epis Sch Greenville SC 1996. mconroy@ainphilips.net

CONSIDINE, H James (NwPa) 11733 SW 17th CT, Miramar FL 33025 B Baraboo WI 9/6/1944 s Harvey James Considine & Ruth Joann. Sterling Coll 1964; BM U of Wisconsin 1967; MM MI SU 1968; MDiv Nash 1975. D 4/26/1975 Bp Charles Thomas Gaskell P 11/1/1975 Bp Frederick Hesley Belden. m 12/28/1971 Linda M Koch. R S Jn's Epis Ch Sharon PA 1986-1992; R Trin Epis Ch Logansport IN 1977-1986; Cur S Barn Ch Warwick RI 1975-1977. iconsidine@earthlink.net

CONSTANT, Donna Rittenhouse (Pa) 167 Hermit Hollow Lane, Middleburg PA 17842 B Geneva IL 2/24/1937 d John Wood Rittenhouse & Angela Mozier. Beloit Coll; U CO; U of New Mex; BA CUA 1987; MDiv VTS 1991. D 6/15/1991 Bp Peter James Lee P 2/12/1992 Bp Robert Poland Atkinson. m

8/29/1959 Richard E Constant c 2. Supply P Dio Cntrl Pennsylvania Harrisburg PA 1998-2000; R Calv Ch Germantown Philadelphia PA 1995-1998; Asst Ch Of The H Cross Dunn Loring VA 1991-1994. dndconstant@directv.net

CONSTANT, Joseph Murrenz (Mass) 3737 Seminary Rd, Alexandria VA 22304 **Spec Coordntr for Haiti Epis Ch Cntr New York NY 2010-; Dir of Racial and Ethnic Mnstrs VTS Alexandria VA 2005-** B Haiti 7/17/1967 BS NEU 1991; Mstr in Div VTS 2003. D 6/7/2003 P 2/1/2004 Bp M(arvil) Thomas Shaw III. m 6/28/1997 Sarah Christine Schwenzfeier c 1. Asst S Tim's Epis Ch Washington DC 2003-2004. Auth, "Bk," *No Turning Back: The Black Presence at VTS*, Evergreen Press, 2009. UBE 2004. Bp's Awd Dio Virginia 2010. JCONSTANT@VTS.EDU

CONTESTABLE, Christine Marie (U) 673 Wall St, Salt Lake City UT 84103 **P S Paul's Ch Salt Lake City UT 2011-** B San Pablo CA 10/7/1964 d Robert Joseph Contestable & Rita Jean. BA U of Tulsa 1989; MDiv CDSP 1995; Ph.D. U of Utah 2010. D 6/10/1995 Bp Robert Reed Shahan P 6/7/1997 Bp William Edwin Swing. Coordntr, Mnstry w YP Dio Utah Salt Lake City UT 1999-2002; Int U Chapl, Epiph Hse Dio Utah Salt Lake City UT 1998-1999; CDSP Berkeley CA 1995-1998; Dir, Online Prog and Prog Associtate, Cntr for Angl Lrng and Ldrshp CDSP Berkeley CA 1995-1998; Assoc S Paul's Ch Oakland CA 1995-1998; P S Paul's Ch Oakland CA 1995-1998; Hosp Chapl, San Francisco Gnrl Hosp Sojourn Multifaith Chapl San Francisco CA 1993-1994; Chapl Intern Virginia Mason Hosp Seattle WA 1993-1994. Auth, "Becoming-Lrng: Rethinking Transformative Educ by Reconceptualizing Learner Agcy and Illuminating the Immanent Dynamism of Classrooms," Proquest, 2010; Co-Auth, "Dancing w the enemy? A man and Wmn talk turkey," *Rocky Mtn Cmncatn Revs*, 2006. christine.contestable@gmail.com

CONTRERAS-RODRIGUEZ, Antonio (LI) 13532 38th Ave, Flushing NY 11354 **S Geo's Par Flushing NY 2011-** B Puerto Rico 8/21/1968 s Bernardo Contreras & Marcolina. BS Sagrado Corazon 1992; MS SUNY@Oswego 1996; PhD Yeshiva U 2005; MDiv The GTS 2007. D 1/18/2007 P 4/25/2008 Bp Orris George Walker Jr. drcontreras2@verizon.net

CONWAY, J Cooper (Nwk) 1514 Palisade Ave, Union City NJ 07087 **S Steph's Ch Millburn NJ 2010-** B New York NY 2/9/1949 d James Shaffrey Conway & Mary Elizabeth. Carnegie Mellon U 1967; Webster Coll 1969; ADS Culinary Inst of Amer 1979; MDiv GTS 1998. D 5/30/1998 Bp John Shelby Spong P 12/12/1998 Bp Jack Marston McKelvey. m 10/5/1974 Peter J Madison c 1. S Alb's Ch Oakland NJ 2008-2010; S Jn's Ch Un City NJ 2003-2008; All SS Ch Harrison NY 2002-2003; Dio Newark Newark NJ 1999; Gr Ch Newark NJ 1998-2002. ACTS-VIM Bd, Dio Newark 2005-2008; Dio Nwk Yth Cmsn 1998-2001. revcoopr@aol.com

CONWAY, Nancy Jean (CPa) 6 Watch Tower Ct, Salem SC 29676 **Pstr Asst H Trin Par Epis Clemson SC 2002-** B Dedham MA 1/30/1933 d Walter H Motte & Elinor Marie. BS U of Massachusetts 1954; MA W Virginia U 1979; MA VTS 1989. D 2/21/1993 P 12/11/1993 Bp Charlie Fuller McNutt Jr. R Trin Ch Jersey Shore PA 1994-2000; Asst R Trin Epis Ch Williamsport PA 1993-1997. Cleric Assn. nconway0130@aol.com

CONWAY, Thomas Bradley (NJ) 22 Wickapecko Dr, Interlaken NJ 07712 B Indianapolis IN 12/8/1940 s John Franklin Conway & Jomyla. BA Indiana U 1963; MDiv Ya Berk 1966; MS Rutgers-The St U 1975. D 6/11/1966 Bp John P Craine P 12/18/1966 Bp Albert Wiencke Van Duzer. c 2. Trin Ch Asbury Pk NJ 2003-2004; Trin Cathd Trenton NJ 2001-2004; Vic Ch Of The H Sprt Lebanon NJ 1968-1971; Cur/Dce Trin Epis Ch Cranford NJ 1966-1968. thomasbconway@verizon.net

COOK, Bob (EC) 5001 Montford Dr, Wilmington NC 28409 B Reading PA 9/6/1933 s Graham Cook & Marcella. Ob 1953; BA U So 1958; BD VTS 1961; BSL NW California Sch of Law 2005. D 6/11/1961 P 12/20/1961 Bp Wilburn Camrock Campbell. m 6/21/1958 Ann Knox c 3. P-in-c S Marys Epis Ch Burgaw NC 1994-2006; COM Dio E Carolina Kinston NC 1987-1991; Chair Conv Com Dio E Carolina Kinston NC 1974-1979; S Jas Par Wilmington NC 1972-1993; BEC Dio W Virginia Charleston WV 1965-1972; R S Jn's Ch Huntington WV 1964-1972; Vic Emm Ch Moorefield WV 1962-1964; Vic Emm Ch Keyser WV 1961-1964. Auth, "90 in 90," 2003. bob-ann@earthlink.net

COOK, Carol Lee (Cal) 2235 3rd St, Livermore CA 94550 B San Jose CA 9/3/1949 d Donn Emery Cook & Barbara Jane. BA Macalester Coll 1971; MA San Francisco St U 1974; MDiv CDSP 1991. D 12/8/1990 P 12/1/1991 Bp William Edwin Swing. R S Barth's Epis Ch Livermore CA 1996-2010; Int S Mk's Epis Ch Palo Alto CA 1993-1995; S Paul's Epis Ch Walnut Creek CA 1991-1993. carollcook@comcast.net

COOK, Charles James (Tex) Po Box 2247, Austin TX 78768 B Pampa TX 8/30/1944 s Charles Buckler Cook & Jeanee Elizabeth. BA Drake U 1966; Theol Stds Ecumencial Inst 1973; MDiv Epis TS of The SW 1974. D 6/8/1974 P 4/1/1975 Bp Willis Ryan Henton. m 6/12/1965 Christine White c 3. Mssn Funding Com Dio Texas Houston TX 1996-2009; The Ch of the Gd Shpd Austin TX 1993-2008; Dir Field Ed Epis TS Of The SW Austin TX 1985-2008; Dio No Carolina Raleigh NC 1979-2009; ExCoun Dio No Carolina Raleigh NC 1979-1985; R Ch Of The Gd Shpd S Louis MO 1979-1984; Chair St Ch Com Dio No Carolina Raleigh NC 1978-1979; Chap Of The Cross Chap Hill NC 1975-1979. ATFE 1985; Assn Practical Theol 1985; Cntr for Par Dvlpmt 1995; PEALL 2005. Sub Chapl Venerable Ord S Jn 1994. ccook@etss.edu

COOK, C(harles) Robert (Neb) 2666 El Rancho Rd, Sidney NE 69162 B Potlatch ID 6/2/1930 s Robert Palmer Cook & Lena Myrtle. BS Chadron St Coll; Med U of Nthrn Colorado. D 9/19/2004 Bp Joe Goodwin Burnett. m 6/7/1953 Marian Elizabeth Stanker c 2.

COOK JR, Charles Sydnor (Va) PO Box 29832, Richmond VA 23242 **Died 5/21/2010** B Danville VA 1/4/1936 s Charles Sydnor Cook & Lillian. BA U of Virginia 1958; MDiv Wesley TS 1961; Cert VTS 1962; CP VTS 1977; VTS 1999. D 6/22/1962 Bp George P Gunn P 6/24/1963 Bp David Shepherd Rose. c 2. Life Mem Viva-Alum Assn 1980; Ord of S Lk; The Jefferson Soc, U of Virginia 1955; Thos Jefferson Soc Alum 2008. Thos Jefferson Soc of Alum U of Virginia 2008; Jefferson Soc Gavel for Publ Spkng U of Virginia Charlottesville VA 1955; Jefferson Soc Cert of Spec Merit U of Virginia Charlottesville VA 1955. cookcb@earthlink.net

COOK, Deborah A (NJ) 47 Birch Dr, Jackson NJ 08527 B Ft Dix NJ 3/27/1961 d John J Kuper & Marilyn Driver. BS Trenton St Coll 1983; MDiv GTS 2007. D 6/9/2007 P 12/22/2007 Bp George Edward Councell. m 7/14/1984 James R Cook c 2. Assoc R Gr Ch In Haddonfield Haddonfield NJ 2007-2010. motherdebbie@gracehaddon.org

COOK, Diane Elizabeth (O) 2521 W Stockwell Ln, Clinton IA 52732 **Trin Ch Coshocton OH 2009-** B Morristown NJ 7/1/1960 d Richard Francis Cook & I Virginia. BS Iowa St U 1982; MDiv SWTS 1995. D 4/1/1995 P 10/1/1995 Bp Carl Christopher Epting. m 10/28/2010 Douglas M Thibaut. R S Paul's Ch Mt Vernon OH 2000-2005; Chr Epis Ch Clinton IA 1995-1999. Ord Of S Helena. DCOOK44@COLUMBUS.RR.COM

COOK, Edward Richard (NJ) 130 Stoneham Dr, Glassboro NJ 08028 **R S Lk's Ch Woodstown NJ 1993-** B Pennsgrove NJ 7/27/1923 s Edward Cook & Frances. BA Cbury Coll 1950; Ya Berk 1958; Ext Educ Prog Trenton NJ 1961. D 4/29/1961 P 10/28/1961 Bp Alfred L Banyard. c 1. R Gr-S Paul's Ch Mercerville NJ 1969-1989; R Chr Ch So Amboy NJ 1964-1969; P-in-c S Steph's Ch Mullica Hill NJ 1962-1964; D-in-c/P-in-c S Ptr's Ch Clarksboro NJ 1961-1964. OHC. COOKYKAY@AOL.COM

COOK, Ellen Piel (SO) 2768 Turpin Oaks Ct, Cincinnati OH 45244 B Woodbury NJ 9/28/1952 d Gerhardt Piel & Mary. BA U Of Toledo Toledo OH 1973; PhD U Of Iowa Iowa City IA 1977; Angl Acad 2006. D 5/13/2006 Bp Kenneth Lester Price. m 5/31/1980 David Piel Cook c 2. ellen.cook@uc.edu

COOK II, Harry Theodore (Mich) 3114 Vinsetta Blvd, Royal Oak MI 48073 B Detroit MI 2/4/1939 s Harry Theodore Cook & Bessie Alice. BA Albion Coll 1961; BD Garrett Evang TS 1964. D 12/23/1967 Bp Richard S M Emrich P 4/27/1968 Bp Archie H Crowley. m 11/3/1979 Susan Chevalier c 2. R S Andr's Ch Clawson MI 1988-2009; R Emm Ch Detroit MI 1969-1979; Asst R Chr Ch Detroit MI 1967-1969. Auth, "Resonance," Polebridge Press, 2011; Auth, "A Humanist Manifesto," Polebridge Press, 2011; Auth, "Asking," WIpf & Stock, 2010; Auth, "Findings," Ch Pub Grp, 2003; Auth, "Seven Sayings Of Jesus," Vintage Press, 2001; Auth, "Devoted Heretic," Cntr For Rational Chrsnty, 1999; Auth, "Chrsnty Beyond Creeds," Cntr For Rational Chrsnty, 1997. Civil Libertarian of the Year Michigan ACLU 1998; Marg Sanger Awd Planned Parenthood of Michigan 1995; Loundy Prize in Hebr Garrett TS 1962. revharrytcook@aol.com

COOK, Harvey Gerald (Az) 20129 N Painted Sky Dr, Surprise AZ 85374 B Chester PA 5/13/1933 s Walter Joseph Cook & Elsie May. BS Penn 1955; M Ed Penn 1956; MDiv SWTS 1965; DMin McCormick TS 1975. D 6/29/1965 P 6/29/1966 Bp Thomas Augustus Fraser Jr. m 11/8/1960 Betty Lou Blackwell c 3. R Chr Ch Of The Ascen Paradise Vlly AZ 1989-1998; Dioc Coun Dio So Carolina Charleston SC 1982-1989; Stndg Com Dio So Carolina Charleston SC 1978-1987; Dioc Coun Dio So Carolina Charleston SC 1975-1978; R Trin Ch Myrtle Bch SC 1970-1989; Asst S Lk's Ch Salisbury NC 1965-1968. Auth, "Vietnam," *Living Ch.* cooksurpri@aol.com

COOK, Heather Elizabeth (Eas) 4325 Cabin Creek-Hurlock Rd, Hurlock MD 21643 **Cn to the Ordnry Dio Easton Easton MD 2005-** B Syracuse NY 9/21/1956 d Halsey Moon Cook & Marcia Mary. BA Queens U, Can 1974; MDiv GTS 1987; Kibbutz Mishmar Ha'Emek Hebr Lang 1988. D 6/20/1987 Bp A(lbert) Theodore Eastman P 4/30/1988 Bp A(rthur) Heath Light. Cn for Mssn Dio Cntrl New York Syracuse NY 2004-2005; R S Andr's Epis Ch York PA 1994-2004; Asst R S Matt's Ch Bedford NY 1990-1994; Chapl Stuart Hall Staunton VA 1987-1990. "Connecting at the Roots," *Estrn Shore Epis*, Dio Easton, 2007; "God Loves a Broken Heart," *The Mssngr*, Dio Cntrl New York, 2005. heather@dioceseofeaston.org

COOK, James Bonham (Kan) 5325 Nieman Rd, Shawnee KS 66203 **Congrl Dvlpmt Cmsn Dio Kansas Topeka KS 2004-; R S Lk's Epis Ch Shawnee KS 1994-** B Charlottesville VA 9/6/1957 s Henry Morgan Cook & Nancy Leontine. BS Trin U San Antonio TX 1980; MDiv VTS 1989. D 6/4/1989 Bp John Herbert MacNaughton P 12/10/1989 Bp Earl Nicholas McArthur Jr. m 4/28/1984 Peggy L Roper c 2. Coun of Trst Dio Kansas Topeka KS

2005-2008; Happ Advsry Bd Dio W Texas San Antonio TX 1990-1992; Asst R St Fran Epis Ch San Antonio TX 1989-1994. rector@stlukes.net

COOK, James Brian (SeFla) 13000 Saint David Road, Minnetonka MN 55305 **R S Mk's Ch Palm Bch Gardens FL 2007-** B Elkhorn WI 7/31/1958 s Robert B Cook & Verone H. BA U of Wisconsin 1980; MA U of Wisconsin 1982; MDiv STUSo 1993. D 6/19/1993 P 1/8/1994 Bp Don Adger Wimberly. m 10/29/1983 Karen A Asmus c 2. Chr Ch Red Wing MN 2002-2003; R The Epis Par Of S Dav Minnetonka MN 1998-2002; R S Lk's Ch Whitewater WI 1995-1998; Assoc R Ch Of The Ascen Frankfort KY 1993-1995. jasbcook@aol.com

COOK, James Harrison (Minn) 317 Franklin St, Red Wing MN 55066 B Red Wing MN 9/6/1920 s Harry Cleveland Cook & Alvida Caroline. BA U MN 1942; Untd TS of the Twin Cities 1977. D 6/30/1969 Bp Hamilton Hyde Kellogg P 6/25/1977 Bp Philip Frederick McNairy. c 3. Long Term Supply S Matt's Epis Ch Chatfield MN 1990-1998; Asst Chr Ch Red Wing MN 1969-1986.

COOK JR, Joe Jr (Mass) 28 Highland Ave, Roxbury MA 02119 B 6/11/1946 D 6/5/1972 Bp Robert Lionne DeWitt P 8/1/1976 Bp Morris Fairchild Arnold.

COOK, Johnny Walter (CGC) 115 S. Conception, Mobile AL 36602 **Dn Chr Ch Cathd Mobile Mobile AL 2003-; Cn S Matt's Cathd Dallas TX 2003-** B Corpus Christi TX 4/23/1946 s Homer Edgar Cook & Floris Lillian. BA U of Texas 1967; MDiv Epis TS of The SW 1984. D 6/26/1984 Bp Gordon Taliaferro Charlton P 1/28/1985 Bp Maurice Manuel Benitez. m 1/27/1968 Mary Potchernick c 4. Stndg Com Dio Cntrl Gulf Coast Pensacola FL 2005-2009; Stndg Com Dio Dallas Dallas TX 2002-2003; Exec Coun Dio Dallas Dallas TX 1998-2002; R S Lk's Epis Ch Dallas TX 1997-2003; R S Cyp's Ch Lufkin TX 1989-1997; Exec Bd Dio Texas Houston TX 1988-1996; Epis TS Of The SW Austin TX 1986-1996; R Trin Epis Ch Jasper TX 1986-1989; Asst R S Jas The Apos Epis Ch Conroe TX 1984-1986. Ord of St. Jn 2001. cook6718@bellsouth.net

COOK, Kay Kellam (U) 2425 Colorado Ave, Boulder CO 80302 **S Aid's Epis Ch Boulder CO 2008-** B Houston TX 10/11/1939 d Glenn Curtis Kellam & Amy Geraldine T. BA Lamar U 1968; MA Lamar U 1972; PhD U CO 1991. D 6/9/2007 P 1/12/2008 Bp Carolyn Tanner Irish. m 6/22/1991 Douglas Burger c 3. kaycook@saintaidans.org

COOK, Lilian Lotus Lee (RG) 2114 Hoffman Dr Ne, Albuquerque NM 87110 B San Francisco CA 12/3/1932 d Frank Eric Russel Lee & Eleanor Katherine. AA Monterey Peninsula Coll 1953. D 5/23/1988 Bp William Davidson. m 4/20/1974 Pleas M Cook. D S Chad's Epis Ch Albuquerque NM 1988-2005. DOK. pclil@aol.com

COOK, Patricia Ann (NAM) PO Box 85, Bluff UT 84512 **Assoc S Jn The Baptizer Bluff UT 2010-; Assoc S Mary Of-The-Moonlight Bluff UT 2010-** B Chicago IL 7/26/1941 d William G Herndon & Linda Alverta R. D 12/13/2005 Bp Mark Lawrence Mac Donald P 8/28/2010 Bp David Earle Bailey. m 5/20/1994 John Bond c 5. cookandbond@msn.com

COOK, Paul Raymond (WMo) No address on file. B Gloucester UK 5/5/1943 s George Raymond Cook & Margaret. ThL Jn Wollaston Theol Coll Au 1966. Trans from Anglican Church Of Australia 2/1/2000 Bp Barry Robert Howe. m 8/9/1986 Yvonne Elizabeth Baker. S Mary's Epis Ch Kansas City MO 2000-2002.

COOK, Peter John Arthur (WLa) 4100 Bayou Rd, Lake Charles LA 70605 **R S Mich And All Ang Lake Chas LA 1991-** B Cambridge UK 5/27/1942 s Alan Jn Cook & Elizabeth F. BA Reading U 1964; MA Brandeis U 1966; Trin TS 1971; PhD Queens U 1981. Trans from Church Of England 7/1/1988 Bp James Barrow Brown. m 7/24/1971 Nancy Nordquist c 4. Epis HS Baton Rouge LA 1988-1991. Auth, "Wolfhard Pannenberg: A Post Enlightenment Theol," *Churchman*; Auth, "Wolfhard Pannenberg," *New Dictionary Of Theol*. nnord@cox-internet.com

COOK, Robert Bradley (Pa) 600 E. Cathedral Road #B-301, Philadelphia PA 19128 **Died 1/31/2010** B Providence RI 6/27/1925 s Arthur Thomas Cook & Gladys S. BA Br 1951; MDiv CDSP 1954. D 6/20/1954 P 3/5/1955 Bp John S Higgins. c 2.

COOK JR, Robert Bruce (NC) 8400 Goose Landing Ct, Browns Summit NC 27214 B Attleboro MA 12/21/1943 s Robert Bruce Cook & Elizabeth Ann. BS Nthrn Michigan U 1967; Wayne 1970; MDiv EDS 1973; DMin STUSo 1979. D 6/30/1973 P 6/25/1974 Bp H Coleman McGehee Jr. m 11/1/1987 Sandra Mastin c 3. S Andr's Ch Greensboro NC 2009-2010; Int S Mary's Epis Ch High Point NC 2008-2009; Chair of Mnstry and Mssn Event Dio No Carolina Raleigh NC 2006-2008; R Ch Of The Epiph Eden NC 2003-2008; R Gr Epis Ch Lexington NC 1997-2001; Chair of Sprtl Formation Cmsn Dio No Carolina Raleigh NC 1991-1996; Sprtl Advsr Curs Dio No Carolina Raleigh NC 1990-1993; S Fran Ch Greensboro NC 1986-2003; Alco & Substnce Abuse Com Dio Cntrl Florida Orlando FL 1983-1986; R S Dav's Epis Ch Lakeland FL 1980-1986; Asst To Bp - Yth Mnstry & Ce Dio SE Florida Miami FL 1977-1980; Educ Com Dio SW Florida Sarasota FL 1975-1977; Cur S Mary's Par Tampa FL 1975-1977; Asst S Jn's Ch Plymouth MI 1973-1975. Auth, "Practical Aspects Rel Educ In Parishes," Sewanee/Vanderbelt Press, 1979; Auth, "Mgmt Theory & Pract," Wayne Press, 1969. Rea. rcookjr@triad.rr.com

COOK, Thomas R (Pa) 301 N. Chester Rd., Swarthmore PA 19081 **R Trin Ch Swarthmore PA 2007-** B Eustis FL 8/29/1963 s Robert Cook & Katherine Elizabeth. BA U of Florida 1985; MDiv STUSo 1997. D 5/31/1997 P 2/10/1998 Bp Charles Farmer Duvall. m 8/11/1990 Britton B Barrs c 3. R Gr Epis Ch Medford MA 2001-2007; Asst R All SS Epis Ch Mobile AL 1997-2001. thomascook12@comcast.net

COOK, William E (Tex) 11245 Shoreline Dr., Apt 308, Tyler TX 75703 **Vic S Lk's Epis Ch Lindale TX 2009-** B DeQueen AR 8/21/1938 s William Elbert Cook & Edith May. BA Rice U 1960; BS Rice U 1961; PhD Van 1969; MDiv Epis TS of The SW 1983. D 6/21/1983 Bp Gordon Taliaferro Charlton P 1/1/1984 Bp Maurice Manuel Benitez. m 4/19/1963 Joan Price c 2. R S Fran Epis Ch Tyler TX 1986-2004; Vic All SS Epis Ch Crockett TX 1983-1986; Vic H Innoc' Epis Ch Madisonville TX 1983-1986. Auth, "A Digital Data Acquisition System for use in Nuclear Med," Van Press, 1969; Auth, "Lot Plot Method of Quality Control," *Quality Control mag*, 1963. wecook@suddenlink.net

COOK OJN, Winifred Rose (Mich) PO Box 287, Onsted MI 49265 B Jackson MI 3/14/1956 d Benjamin Charles Fisher & Joyce Suzanne. Whitaker Inst 2011. D 5/24/2011 Bp Wendell Nathaniel Gibbs Jr. m 8/3/1991 Michael Garry Cook. banditcook3@att.net

COOKE, Barbara Jane (NC) 401 Pinewood Rd, Asheboro NC 27205 **The Epis Ch Of Gd Shpd Asheboro NC 2007-** B Buffalo NY 3/14/1950 d James Arthur Cooke & Katherine Dorothy. MS OH SU 1979; MDiv Methodist TS In Ohio 1994; DAS VTS 2002. D 6/22/2002 Bp Michael Bruce Curry P 4/5/2003 Bp J(ames) Gary Gloster. m 6/9/1973 James Lester Baker c 3. Int S Thos Epis Ch Sanford NC 2007-2009; Int S Paul's Epis Ch Smithfield NC 2006-2007; Vic S Jn's Ch Henderson NC 2002-2006. bjcooke58@gmail.com

COOKE, Bruce Henry (Va) 117 Wagon Wheel Trl, Moneta VA 24121 B Flint MI 6/14/1923 s Herschel Emery Cooke & Alena. BA U MI 1946; STM EDS 1949; Cert U of Maryland 1985; MED U of Maryland 1985. D 7/24/1949 P 2/3/1950 Bp Richard S M Emrich. m 7/14/1984 Janice M Warner c 6. Organizing Pstr Trin Ecum Ch Moneta VA 1988-1991; Asst S Ptr's Epis Ch Arlington VA 1983-1988; Bp Of ArmdF- Epis Ch Cntr New York NY 1975-1980; Dio Iowa Des Moines IA 1970-1980; Excoun Dio Iowa Des Moines IA 1970-1975; Dn Trin Cathd Davenport IA 1969-1973; R Calv Ch Columbia MO 1965-1969; Assoc S Ptr's Epis Ch St Louis MO 1962-1965; Excoun Dio Wyoming Casper WY 1955-1962; R S Alb's Ch Worland WY 1955-1962; R S Jas Ch Riverton WY 1952-1955; Cur Chr Ch Detroit MI 1949-1950. Legion Of Merit USAF 1980. bhcjmc@aol.com

COOKE, Catherine Cornelia Hutton (Vt) 500 South Union, Burlington VT 05401 **Archd Cathd Ch Of S Paul Burlington VT 1989-** B San Antonio TX 1/2/1944 d William Carl Hutton & Catherine Adelaide. U MI 1963; AS Pur 1965; BS Bos 1967; U of Pennsylvania 1974. D 8/24/1988 Bp Daniel Lee Swenson. m 1/20/1968 Roger Lee Cooke c 3. NAAD. ccooke@stpaulscathedralvt.org

COOKE, C(hester) Allen (ETenn) 2124 Carpenter's Grade Road, Maryville TN 37803 B Memphis TN 8/14/1931 s H Brent Cooke & Dorothy. BA Rhodes Coll 1953; MDiv EDS 1956; Fllshp Coll of Preachers 1967. D 7/3/1956 Bp Theodore N Barth P 1/1/1957 Bp John Vander Horst. m 2/2/1960 Sara Dee Goodloe c 3. R Trin Epis Ch Florence AL 1986-1994; R S Geo's Ch Germantown TN 1971-1985; R S Andr's Ch Maryville TN 1967-1971; Asst Ch Of The Gd Shpd Lookout Mtn TN 1961-1963; P-in-c S Thaddaeus' Epis Ch Chattanooga TN 1961-1963; Cur Chr Ch Cathd Nashville TN 1959-1961; P-in-c S Mk's Ch Copperhill TN 1956-1959. revcooke@bellsouth.net

COOKE, Douglas Tasker (Ct) 19 Ridgebrook Dr, West Hartford CT 06107 B Stamford CT 5/19/1934 s Tasker James Cooke & Evelyn Delphine. BA Hob 1956; MDiv Ya Berk 1959. D 6/11/1959 Bp Walter H Gray P 3/5/1960 Bp John Henry Esquirol. m 4/11/1970 Ann B Bussemey c 2. Cn Dio Connecticut Hartford CT 1969-1995; R All SS Epis Ch Oakville CT 1962-1970; Cur S Jn's Ch New Milford CT 1959-1962. Hon Cn Chr Ch Cathd 1995. dougann@comcast.net

COOKE, Hilary Elizabeth (Ind) 1948 Indian Trail Dr, West Lafayette IN 47906 **Asst St Johns Epis Ch Lafayette IN 2008-** B Burlington VT 4/2/1977 d Roger Lee Cooke & Catherine Hutton. BA Bryn 1998; MDiv PrTS 2002. D 6/4/2005 P 5/1/2006 Bp Thomas C Ely. m 8/7/2004 Gregory T Buzzard c 2. hilarycookebmc@yahoo.com

COOKE, Hugh Mabee (EpisSanJ) 67 W Noble St, Stockton CA 95204 **D S Jn's Epis Ch Stockton CA 2000-** B Omaha NE 4/22/1923 s Layton Willard Cooke & Margaret Christie. BS U of Nebraska 1948; MNS Arizona St U 1965; MS Utah St U 1973; BTh Sch for Deacons 1985. D 6/21/1987 Bp Victor Manuel Rivera. m 6/5/1965 Mildred Shannon Cooke. D H Cross Epis Mssn Stockton CA 1987-1999. humila@comcast.net

COOKE JR, James Coffield (EC) 201 Beth St, Greenville NC 27858 **Supply P S Jn's And S Mk's Grifton NC 2004-** B Kinston NC 3/25/1940 s James Coffield Cooke & Iris Henderson. BA U NC 1962; MDiv STUSo 1967. D 6/29/1967 P 1/6/1968 Bp Thomas H Wright. m 12/22/1962 Bonnie Lynn Jones c 2. Supply P Trin Epis Ch Chocowinity NC 2001-2004; R S Anne's Epis Ch Jacksonville NC 1987-2000; Cn for Mnstry Dio Maryland Baltimore MD 1981-1987; Assoc R S Anne's Par Annapolis MD 1975-1981; R S Paul's Epis Ch Clinton NC 1972-1975; Asst R S Jn's Epis Ch Wilmington NC 1967-1972. Chapl Ord of S Lk 1968-2000. jccooke@suddenlink.net

COOKE, James Daniel (Ct) 23 Parsonage Road, HIgganum CT 06441 B New Brunswick NJ 11/17/1967 s George Vaughan Cooke & Priscilla Kathleen. BS Boston Coll 1989; MDiv PrTS 1993; CAS Ya Berk 1996; ThM Yale DS 1996. D 6/20/1998 Bp Herbert Thompson Jr P 1/9/1999 Bp Clarence Nicholas Coleridge. m 11/13/1993 Judith Marie Meyers c 1. Asst S Jn's Epis Ch Essex CT 2000-2001; Cur S Mary's Epis Ch Manchester CT 1998-2000. Assn of CPE 2002; Assn of Profsnl Chapl 2002. cooke.james@sbcglobal.net

COOKE, Mildred Shannon (EpisSanJ) 67 W Noble St, Stockton CA 95204 **Died 11/18/2009** B New Haven CT 7/5/1919 d Frederick William Erlingheuser & Marie Martha. AA San Joaquin Delta Coll 1974; BA California St U 1980; BTh California Sch for Deacons 1985. D 6/21/1987 Bp Victor Manuel Rivera. m 6/5/1965 Hugh Mabee Cooke. NAAD 1988. cookes@mailstation.com

COOKE, Nicholas Francis (EO) Po Box 1001, La Grande OR 97850 **Died 12/11/2009** B Salt Lake City UT 4/9/1932 s Nicholas Francis Cooke & Mary Louisa. Amer Bible Coll; E Oregon U 1980. D 1/18/1983 Bp Rustin Ray Kimsey. Soc Of S Fran.

COOKE, Peter Stanfield (NJ) 16 Brandywyne, Brielle NJ 08730 B New York NY 9/4/1926 s John Bailey Cooke & Cecilia. USNA 1948; Drew U 1951; BA Monmouth U 1962. D 4/19/1969 P 10/25/1969 Bp Alfred L Banyard. m 9/10/1994 Mary Cooke c 2. Int Ch Of S Mich The Archangel Wall Township NJ 1995-1996; Vic S Mk's Epis Ch Keansburg NJ 1992-1995; Int Chr Ch So Amboy NJ 1989-1991; Int S Jn's Ch Eliz NJ 1988-1989; Vic S Jn's Ch Sewaren NJ 1984-1986; R S Raphael The Archangel Brick NJ 1974-1981; Asst The Ch Of S Uriel The Archangel Sea Girt NJ 1969-1973. Lambda Sigma Tau 1962. petercookesr@aol.com

COOKE, Philip Ralph (ECR) 17740 Peak Ave, Morgan Hill CA 95037 **R S Jn The Div Epis Ch Morgan Hill CA 2001-** B Chicago IL 7/11/1950 s Ralph Eugene Cooke & Celesta Nadine. BA U MN 1976; MDiv Nash 1981. D 6/20/1981 P 6/10/1982 Bp A Donald Davies. m 11/23/1977 Karen Gay Bauman c 2. R S Greg's Epis Ch Mansfield TX 1983-1984; Cur S Jn's Ch Ft Worth TX 1981-1983. philipcooke@msn.com

COOL, Opal Mary (Neb) 3525 N. 167Th Cir. Apt. 206, Omaha NE 68116 B Scotts Bay Canada 9/8/1926 d Truman Alfred Corkum & Ruth Helen. EFM STUSo 1996. D 4/7/1999 Bp James Edward Krotz. c 2. cooldeacon@jun.com

COOLEY, Andrew A (Colo) 2200 Loyola Ave, Fort Collins CO 80525 **Int R S Lk's Epis Ch Ft Collins CO 2011-; Dep GC Dio Colorado Denver CO 1997-** B Meeker CO 8/25/1957 s Frank Gideon Cooley & Carolyn. BA U MN 1980; MDiv GTS 1985. D 6/14/1985 P 12/18/1985 Bp William Carl Frey. m 5/18/1985 Teresa Jean Trimboli c 1. Int Chr Epis Ch Aspen CO 2011; R S Mk's Epis Ch Durango CO 1995-2011; S Pat's Epis Ch Pagosa Sprg CO 1985-1987. acooley755@aol.com

COOLIDGE, Edward Cole (Ct) 43 Spruce Ln, Cromwell CT 06416 B Beverly MA 12/8/1929 s William Humphries Coolidge & Elanor. BA Dart 1952; MDiv UTS 1955; Cert GTS 1963. D 6/11/1963 Bp Walter H Gray P 3/21/1964 Bp Joseph Warren Hutchens. m 8/23/1952 Joy Searle c 4. Sr. Mentor Annand Prog Ya Berk New Haven CT 1991-1999; Asst Ch Of S Jn By The Sea W Haven W Haven CT 1989-1991; Asst R Ch Of The H Trin Middletown CT 1983-1989; Cmnty Action For Grtr Middletown Inc E Hampton CT 1971-1983; R Chr Epis Ch Middle Haddam CT 1968-1971; Asst S Paul And S Jas New Haven CT 1963-1968. tedcoolidge2@att.net

COOLIDGE, Robert Tytus (Cal) PO Box 282, Westmount QC H3Z 2T2 Canada B Boston MA 3/30/1933 s Lawrence Coolidge & Victoria Stuart. BA Harv 1955; MA U CA 1957; BLitt Oxf 1966; Cert Montreal TS 2002. D 7/29/1967 Bp John Melville Burgess. Auth, "Adalbero, Bp of Laon," *Stds in Medieval & Renaissance Hist*, U of Nebraska Press, 1965. Amer Soc of Ch Hist 1965; Eccl Hist Soc 1967; Hist Soc of Ch Hist 2000; Integrity Inc 1996; NAAD 1968; RACA 1985. Fell Royal Hist Soc 1968.

COOLIDGE, William McCabe (NC) 118 Cumberland Ave, Asheville NC 28801 B Battle Creek MI 4/16/1943 s John Coolidge & Alice. U CO 1963; BA MI SU 1965; MBA MI SU 1966; MDiv VTS 1972. D 6/24/1972 P 6/23/1973 Bp Thomas Augustus Fraser Jr. m 7/26/1998 Karen Day c 3. R S Barth's Ch Pittsboro NC 1981-1993; R S Paul's Epis Ch Cary NC 1975-1981; Asst Chap Of The Cross Chap Hill NC 1973-1975.

COOLING, David Albert (USC) 801 Yale Ave Apt 630, Swarthmore PA 19081 **P Assoc Trin Cathd Trenton NJ 2005-** B Los Angeles CA 11/21/1939 s Arthur Albert Cooling & Lois. BA Occ 1961; MS USC 1968; MA U CA 1969; MDiv CDSP 1971; EdD GTF/Oxford 2004. D 10/3/1971 P 4/10/1972 Bp Edwin Lani Hanchett. c 2. P Assoc S Paul's Epis Ch Westfield NJ 1992-2004; P Assoc Trin Ch Columbus OH 1986-1991; Chair, Cont Educ Com CDSP Berkeley CA 1983-1985; Co-Chair, VIM Dio El Camino Real Monterey CA 1982-1985; R Trin Cathd San Jose CA 1981-1985; Dn Gr Cathd San Francisco CA 1978-1979; COM Dio California San Francisco CA 1977-1981; Cn Chncllr & Vice Dn Gr Cathd San Francisco CA 1976-1981; Headmaster S Andr's Ch Saratoga CA 1973-1976; Anglical Consult Cmsn Dio Hawaii Honolulu HI 1972-1973; Headmaster Ch Of The H Nativ Honolulu HI 1971-1973. Advancement Dir of the Year Natl Methodist Hosp and Hlth Assn 2001; V.P. Advancement Meth Hm of N.J. 1992; Corp V.P. Ward, Dreshman and Reinhardt 1986. dcooling@aol.com

COOMBER, Matthew J.M. (ND) 4227 South 2nd Street, Moorhead MN 56560 B 9/9/1974 s James Elwood Coomber & Eleanor Ruth. Ph.D. U of Sheffield; M.Div Trin, Toronto TS, U of T 2005. D 6/15/2005 P 12/17/2005 Bp Michael Gene Smith. m 7/31/2004 Sarah Allison Kading c 1. Auth, "Prophets to Profits: How Prophetic Lit Can Address Landownership Abuse in Corp Globalization," *Bible and Justice: Ancient Texts, Mod Challenges*, Equinox, 2010; Guest Ed, "(Spec Ed of Political Theol)," *Political Theol*, Equinox, 2010; Auth, "Exegetical Notes on 1 Kgs. 17.8-16: The Widow of Zarephath," *Expository Times*, Sage Pub, 2007. European Assn of Biblic Stds 2006; SBL 2004; Soc of OT Stds 2007. Gvnr Gnrl's Silver Medal for highest overall Stndg Trin, U Tor 2005; Gordon Kent Steph Memi Prize for highest Stndg in thir Trin, U Tor 2005; McDonald Prize for Gnrl knowledge of the Engl Bible Trin, U Tor 2005; U of Sheffield OSRS full tuition fee waiver U of Sheffield 2005; Trin Prize for highest Stndg in Hebr Trin, U Tor 2004. coombermatthew@gmail.com

COON, David Paul (Haw) Po Box 690, Kamuela HI 96743 B Flint MI 1/3/1928 s Elmer Floyd Coon & Jane Olga. BA Estrn Michigan U 1949; CDSP 1954; MA MI SU 1967. D 6/18/1954 Bp Richard S M Emrich P 12/21/1954 Bp Harry S Kennedy. m 9/11/1953 Joanne F Fleener c 4. Int S Jas Epis Ch Kamuela HI 1996-1998; S Alb's Chap Honolulu HI 1960-1993; Vic S Phil's Ch Maili Waianae HI 1957-1963; Vic S Jas Epis Ch Kamuela HI 1954-1957. DD CDSP 1971. dpjfcoon@hawaii.rr.com

COON, Nancy Galloway (WTex) 200 Crossroads Drive, Dripping Springs TX 78620 B Gulfport MS 12/19/1942 d Morris Galloway Coon & DruEtta Camp. BS Sam Houston St U 1964; MA Sam Houston St U 1965; MDiv Epis TS of The SW 1994. D 5/22/1994 P 12/3/1994 Bp John Herbert MacNaughton. R The Ch Of The H Sprt Dripping Sprg TX 1997-2010; Asst/Assoc S Jn's Ch McAllen TX 1994-1997. nancygcoon@gmail.com

COONEY, Arthur Ernest (WNY) 67 Highland Ave, Salamanca NY 14779 B Ellicotville NY 10/10/1927 s Louis Vincent Cooney & Mary Elizabeth. S Bonaventure Olean NY 1989; H Rood Sem Liberty NY 1990; Epis TS 2001. D 6/7/2003 Bp J Michael Garrison. m 10/9/1947 Wilma H Wyatt. Int S Barn Ch Franklinville NY 2008.

COONEY, James Francis (O) 384 Burr Oak Dr, Kent OH 44240 **Ch Of S Thos Berea OH 2000-** B Lancaster OH 9/22/1928 s Paul Cooney & Mildred C. BA S Chas Sem Columbus OH 1950; STL Gregorian U 1954; PhD OH SU 1966. Rec from Roman Catholic 8/1/1974. m 6/16/1968 Sondra Louise Miley.

COOPER JR, A(llen) William (Alb) 1365 County Route 60, Onchiota NY 12989 **P-in-c S Jn In The Wilderness (Sum Chap) Onchiota NY 2009-; Chapl Dio Albany Albany NY 2004-; P-in-c S Thos Ch Tupper Lake NY 2001-** B Syracuse NY USA 11/30/1942 s Allen William Cooper & A June. BS SUNY 1965; MDiv Ya Berk 1969. D 6/11/1969 P 6/18/1970 Bp Ned Cole. m 7/23/1966 Margo Kelsey c 2. The Ch Of The Mssh Glens Falls NY 1994-2003; R S Jn's Ch Essex NY 1982-1994; Trin Ch Rochester NY 1979-1982; R S Matt's Epis Ch Horseheads NY 1972-1979; Dio Cntrl New York Syracuse NY 1969-1979. Auth, "Evang: Presenting Chr w Clarity," *(Video w Study Guide)*, Dio Alb, 1989; Auth, "When to Baptize Infants and Young Chld," *LivCh*, 1988; Auth, "The Positive Aspects of Evang," *S Andr's Cross*, 1987. Franciscan OHC 2004. twocoops@roadrunner.com

COOPER, Charles Douglas (SC) 252 S Dargan St, Florence SC 29506 B Lancaster SC 12/6/1944 s Calvin Asa Cooper & Georgia Mildred. BA Cit 1968; MA Furman U 1972; MDiv STUSo 1981. D 6/13/1981 P 5/1/1982 Bp William Arthur Beckham. m 6/24/1969 Elizabeth Cooper c 3. R S Jn's Ch Florence SC 1989-2007; R S Cyp's Ch Lufkin TX 1987-1989; R S Dav's Ch Cheraw SC 1983-1987; Asst S Jn's Epis Ch Columbia SC 1981-1983. ccooper33@sc.rr.com

COOPER, Cricket S (NH) 20 Rock Point Circle, Burlington VT 05408 B Baltimore MD 6/7/1961 d Robert Harris Cooper & Marilyn. BA NWU 1983; GTS 1987; MDiv SWTS 1989. D 6/14/1989 Bp Daniel Lee Swenson P 12/15/1989 Bp Robert Marshall Anderson. m 11/27/1999 Thomas Tuthill. Cn for Liturg Dio New Hampshire Concord NH 2007-2011; R S Andr's Ch New London NH 2003-2011; Assoc S Ptr's Epis Ch St Louis MO 2000-2003; Cn for Liturg, Educ and Admin Chr Ch Cathd S Louis MO 1996-2000; Assoc Ch Of The Redeem Chestnut Hill MA 1995-1996; Assoc S Andr's Ch Wellesley MA 1991-1994; Assoc S Jn The Evang S Paul MN 1989-1990. Auth, "assorted meditations," *Finding God Day By Day*, Forw Mvmt, 2010. Prize For Liturg Chanting 1989; Preaching Awd SWTS 1989. cricket.cooper@uvm.edu

COOPER IV, Francis Marion (CGC) Po Box 1677, Santa Rosa Beach FL 32459 **R Chr The King Epis Ch Santa Rosa Bch FL 2004-; BEC Dio E Tennessee Knoxville TN 1998-** B Fort Myers FL 3/28/1948 s Frank Marion Cooper & Mary Katherine. AA S Petersburg Jr Coll 1968; BA U of W Florida

C

1970; MDiv Nash 1973; PhD U of St. Andrews 1981. D 6/24/1973 P 12/28/1973 Bp William Loftin Hargrave. m 8/22/1969 Martha Virginia Magnon c 2. Rgstr, Sch for Deacons Dio Cntrl Gulf Coast Pensacola FL 2008-2011; Dep, GC Dio E Tennessee Knoxville TN 2003-2006; Bp & Coun Dio E Tennessee Knoxville TN 2003-2004; chair, Dio Theol Com Dio E Tennessee Knoxville TN 1997-2004; R S Jn's Epis Ch Johnson City TN 1997-2004; Dn S Mary's Cathd Memphis TN 1991-1997; Dep, GC Dio W Tennessee Memphis TN 1985-1997; BEC Dio W Tennessee Memphis TN 1984-1990; chair, COM Dio W Tennessee Memphis TN 1983-1997; Secy, Bp & Coun and Dio Conv Dio W Tennessee Memphis TN 1983-1997; Cn Dio W Tennessee Memphis TN 1983-1991; Assoc S Mary's Cathd Memphis TN 1981-1983; Vic S Chad's Ch Tampa FL 1975-1978; Cur St Johns Epis Ch Tampa FL 1973-1975. Auth, "Faith Dvlpmt in Chld: A Strtgy for CE"; Auth, "Blessed are the Peacemakers: A Curric for Chld & Adults"; Auth, "The Background & Dvlpmt of Evang Catholicism". Rutherford Prize for Hist Resrch S Mary's Coll 1981. mvmcoop@aol.com

COOPER, Gale Hodkinson (NC) 1636 Headquarters Plantation Drive, Charleston SC 29455 B Windsor UK 10/11/1944 d Sydney Hodkinson & Elizabeth Rae. AA Sullins Coll 1965; BA U Rich 1967; MDiv UTS Richmond VA 1990; Cert VTS 1990. D 6/2/1990 P 4/6/1991 Bp Peter James Lee. m 11/23/1968 Elliot Cooper c 2. Assoc S Jn's Epis Ch Charlotte NC 2004-2009; Assoc S Jn's Epis Ch Charlotte NC 1996-2001; Assoc Epiph Epis Ch Richmond VA 1991-1995. GALEHCOOPER@YAHOO.COM

COOPER, James Herbert (NY) 74 Trinity Pl Fl 25, New York NY 10006 **Trin Par New York NY 2004-** B Orange NJ 10/30/1944 s Herbert Hannan Cooper & Catharine. BA W&L 1967; MDiv VTS 1970; DMin VTS 1993. D 6/13/1970 Bp Leland Stark P 12/27/1970 Bp Allen Webster Brown. m 9/10/1966 Octavia Wood c 2. Chr Epis Ch Ponte Vedra Bch FL 1970-2004; Asst Min S Ptr's Ch Albany NY 1970-1972. Auth, "Liturg and Wrshp: An Invitation to Cmnty," *Bldg Up The Ch*, Forw Mvmt Press, 1997; Auth, "Chr Piety," *Study & Action in the Hm*, 1993; Auth, "Trng Model for Chal Br," *Aware*, 1981. Compass Rose Soc 1982; Intl Rectors and Deans 2006; OHC 1985. jcooper@trinitywallstreet.org

COOPER, Joseph Wiley (EC) 4925 Oriole Dr, Wilmington NC 28403 B Windsor NC 2/6/1944 s John Wheeler Cooper & Rachel. BA Barton Coll 1967; MDiv VTS 1970. D 6/27/1970 P 3/27/1971 Bp Hunley Agee Elebash. Ch Of The Servnt Wilmington NC 1982-2006; S Paul's In The Pines Epis Ch Fayetteville NC 1976-1982; P-in-c S Mary's Ch Gatesville NC 1971-1974; Asst R S Steph's Ch Goldsboro NC 1970-1971. revjcooper@aol.com

COOPER, Michael Edward (Los) 4018 Vista Ct, La Crescenta CA 91214 **P-in-c S Nich Par Encino CA 2010-; DRE And Yth Dio Los Angeles Los Angeles CA 2005-; Dir Of Yth Mnstrs Dio Los Angeles Los Angeles CA 2002-** B Burbank CA 6/4/1964 ThM Loyola U 2000. D 6/19/2004 P 1/22/2005 Bp Joseph Jon Bruno. m 6/26/1999 Leslie Anne Cooper c 2. Dio Los Angeles Los Angeles CA 2004-2009. mnlcooper@sbcglobal.net

COOPER, Michael Scott (CPa) 181 S 2nd St, Hughesville PA 17737 B New York NY 5/19/1952 s Samuel Cooper & Mildred. NYU 1978; BA Hunter Coll 1984; MDiv UTS 1987. D 6/13/1987 P 1/1/1988 Bp Paul Moore Jr. m 1/30/1982 Yvonne Bayza c 4. R S Jas Ch Muncy PA 1995-2000; Int S Jas' Ch Drifton PA 1993-1995; Assoc R S Steph's Ch Whitehall PA 1991-1993; Int S Anth Of Padua Ch Hackensack NJ 1989-1990; R S Paul's And Resurr Ch Wood Ridge NJ 1988-1991. Ord Of S Ben, Probationer Assn H Cross. Un Schlrshp Uts New York NY 1985. BLUEMYSTICPOET@WINDSTREAM.NET

COOPER, Miles Oliver (CFla) 423 Forest Ridge Dr, Aiken SC 29803 B Saint Paul MN 6/27/1932 s Miles Sherman Cooper & Olive Evelyn. BA U MN 1954; MDiv Bex 1966. D 6/29/1966 Bp Philip Frederick McNairy P 3/1/1967 Bp Hamilton Hyde Kellogg. m 10/27/1956 Nancy A Abbott c 3. S Aug Of Cbury Epis Ch Vero Bch FL 1993-1997; Trin Ch Vero Bch FL 1989-1992; Assoc S Paul's Epis Ch New Smyrna Bch FL 1987-1988; R S Mths Epis Ch Toccoa GA 1985-1987; Int S Paul's Epis Ch Jesup GA 1984-1985; Asst Ch Of The Gd Shpd Jacksonville FL 1967-1968; Cur Geth Ch Minneapolis MN 1966-1967. milescooper@bellsouth.net

COOPER, Norbert Milton (SeFla) 11201 Sw 160th St, Miami FL 33157 **R Ch Of The Ascen Miami FL 1989-** B 4/27/1948 s Milton Cooper & Enid. BA S Aug 1973; MDiv Nash 1976. Rec 1/1/1982 as Priest Bp The Bishop Of Nassau. m 2/24/1979 Beryl Pinder c 1. Vic S Mary Epis Ch Chester PA 1986-1989; R S Ptr's Epis Ch Key W FL 1982-1986; S Andr's and Pentecostal Epis Ch Evanston IL 1982. coop4618@bellsouth.net

COOPER, R(ichard) Randolph (Tex) 4805 E Columbary Dr, Rosenberg TX 77471 B Ashland KY 6/24/1940 s Marian Elizabeth. BA U So 1964; MDiv STUSo 1966. D 6/20/1966 Bp William Loftin Hargrave P 1/6/1967 Bp Henry I Louttit. m 7/10/1965 Susan T Tuthill c 2. Cn Dio Texas Houston TX 1986-1995; R S Geo Ch San Antonio TX 1976-1986; R Trin Epis Ch Baytown TX 1972-1976; R S Chris's Ch TAMPA FL 1969-1972; Cur S Chris's Ch TAMPA FL 1968-1969; Asst Gr Epis Ch Of Ocala Ocala FL 1966-1968. Chapl Ord of S Lk 1970; Reg Wrdn 1975-1982; Treas 1983-1987.

COOPER, Robert Marsh (Ark) 2210 Windsor Ct, Little Rock AR 72212 B Salisbury NC 5/19/1935 s Robert Howard Cooper & Mabel Claire. BA Catawba Coll 1957; STB Ya Berk 1960; STM STUSo 1966; MA LSU 1967; Fllshp Coll of Preachers 1969; D.Div. Van 1972; Fllshp Boston Psychoanalytic Inst 1988. D 6/29/1960 Bp Richard Henry Baker P 12/1/1960 Bp Thomas Augustus Fraser Jr. m 7/1/1988 Ann Hedge-Carruthers. Ch Of The Gd Shpd Little Rock AR 2001-2010; Asst Trin Cathd Little Rock AR 1997-2000; The Samar Cntr Clearwater FL 1990-1997; S Lk's On The Lake Epis Ch Austin TX 1981-1982; Epis TS Of The SW Austin TX 1980-1989; S Simon The Fisherman Epis Ch Port Washington WI 1973-1980; Nash Nashotah WI 1971-1980; Chapl S Aug's Chap Nashville TN 1968-1971; Asst Chapl S Alb's Chap & Epis U Cntr Baton Rouge LA 1963-1968; P-in-c All SS Ch Hamlet NC 1960-1963; P-in-c S Dav's Epis Ch Laurinburg NC 1960-1963. Auth, "ATR". AAPC. SAMDAWG@ARISTOTLE.NET

COOPER, Robert Norman (WLa) 1872 Hoffmann Ln, New Braunfels TX 78132 B New Orleans LA 3/2/1937 s John Edward Cooper & Mildred Ann. BS U of Louisiana 1959; MS U of Louisiana 1963; PhD Texas A&M U 1973; STUSo 1999. D 6/7/1999 P 12/11/1999 Bp Robert Jefferson Hargrove Jr. m 12/16/1989 Sallie C Ilseng c 3. Chr Ch S Jos LA 2001-2009; Gr Ch Waterproof LA 2001-2009; The Epis Ch Of The Gd Shpd Vidalia LA 1999-2001.

COOPER, Stephenie Rose (ECR) 1205 Pine Ave, San Jose CA 95125 B Oakland CA 10/30/1952 BTS Epis Sch for Deacons 2006. D 6/5/2010 Bp Mary Gray-Reeves. goib2you@earthlink.net

COOPER-WHITE, Pamela (At) Columbia Theological Seminary, 701 S. Columbia Drive, Decatur GA 30030 **Asst H Trin Par Decatur GA 2011-** B Lynn MA 10/3/1955 d Thomas White & Constance. BA Bos 1977; MDiv Harvard DS 1983; PhD Harv 1983; MA H Name U 1994; PhD Inst for Clincl Soc Wk Chicago IL 2001. D 6/6/1992 P 12/5/1992 Bp William Edwin Swing. m 4/26/1986 Michael Lee Cooper-White c 3. Asst S Barth's Epis Ch Atlanta GA 2008-2010; Asst Ch Of S Mart-In-The-Fields Philadelphia PA 1999-2008; Prof SWTS Evanston IL 1998-1999; Assoc S Mary's Ch Pk Ridge IL 1994-1998; Asst S Paul's Ch Oakland CA 1992-1993. Auth, "Braided Selves: Collected Essays on Multiplicity, God & Persons," *Braided Selves: Collected Essays on Multiplicity, God & Persons*, Cascade Books, 2011; Auth, "Wmn Out of Ord: Risking Change and Creating Care in a Multi-Cultural Wrld," *Complicated Wmn: Multiplicity and Relationality across Gender, Race, and Culture*, Fortress Press, 2009; Auth, "Healing Wisdom: Mnstry in Depth," *Sacr Space and the Psyche: Reflections on Potential Space and the Sacr Built Environ*, Eerdmans, 2009; Auth, "Many Voices: Pstr Psych in Relational and Theol Perspective," *Many Voices: Pstr Psych in Relational and Theol Perspective*, Fortress Press, 2007; Auth, "The Formation of Pstr Counselors: Challenges and Opportunities," *Thick Theory: Psychol, Theoretical Models, and the Formation of Pstr Counselors*, Haworth Press, 2006; Auth, "Shared Wisdom: Use of the Self in Pstr Care & Counslg," *Shared Wisdom: Use of the Self in Pstr Care & Counslg*, Fortress Press, 2004; Auth, "The Cry of Tamar: Violence Against Wmn," *The Cry of Tamar: Violence Against Wmn*, Fortress Press, 1995; Auth, "Schoenberg & the God-Idea: Moses & Aaron," *Schoenberg & the God-Idea: Moses & Aaron*, UMI Resrch Press, 1985. AAR 1990; AAPC 1989; Assn of Epis Healthcare Chapl (AEHC) 1988; ECF (ECF) Fell 1995; IARPP Intl Assn for Relational Psychoanalysis 2007; Resrch Assoc of the Amer Psychoanalytic Assn 2000; Soc for Pstr Theol 1993; Soc of Angl and Luth Theologians (SALT) 2000; Sprtl Dir Intl (SDI) 2009. Sapientia et Doctrina Awd Ford 2012; Sprt Awd for Cmnty Serv Samar Counslg Cntr Philadelphia 2007; Distinguished Achievement in Resrch & Writing (Natl Awd) AAPC 2005; Fac Writing Prize Inst for Clincl Soc Wk 1999; Cert Fell AAPC 1998; Top 10 Bk Awd Acad of Par Cler 1995. cooperwhitep@CTSnet.edu

COOPRIDER, Sheila Carroll (Mich) 3542 Vestal Loop, Broomfield CO 80023 **Lic to Officiate Dio Colorado Denver CO 2010-** B Buffalo NY 5/14/1942 d Kenneth Frederic Carroll & Jean. BA Sweet Briar Coll 1964; MDiv Aquinas Inst of Theol 1992. D 12/1/1989 Bp Donald Maynard Hultstrand P 4/27/1994 Bp Hays H. Rockwell. m 12/26/1964 Charles E Cooprider c 2. Asst Chr Epis Ch Spotsylvania VA 2002-2009; Non-par Dio Virginia Richmond VA 1999-2001; R S Gabr's Epis Ch Eastpointe MI 1995-1998; Asst R S Jn's Ch St Louis MO 1994-1995; Int S Steph's Ch Ferguson MO 1992-1993; D S Geo's Ch Belleville IL 1989-1992. AFP 1982. cscoop246@aol.com

COOTER, Eric Shane (SwFla) 401 S Broadway, Englewood FL 34223 **R S Dav's Epis Ch Englewood FL 2011-; Mem Dioc Coun Dio SW Florida Sarasota FL 2010-** B Greeneville TN 8/18/1965 s Haskell Harold Cooter & Minnie Ruth. BBA E Tennessee St U 1988; MDiv The TS at The U So 2010. D 12/20/2009 P 6/20/2010 Bp Dabney Tyler Smith. m 5/8/1999 Terri Lynn Eros c 1. P-in-c S Dav's Epis Ch Englewood FL 2010-2011; Asst P S Dav's Epis Ch Englewood FL 2010; Pres St. Lk's Cmnty The TS at The U So Sewanee TN 2009-2010; Admin Lamb Of God Epis Ch Ft Myers FL 2005-2007. ecooter@gmail.com

COPE, Jan Naylor (WA) Washington National Cathedral, 3101 Wisconsin Avenue, NW, Washington DC 20016 **Cler Dep to GC Dio Washington Washington DC 2011-; Vic Cathd of St Ptr & St Paul Washington DC 2010-;**

Resolutns Com Dio Washington Washington DC 2010- B Corpus Christi TX 2/9/1956 d Glen Rafe Naylor & Jeannine Withington. BA Trin U San Antonio TX 1978; MDiv Wesley TS 2007. D 6/9/2007 P 1/19/2008 Bp John Chane. m 5/22/1993 John Cope c 1. Assoc R S Dav's Par Washington DC 2007-2010. Compass Rose Soc 1999. jcope@cathedral.org

COPE, Marie Swann (USC) 101 St. Matthew's Ln, Spartanburg SC 29301 B Fletcher NC 3/24/1976 d William Cecil Swann & Brenda Durfee. BA Furman U 1998; MDiv VTS 2002. D 6/8/2002 P 12/21/2002 Bp Robert Hodges Johnson. m 6/15/2002 Hayne Carlisle Cope c 2. Asst S Matt's Epis Ch Spartanburg SC 2009-2010; Assoc Ch Of The H Cross Tryon NC 2006-2008; Ch Of The Redeem Shelby NC 2006. marie.cope@gmail.com

COPELAND, Richard (Dal) 1141 N Loop 1604 E, Suite 105-614, San Antonio TX 78232 B San Angelo TX 1/15/1938 s Gay Yates Copeland & Ester Lou. BA Baylor U 1960; MDiv Nash 1974; DMin Pittsburgh TS 1988. D 6/20/1974 Bp Theodore H McCrea P 12/1/1974 Bp A Donald Davies. m 5/2/1964 Andrea Ball c 2. R The Epis Ch Of The Resurr Dallas TX 1989-1999; R S Andr's Epis Ch Panama City FL 1985-1989; R Gr Epis Ch Of Ocala Ocala FL 1981-1985; R Ch Of The Annunc Lewisville TX 1977-1981; Cur The Epis Ch Of The Resurr Dallas TX 1974-1977. Cmnty Cross Of Nails Ord Of S Lk; Trsfg Retreat Monstry. coaching@richardcopeland.com

COPELAND, Wanda Ruth (Minn) 6581 171st Ln Nw, Ramsey MN 55303 **Asst S Chris's Epis Ch Roseville MN 2007-** B Opelika AL 4/7/1956 d Charles William Copeland & Ina. BA Judson Coll 1977; Cert U MN 1984; MDiv SWTS 1994. D 6/29/1994 Bp James Louis Jelinek P 1/7/1995 Bp Sanford Zangwill Kaye Hampton. m 7/20/1985 Thomas Johnson c 2. H Trin Epis Ch Elk River MN 1994-2006. wcopeland0195@gmail.com

COPENHAVER, Robert Thomas (SwVa) 50 Draper Place, Daleville VA 24083 **Chapl Dio SW Virginia Roanoke VA 2000-** B Roanoke VA 9/28/1932 s Marion Bryan Copenhaver & Rena Morton. BA Roa 1954; BD VTS 1962; DMin S Mary's Sem & U Baltimore MD 1984. D 6/25/1962 P 6/6/1963 Bp William Henry Marmion. m 1/30/1954 Margaret Kidd c 4. Int S Mk's Ch Fincastle VA 2010-2011; Int Trin Epis Ch Rocky Mt VA 2005-2007; Int S Jn's Ch Bedford VA 1998-2000; R S Paul's Epis Ch Salem VA 1969-1997; Assoc The Falls Ch Epis Falls Ch VA 1968-1969; R Chr Epis Ch Buena Vista VA 1962-1968; Vic S Jn's Epis Ch Glasgow VA 1962-1966. Auth, "Aging Together In The Faith Cmnty". Cmnty Builders Awd Untd Way Of Roanoke Vlly 2002; Distinguished Bd Mem Awd Virginia Assn Of Chld'S Hm 1999. aypiper@aol.com

COPENHAVER, William R (WNC) 400 El Bethel Rd, Kings Mountain NC 28086 **Died 8/29/2010** B Colliers WV 7/7/1928 s Bernard W Copenhaver & Anna L. LTh Epis TS In Kentucky 1964. D 6/11/1964 P 12/1/1964 Bp Wilburn Camrock Campbell. c 3.

COPLAND, Edward Mark (SwFla) 5615 Midnight Pass Rd, Sarasota FL 34242 **Int, Consult in Appreciative Inquiry Dio SW Florida Sarasota FL 2011-** B Stamford CT 9/25/1943 s Edward Copland & Marjorie. BA Cor 1965; STB GTS 1968; S Jos's 1972. D 6/11/1968 P 3/25/1969 Bp Walter H Gray. m 6/12/1965 Judith M Mix c 2. Via Media Exec Comm Dio SW Florida Sarasota FL 2003-2008; COM Chair Dio SW Florida Sarasota FL 2001-2008; Cn Dio Pretoria Pretoria 1999-2005; R S Bon Ch Sarasota FL 1991-2011; R S Matt's Ch Evanston IL 1976-1991; Dioc Coun Dio Chicago Chicago IL 1976-1982. Cert in Appreciative Inquiry Cler Ldrshp Inst 2010. emcopland@gmail.com

COPLEY, David Mark (NY) 10 West Elizabeth Street, Tarrytown NY 10591 **Epis Ch Cntr New York NY 2006-** B Notingham England 8/19/1960 s Gordon Anthony Copley & Bridget. RGN/RSCN Sheffield Sch of Nrsng Sheffield GB 1984; VTS 2003. D 6/14/2003 Bp Carol Joy Gallagher P 12/6/2003 Bp David Conner Bane Jr. m 12/17/1993 Susan Kay Leckrone c 1. Asst S Jn's Ch Hampton VA 2003-2006; Exec Coun Appointees New York NY 2003-2005. dcopley@episcopalchurch.org

COPLEY, Susan Kay (NY) 10 W Elizabeth St, Tarrytown NY 10591 **R Chr Epis Ch Tarrytown NY 2007-** B Belleville IL 6/17/1954 d Charles Henry Leckrone & Margaret. BA U of Puget Sound 1976; RN S Vinc's Sch of Nrsng 1986; MDiv VTS 2003. D 6/14/2003 Bp Carol Joy Gallagher P 12/6/2003 Bp David Conner Bane Jr. m 12/17/1993 David Mark Copley c 1. Asst S Jn's Ch Hampton VA 2003-2007. rector@christchurchtny.com

COPP, Ann Humphreys (Md) 444 Garrison Forest Rd, Owings Mills MD 21117 B Memphis TN 11/27/1946 d Edward Harrison Humphreys & Ann. BA Connecticut Coll 1968; MA U of Memphis 1980; MDiv Ya Berk 1995. D 11/30/1997 P 5/1/1998 Bp Stewart Clark Zabriskie. m 11/27/1969 Daniel Noyes Copp c 2. Ch Of The Gd Shpd Ruxton MD 2010-2011; Asst S Thos' Ch Garrison Forest Owings Mills MD 1999-2010. annhcopp@gmail.com

COPPEL JR, Stanley Graham (EpisSanJ) Po Box 146, Jamestown CA 95327 **P Epis Dio San Joaquin Modesto CA 2010-** B Berkeley CA 1/20/1942 s Stanley Graham Coppel & Frances. BA U of San Francisco 1977; Bth Dioc.Calif. Sch for Deacons 1987; CEU's CDSP 2009. D 12/3/1988 Bp William Edwin Swing P 2/28/2009 Bp Jerry Alban Lamb. m 5/9/1971 Rebecca Monroe Venegas c 1. D S Mich And All Ang' Epis Ch Standard CA 2000-2004; D S Eliz's Epis Ch So San Francisco CA 1990-1999; D S Ptr's Epis Ch Redwood City CA 1990. Auth, "Police Chapl - Notification of Death," *Diakonia Nwsltr*, 1989. fatherstan@earthlink.net

COPPEN, Christopher J (Spok) 5108 W Rosewood Ave, Spokane WA 99208 B Ottawa CA 7/24/1959 s Peter John Coppen & Edith Doreen. BA U of Arizona 1981; MDiv EDS 1988; MS Estrn Washington U 2000. D 6/2/1988 P 2/1/1989 Bp Joseph Thomas Heistand. m 6/16/1990 Mary Joan Cowley. R S Ptr's Ch Beverly MA 1995-1998; Vic S Thos Ch Dubois WY 1991-1995; Emm Epis Ch Webster Groves MO 1988-1991. "None". None. coppen.cowley@juno.com

COPPICK, Glendon Cleon (Ky) 851 Live Oak Pl, Owensboro KY 42303 B Stigler OK 3/18/1926 s Cleo Clarence Coppick & Gertie Leela. BA TCU 1952; MDiv CDSP 1955; STD SFTS 1987. D 6/21/1955 P 12/21/1955 Bp Charles A Mason. m 11/21/1954 Shirley Jane Pederson c 3. R Trin Epis Ch Owensboro KY 1959-1991; R Ch Of The Gd Shpd Dallas TX 1955-1959. "The Legacy of Trin Epis Ch," 2008; Auth, "Var arts," 2003. gcoppick@bellsouth.net

COPPINGER, Kristina Yvette (WMo) 107 W Perimeter Dr, San Antonio TX 78227 B New York NY 5/9/1962 d Eino Gabriel Nyberg & Amelia Bertha. BS USAF Acad Colorado Sprg CO 1986; MDiv TESM 1994. D 6/5/1994 P 12/12/1994 Bp Edward Lloyd Salmon Jr. m 5/25/1996 Timothy Ronald Coppinger c 3. Trin Epis Ch Lebanon MO 1997-2001; Asst R S Mich's Epis Ch Charleston SC 1995-1997; Asst R S Paul's Epis Ch Lees Summit MO 1994-1995. kcoppinger@satx.rr.com

COPPINGER, Timothy Ronald (WMo) 107 W Perimeter Dr, San Antonio TX 78227 B Neosho MO 5/14/1965 s Fred Ronald Coppinger & Jennie Loutisha. BS K SU 1988; MDiv TESM 1997. D 6/7/1997 P 12/6/1997 Bp John Clark Buchanan. m 5/25/1996 Kristina Yvette Nyberg c 3. Ch Of S Jn The Div Burkburnett TX 2007-2008; P-in-c S Steph's Epis Ch Wichita Falls TX 2004-2007; R S Geo Epis Ch Camdenton MO 1997-2004. kcoppinger@satx.rr.com

CORAM, James M (NC) 12109 Park Shore Ct, Woodbridge VA 22192 B 1/25/1939 BA Amer U; BD VTS. D 6/8/1968 Bp Robert Bruce Hall P 5/31/1969 Bp Samuel B Chilton. m 8/27/1966 Donna Jean Coram. Dio No Carolina Raleigh NC 1973-1976; S Chris's Epis Ch High Point NC 1972-1985.

CORBETT, Ian Deighton (NAM) Po Box 28, Bluff UT 84512 B Birmingham England 8/24/1942 s Jack Brame Deighton Corbett & Marjorie. BA U of Cambridge 1964; MA U of Cambridge 1967; Westcott Hse Cambridge 1969; MS U of Salford Manchester GB 1983. Trans from Anglican Church of Canada 9/1/2001 Bp Steven Tsosie Plummer Sr. U.R. Vic Navajoland Area Mssn Farmington NM 2001-2008; Utah Reg Bluff UT 2001-2008. "Vanishing Lesotho," *Guardian*, Newspapers, 1991; *Love of the Wrld*, Churchman (UK), 1986. iancorbett123@btinternet.com

CORBETT, James Byron David (Los) 10819 SE Rex St, Portland OR 97266 **Asst All SS Ch Portland OR 2009-** B Indianapolis IN 10/29/1940 s James Byron Corbett & Louise Elizabeth. AB USC 1963; MDiv PDS 1968. D 9/7/1968 P 3/8/1969 Bp Francis E I Bloy. m 5/7/1966 Karen Kristine Banham c 1. Int S Jas Epis Ch Midvale UT 2007-2008; Int S Paul's Ch Akron OH 2006-2007; Int S Mk's Epis Ch Casper WY 2005-2006; Int S Steph's Ch Durham NC 2003-2005; Int S Thos Ch Franklin IN 2002-2003; Int The Epis Ch Of The Epiph So Haven MI 2001-2002; Int S Mk's Ch Yreka CA 2000-2001; P-in-c S Augustines In-The-Woods Epis Par Freeland WA 1999; R S Andr's Epis Ch Ojai CA 1977-1993; LocTen S Jn's And H Chld Wilmington CA 1974-1975; Asst S Mary's Par Laguna Bch CA 1971-1973; P-in-c Gr Epis Ch Lake Havasu City AZ 1970-1971; Cur S Patricks Ch And Day Sch Thousand Oaks CA 1968-1970. frjbdc@live.com

CORBETT, John Philip (NwT) P.O. Box 334, Brownfield TX 79316 **D The Epis Ch Of The Gd Shpd Brownfield TX 2002-** B Phoenix AZ 3/26/1935 s Harry Ledyard Corbett & Miriam Madelyn. BA Estrn New Mex U 1960; MA Estrn New Mex U 1967. D 10/4/1989 Bp Terence Kelshaw P 10/18/2008 Bp C(harles) Wallis Ohl. m 9/4/1994 Eunice F Dickey c 2. D S Paul's Ch Artesia NM 1997-2002; D S Thos A Becket Ch Roswell NM 1989-1996. NAAD 1989-2008.

CORBETT-WELCH, Kathleen Ellen (WA) 2218 Hillhouse Rd, Baltimore MD 21207 **R S Lk's Ch Brighton Brookeville MD 2002-** B Boston MA 7/10/1952 d Thomas Matthew Corbett & Ellen Dorothy. Jn Hopkins Hosp; Mt Auburn Hosp Sch of Nrsng Cambridge MA 1974; MDiv Harvard DS 1993. D 10/3/1997 Bp Geralyn Wolf P 6/1/1998 Bp Jane Hart Holmes Dixon. m 9/15/2005 Ellen Whelan Welch. Asstg P Ch Of The Gd Shpd Ruxton MD 2001-2002; Palliative Care Dio Maryland Baltimore MD 1999-2001; Asstg P Ch Of S Steph And The Incarn Washington DC 1997-1999; Dir, Pstr Care Epis Caring Response To Aids Washington DC 1997-1999. ewcw@comcast.net

CORBISHLEY, Frank J. (SeFla) 921 Sorolla, Coral Gables FL 33134 **Trst Palmer Trin Sch Palmetto Bay FL 2006-; Coll Chapl & P in Charge Chap of the Venerable Bede Coral Gables FL 1994-** B Syracuse NY 8/6/1956 s Bernard Joseph Corbishley & M Kathleen. BS Geo 1978; Mstr of Intl Mgmt Amer Grad Sch of Intl Mgmt Glendal 1980; MDiv GTS 1990. D 6/25/1990 P 12/21/1990 Bp Calvin Onderdonk Schofield Jr. m 11/19/1994 Deborah S Sampieri c 3. Trst Palmer Trin Sch Palmetto Bay FL 1993-1998; Assoc S Andr's Epis Ch Palmetto Bay FL 1990-1994. fcorbishley@miami.edu

CORDINGLEY, Saundra Lee (Md) 23 Seneca Road, Rochester NY 14622 **Assoc S Lk And S Simon Cyrene Rochester NY 2010-** B Sodus NY 4/29/1944 d Edward Cordingley & Betty Jane. Monroe Cmnty Coll; BA St. Jn Fisher Coll 1976; MDiv Colgate Rochester TS 1980. D 6/22/1985 P 4/19/1986 Bp William George Burrill. c 3. R Chr Ch W River MD 1996-2010; R Chr Epis Ch Jordan NY 1990-1996; P-in-c S Jn's Ch Sodus NY 1985-1990. AAPC 1992; EPF. scord1944@aol.com

CORIOLAN, Simpson (Hai) Box 1309, Port-Au-Prince Haiti B 1/29/1947 s Paul M Coriolan & Lise. MDiv ETSC 1974. D 9/29/1974 P 5/1/1975 Bp Luc Anatole Jacques Garnier. m 1/1/1977 Marie Carmen Gilberte Archin. Dio Haiti Ft Lauderdale FL 1974-2004. SIMPSONCO47@YAHOO.COM

CORKERN, Matthew Thomas Locy (Nwk) 41 Woodland Avenue, Summit NJ 07901 **R Calv Epis Ch Summit NJ 2011-** B Brookhaven MS 12/14/1972 s Thomas Locy Corkern & Rebecca Coleman. BA U Rich 1995; Cert in Angl Stds Ya Berk 2001; MA U Rich 2001; MDiv Yale DS 2001. D 6/23/2001 P 12/29/2001 Bp Peter James Lee. m Alice Coke-Corkern c 1. R Trin Epis Ch Mobile AL 2008-2011; Cn Res Chr Ch Cathd Nashville TN 2004-2008; Assoc R For Adult Educ S Jn's Epis Ch McLean VA 2001-2004. The Amer Priory Ord of St. Jn 2004; Vergers' Gld of The Epis Ch 2011. rector@calvary-summit.org

CORKLIN, Stanley Earl (Vt) 744 Parker Road, West Glover VT 05875 B Cheyenne WY 11/15/1941 s Jack Earl Corklin & Alsie Ardeth. BA U of Nthrn Colorado 1964; MDiv Nash 1969. D 6/19/1969 Bp James Winchester Montgomery P 12/20/1969 Bp Gerald Francis Burrill. R S Matt's Ch Enosburg Falls VT 1998-2001; Int S Jn's In The Mountains Stowe VT 1993-1994; R Gr Ch Sterling IL 1983-1992; Fin Rev Dio Chicago Chicago IL 1978-1984; R Chr Ch Streator IL 1978-1983; Vic S Jn The Evang Lockport IL 1972-1978; Cur Chr Ch Waukegan IL 1969-1972. Auth, "Hist of S Matt's Ch Enosburg Falls VT," S Matthews Press, 2002. CBS; OHC. loonsongoldenpond@hotmail.com

CORL, James Alexander (CNY) 7502 Northfield Lane, Manlius NY 13104 B Syracuse NY 5/1/1943 s John Merton Corl & Jane Frances. BA Syr 1965; MDiv EDS 1968; DMin VTS 1992. D 6/10/1968 Bp Walter M Higley P 5/28/1969 Bp Ned Cole. m 6/18/1966 Nancy Jane Duckett c 3. R Chr Ch Manlius NY 2001-2008; Dep GC Dio Cntrl New York Syracuse NY 1982-1997; Assoc S Paul's Ch Endicott NY 1970-1980; No Country Mssn Field Dio Cntrl New York Syracuse NY 1968-1970. Soc of S Marg 1983. jimcorl3@mac.com

CORLETT, Diane Bishop (NC) 6901 Three Bridges Cir, Raleigh NC 27613 **R Ephphatha Ch For The Deaf Raleigh NC 1992-; Coordntr Of Deaf Mnstry Dio No Carolina Raleigh NC 1986-** B Durham NC 7/22/1950 d David Melton Bishop & Rachel. U Durham Durham NC; BS Barton Coll 1972; Med U NC 1980; MDiv GTS 1986. D 6/29/1986 Bp Frank Harris Vest Jr P 6/1/1987 Bp Robert Whitridge Estill. m 8/28/1971 Donald F Corlett c 1. R Ch Of The Nativ Raleigh NC 1992-2009; Chr Ch Cleveland NC 1989-1992; Asst to R All SS' Epis Ch Concord NC 1986-1988. Auth, "Joining The Conversation". P Assoc, CHS. Aclu W.W. Finlater Awd Wale Co. Aclu 2002. diane.corlett@hotmail.com

CORLEY, Kathryn Sue (NY) 97 Underhill Rd, Ossining NY 10562 B Decatur IL 3/2/1957 d Kenneth E Bailey & Carol Ann. D 3/18/2000 P 9/16/2000 Bp Richard Frank Grein. m 6/17/1978 David Wayne Corley c 2. S Mary's Ch Of Scarborough Scarborough NY 2008-2010; Gr Ch Hastings On Hudson NY 2007-2008; S Lk's Ch Somers NY 2006-2007; DCE Ch Of S Mary The Vrgn Chappaqua NY 2000-2001.

CORLEY, Robert Michael (Dal) 10837 Colbert Way, Dallas TX 75218 B Dallas TX 5/28/1970 s Jerry Corely & Jerilyn. BA U of Texas; MDiv STUSo 2006. D 6/24/2006 P 3/26/2007 Bp James Monte Stanton. m 5/14/1994 Laura Elizabeth Norman c 2. Cur S Jn's Epis Ch Dallas TX 2006-2011. corley@stjohnsepiscopal.org

CORMENY III, George Franklin (SC) 3559 Stockton Dr., Mt Pleasant SC 29466 **Ch Of The H Cross Sullivans Island SC 2005-** B Atlanta GA 7/26/1972 s George Franklin Cormeny & Jennifery. BA Cit 1994; MDiv TESM 2002. D 6/3/2002 P 12/15/2002 Bp Edward Lloyd Salmon Jr. m 7/12/1997 Angela Stevenson c 2. The Ch Of The Cross Bluffton SC 2003-2005. "One Ch on Two Campuses," *Seed & Harvest*, TESM, 2004. trip@holycross.net

CORNELIUS, John Dale (Alb) 632 Sw Rand Dr, Burleson TX 76028 **Vic Ch Of The H Cross Burleson TX 1999-** B Olean NY 12/30/1948 s Milfred Charles Cornelius & Betty Jane. BA SUNY 1979; MDiv SWTS 1990. D 6/30/1990 P 2/1/1991 Bp Rogers Sanders Harris. m 11/17/1979 Sharyl Martzolf c 3. Ch Of The H Cross Warrensburg NY 2006-2010; Dio Ft Worth Ft Worth TX 1999-2006; R S Mart's Ch Pawtucket RI 1998-1999; Chapl Cathd Of All SS Albany NY 1994-1998; R Zion Ch Hudson Falls NY 1994-1998; R St Chris's Epis Ch Cobleskill NY 1992-1994; R Chr's Ch Duanesburg NY 1991-1994; Cur S Cathr's Ch Temple Terrace FL 1990-1991. Ccu 1998; SocMary 1996; Ssc 2002. frcorny@yahoo.com

CORNELL, Charles Walton (NCal) 813 Mormon St, Folsom CA 95630 B Marysville CA 7/5/1948 s Woodrow Gordon Cornell & Helen Elizabeth. AA Yuba Coll 1968; BS California St U 1971; MDiv Nash 1989. D 6/21/1989 Bp John Lester Thompson III P 12/1/1989 Bp James Barrow Brown. Trin Ch Folsom CA 1998-2011; S Geo's Ch Bossier City LA 1992-1998; R S Jn's Ch Kenner LA 1989-1992. cornellcharles@att.net

CORNELL, Peter Stuart (NJ) 5 Paterson St, New Brunswick NJ 08901 **D Chr Ch New Brunswick NJ 2007-** B Mt Holly NJ 9/23/1955 BS Trenton St Coll 1977; MBA Rutgers-The St U 1996. D 6/9/2007 Bp George Edward Councell. m 10/11/1980 Nancy Kuntz c 1. pc923@att.net

CORNER, Albert Ellison (Mich) 2345 Oxford #311, Berkley MI 48072 **Died 6/25/2010** B Royal Oak MI 4/30/1918 s William Arthur Corner & Rosa Mattie. NWU 1943; Michigan TS 1971. D 7/1/1971 Bp Archie H Crowley. c 3.

CORNER, Cynthia Ruth (Mich) PO Box 287, Onsted MI 49265 B Detroit MI 10/12/1948 d Albert Ellison Corner & Ida May. MA Siena Heights Coll; Total Mnstry Trng in Dio Michigan; BA Adrian Coll 1970. D 5/24/2011 Bp Wendell Nathaniel Gibbs Jr. ccorner@hudson.k12.mi.us

CORNEY, Richard Warren (NY) 224 W 11th St Apt 3, New York NY 10014 **Prof Emer The GTS New York NY 2001-** B Poughkeepsie NY 11/13/1932 s Richard Field Corney & Mabel Cary. BA Leh 1954; STB GTS 1957; ThD UTS 1970. D 6/11/1957 P 12/21/1957 Bp Horace W B Donegan. m 6/21/1958 Susan S Swarts. Asstg P S Jn's Ch New York NY 2001-2009; Prof The GTS New York NY 1971-2000; Asst Prof The GTS New York NY 1964-1971; Instr The GTS New York NY 1960-1964; Fell; Tutor The GTS New York NY 1957-1960. Auth, "The Bk of Amos," Forw Mvmt, 2008; Auth, "Rod And Stff: A Double Image," *On The Way To Nineveh*, Scholars Press, 1999; Auth, "What Does Literal Meaning Mean," *The ATR*, 1998; Auth, "Isaiah L 10," *Vetus Testamentum*, 1976; Contrib, "Interpreter'S Dictionary Of The Bible," Abingdon, 1962. Amer Schools Of Oriental Resrch 1964-2000; Col Fac Seminar on the Hebr Bible 1971; SBL 1957-2000. corney@gts.edu

CORNMAN, Jane Elizabeth (Pa) St. Marys Episcopal Church, 104 Louella Avenue, Wayne PA 19087 **Yth Advsry Bd Dio Pennsylvania Philadelphia PA 2010-; COM Dio Pennsylvania Philadelphia PA 2008-; Assoc R S Mary's Ch Wayne PA 2005-** B Beverly MA 9/15/1967 d John Frederick Haugh & Elizabeth Ann. BA Mssh Coll 1989; MDiv Ya Berk 2005. D 6/4/2005 P 12/17/2005 Bp Charles Ellsworth Bennison Jr. m 10/19/1991 Douglas Cornman c 2. jane_cornman@hotmail.com

CORNNER, Robert Wyman (Los) 8170 Manitoba St., Unit #1, Playa Del Rey CA 90293 **Dn Chr Ch Par Redondo Bch CA 2001-** B Wichita KS 10/14/1946 s William Benjamin Cornner & Charlotte Helene. BA California St U 1969; ETSBH 1982. D 6/19/1982 P 1/22/1983 Bp Robert C Rusack. m 7/1/1992 Madelyn L Rosen c 2. S Geo's Mssn Hawthorne CA 1991; Supply P Dio Los Angeles Los Angeles CA 1990-2001; S Fran' Par Palos Verdes Estates CA 1989-1990; Asst S Cross By-The-Sea Ch Hermosa Bch CA 1982-1987. rwcornner@aol.com

CORNWELL, Marilyn M (Oly) Church of the Ascension, 2330 Viewmont Way Weat, Seattle WA 98199 **R Ch Of The Ascen Seattle WA 2010-** B Davenport IA 12/23/1952 BA U of Texas 1979; PhD U of Texas 1984; MDiv CDSP 2006. D 6/24/2006 Bp Vincent Waydell Warner P 1/11/2007 Bp Bavi Rivera. m 3/10/1979 Robert Cornwell c 1. S Mk's Cathd Seattle WA 2007-2010; Emm Epis Ch Mercer Island WA 2006-2007; Ch Of The Epiph Seattle WA 2006. co-Auth, "Programmatic Stff Care in an Outpatient Setting," *The Journ of Pstr Care & Counslg*, Journ of Pstr Care Pub, 2005. thecornwells@comcast.net

CORREA, Trino Cortes (EpisSanJ) 3345 Sierra Madre, Clovis CA 93619 B MX 6/4/1950 s Rogelio Romero Correa & Concepcion Arellano. Rec from Roman Catholic 4/19/1997 Bp John-David Mercer Schofield. m 1/18/1983 Robertina A Chavez c 4. Vic Our Lady of Guadalupe Fresno CA 1997-2008.

CORREA AMARILES, Maria Ofelia (Colom) Parroquia San Lucas, Cr 80 No 53A-78, Medellin Antioguia Colombia B Valdivia - Antioquia 1/22/1942 d Javier Correa & Rosario. D 6/16/2007 Bp Francisco Jose Duque-Gomez. m 9/15/1972 Horacio Velez c 3. ofeliacorrea@hotmail.com

CORREA GALVEZ, Jose William (Colom) Carrera 6 No 49-85, Piso 2, Bogota Colombia B Casabianca Tolima 9/7/1965 s Fabio Antonio Correa & Maria Teresa. Teologia Rhema Cebco 2008. D 3/22/2009 Bp Francisco Jose Duque-Gomez. rvdocorrea@yahoo.com

CORRELL, Ruth Elaine (Pgh) Po Box 61554, Potomac MD 20859 B Decatur IN 4/12/1947 d George Merlin Correll & Esther Fame. BS Kent St U 1969; Med Kent St U 1971; MA Trin Evang DS Deerfield IL 1975; EdD NYU 1987; TESM 1995. D 6/12/1999 P 2/24/2000 Bp Robert William Duncan. Asst S Fran Ch Potomac MD 1999-2008. Auth, "Why Teach Bible Stories in the Classroom," *NAES*, 1992. rcorrell@fairpoint.net

CORRIGAN, Candice Lyn (Minn) 506 21st St SW, Austin MN 55912 **P Calv Ch Rochester MN 2010-** B Bayshore NY 7/6/1948 d Robert Calvin Corrigan & Arnella Berry. BA Pur 1972; MS Pur 1973; BS U of Kentucky 1979; MS Idaho St U 1985; PhD U of Kentucky 1988; MDiv The GTS 2010. D 7/23/2009 Bp James Louis Jelinek. m 7/18/2000 Johanna Rose Leuchter c 2. P Chr Ch Austin MN 2011. ACPE (ACPE) 2010; Assn of Profsnl Chapl 2010; Beatitudes Soc 2008; Soc for Anthropology & Rel 1993; Soc for Applied Anthropology 1982; Sprtl Dir Intl 2005. cl GTS 2010. ccorrigan@gts.edu

CORRIGAN, Gertrude Lane (NMich) 809 Michael St, Kingsford MI 49802 B 7/2/1927 D 2/29/2004 Bp James Arthur Kelsey.

CORRIGAN, Michael (Mass) Northfield Mount Hermon School, 1 Lamplighter Way #4702, Mt. Hermon MA 01354 B Baltimore MD 10/15/1945 s Daniel Corrigan & Elizabeth. BA Col 1970; MDiv EDS 1973. D 6/9/1973 Bp Paul Moore Jr P 12/9/1973 Bp Daniel Corrigan. m 1/24/1981 Patricia Vallone c 4. R Ch Of Our Sav Brookline MA 1988-2005; Dio Massachusetts Boston MA 1986-1987; Urban Mssn Com Dio Massachusetts Boston MA 1986-1987; R S Jn's Epis Ch Westwood MA 1983-1988; Dio Massachusetts Boston MA 1979-1983; R Ch Of The Gd Shpd Granite Sprg NY 1975-1979; Cur The Ch Of The H Sprt Lake Forest IL 1973-1975. ESMHE.

CORRY, Richard Stillwell (Va) 214 E King St, Quincy FL 32351 B Quincy FL 12/8/1919 s Arthur Corry & Constance. BA U So 1941; MDiv STUSo 1944; MS Bos 1958. D 12/21/1943 P 11/1/1944 Bp Frank A Juhan. c 3. R Gr Ch Millers Tavern VA 1974-1988; R S Paul's Epis Ch Miller's Tavern VA 1974-1988; Asst Truro Epis Ch Fairfax VA 1966-1973; M-in-c Ch Of Our Sav Arlington MA 1960-1962; Ch Of The Gd Shpd Watertown MA 1950-1953; Vic S Mary's Ch E Providence RI 1949-1950; Vic S Mary's Epis Ch Honolulu HI 1948-1949; Asst Ch Of The Gd Shpd Jacksonville FL 1944-1947. rscorry@tds.net

CORSELLO, Dana Colley (Cal) 1755 Clay St, San Francisco CA 94109 **S Lk's Ch San Francisco CA 2009-** B Midland TX 10/17/1963 d Jack Everett Colley & Reba Eileen. BA U of Missouri 1985; MDiv GTS 1999. D 6/5/1999 P 12/1/1999 Bp C(harles) Wallis Ohl. m 6/26/1999 Andrew K Corsello c 2. S Jas' Ch Richmond VA 2001-2009; S Mary's-In-Tuxedo Tuxedo Pk NY 1999-2001; Intern / Consult Epis Ch Cntr New York NY 1997-1998. revdana@stlukessf.org

CORT, Aubrey Ebenezer (SwFla) 2507 Del Prado Blvd S, Cape Coral FL 33904 **TLC-Mnstrs Ch Of The Epiph Cape Coral FL 2009-** B 7/4/1941 s Charles Cort & Hilda. Paralegal Adel 1981; Cert Theol Fndt Mercer TS 1997. D 10/10/2009 Bp Dabney Tyler Smith. m 8/26/1967 Jean Cort c 2. aubreycort11520@yahoo.com

CORTINAS, Angela Maria (SeFla) 333 Tarpon Dr, Fort Lauderdale FL 33301 **Asst P All SS Prot Epis Ch Ft Lauderdale FL 2010-** B Coral Gables, FL 2/25/1970 d Enrique Luz Cortinas & Teodora. BA Florida Int'l U 1992; Masters U of Memphis 1995; MDiv Epis TS Of The SW 2010. D 12/18/2009 Bp Leopold Frade P 7/10/2010 Bp Calvin Onderdonk Schofield Jr. c 1. angela@allsaintsfl.org

CORTRIGHT, Amy Ethel Marie Chambers (Mo) Christ Church Cathedral, 1210 Locust Street, St. Louis MO 63103 **Vic Chr Ch Cathd S Louis MO 2010-** B Washington DC 8/20/1976 MDiv GTS 2004. D 3/13/2004 P 9/18/2004 Bp Mark Sean Sisk. m 9/23/2005 Joseph Michael Cortright Chambers c 2. Assoc Calv Ch Columbia MO 2006-2010; Asst Ch Of The Incarn New York NY 2004-2006. aecortri@mtholyoke.edu

COSAND, Dale Wayne (CFla) Box 228, Radio City Station, New York NY 10101 B Saint Charles IA 5/4/1922 s Floyd Cosand & Vava Gladys. BA U of Nthrn Iowa 1942; BD SWTS 1945; MS CUNY 1962; PhD Col 1964. D 11/30/1945 P 10/4/1946 Bp Elwood L Haines. Asst S Paul's Ch-In-The-Vill Brooklyn NY 1971-1989; S Eliz's Ch Eliz NJ 1965-1968; Serv S Matt's Ch Woodhaven NY 1959-1971; Serv Ch Of S Alb The Mtyr S Albans NY 1956-1959; P-in-c Gr Epis Ch Inc Port Orange FL 1950-1954; R S Paul's Epis Ch New Smyrna Bch FL 1950-1954; Assoc R Ch Of The H Comf Kenilworth IL 1948-1950; Vic S Steph's Ch Spencer IA 1945-1948. mdwc228@verizon.net

COSBY, Arlinda W (Cal) 36458 Shelley Ct, Newark CA 94560 B Oakland CA 6/24/1942 d Richard Henry Wing & Marjorie. BA San Jose St Coll 1963; MA San Jose St Coll 1973; MDiv CDSP 1979. D 6/30/1979 Bp C Kilmer Myers. c 2. D H Cross Epis Ch Castro Vlly CA 1989-2008; D S Jas Ch Fremont CA 1984-2007; Chapl An Epis Mnstry to Convalescent Hospitals (Aemch) Alameda CA 1981-2007; D S Jas Ch Fremont CA 1979-1981. Associated Parishes; NAAD. S Steph'S Awd Naad 1999. disneyla@pacbell.net

COSENTINO, Eric Fritz (NY) 70 Sunset Rd, Montrose NY 10548 **R Ch Of The Div Love Montrose NY 1987-** B Queens NY 12/8/1956 s Jerry Cosentino & Helga Gertrude. BA CUNY 1979; MDiv GTS 1984. D 6/9/1984 Bp James Stuart Wetmore P 12/16/1984 Bp Walter Decoster Dennis Jr. m 6/28/1980 Melinda Boiko c 4. Cur S Eliz's Ch Ridgewood NJ 1984-1987. CBS.

COSMAN, Sandra Lee (Ct) 220 Prospect St, Torrington CT 06790 **Grtr Hartford Reg Mnstry E Hartford CT 2010-** B Manchester CT 7/24/1963 d Gerald Arthur Cosman & Shirley M. MDiv EDS 2007. D 6/14/2008 Bp Andrew Donnan Smith P 1/31/2009 Bp Laura Ahrens. c 1. Cur Trin Ch Torrington CT 2008-2010; S Jn's Epis Ch Vernon Rock Vernon CT 1990-1994. sandra.cosman@gmail.com

COSTAS, Catherine (Cal) 905 W Middlefield Rd Apt 946, Mountain View CA 94043 **ECD Prog Ch Pension Fund New York NY 2010-; D Dio California San Francisco CA 2007-; Supply D Dio California San Francisco CA 2007-; Assoc D in Res S Ptr's Epis Ch Redwood City CA 2007-** B Ames IA 2/6/1965 d James Allen Stephenson & Naomi Ann. BM U of Iowa 1987; BTS Sch for Deacons 2003. D 12/4/2004 Bp William Edwin Swing. Deacons' Exec Coun Dio California San Francisco CA 2007-2009; D Gd Shpd Epis Ch Belmont CA 2004-2007. NAAD 2000. ccostas@yahoo.com

COSTAS, Janis Kathryn (Ind) 318 Main St, New Harmony IN 47631 **P-in-c S Steph's Epis Ch New Harmony IN 2011-** B Gary IN 12/8/1952 d William P Costas & Angie. M.Div Ya Berk 1991; MSW Bos 1996. D 5/6/2006 P 2/25/2007 Bp Granville Porter Taylor. c 2. R S Mk's Epis Ch Aberdeen SD 2007-2011. revkat@mac.com

COSTIN, Richard Banks (CFla) PO Box 623302, Oviedo FL 32762 B Asheville NC 8/11/1941 s Alphens Boyce Costin & Alice Marie. BA U of Washington 1967; MS Pace U 1981. D 12/11/2010 Bp John Wadsworth Howe. m 10/14/1995 Sandra D'Aries c 3. rcostin@cfl.rr.com

COTTER, Barry Lynn (SO) 1864 Sherman Ave Apt 5SE, Evanston IL 60201 B Los Angeles CA 1/16/1943 s Lawrence L Cotter & Frankie Marie. BA USC 1964; PhD Indiana U 1970; MDiv SWTS 1986. D 6/28/1986 Bp James Russell Moodey P 4/1/1987 Bp Duncan Montgomery Gray Jr. m 6/10/1967 Joan Miller c 1. area Mssnr E Cntrl Ohio Area Mnstry Cambridge OH 2000-2006; area Mssnr, eco cluster S Jn's Epis Ch Cambridge OH 2000-2006; area Mssnr, eco cluster S Paul's Ch Martins Ferry OH 2000-2006; R S Ptr's By The Lake Brandon MS 1992-2000; R S Thos Epis Ch Diamondhead MS 1989-1991; Cur S Jn's Epis Ch Ocean Sprg MS 1986-1989. co-Auth, "Pith, Heart, and Nerve: Truman M. Smith: Horticulture as the Way Back," *Ramsey Cnty Hist*, Ramsey Cnty Hist Soc, 2009; co-Auth, "Pith, Heart, and Nerve: Truman M. Smith: From Banker to Mrkt Gardener," *Ramsey Cnty Hist*, Ramsey Cnty Hist Soc, 2008. cotters1864@sbcglobal.net

COTTRELL, Jan M. (Lex) 1445 Copperfield Court, Lexington KY 40514 **R Ch Of The Resurr Jessamine City Nicholasville KY 1993-** B Covington KY 6/29/1955 d Harry Lloyd Meacham & Joan Miriam. BA U Of Kentucky 1977; MA U of Louisville 1981; MDiv Lexington TS 1991; D. Min TS 2000. D 6/9/1991 P 1/1/1992 Bp Don Adger Wimberly. c 2. Ch S Mich The Archangel Lexington KY 1991-1993; Sem Asst S Jn's Ch Versailles KY 1990-1991. jmcottrell@insightbb.com

COTTRILL, C(harles) David (SO) 3724 Mengel Dr, Kettering OH 45429 **Affiliate S Geo's Epis Ch Dayton OH 2010-** B Columbus OH 7/18/1941 s Charles Cottrill & Ruby Esther. Methodist TS In Ohio 1963; BS OH SU 1963; MDiv Bex 1966; DMin Untd TS Dayton OH 1994. D 6/25/1966 Bp Roger W Blanchard P 12/17/1966 Bp William S Thomas. m 12/16/1962 Martha J Davis c 2. Affiliate S Fran Epis Ch Springboro OH 2007-2010; Chapl Epis Ret. Hms. Deupree Hlth Cmnty Cincinnati OH 1996-2007; Trst Dio Sthrn Ohio Cincinnati OH 1993-1996; Asst R Chr Epis Ch Dayton OH 1992-1996; Chapl, USAF Dio Arizona Phoenix AZ 1973-1993; Chapl, USAF Off Of Bsh For ArmdF New York NY 1973-1993; R S Andr's Ch Glendale AZ 1971-1973; Asst R All SS Ch Cincinnati OH 1967-1971; Cur S Steph's Epis Ch Mckeesport PA 1966-1967. Auth, "A Liturg for Celebration of Ret as Redirection," *Untd TS*, 1994. BSA 2048; Epis Hosp & Chapl Assn 1996-2007; Miami Vlly Epis Russian Ntwk 2008; NOEL 1980; SO Affirmative Aging Cmsn 1989-2000. Meritorious Serv Medal w 5 Oak Leaf Clusters USAF 1981; Commendation Medal w Oak Leaf Cluster USAF 1976. davecottrill@rocketmail.com

COUDRIET, Alan P (NwPa) 10 Woodside Ave, Oil City PA 16301 **P-in-c Emm Ch Corry PA 2011-; Alt to GC, 3x's Dio NW Pennsylvania Erie PA 2004-2012** B Clearfield PA 3/22/1954 s Carl Paul Coudriet & Helen Irene. BA Clarion U of Pennsylvania 1976; MDiv Nash 1995. D 3/22/1995 P 10/4/1995 Bp William Charles Wantland. m 10/7/1989 Karen Lynne Schmidt. Int Ch Of Our Sav DuBois PA 2010-2011; Int Trin Memi Ch Warren PA 2009-2010; Mem, Bp Search Com, 2007 - 2008 Dio NW Pennsylvania Erie PA 2007-2008; Mem, Dioc Coun, 2005 - 2008 Dio NW Pennsylvania Erie PA 2005-2011; Chair, COM, 2005 - 2008 Dio NW Pennsylvania Erie PA 2005-2008; R Chr Epis Ch Oil City PA 2003-2008; Vic S Lk's Ch Spooner WI 2002-2003; Dep to GC, 2003 Dio Eau Claire Eau Claire WI 2001-2003; Admin & Fac, Epis Acad, 2000 - 2003 Dio Eau Claire Eau Claire WI 2000-2003; Exam Chapl, 2000 - 2003 Dio Eau Claire Eau Claire WI 2000-2003; Cler Rep to Dom Mssy Partnership (DMP), 1999 - 2003 Dio Eau Claire Eau Claire WI 1999-2003; Pres, Stndg Com, 1999 - 2001 Dio Eau Claire Eau Claire WI 1999-2001; VP of Dio, 1999 Dio Eau Claire Eau Claire WI 1998-1999; Chapl/Instr, Sum Yth Camps, 1997 - 2002 Dio Eau Claire Eau Claire WI 1997-2003; Chair, Cmte on New & Existing Congregations, 1996 - 2000 Dio Eau Claire Eau Claire WI 1996-2001; Vic S Alb's Ch Spooner WI 1995-2003; Mem, Exec Coun, 1995 - 2001 Dio Eau Claire Eau Claire WI 1995-2001; Vic S Steph's Shell Lake WI 1995-2000. fralan@usachoice.net

COUFAL, M(ary) Lorraine (Ind) 3819 Green Arbor Way #812, Indianapolis IN 46220 B Atkinson NE 3/6/1938 d Edward John Coufal & Helen Mary. BA Regis Coll Denver CO 1964; MA Webster U 1973; MA Seattle U 1980; MDiv Cntrl Bapt TS 1985; DMin GTF 1989; U So 1991. D 11/8/1992 P 6/1/1993 Bp Craig Barry Anderson. Int S Lk's Epis Ch Shelbyville IN 2001-2003; Intern S Tim's Ch Indianapolis IN 2001-2002; Assoc Calv Cathd Sioux Falls SD 1992-1998. Auth of article, ""God's Messages,"" *GTF Fellows YearBook*, GTF, 1989. AEHC 1993; Assn of Profsnl Chapl - Cert Chapl 1982; Int Mnstry

C

Ntwk 2001; Sprtl Dir of Cntrl Indiana Ntwk 2007. Friend of Nrsng Awd Sioux Vlly Hosp Sioux Falls SD 1994. ml600ac@hotmail.com

COUGHLIN, Christopher Anthony (O) 7640 Glenwood Ave, Boardman OH 44512 **S Jn's Epis Ch Bowling Green OH 2011-** B Youngstown OH 6/8/1977 s John Joseph Coughlin & Julie Simons. BA The Coll of Wooster 1999; SWTS 2008; MDiv Bex 2010. D 6/5/2010 Bp Mark Hollingsworth Jr P 4/16/2011 Bp Arthur Benjamin Williams Jr. m 10/8/2005 Lisa M Lucas. Chr Epis Ch Warren OH 2011; Assoc R S Jas Epis Ch Boardman OH 2011. revcoughlin@gmail.com

COUGHLIN, Clark F (Ct) 400 Seabury Dr., Apt. 2126, Bloomfield CT 06002 B Holyoke MA 12/17/1932 s Patrick Aloysius Coughlin & Edna Grow. AS U of New Haven 1952; BS Quinnipiac U 1954; Include in above EDS 1980; MDiv Gordon-Conwell TS 1980. D 10/17/1980 Bp Wilbur Emory Hogg Jr P 6/18/1981 Bp Arthur Edward Walmsley. m 10/4/1969 Joy Elsey. R S Jas' Epis Ch Winsted CT 1983-2000; Asst R Chr Ch Par Epis Watertown CT 1980-1983; Field Educ S Ptr's Ch Beverly MA 1978-1980; Yth, Mus, Tchg S Paul's Ch Brookfield CT 1974-1977. Phi Theta Kappa 1953. Bachelor of Sci Quinnipiac Coll 1954. c.jcoughlin@snet.net

COULTAS OJN, Amy Real (Ky) 612 Myrte St, Louisville KY 40208 **GC Dep, Chair Dio Kentucky Louisville KY 2011-; Presb-Epis Dialog Ecusa / Mssn Personl New York NY 2010-; Cn Mssnr Chr Ch Cathd Louisville KY 2009-; Joint Nomin Com for the Election of a PBp Prov IV 2009-; Trst & Coun Dio Kentucky Louisville KY 2007-; Campus Min Epis Campus Mnstry Louisville KY 2006-** B Louisville KY 7/14/1975 d Paul Carroll Real & Hollis Ann. BFA U of Louisville 1999; MDiv GTS 2006. D 2/24/2006 P 9/9/2006 Bp Edwin Funsten Gulick Jr. m 9/25/1999 Kevin Michael Coultas. Transition Com Dio Kentucky Louisville KY 2008-2011; COM Dio Kentucky Louisville KY 2007-2011; GC Dep Dio Kentucky Louisville KY 2007-2011; Vic S Jas Ch Shelbyville KY 2006-2009. Soc of Cath Priests 2010. amycoultas@gmail.com

COULTER, Clayton Roy (Ore) 7430 Sw Pineridge Ct, Portland OR 97225 B Hartney MT CA 2/2/1931 s Thomas Roy Coulter & Mabel Alice. BA Wstrn Washington U 1952; BD SWTS 1955. D 6/29/1955 P 6/29/1956 Bp Stephen F Bayne Jr. m 12/26/1965 Sharon Louise Towne c 3. Dio Oregon Portland OR 2000-2001; Dn Dio Oregon Portland OR 1993-2000; Epis Par Of S Jn The Bapt Portland OR 1981-2000; R S Paul's Ch Seattle WA 1968-1981; Vic Ch Of The Redeem Kenmore WA 1957-1968; Cur Trin Par Seattle WA 1955-1957. Sis Of S Jn The Bapt 1982; SSJE 1953. sharoy7430@yahoo.com

COULTER, Elizabeth (Ia) 3148 Dubuque St. NE, Iowa City IA 52240 B Champaign IL 4/18/1942 d Lyle Harrison Bean & Elizabeth. BA U of Iowa 1975; MS U of Iowa 1976; MDiv SWTS 1993. D 9/21/1993 P 4/18/1994 Bp Carl Christopher Epting. m 12/16/1961 Charles Roy Coulter c 1. New Song Epis Ch Coralville IA 2001-2004; S Andr's Epis Ch Waverly IA 2001; Dio Iowa Des Moines IA 1994-2000; D Trin Ch Muscatine IA 1993-1994. ecoulter@mchsi.com

COULTER, Joe Carroll (NC) 1111 Greentree Dr, Charlotte NC 28211 **Died 3/28/2011** B Statesville NC 6/26/1932 s Robert Eugene Coulter & Lena. BA U of Maryland 1959; MDiv VTS 1966. D 6/29/1966 P 1/6/1967 Bp Thomas H Wright. c 2. jcoulter@duke-energy.com

COULTER, Sherry Lynn (At) 681 Holt Rd Ne, Marietta GA 30068 B Memphis TN 6/18/1961 d James Coulter & Ellen Janelle. AA Shelby St Cmnty Coll 1983; BA U of Memphis 1988; MDiv STUSo 2000. D 12/16/2000 Bp James Malone Coleman. S Cathr's Epis Ch Marietta GA 2002-2007; Dio W Tennessee Memphis TN 2000-2002; D S Mary's Cathd Memphis TN 2000-2002.

✠ **COUNCELL, Rt Rev George Edward** (NJ) Diocese of New Jersey, 808 West State Street, Trenton NJ 08618 **Bp of New Jersey Dio New Jersey Trenton NJ 2003-** B Detroit MI 10/4/1949 s Graham Duane Councell & Jeannie Doris. BA U CA 1971; MDiv EDS 1975; D.D. GTS 2010. D 6/21/1975 P 12/21/1975 Bp Robert C Rusack Con 10/18/2003 for NJ. m 1/10/1971 Ruth Tietjen c 2. R The Ch Of The H Sprt Lake Forest IL 1995-2003; Cn to Ordnry Dio Wstrn Massachusetts Springfield MA 1986-1995; R S Geo's Ch Riverside CA 1977-1985; Vic S Lk's Mssn Fontana CA 1975-1977. Phi Beta Kappa. gcouncell@aol.com

COUNSELMAN, Robert Lee (NJ) 650 Rahway Ave, Woodbridge NJ 07095 **R Trin Ch Woodbridge NJ 1981-** B Ottawa KS 1/18/1948 s G(eorge) Don Counselman & C(orrine) Hope. BA U of New Mex 1974; MDiv GTS 1976. D 8/6/1976 P 2/15/1977 Bp Richard Mitchell Trelease Jr. m 6/5/1970 Sharon Kay Giffin c 2. Cur Chr Ch Middletown NJ 1976-1980. rector@trinitywoodbridge.org

COUNTRYMAN, L(ouis) William (Cal) 5805 Keith Avenue, Oakland CA 94618 **Assoc The Epis Ch Of The Gd Shpd Berkeley CA 1985-** B Oklahoma City OK 10/21/1941 s Louis Countryman & Bera Sue. BA U Chi 1962; STB GTS 1965; Hebr Un Coll 1968; MA U Chi 1974; PhD U Chi 1977. D 6/20/1965 Bp Chilton Powell P 12/29/1965 Bp Frederick Warren Putnam. c 1. Sherman E. Johnson Prof Emer in Biblic Stds CDSP Berkeley CA 1983-2007; R S Paul's Epis Ch Logan OH 1968-1972; Asst St Phil's Epis Ch Ardmore OK 1965-1967. Auth, "Lovesongs and Reproaches," Morehouse, 2010; Auth, "Dirt, Greed & Sex," Fortress Press, 2007; Auth, "Love, Human and Div," Morehouse, 2005; Ed, "Run, Shepherds, Run," Morehouse, 2005; Auth, "Interpreting the Truth," Trin Press Intl , 2003; Auth, "Gifted by Otherness," Morehouse, 2001; Auth, "The Poetic Imagination," Orbis, 2000; Auth, "Living on the Border of the H," Morehouse Pub, 1999; Auth, "Forgiven & Forgiven," Morehouse Pub, 1998; Auth, "The Mystical Way in the Fourth Gospel," Trin Press Intl , 1994; Auth, "Gd News of Jesus," Trin Press Intl , 1993. rusticus@earthlink.net

COUPER, David Courtland (Mil) 5282 County Road K, Blue Mounds WI 53517 B Little Falls MN 4/5/1938 s John Van Dyke Couper & Elsa. BA U MN 1968; MA U MN 1970; CAS Nash 1994; MA Edgewood Coll 2005. D 12/16/1994 P 6/27/1995 Bp Roger John White. m 12/29/1981 Sabine Lobitz c 3. Vic S Ptr's Ch No Lake WI 2005-2008; P-in-c S Jn The Bapt Portage WI 1996-2004. Auth, "Arrested Dvlpmt: One man's Mssn to improve our nation's police," Dog Ear Pub, 2012; Auth, "Forgiveness In The Cmnty," *Exploring Forgiveness*, U of Wisconsin Press, 1998; Auth, "Quality Policing: The Madison Experience," PERF, Washington DC, 1992; Auth, "How to Rate Your Loc Police," PERF, Washington DC, 1983. davidccouper@aol.com

COUPLAND, Geoffrey D (Va) 5110 Park Ave., Richmond VA 23226 **R Ch Of The H Comf Richmond VA 2009-** B Ottawa CA 10/6/1954 s James George Coupland & Eileen Diane. BA Carleton U 1978; MDiv U Tor 1981. Trans from Anglican Church of Canada 6/1/1996 Bp David Standish Ball. m 12/20/2008 Patricia C Coupland c 1. Int All SS Ch S Louis MO 2007-2009; Int S Lk's Ch Powhatan VA 2006-2007; Brooke-Hancock Cluster Wellsburg WV 2005-2006; R S Mary's Epis Ch Bonita Sprg FL 2002-2004; R S Jn's Ch Ogdensburg NY 1996-2002. hocorector@comcast.net

COURTNEY, Michael David (Ark) 235 Caroline Acres Road, Hot Springs AR 71913 **P-in-c Ch Of The Gd Shpd Little Rock AR 2010-** B Hawthorne CA 12/20/1958 s Alvin Courtney & Frances. AA U of the St of New York; BS Sthrn California U of Hlth Sciences 1978; DC Sthrn California U of Hlth Sciences 1981; STD Sem of the Amer Ch of the E San Jose CA 1995. Rec from Greek Orthodox 7/18/2006 as Priest Bp Larry Earl Maze. m 4/28/1990 Johnna Courtney c 3. Vic Emm Ch Lake Vill AR 870-2652230or8 2006-2009; Vic S Paul's Ch McGehee AR 2006-2009. drmdc64423@aol.com

COURTNEY, Peter (At) 127 Inverness Road, Athens GA 30606 B Boston MA 7/18/1943 s Paul Douglas Courtney & Julia Winchester. BA Hob 1965; STB Ya Berk 1968; Nash 1976. D 6/22/1968 P 12/28/1968 Bp George West Barrett. m 11/28/1986 Deborah T Perry c 2. Int S Aug Of Cbury Ch Augusta GA 2010; Int S Mk's Epis Ch E Longmeadow MA 2008-2009; Int S Dav's Ch Baltimore MD 2007-2008; Int Chr Ch Las Vegas NV 2006-2007; Int S Teresa Acworth GA 2005-2006; R Emm Epis Ch Athens GA 2000-2005; Dn S Andr's Cathd Honolulu HI 1996-2000; R Emm Ch Virginia Bch VA 1984-1996; R Gr Epis Ch Elmira NY 1977-1984; R S Ptr's Epis Ch Henrietta NY 1972-1977; R S Paul's Ch Angelica NY 1970-1972; R S Phil's Ch Belmont NY 1970-1972; Asst Ch Of The Incarn Penfield NY 1968-1970. pc@petercourtney.net

COURTNEY II, Robert Wickliff (La) PO Box 1776, Morgan City LA 70381 **R Trin Epis Ch Morgan City LA 2009-** B Crowley LA 12/5/1972 s Robert W Courtney & Linda Jourdan. BSBA U of Phoenix 2006; MDiv The U So (Sewanee) 2009. D 12/27/2008 P 6/27/2009 Bp Charles Edward Jenkins III. m 5/27/2000 Catherine Davis c 2. Par Admin Chr Ch Cathd New Orleans LA 2003-2006. rwcourtney1972@yahoo.com

COURTNEY JR, Robin Spencer (Tenn) 7872 Harpeth View Dr, Nashville TN 37221 **P-in-c S Jas The Less Madison TN 2007-** B Columbia TN 11/22/1961 s Robin Spencer Courtney & Lucille Frierson. BA Van 1984; MDiv VTS 1996. D 6/16/1996 P 4/6/1997 Bp Bertram Nelson Herlong. Assoc S Mk's Ch Antioch TN 2007; P Gr Ch Sprg Hill TN 2004-2007; Int Dio Tennessee Nashville TN 2003; R S Bede's Epis Ch Manchester TN 1996-2003. fathercourtney@aol.com

COUVILLION, Brian Neff (Chi) 4370 Woodland Ave, Western Springs IL 60558 **R All SS Ch Wstrn Sprg IL 2002-** B Alexandria LA 3/13/1945 s Arthur Bennett Couvillion & Eugenia. BS Louisiana Tech U 1968; MDiv Epis TS of The SW 1987. D 6/13/1987 P 12/12/1987 Bp Willis Ryan Henton. m 7/14/1967 Judith Kathleen Ebright c 3. R S Jas Ch W Dundee IL 1997-2002; Asst R Gr Epis Ch Hinsdale IL 1990-1997; Assoc R S Paul's Epis Ch Shreveport LA 1988-1990; Cur Epis Ch Of The Gd Shpd Lake Chas LA 1987-1988. bncouvillion@comcast.net

COUZZOURT, Beverly Schmidt (NwT) 2516 4th Ave, Canyon TX 79015 **Sacramental P Epis Ch Of S Geo Canyon TX 2006-** B Roswell NM 9/16/1958 d William Irving Schmidt & Frances Miriam. BGS W Texas St U 1981; Certification Primary Montessori Certification 1992. D 9/30/2006 P 4/14/2007 Bp C(harles) Wallis Ohl. m 11/6/1982 James Edward Couzzourt c 2. jcuz@amaonline.com

COVENTRY, Donald Edgar (Spr) 246 Southmoreland Pl, Decatur IL 62521 B Shelbyville IL 12/29/1937 s Kenneth William Coventry & Lelia Nmn. U IL 1975; AAS Rickland Cmnty Coll Decatur IL 1976. D 6/29/2004 Bp Peter Hess Beckwith. m 7/8/1989 Delores Ann Moyer. dncvnt@aol.com

COVER, Michael Benjamin (Dal) 616 Lincolnway E., Mishawaka IN 46544 **D S Paul's Ch Mishawaka IN 2009-** B Boston MA 7/8/1982 s Robin Cover & Janet. AB Harvard Coll 2004; MST Oxf 2005; MDiv Ya Berk 2008. D 6/6/2009 Bp James Monte Stanton P 2/13/2010 Bp Paul Emil Lambert. m 8/4/2007 Susanna Quaile c 1. Dio Nthrn Indiana So Bend IN 2009. mbcover@gmail.com

COVERDALE, John (HB) 6 La Leita Ct, Chico CA 95928 B Madison WI 1/8/1930 s John Francis Bloomer & Marjory Uldene. BA Lawr 1953; Nash 1956. D 5/27/1956 P 12/1/1956 Bp William Hampton Brady. m 6/13/1959 Norma Ellen Sweetser. Stff (Mltry Acad) Ch Of S Jn Chrys Delafield WI 1966-1967; Vic S Geo's Ch Macomb IL 1959-1961; Vic St Jas Epis Ch Mosinee WI 1956-1959.

COVERSTON, Harry Scott (ECR) 630 Roberta Ave, Orlando FL 32803 B West Palm Beach FL 9/1/1953 s Samuel Coverston & Marjorie. AA Lake-Sumter Cmnty Coll 1973; BA U of Florida 1976; JD U of Florida 1981; MDiv CDSP 1995; PhD Florida St U 2000. D 12/21/1994 P 6/22/1995 Bp Richard Lester Shimpfky. m 5/31/1974 Andy Mobley. "Conversation of Content," *Revs of Religous Resrch*, 2008; Auth (Chapt), "Evang Cartons, the Gd and the Bed," *Selling Jesus, Visual Culture and the Mnstry of Chrsnty*, Ed. Dominic Janes, 2008; Auth, "Revs: Deep in Our Hearts," *Turning Wheel*, 2001; Auth, "Sarah," *Living Ch*. Tertiary Ord, Soc of S Fran 1990. frharry@cfl.rr.com

COVERT, Edward Martin (SwVa) Po Box 126, Fort Defiance VA 24437 B Raleigh NC 7/7/1944 s Otis Martin Covert & Ruth. BA U NC 1966; MDiv VTS 1969. D 6/24/1969 P 6/29/1970 Bp Thomas Augustus Fraser Jr. m 6/26/1970 Nan Taylor Rackett c 1. P-in-c Emm Ch Staunton VA 1999; Dep Gc Dio SW Virginia Roanoke VA 1991-1994; Chair Com Dio SW Virginia Roanoke VA 1984-1985; R Chr Ch Martinsville VA 1980-1999; P-in-c S Steph's Epis Ch No Myrtle Bch SC 1974-1980; Asst S Mich's Epis Ch Charleston SC 1971-1974; Asst Ch Of The H Comf Burlington NC 1969-1971. Auth, "Epis". covert@cfw.com

COVINGTON, John E (NY) 410 West 24th Street, Apartment 8K, New York NY 10011 B Charlotte NC 9/10/1946 s William Thomas Covington & Winona Hill. STM GTS; MDiv GTS; U NC; BA Trin Hartford CT 1968. D 5/26/1973 P 11/24/1973 Bp George Alfred Taylor. Int Chr Ch Riverdale Bronx NY 2003-2004; Int Trin Ch Mt Vernon NY 2000-2003; Int S Ptr's Ch Bronx NY 1997-2001; R S Alb's Epis Ch Staten Island NY 1977-1997; S Jn's Ch Larchmont NY 1975-1977; Cur Chr Ch S Ptr's Par Easton MD 1974-1975. john.covington@verizon.net

COWAN, Alice (SO) 4141 South Braeswood Blvd, Apt 424, Houston TX 77025 **Died 1/16/2010** B Dallas,TX 9/18/1936 d Finis Ewing Cowan & Kathleen. BA Rice U 1958; MA SMU 1968; PhD SMU 1975; GTS 1988. D 12/14/1988 Bp Arthur Anton Vogel P 2/1/1990 Bp John Clark Buchanan. c 2. Auth, "Rel Of The Wrld," 1993; Auth, "Rel Of The Wrld," 1988; Auth, "Rel Of The Wrld," 1982; Auth, "Miners," *Merchants & Missionaries*, 1980. EDEO; EWHP; HSEC. acowan@ststephenshouston.org

COWAN, Leonard Chaffee (WMass) 56 Reed St, Agawam MA 01001 **R S Dav's Ch Feeding Hills MA 1984-; Ch Of The Nativ Northborough MA 1981-** B Boston MA 5/28/1952 s Fairman Chaffee Cowan & Martha Logan. BA Trin 1974; Gordon-Conwell TS 1978; MDiv GTS 1979. D 6/1/1979 P 1/1/1980 Bp Alexander Doig Stewart. m 6/19/1976 Hallie Marshall c 2. Cur Chr Ch Fitchburg MA 1979-1981. Ord Of S Lk ,Bro Of S Andr, Curs, NOEL, EPF; Vice Superior Fvc 1997. lencowan1@gmail.com

COWANS, William Marsden (ECR) 900 S Meadows Pkwy Apt 1313, Reno NV 89521 B Redlands CA 11/7/1931 s William Cowans & Agnes Eleanor Mary. BA San Diego St U 1958; MDiv CDSP 1961. D 6/25/1961 P 6/15/1962 Bp James Albert Pike. c 2. R S Thos Epis Ch Sunnyvale CA 1974-1994; Assoc S Thos Epis Ch Sunnyvale CA 1968-1974; P-in-c S Mk's Par Crockett CA 1963-1968; Cur S Mk's Epis Ch Palo Alto CA 1961-1963. wmc711@mac.com

COWARD JR, Milton Edward (At) Po Box 6938, Athens GA 30604 B Savannah GA 2/18/1939 s Milton Edward Coward & Clara Bell. BA Emory U 1960; S Aug's Coll Cbury Gb 1962; ThM VTS 1963; Berry Coll 1975; Med W Georgia Coll 1984; EDS W Georgia Coll 1985. D 5/26/1963 P 5/1/1964 Bp Randolph R Claiborne. m 8/30/1974 Laura Elizabeth Hunter c 1. Dn Cathd Of S Phil Atlanta GA 1970-1973; R S Alb's Ch Elberton GA 1965-1970; Vic S Andr's Ch Hartwell GA 1965-1970; Cur S Mart In The Fields Ch Atlanta GA 1963-1965. Phi Kappa Phi.

COWARDIN, Eustis Barber (ND) 510 E Lake County Rd, Jamestown ND 58401 **Gr Epis Ch Jamestown ND 1999-** B Philadelphia PA 1/3/1935 d William Wyatt Barber & Margaret. BA Wellesley Coll 1956; LPN No Dakota St Coll Of Sci Wahpeton ND 1981. D 12/2/1995 P 6/25/1999 Bp Andrew Hedtler Fairfield. m 6/23/1956 Lewis Cowardin c 4. lcoward@daktel.com

COWARDIN, Stephen Paul (SVa) 8525 Summit Acres Dr, Richmond VA 23235 **R Ch Of The Redeem Midlothian VA 1995-** B Richmond VA 7/24/1947 s John Franklin Cowardin & Maude Elizabeth. BS Old Dominion U 1987; MDiv VTS 1992; DMin VTS 2007. D 6/7/1992 P 12/20/1992 Bp Frank Harris Vest Jr. m 9/11/1980 Susan Malligo c 2. swinepriest@comcast.net

COWDEN, Matthew D (NI) 8385 Luce Ct, Springfield VA 22153 **S Mich And All Ang Ch So Bend IN 2009-** B Washington DC 8/21/1969 s Arthur M Cowden & Marie Anne. BFA Florida St U 1991; MFA U CA 1994; MDiv VTS 2006. D 4/1/2006 P 11/1/2006 Bp Leopold Frade. m 7/11/1992 Melissa T Tomonto c 3. Assoc R Chr Ch Alexandria VA 2006-2009. matthew@matthewcowden.com

COWELL, Curtis Lyle (Kan) 2601 Sw College Ave, Topeka KS 66611 B Bluefield WV 8/22/1938 s Joseph Lyle Cowell & Theodosia Edna. BS VPI 1960; MDiv VTS 1969. D 6/11/1969 P 6/1/1970 Bp Wilburn Camrock Campbell. m 6/24/1966 Elinor Kathryne Schadt c 1. Gr Cathd Topeka KS 1995-2000; The Wheeling Cluster Wheeling WV 1989-1995; R S Andr's Ch Oak Hill WV 1983-1989; Vic Gr Ch Northfork WV 1978-1983; Vic S Lk's Epis Ch Welch WV 1978-1983; Vic S Barn Bridgeport WV 1976-1978; Dio W Virginia Charleston WV 1969-1976. clcowell@cox.net

COWELL, Frank Bourne (Nev) 7300 W Van Giesen St, West Richland WA 99353 **Asst S Mich's Epis Ch Yakima WA 2007-** B Los Angeles CA 6/8/1944 s Henry Cushing Cowell & Olive. AB California St U, Long Bch 1966; MDiv VTS 1983. D 6/21/1983 P 1/20/1984 Bp Leigh Wallace Jr. c 1. R S Paul's Epis Ch Elko NV 2001-2004; Rgnl Dn Dio Hawaii Honolulu HI 1993-1995; Vic Epis Ch On W Kaua'i Eleele HI 1992-2000; RurD H Trin Epis Ch Sunnyside WA 1987-1992; Vic S Jas Epis Ch Brewster WA 1985-1987; Vic S Anne's Ch Omak WA 1983-1987; Ch Of The Trsfg Omak WA 1983-1985. frfrank1@yahoo.com

COWELL, Mark Andrew (WK) 501 W 5th St, Larned KS 67550 **Stndg Com, Pres Dio Wstrn Kansas Hutchinson KS 2009-; Dio Wstrn Kansas Hutchinson KS 2004-; SS Mary And Martha Of Bethany Larned KS 2004-** B Washington DC 3/29/1965 D 11/29/2003 P 6/12/2004 Bp James Marshall Adams Jr. m 11/27/1999 Julie Ann Fletcher c 2. m_a_cowell@yahoo.com

COWPER, Judith Ann (Ct) 54 Dora Dr, Middletown CT 06457 **Pstr Assoc Gr Ch Old Saybrook CT 2005-** B Cambridge MA 7/13/1942 d Harold Paul Knauss & Dorothy Elemine. BA Carleton Coll 1964; MA U of Connecticut 1973; CAS Ya Berk 1992; MDiv mcl Yale DS 1992. D 6/13/1992 Bp Arthur Edward Walmsley P 1/25/1993 Bp Jeffery William Rowthorn. m 9/13/1975 G Clive Cowper. R S Thos Epis Ch Morgantown PA 1999-2002; Int All SS Epis Ch Meriden CT 1999; Int Gr Epis Ch Trumbull CT 1997-1999; P-in-c Ch Of The H Adv Clinton CT 1992-1997. Ord of S Lk, Chapl 1993. judithcowper@sbcglobal.net

COWPERTHWAITE, Robert W (Tenn) 608 Fair St, Franklin TN 37064 **R S Paul's Ch Franklin TN 1988-** B New Brunswick NJ 5/24/1948 s William Gardner Cowperthwaite & June. BA W&L 1970; MDiv VTS 1973. D 6/13/1973 P 5/8/1974 Bp Edward Hamilton West. m 9/28/1974 Susan L Longo c 2. Pstr Off Par of Trin Ch New York NY 1981-1988; Assoc San Jose Epis Ch Jacksonville FL 1976-1981; Asst S Cathr's Ch Jacksonville FL 1973-1976; Vic S Jas Ch Macclenny FL 1973-1976. bob@stpaulsfranklin.com

COX, Anne Elizabeth (Mich) 8 Ridge Rd, Tenants Harbor ME 04860 B Downey CA 10/28/1960 d Donald Nesbit Cox & Judith Anne. BA No Carolina St U 1981; MLa U MI 1984; MDiv UTS 1987. D 6/27/1987 Bp H Coleman McGehee Jr P 3/12/1988 Bp Jose Agustin Gonzalez. Econ Justice Cmsn Dio Michigan Detroit MI 1992-1997; Asst Bp Serv Cmsn Dio Michigan Detroit MI 1992-1994; R Nativ Epis Ch Bloomfield Township MI 1991-1997; Bible T/F Dio Newark Newark NJ 1989-1991; Cntr For Food Action Dio Newark Newark NJ 1988-1991; Asst R S Paul's Ch Englewood NJ 1987-1991. Auth, "Wit," 1996. anne@hedgerowdesign.com

COX IV, Brian (Los) 871 Serenidad Pl, Goleta CA 93117 **R Chr The King Epis Ch Santa Barbara CA 1992-** B Chicago IL 6/25/1950 s Milton James Cox & Mary Louise. BS USC 1972; MDiv EDS 1975; MDR Pepperdine U 2000. D 6/21/1975 P 12/21/1975 Bp Robert C Rusack. m 6/16/1973 Ann Booth c 2. Assoc R Ch Of The Apos Fairfax VA 1986-1992; Assoc R S Jas' Epis Ch Los Angeles CA 1977-1986; Vic S Agnes Mssn Banning CA 1975-1977; R S Steph's Par Beaumont CA 1975-1977. Auth, "Recon Basic Seminar," *Abraham's Ed*, 2008; Auth, "Recon Basic Seminar," *Gaudhian Ed*, 2008; Auth, "Faith-Based Recon," *An Moral Vision that Transforms People and Soc*, 2007; Auth, *Recon Basic Seminar*, 1996. Intl Fndt 1986-2000; Pres Reconciles.net 1996. briancox@cox.net

COX, Catherine Susanna (WMo) 365 E 372nd Rd, Dunnegan MO 65640 **Vic S Alb's In The Ozarks Ch Bolivar MO 2003-; The Rivendell Cmnty Retreat Hse Dunnegan MO 2003-** B NC 2/8/1947 d Clifford Cox & Florence. BS Loretto Heights Coll 1971; MDiv Nazarene TS 1981. D 2/1/2003 P 9/6/2003 Bp Barry Robert Howe. c 5. susanna601@aol.com

COX, Celeste O'Hern (Del) Po Box 1374, Dover DE 19903 **R Chr Ch Dover DE 1999-** B Pittsburgh PA 5/8/1949 d John James O'Hern & Anna Mcelhatten. BS Sthrn Illinois U 1982; CPE 1992; MA S Vinc De Paul Sem 1992; STM GTS 1996. D 9/21/1992 P 9/21/1996 Bp Calvin Onderdonk Schofield Jr. m 11/8/1975 Louis Edward Cox. Assoc The Epis Ch Of Beth-By-The-Sea Palm Bch FL 1994-1999; Dio SE Florida Miami FL 1993-1994. Bd Cert Mem Assn Profsnl Chapl. celeste127@verizon.net

COX, Christopher Edward (NJ) 801 W State St, Trenton NJ 08618 B 5/12/1957 s Edward Cowburn Cox & Joyce. BSC U of Liverpool 1978; New Jersey Sch for Deacons 2009. D 5/16/2009 Bp Sylvestre Donato Romero. m 10/7/1978 Hilary McDonald c 2. christopherecox@aol.com

C

COX JR, Clyde Hoyte (WMass) 677 US RT 1, Stockton Springs ME 04981 B Indianapolis IN 3/14/1931 s Clyde Hoyt Cox & Mary Jane. STB Bos 1955; MDiv Bos 1963. Trans from Anglican Church of Canada 11/22/1994 Bp Robert Scott Denig. m 7/6/1957 Evelyn Bowden c 4. R All SS Ch Worcester MA 1971-1991; Dio Wstrn Massachusetts Springfield MA 1971-1991; R Trin Epis Ch Portland ME 1963-1971; R S Jn's Ch Jamaica Plain MA 1957-1963; Cur S Steph's Meml Ch Lynn MA 1955-1957. Cn Chr Cathd Springfield, Ma 1980; Fell Coll Of Preachers, Washingotn Dc 1980. clydecox@fairpoint.net

COX, Edwin Manuel (NC) 4510 Highberry Rd, Greensboro NC 27410 **Greensboro Convoc Dio No Carolina Raleigh NC 2009-** B Ponce PR 7/17/1944 s Oral Otis Cox & Alicia Francesca. BS USCG Acad New London CT 1966; MDiv STUSo 1979; MEd Coll of Idaho 1987. D 2/24/1984 P 11/17/1984 Bp David Bell Birney IV. m 7/11/1998 Frances Fosbroke c 3. Curs Sprtl Advsr Dio No Carolina Raleigh NC 2007-2009; Int Assoc R S Fran Ch Greensboro NC 2004-2007; Const & Cn Cmte Dio Maine Portland ME 2000-2003; Dioc Coun Dio Maine Portland ME 2000-2002; T/F on Assessment Revs Dio Maine Portland ME 2000-2002; Int R S Sav's Par Bar Harbor ME 1999-2002; Curs Sprtl Advsr Dio Maryland Baltimore MD 1998-1999; EFM Mentor Dio Maryland Baltimore MD 1998-1999; Int R S Jn's Ch Havre De Gr MD 1997-1999; Int R S Paul's Epis Ch Prince Frederick MD 1996-1998; Int R S Jn's Ch Olney MD 1994-1995; Dioc Coun Dio Maryland Baltimore MD 1993-1994; Dir Pstr Care Ch Hosp Corp Baltimore MD 1993; Secy of Conv Dio Maryland Baltimore MD 1992-1996; Int R S Paul's Par Kent Chestertown MD 1992-1993; D Formation Fac Dio Maryland Baltimore MD 1991-1999; Plnng Cmte Dio Maryland Baltimore MD 1991-1996; Liturg & Mus Cmte Dio Maryland Baltimore MD 1990-1996; Hspanic Mnstry Com Dio Maryland Baltimore MD 1989-1992; R S Marg's Epis Ch Baltimore MD 1989-1992; Tri-Ch Par S Mk's Ch Lake City MN 1987-1988; P-in-c H Trin Vale OR 1986-1987; D Formation Fac Dio Idaho Boise ID 1985-1987; EfM Cordinator & Mentor Dio Idaho Boise ID 1985-1987; P-in-c S Lk's Ch Weiser ID 1985-1987; Dioc Coun Dio Idaho Boise ID 1985-1986; Cmncatn Cmte Chair Dio Idaho Boise ID 1985; Liturg Cmte Chair Dio Idaho Boise ID 1984-1986; D & P S Steph's Boise ID 1984-1986. Contrib, "Monograph," *The Ord of Mnstry: Reflections on Direct Ord*, Assn for Ep Deacons (then N Amer Assn for Diac/NAAD), 1996. Assn for Ep Deacons (was NAAD) 1984; Assoc Parishes for Liturg & Mus (AP) 1977-2001; Cmnty of S Mary 1978; Curs 1982; EWC (EWC) 1977; Int Mnstry Ntwk 1994-2004; Md Cler Ass'n, Bd then Pres. 1990-1992; Nat'l Ntwk of Ep Cler Ass'ns 1989-2004; Towson (MD) Area Mnstrl Assn, Pres. 1992-1993; UBE 2005. edwincox@aol.com

COX, Frances Fosbroke (Md) 4510 Highberry Rd, Greensboro NC 27410 B Boston MA 5/12/1948 d Gerald Elton Fosbroke & Kay. BSN U of Maryland 1974; Cert U of Kentucky 1977; MDiv VTS 1981; Cert VTS 1991. D 6/27/1981 Bp David Keller Leighton Sr P 5/11/1985 Bp A(lbert) Theodore Eastman. m 7/11/1998 Edwin Manuel Cox. Int R Ch Of The Epiph Eden NC 2009-2010; Sprtl Advsr to Curs Secretariate Dio No Carolina Raleigh NC 2007-2011; Int Ch Of The Redeem Greensboro NC 2007-2008; Int R S Fran Ch Greensboro NC 2004-2007; Green Cler Ntwk, ME Coun of Ch Dio Maine Portland ME 2001-2004; Mutual Mnstry Consult Dio Maine Portland ME 2001-2004; Int R The Par Of S Mary And S Jude NE Harbor ME 2001-2002; Case Maager for Response Team Dio Maine Portland ME 2000-2004; Int Consult Dio Maine Portland ME 2000-2004; Safe Ch Trnr Dio Maine Portland ME 2000-2004; P in Charge Ch Of The Gd Shpd Houlton ME 2000; Cathd Chapt Dio Maryland Baltimore MD 1997-1999; Comp Dio Relatns - Tokyo Dio Maryland Baltimore MD 1995-1999; Dir, Living into Ptiestly Vocation Prog Dio Maryland Baltimore MD 1994-1999; R Ch Of The Redemp Baltimore MD 1992-1999; Coordntr, Educ for D Formation Dio Maryland Baltimore MD 1992-1999; Sprtl Advsr to Curs Secretariate Dio Maryland Baltimore MD 1992-1998; Chair, Post-Ord Com of COM Dio Maryland Baltimore MD 1992-1994; Eccl Crt Dio Maryland Baltimore MD 1991-1998; COM Dio Maryland Baltimore MD 1988-1994; COM Dio Maryland Baltimore MD 1988-1994; Cntrl Maryland Eccumenical Com Dio Maryland Baltimore MD 1988-1992; D Formation Com Dio Maryland Baltimore MD 1987-1999; NW Reg Pres Dio Maryland Baltimore MD 1987-1989; Cnvnr, Clerica Femina Dio Maryland Baltimore MD 1986-1999; Pstr Counslg & Consult Cntr Bd Dio Maryland Baltimore MD 1986-1992; U of Maryland at Baltimore Chapl Bd Dio Maryland Baltimore MD 1986-1989; Assoc R S Jn's Ch Reisterstown MD 1985-1991; NE Reg Pres Dio Maryland Baltimore MD 1984-1985; D Assoc H Trin Epis Ch Bowie MD 1984-1985; Pres Hargor Reg Dio Maryland Baltimore MD 1982-1995; D Assoc Ch Of The Mssh Baltimore MD 1981-1984; NE Reg VP Dio Maryland Baltimore MD 1981-1983. Associated Parishes 1980; Assn of Epis Deacons (Form NAAD) 1978; Cler Families of Lesbians and Gays 1999; Clerica Femina (Dio MD) 1981-2000; EWC 1978; Integrity 1982; Maryland Cler Assn 1987-1998; No Amer Maritime Mnstry Assn 1992-2006; NE Mnstrl Assn 1981-1984; UBE 2007. ffcox@aol.com

COX, Gary Robert (Chi) 5324 S Kedzie Ave Apt 1B, Chicago IL 60632 **La Iglesia De Nuestra Senora De Las Americas Chicago IL 2011-; Vic Iglesia Epis Santa Teresa De Avila Chicago IL 2009-; Vic Santa Teresa de Avila Chicago IL 2009-** B Chicago IL 9/5/1967 s Maurice Cox & Lorraine. BA Beloit Coll 1989; MA NEU 1997; Med Chicago St U 1999; MDiv Epis TS of The SW 2006. D 6/3/2006 P 12/16/2006 Bp William Dailey Persell. Chr Ch Waukegan IL 2008; Santa Teresa de Avila Chicago IL 2008; Nuestra Senora De Guadalupe Waukegan IL 2006-2008. gary.cox@alum.ssw.edu

COX, James Richard (WK) Po Box 827, Salina KS 67402 B Garden City KS 10/2/1934 s Harold Nmi Cox & Pheobe Faye. BA U of Nthrn Colorado 1959; MDiv Nash 1990. D 5/26/1990 P 11/30/1990 Bp John Forsythe Ashby. m 7/20/1977 Ruth M Cox. Ch Of The Trsfg Bennington KS 1992-2004; Armstrong Meml Chap of S Jn the Evang Salina KS 1990-2004; S Jn's Mltry Sch Salina KS 1990-2004; Asst Chr Cathd Salina KS 1990-1991. CHS; Skcm; SocMary; SocOLW; SSC. Phi Delta Kappa; Phi Alpha Theta. wkcanon@cox.net

COX JR, James Stanley (Ga) 1805 Jeanette St, Valdosta GA 31602 B Washington DC 9/12/1936 s Anna H. BA Pr 1958; BD CDSP 1961; MA Florida St U 1967; PhD Florida St U 1970. D 6/24/1961 P 12/1/1961 Bp Richard Henry Baker. m 6/25/1960 Juanita Oglesby Mixson. S Barn Epis Ch Valdosta GA 1999-2000; S Matt's Epis Ch Houma LA 1995-1996; R S Paul's Ch Abbeville LA 1983-1984; P-in-c S Jas Epis Ch Quitman GA 1966-1970; Vic Gr Ch Pine Bluff AR 1962-1965; Asst Ch Of The Gd Shpd Rocky Mt NC 1961-1962; P-in-c S Jn's Ch Battleboro NC 1961-1962. Auth, "Rel Literacy Criticism". Danforth Assn 1979.

COX, Jason (Los) 6017 Inwood St, Cheverly MD 20785 **Assoc S Columba's Ch Washington DC 2011-** B Silsbee TX 4/13/1978 s Jonathan Cox & Beverly. BA U Of Houston 2001; MDiv VTS 2007. D 5/19/2007 P 1/12/2008 Bp Joseph Jon Bruno. Jubilee Consortium Los Angeles CA 2009-2011; Chapl Cbury Westwood Fndt Los Angeles CA 2009-2010; Epis Urban Intern Prog Los Angeles CA 2007-2009. jsncox@gmail.com

COX, LeRoy E (Ore) 13505 Se River Rd # 243, Portland OR 97222 **Died 9/20/2009** B Glenns Ferry ID 11/9/1919 s Loren P Cox & Mary Elizabeth. BS OR SU 1951; CDSP 1956. D 12/10/1960 P 6/1/1961 Bp James Walmsley Frederic Carman. c 3.

COX, Mildred Louise (Minn) 1210 Washburn Ave N, Minneapolis MN 55411 B Knoxville TN 5/3/1935 d Clyde Edward Wright & Katie Ruth. Msn 1963; Mph 1974; Cert 1981; D Formation Prog 1992. D 11/14/1992 Bp Sanford Zangwill Kaye Hampton P 12/17/1999 Bp James Louis Jelinek. m 4/15/1961 Walter A Cox.

COX, Nancy L J (NC) 525 Lake Concord Road NE, Concord NC 28025 **R, Time-Certain All SS' Epis Ch Concord NC 2010-** B Honolulu HI 4/25/1962 BA Pr 1984; M Pub Aff U of Texas at Austin-LBJ Sch 1987; MDiv VTS 1995. D 7/8/1995 P 1/10/1996 Bp Peter James Lee. m 11/8/1986 Lee Forest Cox c 4. R S Mk's Chap Storrs CT 2002-2010; Asst Trin Epis Ch Southport CT 1998-2002; Asst S Paul's Epis Ch Alexandria VA 1995-1998. nancyljcox@gmail.com

COX, Raymond L (Ct) 461 Mill Hill Ter, Southport CT 06890 B London UK 1/4/1933 s Alfred Cecil Cox & Ellen May. BA U Of Hartford 1970; MDiv STUSo 1979. D 6/9/1979 P 12/15/1979 Bp Morgan Porteus. m 11/13/1954 Dorothy T Gagne c 2. Calv St Geo's Epis Ch Bridgeport CT 1982-1995; Cur S Mk's Ch New Britain CT 1979-1982. frraymond@optimum.net

COX, R. David (SwVa) 107 Lee Ave., Lexington VA 24450 **Dn, Augusta Convocatio Dio SW Virginia Roanoke VA 2010-; R S Lk's Ch Hot Sprg VA 2009-; Dep, GC Dio SW Virginia Roanoke VA 2008-** B Washington DC DC 8/1/1947 s W Russell Cox & Muriel Elizabeth. BA U of Virginia 1969; MDiv Ya Berk 1972; STM Ya Berk 1987; PhD Fndt Hse, Oxford/GTF 2001. D 6/10/1972 P 12/16/1972 Bp Joseph Warren Hutchens. m 6/30/1973 Melissa Anne McCoy c 3. Exec Bd Dio SW Virginia Roanoke VA 2008-2011; P-in-c S Lk's Ch Hot Sprg VA 2006-2009; Int S Alb's Epis Ch Annandale VA 2003-2004; Chairman, D Study Com Dio Virginia Richmond VA 2002-2004; Int Emm Ch At Brook Hill Richmond VA 2002-2003; Int S Mich's Epis Ch Arlington VA 2001-2002; Dep, GC Dio SW Virginia Roanoke VA 1999-2002; Stndg Cttee Dio SW Virginia Roanoke VA 1998-2003; Curs Sec Dio SW Virginia Roanoke VA 1988-1990; R R E Lee Meml Ch (Epis) Lexington VA 1987-2000; Co-Chair Wrld Mssn Com Dio Connecticut Hartford CT 1984-1987; Dn Seabury Deanry Dio Connecticut Hartford CT 1978-1980; Dn Seabury Deanry Dio Connecticut Hartford CT 1978-1980; R S Dav's Ch Gales Ferry CT 1975-1987; Stff Cler S Mk's Ch New Canaan CT 1972-1975. Auth, ",Priesthood In A New Millennium," Ch Pub Inc, 2003; Auth, ",Bond And Cov," Ch Pub Inc, 1999; Auth, "Misc. arts". Merrill Fell Harvard DS 2001; Woods Fell VTS 2000. rdavidcox@earthlink.net

COX, Sean Armer (Tex) 8405 Whiterose Court, College Station TX 77845 **Pres of Stndg Com Dio Texas Houston TX 2011-2012; Chair, ArmdF Cmsn Dio Texas Houston TX 2009-2012; Mem of Stndg Com Dio Texas**

Houston TX 2009-2012; R S Andr's Ch Bryan TX 2006- B Phoenix AZ 4/5/1970 s George Wade Cox & Mary Carolyn. BA U of Arizona 1992; MDiv Epis TS of The SW 1996; DMin VTS 2005. D 6/15/1996 P 6/14/1997 Bp Robert Reed Shahan. m 12/28/1996 Katherine Lynn Shaw c 2. Chair of Transition Com Dio San Diego San Diego CA 2004-2005; COM Dio San Diego San Diego CA 2000-2006; Vic S Thos Epis Ch Temecula CA 2000-2006; Assoc R S Marg's Epis Ch Palm Desert CA 1998-2000; Int Assoc R S Barn On The Desert Scottsdale AZ 1997-1998; Cur Trin Cathd Phoenix AZ 1996-1997. frsean.cox@gmail.com

COXHEAD JR, Stuart Platt (Cal) 2316 Easton Dr, Burlingame CA 94010 **P Assoc (non-stip) All SS Ch Pasadena CA 2005-** B Orange NJ 6/16/1938 s Stuart Platt Coxhead & Margaret Nichols. Cert Defense Lang Inst Frgn Lang Cntr 1961; BA Trin Hartford CT 1964; M. Div. EDS 1967; MA OH SU 1973. D 6/10/1967 P 12/16/1967 Bp Leland Stark. m 9/16/2006 Anne B Breck c 2. Dioc. 2000 Comm. Dio California San Francisco CA 1989-1992; Trst Gr Cathd San Francisco CA 1982-1985; R S Paul's Epis Ch Burlingame CA 1980-2001; Int R S Paul's Ch Columbus OH 1977-1980; Supply P Dio Sthrn Ohio Cincinnati OH 1973-1977; Assoc R S Steph's Epis Ch And U Columbus OH 1969-1972; Cur S Paul's Epis Ch Morris Plains NJ 1967-1969. stuguru2@yahoo.com

COYNE, Margaret (Vt) 14 Church St, Bellows Falls VT 05101 B Skowhegan ME 8/30/1943 d Robert Acheson Crane & Margaret Phyllis. BA Johnson St Coll 1980; MDiv EDS 1994. D 5/31/1994 Bp Mary Adelia Rosamond McLeod P 12/20/1994 Bp Thomas Kreider Ray. m 12/30/2006 Anthony Coyne c 2. Imm Ch Bellows Falls VT 1995-2007; Dio Vermont Burlington VT 1994-1995. mcrane@sover.net

COYNE, William Hugh (WMass) 134 Stonehill Rd, East Longmeadow MA 01028 **Archd Dio Wstrn Massachusetts Springfield MA 1998-; GC Dep Dio Wstrn Massachusetts Springfield MA 1988-2012** B Plainfield NJ 6/19/1953 s Hugh George Coyne & Miriam Joan. BA W Virginia Wesleyan Coll 1975; MDiv GTS 1978. D 6/3/1978 Bp Albert Wiencke Van Duzer P 12/16/1978 Bp Alexander Doig Stewart. m 6/25/1977 Janet S Smith c 3. Dioc Coun Dio Wstrn Massachusetts Springfield MA 1998-2011; Cn Chr Ch Cathd Springfield MA 1989-1995; R Trin Epis Ch Ware MA 1981-1989; Assoc Ch Of The Atone Westfield MA 1978-1981. whcoyne@gmail.com

COZZOLI, John David (Md) 17524 Lincolnshire Rd, Hagerstown MD 21740 **D S Mk's Ch Lappans Boonsboro MD 1999-** B Hagerstown MD 9/23/1937 s Michael Cozzoli & Vera Louise. EFM STUSo; U of Mississippi. D 6/17/1989 Bp A(lbert) Theodore Eastman. m 12/20/1969 Ruth Rittenhouse c 2. D S Anne's Epis Ch Smithsburg MD 1995-1998; Sm Ch Developmennt Dio Maryland Baltimore MD 1993-1994; D S Thos' Par Hancock MD 1989-1993. imjonzoli@yahoo.com

CRABTREE, David (NC) 2911 Hostetler St, Raleigh NC 27609 B 12/17/1949 s Jesse Melvin Crabtree & Sarah Stinson. BS Middleton St. U 1972. D 6/13/2004 Bp Michael Bruce Curry. c 2. D Ch Of The Gd Shpd Raleigh NC 2004-2009. david.crabtree@cgs-raleigh.org

CRAFT, Carolyn M (SVa) 1702 Briery Rd, Farmville VA 23901 **Sprtl Dir Ch Of The Epiph Danville VA 2010-** B Boston MA d James Craft & Carolyn. BA Agnes Scott Coll 1964; MA U of Pennsylvania 1965; PhD U of Pennsylvania 1973; Ya 1975; U of Virginia 1977. D 4/8/1983 P 4/24/1984 Bp Lyman Cunningham Ogilby. Assoc. R; R S Jas Ch Cartersville VA 1998-2009; Assoc. R; R Chr Ch Amelia Crt Hse VA 1998-2004; Assoc. R; R Emm Epis Ch Powhatan VA 1998-2004; P-in-Chg, Vic S Jas Chuch Warfield VA 1989-1996; P-in-Chg, Vic S Jas Ch Emporia VA 1989-1996. Ed Bd, *Cross Currents*, 1976, 1996; Reviewer, *Libr Journ*. AAR 1975. UVA Vstng Schlr U of Virginia 1977; Yale PD Fllshp Ya 1974; Phi Kappa Phi. craftcm@longwood.edu

CRAFT, John Harvey (La) 4505 S Claiborne Ave, New Orleans LA 70125 B Hattiesburg MS 12/20/1953 s Harvey Milton Craft & Mary Beth S. BA Tul 1975; JD Tul 1979; MPS Loyola U - New Orleans 2008. D 2/2/2011 P 8/27/2011 Bp Morris King Thompson Jr. m 12/21/1974 Nancy Crackere c 5. jhcraft@dellsouth.net

CRAFT, Mart Kenneth (Spok) 127 E 12th Ave, Spokane WA 99202 **Died 2/5/2011** B Sunnyside WA 8/28/1939 s Jean Kenneth Craft & Katherine Delores. BA WA SU 1961; MDiv CDSP 1964. D 8/23/1964 P 6/1/1965 Bp Russell S Hubbard. c 3. Associated Parishes. martkcraft@comcast.net

CRAFT, Stephen Frank (La) 3101 Plymouth Pl, New Orleans LA 70131 **S Phil's Ch New Orleans LA 2004-** B Hattiesburg MS 10/9/1958 s Harvey Milton Craft & Mary Beth. BD Tul 1985; MDiv Epis TS of The SW 1992. D 6/13/1992 P 12/13/1992 Bp James Barrow Brown. m 6/26/1993 Martha Bearfield. Vic S Andr's Ch Clinton LA 1992-2000; Vic S Pat's Ch Zachary LA 1992-2000. craft9527@bellsouth.net

CRAFTON, Barbara Cawthorne (NY) 387 Middlesex Ave, Metuchen NJ 08840 **Int Ch Of The Atone Stratford NJ 1985-** B Mora MN 3/28/1951 d D M Cawthorne & Aida Lorain. BA Rutgers-The St U 1977; MDiv GTS 1980. D 6/7/1980 Bp Albert Wiencke Van Duzer P 12/1/1980 Bp George Phelps Mellick Belshaw. m 11/25/1989 Richard Edgecomb Quaintance c 2. S Jas Epis Ch Firenze IA IT 2008-2009; The Geranium Farm Metuchen NJ 2008-2009; R S Clem's Ch New York NY 1996-2002; Seamens Ch Inst Income New York NY 1993-1996; Trin Educ Fund New York NY 1991; Corp Of Trin Ch New York NY 1990; Seamens Ch Inst Income New York NY 1983-1989; S Lk's Epis Ch Metuchen NJ 1981-1983. Auth, "Numerous arts & Revs"; Auth, "Sewing Room"; Auth, "Blessed Paradoxes". Cmnty H Sprt. bccrafton@geraniumfarm.org

C

CRAFTS JR, Robert (SanD) 13030 Birch Ln, Poway CA 92064 **Vic S Eliz's Epis Ch San Diego CA 2001-** B Cleveland OH 5/4/1935 s Robert Crafts & Glenna Marie. BA Ya 1957; MD Case Wstrn Reserve U 1962; MDiv Nash 1989. D 6/24/1989 P 12/27/1989 Bp Charles Brinkley Morton. m 7/6/1963 Carol Ann Bilhardt c 2. Bd Of Trst Nash Nashotah WI 2000-2004; Mssnr S Mk's Ch San Diego CA 1999-2001; P-in-c S Mary's In The Vlly Ch Ramona CA 1999; Asst All SS Ch Vista CA 1998; Dio San Diego San Diego CA 1992-2000; P-in-c S Jn's Ch Indio CA 1989-1998. Conf Of S Ben 1978. rcrafts@cox.net

CRAGER, H(arry) Dillon (FdL) 3360 County Rd E, Baileys Harbor WI 54202 **D S Lk's Sis Bay WI 2003-** B Philadelphia PA 12/11/1943 s Russell Harry Crager & Edith Mary. BA Elizabethtown Coll 1966; MS U Pgh 1969. D 8/30/2003 Bp Russell Edward Jacobus. m 8/29/1964 Suzanne F Hamell c 1. flyfisher@isp.com

CRAGON JR, Miller M. (Chi) 5555 N Sheridan Rd Apt 810, Chicago IL 60640 **Asstg Cathd Of S Jas Chicago IL 2002-** B Ruston LA 6/29/1924 s Miller Cragon & Lou Willie. BA Tul 1944; MDiv STUSo 1947; S Aug's Coll Cbury GB 1954; MA SMU 1960. D 12/29/1946 Bp John L Jackson P 12/21/1950 Bp Girault M Jones. m 9/6/2011 Gregorio Aluarado. Coordntr Sch for Diac Mnstry Dio Chicago Chicago IL 1984-1989; Cn Ordnry Dio Chicago Chicago IL 1978-1989; Seamens Ch Inst Income New York NY 1970-1978; Seamans Inst Bonus 4 Per Cent New York NY 1970-1976; Seaman's Ch Inst Bonus 11 Per Cent New York NY 1970-1976; Exec Dir DeptCE Dio New York New York City NY 1961-1969; DRE S Mich And All Ang Ch Dallas TX 1954-1961; R Chr Ch Covington LA 1950-1953; Cur S Andr's Epis Ch New Orleans LA 1947-1948. Auth, *Rel Educ*. gregnmill67@aol.com

CRAIG, Carolyn (EC) 201 S Eastern St., Greenville NC 27858 B Sewanee TN 11/1/1957 d C Phillip Craig & Nancy Taylor. BA U CO 1985; Harv 1988; Duke 1990; MDiv CDSP 1992. D 6/20/1992 Bp Hunley Agee Elebash P 5/1/1993 Bp Brice Sidney Sanders. Dir of Chr Formation and Educ S Paul's Epis Ch Greenville NC 2007-2011; Dio E Carolina Kinston NC 2005-2006; P S Paul's Ch Vanceboro NC 2000-2003; S Tim's Epis Ch Greenville NC 1994-1996. lilly031@gmail.com

CRAIG SR, Claude Phillip (EC) Po Box 1336, Kinston NC 28503 **Dio E Carolina Kinston NC 2000-; Cdo Dio E Carolina Kinston NC 2000-** B Oklahoma City OK 6/1/1936 s Harold Houston Craig & Mary Taylor. BA U So 1958; BD STUSo 1962. D 6/29/1962 Bp Thomas Augustus Fraser Jr P 6/29/1963 Bp Richard Henry Baker. m 9/8/1956 Nancy Dibble. Cn Ordnry Dio E Carolina Kinston NC 1998-2000; Dio E Carolina Kinston NC 1997-1999; Chair Dio E Carolina Kinston NC 1990-1998; R S Mary's Ch Kinston NC 1986-1997; Const & Cns Cmsn Dio No Carolina Raleigh NC 1984-1985; Chair Dept Msnns Dio No Carolina Raleigh NC 1983-1985; R The Epis Ch Of Gd Shpd Asheboro NC 1981-1985; Educ & Trng Com Dio No Carolina Raleigh NC 1978-1983; R Emm Ch Warrenton NC 1978-1980; S Matt's Ch Pampa TX 1974-1976. Oblate Ord Julian Of Norwich 1994. nanphil@suddenlink.net

CRAIG JR, Claude Phillip (Va) 6300 SW Nicol Road, Portland OR 97223 **P Ascen Par Portland OR 2011-; Chapl Oregon Epis Sch Portland OR 2011-** B Greensboro NC 11/22/1967 s Claude Phillip Craig & Nancy. BA U NC 1991; MDiv VTS 1995. D 6/3/1995 P 12/10/1995 Bp Brice Sidney Sanders. m 9/24/1994 Jennifer Lynn Bosworth. Chapl Epis HS Alexandria VA 1997-2007; Asst R S Jn's Epis Ch Wilmington NC 1995-1997. craigp@oes.edu

CRAIG JR, Harry Walter (Kan) 5041 Sw Fairlawn Rd, Topeka KS 66610 **D S Dav's Epis Ch Topeka KS 1986-** B Lawrence KS 5/11/1939 s Harry Walter Craig & Lola. BA U of Kansas 1961; LLB U of Kansas 1964. D 10/24/1986 Bp Richard Frank Grein. m 4/30/1960 Karen May Martin c 4. hcraig@martintractor.com

CRAIG, Hugh Burnette (NC) No address on file. B 11/12/1936 D 6/29/1962 P 6/29/1963 Bp Richard Henry Baker.

CRAIG, Idalia Simmons (NJ) 212 N Main St, Glassboro NJ 08028 **S Thos' Epis Ch Glassboro NJ 2006-** B Goldsboro NC 4/7/1952 d Clifton E Simmons & Etla. D 5/20/2000 P 12/9/2000 Bp David B(ruce) Joslin. m 8/29/2005 Peyton Craig c 1. Assoc R S Ptr's Ch Freehold NJ 2000-2006. revidaliacraig@yahoo.com

CRAIG III, James O (WMass) 11 Cotton St, Leominster MA 01453 **Dioc Coun Dio Wstrn Massachusetts Springfield MA 2007-2012; R S Mk's Ch Leominster MA 1996-** B Manchester CT 6/28/1953 s James Orville Craig & Ruth. BA Southampton Coll Southampton NY 1976; MDiv Bex 1992. D 6/13/1992 P 12/19/1992 Bp William George Burrill. m 8/16/1975 Cynthia Jeanne

Keough c 4. Dn, No Worcester Dnry Dio Wstrn Massachusetts Springfield MA 1998-2004; D/R S Geo's Ch Hilton NY 1992-1996. j.o.craig@verizon.net

CRAIG III, Richard Edwin (Mil) 4417 Westway Ave, Racine WI 53405 B Atlanta GA 11/6/1945 s Richard Edwin Craig & Nettie Beatrice. BA Georgia St U 1969. D 6/3/1990 Bp Earl Nicholas McArthur Jr P 2/17/1991 Bp John Herbert MacNaughton. m 6/23/1967 Marie Pascoe c 3. R S Jn The Bapt Portage WI 2008-2010; Int R S Mk's Ch Milwaukee WI 2007-2008; R S Lk's Ch Racine WI 2002-2006; Vic S Andr's Epis Ch Corpus Christi TX 2001-2002; Vic S Thos And S Mart's Ch Corpus Christi TX 1998-2002; Vic Ch Of Our Sav Aransas Pass TX 1998-2001; Asst to R S Andr's Epis Ch San Antonio TX 1990-1997. Auth, "Questions of the Bible: Who? What? Where? When? Why?," PublishAmerica, 2006; Auth, "What Do We Do w Lk 6?," PublisherAmerica, 2004. recraigiii@mac.com

CRAIGHEAD JR, J(ohn) Thomas (Oly) 23404 107th Ave SW, Vashon WA 98070 B New York NY 3/5/1951 s John Thomas Craighead & Mary. Coll of Wooster 1971; BA U of Montana 1975; MDiv GTS 1982; MSW Syr 1994. D 6/5/1982 Bp William Moultrie Moore Jr P 12/9/1982 Bp Harold B Robinson. m 11/26/1982 Lorna Walker c 2. St Bede Epis Ch Port Orchard WA 1995-2001; S Andr's Epis Ch Colchester VT 1986-1992; Cn S Paul's Cathd Buffalo NY 1982-1985. Sprtl Dir Intl 2001. craigheadwalker@juno.com

CRAIGHILL, Peyton Gardner (Pa) 25 Sycamore Lane, Lexington VA 24450 B Nanchang China 10/24/1929 s Lloyd Rutherford Craighill & Marian Gardner. BA Ya 1951; BD VTS 1954; STM GTS 1965; PhD PrTS 1973. D 7/10/1954 P 3/31/1955 Bp Lloyd Rutherford Craighill. m 4/24/1962 Mary Roberts c 2. Assoc Ch Of The Redeem Bryn Mawr PA 2002-2008; Epis Cmnty Serv Philadelphia PA 1989-1994; Dio Pennsylvania Philadelphia PA 1988-1994; Assoc The Ch Of The H Trin Rittenhouse Philadelphia PA 1988-1989; The TS at The U So Sewanee TN 1980-1982; The U So (Sewanee) Sewanee TN 1980-1982; Asst The Ch Of The Redeem Baltimore MD 1954-1957. Ed, "Diac Mnstry, Past, Present and Future," NAAD, 1998. Cntr for Baptismal Living 1998-2008; Episcopalians on Baptismal Mssn 2010; Mem Mssn 2006; NAAD 1989-1998; SE Asia Assn for Theol Educ 1961-1978; Taiwan Chr Consultative Coun 1961-1978. peyton.g@comcast.net

CRAIN II, Lee Bryan (LI) 518 Brooklyn Blvd, Brightwaters NY 11718 B Flushing NY 2/14/1951 s Michael Crain & Norma Olga. D 7/19/1987 Bp Henry Boyd Hucles III. m 7/30/1983 Allison Jill Boyd.

CRAIN, William Henry (WMo) 9208 Wenonga Rd, Leawood KS 66206 **Chapl Bp Spencer Place Inc Kansas City MO 2004-; St Lk's So Chap Overland Pk KS 2004-** B Atlanta GA 10/17/1941 s Dorothy Jewel. BA Olivet Nazarene U 1963; MS Creighton U 1968. D 2/7/2004 Bp Barry Robert Howe. m 6/29/1985 Rebecca Lee Crain c 1. whcrain@swbell.net

CRAM, Don (RG) Po Box 45000, Rio Rancho NM 87174 B Glendale CA 7/31/1949 s Owen B Cram & Doris Grace. BS USC 1971; MDiv NW Bapt Sem Tacoma WA 1976; Brigham Young U 1996. D 11/17/1999 P 4/25/2001 Bp Terence Kelshaw. m 6/13/1970 Carol Linda Lawton c 4. Cn S Jn's Cathd Albuquerque NM 2006-2007; Hope in the Desert Eps Ch Albuquerque NM 2004-2005; Vic Epis Ch Of The H Fam Santa Fe NM 2004; Vic Epis Ch Of The Epiph Socorro NM 2001-2003; D S Fran Ch Rio Rancho NM 1999-2001. Bro of S Andr. doncram@mac.com

CRAM JR, Norman Lee (NCal) Po Box 224, Vineburg CA 95487 B Waukegan IL 8/24/1937 s Norman Lee Cram & Charlotte Fleming. BA Wms 1959; BD CDSP 1962; MA Grad Theol Un 1976. D 8/12/1962 P 5/1/1963 Bp William F Lewis. m 7/21/1962 Deirdre Elizabeth Field c 2. P-in-c St Johns Epis Ch Petaluma CA 2007-2009; P-in-c S Steph's Epis Ch Sebastopol CA 1999-2000; Chapl Off Of Bsh For ArmdF New York NY 1964-1994; Cur S Jn's Epis Ch Olympia WA 1962-1964. Meritorious Serv Medal US Navy 1994; USCoast Guard Commendation Medal US Coast Gaurd 1986; Joint Serv Commendation Medal US Navy 1969; USNavy Commendation Medal US Navy 1967; Gold Star in Lieu of 5th Awd US Navy 1964. dootscram@aol.com

CRAMER, Alfred Anthony (Vt) 47 Morningside Commons, Brattleboro VT 05301 B Somerville MA 11/30/1933 s Alfred Cramer & Irene Marie. BA Bos 1957; MDiv EDS 1962; MSW Smith 1991. D 7/15/1962 P 1/25/1963 Bp William F Lewis. m 6/18/1988 Janet French Thompson c 4. R Chr Epis Ch Burlington IA 1978-1983; R S Lk's Ch Des Moines IA 1969-1978; Vic S Matthews Auburn WA 1964-1965; Cur S Mk's Cathd Seattle WA 1962-1964. Amer Assn for Marriages Fam Ther 1979. aacramer@sover.net

CRAMER, Jared C (WMich) 524 Washington Ave, Grand Haven MI 49417 **Faith & Ord Cmssnr Natl Coun Of Ch New York NY 2011-; Dn (of Dnry) Dio Wstrn Michigan Kalamazoo MI 2010-; R S Jn's Epis Ch Grand Haven MI 2010-** B Owosso MI 9/14/1981 s Gerald Clair Cramer & Susan Leigh. BS Rochester Coll 2004; MDiv Abilene Chr U 2007; STM TS 2008. D 4/20/2008 P 12/14/2008 Bp C(harles) Wallis Ohl. m 11/8/2008 Bethany Anne Switter. Cler Res Chr Ch Alexandria VA 2008-2010. jared.c.cramer@gmail.com

CRAMER, Roger W (Mass) 16 Aubin Street, Amesbury MA 01913 B Mansfield OH 2/29/1944 s Stanley L Cramer & Annabel. Drew U; BA OH SU 1966; ThM U Chi 1969; DMin U Chi 1971. D 6/18/1972 P 12/1/1972 Bp David Keller Leighton Sr. m 10/28/1978 Louise Sabolchy c 2. R S Paul's Ch Newburyport MA 1979-2005; Assoc Trin Ch Princeton NJ 1976-1979; Chr Ch Columbia MD 1973-1976. Phillips Brooks Cler Club Of Boston. rogercramer6@comcast.net

CRAMMER, Margaret Corinne (Chi) 927 Scott Blvd Apt 205, Decatur GA 30030 **Cler Assoc All SS Epis Ch Atlanta GA 2007-** B Omaha NE 10/8/1950 d Adrain Crammer & Ruth L. ABD Emory U; Garrett Evang TS; U Chi; BA NWU 1980; MA NWU 1983; MDiv Ya Berk 1995. D 6/17/1995 P 12/1/1995 Bp Frank Tracy Griswold III. Int S Paul's Epis Ch Newnan GA 1997-2000; Asst to R S Jos's Epis Ch McDonough GA 1996-1997. Norenberg Preaching Prize Yale - Berkely DS 1994. crammer@bellsouth.net

CRAMPTON, Barbara Amelia (Ga) 703 E 48th St, Savannah GA 31405 **D S Mich And All Ang Savannah GA 2000-** B Monticello NY 2/7/1925 d Chester Wright Couch & Winifred Charlotte. BS The Coll of S Rose 1975; Dio Albany Diac Prog Albany NY 1983. D 6/18/1983 Bp Wilbur Emory Hogg Jr. m 5/15/1948 Gordon Kelsey Crampton c 2. D The Epis Ch Of S Jn Bapt Thomaston ME 1984-2000; D S Andr's Ch Scotia NY 1983-1984. NAAD 1982. dcnbarbatsav@hotmail.com

CRAMPTON, Susan H (WMass) 54 Grandview Dr, Williamstown MA 01267 B Denver CO 4/5/1938 d Jack Ramsay Harris & Ellen Margaret. BA Smith 1960; MDiv EDS 1977. D 6/18/1977 P 2/4/1978 Bp Alexander Doig Stewart. m 12/29/1961 Stuart Crampton c 3. R Chr Epis Ch Sheffield MA 1994-2003; Assoc R S Andr's Ch Longmeadow MA 1991-1993; Dio Wstrn Massachusetts Springfield MA 1984-2003; Vic S Jn's Ch Ashfield MA 1984-1991; Asst The Amer Cathd of the H Trin Paris 75008 FR 1982-1983; Assoc S Jn's Ch Williamstown MA 1978-1984; Intern Gr Ch Amherst MA 1977-1978. Fllshp of the Way of the Cross 1982; SCHC 1978. shcrampt@williams.edu

CRANDALL, Harry Wilson (SVa) PO Box 275, 9115 Franktown Road, Franktown VA 23354 **R Emer Hungars Par Eastville VA 2002-** B Portland ME 3/30/1932 s Harry Wells Crandall & Ada Elizabeth. BS USMA at W Point 1956; MDiv STUSo 1983. D 7/6/1983 P 4/7/1984 Bp C(laude) Charles Vache. m 9/7/1963 Catherine Dishman c 2. Dn Dio Sthrn Virginia Norfolk VA 1987-1991; R Hungars Par Eastville VA 1983-2002. Treas Natl ECom 1989-1998. Janette Pierce Awd ECom 1998; Polly Bond Awd ECom 1998. hcrandall@verizon.net

CRANDALL, John Davin (Mass) 404 Juniper Way, Tavares FL 32778 **Asst S Edw The Confessor Mt Dora FL 2008-** B Harrisburg PA 5/25/1937 s John Milton Crandall & Elizabeth. BA Trin Hartford CT 1958; MDiv VTS 1969. D 6/4/1969 P 12/6/1969 Bp Dean T Stevenson. m 10/6/2007 Mary Beth Whitcher c 3. Par Dev Comm Dio Massachusetts Boston MA 1986-1989; R All SS Epis Ch Attleboro MA 1984-1999; Dioc Coun Dio Minnesota Minneapolis MN 1980-1984; R Chr Ch Albert Lea MN 1979-1984; Dn Lay Acad Dio Bethlehem Bethlehem PA 1976-1979; Cn Cathd Ch Of The Nativ Bethlehem PA 1975-1979; Vic Chr Ch Berwick PA 1971-1975; Cur The Epis Ch Of S Jn The Bapt York PA 1969-1971. ACPE; Bd Dir Acad Par Cleric. mlcjdc@aol.com

CRANDELL, Herbert Charles (EMich) 3191 Hospers St, Grand Blanc MI 48439 B Ann Arbor MI 11/11/1931 s Herbert Charles Crandell & Vera Marion. BS U MI 1953; MDiv VTS 1963. D 6/29/1963 Bp Archie H Crowley P 2/29/1964 Bp Richard S M Emrich. m 12/6/1986 Janet Bignall c 3. R S Jude's Epis Ch Fenton MI 1965-1974; Asst S Paul's Epis Ch Flint MI 1963-1965. hccjr@umich.edu

CRANE, Charles Tarleton (Haw) 6220 E Broadway Rd # 309, Mesa AZ 85206 **Supply Dio Arizona Phoenix AZ 1995-** B Honolulu HI 4/11/1928 s Ezra Crane & Frances Erma. BD Iowa St U 1951; MDiv CDSP 1957; Chichester Theol Coll 1977. D 6/23/1957 Bp Russell S Hubbard P 12/23/1957 Bp Harry S Kennedy. m 8/26/2006 Marie Elaine Hohm c 3. Mem, Dioc Coun Dio Hawaii Honolulu HI 1986-1988; Trst CDSP Berkeley CA 1981-1988; Mem, Stndg Com Dio Hawaii Honolulu HI 1981-1985; Ch Of The H Nativ Honolulu HI 1968-1988; R All SS Ch Kapaa HI 1959-1966; Yth DCE S Andr's Cathd Honolulu HI 1957-1959. Auth, "The Cler Search Dilemma," 1991. azkanaka@aol.com

CRANE, Gordon Albert (CFla) 594 Comanche Ave, Melbourne FL 32935 **D H Trin Epis Ch Melbourne FL 2007-** B Binghamton NY 8/23/1920 s Albert Wallace Crane & Georgianna Elizabeth. SUNY 1950; Florida Inst of Tech 1970; AS Brevard Cmnty Coll 1975. D 2/2/1987 Bp William Hopkins Folwell. m 3/27/1956 Dorothy Violet Beddows c 4. D H Trin Epis Ch Melbourne FL 1987-2000. Ord Of S Lk.

CRANE, Linda Sue (EMich) 1213 6th St, Port Huron MI 48060 B St Clair MI 2/14/1953 d James Henry Prince & Ruth Irene. Nrsng St Clair Cnty Cmnty 1980. D 11/18/2006 Bp Edwin Max Leidel Jr. c 4. crane-linda@sbc.global.net

CRANE, Rebecca Mai (Mass) 13 Trinity St., Danvers MA 01923 B Salem MA 2/19/1965 d Barney Murphree & Shirley. BA U of Massachusetts Amherst 1987; MEd Salem St Coll Salem MA 2003; Cert. in Angl Stds D Progam Dio Massachusetts 2008. D 6/7/2008 Bp M(arvil) Thomas Shaw III. m 6/6/1987 Eric Crane c 2. deaconcrane@gmail.com

CRANSTON, Dale Lawrence (NY) 21 Stone Fence Road, Mahwah NJ 07430 B Paterson NJ 1/22/1946 s Lawrence Cranston & Marie W. BA Grove City

Coll 1968; MDiv EDS 1972. D 6/10/1972 Bp Leland Stark P 4/26/1975 Bp George E Rath. Chr Ch Of Ramapo Suffern NY 2004-2009; Assoc All SS' Epis Ch Glen Rock NJ 1972-1988. dale.cranston@gmail.com

CRANSTON, Pamela Lee (Cal) 207 Taurus Ave, Oakland CA 94611 **Vic S Cuth's Epis Ch Oakland CA 2011-** B New York NY 10/21/1950 d Day Lee & Nancy Arabel. Cert Ch Army Trng Coll 1972; BA San Francisco St U 1984; MDiv CDSP 1988. D 6/3/1989 P 6/9/1990 Bp William Edwin Swing. m 8/18/1984 Edward Eugene Cranston. Long-term Int S Cuth's Epis Ch Oakland CA 2006-2011; Field Educ Supvsr CDSP Berkeley CA 1995-2004; Assoc R All Souls Par In Berkeley Berkeley CA 1995-1997; Cler Wellness Cmsn, Chair Dio California San Francisco CA 1992-2009; Asst R S Tim's Ch Danville CA 1990-1994; Asst to Cn Pstr Gr Cathd San Francisco CA 1988-1990; Exec Dir - Vol Corps Epis Ch Cntr New York NY 1972-1973. Auth, "Rosing From the Dead: Poems of Paul J. Willis," *ATR*, ATR, Inc., 2010; Auth, "Poetry," *ATR*, ATR, Inc., 2010; Auth, "Love Was His Meaning: An Intro to Julian of Norwich," Forw Mvmt, 2008; Auth, "Psalm Writing A Playbox for Bldg Beloved Cmnty," *Playbox CD - for Bldg the Beloved Cmnty*, Dio CA, 2008; Auth, "Essay: Poetry and Priesthood," *The Angl: A Journ of Angl Identity*, Angl Soc - GTS, 2006; Auth, "Coming to Treeline: Adirondack Poems," St. Huberts Press, 2005; Auth, "The Poet as Archbp: The Poems of Rowan Williams," *The Angl: A Journ of Angl Identity*, Angl Soc - GTS, 2005; Auth, "The Madonna Murders," St. Huberts Press, 2003; Auth, "Coming To Treeline - poem," *Blueline Anthology*, Syr Press, 2003; Auth, "Poetry," *Penwood Revs*, 2002; Auth, "A Sprtl Journey w Jn Donne," Forw Mvmt, 2001; Auth, "Searching For Nova Albion," *ATR*, ATR, Inc., 2001; Auth, "Cler Wellness & Mutual Mnstry," O'Brien & Whitaker Pub, 2000; Auth, "Poetry," *Adirondack Revs*, 2000; Auth, "Resurr," *Wmn Healing and Empowering*, ELCA Pub, 1996. Amer Acad of Poets 2000-2005; Cal Cler Assn Bd Mem 1995-1997; Dio Cal Cleric Compnstn T/F Mem 1996-2000; Kilvert Soc 1993. MDiv w hon CDSP 1988. pcranstn@pacbell.net

CRAPSEY II, Marcus Trowbridge (Mass) 13 Manor Drive Apt A, Groveland MA 01834 **Int S Jn's Epis Ch Gloucester MA 2010-; Int S Jn's Epis Ch Gloucester MA 1979-** B New York NY 12/23/1950 s Marcus Trowbridge Crapsey & Rosemary Ward. BA U of Connecticut 1972; MSW U of Connecticut 1976; MDiv GTS 1979. D 6/9/1979 Bp Morgan Porteus P 5/10/1980 Bp Richard Beamon Martin. m 8/12/1972 Linda Ericsson c 2. Int S Mary's Epis Par Northfield VT 2009-2010; R Trin Epis Ch Haverhill MA 1989-2009; Vic S Geo's Ch Middlebury CT 1982-1989; Asst S Mk's Ch Westhampton Bch NY 1979-1982. marcus.crapsey42@gmail.com

CRARY, Kathleen (Cal) 169 Pearce, Hercules CA 94547 **R Chr Ch Alameda CA 2010-** B Lawrence KS 6/13/1951 Rec from Evangelical Lutheran Church in America 12/1/2001 Bp William Edwin Swing. Int S Jas Ch Fremont CA 2008-2010; Assoc Ch Of The H Trin Richmond CA 2005-2008; Assoc Chr The Lord Epis Ch Pinole CA 2002-2005. kathycrary@gmail.com

CRASE, Jane Lieberg (Los) 56312 Onaga Trl, Yucca Valley CA 92284 **S Jos Of Arimathea Mssn Yucca Vlly CA 2011-** B Pasadena CA 10/27/1945 d Elan R Lieberg. Paralegal Cert USC 1976; AA Mt San Antonio Coll 1986. D 6/4/2011 Bp Joseph Jon Bruno. m 1/8/1983 Gary Crase. dmtjane@aol.com

CRAUN, Christopher Brooke (Ore) 3236 NE Alberta St., Portland OR 97211 **R S Mich And All Ang Ch Portland OR 2009-** B Berkeley CA 4/30/1980 s Raymond Craun & Carol. BA U CA 2002; CTh CDSP 2003; MDiv GTS 2006. D 6/3/2006 Bp William Edwin Swing P 12/2/2006 Bp Marc Handley Andrus. m Michelle Nixon. Asst S Jas's Ch W Hartford CT 2006-2009; Dio California San Francisco CA 2002-2003. cbcraun@yahoo.com

CRAVEN III, James Braxton (NC) 17 Marchmont Ct, Durham NC 27705 **Prison Cmsn Dio No Carolina Raleigh NC 2010-; P Assoc S Lk's Epis Ch Durham NC 1992-** B Portsmouth VA 12/8/1942 s James Braxton Craven & Mary Kistler. Coll of Preachers; USNA 1960; BA U NC 1964; JD Duke 1967; MDiv Duke 1981. D 12/14/1985 Bp Robert Whitridge Estill P 12/29/1995 Bp Charles Lovett Keyser. m 8/22/1964 Sara Ann Harris c 3. Chair, Dioc Cmsn on the ArmdF Dio No Carolina Raleigh NC 1992-1999; Asst S Jos's Ch Durham NC 1985-1992. Auth, "arts," *Living Ch*, Living Ch, 1985. LCDR, USN(Ret) US Navy 1996. jbc64@mindspring.com

CRAVEN, Sam (Tex) 6221 Main St, Houston TX 77030 **Palmer Memi Ch Houston TX 2005-** B Andalusia AL 9/14/1946 s Harold Craven & Virginia Beatrice. BS U of Alabama 1968; JD Loyola U 1971; MDiv Epis TS of The SW 2003. D 6/7/2003 P 4/1/2004 Bp D(avid) Bruce Mac Pherson. m 2/14/1987 Irma Louise Craven c 3. S Cuth's Epis Ch Houston TX 2003-2005. scraven@palmerchurch.org

CRAVENS, James Owen (Spr) 4 Canterbury Ln, Lincoln IL 62656 **Ch Of S Jn The Bapt Lincoln IL 1996-** B Pueblo CO 8/17/1954 s Jackson R Cravens & Barbara Ellen. BA Ft Lewis Coll 1976; MDiv UTS 1980. D 6/14/1980 P 12/1/1980 Bp John Shelby Spong. c 2. Trin Ch Lincoln IL 1996-2010; R S Mart's Ch Pawtucket RI 1987-1996; Assoc S Steph's Ch Ridgefield CT 1982-1987; Cur Chr Ch Ridgewood NJ 1980-1982. Auth, "Recent Trends In Epis Stwdshp". chcusnr@yahoo.com

CRAVER III, Marshall Pinnix (CGC) 613 Highland Woods Dr E, Mobile AL 36608 **Assoc R S Paul's Ch Mobile AL 2003-** B Brewton AL 10/20/1953 s Marshall Pinnix Craver & Ellen. BS Auburn U 1977; MDiv STUSo 1984. D 6/1/1984 P 5/1/1985 Bp Charles Farmer Duvall. m 12/16/1978 Jan Pullen c 3. Int S Steph's Ch Brewton AL 2002-2003; R S Jas' Epis Ch Alexander City AL 1995-2002; Chr The Redeem Ch Montgomery AL 1988-1995; The Ch Of The Redeem MOBILE AL 1988-1995; Chr Ch Cathd Mobile Mobile AL 1984-1988. marshallcraver@bellsouth.net

CRAWFORD, Alicia Leu Lydon (Chi) 550 N Green Bay Rd, Lake Forest IL 60045 B Saint Louis MO 1/9/1950 d Alicia Hafner. BA Amer U 1972; MDiv SWTS 1986. D 6/14/1986 Bp James Winchester Montgomery P 12/12/1987 Bp Frank Tracy Griswold III. m 12/22/1969 James Ellis Crawford c 2. Cur S Mk's Ch Evanston IL 1986-1987. Soc of S Jn the Evang. aliciallcrawford@aol.com

CRAWFORD, Grady J (At) 2602 Oglethorpe Cir NE, Atlanta GA 30319 **Cathd Of S Phil Atlanta GA 2009-** B Waycross GA 10/31/1959 s Grady J Crawford & Patricia L. BA,BS U of So Alabama; MDiv Candler TS 2009. D 12/20/2008 P 6/28/2009 Bp J(ohn) Neil Alexander. buddy.crawford@mindspring.com

CRAWFORD, Hayden G (SeFla) 701 45th Ave S, Saint Petersburg FL 33705 **R Ch Of The Incarn Miami FL 2010-** B Gainesville FL 11/9/1948 s Jackson Collier Crawford & Marion. BS Florida A&M U 1973; MDiv Interdenominational Theol Cntr 1978. D 5/3/1980 P 12/17/1980 Bp Furman Stough. m 4/8/1989 Alexis M Campbell c 2. P-in-c S Alb's Epis Ch St Pete Bch FL 2008-2010; Assoc Ch Of S Mich And All Ang Sanibel FL 2007; Assoc Chr Ch Bradenton FL 2005-2007; Jubilee Mnstry Advsry Exec Coun Appointees New York NY 2000-2003; Stndg Com Dio SW Florida Sarasota FL 1997-2003; R S Aug's Epis Ch St Petersburg FL 1996-2005; R S Aug And S Mart Ch Boston MA 1992-1996; R Ch Of Our Merc Sav Louisville KY 1987-1992; Exec Coun Dio Mississippi Jackson MS 1985-1986; R S Mk's Ch Jackson MS 1984-1986; R S Simon The Cyrenian Ch Philadelphia PA 1983-1984; Vic Gd Shpd Ch Montgomery AL 1980-1983. CPE Advsry Bd; NAACP; UBE. Cntrl Cmnty Cntr Awd Louisville KY 1987; Ldrshp Awd Naacp 1982; Young Men Of Amer 1979; Rel Awd Phi Beta Sigma. frhayden1980@msn.com

CRAWFORD, Katherine Carlsen (Az) 15758 W Latham St, Goodyear AZ 85338 B Douglas WY 5/6/1985 d Kent Holmes Crawford & Christine Carlsen. BA L&C 2007; MDiv VTS 2012. D 6/11/2011 Bp Kirk Stevan Smith. katie.c.crawford@gmail.com

CRAWFORD JR, Kelly Allen (Los) 1622 Dalmatia Dr, San Pedro CA 90732 **Exec Dir Sci Dio Los Angeles Los Angeles CA 1991-; Seamens Ch Inst Of Los Angeles San Pedro CA 1991-** B Farmington NM 4/18/1946 s Kelly Allen Crawford & Evelyn. BD U of New Mex 1982; MDiv CDSP 1989. D 7/22/1989 Bp Terence Kelshaw P 5/15/1990 Bp Donald Purple Hart. c 1. Epis Ch On W Kaua'i Eleele HI 1989-1991; S Jn's Ch Eleele HI 1989-1991. kelly.crawford@sealanes.org

CRAWFORD, Lee Alison (Vt) POB 67, Plymouth VT 05056 **Trin Ch Rutland VT 2008-; GC Dep Dio Vermont Burlington VT 1997-** B Norwalk CT 5/10/1957 d Arthur James Crawford & Jean Alice. BA Smith 1979; MA Pr 1983; PhD Pr 1991; MDiv GTS 1993. D 6/12/1993 Bp George Phelps Mellick Belshaw P 1/29/1994 Bp Joe Morris Doss. m 8/25/2000 Anne Clarke Brown. R S Mary's Epis Par Northfield VT 1994-2008; Asst Gr-S Paul's Ch Mercerville NJ 1993-1994; Asst H Trin Ch So River NJ 1993-1994; Asst Seamens Ch Inst Income New York NY 1993-1994. Auth, "The Mtn Echo"; Auth, "Wit". Cler Ldrshp Proj Class Ix 1997-2000; EWC 1988; Fundacion Cristosal 2000; Integrity; Ord Of S Helena 1988. Pilgrim Min to Israel Knights Templar 2011. lacinvt94@aol.com

CRAWFORD, Leo Lester (SwFla) 2694 Grove Park Rd, Palm Harbor FL 34583 B Jonesville LA 4/30/1941 s Leo F Crawford & Mabel A. BD LSU 1964; MDiv Nash 1988. D 6/4/1988 P 12/10/1988 Bp Willis Ryan Henton. m 4/28/1973 Ann R Skyrmes c 3. R Gd Samar Epis Ch Clearwater FL 2000-2008; Chr Ch Bastrop LA 1988-2000. leocrawford@gmail.com

CRAWFORD, Malia (Mass) 133 School St, New Bedford MA 02740 **Cur Gr Ch New Bedford MA 2008-** B Honolulu HI 5/2/1974 d James Aloysius Crawford & Nola. SB MIT 1996; MDiv Harvard DS 2005. D 6/7/2008 Bp M(arvil) Thomas Shaw III. m 10/4/2008 Amy LaVertu. Admin Asst for Worhsip and Pstr Care Trin Ch In The City Of Boston Boston MA 2005-2008. mcrawford@post.harvard.edu

CRAWFORD, Mark Taylor (Tex) PO Box 20269, Houston TX 77225 B New Orleans LA 8/25/1954 s William Neilly Crawford & Jeanette Ruth. BA SMU 1976; BA Oxf 1978; MA Oxf 1983; M.A. Wycliffe Hall, Oxford 1983; Cntrl Texas Pstr Cntr TX 1992; D.Min Austin Presb TS 2001. D 12/21/1980 P 9/16/1981 Bp The Bishop Of Paraguay. m 6/16/1979 Jean Eddison c 3. Campus Mssnr Palmer Memi Ch Houston TX 2004-2008; R Gr Epis Ch Alvin TX 1999-2003; GBEC Dio Texas Houston TX 1997-2009; R Epis Ch Of The H Sprt Waco TX 1990-1996; Vic Gr Epis Ch Georgetown TX 1985-1987; Vic S Jas' Ch Taylor TX 1985-1986; Asst Ch Of The Ascen Houston TX 1983-1985. Auth, "Doctoral Proj," *Called To Serve: /Exam The Process Of Ord*, Austin

Presb TS, 2000; Auth, "Bk Revs," *Susana Wesley: The Complete Writings*, 1999. Assn of Epis Hlth Care Chapl 2008. mtc5401@aol.com

CRAWFORD, Nancy Rogers (Ore) 1595 E 31st Ave, Eugene OR 97405 **S Mary's Epis Ch Eugene OR 2010-** B Agana Guam 3/19/1949 d James Graves Rogers & Virginia Boyd. Bachelor of Sci U of Louisiana at Monroe 1971. D 10/21/2006 Bp Johncy Itty. m 3/19/1982 Phillip Crawford c 2. Dio Oregon Portland OR 2006-2008; S Mary's Epis Ch Eugene OR 2000-2006.

CRAWFORD, Robert Lee (NY) Po Box 1415, Camden ME 04843 B Toledo OH 10/14/1938 s Lee R Crawford & Dorcas. BA NWU 1960; STB GTS 1966; MA U of Pennsylvania 1971. D 6/4/1966 P 12/1/1966 Bp Horace W B Donegan. m 6/18/1960 Kathryn Wakefield Shearer c 2. Ch Of The Gd Shpd Waban MA 1994-2004; S Geo's Ch Portsmouth RI 1966-1969. rcrawford_emeriti@andover.edu

CRAWFORD, Sidnie White (Neb) 925 Piedmont Rd, Lincoln NE 68510 **P Assoc S Mk's On The Campus Lincoln NE 2011-** B Greenwich CT 1/8/1960 d Earle William White & Mildred Ottilie. MTS Harvard DS 1984; PhD Harv 1988. D 9/2/2004 P 10/15/2005 Bp Joe Goodwin Burnett. m 6/11/1994 Dan Duvall Crawford. Angl Assn of Biblic Scholars 2003. scrawford1@url.edu

CRAWFORD, Susan Kaye (Miss) 1026 S Washington Ave, Greenville MS 38701 **S Jas Ch Greenville MS 2009-** B Kennett MO 10/9/1948 d Carl Freeman Crawford & Marie. BS Evangeligal 1970; MDiv STUSo 1989. D 6/3/1989 P 3/24/1990 Bp Alex Dockery Dickson. Int S Mart's Ch Ellisville MO 2007-2009; S Lk's Epis Ch Jackson TN 2004-2006; Assoc S Geo's Ch Germantown TN 1992-2004; Dio W Tennessee Memphis TN 1989-1992; D-In-Trng S Jn's Ch Mart TN 1989-1990. Auth, "mag'S 2000 List Of Wmn Who Make A Difference". Dioc Coordntng Cmsn; Wmn Kairos Prison Mnstry. skcyorkie2@aol.com

CRAWLEY, Clayton D (ECR) 90 West St Apt 21P, New York NY 10006 **EVP, CIO The CPG New York NY 2011-; Bd Mem EDS Cambridge MA 2008-; Non-Stipendiary Cler Par of Trin Ch New York NY 2007-; Non-Stipendiary Cler S Barth's Ch New York NY 2002-** B Atlanta GA 10/15/1964 s Harvey Darrell Crawley & Beverly Conner. BM Samford U 1987; CAS CDSP 1990; MDiv CDSP 1994. D 4/23/1994 P 11/12/1994 Bp Richard Lester Shimpfky. SVP, CIO The CPG New York NY 2004-2011; VP, CIO Ch Pension Fund New York NY 2002-2003; Non-Stipendiary Cler The Ch Of S Lk In The Fields New York NY 2000-2002; VP The CPG New York NY 1999-2002; Assoc R All SS Epis Ch Palo Alto CA 1997-1999; Non-Stipendiary Cler The Epis Ch Of S Jn The Evang San Francisco CA 1996-1997; D All SS Epis Ch Palo Alto CA 1994-1995. Associated Parishes Coun, Exec Com 1999-2001; Associated Parishes Coun, Pres 2001-2003; AP, Coun Mem 1996-2005; GTNG Core Team 1998-2000. clayton@crawley.net

CREAMER JR, Francis Bunnell (LI) 715 Friendship Rd, Waldoboro ME 04572 B Detroit MI 2/24/1937 s Francis Bunnell Creamer & Margaret Welch. BA Trin Hartford CT 1958; STB Ya Berk 1963; Fllshp Trin, U. of Toronto 1964. D 6/11/1963 Bp Walter H Gray P 6/1/1964 Bp John Henry Esquirol. m 11/28/1959 Ann L Lichty c 2. R S Lk's Ch E Hampton NY 1978-1997; R S Andr's Ch New London NH 1971-1978; Asst Ch Of The Heav Rest New York NY 1966-1971; Cur S Jas's Ch W Hartford CT 1964-1966. Sidney Chld Fell Trin, U Tor, Can Can 1964. fcreamer@midcoast.com

CREAMER, Frank Charles (SwFla) 3035 Edgemoor Dr, Palm Harbor FL 34685 **R All SS Ch Tarpon Sprg FL 1993-** B Boone IA 5/20/1954 s Frank Hobson Creamer & Ruth Eileen. BA Florida Intl U 1978; MDiv STUSo 1981. D 5/31/1981 P 2/1/1982 Bp Calvin Onderdonk Schofield Jr. m 9/5/1980 Jean F Fatool c 1. R Ch Of The Intsn Ft Lauderdale FL 1984-1993; Trin Cathd Miami FL 1982-1984. Exemplary Serv Hurricane Andr Relief Dio SE Florida 1993; Clergyman of The Year Kiwanis Intl FL 1988. jean_creamer@yahoo.com

CREAN, Charleen (WMich) 931 E. Walnut St. #114, Pasadena CA 91106 **Par D Ch of the H Sprt Belmont MI 2011-** B Fort Rucker AL 7/26/1951 d Frank McCoy & Frances Wynona. BA U of Hawaii 1985; MSW U of Hawaii 1995. D 12/14/1986 Bp Donald Purple Hart. m 9/19/1985 John Edward Crean. Par D S Paul's Epis Ch Grand Rapids MI 1996-2004. charleenc@aol.com

CREAN JR, John Edward (Los) 931 E Walnut St #114, Pasadena CA 91106 **Int Pstr S Lk's Par Monrovia CA 2012-; Adj Assoc All SS Ch Pasadena CA 2010-** B New York NY 11/15/1939 s John Edward Crean & Agnes Gertrude. BA H Cross Coll 1962; MA Ya 1964; PhD Ya 1966. D 4/28/1974 P 11/30/1974 Bp Edwin Lani Hanchett. m 9/19/1985 Charleen McCoy. R-under-Contract S Jn the Apos Epis Ch Ionia MI 2008-2010; R-under-Contract S Alb's Mssn Muskegon MI 2007; Dir of Vocational Formation Dio Wstrn Michigan Kalamazoo MI 2005-2009; R S Paul's Epis Ch Grand Rapids MI 1996-2005; Dn - W Oahu Dnry Dio Hawaii Honolulu HI 1989-1993; Stndg Com Dio Hawaii Honolulu HI 1985-1986; R S Geo's Epis Ch Honolulu HI 1983-1996; Dioc Sprtl Dir Dio Hawaii Honolulu HI 1980-1982; Asst The Par Of S Clem Honolulu HI 1977-1982; Assoc S Steph's Ch Wahiawa HI 1974-1977. Auth, "arts," *Magistra:Wmn Sprtlty In Hist*, 1995; Auth, "Altenburg Rule Of Ben (Ed)," Eos Verlag, Germany, 1992; Auth, "arts," *LivCh*, 1971. Confrater, Ord Of S Ben 1996; Oblate, Benediktinerabtei Sankt Bonifaz, Munich, Germany 2004; P Assoc, OHC 1974. jcreanjr@att.net

CREASY, James A (Ala) 712 Sixth Ave., Opelika AL 36801 B Florence AL 3/17/1947 s James Eulis Creasy & Nancy. BA U of No Alabama 1970; PDS 1973; MDiv EDS 1975. D 5/31/1975 P 12/20/1975 Bp Furman Stough. m 4/8/1972 Charleen Marie Forman c 1. R Emm Epis Ch Opelika AL 1997-2002; R S Jn's Ch Bedford VA 1992-1997; Exec Bd Dio SW Virginia Roanoke VA 1989-1992; R Chr Epis Ch Marion VA 1987-1992; Cur S Andr's Epis Ch Palmetto Bay FL 1985-1987; Cur S Geo's Epis Ch Griffin GA 1982-1985; Cur Dio Micronesia Tumon Bay GU GU 1980-1981; Exec Coun Appointees New York NY 1980-1981; R S Mk's Ch Prattville AL 1976-1980; D S Barth's Epis Ch Florence AL 1975-1976. trisk47@gmail.com

CREASY, Robert Edward (WTex) 3605 Gamble, Schertz TX 78154 B Richmond VA 2/26/1929 s James Allen Creasy & Ellen Rebecca. BA U Rich 1953; BD Epis TS of The SW 1955; STM Epis TS of The SW 1973. D 6/11/1955 P 1/1/1956 Bp Everett H Jones. m 6/24/1958 Carolyn J Virden. S Matt's Epis Ch Universal City TX 1966-1998; R S Jn's Ch New Braunfels TX 1960-1966; Asst Ch Of The Gd Shpd Corpus Christi TX 1958-1960; Vic S Andr's Epis Ch Corpus Christi TX 1955-1958. Hon Citation Bp & Coun 1968. recjc1@juno.com

CREASY, William Charles (O) 65 E Maple Ave, New Concord OH 43762 B Massillon OH 2/17/1927 s Steven Ernest Creasy & Ella Arlene. BA Coll of Wooster 1949; Kent St U 1950; BD Ob 1954; D.Div Van 1971. D 3/27/1960 P 10/16/1960 Bp Nelson Marigold Burroughs. c 1. R All SS Ch Parma OH 1963-1968; D/R Adv Epis Ch Westlake OH 1960-1963. Auth, "Popular Motives of the Early Disciples of Chr," 1971.

CREED, Christopher DuFlon (ECR) 1769 Forest View Ave, Burlingame CA 94010 B Baltimore MD 5/20/1943 s Eugene Creed & Jeanne. BA JHU 1965; JD Harv 1968; MBA Stan 1975; MDiv CDSP 1993. D 6/3/1995 P 6/1/1996 Bp William Edwin Swing. m 6/10/1967 Barbara Ann Bywater. R S Fran Epis Ch San Jose CA 2000-2011; Int Trin Par Menlo Pk CA 1998-1999; Int Chr Ch Portola Vlly CA 1996-1998; Asst R S Ambr Epis Ch Foster City CA 1995-1996. Phi Beta Kappa JHU Baltimore MD 1965. frcreed@aol.com

✠ **CREIGHTON, Rt Rev Michael Whittington** (CPa) 2716 Gingerview Lane, Annapolis MD 21401 B Saint Paul MN 11/30/1940 s William Foreman Creighton & Marie- Louise. BA Trin Hartford CT 1962; MDiv EDS 1968. D 6/29/1968 Bp William Foreman Creighton P 1/25/1969 Bp C Kilmer Myers Con 11/18/1995 for CPa. m 12/30/1966 Elizabeth Hampton Goodridge c 2. Dio Cntrl Pennsylvania Harrisburg PA 1995-2006; R S Steph's Epis Ch Seattle WA 1981-1995; The Epis Ch In Almaden San Jose CA 1973-1981; Assoc The Epis Ch Of S Mary The Vrgn San Francisco CA 1968-1973. Auth, *For Starters Volumes I & II*, Forw Mvmt, 1988. mwcegc0990@aol.com

CREIGHTON, Susan (Oly) 48 Sudden Vly, Bellingham WA 98229 **Anchorite Dio Olympia Seattle WA 1995-** B Flagstaff AZ 1/29/1943 d Carroll Clark Creighton & Edith. BS Colorado St U 1965; MDiv CDSP 1979. D 6/24/1979 Bp Matthew Paul Bigliardi P 6/1/1981 Bp Paul Moore Jr. TS Dio Olympia Seattle WA 1990-1995; Campus Mnstry Dio Wstrn Michigan Kalamazoo MI 1987-1989; Dio Olympia Seattle WA 1985-1987; Trial Crt Dio Olympia Seattle WA 1985-1987; Bp Educ Com Dio Olympia Seattle WA 1984-1987; Vic S Marg's Ch Seattle WA 1984-1987. Auth, "poetry, essays," *Voices Weaving*, 1996; Auth, "Revs," *Cntr Bulletin*, Theol & Natural Sciences Cntr, Berkeley, CA, 1993; Auth, "DeepLight Hill--A Personal Sprtlty of Creation," *Earth Letter*, Earth Mnstry, Seattle, WA, 1993; Auth, "Wmn Ways of Knowing-Sprtl Gifts of Wisdom & Knowledge," *The Royal Cross- DOK*, 1992; Auth, "essays," *St Helena*, OSH, Vales Gate, NY, 1979. Ord of S Helena, D 1979-1981; Ord of S Helena, P 1981-1984. Beta Beta Beta Coll of Agriculture-Colo.St.Univ. 1965; Gamma Sigma Delta Coll of Agriculture-Colo.St.Univ. 1965. anchorhold@comcast.net

CRELLIN, Timothy Edward (Mass) 25 Boylston St, Jamaica Plain MA 02130 **Dio Massachusetts Boston MA 1999-; Vic S Steph's Epis Ch Boston MA 1999-** B Oswego NY 1/27/1968 s David Warren Crellin & Barbara. BA Br 1990; MDiv Harvard DS 1996. D 9/8/1996 Bp M(arvil) Thomas Shaw III P 4/13/1997 Bp Robert Wilkes Ihloff. m 6/29/1996 Jennifer A Sazama c 1. Assoc Ch Of The Redeem Chestnut Hill MA 1996-1999. SSM 2008. Robert Tobin Awd for Soc Justice Epis City Mssn, Boston 2008. tecrellin@aol.com

CRERAR, Patrick T (Va) 3601 Russel Rd, Alexandria VA 22305 **Assoc Gr Epis Ch Alexandria VA 2008-** B Ft Leavenworth KA 11/17/1968 s John H Crerar & Katherine C. BS Geo Mason U 1991; MDiv VTS 2008. D 5/24/2008 P 12/14/2008 Bp Peter James Lee. m 5/6/2000 Christina A Crerar. cl VTS 2008. ptcrerar@comcast.net

CRESPO, Wilfredo (SanD) 10125 Azuaga St, San Diego CA 92129 **R S Tim's Ch San Diego CA 2007-** B New York NY 9/18/1952 s Joseph Angel Crespo & Gladys. BA Coll of New Rochelle 1980; MA NYU 1984; MDiv NYTS 1986; MA U of Phoenix 1999; DMin SWTS 2005. D 3/17/1994 P 9/21/1994 Bp Gethin Benwil Hughes. m 6/24/2000 Maria Tillmanns c 2. Fed Bureau of Prison Off Of Bsh For ArmdF New York NY 1995-2008. Amer Assn of Profsnl Chapl; Coll Of Chapl, Amer Correctional Chapl Assn. frwillycrespo@aol.com

CRESS, Katherine Elizabeth (Mass) 28 Pleasant St., Medfield MA 02052 **Ch Of Our Sav Somerset MA 2009-** B Fairborn OH 10/8/1960 d Donald Raymond Cress & Diana. BA Georgetown Unversity 1982; MAT Br 1984; EdD Harvard Grad Sch of Educ 2000; MDiv Boston Univ Sch Of Theo 2009. D 6/6/2009 Bp M(arvil) Thomas Shaw III. m 12/29/1989 Samuel Kauffmann c 2. katecress@yahoo.com

CRESSMAN, Lisa Suzanne Kraske (Minn) 4731 Lily Ave N, Lake Elmo MN 55042 **Asst P S Mary's Basswood Grove Hastings MN 2008-** B Detroit MI 11/18/1962 d Robert Lee Kraske & Elizabeth Joanne. B.S.N. U of Wisconsin 1985; MDiv CDSP 1992; DMin Chr TS 2000. D 5/31/1992 Bp George Edmonds Bates P 3/13/1993 Bp Edward Witker Jones. m 9/26/1987 Erik N Cressman c 2. Assoc P S Mary's Basswood Grove Hastings MN 2006-2007; R S Thos Ch Franklin IN 1999-2002; Assoc R Trin Ch Indianapolis IN 1992-1999. Auth, "Journey Into Compassion (sermon)," *Preaching through the Year of Mk: Sermons that Wk VIII*, Morehouse Pub, 1999; Auth, "How Can This Be ? (sermon), Preaching as Image," *Story and Idea: Sermons that Wk VII*, Morehouse Pub, 1998. cressman_lisa@comcast.net

CRESSMAN, Louisel A (NJ) 25 Lakeshore Dr, Hammonton NJ 08037 B Philadelphia PA 3/2/1948 d Louis Gentner Cressman & Elizabeth James. BA Juniata Coll 1971; MS Bryn 1991. D 4/13/1985 Bp George Phelps Mellick Belshaw. m 12/31/1976 David Michael Watral c 3. The Evergreens Moorestown NJ 1988-1989.

CRESWELL, C(arl) Edward (NwT) 2113 S Lipscomb St, Amarillo TX 79109 B Toledo OH 10/6/1934 s George Tonson Creswell & Ruth Lorraine. BA Cntrl Michigan U 1961; BD Bex 1964; MA Cntrl Michigan U 1974; JD Texas Tech U 1981. D 6/13/1964 P 12/1/1964 Bp Roger W Blanchard. m 9/1/1989 Cynthia Carroll c 5. S Jn The Bapt Epis Clarendon TX 1987-2000; R S Andr's Epis Ch Emporia KS 1969-1971; Actg R S Mk's Epis Ch Dayton OH 1968-1969; Cur Chr Epis Ch Dayton OH 1964-1966. Auth, *Privileged Communicants & The Mltry Chapl*; Auth, *Substituted Judgement For The Terminally Ill Incompetent*; Auth, *The Short Term Counslg Contract*. Conf of Ord of S Ben 1964. fatherned@yahoo.com

CRESWELL, Jennifer Marin (Ore) 4411 NE Beech St., Portland OR 97213 **S Lk's Epis Ch Gresham OR 2008-** B Portland OR 2/3/1979 d Jeffrey Creswell & Sarah. BA Mt Holyoke Coll 2001; MDiv Ya Berk 2005. D 10/8/2005 Bp Johncy Itty P 4/8/2006 Bp Catherine Scimeca Roskam. m 8/4/2002 Ian H Doescher c 2. Gr Ch Millbrook NY 2005-2007. jennifermcrfeswell@yahoo.com

CRETEN, C(laude) Dan (NMich) E4929 State Highway M35, Escanaba MI 49829 **D S Steph's Ch Escanaba MI 2003-** B Escanaba MI 11/14/1941 D 5/4/2003 Bp James Arthur Kelsey. m 7/24/1965 Kathleen Ann La Porte.

CREWDSON, Robert Henry (SwVa) 6 Miley Ct, Lexington VA 24450 B Ridley Park PA 1/29/1933 s Henry Crewdson & Kathryn Irene. BS VPI 1955; MDiv VTS 1960; STM UTS Richmond VA 1971; DMin UTS Richmond VA 1974. D 6/28/1960 Bp Frederick D Goodwin P 7/1/1961 Bp Samuel B Chilton. m 8/5/1956 Lois Perkins c 2. Chapl R E Lee Meml Ch (Epis) Lexington VA 2008-2011; R S Andr's Ch Clifton Forge VA 2000-2008; Ecum Off Dio SW Virginia Roanoke VA 1999-2009; R Par Of The H Comm Glendale Sprg NC 1989-1998; Prince Geo Winyah Epis Preschool Georgetown SC 1985-1989; R Prince Geo Winyah Epis Ch Georgetown SC 1985-1989; R S Paul's Ch Haymarket VA 1970-1985; R Chr Epis Ch Brandy Sta VA 1964-1970; R S Lk's Ch Remington VA 1964-1970. Auth, "Love & War: A Sthrn Soldier's Struggle Between Love & Duty," Mariner Companies, Inc., 2009; Auth, "Ecum & the Corinthian Correspondence (2nd Ed)," Mariner Companies, Inc., 2008; Auth, "Ecum & the Corinthian Correspondence," Mariner Companies, Inc., 2007. Woods Fell VTS 1996; Rec The Allin Fllshp 1992. athiker@embarqmail.com

CREWE, Hayward Benaiah (Vt) 169 Woodhaven Dr Unit 2e, White River Junction VT 05001 B Saratoga Sprgs NY 4/30/1925 s Benaiah Hudson Crewe & Lena Pearl. BA Wayne 1948; LTh GTS 1951; MDiv GTS 1972; MA U of Vermont 1972. D 6/29/1951 Bp Richard S M Emrich P 2/2/1952 Bp Russell S Hubbard. Vic S Barn Ch Norwich VT 1962-1966; Vic S Mart's Epis Ch Fairlee VT 1962-1966; Vic Gr Epis Ch Brandon VT 1958-1962; R S Thos' Epis Ch Brandon VT 1958-1962; Asst Ch Of The Gd Samar Paoli PA 1957-1958; Vic Trin Ch Gulph Mills King Of Prussia PA 1956-1957; Asst The Ch Of The Gd Shpd Bryn Mawr PA 1953-1955; Vic S Steph's Epis Ch Hobart IN 1952-1953. hayward.b.crewe@valley.net

CREWS, Norman Andrew (SwVa) 1125 Spindle Xing, Virginia Beach VA 23455 B Sapulpa OK 8/11/1935 s Norman Andrew Hayter & Mildred Irene. BS U of Nebraska 1970; MDiv GTS 1985. D 5/25/1985 P 3/1/1986 Bp C(laude) Charles Vache. m 5/25/1957 Nordleen S Johnson c 3. Chapl Boys Hm Covington VA 1997-1998; R Emm Ch Covington VA 1988-1997; R Calv Ch Bath Par Dinwiddie VA 1985-1988; R Ch Of The Gd Shpd Bath Par Mc Kenney VA 1985-1988. ncrews1@cox.net

CREWS, Norman Dale (CPa) 201 Porter Dr, Annapolis MD 21401 B Louisville KY 7/24/1937 s Maurice Veatch Crews & Alleta Doris. BS Ball St U 1959; LTh STUSo 1964. D 7/20/1964 P 1/1/1965 Bp Joseph Thomas Heistand. m 7/11/1964 Dianne MacKinnon. Annapolis Yth Ctr Inc Annapolis MD 1975-1976; R S Jn's Epis Ch Huntingdon PA 1965-1972; Cur S Andr's Epis Ch York PA 1964-1965.

CREWS, Richard Edwin (Ct) Po Box 46, South Kent CT 06785 B Independence MO 3/28/1930 s Marion Payne Crews & Mildred Claire. BS Cor 1953; MDiv Ya Berk 1962; STM Ya Berk 1969; Fllshp Coll of Preachers 1975; MA Cor 1989. D 6/23/1962 Bp Walter H Gray P 3/1/1963 Bp Joseph Warren Hutchens. m 6/4/1954 Joan E Dinkel c 2. P-in-c S Andr's Epis Ch New Preston Marble Dale CT 1995-2001; Int Vic S Thos of Cbury New Fairfield CT 1988-1992; Ch Of St Thos Of Cantebury Kent CT 1988-1991; So Kent Sch So Kent CT 1982-1994; Cur S Andr's Epis Ch New Preston Marble Dale CT 1962-1964; Cur S Jn's Ch New Milford CT 1962-1964. rjcrews@charter.net

CREWS, Warren Earl (Mo) 2 Algonquin Wood, Saint Louis MO 63122 **Chair, Dioc BEC Dio Missouri S Louis MO 2010-; Chair, Dioc Nomin Com Dio Missouri S Louis MO 2007-** B Guthrie OK 8/11/1940 s Earl William Crews & Judith Dyrth. BA Ya 1962; BD EDS 1965; MA Oklahoma City U 1976; PhD S Louis U 1995. D 6/20/1965 P 12/1/1965 Bp Chilton Powell. m 7/28/1967 Mary McCall c 2. Dio Missouri S Louis MO 1998-2003; Emm Epis Ch Webster Groves MO 1996-2007; Ch Of The Epiph Kirkwood S Louis MO 1996; R S Tim's Epis Ch Creve Coeur MO 1986-1991; Sub-Dn Trin Cathd Little Rock AR 1981-1986; Dio Arkansas Little Rock AR 1977-1980; Asst S Jn's Ch Oklahoma City OK 1971-1974; Asst Vic S Edw Chap Oklahoma City OK 1967-1976; Asst S Paul's Cathd Oklahoma City OK 1967-1971; R S Thos Ch Pawhuska OK 1966-1967; Cur S Matt's Ch Enid OK 1965-1966; S Steph's Alva Alva OK 1965-1966. Pres Interfaith Partnership of St. Louis 2002; Pres EDEO 1982. wecrews@sbcglobal.net

CREWS, William Eugene (Colo) 1640 Coyote Rd, 4042 Xerxes Ave. S., Minneapolis MN 55410 B Tulsa OK 12/20/1933 s Ira David Crews & Ruth. W&L 1953; BA U of Oklahoma 1955; BD CDSP 1958; Grad Stds Grad Theol Un 1982. D 5/16/1958 P 11/29/1958 Bp Chilton Powell. m 11/8/1958 Ann Louisa Hanson c 2. P-in-c Trin Epis Ch Kingman AZ 2003-2007; P-in-c Epis Ch Of S Ptr And S Mary Denver CO 1987-1997; Colorado Epis Fndt Denver CO 1986-1997; R S Dav's Epis Ch Topeka KS 1982-1986; S Thos Of Cbury Epis Ch Albuquerque NM 1973-1981; S Bede's Epis Ch Santa Fe NM 1961-1967; Asst Ch of the H Faith Santa Fe NM 1961-1962; P-in-c S Edm's Ch Bronx NY 1959-1961; Vic S Barn Ch Foreman AR 1959; Vic S Jas Ch Antlers OK 1958-1959; Vic S Lk The Beloved Physcn Idabel OK 1958-1959; Vic S Mk's Ch Hugo OK 1958-1959. Associated Parishes Coun. Commencement Speaker CDSP 1963. williamcrews5@gmail.com

CRIM, Burritt Shepard (Ore) 357 Sw Butterfield Pl, Corvallis OR 97333 **Chapl The Epis Ch Of The Gd Samar Corvallis OR 1995-** B Detroit MI 10/7/1927 s William Doolittle Crim & Margaret. BS Montana St U 1952; BD CDSP 1958. D 8/3/1958 P 7/16/1959 Bp Chandler W Sterling. m 8/26/1950 JoAnn May Peck c 4. Vic Ch Of The Ascen Neodesha KS 1990-1992; R Ch Of The Epiph Independence KS 1990-1992; Bp Dep Dio Kansas Topeka KS 1987-1990; Exec Coun Appointees New York NY 1987-1990; St. Jn The Div Epis Ch Tumon Bay 1987-1990; RurD NW Convoc Dio Kansas Topeka KS 1984-1987; S Lk's Ch Wamego KS 1984-1987; S Ptr's Par Santa Maria CA 1982-1984; Vic Calv Ch Bunkie LA 1978-1982; Vic H Comf Ch Ball LA 1978-1982; S Mich's Epis Ch Pineville LA 1978-1982; Vic Trin Epis Ch Ball LA 1978-1982; Epis Dio San Joaquin Modesto CA 1976-1977; S Jn's Epis Ch Tulare CA 1976-1977; Dio Estrn Oregon The Dalles OR 1970-1976; R The Ch Of The Trin Coatesville PA 1967-1970; Vic Ch Of The Ascen Parkesburg PA 1966-1967; Cur Madison Cnty MT Dio Montana Helena MT 1958-1959. goodshepard@msn.com

CRIMI, Lynne B (Alb) 7 Sweet Rd, Stillwater NY 12170 B Virginia 11/23/1944 d William Bennett & Doris. BA Russell Sage Coll 1966; MS Rutgers-The St U 1989. D 6/11/2005 Bp Daniel William Herzog. m 8/7/1965 Dennis Crimi c 3. lynncrimi@verizon.net

CRIPPEN, David Wells (ETenn) 19741 Highway 11, Wildwood GA 30757 B Chester PA 5/13/1936 s Lynn Thompson Crippen & Rebekah. BS U of Tampa 1962; MA U of So Florida 1965; MA Scarritt Coll 1967; PhD Peabody Coll 1973; MDiv STUSo 1986. D 6/10/1986 Bp William Hopkins Folwell P 5/31/1987 Bp George Lazenby Reynolds Jr. m 7/23/1961 Karen Lou Baumann c 3. Int S Mart Of Tours Epis Ch Chattanooga TN 2008-2010; Int Chr Epis Ch Albertville AL 2008; R S Jos's On-The-Mtn Mentone AL 2001-2008; S Mich And All Ang Anniston AL 1999-2001; S Jas Epis Ch of Greeneville Greeneville TN 1998-1999; S Andr's Epis Ch Douglas GA 1998; Hosanna Wildwood GA 1992-1997; Chr Epis Ch Tracy City TN 1989-1992; Dio Cntrl Florida Orlando FL 1986-1987. Auth, "2 Sides of the River," Abingdon Press, 1976; Auth, "New Approaches in Rel Educ"; Auth, "Written Lesson: 4 Methods of Presentation," Elem Sch Journ. sunnihill@charter.net

CRIPPEN, Stephen Daniel (Oly) 1245 10th Ave E, Seattle WA 98102 **Chair, BEC Dio Olympia Seattle WA 2011-; Mem, COM Dio Olympia Seattle WA 2011-; D S Mk's Cathd Seattle WA 2011-; Consult, Congrl Consulting Ntwk Dio Olympia Seattle WA 2010-; Trnr, Coll for Congrl Dvlpmt Dio Olympia Seattle WA 2010-** B Worthington MN 8/17/1970 s Gary Lee

Crippen & Nancy Katherine. BA Augsburg Coll 1992; MA Pacific Luth U 1999; Diac Cert Seattle U 2011. D 10/29/2010 Bp Gregory Harold Rickel. Mem, BEC Dio Olympia Seattle WA 2011; Trnr, Coll for Congrl Dvlpmt Dio Olympia Seattle WA 2010-2011; D S Steph's Epis Ch Seattle WA 2010-2011. stephen@stephencrippen.com

CRIPPS, David Richard (Roch) 139 Lake Bluff Rd, Rochester NY 14622 B Rochester NY 4/13/1955 s Richard Charles Cripps & Florence Martha. BA St. Jn Fisher Coll 1977; MDiv TESM 1980; MS Nazareth Coll 1983. D 8/10/1991 P 5/1/1992 Bp William George Burrill. m 12/15/1984 Kathleen Ann Dobberstein.

CRISE, Rebecca Ann (WMich) Saint Mark's Episcopal Church, 201 W. Michigan Ave., Paw Paw MI 49079 **Dn, St. Jos Dnry Dio Wstrn Michigan Kalamazoo MI 2010-; Mem, Dioc Coun Dio Wstrn Michigan Kalamazoo MI 2010-; R S Mk's Epis Ch Paw Paw MI 2007-** B Chicago IL 3/2/1951 d Roger Julian Crise & Helen Beatrice. DVM Pur 1975; MDiv SWTS 2005. D 4/15/2005 P 11/18/2005 Bp Edward Stuart Little II. Cur Chr Ch Waukegan IL 2005-2007. stmarksrectorpawpaw@gmail.com

CRISP, Sheila L A (Oly) PO Box 88550, Steilacoom WA 98388 **P-in-c S Jos And S Jn Ch Steilacoom WA 2011-** B Coronado CA 11/27/1960 d Daniel Graham Crisp & Jo Ann M. AA So Puget Sound Cmnty Coll 2004; BA U of Washington 2006; MDiv CDSP 2010. D 4/17/2010 Bp Gregory Harold Rickel. c 2. D Chr Ch Tacoma WA 2010-2011; Asst CDSP Berkeley CA 2010. scrisp3920@msn.com

CRISS, Carthur Paul (Kan) 4138 E 24th St N, Wichita KS 67220 B Kansas City KS 6/5/1932 s Paul Edwin Criss & Ellen Elizabeth. BA U IL 1954; MDiv SWTS 1957; STM STUSo 1971. D 7/11/1957 P 11/1/1958 Bp William Henry Marmion. m 6/3/1977 Marybeth True Cupp c 2. Int S Jas Ch Wichita KS 2001-2003; Int S Andr's Ch Derby KS 1998-2001; Dio Kansas Topeka KS 1984-1987; Cn To Ordnry Dio Kansas Topeka KS 1983-1993; R S Alb's Epis Ch Wichita KS 1978-1997; Wichita St Univ Campus Mssn Topeka KS 1970-1978; R Gr Epis Ch Winfield KS 1961-1965. cpcr@aol.com

CRIST, John Frederick (Chi) P.O. Box, 131 Fifth St., McNabb IL 61335 B Muncie IN 8/17/1942 s Robert Frederick Crist & Armella June. BA MI SU 1965; BD SWTS 1968; MA Edgewood Coll 1991. D 6/29/1968 Bp Archie H Crowley P 3/15/1969 Bp Richard S M Emrich. m 9/2/1967 Maryfrances Press. S Paul's Ch La Salle IL 2000-2010; Chr Epis Ch Ottawa IL 1999-2010; Chr Ch Streator IL 1998-2010; R S Mart's Epis Ch Fairmont MN 1990-1998; R Trin Ch Janesville WI 1984-1990; R Ch Of The Epiph Forestville MD 1980-1984; Asst S Thos Epis Ch Battle Creek MI 1976-1980; Cur Trin Ch Indianapolis IN 1973-1976; Asst S Lk's Epis Ch Rochester MN 1971-1973; Assoc Min Chr Ch Cathd Eau Claire WI 1969-1971; S Lk's Ch Altoona WI 1969-1971. Auth, "Change in the Ch," *Acad of Par Cler Journ*, 1970. mjcrist@crtelco.com

CRIST, Roy Gene (WVa) Box 602, 19958 Midland Trail, Ansted WV 25812 **Mssnr S Andr's Ch Oak Hill WV 2002-** B Beckley WV 5/2/1939 s Eugene Stanton Crist & Hazel Nyra. BA W Virginia U Inst of Tech 1987. D 12/12/1987 P 12/4/1988 Bp Robert Poland Atkinson. m 4/6/1978 Jane Nuckols c 3. The New River Epis Mnstry Hansford WV 1990-2011; P-in-c Ch Of The Redeem Ansted WV 1988-2002. Land 1992. rgcrist@msn.com

CRIST JR, William Harold (Los) 2091 Business Center Dr Ste 130, Irvine CA 92612 B Edinburg TX 10/5/1946 s William Harold Crist & Larayne Evelyn. BA TCU 1969; MDiv EDS 1974; MA U of Massachusetts 1988. D 5/23/1974 Bp Harold Cornelius Gosnell P 11/1/1974 Bp Richard Earl Dicus. m 6/4/1977 Mary Frances Jenson. Assoc S Geo's Epis Ch Laguna Hills CA 1992-1994; Supply P Dio Wstrn Massachusetts Springfield MA 1988-1992; Asst S Mk's Epis Ch San Antonio TX 1978-1981; Vic S Matt's Ch Edinburg TX 1974-1977. Klingenstein Fllshp Col 1984. willcrist@willcrist.com

CRISTE-TROUTMAN, Robert Joseph (Nwk) 131 Broad St, Washington NJ 07882 **P-in-c Trin Epis Ch Mt Pocono PA 2011-; P-in-c Trin Epis Ch Mt Pocono PA 2011-** B Bourne MA 6/5/1951 s Lawrence Edward Criste & Dorothy. AA Concordia Coll 1971; BA Concordia Coll 1973; MDiv Luth TS at Gettysburg 1979. D 3/21/1998 Bp Jack Marston McKelvey P 10/31/1998 Bp John Shelby Spong. m Neil I Criste-Troutman c 2. R S Ptr's Ch Washington NJ 2001-2011; Supply S Ptr's Ch Washington NJ 2000-2001; D S Jas Ch Upper Montclair NJ 1998-1999. frbob127@yahoo.com

CRISTOBAL, Robert S (Chi) 1000 West Rt 64, Oregon IL 61061 **P-in-c S Bride's Epis Ch Oregon IL 2008-** B Moline IL 5/21/1979 s Reynaldo Lanuza Cristobal & Maria Paz Salamat. BA Monmouth Coll Monmouth IL 2001; MDiv SWTS 2005. D 6/3/2006 P 12/16/2006 Bp William Dailey Persell. rfs.cristobal@gmail.com

CRITCHFIELD, Margot D (Mass) St. Stephen's Church, 16 Highland Ave., Cohasset MA 02025 **R S Steph's Ch Cohasset MA 2008-** B Huntington CT 7/13/1955 d Wallace Brown Dunlap & Margaret Helen. BA GW 1978; MDiv VTS 2001. D 6/9/2001 P 2/9/2002 Bp Jane Hart Holmes Dixon. m 5/31/1987 Donald Dow Critchfield c 1. Assoc S Alb's Par Washington DC 2001-2008. mcritchfield@ststephenscohasset.org

CRITCHLOW II, Fitzgerald St Clair (Jerry) (NCal) 5609 Phlox Ct, Sacramento CA 95842 **Serv All SS Memi Sacramento CA 2001-** B Brooklyn NY 12/14/1944 s Fitzgerald St Clair Critchlow & Frances Helen. BA Natl U 1985; Cert Natl U 1986; MA Natl U 1988; BA D Formation Prog 1995. D 6/3/1995 Bp Jerry Alban Lamb. m 7/29/1983 Mary Jo Alfonso Rousey c 2. D S Matt's Epis Ch Sacramento CA 1995-2000. Prince Hall Masons 1973; Prince Hall Shiners 1978; Scotish Rite Masons 1976. fcritchlow@earthlink.net

CRITELLI, Robert J (NJ) 13 King Arthurs Ct, Sicklerville NJ 08081 B Jersey City NJ 4/21/1937 s John Louis Critelli & Irene Elizabeth. Epiph Apostolic Coll; BA Immac Concep Sem 1959; MS Iona Coll 1971. Rec from Roman Catholic 6/1/1985 as Deacon Bp George Phelps Mellick Belshaw. m 11/4/1972 Victoria Hughes c 2. Chr Ch Magnolia NJ 2007-2009; Chr Ch Collingswood NJ 2004; R Ch Of The Atone Stratford NJ 1985-1990. rjcekw@earthlink.net

CRITES, Karry Dean (Nev) 1035 Munley Dr, Reno NV 89503 B Louisville KY 3/6/1953 s Cyrus Daniel Crites & Joycelynn Marie. BS U of Missouri 1987; MDiv CDSP 1990. D 4/25/1990 P 11/6/1990 Bp Stewart Clark Zabriskie. m 4/7/1979 Dale Austin c 2. ELM Cmnty Ch Reno NV 2002-2009; Gr-St Fran Cmnty Ch Lovelock NV 1990-1996; Dio Nevada Las Vegas NV 1990-1994. Angl Comm Ntwk; ERM. frkarryelm@aol.com

CRITES, Rebecca Tuck (SwVa) St Johns Episcopal Church, P O Box 607, Glasgow VA 24555 **EDEIO Dio SW Virginia Roanoke VA 2008-; S Jn's Epis Ch Glasgow VA 2008-; R S Thos Ch Bedford VA 2007-** B Arlington VA 6/5/1957 d Anthony Vance Tuck & Elnora Thompson. BS Longwood Coll 1979; Masters Wk Virginia Commonwealth U 1982; MDiv VTS 2007; Certification SMU 2011. D 6/10/2007 Bp A(rthur) Heath Light P 12/15/2007 Bp Frank Neff Powell. m 8/13/1977 James William Crites c 3. S Jas Ch Roanoke VA 2007. beckett605@cox.net

CRITTENDEN, F. Thomas Glasgow (SwVa) 123 W. Washinton St., Lexington VA 24450 **R R E Lee Memi Ch (Epis) Lexington VA 2007-** B Honolulu HI 11/4/1953 s William Cunningham Crittenden & Conde Glasgow. BA Lawr 1976; MDiv CDSP 1984. D 6/5/1984 P 12/18/1984 Bp Furman Stough. m 10/8/1988 Christianna H Haymes c 3. R Ch Of The H Comf Tallahassee FL 1994-2007; Assoc S Mart's Ch Ellisville MO 1991-1994; R Trin Ch Wetumpka AL 1986-1990; Cur Chr Ch Tuscaloosa AL 1984-1986. office@releechurch.org

CRITTENDEN, William Setchel (WNY) Po Box 93, Chautauqua NY 14722 B Hazelton PA 11/24/1932 s William Crittenden & Eleanor. Hur; BA Gannon U 1961. D 6/13/1964 P 3/1/1965 Bp William Crittenden. m 9/7/1963 Charlotte Victoria Doeright. Supply P Dio NW Pennsylvania Erie PA 1991-1999; Vic S Barn Ch Franklinville NY 1989-1990; Vic S Jn's Epis Ch Ellicottville NY 1989-1990; Vic Ch Of The H Cross No E PA 1974-1976; R S Matt's Epis Ch Horseheads NY 1969-1971; Assoc Zion Ch Rome NY 1966-1969; Stff S Mk's Ch New Canaan CT 1964-1966.

CROCKER, Byron Grey (Tex) 2025 Hanover Cir, Beaumont TX 77706 B Newton KS 12/8/1935 s H Mason Crocker & Florabel Eudora. BA U of Texas 1957; MDiv CDSP 1966; Oxf 1984. D 7/11/1966 Bp Everett H Jones P 1/1/1967 Bp Richard Earl Dicus. m 8/23/1957 Ann Duggan. S Mk's Ch Beaumont TX 1992-1998; R S Steph's Ch Beaumont TX 1971-1991; Assoc S Mk's Epis Ch San Antonio TX 1968-1971; Asst Ch Of The Adv Brownsville TX 1966-1968. adcbgc@sbcglobal.net

CROCKER, George Neville (Ct) 29 Powder Horn Hl, Brookfield CT 06804 **R Emer S Paul's Ch Brookfield CT 2003-** B New York,NY 1/21/1933 s Neville Minor Crocker & Katherine Gertrude. BS Sthrn Connecticut St U 1964; MDiv Ya Berk 1967; MS Iona Coll 1982; DMin Ecum Theol Cntr Detroit MI 1987. D 6/13/1967 Bp Walter H Gray P 4/6/1968 Bp Joseph Warren Hutchens. R S Paul's Ch Brookfield CT 1970-2002; Vic Imm Ch Ansonia CT 1969-1970; Cur Chr Ch Ansonia CT 1967-1970. CHS 1980; OHC. revg@snet.net

CROCKER JR, John (NJ) 99 Colorado Ave, Warwick RI 02888 B Oxford Oxfordshire UK 10/19/1923 s John Crocker & Mary Bowditch. BA Harv 1948; STM EDS 1954; MA Br 1969. D 6/19/1954 P 5/15/1955 Bp Norman B Nash. c 3. Trst The GTS New York NY 1979-1985; R Trin Ch Princeton NJ 1977-1989; Dio Massachusetts Boston MA 1969-1977; Cur Trin Ch In The City Of Boston Boston MA 1954-1958. "A New Birth of Freedom: The calling for an Amer Hist; Thos P. Govan," X libris, 2005. Bd Dir Cross-Currents.

CROCKER JR, J(ohn) A(lexander) Frazer (U) 3541 Ocean View Dr, Florence OR 97439 **Asst S Andr's Epis Ch Florence OR 1996-** B Detroit MI 10/4/1935 s John A(lexander) Frazer Crocker & Marjorie Olieva. AB Ken 1957; MDiv CDSP 1960; MSW U of Utah 1974; DMin GTF 1992. D 6/29/1960 Bp Richard S M Emrich P 12/30/1960 Bp Gordon V Smith. m 6/4/1977 Diana Worden c 2. Exec Dir Epis Soc & Pstr Mnstrs Dio Utah Salt Lake City UT 1991-1995; Epis Cmnty Serv Inc Salt Lake City UT 1991-1995; Bp Of U Dep For Pstrl Care & Mnstry Enablement Dio Utah Salt Lake City UT 1988-1990; Chapl St Marks Hosp Salt Lake City UT 1983; R S Mary's Ch Provo UT 1967-1972; Assoc R Gr Ch Jamaica NY 1964-1967; Vic S Paul's Indn Mssn Sioux City IA 1961-1964; Cn Trin Cathd Davenport IA 1960-1961. Cath Fllshp Epis Ch; OHC. jafcjr@charter.net

CROCKER, Ronald Conrad (Va) 3 Hamilton Court, Uxbridge MA 01569 B Quincy MA 2/4/1944 s Rendell Conrad Crocker & Margaret. BA U of Massachusetts 1965; MDiv CDSP 1968. D 6/30/1968 Bp Anson Phelps Stokes Jr P 5/17/1969 Bp Frederic Cunningham Lawrence. m 8/19/1967 Donna G Garrison c 4. R S Geo's Epis Ch Arlington VA 1997-2009; Cn to Ordnry Dio Rhode Island Providence RI 1991-1997; R Chr Ch In Lonsdale Lincoln RI 1979-1990; R S Ptr's Ch Dartmouth MA 1970-1979; Cur S Paul's Ch Boston MA 1968-1970. Auth, *Passion & Death of Jesus*, Priv, 1971; Auth, "Psalm 80," *Psalm 80*, Priv, 1968. ronald.crocker@verizon.net

CROCKETT, Daniel Lee (At) PO Box 102, Conyers GA 30012 **S Aid's Ch San Francisco CA 2003-; R S Simon's Epis Ch Conyers GA 2003-** B Ottawa KS 11/2/1954 s James David Crockett & Leta Helen. BA Coll of the Ozarks 1991; MDiv VTS 1994. D 6/4/1994 Bp John Clark Buchanan P 1/6/1995 Bp Edwin Funsten Gulick Jr. m 6/24/1995 Star Ann Shank c 2. R S Mk's Epis Ch Jonesboro AR 2000-2003; R S Ptr's Epis Ch Monroe CT 1996-2000; Barren River Area Russellville KY 1994-1996; Vic Trin Ch Russellville KY 1994-1996. Weekly Rel Columnist, *Rockdale Citizen*, 2004 - 2008. fatherdan@bellsouth.net

CROCKETT, Jennie L (SO) 2700 Kenview Rd S, Columbus OH 43209 B Franklin County 6/25/1939 d Helen. BA Capital U 1985; MDiv The Angl Acad Columbia OH 2006. D 5/13/2006 Bp Kenneth Lester Price. m 7/15/1961 Kenneth Crockett c 2. jencrockett@sbcglobal.net

CROCKETT, Larry Joe (Minn) 4525 Alicia Dr, Inver Grove Heights MN 55077 B Dayton OH 7/6/1949 s Fred Carson Crockett & Amelia Faye. BA Pacific Luth U 1971; MDiv Luther TS 1977; PhD U MN 1990. D 12/17/1999 Bp James Louis Jelinek P 8/10/2000 Bp Daniel Lee Swenson. m 3/21/1981 Cheryl Diane Solomonson c 2. P-in-c S Mary's Basswood Grove Hastings MN 2001-2010. Auth, *Turing Test and the Frame Problem*, Ablex, 1994; Auth, *Universal Assembly Lang*, McGraw-Hill, 1986. Honored Fac Awd Augsburg Coll 1996; Outstanding Tchg Awd Metro St U 1987. frlarry@stmaryschurch.us

CROES, John Rodney (NJ) 20 Claremont Ave, South River NJ 08882 B New Brunswick NJ 12/25/1942 s John R Croes & Evelyn C. BA Rutgers-The St U 1966; MDiv PDS 1974. D 4/27/1974 P 12/1/1974 Bp Albert Wiencke Van Duzer. m 11/16/2008 Margaret P Prinz c 3. R S Ptr's Ch Perth Amboy NJ 1977-2008; R St Jn the Bapt Epis Ch Linden NJ 1976-1977; Cur S Ptr's Ch Perth Amboy NJ 1974-1976. rodcapedory@verizon.net

CROFT, Charles Carter (RG) 615 N Texas St, Silver City NM 88061 B Lohngsthal NY DE 4/1/1955 s Eldred Carter Croft & Mary Ann. BA Acadia U 1977; MDiv Nash 1990; Cert Advncd CPE 1991. D 6/30/1990 P 2/1/1991 Bp Rogers Sanders Harris. m 9/11/1999 Ann H Hollingsworth c 1. R Ch Of The Gd Shpd Silver City NM 2008-2010; Int Epis Ch Of The Sav Hanford CA 2007-2008; Asst S Jas Epis Cathd Fresno CA 2003-2007; S Mary's Ch Charleroi PA 2001-2003; S Andr's Ch Breckenridge TX 1996-2001; Ch Of The Redeem Sarasota FL 1991-1996; Dio SW Florida Sarasota FL 1990-1991. silvercityrev@gmail.com

CROFT, Jay Leslie (Ala) 1431 Magnolia Curv, Montgomery AL 36106 **P Assoc Ch Of The H Comf Montgomery AL 2011-** B Hartford CT 2/24/1942 s Enoch Eustis Croft & Lila Goodrich. BA Simpson Coll Indianola IA 1965; MDiv UTS 1970. D 6/7/1969 P 12/6/1969 Bp Horace W B Donegan. m 9/7/1968 Frances Week Ralston c 1. P-in-c S Mk's For The Deaf Mobile AL 2006-2009; Archd Deaf Dio Alabama Birmingham AL 1996-2005; R S Jn's Epis Deaf Ch Birmingham AL 1996-2005; Dio Washington Washington DC 1996; Vic S Barn' Epis Ch of The Deaf Chevy Chase MD 1980-1996; Vic For Deaf Wk Dio Ohio Cleveland OH 1974-1979; Vic S Ann's Ch For The Deaf New York NY 1969-1974. Epis Conf Of The Deaf Of The Epis Ch In The 1984. Meritorious Serv Awd ECD 1992. jlcroft@knology.net

CROMEY, Edwin Harry (NY) St. Luke's Church, 850 Wolcott Ave. Box 507, Beacon NY 12508 **Int S Lk's Ch Beacon NY 2006-** B Brooklyn NY 5/26/1934 s Edward Warren Cromey & Helen Louise. BA Adel 1956; MDiv GTS 1962; DMin Drew U 1997. D 4/28/1962 P 12/21/1962 Bp James P De Wolfe. m 8/11/1972 Pamela Bock c 2. S Mary's-In-Tuxedo Tuxedo Pk NY 1981-2006; P-in-c S Jn's Arden NY 1980-2006; Int Ch of S Jn on the Mtn Bernardsville NJ 1979-1980; St Jn The Bapt Sch Mendham NJ 1978-1980; P-in-c S Jn Jersey City NJ 1973-1976; R S Ann's Ch Sayville NY 1964-1970; Asst Cathd Of The Incarn Garden City NY 1962-1964. Auth, "Faith is There," *Let Us Get on w the Works*; Auth, *S Jn Bapt Sch 1880-1980*; Auth, *Ultimate in Educ*. Cmnty of S Jn the Bapt 1975. ecromey@optonline.net

CROMEY, Robert Warren (Cal) 3839 - 20th, San Francisco CA 94114 B Brooklyn NY 2/16/1931 s Edward Warren Cromey & Helen Louise. Fllshp Coll of Preachers; Fllshp Esalen Inst; BA NYU 1953; MDiv GTS 1956. D 6/3/1956 P 12/17/1956 Bp Horace W B Donegan. m 8/14/1983 Elizabeth Garbett c 3. R Trin Ch San Francisco CA 1981-2002; S Eliz's Epis Ch So San Francisco CA 1981; Vic S Aid's Ch San Francisco CA 1965-1970; Cn Ordnry Dio California San Francisco CA 1962-1965; R Ch Of The H Nativ Bronx NY 1958-1962; Cur Chr Ch Bronxville NY 1956-1958. "So You Want to Get m," *Self-Pub*, Lulu.com, 2007; Auth, *In God's Image*, Alamo Sq Press, 1992; Auth, "Feeding Prog," *Wit*, 1972; Auth, "Sex and the Unmarried," *Wit*, 1972; Auth, "Soc Relatns as Evang," *Wit*, 1968; Auth, "I Can't Pray," *Wit*, 1968; Auth, "Mnstry to Homosexuals," *LivCh*, 1964. Bd Trst, GTS 1991-1994; Ethics Com U CA Med Cntr San Francisco CA 1997-1999. SS Alive Awd MCC, San Francisco 1995; Ldrshp in GLT Rts Cable Car Awards 1990; Care of Homeless Awd San Francisco Bd. of Supervisors 1985. twocromeys@earthlink.net

CROMMELIN-DELL, Sue (SVa) 500 Court St., Portsmouth VA 23704 **Assoc Estrn Shore Chap Virginia Bch VA 2010-** B San Diego CA 11/14/1938 d Henry Crommelin & Sally Huntress. BA Wellesley Coll 1960; MSW U of Houston Grad Sch of Soc Wk 1978; MDiv EDS 2008. D 2/1/2008 P 8/1/2008 Bp John Clark Buchanan. m 1/26/1980 Paul F Dell c 4. crommelin@aol.com

CROMPTON, Sherry (Pa) 2717 Shelburne Road, Downingtown PA 19335 **R The Ch Of The Trin Coatesville PA 2003-** B Hanover PA 4/7/1964 d Barry Jude Bealing & Nancy Jean. AS Brandywine Coll 1984; BS Widener U 1990; MDiv GTS 2002; MS Neumann U 2011. D 6/22/2002 P 5/31/2003 Bp Charles Ellsworth Bennison Jr. m 6/18/1988 Richard Hale Crompton c 1. Dio Pennsylvania Philadelphia PA 2002-2003. revcrompton@aol.com

CROMWELL, Richard (NJ) 305 N Broadway, Pennsville NJ 08070 **P-in-c S Geo's Ch Pennsville NJ 2011-** B Bronx NY 12/13/1947 s Richard K Cromwell & Corinne. BA Drew U 1970; MDiv PDS 1973; Andover Newton TS 1985. D 6/9/1973 Bp Leland Stark P 6/1/1974 Bp George E Rath. m 6/6/1970 Margaret Monahan. Assoc S Dav's Ch Cranbury NJ 1997-2004; Asst Ch Of The Gd Shpd Waban MA 1981-1982; Int All SS Ch Stoneham MA 1979-1980; R Ch Of The H Comm Norwood NJ 1975-1979; Cur S Paul's Epis Ch Morris Plains NJ 1973-1974. ACPE, AAPC, Ord Of S Lk. arcy1947@yahoo.com

✠ **CRONEBERGER, Rt Rev John Palmer** (Be) 1079 Old Bernville Rd, Reading PA 19605 **Ret Bp of Newark Dio Bethlehem Bethlehem PA 2009-** B Pottsville PA 8/25/1938 s Robert Bruce Croneberger & Ethel Elizabeth. BA Leh 1960; MDiv VTS 1963. D 6/15/1963 P 3/1/1964 Bp Frederick J Warnecke Con 11/21/1998 for Nwk. m 8/28/1965 Marilyn A Muehleisen c 5. Bp Dioc Dio Newark Newark NJ 2000-2007; Bp Dio Newark Newark NJ 1998-2007; Bp Coadj Dio Newark Newark NJ 1998-2000; Stndg Com Dio Newark Newark NJ 1993-1998; Pres, Newark Cler Assn Dio Newark Newark NJ 1992-1998; Dep, GC Dio Newark Newark NJ 1991-1997; Dioc Coun Dio Newark Newark NJ 1983-1985; R Ch Of The Atone Tenafly NJ 1980-1998; Chair, Evang Com Dio Bethlehem Bethlehem PA 1977-1979; R S Mary's Epis Ch Reading PA 1974-1980; Exec Coun Dio Bethlehem Bethlehem PA 1967-1973. Auth, "Spkng the Truth About Doing the Truth," *The Voice of Integrity*. DD VTS Alexandria VA 1999; Hon Lifetime Cn Dio Newark 1996; Dioc Cbury Schlr Dio Newark 1992. bishopjpc@epix.net

CROOK, Clifford (Minn) 3055 Timberwood Trail, Eagan MN 55121 B New Bedford MA 11/19/1927 s John Jesse Dean Crook & Margaret Ellen. AS Cambridge Jr Coll 1948; BS Mar 1950; STB EDS 1959. D 6/19/1959 Bp Henry W Hobson P 12/1/1959 Bp Roger W Blanchard. m 1/12/1990 Denise Dugdale Erickson c 4. Assoc S Ptr's Ch Casa Grande AZ 2000-2009; R H Trin Epis Ch Elk River MN 1986-1988; P-in-c S Jn's Ch Aitkin MN 1983-1986; R Ch Of Our Sav Little Falls MN 1981-1983; R S Lk's Epis Ch Hastings MN 1971-1981; R Emm Ch Corry PA 1968-1971; Asst Chr Epis Ch Dayton OH 1962-1964; R S Jn's Ch Columbus OH 1960-1962. Cleric of Year Natl Coun BSA; Silver Beaver Awd Natl Coun BSA; Paul Harris Fell Rotary Intl .

CROOK II, Jerry V (Ga) 4027 Dumaine Way, Memphis TN 38117 B Memphis TN 10/10/1946 s Jerry Vardaman Crook & Mary Francis (Richartz). BS Lambeth Coll 1969; MDiv GTS 1976. D 4/21/1976 P 11/1/1976 Bp (George) Paul Reeves. Asst S Geo's Ch Germantown TN 2006-2011; S Eliz's Epis Ch Richmond Hill GA 2004-2005; S Phil's Ch Hinesville Hinesville GA 1985-1990; Calv Ch Americus GA 1978-1983; The Ch Of The Gd Shpd Augusta GA 1976-1978. jvcrook@earthlink.net

CROOK, Senter Cawthon (WTenn) 2796 Lombardy Ave, Memphis TN 38111 B Memphis TN 10/23/1943 d Jere Lawrence Crook & Janie Williams. Bradford Coll; Pacifica Grad Inst; BA SW at Memphis 1965; MDiv STUSo 1988. D 6/26/1988 P 5/20/1989 Bp Alex Dockery Dickson. m 12/5/1998 Isaac Joseph McFadden c 3. Asstg P S Mary's Cathd Memphis TN 1996-1998; Assoc S Elis's Epis Ch Memphis TN 1993-1995; Int Ch of the H Apos Collierville TN 1990; Assoc Ch of the H Apos Collierville TN 1988-1989. sentercc@bellsouth.net

CROOM, James (WMich) 2795 Riley Ridge Road, Holland MI 49424 **Grand Vlly Dnry Dio Wstrn Michigan Kalamazoo MI 2010-; R H Trin Epis Ch Wyoming MI 2008-** B Fort Hood TX 10/3/1949 s H(orace) C Croom & Irene Areatus. B Mus U NC 1973; M Mus U NC 1977; MDiv CDSP 2001; DMin Wstrn Theol Seminsry 2013. D 6/2/2001 P 12/1/2001 Bp William Edwin Swing. m 4/8/1995 Stephanie B Batson c 1. Chair, COM Dio Wstrn Michigan Kalamazoo MI 2009-2011; COM Dio Wstrn Michigan Kalamazoo MI 2008-2011; Par Assoc for Pstr Care Gr Ch Grand Rapids MI 2008-2010; Int S Lk's Par Kalamazoo MI 2007-2008; Epis Sr Communities Walnut Creek CA 2006-2007; Ch Of Our Sav Mill Vlly CA 2004-2006; Int Gr Ch Martinez CA

2002-2004; Cur S Bede's Epis Ch Menlo Pk CA 2001-2002. revjimcroom@yahoo.com

CROOM, Letitia Church (EO) PO Box 292, Cove OR 97824 B Savannah GA 2/24/1925 d Hardy Croom & Lettie. BA Florida St U 1946; Cert GTS 1948; MA UTS 1948. D 11/21/1971 Bp Norman L Foote P 1/16/1977 Bp William Benjamin Spofford. The Oregon Trail Trin Ogallala NE 1990; Dio Estrn Oregon The Dalles OR 1989-1991; Vic S Paul's Epis Ch Nyssa OR 1974-1988; Vic H Trin Vale OR 1974-1985; Asst Ch Of H Nativ Meridian ID 1972-1974. tishc@coveoregon.com

CROSBY, Derrill Plummer (NH) 11 Central St, Peterborough NH 03458 B Providence RI 10/17/1923 s Gordon Eugene Crosby & Florence Maria. BA U of Maryland 1971; MDiv VTS 1977; Ldrshp Acad for New Directions 1981. D 5/21/1977 Bp Robert Bruce Hall P 11/1/1977 Bp Charles Gresham Marmion. m 2/20/1988 Janice Mary Crosby c 3. Chair - Dioc Subcommittee Ret Cler & Fams Dio New Hampshire Concord NH 1991-1995; Dioc Renwl & Evang Com Dio New Hampshire Concord NH 1988-1989; Sprtl Dir Curs Sec Dio New Hampshire Concord NH 1984-1986; R Ch Of The Epiph Newport NH 1983-1990; Exec Dir Newport Area Assn Chs Dio New Hampshire Concord NH 1983-1990; Dn Roanoke Cler Dio SW Virginia Roanoke VA 1978-1981; R Trin Ch Buchanan VA 1977-1983. Auth, "arts". Bro Of S Andr; Ord Of S Lk. derrill1@msn.com

CROSBY, James Pennington (Fla) 1932 Sweet Briar Ln, Jacksonville FL 32217 B Queens NY 12/31/1931 s Watson Pennington Crosby & Adelaide Augusta. BA Adams St Coll 1954; Long Island Dioc TS 1957; Coll of Preachers 1975. D 6/22/1957 P 12/1/1957 Bp James P De Wolfe. m 5/31/1968 Marian Knight Rogers. S Geo's Epis Ch Jacksonville FL 1977-1980; Asst Chr Ch Bradenton FL 1969-1973; R S Paul's Ch Bennettsville SC 1968-1969; Vic Ch Of The Gd Shpd Helena MT 1964-1967; Vic S Alb's Epis Ch Laurel MT 1964-1967; Vic Chr Ch Brentwood NY 1957-1959. Auth, "When The P Becomes A Widower". Intl Conf Of Police Chapl. jimmimi@comcast.net

CROSBY, Karen Ann (Md) 52 S Broadway, Frostburg MD 21532 B Cumberland MD 8/10/1956 d Ernest Preston Ogden & Ruth Sylvia Wolff. BA Frostburg St Coll 1978; MSW W Virginia U 1980; Luth TS Gettysburg PA 2011. D 7/6/2008 P 2/14/2009 Bp John Leslie Rabb. m 8/8/1981 Anthony E Crosby. kcrosby@ang-md.org

CROSBY, William Franklin (RG) 6344 Gray St, Arvada CO 80003 B Middletown NY 4/1/1932 s Samuel Crosby & Marie Olive. BA Leh 1953; STB GTS 1959; PhD Adams St Coll 1967. D 8/1/1959 P 12/21/1959 Bp James P De Wolfe. Int S Paul's/Peace Ch Las Vegas NM 1999; Assoc P S Bede's Epis Ch Santa Fe NM 1988-1990; Ch Of S Mary The Vrgn New York NY 1988-1989; Assoc P Ch Of S Mary The Vrgn New York NY 1985-1988; Asst Ch Of The Resurr E Elmhurst NY 1966-1994; Vic S Dav's Epis Ch Cambria Heights NY 1959-1963.

CROSS II, Eugenia Sealy (NC) 1032 Wessyngton Rd, Winston Salem NC 27104 **Vic Ch Of The Ascen At Fork Advance NC 2007-** B Marion NC 2/13/1949 d Oliver Roane Cross & Eugenia Sealy. BA Meredith Coll 1974; MDiv VTS 1992. D 6/15/1992 Bp Robert Whitridge Estill P 6/1/1993 Bp Huntington Williams Jr. Assoc R S Tim's Epis Ch Winston Salem NC 1992-2006. vicarsealy@bellsouth.net

CROSS JR, Freeman Grant (Ga) 5424 Hill Rd, Albany GA 31705 B Knoxville TN 5/22/1935 s Freeman Grant Cross & Jean. BS USMA At W Point 1957; MS U IL 1962; MDiv SWTS 1989. D 6/10/1989 P 3/1/1990 Bp Harry Woolston Shipps. m 12/6/1961 Emilie Wognum c 2. Ch Of The H Sprt Dawson GA 1997-2007; S Fran Ch Camilla GA 1997-2007; S Marg Of Scotland Epis Ch Moultrie GA 1995-1996; Vic S Matt's Epis Ch Fitzgerald GA 1989-1993. fgcross@aol.com

CROSS, Kevin Michael (Eas) P.O. Box 387, Oxford MD 21654 **Dioc Coun Mem Dio Easton Easton MD 2011-; R Ch Of The H Trin Oxford MD 2010-** B Grosse Pointe, MI 5/23/1952 s Harold Earl Cross & Loretta Mulvihill. BA Tufts U 1974; MSW Boston Coll 1977; M. Div EDS 2008. Trans from Anglican Church of Canada 3/31/2010 Bp James Joseph Shand. m 8/18/1974 Barbara A Bicknell c 2. Soc Justice Awd EDS 2008. kevinmichaelc@gmail.com

CROSS, Myrick Tyler (SO) 318 E 4th St, Cincinnati OH 45202 **Cn Vic Epis Soc of Chr Ch Cincinnati OH 2005-** B Belfast ME 4/9/1943 s Stephen Myrick Cross & Hazel Annie. BA Wheaton Coll 1965; Med U of Maine 1969; EdD Ball St U 1976; MDiv GTS 1983. D 5/28/1983 P 12/1/1983 Bp Frederick Barton Wolf. m 8/1/1970 Amy Cole c 2. Epis Soc Of Chr Ch Cincinnati OH 2005-2010; S Jas Ch Old Town ME 2005; S Pat's Ch Brewer ME 2004-2005; R S Fran By The Sea Blue Hill ME 2001-2003; R Ch Of The Mssh Woods Hole MA 1989-2001; Assoc The Ch Of The Redeem Baltimore MD 1986-1989; R Chr Ch Biddeford ME 1983-1986. myrickcross@gmail.com

CROSS, Samuel Otis (LI) 224 W 11th St Apt 4, New York NY 10014 **Asst S Jn's Ch New York NY 1993-** B Memphis TN 12/13/1947 s Ruben Otis Cross & Anne Lois. BS U of Memphis 1971; MDiv GTS 1976; STM GTS 1981. D 6/26/1976 Bp John Vander Horst P 4/24/1977 Bp William Evan Sanders. Epis Mssn Soc New York NY 1989-1991; R Ch Of The H Apos Brooklyn NY 1986-1993; R S Paul's Ch Brooklyn NY 1982-1986; Ch Of The Annunc Ridgewood NY 1982-1983; Vic Bp Otey Memi Ch Memphis TN 1977-1979; D-in-Trng Ch Of The Gd Shpd Lookout Mtn TN 1976-1977.

CROSSETT, Judith Hale Wallace (Ia) 320 E College St, Iowa City IA 52240 **D Trin Ch Iowa City IA 2009-** B Chicago IL 2/18/1947 d David Dickson Wallace & Joan Hillmer. BA Gri 1968; MA U Tor Toronto ON CA 1970; PhD U of Iowa 1977; MD U of Iowa 1984; MS U of Iowa 1988. D 2/8/2009 Bp Alan Scarfe. c 1. judith-crossett@uiowa.edu

CROSSNOE, Marshall E (Mo) 217 ADAMS ST, JEFFERSON CITY MO 65101 **S Alb's Epis Ch Fulton MO 2008-; Full Time S Mk's Epis Ch Portland MO 2008-** B Abilene TX 5/12/1960 s Floyd Valton Crossnoe & Barbara Joyce. MABS Dallas TS 1986; MA U of Texas 1989; Dr U of Wisconsin 1996. D 12/21/2007 P 6/21/2008 Bp George Wayne Smith. m 12/19/1987 Debra Sue Maddox c 2. crossnoe@gmail.com

CROSSWAITE, John Joseph (Mil) 700 Quinlan Dr., Pewaukee WI 53072 B Elkhorn WI 3/20/1949 s John William & Mary F. MDiv St Fran Sem 1978; MAS U of San Francisco 1984. Rec from Roman Catholic 7/8/2008 Bp Steven Andrew Miller. m 5/6/2000 Elizabeth Yunker c 2. jcrosswaite@wi.rr.com

CROSTHWAIT, Gregory Lloyd (Dal) PO Box 1837, Mt Pleasant TX 75456 **R S Dav's Ch Gilmer TX 2008-; R Trin NE Texas Epis Ch Mt Pleasant TX 2008-** B Garland TX 7/13/1970 BA U of Texas at Dallas 1994; Th.M. Dallas TS 2002. D 1/31/2004 P 7/29/2004 Bp James Monte Stanton. m 11/22/1997 Emily Kaylene Crosthwait c 3. S Ptr's By The Lake Ch The Colony TX 2007-2008; R The Epis Ch of the Intsn Carrollton TX 2005-2007; Pstr For Adult Mnstrs S Nich Ch Flower Mound TX 2004-2005. fr.crosthwait@gmail.com

CROTHERS, John-Michael (NY) 214 Burntwood Trl, Toms River NJ 08753 B Vancouver BC CA 10/24/1938 s Donald Crothers & Helene. BA Concordia U 1963; MDiv GTS 1966. D 6/16/1966 P 12/21/1966 Bp Jonathan Goodhue Sherman. R S Jn's Ch Staten Island NY 1978-1999; Ch Of S Alb The Mtyr S Albans NY 1977; Ord Of St Vinc Little Neck NY 1976-1978; Zion Ch Douglaston NY 1976-1978; ACU Oakland CA 1974-1976; Cur S Paul's Ch Brooklyn NY 1968-1974; S Thos' Epis Ch Bellerose Vill NY 1967-1968; Epis Ch of The Resurr Williston Pk NY 1966-1967. CCU 1968; GAS 2001; SocMary 1999; SSC 1991. DD Ign U, Indianapolis, IN 1999. frj-mcssc@comcast.net

CROTHERS, Kenneth Delbert (Ida) Po Box 374, Shoshone ID 83352 **D Chr Ch Shoshone ID 1988-** B Jerome ID 2/20/1925 s Delbert Crothers & Olive Irene. BS Idaho St U 1949; MS U of Idaho Moscow 1955. D 11/6/1988 Bp David Bell Birney IV. m 8/27/1950 Inez Marie Burkhalter c 3.

CROUCH, Billy Gene (NY) 3604 Balcones Dr, Austin TX 78731 B Port Lavaca TX 5/14/1930 s Lemuel Wade Crouch & Lillian. BS Baylor U 1954; MS Baylor U 1955; PhD U of Tennessee 1958. D 12/24/1961 Bp James Albert Pike. Asst Ch Of The Resurr New York NY 1965-1995; Asst S Jn's Ch Cohoes NY 1964-1965; Asst Gr Cathd San Francisco CA 1961-1963.

CROUCH, Emily Schwartz (Ky) 821 S 4th St, Louisville KY 40203 **S Matt's Epis Ch Louisville KY 2009-** B Tallahassee FL 1/5/1980 d Geoffrey Schwartz & Victoria. BA Rhodes Coll 2002; MS Louisville Presb Sem 2007; MDiv GTS 2008. D 9/5/2008 P 3/25/2009 Bp Edwin Funsten Gulick Jr. m 5/30/2010 Zachary James Crouch. Asst Calv Ch Louisville KY 2008-2009. ecrouch@stmatt-ky.org

CROW, Lynda Diane (Los) 1145 W Valencia Mesa Dr, Fullerton CA 92833 **Assoc R Emm Par Fullerton CA 1995-** B Toronto Ontario Canada 7/4/1947 d Leslie William Cunninghame & Bessie Eleanor. AS Mt San Antonio Coll 1967; BA U of La Verne CA 1984; MDiv CDSP 1995. D 6/10/1995 Bp Robert Marshall Anderson P 1/13/1996 Bp Chester Lovelle Talton. m 11/2/1968 Donald Robert Crow c 2. molyn11396@aol.com

CROW, Robert B (Ga) St. Andrews By-the-Sea Episcopal Church, PO Box 1658, Destin FL 32540 **S Andr's By The Sea Epis Ch Destin FL 2011-** B Jackson MS 9/22/1963 s Robert Neal Crow & Margaret Ann Taylor. BS U of Alabama at Birmingham 1986; MBA Samford U 1993; MDiv The TS at the U So 2011. D 5/14/2011 Bp Scott Anson Benhase. m 10/28/2011 Kathryn Ann B Kathryn Ann Brymer. rbarrycrow@gmail.com

CROWDER, James Robert (Md) 13801 York Rd Apt E9, Cockeysville MD 21030 **Dio Maryland Baltimore MD 2002-** B Ellisville MS 10/23/1933 s Walter Byron Crowder & Sadie. BS Mississippi St U 1955; MDiv VTS 1959. D 6/16/1959 P 12/17/1959 Bp Duncan Montgomery Gray. m 6/6/1958 Suzanne Buckson c 4. Chair, T/F of Corp Dio Maryland Baltimore MD 1998-2000; S Jn's Ch Ellicott City MD 1996; Human Sxlty Com Dio Maryland Baltimore MD 1990-1992; Sr Assoc The Ch Of The Redeem Baltimore MD 1989-1996; Fin Com Dio Connecticut Hartford CT 1984-1986; Chair Structure Evaltn Com Dio Connecticut Hartford CT 1980-1982; R S Jas Epis Ch Farmington CT 1976-1989; Dioc Coun Dio Maryland Baltimore MD 1971-1973; Epiph Ch Dulaney Vlly Timonium MD 1966-1976; R S Jn's Ch Mt Washington Baltimore MD 1961-1966; Asst S Paul's Epis Ch Meridian MS 1959-1961. jandscrowder@comcast.net

CROWE, Kathleen A (ECR) Holy Spirit Episcopal Church, 65 W Rincon Ave, Campbell CA 95008 **D Ch Of The H Sprt Campbell CA 2007-** B Siox City Iowa 4/5/1945 d William Crowe Crowe & Helen Marie. Cert in Behavioral Sci; BA California Sch for Deacons 2007. D 9/8/2007 Bp Sylvestre Donato Romero. S Edw The Confessor Epis Ch San Jose CA 2007-2009. office@stedwards.org

CROWELL, Larry A (SO) 7015 Ballantrae Loop, Dublin OH 43016 B Philipsburg PA 2/1/1953 s Jules Crowell & Helen. BBA Elizabethtown Coll 1976; MPA Penn 1985; MDiv TESM 2004. D 6/12/2004 P 12/12/2004 Bp Robert William Duncan. m 3/2/1974 Deborah Crowell. S Lk's Ch Powhatan VA 2007-2011; Galilee Epis Ch Virginia Bch VA 2005-2007; Angl Comm. Ntwk Of Dio And Parishes Pittsburgh PA 2004-2005. lcrowell@lssco.org

CROWELL, Paul L (Az) 2800 Huntsman Ct, Jamestown NC 27282 B Denver CO 12/20/1942 s Paul Crowell & Mary Louise. BA Cornell Coll 1965; MDiv Nash 1981; DMin Fuller TS 1997. D 5/26/1981 P 11/30/1981 Bp Walter Cameron Righter. m 8/15/1965 Patricia Lea c 3. R S Lk's Ch Prescott AZ 1990-2006; Assoc R All SS Ch Of Winter Pk Winter Pk FL 1985-1990; Vic S Geo's Ch Sidney NE 1981-1985; Vic S Paul's Ch Ogallala NE 1981-1985. Auth, *BRF SALT*. OHC 1981. pcrowell3@triad.rr.com

CROWELL, Richard Stockton (Mass) 2 Esker Place, North Falmouth MA 02556 B Melrose MA 9/22/1929 s Stewart Preston Crowell & Helen. BS Tufts U 1952; STB Ya Berk 1956. D 6/23/1956 Bp Norman B Nash P 2/1/1957 Bp Anson Phelps Stokes Jr. c 4. R S Barn Ch Falmouth MA 1961-1991; Asst to R S Mk's Ch New Canaan CT 1956-1961. birderdick@aol.com

CROWLE, Wesley Edward (Minn) 1545 Northeast 7 1/2 Avenue NE, Rochester MN 55906 **Pstr Asst S Lk's Epis Ch Rochester MN 1990-** B Three Hills AB CA 2/22/1922 s Harold Edward Crowle & Ida Pearl. BA U of Alberta Edmonton AB CA 1948; BD/LTH U Tor 1951; CPE Advncd CPE 1962. Trans from Anglican Church of Canada 9/1/1965 as Priest Bp Hamilton Hyde Kellogg. m 1/21/1956 Dorothy Irene Griffiths c 3. Int S Lk's Epis Ch Rochester MN 1988-1989; Dio Minnesota Minneapolis MN 1965-1988. APHA 1971-1989; Assembly of Epis Hosp & Chapl 1981-1989; Assn of Profsnl Chapl 1998-1989; Coll of Chapl 1971-1989. Chapl Emer Coll of Chapl APHA 1989. wesdotcrowle@aol.com

CROWLEY, Daniel Fenwick (Mass) 76 Olde Towne Lane, West Chatham MA 02669 B Lawrence MA 7/8/1940 s Archie H Crowley & Jean. BA Wms 1962; MA Col 1963; BD EDS 1970. D 6/20/1970 P 1/29/1971 Bp Archie H Crowley. m 8/17/1963 Susan L Leicht c 3. Int S Jn's Epis Ch Saugus MA 2008-2009; Int S Paul's Epis Ch No Andover MA 2006-2007; Assoc Ch Of The H Sprt Mattapan MA 2000-2004; Assoc R S Jn's Ch Ellicott City MD 1997-2000; R S Jn's Ch Bridgeport CT 1984-1997; R S Mart's Epis Ch New Bedford MA 1974-1984; Cur S Ptr's Epis Ch Lakewood OH 1970-1974. Phillips Brook Soc 2000-2003. crowleysukidan@aol.com

CROWSON, Steven Franklin (LI) Po Box 22, Leeds ME 04263 **Dio Maine Portland ME 2008-; R Trin Epis Ch Lewiston ME 2008-** B Birmingham AL 11/12/1939 s Cecil Franklin Crowson & Selamarie Arita. BS Auburn U 1963; MDiv Gordon-Conwell TS 1974; DMin Bos 1987. D 6/9/1976 P 12/5/1976 Bp Morris Fairchild Arnold. c 1. R S Mary's Epis Ch Shltr Island NY 1995-2006; R Gr Ch Salem MA 1979-1995; Cur S Paul's Ch Boston MA 1976-1978. frstevec@gmail.com

✠ CROWTHER, Rt Rev CE (Los) 289 Moreton Bay Ln Apt 2, Goleta CA 93117 B Bradford Yorkshire UK 3/4/1929 s Joseph Austin Crowther & Margaret Edith. BA U Of Leeds Leeds Gb 1950; LLB U Of Leeds Leeds Gb 1952; LLM U Of Leeds Leeds Gb 1953; GOE Cuddesdon Theol Coll, Oxford 1956; PhD U CA 1975. Trans from Church Of England 4/1/1959 as Priest Bp Francis E I Bloy Con 1/1/1965 for Diocese of Kimberley & Kuruman. m 12/18/1994 Claudette Y Crowther. Collegial Bp Of Ecr Dio El Camino Real Monterey CA 1984-1986; Dio California San Francisco CA 1971-1977; Asstg Bp Of Cal Dio California San Francisco CA 1970-1984. Auth, "Where Rel Gets Lost In The Ch," Morehouse Barlow; Auth, "Face Of Apartheid," U Of New Zealand Press; Auth, "Rel Trusts: Their Dvlpmt," *Scope & Meaning*, Geo Ronald - Oxford; Auth, "Intimacy," *Strtgies For Successful Relationships*, Capra Press. Dplma AAPC, Life Clini. drecrowther@cox.net

CROWTHER JR, James Pollard (Ga) 398 Laurel Mountain Trl # 999, Saluda NC 28773 B New York NY 2/12/1933 s James Pollard Crowther & Lottie. BS Florida St U 1954; Harv 1966; MDiv STUSo 1971; MS STUSo 1973. D 6/17/1957 P 2/1/1961 Bp Albert R Stuart. S Fran Ch Camilla GA 1983-1986; Cur All SS Epis Ch Thomasville GA 1982-1983; Chr Ch Greenville SC 1978-1980; S Steph's Ch S Steph SC 1968-1977; R Trin Epis Ch Pinopolis SC 1968-1977; Cur H Trin Epis Ch Charleston SC 1966-1968; Cur The Ch Of The Gd Shpd Augusta GA 1960-1963; Vic Ch Of The Gd Shpd Swainsboro GA 1957-1958; Vic The Epis Ch Of The Annunc Vidalia GA 1957-1958. Auth, "How To Teach Rel (The Old-Fashioned And Proven Way)"; Auth, "A Study Course On The Miracles In The NT," *A Few Portraits Of Jesus Chr In The NT*; Auth, "A Study Course On The Bk Of Revelation," *H Cross*; Auth, "A Study Course On The Original Twelve Apos - Plua Study Course On The Original Twelve Apos - Plus One," *What Happened At The Reformation (An Ang.*

CROZIER, Richard Lee (USC) 125 Pendleton St Sw, Aiken SC 29801 B San Diego CA 1/19/1956 s Robert Calvin Crozier & Carolyn Redfern. BA San Diego St U 1981; MDiv SWTS 1984. D 8/24/1984 Bp Charles Brinkley Morton P 5/1/1985 Bp Richard Mitchell Trelease Jr. m 6/25/1982 Rita Ann Stanley. S Barn Ch Jenkinsville SC 2001; S Thad Epis Ch Aiken SC 1998-2000; Off Of Bsh For ArmdF New York NY 1993-1998; Vic S Mk's Ch Chester SC 1987-1993; Vic S Ptr's Ch Great Falls SC 1987-1993; R S Mk's Epis Ch Pecos TX 1985-1986; Cur S Andr's Ch Roswell NM 1984-1985. SHN.

CRUIKSHANK, Charles Clark (CPa) 212 Penn St, Huntingdon PA 16652 B Jewickley PA 8/25/1956 s Charles Clark Cruikshank & Lois Jane. BS The Penn 1979. D 10/31/2010 Bp Nathan Dwight Baxter. m 10/27/1979 Patricia Patricia Ann Miller c 2. charliecruikshank@gmail.com

CRUM JR, G(eorge) Milton (USC) 915 Saddle Drive, Apt 124, Helena MT 59601 B Orangeburg SC 4/13/1924 s G(eorge) Milton Crum & Sadelle. Clemson U 1943; BS U of Nebraska 1945; MDiv STUSo 1951; DIP S Aug's Coll Cbury GB 1957; Cert CUA 1970. D 6/28/1951 P 2/1/1952 Bp Thomas N Carruthers. m 8/22/1987 Kathe Hegnsle. Prof VTS Alexandria VA 1972-1989; Asst Prof VTS Alexandria VA 1966-1969; R Ch Of The H Comm Allendale SC 1951-1960. Auth, "Evil, Anger, and God," WingSpan Press, 2008; Auth, "Confessions of a Recovering Racist," *The Virginia Sem Journ*, VTS, 1997; Auth, "The Sundays after Pentecost," *Breaking the Word*, Ch Hymnal Corp, 1994; Auth, "Manual on Preaching," Morehouse-Barlow, 1988; Auth, "If Ordnry People Had Gone to Ch," *St. Lk's Journ of Theol*, Sewanee TS, 1984; Co-Auth, "Lesser Festivals 3: SS' Days and Spec Occasions," Fortress Press, 1981; Auth, "Manual on Preaching," Judson Press, 1977; Auth, "Our Approach to the Ch Year," *Wrshp*, St Johns Abbey, 1977. 2crums@bresnan.net

CRUM, Robert James Howard (EO) 700 SW Eastman Pkwy Ste B110, Gresham OR 97080 B Portland OR 12/9/1945 s Howard Alvin Crum & Mary Helen. BA Mt Ang Abbey 1967; MDiv S Thos Sem 1971. Rec from Roman Catholic 1/25/1984 as Priest Bp Matthew Paul Bigliardi. m 11/29/1975 Gayle Frances Spulniak. Vic Dio Estrn Oregon The Dalles OR 1989-1991; Vic S Alb's Epis Ch Redmond OR 1989-1991; Vic S Mk's Epis and Gd Shpd Luth Madras OR 1989-1991; Mssy Exec Coun Appointees New York NY 1985-1989; Vic St Andrews Ch Agat GU 1985-1988; Assoc S Fran Of Assisi Epis Wilsonville OR 1982-1984. robert.crum2@frontier.com

CRUM, Thomas Lee (Mass) Martha Crum, 507 4th St, Brooklyn NY 11215 **Died 11/20/2010** B Bushnell FL 2/20/1923 s Charlie Eddie Crum & Mary. BA U of Florida 1947; BD EDS 1951. D 7/3/1951 P 2/18/1952 Bp Thomas N Carruthers. c 3.

CRUMB, Lawrence Nelson (Ore) 1674 Washington St, Eugene OR 97401 **Int Vic S Andr's Ch Cottage Grove OR 2009-** B Palo Alto CA 5/19/1937 s Fred Wells Crumb & Esther Carol. BA Pomona Coll 1958; MDiv Nash 1961; GTS 1962; MA U of Wisconsin 1967; STM Nash 1973. D 9/7/1961 Bp Francis E I Bloy P 6/16/1962 Bp Daniel Corrigan. m 7/31/1968 Ellen Adele Locke c 1. Int S Tim's Epis Ch Salem OR 2005-2007; S Geo's Epis Ch Roseburg OR 2003-2004; Int Trin Ch S Louis MO 2000-2001; Int R S Alb's Epis Ch Tillamook OR 1999; S Alb's Epis Ch Tillamook OR 1995; Instr Sch Theol & Mnstry Dio Oregon Portland OR 1990-1992; P-in-c S Mary Ch Gardiner OR 1981-1982; St Marys Ch Reedsport OR 1981-1982; S Andr's Ch Cottage Grove OR 1980-1981; S Dav's Ch Drain OR 1980-1981; S Mary's Epis Ch Eugene OR 1978-1995; S Lk's Ch Racine WI 1978; S Steph's Ch Racine WI 1970-1978; Asst Libr, NT Gk Instr Nash Nashotah WI 1965-1970; Cur St Johns Epis Ch Lafayette IN 1964-1965; Cur S Jn The Evang Ch Elkhart IN 1962-1964; Asst Gr Ch Un City NJ 1961-1962. Auth, "2nd ed. (Oxford Mvmt)," *2nd ed. (Oxford Mvmt)*, Scarecrow, 2009; Auth, "Supplement (Oxford Mvmt)," *Supplement (Oxford Mvmt)*, Scarecrow, 1993; Auth, "The Oxford Mvmt & Its Leaders," *The Oxford Mvmt & Its Leaders*, Scarecrow, 1988; Auth, "Historic Preservation in the Pacific NW," *Historic Preservation in the Pacific NW*, Coun of Plnng Librarians, 1979. Affirming Catholicism; HSEC. lcrumb@uoregon.edu

CRUMBAUGH III, Frank B (NJ) 410 S Atlantic Ave, Beach Haven NJ 08008 **Intake Off Dio New Jersey Trenton NJ 2011-2012; R The Ch Of The H Innoc Bch Haven NJ 1997-** B Memphis TN 1/7/1953 s Frank Boyd Crumbaugh & Jennie Sue. BA Cntr Coll 1974; MDiv GTS 1984. D 2/20/1988 P 9/28/1988 Bp John Shelby Spong. m 8/11/1984 Gretchen Densmore Zimmerman c 3. T/F on Restructure Dio New Jersey Trenton NJ 2009-2010; Trial Crt Dio New Jersey Trenton NJ 2005-2008; Loan & Grant Com Dio New Jersey Trenton NJ 2004-2006; R S Tim's Epis Ch Creve Coeur MO 1992-1997; S Mary's Ch Belvidere NJ 1988-1992; S Ptr's Ch Washington NJ 1988-1992. CLP 2000-2003; F&AM 1977; OGS 1995; Phi Delta Theta 1971; SAR 2002. Eagle Scout BSA 1968. crumbaugh@msn.com

CRUMLEY, Carole Anne (WA) 3039 Beech St Nw, Washington DC 20015 **Shalem Inst For Sprtl Formation Washington DC 1999-** B Johnson City TN 2/3/1944 d Harry Lewis Crumely & Margaret Nola. BA Duke 1966; MA U NC 1969; MDiv Inter/Met Sem 1976. D 6/26/1976 P 1/8/1977 Bp William Foreman Creighton. m 2/4/1995 Clark Elliot Lobenstine. Cathd of St Ptr & St Paul Washington DC 1981-1997; S Jn's Ch Georgetown Par Washington DC

1980-1982; Ch Of The Ascen Gaithersburg MD 1979-1980; Cur Chr Ch Capitol Hill Washington DC 1976-1978. Auth, "Meaning In The Midst Of Chaos". carole@shalem.org

CRUMMEY, Rebecca Jo (Colo) 967 Marion St Apt 7, Denver CO 80218 **S Jn's Cathd Denver CO 2010-** B London England 10/29/1967 BA U IL. D 6/8/2003 Bp Peter Hess Beckwith P 3/25/2004 Bp Robert John O'Neill. Cur S Jn's Cathd Denver CO 2003-2009. RJCRUMMEY@YAHOO.COM

CRUMP, David Archelaus (Los) Po Box 371645, Montara CA 94037 B Saugerties NY 8/15/1927 s Benjamin Franklin Crump & Frances May. BA Alfred U 1950; MDiv VTS 1953. D 6/23/1953 P 12/23/1953 Bp Dudley S Stark. m 5/22/1983 Annely Crump-Garay c 1. Assoc R S Jas' Epis Ch Los Angeles CA 1966-1970; Vic Ch Of S Jude The Apos Cupertino CA 1962-1965; R S Lk's Ch Brockport NY 1953-1956. Auth, *Forth.* acrumpgaray@yahoo.com

CRUMPTON IV, Alvin Briggs (Ga) PO Box 1155, Brunswick GA 31521 **P S Mk's Ch Brunswick GA 2011-** B Americus GA 9/11/1970 s Alvin Briggs Crumpton & Brenda June. BBA Georgia SW St U 1994; MDiv The TS at Sewanee 2011. D 2/11/2011 P 10/1/2011 Bp Scott Anson Benhase. m 12/4/2006 Valerie T Tan c 1. albcrumpton@hotmail.com

CRUPI OJN, Hilary (FdL) Julian House Monastery, 2812 Summit Ave., Waukesha WI 53188 B San Diego CA 6/5/1961 d Robert Louis Crupi & Kathleen Mary. BA California St U 1986. D 5/10/2002 P 12/21/2002 Bp Russell Edward Jacobus. ojn@orderofjulian.org

CRUSE, John Woolfolk (Ala) 4941 Montevallo Rd, Birmingham AL 35210 **P Assoc Gr Ch Birmingham AL 2002-** B Tuscaloosa AL 10/22/1945 s Joseph Woolfolk Cruse & Johnnie. BA U So 1967; MA U of Virginia 1968; MDiv STUSo 1973. D 6/8/1973 P 12/1/1973 Bp Furman Stough. S Martins-In-The-Pines Ret Comm Birmingham AL 2002-2009; Trin Ch Wetumpka AL 2001; S Paul's Epis Ch Lowndesboro AL 1996-1999; Chapl S Dunst's: The Epis Ch at Auburn U Auburn AL 1995-2000; All SS Ch Montgomery AL 1995-1996; H Comf Ch Gadsden AL 1987-1995; R S Alb's Ch Birmingham AL 1983-1986; R Gr Epis Ch Mt Meigs AL 1981-1983; S Paul's Ch Selma AL 1980-1981; Dio Alabama Birmingham AL 1978-1999; Ch Of The H Comf Montgomery AL 1973-1978. Kappa Sigma; Omicron Delta Kappa; Phi Beta Kappa. JOHN@JOHNCRUSE.NET

CRYSLER JR, Fred (Ct) PO Box 9324, Louisville KY 40209 B Wabash IN 3/12/1941 s Frederick S Crysler & Emma Lou. BA Br 1963; MDiv EDS 1968. D 6/6/1968 P 3/1/1969 Bp Robert Lionne DeWitt. m 12/6/2002 Elizabeth Kay Crysler c 2. R Chr Ch Sharon CT 2003-2006; R Resurr Ch Louisville KY 1988-2002; Vic S Chad's Ch Tampa FL 1983-1988; Int Trin Ch Covington KY 1982-1983; Assoc S Jn's Ch Bala Cynwyd PA 1976-1977; Assoc Chapl for Prison Mnstry Dio Pennsylvania Philadelphia PA 1972-1975; Cur The Epis Ch Of The Adv Kennett Sq PA 1968-1970. EPF, WON, Natl Assn for the S 1968-1975. fred41@mohawk.net

CRYSLER, Kenneth (EO) 67794 Highway 395 S, Pendleton OR 97801 B 6/9/1939 D 9/29/1976 P 6/19/1977 Bp William Benjamin Spofford. m 7/18/1964 Sabra J Crysler c 2. Ch Of The Redeem Pendleton OR 1999-2004; S Steph's Baker City OR 1997-2001. papaken@uci.net

CUBINE, James W (WTenn) 7910 Gayle Ln, Memphis TN 38138 B Chattano GA 12/22/1947 s Thomas A Cubine & Jo. BA U of Tennessee 1971; MA U of Kansas 1973; MDiv SWTS 1981. D 6/21/1981 Bp William F Gates Jr P 5/1/1982 Bp William Evan Sanders. m 12/22/1973 Carroll Luck c 2. S Anne's Ch Millington TN 2004-2010; S Andr's Epis Ch Collierville TN 1988-2000; S Jas Epis Ch Zanesville OH 1987-1988; Dio W Tennessee Memphis TN 1986-1987; S Geo's Ch Germantown TN 1981-1983. JCUBINE@AOL.COM

CUDD, Anne (Ida) 3024 SW 98th Way, Gainesville FL 32608 B Troy NY 2/5/1940 d Horace John Grover & Alice Elizabeth. BS Denison U 1961; MD OH SU 1967; MS U of Delaware Newark 1975; MDiv STUSo 1991. D 11/22/1986 P 8/4/1990 Bp David Bell Birney IV. m 8/28/1969 Kermit George Cudd. Asst S Fran Epis Ch Coll Sta TX 2007-2009; Vic S Dav's Epis Ch Caldwell ID 1999-2005; P-in-c S Agnes' Mssn Cowan TN 1990-1999; D Trin Epis Ch Pocatello ID 1986-1988. Phi Beta Kappa Denison U Granville OH 1961. agcudd@gmail.com

CUDWORTH, Robert Wallace (Ct) 400 Seabury Dr Apt 3142, Bloomfield CT 06002 B West Hartford CT 9/20/1923 s Abel Wallace Cudworth & Ruth. BA Trin Hartford CT 1949; U of Connecticut 1956; S Jos's Coll 1986. D 12/1/1990 Bp Arthur Edward Walmsley. m 7/29/1978 Dorothy Jorgensen c 4. D S Jn's Ch W Hartford CT 1996-2001; D Gr Ch Newington CT 1993-1996; D Trin Ch Portland CT 1991-1993; D S Jn The Evang Yalesville CT 1990-1991. "Anglicanism," *Understanding Your Neighbor's Faith*, KTAV Pub Hse, 2004.

CUFF, Stephen James (SO) 5238 Crested Owl Ct., Morrow OH 45152 **Dir of Sprtl Svcs. Epis Ret. Hms. Deupree Hlth Cmnty Cincinnati OH 2007-; Chapl Marjorie P Lee Ret Cmnty Cincinnati OH 2007-** B Buffalo NY 7/17/1960 s Robert John Cuff & Dessie Carolyn. BA SUNY at Buffalo 1982; Nash 1991; MDiv STUSo 1993. D 6/19/1993 Bp John Wadsworth Howe P 6/11/1994 Bp John H(enry) Smith. m 2/4/1984 Beth Ellen Rhoades c 2. Vic S Andr's Epis Ch Washington Crt Hse OH 1999-2007; Sum Camp Dir Dio Sthrn Ohio Cincinnati OH 1999-2002; R S Mk's Epis Ch Berkeley Sprg WV 1994-1999; Cur Trin Ch Parkersburg WV 1993-1994. Assn of Profsnl Chapl 2009. cuffsj@hotmail.com

CUFF, Victoria Slater Smith (NJ) 45 2nd St, Keyport NJ 07735 **Archd Chr Ch Middletown NJ 1995-** B Orange NJ 1/19/1943 d William Algy Smith & Constance Eastman. BS Simmons Coll 1965. D 10/31/1998 Bp Joe Morris Doss. m 12/21/1966 William Cuff c 3. D Chr Ch Middletown NJ 1998-2011; Trin Ch Princeton NJ 1986-1994. NACED 2006; NAAD; Rel Educ Assn. victoriacuff@yahoo.com

CULBERTSON, David Paul (CPa) 210 S Washington St, Muncy PA 17756 **R-Full Time S Jas Ch Muncy PA 2004-** B Carlisle PA 9/4/1968 BA Wilson Coll. D 6/20/2004 P 1/29/2005 Bp Michael Whittington Creighton. m 10/6/1994 Diane Lyn Spangler c 2.

CULBERTSON, Philip Leroy (O) 2101 North Berne Drive, Palm Springs CA 92262 B Bartlesville OK 10/10/1944 s Walter Leroy Culbertson & Wanda Miriam. BA Washington U 1966; MDiv GTS 1970; Hebr U-Jerusalem IL 1976; PhD NYU 1977; WCC 1992. D 6/6/1970 Bp Horace W B Donegan P 12/14/1970 Bp Paul Moore Jr. c 2. Prof Coll Of St Jn The Evang 1992-2007; Prof The TS at The U So Sewanee TN 1985-1992; R Chr Ch Oberlin OH 1976-1985; Asst Ch Of The H Trin New York NY 1970-1974. Auth, "Sprt Possession, Theol, Identity," ATF Press, 2010; Auth, "Bible in/and Popular Culture," SBL Press, 2010; Auth, "New Proclamation, Year C 2010," Fortress Press, 2009; Auth, "Penina Uliuli: Contemporary Changes in Mntl Hlth," U of Hawaii Press, 2007; Auth, "The Sprtlty of Men," Fortress Press, 2002; Auth, "Caring For God's People," Fortress Press, 2000; Auth, "Counslg Issues So Pacific Cmnty," Accent Books, 1997; Auth, "A Word Fitly Spoken: The Parables Of Jesus," Suny Press, 1995; Auth, "Counslg Men," Fortress Press, 1994; Auth, "New Adam: Future Of Masculine Sprtlty," Fortress Press, 1992; Auth, "The Pstr: Readings In The Patristic Period," Fortress Press, 1990. p. culbertson@auckland.ac.nz

CULBERTSON, Thomas Leon (Md) 6 Yearling Way, Lutherville MD 21093 B Oil City PA 1/3/1939 s Russell Grant Culbertson & Frances Sarah. BA Baldwin-Wallace Coll 1962; Oberlin Grad Sch 1963; MDiv EDS 1966; DMin Ashland TS 1977; PhD GTF 2000. D 6/25/1966 P 1/27/1967 Bp Nelson Marigold Burroughs. m 6/11/1966 Deborah R Ridlon c 2. Com on Cn, Dn, Exam Chapl Dio Maryland Baltimore MD 2000-2005; Emm Ch Baltimore MD 1986-2005; Ecum Off Dio SW Virginia Roanoke VA 1983-1985; R S Paul's Epis Ch Lynchburg VA 1982-1985; Dioc Coun Dio Ohio Cleveland OH 1976-1979; Assoc S Paul's Epis Ch Cleveland Heights OH 1972-1982; R S Paul's Ch Oregon OH 1968-1972; Cur S Michaels In The Hills Toledo OH 1966-1968. Auth, "Mntl Illness and Psych Treatment A Guide for Pstr Counselors," The Haworth Press, 2003. The Soc for Values in Higher Educ 2007. tlcdrc@Gmail.com

CULLEN, Kathleen Mary (NH) 1035 Lafayette Rd., Portsmouth NH 03801 **P-in-c Chr Ch Portsmouth NH 2011-; P-in-c Trin Ch Hampton NH 2011-** B Manchester NH 3/12/1948 d Edward H Cullen & Dorothy Katherine. BA U of New Hampshire 1973; MDiv Andover Newton TS 2003; Post Study EDS 2005; Cert/ Shalem Inst for Sprtl Formation 2006. D 8/26/2007 P 6/4/2008 Bp V Gene Robinson. m 10/26/2011 Mary J Young. Assoc P Gr Ch Manchester NH 2011; Pstr Assoc S Matt's Ch Goffstown NH 2008-2011. Pryr Grp & Retreat Ldrshp Shalem Inst of Sprtl Formation 2006; mcl Andover Newton Theol 2003. kathcullen@gmail.com

CULLEN, Peter (LI) 199 Carroll St, Brooklyn NY 11231 **R S Paul's Ch Brooklyn NY 1987-** B Ancon PA 2/24/1951 s James C Cullen & Evelyn E. BA Florida Sthrn Coll 1973; MDiv GTS 1978; STM GTS 1982. D 6/24/1978 P 6/1/1979 Bp William Gillette Weinhauer. Assoc R S Ptr's by-the-Sea Epis Ch Bay Shore NY 1982-1987; Int Ch Of The Ascen Hickory NC 1980-1981; D-In-Trng Ch Of The Ascen Hickory NC 1978-1979. pmtownsend@aol.com

CULLINANE, Kathleen Jean (EpisSanJ) 1528 Oakdale Rd, Modesto CA 95355 **Epis Dio San Joaquin Modesto CA 2011-** B Cape May Courthouse NJ 6/2/1955 d Daniel Cullinane & Jeanette. U CA 1974; Goldenwest Huntington Bch CA 1975; BS Loyola Marymount U 1977; Cert Theol Bp Tucker Theol Coll Mukono Ug 1988; MDiv/STM GTS 1989. D 6/10/1989 P 1/13/1990 Bp Frederick Houk Borsch. Int S Fran In The Fields Zionsville IN 2009-2010; Cn Chr Ch Cathd Indianapolis IN 2000-2008; R S Mary's Epis Ch Los Angeles CA 1989-2000. kcullinane@diosanjoaquin.org

CULLIPHER III, James Robert (USC) 800 Stillpoint Way, Balsam Grove NC 28708 B Monroe LA 11/9/1934 s James Robert Cullipher & Lois Welch. BS U of Louisiana at Monroe 1957; MDiv STUSo 1970. D 6/30/1970 Bp William Evan Sanders P 5/30/1971 Bp John Vander Horst. m 8/13/1955 Annette Moak c 2. Journey Into Wholeness Inc Balsam Grove NC 1988-1999; Asst R Chr Ch Greenville SC 1984-1987; R The Epis Ch of The Redeem Jacksonville FL 1977-1984; Asst S Ptr's Ch Jacksonville FL 1975-1976; P-in-c S Mary Magd Ch Fayetteville TN 1971-1975; D-in-trng S Jn's Epis Cathd Knoxville TN 1970-1971. jim@journeyintowholeness.org

CULMER, Ronald D (Cal) 3350 Hopyard Rd, Pleasanton CA 94588 **R S Clare's Epis Ch Pleasanton CA 2004-** B Mildenhall UK 3/27/1964 s Henry Douglas Culmer & Sonia Antionette. BA California Luth U 1990; MDiv

CDSP 1994. D 6/4/1994 Bp Chester Lovelle Talton P 1/14/1995 Bp Frederick Houk Borsch. m 8/5/1995 Diana H Culmer c 2. R S Mart-In-The-Fields Par Winnetka CA 1997-2004; Asst S Steph's Epis Ch Santa Clarita CA 1994-1996. onebreadonecup@msn.com

CULP JR, Robert S (Roch) 19 Arbor Ct, Fairport NY 14450 B Long Beach CA 10/13/1938 s Robert S Culp & Margaret Edna. BS USMA At W Point 1962; Med Bos 1976; MDiv Bex 1980. D 3/22/1981 P 5/1/1982 Bp Robert Rae Spears Jr. m 11/16/2002 Karen Joyce Kipnes c 3. Chapl The Chap of the Gd Shpd Rochester NY 1998-2000; P-in-c S Jn's Ch Mt Morris NY 1986-1998; P-in-c The Ch Of The H Apos - Epis Perry NY 1986-1998. bobculp@hotmail.com

CULPEPPER, Charles Leland (Miss) 1832 Saint Ann St, Jackson MS 39202 **S Alexis Ch Jackson MS 2006-** B Meridian MS 4/11/1950 s Arlas Leland Culpepper & Virginia Claire. BA Millsaps Coll 1972; JD U of Mississippi 1978; MDiv Epis TS of The SW 1989. D 5/30/1998 P 1/30/1999 Bp Alfred Clark Marble Jr. m 12/30/1978 Mary Katherine Johnson c 1. Dio Mississippi Jackson MS 2001-2005; Cn to Yth & Col Mnstrys Dio Mississippi Jackson MS 2000-2006; Cur S Paul's Epis Ch Meridian MS 1998-2000. kculpep343@aol.com

CULPEPPER, Judith Anne (Ind) 6736 Prince Regent Ct, Indianapolis IN 46250 B Fort Jackson SC 7/29/1952 d Julius Marlin Culpepper & Evelyn Sykes. BS U of So Carolina 1973; MD U of Virginia 1977; MDiv Chr TS 1994; CAS SWTS 1994. D 6/24/1994 P 6/1/1995 Bp Edward Witker Jones. S Thos Ch Franklin IN 2005-2008; S Paul's Epis Ch Gas City IN 2005-2007; Vic S Steph's Elwood IN 1999-2008; Asst Trin Epis Ch Bloomington IN 1997-2000; Assoc S Thos Ch Franklin IN 1994-1997. kitties@ori.net

CULPEPPER, Polk (Ind) 1015 E Main St, New Albany IN 47150 B Alexandria LA 5/12/1948 s W A Culpepper & Thelma. BA LSU 1970; JD LSU 1973; MDiv STUSo 1987. D 6/20/1987 P 12/15/1987 Bp Willis Ryan Henton. m 4/7/1973 Catherine Connell c 2. R S Paul's Epis Ch New Albany IN 2005-2010; S Jas Ch Shelbyville KY 2004-2005; Calv Ch Louisville KY 2001-2003; Ch Of The Gd Shpd Cashiers NC 1994-2001; R Ch Of The Ascen Mt Sterling KY 1988-1994; Asst Gr Epis Ch Monroe LA 1987-1988. PLOK@INSIGHTBB.COM

CULTON, Douglas (Del) 1212 E Holly St, Goldsboro NC 27530 **P-in-c S Fran Ch Goldsboro NC 2011-** B Providence RI 12/31/1950 s Donald Fraser Culton & Melva Anna. BA Drury U 1973; MDiv GTS 1977; Cert St. Mary's Sem Univ Baltimore MD 1987. D 9/10/1977 P 3/1/1978 Bp Robert Bracewell Appleyard. c 3. Int S Anne's Epis Ch Jacksonville NC 2007-2008; Int Chr Epis Ch Tarrytown NY 2004-2006; R S Ptr's Ch Lewes DE 1984-2003; R S Jas Epis Ch Arlington VT 1979-1983; Asst Fox Chap Epis Ch Pittsburgh PA 1977-1979. dculton@nc.rr.com

CULVER, Carson Kies (Mil) 590 N Church St, Richland Center WI 53581 **P-in-c H Trin Epis Ch Prairie Du Chien WI 2002-** B Detroit MI 12/23/1944 s Ernest Delos Culver & Genevieve Mae. BS U of Wisconsin 1967; MS U of Wisconsin 1979; MDiv U Of Dubuque 1985; Cert Nash 1989. D 8/6/1989 P 2/1/1990 Bp Roger John White. m 8/19/1967 Marilyn Irish c 2. P-in-c Trin Epis Ch Platteville WI 1991-2000; S Barn Richland Cntr WI 1989-2009. Richland Cnty Mnstry Assn 1989. stbarnabas@mwt.net

CULVER, Douglas Eugene (Eau) 1840 N Prospect Ave Apt 214, Milwaukee WI 53202 **Died 12/16/2010** B Chicago IL 10/15/1919 s Francis Norwood Culver & Mary. BS Illinois St U 1964; MDiv SWTS 1967. D 6/3/1967 Bp Albert A Chambers P 12/1/1967 Bp William W Horstick. c 2.

CULVER, Esme Jo R (Ore) Grace Memorial Church, 1535 Ne 17th Ave, Portland OR 97232 **Gr Meml Portland OR 2007-** B Cheltenham Brigtain 6/6/1943 d Geoffrey Grover Rymer & Kathleen. BA Portland St U 1981; MDiv CDSP 2007. D 7/13/2006 P 4/14/2007 Bp Johncy Itty. c 3. Assoc. For Mssn & Mnstry Gr Meml Portland OR 1982-2001. esmec@grace-memorial.org

CUMBERLAND ELLIOTT, Annie Kay (Miss) P.O. Box 23107, Jackson MS 39225 **Int Chapl S Andr's Epis Sch Ridgeland MS 2012-; Coordntr for Yth Mnstrs Dio Mississippi Jackson MS 2009-; Assoc S Andr's Cathd Jackson MS 2008-** B Meridian MS 8/13/1981 d Luke Kaylor Cumberland & Susan Martin. BA Van 2003; MDiv VTS 2008. D 6/7/2008 P 2/1/2009 Bp Duncan Montgomery Gray III. m 9/24/2010 Gates Safford Elliott. annie.kay.elliott@gmail.com

CUMBIE II, W(alter) Kenneth (CGC) 172 Hannon Ave, Moile AL 36604 **S Lk's Epis Ch Mobile AL 2005-** B San Antonio TX 12/10/1952 s Walter Kenneth Cumbie & Joyce Maxinne. BA U of Mobile 1974; MDIV/MRE MidWestern Bapt TS 1980; CPE CPE 1983; DMin GTF 1989. D 1/23/1993 P 7/24/1993 Bp John Clark Buchanan. m 8/29/2007 Joan Cumbie c 2. R H Sprt Epis Ch Gulf Shores AL 2000-2005; R Ch Of The Gd Shpd Mobile AL 1996-2000. Cert Fell Coll of Chapl 1985; Cmdr, US Navy (Reserves) 1986. kcumbie3@aol.com

CUMMER, Edwin West (SwFla) 641 Corwood Dr, Sarasota FL 34234 B 9/20/1917 D 6/29/1972 Bp William Loftin Hargrave.

CUMMING, Jane (NY) 163 Todd Road, Katonah NY 10536 B Basingstoke Hampshire UK 2/27/1927 d Leslie George Housden & Esther Josephine. BA SUNY 1982; MDiv GTS 1983. D 6/4/1983 Bp Paul Moore Jr P 7/1/1984 Bp James Stuart Wetmore. m 2/2/1957 Ian J Cumming c 2. Mnstry Of Persons w Disabil Rye NY 1987-1988.

CUMMINGS, Carolsue (NJ) 322 So Second St, Surf City NJ 08008 B Camden NJ 12/21/1944 d John Ellsworth Jones & Mary Jane. BS Penn Hall Coll Chambersburg PA 1966. D 6/9/1990 Bp George Phelps Mellick Belshaw. m 4/29/1967 Donald Cummings c 3. D S Steph's Ch Waretown NJ 1999-2009. deaconcjc@yahoo.com

CUMMINGS, Dorothy Stacey (WMo) 1601 South Ave # B, Springfield MO 65807 B Protem MO 3/7/1924 d Albert Henry Stacey & Ruth Marie. BS SW Missouri St U 1956; MA U of Arkansas 1966; PhD U of Arkansas 1975. D 12/13/1980 Bp Arthur Anton Vogel. D Shpd Of The Hills Branson MO 1980-1985. Auth, "Delta Kappa Gamma Intl News".

CUMMINGS, George William (Los) 1380 S Marengo Ave, Pasadena CA 91106 B Brooklyn NY 3/25/1927 s Arthur Roland Cummings & Kathryn Louise. BS USNA 1949; MDiv CDSP 1961. D 9/7/1961 P 3/1/1962 Bp Francis E I Bloy. c 4. Dio Los Angeles Los Angeles CA 1989-1999; Epis Hm For The Aged Camp Hill PA 1972-1999; The Epis Hm Communities Pasadena CA 1972-1999; Assoc Ch Of Our Sav Par San Gabr CA 1964-1965; Asst S Fran' Par Palos Verdes Estates CA 1961-1964. *What Ever Happened to Levi*, (Self Pub), 2002. gwcummings1@att.net

CUMMINGS, Patricia Lynn Higgins (Cal) 110 Wood Rd Apt C-104, Los Gatos CA 95030 B Palo Alto CA 5/7/1935 d Howard Earle Higgins & Dorothy Lynn. BA California St U 1957; MDiv CDSP 1980. D 9/15/1980 P 1/6/1982 Bp William Edwin Swing. c 3. S Aug's Ch Oakland CA 1999-2004; Int S Aid's Ch San Francisco CA 1984-1985; Asst H Cross Epis Ch Castro Vlly CA 1982-1984; Assoc S Paul's Ch Oakland CA 1980-1982. Hesed Comm Oakland 1990; OHC 1980. revplc@aol.com

CUMMINGS, Robert Charles (RI) 111 Black Pond Rd, Charlestown RI 02813 B Flushing NY 2/14/1948 s Jack Stanion Cummings & Marjorie. U of Connecticut; MDiv VTS 1973. D 6/9/1973 P 12/22/1973 Bp Joseph Warren Hutchens. m Sonita Weber c 2. Vic S Eliz's Ch Hope Vlly RI 1994-2008; Dir S Paul's Ch No Kingstown RI 1982-1990; Dir Yth Mnstrs S Mk's Ch Mystic CT 1980-1982; R S Jas' Ch New Haven CT 1976-1979; Vic S Paul's Ch Windham CT 1973-1976; Asst R S Paul's Epis Ch Willimantic CT 1973-1975. Auth, *Collared*, Morris Pub, 2002.

CUMMINGS, Robert Joseph (CFla) Prescott M-249, Deerfield Beach FL 33442 **Died 9/20/2010** B Providence RI 4/27/1924 s William Joseph Cummings & Mary Joseph. BA U of Rhode Island 1960; MDiv Ya Berk 1963; MPA/DPA Nova U 1978. D 6/26/1963 P 6/1/1964 Bp William Henry Marmion. c 2. rjc33442@peoplepc.com

CUMMINGS, Ruth Lindberg (At) 1501 Dinglewood Dr, Columbus GA 31906 **Assoc S Anne's Epis Ch Atlanta GA 2009-** B Pittsburgh PA 11/27/1958 d William Edward Lindberg & Lucille Ruth. BS Indiana U 1980; TESM 1984; MDiv Candler TS Emory U 1994. D 6/4/1994 P 12/1/1994 Bp Frank Kellogg Allan. m 5/29/1988 David Cummings c 3. Chld's Chr Ed Dir S Thos Epis Ch Columbus GA 2008-2009; Assoc Trin Epis Ch Columbus GA 1999-2003. rcummings@saintannes.com

CUMMINGS, Sally Ann (Minn) 520 N Pokegama Ave, Grand Rapids MN 55744 B Minneapolis MN 7/7/1957 d John Mangold & Ruth. AS No Hennepin Cmnty Coll 1978. D 6/21/2009 Bp James Louis Jelinek. m 5/21/1988 Gary Cummings c 2. sagecumm@msn.com

CUMMINGS, Sudduth Rea (NC) 3990 Meandering Ln., Tallahassee FL 32308 B Kansas City MO 10/8/1946 s Robert John Cummings & Pamelia Nell. BA Phillips U 1968; MDiv GTS 1971; DMin SMU 1979. D 6/29/1971 P 12/21/1971 Bp Chilton Powell. m 6/6/1969 Charlotte Chase. Int S Jn's Epis Ch Charlotte NC 2008-2009; Int S Jn's Ch New Haven CT 2006-2009; Int S Paul's By-The-Sea Epis Ch Jacksonville Bch FL 2002-2006; Int S Lk's Ch Ft Myers FL 2001-2002; Prof TESM Ambridge PA 1998-2001; R S Tim's Ch Catonsville MD 1991-1998; R S Mk's Epis Ch San Antonio TX 1980-1991; Asst Ch Of The Incarn Dallas TX 1977-1980; R S Jn's Ch Durant OK 1974-1976; Int Gr Ch Muskogee OK 1971-1972. Auth, "Bible Stds," *Journey in the Word*, BRF. Paul Harris Fell Rotary Club Intl 1986. scummings206@comcast.net

CUMMINS, Thomas Woodrow (Ore) 11100 Sw Riverwood Rd, Portland OR 97219 B New York NY 11/18/1918 s John Francis Cummins & Florence Louise. BS U of Connecticut 1943; STD CDSP 1971; DMin Jesuit TS 1984. D 6/17/1973 P 10/4/1974 Bp George Richard Millard. m 7/31/1943 Emily Mary Murray c 4. Chr Ch Par Lake Oswego OR 1998-2000; Chr Ch Par Lake Oswego OR 1991-1993; R S Fran Of Assisi Epis Wilsonville OR 1987-1991; P S Fran Of Assisi Epis Wilsonville OR 1979-1980; Assoc Chr Ch Par Lake Oswego OR 1975-1977; S Andr's Ch Saratoga CA 1974-1976. Collegiality in Ch Ldrshp Jesuit TS 1976. cummins11100@comcast.net

CUNDIFF, Edward N (CFla) 181 Mallard Pond Cir, Alto GA 30510 **D Ch of the Resurr Sautee Nacoochee GA 2009-** B Paintsville KY 9/2/1951 s Eddie M Cundiff & Martha. AA Belhaven Coll 2001; Inst for Chr Stds Florida 2003.

D 12/18/2004 Bp John Wadsworth Howe. m 9/5/1969 Paula R Hollingsworth c 2. ENCCCDI@WINDSTREAM.NET

CUNIFF, Wanda Wood (Tex) Christ Episcopal Church, 1320 Mound St., Nacogdoches TX 75961 **Com for the Diac Dio Texas Houston TX 2008-; D Chr Ch Nacogdoches TX 2007-** B Galveston TX 6/4/1949 d Robert Alexander Wood & Dorothy Linthwaite. BA Steph F. Austin St. U 1970; MLS U of Texas at Austin 1974; Cert Iona Sch of Mnstry 2007. D 2/9/2007 Bp Don Adger Wimberly. m 1/31/1970 Troy Cuniff c 2. The OSL 1998. wcuniff@gmail.com

CUNNINGHAM, Arthur Leland (Mil) 1320 Mill Rd, Delafield WI 53018 B Kingfisher OK 1/12/1941 s James Owen Cunningham & Pauline. BA Coll of Emporia 1963; MDiv SWTS 1968. D 6/1/1968 Bp Edward Clark Turner P 5/16/1969 Bp C Kilmer Myers. m 8/24/1968 Mary Taylor c 1. Ecum Com Dio Milwaukee Milwaukee WI 1996-2000; Prov Syn Dio Milwaukee Milwaukee WI 1995-1998; R Zion Epis Ch Oconomowoc WI 1989-2000; Dn, Nash Deanry Dio Milwaukee Milwaukee WI 1989-1993; R S Matt's Ch Enid OK 1981-1989; Dioc Coun Dio Oklahoma Oklahoma City OK 1981-1983; Epis Dio San Joaquin Modesto CA 1978-1980; Vic S Dunstans Epis Ch Modesto CA 1978-1980; R S Jas' Ch Monterey CA 1971-1978; Cur All SS Ch Carmel CA 1968-1971. howso@wi.rr.com

CUNNINGHAM JR, Carleton Sewell (ETenn) 675 Willowcrest Place, Kingsport TN 37660 B Toledo OH 1/13/1933 s Carleton Sewell Cunningham & Ethel Hales. BA U So 1957; MDiv VTS 1971. D 6/27/1971 Bp William Evan Sanders P 3/25/1972 Bp John Vander Horst. m 3/25/1961 Nelia Daggett c 2. Ch Of The H Cross Valle Crucis NC 2000-2002; R St Jas Epis Ch at Knoxville Knoxville TN 1983-1995; S Chris's Ch Kingsport TN 1978-1983; The Epis Ch Of The Mssh Pulaski TN 1977-1978; P The Epis Ch Of The Mssh Pulaski TN 1972-1976; D & Asst P S Lk's Ch Cleveland TN 1971-1972. neliacarl@skybest.com

CUNNINGHAM, Chris (SVa) 400 High St, Farmville VA 23901 **Dn, Convoc VIII Dio Sthrn Virginia Norfolk VA 2010-; Mem, COM Dio Sthrn Virginia Norfolk VA 2010-; Mem, Prog, Bdgt and Revs Cte Dio Sthrn Virginia Norfolk VA 2010-; R Johns Memi Epis Ch Farmville VA 2008-** B Frankfurt DE 5/3/1961 s Richard Joseph Cunningham & Elisabeth Aimee. BA GW 1983; MDiv Wesley TS 2005. D 6/18/2005 P 12/18/2005 Bp Peter James Lee. m 6/29/1985 Jeunee Jerman c 3. Vic Ch Of The Gd Shpd Bluemont VA 2007-2008; Asst S Ptr's Epis Ch Purcellville VA 2005-2008; D Trin Ch Manassas VA 2005. ctcunningham61@gmail.com

CUNNINGHAM, James Earl (Tex) 2227 Woodland Springs Dr, Houston TX 77077 **D S Mart's Epis Ch Houston TX 2007-** B Cleveland OH 4/4/1928 s Thomas Earl Cunningham & Dorothy Luella. BS U of Texas 1957; MS SMU 1966; Iona Sch for Mnstry 2007. D 2/9/2007 Bp Don Adger Wimberly. c 3. D S Mart's Epis Chld's Cntr Houston TX 2007. jcunningham@stmartinsepiscopal.org

CUNNINGHAM, James Harry (SwVa) 14314 Climbing Rose Way #102, Centreville VA 22021 B Wheeling WV 5/17/1924 s James Elmer Cunningham & Mildred Maria. BD Geo 1946; MDiv VTS 1960. D 6/28/1960 Bp Frederick D Goodwin P 6/24/1961 Bp Samuel B Chilton. R S Lk's Ch Hot Sprg VA 1980-1991; S Anne's-Belfield Sch Charlottesville VA 1969-1970; Ch Of Our Sav Charlottesville VA 1961-1980. R Emer S Lk's Ch 1991.

CUNNINGHAM, Jeunee Jerman (SVa) 600 Talbot Hall Rd, Norfolk VA 23505 **Congrl Dvlpmt Dio Sthrn Virginia Norfolk VA 2010-; Campus Min Johns Memi Epis Ch Farmville VA 2010-; R S Anne's Ch Appomattox VA 2009-** B San Gabriel CA 1/11/1963 d Jerry Luther Jerman & Eleanor Mae. BS Geo 1985; MDiv VTS 2000. D 6/24/2000 P 2/6/2001 Bp Peter James Lee. m 6/29/1985 Chris Cunningham c 4. Founding Vic S Gabr's Epis Ch Leesburg VA 2003-2008; Asst S Jas' Epis Ch Leesburg VA 2000-2002. jeunee@earthlink.net

CUNNINGHAM, Lynn Edward (Wyo) 3403 Ordway St Nw, Washington DC 20016 **Adj S Marg's Ch Washington DC 1986-** B Ithaca NY 6/28/1944 s Lowell Clem Cunningham & Marie. BA Cor 1966; BD UTS 1969; JD Col 1972. D 2/10/1970 Bp Leland Stark P 12/12/1970 Bp George E Rath. Asst Ch Of S Steph And The Incarn Washington DC 1975-1986; Asst S Mary's Manhattanville Epis Ch New York NY 1970-1975.

CUNNINGHAM, Marcus Thomas (Kan) 309 W Elm St, Sedan KS 67361 **Ch Of The Epiph Sedan KS 2009-** B Evergreen Park IL 7/6/1963 s Marcus Cunningham & Elizabeth. Marq 1983; BS U of Wisconsin 1987; MDiv U So 2006. D 1/25/2006 P 9/11/2006 Bp Edward Stuart Little II. m 7/22/1989 Anne-Marie D Berube c 5. New Life Epis Ch Uniontown OH 2009; D S Matt's Epis Ch Brecksville OH 2006-2009. TATANKAMARCUS@YAHOO.COM

CUNNINGHAM, Margaret Taylor (Pa) 138 Rose Ln, Haverford PA 19041 B Pasadena CA 12/28/1940 d Daniel Dwight Taylor & Sarah Kellogg. Vas 1961; BA U CA 1982; MA U CA 1984; MDiv EDS 1996. D 6/18/1996 P 1/18/1997 Bp Frederick Houk Borsch. c 3. Ch Of The Redeem Bryn Mawr PA 2001-2004; Assoc R Ch Of The Redeem Bryn Mawr PA 2000; All SS Ch Pasadena CA 1996-2001. mwthc@comcast.net

CUNNINGHAM, Michael Ray (Los) St Marys Episcopal Church, 2800 Harris Grade Rd, Lompoc CA 93436 **R S Mary's Par Lompoc CA 2007-; Dio Los Angeles Los Angeles CA 1994-** B Dallas TX 7/1/1954 s Donald Ray Cunningham & Irene Carol. BA U of Texas 1976. D 5/2/2007 P 11/19/2007 Bp Joseph Jon Bruno. m 1/1/2001 Deborah Dunn c 2. rector@stmaryslompoc.org

CUNNINGHAM, Patricia S (Ct) 51 Summit Rd, Riverside CT 06878 **Int S Jn's Epis Ch Boulder CO 2011-** B Vancouver BC 7/10/1958 d Edward Starrs & Daisy. MA Emory U 2000; MS The London Sch of Econ and Political Sci 2002; MA Berkeley Bapt DS 2007. D 6/9/2007 P 12/15/2007 Bp Andrew Donnan Smith. m 5/27/1984 David Cunningham c 8. Chr Epis Ch Norwich CT 2009-2010; Chr Ch Roxbury CT 2008-2009; Cur S Paul's Ch Riverside CT 2007-2008. trish.cunningham@ymail.com

CUNNINGHAM, Philip John (WTex) 2500 N. 10th St., McAllen TX 78501 **Vic S Marg's Epis Ch San Antonio TX 2010-** B Fresno CA 5/7/1970 s Daniel Nelson Cunningham & Melinda. BA Santa Clara U 1992; MBA Van 1996; MDiv Nash 2008. D 6/25/2008 Bp David Mitchell Reed P 6/8/2009 Bp Gary Richard Lillibridge. m 6/15/1996 Amy Thompson c 2. Asst S Jn's Ch McAllen TX 2008-2010. pjcunningham4@yahoo.com

CUNNINGHAM, Steven Lee (Colo) 307 Biscayne Ct, Lafayette CO 80026 B Denver CO 7/12/1951 s Carl Cunningham & Helen Eileen. BA U CO 1975. D 6/29/1979 P 1/26/1980 Bp William Carl Frey. m 12/22/1973 Deborah Ellen Neavor. All SS Epis Ch Denver CO 2004-2005; Asstg P Ch Of The H Comf Broomfield CO 1993-2003; P Dio Colorado Denver CO 1983-1992; Asst S Aid's Epis Ch Boulder CO 1981-1983; Cur S Tim's Epis Ch Centennial CO 1980-1981; Cur The Ch Of Chr The King (Epis) Arvada CO 1979. Auth, "Cnfrmtn: Workbook". frstevec@aol.com

CUNNINGHAM, William Wallace (Ala) 4080 Rose Hill Ct, Millbrook AL 36054 B Nashville TN 7/24/1942 s William W Cunningham & Elizabeth Naomi. Diac Sch Birmingham AL; EFM; BBA Lamar U. D 10/30/2004 Bp Marc Handley Andrus. m 10/4/1964 Sharrell Baxter c 5.

CUPP, Jean Carol (EO) 1239 Nw Ingram Ave, Pendleton OR 97801 **D Ch Of The Redeem Pendleton OR 1999-** B Chicago IL 12/26/1943 D 9/26/1999 Bp Rustin Ray Kimsey. m 9/26/1964 William Franklyn Cupp c 3.

CURL, James Fair (WNC) 461 Crowfields Dr., Asheville NC 28803 **Allegany Cnty Mnstry Belmont NY 2002-** B Millen GA 10/22/1944 s William White Curl & Carolyn Margaret. BA Davidson Coll 1966; MA NWU 1968; PhD U Pgh 1974; Cert Dioc Sch For Total Common Mnstry 2002. D 12/8/2001 P 10/22/2002 Bp Jack Marston McKelvey. m 8/23/1968 Kathryn W Chatham c 2. fcurl@aldred.edu

CURNS, Mary S (EC) 4907 Briarhill Rd, New Bern NC 28562 **R S Anne's Epis Ch Jacksonville NC 2009-** B Elmira NY 9/7/1956 d Andrew Strong & Berdena. BS Mansfield U of Pennsylvania 1979; MS Elmira Coll 1985; MDiv GTS 2004. D 6/9/2004 Bp Gladstone Bailey Adams III P 1/6/2005 Bp Clifton Daniel III. c 2. Asst Chr Ch New Bern NC 2004-2009. epiphany2005@embarqmail.com

CURRAN JR, Charles Daniel (SwVa) 1011 Francisco Road, Henrico VA 23229 B Ancon Panama 10/27/1934 s Charles Daniel Curran & Virginia. A.B. Earlham Coll 1958; Amer U 1960; MDiv STUSo 1967. D 6/21/1967 Bp Henry I Louttit P 12/22/1967 Bp James Loughlin Duncan. m 9/10/1977 Anne Gordon Cooke c 6. Ch Of The Sprt Alexandria VA 1992-1993; Kingston Par Epis Ch Mathews VA 1992-1993; Assoc P S Steph's Ch Richmond VA 1991-1995; Supply P Dio Virginia Richmond VA 1980-1998; Asst S Marg's Ch Woodbridge VA 1974-1975; R S Jn's Epis Ch Homestead FL 1968-1971; Cur H Trin Epis Ch W Palm Bch FL 1967-1968. charliegang@comcast.net

CURRAN, Michael Joseph (Ak) 4024 Ridge Way, Juneau AK 99801 B Derby CT 8/10/1947 s Robert Joseph Curran & Ruth Elaine. Cert U So 1999. D 12/18/1999 P 6/18/2000 Bp Mark Lawrence Mac Donald. m 8/6/1977 Cynthia Ann Dolmas c 2. S Brendan's Epis Ch Juneau AK 2004-2005; R S Phil's Ch Wrangell AK 2000-2004. mjcurran@gci.net

CURREA, Luis Alejandro (SwFla) Po Box 9332, Tampa FL 33674 B Bogota CO 11/14/1934 s Alejandro Currea & Elisa. Cert Sem Mayor De Bogota 1960; BA Florida Intl U 1977; DIT VTS 1986. Rec from Roman Catholic 9/1/1986 as Priest Bp Calvin Onderdonk Schofield Jr. c 3. S Fran Ch Tampa FL 1992-1999; Dio SW Florida Sarasota FL 1988-1991; Iglesia Epis De Todos Los Santos Miami FL 1988; Cur All Ang Ch Miami Sprg FL 1986-1988. lcurrea@schwob.com

CURRIER, Jonathan Edwin (CPa) 301 Saint Thomas Rd, Lancaster PA 17601 **R S Thos Ch Lancaster PA 2009-** B Braintree MA 1/18/1957 s Terrence Parkman Currier & Janet Ruth. BA Harv 1979; MDiv UTS 1979. D 6/10/1989 Bp Paul Moore Jr P 12/13/1990 Bp Peter James Lee. m 7/22/1982 Ann S Wheaton c 2. R S Chris's Ch New Carrollton MD 1993-2009; Asst S Ptr's Ch Albany NY 1990-1993; Yth S Paul's Memi Charlottesville VA 1989-1990. Auth, "Sermon," *Preaching as the Art of Sacr Conversation: Sermons That Wk VI*, Morehouse Pub, 1997. Fell, winter term Coll of Preachers 2001; 1st Prize Winner, Sermon Competition Epis Evang Fndt 1996. jonathanecurrier@aol.com

CURRIN JR, Beverly Madison (CGC) 510 N 20th Ave, Pensacola FL 32501 B Greensboro NC 6/28/1931 s Beverly Madison Currin & Gertrude. BA Elon U 1953; MDiv Duke 1956; ThM UTS Richmond VA 1957; PhD UTS Richmond VA 1958. D 10/26/1958 Bp Frederick D Goodwin P 11/1/1959 Bp Robert Fisher Gibson Jr. m 8/4/1962 Eleanor McCall Lachicotte c 3. R Chr Ch Par Pensacola FL 1966-2002; R Cathd Of S Lk And S Paul Charleston SC 1961-1963; Asst Gr & H Trin Epis Ch Richmond VA 1958-1961. Auth, *The Chr Ch Bk*, 2002; Auth, *Search for the Lost Rectors*, 1999; Auth, *The Vision Glorious*, 1996; Auth, *Decision in Crisis*, 1995; Auth, *The Faith That Never Disappoints*, Abingdon, 1983; Auth, *From One Generation to Another*, 1979; Auth, *If Man is to Live*, Abingdon, 1969. DECONS 1977-1997. Hon Cn The Cathd Ch of St. Lk and St. Paul Charleston S.C. 2003; Fell Coll of Preachers Washington DC 1980. mattcurrin31@aol.com

CURRY, Dorothy Reed (Cal) 6 Manning Place, Queens Road, Richmond Great Britain (UK) **Cn for Pstr Care Cathd Ch Of S Paul San Diego CA 2006-** B Seattle WA 7/19/1934 d Elmer Edwin Reed & Elise Dorothy Menkus. BA U of Washington 1956; MDiv CDSP 1982. D 11/22/1981 P 12/11/1982 Bp William Edwin Swing. c 2. The Epis Ch Of S Andr Encinitas CA 1999; R Ch Of The H Trin Richmond CA 1986-1996; Chr Ch Portola Vlly CA 1984-1986; S Jas Ch Fremont CA 1983-1984; S Edm's Epis Ch Pacifica CA 1982-1983. revdrcb@cox.net

CURRY, Gene Edward (Mich) 2735 Manchester Rd, Ann Arbor MI 48104 B Colville WA 8/12/1936 s Elliot Curry & Jessie Claire. BS California St Polytechnic U 1958; MDiv Bex 1961. D 6/25/1961 Bp James Albert Pike P 1/25/1962 Bp George Henry Quarterman. m 10/14/2004 Ruth Evelyn Hartzler c 2. S Mich And All Ang Epis Ch Lincoln Pk MI 2002-2007; S Matt's Epis Ch Rockwood MI 1990-1999; S Jn's Ch Westland MI 1988; P-in-c S Clem's Epis Ch Inkster MI 1987-1988; P-in-c S Columba Ch Detroit MI 1986-1987; P-in-c S Hilda's Epis Ch River Rouge MI 1975-1979; Assoc S Mart Ch Detroit MI 1966-1975; Cur S Nich' Epis Ch Midland TX 1961-1964. gec1936@comcast.net

CURRY, Glenda Sharp (Ala) 2670 Southgate Dr, Birmingham AL 35243 **R All SS Epis Ch Birmingham AL 2004-** B Fort Stockton TX 6/20/1953 d Dalton Glenn Sharp & Mac Van. MDiv STUSo 2002. D 5/29/2002 P 12/3/2002 Bp Henry Nutt Parsley Jr. m 6/3/1995 William A Curry. R Epis Ch Of The Epiph Leeds AL 2002-2004.

✠ **CURRY, Rt Rev James Elliot** (Ct) 14 Linwold Dr, West Hartford CT 06107 **Cn Ordnry Dio Connecticut Hartford CT 1998-** B Oak Park IL 7/15/1948 s Warren Blount Curry & Clemence Ann. BA Amh 1970; Med U of Massachusetts 1979; MDiv Ya Berk 1985. D 6/8/1985 Bp Arthur Edward Walmsley P 12/10/1985 Bp Clarence Nicholas Coleridge Con 10/14/2000 for Ct. m 1/17/1970 Kathleen McIntosh c 3. R Trin Ch Portland CT 1988-1998; Asst Trin Ch Torrington CT 1985-1988. DD Berk 2006. jamesecurry1@att.net

✠ CURRY, Rt Rev Michael Bruce (NC) 200 W Morgan St Ste 300, Raleigh NC 27601 **Bp of NC Dio No Carolina Raleigh NC 2000-** B Chicago IL 3/13/1953 s Kenneth Stewart Lee Curry & Dorothy Ada. BA Hob 1975; MDiv Yale DS 1978; Ya Berk 2001; U So 2001. D 6/3/1978 Bp Harold B Robinson P 12/1/1978 Bp John Melville Burgess Con 6/17/2000 for NC. m 6/20/1981 Sharon Elizabeth Clement c 1. R S Jas' Epis Ch Baltimore MD 1988-2000; R S Simon Of Cyrene Epis Ch Cincinnati OH 1982-1988; R S Steph's Epis Ch Winston Salem NC 1978-1982. Auth, *Sermons That Wk*. Soc Trsfg. michaelsharonc@aol.com

CURRY, Norval Henry (Minn) 25252 162nd St, Paynesville MN 56362 B Chicopee MA 11/13/1927 s Archie Curry & Elizabeth. BBA W New Engl 1954; S Chad 1958. Trans from Anglican Church of Canada 7/28/1966 Bp Hamilton Hyde Kellogg. c 2. S Matt's Ch Glendive MT 1985-1989; R Chr Ch Epis Beatrice NE 1982-1984; R S Steph's Epis Ch Paynesville MN 1981-1982; R S Lk's Ch Willmar MN 1975-1981; R Bp Whipple Mssn Morton MN 1972-1975; R S Jn Hutchinson MN 1972-1975; R Ch Of The Gd Samar Sauk Cntr MN 1969-1972; R S Steph's Epis Ch Paynesville MN 1969-1972.

CURT, George (SwFla) 1204 Westlake Blvd, Naples FL 34103 **Assoc S Mary's Epis Ch Bonita Sprg FL 2003-** B Detroit MI 5/12/1927 s Karl Curt & Margaret. LTh STUSo 1975; MDiv STUSo 1987. D 5/18/1975 P 11/1/1975 Bp Addison Hosea. m 11/18/1975 Vivi Sahagian. R S Dav's Epis Ch Englewood FL 1983-1990; Vic S Chad's Ch Tampa FL 1978-1983; Vic S Bede's Ch St Petersburg FL 1977-1978; All SS Ch Cold Sprg KY 1975-1977. Ord Of S Lk. vivicurt@juno.com

CURTIN, Anne Fahy (Alb) PO Box 9, Adirondack NY 12808 B Southampton NY 4/26/1947 d James Thomas Fahy & Anna Rita. BS Le Moyne Coll 1968; MA Colg 1970; JD Albany Law Sch Un U 1982; MT St. Bern's Inst Rochester NY 2002. D 6/9/2001 P 12/8/2001 Bp Daniel William Herzog. m 11/28/1970 Daniel John Curtin c 2. Vic Ch Of The H Cross Troy NY 2001-2007. Captial Dist Wmn Bar Assn 1983; Healing a Wmn's Soul, Inc. 2007; Wmn Bar Assn of New York St 1983. motheranne@berk.com

CURTIN, Ernest A (Pa) St Luke's Episcopal Church, 100 E Washington Ave, Newtown PA 18940 **Dioc Coun Dio Pennsylvania Philadelphia PA 2010-2013; R S Lk's Ch In The Cnty Of Buck Newtown PA 2007-** B Trenton NJ 3/9/1949 s Ernest Albert Curtin & Doris Stout. BA Wilyan and Mary 1971; MTS VTS 1973; MAT Coll of NJ 1975. D 9/2/2006 Bp Keith Lynn Ackerman P 12/16/2006 Bp Charles Ellsworth Bennison Jr. SocMary 1975-2021. ecurtin@msn.com

CURTIS, Charles Edward (EMich) 3260 E Midland Rd, Bay City MI 48706 **Dio Estrn Michigan Saginaw MI 2000-** B Cooperstown NY 2/2/1943 s Edward Romine Curtis & Lucy May. BA MI SU 1964; STB EDS 1967. D 6/29/1967 Bp Richard S M Emrich P 3/26/1968 Bp Archie H Crowley. m 1/17/1981 Jayne N Newcomb c 1. R S Albans Epis Ch Bay City MI 1986-2001; R All SS Ch Nevada MO 1980-1986; Asst S Jn's Ch Royal Oak MI 1977-1980; Vic Chr The King Epis Ch Taylor MI 1969-1977; Asst S Thos Ch Trenton MI 1967-1969. cecpr68@yahoo.com

CURTIS, Edward Wells (Chi) 637 S Dearborn St Ste 1, Chicago IL 60605 **R Gr Ch Chicago IL 1991-** B Cambridgeshire UK 10/1/1953 s Douglas Craig Curtis & Beryl Henley. BA W&L 1975; EdM Bos 1979; MDiv GTS 1984; DMin SWTS 2001. D 6/2/1984 Bp C(laude) Charles Vache P 12/7/1984 Bp Charles Thomas Gaskell. Cn Trin Cathd Cleveland OH 1987-1991; S Paul's Ch Milwaukee WI 1984-1987. EPF 1988. grizchic@aol.com

CURTIS, Frederick L (Alb) 262 Main St N, Southbury CT 06488 B Norwalk,CT 4/5/1947 s Frederick W Curtis & Nancy Cb. MDiv EDS 1974. D 6/8/1974 P 2/22/1975 Bp Joseph Warren Hutchens. m 7/19/1969 Phyllis R Riggs. R Ch Of The Epiph Southbury CT 1977-2004; Cur S Andr's Ch Meriden CT 1974-1977. SSC. phylcurt25@aol.com

CURTIS, James Dabney (At) 1100 Hampton Way NE, Atlanta GA 30324 B Memphis TN 12/16/1938 s Dana Carlton Curtis & Virginia. BA Rhodes Coll 1960; BD VTS 1964; CPE Georgia Mntl Hlth Inst Atlanta GA 1971; ThD (scl) Emory U 1975; Fllshp Oxf 1976. D 6/22/1964 Bp John Vander Horst P 5/29/1965 Bp William Evan Sanders. c 2. Int S Jn's Coll Pk GA 2007-2010; Artist in Res EDS Cambridge MA 2004-2005; Int S Bede's Ch Atlanta GA 2002-2004; Int S Barth's Epis Ch Atlanta GA 2001-2002; All SS Epis Ch Atlanta GA 1999-2001; Dio Atlanta Atlanta GA 1998-1999; Int S Jas Epis Ch Marietta GA 1996-1998; Int S Edw's Epis Ch Lawrenceville GA 1995-1996; Int S Jos's Epis Ch McDonough GA 1995; R Gr Ch Chattanooga TN 1979-1994; Vic Ch Of The Gd Samar Knoxville TN 1965-1969; D Ch Of The Ascen Knoxville TN 1964-1965. ECVA 2003. Procter Fllshp Epis Div. Sch 2004; Braitmyer Fllshp Natl. Assn Indep Schools 1978. jcurtis3@bellsouth.net

CURTIS, Kenton James (NY) 207 W 80th St Apt 3a, New York NY 10024 **All SS Ch New York NY 1997-** B Loveland CO 10/3/1960 s Malcolm James Curtis & Geraldine Susan. BA U of Nthrn Colorado 1985; MS Colorado St U 1989; Dio Colo Diac Prog CO 1996. D 11/2/1996 Bp William Jerry Winterrowd. S Lk's Ch Denver CO 1997-2003. NAAD. kjcco@aol.com

CURTIS, Lynne Marsh Piret (Alb) 912 Route 146, Clifton Park NY 12065 B New York City NY 6/27/1945 d George Alfred Piret & Pauline Marsh. BA Wm Smith 1967; MSW Sch fo Soc Welf 1982. D 11/30/1991 Bp David Standish Ball. m 6/24/1967 Clark Sanford Curtis c 4. lynneclark@spa.net

CURTIS, Mary Page (NC) 212 Edinboro Dr, Southern Pines NC 28387 B Montgomery AL 10/30/1942 d William Tyler Page & Mary Elizabeth-Hearn. BS Geo Mason U 1987; MDiv VTS 1991. D 6/15/1991 P 2/2/1992 Bp Peter James Lee. m 2/8/1999 Frank Curtis c 2. Assoc R S Thos Epis Ch Sanford NC 2000-2008; Asst R Emm Par Epis Ch And Day Sch Sthrn Pines NC 1993-1999; Assoc R S Andr's Epis Ch Ft Pierce FL 1991-1993. mfcurtis136@gmail.com

CURTIS, Patricia Harris (WNC) St John's Episcopal Church, PO Box 175, Sylva NC 28779 **S Jn's Ch Sylva NC 2007-** B Jacksonville FL 11/25/1951 d John Robert Harris & Mary Patricia. BA U of Cntrl Florida 1982; JD Florida St U Coll Of Law Tallahassee FL 1986; MA U NC 1996; MDiv The GTS 2007. D 6/9/2007 Bp Granville Porter Taylor. pcurtis@gts.edu

CURTIS, Sandra King (Roch) 10 Shether St # 272, Hammondsport NY 14840 **S Jas Ch Hammondsport NY 1995-** B Corning NY 10/18/1943 d Leland Edson King & Honor Grace. BS SUNY 1965; Med Nazareth Coll 1979; MDiv St. Bern's Inst Rochester NY 1991. D 8/10/1991 P 2/23/1992 Bp William George Burrill. m 6/15/1963 Crocker Curtis c 2. Ch of the Redeem Addison NY 1991-2005. Auth, "The Cursive Approach To Readiness & Reading," 1981. motherc@citilink.net

CURTIS JR, W(illiam) Shepley (Nev) 1654 County Rd, Minden NV 89423 B Abilene TX 4/10/1943 s William Shepley Curtis & Frances Lois. BA Dart 1965; U CO 1966; MDIV CDSP 1969; Advncd CPE 1980. D 6/24/1969 P 10/28/1970 Bp Edwin B Thayer. m 4/4/1982 Joy Marcia Peterson c 4. Ch Of Coventry Cross Minden NV 2007-2008; All SS Of The Sierras So Lake Tahoe CA 1984-1988; Trin Ch Trinidad CO 1983-1984; Cur S Lk's Ch Billings MT 1978-1979; Asst Ch Of S Phil And S Jas Denver CO 1975-1977; S Mich's Ch Telluride CO 1971-1975; Vic S Paul's Ch Montrose CO 1971-1975; S Jn's Epis Ch Ouray CO 1971-1974; Cur Ch Of Our Sav Colorado Sprg CO 1969-1970. shepandjoy@gmail.com

CURTIS, Yvonne Marie (WNY) PO Box 14, Dunkirk NY 14048 B Gowanda NY 3/29/1942 d Lawrence Small & Bernice. BS U of Nevada 1964; MS U of

Nevada 1966; PhD U CA 1972. D 4/14/2009 P 11/8/2009 Bp J Michael Garrison. c 2. ycurtis@verizon.net

CURTISS, Geoffrey (Nwk) 1238 Park Ave, Hoboken NJ 07030 **All SS Epis Par Hoboken NJ 1984-** B Paterson NJ 7/18/1948 s Edgar O Curtiss & Ann. BA Ge 1970; MDiv Gettysburg Luth TS 1975. D 6/14/1975 P 12/14/1975 Bp George E Rath. m 2/6/1971 Linda W Wiggins c 2. Hoboken Urban Mssn And Dioc Yth Hoboken NJ 1980-1983; Asst Trin And S Phil's Cathd Newark NJ 1975-1979. lindacurtiss@gmail.com

CUSHING, Nan Chenault Marshall (NC) 69 Crystal Oaks Ct, Durham NC 27707 **D Dio No Carolina Raleigh NC 2002-; Pstr Response Team Dio No Carolina Raleigh NC 2002-; D Dio No Carolina Raleigh NC 1995-** B New York NY 5/27/1935 d Gerard Farrar Marshall & Nan Burgess. BFA Rhode Island Sch of Design 1957; Cert Appalachian Mnstry Educ Resource Cntr 1986; MA TESM 1989. D 4/29/1995 Bp Huntington Williams Jr. c 2. D S Andr's Ch Haw River NC 2002-2009; Archd Dio No Carolina Raleigh NC 2001-2006; Archd Dio No Carolina Raleigh NC 2001-2006; D S Tit Epis Ch Durham NC 1995-1998. NAAD 1994. nancmc@verizon.net

CUSHINOTTO, Susan Elizabeth (NJ) 9425 3rd Ave, Stone Harbor NJ 08247 **D S Mary's Epis Ch Stone Harbor NJ 2009-** B Camden NJ 6/12/1956 d Frank Andrew Applegate & Margaret Brittin. D 5/16/2009 Bp Sylvestre Donato Romero. m 1/10/1976 Richard Cushinotto c 3. susan.cushinotto@gmail.com

CUSHMAN, Mary (NY) PO Box 211, Chebeague Island ME 04017 B New York NY 9/30/1942 d John Latham Toohey & Virginia. BS U of Sthrn Maine 1976; MDiv Ya Berk 1988. D 6/4/1988 P 5/1/1989 Bp Edward Cole Chalfant. m 6/1/1985 Thomas Spaulding Cushman. Assoc S Jas Ch New York NY 1993-1997; Assoc To R Chr Ch Alexandria VA 1988-1993.

CUSHMAN, Thomas Spaulding (NY) 6 Huddum Cir, Chebeague Island ME 04017 B Meriden CT 10/27/1942 s Robert Earl Cushman & Barbara. BA Randolph-Macon Coll 1967; Med U of Maine 1976; MDiv Ya Berk 1988. D 6/4/1988 P 5/1/1989 Bp Edward Cole Chalfant. m 6/1/1985 Mary Toohey. Assoc S Jas Ch New York NY 1993-1997; Assoc To R Chr Ch Alexandria VA 1988-1993.

CUSIC, Georgeanne Hill (FdL) 1510 N Broadway Ave, Marshfield WI 54449 **D S Alb's Epis Ch Marshfield WI 2004-** B Dayton OH 3/25/1946 Dio Fond Du Lac; BA U of Wisconsin 1969; Sch Of Chr Stds 2003. D 6/19/2004 Bp Russell Edward Jacobus. m 9/3/1966 Marshall Edward Cusic c 3. ghcusic@msn.com

CUSICK, Lorraine A (LI) 634 N Fulton Ave, Lindenhurst NY 11757 **Cnvnr of Deacons Dio Long Island Garden City NY 2007-** B Montreal Canada 8/16/1948 d Daniel Cusick & Irene C. BA Molloy Coll 1971; MA St. Johns U 1973; JD Hofstra U 1980; Cert Geo Mercer Jr. Memi TS 2006. D 10/23/2006 Bp Orris George Walker Jr. D S Anselm's Ch Shoreham NY 2006-2008. Assn for Epis Deacons 2006. lcusick@optonline.net

CUSTER, Margaret (Peg) Gardiner (NH) 356 Deer Hill Road, Chocorua NH 03817 B Washington DC 7/29/1930 d Donald Alfred Gardiner & Margaret May. MRE CUA 1979; MDiv S Mary's TS & U 1983; CAS VTS 1986. D 6/14/1986 Bp John Thomas Walker P 6/14/1987 Bp Ronald Hayward Haines. m 5/26/1951 Roland Lee Custer c 5. Chr Ch Portsmouth NH 2010-2011; P-in-c Trin Epis Ch Tilton NH 2005-2007; Vic Chr Ch Portsmouth NH 2003-2005; R S Andr's-In-The-Vlly Tamworth NH 1992-2002; Int S Paul's Epis Ch Piney Waldorf MD 1991-1992; Int S Jn's Ch Oakland MD 1990-1991; Int S Edw's Epis Ch Lancaster PA 1989-1990; Int Epis Ch Of Our Sav Midlothian VA 1988-1989; Asst Gr Epis Ch Silver Sprg MD 1986-1988. Co-Auth/Ed, "Act Now"; Auth, "Young At Heart; Ideas & Illustrations". deerhill356@roadrunner.com

CUSTER, Raymond Dale (SVa) 14404 Roberts Mill Court, Midlothian VA 23113 **R S Jn's Ch Chester VA 2004-** B South Boston VA 6/22/1970 s Raymond Custer & Emily. BS Virginia Tech 1994; MS Virginia Tech 1996; MDiv VTS 2000. D 5/27/2000 Bp Donald Purple Hart P 12/7/2000 Bp David Conner Bane Jr. m 11/15/2009 Doris D DeLauder c 1. S Mart's Epis Ch Williamsburg VA 2002-2004; Ch Of The Redeem Midlothian VA 2000-2002. rdalecuster@gmail.com

CUTAIAR, Michael Louis (NMich) 932 Carney Blvd, Marinette WI 54143 B Detroit MI 11/17/1957 s Donald Cutaiar & Elaine. D 6/4/2006 Bp James Arthur Kelsey. m 2/19/2007 Luann Hay. mcutaiar@new.rr.com

CUTIE, Alberto Ricardo (SeFla) 11173 Griffing Blvd, Miami FL 33161 B San Juan PR 4/29/1969 s Alberto Cutie & Yolanda B. BA S Johns Vianney Sem 1991; MA St Vinc DePaul Reg Sem 1994; MDiv St Vinc DePaul Reg Sem 1995; DMin The U So (Sewanee) 2014. Rec from Roman Catholic 5/29/2010 Bp Leopold Frade. m 6/26/2010 Ruhama Buni Cutie c 2. P-in-c Ch Of The Resurr Biscayne Pk FL 2010; LP Ch Of The Resurr Biscayne Pk FL 2009-2010. fatherac@gmail.com

CUTLER, Donald Robert (NY) 38 Chestnut St, Salem MA 01970 B Sharon PA 11/20/1931 s John Bingham Cutler & Elmo Wilhelmina. BA Penn 1953; ThM VTS 1957; PhD Harv 1965. D 6/7/1957 P 12/14/1957 Bp John T Heistand. m 6/20/1958 Virginia Cutler c 3. R The Ch Of S Jos Of Arimathea White Plains NY 1971-1991; Asst S Andr's Ch St Coll PA 1957-1959. Fell Harv 1959; Phi Beta Kappa. dbookmark@covad.net

CUTLER, E Clifford (Pa) 18 E Chestnut Hill Ave, Philadelphia PA 19118 **R S Paul's Ch Philadelphia PA 2006-** B Philadelphia PA 4/10/1949 s Edward C Cutler & Catherine C. BS Trin 1971; MDiv EDS 1976. D 6/12/1976 P 5/1/1977 Bp Lyman Cunningham Ogilby. m 12/22/1973 Amy Johnston c 2. R S Steph's Ch Cohasset MA 1985-2006; St Lukes Ch Philadelphia PA 1978-1985; Cur Nevil Memi Ch Of S Geo Ardmore PA 1976-1978. Fllshp S Alb & Sergius, Philadelphia Cler. ccutler@stpaulschestnuthill.org

CUTLER, Howard Taylor (HB) 614 Appeldoorn Cir, Asheville NC 28803 B Princess Ann County VA 11/9/1935 s Julian A Cutler & Idell. BS E Carolina U 1959; BD VTS 1962. D 6/28/1962 P 1/1/1963 Bp Thomas H Wright. m 8/2/1991 Joy Cutler c 5. R S Andr's Mssn Charleston SC 1967-1973. jycutler@gmail.com

CUTLER, Paul Colman (NMich) Hc 1 Box 646, Wetmore MI 49895 B Buffalo NY 6/26/1928 s Paul Colman Cutler & Frances Boxhorn. BS Baldwin-Wallace Coll 1952; MS Case Wstrn Reserve U 1954. D 9/8/1996 Bp Thomas Kreider Ray. m 2/22/1952 Shirley Jane Hanson.

CUTOLO, Mark Anthony (WNY) No address on file. B Buffalo NY 12/5/1983 s Anthony Cutolo & Laudi. BA U at Buffalo 2005; MDiv Yale DS 2008. D 12/22/2007 P 6/21/2009 Bp J Michael Garrison. MorningRain1205@aol.com

CUTTER IV, Irving Taylor (Okla) 4200 S Atlanta Pl, Tulsa OK 74105 **R S Jn's Epis Ch Tulsa OK 2006-** B Austin TX 2/7/1966 s Irving Taylor Cutter & Hilde Dauner. BA Rice U 1987; MDiv VTS 1998. D 6/20/1998 Bp Claude Edward Payne P 6/26/1999 Bp Leopoldo Jesus Alard. m 10/12/2002 Andrea Elizabeth Treiber c 1. R S Jas Epis Ch Houston TX 2001-2006; S Mk's Ch Beaumont TX 1998-2001. Dudley Speech Prize VTS Alexandria VA 1998. irv.cutter@gmail.com

CYR, Gary Alan (Me) 3 J St, Bangor ME 04401 B Caribou ME 8/13/1962 s Alphy J Cyr & Viola G. BA St. Jos's Coll 2008; MDiv Bangor Theol 2010. D 6/19/2010 Bp Stephen Taylor Lane. gcyr0001@roadrunner.com

CYR, Mark Bernard (NY) 25 Addy Road, P.O. Box 191, Bethany Beach DE 19930 **S Martha's Epis Ch Bethany Bch DE 2010-** B Van Buren ME 8/2/1956 s Bernard Roger Cyr & Aline. Concordia U 1977; BA U of Utah 1984; MDiv EDS 1988; DMin SWTS 2005. D 9/9/1989 P 6/10/1990 Bp Otis Charles. m 8/21/1993 Margie Kirby c 3. P-in-c Gr Epis Ch - Wicomico Par Easton MD 2009-2010; Dioc Stff Dio New York New York City NY 2000-2009; R Chr Ch Warwick NY 1993-2000; R S Jn's Epis Ch Holbrook MA 1991-1993; Asst to R Par Of The Epiph Winchester MA 1989-1991. mark@25addyroad.org

CZARNETZKY, Sylvia Yale (Miss) 148 French Br, Madison MS 39110 **S Jn's Ch Aberdeen MS 2009-** B Greenville MS 8/25/1958 d James Robertshaw & Sylvia Yale. BA U So 1980; JD Tul 1984; MA U of Mississippi 1993; MDiv SWTS 1998. D 8/29/1998 P 3/24/1999 Bp Alfred Clark Marble Jr. m 9/25/1999 John M Czarnetzky. The Chap Of The Cross Madison MS 2006-2009; D Ch Of The Adv Sumner MS 1998-2006. sylviac@ms.metrocast.net

CZOLGOSZ, Joseph Tamborini (Chi) 707 S Chester Ave, Park Ridge IL 60068 B Saginaw MI 10/9/1950 s Joseph Czolgosz & Edna. BA U of St. Thos 1972; MA CUA 1975; MDiv Anderson U TS 1992; DMin SWTS 2008. Rec from Roman Catholic 9/24/2003 as Priest Bp William Dailey Persell. m 9/4/1993 Susan T Czolgosz c 1. S Mary's Ch Pk Ridge IL. "Healing Stories, Past, Present and Future: A Framework for Par Nrsng," *Proceedings of the Eighth Annual Westberg Symposium*, Natl Par Nurse Resource Cntr, 1994. BroSA 2003. Summit Ldrshp Advoc Hlth Care 2005. czolgosz@sbcglobal.net

D

DAGE JR, Raymond Ellison (SwFla) 5326 Charles St, New Port Richey FL 34652 B Kearney NE 11/10/1942 s Raymond Ellison Dage & Ruth Mary. U of Nebraska 1961; BA U of Nebraska 1965; MA U Of Florida 1972; MA Nash 1976. D 5/1/1976 Bp Stanley Hamilton Atkins P 11/1/1976 Bp Emerson Paul Haynes. m 7/15/1967 Jacqueline Heinecken. R S Steph's Ch New Port Richey FL 1997-2009; R S Jn's Epis Ch Brooksville FL 1989-1997; S Edm's Epis Ch Arcadia FL 1984-1989; R S Alb's Epis Ch Ft Wayne IN 1981-1982; Cur S Lk's Ch Ft Myers FL 1976-1981. Auth, "Nashotah Revs". rdage42@hotmail.com

DAGG, Margaret Kathleen (Kan) 1427 SW Macvicar Ave, Topeka KS 66604 **Int S Mart-In-The-Fields Edwardsville KS 2008-** B Topeka KS 7/5/1949 d Richard M McKinney & Margaret Alice. BA Washburn U 1975; MA U of Kansas 1986; MDiv VTS 2002. D 4/6/2002 P 10/5/2002 Bp William Edward Smalley. m 9/26/1992 Adam Leroy Dagg c 2. P-in-c S Phil's Epis Ch Topeka KS 2004-2007; Vic S Aid's Ch Olathe KS 2002-2004. kay.dagg@sbcglobal.net

DAGGETT, Paul Edward (SO) 115 North 6th Street, Hamilton OH 45011 **Trin Ch Hamilton OH 2000-** B Providence RI 2/28/1943 s Edward Martin Daggett & Myra Estell. BA Bos 1965; MDiv Epis TS of The SW 1970. D 6/19/1970 Bp Frederick P Goddard P 6/1/1971 Bp J Milton Richardson. m 12/

21/1969 Mary J Douglas c 2. Stndg Cmsn Dio Delaware Wilmington DE 1993-1999; R S Alb's Wilmington DE 1991-2000; R S Paul's Ch Mt Vernon OH 1984-1991; Plnng Com Dio Ohio Cleveland OH 1984-1988; Chair - Dept. of Mssn & Mnstry Dio W Virginia Charleston WV 1982-1983; R Chr Ch Point Pleasant WV 1977-1983; Yth Dir Dio W Virginia Charleston WV 1976-1978; R S Thos' Epis Ch Weirton WV 1973-1977; Dio Texas Houston TX 1970-1973; S Jn's Epis Ch Carthage TX 1970-1973; Vic-in-Charge S Jn's Epis Ch Cntr TX 1970-1973. Paul Harris Fell 1991. mdagg@earthlink.net

DAHARSH, Floyd Arthur (Okla) 112 West 9th Street, Hugoton KS 67951 **S Jn's Ch Ulysses KS 2003-; P-in-c S Steph's Ch Guymon OK 2003-** B Americus KS 11/2/1936 s Frank Arthur Daharsh & Della Fern. BS Emporia St U 1960; MS Emporia St U 1966. D 9/9/1990 P 11/30/1991 Bp John Forsythe Ashby. m 3/1/1963 Edwina Berniel Sehl.

DAHILL, Laurel Anne (WMich) 323 S. State St., Big Rapids MI 49307 **R S Andr's Ch Big Rapids MI 2008-** B Arlington MA 6/28/1971 d Charles Ireland Dahill & Eileen Marie. BA SUNY 1994; MFA VPI & St U 1997; MDiv SWTS 2007; MTS SWTS 2008. D 6/7/2008 Bp Jeffrey Dean Lee P 12/6/2008 Bp Robert R Gepert. m 5/19/2001 Kathryn Latterell. Contrib, "Freedom and Liberty," *Recon & Healing*, Preaching Excellence Prog, 2007. ldahill@juno.com

DAHL, Joan Elizabeth (Spok) 8991 State Route 24, Moxee WA 98936 **D Chr Epis Ch Zillah WA 2000-** B Seattle WA 12/1/1946 d William Taylor Rogers & Dorothy Vivian. U of Washington; AAS/RN Shoreline Cmnty Coll 1968. D 10/16/1999 Bp John Stuart Thornton. m 8/17/1968 Joseph Miller Dahl c 2. Lower Yakima Vlly Mutual Mnstry 2000.

DAIGLE, Deborah Heft (Tex) PO Box 1344, Madisonville TX 77864 B Cleveland OH 8/7/1948 d Ronald Heft & Mary Hall. Bi-Vocational Iona Sch of Mnstry 2010. D 6/19/2010 Bp C(harles) Andrew Doyle. c 2. daigle.deborah@yahoo.com

DAILEY, Beulah Huffman (Dal) 2929 Hickory St, Dallas TX 75226 **Asst S Jas Ch Dallas TX 2002-** B Marion NC 7/14/1936 d Aaron Lee Huffman & Lola. Clevenger Coll Of Bus; LST GTS 1985. D 6/14/1986 Bp Donis Dean Patterson P 3/1/1996 Bp James Monte Stanton. m 6/13/1987 Harry Edward Dailey. S Jas Ch Dallas TX 1998-2000; Asst S Paul's Epis Ch Waxahachie TX 1992-1998; Asst Ch Of The Gd Shpd Cedar Hill TX 1986-1992. DOK 1989; Ord Of S Lk 1976; S Steph Mnstry 1999. High Profile Dallas Morning News 2002; Serv To Mankind Awd Sertoma Club Of Dallas Texas 2002; Ex. Dir Of The Year Texas Homeless Ntwk 2002; Participated In Pres. G.W. Bush Inaguration Serv 2000; Heart Of Gold Awd Leukemia Soc 1997. shelterspk@aol.com

DAILEY, Douglas Grant (At) 422 Brenau Ave, Gainesville GA 30501 **R Gr Epis Ch Gainesville GA 2002-** B Columbus OH 9/19/1956 s Alan Ward Dailey & Vivian Louise. Emory U 1978; LTh Lincoln Theol Coll 1988; BTh U of Nottingham 1988. Trans from Church Of England 4/1/1992 Bp Robert Hodges Johnson. m 8/23/1980 Judith Ann Browning c 3. R Trin Epis Ch Statesville NC 1993-2002; Assoc R Ch Of The Ascen Hickory NC 1991-1993. douglasdailey@charter.net

DAILEY, Harry Edward (Dal) 2650 Cedar Springs Rd Apt 6638, Dallas TX 75201 B Columbus OH 7/6/1951 s Harry Dailey & Patricia. Cert of Study Advantage Hlth Serv 1992; Cert of Study Hazelden SW 1999; Lic Angl TS 2002. D 6/3/2000 P 10/11/2003 Bp James Monte Stanton. m 6/13/1987 Beulah Huffman Dailey c 1. As Told to Russ Pate Biography, "Heaven Sent," *The Bubba and Harry Dailey Story*, Auth Hse, 2004. Bro of St. Andr 1988-2009; Chaplin Verger's Gld 2007-2009. therevsdailey@sbcglobal.net

DAILY JR, Charles Wendell (FdL) N 6945 Ash Road, Shawano WI 54166 **D S Jn's Ch Shawano WI 2003-** B Oakland CA 11/2/1943 s Charles Wendell Daily & June Alberta. BA U Denv 1969; MSW U Denv 1971; MChSpr Creighton U 1990. Rec from Roman Catholic 4/12/2003 as Deacon Bp Russell Edward Jacobus. m 8/6/2002 Pamela M Kerry. Angl Comm Ntwk 2006. stjohnshawano@gmail.com

DAILY, Teresa Wooten (Ark) 925 Mitchell St, Conway AR 72034 **D-in-c S Ptr's Ch Conway AR 2008-** B Atlanta GA 6/16/1966 d Ernest A Wooten & Virginia Parkerson. BS Duke 1988; MD Ya Sch of Medecine 1992; MDiv Epis TS of the SW 2008. D 3/15/2008 P 9/20/2008 Bp Larry R Benfield. m 6/7/1992 David W Daily c 2. tlwdaily@yahoo.com

DAKAN, Karen Nugent (SwFla) 14 Sandy Hook Rd N, Sarasota FL 34242 B Chicago IL 1/26/1942 d Martin Burton Nugent & Marie Agnes. BA Br 1964; MA U of So Florida 1975. D 11/30/1986 Bp Emerson Paul Haynes. m 4/20/1963 Stephen Lee Dakan c 2. Asst S Bon Ch Sarasota FL 1986-2000. kdakan@comcast.net

DALABA, Elizabeth Mahrer (U) 1086 E Bedford St, Kaysville UT 84037 B Wilmington DE 7/10/1919 d Joseph Louis Mahrer & Mary Virginia. BS U of Maryland 1941. D 7/22/1980 P 4/5/1981 Bp Otis Charles. m 2/26/1950 Carl Henry Dalaba. Assoc S Ptr's Ch Clearfield UT 1981-2006. DOK.

DALBY, Mary Martin Douglass (Ark) 710 Quapaw Ave, Hot Springs National Park AR 71901 **Exec Coun Dio Arkansas Little Rock AR 2010-; Camp Mitchell Bd Trst Dio Arkansas Little Rock AR 2009-; S Fran Ch Heber Sprg AR 2009-; Bd Trst Dio Arkansas Little Rock AR 2008-; ECW Bd Dio Arkansas Little Rock AR 2002-** B Little Rock AR 11/14/1958 BSBA LSU 1981; Mstr of DS of Theol 2006. D 7/9/2005 P 2/4/2006 Bp Larry Earl Maze. m 4/27/1985 Robert E Dalby c 3. Del to ECW Trien Dio Arkansas Little Rock AR 2009; S Jn's Epis Ch Ft Smith AR 2006-2009; Del to ECW Trien Dio Arkansas Little Rock AR 2006. surprisedbygrace@yahoo.com

D'ALCARAVELA, Joao Antonio Alpalhao (Mass) Palmoinho, Serra do Louro, Palmela 2950-305 Portugal B Sardoal Portugal 10/5/1931 s Antonio Daniel Alpalhao & Patrocinia Maria. Cert Seminario da Luz Lisbon PT 1958; BD Dominican U Ottawa CA 1974; Med U of Montreal 1976; Fllshp EDS 1987; PhD U of Montreal 1987; EDS 1988. Rec from Roman Catholic 9/29/1990 as Priest Bp David Bell Birney IV. m 6/13/1987 Carol Blanchard c 2. Ethno Fam Serv New Bedford MA 1993-1994; Dio Massachusetts Boston MA 1990-1993. Auth, "A Minority in a Changing Soc:The Portuguese Communities of Quebec," *in Engl*, U of Ottawa Press, 1980. Jadalcaravela@gmail.com

D

DALE, Anne Edge (EC) 209 Puddin Ridge Rd, Moyock NC 27958 B Norfolk VA 9/7/1955 d James Norwood Edge & Coraleigh Scott. BA Meredith Coll 1977; MEd No Carolina St U 1983; MDiv VTS 2011. D 6/11/2011 Bp Clifton Daniel III. m 4/17/1982 Roland Ward Dale c 2. annedale4@gmail.com

DALE, Kathleen Askew (Los) St. Margaret's Episcopal Church, 47-535 HWY 74 at Haystack Rd., Palm Desert CA 92260 **Dir of Counslg S Marg's Epis Ch Palm Desert CA 2008-** B Hahira GA 11/6/1948 d Robert Lee Dale & Hazel. BA Bos 1970; MDiv Harvard DS 1977; MA Antioch U 1985. D 6/11/1978 Bp Morris Fairchild Arnold P 2/11/1979 Bp Robert C Rusack. Assoc All SS Par Beverly Hills CA 1984-1990; Assoc S Mich and All Ang Epis Ch Studio City CA 1980-1984; Cur All SS Ch Pasadena CA 1978-1980. kathleenadale@earthlink.net

DALES, Randolph Kent (NH) Po Box 359, Wolfeboro NH 03894 **Bd Trst Dio New Hampshire Concord NH 2010-; Bd Trst The Holderness Sch Plymouth NH 2008-; R All SS Epis Ch Wolfeboro NH 1978-** B Los Angeles CA 9/30/1941 s John Leighton Dales & Freda Elizabeth. BA Stan 1963; MDiv VTS 1966. D 9/10/1966 P 3/11/1967 Bp Francis E I Bloy. m 4/15/1994 Lynn Tyler c 3. S Gabr's Epis Ch Marion MA 1977-1978; S Gabr's Epis Ch Marion MA 1976; Vic Trin Ch Meredith NH 1972-1978; The Holderness Sch Plymouth NH 1971-1978; Cur Chr Ch Exeter NH 1969-1971; Cur S Dav's Par Los Angeles CA 1967-1969. allsaints@metrocast.net

D'ALESANDRE, Peter John (O) 84 Lake Washington Dr # 2814, Chepachet RI 02814 **Vic Gr Epis Ch Yantic CT 2005-** B New York NY 9/21/1943 s John James D'Alesandre & Marie Elizabeth. BA Leh 1965; BD Nash 1970; MA U of Connecticut 1998; Nat'l Taiwan Normal U 1999. D 6/6/1970 Bp Horace W B Donegan P 12/21/1970 Bp Donald H V Hallock. m 12/21/1968 Janet Helen Judge c 4. S Matt's Ch Ashland OH 1988-1996; Cur S Barn Ch Warwick RI 1981-1988; Vic Chr The King Epis Ch Huntington IN 1975-1980; Cur All SS Epis Ch Kansas City MO 1971-1975; Asst Chr Epis Ch Of Delavan Delavan WI 1970-1971. CCU, CBS; P AssociateComTransfiguration 1992. fatherpeterofyantic@gmail.com

DALEY, Alexander Spotswood (Mass) 81 Mill Pond, North Andover MA 01845 B Boston MA 4/4/1935 s Robert Francis Daley & Louisa. BA Harv 1957; STB EDS 1971; DMin Pittsburgh TS 1984. D 6/26/1971 P 1/20/1972 Bp John Melville Burgess. Cler Convenr Dio Massachusetts Boston MA 1994-1999; S Aid's Chap So Dartmouth MA 1991-1995; R S Paul's Epis Ch No Andover MA 1976-2005; Asst S Geo's Epis Ch Dayton OH 1971-1973. EvangES; Ord Of S Lk.

DALEY, Joy Anne (Dal) 7114 Alpha Rd, Dallas TX 75240 **Vic The Epis Ch Of The Trsfg Dallas TX 2001-** B Beverly MA 3/27/1953 d Henry A Belanger & Theresa M. BA Bridgewater Coll 1975; MA Assumption Coll 1980; MDiv Brite DS 2001. D 6/9/2001 P 5/25/2002 Bp James Monte Stanton. c 2. jdaley@transfiguration.net

DALFERES, Craig Douglas (La) 624 Winfield Blvd, Houma LA 70360 **R S Matt's Epis Ch Houma LA 2004-** B Baton Rouge LA 7/11/1968 s Joseph Lee Dalferes & Linda. BS Centenary Coll 1990; MDiv Nash 1998. D 5/30/1998 P 12/12/1998 Bp Charles Edward Jenkins III. m 9/24/1994 Jennifer Lynn Dalferes c 2. Assoc R Trin Epis Ch Baton Rouge LA 1998-2004. cdalferes@aol.com

DALGLISH, William Anthony (Tenn) 1911 Hampton Dr, Lebanon TN 37087 **Vic Emer Ch of the H Cross Murfreesboro TN 2011-** B Saint Paul MN 1/13/1941 s James J Dalglish & Mary Theresa. BA S Paul TS 1963; MA Scarritt Grad Sch 1969; MDiv S Meinrad TS 1971; DMin Van 1979; Cfp Coll for Fin Plnng 1983; Postdoc STUSo 1985. Rec from Roman Catholic 6/1/1985 as Priest Bp William Evan Sanders. m 11/2/1974 Carol Solomon c 1. Int Vic Ch of the H Cross Murfreesboro TN 2008-2011; Affirmative Aging Dir Dio Tennessee Nashville TN 1999; Vic S Jn's Epis Ch Mt Juliet TN 1996-1998; Dandridge Trust - Trst, Treas Dio Tennessee Nashville TN 1987-1993; Vic The Ch Of The Epiph Lebanon TN 1985-1998. Auth, "Models For Catechetical Mnstry In The Rural Par," Conf Of Cath Bishops, 1982; Auth, "Fam Centered Model As Option For CE," Meth Bd Discipleship, 1974; Auth,

"Media For Chr Formation (3 Volumes)," Pflaum, 1970. First Epis P In Tennessee Approved As Pstr Of Luthern (Elca) Ch 2001. bdalglish@aol.com

DALLY, John Addison (Chi) 2650 N Lakeview Ave Apt 2501, Chicago IL 60614 **Artist-in-Res S Ptr's Epis Ch Chicago IL 2011-; Prof of Theol and Culture SWTS Evanston IL 2011-** B Park Ridge IL 4/23/1957 s Addison Barber Dally & Betty Jane. BA U CA 1978; MDiv Yale DS 1981; PhD U Chi 1994. D 6/19/1982 P 1/20/1983 Bp Robert C Rusack. m 8/1/2008 Todd Marcus Young. S Ptr's Epis Ch Chicago IL 2007; SWTS Evanston IL 2006-2009; S Dunst's Epis Ch Westchester IL 1995-2000; Epis Luth Mnstry Evanston IL 1994-1995; S Mary's Ch Pk Ridge IL 1989-1992; Dio Chicago Chicago IL 1989; S Paul's Epis Ch Tustin CA 1986-1987; The ETS At Claremont Claremont CA 1986-1987; Assoc R Trin Epis Ch Santa Barbara CA 1982-1986. Auth, "Choosing the Kingdom: Missional Preaching for the Household of God," Alb Inst, 2008; Auth, "Myths And Fictions," E. J. Brill, 1993; Ed, "Monasticism & The Arts," Syr Press, 1983; Compsr, "Var Choral Works"; Auth, "Var Plays". Galler Prize U Chi 1994; Fllshp Inst For The Advncd Study Of Rel, Unversity Of Chic 1992; Fell ECF U Chi 1988; Phi Beta Kappa U CA, Irvine 1978. john.dally@seabury.edu

DALMASSO, Gary Lee (Q) 215 29th Ave, East Moline IL 61244 B Canton IL 10/4/1942 s Joseph Dalmasso & Maxine. BA U of Iowa 1964; BA GTS 1967. D 4/1/1967 P 10/28/1967 Bp Francis W Lickfield. m 6/28/1969 Judith Connie Dalmasso c 4. Chr Epis Ch Clinton IA 2003-2005; Renwl In Chr Mnstrs E Moline IL 1995-2003; Vic S Jn's Epis Ch Peoria IL 1990-1994; Vic S Mk's Epis Ch Peoria IL 1967-1975. Fllshp Of Epis Evangelicals, Pews Action. ricmadm@aol.com

DALMASSO, Judith Connie (Ia) Renewal in Christ Ministries, PO Box 94, East Moline IL 61244 **Trin Cathd Davenport IA 2010-; Renwl In Chr Mnstrs E Moline IL 2007-** B Moline IL 2/15/1946 d Conrad I Wilson & Marion A. BA Augustana Colloge 1987; MTS Nash 2006. D 6/23/2007 P 1/6/2008 Bp Alan Scarfe. m 6/28/1969 Gary Lee Dalmasso c 4. ricmadm@aol.com

DALTON, Franklin Bruce (NCal) 401 Sandstone Dr, Vallejo CA 94589 **Died 7/17/2011** B Council Bluffs IA 12/6/1925 s Charles Ray Dalton & Minnie Christine. AA U of Nebraska 1963. D 2/24/1966 P 12/6/1966 Bp Russell T Rauscher. c 3. franklindalton@msn.com

DALTON, Harlon Leigh (Ct) Episcopal Diocese of Connecticut, 1335 Asylum Avenue, Hartford CT 06105 B Cleveland OH 12/25/1947 s John W Dalton & Louise L. read for Ord; BA Harv 1969; JD Ya 1973; Angl Cert Ya Berk 2001. D 6/8/2002 P 1/4/2003 Bp Andrew Donnan Smith. m 9/6/1986 Jill M Berlenbach. Com 2, COM Dio Connecticut Hartford CT 2011; Int S Ann's Epis Ch Old Lyme CT 2010; Stndg Com Dio Connecticut Hartford CT 2007-2011; Prog & Bdgt Com Dio Connecticut Hartford CT 2006-2011; Com 1, COM Dio Connecticut Hartford CT 2005-2011; Assoc R S Paul And S Jas New Haven CT 2002-2010. "Racial Healing," Doubleday, 1995. hdalton@ctdiocese.org

DALTON JR, James Albert (Ark) 94 Cherrywood Dr., Cabot AR 72023 **P S Steph's Epis Ch Jacksonville AR 2006-** B Charleston AR 11/4/1953 s James Albert Dalton & Doris Jean. BSE Arkansas Tech 1975; MSE U of Cntrl Arkansas 1989. D 6/3/2006 P 12/9/2006 Bp Larry Earl Maze. m 6/16/1973 Joyce Foley Joyce Rae Foley c 2. jdalton@classicnet.net

DALTON, Joyce Foley (Ark) St Stephen's Episcopal Church, 2413 Northeastern Ave, Jacksonville AR 72076 B Ft Smith AR 2/15/1953 d Charles R Foley & Loretta. BA Arkansas Polytechnic Coll 1975; Med U of Arkansas 1983. D 6/3/2006 Bp Larry Earl Maze. m 6/16/1973 James Albert Dalton c 2. jdalton@classicnet.net

DALTON, William Thomas (Dal) 311 W. 5th St., Bonham TX 75418 B University City MO 7/17/1933 s Harry Vernon Dalton & Virginia A. BA U of No Texas 1958; MDiv Epis TS In Kentucky 1964. D 6/18/1964 Bp Theodore H McCrea P 9/18/2004 Bp James Monte Stanton. m 11/23/1967 Lois Charlene Forbus. Vic Ch Of The H Trin Bonham TX 2004-2008. fatherbill@verizon.net

DALTON-THOMPSON, James Philip (Me) 43 Foreside Road, Falmouth ME 04105 **Died 12/1/2010** B Detroit MI 10/3/1950 s James Philip Thompson & Shirley Jane. BA MI SU 1972; MA Mid 1978; MDiv EDS 1983. D 6/18/1983 Bp Henry Irving Mayson P 12/18/1983 Bp Henry Boyd Hucles III. Auth and Ed, "Le Livre de la Priere Commune," Ch Pub; Auth, "Johnny Can Read, but can he lead?," *Boarding Schools Quarterly*. jpd_t@hotmail.com

DALY, Joseph Erin (WLa) 1030 Johnston St, Lafayette LA 70501 B Truro NS CA 11/1/1971 s George Sansom Daly & Carol Janice. PhD McGill U; Regent Coll Vancouver Bc CA 1996; MDiv Samford U 1998. D 10/26/2002 P 6/3/2003 Bp Daniel William Herzog. m 6/30/1995 Angela Adele Duplantis c 2. Ch Of The Ascen Lafayette LA 2003-2009; S Andr's Epis Ch Douglas GA 2003-2009; Trin Ch Plattsburgh NY 2002-2003. ascensionrector@yahoo.com

DALY III, Raymond Ernest (Fla) 160 Sea Island Dr, Ponte Vedra Beach FL 32082 **Assoc S Geo's Epis Ch Jacksonville FL 2000-** B Chicago IL 2/6/1929 s Raymond Ernest Daly & Catherine. Nash; BA DePaul U 1950; PhD Unversity Of Lausanne Ch 1972. D 4/19/1986 Bp Charles Brinkley Morton. Assoc - Mssn Hse Dio Florida Jacksonville FL 1995-2000; Assoc S Mary Of The Hills Epis Par Blowing Rock NC 1992-1995; Asst To Bp Dio Wstrn No Carolina Asheville NC 1990-1992; Assoc S Ptr's Epis Ch Del Mar CA 1986-1989; Consult To Congs Dio Olympia Seattle WA 1983-1984. Auth, "Intl Money Mgmt". Compass Rose Soc 1999.

DALY, Richard R (Dal) 5323 N Mulligan Ave, Chicago IL 60630 **S Paul's Par Riverside IL 2002-** B Chicago IL 2/16/1962 s Ernest Edgar Daly & Lucille Stella. BA Loyola U 1985; MDiv Nash 1991; Post Grad Study Cntr for Rel & Psych Chicago IL 1995. D 12/1/1990 P 6/14/1991 Bp William L Stevens. m 10/23/2004 Diana Lyn Fairchild c 3. Int S Raphael The Archangel Oak Lawn IL 1999-2002; R S Steph's Epis Ch Sherman TX 1996-1998; R S Ptr's Epis Ch Sheboygan Falls WI 1993-1996; Cur Trin Ch Wauwatosa WI 1991-1993; Asst S Anskar's Epis Ch Hartland WI 1990-1991. Socitey of the H Cross 1997. richd17062@hotmail.com

DALY JR, Robert Edmund (Md) 2610 Sarah Ln, Baltimore MD 21234 B Baltimore MD 8/24/1936 s Robert Edmund Daly & Virginia Delilah. BS Jn Hopkins U 1966; MDiv EDS 1969. D 6/23/1969 Bp David Keller Leighton Sr P 6/3/1970 Bp Harry Lee Doll. m 12/30/1967 Anne Elizabeth Limpert c 2. Endwmt Grants Comittee Dio Maryland Baltimore MD 1997-2000; Stndg Com Dio Maryland Baltimore MD 1991-1994; Chair - Stwdshp Com Dio Maryland Baltimore MD 1988-1991; Dioc Coun Dio Maryland Baltimore MD 1983-1986; R Ch Of The Mssh Baltimore MD 1981-2001; Int St Matthews Epis Ch Seat Pleasant MD 1980-1981; P-in-c S Jn's Ch Chevy Chase MD 1979-1980; Asst S Jn's Ch Chevy Chase MD 1973-1979; R S Thos' Par Hancock MD 1971-1973; Asst S Geo's Ch Perryman MD 1969-1971. robertdaly2@comcast.net

DALZON, Wilfrid (Hai) No address on file. B 7/13/1940 STB ETSC 1964. D 5/14/1964 Bp Charles Alfred Voegeli P 12/1/1964 Bp James Loughlin Duncan.

D'AMARIO, Matthew Justin (Md) 3009 Greenmount Ave., Baltimore MD 21218 B Westminster MD 10/17/1970 s Raymond Andrew D'Amario & Evelyn Dolores Manger. BA Jn Hopkins U 1992; MDIV St. Mary's Sem 1998. Rec from Roman Catholic 9/29/2009 Bp John Leslie Rabb. craigmatthew3801@gmail.com

DAMBROT, Donna Lise (SeFla) 738 NE 7th Ave, Fort Lauderdale FL 33304 **Pres & Exec Dir Epis Chars of SE Florida Palm Bch Gardens FL 2009-** B New York NY 4/7/1958 d Irwin Dambrot & Pearl. BA Queens Coll, CUNY 1980; JD S Jn's Law Sch Jamaica NY 1984; MDiv GTS 2000. D 5/20/2000 Bp Richard Frank Grein P 2/4/2003 Bp Mark Sean Sisk. Assoc Dir Dio New York New York City NY 2007-2009; R S Jas Ch Langhorne PA 2006-2007; Asst All SS Ch New York NY 2005-2006; Assoc The Ch Of S Lk In The Fields New York NY 2001-2005; D The Ch Of S Lk In The Fields New York NY 2000-2001; D Ch Of The H Trin New York NY 2000. ddambrot@aol.com

D'AMICO, Samuel Robert (Los) 23442 El Toro Rd # 368, Lake Forest CA 92630 B Wakefield MA 3/12/1918 s Anthony D'Amico & Annie. BA Harv 1939; MDiv EDS 1943; Harv 1943; PhD Grad Theol Un 1972. D 9/15/1943 P 5/31/1944 Bp Raymond A Heron. m 7/20/1946 Alice Virginia Shepard c 3. Netwk Off PBFWR Epis Ch Cntr New York NY 1982-1985; S Jas Par Los Angeles CA 1963-1982; R H Faith Par Inglewood CA 1953-1963; Exec DRE Dio Los Angeles Los Angeles CA 1953-1958; R Cong Of S Athan Los Angeles CA 1947-1953; Cn Cathd Of S Jn Providence RI 1944-1947; Exec DRE Dio Rhode Island Providence RI 1944-1947.

DAMON, David Reid (Fla) 7930 Bellemeade Blvd S, Jacksonville FL 32211 B Baltimore MD 1/26/1926 s Samuel Reed Damon & Jeannie Douglas. BS USMMA 1947; BS Pur 1950; MDiv STUSo 1950; D.Min Van 1974. D 6/16/1955 Bp Frank A Juhan P 2/1/1956 Bp Edward Hamilton West. c 3. R S Andr's Ch Jacksonville FL 1969-1979; D H Nativ Epis Ch Panama City FL 1955-1956. Auth, *JD*; Auth, *TA & Some Rel Applications*. davdamone@aol.com

DAMROSCH, Thomas Hammond (WMass) PO Box 612, Stockbridge MA 01262 **R S Paul's Epis Ch Stockbridge MA 2007-** B Manila Phillipines 11/4/1949 s Leopold Damrosch & Elizabeth Brotherton. Dplma NYU 1979; BA SUNY 1986; MDiv GTS 1989. D 6/10/1989 Bp Paul Moore Jr P 12/9/1989 Bp Richard Frank Grein. m 2/12/1977 Marthe Emily Turner c 1. R S Paul's Ch Naples FL 2001-2007; Cn Mssnr Dio Cntrl New York Syracuse NY 1999-2001; Precentor Dio Cntrl New York Syracuse NY 1996-1998; R S Paul's Ch Brownville NY 1995-2001; R Gr Ch Dalton MA 1991-1995; Ltrgcl & Mus Cmsn Dio New York New York City NY 1989-1995; Team Monticello NY 1989-1991. frtomd@juno.com

DAMUS, Pierre Gasner (LI) 1227 Pacific St, Brooklyn NY 11216 **P-in-c S Barth's Ch Brooklyn NY 2005-; Asstg P S Paul's Ch-In-The-Vill Brooklyn NY 1998-** B 7/5/1961 s Prince Damus & Victorie. BA Sem Theol of Haiti 1989. D 7/30/1989 P 2/14/1990 Bp Luc Anatole Jacques Garnier. m 9/22/1998 Magdala Damus c 4. Asstg P Gr Ch Jamaica NY 2001-2005; P-in-c Dio Haiti Ft Lauderdale FL 1989-1997. gdamus@verizon.net

DANDRIDGE, Robert Floyd (WLa) 702 Elm St, Minden LA 71055 B Minden LA 9/19/1937 s Floyd E Dandridge & Nellie O. TS; BS NW St U 1959; U So 1989; Int Mnstry Prog 2002. D 3/1/2000 P 11/12/2000 Bp Robert Jefferson Hargrove Jr. m 8/4/1961 Evelyn Virginia Greene.

DANFORD, Nicholas Chase (Tex) 4 Fountain Sq, Larchmont NY 10538 **S Jn's Ch Larchmont NY 2011-** B Corsicana TX 3/6/1982 s Jimmy Lester Danford & Dana Jo. BA Rice U 2004; MDiv VTS 2011. D 6/18/2011 Bp C(harles) Andrew Doyle. chase.danford@gmail.com

DANFORTH, John Claggett (Mo) 911 Tirrill Farms Rd, Saint Louis MO 63124 **Assoc Ch Of The H Comm U City MO 1995-** B Saint Louis MO 9/5/1936 s Donald Danforth & Dorothy. BA Pr 1958; BD/LLB Ya 1963. D 9/15/1963 P 3/1/1964 Bp George Leslie Cadigan. m 9/7/1957 Sally Baird Dobson. Assoc S Alb's Par Washington DC 1977-1994; Assoc Gr Ch Jefferson City MO 1969-1976; Asst The Ch Of The Epiph New York NY 1963-1966.

DANGELO, Michael Bradley (Mass) 17 Helen St, Hull MA 02045 B Harrogate North Yorkshire UK 6/24/1976 BA Wheaton Coll 1998; DAS Ya Berk 2004; MDiv Ya Berk 2004. D 6/12/2004 P 1/8/2005 Bp M(arvil) Thomas Shaw III. m 6/10/2000 Faye S Dangelo c 1. S Paul's Ch Lynnfield MA 2004-2008; Asst Trin Ch In The City Of Boston Boston MA 2004-2008. mdangelo@stpaulslynnfield.org

D'ANGIO, Peter David (Be) 311 Wheeler Ave., Scranton PA 18510 **P-in-c S Lk's Ch Scranton PA 2007-** B Boston MA 6/18/1959 s Giulio John D'Angio & Jean. BA U of Pennsylvania 1981; MA U of Pennsylvania 1985; MDiv GTS 1994; MS Coll of Preachers 2000. D 6/29/1994 Bp Sanford Zangwill Kaye Hampton P 1/6/1995 Bp James Louis Jelinek. m Gregory Scott Hinson. Int Trin Epis Ch Pottsville PA 2006; Int S Andr's Epis Ch Glenwood MD 2003-2004; Int S Jas Ch Lancaster PA 2002-2003; Int Imm Epis Ch Glencoe MD 2001-2002; Int Chr Ch Columbia MD 1999-2001; R S Mths' Epis Ch Baltimore MD 1997-1999; Vic Chr Ch Harrison NJ 1995-1996. Auth, "Liturg Conf". Epis Carmel of St. Teresa (Assoc) 2007. peterstlukes@verizon.net

✠ **DANIEL III, Rt Rev Clifton** (EC) 1800 E 5th St, Greenville NC 27858 **Bp of E Carolina Dio E Carolina Kinston NC 1996-** B Goldsboro NC 7/4/1947 s Clifton Daniel & Evelyn Vann. BA U NC 1969; MDiv VTS 1972; S Geo's Coll Jerusalem IL 1977; Coll of Preachers 1980; Grad Theol Un 1984; St Petersburg Theol Acad, Russia 1992; Angl Cntr In Rome Rome It 1993. D 6/29/1972 P 4/14/1973 Bp Hunley Agee Elebash Con 9/21/1996 for EC. m 8/19/1978 Anne M Miller c 3. Dep Gc Dio Rhode Island Providence RI 1991-1994; R S Mich's Ch Bristol RI 1984-1996; Assoc S Paul's Epis Ch Dayton OH 1980-1984; Chair, Dept, Chr Educ Dio E Carolina Kinston NC 1977-1980; R S Thos' Epis Ch Ahoskie NC 1975-1980; Asst S Mary's Ch Kinston NC 1972-1975. DD TS U So 1997; DD VTS 1997. cdaniel@diocese-eastcarolina.org

DANIEL, Wilfred Arthnel (VI) 112 Estate La Reine, Christiansted, Saint Croix VI B Saint Kitts West Indies 12/29/1945 s Alfred Daniel & Albertha. Trans from Church Of England 9/1/2000 Bp Theodore Athelbert Daniels. m 10/17/1968 Gwendolyn Adams c 2. R S Jn's Ch Christiansted VI 2000-2009. fuzzdaniel@yahoo.com

DANIELEY, Teresa Kathryn Mithen (Mo) 3664 Arsenal St, Saint Louis MO 63116 **R S Jn's Ch St Louis MO 2004-** B St Louis MO 3/25/1977 d Francis Andrew Mithen & Phyllis Agnes. BA Ya 1998; MA U Chi 2001; MDiv GTS 2004. D 12/19/2003 P 6/25/2004 Bp George Wayne Smith. m 9/26/2009 Jonathan Danieley c 1. YA Cmnty Serv Awd Untd Ch Wmn of Connecticut 1998. tkmithen@aya.yale.edu

DANIELL JR, Hal S(hipley) (Ga) 335 Brockinton Marsh, Saint Simons Island GA 31522 **Died 7/25/2009** B Emory GA 6/28/1930 s Hal Shipley Daniell & Mary Elizabeth. BS Georgia Inst of Tech 1957; BD Epis TS of The SW 1960; STM Nash 1979; DD Epis TS In Kentucky 1981. D 6/18/1960 P 12/20/1960 Bp Randolph R Claiborne. NCCJ Annual Awd Lexington KY 1987; Hon Cn 1983; Serv to Mankind Awd Sertoma Intl 1981.

DANIELS, Joel C (NY) 202 W 58th St Apt 5NE, New York NY 10019 **Asst S Thos Ch New York NY 2010-** B St. Augustine FL 2/7/1978 s James Edward Daniels & Ginger Cook. BA Col 2000; MDiv GTS 2007. D 3/10/2007 P 9/15/2007 Bp Mark Sean Sisk. m 9/19/2003 Lystra Batchoo. Int S Barn Ch Irvington on Hudson NY 2007-2009. joelcdaniels@gmail.com

DANIELS, John Derek (WA) 1001 E Lincoln Hwy, Exton PA 19341 **CFS The Sch At Ch Farm Exton PA 2011-** B Doylestown PA 1/15/1960 s Beverly Francis Hearns & Winifred D. W Los Angeles Coll; BS U of Phoenix 2002; MDiv VTS 2007. D 6/4/2011 Bp John Chane. m 11/6/1993 Lori L Martin c 4. jdaniels@goctg.net

✠ **DANIELS, Rt Rev Theodore Athelbert** (VI) 3208 Prairie Clover Path, Austin TX 78732 B Ancon PA 11/3/1944 s Ethelridge Daniels & Carlotta Leotta. AAS/ AA Canal Zone Coll 1971; MDiv ETSC 1975; BS Florida St U 1976; Oklahoma St U 1978; Cntr for Addiction Trng and Educ 1989; St. Eliz Hosp 1989; Bowie St U 1990; Institue for Pstr Psych 1994; Fielding Grad Inst 1998; D.D. GTS 2002; Dispute Resolution Cntr 2005; Dispute Resolution Cntr 2008; Employer Spprt of Guard and Reserve (ESGR) 2008; Employer Spprt of Guard and Reserve (ESGR) 2010. D 6/7/1969 P 12/1/1969 Bp Robert B Gooden Con 6/30/1997 for VI. m 10/21/1972 Cristina Strickland c 3. Asst Bp Dio Texas Houston TX 2003-2005; Abundance Com Ch Pension Fund New York NY 2001-2003; Bp Of VI Dio Vrgn Islands St Thos VI VI 1997-2003; Chapl, CAP Bp Of ArmdF- Epis Ch Cntr New York NY 1994-2004; R Calv Ch Washington DC 1992-1997; Vic H Redeem Mssn Capitol Heights MD 1985-1992; R S Lk's Epis Ch Columbia SC 1980-1985; R St Christophers Ch 1971-1980; P-in-c Ch Of The Trsfg 1971-1972; P-in-c St Georges Ch 1971-1972; Dio Panama 1969-1980. Life Mem Ord S Vinc Gld of Acolytes 1970; Ord Of S Lk, Bro Of S Andr 1974. DD The GTS 2002; Citation from Coun of Dist of Columbia Coun of Dist of Columbia 1997; Citation from Gvnr of St of Maryland Gvnr of St of Maryland 1997; Citation from Maryland Gnrl Assembly Maryland Gnrl Assembly 1997; Citation from Maryland Hse of Representatives Maryland Hse of Rep 1997; Proclamation of Theo A. Daniels Day Mayor of the Dist of Columbia 1997; Ord of the Palmeto Gvnr of the St of So Carolina 1985; Phi Theta Kappa Delta Omega Chapt, Canal Zone Coll 1964; Natl Hon Soc Copley HS 1962. THEODORE.DANIELS@SBCGLOBAL.NET

DANIELS, William Greer (ETenn) 308 Fey Rd., Chestertown MD 21620 **Died 1/24/2011** B Chattanooga TN 7/19/1935 s William James Daniels & Jo. BA U Of Chattanooga 1958; STB Ya Berk 1961; Van 1964. D 6/22/1961 P 2/1/1962 Bp John Vander Horst. c 4. daniels@chesapeake.net

DANIELSON JR, Paul Everett (ECR) 22481 Ferdinand Dr, Salinas CA 93908 B Santa Barbara CA 8/18/1938 s Paul Everett Danielson & Katharine Elizabeth. BA Pr 1960; MDiv UTS 1963; CAS EDS 1964. D 6/6/1964 Bp Walter M Higley P 6/16/1965 Bp Ned Cole. m 6/25/1966 Margaret Elizabeth Entwisle c 1. All SS' Epis Day Sch Carmel CA 1984-2001; R Epis Ch Of The Gd Shpd Salinas CA 1969-1984; Cur Calv Epis Ch Santa Cruz CA 1967-1968; Cur S Paul's Ch Endicott NY 1964-1967. paul_danielson@hotmail.com

DANIEL-TURK, Patricia Daniel-Turk (Fla) 15 East Manor, Beaufort SC 29906 B Goldsboro NC 5/24/1949 d Clifton Daniel & Evelyn Vann. BA No Carolina Wesleyan Coll 1971; MDiv VTS 1985. D 12/18/1986 Bp Frank Harris Vest Jr P 12/21/1987 Bp Robert Whitridge Estill. m 12/30/1983 James Turk c 1. R St Pat's Epis Ch S Johns Fl 2008-2010; Assoc Ch Of Our Sav Jacksonville FL 2001-2008; S Mk's Epis Ch Jacksonville FL 1994-2001; Asst Emm Ch Orlando FL 1989-1993; S Jn's Epis Ch Charlotte NC 1987-1988. turkpdt@aol.com

D'ANIERI, Margaret Clare (O) 18369 State Route 58, Wellington OH 44090 **R S Paul Epis Ch Norwalk OH 2009-; Dn, No Cntrl Mssn Area Dio Ohio Cleveland OH 2007-; Zion Ch Monroeville OH 2002-** B Schenectady NY 6/18/1960 d John Eugene D'Anieri & Mary Rae. BA U of Virginia 1982; Bex 2001; Trin Luth Sem 2001; MDiv GTS 2002. D 6/8/2002 P 12/14/2002 Bp Arthur Benjamin Williams Jr. m 5/23/1992 Chester John Bowling. Chr Epis Ch Geneva OH 2009; Trst of the Dio Dio Ohio Cleveland OH 2003-2008; COM Dio Ohio Cleveland OH 2003-2007; No Cntrl Epis Shared Mnstry Port Clinton OH 2002-2009; Assoc No Cntrl Epis Shared Mnstry Port Clinton OH 2002-2004; Assoc R No Cntrl Epis Shared Mnstry Port Clinton OH 2002-2004. niskayuna1960@gmail.com

DANITSCHEK, Thomas Kent (Colo) 6930 E 4th Ave, Denver CO 80220 B Omaha NE 3/6/1962 s Edgar W Danitschek & Alice Lorraine. TESM; BS U CO 1987. D 6/9/2001 P 12/29/2001 Bp William Jerry Winterrowd. Assoc Chr Epis Ch Denver CO 2001-2011. tkentd@gmail.com

DANKEL, S. Rainey Gamble (EC) 1024 Summerlin Falls Ct., Wilmington NC 28412 B Whitmire SC 12/16/1946 d Connolly C Gamble & Melba B. BA Mary Baldwin Coll 1968; Angl Stds Ya Berk 2011; MDiv Yale DS 2011. D 6/12/1999 P 6/18/2011 Bp Clifton Daniel III. D Ch Of The Servnt Wilmington NC 1999-2008. dankel@ec.rr.com

DANNALS, James Clark (Va) 905 Princess Anne St, Fredericksburg VA 22401 **R S Geo's Ch Fredericksburg VA 2004-** B Huntsville AL 7/12/1953 s George Clark Dannals & Cortez. BS Florida St U 1975; MDiv Yale DS 1979. D 6/25/1979 P 1/6/1980 Bp William Hopkins Folwell. m 9/7/1974 Carolyn Hoffman c 3. Dio Wstrn Massachusetts Springfield MA 2002-2004; R S Steph's Ch Pittsfield MA 2002-2004; Stndg Com Dio Wstrn No Carolina Asheville NC 1999-2002; R S Lk's Ch Boone NC 1997-2002; Stndg Com Dio Florida Jacksonville FL 1994-1997; R Ch Of The Gd Shpd Jacksonville FL 1989-1997; Vic Ch Of Our Sav Palm Bay FL 1982-1989; Asst S Jn's Ch Melbourne FL 1979-1982. Auth, "Love That Endures," *LivCh*, 1988. Publ Spkng Berk 1979. jdannals@verizon.net

DANNALS, Robert Samuel (Dal) 8011 Douglas @ Colgate, Dallas, TX 75229 **R S Mich And All Ang Ch Dallas TX 2007-** B Orlando FL 11/24/1955 s George Clark Dannals & Corky. BA Florida St U 1977; MDiv VTS 1981; DMin Drew U 1989; PhD GTF 2005. D 6/21/1981 P 1/17/1982 Bp William Hopkins Folwell. m 6/23/1991 Valerie Robie c 3. R Chr Ch Greenville SC 1997-2007; R Chr Ch New Bern NC 1992-1997; R Trin Epis Ch Statesville NC 1985-1992; Assoc R Chr Ch Charlotte NC 1981-1985. "Aspects Of The Imitation Of Chr In The Moral Christology Of Dietrich Bonhoeffer," Grad Theol Press, 2005; "A Theol Chr Mar," Drew U Press, 1989. Compass Rose Soc; Spck/Usa. bdannals@saintmichael.org

DANNELLEY, James Preston (Tex) 1205 Flag St, Llano TX 78643 B Laredo TX 12/9/1928 s Preston Dannelley & Bernice Cecilia. MDiv Epis TS of The SW 1961. D 7/18/1961 Bp Everett H Jones P 1/1/1962 Bp Richard Earl Dicus. m 6/3/1950 Laura Eloise Kelly c 2. Ch Of The Gd Shpd Houston TX

1977-1984; Vic S Phil's Ch Hearne TX 1974-1977; R Chr Ch Eagle Lake TX 1962-1965; D-in-c Trin Ch Jct TX 1961-1962.

DANNER, David Lawrence (SwFla) All Angels by the Sea Episcopal Church, 563 Bay Isles Rd, Longboat Key FL 34228 **R All Ang By The Sea Longboat Key FL 2005-** B Rockford IL 1/15/1951 s Edward James Danner & Olive Alice. BA Lawr 1973; MDiv Trin, Toronto 1976; MA U Tor 1978; DMin Luth TS at Gettysburg 1997. Trans from Anglican Church of Canada 12/1/1986 as Priest Bp Emerson Paul Haynes. m 8/25/1979 Wafa Farah c 2. R Trin Ch Newton Cntr MA 1995-2005; R Emm Ch Quakertown PA 1988-1995; Asst Calv Ch Indn Rocks Bch FL 1986-1988. Auth, "The Parting Of The Ways For Lutherans & Episcopalians," *Angl & Epis Hist*, 1999; Auth, "Flo-A Study In Hope," *Journ Of Humane Med*, 1986; Auth, "Gown," *Trin Revs*, 1976. Phi Beta Kappa 1973. david.danner@allangelslbk.org

DANSDILL, Dorothy Newton (NMich) 501 N Ravine St, Sault Sainte Marie MI 49783 **R S Jas Ch Of Sault S Marie Sault Ste Marie MI 2006-** B 10/18/1947 d Arthur Henry Newton & Dortothy Margaret. BA U MI 1969; MA U MI 1970. D P 5/28/2006 Bp James Arthur Kelsey. m 7/28/1973 John Newton Dansdill c 2. ddansdill@hotmail.com

DANSON, Michelle A(nne) (Colo) 7776 Country Creek Dr, Longmont CO 80503 B Bradford England 2/7/1952 d John Giblin & Kathleen. B.Sc Dur, Engl 1973; PGCE Dur, Engl 1974; M.Div Iliff TS 2002; CCS GTS 2007. D 6/8/2002 P 6/22/2003 Bp William Jerry Winterrowd. m 8/7/2004 David Alan Plume c 4. H Apos Epis Ch Englewood CO 2005-2006; Asst P/ Par Sprtl Dir Ch Of The H Trin New York NY 2003-2004; D/part time H Apos Epis Ch Englewood CO 2002-2003. madanson@cs.com

DANTONE, Janet Wiley (Tex) 3514 Gannett St, Houston TX 77025 **Assoc S Jn The Div Houston TX 2006-** B Sherman, TX 6/13/1959 d Thomas Wiley & Paula F. BS USAF Acad 1981; MS Troy St U 1984; MDiv TESM 2006. D 6/24/2006 P 1/25/2007 Bp Don Adger Wimberly. m 8/2/2008 Harold Dantone c 3. jdantone@sjd.org

DANZEY, Charles Stephen (Dal) 4414 Abbott Ave, Dallas TX 75205 **Asst Epis Ch Of The Redeem Irving TX 2008-** B Fort Jackson SC 5/17/1957 s Charles W Danzey & Opal. BA Samford U 1980; PhD SW Bapt TS 1995; MDiv SW Bapt TS 1998. D 6/24/2006 Bp James Monte Stanton P 11/6/2008 Bp Paul Emil Lambert. c 1. Ch Of The Incarn Dallas TX 2006; Ch Of The Incarn Dallas TX 2005-2006. sdanzey@yahoo.com

D'AOUST, Jean-Jacques (Colo) 1543 S Estrella Ave, Loveland CO 80537 **Ch Of The H Comf Broomfield CO 2003-; Asst All SS Ch Loveland CO 2002-** B Alfred ON CA 1/3/1924 s Henri Joseph D'Aoust & Aurore. BA/BPH U of Ottawa 1946; MA S Vinc's Sem 1957; Pontifical Inst For Mediaeval Stds CA 1963; MA Ya 1966; MA Ya 1967; PhD Ya 1968; MA Slippery Rock U 1987. Rec from Roman Catholic 12/26/1966 as Deacon Bp John Melville Burgess. m 10/31/1987 Susan Anderson. Int S Andr's in the Vill Ch Barboursville WV 1996-2001; Assoc R Trin Ch Huntington WV 1994-1996; Fox Chap Epis Ch Pittsburgh PA 1983-1987; Ch Of The Epiph Grove City PA 1981-1982; Dio Maryland Baltimore MD 1978-1980; Shared Cmnty Mnstry Cortland A A Homer NY 1975-1978. Auth, "The Wrld Of Teilhard De Chardin," 1960; Auth, "Energetics Of Cosmic Love". AAR 1967; APA 1987; Amer Psychol Soc 1987; Soc For Values In Higher Educ 1964; Wester Inst 1999. Natl Tchg Fllshp 1967; Can Coun Fllshp 1966; Kent Fllshp 1964; Fllshp Ya 1964. jdaoust@ecoisp.com

DARBY, Steven Lanier (Ga) 114 W Mockingbird Ln, Statesboro GA 30461 B Jacksonville FL 4/22/1947 s Jack W Darby & Jean Allen. BA Georgia St U 1971; GTS 1974; MA Georgia St U 1978. D 2/22/2006 Bp Henry Irving Louttit. m 6/6/1976 Regina Edwards c 1. slanierdarby@yahoo.com

DARDEN, John Webster (Dal) 705 Williams St, Pasadena TX 77506 B Tyler TX 3/11/1932 s Robert Webster Darden & Willie Oleta. BBA U of Texas 1959; GTS 1963. D 9/21/1963 P 3/1/1964 Bp Theodore H McCrea. m 6/15/1957 Helen Burrer. Rural D Dio Dallas Dallas TX 1967-1971; R Ch Of The Gd Shpd Brownwood TX 1966-1971; Vic Ch Of The Gd Shpd Dallas TX 1964-1966; Vic Ch Of The H Cross Burleson TX 1963-1964. JDARDEN@SDARDEN.NET

DARISME, Joseph Wilkie (Hai) Boite Postale 1309, Port-Au-Prince Haiti B Arcahaie HT 12/22/1943 s adopted Amila & Alvert Darisme. STB ETSC 1969. D 11/30/1968 Bp Charles Alfred Voegeli.

DARKO, Daniel Dodoo (WA) 1510 Erskine St, Takoma Park MD 20912 B Accra GH 5/13/1942 s Wallestine Godwin Dako & Paulina Dorothy. Cert U of Ibadan Ibadan NG 1965; Cert Ghana Inst of Mgmt & Publ Administrion Legon 1982; DipTh U of Ghana Sem Legon GH 1982; BA SUNY 1987; MA SUNY 1988. Trans 2/1/1987 as Priest Bp Paul Moore Jr. m 4/25/1970 Juliana E Nmai c 3. R S Monica's Epis Ch Washington DC 1992-2007; Asst All SS Ch Staten Island NY 1990-1991; UTO Grants Admin Epis Ch Cntr New York NY 1989-1992; R Hse Of Pryr Epis Ch Newark NJ 1987-1989; Cur The Ch of S Matt And S Tim New York NY 1986-1987. OHC 1980. Hon Cn and Commissary Dio Cape Coast Ghana W Afr 1994. dodoodarko@verizon.net

DARLING, Elizabeth Ann (WNC) 118 Clubwood Ct, Asheville NC 28803 B Ann Arbor MI 1/24/1954 d James Sands Darling & Mary Lee. MDiv McCormick TS 1982; MLS U Chi 1982; ThM Luth TS at Chicago 1985; CAS EDS 1992. D 10/8/1992 Bp William Walter Wiedrich P 6/5/1993 Bp Robert Hodges Johnson. m 12/15/2000 Edward Morgan Gardner. Assoc R & Int S Jas Ch Black Mtn NC 1999-2003; Assoc R S Mk's Ch Gastonia NC 1992-1999. badarling@charter.net

DARLING, Mary (Roch) 2704 Darnby Dr, Oakland CA 94611 B Corning NY 5/20/1964 d Arthur Perry Darling & Anne Elizabeth. BA Hav 1986; MBA NWU 1993; MDiv CDSP 1999. D 6/5/1999 Bp William George Burrill P 9/29/2000 Bp Jack Marston McKelvey. S Jn's Epis Ch Oakland CA 2001-2010. darlingmolly@gmail.com

DARROW, R(obert) Michael (Colo) 3275 S Pontiac St, Denver CO 80224 B Denver CO 5/22/1937 s Robert Irving Darrow & Alice M. Wms 1957; BA U Denv 1959; MDiv Nash 1962; Int Mnstry Prog 1998. D 6/18/1962 P 12/21/1962 Bp Joseph Summerville Minnis. chair Com on Mnstry Dio Milwaukee Milwaukee WI 1985-1995; R S Jas Ch W Bend WI 1980-1999; chair Com on Mnstry Dio Colorado Denver CO 1977-1980; R S Tim's Epis Ch Centennial CO 1967-1979; Reorgnztn Com Dio Nthrn Indiana So Bend IN 1965-1967; Vic S Ptr's Ch Rensselaer IN 1965-1967; Cur S Lk's Epis Ch Ft Collins CO 1962-1965. frd3275@comcast.net

DARVES-BORNOZ, Derek Yves (Ore) 525 E 68th St, NY New York 10065 **Assoc for Pstr Care and Ch Resrch The CPG New York NY 2011-** B Montreal Canada 3/29/1978 s Gilles Pierre-Albert Darves-Bornoz & Bonnie Jean. BA Reed Coll 2001; MS U of Oregon 2003; PhD U of Oregon 2006; MDiv The GTS 2009; Bd Cert Chapl Assn of Profsnl Chapl 2010. D 5/30/2009 Bp Sanford Zangwill Kaye Hampton P 12/4/2009 Bp Catherine Scimeca Roskam. m 10/20/2011 Phaedra Darves c 1. P Assoc The Ch Of The Epiph New York NY 2010-2011. Coauthor, "Corp Unity in Amer Trade Plcy: A Ntwk Analysis of Corp-Dyad Political Action," *Amer Journ of Sociol*, U Chi Press, 2011. ddarves@cpg.org

DASS, Stephen (CFla) PO Box 1962, Ocala FL 34478 **P-in-c Coventry Epis Ch Ocala FL 2009-** B Singapore 9/7/1968 s Francis Dass & Daisy. LTH Montreal Dioc Theol Coll 2004. Trans from Igreja Episcopal Anglicana do Brasil 5/1/2009 as Priest Bp John Wadsworth Howe. m 8/19/1995 Mary Partridge. fr.stephendass@gmail.com

DAUER-CARDASIS, Joade A (NY) 227 E 87th St Apt 1B, New York NY 10128 **R S Ptr's Ch Bronx NY 2008-** B New York NY 2/10/1947 d John Joseph Dauer & Adeline. BA Marymount Coll 1968; Iona Coll 1974; NYU 1976; MDiv Ya Berk 1990. D 6/9/1990 P 2/1/1991 Bp Arthur Edward Walmsley. m 10/17/1970 James J Cardasis c 4. Dio Long Island Garden City NY 2001-2002; S Ann And The H Trin Brooklyn NY 1999-2001; Dio Vermont Burlington VT 1997-1999; S Jn's In The Mountains Stowe VT 1994-1999; S Fran Ch Stamford CT 1990-1994. jamdc1@gmail.com

DAUGHERTY II, Charles Raymond Cotton (WA) 45020 Nolan Ct, Hollywood MD 20636 B Rapid City SD 10/5/1920 s Charles Raymond Cotton Daugherty & Laura May. BA GW 1944; MA GW 1949; STB EDS 1952; Fllshp Coll of Preachers 1960; S Aug's Coll Cbury GB 1963; STM STUSo 1967. D 6/14/1952 P 12/23/1952 Bp Angus Dun. m 3/2/1957 Mary Turner Wise c 3. R The Ch Of The Ascen Lexington Pk MD 1969-1986; BEC Dio Washington Washington DC 1957-1967; Vic The Ch Of The Ascen Lexington Pk MD 1952-1968; R S Andr's Ch Leonardtown California MD 1952-1964. Auth, *Heritage & Destiny of Epis Ch*, Self-Pub, 1994.

DAUGHERTY, William King (RG) 12836 Balez Dr, Frisco TX 75035 **Died 2/24/2010** B Denton TX 1/13/1931 s Bill Daugherty & Ruth Hazel. BBA U of Texas 1957; MBA Texas Tech U 1964; PhD U of Texas 1969; Prchr Lewis Sch Of Mnstry 1984; BA Sul Ross St U 1999. D 2/3/1986 P 10/21/1986 Bp Richard Mitchell Trelease Jr. Intl Ord Of S Lk The Physcn 1997. Phi Kappa Phi U Of Texas Austin TX 1966. wkd@wcc.net

DAUGHTRY, James Robert (RG) 205 Augusta Way, Melbourne FL 32940 B Roswell NM 11/12/1931 s Robert Edward Daughtry & Blaine Johnson. BS Geo 1954; STB GTS 1960. D 6/26/1960 Bp William Francis Moses P 12/29/1960 Bp Henry I Louttit. Asstg Cler S Mary's Epis Ch Albuquerque NM 1993-1994; Ch of the H Faith Santa Fe NM 1989-1991; S Paul's Par Washington DC 1974-1989; R S Paul's Rock Creek Washington DC 1974-1989; Ch Of The Resurr Tucson AZ 1963-1974; Cur S Phil's Ch Coral Gables FL 1960-1963. Hon Cn S Cyp the Mtyr Kusami Ghana 1983. jdaughtry@cfl.rr.com

DAUGHTRY, Susan Laurel (Va) 1325 Nottoway Ave, Apt. A, Richmond VA 23227 **Asst S Thos' Ch Richmond VA 2008-** B Waynesboro VA 8/11/1981 d Robert Purcell Daughtry & Judith Pettit. BA U of Virginia 2003; MDiv VTS 2006. D 6/24/2006 P 2/3/2007 Bp Peter James Lee. Stndg Com Dio Virginia Richmond VA 2007-2010; Assoc R Ch Of The H Comf Vienna VA 2006-2008. sldaughtry@gmail.com

DAUM, J(ohn) William (Los) 25662 Crestfield Cir, Castro Valley CA 94552 **Died 8/26/2010** B Tucson AZ 10/16/1925 s George Marion Daum & Anna Belle. BA U of Arizona; Fuller TS 1950; Med U of Arizona 1950; MDiv Denver Sem 1955; CDSP 1959. D 6/22/1959 P 2/16/1960 Bp Francis E I Bloy. c 3. thedaums@yahoo.com

DAUNT, Francis Thomas (La) 815 E Guenther St, San Antonio TX 78210 B Enniskeane County Cork IE 5/25/1945 s Albert Nelson Daunt & Hilda May. BA U So 1967; MDiv GTS 1970. D 6/11/1970 Bp (George) Paul Reeves P 3/24/1971 Bp Albert R Stuart. m 2/4/1995 Jane Bowles c 2. R S Mary's Ch Franklin LA 1994-2010; Stndg Com Dio Louisiana Baton Rouge LA 1992-1995; R S Jas Epis Ch Baton Rouge LA 1989-1993; R H Trin Par Decatur GA 1980-1989; R S Mk's Ch Brunswick GA 1975-1980; Vic Trin Ch Statesboro GA 1972-1975; Vic Trin Ch Cochran GA 1970-1972. ftdaunt@gmail.com

DAUPHIN, Joanne Coyle (Eur) 51 rue d'Amsterdam, Paris 75008 France **Ecum Off for France Convoc of Amer Ch in Europe Paris FR 2011-; Ecum Rep Convoc of Amer Ch in Europe Paris FR 2003-; D Convoc of Amer Ch in Europe Paris FR 1994-** B White Plains NY 3/31/1936 d Hugh Smith Coyle & Marie Fitzpatrick. BA Wellesley Coll 1957; MA Tufts U 1958; MA Tufts U 1959; PhD Tufts U 1963; CertificateofHigherE U of Wales, Bangor 2003. D 6/7/2003 Bp Pierre W Whalon. m 7/13/1963 Patrick Dauphin. j.dauphin@noos.fr

DAUTEL, Terrence Pickands (O) Po Box 62, Gates Mills OH 44040 **S Mart's Ch Chagrin Falls OH 2008-** B Cleveland OH 8/20/1943 s Charles Poe Dautel & Seville Jeanne. BA Kenyon Adelbert 1968; MA Wstrn Carolina U 1973; MA Wstrn Carolina U 1975; MDiv Bex 1978. D 3/4/1979 P 9/1/1980 Bp John Harris Burt. The Cluster Of Ch In Ne Oh Ashtabula OH 1997-1999; S Mart's Ch Chagrin Falls OH 1981-1983; S Hubert's Epis Ch Mentor OH 1980-1996; S Barth's Ch Mayfield Vill OH 1979-1980.

DAVENPORT, carrol kimsey (Mo) 17 Broadview, Kirksville MO 63501 **Assoc Trin Epis Ch Kirksville MO 2005-** B Norfolk VA 3/22/1959 d Aubrey Carrol Davenport & Mary Louise Sherman. BA Averett U 1981; MDiv Sthrn Bapt TS Louisville KY 1986. D 12/21/2005 P 6/29/2006 Bp George Wayne Smith. m 1/7/1984 William Michael Ashcraft c 2. davenport1959@yahoo.com

DAVENPORT, David Wendell (SVa) 6051 River Road Pt, Norfolk VA 23505 **R Ch Of The Ascen Norfolk VA 1997-** B Miami FL 4/6/1948 s Luther Marchant Davenport & Dorothye. BA Furman U 1970; MDiv VTS 1973. D 6/23/1973 Bp Milton LeGrand Wood P 4/1/1974 Bp Bennett Jones Sims. m 8/5/1988 Lillian Haynes c 2. Coordntr Yth Mnstrs Dio Sthrn Virginia Norfolk VA 1978-1986; Ch Of The Ascen Norfolk VA 1976-1991; Dio Sthrn Virginia Norfolk VA 1975-1986; Asst R Chr Ch Macon GA 1973-1975. dw1davenport@msn.com

DAVENPORT, Elizabeth Jayne Louise (Chi) 1413 Pine Woods Ct, University Park IL 60484 B Potters Bar Hertfordshire UK 10/30/1955 d Ian David Hill & Esme. BA Oxf 1977; MA Oxf 1981; DIT Nthrn Ord Course Manchester Gb 1982; ThM Fuller TS 1989; PhD USC 2003. Trans from Church Of England 1/1/1991 Bp Frederick Houk Borsch. m 6/22/2008 Anne Cecilia Benvenuti. Dio Los Angeles Los Angeles CA 1991-1993; Assoc St Johns Pro-Cathd Los Angeles CA 1991-1993; All SS Ch Pasadena CA 1991. ejld@uchicago.edu

DAVENPORT, Lane John (WA) 1217 Massachusetts Ave Nw, Washington DC 20005 **R Ch Of The Ascen And S Agnes Washington DC 1997-** B Greenbrae CA 8/3/1965 s Charles Davenport & Gail. BA U CA 1987; BA Oxf 1992; MA Oxf 1998. D 9/21/1993 P 3/26/1994 Bp Edward Harding MacBurney. m Amy Wilkins c 1. P-in-c Ch Of The Ascen And S Agnes Washington DC 1994-1996; Cur Ch Of The Ascen And S Agnes Washington DC 1993-1994.

DAVENPORT, Marcia Ellen McC (SwFla) 1606 Chickasaw Rd, Arnold MD 21012 B Detroit MI 5/27/1947 d Jay William McCormick & Elizabeth Mcneill. Antioch Coll 1967; BA Bloomfield Coll 1973; MA Montclair St U 1975; MS Loyola U 1984; MDiv VTS 1990; Cert Loyola U 1997. D 6/16/1990 P 1/30/1991 Bp A(lbert) Theodore Eastman. m 5/26/1995 Robert Davenport c 1. Chapl/Asst St Johns Epis Ch Tampa FL 2002-2009; Gr Ch Brunswick MD 2000-2002; St. Anne's Day Sch Annapolis MD 1999-2000; R S Paul's Ch Trappe MD 1996-1999; Int Trin Cathd Easton MD 1994-1995; Pstrl Assoc S Anne's Par Annapolis MD 1990-1994. Int Mnstry Ntwk 1996-2000. marciarev@aol.com

DAVENPORT, Robert Atkinson (SVa) 1509 N Shore Rd, Norfolk VA 23505 **R Ch Of The Gd Shpd Norfolk VA 2004-** B Salem MA 3/9/1951 s Stephen R Davenport & Susan. BA U So 1973; MDiv VTS 1985. D 9/15/1985 Bp David Reed P 4/1/1986 Bp A(rthur) Heath Light. m 1/3/2004 Elizabeth Davenport c 5. R Trin Ch Upperville VA 1993-2004; Assoc Trin Ch Upperville VA 1990-2004; Nelson Par Cluster Howardsville VA 1985-1989. robert@goodshepherdnorfolk.org

DAVENPORT III, Stephen Rintoul (WA) 4700 Whitehaven Pkwy Nw, Washington DC 20007 B Charlottesville VA 11/2/1942 s Stephen R Davenport & Susan. BA W&L 1964; MDiv VTS 1970. D 7/23/1970 P 7/1/1972 Bp Charles Gresham Marmion. m 8/13/1966 Tracy Ann Bruce. Assoc R S Pat's Ch Washington DC 1980-1993; S Jn's Ch Murray KY 1975-1980; The Untd Campus Mnstry Murray KY 1975-1980; Mssn Partnr Dio Haiti Ft Lauderdale FL 1970-2003. Rgnl Serv Awd Murray St U 1976.

DAVEY, Jan (RG) 639 Frederico Blvd, Belen NM 87002 **Vic S Phil's Ch Belen NM 2004-** B United Kingdom 3/19/1932 d Reginald Thurley & Mabel. NYU 1977; Dioc Trng 1982. D 1/8/1982 Bp Richard Mitchell Trelease Jr P 8/10/1982 Bp George R Selway. m 7/3/1954 George Davey William c 2. fr.jan@msn.com

DAVID, Charles Laskin (Mass) 6390 Sagewood Way, Delray Beach FL 33484 B Klamath Falls OR 1/21/1949 BA Goddard Coll 1979; MDiv EDS 2003. D 6/7/2003 P 6/5/2004 Bp M(arvil) Thomas Shaw III. S Jn's Chap Cambridge MA 2005; S Mary's Epis Ch Dorchester MA 2004-2005. tippidog@msn.com

DAVID, Christopher Leyshon (LI) PO Box 110, Salem NY 12865 B Llwyn-y-pia Glamorganshire GB 1/8/1947 s Stanley Leyshon David & Mary. Doctoral ABD NYU; BA NYU 1969; MDiv/STB GTS 1972. D 6/2/1972 P 12/9/1972 Bp Paul Moore Jr. m 4/29/1978 Kathleen Tuite c 3. Dn of Peconic Dio Long Island Garden City NY 2003-2010; R S Mk's Ch Westhampton Bch NY 2001-2011; Chairperson, The Migrant Mnstry Com Ecusa / Mssn Personl New York NY 1988-2002; R Ch Of The Gd Shpd Midland Pk NJ 1987-2001; Pres Mid Hudson Catskill Rural and Migrant Min Poughkeepsie NY 1980-1987; R S Jn's Epis Ch Kingston NY 1978-1987; Vic S Anne's Ch Washingtonville NY 1975-1978; Vic S Dav's Ch Highland Mills NY 1975-1978; Asst Min Gr Epis Ch New York NY 1972-1975. cldavid@aol.com

DAVID, Jacob Thandasseril (Nwk) 1 Paddock Court, Dayton NJ 08810 B Kottayam Kerala IN 1/22/1941 s Thandasseril Joseph David & Mariamma. BS U Kerala IN 1961; MDiv VTS 1984. Trans from Church of South India 5/1/1991 Bp John Shelby Spong. m 1/20/1972 Shanta Phillips. S Paul's And Resurr Ch Wood Ridge NJ 1991-2011. revjdavid@yahoo.com

DAVID, John Spencer (WMich) 4864 River Rd, Twin Lake MI 49457 **R Chr Epis Ch Charlevoix MI 2006-** B Aurora IL 1/20/1943 s John David & Blanche. BA DePauw U 1965; MDiv STUSo 1983. D 6/24/1983 P 1/1/1984 Bp William Hopkins Folwell. m 6/15/1968 Susan Lewis Carr c 4. R S Greg's Epis Ch Muskegon MI 1995-2005; S Ptr's By-The-Sea Sitka AK 1991-1994; R Ch Of The Redeem Ruston LA 1987-1991; R S Fran' Ch Norris TN 1984-1987; All SS Epis Ch Lakeland FL 1983-1984.

DAVID, Ronald (Los) 1225 Wilshire Blvd, Los Angeles CA 90017 **Chapl Gd Samar Hosp Los Angeles CA 2007-** B New York NY 9/29/1948 s Reginald David & Hentlyn Jeanette. BA SUNY 1971; MD SUNY 1975; MDiv VTS 2003. D 12/19/2005 P 7/15/2006 Bp Joseph Jon Bruno. m 12/30/2000 Deborah Springpeace c 3. rdavid@goodsam.org

DAVIDS, Peter Hugh (Pgh) Schloss Mittersill, Thalbach 1 Austria B Syracuse NY 11/22/1947 s Hugh Harold Davids & Doris Marie. BA Wheaton Coll 1968; MDiv TESM 1971; PhD U of Manchester 1974. D 6/9/1979 P 10/1/1979 Bp Robert Bracewell Appleyard. m 8/19/1967 Judith Lee Bouchillon. Auth, "Jas (Nibc 15)"; Auth, "First Epistle Of Ptr (Nicnt)". SBL, Snts.

DAVIDSON, Charles Alexander (Ct) PO Box 1921, Hartford CT 06144 **R S Monica's Ch Hartford CT 2007-; S Vinc's Epis Ch St Petersburg FL 2007-** B Mackenzie GY 1/31/1954 s Albert Oscar Davidson & Marjorie. BA Codrington Coll, Barbados 1977. Trans from Church in the Province Of The West Indies 2/1/1998 Bp Joe Morris Doss. m 6/22/1996 Maureen Grant. R S Vinc's Epis Ch St Petersburg FL 2003-2007; S Aug's Epis Ch Asbury Pk NJ 1997-2003; P-in-c All Souls Ch New York NY 1996-1997. AFP 1987. cadpriest@gmail.com

DAVIDSON, Donald Frederick (Kan) 1809 Sw Webster Ave, Topeka KS 66604 **R S Dav's Epis Ch Topeka KS 2004-** B Bellefontaine OH 10/1/1957 s George William Davidson & Thelma Jane. OH SU; BS Rio Grande Rio Grande OH 1981; MDiv SWTS 1984; DMin SWTS 1996. D 9/9/1984 Bp William Grant Black P 5/1/1985 Bp John Forsythe Ashby. m 5/20/2006 Marcella Gwaltney. St Thos The Apos Overland Pk KS 2003; US-A Pension Fund Mltry New York NY 2002-2003; R S Thos The Apos Ch Overland Pk KS 1997-2004; Vic S Lk's Ch Wymore NE 1992-1997; R Chr Ch Epis Beatrice NE 1989-1997; Vic Epis Ch Of The Incarn Salina KS 1988-1989; Chapl S Jn's Mltry Sch Salina KS 1984-1989. Ord of S Helena - Assoc 1984. The Bp's Cross Dio Kansas 2011. frdon@stdavidschurch.com

DAVIDSON, George Bell (Nwk) 209 Laurel Rd Apt 234, Voorhees NJ 08043 **Died 11/11/2009** B Bangalore Karnataka IN 4/26/1913 s Benjamin Davidson & Alice Annie Wemyss. OH SU 1934; U Tor 1946. Trans from Anglican Church of Canada 6/1/1948. c 2.

DAVIDSON, Jon Paul (Nev) PO Box 8822, Incline Village NV 89452 B Los Angeles CA 5/3/1935 s Paul Randolph Davidson & Celo Ellen. BA U CA 1959; MDiv CDSP 1962; MA U of Pennsylvania 1970. D 6/30/1962 Bp Charles F Hall P 6/5/1963 Bp George Richard Millard. m 6/27/1964 Elizabeth Simmons c 1. S Pat's Ch Incline Vill NV 1984-1986; Cur Gr Ch Manchester NH 1962-1964. Auth, "Living A Biblic Story," *TV (Video) Prog*, CDSP, 1986; Auth, "Introducing Students to the Natural Sciences," *TV (Broadcast & Video) Prog*, U.S.D.A. Forest Serv, 1985; Auth, "We Gather Together," *TV (Video) Prog*, The Epis Ch Gnrl Conv., 1982; Auth, "Your Leaders Are Listening," *TV (Video) Prog*, The Epis Ch (Hse of Bps), 1981; Auth, "Welcome to the Dio Nevada," *Website*, www.nvdiocese.org/profile, 1970. imagepro@concentric.net

DAVIDSON, Patricia Foote (Ct) 65 Parker Hill Road Ext, Killingworth CT 06419 **Assoc P S Ann's Epis Ch Old Lyme CT 1998-** B Brooklyn NY 10/30/

1929 d Merrill Newton Foote & Ruth Harriet. BA Mt Holyoke Coll 1951; MDiv GTS 1983. D 6/13/1983 Bp Robert Campbell Witcher Sr P 6/17/1984 Bp Arthur Edward Walmsley. m 4/7/1956 Robert Treat Hooker Davidson c 1. Int S Ann's Epis Ch Old Lyme CT 1991-1992; Int The Par Of Emm Ch Weston CT 1987-1988; Middlesex Area Cluster Mnstry Higganum CT 1983-1994; Asst Dio Connecticut Hartford CT 1983-1987. Auth, "Jewelry in the Brooklyn Museum," *The Brooklyn Museum*, 1984; Auth, "The Bastis Gold," *The Brooklyn Museum Annual*, 1967; Auth, "Gk Gold Jewelry from the Age of Alexander," Museum of Fine Arts, 1965. CPFD7@AOL.COM

D

DAVIDSON, Robert Michael (Pa) 22 E Chestnut Hill Ave, Philadelphia PA 19118 **Liturg Cmsn Dio Pennsylvania Philadelphia PA 2011-; D S Paul's Ch Philadelphia PA 2010-** B Philadelphia PA 8/14/1941 s William Maurice Davidson & Sarah Frye. BA Leh 1963; MDiv Luth Theol 2008. D 6/6/2009 Bp Edward Lewis Lee Jr. m 12/17/1966 Pamela Hermann c 4. Dioc Revs Bd Dio Pennsylvania Philadelphia PA 2010-2011; D Calv Epis Ch Nthrn Liberty Philadelphia PA 2009-2010; Chairman Stwdshp Com Dio Pennsylvania Philadelphia PA 1990-1993. rob@4suns.com

DAVIDSON, Susan La Mothe (La) 8216 Baylor Drive, Tyler TX 75703 **P-in-c All SS Ch Wolcott CT 2011-** B Buffalo NY 2/16/1942 d Theodore La Mothe & Helen Hazel. BA SUNY at Buffalo 1965; SMM UTS 1969; MDiv GTS 1994. D 8/15/1994 P 2/24/1995 Bp Larry Earl Maze. m 5/21/1969 Jerry Frank Davidson c 2. Dn, Jefferson Dnry Dio Louisiana Baton Rouge LA 2005-2008; R All SS Epis Ch River Ridge LA 1998-2008; Exec Coun Dio Arkansas Little Rock AR 1996-1998; Vic S Mich's Epis Ch Little Rock AR 1994-1998. AGO 1963-1992. motherdavidson@gmail.com

DAVIDSON, Thomas Walter (Az) 4015 E. Lincoln Drive, Paradise Valley AZ 85253 **Assoc Chr Ch Of The Ascen Paradise Vlly AZ 2008-** B Denver CO 6/10/1937 s Norris Dunbar Davidson & Ruth. BA Indiana U 1959. D 6/11/1994 Bp Robert Reed Shahan P 1/23/2005 Bp Kirk Stevan Smith. m 6/12/1999 Jacynth Wilson c 2. All SS Ch Phoenix AZ 2000-2007; Dio Arizona Phoenix AZ 1994-1996; Chair, Stwdshp Cmsn Dio Arizona Phoenix AZ 1968-1972. ESMA 1995-2005; NAAD 1996-2005. thomas.davidson@ccaaz.org

DAVIDSON, William Albert (Vt) 2260 County Route 12, Whitehall NY 12887 B Pittsburgh PA 12/2/1939 s William Albert Davidson & Ruth. BA U Pgh 1961; MDiv Nash 1964; Cert Inst for Advncd Supervision 1979. D 6/20/1964 P 12/21/1964 Bp James P De Wolfe. Trst Cathd Of St Jn The Div New York NY 1997-2000; Chair Jewish-Chr Comm. Dio New York New York City NY 1994-2002; Int Consult Dio New York New York City NY 1993-1997; R Chr Ch Riverdale Bronx NY 1985-2002; Prof The GTS New York NY 1976-1985; R Ch Of The Ascen Greenpoint Brooklyn NY 1966-1976; Cur S Paul's Ch-In-The-Vill Brooklyn NY 1964-1966. therevwad@aol.com

DAVIDSON-METHOT, David Glenn (Los) 1101 Nina Dr, Oxnard CA 93030 B Dearborn MI 9/11/1953 s Theodore F Davidson & Maxine H. BA Nthrn Arizona U 1975; MDiv CDSP 1979; PhD Pacifica Grad Inst Carpinteria CA 2000. D 6/17/1979 Bp Joseph Thomas Heistand P 12/21/1979 Bp William Edwin Swing. m 12/29/1988 Teresa Maria Greth c 2. All SS Epis Ch Oxnard CA 1999-2001; Com Dio Los Angeles Los Angeles CA 1992-1994; R S Patricks Ch And Day Sch Thousand Oaks CA 1990-1998; St Of The Ch Dio Nthrn California Sacramento CA 1988-1990; R Emm Epis Ch Grass Vlly CA 1983-1990; Int Epis Ch Of Our Sav Placerville CA 1982-1983; Cur S Paul's Epis Ch Walnut Creek CA 1979-1982. Auth, "An Early Amer Sampler: Being A Collection Of Early Amer Hymns For Use In Publ Wrshp," All SS Press. San Francisco, 1981; Auth, "Log Bldg In The San Francisco Peaks Area Of Nthrn Arizona," SW Folklore, 1979; Auth, "Calibrating The Compass," *Residential Treatment For Chld And Yth*. APA 1995. threed.doc@verizon.net

DAVIES, Ian E (Los) 7501 Hollywood Blvd, Los Angeles CA 90046 **S Thos The Apos Hollywood Los Angeles CA 2002-** B Merthyr Tydfil Wales 3/5/1964 BD U of Wales 1985; Post Grad Cert Theol U of Cambridge 1988. Trans from Church Of England 1/16/2002 as Priest Bp Joseph Jon Bruno. "Club" (for Theol Stds) Athenaeum, London 1998; British & European Societies for Philos of Rel 1987-2002; Mem of the Royal Inst of Philos 1985-2002; Soc for the Study of Theol 1986. frdavies@saintthomashollywood.org

DAVIES JR, Richard Wood (Pgh) 217 Allenberry Cir, Pittsburgh PA 15234 **Vic Old S Lk's Pittsburgh PA 1988-** B Pittsburgh PA 2/18/1927 s Richard Wood Davies & Hannah Jane. BA U Pgh 1952; MDiv VTS 1955; Med U Pgh 1972. D 6/25/1955 P 12/21/1955 Bp Austin Pardue. m 8/18/1951 Doris J Krebs c 2. Asst S Paul's Epis Ch Pittsburgh PA 1987-2010; Cn Dio Pittsburgh Monroeville PA 1983-1987; R S Ptr's Epis Ch Brentwood Pittsburgh PA 1957-1982; Min in charge S Paul's Ch Monongahela PA 1955-1957. Auth, "Hist of the Cong," *Rebellion & Revelation - The Hist of Old S Lk Ch*, 1996; Auth, "One act play," *A Burning Faith- The 1794 Whiskey Rebellion*, 1995. Canrichdavies@aol.com

DAVIES-ARYEEQUAYE, Eliza Ayorkor (NY) 23 Water Grant St. Apt. 9E, Yonkers NY 10701 **D S Martha's Ch Bronx NY 2008-** B Accra Ghana 8/11/1949 d Daniel Cofie Aryeequaye & Alice Adobea. B.A. U of Houston 1986; Non-Degree NY Dio Deaconate Trng 2005. D 5/14/2005 Bp Mark Sean Sisk. c 1. D S Paul's Ch Yonkers NY 2005-2008; Mem Bp's Com S Jas Epis Ch Fordham Bronx NY 1992-2002. New York AltGld 2009. edaviesprof@yahoo.com

DAVIES-JONES, Max L (NY) 26-Q Weed Hill Ave, Stamford CT 06907 B Bathurst GM 9/8/1931 s Max Leslie Jones & Mary Cecilia. DIT Codrington Coll 1958; Mirfield Coll Gb 1959; Cert Grassland New York Pstr Counslg 1974; Blanton-Peale Grad Inst 1977; MS Iona Coll 1984; MS Yeshiva U 1991. D 12/1/1958 Bp The Bishop Of Barbados. m 8/30/1969 Ina R Richarson. R S Simeon's Ch Bronx NY 1977-1980; Asst Gr Ch White Plains NY 1969-1970.

DAVILA, Mary B (Va) 117 Rivana Terr SW, Leesburg VA 20175 **S Jas' Epis Ch Leesburg VA 2005-; Trin Epis Ch Columbus GA 2005-** B Lexington NC 9/6/1976 d Donald W Fisher & Talmadge Russell. BA U Rich 1998; MDiv VTS 2005. D 6/18/2005 P 12/18/2005 Bp Peter James Lee. m 8/7/2004 Christopher Davila. Dir. Chld'S Mnstrs S Steph's Ch Richmond VA 1999-2002. MARY@STJAMESLEESBURG.ORG

DAVILA, Willie Rodriguez (SeFla) 1063 Haverhill Rd N, Haverhill FL 33417 **S Christophers Ch Haverhill FL 2010-** B San Antonio TX 6/3/1951 s Guadalupe Aguilar Davila & Reducinda. U of Texas; BS Trin U San Antonio TX 1977; MDiv Epis TS of The SW 1986. D 6/15/1986 Bp John Herbert MacNaughton P 1/1/1987 Bp Stanley Fillmore Hauser. m 12/29/1973 Teresita G Gonzales c 2. Vic The Ch Of The Recon Corpus Christi TX 1991-2010; Asst R Ch Of The Gd Shpd Corpus Christi TX 1987-1991; Dio W Texas San Antonio TX 1986-1991; Asst R S Mk's Ch San Marcos TX 1986-1987. Auth, "Moments Of Gr," *Ratherview*, Ets-Austin, 1987. wrdavila@infionline.net

DAVILA VASQUEZ, Jaime Alirio (EcuC) Cdla Primavera Mz-A-3, Villa 8, Duran Ecuador **P Iglesia de Jesus Obrero de Duran Primavera #1 Guayaquil EC 1992-; Litoral Dio Ecuador Guayaquil EQ EC 1988-** B Guayaquil EC 4/1/1948 s Luz Elena. Sete 1988. D 3/12/1988 Bp Adrian Delio Caceres-Villavicencio P 6/1/1992 Bp Martiniano Garcia-Montiel. m 11/30/1971 Lilian Virginia Plaza.

DAVINICH, George Davinich (Mich) 945 Palmer St, Plymouth MI 48170 **R Gr Epis Ch Southgate MI 2006-** B Detroit MI 7/14/1953 s Michael Davinich & Rachel. BS U MI 1994; MDiv SWTS 2004. D 12/20/2003 P 6/26/2004 Bp Wendell Nathaniel Gibbs Jr. m 2/1/1985 Mary Suzanne Leslie c 3. Asst R All SS Ch E Lansing MI 2004-2006. revdavinich@gmail.com

DAVIOU, Albert G (At) 432 Noelle Lane, Dahlonega GA 30533 **R S Eliz's Epis Ch Dahlonega GA 2007-** B Hackensack NJ 11/12/1948 s Albert Daviou & Evelyn. BA Calvin Coll 1972; MDiv SWTS 1984. D 6/11/1984 Bp Charles Ellsworth Bennison Jr P 12/21/1984 Bp Howard Samuel Meeks. m 12/29/1973 Patricia Prince c 2. The Ch Of The Gd Shpd Acton MA 2004-2005; Dio Atlanta Atlanta GA 1996; Ch Of The Annunc Marietta GA 1994-1996; Assoc S Mk's Ch Grand Rapids MI 1988-1993; S Jn's Ch Fremont MI 1984-1988; R S Mk's Ch Newaygo MI 1984-1988. agdaviou@windstream.net

DAVIS JR, Albin P (Los) 209 S. Detroit St., Los Angeles CA 90036 B Baltimore MD 5/11/1920 s Albin P Davis & Irene E. JD U of Maryland 1951; ETSBH 1963. D 9/5/1963 P 3/1/1964 Bp Francis E I Bloy. m 8/28/1943 Martha C Wilson c 3. Assoc S Jas Par Los Angeles CA 1988-2007. karenw@ix.netcom.com

DAVIS, Alice Downing (Va) P.O. Box 622, Luray VA 22835 B Richmond VA 11/27/1940 d John William Downing & Evelyn Jordan. BFA Richmond Profsnl Inst 1963; MDiv VTS 1984; DMin VTS 1993. D 1/6/1985 Bp Peter James Lee P 10/1/1985 Bp A(lbert) Theodore Eastman. m 10/12/1974 Joseph Claiborne Davis. Vic S Paul's Ch Shenandoah VA 2000-2003; Dio Virginia Richmond VA 2000-2001; Vic Chr Epis Ch Lucketts Leesburg VA 1995-1998; Vic Ch Of The Gd Shpd Bluemont VA 1987-1990; D S Paul's Epis Par Point Of Rocks MD 1985-1986. alice.davis10@gmail.com

DAVIS, Angus Kenneth (Pa) PO Box 329, Kimberton PA 19442 B Charleston SC 6/2/1948 s Kenneth Davis & Judith. BA Col 1971; MA U Of Delaware Newark 1973; MDiv GTS 1985; MA Tem 1990. D 6/15/1985 P 6/1/1986 Bp Lyman Cunningham Ogilby. m 6/23/1985 Tamara Rose Burk. The Epis Ch Of The Adv Kennett Sq PA 1998; Asst S Christophers Epis Ch Oxford PA 1995-1997; Vic S Geo S Barn Ch Philadelphia PA 1993-1995; Dio Pennsylvania Philadelphia PA 1990-1995; Asst to R The Ch Of The H Trin Rittenhouse Philadelphia PA 1986-1988; D-In-Trng Ch Of S Jn The Evang Philadelphia PA 1985-1986. Soc Of S Jn The Evang. akd3@earthlink.net

DAVIS, Ann Black (Va) PO Box 100, Gum Spring VA 23065 **R S Jas Epis Ch Louisa VA 2007-** B Spartanburg SC 11/1/1945 d Sam Orr Black & Nancy. BA Queens Coll 1968; MDiv STUSo 1988. D 6/11/1988 P 5/20/1989 Bp William Arthur Beckham. c 3. Asst R S Fran Ch Greenville SC 1989-1999. revabdavis@yahoo.com

DAVIS, Bancroft Gherardi (Pa) 809 Bryn Mawr Ave, Newtown Square PA 19073 B New York NY 10/15/1950 s Bancroft Gherardi Davis & Marguerite Pryce. PsyD Chestnut Hill Coll; BA Jn Hopkins U 1973; MLS Wesl 1984; MDiv Ya Berk 1991; MSW Virginia Commonwealth U 2001. D 6/13/1992 Bp Arthur Edward Walmsley P 6/20/1993 Bp Jeffery William Rowthorn. m 9/3/1977 Rebecca Davis c 2. Assoc R Ch Of The Redeem Bryn Mawr PA 2004-2007; P-in-c S Dunstans Ch Blue Bell PA 2001-2004; Virginia Epis Sch Lynchburg VA 1996-1999; Assoc R S Paul's Epis Ch Lynchburg VA

1993-1996; Chapl S Thos's Ch New Haven CT 1992-1993; S Thos's Day Sch New Haven CT 1992-1993; D S Tim's Ch Fairfield CT 1992-1993. gherardi3@comcast.net

DAVIS, Calvin Lee (SwFla) 725 Nokomis Ave S, Venice FL 34285 B Staunton VA 8/17/1939 s Reuben Frank Davis & Mary Janet. AA Palm Bch Jr Coll 1960; BS Jas Madison U 1962; MA Jas Madison U 1965; BD/MDiv Bex 1968. D 6/23/1968 Bp James Loughlin Duncan P 12/1/1968 Bp Albert Ervine Swift. m 6/26/1965 Sandra Sparks c 2. S Mk's Epis Ch Venice FL 1970-1990; Cur S Mary's Par Tampa FL 1968-1970. cdavis9626@aol.com

DAVIS, Catherine Ward (EC) St James Parish, 25 S 3rd St, Wilmington NC 28401 B Wilmington NC 3/5/1952 d Edward Lee Ward & Adelaide Scales. BA Duke 1974; MA U NC Wilmington 1999. D 6/3/2006 Bp Clifton Daniel III. m 10/11/1975 Michael C Davis c 2. kitty@stjamesp.org

DAVIS, Charles Lee (Ak) ST MATTHEW'S EPISCOPAL CHURCH, 1030 2ND AVE, FAIRBANKS AK 99701 B Anchorage AK 7/24/1940 s Edward V Davis & DeEtte C. LLB U of Idaho 1966. D 7/23/2006 P 6/28/2007 Bp Mark Lawrence Mac Donald. m 1/1/1963 Mary Margaret Walker c 1. cleedavis@acsalaska.net

DAVIS SR, Charles Meyer (USC) 232 Elstow Rd, Irmo SC 29206 **Assoc Trin Cathd Columbia SC 2009-; P S Ptr's Ch Great Falls SC 2002-** B Macon GA 2/18/1932 s James Cecil Davis & Hilda Gertrude. BS U GA 1958; MDiv STUSo 1973. D 6/25/1973 P 2/25/1974 Bp (George) Paul Reeves. c 2. P-in-c Epis Ch Of S Simon And S Jude Irmo SC 2004-2008; R S Jn's Epis Ch Congaree Hopkins SC 1994-2001; R S Mths Epis Ch Toccoa GA 1988-1992; Mikell C&C Toccoa GA 1979-1987; Georgia Epis Conf Cntr At H Waverly GA 1976-1979; Vic H Cross Ch Thomson GA 1973-1976; Vic Trin Ch Harlem Augusta GA 1973-1976. frcharles2@yahoo.com

DAVIS JR, Charles Meyer (USC) 3709 Greenbriar Dr, Columbia SC 29206 **Trin Cathd Columbia SC 2001-** B Decatur GA 10/19/1955 s Charles Meyer Davis & Wilmarose. BA Valdosta St U 1979; MDiv GTS 1985. D 6/8/1985 P 5/31/1986 Bp Charles Judson Child Jr. m 12/28/1985 Alicia P Portwood c 2. S Chris's Ch Spartanburg SC 1997-2001; R S Jn's Epis Ch Ocean Sprg MS 1993-1996; R S Simon's Epis Ch Conyers GA 1989-1993; Asst S Thad Epis Ch Aiken SC 1986-1989; Asst S Mk's Ch Dalton GA 1985-1986. davis@trinitysc.org

DAVIS, Charlotte Murray (NC) 3120 Sunnybrook Dr, Charlotte NC 28210 B Huntington NY 11/29/1946 d Andrew Hawirt Murray & Alice Cecelia. BA Mt Holyoke Coll 1969. D 5/31/1992 Bp Robert Whitridge Estill. m 9/20/1969 John Macnutt Davis.

DAVIS, Clifford Bruce (Kan) No address on file. **D S Thos The Apos Ch Overland Pk KS 2000-** B Edina MO 7/20/1957 s Bert Clifford Davis & Fonda Lorene. BTh Hannibal-Lagrange Coll 1979; MDiv SW Bapt TS 1981; DD Midwest TS Kansas City MO 1988. D 10/19/1998 Bp William Edward Smalley. m 8/19/1978 Terri Lynn Cusimano. Auth, "Working Grief". cliff_davis_az@msn.com

DAVIS, David Joseph (EC) 208 Country Club Dr., Shallotte NC 28470 **R S Jas The Fisherman Epis Ch Shallotte NC 2004-** B New York NY 8/1/1951 s David J Davis & Marilyn Florence. BA VMI 1973; Command and Gnrl Stff Coll 1986; MBA Webster U 1988; Cert Dio EC Diac Trng Sch 1996; MDiv STUSo 2004. D 4/26/1997 Bp Brice Sidney Sanders P 7/19/2004 Bp Clifton Daniel III. m 12/29/1972 Patricia Jean Vandergrift c 2. D H Trin Epis Ch Fayetteville NC 1997-2001. BroSA 1991; OSL 1994. fatherdave@stjamesthefisherman.net

DAVIS, Donald Henry Kortright (WA) 11414 Woodson Ave, Kensington MD 20895 **R Ch Of The H Comf Washington DC 1987-** B 8/24/1941 s Cecil H Davis & Florence Edna. BD Codrington Coll 1965; MA U of The W Indies 1976; PhD U of Sussex 1979. Rec 11/1/1986 as Priest Bp John Thomas Walker. m 1/18/1967 Joan Thompson c 3. Auth, "Mssn For Caribbean Change"; Auth, "Emancipation Still Comin". Arcic Ii, Uspg.

DAVIS, Doyal (Okla) P.O. Box 1905, Shawnee OK 74802 B Midlothian OK 7/21/1940 s William Otis Davis & Grace Mae. MA U of Hawaii; BA U of Hawaii. D 6/20/2009 Bp Edward Joseph Konieczny. layod@sbcglobal.net

DAVIS III, Edward Braxton (SC) 1272 Winchester Dr, Charleston SC 29407 **D S Andr's Mssn Charleston SC 2009-** B Dinwiddie County VA 1/6/1938 s Edward Braxton Davis & Edith Virginia. BA VMI 1960; PhD U of Virginia 1970. D 9/10/2005 Bp Edward Lloyd Salmon Jr. m 6/15/1963 Sheila Mcclarren Davis c 2. D Cathd Of S Lk And S Paul Charleston SC 2005-2009. davis1106@bellsouth.net

DAVIS, Emily Hillquist (Mo) 9441 Engel Ln, St. Louis MO 63132 **Asst S Mart's Ch Ellisville MO 2011-; Vic S Thos Ch For The Deaf St Louis MO 2011-** B Richmond VA 7/6/1967 d David K Hillquist & Catherine Rinker. BA Indiana U 1989; MA Washington U 1992; PhD Washington U 2002; MDiv Eden TS 2007. D 12/20/2006 P 6/29/2007 Bp George Wayne Smith. m 12/29/1990 Warren Davis c 3. Cur Gr Ch Kirkwood MO 2007-2011. revemilyhd@gmail.com

DAVIS, Fred Richard (Mo) 9345 Ewers Dr, Saint Louis MO 63126 B Trenton MO 8/29/1935 s Muriel Orville Davis & Thelma Alberta. BA TCU; Ya Berk 1961; Cert U of Missouri 1993. D 6/20/1961 P 12/1/1961 Bp Charles A Mason. m 2/14/1993 Diane Dewey c 5. Ch Of The Adv S Louis MO 1978-1991; R S Chris's Ch And Sch Ft Worth TX 1965-1977; Cur All SS' Epis Ch Ft Worth TX 1962-1965; Vic All SS Ch Atlanta TX 1961-1962; Vic S Chas The Mtyr DAINGERFIELD TX 1961-1962. freddavis829@yahoo.com

DAVIS, Gail E (Kan) 3259, Walnut Hill Dr, San Angelo TX 76904 **Emm Epis Ch San Angelo TX 2011-** B Saint Louis MO 12/28/1945 d William Davis & Mary. BFA U of Kansas 1970; BA U of Kansas 1978; MS Nova SE U 1990; MDiv Epis TS of The SW 2001. D 3/17/2001 P 10/27/2001 Bp William Edward Smalley. m 11/16/1996 Jeffrey B Stephens c 2. Trst Dio Kansas Topeka KS 2008-2011; Gr Epis Ch Ottawa KS 2007-2010; Trst Epis TS Of The SW Austin TX 2004-2008; S Fran Cmnty Serv Inc. Salina KS 2001-2007. Fllshp of SSJE 1996. evensongs@gmail.com

DAVIS, Gena Lynn (Tex) 5010 N Main St, Baytown TX 77521 **Vic Gr Epis Ch Houston TX 2011-** B Kingsville TX 7/25/1963 d Richard Allan Lassmann & Margie. BBA U of Houston 1985; MBA U of Texas 1990; MDiv Epis TS Of The SW 2009. D 6/20/2009 P 1/10/2010 Bp C(harles) Andrew Doyle. m 2/22/1999 Gary Richard Davis c 1. Cur Trin Epis Ch Baytown TX 2009-2011. genaldavis@yahoo.com

DAVIS, George Miller (NI) 1921 NW O'Brien Rd., Lee's Summit MO 64081 B Broken Bow OK 1/14/1925 s Miller Abbot Davis & Johnnie Bird. BS U of No Texas 1949; Med U of No Texas 1955; SS GTS 1959. D 9/5/1959 P 3/20/1960 Bp J(ohn) Joseph Meakins Harte. m 6/22/1991 Mary Davis c 4. R S Andr Epis Ch Kokomo IN 1973-1991; Asst Trin Ch Ft Wayne IN 1967-1973; Vic S Laurence Epis Ch Grapevine TX 1959-1960; Vic S Mk's Ch Arlington TX 1959-1960. droamers@aol.com

DAVIS, Gordon Bell (Va) 1410 Runnymede Rd, Norfolk VA 23505 **Par Assoc Chr and S Lk's Epis Ch Norfolk VA 1992-** B Beaufort NC 1/3/1926 s Clarence Leslie Davis & Claudia. BS E Carolina U 1948; VTS 1954; S Aug's Coll Cbury Gb 1965. D 6/4/1954 P 6/1/1955 Bp George P Gunn. m 2/16/1963 Virginia Ritchie. Chr Epis Ch Gordonsville VA 1971-1989; Assoc All SS Ch Richmond VA 1965-1971; R Gr Ch Yorktown Yorktown VA 1957-1964; D S Jn's Ch Chester VA 1954-1957. Who'S Who Rel; Stdt/P Awd Amer Com 64-65 S Aug Coll Engl. va1967@msn.com

DAVIS, Holly Ann (NwPa) PO Box 550, Franklin PA 16323 **R S Jn's Ch Franklin PA 2008-** B Norfolk VA 11/18/1967 d Peter Allen Davis. BA Transylvania U 1989; MDiv VTS 2008. D 1/24/2008 Bp Stacy F Sauls P 10/18/2008 Bp Sean Walter Rowe. therevhadavis@gmail.com

DAVIS, James Howard (Ida) 4705 Savannah Ln., Boise ID 83714 B Saint Louis MO 2/27/1928 s Robert Willis Davis & Lee Zimrude. BSME U of Nevada at Reno 1951; MDiv CDSP 1954. D 7/29/1954 P 2/9/1955 Bp William F Lewis. c 2. S Gabr's Epis Ch Philadelphia PA 1986-1989; No Par Epis Ch Frackville PA 1984-1985; Trin Ch Newtown CT 1982-1984; S Steph's Boise ID 1963-1989; R S Mary's Ch Emmett ID 1956-1962; Cur Trin Epis Ch Reno NV 1954-1956. jdavisprst@cableone.net

DAVIS, James Lloyd (Mil) 6617 Romford Ct, Johnston IA 50131 B Wilkes-Barre PA 7/31/1951 s William John Davis & Hannah. PhD Candidate U of Wisconsin; BA Wilkes Coll 1976; MDiv Bex 1981; DMin Estrn Bapt TS 1989. D 6/13/1981 P 3/17/1982 Bp Lloyd Edward Gressle. m 6/2/1978 Mary Paul c 1. Dio Iowa Des Moines IA 2003-2006; S Andr's Ch Madison WI 1989-1996; S Gabr's Epis Ch Philadelphia PA 1985-1989; No Par Epis Ch Frackville PA 1984-1985; Trin Ch Newtown CT 1982-1984; Ch Of The Epiph Glenburn Clarks Summit PA 1981-1982. Auth, "Boundaries: The Pstr'S Role," *Integration*. jim.davis6617@yahoo.com

DAVIS, John Bartley (ND) 7940 45r Street Southeast, Jamestown ND 58401 **Assoc Gr Epis Ch Jamestown ND 1996-** B Aberdeen SD 11/3/1948 s Edwin Davis & Mary Elizabeth. BS No Dakota St U 1974. D 12/1/1995 P 10/1/1996 Bp Andrew Hedtler Fairfield. m 6/25/1977 Katherine Marion McElroy.

DAVIS JR, Johnnie Manly (USC) PO Box 2959, West Columbia SC 29171 **Dioc Exec Coun Dio Upper So Carolina Columbia SC 2011-; Chapl So Carolina Epis Hm At Still Hopes W Columbia SC 2009-** B Hartsville SC 11/25/1944 s Johnie Manly Davis & Lucy Lee. U of So Carolina 1969; BS Fran Marion U 1972; MDiv SE Bapt TS Wake Forest NC 1976; CAS STUSo 1997. D 6/1/1997 P 12/1/1997 Bp Edward Lloyd Salmon Jr. m 5/15/1965 Carol P Puleo c 1. Vic And P-in-c Epis Ch Of The H Trin Ridgeland SC 1997-2009. OHC - Assoc 1988. frharley@earthlink.net

DAVIS, John Rogers (Los) 640 Alta Vista #314, Santa Fe NM 87501 **Died 12/8/2009** B Hollywood CA 4/10/1925 s Elias Davis & Elisabeth. MA Stan 1948; BD EDS 1952. D 7/27/1952 P 3/1/1953 Bp Donald J Campbell. c 4. jrogersdavis@cybermesa.com

DAVIS, John William Sutphin (NC) 300 N Ridge Rd, Apt 68, RICHMOND VA 23229 B Henderson NC 6/17/1923 s Robert Green Davis & Mary Campbell. BS U NC 1947; BD, M Div VTS 1955. D 6/18/1955 Bp Richard Henry Baker P 12/21/1955 Bp Edwin A Penick. m 5/12/1945 Sarah Dawson c 2. Ch Of The Gd Shpd Rocky Mt NC 1991; The Ch Of The H Innoc Henderson NC 1975-1980. john.davis@mma1.com

DAVIS, Jon (CFla) 1412 Palomino Way, Oviedo FL 32765 **Cbury Retreat And Conf Cntr Oviedo FL 2009-; Vic Ch of the Incarn Oviedo FL 2006-** B Fort McPherson GA 9/4/1959 s Millard Quillian Davis & June Lucille. BA Berry Coll 1982; MDiv Reformed TS 2000; TESM 2000. D 3/3/2001 P 10/20/2001 Bp John Wadsworth Howe. m 12/27/1991 Beth B Broadus. All SS Ch Of Winter Pk Winter Pk FL 2003-2006; Dio Cntrl Florida Orlando FL 2001-2003; Cn for Yth Mnstry Dio Cntrl Florida Orlando FL 1991-2003. jon@incarnationoviedo.com

D

DAVIS, Joseph Norman (Tenn) 8215 Planters Grove Dr, Cordova TN 38018 **The Epis Ch Of The Resurr Franklin TN 2007-** B Nashville TN 4/10/1957 s Maclin Paschall Davis & Dorothy. BA U So 1979; W&L 1980; MDiv Nash 1986. D 6/21/1986 Bp George Lazenby Reynolds Jr P 1/1/1987 Bp Donis Dean Patterson. m 5/26/1984 Cynthia H Hill c 2. R S Phil Ch Bartlett TN 1994-2007; Assoc R S Jn's Epis Ch Memphis TN 1990-1994; R Ch Of The H Sprt Graham TX 1988-1990; Vic S Ptr By The Lake Graford TX 1988-1990; Yth Min Ch Of The Incarn Dallas TX 1986-1988. fatherjoe4@comcast.net

DAVIS, Judith Anne (Mass) 671 Route 28, Harwich Port MA 02646 **R Chr Ch Epis Harwich Port MA 2008-** B Henderson NC 5/25/1947 d Herbert Archie Davis & Estelle. BS High Point U 1969; PhD U Of Florida 1980; Ds Duke 1989; MDiv Ya Berk 1991; STM Yale DS 1995. D 6/22/1991 Bp Huntington Williams Jr P 6/27/1992 Bp George Nelson Hunt III. m 12/30/1995 Anne Elizabeth Gilson c 1. Chair of Cmsn on Liturg Dio Washington Washington DC 1998-2006; R Chr Ch Capitol Hill Washington DC 1996-2008; Trst and Secy of Bd Trst Ya Berk New Haven CT 1994-2008; Dioc Coun Dio Rhode Island Providence RI 1992-1996; Asst S Mich's Ch Bristol RI 1992-1996; D Ch Of S Jas The Apos New Haven CT 1991-1992; Cur S Jas' Ch New Haven CT 1991-1992; Chapl S Thos's Day Sch New Haven CT 1991-1992. Contrib, "two chapters," *Visio Divina: A Rdr in Faith and Visual Arts*, LeaderResources, 2009. Christians in the Visual Arts 2000; Epis Ch and the Visual Arts -artist Mem 1996. Phi Kappa Phi U of Florida 1977. motherjude@comcast.net

DAVIS, Judith Anne (Chi) 1534 Clear Dr, Bolingbrook IL 60490 **D Ch Of S Ben Bolingbrook IL 2001-** B Chicago IL 2/23/1937 d Charles Robert Swinehart & Phebe (sic) Catherine. BS U IL 1958; Cert Chicago Sch Of Diac Mnstry Chicago IL 1989. D 12/2/1989 Bp Frank Tracy Griswold III. D S Hilary's Ch Prospect Hts IL 1989-2000. Auth, "Pstr Care Of The Mentally Ill; A Handbook For Pastors," Universal Pub, 2000. NAAD; Ord Julian Of Norwich. dnjadavis@aol.com

DAVIS, Leverett B (Me) 35 Schooner St Apt 113, Damariscotta ME 04543 B Hartford CT 4/3/1914 s John Henry Kelso Davis & Edith Hollister. BA Wms 1936; BD/MDiv VTS 1942; EdM Harv 1964. D 8/10/1942 Bp Frederick G Budlong P 12/7/1942 Bp Walter H Gray. R Chr Ch Exeter NH 1944-1951; Cur S Jn's Epis Par Waterbury CT 1942-1944. Ch Soc for Coll Week.

DAVIS, M(alcolm) (Oly) 4490 Smugglers Cove Rd, Freeland WA 98249 B Cleveland OH 9/20/1935 s Kenneth Culp Davis & Carol Margaret. BA Harv 1958; MDiv CDSP 1961. D 6/12/1961 P 12/16/1961 Bp Sumner Walters. m 8/15/1959 Jane Elizabeth Nilan c 4. Dio Olympia Seattle WA 1998-2000; R S Thos Ch Medina WA 1989-2000; Chair Dvlpmt Com Dio Olympia Seattle WA 1989-1993; R & Headmaster S Patricks Ch And Day Sch Thousand Oaks CA 1984-1989; S Anselm Of Cbury Par Garden Grove CA 1978-1984; R S Columba Ch Fresno CA 1969-1978; R S Jn's Par Porterville CA 1964-1968; Vic Chr Ch Lemoore CA 1961-1964. Auth, *How to Resettle a Refugee Fam*; Auth, *Of Foxes & Birds & s Man*. OHC 1962. davises@whidbey.com

DAVIS, Mary Alice (Okla) 3200 Shady Brook Rd, Woodward OK 73801 **Dio Oklahoma Oklahoma City OK 1996-; Vic S Jn's Epis Ch Woodward OK 1996-** B Berwyn IL 1/25/1953 d Chester Davis & Mabel. BD U MN 1980; MDiv SWTS 1992. D 6/24/1992 P 3/6/1993 Bp Robert Marshall Anderson. m 9/6/1998 Mac Benbrook. Int S Bede's Ch Cleveland OK 1994-1996. revmaryd@sbcglobal.net

DAVIS, Mary Elizabeth (Nwk) 31 Woodland Ave, Summit NJ 07901 **S Paul's Epis Ch Chatham NJ 2011-; Asst R Calv Epis Ch Summit NJ 2010-** B Ashland KY 6/6/1966 d Stephen Ernest Berger & Elizabeth Crawford. BA U So 1988; MA Col Tchr's Coll 1992; MDiv Drew U TS 2009. D 6/5/2010 P 12/11/2010 Bp Mark M Beckwith. m 6/18/1988 Walter J Davis c 3. davisteam@comcast.net

DAVIS, Matthew Steven (EpisSanJ) 1710 Verde St, Bakersfield CA 93304 B Gardena CA 10/11/1951 s William Davis & Christine. BA California St U 1973; Theol TS 1983; MA U Of Greece 1983; TS, Fresno 2005. Rec from Greek Orthodox 5/21/2006 Bp John-David Mercer Schofield. m 9/10/1998 562-66-1693 Hathaway-Lucas. S Mk's Ch Shafter CA 2006-2008. christinehiswife@msn.com

DAVIS, Michael McKean (WTex) 8401 Kearsarge Dr, Austin TX 78745 B Chicago IL 5/10/1938 s David M Davis & Margaret W. BA Ken 1960; MDiv CDSP 1966; MA U of Texas 1974. D 7/14/1966 Bp Everett H Jones P 1/25/1967 Bp Richard Earl Dicus. m 12/27/2008 Patricia Ann Rose. S Andr's Ch Brackettville TX 1998; S Mich's Ch Sandia TX 1997-1998; Texas Mltry Inst San Antonio TX 1992-1994; S Geo Ch San Antonio TX 1991; S Matt's Epis Ch Universal City TX 1988-1990; S Matt's Epis Ch Kenedy TX 1987-1989; S Steph's Ch Goliad TX 1987-1988; R All SS Epis Ch San Benito TX 1983-1987; Trin Ch Marshall TX 1982-1983; Trin Epis Sch Marshall TX 1979-1983; Asst Ch Of The Ascen Houston TX 1976-1979; Asst Ch Of The Epiph Kingsville TX 1966-1968. mmdavis09@att.net

DAVIS, Milbrew (WTex) 338 Hub Ave, San Antonio TX 78220 B La Grange TX 11/4/1930 s George W Davis & Victoria. BA Prairie View A&M U 1952; MS Our Lady of the Lake U San Antonio TX 1960; MDiv Epis TS of The SW 1970; DMin SFTS 1985. D 6/2/1970 Bp Harold Cornelius Gosnell P 12/1/1970 Bp Richard Earl Dicus. m 7/25/1953 Shirley M Fears c 3. S Phil's Ch San Antonio TX 1975-1997; D S Thos And S Mart's Ch Corpus Christi TX 1970-1972. Auth, *Hist of S Phil's Epis Ch San Antonio TX 1895-1985*, 1985. Coll of Chapl 1973; Natl Assn of Soc Wk 1960; Phi Beta Sigma Fraternity, Inc. 1952. MDavis002@satx.rr.com

DAVIS, Molly Boscher (CFla) 251 E Lake Brantley Dr, Longwood FL 32779 **Chapl Sweetwater Epis Acad Longwood FL 2008-** B Lansing Michigan 7/18/1975 d David Bruce Bosscher & Mary Slotman. BA U of Virginia 2003; MDiv The U So (Sewanee) 2008. D 5/24/2008 Bp Peter James Lee P 12/10/2008 Bp John Wadsworth Howe. m 3/9/1996 Creston Davis c 2. davis.molly@gmail.com

DAVIS, Orion Woods (Nwk) 2 Pasadena St, Canton NC 28716 B Aiken SC 3/20/1943 s Orion Woods Davis & Ruth. BA Clemson U 1965; MDiv STUSo 1968. D 6/23/1968 P 5/15/1969 Bp John Adams Pinckney. m 9/3/1966 Pamela N Newberry c 2. R S Mary's Ch Sparta NJ 2004-2011; R S Jas Ch Upper Montclair NJ 1994-2004; R Ch Of The Epiph Allendale NJ 1989-1994; R S Elis's Epis Ch Memphis TN 1982-1989; R S Steph's Ch Pearl River NY 1976-1982; R Chr Ch Red Hook NY 1971-1976; Asst Gr Epis Ch Nyack NY 1969-1971; Asst Ch Of The Resurr Greenwood SC 1968-1969. frorion@charter.net

DAVIS, Patricia Rhoads (SVa) 1109 Pickwick Rd, Virginia Beach VA 23455 **D Chr and S Lk's Epis Ch Norfolk VA 2009-** B Macon GA 9/29/1948 d Walter Daniel Rhoads & Genevieve June. BA Roa 1970; Cert EFM 1992; Cert Virginia Inst. for Sprtl Dir. Smithfield VA 1995; D Formation Prog, NC 1999. D 6/19/1999 Bp David Conner Bane Jr. m 7/10/1971 Rodney Michael Davis c 2. D, Int Galilee Epis Ch Virginia Bch VA 2008-2009; D The Epis Ch Of The Adv Norfolk VA 2003-2007; Archd Dio Sthrn Virginia Norfolk VA 2002-2008; D S Paul's Ch Norfolk VA 1999-2003. Co-Auth, "Searching the Heart of God," Greene Tree Press, 2003; Auth, "Reflections of Jesus," *Prisms of the Soul*, Morehouse Pub, 1996. Alzheimers Assn 1999-2001; Dio SVa Cmsn on Aging 1999-2001; NAAD 1999; Sthrn Virginia Epis Cler Assn 2000. Jn Hines Preaching Awd VTS 2006.

DAVIS, Philip Arthur (SwFla) 1603 52nd St W, Bradenton FL 34209 B Salem MA 7/1/1935 s Chester R Davis & Esther A. BS NEU 1958; BA NEU 1958. D 6/14/1997 Bp Rogers Sanders Harris. m 6/10/1969 Janet E Halverson.

DAVIS, Rodney (NCal) 2140 Mission Ave., Carmichael CA 95608 **Trst CDSP Berkeley CA 2010-; Chair, Const & Cn Com Dio Nthrn California Sacramento CA 2010-; Assoc for Adult Sprtl Formation S Mich's Epis Ch Carmichael CA 2009-** B Sacramento CA 2/14/1949 s Lester Thomas Davis & Pauline Lillian. BA UC Davis 1971; JD UC Hastings Coll of Law 1974; MPA USC 1979; MDIV CDSP 2009. D 6/13/2009 P 1/9/2010 Bp Barry Leigh Beisner. m 8/10/1974 Susan Baxter c 2. roddavis@winfirst.com

DAVIS, Ronald (Fla) PO Box 13872, Tallahassee FL 32317 B 5/11/1938 D 6/24/1965 P 3/30/1966 Bp Edward Hamilton West. m 8/15/1964 Jean P Peyton. Ch Of The Adv Tallahassee FL 1988-1993; All SS Epis Ch Lakeland FL 1979-1988; S Chris's Ch Pensacola FL 1975-1978. RONALDDAVIS1@JUNO.COM

DAVIS, Ronald Lee (SeFla) 140 S.E. 28Th Ave, Pompano Beach FL **S Andr's Epis Ch Of Hollywood Dania Bch FL 2010-** B Abingdon VA 12/16/1969 s Ronald Lee Davis & Suzane. BB Amer Intl 2004; MDiv Bex 2009. D 12/27/2008 P 6/27/2009 Bp Leopold Frade. leedavis1416@bellsouth.net

DAVIS, Thomas Anthony (Spr) 5063 Cartter Rd, Kell IL 62853 B New York NY 5/8/1939 s Thomas Lincoln Davis & Roxanna Saunders. AS Kaskaskia Coll 1984; BS Sthrn Illinois U 1986; MS Sthrn Illinois U 1999. D 10/23/1998 P 6/8/2003 Bp Peter Hess Beckwith. m 8/19/1978 Karen Burton c 2. Vic S Thos Ch Salem IL 2002-2010. NAAD. tomdedcn@yahoo.com

DAVIS JR, Thomas Clark (USC) 102 Carteret Court, Clemson SC 29631 B Forty-Fort PA 8/21/1929 s Thomas Clark Davis & Frances Harrison. BA Brothers 1951; MDiv Drew U 1954. D 12/17/1957 P 6/17/1958 Bp Frederick J Warnecke. c 4. Int S Jas Epis Ch Greenville SC 2007-2008; Int S Fran Ch Greenville SC 2001-2002; Int Gr Epis Ch Anderson SC 1998-1999; Int Ch Of The Resurr Greenwood SC 1996-1997; R H Trin Par Epis Clemson SC 1970-1995; Asst S Steph's Epis Ch Wilkes Barre PA 1957-1958. tomdavis2@bellsouth.net

DAVIS, Thomas Preston (USC) 30 Lyme Bay Road, Columbia SC 29210 B South Bend IN 8/22/1945 s Daniel L Davis & Mary B. MDiv UTS; BS U Cinc. D 9/10/1972 Bp Frederick Warren Putnam P 3/1/1973 Bp John Mc Gill Krumm. m 12/17/1966 Judith Baston. Ccn.

DAVIS, Vicki (Ct) 543 Old Mill Rd, Fairfield CT 06824 B Highland IL 9/18/1954 d Thomas Joseph Knebel & Mary Louise. BA U of Missouri 1976; JD Col 1981; MDiv Ya Berk 1999. D 6/9/2001 P 5/25/2002 Bp Andrew Donnan Smith. c 3. Cur S Mk's Ch New Canaan CT 2002-2007; Asst Chr Ch Stratford CT 1999-2001. davis-vicki@sbcglobal.net

DAVIS, West Richard (Oly) 790 Smugglers Cove Rd, Friday Harbor WA 98250 B Minneapolis MN 12/15/1936 s West Cowan Davis & Evelyn. BA San Jose St U 1961; MDiv EDS 1965; Cert SWTS 2005. D 12/18/1965 P 7/1/1966 Bp James Albert Pike. m 5/2/1970 M Suzanne Taylor. R S Dav's Epis Ch Friday Harbor WA 1993-2001; R S Andr's Epis Ch Tacoma WA 1978-1993; R S Edw The Confessor Epis Ch San Jose CA 1969-1971; Assoc S Andr's Ch Saratoga CA 1965-1969. westerly@rockisland.com

DAVIS III, Zabron A (WTenn) 2225 Jefferson Ave, Memphis TN 38104 **Cn Dio W Tennessee Memphis TN 2010-** B Little Rock AR 9/4/1947 s Z A Davis & Mary Elizabeth. BS Mississippi Coll 1969; JD U of Mississippi 1975; MDiv SWTS 1990. D 5/12/1990 P 12/5/1990 Bp Duncan Montgomery Gray Jr. m 5/26/1973 Cathleen Coers c 2. Dio Atlanta Atlanta GA 2010; Vic St Ben's Epis Ch Smyrna GA 2009-2010; R Trin Ch Natchez MS 1997-2009; Vic H Innoc' Epis Ch Como MS 1992-1997; Vic Ch Of The Redeem Greenville MS 1990-1992; Cur S Jas Ch Greenville MS 1990-1992. cdavis@episwtn.org

DAVIS-HELLER, Lisa Ann (WVa) 266 Paw Paw Ln, Saint Marys WV 26170 **Ohio Vlly Epis Cluster Williamstown WV 2002-** B 12/20/1957 D 9/20/2001 Bp C(laude) Charles Vache P 6/8/2002 Bp William Michie Klusmeyer. m 4/5/1986 Richard Charles Heller c 2. ladh@frontiernet.net

DAVIS-LAWSON, Karen DM (LI) 1420 27th Ave, Astoria NY 11102 B 3/14/1961 d Beresford S Davis & Eileen C. MA Brooklyn Coll; BA Brooklyn Coll 1982; MS Brooklyn Coll 1997; MDiv The GTS 2009. D 6/22/2009 Bp James Hamilton Ottley P 1/16/2010 Bp Lawrence C Provenzano. m 8/18/2007 Noel Lawson. P Ch Of The Redeem Astoria NY 2010-2011; P S Geo's Ch Astoria NY 2010-2011; D Ch Of The Redeem Astoria NY 2009-2010; D S Geo's Ch Astoria NY 2009-2010. revkdl@gmail.com

DAVISON, Arienne S (Oly) 801 Pine St Apt 8d, Seattle WA 98101 **Gr Ch Bainbridge Island WA 2010-** B Seattle WA 6/3/1979 d Eric Lyman Davison & Sara Mae Chan. BS U Of Washington Seattle WA 2002; MDiv VTS 2007. D 6/30/2007 Bp Bavi Rivera P 1/26/2008 Bp Gregory Harold Rickel. Assoc R for Fam Mnstrs Emm Epis Ch Mercer Island WA 2007-2010. aridavison@gmail.com

DAVIS-SHOEMAKER, Courtney Elizabeth (Mass) 1019 E Willowbrook Drive, Burlington NC 27215 B Nashville TN 9/27/1975 d Hugh Steven Davis & Jan Stanfield. BA Dickinson Coll 1997; MDiv The GTS 2008. D 6/7/2008 Bp M(arvil) Thomas Shaw III P 1/10/2009 Bp Roy Frederick Cederholm Jr. m 5/31/2008 Adam James Shoemaker. Asst S Steph's Memi Ch Lynn MA 2008-2011. cedavis0927@gmail.com

DAVISSON, Mary Thomsen (Md) 2363 Hamiltowne Cir., Baltimore MD 21237 **Assoc Ch Of The Redemp Baltimore MD 2004-** B Baltimore MD 12/5/1952 d John S Thomsen & Helen S. BA/MA Br 1974; PhD U CA, Berkeley 1979; MDiv VTS 2004. D 6/12/2004 Bp John Leslie Rabb P 1/8/2005 Bp Robert Wilkes Ihloff. m 3/22/1980 Edwin Orlando Davisson c 3. "Chapl to Seafarers," *Virginia Sem Journ*, 2007; "The Observers of Daedalus in Ovid," *Classical Wrld 90*, 1997; "Mythological Examples in Ovid's Remedia," *Phoenix 50*, 1996; "Tristia 5.13 and Ovid's Use of Epistolary Form," *Classical Journ 80*, 1985. Ord of Urban Missioners 1999. maryhtdavisson@aol.com

DAVY, Brian Kendall (At) 589 Martins Grove Rd, Dahlonega GA 30533 **S Lk's Ch Ft Vlly GA 2008-; S Thos Of Cbury Thomaston GA 2004-** B 5/16/1947 s Martin Edward Davy & Dorothy Helen. BA Georgia St U 1982; MDiv STUSo 1991. D 6/6/1991 P 1/1/1992 Bp Frank Kellogg Allan. m 12/15/1990 Susan C Callender c 1. Chr Ch Macon GA 2002-2003; S Eliz's Epis Ch Dahlonega GA 1994-2001; Asst R Ch Of The Epiph Atlanta GA 1991-1993. bkd@windstream.net

DAW JR, Carl Pickens (Ct) 171 Highland Ave, Watertown MA 02472 B Louisville KY 3/18/1944 s Carl Pickens Daw & Sara Ruth. BA Rice U 1966; MA U of Virginia 1967; PhD U of Virginia 1970; MDiv STUSo 1981. D 6/14/1981 P 3/18/1982 Bp C(laude) Charles Vache. m 5/31/1969 May Bates c 1. Int S Thos Memi Epis Ch Oakmont PA 1993-1994; Vic/Chapl S Mk's Chap Storrs CT 1984-1993; Asst Chr And Gr Ch Petersburg VA 1981-1984. Co-Auth, "A HymnTune Psalter, RCL Ed, v. 1-2," Ch Pub, Inc., 2007; Co-Auth, "Liturg Mus for the RCL, Years A,B,C," Ch Pub, Inc., 2007; Auth, "Gathered for Wrshp," Hope Pub Co., 2006; Co-Auth, "A HymnTune Psalter v. 1-2," Ch Pub, Inc., 1998; Auth, "New Psalms and Hymns and Sprtl Songs," Hope Pub Co., 1996; Auth, "Breaking the Word," Ch Pub Inc., 1994; Auth, "To Sing God's Praise," Hope Pub Co., 1992; Auth, "A Year of Gr," Hope Pub Co., 1990. Hymn Soc US & Can. Fell RSCM 2011; D.D. VTS 2009; Fell Hymn Soc in the US & Can 2007. cpdaw@bu.edu

DAWSON, Adrien Portia (Md) 4412 Eastway, Baltimore MD 21218 **R Ch Of S Marks On The Hill Pikesville MD 2007-** B Charlottesville VA 5/3/1975 d Richard Eric Gehring & Susan Jane. BA St. Jn's Coll Annapolis MD 1996; MDiv GTS 2002. D 6/8/2002 Bp John Leslie Rabb P 12/6/2002 Bp Robert Wilkes Ihloff. m 5/20/2000 Sean Frederick Dawson. Asst Trin Ch Towson MD 2002-2007. revdawson@comcast.net

DAWSON, Barbara Louise (Cal) 399 Gregory Ln, Pleasant Hill CA 94523 **D Ch Of The Resurr Pleasant Hill CA 1988-** B Omaha NE 2/3/1952 d Charles Baxter Schwellenbach & Harriet Mae. BS San Diego St U 1975. D 3/14/1985 Bp Otis Charles. m 6/9/1973 David Lanford Dawson c 2. D Dio Utah Salt Lake City UT 1985-1988. dawsonfam@astound.net

DAWSON, Eric Emmanuel (VI) 19-5 Hope, Saint Thomas VI 00801 B Saint Thomas VI 12/26/1937 s Joseph E Dawson & Ann Oliver. BS NYU 1964. D 3/25/1974 Bp Edward Mason Turner. m 6/11/1966 Betty J Vanterpool c 2.

DAWSON JR, Frank Prescott (Md) No address on file. **D Dio Maryland Baltimore MD 1983-** B Chicago IL 9/18/1924 s Frank P Dawson & Kathryn M. U of Wisconsin 1948; BS Roosevelt U 1954. D 6/26/1983 Bp David Keller Leighton Sr. m 11/12/1977 Mickey Colin. Voc D S Ptr's Epis Ch Ellicott City MD 1991-1993; D Ch Of The H Cov Baltimore MD 1986-1987; Voc D S Ptr's Epis Ch Ellicott City MD 1983-1986. Irenaeus Soc Of Priests & Deacons. fpdmcd@aol.com

DAWSON, George Henry (WTex) 4426 Dolphin Pl, Corpus Christi TX 78411 B Baltimore MD 6/4/1932 s George Henry Dawson & Anna Price. BSinME Duke 1954; MDiv VTS 1961. D 7/11/1961 Bp Everett H Jones P 1/1/1962 Bp Richard Earl Dicus. m 12/3/1955 Lorraine Johnson c 2. Int S Jas Epis Ch Hebbronville TX 1990-1993; P-in-c Ch Of Our Sav Aransas Pass TX 1987-1990; P-in-c Ch Of The Ascen Refugio TX 1986-1990; P-in-c S Thos And S Mart's Ch Corpus Christi TX 1973-1987; Actg/Assoc. R Ch Of The Gd Shpd Corpus Christi TX 1969-1971; Asst R Ch Of The Gd Shpd Corpus Christi TX 1965-1968; P-in-c S Chris's By The Sea Portland TX 1965-1968; Asst S Lk's Ch Alexandria VA 1964-1965; Vic S Chris's Ch Bandera TX 1961-1964. Auth, *A Plan for Bldg an Integrated Total Distribution Co*, Self, 1972; Auth, "Transportation Concerns," *Choices Facing Corpus Christi*, 1972. Mssn to Seafarers 1976. Meritorious Publ Serv Citation Commandant, U.S. Coast Guard 1994. ghdawson@swbell.net

DAWSON, Margaret Grantham (La) 320 Sena Dr, Metairie LA 70005 **D S Mart's Epis Ch Metairie LA 2003-** B 9/1/1942 D 9/13/2003 Bp Charles Edward Jenkins III. m 7/29/1989 Anthony Michael Dawson. mgdrake@juno.com

DAWSON JR, Marshall Allen (Lex) 1375 Weisenberger Mill Rd, Midway KY 40347 **D Dio Lexington Lexington KY 1985-** B Versailles KY 3/22/1938 s Marshall Allen Dawson & Mary Flowers. BS U Of Kentucky 1960; MD U Of Kentucky 1964; Epis TS In Kentucky 1986. D 6/4/1985 Bp Don Adger Wimberly. m 8/5/1961 Nancy Ann Barnett c 2. madawson@pol.net

DAWSON, Paul Sweeting (Md) 145 Main St., Apt. A1, Vineyard Haven MA 02568 B Baltimore MD 6/27/1930 s Jesse Potter Dawson & Blanche. MS Loyola U; BA McDaniel Coll 1953; Drew U 1956; GTS 1957. D 3/29/1958 P 1/1/1959 Bp Noble C Powell. m 6/25/1960 Marilyn Hardester c 1. P-in-c S Judes Epis Ch Franklin NH 1996-1999; P-in-c Trin Epis Ch Tilton NH 1996-1998; Fairhaven Sykesville MD 1982-1991; Ch Hosp Corp Baltimore MD 1972-1982; Cur S Mich And All Ang Ch Baltimore MD 1969-1972; R S Jn's Ch Kingsville MD 1962-1969. Auth, "Poems: After Tao," *Trst-ATR*, 1976; Auth, "A Hospice Handbook Chapt 7"; Auth, "Hospice: Complete Care For Terminally Ill Chapt 5". pdpriest@gmail.com

DAWSON JR, Tucker Edward (La) 321 State St, Bay Saint Louis MS 39520 B Baton Rouge LA 12/31/1934 s Tucker Edward Dawson & Evelyn Winston. BS LSU 1957; MDiv STUSo 1962; Med U of New Orleans 1971. D 6/29/1962 Bp Girault M Jones P 6/1/1963 Bp Iveson Batchelor Noland. m 2/27/1965 Margene Sweitzer c 1. R S Andr's Epis Ch New Orleans LA 1988-1998; Mem, Stndg Com Dio Kansas Topeka KS 1981-1985; R S Thos The Apos Ch Overland Pk KS 1975-1988; R Chr Ch Slidell LA 1969-1975. FRIRTUK@MCHSI.COM

DAWSON, Walter Wesley (Mich) 331 Elkin Ct, Commerce Township MI 48382 B Detroit MI 9/15/1945 s Donald Lloyd Dawson & Lois Irene. BS in Ed Cntrl Michigan U 1968; MDiv VTS 1973. D 9/2/1973 P 6/23/1974 Bp H Coleman McGehee Jr. m 2/27/1971 Laura Dawson c 3. R S Geo's Ch Milford MI 1997-2011; R S Jas Epis Ch Hibbing MN 1990-1997; R Emm Ch Staunton VA 1986-1990; Chapl Epis U Mnstry Johnson City TN 1980-1986; Asst S Jn's Epis Ch Johnson City TN 1980-1985; Vic S Fran Epis Ch Grayling MI 1975-1980; Cur All SS Ch E Lansing MI 1973-1975. Pi Kappa Delta (Hon Forensics). wingandaprayer3@gmail.com

DAY III, Charles V. (Be) 3908 Eisenhower Way, Tobyhanna PA 18466 B Cartersville GA 1/2/1936 s Charles Van Day & Mary Lou. BA/BS Stetson U 1965; MDiv STUSo 1967. D 6/13/1967 Bp James Loughlin Duncan P 12/20/1967 Bp William Loftin Hargrave. m 3/31/1981 Virginia Rex c 4. Strng Com Epis Peace & Justice Netwrk Dio Bethlehem Bethlehem PA 1989-1993; R S Geo's Epis Ch Hellertown PA 1986-1995; Vic S Tim's Ch Macedonia OH 1982-1986; R Aug Par Chesapeake City MD 1981-1982; R S Jn's Ch Naples FL 1976-1981; R H Innoc Epis Ch Valrico FL 1969-1976; Asst Ch Of The Gd Shpd Dunedin FL 1967-1969. Auth, "The Chapl Becomes a Patient," *Chapl Today*, Asso. of Profsnl Chapl, 2008; Auth, "Bk Revs," *Living Ch*, Living Ch Fndt, 2006; Ed, "Nwsltr - Assembly Of Epis Hospitals And Chapl," *Assembly* *of Epis. Hosps. & Chapl*, AEHC, 1975; Assoc Ed, "S Lk Journ Of Theol," *St. Lk's Journ of Theol*, TS, Univ of So, 1965. Assn Of Profsnl Chapl - Bd Cert Chaplai 1999. Bd Cert Chapl Assn of Profsnl Chapl 1999. cday18344@yahoo.com

DAY, Christine Jane (CNY) 35 Second St, Johnson City NY 13790 **R All SS Epis Ch Johnson City NY 2004-** B North Tonawanda NY 10/25/1953 d Elmer Walter Day & Mary Jane Brown. BA Cor 1975; MS Indiana U 1977; MDiv GTS 1999. D 6/12/1999 P 12/18/1999 Bp David B(ruce) Joslin. S Paul's Cathd Syracuse NY 2004; S Dav's Ch De Witt NY 2002; Campus Mnstry Mssnr Dio Cntrl New York Syracuse NY 2001-2003; Dio Cntrl New York Syracuse NY 1999-2003; Spec Asst to Bp Dio Cntrl New York Syracuse NY 1999-2001. Bd Nazareth Proj 1995-2007; ESMHE 1999-2003. revchristinejday@aol.com

DAY, Dennis Lee (CGC) Po Box 2066, Fairhope AL 36533 B Chicago IL 1/9/1936 s Elden William Day & Leona Katherine. BA Pr 1958; Nash 1960; BD SWTS 1961; MA U of Wisconsin 1970; PhD U of Wisconsin 1975; MEd U of So Alabama 1980; EdS U of So Alabama 1989. D 6/10/1961 P 12/1/1961 Bp Horace W B Donegan. m 11/17/1979 Marjorie Sellers c 2. Assoc All SS Epis Ch Mobile AL 1993-1996; Assoc All SS Epis Ch Mobile AL 1982-1984; Serv S Jn The Evang Robertsdale AL 1978-1981; P-in-c H Cross Epis Ch Wisconsin Dells WI 1972-1975; Assoc S Matt's Ch Kenosha WI 1967-1969; R S Andr's Ch Kenosha WI 1963-1966; Cur S Jn The Evang Ch Elkhart IN 1961-1963. Outstanding Secondary Tchr S ate 95 AL 1995; Woodrow Wilson Fndt Fllshp 1992. dlday199@lycos.com

DAY, Jeremiah Carroll (EC) 109 Skipper Circle, Oriental NC 28571 **P S Thos Ch Oriental NC 1999-** B Fort Knox KY 1/3/1953 s Jeremiah Carol Day & Anna. BS USNA 1975; MDiv VTS 1990. D 6/16/1990 P 12/22/1990 Bp Brice Sidney Sanders. m 6/7/1975 Marian Dietz c 3. Off Of Bsh For ArmdF New York NY 1994-2000; Trin Epis Ch Chocowinity NC 1990-1994; Zion Epis Ch Washington NC 1990. jeremiah@coastalnet.com

DAY, John Edward (Spok) 9843 Derby Way, Elk Grove CA 95757 **Bd Chair, Epis Comm Fed Credit Un Dio Los Angeles Los Angeles CA 1999-** B Salt Lake City UT 2/21/1951 s Jack Rampton Day & Frances Purton. BS U of Utah 1988; MDiv CDSP 1991; DMin SWTS 2001. D 6/2/1991 P 12/7/1991 Bp George Edmonds Bates. m 9/11/1973 Gail Kibbe c 2. R S Mk's Epis Ch Moscow ID 2004-2006; R S Geo's Par La Can CA 1995-2004; Vic Gr Epis Ch St Geo UT 1992-1995; Cur Cathd Ch Of S Mk Salt Lake City UT 1991-1992. Assoc, OHC. Hon Cn Dio Los Angelels 2003. revjohnandgail@gmail.com

DAY JR, John Warren (Wyo) 441 Highland Dr, Bellingham WA 98225 B Sapulpa OK 9/24/1922 s John Warren Day & Harriet Mason. BA Antioch Coll 1949; BD UTS 1958; Brigham Young U 1974. D 9/16/1958 P 3/1/1959 Bp James W Hunter. c 2. R S Jas Ch Riverton WY 1960-1970; In-Charge All SS Ch Wheatland WY 1958-1960; In-Charge Ch Of Our Sav Hartville WY 1958-1960; In-Charge S Jn The Bapt Ch Glendo WY 1958-1960.

DAY, Katherine Browning Lufkin (CNY) 106 Ardsley Dr, Syracuse NY 13214 B Saint Paul MN 9/20/1954 d James Markham Lufkin & Rosemarie Johanna. BA S Jn's Coll 1976; MA Untd TS 1983; MDiv GTS 1989. D 6/10/1989 Bp Paul Moore Jr P 12/9/1989 Bp Douglas Edwin Theuner. m 6/23/1979 William Blaine Day c 2. Dio Cntrl New York Syracuse NY 2005; R Chr Epis Ch Jordan NY 1997-2010; R H Trin Ch So River NJ 1994-1997; Assoc S Lk's Ch Gladstone NJ 1991-1993; Asst S Andr's Ch New London NH 1989-1991. Cmnty S Jn Bapt. kblday@gmail.com

DAY, Margaret Ann (Me) 777 Stillwater Ave Lot 63, Old Town ME 04468 **Serv Dio Maine Portland ME 1990-** B Bangor ME 11/22/1951 d William Roy Gorrill & Jean Elizabeth. BSW U of Maine 1990; MS U of Maine 1996. D 10/25/1990 Bp Edward Cole Chalfant. m 6/9/1973 Lloyd Wesley Day. Auth, *Discerning the Call to Soc Mnstry*, Alb Inst. St. Steph's Awd NAAD 2005. pegday@gwi.net

DAY, Michael Henry (SwFla) 1070 54th St N, Saint Petersburg FL 33710 B Tampa FL 2/6/1941 s Frank Perritt Day & Winfred Nell. BA U of So Florida 1964; MDiv GTS 1967. D 6/17/1967 Bp William Loftin Hargrave P 12/1/1967 Bp Henry I Louttit. m 11/16/2006 Julianna V Day c 2. S Vinc's Epis Ch St Petersburg FL 1976-2001; R S Mary's Epis Ch Palmetto FL 1970-1976; Cur S Mich's Ch Orlando FL 1967-1970. frmikeday@gmail.com

DAY, Randall Carl Kidder (Los) 2901 Nojoqui Avenue, P.O. Box 39, Los Olivos CA 93441 **R S Mk's-In-The-Vlly Epis Los Olivos CA 2008-** B Brazil IN 5/23/1955 s Robert Bryson Day & Marion Elizabeth. BA Oral Roberts U 1977; MA U of Tulsa 1980; MDiv Nash 1985; DMin SWTS 2010. D 6/15/1985 Bp Frank Tracy Griswold III P 12/19/1985 Bp James Winchester Montgomery. m 1/1/2000 William R Hurbaugh. COM Dio Newark Newark NJ 2006-2008; GC Alt Dep Dio Newark Newark NJ 2006; Bp Nomin Com Dio Newark Newark NJ 2005-2006; Profile Com Co-Chair Dio Newark Newark NJ 2005-2006; COM Lay Mnstry Com Dio Newark Newark NJ 2004-2008; Ward J. Herbert Fund Bd Dio Newark Newark NJ 2004-2008; Dioc Coun Dio Newark Newark NJ 2000-2004; R S Mk's Ch Teaneck NJ 1998-2008; Asstg Cler Cathd of St Ptr & St Paul Washington DC 1993-1997; Int S Monica's Epis Ch Washington DC 1991-1992; Exec Dir The Friends Of Cbury Cathd In The Untd States Washington DC 1989-1997; Int S Geo's Ch Glenn Dale MD 1989-1990; P-in-c S Andr's Ch Downers Grove IL 1985-1988. Auth, "Sewanee Theol Revs," 1994. Mem Bd, Los Olivos Bus Orgnztn 2011; Mem Bd, Santa Ynez Vlly Cottage Hosp Fndt 2011; Coun Mem Township of Teaneck 2006; Mem Med Ethics Com, H Name Hosp 2004; Pres Teaneck Interfaith Cler Coun 2000; Hon Chapl Untd States Hse Of Representatives 1995. randallday@mac.com

DAY, Robert Charles (Mass) 47 Willow Tree Hollow, PO Box 3000 PMB 3124, West Tisbury MA 02575 B Hackensack NJ 7/29/1927 s Harvey Carter Day & Sophie Therese. BA U of Delaware Newark 1949; MA Oxf, Engl 1959; MDiv EDS 1965. D 6/12/1965 Bp Charles F Hall P 12/1/1965 Bp John Melville Burgess. m 12/21/1963 Barbara Whidden c 3. The Adv Sch Boston MA 1965-1995; The Ch Of The Adv Boston MA 1965-1977.

DAY, Thomas Leighton (Tex) 320 N Kansas Ave, League City TX 77573 **R S Chris's Ch League City TX 2002-** B Bristol VA 3/28/1950 s Frank Patterson Day & Sarah Elizabeth. BS U of Tennessee 1973; MDiv STUSo 1990; DMin SWTS 2001. D 6/16/1990 P 1/9/1991 Bp Maurice Manuel Benitez. m 6/9/1973 Madeline Kimball McVeigh c 3. R S Tim's Epis Ch Houston TX 1992-2002; All SS Epis Ch Stafford TX 1990-1992. OSL 1985. tom@stchrischurch.org

DAY, Virginia Rex (Be) 3908 Eisenhower Way, Tobyhanna PA 18466 B Holyoke MA 10/8/1940 d Percy Fielitz Rex & Ruth Irwin. BA Smith 1962; Moravian TS 1993; MDiv GTS 1994; STM GTS 2006. D 4/23/1994 P 10/29/1994 Bp James Michael Mark Dyer. m 3/31/1981 Charles V. Day c 2. R Trin Epis Ch Mt Pocono PA 1999-2008; Cn Mssnr Cathd Ch Of The Nativ Bethlehem PA 1994-1999. grexday@msn.com

DAYTON, Douglas Kennedy (NwPa) 3600 Mcconnell Rd, Hermitage PA 16148 B North Tonawanda NY 10/6/1942 s William Kennedy Dayton & Virginia Roth. BS SUNY 1964; MS SUNY 1969; MDiv TESM 1989. D 6/29/1989 Bp C(hristopher) FitzSimons Allison P 4/1/1991 Bp Robert Deane Rowley Jr. m 8/16/1969 Kathleen Dayton c 2. Dioc Coun Dio NW Pennsylvania Erie PA 2006-2008; Stndg Com Dio NW Pennsylvania Erie PA 1998-2003; Dioc Coun Dio NW Pennsylvania Erie PA 1997-2000; S Jn's Epis Ch Sharon PA 1989-2009.

DE ACETIS, Joseph Lewis (Be) 58 Deer Path Dr, Flanders NJ 07836 B Brooklyn NY 6/8/1927 s Fiore De Acetis & Margaret. BS S Mary Coll Leavenworth KS 1951; Mt St. Alphonsus 1955. Rec from Roman Catholic 6/1/1997 as Priest Bp Paul Victor Marshall. m 7/18/1970 Joan Marie Bosch. Trin Ch Easton PA 1997-2002. Fed Of Chr Ministers.

DEACON JR, Charles Alexander (WNY) 34 Beattie Avenue, 84 Rosedale Blvd., Amherst NY 14226 B Quincy MA 5/12/1932 s Charles Alexander Deacon & Winnifred Dean. BA Bos 1954; MDiv PDS 1962. D 10/13/1962 Bp Anson Phelps Stokes Jr P 4/27/1963 Bp Lewis B Whittemore. c 3. Stndg Com Dio Wstrn New York Tonawanda NY 2001-2002; Int S Jn's Gr Ch Buffalo NY 2000-2002; S Matt's Ch Buffalo NY 1997-1998; VP Niagara Dnry Dio Wstrn New York Tonawanda NY 1992-1993; Dioce Coun Dio Wstrn New York Tonawanda NY 1982-1984; All SS Ch Lockport NY 1970-1979; Cur Ch Of The Adv Kenmore NY 1966-1970; Vic S Andr's Ch Friendship NY 1965-1966; P-in-c S Paul's Ch Angelica NY 1965-1966; Cur Chr Ch Rochester NY 1962-1965. deaconac@roadrunner.com

DEACON, Jonathan (NJ) 12 Bryan Dr, Voorhees NJ 08043 B Auckland NZ 11/9/1949 s Owen Joseph Deacon & Joyce. BA U of Auckland 1969; BTh S Jn Angl Sem 1978; BS U of Auckland 1979; MDiv S Jn Angl Sem 1995; PhD S Jn Angl Sem/ Auckland U. 2000. Trans from Anglican Church in Aotearoa, New Zealand and Polynesia 2/1/1996 Bp Joe Morris Doss. m 4/18/1998 Margaret Klein c 2. R Trin Epis Old Swedes Ch Swedesboro NJ 1996. Intl Police Chapl Conf Untd States of Ameri 1992-1995. Hon Cn Trin Cathd Auckland New Zealand 1995. safehavenpcs@aol.com

DEACON, Robert (CNY) 9 Lockwood St, Bellows Falls VT 05101 B Philadelphia PA 10/5/1930 s Robert Deacon & Agnes. Dropsie Coll; BA U of Pennsylvania 1952; BD ETS 1957. D 6/22/1957 Bp Joseph Gillespie Armstrong P 12/21/1957 Bp Oliver J Hart. m 6/8/1957 Martha Joan Hesthal c 4. Emm Ch Norwich NY 1988-1995; Imm Ch Bellows Falls VT 1980-1988; S Jas (Old Swedes) Ch of Kingsessing Philadelphia PA 1966-1980; Gr Ch And The Incarn Philadelphia PA 1958-1962; Trin Ch Swarthmore PA 1957-1958. bobdkn@gmail.com

DEADERICK, Dianna LaMance (USC) 1300 Pine St, Columbia SC 29204 B Pontiac MI 9/5/1958 d Ralph Lee LaMance & Nancy Hoff. BA Berea Coll 1980; MA U of So Carolina 1996; Sch for Mnstry 2008. D 5/21/2011 Bp W(illiam) Andrew Waldo. m 1/17/1981 Douglas Deaderick c 2. diannald@sc.rr.com

DEAKLE, David Wayne (La) 4350 SE Brooklyn St, Portland OR 97206 B Mobile AL 11/18/1955 s Jackson Zebulon Deakle & Katherine Inez. BA U of Mobile 1977; MDiv New Orleans Bapt TS 1979; MA U of New Orleans 1982; ThD New Orleans Bapt TS 1985; MA Notre Dame Sem 1987; PhD S Louis U 1991. D 6/17/1989 P 1/18/1990 Bp James Barrow Brown. m 11/17/1979 Guadalupe Brenes. Prof of NT & Patristics Nash Nashotah WI 1992-2005; P-in-c S Ptr's Ch No Lake WI 1992-2005; Asst R S Jn's Ch Norristown PA 1989-1992. Cath Biblic Assn 1990. dwdeakle@execpc.com

DEAN, Bobby Wayne (CGC) PO Box 1677, Santa Rosa Beach FL 32459 B Wake County NC 8/19/1938 s Hursel Grant & Mary. BA Wstrn Carolina U 1964. D 2/10/2011 Bp Philip Menzie Duncan II. m 8/8/1981 Patricia Hoskins c 3. bobdean@gnt.net

DEAN, Gordon Joy (WMass) 10 Fox Rd, Shelburne Falls MA 01370 B Fall River MA 10/27/1932 s Arthur Franklin Dean & Gladys Evelyn. BU; BM Bos 1954; MM Bos 1955; MDiv EDS 1961. D 6/25/1961 Bp Anson Phelps Stokes Jr P 1/5/1962 Bp Roger W Blanchard. c 4. Vic S Jn's Ch Ashfield MA 1999-2002; Dir of Mus S Lk's Par Darien CT 1988-1995; Massachusetts Coun Of Ch Boston MA 1977-1979; Chair, Dioc Revs Com, Dioc Coun Dio Wstrn Massachusetts Springfield MA 1976-1977; R S Barn And All SS Ch Springfield MA 1973-1977; Assoc for Lay Mnstry Gr Ch Amherst MA 1969-1973; Assoc S Steph's Epis Ch And U Columbus OH 1961-1969. Auth, "Sermon As Intervention: A Tool for Change," ACC, 1976; Auth, "Yth Culture," *Resrch Paper as Fell, Coll of Preachers*, 1967; Auth, "Theol Of Hymnal 1940," *Thesis, ETS*, 1961. Associated Parishes; ACC: Cert Practitioner; Orgnztn Dvlpmt Ntwk. Fell Coll Of Preachers 1967. gdean@valinet.com

DEAN, Jay Judson (Me) 33 Baker St, Dover NH 03820 B Ipswich MA 10/19/1930 s William Judson Dean & Amy. BS U of New Hampshire 1953; MDiv Ya Berk 1964; MS U of Maine 1976; DMin Bos 1980. D 6/20/1964 Bp Anson Phelps Stokes Jr P 6/12/1965 Bp Oliver L Loring. m 2/12/1981 Claire Hope Elliott c 4. Int Chr Ch Norway ME 1979-1980; P-in-c S Ann's Epis Ch Windham Windham ME 1974-1976; P-in-c S Steph The Mtyr Epis Ch E Waterboro ME 1966-1974; Cur Trin Epis Ch Portland ME 1964-1965. Auth, *How Damage is Done in Name of Chr!*.

DEAN, Rebecca Anderson (SVa) 985 Huguenot Trl, Midlothian VA 23113 **D Manakin Epis Ch Midlothian VA 2007-** B Salem OR 5/12/1947 d Gene Clair Anderson & Betty Virginia. Dioc Of No Carolina D Formation Prog Durham NC. D 6/9/2007 Bp John Clark Buchanan. m 8/26/1967 Kerry Dean c 2. beckidean@verizon.net

DEAN, Robert C(hollar) (RG) 1880 Courthouse Rd, Stafford VA 22554 B Cleveland OH 2/24/1921 s Robert Charles Dean & Ella Mary. BS Case Wstrn Reserve U 1942; BD Bex 1953; MDiv CRDS 1973. D 6/9/1953 P 12/16/1953 Bp Nelson Marigold Burroughs. c 3. Vol Pstrl Assoc S Geo's Ch Fredericksburg VA 1997-2005; R S Jn's Ch Farmington NM 1981-1988; Dio Ohio Cleveland OH 1979; Dio Ohio Cleveland OH 1977-1978; Ch Of The Gd Shpd Beachwood OH 1953-1976. Associated Parishes 1953; HSEC 1953; Ptr Tare Inc 1945; Pt Boats, Inc. 1945. Fllshp Coll Of Preachers Washington DC 1967; Wates Seabury Exch Fellowowship Par Of Tunbridge Kent Engl 1964. tocnniebanaie@yahoo.com

DEAN, Steven Jay (Los) 25211 Via Tanara, Santa Clarita CA 91355 **Vic S Fran Of Assisi Epis Ch Simi Vlly CA 2002-** B Tacoma WA 10/5/1945 s Jay O Dean & Ruth. BS California St U 1972; MDiv Claremont TS 1998. D 6/15/1996 P 1/1/1997 Bp Chester Lovelle Talton. m 12/17/1966 Dorothy Dean c 3. S Marg's Epis Ch So Gate CA 1998-2002; S Simon's Par San Fernando CA 1996-1998. sjdean.sr@att.net

DEAN, Susan Chanda (Oly) 3714 90th Avenue SE, Mercer Island WA 98040 B Washington DC 6/2/1945 d John Chanda & Ruth Evelyn. BA Clark U 1967; MDiv CDSP 2002. D 6/29/2002 Bp Sanford Zangwill Kaye Hampton P 1/25/2003 Bp Vincent Waydell Warner. m 6/10/1978 David Joseph Dean c 1. D/P Assoc Emm Epis Ch Mercer Island WA 2002-2004. susndean@juno.com

DE ANAYA, Nilda Lucca (PR) 2100 Washington Ave Apt 2c, Silver Spring MD 20910 B 8/15/1927 D 8/15/1982 P 2/8/1983 Bp Francisco Reus-Froylan. Dio Puerto Rico S Just PR 1982-1997.

DEANE SR, Warren Herbert (Roch) 418 Sherburne Rd, Portsmouth NH 03801 B Dorchester MA 2/10/1928 s Barnabas Herbert Deane & Victoria Elizabeth. BS Bos 1949; EdM Bos 1953; EDS 1956; MDiv ETS 1971; DMin Andover Newton TS 1977; ThM CRDS 1978; Cert Portsmouth Inst Psych 1982; Bex 1986; Bex 1991. D 6/23/1956 P 12/23/1956 Bp Norman B Nash. m 3/10/1991 Jeannine Rita Jacques c 6. R Trin Ch Hampton NH 1985-2000; R S Jn's Epis Ch Honeoye Falls NY 1962-1974; Asst Min Emm Epis Ch Webster Groves MO 1958-1961; Cur Chr Ch Waltham MA 1956-1958. WHDSR49@comcast.net

DEANE JR, William Boyd (Pa) No address on file. B Fort Bragg NC 9/14/1947 s William B Deane & Alma Elizabeth. MDiv EDS; BS Oklahoma St U; PhD U of Pennsylvania. D 6/23/1973 P 3/22/1974 Bp Robert Lionne DeWitt. Auth, "The Runaway & The Law".

DEAR, Arthur Tyrrel (CFla) Po Box 668, New Smyrna FL 32170 B Hackensack NJ 12/1/1938 s Arthur Tyrrel Dear & Dorothea. BS Florida St U 1960; STB GTS 1963; Ntl Profsnl Dvlpmt Prog 1974. D 6/10/1963 Bp Henry I Louttit P 12/1/1963 Bp James Loughlin Duncan. m 12/27/1958 Roxanna Banks. Int Ch Of S Dav's By The Sea Cocoa Bch FL 1997-1998; Int S Edw The Confessor Mt Dora FL 1996; Assoc Gr Epis Ch Inc Port Orange FL 1993-2010; Int Chr Ch Ft Meade FL 1990-1992; Int Ch Of Our Sav Palm Bay FL 1989-1990; Vic S Ptr The Fisherman Epis Ch New Smyrna Bch FL 1987; Asst S Paul's Epis Ch New Smyrna Bch FL 1985-1986; Asst S Phil's Ch Coral Gables FL 1977-1978; R S Margarets Epis Ch Miami Lakes FL 1975-1977; Cn Dio SE Florida Miami FL 1969-1975; Vic Ch Of The Incarn Miami FL 1966-1969; Asst S Steph's Ch Coconut Grove Coconut Grove FL 1963-1966. Who'S Who Rel Amer 1975. tdear123@gmail.com

DEARING, Trevor (Oly) 4 Rock House Gardens, Radcliffe Road, Stamford PE9 1AS Great Britain (UK) B Hull Yorkshire UK 9/14/1933 s Walter Edward Dearing & Hilda. BD Lon 1956; MA U of Birmingham 1963. Trans from Church Of England 4/22/1981 Bp Robert Hume Cochrane. m 6/22/1957 Harriet Anne Steele c 4. R S Lk's Epis Ch Seattle WA 1981-1983. Auth, *A People of Power*; Auth, *God & Healing of the Mind*; Auth, *Its True*; Auth, *Supernatural Healing Today*; Auth, *Supernatural Superpowers*; Auth, *Total Healing*; Auth, *Wesleyan & Tractarian Wrshp*. Chapl Ord of S Lk Physcn 1996.

D

DEARMAN, David Coy (Tex) 46 W Dansby Dr, Galveston TX 77551 **Hd of Sch Trin Ch Galveston TX 2002-** B Baton Rouge LA 1/4/1960 s William Arthur Dearman & Melvie Fay. BS U So 1982; MEd Mississippi Coll 1984; MDiv VTS 1987. D 6/11/1987 P 4/28/1988 Bp James Barrow Brown. m 8/15/1981 Corey Morgan c 3. Hd of Sch All SS' Epis Sch Morristown TN 1996-2002; Dn of Students All SS' Epis Sch Vicksburg MS 1990-1996; Chapl Chr Ch Covington LA 1987-1990. dcdearman@comcast.net

DEARMAN JR, William Benjamin (NY) 7 Oakridge Pkwy, Peekskill NY 10566 B Lumberton MS 9/29/1926 s William B Dearman & Maxie McCastle. BS Tul 1949; MDiv Epis TS of The SW 1958. D 4/9/1960 P 10/18/1960 Bp Charles F Hall. m 6/30/1962 Mary J Anderson c 3. P in charge S Jn's In The Wilderness Stony Point NY 1997-2003; St Marys Sch Peekskill NY 1974-1977; Vic Ch Of The Epiph Lisbon Lisbon NH 1971-1973; Vic S Dav's Ch Salem NH 1961-1965; Assoc Gr Ch Manchester NH 1959-1961. frbill@esym.net

DEATON JR, Charles Milton (Miss) 1616 52nd Ct, Meridian MS 39305 **R S Ptr's By The Lake Brandon MS 2006-** B Greenwood MS 6/16/1970 s Charles Milton Deaton & Mary Dent. BA Millsaps Coll 1992; MDiv STUSo 1997. D 5/29/1997 P 2/1/1998 Bp Alfred Clark Marble Jr. m 5/18/1996 Jennifer Deaton Melnyk c 1. S Paul's Epis Ch Meridian MS 2005-2006; S Jn's Ch Laurel MS 2004-2005; Asst S Aug's Epis Ch Croton On Hudson NY 2003-2004; The GTS New York NY 2002-2004; S Ptr's Ch Oxford MS 1997-2001. charliedeaton123@aol.com

DEATON, Jennifer Deaton (Miss) PO Box 23107, Jackson MS 39225 B Heidelberg Germany 12/16/1971 d W(alter) William Melnyk & Catherine Cleveland. BA Emory U 1996; Med U of Mississippi 1999; MDiv GTS 2004. D 6/24/2004 P 2/5/2005 Bp Duncan Montgomery Gray III. m 5/18/1996 Charles Milton Deaton c 1. Cur S Paul's Epis Ch Meridian MS 2004-2006. jendeaton@comcast.net

DEATRICK, George Edward (NJ) 215 Philadelphia Blvd, Sea Girt NJ 08750 B Defiance OH 5/17/1952 s John Frederick Deatrick & Alma Gertrude. BA Heidelberg Coll 1973; MDiv SWTS 1976. D 6/19/1976 Bp John Harris Burt P 1/18/1977 Bp James Winchester Montgomery. m 9/15/2001 Jean Rodgers. P-in-c Ch Of S Mk And All SS Absecon Galloway NJ 2005-2007; R S Helena's Ch Willowbrook IL 2001-2005; Int Ch Of The Medtr Chicago IL 2000-2001; Int The Ch Of S Uriel The Archangel Sea Girt NJ 1998-2000; Int Santa Teresa de Avila Chicago IL 1996-1997; Int Dio Chicago Chicago IL 1995-1998; SWTS Evanston IL 1995-1998; R Ch Of S Mich The Archangel Wall Township NJ 1993-1995; Cn S Paul's Cathd Peoria IL 1992-1993; R S Jas Epis Ch Newport Newport DE 1990-1992; Vic S Dunst's Epis Ch Westchester IL 1988-1990; Interin R Gr Epis Ch Hinsdale IL 1987-1988; R S Andr's Ch Downers Grove IL 1980-1987; Assoc S Andr's Ch Downers Grove IL 1978-1980; Cur The Epis Ch Of S Jas The Less Northfield IL 1976-1978. Bro Of S Andr 1982. rectorydoor@aol.com

DEATS, Cathy Leigh (Nwk) 10 Schoolhouse Ln, Flanders NJ 07836 **Pres Stndg Com Dio Newark Newark NJ 2011-; Dep to GC Dio Newark Newark NJ 2008-; R S Jas' Epis Ch Hackettstown NJ 2001-; Co-Chair Deaf Mnstry Dio Newark Newark NJ 1993-** B Greenwich CT 12/29/1949 d William Edward Smith & Irene Marion. BS U of Connecticut 1971; MS U of Connecticut 1977; DSW CUNY 1990; MDiv Drew U 1996. D 6/1/1996 Bp John Shelby Spong P 12/6/1996 Bp Jack Marston McKelvey. m 5/14/1977 Theodore Levi Deats c 1. Pres Stndg Com Dio Newark Newark NJ 2009-2010; Co-Chair Title IV Plcy Com Dio Newark Newark NJ 2008-2009; COM Dio Newark Newark NJ 1998-2004; Cur S Paul's Ch Englewood NJ 1996-2001. CHS 1991; NASW 1976. Preaching Awd Drew Univ TS 1996; Preaching Awd Drew Univ TS 1996. cathydeats@optonline.net

DEAVOURS, Cipher Alston (NJ) 112 Union St, Montclair NJ 07042 **D S Jn's Ch Eliz NJ 2005-** B Lebanon TN 1/15/1941 s Burns Moore Deavours & Lucile. SCM Br 1966; ScD U of Virginia 1969. D 6/4/2005 Bp George Edward Councell. m 6/19/2004 Lyn Headley. edeavors@kean.edu

DE BARY, Edward Oscar (Miss) 11 Wakefield Dr Apt 2105, Asheville NC 28803 B Antwerp Belgium 12/1/1938 s Edmond Theodore de Bary & Anne Marie Sophie. BA U So 1961; MDiv STUSo 1968; STL U of Louvain 1978; PhD U of Louvain 1983; STD U of Louvain 1984. D 6/22/1968 Bp George P

Gunn P 9/21/1969 Bp David Shepherd Rose. m 5/29/1974 Marcia Gladys Huff. R S Paul's Ch Columbus MS 2005; Trin Ch Winchester TN 2001; S Barn Ch Tullahoma TN 1997-1998; S Bede's Epis Ch Manchester TN 1995-1996; Dir EFM The TS at The U So Sewanee TN 1982-2004; Vic Epis Ch Of The Incarn W Point MS 1978-1982; Ch Of The Resurr Starkville MS 1974-1976; P-in-c Ch Of The Ascen Brooksville MS 1971-1976; P-in-c Ch Of The Nativ Macon MS 1971-1976. "Theol Reflection," Liturg Prfess, 2003; Gnrl Ed, *EFM Year 4*, 2002; Auth, "EFM," *Creative Transformation*, 2001; Gnrl Ed, *EFM Year 3*, 2001; Gnrl Ed, *EFM Year 2*, 2000; Gnrl Ed, *EFM Year 1*, 1999; Auth, "A Hist of the EFM Prog," *Sewanee Theol Revs*, 1999; Auth, "Common Lessons and Supporting Materials," *EFM*, 1998. emdeb@charter.net

DEBBOLI, Walter Anthony (Ct) 80 Rockwell Ave, Plainville CT 06062 B Troy NY 12/14/1929 s Anthony A Debboli & Eleanor P. BA Siena Coll 1952; MDiv Ya Berk 1955; DMin Bible Inst Sem 1979; MS U of Hartford 1983. D 5/29/1955 P 12/1/1955 Bp David Emrys Richards. m 6/6/1954 Gertrude O Ostwald. Ch of our Sav Plainville CT 1960-1984; Cur S Jn's Ch Larchmont NY 1955-1956. Auth, *Systematic Phoebic Desensitization*.

DE BECK, Ward Foster (Los) Po Box 169, Salem OR 97308 B Vancouver BC CA 11/12/1913 s Edwin Keary De Beck & Maria Anne. BA U Of British Columbia Vancouver Bc CA 1938; LTh ATC 1941. Trans from Anglican Church of Canada 1/1/1942. c 4. Asst S Paul's Epis Ch Salem OR 1980-2000; Vic S Thos' Mssn Hacienda Heights CA 1968-1979; Assoc Chr Ch Coronado CA 1959-1968; R S Mk's Par Downey CA 1951-1959; Cur S Jas By The Sea La Jolla CA 1949-1951; Cn Cathd Of S Jn The Evang Spokane WA 1947-1949; R Gr Ch Ellensburg WA 1946-1947. Navy League- Coronado Chapt 1963-1968; Rotary Intl Lo Piuente- Industry 1969-1979; Rotary Intl Of Coronado Ca 1960-1968; Rotary Intl Of Downey Ca 1952-1959; Rotary Intl Of Keizer Or 1980-2002. Paul Harris Fell 1984; Citizenship Awd Sar 1966.

DE BEER, John Michael (Mass) 12 White Pine Ln, Lexington MA 02421 **R S Mk's Epis Ch Burlington MA 2008-** B Johannesburg ZA 7/13/1945 s Charles Max De Beer & Sheila Laura. BS U Witwaters Rand 1967; MA Oxf 1969; DMin SWTS 2005. D 12/17/1972 P 12/1/1973 Bp The Bishop Of Johannesburg. m 7/10/1970 Patricia Jean Worrell c 1. P-in-c S Mk's Epis Ch Burlington MA 2005-2007; Int S Ptr's Ch Weston MA 2005-2006; R St Martins-In-The-Field Ch Severna Pk MD 1992-2005; Congrl Dvlpmt Dio SE Florida Miami FL 1991-1992; Asst S Phil's Ch Coral Gables FL 1988-1990; Int Hd of Sch S Phil's Epis Sch Coral Gables FL 1988-1989; Dir of Educ for EfM The TS at The U So Sewanee TN 1980-1988. Auth, "The Art of Theol Reflection," Crossroad, 1994; Auth, "Until We Are Free-A Study Guide on So Afr," Friendship Press, 1988; Auth, "Everyday Theol," *Chicago Stds*, 1983. EPF. connect.john@gmail.org

DE BEER, Patricia Jean (Mass) 14 Saint Marks Rd, Burlington MA 01803 **Ch Of Our Sav Arlington MA 2000-** B Los Angleles CA 4/26/1949 d Jack Mandeville Worrell & Frances Wilma. BA U CA 1971; MDiv Chicago TS 1980; Cert Shalem Inst Washington DC 1984; DMin STUSo 1990. D 4/24/1987 P 12/4/1987 Bp George Lazenby Reynolds Jr. m 7/10/1970 John Michael De Beer c 1. R The Ch Of Our Redeem Lexington MA 2005-2009; Chair, Cmsn of Mnstry Dio Maryland Baltimore MD 1994-2000; Bp's Search Com Dio Maryland Baltimore MD 1993-1994; R St Martins-In-The-Field Ch Severna Pk MD 1992-2005; Bd Trst The U So (Sewanee) Sewanee TN 1990-1992; Int S Phil's Ch Coral Gables FL 1988-1992; P in Charge Dio Tennessee Nashville TN 1987-1988. Auth, *Plnng for Mnstry*; Auth, *Study Guide on So Afr*; Auth, *Until We Are Free*. EPF; Ord of S Lk. debeer.tricia@gmail.com

DEBENHAM JR, M(artin) Warren (Cal) 143 Arlington Ave, Berkeley CA 94707 B San Francisco CO 1/20/1933 s Martin Warren Debenham & Josephine Osmund. BA Stan 1955; BD CDSP 1958. D 6/29/1958 Bp Henry H Shires P 3/1/1959 Bp James Albert Pike. m 5/25/1957 Sally F Kuechler c 3. R S Alb's Ch Albany CA 1975-1985; P-in-c S Alb's Ch Albany CA 1973-1974; Vic S Thos Epis Ch Sunnyvale CA 1960-1965; Asst Trin Cathd San Jose CA 1958-1960. "Laughter On Record," Scarecrow Press, 1988.

DE BONVILLE, John Henry (WMass) 62 Charter Oak Dr, Feeding Hills MA 01030 **R Ch Of The Gd Shpd W Springfield MA 2007-** B Keene NH 2/23/1948 s Hervey J DeBonville & Rita E. Andover Newton TS; TESM; BA Providence Coll 1970; MBA Wstrn New Engl Coll 1978. D 10/9/1981 Bp Alexander Doig Stewart P 6/10/2006 Bp Gordon Paul Scruton. m 6/12/1971 Cathy J MacKay c 2. D S Ptr's Ch Springfield MA 1996-2002; D S Andr's Ch Longmeadow MA 1981-1988. john.debonville@aic.edu

DEBOW, Rebecca Stephenson (Ala) 3519 W Lakeside Dr, Birmingham AL 35243 **S Lk's Epis Ch Birmingham AL 2006-** B Omaha NE 12/15/1955 d Ottis Virgil Stephenson & Sarah Elizabeth. BA Huntingdon Coll 1977; MDiv Candler TS Emory U 1995. D 2/25/1995 P 8/1/1995 Bp Robert Oran Miller. m 8/29/1981 Michael Eugene DeBow c 2. R The Epis Ch Of S Fran Of Assisi Indn Sprg Vill AL 1996-2006; Cur S Steph's Epis Ch Birmingham AL 1995-1996.

DE BRUYN, Richard Arthur (ECR) 448 Hansen Hill Rd, Arroyo Grande CA 93420 **Died 12/4/2010** B Grand Rapids MI 7/5/1925 s Neil De Bruyn & Hilda Elizabeth. Long Bch City Coll 1953; BA Sch for Deacons 1993. D 12/18/1993 Bp Richard Lester Shimpfky. c 5. deacond@neteze.com

DEBUSSY, Muriel S (NJ) 825 Summerset Dr, Hockessin DE 19707 B Scranton PA 10/17/1936 d Ellson Searfass & Virgina. AA Keystone Jr Coll 1956; BS Rutgers-The St U 1987; MDiv GTS 1994. D 6/11/1994 Bp George Phelps Mellick Belshaw P 12/1/1994 Bp Joe Morris Doss. m 8/6/2005 Robert Paul De Bussy c 1. S Thos' Epis Ch Glassboro NJ 2001-2005; Asst S Ptr's Ch Spotswood NJ 1994-2001. revmhubert@aol.com

DEBUYS III, John Forrester (Ala) 2501 Country Club Cir, Birmingham AL 35223 B Tuscaloosa AL 9/26/1966 s John Forrester DeBuys & Maida Louise. BA Hampden-Sydney Coll 1988; MDiv STUSo 2004. D 5/21/2005 P 12/13/2005 Bp Henry Nutt Parsley Jr. m 5/1/1993 Katherine DeBuys c 3. All SS Epis Ch Birmingham AL 2005-2007. fdebuys@allsaintsbirmingham.org

DECARLEN, Marya Louise (Mass) 35 King George Dr # 1921, Boxford MA 01921 **R S Jas Ch Groveland Groveland MA 2003-** B Green Bay WI 8/20/1956 d Clifford Patrick Tatro & Carla Mae. BA Stephens Coll 1977; MDiv EDS 1983. D 6/8/1983 P 1/1/1984 Bp Walter Cameron Righter. m 10/8/1999 Donald Bumiller c 2. Wyman Memi Ch of St Andr Marblehead MA 1999-2003; Wyman Memi Ch of St Andr Marblehead MA 1992-1995; Vic S Mk's Ch Maquoketa IA 1985-1989; Asst R S Thos' Epis Ch Sioux City IA 1983-1985. mdecarlen@comcast.net

DECARVALHO, Maria Elena (RI) 18 Vassar Ave, Providence RI 02906 B Providence RI 5/13/1954 d Manuel Alves Decarvalho & Mary Evelyn. BA Ya 1976; MDiv Weston Jesuit TS 1990. D 6/23/1990 P 2/9/1991 Bp George Nelson Hunt III. m 10/17/1981 Ashbel Tingley Wall c 2. Dn Cathd Of S Jn Providence RI 1998-2004; Asst R Gr Ch In Providence Providence RI 1990-1996. mariadec@cox.net

DE CHAMBEAU, Franck Alsid (Ct) 163 Belgo Rd, P.O. Box 391, Lakeville CT 06039 B Marinette WI 12/7/1936 s Alsid Joseph De Chambeau & Viola Bertha. BS U of Wisconsin 1958; M.Div. GTS 1961; MA Col 1976; EdD Col 1977. D 6/18/1961 Bp William Hampton Brady P 4/7/1962 Bp Joseph Warren Hutchens. m 11/17/2008 Richard D Spoor. Asst S Jn's Ch Salisbury CT 2002; Asst Trin Ch Lakeville CT 2002; Cur S Mk's Ch Jackson Heights NY 1963-1964; Cur S Ptr's Epis Ch Cheshire CT 1961-1963. Auth, "Keeping the Corp Tall Ships Afloat," *Bus Week*; Auth, "Concrete Approaches to a Philos of Adult Lrng," *Doctoral Thesis*; Auth, "Positioning Multi-Nationals for New Global Strategies," *Leaders*. Acad of Mgmt 1985; HR Plnng Soc 1977; Strategic Mgmt Soc 1990; The Berkshire Choral Fest 2000; The Conf Bd, Orgnztn & Mgmt Coun 1982; The Grp for Strategic Orgnztn Effectiveness 1983; The Salisbury Forum 2005. litchview@sbcglobal.net

DE CHAMPLAIN, Mitties McDonald (NY) 175 9th Ave, New York NY 10011 **S Clem's Ch New York NY 2009-; The GTS New York NY 1998-** B Pasadena CA 10/23/1948 d Edgar Lee McDonald & Caroline Louise. AA Palomar Coll 1968; BS NWU 1970; MA NWU 1971; PhD USC 1987. D 6/10/1995 P 1/1/1996 Bp Frederick Houk Borsch. dechamplain@gts.edu

DECKENBACH, Paul Conover (Nwk) 1551 26th Ave, San Francisco CA 94122 B Newark NJ 4/22/1927 s Peter Ritte' Deckenbach & Eleanor. BA U of Virginia 1951; STB GTS 1964. D 6/12/1954 P 12/18/1954 Bp Benjamin M Washburn. c 2. Asst S Ptr's Epis Ch San Francisco CA 1986-1994; Dioc Coun Dio Newark Newark NJ 1969-1973; R S Andr's Ch Harrington Pk NJ 1966-1981; R S Jn's Epis Ch Boonton NJ 1957-1963; Cur Gr Ch Newark NJ 1954-1957. Cmnty of S Jn the Bapt. herbalj@yahoo.com

DECKER, Alva George (Ct) 122 Tromley Rd, East Windsor CT 06088 **Died 3/24/2011** B Newark NJ 9/20/1929 s George Henry Decker & Louise. MDiv STUSo 1954; BA FD 1957; STB Ya Berk 1960. D 6/11/1960 Bp Benjamin M Washburn P 12/17/1960 Bp Donald MacAdie. Auth, "Instead Of A Pageant," *Living Ch*, 1966. Cmnty Of S Jn The Bapt.

DECKER, Clarence Ferdinand (SO) 545 Woodsfield Dr, Columbus OH 43214 B Taintor IA 11/9/1925 s Richard William Decker & Marie Wilhelmena. BS Wstrn Michigan U 1950; MS MI SU 1952; PhD MI SU 1954; MDiv SWTS 1967. D 6/12/1965 Bp James Winchester Montgomery P 12/18/1965 Bp Gerald Francis Burrill. m 8/15/1948 Lucielle Ellen Thompson c 2. Int Trin Ch Newark OH 1997-1998; Int S Paul's Ch Marion OH 1996-1997; Int S Paul's Ch Chillicothe OH 1992-1993; Supply P Dio Sthrn Ohio Cincinnati OH 1990-1991; Epis Ret HmInc. Cincinnati OH 1984-1990; Ch Of S Edw Columbus OH 1982-1983; S Phil's Ch Columbus OH 1979-1981; Cmsn Higher Educ Dio Pittsburgh Monroeville PA 1970-1975; Cur Trin Ch Highland Pk IL 1965-1967. Auth, *arts Sci Journ*. Soc of St. Mary 1965; Soc of St. Simeon and St. Anna 1995. cdecker614@aol.com

DECKER, Dallas B (Haw) PO Box 7105, Ocean View HI 96737 B Elmira NY 8/10/1939 s George Bentley Decker & Theodora Gertrude. BS SUNY 1975; Mercer TS 1977. D 6/5/1976 P 12/21/1976 Bp Jonathan Goodhue Sherman. c 4. Vic S Jude's Hawaiian Ocean View Ocean View HI 2008-2011; Int Ch Of The Recon Webster MA 2006-2008; Supply S Mich And All Ang Seaford NY 2000-2006; Assoc S Ann's Ch Sayville NY 1997-2000; Int S Paul's Ch Glen Cove NY 1996-1997; Assoc S Paul's Ch Glen Cove NY 1995-1996; Assoc S Thos Ch Farmingdale NY 1994-1997; Assoc S Ann's Ch Sayville NY

1990-1994; R Zion Ch Douglaston NY 1987-1990; R Ch Of The H Sprt Gallup NM 1983-1987; Vic Ch Of The Gd Shpd Helena MT 1978-1983; Vic S Alb's Epis Ch Laurel MT 1978-1983; Vic S Thos Ch Hardin MT 1978-1983; Vic S Mths Epis Ch No Bellmore NY 1977-1978; Vic S Paul's Ch Roosevelt NY 1977-1978; Asst S Mk's Ch Westhampton Bch NY 1976-1977. Ord Of Ascen; OHF. cytodb@aol.com

DECKER, Georgia Ann (WK) 509 16th Ter, Hutchinson KS 67501 **Gr Epis Ch Hutchinson KS 2003-** B Hutchinson KS 3/21/1936 D 11/29/2003 Bp James Marshall Adams Jr. c 3. deckerg@sbcglobal.net

DECKER, Linda McCullough (Haw) 307 S Alu Rd, Wailuku HI 96793 B Wichita Falls, TX 10/29/1937 d Marvin E McCullough & Adaline T. Rad 1958; MDiv Weston Jesuit TS 1981. D 5/16/2010 P 12/4/2010 Bp Robert LeRoy Fitzpatrick. m 12/30/1957 John A Decker c 1. lmctrigg@clearwire.net

DECKER, Margaret Sharp (SanD) 1651 S Juniper St Unit 26, Escondido CA 92025 **Dioc Corp Dio San Diego San Diego CA 2005-; R Trin Ch Escondido CA 1995-** B Reno NV 8/2/1962 d Milton Lewis Sharp & Beverly Hug. BA U of Nevada at Reno 1984; MDiv CDSP 1990. D 5/1/1990 P 11/15/1990 Bp Stewart Clark Zabriskie. c 1. Stndg Com Dio San Diego San Diego CA 1996-2001; Asst S Dunst's Epis Ch San Diego CA 1993-1995; Dioc Corp Dio San Diego San Diego CA 1992-1995; Cur Trin Ch Escondido CA 1990-1992. rector@trinityescondido.org

DECKER, Prince A (WA) 3918 Wendy Ln, Silver Spring MD 20906 **Calv Ch Washington DC 2007-** B Freetown Sierra Leone 8/25/1952 s Jonathan Decker & Millicent. Mindolo Ecummenical Coll; Hndip London Inst Of Commerce 1975; Fbc U Of Sierra Leone 1980. Trans from Church of the Province of West Africa 1/3/2005 Bp John Chane. m 12/29/1984 Kadi Decker c 3. S Paul's Rock Creek Washington DC 2005-2007. juniseprince@hotmail.com

DECOSS, Donald Albion (Cal) 26 Overlake Ct, Oakland CA 94611 B Oakland CA 6/24/1920 s Bertram A DeCoss & Alma Nielsen. Golden Gate U. D 12/24/1960 Bp James Albert Pike. m 10/3/1947 Catherine Francis Scheimer c 1. D/Asst S Clem's Ch Berkeley CA 1962-1989; D/Asst S Anne's Ch Fremont CA 1960-1962; D/Asst S Jn's Epis Ch Oakland CA 1960-1962.

DEDDE, Joseph Colin (WNY) 233 Brantwood Rd, Amherst NY 14226 B Mount Kisco NY 2/3/1939 s Joseph N Dedde & Grace. AS Dn Coll 1960; BA Juniata Coll 1963; MDiv Ya Berk 1966. D 6/4/1966 P 12/1/1966 Bp Horace W B Donegan. m 12/31/1966 Cynthia Margaret Kirby. R S Mich And All Ang Buffalo NY 1977-2001; R S Mk's Epis Ch Yonkers NY 1969-1977; Asst S Mary's Ch Mohegan Lake NY 1967-1969; Cur Gr Ch In Providence Providence RI 1966-1967. Cwc. cdedde@adelphi.net

DEDMON JR, Robert Aaron (Q) 3601 North North, Peoria IL 61604 **Chair, Com to Reorganize Dio Quincy Peoria IL 2009-; Dn And R S Paul's Cathd Peoria IL 2005-** B Dyersburg TN 11/23/1947 s Robert Aaron Dedmon & Mary Elizabeth. BA Un U Jackson TN 1969; MA U of Tennessee 1970; PhD U of Tennessee 1975; MDiv STUSo 1982. D 6/20/1982 P 4/20/1983 Bp William Evan Sanders. m 8/30/1969 Judy S Smith c 3. Stndg Com Dio Quincy Peoria IL 2006-2007; Cn To Ordnry Dio Tennessee Nashville TN 1994-2005; Episcopate Com Dio Tennessee Nashville TN 1992-1993; S Mk's Ch Antioch TN 1989-1994; Vic S Bede's Epis Ch Manchester TN 1983-1986; Trst The TS at The U So Sewanee TN 1982-1987; D S Paul's Epis Ch Chattanooga TN 1982-1983. Auth, "Job As Holocaust Survivor," *S Lk Journ Of Theol*, 1984. frdedmon@stpaulspeoria.com

DEDRICK, Royal Fred (NC) 2133 Wildlife Rd, Charlotte NC 28214 **Died 1/15/2011** B Wharton NJ 7/4/1928 s Fred Roy Dedrick & Marguerite Teresa. BA Ups 1955; Clu 1970; New Jersey Theol Sem 1975; Chfc 1985. D 12/20/1975 P 8/13/1977 Bp Albert Wiencke Van Duzer. c 4. OHC 1963. dedrickroy@juno.com

DEEGAN, Virginia Edna (CFla) 210 Fallen Timber Trl, Deland FL 32724 B Chicago IL 3/2/1935 d Phillip Joseph Deegan & Edna Mae. BEd U of Miami 1956; Med Florida Atlantic U 1970; 1975; EdD U of Florida 1988. D 6/15/1975 Bp William Hopkins Folwell. c 1. Who's Who in Educ 2007; Who's Who in Amer Wmn.

DEERY, Laurel Pierson (Mass) 44 School St, Manchester MA 01944 B Stamford CT 12/14/1948 BA Buc 1970; Med U of New So Wales 1986. D 6/3/2006 Bp M(arvil) Thomas Shaw III. m 1/24/1970 Craig Deery c 2. laurelpd@verizon.net

DEETHS, Margaret Edith (Cal) 576 Cedarberry Ln, San Rafael CA 94903 B London England 6/30/1934 BA Sch for Deacons 2003. D 12/6/2003 Bp William Edwin Swing. c 3. D Gr Cathd San Francisco CA 2003-2011.

DEETZ, Susan Maureen (Minn) 4210 Robinson St, Duluth MN 55804 B 6/21/1955 D 6/17/2001 Bp James Louis Jelinek. m 6/23/1978 William Harold Deetz c 3. S Paul's Epis Ch Duluth MN 2001-2004. sdeetz@charter.net

DE FONTAINE-STRATTON, James (NY) 161 Mansion St, Poughkeepsie NY 12601 B Farnborough Kent UK 7/19/1932 s Eric Bruce Stratton & Winifred Tate. Certtificate of Ed London St Mk & St Jn 1959; Cert of Ed London, St Mk & St Jn 1965; BA (Hons) London Univ. Golsmiths Coll 1971; Dplma in Educ London Univ. Inst of Educ 1972; MA Col, TC NYC 1975; MEd Columbia Univercity, TC NYC 1977. D 1/14/1979 P 1/16/1980 Bp Charles Lee Burgreen. m 10/1/1967 Dorothy Elaine McKoy c 3. Int P S Lk's Ch Somers NY 2005-2006; Dio New York New York City NY 1998-2004; P-in-c S Paul's Ch Poughkeepsie NY 1998-2004; Int Ch Of The Gd Shpd Wakefield Bronx NY 1997-1998; Dn Dio New York New York City NY 1993-1994; Ch Of The H Nativ Bronx NY 1990-1994; S Hilda's And S Hugh's Sch New York NY 1985-1988; Assoc Ch Of The Atone Bronx NY 1982-1983; Asst Ch Of The H Nativ Bronx NY 1982-1983; Assoc The Epis Ch of S Jn the Div Tamuning GU 1980-1982; Dio Micronesia Tumon Bay GU GU 1979-1982. jbdefs@gmail.com

DEFOOR II, J Allison (SeFla) 359 River Plantation Rd, Crawfordville FL 32327 B Coral Gables FL 12/5/1953 s James Allison DeFoor & Marjorie. BA U of So Florida 1976; JD Stetson U Coll Of Law 1979; MA U of So Florida 1979; M. Div. Florida Cntr for Theol Sutdies 2001; D. Min. Florida Cntr for Theol Stds 2005. D 9/9/2006 P 3/6/2007 Bp Leopold Frade. m 6/24/1977 Terry White c 3. STD Florida Cntr for Theol Stds. adefoor@earthbalance.com

DEFOREST, John William (Tex) 3535 Whittaker Ln, Beaumont TX 77706 B Sewanee TN 12/5/1946 s John Theophilus De Forest & Anne. BS SW U Georgetown TX 1969; MA U of Houston 1972; MDiv VTS 1996. D 6/22/1996 Bp Claude Edward Payne P 1/6/1997 Bp William Elwood Sterling. m 8/30/1969 Nancy VanKleef c 2. Int R S Jas Epis Ch Houston TX 2007-2008; Int R S Chris's Ch Houston TX 2005-2007; P-t Supply H Trin Epis Ch Dickinson TX 2005; R S Jn's Ch La Porte TX 2003-2004; Vic Ch Of The Incarn Houston TX 1998-2003; Asst R S Steph's Epis Ch Houston TX 1996-1998. billdeforest@sbcglobal.net

DEFOREST, Nancy (Tex) 3535 Whittaker Ln, Beaumont TX 77706 **R S Steph's Ch Beaumont TX 2008-** B Minneapolis MN 11/29/1948 d William John Van Kleef & Alfhild Matilda. U of Texas 1967; BS U of Houston 1970; MS U of Houston Clear Lake 1978; MDiv VTS 1996. D 6/22/1996 Bp Claude Edward Payne P 1/6/1997 Bp William Elwood Sterling. m 8/30/1969 John William DeForest c 2. S Ptr's Epis Ch Brenham TX 2007; Asst R S Jn The Div Houston TX 1996-2006. billdeforest@sbcglobal.net

DEFRANCO JR, Peter (Nwk) 396 Clifton Ave, Clifton NJ 07011 **R S Ptr's Ch Clifton NJ 2005-** B Paterson NJ 12/29/1952 s Peter De Franco & Gisella Ann. BA Don Bosco Coll 1975; MDiv Drew U 2002; GTS 2002. D 5/31/2003 Bp John Palmer Croneberger P 12/6/2003 Bp Rufus T Brome. Gr Ch Nutley NJ 2004-2005; Assoc for Chr Formation Gr Ch Madison NJ 2003-2004. pdfjr2010@gmail.com

DEFRIEST, Jeannette (Chi) 400 Main St Apt 5A, Evanston IL 60202 **S Lk's Ch Evanston IL 2004-; Alt Dep GC Dio Newark Newark NJ 2000-** B Pasadena CA 6/24/1956 d J DeFriest & Mary. California St Polytechnic U; MDiv EDS 1988; Cert The Ch Dvlpmt Inst 1998; DMin SWTS 2004. D 12/22/1990 P 6/22/1991 Bp Daniel Lee Swenson. R Ch Of The Mssh Chester NJ 2002-2004; Alum Exec Com EDS Cambridge MA 1993-2004; P-in-c Ch Of The Mssh Chester NJ 1993-1999; Asst R S Lk's Epis Ch Montclair NJ 1991-1993. jdfrst@hotmail.com

DEGAVRE, Susan Williams (Va) 7120 S. Wenatchee Way Unit C, Aurora CO 80016 B San Antonio TX 5/27/1942 d William Allen Williams & Hazel. BA Randolph-Macon Wmn's Coll 1963; MDiv VTS 1991. D 6/15/1991 Bp Peter James Lee P 1/12/1992 Bp Frank Harris Vest Jr. c 3. Int S Steph's Epis Ch Aurora CO 2007-2008; Int S Jas Epis Ch Essex Jct VT 2004-2007; Assoc Ch Of S Jn The Evang Hingham MA 2001-2004; R Imm Ch King and Queen Courthouse VA 1997-2001; R S Jn's Ch W Point VA 1997-2000; Assoc R S Thos' Ch Whitemarsh Ft Washington PA 1996-1997; Asst R Estrn Shore Chap Virginia Bch VA 1991-1996. susandegavre@comcast.net

DE GOLIER, James Richard (Mil) 7707 N Brookline Dr Apt 309, Madison WI 53719 **Died 6/19/2011** B Elkhart IN 8/26/1921 s Avery De Golier & Aline Erma. MDiv Nash 1946; BA Carroll Coll 1947; DD Nash 1974. D 4/6/1946 P 4/1/1947 Bp James R Mallett. c 2. Cmnty Of S Mary. P Of Year Dio Mil 1985. degskpi@merr.com

DEGOOYER, Bruce Underwood (Spr) 2816 Greenfield Rd, Bloomington IL 61704 **S Matt's Epis Ch Bloomington IL 2004-** B Fort Leavenworth KS 1/20/1952 s Louis Cornelius DeGooyer & Mary Winifred Priscilla. BA WA St U 1974; MPA The Evergreen St Coll 1986; Olympia TS 1993. D 6/29/2004 Bp Peter Hess Beckwith. m 10/9/1976 Sylvia Hoffman c 2. No Amer Assoc. for the Diac 2004. deaconbruce@aol.com

DE GRAVELLES, Charles Nattons (La) 3651 Broussard St, Baton Rouge LA 70808 **Epis HS Baton Rouge LA 2002-** B Lafayette LA 11/2/1949 s Charles Camile deGravelles & Mary Virginia. BA LSU 1971. D 6/10/1995 Bp James Barrow Brown. m 12/19/1970 Angela Margaret Winder c 3.

DE GWECK, Stephen William (Ala) 3736 Montrose Rd, Birmingham AL 35213 **Assoc S Lk's Epis Ch Birmingham AL 2004-** B Staten Island NY 6/29/1949 s William Joseph De Gweck & Elaine Marilyn. BA Wag 1970; MDiv Trin Luth Sem 1975; DMin GTF 1988. D 6/13/1992 P 1/8/1993 Bp Robert Oran Miller. m 3/30/1972 Dawn Louise Asquith c 2. R S Mk's Ch Prattville AL 1996-2004; Chapl Off Of Bsh For ArmdF New York NY 1992-1996. sdegweck@saint-lukes.com

DEHETRE, Donna B (Chi) 31 Edgehill Rd, New Haven CT 06511 B Washington DC 7/6/1941 d William Thompson Bayless & Mildred. BA Wheaton Coll 1962; MDiv SWTS 1980. D 6/15/1981 Bp James Winchester Montgomery P 11/19/1983 Bp Quintin Ebenezer Primo Jr. m 12/22/2005 Claudia R Libertin c 3. Ch Of S Jn By The Sea W Haven W Haven CT 2001-2003; No Cntrl Reg Mnstry Enfield CT 1997; Assoc S Thos's Ch New Haven CT 1996-2001; Int Ch Of The H Fam Lake Villa IL 1990-1994; Int S Chad Epis Ch Loves Pk IL 1989-1990; Int S Bride's Epis Ch Oregon IL 1988-1989; Asst The Epis Ch Of S Jas The Less Northfield IL 1981-1986; Asst To Dir Field Educ SWTS Evanston IL 1981-1983. AAPC 1990. dbdehetre@gmail.com

DE HOPE, Gary Joseph (CNY) Po Box 13555, San Juan PR 00908 **Died 8/9/2011** B Scranton PA 6/15/1939 s Garry DeHope & Alice Martha. BS Wilkes Coll 1962; MS SUNY 1968; BD EDS 1970; MS Dowling Coll 1990. D 6/14/1970 Bp Ned Cole P 12/19/1970 Bp Francisco Reus-Froylan. NAES. Pres Middle St Assoc Of Colleges And Schools Philadephia PA 1994.

DEJOHN, Kathleen Ann Gillespie (NJ) 138 Rector St, Perth Amboy NJ 08861 **S Ptr's Ch Perth Amboy NJ 1998-** B Perth Amboy NJ 1/25/1951 d William Warner Gillespie & Audrey Margaret. Allentown Hosp Sch Of Nrsng 1972. D 10/31/1998 Bp Joe Morris Doss. m 6/9/1973 Gennaro De John.

DE KAY, Charles Augustus (Chi) 462 Oak Avenue, Aurora IL 60506 **S Matt's Ch Evanston IL 2011-** B New York NY 2/28/1963 s George Colman de Kay & Mary Elliman. New Sch for Soc Resrch; Vas; BA Tem 1988; MDiv SWTS 2004. D 6/19/2004 Bp Carolyn Tanner Irish P 12/18/2004 Bp William Dailey Persell. m 9/18/2004 Christina Teresa Padilla c 3. R Trin Epis Ch Aurora IL 2006-2011; Cur The Epis Ch Of S Jas The Less Northfield IL 2004-2006. c_de_kay@hotmail.com

DEKAY, Eckford James (ECR) 1670 White Creek Ln, San Jose CA 95125 B New York NY 12/19/1923 s Eckford Craven de Kay & Kathleen Eleanor. BA Cor 1949; MDiv CDSP 1966. D 6/11/1966 P 12/18/1966 Bp Albert A Chambers. c 2. R S Fran Epis Ch San Jose CA 1983-1992; Dn The Cathd Ch Of S Paul Springfield IL 1971-1983; Archd Dio Springfield Springfield IL 1966-1971; Vic S Jas Epis Ch McLeansboro IL 1966-1971; Vic Trin Ch Mt Vernon IL 1966-1971. Auth, *Heraldry In The Epis Ch*, Acorn Press, 1996. eckford@aol.com

DEKKER, Robert Peter (Chi) 611 S. Evergreen Ave, Arlington Heights IL 60005 **R S Simons Ch Arlington Heights IL 1991-** B Sheboygan WI 7/15/1944 s Peter Nick Dekker & Bernice Frieda. BA California St U, L.A. 1972; MA, Ed. California St U, S.B. 1979; MA Claremont TS 1986. D 6/22/1986 Bp Robert C Rusack P 1/17/1987 Bp Oliver Bailey Garver Jr. m 6/29/1968 Helen Childs c 1. Dn - Elgin Dnry Dio Chicago Chicago IL 1996-2002; Cathd Chapt Dio Chicago Chicago IL 1995-1998; Asst R All SS-By-The-Sea Par Santa Barbara CA 1988-1991; Cur S Greg's Par Long Bch CA 1986-1988. Ord of H Cross, Assoc 2003. bob.helen.dekker@gmail.com

DE LA CRUZ REYES, Rafael Antonio (DR) Calle Santiago #114 Gazcue, Santo Domingo Dominican Republic B 1/28/1941 s Eleuterio De La Cruz & Carmela. Rec from Roman Catholic 1/1/1998 as Priest Bp Julio Cesar Holguin-Khoury. m 11/18/1982 Lourdes Josefina Compres De La Cruz. Dio The Dominican Republic (Iglesia Epis Dominicana) Santo Domingo DO 1999-2010. IGLEPIDOM@CODETEL.NET.DO

DELAFIELD, Audrey Sawtelle (Me) 32 Ship Channel Rd, South Portland ME 04106 **D S Alb's Ch Cape Eliz ME 1988-** B Boston MA 12/8/1941 d Egerton Burpee Sawtelle & Muriel Florence. AA Bradford Jr Coll 1962; BA McGill U 1964. D 5/20/1988 Bp Edward Cole Chalfant. m 11/27/1965 Joseph Livingston Delafield c 3. jdelafie@maine.rr.com

DELAMATER, Joan (Minn) 6287 Crackleberry Trl, Woodbury MN 55129 **S Jn In The Wilderness White Bear Lake MN 2004-** B Cadillac MI 3/17/1953 d James Eugene Potvin & Mariette. MDiv SWTS; MDiv Untd TS Of The Twin Cities; BA The Coll of St. Cathr 1975; MA U of St. Thos 1977. D 12/20/2001 P 6/20/2002 Bp James Louis Jelinek. m 9/22/1979 James R Delamater c 2. Ch Of The Ascen Stillwater MN 2002-2004. revjoanie@comcast.net

DE LANEROLLE, Nihal Chandra (Ct) 500 Prospect St Apt 2-F, New Haven CT 06511 **Middlesex Area Cluster Mnstry Higganum CT 2000-** B Colombo LK 4/16/1945 s Leslie Barnes DeLanerolle & May Adelaide. BS U Of Ceylon Colombo Lk 1967; PhD U of Sussex 1972; BA U of Cambridge 1974; MA U of Cambridge 1981. D 5/31/1977 Bp Philip Frederick McNairy P 7/11/1978 Bp Robert Marshall Anderson. P S Paul And S Jas New Haven CT 1987-1993; P S Matt's Epis Ch Minneapolis MN 1977-1978. Dsc U Of Sussex Engl 1995. nihal.delanerolle@yale.edu

DELANEY, James William (Nwk) 26 Prescott Rd, Ho Ho Kus NJ 07423 **Gr Epis Ch Westwood NJ 1988-** B Passaic NJ 12/11/1928 s John William Delaney & Vera. BBA Pace U 1951. D 12/21/1975 Bp Leland Stark. m 5/21/1967 Janet Kirwan c 1. D Ch Of The H Comm Paterson NJ 1975-1990.

DELANEY, Mary Joan (Az) 5611E Alta Vista St, Tucson AZ 85712 **Dio Estrn Michigan Saginaw MI 2006-; Assoc S Jn's Cathd Denver CO 1996-** B Faribault MN 1/6/1931 d Hobson George Savoie & Marguerite. BA California St U 1980; MA Azusa Pacific U 1982; MDiv Fuller TS 1992. D 6/13/1992 Bp Chester Lovelle Talton P 1/1/1993 Bp Frederick Houk Borsch. m 4/19/1952 Daniel Joseph Delaney c 7. Assoc Ch Of Our Sav Par San Gabr CA 1992-1993. ddmare@cox.net

DELANEY, Mary T (EMich) 1038 W Center St, Alma MI 40001 **R S Jn's Epis Ch Alma MI 2008-; R S Jn's Epis Ch Alma MI 2008-** B Detroit MI 10/15/1937 d George Daniel Delaney & Dorothy Claire. BSN U of Detroit Mercy 1961; MSN Wayne 1972; PhD NWU 1991; CTh SWTS 2002. D 5/4/2002 P 11/2/2002 Bp Edwin Max Leidel Jr. S Jn's Epis Ch Alma MI 2005-2009; Dio Estrn Michigan Saginaw MI 2004-2009; Leap Harrisville MI 2002-2005; Chr Epis Ch E Tawas MI 2002-2003; S Andrews-By-The-Lake Epis Ch Harrisville MI 2002-2003. mtdelaney@charter.net

DELANEY, Michael Francis (NY) 780 Greenwich Street #4M, New York NY 10014 **R S Andr's Epis Ch Staten Island NY 2001-** B Jersey City NJ 1/3/1957 s Keiran Joseph Delaney & Marie Annette. BA Seton Hall U 1994; MDiv UTS 1998. Trans 9/29/2003 Bp John Palmer Croneberger. Chr Hosp Jersey City NJ 1999-2001; P-in-c S Ptr's Ch Washington NJ 1998-1999. Co-Auth, "Rel Educ," *Exploring the Pathways of Faith*, Brown-Roa, 1997. Natl Assn of Pstr Mus 1977. frmichaelstandrew@mac.com

DELAUTER, Joe H (CPa) 598 Longbarn Rd, State College PA 16803 **D S Andr's Ch St Coll PA 2005-** B State College PA 3/13/1945 s Joseph Cyrus DeLauter & Lettie Knutsen. BS Penn 1976. D 9/19/2005 Bp Michael Whittington Creighton. m 12/22/1965 Sandra DeLauter c 2. Soc of Cert Sr Advisors 2011. JOE.DELAUTER@HOMEINSTEAD.COM

DE LA VARS, Gordon John (WNY) 115 S Erie St, Mayville NY 14757 **R S Paul's Epis Ch Mayville NY 1999-** B Elyria OH 11/19/1950 s Gordon LaGrand & Elizabeth Josephine. BS Kent St U 1974; MA U Of Akron 1980; PhD OH SU 1985; MDiv Bex 1998. D 6/6/1998 P 12/1/1998 Bp David Charles Bowman. m 10/13/1984 Lauren Helen Pringle. Vic Chap Of The Gd Shpd Chautauqua NY 1999; Ch Of The Adv Kenmore NY 1998-1999. Auth, "Testament Of Yth"; Auth, "Heritage Restored: Franciscanism In The Angl Comm". Conf On Chrsnty & Lit.

DEL BENE, Ronald Norman (Ala) 2841 Floyd Bradford Rd, Trussville AL 35173 **Int Epis Soc of Chr Ch Cincinnati OH 2010-** B Warren OH 9/18/1942 s Donald James Del Bene & Virginia Louise. BA Gannon U 1963; MA Marq 1966; STUSo 1979; DMin U of Creation Sprtlty Oakland CA 2002. D 3/9/1979 P 12/11/1979 Bp Emerson Paul Haynes. m 7/6/1968 Eleanor M Del Bene c 2. Int Gr - S Lk's Ch Memphis TN 2008-2010; Int S Mary's Cathd Memphis TN 2006-2007; Int Ch Of The H Comm Memphis TN 2005-2006; Int The Chap Of The Cross Madison MS 2004-2005; Int All SS Epis Ch Birmingham AL 2002-2004; R S Mich's Epis Ch Birmingham AL 1996-2002; Exec S Lk's Epis Ch Birmingham AL 1988-1992; Mssnr Dio Alabama Birmingham AL 1987-1990; R H Cross Trussville AL 1980-1986; Asst S Bon Ch Sarasota FL 1979-1980. Auth, *Into the Light*, Wipf&Stock, 2007; Auth, *Alone w God*, Wipf&Stock, 2005; Auth, *Hunger of the Heart*, Wipf&Stock, 2005; Auth, *The Breath of Life*, Wipf&Stock, 2005. ron@delbene.org

DEL CASTILLO, Gloria Rosa (Cal) 622 Lois Lane, El Sobrante CA 94803 **Vic Iglesia Epis Del Buen Samaritano San Francisco CA 2002-** B 7/12/1950 d Jorge Roberto Del Castillo & Berthina. BA U Fed erico Villarreal 1975; MA U Federico Villarreal 1977; BS Contra Costa Coll 1984; Anglicanism CDSP 1996; Bachelor of Theol Stds The Sch for Deacons 1996. D 6/6/1998 P 12/5/1998 Bp William Edwin Swing. REDHISPANA@AOL.COM

DELCUZE, Mark Stewart (Mass) 351 Main St, Ridgefield CT 06877 **R S Jn's Ch Beverly Farms MA 2010-** B Quantico VA 3/17/1958 s Godfrey Stewart Delcuze & Patricia Ann. BA U of Virginia 1980; MDiv EDS 1985. D 6/5/1985 P 1/6/1986 Bp Robert Poland Atkinson. m 9/10/1983 Mary Jerome c 2. R S Steph's Ch Ridgefield CT 2005-2010; Assoc Estrn Shore Chap Virginia Bch VA 1997-2005; R Ch Of The Ascen Norfolk VA 1992-1997; Asst R Gr Ch Kilmarnock VA 1989-1992; R Trin Ch Moundsville WV 1986-1989; Asst R Trin Ch Parkersburg WV 1985-1986. markdelcuze17@gmail.com

DELEERY, Seth Mabry (Tex) 9002 Clithea Cv, Austin TX 78759 B Galveston,TX 10/11/1946 s Joseph Sutherland Deleery & Mildred Nmn. BA U Of Houston 1969; MDiv Epis TS of The SW 1974; MS U Of Houston 1980; ThM Harvard DS 1990. D 6/19/1974 Bp Scott Field Bailey P 6/18/1975 Bp J Milton Richardson. m 11/14/1992 Elizabeth Gibson c 2. R S Richard's Of Round Rock Round Rock TX 1993-2004; Cn To Ordnry Dio Texas Houston TX 1991-1993; Dio Texas Houston TX 1981-1989; Vic S Jn's Epis Ch Austin TX 1981-1984; R S Mich's Ch La Marque TX 1978-1981; Locten Trin Ch Houston TX 1977-1978; Trin Ch Jacksonville TX 1976-1977; Dio Iran New York NY 1976; Asst S Mart's Epis Ch Houston TX 1974-1976. Auth, "Chr Socialist Mvmt In Engl 1848-1854". Hal Perry Awd Epis TS 2004. sethdeleery@att.net

DE LEEUW, Gawain Frederik (NY) 95 Ralph Ave, White Plains NY 10606 **R S Barth's Ch In The Highland White Plains NY 2001-** B Rochester NY 5/16/1969 s Hendrik Mcwilliams de Leeuw & Shreela. BA Ob 1991; MDiv U Chi 1995; CAS GTS 1996; DMin SWTS 2010. D 12/9/1995 P 6/15/1996 Bp William George Burrill. Cur Gr Ch White Plains NY 1998-2001; Assoc P Santa Rosa Mssn at Gr Ch White Plains NY 1998-2001. Auth, "Counting Treasures," *Volume 89*, ATR, 2007. Affirming Catholicism; SBL; Soc of Cath Priests 2011. Luce Schlr Henry Luce Schlr 1996. fathergawain@yahoo.com

DELEUSE, **Betsey Wilder** (Me) 27 Arlington St. Unit 1, Portland ME 04101 **Cler Mem, Com on H Ord Dio Maine Portland ME 2008-; D Cathd Ch Of S Lk Portland ME 2001-** B Lexington KY 6/11/1936 d Newell Morris Wilder & Gertrude. BA Hartwick Coll 1958; EFM The U So, Sch of Theoloby 1999. D 12/1/2001 Bp Chilton Abbie Richardson Knudsen. c 3. hunnybee7@gwi.net

DELEVETT, Aimee Ellen Sanders (Chi) 412 55th St, Clarendon Hills IL 60514 **R Ch Of The H Nativ Clarendon Hills IL 2006-** B Indianapolis IN 11/26/1972 D 6/5/2004 P 12/10/2004 Bp J(ohn) Neil Alexander. S Mary's Ch Pk Ridge IL 2004-2006. aimee.delevett@gmail.com

DELFS SSG, Carin Bridgit (SO) 109 John St, Louisburg NC 27549 **Asst S Ptr's Epis Ch Delaware OH 2011-** B Holyoke MA 9/24/1944 d Bernard August Delfs & Ruth Irene. Hudson Vlly Cmnty Coll; BA Salem Coll Winston Salem NC 2002; MDiv Wake Forest U 2005. D 10/10/1994 Bp David Standish Ball P 10/29/2005 Bp Michael Bruce Curry. c 2. Vic S Paul's Ch Louisburg NC 2007; Dio No Carolina Raleigh NC 2005-2007; P Asst Winston-Salem Area Colleges Mnstry Winston Salem NC 2005-2007; Asst S Paul's Epis Ch Winston Salem NC 2002-2007; D Asst Dio No Carolina Raleigh NC 2001-2002; Asst S Anne's Ch Winston Salem NC 1999-2000; Asst Cathd Of All SS Albany NY 1997-1998; Asst S Paul's Epis Ch Albany NY 1994-1997. Odk 2001; Ssg 1996; Theta Alpha Kappa Natl hon Soc For Rel Stds 2002. delfs.carin@yahoo.com

DELGADILLO, Ralph L (NC) 4002 Oak Grove Ave, Greensboro NC 27405 B Litchfield Park AZ 9/10/1940 s Antonio A Delgadillo & Maria Duarte. BA Arizona St U 1966; MPA Arizona St U 1985; EDS 1991; Cert Epis TS of The SW 1992. D 5/30/1999 Bp Robert Hodges Johnson P 11/30/1999 Bp Robert Carroll Johnson Jr. m 1/9/2002 Gloria Yolanda Delgadillo c 2. Vic Galloway Memi Chap Elkin NC 2006-2010; Int S Barn' Ch Greensboro NC 2001-2002; Hisp Mssnr Ch Of The Gd Shpd Raleigh NC 2000-2001; Asst R S Paul's Epis Ch Smithfield NC 2000-2001. frdelgadillo@aol.com

DELGADO-MARKSMAN, Adams Felipe (Ve) Calle Roscio #63, Salida Caratal, Edo. Bolivar 1000 Venezuela **Dio Venezuela Colinas De Bello Monte Caracas 10-42-A VE 2004-** B 8/23/1957 D P. CARATAL1857@HOTMAIL.COM

DELGADO-MILLER, Diego Antonio (NY) 260 W 231st St, Bronx NY 10460 **Dioc Trng Cntr New York NY 2007-** B 12/25/1944 s Mario Delgado & Amanda. Inst Comercial 1962; Jr Coll 1966; Universidad Autonoma De Santo Domingo Santo Domingo Do 1969; NYTS 1982; Inst Pstrl Hispano 1986. D 11/23/1987 Bp Paul Moore Jr P 11/1/1989 Bp Walter Decoster Dennis Jr. c 1. Ch Of The Medtr Bronx NY 2004; Dio New York New York City NY 2001-2004; Asst P S Jas Epis Ch Fordham Bronx NY 1998-2001; New York Spec Account New York NY 1998-2000; Diocn Msnry & Ch Extntn Socty New York NY 1997; Hisp Mnstry New York NY 1990-1992.

DE LION, Lawrence Raymond (LI) 15 Greenwich Rd, Smithtown NY 11787 **Pres of Revs Com Dio Long Island Garden City NY 2010-; Cathd Chapt Dio Long Island Garden City NY 2008-; Dn of Suffolk No Shore Dio Long Island Garden City NY 2007-; Revs Com Dio Long Island Garden City NY 2007-; Cn Com Dio Long Island Garden City NY 2006-; Prof Geo Mercer TS Garden City NY 2006-; R S Thos Of Cbury Ch Smithtown NY 2003-** B Alliance OH 9/5/1952 BA Mt Un Coll 1974; MDiv Yale DS 1977; MDiv Ya 1977. D 6/25/1983 P 11/1/1983 Bp John Harris Burt. Cathd Chapt Dio Long Island Garden City NY 2008-2009; Assistan Secy to Dioc Conv Dio Long Island Garden City NY 2006-2009; Asst Secy to Dioc Coun Dio Long Island Garden City NY 2006-2009; Chair Yth Issues Com Dio Chicago Chicago IL 1992-1994; Dioc Coun Dio Chicago Chicago IL 1991-1994; Dioc Yth Coun Dio Chicago Chicago IL 1990-1993; for YouthCommittee on Sprtl Formation Dio Chicago Chicago IL 1990-1993; Dnry Chair for CE Dio Chicago Chicago IL 1989-2003; R S Alb's Ch Chicago IL 1989-2003; Supvsr for Lay Chapl Bp Anderson Inst Dio Chicago Chicago IL 1989-1996; Cmsn on EFM and Mssn Dio Chicago Chicago IL 1989-1994; EUC Dio Chicago Chicago IL 1989-1994; Racism Com Dio Chicago Chicago IL 1989-1994; Fac S Greg's Epis Sch Chicago IL 1989; Ldrshp Trng Div Dio Ohio Cleveland OH 1986-1989; Reg Assoc in CE Dio Ohio Cleveland OH 1986-1989; CE Cmsn Dio Ohio Cleveland OH 1985-1989; R S Andr Ch Canfield OH 1985-1989; EFM Mentor Dio Wstrn Kansas Hutchinson KS 1984-1985, Supvsr for D in Trng Dio Wstrn Kansas Hutchinson KS 1984-1985; P S Paul's Epis Ch Goodland KS 1984-1985; Asst Chr Epis Ch Warren OH 1983-1984; Host for Dioc Yth Conv Dio Ohio Cleveland OH 1983-1984. Amer Cancer Soc Chairman Bd Dir 1990-2000; Co-Chair Crop Walk for Wrld Hunger 1990-1994; HIV/AIDS Pstr Care 1989-2003; Rotary Club Grp Study Exch Columbia, So Amer 1986-1986; Rotary Club of Smithtown Bd Dir 2008; Rotary Club of Smithtown Pres Elect 2011; Rotary Club of Smithtown Secy 2009-2010; Rotary Club of Smithtown VP 2010-2011; Rotary Club of Smithtown, New York 2003; Vstng Nurses Bd Dir 1985-1989. Paul Harris Fell Rotary Club of Smithtown New York 2010. lawrencedelion@optonline.net

DELK, Michael L (SVa) 205 Castle Ln, Williamsburg VA 23185 **R Hickory Neck Ch Toano VA 2002-** B Russellville KY 6/22/1972 s Clyde Delk & Nancy Lou. BA Transylvania U 1994; MDiv VTS 1997. D 6/21/1997 P 12/22/1997 Bp Don Adger Wimberly. m 6/6/1998 Stephanie L Taylor c 2. Cn for YA & Cmncatn Cathd Of S Phil Atlanta GA 1999-2002; Asst to the R Ch Of The Gd Shpd Lexington KY 1997-1999. mdelk@hickoryneck.org

DELL JR, Edward Thomas (Mass) Po Box 44, West Peterborough NH 03468 **Dio Pennsylvania Philadelphia PA 1971-** B Atlanta GA 2/12/1923 s Edward Thomas Dell & Virginia Prue. BA Estrn Nazarene Coll 1947; BTh Estrn Nazarene Coll 1948; MDiv EDS 1955. D 6/25/1955 Bp Norman B Nash P 2/4/1956 Bp Anson Phelps Stokes Jr. c 3. P S Paul's Ch Boston MA 1956-1961; Cur S Jn's S Jas Epis Ch Roxbury MA 1955-1956. Auth, *A Handbook for Ch Weddings*, MoreHouse - Barlow, 1964. edthomwards3@gmail.com

D

DELL, Jacob William (Alb) 1674 3rd Ave Apt 3D, New York NY 10128 **Mgr, Digital Marketing and Advert Epis Ch Cntr New York NY 2011-** B Orange NJ 2/18/1973 s William Curtis Dell & Joanne. BA Ya 1995; MA Nash 2008; Cert in Angl Stds Nash 2010. D 12/12/2009 Bp William Howard Love. c 3. jakedell@gmail.com

DELL, Mary Lynn (O) 2741 Sherbrooke Road, Shaker Heights OH 44122 B Valley Forge PA 9/12/1959 BS Milligan Coll 1981; MD Indiana U 1985; MTS Candler TS Emory U 1993; ThM Candler TS Emory U 1995; DAS VTS 2002. D 6/14/2003 P 12/20/2003 Bp Peter James Lee. m 5/29/1999 David Vandermeulen c 2. Chr Ch Alexandria VA 2003-2004. Mary.Dell@UHhospitals.org

DELLARIA, Kevin (WTex) St. Andrew's Episcopal Church, 201 E. Nolte, Seguin TX 78155 **Exec Bd Dio W Texas San Antonio TX 2011-; Hlth Ins Com Dio W Texas San Antonio TX 2009-; R S Andr's Epis Ch Seguin TX 2009-** B Houston TX 8/1/1972 s Charles Dellaria & Shirley. BA Hardin-Simmons U 1996; MA Hardin-Simmons U 2001; MDiv Epis TS of the SW 2008. D 12/20/2007 Bp C(harles) Wallis Ohl. m 11/23/1996 Donna K Smith c 2. Nomin Com (Chair) Dio W Texas San Antonio TX 2010-2011; Hlth Ins Com Dio W Texas San Antonio TX 2009-2011; Nomin Com Dio W Texas San Antonio TX 2009-2011; Asst Trin Ch Victoria TX 2008-2009. Co-Auth, "The Bible and the 'Other': Fndt for Theologizing in a Global Context," *Revs & Expositor*, 1997. frkevin@standrewseguin.org

DELMAS, Hailey Lynne (Cal) 28 Cobblestone Ln, Belmont CA 94002 **D Ch Of The Epiph San Carlos CA 2000-** B Redwood City CA 4/20/1967 d Daniel Williard Bellack & Judith. BA U CA 1989; Cert Mercer TS 1999. D 6/23/1999 Bp Orris George Walker Jr. D Ch Of The Adv Westbury NY 1999-2000. hailey@cyberdeacon.com

DELOACH III, Albertus Lee (La) 1444 Basswood Dr, Denham Springs LA 70726 **Died 7/14/2010** B West Monroe LA 2/4/1931 s Albertus Lee DeLoach & Helen Gray. BA NE LSU 1956; BD STUSo 1959; STM STUSo 1973; MS Tul 1979. D 6/24/1959 Bp Iveson Batchelor Noland P 5/16/1960 Bp Girault M Jones. c 2. bertfrances@att.net

DEL VALLE-ORTIZ, Efrain Edgardo (PR) Mansiones de San Martin #26 Las Villas, San Juan RP 00924 Puerto Rico B San Juan PR 9/4/1957 s Efrain Del Valle-Roman & Fidelina. D 6/30/2007 P 7/6/2008 Bp David Andres Alvarez-Velazquez. m 3/22/2002 Okichie Delgado-Ocasio c 4. efrainedgardo@yahoo.com

DELZELL, Constance Kay Clawson (Colo) 3 Calle de Montanas, Santa Fe NM 87507 B Carmi IL 12/31/1941 d Darrell Benton Clawson & Gertrude Edith. SWTS; BA U CO 1979; MA Iliff TS 1981. D 6/4/1983 Bp William Carl Frey P 12/1/1983 Bp William Harvey Wolfrum. m 2/23/1962 David Delzell. S Andr's Ch Denver CO 1999-2007; S Jn's Cathd Denver CO 1992-1998; Vic S Mary Magd Ch Boulder CO 1986-1990; S Jn's Epis Ch Boulder CO 1983-1987. AAPC. delzelld@comcast.net

DEMAREST, Richard Alan (Ida) 518 N. Eighth Street, Boise ID 83702 **Dn S Mich's Cathd Boise ID 1998-** B Paterson NJ 12/17/1956 s Harrison B Demarest & Ruth H. BA Montclair St U 1984; MDiv CRDS 1987; MA Geo Fox U, Newburgh, Oregon 2004. D 5/30/1987 P 12/5/1987 Bp John Shelby Spong. m 1/4/1986 Diane Lorraine Steiner. Dioc Coun Dio Idaho Boise ID 2004-2006; Cn Trin Cathd Pittsburgh PA 1993-1998; R S Andr's Ch Harrington Pk NJ 1989-1993; Dept of Missions Dio Newark Newark NJ 1989-1991; Asst Calv Epis Ch Summit NJ 1987-1989; Bp's T/F on the Bible Dio Newark Newark NJ 1987-1988. Boise Downtown Rotary. Inter-Angl Stds Prog Oxford Engl 1991; Rossiter Fell Bex 1990. diaconos@aol.com

DE MEL, Chitral Suranjith (Mass) 25 Sunset Dr, Douglas MA 01516 B Sri Lanka 10/9/1957 LLD Law Coll Colombo Lk 1984; MS Clarion U of Pennsylvania 1992; MDiv EDS 2005. D 6/4/2005 P 1/7/2006 Bp M(arvil) Thomas Shaw III. m 12/29/1984 Vyonni De Mel c 1. Urban Res S Anne's Ch Lowell MA 2008-2011; S Mary's Epis Ch Dorchester MA 2006. cdemel1771@aol.com

DEMENT, Thomas Erik (Oly) 1118 E Baldwin Ave, Spokane WA 99207 B Portland OR 2/19/1946 s Karl Adams Dement & Margaret Dacotah. Willamette U 1966; BA Stan 1968; MA Stan 1974; MDiv CDSP 1977. D 6/25/1977 Bp C Kilmer Myers P 5/17/1978 Bp Matthew Paul Bigliardi. m 1/1/1979 Meredith Barthelemy c 1. S Dunst-The Highlands Shoreline WA 1986-2008; R S Dunst's Ch w the Henry Memi Chap Shoreline WA 1986-2008; Vic S Tim's Ch Brookings OR 1980-1986; Cur S Barth's Ch Beaverton OR 1979; Legacy

Gd Samar Hosp Portland OR 1977-1978. A.B. "w dist" andDepartmental hon (Hist) Stan 1968. tmdement@q.com

DEMERCHANT, Barton Wilson Blaise (Chi) 42522 Woodward Avenue, Condo #B, Bloomfield Hills MI 48304 **Died 12/3/2010** B Royal Oak MI 4/23/1935 s Eugene Estey DeMerchant & Hazel Adelaide. BA U of Detroit 1960; MA Marq 1968; STM Nash 1973; DMin VTS 1987. D 6/30/1973 P 1/1/1974 Bp H Coleman McGehee Jr. c 1. Auth, *A Theol of Pryr*, Ford Press; Auth, *Pryr & Renwl*, Ford Press; Auth, *The Euch as the Fndt of Fidelity in Cmnty*, Ford Press. Oblate Ord of S Ben 1977. bdemerchant@comcast.net

DEMERE, Charles Clapp (WA) 20 Shoreland Drive, Belfast MD 04915 B Savannah GA 10/30/1928 s Raymond McAlister Demere & Josephine. BA Ya 1950; MDiv VTS 1954. D 6/27/1954 Bp Middleton S Barnwell P 4/1/1955 Bp Albert R Stuart. m 9/1/1953 Margaret Birney Crawford c 4. Assoc R S Alb's Par Washington DC 1964-1965; Vic S Bede's Ch Atlanta GA 1960-1964; Asst R S Jas Epis Ch Marietta GA 1958-1960; Vic S Anne's Ch Tifton GA 1954-1957.

DEMING, Nancy James (Pa) 518 Hilaire Rd, Saint Davids PA 19087 **Dio Pennsylvania Philadelphia PA 2004-** B Lynn MA 6/23/1957 BA Simmons Coll 1979; MA Luth TS 2000; GTS 2004. D 6/24/2000 P 5/29/2004 Bp Charles Ellsworth Bennison Jr. m 6/20/1981 Philip Schyler Deming. nancyjd610@aol.com

DEMING, Robert (Ct) 20 Shepherd Ln, Orange CT 06477 B Providence RI 1/26/1942 s Edwin Albert Deming & Violet Elizabeth. BA Wag 1964; MDiv GTS 1967. D 6/17/1967 P 3/1/1968 Bp John S Higgins. m 5/18/1968 Carolyn Evans c 2. R Ch Of The Gd Shpd Orange CT 1974-2008; Vic S Mk's Ch Groveton NH 1970-1974; R S Paul's Ch Lancaster NH 1970-1974; Cur S Paul's Ch Pawtucket RI 1967-1970. Paul Harris Fell Rotary Intl . goodshepherd@snet.net

DEMING, William Bower (ECR) 20250 Franciscan Ct, Salinas CA 93908 **D Epis Ch Of The Gd Shpd Salinas CA 1993-** B Yonkers NY 8/15/1930 s Leroy C Deming & Irene. BA Sch for Deacons 1992. D 5/22/1993 Bp Richard Lester Shimpfky. m 8/26/1982 Heather Barbara Martin. deming2@sbcglobal.net

DE MIRANDA, Mario Eugenio (SeFla) 15650 Miami Lakeway N, Miami Lakes FL 33014 B 11/15/1945 s Jose De Miranda & Juana. Trans from Iglesia Episcopal de Cuba 10/20/1993 Bp Julio Cesar Holguin-Khoury. m 8/28/1968 Romelia Calviz c 3. San Francisco de Asis Miami Lakes FL 2006-2009.

DEMLER, Maureen Ann (Alb) 912 Route 146, Clifton Park NY 12065 B Yonkers NY 5/13/1949 d Margaret Brett McDermott. MA SUNY 1972; BS Albany Coll of Pharm 1979. D 5/30/2009 Bp William Howard Love. m 5/31/1971 Randall Demler c 3. mdemler@nycap.rr.com

DEMMLER, Mary Reynolds (At) 995 E Tugalo St, Toccoa GA 30577 **R S Mths Epis Ch Toccoa GA 2009-** B Greenvile SC 2/2/1977 d John Lee Hemmer & Jane Reynolds. BA W&L 1999; MDiv Duke 2003. D 9/8/2003 P 3/30/2004 Bp Henry Irving Louttit. m 9/30/2005 Derek J Demmler c 2. S Ptr's Epis Ch Arlington VA 2006-2009; Chr Ch Valdosta GA 2004-2006; S Barn Epis Ch Valdosta GA 2004-2006. mdemmler@windstream.net

DEMMON, Michael David Scott (Colo) 2000 Stover St, Fort Collins CO 80525 **Assoc R S Lk's Epis Ch Ft Collins CO 2008-** B Norfolk VA 6/5/1983 s William J R Demmon & Elisabeth S J. BA U CO 2005; MDiv TESM 2008. D 5/31/2008 P 1/10/2009 Bp Robert John O'Neill. m 8/23/2007 Elizabeth Hoskinsen c 1. Asst TESM Ambridge PA 2007-2008. michael.demmon@yahoo.com

DEMO, Gar Raymond Tarrant (Kan) 2745 Silver Crest Dr, Conway AR 72034 **R S Thos The Apos Ch Overland Pk KS 2006-** B Austin TX 6/7/1969 s Jerry Rolland Demo & Sondra Sue. BA Wichita St U 1994; MDiv Epis TS of The SW 1997. D 6/7/1997 P 12/1/1997 Bp William Edward Smalley. m 6/4/1994 Kelly Marie Hamilton c 2. Vic S Ptr's Ch Conway AR 2002-2006; Asst R S Mich And All Ang Ch Mssn KS 1998-2002; Dio Kansas Topeka KS 1997-1998. gardemo@gmail.com

DEMO, Kelly Marie (Kan) 2745 Silver Crest Dr, Conway AR 72034 **Cn For Yth Mnstrs Dio Arkansas Little Rock AR 2001-** B Topeka KS 2/17/1968 d Hudson Houston Hamilton & Carol Ann. BD U of Kansas 1993; Epis TS of The SW 1997. D 6/7/1997 P 12/6/1997 Bp William Edward Smalley. m 6/4/1994 Gar Raymond Tarrant Demo c 2. Cn Dio Arkansas Little Rock AR 2002-2006; Dio Kansas Topeka KS 2000-2002; Yth Off Dio Kansas Topeka KS 1999-2000; Assoc R Trin Ch Lawr KS 1997-1999. kellydemo@aol.com

DE MONTMOLLIN, D(ee) Ann (WNC) 394 N. Main Street, Rutherfordton NC 28139 **R Ch Of The Annunc Holmes Bch FL 2010-** B Lawtey FL 1/1/1947 d Ina. BD Barry U 1988; MS St. Thos U Miami FL 1991; MDiv Ya Berk 2001. D 6/16/2001 P 12/15/2001 Bp Leopold Frade. m 8/10/1968 Phil de Montmollin c 2. R S Fran' Epis Ch Rutherfordton NC 2003-2010; Asst R S Thos Epis Par Coral Gables FL 2001-2003. dee@tampabay.rr.com

DEMOTT, Richard Arthur (Va) 784 Alpine Dr, Seven Devils, Banner Elk NC 28604 **Adj Cler S Mary Of The Hills Epis Par Blowing Rock NC 1999-** B Rockville Center NY 1/17/1930 s Arthur Daniel DeMott & Eva Belle. BS Un Coll Schenectady NY 1952; MDiv Yale DS 1955; STM Luth TS at Philadelphia 1966; GTS 1975. D 8/21/1976 Bp George E Rath P 12/21/1976 Bp John Shelby Spong. c 5. P-in-c The Sav Epis Ch Newland NC 1996-2001; S Matt's Epis Ch Sterling VA 1979-1995; Assoc S Tim's Ch Herndon VA 1977-1979.

DEMPESY, Catherine Biggs (WNY) St Pauls Cathedral, 128 Pearl St, Buffalo NY 14202 **The Epis Ch Of The Gd Shpd Buffalo NY 2010-** B Chicago IL 6/15/1961 d George Huling Dempesy & Elaine Biggs. BA Lawr 1982; MS Benedictine U 1989; MDiv Bex 2008. D 12/1/2007 Bp J Michael Garrison. S Paul's Cathd Buffalo NY 2008-2010. cbdemp@gmail.com

DEMPSEY, John Knowles (Spok) 517 N Sargent Rd, Spokane Valley WA 99212 B San Bernardino CA 9/18/1936 s John Knowles Dempsey & Mary Virginia. MDiv CDSP 1967; BBA Golden Gate U 1967; DMin SFTS 1991. D 5/20/1967 Bp George Richard Millard P 12/1/1967 Bp John Raymond Wyatt. m 7/8/1972 Rosemeri Fairchild c 4. R Epis Ch of the Nativ Lewiston ID 1992-1998; R All SS Ch Spokane WA 1987-1992; Exec Coun Appointees New York NY 1982-1987; Vic H Trin Epis Ch Wallace ID 1969-1972; Vic S Mk's Ch Ritzville WA 1967-1969. Auth, *The New Okinawa: Where Is It?*, 1983; Auth, *Original Angl Mssn in Inland No W*. SSC. "Who's Who in the Wrld". jackandlase@phmefish.com

DEMPZ, Julia A (Mich) 61 Grosse Pointe Blvd, Grosse Pointe Farms MI 48236 B Jackson MI 1/29/1948 d Williard Ray Adams & Barbara Carter. BA Wstrn Coll of Mia in Ohio 1970; S Jn's Prov Sem 1988; MDiv U Tor 1989; DMin Ecum TS 1997. D 6/23/1990 P 1/5/1991 Bp R(aymond) Stewart Wood Jr. m 8/8/1987 Charles Dempz. Nativ Epis Ch Bloomfield Township MI 2002-2009; R Nativ Epis Ch Bloomfield Township MI 2000; Assoc Chr Ch Grosse Pointe Grosse Pointe Farms MI 1994-2002; S Jas Epis Ch Birmingham MI 1990-1994. juliadempz@sbcglobal.net

DEMURA, Christine A (Oly) 10042 Main St Apt 410, Bellevue WA 98004 **Assoc S Marg's Epis Ch Bellevue WA 2002-** B Seattle WA 12/3/1954 Trans from Anglican Communion in Japan 6/10/2002 Bp Vincent Waydell Warner. c 2. cdemura@saintmargarets.org

DENARO, John Edward (NY) 1988 3rd Ave Apt 3, New York NY 10029 **P-in-c S Ann And The H Trin Brooklyn NY 2011-; P-in-c S Ann And The H Trin Brooklyn NY 2011-** B BronxNY 5/7/1963 s Gabriel Santo Denaro & Elisa. BA Wms 1981; MDiv Ya Berk 1991. Rec from Roman Catholic 3/10/1987 Bp Arthur Edward Walmsley. Int Asst Ch Of The H Apos New York NY 2008-2009; Int S Mk's Ch In The Bowery New York NY 2007-2008; Epis Ch Cntr New York NY 2003-2011; Trin Par New York NY 2001-2003; Pstr The Ch of S Edw The Mtyr New York NY 1998-2001; Int Chr And S Steph's Ch New York NY 1997-1998; Int Gr Ch Middletown NY 1996-1997; Vic Calv and St Geo New York NY 1994-1996; Assoc S Ptr's Ch New York NY 1992-1993. Berk Grad Soc 2005. johnny.juanny@me.com

DENDTLER, Robert Blanchard (At) 1011 Cedar Ridge, Greensboro GA 30642 B Buffalo NY 5/7/1936 s Hilmar Dendtler & Genevieve Ruth. BS U of Pennsylvania 1958; MS U of Tennessee 1963; MDiv VTS 1983; ThM PrTS 1990. D 6/18/1983 Bp Robert Bruce Hall P 12/20/1983 Bp John Shelby Spong. m 6/18/1960 Charlotte Anne Wheatley c 3. Int S Jn's Ch Christiansted VI 2009-2010; R Chr Epis Ch Kennesaw GA 1993-2000; R S Mary's Ch Sparta NJ 1986-1993; R Trin Epis Ch Kearny NJ 1983-1986. frbob@plantationcable.net

DENEAU, Elizabeth Ann (NMich) 500 Ogden Ave, Escanaba MI 49829 B St Louis MO 11/4/1943 d Norman Slough & Norma. BS Nthrn Michigan U 1978. D 9/19/2010 Bp Thomas Kreider Ray. m 8/27/1962 Walter Deneau c 2.

DENEKE, William Thomas (At) 515 E Ponce De Leon Ave, Decatur GA 30030 B San Antonio TX 10/13/1943 s William Crittenden Deneke & Ella Snow. BS U of Texas 1965; MDiv Sthrn Bapt TS Louisville KY 1969; ThM Sthrn Bapt TS Louisville KY 1970; VTS 1971. D 6/13/1971 Bp Charles Gresham Marmion P 12/1/1971 Bp William G Wright. m 1/27/1990 Deborah Lee Silver c 1. R H Trin Par Decatur GA 2000-2010; R Ch Of Our Sav Martinez GA 1979-2000; R All SS Ch Alexandria VA 1977-1978; R S Phil's Ch Southport NC 1974-1977; Asst S Ptr's Epis Ch Washington NC 1971-1974. deneke-silver@mindspring.com

DENG DENG, William (Oly) 4759 Shattuck Pl S Unit B101, Renton WA 98055 B Sudan 1/1/1977 s Deng Majuk & Amir. Trans from The Episcopal Church of the Sudan 3/13/2003 Bp Vincent Waydell Warner. c 1. dengwilliam@hotmail.com

DENHAM, John (WA) 767 N Cambridge Way, Claremont CA 91711 B Jacksonville FL 6/26/1930 s Thompson Brooks Simkins Denham & Leila. BA U NC 1952; MDiv VTS 1956; MS CUA 1981. D 6/12/1956 Bp Richard Henry Baker P 8/10/1957 Bp Edwin A Penick. m 11/6/1971 Maxine McKinley. Pstr Counslr S Alb's Par Washington DC 1988-1990; Pstr Counslr Ch Of The Resurr Alexandria VA 1981-1990; Exec Dir Mid-Atlantic Assoc For Train & Consult Washington DC 1968-1979; Dir of Chr Trng & Educ Dio Maryland Baltimore MD 1961-1968; Assoc S Jn's Par Hagerstown MD 1959-1961; P-in-c Ch Of The Mssh Mayodan NC 1957-1959; Asst S Phil's Ch Durham NC 1956-1957. Diplomate NASW 1986-1990; Diplomate-Amer Bd Examiners in Clincl Soc Wk 1988-1990. jmtdenham@verizon.net

DENISON, Charles Wayne (Wyo) 2502 Overland Road, Laramie WY 82070 B Arlington TX 1/4/1961 s Michael Revo Denison & Donnie. BBA Texas Wesl 1984; MDiv Fuller TS 1987; PhD U Denv 1994. D 6/24/1996 Bp Bob Gordon Jones P 1/28/1997 Bp William Harvey Wolfrum. m 1/7/1984 Bodwin W Wolle c 2. S Matt's Epis Cathd Laramie WY 2000-2002. Auth, "The Chld Of Est". chuckdenison@mac.com

DENISON JR, Raleigh Edmond (Dal) 1504 S Ash St, Georgetown TX 78626 **P-in-c Ch Of S Andr's In The Pines Pinedale WY 1971-** B Alpine TX 6/15/1935 s Raleigh Edmond Denison & Carolyn. BA U of Texas 1956; STB Ya Berk 1959; MA U of Texas 1964. D 6/21/1959 Bp John E Hines P 12/1/1959 Bp James W Hunter. m 6/9/1956 Mary Bert Hewitt c 2. P-in-c H Trin Ch Eastland TX 1971-1982; P-in-c Trin Ch Dublin TX 1967-1982; Cleric St Jn the Bapt Epis Ch Big Piney WY 1959-1962.

DENMAN, Scott Lester (Cal) 7917 Outlook Ave, Oakland CA 94605 **R S Jn's Epis Ch Oakland CA 1996-** B Denver CO 12/7/1955 s Victor Winfield Denman & Janet Milhouse. BA Colorado Coll 1978; MA Harvard DS 1981; MDiv Gordon-Conwell TS 1992; EDS 1994. D 6/4/1994 Bp David Elliot Johnson P 6/24/1995 Bp Barbara Clementine Harris. m 12/30/1978 Kamilla Lee Sparks. Dio Massachusetts Boston MA 1994-1996; Serv The Cathd Ch Of S Paul Boston MA 1994-1996. scott@stjohnsoakland.org

DENNEY, Curtis Stetson (Alb) 9650 State Highway, Ogdensburg NY 13669 **P S Phil's Ch Norwood NY 2007-** B Utica NY 5/16/1932 s Lucien Curtis Denney & Helen Catherine. BA SUNY 1960; MDiv GTS 1963. D 6/15/1963 Bp Allen Webster Brown P 12/21/1963 Bp Charles Bowen Persell Jr. m 1/27/1951 Mary Elizabeth Pickett c 3. Chr Ch Morristown NY 1989-1992; RurD Dio Albany Albany NY 1980-1986; Stndg Com Dio Albany Albany NY 1970-1976; R Gr Epis Ch Canton NY 1969-1988; R S Lk's Ch Mechanicville NY 1967-1969; P-in-c Trin Ch Schaghticoke NY 1967-1969; Assoc Chr Ch Cooperstown NY 1963-1967. Soc of S Marg 1991. Hon Cn Cathd of All SS Albany NY 2003. curtmary@northnet.org

DENNEY, Shawn W (Spr) 3813 Bergamot Dr, Springfield IL 62712 **Stndg Com Dio Springfield Springfield IL 2008-; Vic S Lk's Ch Springfield IL 1999-** B Jacksonville IL 4/5/1951 s Ray Denney & Marilyn. BA MacMurray Coll 1973; JD U IL 1976. D 6/1/1997 P 5/26/1998 Bp Peter Hess Beckwith. m 2/8/1997 Mary Ann Narve c 1. P-in-c S Lk's Ch Springfield IL 1998-1999. CBS; SKCM; SocMary. archdeacon@episcopalspringfield.org

DENNEY, Shelley Booth (Los) PO Box 1317, Lake Arrowhead CA 92352 **P-in-c S Richard's Epis Ch Lake Arrowhead CA 2008-** B Nashville TN 11/15/1950 d John Edmunds Booth & Edith G. BA University of California 1972; MA San Jose St U 1975; MDiv CDSP 2008. D 6/21/2008 Bp Mary Gray-Reeves P 12/21/2008 Bp Chester Lovelle Talton. m 10/4/2008 David H Starr c 3. shelleydenney@gmail.com

DENNEY-ZUNIGA, Amy E (ECR) 3080 Santa Ana Valley Rd, Hollister CA 95023 **P-in-c S Lk's Ch Hollister CA 2009-** B Los Gatos CA 11/8/1977 d Robert Harris Denney & Shelley Booth. BS U CA 2001; BA U CA 2001; MDiv Ya 2005. D 6/24/2005 P 12/27/2005 Bp Jerry Alban Lamb. m 8/21/2004 Vincent M Zuniga c 1. Dom And Frgn Mssy Soc- Epis Ch Cntr New York NY 2008; Exec Coun Appointees New York NY 2008. amydenneyzuniga@gmail.com

DENNIS, Alan Godfrey (NY) 346 W 20th St, New York NY 10011 **S Ptr's Ch New York NY 2010-** B Cape Town Cape ZA 6/4/1955 s Benjamin Raymond Dennis & Mary Johanna. D.TH (hon) S Ptr's Coll Fed TS 1978. Trans from Church of the Province of Southern Africa 7/30/1999 Bp Clarence Nicholas Coleridge. m 4/16/1979 Jennifer Abrahams c 2. Par Of Chr The Redeem Pelham NY 2009-2010; Cathd Of St Jn The Div New York NY 2006-2009; Dn S Jn's Cathd Albuquerque NM 2003-2006; R S Jn's Ch Bridgeport CT 1999-2003; Asst S Lk's Par Darien CT 1996-1999. Auth, "Towers Of Hope (1 Chapt)," 2002; Auth, "Life & Teachings Of S Aug," 1992; Auth, "Between Sea & Mtn," 1986; Auth, "Suffering Servnt As Contemporary Figure," 1977. Assoc OHC 2004; Comp Cmnty Of The Resurrect 1976. ajdennis56@aol.com

DENNIS, Fredrick Hogarth (Alb) 455 Park Ave, Saranac Lake NY 12983 B Washington DC 9/14/1939 s Lynwood S Dennis & Muriel Ellen R. BA U of Virginia 1962; MDiv VTS 1965. D 6/9/1965 P 12/15/1965 Bp Wilburn Camrock Campbell. m 6/23/1977 Dorothy Barrett. R The Ch of St Lk The Beloved Physcn Saranac Lake NY 1985-2005; Assoc R The Cathd Of All Souls Asheville NC 1975-1985; R S Jn Wheeling WV 1973-1975; Asst Trin Ch Huntington WV 1967-1973. conrick@verizon.net

DENNIS, Gladys Inez Hendren (RG) PO Box 146, Marfa TX 79843 **Vic S Steph's Epis Ch Ft Stockton TX 2005-** B Brownsville TN 3/2/1946 d Julian Thomas Hendren & Gladys Inez. Lindenwood U 1966; BS Texas Tech U 1970; MDiv UTS 1994. D 6/4/1994 Bp Jack Marston McKelvey P 12/1/1994 Bp John Shelby Spong. c 1. Supply P S Mk's Epis Ch Pecos TX 2003-2005; Other Cler Position Ch Of S Nich Pompano Bch FL 1999-2003; R Ch Of The Intsn Ft Lauderdale FL 1997-1999; Asst All SS Ch Bergenfield NJ 1994-1996; Asst S Lk's Epis Ch Haworth NJ 1994-1996.

DENNIS, Loretta Anne (Roch) 240 S 4th St, Philadelphia PA 19106 B Rochester NY 1/29/1947 d Bernard P Dennis & Carmella. BA Nazareth Coll 1970; MDiv CDSP 1980. D 9/29/1980 P 10/1/1981 Bp Robert Rae Spears Jr. Assoc Ch Of The Ascen Rochester NY 1984-1986; Asst S Paul's Ch Rochester NY 1980-1983.

DENNIS, William Joseph (WLa) 501 Springfield Ave, Eutaw AL 35462 B Rockford IL 9/10/1933 s Joseph Merlin Dennis & Winona West. LTh Epis TS In Kentucky 1964; BA U of Wisconsin 1970; MDiv Epis TS In Kentucky 1973. D 5/30/1964 Bp William R Moody P 3/25/1965 Bp Albert A Chambers. c 1. R Chr Ch S Jos LA 1995-2000; R Gr Ch Waterproof LA 1995-2000; S Lk's Ch Hot Sprg VA 1992-1995; S Patricks Ch Albany GA 1986-1991; R S Lk's Epis Ch Jacksonville AL 1983-1986; R S Steph's Ch Eutaw AL 1974-1982; R S Andr's Ch Kenosha WI 1967-1974; Cn/Cur The Cathd Ch Of S Paul Springfield IL 1964-1967. The Franciscan Ord of the Div Compassion (Oblate P) 1997; The SocMary (Mem).

DENNISTON, Marjanne Manlove (Spok) 6232 E English Point Rd, Hayden Lake ID 83835 B Newburgh NY 11/25/1927 d Stanley Thorpe Manlove & Marjorie Anna. Gonzaga U; AA Ladycliff Coll; BA U CA. D 4/29/1981 Bp Leigh Wallace Jr P 1/8/1997 Bp Frank Jeffrey Terry. m 6/6/1946 Clyde R Denniston, Jr. Asst S Lk's Ch Coeur D Alene ID 1992-1997; Asst S Steph's Epis Ch Spokane WA 1984-1992; Asst Ch Of The H Sprt Vashon WA 1981-1983. Auth, "Prism Of The Soul," Morehouse Pub. marjdenn@intermaxnetworks.com

DENNLER, William David (Tenn) 615 6th Ave. S., Nashville TN 37203 **D in Charge Ch Of The H Trin Nashville TN 2009-** B Middletown CT 1/21/1954 s Albert Charles Dennler & Sally Jean. AA Los Angeles City Coll 1977; BA Indiana U 2005; MDiv Nash 2009. D 6/6/2009 P 12/6/2009 Bp John Crawford Bauerschmidt. c 2. wdennler@gmail.com

DENNY, Stephen Michael (Ore) 10143 Se 49th Ave, Milwaukie OR 97222 **D S Jn The Evang Ch Milwaukie OR 1993-** B Portland OR 11/6/1953 s John Lewis Denny & Rosalie. Cert Clackamas Cmnty Coll 1973; Oregon Cntr for the Diac 1993. D 10/4/1993 Bp Robert Louis Ladehoff. m 11/21/1973 Betty Alice Wills. dcadenny@aol.com

DENSON JR, John Eley (Ind) 5 Granite St, Exeter NH 03833 **R S Paul's Epis Ch Indianapolis IN 2011-** B Richmond VA 10/6/1962 s John Eley Denson & Barbara. BA W&M 1984; MDiv SWTS 1992; DMIn SWTS 2009. D 6/13/1992 Bp Allen Lyman Bartlett Jr P 12/19/1992 Bp Frank Tracy Griswold III. m 8/16/1986 Stephanie Doss Wright c 2. R Chr Ch Exeter NH 1999-2011; Ch Of The H Comf Kenilworth IL 1992-1999. Auth, "For God Alone My Soul in Silence Waits," *New Hampshire Epis News*, 2009; Auth, "The Chr Pract of Hosp," *New Hampshire Epis News*, 2008. Henry Benjamin Whipple Schlr SWTS 1992; Dramatics Awd SWTS 1992; HN Moss Bk Awd SWTS 1991. jdenson@stpualsindy.org

DENSON III, John Lane (Tenn) 3105 Overlook Dr, Nashville TN 37212 **P Assoc S Ann's Ch Nashville TN 2003-** B Temple TX 2/4/1923 s John Lane Denson & Ruth Isabella. BA U of Texas 1949; MA U of Texas 1950; MDiv Epis TS of The SW 1954. D 7/1/1954 Bp John E Hines P 7/12/1955 Bp Clinton Simon Quin. m 5/25/1985 Caroline Stark c 4. Asstg P S Aug's Chap Nashville TN 1995-2000; Int S Aug's Chap Nashville TN 1987-1988; S Johns Ch Old Hickory TN 1980-1987; R Chr Ch Cathd Nashville TN 1965-1970. "arts In Ch mag Issues Of Select Sermons," 2003. Cmnty Of S Mary 1983. densonlane@bellsouth.net

DENTON, Edna Marguerite (SO) 1021 Crede Way, Waynesville OH 45068 **D S Fran Epis Ch Springboro OH 2002-** B Chicago IL 9/12/1932 d Thomas Joseph Layden & Edna Marguerite. Angl Acad 2002. D 10/26/2002 Bp Herbert Thompson Jr. m 1/31/1953 John Louis Denton.

DENTON, Jean Margaret (Ind) 1210 E 71st St, Indianapolis IN 46220 **Sr. Assoc R S Paul's Epis Ch Indianapolis IN 2006-; Dir of Hlth Mnstrs S Paul's Epis Ch Indianapolis IN 1992-** B Brooklyn NY 7/8/1946 d Cornelius Denton & Janet B. BSN Cor 1968; MA Col 1971; Dio Indiana Sch of Mnstry IN 1992. D 6/24/1992 Bp Edward Witker Jones P 7/17/2005 Bp Catherine Elizabeth Maples Waynick. m 1/1/1994 Thomas C Barnes c 2. Par Nrsng Consult to Congreg Mnstrs Cluster Epis Ch Cntr New York NY 1996-2001. Auth, "Gd is the Flesh," Morehouse, 2005; "An Epis Answers Questions about Par Nrsng," *Natl Epis Hlth Mnstrs*, 2001; Auth, "Steps to a Hlth Mnstry in Your Epis Cong," *Natl Epis Hlth Mnstrs*, 2001. Hlth Mnstrs Assn 1989. jeandenton@aol.com

DENTON, Maria Anna (Colo) 7068 Kiowa Rd, Larkspur CO 80118 B Boston MA 3/15/1940 D 11/10/2001 Bp William Jerry Winterrowd. c 2. mdstar@earthlink.net

DEPHOUSE, Jonathan Richard (Los) 1325 Monterey Rd, South Pasadena CA 91030 **Assoc D S Jas' Par So Pasadena CA 2009-** B Muskegon MI 7/24/1980 s James Martin Dephouse & Cathleen Dawn. BA Cornerstone U; MA Fuller TS 2005; MDiv VTS 2009. D 6/6/2009 P 1/9/2010 Bp Sergio Carranza-Gomez. m 12/23/2005 Sarah Lynn Baird c 1. jondephouse@gmail.com

DEPPE, Thomas Walter (Fla) 250 River Hills Dr, Jacksonville FL 32216 **R All SS Epis Ch Jacksonville FL 2006-** B Carthage TX 2/20/1958 s Walter Frank Deppe & Nell Louella. BS USNA 1980; MA Naval War Coll 1993; MDiv Epis TS of the SW 2003. D 6/21/2003 P 5/15/2004 Bp Philip Menzie

Duncan II. m 7/17/1982 Deborah S Timpte c 3. D-In-Trng/P Associte S Paul's Ch Mobile AL 2003-2006. Masters w dist Naval War Coll 1993. tdeppe@allsaints.jax.org

DEPPEN, G(ehret) David (NJ) 35 Queens Way, Wellfleet MA 02667 B Reading PA 5/22/1931 s Charles Gehret Deppen & Helen Anna. BA Cor 1953; MA U of Wisconsin 1956; STB GTS 1959; STM GTS 1964. D 6/20/1959 P 12/19/1959 Bp Charles L Street. m 7/11/1959 Gertrude Stottlemyer c 2. Int Gr Ch New Bedford MA 1993-1994; Dio New Jersey Trenton NJ 1984-1987; R S Paul's Epis Ch Westfield NJ 1982-1992; Ch Of The H Comm U City MO 1970-1982; Dio Missouri S Louis MO 1970-1979; Vic S Lk's Ch Madison WI 1964-1965; Cur The Ch Of S Jn The Evang Flossmoor IL 1959-1962. Auth, *My Dear People: Letters to a Cong*, Mnstry Press, 1990. daviddeppen@comcast.net

DEPRIEST, Sandra Moss (Miss) 510 7th St N, Columbus MS 39701 **Vic The Epis Ch Of The Gd Shpd Columbus MS 2006-** B 1/21/1954 d Charles J Moss & Edith Laverne. BS K SU 1976; JD Washburn U 1978; MDiv VTS 1999. D 8/6/1999 Bp Alfred Clark Marble Jr P 2/11/2000 Bp Henry Nutt Parsley Jr. m 1/21/1984 Donald R DePriest c 3. Vic S Jn's Ch Aberdeen MS 2001-2003; Vic The Epis Ch Of The Gd Shpd Columbus MS 2001-2003; Asst R Chr Ch Tuscaloosa AL 1999-2001. sdepr@aol.com

DEPUE, (Karen Lynn) Joanna (NY) 7 Heather Ln, Orangeburg NY 10962 B Morristown NJ 8/29/1950 d Harold Depue & Constance. Dio New York D Trng Prog NY 1993. D 6/15/1993 Bp Walter Decoster Dennis Jr. D S Barth's Ch In The Highland White Plains NY 2002-2005; D Gr Ch Hastings On Hudson NY 1996-1998; D Chr Epis Ch Sparkill NY 1994-1995. NAAD 1994. molc@geraniumfarm.org

DE PUY KERSHAW, Susan Lynn (NH) P.O. Box 485, Walpole NH 03608 **R S Jn's Ch Walpole NH 2004-** B Lakewood NJ 11/28/1954 BA Tem 1976; MDiv Estrn Bapt TS 1980; ThM PrTS 1985; CAS EDS 2002. D 3/27/2004 P 11/6/2004 Bp V Gene Robinson. Par Of S Jas Ch Keene NH 2002-2004. sdkershaw@myfairpoint.net

DERAGON, Russell Lelan (Ct) 871 N Indian River Dr, Cocoa FL 32922 B Worcester MA 2/1/1927 s Lelan Stanley Deragon & Margaret Mary. BA McDaniel Coll 1951; MDiv Ya Berk 1954; MA U of Rhode Island 1974. D 6/2/1954 Bp Walter H Gray P 12/18/1954 Bp Robert McConnell Hatch. m 6/12/1954 Desdemona Alice Simpson c 2. Asst Bp Seabury Ch Groton CT 1997-2005; Vic S Paul's Ch Westbrook CT 1974-1979; R Cathd Of S Jn Providence RI 1970-1972; R Trin Epis Ch Bristol CT 1962-1970; R S Jas Ch The Par Of N Providence RI 1959-1961.

DERAVIL, Jean-Jacques (Hai) Diquini 63b #8, Carrefour Haiti **Dio Haiti Ft Lauderdale FL 2002-** B Haiti 8/3/1959 LTh Codrington Coll. D 10/18/1998 P 4/25/1999 Bp Jean Zache Duracin. m 5/29/1993 Turin Marie Deravil c 1. St. Croix Par Ch 2002-2007; St. Thos Ch 2002-2007. jackdera@hotmail.com

DERBY, Glenn Evans (Minn) 408 N 7th St, Brainerd MN 56401 B Sewickley PA 8/9/1943 s John Leslie Derby & Mary. BS Montana St U 1975; MDiv Nash 1983. D 5/27/1983 P 2/2/1984 Bp Jackson Earle Gilliam. m 6/26/1996 Alison Conlon. R S Paul's Ch Brainerd MN 1998-2006; S Alb's Ch Sussex WI 1986-1998; Cur Zion Epis Ch Oconomowoc WI 1983-1985. glenn@agderby.org

DERBY, Roger Sherman (Mich) 34 Niagara Ave, Pontiac MI 48341 B Brooklyn NY 3/15/1935 s Irving Marsh Derby & Helen Georgia. BA Ham 1957; BD EDS 1960. D 6/15/1960 P 3/25/1961 Bp Dudley S Stark. m 1/7/1961 Nancy Elizabeth Tyner c 2. Int Nativ Epis Ch Bloomfield Township MI 1997-1998; Int S Jn's Ch Plymouth MI 1995-1997; Int S Jas Ch Grosse Ile MI 1993-1994; Int Chr Ch Dearborn MI 1992-1993; R All SS Epis Ch Pontiac MI 1974-1992; R Calv Ch Syracuse NY 1969-1974; R The Ch Of The Epiph Rochester NY 1964-1969; Vic S Andr's Ch Friendship NY 1962-1964; Vic S Paul's Ch Angelica NY 1962-1964; Cur Chr Ch Pittsford NY 1960-1962. rnderby@aol.com

DERBY, William Vinton (NY) 14 E 109th St, New York NY 10029 **R The Ch of S Edw The Mtyr New York NY 2010-** B 9/27/1946 MDiv EDS 1972; STM GTS 1988. D 6/3/1972 Bp Paul Moore Jr P 1/6/1973 Bp James Stuart Wetmore. R S Thos Angl Ch Vancouver BC 2007-2010; Int S Jas Ch Vancouver BC 2004-2006; R St Mich All Ang Ch 1994-2004. OGS 1991. PhiBetaKappa Rutgers U 1967. wvderby@uniserve.com

DERBYSHIRE, John Edward (CNY) 229 Twin Hills Dr, Syracuse NY 13207 B New York NY 11/3/1927 s Ivan Russel Derbyshire & Madeline Grace. BS Wayne 1951; MDiv Bex 2003. D 12/9/1989 Bp David Charles Bowman. c 6. D S Paul's Cathd Syracuse NY 1998-2003; D S Paul's Cathd Buffalo NY 1991-1998; D S Mich And All Ang Buffalo NY 1989-1990. john@kew.com

DE RIJK OSB, Cornelis Johannes (Az) 28 W Pasadena Ave, Phoenix AZ 85013 B Utrecht Holland NL 9/6/1936 s Godefridus Petrus de Rijk & Cornelia Johanna. BA Arizona St U 1971; MS Arizona St U 1973; MDiv Nash 1976. D P 1/18/1977 Bp J(ohn) Joseph Meakins Harte. Assoc S Mary's Epis Ch Phoenix AZ 1982-1985; Vic Ch Of The Resurr Tucson AZ 1977-1979; Epis Par Of S Mich And All Ang Tucson AZ 1977-1979; Epis Cmnty Serv Phoenix AZ 1976-1977. "factors during hemodialysis and their implications of Soc Wk"; *Mstr Thesis - Identification of Specific stress factors during hemodia lysis and their implications for Soc Wk.*. cderijk@cox.net

DERKITS III, J James (Tex) St Mark's Episcopal Church, 3816 Bellaire Blvd, Houston TX 77025 **Assoc S Mk's Ch Houston TX 2006-** B Beaumont TX 1/24/1977 s John Derkits & Bonnie. BS Texas St U San Marcos TX 1999; MDiv VTS 2006. D 6/24/2006 Bp Don Adger Wimberly P 1/6/2007 Bp Rayford Baines High Jr. m 1/8/2000 Laura K Derkits c 1. Asst R S Mary's Epis Ch Cypress TX 2006-2008; Yth Dir Chr Ch Cathd Houston TX 2000-2003. jderkits@gmail.com

DEROSE, Kathryn Pitkin (Los) 2621 6th St Apt 5, Santa Monica CA 90405 **D H Faith Par Inglewood CA 1998-** B Iowa City IA 3/11/1963 d Roy Macbeth Pitkin & Marcia Alice. PhD U CA; BA Duke 1985; MA U CA 1992. D 6/27/1998 Bp Chester Lovelle Talton. m 4/10/1999 Stephen Francis Derose. Auth, "Dealing w Diversity: Recruiting Ch & Wmn For Randomized Trial Of Mam"; Auth, "Breast Cancer Screening Adherence: Does Ch Attendan," *Breast Cancer Screening Adherence: Does Ch Attendance Matter*; Auth, "Ch-Based Telephone Mamography Counslg w Peer Counselors," *Hlth Cmncatn*; Auth, "Networks Of Care: How Latina Immigrants Find Their Way To & Through A Cmnty Hosp," *Journ Of Immigrant Hlth*; Auth, "Limited Engl Proficiency & Latinos' Use Of Physicians Serv," *Med Care Resrch & Revs*. Hlth Ministers Assn, Caucus On Publ Hlth & The 4th Cmnty. kpitkin@ucla.edu

DERSNAH, Donald (Mich) 3532 Terhune Rd, Ann Arbor MI 48104 **Trst Dio Michigan Detroit MI 2008-** B Gladwin MI 11/28/1947 s William Robert Dersnah & Ruth Elaine. BA U MI 1969; U MI 1974; Cert Whitaker TS 1997. D 10/11/1997 Bp R(aymond) Stewart Wood Jr. m 12/21/1968 Patricia Lee McCoy c 2. D S Jn's Ch Howell MI 2001-2009; Dioc Com Dio Michigan Detroit MI 2000-2003; D S Clare Of Assisi Epis Ch Ann Arbor MI 1997-2001; Cathd Chapt Dio Michigan Detroit MI 1997-2000. DersnahD@michigan.gov

DE RUFF, Elizabeth Anslow (Cal) PO Box 1137, Ross CA 94957 **Liturg and Mus Cmsn Dio California San Francisco CA 1998-** B Boston MA 3/24/1962 d Robert Edward Anslow & Carolyn Clare. BS USC 1984; MDiv CDSP 1998. D 6/5/1999 P 11/26/1999 Bp William Edwin Swing. m 5/28/1988 David Alan De Ruff c 3. Assoc P Chr Ch Sausalito CA 2001-2003; Liturg and Mus Cmsn Dio California San Francisco CA 1998-2010; P S Greg Of Nyssa Ch San Francisco CA 1998-2000. Auth, "Including Henry," *God's Friends*. Creative Mnstrs Grant Dio California Creative Mnstrs Dept 2005. betsy@deruff.com

DESALVO, David Paul (Del) 350 Noxontown Rd, Middletown DE 19709 **S Andrews Sch Of Delaware Inc Middletown DE 2011-** B Winchester MA 8/29/1953 BA U So. D 12/13/2003 P 1/15/2005 Bp Wayne Parker Wright. m 7/19/1981 Mary Park c 2. Assoc S Andr's Sch Chap Middletown DE 2003-2011.

DESAULNIERS, John J (Va) 406 Haven Lake Ave, Milford DE 19963 B Boston MA 6/16/1931 s George Edward Desaulniers & Genevieve Catherine. BS U of Maryland 1972; MDiv VTS 1985. D 6/22/1985 P 4/1/1986 Bp Peter James Lee. m 8/26/1978 Charlotte Elizabeth Caldwell c 3. P-in-c All SS Epis Ch Delmar DE 2000-2003; Little Fork Epis Ch Rixeyville VA 1985-1999. john.desaulniers@verizon.net

DESCHAINE, Thomas Charles (Me) Po Box 467, Augusta ME 04332 B Augusta ME 5/4/1943 BS U of Maine 1965; Med Providence Coll 1973; Cert STUSo 2001. D 6/5/2004 Bp Chilton Abbie Richardson Knudsen. m 8/13/1966 Carlene Preble c 2. tcdesch966@aol.com

DESHAIES, Robert Joseph (SeFla) 7461 Nw 13th Ct, Plantation FL 33313 **R S Benedicts Ch Plantation FL 1995-** B Waterbury CT 8/17/1948 s Germain Alfred Deshaies & Rose. BA Assumption Coll 1970; MDiv S Jn's Sem Brighton MA 1975. Rec from Roman Catholic 10/4/1991 as Priest Bp Calvin Onderdonk Schofield Jr. m 7/11/1987 Deborah Cabral Lapetina c 3. R S Tim's Ch Griffith IN 1992-1995; Asstg S Jos's Epis Ch Boynton Bch FL 1991-1992. Bro of S Andr 1995. revdeshaies@saintbenedicts.org

DES HARNAIS, Gabriel Alfred (Mich) 5500 Old Noble Rd, Cedar Grove NC 27231 B River Rouge MI 9/1/1933 s Armand Francois Desharnais & Therese Ubaldine. BA Sacr Heart Sem Coll Detroit MI 1955; MSW Wayne 1969; PhD Wayne 1979; MDiv St. Jn's Prov Sem Plymouth MI 1980. Rec from Roman Catholic 12/10/1988 as Priest Bp H Coleman McGehee Jr. m 3/22/1968 Mary Bernadette LaJeunesse c 2. Int Trin Ch Fuquay Varina NC 2001-2002; Supply Dio No Carolina Raleigh NC 1997-2002; Prchr Dio Michigan Detroit MI 1996-1997; S Alfred's Ch Oxford MI 1993-1995; Supply Dio Michigan Detroit MI 1989-1995; S Steph's Ch Troy MI 1989-1990. "Ther Expectancy Inventory: Dvlpmt and Preliminary Validation," *Psychol Reports*, vol.52 479-487, 1983. margub@mindspring.com

DESHAW OJN, Glen (Oly) 11380 NE 36th Pl Apt B135, Bellevue WA 98004 **S Jn's Ch Kirkland WA 2008-** B Seattle WA 7/28/1949 BA U of Washington 1983; MDiv Nash 2005. D 6/25/2005 Bp Vincent Waydell Warner P 12/18/2005 Bp Jeffrey Neil Steenson. m 3/18/1972 Rebecca S Young c 2. S Jn's Epis Ch Olympia WA 2008-2011; R S Paul's Ch Artesia NM 2005-2008; Vic S Thos A Becket Ch Roswell NM 2005-2006. Auth, "Stem Cell Confusion," *Nwsltr of NOEL*, Nat'l Org. of Episcopalians for Life, 2007. Assoc, Ord of Julian of Norwich 2004; Mem, Ord of St Lk 2005. revajd@gmail.com

DE SHEPLO, Louis John (NJ) 551 Saint Kitts Dr, Williamstown NJ 08094 **D S Thos' Epis Ch Glassboro NJ 2009-** B Long Beach NJ 10/4/1943 s John De Sheplo & Caroline Johnson-Donnelly. BA Glassboro St U 1972; MA Rowan U 1974. D 10/31/1998 Bp Joe Morris Doss. m 10/26/1968 Marie Grant c 3. D S Mk's At The Crossing Ch Williamstown NJ 1998-2008. ldeshepb@aol.com

DE SILVA, Sumith (Az) 9533 E. Kokopelli Circle, Tucson AZ 85748 **Assoc R S Alb's Epis Ch Tucson AZ 2000-** B Kotte LK 9/11/1942 s Edward Solomon DeSilva & Silta Perlyn. Gce Wesley Coll 1964; DIT Theol Coll Of Lanka 1973; Dplma in Preaching Coll of Preachers, Washington D.C. 1991. D 12/1/1972 P 12/1/1973 Bp The Bishop Of Colombo. m 8/31/1974 Shanthi Malani Meniknayake c 2. Curs Mvmt Sprtl Dir Dio Arizona Phoenix AZ 2009-2011; R S Jn The Bapt Globe AZ 1994-1999; RurD Big Sky Dnry Dio Montana Helena MT 1990-1992; Vic S Paul's Ch Ft Benton MT 1989-1999; Chair of Ch and Soc Com and Comp Dio Dio Montana Helena MT 1988-1992; Refugee Resettlement Off and P.B.'s Fund for Wrld Relief Dio Montana Helena MT 1988-1992; R S Fran Epis Ch Great Falls MT 1986-1993; Assoc Ch Of The Incarn Great Falls MT 1986-1989; Vic Calv Epis Ch Roundup MT 1983-1986; P Counslr Epis Cmnty Serv Phoenix AZ 1980-1982. Ch & Soc Cmsn Ntwk, PBFWR. sumisdes@hotmail.com

DESIR, Jean Nephtaly (DR) Iglesia Episcopal Dominicana, Apartado 764, Santo Domingo Dominican Republic **Dio The Dominican Republic (Iglesia Epis Dominicana) Santo Domingo DO 1992-** B Gressier Port-au-Prince HT 9/2/1960 s Aurel Desir & Servilia. 1986; TS Grad 1991. D 6/7/1992 P 12/1/1993 Bp Julio Cesar Holguin-Khoury. c 1.

DESIR, St Clair Roger (Hai) Box 13224, Port-Au-Prince Haiti B 8/12/1929 s Alphonse Canis Desir & Emmanuella O. BA Lycee Petion Hai Ht 1947; Epis TS 1951; MA Wayne 1953. D 6/17/1951 P 8/1/1953 Bp Charles Alfred Voegeli. m 6/8/1962 Marie-Mathilde Joseph c 3. Gladwyne Presb Ch Gladwyne PA 1990-1992; ABS New York NY 1969-1989. Auth, "The Process Of Urbanization At Port-Au-Prince"; Auth, "Etudes Creoles"; Auth, "The Other Side"; Auth, "Tetansanm/Comm". Haitian Bible Soc, Untd Bible Soc. rogersainclair@yahoo.com

DESMARAIS, Camille Leonile (Ala) 615 Lee St, Saraland AL 36571 **Died 4/13/2011** B Saint Johnsbury VT 8/28/1931 s Onile Willie Desmarais & Yvonne. BS Gallaudet U 1963; MDiv VTS 1966. D 6/17/1966 Bp George Mosley Murray P 12/18/1966 Bp Walter H Gray. c 3. Auth, "Mnstry Vocation for Deaf Men". Pres, Epis Conf of the Deaf of the Epis Ch 1978-1984.

DESMARAIS, Susanna (Neb) 2729 Hall St, Endwell NY 13760 **R Ch Of The H Trin Lincoln NE 2010-; Mem, Eccl Trial Crt Dio Cntrl New York Syracuse NY 2007-; Mus and Liturg Cmsn Dio Cntrl New York Syracuse NY 2007-** B Boston MA 5/21/1954 d Paul DesMarais & Phoebe. BA California St U 1978; MBA California St U 1984; MLS San Jose St U 1992; MDiv CDSP 2003. D 6/28/2003 P 1/12/2004 Bp Richard Lester Shimpfky. c 2. R S Paul's Ch Endicott NY 2006-2010; All SS Epis Ch Omaha NE 2003-2006. revsusanna@gmail.com

DESMITH, David John (Nwk) 90 Kiel Ave, Kinnelon NJ 07405 **R S Dav's Ch Kinnelon NJ 2003-** B Canandaigua NY 1/2/1951 s Elmer Z DeSmith & Ruth M. BA SUNY 1973; MDiv Bex 1990. D 6/16/1990 Bp William George Burrill P 2/1/1991 Bp Andrew Frederick Wissemann. c 2. Int Trin Cathd Easton MD 2002-2003; Dio Wstrn Massachusetts Springfield MA 2000-2002; Assoc S Steph's Ch Pittsfield MA 1998-2000; Dio Wstrn Massachusetts Springfield MA 1998-1999; R Chr Ch Rochdale MA 1993-1997; Dio Wstrn Massachusetts Springfield MA 1990-1997; Cur Ch Of The Atone Westfield MA 1990-1993. david.desmith@stdavidskinnelon.org

DESROSIERS JR, Norman (CFla) Holy Apostles Church, 505 Grant Ave, Satellite Beach FL 32937 **R Epis Ch Of The H Apos Satellite Bch FL 2006-** B Fall River MA 12/11/1946 s Norman Desrosiers & Rose Anna. BA Barrington Coll 1975; MDiv EDS 1980; MS/MA Command and Gnrl Stff Coll 1999. D 6/7/1980 Bp Morris Fairchild Arnold P 6/1/1981 Bp George Nelson Hunt III. m 5/31/1969 Barbara Lorraine Stedman c 2. Off Of Bsh For ArmdF New York NY 1989-2006; S Mths Ch Coventry RI 1984-1989; S Paul's Ch No Kingstown RI 1980-1984. sheplead@hotmail.com

DESUEZA, Edmond (NY) 271 Broadway, Newburgh NY 12550 B San Pedro de Macoris DO 7/31/1934 s Frank Emmanuel Lake Desueza & Ellen Andrea. D 6/10/1961 P 1/14/1962 Bp Paul Axtell Kellogg. m 8/17/1979 Isha Rojas Delgado c 3. P-in-c Ch Of The Gd Shpd Newburgh NY 2002-2006; Cntrl Epis Dnry New Britain CT 2000-2001; P S Matt's Ch Henderson TX 1998-2002; P S Chris's Ch League City TX 1997-1998; P S Fran Ch Houston TX 1996-1997; Novena Provincia Iglesia Epis 1994-2000; Dio El Salvador Ambato 18-01-525 Tu EC 1993; Dio The Dominican Republic (Iglesia Epis Dominicana) Santo Domingo DO 1975-1976. edesuezaf@hotmail.com

DESUEZA SAVINON, Edmond Guillermo (PR) Calle Santiago 114, Santo Domingo Dominican Republic B Santo Domingo Dominican Republic 7/14/1961 s William Desueza Fleury & Carmen Marina. BA 1979; MD 1984; BTh 1987. D 5/3/1987 P 5/29/1988 Bp Telesforo A Isaac. m 7/14/1987 Hortensia Marina. Dio The Dominican Republic (Iglesia Epis Dominicana) Santo Domingo DO 1987-1995. dmond@coqui.net

DETTWEILER, Walther Richard (CPa) 2654 Northfield Dr, East Petersburg PA 17520 B Newark NJ 2/27/1933 s Walther Dettweiler & Olga Anna. Fllshp Coll of Preachers; BA Rutgers-The St U 1954; MDiv Ya Berk 1957; Cert Profsnl Hosp Chapl 1967. D 6/15/1957 P 12/21/1957 Bp Benjamin M Washburn. m 6/27/1959 Marcia Ann Henriksen c 3. P-in-c S Lk's Epis Ch Mt Joy PA 1993-1995; P-in-c Ch Of The Crucif Philadelphia PA 1992; S Nathanaels Ch Philadelphia PA 1991-1992; P-in-c S Barth's Ch Philadelphia PA 1988-1991; Asst All SS' Epis Ch Scotch Plains NJ 1982-1987. Auth, "Nothing Is Lost; Everything Is Recoverable," *Clean & Sober Times*; Auth, "More Than A Friend, Less Than A Lover," *The Boundaries Counslg*. Coll Of Chapl; RACA. therapistwalt@earthlink.net

DETTWILLER II, George Frederick (Tenn) 108 Savoy Cir., Nashville TN 37205 B Memphis TN 10/8/1932 s Edgar Ellis Dettwiller & Elsie Mae. BA Van 1954. D 2/14/2004 P 10/24/2004 Bp Bertram Nelson Herlong. m 6/19/1987 Kathryn King c 4. S Phil's Ch Nashville TN 2004-2005. fatherfred@detdist.com

DETWEILER, William Raymond (HB) 6631 Wakefield Dr Apt 903, Alexandria VA 22307 B Chalfont PA 10/27/1929 s Raymond Swartley Detweiler & Anna May. BA Penn 1951; MDiv CDSP 1960. D 6/11/1960 P 12/14/1960 Bp John P Craine. m 8/3/1963 Mary Josephine Holmes c 2. Asst Trin Ch New Orleans LA 1965-1970; Cur Gr Ch Muncie IN 1960-1963. detweilersw-mj@juno.com

DEUEL, Ellen Mighells Cook (SanD) 1212 H St Spc 219, Ramona CA 92065 **D S Mary's In The Vlly Ch Ramona CA 2000-; D S Fran' Epis Ch Turlock CA 1995-** B Buffalo NY 11/2/1932 d Harold Jewett Cook & Harriet Geraldine. Mt Holyoke Coll; Pratt Inst. D 6/10/1995 Bp Calvin Onderdonk Schofield Jr. m 12/30/1961 Starr Alfred Deuel. Ed, "California Quarterly," Orange Cnty Geneological Soc. CT 1960. edeuel@yahoo.com

DEVALL IV, Frederick D (La) St. Martin's Episcopal Church, 2216 Metairie Road, Metairie LA 70001 **Chairman, Bd Trst S Mart's Epis Sch Metairie LA 2010-2012; Exec Bd Dio Louisiana Baton Rouge LA 2010-; R S Mart's Epis Ch Metairie LA 2004-** B New Orleans LA 6/30/1969 s Frederick DuMontier Devall & Ruth Margaret. BS U So 1991; MDiv VTS 1996. D 6/15/1996 P 12/21/1996 Bp James Barrow Brown. m 6/22/1996 Lisa J Underhill c 2. Pres, Stndg Com Dio Louisiana Baton Rouge LA 2005-2006; Vic Chap Of The H Comf New Orleans LA 1998-2004; Cur S Lk's Ch Baton Rouge LA 1996-1998. fddstm@bellsouth.net

DEVATY, Jean Marie (SC) 50 Pope Ave, Hilton Head SC 29928 **Assoc R S Lk's Epis Ch Hilton Hd SC 2008-** B Pittsburgh PA 5/3/1958 d Joseph Frank DeVaty & Dorothy Anna. BA Wheaton Coll 1980; MA Wheaton Grad Sch 1991; MDiv TESM 2005. D 6/11/2005 P 12/11/2005 Bp Robert William Duncan. Asst. R Ch Of The Ascen Pittsburgh PA 2005-2007. devaty@gmail.com

DEVAUL, Philip Hart (Los) 31641 La Novia Ave, San Juan Capistrano CA 92675 **Chapl S Marg Of Scotland Par San Juan Capistrano CA 2010-** B Orange CA 7/17/1979 s Gary Allen DeVaul & Marcia L. BA Tufts U 2001; MDiv VTS 2010. D 6/12/2010 Bp Diane M Jardine Bruce P 1/8/2011 Bp Mary Douglas Glasspool. m 7/19/2008 Krista Ward Thelford. pdevaul@hotmail.com

DEVEAU, Peter Jay (Oly) 3824 34th Ave Sw, Seattle WA 98126 **Dn Gr And H Trin Cathd Kansas City MO 2012-; R S Jn The Bapt Epis Ch Seattle WA 1997-** B Rye NY 7/21/1953 s Richard Jay DeVeau & Marie Ellen. SUNY; BA SUNY 1982; MDiv Ya Berk 1986. D 6/7/1986 Bp Paul Moore Jr P 12/14/1986 Bp Arthur Anton Vogel. m 10/4/1980 Mary Agnes Purcell c 1. Assoc Gr And H Trin Cathd Kansas City MO 1990-1996; Asst Chr Epis Ch Springfield MO 1986-1990. pjdeveau80@gmail.com

DEVENS, Philip (RI) 111 Greenwich Ave # 2886, Warwick RI 02886 **R All SS Ch Warwick RI 2000-** B Boston MA 11/13/1952 s Richard Mather Devens & Sylvia. BA Roa 1975; MDiv EDS 1984. D 6/2/1984 Bp John Bowen Coburn P 6/22/1985 Bp George Nelson Hunt III. m 6/1/1985 Barbara Lewis. Ch Of The H Sprt Charlestown RI 1986-2000; Cur S Paul's Ch Pawtucket RI 1984-1986. Soc Of S Jn The Evang 1980. revdev@bryant.edu

DEVINE, Michael Francis (WMass) 47 Ruskin St, Springfield MA 01108 **Cn Chr Ch Cathd Springfield MA 2003-** B Davenport IA 11/7/1946 s Ralph William DeVine & Elizabeth Ann. Concordia Coll 1966; BA Augustana Coll 1968; MDiv VTS 1977. D 9/10/1977 P 1/6/1979 Bp George Phelps Mellick Belshaw. m 12/23/1972 Mariana Bauman c 2. R S Geo And San Jorge Cntrl Falls RI 1989-2003; Vic Ch Of S Andr The Apos Camden NJ 1981-1989; Hisp Mssnr Dio New Jersey Trenton NJ 1977-1980. ap735@earthlink.net

DEVINE, Whitney Alford Jones (Oly) 4420 - 137th Avenue Northeast, Bellevue WA 98005 B Memphis TN 4/13/1957 d Frank Aubrey Jones & Dorothy Whitney. BD Van 1980; ThM Fuller TS 1986; MDiv VTS 1988. D 6/18/1988 Bp Alex Dockery Dickson P 6/26/1991 Bp Vincent Waydell Warner. m 6/25/1988 Craig Richard Devine c 4. Assoc Ch Of The Resurr Bellevue WA 2001-2007; Vic Gr Ch Duvall WA 1997-2000; Asst Ch Of The Epiph Seattle WA 1992-1997; Assoc S Fran Epis Ch Mill Creek WA 1989-1992; Cur Chap of S Martha and S Mary of Bethany Seattle WA 1988-1989.

DE VRIES, Charles G(osse) (RG) 3045 Buena Vida Cir Apt 113, Las Cruces NM 88011 **Died 8/29/2011** B Wheeling WV 6/27/1919 s Gosse Bote de Vries

& Ruth. BA W Virginia U 1941; MS LSU 1948; PhD LSU 1949; CDSP 1953. D 5/31/1953 Bp Thomas Casady P 12/16/1953 Bp Chilton Powell. c 3. Auth, *Rational Chr Behavior Theory & Pract*; Auth, *Study Manuals*. Hon Cn S Jn Cathd Albuquerque MM 1994. CLDEVRIES@ZIANET.COM

DEWEES, Herbert Reed (Dal) 9511 Meadowknoll Dr, Dallas TX 75243 **Ret S Jn's Epis Ch Dallas TX 2011-** B Stockton CA 5/22/1942 s Russell Joseph DeWees & Aletha Anna. BS Austin Coll 1965; MDiv TESM 2000. D 6/3/2000 Bp D(avid) Bruce Mac Pherson P 6/7/2001 Bp Clifton Daniel III. m 7/1/1965 Emily Jean Lippke. Assoc R Ch Of The Gd Shpd Dallas TX 2003-2010; Cur S Lk's Epis Ch Dallas TX 2000-2003. herbknep@yahoo.com

D

DE WETTER, Robert Emerson (CNY) PO Box 5310, Snowmass Village CO 81615 **Sr Pstr Snowmass Chap Snowmass Vill CO 2009-** B El Paso TX 2/20/1960 s Peter deWetter & Margaret. BA U CA 1981; MA U CA 1985; PhD U CA 1987; MDiv STUSo 1999. D 5/23/1999 Bp Terence Kelshaw P 12/11/1999 Bp Douglas Edwin Theuner. m 4/1/1989 Regina Ann Vonlgnatius c 3. R S Jame's Ch Skaneateles NY 2002-2009; Asst to R S Paul's Ch Concord NH 1999-2002. Woods Ldrshp Awd U So Sewanee TN 1997. robert@snowmasschapel.org

DEWEY, E Robinson (SC) 598 E Hobcaw Dr, Mount Pleasant SC 29464 **Costal Crisis Chapl Charleston SC 2001-** B Memphis TN 12/29/1952 s Edward Robinson Dewey & Laurie Barton. BA Mars Hill Coll 1977; MDiv TESM 1983; Spec. Study U So 1983; FBI Chapl Trng 1993. D 6/25/1983 P 5/1/1984 Bp Alex Dockery Dickson. m 4/20/2001 Kathryn Rentiers Dewey. Dio So Carolina Charleston SC 1991-1997; Asst R S Jn's Epis Par Johns Island SC 1989-1991; Assoc R Chr Epis Ch San Antonio TX 1987-1989; Assoc R All SS Epis Ch Birmingham AL 1985-1986; Assoc R Gr - S Lk's Ch Memphis TN 1983-1985. Auth, "Pstr Crisis Intervention II," Icisf/Chevron, 2002; Auth, "Pstr Crisis Intervention I," Icisf/Chevron, 2001. Chr Rotary Club 1994; Intl Conf Of Police Chapl 1991. Citizen Of Year Breakfast Rotary Club Charleston 1995. ccc@coastalcrisischaplain.org

DEWEY JR, S(anford) Dayton (NY) B908 New Providence Wharf, 1 Fairmont Ave, London E14 9PB U.K. Great Britain (UK) B Hampton VA 11/29/1944 s Sanford Dayton Dewey & Betty. BA Syr 1967; MA Syr 1972; MDiv GTS 1979. D 6/2/1979 Bp Paul Moore Jr P 3/1/1980 Bp Ned Cole. Dpt Of Missions Ny Income New York NY 1980-1986; S Lk's-Roosevelt Hosp Cntr New York NY 1980-1986. Auth, "Living," *Lrng & Loving*. daytondewey@gmail.com

DEWITT, Edward Leonard (NMich) 90 Croix St Apt 2, Negaunee MI 49866 B 10/10/1935 s William Alexander. BS Nthrn Michigan U 1995. D 11/4/2007 Bp Rustin Ray Kimsey. m 11/20/1954 Phyllis M Marley c 4. lendewitt@sbcglobal.net

DEWITT, Phyllis M (NMich) 301 N 1st St, Ishpeming MI 49849 B Detroit MI 12/14/1934 d Henry Marley & Alma. Nthrn Michigan U. D 5/2/2007 Bp James Arthur Kelsey P 11/4/2007 Bp Rustin Ray Kimsey. m 11/20/1954 Edward Leonard DeWitt c 4. phyllisdew@sbcglobal.net

DEWLEN, Janet Marie (Colo) 2500 22nd Drive, Longmont CO 80503 **D S Steph's Ch Longmont CO 1999-** B Minneapolis MN 3/10/1954 d Clifford W Swartout & Alice J. Cert Sch of Radiologic Tech Denver CO 1974; Colorado Sch of Diac Trng Denver CO 1999. D 11/6/1999 Bp William Jerry Winterrowd. m 5/14/1977 Gerald Edwin Dewlen c 2. Mem COM Dio Colorado Denver CO 2007-2011. NAAD (NAAD) 1998. jan.dewlen@gmail.com

DE WOLF, Mark Anthony (Ct) 9 Weetamoe Farm Druve, Bristol RI 02809 B Flushing NY 4/21/1932 s Mark Anthony DeWolf & Elizabeth Tillinghast. BA Ripon Coll Ripon WI 1955; MDiv Ely Theol Coll, Cambridge, UK 1959. P 6/1/1960 Bp The Bishop of London. m 6/5/1965 Jennifer M MacDonald c 3. S Andr's Ch Stamford CT 1975-1997; R S Mary's Ch Amityville NY 1967-1975; P-in-c Emm Epis Ch Of Sheepshead Bay Brooklyn NY 1964-1966; P-in-c S Jn's Epis Chap Brooklyn NY 1964-1966. JENMARKDEWOLF@AOL.COM

DEWOLFE, Robert Francis (WTex) 3412 Pebblebrook Dr, Tyler TX 75707 **Int S Fran Epis Ch Tyler TX 2010-; Gr Ch Port Lavaca TX 1996-** B Providence RI 10/28/1939 s Fred Ashley DeWolfe & Amy Dorothy. So Dakota St U; BEd Rhode Island Coll 1965; MA Chapman U 1974; MDiv STUSo 1980; DMin SMU 1998. D 6/18/1980 Bp Stanley Fillmore Hauser P 12/19/1980 Bp Scott Field Bailey. m 10/28/1961 Jo-Anne Boyce c 4. Vic S Marg's Epis Ch San Antonio TX 2005-2009; Partnr In Mnstry Estrn Convoc Kennedy TX 2000-2005; Cn Mssr- Partnr in Mnstry Dio W Texas San Antonio TX 1995-2005; Dio W Texas San Antonio TX 1995-1999; R Trin Epis Ch Pharr TX 1990-1995; Vic S Chris's By The Sea Portland TX 1985-1990; St Andrews Ch Robstown TX 1982; Vic Ch Of Our Sav Aransas Pass TX 1980-1987; Vic S Andr's Epis Ch Corpus Christi TX 1980-1982. Bro Of S Andr 1993; OHC 1976. frbobdew@yahoo.com

DEWOLFE, Robert Haydon (Haw) 1515 Wilder Ave # 2, Honolulu HI 96822 B Brattleboro VT 3/15/1942 s Daniel Charles DeWolfe & Edith Hooper. BA Marlboro Coll 1966; MDiv Ya Berk 1971. D 6/5/1971 Bp Harvey D Butterfield P 12/18/1971 Bp Frederick Barton Wolf. c 2. R Gd Samar Epis Ch Honolulu HI 1999-2004; S Andr's Epis Ch St Johnsbury VT 1994-1999; P S Barn Ch Rumford ME 1987-1993; Trin Ch Saco ME 1976-1983; Vic S Steph The Mtyr Epis Ch E Waterboro ME 1972-1976; Vic Trin Ch Castine ME 1972-1976; Cur Gr Epis Ch Bath ME 1971-1972. Ord of S Helena 1990. Leo L Pelletier Awd. sawasdeerob@gmail.com

DEWS, John D (Lex) 545 W Wellington Ave Apt 2n, Chicago IL 60657 B Tiffin OH 2/11/1956 s Dale Arthur Dews & Mae Elizabeth. Lic Epis TS In Kentucky 1990. D 12/19/1990 P 8/9/1995 Bp Don Adger Wimberly. R Ch Of The Ascen Mt Sterling KY 1995-2006. dews.john@gmail.com

DEXTER, Beverly Liebherr (SanD) 325 Kempton St Apt 104, Spring Valley CA 91977 B Toledo OH 9/6/1943 d Richard John Liebherr & Georgiana Martha. BS OH SU 1961; Med Georgia St U 1969; EDS Georgia St U 1973; EdD Duke 1975; MDiv Ya Berk 1990. D 6/16/1990 P 12/15/1990 Bp Charles Brinkley Morton. Assoc R S Ptr's Epis Ch Del Mar CA 2005-2010; Asstg P The Epis Ch Of S Andr Encinitas CA 2005; Asst R S Barth's Epis Ch Poway CA 2002-2005; Assoc R S Dunst's Epis Ch San Diego CA 1999-2000; Chapl S Jas By The Sea La Jolla CA 1998-1999; Priory Sch Chapl S Andr's Cathd Honolulu HI 1992-1998; Chapl S Andr's Priory Sch Honolulu HI 1992-1998; Asst to R Ch Of The Gd Samar San Diego CA 1990-1992. Auth, *Spec Educ & the Classroom Tchr*, Chas C. Thos, 1977. CT 1994. revbev90@yahoo.com

DEXTER, Raymond Arthur (Ak) 1634 Stanton Ave, Anchorage AK 99508 B Hartford CT 12/11/1923 s Lyman A Dexter & Mona V. BS/MS MIT 1947; Trin 1949; EdD Stan 1962. D 10/3/1976 P 3/1/1977 Bp David Rea Cochran. m 8/8/1975 Kathleen E Ferguson. Auth, "Off Trng In Salvation Army". Msa US-A.

DEY, Charlotte Jane (EO) 8090 Granite Falls Ct, Redmond OR 97756 **D Epis Ch Of The Trsfg Sis OR 2004-** B Benson MN 12/14/1927 d Elmer Ellsworth Bowers & Charlotte Iona. RN S Lk's Hosp Nrsng Sch 1948; BD U of Kansas 1970; MPA U of Missouri 1975; W Missouri Sch of Mnstry 1992. D 2/27/1993 Bp Hays H. Rockwell. c 2. D Gr Ch Jefferson City MO 1993-2004. NAAD 1993. janedey@handcable.com

DEYOUNG, Lily (Mass) 12408 Main Campus Drive, Lexington MA 02421 B Red Bank NJ 4/1/1955 d Roderick N DeYoung & Lois I. BA Rutgers-The St U 1978; JD Seton Hall U 1983; MDiv EDS 2000; MA Weston Jesuit TS 2001. D 6/10/2000 P 2/24/2001 Bp John Palmer Croneberger. R Ch Of Our Sav Arlington MA 2007-2010; The Epis Ch Of S Mary The Vrgn San Francisco CA 2003-2005; Asst Trin Ch Concord MA 2001-2003. lilydeyoung@aol.com

DIAMOND, Caroline (Los) 1050 E Ramon Rd Unit 125, Palm Springs CA 92264 B Baltimore MD 4/11/1950 d Carroll Janofsky & Bernice Jacobs. BS Towson U 1981; MDiv VTS 1987. D 6/20/1987 P 5/14/1988 Bp A(lbert) Theodore Eastman. m 9/17/1999 William Jessie Redmon. Vic S Richard's Epis Ch Lake Arrowhead CA 2001-2005; R S Andr's Ch Methuen MA 1999-2001; Assoc Ch Of The Gd Samar San Diego CA 1995-1999; Assoc S Jas' Epis Ch Parkton MD 1992-1995; Asst S Jn's Ch Reisterstown MD 1992-1995; Asst Min Emm Ch Baltimore MD 1989-1992; Dio Maryland Baltimore MD 1987-1989; Cur Emm Ch Cumberland MD 1987-1989. carolinediamond8888@gmail.com

DIAMOND, James Alan (SO) 318 E 4th St, Cincinnati OH 45202 **Died 7/21/2011** B Rochester NY 3/7/1945 s Jerome Diamond & Edith. ABS Br 1966; STB Harvard DS 1971. D 6/26/1971 P 2/19/1972 Bp John Melville Burgess. c 1. Auth, *Cand for Cults: Adolescent in Par Ch*. Cmnty of Resurr; Cmnty of the Cross of Nails; CEEP; EPF; ESMHE. Thompson Humanitarian Awd Cincinnati Human Rts Cmsn 2007; Comp of Cross of Nails Coventry Cathd 2004. diamond.ja@gmail.com

DIAZ, George Diaz (NY) 257 Clinton St Apt 19n, New York NY 10002 **D The Ch of S Matt And S Tim New York NY 2005-** B New York NY 7/19/1950 s Domingo Diaz-Medina & Paulita. BA SUNY 1975. D 5/14/2005 Bp Mark Sean Sisk. m 9/9/1977 Magdalena Perez c 2. gdiaz@nyc.rr.com

DIAZ, Gladys (NY) Po Box 617, Bronx NY 10473 **Dioc Trng Cntr New York NY 2010-** B Puerto Rico 2/28/1957 BS SUNY 2004; MDiv GTS 2006. D 3/11/2006 P 9/23/2006 Bp Mark Sean Sisk. Gr Ch White Plains NY 2009-2010. gdiaz0228@optonline.net

DIAZ, Jose A (Ct) 15 Robert St., Bridgeport CT 06606 **Mssnr Dio Connecticut Hartford CT 2003-** B Fajardo Puerto Rico 8/2/1951 Cert ETSC 1985; BBA U of Puerto Rico 1989; MBA U of Phoenix 1993. Trans from Province IX 11/4/2003 Bp Andrew Donnan Smith. m 1/30/2008 Marjorie Diaz c 3. Dio Puerto Rico S Just PR 1990-2003. jdmmsr@sbcglobal.net

DIAZ, Joseph Herbert (SwFla) 3396 Deerfield Ln, Clearwater FL 33761 **R H Trin Epis Ch In Countryside Clearwater FL 1989-** B Tampa FL 6/3/1939 s Sergio Diaz & Evelia. AA U of Tampa 1967; BS U of Tampa 1981; MDiv STUSo 1985. D 6/22/1985 P 12/28/1985 Bp Emerson Paul Haynes. m 9/13/1959 Janet Yuill c 1. R H Trin Epis Ch In Countryside Clearwater FL 1989-2010; Cathd Ch Of S Ptr St Petersburg FL 1985-1989. joed39@verizon.net

DIAZ, Narciso Antonio (Chi) 2415 N Butrick St, Waukegan IL 60087 **Nuestra Senora De Guadalupe Waukegan IL 2000-** B DO 1/30/1965 s Jose Juaquin Diaz Baes & Rita E Castillo. BA Universidad Del Valle Mx 1997; BA San Andres Angl Sem Mex City Df Mx 1998. Trans from La Iglesia Anglicana de

Mex 1/1/2000. m 7/14/1994 Olivia Denis c 1. Dio Chicago Chicago IL 2000-2002.

DICARLO, Michael Joseph (Los) 1400 W. 13th St. Spc 139, Upland CA 91786 B Los Angeles CA 2/21/1948 s Donald Joseph Carll & Muriel Ilene. BA California St U 1974; MDiv GTS 1980; ASN Coll of Canyons 1996; MHA U of La Verne 2004. D 6/21/1980 P 1/1/1981 Bp Robert C Rusack. m 4/19/1983 Cheryl Reid c 2. R S Nich Par Encino CA 1982-1993; Assoc Prince Of Peace Epis Ch Woodland Hills CA 1980-1982. OHC. dicarlo48@msn.com

DICK, Brandt Allen (Miss) 506 Washington St, Natchez MS 39120 **Trin Epis Day Sch Natchez MS 2009-; Chapl Trin Ch Natchez MS 2005-** B McComb MS 3/1/1968 s Donald Allen Dick & Shirley. BS Mississippi Coll 1990; MDiv STUSo 2005. D 6/1/2005 P 12/14/2005 Bp Duncan Montgomery Gray III. m 6/27/1998 Erica Pope c 1. frbrandt@cableone.net

DICKEY, Charles Prewitt (Ore) 75718 London Rd, Cottage Grove OR 97424 **Died 11/18/2010** B Oakland CA 1/19/1929 s Walter Fish Dickey & Christine Bell. BA U CA 1951; MA U CA 1954; Stan 1959; MDiv CDSP 1961. D 6/25/1961 P 3/25/1962 Bp James Albert Pike. c 2.

DICKEY, Robert William (Va) 108 Forest Garden Rd, Stevensville MD 21666 B Lexington VA 4/15/1932 s Robert William Dickey & Elizabeth Cribbins. W&L 1952; BA Duke 1956; BD VTS 1960. D 5/21/1960 Bp John Brooke Mosley P 11/22/1960 Bp James W Hunter. m 6/22/1957 Carolyn Weimer c 3. Reg Dn Dio Virginia Richmond VA 1976-1978; R S Thos Epis Ch McLean VA 1969-1987; R S Phil's Ch Laurel DE 1965-1969; Assoc S Marg's Ch Washington DC 1963-1965; Vic Ch Of The Gd Shpd Sundance WY 1960-1963. Reg Dn Dio Virginia 1976. bcdickey@friend.ly.net

DICKINSON, A Hugh (Pa) 2510 Lake Michigan Dr, NW Apt. A-205, Grand Rapids MI 49504 **Supply P S Phil's Epis Ch Grand Rapids MI 2009-** B Wilmington DE 4/1/1934 s Albert Hughes Dickinson & Margaret Elisabeth. BA Trin Hartford CT 1955; STB EDS 1958; DMin Estrn Bapt TS 1981. D 5/31/1958 P 6/6/1959 Bp John Brooke Mosley. m 7/30/2005 Margery Livingston c 3. Supply P Emm Ch Hastings MI 2007-2009; Int S Barn By The Bay Villas NJ 1999-2002; R S Jn The Evang Ch Lansdowne PA 1976-1997; R S Phil's Ch Laurel DE 1960-1964; Cur S Jas Ch Wilmington DE 1958-1960. hughdickinson@yahoo.com

DICKINSON, Garrin William (Dal) 3804 Carrizo Dr, Plano TX 75074 **R The Epis Ch Of The H Nativ Plano TX 2005-** B Ann Arbor MI 9/18/1969 s Robert William Dickinson & Ann Marie. BA U Pgh 1995; MDiv TESM 2000. D 11/9/2001 P 5/25/2002 Bp Robert William Duncan. m 9/4/1999 Jennifer Elizabeth Higgins c 3. Nthrn Convoc Chairman Dio Dallas Dallas TX 2006-2008; The Ch Of The Gd Shpd Bryn Mawr PA 2001-2002. "The Subversion of Middle-Earth," *Touchstone*, The Fllshp of St. Jas, 2002. rector@holynativity.org

DICKINSON IV, Robert Peet (SC) 1319 Winchester Drive, Charleston SC 29407 **Cathd Of S Lk And S Paul Charleston SC 2009-** B Falls Church VA 8/6/1973 BA Wake Forest U 1995; BTh Oxf 2003. D 6/18/2003 P 1/10/2004 Bp Edward Lloyd Salmon Jr. m 4/18/1998 Jennifer Barrett Macomson. S Mich's Epis Ch Charleston SC 2003-2009. PEET@YOUR-CATHERDRAL.ORG

DICKS, Paul Richard (Spr) 422 E 1st South St, Carlinville IL 62626 B Oto IA 8/14/1937 s Paul Ray Dicks & Edith Belle. BA Morningside Coll 1959; BD EDS 1962. D P 12/1/1962 Bp Gordon V Smith. m 9/24/1988 Christine Ann Garavet c 2. Vic S Ptr's Ch Carlinville IL 1996-2002; S Paul's Epis Ch Carlinville IL 1996-2001; P Ch Of The Gd Shpd Sun Prairie WI 1993-1996; S Chad's Ch Sun Prairie WI 1988-1993; R S Anskar's Epis Ch Hartland WI 1981-1988; Asst Chr Ch Cathd Eau Claire WI 1978-1981; S Lk's Ch Altoona WI 1978-1981; R S Alb's Ch Superior WI 1972-1973; R S Jn's Ch Shenandoah IA 1966-1969; R S Barth's Ch Granite City IL 1964-1966; R S Thos Epis Ch Glen Carbon IL 1964-1966; Vic S Alb's Ch Sprt Lake IA 1962-1964. SHN, SocMary, Amer Angl Coun. pdicks@wi.rr.com

✠ DICKSON, Rt Rev Alex Dockery (WTenn) 1F Vendue Range, Charleston SC 29401 **Ret Bp of W Tennessee S Mich's Epis Ch Charleston SC 2008-; Ret Bp of WTenn Dio W Tennessee Memphis TN 1994-** B Alligator MS 9/9/1926 s Alex Dockery Dickson & Georgie Wicks. BBA U of Mississippi 1949; MDiv STUSo 1958; Med Mississippi Coll 1971; DD STUSo 1985. D 5/31/1958 P 12/2/1958 Bp Duncan Montgomery Gray Con 4/9/1983 for WTenn. m 1/2/1999 Jane G Carver c 2. Bp of WTenn Dio W Tennessee Memphis TN 1983-1994; COM Hse Deps Dio Mississippi Jackson MS 1976-1982; St of Ch Com Dio Mississippi Jackson MS 1976-1982; All SS' Epis Sch Vicksburg MS 1968-1983; Stndg Com Dio Mississippi Jackson MS 1965-1968; Dep GC Dio Mississippi Jackson MS 1964-1982; Chair Dept Yth Dio Mississippi Jackson MS 1963-1965; R S Columb's Ch Ridgeland MS 1962-1968; R Chap Of The Cross ROLLING FORK MS 1958-1962; Vic S Paul's Ch Hollandale MS 1958-1962. alexjanedickson@bellsouth.net

DICKSON JR, E(lton) Robert (Mass) 6102 Buckhorn Rd, Greensboro NC 27410 B Binghamton NY 4/4/1929 s Elton Robert Dickson & Florence Marie. BA Harpur Binghamton NY 1952; STB EDS 1957. D 6/29/1957 Bp Walter M Higley P 6/13/1958 Bp Malcolm E Peabody. c 4. R S Jn's Epis Ch Holbrook MA 1964-1988; Asst Zion Ch Rome NY 1960-1964; S Jas Ch Cleveland NY 1957-1960; Mssy-in-c Trin Ch Camden NY 1957-1960.

DICKSON, Jacqueline Scott (Spok) 14820 E 8th Ave, Spokane Valley WA 99037 **Died 7/13/2010** B Methuen MA 7/30/1939 d Carl Hastings Lesure & Anna Ruth. RN Bp Johnson Coll of Nrsng / UCLA 1961; MDiv CDSP 1979; DMin SFTS 1992. D 6/17/1979 P 3/25/1980 Bp Joseph Thomas Heistand. c 2. Auth, "Role of the Profsnl Nurse in Radiation Oncology"; Auth, "Journey in the Wilderness: A Critical Study of Low Self-Esteem as a Barrier to Mutual Mnstry". AAPC 1994; Amer Psych Assn 1989; WMHCA 1989. Fell APA 2007; Fell AAPC 1994. jackie@cet.com

DICKSON, M(arkham) Allen (WLa) PO Box 51367, Shreveport LA 71135 B Shreveport LA 6/10/1922 s Claudius Markham Dickson & Marjorie Ross Fields. MS California Inst of Tech; DD Cranmer Theol Hse; BS MIT; DD Nashota Hse. D 8/14/1961 Bp Girault M Jones P 8/26/1973 Bp Iveson Batchelor Noland. m 9/4/1943 June Baldwin c 4. Asst Ch Of The H Cross Shreveport LA 1980-1988; Asst S Mk's Ch Gladewater TX 1979-1980; Asst S Paul's Epis Ch Shreveport LA 1961-1979. revadickson@cranmerhouse.edu

DICKSON, Patricia Joan (Va) 3883 Connecticut Ave NW Apt 715, Washington DC 20008 **P Assoc For Wrshp Cathd of St Ptr & St Paul Washington DC 2002-** B Somers Point NJ 10/3/1952 d Richard Dickson & Bernice Elizabeth. BS Mt St. Mary's Sem 1975; MA Mt St. Mary's Sem 1976; MDiv S Vinc Sem Latrobe PA 1985. D 11/17/2001 Bp Peter James Lee P 5/18/2002 Bp Duncan Montgomery Gray III. m 3/20/1987 Christopher Patrick Hoff. S Jas Ch Potomac MD 2007-2008. pdickson@cathedral.org

DICKSON, Paul Abbott (Spok) No address on file. B Fairfield CT 1/10/1931 D 6/14/1964 Bp Russell S Hubbard.

DIEBEL, Mark Heberton (Alb) 68 Troy Rd., East Greenbush NY 12061 **R Chr Ch Greenville NY 2010-** B Colorado Springs CO 11/16/1955 s Wendel Hobart Diebel & Thayer. BS Colorado St U 1979; MDiv Epis TS of The SW 1988. D 6/11/1988 Bp William Carl Frey P 12/14/1988 Bp James Daniel Warner. m 8/12/1978 Beth Ann Kasic c 2. Par Admin S Andr's Epis Ch Albany NY 2007-2010; R S Jn The Evang Columbiaville NY 1991-2007; Cur S Matt's Ch Lincoln NE 1988-1991. mark.diebel@gmail.com

DIEFENBACHER, Fred H (SwFla) 3824 Twilight Dr, Valrico FL 33594 B Mineola NY 1/20/1932 s Carl H Diefenbacher & Marie Anna. BA Juniata Coll 1954; MDiv Dubuque TS 1958; MS U of Iowa 1968. D 6/1/1979 Bp Edward Mason Turner P 11/1/1980 Bp Emerson Paul Haynes. m 7/29/1956 Anne Shoeman. S Cecilia's Ch Tampa FL 1991-1992; Dio SW Florida Sarasota FL 1986-1991; S Barth's Ch St Petersburg FL 1985-1986; Asst Ch Of The Epiph Cape Coral FL 1983-1985. Mnstrl Fllshp.

DIEGUE, Joseph Tancrel (Hai) Box 1309, Port-Au-Prince Haiti **Dio Haiti Ft Lauderdale FL 1983-** B Leogane HT 4/3/1954 Epis TS. D 1/23/1983 P 7/1/1983 Bp Luc Anatole Jacques Garnier.

DIEHL, Jane Cornell (EMich) 3201 Gratiot Ave, Port Huron MI 48060 **D S Paul's Epis Ch Port Huron MI 2008-** B Durham NC 11/23/1946 d William Townsend Davison & Milared. BA Wayne 1975; MSW MI SU 1989. D 12/13/2008 Bp S(teven) Todd Ousley. m 5/1/1971 Robert Edward Diehl c 2. jcdiehl5171@att.net

DIEHL, Robert Edward (EMich) 3201 Gratiot Ave, Port Huron MI 48060 **Assoc S Paul's Epis Ch Port Huron MI 2008-** B Detroit MI 12/29/1941 s Robert August Diehl & MaryLouise Camilla Bonneau. BA Wayne St Univesity 1964; MA Estrn Michigan U 1973. D 6/7/2008 P 12/13/2008 Bp S(teven) Todd Ousley. m 5/1/1971 Jane Cornell Diehl c 2. rediehl5171@aol.com

DIELY, Elizabeth Barrett Hanning (Be) 629 Glenwood St, Emmaus PA 18049 **Asstg P S Marg's Ch Emmaus PA 2002-** B York PA 3/15/1942 d Norman Walter Hanning & Eva Viola. BA Wilson Coll 1964; MA GW 1968. D 10/23/2001 P 10/6/2002 Bp Paul Victor Marshall. m 6/21/1969 Paul Rockwell Diely c 1. S Mary's Epis Ch Reading PA 2004. barrett42@fast.net

DIERICK, Frances Lorraine (Oly) 102 Glenn Ln, Montesano WA 98563 **P S Mk's Epis Ch Montesano WA 1993-** B Aberdeen WA 1/15/1936 d George Bernard Barber & Lena Elizabeth. Gn Coll. D 8/29/1992 P 3/27/1993 Bp Vincent Waydell Warner. m 11/4/1954 Robert Louis Dierick. Montesano Mnstrl Assn.

DIETEL, Robert G. (Oly) 1331 Rucker Ave, Everett WA 98201 **Vic S Ald's Epis Ch Camano Island WA 1999-; P-in-c S Mart And S Fran Epis Rockport WA 1994-** B Palo Alto CA 5/11/1944 s Howard Richard Dietel & Lila Grace. BA Walla Walla Coll 1966; PhD U of Washington 1986; MDiv CDSP 1992. D 6/26/1992 P 6/22/1993 Bp Vincent Waydell Warner. m 7/22/1978 Lorraine Cecille Meier c 2. P-in-c Ch Of The Trsfg Darrington WA 1994-2002; Asst S Hilda's - S Pat's Epis Ch Edmonds WA 1992-1994. Auth, "Ancient Akkadian Grammatical Concepts," 1986; Auth, "Current Issues in Linguistics," 1985; Auth, "Salix of Alaska," *Flora No Amer*, 1973. Cath Biblic Assn; SBL. Who's Who in Amer Botany Carnegie-Mellon U 1973. dietelb@yahoo.com

DIETER, David Dean (Mich) 847 Grand Marais St, Grosse Pointe Park MI 48230 **Sr Assoc Chr Ch Grosse Pointe Grosse Pointe Farms MI 2003-** B Easton MD 10/21/1954 s Paul David Dieter & Clara Jane. BS Indiana Wesl

1976; MDiv GTS 2003; DMin GTF/Oxford Prog 2009. D 12/21/2002 P 6/24/2003 Bp Wendell Nathaniel Gibbs Jr. m 4/11/1983 Richard P Thomas. Epis Soc for Mnstry on Aging 1988-1997. Sprt of Detroit Awd Detroit City Coun, Mayor, MI Gvnr 2009. ddieter@mindspring.com

DIETERLE, Ann M (Chi) 222 Kenilworth Ave, Kenilworth IL 60043 **S Jas' Ch Richmond VA 2010-** B Patchogue NY 5/11/1976 BS Florida St U 1998; MDiv STUSo 2005. D 6/5/2005 Bp Samuel Johnson Howard P 12/10/2005 Bp David Conner Bane Jr. Assoc R Ch Of The H Comf Kenilworth IL 2008-2010; Assoc Hickory Neck Ch Toano VA 2005-2008. anndieterle@mac.com

DIETRICH, Seth A (Mil) 4234 N Larkin St, Milwaukee WI 53211 **Chr Ch Whitefish Bay WI 2007-** B Austin TX 5/24/1974 s William Dietrich & Elizabeth. BA Wheaton Coll 1996; MDiv VTS 2007. D 6/2/2007 P 1/12/2008 Bp Steven Andrew Miller. m Margaret Dietrich c 2. dietrichsfour@att.net

DIETSCHE, Andrew Marion Lenow (NY) 1047 Amsterdam Ave, New York NY 10025 **Cn For Pstr Care Dio New York New York City NY 2001-** B Frankfurt DE 11/9/1953 s Raymond Oscar Dietsche & Jane Elizabeth. California St Polytechnic U 1974; BA U CA 1976; MDiv SWTS 1987. D 6/13/1987 Bp Charles Brinkley Morton P 12/12/1987 Bp Frank Tracy Griswold III. m 3/26/1977 Margaret Mahoney c 2. Pres of BEC Dio Wstrn Massachusetts Springfield MA 2000-2001; Mem of Stndg Com Dio Wstrn Massachusetts Springfield MA 1998-2001; Mem of COM Dio Wstrn Massachusetts Springfield MA 1997-2001; Cn of Chr Ch Cathd Dio Wstrn Massachusetts Springfield MA 1996-2001; Dn of Hampden Dnry Dio Wstrn Massachusetts Springfield MA 1994-2000; Mem of BEC Dio Wstrn Massachusetts Springfield MA 1992-1999; Chairman of Cmncatn Com Dio Wstrn Massachusetts Springfield MA 1992-1995; R Ch Of The Gd Shpd W Springfield MA 1990-2001; Asst Chr Ch Winnetka IL 1987-1990. adietsche@dioceseny.org

DIETZ, Joseph Bland (Pa) 2619 N Charlotte St, Pottstown PA 19464 **D S Ptr's Ch Phoenixville PA 2010-** B Easton PA 11/28/1937 s Luther Calvin Dietz & Mary Brusstar. BS Lebanon Vlly Coll 1960; AA Penn 1980; Cert Pennsylvania Diac Sch 1994. D 10/8/1994 Bp Allen Lyman Bartlett Jr. m 7/15/1961 Shirley Ann Landis c 2. D Trin Epis Ch Ambler PA 2009-2010; D Ch Of The Epiph Royersford PA 2006-2009; D Emm Ch Quakertown PA 2003-2006; S Ptr's Ch Phoenixville PA 2000-2001; D The Ch Of The Trin Coatesville PA 1996-1999; D S Ptr's Ch Phoenixville PA 1994-1996. NAAD 1994. joesframes@comcast.net

DIGGS, Thomas Tucker (USC) 2313 Kestrel Dr, Rock Hill SC 29732 B Richmond VA 5/19/1934 s John Roger Diggs & Dorothy Farrington. BBA U of Miami 1956; MDiv VTS 1959. D 11/14/1959 Bp Charles L Street P 6/18/1960 Bp John S Higgins. m 6/10/1959 Doris R Reuther c 2. Vic S Mk's Ch Chester SC 1995-2002; Dioc Coun Dio Connecticut Hartford CT 1989-1992; CT Cathd Chapt Dio Connecticut Hartford CT 1987-1990; R Chr Ch Stratford CT 1986-1994; Chair Stwdshp Com Dio Wstrn Massachusetts Springfield MA 1982-1986; Dn E Worcester Dnry Dio Wstrn Massachusetts Springfield MA 1980-1984; Dioc Coun Dio Wstrn Massachusetts Springfield MA 1979-1985; R Ch Of The Gd Shpd Clinton MA 1977-1986; Dept Evang Dio Wstrn Massachusetts Springfield MA 1977-1980; Assoc S Pat's Ch Washington DC 1975-1977; Dioc Coun Dio Georgia Savannah GA 1973-1975; Vic Gr Epis Ch Sandersville GA 1972-1975; Asst Trin Ch Newport RI 1965-1970; Ch Of The Resurr Warwick RI 1962-1965; R Ch Of The H Trin Tiverton RI 1959-1962.

DILEO, John Michael (Fla) 16921 W Newberry Rd, Newberry FL 32669 B Port Chester NY 3/9/1955 s Joseph Cosmo Di Leo & Emily. BA Duke 1977; Med U of Florida 1980; MDiv VTS 1989. D 6/24/1989 Bp Gerald Francis Burrill P 12/1/1989 Bp Rogers Sanders Harris. m 1/3/1981 Lucinda Field Palmer c 1. R S Jos's Ch Newberry FL 1994-2009; Asst to R St Johns Epis Ch Tampa FL 1989-1994. jdileo1230@aol.com

DILG, Arthur Charles (Pgh) 1371 Washington St, Indiana PA 15701 **Vic S Ptr's Epis Ch Blairsville PA 2004-** B New York NY 7/8/1936 s Charles Arthur Dilg & Emma Elizabeth. BA Bethany Coll 1959; BD Bex 1962; MA Duquesne U 1990. D 6/16/1962 Bp William S Thomas P 12/12/1962 Bp Austin Pardue. m 9/9/1961 Marilyn A Meyers c 2. Int S Alb's Epis Ch Murrysville PA 2002-2004; Int S Thos Ch In The Fields Gibsonia PA 2000-2002; Int S Alb's Epis Ch Murrysville PA 1998-1999; R Chr Epis Ch Indiana PA 1969-1998; Asst R Ch Of The Ascen Pittsburgh PA 1965-1969. Alb Inst, AFP, Trustsee 1997-2003; Assoc, All SS Sis of the Poor 2005; Dioc Chapl to the Ret 2000; Int Mnstry Ntwk 1998-2005. dilgarthur@gmail.com

DILL, David Stone (Ala) 206 Clarendon St., Boston MA 02116 **R Gd Shpd Decatur AL 2011-** B Birmingham AL 4/22/1970 s Ralph Laurence Dill & Peggy Stone. BA Birmingham-Sthrn Coll 1992; MDiv Ya Berk 2008. D 6/14/2008 P 1/24/2009 Bp John Chane. m 5/3/1997 Mary A Tampary c 2. Asst Trin Ch In The City Of Boston Boston MA 2008-2011. dsdill@me.com

DILL, Todd R (NC) 8515 Rea Rd, Waxhaw NC 28173 **S Marg's Epis Ch Waxhaw NC 2008-** B Portsmouth VA 12/19/1966 BM U Cinc 1991; MM U Cinc 1994; MDiv STUSo 2004. D 6/5/2004 P 1/15/2005 Bp J(ohn) Neil Alexander. m 8/24/1991 Regina O Dill c 2. S Dav's Ch Roswell GA 2004-2008. dill@saintmargarets.net

DILLARD JR, Starke (Spotswood) (NC) 45 Springmoor Ct., Raleigh NC 27615 B Charlotte NC 4/4/1928 s Starke Spotswood Dillard & Alice. BA U NC 1949; BD VTS 1953. D 6/24/1953 Bp Richard Henry Baker P 10/23/1954 Bp Edwin A Penick. m 9/1/1951 Angela W Hamer c 3. Asst Chr Epis Ch Raleigh NC 1985-1991; Chapl S Mary's Chap Sch Raleigh NC 1977-1984; S Jn's Ch Worthington OH 1971-1976; R S Alb's Ch Harlingen TX 1969-1971; Assoc R Chr Ch Charlotte NC 1965-1969; R S Paul's Epis Ch Smithfield NC 1960-1965; M-in-c S Matt Ch Salisbury NC 1953-1955. Auth, *Ch Needlepoint*, 1991. SFJ 1984.

DILLARD JR, Thomas A (NY) 345 Town View Dr, Wappingers Falls NY 12590 **Died 3/21/2011** B Pittsfield MA 8/17/1938 s Thomas A Dillard & Gertrude. BA Norwich U 1963; STB Ya Berk 1966; STM NYTS 1971; MS Ford 1974. D 6/23/1966 P 12/1/1966 Bp Robert McConnell Hatch. Outstanding Young Men Amer Awd 1976; Intl Men Achievement Awd 77; Who'S Who Black Amer 75-76.

DILLARD, Walter Scott (Va) Sr 666, Box 96, Wicomico Church VA 22579 B Greenville SC 4/27/1939 s Walter Willimon Dillard & Mildred. BS USMA At W Point 1961; MA U of Washington 1969; PhD U of Washington 1972; MDiv VTS 1993. D 6/12/1993 P 12/1/1993 Bp Peter James Lee. m 5/21/1986 Pauletta Johnson c 2. Wicomico Par Ch Wicomico Ch VA 1993-2011. Auth, "Sixty Days To Peace". Int Mnstry Ntwk; RWF. coloneldillard@gmail.com

DILLER, Sallie Winch (NMich) 733n E Gulliver Lake Rd, Gulliver MI 49840 B Hartford CT 2/20/1930 d Winch Simpson & Josephine Eldridge. D 9/30/2006 Bp James Arthur Kelsey. c 2. swdiller@up.net

DILLEY, John S (HB) 519 N Elmwood Ave, Traverse City MI 49684 B 12/9/1928 D 5/19/1955 Bp William Crittenden P 12/21/1955 Bp Stephen E Keeler. m 4/30/1949 Frances A Dilley. dilleyjack@yahoo.com

DILLIPLANE, Nancy Burton (Md) 1022 Main St., Darlington MD 21034 **R Gr Epis Ch Darlington MD 2010-** B Arlington PA 2/26/1961 d Kenneth Burton & Marjorie. BA Swarthmore Coll 1983; MS Nova SE U 1987; MDiv GTS 2006. D 6/10/2006 P 12/16/2006 Bp Charles Ellsworth Bennison Jr. m 6/30/1984 Steven Burton Dilliplane c 3. Asst S Paul's Ch Philadelphia PA 2007-2010; Asst Chr Ch Prince Geo's Par Rockville MD 2006-2007; Dir of Chr Formation S Andr's Ch Yardley PA 1999-2004. nancy.dilliplane@gmail.com

DILLON, Gwendolyn J (Chi) 446 E 95th St, Chicago IL 60619 **D S Geo/S Mths Ch Chicago IL 1989-** B Minneapolis MN 2/21/1926 d Henry F Schofield & Lillian L. D 12/2/1989 Bp Frank Tracy Griswold III. m 8/31/1958 Webster Dillon. Tertiary Of The Soc Of S Fran.

DILLON, John Lawrence (U) 8738 Oakwood Park Cir, Sandy UT 84094 **Asstg P S Jas Epis Ch Midvale UT 2000-** B UK 5/22/1935 s Joseph Dillon & Mabel. D 3/14/1985 P 5/26/1996 Bp George Edmonds Bates. m 12/14/1963 Mary Lilian Shutter. Sexton S Jas Epis Ch Midvale UT 1985-1998. jmldil@q.com

DILLON II, Tommy J (Cal) 561 Burnett #1, San Francisco CA 94131 **Bd Mem San Francisco Night Mnstry San Francisco CA 2011-; SOJOURN Chapl to SF Gnrl Hosp Dio California San Francisco CA 2006-; R S Aid's Ch San Francisco CA 2006-** B Baton Rouge LA 6/18/1969 s Tommy Joe Dillon & Linda Mary. BA LSU 1992; MDiv Ya Berk 1995; STM GTS 1996. D 7/24/2003 Bp Charles Edward Jenkins III P 2/20/2004 Bp Robert Campbell Witcher Sr. SOJOURN Chapl to SF Gnrl Hosp Dio California San Francisco CA 2006-2008; The Edge, Campus Mnstry at San Francisco St U Dio California San Francisco CA 2006-2008; Cmsn on Liturg and Mus Dio Louisiana Baton Rouge LA 2004-2005; Chair, Undoing Racism Com Dio Louisiana Baton Rouge LA 2003-2005; Lay Vic S Aug's Ch Baton Rouge LA 2000-2003. rectorsaintaidan@aol.com

DILLS, (Robert) Scott (Oly) 919 - 21st Avenue East, Seattle WA 98112 B Tulsa OK 9/1/1935 s Robert William Dills & Evelyn. BA Harv 1957; MDiv CDSP 1965. D 8/29/1965 Bp Hal Raymond Gross P 6/1/1966 Bp Russell S Hubbard. m 6/25/1965 Eleanor Louise Pollock c 2. Admin S Mk's Cathd Seattle WA 1993-1996; R Epis Ch of the Nativ Lewiston ID 1968-1970; Asst R S Tim's Epis Ch Yakima WA 1965-1968. rsdills@msn.com

DI LORENZO, Anthony (LI) 7 Warner Ln, Lake Ronkonkoma NY 11779 B Brooklyn NY 8/4/1939 s Antonio DiLorenzo & Angelina. Pratt Inst 1957; S Mary Coll S Mary KY 1962; BA Mt St. Mary's Sem 1964; MDiv Mt St. Mary's Sem 1968; DAS GTS 1993. Rec from Roman Catholic 2/1/1994 as Priest Bp Orris George Walker Jr. m 5/21/1994 Myriam Dempster c 3. R S Mary's Ch Lake Ronkonkoma NY 1998-2011; P-in-c S Jn's Ch Flushing NY 1995-1998; P-in-c S Paul's Ch Coll Point NY 1995-1998; Vic Ch Of The H Cross Brooklyn NY 1994-1995; Dio Long Island Garden City NY 1994-1995; Assoc S Ann And The H Trin Brooklyn NY 1993-1994. fatherd@optonline.net

DIMARCO, Thomas Edgar (USC) PO Box 206, Trenton SC 29847 **Ch Of The Ridge Trenton SC 2011-** B Spartanburg SC 10/21/1959 s Joseph John DiMarco & Caroline Cromer. BA The Coll of Charleston 1981; MDiv The TS at The U So 2011. D 6/4/2011 Bp W(illiam) Andrew Waldo. m 3/21/1982 Miranda Gail S Somers c 2. tom@churchoftheridge.org

DIMMICK, Kenneth Ray (Tex) Lorenzstaffel 8, Stuttgart 70182 Germany **Dio Mssnry, Vic, St Cathr's Ang Chplncy, Stuttgart Dio Texas Houston TX 2009-; Dio Mssnry, Vic, St Cathr's Ang Chplncy, Stuttgart Dio Texas Houston TX 2009-; S Jas Hse Of Baytown Baytown TX 2005-** B Douglas WY 1/14/1955 s Raymond Ivan Dimmick & Janet Louise. BA Texas A&M U 1977; MDiv Nash 1984. D 6/9/1984 P 12/21/1984 Bp Willis Ryan Henton. Assoc R Palmer Memi Ch Houston TX 2000-2005; R Gr Ch Of W Feliciana S Francisville LA 1987-2000; Vic S Jn Mssn Laurel Hill S Francisville LA 1987-1999; Cur S Mths Epis Ch Shreveport LA 1984-1986. Auth, "A Letter From Engl," *Angl & Epis Hist*, Hist Soc Of The Epsicopal Ch, 2001. CAECG [Coun of Angl and Epis Ch in Germany] 2006; HSEC 1987; SHN 1983; SocMary 1996. kennethrdimmick@yahoo.com

DINAN, Rebecca Lynn Willoughby (Me) 55 Bayview Dr, Northport ME 04849 B Appalachia VA 4/19/1942 d Harry James Willoughby & Irma Ruth. BA Radford U 1963; MA S Mary's Sem U 1978; MDiv VTS 1980. D 6/28/1980 P 12/28/1980 Bp David Keller Leighton Sr. m 1/29/1966 Joseph Patrick Dinan. VTS Alexandria VA 1984-1986; Int Trin Ch Towson MD 1983; Gr Ch Elkridge MD 1982-1983; Dio Maryland Baltimore MD 1980-1982.

DINGES, John Albert (Mil) Box 27671, West Allis WI 53227 B Chicago IL 6/21/1938 s Charles Dinges & Grace C. Nash 1975. D 2/2/1976 Bp Charles Thomas Gaskell. m 3/1/1958 Marlene Elza c 2. Conf Of S Ben, S Greg Abbey.

DINGLE, John Hausmann (NY) 143 Kent I, Century Village, West Palm Beach FL 33417 B Runnemede NJ 1/24/1921 GTS 1956. D 3/24/1956 P 12/1/1956 Bp Benjamin M Washburn. m 2/1/1973 Suni Hatil c 2. R Ch Of The Crucif Philadelphia PA 1958-1959; Asst Trin Ch Montclair NJ 1956. Chapl Ord Of S Lk. fatherdingle@hotmail.com

DINGLEY, Alison M. (EO) Episcopal Church of the Redeemer, 241 SE Second St., Pendleton OR 97801 **Int R Ch Of The Redeem Pendleton OR 2011-; P-in-c S Paul's Ch Klamath Falls OR 2008-** B Hilo HI 2/17/1949 d Leighton Alden Dingley & Helen Cowley. BA Shimer Coll 1970; MDiv Untd TS Of The Twin Cities 1976. D 4/25/1978 Bp Philip Frederick McNairy P 11/1/1978 Bp Robert Marshall Anderson. m 8/15/1998 Willis HA Moore. Dioc Coun Dio Estrn Oregon The Dalles OR 2008-2011; Stndg Com Dio Estrn Oregon The Dalles OR 2008-2011; Int S Pauls Epis Ch The Dalles OR 2006-2008; P-in-c S Steph's Ch Wahiawa HI 2001-2006; Dioc Coun Dio Hawaii Honolulu HI 2001-2005; R S Lk's Epis Ch Honolulu HI 1999-2000; Vic Waikiki Chap Honolulu HI 1996-1999; Bp's Search Com Dio Hawaii Honolulu HI 1994-1996; Vic S Matt's Epis Ch Waimanalo HI 1987-1989; Pastr Asst S Eliz's Ch Honolulu HI 1986-1987. alison.dingley@gmail.com

DINGMAN, Joel Andrews (Wyo) 807 10th St, Wheatland WY 82201 **Dio Wyoming Casper WY 2010-** B Jackson MN 7/25/1957 s Donald Dingman & Carol. D 8/23/2000 P 3/17/2001 Bp Bruce Edward Caldwell. m 2/21/1976 Nancy Jo Ingebrighton. P All SS Ch Wheatland WY 2001-2008.

DINGWALL, David Allan (Eas) 3744 Algonquin Trl, Snow Hill MD 21863 **R Ch Of S Paul's By The Sea Ocean City MD 2005-** B BC Canada 12/26/1962 s Donald Dingwall & Margaret. BA U of Victoria 1984; MDiv The Coll of Emm and St. Chad 1985. Trans from Anglican Church of Canada 1/18/2005 Bp James Joseph Shand. m 6/26/1999 Brenda Dingwall c 1. david.dingwall@me.com

DINOTO, Anthony Charles (Ct) 196 Main St., Durham CT 06422 **Int Ch Of The Epiph Durham CT 2011-** B Westerly RI 6/20/1950 s Angelo Thomas Dinoto & Irene. AS Amer Acad McAllister Inst of Funeral Serv 1977; BS SUNY 1998; MDiv GTS 1999. D 6/12/1999 Bp Clarence Nicholas Coleridge P 1/8/2000 Bp Andrew Donnan Smith. m 10/1/1977 Susan Stockwell Payne c 3. Int Chr Ch Guilford CT 2008-2010; Vic S Alb's Ch Danielson CT 2002-2008; Asst Chr Ch Greenwich CT 1999-2000.

DINOVO, D Rebecca (SanD) St Alban's Episcopal Church, 490 Farragut Cir, El Cajon CA 92020 **Assoc Gr Ch Kirkwood MO 2011-** B Sacramento CA 10/16/1972 BA Whitworth U 1995; M.Div. CDSP 1999; STM Nash 2003. D 4/30/2003 P 11/23/2003 Bp Wendell Nathaniel Gibbs Jr. m 6/23/2007 Salvatore A Dinovo c 1. R S Alb's Epis Ch El Cajon CA 2007-2011; Assoc R S Jn's Ch Worthington OH 2004-2007; Cbury Hse Ann Arbor MI 2003-2004; Cbury Hse Laramie WY 2003-2004. rebecca.dinovo@gracekirkwood.org

DINSMORE, Taylor Whitehead (ETenn) 9125 Candlewood Dr, Knoxville TN 37923 **Asst R Ch Of The Gd Samar Knoxville TN 2005-** B Chattanooga TN 5/27/1952 d James Whitehead & Mary. BA U of Tennessee 1975; MDiv STUSo 2005. D 6/18/2005 P 1/6/2006 Bp Charles Glenn VonRosenberg. m 7/28/1979 Ervin Whitehead Dinsmore c 2. taylordins@aol.com

DINSMORE, Virginia Carol (Nwk) 232 E Main Rd, Portsmouth RI 02871 B Lynchburg VA 10/6/1960 d Clyde Joseph Baker & Kathleen Myrtle. AS Harvard DS 1993; BA Tennessee Wesleyan Coll 2000; MDiv Drew U 2003; Cert GTS 2004; STM GTS 2005. D 9/11/2005 P 3/26/2006 Bp John Palmer Croneberger. c 1. P-in-c S Dunst's Epis Ch Succasunna NJ 2008; Asst to the R & Coordntr for Chr Formatio S Mary's Ch Portsmouth RI 2005-2008. revginny@optonline.net

DINWIDDIE, Donald (Dal) 532 Redberry Ln, St. Johns FL 32259 B Crawfordsville IN 8/29/1934 s Ernest Lee Dinwiddie & Catharine Whittington. BA Wabash Coll 1956; Oral Robert's TS 1968; MDiv Epis TS of The SW 1972; Med U of No Texas 1994. D 7/1/1972 Bp Chilton Powell P 12/20/1972 Bp Frederick Warren Putnam. c 5. P-in-c Ch Of The H Comf Cres City FL 2001; S Paul's Epis Ch Greenville TX 1995-2001; R Chr The King Epis Ch Ft Worth TX 1986-1995; Vic S Mart's Ch Pryor OK 1983-1986; Dioc Coun Dio Oklahoma Oklahoma City OK 1979-1982; S Matt's Ch Sand Sprg OK 1975-1976; Cur St Phil's Epis Ch Ardmore OK 1972-1973. donaldbdinwiddie@bellsouth.net

DINWIDDIE, Philip Matthew (Mich) 25150 East River, Grosse Ile MI 48138 **R S Jas Ch Grosse Ile MI 2004-** B Beeville TX 6/25/1974 s Brian Dinwiddie & Lucy. Illinois Inst of Tech 1992; BSW Jane Addams Coll of Soc Wk at U IL 1997; MS U MI 1998; MDiv VTS 2002. D 12/22/2001 P 6/26/2002 Bp Wendell Nathaniel Gibbs Jr. Asst All SS Ch E Lansing MI 2002-2004. Cmnty of Celebration 2001. rector@saintjamesgi.net

DIRADDO, Joseph Andrew (WTex) 1 Bishop Gadsden Way #329, Charleston SC 29412 **Int S Jn's Ch Charleston SC 2002-** B Camden NJ 9/11/1929 s Nicholas Anthony DiRaddo & Florence Alberta. BA U of Pennsylvania 1951; STB GTS 1954. D 5/8/1954 Bp Wallace J Gardner P 11/15/1954 Bp Alfred L Banyard. m 7/15/1954 Mary Goode Geer c 5. R S Lk's Epis Ch San Antonio TX 1982-1996; Dept Stwrdshp Dio Texas Houston TX 1977-1982; R Ch Of The Epiph Houston TX 1969-1982; R S Paul's Epis Ch Orange TX 1966-1969; R Ch Of The Resurr Austin TX 1963-1965; Vic S Jas Ch Austin TX 1963-1964; Asst Trin Cathd Columbia SC 1962-1963; R All SS Ch Florence SC 1958-1960; Asst S Jn's Ch Florence SC 1957-1958; Vic S Andr's Epis Ch Lincoln Pk NJ 1954-1957. jadmgd@comcast.net

DIRBAS, Joseph James (SanD) PO Box 336, Del Mar CA 92014 **Assoc S Ptr's Epis Ch Del Mar CA 2010-** B Livonia MI 10/12/1966 s George Dirbas & Tajmahal. BSBL California Polytechnic St U 1988; MSEE California St U, Fullerton 1992; MDiv The GTS 2010. D 6/19/2010 P 12/18/2010 Bp James Robert Mathes. m 8/15/2010 Terry Shields Terry Lyon Shields. jdirbas@mac.com

DIRBAS, Terry Shields (EC) 1114 9th St, Coronado CA 92118 **Assoc Chr Ch Coronado CA 2010-** B Fayetteville NC 8/21/1983 d Alfred Holton Shields & Pawley Thomas. BA Duke 2006; MDiv The GTS 2010. D 6/12/2010 Bp Clifton Daniel III P 12/18/2010 Bp James Robert Mathes. m 8/15/2010 Joseph James Dirbas. TERRYDIRBAS@GMAIL.COM

DIRGHALLI, S George (CNY) 131 Durston Ave, Syracuse NY 13203 B Detroit MI 12/1/1926 s George Moses Dirghalli & Lulu A. Drew U; Harv; BS U of Florida 1950; MS U of Florida 1951; MDiv EDS 1964. D 6/17/1964 P 12/21/1964 Bp John P Craine. m 4/22/1967 Kira Siewert c 2. Calv Ch Syracuse NY 1968-1988; Asst Gr Ch Cortland NY 1964-1968. Auth, *A Theol of Mnstry*; Auth, *The Origin & Dvlpmt of Creedal Confession in the Life of the Primitive Ch*. dirghallig@aol.com

DISBROW, Jimme Lynn (Okla) 1737 Churchill Way, Oklahoma City OK 73120 B Blackwell OK 4/17/1938 s James A Disbrow & Lilla M. GTS; BS Oklahoma Bapt U 1960; Med NWU 1965; EdD Oklahoma St U 1971; MAR Epis TS of The SW 1985; Med Cntrl St U 1988. D 6/20/1973 Bp Chilton Powell P 7/1/1985 Bp Gerald Nicholas McAllister. m 8/25/1966 Laura Lou Reeves c 2. Vic S Tim's Epis Ch Pauls Vlly OK 1978-1983; D S Lk's Epis Ch Ada OK 1974-1978. Auth, *Abstracts of Engl Stds*. Sigma Tau Delta. j.disbrow@sbcglobal.net

DISCAVAGE, Thomas Damian (Los) 1830 Taft Ave Apt 202, Los Angeles CA 90028 **Vic for Admin S Jas Par Los Angeles CA 2008-** B Buffalo NY 12/19/1962 s Robert Discavage & Lillian. BS Canisius Coll 1984; MDiv Chr The King Sem 1988. Rec from Roman Catholic 5/3/2002 as Priest Bp J Michael Garrison. R S Barn' Epis Ch Los Angeles CA 2004-2008; Actg R Chr Ch Albion NY 2002-2003. tdd1262@mac.com

DISCH III, William John (Tex) 119 Fox Home Ln, Georgetown TX 78633 B Austin TX 10/13/1941 s William John Disch & Mary Helen. BA U of Texas 1966; MDiv TESM 1986. D 6/24/1986 Bp Maurice Manuel Benitez P 3/23/1987 Bp Anselmo Carral-Solar. m 6/6/1964 Alice Mayo c 3. P-in-c S Jas' Ch Taylor TX 2004-2005; R H Trin Epis Ch Austin TX 1992-2004; R Ch Of The H Comf Angleton TX 1989-1992; Asst R S Alb's Epis Ch Waco TX 1986-1989. wjdisch@aol.com

DISHAROON, Susan Clay (Miss) 3030 Highway 547, Port Gibson MS 39150 B Champaign IL 1/3/1935 d Robert Pepper Clay & Mary Martha. BA Sweet Briar Coll 1956. D 1/4/2003 Bp Alfred Clark Marble Jr. m 6/10/1959 Benjamin Magruder Disharoon c 4. D Chr Epis Ch Vicksburg MS 2005-2010.

DISTANISLAO, Virginia Gates (SVa) 512 S. Broad St., Kenbridge VA 23944 **P-in-c Epis Ch Of S Paul And S Andr Kenbridge VA 2008-** B Richmond VA 4/24/1962 d Ernest Plesants Gates & Virginia Yonee. BS Mary Baldwin Coll 1984; Cert Sch of Mnstry Formation 2008. D 2/1/2008 P 8/1/2008 Bp John Clark Buchanan. m 10/26/1985 Phillip Thomas DiStanislao c 2. gini@bonairtitle.com

DITTERLINE, Richard Charles (Pa) 1350 Spring Valley Rd, Bethlehem PA 18015 **Trin Ch Bethlehem PA 2006-** B Bethlehem PA 6/1/1937 s Roy Edwin Ditterline & Anna Marguerite. BA Moravian TS 1967; MDiv Berkeley Bapt

DS 1970; DMin Drew U 1996. D 6/27/1970 Bp Frederick J Warnecke P 3/13/1971 Bp Richard S M Emrich. m 6/19/1965 Susan Yolan Pecsek c 2. Chair Chapl Coun Dio Pennsylvania Philadelphia PA 1996-2000; Secy Curs Dio Pennsylvania Philadelphia PA 1985-1988; Dn Bucks Deanry Dio Pennsylvania Philadelphia PA 1982-1985; Chair Chapl Coun Dio Pennsylvania Philadelphia PA 1979-1982; Secy Curs Dio Pennsylvania Philadelphia PA 1977-1980; R Gr Epis Ch Hulmeville PA 1976-2000; Cn Geth Cathd Fargo ND 1974-1976; Vic S Paul's Epis Ch Harsens Island MI 1970-1974. Auth, *Trng Lay Visitation Team for Par Shut-Ins*, UMI, 1996. rcditterline@ptd.net

DITZENBERGER, Christopher Steven (Colo) 6190 E. Quincy Avenue, Englewood CO 80112 B Denver CO 4/24/1966 s James Warren Ditzenberger & Joanne Claire. BA Gordon Coll 1988; MA Gordon-Conwell TS 1995; MDiv VTS 1999. D 6/19/1999 P 2/19/2000 Bp Peter James Lee. m 8/27/1993 Chungjoo L Lee c 2. Chr Ch Greenville SC 2001-2005; S Mary's Fleeton Reedville VA 1999-2001; S Steph's Ch Heathsville VA 1999-2001. cjditzenberger@gmail.com

DIVINE, Betty Baird (Tex) 1616 Fountainview Dr #203, Houston TX 77057 **D S Jas Epis Ch Houston TX 2010-** B Houston TX 6/30/1944 d Russell Sterling Barnett & Lucy Hawkins. BS Universtiy of Texas 1966; Mstr in Educ U of St. Thos 1999; Iona Sch for Mnstry 2007. D 2/9/2007 Bp Don Adger Wimberly. m 1/16/1999 Thomas McCallie Divine c 3. D S Mk's Ch Houston TX 2007-2010. bbdivine@comcast.net

DIVIS, Mary Lou (Be) 408 E Main St, Nanticoke PA 18634 B Buffalo NY 4/24/1949 d Robert Hoover & Alice Moran. BEd Hastings Coll 1972; MEd Sacr Heart U 1992; M Th U of Scranton 2003; Cert. in Angl Stds The GTS 2006. D 5/17/2006 Bp Paul Victor Marshall. m 9/23/2000 Wayne George Divis c 4. S Geo's Ch Nanticoke PA 2008-2009. ldivis@epix.net

✠ **DIXON, Rt Rev Jane Hart Holmes** (WA) 2801 New Mexico Ave NW Apt208, Washington DC 20007 B Winona MS 7/24/1937 d Edward Warren Holmes & Mary Laura. BA Van 1959; MA Van 1962; MDiv VTS 1981. D 6/20/1981 P 1/16/1982 Bp John Thomas Walker Con 11/19/1992 for WA. m 8/6/1960 David M Dixon c 3. Trst VTS Alexandria VA 1994-2002; Dio Washington Washington DC 1992-2002; R S Phil's Epis Ch Laurel MD 1986-1992; Exec Bd Alum Assn VTS Alexandria VA 1984-1987; Assoc S Alb's Par Washington DC 1984-1986; Assoc Ch Of The Gd Shpd Burke VA 1981-1984. DD VTS Alexandria VA 1983. jhdwash@gmail.com

DIXON JR, John Henry (RG) Av. C. Leon de Nicaragua 1, Esc. 3, 1-B, Alicante 03015 Spain B Fort Hood TX 12/22/1949 s John Henry Dixon & Mary Frances. BA U of Texas 1971; MDiv Trin Evang DS Deerfield IL 1979; MA U of Texas 1989. D 8/6/1979 P 5/1/1980 Bp Richard Mitchell Trelease Jr. m 8/6/1976 Ninfa Duran c 3. SAMS Ambridge PA 1991-2009; Dio The Rio Grande Albuquerque NM 1990-1991; Global Teams Forest City NC 1988-1989; S Paul's Ch El Paso TX 1979-1987; Cur All SS Epis Ch El Paso TX 1979-1981. SAMS 1989. johnelpaso@yahoo.es

DIXON, Mary Lenn (Tex) 1101 Rock Prairie Rd, College Station TX 77845 B Hamilton TX 9/18/1947 d Robert Bernard Miller & Mavis McKinley. no degree Iona Sch for Mnstry 2011. D 6/18/2011 Bp C(harles) Andrew Doyle. m 2/10/1975 Warren A Dixon c 2. marylenndixon@gmail.com

DIXON, Robert Keith (Nwk) 73 Fernbank Ave, Delmar NY 12054 B Albany NY 8/8/1936 s Harry W Dixon & Rebekah Louise. BA Ham 1958; STB GTS 1961. D 6/10/1961 P 12/1/1961 Bp Leland Stark. m 7/8/1961 Linda Silance c 3. S Jn's Ch Cohoes NY 1997-2002; Cathd Of All SS Albany NY 1992-1997; R S Jn's Ch Passaic NJ 1966-1981; Cur Ch Of The H Trin New York NY 1963-1966; Cur Calv Epis Ch Summit NJ 1961-1962.

DIXON, Valerie Wilde (Ct) 23 Bayview Ave, Niantic CT 06357 **S Jn's Epis Ch Niantic CT 2009-** B Berkeley CA 1/14/1944 d Robert Ernest Wilde & Mary Jeanette. BA Stan 1966; MA CUA 1970; MDiv EDS 2002. D 6/8/2002 P 6/21/2003 Bp Andrew Donnan Smith. m 4/20/1968 Gregg Woodford Dixon c 3. S Jas Ch Preston CT 2002-2008. VALERIEDIXON1@YAHOO.COM

DOAR, Katherine Baginski (ECR) 1225 Pine Ave, San Jose CA 95125 **D S Fran Epis Ch San Jose CA 2002-** B Washington DC 4/3/1967 d Joseph Michael Baginski & Linda Christine. BA U CA 1990; MA Harvard DS 1998; CAS CDSP 2002. D 6/22/2002 P 3/1/2003 Bp Richard Lester Shimpfky. m 4/22/1995 Matthew Doar c 3. kdoar@pobox.com

DOBBIN, Robert A (Cal) 24 Van Gordon Pl, Danville CA 94526 B Baltimore MD 6/12/1946 s Tilton H Dobbin & Julia B. BA Dart 1967; JD Willamette U 1975; LLM Geo 1978; BD The Sch For Deacons Berkeley 2006. D 12/2/2006 Bp Marc Handley Andrus. m 7/10/1971 Patricia A Marenco c 3. dobbin1982@hotmail.com

DOBBINS, Burford C (WTex) 1501 N. Glass St., Victoria TX 77901 **Trin Ch Victoria TX 2006-** B 10/22/1961 BA U So 1984; JD So Texas Coll of Law 1987; M.Div. TS 2003. D 6/9/2003 Bp Robert Boyd Hibbs P 1/6/2004 Bp James Edward Folts. m 3/29/2005 Melissa Gallander Dobbins c 2. St Ptr & St Paul Ch Mssn TX 2003-2006. bur@dobbins.cc

DOBBINS, Timothy Dean (Pa) 292 Militia Dr, Radnor PA 19087 B Camp Lejeune NC 1/24/1954 s Peter Mullin Dobbins & Christine. BA U Of Florida 1976; MDiv VTS 1981. D 6/7/1981 Bp Frank Stanley Cerveny P 12/1/1981 Bp John Thomas Walker. c 2. Ch Of The Redeem Bryn Mawr PA 1990-1998; R S Jn's Epis Ch Gloucester MA 1984-1990; Asst S Jn's Ch Lafayette Sq Washington DC 1981-1984. Auth, ",Stepping Up: Bus Decisions That Matter," Harper Collins, 2006; Auth, ",Bus Comp," Random Hse, 2002; Auth, "Aware"; Auth, "Signs Of Gr: Mnstry For The 21st Century". tdobbins@culturalarchitects.com

DOBBINS JR, W(illiam) David (Ct) 23 Litchfield Ponds, Litchfield CT 06759 **R S Paul's Ch No Kingstown RI 2010-** B Torrington CT 9/25/1956 s William David Dobbins & Agatha Elizabeth. BS U of Virginia 1978; Oak Hill Theol Coll 1981; STM GTS 1987; MDiv GTS 1987; Cert Blanton-Peale Grad Inst 1992. D 6/13/1987 Bp Arthur Edward Walmsley P 2/1/1988 Bp Jeffery William Rowthorn. m 4/23/1994 Jane Dobbins. Int Trin Ch Newport RI 2008-2010; S Mich's Ch Bristol RI 2005-2008; S Jn's Ch Walpole NH 2004; Int S Jn's Ch Walpole NH 2003-2004; Greenwoods Counslg Serv Litchfield CT 1994-1995; Asst to R S Jn's Of Lattingtown Locust Vlly NY 1987-1989. AAPC 1991; Int Mnstry Ntwk 2001. oskardobbs@gmail.com

DOBROSKY, Mike (Miss) 117 Stonebridge Ln, Clinton MS 39056 **Died 1/2/2011** B Lorain OH 5/30/1941 s Peter John Dobrosky & Mary. BS U of Sthrn Mississippi 1983; MDiv SWTS 1986. D 6/7/1986 P 2/1/1987 Bp Duncan Montgomery Gray Jr. dobroskym@bellsouth.net

DOBSON, Marc A (Dal) 2007 Stagecoach Trail, Heartland TX 75126 **Instr at the Stanton Cntr for Theol Educ Dio Dallas Dallas TX 2010-; Vic Gr Ch Mesquite TX 2008-** B Pittsburgh PA 6/9/1959 AA Edinboro U 1987; BS Geneva Coll 1991; MDiv TESM 2003. D 6/12/2004 Bp Robert William Duncan P 12/19/2004 Bp Henry William Scriven. c 3. R S Mary's Ch Warwick RI 2005-2007; Asst Prince Of Peace Epis Ch Aliquippa PA 2004-2005. mdobson10@yahoo.com

DOBYNS, N(ancy) (Ind) 1021 Sw 15th St, Richmond IN 47374 **Exec Coun Mem Dio Indianapolis Indianapolis IN 2009-; Dio Indianapolis Indianapolis IN 2008-; S Lk's Epis Ch Shelbyville IN 2008-** B Charleston WVa 12/30/1949 d Samuel Crocker Lawrence & Julia Belle. AAS Seattle Cmnty Coll 1972; BA Fairhaven Coll 1975; MDiv Earlham Sch of Rel 1997; CAS Bex 2005. D 6/18/2005 P 7/8/2006 Bp Catherine Elizabeth Maples Waynick. m 3/19/1972 R(ichard) Dobyns c 3. Asst Gr Ch Muncie IN 2006-2008; D S Lk's Epis Ch Shelbyville IN 2005-2006. dobynskr@gmail.com

DOBYNS, R(ichard) (Ind) 1021 Sw 15th St, Richmond IN 47374 **Dio Indianapolis Indianapolis IN 2008-** B Bethesda MD 2/17/1949 s Donald Keith Dobyns & Kathleen Eady. BS Wstrn Washington U 1976; DO Des Moines U 1978; MDiv Earlham Sch of Rel 1998; CAS Bex 2005. D 6/18/2005 P 7/8/2006 Bp Catherine Elizabeth Maples Waynick. m 3/19/1972 N(ancy) Lawrence c 2. Asst Gr Ch Muncie IN 2006-2008. kdobyns@yahoo.com

DOCKER JR, John Thornley (NY) 631 Sandy Bay Road, RR 7, Dunnville, Ontario N1A 2W6 Canada B Reading PA 6/2/1937 s John Thornley Docker & Evelyn Clara. W Chester St Teachers Coll 1957; BA Leh 1960; MDiv GTS 1963; DMin Bex 1987. D 6/15/1963 P 3/7/1964 Bp Frederick J Warnecke. m 12/31/1968 Georgie Elizabeth Dawson c 2. Hon Asst S Pauls On The Hill Epis Ch Ossining NY 1983-1998; Stff Off - Mnstry Dev. Epis Ch Cntr New York NY 1982-1998; Prog Dir Dio Bethlehem Bethlehem PA 1976-1982; Cn Mssnr Chr Ch Rochester NY 1974-1976; R Ch of the Nativ-St Steph Newport PA 1968-1974; Prog Asst. Dio Cntrl Pennsylvania Harrisburg PA 1968-1974; Vic S Mary's Epis Ch Wind Gap PA 1963-1968. Auth, *Dunville Heroes*, Dunnville Dist Heritage Assn, 2003; Auth, *Grand Naval River Depot*, Dunnville Dist Heritage Assn, 2001; Auth, *Fluffing the Tangled Skein*, Epis Ch Cntr, 1990; Auth, *Toward a Totally Ministering Ch*, Epis Ch Cntr, 1987. Scadding Awd Ontario Hist Soc 2002; Barkhausen Awd Assn for Great Lakes Maritime Hist 2001. jtdocker@yahoo.ca

DOCKERY, Nancy Lynn (Nev) 501 Bianca Bay St, Las Vegas NV 89144 B Colorado Springs CO 1/12/1956 d Eldon Glen Cole & Billie Ann. AAS Comm Coll of S Nevada 1992. D 12/3/1995 Bp Stewart Clark Zabriskie. m 9/27/1980 Jan Theodore Dockery c 2.

DOCKERY JR, William Dee (Dal) 7223 Colgate Ave, Dallas TX 75225 B Greenville TX 11/2/1934 s William Dee Dockery & Alice Morris. BA U of Texas 1958; MDiv VTS 1992. D 6/20/1992 Bp Donis Dean Patterson P 4/21/1993 Bp James Monte Stanton. m 5/28/1994 Sharon Sue Sears McLain c 2. R S Dav's Ch Garland TX 1996-2000; Asst S Mich And All Ang Ch Dallas TX 1995-1996; Dn Of Anglcn Schl Of Theol Dio Dallas Dallas TX 1993-1995; S Matt's Cathd Dallas TX 1992-1995. ssd227@sbcglobal.net

DOCTOR, Virginia Carol (Ak) P.O. Box 93, Tanana AK 99777 **Dio Alaska Fairbanks AK 2001-; Cn To The Ordnry Dio Alaska Fairbanks AK 2000-** B Syracuse NY 2/23/1950 d Alfred Laverne Doctor & Birdie Virginia. Onondaga Cmnty Coll 1971; SUNY 1973. D 9/2/2000 P 7/15/2001 Bp Mark Lawrence Mac Donald. Exec Coun Appointees New York NY 2005-2008. gindoctor@aol.com

DOD, David Stockton (ECR) 8294 Carmelita Ave, Atascadero CA 93422 B Klamath Falls OR 7/11/1944 s Donald Dungan Dod & Annabelle Jean. AA Warren Wilson Coll 1964; BA Trin U San Antonio TX 1966; MDiv ETSC 1971. D 5/31/1971 P 12/21/1971 Bp Francisco Reus-Froylan. m 6/19/1966

Judith Hinshaw c 2. Hisp Min Sthrn Reg Dio El Camino Real Monterey CA 1990-1992; Vic S Mk's Ch KING CITY CA 1986-1990; Chr And S Ambr Ch Philadelphia PA 1981-1986; Asst To Hisp Mnstry Dio Pennsylvania Philadelphia PA 1981-1986; Dio Panama 1979-1981; Chr Ch By The Sea 1978-1981; P Ch Of S Mths Asheville NC 1975-1977.

DODD, Debra (Dee) Anne (Ct) 37 Bailey Dr, North Branford CT 06471 **S Paul's Ch Wallingford CT 2009-** B Pineville WV 6/5/1958 d Robert Lowell Dodd & Rosemary Alice. BS Ohio U 1980; MDiv UTS 1988; STM GTS 1991. D 6/10/1989 P 3/24/1990 Bp Arthur Edward Walmsley. m 7/20/1983 Brad Schide c 2. Vic Zion Epis Ch No Branford CT 1994-2009; Asst R S Mary's Epis Ch Manchester CT 1989-1994. Producer/Co-Writer, "Let Them Eat Missiles," 1985; Writer/Ed, "Hunger & Militarism: A Guide To Study Reflection & Action," 1984. revdadodd@aol.com

DODD, Jean Carrison (Fla) 1860 Edgewood Ave S, Jacksonville FL 32205 **D S Jn's Cathd Jacksonville FL 2011-; San Jose Epis Ch Jacksonville FL 2000-** B Tampa FL 4/7/1941 D 9/21/2003 Bp Stephen Hays Jecko. m 2/8/1991 Arthur Robert Dodd c 4.

DODDEMA, Peter (Kan) 118 West Poplar Street, Harrodsburg KY 40330 **P-in-c S Phil's Ch Harrodsburg KY 2011-** B Cedar Falls IA 11/16/1973 s Paul Eugene Doddema & Margaret Ella. BA U of Kansas 2001; MDiv VTS 2011. D 6/11/2011 Bp Dean Elliott Wolfe. m 7/10/1999 Michele Nicole Burchinal c 1. stphilipclergy@bellsouth.net

DODDS, Doris Ann (Minn) 715 Paine Dr, Paynesville MN 56362 B Milwaukee WI 3/13/1933 d Estella. Milwaukee St Teachers Coll. D 5/6/2003 Bp Daniel Lee Swenson P 11/11/2003 Bp James Louis Jelinek. P S Steph's Epis Ch Paynesville MN 2003-2011.

DODGE, Robin Dennis (WA) 5150 Macomb Street, N.W., Washington DC 20016 **R S Dav's Par Washington DC 2005-** B Springfield VT 8/15/1958 s Kenneth C Dodge & Bea B. BA Cor 1980; JD Bos 1983; MDiv VTS 1999. D 4/14/1998 P 5/22/1999 Bp Leopold Frade. m 9/20/1986 Therese Saint-Andre c 2. Assoc R S Mary's Epis Ch Arlington VA 1999-2002. fr.rdodge@gmail.com

DODSON, Wayne (NY) 9 W 130th St, New York NY 10037 **R S Ambr Epis Ch New York NY 1999-** B BB 5/3/1952 s Darnley Dodson & Eula. BS CUNY 1981; MDiv GTS 1994; STM GTS 1996. D 2/14/1994 P 9/1/1994 Bp Orris George Walker Jr. m 8/29/1993 Maurina Welch c 1. Asst to R Gr Ch Jamaica NY 1994-1999.

DOERR, Nan Lewis (Tex) 901 S. Johnson, Alvin TX 77511 **Int R S Jn's Ch La Porte TX 2011-** B San Antonio TX 9/1/1944 d Andrew Bradley Lewis & Jimmie Lea. BME Sam Houston St U 1967; MDiv Epis TS of The SW 2000. D 6/17/2000 Bp Claude Edward Payne P 6/17/2001 Bp Leopoldo Jesus Alard. m 4/27/1968 Samuel Doerr c 2. R Ch Of The Redeem Houston TX 2006-2010; Asst & Mssnr Campus Mnstry S Steph's Ch Huntsville TX 2000-2006. "Praying w Beads," Eerdmans, 2007. nan@doerrworks.com

DOERSAM, H(arry) Arthur (CNY) 725 Lee Cir, Johnson City NY 13790 B Saginaw MI 4/4/1928 s Harry Charles Doersam & Mary Ann. BA U MI 1950; MDiv VTS 1953; Moravian TS 1975. D 6/27/1953 P 6/24/1954 Bp Richard S M Emrich. m 12/15/1973 Marilyn S Bennett c 6. R Trin Memi Ch Binghamton NY 1976-1993; Dio Bethlehem Bethlehem PA 1976; Dep GC Dio Bethlehem Bethlehem PA 1967-1976; R Ch Of The Epiph Glenburn Clarks Summit PA 1959-1967; Asst Chr Ch Greenville Wilmington DE 1955-1959; Cur Chr Ch Grosse Pointe Grosse Pointe Farms MI 1953-1955. grandmad@sprynet.com

DOGARU, Vickie A (Oly) 22405 Ne 182nd Ave, Battle Ground WA 98604 **Assoc. Adult Sprtl Dvlpmt and Yth Mnstry S Lk's Epis Ch Vancouver WA 2007-** B Salem Oregon 8/6/1951 d Dale Neal Wilkerson & Violet Mae. BS U of Oregon 1973; MDiv Seattle U 2005. D 6/24/2006 Bp Vincent Waydell Warner P 2/17/2007 Bp Bavi Rivera. m 9/9/1978 Emil Dogaru c 2. vickie@stlukesvancouver.com

DOGGETT, William Jordan (Cal) 1209 East Capitol Street SE, Washington DC 20003 B Woodland CA 11/13/1956 s James Nielsen Doggett & Muriel Ann. BA U CA 1978; MDiv CDSP 1995; PhD Grad Theol Un 2005. D 12/2/1995 P 12/6/1996 Bp William Edwin Swing. c 2. Chr Ch Capitol Hill Washington DC 2001-2010; Liturg And Mus Dir S Ptr's Epis Ch Redwood City CA 1997-1998. Compsr, "Mus By Heart: Paperless Songs for Evening Wrshp," Ch Pub, 2008; Auth, "New Proclamation Commentary on Feasts: H Days and Other Celebrations," Augsburg/Fortress, 2007; Auth, "Make Believe," Klutz Press, 1991. billdoggett@hotmail.com

DOHERTY, Anna Clay (Mil) 670 E Monroe Ave, Hartford WI 53027 **Stndg Com, Dio Milwaukee S Aidans Ch Hartford WI 2011-** B Fort Madison IA 1/4/1983 d Jerry Clay Doherty & Sheila Doherty. BA Cornell Coll 2005; MDiv Ya Berk 2008. D 7/26/2007 P 7/8/2008 Bp James Louis Jelinek. m 6/23/2007 Jeremy R Deaner. Asst S Paul's Ch Milwaukee WI 2008-2009; D S Mk's Ch New Britain CT 2007-2008. a-doherty@hotmail.com

DOHERTY, Jerry Clay (Minn) 201 Bayberry Avenue Ct, Stillwater MN 55082 **Chapl U Epis Ch Minneapolis MN 2011-** B Des Moines IA 1/2/1949 s Joe William Doherty & Nia Myrta. BS Iowa St U 1971; MDiv SWTS 1974; DMin SWTS 1998. D 6/14/1975 P 12/1/1975 Bp Walter Cameron Righter. m 4/23/1982 Sheila Maybanks c 2. R Ch Of The Ascen Stillwater MN 1992-2008; R Ch Of The Incarn Great Falls MT 1985-1992; R S Lk's Ch Ft Madison IA 1979-1985; Cur S Tim's Epis Ch W Des Moines IA 1978-1979; Asst S Jn's Ch Mason City IA 1975-1978. Auth, *A Celtic Model of Mnstry*, The Liturg Press, 2003; Auth, *Crossroads*. doher4@comcast.net

DOHERTY, John S (Ia) CATHEDRAL CHURCH OF ST PAUL, 815 HIGH ST, DES MOINES IA 50309 **Coord. of Fin & Mnstry The Cathd Ch Of S Paul Des Moines IA 2008-** B Des Moines IA 8/5/1953 s Joe William & Nia. D 10/8/2007 Bp Alan Scarfe. m 6/8/1974 Janet Cate c 2. bloom2u@aol.com

DOHERTY, Maureen Catherine (Ia) 417 Olive St, Cedar Falls IA 50613 **no Trin Epis Par Waterloo IA 2011-; Dio Iowa Des Moines IA 2009-** B Albuquerque NM 6/7/1946 d Jerome J Doherty & Margaret Ruth. Xavier U; BA Coll of Mt St. Jos 1971; MDiv Epis TS of The SW 2001. Rec from Roman Catholic 8/15/1996 Bp Terence Kelshaw. m 5/8/2009 Joan Farstad c 1. R S Andr's Epis Ch Waverly IA 2002-2009; Int S Aid's Epis Ch Tulsa OK 2001-2002. mcdiniowa@aol.com

DOHERTY, Noel James (Okla) 6910 E 62nd St, Tulsa OK 74133 B Redding CA 9/18/1941 s Robert Timothy Doherty & Ella Kristine. BA Bethany U 1963; MDiv GTS 1971. D 6/29/1971 P 12/19/1971 Bp Chilton Powell. R S Dunst's Ch Tulsa OK 2001-2008; R All SS Epis Ch Miami OK 1980-2001; Cur S Jn's Epis Ch Tulsa OK 1973-1979; Cur Trin Ch Tulsa OK 1971-1973. ndoherty1@cox.net

DOHERTY-OGEA, Kathleen Lambert (WLa) 206 South Street, Bastrop LA 71220 B Battle Creek MI 4/5/1944 d Glenn Lambert Doherty & Edith Brewster. D 6/3/2000 P 12/16/2000 Bp Robert Jefferson Hargrove Jr. m 4/2/1994 Herman Joseph Ogea. D Chr Ch Bastrop LA 2000-2002.

DOHLE, Robert Joseph (Tex) St Paul's Episcopal Church, 1307 W 5th St, Freeport TX 77541 **Vic S Paul's Epis Ch Freeport TX 2008-** B Steelville MO 9/4/1947 s Robert Joseph Dohle & Venita G. N/A Iona Sch for Mnstry. D 6/23/2007 Bp Don Adger Wimberly P 1/26/2008 Bp Rayford Baines High Jr. m 10/15/1971 Patricia Anne Dohle c 2. pdohle@comcast.net

DOHONEY, Edmund Luther (WTex) 14906 Grayoak Frst, San Antonio TX 78248 B Shreveport LA 7/30/1941 s Alfred Walker Dohoney & Sally May. BA U of Arkansas 1964; MDiv STUSo 1977. D 6/14/1977 P 5/1/1978 Bp James Barrow Brown. m 3/31/1978 Christine Harrison c 3. R The Epis Ch Of The Epiph New Iberia LA 1999-2001; Int Epis Ch Of The Mssh Gonzales TX 1993; Int All SS Epis Ch Corpus Christi TX 1990-1991; Cn to the Ordnry Dio W Texas San Antonio TX 1988-1999; COM Dio W Texas San Antonio TX 1985-1988; Chair, Compstn Com Dio W Texas San Antonio TX 1984; R S Andr's Epis Ch Seguin TX 1983-1988; R Epis Ch Of The Mssh Gonzales TX 1979-1983; Vic S Jas Ch Hallettsville TX 1979-1982; Asst S Lk's Epis Ch San Antonio TX 1978-1979; Cur S Phil's Ch New Orleans LA 1977-1978. CODE 1989-1998. edmunddohoney@sbcglobal.net

DOING JR, Robert Burns (SwFla) 36 Barkley Circle Apt 205, Fort Myers FL 33907 B Brooklyn NY 12/14/1929 s Robert Burns Doing & Louisa Richardson. BA Trin, Hartford CT 1951; LTh GTS 1954. D 4/24/1954 P 11/13/1954 Bp James P De Wolfe. m 9/4/1954 Susan Wakeman c 3. R S Anselm Epis Ch Lehigh Acres FL 1982-1994; R S Jas' Epis Ch Winsted CT 1962-1982; Cur Trin Epis Ch Roslyn NY 1954-1956. rdoing@embarqmail.com

DOLACK, Craig A (SwVa) P.O. Box 277, Fincastle VA 24090 B Cortez CO 6/22/1971 s Gary Dolack & Elizabeth. BA No Carolina St U 1994; MDiv STUSo 2006. D 5/11/2006 Bp Richard Sui On Chang P 11/15/2006 Bp Henry Irving Louttit. m 12/16/2000 Sharon W Walton c 2. S Mk's Ch Fincastle VA 2008-2011; Asst S Thos Ch Savannah GA 2006-2008. One Epis 2007; The Epis Majority 2007; The Epis Publ Plcy Ntwk 2007. craig_dolack@yahoo.com

DOLAN, John Richard (Chi) 3925 Central Ave, Western Springs IL 60558 B Oxford UK 10/29/1942 s Walter Henry Dolan & Joan. BS Lon 1969. D 2/3/1996 Bp Frank Tracy Griswold III. m 7/5/1975 Karen Joyce Berg c 2. D Emm Epis Ch La Grange IL 1996-2011. Auth, "The Mushroom Farm," *The Mushroom Farm*, Signalman Pub, 2011. Inst Chart Acct 1968. johnrdolan@aol.com

DOLAN, Mary Ellen (Eur) Frankfurter Strasse 3, Wiesbaden 65189 Germany **All SS Epis Ch Braine-l'Alleud 1420 BE 2010-; Int Ch of S Aug of Cbury 65189 Wiesbaden DE 2007-** B Framingham MA 6/5/1944 d Matthew Leo Dolan & Helen Nila. BS S Jos Sem & Coll 1968; Dplma Inst De Med Tropicale BE 1972; Dplma Inst D'Enseignment Med-RDC 1974; MA St. Johns U 1986; STM GTS 1990. D 6/24/1995 Bp J Clark Grew II P 12/30/1995 Bp Craig Barry Anderson. Amer Ch In Europe 2007-2010; Chr Ch Westerly RI 2002-2006; Ch of the Epiph Rumford RI 2000-2001; St Mich & Gr Ch Rumford RI 2000-2001; S Mary's Ch Portsmouth RI 1997-1998. CAECG 2007; EPGM 1998-2006; Réseau Francophone de la Comm Anglicane 1990; TMEC 2008. priest1295@yahoo.fr

DOLAN, Pamela Elisabeth (Mo) 9 S Bompart Ave, Saint Louis MO 63119 **Dir of Chr Formation/Cmncatn Asst Emm Epis Ch Webster Groves MO 2006-** B Oakland CA 7/2/1968 d David William Lowe & Patricia Bradley. BA U CA-Berkeley 1990; MTS Harvard DS 1995. D 12/18/2009 P 6/19/2010 Bp George Wayne Smith. m 7/16/1994 John Dolan c 2. peldolan@yahoo.com

DOLAN-HENDERSON, Susan (Tex) 3104 Harris Park Ave, Austin TX 78705 B Flushing NY 11/21/1957 d Michael Joseph Dolan & Irene. BD Boston Coll

1979; MDiv Ya Berk 1985; PhD Emory U 1994. D 11/1/1994 Bp Maurice Manuel Benitez P 5/1/1995 Bp Claude Edward Payne. m 10/27/1990 Alvin Augustus Henderson c 1. Epis TS Of The SW Austin TX 1995-2007. Auth, "Our Common Life & Heritage"; Auth, "Dictionary Feminist Theologies". AAR, Soc Chr Ethics. adh9927@gmail.com

DOLEN, William Kennedy (Ga) 605 Reynolds St, Augusta GA 30901 **Asstg P S Paul's Ch Augusta GA 2010-; Asstg P S Paul's Ch Augusta GA 2010-; D S Paul's Ch Augusta GA 2010-** B Memphis TN 10/16/1952 s William Smith Dolen & Dorothy Dewitt. BS Rhodes Coll 1974; MD U of TN Cntr for Hlth Serv 1977. D 2/6/2010 P 8/21/2010 Bp Scott Anson Benhase. m 12/21/1974 Carolyn Canon c 2. bdolen@mcg.edu

D

DOLL, M(ary) Chotard (Spok) 441 Highland Ave, Fort Thomas KY 41075 **P in Res S Paul's Ch Newport KY 2007-** B Washington DC 5/1/1939 d Harry Lee Doll & Delia Frances. BA Ob 1961; MDiv VTS 1978. D 6/14/1978 P 4/7/1979 Bp John Mc Gill Krumm. m 10/4/1985 Bernard Fenik. Supply P Gr Ch Dayton WA 2002-2007; R S Ptr's Ch La Grande OR 1989-1998; R Calv Ch Cincinnati OH 1980-1989; Asst S Geo's Epis Ch Dayton OH 1978-1980. dolfen@insightbb.com

DOLLAHITE, Damian DeWitt Gene (Dal) 226 Oakhaven Dr, Grand Prairie TX 75050 B Yukon OK 11/2/1939 s Louis C Dollahite & Mabel Lucille. AA Coll of Marin 1971; BA Antioch Coll W San Francisco CA 1976; MDiv CDSP 1981. D 10/24/1973 Bp C Kilmer Myers P 5/1/1981 Bp William Edwin Swing. c 1. R S Mary's Epis Ch And Sch Irving TX 1995-2008; Exec Coun Dio Wstrn Michigan Kalamazoo MI 1988-1995; R S Phil's Ch Beulah MI 1987-1995; P-in-c S Geo's Ch Lusk WY 1986-1987; Ch Of S Andr's In The Pines Pinedale WY 1982-1985; Vic S Hubert The Hunter Bonduran Jackson WY 1982-1985; St Jn the Bapt Epis Ch Big Piney WY 1982-1985; Yth Min Ch Of The H Innoc Corte Madera CA 1961-1978. Angl Eucharistic League; Chapl Ord Of S Lk, Ohca, CBS, NOEL, Epis Untd. frdamian1@aol.com

DOLNIKOWSKI, Edith Wilks (Mass) St. Andrew's Church, 79 Denton Rd, Wellesley MA 02482 **Par Admin S Andr's Ch Wellesley MA 1998-** B Pittsburgh PA 7/21/1959 d Joseph John Wilks & June Edith. BA Coll of Wooster 1981; MA MI SU 1984; PhD MI SU 1989; MDiv EDS 1994. D 6/3/1995 Bp Barbara Clementine Harris P 5/23/1996 Bp M(arvil) Thomas Shaw III. m 12/30/1980 Gregory G Dolnikowski. Asst Ch Of Our Sav Brookline MA 1995-2003. Amer Soc of Ch Hist 1990; MA Epis Cleric Assn 1995. gregory.dolnikowski@tufts.edu

DOLPH, Scott Marshall Michael (Ore) 4233 S. E. Ash Street, Portland OR 97215 **Assoc Chapl Legacy Gd Samar Hosp Portland OR 1995-; R S Aid's Epis Ch Gresham OR 1994-** B Tucson AZ 8/27/1957 s Wilbert Emery Dolph & Shirley Ann. BA U of Arizona 1980; MDiv GTS 1995. D 6/11/1985 Bp Joseph Thomas Heistand P 12/27/1985 Bp Emerson Paul Haynes. Cur Trin Epis Cathd Portland OR 1988-1993; Cur S Jn's Epis Ch Clearwater FL 1985-1987. Auth, "Maintenance," *Tucson Preservation Primer*. wolf482246@yahoo.com

DOLS, Timothy Walters (Va) 5705 Oak Bluff Ln, Wilmington NC 28409 B Baltimore MD 7/6/1942 s William Ludwig Dols & Isabel Louise. BA W&L 1964; MDiv VTS 1967; DMin Wesley Sem 1985. D 6/20/1967 P 6/1/1968 Bp Harry Lee Doll. m 8/22/1964 Anne S Stahl c 2. R S Ptr's Epis Ch Arlington VA 1975-2001; R Sherwood Epis Ch Cockeysville MD 1969-1975; Asst S Tim's Ch Catonsville MD 1967-1968. tdols@juno.com

DOLS JR, William Ludwig (Va) 300 Aspen St, Alexandria VA 22305 B Baltimore MD 4/17/1933 s William Ludwig Dols & Isabel Louise. BA W&L 1955; MDiv VTS 1958; Fllshp Coll of Preachers 1983; PhD Grad Theol Un 1988. D 6/17/1958 Bp Harry Lee Doll P 1/1/1959 Bp Noble C Powell. m 9/7/1957 Shirley Spoerry c 2. Exec Coun Dio Virginia Richmond VA 1972-1983; R Imm Ch-On-The-Hill Alexandria VA 1972-1983; Exec Coun Dio E Carolina Kinston NC 1967-1969; R S Jas Par Wilmington NC 1965-1972; Vic S Jn's Epis Ch Arlington VA 1961-1965; Cur S Thos' Ch Garrison Forest Owings Mills MD 1958-1960. Auth, "Finding Jesus, Discovering Self," Morehouse, 2006; Auth, "Just Because It Didn'T Happen: Sermons And Prayers As Story," Myers Pk Bapt Ch, 2001; Auth, "Awakening The Fire Within: A Primer For Issue-Centered Educ," The Educational Cntr, 1994; Auth, "The Ch As Crucible For Transformation," *Jung's Challenge To Contemporary Rel*, Chiron, 1987; Auth, "3-Dimensional Man: A Collection Of Sermons," 1968. wdols@aol.com

DOMBEK, Timothy M (Az) 11242 N 50th Ave, Glendale AZ 85304 **Cn to the Ordnry Dio Arizona Phoenix AZ 2007-** B Warsaw IN 12/10/1958 s Loddy Joe Dombek & Olive Lillian. Anderson U; BA Bethel Coll 1989; MDiv SWTS 1992. D 4/25/1992 P 12/9/1992 Bp Francis Campbell Gray. m 6/9/1990 Beth Ann Bittner c 1. R S Jas Epis Ch Greenville SC 2000-2007; Chapl Heathwood Hall Epis Sch Columbia SC 1996-2000; P-in-c S Barn Ch Jenkinsville SC 1996-2000; Assoc The Epis Ch Of The Trsfg Dallas TX 1992-1996. Auth, "E-Prime & Euch: Theol/Semantic Consideration," *E-Prime III! Third Anthology*, Int'l Soc for Gnrl Semantics, 1997. Natl Forensic League 1997-2000. timothy.dombek@gmail.org

DOMENICK JR, W(arren) L(ee) (Ga) 13216 Detroit Ave, Lakewood OH 44107 **R S Paul's Epis Ch Jesup GA 2008-** B Fort Ord CA 12/8/1966 s Warren Lee Domenick & Elaine. BA Shaw U 1997; MDiv STUSo 2000. D 6/24/2000 P 2/17/2001 Bp Clifton Daniel III. m 12/12/1992 Julia J Joyce c 1. R Ch Of The Ascen Lakewood OH 2002-2008; Asst to R Chr Ch New Bern NC 2000-2002. CE Awd For Creativity And Excellence In Biblic Tchg ABS 2000. leedomenick@ameritech.net

DOMIENIK, Steven B (SO) A, 13 Saint Johns Rd., Cambridge MA 02138 B Detroit MI 7/26/1961 s Bernard E Domienik & Katherine. BA U of Detroit 1984; MA U Cinc 1991; MDiv EDS 2009. D 6/14/2008 P 6/20/2009 Bp Thomas Edward Breidenthal. c 2. Ch Of The Gd Shpd Athens OH 2009-2010. sdomienik@gmail.com

DONAHOE, Melanie (Cal) Church of the Epiphany, 1839 Arroyo Avenue, San Carlos CA 94070 **R Ch Of The Epiph San Carlos CA 2009-** B San Rafael CA 11/14/1953 d Stephen Norton Donahoe & Virginia. BA Stan 1975; MA Geo 1987; MA Washington Theol Un 1989; CAS CDSP 2004. D 4/30/2005 P 11/12/2005 Bp Sylvestre Donato Romero. m 5/29/1983 Henry Tenenbaum c 2. Assoc Trsfg Epis Ch San Mateo CA 2005-2009. henry@henrymail.com

DONAHUE, Lawrence Charles (NwPa) 204 Jackson Ave, Bradford PA 16701 B Bronx NY 7/9/1941 s Lawrence Anthony Donahue & Grace Josephine. BA Niagara U 1966; MDiv Niagara U 1970. Rec from Roman Catholic 5/1/1979 as Priest Bp Robert Campbell Witcher Sr. m 11/13/1982 Patricia Ann Rielly. R Ch Of The Ascen Bradford PA 1998-2007; S Cuth's Epis Ch Selden NY 1982-1998; Cur H Trin Epis Ch Hicksville NY 1979-1982. patlarry@penn.com

DONAHUE, Ray Lawrence (Alb) 24929 State Highway 206, Downsville NY 13755 **Chapl Lake Delaware Boys Camp Delhi NY 1969-** B Elmira NY 2/23/1929 s James B Donahue & Laura S. BA Hob 1951; STB GTS 1954. D 6/6/1954 Bp Frederick Lehrle Barry P 12/18/1954 Bp David Emrys Richards. P-in-c S Marg's Ch Sidney NY 1956-2001; P-in-c S Mary's Ch Downsville NY 1956-2001; Asst S Paul's Schoharie NY 1954-1956; Asst The Ch Of The Gd Shpd Canajoharie NY 1954-1956.

DONALD, James (WA) 1 Peachtree Battle Ave. , NW #5, Unit #5, Atlanta GA 30305 **Cler Assoc All SS Epis Ch Atlanta GA 2007-** B Hackensack NJ 7/30/1944 s Joseph Edward Donald & Marion Agnes. BA S Michaels Coll Winooski VT 1966; MAT U of Notre Dame 1967; MDiv GTS 1978; DMin Fuller TS 1997. D 6/9/1978 Bp Robert Shaw Kerr P 2/9/1979 Bp John Thomas Walker. m 6/10/1967 Kathryn Wyman c 2. R S Columba's Ch Washington DC 1995-2005; R S Matt's Ch Charleston WV 1984-1995; Mem, Stwdshp Cmsn Dio W Virginia Charleston WV 1984-1994; Dep to the Bp Dio So Carolina Charleston SC 1981-1984; Asst Gr Epis Ch Silver Sprg MD 1979-1981; St. Albans Sch Cathd of St Ptr & St Paul Washington DC 1978-1979. Auth, "arts," 2003. Jn Hines Preaching Awd VTS 2000. jasdonald@aol.com

DONALD, Kenneth (USC) 203 Heathwood Pl, Easley SC 29640 B Fernie BC CA 2/16/1921 s John Clinton Donald & Elizabeth Robertson. No Carolina St U 1943; Cert STUSo 1953; Ssas Yale DS 1955. D 6/26/1953 P 3/24/1954 Bp Thomas N Carruthers. Vic S Mich's Epis Ch Easley SC 1980-1985; Asst Ch Of The H Comf Sumter SC 1975-1979; Vic All SS Epis Ch Hampton SC 1970-1975; Vic Ch Of The H Comm Allendale SC 1970-1975; R Epis Ch Of The H Sprt Apopka FL 1964-1970; R S Jas Ch Black Mtn NC 1956-1964; V-Chair Com Alco Dio So Carolina Charleston SC 1955-1956; R The Ch Of The Epiph Eutawville SC 1954-1956; R S Matt's Ch (Ft Motte) S Matthews SC 1953-1956.

DONALDSON, Audley (LI) 1345 President St, Brooklyn NY 11213 **Ch Of SS Steph And Mart Brooklyn NY 2007-** B Negril Jama CA 1/9/1957 s Lester Donaldson & Lena. BA U of The W Indies 1980; DMin W Indies Untd Theol Coll Kingston Jm 1980; STM Ya Berk 1985; Ya 1985. Rec 1/1/1987 as Priest Bp C(hristopher) FitzSimons Allison. Ch Of The Redeem Brooklyn NY 2007-2010; S Mk's Ch Brooklyn NY 2004-2007; Voorhees Coll Denmark SC 1987; Asst S Mk's Ch Brooklyn NY 1985-1986. revauds@aol.com

DONALDSON, Walter Alexander (Los) 7631 Klusman Ave, Rancho Cucamonga CA 91730 **Asst Chr Ch Par Ontario CA 1975-** B New Castle PA 11/12/1937 s Harold Alton Donaldson & Dorothy. BA U CA 1966; Med U of Redlands 1971; DIT ETSBH 1976. D 6/18/1977 P 1/14/1978 Bp Robert C Rusack. m 4/20/1966 Dolly Ruth Thacker. Auth, *Chance to be a Chld.*

DONATELLI, Todd Matthew (WNC) Cathedral of All Souls, 9 Swan St, Asheville NC 28803 **Dn The Cathd Of All Souls Asheville NC 1997-** B Oak Park IL 11/21/1956 s Henry Dominick Donatelli & Audrey Louise. ABJ U GA 1979; MDiv VTS 1987. D 6/6/1987 P 4/23/1988 Bp Charles Judson Child Jr. m 12/29/1979 Rebecca Louise Ferguson c 1. Dio Wstrn No Carolina Asheville NC 1999-2002; Dio Mississippi Jackson MS 1996-2002; Cn S Andr's Cathd Jackson MS 1990-1997; Dioc Educ Cmsn Dio Mississippi Jackson MS 1990-1993; Asst to R S Barth's Epis Ch Atlanta GA 1987-1990. Auth, "The Fruitful Mar," *Mississippi mag*, 1995. Guest Prchr "The Prot Hour" Series Of Four Sermons 2001. tdonatelli@allsoulscathedral.org

DONATHAN, W(illiam) Larry (WA) 105 15th Street SE, Washington DC 20003 B Alexandria VA 5/20/1966 s Foley Jack Donathan & Frances Caroline.

BA Geo Mason U 1989; MDiv VTS 1994; MA Amer U 2005. D 6/11/1994 P 12/14/1994 Bp Peter James Lee. Dio Washington Washington DC 2003; R S Jn's Epis/Angl Ch Mt Rainier MD 1997-2003; Asst R S Mary's Ch Wayne PA 1995-1997; Asst R Gr Ch Anniston AL 1994-1995. SocMary 1989. RevWLD@aol.com

DONDERO, Christina Downs (At) 879 Clifton Rd Ne, Atlanta GA 30307 **D S Barth's Epis Ch Atlanta GA 2006-** B Doylestown PA 1/4/1948 d Raymond Cloyd Downs & Elizabeth Holmquist. BA Connecticut Coll 1969; Candler TS Emory U 1999. D 8/6/2006 Bp J(ohn) Neil Alexander. m 7/6/1968 Timothy Joseph Dondero c 5. christinadondero@bellsouth.net

DONECKER, Paul Clayton (CPa) 351 Bull Run Crossing, Lewisburg PA 17837 B Philadelphia PA 11/26/1948 s John Jacob Donecker & Mary Elizabeth. BA Buc 1970; MDiv VTS 1976. D 6/11/1977 P 7/9/1978 Bp Lyman Cunningham Ogilby. m 12/22/1973 Leigh Hewitt Doane c 2. Sabbitical Supply P Chr Ch Williamsport PA 2011; Int R Trin Memi Ch Binghamton NY 2007-2011; Archd Congrl Dev & Deplymt Dio Cntrl Pennsylvania Harrisburg PA 1996-2007; R S Andr's Epis Ch Lewisburg PA 1979-1996; Cur Chr Ch Stratford CT 1978-1979. Cler Asociation 1979; Int Mnstry Ntwk 2008. archdpcd@aol.com

DONELSON JR, Frank T(aylor) (WTenn) 475 N Highland St Apt 7e, Memphis TN 38122 B Memphis TN 4/9/1924 s Frank Taylor Donelson & Mildred. BA Van 1948. D 3/25/1969 Bp William F Gates Jr. m 8/26/1950 Virginia Parker c 3. D S Jn's Epis Ch Memphis TN 1969-2009. thedonelsons@iopener.net

DONNELLY, Ellen Alston (Nwk) 852 Bullet Hill Rd, Southbury CT 06488 B Pittsburg CA 10/7/1944 d William Payne Alston & Mary Frances. BA U MI 1969; MDiv VTS 1982. D 6/27/1982 P 4/1/1983 Bp Robert Rae Spears Jr. m 10/31/1981 John Allen Donnelly c 2. R S Mich's Epis Ch Wayne NJ 1991-2011; R Calv Ch Stonington CT 1986-1991; Asst Min Chr Ch Greenwich CT 1983-1986; Asst S Thos Epis Ch Rochester NY 1982-1983. fedonnelly@gmail.com

DONNELLY, Jeffrey Joseph (Cal) St. James Parish, 65 Church St Apt 301, Toronto ON MSC 2E9 Canada B Albany NY 10/13/1963 s Joseph Donnelly & Betty. BA Gordon Coll 1990; MA Tem 1995; MDiv U Tor 2006. D 6/3/2006 Bp William Edwin Swing P 12/2/2006 Bp Marc Handley Andrus. jeffreyjdonnelly@yahoo.com.au

DONNELLY, John Allen (Nwk) 470 Quaker Farms Road, Oxford CT 06478 **R Chr Ch Oxford CT 2011-** B Cincinnati OH 8/25/1953 s Cecil B Donnelly & Jean A. BA U Cinc 1976; BS U Cinc 1976; MDiv VTS 1981; DMin Kingsway Chr Coll and Sem 1999; Cert Drew U 2000. D 6/27/1981 Bp William Grant Black P 6/27/1982 Bp Robert Rae Spears Jr. m 10/31/1981 Ellen Alston c 2. R S Mich's Epis Ch Wayne NJ 1991-2011; R Calv Ch Stonington CT 1986-1991; Asst Min Chr Ch Greenwich CT 1983-1986; P-in-c S Thos Epis Ch Rochester NY 1981-1983. Auth, "Its A Miracle," *A Journ of Chr Healing*, 2006; Auth, "The Healing Continues," *A Journ of Chr Healing*, 2000. NJ Hospice Chapl of the Year NJ Hospice and Palliative Care Orgnztn 2011; US Congressional Cert of Spec Recognition 2001; Phi Beta Kappa 1976. jdonnellyccqf@aol.com

DONNELLY, J(ohn) Kevin (Az) 609 Oliver Cir, Bisbee AZ 85603 B San Diego CA 2/8/1940 s Donald James Donnelly & Evelyn Elizabeth. San Diego St Coll 1959; Carmelite Sem Oakville CA 1961; S Mary Coll Dublin Ie 1963; BA Teresianum Pontifical Fac It 1965; STL Teresianum Pontifical Fac It 1968. Rec from Roman Catholic 12/1/1987 as Priest Bp Charles Shannon Mallory. m 12/24/1973 Susan Mullaney. R Epis Ch Of The Trsfg Mesa AZ 1989-1994; Asst S Alb's Epis Ch Tucson AZ 1988-1989.

DONNELLY, Richard Colonel (Ct) 430 Quaker Drive, York PA 17402 B Albany NY 12/15/1927 s Henry Ellis Donnelly & Lena Elizabeth. Berea Coll 1955; BA Hartwick Coll 1957; MA Syr 1958; BD Harvard DS 1961; MDiv EDS 1972. D 6/16/1962 Bp Allen Webster Brown P 12/22/1962 Bp Donald MacAdie. m 1/14/2006 Frances Allison c 3. R Chr Ch Ansonia CT 1982-1987; Assoc S Jas Epis Ch Danbury CT 1979-1982; R Zion Epis Ch Wappingers Falls NY 1971-1977; R S Andr's Epis Ch York PA 1965-1971; Asst Trin Epis Ch Roslyn NY 1963-1965; Cur Chr Epis Ch E Orange NJ 1962-1963. The AAPC 1975. rdonnell@ycp.edu

DONOGHUE, Larry James (Colo) 937 Jersey St, Denver CO 80220 **Died 3/9/2011** B Denver CO 3/18/1941 s James Donoghue & Marie. BA Hob 1963; MS Nash 1969. D 3/1/1969 Bp Donald H V Hallock P 9/29/1969 Bp Edwin B Thayer. Integrity 1990. ljd@tde.com

DONOHUE, Janie (Mass) 12 Arden St, New Haven CT 06512 **Dio Massachusetts Boston MA 2010-** B Manchester CT 8/2/1968 d Ralph Donohue & Judith. BS NWU Evanston IL 1994; MA TESM 1994; MDiv Yale DS 2004. D 6/9/2007 Bp Andrew Donnan Smith. m Lauren Patalak c 1. Asst S Ann's Epis Ch Old Lyme CT 2007-2010. Meuhl Preaching Prize Berkeley Grad Soc 2004. jdonohue@mit.edu

DONOHUE-ADAMS, Amy (Tex) 11703 Oakwood Dr, Austin TX 78753 B Chicago IL 11/30/1946 d Daniel Charles Donohue & Bernice. BS S Mary Of The Woods Coll S Mary Of The Woods IN 1969; MDiv Epis TS of The SW 1993. D 6/21/1993 Bp William Jackson Cox P 3/14/1994 Bp Claude Edward Payne. m 6/3/1995 William Seth Adams. Chapl S Jas Ch Austin TX 1998-2004; Vic S Ptr's Epis Ch Lago Vista TX 1995-1996; Asst S Fran Ch Houston TX 1993-1995. amylfp@gmail.com

✠ **DONOVAN JR, Rt Rev Herbert Alcorn** (NY) 152 Broadway # 8, Dobbs Ferry NY 10522 B Washington DC 7/14/1931 s Herbert Alcorn Donovan & Marion Mitchell. BA U of Virginia 1954; MDiv VTS 1957; Fllshp Coll of Preachers 1976; Fllshp Harvard DS 1987. D 6/10/1957 Bp Frederick D Goodwin P 12/10/1957 Bp James W Hunter Con 9/22/1980 for Ark. m 7/7/1959 Mary Sudman c 3. Consult to P.B. Epis Ch Cntr New York NY 2000-2001; Asstg Bp of NJ Dio New Jersey Trenton NJ 1999-2000; Provsnl Bp of Chi Dio Chicago Chicago IL 1998-1999; Ret Bp of Ark Dio Arkansas Little Rock AR 1993-2003; Asstg Dio New York New York City NY 1993-1997; Vic Par of Trin Ch New York NY 1993-1997; Epis Ch Cntr New York NY 1990; Dio Arkansas Little Rock AR 1984-1990; Bp Coadj of Ark Dio Arkansas Little Rock AR 1980-1981; Stndg Com Dio Newark Newark NJ 1972-1977; R S Lk's Epis Ch Montclair NJ 1970-1980; Cn Chr Ch Cathd Louisville KY 1964-1970; Exec Off Dio Kentucky Louisville KY 1964-1970; Vic S Andr's Ch Basin WY 1959-1964; R S Jn's Ch Green River WY 1957-1959. Auth, "Var Tracts," *Forw Mvmt*, 1973. DD Berk atYale New Haven CT 2003; DD U So Sewanee TN 1984; DD VTS Alexandria VA 1981. msdonovan@msn.com

DONOVAN, John Carl (Tex) 2908 Avenue O Apt 1, Galveston TX 77550 B Muncie IN 7/20/1930 s Carl Edwin Donovan & Eleanor Law. BA U of Texas 1952; LLB U of Texas 1954; BD Epis TS of The SW 1957; Fllshp Coll of Preachers 1970. D 6/20/1957 P 5/24/1958 Bp James Parker Clements. m 2/3/1962 Joal Harris c 3. R Trin Ch Galveston TX 1976-1995; BEC Dio Texas Houston TX 1971-1995; R S Steph's Ch Beaumont TX 1965-1971; Assoc Trin Ch Galveston TX 1963-1965; Vic Chr Epis Ch Mexia Mexia TX 1957-1962. Phi Beta Kappa. joaldonovan@hotmail.com

DONOVAN, Nancy Lu (SD) 9412 Saint Joseph St, Silver City SD 57702 **D S Matt's Epis Ch Rapid City SD 2001-; D S Dav Of Wales Epis Ch Lincoln NE 1996-** B Hot Springs SD 10/14/1935 d Glenn Harrison Frary & Verda June. Stephens Coll; U Denv 1957. D 5/24/1996 Bp James Edward Krotz. m 2/1/1958 Uhl Dean Donovan c 3. Oblate Ord Of S Ben. uhlnancy@aol.com

DONOVAN, William Patrick (Minn) 684 Mississippi River Blvd S, Saint Paul MN 55116 **Cn Cathd Ch Of S Mk Minneapolis MN 1978-** B Saint Louis MO 12/2/1929 s John Elmer Donovan & Dorothy. BA Washington U 1951; MA Washington U 1952; PhD U Cinc 1961; Westcott Hse Cambridge 1968. D 5/10/1971 P 2/13/1972 Bp Philip Frederick McNairy. m 6/15/1955 Patricia Ann O'Keefe c 2. Asst S Geo's Ch St Louis Pk MN 1971-1974. Auth, *Excavations at Nichoria*; Auth, *Palace of Nestor*. wpdonovan@prodigy.net

DOOLEY, Martha Mae (NJ) 4735 Cedar Ave, Philadelphia PA 19143 **D Ch Of S Jn-In-The-Wilderness Gibbsboro NJ 2005-** B York Harbor ME 3/25/1949 d George Hadley Dooley & Eugenia Triplett. BSN U of Maryland 1972; MSN U of Pennsylvania 1983. D 6/11/2005 Bp George Edward Councell. m 7/17/1996 Kathleen Murray. Integrity 1994. martha.dooley@verizon.net

DOOLITTLE, Geoffrey Douglas (CNY) 2647 N Van Dorn St Apt 12, Alexandria VA 22302 **S Paul's Ch Owego NY 2010-** B Binghamton NY 11/23/1960 s Raymond L Doolittle & Barbara L. AAS Broome Cmnty Coll 1980; MDiv VTS 2010. D 12/19/2009 P 11/3/2010 Bp Gladstone Bailey Adams III. m 5/24/1980 Joann E Doolittle c 3. gd07867@hotmail.com

DOOLY, Robert Wallace Bernard (Fla) 9140 Mellon Ct, Saint Augustine FL 32080 B Cork IE 6/26/1940 s Timothy Dooly & May. BA St. Pat's Coll Thurles Tipperary IE 1965; STL CUA 1967; STD The Ponitifical Lateran U 1972. Rec from Roman Catholic 12/1/1976 as Priest Bp Frank Stanley Cerveny. m 2/13/1976 Marcia Riley. Cn S Jn's Cathd Jacksonville FL 1994-2001; Dio Florida Jacksonville FL 1979-1994; Chapl Resurr Chap Tallahassee FL 1979-1994; Trin Epis Ch St Aug FL 1977-1979. b.dody@yahoo.com

DOPP, William Floyd (SwFla) 818 Chamise Ct, San Marcos CA 92069 B Watertown WI 4/30/1942 s William M Dopp & June K. San Diego St U; BS Indiana U 1969; MDiv Claremont TS 1994; DMin SWTS 2001. D 6/11/1994 P 2/24/1995 Bp Gethin Benwil Hughes. m 9/8/1962 Janet Dopp. R S Mart's Epis Ch Hudson FL 2005-2009; Cmncatn Off Dio San Diego San Diego CA 1999-2002; Vic S Columba's Epis Ch Santee CA 1995-1999; Dio San Diego San Diego CA 1994-2005; Trin Ch Escondido CA 1994. Auth, "Tale of Two Ch," 2009; Auth, "The Archd's Column," *The Ch Times*, 2002; Auth, "The Ed'S Notebook," *The Ch Times*, 1994; Auth, "Copy Writers Idea Bk," 1982. Bro Of S Andr 1982; OSL 2006. Ord Of Constantine Sigma Chi Fraternity Alum 2001; Polly Bond Cert For "Spec Lambeth Ed" ECom 1998. frdopp@aol.com

DORAN, Judith Ann (SO) 256 Chatham Dr, Fairborn OH 45324 **P Trin Epis Ch Troy OH 2011-** B Chicago IL 6/18/1953 d Walter S Grabowski & Catherine V. BA Chapman U 1983; MDiv Bex 2006. D 5/14/2005 Bp Herbert Thompson Jr P 6/24/2006 Bp Kenneth Lester Price. m 5/6/1978 Patrick Doran c 2. P S Andr's Ch Dayton OH 2011; P S Jas Ch Piqua OH 2010; Asst S Paul's Epis Ch Dayton OH 2006-2010. judithadoran@aol.com

DORAN, Michelle Stuart (Md) Christ Church, 220 Owensville Rd., West River MD 20778 B Oil City PA 1/8/1947 d Charles Franklin Stuart & Mary Stewart.

BA SUNY 1969; MEd U of Maryland 1975. D 6/2/2007 Bp John Leslie Rabb. m 8/25/1973 Richard Doran c 2. N.A.A.D. 2007. msdoranl@comcast.net

DORN, Christy Michelle (Los) 12341 Semora Pl, Cerritos CA 90703 B Oakland CA 7/23/1949 d Lewis Robert Dorn & Eleanor Elizabeth. BA U of Arizona 1972; MDiv CDSP 1991. D 12/5/1992 Bp William Edwin Swing P 11/1/1993 Bp John Lester Thompson III. m 6/11/1994 Lawrence Glen Ehren. Assoc S Wilfrid Of York Epis Ch Huntington Bch CA 2006-2011; S Mk's Ch Grand Rapids MI 2002-2005; Ch Of The Gd Shpd Lexington KY 2001-2002; Komo Kulshan Cluster Mt Vernon WA 2000; S Andr's Ch Seattle WA 1998-1999; Assoc S Paul Epis Ch Bellingham WA 1995-1997; Epis Soc Of Chr Ch Cincinnati OH 1993-1995. families@stwilfridschurch.org

DORN III, James M (Fla) PO Box 370, Palatka FL 32178 **R S Mk's Ch Palatka FL 2005-** B Charleston SC 9/20/1961 s James Marion Dorn & Mary Sutton. BS Presb Coll, Clinton SC 1983; MDiv TS 2002. D 12/14/2002 Bp Dorsey Felix Henderson P 12/19/2003 Bp Henry Irving Louttit. m 1/4/1986 Janette Sue McIntosh c 3. Asst R S Thos Ch Savannah GA 2002-2005. jmdorn3@gmail.com

DORNEMANN, Deanna Maxine (EC) 60 Bethlehem Pike Rm 1401, Philadelphia PA 19118 **S Paul Ch Exton PA 2008-** B 7/26/1944 d Alton L Maddox & Maudine. BS Wesl 1966; MDiv STUSo 1990. D 6/16/1990 P 12/27/1990 Bp Brice Sidney Sanders. Ch Of The Incarn Morrisville PA 2001-2003; S Paul's Ch Philadelphia PA 1993-1999. dmmaddox@aol.com

DORNER, Mary Anne (SwFla) 27127 Fordham Dr, Wesley Chapel FL 33543 B Chicago IL 9/13/1945 d James L Soens & Anne L. Cert Coll of Preachers; Lancaster TS; BA Neumann Coll Aston PA 1984; MDiv VTS 1989. D 6/24/1989 P 6/22/1991 Bp Cabell Tennis. m 8/1/1964 Theodore M Dorner. S Jn The Div Epis Ch Sun City Cntr FL 2004-2006; Vic Resurr Epis Ch Naples FL 1998-2002; Assoc R Ch Of The Gd Shpd Dunedin FL 1994-1998; Dioc Coun Dio Delaware Wilmington DE 1991-1994; Asst Gr Epis Ch Wilmington DE 1990-1991; D & DRE S Mart's Ch Radnor PA 1989-1990. Auth, "Brandywine Baptism Progran Ldr'S Manual & Parents Guide". Epis Soc For Mnstry To Aging 1992-1995. revdorner@tampabay.rr.com

DOROW, Robert Michael (Pgh) 15023 Oakwood Drive, Big Rapids MI 49307 B Pittsburgh PA 5/21/1969 s Ernest Baxter Dorow & Arlene Thelma. MDiv TESM 2002. D 6/14/2003 P 3/6/2005 Bp Robert William Duncan. m 8/11/2007 Tracey Bloodworth c 2. Bread of Life Luth Ch Hudsonville MI 2008-2011; Int Bread of Life Luthern Ch Hudsonville MI 2008-2011; P-in-res Trin Cathd Pittsburgh PA 2005-2007. robdorow@hotmail.com

DORR JR, E(rwin) John (Ind) 256 51st St Cir E, Palmetto FL 34221 B Farina IL 3/16/1930 s Erwin John Dorr & Edna Christine. BA U IL 1952; MA Ya 1955. D 10/14/1959 P 5/5/1960 Bp Chilton Powell. m 12/31/1991 Marion Schneider c 2. P-in-c S Mths Ch Rushville IN 1974-1982; R S Jas Ch New Castle IN 1970-1973; R Gr Epis Ch Chadron NE 1962-1970; Vic Ch Of The Ascen Pawnee OK 1959-1962; Cur S Andr's Ch Stillwater OK 1959-1962. billybrucewagener@gmail.com

DORR, Guy Edward (LI) 320 Great River Road, Great River NY 11739 **R Emm Epis Ch Great River NY 1992-** B Fort Worth TX 11/22/1939 s Otis Edward Dorr & Jenlee Margaret. BS Arizona St U 1963; MA U of Arkansas 1977; BA U of Tennessee 1983; MDiv Yale DS 1988; STM Yale DS 1989. D 6/8/1989 P 12/1/1989 Bp Robert Oran Miller. m 4/28/1990 Kathleen Elaine Anderson-Gillespie c 4. Emm Epis Ch Great River NY 1991-2003; R Ch Of The Mssh Heflin AL 1990-1991; Epis Black Belt Mnstry Demopolis AL 1990; Dio Alabama Birmingham AL 1989.

DORR, Kathleen Elaine (Ct) 39 Whalers Pt, East Haven CT 06512 **Asst Chr Ch New Haven CT 1999-** B Wyandotte MI 6/26/1952 d Robert Earl Anderson & Beatrice Josephine. BA OH SU 1977; MDiv Ya Berk 1989. D 6/23/1995 Bp Orris George Walker Jr P 9/1/1996 Bp Charles Lovett Keyser. m 4/28/1990 Guy Edward Dorr c 2. Seabury Ret Cmnty Bloomfield CT 2003-2008; Int Chr Ch Bay Ridge Brooklyn NY 1998-1999; Asst S Matt's Cathd Dallas TX 1996-1998.

DORRIEN, Gary John (NY) Union Theological Seminary, 3041 Broadway, New York NY 10027 B Midland MI 3/21/1952 s John Ellis Dorrien & Virginia Catherine. Harv; BA Alma Coll 1974; MA PrTS 1978; MDiv UTS 1978; ThM PrTS 1979; PhD Un Grad Sch New York NY 1989. D 6/19/1982 P 12/1/1982 Bp Wilbur Emory Hogg Jr. m 8/4/1979 Brenda Louise Biggs. Dio Albany Albany NY 1986-1987; S Andr's Epis Ch Albany NY 1982-1987; Doane Stuart Sch Albany NY 1982-1985. Auth, "The Making Of Amer Liberal Theol: Idealism, Realism," *And Modernity 1900-1950*, 2003; Auth, "The Making Of Amer Liberal Theol: Imagining Progressive Rel 1805-1900," 2001; Auth, "The Barthian Revolt In Mod Tech," 2000; Auth, "The Neoconservative Mind," 1993; Auth, "The Democratic Socialist Vision," 1986; Auth, "Logic & Consciousness"; Auth, "Reconstructing The Common Gd"; Auth, "Soul In Soc"; Auth, "The Word As True Myth"; Auth, "Remaking Evang Theol". Omicron Delta Kappa hon Soc 1973; Phi Beta Kappa, Sw Mi Chapt 1999. Florence J. Lucasse Awd For Outstanding Schlrshp Kalamazoo Coll 1994; U Chi Prog On Secondary Sch Tchg 1987.

DORSCH, Kenneth John (Ore) 15625 Nw Norwich St, Beaverton OR 97006 **Int All SS Ch Portland OR 2010-** B Newark NJ 12/28/1945 s Harold Robert Dorsch & Marie Caroline. BA Rutgers-The St U 1967; Fllshp Fulbright Schlr 1968; MDiv Ya Berk 1971; Fllshp ECF Fllshp 1979; DMin SWTS 2005. D 6/12/1971 Bp Leland Stark P 12/1/1971 Bp George E Rath. m 6/11/1977 Joy Swickard. R S Barth's Ch Beaverton OR 2000-2009; R S Jn's Par Hagerstown MD 1992-1999; R S Jn The Div Ch Saunderstown RI 1990-1992; Asst and Dir of Mus Ch Of The H Comf Kenilworth IL 1985-1990; Asst & Dir Of Mus Trin Epis Ch Wheaton IL 1979-1984; Int Mssh-S Barth Epis Ch Chicago IL 1978-1979; P-t Fac Nash Nashotah WI 1975-1978; Cur Par of St Paul's Ch Norwalk Norwalk CT 1971-1975. Soc Of S Jn The Evang 1970-1991. Fllshp ECF 1979; Fulbright Schlr U. S. Govt 1967. kjdorsch@gmail.com

DORSEE, Ballard (Ct) 461 Mill Hill Ter, Southport CT 06890 **P in charge Ch Of The Gd Shpd Shelton CT 1999-** B Detroit MI 6/11/1929 s Edmund Ballard Dorsee & Alice Emma. LTh VTS; BA U of Maryland 1951. D 6/24/1967 P 6/1/1969 Bp William Foreman Creighton. m 11/9/1974 Roberta Dorsee c 5. Clerk of the Works S Jn's Ch W Hartford CT 1993-1996; Stndg Com Dio Connecticut Hartford CT 1982-1987; R Gr Epis Ch Norwalk CT 1977-1991; R S Jas Ch Hartford CT 1969-1977; Asst S Phil's Epis Ch Laurel MD 1967-1969. bddseao@aol.com

DORSEY, James Claypoole (Pa) 257 W Somerville Ave, Philadelphia PA 19120 B Baltimore MD 8/21/1932 s Brice Marden Dorsey & Mary Elizabeth. BA Loyola Coll 1955; STB PDS 1958. D 6/17/1958 P 3/14/1959 Bp Harry Lee Doll. R S Alb's Ch Philadelphia PA 1960-2003; Asst To Dn S Paul's Cathd Fond du Lac WI 1959-1960; Cur H Trin Epis Ch Baltimore MD 1958-1959. Co-Ed, "Catalog Of Hist Mus," 1974. AGO 1970-2003; Chairman Grants Com 1974-1991; Coun/Dir CBS 1967-1991; GAS, Wrdn 1970-1988; SHN; Soc Advancement Of Chr In Pennsylvania 1967-2003; SocMary 1968-1976; Wrdn Emer 1991. Hon Cn Iglesia Cateral Del Redentor Madrid Espana 1989.

DORSEY, Laura Miller (Eas) 28333 Mount Vernon Rd, Princess Anne MD 21853 B Catonsville MD 11/24/1950 D 9/15/2001 Bp Martin Gough Townsend P 10/5/2002 Bp Charles Lindsay Longest. c 1.

DOSCHER SR, Richard Carl (SwFla) 1601 Curlew Rd, Palm Harbor FL 34683 **R S Alfred's Epis Ch Palm Harbor FL 2005-** B Bronx NY 9/2/1952 s Carl Peter Doscher & Grace Lillian. BA Curry Coll Milton MA 1975; MDiv Maryknoll Inst Of Theol Maryknoll NY 1979; DAS GTS 1990. Rec from Roman Catholic 7/15/1990 as Deacon. m 11/27/1982 M Julia Doscher c 3. R S Phil's Ch Brooklyn NY 1999-2005; All SS Ch Great Neck NY 1998-1999; R S Pat's Ch Deer Pk NY 1993-1995; Asst to R S Mary's Ch Lake Ronkonkoma NY 1990-1993.

✠ **DOSS, Rt Rev Joe Morris** (NJ) 15 Front St, Mandeville LA 70448 B Mobile AL 3/29/1943 s Morris Doss & Frances. BA LSU 1965; JD LSU 1968; STB GTS 1971; DD GTS 1981. D 6/21/1971 P 1/1/1972 Bp Iveson Batchelor Noland Con 10/31/1993 for NJ. m 2/15/1975 Susan T Terkuhle c 2. Bp Dio New Jersey Trenton NJ 1995-2001; Bp Coadj Dio New Jersey Trenton NJ 1993-1994; S Mk's Epis Ch Palo Alto CA 1985-1993; Dep GC Dio Louisiana Baton Rouge LA 1979; R Gr Ch New Orleans LA 1973-1985; D Epis Ch Of The Gd Shpd Lake Chas LA 1971-1973; Spec Consult Dio Louisiana Baton Rouge LA 1969-1972. Auth, *Law & Morality: Capital Punishment*; Auth, *Let the Bastards Go: From Cuba to Freedom--Or God's Mercy*; Auth, *The Songs of the Mothers: Messages of Promise for the Future Ch*. bishop.doss@gmail.com

DOSS, Matthew Brian (Ala) 1311 Toney Dr SE, Huntsville AL 35802 **R St Thos Epis Ch Huntsville AL 2009-** B 8/5/1971 D 5/26/2004 P 12/2/2004 Bp Henry Nutt Parsley Jr. m 5/27/1995 Jennifer Doss c 2. R S Lk's Ch Scottsboro AL 2007-2009; Assoc S Lk's Epis Ch Birmingham AL 2004-2007. mdoss@sthomashuntsville.org

DOSTAL FELL, Margaret Ann (Minn) 1765 Upper 55th St E, Inver Grove Heights MN 55077 B Jackson MN 4/8/1947 d Louis Leslie Dostal & Clara Marie. BA U MN 1970; MDiv Untd TS 2002. D 6/12/2003 P 12/18/2003 Bp James Louis Jelinek. m 12/31/2002 George Mansfield Fell. mdf@mm.com

DOSTER, Daniel Harris (Ga) 724 Victoria Cir, Dublin GA 31021 **Respite P Dio Georgia Savannah GA 1997-** B Moultrie GA 12/15/1934 s Percy James Doster & Juanita. BA Florida St U 1961; MS Ft Vlly St U 1984. D 12/3/1980 Bp (George) Paul Reeves P 11/22/1997 Bp Henry Irving Louttit. m 3/29/1964 Robin Baker. D'S Advsry Com Dio Georgia Savannah GA 1996-1997; Cmsn Alcosm & Drug Abuse Dio Georgia Savannah GA 1985-1988; D Chr Epis Ch Dublin GA 1980-1997. ddoster13@hotmail.net

DOTY, D(avid) Michael (WNC) 143 Caledonia Rd, Landrum SC 29356 **R Ch Of The H Cross Tryon NC 2002-** B Greeneville TN 1/19/1952 s Isaac Lafayette Doty & Opal Morelock. BA Carson-Newman Coll 1976; MDiv STUSo 1990; DMin STUSo 1997. D 6/18/1990 P 12/21/1990 Bp William Evan Sanders. m 5/20/1972 Pamela Dye c 1. R S Paul's Ch Athens TN 1994-2000; Alt Dep to GC Dio E Tennessee Knoxville TN 1994-1996; Wm E. Sanders Minorities Schlrshp Fund, Chair Dio E Tennessee Knoxville TN 1992-2002; Bd Dir and Chair EAM Knoxville TN 1992-1995; Sm Ch Off Dio E Tennessee

Knoxville TN 1990-1996; Vic S Thos Ch Elizabethton TN 1990-1994; Bp and Coun Dio E Tennessee Knoxville TN 1990-1993; Opportunity Fund Grants and Loans Com Dio E Tennessee Knoxville TN 1990-1993. Auth, "Anglicanism in Appalachia: The Formation of the Epis Ch in E Tennessee," *DMin Dissertation Proj STUSo*, Dio E Tennessee, 1997; Auth, "Anglicanism in Appalachia," *Appalachian Stds Conf*, Virginia Tech, Blacksburg, VA, 1995; Auth, "Epis Ch & Baptismal Tradition: Examination of Faith Perspectives," *Sewanee Theol Revs*, U So, 1995. CODE 2000-2001. mdoty@holycrosstryon.org

DOTY, Phyllis Marie (Fla) P.O. Box 4366, Dowling Park FL 32064 B Colorado Springs CO 4/11/1940 d Theodore Millet Doty & Isabel. Angl TS; BA Col Bible Coll 1969; MA Uta-Arlington 1981; Lic Angl Sem 1991. D 6/20/1992 Bp Donis Dean Patterson. D for Hisp Mnstrs S Matt's Cathd Dallas TX 2000-2008; Ch Of The Gd Shpd Cedar Hill TX 1992-1994. phylis01@windstream.net

DOUBLEDAY, William Alan (NY) 278 Burns Street, Forest Hills NY 11375 **Assoc S Lk's Ch Forest Hills NY 2005-** B Northamton MA 2/9/1951 s Elwyn John Doubleday & Margret Ann. BA Amh 1972; MDiv EDS 1976. D 6/14/1980 P 12/12/1980 Bp Alexander Doig Stewart. Int Dn Bex Columbus OH 2009-2011; Assoc Dn Bex Columbus OH 2006-2009; Vstng Prof Bex Columbus OH 2005-2006; Prof The GTS New York NY 1986-2006; Chapl S Lk's-Roosevelt Hosp Cntr New York NY 1983-1986; Chapl Morningside Hse Nrsng Hm Bronx NY 1980-1982; Cur S Jas Ch Great Barrington MA 1979-1980. Auth, "Fighting Aids & Hiv Together," *Envisioning The New City: A Rdr On Urban Mnstry*, Westmin/Jknox, 1992; Contrib, "The Gospel Imperative In The Midst Of Aids," Morehouse-Barlow, 1988; Contrib, "Aids: Facts & Issues," Rutgers U Pr, 1986. Hon Cn Dio the Highveld, So Afr 2003. wdoubleday@nyc.rr.com

DOUCETTE OSB, Lee Francis (Minn) 7213 W Shore Dr, Edina MN 55435 B Minneapolis MN 1/21/1936 s Clifford H Doucette & Frances. BS U MN 1973; MA Untd TS of the Twin Cities 1983; DMin Untd TS of the Twin Cities 1986. Rec from Roman Catholic 6/22/1978 as Deacon Bp Robert Marshall Anderson. m 7/14/1956 Vivian E Thielman c 2. Asst S Steph The Mtyr Ch Minneapolis MN 2005-2008; Dio Minnesota Minneapolis MN 2003-2004; Int Mssh Epis Ch S Paul MN 2003-2004; S Steph The Mtyr Ch Minneapolis MN 1993-2003; Geth Ch Minneapolis MN 1991. ldoucette7213@comcast.net

DOUGHARTY, Philip Wilmot (WNY) 51 Colonial Cir, Buffalo NY 14222 **R S Jn's Gr Ch Buffalo NY 2002-** B Fort Worth TX 6/7/1950 s Bernard Wilmot Dougharty & Margaret Ruth. BME Oklahoma Bapt U 1972; MM U of New Mex 1982; MDiv UTS 1995. D 6/10/2000 P 2/10/2001 Bp John Palmer Croneberger. c 1. Asst Trin And S Phil's Cathd Newark NJ 2001-2002. hartph@hotmail.com

DOUGHERTY JR, Edward Archer (SeFla) 8 Sky Hollow Dr, Albany NY 12204 **Assoc S Paul's Epis Ch Albany NY 2010-** B Glen Ridge NJ 10/8/1939 s Edward Archer Dougherty & Elisabeth. BA Wms 1962; BD Harvard DS 1965; Med Ohio U 1969; PhD U MI 1972. D 6/26/1965 P 1/16/1966 Bp Roger W Blanchard. m 6/17/1961 Barbey Dougherty c 3. Asst Cathd Of All SS Albany NY 1995-1998; Asst S Clare Of Assisi Epis Ch Ann Arbor MI 1974-1983; S Clare Of Assisi Epis Ch Ann Arbor MI 1972; Untd Campus Mnstry Athens OH 1968-1972; Vic Ch Of The Epiph Nelsonville OH 1966-1968; Ch Of The Gd Shpd Athens OH 1965-1968. ned.dougherty@gmail.com

DOUGHERTY, Jan (Minn) 5844 Deer Trail Cir, Woodbury MN 55129 **D Cathd Ch Of S Mk Minneapolis MN 1997-** B Mount Pleasant IA 6/15/1940 d Ernest Hayes & Ruth. Pomona Coll 1960; BS U of Iowa 1962. D 1/5/1989 Bp Robert Marshall Anderson. m 8/26/1961 Richard Dougherty c 4. janhayesd@comcast.net

DOUGLAS, Alan David (Colo) 5409 Fossil Creek Dr, Fort Collins CO 80526 B San Antonio TX 8/15/1936 s Leslie Allyn Douglas & Avis. BA Stetson U 1958; MDiv TCU 1961; ThM TCU 1965. D 6/26/1966 Bp Everett H Jones P 12/1/1966 Bp Richard Earl Dicus. m 4/27/1957 Patricia Pipkin c 6. S Lk's Epis Ch Ft Collins CO 1982-1999; R Ch Of The Gd Shpd Brownwood TX 1971-1982; P-in-c Ch Of Our Sav Aransas Pass TX 1968-1971; P-in-c Trin-By-The-Sea Port Aransas TX 1968-1971; Assoc R S Dav's Epis Ch San Antonio TX 1966-1968. rabriver@aol.com

DOUGLAS, Ann Leslie (NY) 85 E Main St, Mount Kisco NY 10549 B 2/17/1946 d Gordon Derham & Constance. D 5/2/2009 Bp Mark Sean Sisk. m 10/14/1967 Dwight Hendee Douglas c 3. threave04@yahoo.com

DOUGLAS, Carole Robinson (Md) 7521 Rockridge Rd, Pikesville MD 21208 **Asstg P S Jas' Epis Ch Baltimore MD 2009-** B Fort Meade MD 9/23/1958 d John Coker Robinson & Catherine Marie. BD U of Maryland 1984; MDiv VTS 1997. D 6/7/1997 P 12/1/1997 Bp Robert Wilkes Ihloff. m 11/1/1996 John Allen Douglas c 1. Ch Of The H Nativ Baltimore MD 2006-2008; S Mich And All Ang Ch Baltimore MD 2001; Asst S Jas' Epis Ch Baltimore MD 1997-1999. cfrdouglas@juno.com

DOUGLAS, Dorothy Ruth (CGC) 5904 Woodvale Dr, Mobile AL 36608 B Birmingham AL 6/26/1941 d Ralph Winfred Douglas & Mildred Louise. Birmingham-Sthrn Coll 1962; BA Emory U 1963; MA U of Alabama 1966; EdD U of Alabama 1969; Cert STUSo 1997. D 8/24/1997 P 3/21/1998 Bp Charles Farmer Duvall. Ch Of The Gd Shpd Mobile AL 2005-2008; S Mk's For The Deaf Mobile AL 2005-2006; S Thos Ch Citronelle AL 2005-2006; S Ptr's Ch Jackson AL 2002-2004; Vic S Thos Ch Citronelle AL 1997-2002; Dio Cntrl Gulf Coast Pensacola FL 1997-1998. dottie1@us.inter.net

DOUGLAS JR, Harry Bell (SeFla) 33 Kathy Ann Dr, Crawfordville FL 32327 B Augusta GA 2/18/1925 s Harry Bell Douglas & Frances Simspon. BA U So 1948; MDiv STUSo 1952. D 6/23/1952 P 12/17/1952 Bp Frank A Juhan. m 7/31/1971 Lianne Heckman Douglas c 3. Vic Ch Of The Ascen Carrabelle FL 2005-2009; Asst to R S Jn's Epis Ch Tallahassee FL 1993-2000; R All SS Prot Epis Ch Ft Lauderdale FL 1978-1988; R Ch Of The Gd Shpd Jacksonville FL 1968-1970; Vic Ch Of The Adv Tallahassee FL 1959-1962; Exec Dir Yth And Camp Weed Dio Florida Jacksonville FL 1954-1959; Vic S Jas' Epis Ch Port S Joe FL 1952-1954. Hon Cn Dio Florida 2006. harrybell2@aol.com

✠ DOUGLAS, Rt Rev Ian Theodore (Ct) Episcopal Diocese Of Connecticut, 1335 Asylum Ave, Hartford CT 06105 **Bp of Connecticut Dio Connecticut Hartford CT 2010-** B Fitchburg MA 5/20/1958 s Duncan Douglas & Gladys Mary. BA Mid 1980; EdM Harv 1982; MDiv Harvard DS 1983; PhD Bos 1993. D 6/11/1988 P 6/24/1989 Bp Andrew Frederick Wissemann Con 4/17/2010 for Ct. m 10/13/1984 Kristin Harris c 3. Angus Dun Prof of Mssn and Wrld Chrsnty EDS Cambridge MA 1991-2010; Adj Prof EDS Cambridge MA 1989-1991; S Jas' Epis Ch Cambridge MA 1989-1990. "Inculturation and Angl Wrshp," *Oxford Guide to BCP*, Oxf Press, 2006; "Authority, Unity and Mssn in the Windsor Report," *ATR 87*, 2005; Auth, "GThankful for their Offerings: Wmn in the Frgn Mssn of the Epis Ch in the 20th Centur," *Deeper Joy: Laywomen and Vocation in the 20th-Century Epis Ch*, Ch Pub, 2005; "An Amer Reflects on the Windsor Report," *Journ of Angl Stds 3.2*, 2005; "Anglicans Gathering for Gods Mssn: A Missiological Ecclesiology for the Angl Comm," *Journ of Angl Stds 2.2*, 2004; Auth, *Waging Recon: God's Mssn in a Time of Globalization and Change*, Ch Pub, 2002; Co-Ed, *Beyond Colonial Anglicanism: The Angl Comm in the Twenth-First Century*, Ch Pub Inc, 2001; Auth, "Angl Identity and the Missio Dei: Implications for the Amer Convoc of Ch in Europe," *ATR 82*, 2000; Auth, "Whither the Natl Ch? Reconsidering the Mssn Structures of the Epis Ch," *A New Conversation: Essays on the Future of Theol and th*, Ch Pub Inc, 1999; Auth, "Baptized into Mssn: Mnstry and H Ord Reconsidered," *Sewanee Theol Revs 40*, Michaelmas, 1997; Auth, "Lambeth 1998 and the Challenge of Pluralism," *The Angl 26*, 1997; Auth, *Fling Out the Banner: The Natl Ch Ideal and the Frgn Mssn of the Epis Ch*, Ch Hymnal, 1996. Amer Soc for Missiology 1986; Angl Contextual Theologians Ntwk 2003; Dep to GC 2000-2006; Epis Partnership for Global Mssn 1990; EWHP 1993; Hist Soc of Epis Ch 1992; HOB Theol Com 2000-2006; Inter-Angl Stndg Cmsn on Mssn and Evang 2001-2006; Sem Consult on Mssn 1994; SCWM, The GC of 1992-1997. Angl Consultative Coun Exec Coun 2007; Spec Cmsn on the Epis Ch and the Angl Com GC 2006; Execuive Coun GC 2006; Design Grp for Lamberth Conf of Angl Bishops 2008 Archbp of Cbury 2005; Ed Bd Journ of Angl Stds 2002; Fllshp Epis Ch Foundations 1986. itdouglas@ctdiocese.org

DOUGLAS, Jeffrey Allen (EC) 904 N Colony Avenue, Ahoskie NC 27910 **S Thos' Epis Ch Ahoskie NC 2002-** B Eugene OR 2/20/1957 s Allen Lee Douglas & Phyllis Jean. BA U So 1979; MDiv GTS 1989. D 6/10/1989 Bp John Thomas Walker P 1/1/1990 Bp Brice Sidney Sanders. m 6/12/1982 Elizabeth Covert c 1. R Ch of the H Cross Mt Holly NC 1998-2002; R S Andr Ch Mt Holly NC 1998-2001; R H Trin Epis Ch Hampstead NC 1993-1998; P-in-c Ch Of The H Innoc Seven Sprg NC 1991-1993; Asst to R S Mary's Ch Kinston NC 1989-1993. jeff@saintthomasahoskie.com

DOUGLAS, Philip Carlton (Mass) 34 Meriam St, New Bedford MA 02740 **Died 8/4/2011** B Gloucester MA 10/11/1922 s Louis Richard Douglas & Ethel Gertrude. BA Tufts U 1945; STB EDS 1948. D 6/2/1948 P 12/1/1948 Bp Norman B Nash. c 2. Fllshp Coll of Preachers; Bp Nash Fllshp Dio Massachusetts MA.

DOUGLAS, Roger Owen (Az) 47280 Amir Dr, Palm Desert CA 92260 B New York NY 6/5/1932 s Milton Douglas & Veola. BA Trin 1953; STB Ya Berk 1956; STM Ya Berk 1971; Ya 1972; DMin VTS 1979. D 6/9/1956 P 12/1/1956 Bp Benjamin M Washburn. m 10/25/1958 Margaret Atchison c 3. R S Phil's In The Hills Tucson AZ 1977-2001; R S Matt's Epis Ch Wilton CT 1966-1977; Vic The Ch Of The Sav Denville NJ 1960-1966. Auth, "The Pilgrim Season," Forw Mvmt; Auth, "Selected Sermons"; Auth, "Chapt From Chap To Reg Ch," *Cntr City Ch: The New Urban Frontier*.

DOUGLAS, Susan McKee (CGC) PO Box 29, Bon Secour AL 36511 **Cmsn on Curs Dio Cntrl Gulf Coast Pensacola FL 2011-; D S Paul's Chap Magnolia Sprg AL 2011-; D S Ptr's Epis Ch Bon Secour AL 2011-** B Waterbury CT 9/25/1954 d John Conway McKee & Helen Elizabeth. AS/DH U of Bridgeport 1974. D 2/10/2011 Bp Philip Menzie Duncan II. m 7/17/2003 Scott C Douglas c 3. The Epis Cmnty 2011. foleysue@gulftel.com

DOUGLAS, William Savage (Tex) 9404 Yellow Stone Rd, Waco TX 76712 **Asst S Paul's Ch Waco TX 2002-** B San Antonio TX 9/12/1927 s Raymond C Nipper Douglas & Mae Savage. BS U Pgh 1950; MDiv VTS 1953. D 7/14/

1953 P 3/12/1954 Bp Everett H Jones. m 7/9/1955 Marion Boone c 3. St Lk's Epis Hosp Houston TX 1983-1992; R Trin Ch Marshall TX 1971-1983; R The Epis Ch Of The Adv Alice TX 1967-1971; R S Paul's Ch Brady TX 1962-1967; Asst Ch Of The Heav Rest Abilene TX 1959-1962; Asst S Steph's Epis Ch Houston TX 1957-1959; P-in-c S Jas Ch Hallettsville TX 1953-1957; P-in-c Trin Epis Ch Edna TX 1953-1957. Ord Of S Lk 1976-1992. wsd14@grandecom.net

D

DOUGLASS, David George (NI) 6085 N 190 W, Howe IN 46746 **D All SS Chap Howe IN 2003-; D S Mk's Par Howe IN 2003-** B East Cleveland OH 7/27/1942 s David Mowery Douglass & Jessadale. Montreal TS; BA Heidelberg Coll 1964; MA Kent St U 1971. D 1/8/2003 Bp Edward Stuart Little II. m 4/19/1969 Nancy Jo Kackley c 3. ddouglass@howemilitary.com

DOUGLASS, James Herford (La) Po Box 523900, Miami FL 33152 B DeQuincy LA 1/8/1927 s Robert Leroy Douglass & Frankie. BA Centenary Coll 1950; ThB STUSo 1953; MS Tul 1972. D 6/23/1953 Bp Girault M Jones P 5/1/1954 Bp Iveson Batchelor Noland. c 1. Vic S Mich's Ch Baton Rouge LA 1984-1991; Exec Coun Appointees New York NY 1972-1984; R Chr Ch S Jos LA 1963-1966; P-in-c Gr Ch Waterproof LA 1963-1966; R Trin Epis Ch Morgan City LA 1955-1957. jdouglas71@hotmail.com

DOUTHITT, William Patrick (Okla) 4818 E 9th St, Tulsa OK 74112 **Died 4/3/2011** B Manhattan KS 12/17/1946 s John Leroy Douthitt & Ann Rosalie. BS U of Oklahoma 1970; MDiv Nash 1973. D 6/16/1973 Bp Chilton Powell P 1/1/1974 Bp James Winchester Montgomery.

DOVE JR, Mifflin (Tex) 5702 Coyote Call Ct, Katy TX 77449 B Corpus Christi TX 10/31/1966 s Mifflin Hawley Dove & Sharon Louise. Texas A&M U 1986; Del Mar Coll 1987; BBA Texas A&M U 1989; MDiv VTS 1995. D 6/18/1995 Bp John Herbert MacNaughton P 12/18/1995 Bp James Edward Folts. m 5/1/2004 Rebecca Lyn Phillips c 2. R S Paul's Ch Katy TX 2006-2011; R S Geo's Epis Ch Texas City TX 2000-2006; Asst S Geo Ch San Antonio TX 1997-2000; Vic Gr Ch Llano TX 1995-1997. Soc of S Jn the Evang 1993. miffdove@gmail.com

DOVER III, John Randolph (SC) 231 Cedar Berry Ln, Chapel Hill NC 27517 B Shelby NC 9/12/1926 s John Randolph Dover & Elaine. BA U NC 1960; JD U NC 1962; Cert GTS 1978. D 6/1/1978 P 5/1/1979 Bp William Gillette Weinhauer. c 3. P Assoc Ch Of Our Sav Johns Island SC 1992-2003; Int Ch Of Our Sav Johns Island SC 1991; Trin Epis Ch Orange CA 1978-1984. jdover6728@aol.com

DOVER, Sara Harned (Be) 226 Ridings Cir, Macungie PA 18062 B Allentown PA 3/26/1935 d Robert Van Horn Harned & Estelle Victoria. BA Cedar Crest Coll 1983; MDiv VTS 1987. D 6/30/1987 P 2/1/1988 Bp James Michael Mark Dyer. Asst S Anne's Epis Ch Trexlertown PA 1999-2000; Int Trin Ch Bethlehem PA 1997-1998; Chr Epis Ch Buena Vista VA 1990-1995; No Par Epis Ch Frackville PA 1987-1990.

DOW, Neal Hulce (Colo) 3296 S Heather Gardens Way, Aurora CO 80014 B Washington DC 8/31/1933 s Carl Smith Dow & Alice Mary. BS Cntrl Michigan U 1958; MDiv Nash 1964. D 6/17/1964 Bp John P Craine P 12/21/1964 Bp Donald H V Hallock. m 12/13/1952 Marjorie H Hathcock c 5. R S Steph's Epis Ch Aurora CO 1972-1985; R S Alb's Ch Sussex WI 1966-1972; Vic S Ptr's Ch No Lake WI 1966-1972; Cur S Matt's Ch Kenosha WI 1964-1966. CCU; Clowns Of Amer, Intl ; Fllshp Of Chr Magicians; Fllshp Of Merry Christians; Wrld Clown Assn. S Geo Awd; Silver Beaver Awd Bsa S Geo Awd Epis Ch Com On Bro Of S Andr; God And Serv Awd Epis Ch Com On Yth. mndow@msn.com

DOWARD, Amonteen Ravenden (VI) PO Box 486, Christiansted VI 00821 B Anguilla, BWI 6/12/1941 d Alfred Livingston Bryan & Isolen Beatrice. BA U of the Vrgn Islands 1984. D 3/6/2010 Bp Edward Ambrose Gumbs. c 3. ardoward@vipowernet.net

DOWDESWELL, Eugenia Hedden (WNC) Po Box 132, Flat Rock NC 28731 B Fort Bragg NC 7/24/1944 d Julius Clyde Hedden & Elizabeth Eugenia. BA Mary Baldwin Coll 1966. D 10/27/1990 Bp Robert Hodges Johnson. m 6/26/1970 Robert Horton Dowdeswell c 2. Archd The Cathd Of All Souls Asheville NC 2005-2011; D S Jas Epis Ch Hendersonville NC 1990-2004. Honored Wmn Awd Natl ECW at Trienniel 2000. geniad@bellsouth.net

DOWDLE, Cathey (SanD) 726 2nd Ave, Chula Vista CA 91910 **P-in-c The Ch Of Chr The King Alpine CA 2007-** B Salem OR 1/15/1955 d Gordon Dennis Bolton & Iris Beverly. BA Lewis & Clark Coll 1977; MDiv ETSBH 2007. D 12/21/2006 P 6/9/2007 Bp James Robert Mathes. m 9/23/1978 Timothy Dowdle. revcat@gmail.com

DOWER, Ronny W (NJ) 3500 Penny Ln, Zanesville OH 43701 B Huntington WV 8/20/1943 s Frederick Warren Dower & Deannie. BA Marshall U 1975; MDiv STUSo 1980; DMin STUSo 1993. D 6/4/1980 P 6/1/1981 Bp Robert Poland Atkinson. m 6/27/1964 Vivian Irene Mullens c 3. P-in-c S Jn's Epis Ch Maple Shade NJ 2002-2009; Trin Ch Moorestown NJ 2001-2002; S Mary's Ch Haddon Heights NJ 1997-2000; S Steph's Epis Ch Forest VA 1994-1997; Geth Epis Ch Marion IN 1990-1994; CE Com Dio W Virginia Charleston WV 1984-1990; S Ann's Ch New Martinsville WV 1981-1990; S Jn's Ch Huntington WV 1980. Auth, "Common Pryr In Concord: A Practical Approach To The L/E Concordat". ronnywdower@juno.com

DOWER, Sandra Nichols (WNY) Po Box 612, Bemus Point NY 14712 B Westerly RI 2/10/1935 d Thomas Pitman Nichols & Helen. BA Edinboro U 1973; MS SUNY 1985; MDiv Bex 2004. D 12/20/2003 P 11/13/2004 Bp J Michael Garrison. m 5/21/1955 David M Dower c 3. P-in-c S Ptr's Ch Westfield NY 2009-2010; P-in-c Gr Ch Randolph NY 2006-2007. s_dower@hotmail.com

DOWLING-SENDOR, Elizabeth (NC) 6 Davie Cir, Chapel Hill NC 27514 **Co-Chair - COM Dio No Carolina Raleigh NC 2002-; Pstr Response Team Dio No Carolina Raleigh NC 2002-** B Beaufort SC 3/14/1952 d Grafton Geddes Dowling & Edith. BA Harv 1973; MDiv Duke 1998; Cert VTS 1998. D 6/20/1998 Bp Robert Carroll Johnson Jr P 5/1/1999 Bp J(ames) Gary Gloster. m 6/18/1978 Benjamin Dowling-Sendor c 3. Assoc Ch Of The H Fam Chap Hill NC 2002-2004; COM Dio No Carolina Raleigh NC 2000-2007; Dio No Carolina Raleigh NC 2000-2006; Assoc R S Phil's Ch Durham NC 1998-2001. lizds@bellsouth.net

DOWNER, Gretchen Marie (Ida) 1419 Butte View Cir, Emmett ID 83617 B Livingston MT 2/14/1942 d Alfred Martin Lueck & Doris K Wade. Lewis & Clark Coll 1962; BS Albertson Coll 1964; MA Cntrl Michigan U 1978. D 12/15/1996 P 11/29/1997 Bp John Stuart Thornton. m 9/4/1962 Larry Vinton Downer c 2. D S Mary's Ch Emmett ID 1996-1999. gmdowner@gmail.com

DOWNES, Richard Hill (Mass) 71 Saint Marys St Apt 1, Brookline MA 02446 **Assoc Ch Of S Jn The Evang Boston MA 2004-** B Haverhill MA 7/22/1938 s Richard Downes & Irene Wilson. BA Bow 1960; MDiv GTS 1967. D 6/24/1967 P 5/25/1968 Bp Anson Phelps Stokes Jr. m 3/19/1976 Sherrell B Bland. R Ch Of The Redeem Chestnut Hill MA 1995-2003; S Paul's Ch Brunswick ME 1993; S Pat's Ch Washington DC 1986-1987; Cathd of St Ptr & St Paul Washington DC 1969-1978. Soc Of S Jn The Evang. rhdownes@comcast.net

DOWNEY, John Paul (NwPa) 220 W 41st St, Erie PA 16508 **Dn Cathd Of S Paul Erie PA 1987-** B Corry PA 1/12/1954 s John Joseph Downey & Jean. BA Grove City Coll 1975; MDiv SWTS 1980. D 6/11/1980 P 12/20/1980 Bp Donald James Davis. m 6/7/2002 Sharon Ann Downey c 3. R Gr Epis Ch Ridgway PA 1983-1986; Vic Ch Of The H Trin Houtzdale PA 1980-1982; Vic S Lawr Ch Osceola Mills PA 1980-1982. jpdowney@aol.com

DOWNIE, Elizabeth Morris (EMich) 617 Forest Dr, Fenton MI 48430 **Assoc S Christophers Epis Ch Grand Blanc MI 2004-** B Columbus OH 12/19/1935 d Donald Mcleod Pond & Mary Elizabeth. BA Wellesley Coll 1957; Ya Berk 1959; MA U MI 1973; U So 1991. D 6/21/1991 Bp Henry Irving Mayson P 2/1/1992 Bp R(aymond) Stewart Wood Jr. c 2. Pres Dio Estrn Michigan Saginaw MI 1996-1998; R S Jude's Epis Ch Fenton MI 1992-2004; All SS Ch E Lansing MI 1992-1993; Sccm Epis Ch Cntr New York NY 1975-1994. Auth, "The Hymnal 1982 Serv Mus"; Auth, "A Guide For The Selection & Employment Of Ch Mus"; Auth, "A Survey Of Serv Mus," *The Hymnal 1982 Comp.* Associated Parishes 1980; AAM 1977; Assn Of Dioc Liturg & Mus Committees 1976; Epis Ntwk For Economical Justice; EPF 1980; EWC 1994; Naac; NNLP; Oblate Of S Ben 1981. emdownie@gmail.com

DOWNIE, Paul Scoville (Mich) 1346 Wolf Ct, East Lansing MI 48823 **Died 8/17/2010** B Detroit MI 7/24/1930 s Lester Reid Downie & Gladys Hortense. BA U MI 1952; MA U MI 1956; MDiv Ya Berk 1959. D 6/28/1959 P 12/29/1959 Bp Richard S M Emrich. c 2. Auth, *God's Rainbow: An Inclusive Affirmation of Our Gay and Lesbian Brothers and Sis (rev.)*, 2000; Auth, "Pstr Paul monthly Rel column," *LGBT News*, 1998. Straight Ally of the Year Lansing Assn for Human Rts Lansing MI 2000. mary.downie@gmail.com

DOWNING, George L (WNC) 21 Indigo Way, Hendersonville NC 28739 B Jacksonville FL 2/6/1944 s Frank Langford Downing & Doris. BA Marshall U 1968; MDiv VTS 1971. D 6/11/1971 P 2/1/1972 Bp Wilburn Camrock Campbell. m 9/14/1963 Marsha R Racer. Imterim R Ch Of The H Nativ Honolulu HI 2002-2006; Assoc Calv Ch Memphis TN 2001-2002; Ch Of The Ridge Trenton SC 1996-2001; Dio Upper So Carolina Columbia SC 1996-2001; Vic Our Sav Epis Ch Trenton SC 1993-2001; Vic Trin Ch Edgefield SC 1993-2001; R The Ch Of The Gd Shpd Augusta GA 1982-1992; Kanuga Confererences Inc Hendersonville NC 1980-1982; R S Jn's Epis Ch Wilmington NC 1976-1980; Assoc S Jas Par Wilmington NC 1973-1976; R S Ptr's Ch Huntington WV 1972-1973. laruedowning@gmail.com

DOWNING, John W (Mil) 18735 Monastery Dr, Eagle River AK 99577 B 4/15/1932 D 5/27/1958 P 12/19/1958 Bp William F Lewis. m 4/15/1973 Nancy Lee c 2. S Mk's Par Glendale CA 1989-1990; Dio Milwaukee Milwaukee WI 1986-1989; Trin Epis Ch Platteville WI 1986-1989; S Mk's Ch KING CITY CA 1985-1986. frjohndowning@yahoo.com

DOWNING, Patricia S (Del) 1108 N Adams St, Wilmington DE 19801 **R Trin Par Wilmington DE 2008-** B Cheverly MD 10/26/1966 d Charles Steinecke & Maureen Ann. BA U of Vermont 1988; MDiv GTS 1995. D 6/17/1995 Bp Jane Hart Holmes Dixon P 1/18/1996 Bp Ronald Hayward Haines. m 10/8/1995 Richard E Downing. R Gd Shpd Epis Ch Silver Sprg MD 1997-2008; Asst S Paul's Epis Ch Piney Waldorf MD 1995-1997. patricia@trinityparishde.org

DOWNING, Richard E (WA) 222 8th St Ne, Washington DC 20002 B Allegan MI 7/27/1944 s Ernest E Downing & Donna Isabel. STB GTS; BD Geo 1966. D 6/28/1969 P 6/14/1970 Bp William Foreman Creighton. m 10/8/1995 Patricia S Steinecke. Par of St Monica & St Jas Washington DC 1976-2008; S Paul's Par Prince Geo's Cnty Brandywine MD 1972-1976; D-in-Trng Nativ Epis Ch Temple Hills MD 1969-1971. Capitol Hill Grp Mnstry; Pres/Secy, Cath Fllshp Epis Ch 1986-1994. FATHERDOWNING@GMAIL.COM

DOWNS, Alice Lacey (NJ) 64 Pape Dr, Atlantic Highlands NJ 07716 B Hartford CT 9/30/1952 d Norton Downs & Mary Marguerite. AA Bradford Jr Coll 1972; BA Bradford Coll 1973; MA Geo 1982; MDiv GTS 1987. D 6/6/1987 P 2/1/1988 Bp Edward Cole Chalfant. m 10/1/1988 Dean Henry. P-in-c S Mk's Epis Ch Keansburg NJ 2001-2010; Int S Lk's Epis Ch Metuchen NJ 1998-2000; Int S Jn's Ch Somerville NJ 1996-1998; New Jersey Coun Of Ch Trenton NJ 1995-1996; Assoc Chr Ch Middletown NJ 1994-1996; The GTS New York NY 1991-1994; Assoc Chr Ch Epis Shrewsbury NJ 1989-1993; S Peters Luth Ch New York NY 1988-1990. Auth, "Leaven For Our Lives: Conversations On Faith," *Bread And Comp*, Cowley, 2002; Auth, "Jubilee," 1985. henrydowns@myfairpoint.net

DOWNS, Andrew David (At) 576 Roscoe Rd., Newnan GA 30263 **S Dav's Ch Lansing MI 2007-** B Wyanndotte 1/30/1978 s Joseph Thomas Downs & Merrill Lynn. BA Alma Coll 1999; Emerson Coll Boston MA 2000; MDiv Huron U Coll London Ontario 2007. D 6/16/2007 P 5/17/2008 Bp S(teven) Todd Ousley. m 5/20/2005 Rose Renee McKellar-Downs c 1. S Paul's Epis Ch Newnan GA 2009-2011. drewdowns07@yahoo.com

DOWNS, Dalton Dalzell (WA) 703 Carmel Lane, Poinciana FL 34759 B Corn Island NI 1/28/1936 s Alexander Emmanuel Downs & Brunella Clotilda. CPA Escuela Practica de Comercio PA 1957; BA U Nac'l Panama 1961; MDiv ETSC 1964. D 6/20/1964 P 1/1/1965 Bp Reginald Heber Gooden. m 6/8/1968 Ana Jo Byron c 2. R S Tim's Epis Ch Washington DC 1986-2006; Ch Of The Trsfg Cleveland OH 1967-1980; Asst S Andr's Ch Cleveland OH 1967-1968. Hon Cn 89 Gd Shpd San Pedro Sula Hond 1989; Urban Consult/Orgnzr Campbell Awd CS4 Ohio Coun of Ch 1977. ddalzell36@gmail.com

DOWNS, Donna Marie (Ct) 64 Philip Dr, Shelton CT 06484 **R S Paul's Ch Woodbury CT 2009-** B Bridgeport CT 9/8/1955 MDiv Ya Berk 1987. D 6/21/2003 P 1/3/2004 Bp Andrew Donnan Smith. m 8/29/1981 Allen Gybbon Downs c 3. Assoc Par of St Paul's Ch Norwalk Norwalk CT 2004-2009; Cur S Ptr's-Trin Ch Thomaston CT 2003-2004. donna.downs@snet.net

DOWNS, Edward Alley (WNC) 46 Wagon Trl, Black Mountain NC 28711 **Died 11/4/2010** B Orange NJ 11/10/1928 s Winfield Scott Downs & Esther Alley. BA Harv 1950; MD GW 1954; Priv Tutoring under Bp Willis Henton and Rev. Kenneth 1975. D 6/9/1974 P 4/5/1975 Bp Willis Ryan Henton. c 4. NASSAM 1975.

DOWNS JR, Joseph Thomas (EMich) 3225 N Branch Dr, Beaverton MI 48612 **P-in-c S Paul's Epis Ch Gladwin MI 2010-** B Morenci AZ 12/26/1948 s Joseph Thomas Downs & Harriet Amagene. BS Cntrl Michigan U 1970; MDiv VTS 1974. D 6/15/1974 P 6/1/1975 Bp H Coleman McGehee Jr. m 9/7/1969 Merrill L Faustman c 2. GC, Pension Com, VP Dio Estrn Michigan Saginaw MI 2009; P-in-c H Fam Epis Ch Midland MI 2008-2009; Cmncatn Dir Dio Estrn Michigan Saginaw MI 2000-2010; GC Dep, chair of deputation Dio Estrn Michigan Saginaw MI 1997-2010; Stndg Com, Secy Dio Estrn Michigan Saginaw MI 1995-2000; R Trin Epis Ch Alpena MI 1981-2000; Vic Gr Epis Ch Southgate MI 1977-1981; Asst S Paul's Epis Ch Lansing MI 1974-1977. tdowns@eastmich.org

DOWNS, Lee Daniel (Mil) 8620 N Port Washington Rd, Apt 208, Fox Point WI 53217 B Richland Center WI 10/21/1944 s Dan H Downs & Alice Ruth. BS U of Wisconsin 1968; ThM Bos 1972; DMin Bos 1975. D 9/12/1986 P 1/10/1987 Bp Roger John White. c 3. R Chr Ch Whitefish Bay WI 2002-2009; Supply S Jn In The Wilderness Elkhorn WI 1999-2001; P-in-c S Nich Epis Ch Racine WI 1995-1998; P-in-c S Andr's Ch Kenosha WI 1991-1994; Asst S Matt's Ch Kenosha WI 1986-1991. CBS 1987. kb9gzg@wi.rr.com

DOWNS, Thomas Alexander (CFla) 390 Lake Lenelle Drive, Chuluota FL 32766 B Superior WI 4/7/1938 s Alexander Downs & Eleanor. BA S Paul Sem RC St. Paul MN 1960; MA S Paul Sem RC St. Paul MN 1964; MA S Paul Sem St. Paul MN 1964; MA U of Notre Dame 1970; DMin Grad Theol Un 1978. Rec from Roman Catholic 9/21/1982 as Priest Bp William Hopkins Folwell. m 7/3/1970 Bernice A Blaese c 3. R S Richard's Ch Winter Pk FL 2004-2010; R S Paul's Ch Albany GA 1992-2003; Dio Cntrl Florida Orlando FL 1985-1992; Cathd Ch Of S Lk Orlando FL 1982-1985; Cn Dio Cntrl Florida Orlando FL 1982-1985. Auth, *The Par as Lrng Cmnty*, Paulist, 1979; Auth, *A Journey to Self Through Dialogue (23rd Pub)*, 23rd Pub, 1977. Serv to Mankind Sertoma 1994. t.downs@cfl.rr.com

✠ DOYLE, Rt Rev C(harles) Andrew (Tex) 2328 Blue Bonnet, Houston TX 77030 **Bp of Texas Dio Texas Houston TX 2009-** B Carbondale IL 5/31/1966 s Charles Franklin Doyle & Sylvia Ann. BFA U of No Texas 1990; MDiv VTS 1995. D 6/17/1995 Bp Claude Edward Payne P 1/23/1996 Bp Christine Marie Faulstich Con 11/22/2008 for Tex. m 5/19/1990 JoAnne Christine Pearson c 2. Bp Coadj Dio Texas Houston TX 2008-2009; Cn Dio Texas Houston TX 2003-2008; Dio Texas Houston TX 1997-2003; Cur Chr Epis Ch Temple TX 1995-1997. adoyle@epicenter.org

DOYLE, Henry Lovelle (Minn) 1000 Shumway Ave, Faribault MN 55021 **Shattuck-S Mary's Sch Faribault MN 1989-** B Tampa FL 9/7/1951 s Robert Lee Doyle & Muriel Antoinette Yvonne. BA Colorado Coll 1973; Med Colorado St U 1981; MDiv Nash 1981. D 7/17/1989 Bp William Harvey Wolfrum P 1/27/1990 Bp Sanford Zangwill Kaye Hampton. *Freshman Drinking Patterns*, 1981. SHN 1987. henry.doyle@s-sm.org

DOYLE, Ralph Thomas (Mo) 1432 Kearney St, El Cerrito CA 94530 B Boston MA 3/2/1944 s Ralph Thomas Doyle & Marion Blanche. Cert Managment Consult; CDSP 1975; Notre Dame Coll 1978. D 6/28/1975 P 5/1/1976 Bp C Kilmer Myers. Int Dio Missouri S Louis MO 2000-2002; Cn to the Ordnry Dio San Diego San Diego CA 1989-1995; Founding Vic S Ben's Par Los Osos CA 1986-1988; Int S Jas Ch Paso Robles CA 1985-1986; Assoc S Fran' Epis Ch San Francisco CA 1982-1985. Coauthor, "Rev: 3 Critical Questions," *Imagery in the Bk of Revelation*, Peeters, 2011; Coauthor, "Audio-Visual Motif in Apocalypse of Jn," *Journ of Biblic & Pneumatological Resrch*, Wipf & Stock, 2011; Coauthor, "Lion/Lamb in Revelation," *Currents in Biblic Resrch*, Sage, 2009; Coauhor, "Violence in the Apocalypse of Jn," *Currents in Biblic Resrch*, Sage, 2007. Amer Assn of Chr Counselors 1985; Cath Conf on Alcoholiam 1990. metanoia1549@sbcglobal.net

DOYLE, Seamus Patrick (Ark) 1802 W Cambridge Dr, Harrison AR 72601 B Bellaghy County Derry IE 10/14/1946 s Harry Doyle & Annie. MDiv H Ghost Mssy Coll Dublin IE 1973; Cert Catechetical & Pstr Cntr Dundalk IE 1974; DMin STUSo 1997. Rec from Roman Catholic 5/1/1991 as Priest Bp David Reed. m 8/13/1988 Margaret Ernesta Hines c 2. R S Jn's Ch Harrison AR 2005-2011; Vic S Barn Ch Moberly MO 2003-2004; Mid Missouri Cluster Fulton MO 2000-2005; Vic S Alb's Epis Ch Fulton MO 2000-2005; Vic S Mk's Epis Ch Portland MO 2000-2005; Pstr S Matt's Epis Ch Mex MO 2000-2002; Purchase Area Reg Mnstry Mayfield KY 1992-1999; Vic / Area Min S Mart's-In-The-Fields Mayfield KY 1992-1999; Vic / Area Min S Paul's Ch Hickman KY 1992-1999; Vic / Area Min S Ptr's of the Lakes Gilbertsville KY 1992-1999; Vic / Area Min Trin Epis Ch Fulton KY 1992-1999. Auth, *Do this in Remembrance of Me*, Liquori, 2003; Auth, *A Way of Life: Fourteen Moments in the Life of Jesus*, Liquori, 2002; Auth, "Magdala- The Wmn of the Well," *Chr Singles mag*, 1987; Auth, "Short Stories," *The Best of Lafayette*, 1976. CASA 2008; Ecum Mnstrs, Chair of Bd 2000; Rotary Intl 2001. spdirish@yahoo.com

DRACHLIS, David Bernard (Ala) 1103 Shades Cir Se, Huntsville AL 35803 **Cmncatn Coordntr Dio Alabama Birmingham AL 2009-** B Los Angeles CA 8/19/1948 s Irving Bernard Drachlis & Virginia M. D 10/30/2004 Bp Henry Nutt Parsley Jr. m 2/27/1988 Sharon Fay Baumgardner. ddrachlis@dioala.org

DRAEGER JR, Walter Raymond (WMich) 3957 Sherwood Forest Dr, Traverse City MI 49686 B Racine WI 10/19/1929 s Walter Raymond Draeger & Lulu Marie. Marq; U of Arizona; U of Wisconsin; LTh SWTS 1979. D 6/9/1979 Bp Quintin Ebenezer Primo Jr P 12/1/1979 Bp James Winchester Montgomery. m 1/5/1952 Sally Clarke c 5. Int R S Phil's Ch Beulah MI 1995-1998; Emm Ch Petoskey MI 1990-1994; R S Jn's Ch Howell MI 1987-1990; S Dav's Ch Lansing MI 1981-1987; Cur S Simons Ch Arlington Heights IL 1979-1981. holydad@earthlink.com

DRAESEL JR, Herbert Gustav (NY) 215 W 84th St #515, New York NY 10024 B Jersey City NJ 3/14/1940 s Herbert Gustav Draesel & Irene Louise. BA Trin Hartford CT 1961; BD GTS 1964. D 6/13/1964 Bp Dudley S Stark P 12/1/1964 Bp George E Rath. m 1/1/1967 Ada Morey c 2. SCCM Dio New York New York City NY 1988-1990; R Ch Of The H Trin New York NY 1984-2003; R Gr Ch White Plains NY 1975-1984; R Ch Of S Mary The Vrgn Chappaqua NY 1972-1975; Cur Hse Of Pryr Epis Ch Newark NJ 1964-1965. Auth, *Celebration*; Auth, *Everyman: The Mus*; Auth, *Praise & Jubilee*; Auth, *Rejoice*; Auth, *Troubadour*. hdraeseh@aol.com

DRAKE, Betty Lorraine Miller (Fla) 100 S Palmetto Ave, Green Cove Springs FL 32043 B Charleston WV 8/23/1931 d Leonard Thomas Miller & Beatrice. Marshall U; S Fran Sch Nrsng San Fran WV; W Virginia St Fire Sch; W Virginia St Fire Sch. D 2/18/1990 Bp Frank Stanley Cerveny. m 4/12/1949 Robert Theodore Drake c 4. Cn S Jn's Cathd Jacksonville FL 1991-2001. bbldrake@aol.com

DRAKE, Deborah Rucki (Nwk) 380 Clifton Ave, Clifton NJ 07011 B Jersey City NJ 2/11/1954 d Zigmunt Rucki & Dorothy. Cert Rel Stds Felician Coll 1996; MPA Seton Hall U 2000. D 6/9/2007 Bp Mark M Beckwith. m 11/6/1983 Theodore Drake. deborahdrake@optonline.net

DRAKE, Jo-Ann Jane (RI) 655 Hope St, Providence RI 02906 **R Ch Of The Redeem Providence RI 1993-** B Providence RI 1/3/1949 d Daniel Edward Drake & Edith Antonetta. AS Johnson & Wales U 1971; BA Rhode Island Coll 1974; MDiv EDS 1977. D 8/27/1977 P 10/1/1978 Bp Frederick Hesley Belden. Assoc R S Matt's Ch Maple Glen PA 1989-1993; Spec Asst S Paul's Ch Elkins Pk PA 1985-1989; Vic S Gabr's Epis Ch Philadelphia PA

1982-1985; Asst Par Of S Jas Ch Keene NH 1979-1981; Asst S Ptr's Ch Glenside PA 1977-1979. redeemer-prov@cox.net

DRAKE JR, John William (Dal) 2706 Spring Lake Dr, Richardson TX 75082 **Died 7/25/2011** B Spartanburg SC 4/5/1923 s John William Drake & Josephine Glascow. BS Wake Forest U 1943; MDiv STUSo 1945; STM STUSo 1965; S Aug's Coll Cbury Gb 1966; Cert U of Texas 1981; Cert Pstr Care Educational Cntr Dallas TX 1992. D 11/25/1945 P 4/9/1947 Bp Edwin A Penick. c 4. Advsry Bd Cathd Gardens 1998; Amer Soc On Aging 1988; Cmsn On Positive Aginng Dio Dallas (Chair 1998-2002) 1998; Natl Coun On Aging 1998; Seniorr Citizens Of Grtr Dallas 1998; SW Soc On Aging 1998. jwdrake2@comcast.net

DRAKE, Lesley-Ann (At) 2160 Cooper Lake Rd SE, Smyrna GA 30080 B Norbury England 5/15/1958 d Derek John Milford & Judith Wortley. OND E Surrey Coll 1977. D 8/6/2011 Bp J(ohn) Neil Alexander. m 6/11/1989 Bob Drake c 2. lesleyanndrake@hotmail.com

DRAKE, Leslie Sargent (USC) 1630 Silver Bluff Rd., Aiken SC 29803 **S Aug Of Cbury Aiken SC 2009-** B Melrose MA 5/13/1947 s Edward Curnick Drake & Emily S. Trans from Church Of England 7/2/2009 Bp Dorsey Felix Henderson. m 9/6/2006 Yolande Patricia Stewart. FRLDRAKE@BELLSOUTH.NET

DRAPER, Richard Thorp (Ind) 11974 State Highway M26, Eagle Harbor MI 49950 B Rocky Mount NC 1/2/1947 s William Livingston Draper & Mildred Clay. BA U NC 1969; MDiv VTS 1973; S Geo's Coll Jerusalem 1986. D 6/23/1973 Bp Thomas Augustus Fraser Jr P 1/13/1974 Bp William J Gordon Jr. m 9/6/1993 Sherry R Mattson c 3. R Chr Ch Madison IN 1998-2010; Int Vic Trin Ch So Hill VA 1995-1997; Int R Chr Ascen Ch Richmond VA 1994; Int Vic Trin Ch Highland Sprg VA 1992-1993; R Emm Ch Callaville FREEMAN VA 1976-1992; R S Andr's Lawrenceville VA 1976-1992; R Trin / S Mk's Alberta VA 1976-1987; Dn of the Arctic Coast Dio Alaska Fairbanks AK 1974-1976; Vic S Geo In The Arctic Kotzebue AK 1973-1976. rick_draper@juno.com

DRAWDY, Joseph Guydon (SwFla) 314 Bloomingfield Dr, Brandon FL 33511 **Died 7/18/2010** B Orlando FL 5/27/1931 s Joseph Levi Drawdy & Martha Rae. BA Stetson U 1959; BD STUSo 1962; MA U of So Florida 1977. D 6/29/1962 Bp Henry I Louttit P 12/1/1962 Bp William Loftin Hargrave. c 2.

DRAZDOWSKI, Edna Jean (Ga) 202 Starmount Dr, Valdosta GA 31605 **Chr Ch Valdosta GA 2009-** B Arlington VA 12/15/1955 d Joseph Cummings & Ellen Amanda. MDiv Vancouver TS; Vancouver TS; U of Maryland 1974; BS Valdosta St U 1979; Med Valdosta St U 1988; Med Valdosta St U 1992; Valdosta St U 1995; STUSo 2002. D 2/4/2006 P 11/11/2006 Bp Henry Irving Louttit. m 9/11/1977 James Drazdowski c 2. tdraz@bellsouth.net

DREBERT, David A. (CNY) Trinity Memorial Church, 44 Main St, Binghamton NY 13905 **R Trin Meml Ch Binghamton NY 2011-** B Cambridge MA 1/12/1949 s William Drebert & Lillian. BA U of Vermont 1970; MS U of Vermont 1973; MBA U of Sthrn Maine 1991; MA SWTS 2002; D.Min SWTS 2008. D 9/11/1998 P 12/15/2001 Bp Russell Edward Jacobus. m 6/24/2000 Kay Marie Halle c 4. S Jas Epis Ch Milwaukee WI 2010-2011; Int All SS' Cathd Milwaukee WI 2009-2010; R S Anskar's Epis Ch Hartland WI 2006-2010; Vic Chr the King/H Nativ (Sturgeon Bay) Sturgeon Bay WI 2002-2006; D S Paul's Ch Marinette WI 1998-2001. Ord of Julian of Norwich 2003. kestreldave@yahoo.com

DREBERT, Kay Marie (Mil) 227 W Walnut Dr, Sturgeon Bay WI 54235 B Plymouth WI 6/24/1957 BA Lakeland Coll 1984. D 10/2/1994 Bp Russell Edward Jacobus. m 6/24/2000 David A. Drebert c 2. S Anskar's Epis Ch Hartland WI 2006-2009. dcnkay@yahoo.com

DREIBELBIS, John LaVerne (Chi) 3317 Grant St, Evanston IL 60201 B Miles City MT 12/1/1934 s John Calvin Dreibelbis & Regina Theresa. U Chi 1956; MDiv SWTS 1959; PhD U Chi 1990. D 6/20/1959 P 12/1/1959 Bp Charles L Street. m 6/11/1960 Patricia A Dreibelbis c 4. SWTS Evanston IL 1994-2004; Epis Ch Coun U Chi Chicago IL 1976-1977; R Gr Epis Ch Huron SD 1971-1975; S Chrys's Ch Chicago IL 1964-1971; Cur S Matt's Ch Evanston IL 1959-1960. "Beyond Wish Lists for Pstr Ldrshp," *Theol Educ, Vol. 40 Supplement*, 2005. Serv Awd Seabury-Wstrn Alum/AE Assn 2004; Prncpl Investigator Lilly Endwmt Resrch Proj "Toward A Higher Quality" 1999; Seabury Cross, honoris causa Seabury-Wstrn Stdt body 1999. john.dreibelbis@aol.com

DRENNEN, Zachary Polk (WVa) Elewana Education Project, 168 Meadow Ridge Dr., Shepherdstown WV 25443 **Exec Coun Appointees New York NY 2008-** B Washington DC 9/15/1970 s William Miller Drennan & Sarah Polk. BA Colorado Coll 1993; MDiv Harvard DS 2002. D 6/8/2002 P 12/14/2002 Bp William Michie Klusmeyer. The Meml Ch Of The Gd Shpd Parkersburg WV 2002-2004. zachdrennen@elewana.org

DRESBACH, Michael Garrick (ECR) Iglesia Episcopal de Panama, Apartado R, Balboa 94709 Panama **Exec Coun Appointees New York NY 2002-; Dio Panama 1999-** B Oakland CA 4/19/1954 s James Maurice Dresbach & Constance Robina. BS U of San Francisco 1994; MDiv CDSP 2000; MA Grad Theol Un 2000. D 6/21/1997 P 12/22/1997 Bp Richard Lester Shimpfky. m 3/18/1978 Mona Lyn Neimoyer c 2. Assoc P S Phil's Ch San Jose CA 1997. mgbach@gmail.com

DRESCHER, Kenneth Gordon (NY) 5950 N Fountains Ave Apt 9102, Tucson AZ 85704 **Died 9/20/2010** B Staten Island NY 9/17/1922 s Kenneth Louis Drescher & Mary. BA Hob 1948; MDiv GTS 1958; STM NYTS 1970. D 6/10/1951 P 12/12/1951 Bp Horace W B Donegan. c 4. evelyna22@earthlink.net

DRESSEL, Marilyn McConkey (EMich) 3725 Woodside Dr, Traverse City MI 49684 B Cass City MI 10/1/1939 d Keith Dudley McConkey & Mildred Martha. MI SU 1961; BS Cntrl Michigan U 1962; Cert Whitaker TS 1978; Bex 1989. D 10/22/1978 Bp William J Gordon Jr P 7/15/1989 Bp H Coleman McGehee Jr. m 8/21/1960 Joseph Charles Dressel c 3. Supply P Gr Epis Ch Traverse City MI 2000-2002; Gr Epis Ch Traverse City MI 1997-1998; Supply P S Jn's Epis Ch Midland MI 1995-2000; Epis Tri Par Cluster Gladwin MI 1994-1995; P/Admin Gr Epis Ch Standish MI 1994-1995; P/Admin S Paul's Epis Ch Gladwin MI 1994-1995; Asst S Jn's Epis Ch Midland MI 1989-1993; Asst S Jn's Epis Ch Midland MI 1978-1988.

DRESSER, Deborah Metcalf (NY) 105 Grand St, Newburgh NY 12550 B Boston MA 12/18/1943 d Richard Carter Metcalf & Elizabeth Raglan. BA Manhattanville Coll 1980; MDiv UTS 1984; DMin NYTS 1994. D 6/9/1984 Bp James Stuart Wetmore P 1/13/1985 Bp Paul Moore Jr. m 6/22/1980 Robert Merrill Dresser c 2. S Geo's Epis Ch Newburgh NY 2010; Chr Epis Ch Sparkill NY 1995-1996; Chap Of S Jn The Div Tomkins Cove NY 1992-1996; Reg II Yth Mnstrs Tomkins Cove NY 1990-1992; Gr Ch White Plains NY 1987-1990; Int S Mary's Ch Mohegan Lake NY 1986-1987; Cur S Andr's Ch Brewster NY 1984-1986. Auth, "Into The Wrld," *Reflections*. Leaveners. deborahdresser@gmail.com

DRESSER, Robert Merrill (NY) 375 Grand St, Newburgh NY 12550 B Cambridge MA 2/13/1931 s Allen Trafton Dresser & Mildred Louise. BA Ya 1952; BD Yale DS 1955; MA U of Connecticut 1980; PhD Ford 1990. D 9/10/1955 Bp Raymond A Heron P 3/1/1956 Bp Charles F Hall. m 6/22/1980 Deborah Metcalf Dresser c 2. Int S Geo's Epis Ch Newburgh NY 1995-1996; Hudson Vlly Mnstrs New Windsor NY 1995; Ch Of The Gd Shpd Granite Sprg NY 1980-1995; R Ch Of The Gd Shpd Newburgh NY 1980-1995; R Chr's Ch Rye NY 1977-1978; R S Fran Ch Stamford CT 1965-1977; R Bp Seabury Ch Groton CT 1959-1965; Cur All SS Ch Worcester MA 1955-1957. Auth, "Rhetoric & Substance In Bern Of Clairvaux"; Auth, "Sermons On The Song"; Auth, "Stds In Medieval Cistercian Hist". Soc Of S Jn The Evang. robert.dresser@verizon.net

DREWRY, John Colin (EC) 2513 Confederate Dr, Wilmington NC 28403 B Raleigh NC 7/31/1932 s John C Drewry & Mary. BA U NC 1958; U NC 1959. D 10/21/1998 Bp Clifton Daniel III. m 8/27/1955 Gail Farthing c 3.

DRINKWATER, Gary G (Me) 132 Montello St., Lewiston ME 04240 **D Chr Ch Gardiner ME 2002-** B Portland ME 12/18/1949 s Gilman Rupert Drinkwater & Ruth Shirley. D 12/1/2001 Bp Chilton Abbie Richardson Knudsen. m 10/2/1972 Diane Marie Rivard. D Trin Epis Ch Lewiston ME 2001-2002.

DRINO, Jerry William (ECR) 14801 Whipple Ct, San Jose CA 95127 **Sudanese Mnstry Trin Cathd San Jose CA 2002-** B Monterey Park CA 3/19/1941 s Louie Thomas Drino & Winifred May. BA U CA 1963; MDiv CDSP 1967; DD CDSP 2002. D 9/10/1966 P 9/11/1967 Bp Francis E I Bloy. m 6/25/1966 Marilyn Koppel c 2. Exec Dir Prov VIII Tagard OR 1989-2006; Stndg Com Dio El Camino Real Monterey CA 1987-1991; Alt Dep GC Dio El Camino Real Monterey CA 1984-1987; COM Dio El Camino Real Monterey CA 1980-1987; Dept of Missions Dio California San Francisco CA 1975-1979; R S Phil's Ch San Jose CA 1971-1999; Chapl/Yout Dir S Andr's Ch Saratoga CA 1967-1971; Yth Dir S Steph's Par Belvedere CA 1966-1967. Auth, "Meeting on New Ground," *Cultural Sensitivity in the Ord Process*, Ch Pub, 2007; Contributing Auth, "Celtic Liturg," *From Shore to Shore*, Soc for the Propagation of the Gospel, 2003; Contributing Auth, "Vision for Mssn in Matt & Lk," *Global Mssn*, Untd Soc for the Propagation of theGospel, 2002; Co-Auth, "Mart Luther King Day Dialogues," *(Same)*, Ch Pub, 1999; Auth, "Reclaiming The Beloved Cmnty," *(Same)*, Prov Viii, 1998; Auth, "Resource In Cultural Sensitivity in the Ord Process," *(Same)*, Ch Pub, 1992; Contributing Ed, "Records Of The Life Of Jesus (Rsv)," *(Same)*, Gld For Psychol Stds, San Francisco, 1991. Amer Friends of the Epis Ch in the Sudan 2005; Four Sprg Seminars 1998; Gld For Psychol Stds 1971-1992; Hope w Sudan 2003. Jefferson Awd 2010; Jefferson Awd for Publ Serv Natl Jefferson Awards 2010; Bp's Cross Dio El Camino Real 2008; DD CDSP 2002. jdrino@hopewithsudan.org

DRIVER, Bess D (Az) 2137 W. University Ave., Flagstaff AZ 86001 **D Ch Of The Epiph Flagstaff AZ 2004-** B Muskegee MI 4/7/1935 d Edgar Lester Driver & Bonnie M. D 10/14/2006 Bp Kirk Stevan Smith. bdriver44@yahoo.com

DROBIN, Frederick Anthony (NY) PO Box 147, Rhinebeck NY 12572 **Vic La Misión Epis Santiago Apóstol [La MESA] Dover Plains NY 2007-** B Utica NY 9/3/1941 s Joseph Francis Drobin & Stella Joan. BA S Anth Coll Hudson NH 1966; BD Capuchin TS 1969; MA Maryknoll TS 1970; MA NYU 1978; Cert Inst Of Relationships Ther New York NY 1985; Cert Inst Of

Relationships Ther New York NY 1986; MPhil UTS 1992; PhD UTS 1996. Rec from Roman Catholic 6/1/1985 as Priest Bp Paul Moore Jr. Ch Of The Gd Shpd Greenwood Lake NY 2005-2007; Assist Gr Epis Ch Nyack NY 1989-2004; S Jas Ch New York NY 1985-2004; Pstr S Jas Ch New York NY 1981-1982. Auth, "Sprtlty, the New Opiate,Journ Of Rel & Hlth," 1999; Auth, "Reflections of a Psychoanalyst at Mass,Journ Of Rel & Hlth," 1997; Auth, "Tribute To Ann Belford Ulanov," *Un Sem Quarterly Revs A Festschrift For Ann Ulanov*, 1997; Auth, "Tribute to Ann Belford Ulanov,Un Sem Quarterly Revs: A festschrift for Ann Ulanov". drdrobin9@aol.com

DROPPERS, Thomas (NC) 1503 Pepper Hill Rd, Greensboro NC 27407 B Albany NY 3/30/1931 s Seton Rand Droppers & Margaret Evelyn. BA Ham 1953; STB GTS 1956; MLS U NC 1998. D 5/27/1956 P 12/8/1956 Bp Frederick Lehrle Barry. m 6/27/1959 Mary Ellen Anderson c 4. P-in-c S Andr's Ch Greensboro NC 2000-2001; R All SS Ch Greensboro NC 1984-1994; R S Mk's Epis Ch Huntersville NC 1969-1984; R S Jas Ch Black Mtn NC 1964-1969; Trin Ch Kings Mtn NC 1959-1964; Asst S Geo's Epis Ch Schenectady NY 1956-1959. tdrops@triad.rr.com

DROST, Patricia May (Md) 3406 Henry Harford Dr, Abingdon MD 21009 B Indianapolis IN 5/6/1947 D 6/14/2003 Bp Robert Wilkes Ihloff P 1/6/2004 Bp John Leslie Rabb. Int S Paul's Epis Ch Mt Airy MD 2010-2011; Gr Epis Ch Darlington MD 2008-2009; S Mary's Ch Abingdon MD 2004-2005. drostmeister@aol.com

DROSTE, Robert Edward (Cal) 911 Dowling Blvd, San Leandro CA 94577 **R All SS Epis Ch San Leandro CA 2002-** B Syracuse NY 5/4/1962 s Ronald Edward Droste & Susan. BA Coll of Charleston 1984; MDiv CDSP 2000; DMin SWTS 2010. D 6/2/2000 Bp Robert Louis Ladehoff P 12/2/2000 Bp William Edwin Swing. m 5/13/1995 Karla Jean Krouse. Assoc Trin Ch San Francisco CA 2000-2002. robdroste@sbcglobal.net

DRUBE, Bruce James (Ala) 1219 Quail Run Dr Sw, Jacksonville AL 36265 **D S Mich And All Ang Anniston AL 2005-** B Clearlake SD 6/19/1952 s Donald Drube & Frances. D 10/30/2004 Bp Henry Nutt Parsley Jr. m 8/7/1976 Sharon Lynn Seipel c 3.

DRUCE, Glenn Edward (NJ) Calle Meteoro 1169, Secc Jardines, Las Playas, Tijuana Baja California 22500 Mexico B Camden NJ 8/7/1947 s Albert Druce & Margaret. BS Alderson-Broaddus Coll 1969; MDiv GTS 1972. D 6/5/1972 P 2/16/1973 Bp Wilburn Camrock Campbell. Dio New Jersey Trenton NJ 1998-2003; Cn To Ordnry Dio New Jersey Trenton NJ 1998-2003; Ch Of S Mk And All SS Absecon Galloway NJ 1974-1997; Vic S Andr's Ch Mullens WV 1972-1974. winstonmadison@yahoo.com

DRURY, Joanne Christine (SD) 2702 Grandview Dr, Rapid City SD 57701 **D Emm Epis Par Rapid City SD 2002-** B Danville PA 6/19/1953 d George Henry Neff & Anna Davis. D 4/5/2002 Bp Creighton Leland Robertson.

DRURY, Susan Rollins (Kan) 7311 Legler Road, Shawnee KS 66217 **D S Mich And All Ang Ch Mssn KS 2004-** B Boston MA USA 11/29/1943 d Charles Lucian Drury & Phyllis Rollins. BSN Ferris St U 1987; MA Webster U 1992. D 2/2/1997 Bp William Edward Smalley. m 9/30/2006 Ronald Ellis Donnelly c 2. D S Dav's Epis Ch Topeka KS 2002-2004; D S Mich And All Ang Ch Mssn KS 1997-2002. NAAD 1997; PEO 2005; Sigma Theta Tau 1989. Archd's Cross Dio Kansas, Topeka, KS 2008; Vision Awd Bp, Dio Kansas 2004. deaconsuzi@kc.rr.com

DRYMON, John Aaron (Ark) P.O. Box 2255, Batesville AR 72503 **S Paul's Epis Ch Batesville AR 2009-** B Little Rock AR 1/12/1984 s John Doyle Drymon & Patricia Ann G. AB Colg 2006; MDiv The GTS 2009. D 3/21/2009 Bp Larry Earl Maze P 9/22/2009 Bp Larry R Benfield. jdrymon@gmail.com

DRYNAN, Thomas Steele (Ore) 6431 Ganon St Se, Salem OR 97317 B Salem OR 8/14/1937 s Thomas Johnston Drynan & Dehlia Naomi. OR SU; AS Chemeketa Cmnty Coll Salem OR 1970. D 6/10/1990 Bp Robert Louis Ladehoff. m 8/31/1957 Marilynne Maurer c 2. Silver Beaver BSA; Eagle Scout BSA.

DRYSDALE, Jessie Cookson (Me) 136 Butterfield Landing Rd., Weston ME 04424 B Framingham MA 8/20/1935 d Frederick Appleby Cookson & Andrena Christine. Lic Katharine Gibbs Sch. D 5/3/2003 Bp Chilton Abbie Richardson Knudsen. m 9/2/1955 David Thomas Drysdale c 2. D Ch Of The Gd Shpd Houlton ME 2003-2011.

DUBAY, David Michael (SC) 95 Folly Road Blvd., Charleston SC 29407 **Vic H Trin Epis Ch Charleston SC 2009-** B Enid OK 4/13/1964 s Peter King Dubay & Karen Harvey. BA Coll of Charleston 1989; MDiv STUSo 2005. D 6/23/2005 P 12/3/2005 Bp Edward Lloyd Salmon Jr. m 6/22/1992 Lisa C Dubay c 3. Asst R S Phil's Ch Charleston SC 2005-2008. frdavid@bellsouth.net

DUBAY, Joseph Arthur (Ore) 1805 NW 34th Ave, Portland OR 97210 B Cambridge MA 10/4/1931 s Joseph Arthur Dubay & Jessie Stokes. BA Harv 1953; MA Harv 1954; MDiv CDSP 1963. D 6/24/1963 P 1/5/1964 Bp James Walmsley Frederic Carman. m 7/8/1959 Inga S Shipstead c 3. All SS Ch Hillsboro OR 1994-1996; Wm Temple Hse Portland OR 1992-1993; Trin Epis Cathd Portland OR 1976-1996; R Trin Epis Ch Ashland Ashland OR 1965-1968; Cur Emm Ch Coos Bay OR 1963-1965. Phi Beta Kappa Harvard Coll 1953; Peace Awd. dubay@teleport.com

DUBOIS, Charles Holgate (NJ) 33509 Anns Choice Way, Warminster PA 18974 B Woodbury NJ 8/4/1932 s Carl F DuBois & Margaret Fisler. BA Dickinson Coll 1955; STB Ya Berk 1958; Cert Pstr Trng Inst Philadelphia PA 1980; DMin Estrn Bapt TS 1983. D 4/26/1958 P 11/1/1958 Bp Alfred L Banyard. m 6/9/1960 Ruth Alice Jarvis c 2. The TS at The U So Sewanee TN 1986-1997; COM Dio New Jersey Trenton NJ 1983-1986; Alt / Dep GC Dio New Jersey Trenton NJ 1979-1985; R Ch Of The Gd Shpd Pitman NJ 1968-1986; R Dio NW Pennsylvania Erie PA 1964-1968; Cur Trin Ch Moorestown NJ 1958-1964. chdubois32@email.com

DUBOIS, Nancy Angell (Vt) 466 Partridge Hl, Randolph VT 05060 B Randolph VT 7/13/1930 d Wilmer Webster Angell & Margaret Kaulbeck. BA Skidmore Coll 1953; Dioc Study Prog 1988. D 10/9/1988 Bp Daniel Lee Swenson. m 8/1/1953 Richard Earl Dubois c 4. NAAD.

DUBOSE, Georgia Isobel (WVa) Po Box 999, Harpers Ferry WV 25425 **S Jn's Ch Harpers Ferry WV 2008-; Nelson Cluster Of Epis Ch Rippon WV 2005-** B Rockford IL 7/31/1947 d Henry Hanson Caldwell & Christina Isobel. BA U of Missouri 1969; Cert of Pstr Ldrshp Bex Sem 2003. D 12/10/2005 P 6/10/2006 Bp William Michie Klusmeyer. m 1/3/1998 Robert Du Bose c 2. georgiad@citlink.net

DUBOSE, Jerry Davis (SC) 9540 Marlboro Ave, Barnwell SC 29812 B Manning SC 3/30/1954 s Kelly Joe DuBose & Talberta Faye. BA Clemson U 1977; MBA Duke 1992; MDiv STUSo 2003. D 6/14/2003 P 6/3/2004 Bp Dorsey Felix Henderson. m 6/5/1999 Anna DuBose c 1. Ch Of The H Apos Barnwell SC 2005-2010; S Thad Epis Ch Aiken SC 2003-2005. OSL 2007. dubosejs@aol.com

DUCKWORTH, Bonnie Wagner (NC) 512 Western Blvd, Lexington NC 27295 **D Gr Epis Ch Lexington NC 2005-** B Lexington NC 7/20/1949 D 6/13/2004 Bp Michael Bruce Curry. m 6/19/1971 Marion Eugene Duckworth c 2. D Yadkin Vlly Cluster Salisbury NC 2004-2005; Lay Par Asst Gr Epis Ch Lexington NC 1981-1993. gduckworth@lexcominc.net

DUCKWORTH, Penelope Tulleys (Cal) Christ Episcopal Church, Sei Ko Kai, 2140 Pierce St., San Francisco CA 94115 B Columbus OH 3/27/1947 d Benton Raymond Duckworth & Alice Josephine. BA U CA 1970; MDiv CDSP 1978; MFA SFSU 1998. D 5/29/1982 Bp Charles Shannon Mallory P 9/1/1983 Bp William Edwin Swing. m 11/19/1983 Dennis Gordon c 1. Chr Epis Ch Sei Ko Kai San Francisco CA 2006-2008; Calv Epis Ch Santa Cruz CA 2002-2004; Stanford Cbury Fndt Standford CA 1985-2002; S Paul's Epis Ch Burlingame CA 1983-1985. Auth, *Mary: The Imagination of Her Heart*, Cowley, 2004; Auth, *I Am: Sermons On the Incarn*, Abingdon, 1996; Auth, "Disbelief for Joy," *Best Sermons III*, Harper and Row, 1990; "poetry," *The Amer Schlr, The ATR, The Chr Century, Theol Today, Poetry NW, and others*. EPF 2005; ESMHE 1985-2002. penelope.duckworth@yahoo.com

DUDLEY, Crayton T (Ct) 244 Silver Springs Cir Sw, Atlanta GA 30310 B 2/23/1928 BA Clark Atlanta U. D 6/17/1968 Bp Harry Lee Doll P 5/1/1969 Bp David Keller Leighton Sr. m 10/9/1952 Allegra L Dudley c 2. S Mk's Ch Bridgeport CT 1987-1993; S Aug's Epis Ch St Petersburg FL 1980-1987; Ch Of The H Trin Nashville TN 1974-1980. Auth, "Wrld Rel," *Wilson Libr Bulletin*. Phi Beta Sigma. stercour01@aol.com

DUDLEY, Michael (O) 32 Alton Rd, Quincy MA 02169 **P-in-c S Jas Epis Ch Teele Sq Somerville MA 2005-** B Sandusky OH 4/13/1941 s William Oliver Dudley & Doris Josephine. BS Otterbein Coll 1964; MA U of Mississippi 1969; MDiv SWTS 1981. D 6/27/1981 P 1/26/1982 Bp John Harris Burt. m 2/14/2006 David Hefling. S Paul's Epis Ch Cleveland Heights OH 2003-2005; Int Gr Ch Madison WI 2002-2003; Vic Cathd Of S Jas Chicago IL 2001-2002; Ch Of Our Sav Akron OH 1991-2001; Liturg Com Dio Ohio Cleveland OH 1990-1997; R S Paul's Ch Steubenville OH 1987-1991; Asst S Lk's Ch San Francisco CA 1984-1987; Asst R S Jn's Ch Youngstown OH 1981-1984. Soc Of S Jn The Evang. ddudley344@aol.com

DUDLEY JR, Thomas Lee (Va) 134 Boscawen, Winchester VA 22601 **R S Mich's Epis Ch Easley SC 2011-; Off Of Bsh For ArmdF New York NY 1985-** B Fayetteville NC 2/11/1950 s Thomas Lee Dudley & Josephine. BA U of Maryland 1976; MDiv VTS 1982. D 6/7/1982 Bp Hunley Agee Elebash P 5/1/1983 Bp David Henry Lewis Jr. m 1/29/1977 Martha Elizabeth McCullen c 1. Chr Epis Ch Winchester VA 1982-1985.

DUER, Don Rey (CFla) 2005 Harrison Ave, Orlando FL 32804 **D Cathd Ch Of S Lk Orlando FL 2000-** B Ocala FL 11/17/1936 s Roy Judson Duer & Margaret. BA U of Florida 1966; Cert Inst for Chr Stds Florida 1990. D 12/9/2000 Bp John Wadsworth Howe. m 2/14/1985 Christine Eleanor Bleddyn c 1. "Bldg for Chr," *Cntrl Flordia (Series of arts)*, 2002.

DUERR, Robert Edward (Mass) 9 Pleasant St, Salem MA 01970 B Pittsburgh PA 10/3/1949 s Elmer Edward Duerr & Philomena. BA U Pgh 1971; PDS 1974; MDiv EDS 1976. D 8/29/1976 P 4/1/1977 Bp Robert Bracewell Appleyard. m 12/19/1970 Nancylee P Cunningham. Cur S Paul's Ch Newburyport MA 1976-1978.

DUFF, Eric Towle Moore (NCal) 1318 27th Street, Sacramento CA 95816 B Cincinnati OH 10/20/1957 s Edward Roy Duff & Janet Appleby. BA Colby Coll 1979; MS Col 1984; MDiv UTS 1984; Lic LCSW CA 1990. D 6/8/1985 P 1/25/1986 Bp William Grant Black. m 6/17/1994 Betty J Moore c 3. Epis Cmnty Serv Sacramento CA 2009-2010; Dir, ECS Dio Nthrn California Sacramento CA 2006-2009; R S Alb's Ch Arcata CA 1990-2006; Assoc Chr Ch Eureka CA 1989-1990; Apos Hse Newark NJ 1985-1988; Assoc Hse Of Pryr Epis Ch Newark NJ 1984-1988. Interview, "Eric Duff," *Do Unto Others*, Westview Pres, 2003. Cmnty of theTransfiguration 1990. Cmndatn Nwk City Coun 1988. bemd@suddenlink.net

D

DUFF, Lyndie (Wyo) 1117 West Ramshorn Boulevard, Box 844, Dubois WY 82513 **D S Thos Ch Dubois WY 1991-** B San Francisco CA 5/4/1940 d John Thomas Wallace & Norma Belle. STUSo 1987; Ldrshp Acad for New Directions 1990; S Lk's Hosp Aberdeen SD 1990. D 1/25/1991 Bp Bob Gordon Jones. m 11/15/1958 Carroll Elmore c 4.

DUFFEY, Ben Rosebro (SVa) 232 Southampton Rd, Franklin VA 23851 **S Mk Ch Roanoke Rapids NC 1991-** B Richmond VA 8/25/1927 s Parks Pegram Duffey & Frances Melvin. U of Virginia 1951; VTS 1966. D 6/24/1966 P 6/1/1967 Bp George P Gunn. m 7/15/1977 Suzanne Stirling c 3. Emm Ch Franklin VA 1970-1989; Cur Estrn Shore Chap Virginia Bch VA 1966-1970. suzduf@whro.net

DUFFEY, William (Pa) 3300 Darby Road, Haverford PA 19041 **Assoc R S Dav's Ch Wayne PA 2008-** B Lincoln NE 6/9/1937 s Floyd Leroy Duffey & Lorna Dorene. BS U of Nebraska 1960; MA U of Nebraska 1967; Med Col 1972; EdD Col 1976; CAS GTS 1983. D 6/11/1983 P 6/12/1984 Bp Lyman Cunningham Ogilby. m 4/15/1967 Betty A McCorkle c 2. Cleric Nevil Memi Ch Of S Geo Ardmore PA 1996-2008; R S Jas Epis Ch Prospect Pk PA 1990-1996; Asst S Mart's Ch Radnor PA 1985-1990; Asst S Clements Ch Philadelphia PA 1984-1985; Cur The Ch Of The Trin Coatesville PA 1984. Auth, "Living Ch". Cmnty Of S Mary, CBS. stgeorgebd@aol.com

DUFFIELD, Suzanne Elaine Menard (U) St Eliizabeth Episcopal Church, PO Box 100, Whiterocks UT 84085 **Vic S Eliz's Ch Whiterocks UT 2002-** B Darien CT 6/19/1942 d Roland Joseph Menard & Doris Elaine. U of Connecticut 1960; BA Florida Atlantic U 1988; MDiv STUSo 1992. D 6/29/1992 P 12/19/1992 Bp Calvin Onderdonk Schofield Jr. m 10/28/1961 James Duffield c 2. Stndg Commitee, VP Dio Utah Salt Lake City UT 2008-2011; Coun Dio Utah Salt Lake City UT 2003-2007; Int S Mths Epis Ch Toccoa GA 2002; Int Gr-Calv Epis Ch Clarkesville GA 2001; Int S Jas Epis Ch Clayton GA 2000-2001; Assoc Ch of the Resurr Sautee Nacoochee GA 1999-2000; Assoc The Epis Ch Of S Ptr And S Paul Marietta GA 1992-2000. Eli Lilly Endwmt Grant 2008. sedjed@ubtanet.com

DUFFTY, Bryan (ECR) 3020 Daurine Ct, Gilroy CA 95020 B Leeds Yorkshire UK 7/16/1933 s John William Duffty & Olive. Leeds Coll Of Tech Gb; BA Sch for Deacons 1983. D 5/26/1985 Bp Charles Shannon Mallory. m 2/7/1959 Ann Russell c 2. D S Steph's In-The-Field Epis Ch San Jose CA 1996-1999; D S Jn The Div Epis Ch Morgan Hill CA 1985-1990.

DUFFUS, Cynthia Slaughter (Lex) 48 W High St, Mt Sterling KY 40353 **Reverend Ch Of The Ascen Mt Sterling KY 2009-** B Pittsburgh PA 11/2/1954 d Pendleton Jett Slaughter & Mary Fisher. BA U of Virginia 1976; MS Virginia Commonwealth U 1991; MDiv The TS at The U So 2009. D 6/13/2009 Bp Herman Hollerith IV P 12/21/2009 Bp James Joseph Shand. m 8/25/1979 Gordon Douglas Duffus c 1. cduffus@att.net

DUFFY, Christopher Gregory (NJ) 338 Ewingville Rd., Trenton NJ 08628 B Staten Island NY 5/19/1943 s Gregory O Duffy & Rose. BA St. Fran Coll Brooklyn NY 1965; MA Indiana U 1966; EdD Indiana U 1970; PrTS 1979; GTS 1982; Cert Coll Of NJ 1983; GTF 1987. D 6/4/1983 P 1/14/1984 Bp George Phelps Mellick Belshaw. m 8/13/1967 Barbara Ann Miller c 1. S Matt's Ch Pennington NJ 2001; S Thos Ch Alexandria Pittstown NJ 1999-2000; Trin Cathd Trenton NJ 1994-1995; Assoc S Lk's Ch Ewing NJ 1988-1994; R Ch Of Our Merc Sav Penns Grove NJ 1985-1987; Int The Ch Of The H Innoc Bch Haven NJ 1985; Epis Cmnty Serv Philadelphia PA 1984-1985; Asst Ch Of The H Sprt Lebanon NJ 1983-1984. Honoray Cn Trin Cathd Trenton NJ 1995; Phi Delta Kappa. bdcd@verizon.net

DUFFY, Glenn Alan (Eas) 63 Battersea Rd., Berlin MD 21811 B Jamaica NY 10/30/1940 s Philip Frederick Duffy & Ernestine. Mercer TS 1975. D 6/29/1974 P 1/25/1975 Bp Jonathan Goodhue Sherman. m 7/2/1960 Marie D Dietrich c 2. R S Pat's Ch Deer Pk NY 1998-2003; R Chr Epis Ch Lynbrook NY 1981-1998; D Par Of S Jas Of Jerusalem By The Sea Long Bch NY 1974-1975. Who'S Who In Rel 1981; Who'S Who In Fin And Industry 1979. gaduffy@mchsi.com

DUFFY, Kirk Mallory (Ga) PO Box 22395, Savannah GA 31403 **D S Thos Ch Savannah GA 2008-** B Bronxville NY 11/2/1948 s Robert Francis Duffy & Jane Kirk. BA Amh 1971; MBA NYU 1977. D 8/15/2007 Bp Henry Irving Louttit. m 9/18/1999 Christina Hurst c 2. titusonenine@kirkduffy.net

DUFORD, Donald John (Mich) 16889 Club Drive, Southgate MI 48195 B Detroit MI 5/24/1944 s George Gilbert Duford & Florence Irene. Sacr Heart Sem 1986; BA Madonna U 1992; MBA GTF 1993; DMin GTF 1995. Rec from Roman Catholic 6/1/1995 as Deacon Bp R(aymond) Stewart Wood Jr. m 7/7/1965 Kathleen M Kramer c 3. R Ch Of The Resurr Clarkston MI 2004-2007; Asst Chr Ch Cranbrook Bloomfield Hills MI 2002-2004; R S Dav's Ch Southfield MI 2000-2002; R Dream Cluster Taylor MI 1998-2000; P-in-c Gr Epis Ch Southgate MI 1996-1997; Chapl Off Of Bsh For ArmdF New York NY 1995-1998. Auth, "Addiction," *Peacemaker Bible*, Intl Bible Soc, 2007. Amer Counslg Assn 1996; Mltry Chapl Associations 1995; SSC 2005. Mem Mortuary Sci Exam Bd-Michigan 2004. frduford@yahoo.com

DUGAN II, Haynes Webster (Okla) 152795 Cr 208, Blair OK 73526 B Shreveport LA 1/8/1939 s Haynes Webster Dugan & Helen Grace. BBA Texas A&M U 1961; MDiv VTS 1968. D 6/24/1968 Bp Girault M Jones P 1/1/1969 Bp Iveson Batchelor Noland. m Emilie Weigel c 2. R S Paul's Ch Altus OK 1998-2006; Off Of Bsh For ArmdF New York NY 1978-1998; R S Geo's Ch Bossier City LA 1976-1978; P Dio W Texas San Antonio TX 1974-1976; R Trin Epis Ch Pharr TX 1971-1974; Cur Epis Ch Of The Gd Shpd Lake Chas LA 1970-1971; Vic Ch Of The Incarn Amite LA 1968-1970; Cur Gr Memi Hammond LA 1968-1970. Legion Of Merit. Legion Of Merit Us Army 1998.

DUGAN, Jeffrey Scott (Ct) 345 Seabury Drive, Bloomfield CT 06002 B Boston MA 2/9/1954 s Michael Harry Dugan & Priscilla. BA Dart 1976; MDiv Ya Berk 1980. D 5/31/1980 Bp Frederick Barton Wolf P 11/29/1980 Bp H Coleman McGehee Jr. m 7/6/2002 Elizabeth Hall c 4. R S Jas Epis Ch Farmington CT 1990-2010; Int Chr And H Trin Ch Westport CT 1989-1990; Int S Jn's Epis Par Waterbury CT 1988-1989; Assoc R Bruton Par Williamsburg VA 1983-1987; Assoc R Chr Ch Grosse Pointe Grosse Pointe Farms MI 1980-1983. Auth, "Chris's Sum," Cumberland Hse, 2001. jeffdugan@comcast.net

DUGAN, Raymond P (Az) 534 W Wilshire Dr, Phoenix AZ 85003 **Int S Andr's Ch Glendale AZ 2010-** B Temuco Chile South America 2/17/1935 s Walter Howard Dugan & Marguerita. BS Arizona St U 1957; MDiv Epis TS of The SW 1960. D 6/12/1960 P 12/11/1960 Bp Arthur Kinsolving. m 6/9/1954 Nancy H Hansen c 2. Assoc Trin Cathd Phoenix AZ 2008-2010; Asst Gd Shpd Of The Hills Cave Creek AZ 2006-2007; Int S Ptr's Ch Casa Grande AZ 2003-2006; R Epis Ch Of The Trsfg Mesa AZ 1994-2002; Int S Ptr's Ch Litchfield Pk AZ 1992-1993; Vic S Lk's At The Mtn Phoenix AZ 1979-1992; Cmnty Coun Phoenix AZ 1970-1976; Cn Pstr Trin Cathd Phoenix AZ 1964-1970; Vic S Dav's Epis Page AZ 1960-1964; Vic S Jn's Ch Williams AZ 1960-1964. rdugan2@cox.net

DUGAT JR, William Dennis (WTex) 306 S Acorn St, Fredericksburg TX 78624 **S Barn Epis Ch Fredericksburg TX 2005-** B Beeville TX 1/12/1934 s W D Dugat & Francis. BS Texas A&M U 1955. D 3/25/1988 Bp John Herbert MacNaughton P 9/30/1988 Bp Earl Nicholas McArthur Jr. c 3. poppyg@austin.rr.com

DUGGAN, Joe F (Nev) 1644 Shadow Wood Road, Reno NV 93103 B Bronx NY 6/1/1956 s James Duggan & Catherine. BS Manhattan Coll Bronx NY 1978; MA EDS 2006; PhD 2010. D 6/3/2006 P 1/6/2007 Bp Joseph Jon Bruno. m 11/15/2003 Stefani S Schatz. "The Postcolonial Paradox," *Journ of Angl Stds*, Camb Press, 2009. Acad Fllshp Partnr ECF 2008. nyclaman@gmail.com

DUGGAR, Marilyn Elaine (Ak) St Mark's Episcopal Church, PO Box 469, Nenana AK 99760 B Fairbanks AK 4/6/1954 d Robert A Coghill & Gladys A. BA U of Alaska 1976. D 4/25/2007 Bp Mark Lawrence Mac Donald. m 12/22/1984 Morgan Hilton Duggar c 2. meduggar@matonline.net

DUGGER, Clinton George (Alb) Po Box 148, New Lebanon NY 12125 **P-in-c Ch Of Our Sav New Lebanon NY 2000-** B Beacon NY 9/8/1929 s William Dugger & Mary. BA S Aug 1959; STB PDS 1962; MS SUNY 1967. D 6/9/1962 Bp Horace W B Donegan P 12/15/1962 Bp Allen Webster Brown. m 11/24/1962 Virginia McLean c 1. Cathd Chapt Dio Albany Albany NY 1998-2002; Ch Of The Redeem Rensselaer NY 1985-1997; Vic S Lk's Ch Chatham NY 1973-1985. Sigma Rho Sigma 1958. Chapl Emer Hoosac Sch 1988; Who's Who in Rel 1975; Man of the Year Awd Nthrn Columbia Rotarians 1975; Hon Cn All SS Cathd Albany NY 1968. clint14401@webtv.net

DUGGER, Rita Jacqueline Carney (WNY) 24 Linwood Ave, Buffalo NY 14209 B Buffalo NY 11/2/1927 d John A Carney & Anne May. Basic Interp Trng Prog; Rochester Inst Of Tech Natl Tech Institu 1986. D 6/7/1980 Bp Harold B Robinson. m 6/21/1946 Raymond Emerson Dugger c 4. Cwc; Natl Epis Ch Of The Deaf.

DUGGIN, Sarah Helene (WA) 3240 O St NW, Washington DC 20007 **Asst R S Jn's Ch Georgetown Par Washington DC 2009-** B Philadelphia PA 6/22/1954 d John Duggin & Kathryn White. AB Smith 1976; JD U of Pennsylvnia Law Sch 1979; MDiv Wesley TS 2009. D 6/13/2009 P 1/16/2010 Bp John Chane. m 9/8/1984 Kirk Renaud c 2. duggin@law.edu

DUGGINS, Dave (Miss) 11598 Azalea Trce, Gulfport MS 39503 **D S Thos Epis Ch Diamondhead MS 2009-** B Ajo AZ 7/11/1943 s Amos Dwight Duggins & Florence Senf. BS U of Maryland 1986. D 1/17/2004 Bp Duncan Montgomery Gray III. m 10/17/1987 Mary L Hinsdale c 2. deacondaved@bellsouth.net

DUGGINS, Gordon Hayes (NY) P.O. Box 670, Colfax NC 27235 **Assoc S Mary's Manhattanville Epis Ch New York NY 1993-** B Winston-Salem NC

11/29/1950 s Hayes Duggins & Pencie Victoria. BA Duke 1973; MDiv cl VTS 1976; ThM cl Harvard DS 1977; ThD Harvard DS 1982. Rec 6/1/1985 as Priest Bp Paul Moore Jr. m 11/26/2008 Armando Tejeda Dunn c 1. Vic Trin Epis Ch Litchfield CT 1988-1992; Cur S Thos Ch New York NY 1981-1984. Rec Campbell Schlrshp, Harvard 1978; Fell ECF 1978; Rec WN Reynolds Schlrshp, Duke 1969. gordonduggins@aol.com

DUGHI, Lorraine Mazuy (Nwk) 7 Canal Ln # 300, Hackettstown NJ 07840 B Newton NJ 10/2/1925 D 6/12/2004 P 3/25/2006 Bp John Palmer Croneberger. l.dughi@att.net

DUH, Michael Yung-che (Tai) 952 Sec 2 Chading Road Chading, Kaohsiung Hsien 85202, Taiwan China B 9/28/1955 s Dau-sheng Duh & Shyuee-lii. BA Natl Cheng-Chi U 1979; MDiv Taiwan TS Tw 1984. D 7/15/1984 P 8/1/1985 Bp Pui-Yeung Cheung. m 7/23/1981 Shiang-liin Lii.

DUKE, Cecilia Bliley (At) 597 Haralson Dr Sw, Lilburn GA 30047 **R Chr Ch Norcross GA 2009-** B Richmond VA 6/9/1953 d Joseph Wilfred Biliey & Catherine Cecilia. BA VPI 1975; M.Ed. Georgia St U 1981; EDS Georgia St U 1991; MDiv Candler TS Emory U 1999. D 6/5/1999 Bp Onell Asiselo Soto P 2/5/2000 Bp Frank Kellogg Allan. m 8/12/1978 David H Duke c 2. Assoc R The Epis Ch Of S Ptr And S Paul Marietta GA 2005-2008; Assoc R S Mich And All Ang Ch Stone Mtn GA 2001-2005; Stndg Commision on Educ Dio Atlanta Atlanta GA 2000-2003; Stndg Commision on Mnstry Dio Atlanta Atlanta GA 2000-2003; Assoc R S Pat's Epis Ch Atlanta GA 1999-2001. Bd Emmaus Hse 2009; Delta Kappa Gamma 1979-1994; EFM 2002; Green Bough Hse of Pryr, Adrian, GA 1993; Kappa Delta Phi 1983-1995; Ldrshp Trng Inst 2000-2005; The SSAP 2006. dukec@mindspring.com

DUKENSKI, Carolyn Perry (Ct) 350 Westside Rd, Goshen CT 06756 B Pasadena CA 10/6/1949 d Donald Edward Perry & Winifred. BA Hood Coll 1971; MS U of Bridgeport 1976; MDiv Ya Berk 1996. D 6/14/1997 Bp Clarence Nicholas Coleridge P 1/3/1998 Bp Andrew Donnan Smith. m 6/5/1971 Ronald Henry Dukenski c 2. Vic S Ptr's Epis Ch Oxford CT 2000-2004; Asst S Jas Epis Ch Danbury CT 1998-2000; Asst Ch of our Sav Plainville CT 1997-1998; Asst St Gabr's Ch E Berlin CT 1997-1998.

DUKES, John Edmund (At) 1964 Gratis Rd Nw, Monroe GA 30656 B Montgomery AL 3/17/1950 s Arthur Dow Dukes & Flora Grant. BA Auburn U 1972; MDiv STUSo 1981. D 5/28/1981 P 12/1/1981 Bp Furman Stough. m 12/12/1987 Ethel Lee Jones c 1. Vic S Anth's Epis Ch Winder GA 2002-2005; S Edw's Epis Ch Lawrenceville GA 1996; S Mary And S Martha Ch Buford GA 1993-1995; Dio Atlanta Atlanta GA 1992-1993; Asst to R The Ch Of S Matt Snellville GA 1990-1992; R S Phil's Ch Ft Payne AL 1982-1984; Cur Ch Of The H Comf Montgomery AL 1981-1982. JOHNEDUKES@HOTMAIL.COM

DUKES, Lynne Adair (Slane) (WMich) 115 3rd St S Apt 913, Jacksonville Beach FL 32250 B Los Angeles CA 6/3/1941 d Henry Ladoyle Slane & Jean Leone. BA Jacksonville U 1997; MDiv Epis TS of The SW 2000. D 6/11/2000 P 12/10/2000 Bp Stephen Hays Jecko. c 2. P Trin Ch Three Rivers MI 2001-2006. revlynnedukes@comcast.net

DULANY, Susan Strobhar (Ga) 18 Abercorn St, Savannah GA 31401 **Died 2/20/2011** B Savannah GA 5/13/1943 d Arthur Douglass Strobhar & Katherine. Armstrong Atlantic St Coll. D 4/8/1989 Bp Harry Woolston Shipps.

DULFER, John Guidi (NY) 110 W 15th St Apt 1, New York NY 10011 B Broken Hill NSW AU 9/30/1937 s Jack Dulfer & Maybell Ulando. Tstc Ballarat & Melbourne Art Schools Melbourne Au 1957; Lichfield Theol Coll 1964. Trans from Church Of England 10/1/1984. P-in-c S Mary's Castleton Staten Island NY 2001-2002; Int Ch Of The Resurr New York NY 2000-2001; S Jn Jersey City NJ 1985-1986; S Matt's Ch Jersey City NJ 1985-1986; Dio Newark Newark NJ 1984.

DULGAR, Sandra (Nev) PO Box 111, Nezperce ID 83543 B Sandpoint ID 6/11/1941 d Guy G Raynor & Louise E. D 11/15/1997 Bp Stewart Clark Zabriskie. m 7/20/1984 James R Dulgar. D S Mk's Ch Tonopah NV 1997-2002.

DULL, Stanley Lynn (Pa) 2215 Palm Tree Dr, Punta Gorda FL 33950 B Midland MI 5/11/1942 s Orville Dull & Barbara. BS Cntrl Michigan U 1969; MDiv PDS 1974; MA Immaculata U 1993; PsyD Immaculata U 1999. D 6/15/1974 P 8/15/1975 Bp Lyman Cunningham Ogilby. m 8/15/2008 Mary Margaret Dull c 5. Ch Of The Epiph Cape Coral FL 2000-2008; Ch Of The Ascen Parkesburg PA 1975-2000. dullstan@aol.com

DUMKE, Barbara A (Colo) 11684 Eldorado St Nw, Coon Rapids MN 55433 **Ch of the Gd Shpd Colorado Sprg CO 2007-** B Oshkosh WI 5/27/1946 d Robert William Dumke & Florence Rose. BA U of Wisconsin 1968; MA U Pgh 1970; MDiv Untd TS Of The Twin Cities 1985; MA CDSP 1987. D 6/24/1987 P 5/1/1988 Bp Robert Marshall Anderson. m 9/17/1988 Eugene Richard Wahl. Trin Ch Anoka MN 1992-2000; The Epis Cathd Of Our Merc Sav Faribault MN 1992; Assoc R St Johns Epis Ch Ross CA 1989-1992; Asst S Aid's Ch San Francisco CA 1987-1988. Auth, "Cath Dig"; Auth, "Soundings". barbaraanndumke@yahoo.com

DUMKE, Edward John (Cal) 805 Barneson Ave, San Mateo CA 94402 B San Mateo CA 3/10/1946 s Donald S Dumke & Dorothy L. San Francisco St U; BA San Francisco St U 1968; MDiv CDSP 1975. D 6/28/1975 Bp C Kilmer Myers P 4/1/1976 Bp Clarence Rupert Haden Jr. Trin Cathd Sacramento CA 1975-1977; Field Worker Trsfg Epis Ch San Mateo CA 1974-1975.

DUMOLT, Elizabeth Ann (Los) 555 E Mountain View Ave, Glendora CA 91741 **D Gr Epis Ch Glendora CA 2010-** B San Diego, CA 3/16/1956 d Raymond T DuMolt & Gloria A. Cert. in Diac Stds Epis TS at Claremont; U of San Diego 1979; M Div. Claremont TS 2013. D 5/22/2010 Bp Chester Lovelle Talton. adumolt@msn.com

DUNAGAN, Joe Kimbell (At) 116 Alabama Ave, Macon GA 31204 **P in Charge S Chris's At-The-Crossroads Epis Perry GA 2010-** B Haw Kinsville GA 1/24/1955 s Joe A Dunagan & Bettie O. BA Berry Coll 1976; MDiv Emory U 1980. D 12/19/2009 Bp J(ohn) Neil Alexander. m 10/25/2009 Katherine Torbert Kelly c 1. joe.dunagan@gmail.com

DUNBAR, Donald Machell (Mass) 160 Longmeadow Rd, Fairfield CT 06824 B New York NY 4/19/1934 s Howard Riley Dunbar & Alice ELizabeth Goode. BA Colby Coll 1956; MDiv EDS 1959; MLS Wesl 1973; Med Boston Coll 1980. D 6/20/1959 P 12/1/1959 Bp Anson Phelps Stokes Jr. m 8/27/1966 Susan Morrill Finlay c 1. Dir Chr Ch Waltham MA 1976-1979; Dir S Ptr's Ch Weston MA 1970-1979; Asst Min S Ptr's Ch Weston MA 1963-1966; Cur Trin Par Melrose MA 1959-1961. "What You Don't Know Can Keep You Out of Coll," Penguin-Gotham, 2007. St. Jn's Soc 2007. DDUNBAR@DUNBARCONSULTANTS.COM

DUNBAR, Gavin Gunning (Ga) 1 W Macon St, Savannah GA 31401 **R S Jn's Ch Savannah GA 2006-; Assoc S Jn's Ch Savannah GA 1997-** B Toronto ON CA 9/11/1961 s Addison Carlyle Dunbar & Phyllis Lorraine. Dalhousie U; BA U Tor 1984; MDiv U Tor 1991. Trans from Anglican Church of Canada 7/1/1997 Bp Henry Irving Louttit. PB Soc of the U. S. A. 2000. gdunbar@stjohnssav.org

DUNBAR, Julia Brown (Mass) 20 Whitney Ave, Cambridge MA 02139 **Assoc All SS Par Brookline MA 2011-** B Washington DC 5/10/1949 D 6/12/2004 P 1/8/2005 Bp M(arvil) Thomas Shaw III. c 2. jbdun@comcast.net

DUNBAR, Pamela Virginia Waite (Dal) 9221 Flickering Shadow Dr, Dallas TX 75243 **Mssnr Dio Dallas Dallas TX 1999-** B San Francisco CA 6/8/1947 d Noble Lloyd Waite & Isabelle. Dio NW TS For Deacons; Texas Tech U; BA California St U 1969. D 10/25/1985 Bp Sam Byron Hulsey. m 5/1/1970 David W Dunbar c 2. D S Nich' Epis Ch Midland TX 1985-1999. CHS.

DUNBAR, Philip Craig (CFla) 2505 Gramercy Dr, Deltona FL 32738 **D All SS Epis Ch Enterprise FL 2001-** B Brockton MA 10/31/1942 s Donald Cogan Dunbar & Hazel Marie. BA/BA Florida St U 1970; Inst For Chr Stds, Orlando, FL 1976; MA Rol 1983. D 5/14/1977 Bp William Hopkins Folwell. m 7/3/1966 Judy Ann Williams c 4. D S Barn Ch Deland FL 1981-2000; Asst All SS Epis Ch Enterprise FL 1977-1981. revpcd@yahoo.com

DUNBAR, Robert Barron (USC) PO Box 36155, Rock Hill SC 29732 **Asst Ch Of Our Sav Rock Hill SC 2009-** B Chester SC 1/25/1932 s James Irwin Dunbar & Louise. BA Davidson Coll 1954; MDiv UTS Richmond VA 1957; MA Prcsb Sch CE Richmond VA 1964; STUSo 1965; Harvard DS 1987. D 4/2/1966 P 4/1/1967 Bp John Adams Pinckney. c 1. Asst Ch Of Our Sav Rock Hill SC 1995-2008; Assoc Par Ch of St. Helena Beaufort SC 1989-1993; R S Ptr's Epis Ch Cambridge MA 1980-1989; Vic Ch Of S Jn The Evang Boston MA 1977-1980; Cn Dio Upper So Carolina Columbia SC 1968-1977; Vic Calv Ch Pauline SC 1968-1976; D Epis Ch Of The Redeem Greenville SC 1966-1968. FAUTEDEMIEUX@COMPORIUM.NET

DUNCAN, Barbara Tompkins (WA) 8103 Langley Dr, Glen Allen VA 23060 **Assoc Emm Ch At Brook Hill Richmond VA 2006-** B Richmond VA 1/4/1942 d Brown Tompkins & Ada. BS Virginia St U 1962; MM W Chester U of Pennsylvania 1979; MDiv Lancaster TS 1987; DMin GTF 1992. D 2/28/1987 P 2/1/1988 Bp Cabell Tennis. c 4. S Nich' Epis Ch Newark DE 2002; Cn Mssnr/Pstr Cathd of St Ptr & St Paul Washington DC 1997-2002; Epis Cmnty Serv Philadelphia PA 1995-1997; Assoc R S Columba's Ch Washington DC 1993-1995; Assoc R Chr Ch Greenville Wilmington DE 1990-1992; Int Ch of St Andrews & St Matthews Wilmington DE 1988-1990; Dio Delaware Wilmington DE 1987-1990; Bp's D to City Cathd Ch Of S Jn Wilmington DE 1987-1988. NAAD 2005. btd04@aol.com

DUNCAN, Carol Craig (O) 629 46th St Nw, Canton OH 44709 **D Trin Ch Allnce OH 1996** B Macon GA 9/28/1945 d William Sloan Kinney & Catherine. BA Smith 1967. D 11/8/1996 Bp J Clark Grew II. m 10/28/1967 James Robert Duncan.

DUNCAN, Christopher Ray (Tex) PO Box 5176, Austin TX 78763 **Cur The Ch of the Gd Shpd Austin TX 2009-** B Houston TX 11/7/1981 s Mark Oliver Duncan & Dianne Michel. BA Texas A & M U 2004; MDiv VTS 2009. D 6/20/2009 Bp C(harles) Andrew Doyle P 1/20/2010 Bp Dena Arnall Harrison. m 6/24/2006 Casey Rush c 1. chris@gsaustin.org

DUNCAN, Daniel Lester (NwPa) 1600 N Keel Ridge Rd, Hermitage PA 16148 **Died 9/10/2011** B Cumberland MD 12/8/1948 D 6/24/2002 Bp Gladstone Bailey Adams III. c 6.

DUNCAN, David (Los) 4640 Woodduck Ln, Salt Lake City UT 84117 **Ch Of The H Trin and S Ben Alhambra CA 2004-** B Brooklyn NY 1/10/1948 s Donald Stuart Duncan & Jean Ingraham. BA Swarthmore Coll 1969; MA

Claremont Coll 1974; MA Claremont Coll 1976; MDiv GTS 1979. D 6/23/1979 P 1/1/1980 Bp Robert C Rusack. c 2. S Martha's Epis Ch W Covina CA 2001-2004; Chr Ch Par Redondo Bch CA 2000-2001; S Thos The Apos Hollywood Los Angeles CA 2000; S Mk's Par Downey CA 1997-2000; Cathd Cntr Of S Paul Cong Los Angeles CA 1995-1997; Assoc S Cross By-The-Sea Ch Hermosa Bch CA 1994-1995; R The Par Ch Of S Lk Long Bch CA 1992-1994; S Anselm Of Cbury Par Garden Grove CA 1989-1992; Trin Epis Par Los Angeles CA 1982-1989; The ETS At Claremont Claremont CA 1981-1991; Dio Los Angeles Los Angeles CA 1979-1982. Auth, *Wit.* manchesternorthroad@yahoo.com

DUNCAN, Hugh C (Ida) 5120 W Overland Rd PMB-276, Boise ID 83705 B Greenville NC 12/25/1938 s Fitzhugh D Duncan & Elizabeth C. BS USNA 1961; MDiv Epis TS of The SW 1981. D 6/24/1981 P 1/1/1982 Bp Leigh Wallace Jr. m 9/17/1965 Beverly L Foster c 2. R All SS Epis Ch Boise ID 1989-1998; Stndg Com Dio Idaho Boise ID 1988-1993; COM Dio Spokane Spokane WA 1982-1988; R S Mart's Ch Moses Lake WA 1981-1989; S Mk's Ch Ritzville WA 1981-1982. hduncan4@cox.net

DUNCAN, J(ames) Bruce (Los) 45 Chestnut St Unit A, North Adams MA 01247 B Elgin IL 4/20/1937 s Delbert James Duncan & Elizabeth Ann. U CO 1957; BA San Francisco St Coll 1959; Cert STUSo 1987; MDiv GTS 1990; Nash 1992; STM GTS 1994; U Tor 1996; Cert The Ch Dvlpmt Inst 1998. Trans from Anglican Church of Canada 11/1/1996 Bp Frederick Houk Borsch. m 7/13/1973 Ruth K Lemmert. St Fran Cong Alhambra CA 2000-2001; Dio Los Angeles Los Angeles CA 1999-2001; Int Epis Chap Of S Fran Los Angeles CA 1999-2001; Vic S Alb's Epis Ch Yucaipa CA 1996-1999. AAR 1990; Angl Soc 1996; Integrity Inc 1990; SBL 1990. Seymour Prize Extemporaneous Preaching GTS 1988.

DUNCAN, Janice Eileen (NwPa) 870 N Buhl Farm Dr, Hermitage PA 16148 B Sharon PA 12/20/1942 d Charles Peter Metz & Mildred Leona. Edinboro U; BA Grove City Coll 1993; MDiv STUSo 1996. D 7/10/1996 P 1/19/1997 Bp Robert Deane Rowley Jr. c 6. S Matt's Ch Moravia NY 2002-2008; Tri Cnty Cluster Moravia NY 2001-2002; Chr Epis Ch Oil City PA 1997-2001. no

DUNCAN, John L (NCal) 110 San Benito Avenue, Aptos CA 95003 B San Jose CA 6/21/1939 s John Parker Duncan & Frances Ruth. CDSP; BA San Jose St U 1962; MDiv PSR 1966. D 6/29/1966 P 5/19/1967 Bp Clarence Rupert Haden Jr. m 4/8/1961 Janet Gay Meckler c 3. R Gr Epis Ch Fairfield CA 1983-2000; Assoc All SS Epis Ch Watsonville CA 1970-1983; Vic S Andr's In The Highlands Mssn Antelope CA 1967-1969; Cur Trin Cathd Sacramento CA 1966-1967. jnjduncan@yahoo.com

✠ **DUNCAN II, Rt Rev Philip Menzie** (CGC) Diocese Of The Central Gulf Coast, P.O. Box 13330, Pensacola FL 32591 **Bp of Cntrl Gulf Coast Dio Cntrl Gulf Coast Pensacola FL 2001-** B Glen Cove NY 12/6/1944 s Philip Menzie Duncan & Jessie. BA Baldwin-Wallace Coll 1967; MDiv/STB GTS 1970; St. Geo's Coll Jerusalem 1977; PrTS 1984; DMin VTS 1990. D 6/13/1970 P 12/19/1970 Bp Jonathan Goodhue Sherman Con 5/12/2001 for CGC. m 6/20/1970 Kathlyn Cowie c 2. Dn S Matt's Cathd Dallas TX 1993-2001; Bd Angl TS Dio Dallas Dallas TX 1993-2000; Chair Epis Migration Mnstry Dio SW Florida Sarasota FL 1990-1993; VP Ecum Bd Dio SW Florida Sarasota FL 1982-1983; Dioc Coun Dio SW Florida Sarasota FL 1979-1984; R S Jn's Epis Ch Clearwater FL 1972-1993; Cur Chr Ch Ridgewood NJ 1970-1972. Fllshp of the Soc of S Jn the Evang 1978; Ord of S Jn of Jerusalem 1996. DD The U So TS 2003; DD The GTS 2002; DD The VTS 2002. bishopduncan@diocgc.org

DUNCAN, Rosemarie (WA) 1329 Hamilton St Nw, Washington DC 20011 **Assoc S Columba's Ch Washington DC 2005-** B Washington DC 11/27/1959 d William Wilkins Duncan & Falva Joan. BS How 1985; MS How 1989; PhD How 1999; MDiv VTS 2005. D 6/11/2005 P 1/21/2006 Bp John Chane. m 8/24/2010 Judith Hutchinson. rduncan@columba.org

DUNCAN, Rudolph Atherton (Haw) 46-082 Puulena St Apt 1221, Kaneohe HI 96744 B Honolulu HI 2/13/1926 s Rudolph William Duncan & Gladys Laura. BS U CA 1949; MDiv CDSP 1968. D 5/10/1968 Bp Edwin Lani Hanchett P 12/18/1968 Bp Harry S Kennedy. m 6/9/1951 Kathleen Ululani Hopkins c 3. Treas Dio Hawaii Honolulu HI 1979-1991; S Mary's Epis Ch Honolulu HI 1968-1978.

DUNCAN, Shawn Patrick (WNY) 264 Water St Apt 6D, New York NY 10038 **Committe on Cn Dio Long Island Garden City NY 2011-; Int S Geo's Par Flushing NY 2010-** B Anaheim CA 6/26/1962 s Fred William Duncan & Linda Louise. BA U CA 1985; MDiv CDSP 1992. D 5/26/1992 P 12/4/1992 Bp Jerry Alban Lamb. m 6/30/1991 Victoria Dean c 2. Int All SS' Epis Ch Briarcliff Manor NY 2009-2010; Const & Cn Com - Chair Dio Wstrn New York Tonawanda NY 2008-2009; Mssn Ldrshp and Mgmt Team — Chair Dio Wstrn New York Tonawanda NY 2008-2009; Stndg Com Dio Wstrn New York Tonawanda NY 2008-2009; Reg Dn Dio Wstrn New York Tonawanda NY 2007-2009; Dep to GC Dio Wstrn New York Tonawanda NY 2004-2009; R Trin Epis Ch Hamburg NY 1999-2009; Personl Com Dio Wstrn New York Tonawanda NY 1999-2004; R S Paul's Epis Ch Elko NV 1995-1999; Dioc Coun Dio Nevada Las Vegas NV 1995-1998; S Mich's Epis Ch Carmichael CA 1992-1995. Alb Inst 1992. shawn@c3design.org

DUNCAN, Victoria (WNY) Episcopal Diocese of Western New York, 1114 Delaware Avenue, Buffalo NY 14209 **Mssnr for Transition Mnstry Epis Ch Cntr New York NY 2009-** B Berkeley CA 5/13/1958 d Dawson Frank Dean & Ruth Woods. BA Mt Holyoke Coll 1980; MDiv CDSP 1991. D 10/6/2000 P 4/7/2001 Bp J Michael Garrison. m 6/30/1991 Shawn Patrick Duncan c 2. Cn for Mssn & Mnstry and Dioc Deploy Off Dio Wstrn New York Tonawanda NY 2003-2009; Assoc R S Mk's Ch Orchard Pk NY 2000-2002; COM Dio Nevada Las Vegas NV 1996-1997; COM Dio Nthrn California Sacramento CA 1992-1995. vduncan@episcopalchurch.org

DUNCAN-O'NEAL III, Bill M. (Ark) 9669 Wedd St, Overland Park KS 66212 B Cleveland OH 11/18/1934 s William McKinley Duncan & Mary Louisa. BA U of Texas 1956; BD VTS 1962; MDiv VTS 1970; MLS U of Texas 1971. D 7/20/1962 Bp Everett H Jones P 2/15/1963 Bp Richard Earl Dicus. m 2/14/1994 Jan Irving c 2. Dn, SW Convoc Dio Arkansas Little Rock AR 1968-1969; R S Jn's Ch Camden AR 1966-1969; Cur The Falls Ch Epis Falls Ch VA 1964-1966; Dn, Sthrn Convoc Dio W Texas San Antonio TX 1963-1964.

DUNCAN-PROBE, DeDe (Va) 11544 Clara Barton Dr., Fairfax Station VA 22039 **Vic S Peters-In-The-Woods Epis Ch Fairfax Sta VA 2009-** B Ft Worth TX 5/4/1962 BS Steph F. Austin St U 1985; MA Pepperdine U 1993; MDiv GTS 2003. D 6/28/2003 P 1/19/2004 Bp Richard Lester Shimpfky. m 2/12/1994 Christopher A Probe c 3. P-in-c All SS Ch Stoneham MA 2007-2008; Int S Jn's Epis Ch McLean VA 2006-2007; Assoc R Ch Of The H Comf Vienna VA 2003-2006; All SS Par Beverly Hills CA 1992-1994. dduncanprobe@yahoo.com

DUNCANSON, Frederick Philip (NY) 6 Long Meadow Dr, Monsey NY 10952 **Off Dio Newark Newark NJ 2000-; Chapl for Healing S Mich's Epis Ch Wayne NJ 1998-** B Everett MA 8/7/1952 s Frederick Julian Duncanson & Rita Dolores. NYTS; BS MIT 1974; MD Mt Sinai Sch of Med 1978; S Jn's-Div Inst Theol New York NY 1984. D 6/11/1988 P 12/11/1988 Bp Paul Moore Jr. m 6/25/1988 Jeanne Antoinette Eenkhoorn. Cur Chr Ch Of Ramapo Suffern NY 1988-1998. Auth, "A Leper Came to Him," *Sharing*, 1986. Amer Angl Coun 2000; Ord of S Lk, ERM, CCL, Cursill; Wrld Revival Ntwk 2000. Fllshp Infectious Diseases Soc of Amer 1982. fduncanson@pol.net

DUNHAM, John Spofford (WTex) 3408 Packsaddle Dr, Horseshoe Bay TX 78657 B San Antonio TX 11/15/1924 s Walter Megonogel Dunham & Katharine Parker. BBA U of Texas 1950; MDiv Epis TS of The SW 1971. D 6/20/1971 Bp Harold Cornelius Gosnell P 12/1/1971 Bp Richard Earl Dicus. c 2. Vic Gr Ch Llano TX 1983-1995; Vic Epis Ch Of The Gd Shepard Geo W TX 1973-1983; R S Phil's Ch Beeville TX 1973-1983; Vic Epiph Epis Ch Raymondville TX 1971-1973. frjsd1@nctv.com

DUNHAM, Richard Eldon (WTex) PO Box 314, Bandera TX 78003 B Corpus Christi TX 12/25/1949 s Walter Dunham & Virginia. BA U of Texas 1972; MDiv Epis TS of the SW 1979. D 6/12/1979 Bp Scott Field Bailey P 12/12/1979 Bp Stanley Fillmore Hauser. c 1. R S Chris's Ch Bandera TX 2002-2010; S Mk's Epis Ch Moscow ID 1988-2002; The Epis Ch Of The Adv Alice TX 1983-1988; S Peters Epis Sch Kerrville TX 1979-1983; S Ptr's Epis Ch Kerrville TX 1979-1983. rdunhamcc@att.net

DUNKEL, Lisa Marie (Cal) 778 Cumberland Dr, Pleasant Hill CA 94523 **Died 6/21/2010** B Hamelin DE 8/14/1934 d Willie Dunkel & Irma. BA U CA 1970; MLS U CA 1971; MA U CA 1978; BA Sch for Deacons 1997. D 12/6/1997 Bp William Edwin Swing. lisa@st-timothy.org

DUNKERLEY, James Hobson (Chi) 621 W Belmont Ave, Chicago IL 60657 B Manchester UK 12/4/1939 s James Dunkerley & Elsie. Kelham Theol Coll 1964; BD SWTS 1969; STM SWTS 1970. Trans from Church Of England 10/28/1970 as Priest Bp Gerald Francis Burrill. Dn Dio Chicago Chicago IL 2004-2006; Dioc Coun Mem Dio Chicago Chicago IL 2000-2005; Dioc Coun Mem Dio Chicago Chicago IL 1984-1989; R S Ptr's Epis Ch Chicago IL 1970-2007. CCU 1965; Soc of the Sacr Mssn (Assoc) 1958. rector@stpetrschicago.org

DUNKLE, Kurt Hughes (Fla) 1038 River Road, Orange Park FL 32073 **Gr Epis Ch Orange Pk FL 2008-** B Saint Petersburg FL 8/23/1961 s Harry Dunkle & Caroline. BA Duke 1983; JD U Of Florida 1987; MDiv GTS 2004. D 5/30/2004 P 12/5/2004 Bp Samuel Johnson Howard. m 5/16/1987 Cathleen Dunkle c 3. Cn Dio Florida Jacksonville FL 2004-2008. Auth, "Stwdshp," *LivCh*, 2008. kurt@dunkle.net

DUNKS, Andrew A (SwVa) 4010 Ves Road, Lynchburg VA 24503 **Christchurch Sch Christchurch VA 2010-** B Bryan TX 3/17/1962 s Wallace Edwin Dunks & Ginger Ray. BA Texas A&M U 1984; MA U of Notre Dame 1986; MDiv Epis TS of The SW 1989. D 2/8/1990 Bp William Elwood Sterling P 8/1/1990 Bp Earl Nicholas McArthur Jr. m 1/20/1990 Julia McBee c 2. Virginia Epis Sch Lynchburg VA 2002-2010; Vic S Mich's Epis Ch San Antonio TX 1994-2002; Asst R S Barth's Ch Corpus Christi TX 1990-1993. ERM. adunks@ves.org

DUNLAP, Daniel K (Tex) 715 Carrell St., Tomball TX 77375 **Actg R Ch Of The Gd Shpd Tomball TX 2009-** B Philadelphia PA 9/25/1963 s David Parker Dunlap & Patricia G. BS Penn 1986; MA,MDiv Biblic TS 1989; PhD Wycliffe Hall 2001. D 6/23/2007 Bp Don Adger Wimberly P 1/9/2008 Bp Rayford Baines High Jr. m 6/27/1987 Donna G Donna Marie Grow c 3. lexorandi@sbcglobal.net

DUNLAP, D(ennis) Joe (Chi) 326 W. Northland Ave, Peoria IL 61614 B Bloomington IL 5/7/1949 s Everett Ivan Dunlap & Gladys Velma. BA Illinois St U 1970; MA Illinois St U 1971; MDiv Nash 1974. D 5/14/1974 P 5/24/1975 Bp Albert William Hillestad. R S Paul's Ch McHenry IL 2004-2006; R All SS Ch Morton IL 1996-2004; R St Johns Epis Ch Wisconsin Rapids WI 1983-1996; Cn S Paul's Cathd Fond du Lac WI 1977-1983; Cntrl Dio Ecuador EC 1975-1977; Mssy Appointee by PB Dom And Frgn Mssy Soc- Epis Ch Cntr New York NY 1975-1977; Cur Ch Of The Trsfg Freeport NY 1974-1975. AGO 1976; Organ Hist Soc 1977; SHN 1978. joeperscc@comcast.net

DUNLAP, Eunice Rosalie (WNC) 403 Northview Dr, Fayetteville NC 28303 **Asst R S Jas Epis Ch Hendersonville NC 2007-** B New York NY 7/4/1961 d John Zieley & Margarete. MDiv Bangor TS 1997; BS SUNY 1997; DAS VTS 2002. D 4/10/2002 P 2/25/2003 Bp Clifton Daniel III. m 8/11/1984 George Mackenzie Dunlap c 3. H Trin Epis Ch Fayetteville NC 2002-2006. eunicerdunlap@gmail.com

DUNLAP, Garland Edward (Va) 207 Branner Ave, Winchester VA 22601 B Winchester VA 8/17/1942 s Charles Dunlap & Anna. BA Virginia Commonwealth U 1969; MDiv VTS 1972. D 5/27/1972 Bp Charles F Hall P 5/1/1973 Bp Robert Fisher Gibson Jr. m 12/18/1966 Donna Ploss c 1. R S Paul's On-The-Hill Winchester VA 2000-2003; R Varina Epis Ch Richmond VA 1997-2000; S Paul's Epis Ch Wilmington NC 1995-1996; R S Fran Ch Goldsboro NC 1980-1994; R S Phil's Ch Southport NC 1978-1980; Asst S S Jas' Ch Richmond VA 1974-1978; Asst S S Thos' Ch Richmond VA 1972-1974. ged42@bellsouth.net

DUNLAP, Joseph Lacy (SC) 3608 Providence Pl, Winterville NC 28590 B Wilmington DE 7/28/1946 s Harmon Richard Dunlap & Margaret. BS No Carolina St U 1969; MDiv VTS 1977. D 6/18/1977 P 2/1/1978 Bp Hunley Agee Elebash. m 12/22/1972 Barbara Joyner. S Chris's Ch Sumter SC 1987-1988; Asst R Chr Ch New Bern NC 1986-1987; Ch Of The H Innoc Seven Sprg NC 1977-1978.

DUNLOP, Judith Goldsborough (Cal) 735 Sapphire St., Redwood City CA 94061 **Assoc Ch Of The Epiph San Carlos CA 2011-** B New York NY 1/20/1938 d Francis Farrar Goldsborough & Marjorie. BS Col 1961; MA Col 1966; MDiv CDSP 1990; D.D. CDSP 2011. D 12/8/1990 P 9/1/1991 Bp William Edwin Swing. c 2. Assoc All SS' Ch San Francisco CA 2004-2011; Int R Ch Of The Epiph San Carlos CA 2001-2004; Int R Chr Epis Ch Los Altos CA 1999-2001; Vic S Cyp's Ch San Francisco CA 1997-1999; Assoc All SS' Ch San Francisco CA 1992-1997; Dn Epis Sch For Deacons Berkeley CA 1990-1998. Auth, "sev arts". thevrm@comcast.net

DUNN, Deborah (Los) 1031 Bienveneda Ave, Pacific Palisades CA 90272 **P-in-c S Ptr's Par Santa Maria CA 2007-** B Angleton TX 8/10/1951 d John Wallace Dunn & Ella Lee. BFA U of Texas 1976; California St U 1987; ETSBH 1988; MDiv GTS 1991. D 6/15/1991 P 1/1/1992 Bp Frederick Houk Borsch. m 1/1/2001 Michael Ray Cunningham c 2. Vic S Thos' Mssn Hacienda Heights CA 1999-2007; The Par Of S Matt Pacific Palisades CA 1995-1999; Dio Los Angeles Los Angeles CA 1993-1995; Asst S Cross By-The-Sea Ch Hermosa Bch CA 1992-1993; S Fran' Par Palos Verdes Estates CA 1991-1992. revdunn@aol.com

DUNN III, D(ouglas) (SVa) 2000 Huguenot Trl, Powhatan VA 23139 **Gr Epis Ch Hinsdale IL 2010-** B Norfolk VA 3/31/1951 s Douglas Donald Dunn & Nira Lee. UTS Richmond VA; U Sydney TS 1972; BS Oklahoma St U 1974; Med Coll of Virginia 1976; S Geo's Coll Jerusalem IL 1977; MDiv VTS 1978; S Jn Coll GB 1986. D 5/25/1978 P 11/1/1978 Bp C(laude) Charles Vache. m 12/27/1989 Mary Ann Slater. Int S Lk's Ch Powhatan VA 1998-1999; Int S Mart's Epis Ch Henrico VA 1997; Int S Mk's Ch Richmond VA 1995-1997; Int S Barn Epis Ch Richmond VA 1994-1995; S Paul's Ch Petersburg VA 1992-1994; Int The Fork Ch Doswell VA 1992; Int S Lk's Ch Blackstone VA 1990-1991; Int Ch Of The Gd Shpd Richmond VA 1989-1990; Int Gr Ch Yorktown Yorktown VA 1988-1989; S Jn's Ch Suffolk VA 1987-1988; R Trin Epis Ch Beaver PA 1982-1983; All SS Ch Richmond VA 1979-1982; D Chr Ch Amelia Crt Hse VA 1978-1979; D Emm Epis Ch Powhatan VA 1978-1979; Pac Cure Par Cartersville VA 1978-1979; D S Jas Ch Cartersville VA 1978-1979. Societas Liturgica. Woods Fell VTS 1985. dddunniii@verizon.net

DUNN, Douglas Robert (Colo) 1270 Poplar St, Denver CO 80220 **R S Lk's Ch Denver CO 1993-** B Sioux Falls SD 8/14/1953 s Robert William Dunn & Shirley Rose. BS So Dakota St U 1979; MDiv Nash 1984; DMin SWTS 2001. D 5/31/1984 Bp Conrad Gesner P 11/30/1984 Bp Craig Barry Anderson. m 8/11/1979 Janet Beecher c 3. Reg Mssnr Dio Colorado Denver CO 2005-2009; S Dav Of Wales Ch New Berlin WI 1985-1993; Vic Ch Of The Incarn Greg SD 1984-1985; Supvsr Mnstry Dvlpmt Prog Dio So Dakota Sioux Falls SD 1984-1985; Educ Coordntr S Paul's Ch Milwaukee WI 1983-1984. doug@lukeonline.org

DUNN, Frank (WA) St Stephen and the Incarnation Parish, 1525 Newton St NW, Washington DC 20010 **Sr P Ch Of S Steph And The Incarn Washington DC 2010-** B Conway, SC 5/30/1945 s Otis Gasque Dunn & Dora Theresa. BA Randolph-Macon Coll 1967; BD PrTS 1970; GTS 1971. D 6/4/1971 P 12/1/1971 Bp William Henry Marmion. c 2. R S Jn's Ch Lynchburg VA 1992-2004; R Trin Ch Newtown CT 1979-1992; R S Andr's Epis Ch Charlotte NC 1975-1979; Cur S Mart's Epis Ch Charlotte NC 1971-1974. Auth, "Bldg Faith In Families," Morehouse, 1986. ioprete@verizon.net

DUNN, G(eorge) Mervyn (Ga) 8 Woodbridge Crescent, Kanata ON K2M 2N6 Canada B Belfast Northern Ireland 2/22/1941 s George Dunn & Alice. LTh Ch of Ireland Theol Coll 1973. Trans from Church Of England 2/1/1998 as Priest Bp Edward Lloyd Salmon Jr. m 2/1/1964 Margaret Jennifer Fitzroy Cairns c 3. Assoc R Chr Ch Frederica St Simons Island GA 2007-2010; Asst R Ch Of The Ascen Knoxville TN 2001-2006; Vic S Barn Ch Dillon SC 1998-2001. jenmerv64@yahoo.com

DUNN, Matilda Eleeen Greene (ETenn) 7013 Rocky Trl, Chattanooga TN 37421 B Greenville LR 6/13/1952 d Judson H Greene & Rachel R. BA Bloomfield Coll 1974; MS Sthrn Illinois U 1976; MDiv STUSo 1994. D 8/6/1994 Bp Bertram Nelson Herlong P 5/1/1995 Bp Robert Gould Tharp. m 1/30/1970 Daniel Elwood Dunn. Dio E Tennessee Knoxville TN 2001-2005; Epis. Comm. Of Se Tennessee Signal Mtn TN 1998-2001; Gr Ch Chattanooga TN 1996-1998; Assoc S Ptr's Ch Chattanooga TN 1995-1996. Cmnty Cross Nails; Cmnty Of S Mary; EWHP; Eshme; UBE.

DUNN, Patrick Hall (Miss) 4030 Perch Point Dr, Mobile AL 36605 B Florence AL 4/4/1938 s Julius Ethelbert Dunn & Emma Margaret. BA U of Alabama 1960; BD VTS 1968. D 6/14/1968 P 6/1/1969 Bp George Mosley Murray. m 7/14/1963 Phyllis Warren c 2. Int S Paul's Epis Ch Daphne AL 2008; Int S Jas Ch Fairhope AL 1999-2002; Par Of The Medtr-Redeem McComb MS 1985-1993; R S Andr's Ch Mobile AL 1969-1984; Vic H Cross Trussville AL 1968-1969. "Mullet -Mugill Cephalus Manuscript," Self Pub, 2000. phylsdunn@aol.com

DUNN, Prentiss Carroll (La) No address on file. B Bastrop LA 11/22/1944 s Prentiss Franklin Dunn & Bennie Louise. BA Baylor U 1967; Acad Mus & Dramatic Arts Vienna At 1972; MA Indiana U 1973. D 6/6/1982 P 12/1/1983 Bp James Barrow Brown. Trin Epis Ch Baton Rouge LA 1983-1984; Trin Ch New Orleans LA 1982-1983. 631-287-4190

DUNN, Robert Ellis (Oly) Po Box 1377, Granite Falls WA 98252 B Bloomington IL 4/19/1938 s William Ellis Dunn & Lillie Jane. Dplma Burnley Sch of Art 1960; BTh Vancouver TS 1973. D 7/17/1973 P 7/10/1974 Bp Ivol I Curtis. m 1/21/1959 Gaye M Gates c 4. Asst S Phil Ch Marysville WA 2002-2007; Vic Ch Of Our Sav Monroe WA 1997-1998; R S Steph's Epis Ch Spokane WA 1991-1997; R S Fran' Par Palos Verdes Estates CA 1988-1991; R S Jn's Ch Kirkland WA 1978-1988; R Ch Of The H Trin Hoquiam WA 1975-1978; R H Trin Ch Seattle WA 1975-1978; Vic S Christophers Epis Ch Westport WA 1975-1978; Cur Trin Epis Ch Everett WA 1973-1975. bob@bobdunnartist.com

DUNN, Sharon Kay Estey (Nev) 3500 San Mateo Ave, Reno NV 89509 **P S Steph's Epis Ch Reno NV 1995-** B Bartlesville OK 2/20/1937 d Clarence Leroy Estey & Irma Jean. BA U of Kansas 1959; MA Stan 1963; U of Arizona 1979; CDSP 1993. D 8/14/1994 P 2/17/1995 Bp Stewart Clark Zabriskie. m 9/6/1959 Peter Graves Dunn. Edtr Dio Nevada Las Vegas NV 1992-1995. Auth, "Pryr," *Race And Pryr*, Morehouse, 2003; Auth, "Poem And Pryr," *Wmn Uncommon Pryr*, Morehouse, 2000. Ord Of S Lk 1986. revmum@gbis.com

DUNN, Virginia Davis (CPa) 5 Redbud Dr, Mechanicsburg PA 17050 **Died 5/26/2010** B Phoenixville PA 7/28/1923 d Robert Stanley Davis & Jennie. RN Bryn Mawr Hosp Sch of Nrsng 1944; BS Mssh Coll 1972. D 3/25/2007 Bp Nathan Dwight Baxter. c 3. sailpa@aol.com

DUNN, William Edward (Los) 1803 Highland Hollow Dr # 559, Conroe TX 77304 **S Steph's Par Beaumont CA 2010-** B Freeport TX 8/11/1957 s John Wallace Dunn & Ella Lee. BA Steph F. Austin St U 1978; SW Texas St U San Marcos 1987; MDiv Epis TS of The SW 1998. D 6/20/1998 Bp Claude Edward Payne P 6/22/1999 Bp Leopoldo Jesus Alard. m 2/1/1991 Sharron H Hodde c 4. S Mich's Epis Ch Riverside CA 2009-2010; Chr The King Epis Ch Humble TX 2001-2005; Asst S Jas The Apos Epis Ch Conroe TX 1998-2001.

DUNNAM, Thomas Mark (Eur) Via Bernardo Rucellai 9, Firenze 50123 Italy **S Jas Epis Ch Firenze IA IT 2009-** B Mobile AL 11/17/1946 s Ernest Hays Dunnam & Kitty Williams. BA Birmingham-Sthrn Coll 1969; MDiv GTS 1972. D 6/11/1972 P 4/1/1973 Bp John M Allin. m 1/3/1981 Emily Kling c 1. Dioc Coordntr Dio Cntrl Gulf Coast Pensacola FL 1987-2009; S Mk's For The Deaf Mobile AL 1982-1987; R Ch Of The Gd Shpd Mobile AL 1981-1987; Cur S Andr's Epis Ch New Orleans LA 1973-1976; Dio Mississippi Jackson MS 1972-1973; Cur S Jn's Epis Ch Pascagoula MS 1972-1973. RECTOR@STJAMES.IT

DUNNAN, Donald Stuart (Md) Saint James School, Saint James MD 21781 **S Jas Sch St Jas MD 1992-** B Washington DC 3/3/1959 s Weaver White

Dunnan & Diana Barrett. BA/MA Harv 1981; BA Oxf 1985; Cert GTS 1986; MA Oxf 1990; PhD Oxf 1991. D 6/21/1986 P 1/1/1987 Bp Oliver Bailey Garver Jr. Harvard-Westlake Sch N Hollywood CA 1986-1987. dsdunnan@stjames.edu

DUNNAVANT, Charles Randall (Tenn) 817 Stonebrook Blvd, Nolensville TN 37135 **R Ch Of The Gd Shpd Brentwood TN 1998-** B Pulaski TN 7/8/1953 s Charles Mahlon Dunnavant & Bettye Jim. BS Middle Tennessee St U 1985; MDiv STUSo 1988. D 6/25/1988 P 1/21/1989 Bp George Lazenby Reynolds Jr. m 2/14/1976 Lannette I Ikard c 1. Vic Dio Tennessee Nashville TN 1995-1997; R S Mary Magd Ch Fayetteville TN 1992-1995; D-in-Trng S Mary Magd Ch Fayetteville TN 1988-1989. Citizen of Year 94 Natl Grand Elks Lodge 1994; Silver Beaver Awd for Distinguished Serv BSA 1993. crdunnavant@comcast.net

D

DUNNETT, Walter McGregor (Chi) 2127 Hallmark Ct, Wheaton IL 60187 **Asstg P S Mk's Epis Ch Glen Ellyn IL 1998-** B Tayport Scotland GB 7/5/1924 s Daniel McDougall Dunnett & Jemima Kinnaird. BA Wheaton Coll 1949; MA Wheaton Coll 1950; BD Wheaton Coll 1953; PhD Case Wstrn Reserve U 1967; STM Luther TS 1980; DWS Inst for Wrshp Stds Orange Pk FL 2004. D 6/24/1991 Bp Robert Marshall Anderson P 1/22/1992 Bp Sanford Zangwill Kaye Hampton. m 7/8/1944 Dolores R Eddy c 2. P Mssh Mssh Epis Ch S Paul MN 1992-1997. Auth, "NT Survey," *NT Survey*, Eerdmans, 1985; Auth, "The Interp of H Scripture," *The Interp of H Scripture*, Thos Nelson, 1984; Auth, "The Bk of Acts," *The Bk of Acts*, Baker, 1981; Auth, "Revelation," *Revelation: God's Final Word to Man*, Meridian, 1967; Auth, "NT Survey," *NT Survey*, E.T.T.A., 1963; Auth, "An Outline of N.T. Survey," *An Outline of NT Survey*, Moody Press, 1960. Evang Theol Soc, Pres 1987. Pi Gamma Mu Wheaton Coll 1948. w.mcgregor_d@juno.com

DUNNING, David (Oly) 4223 Ne 33rd St, Seattle WA 98105 B Cleveland OH 3/15/1936 s Frank Dunning & Marie. BS OH SU 1958; MDiv Bex 1964; MA GW 1972; PhD Fielding Inst 1982. D 6/13/1964 P 12/1/1964 Bp Roger W Blanchard. m 5/15/1959 Donna George. R S Steph's Epis Ch Seattle WA 1972-1980; R Chr Ch Capitol Hill Washington DC 1968-1972; Asst Trin Ch Columbus OH 1964-1968. Auth, "Study Of Effective Epis Priests". david@effectiveleader.com

DUNNING, Jane Romeyn (WMass) 44 Main St, Shelburne Falls MA 01370 B Detroit MI 8/12/1938 d Hendrik Romeyn & Margery. BA Manhattanville Coll 1987; MDiv GTS 1991. D 6/8/1991 P 12/14/1991 Bp Richard Frank Grein. m 2/13/1960 Harry Martin Dunning c 2. Vic S Jn's Ch Ashfield MA 2002-2006; S Mk's Ch Adams MA 2000-2006; Vic S Helena's Epis Ch Lenox MA 1993-2000; Cur S Jn's Ch Larchmont NY 1991-1993. vicarjane@comcast.net

DUNNING, William Melbourne (Md) 1612 Trebor Ct, Lutherville MD 21093 B Worcester MA 12/6/1936 s Elmer Carlton Dunning & Marion Villna. BA Bos 1959; MDiv GTS 1962. D 6/22/1962 Bp Robert McConnell Hatch P 12/22/1962 Bp Leland Stark. m 8/6/1965 Margaret S Searing. Int R S Thos Epis Ch Towson MD 2008-2011; P-in-c Ch Of S Marks On The Hill Pikesville MD 2004-2007; Int Imm Ch Highlands Wilmington DE 2002-2004; Int S Jas' Epis Ch Downingtown PA 2001-2002; Int S Fran-In-The-Fields Malvern PA 1999-2001; Int The Ch Of The H Trin W Chester PA 1998-1999; R S Mich And All Ang Ch Baltimore MD 1988-1998; R Trin Epis Ch Haverhill MA 1981-1988; R Chr Ch Waterbury CT 1975-1981; Asst S Thos Epis Ch Rochester NY 1966-1971; Vic Gr Ch Oxford MA 1964-1966; Cur S Jn's Ch Dover NJ 1962-1964. dunn36@verizon.net

DUNNINGTON, Michael Gerard (Mo) 1620 Forestview Ridge Ln, Ballwin MO 63021 **P-in-c All SS Ch S Louis MO 2010-** B Saint Louis MO 1/14/1946 s Joseph Anthony Dunnington & Olive Minette. BA S Louis U 1969; MA S Louis U 1970; MBA Sthrn Illinois U 1975; MDiv TS 1996. D 6/29/1996 P 6/1/1997 Bp Robert Carroll Johnson Jr. m 8/3/2000 Leslie Holdsworth c 2. P-in-c Ch Of The Ascen S Louis MO 2004-2007; R The Ch Of The H Innoc Henderson NC 1998-1999; Asst Ch Of The H Comf Burlington NC 1996-1998. Cath Fllshp of the Epis Ch 1993-1997. cvlwrnut@sbcglobal.net

DUNPHY, Martha-Jane (NY) 190 Pinewood Rd Apt 78, Hartsdale NY 10530 **D Gr Ch White Plains NY 1997-; D Santa Rosa Mssn at Gr Ch White Plains NY 1997-** B White Plains NY 10/11/1945 d William E Dunphy & Jane Adelaide. SUNY; The Coll of Westchester 1968. D 4/26/1997 Bp Richard Frank Grein. NAAD.

DUNST, Earl Walter (Mil) 8121 N Seneca Rd, Milwaukee WI 53217 B Milwaukee WI 11/29/1915 s Albert Otto Dunst & Marie Thelkla. D 12/22/1956 Bp Donald H V Hallock. m 10/19/1946 Jane Lango c 3. Asst S Paul's Ch Milwaukee WI 1956-1996.

DUPLANTIER, David Allard (La) 2037 South Carrollton Avenue, New Orleans LA 70118 **Dn Chr Ch Cathd New Orleans LA 2002-** B Louisville KY 3/15/1961 s Donald Allard duPlantier & Lucy Stites. BA Mia 1983; MDiv GTS 1993. D 6/26/1993 P 9/21/1994 Bp Herbert Thompson Jr. c 2. Asst The Ch of the Redeem Cincinnati OH 1997-2002; R Gr Ch Pomeroy OH 1994-1997; Cur Ch Of The Gd Shpd Athens OH 1993-1994. CT (assoc) 1995; Soc of the Cincinnati (Virginia) 2011. Distinguished Alum Gnrl Sem 2009. cccdean@aol.com

DUPLESSIE, Thomas Frederick (Me) 27 Butters Rd, Exeter ME 04435 **Dioc Coun Mem Dio Maine Portland ME 2002-** B Waterville ME 5/30/1942 s Emile Phillip Duplessie & Christine Andelina. AA Thos Jr Coll 1963; BA U of Maine 1971; MS SUNY 1993; Cert Bangor TS 2002. D 6/20/2004 Bp Chilton Abbie Richardson Knudsen. c 2. NADD 2004. duplessietom@hotmail.com

DUPREE, Charles T (Ind) 111 S. Grant St., Bloomington IN 47408 **R Trin Epis Ch Bloomington IN 2008-** B Tarboro NC 12/21/1969 s Joseph Lee Dupree & Sara. BFA E Carolina U 1993; MDiv VTS 1999. D 6/12/1999 P 5/2/2000 Bp Clifton Daniel III. m 6/29/2004 Matthew Cole. S Greg's Epis Ch Woodstock NY 2004-2008; Assoc R S Paul's Epis Ch Greenville NC 1999-2004. ctdupree@trinitybloomington.org

DUPREE, H(ugh) Douglas (Ga) Balliol College, Oxford OX1 3BJ Great Britain (UK) B Dothan AL 1/25/1950 s Hubert O Dupree & Ann. BA U So 1972; MDiv VTS 1975; MA Oxf 1986; PhD Oxf 1988. D 6/8/1975 Bp Frank Stanley Cerveny P 2/1/1976 Bp (George) Paul Reeves. Assoc S Jn's Ch Savannah GA 1975-1980. Hon Cur S Mich's Ch/Oxford Oxford Engl 1980. douglas.dupree@balliol.ox.ac.uk

DUPREY, David Luke (Wyo) 1 S Tschirgi St, Sheridan WY 82801 **Off Of Bsh For ArmdF New York NY 2008-** B Norwich CT 9/30/1962 s Richard Henry Duprey & Mary Ann. Wright St U 1980; OH SU 1983; BD Capital U 1985; MDiv TESM 1988. D 6/24/1988 P 1/6/1999 Bp Bob Gordon Jones. c 3. R S Ptr's Epis Ch Sheridan WY 1992-2008; St Jn the Bapt Epis Ch Big Piney WY 1988-1992. "Full of Gr and Truth," *self Pub*, self Pub, 1998. dld@fiberpipe.net

DU PRIEST, Travis Talmadge (Mil) 508 DeKoven, Racine WI 53403 B Richmond VA 8/15/1944 s Travis Talmadge Du Priest & Mildred Abbitt. BA U Rich 1966; PhD U of Kentucky 1972; no degree sought St. Chad's Coll, U of Durham 1973; MTS Harvard DS 1974; no degree sought U of Cambridge 1982. D 6/1/1974 P 6/16/1975 Bp Addison Hosea. m 9/1/1972 Mabel B Benson c 2. Exec Dir Dekoven Fndt for Ch Wk Racine WI 1991-2006; Asstg P S Lk's Ch Racine WI 1988-1997. Auth, "To Hear Celestial Harmonies: Jas DeKoven and The DeKoven Cntr," *Co-edited*, Foreward Mvmt Pub, 2002; Ed, "Poems by Kath Philips," *Intro*, Schlr's Facsimiles and Reprints, 1988; Auth, "Measure & Off of Friendship by Jeremy Taylor," *Intro*, Schlr's Facsimiles and Reprints, 1986; "numerous poems and arts," TLC, ATR, and others; "A Heart for the Future," *Chapt*, Ch Pub; Ed, "A New Conversation," *Chapt*, Ch Pub; Co-Ed, "Engaging the Sprt," *Chapt*, Ch Pub; "Sum Storm on the Jas," *Long Poem*, Telstar Pub; "Noon at Smyrna," *Poetry Chapbook*, Can; "Soapstone Wall," *Poetry Chapbook*, Wolfsong Pub. Cmnty of S Mary, P Assoc. 1977; Natl Huguenot Soc, Hon. Pres. Gnrl 1985; Venerable Ord of S Jn 1995. Distinguished Tchr Year Awd Carthage Coll 1980; Fell Danforth 1977; Fell Rockerfeller 1971; Fell NDEA 1967; Vstng Fell Cntr for Renaissance & Reformation Stds, Victoria Coll,; Best Paper at Conf Chrsnty & Lit: SE Reg; Fell Coll of Preachers; Moon Fell Dio Milwaukee Fllshp; Mid-W Fac Fllshp Univ. of Chicago; Allin Fllshp U So; Resrch Fell Wm. A. Clark Libr, UCLA. tdupriest@wi.rr.com

✠ DUQUE-GOMEZ, Rt Rev Francisco Jose (Colom) Calle 122-A #1211, Bogota Colombia **Bp Of Colombia Dio Colombia Bogota CO 2002-; Bp of Colombia Iglesia Epis En Colombia 1988-** B 9/17/1950 s Jose Maria Duque & Oliva. Cert ETSC; JD Universidad Libre De Colombia; Unv Javeriana. D 12/8/1988 P 12/1/1991 Bp Bernardo Merino-Botero Con 7/14/2001 for Colom. m 12/16/1983 Blanca Lucia Echeverry.

✠ DURACIN, Rt Rev Jean Zache (Hai) Box 1309, Port-Au-Prince Haiti **Bp of Haiti Dio Haiti Ft Lauderdale FL 1977-** B 2/20/1947 s Montas Duracin & Camenise. BD Lycee A Petion; Sem Epis Ch Hai 1977. D 9/18/1977 P 5/1/1978 Bp Luc Anatole Jacques Garnier Con 6/2/1993 for Hai. m 12/18/1979 Marie Edithe Louis-Jean. epihaiti@globelsud.net

DURAIKANNU, Yesupathan (Colo) 15 Walnut St, Walden NY 12586 **Ch Of The Ascen Salida CO 2007-; P-in-c S Andr's Ch Walden NY 2002-** B Eachambadi IN 7/25/1958 s S. Duraikannu & A. BD Bp's Theol Coll, Calcutta; BTh So India Biblic Sem Bangarpet Ks IN; DMin STUSo 2003. Trans from Church of South India 3/14/2001 Bp Bertram Nelson Herlong. m 12/27/1994 Suchita Mir c 2. Mem -Fin Com Dio New York New York City NY 2004-2006; P-in-c St Fran of Assisi Montgomery NY 2002-2006; Asst R S Ptr's Ch Columbia TN 2001-2002. fryesu25@yahoo.com

DURAND, Sally Elaine (Az) 7813 N. Via De La Luna, Scottsdale AZ 85258 **Hisp Mnstrs Dio Arizona Phoenix AZ 2009-; D Trin Cathd Phoenix AZ 2009-; Asst Iglesia Epis De San Pablo Phoenix AZ 2007-** B Santa Fe NM 4/29/1953 d Harvey Stowe Durand & Gratia Antonia. BA New Mex St U. 1975; MA U of San Diego 1992; CTh ETSBH 2000. D 6/9/2001 Bp Gethin Benwil Hughes. Asst S Lk's Ch San Diego CA 2004-2007; S Lk's Ch San Diego CA 2002-2004; S Eliz's Epis Ch San Diego CA 2001-2008; Dio San Diego San Diego CA 2001-2005. Soc of S Jn the Evang (Assoc) 1996. sallydurand@cox.net

DURANT, Jack Davis (NC) 3001 Old Orchard Rd, Raleigh NC 27607 B Birmingham AL 9/7/1930 s Kyle Hobson Durant & Benalie. BA Maryville Coll

1953; MA U of Tennessee 1955; PhD U of Tennessee 1963. D 4/29/1995 Bp Huntington Williams Jr. c 2. deaconjack@msn.com

DURANT, Jennifer Ronan (NC) 1165 Rio Rd E, Charlottesville VA 22901 **Asst Ch Of Our Sav Charlottesville VA 2011-** B Boston MA 8/1/1968 d Donald Abell Ronan & Linda Hollis. BBA U of Masschusetts 1990; MDiv VTS 2011. D 6/18/2011 Bp Michael Bruce Curry. m 6/30/1990 Matthew Durant c 2. durrant.jennifer@gmail.com

D'URBANO, Faith Jeanne (Be) 340 W. Orange Street, Lancaster PA 17603 B Bryn Mawr PA 12/17/1950 d John Robert Felice & Susanne Florence. BA W Chester St Coll 1971; MA Villanova U 1976; MDiv GTS 2000. D 4/29/2000 P 3/26/2001 Bp Paul Victor Marshall. c 2. Asst S Gabr's Ch Douglassville PA 2000-2005. faith_d_urbano@yahoo.com

DURE, Lucy Ann Craig (Nwk) 46 Montrose Ave, Verona NJ 07044 **R Ch Of The H Sprt Verona NJ 2000-** B Fort Sill OK 12/1/1954 d Richard Stirling Craig & Mary Gay. BA Ford 1987; MDiv Ya Berk 1991. D 5/30/1998 Bp Jack Marston McKelvey P 12/5/1998 Bp John Palmer Croneberger. m 12/30/1989 Davis Oakford Dure. Asst S Lk's Epis Ch Montclair NJ 1998-2000. ladure@aol.com

DURGIN, Ralph Thayer (Ct) 250 Old Field Ln # 823, Eastham MA 02642 B Weymouth MA 7/4/1928 s Chester Eugene Durgin & Emma Louise. BA Bos 1952; Cert Merc TS 1973. D 6/17/1972 P 12/1/1972 Bp Jonathan Goodhue Sherman. m 4/21/1947 Kathleen Mahoney. Int Ch Of The Ascen Fall River MA 2000-2002; R S Jas' Ch New Haven CT 1980-1994; S Jas Ch Old Town ME 1974-1980; S Pat's Ch Brewer ME 1974-1980; Asst S Bon Epis Ch Lindenhurst NY 1972-1974. Int Mnstry Ntwk 1998. rkdurg@gis.net

DURHAM, Eugenia M (Az) 1275 S Heritage Pl, Safford AZ 85546 B Little Rock AR 3/14/1939 d Paul Saunders Miller & Marjorie Jane. BA Maryville Coll 1961; MA Luther TS 1990; CAS SWTS 1993; DMin SWTS 2006. D 6/24/1993 Bp Robert Marshall Anderson P 1/6/1994 Bp Sanford Zangwill Kaye Hampton. c 2. Dioc Coun Dio Arizona Phoenix AZ 1996-1999; Dio Arizona Phoenix AZ 1993-2011; P Mssnr All SS Epis Ch Safford AZ 1993-1995; S Matt's Ch St Paul MN 1993-1995; P Mssnr SS Phil And Jas Morenci AZ 1993-1995. emdurham@cableone.net

DURHAM, Martha Hemenway (Chi) St Mary's Episcopal Church, 306 S Prospect Ave, Park Ridge IL 60068 **D S Mary's Ch Pk Ridge IL 2007-** B Westfield NY 12/25/1955 d Richard Ernest Hemenway & Marjorie A. BSS Cornell Coll 1978; Sch for Deacons Dio Chicago 2007. D 1/19/2008 Bp Victor Alfonso Scantlebury. m 5/5/1984 Thomas Durham c 2. Dir Rel Educ S Mary's Ch Pk Ridge IL 1993-1996. marthasmessages@comcast.net

DURKEE II, Frank Leo (WA) 130 Castle Rock Rd Unit 119, Sedona AZ 86351 **Died 3/25/2011** B Ouray CO 10/19/1932 s Frank Leo Kurkee & Lillian Maxfiels. BA Pr 1954; BD VTS 1962. D 6/16/1962 P 12/22/1962 Bp William Foreman Creighton. durks2@yahoo.com

DURKEE, Robert Melvin (Mass) 10 Mountain Laurels Dr Apt 302, Nashua NH 03062 B Cambridge MA 11/8/1926 s Melvin R Durkee & Elizabeth. BA Tufts U 1950; STB Bos 1955; STM Bos 1957; EDS 1964; Command and Gnrl Stff Coll 1975; DD Lon 1979. D 5/7/1964 P 9/1/1964 Bp John Melville Burgess. m 1/5/2008 Elaine F Durkee. Gr Epis Ch Medford MA 1964-1989. Auth, "Changing Modes of Chapl"; Auth, "On Conscientious Participants". Mltry Chapl Assn.

DURNING, Michael Peter (SwFla) 12002 Summer Meadow Dr, Bradenton FL 34202 **Cn to the Ordnry Dio SW Florida Sarasota FL 2001-; Cn Dio SW Florida Sarasota FL 1997-; Cong Dvlpmt Dio SW Florida Sarasota FL 1997-** B Philadelphia PA 5/5/1951 s Francis Peter Durning & Catherine Theresa. BFA U of the Arts Philadelphia PA 1973; MDiv GTS 1987. D 6/11/1988 Bp Allen Lyman Bartlett Jr P 5/27/1989 Bp Frank Stanley Cerveny. m 11/17/1973 Bonnie Jean MacDonald c 3. S Mk's Ch Marco Island FL 1992-1997; Asst S Jn's Ch Naples FL 1988-1992; S Fran-In-The-Fields Malvern PA 1987-1988. CODE 1997. mdurning@aol.com

DURREN, Paula Ellen (WMich) 19 S Jameson St, New Buffalo MI 49117 **Ch Of The Medtr Harbert MI 2002-** B Columbus IN 3/11/1953 d Charles Ronald Bassett & Marjorie Marie. BSW Geo Wms of Aurora U 1976; MS Indiana U 1985; MDiv SWTS 2002. D 5/26/2002 Bp Edward Lewis Lee Jr P 12/14/2002 Bp Robert R Gepert. m 1/6/1973 Michael Jerry Durren c 2.

DURST, Lester Earle (CGC) 5409 Twin Creeks Dr, Valrico FL 33596 **Asst S Mary's Par Tampa FL 2010-** B Sarasota FL 1/7/1951 s Marion Earle Durst & Mildred. BA Stetson U 1973; JD U of Florida 1976; MDiv VTS 1990. D 6/30/1990 P 1/18/1991 Bp Rogers Sanders Harris. m 6/9/1973 Carolyn Fleischman c 2. R S Chris's Ch Pensacola FL 2002-2008; R S Ptr's Ch Plant City FL 1995-2002; Asst St Johns Epis Ch Tampa FL 1993-1995; Asst Ch Of The Redeem Sarasota FL 1990-1992. Contrib, *Gd News Daily*. Chapl Ord of S Lk 1992. lester.durst@gmail.com

DURST, Ted E (Chi) 4900 N Marine Dr Apt 411, Chicago IL 60640 **Asstg Epis Ch Of The Atone Chicago IL 2011-** B Brady TX 4/19/1952 s Clinton Durst & Anna Grace. BBA Angelo St U 1974; MDiv SWTS 1995. D 6/12/1995 Bp James Edward Folts P 12/16/1995 Bp Frank Tracy Griswold III. m 7/19/2000 Mark D Britt c 1. P-in-c The Ch Of The H Innoc Hoffman Schaumburg IL 2004-2006; R Trin Epis Ch Houghton MI 2001-2004; Asstg S Ptr's Epis Ch Chicago IL 2000-2001; Assoc R Emm Epis Ch Rockford IL 1996-1997; Asst to Exec. Dir. Cathd Shltr Chicago IL 1995-1996. tedur@aol.com

DUTCHER, Katherine Grant (Okla) St Andrew's Episcopal Church, PO Box 1256, Lawton OK 73502 **D S Andr's Epis Ch Lawton OK 2007-** B Ft Arbuckle OK 2/28/1934 d Thomas Stephen Grant & Katie Belle. D 6/16/2007 Bp Robert Manning Moody. m 3/29/1956 Joe Blake Dutcher c 7. K22834@sbcglobal.net

DUTTON-GILLETT, Matthew Richard (Cal) 330 Ravenswood, Menlo Park CA 94025 **R Trin Par Menlo Pk CA 2009-** B Cleveland OH 6/27/1966 s Carl Robert Gillett & Marilyn Anne. BA MI SU 1987; MDiv EDS 1991. D 6/21/1991 Bp Henry Irving Mayson P 1/18/1992 Bp R(aymond) Stewart Wood Jr. m 9/2/1989 Katherine Sydney Dutton c 2. R S Eliz's Epis Ch Knoxville TN 1999-2009; R S Ptr's Epis Ch Sycamore IL 1995-1999; Assoc To R S Ptr's Epis Ch St Louis MO 1991-1995. "Homilies On A Gd Life," (Priv Pub), 2004. matthew@trinitymenlopark.org

DUVAL, Linda Marie (NY) 16 Boulder Ave, Kingston NY 12401 B Newburgh NY 7/5/1955 d Norman P Bouchard & Helen Rose. D 5/20/2000 Bp Richard Frank Grein. m 6/4/1977 Gary Joseph Duval.

DUVAL JR, Richard Henri (EpisSanJ) 813 Lassen View Dr, Lake Almanor CA 96137 B Buffalo NY 4/26/1930 s Richard Henri Duval & Isobel Irene. BA Claremont Coll 1951; MDiv CDSP 1956. D 6/25/1956 Bp Francis E I Bloy P 2/26/1957 Bp Donald J Campbell. m 12/20/1952 Bernice A Sprau c 7. Int S Matt's Ch San Andreas CA 1999-2001; R S Mich The Archangel Par El Segundo CA 1972-1992; Vic All SS Epis Ch Brawley CA 1966-1972; Vic S Paul's Par Lancaster CA 1957-1966; Cur S Mk's Par Altadena CA 1956-1957.

DUVAL, Robert Joseph (Ct) 3121 St. Stephens Ln., Whitehall PA 18052 B Bristol CT 3/13/1939 s Joseph Antonio Duval & Juliette Aurore. BA Trin Hartford CT 1960; MDiv STUSo 1986. D 6/14/1986 Bp Arthur Edward Walmsley P 12/20/1986 Bp Clarence Nicholas Coleridge. m 5/2/1959 Gloria Jean Coe c 2. R S Ptr's Epis Ch Hebron CT 1997-2003; R Chr Ch Trumbull CT 1986-1997. bobduval@me.com

✠ **DUVALL, Rt Rev Charles Farmer** (CGC) 104 Wildeoak Trl, Columbia SC 29223 **Ret Bp Of Cntrl Gulf Coast Dio Cntrl Gulf Coast Pensacola FL 2001-** B Bennettsville SC 11/18/1935 s Henry Powe Duvall & Elizabeth Phoebe. BA Cit 1957; MDiv VTS 1960. D 6/18/1960 Bp Albert S Thomas P 3/24/1961 Bp Gray Temple Con 4/11/1981 for CGC. m 6/2/1957 Nancy Rice c 3. Bd Rgnts The TS at The U So Sewanee TN 1995-2001; Bp Dio Cntrl Gulf Coast Pensacola FL 1981-2001; R Ch Of The Adv Spartanburg SC 1977-1980; R H Trin Epis Ch Fayetteville NC 1970-1977; Dep Gc Dio So Carolina Charleston SC 1967-1969; Chair, Dept. of CE Dio So Carolina Charleston SC 1964-1967; R S Jas Ch Charleston SC 1962-1970. EvangES. Hon Doctor TS, U fo the So 1986; Hon Doctor VTS 1982. cfdbish8101@aol.com

DUVALL, Robert Welsh (Va) 704 Holloway Circle N, North Myrtle Beach SC 29582 **S Jn's Ch Sewaren NJ 1994-** B Cheraw SC 1/21/1928 s Gideon Walker Duvall & Mary IsaBelle. BS Clemson U 1951; MDiv TS, Univ of the So 1962. D 7/11/1962 Bp Clarence Alfred Cole P 6/24/1963 Bp Robert E Gribbin. m 9/29/1948 Ann Trively c 3. Asst Trin Cathd Columbia SC 1964-1967; Vic S Ptr's Ch Great Falls SC 1963-1964; Vic S Steph's Epis Ch Ridgeway SC 1963-1964. EPF 2003. rduvall@alumni.sewanee.edu

DUVALL, Theodore W (SC) 1642 William Hapton Way, Mt. Pleasant SC 29466 **R Chr Epis Ch Mt Pleasant SC 2011-** B Savannah GA 12/29/1961 s Charles Farmer Duvall & Ann. BA U NC 1983; MDiv VTS 1989. D 6/10/1989 P 5/19/1990 Bp William Arthur Beckham. m 9/15/1984 Katherine Dubose c 2. Chr Ch Greenville SC 2005-2011; R S Barth's Epis Ch Hartsville SC 1995-2005; Assoc S Aug Of Cbury Ch Augusta GA 1991-1995; Assoc Epis Ch Of The Redeem Greenville SC 1989-1991. tduvall@christch.org

DUVEAUX, Irnel (Hai) Box 1309, Port-Au-Prince Haiti B Cap Haitien HT 5/6/1961 s Marie Elizabeth. Montrouis TS 1987. D 6/12/1988 P 12/1/1988 Bp Luc Anatole Jacques Garnier. Dio Haiti Ft Lauderdale FL 1989-1998.

DUVERT, Pierre-Andre (LI) 331 Hawthorne St, Brooklyn NY 11225 **Ch Of The Resurr E Elmhurst NY 1999-** B 6/2/1964 s Andre B Duvert & Paunie. BA SUNY 1989; MDiv GTS 1992; STM GTS 1996. D 6/8/1991 P 12/1/1991 Bp Richard Frank Grein. m 4/25/1992 Elourdes Isidore c 3. S Gabr's Ch Brooklyn NY 1995-1999. paduvert@verizon.net

DWARF, Lindsey Craig (ND) PO Box 781, Fort Yates ND 58538 **Dio No Dakota Fargo ND 2006-; Asst S Lk's Ch Ft Yates ND 2003-** B Fort Yates ND 8/30/1962 D 6/12/2003 P 12/13/2003 Bp Andrew Hedtler Fairfield. m 7/1/2002 Kimberly Standing Crow c 4.

DWIGHT, Robert Bolman (SO) 115 W Monument Ave, #1201, Dayton OH 45402 **Chr Epis Ch Dayton OH 1971-** B Visalia CA 12/18/1935 s Herbert McGilvray Dwight & Marian Dewolfe. BA Stan 1958; BD 1962; MS U of Oregon 1969; PhD U of Oregon 1971. D 6/13/1962 P 12/19/1962 Bp James Walmsley Frederic Carman. m 12/29/1962 Rose Bowen c 2. Int Trin Epis Ch Troy OH 2002-2003; Int Trin Epis Ch Troy OH 1986-1987; P-in-c S Dav

Vandalia OH 1978-1981; R Ch Of The Resurr Eugene OR 1966-1968; Cur S Mary's Epis Ch Eugene OR 1962-1966. rdwight@woh.rr.com

D'WOLF JR, James Francis (Kan) 6976 Pintail Dr # 113, Fishers IN 46038 B Saint Louis MO 2/18/1927 s James Francis D'Wolf & Leone Louise. BA U of Missouri 1950; STB ETS, Cambridge MA 1955. D 6/18/1955 P 12/18/1955 Bp Arthur C Lichtenberger. m 4/18/1958 Jean Lee Sampson c 3. Assoc R S Mich & S Geo Clayton MO 1990-2005; P-in-c S Paul's Ch Palmyra MO 1989-1990; Int S Matt's Epis Cathd Laramie WY 1985-1986; Int S Steph's Ch Casper WY 1984-1985; R S Paul's Ch Manhattan KS 1971-1983; R Trin Epis Ch El Dorado KS 1963-1971; Vic S Lk and S Jn's Caruthersville MO 1955-1962. Auth, "Heav Food II," 1995; Auth, "Heav Food I," 1978.

DWYER, John F (NY) 1772 Church St Nw, Washington DC 20036 **Mem, Personl Com Dio Minnesota Minneapolis MN 2011-; R S Chris's Epis Ch Roseville MN 2011-** B Mt Vernon NY 8/23/1960 s James E Dwyer & Mary G. BA Fairfield U 1982; JD St Jn's Univ Sch Of Law 1986; MDiv VTS 2007. D 3/10/2007 P 9/15/2007 Bp Mark Sean Sisk. P-in-c S Anne's Ch Damascus MD 2011; Mem, Fin Com Dio Washington Washington DC 2008-2011; Asst S Thos' Par Washington DC 2007-2010. Auth, "Those 7 References: A study of the 7 References to Homosexuality in the Bible," Bk Surge, 2007. dwyerjohnf@gmail.com

DWYER, Martin James (Ida) 3 Park Pl, Garden Valley ID 83622 B South Bend IN 10/15/1926 s Martin James Dwyer & Martha Louise. BA Ripon Coll Ripon WI 1954; STM Ya Berk 1957; MA U of Nthrn Iowa 1972. D 6/29/1957 P 1/25/1958 Bp Conrad Gesner. m 6/21/1980 Rebecca Ann Copple c 1. Dn S Mich's Cathd Boise ID 1979-1988; R S Andr's Epis Ch Minneapolis MN 1973-1979; R Trin Epis Par Waterloo IA 1968-1973; R S Steph's Epis Ch Aurora CO 1964-1967; Cur Emm Epis Par Rapid City SD 1961-1964; P-in-c Geth Epis Ch Sisseton SD 1957-1961. bckjm@earthlink.net

DWYER, Michael William (NI) 12718 Marshall St, Crown Point IN 46307 B Chicago IL 3/22/1948 BA Loyola U 1972; MHA Gvnr St U 1979; MAPS Cath Theol Un 2011. D 9/2/2011 Bp Edward Stuart Little II. m 7/4/1996 Jane Ann Dwyer c 5. mdwyer207@aol.com

DWYER, Patricia Marie (Be) 711 S 83rd Way, Mesa AZ 85208 B Waterbury CT 10/13/1939 d George Smith McCormick & Kathleen Marie. BS Alverno Coll 1961; MA La Salle U 1983; DMin Estrn Bapt TS 1985; MA La Salle U 1985. D 4/17/2004 P 10/31/2004 Bp Paul Victor Marshall. c 2. R S Jos's Ch Pen Argyl PA 2006-2009; R S Mary's Epis Ch Wind Gap PA 2006-2009; supply P Trin Epis Ch Pottsville PA 2005-2006. revpdwyer@gmail.com

DWYER, Thomas Patrick Jonathan (CGC) 800 22nd St, Port St Joe FL 32456 **Cmsn on Fin Dio Cntrl Gulf Coast Pensacola FL 2011-; Dioc Disciplinary Bd Dio Cntrl Gulf Coast Pensacola FL 2011-; S Jas' Epis Ch Port S Joe FL 2009-** B Dorchester MA 1/16/1949 s Robert Patrick Dwyer & Barbara Ellen. BS Palm Bch Atlantic U 1998; MDiv VTS 2003. D 12/18/2003 Bp James Hamilton Ottley P 7/17/2004 Bp Leopold Frade. m 12/7/1968 Lynn Anne Sickels. Vic S Steph's Epis Ch Ridgeway SC 2004-2009; Epis Ch Of The Adv Palm City FL 2004. BSA 2010; Rotary Intl 2010. vetelover@gmail.com

DWYER, William Daniels (WMass) 936 Grayson Dr #118, Springfield MA 01119 B New York NY 4/28/1930 s William Joseph Dwyer & Clara Virginia. MDiv GTS 1955; Assoc Sem Dubuque IA 1977; EDS 1980; Cert Hartford Sem 1998. D 6/11/1955 P 12/18/1955 Bp Benjamin M Washburn. m 8/5/1961 Utako Shiraishi c 3. Assoc S Ptr's Ch Springfield MA 1997-2003; Hisp Mnstry Chr Ch Cathd Springfield MA 1992-1998; Mssnr S Paul's Ch Holyoke MA 1992-1995; Dio Wstrn Massachusetts Springfield MA 1981-1992; R S Ptr's Ch Springfield MA 1981-1992; S Steph's Epis Ch Boston MA 1972-1981; Cur Ch Of The Redeem Morristown NJ 1955-1956. Auth, "Chapt on S Steph's Ch, Boston," *Models of Metropltn Mnstry*, Broadman, 1979. Fllshp of the Way of the Cross 1988; Ord of H Cross 1983. Hon Cn Chr Ch Cathd Springfield MA 1986; Nash Fllshp Dio Massachusetts 1978. uandwdwyer@comcast.net

DYAKIW, Alexander Raymond (CPa) St John's Episc Ch, 120 W Lamb St, Bellefonte PA 16823 B New York City NY 3/29/1951 s Mykola Dyakiw & Anna. D 6/9/2007 Bp Nathan Dwight Baxter. m 11/25/1972 Ellen P Parmenter. deacon@comcast.net

DYCHE, Bradley Callaway (NY) 6 Old Post Road North, Croton on Hudson NY 10520 **R S Aug's Epis Ch Croton On Hudson NY 2006-** B Enid OK 2/17/1976 s Steven Lee Dyche & Kathie Louise. BA U of Oklahoma 1998; MDiv GTS 2002. D 6/29/2002 Bp Robert Manning Moody P 12/28/2002 Bp Catherine Scimeca Roskam. Cur S Jn's Ch Larchmont NY 2002-2006. Mnstry Fell The Fund For Theol Educ 1999. bdyche@bestweb.net

DYCKMAN, Edward Joseph (SC) 104 Line St, Charleston SC 29403 B Jersey City NJ 5/31/1947 s Warren Joseph Dyckman & Virginia Louise. Cert Dio SC D Sch; BS Prett Inst 1969; MA U of Maryland 1975. D 9/11/2010 Bp Mark Joseph Lawrence. m 7/5/1969 Lucy Trask. dyckman.edward@gmail.com

DYER, Alex (Ct) 51 Crown St, New Haven CT 06510 **S Paul And S Jas New Haven CT 2010-** B Kingsport TN 6/2/1979 s Charles Wayne Dyer & Carol Lindeman. MDiv GTS; BA Randolph-Macon Coll. D 6/15/2005 Bp James Louis Jelinek P 1/7/2006 Bp E(gbert) Don Taylor. m Ryan B DeLoach. Assoc Trin Ch On The Green New Haven CT 2007-2010; The Ch Of S Lk In The Fields New York NY 2006; Web Serv Spec Epis Ch Cntr New York NY 2005-2007; Epis Ch Cntr New York NY 2005-2006. ECom 2005-2007. ryandeloach@gmail.com

DYER, Edward John (Fla) 23 Kingslan Ct, Savannah GA 31419 B Wilmington DE 6/24/1927 s Frederick A Dyer & Ethel. BS U Of Delaware Newark 1952; MS U Of Delaware Newark 1954; BD VTS 1957; EdD Tem 1964. D 6/15/1957 P 5/1/1958 Bp John Brooke Mosley. m 6/19/1988 Vickie R Swicegood. S Mk's Ch Palatka FL 1987-1988; R The Epis Ch of The Redeem Jacksonville FL 1984-1987; Jacksonville Epis HS Jacksonville FL 1981-1984; Cn The Epis Cathd Of Our Merc Sav Faribault MN 1977-1981; Shattuck-S Mary's Sch Faribault MN 1974-1981; R Chr Ch Milford DE 1960-1966; Asst Cathd Ch Of S Jn Wilmington DE 1957-1960. Auth, "The Cost Of Educ Of A Clergyman"; Auth, "Priestar P & Chr Teachers"; Auth, "Cont Educ Of The Cler"; Auth, "Ch & Sch Educ"; Auth, "Indep Educ In Mn". ejohndyer@charter.net

✠ DYER, Rt Rev James Michael Mark (Be) 3737 Seminary Rd, Alexandria VA 22304 B Manchester NH 6/7/1930 s James Michael Dyer & Anna Dorothy. DD Epis TS of The SW; DD Muhlenberg Coll; BA S Anselm Coll Manchester NH 1959; ThM S Paul's Coll Lawrenceville VA 1965; STL U of Ottawa 1965. Rec from Roman Catholic 6/1/1971 as Priest Bp John Melville Burgess Con 11/6/1982 for Be. m 4/30/2004 Amelia J Dyer. VTS Alexandria VA 1996-2002; Bp of Be Dio Bethlehem Bethlehem PA 1983-1995; Dio Bethlehem Bethlehem PA 1982-1995; Bp Coadj of Be Dio Bethlehem Bethlehem PA 1982-1983; R Chr Ch So Hamilton MA 1978-1982; Dio Massachusetts Boston MA 1973-1978; Mssnr Dio Massachusetts Boston MA 1971-1978. Prof Emer VTS 2006; DD Epis TS of the SW; DD Muhlenberg. mdyer@vts.edu

DYER, Susan Jeinine (Wyo) p.o. box 399, Saratoga WY 82331 B Denver CO 12/1/1946 D 11/11/2000 Bp William Jerry Winterrowd. m 10/29/1994 Stephen Dyer c 3. sandsdyer@aol.com

DYKE, Nicolas Roger David (Tex) 3815 Echo Mountain Dr, Humble TX 77345 B London UK 12/5/1937 s John B Hirst & Mary Diana. BBA Texas A&M U 1961; So Texas Coll of Law 1967; MDiv Epis TS of The SW 1977. D 6/30/1977 Bp Roger Howard Cilley P 6/1/1978 Bp J Milton Richardson. m 6/2/1984 Karoline Kathleen Dyke c 2. R S Andr's Ch Bryan TX 1988-2004; S Phil's Ch Hearne TX 1988-2003; H Comf Epis Ch Sprg TX 1986-1988; R H Comf Epis Ch Sprg TX 1977-1986.

DYKES, Deborah White (Miss) 3524 Old Canton Rd, Jackson MS 39216 B Shreveport LA 10/10/1951 d Ruben Eugene White & Elizabeth Raye. Mstr Mississippi St U 1977; Cert Dio Colorado Diac Formation Prog 2001; Iliff TS 2001. D 11/10/2001 Bp William Jerry Winterrowd. m 12/9/1992 David R Dykes c 4. Dir of Cntr for Formation & Mssn Dio Mississippi Jackson MS 2005-2009; Cn for Sprtl Formation for Adults & Chld S Andr's Cathd Jackson MS 2002-2005; Dir of Yth Mnstry S Jn's Cathd Denver CO 2001-2002; Dir of Yth Mnstry S Jn's Cathd Denver CO 1992-2002. debodykes@mac.com

DYNER, Marthe F (NH) Po Box 347, Charlestown NH 03603 **R S Lk's Ch Charlestown NH 2004-; R Un Ch Claremont NH 2004-** B New York NY 3/30/1937 d Jesse Robinson Fillman & Elizabeth Younce. Rad 1956; BA Bryn 1958; U of Utah 1976; MDiv EDS 1988. D 6/12/1988 Bp George Edmonds Bates P 5/8/1989 Bp Douglas Edwin Theuner. m 6/17/1989 Charles Meader. Int S Ptr's Epis Ch Londonderry NH 2004; Assoc S Paul's Ch Concord NH 1998-2003; Cn for Mnstry Resources Dio New Hampshire Concord NH 1993-2007; Asst R Ch Of The Gd Shpd Nashua NH 1988-1993. mfdinnh@aol.com

DYSON, Elizabeth Wheatley (Mass) 451 Birchbark Dr, Hanson MA 02341 **Dn of So Shore S Andr's Ch Hanover MA 2011-; R S Andr's Ch Hanover MA 2007-** B New Bedford MA 12/30/1956 d William Harris Rapp & Alice Lee. BA U of Massachusetts 1978; MA Bridgewater St Coll 1992; MDiv Andover Newton TS 2002. D 6/15/2002 P 5/31/2003 Bp M(arvil) Thomas Shaw III. m 7/14/1984 David Dyson c 3. Asst R S Steph's Ch Cohasset MA 2002-2007. revbaka@yahoo.com

DYSON, Martha Lynn (Vt) 1417 Sw Dolph St, Portland OR 97219 B Houston TX 7/24/1958 d Jeff Arnold Dyson & Shirley Ann. U Of Houston 1980; BFA Steph F. Austin St U 1981; MA Oral Roberts U 1987; MA Drew U 1992. D 6/5/1993 Bp John Shelby Spong P 4/23/1994 Bp Jack Marston McKelvey. Cathd Ch Of S Paul Burlington VT 1997-2001. rev.docmartha@gmail.com

DYSON, Thack Harris (CGC) 28788 N Main St, Daphne AL 36526 **GC Dep Dio Cntrl Gulf Coast Pensacola FL 2009-; Stndg Com Dio Cntrl Gulf Coast Pensacola FL 2009-; R S Paul's Epis Ch Daphne AL 2001-** B Pensacola FL 9/24/1955 s Bromley Clegg Dyson & Nina. BA U of Alabama 1977; JD Cumberland Law Sch, Samford U 1982; MDiv VTS 1996. D 6/1/1996 P 2/2/1997 Bp Charles Farmer Duvall. m 8/13/1977 Rebecca Ann Poole c 1. GC Dep Dio Cntrl Gulf Coast Pensacola FL 2009; COM Dio Cntrl Gulf Coast Pensacola FL 2007-2011; Stndg Com Dio Cntrl Gulf Coast Pensacola FL 2004-2007; Stndg Com Dio Cntrl Gulf Coast Pensacola FL 1999-2002; R S Mk's Epis Ch Troy AL 1999-2001; Assoc R S Chris's Ch Pensacola FL 1996-1999. tdyson1996@aol.com

E

EADE, Christopher Kevin (Los) 1031 Bienveneda Ave, Pacific Palisades CA 90272 **S Mart-In-The-Fields Par Winnetka CA 2004-** B San Jose CA 10/6/1952 s Kenneth Charles Eade & Doris. New Mex St U. 1975; MDiv Nash 1978. D 6/3/1978 Bp John Alfred Baden P 5/1/1979 Bp Robert Bruce Hall. c 2. S Mk's Par Downey CA 1995-1996; The Par Of S Matt Pacific Palisades CA 1991-1995; Asst P All SS Par Beverly Hills CA 1989-1991; Harvard-Westlake Sch N Hollywood CA 1987-1991; R S Ptr's Ch Altavista VA 1984-1987; Virginia Epis Sch Lynchburg VA 1982-1987; Vic S Lk's Epis Hawkinsville GA 1980-1982; Asst Pohick Epis Ch Lorton VA 1978-1980.

EADE, Kenneth Charles (Va) 6465 Calamar Dr, Cumming GA 30040 B Hanna AB CA 4/19/1921 s Charles John Eade & Maud Susan. BA Occ 1948; BD CDSP 1951; Claremont Coll 1953; S Aug's Coll Cbury Gb 1959. D 8/4/1951 P 2/1/1952 Bp Karl M Block. m 8/20/1951 Doris Church c 3. S Mary's Epis Ch Arlington VA 1972-1983; R S Lk's Epis Ch Anth NM 1962-1972; Cur Ch Of The H Trin Midland TX 1958-1962; Vic S Thos Epis Ch Sunnyvale CA 1952-1953. 21kce@adelphia.net

EADES JR, Charles Hubert (Miss) 50 Hillcrest Rd, Mountain Lakes NJ 07046 **Asst P S Ptr's Ch Mtn Lakes NJ 1992-** B Dallas TX 7/19/1916 s Charles Hubert Eades & Ewell. BS SMU 1938; MA U of Texas 1940; PhD U IL 1948. D 6/13/1964 Bp Leland Stark P 4/1/1984 Bp John Shelby Spong. m 8/29/1942 Elizabeth Pearl Jones. D Ch Of The Gd Shpd Ringwood NJ 1982-1984; Asst Ch Of The Redeem Morristown NJ 1980-1982; Asst S Jn's Ch Dover NJ 1966-1980; Asstg P S Ptr's Ch Mtn Lakes NJ 1964-1966. Auth, "Sci arts".

EADES, Susan Tindall (Ia) 1351 Ridgecrest Dr, Clinton IA 52732 **Dioc Coun Dio Montana Helena MT 2011-; R St Jas Epis Ch Dillon MT 2011-** B Lewistown MT 11/10/1953 d Herbert Byron Tindall & Betty Lou. NW Cmnty Coll 1995; BTh The Coll of Emm and St. Chad 2000; U of Great Falls 2003. D 12/11/1999 P 6/17/2000 Bp Charles Jones III. c 2. Bd Dir Dio Iowa Des Moines IA 2007-2010; Congrl Developement Com Dio Iowa Des Moines IA 2006-2008; R Chr Epis Ch Clinton IA 2005-2010; Assoc Ch Of The Incarn Great Falls MT 2004-2005; Stwdshp Chair Dio Montana Helena MT 2004-2005; Ecum Off Dio Montana Helena MT 2001-2005; Vic S Fran Epis Ch Great Falls MT 2000-2004. blessings3@msn.com

EADS, Charles Carroll (Md) 16 Swantamont Rd, Swanton MD 21561 B Baltimore MD 1/14/1924 s John Mcclelland Eads & Rosina Naomi. BA U of Maryland 1947; MDiv VTS 1947. D 3/17/1947 P 6/1/1948 Bp Noble C Powell. Chr Ch Forest Hill MD 1949-1989; H Cross Ch St MD 1949-1989.

EAGER, Donald Bates (SO) 2102 Scenic Dr Ne, Lancaster OH 43130 **D S Phil's Ch Circleville OH 2004-** B Clarksville TN 12/18/1946 s Orlo Robert Eager & Mary Betty. BS Kent St U 1976. D 6/12/2004 Bp Herbert Thompson Jr. m 1/1/1997 Linda Sue Kyle c 3. deager@columbus.rr.com

EAGLEBULL, Harold L (Minn) Po Box 1149, Cass Lake MN 56633 **Int. Vic S Johns/Epis Ch Onigum Mssn Walker MN 2002-; S Ptr's Ch Cass Lake MN 2002-** B Pine Ridge SD 10/13/1945 s Ross Charles Henry & Emma Florence. Cert Cook Coll & TS Tempe AZ 1981; Rio Salado Coll 1981; MDiv Untd TS Of The Twin Cities 1983. D 6/23/1984 Bp Harold Stephen Jones P 3/1/1986 Bp Harold Anthony Hopkins Jr. m 5/14/1999 Charlette Good Shield c 4. Dio Wyoming Casper WY 1999-2002; Mssr Our Fr's Hse Ft Washakie WY 1999-2001; Supply P S Alb's Epis Ch Porcupine SD 1988-1999; Supply P S Julia's Epis Ch Mart SD 1988-1999; Supply P S Thos Ch Porcupine SD 1988-1999; Dio No Dakota Fargo ND 1986-1988; Vic S Jas Ch Ft Yates ND 1985-1988; Dio Minnesota Minneapolis MN 1985-1986; Vic Ch Of The Mssh Prairie Island Welch MN 1984-1985; D Ch Of The Mssh Wounded Knee SD 1984. 82nd Airborne Div Assn; Airborne Static Line; Amer Indn Veterans; Nata Alum. stmichaelsmission@onewest.net

EAKINS, Bill (Ct) 25 Scarborough St, Hartford CT 06105 **S Jas Epis Ch Farmington CT 2010-** B Atlanta GA 11/15/1944 s William Joseph Eakins & Ruth Elizabeth. BA Trin 1966; BA Oxf 1968; BD EDS 1970; MA Oxf 1972. D 6/20/1969 Bp Robert McConnell Hatch P 1/1/1970 Bp Donald J Campbell. m 5/11/1996 Hope Howlett c 3. R Trin Epis Ch Hartford CT 1984-2002; R All SS Ch So Hadley MA 1980-1984; Vic Ch Of The Nativ Northborough MA 1973-1980; D-Intern Chr Ch Cathd Springfield MA 1969-1971. "Faith and Hearing," *Faith and Form*, 2007; Auth, *Lord Ptr Wimsey Cookbook*, Ticknor and Fields, 1982. w.j.eakins@gmail.com

EAKINS, Hope Howlett (Ct) 25 Scarborough St, Hartford CT 06105 **S Jas Epis Ch Farmington CT 2010-** B Wilmington DE 5/30/1942 d Harold Henry Howlett & Helen. BA NWU 1963; MS Sarah Lawr Coll 1971; MDiv Yale DS 1989. D 6/10/1989 Bp Arthur Edward Walmsley P 12/19/1989 Bp Jeffery William Rowthorn. m 5/11/1996 Bill Eakins c 3. R S Jn's Epis Ch Essex CT 1993-2002; Assoc Trin Epis Ch Hartford CT 1989-1993. Auth, *Human Anatomy and Physiology*, Macmillan, 1990. eakinses@gmail.com

EAMES, Marc Gilbert (Mass) 379 Hammond St, Church Of The Redeemer, Chestnut Hill MA 02467 **Cur Ch Of The Redeem Chestnut Hill MA 2007-** B Springfield MA 3/13/1979 s John Stanley Eames & Guylene Kay. BA U of Connecticut 2001; MDiv Berkeley Bapt DS 2007. D 6/2/2007 P 1/12/2008 Bp M(arvil) Thomas Shaw III. m 9/21/2002 Gretchen Eames c 1. meames@redeemerchestnuthill.org

EARL, John Keith (WNC) 1650 5th St Nw, Hickory NC 28601 B Tulsa OK 5/18/1946 s Gene Markley Earl & Marjorie Jean. MD U of Oklahoma 1968; U of Virginia 1976. D 11/10/1985 Bp William Gillette Weinhauer. m Jane Sarah c 4. D S Alb's Ch Hickory NC 1985-2010. jkedeacdoc@aol.com

EARLE, Charles Douglas (WTex) 7302 Robin Rest Dr, San Antonio TX 78209 **R S Paul's Epis Ch San Antonio TX 1999-** B San Antonio TX 1/6/1949 s Charles Thomas Earle & Nila Keese. BBA U Americas Puebla MX 1972; MDiv Epis TS of The SW 1984. D 6/8/1984 P 12/11/2000 Bp Scott Field Bailey. m 8/21/1971 Mary Colbert c 2. Int S Paul's Ch Brady TX 1998; Int Ch Of Recon San Antonio TX 1995-1998; Chair COM Dio W Texas San Antonio TX 1990-1994; Vic S Mths Devine TX 1989-1990; Vic All SS Epis Ch Pleasanton TX 1987-1990; Area Mssnr S Matt's Epis Ch Kenedy TX 1984-1987; Area Mssnr S Steph's Ch Goliad TX 1984-1987; Asst Trin Ch Victoria TX 1984-1987; Area Mssnr Trin Epis Ch Edna TX 1984-1987. dougearle09@gmail.com

EARLE, Leigh Christensen (Wyo) 1745 Westridge Cir, Casper WY 82604 **D Chr Epis Ch Glenrock WY 2010-; COM Mem Dio Wyoming Casper WY 2006-; D S Mk's Epis Ch Casper WY 2005-** B TX 10/17/1952 d Joe Smith Powell & Dorothy Jean. AS Casper Coll 1987; BS U of Wyoming 1990; MS U of Wyoming 1996. D 5/31/2005 Bp Bruce Edward Caldwell. m 5/31/1986 Ralph Theodore Earle. Auth, "Benefits and Barriers to Well-Chld Care: Perceptions of Mothers in a Rural St," *Publ Hlth Nrsng*, Blackwell Sci, Inc., 1998. Amer Acad of Nurse Practitioners 1996; Assn of Epis Deacons 2004; Natl Epis Hlth Mnstrs 2004; Off of Bp Suffr for Chaplaincies 2006; OSL the Physcn 2003. raleigh509@msn.com

EARLE, Mary Colbert (WTex) 7302 Robin Rest Dr, San Antonio TX 78209 B San Antonio TX 11/30/1948 d Gene Edward Colbert & Mary. BA U of Texas 1970; MA U of Texas 1975; MA Epis TS of The SW 1984; MDiv Epis TS of The SW 1986. D 2/2/1987 P 9/4/1987 Bp John Herbert MacNaughton. m 8/21/1971 Charles Douglas Earle c 2. Instr in Pstr Mnstry Epis TS Of The SW Austin TX 2000-2004; Asst R S Mk's Epis Ch San Antonio TX 1999-2004; Ch Of Recon San Antonio TX 1990-1998; Texas Mltry Inst San Antonio TX 1989-1990; Vic S Mths Devine TX 1987-1989. Auth, "Celtic Chr Sprtlty," SkyLight Paths, 2011; Auth, "Days of Gr: Meditations and Practices for Living w Illness," Morehouse, 2009; Auth, "The Desert Mothers," Morehouse, 2007; Auth, "Beginning Again: Benedictine Wisdom for Living w Illness," Morehouse, 2004; Auth, "H Comp: Sprtl Practices from the Celtic SS," Morehouse, 2004; Auth, "Broken Body, Healing Sprt: Lectio Divina and Living w Illness," Morehouse, 2003; Auth, "Praying w the Celtic SS," S Mary's Press, 2000. Amer Academy of Rel 1999; Soc for the Study of Chr Sprtlty 1997; Sprtl Dir Intl 1997. Phi Beta Kappa U of Texas at Austin 1970. mcearle48@gmail.com

EARLE, Patty Ann Trapp (NC) Po Box 1103, Statesville NC 28687 B Akron OH 3/23/1931 d Edward U Trapp & Geneva Mae. MA Kent St U 1958; PhD U NC 1978; MDiv Duke 1989; CAS VTS 1989. D 6/3/1989 Bp Robert Whitridge Estill P 6/1/1990 Bp Huntington Williams Jr. S Anne's Ch Winston Salem NC 2000-2001; Ch Of The Mssh Mayodan NC 1989-2000; Sem Asst S Andr's Ch Greensboro NC 1987-1988. Auth, "Var arts," *Pub & Books 64-88.* Vts Mssy Soc.

EARLE III, Richard Tilghman (SwFla) 555 13th Avenue NE, Saint Petersburg FL 33701 **Const and Cn Com Dio SW Florida Sarasota FL 2003-; D Cathd Ch Of S Ptr St Petersburg FL 2002-** B Saint Petersburg FL 3/18/1942 B.A. The U So 1963; J.D. The U of Forida 1966. D 1/18/2002 Bp John Bailey Lipscomb. m 5/13/1989 Shirley Sipe c 2. REARLE@EDS.EDU

EARLS, John G (USC) 405 S Chapel St, Baltimore MD 21231 **S Jn's Ch Columbus OH 2004-** B Gaffney SC 5/7/1962 s Larry Steve Earls & Rose Mary. BS Clemson U 1984; MDiv VTS 2004. D 6/12/2004 P 5/12/2005 Bp Dorsey Felix Henderson. Asst S Barth's Ch No Augusta SC 2004-2005. jgearls@aol.com

EARLY, Nancy Davis (WA) 402 Montrose Ave, Catonsville MD 21228 B New York NY 2/5/1958 d John Collins Early & Eleanor Davis. BA U of Vermont 1982; MDiv Harvard DS 1986. D 6/11/1988 Bp David Elliot Johnson P 5/1/1989 Bp John Thomas Walker. c 2. Assoc R S Columba's Ch Washington DC 2000-2002; R S Lk's Ch Brighton Brookeville MD 1992-2000; S Jn's Ch Georgetown Par Washington DC 1988-1991. nancyearly@post.harvard.edu

EASLEY, Alexander Hufford (SVa) 10240 Hendley Rd Apt 326, Manassas VA 20110 **Died 7/27/2011** B Richmond VA 11/19/1918 s Alexander Easley & Nella. BA S Aug 1941; MDiv VTS 1944. D 6/6/1944 P 6/1/1945 Bp Wiley R Mason. c 3.

EASLEY, Barbara Ann (Ia) 605 Avenue E, Fort Madison IA 52627 B Brookfield MO 11/4/1934 d Eugene Bagley & Marjorie. D 10/25/2009 Bp Alan Scarfe. c 3. sameasley@mchsi.com

EASLEY, Julia Kathleen (Ia) 26 E Market St, Iowa City IA 52245 B Fort Madison IA 2/19/1963 d Norris Easley & Barbara Ann. BA U of Notre Dame 1985; MDiv SWTS 1990. D 5/12/1990 P 12/14/1990 Bp Carl Christopher

Epting. c 1. U Of Iowa Chapl Iowa City IA 1992-2008; Dio Iowa Des Moines IA 1992-2007; Int Cbury At Kansas U Lawr KS 1991-1992; Dio Kansas Topeka KS 1991-1992; S Paul's Ch Milwaukee WI 1990-1991. Auth, "Evang w YA," *Plumbline*. ESMHE 1991-2005. jkeasley@inav.net

EASTER, James Hamilton (Okla) 11308 N Miller Ave, Oklahoma City OK 73120 **D All Souls Epis Ch Oklahoma City OK 2004-** B Baltimore MD 3/25/1931 s James Angle Easter & Mary Teresa. BA Bowling Green St U 1953. D 7/14/1968 Bp Chilton Powell. m 1/31/1953 Colleen Jean Irish c 2. D S Jas Epis Ch Oklahoma City OK 1993-2004; Asst S Aug Of Cbury Oklahoma City OK 1982-1993. JANDCEASTER@SBCGLOBAL.NET

EASTER, Mary Kathleen (WMo) 973 Evergreen Ave, Hollister MO 65672 **D Shpd Of The Hills Branson MO 1997-** B Londonderry IE 1/1/1947 d Leslie Jarvis & Margaret Maud. BSW Missouri Wstrn St U 1987. D 2/1/1997 Bp John Clark Buchanan. m 10/19/1991 James Dennis Easter.

EASTER, William Burton (Chi) 594 Eastlake Dr Se, Rio Rancho NM 87124 B Grosse Pointe Farms MI 11/6/1926 s William Burton Easter & Marvel Theresa. BA Ripon Coll Ripon WI 1953; BD VTS 1959. D 6/20/1959 P 12/19/1959 Bp Charles L Street. c 5. Int Epis Ch Of The Epiph Socorro NM 1995-1996; Int Gr Ch Sterling IL 1992-1993; Int Ch Of The Trsfg Palos Pk IL 1991; S Jn The Evang Lockport IL 1990; Assoc S Paul's On The Plains Epis Ch Lubbock TX 1965-1970; ExCoun Dio W Texas San Antonio TX 1963-1965; R S Alb's Ch Harlingen TX 1962-1965; R S Thos And S Mart's Ch Corpus Christi TX 1960-1962; Cur Gr Ch Oak Pk IL 1959-1960. Auth, "The Professionalizing Process," *Journ of Par Cler*; Auth, "Time for a Hse of P?," *Profsnl Supplement Epis Life Predecessor*. Associated Parishes; Silver Eagles; Westar Inst. paques@mindspring.com

EASTERDAY, Pamela Kay (CFla) 3524 Pineda Crossing Dr, 1830 s Babcock St, Melbourne FL 32901 **Co-R H Trin Epis Ch Melbourne FL 2006-** B Marion IN 10/12/1961 d James Holbrook Oakerson & Betty Irene. Manchester Coll 1982; BS Indiana St U 1984; MDiv CDSP 1992. D 5/26/1992 Bp Edward Witker Jones P 11/29/1992 Bp John Stuart Thornton. m 6/2/1982 Stephen Wayne Easterday c 2. Dn Geth Cathd Fargo ND 1998-2006; Cn Ordnry Dio Idaho Boise ID 1997-1998; Epis Ch In Minidoka & Cassia Cnty Rupert ID 1994-1997; Co-Vic S Jas Ch Burley ID 1992-1997; Co-Vic St Matthews Epis Ch Rupert ID 1992-1997; Cntrl Dnry Cluster Shoshone ID 1992-1993. FA 2009; Ord of S Lk 2000. revpam@holytrinitymelbourne.org

EASTERDAY, Stephen Wayne (CFla) 1830 S. Babcock St., Melbourne FL 32901 **Co-R H Trin Epis Ch Melbourne FL 2006-** B Marion IN 4/2/1962 s Wayne Gilbert Easterday & Dorothy May. BS Rose-Hulman Inst for Tech 1984; MDiv CDSP 1992. D 5/26/1992 Bp Edward Witker Jones P 11/29/1992 Bp John Stuart Thornton. m 6/2/1982 Pamela Kay Oakerson c 2. Dn Geth Cathd Fargo ND 1998-2006; Dio Idaho Boise ID 1997; Epis Ch In Minidoka & Cassia Cnty Rupert ID 1994-1998; Co-Vic S Jas Ch Burley ID 1992-1997; Co-Vic St Matthews Epis Ch Rupert ID 1992-1997; Cntrl Dnry Cluster Shoshone ID 1992-1993. EvangES; Ord of S Lk 2000. frsteve@holytrinitymelbourne.org

EASTERLING JR, Richard Brooks (La) 1315 Jackson Ave, New Orleans LA 70130 **Int S Lk's Ch New Orleans LA 2007-; Trin Ch New Orleans LA 2006-** B Alexandria LA 5/11/1977 s Richard Brooks Easterling & Michelle Howse. BA LSU 1999; MDiv SWTS 2003. D 12/28/2002 P 7/6/2003 Bp Charles Edward Jenkins III. Chr Ch Slidell LA 2011; Cur S Augustines Ch Metairie LA 2003-2005. Our Lady of Walsingham 2008. easterling@mac.com

EASTERLING SR, William Ramsay (WLa) 405 Glenmar, Monroe LA 71201 **Int Gr Epis Ch Monroe LA 2011-** B Little Rock AR 10/30/1948 s Thomas Grayson Easterling & Gladys Ramsay. Gnrl Stds L.S.U. 1975; BS Iowa Wesleyan 1986; MTS Nash 2007. D 12/7/2006 P 6/30/2007 Bp Keith Lynn Ackerman. m 8/9/1975 Catherine G Easterling c 3. Assoc Nash Nashotah WI 2007-2011. beasterling@nashotah.edu

EASTES, Suzanne Hardey (Mo) 15826 Clayton Rd Apt 131, Ellisville MO 63011 **Assoc S Tim's Epis Ch Creve Coeur MO 2006-** B Indianapolis IN 6/1/1936 d Karl William Hardey & Jane. BS Pur 1958; MBA U MN 1977; MDiv Nash 1985. D 6/24/1985 Bp Robert Marshall Anderson P 2/2/1986 Bp William Augustus Jones Jr. c 2. Gr Ch Kirkwood MO 1993-2006; Assoc R S Augustines Ch S Louis MO 1991-1993; Int S Andr's Epis Ch Edwardsville IL 1990-1991; Trin Ch S Louis MO 1985-1987. sueeastes@gmail.com

✠ **EASTMAN, Rt Rev A(lbert) Theodore** (Md) 3440 S Jefferson St, #1481, Falls Church VA 22041 B San Mateo CA 11/20/1928 s Carl John Eastman & Inette Therese. BA Hav 1950; MDiv VTS 1953; Fllshp Epis TS of The SW 1963; Fllshp Coll of Preachers 1972; Fllshp Epis TS of The SW 1980. D 7/15/1953 Bp Henry H Shires P 1/25/1954 Bp Karl M Block Con 6/26/1982 for Md. m 6/13/1953 Sarah Veronica Tice c 3. Bp of Md Dio Maryland Baltimore MD 1986-1995; Bp Coadj of Md Dio Maryland Baltimore MD 1982-1985; R S Alb's Par Washington DC 1973-1982; R The Epis Ch Of The Medtr Allentown PA 1969-1973; Exec Secy, Ovrs Mssn Soc Dio Washington Washington DC 1956-1979; Vic Trin Ch Gonzales CA 1953-1956. Auth, "The Mssn of Chr in Urban Amer," *Crossroads are for Meeting*, SPCK/USA, 1986; Auth, "The Baptizing Cmnty: Chr Initiation and the Loc Cong," Seabury Press, 1982; Auth, "Mssn: In or Out," Friendship Press, 1967; Auth, "Chr Responsibility in One Wrld," Seabury Press, 1965; Auth, "Chosen And Sent: Calling the Ch to Mssn," Eerdmans, 1965; Auth, "Letters from the Rim of E Asia," The Natl Coun, 1963. DD S Mary Sem & U 1994; DD VTS 1983; LHD Epis TS of the SW 1982. east1128@aol.com

EASTMAN, Susan Grove (NC) 4604 Brodog Ter, Hurdle Mills NC 27541 B Tucson AZ 9/20/1952 d George Thomas Grove & Patricia. BA Pomona Coll 1974; MDiv Yale DS 1978; Ph.D. Duke DS 2003. D 6/5/1982 Bp Paul Moore Jr P 1/1/1983 Bp George Clinton Harris. m 7/20/1986 Edward Warren Eastman c 2. Asst S Steph's Ch Durham NC 1997-1998; Dio Oregon Portland OR 1991-1995; Vic The Epis Ch Of The Prince Of Peace Salem OR 1991-1995; Dio Alaska Fairbanks AK 1982-1986; Vic S Andr's Epis Ch Petersburg AK 1982-1986. Auth, "Incarn as Mimetic Participation," *Journ for the Study of Paul and His Letters*, Journ, 2011; Auth, "Israel and the Mercy of God: a re-reading of Galatians 6:16 and Romans 9-11," *NT Stds*, Journ, 2010; Auth, "Imitating Chr Imitating Us," *The Word Leaps the Gap*, Eerdmans, 2008; Auth, "Recovering Paul's Mo Tongue," *Bk*, Eerdmans, 2007; Auth, "Cast out the slave Wmn and her son," *Journ for the Study of the NT*, Journ, 2006; Auth, "The Foolish Fr and the Econ of Gr," *The Expository Times*, Journ, 2006; Auth, "Whose Apocalypse? The Identity of the Sons of God in Romans 8:19," *Journ of Biblic Lit*, Journ, 2002. seastman@div.duke.edu

EASTON, Elizabeth Lavender (Neb) 9302 Blondo St., Omaha NE 68134 **Cur All SS Epis Ch Omaha NE 2009-** B Seattle WA 3/7/1983 d David Alvin Easton & Marilyn Lavender. BA Wstrn Washington U 2005; MDiv CDSP 2009. D 4/17/2009 Bp Gregory Harold Rickel P 11/17/2009 Bp Joe Goodwin Burnett. ELIZABETH.EASTON@GMAIL.COM

EASTON, Stanley Evan (Ala) 1104 Church Avenue Northeast, Jacksonville AL 36265 **D S Lk's Epis Ch Jacksonville AL 1991-** B Spokane WA 5/30/1936 s Arthur Lee Easton & Nellie Virginia. Whitworth U 1955; BA WA SU 1958; Med LSU 1967; EdD LSU 1970. D 10/6/1990 Bp Charles Jones III. m 5/30/1981 Tien-Han Ma c 1. S Lk's Epis Ch Jacksonville AL 1998-1999. Assn for Epis Deacons 1990. seaston@mac.com

EASTWOOD, John Harrison (Cal) 30 Ogden Ave, San Francisco CA 94110 **Pres Prov VIII Tagard OR 2006-2012** B Chester PA 5/13/1943 s John Harrison Eastwood & Margaret. BA Pur 1966; STB GTS 1971; DMin Chr TS 1981. D 6/12/1971 P 12/15/1971 Bp John P Craine. m 9/12/1970 Judith A Deletti c 2. R S Paul's Ch Oakland CA 1993-2007; R The Epis Ch Of S Jn The Evang San Francisco CA 1985-1993; Assoc R All SS Ch Indianapolis IN 1973-1985; Asst S Thos Ch Franklin IN 1971-1973; Asst S Tim's Ch Indianapolis IN 1971-1973. AAPC. jhebernal@gmail.com

EATON, Albert Edward (EC) 502 Main Street Ext Apt 108, Swansboro NC 28584 **S Ptr's By-The-Sea Swansboro NC 2004-** B Pittsburgh PA 7/2/1946 s Edward Hough Eaton & Judith. Leh; BS Indiana U 1968; MBA Indiana U 1970; MDiv STUSo 1995. D 5/24/1995 P 12/2/1995 Bp Robert Hodges Johnson. m 7/15/1967 Carol A Lusher c 3. S Andr's Ch Bessemer City NC 1997-2004; Ch Of The Redeem Shelby NC 1995-1996. frbert@bizec.rr.com

EATON, Donald Barnett (Ore) 7675 Sw Taylors Ferry Rd, Portland OR 97223 B Oakland CA 3/10/1931 s Clarence Albert Eaton & Grace Ethel. BA San Jose St U 1952; MDiv CDSP 1955. D 6/10/1955 P 12/17/1955 Bp Benjamin D Dagwell. m 9/12/1999 Joyce M Thompson c 4. Dio Oregon Portland OR 1988-1991; Vic S Paul's Epis Mssn Powers OR 1986-1991; S Jas' Epis Ch Coquille OR 1986-1987; S Mk's Ch Myrtle Point OR 1986-1987; Samar Hlth Serv Corvallis OR 1982-1986; Asst The Epis Ch Of The Gd Samar Corvallis OR 1979-1983; Epis Ch Coun Tulsa OK 1976-1979; Vic S Matt's Epis Ch Eugene OR 1964-1967; R Calv Ch Seaside OR 1958-1963; Vic S Mary's Ch Woodburn OR 1956-1958; Cur Trin Epis Cathd Portland OR 1955-1956. Ord Of S Lk. revfrcol@aol.com

EATON, Laura Mary (NMich) PO Box 27, Calumet MI 49913 **Epis P Chr Ch Calumet Laurium MI 2006-; Epis P S Ptr's-By-The-Sea Eagle Harbor MI 2006-; Epis P Trin Epis Ch Houghton MI 2006-** B Laurium MI 5/17/1948 d Beverly Clarice. Michigan Tech U; Non Sem/Stds Through Dio N. Michigan; AD Nthrn Michigan U 1970. D 8/17/2005 P 2/28/2006 Bp James Arthur Kelsey. c 4. leaton48@yahoo.com

EATON, Peter David (Colo) 1350 Washington St, Denver CO 80203 **Dn S Jn's Cathd Denver CO 2002-** B Washington DC USA 8/28/1958 s Alfred Wade Eaton & Judith Mary. BA Lon 1982; BA U of Cambridge 1985; CTh Westcott Hse Cambridge 1986; MA U of Cambridge 1989; MA Oxf 1990; Fell in Res U So 1995. Trans from Church Of England 5/20/1991 as Priest Bp George Edmonds Bates. m 9/25/2004 Katherine Kimball Gleason. R S Jas Ch Lancaster PA 1995-2001; Assoc R S Paul's Ch Salt Lake City UT 1991-1995. Contrib, "Remembering Jn Krumm," *Remembering Jn Krumm*, Forw Mvmt, 1998; Contrib, "Oxf Dictionary of the Chr Ch 3rd Ed," *Oxf Dictionary of the Chr Ch 3rd Ed*, OUP, 1997; Ed, "Bp Paul Jones," *Bp Paul Jones*, Forw Mvmt, 1992; Ed, "The Trial of Faith," *The Trial of Faith*, Morehouse, 1988; Auth, "Journ," *arts & Revs*, Var. Alcuin Club 1985; Assoc OHC 1975; Eccl Law Soc 2008; Nikaean Club 1985; Soc of Cath Priests 2010. Advancing Lrng in

Lancaster Sch Dist of Lancaster 2002; Publ Serv Awd Utah AIDS Fndt UT 1994. peter@sjcathedral.org

EATON, Robert Gordon (EpisSanJ) 1571 E Glenwood Ave, Tulare CA 93274 **R S Jn's Epis Ch Tulare CA 1989-** B Portland OR 10/23/1955 s Donald Barnett Eaton & Joan Carolyn. BMusic U of Oregon 1977; MDiv CDSP 1984. D 6/29/1984 Bp Robert Hume Cochrane P 6/1/1985 Bp Matthew Paul Bigliardi. m 6/23/1978 Angela Burnett c 2. Epis Dio San Joaquin Modesto CA 1994-1995; Assoc S Paul's Epis Ch Salem OR 1984-1989; Yth Min S Paul's Epis Ch Salem OR 1984-1989; Sem Intern St Johns Epis Ch Roseville CA 1982-1983. "How to Motivate, Train and Nurture Acolytes," Morehouse, 2002; *Sm Ch Wk Series*, "Houses of Wrshp" website, 1999. ERM 1983; Fllshp of S. Jn Evang 1978-1985; OSL 1975-1989. rgeaton@rocketmail.com

EATON, William Albert (SeFla) 10914 Nw 8th Ct, Plantation FL 33324 **Asstg H Sacr Pembroke Pines FL 2002-** B Pittsburgh PA 10/28/1934 s William Albert Eaton & Edith Barbera. Muskingum Coll; Pittsburgh Pstr Inst 1977; Pittsburgh Tpm 1977; TESM 1984. D 6/25/1977 Bp Robert Bracewell Appleyard P 12/1/1984 Bp Alden Moinet Hathaway. m 10/2/1954 Ruth Heinike c 3. Ch Of The Resurr Cranberry Twp PA 1984-1995; Asst S Mart's Epis Ch Monroeville PA 1977-1984. Ord Of S Lk.

EAVES, Lindon John (Va) 10835 Old Prescott Rd, Richmond VA 23238 **P S Thos' Ch Richmond VA 2002-** B 9/23/1944 s Kenneth Lindon Eaves & Winifred. BS U Of Birmingham Gb 1966; GOE Ripon Coll Cuddesdon 1968; PhD U Of Birmingham Birmingham Gb 1970; MA Oxf 1979; Ds Oxf 1980. Trans 1/1/1995 Bp Peter James Lee. m 6/29/1968 Susan Nuthall Eaves. P-In-Res Ch Of The H Comf Richmond VA 1985-1997. Auth, "Genes Culture & Personality," 1989. Pres Behavior Genetics Assn 1993. Doctor, Honoraryoris Causa Vrije Universiteit 2000; Dobzhansky Lifetime Achievement Awd Behavioral Genetics Assn 1998; Paul Hoch Awd Amer Psych Assn 1992.

EAVES, Susan Nuthall (Va) 3207 Hawthorne Ave, Richmond VA 23222 **T/F on Giving Dio Virginia Richmond VA 2011-; R S Thos' Ch Richmond VA 2001-** B Birmingham UK 4/29/1947 d Norman Alan Nuthall & Lilian. Cert, Oxford Lady Spencer Churchill Coll of Educ 1968; Cert VTS 1991; MA U Rich 1992. D 12/12/1991 P 9/1/1992 Bp Peter James Lee. m 6/29/1968 Lindon John Eaves c 3. Windsor Dialogue Co-Chair Dio Virginia Richmond VA 2008-2009; GC Dep Dio Virginia Richmond VA 2000-2009; Pres, Stndg Com Dio Virginia Richmond VA 2000; Stndg Com Dio Virginia Richmond VA 1998-2000; Assoc R S Jas' Ch Richmond VA 1996-2001; P-in-res Ch Of The H Comf Richmond VA 1991-1994. seaves@sthomasrichmond.org

EBEL, Ann Teresa (PR) 946 Oxford St, Berkeley CA 94707 B 10/20/1940 D 12/23/1978 Bp C Kilmer Myers P 6/5/1980 Bp William Edwin Swing. S Mk's Par Berkeley CA 1987-1990; Epis Ch Of Our Sav Oakland CA 1979-1980; Epis Ch Of Our Sav Oakland CA 1978-1979.

EBENS, Richard Frank (Mass) 4-C Autumn Dr, Hudson MA 01749 B Somerville MA 12/6/1929 s Frank Joseph Ebens & Dorothy. BS NEU 1952; STB Ya Berk 1958. D 6/21/1958 Bp Frederic Cunningham Lawrence P 12/1/1958 Bp Anson Phelps Stokes Jr. m 6/5/1965 Mary J Smith c 2. R S Lk's Ch Hudson MA 1966-1990; Assoc S Jn's Ch Norristown PA 1965-1966; Cur Ch Of S Jn The Evang Hingham MA 1958-1961. richebens@verizon.net

EBERHARDT, Bruce Allan (WA) 9907 Dale Dr, Upper Marlboro MD 20772 B New York NY 3/12/1932 s Paul Ernest Eberhardt & Florence Agnes. BS Newark Coll of Engr 1960; BD Epis TS of The SW 1967; STM Epis TS of The SW 1968. D 6/23/1967 Bp J Milton Richardson P 5/29/1968 Bp Frederick P Goddard. m 5/30/1953 Janet C Becker c 3. R Nativ Epis Ch Temple Hills MD 1977-1997; Assoc S Fran Ch Houston TX 1974-1977; Asst S Geo's Ch Austin TX 1967-1968. Fllshp ECF 1967. eberhardtbj@gmail.com

EBERHARDT, Karen Anne (Nwk) PO Box 104, Morris Plains NJ 07950 B Denver CO 10/14/1947 d Friend Arthur Hasenkamp & Doris Evelyn. U of New Mex; BA Thos Edison St. Coll 1995; MDiv Drew U 1999. D 12/9/2006 Bp Carol Joy Gallagher. c 2. D S Paul's Epis Ch Morris Plains NJ 2007-2009. kkawe@optonline.net

EBERHARDT, Timothy Charles (Vt) 4 Prospect Ave, Randolph VT 05060 B Morristown NJ 12/4/1945 s Charles Richard Eberhardt & Dorothy. BA Bow 1968; MDiv Bangor TS 1977. D 6/4/1977 P 12/5/1977 Bp Frederick Barton Wolf. c 2. R S Jn's Epis Ch Randolph VT 1981-2010; R S Barn Ch Rumford ME 1977-1980.

EBERLE, Bill (Va) P.O. Box 367, Rixeyville VA 22737 **R Little Fork Epis Ch Rixeyville VA 2008-** B Orange NJ 12/20/1947 s Edward Radcliffe Eberle & Jane. DMin Candidate Asbury TS; BA Ya 1970; MDiv UTS 1974. D 6/8/1974 Bp George E Rath P 1/26/1975 Bp David Keller Leighton Sr. m 6/21/1969 Linda Sue Cornell c 3. R S Thos Ch Lancaster PA 1998-2008; Stndg Com Dio El Camino Real Monterey CA 1988-1990; R S Edw The Confessor Epis Ch San Jose CA 1983-1998; R S Lk's Ch Phillipsburg NJ 1978-1983; Dioc Coun Dio Maryland Baltimore MD 1976-1978; Asst The Ch Of The Redeem Baltimore MD 1974-1978. frbilleberle@aol.com

EBERLY, G(eorge) Douglas (NJ) 500 19th St, Ocean City NJ 08226 B Philadelphia PA 12/19/1946 s Charles Clayton Eberly & Charlotte Milburn. Westminster Coll 1965; BA SMU 1968; MDiv SWTS 1971. D 6/22/1971 Bp A Donald Davies P 12/23/1971 Bp Theodore H McCrea. R Epis Ch Of The Epiph Ventnor City NJ 1997-2005; H Trin Epis Ch Ocean City NJ 1995-1997; Gr Epis Ch Glendora CA 1991-1995; Epis Ch Of The Redeem Irving TX 1976-1991; R S Ptr's Ch McKinney TX 1974-1976; Cur S Jas Ch Dallas TX 1972-1973. AAM; Dioc Liturg & Mus Commissions; SocMary. Fr. Tom Schiawo Bro Awd Judea-Chr 2005; Who'S Who In Amer Rel. frgeodoug@aol.com

EBERMAN, John Fowler (WA) 703 Agawam St, Elizabeth City NC 27909 B Norfolk VA 12/2/1933 s John Hopkins Eberman & Eloise Virginia. BS VPI 1958; MDiv VTS 1961. D 6/26/1961 P 6/27/1962 Bp William Henry Marmion. m 6/17/1961 Betty Jo Griffith c 2. Int P S Thos Ch Oriental NC 1998-1999; Supply P S Andr's Ch Columbia NC 1997-2011; R S Paul's Par Prince Geo's Cnty Brandywine MD 1989-1996; R S Jn's Epis Ch Crawfordsville IN 1981-1989; Vic Chr Ch Elizabethtown KY 1968-1981; Vic H Trin Ch Brandenburg KY 1968-1979; Asst S Jn's Ch Roanoke VA 1964-1968. bjandj61@embarqmail.com

EBERT, Bernhard (Colo) 802 Raton Ave, La Junta CO 81050 B Port Colborne Ontario CA 8/7/1958 s Erich Ebert & Emma. BMusA U of Wstrn Ontario 1980; MDiv U Tor 2000. D 6/9/2001 P 12/1/2001 Bp William Jerry Winterrowd. m 6/5/1993 Angelika Ermel c 1. R S Andr's Ch La Junta CO 2001-2011; S Andr's Ch La Junta CO 2000-2001. asharpbflat@centurytel.net

EBRIGHT, Howard Sefton (Colo) 314 Country Club Park Rd, Grand Junction CO 81503 B Denver CO 4/15/1923 s Frank Brookfield Ebright & Margaret Ella. BS Colorado St U 1947; MS U MI 1949; Cert Dioc TS 1968; MS U MI 1973. D 6/29/1968 Bp Archie H Crowley P 9/19/1969 Bp Richard S M Emrich. m 10/17/1946 Marjorie Kathleen Skitch. Assoc S Matt's Ch Grand Jct CO 1976-1979; Fndg P Ch Of The Nativ Grand Jct CO 1971-1976; P-in-c S Alfred's Ch Oxford MI 1970-1971; P-in-c S Andr's Ch Clawson MI 1968-1970. Ord Of S Paul The Tentmaker.

ECCLES, Margot E (Chi) St Simon's Episcopal Church, 717 W Kirchhoff Rd, Arlington Heights IL 60005 **Assoc S Simons Ch Arlington Heights IL 2007-** B Tucson AZ 4/24/1969 d Robert Stuart Eccles & Margot Lacy. BA Lake Forest Coll 1991; MTS SWTS 2003; MAPC Loyola U 2005; MDiv SWTS 2007. D 6/2/2007 Bp William Dailey Persell P 12/15/2007 Bp Victor Alfonso Scantlebury. m 11/5/2009 Kathleen E Eccles. stsimonassociate@yahoo.com

ECCLES, Mark Eldon (Ia) 1619 21st St Nw, Cedar Rapids IA 52405 **Stff D Chr Ch Cedar Rapids IA 1996-** B Fort Dodge IA 1/21/1951 s Guy E Eccles & Mary Ellen. BA U of Nthrn Iowa 1973. D 12/3/1995 Bp Carl Christopher Epting. m 8/28/1971 Mary Fay Walkenhauer c 1. meeccles@att.net

ECHOLS, Janet Lyn (SC) No address on file. B Conway SC 8/21/1958 d E P Roberts & Eunice May. BA Coll of Charleston 1982; MDiv TESM 1995. D 9/9/1995 P 5/1/1996 Bp Edward Lloyd Salmon Jr. Chr Epis Ch Mt Pleasant SC 1995-1996. Dok.

ECHOLS, Mary W (SwFla) 917 11th St N, Naples FL 34102 **D Trin By The Cove Naples FL 2004-; Asstg D The Epis Ch Of The Trsfg Dallas TX 1996-; Off Of Bsh For ArmdF New York NY 1994-** B Pittsfield IL 6/29/1942 d Roy J Wade & Elma C. BS U IL 1964; USC 1965; LST Angl TS 1986. D 6/13/1987 Bp Donis Dean Patterson. m 7/6/1965 Ronald Echols c 2. Asstg D Ch Of The Annunc Lewisville TX 1992-1994; Asstg D Epis Ch Of The Redeem Irving TX 1987-1992. Epis Cleric Un. deaconmary@aol.com

ECHOLS, William Joseph (WLa) 104 Ingram St, Lake Providence LA 71254 **Trin Ch Tallulah LA 1999-** B Moticello AR 9/28/1951 s Don Henry Echols & Betty Jane. BBA NE Louisiana U 1978; MDiv STUSo 1987. D 5/30/1987 P 12/1/1987 Bp Willis Ryan Henton. m 12/29/1999 Linda Gail Mcdonald Locantro c 3. Gr Ch Lake Providence LA 1995-2003; R S Thos' Ch Monroe LA 1990-1994; Cur S Mths Epis Ch Shreveport LA 1987-1990.

ECKARDT, Robert Remick (At) 720 Whitemere Ct Nw, Atlanta GA 30327 **D S Anne's Epis Ch Atlanta GA 1996-** B Brooklyn NY 6/6/1933 s Richard Eckardt & Ruth Bass. BA Amh 1955. D 10/28/1995 Bp Frank Kellogg Allan. m 6/1/1996 Eve Foy c 4.

ECKART JR, Richard Joseph (Roch) 38 Dale Rd, Rochester NY 14625 **Assoc S Mich's Ch Geneseo NY 2000-** B New York NY 8/7/1934 s Richard Joseph Eckart & Mary. BA Ya 1956; MDiv VTS 1961; Cert Onondaga Cmnty Coll 1982. D 10/14/1961 Bp William Foreman Creighton P 4/1/1962 Bp Angus Dun. m 9/16/1961 Renate Gertrude Hanoche c 2. R S Mk's And S Jn's Epis Ch Rochester NY 1980-1999; Emm Ch E Syracuse NY 1980; Dio Cntrl New York Syracuse NY 1979-1980; Groton Sch Groton MA 1970-1976; R Ch Of The H Comf Washington DC 1963-1970; Cur S Tim's Epis Ch Washington DC 1961-1963. Auth, "To Complete A Par," *Aware*. reckart@rochester.rr

ECKEL, Malcolm David (Mass) 11 Griggs Ter., Brookline MA 02446 **Assoc Ch Of Our Sav Boston MA 1995-** B Albany NY 9/19/1946 s Malcolm William Eckel & Mary Constance. BA Harv 1968; EDS 1969; BA Oxf 1971; MA Oxf 1976; PhD Harv 1980. D 3/31/1974 P 3/1/1975 Bp Alexander Doig Stewart. m 6/25/1995 Sarah Vance c 1. Auth, "Bhaviveka and His Buddhist Opponents," Harv Press, 2008; Auth, "Buddhism," Oxf Press, 2002; Auth, "To See The Buddha," Pr Press, 1994; Auth, "Jnanagarbha on The dist Between The Two Truths". Distinguished Tchg Prof of the Hmnts Bos 2003; Metcalf Awd for Tchg Excellence Bos 1998. mdeckel@bu.edu

ECKHOLM, Vincent Joseph (Chi) 81 Rotterdam Dr, Antioch IL 60002 B Evanston IL 1/12/1942 s Vincent James Eckholm & Lillian Clair. BA S Mary-Lake Sem Mundelein IL 1963; ThM S Mary-Lake Sem Mundelein IL 1966. Rec from Roman Catholic 1/1/1975 as Priest Bp James Winchester Montgomery. m 7/11/2004 Cynthia Tobolodt. R S Ign Of Antioch Ch Antioch IL 1985-2006; Lawr Hall Sch Chicago IL 1981-1985; Dir Gr Ch Oak Pk IL 1981-1983; R S Jn's Epis Ch Chicago IL 1979-1980; R S Jn's Ch Shenandoah IA 1975-1979. cynthia.eckholm@trustmarkins.com

ECKIAN, Deirdre (WA) 132 F Street SE, Washington DC 20003 **Asst to the R Chr Ch Georgetown Washington DC 2006-** B Orlando FL 7/17/1975 BA Ya 1997; MDiv Ya Berk 2003. D 6/10/2006 P 1/20/2007 Bp John Chane. m 5/24/2008 James Leslie. deirdre_eckian@yahoo.com

ECKMAN JR, Daniel Willard (Va) 3160 Grovehurst Pl, Moved to SC in August 2011, Alexandria VA 22310 **Supvsr Field Educ VTS Alexandria VA 2001-** B Baltimore MD 5/31/1946 s Daniel Willard Eckman & Ada. BS U of Maryland 1969; MDiv VTS 1972; PrTS 1998. D 5/25/1972 P 2/3/1973 Bp David Keller Leighton Sr. m 5/28/1970 Barbara R Eckman c 3. R Emm Epis Ch Alexandria VA 1998-2011; S Phil's Epis Ch Greenville SC 1997-1998; Dir of Dvlpmt Chr Ch Greenville SC 1995-1998; Dir of Dvlpmt S Andr's Chap S Andrews TN 1991-1995; R St Martins-In-The-Field Ch Severna Pk MD 1978-1990; S Jn's Ch Mt Washington Baltimore MD 1974-1978. aceeckman@aol.com

ECKSTEIN, Carol Garvey (NCal) Po Box 534, Bayside CA 95524 **D Chr Ch Eureka CA 1998-** B Sacramento CA 4/20/1947 d Albert George Garvey & Emily Jane. EFM STUSo; AA Sacramento City Coll 1977; EFM San Francisco St U 1979; Coll of the Redwoods 2002. D 11/2/1996 Bp William Jerry Winterrowd. m 7/29/1986 Conrad Eckstein c 1. D S Laurence's Epis Mssn Conifer CO 1996-1997. garvey@humboldt1.com

EDDY, Charles H. (Ak) P.O. Box 747, Willow AK 99688 B Cincinnati OH 1/24/1939 s William Henry Eddy & Catherine Dean. BA Hanover Coll 1962; MDiv VTS 1966. D 6/5/1966 Bp William R Moody P 12/1/1966 Bp William J Gordon Jr. c 2. S Mary's Ch Anchorage AK 1972-2000; Asst The Ch Of The H Trin Juneau AK 1966-1969. chuckeddy85@gmail.com

EDDY, Diane Lynn (Ia) 1458 Locust St, Dubuque IA 52001 B Mendota IL 2/24/1960 d Eugene Paul Clark & Margaret Louise. D 2/22/2009 Bp Alan Scarfe. m 7/28/1990 David Ross Eddy c 1. ladyhummer1@peoplepc.com

EDDY, Elizabeth (NJ) 1111 Parsippany Blvd Apt 130, Parsippany NJ 07054 **Supply P Dio Newark Newark NJ 2010-** B Sullivan's Island SC 9/2/1943 d Robert Anthony Brandewie & Vada Orion. BA Florida St U 1964; MA Florida St U 1968; PhD Florida St U 1970; MDiv Nash 1982. D 6/20/1982 Bp H Coleman McGehee Jr P 3/2/1984 Bp John Shelby Spong. c 1. S Jn's Ch Eliz NJ 2001-2009; Supply P Dio New Jersey Trenton NJ 1997-2001; Supply P Dio Newark Newark NJ 1997-2001; S Jn's Ch Fords NJ 1987-1997; Asst Ch Of The Atone Tenafly NJ 1984-1986; Asst S Paul's Ch Englewood NJ 1984-1985; Asst S Steph's Ch Hamburg MI 1982-1983. Contemplative Outreach 1986; Curs 1977; DOK 1977; Kairos 1987; Tres Dias 1984. brandyweave@gmail.com

EDDY, William Welles (Mass) Po Box 3615, Waquoit MA 02536 **Trin Epis Ch Wrentham MA 2009-** B Hartford CT 9/14/1946 s Welles Eddy & Elizabeth. BA Ya 1968; Epis TS of The SW 1975; New York Inst of Tech 1976. D 6/11/1977 P 6/28/1978 Bp Paul Moore Jr. m 4/8/1994 Eileen Walsh c 2. Int Par Of The Epiph Winchester MA 2008; S Paul's Ch In Nantucket Nantucket MA 2007-2008; Ch Of S Jn The Evang Duxbury MA 2005-2007; S Mary's Epis Ch Barnstable MA 2004; Trin Epis Ch Weymouth MA 2002-2004; Chr Ch Epis Harwich Port MA 2000-2002; Int S Andr's Ch Hanover MA 1998-2000; Sabbatical P S Steph's Ch Cohasset MA 1997; Ch Of The Gd Shpd Wareham MA 1995-1997; Int S Jn's Ch Sandwich MA 1994-1995; Int All SS Ch Whitman MA 1992-1994; S Andr's Ch Edgartown MA 1987-1991; S Ptr's Ch On The Canal Buzzards Bay MA 1987; Int R S Andr's Ch Edgartown MA 1984-1986; S Jn's Ch Jamaica Plain MA 1981-1984; All SS' Ch Sthrn Shores NC 1979-1982; Gr Ch Vineyard Haven MA 1977-1978. wmweddy@comcast.net

EDELMAN, Walter Lucian (SanD) 17427 Gibraltar Ct, San Diego CA 92128 B White Plains NY 1/11/1937 s Walter Leon Edelman & Mary Emma. BA Ken 1958; U Of Paris-Sorbonne Fr 1958; U Of Strasbourg Fr 1959; MDiv GTS 1962. D 6/9/1962 P 12/22/1962 Bp Horace W B Donegan. P-in-c H Cross Mssn Carlsbad CA 1996-1999; R Chr Ch Coronado CA 1978-1995; The Bp's Sch La Jolla CA 1976-1978; Assoc Chr Ch Coronado CA 1973-1976; R Ch Of The Medtr Bronx NY 1967-1973; Cur Chr Epis Ch Tarrytown NY 1962-1965.

EDEN, Jonathan T (Mass) 865 Madison Ave, New York NY 10021 **Chr Ch Cambridge Cambridge MA 2009-** B Chicago, IL 10/1/1974 s C(harles) Clifton Eden & Anne T. BS Bates Coll 1996; MBA Boston Coll 2002; MDiv Andover Newton TS 2006. D 6/2/2007 P 1/12/2008 Bp M(arvil) Thomas Shaw III. Lilly Fell S Jas Ch New York NY 2007-2009. jeden@cccambridge.org

EDEN, Kathryn O (CNY) 120 W 5th St, Oswego NY 13126 B Utica NY 3/16/1947 d William Elliott Eden & Kathryn Jane. AA Mohawk Vlly Cmnty Coll 1966; BA Utica Coll 1968; MS SUNY 1973; MDiv Bex 1979. D 6/23/1979 P 5/28/1980 Bp Ned Cole. R Ch Of The Resurr Oswego NY 2000-2009; Vic S Paul's Ch (Sum Chap) Waterville NY 1992-2000; R S Steph's Ch New Hartford NY 1992-2000; Ch Of The Gd Shpd Rangeley ME 1984-1992; St Andrews Epis Ch Rome NY 1981-1984; Cur Trin Memi Ch Binghamton NY 1979-1981. heden80@aol.com

EDENS III, Henry Harman (NC) 8011 Douglas Ave, Dallas TX 75225 **Chr Ch Charlotte NC 2006-** B Richmond VA 6/12/1970 s Henry Harman Edens & Jane Reed. BA Hampden-Sydney Coll 1992; MDiv Ya Berk 1996. D 6/15/1996 Bp Peter James Lee P 1/1/1997 Bp Frank Clayton Matthews. m 2/10/2000 Beverly Thagard c 2. Assoc R S Mich And All Ang Ch Dallas TX 2002-2006; Assoc R S Paul's Ch Ivy VA 1998-2002; Asst R S Paul's Ch Augusta GA 1996-1998; Par Assoc R E Lee Memi Ch (Epis) Lexington VA 1994-1995. chip.edens@yahoo.com

EDER, Craig Eduard (WA) 3103 Cathedral Ave Nw, Washington DC 20008 **Died 11/22/2009** B Ridley Park PA 9/6/1919 s Charles Eduard Eder & Wilhilmina Frederika. BA Harv 1942; BD VTS 1944. D 6/3/1944 Bp Oliver J Hart P 1/25/1945 Bp Angus Dun. "A Flash Of Bright Air," Other Worlds Press, 2001. Friends Of St. Ben - Chairman Of The Bd 1984-2005.

EDGAR, Barbara Look (Mass) 295 Sudbury Lane, Hyannis MA 02601 **Died 12/24/2009** B New York,NY 7/27/1936 d Allen MacMartin Look & Maria Sloan. AA Bradford Jr Coll 1956; BS Col 1959; MDiv Harvard DS 1987. D 6/11/1988 Bp David Elliot Johnson P 5/1/1989 Bp Barbara Clementine Harris. c 3. The Fllshp of S Jn. bw1@gis.net

EDGERTON, Richard Triem (Wyo) 2457 Barrington Way Unit 303, Wooster OH 44691 B Salem OH 10/17/1928 s Gilbert Edgerton & Harriet A. BS Ohio Nthrn U 1952; MDiv VTS 1982. D 6/26/1982 P 4/1/1983 Bp John Harris Burt. m 6/18/1949 Beverly Stouell c 2. S Lk's Epis Ch Buffalo WY 1991-1997; Int S Ptr's Epis Ch Sheridan WY 1989-1990; R S Ptr's Ch Tecumseh MI 1983-1988; Asst S Andr Epis Ch Mentor OH 1982-1983. rev-bev@trib.com

EDINGTON, Mark David Wheeler (Mass) 26 Plympton St, Cambridge MA 02138 **S Jn's Ch Newtonville MA 2009-** B Lansing MI 3/15/1961 s Edgar David Edington & Patricia Constance. D 5/27/2000 Bp M(arvil) Thomas Shaw III P 5/26/2001 Bp Barbara Clementine Harris. m 8/20/1983 Judith Hadden. D S Dunstans Epis Ch Dover MA 2000-2009. mark_edington@harvard.edu

EDLEMAN JR, Samuel Warren (Md) 1257 Weller Way, Westminster MD 21158 B Savannah GA 3/12/1936 s Samuel Warren Edleman & Adelaide Elizabeth. BA Oglethorpe U 1957; STB GTS 1960. D 6/5/1960 P 4/25/1961 Bp Albert R Stuart. m 6/7/1960 Margaret Frances Young c 3. Asst Ch Of The Ascen Westminster MD 1999; Int S Phil's Ch Annapolis MD 1997-1999; Int S Lk's Ch E Hampton NY 1996-1997; Int Gr Ch Brunswick MD 1994-1995; Garrett Cnty Epis Ch Oakland MD 1992; P-in-c All SS Ch Annapolis Jct MD 1982-1991; R S Mk's Ch Highland MD 1975-1981; Asst R S Paul's Ch Augusta GA 1965-1975; Vic Chr Epis Ch Dublin GA 1961-1965; P-in-c Gr Epis Ch Sandersville GA 1961-1965; P-in-c S Lk's Epis Hawkinsville GA 1960-1961; D Trin Ch Cochran GA 1960-1961. sedleman@yahoo.com

EDLER, John Richard (Nwk) 130 Cleaves Point Rd, East Marion NY 11939 B Brooklyn NY 6/16/1924 s George Olaf Edler & Frances Croly. BA Trin 1945; STB Ya Berk 1948. D 3/18/1948 P 12/1/1948 Bp James P De Wolfe. m 6/4/1949 Jean Palmer c 4. Vic S Alb's Ch Oakland NJ 1966-1983; R Trin Ch Irvington NJ 1951-1966; P-in-c Ch Of The Redeem Mattituck NY 1948-1949; P-in-c S Mary's Ch Hampton Bays NY 1948-1949. jedler1@optonline.net

EDMAN, David Arthur (FtW) HC 70 Box 206, Ardmore OK 73401 B Worcester MA 1/9/1930 s Victor Raymond Edman & Edith Marie. BA Wheaton Coll 1955; MA Col 1958; BD UTS 1959. D 1/10/1959 P 7/1/1959 Bp Charles Francis Boynton. m 9/14/1986 Rita J Hayward. Int S Paul's Epis Ch Gainesville TX 2008-2010; R Ch Of S Thos Camden ME 1984-1991; R Gr Ch Scottsville NY 1969-1984; Cn Chr Ch Rochester NY 1965-1968; Cur Chr Ch Bronxville NY 1959-1962. Auth, "Your Weaknesses Are Your Strengths," Loyola U Press, 1993; Auth, "Once Upon an Eternity," Resource Pub, 1984; Auth, "Of Wise Men & Fools: Realism in the Bible," DoubleDay, 1972. daedman@earthlink.net

EDMAN, Elizabeth Marie (Chi) 703 Hinman Ave #3N, Evanston IL 60202 B Fort Smith AR 12/20/1962 d Norman Edman & Martha Rose. BA Franklin & Marshall Coll 1985; MDiv UTS 1991. D 6/4/2005 P 8/5/2006 Bp Thomas C Ely. c 2. Epis Coun At Nthrn Illinois U Evanston IL 2006-2009; Cathd Ch Of S Paul Burlington VT 2005-2006. liz.edman@gmail.com

EDMANDS II, Frank A (SO) 3984 Wynding Dr, Columbus OH 43214 **P Trin Epis Ch London OH 2008-** B Newton MA 5/16/1946 s Lawrence Edmands & Dorothy Diller. BA California St U 1976; MA California St U 1981; MDiv GTS 1990. D 6/16/1990 Bp Frederick Houk Borsch P 1/18/1991 Bp William George Burrill. m 5/2/1981 Lynn Carter-Edmands. S Andr's Ch Pickerington OH 2007-2008; R Chr Memi Epis Ch Danville PA 2000-2006; P-in-c All SS Epis Ch Williamsport PA 1998-2000; Trin Epis Ch Williamsport PA 1998-1999; Sch Min Ch Of The H Trin Pawling NY 1994-1997; Vic Ch Of The Gd Shpd Savona NY 1992-1994; R S Jas Ch Hammondsport NY 1992-1994; Asst R Chr Ch Pittsford NY 1990-1992. fedmands@sbcglobal.net

EDMINSTER, Beverley Beadle (Az) 1810 E Camino Cresta, Tucson AZ 85718 **D S Phil's In The Hills Tucson AZ 2000-** B Atlantic IA 10/29/1931 d Howard Owen Beadle & Frances Maxine. BA U of Tulsa 1953; Med U of Arizona 1966. D 10/14/2000 Bp Robert Reed Shahan. c 2. Benedictine Ord 1993-2003; Ssje,Cambridge Mass 1994. bevedminster@comcast.net

EDMISTON, Alan James (LI) 3939 Ocean Dr, Vero Beach FL 32963 B Bay Shore NY 7/2/1940 s Ralph William Edmiston & Helen Radford. BS Rider Coll 1963; STB PDS 1967. D 4/22/1967 P 10/1/1967 Bp Alfred L Banyard. R All SS Ch Bayside NY 1982-1999; S Ptr's by-the-Sea Epis Ch Bay Shore NY 1970-1982; Cur Gr Epis Ch Plainfield NJ 1967-1970. montauksouth@aol.com

EDMONDS, Curtis M (Nev) Po Box 70342, Las Vegas NV 89170 B Des Moines IA 9/24/1944 s Augustus Hill Edmonds & Leone Margret. BS U of Nevada at Reno 1980. D 5/18/1987 P 12/1/1987 Bp Stewart Clark Zabriskie. Assoc S Tim's Epis Ch Henderson NV 1987-1992.

EDMONDS, John B (NY) Po Box 1535, Blue Hill ME 04614 B Concord NH 3/26/1942 s John Bulkeley Edmonds & Katherine Temple. BA Carleton Coll 1964; BD EDS 1968. D 6/22/1968 P 6/14/1969 Bp Anson Phelps Stokes Jr. Assoc P S Mk's Ch Taunton MA 1998-2002; Supt Seamens Ch Inst Newport RI 1994-2002; Pstr Co-ordinator Team Monticello NY 1993-1994; Vic S Eliz's Ch Hope Vlly RI 1987-1992; Vic S Thos' Alton Wood River Jct RI 1987-1992; Dir/Sch for Deacons Dio Rhode Island Providence RI 1981-1992; Chapl Delaware St Hosp New Castle DE 1975-1977; Cur Ch Of The H Nativ So Weymouth MA 1968-1970. moosoneek@gmail.com

EDMONDSON, Emily Fisher (SwVa) 37367 Rafferty Rd, Chilhowie VA 24319 **Asst The Tazewell Cnty Cluster Of Epis Parishes Tazewell VA 2010-** B New Milford, CT 12/23/1951 d Benjamin Lang Barringer & Anne Allen. BS U of Tennessee 1973. D 3/13/2010 P 10/2/2010 Bp Frank Neff Powell. m 6/15/2002 Keith Everett Edmondson c 2. emilye@centurylink.net

EDMONDSON, Stephen Bud (Va) 3939 Seminary Rd, Alexandria VA 22304 **R S Thos Epis Ch McLean VA 2007-** B Munich DE 4/13/1962 s Elmer Bud Edmondson & Clarice Marie. BA Stan 1984; MDiv Ya Berk 1988. D 12/29/1988 Bp Gordon Taliaferro Charlton P 7/1/1989 Bp Maurice Manuel Benitez. c 2. Middlesex Area Cluster Mnstry Higganum CT 1992-1998; S Cyp's Ch Lufkin TX 1989-1991. STTHOM1RECTOR@COX.NET

EDMONSON, Harold W (NAM) 716 S Cedar Ave, Roswell NM 88203 B Clayton IN 8/16/1925 s Willard Franklin Edmonson & Ruth. 10 other institutions; BS Cbury Coll 1949; MS Indiana U 1952; Cuttington U Coll 1958; MDiv Epis TS of The SW 1961. D 7/18/1961 Bp Richard Earl Dicus P 1/24/1962 Bp Everett H Jones. m 12/24/1947 Ava Villars c 3. The Epis Ch In Navajoland Coun Farmington NM 1981-1987; Pro Cathd Epis Ch Of S Clem El Paso TX 1975-1980; R S Mich's Ch Tucumcari NM 1969-1975; R S Paul's/Peace Ch Las Vegas NM 1969-1975; Assoc Ch of the H Faith Santa Fe NM 1968-1969; R S Ptr's Epis Ch Rockport TX 1964-1968; R Epis Ch Of The Mssh Gonzales TX 1961-1964. Frgn Mssy Dept., ECUSA 1956-1959; Soc of Form Spec Agents of FBI. Who's Who in Rel, First Ed 1991; Commendation Pope Jn Paul II on his 25th Anniv. avaedmon@dfn.com

EDMUNDS, Robert Douglas (Mass) PO Box 1287, Edgartown MA 02539 **Epis Ch Cntr New York NY 2011-** B Boston MA 1/1/1955 s Verne Cheney Edmunds & Carolyn Jane. AA Quinsigamund Cmnty Coll 1975; BA U of Massachusetts 1977; MDiv Yale DS 1984. D 6/13/1984 P 2/27/1985 Bp Andrew Frederick Wissemann. m 8/20/1977 Deborah Schuller c 2. Exec Coun Appointees New York NY 2008-2011; R S Andr's Ch Edgartown MA 1992-2008; Dioc Coun Mem Dio Wstrn New York Tonawanda NY 1989-1992; R S Paul's Epis Ch Mayville NY 1987-1992; Dir - Hunger T/F Dio Wstrn New York Tonawanda NY 1985-1990; Cur S Lk's Epis Ch Jamestown NY 1984-1987. "Selective Divestment: Bringing Econ pressure on the Govt of Israel," *LivCh*, LivCh Fndt, 2006; "Israel's Actions Can't be Ignored," *LivCh*, LivCh Fndt, 2005. rde111@hotmail.com

EDSALL, Hugh Crichton (Fla) 31 Aledo Ct, Saint Augustine FL 32086 B Princeton NJ 5/20/1931 s Preston William Edsall & Katherine Crichton. BA Swarthmore Coll 1953; MDiv GTS 1956. D 6/15/1956 Bp Edwin A Penick P 12/21/1956 Bp Richard Henry Baker. m 9/12/1969 Judith E Loeser c 6. Assoc S Lk's Epis Ch Live Oak FL 2001-2007; Int Ch Of The Redeem Asheville NC 1996-2000; Pres Stndg Com Dio Florida Jacksonville FL 1990-1994; Pres, Stndg Com Dio Florida Jacksonville FL 1986-1989; P-in-c S Jos's Ch Newberry FL 1982-1993; Mssn Area Supvsr Convoc Dio Florida Jacksonville FL 1980-1984; Assoc S Mich's Ch Gainesville FL 1980-1982; Stndg Com Dio Wstrn No Carolina Asheville NC 1974-1976; R Ch Of The Redeem Asheville NC 1971-1980; R S Mich And All Ang Ch So Bend IN 1963-1969; Cn Mssnr Dio Nthrn Indiana So Bend IN 1961-1963; R Trin Epis Ch Logansport IN 1959-1961; Asst Ch Of The Redeem Sarasota FL 1958-1959; Cur S Mart's Epis Ch Charlotte NC 1956-1958. "Whole Chrsnty," *Whole Chrsnty*, The Angl Bookstore, 2004. hughedsall3@gmail.com

EDSON, Heidi Louise (Haw) PO Box 157, Hoolehua HI 96729 **Cler-in-Charge Gr Ch Hoolehua HI 2010-** B Germany 1/11/1955 d Ella. AA Young Harris Coll 1975; BM Georgia Sthrn U 1977; MDiv CDSP 2010. D 6/12/2010 P 12/11/2010 Bp Robert LeRoy Fitzpatrick. m 4/29/2000 Douglas Allen Edson. edson.heidi@gmail.com

EDSON, John B (CPa) 622 S York Rd, Dillsburg PA 17019 B West Point,NY 5/6/1938 s Holt Faifield Butt & Elizabeth Edson. BA Tusculum Coll 1966; STB Ya Berk 1970. D 6/27/1970 Bp William Foreman Creighton P 3/13/1971 Bp John Harris Burt. Hope Epis Ch Manheim PA 2001-2003; R Trin Epis Ch Monroe MI 1998-2001; S Lk's Epis Ch Mechanicsburg PA 1997-1998; Dio Wstrn Massachusetts Springfield MA 1996-1997; Int S Jas Epis Ch At Woonsocket Woonsocket RI 1995-1996; Trin Ch Potsdam NY 1994-1995; Zion Ch Hudson Falls NY 1992-1994; Int S Jas Epis Ch Essex Jct VT 1991-1992; Int S Paul's Ch Winona MN 1990-1991; Int Chr Ch Austin MN 1989-1990; R Chr Ch Albert Lea MN 1986-1989; Dio Spokane Spokane WA 1980-1985; R All SS Ch Spokane WA 1979-1986; R S Lk's Epis Ch Niles OH 1974-1979; P-in-c S Paul's Ch Bellevue OH 1972-1974; Mem, COM Dio Ohio Cleveland OH 1971-1974; Cur S Barn Ch Bay Vill OH 1970-1972. "In Gratitude for Lutherans," *LivCh*, January 23, 2007, 2007. Citation ARC 1976.

EDSON, Larry (Eau) 608 Madison St, Stanley WI 54768 **Cmncatn Com Dio Eau Claire Eau Claire WI 2008-** B Kansas City MO 8/9/1939 s James Lionel Edson & Edythe. BS Cntrl Missouri St U 1965; MS Cntrl Missouri St U 1966; DO Kirksville Coll 1974. D 11/30/1989 Bp William Charles Wantland P 3/29/2003 Bp Keith Bernard Whitmore. m 9/17/1960 Marilyn June Twenter c 3. H Trin Ch Conrath WI 2005-2009. ESA. lmedson@charter.net

EDSON, Robert Bruce (Mass) 4 Home Meadows Ln, Hingham MA 02043 **part time Emm Ch W Roxbury MA 2011-; Part Time S Jn's Epis Ch Franklin MA 2008-** B West Point NY 4/6/1941 s Holt Fairfield Butt & Elizabeth. BA Tusculum Coll 1963; MDiv EDS 1966. D 6/25/1966 P 5/27/1967 Bp William Foreman Creighton. c 2. Chair Recently Ord Cler Dio Massachusetts Boston MA 1985-1996; R Ch Of S Jn The Evang Hingham MA 1981-2007; Vacancy Consult Dio Washington Washington DC 1980-1981; R Trin Ch Washington DC 1976-1981; R S Jn's Ch Cornwall NY 1970-1976; full time S Jn's Ch Chevy Chase MD 1966-1970. edsonrb@aol.com

EDWARD, Baskaran John (NY) 8 Sunnyside Ave, Pleasantville NY 10570 B Kelang Malaysia 5/31/1964 s Edward Thomas Chelliah & Sushila Mary. BTh Un Biblic Sem, Pune, India 1988; BD/MDiv Un Biblic Sem, Pune, India 1990; ThM PrTS 2002. Trans from Church of the Province of South East Asia 5/3/2004 Bp John Palmer Croneberger. m 8/28/1995 Addaline Princet Suja Godwin c 3. P S Jn's Ch Pleasantville NY 2006-2010; Ch Of The H Trin W Orange NJ 2004-2006. frjohnpvlle@optonline.net

EDWARD, Gadi Michael (ND) 120 8th St S, Moorhead MN 56560 B 1/1/1963 s Michael Afkey Edward & Yomama Toba. D 6/23/2007 Bp Michael Gene Smith. m 10/28/1998 Charity Justin Dudu c 2.

EDWARDS, Bonnie Ellen (Los) 34 Via Jolitas, Rancho Santa Margarita CA 92688 **P-in-c S Thos Of Cbury Par Long Bch CA 2010-** B Tyler TX 10/3/1961 d Tilton Orren Edwards & Mildred I. BA U of No Texas 1987; MDiv Epis TS of The SW 2007. D 6/23/2007 Bp Don Adger Wimberly P 8/8/2009 Bp Joseph Jon Bruno. S Clem's-By-The-Sea Par San Clemente CA 2009; Transitional D S Clem's-By-The-Sea Par San Clemente CA 2008-2009; Asst S Steph's Ch Huntsville TX 2007-2008. revbonniee@gmail.com

EDWARDS, Carl Norris (Md) 1509 Glencoe Rd, Sparks MD 21152 B Asheville NC 11/19/1933 s Lee Henry Edwards & Elia Rand. BA Duke 1955; MDiv UTS 1960. D 6/29/1965 P 5/1/1966 Bp Thomas Augustus Fraser Jr. m 9/3/1955 Janet P Ray c 3. Vic S Barth's Ch Pittsboro NC 2007-2011; P-in-c S Paul's Ch Louisburg NC 2002-2007; R Imm Epis Ch Glencoe MD 1979-2001; Asst S Paul's Par Baltimore MD 1976-1979. Soc for Values in Higher Educ 1961. Bp's Awd for Outstanding Ord Mnstry Dio Maryland 2000. carljanet@bellsouth.net

✠ **EDWARDS, Rt Rev Dan Thomas** (Nev) 9480 S Eastern Ave Ste 236, Las Vegas NV 89123 **Bp of Nevada Dio Nevada Las Vegas NV 2008-** B Texarkana AR 1/20/1950 s Jewel Sumpter Edwards & Verdi Ruth. BA U of Texas 1972; JD U of Texas 1975; MDiv GTS 1990; STM GTS 1992. D 8/6/1990 Bp David Bell Birney IV P 5/1/1991 Bp Frank Kellogg Allan. m 10/31/1977 Linda H Holdeman c 2. R S Fran Ch Macon GA 1994-2007; Asst to R Chr Ch Macon GA 1990-1994. Auth, "Study Guides Pb Sprtlty Reflections On"; Auth, "Tx Law Revs". AAR. dan@episcopalnevada.org

EDWARDS, Don Raby (Va) 106 Dunstan Ct, Morehead City NC 28557 B Edgecomb NC 6/13/1931 s Charles Kenneth Edwards & Mabel. BA E Carolina U 1955; MDiv VTS 1958. D 6/25/1958 P 2/28/1959 Bp Thomas H Wright. m 6/3/1957 Jane Credle c 2. Cler Compstn Com Dio Virginia Richmond VA 1986-1994; Stndg Com Dio Virginia Richmond VA 1981-1984; Dep Gc Dio E Carolina Kinston NC 1979-1985; Gc Futures Sites Dio E Carolina Kinston NC 1979-1985; Gc Futures Sites Dio E Carolina Kinston NC 1979-1985; Dn Reg 12 Dio Virginia Richmond VA 1978-1982; Stndg Com Dio Virginia Richmond VA 1976-1979; Exec Com VTS Alexandria VA 1975-1979; R S Steph's Ch Richmond VA 1973-1993; Chair Vacancy Consult & Par Dvlpmt Dio Virginia Richmond VA 1973-1976; Chair Vacancy Consult & Par Dvlpmt Dio Virginia Richmond VA 1973-1976; Com Dio Virginia Richmond VA 1973-1976; Stndg Com Cathd Of S Phil Atlanta GA

1972-1973; Excoun Cathd Of S Phil Atlanta GA 1969-1971; Gc Com St Ch Dio E Carolina Kinston NC 1967-1969; Stndg Com Dio E Carolina Kinston NC 1967-1968; Chair Deptce Dio E Carolina Kinston NC 1964-1967; R S Steph's Ch Goldsboro NC 1963-1968; Bec Dio E Carolina Kinston NC 1962-1968; Dep Gc Dio E Carolina Kinston NC 1961-1967; R S Paul's Epis Ch Wilmington NC 1961-1963; Excoun Dio E Carolina Kinston NC 1960-1967; Vic S Chris's Ch Havelock NC 1958-1961. Auth, "Conversations w Seward Hiltner"; Auth, "Cassette Conversations w Seward Hiltner". DD VTS Alexandria VA 1979; Fell VTS Alexandria VA 1971; Hon Cn Dio Bukedi Uganda; Hon Cn Dio Guatemala. ducks12@embarqmail.com

EDWARDS, Douglas Brian (Los) 4255 Harbour Island Ln, Oxnard CA 93035 **Hsng Cmsn Dio Los Angeles Los Angeles CA 1993-; Chair Immigration & CitizenshipComm Dio Los Angeles Los Angeles CA 1987-; Stwdshp & Fin Dio Los Angeles Los Angeles CA 1985-** B Orange CA 9/10/1956 s Harold Kenneth Edwards & Mary Louise. MDiv GTS 1984; BS Newport U 1984; DMin GTF 1997. D 6/16/1984 P 12/19/1984 Bp Robert C Rusack. m 4/18/1982 Lynn Stopher c 2. R S Ambr Par Claremont CA 1990-2004; Trin Epis Ch Orange CA 1984-1990. "Questions from the Pew," *LA Times Weekly Column*, 2003; Auth, "Abortion: Does the Epis Ch Have a Plcy?," *Living Ch*, 1984. Hon Archd Dio Senyani 2004. canondougedwards@yahoo.com

EDWARDS, Dwight Woodbury (ECR) Po Box 853, Pacific Grove CA 93950 **Vol Chapl for Ret Cler Dio El Camino Real Monterey CA 2006-** B Oakland CA 6/11/1930 s Maurice Woodbury Edwards & Ruth Evelyn. BA U CA 1951; CDSP 1955. D 6/12/1955 P 12/17/1955 Bp Karl M Block. m 1/1/1991 Rose J Jansson. Pres, Stndg Com Dio California San Francisco CA 1976-1977; R Ch of S Mary's by the Sea Pacific Grove CA 1973-1998; R S Tim's Epis Ch Mtn View CA 1963-1973; Vic S Tim's Epis Ch Mtn View CA 1955-1963; Sem-in-charge S Lk's Ch Jolon CA 1953-1955; Sem-in-charge S Matt's Ch San Ardo CA 1953-1955. DD CDSP 1993; Par Hall Named Dedication S Mary, Pacific Grove CA Pacific Grove CA 1993; Par Hall Named Dedication S Tim, Mtn View CA 1976. dwightandrosi@redshift.com

EDWARDS, Fitzroy Foster (NY) 72 Carnegie Ave, Elmont NY 11003 **D S Phil's Ch New York NY 1998-** B Saint John's Antigua AG 6/15/1941 s Joseph Foster Edwards & Susanna Jestina. BS CUNY 1965; MS U of the Incarnate Word 1970. D 5/16/1998 Bp Richard Frank Grein. m 7/16/1966 Yvonne Monica Arnott c 3. Auth, "Journ Of Clincl Microbiology". Amer Soc For Microbiology; Med Mycology Soc Of New York; Norad.

EDWARDS, Halbert Daniel (Okla) 1728 NW 42nd St, Oklahoma City OK 73118 B Oklahoma City OK 2/28/1940 s Joseph Henry Edward & Clara Elma. BA U of Oklahoma 1961; BD Nash 1964; DDS U of Oklahoma 1982. D 6/20/1964 P 12/21/1964 Bp Chilton Powell. m 8/12/1967 Lillian Ann Overstreet c 2. Dio Colorado Denver CO 1971-1978; Asst S Mary's Ch Edmond OK 1968-1971; Vic S Barn Ch Poteau OK 1964-1968. sailprozac@cox.net

EDWARDS, James Dennison (LI) 700 Trutt Rd, Winfield PA 17889 B Endicott NY 6/23/1940 s Floyd Marvin Edwards & Marguerite Beatrice. AAS SUNY 1960; BA Dakota Wesl 1964; MDiv GTS 1970; MSW Yeshiva U 1982. D 3/14/1970 P 12/19/1970 Bp Frederick J Warnecke. m 7/19/2009 John Xavier Jobson. Vic Ch Of The Redeem Mattituck NY 1990-2002; Sr. Ther Epis Cmnty Serv Long Island 1927 Garden City NY 1985-1986; Assoc Gr Epis Ch Massapequa NY 1981-1984; Vic St Christophers Ch Massapequa NY 1976-1981; Cur S Lk's Ch Forest Hills NY 1972-1974; Cur Ch of St Andrews & St Matthews Wilmington DE 1971-1972; D-in-trng Trin Ch Bethlehem PA 1970-1971. SocMary 1990. edwards2@ptd.net

EDWARDS, James Lloyd (USC) 4628 Datura Rd, Columbia SC 29205 **P-in-c Ch Of The Cross Columbia SC 1993-** B Morgan City LA 9/9/1941 s James Lucius Edwards & Nelwya Louise. BS LSU 1962; PhD LSU 1971; MDiv Nash 1974. D 6/30/1974 Bp William Evan Sanders P 5/1/1975 Bp John Vander Horst. m 6/25/1988 Curry Verner c 1. Cn Pstr Trin Cathd Columbia SC 1982-1993; Dio Tennessee Nashville TN 1978-1982; Vic S Thos Epis Ch Knoxville TN 1978-1982; Asst S Geo's Ch Nashville TN 1974-1978; Dio Tennessee Nashville TN 1973-1975; Bte Dio Tennessee Nashville TN 1973-1975. Auth, "How We Belong," *Fight & Pray*, The Alb Inst, 1993; Auth, "Discovering Your Sprtl Gifts," Cowley Press, 1988. lloyde@sc.rr.com

EDWARDS, James Paul (Nev) 1400 Ebbetts Dr, Reno NV 89503 **Assoc Trin Epis Ch Reno NV 2002-** B Salinas CA 10/4/1931 s Joseph Hiram Edwards & Catherine Constance. MA U of San Francisco; W Baden Coll; BA Gonzaga U 1955; BA Gonzaga U 1956. D 2/12/2002 P 9/14/2002 Bp Katharine Jefferts Schori. m 2/2/1963 Joan Irene Vertin. lviejo@juno.com

EDWARDS JR, John Richard (Ark) 6850 Rosefield Dr, La Mesa CA 91941 B Beloit WI 3/11/1929 s John Richard Edwards & Thelma Louise. BA Beloit Coll 1951; MDiv Nash 1960. D 10/31/1953 P 6/1/1954 Bp Donald H V Hallock. m 6/24/1950 Doris Koebel c 2. Int S Mk's Epis Ch Jonesboro AR 1999-2000; Int S Paul's Epis Ch Batesville AR 1997-1998; Int Trin Epis Ch Mineral Point WI 1996-1997; Int S Paul's Ch Fayetteville AR 1991-1993; S Barn' Epis Ch Los Angeles CA 1986-1989; Assoc R S Paul's Epis Ch Tustin CA 1983-1986; Off Of Bsh For ArmdF New York NY 1961-1969; P-in-c Trin Epis Ch Mineral Point WI 1954-1956. Angl Priests Euch League; Oblate OHC; Soc Of S Mary. dogwoodhouse@hotmail.com

EDWARDS II, J(ustin) Sargent (EpisSanJ) 765 Mesa View Dr Spc 98, Arroyo Grande CA 93420 B Denver CO 7/25/1933 s Justin Sargent Edwards & Virginia. BA U of Washington 1955; MDiv CDSP 1966; DMin Fuller TS 1988. D 6/29/1966 Bp Ivol I Curtis P 3/17/1967 Bp George Richard Millard. m 7/3/1994 Nancy Edwards c 3. R Calv Epis Ch Kaneohe HI 1978-1995; R S Steph's Ch Gilroy CA 1969-1978; Asst All SS Epis Ch San Leandro CA 1966-1969. Auth, *Hm Groups in Ch Renwl*, 1988. sargenancy@earthlink.net

EDWARDS, Laura MacFarland (WA) 13118 Collingwood Ter, Silver Spring MD 20904 B Dallas TX 5/13/1956 d R(obert) K(emerer) Edwards & Phoebe Lee. Hobart and Wm Smith Colleges 1976; BA U of Pennsylvania 1979; MDiv GTS 1984. D 6/2/1984 P 4/25/1985 Bp George Phelps Mellick Belshaw. c 3. Asst S Steph's Ch Newport News VA 1986-1988; Assoc S Mk's Ch In The Bowery New York NY 1984-1985. lmel54@yahoo.com

EDWARDS, Lydia A (NJ) 81 Hillside Ave, Metuchen NJ 08840 B Baltimore MD 12/29/1950 d Jack Gold & Jeter Grace. BA U of Maryland 1972; U of Wisconsin 1974; MDiv GTS 1982; BA Rutgers-The St U 2001. D 6/5/1982 Bp Albert Wiencke Van Duzer P 1/22/1983 Bp George Phelps Mellick Belshaw. m 6/20/1971 Paul Clemens c 1. S Lk And All SS' Ch Un NJ 1993-2004; Int S Lk And All SS' Ch Un NJ 1990-1991; New Brunswick Episurban Wk Com No Brunswick NJ 1984-1986; Chapl The Epis Campus Mnstry at Rutgers New Brunswick NJ 1982-1983; The Wm Alexander Procter Fndt Trenton NJ 1982-1983. Auth, "Study guide for The Mtn That Loved a Bird," 1985. OHC 1990. lydias.mailbox@gmail.com

EDWARDS, Lynn Chester (Pgh) 611 West St, Pittsburgh PA 15221 **COM Dio Pittsburgh Monroeville PA 2010-; P Assoc Trin Cathd Pittsburgh PA 2003-; Chr Epis Ch No Hills Pittsburgh PA 2000-** B Pittsburgh PA 10/30/1940 s Chester John Edwards & Eleanor. BSed. U of Pennsylvania 1963; MDiv GTS 1966. D 5/28/1966 Bp William S Thomas P 12/1/1966 Bp Austin Pardue. Vic Ch Of The Gd Shpd Pittsburgh PA 1971-1998; Vic S Jn's Epis Ch Donora PA 1966-1971. CBS, ECF, GAS; Ord Of S Ben, Comt, SocOLW. lynnchesedwards@cs.com

EDWARDS, Nancy Beltz (NCal) 215 Finch Pl SW Apt 305, Bainbridge Is WA 98110 B Tillamook OR 11/22/1927 d Fredrich R Beltz & Naomi Amy. BA U of Oregon 1949; MDiv CDSP 1984. D 6/10/1984 P 1/6/1985 Bp John Lester Thompson III. Organizing Vic S Jas Of Jerusalem Epis Ch Yuba City CA 1985-1986; Asst Min S Jn's Epis Ch Marysville CA 1984-1986. revnbe@hotmail.com

EDWARDS JR, O(tis) C(arl) (WNC) 115 Murphy Hill Rd, Weaverville NC 28787 **Adj P Epis Ch Of The H Sprt Mars Hill NC 2002-; P Assoc S Mary's Ch Asheville NC 1999-** B Bienville LA 6/15/1928 s Otis Carl Edwards & Margaret Lee. BA Centenary Coll 1949; STB GTS 1952; STM SMU 1962; MA U Chi 1963; PhD U Chi 1971; DD Nash 1976; DD U So 2006. D 5/28/1953 Bp Iveson Batchelor Noland P 4/28/1954 Bp Girault M Jones. m 2/19/1957 Jane T Trufant c 3. Prof SWTS Evanston IL 1983-1993; Dn SWTS Evanston IL 1974-1983; Prof Nash Nashotah WI 1964-1974; Vic Gr Ch Chicago IL 1961-1963; Vic S Paul's Epis Ch Waxahachie TX 1960-1961; Vic S Thos Ch Ennis TX 1960-1961; R Trin Epis Ch Morgan City LA 1957-1960; Vic S Paul's Ch Abbeville LA 1954-1957; Cur Trin Epis Ch Baton Rouge LA 1953-1954. Auth, *Elements of Homil*, Pueblo, 1981; Auth, *Lk's Story of Jesus*, Fortress, 1981; Auth, *The Bible for Today's Ch*, Seabury, 1980. Jos Cardinal Bernardin Natl Coun of Ch 2008; Lifetime Achievement Acad of Homil 2007; Bk of the Year Acad of Par Cler 2005; Raven Mystery Writers of Amer 1965. ocejunr@gmail.com

EDWARDS, Paul David (Los) 734 W Maplewood Ave, Fullerton CA 92832 B New York NY 4/27/1932 s George William Edwards & Louise Francis. BA U So 1954; BD UTS 1957; STM STUSo 1968; MA Chapman U 1981. D 6/17/1957 P 12/21/1957 Bp Horace W B Donegan. m 6/22/1957 Anita Soule c 3. Assiting Cler Trin Epis Ch Orange CA 2002-2007; Emm Par Fullerton CA 1963-1994; Cur S Jn's Ch Getty Sq Yonkers NY 1957-1958. Auth, "Sprtl Intelligence Handbook," Morris Pub, 1998. Aamft. paulnanita@sbcglobal.net

EDWARDS, Ralph (Alb) 50 Dana Ave Apt 205, Wynantskill NY 12198 **Adirondack Missions Brant Lake NY 1969-** B Philadelphia PA 6/29/1927 s Wilfred Edwards & Anna Humphrey. BA Tem 1956; STM PDS 1960. D 5/14/1960 Bp Oliver J Hart P 11/1/1960 Bp Joseph Gillespie Armstrong. Chr Ch Schenectady NY 1977; P-in-c + surrounding Mssn Ch S Jn The Evang Columbiaville NY 1970-1974; Vic Ch Of S Clem Of Rome Belford NJ 1961-1969; Cur Chr Ch Reading PA 1960-1961.

EDWARDS, Rebecca Nelson (ETenn) 4321 Eastgate Mall, San Diego CA 92121 **Ch Of The Gd Samar San Diego CA 2011-** B Reno NV 9/16/1978 d James Donovan Nelson & Georgia Morse. BA Wellesley Coll 2001; MDiv VTS 2011. D 6/4/2011 Bp Charles Glenn VonRosenberg. m 11/26/2003 Joshua Edwards. rebbles@gmail.com

EDWARDS, Robert Daniel (Los) 416 S Broadway, Redondo Beach CA 90277 **R S Marg Of Scotland Par San Juan Capistrano CA 1999-** B Augusta GA 7/22/1959 s Paul David Edwards & Anita. BA California St U 1982; MDiv

GTS 1987. D 6/20/1987 Bp Oliver Bailey Garver Jr P 5/1/1988 Bp William Carl Frey. m 8/6/1988 Michele Ann Manning. R Chr Ch Par Redondo Bch CA 1990-1999; Cur S Marg Of Scotland Par San Juan Capistrano CA 1987-1990. RMEDWARDS7@ATT.NET

EDWARDS JR, Theodore Whitfield (SwFla) 9211 31st Street Court East, Parrish FL 34219 B Glen Ridge NJ 12/14/1947 s Theodore Whitfield Edwards & Dorothy Ann. BA Hob 1970; MDiv VTS 1977; MA Webster U 1985; STM Yale DS 2001. Trans 9/10/2003 Bp Stephen Hays Jecko. m 1/3/1970 Carol Henseler c 2. P-in-c S Geo's Epis Ch Bradenton FL 2006-2010; R S Jn's Ch Ogdensburg NY 2003-2005; Chapl Off Of Bsh For ArmdF New York NY 1983-2003; Vic Ch Of The Trsfg Towaco NJ 1980-1983. Auth, "Refuge and Strength," Ch Pub Grp, 2008. Joint Serv Conf On Profsnl Ethics 2001-2004; Mltry Chapl Assn 1983-2004. NATO Medal US Marine Corps 1997; Meritorious Serv Medal (3) US Navy 1997; NATO Medal Royal Navy 1993; Coast Guard Commendation Medal US Coast Guard 1991; Coast Guard Achievement Medal US Coast Guard 1991; Navy Commendation Medal (2) US Navy 1989. twedwards@gmail.com

EDWARDS III, Tilden Hampton (WA) 9615 Page Ave, Bethesda MD 20814 B Austin TX 9/21/1935 s Tilden Hampton Edwards & Marie Mildred. BA Stan 1957; MDiv Harvard DS 1961; CAS EDS 1962; PhD Un Grad Sch Cincinnati OH 1979. D 6/16/1962 P 12/16/1962 Bp William Foreman Creighton. m 7/3/1999 Mary Lyon c 2. Cur Ch Of S Steph And The Incarn Washington DC 1962-1966. Auth, "Sprtl Dir, Sprtl Comp," Paulist Press, 2001; Auth, "Living Simply Through the Day (Revised; 1st Ed 1977)," Paulist Press, 1998; Auth, "Sabbath Time (revised 1st. ed 1980))," Upper Room, 1992; Auth, "Living in the Presence," Harper San Francisco, 1987; Ed, "Living w Apocalypse," Harper San Francisco, 1984; Auth, "All God's Chld," Abingdon Press, 1982; Auth, "Sprtl Friend," Paulist Press, 1980. DD VTS 2002; Phi Beta Kappa Stan 1957. tilden@erols.com

EDWARDS, Tom Turney (SwFla) 2033 Albert Cir, Wilmington NC 28403 B Winston-Salem NC 4/21/1921 s E Franklin Edwards & Sarah Elizabeth. BA U So 1942; BD EDS 1948; STM Harvard DS 1961; PhD Harv 1961. D 6/13/1948 P 1/1/1949 Bp Edwin A Penick. m 8/9/1944 Rosemary C Cody c 1. Cn The Amer Cathd of the H Trin Paris 75008 FR 1988-1990; R Ch Of The Ascen Clearwater FL 1975-1986; R S Paul's Ch Philadelphia PA 1956-1975; R S Phil's Ch Durham NC 1951-1956; Cn The Amer Cathd of the H Trin Paris 75008 FR 1950-1951; P-in-c S Gabr's Epis Ch Marion MA 1949-1950; Min in charge Ch Of The Adv Enfield NC 1948-1949.

EDWARDS JR, Walter Dewey (NC) Po Box 2346, Bryson City NC 28713 B Tryon NC 5/24/1928 s Walter Dewey Edwards & Maudie Leona. Roa 1946; BA Wheaton Coll 1952; MDiv STUSo 1955. D 4/20/1955 P 11/22/1955 Bp William Henry Marmion. m 5/22/1999 Lynda Schumacher c 3. Vic All SS Epis Ch Charlotte NC 1978-1992; Vic S Eliz's Ch Roanoke VA 1958-1961; Vic Chr Ch Pearisburg VA 1955-1958. Ed, *All SS Curric*, 1982. Meritorious Serv Medal US AF 1978; Humanitarian Serv Medal US AF 1975; Bronze Star Medal US AF 1970. whmbo@hughes.net

EDWARDS, William Glover (WNC) 38 Wildwood Ave, Asheville NC 28804 B Tarboro NC 6/1/1933 s Solomon Henry Edwards & Elizabeth Quince. BA U No Carolina 1955; MDiv GTS 1958; DMin GTF 1996. D 6/29/1958 Bp Edwin A Penick P 5/23/1959 Bp Richard Henry Baker. m 5/5/1972 Margret Louise Murphy c 2. Int P S Lk's Epis Ch Asheville NC 2004-2005; Int P Trin Ch Spruce Pine NC 2002-2003; Dioc Conv Secy Dio Wstrn No Carolina Asheville NC 2001-2008; Int P S Fran' Epis Ch Rutherfordton NC 2000-2001; Chair - Prov Iv Commisions on Min Dio Wstrn No Carolina Asheville NC 1988-1994; Dep - GC Dio Wstrn No Carolina Asheville NC 1969-1997; R Gr Ch Asheville NC 1968-1999; R S Fran' Epis Ch Rutherfordton NC 1961-1968. Intl Enneagram Assn; Intl Transactional Analysis Assn; Sprtl Dir Intl . williamglover@yahoo.com

EDWARDS, William Patrick (Mil) 12663 Perkins Rd, Baton Rouge LA 70810 **Epis HS Baton Rouge LA 2011-; P-in-c S Marg's Epis Ch Baton Rouge LA 2011-** B Melbourne FL 9/29/1962 s Gerald Linwood Edwards & Bernice Miller Edmondson. BALS scl Oglethorpe U; MDiv cl Nash 2011. D 6/4/2011 Bp Steven Andrew Miller. m 8/3/2003 Deborah Abbott c 4. EPISCOPALPATRICK@CENTURYTEL.NET

EDWARDS-ACTON, James Kendall (Los) 727 Olympic Ave, Costa Mesa CA 92626 **Jubilee Consortium Los Angeles CA 2006-; R S Steph's Par Los Angeles CA 1999-** B Hemet CA 7/24/1964 s Sidney Guy Acton & Jane Lowrey. BS U CA 1994; MDiv Epis TS of The SW 1997. D 6/7/1997 Bp Chester Lovelle Talton P 1/1/1998 Bp Frederick Houk Borsch. m 5/14/1994 Suzanne Marie Edwards. S Mich And All Ang Par Corona Del Mar CA 1997-1999. sumijaime@aol.com

EFFINGER, Richard Wayne (SeFla) 141 S County Rd, Palm Beach FL 33480 **The Epis Ch Of Beth-By-The-Sea Palm Bch FL 2010-** B Cleveland OH 1/1/1951 s Richard Walter Effinger & Helen Aphrodite. BA OH SU 1974; MA OH SU 1978; MDiv GTS 2010. D 12/18/2009 P 6/19/2010 Bp Leopold Frade. effinger@bbts.org

EGAN, Adam DJ (Alb) 16 Elsmere Ave, Delmar NY 12054 **R S Steph's Ch Delmar NY 2010-** B Baltimore MD 7/7/1980 s Colleen Kelly. Bangor TS; BA La Roche Coll; Savonarola Sem 2008. Rec from Polish National Catholic Church 2/27/2010 Bp William Howard Love. m 8/17/2002 Jeanne Novak c 1. adamegan@comcast.net

EGBERT, David Allen (Okla) 2817 Natchez Trl, Edmond OK 73012 B 6/30/1941 s David Allen Egbert & Ada Marion. BS SW Oklahoma St U 1963; MDiv SWTS 1969. D 6/17/1969 Bp Frederick Warren Putnam P 12/1/1969 Bp Chilton Powell. m 6/1/1963 Norma Tidwell c 2. Int R S Mich's Epis Ch Norman OK 2009-2010; Int R S Jn's Ch Norman OK 2003-2004; S Mary's Ch Edmond OK 1981-2001; R Ch Of The Redeem Kansas City MO 1975-1981; Dio W Missouri Kansas City MO 1975-1981; Asst S Jn's Ch Norman OK 1972-1975. Int Mnstry Ntwk 2000. Distinguished Mnstry Awd Dio Oklahoma 2002; Cn Dio Oklahoma 2001. eghouse@cox.net

EGBERT, Paula Sue (Ida) 5780 Millwright Ave, Boise ID 83714 **D Ch Of H Nativ Meridian ID 1989-** B Monterey CA 10/23/1944 d Paul Leonard Baker & Betty Mary. LPN Boise St U 1977. D 5/6/1989 Bp David Bell Birney IV. m 10/23/1987 Richard G Egbert.

EGELHOFF, William Frederick (SVa) 1500 Westbrook Ct Apt 1104, Richmond VA 23227 B Buffalo NY 2/27/1918 s Robert F Egelhoff & Shirley M. BA Wms 1940; MBA Harv 1943; MDiv VTS 1957; S Aug's Coll Cbury GB 1963. D 6/17/1957 P 12/1/1957 Bp George P Gunn. m 11/30/1974 Dorothy P Lumpkin c 4. Vic S Mart's Epis Ch Williamsburg VA 1963-1971; R Emm Ch Oak Hall VA 1957-1962; R H Trin Prot Epis Ch Onancock VA 1957-1962. ESMA Bd Dir/ 1981-1987; SCHC Chapl 1977-1980. begel1918@gmail.com

EGERTON, Karen Campbell (CFla) 1404 Chapman Cir, Winter Park FL 32789 B Steubenville OH 10/10/1945 d Alfred Cooper Campbell & Phyllis Elizabeth. Reformed TS; BA U of Florida 1967; MDiv STUSo 2002. D 12/13/1997 P 6/29/2002 Bp John Wadsworth Howe. m 6/15/1968 Charles Henry Egerton c 4. Asst All SS Ch Of Winter Pk Winter Pk FL 2002-2007; D Epis Ch Of The Ascen Orlando FL 1997-2001. mtrkarene@allsaintswp.com

EGGENSCHILLER, Robert Emil (Alb) 20141 Ian Ct Unit 106, Estero FL 33928 **Died 9/2/2010** B Paterson NJ 1/2/1940 s Marcel Francis Eggenschiller & Jean Rose. BA Amer U 1961; STM EDS 1964. D 6/13/1964 P 12/1/1964 Bp Leland Stark. c 2. Who'S Who In Amer Rel; Citizen Of The Year. frbob2k@gmail.com

EGGER, Jon Anthony (WMo) 209 SE Mount Vernon Drive, Blue Springs MO 64014 **D Trin Ch Independence MO 2009-** B Virginia MN 6/13/1958 s Joseph Louis Egger & Margaret Ann. A.D.N Hibbing Cmnty Coll 1979; Dplma W Missouri Sch of Mnstry 2002. D 2/1/2003 Bp Barry Robert Howe. m 10/13/2007 Dawn Ann Tish c 2. D Ch Of The Resurr Blue Sprg MO 2003-2006. NAAD 2003; RACA 2006. revegger@gmail.com

EHMER, J(oseph) Michael (WTenn) CREDO Institute, 266 S Front St, Suite 204, Memphis TN 38103 **Assoc Dir Credo Inst Inc. Memphis TN 2007-** B Miami FL 3/18/1952 s Joseph Francis Ehmer & Virgilee Benton. BS U Of Florida 1974; MBA RPI 1982; MDiv Epis TS of the SW 1999. D 3/13/1999 P 10/2/1999 Bp C(harles) Wallis Ohl. m 4/19/1975 Sue-Ann Ehmer c 2. Cn To The Ordnry Dio NW Texas Lubbock TX 2002-2006; Reg Vic S Jn's Ch Lamesa TX 1999-2003; Reg Vic S Lk's Epis Ch Levelland TX 1999-2003; Reg Vic The Epis Ch Of The Gd Shpd Brownfield TX 1999-2003. mehmer@comcast.net

EHRICH, Thomas Lindley (NC) 505 W 54th St Apt 812, New York NY 10019 B Evansville IN 10/16/1945 s William Reed Ehrich & Sarah Ruth. BA Wms 1967; MS Col 1968; MDiv EDS 1977. D 6/18/1977 Bp John P Craine P 12/1/1977 Bp Edward Witker Jones. m 6/11/1977 Helen Ehrich c 3. S Barth's Ch New York NY 2007-2008; R S Paul's Epis Ch Winston Salem NC 1993-1995; R S Mart's Epis Ch Charlotte NC 1988-1993; R S Steph's Ch Ferguson MO 1985-1988; Vic S Fran In The Fields Zionsville IN 1979-1985; Dio Indianapolis Indianapolis IN 1977-1979; Vic S Steph's Elwood IN 1977-1979. Auth, "Ch Wellness," Ch Pub Corp., 2008; Auth, "Just Wondering, Jesus," Ch Pub Corp., 2005; Auth, "w Scripture as My Compass," Abingdon Press, 2003; Auth, "Journey," Crossroad Pub, 1995; Auth, "New Perspectives On Epis Seminaries"; Auth, "Foward Day-By-Day," FMP; Auth, "On A Journey 93-," Morning Walk Media Inc. tom.ehrich@morningwalkmedia.com

EIBIN, Julian Raymond (Nwk) 284 Island Ave., Ramsey NJ 07446 **Com on the Priesthood Dio Newark Newark NJ 2011-; Dist Conveener Dio Newark Newark NJ 2011-; Newark ACTS Bd Dir Dio Newark Newark NJ 2010-; R S Jn's Memi Ch Ramsey NJ 2009-** B Amersham UK 5/31/1951 s Karol Eibin & Janina. BA S Mary Sem Coll Baltimore MD 1973; MA CUA 1977; Cert SWTS 2003. Rec from Roman Catholic 5/28/1983 as Priest Bp Otis Charles. m 8/6/2005 Deborah Macoy Jones c 3. Congrl Dvlpmt Commision Dio Ohio Cleveland OH 2006-2009; R S Paul's Ch Mt Vernon OH 2006-2009; Ch of the Nativ-St Steph Newport PA 2005; Ch Planter Dio Cntrl Pennsylvania Harrisburg PA 2002-2005; Dio Arkansas Little Rock AR 2002; Vic S Thos Ch Springdale AR 1999-2002; R Ch Of The Trsfg Braddock Heights MD 1991-1999; R S Andr's Epis Ch Enfield CT 1985-1991; Asst To

Bp For Mnstry Dio Utah Salt Lake City UT 1983-1985; Pstr Team S Steph's Ch W Vlly City UT 1983-1985. jeibin@verizon.net

EICH III, W Foster (Ala) St Bartholomew's Episcopal Church, 1600 Darby Dr, Florence AL 35630 **Assoc S Barth's Epis Ch Florence AL 1981-** B Tuskegee AL 6/26/1938 s Wilbur Foster Eich & Lula Olivia. BA Huntingdon Coll 1960; MD Tul 1964. D 6/6/1980 P 12/15/1981 Bp Furman Stough. m 5/31/1963 Eugenia Graves c 3. wfeich@comcast.net

EICHENLAUB, Patricia (Mich) 2745 Lake Pine Path Apt 219, Saint Joseph MI 49085 B South San Gabriel CA 2/6/1940 d Arthur Bertram Smith & Bette Louise. BA U CA, Santa Barbara 1961; MA Arizona St U 1967; EdD Utah St U 1974; MDiv SWTS 1977. D 6/11/1977 Bp James Winchester Montgomery P 2/5/1978 Bp William Henry Marmion. m 3/19/1967 Frank J Eichenlaub c 2. R S Geo's Epis Ch Warren MI 1998-2003; R S Pat's Epis Ch Madison Heights MI 1998-2003; Vic Ch of the Gd Shpd Dearborn MI 1987-1998. Ed, *Quarterly Revs*. pfeichenlaub@hotmail.com

EICHLER, Stephen (ETenn) 1400 Riverside Dr, Coral Springs FL 33071 B New York NY 12/12/1950 s Frederick Vincent Eichler & Dorothy Helen. BA Florida Atlantic U 1975; MDiv STUSo 1984. D 6/11/1984 P 12/21/1984 Bp Calvin Onderdonk Schofield Jr. m 2/22/1979 Dolores Kovach c 2. Chr Ch Epis So Pittsburg TN 2004-2010; R S Mary Magd Epis Ch Coral Sprg FL 1993-2002; R S Alb's Epis Ch Hixson TN 1986-1993; Asst To Dn Trin Cathd Miami FL 1984-1986. stepheneichler@hotmail.com

EICHNER, James F (Oly) **R Ch Of The H Cross Redmond WA 2002-** D 8/18/1996 Bp Andrew Hedtler Fairfield P 4/8/1997 Bp Edward Lloyd Salmon Jr.

EICK, John David (WMo) 8030 Ward Pkwy, Kansas City MO 64114 B Niagara Falls NY 6/27/1939 s Norman John Eick & Laura Marian. BS U MI 1963; MS GW 1966; PhD SUNY 1971. D 10/28/1988 Bp Richard Frank Grein. m 7/10/1960 Mary Elizabeth Warren c 3. EFM, NAAD.

EICKWORT, Kathleen Ruth (WMich) 501 Se 50th Ave, Ocala FL 34471 B Baltimore MD 1/3/1945 d George Robert Hoddinott & June Meredith. BS MI SU 1965; MA U of Kansas 1967; PhD Cor 1971; Bex 1983; Cert Onondaga Cmnty Coll 1983. D 6/11/1983 Bp Ned Cole P 5/31/1984 Bp O'Kelley Whitaker. c 3. R S Alb's Mssn Muskegon MI 1993-1996; R Ch Of The Epiph Trumansburg NY 1986-1993; Assoc Schuyler Cnty Episc Parishes Watkins Glen NY 1984-1986; Assoc S Jas' Epis Ch Watkins Glen NY 1983-1986; Assoc S Jn's Epis Ch Watkins Glen NY 1983-1986; Assoc S Paul's Ch Montour Falls NY 1983-1986; Dir S Jn's Ch Ithaca NY 1983-1985. Assn Chr Therapists 1985; Franciscan Ord Of Celi De - Chapl 1997; Ord Of S Lk 1978. kathleen_e@usa.net

EIDAM JR, John Mahlon (SVa) 224 S Military Hwy, Norfolk VA 23502 **R S Ptr's Epis Ch Norfolk VA 1997-** B West Reading PA 7/1/1948 s John Mahlon Eidam & Jeanette May. BS W Chester St Coll 1970; MEd W Chester St Coll 1976; MDiv VTS 1990. D 6/16/1990 Bp Allen Lyman Bartlett Jr P 9/28/1991 Bp Donis Dean Patterson. c 2. Assoc R Ch Of The Gd Shpd Norfolk VA 1993-1997; Asst R Chr Epis Ch Plano TX 1990-1993. johneidam48@verizon.net

EIDSON, Robert George (Mich) 1167 Timberview Trl, Bloomfield Hills MI 48304 B Niles MI 1/11/1929 s Duane H Eidson & Helen Margaret. BBA U MI 1950; LLB U MI 1952; BD VTS 1961. D 6/29/1961 Bp Richard S M Emrich P 1/1/1962 Bp Archie H Crowley. m 9/20/1958 Janet Margaret Allison Hardie c 2. R S Jn's Ch Royal Oak MI 1973-1990; R Trin Epis Ch Flushing MI 1967-1972; R S Paul's Epis Ch Brighton MI 1961-1967. rmeidson@sbcglobal.net

EILERTSEN, Edwin John (Minn) 1715 Weston Ln N, Plymouth MN 55447 B Brooklyn NY 3/15/1925 s Jack Eilertsen & Camilla. BA U MN 1948; MDiv Ya Berk 1952. D 6/21/1952 P 12/1/1952 Bp Stephen E Keeler. m 6/12/1950 Judith Bennett c 3. S Mart's By The Lake Epis Minnetonka Bch MN 1966-1989; Dept of CE Dio Minnesota Minneapolis MN 1959-1962; R S Nich Ch Richfield MN 1955-1959; Vic Emm Epis Ch Alexandria MN 1952-1955. Auth, "Intimate Journey," Addison-Wesley Pub, 1987; Auth, "We Gather Together To Ask the Lord's Blessing," S Mart's Par Pub, 1982; Auth, "Helping a Cong to Study Itself". DD Sebury-Wstrn TS.

EILERTSEN, Martha Hay (Spok) 132 Warwick Dr, Pittsburgh PA 15241 B Dillon MT 2/13/1962 D 6/14/2003 P 12/22/2003 Bp Robert William Duncan. m 11/24/1984 Jeffrey Ragle Eilertsen c 2. S Thos' Epis Ch Canonsburg PA 2004-2007; S Paul's Epis Ch Pittsburgh PA 2003.

EIMAN, Amanda B (Va) 1608 Russell Rd, Alexandria VA 22301 **S Jas Ch Wichita KS 2010-** B Ridgewood NJ 2/16/1981 d Stephen Eiman & Alice. BA Drew U 2004; MDiv VTS 2007. D 9/6/2008 Bp Mark M Beckwith. Asst Emm Epis Ch Alexandria VA 2008-2010. amandabrayton@yahoo.com

EINERSON, Dean Alfred (FdL) 29 S Pelham St, Rhinelander WI 54501 **R S Aug's Epis Ch Rhinelander WI 2002-** B Dubuque IA 4/17/1948 s Dean Swiggum Einerson & Mary Louise. BS U of Wisconsin 1971; MDiv SWTS 1999. D 8/25/1984 Bp Charles Thomas Gaskell P 5/29/1999 Bp Roger John White. m 8/14/1971 Barbara J Portman c 2. P-in-c Trin Epis Ch Platteville WI 1999-2002; D S Jas Ch W Bend WI 1984-1996. deanaeinerson@hotmail.com

EISENSTADT-EVANS, Elizabeth (Pa) 50 Fleming Drive, Glenmoore PA 19343 B New York NY 2/21/1955 d Abraham Selden Eisenstadt & Paulette. BA Kirkland Coll 1976; MDiv PrTS 1980; GTS 1984. D 6/16/1984 P 7/1/1985 Bp Lyman Cunningham Ogilby. m 9/19/1992 Haydn Barry Evans c 2. S Mk's Ch Honey Brook PA 2010-2011; Int R Calv Ch Glen Riddle PA 2009; Dio Pennsylvania Philadelphia PA 2002; Assoc Ch Of The Gd Samar Paoli PA 1995-2002; Int Calv And S Paul Philadelphia PA 1993-1995; The Philadelphia Theo Inst Lansdowne PA 1992; Epis Ch Cntr New York NY 1988-1990; S Mary's Ch Hamilton Vill Philadelphia PA 1985-1987; S Dav's Ch Philadelphia PA 1984-1985. Online Contrib, "GetReligion," *www.getreligion.org*. Assoc of SSM. Polly Bond Awd 1992; Polly Bond Awd For Merit 1989; Awd For Merit Associated Ch Presses 1989. eeevans269@aol.com

EKEVAG, Ellen Poole (Ky) 209 N Pine St, New Lenox IL 60451 **Vic Gr Epis Ch New Lenox IL 2010-** B Fulton KY 4/9/1980 d John Michael Poole & Roslyn Lobred. BA Ham 2002; MDiv VTS 2006. D 2/24/2006 P 9/9/2006 Bp Edwin Funsten Gulick Jr. m 5/23/2006 Per Ekevag. Trin Epis Ch Fulton KY 2010; Asst Gr Ch Paducah KY 2006-2009. eekevag@gmail.com

EKIZIAN, Hagop J (NY) 137 N Division St, Peekskill NY 10566 B New York NY 1/13/1926 s Mardiros Ekizian & Vehanoush. BS Hartwick Coll 1950. D 6/8/1968 Bp Horace W B Donegan. m 8/30/1947 Grace Link c 4. D S Ptr's Epis Ch Peekskill NY 1968-2007.

EKLO, Thomas J (Minn) 8064 Golden Valley Rd, Golden Valley MN 55427 **R S Nich Ch Richfield MN 2005-** B Minneapolis MN 10/8/1951 MA The Coll of St. Cathr 1993; MDiv GTS 2004. D 6/10/2004 P 12/16/2004 Bp James Louis Jelinek. Int S Matt's Ch St Paul MN 2004-2005. tjeklo@yahoo.com

EKLUND, Carolyn Hassig (NJ) 600 Cleveland Ave, Plainfield NJ 07060 **R Gr Epis Ch Plainfield NJ 2001-** B Kansas City KS 8/5/1955 d Robert Charles Hassig & Carol Mayer. BA U of Kansas 1978; BS U of Kansas 1979; MDiv GTS 1998. D 6/20/1998 P 6/19/1999 Bp Robert Carroll Johnson Jr. Asst Yth & Ce Ch Of The Gd Shpd Rocky Mt NC 1998-2001. Ord Of S Helena 1999. eklundgrace@comcast.net

EKLUND, Virginia Jane Rouleau (Lex) 130 Winterhawk Rd, Danville KY 40422 **Ch S Mich The Archangel Lexington KY 1988-** B Clinton MA 2/21/1943 d Robert Alexander Rouleau & Emeline Gertrude. BA Mid 1965; MA U MN 1969; MS U of Kentucky 1992. D 6/12/1988 Bp Don Adger Wimberly. m 8/9/1969 Neil Andrew Eklund c 2. D Epis Ch of Our Sav Richmond KY 1990-1998; D Trin Epis Ch Danville KY 1988-1990. nveklund@roadrunner.com

EKREM, Katherine Boyle (Mass) 150 Chapel St, Norwood MA 02062 **P-in-c The Ch Of Our Redeem Lexington MA 2009-** B Greenwich CT 4/12/1969 d Howarth Perry Boyle & Esther Fleming. BA Wms 1991; MDiv GTS 2000. D 3/18/2000 P 9/16/2000 Bp Richard Frank Grein. m 5/13/1995 David N Ekrem c 3. R Gr Ch Norwood MA 2003-2009; Asst S Barn Ch Irvington on Hudson NY 2000-2002. kate.b.ekrem@gmail.com

EKSTROM, Ellen Louise (Cal) 1017 Virginia Street, Berkeley CA 94710 B Vallejo CA 5/12/1953 d Alvin James Ekstrom & Jeannette Frances. AA Contra Costa Coll 1975; BA Sch for Deacons 2002. D 12/7/2002 Bp William Edwin Swing. m 6/28/1982 Carlos A Fernandez c 3. Eccl Crt Dio California San Francisco CA 2010-2011; D S Mk's Par Berkeley CA 2002-2011. Auth, "A Knight on Horseback," ireadiwrite Pub LLC, 2011; Auth, "Tallis' Third Tune," ireadiwrite Pub LLC, 2011; Auth, "Armor of Light," ireadiwrite Pub LLC, 2009; Auth, "The Legacy," *Digital Ed*, ireadiwrite Pub LLC, 2009; Auth, "The Legacy," Trivium Pub, 2004. The Iona Cmnty 2007. Chr Ethics Sch for Deacons 2001; Chr Mythos Sch for Deacons 2000. reverendella@gmail.com

ELAM II, Walter L (CGC) 153 Orange Ave, Fairhope AL 36532 B Birmingham,AL 10/1/1946 s Walter Leroy Elam & Virginia Towen. BA Jacksonville St U 1978; MDiv STUSo 1982; DMin STUSo 1994. D 6/2/1982 P 12/1/1982 Bp Furman Stough. c 1. S Fran Ch Dauphin Island AL 2000-2008; Ch Of The H Comf Montgomery AL 1985-1999; R S Jas' Ch Livingston AL 1982-1985. Auth, "Pstr Or Profsnl"; Auth, "The Use Of Psychotherapeutic Technique In The Priestly Off". AAPC; Assn For Sprtl Ethical & Rel Values In Counslg; Lic Profsnl Counslr, Lic Mar Fam Ther. wlelam@bellsouth.net

ELBERFELD, Katherine Ann Fockele (At) 123 Church St NE # 150, Marietta GA 30060 B Daytona Bch FL 3/22/1949 d Louis Ray Fockele & Jean Ann. Coll of Preachers; Stetson U 1969; BA U So 1971; MA Amer U 1974; MDiv VTS 1993. D 6/19/1993 P 1/6/1994 Bp Don Adger Wimberly. c 1. PBp'S T/F On Ldrshp Epis Ch Cntr New York NY 2001; Adj Instr VTS Alexandria VA 1999-2002; Pres Servnt-Ldr Dvlpmt Cntr Inc Alexandria VA 1999-2000; Assoc S Geo's Epis Ch Arlington VA 1997-1998; Asst S Aid's Ch Alexandria VA 1993-1996; COM Dio Lexington Lexington KY 1987-1990. Co-Auth, "Green by Design," *Green by Design*, Gabr Cntr for Servnt-Ldrshp, 2008; Auth, "In the Midst of Sunflowers," *In the Midst of Sunflowers*, Servnt-Ldr Publicatioons, 2006; Auth, "Reaching For Peace," *Concepts In Human Dvlpmt*, 2003; Auth, "To Speak of Love," *To Speak of Love*, Servnt-Ldr Pub, 2003; Auth, "To Speak Of Love," *Concepts In Human Dvlpmt; Var Dioc Newspapers*, 2002; Auth, "Serv Is The Truest Form Of Ldrshp," *Ldrshp In*

Action, 2002; Auth, "Servnt-Ldrshp: The Doorway To Cmnty," *New Ther; Concepts In Human Dvlpmt*, 2002; Auth, "The Hats," *Appalachian Heritage*, 1987; Auth, "Brotherly Love," *Appalachian Heritage*, 1986; Auth, "Jordan To Jerusalem," Forw Mvmt Pubs, 1979. Bd Trst Uso Sewanee Tn 1999-2002; Solo Flight, Stff Mem 1999-2000. Nomin For 1993 Dav H.C. Read Prchr/Schlr Awd VTS 1993; Poly Bond Awd ECom 1989; Phi Beta Kappa U So 1971; Ord Of The Gownsmen, Acad hon Soc U So 1969. kae@gabrielcenter.org

ELBERFELD, Richard Bradford (NwPa) 3105 Springland Terrace, Erie PA 16506 B Columbus OH 11/12/1948 s Richard Bradford Elberfeld & Mildred. BA U So 1970; MDiv VTS 1977; DMin STUSo 1987. D 5/21/1977 Bp Robert Bruce Hall P 12/18/1977 Bp Arthur Anton Vogel. m 2/8/1997 Sung Hui Yu c 4. Vic S Mary's Ch Erie PA 1998-2005; R S Mk's Ch Erie PA 1996-2009; P-in-c Trin Epis Ch Clanton AL 1995-1996; Off Of Bsh For ArmdF New York NY 1990-1996; Epis Ch of Our Sav Richmond KY 1985-1990; Chair Liturg Cmsn Dio Lexington Lexington KY 1985-1987; Dio W Missouri Kansas City MO 1981-1985; R Chr Ch Epis Boonville MO 1981-1984; Asst Gr And H Trin Cathd Kansas City MO 1979-1981; Cur S Ptr's Epis Ch Kansas City MO 1977-1979. relberfeldjr@roadrunner.com

ELCOCK, Frank Ulric (LI) 257 Leaf Ave, Central Islip NY 11722 **Vic Ch Of The Mssh Cntrl Islip NY 2003-** B Panama City PA 6/21/1931 s Clyde Lemont Elcock & Edith Gertrude. Cert Mercer TS 1986; BS Liberty U 1990; MA Liberty U 1999. D 1/16/1991 P 1/4/1992 Bp Orris George Walker Jr. m 2/27/1960 Elvia Jesticia Blake c 4. Asst Caroline Ch Of Brookhaven Setauket NY 2000-2004; Vic S Mths Epis Ch No Bellmore NY 1999-2004; Assoc S Ann's Ch Sayville NY 1993-1997; Int Caroline Ch Of Brookhaven Setauket NY 1992-1993; D Ch Of The Mssh Cntrl Islip NY 1991-1992.

ELDER, Clayton Lee (WTex) 311 E Corpus Christi St, Beeville TX 78102 **R S Phil's Ch Beeville TX 2010-** B Victoria TX 9/5/1972 s Donald Albert Elder & Elizabeth Josephine. BA SMU 1995; MAIB Webster U 1998; MDiv Perkins TS 2008. D 10/18/2008 Bp James Monte Stanton P 4/18/2009 Bp Paul Emil Lambert. m 8/16/2003 Jodie L Elder c 1. Cur S Lk's Epis Ch Dallas TX 2008-2010. elder_clayton@hotmail.com

ELDER, Robert Macrum (Va) 218 2nd St, Huntingdon PA 16652 B Baltimore MD 7/17/1925 s George Howard Elder & Anna. BA Washington Coll WA 1951; BD Bex 1954. D 6/25/1954 P 3/1/1955 Bp Noble C Powell. R Emm Ch Rapidan VA 1985-1990; Off Of Bsh For ArmdF New York NY 1958-1969; Cur S Jas Ch Monkton MD 1954-1955; Cur S Jas' Epis Ch Parkton MD 1954-1955.

ELDER-HOLIFIELD, Donna Ellen Carter (ECR) 64 San Pedro St, Salinas CA 93901 B Chicago IL 9/19/1940 d Herbert Ray Carter & Elizabeth Agnes. BA/MA U of Arkansas 1960; U MI 1963; Cert U of Paris-Sorbourne Paris FR 1983; BS Sch for Deacons 1992. D 6/22/1994 Bp Richard Lester Shimpfky. m 7/7/2003 Richard C Holifield. CA Teachers of Frgn Languages; NAAD. Dedicated Unionist Awd CA Fed of Teachers 2002. bonprofesseur@yahoo.com

ELDRIDGE, Barbara Adelle (CFla) 2143 Kings Cross St, Titusville FL 32796 **D S Giles Chap Deerfield Asheville NC 2000-** B Ardsley PA 1/7/1938 d Newton Ellesworth Blue & Eva Agnes. BA Barry U 1959. D 12/18/1993 Bp John Wadsworth Howe. m 1/29/1960 Radford Washington Eldridge. D S Tim's Epis Ch Daytona Bch FL 1993-2000. Ord Dok; Ord Of S Lk.

ELDRIDGE JR, Robert William (Ga) Hq Forscom, 1777 Hardee Ave Sw, Fort Mcpherson GA 30330 **Off Of Bsh For ArmdF New York NY 1999-** B Melrose MA 1/2/1946 s Robert William Eldridge & Florence Esther. BA Bos 1965; ThM Bos 1973. D 11/14/1998 P 5/1/1999 Bp Henry Irving Louttit. m 8/17/1968 Leona Marion Haskell.

ELEK, Hentzi (Pa) 3625 Chapel Rd, Newtown Square PA 19073 **R S Alb's Ch Newtown Sq PA 2001-** B Philadelphia PA 2/8/1965 s Peter Stephen Elek & Mary. BA Harv 1988; MDiv Ya Berk 1995. D 6/10/1995 Bp Allen Lyman Bartlett Jr P 1/10/1996 Bp Peter James Lee. m 12/28/1990 Sarah Francis Barton c 2. Asst R S Fran Epis Ch Great Falls VA 1997-2001; Asst R S Paul's Epis Ch Alexandria VA 1995-1997. Soc Of S Jn The Evang 1985. father.hentzi@verizon.net

ELEY, Gary W (Vt) 35 Adams Ct, Burlington VT 05401 B Altus OK 7/7/1944 s Carl W Eley & Margaret Sue. Med U of Vermont; BA Oklahoma St U 1966; MDiv Drew U 1969; Cert CDSP 1970. D 5/31/1970 Bp George Richard Millard P 12/1/1970 Bp Leland Stark. m 1/23/1983 Sidney L Eley c 1. All SS' Epis Ch S Burlington VT 1973-1989; Cur S Ptr's Ch Morristown NJ 1970-1973. garyeley@eleymgt.com

ELFERT, Martin O (Spok) 127 E 12th Ave, Spokane WA 99202 **Cathd Of S Jn The Evang Spokane WA 2011-** B Vancouver BC 10/21/1972 s Frank Elfert & Helen. BFA U of British Columbia Vancouver BC CA 1995; MDiv CDSP 2011. D 8/14/2011 Bp James Edward Waggoner. m 4/7/2004 Phoebe R MacRae c 2. MARTIN.OFR.ELFECT@GMAIL.COM

ELFVIN, Robert Roger (Ia) 2816 Eula Dr, Des Moines IA 50322 B Charleston SC 1/25/1945 s Charles Donald Elfvin & Gloria Audrey. BA OH SU 1966; MDiv Ya Berk 1969. D 6/14/1969 P 5/8/1970 Bp John Harris Burt. m 3/5/1966 Karon Kerber c 4. R S Lk's Ch Des Moines IA 1978-2009; R Trin Ch Findlay OH 1971-1978; Asst Chr Ch Lima OH 1969-1971. stlukes1@juno.com

ELIN, Darren Richard Strawn (SO) 100 Miami Ave, Terrace Park OH 45174 **Strtgy Team for Healthy Congregations Dio Sthrn Ohio Cincinnati OH 2011-; Safe Ch Trng Prog Coordntr Dio Sthrn Ohio Cincinnati OH 2010-; R S Thos Epis Ch Terrace Pk OH 2010-** B Stockton CA 8/20/1970 s Rhoderick Jack Elin & Andrea. BA California St U 1992; DAS Ya Berk 1998; MDiv Yale DS 1998; Cert Yale Inst of Sacr Mus 1998. D 6/26/1999 Bp Sanford Zangwill Kaye Hampton P 12/17/1999 Bp Andrew Donnan Smith. m 11/21/2009 Sarah Julie Strawn c 2. Mutual Mnstry Dvlpmt Team Dio Estrn Michigan Saginaw MI 2007-2010; Pstr Response Team Dio Estrn Michigan Saginaw MI 2007-2010; Dioc Exam Chapl Dio Estrn Michigan Saginaw MI 2006-2010; Personl Com Dio Estrn Michigan Saginaw MI 2005-2010; R S Jn's Epis Ch Saginaw MI 2004-2010; Assoc R S Jn's Ch Barrington RI 2002-2004; P-in-c S Dav's Epis Ch Halifax MA 2000-2002; Cur S Matt's Epis Ch Wilton CT 1998-2000. Thos Philips Memi Awd in Liturg Ya Berk 1998. darren.elin@me.com

E

ELIOT, Mary Ashley (Md) 6800 Oakland Mills Rd, Columbia MD 21045 **Epis Ch Of Chr The King Windsor Mill MD 2009-** B Evanston IL 5/17/1967 d John Eliot & Sylvia H. BS U of Maryland 1989; EdM Harv 1993; MA Washington Theol Un 1998; DAS GTS 1999. D 6/26/2004 Bp Peter James Lee P 1/15/2005 Bp Robert Wilkes Ihloff. m 1/29/2005 Jeffrey K Staples c 2. Assoc R Chr Ch Columbia MD 2004-2009; S Dunst's McLean VA 1999-2004. revmeliot@gmail.com

ELISEE, Jean R (NY) 33 Mount Pleasant Ave Rm 120, West Orange NJ 07052 B Haiti 9/26/1927 D 6/8/1952 P 12/8/1952 Bp Charles Alfred Voegeli Con 1/1/1972 for Hai. m 12/20/1961 Anita Elisee. Diocn Msnry & Ch Extntn Socty New York NY 1988-1989; Dpt Of Missions Ny Income New York NY 1988-1989; Exec Coun Appointees New York NY 1980-1987.

ELKINS-WILLIAMS, Stephen John (NC) 100 Black Oak Pl, Chapel Hill NC 27517 **Assoc Chap Of The Cross Chap Hill NC 1982-** B Bakersfield CA 6/9/1944 s Harold Richard Williams & Agnes Mary. BA Gonzaga U 1969; MDiv Regis Coll Toronto ON CA 1975. Rec from Roman Catholic 5/26/1982 as Priest Bp Robert Hume Cochrane. m 12/20/1978 Elizabeth Coolidge Elkins c 2. S Steph's Epis Ch Seattle WA 1982; S Steph's Epis Ch Seattle WA 1978-1982. Auth, "Oh It's You Again! in Preaching Through the Years of Lk," *Sermons That Wk IX*, 2000; Auth, "Lost in Wonder, Love and Praise," *Angl Dig*, 1999; Auth, "Ch-Going," *Angl Dig*, 1999. sew@thechapelofthecross.org

ELL, Marianne Sorge (ND) 4751 Highway 1804, Williston ND 58801 **R S Ptr's Epis Ch Williston ND 1995-** B Fargo ND 2/5/1963 d Elliott Lorenz Sorge & Marjorie Aline. BA DePauw U 1984; MDiv Epis TS of The SW 1989. D 6/3/1989 P 1/6/1990 Bp Elliott Lorenz Sorge. m 12/1/1990 John William Ell c 1. Dio No Dakota Fargo ND 2000-2010; R S Mich's and All Ang' Ch Fairview MT 1995-1999; Vic S Paul's Ch S Jn's Hillsboro MD 1990-1995; Cur Chr Ch S Ptr's Par Easton MD 1989-1990. marianne@dia.net

ELLEDGE II, C Clyde (Mass) 54 Robert Road, Marblehead MA 01945 **R Wyman Memi Ch of St Andr Marblehead MA 2011-** B Tacoma WA 12/15/1962 s C Ray Elledge & Marjorie Jean. BA U of Kansas 1986; MDiv SWTS 1993. D 6/27/1993 Bp Peter Hess Beckwith P 5/1/1994 Bp Donald Purple Hart. m 6/10/1995 Kathryn Nesbit c 2. R The Annunc Of Our Lady Gurnee IL 2000-2011; Asst S Chris's By-The River Gates Mills OH 1997-2000; R All SS Ch Brooklyn MI 1995-1997; Chapl S Andr's Priory Sch Honolulu HI 1993-1995. Contrib, "Effective Orgnztn for Congrl Renwl," Acta Pub., 2008. elclyde@gmail.com

ELLEDGE JR, John Harrol (Md) 708 Teal Ct, Havre De Grace MD 21078 **Died 12/13/2009** B Hattiesburg MS 3/31/1939 s John Harrol Elledge & Lucille. Cert Syr 1960; Cert Syr 1960; BA OH SU 1967; BA OH SU 1967; Cert USAF 1973; Cert USAF 1973; MDiv STUSo 1977; MDiv STUSo 1977; Cert USAF 1988; USAF 1988; USAF 1989; USAF 1989; USAF 1994. D 5/23/1977 P 12/14/1977 Bp Furman Stough. c 2. Auth, "Pryr," *The Angl Dig*, 2002; Auth, "Var arts," *Living Ch*. Assn Bible Tchrs; Cmnty Of S Mary; ERM; Ord Of S Lk. Legion Of Merit Usaf 1999; Meritorious Serv Med Usaf 1995; Joint Serv Commendation Medal Mac/V 1975; Omicron Delta Epsilon; Omicron Delta Epsilon; Meritor Serv Medal Usaf; Joint Serv Commend Medal Usaf. fijn33@comcast.net

ELLEDGE, Kathryn Nesbit (Chi) 54 Robert Road, Marblehead MA 01945 B Arlington IL 10/17/1962 d Robert G Nesbit & Janet P. BA U of Missouri 1982; MDIV/MSW U Chi 1990; CAS SWTS 1991. D 6/15/1991 P 12/1/1991 Bp Frank Tracy Griswold III. m 6/10/1995 C Clyde Elledge c 2. The Annunc Of Our Lady Gurnee IL 2007-2011; Long-term supply Dio Ohio Cleveland OH 1997-2001; Long-term supply Dio Michigan Detroit MI 1995-1997. KNELLEDGE@GMAIL.COM

ELLER, Ruth Elizabeth (U) 700 S Silver Ridge St Spc 85, Ridgecrest CA 93555 B Tac WA 6/12/1943 d Henry Eller & Victoria. BA Vas 1965; MA Smith 1967; PhD U CA 1980; MDiv CDSP 1989. D 6/3/1989 P 6/9/1990 Bp William Edwin Swing. Int Pstr Ch Of The Resurr Centerville UT 2008-2009; R S Jn's Epis Ch Logan UT 1999-2008; Dioc Mssnr Dio California San

Francisco CA 1996-1999; Int Pstr S Thos Epis Ch Sunnyvale CA 1995-1996; Int Pstr Ch Of S Jn The Bapt Aptos CA 1994-1995; Int Pstr All SS Epis Ch Palo Alto CA 1993-1994; Int Pstr S Lk's Ch Los Gatos CA 1992-1993; Pstr Assoc S Lk's Ch Los Gatos CA 1990-1992; Pstr Asst S Lk's Ch Los Gatos CA 1989-1990. reeller@aol.com

ELLERY, Celia (NwT) 2661 Yale Ave, San Angelo TX 76904 **Dn, Eagle Cove Dnry Dio NW Texas Lubbock TX 2010-; R Epis Ch Of The Gd Shpd San Angelo TX 2009-** B Tulsa OK 10/17/1955 d Harold Jackson Norman & Barbara JoAnn. BA Arkansas Tech U 1977; MA SW Texas St U San Marcos 1982; MDiv Epis TS of The SW 2005. D 12/18/2004 P 6/18/2005 Bp C(harles) Wallis Ohl. m 8/9/1975 Jon Christopher Ellery c 3. Secy of Stndg Com Dio NW Texas Lubbock TX 2009-2011; Ecum Off Dio NW Texas Lubbock TX 2008-2009; P-in-c Epis Ch Of The Gd Shpd San Angelo TX 2007-2009; Asst Epis Ch Of The Gd Shpd San Angelo TX 2005-2006. EDEIO 2008-2009. celiaellery@gmail.com

ELLESTAD, Charles Dwight (Lex) Po Box 482, Frankfort KY 40602 B Madison WI 10/7/1945 s Elver Theodore Ellestad & Eleanor Celene. BS U of Wisconsin 1967; MA U of Wisconsin 1971; MA Westminster Coll 1977; MDiv Nash 1983. D 11/27/1982 Bp Charles Thomas Gaskell P 6/1/1983 Bp Addison Hosea. m 4/24/1981 Jean Rowley c 2. S Jos Mssn Salvisa KY 1993-2006; R Ch Of The Ascen Frankfort KY 1989-2006; Cn To Ordnry Dio Easton Easton MD 1987-1989; Assoc Chr Ch Cathd Lexington KY 1983-1987. cdellestad@aol.com

ELLEY, Eric M (WMass) PO Box 528, Somersville CT 06072 **D S Jn's Ch Northampton MA 2006-** B Trenton NJ 9/2/1970 s Svend Elley & Irene. AAS Pennco Tech Bristol PA; D Formation Prog 2000. D 10/21/2000 Bp David B(ruce) Joslin. m 2/18/2005 Graham Van Keuren. Dio New Jersey Trenton NJ 2000-2005. eelley@gmail.com

ELLGREN, Neysa Anne (Ore) 11800 SW Military Ln, Portland OR 97219 **Cn Dio Oregon Portland OR 2010-** B Blue Earth MN 7/12/1959 d Stanley Eugene Studer & Mary Therese. BS Minnesota St U Mankato 1981; MDiv Iliff TS 1997; DMin SWTS 2005. D 6/7/1997 P 1/3/1998 Bp William Jerry Winterrowd. m 2/13/1982 David Ellgren c 4. Int S Jn The Evang S Paul MN 2010; R Ch Of The Epiph Epis Plymouth MN 2000-2010; Assoc S Aid's Epis Ch Boulder CO 1997-1999. ESMHE/Strng Com 1997-1999; Natl Nework of Epis Cler Associations (NNECA) 2007. neysa.anne@gmail.com

ELLINGBOE, Shirley Kay (RG) 5794 Ndcbu, Taos NM 87571 **Int St Thos Ch Hanalei HI 2009-** B Colfax WI 11/8/1940 d Lawrence Oliver Christianson & Marie Louise. BSW Avila Coll 1989; MDiv SWTS 1993. D 1/25/1984 Bp Robert Marshall Anderson P 5/8/1993 Bp William Edward Smalley. m 4/15/1977 John Ellingboe c 2. Dioc Coun Dio The Rio Grande Albuquerque NM 1998-2000; R S Jas Epis Ch Taos NM 1995-2006; Growth & Effective Cmte Dio The Rio Grande Albuquerque NM 1995-2000; Assoc S Thos The Apos Ch Overland Pk KS 1993-1995; D S Thos The Apos Ch Overland Pk KS 1987-1993; D The Epis Ch Of The Adv W Bloomfield MI 1984-1987. scl Avila Coll 1989. shirleyellingboe@gmail.com

ELLINGTON, Meta Louise Turkelson (NC) 521 Marlowe Rd, Raleigh NC 27609 **D S Mich's Ch Raleigh NC 2008-** B Reidsville NC 10/31/1945 d Richard Wesley Turkelson & Lillian Meador. BA U NC 1966. D 10/2/1988 Bp Robert Whitridge Estill. m 8/6/1966 William Woolcott Ellington c 2. D Ch Of The Gd Shpd Raleigh NC 1998-2000; D Chr Epis Ch Raleigh NC 1994-1998; Chapl S Mary's Chap Sch Raleigh NC 1994-1998; S Mary's Sch Raleigh NC 1994-1998; D-In-C St Elizabeths Epis Ch Apex NC 1993-1994; D S Cyp's Ch Oxford NC 1992-1993; D S Tim's Ch Raleigh NC 1988-1992. tometa@nc.rr.com

ELLINGTON, William Ferrell (Cal) 303 N West St, Mcalester OK 74501 **P-in-c Trin Ch Eufaula OK 2008-** B Arlington TX 9/20/1934 s Bennett Ferrell Ellington & Irene. MDiv SWTS; BA U of Texas 1961; U of Oklahoma 1974; PhD Pacific Grad Inst 1998. D 6/18/1964 P 12/1/1964 Bp Theodore H McCrea. m 6/18/1977 Patricia Ellen Dearing c 2. R Trin Par Fillmore CA 1995-2000; Vic S Paul's Mssn Barstow CA 1991-1995; Int S Jn The Bapt Par Corona CA 1990-1991; R S Jos's Par Buena Pk CA 1987-1990; R S Paul's Epis Ch Evanston WY 1979-1987; Vic S Mart's Ch Pryor OK 1973-1977; Vic S Jn's Epis Ch Vinita OK 1973-1974; R S Jas Epis Ch Oklahoma City OK 1970-1972; R S Andr's Ch Breckenridge TX 1966-1969; Vic S Phil's Epis Ch Sulphur Sprg TX 1965-1966. Hon Cn S Matt Cathd Dallas TX 1969. bill@ellingtonok.com

ELLIOTT, Beverley Florence (At) 5458 E Mountain St, Stone Mountain GA 30083 **S Barth's Epis Ch Atlanta GA 2002-** B Hobart Tasmania AU 12/29/1952 d John Roland Grubb & Joan Beverly. DAS Queensland U 1982; MDiv Candler TS Emory U 1997; GTS 2001. D 6/9/2001 Bp Robert Gould Tharp P 1/21/2002 Bp J(ohn) Neil Alexander. m 10/11/1980 Paul Alexander Elliott. beverley@stbartsatlanta.org

ELLIOTT III, David Augustus (Miss) 3921 Oakridge Dr, Jackson MS 39216 B Meridian MS 2/24/1940 s David Augustus Elliott & Mary. BA U So 1961; MDiv 1969. D 6/23/1969 P 5/24/1970 Bp John M Allin. m 4/27/1959 Gay Rawlings c 4. Assoc R S Jas Ch Jackson MS 2000-2007; R Ch of the H Trin Vicksburg MS 1994-2000; R S Jas Ch Greenville MS 1984-1994; R S Tim's Ch Signal Mtn TN 1980-1983; Cn S Andr's Cathd Jackson MS 1975-1980. Auth, "Var Bk Revs," *S Lk Journ.* gelliott1@comcast.net

ELLIOTT, Gates Safford (Miss) 674 Mannsdale Rd, Madison MS 39110 **Asst R The Chap Of The Cross Madison MS 2010-** B Houston TX 10/1/1973 s David James Elliott & Elizabeth Safford. BBA U of Houston 2001; MDiv VTS 2009. D 6/20/2009 Bp C(harles) Andrew Doyle P 1/7/2010 Bp Rayford Baines High Jr. m 9/24/2010 Annie Kay Cumberland. Cur S Steph's Ch Beaumont TX 2009-2010. gates.elliott@gmail.com

ELLIOTT III, Harry Arnold (Ct) 41 Park St, Manchester CT 06040 **R Gr Epis Ch Windsor CT 2011-** B Buffalo NY 8/28/1953 s Harry Arnold Elliott & Joy Marilyn. BA SUNY 1976; MDiv Bex 1990. D 2/28/1987 P 5/12/1990 Bp David Charles Bowman. m 8/28/1976 Susan Elaine Minch c 3. Cler Conf Plnng Com Dio Connecticut Hartford CT 2001-2004; Dn, Hartford Dnry Dio Connecticut Hartford CT 1999-2000; R S Mary's Epis Ch Manchester CT 1998-2007; Cmncatn Com Dio Wstrn New York Tonawanda NY 1991-1998; Outreach Grants Com Dio Wstrn New York Tonawanda NY 1991-1998; COM Dio Wstrn New York Tonawanda NY 1991-1997; R S Ptr's Ch Westfield NY 1990-1998; Fin Com Dio Wstrn New York Tonawanda NY 1987-1991; Asst Ch Of The Adv Kenmore NY 1986-1988; Prison Chapl Dio Wstrn New York Tonawanda NY 1986-1988. "From Death Comes Life," The Journ/Hearst, 1994; "The Real Meaning of All Souls and All SS," Westfield Republican/Hearst, 1991. Cler Conf Plnng Com Dio Ct 1999; Dn Dio Ct Hartford Dnry 1999; Supvsr, OTP Prog Dio Ct 1998. chipe@pobox.com

ELLIOTT JR, James Edward (Ala) 2714 Hilltop Cir, Gadsden AL 35904 **P-in-c Calv Ch Oneonta AL 2011-** B Fayette AL 8/3/1942 s James Edward Elliott & Ruby Nell. BS Auburn U 1963; MDiv Candler TS Emory U 1967; U of Alabama 1986; CAS STUSo 1987. D 5/26/1987 Bp Robert Oran Miller P 12/17/1987 Bp Furman Stough. m 6/6/1962 Jane P Elliott c 2. Int Chr Epis Ch Albertville AL 2008; Int S Paul's Ch Selma AL 2008; Ecum and Interfaith Off Dio Alabama Birmingham AL 2005-2010; Dn of Mtn Convoc Dio Alabama Birmingham AL 2002-2008; R H Comf Ch Gadsden AL 1996-2008; Secy of the Dio Dio Alabama Birmingham AL 1994-1997; R H Cross Trussville AL 1990-1996; R S Mich And All Ang Millbrook AL 1987-1990. jim2714@bellsouth.net

ELLIOTT, James Lawrence (Ga) 1521 N Patterson St, Valdosta GA 31602 **P-in-c S Jas Epis Ch Quitman GA 2011-; Asstg P Chr Ch Valdosta GA 2010-; Chncllr Dio Georgia Savannah GA 2004-** B Thomasville GA 11/19/1959 s William Gus Elliott & Walton Carpenter. AB Davidson Coll 1982; JD U GA Sch of Law 1985. D 11/7/2009 Bp Henry Irving Louttit P 8/21/2010 Bp Scott Anson Benhase. m 5/25/1985 Susan Thomas c 3. jelliott@ebbglaw.com

ELLIOTT, James Thom (NCal) 36414 SE Forest St, Snoqualmie WA 98065 B Bremerton WA 1/20/1935 s George William Elliott & Alma Bertha Anna. BMus U of Puget Sound 1957; SMM UTS 1961; MDiv CDSP 1965; DMin SFTS 1992. D 9/11/1965 P 3/26/1966 Bp Ivol I Curtis. m 9/17/1994 Anne Scholes c 2. Int S Matt's Epis Ch Sacramento CA 1986; R Epis Ch Of The Epiph Vacaville CA 1978-1985; Vic S Geo's Ch Seattle WA 1968-1978; Cur S Jn's Epis Ch Olympia WA 1965-1968. elliottjt@centurytel.net

ELLIOTT JR, Nathaniel Rutter (NJ) 506 Devon Rd, Haddonfield NJ 08033 **P Asst Gr Ch In Haddonfield Haddonfield NJ 1998-; P in charge S Mary's Ch Haddon Heights NJ 1997-** B Wilkes-Barre PA 11/9/1929 s Nathaniel Rutter Elliott & Elizabeth. BA U of Pennsylvania 1953. D 4/25/1964 P 10/31/1964 Bp Alfred L Banyard. m 4/14/1952 Barbara Jane Acomb c 2. P S Mary's Ch Haddon Heights NJ 1990-1996; Int S Mary's Ch Haddon Heights NJ 1989-1990; P S Mary's Ch Haddon Heights NJ 1986-1989; P S Jn's Epis Ch Maple Shade NJ 1978-1984; P Chr Ch Magnolia NJ 1976-1978; P S Jas Epis Ch Cape May NJ 1974-1975; P Chr Ch Millville NJ 1973-1975; Ch Of Our Sav Camden NJ 1969-1970. AGO 2007.

ELLIOTT, Norman Henry Victor (Ak) 2401 Galewood St, Anchorage AK 99508 **Archd of So Cntrl Alaska Dio Alaska Fairbanks AK 1997-; R Emer All SS' Epis Ch Anchorage AK 1990-; Hon Chapl to the ArmdF of Alaska Bp Of ArmdF- Epis Ch Cntr New York NY 1963-** B Plymouth England 2/2/1919 s Sidney Norman Elliott & Laura Charlotte. BA Detroit Inst of Tech 1948; BD VTS 1951; S Aug's Coll 1956; MDiv VTS 1971; Oxf 1986. D 6/30/1951 Bp Russell S Hubbard P 2/17/1952 Bp William J Gordon Jr. c 3. R All SS' Epis Ch Anchorage AK 1962-1989; R S Jn's Ch Ketchikan AK 1958-1962; Archd of the Yukon Dio Alaska Fairbanks AK 1957-1958; R S Matt's Epis Ch Fairbanks AK 1954-1955; Mssy-in-charge S Steph's Ch Ft Yukon AK 1952-1953; D S Mk's Ch Nenana AK 1951-1952. Auth, *Living Ch.* Mssn to Seafarers, U.K. 1962; SSC 1989. Soc of SS Simeon and Anna Epis Dio Alaska 1990; Hon Chapl ArmdF Chapl 1963. nelliott@gci.net

ELLIOTT, Paul Alexander (At) 5458 E Mountain St, Stone Mountain GA 30083 **R S Mich And All Ang Ch Stone Mtn GA 2000-** B 2/24/1952 BA Cntrl Queensland U Rockhampton Qld Au 1981; Grad. Dip. Teach. U Of Sthrn Queensland Brisbane Qld Aus 1982; BTh Brisbane Coll of Theol 1985; ThD Candler TS Emory U 2004. Trans from Anglican Church Of Australia 10/31/

2000 Bp Frank Kellogg Allan. m 10/11/1980 Beverley Florence Elliott. paulos.elliott@gmail.com

ELLIOTT, Paul C (At) 210 Redding Rdg, Peachtree City GA 30269 **S Andr's In-The-Pines Epis Ch Peachtree City GA 2007-** B Huntsville AL 2/4/1967 s Paul James Elliott & Judith Ann. BA Birmingham-Sthrn Coll 1990; MDiv GTS 1996. D 6/8/1996 P 12/1/1996 Bp Frank Kellogg Allan. m 8/19/1995 Susan Farmer Langley c 3. S Mart In The Fields Ch Atlanta GA 1996-2002. revelliott@mnc.com

ELLIOTT III, Richard G (EC) 2322 Metts Ave, Wilmington NC 28403 **Compstn and Benefits Com Dio E Carolina Kinston NC 2010-; Commision on Const and Cn Dio E Carolina Kinston NC 2009-; R S Andr's On The Sound Ch Wilmington NC 2002-** B Lexington KY 3/20/1953 s Richard Gill Elliott & Virginia Tobin. BA Cntr Coll 1975; MDiv STUSo 1979. D 5/13/1979 Bp Addison Hosea P 5/19/1980 Bp William Arthur Beckham. m 8/28/1982 Giles Singleton c 1. R S Geo Ch Anderson SC 1995-2001; Dio Lexington Lexington KY 1986-1995; Vic S Aug's Chap Lexington KY 1985-1995; Asst R S Mk's Epis Ch Venice FL 1983-1985; Cur H Trin Par Epis Clemson SC 1979-1983. richard.elliott@standrewsonthesound.org

ELLIOTT, Robert James (O) 8710 Thornwood Ln, Tampa FL 33615 B Coshocton OH 12/8/1924 s Frank Elliott & Ruby Pearl. BA Muskingum Coll 1953; Cert Bex 1956; Accredited Int Spec 1990. D 6/23/1956 P 12/23/1956 Bp Nelson Marigold Burroughs. m 10/31/1981 Janis Ford c 2. Int S Clem Epis Ch Tampa FL 1996-1997; Asst St Johns Epis Ch Tampa FL 1995-2005; Int All SS Ch Parma OH 1994-1995; Int Chr Epis Ch Warren OH 1992-1994; Int Ch Of The Epiph Euclid OH 1990-1992; Int S Ptr's Ch Ashtabula OH 1989-1990; Int Gr Epis Ch Willoughby OH 1987-1988; R S Mk's Ch Cleveland OH 1974-1984; R S Paul's Ch Marion OH 1961-1973; Min in charge Gr Ch Galion OH 1956-1959. Auth, *Evang in the Epis Ch*. Natl Int Mnstry Ntwk 1987-1997. janbobtam@aol.com

ELLIOTT, R(odger) (Minn) 1262 Birch Pond Trail, White Bear Lake MN 55110 **U Epis Ch Minneapolis MN 2000-** B Newton KS 12/28/1956 s Rodger Neil Elliott & Mary June. BA Pepperdine U 1978; MDiv PrTS 1983; PhD PrTS 1989; CAS SWTS 2002. D 6/15/2002 P 12/17/2002 Bp James Louis Jelinek. m 8/22/1998 Mary Ellen Beal c 2. U Epis Cntr Minneapolis MN 2004-2005; Dio Minnesota Minneapolis MN 2002-2003. Coeditor, "Documents and Images for the Study of Paul," Fortress Press, 2010; Auth, "Paul and Marxist Interp," *Paul in Postcolonial Perspective*, Forttress Press, 2010; Auth, "Ideology and the Chr Event," *S Paul's Journey into Philos*, Wipf & Stock, 2009; Auth, "The Arrogance of Nations: Reading Romans in the Shadow of Empire," Fortress Press, 2008; Auth, "A Famine of the Word: Stringfellowian Reflection," *The Bible in the Publ Sq*, Fortress Press, 2008; Auth, "The Bible and Empire," *The Peoples' Bible*, Fortress Press, 2008; Auth, "The Rhetoric of Romans," Sheffield 1990; Fortress Press, 2006; Auth, "Liberating Paul: The Justice of God and the Politics of the Apos," Orbis 1994; Fortress Press, 2005. Assn of Angl Biblic Scholars 1998; EPF 1990. Breaking the Silence Awd GLBT Prog Off, U MN 2005. neilelliott@msn.com

ELLIOTT, Scott Fuller (Chi) 2222 W Belmont Ave, # 205, Chicago IL 60618 **D S Alb's Ch Chicago IL 2010-** B Norfolk VA 9/24/1955 s Thomas Elliott & Dorothy Jean. AA Harper Cmnty Coll Palatine IL 1975; BA U of Iowa 1977. D 2/7/1998 Bp Herbert Alcorn Donovan Jr. m 5/21/2005 Cynthia Ann Cheski. D S Ptr's Epis Ch Chicago IL 1998-2010. deaconse@gmail.com

ELLIOTT, William Tate (EMich) 6757 Middle Rd, Hope MI 48628 B Detroit MI 7/5/1924 s Chester Earl Elliott & Bessie Hazel. BA Wayne 1950; MDiv VTS 1951. D 7/7/1951 Bp Richard S M Emrich P 1/19/1952 Bp Russell S Hubbard. c 2. R S Jn's Epis Ch Midland MI 1960-1984; R Trin Epis Ch Flushing MI 1957-1960; Vic S Paul's Epis Ch Gladwin MI 1951-1956; Vic Gr Epis Ch Standish MI 1951-1954. Auth, "25 Days to Christmas," *An Adv Journey*, Forw Mvmt, 2003; Auth, *The Forty Days of Lent*, Forw Mvmt, 2002. elliottwt@aol.com

ELLIS, Jane Fielding (Nwk) 556 Mohave Cir, Huntington CT 06484 **D S Jn's Ch Bridgeport CT 2002-** B Montgomery AL 11/4/1947 d Frank Fielding Ellis & Dorothy Breitting. BA Judson Coll 1970; MS Troy St U-Troy AL 1976; U of Alabama 1985; MFA Auburn U Montgomery 1987. D 12/9/2000 Bp Andrew Donnan Smith. Wmn Of dist Awd GSA 2002; Wmn Of Substance Connecticut 2001; hon Soc Pi Sigma Alpha Auburn U 1987; Outstanding Young Wmn Of Amer 1981; hon Soc Chi Delta Phi Judson Coll 1970. jellis@suhs-ct.org

ELLIS, Kassinda Rosalinda (LI) 13927 Caney Ln, Fl 2, Rosedale NY 11422 **P-in-c Ch Of S Thos Brooklyn NY 2009-** B Long Island, NY 1/1/1979 d Randolph Ellis & Perpetua. BA Hofstra U 2001; MDiv SWTS 2005. D 1/25/2006 Bp Rodney Rae Michel P 6/14/2007 Bp Orris George Walker Jr. S Aug's Epis Ch Brooklyn NY 2006-2009; SWTS Evanston IL 2002-2005. darevkellis@gmail.com

ELLIS, Malcolm A (Md) 232 Saint Thomas Ln, Owings Mills MD 21117 **S Thos' Ch Garrison Forest Owings Mills MD 2009-** B Durban Natal ZA 11/12/1951 s Leslie Norman Ellis & Kathleen Elizabeth. DIT S Paul Theol Coll 1974; MDiv Chicago TS 1978; DMin Chicago TS 1979. Trans from Church of the Province of Southern Africa 7/1/1989 Bp Frank Tracy Griswold III. m 7/3/1976 Teresa A Scott Stokes c 4. R S Lk's Epis Ch San Antonio TX 2002-2009; R Mssh Epis Ch S Paul MN 1994-2002; R S Mary's Epis Ch Palmetto FL 1990-1994; Assoc The Ch Of The H Sprt Lake Forest IL 1987-1990. rev.m.ellis@gmail.com

ELLIS, Marshall Johnston (Oly) 2460 Persian Dr Apt 20, Clearwater FL 33763 **Died 8/26/2009** B Macon GA 4/12/1920 s Marshall Johnston Ellis & Martha Ross. BA U So 1941; MDiv UTS 1944; Oxf 1956; MLS U of Washington 1971. D 1/7/1944 Bp Middleton S Barnwell P 9/1/1944 Bp John M Walker Jr. c 2. Ord of S Lk.

ELLIS, Michael Elwin (Fla) 6126 Cherry Lake Dr N, Jacksonville FL 32258 **St Fran in the Field Ponte Vedra FL 2005-** B Cocoa FL 9/12/1951 s Basil Elwin Ellis & Doris Clotile. BS Florida St U 1976; MDiv SWTS 1981. D 6/7/1981 P 12/20/1981 Bp Frank Stanley Cerveny. m 2/11/2006 Joan Barnwell Ellis c 2. S Eliz's Epis Ch Jacksonville FL 2004-2005; R S Barth's Ch Bristol TN 1999-2003; Epis Ch Of The H Sprt Tallahassee FL 1985-1999; Ch Of The Epiph Jacksonville FL 1981-1985. frmellis@gmail.com

ELLIS, Michael Warren (Md) 4803 Leybourne Dr, Hilliard OH 43026 B Cambridge MA 9/24/1937 s Stanley Warren Ellis & Frances. BA Pr 1959; STB GTS 1962; MSW Wayne 1973. D 6/23/1962 Bp Anson Phelps Stokes Jr P 6/1/1963 Bp George West Barrett. m 8/31/1963 Anice R Rutters c 2. R S Jn's Ch Frostburg MD 1988-1997; Supply P Dio Cntrl Pennsylvania Harrisburg PA 1974-1988; Asst Chr Ch Grosse Pointe Grosse Pointe Farms MI 1967-1968; S Jas Ch Sullivan MO 1964-1967; Cur Chr Ch Corning NY 1962-1964. Curs 1982-1997. michaellisw@aol.com

ELLIS, Richard Alvin (Ct) 15 Piper Rd Apt J313, Scarborough ME 04074 B Medford MA 5/13/1930 s Lewis Wilson Ellis & Doris. BA Dart 1952; MS Ya Berk 1955. D 2/23/1957 Bp Charles F Hall P 2/26/1958 Bp Robert McConnell Hatch. m 6/28/1958 Monica Wright c 3. Chr Ch Harwinton CT 1974-1978; R S Jn's Ch Pine Meadow CT 1971-1992; Vic Ch Of The H Comm Lakeview NY 1964-1970; Vic S Mart's Ch Pittsfield MA 1960-1964; Cur All SS Ch Worcester MA 1957-1960. monical_ellis@hotmail.com

ELLIS, Russell Ray (Vt) 328 Shore Rd, Burlington VT 05408 B Plymouth WI 7/16/1927 s Ray Dean Ellis & Hyldanna. BA Lawr 1950; BD SWTS 1954; STM UTS 1965. D 6/19/1954 P 12/20/1954 Bp Gerald Francis Burrill. m 6/14/1955 Nancy E Carpenter c 4. Rock Point Sch Burlington VT 1969-1992; R S Steph's Ch Middlebury VT 1956-1969; Cur S Paul's By The Lake Chicago IL 1954-1956. Phi Beta Kappa Lawr Coll. rrellis@burlingtontelecom.net

ELLIS, Steven MacDonald (ECR) 318 Lee St, Santa Cruz CA 95060 **R Ch Of S Jn The Bapt Aptos CA 1995-** B Fresno CA 1/5/1951 s Donald Stanley Ellis & Virginia Ann. BA California St U 1974; MDiv CDSP 1978. D 7/2/1978 P 6/1/1979 Bp Victor Manuel Rivera. m 2/22/2003 Robin Ellis c 5. Epis Ch Of S Anne Stockton CA 1986-1995; Cur S Paul's Epis Ch Modesto CA 1978-1985. silleevets@gmail.com

ELLIS, Walter L. (Tex) 2525 Seagler Rd, Houston TX 77042 B McKinney TX 10/22/1941 s Erwin Ballard Ellis & Mary Edra. BA U of No Texas 1964; MA U of No Texas 1966; MDiv VTS 1977; DMin Auston Presb TS 1993. D 6/17/1977 Bp Roger Howard Cilley P 6/12/1978 Bp J Milton Richardson. m 11/23/1960 Susan Elder c 3. R Ch Of The Ascen Houston TX 2001-2010; Ed Bd Dio Texas Houston TX 1998; Dioc Curs Sec Dio Texas Houston TX 1997; Stndg Com Dio Texas Houston TX 1996; Chair Dept Environ Dio Texas Houston TX 1993-1995; Stwdshp Consult Dio Texas Houston TX 1990; Coordntr Dioc FA Dio Texas Houston TX 1987-1989; R S Chris's Ch League City TX 1982-2001; R S Mich And All Ang' Epis Ch Longview TX 1977-1982; Vic S Mk's Ch Gladewater TX 1977-1979. Auth, "Baptismal Study Text"; Auth, "Numerous Rel & Sci arts Baptismal Study Text". Loc Mnstrl Associations 1977. Who'S Who In Rel 1992; Paul Harris Fellowowship. ninian98@att.net

ELLIS, Wilbur Richard (O) 2960 Hayes St, Avon OH 44011 B Brooklyn NY 7/4/1922 s Harry Greismer Ellis & Caroline Dorothy. MS Stevens Inst Of Tech 1949; BD Bex 1959. D 6/13/1959 P 3/1/1960 Bp Nelson Marigold Burroughs. c 3. S Jn's Ch Cleveland OH 1974-1985; In-Charge Ch Of The H Trin Epis Bellefontaine OH 1959-1962; In-Charge S Mk's Ch Sidney OH 1959-1962. Auth, "Automation mag".

ELLIS, William Joseph (NwPa) 222 Brisbin St, Houtzdale PA 16651 **Vic - nonstipendiary Ch Of The H Trin Houtzdale PA 2008-** B Philipsburg PA 4/15/1951 s Joseph Paul Ellis & Gail Marie. D 11/17/2006 Bp Arthur Benjamin Williams Jr P 1/19/2008 Bp Sean Walter Rowe. m 5/15/1971 Donna Marie Donna Marie Fish c 2. fr.billellis@comcast.net

ELLIS JR, William Robert (Spok) 128 E 12th Ave, Spokane WA 99202 **Stndg Com Dio Spokane Spokane WA 2009-; Dep, GC Dio Spokane Spokane WA 2008-; COM Dio Spokane Spokane WA 2007-; Dn Cathd Of S Jn The Evang Spokane WA 2006-** B Portland OR 2/23/1954 s William Robert Ellis & Nancy Anne. BA U of Oregon 1976; MDiv CDSP 1982. D 6/29/1982 P 5/25/1983 Bp Matthew Paul Bigliardi. m 6/24/1978 Beth Schindele c 2. COM Dio Estrn Oregon The Dalles OR 2002-2005; Dep, GC Dio Estrn Oregon The Dalles OR 1997-2006; Stndt Com Dio Estrn Oregon The Dalles OR 1994-2000; R Trin Ch Bend OR 1992-2006; Dioc Coun Dio

Oregon Portland OR 1990-1992; Vic S Bede's Ch Forest Grove OR 1984-1992; Cur Emm Ch Coos Bay OR 1982-1984; Vic S Mary Ch Gardiner OR 1982-1984. DD CDSP 2009; Phi Beta Kappa Alpha of Oregon Chapt 1976. bnbellis@comcast.net

ELLISON, Monique A (Mich) 5253 Harvard Rd, Detroit MI 48224 **S Chris Epis Ch Linthicum Heights MD 2011-** B Wayne MI 3/25/1970 d James Curtis Ellison & Della Mae. BS U Of Detroit 1994; MDiv SWTS 2002. D 12/22/2001 P 6/27/2002 Bp Wendell Nathaniel Gibbs Jr. S Ptr's Ch Philadelphia PA 2005-2007; Asst S Paul's Epis Ch Lansing MI 2002-2005. monique.ellison@gmail.com

E

ELLISOR, James Dillard (WLa) 4512 Fern Ave, Shreveport LA 71105 **Died 12/9/2009** B Andalusia AL 11/5/1928 s John Oscar Ellisor & Ethel Leone. BA U of Alabama 1951; BD Candler TS Emory U 1954; MRE Loyola U 1990. D 6/14/1961 P 12/19/1961 Bp Edward Hamilton West. c 3. Asst R Emer St. Paul's, Shreveport, LA 1993. ejde1105@aol.com

ELLSWORTH, Bradford Edwin (WMo) Po Box 160, Cabool MO 65689 **Vic Ch Of The Trsfg Mtn Grove MO 1997-** B Oakland CA 2/4/1939 s George Inness Ellsworth & Edwina Reed. U CA; BA U CA 1961; W Missouri Sch of Mnstry 1994. D 2/4/1995 P 8/31/1997 Bp John Clark Buchanan. m 6/13/1959 Jean Elaine McGuigan. NAAD. judge@train.missouri.org

ELLSWORTH, Eleanor L (SanD) 2205 Caminito Del Barco, Del Mar CA 92014 **Assoc S Jas By The Sea La Jolla CA 2007-; Chapl Cathd of St Ptr & St Paul Washington DC 1993-** B Biloxi MS 4/20/1948 d John Francis Lynch & Mary Eleanor. BA U of Tennessee 1970; MLS U of Tennessee 1972; MPA U of Tennessee 1976; MDiv VTS 1990. D 6/9/1990 P 12/9/1990 Bp Ronald Hayward Haines. c 2. S Mary's Epis Sch Memphis TN 2000-2002; Chr Ch Par Kensington MD 1996-1999; S Paul's Epis Par Point Of Rocks MD 1995-1996; Assoc R & Chapl Chr Ch Prince Geo's Par Rockville MD 1990-1994. Auth, "Column Ed," *Journ Of Rehab*, 1983; Auth, "Motivation And Stff Dvlpmt," *Journ Of Libr Admin*, 1982; Auth, "Natl Rehab Info Cntr," *Rehab Journ/Newsletters*, 1980; Auth, "Photograph," *Sch Libr Journ*, 1973. Cathd Fund (Chair: 1997)/ Washington Natl Cathd 1996-2000; Cath Fllshp Of The Epis Ch 1990-1994; Friends Of S Ben 1996; NAES, Bd Gvnr 2001; OSL (Chapl, 1997-8) 1996-1999; Sead 1990-1996. Shirley Olefson Awd Jr Members Round Table/ Amer Libr Assn 1972. elellsworth@earthlink.net

ELLSWORTH JR, Phillip Channing (WA) 10033 River Rd, Potomac MD 20854 **Cler Supply S Jn's Ch Harbor Sprg MI 2003-; Assoc R S Fran Ch Potomac MD 1998-** B El Paso TX 5/18/1959 s Phillip Channing Ellsworth & Akiko. BA Wheaton Coll 1982; MA Wheaton Coll 1987; Dipl. Ya Berk 1995; M.Div. Yale DS 1995. D 6/24/1995 Bp J Clark Grew II P 1/6/1996 Bp Craig Barry Anderson. m 6/28/1980 Victoria M White c 4. Assoc R S Barth's Ch New York NY 1995-1998. The Wolcott Calkins Prize Ya 1995.

ELLSWORTH, Scott Anthony (Ida) 2887 Snowflake Dr, Boise ID 83706 **COM Dio Idaho Boise ID 2003-; D S Steph's Boise ID 1998-** B Mankato MN 6/14/1956 s Richard Anthony Ellsworth & Nancy Ann. U MN; BS OR SU 1981. D 1/31/1998 Bp John Stuart Thornton. m 12/28/1981 Susan Ann Lomax c 3. NAAD 1998. twosae@cableone.net

ELMER-ANTHONY, Betty Lou (Ak) 11641 Hebron Dr, Eagle River AK 99577 **D H Sprt Epis Ch Eagle River AK 1998-** B San Diego CA 9/13/1929 d Joseph Mathias Elmer & Isabell Catherine. Anchorage Cmnty Coll; U of Alaska; EFM STUSo 1986. D 6/1/1984 Bp George Clinton Harris. m 5/18/1990 Richard David Anthony c 3. D S Christophers Ch Anchorage AK 1984-1997. Auth, "We have a whale!," *Alaska mag*; "A Century of Faith: Centennial Commemorative, 1885-1995, Epis Dio Alaska," *Centennial Press*. Soc of S Anne and S Simeon 1992.

ELSBERRY, Terence Lynn (NY) PO Box 293, Bedford NY 10506 **R S Matt's Ch Bedford NY 1994-** B Marshalltown IA 4/3/1943 s Lynn Jefferson Elsberry & Adaline Ruth. BA Drake U 1966; MDiv VTS 1984. D 5/26/1984 Bp Walter Cameron Righter P 12/1/1984 Bp William Foreman Creighton. m 11/23/1989 Nancy O Olds c 2. Sr Assoc R Chr Ch Greenwich CT 1986-1994; Asst Min S Jn's Ch Lafayette Sq Washington DC 1984-1986. Auth, "Marie of Romania".

ELSE, John David (Pgh) 272 Caryl Dr, Pittsburgh PA 15236 **Supply The Ch Of The Adv Jeannette PA 2005-** B Pittsburgh PA 3/4/1933 s Harry Calvin Else & Esther Irene. BS Penn 1955; Nash 1965. D 5/22/1965 Bp William S Thomas P 12/18/1965 Bp Austin Pardue. m 6/6/1953 Patricia Schneider c 3. Supply S Jn's Epis Ch Donora PA 2000-2005; Consult Trin Cathd Pittsburgh PA 1984-1988; Min In Charge S Geo's Ch Waynesburg PA 1965-1970; Min in charge S Thos' Epis Ch Canonsburg PA 1965-1968. Auth, "Recovering Recovery, Journ Of Mnstry In Addiction And Recovery," *Volume 6 (2)*, 1999; Auth, "In Giving We Rescue: The View From Russia, Journ Of Mnstry In Addiction And Recovery," *Volume 1 (2)*, 1994; Auth, "Life Is A Journey Back Hm," Centering, 1993; Auth, "Two Plus Two Equals One," Chem People Inst, 1984. Pres Of NECAD 1985-1987. cfs12step@aol.com

ELSENSOHN, David Dirk (Ak) 1714 Edgecumbe Dr, Sitka AK 99835 **R S Ptr's By-The-Sea Sitka AK 1995-** B Portland OR 3/8/1948 s Harold Keith Elsensohn & Patricia. BA Marylhurst U 1988; Cert Marylhurst U 1988; Cert Dio AK Prog Juneau AK 1993; MDiv Vancouver TS 2001. D 4/11/1993 P 12/6/1993 Bp Steven Charleston. m 3/14/1981 Bonnie Maurine Joseph c 2. Asst to R The Ch Of The H Trin Juneau AK 1993-1995. david.elsensohn@yahoo.com

ELVIN, Peter Thurston (WMass) 35 Park St, Williamstown MA 01267 **S Jn's Ch Williamstown MA 1978-** B Cranston RI 1/20/1947 s Arthur Leishman Elvin & Margaret. BA Trin Hartford CT 1969; MDiv GTS 1973. D 6/16/1973 Bp Frederick Hesley Belden P 1/5/1974 Bp Conrad Gesner. m 6/22/1974 Diana Malootian c 2. Dep Gc Dio Wstrn Massachusetts Springfield MA 1988-2000; Dn Dio Wstrn Massachusetts Springfield MA 1988-1994; Com Dio Wstrn Massachusetts Springfield MA 1985-1995; Bec Dio Wstrn Massachusetts Springfield MA 1983-1990; Chair Ce Cmsn Dio Wstrn Massachusetts Springfield MA 1979-1982; R S Lk's Ch Worcester MA 1978-1986; Dio Wstrn Massachusetts Springfield MA 1978-1982; R S Phil's Ch Easthampton MA 1976-1978; Asst S Andr's Ch Longmeadow MA 1973-1976. ptelvin@roadrunner.com

ELWELL, Pamela (SO) 321 East Kanawha Ave, Columbus OH 43214 **D S Steph's Epis Ch And U Columbus OH 2006-** B Richmond VA 7/18/1935 d Horace Clayton McSwain & Isabel Smith. BA W&M 1963; MLS Case Wstrn Reserve U 1970. D 5/13/2006 Bp Kenneth Lester Price. m 8/24/1963 William Edwin Elwell c 2. pamelwell@gmail.com

ELWOOD, Fred(erick) Campbell (Mich) 1334 Riverside Dr, Buhl ID 83316 B Wichita KS 7/20/1948 s Harold Campbell Elwood & Mary Elizabeth. BA Wichita St U 1970; MA U CA 1975; MDiv GTS 1979; STM GTS 1988. D 6/23/1979 P 1/12/1980 Bp Robert C Rusack. m 5/29/1971 Alice A Akin c 2. R S Jas Epis Ch Birmingham MI 2001-2011; R S Jn's Epis Ch Olympia WA 1993-2001; R S Andr's Epis Ch Staten Island NY 1991-1993; R Ch Of The Ascen Twin Falls ID 1982-1991; Assoc S Paul's Epis Ch Ventura CA 1979-1982. Auth, *Sharing Biblic Dialogues: Lectionary Readings for Groups*, Ch Pub, 2002; Auth, *In the Shadows of H Week: The Off of Tenebrae*, Ch Pub, 1996. fred.elwood@gmail.com

ELWOOD, Richard Hugh (Tex) 308 E San Antonio St, Fredericksburg TX 78624 **R S Barn Epis Ch Fredericksburg TX 2004-** B Fort Riley KS 5/11/1939 s Ernest Anthony Elwood & Madeline. BA Baylor U 1961; BD STUSo 1966. D 6/26/1966 Bp J Milton Richardson P 6/6/1967 Bp Frederick P Goddard. m 8/10/1990 Ellen Jane Leister c 2. S Mart's Epis Ch Houston TX 2000-2005; S Mk's Ch Beaumont TX 1984-2000; Ch Of The Gd Shpd Kingwood TX 1979-1984; R Palmer Memi Ch Houston TX 1977-1979; R Chr Epis Ch Tyler TX 1971-1977; Chapl S Jos's Chap at the Kent Sch Kent CT 1970-1971; Asst Palmer Memi Ch Houston TX 1966-1970. Auth, "Mart in the Narthex by Mart the Dog," *Shearer Pub*, 2011; Auth, "Rel Column Kingwood Observer". Moonbeam's Chld's Bk Awd Indep Pub Assn of Amer 2011; Moonbeam Chld's Bk Awd Indep Pub Assn of Amer 2011. dickelwood@gmail.com

ELY, Elizabeth Wickenberg (NC) "Dunwyck", 64 Peniel Road, Columbus NC 28722 **GC Deputation Chair Dio No Carolina Raleigh NC 2010-; Cn for Reg Mnstry Dio No Carolina Raleigh NC 2009-; Prov IV, Eccl Crt Epis Ch Cntr New York NY 2009-; GBEC Ed Epis Ch Cntr New York NY 2005-** B Columbia SC 6/14/1953 d Charles Herbert Wickenberg & Margaret Gall. BA Agnes Scott Coll 1975; MS Col 1976; MDiv, cl GTS 1989; PhD GTF 2012. D 5/19/1989 Bp Allen Lyman Bartlett Jr P 5/23/1990 Bp Huntington Williams Jr. m 6/14/1984 Duncan Cairnes Ely c 1. Vic S Phil's Epis Ch Greenville SC 2000-2009; Dn of Reedy River Convoc Dio Upper So Carolina Columbia SC 2000-2004; Prov IV, Com to Elect PBp Epis Ch Cntr New York NY 2000-2003; Dioc Coun Dio Upper So Carolina Columbia SC 1999-2003; BEC Dio Upper So Carolina Columbia SC 1998-2009; GC Dep Dio Upper So Carolina Columbia SC 1998-2009; Dioc Cmncatns Com Chair Dio Upper So Carolina Columbia SC 1998-1999; Stdng Com Pres Dio Upper So Carolina Columbia SC 1997-1999; Assoc R Ch Of The Adv Spartanburg SC 1996-1999; Suffr Com Search Com Secy Dio No Carolina Raleigh NC 1995-1996; Vic All SS Epis Ch Charlotte NC 1993-1996; Dioc Coun Secy Dio No Carolina Raleigh NC 1993-1996; Vic S Pat's Mssn Mooresville NC 1992-1996; COM, Secy Dio No Carolina Raleigh NC 1991-1996; Assoc R S Jn's Epis Ch Charlotte NC 1989-1992. Auth, "Chrsnty and Politics: A Consideration of Apartheid," *Fndt Theol Monograph 2009*, GTF, 2009; Auth, "It's Your Turn to Carry the Chld," *Preaching as the Art of Sacr Conversation: Sermons that Wk VI*, Morehouse, 1997; Auth, "A Manual for Eucharistic Visitors," Morehouse, 1991. ECom 1997-2000. Oxford Fndt Fell GTF 1999; Sewanee Fell U So 1999. beth.ely@episdionc.org

ELY, James Everett (Tex) 1700 Golden Ave, Bay City TX 77414 B Stillwater OK 10/20/1946 s Delbert Richard Ely & Lohoma Joyce. BS U of Missouri 1978; MD U of Missouri 1983. D 2/3/2002 Bp Claude Edward Payne P 11/16/2002 Bp Don Adger Wimberly. m 6/28/1968 Linda Louise Lawkin c 3.

✠ **ELY, Rt Rev Thomas C** (Vt) 11 Rock Point Rd, Burlington VT 05408 **Trst EDS Cambridge MA 2009-; Bp of Vermont Dio Vermont Burlington VT 2001-** B Norwalk CT 12/14/1951 s Leonard Clark Ely & Shirley Marie. BA Wstrn Connecticut St U 1976; MDiv STUSo 1980. D 6/14/1980 Bp Morgan Porteus P 12/13/1980 Bp Arthur Edward Walmsley Con 4/28/2001 for Vt. m

5/22/1976 Martha Ann Wiggins c 2. Mssnr Grtr Hartford Reg Mnstry Grtr Hartford Reg Mnstry E Hartford CT 1991-2001; Dir of Yth Mnstrs Dio CT Dio Connecticut Hartford CT 1985-1991; Asst Mssnr Middlesex Area Cluster Mnstry Middlesex Area Cluster Mnstry Higganum CT 1980-1984. Cranmer Cup 2000; LAND 1981; Living Stones 2001. Hon Doctorate of Mnstry U So 2002. tely@svcable.net

EMBRY, F Alvin (Mont) 2700 N A W Grimes Blvd Apt 714, Round Rock TX 78665 B Atlanta GA 12/4/1941 s Foster Alvin Embry & Martha Lucille. BA Georgia St U 1963; BD Duke 1966; ThM Duke 1967. D 6/28/1975 P 11/1/1975 Bp John Mc Gill Krumm. m 12/21/1990 Mary Lydia Harvey c 2. St Lk's Epis Hosp Houston TX 1979-1984. AEMBRY@AUSTIN.RR.COM

EMENHEISER, D(avid) Edward (WMich) 174 Wakulat Ln, Traverse City MI 49686 B Hanover PA 5/8/1941 s Paul D Emenheiser & Esther L. BA U So 1963; MDiv GTS 1966. D 4/16/1966 P 10/18/1966 Bp Francis W Lickfield. m 6/11/1966 Ann Minteer c 2. R Gr Epis Ch Traverse City MI 1994-2007; R H Trin Epis Ch Wyoming MI 1976-1994; S Jn's Epis Ch Kewanee IL 1975-1976; Vic H Trin Epis Ch Peoria IL 1974-1976; Vic Trin Epis Ch Peoria IL 1969-1972; S Fran Epis Ch Dunlap IL 1966-1969; Vic S Jn's Ch Peoria IL 1966-1969. eemenheiser@aol.com

EMERSON, E(lmarie) Angela (Vt) 747 Hartford Ave. Suite 1, White River Junction VT 05001 **Min of Stwdshp Dvlpmt Dio Vermont Burlington VT 2008-** B 3/29/1952 d Samuel Burt Emerson & Elmarie Constance. BA U of Tennessee 1974; JD Woodrow Wilson Coll of Law 1977; MDiv Epis TS of the SW 2006. D 12/21/2005 P 6/25/2006 Bp J(ohn) Neil Alexander. Cur and Sch Chapl Epis Par Of S Mich And All Ang Tucson AZ 2006-2007. Lettie Pate Whitehead Evans Awd for Lay Ldrshp VTS 2001. aemerson@dioceseofvermont.org

EMERSON, James Carson (Q) 1625 Hershey Ct, Columbia MO 65202 B Quincy IL 11/9/1939 s James Marion Emerson & Dorothy Eloise. BA U of Missouri 1962; MDiv VTS 1969; Ldrshp Acad for New Directions 1984. D 6/21/1969 Bp Lauriston L Scaife P 12/1/1969 Bp Harold B Robinson. Vic S Jas Epis Ch Griggsville IL 1995-1999; Cn to the Ordnry Dio Quincy Peoria IL 1988-1995; Dioc Healthcare Mssn Coordntr/Chapl Dio Quincy Peoria IL 1987-1995; Ecum Off Dio Quincy Peoria IL 1985-1995; R S Ptr's Ch Peoria IL 1985-1995; Vic S Andr's Ch Hays Hays KS 1982-1985; Dio Wstrn Kansas Hutchinson KS 1980-1985; Vic S Eliz's Ch Russell KS 1980-1985; Dio W Missouri Kansas City MO 1973-1980; Vic S Mary's Ch Fayette MO 1973-1980; Vic Trin Epis Ch Marshall MO 1973-1980; Vic S Andr's Ch Newfane Burt NY 1971-1973; Vic S Jn's Ch Wilson NY 1971-1973; Cur S Jn's Gr Ch Buffalo NY 1969-1971. Alum Recognition Awd Missouri Chapt of Delta Upsilon Intl Fraternity 2010; Man-Of-Yr Finalist Russell Cnty Ks 1983. jayce0b05@yahoo.com

EMERSON, Jason Daniel (Neb) 9932 Bedford Ave., Omaha NE 68134 **R Ch Of The Resurr Omaha NE 2009-** B Corinth MS 9/21/1976 s Isaac Daniel Emerson & Eula Mande. BA Middle Tennessee St U 1999; MA U Cinc 2001; MDiv GTS 2005. D 5/30/2005 P 1/21/2006 Bp Joe Goodwin Burnett. m 6/12/2004 Jodie L Emerson. All SS Epis Ch Omaha NE 2007-2009; Min for Yth and YA Dio Nebraska Omaha NE 2005-2007. fatherjason@gmail.com

EMERSON, Keith Roger (SVa) St. Paul's Church, 213 N. Main Street, Suffolk VA 23434 **R S Paul's Epis Ch Suffolk VA 2007-** B Pittsburgh PA 10/10/1959 s Roger Emerson & Jane. BA Grove City Coll 1982; Gordon-Conwell TS 1985; MDiv VTS 1987; DMin Un Theol Seminaunion TS & Presbyt 2005. D 6/27/1987 P 5/13/1988 Bp James Russell Moodey. c 2. R Epiph Epis Ch Richmond VA 1997-2007; R S Jn's Ch Keokuk IA 1993-1997; Asst Chr Ch Epis Hudson OH 1989-1993; Asst S Ptr's Epis Ch Lakewood OH 1987-1989. keith@saintpauls-suffolk.org

EMERSON, Mary Beth (Va) 2217 Columbia Pike, Arlington VA 22204 **Cmsn on Chr Formation Dio Virginia Richmond VA 2011-; D Trin Ch Arlington VA 2010-** B Newark NJ 11/18/1955 d Joseph James & Christina. MA U GA 1986; Advncd Cert Epis Sem of the SW 2002; Diac Formation Inst Dio Virginia 2010. D 2/5/2011 Bp Shannon Sherwood Johnston. m 5/20/1983 Warren K Emerson c 3. deacon@tecarl.org

EMERSON, R Clark (ECR) 1412 Maysun Ct, Campbell CA 95008 **Asst S Lk's Ch Los Gatos CA 1985-** B Los Angeles CA 3/9/1945 s George Heins Emerson & Irma Furney. AA Foothill Coll 1964; BA San Jose St U San Jose CA 1966; Cert San Jose St U San Jose CA 1967; MDiv CDSP 1972. D 6/24/1972 P 1/6/1973 Bp George Richard Millard. Asst St Johns Pro-Cathd Los Angeles CA 1976-1985; Asst S Fran' Par Palos Verdes Estates CA 1972-1976.

EMERY, Dana Karen (Minn) 1400 Corbett Rd, Detroit Lakes MN 56501 B Fargo ND 5/29/1947 d Marvin Theodore Anderson & Helen Marie Mattson. BA St U MN 1988; Cert Engl Sch of Gardening 1996; MDiv Untd Theol Sem Twin Cities 2008. D 12/11/2008 P 6/27/2009 Bp James Louis Jelinek. m 8/12/1967 John Richard Emery c 3. danakaren@arvig.net

EMERY, Harold Alfred (SVa) 2363 Chapel Ridge Pl Apt 2B, Salina KS 67401 B Scranton PA 3/13/1932 s Harold Alfred Emery & Ellen Gertrude. BA Un Coll Barbourville KY 1953; STB PDS 1960. D 6/16/1960 P 12/22/1960 Bp Frederick J Warnecke. m 1/13/2007 Karen Anne Reboul c 5. Cntrl Mecklenburg Cure Boydton VA 1992-1997; R Gr Epis Ch Drakes Branch VA 1992-1997; R S Jn's Epis Ch Chase City VA 1992-1997; R S Tim's Epis Ch Clarksville VA 1992-1997; R S Phil's Ch Coraopolis PA 1982-1992; S Fran Cmnty Serv Inc. Salina KS 1974-1982; R S Jn's Epis Ch Bellefonte PA 1968-1973; Asst Ch Of The Gd Samar Paoli PA 1962-1965; In-C Epis Par Of S Mk And S Jn Jim Thorpe PA 1960-1962.

EMMERT, John H (CPa) 648 Laurel View Dr., Manheim PA 17545 B Kendallville IN 6/29/1941 s Howard W Emmert & E Gwendolyn. BA U MI 1963; MDiv VTS 1970; DMin Palmer TS 1995. D 6/29/1970 Bp George P Gunn P 5/1/1971 Bp David Shepherd Rose. m 12/19/1964 Kathryn E Klontz c 2. R S Jn's Epis Ch Lancaster PA 1996-2004; R Old Donation Ch Virginia Bch VA 1985-1996; Asst Galilee Epis Ch Virginia Bch VA 1980-1985; P-in-c Ch Of The Epiph - Luth Valdez AK 1973-1975; Dio Sthrn Virginia Norfolk VA 1970-1980; Cur Bruton Par Williamsburg VA 1970-1973. john.emmert1@gmail.com

EMRICH III, Frederick Ernest (WMass) 7 Smith St, P.O. Box 318, North Haven ME 04853 **Assoc All Ang By The Sea Longboat Key FL 2010-; S Paul's Epis Ch No Andover MA 2002-** B Boston MA 1/16/1940 s Richard Stanley Merrill Emrich & Beatrice Anne. BA Harv 1961; BD EDS 1968. D 6/22/1968 Bp Anson Phelps Stokes Jr P 5/1/1969 Bp Richard S M Emrich. m 6/7/2008 Diana Emrich c 4. Brooks Sch Chap No Andover MA 2002-2008; Ch Of The H Trin Pawling NY 1999-2000; Dio Wstrn Massachusetts Springfield MA 1987-1998; R S Jas' Ch Greenfield MA 1987-1998; R Trin Ch Washington DC 1982-1987; R Ch Of The Gd Shpd Reading MA 1971-1982; Cur S Ptr's Ch Beverly MA 1968-1971. FEEmrich@aol.com

EMRICH III, Richard S M (CNY) 190 Quaker Point Rd, West Bath ME 04530 B Boston MA 9/12/1938 s Richard S M Emrich & Beatrice. BA Harv 1960; JD U MI 1964; MDiv SWTS 1992. D 6/27/1992 Bp Richard S M Emrich P 1/1/1993 Bp Henry Irving Mayson. m 1/22/1980 Mary Sherwood Condon c 2. R Zion Ch Rome NY 1994-2002; Asst To Dn Cathd Ch Of S Paul Detroit MI 1992-1994. rsmemrich@aol.com

EMRY, Anne D (Mass) 172 Main St, Hingham MA 02043 **Cur Ch Of S Jn The Evang Hingham MA 2010-** B Greenwich CT 11/16/1958 d Tibo de Cholnolg & Nancy T. BA NWU 1980; MDiv CDSP 2010. D 6/5/2010 Bp Marc Handley Andrus P 1/8/2011 Bp M(arvil) Thomas Shaw III. m 7/31/1988 Steve Emry. mtranne@stjohns-hingham.org

ENCARNACION-CARABALLO, Felix Antonio (DR) C/Santiago 114, Santo Iomingo Dominican Republic **Dio The Dominican Republic (Iglesia Epis Dominicana) Santo Domingo DO 2000-** B La Romana 8/6/1966 D 4/10/1999 P 5/13/2000 Bp Julio Cesar Holguin-Khoury. m 8/29/1998 Berkys Herrera c 3.

ENCINOSA, Christina Dolores (SeFla) 68 Paxford Ln, Boynton Beach FL 33426 **P-in-c Ch Of The H Redeem Lake Worth FL 2004-** B Miami FL 2/4/1978 d Jose Luis Encinosa & Dolores. BA U of Miami 1999; MDiv GTS 2004. D 4/17/2004 P 10/17/2004 Bp Leopold Frade. m 5/14/2011 Gerhardt Witt. Ch And Soc Prize The GTS 2004. revencinosa@bellsouth.net

ENDICOTT, Rachel Faith (Oly) 15114 SE 48th Dr., Bellevue WA 98006 B London UK 8/4/1963 d Oliver Brian Endicott & Yvonne Mary. BA Scripps Coll 1985; MBA Natl U 1987; MDiv VTS 1997. D 6/14/1997 P 12/21/1997 Bp Gethin Benwil Hughes. c 1. Assoc R Trin Par Seattle WA 2006-2009; Int S Alb's Ch Edmonds WA 2005-2006; Assoc R S Marg's Epis Ch Bellevue WA 1997-2003. Auth, "The Many Faces Of Rachel," *Wmn Uncommon Prayers: Our Lives Revealed, Nurtured, Celebrated*, Morehouse Pub, 2000. rendicott@comcast.net

ENG, Lincoln Paul (Ore) 5120 Sw 182nd Ave, Beaverton OR 97007 B Seattle WA 10/18/1921 s Arthur Wing Eng & Koon Hay. BS U of Washington 1949; BD CDSP 1952. D 6/24/1952 P 6/29/1953 Bp Stephen F Bayne Jr. m 8/27/1949 Mabel Luke c 5. Int S Fran Of Assisi Epis Wilsonville OR 2001-2002; Int S Paul's Par Oregon City OR 1999-2000; Int S Steph's Epis Par Portland OR 1998-1999; Int H Trin Epis Ch Spokane WA 1996-1997; Int S Jas Epis Ch Tigard OR 1995-1996; Int S Chris's Ch Port Orford OR 1992-1993; Int S Jn-By-The-Sea Epis Ch Bandon OR 1991-1992; Int Chr Ch S Helens OR 1989-1990; Int The Epis Ch Of The Gd Samar Corvallis OR 1988-1989; Int S Steph's Epis Ch Longview WA 1987-1988; Archd Dio Oregon Portland OR 1979-1986; R S Barth's Ch Beaverton OR 1971-1979; Vic S Geo's Ch Seattle WA 1961-1965; Vic St Ptr's Epis Par Seattle WA 1955-1961. lpeng2@juno.com

ENGBLOM, Marcia Gayle (NCal) 6931 Lincoln Avenue, Carmichael CA 95608 **Died 10/28/2011** B Truth or Consequences NM 10/31/1953 d Ronald Lloyd Wynn & Marilyn Jean. BA Wstrn Oregon U 1977; MDiv CDSP 1994. D 5/26/1994 Bp Robert Louis Ladehoff P 12/10/1994 Bp Jerry Alban Lamb. c 2. robert.engblom@gmail.com

ENGDAHL JR, Frederick Robert (Mich) 6490 Clarkston Rd., Clarkston MI 48346 B Escanaba MI 3/27/1956 s Frederick Robert Engdahl & Margaret Laverne. BS Cntrl Michigan U 1980; LTh SWTS 1983; MDiv SWTS 1985. D 6/29/1985 Bp H Coleman McGehee Jr P 12/15/1985 Bp Frank Stanley Cerveny. m 6/21/1980 Gail Carolyn Simula c 2. Ch Of The Resurr Clarkston MI 2008-2009; S Lk's Ch Marietta OH 2005-2008; R Gr Ch Rice Lake WI

2000-2005; R S Mk's Epis Ch Aberdeen SD 1997-1998; S Mk's Ch Lake City MN 1994-1997; R S Paul's Epis Ch St. Clair MI 1989-1991; R S Steph's Baker City OR 1987-1989; Asst Chr Epis Ch Ponte Vedra Bch FL 1985-1987. fengdahl@parishmail.com

ENGELS, Allen Robert (Colo) 3081 Evanston Ave, Grand Junction CO 81504 B Martinez CA 5/29/1939 s Allen Engels & Ann Delores. Cmnty Coll Of Af. D 1/22/2000 P 7/29/2000 Bp William Jerry Winterrowd. m 6/16/1962 Carolyn Beatrice Strickland c 3. P Ch Of The Nativ Grand Jct CO 2000-2007.

ENGELS, jimichael (Mass) 1190 Adams St Apt 213, Dorchester Center MA 02124 B Salt Lake City UT 9/21/1936 s Kenneth John Engels & Rebecca Karyl. BA Dart 1958; MA U Tor 1963; Nash 1967; MDiv U Tor 1968. D 9/7/1968 P 3/8/1969 Bp Francis E I Bloy. m 4/27/1968 Margaret F Engels c 3. Gr Ch Everett MA 1998-2002; Supply P Dio Massachusetts Boston MA 1991-1997; St Johns Ch Taunton MA 1989-1992; R S Jn The Evang Taunton MA 1989-1991; Int S Jn's Epis Ch Peoria IL 1988-1989; Trin Ch Muscatine IA 1985-1987; R S Steph's Par Whittier CA 1977-1985; Assoc S Jas Par Los Angeles CA 1972-1975; P-in-c Ch Of The Ang Pasadena CA 1970-1972; Cur All SS Par Los Angeles CA 1968-1970. Auth, "Poem A Friend Ship," 2002; Auth, "Poem Trin 2002," 2002; Auth, "Poem 4 Verbal Icons," 2001; Auth, "Poem Trilogue," 2000; Auth, "Poem Quartet," 1997. margaretfaith.engles@verizon.net

ENGLAND, Edward Gary (ETenn) 699 Pittman Rd, Whitwell TN 37397 B Springfield IL 10/28/1939 s Edward Garret England & Pauline Coe. BS Georgia St U 1967. D 1/7/2006 Bp Charles Glenn VonRosenberg. m 6/15/1963 Virginia Stanley c 3. gary.england@christchurchsp.org

ENGLAND, Gary William (Ky) 6710 Wolf Pen Branch Rd, Harrods Creek KY 40027 B Birmingham AL 6/9/1952 s William Oscar England & Laura Mae. BS U of Alabama 1974; MA U of Alabama 1975; JD Cumberland Sch of Law at Samford U 1981. D 8/27/2011 Bp Terry Allen White. m 11/11/1989 Maria Nicolette Sorolis c 3. genglandesq@insightbb.com

ENGLAND, Loy David (WTex) Po Box 1025, Pflugerville TX 78691 B Texarkana AR 3/11/1931 s Loy D England & Natalie. BS U of Arkansas 1953; MDiv Epis TS of The SW 1960; MA U of Texas 1966. D 6/6/1974 Bp Harold Cornelius Gosnell P 12/1/1974 Bp Richard Earl Dicus. m 12/31/1955 Margaret Penelope Carsen. P-in-c S Mich And All Ang Epis Ch Blanco TX 1974-1988. Auth, "Var Tech arts". Apwa.

ENGLAND, Margaret Jefferson (Az) 11058 Portobelo Dr, San Diego CA 92124 B Liverpool UK 10/25/1930 d Herbert David Waghorn & Margaret Jane. Cert Avery Hill Coll 1955; Lon 1955; Cert Westminster Coll 1955; CTh Claremont TS 1980. D 11/7/1992 Bp Robert Reed Shahan. m 4/5/1958 James Norman England c 2. D S Dav's Epis Ch San Diego CA 1998-1999; S Steph's Ch Phoenix AZ 1993-1997. SCHC 1982. ourmarg1@earthlink.net

ENGLAND JR, Nick Arnold (WVa) 411 Prichard St, Williamson WV 25661 B Pikeville KY 11/3/1945 s Nick Arnold England & Nanna. BS Pikeville Coll 1968; DMD U of Louisville 1977. D 11/22/2004 P 11/5/2005 Bp William Michie Klusmeyer. m 5/21/1983 Mary Jane McCoy c 3. D S Pauls Epis Ch Williamson WV 2004-2005. naejr@mikrotec.com

ENGLAND, O(tis) Bryan (WMo) 315 E Partridge Ave, Independence MO 64055 B Mammoth Sprgs AR 1/28/1949 s Otis Thomas England & Lola Pearl. Weatherford Coll 1974; BA U of Texas 1976; MA U of Texas 1981. D 4/10/1994 Bp Carl Christopher Epting. m 8/16/1986 Linda Marie Dealey c 2. COM Dio W Missouri Kansas City MO 2006-2010; D Gr And H Trin Cathd Kansas City MO 2003-2010; D Chr Epis Ch Clinton IA 1998-2000; COM Dio Iowa Des Moines IA 1996-2001; D S Ptr's Ch Bettendorf IA 1994-2002; D S Alb's Ch Davenport IA 1994-1998. Assn for Epis Deacons 1994. bryan_england@yahoo.com

ENGLE, Cynthia L (Tex) 680 Calder St, Beaumont TX 77701 **S Fran Of Assisi Epis Prairie View TX 2011-; S Paul's Ch Navasota TX 2011-** B Waco TX 4/11/1953 d Harvey C Lanham & Neal C. BM Texas A & M U 1983; MDiv TESM 1995; PhD U of Cambridge 2006. D 12/6/2008 Bp Kirk Stevan Smith P 12/9/2009 Bp Dena Arnall Harrison. m 12/2/1972 B Lee Engle c 2. S Mk's Ch Beaumont TX 2009-2011; Adult Educ Dir Chr Ch Of The Ascen Paradise Vlly AZ 2008-2009; Asst Gd Shpd Of The Hills Cave Creek AZ 1995-1997. clengle@cox.net

ENGLE SR, Mark (NMich) 22975 Pine Lake Rd, Battle Creek MI 49014 B Denver CO 8/21/1948 s VV Engle & Catharine Patricia. BA Alma Coll 1970; MDiv SWTS 1973; DMin STUSo 1982. D 5/19/1973 Bp Charles Ellsworth Bennison Jr P 1/26/1974 Bp Charles Bennison. m 3/20/1970 Sharon Speas c 3. S Andr's Ch Lexington KY 2000-2007; S Paul's Ch Marquette MI 1988-2006; S Paul's Jeffersonville IN 1981-1988; Cn S Paul's Cathd Buffalo NY 1978-1981; S Andr's-Sewanee Sch Sewanee TN 1975-1978; Cur S Lk's Par Kalamazoo MI 1973-1974. cousinsisland@gmail.com

ENGLEBY, Matthew S (NJ) 379 Mount Harmony Rd, Bernardsville NJ 07924 **Exec Coun Appointees New York NY 2011-** B Roanoke VA 3/23/1962 s Jane E. BA U So 1984; MDiv GTS 1991. D 6/9/1991 Bp Arthur Edward Walmsley P 5/1/1992 Bp Allen Lyman Bartlett Jr. m 8/4/1990 Linda Nash c 3. The Ch Of The Sav Denville NJ 2009-2011; R Ch of S Jn on the Mtn Bernardsville NJ 1999-2009; S Andr's Epis Sch Potomac MD 1998-1999; Asst Ch Of The Redeem Bryn Mawr PA 1991-1993. matthew@engleby.org

ENGLISH, Ann Cantwell (Spok) Rr 1 Box 241-B, Touchet WA 99360 B Indianapolis IN 12/10/1943 d John Edgar Cantwell & Betty Cole. BA U GA. D 3/19/1987 Bp Leigh Wallace Jr. m 11/26/1964 William Howard c 2. ahoward@bmi.net

ENGLISH, Carrie Russeau (Fla) 11601 Longwood Key Dr W, Jacksonville FL 32218 **D Resurr Epis Ch Jacksonville FL 2006-** B Jacksonville FL 8/9/1948 d James Russeau & Myrtle Laura. BS Tennessee St U 1970; MA U of No Florida 1979; Angl Inst Live Oak FL 2004. D 6/5/2005 Bp Samuel Johnson Howard. m 11/27/1976 Jeffery English c 2. englishc0809@bellsouth.net

ENGLISH JR, James Jones (SwFla) 1255 Florida Ave, Fort Myers FL 33901 B Wilmington DE 3/24/1927 s James Jones English & Gertrude. BA Hob 1949; ThB PDS 1953; MS U of Pennsylvania 1959; PhD Ford 1974. D 4/25/1953 P 10/25/1953 Bp Wallace J Gardner. m 2/12/1966 Van Palmer Yelvington. Chair Schs Com Dio SW Florida Sarasota FL 1986-1993; EDEO Ft Meyers FL 1986-1992; S Lk's Ch Ft Myers FL 1981-1993; Ce Cmsn Dio SW Florida Sarasota FL 1981-1984; R S Ambr Epis Ch Ft Lauderdale FL 1980-1981; Yth Cmsn Dio SE Florida Miami FL 1977-1981; Cur S Paul's Ch Delray Bch FL 1977-1980; Vic S Andr The Apos Highland Highlands NJ 1957-1960; Chapl S Marks Sch Of Texas Dallas TX 1956-1957; Pstr Cathd Of St Jn The Div New York NY 1955-1966; Cur The Ch Of S Uriel The Archangel Sea Girt NJ 1953-1955. Auth, "Developing Curric For Educational Renwl"; Auth, "Authority & Arcic Dialogue"; Auth, "Ethical Aspects Of Living Wills". EDEO 1981-1993; SSC 1986. jje1@comcast.net

ENGLISH, John Lyle (WMich) 1045 Woodrow Ave Nw, Grand Rapids MI 49504 **Contract Cler S Phil's Epis Ch Grand Rapids MI 2003-** B Detroit MI 7/19/1930 s William Lowell English & Viola Marie. BA MI SU 1955; LTh SWTS 1959. D 5/29/1959 Bp Charles L Street P 11/28/1959 Bp William W Horstick. m 8/25/1956 Jeanette M DeClercq c 4. R S Paul's Epis Ch Grand Rapids MI 1980-1995; R S Andr's Ch Big Rapids MI 1975-1980; R S Paul's Epis Ch Grand Rapids MI 1963-1975; R S Kath's Ch Owen WI 1959-1963. jenglishes@hotmail.com

ENGLISH, Linda Jean (WK) 114 W Roosevelt, Phoenix AZ 85003 **S Mich's Ch Hays KS 2010-; Vic S Geo's Epis Ch Holbrook AZ 2007-** B Kansas City MO 7/20/1946 d Rodger Clifford English & Lila Lee. BS Upper Iowa U 2001; MDiv SWTS 2004. D 12/20/2003 P 6/26/2004 Bp Dean Elliott Wolfe. m 11/9/1991 Robert Lee Cook c 3. Dio Arizona Phoenix AZ 2007-2009; S Fran Cmnty Serv Inc. Salina KS 2004-2007. EPF 2006. englishcook@cox.net

ENGLISH, Thomas Ronald (Ore) 2530 Fairmount Blvd, Eugene OR 97403 **D S Mary's Epis Ch Eugene OR 2000-** B Salt Lake City UT 6/17/1943 s Thomas John English & Rosemary Claire. BA U of Oregon 1966; MA U of Oregon 1978. D 10/4/1999 Bp Robert Louis Ladehoff. m 5/26/1984 Nancy Alice Mote c 2. Rotary Intl 2001; W Cascade Returned Peace Corps Vol 2000. Voulenteer of the year Ln Cnty Sheriff 2005. english@riousa.com

ENGLISH, Tristan Clifford (Wyo) 4700 S Poplar St, Casper WY 82601 **COM Dio Wyoming Casper WY 2011-; HR Camp Fndt Dio Wyoming Casper WY 2010-** B Decorah IA 9/12/1971 s Clifford John English & Martha Anne. BA Ursinus Coll 1994. D 3/13/2010 Bp Bruce Edward Caldwell P 9/29/2010 Bp John Sheridan Smylie. m 2/10/2001 Debra L Watson. trisenglish@hotmail.com

ENGLISH, William H (Roch) 248 Commons Lane, Foster City CA 94404 B Corning NY 5/21/1939 s Floyd W English & Marian D. BS St Univ. of N. Y. at Buffalo 1961; JD St Univ. of N.Y. at Buffalo Law Sch 1964; MDiv EDS 1969. D 6/21/1969 P 12/1/1969 Bp George West Barrett. m 8/18/1962 Elizabeth Margaret English c 1. R Zion Ch Avon NY 1991-1994; Asst for Pstr Mnstry S Paul's Ch Rochester NY 1972-1991; P-in-c Chr Ch Sodus Point NY 1969-1972; P-in-c S Steph's Ch Wolcott NY 1969-1972. WHENGLISH@YAHOO.COM

ENGLISH, William Lawson (NY) 605 Radiance Dr, Cambridge MD 21613 B Cambridge MD 7/19/1936 s William Marion English & Mary Stewart. BA Amer U 1960; STB GTS 1965. D 6/12/1965 P 12/21/1965 Bp Allen J Miller. S Mary's Castleton Staten Island NY 1967-1999; R S Andr's Hurlock MD 1965-1967; R S Steph's Epis Ch E New Mrkt MD 1965-1967.

ENGLUND, David (NCal) 1624 10th St, Oroville CA 95965 **P-in-c S Paul's Epis Ch Oroville CA 2007-** B Kansas City MO 7/25/1949 s Vernon E Englund & Emma F. BA Azusa Pacific U 1971; MDiv Fuller TS 1979; DMin SWTS 2009. D 4/18/2004 P 10/17/2004 Bp Jerry Alban Lamb. m 12/31/1998 Susan Jean Doughty c 2. englund@oro-mail.com

ENGLUND, Henry C (NJ) 424 Windrow Clusters Dr, Moorestown NJ 08057 B Trenton NJ 8/21/1943 s Gustaf Henny Englund & Louise E. BS U of Virginia 1965; MDiv PDS 1968; STM NYTS 1980; MBA La Salle U 1984. D 4/20/1968 P 10/26/1968 Bp Alfred L Banyard. m 8/30/2001 Judith R Goodwin c 1. Trin Ch Moorestown NJ 1995-2004; Evergreens Chap Moorestown NJ 1979-2003; R S Paul's Epis Ch Bound Brook NJ 1972-1979. henglund313@gmail.com

ENGSTROM, Marilyn Jean (Wyo) 1714 Mitchell St, Laramie WY 82072 **Dn S Matt's Epis Cathd Laramie WY 2002-** B Rawlins WY 10/4/1950 d Louis Walfred Engstrom & Mary Virginia. BA U of Wyoming 1973; MDiv TESM 1989. D 6/14/1989 P 12/5/1989 Bp Bob Gordon Jones. R H Trin Epis Ch Gillette WY 1994-2002; Dio Wyoming Casper WY 1991-1994; R S Geo's Ch Lusk WY 1989-1991. marengstrom104@gmail.com

ENNIS, Kathleen Knox (SwFla) 6180 Golden Oaks Ln, Naples FL 34119 B Wichita KS 10/19/1938 d Van William Knox & Katherine. Smith-Study Abroad Madrid ES 1959; Phi Beta Kappa Sweet Briar Coll 1960; BA Sweet Briar Coll 1960. D 6/13/1998 Bp John Bailey Lipscomb. m 10/14/1961 Hugh Richard Ennis c 4. Iona Hope Epis Ch Ft Myers FL 1998-2009. Auth, "Washed Clean: the Value of Sacramental Confession," *LivCh*, LivCh Fndt, Inc., 12-10-2000; Auth, "The Atone," *LivCh*, LivCh Fndt, Inc., 3-5-2000. KKE@aol.com

ENSOR, A(melia) Jeanne (Oly) 8235 36th Ave Ne, Seattle WA 98115 B Seattle WA 3/10/1948 d Glenn W Smith & Maxine E. AA Shoreline Cmnty Coll 1982. D 7/9/1994 Bp Vincent Waydell Warner. m 11/4/1967 Harold Carl Ensor c 2. D Chr Ch SEATTLE WA 2007-2009. Hlth Ministers Assn; NAAD.

ENSOR, Peter Crane (Los) 111 Westview Drive, Dubois WY 82513 B Cambridge MA 3/13/1938 s Howard Reginald Ensor & Florence Crane. BA Ham 1960; BD EDS 1963. D 6/22/1963 Bp Anson Phelps Stokes Jr P 5/1/1964 Bp John Brooke Mosley. m 6/30/1962 Jean D Donnelley. R S Thos Ch Dubois WY 2000-2002; S Jas' Par So Pasadena CA 1989-1999; Vic S Marg Of Scotland Par San Juan Capistrano CA 1985-1989; R Epis Ch Of The Ascen Dallas TX 1981-1985; The Oakridge Sch Ft Worth TX 1979-1981; White Lake Sch Ft Worth TX 1978; S Mk's Cathd Shreveport LA 1975-1978. houdon@wyoming.com

EOYANG JR, Thomas Tee (Pa) 1530 Spruce St Apt 805, Philadelphia PA 19102 B New York NY 2/7/1951 s Thomas Tsao Eoyang & Ellen Tsao. BA Harv 1972; MA Stan 1975; MDiv EDS 2003. D 6/19/2004 P 12/18/2004 Bp Charles Ellsworth Bennison Jr. R Gr Epiph Ch Philadelphia PA 2007; Int Trin Memi Ch Philadelphia PA 2005-2007; S Ptr's Ch Glenside PA 2004-2005. "Why This Story Yet Again," Morehouse Pub, 2005; "The Ethics Of Healthcare For Profit (Guest Ed)," Journey Of Profsnl Nrsng, 2001; "The Illness Experience," Sorensen & Luckmann'S Basic Nrsng; Saunders, 1994. Frederick Meggee Adams Prize EDS 2003; Wm C. Winslow Prize EDS 2003; Wm H. Lincoln Prize EDS 2002; Class Of 1936 Prize EDS 2001. thoseoyang@aol.com

EPES, Gail Elliot Allinson (Va) 1200 N Quaker Ln, Alexandria VA 22302 B Lawrence KS 1/4/1946 d Edward Page Allinson & Louise Elliot. BA GW 1968; Med U of Virginia 1969; MDiv VTS 1987. D 6/13/1987 P 4/27/1988 Bp Peter James Lee. m 8/24/1968 William Epes. P Ch Of The Gd Shpd Burke VA 1987-1991. gae@episcopalhighschool.org

EPPERSON, Christopher (SVa) PO Box 3520, Williamsburg VA 23187 **Bruton Par Williamsburg VA 2011-** B Cleveland TN 3/29/1970 s Robert Larry Epperson & Armen Harriet. BS U of Tennessee 1996; MDiv GTS 1999. D 6/19/1999 P 2/26/2000 Bp Charles Glenn VonRosenberg. m 12/31/1996 Laura B Burbank c 3. S Columba's Chap Middletown RI 2006-2011; Assoc R - Adult Formation / Pstr Care All SS Epis Ch Atlanta GA 2001-2006; S Jn's Epis Ch Johnson City TN 1999-2001. frepperson@gmail.com

EPPES JR, Robertson (WTenn) 3630 Northwood Dr, Memphis TN 38111 B Greenville SC 9/6/1922 s Robertson Eppes & Alice Prioleau. BD No Carolina St U 1943; BD VTS 1952. D 7/15/1952 Bp Edmund P Dandridge P 2/28/1953 Bp Theodore N Barth. m 10/21/1953 Nelsie McGehee c 2. R All SS Epis Ch Memphis TN 1960-1983; Asst S Mary's Cathd Memphis TN 1952-1953.

EPPLE, Jogues Fred (Okla) 2523 Portland Ave Apt 2210, Minneapolis MN 55404 B Cleveland OH 2/2/1930 s Fred Epple & Caroline. MDiv Cath Theol U 1957; MA CUA 1967. Rec from Roman Catholic 6/24/1983 as Priest Bp James Daniel Warner. Vic S Paul's Ch Clinton OK 1987-1989; R Calv Ch Hyannis NE 1984-1987; Vic S Jos's Ch Mullen NE 1984-1987; Chr Ch Cntrl City NE 1983-1984. Auth, *Exploring Gray: Value of Depression*; Auth, *Gigapop Opportunities of Aging*; Auth, *Tour: Intro to Internet 2*. fatherjogues@yahoo.com

EPPLY-SCHMIDT, Joanne (NJ) 26 Nelson Ridge Rd, Princeton NJ 08540 **Assoc Trin Ch Princeton NJ 2005-; Supply Dio New Jersey Trenton NJ 2000-** B Hartford CT 10/27/1955 d William Robert Epply & Loraine. BA Pr 1982; MDiv Ya Berk 1988. D 6/10/1989 Bp George Phelps Mellick Belshaw P 10/27/1990 Bp Albert Wiencke Van Duzer. m 5/17/1986 Paul Erick Epply-Schmidt c 2. Asst S Matt's Ch Pennington NJ 1990-2000; Asst S Bern's Ch Bernardsville NJ 1989-1990. revjes1@yahoo.com

✠ **EPTING, Rt Rev Carl Christopher** (Ia) 3026 Middle Rd, Davenport IA 52803 B GreenvilleSC 11/26/1946 s Carl Edward Epting & Margaret. BA U of Florida 1969; MDiv SWTS 1972; STM GTS 1984. D 4/29/1972 Bp James Winchester Montgomery P 11/8/1972 Bp William Hopkins Folwell Con 9/27/1988 for Ia. m 11/9/2001 Susanne K Freyermuth c 3. PBp Epis Ch Cntr New York NY 2001-2009; Ecum Off Epis Ch Cntr New York NY 2001-2009; Ret Bp of Iowa Dio Iowa Des Moines IA 1988-2001; R S Mk's Ch Cocoa FL 1981-1988; Cn S Jn's Cathd Jacksonville FL 1978-1980; Vic S Lk The Evang Ch Mulberry FL 1974-1978; Vic S Steph's Ch Lakeland FL 1974-1978; Cur H Trin Epis Ch Melbourne FL 1972-1974. "Var arts," *Ecum Trends, LivCh, Epis Life*. Bp Visitor - Cmnty of Celebration; Bp Visitor - CT Cincinnati Oh; OHC. DD Wartburg TS 2001; DD SWTS 1988. ccepting@aol.com

ERAZO-LOPEZ, Juan (ECR) 132 winhamSt, Salinas CA 93901 B Quito Ecuador 5/17/1947 s Juan Eduardo Erazo & Maria Lopez. Colegio Eloy Alfaro; Seminario Continuo Epis. D 12/18/1988 P 12/1/1989 Bp Adrian Delio Caceres-Villavicencio. m 4/3/1972 Ruth Cecilia Monge-Teran c 3. Dio El Camino Real Monterey CA 2009; S Paul's Epis Ch Salinas CA 2003-2009; Ch Of The Mssh Santa Ana CA 2002-2003; Ch Of The Ascen Tujunga CA 1998-2000; Iglesia Epis Del Ecuador Ecuador 1996-1998. Entrega Honorifica Del Periodico Latinoamercinan En Roma Sa Ese 2005; Otorgado Por La Iglesia Episcopla "Mssn Latinoamericana". juan_erazo@sbcglobal.net

ERAZO-LOPEZ, Ruth Cecilia (ECR) 132 Winham St, Salinas CA 93901 B Quito Ecuador 8/19/1953 d Hector Eduardo Monge & Blanca Marina. Bachiller Ciencias Sociales Colegio 13 de Abril Ecuador; Seminario Continuo Epis. D 5/19/1990 Bp Adrian Delio Caceres-Villavicencio P 11/3/1996 Bp J Neptali Larrea-Moreno. m 4/3/1972 Juan Erazo c 3. S Barth's Mssn Pico Rivera CA 2001-2003; Dio Los Angeles Los Angeles CA 1998-2000; Iglesia Epis Del Ecuador Ecuador 1996-1998.

ERB, Edward Kenneth (Be) 827 Church St., Honesdale PA 18431 **R Gr Epis Ch Honesdale PA 2008-** B Lock Haven PA 4/26/1957 s Walter Kenneth Erb & Margaret Jane. BA Lycoming Coll 1979; MDiv GTS 1997. D 6/6/1997 P 6/27/1998 Bp Michael Whittington Creighton. m 8/17/1980 Susan Renee Shadle. Hon Cn for Liturg and Mus Dio Bethlehem Bethlehem PA 2002-2004; S Jn's Epis Ch Hamlin PA 1998-2007. H Cross Monstry in W Pk, NY. edwardkerb@aol.com

ERDMAN, Daniel Le Roy (Mich) 929 E Hawthorne Loop, Webb City MO 64870 **Chapl S Lk Nrsng Cntr Carthage MO 2008-; Vic S Jn's Ch Neosho MO 2007-** B York PA 11/5/1944 s Marlin H Erdman & Mabel. BA Wheaton Coll 1968; MA Yale DS 1971; MDiv Yale DS 1973. D 6/8/1973 P 12/15/1973 Bp Dean T Stevenson. m 12/31/1974 Susan Erdman. R Trin Epis Ch Farmington Hills MI 2001-2006; R S Phil's Ch Joplin MO 1996-2001; R Chr Ch Rolla MO 1992-1996; R S Lk's Epis Ch Mt Joy PA 1984-1992; R Chr Memi Epis Ch Danville PA 1981-1984; Chr Ch Berwick PA 1975-1981; Vic All SS Ch Selinsgrove PA 1974-1975; Vic S Mk's Epis Ch Northumberland PA 1974-1975. erddan@hotmail.com

ERDMAN, Jonathan Mark (Ky) 821 S 4th St, Louisville KY 40203 **Calv Ch Louisville KY 2010-** B 10/5/1978 D 12/19/2003 P 6/25/2004 Bp George Wayne Smith. m 7/15/2004 Andrea Benson. Yth Min S Thos Ch New York NY 2005-2010; Emm Epis Ch Webster Groves MO 2004-2005. jmferdman@addressisp.com

ERHARD, Michael Edward Charles (Cal) 2300 Bay St Apt 302, San Francisco CA 94123 **D Gr Ch S Helena CA 2004-** B Chicago IL 6/18/1953 s Edward Charles Erhard & Mary Ann. BA NWU 1975; MPA NWU 1977; BA Sch for Deacons 1984. D 12/7/1985 Bp William Edwin Swing. Int Assoc S Mk's Epis Ch Palo Alto CA 1994-1996; S Lk's Ch San Francisco CA 1993-2004; D S Clem's Epis Ch Seattle WA 1990-1992; D Gr Cathd San Francisco CA 1987-1989; Trsfg Epis Ch San Mateo CA 1985-1987. mecerhard@cpcmg.com

ERICKSON JR, Charles J(ohn) (ECR) 424 Bernardo, Morro Bay CA 93442 **R Emer S Ptr's By-The-Sea Epis Ch Morro Bay CA 1996-** B Evansville IN 3/3/1924 s Charles John Erickson & Hannah Madora. OD Nthrn Illinois U 1948; BD U Chi 1958. D 9/20/1958 Bp Henry H Shires P 3/20/1959 Bp James Albert Pike. m 6/15/1957 Lenore Anderson c 2. Dioc Coun Dio El Camino Real Monterey CA 1986-1990; COM Dio El Camino Real Monterey CA 1981-1986; S Lk's Ch Atascadero CA 1968-1978; S Ptr's By-The-Sea Epis Ch Morro Bay CA 1962-1991; Vic S Jn The Div Epis Ch Morgan Hill CA 1958-1962. lenore@joimail.com

ERICKSON, David Lyle (Los) 1818 Monterey Blvd, Hermosa Beach CA 90254 **Assoc S Cross By-The-Sea Ch Hermosa Bch CA 2011-** B Decorah IA 7/27/1976 s Kenneth Paul Erickson & Carol Lee. BFA U CO at Boulder 2001; MDiv VTS 2011. D 6/21/2011 Bp Mary Douglas Glasspool. m 7/1/2006 Heather Beth Erickson c 1. davidlyleerickson@gmail.com

ERICKSON, Frederick David (Los) 219 Hortter Street, Philadelphia PA 19144 B Rhinelander WI 11/12/1941 s Lennart Erickson & Marie. BA NWU 1963; MA NWU 1964; PhD NWU 1969. D 6/14/1975 Bp John Melville Burgess. m 8/31/1968 Joanne Straceski c 2. Asst Ch Of S Jn The Evang Boston MA 1975-1978; Asst Par Of S Mary In Palms Los Angeles CA 1975-1978. Auth, "Qualitative Methods In Resrch On Tchg"; Auth, "The Counslr As Gatekeeper: Interaction In Counslg Encounters".

ERICKSON, Gregory Charles (WNC) 1359 Lamb Mountain Rd, Hendersonville NC 28792 B Jamestown NY 1/31/1952 s Frank Erickson & Carol Mae. BS Cit 1974. D 1/28/2006 Bp Granville Porter Taylor. m 8/13/1977 Robin Erickson c 1. greg.erickson@volvo.com

ERICKSON JR, Joseph Austin (Los) 764 Valparaiso Dr, Claremont CA 91711 B Cambridge MA 4/30/1924 s Joseph Austin Erickson & Esther Reese. BA

Harv 1945; STB EDS 1951; ThD TS at Claremont 1965. D 1/6/1951 Bp Raymond A Heron P 7/15/1951 Bp Donald J Campbell. m 6/13/1970 Catherine Henley Erickson c 4. Pstr Coun S Martha's Epis Ch W Covina CA 1964-1971; R S Mk's Epis Ch Upland CA 1953-1963; Cur All SS Ch Pasadena CA 1951-1953. derick2727@aol.com

ERICKSON, Kenneth Lawrence (Chi) 1102 Ash St, Winnetka IL 60093 **Asst S Greg's Epis Ch Deerfield IL 2008-** B Chicago IL 4/28/1966 s Richard A Erickson & John L. BA Wheaton Coll 1988; MDiv Duke 1995; GTS 2001. D 6/23/2001 Bp Michael Bruce Curry P 1/20/2002 Bp Robert Louis Ladehoff. m 10/20/1990 Katherine J McCalla c 1. S Greg's Epis Sch Chicago IL 2008-2010; Ch Of The H Comf Kenilworth IL 2005-2007; S Ann's Ch Woodstock IL 2004-2005; S Paul's Epis Ch Salem OR 2004; Dio Oregon Portland OR 2002-2003. ken@christchurchwinnetka.org

ERICKSON, Lori Jean (Ia) 222 Fairview Ave, Iowa City IA 52245 **D Trin Ch Iowa City IA 2005-** B Waukon IA 5/21/1961 BA Luther Coll 1983; MA U of Iowa 1985. D 4/16/2005 Bp Alan Scarfe. m 9/5/1987 Robert Sessions c 2. erickson@avalon.net

ERICKSON, Mary Cobb (Wyo) PO Box 1690, Jackson WY 83001 **Ch Of The Trsfg Jackson WY 2009-** B Berkeley CA 12/9/1963 d Miles Alan Cobb & Beth Cobb. BA U CA, Berkeley 1988; MDiv Harvard DS 1994. D 11/1/2009 Bp Bruce Edward Caldwell P 8/10/2010 Bp John Sheridan Smylie. m 8/29/1999 Bruce Alan Erickson c 2. Asst S Jn's Epis Ch Jackson WY 2007-2009. mary@stjohnsjackson.org

ERICKSON, Mary Kahrs (At) 4 Jones St, Cartersville GA 30120 **Ch Of The Ascen Cartersville GA 2010-** B Traverse City MI 12/23/1953 d Edward Carl Kahrs & Eunice Mae. BSN U MI 1976; MBA Berry Coll 1983; MDiv Candler TS Emory U 2004. D 6/5/2004 P 2/12/2005 Bp J(ohn) Neil Alexander. m 11/28/1981 Stephen W Erickson c 4. Assoc S Mart In The Fields Ch Atlanta GA 2005-2010. mskahrs@bellsouth.net

ERICKSON, Richard Paul (Alb) 901 Ridge View Circle, Castleton-On-Hudson NY 12033 B Hudson NY 4/27/1964 s Richard Erickson & Elaine. AA Columbia-Greene Cmnty Coll 1984; AS Columbia-Greene Cmnty Coll 1986; AAS Maria Coll 1996. D 6/10/2006 Bp Daniel William Herzog. m 5/30/1998 Theresa Erickson. richard.theresa@verizon.net

ERICKSON, Scott (WA) 1741 Q St NW Apt B, Washington DC 20009 B Fort Dodge IA 5/26/1967 s Rubert Ernest Erickson & Doris Ann. MDiv No Pk TS 1989; BA No Pk U 1989; ThD Uppsala U 1996; PostDoc Harv 1998. D 11/1/2001 P 5/19/2002 Bp Douglas Edwin Theuner. m 9/9/2010 Ryan Banks-Erickson. Cathd of St Ptr & St Paul Washington DC 2008-2011; Prot Epis Cathd Fndt Washington DC 2007. Ed, "Sch Chap Serv & Prayers," Ch Pub, 2007; Auth, "The Anatomy of Immigrant Hymnody," *Hymnody in Amer Protestanism*, Oxf Press, 2003; Auth, "Immigrants, Pilgrims and People of Faith," *Essays in Memory of Zenos Hawkinson*, Cov Press, 2001; Auth, "Ethnicity and Rel in the Twin Cities," *Swedes in the Twin Cities*, Minnesota Hist Press, 2001; Auth, "The Ch as Ext of the Homeland," *Migrants and the Homeland*, Cntr for Multiethnic Resrch, 2000; Auth, "The Ch w the Soul of a Nation," *The Cov Quarterly*, 2000; Auth, "The Nature of Amer Rel Influences on the Swedish Mssn Cov Ch," *Amer Rel Influences in Sweden*, Ch of Sweden Resrch Dep't, 1996. AAR 1993; Amer Soc of Ch Hist 1993; Assn of Boarding Schools 1998; Cbury Shaker Vill 2000; Cmnty of the Cross of Nails 1999; HSEC 1999; NAES 1998; Orgnztn of Amer Historians 1998; Soc for the Advancement of Scandinavian Study 1996; Swedish-Amer Hist Soc 1997. Post-Doctoral Resrch Fllshp The Bank of Sweden Tercentenary Fund Harvard MA 1997; Dissertation Fllshp C.E. Wikstrom Meml Fund Stockholm SE 1996; Dissertation Fllshp Olavus Petri Fund Uppsala SE 1995; Doctoral Fllshp Amer-Scandanavian Fndt New York NY 1994; Doctoral Fllshp Ecum Fund for the Stds of the Swedish Free Ch Move Stockholm SE 1993; Alfred Ahnfeldt Medallion for Acad achievement No Pk TS 1993; The Most Outstanding Sr Alum Assn of No Pk U 1989; Stdt Laureate Awd Lincoln Academy of Illinois Springfield IL 1988. serickson@phillipsbrooks.org

ERICKSON, Winifred Jean (NMich) 1506 Us #2 Highway West, Crystal Falls MI 49920 B London UK 1/14/1922 d Robert Kitford & Harriet. D 5/20/1990 Bp Thomas Kreider Ray. m 11/6/1971 Donald Arnold Erickson c 3. D S Mk's Ch Crystal Falls MI 1990-2008; D Dio Nthrn Michigan Marquette MI 1990-2002.

ERICSON, William Delmer (Mich) Po Box 267, Dewitt MI 48820 **Supply P Emm Ch Hastings MI 2009-** B Glenwood Sprgs CO 9/28/1939 s Earl Edward Ericson & Dagmer Gunheld. Mesa Cmnty Coll 1965; BA Wstrn St Coll of Colorado 1967; MDiv SWTS 1977. D 7/3/1977 P 1/6/1978 Bp William Hopkins Folwell. m 6/12/1964 Mildred P Powe c 3. S Mich's Epis Ch Lansing MI 2002; S Aug Of Cbury Mason MI 1999-2001; Dio Michigan Detroit MI 1999; S Annes Ch Dewitt MI 1991-1999; Chr Epis Ch Owosso MI 1990-1991; Assoc S Paul's Epis Ch Lansing MI 1987-1989; R S Matt's Epis Ch Saginaw MI 1983-1987; Asst S Andr Epis Ch Mentor OH 1978-1983; Cur All SS Ch Of Winter Pk Winter Pk FL 1977-1978. billericson@yahoo.com

ERIXSON, Lorna Lloyd (At) 2100 Hilton Ave, Columbus GA 31906 **Assoc S Thos Epis Ch Columbus GA 2011-** B Ireland 9/26/1952 d Gilbert Arthur Lloyd & Jean. BA U of Ulster 1974; PGCE Camb 1975; MSc Troy St U 1987; MDiv The TS at The U So 2010. D 12/19/2009 P 6/26/2011 Bp J(ohn) Neil Alexander. c 2. lerixson@cantab.net

ERLANDSON, Ronald Ivan (Los) 2929 Waverly Dr Apt 209, Los Angeles CA 90039 **Died 11/30/2009** B Rockford,IL 8/21/1937 s O Ivan Erlandson & Lucia Edna. BA Augustana Coll 1959; U Chi 1961; MDiv SWTS 1970; MS U Of La Verne La Verne CA 1980. D 6/13/1970 Bp James Winchester Montgomery P 12/1/1970 Bp Gerald Francis Burrill. OHC. rierlandson@pacbell.net

ERNEST, Warren Taylor (NY) 99 River Rd, Mystic CT 06355 B Brookville MA 1/17/1933 s Wentworth Allan Ernest & Gertrude Eva Taylor. BA DePaul U 1954; BD Nash 1958; Ford 1972. D 6/20/1957 Bp Charles A Mason P 12/21/1957 Bp J(ohn) Joseph Meakins Harte. c 2. R S Lk's Ch Eastchester NY 1973-1998; Vic All SS Epis Ch Safford AZ 1963-1969; LocTen S Mich's Ch Richland Hills Richland Hills TX 1962-1963; Vic Trin Ch Henrietta TX 1958-1962; Cur S Lk's Ch Denison TX 1957-1958.

ERON, James Phillip (SanD) 12426 W Mesa Verde Dr, Sun City West AZ 85375 B WI Rapids WI 12/21/1932 s Phillip Anthony Eron & Lavina Christine. MA Universidad de Guadalajara; BA H Cross Sem 1955; STL CUA 1959. Rec from Roman Catholic 11/1/1980 as Priest Bp Edmond Lee Browning. m 5/26/2005 Marinell Rea Hale. Int S Chris's Ch Sun City AZ 2000-2001; S Mary's In The Vlly Ch Ramona CA 1999-2000; Chr Meml Ch Kilauea HI 1984-1992; Asst H Innoc' Epis Ch Lahaina HI 1982-1983. Auth, "Superceding Creation," *LivCh*, 1998. eronjm@wmconnect.com

ERQUIAGA, Trudel Nada (Nev) 1128 Green Valley Drive, Fallon NV 89406 B White Pine County NV 2/19/1957 d Robert Gilbert Linnell & Katherine. BS U of Nevada at Reno 1979. D 10/11/2002 P 5/24/2003 Bp Katharine Jefferts Schori. m 8/15/1981 David Erquiaga c 2. D H Trin Epis Ch Fallon NV 2002-2003. erq@charter.net

ERSKINE, John (Jack) Arthur (EO) 60960 Creekstone Loop, Bend OR 97702 B Lewiston ID 11/15/1949 s Sewell Thomas Erskine & Juliana. BEd Wstrn Washington U 1972; MDiv CDSP 1976; Cert Ripon Coll Cuddesdon Oxford GB 1989. D 12/5/1979 P 1/1/1981 Bp Robert Hume Cochrane. m 6/8/1996 Christine Elaine Close c 3. Ch Of The H Sprt Episco Battle Ground WA 2006; Ch Of The Gd Shpd Vancouver WA 1998-2008; S Steph's Epis Ch Longview WA 1997; Vic S Columba's Epis Ch And Chilren's Sch Kent WA 1992-1994; Asst R S Barn Epis Ch Bainbridge Island WA 1989-1992. Ord of S Ben 1983. jerskine15@msn.com

ERVIN, Robert Shearer (NH) 177 Mount Vernon St, Dover NH 03820 **Died 3/10/2010** B Washington DC 11/17/1945 s John Shearer Ervin & Jean. BA Dart 1967; MDiv Harvard DS 1970; DMin Bangor TS 1994. D 6/20/1970 P 12/20/1970 Bp John Melville Burgess. c 2. Ed, "Angl RC Soundings," 1990. robtservin@ttlc.net

ERVOLINA, Timothy Mark (USC) 120 Ridgewood Cir, Greenwood SC 29649 **D Ch Of The Resurr Greenwood SC 2002-** B Pt Hueneme CA 11/23/1954 s Kenneth Dominic Ervolina & Dorothy Ann. BA SE Coll Assembly Of God Lakeland FL 1989; MA Faith Evang Luth Sem 1994. D 12/11/1999 Bp John Wadsworth Howe. m 6/25/1994 Suzanne Crump c 3. D S Dav's Epis Ch Lakeland FL 1999-2002. tervolina@earthlink.net

ERWIN JR, James Walter (NC) 200 Riverside Ave, Riverside CT 06878 **Cur S Paul's Ch Riverside CT 2010-** B Savannah, GA 3/25/1960 s James Walter Erwin & Harriet Bell. Assoc Young Harris Jr Coll 1980; BA U GA 1982; MDiv The GTS 2009. D 12/15/2009 Bp Michael Bruce Curry P 6/26/2010 Bp Ian Theodore Douglas. c 2. jim.erwin@stpaulsriverside.org

ERWIN, Virginia Gilbert (Los) 2157 Birdie Dr, Banning CA 92220 B Long Island NY 8/11/1945 d John Gilbert & Ruth R. BS U of Nevada at Reno 1967; MS Pepperdine U 1975; MA ETSBH 1986. D 6/22/1986 Bp Robert C Rusack P 1/11/1987 Bp Oliver Bailey Garver Jr. c 2. R Trin Epis Ch Orange CA 1991-2006; Archd for Cler Deploy & Dvlpmt Dio Los Angeles Los Angeles CA 1988-1991; Cur S Jas Par Los Angeles CA 1986-1988. revginny@aol.com

ERWIN, William Portwood (Mich) 5316 Heritage Ct, Rocklin CA 95765 B Dallas TX 10/12/1927 s William Portwood Erwin & Constance Sarah. MDiv Epis TS of The SW; MS Wayne; BA Harv 1950; MA Westminster Choir Coll of Rider U 1952. D 6/27/1957 P 4/1/1958 Bp Edward Hamilton West. m 12/14/1985 Yong Joo Erwin c 4. St Mths Ch Detroit MI 1974-1978; R S Paul's Ch Muskegon MI 1966-1972; Vic S Mary's Epis Ch Green Cove Sprg FL 1963-1965; Cn Precentor S Jn's Cathd Jacksonville FL 1962-1963; Vic S Andr's By The Sea Epis Ch Destin FL 1957-1962. Auth, "Carol Of S Jos'S Dream".

ESBENSHADE, Burnell True (Mo) 1116 E Linden Ave, Saint Louis MO 63117 B Louisville KY 10/7/1943 d Burlyn Pike & Nell Sanders. BA Cntr Coll 1965; MA Van 1966; Epis Sch for Mnstry 2006. D 2/7/2007 Bp George Wayne Smith. m 6/26/1971 Donald H Esbenshade c 2. desbenshad@aol.com

ESCOTT, Raymond Philip (WNC) 12 Misti Leigh Ln, Waynesville NC 28786 B Warren OH 10/12/1950 s Phillip Escott & Janice. D 1/28/2006 Bp Granville Porter Taylor. m 9/2/1972 Peggy Chapman c 3. SSF, Third Ord 1994. raydeacon@peoplepc.com

ESONU, Clinton Chukwuemeka (WA) 2031 Powhatan Rd, Hyattsville MD 20782 **All SS Igbo Angl Ch Lanham MD 2007-** B Nigeria 2/14/1951 s Christopher A Esonu & Cathrine. BS U of Nigeria 1979; BA London TS 1987; MA London TS 1988; MA VTS 1998. Trans from Church Of Nigeria 1/3/2005 Bp John Chane. m 10/3/1981 Ngozi Esonu c 3. S Mich And All Ang Adelphi MD 2005-2006. ccesonu@yahoo.com

ESPESETH, Cynthia Anne (Oly) 19015 244th Ave Ne, Woodinville WA 98077 **Cmsn for Outdoor Mnstry and Hosp Dio Olympia Seattle WA 2011-; Vic S Hilda's - S Pat's Epis Ch Edmonds WA 2007-; Chapl, Oprtns Com for Huston C&C Dio Olympia Seattle WA 2002-** B Durango CO 8/14/1959 d Ernest Leon Hunsaker & Dorothy Anne. BA U CO 1981; MDiv SWTS 2001. D 6/23/2001 P 1/13/2002 Bp Vincent Waydell Warner. m 8/5/1989 Robert Evan Espeseth c 2. Cmsn for Evang Dio Olympia Seattle WA 2007-2009; Asst S Steph's Epis Ch Seattle WA 2006-2007; Cmsn for Personl Dio Olympia Seattle WA 2005-2009; P-in-c All SS Ch Bellevue WA 2004-2005; Bp Suffr Search Com Dio Olympia Seattle WA 2003-2004; Cler Assn Bd Dio Olympia Seattle WA 2002-2005; Asst All SS Ch Bellevue WA 2001-2006. cynthia.espeseth@gmail.com

ESPINOSA-AREVALO, Carlos (EcuC) Calle Uruguay 649, Ingahurco, Ambato Ecuador B Tabacundo Pichincha EC 6/19/1937 s Jose Miguel Espinosa Saavedra & Ana Arevalo. BA. m 2/17/1964 Teresa Endara c 4. Iglesia Epis Del Ecuador Ecuador 1973-1996. Auth, "The Ch & The Dynamics Of Evang".

ESPINOSA-ENDARA, Juan Carlos (EcuC) Avenida Quito 8-71, Santo Domingo Ecuador B Atuntaqui EC 11/22/1964 s Carlos Espinosa Arevalo & Alicia Teresa. Conservatorio De Musica; Pontificia Universidad Catolica Del Ecu; BA Colegio Nacional Bolivar 1984; BA Colegio Luis Ulpiano De La Torre 1986. D 12/20/1992 Bp J Neptali Larrea-Moreno. m 7/10/1987 Maria Irene Aracelly Fernandez.

ESPOSITO, Catherine Patricia (NJ) 14 Edgemere Dr, Matawan NJ 07747 **S Ptr's Ch Freehold NJ 2000-** B Kearny NJ 12/31/1955 d Charles Tronicke & Patricia Kearns. BA Rutgers-The St U 1984. D 6/11/2005 Bp George Edward Councell. m 4/26/1991 Phillip M Esposito c 1. cath_esposito@hotmail.com

ESTES, Diane Manguno (La) 9929 Elm Pl, New Orleans LA 70123 **S Andr's Epis Sch New Orleans LA 2002-** B Fort Eustis VA 2/25/1956 d Larry Wayne Manguno & Arlene Jean Johnson. BA U of Texas 1978; PhD U of Texas 1985; Sch For Mnstry Dio Louisiana 2002. D 7/24/2003 P 5/23/2004 Bp Charles Edward Jenkins III. m 7/30/1977 David Anderson Estes c 3. S Andr's Epis Ch New Orleans LA 2005-2010; Co-Dir, Chr Formation All SS Epis Ch River Ridge LA 1997-1999. dae1977@email.msn.com

ESTES JR, George Colquitt (SVa) 18 Marshall St, Petersburg VA 23803 B Waco TX 7/30/1924 s George Colquitt Estes & Elmeda Pearl. BA U So 1948; BD STUSo 1951. D 7/3/1951 Bp Clinton Simon Quin P 6/16/1952 Bp John E Hines. m 4/22/1954 Mary Brooke S Steele c 3. R S Jn's Ch Centreville VA 1990-1991; Dep Gc Dio Sthrn Virginia Norfolk VA 1985-1988; Archd Dio Sthrn Virginia Norfolk VA 1982-1989; R S Paul's Ch Newport News VA 1968-1981; Min in charge Chr and S Lk's Epis Ch Norfolk VA 1967-1968; Mssnr Iglesia Epis Trinidad Cali CO 1964-1967; R S Patricks Ch Falls Ch VA 1959-1964; R S Thos Epis Ch Orange VA 1954-1955; Asst S Mk's Ch Houston TX 1952-1954; Min in charge Chr Ch San Aug TX 1951-1952; Min In Charge Trin Epis Ch Jasper TX 1951-1952. georgecolquitt@aol.com

ESTES, James Gray (SanD) 1427 Rimrock Dr, Escondido CA 92027 B Concord NH 8/24/1934 s Josiah Gray Estes & Delphine. BA New Engl Coll 1958; MDiv Yale DS 1961. D 6/10/1961 P 12/13/1961 Bp Charles F Hall. m 3/18/1961 Virginia D Darneille c 3. Chair Wrld Mssn Com Dio San Diego San Diego CA 1988-1990; Chair Cler Dio San Diego San Diego CA 1988-1989; COM Dio San Diego San Diego CA 1986-1992; S Fran Ch Pauma Vlly CA 1985-2002; Stndg Com Dio The Rio Grande Albuquerque NM 1981-1982; Chair Dio The Rio Grande Albuquerque NM 1978-1981; R Gr Ch Carlsbad NM 1977-1985; Chair Dio The Rio Grande Albuquerque NM 1976-1981; Prov VII CE Com Dio The Rio Grande Albuquerque NM 1976-1981; Untd Campus Mnstry Silver City NM 1976-1977; Cur Par Of S Jas Ch Keene NH 1961-1963; Vic S Jn's Ch Walpole NH 1961-1963. Auth, *Does Your Par Need a Columbarium?*. Valedictorian New Engl Coll Henniker NH 1958. jvestes@sbcglobal.net

ESTES, Robert Theodore (WMo) 425 East Cherry St, Nevada MO 64772 **D in Charge All SS Ch Nevada MO 2008-** B Joplin MO 2/13/1955 s Robert Theodore Estes & Josephine Marie. BSE Missouri Sthrn St Coll 1977; MS Pittsburgh St U 1983. D 6/7/2008 Bp Barry Robert Howe. m 11/7/2003 Melinda Schesser c 3. S Lk Nrsng Cntr Carthage MO 2005-2008. estescrtlg@suddenlink.net

ESTES, William Thomas (FtW) Grace Church, 405 Glenmar Ave, Monroe LA 71201 B Memphis TN 5/17/1966 s Thomas Henry Estes & Carol Ann. AS Jas H. Faulkner St Cmnty Coll 1992; BA U of Memphis 1995; MA Nash 2006. D 9/30/2006 P 6/25/2007 Bp Jack Leo Iker. m 6/20/1992 Lisa M Powers c 5. Gr Epis Ch Monroe LA 2006-2008. Angl Comm Ntwk 2006; CBS 2005; Forw in Faith 2005; Pusey Gld 2005-2006. curateWTE@graceepiscopal.org

ESTEY, Lawrence Mitchell (Me) 3 Greenhead Lane, P O Box 646, ME ME 04681 B Trenton NJ 3/12/1941 s L(awrence) Wendell Estey & Audree. BS Col 1966; MDiv UTS 1969. D 6/7/1969 P 12/20/1969 Bp Horace W B Donegan. m 3/19/2009 Elizabeth Singer c 1. R S Brendan's Epis Ch Stonington ME 2003-2006; S Brendan's Epis Ch Stonington ME 2000; R S Jn's Epis Ch Troy NY 1988-2000; Assoc The Ch Of The Redeem Baltimore MD 1977-1988; R Ch Of The Gd Shpd Wareham MA 1972-1977; Cur Chr Ch So Hamilton MA 1969-1971. Fell Coll of Preachers Washington DC 1982. lestey@roadrunner.com

ESTIL, Colbert (Hai) c/o Diocese of Haiti, Boite Postale 1309 Haiti B 4/8/1972 s Is Fraus Estil & Avril. D 1/25/2006 P 2/18/2007 Bp Jean Zache Duracin. m 4/22/2008 Rene Marie R Rene Marie Monese c 1. collestibert@yahoo.fr

✠ ESTILL, Rt Rev Robert Whitridge (NC) 3224 Landor Rd, Raleigh NC 27609 B Lexington KY 9/7/1927 s Robert Julian Estill & Elizabeth Pierpont. BA U of Kentucky 1949; BD EDS 1952; STM STUSo 1960; DMin STUSo 1970; Fllshp VTS 1973; DD VTS 1980; DD STUSo 1984; LHD S Aug's Coll Raleigh NC 1992. D 6/27/1952 P 12/12/1952 Bp William R Moody Con 3/15/1980 for NC. m 6/17/1950 Joyce Haynes c 2. Ret Bp of NC Dio No Carolina Raleigh NC 1994; Pres Prov IV Dio No Carolina Raleigh NC 1990-1994; Bd Trsts The GTS New York NY 1985-1992; Bp of NC Dio No Carolina Raleigh NC 1983-1994; Bp Coadj of NC Dio No Carolina Raleigh NC 1980-1982; R S Mich And All Ang Ch Dallas TX 1976-1980; Fac VTS Alexandria VA 1971-1976; R S Alb's Par Washington DC 1969-1973; R Chr Ch Cathd Lexington KY 1955-1963; R S Mary's Epis Ch Middlesboro KY 1952-1955. Fell, Soc of S Jn the Evang; OHC. Jessie Ball DuPont Awd. jobo617@aol.com

ESTRADA, Carolyn Sullivan (Los) 2516 E Willow St Unit 108, Signal Hill CA 90755 **Assoc R Ch Of The Mssh Santa Ana CA 2001-** B Dallas TX 3/13/1942 d Glenn Raymond Sullivan & Jessie May. BA Whittier Coll 1963; MA Whittier Coll 1976; MDiv Claremont TS 2001. D 6/9/2001 Bp Joseph Jon Bruno P 1/12/2002 Bp Frederick Houk Borsch. pokol3@aol.com

ESWEIN, Nancy G (Cal) 27 Grand View Ave, San Francisco CA 94114 **CDSP Berkeley CA 2004-** B San Mateo CA 5/13/1955 d Bruce James Eswein & Janet Gordon. BA U CA 1978; BTS Sch for Deacons 1993; MTS CDSP 1997. D 6/4/1994 Bp William Edwin Swing. m 9/25/1997 Zona Sage Esq. Ch Of The H Innoc San Francisco CA 2001-2004; Sojourn Multifaith Chapl San Francisco CA 1999-2004; Dio California San Francisco CA 1999-2002; Ch Of The Adv Of Chr The King San Francisco CA 1996-1999. Auth, "When Worlds Collide: An Encounter between an Anglo-Cath Par & a Homeless Shltr," 1997. Affirming Catholicism 1996; ATR Bd 2006; Assoc. Theol Field Educators 2004; Assoc. of Practical Theol 2004. revneswein@sbcglobal.net

ETEMAD, Sandra L (Pa) 5603 N Charles St, Baltimore MD 21210 **All SS Ch Norristown PA 2010-; Ch of the Redeem Par Day Sch Baltimore MD 2006-** B 11/14/1962 d Jon L Lawrence & Louise. BA Humboldt St U 1992; MDiv VTS 2006. D 6/3/2006 Bp Jerry Alban Lamb P 12/9/2006 Bp Robert Wilkes Ihloff. m 7/26/2008 Majid Etemad c 2. Assoc R The Ch Of The Redeem Baltimore MD 2006-2010. mothersandra@ymail.com

ETHELSTON, Frank Geoffrey (Oly) 17543 102nd Ave NE Apt 138, Bothell WA 98011 B 2/14/1927 s Frank Percy Ethelston & Hilda S. TS Dio Olympia 1969. D 5/26/1973 Bp Lane W Barton P 1/1/1980 Bp Robert Hume Cochrane. c 4. P-in-c Gr Ch Duvall WA 1993-1996; Dio Olympia Seattle WA 1991-1992; D & P Assoc S Jn's Ch Kirkland WA 1974-1990. ETHELSTONS@LIVE.COM

ETHRIDGE, Forrest Eugene (Ga) 2408 Forest Ave NW, Fort Payne AL 35967 **Assoc S Phil's Ch Ft Payne AL 1992-** B Atlanta GA 5/13/1923 s Eugene Wright Ethridge & Addie Lee. Cert U Chi 1943; BS Georgia Tech 1949; MDiv Nash 1967. D 6/10/1967 P 1/25/1968 Bp Albert R Stuart. c 1. Vic H Cross Ch Thomson GA 1983-1991; Vic Trin Ch Harlem Augusta GA 1983-1991; Dioc Coun Dio Georgia Savannah GA 1973-1976; R S Mich's Ch Waynesboro GA 1969-1983; Vic S Phil's Ch Hinesville Hinesville GA 1968-1969. treesplus@boonlink.net

ETTENHOFER, Karen Ruth (NMich) 500 Ogden Ave, Escanaba MI 49829 B Escanaba MI 8/22/1952 d Lloyd William Hendrickson & Laverne Margaret. D 9/19/2010 Bp Thomas Kreider Ray. m 4/8/1972 Francis Ettenhofer c 2. ketten@chartermi.net

ETTLING, Albert John (Tex) 4383 Varsity Ln, Houston TX 77004 B Lake Charles LA 12/27/1919 s Albert Joseph Ettling & Dorothy Bourk. BA Washington U 1940; UTS 1942; MDiv EDS 1943. D 5/29/1942 P 2/27/1943 Bp William Scarlett. m 1/30/1943 Emily Tucker c 5. Chair, COM Dio Texas Houston TX 1964-1971; Dio Texas Houston TX 1960-1985; Gr Epis Ch Houston TX 1960-1969.

EUNSON, Lisa Kei (Cal) St Ternan's Rectory, High Street, Banchory - AB31 5TB Great Britain (UK) B Tokyo Japan 5/18/1954 d Robert C R Eunson & Katherine. BA San Francisco St U 1978; MDiv CDSP 2001. D 12/1/2001 P 6/1/2002 Bp William Edwin Swing. Assoc R S Paul's Epis Ch Burlingame CA 2001-2006. rev_lisa_eunson@yahoo.com

EUSTACE, Warren Paul (ECR) 812 Bay St, Mountain View CA 94041 **D S Thos Epis Ch Sunnyvale CA 2005-** B San Jose CA 4/21/1955 s Warren G

Eustace & Lynda Elaine. BA Sch for Deacons 2005. D 6/18/2005 Bp Sylvestre Donato Romero. m 7/17/1993 Kindra L Fish c 1. warren@sgi.com

EUSTIS, Patricia Eustis (Oly) 555 SE Regatta Dr, Oak Harbor WA 98277 **Dio Olympia Seattle WA 2010-** B Philadelphia PA 6/18/1945 d George Lawrence Moran & Anna Margaret. U of Maryland; MDiv EDS 1998. D 6/5/1999 P 6/3/2000 Bp M(arvil) Thomas Shaw III. m 5/19/1990 Augustus W Eustis c 3. R St Steph's Epis Ch Oak Harbor WA 2010; Int S Barn Ch Falmouth MA 2007-2009; R Trin Epis Ch Cranford NJ 2004-2007; Assoc S Phil's Epis Ch Laurel MD 2003-2004; R Sherwood Epis Ch Cockeysville MD 2001-2003; Asst R Trin Ch Concord MA 1999-2001. Co-Auth, "Dom Violence T/F Report," *Med Educ Journ*, City of Boston, 1996; Co-Auth, "Dom Violence & The Healer's Responsee:Strategies for Identifying and Treating People Who Experienced Dom Violence," *Ohio St Med Assn Journel*, Ohio St Med Assn, 1996; Co-Auth, "Intimate Violence and the Healer's Response," *Harv Ldrshp Forum*, Harv, 1995; Auth, "hon You, hon Me ,Conflict Resolution," *Safe Nbrhd*, City Of Boston, 1993. Co-Cnvnr Concord River Dnry 2000-2001; Dio Ma Wmn Crisis Com; Chair 1997-2001; Ma Epis Cleric Assn; Bd Mem 1999. Allison Cheek Feminist Liberation Theol Prize EDS Cambridge MA. pateustis@gmail.com

EVANS, Aaron Jay (WMich) 1115 W Summit Ave, Muskegon MI 49441 **R Trin Epis Ch Grand Ledge MI 2010-** B San Antonio TX 5/10/1977 s Robbie Evans & Nan. BA E Texas Bapt U 1999; MALS Valparaiso U 2003; MDiv The TS at The U So 2008. D 12/15/2007 P 7/2/2008 Bp Edward Stuart Little II. m 4/6/2002 Rachael Nichole Johnson. Supply P Leonidas Polk Memi Epis Mssn Leesville LA 2008-2009; Co-Yth Pstr S Jn The Evang Ch Elkhart IN 2003-2005; Yth Pstr S Paul's Ch Kilgore TX 2001-2002. The Soc of Cath Priests 2010. fatheraaronevans@gmail.com

EVANS, Amber Stancliffe (Cal) 1357 Natoma St, San Francisco CA 94103 **Assoc S Greg Of Nyssa Ch San Francisco CA 2008-; S Matt's Epis Ch San Mateo CA 2006-** B Topeka 11/10/1979 BA Washington U 2001; MDiv CDSP 2005; MA CDSP 2007. D 6/3/2006 Bp William Edwin Swing P 12/2/2006 Bp Marc Handley Andrus. m 10/8/2005 Colin H Evans. Ch Of The Epiph San Carlos CA 2006-2008; S Matt's Epis Day Sch San Mateo CA 2006-2008. amber_stancliffe@yahoo.com

EVANS, Carol S (O) 246 Cedar Ave, Ravenna OH 44266 **R Gr Ch Ravenna OH 1998-** B Hannibal MO 6/21/1957 d Virgil W Harsell & Virginia M. BA Truman St U Kirksville MO 1988; MA Louisville Presb TS 1991; MDiv CDSP 1995. D 6/24/1995 P 12/27/1995 Bp Richard Lester Shimpfky. m 6/7/1991 Maynard B Evans. P S Steph's Epis Ch San Luis Obispo CA 1995-1996. Aamft. cse1802@aol.com

EVANS II, C David (NwPa) 506 Young Rd, Erie PA 16509 B Elkhart IN 10/23/1945 s Clifford David Evans & Flora Louise. BS Pur 1968; MDiv Nash 1989; The Ch Dvlpmt Inst 1999; Ncd Trng Level 1 & 2 2005; Clp Class 17 2006. D 12/17/1988 P 6/20/1989 Bp Francis Campbell Gray. m 6/19/1966 Lorraine Greene c 4. Dio NW Pennsylvania Erie PA 2004-2007; R Ch Of The H Sprt Erie PA 1992-2004; S Ptr's Ch Bainbridge NY 1990-1992. cdevans@erie.net

EVANS, David Edmund (WMass) 300 Basin Rd, Vernon VT 05354 **Died 3/2/2011** B Providence RI 7/9/1916 s Irving Andrew Evans & Emily Howard. BA Br 1939; ThB PDS 1942; Fllshp Coll of Preachers 1948. D 9/29/1942 P 5/1/1943 Bp James D Perry. c 5. Auth, *There Is a Whisper*, 1981; Auth, *Sun This Day*; Auth, *Trsfg*. maiden-england@comcast.net

EVANS, David Hugh (Mich) 1926 Morris St, Sarasota FL 34239 B Detroit MI 8/4/1934 s Robert L Evans & Doris Mildred. BA U MI 1957; MDiv SWTS 1964. D 6/29/1964 Bp C Kilmer Myers P 4/10/1965 Bp Richard S M Emrich. m 2/21/1983 Nancy Ann Conrad. R Gr Ch Mt Clemens MI 1967-1977; Vic S Barth's Ch Swartz Creek MI 1964-1966. nadaevans@comcast.net

EVANS, Deedee (Kan) St. James Episcopal Church, 3750 E. Douglas, Wichita KS 67208 **D S Jas Ch Wichita KS 1986-** B Everett WA 5/10/1936 d William Harold Smith & Bellva Elizabeth. BS Friends U 1993. D 10/24/1986 Bp Richard Frank Grein. m 1/28/1955 Dennis Leigh Evans c 2. OHC 1984-2004. deedeeevans@cox.net

EVANS, Dolores Elaine (Be) 246 Colonial Crest Dr, Lancaster PA 17601 B Lancaster PA 3/9/1944 d Franklin L Eckman & Beatrice E. D 9/29/2007 P 8/15/2008 Bp Paul Victor Marshall. c 2. devans1962@comcast.net

EVANS, Donald Earl (CPa) 12 Wilson St., Corning NY 14830 B Harrisburg PA 3/18/1933 s Earl Edwin Evans & Helene Natalie. BS Carnegie Mellon U 1978; MDiv VTS 1979. D 5/29/1968 P 1/25/1969 Bp Dean T Stevenson. m 2/24/1968 JoAnn Fae Stewart c 1. R Ch of the Redeem Addison NY 2005-2010; Int S Thos' Ch Bath NY 2002-2004; Int S Paul's Ch Manheim PA 1998-2000; Vic S Jn's Epis Ch Huntingdon PA 1990-1996; R S Mk's Epis Ch Lewistown PA 1984-1990; Vic Hope Epis Ch Manheim PA 1972-1976; Asstg R S Andr's Ch St Coll PA 1968-1972. Hon Cn Dio of Cntrl Pennsylvania 1970. devans7@stny.rr.com

EVANS, Gareth Clive (Mass) 106 13th St Apt 113, Charlestown MA 02129 **The Ch Of The Gd Shpd Acton MA 2010-; Par Of The Mssh Auburndale MA 2004-** B Lancashire England 7/10/1968 Trans from Church Of England 6/25/2004 Bp M(arvil) Thomas Shaw III. m 6/1/2010 Frances E Bean c 1. R S Jn's Ch Charlestown (Boston) Charlestown MA 2004-2010. garethcevans@gmail.com

EVANS, Gary (NMich) 115 W Douglass Ave, Houghton MI 49931 B El Paso TX 12/30/1940 s Thomas Jay Evans & Evelyn. BA U of Montevallo 1962; MA SWTS 1967; MDiv SWTS 1980. D 7/27/1985 P 2/1/1986 Bp Thomas Kreider Ray. m 9/26/2011 Philip John Nancarrow. P-in-res Ch Of The Trsfg Ironwood MI 1988-1991; Asst to Bp Dio Nthrn Michigan Marquette MI 1984-1988. Contrib, *Living Simply*, Seabury Press, 1981; Co-Auth, *Equipping God's People*, Seabury Press, 1979. Epis Mnstry Dvlpmt Cltn 1986-1989. gevans1@chartermi.net

EVANS, Geoffrey (SeFla) 2250 Sw 31st Ave, Fort Lauderdale FL 33312 **Died 9/18/2011** B London UK 3/14/1938 s Donald Thomas Evans & Lillian May. BA Duke 1958; BD Epis TS In Kentucky 1963; U So 1968. D 6/1/1963 P 12/1/1963 Bp William R Moody. geoffmarge@aol.com

EVANS, Geoffrey Parker (Ala) 1910 12th Ave S, Birmingham AL 35205 **Asst to the R S Mary's-On-The-Highlands Epis Ch Birmingham AL 2010-** B Huntsville AL 2/25/1984 s Ronald Dewayne Evans & Claudia Goodwin. BA U of Alabama, Birmingham 2006; MDiv VTS 2010. D 6/2/2010 Bp John McKee Sloan P 12/7/2010 Bp Henry Nutt Parsley Jr. m 6/26/2010 Emily Robertson Emily Claire Robertson. geoffevans1@gmail.com

EVANS, Haydn Barry (Pa) 487 Cassatt Court, West Chester PA 19380 B Washington DC 5/3/1936 s Haydn Lewis Evans & Laura Daisy. BA Br 1959; Westcott Hse Cambridge 1961; MDiv VTS 1962. D 10/6/1962 Bp A H Blankingship P 1/1/1964 Bp William Foreman Creighton. m 9/19/1992 Elizabeth Eisenstadt-Evans c 4. The Ch Of The H Comf Drexel Hill PA 2006-2007; S Mart's Ch Radnor PA 2005-2006; S Paul Ch Exton PA 2003-2005; Int Trin Ch Gulph Mills King Of Prussia PA 2001-2003; S Alb's Ch Newtown Sq PA 2001; Int S Mary's Ch Wayne PA 1999-2000; Int Trin Epis Ch Ambler PA 1996-1999; The Grubb Inst Wayne PA 1994-1999; The Grubb Inst Washington DC 1984; Cathd of St Ptr & St Paul Washington DC 1970-1983; Cur Ch Of S Steph And The Incarn Washington DC 1963-1970. Auth, "Excellence in Mnstry," *Personal & Profsnl Dvlpmt Needs of Cler of the Epis Ch*, ECF, 1988; Auth, "Success & Failure of a Rel Club," *Bldg Effective Mnstry*, Harper & Row, 1983; Auth, "Homil," *A Revs of Rel Cmncatn*, Acad of Homil, 1976. hbevans@comcast.net

EVANS, Holly Sue (CNY) PO Box 319, Copenhagen NY 13626 **Gr Ch Copenhagen NY 2009-; Shared Epis Mnstry E Carthage NY 2006-** B Dover NH 10/15/1949 d David Edmund Evans & Ruth Alice. Formation Prog Of The Dio Cntrl New York; BA Wm Smith 1971; Med SUNY 1988. D 10/7/2006 Bp Gladstone Bailey Adams III. c 3. hevans@ccsknights.org

EVANS, James Eston (Pa) 2 Emmett St, Phoenixville PA 19460 B Grand Rapdis MI 8/14/1942 s James E Evans & Helen. BA IL Wesl 1965; BD Nash 1968. D 6/15/1968 P 12/1/1968 Bp James Winchester Montgomery. m 10/31/2011 Nancy B Evans c 4. Int S Mary's Ch Wayne PA 1999-2002; Vic Chr Ch Bridgeport PA 1991-2001; St Peters Place Phoenixville PA 1990-1998; R S Ptr's Ch Phoenixville PA 1974-1990; Vic The Blessed Sacr Ch Green Bay WI 1970-1974; Cur S Thos Ch Menasha WI 1968-1970. jevans@stpetersplace.com

EVANS, James W (Dal) 200 W College St, Terrell TX 75160 B Durham NC 10/29/1981 s Jim H Evans & Melinda I. BS U NC; ThM Dallas TS 2009; Angl Stds Cert Nash 2010. D 1/25/2011 Bp James Monte Stanton. m 7/22/2007 Alicia Marsh. Cur Ch Of The Gd Shpd Terrell TX 2011. rev.wesleyevans@gmail.com

EVANS, James Walker (Spr) 253 Depew Ave, Buffalo NY 14214 **Asst Chapl Epis Ch Hm Buffalo NY 2000-** B Saint Louis MO 8/20/1930 s Charles D Evans & Alma Jeanette. BA U of Missouri 1956; BD CDSP 1959; STM Eden TS 1970. D 5/30/1959 Bp Clarence Rupert Haden Jr P 12/1/1959 Bp George Leslie Cadigan. m 6/16/1956 Margaret B Bolsterli c 2. P-in-c S Paul's Epis Ch Stafford NY 1996-1998; Int St Johns Epis Youngstown NY 1992-1993; S Tim's Ch Indianapolis IN 1991-1992; R Emm Memi Epis Ch Champaign IL 1973-1985; R S Augustines Ch S Louis MO 1971-1973; Cn Chr Ch Cathd S Louis MO 1968-1971; R S Augustines Ch S Louis MO 1964-1968; Vic S Jas Ch Sullivan MO 1959-1964; Vic St Johns & St Jas Ch Sullivan MO 1959-1964. AAPC 1972.

EVANS, John Frederick (WA) 10450 Lottsford Rd Apt 3115, Mitchellville MD 20721 B Dunmore PA 6/18/1921 s Clarence Frederick Evans & Marguerite Evelyn. BA Ob 1943; MA Harv 1947; MDiv VTS 1962. D 6/9/1962 Bp Robert Fisher Gibson Jr P 6/22/1963 Bp Samuel B Chilton. m 8/27/1943 Mary R Richardson c 2. P-in-c Ch Of Our Sav Silver Sprg MD 1998-1999; Int Gr Epis Ch Silver Sprg MD 1996-1997; Int S Mary's Epis Ch Foggy Bottom Washington DC 1988-1990; Dio Washington Washington DC 1979-1988; R Ch Of The Ascen Silver Sprg MD 1975-1979; R Ch Of Our Sav Washington DC 1968-1975; Asst Min S Jn's Ch Lafayette Sq Washington DC 1965-1968. Natl Interfaith Cltn on Aging 1980. Sprtlty and Aging Awd Natl Interfaith Cltn of Aging 2004; Phi Beta Kappa. jemeco8@hotmail.com

EVANS, John Howard (NH) 1215 Main Rd Apt 211, Tiverton RI 02878 B Providence RI 12/2/1917 s Irving Andrew Evans & Emily Howard. BA Br

1940; MDiv Ya Berk 1943. D 10/24/1943 Bp James D Perry P 6/11/1944 Bp William A Lawrence. R S Lk's Ch Charlestown NH 1970-1979; Un Ch Claremont NH 1970-1979; R S Jas Ch The Par Of N Providence RI 1964-1970; Vic S Matt's Ch Paramus NJ 1960-1964; R Ch Of The H Cross Troy NY 1957-1960; Asst S Paul's Ch Englewood NJ 1954-1956; Chapl Seamens Ch Inst Income New York NY 1948-1954; R Ch Of The Gd Shpd Fitchburg MA 1945-1948; Vic The Chap Of All SS Leominster MA 1945-1948; Asst S Steph's Ch Pittsfield MA 1943-1945. Auth, *Vignettes of New Engl*, Connell Sullivan Press, 1958.

EVANS, John Miles (Md) PO Box 1272, Portsmouth NH 03802 B Chicago IL 6/25/1939 s Mydrim Miles Evans & Gladyce Pauline. BA Ya 1961; BA U of Cambridge 1964; JD Ya 1967; MA U of Cambridge 1968; MDiv NYTS 1993. Trans from Scottish Episcopal Church 4/1/1999 Bp Robert Wilkes Ihloff. c 1. R All Hallows Par So River Davidsonville MD 1999-2006; Int Chr Epis Ch Lynbrook NY 1998-1999; Com Cn Dio New York New York City NY 1979-1983. Bd Mem Affirming Catholicism 2001; Ecum Soc Blessed Vrgn Mary 1993; Knight of Justice, Ord of of St. Jn 1973; Soc for Values in Higher Educ 1961; Soc of Cath Priests 2010. johnmilesevans@comcast.net

EVANS, Karen Patricia (At) 675 Holly Drive, Marietta GA 30064 B Memphis TN 10/24/1944 d Kurt Adler & Edna Mae. BA Wilson Coll 1965; MA Jn Hopkins U 1967; MDiv S Jn's Prov Sem Plymouth MI 1984. D 6/30/1984 Bp Henry Irving Mayson P 5/25/1985 Bp H Coleman McGehee Jr. m 12/23/1967 WILLIAM LEE EVANS c 2. R S Jas Epis Ch Marietta GA 1998-2009; R Emm Epis Ch Alexandria VA 1991-1998; R S Paul's Ch S Louis MO 1988-1991; Asst S Steph's Ch Ferguson MO 1986-1988; Asst S Mich's Ch Grosse Pointe Woods MI 1984-1986. k-evans2001@comcast.net

EVANS, Katharine Cope (Mass) 18 Lafayette Rd, Ipswich MA 01938 B Bryn Mawr PA 10/22/1946 d Francis Cope Evans & Rachel Worthington. BA Wellesley Coll 1968; MAT Br 1969; MDiv EDS 1995. D 9/8/1996 Bp M(arvil) Thomas Shaw III P 5/8/1997 Bp Donald Purple Hart. c 2. R Emm Epis Ch Wakefield MA 1999-2005; Asst S Paul's Ch Dedham MA 1996-1999. Fllshp of S Jn 1992; SCHC 1985. NDEA Fell Br Providence RI 1968; Durant Schlr Wellesley Coll Wellesley MA 1968; Pendleton Schlr Wellesley Coll Wellesley MA 1964. KAYEVANS1@JUNO.COM

EVANS, Leonard D (U) 515 S 1000 E Apt 506, Salt Lake City UT 84102 **Asst S Paul's Ch Salt Lake City UT 2009-** B Jacksonville FL 11/18/1943 s Leonard Evans & Margaret Amilia. BA Arizona St U 1965; MDiv PDS 1968. D 6/22/1968 Bp Russell S Hubbard P 7/1/1969 Bp J(ohn) Joseph Meakins Harte. m 2/7/1981 Vicki C Corcoran c 1. Int All SS Ch Phoenix AZ 2008-2009; Int S Barn EpiscopalChurch Tooele UT 2007-2008; Int S Jude's Ch Cedar City UT 2006; Dio Utah Salt Lake City UT 2004-2008; Int Gr Epis Ch St Geo UT 2004-2005; Int S Mary's Ch Provo UT 2004; Int Ch Of The Resurr Centerville UT 2002-2004; Int S Mich's Ch Brigham City UT 2001-2002; Dio Arizona Phoenix AZ 2001; Int Epis Ch of the H Sprt Phoenix AZ 2001; R S Paul's Ch Phoenix AZ 1993-2001; Cn Gr Cathd Topeka KS 1989-1993; R Trin Epis Ch El Dorado KS 1984-1989; Vic S Geo's Epis Ch Holbrook AZ 1977-1984; R S Paul's Epis Ch Winslow AZ 1977-1984; S Raphael In The Vlly Mssn Benson AZ 1976-1977; R S Andr's Epis Ch Nogales AZ 1973-1975; Cur S Jas Epis Ch Danbury CT 1970-1973; Cur S Andr's Ch Stamford CT 1969-1970; D S Clements Ch Philadelphia PA 1968-1969. levans@fastq.com

EVANS, Leslie Elizabeth (Be) 52 W Elizabeth Ave, Bethlehem PA 18018 **Died 11/2/2010** B Bethlehem PA 10/26/1946 d Cary Grayson Evans & Elizabeth Radcliffe. BSN Tem 1971; MDiv Luth TS at Philadelphia 1982. D 6/12/1982 P 6/22/1983 Bp Lyman Cunningham Ogilby. c 2. Int Mnstry Ntwk 1992-1995. Dn Pennypack Dnry 1998. e.leslie72@yahoo.com

EVANS, Mark Eugene (FdL) 402 Pekin St., P.O. Box 386, Lincoln IL 62656 **R Trin Ch Lincoln IL 2011-** B Mason City IA 7/13/1959 s E Eugene Evans & Dorothy. BA Luther Coll 1981; MBA Drake U 1983; MDiv Nash 2009. D 12/20/2008 P 6/27/2009 Bp Russell Edward Jacobus. m 7/29/2006 Sandra Moore c 3. Dir. of Ch Relatns Nash Nashotah WI 2010-2011. mevans_cfa@hotmail.com

EVANS, N. Dean (Pa) 304 Lexington, Media PA 19063 B Springfield PA 3/22/1925 s Norman Harrison Evans & Mae Agnes. BA Ursinus Coll 1948; MS U of Pennsylvania 1951; EdD Tem 1958; MA PrTS 1975. D 1/11/1958 Bp Andrew Tsu P 10/28/1972 Bp Alfred L Banyard. m 6/23/1951 Jacqueline Lentz. Supply P Dio Pennsylvania Philadelphia PA 1997-2003; Int The Epis Ch Of The Adv Kennett Sq PA 1996-1997; Int Ch Of S Mart-In-The-Fields Philadelphia PA 1994-1995; Chair Pa Cmsn For Mnstry In Higher Educ Dio Pennsylvania Philadelphia PA 1990-1995; Int The Ch Of The H Trin Rittenhouse Philadelphia PA 1983-1984; Dce Dio New Jersey Trenton NJ 1973-1978; Assoc S Ptr's Ch Medford NJ 1972-1978; Asst Ch Of The Redeem Springfield PA 1958-1967. Auth, "Plnng & Dvlpmt Of Innovative Cmnty Colleges," Prentice Hall, 1973; Auth, "Handbook For Effective Curric Dvlpmt," Prentice Hall, 1967; Auth, "Handbook For The Effective Supervision Of Instrn," Prentice Hall, 1964. OHC 1970. Bp Albert Van Duzer Bp'S Medal Dio New Jersey 1973. deanandjackie@juno.com

EVANS, Noah Hearne (Mass) 28 Hillcrest Street, Waltham MA 02451 **Together Now Capital Cmpgn Com Dio Massachusetts Boston MA 2011-; Chair, Bd Epis City Mssn Boston MA 2011-; R Gr Epis Ch Medford MA 2008-; VP, Barbara C. Harris Camp and Confernce Cntr Dio Massachusetts Boston MA 2006-** B Lansing MI 8/27/1977 s Richard W Evans & Carol A. BA Washington U, St. Louis 2000; MDiv GTS 2004. D 6/12/2004 Bp M(arvil) Thomas Shaw III P 1/8/2005 Bp Gayle Elizabeth Harris. m 2/15/2003 Sara Hariett Irwin c 2. VP, Barbara C. Harris Camp and Confernce Cntr Dio Massachusetts Boston MA 2006-2009; Bd Mem Epis City Mssn Boston MA 2005-2011; Assoc R S Anne's In The Fields Epis Ch Lincoln MA 2004-2008; Sem Trin Ch Of Morrisania Bronx NY 2003-2004; Sem Ch Of S Mary The Vrgn New York NY 2002-2003. Seymour Prize for Preaching GTS 2003. noah@irwinevans.com

EVANS, Paul Fredric (Cal) 858 Church Street, Saratoga Springs NY B Elizabeth NJ 6/3/1937 s Paul Alexander Evans & A Mildred. BA U of Buffalo 1960; STB Ya Berk 1963. D 6/15/1963 Bp Lauriston L Scaife P 6/22/1968 Bp C Kilmer Myers. Ch Of Beth Saratoga Sprg NY 1999-2002; Ch Of Beth Saratoga Sprg NY 1982-1984; Int Trin Ch San Francisco CA 1980-1981; Assoc The Epis Ch Of S Jn The Evang San Francisco CA 1976-1982; Assoc Gr Cathd San Francisco CA 1968-1982; Spec Asst to Bp Suffr Dio California San Francisco CA 1968-1969; Cur S Paul's Cathd Buffalo NY 1963-1964. Auth, *Art Pottery of US*, Scribner's, 1974; Ed, *Pacific Churchman*, 1969; Auth, *Living Ch*; Auth, *Var Museum and Resrch Pub*. Angl Soc; Ch Hist Soc. Resrch Libraries in hon Of: Winterthur Museum, Del. Delaware 2000; Oakland CA Art Museum 1991; Who's Who Amer Art. AnglicanBk@aol.com

EVANS, Rachael Nichole (WMich) 1115 W Summit Ave, Muskegon MI 49441 **R S Greg's Epis Ch Muskegon MI 2009-** B Eau Claire WI 2/18/1980 d David Alan Gunnes & Karen Marie. BA Valparaiso U 2002; MDiv The TS at The U So 2008. D 12/15/2007 P 7/2/2008 Bp Edward Stuart Little II. m 4/6/2002 Aaron Jay Evans. Cur S Jas Epis Ch Alexandria LA 2008-2009; Co-Yth Pstr S Jn The Evang Ch Elkhart IN 2003-2005. The Soc of Cath Priests 2010. aj.rn.evans@gmail.com

EVANS JR, Ralph Easen (CFla) 2804 Coral Shores Dr, Fort Lauderdale FL 33306 B Harrisburg PA 4/4/1948 s Ralph Easen Evans & Jean Ury. BA Penn 1976; MDiv Nash 1980. D 6/13/1980 P 12/1/1980 Bp Dean T Stevenson. m 7/24/1971 Patricia Winters c 2. R S Sebastian's By The Sea Melbourne Bch FL 2005-2010; R S Mk The Evang Ft Lauderdale FL 1990-2005; R S Steph's Ch Longmont CO 1983-1990; Vic S Aug's Ch Creede CO 1981-1983; Vic S Steph The Mtyr Epis Ch Monte Vista CO 1981-1983; Cur S Mary's Ch Wayne PA 1980-1981. evsays@aol.com

EVANS, Robert Raphael (Okla) 2512 Glynnwood Dr, Bartlesville OK 74006 B Berkeley CA 2/12/1924 s Kenneth Raphael Evans & Naomi Ida. BA U CA 1949; MDiv Nash 1964. D 6/20/1964 P 12/20/1964 Bp Chilton Powell. m 9/3/1949 Anne Lee c 4. R Chr Ch Whitefish Bay WI 1977-1991; Secy, Stndg Com Dio Oklahoma Oklahoma City OK 1972-1973; Bp's Coun Dio Oklahoma Oklahoma City OK 1971-1975; R S Lk's Epis Ch Bartlesville OK 1966-1977; Vic S Mich And All Ang Ch Lindsay OK 1964-1966; Vic S Tim's Epis Ch Pauls Vlly OK 1964-1966. Hon Cn Dio Milwaukee 1996.

EVANS, Scott Charles (Alb) 15 W High St, Ballston Spa NY 12020 B Newton NJ 10/9/1967 s John M Evans & Helen. BSEE Virginia Tech U 1990; MS/EE U of Connecticut 1998; PhD,EE Rensselaer Polythecnic Inst 2003; MA Nash 2009. D 5/30/2009 P 1/9/2010 Bp William Howard Love. m 7/13/1991 Stephanie Beth Evans c 4. evans@research.ge.com

EVANS, Steve Armitage (Ga) 4625 Sussex Pl, Savannah GA 31405 B Wilmington DE 1/14/1949 s Evan Franklin Evans & Barbara. BA Duke 1984; MDiv STUSo 1992. D 6/20/1992 Bp Brice Sidney Sanders P 1/25/1993 Bp Harry Woolston Shipps. m 7/19/2008 Eunice Evans c 2. Asst R Chr Ch Epis Savannah GA 1992-2005. Auth, "Matters of the Heart," *A Workbook for Personal Transformation*, Forerunner Press, 2009. SAMS 1985-1986. stevenaevans@gmail.com

EVANS, Theodore H. (WMass) 235 Walker St. Apt. 236, Lenox MA 01240 **Assoc S Ptr's Ch Weston MA 1999-** B Tuscaloosa AL 6/18/1933 s Theodore Hubbard Evans & Jean. AB Harv 1957; MDiv VTS 1961. D 6/23/1961 Bp Robert Fisher Gibson Jr P 4/19/1962 Bp The Bishop of Hong Kong. m 10/31/1963 Valerie Wilson c 2. Vstng P S Ptr's Ch Weston MA 1996-1997; Dio Wstrn Massachusetts Springfield MA 1974-1995; R S Paul's Epis Ch Stockbridge MA 1974-1995; Epis Chapl At Harvard & Radcliffe Cambridge MA 1967-1974. Contrib, "The Application of Love," *The Vietnam War: Chr Perspectives*, Eerdmans, 1967. tvevans@gis.net

EVANS JR, V(ernon) Creighton (SC) PO Box 9, Eutawville SC 29048 B Charleston SC 6/17/1953 s V Creighton Evans & Joan. BS Coll of Charleston 1977; MDiv TESM 1994. D 6/18/1994 P 1/4/1995 Bp Edward Lloyd Salmon Jr. m 7/1/1978 Nina Elizabeth Ash c 2. The Ch Of The Epiph Eutawville SC 2010-2011; Vic All Souls Epis Ch No Ft Myers FL 1998-2010; Vic S Mths Epis Ch Summerton SC 1994-1998. creighton.evans@gmail.com

EVANS III, William Dunbar (Ala) 315 Clanton Ave, Montgomery AL 36104 B Lexington VA 5/29/1945 s William D Evans & Agnes Rowan. BA U So 1967;

MDiv VTS 1975. D 5/27/1975 P 6/1/1976 Bp David Shepherd Rose. m 5/10/1969 Mary Inge Hampson c 2. S Paul's Epis Ch Lowndesboro AL 1999-2000; Ch Of The Ascen Montgomery AL 1993-1999; R Ch Of The H Redeem Lake Worth FL 1988-1993; S Eliz's Ch Schnecksville PA 1985-1988; The Epis Ch Of The Medtr Allentown PA 1981-1985; Cur S Tim's Ch Catonsville MD 1978-1981; R Calv Ch Bath Par Dinwiddie VA 1977-1978; Asst Ch Of The Gd Shpd Norfolk VA 1975-1976. Ord Of S Lk; Soc Of The Poor.

EVANS, WILLIAM LEE (Ga) 675 Holly Drive, Marietta GA 30064 B Kalamazoo MI 6/22/1944 s Robert James Evans & Mabel. BA MI SU 1966; SAIS Jn Hopkins U 1967; Cntr for European Stds Bologna IT 1968; MDiv Hur 1974. D 6/15/1974 P 6/9/1975 Bp H Coleman McGehee Jr. m 12/23/1967 Karen Patricia Adler c 2. Ch Of The H Cross Decatur GA 2004-2005; Int Chr Ch Macon GA 2002-2003; Epis Ch Of The H Sprt Cumming GA 2001-2002; S Dav's Ch Roswell GA 2000-2001; Int S Mich And All Ang Ch Stone Mtn GA 1999-2000; Int S Anne's Epis Ch Atlanta GA 1998-1999; Int Ch Of Our Sav Silver Sprg MD 1997-1998; Int Gr Epis Ch Silver Sprg MD 1995-1997; Int Imm Ch-On-The-Hill Alexandria VA 1994-1995; Int Ch Of The H Comf Vienna VA 1993-1994; Int S Jas' Epis Ch Alexandria VA 1992-1993; S Ptr's Epis Ch St Louis MO 1986-1991; S Andr's Ch Waterford MI 1979-1986; Asst S Jas Ch Grosse Ile MI 1976-1979; Cur Trin Epis Ch Alpena MI 1974-1976. billyleeevans@gmail.com

EVENSON, Bruce John (SC) 214 Wentworth St, Charleston SC 29401 B New York NY 8/14/1946 s Swen Ninus Evenson & Aina Adele. BA Witt 1968; MDiv Luth TS at Chicago 1972. D 1/21/1998 P 9/1/1998 Bp Edward Lloyd Salmon Jr. m 8/15/1987 Johanna Helander c 1. St Johannes Luth Ch Charleston SC 2007-2011; Chapl Porter-Gaud Sch Charleston SC 2001-2002; Assoc Gr Ch Charleston SC 2001; Assoc Gr Ch Charleston SC 1998-2000. ebruceven@comcast.net

EVERETT, Sherman Bradley (SO) 3206 Brandon Rd, Columbus OH 43221 **Trin Ch Columbus OH 1999-** B Portland OR 10/2/1936 D 10/30/1999 Bp Herbert Thompson Jr. m 8/30/1963 Joan Everett c 2. severet@columbus.rr.com

EVERHARD, Darby Oliver (NC) 520 Summit Street, Winston Salem NC 27101 **S Paul's Epis Ch Winston Salem NC 2009-; S Jas Ch W Dundee IL 2004-** B Natick MA 7/28/1949 BS Indiana U 1971; MDiv Bex 2004. D 10/25/2003 Bp Herbert Thompson Jr P 6/19/2004 Bp Kenneth Lester Price. m 5/29/1999 Thomas Charles Everhard c 3. Cur S Thos Epis Ch Terrace Pk OH 2004-2009. darbo@eos.net

EVERSLEY, Walter VL (Md) 2013 Saint Paul St, Baltimore MD 21218 B Georgetown GY 9/14/1940 s Walter Eustace Eversley & Sarah Gwendolyn. BA Moravian TS 1969; MA Harv 1974; PhD Harv 1976; JD Col 1981. D 6/11/1988 P 12/11/1988 Bp Paul Moore Jr. m 8/5/1963 Daphne Greene c 3. R S Mich And All Ang Ch Baltimore MD 2001-2009; Theo-in-Res S Mary's Epis Ch Foggy Bottom Washington DC 2000-2001; Int Trin Ch Washington DC 1998-2000; Prof VTS Alexandria VA 1996-2002; Assoc S Mary's Epis Ch Arlington VA 1989-1998; Asst Prof VTS Alexandria VA 1988-1991. "Answered Prayers," *In Pursuit of a Useful Life*, New Visions Inst Pub, 2008; Auth, "The Pstr (Jonathan Edwards) as Revivalist," *Edwards in Our Time*, Erdman, 1999; Auth, *Handbook of Angl Theol*, 1998; Auth, "Jn Donne," *Soc of Promoting Chr Knowledge Handbook Angl Theol*, 1998; Auth, "Jesus & Culture," *Truth About Jesus*, 1998. AAR; Angl Theol Conf; SEAD, Jn Donne Soc. Resrch Fell Oxf Oxford Engl 1996. DEVERSLEY@AOL.COM

EVERSMAN, Karen Lynn (O) 2041 W. Reserve Cir., Avon OH 44011 B Bethesda MD 2/3/1952 d James Richard Eversman & Mary Virginia. BBA Ohio U 1973; MDiv EDS 1976. D 11/25/1978 P 11/4/1979 Bp John Mc Gill Krumm. P Calv Ch Sandusky OH 2000-2002; Int S Ptr's Epis Ch Lakewood OH 1999-2000; P Epis Shared Minist Of Nwohio Sherwood OH 1998; P S Jas Bucyrus OH 1991-1995; Int Chr Ch Lima OH 1988-1989; R Gr Ch Galion OH 1983-1987; Assoc S Ptr's Epis Ch Delaware OH 1980-1983; Serv Gr Ch Cincinnati OH 1978-1980.

EVETT, Douglas Paul (Mich) 5439 Pine View Dr, Ypsilanti MI 48197 B Denver CO 4/17/1938 s Paul Loyd Evett & Mary Louise. BA U So 1960; BD EDS 1963. D 6/11/1963 Bp Charles Ellsworth Bennison Jr P 12/1/1963 Bp Charles Bennison. c 4. Dio Michigan Detroit MI 1990-1994; R S Clare Of Assisi Epis Ch Ann Arbor MI 1972-2001; Assoc Gr Ch Grand Rapids MI 1965-1972; Vic S Jas' Epis Ch Of Pentwater Pentwater MI 1963-1965. devett@umich.edu

EWART, Craig Kimball (NY) 6981 Colonial Dr, Fayetteville NY 13066 B Columbus OH 11/14/1943 s Cyril G Ewart & Helen Arlene. BA Coll of Wooster 1965; STB PDS 1968; PhD Stan 1978. D 2/10/1969 P 12/1/1969 Bp Horace W B Donegan. c 2. P-t Asst S Barth's Ch New York NY 1971-1974; Cur S Aug's Ch New York NY 1969-2004. Homil Awd Chr Ch, Oxford, PA 1968. ckewart@syr.edu

EWING, Judith Lynette (SC) 203 Magnolia Bluff Dr, Columbia SC 29229 **Chr Epis Ch Mt Pleasant SC 2006-** B Scarborough UK 11/3/1941 d Philip Thomas Gylby Garner & Veronica. BEd Manchester Coll 1976; BSW Limestone Coll 1996; MS U of So Carolina 2003. D 12/14/2002 Bp Dorsey Felix Henderson.

EWING, Ward Burleson (ETenn) 175 9th Ave, New York NY 10011 B Johnson City TN 7/22/1942 s John Arthur Ewing & Frances Mory. BA Trin 1964; STB GTS 1967. D 7/1/1967 Bp William F Gates Jr P 4/1/1968 Bp William Evan Sanders. m 5/11/1968 Jennings Emison c 3. Dn & Pres The GTS New York NY 1998-2009; R Trin Epis Ch Buffalo NY 1985-1998; Vic S Ptr's Epis Ch Louisville KY 1975-1985; Cn S Jn's Cathd Jacksonville FL 1973-1975; Vic S Columba's Epis Ch Bristol TN 1968-1972; D-In-Trng Calv Ch Memphis TN 1967-1968. Auth, "Job: A Vision Of God"; Auth, "The Power Of The Lamb: Revelations Theol Of Liberation For You"; Auth, "Mnstry, Power," *& Chr.* D.D. U So. ewing@gts.edu

EXLEY-STIEGLER, George Ebdon (Roch) 168 Dalaker Dr, Rochester NY 14624 B Flushing NY 8/2/1916 s Julius Christian Stiegler & Alice Gwendolyn. BS Syr 1951; STM Ya Berk 1953; Urban Trng Cntr 1965; Centro Informacion De Documentacion Cueravaca MX 1974; Oxf 1979; Oxf 1980. D 6/29/1953 Bp Malcolm E Peabody P 3/22/1954 Bp Walter M Higley. m 1/8/1978 Anna Exley-Stiegler c 2. Cn of Metropltn Mnstry Dio Rochester Rochester NY 1968-1982; R Calv/St Andr's Par Rochester NY 1964-1978; Div of Metropltn Mnstry Dio Rochester Rochester NY 1964-1967; R S Lk's Ch Brockport NY 1957-1964; Dept CE Dio Rochester Rochester NY 1957-1960; R S Jas Ch Cleveland NY 1953-1954; R Trin Ch Camden NY 1953-1954. GEOES@frontiernet.net

EXNER, William Edward (NH) 19 W Union St, Goffstown NH 03045 **S Matt's Ch Goffstown NH 1985-** B Clifton Sprgs NY 4/8/1954 s Edward Burton Exner & Elizabeth Janekka. Rochester Inst Of Tech 1974; Cor 1975; BA Ithaca Coll 1976; MDiv EDS 1982. D 6/26/1982 P 5/1/1983 Bp Robert Rae Spears Jr. m 7/12/1975 Jane B Bluhm c 3. Vic Chr Ch Sackets Harbor NY 1982-1985; Cur Trin Epis Ch Watertown NY 1982-1985. EPF. exner@comcast.net

EYBERG, Carl Joseph (Pgh) 1842 E Richmond Pl, Springfield MO 65804 B Rolla MO 7/7/1952 D 6/12/2004 Bp Robert William Duncan P 12/21/2004 Bp Henry William Scriven. m 3/12/1988 Janet S Eyberg c 5. carleyberg@hotmail.com

EYLERS, David Edward (NY) PO Box 352, Harwinton CT 06791 B Poughkeepsie NY 6/12/1940 s Dirk Eylers & Emily Jane. BA Mar 1962; MDiv GTS 1965. D 6/12/1965 P 12/18/1965 Bp Horace W B Donegan. m 8/5/1967 Carla Peterson c 3. S Lk's Ch Beacon NY 1999-2006; S Lk's Ch Beacon NY 1980-1998; R S Mary's Ch Mohegan Lake NY 1971-1980; R S Thos Epis Ch New Windsor NY 1967-1971; Cur S Alb's Ch Simsbury CT 1965-1967. eylersdavid@sbcglobal.net

EYTCHESON, Gerald Leonard (Kan) 2400 Gary Ave, Independence KS 67301 **Vic Ch Of The Epiph Independence KS 1993-** B Independence KS 6/21/1944 s Benjamin Leonard Eytcheson & Rose Ellen. AA Independence Cmnty Coll 1964; BS Pittsburgh St U 1966; MS Pittsburgh St U 1973; Dio Kansas Sch For Mnstry KS 1993. D 10/30/1987 Bp Richard Frank Grein P 6/23/1993 Bp William Edward Smalley. m 7/26/1975 Linda Marie Gillis c 5. Vic Ch Of The Ascen Neodesha KS 1987-1993. gerald@eytcheson.com

EZELL II, James V (ECR) 105 Dogwood Trl, Elizabeth City NC 27909 **S Paul's Epis Ch Salinas CA 2007-** B Tulsa OK 9/9/1952 s James Vance Ezell & Carol Ann. BA Alfred U 1975; MDiv SWTS 1979. D 6/9/1979 P 12/1/1979 Bp Robert Bracewell Appleyard. m 11/20/2007 Marylyn L Linsley. The Morgan Sch Lenoir NC 1991-1993; S Lk's Epis Ch Asheville NC 1985-1991; Trin Epis Ch Asheville NC 1982-1985; Asst Chr Ch Greensburg PA 1979-1982; S Barth's Ch Scottdale PA 1979-1982. Ord Of S Lk. ezells_in_salinas@yahoo.com

F

FAASS, Peter (O) 3566 Avalon Rd, Shaker Heights OH 44120 **Pres, Stndg Com Dio Ohio Cleveland OH 2011-; R Chr Ch Shaker Heights OH 2006-** B Delft NL 9/4/1954 s Cornelius Pieter Faass & Margaret Gertruida. BA Wstrn Connecticut St U 1977; MDiv GTS 1999. D 6/12/1999 Bp Clarence Nicholas Coleridge P 12/18/1999 Bp Andrew Donnan Smith. R The Epis Ch Of S Jn The Bapt Sanbornville NH 2001-2006; Cur Trin Ch Torrington CT 1999-2001. priest@cometochristchurch.org

FABIAN, Richard Gardner (Cal) 2525 Lyon St, San Francisco CA 94123 B Evanston IL 10/1/1942 s Francis Gordon Fabian & Gretchen. BA Ya 1965; MA U of Cambridge 1967; Coll of the Resurr 1969; MDiv GTS 1970. D 6/18/1970 Bp Theodore H McCrea P 1/30/1971 Bp Paul Moore Jr. S Greg Of Nyssa Ch San Francisco CA 1980-2007; Dio California San Francisco CA 1976-1977. Auth, "Norris's Razor," *ATR*, ATR, 2008; Compsr, "Mus in," *Mus for Liturg II*, All SS Co, 1999; Compsr, "Mus in," *Ch Hymnal Series 5: Congrl Mus for Euch*; Compsr, "Mus Hymnal 82, Mus in Wonder," *Love & Praise*. All SS Comp Founding Dir 1974; Intl Angl Liturg Consult 1989; NAAL 1981; Societas Liturgica 1987. Jones Lectures Sewanee DS 2006; Distinguished Alum GTS 2004. rick@allsaintscompany.org

FABRE, John Peter (Az) 18083 W Douglas Way, Surprise AZ 85374 **P-in-c S Chris's Ch Sun City AZ 2011-** B 1/2/1944 s Gabriel Gaston Fabre & Virginia Jane Wilson. BS Florida Sthrn Coll 1981; DTS Epis TS Of The SW 2009. D 6/6/2009 P 1/3/2010 Bp Kirk Stevan Smith. m 7/24/1967 Barbara Burrous c 3. Hisp Mnstry S Chris's Ch Sun City AZ 2010-2011. jpfabre@cox.net

FABRE, Julie Kilbride (U) 38105 Redwood Road #2191, West Valley City UT 84119 B 3/7/1953 d Harold Anthony Fabre & Jo Orbon. BA Harv 1979; MDiv CDSP 1985. D 5/25/1996 Bp George Edmonds Bates. m 7/17/2003 John Dickson Stewart. Epis Cmnty Serv Inc Salt Lake City UT 2002-2003; Dio Utah Salt Lake City UT 1996-2002.

FACKLER, Phillip Joseph Augustine (Chi) 1700 Le Roy Ave Apt 5, Berkeley CA 94709 B St Louis MO 10/3/1980 s James David Fackler & Joan Ruth. BS U IL Urbana 2003; MDiv CDSP 2008; MA Grad Theol Un 2009. D 6/7/2008 P 12/6/2008 Bp Jeffrey Dean Lee. m 9/4/2005 Callie Estelle Swanlund. Asst Ch Of The H Innoc San Francisco CA 2008-2009. Traebert-Graebner Gk Scriptural Scholars Awd CDSP 2006; Mercer Schlrshp Mercer Schlrshp Fund 2006; Soc for Increase in Minstiry Schlrshp Soc for the Increase in Mnstry 2006. phfackler@hotmail.com

FACTOR, Beverly A (Los) 1404 Durham Dr, Herculaneum MO 63048 B Paden City,WV 9/26/1939 d Charles Arthur Woodburn & Geraldine Virginia. MDiv GTS 1995; BSLA Rgnts Coll SUNY Albany 1995; DMin SWTS 2004. D 7/25/1992 P 5/15/1993 Bp Herbert Thompson Jr. m 9/13/2007 Joseph Joel Elterman c 2. New Ch Plant - Mssnr for Monroe Cnty Dio Springfield Springfield IL 2002-2003; Sexual Misconduct Off Dio Los Angeles Los Angeles CA 2001-2002; Int S Patricks Ch And Day Sch Thousand Oaks CA 2001-2002; Int S Ptr's Par Santa Maria CA 2000-2001; Prevention of Misconduct and Chld Sexual Abuse Workshop Fac Dio Los Angeles Los Angeles CA 1999-2002; Int S Mary's Par Lompoc CA 1998-2000; Vic S Fran Epis Ch Eureka MO 1995-1997; Advsry Com on Pension and Benefits Dio Sthrn Ohio Cincinnati OH 1994-1995; Com on Pension and Benefits Dio Sthrn Ohio Cincinnati OH 1994-1995; Lay Eucharistic Min Trnr Dio Sthrn Ohio Cincinnati OH 1994-1995; Prevention of Chld Sexual Abuse Workshop Fac Dio Sthrn Ohio Cincinnati OH 1994-1995; COM Dio Sthrn Ohio Cincinnati OH 1993-1995; Cur Gr Ch Cincinnati OH 1992-1994. revbev1992@sbcglobal.net

FAETH, Margaret Ann (Va) 4529 Peacock Ave, Alexandria VA 22304 **Asst R Imm Ch-On-The-Hill Alexandria VA 1996-** B Washington DC 8/2/1959 d William Kramer Bishop & Mary Ellen. BS U Of Florida 1981; MBA MWC 1988; MDiv VTS 1996. D 6/15/1996 P 1/1/1997 Bp Peter James Lee. m 8/29/1981 Paul Eugene Faeth c 2. mafaeth@icon.net

FAGEOL, Suzanne Antoinette (Oly) Po Box 303, Langley WA 98260 B Akron OK 12/2/1949 d William Bertram Fageol & Suzanne. BA U of Vermont 1971; Hartford Sem 1973; U Chi 1977; MDiv SWTS 1979; U Of Aberdeen Aberdeen Gb 1987. D 6/4/1979 Bp James Winchester Montgomery P 7/11/1980 Bp Leland Stark. The Epis Ch Of S Jas The Less Northfield IL 1979-1980. Ed, "Who Are You Looking For," Wmn In Theol, 1998; Auth, "Sprtl Direction For The New Millenium," *Convergence 11:2*, Spr, 1998; Auth, "How To Set Up And Maintain A Sprtl Pract," *Convergence 8:2*, Spr, 1995; Auth, "Celebrating Experience," *Wmn Included*, Spck, 1990. Ecum Yth Coun Of Europe; Inst Of Noetic Sciences; Sprtl Dir Intl ; Wmn In Theol, Mvmt For The Ord Of Wmn; Womens Working Grp. Fellowowship Heythrop Coll Of The Lon London Engl 1990. spirit@whidbey.com

FAGG, Randy Jay (Ida) PO Box 324, Rupert ID 83350 **P St Matthews Epis Ch Rupert ID 2007-** B 2/17/1948 s Ronald Merel Fagg & Gladyce Arndt. BS U Of Idaho 1971. D 10/22/2006 P 5/4/2007 Bp Harry Brown Bainbridge III. rfagg@pmt.org

FAHRNER, Pamela Henry (Md) Saint John's Episcopal Church, 5234 Maryland Hwy, Deer Park MD 21550 **P S Jn's Ch Oakland MD 2009-; Fac for Agape A Gathering of Wmn S Matt's Par Oakland MD 2008-** B Chicago IL 6/6/1946 d Clyde E Henry & Janis. AA Cerritos Coll Norwalk CA/UCLA 1977. D 7/5/2008 P 6/27/2009 Bp John Leslie Rabb. m 11/27/1963 Jeffrey Fahrner c 2. D S Jn's Ch Oakland MD 2008-2009. phfahrner@comcast.net

FAIN, Beth Jernigan (Tex) 10515 Laneview Dr, Houston TX 77070 **R S Mary's Epis Ch Cypress TX 1997-** B Waco TX 9/26/1951 d Austin Jackson Jernigan & Elizabeth Jean Gibson. BS Texas Wmn's U-Denton 1973; Med Texas Wmn's U-Denton 1976; U of St. Thos 1983; Cert Epis TS of The SW 1992; MDiv Houston Grad TS 1992. D 6/27/1992 P 1/25/1993 Bp Maurice Manuel Benitez. m 10/18/1968 Jay Lindsey Fain c 2. Asst to R S Dunst's Epis Ch Houston TX 1992-1997. DOK, Steph Mnstry. revdbeth@aol.com

FAIN, Robert Duncan (Ga) 2230 Walton Way, Augusta GA 30904 **Dn Dio Georgia Savannah GA 2003-; Trst The TS at The U So Sewanee TN 1992-; The Ch Of The Gd Shpd Augusta GA 1983-** B Hendersonville NC 1/16/1955 s James Toole Fain & Thomasina Shepherd. BA Cit 1977; MDiv STUSo 1983. D 6/25/1983 P 2/24/1984 Bp William Gillette Weinhauer. m 12/31/1977 Debra Aiken c 2. Auth, "Christmas," *The chorister(dec/Jan)*, 2002; Auth, "Reservists Help Bridge the Gap," *Proceedings (June)*, US Naval Inst, 2000. Alum Coun STUSo; Bd Rgnts, the UOS 2004-2007; Kanuga Conferences Prog Com 1999; Naval Reserve Chapl 1985-1999; Trst Univ. Of the So 1995-2001; V-P Ch Relatns- Assoc Alumuni 2002-2005. rdfain@goodshepherd_agusta.net

FAIR, Verna Maria (Chi) 1134 Highpointe Dr, Dekalb IL 60115 **R S Jn's Epis Ch Naperville IL 2006-** B Chicago IL 10/28/1954 d Walter Fredrick White & Dorothy Esther. BS U IL 1977; MDiv McCormick TS 1982. D 6/19/1982 P 3/1/1983 Bp Quintin Ebenezer Primo Jr. m 10/16/1996 Rodney Dana Fair c 1. Gr Ch Sterling IL 2003-2006; S Lk's Ch Dixon IL 2003-2006; Off Of Bsh For ArmdF New York NY 1994-1999; Ch Of The H Cross Chicago IL 1985-1994; Dio Chicago Chicago IL 1982-1984. elshaddai54@yahoo.com

FAIRBANKS, Barbara Jean (Minn) 3044 Longfellow Ave, Minneapolis MN 55407 B Wagner SD 9/13/1954 d Phillip C Dudley & Eva P. BS Dakota Coll 1979; MEd So Dakota St U 1980; MDiv Untd Theol Sem Twin Cities 2009. D 12/11/2008 P 6/27/2009 Bp James Louis Jelinek. m 6/9/2001 Guy Fairbanks c 2. barb.fairbanks20@comcast.net

FAIRFIELD, Roger Louis (EO) 69793 Pine Glen Rd, Sisters OR 97759 B Long Beach CA 8/10/1942 s Robert Fairfield & Margaret. BS OR SU 1964; MS U CA 1966. D 6/10/2006 Bp William O Gregg. m 6/13/1964 Dixie Fairfield c 2. rfairfield@bendcable.com

FAIRLESS, Caroline S (NH) 8 Whispering Pines Rd, Wilmont NH 03287 **S Andr's Ch New London NH 2008-** B Pittsburgh PA 5/1/1947 d Blaine Franklin Fairless & Caroline Sproul. AA Centenary Coll 1967; BA Barnard Coll of Col 1971; MDiv CDSP 1989. D 6/3/1989 P 6/9/1990 Bp William Edwin Swing. m 12/8/2001 James Rollins Sims. S Jas Epis Ch Bowie MD 2004-2007; S Jn's Ch Roanoke VA 1999-2000; Vic Ch Of The H Fam Half Moon Bay CA 1993-1999; Assoc S Paul's Epis Ch San Rafael CA 1989-1992. Auth, "The Space Between Ch & Not-Ch ~ A Sacramental Vision for the Healing of our Planet," U Press of Amer, 2011; Auth, "Hambone," Ch Pub, 2001; Auth, "New Voices/Ancient Words: Dramatic Adaptions Of Scripture," Ch Pub, 2001; Auth, "Confessions Of A Fake P," Ch Pub, 2001; Auth, "Chld At Wrshp: Congregations In Bloom," Ch Pub, 2000. fairless@comcast.net

FAIRMAN, Henry Francis (RI) 73 Touisset Ave, Swansea MA 02777 B Providence RI 6/22/1934 s John Arthur Fairman & Emily Loretta. BA Bos 1956; MDiv Ya Berk 1959; MS Marywood U 1980. D 6/20/1959 P 12/19/1959 Bp John S Higgins. m 6/6/1958 Janis L O'Brien c 4. Neponset Cmnty Serv Dorchester MA 1994-1995; Int S Lk's Ch Pawtucket RI 1985-1986; S Mk's Epis Ch Riverside RI 1985; Int S Mk's Epis Ch Riverside RI 1982-1983; H Cross Epis Ch Wilkes Barre PA 1974-1978; R Trin Epis Ch W Pittston PA 1974-1978; Coordntr Dio Bethlehem Bethlehem PA 1972-1973; R S Lk's Ch Lebanon PA 1970-1972; R S Ptr's Epis Ch Hazleton PA 1965-1970; Asst S Steph's Epis Ch Wilkes Barre PA 1962-1965; Vic The Epis Ch Of S Clem And S Ptr Wilkes Barre PA 1962-1965; Vic S Thos' Alton Wood River Jct RI 1959-1961. Who's Who in Rel 1976.

FAIRWEATHER, Carolynne Marie (Ore) 305 Myrtlewood Ct, Newberg OR 97132 **Cnvnr - Ecum and Interfaith Cmsn Dio Oregon Portland OR 2011-; Asst Chr Ch Par Lake Oswego OR 2005-** B Grimsby England 2/26/1945 d Robert Harvey Burdge & June. BA Paterson St Coll 1966; BA WPC 1982; MDiv Drew U 1986; DMin Drew U 1995. D 4/30/2003 Bp Robert Louis Ladehoff P 10/18/2003 Bp Johncy Itty. m 9/7/1996 Roger William Weeks c 2. Assembly of Epis Healthcare Chapl 2004; Assn of Profsnl Chapl 2000. revcmf1@comcast.net

FAISON, Dee Doheny (Pa) 405 Warren Rd, West Chester PA 19382 B Darby PA 2/17/1947 d Joseph Aloysius Ignatius Doheny & Dorothy Eleanor. BA Rosemont Coll 1979; MDiv Luth TS 1987; Samatan Counslg Cntr 1993; Pennsylvania Coun Religionations 1997. D 6/20/1987 Bp Allen Lyman Bartlett Jr. m 9/7/1968 Paul Lloyd Faison c 3. S Jn The Evang Ch Lansdowne PA 1991-2004; D Ch Of The Redeem Bryn Mawr PA 1990-1991; D S Mart's Epis Ch Upper Chichester PA 1987-1989. deesnsh01@msn.com

FAIT JR, Harold Charles (Minn) D 11/30/1974 Bp Philip Frederick McNairy P 2/24/1993 Bp Sanford Zangwill Kaye Hampton.

FALBY, Chester Edward (Ore) 11660 Ernst Ct, Nehalem OR 97131 **Chapl to No Coast Dioc Ret Cler Dio Oregon Portland OR 2009-** B Berlin MA 5/27/1927 s Vern Frederick Falby & Blanche Jennette. BA U of Massachusetts 1948; MDiv CDSP 1951; STM GTS 1960. D 6/29/1951 P 6/24/1952 Bp Stephen F Bayne Jr. m 8/25/1951 Laurel Deanne Bowman c 6. Int S Cathr Of Alexandria Manzanita OR 2000-2002; Int Calv Ch Seaside OR 1998-1999; Vic Ch Of The Ascen Riddle OR 1979-1992; Vic Ch Of The H Sprt Sutherlin OR 1979-1992; R S Geo's Epis Ch Roseburg OR 1979-1992; R All SS Ch Hillsboro OR 1966-1979; R S Agnes Ch Little Falls NJ 1954-1962; LocTen S Andr's Ch Brewster NY 1953-1954; Asst Min S Paul's Ch Seattle WA 1952-1953; Vic S Jas Ch Sedro-Woolley WA 1951-1952. Cler Presenting Team Mar Encounter 1977-1992; Ord of S Lk - Chapl 1977-1992. cfalby@nehalemtel.net

FALCIANI, Justin Anthony (NJ) 16 W. Wilmont Ave, Somers Point NJ 08244 **R Chr Ch Somers Point NJ 2010-** B Vineland NJ 12/7/1976 s Anthony Falciani & Mary Ann. BA Cabrini Coll 1999; MA UTS New York NY 2001; MDiv VTS 2008. D 6/7/2008 Bp George Edward Councell P 12/7/2008 Bp Sylvestre Donato Romero. Vic S Mk's At The Crossing Ch

Williamstown NJ 2008-2010. Contrib, "Ecum in the 21st Century: Discovering out Common Baptism," *Ecum Trends*, Graymoor Ecum and Inter-Rel Inst, 2007. Phi Alpha Theta- Intl hon Soc 1998; Theta Alpha Kappa- Natl hon Soc of Rel Stds/Theol 1999. 2007 Natl Sem Essay Contest Epis Dioc Ecum and Inter-Rel Off 2007. gratian76@aol.com

FALCONE, John Francis (O) 7513 W 33rd St, Tulsa OK 74107 B Washington DC 7/27/1931 s Anthony Falcone & Minerva. BA S Mary's Coll Raleigh NC 1953; MDiv U of Louvain 1957; MA GW 1968; EDS 1970; DMin Oral Roberts U 2000. Rec from Roman Catholic 7/1/1980 Bp Robert Bruce Hall. m 4/17/1976 Diana Wright Carey c 1. Vic S Anne's In The Field Madison OH 1987-1989; R S Jn's Epis Ch Arlington VA 1980-1987.

FALCONER, Allan (Miss) 11593 Avondale Dr, Fairfax VA 22030 B Derby UK 7/5/1944 s Allan Falconer & Ada. BS U of Durham Durham GB 1965; PhD U of Durham GB 1970; DIT S Fran Coll Brisbane AU 1982. Trans from Anglican Church Of Kenya 8/10/1991 Bp George Edmonds Bates. m 1/2/1967 Renee Cowley c 2. Vic S Eliz's Mssn Collins MS 2003-2004; Permission to officiate Ch Of The Ascen Hattiesburg MS 1998-2006; Assoc S Jn's Epis Ch Logan UT 1991-1997. allanfalconer@aol.com

FALES, Stephen Abbott (Ind) 1440 W Main St, Carmel IN 46032 **R S Chris's Epis Ch Carmel IN 2002-** B Providence RI 2/10/1952 s Lester Parmenter Fales & Virginia. BA Hartwick Coll 1974; MDiv Yale DS 1978. D 6/17/1978 P 12/17/1978 Bp Frederick Hesley Belden. m 5/8/1976 Marian F Dzierwa c 2. R S Ptr's Epis Ch Cheshire CT 1990-2002; R S Andr The Apos Rocky Hill CT 1982-1990; Asst Ch Of The H Comf Vienna VA 1981-1982; Cur S Mich's Ch Bristol RI 1978-1981. frsteve@stchriscarmel.com

FALKOWSKI, Lawrence S (Ore) 2305 Cedar Village Blvd, East Brunswick NJ 08816 **Died 12/26/2010** B Bayonne NJ 1/9/1949 s Walter A Falkowski & Alice T. BS S Ptr's Coll Jersey City NJ 1970; MA FD 1972; PhD Rutgers-The St U 1976; MDiv VTS 1994. D 6/11/1994 Bp James Barrow Brown P 12/1/1994 Bp John Shelby Spong. c 2. Auth, *Pyschol Models in Intl Politics*, Westview, 1980; Auth, "Presidents," *Secretaries of St & Crisis in US Frgn Plcy*, Westview, 1977. Chrsnty for 3rd Millenium. lsfalkowski@comcast.net

FALLON, Amy L (O) 125 E. Market St, Tiffin OH 44883 **R Old Trin Epis Ch Tiffin OH 2010-** B Nashua NH 8/17/1962 d John William Fallon & Kathleen Winifred. BA Bryn 1984; MDiv Weston Jesuit TS 1988. D 7/25/1998 Bp Arthur Edward Walmsley P 2/20/1999 Bp Douglas Edwin Theuner. Vic S Mk's Chap Storrs CT 2001-2010; Asst Trin Epis Ch Hartford CT 1998-2001. amy.fallon08@gmail.com

FALLOWFIELD, William Harris (Md) 2622 N Calvert St, Baltimore MD 21218 B Chestertown MD 8/27/1938 s Harry Wallace Fallowfield & Sara Harris. BS Towson U 1960; BD VTS 1965. D 6/22/1965 P 6/1/1966 Bp Harry Lee Doll. m 10/18/1986 Faye Houston c 2. S Jas Ch Irvington Baltimore MD 1994-1998; Int S Geo's And S Matthews Ch Baltimore MD 1993-1994; Bp Clagget Cntr Buckeystown MD 1974-1989; R S Mary's Epis Ch Woodlawn Baltimore MD 1967-1974; Asst S S Jn's Par Hagerstown MD 1966-1967. Auth, "Sacr Ground, Sacr Stories: Slave Monologues from 1840," 2011; Auth, "Lectionary Bible Plays for Chld and Yth," 2004; Auth, "Claggett Cntr: A Personal View & Guide," 1980. Bp's Awd For Distinguished Serv 1989. wmhfallo@hotmail.com

FALLS, Michael Lee (Tex) 5831 Secrest Dr, Austin TX 78759 B Bemidji MN 3/3/1934 s Harry Victor Falls & Agnes. U MN; Epis TS of The SW 1970. D 6/17/1970 Bp Scott Field Bailey P 7/1/1971 Bp J Milton Richardson. m 7/12/1997 Beth W Wright. S Dav's Ch Austin TX 1990-1993; Asst R Palmer Memi Ch Houston TX 1970-1975. mikeandbethfalls@sbcglobal.net

FAMULARE JR, Joseph Anthony (Alb) 119 Southern Ave, Little Falls NY 13365 **Trin And S Mich's Ch Albany NY 2005-** B Herkimer NY 9/15/1967 s Joseph Anthony Famulare & Jean Ann. D 6/15/2002 P 4/22/2006 Bp David John Bena. m 10/3/1992 Christine Leskovar c 1. jcmelody@yahoo.com

FANGUY, Mabel Matheny (Pgh) 1114 1st St, Canonsburg PA 15317 **Asst S Paul's Epis Ch Pittsburgh PA 2009-** B Poughkeepsie NY 11/19/1958 d James Harnley Matheny & Dania Elizabeth. BS California St U 1982; MDiv VTS 1999. D 2/28/1999 Bp Charles Edward Jenkins III P 9/11/1999 Bp Robert William Duncan. m 11/26/1986 David Lawrence Fanguy c 2. R S Thos' Epis Ch Canonsburg PA 1999-2004. revmabel@comcast.net

FANNING, Thomas H (Miss) 24 Greystone Dr, Madison MS 39110 **R S Lk's Ch Brandon MS 2006-** B Jackson MS 5/5/1962 s William Fanning & Marjorie. BS Belhaven Coll 1985; MDiv STUSo 2006. D 5/31/2006 P 2/17/2007 Bp Duncan Montgomery Gray III. m 8/2/1986 Marjorie Goodsell Fanning c 1. thfanning@hotmail.com

FARABEE, Allen Waldo (WNY) 310 Norwood Ave, Buffalo NY 14222 **S Dav's Epis Ch W Seneca NY 1975-** B Fort Myers FL 12/10/1946 s A Waldo Farabee & Marion Belle. BS Indiana U 1969; MDiv Yale DS 1972; STM Nash 1979; JD U of Connecticut 1993. D 6/2/1974 Bp Albert Ervine Swift P 3/1/1975 Bp James Loughlin Duncan. m 10/26/2011 Galen Granquist. S Jas' Ch Batavia NY 2005-2006; S Paul's Cathd Buffalo NY 1995-2005; R S Mich's Ch Litchfield CT 1985-1995; S Paul's/Trin Chap Alton IL 1981-1984; R S Paul's Ch Marinette WI 1977-1981; Asst All SS Prot Epis Ch Ft Lauderdale FL 1975-1977. Phi Eta Sigma; Pi Kappa Lamda. MDIVJD@AOL.COM

FARAMELLI, Norman Joseph (Mass) 29 Harris St, Waltham MA 02452 B Wilkes-Barre PA 8/26/1932 s Guido Faramelli & Clara. BS Buc 1955; STB PDS 1960; PhD Tem 1967. D 5/14/1960 P 12/1/1960 Bp Oliver J Hart. m 4/27/1957 Lucie Marie Schaffer c 2. Int S Lk's/San Lucas Epis Ch Chelsea MA 2000; S Lk's/San Lucas Epis Ch Chelsea MA 1995-1998; S Paul's Ch Newburyport MA 1994; S Lk's And S Marg's Ch Allston MA 1992-1993; S Eliz's Ch Sudbury MA 1990-1991; Gr Ch Lawr MA 1989-1990; Gr Ch Newton MA 1983-1984; Epis City Mssn Boston MA 1981; S Dunstans Epis Ch Dover MA 1979; Boston Indstrl Mssn Cambridge MA 1967-1976; Dir S Paul's Epis Ch Westfield NJ 1960-1963. Auth, "Technethics: Chr Mssn In An Age Of Tech".

FARBER, Joseph Wade (Okla) 1420 E Dewey Ave, Sapulpa OK 74066 B Oklahoma City OK 11/12/1957 s Clyde Grant Farber & Clara Fay Thompson. BA U Chi 1980; JD U of Oklahoma 1984; MDiv The U So (Sewanee) 2010. D 1/23/2010 P 7/24/2010 Bp Edward Joseph Konieczny. m 8/7/2004 Janice F Farber c 3. P-in-c Gd Shpd Epis Ch Sapulpa OK 2010-2011. jwfarber@gmail.com

FARGO, David Rolland (NC) 3081 Golfside Ln, Hendersonville NC 28739 B Memphis TN 7/28/1945 s Robert Rolland Fargo & Mary Ann. BA Van 1967; MDiv GTS 1970. D 6/24/1970 Bp William F Gates Jr P 3/28/1971 Bp William Evan Sanders. m 8/26/1967 Sally Sue Blood c 2. COM Dio Louisiana Baton Rouge LA 1993-1996; Stndg Com Dio Louisiana Baton Rouge LA 1988-1991; R Chr Ch Slidell LA 1982-2000; Assoc H Trin Epis Ch Greensboro NC 1977-1982; Dio No Carolina Raleigh NC 1973-1976; Vic S Anne's Ch Winston Salem NC 1972-1977; D-in-trng S Steph's Epis Ch Oak Ridge TN 1970-1971. fargo.dr@gmail.com

FARIA III, Manuel Pinheiro (Mass) 4 Ocean St, Beverly MA 01915 **Congrl Coach Dio Massachusetts Boston MA 2006-; R S Ptr's Ch Beverly MA 1999-** B Danbury CT 5/2/1954 s Manuel Pinheiro Faria & Mary. BS Bos 1976; MDiv Yale DS 1996. D 6/8/1996 Bp Clarence Nicholas Coleridge P 12/21/1996 Bp Gordon Paul Scruton. m 10/22/1988 Louise A Seelig c 2. Congrl Coach Dio Massachusetts Boston MA 2006-2007; Conv Resolutns Com Dio Massachusetts Boston MA 2004-2007; Asst S Steph's Ch Pittsfield MA 1996-1999. revfaria@gmail.com

FARINA, Gaspar Miran (Mil) 154 Club Wildwood, Hudson FL 33568 B Beloit WI 10/25/1915 s Michael Farina & Sarah. BD U of Wisconsin-Whitewater 1938; MS Marq 1950. D 12/22/1956 Bp Donald H V Hallock. m 6/21/1941 Jane K Lord c 4. Asst S Edmunds Ch Milwaukee WI 1963-1976; Asst St Mths Epis Ch Waukesha WI 1956-1963.

FARKAS, Hazel Daphne Martin (SVa) 111 Montrose, Williamsburg VA 23188 **D S Mart's Epis Ch Williamsburg VA 2000-** B Saint Albans Hertfordshire UK 4/17/1937 d George Martin & Lucie Margaret Victoria. Maryland; M.B.Ch.B U of Edinburgh Edinburgh GB 1962; Cert STUSo 1979. D 6/26/1983 Bp David Keller Leighton Sr. m 4/27/1963 Hanson Farkas c 3. D Gr Ch Utica NY 1988-1998; D S Jas' Ch Clinton NY 1985-1989; D The Ch Of The H Apos Halethorpe MD 1983-1984; Consult Psych S Tim's Ch Catonsville MD 1973-1984. Auth, "Var arts," *Psych Journ*, Amer Psych Assn. Ord of S Lk 1985. hazel413@cox.net

FARLEY, Nancy Stone (Lex) 151 Vine St, Sadieville KY 40370 B Burbank CA 3/9/1955 d Robert Clark Stone & Eugenia Loretta. BD U Of Kentucky 1977; MA Estrn Kentucky U 1981; MDiv GTS 1994. D 6/25/1994 P 1/18/1995 Bp Rogers Sanders Harris. c 2. R Ch Of The H Trin Georgetown KY 2002-2005; R S Eliz's Epis Ch Zephyrhills FL 1997-2002; Asst & Sch Chapl S Mary's Par Tampa FL 1996-1997; S Andr's Epis Ch Tampa FL 1994-1996. mothernanc@aol.com

FARMER, Edward Dean (Wyo) PO Box 385, Meeteetse WY 82433 **S Alb's Ch Worland WY 2011-** B Cody WY 12/12/1950 D 8/27/2005 Bp Bruce Edward Caldwell. m 6/28/1974 Rita Farmer c 1. farmer@tctwest.net

FARMER, Eyleen Hamner (Md) 102 N 2nd St, Memphis TN 38103 **Assoc Calv Ch Memphis TN 2010-** B Boulder CO 10/31/1950 d Martin Hamner & Barbara. BA U of Memphis 1983; MA U of Memphis 1986; MDiv Van 1992. D 6/10/2006 P 1/6/2007 Bp Don Edward Johnson. m 11/13/2004 Thomas A Momberg c 2. Int S Jn's Par Hagerstown MD 2010; Assoc Gr - S Lk's Ch Memphis TN 2008-2009; Assoc R Calv Ch Memphis TN 2006-2008. reveyleen@gmail.com

FARMER, Gary Clayton (WNC) Po Box 633, Arden NC 28704 B Hickory NC 10/13/1934 s Earl Vennoy Farmer & Mattie Lee. New Sch for Soc Resrch; BA Duke 1957; MDiv GTS 1965. D 6/22/1965 Bp William Loftin Hargrave P 12/28/1965 Bp James Loughlin Duncan. c 2. Deerfield Hm Asheville NC 1984-2000; S Steph's Ch Richmond VA 1975-1977; ExCouncil Dio Wstrn No Carolina Asheville NC 1972-1973; P-in-c Ch Of The Epiph Newton NC 1967-1976; Asst Ch Of The Gd Shpd Dunedin FL 1965-1967. Amer Assn for Counslg and Develpment; Clincl Memi Intl Acad of Behavioral Med; Dplma for Amer Psych Assn. barley633@gmail.com

FARMER, Jennie Marietta (EMich) 453 S 26th St, Saginaw MI 48601 B Saginaw MI 2/10/1921 d James Black & Irene Elizabeth. Delta Coll U Cntr MI; Cert Michigan TS 1982. D 6/15/1982 Bp William J Gordon Jr. m 6/14/1942 Thomas Owen Farmer c 1. Asst S Paul's Epis Ch Saginaw MI 1982-1990. Ord Of S Lk.

FARMER, Marjorie Louise Nichols (Pa) 222 Linden Dr, Elkins Park PA 19027 B Hartford CT 3/17/1922 d Edward Kingston Nichols & Laura Ella. BA Tem 1946; MA Tem 1954; Med Tem 1958; EdD Tem 1975; MA Luth TS 1983. D 6/20/1987 P 5/1/1988 Bp Allen Lyman Bartlett Jr. m 4/12/1943 Clarence Farmer. Auth, "Composition & Grammar"; Auth, "Consensus & Dissent". SCHC. The DSA Natl Coun Of Tchrs Engl 1981.

FARQUHAR-MAYES, Alice F(ay) (Ida) 1560 Lenz Ln, Boise ID 83712 B Passaic NJ 1/3/1945 d William Henry Farquhar-Mayes & Frances Alexandra. RN New Engl Bapt Hosp 1965; BA U Of Hartford 1973; MS Ya 1975; Cnm Ya 1975; MDiv GTS 1982. D 6/12/1982 P 5/6/1983 Bp Arthur Edward Walmsley. m 5/16/1981 Thomas Farquhar-Mayes. Ch Of H Nativ Meridian ID 2007-2009; Cn S Mich's Cathd Boise ID 2001-2007; Serv S Steph's Boise ID 1992-2001; S Jas Ch Mtn Hm ID 1988; Assoc S Lk's Par Darien CT 1985-1987; Cur S Paul's Ch Fairfield CT 1982-1985. Auth, "Ethical Considerations In Use Of Neuromuscular Blockades," *Ccnq*. Amer Soc For Bioethics & Hmnts 1999; Assn Of Profsnl Chapl 1989; Bd Cert Chapl 1989. Pres'S Awd S Lk'S Rmc Boise ID 1994; Outstanding St Ldr Assn Of Profsnl Chapl. scotslass1@msn.com

FARQUHAR-MAYES, Thomas (Ida) 1115 W Clarinda Dr, Meridian ID 83642 B St. Louis MO 12/4/1938 D 11/12/1983 P 6/13/1984 Bp David Bell Birney IV. m 5/16/1981 Alice F(ay) Farquhar-Mayes c 1. Emm Epis Ch Stamford CT 1984-1986. scotslassl@msn.com

FARR, Beau Anthony (At) 5685 Highway 332, Hoschton GA 30548 B Winder GA 9/19/1960 D 6/5/2004 P 10/1/2005 Bp J(ohn) Neil Alexander. S Anth's Epis Ch Winder GA 2005-2009. bafarrr@worldnet.att.net

FARRAR, Charles Thomas (Me) 79 Mallard Dr, Richmond ME 04357 B New York NY 4/29/1941 s Clayton Adelbert Farrar & Elisabeth. MDiv GTS; BA U So. D 6/7/1968 P 12/1/1969 Bp Horace W B Donegan. c 1. S Matt's Epis Ch Hallowell ME 1979-1983; S Johns Epis Hosp Far Rockaway NY 1973-1976; Asst S Paul And S Jas New Haven CT 1970-1971; Asst Min S Jn's Ch Stamford CT 1968-1970.

FARRAR III, Holway Dean (Los) 4091 E La Cara St, Long Beach CA 90815 **Asst The Par Ch Of S Lk Long Bch CA 2006-** B San Diego CA 6/10/1949 s Holway Dean Farrar & Bonnie Louise. BA U CA, San Diego 1971; MDiv EDS 1975. D 6/21/1975 P 2/21/1976 Bp Robert C Rusack. R S Fran' Par Palos Verdes Estates CA 1993-2006; Vic S Thos' Mssn Hacienda Heights CA 1979-1993; Asst S Geo's Epis Ch Laguna Hills CA 1976-1979; Dio Los Angeles Los Angeles CA 1975-1976. dean90815@verizon.net

FARRELL, John T (LI) 1155 Warburton Ave, Apt 4D, Yonkers NY 10701 B Glen Cove NY 1/27/1948 s D(aniel) Harmon Farrell & Lydia Marie. BA Belmont Abbey Coll 1970; MA Ball St U 1972; PhD U Of Delaware Newark 1983; Dplma Ya Berk 1990; MDiv Yale DS 1990. D 6/8/1991 P 6/13/1992 Bp Cabell Tennis. Vic Dio Long Island Garden City NY 2008-2010; Vic S Jas Ch Elmhurst NY 2008-2010; P-in-c Chr Ch Bay Ridge Brooklyn NY 2003-2008; R S Paul's Epis Ch Prince Frederick MD 1998-2003; Vic Mt Olivet Epis Ch New Orleans LA 1996-1998; Chapl S Mart's Epis Sch Metairie LA 1995-1998; Asst Chr Ch Cathd New Orleans LA 1995-1996; P-in-c S Dav's Ch Philadelphia PA 1992-1995. Auth, "Sought Through Pryr and Meditation," Cntrl Recovery Press, 2013; Auth, "Guide Me in My Recovery," Cntrl Recovery Press, 2011; Auth, "Writing for Bus: A Casebook," Kendall Hunt, 1995; Auth, "Numerous arts". Ord Of Urban Missioners 1999. Paul Harris Fell rotary Intl 2001. johnfarrell@aya.yale.edu

FARRELL JR, Reid Dwyer (Vt) PO Box 273, Swanton VT 05488 **Cler Dep to GC 2012 Dio Vermont Burlington VT 2010-; R H Trin Epis Ch Swanton VT 2004-** B New Orleans LA 1/2/1952 s Reid Dwyer Farrell & Adelaide Jacqueline. PhD U Of Florida; BS U Of Florida 1977; MDiv GTS 1982. D 5/31/1982 P 1/1/1983 Bp Emerson Paul Haynes. m 10/20/2009 Dale Lee Willard. First Alt Cler Dep to GC 2009 Dio Vermont Burlington VT 2008-2010; Dioc Coun Dio Vermont Burlington VT 2006-2011; R Gr Epis Ch Southgate MI 1999-2004; P-in-c S Thos Ch Mamaroneck NY 1999; P-in-c Gr Ch Cincinnati OH 1997-1999; Assoc R S Bon Ch Sarasota FL 1986-1997; Asst H Trin Ch Gainesville FL 1985-1986; Cur Ch Of The Gd Shpd Punta Gorda FL 1982-1984. Auth, "Var arts & Presentations". Soc Of S Jn The Evang 1979. holytrinityrector@myfairpoint.net

FARROW, Donald Lester (SO) 5555 Copenhagen Dr, Westerville OH 43081 B Bryn Mawr PA 10/13/1928 s Henry William Farrow & Marian. BA Trin Hartford CT 1950; MDiv VTS 1953. D 6/13/1953 Bp Joseph Gillespie Armstrong P 12/12/1953 Bp Oliver J Hart. m 9/6/1952 Carolyn Lincoln Taylor c 5. Whetstone Care Cntr Columbus OH 1993-1998; Int S Matt's Ch Westerville OH 1992-1993; P-in-c Gd Shpd Ch Montgomery AL 1984-1985; CE Dio Pennsylvania Philadelphia PA 1955-1967; Vic S Andr's In The Field Ch Philadelphia PA 1955-1957. dfar555@aol.com

FARWELL JR, James William (At) Bethany College, Bethany WV 26032 B Jacksonville FL 8/1/1960 s James William Farwell & Dorothy Louise. BA CUA 1984; MDiv GTS 1989; PhD Emory U 2001. D 6/11/1989 P 12/10/1989 Bp Frank Stanley Cerveny. m 12/15/1984 Rita C Faulkner c 2. The GTS New York NY 2002-2007; Cn Theol Cathd Of S Phil Atlanta GA 1999-2002; S Barth's Epis Ch Atlanta GA 1995-1997; S Steph's Ch Coconut Grove Coconut Grove FL 1990-1993; Asst R S Andr's Ch Jacksonville FL 1989-1990. "This is the Night: Suffering Salvation and the Liturgies of H Week," T & T Clark/ Continuum, 2005; "The Study of Liturg and Postmodernism," Proceedings of the NAAL, 2005; "Baptism, Euch, and the Hosp of Jesus," ATR, 2004; "Salvation, Bishops, FD Maurice," *Encyclopedia of Protestantism*, Routledge, 2003. AAR 1995; No Amer Acad of Liturg 2006; Soc for Buddhist-Chr Stds 1997. jfarwell@bethanywv.edu

FASEL, William Jay (WMo) 824 W 62nd St, Kansas City MO 64113 **Cn Mssnr, NE Epis Reg Mnstry Dio W Missouri Kansas City MO 2001-; NE Reg Mnstry Lexington MO 2001-** B Wharton TX 2/2/1954 s Joseph Henry Fasel & Lois Watts. BS USCG Acad New London CT 1976; Geo Mason U 1981; MBA U of Texas at San Antonio 1985; MDiv STUSo 1990; DMin SWTS 1998. D 5/26/1990 Bp Earl Nicholas McArthur Jr P 12/2/1990 Bp John Herbert MacNaughton. m 7/3/1985 Michelle P Boyd c 4. R Shpd Of The Hills Branson MO 1993-2001; Vic All SS Epis Ch Pleasanton TX 1990-1993; Vic S Mths Devine TX 1990-1993. frbillnerm@hotmail.com

FAST SR, Todd Howard (Oly) 8756 Sylvan Pl Nw, Seattle WA 98117 B Lima OH 10/12/1926 s Harley J Fast & Rose F. BA Denison U 1949; Cert ETSBH 1967. D 9/10/1966 P 3/1/1967 Bp Francis E I Bloy. m 9/10/1949 Josephine Staats c 6. Asstg P S Lk's Epis Ch Seattle WA 1994-1995; Int S Chas Angl Par Poulsbo WA 1989-1991; Assoc S Lk's Epis Ch Seattle WA 1974-1977; R S Clem's Mssn Huntington Pk CA 1970-1974; Asst S Anselm Of Cbury Par Garden Grove CA 1966-1970. toddnjofast@msn.com

FAUCETTE, Chip (At) 2998 Kodiak Ct, Marietta GA 30062 **D The Epis Ch Of S Ptr And S Paul Marietta GA 2006-** B Chattanooga TN 1/19/1947 s Robert Faucette & Betty. BS U Of Tennessee Knoxville TX 1970. D 8/6/2006 Bp J(ohn) Neil Alexander. c 3. Bro of St. Andrewsd 2001. cfaucette@earthlink.net

FAULKNER, David Michael (Dal) Saint James' Church, 413 Olive Street, Texarkana TX 75501 **Cur S Jas Epis Ch Texarkana TX 2011-** B Dallas TX 3/28/1983 s Albert G Faulkner & Rebecca J. MDiv Beeson DS 2008; BA Wheaton Coll 2009; DAS Epis TS Of The SW 2010. D 6/26/2010 P 4/8/2011 Bp Paul Emil Lambert. m 12/30/2006 Laura Jones. Cur H Trin Ch Rockwall TX 2010-2011. davidmfaulkner@gmail.com

FAULKNER, Thomas Dickson (NY) 131 E 66th St Apt 10b, New York NY 10065 **Vic Chr Epis Ch Sparkill NY 2006-** B Nyack NY 11/4/1943 s John Edward Faulkner & Viola Emily. BA Dart 1967; MDiv EDS 1974; MFA Pratt Inst 1978. D 6/8/1974 P 12/1/1977 Bp Paul Moore Jr. m 7/29/1995 Brenda G Husson c 1. Assoc S Jas Ch New York NY 2000-2005; Ch Of The Ascen Mt Vernon NY 1997-1998; Int H Innoc Highland Falls NY 1995-1997; S Thos Epis Ch New Windsor NY 1995-1996; Gr Ch White Plains NY 1994; Dir Peace/Disarmament Dio New York New York City NY 1982-1984; Diocn Msnry & Ch Extntn Socty New York NY 1982-1984; Dpt Of Missions Ny Income New York NY 1982-1984; Asst S Ann And The H Trin Brooklyn NY 1978-1982; Asst S Phil's Ch Brooklyn NY 1977-1978; Asst Gr Epis Ch Nyack NY 1976-1977. Contrib, "On the Ground After 9/11," Haworth Press, 2005. metrohope@mac.com

FAULSTICH, Christine Marie (Tex) 8134 Mesa Dr, Austin TX 78759 **Cur S Matt's Ch Austin TX 2010-** B Olympia Fields IL 6/17/1984 d John Thomas Faulstich & Lynne Head. BA Rice U 2006; MDiv VTS 2010. D 6/19/2010 Bp C(harles) Andrew Doyle P. CFAULSTICH@GMAIL.COM

FAULSTICH, Matthew (SeFla) 1704 Buchanan St, Hollywood FL 33020 **R S Jn's Ch Hollywood FL 1997-** B Winamac IN 3/18/1951 s Lawrence George Faulstich & Rita Lucille. BA Pur 1973; S Meinrad RC Sem 1974; MDiv cl S Vinc Depaul RC Sem 1977; Moreau RC Sem At U Of Notre Dame 1978; CAS SWTS 1989. Rec from Roman Catholic 5/19/1989 Bp Francis Campbell Gray. m 9/17/1983 Cheryl Rankin c 3. Vic S Jn's Ch Centralia IL 1989-1997; Vic S Thos Ch Salem IL 1989-1997. M Div cl St. Vinc de Paul Sem 1977. mattncheryl@bellsouth.net

FAUPEL, David William (Lex) 4500 Massachusetts Ave Nw, Washington DC 20016 **Int R S Jn's Ch Versailles KY 2002-** B Cass City MI 5/28/1944 s David Henry Faupel & Clara Edith. BA Cntrl Bible Coll Springfield MO 1966; BA Evang Bible Coll 1968; MDiv Asbury TS 1971; MS U Of Kentucky 1972; PhD U Of Birmingham Birmingham Gb 1989. D 12/17/1978 P 12/1/1979 Bp Addison Hosea. m 6/27/1992 Bonnie Elliott. Asst R S Jn's Ch Versailles KY 2000-2002; P-in-c S Phil's Ch Harrodsburg KY 1996-1999; Asst P Ch Of The Gd Shpd Lexington KY 1992-1993; Supply P S Jas Epis Ch Prestonsburg KY 1991-1992; LocTen S Jn's Ch Versailles KY 1990-1991; Asst P Chr Ch Cathd Lexington KY 1987-1988; P-in-c S Andr's Ch Lexington KY 1985-1986; Cur S Jn's Ch Versailles KY 1980-1982; Asst Trin Epis Ch Danville KY 1978-1979. Auth, "Amer Pentecostal Mvmt: A Bibliographical Essay"; Auth, "The Everlasting Gospel"; Auth, "The Higher Chr Life". Amer Theol Libr

Assn 1967; Kentucky Libr Assn 1974; Soc For Pentecostal Stds 1970; Wesleyan Theol Scoiety 1979; Wrld Methodist Hist Soc 1998. bill_faupel@ats.wilmore.ky.us

FAUSAK, Frederick Emil (NY) 41 Alter Ave, Staten Island NY 10304 **D S Andr's Epis Ch Staten Island NY 2002-** B Jersey City NJ 7/9/1936 s Albert Fausak & Martha. BA CUNY 1979. D 4/26/1997 Bp Richard Frank Grein. m 6/6/1961 Theresa Ann Fausak c 3. D S Mary's Castleton Staten Island NY 2001; D S Andr's Epis Ch Staten Island NY 1997-2000. fredfausak@aol.com

FAUST, Andrew S (CFla) 92 North St., Saco ME 04072 **R The Ch Of S Lk And S Ptr S Cloud FL 2005-** B Washington D.C. 12/29/1946 s George T Faust & Ruth. Montgomery Coll; Montreal TS 1998. Trans from Scottish Episcopal Church 9/27/2001 Bp John Wadsworth Howe. m 12/28/1985 Brenda L Laresen. R S Jude's Ch Orange City FL 2001-2005. afaust@maine.rr.com

F

FAUST III, Frank Lawrence (La) 1921 Cammie Ave, Metairie LA 70003 B New Orleans LA 12/29/1941 s Frank Lawrence Faust & Mary Ina. BA Tul 1963; MDiv SWTS 1966; EdD U of New Orleans 1980. D 6/24/1966 Bp Girault M Jones P 6/16/1967 Bp Iveson Batchelor Noland. m 6/26/1965 Patricia Faust. Cur Trin Epis Ch Baton Rouge LA 1966-1967. Auth, "Amer Sch Bd Journ"; Auth, "Il Princapello Di Seville, Or In Educ Survival'S The Name Of The Game," *Amer Sch Bd Journ*; Auth, "El Superentenda En Hades, Or The Bd Meeting'S About To Begin," *Amer Sch Bd Journ*; Auth, "Revs Of Recent Stds Of Stdt Attitudes Towards Innovation," *Clearing Hse*; Auth, "El Superentenda En Hades," *Or The Bd Meeting'S About To Begin*. The Polly Bond Awd Epis Cmncatn 1997. flfaust3@cox.net

FAY, Michael (Mont) 514 Whatley Road, Nashua MT 59248 B Denver CO 11/12/1946 s John William Fay & Gladys Vivian. MD Geo 1977; BS USMA at W Point 1977; GD Trin Melbourne AUS 2003; DMinn TS 2010. D 10/2/1999 P 4/1/2000 Bp Charles Jones III. m 6/14/1970 Samar Freemon c 2. fr.mike.fay@gmail.com

FAY, Susan Delia (NCal) 3878 River Rd, Colusa CA 95932 **Mssnr S Paul's Epis Ch Oroville CA 2002-; Dio Nthrn California Sacramento CA 1999-** B Oxford MI 8/24/1963 d Louis Elwyn Fay & Alice Dickinson. MDiv STUSo 1991. D 6/22/1993 P 5/1/1994 Bp John Stuart Thornton. Mssnr S Steph's Epis Ch Colusa CA 2002-2003; Reg Mssnr H Trin Epis Ch Willows CA 1999; Mssnr S Tim's Ch Gridley CA 1999; S Geo's Ch Lusk WY 1996-1999; Dio Idaho Boise ID 1993-1999. Auth, "I Call Them Ang". Ord Of S Helena. gardenpriest@comcast.net

FAY, William Merrill (Cal) 955 Mendocino Ave, Berkeley CA 94707 **Died 8/5/2011** B Berkeley CA 12/11/1923 s Percival Bradshaw Fay & Esther Frances. BA U CA 1948; BD VTS 1951. D 8/4/1951 P 2/23/1952 Bp Karl M Block. c 4.

FAYETTE, Shelly Lynn (Oly) 805 SE Ellsworth Rd, Vancouver WA 98664 **Assoc Pstr Ch Of The Gd Shpd Vancouver WA 2009-** B Yakima WA 7/15/1980 d Fred William Fayette & Louise Ann Kohn. BA Seattle U 2003; MDIV UTS 2009. D 4/17/2009 Bp Gregory Harold Rickel P 1/9/2010 Bp Bavi Rivera. Dioc Intern Dio Estrn Oregon The Dalles OR 2009. SHELLYF@GOODSHEPHERDVANCOUVER.ORG

FEAGIN JR, Jerre Willis (WNY) 70 Westchester Rd, Williamsville NY 14221 **Int S Mths Epis Ch E Aurora NY 2011-** B Macon GA 1/16/1944 s Jerre Willis Feagin & Frances Ione. BS Auburn U 1966; MDiv GTS 1973. D 6/5/1973 P 12/21/1973 Bp William Henry Marmion. m 10/9/2010 Amy Feagin c 2. R St Mk Epis Ch No Tonawanda NY 1999-2010; P-in-c S Ptr's Epis Ch Eggertsville NY 1993-1999; R Calv Epis Ch Williamsville NY 1982-1992; Exec Dir COM Dio Wstrn New York Tonawanda NY 1979-1985; R The Epis Ch Of The Gd Shpd Buffalo NY 1978-1982; Asst S Jn's Of Lattingtown Locust Vlly NY 1975-1978; Asst S Jn's Ch Roanoke VA 1973-1974. jerrefeagin12@gmail.com

FEAMSTER JR, Thomas Otey (NC) 1805 Virginia Ct, Tavares FL 32778 B Newport News VA 10/23/1930 s Thomas Otey Feamster & Gladys Virginia. Florida St U 1956; MDiv STUSo 1972. D 6/16/1972 P 6/1/1973 Bp Edward Hamilton West. m 1/8/1983 Betty Baldwin c 3. P Dio No Carolina Raleigh NC 1993-1995; P-in-c S Mths Ch Louisburg NC 1986-1995; R S Paul's Ch Louisburg NC 1985-1995; R Chr Ch Hackensack NJ 1983-1985; R Gr Epis Ch Paris TN 1979-1982; P-in-c S Anne's Epis Ch Keystone Heights FL 1972-1979. feamster.tom@gmail.com

FEATHER, Mark Randolph (Ky) 7009 Hadley Ct, Louisville KY 40241 **R S Paul's Ch Louisville KY 2003-** B Troy NY 9/7/1955 s Arthur Philip Feather & Wanda Agnes. BS U Of Kentucky 1977; JD Stan 1980; MDiv VTS 2001. D 6/3/2001 P 6/8/2002 Bp Edwin Funsten Gulick Jr. m 8/22/1981 Marilyn S Schlapbach c 2. Mem Eccl Crt Dio Kentucky Louisville KY 2008-2011; Cur S Mk's Epis Ch Louisville KY 2002-2003; Campus Min Dio Kentucky Louisville KY 2001-2003; Cur Ch Of The Adv Louisville KY 2001-2002. Kentucky Bar Assn 1980. revmarkfeather@insightbb.com

FEATHERSTON, William Roger (Eur) Via B. Rucellai 09, Florence 50123 Italy B Melbourne Australia 10/12/1943 s William Featherston & Ada. S Mich's Hse Crafers Au 1967; BA U of Melbourne 1987. Trans from Anglican Church Of Australia 5/22/2005 Bp Pierre W Whalon. m 12/15/1969 Finola Elizabeth James c 3. S Jas Epis Ch Firenze IA IT 2005-2008. rogerfeatherston@hotmail.com

FEDEWA, Michael Carl (WMich) 1025 3 Mile Rd Ne, Grand Rapids MI 49505 **R S Andr's Ch Grand Rapids MI 1992-** B Lansing MI 7/5/1955 s Vernon Carl Fedewa & Beverly Anne. Aquinas Coll; BA S Thos Sem 1977; STB Gregorian U 1980; Cert GTS 1986. Rec from Roman Catholic 9/7/1986 Bp Howard Samuel Meeks. m 6/22/1984 Linda Ann Houswerth c 1. R Chr Ch Lockport NY 1990-1992; Asst S Thos Epis Ch Battle Creek MI 1986-1990. mfedewa@sbcglobal.net

FEDOCK, Maria Michele (Md) 2115 Southland Rd, Baltimore MD 21207 **D S Barth's Ch Baltimore MD 1984-** B Baltimore MD 3/12/1942 d Michael John Fedock & Thelma E. Cmnty Coll of Baltimore Baltimore MD 1961; Loyola Coll 1976. D 5/12/1979 Bp David Keller Leighton Sr. D Ch Of The H Nativ Baltimore MD 1979-1983. mitchiepool@verizon.net

FEDORCHAK, Karen (Ct) 48 S Hawthorne St, Manchester CT 06040 **D S Mary's Epis Ch Manchester CT 2002-** B Wilmington DE 9/2/1936 d Francis E Russell & Dorothy S. BS U Of Delaware Newark 1958. D 12/1/1990 Bp Arthur Edward Walmsley. m 5/16/1959 John Adam Fedorchak c 3. D S Jas's Ch W Hartford CT 1996-2001; D S Mary's Epis Ch Manchester CT 1990-1996. dn.k.fedorchak@cox.net

FEDOSUK, James Henry (Spr) 415 N Plum St, Havana IL 62644 B Hillsdale MI 11/30/1931 s George Fedor Fedosuk & Mary Elizabeth. MDiv Nash; BA Bradley U 1962. D 3/13/1965 P 9/1/1965 Bp Francis W Lickfield. S Jas Epis Ch Lewistown IL 1985-1994; R S Barn Ch Havana IL 1968-1994; Asst Trin Epis Ch Peoria IL 1965-1968. S Ben's Abbey (Oblate) 2003.

FEELY, Mary Josephine (Minn) 8055 Morgan Ave N, Stillwater MN 55082 **Mssnr for the Diac Dio Minnesota Minneapolis MN 2009-** B Saint Cloud MN 4/7/1956 d Francis Hilmer Voelker & Ludmila Angela. BSN U MN 1978; Dio Minnesota Diac Prog MN 1994. D 9/8/1994 Bp Sanford Zangwill Kaye Hampton. m 9/2/1978 John Patrick Feely c 2. D La Mision El Santo Nino Jesus S Paul MN 1998-2001; D Chr Ch S Paul MN 1994-1998. Intl OSL the Physcn 2005; Natl Epis Hlth Mnstrs 2005. revmaryjo@gmail.com

FEERER, Jane Elizabeth (CNY) PO Box 3647, Coeur D Alene ID 83816 B Dayton OH 9/16/1954 d Eugene Kenneth Feerer & Gail Elizabeth. BA MI SU 1977; MDiv SWTS 1980; MBA U of Phoenix 2005. D 6/27/1980 Bp H Coleman McGehee Jr P 7/1/1981 Bp Henry Irving Mayson. Chapl Off Of Bsh For ArmdF New York NY 1988-1992; R Chr Ch Wellsburg NY 1983-1988; R Gr Ch Waverly NY 1983-1988; Cur S Mart Ch Detroit MI 1980-1981. Auth, "Compsr Promise," *Sonrise Folk Masses*.

FEHR, Thomas James (SO) 10011 Armitage Rd, Athens OH 45701 **P-in-c Gr Ch Pomeroy OH 2011-** B Shelbyville KY 7/19/1959 s James Paul Fehr & Joyce Marie. BS U of Kentucky 1982; MAR Athenaeum of Ohio 1999; MDiv Bex 2009. D 6/14/2008 P 6/20/2009 Bp Thomas Edward Breidenthal. Asst S Lk's Ch Granville OH 2009-2011; D All SS Ch Cincinnati OH 2008-2009. tjfehr@gmail.com

FEHR, Wayne L (Mil) 8220 Harwood Ave Apt 334, Wauwatosa WI 53213 B Covington KY 4/23/1938 s Peter George Fehr & Bernetta Mary. BA Xavier U 1959; MA Loyola U 1966; STL Hochschule Sankt Georgen Frankfurt DE 1970; PhD Ya 1978. Rec from Roman Catholic 6/21/1988 as Priest Bp Roger John White. R S Thos Of Cbury Ch Greendale WI 1999-2005; P-in-c S Jn The Div Epis Ch Burlington WI 1999; P-in-c S Paul's Ch Ashippun Oconomowoc WI 1994-1998; Int S Paul's Ch Milwaukee WI 1993-1994. Auth, *Sprtl Wholeness for Cler*, Alb Inst, 1993; Auth, *The Birth of the Cath Tubingen Sch*, Scholars Press, 1981. waynefehr@tds.net

FEICK, Donald Harger (CPa) 22 Black Oak Cir, Crossville TN 38558 B Avalon PA 8/4/1920 s Harry William Feick & Pearl Rachel. BS Grove City Coll 1942; U So 1949. D 7/1/1959 P 6/29/1960 Bp John T Heistand. m 7/1/1989 Geraldine Stansbery c 3. Vic Chr Ch Rugby TN 1996-2000; R Trin Ch Coshocton OH 1993-1994; R Trin Epis Ch Chambersburg PA 1975-1986; Vic All SS Ch Coudersport PA 1971-1975; R Chr Ch Coudersport PA 1971-1975; Chair Dio Delaware Wilmington DE 1970-1971; R S Ptr's Ch Smyrna DE 1966-1971; R S Lk's Epis Ch Mt Joy PA 1962-1966; Vic Ch of the Nativ-St Steph Newport PA 1959-1962; Vic St Stephens Epis Ch Thompsontown PA 1959-1962. dongere@fairfieldglade.com

FEIDER, Paul A (FdL) 1511 Cedarhurst Dr, New London WI 54961 **Vic S Jn's Epis Ch New London WI 1997-** B Sheboygan WI 2/20/1951 s Wilmer Nicholas Feider & Marcella Loretta. BA U of Innsbruck Austria 1973; MA S Fran Sem 1977; CAS Nash 1995. Rec 5/21/1995 as Priest Bp Russell Edward Jacobus. m 5/27/1995 Julie J Murray c 2. Vic S Jn's Ch Shawano WI 1997-2003; Vic Ch Of The Heav Rest Princeton WV 1995-1997. Auth, "Resting in the Heart," 2001; Auth, "Sacraments: Encountering the Risen Lord," 1986; Auth, "Journey to Inner Peace," 1984; Auth, "Paul's Letters for Today's Chr," 1982; Auth, "Healing & Suffering," 1980. Assn of Chr Therapists 1979; Ord of S Lk 1996. frfeider@juno.com

FELICETTI, Elizabeth Marshall (SVa) 1217 Yarbrough Way, Virginia Beach VA 23455 **R S Dav's Epis Ch Richmond VA 2011-** B Phoenix AZ 2/23/1968 d James Rutherland Lord Marshall & Betty Udell. BA U of Arizona 1990;

MDiv VTS 2007. D 6/9/2007 P 12/8/2007 Bp John Clark Buchanan. m 10/19/1996 Gary Felicetti. Assoc Old Donation Ch Virginia Bch VA 2007-2011. efelicetti@cox.net

FELLHAUER, Edward (Miss) 1165 Columbine Cir, Salina KS 67401 **Dn/Pres S Fran Cmnty Serv Inc. Salina KS 2002-** B Kansas City MO 11/18/1946 s William Howard Fellhauer & Maxine Rose. BA U of Missouri 1968; MA U of Missouri 1970; MDiv Epis TS of The SW 1987. D 6/3/1987 Bp Richard Frank Grein P 12/21/1987 Bp John Herbert MacNaughton. m 1/28/1989 Sheila Rose Barber c 2. Reg VP S Fran Acad Inc. Salina KS 1994-2002; Chapl S Fran Acad Inc. Salina KS 1993-1994; St. Bede's Vic Dio Oklahoma Oklahoma City OK 1991-1994; Int S Matt's Ch Enid OK 1989-1990; Asst R S Alb's Ch Harlingen TX 1987-1989. Auth, "Column," *SFCS Web-site Highlights*, St. Fran Com Serv, 2011; Auth, "Column," *SFCS Web-site*, St. Franics Com Serv, 2010; Auth, "Pres's Report," *Highlights*, St. Fran Com Serv, 2009; Auth, "Pres's Column," *Highlights*, St Fran Com Serv, 2008; Auth, "Pres's column," *Highlights*, St Fran Cmnty Serv, 2007; Auth, "Cir ," *Highlights*, St. Fran Com Serv, 2006; Auth, "Cir ," *Highlights*, St. Fran Com Serv, 2005; Auth, "Cir ," *Highlights*, SFA, 2004; Auth, "Cir ," *Highlights*, SFA, 2003; Auth, "Pres's Cir ," *Highlights mag*, The S Fran Acad, 2002; Auth, "Preventing Abuse," *Preventing Chld Sexual Abuse: Creating Safer Environ*, The S Fran Acad, 1997; Auth, "Developmental Disabil," *Paradigm mag*, The S Fran Acad, 1995; Auth, "Corporal Punishment - Blistering Issue or Wrong Tool?," *AHEC News*, AHEC, 1991. Chld Welf League of Amer 2002; Epis Cmnty Serv 2002; MS Assn Chld Care Agencies 1995-2003; Natl Assn Hm & Serv for Chld 1996-2000. Serv Awd St. Fran Cmnty Serv 2010; Excellence In Action St. Fran Cmnty Serv 2010; Serv Awd The S Fran Acad 2004; Serv Awd St. Matt's Enid Okalhama 1991; Bd Awd The Shpd Cntr,Texas 1989. edf@st-francis.org

FELLHAUER, Sheila Rose (Miss) 1165 Columbine Cir, Salina KS 67401 **Chapl for Sprtl Wellness S Fran Cmnty Serv Inc. Salina KS 2004-** B Saint Louis MO 12/18/1945 d George Emory Barber & Alpha Lorraine. MA U of Missouri 1967; BA U of Missouri 1967; MDiv Epis TS of The SW 1987. D 6/20/1987 P 3/1/1988 Bp Gerald Nicholas McAllister. m 1/28/1989 Edward Fellhauer c 2. P-in-c Epis Ch Of The Incarn Salina KS 2004-2008; R S Paul's Epis Ch Picayune MS 2000-2003; Int R The Epis Ch Of The Medtr Meridian MS 1997-1998; Chapl S Fran Acad Inc. Salina KS 1996-1999; P-in-c S Dunst's Ch Tulsa OK 1991-1995; Vic S Jn's Epis Ch Woodward OK 1987-1991. Auth, "Come Join in The Search: Lenten Meditations," *S Fran Cmnty Serv*, SFCS Pub, 2011; Auth, "Can I Walk My Dog In Heaven?: Chld's Spiritually," *S Fran Cmnty Serv*, SFCS Pub, 2010; Auth, "Alleluia! Chr Is Risen!: Eastertide Meditations," *S Fran Cmnty Serv*, SFCS Pub, 2009; Auth, "Ther In Chr," *S Fran Cmnty Serv*, SFCS Pub, 2009; Auth, "Unto Us A Chld is b: Christmastide Mediations," *S Fran Cmnty Serv*, SFCS Pub, 2007; Auth, "On the Path of God's Ways/ A Lenten Journey: Lenten Mediations," *S Fran Cmnty Serv*, SFCS Pub, 2007; Auth, "All Creatures of Our God and King, Lift Up Your Voices, Let us Sing!," *The S Fran Acad*, The S Fran Acad, 2006; Auth, "Sing Alleluia Above the Treetops! Sing Alleluia to the Sun!," *The S Fran Acad*, The S Fran Acad, 2005; Auth, "Lord Make Me an Instrument of your Peace," *The S Fran Acad*, The S Fran Acad, 2004; Auth, "Twelve Gifts of Christmas: Christmastide Mediations," *The S Fran Acad*, The S Fran Acad, 2004. sheila.fellhauer@st-francis.org

FELLOWS, Richard Greer (SwFla) 15801 Country Lake Drive, Tampa FL 33624 **P-in-c S Jn's Epis Ch Brooksville FL 2011-** B Douglas AZ 5/4/1958 s William Greer Fellows & Helen Elizabeth. BS U of Arizona 1980; MDiv VTS 1983. D 5/29/1983 P 12/14/1983 Bp Joseph Thomas Heistand. m 1/17/2006 Laura M Magnon c 2. Cur S Mary's Par Tampa FL 2005-2010; R Ch Of The Annunc Holmes Bch FL 1989-2000; Vic S Jn's Ch Centralia IL 1985-1988; Vic S Thos Ch Salem IL 1985-1988; Assoc R Chr Ch Springfield IL 1983-1985. richardgfellows@me.com

FELLOWS, Robert Hayden (Okla) 516 West 3rd, Stillwater OK 74074 B Tulsa OK 11/16/1944 s Charles Ray Fellows & Evelyn Hayden. BA U of Tulsa 1967; MDiv Epis TS of The SW 1970. D 6/20/1970 P 12/20/1970 Bp Chilton Powell. m 6/21/1968 Kathryn Dains c 2. R S Andr's Ch Stillwater OK 1988-2011; R The Epis Ch Of The H Apos Moore OK 1978-1988; S Elis's Ch Oklahoma City OK 1971-1975; Cur S Lk's Epis Ch Bartlesville OK 1970-1978. fellows@bright.ok.net

FELS, Charles Wentworth Baker (ETenn) 850 Volunteer Landing Ln, Knoxville TN 37915 **R Ch Of The Gd Shpd Knoxville TN 2006-** B Cincinnati OH 2/26/1943 s Rendgis Thomas Fels & Beatrice Baker. VTS; BA Stan 1965; MA Van 1972; JD Van 1974; MDiv EDS 2005. D 6/18/2005 P 1/28/2006 Bp Charles Glenn VonRosenberg. m 5/20/2005 Susan Sgarlat c 2. Adj D and P S Barth's Ch New York NY 2005-2006; Sem S Alb's Par Washington DC 2003-2005. charlesfels@mac.com

FELSOVANYI, Andrea (NCal) 4 Bishop Ln, Menlo Park CA 94025 B Chicago IL 4/18/1947 d Anthony Felsovanyi & Shirley. BS MI SU 1973; JD Antioch Sch Law 1976; MDiv Ya Berk 1995; STM Ya Berk 1998. D 6/13/1998 Bp Clarence Nicholas Coleridge P 1/1/1999 Bp Richard Lester Shimpfky. Ch Of Our Sav Mill Vlly CA 2005-2006; S Aid's Ch San Francisco CA 2004-2005; Ch Of The Ascen Vallejo CA 2003-2005; H Cross Epis Ch Castro Vlly CA 2001-2002; Epis Sr Communities Walnut Creek CA 1999-2001; S Lk's Ch Los Gatos CA 1999-2001. SCHC.

FELTON, Paul D (Tex) 707 Venice St, Sugar Land TX 77478 B Chicago IL 5/20/1924 s Henry Dunbar Felton & Lucy. BA Ripon Coll Ripon WI 1949; BD Nash 1952; PhD Marq 1968. D 7/1/1952 P 12/1/1952 Bp Wallace E Conkling. m 6/7/1952 Mary Yerkish c 5. All SS Epis Ch Stafford TX 1992-1993; Ch Of The Redeem Houston TX 1982-1992; Asst Ch Of The Redeem Houston TX 1972-1974; Cur The Ch Of The H Sprt Lake Forest IL 1952-1954. Auth, "Renwl," *Theol Renwl & Towards Renwl*. pdfelton@academicplanet.com

FELTY, Rose Ann (Alb) PO Box 114, Columbiaville NY 12050 **S Jn The Evang Columbiaville NY 2010-** B San Antonio TX 11/12/1954 d Fred C Felty & Erma D. BA St Mary's U 1977; MDiv Nash Theol Sem 2010. D 6/5/2010 Bp William Howard Love. feltyroseann@yahoo.com

FENHAGEN II, James Corner (NY) 395 Timberview Ct, Pawleys Island SC 29585 B 11/4/1929 s Frank Fenhagen & Mary. BA U So 1951; BD VTS 1954. D 6/25/1954 P 3/31/1955 Bp Noble C Powell. m 7/14/1950 Eulalie McFall c 3. ECF Inc New York NY 1992-1994; Dn The GTS New York NY 1978-1992; Dce Dio Washington Washington DC 1963-1967; Cur Ch Of The H Nativ Baltimore MD 1954-1955. Auth, "More Than Wanderers"; Auth, "Mutual Mnstry"; Auth, "Invitation To Holiness"; Auth, "Mnstry & Solitude"; Auth, "Mnstry For New Time". DD Washington And Lee 1990; DD U So 1986; DD Virgina TS 1978. efenhagen@yahoo.com

FENLON, Mathew Charles (CFla) PO Box 605, Gladstone NJ 07934 **S Jn The Div Houston TX 2010-** B Dayton OH 4/27/1979 s William Fenlon & Linda. BSS Ohio U 2003; MDiv TESM 2008. D 5/31/2008 Bp John Wadsworth Howe P 5/2/2009 Bp George Edward Councell. m 10/8/2010 Jessica Fenlon. Cur S Lk's Ch Gladstone NJ 2008-2010. mfenlon@sjd.org

FENN, Richard Kimball (Pa) 34 Edgehill St., Princeton NJ 08540 B Oberlin OH 1/5/1934 s Percy Thomas Fenn & Caroline Elizabeth. BA Ya 1955; BD EDS 1958; ThM PrTS 1966; PhD Bryn 1970. D 5/30/1958 P 12/1/1958 Bp Nelson Marigold Burroughs. m 6/1/1956 Caroline Yale White c 3. P-in-c S Phil's Ch New Hope PA 1966-1970; Vic Ch Of The Epiph Royersford PA 1963-1966; Cur Ch Of Our Sav Akron OH 1958-1960. Auth, "The Death Of Herod"; Auth, "The End Of Time".

FENN, Richard Lewis (WNY) RR 1 Box 323, Edgartown MA 02539 B Cleveland OH 3/2/1934 s Fred M Fenn & Sarah. Oxf; BA Ken 1957; BD EDS 1964. D 6/20/1964 P 1/1/1965 Bp Robert McConnell Hatch. m 5/19/1984 Marcia K Sullivan c 2. Dn Dio Wstrn New York Tonawanda NY 1984-1998; R S Lk's Epis Ch Jamestown NY 1976-1998; Dn Dio Wstrn Massachusetts Springfield MA 1972-1973; R Epis Ch Of The Epiph Wilbraham MA 1967-1976; Cur S Steph's Ch Pittsfield MA 1964-1967. msfenn@comcast.net

FENNER, Renee Lynette (Mo) 1012 Advocate Ct, Florissant MO 63034 **COM Dio Missouri S Louis MO 2011-; R S Barn Ch Florissant MO 2010-** B Saint Louis MO 8/2/1954 d Walter Fenner & Irene. BA Webster U 1976; MDiv GTS 2005. D 12/22/2004 P 6/24/2005 Bp George Wayne Smith. Cn Pstr, Liturg, Adult Formation Chr Ch Cathd S Louis MO 2005-2010. rfennersbarnabas@sbcglobal.net

FENTERS JR, LaVerne Harold (SC) 1915 Pinopolis Road, Pinopolis SC 29469 **R Trin Epis Ch Pinopolis SC 2004-** B Florence SC 9/30/1951 s LaVerne Harold Fenters & Dorothy Elwyne. BS Cit 1973; MDiv STUSo 1999. D 6/6/1999 P 12/5/1999 Bp Edward Lloyd Salmon Jr. m 6/12/1982 Laura Elizabeth Dekle c 2. Assoc R Old S Andr's Par Ch Charleston SC 1999-2004.

FENTON, Arnold Aidan (SanD) 9815 Circa Valle Verde, El Cajon CA 92021 B Westfield NJ 3/28/1927 s Arnold Alexander Fenton & Carla. BA Laf 1948; MDiv GTS 1951. D 6/10/1951 Bp Horace W B Donegan P 12/15/1951 Bp William A Lawrence. m 12/4/1974 Barbara B Burrows c 3. P-in-c S Dav's Epis Ch San Diego CA 2000-2001; R The Par Of S Matt Pacific Palisades CA 1979-1990; R All Souls' Epis Ch San Diego CA 1973-1979; R Chr Ch Grosse Pointe Grosse Pointe Farms MI 1969-1973; R Chr Ch Tacoma WA 1961-1969; R S Steph's Epis Ch Longview WA 1955-1961; Cur Chr Ch Cathd Springfield MA 1951-1953. bfentonbbf@aol.com

FENTON, David Henry (SanD) 3962 Josh St, Eugene OR 97402 B Los Angeles CA 2/23/1931 s Melville Fenton & Helen Grace. BA U of Redlands 1952; MDiv Nash 1969. D 9/13/1969 P 3/21/1970 Bp Francis E I Bloy. m 8/23/1952 Jean Burnight c 2. Cler Salary Revs Dio San Diego San Diego CA 1974-1994; R S Jn's Ch Fallbrook CA 1972-1996; Cur S Lk's Of The Mountains La Crescenta CA 1969-1972. Auth, "The 1940-1982 Hymnal Cross-Reference"; Auth, *Bdgt Press Calendar*; Auth, *Liturg Desk Calendar*, Franklin X. McCormick. fentondh@aol.com

FENTON, Eric Denis (WTex) 14207 Bold Ruler St, San Antonio TX 78248 **R Gr Ch Cuero TX 2011-** B Croswell MI 8/15/1948 s Omar Mills Fenton & Jeane Denison. BA MI SU 1975; MDiv TESM 1981. D 6/21/1981 P 5/9/1982 Bp Charles Farmer Duvall. m 7/2/1988 Janet Etzwiler c 5. P-in-c Chr Ch in the Hill Country Bulverde TX 2008-2009; Asst R Chr Epis Ch San Antonio TX 2003-2007; Chapl Off Of Bsh For ArmdF New York NY 1987-2003; Vic All

SS Ch Prudenville MI 1983-1986; Vic S Eliz's Epis Ch Roscommon MI 1983-1986; Cur S Andr's Epis Ch Panama City FL 1981-1983. Meritorious Serv Medal USAF 2001. efenton1@me.com

FENTON, Fred Arthur (Cal) 4726 Curletto Dr, Concord CA 94521 B Los Angeles CA 4/5/1935 s Melville Fenton & Helen. BA Harv 1958; STB EDS 1961. D 9/7/1961 P 3/27/1962 Bp Francis E I Bloy. m 9/12/1954 Billie L Loit c 3. R S Jas Epis Ch Baton Rouge LA 1994-2001; Dio Louisiana Baton Rouge LA 1990-1992; R S Aug By-The-Sea Par Santa Monica CA 1971-1994; R S Mk's Epis Ch Upland CA 1969-1971; R S Jn's Epis Ch Chula Vista CA 1966-1969; Vic S Mary's/Santa Maria Virgen Imperial Bch CA 1962-1966; Cur S Jude's Epis Par Burbank CA 1961-1962. Auth, "Make invisible visible," *Epis Life*, 2009; Auth, "Foreword," *Beyond Words*, Morehouse, 2004; Auth, "Nuts and Bolts of a Stwardship Cmpgn," *The Livivng Ch*, 1996; Auth, "A New Approach for Bishops," *LivCh*, 1992; Auth, "Decade of Evang: Something seems to be Missing," *LivCh*, 1992; Auth, "Baby Boomers: How have people of this Generation been brought back to Ch?," *LivCh*, 1988; Auth, "Age of the Laity," *The Epis News*, 1973. OHC 1962; Our Lady of Walsingham 1982; SHN 1964. Fr Fred Fenton Day City of Baton Rouge 2000; Sch Chair w Plaque Crossroads Sch 1994; L.A. Cnty Recognition Bd Supervisors 1991; Mayor's Commendation City of Santa Monica 1991; Sch Chair EDS 1989; Sch Chair w Plaque EDS 1989. fentons925@sbcglobal.net

FENTON, Gordon Douglas (NY) 102-1435 Nelson Street, Vancouver BC V6G 2Z3 Canada **Dir for Mssn & Mnstry Dio New Westminster Vancouver BRITISH COLUMBIA 2011-; Campus Mnstry Com Dio New York New York City NY 2005-** B Fort Frances Ontario CA 1/4/1956 s James William Fenton & Ethel Janet. BA U of Manitoba 1977; Cert. Drug & Alco Counselling Smith Clnc, St Jos's Hosp, Thunder Bay, ON 1981; MDiv St. Jn's Coll Winnipeg CA 1981. Trans from Anglican Church of Canada 12/11/2002 Bp Mark Sean Sisk. m 8/18/2003 Keith S Landherr. Assoc Chr And S Steph's Ch New York NY 2009-2011; Asst The Ch Of S Lk In The Fields New York NY 2004-2008; Prog Off for YA & Campus Mnstrs Epis Ch Cntr New York NY 2002-2011. Auth, "In the Batey," *People of God*, Angl Ch of Can, 1994; Auth, "When the Words Stop Working," *Plumbline*, Journ of MHE, 1994; Auth, "Hope is Found in the Struggle," *People of God*, Angl Ch of Can, 1993; Auth, "From the Down Side Up," *In Lumine*, St Jn's Coll, 1992; Co-Auth, "The Jos Proj," *The Jos Proj*, Angl Ch of Can, 1984. Affirming Angl Catholicism 1998; Conf of St Ben 1979; Fllshp of St Jn the Evang 2004; Friends of the Angl Cntr-Rome 2006. Distinguished Ldrshp Awd Epis Campus Chapl 2011. gdfenton@gmail.com

FENTON, Graham R C (Minn) 4720 Zenith Ave S, Minneapolis MN 55410 B Kroonstad ZA 7/13/1949 s Albert George Fenton & Izetta Evelyn. BS U of Natal 1971; GOE S Jn's TS 1974. Trans from Church of the Province of Southern Africa 5/1/1984. m 6/15/1974 Gillian Margaret Blatch c 2. Assoc S Steph The Mtyr Ch Minneapolis MN 1993-2009; R Chr Epis Ch Grand Rapids MN 1984-1993. grcfenton@gmail.com

FENWICK, Robert Donald (SO) 6439 Bethany Village Dr., Box 307, Centerville OH 45459 B Great Falls MT 6/4/1930 s John Leopold Fenwick & Amy William. BS Winona St U 1953; MDiv Bex 1959; DD S Paul's Coll 1979. D 6/20/1959 P 12/21/1959 Bp Hamilton Hyde Kellogg. m 8/3/1952 Lois Bowen c 2. R S Paul's Epis Ch Dayton OH 1975-1995; R S Lk's Epis Ch Rochester MN 1964-1975; Assoc R Calv Ch Rochester MN 1962-1963. Hon DD S Paul'S Collete Lawrenceville VA 1979.

FEREBEE, Randolph Curtis (WNC) 127 42nd Avenue Dr NW, Hickory NC 28601 B Spartanburg SC 6/7/1947 s Curtis Audrey Ferebee & Sara Elizabeth. BA Belmont Abbey Coll 1969; MDiv VTS 1973; DMin STUSo 1999. D 5/20/1973 Bp Matthew G Henry P 11/25/1973 Bp William Gillette Weinhauer. m 5/1/1970 Judith Anne Raxter c 2. R S Alb's Ch Hickory NC 1975-2009; Assoc Ch Of The Ascen Hickory NC 1973-1975. ferebee@charter.net

FERGUESON, John Frederick (Oly) 14449 90th Ct Ne, Bothell WA 98011 **R Ch Of The Redeem Kenmore WA 1983-** B Jackson MI 8/6/1944 s Carl Fergueson & Doris. BA Albion Coll 1966; MDiv SWTS 1972. D 5/27/1972 Bp Charles Ellsworth Bennison Jr P 12/1/1972 Bp Charles Bennison. m 2/4/1967 Virginia Amrein. R Emm Ch Hastings MI 1979-1983; Dio Wstrn Michigan Kalamazoo MI 1976-1979; S Mich's Ch Grand Rapids MI 1972-1976. Auth, "A Man Of Sorrows," *Familar w Suffering*. Natl Conf Viet Nam Veteran Ministers. JFERGUESON@AOL.COM

FERGUSON, Anthony David (Fla) St. Peter's Church, 5042 Timuquana Road, Jacksonville FL 32210 **R S Ptr's Ch Jacksonville FL 1993-** B London UK 4/10/1951 s Norman Malcolm Ferguson & Stella Marie-Therese. HNC1 Ewell Coll 1972; CTh Oxf 1978. Trans from Church Of England 7/1/1980 as Priest Bp William Gillette Weinhauer. m 9/7/1985 Norma Glennon c 3. Sm Ch Cmsn Dio No Carolina Raleigh NC 1984-1993; R S Marg's Epis Ch Waxhaw NC 1984-1993; R S Jn's Epis Ch Marion NC 1980-1984. adnf51@hotmail.com

FERGUSON, Dina McMullin (Los) 1818 Monterey Blvd, Hermosa Beach CA 90254 B Inglewood CA 3/3/1951 d Patricia. BA USC 1973; MS USC 1977; DMin Untd TS 2007; CAS Chuch DS of the Pacific 2008. D 1/21/2009 P 7/25/2009 Bp Joseph Jon Bruno. m 7/2/1972 David Ferguson c 2. dmferguson@earthlink.net

FERGUSON, Dru (NwT) 510 Newell Ave, Dallas TX 75223 B Las Vegas NM 7/24/1943 d Cloma Alexander Huffman & Nancy Ann. BA Arizona St U 1965; Med Arizona St U 1969; MDiv Epis TS of The SW 1994. D 6/25/1994 P 6/24/1995 Bp James Monte Stanton. m 11/10/1973 Ronald Dean Ferguson c 1. S Ptr's Epis Ch Amarillo TX 2007-2009; Asst for Pstr Care S Andr's Epis Ch Amarillo TX 2004-2006; S Ptr's Epis Ch Amarillo TX 2004-2006; S Paul's Epis Ch Dallas TX 2003-2004; Cbury Epis Sch Desoto TX 1998-2003; Int S Mths' Epis Ch Athens TX 1998-1999; Asst The Epis Ch Of The Trsfg Dallas TX 1996-1998; Cur S Paul's Epis Ch Dallas TX 1994-1996. DOK 1992; NECA 1994-2000; NEAC 1994-2001; Ord Of S Lk 2000. mtrdru@yahoo.com

FERGUSON, Fred-Munro (Alb) 6 Spences Trce, Harwich MA 02645 B Montclair NJ 5/14/1934 s Allan Nixon Ferguson & Gizella Angela. BA Westminster Choir Coll of Rider U 1956; PDS 1958. D 5/23/1959 P 12/19/1959 Bp Donald MacAdie. R Ch Of S Sacrement Bolton Landing NY 1980-1993; Trst Dio Dio Albany Albany NY 1980-1984; COM Dio Albany Albany NY 1980-1983; Mus Cmsn Dio Albany Albany NY 1975-1979; R S Mk's Epis Ch Philmont NY 1975-1979; Secy to Bp Dio Albany Albany NY 1974-1979; Cur S Lk's Ch Catskill NY 1971-1975; Ch Of The Trsfg No Bergen NJ 1966-1971; Ch Of The Trsfg No Bergen NJ 1960-1962; Cur S Jas Ch Upper Montclair NJ 1959-1960. Osf 1964-1965; SSC 1984; Ssc. frfergusonssc@comcast.net

FERGUSON, Judith Ann (NY) 391 Main St, Highland Falls NY 10928 **R H Innoc Highland Falls NY 2001-** B Drexel Hill PA 7/12/1952 d Robert Warren Ferguson & Pauline Lillian. AA/BS Philadelphia Coll of Bible 1974; MFA NYU 1980; MDiv STUSo 1996. D 6/1/1996 P 12/7/1996 Bp Richard Frank Grein. Cur S Jn's Ch Larchmont NY 1997-2001; Cur Ch Of S Mary The Vrgn Chappaqua NY 1997; D S Mk's Ch Honey Brook PA 1996. Assessment Bd 2008-2009; Com of Campus Mnstry-Chapl to USMA 2002; Com to Elect a Bp 2010-2011; Congrl Spprt Plan Com 2010; Congrl Spprt Plan Committtee 2006-2008; Mid-Hudson Reg Coun 2003-2004; Prov Syn Dep 2001-2003. tobyferg@hotmail.com

FERGUSON JR, Lawrence C (EO) Po Box 1344, Prineville OR 97754 B Pittsfield MA 11/20/1934 s Lawrence Cooley Ferguson & Effie Stella. BA Hav 1957; STB EDS 1960. D 6/4/1960 Bp William A Lawrence P 12/9/1960 Bp Lane W Barton. m 6/28/1959 Anna Rita Stiles c 3. Cntrl OR Mssnr Dio Estrn Oregon The Dalles OR 1992-1996; Dio Estrn Oregon The Dalles OR 1991-1996; COM Dio Estrn Oregon The Dalles OR 1988-1994; S Andr's Epis Ch Prineville OR 1986-1991; R The Par Of S Mk The Evang Hood River OR 1968-1986; Vic S Mk's Epis and Gd Shpd Luth Madras OR 1960-1968; Vic S Alb's Epis Ch Redmond OR 1960-1961. laranna@crestviewcable.com

FERGUSON, Leslie Clark (SVa) 5537 Greenefield Dr S, Portsmouth VA 23703 **R S Jn's Ch Suffolk VA 2010-** B Long Beach, CA 12/8/1962 s Michael Blackburn Ferguson & Carolyn Rose. BS OR SU 1985; MS Naval Post Grad Sch 1993; MA NAVAC War Coll 2002; MDiv VTS 2010. D 6/12/2010 P 12/18/2010 Bp Herman Hollerith IV. m 10/1/1983 Kathleen Mary Kathleen Mary Thomas. les.ferguson62@verizon.net

FERGUSON SR, Michael Blackburn (SVa) 900 Fleet Drive #287, Virginia Beach VA 23454 **Co-Pstr Ch Of H Apos Virginia Bch VA 2009-** B Baker City OR 4/8/1939 s Harold Leslie Ferguson & Vivienne Charlotte. BS Estrn Oregon U 1960; MDiv VTS 1993. D 6/12/1993 Bp Peter James Lee P 12/18/1993 Bp Donald Purple Hart. m 12/27/1959 Carolyn Rose Muller c 3. Stndg Com Dio Sthrn Virginia Norfolk VA 2008-2011; R S Anne's Ch Appomattox VA 1996-2008; Vic S Annes Ch Mililani HI 1993-1996. Auth, "Ethical Implications of Fetal Tissue Cell Resrch & Ther," *Harris Prize Essay*, 1994; Auth, *ATR*. mferguson2@cox.net

FERGUSON, Raymond Arthur (Ore) 3602 Hawthorne Ln, Tillamook OR 97141 **Died 9/26/2010** B Cheshire MA 11/24/1936 s Lawrence Cooley Ferguson & Effie. Amer Intl Coll. D 9/6/1967 P 4/1/1968 Bp Lane W Barton. c 3. fergray55@embarqmail.com

FERGUSON, Ronald L (Chi) 818 Metz Ln, Rockton IL 61072 B Chicago IL 12/10/1935 s Earl Ferguson & Lucile. AA Gateway Tech Kenosha WI 1964; Sem Chicago IL 1991. D 12/7/1991 Bp Frank Tracy Griswold III. m 8/15/1981 Christine Ulmer. ferguson01@charter.net

FERGUSON, Ruth Ephgrave (Roch) 377 Rector Pl Apt 95, New York NY 10280 **R Chr Ch Rochester NY 2008-** B Murfreesboro TN 6/5/1968 d Franklin Cole Ferguson & Elizabeth Ewel. BA Warren Wilson Coll 1991; MDiv GTS 1997. D 5/31/1997 P 4/1/1998 Bp William George Burrill. m 6/22/1991 Samuel Alexander Sommers c 2. The Ch Of S Lk In The Fields New York NY 1999-2002; Asst R S Jn's Ch Olney MD 1997-1999. rutheph@aol.com

FERGUSON, Sheila Louise Ellen (Chi) 1709 Indian Knoll Rd, Naperville IL 60565 B Windsor ON CA 8/26/1944 d Eric Bertram Saward & Mary Forsythe. Cert London Teachers Coll GB 1964; BS U MI 1969; MA U MI 1971; MDiv SWTS 1989. D 8/19/1989 Bp William Grant Black P 3/8/1990 Bp Frank Tracy Griswold III. m 8/29/1970 Ronald J Ferguson c 3. Calv Ch Lombard IL 2006-2008; S Mk's Epis Ch Glen Ellyn IL 2004-2006; Assoc Dio Chicago Chicago IL 2003-2004; Cong Dvlpmt Dio Chicago Chicago IL 1998-2002; S

Hugh Of Lincoln Epis Ch Elgin IL 1990-1991; S Barn' Epis Ch Glen Ellyn IL 1989-1997. RFerguson9@aol.com

FERGUSON, Stephen Keith (Tex) PO Box 20269, Mail Code 4-184, Houston TX 77225 B Shreveport LA 8/17/1949 s Mason Lavelle Ferguson & Wil-ladene. BS NE Louisiana U 1971; MDiv Epis TS of The SW 1994. D 6/17/1995 Bp Claude Edward Payne P 1/11/1996 Bp William Elwood Sterling. m 8/9/1969 Sandra W Willis c 3. R H Comf Epis Ch Sprg TX 1998-2011; Sprtl Dir - Curs Dio Texas Houston TX 1997-1999; Assoc S Lk's On The Lake Epis Ch Austin TX 1995-1998; Asst Chr Epis Ch Temple TX 1994-1995. 0rder of St. Lk the Physcn 1987; BroSA 1995. sonfergus@aol.com

FERGUSON, Thomas Charles (Mil) Episcopal Church Center, 815 2nd Ave., New York NY 10017 **Dn Bex Columbus OH 2011-; Epis Ch Cntr New York NY 2009-** B Weymouth MA 5/26/1969 s Donald Ferguson & Barbara. BA Wesl 1991; MDiv Ya Berk 1994; ThM H Cross TS 1997; PhD Ch DS of Pacific 2002. D 6/6/2009 Bp Mary G Miller. m 9/4/1999 Shannon Kelly c 1. Epis Ch Cntr New York NY 2009-2011. tferguson@bexley.edu

FERGUSON, Vergie Rae (Az) 1650 W Glendale Ave Apt 4103, Phoenix AZ 85021 B Phoenix AZ 1/5/1929 d Arthur Elmore Vest & Garnet Vergie. U of Arizona; BS Nthrn Arizona U 1979. D 11/7/1992 Bp Joseph Thomas Heistand. m 6/11/1947 Jay Edward Ferguson. D S Jn The Bapt Globe AZ 1999-2006; D Ch Of The Epiph Flagstaff AZ 1992-1999. DOK 1992. vergief@gmail.com

FERGUSON, Virginia Alice (Nev) 6773 W Charleston Blvd, Las Vegas NV 89146 B San Francisco CA 2/4/1932 d George Richard McGrath & Virginia Alice. D 5/28/1983 Bp Wesley Frensdorff. D S Thos Ch Las Vegas NV 1983-1988. vaf32@aol.com

FERGUSON-WAGSTAFF, Cecil Clifford (CNY) 107 Saint Ives N, Lansing MI 48906 B Meriden CT 6/22/1920 s Clifford William Wagstaff & Cora Catherine. BA U of Tennessee 1944; BD Amer Bapt Sem Chicago IL 1950; MA SWTS 1963; ThD Covington TS 1986. D 6/15/1963 Bp James Winchester Montgomery P 10/18/1963 Bp Charles Gresham Marmion. c 3. P-in-c Emm Ch Adams NY 1982-1988; P-in-c Zion Ch Adams NY 1982-1988; Gr Epis Ch Traverse City MI 1973-1982; Assoc Trin Epis Ch Grand Ledge MI 1973-1982; Gr Epis Ch Menominee MI 1964-1967; Asst S Andr's Ch Louisville KY 1963-1964. Auth, *Spectrum of Mar*, C & M Pub, 1969; Auth, *The Littlest Snow Flake*, C & M Pub, 1964. cecilcfw.1@juno.com

FERGUSSON, Margaret Austin (WNC) 200 Tabernacle Rd, Black Mountain NC 28711 B Palo Alto CA 9/20/1919 d William Grafton Austin & Frances Alice. BA Pomona Coll 1941. D 12/21/1985 Bp William Gillette Weinhauer. m 5/7/1942 John Fergusson c 4.

FERLO, Roger Albert (NY) 3737 Seminary Rd, Alexandria VA 22304 **Assoc Dn and Dir for the Inst for Chr VTS Alexandria VA 2004-** B Rome NY 10/21/1951 s Albert Mario Ferlo & Nathaline Marie. AB Colg 1973; MA Ya 1974; M.Phil. Ya 1975; PhD Ya 1979; CAS GTS 1985. D 6/8/1985 P 2/5/1986 Bp Arthur Edward Walmsley. m 7/31/1977 Anne C Harlan c 1. Trst Cathd Of St Jn The Div New York NY 2000-2005; Dep GC Dio New York New York City NY 2000-2003; R The Ch Of S Lk In The Fields New York NY 1994-2003; Pres Dioc Coun Dio Pittsburgh Monroeville PA 1989-1990; R The Ch Of The Redeem Pittsburgh PA 1987-1993; Asst and Day Sch Chapl The Ch Of The Gd Shpd Augusta GA 1985-1987. Ed, "Heaven," Seabury Press, 2007; Auth, "Sensing God," Cowley Press/Rowman and Littlefield, 2002; Auth, "This Christmas in New York," *The Tablet*, 2001; Auth, "Opening The Bible," Cowley Press/Rowman and Littlefield, 1997. DD Colg 2010; Cler Renwl Grant Lilly Endwmt 2000; Distinguished Tchg Prize Ya 1981; Whiting Fllshp in Hmnts Mrs. Giles Whiting Fndt 1976; Danforth Grad Fell Danforth Fndt 1973; Phi Beta Kappa Colg 1972. roger.ferlo@gmail.com

FERNANDEZ, Jose Pascual (NY) 107 Se Superior Way, Stuart FL 34997 **P H Faith Epis Ch Port S Lucie FL 1998-** B Guantanamo-Oriente CU 5/17/1929 s Manuel Fernandez & Carmen. BTh Seminar Pont S Basilio Magno; BTh Semina Rio U 1954; Epis TS of The SW 1982. Rec from Roman Catholic 6/1/1982 as Priest Bp Calvin Onderdonk Schofield Jr. m 9/11/1977 Olga Fernandez c 2. Vic Chr Ch Trenton NJ 1988-1994; Hisp Epis Cntr San Andres Ch Yonkers NY 1983-1988; Hisp Vic Chr Epis Ch Tarrytown NY 1982-1988; Hisp Vic Gr Ch White Plains NY 1982-1988; H Cross Epis Ch Miami FL 1982; Asst H Cross Epis Ch Miami FL 1978-1981. Auth, "Catechism For Sunday Sch At The Epis Ch"; Auth, "Conozca La Iglesia Epis"; Auth, "The Mssn". Assn Of Natl Profsnl Hispanics.

FERNANDEZ, Linda Jean Pell (Md) 1930 Brookdale Rd, Baltimore MD 21244 B Exeter NH 6/11/1955 d Arthur Bowker Pell & Beryle Wynn. BS Cntr Coll 1977; MDiv SWTS 1981; MS U IL 1984. D 6/13/1981 Bp Addison Hosea P 7/1/1982 Bp Quintin Ebenezer Primo Jr. m 9/5/1980 Rodolfo Fernandez c 3. S Thos Epis Ch Towson MD 2009-2011; Gr Luth Ch Westminster MD 2004-2005; R Epis Ch Of Chr The King Windsor Mill MD 1997-2004; P-in-c Gr Ch Everett MA 1992-1996; Assoc S Paul's Ch Malden MA 1990-1992; Ch Of The H Trin Marlborough MA 1989; Assoc S Paul's Ch Lynnfield MA 1988-1990; R S Bride's Epis Ch Oregon IL 1986-1988; St Barn Urban Cntr Chicago IL 1985; Cathd Shltr Chicago IL 1981-1983; Asst S Mart's Ch Chicago IL 1981-1983. Auth, "A Handbook On Dom Violence For Cler". Mec Sec Convenor. Natl Assn Female Execs. ecctk@erols.com

FERNANDEZ-LIRANZO, Hipolito Secundino (DR) Calle 10 No. 30, Villa Olga, Santiago Dominican Republic B Salcedo 3/30/1929 s Secundino Fernandez Camilo & Ana Rosa. BTh Sem Pontificio Sto Tomas de Aquino 1958; U Nacl Pedro Henriquez Urena 1972. Rec from Roman Catholic 10/1/1984 as Priest Bp Telesforo A Isaac. m 12/25/1971 Dulcina Natividad Tejada c 3. Vic Iglesia Epis San Lucas Santiago CL 1989-2002; Dio The Dominican Republic (Iglesia Epis Dominicana) Santo Domingo DO 1984-2000; Iglesia Epis Cristo el Rey San Felipe de Puerto Plat DO 1984-1988. nativi_04@yahoo.com

FERNANDEZ-POLA, Rosali (PR) PO Box 23, Peñuelas PR 00624 B Ponce Puerto Rico 10/28/1945 s Francisco Fernandez Rodriguez & Emma. D 8/12/1972 P 5/5/1993 Bp Francisco Reus-Froylan. m 12/24/1974 Ida Rosario.

FERNANDEZ REINA, Hipolito (DR) Jesus Nazareno, Calle La Cruz Esq Ingeniero Guzman Abrea, San Francisco De Maloris Dominican Republic **Dio The Dominican Republic (Iglesia Epis Dominicana) Santo Domingo DO 2006-** B Santiago DR 2/25/1974 D 2/5/2005 P 2/12/2006 Bp Julio Cesar Holguin-Khoury. m 12/25/1996 Lilian Mercedes Perez c 3. schizzo28@msn.com

FERNER, David Raymond (Ind) 201 W King St, Franklin IN 46131 **R S Thos Ch Franklin IN 2003-** B Newark NJ 10/1/1947 s Arthur Ferner & Hazel. BA Montclair St U 1969; MDiv EDS 1972; DMin Bos 1995. D 6/10/1972 Bp Leland Stark P 12/20/1972 Bp Morris Fairchild Arnold. m 8/29/1970 Betty Gemmer c 3. Dnry Dn Dio Indianapolis Indianapolis IN 2006-2011; COM Dio Indianapolis Indianapolis IN 2003-2009; R Dio Upper So Carolina Columbia SC 1998-2003; R H Trin Par Epis Clemson SC 1998-2003; S Paul's Pendleton Clemson SC 1997-2003; R All SS Ch Chelmsford MA 1988-1998; COM Dio Bethlehem Bethlehem PA 1984-1987; R All SS Epis Ch Lehighton PA 1981-1988; R S Jn's Epis Ch Palmerton PA 1981-1988; Dioc Coun Dio Massachusetts Boston MA 1979-1981; R Trin Ch Marshfield Hills MA 1976-1981; Asst Chr Ch Needham MA 1972-1975. Fllshp Soc Of S Jn The Evang 1992. drferner47@gmail.com

FERREL, Artis Louise (Ia) 15102 Pinehurst Dr, Council Bluffs IA 51503 B Council Bluffs IA 7/11/1929 d Arthur Leslie Rowley & Olga Josephine. Mnstry Formation Prog 2000. D 6/3/2000 P 12/9/2000 Bp Carl Christopher Epting. m 10/7/1974 Carl Dewayne Ferrel.

FERRELL, Davis Marion (NCal) 515 Nursery St, Nevada City CA 95959 **D H Trin Ch NEVADA CITY CA 1998-** B Long Beach CA 2/6/1937 s Harold Marion Ferrell & Ruth Davis. BA California St U 1966; MA Chapman U 1972; CDSP 1986. D 5/10/1998 Bp Jerry Alban Lamb. m 8/8/1959 Doretta Gladys Rowell c 2. xcpodave@sbcglobal.net

FERRELL, Nathan Wilson (NJ) 424 East Third St, Moorestown NJ 08057 **R Ch Of The Ascen Gloucester City NJ 2009-; Vic of Shared Mnstry H Sprt Bellmawr NJ 2009-** B Mount Holly, New Jersey 8/10/1972 s Robert William Ferrell & Desma Wilson. BA U of Vermont 1995; MDiv Bapt TS at Richmond 1998. D 6/15/2002 P 12/16/2002 Bp Peter James Lee. m 6/25/1994 Erin McGee c 3. Vic of Shared Mnstry S Lk's Ch Westville NJ 2009-2011; Trin Ch Topsfield MA 2003-2005; Assoc R S Geo's Ch Fredericksburg VA 2002-2003. nathanferrell@msn.com

FERRELL, Sean Daniel (WTenn) 309 E Baltimore St, Jackson TN 38301 **Chair of COM Dio W Tennessee Memphis TN 2009-; S Lk's Epis Ch Jackson TN 2006-** B Kansas City KS 1/26/1972 s Max Albert Ferrell & Kay. BA Ottawa U 1996; MDiv STUSo 1999. D 6/26/1999 Bp Barry Robert Howe P 2/5/2000 Bp Frank Kellogg Allan. m 2/6/1999 Kiezha Nichole Smith c 2. Cbury MI SU E Lansing MI 2003-2006; Chapl Emm Epis Ch Athens GA 1999-2002; Chapl S Mary's Chap Athens GA 1999-2002. ferrellsd@mindspring.com

FERRER, Gabriel Vincente (Los) All Saints Parish, 504 N Camden Dr, Beverly Hills CA 90210 **Sr Assoc R All SS Par Beverly Hills CA 2006-** B Santa Monica CA 8/1/1957 s Jose Ferrer & Rosemary. D 6/3/2006 P 1/6/2007 Bp Joseph Jon Bruno. m 9/1/1979 Debby Ferrer c 4. Assoc All SS Par Beverly Hills CA 1997-2006. gferrer@allsaintsbh.org

FERRIANI, Nancy Ann (Ind) 5010 Washington Blvd, Indianapolis IN 46205 **Sr Assoc Trin Ch Indianapolis IN 1988-** B Winthrop MA 1/23/1938 d George Reed & Elinor M. Cert SWTS; BD U of Kansas 1982; MDiv Chr TS 1986. D 6/24/1986 P 4/4/1997 Bp Edward Witker Jones. m 7/27/1956 Robert Ferriani. Dep Gc Dio Indianapolis Indianapolis IN 1994-2000; Trin Ch Indianapolis IN 1986-2009; Stndg Com Dio Indianapolis Indianapolis IN 1986-1998. OA. nferriani@aol.com

FERRITO, Michael Louis (ECR) 1391 Market St, Santa Clara CA 95050 **Vic Ch Of The H Sprt Campbell CA 2001-** B San Jose CA 6/28/1951 s Joseph Ferrito & Josephine. BA San Jose St U 1971; Mstr of Div CDSP 2001. D 6/26/1999 P 6/14/2000 Bp Richard Lester Shimpfky. m 1/20/1972 Gwen S Bonney c 3. Assoc S Thos Epis Ch Sunnyvale CA 1999-2001. revmikehs@hotmail.com

FERRO, Mauricio (Colom) Carrera 16 #94-A-30, Bogota Colombia B Bogota CO 10/14/1942 s Cesar Ferro & Isabel Calvo. ABD Harv; ThM Leopold

Franzens U At; ThD Pontifical Liturg Inst Rome It; U De Comillas Es. Rec from Roman Catholic 8/1/1995. m 3/15/1997 Olga Moreno.

FERRY, Daniel Whitney (NH) 1465 Hooksett Rd Unit 280, Hooksett NH 03106 B Hackensack NJ 8/13/1937 s Arthur Nichols Ferry & Agnus. BS VPI 1960; BD EDS 1965; MBA Rivier Coll 1998. D 6/26/1965 Bp John Melville Burgess P 6/1/1966 Bp Frederic Cunningham Lawrence. m 10/5/1996 Janet Conway Quiet c 4. P Northwood Epis Mssn Northwood NH 1993-1995; P Dio New Hampshire Concord NH 1991-1993; P Gr Ch Manchester NH 1988-1989; R Ch Of Our Sav Milford NH 1968-1986. ferrydw@aol.com

FERRY, Margaret Lee (Vt) 16 Pearl St, East Bridgewater MA 02333 **P-in-c S Jn The Bapt Epis Hardwick VT 2009-** B Abington PA 9/23/1950 d John Stiger Ferry & Margaret Darling. MDiv EDS; BA Mid. D 6/17/1976 P 5/1/1977 Bp Lloyd Edward Gressle. m 7/21/1984 Charles Colburn Wohlers. Int S Thos' Epis Ch Brandon VT 2006-2009; S Dav's Epis Ch Halifax MA 1993-1997; S Jn's/S Steph's Ch Fall River MA 1984-1985; Trin Ch Concord MA 1979-1983; Mssnr To YA All SS Par Brookline MA 1978-1979.

FERTIG, Gary P (Chi) 1133 N La Salle Dr, Chicago IL 60610 **R Ch Of The Ascen Chicago IL 1996-** B Bronx NY 11/6/1951 s Peter Fertig & Isabelle. BA Iona Coll 1973; MDiv Nash 1976. D 6/5/1976 P 12/18/1976 Bp Jonathan Goodhue Sherman. Vic S Thos Ch New York NY 1977-1995; Asst to Dn Nash Nashotah WI 1976-1977. gpfertig@sbcglobal.net

FESQ, John Alfred (Mass) 35 High St Apt 14, Marlborough MA 01752 B Bronx NY 3/8/1931 s Robert Maxwell Fesq & Emilie. BA FD 1964; MDiv VTS 1967. D 6/10/1967 Bp Leland Stark P 12/13/1967 Bp George E Rath. m 6/13/1964 Joan E Johnson c 1. Supplement Accounts Boston MA 1971-1977; R Ch Of The Gd Shpd Dedham MA 1969-1997; Cur Chr Ch Quincy MA 1967-1969. yyolowl@aol.com

FESSLER, Robert H (Mil) 2275 De Carlin Dr, Brookfield WI 53045 B Milwaukee WI 7/8/1939 s Henry Leo Fessler & Jeanette Elizabeth. BA S Fran Major Sem 1961. Rec from Roman Catholic 10/1/1986 Bp Roger John White. m 8/17/1974 Patricia Janusz. S Tim's Ch Milwaukee WI 1991-2011. rffrpapa@wi.rr.com

FETTERHOFF, Ira Lincoln (Md) 111450 Asbury Circle #333, Solomons MD 20688 **Died 3/5/2011** B Baltimore,MD 10/5/1928 s Ira Lincoln Fetterhoff & Mary Alice. BA Carroll Coll 1951; Nash 1952; MDiv PDS 1954; MD U of Maryland 1967. D 6/25/1954 P 3/31/1955 Bp Noble C Powell. c 2. fetterhoff.barbara@comcast.net

FETTERMAN, James Harry (WLa) 11130 122nd Street, South Ozone Park NY 11420 B Bloomsburg PA 12/6/1945 s Lawrence Edgar Fetterman & Eleanor Esther. BA Bloomsburg U of Pennsylvania 1978; MDiv VTS 1981. D 6/12/1981 Bp Dean T Stevenson P 12/1/1981 Bp Charlie Fuller McNutt Jr. m 9/10/2011 Ildefonso Gonzalez-Rivera. Int Trin Epis Ch Roslyn NY 2003; Cn S Mk's Cathd Shreveport LA 1998-2002; R Chr Memi Epis Ch Danville PA 1985-1998; Vic All SS Ch Selinsgrove PA 1981-1985; Vic S Mk's Epis Ch Northumberland PA 1981-1985. FATHERFET2@AOL.COM

FETTERMAN, John J (Pgh) 1446 Maple Ave, Verona PA 15147 B Harrisburg PA 7/4/1937 s John Joseph Fetterman & Frances Genevieve. BA S Chas Sem Philadelphia PA 1959; STL Gregorian U 1963; MA U Pgh 1972; MLS U Pgh 1975. Rec from Roman Catholic 3/23/1978 as Priest Bp Robert Bracewell Appleyard. m 10/20/1975 Catherine Sands c 1. R Gr Ch Madison WI 1991-2002. jkfetter@comcast.net

FETZ, Robert Derrick (WMass) 1419 Grimes Cir, Urbana OH 43078 B Springfield OH 12/18/1980 s Robert Dix Fetz & Sheila. MDiv SWTS; BA Otterbein Coll 2004. D 5/13/2006 Bp Kenneth Lester Price P 6/16/2007 Bp Thomas Edward Breidenthal. m 6/21/2008 Jamie Ann Fetz. S Mary Magd Ch Maineville OH 2009-2011; E Cntrl Ohio Area Mnstry Cambridge OH 2007-2008. derrick.fetz@gmail.com

FEUERSTEIN, Paul Bruck (NY) 431 E 118th St, New York NY 10035 **Pres/CEO Barrier Free Living New York NY 2009-; Assoc Ch Of The H Trin New York NY 1977-** B Jersey City NJ 12/22/1947 s Charles Philip Feuerstein & Helen. BA Concordia Sr Coll 1969; Concordia TS 1970; MA NYU 1971; STM GTS 1973; MSW CUNY 1982. D 6/9/1973 Bp Paul Moore Jr P 12/7/1973 Bp James Stuart Wetmore. m 9/15/1979 Rebecca Ruth Eddy c 3. Chapl S Albans Sch Washington DC 1976-1977; Asst Ch Of The H Trin New York NY 1974-1976. Auth, "Disabled Wmn and Dom Violence: Notes from the Field," *Serv Delivery for Vulnerable Populations*, Springer Pub Co, 2011; Auth, "9/11 and People w Disabil," *On the Ground After September 11: Mntl Hlth Responses and Practical Knowledge Gained*, Haworth Maltreatment and Trauma Press, 2005; Auth, "Empowering Fam Ther," *Sometimes You Just Want To Feel Like a Human Being: Case Stds of Empowering Psych w People w Disabil*, Paul H Brooks, 1995; Auth, "Wmn and Chld w Disabil and Dom Violence," Milbank Memi Fund, 1986. Assoc of OHC 1971. Fell Brookdale Cntr For The Aging 1989. pbfeuerstein@gmail.com

FEUS, William Frederick (NJ) 88 Claremont Rd., Bernardsville NJ 07924 **R S Bern's Ch Bernardsville NJ 2008-** B Englewood NJ 8/11/1965 s Frederick William Feus & Gloria Redeke. BA New Sch U 1992; MDiv GTS 2004. D 6/12/2004 Bp John Palmer Croneberger P 12/18/2004 Bp Vincent King Pettit. m 9/8/1990 Kimberley Mary Vere c 2. Cur S Geo's-By-The-River Rumson NJ 2004-2008. wffeus@yahoo.com

FEYERHERM, Elise Anne (SO) 3400 Calumet St, Columbus OH 43214 **Prof Bex Columbus OH 2009-; Assoc S Jas Epis Ch Columbus OH 2009-** B Camden NJ 11/21/1960 d Marvin Feyerherm & Miriam. AB Earlham Coll 1982; MDiv Ya Berk 1986; PhD Boston Coll 2001. D 6/13/2009 P 6/19/2010 Bp Thomas Edward Breidenthal. m 8/15/1998 John Clabeaux. elisefeyerherm@sbcglobal.net

FEYRER, David Allport (Ct) 70 S. Dogwood Trail, Southern Shores NC 27949 B Allentown PA 4/20/1941 s Albert Donald Feyrer & Margaret. ABS Muhlenberg Coll 1963; MDiv PDS 1969. D 6/29/1969 P 5/16/1970 Bp Frederick J Warnecke. m 5/9/1964 Sandra Franklin c 6. R The Par Of Emm Ch Weston CT 2002-2010; P-in-c Chr Ch Norwalk CT 1998-2002; Assoc S Steph's Epis Ch Wilkes Barre PA 1973-1980. dfeyrer@feyrerobx.com

FHUERE, Brenda Lee (Colo) 520 Jaylee St Unit A, Clifton CO 81520 B Oberlin KS 9/23/1942 d Melvin Lloyd Stimbert & Lois Floy. BA Mesa St Coll, Colorado 1995. D 1/22/2000 P 7/29/2000 Bp William Jerry Winterrowd. c 3. Ch Of The Nativ Grand Jct CO 2005-2007; Epis Par Of S Jn The Bapt Portland OR 2005. bfhuere@wic.net

FICHTER JR, Richard E (Va) PO Box 588, Gordonsville VA 22942 **P-in-c Chr Epis Ch Gordonsville VA 2008-** B Fairfax VA 1/3/1968 s Richard Edward Fichter & Suzanne Butler Bell. BS Virginia Tech 1990; MDiv VTS 2001. D 6/23/2001 P 12/29/2001 Bp Peter James Lee. Int Asst R Chr Epis Ch Winchester VA 2006-2008; Asst R Gr Ch Kilmarnock VA 2002-2006; Assoc S Paul's Ch Beaufort NC 2001-2002. rfichterjr@msn.com

FICKS III, Robert Leslie (Ct) 8166 Mount Air Place, Columbus OH 43235 B Cincinnati OH 6/17/1944 s Robert Leslie Ficks & Virginia. BA Ken 1970; MDiv Ya Berk 1984. D 6/9/1984 P 4/25/1985 Bp Arthur Edward Walmsley. m 8/16/1969 Ann Longbotham c 4. R S Andr's Ch Millinocket ME 2007-2010; R S Jn's Ch Washington CT 1988-2007; Trst Ya Berk New Haven CT 1987-1997; Com for Pstr Care Cler Dio Connecticut Hartford CT 1986-1990; Asst R Chr And H Trin Ch Westport CT 1984-1988. rficks@snet.net

FIDDLER, Andrew (Ct) 215 Highland St, New Haven CT 06511 B New York NY 5/4/1943 s Charles Norman Fiddler & Hannah Phoebe. BA Pr 1964; MDiv EDS 1968. D 6/8/1968 P 12/15/1968 Bp Leland Stark. m 2/16/1974 Paulann T Taylor c 1. Trin Ch On The Green New Haven CT 1970-2009; Cur Chr Ch Ridgewood NJ 1968-1970. afiddler@snet.net

FIDLER, Brian Ernest (Mass) 7607 La Jolla Boulevard, La Jolla CA 92037 **Chapl The Bp's Sch La Jolla CA 2011-** B Plainfield NJ 11/19/1955 s William Larch Fidler & Beryl. BA Coll of Wooster 1977; MDiv Ya Berk 1981. D 6/6/1981 Bp Albert Wiencke Van Duzer P 1/16/1982 Bp George Phelps Mellick Belshaw. m 6/21/1980 Joanne Shirley Blake. Chapl Groton Sch Groton MA 2000-2011; Chapl Trin-Pawling Sch Pawling NY 1984-1993; Asst Trin Ch Moorestown NJ 1981-1984. Auth, "The Prophetic Voice," CRIS, 1991. fidlerb@bishops.net

FIEBKE, Edward John (Alb) 6014 7th Ave W, Bradenton FL 34209 **Asst S Mary Magd Lakewood Ranch FL 2009-** B Antigo WI 9/5/1933 s Nicholas Christian Hugo Fiebke & Ruth Elida. BA SUNY 1955; STB GTS 1959. D 5/23/1959 P 11/28/1959 Bp Frederick Lehrle Barry. m 4/25/1998 Linda M Dubay c 2. Asstg Chr Ch Bradenton FL 1997-2003; R S Paul's Ch Kinderhook NY 1967-1995; R S Mk's Ch Malone NY 1961-1967; Cur S Jn's Ch Ogdensburg NY 1959-1961. efiebke@tampabay.rr.com

✠ FIELD, Rt Rev Martin Scott (WMo) P. O. Box 413227, Kansas City MO 64141 **Bp of W Missouri Dio W Missouri Kansas City MO 2011-** B Salem OH 9/13/1956 s Lewell Gordon Field & Helen Louise. BA Bethany Coll 1978; MDiv Lexington TS 1983. D 10/10/1991 Bp Charles Lovett Keyser P 5/2/1992 Bp Donald Purple Hart Con 3/5/2011 for WMo. m 8/4/1979 Donna C Cassarino c 2. Dio Estrn Michigan Saginaw MI 2005-2010; R S Paul's Epis Ch Flint MI 2003-2011; Assoc S Lk's Epis Ch Jackson TN 1998-2003; Int S Anne's Ch Millington TN 1996-1997; Int S Matt's Ch Covington TN 1994-1996; Off Of Bsh For ArmdF New York NY 1992-1996; Yth Mnstr S Jn's Ch Chevy Chase MD 1985-1989. bishopfield@ediowestmo.org

FIELD, Norman Grover (NwPa) 747 E 41st St, Erie PA 16504 B Erie PA 10/11/1948 s Claud Melvin Field Field & Beautrice Lucille. D 3/30/1996 P 12/1/1996 Bp Robert Deane Rowley Jr. m 11/22/1969 Joyce Anne Mosier.

FIELD, Robert Durning (WNC) 256 E. Main St., Brevard NC 28712 **Fresh Start Fac Dio Wstrn No Carolina Asheville NC 2010-; R S Phil's Ch Brevard NC 1997-** B Brunswick ME 4/3/1963 s John Henry Field & Elizabeth Blynn. BA Dart 1985; MDiv STUSo 1993; DMin TS 2008. D 6/29/1993 P 12/1/1993 Bp Robert Hodges Johnson. m 8/22/1987 Jayne Gloster c 2. COM Dio Wstrn No Carolina Asheville NC 2001-2007; Dioc Nwspr Bd Dio Wstrn No Carolina Asheville NC 1994-1997; Assoc S Alb's Ch Hickory NC 1993-1997. rdfield@comporium.net

FIELD, William Overstreet (Del) 1611 Spring Dr Apt 5B, Louisville KY 40205 B Lexington KY 8/4/1933 s Robert Edwin Field & Helen. BA S Mary's Sem Baltimore MD 1955; STB S Mary's Sem & U Baltimore MD 1957; Med Xavier U 1970; JD U Of Kentucky 1984; DAS STUSo 1999. Rec from Roman

Catholic 3/11/2000 Bp Robert Jefferson Hargrove Jr. m 3/6/1973 Barbara H Hoffman. Int S Lk's Ch Marietta OH 2009; Chr Ch Greenville Wilmington DE 2004-2005; Ch Of The Gd Shpd Ruxton MD 2002-2004; S Jas Epis Ch Alexandria LA 2000-2002. billandbarbarafield@yahoo.com

FIELDS, Cyprian William (Los) 5900 Canterbury Dr Apt A220, Culver City CA 90230 B San Antonio TX 8/28/1924 s William Fields & Ruby Agnes. BS Sthrn U Baton Rouge LA 1945; BA U CA 1969; LTh Untd Theol Coll Of The W Indies Kingston Jm 1976. D 5/1/1975 P 6/1/1976 Bp The Bishop Of Jamaica. Cleric Chr The Gd Shpd Par Los Angeles CA 1995-1996; R S Lk's Ch New Orleans LA 1993-1995; Asst S Tim's Epis Ch Washington DC 1990-1993; Dio Washington Washington DC 1988-1993; Dpt Of Missions Ny Income New York NY 1986-1988; S Lk's-Roosevelt Hosp Cntr New York NY 1986-1988; Assoc P S Phil's Ch New York NY 1986-1988; Vic S Agnes And S Paul's Ch E Orange NJ 1980-1986; R All Souls Ch New York NY 1978-1980; P-in-c S Andr's Ch New York NY 1976-1977. Humanitarian Awd Los Angeles Chapt UBE 2005. cfields138@aol.com

FIELDS, Kenneth L (Tex) 717 Sage Rd, Houston TX 77056 **Vice R S Mart's Epis Ch Houston TX 2008-** B Tampa FL 10/8/1945 s Eugene Roscoe Fields & Pauline. BA U Of Florida 1966; MA U Of Florida 1968. D 6/29/1981 Bp Emerson Paul Haynes P 3/25/1988 Bp Robert Oran Miller. m 12/20/1969 Mary A Smith c 1. Stndg Com Dio Alabama Birmingham AL 2002-2006; R Cbury Chap and Coll Cntr Tuscaloosa AL 1997-2008; S Thos Epis Ch Birmingham AL 1992-1996; Dio Alabama Birmingham AL 1991-1992; S Jn's Ch Montgomery AL 1988-1991; Coordntr Educ Progs Ch Of The H Comf Montgomery AL 1982-1984. Auth, "The Apos," 1997; Auth, "Trausept Trivia"; Ed, "Dio Nwspr". fields45@comcast.net

FIELDS, Laddie B (Tex) 431 Pace Rd, Hendersonville NC 28792 B Sentinel OK 2/14/1925 s Ross Stelzer Fields & Tressie Gladys. Epis TS of The SW; BS U of Oklahoma 1948. D 1/3/1982 Bp William Carl Frey P 9/28/1982 Bp Gordon Taliaferro Charlton. m 5/13/1990 Ellen H Wood c 4. P-in-c S Paul's Ch Edneyville NC 1997-2004; Int S Alb's Ch Houston TX 1994-1995; Ch Of The Redeem Houston TX 1982-1993; Admin Redeem Dio Texas Houston TX 1982-1984. laddandellen@bellsount.net

FIELDSTON, Heidi A (Mass) 24 Court St, Dedham MA 02026 **Int Trin Ch Randolph MA 2010-; Assoc Chr Ch Needham MA 2007-** B Boston MA 2/27/1946 d Joseph Fieldston & Rosely. BA Smith 1968; MBA Ya 1980; Harvard DS 1993; MDiv EDS 1996. D 6/6/1998 P 5/1/1999 Bp M(arvil) Thomas Shaw III. m 5/22/1983 Howard Ostroff c 1. S Eliz's Ch Sudbury MA 2006; First Luth Ch Malden MA 2005; S Paul's Ch Dedham MA 1999-2005; D S Dunstans Epis Ch Dover MA 1998-1999. hfieldston@mac.com

FIFE, Richard (SwVa) 2250 Maiden Ln Sw, Roanoke VA 24015 **Disciplinary Bd Revs Pres Dio SW Virginia Roanoke VA 2011-2015; Ldrshp Dvlpmt Com Dio SW Virginia Roanoke VA 2010-2012; R S Eliz's Ch Roanoke VA 1999-** B Charlottesville VA USA 4/19/1953 s Francis Harrison Fife & Virginia. BA U of Virginia 1975; AAS Piedmont Virginia Cmnty Coll 1980; Cert St. Geo's Coll Jerusalem Israel 1984; MDiv VTS 1985; Cert Int Mnstry Ntwk 1994; Coursework VTS 2005; Cert Cler Ldrshp Inst 2006. D 6/22/1985 Bp Peter James Lee P 5/8/1986 Bp O'Kelley Whitaker. m 6/12/1999 Jenny G Garrett c 2. Long Range Plnng Com Dio SW Virginia Roanoke VA 2007-2008; Mutual Mnstry Revs Com Dio SW Virginia Roanoke VA 2006-2007; Cnvnr of the Roanoke Convoc Cler Dio SW Virginia Roanoke VA 2005-2008; Dn of the Roanoke Convoc Dio SW Virginia Roanoke VA 2005-2008; St. Eliz's Epis Day Sch S Eliz's Ch Roanoke VA 2001-2005; Exec Bd Dio SW Virginia Roanoke VA 2001-2004; Exec Bd Personl Com Dio SW Virginia Roanoke VA 2001-2004; After Sch Acceleration Prog Bd Chair S Eliz's Ch Roanoke VA 2000-2007; R Chr Ch Palmyra NJ 1998-1999; R Riverfront Epis Team Mnstry Riverside NJ 1998-1999; R S Steph's Ch Riverside NJ 1995-1999; R H Trin Ch Collingswood NJ 1990-1995; R Ch of the Gd Shpd Syracuse NY 1985-1990; Paris Cluster/Area Mnstry Cler Team Dio Cntrl New York Syracuse NY 1985-1990; R Gr Epis Ch Waterville NY 1985-1990. Alb Inst 1986-1996; Associated Parishes 1986-1995; Assn of Dioc Liturg & Mus Commisions 1990-1995; Int Mnstry Ntwk 1994-1999; Ldrshp Acad for New Directions 1986-1990; Liturg done well Ntwk 2001; Natl Ntwk of Epis Cler 1990-1994; Sophia Ntwk 2001 2005. rhfife@mindspring.com

FIGGE, Diane Marie (RG) 3900 Trinity Dr, Los Alamos NM 87544 **Trin On The Hill Epis Ch Los Alamos NM 2010-** B St Louis MO 6/4/1951 d Harold George Figge & Anita Maria. BSN Avila; Cert of Basic Chr Stds Dio Rio Grande Sch fro Mnstry. D 9/19/2009 P 9/24/2010 Bp William Carl Frey. dfigge@juno.com

FIKE, Christopher John (Mass) 24 Oakland St, Medford MA 02155 **Chr Ch Somerville MA 2006-** B Minneapolis MN 1/28/1965 s David Duane Fike & Mary Jean. BA Ken 1987; MS Simmons Coll 1993; MDiv EDS 1999. D 6/5/1999 P 6/3/2000 Bp M(arvil) Thomas Shaw III. c 2. Dio Massachusetts Boston MA 1999-2003; Cox Fell The Cathd Ch Of S Paul Boston MA 1999-2002. sfike@diomass.org

FIKES, G(erald) David (Tex) PO Box 100014, Arlington VA 22210 B Pine Bluff AR 12/28/1954 s Conley Newton Fikes & Berta Marie. BA U of Arkansas 1976; MDiv Candler TS Emory U 1981. D 6/7/1986 P 11/15/1986 Bp Charles Judson Child Jr. m 9/20/2008 Lisa Elizabeth Navarra c 2. The Ch of the Gd Shpd Austin TX 2000-2007; R Gr - S Lk's Ch Memphis TN 1992-2000; Asst All SS Epis Ch Atlanta GA 1987-1991; D S Anne's Epis Ch Atlanta GA 1986-1987. Theta Pi 1981. gdavidfikes@yahoo.com

FILBERT, Brandon Lee (Ore) 2090 High St. SE, Salem OR 97302 **Stndg Com Dio Oregon Portland OR 2008-; R S Tim's Epis Ch Salem OR 2007-** B Corvallis OR 2/7/1964 s John Wesley Filbert & Genevieve Inez. BA Willamette U 1986; MDiv GTS 1993. D 5/30/1993 P 11/30/1993 Bp Robert Louis Ladehoff. m 5/17/1986 Pamela Athearn Wagner c 2. Vic S Bede's Ch Forest Grove OR 1993-2007; Full-time Sem intern Gr Ch Brooklyn NY 1991-1992. filberts@sainttimothys.org

FILER, Judy Kathleen (Tex) St John's Episcopal Church, 514 Carter St, Marlin TX 76661 **R S Jn's Epis Ch Marlin TX 2007-** B Boise ID 2/27/1947 d Charles Walter Winters & Mary Rice. BS OR SU 1969; Iona Sch of Mnstry 2006. D 6/24/2006 Bp Don Adger Wimberly P 1/20/2007 Bp Rayford Baines High Jr. m 7/10/1971 Wesley Joseph Filer c 1. jwfiler@aol.com

F

FILL, Michael (Be) 1919 Chestnut St Apt 2212, Philadelphia PA 19103 B Passaic NJ 10/6/1938 s Michael Fill & Mary Kathryn. BS U of Scranton 1962; MDiv PDS 1965. D 6/26/1965 P 3/5/1966 Bp Frederick J Warnecke. Int S Ptr's Epis Ch Tunkhannock PA 2001-2003; Int Ch Of The Gd Shpd Scranton PA 1996-1997; Vic S Jn's Epis Ch Hamlin PA 1993-1994; R Gr Epis Ch Honesdale PA 1975-1992; R S Mich's Epis Ch Bethlehem PA 1974-1975. Soc of S Jn the Evang 1993. poconopadre@aol.com

FILLER, John Arthur (U) 807 E Ave, Coronado CA 92118 B Grass Valley CA 5/7/1938 s John Calvin Filler & Mayme L. BA U of Hawaii 1971; MDiv CDSP 1974. D 2/16/1975 Bp C Kilmer Myers P 10/16/1976 Bp Edmond Lee Browning. m 6/24/1989 Mary JoAnne Basile c 1. R S Ptr's Ch Clearfield UT 2000-2004; COM Dio Utah Salt Lake City UT 1999-2002; Int S Ptr's Ch Clearfield UT 1990-1993; Int S Edm's Epis Ch Pacifica CA 1988-1989; Int S Geo's Epis Ch Antioch CA 1984; Vic S Aug's Epis Chap Kapaau HI 1976-1984. RACA 1972. johnfiller@me.com

FINAN, A(lice) Jeanne (WNC) 427 Dutch Creek Rd, Banner Elk NC 28604 **R S Jn's Ch Asheville NC 2007-** B Tokyo JP 10/7/1949 d John Joseph Finan & Mary Alice. BA U NC 1970; MDiv VTS 2003; MA U of Wales 2005. D 5/31/2003 P 12/20/2003 Bp Robert Hodges Johnson. m 3/4/1975 Thomas Wade Eshelman c 2. Chair, COM Dio Wstrn No Carolina Asheville NC 2005-2011; Assoc R S Mary Of The Hills Epis Par Blowing Rock NC 2003-2007. Auth, "Remember Your Baptism: Ten Meditations," Cowley, 2004. Dir's Awd Epis EvangES 2002. jeannefinan@gmail.com

FINCH, Barbara Jo (Ore) PO Box 447, Lake Oswego OR 97034 B Eugene OR 2/27/1952 d Douglas Burton Finch & Lucille. BS U of Oregon 1974. D 11/1/1996 Bp Robert Louis Ladehoff. D Chr Ch Par Lake Oswego OR 1996-2011. deaconbj@hotmail.com

FINCH JR, Floyd William (SC) One Bishop Gadsden Way, A-119, Charleston SC 29412 **Chapl to Ret Cler and spouses Dio So Carolina Charleston SC 2007-** B Arden NC 4/22/1929 s Floyd William Finch & Ruth. BA Berea Coll 1951; MDiv VTS 1954; MA Appalachian St U 1968. D 6/8/1954 P 6/10/1955 Bp Matthew G Henry. m 9/4/1954 Leona Iris Sutherland c 4. Assoc S Jas Ch Charleston SC 1996-2003; Bp's Representive to Curs Dio So Carolina Charleston SC 1993-2007; Int Vic Ch Of The H Fam Moncks Corner SC 1993-1996; Chrmn St of Ch Comm Dio So Carolina Charleston SC 1992-1994; Vic All SS Epis Ch Hampton SC 1988-1993; R Epis Ch Of The H Trin Ridgeland SC 1988-1993; R Trin Epis Ch Columbus GA 1981-1986; R S Paul's Epis Ch Summerville SC 1976-1981; Hd Mstr The Patterson Sch Lenoir NC 1968-1976; Stndg Com, Trst F Crittenden Hm Dio No Carolina Raleigh NC 1966-1967; Com Evang Dio No Carolina Raleigh NC 1965-1967; Pres Mecklenburg Convoc Dio No Carolina Raleigh NC 1960-1961; R Ch Of The H Comf Charlotte NC 1959-1967; R S Jas Epis Ch Lenoir NC 1956-1959; P-in-c Trin Ch Kings Mtn NC 1955-1956; P-in-c S Andr's Ch Bessemer City NC 1954-1956. Natl Register of Prominent Americans 1973; Personalities of the So 1972; 1,000 Men of Achievement 1969; Who's Who in the So and SW 1969; Royal Blue Bk, London 1968; Who's Who in Rel 1968; Dictionary of Intl. Biography 1967, Who's Who in Amer Colleges and Universities 1951. fwfjr@juno.com

FINCH, Robin Lee (Ida) All Saints' Episcopal Church, 704 S Latah St, Boise ID 83705 B Lewiston ID 4/6/1955 d Gordon Shore & Alice Marie. Boise St U; BS U Of Idaho Moscow 1979. D 1/6/1996 Bp John Stuart Thornton P 5/22/2005 Bp Harry Brown Bainbridge III. m 2/29/1992 Douglas Finch.

FINCHER, Michael Kevin (Los) 439 S. 4th St., Redlands CA 92373 **Assoc R Trin Epis Ch Redlands CA 2009-** B Las Vegas NV 10/19/1961 s Nelson Ray Fincher & Mary. BA U CA 1984; MDiv SWTS 2006. D 6/3/2006 P 1/6/2007 Bp Joseph Jon Bruno. Chapl Cbury Westwood Fndt Los Angeles CA 2006-2009; Cur S Alb's Epis Ch Los Angeles CA 2006-2009. mkfincher@gmail.com

FINEANGANOFO, Sosaia Ala (Cal) 2565 Redbridge Rd, Tracy CA 95377 **Asst S Mk's Epis Ch French Camp CA 2008-; P Assoc S Paul's Epis Ch**

Burlingame CA 1987- B Nukualofa To GA 11/11/1935 d Mosese Hopoi Fineanganofo & Susana. S Johns TS Fj. Trans 9/1/1993 Bp JL Bryce. m 6/27/1959 Lavinia Iongi c 4.

FINEOUT, William High (Mich) St. Pauls Episcopal Church, 218 W Ottawa St, Lansing MI 48933 **D S Paul's Epis Ch Lansing MI 2008-** B Lansing MI 3/24/1947 s Donald S Fineout & Jane Ann. BA Estrn Michigan U 1969; MA Estrn Michigan U 1974. D 6/21/2008 Bp Wendell Nathaniel Gibbs Jr. m 6/14/1985 Shannon Drotar c 2. fineout@comcast.net

FINKENSTAEDT JR, Harry Seymour (WMass) 13761 Charismatic Way, Gainesville VA 20155 B Grosse Pt E MI 9/28/1923 s Harry Seymour Finkenstaedt & Eliza Moody. BA Ya 1948; BD EDS 1953; MA U of Massachusetts 1968; Cert U of Massachusetts 1970. D 5/31/1953 Bp Horace W B Donegan P 1/6/1954 Bp Harry S Kennedy. m 4/19/1960 Anne M Williams c 4. R S Jn's Ch Athol MA 1962-1967; Asst Ch Of The H Trin New York NY 1956-1957; Mssy Dio Hawaii Honolulu HI 1953-1958; Dio Hawaii Honolulu HI 1953-1956; Vic S Matt's Epis Ch Waimanalo HI 1953-1954. annefink@comcast.net

FINLEY IV, John Huston (Mass) 717 Atlantic Ave Apt 3B, Boston MA 02111 **S Mk's Ch Dorchester MA 2008-; Epiph Sch Boston MA 2006-** B Boston 6/15/1970 s John Huston Finley & Margot Gerrity. BA Harv 1992. D 1/7/2006 Bp M(arvil) Thomas Shaw III P 1/6/2007 Bp Gayle Elizabeth Harris. m 11/12/2005 Carl Stanley McGee. jfinley@epiphanyschool.com

FINLEY, Rosamond Stelle (Los) 212 W Franklin St, Tucson AZ 85701 B Kansas City KS 2/26/1979 BA Van 2001; MDiv Claremont TS 2005. D 6/11/2005 Bp Chester Lovelle Talton. Asst S Ptr's Par San Pedro CA 2005. rosamond@stpertsanpedro.org

FINN, Anne Marie (NwT) 2630 S 11th St, Abilene TX 79605 B Houston TX 2/28/1941 d Edwin E Finn & Marie Genevieve. BA Dominican Coll 1967; MA S Thos U Miami FL 1972; MA S Mary U 1985; CTh Epis TS of The SW 1989. D 1/20/1989 Bp Earl Nicholas McArthur Jr P 7/1/1989 Bp John Herbert MacNaughton. S Mk's Epis Ch Abilene TX 1994-1996; S Mk's Epis Ch Coleman TX 1993-1994; R Epis Ch Of The Mssh Gonzales TX 1989-1993. Assn Rel & Value Issues In Counslg; Sw Ntwk Womens Ministers, Amer Assn Counslg And Dvlpmt. Distinguished Grad S Mary U 1985.

FINN, Michael John (Roch) 1245 Culver Rd, Rochester NY 14609 B Rochester NY 5/13/1947 s John Joseph Finn & Helen Ann. BA St. Jn Fisher Coll 1974; MPA SUNY Brockport 1994. D 5/2/2009 Bp Prince Grenville Singh. m 5/14/1983 Jane Lyon c 3. mikefinn@infionline.net

FINN, Patrick Shawn (SVa) 3011 Maritime Forest Dr, Johns Island SC 29455 **Off Of Bsh For ArmdF New York NY 2008-** B Detroit MI 4/29/1958 s Bernard James Finn & Marie Germaine. Trin-Dublin, Ireland 1978; BA Educ/Psychol U MI 1982; MDiv EDS 1987. D 6/27/1987 Bp H Coleman McGehee Jr P 2/1/1988 Bp David Charles Bowman. m 5/24/1980 Leslie Dean c 3. Spec Mobilization Spprt Plan Washington DC 2009; Pension Fund Mltry New York NY 2008; R Ch Of Our Sav Johns Island SC 2002-2007; Dio Utah Salt Lake City UT 1995-2002; Vic S Lk's Ch Pk City UT 1995-2000; R S Mk's Ch Alexandria VA 1989-1995; R Trin Ch Warsaw NY 1987-1989. Chapl, "Sprtl Resiliency," *Warrior Resiliency/Staying Green*, US NAVY, 2008. Aikido Shodan (Black Belt) Tokyo Japan 2001. Meritorious Serv Medal UnitedStates Navy 2011. ofinns@bellsouth.net

FINN, Robert Patrick (EMich) PO Box 83, West Branch MI 48661 B Detroit MI 8/28/1936 s Patrick V Finn & Ethel L. MS Cntrl Michigan U 1970. D 9/13/2008 Bp S(teven) Todd Ousley. m 8/12/1961 Janet Finn c 2. rjfinn@voyager.net

FINNIN, Nathan McBride (EC) St. Mary's Episcopal Church, 800 Rountree Ave., Kinston NC 28501 **Cbury Sch Greensboro NC 2010-** B Boston MA 2/23/1982 s Timothy Francis Finnin & Laura McBride. BA The U NC at Chap Hill 2004; BA The U NC at Chap Hill 2004; Dplma Ya Berk 2008; M.DIV. Yale DS 2008. D 6/14/2008 P 2/21/2009 Bp Clifton Daniel III. Asst S Mary's Ch Kinston NC 2008-2010. nathan.finnin@aya.yale.edu

FINSTER, Mary Ruth (NI) 1817 W Monroe St, Kokomo IN 46901 B Fort Wayne IN 11/3/1922 d Charles Madison Pfeiffer & Mary Ruth. BS Manchester Coll 1944; MA Colorado St Coll 1949. D 5/8/1990 Bp Francis Campbell Gray. D S Andr Epis Ch Kokomo IN 1990-2005.

FIRTH, Harry Warren (WMo) 4024 W 100th Ter, Overland Park KS 66207 B Topeka KS 7/4/1934 s Charles Bennett Firth & Edna Annette. BA Kansas St Teachers Coll 1956; BD SWTS 1959; Tchg Cert Can Montessori Assn Calgary CA 1964. D 6/6/1959 P 12/5/1959 Bp Edward Clark Turner. Cn to the Ordnry Dio W Missouri Kansas City MO 1995-1998; Hon Cn Gr And H Trin Cathd Kansas City MO 1994-1995; R All SS Epis Ch Kansas City MO 1970-1994; R Trin Ch Arkansas City KS 1968-1970; Cur S Mich And All Ang Ch Mssn KS 1964-1968; Vic Ch Of The Ascen Neodesha KS 1959-1964. Bp's Shield Dio W Missouri 1993. hwfirth@swbell.net

FISCHBECK, Lisa Galen (NC) 8410 Merin Rd, Chapel Hill NC 27516 **Dioc Coun Dio No Carolina Raleigh NC 2011-; Founding Vic Ch Of The Advoc Carrboro NC 2003-** B Philadelphia PA 5/3/1956 d Kenneth Henry Fischbeck & Rita Helen. BA Duke 1977; MA U of Virginia 1981; MDiv Duke 1991; Cert VTS 1992. D 1/18/1992 Bp Robert Whitridge Estill P 1/23/1993 Bp Huntington Williams Jr. m 9/2/1989 Robert Lamar Bland c 1. Dep to GC Dio No Carolina Raleigh NC 2008-2011; Stndg Com Dio No Carolina Raleigh NC 2007-2010; Mssn Implementation Team Chair Dio No Carolina Raleigh NC 2005-2006; Strategic Plnng Com Dio No Carolina Raleigh NC 2003-2005; Bd of Epis Farmworker Mnstry Dio No Carolina Raleigh NC 1999-2002; Bd of Epis Farmworker Mnstry Dio No Carolina Raleigh NC 1999-2002; Bd Dir - Chair 2001 Epis Farmworker Mnstry Newton Grove NC 1999-2002; Dn of Durham Convoc Dio No Carolina Raleigh NC 1998-2005; Asst to R Ch Of The H Fam Chap Hill NC 1997-2002; Chair Dept Mnstry & Higher Educ Dio No Carolina Raleigh NC 1996-1998; Dioc Coun Dio No Carolina Raleigh NC 1996-1998; Asst to R S Steph's Ch Durham NC 1992-1997; D Dio No Carolina Raleigh NC 1992; Campus Min Chap Of The Cross Chap Hill NC 1989-1990. Auth, "Epistle for Christmas and Epiph," *Feasting on the Word: Year A, Volume One*, Westminster-Knox, 2010; Auth, "Baptism by Immersion," *LivCh*, LivCh, 2007. lisa.fischbeck@gmail.com

FISCHER III, Charles Leonard (At) 3737 Seminary Rd, Alexandria VA 22304 **S Paul's Epis Ch Atlanta GA 2011-; Dir VTS Alexandria VA 2009-** B Neptune NJ 6/25/1975 s Charles L Fischer & Marilyn B. BA Morehouse Coll 1997; MDiv VTS 2009. D 12/20/2008 P 6/28/2009 Bp J(ohn) Neil Alexander. m 10/9/2004 Rhonda D Pelham c 1. clfischer3@gmail.com

FISCHER, John Denny (Mil) 920 E Courtland Pl, Milwaukee WI 53211 B 8/20/1932 s Percy Theodore Fischer & Mabel Madora. BA St. Ambr U Davenport IA 1953; MA U IL 1954; PhD U IL 1958. D 5/27/1965 P 6/1/1966 Bp Donald H V Hallock. Chr Ch Whitefish Bay WI 1996-2000.

FISCHER III, Louis Cappel (SwVa) 192 Bishops Ln, Lynchburg VA 24503 B Atlanta GA 9/15/1934 s Louis Cappel Fischer & Adele R. BS Coll of Charleston 1956; BD VTS 1959; Fell Coll of Preachers 1975; Fllshp Con-Ed VTS 1980; Med Lynchburg Coll 1992. D 6/11/1959 P 5/16/1960 Bp Thomas N Carruthers. m 6/19/1959 Charlotte A Alexander c 2. Exec Bd Dio SW Virginia Roanoke VA 2000-2004; R S Ptr's Ch Altavista VA 1989-1999; R S Thos Ch Bedford VA 1989-1999; Exec Bd Dio SW Virginia Roanoke VA 1979-1982; Com Dio SW Virginia Roanoke VA 1973-1978; S Steph's Epis Ch Forest VA 1968-1989; Chr Epis Ch Buena Vista VA 1968-1970; Chair Dio Upper So Carolina Columbia SC 1967-1968; Vic Ch Of The Epiph Laurens SC 1964-1968; Asst Ch Of The Adv Spartanburg SC 1961-1964; Vic S Barn Ch Dillon SC 1959-1961. Auth, "Pstr Implications," *Lectionary Homil*, 1999; Auth, "Mega Prog For A Mini-Ch," *Action Info*, The Alb Inst, 1993. AAPC 1982. lcfischer@ntelos.net

FISCHER, Sara (Ore) 2800 SE Harrison Street, Portland OR 97214 **GC Dep Dio Oregon Portland OR 2012; R S Dav's Epis Ch Portland OR 2009-** B Redwood City CA 8/5/1959 d George Yuri Fischer & Elinor. BA U of Massachusetts 1984; MDiv GTS 2003. D 6/14/2003 Bp Robert Louis Ladehoff P 12/17/2003 Bp Johncy Itty. m 7/27/1996 Mark G Faust c 1. Bp's Search Com Dio Oregon Portland OR 2009-2010; GC Dep Dio Oregon Portland OR 2009; COM Dio Oregon Portland OR 2006-2010; R S Jn The Evang Ch Milwaukie OR 2005-2009; Dioc Coun Dio Oregon Portland OR 2004-2006; Assoc Gr Memi Portland OR 2003-2005. mothersara@gmail.com

FISCHER, Susan Krueger (U) 1579 S State St, Clearfield UT 84015 **Asst S Paul's Ch Salt Lake City UT 2011-; Epis Cmnty Serv Inc Salt Lake City UT 2010-** B Oklahoma City TX 1/19/1949 d William Ryan Krueger & Harriett Ann. Dplma Theol Stds Epis TS Of The SW 2010. D 6/12/2010 Bp Carolyn Tanner Irish P 6/18/2011 Bp Scott Byron Hayashi. c 2. Epis Cmnty Serv Inc Salt Lake City UT 1999-2009. susankfischer09@gmail.com

FISCHER-DAVIES, Clare Ilene (RI) 50 Orchard Ave, Providence RI 02906 **R S Mart's Ch Providence RI 2005-** B Saint Louis MO 1/19/1956 d George Ludwig Fischer & Mary Lou. BA New Engl Conservatory of Mus 1977; MDiv EDS 1983. D 6/5/1983 P 12/1/1983 Bp A(rthur) Heath Light. c 2. R Chr Ch Blacksburg VA 1994-2005; Asst Gr Ch Manchester NH 1990-1994; R S Andr's-In-The-Vlly Tamworth NH 1986-1990; Cur S Lk's Epis Ch Metuchen NJ 1983-1986. rector.stmartins@gmail.com

FISH, Cameron Hoover (CNY) 6 Perry Cir Apt D, Annapolis MD 21402 **Off Of Bsh For ArmdF New York NY 1997-** B Wilmington DE 11/21/1958 s Floyd Hamilton Fish & Jean Lincoln. BA Cor 1982; MDiv VTS 1989; ThM PrTS 2003. D 6/17/1989 P 6/23/1990 Bp O'Kelley Whitaker. m 5/27/1995 Paulette Elaine Thesier c 1. R Gr Ch Carthage NY 1991-1997; R S Jn's Ch Black River NY 1991-1997; Dio Cntrl New York Syracuse NY 1989-1991; Dioc Intern Gr Ch Baldwinsville NY 1989-1991. Cbury Way CNY 1993-1997. fastpast89@aol.com

FISH, Charles (Tad) Cramer (Ct) PO Box 67724, Albuquerque NM 87193 B San Jose CR 3/31/1950 s Charles Elmer Fish & Elizabeth Cecil. BS Estrn New Mex U 1972; MA Fuller TS 1984; MDiv STUSo 1991. D 6/29/1991 Bp Terence Kelshaw P 1/18/1993 Bp Reginald Heber Gooden. m 8/4/1991 Sonnie Eriksen. Asst All SS Ch Wolcott CT 2003-2005; Grtr Waterbury Mnstry Middlebury CT 2003-2005; Asst S Geo's Ch Middlebury CT 2003-2005; Int Calv Epis Ch Bridgeport CT 2001-2002; Int Calv St Geo's Epis Ch Bridgeport CT 2001-2002; R H Trin Epis Ch Hollidaysburg PA 1999-2000; Dio San

Diego San Diego CA 1998-1999; Vic S Anth Of The Desert Desert Hot Sprg CA 1998-1999; R S Jn's Ch Indio CA 1998-1999; Asst S Mary's Epis Ch Manchester CT 1995-1998; Dio NW Texas Lubbock TX 1993-1995; Asst S Jn's Epis Ch Odessa TX 1992-1993; Yth Min/ CE Par Ch of St. Helena Beaufort SC 1991-1992. fishalbq@aol.com

FISH, Gloria Hoyer (Roch) 46 Azalea Rd, Rochester NY 14620 **Assoc S Steph's Ch Rochester NY 1980-** B Dayton OH 7/20/1941 d Albert C Hoyer & Z Roberta. BS Kent St U 1963; MDiv Bex 1979; DMin CRDS 1990. D 6/30/1979 P 5/1/1980 Bp Robert Rae Spears Jr. m 10/13/1984 Wilfred Kenneth Cauthen. EWC.

FISH SR, Laurence Dean (NJ) 90 S Main St, Cranbury NJ 08512 **Died 7/26/2010** B Elizabeth NJ 6/2/1929 s Vincent Paris Fish & Evelyn Horton. BS Trenton St Coll 1951; MDiv PDS 1963; STM NYTS 1976. D 4/27/1963 P 11/2/1963 Bp Alfred L Banyard. c 4. Auth, "Biography Of Bp Wm Odenheimer," *New Jersey Dioc Journ*; Auth, "Biography Of Jn Croes: First Bp Of Nj," *New Jersey Dioc Journ*; Auth, "The 1789 GC: Unity Through Compromise & Toleration," *The Hstgr*. Natl Epis Historians And Archivists. lfish@newjersey.anglican.org

FISH, Sonnie Eriksen (Ct) PO Box 67724, Albuquerque NM 87193 **Luth Ch Of The Servnt Santa Fe NM 2007-; All SS Ch Wolcott CT 2001-** B Brooklyn NY 7/9/1952 d Erik Eriksen & Sonny Moller. BA Florida Intl U 1973; MS Florida Intl U 1979; MDiv STUSo 1992. D 6/28/1992 Bp Joseph Thomas Heistand P 1/18/1993 Bp Reginald Heber Gooden. m 8/4/1991 Charles (Tad) Cramer Fish. Grtr Waterbury Mnstry Middlebury CT 2001-2005; S Geo's Ch Middlebury CT 2001; Mt Zion Ch Glasgow PA 2000-2001; Dio San Diego San Diego CA 1998-1999; Asst Vic S Anth Of The Desert Desert Hot Sprg CA 1998-1999; Asst S Jn's Ch Indio CA 1998-1999; Grtr Hartford Reg Mnstry E Hartford CT 1995-1998; Dio NW Texas Lubbock TX 1993-1995; S Jn's Epis Ch Odessa TX 1993. fishalbq@aol.com

FISHBAUGH-LOONEY, Kristen Fishbaugh (Md) 11232 Falls Rd, Timonium MD 21093 **S Pauls Sch for Girls Lutherville MD 2008-; S Paul's Sch Brooklandville MD 2008-** B Carthage NY 8/2/1967 d James Allen Fishbaugh & Roslyn. BA Coll of Wooster 1989; MDiv Yale DS 1994. D 10/29/2005 Bp Robert Wilkes Ihloff P 4/29/2006 Bp John Leslie Rabb. m 8/17/1991 Mark Looney c 2. S Tim's Sch Stevenson MD 2005-2008. klooney@stt.org

FISHBECK, Nadine B (Tenn) 1100 Saint Marys Ln., Sewanee TN 37375 **P-St. Mary's Chap Sis of St Mary Sewanee TN 2008-** B Plattsburgh NY 6/9/1951 d Howard Fishbeck & Braunda. BA Indiana St U 1973; BS U of No Dakota 1984. D 3/29/2003 P 6/12/2004 Bp William Michie Klusmeyer. Nelson Cluster Of Epis Ch Rippon WV 2004-2007. fishbeck.julian037@gmail.com

FISHBURNE, Donald (ETenn) 3488 Reflecting Drive, Chattanooga TN 37415 **R S Paul's Epis Ch Chattanooga TN 2008-; Bd Rgnts The U So (Sewanee) Sewanee TN 2008-** B Charleston SC 8/1/1951 s Henry Burnett Fishburne & Amy Perry. BA U So 1973; MDiv VTS 1979; DMin STUSo 1998. D 6/16/1979 P 12/21/1979 Bp Gray Temple. m 5/24/1986 Sarah Vann c 2. Bp Search Com Dio E Tennessee Knoxville TN 2011; R Ch Of S Mich And All Ang Sanibel FL 2001-2008; Dioc Congrl Dvlpmt Cmns Dio Georgia Savannah GA 1996-1998; R S Paul's Ch Augusta GA 1990-2000; Bd Dio Conf Cntr Dio No Carolina Raleigh NC 1988-1990; Assoc R Chr Ch Charlotte NC 1987-1990; R S Matt's Epis Ch Darlington SC 1984-1987; Dioc Dept Ce Dio So Carolina Charleston SC 1982-1985; Asst R S Mich's Epis Ch Charleston SC 1981-1984; P S Mths Epis Ch Summerton SC 1979-1981. Auth, "New Cler Dvlpmt Handbook". donaldfishburne@gmail.com

FISHER, David Hickman (Chi) 1012 Churchill Dr, Naperville IL 60563 B San Bernadino CA 8/28/1943 s Hickman Young Fisher & Julia. Col; BA Carleton Coll 1965; MA UTS 1967; MA Van 1973; PhD Van 1976. D 2/24/1973 Bp William F Gates Jr P 9/23/1973 Bp John Vander Horst. m 6/1/1990 Sarah B Fowler c 3. Asst Trin Epis Ch Wheaton IL 2002-2006; Ch Of The H Nativ Clarendon Hills IL 1998-1999; S Chris's Epis Ch Oak Pk IL 1996-1997; Emm Epis Ch La Grange IL 1989-1993; LocTen S Phil's Epis Palatine IL 1985-1986; LocTen All SS Ch Wstrn Sprg IL 1983-1985; LocTen S Jn's Epis Ch Chicago IL 1980-1982; S Annes Epis Ch Caseyville IL 1979-1980; LocTen Emm Ch Hastings MI 1977-1978; LocTen S Jn the Apos Epis Ch Ionia MI 1977-1978; LocTen S Mary Magd Ch Fayetteville TN 1975-1976; Instr Theol & Asst to Dn The TS at The U So Sewanee TN 1974-1976; Asst S Geo's Ch Nashville TN 1973-1974. Auth, "Theory," *Oxford Encyclopedia of Aesthetics*, 1998; Auth, *Loyalty Tolerance & Recognition in J Val Inq*, 1997; Auth, "Self in Text," *Text in Self in Semeia*, 1990. Clarence Dissingen Tchg Excellence No Cntrl Coll. dhfisher@noctrl.edu

FISHER, Davis Lee (Chi) 1316 Maple Avenue, Apt. A-1, Evanston IL 60201 **Assoc S Lk's Ch Evanston IL 2007-** B Oak Park IL 4/2/1942 s Frank Theodore Fisher & Helen Annabelle. Cert Goethe Inst 1963; BA Lawr 1964; MDiv GTS 1967; MBA U Chi 1972; MTS Garrett-Evang TS 1998. D 6/17/1967 Bp James Winchester Montgomery P 12/16/1967 Bp Gerald Francis Burrill. c 3. Assoc S Raphael The Archangel Oak Lawn IL 2005-2006; Assoc S Aug's Epis Ch Wilmette IL 1996-2005; Cathd Shltr Chicago IL 1996-1997; Assoc S Matt's Ch Evanston IL 1980-1995; Asst Ch Of Our Sav Chicago IL 1969-1980; Cur Ch Of The H Comf Kenilworth IL 1967-1969. davisfishr@aol.com

FISHER, Donald Michael (Cal) 2395 Francisco St., #102, San Francisco CA 94123 B Marquette MI 5/1/1938 Rec from Roman Catholic 12/1/2001 Bp William Edwin Swing. c 2. Vic S Cyp's Ch San Francisco CA 2002-2009. donfl@aol.com

FISHER, Douglas John (NY) PO Box 974, Millbrook NY 12545 **R Gr Ch Millbrook NY 2000-** B Baltimore MD 12/7/1954 s Thomas John Fisher & Louisa T. BA St. Johns U 1976; MDiv Immac Concep Sem 1980. Rec from Roman Catholic 6/7/1997 as Priest Bp Catherine Scimeca Roskam. m 7/1/1984 Elizabeth Byrne c 3. Pstr H Innoc Highland Falls NY 1997-2000. revdougfisher@msn.com

FISHER, Elizabeth Byrne (NY) Po Box 974, Millbrook NY 12545 **S Thos Ch Amenia Un Amenia NY 2010-; St Thos Ch Amenia NY 2010-** B Rockville Centre NY 9/10/1956 d William F X Byrne & Eileen Mary. BA Amer U 1978; MPS New York Inst of Tech 1986; MDiv Ya Berk 2004. D 3/13/2004 P 9/18/2004 Bp Mark Sean Sisk. m 7/1/1984 Douglas John Fisher c 3. Asst. Min S Matt's Ch Bedford NY 2005-2007. elizfisher@msn.com

FISHER, Ernest Wilkin (SwFla) 6658 - 31 Way South, Saint Petersburg FL 33712 B Sheridan WY 8/18/1942 s Ernest Brayton Fisher & Helen Elizabeth. BA Col 1965; Med Natl-Louis U 2000. D 10/22/1988 Bp Gerald Francis Burrill. m 12/31/1985 Patricia Ann Allison Cooksey c 4. D S Barth's Ch St Petersburg FL 2001-2006; D S Matt's Ch St Petersburg FL 1998-2000; D S Aug's Epis Ch St Petersburg FL 1994-1997; Asst S Matt's Ch St Petersburg FL 1988-1994. ewf10@columbia.edu

FISHER, James A(lfred) (NJ) 15 Maple Street, South Seaville NJ 08246 B Los Angeles CA 3/27/1942 s Alfred James Fisher & Angela. BS USNA 1963; MDiv STUSo 1981; DMin Estrn Bapt TS 1991. D 6/15/1981 Bp William Grant Black P 12/15/1981 Bp A(rthur) Heath Light. m 9/16/1989 Gail Diane Hinkle. Ch Of The Adv Cape May NJ 1995-2007; H Trin Epis Ch Ocean City NJ 1990-1992; Chapl Cathd of St Ptr & St Paul Washington DC 1989-1990; R All Hallow's Ch Snow Hill MD 1984-1989; R Chr Ch Pearisburg VA 1981-1984. AAPC 1991; Fell. jafisher42@verizon.net

FISHER, Jeff Wright (Tex) 305 N 30th St, Waco TX 76710 **Stndg Com Dio Texas Houston TX 2011-; R S Alb's Epis Ch Waco TX 2006-** B Houston TX 2/15/1964 s Nelson Augustus Fisher & Nancy Wright. BBA U of Texas 1986; MDiv VTS 2004. D 6/12/2004 P 12/21/2004 Bp Don Adger Wimberly. m 6/17/1989 Susan S Stephenson c 2. Assoc R S Mary's Epis Ch Cypress TX 2004-2006. jeff@stalbanswaco.org

FISHER, Jerry William (NC) 635 Galashiels Place, Wake Forest NC 27587 B Cleveland OH 1/8/1945 s Fred Parish Fisher & Helen Jane. BA OH SU 1969; MDiv VTS 1978. D 6/24/1978 P 5/19/1979 Bp John Harris Burt. m 12/20/1967 Sarah Holsinger c 5. P-in-c Calv Ch Tarboro NC 2011; Int S Anne's Ch Winston Salem NC 2009-2011; R S Johns Epis Ch Wake Forest NC 1993-2009; Int S Steph's Ch Goldsboro NC 1992-1993; Int Emm Par Epis Ch And Day Sch Sthrn Pines NC 1991-1992; Int S Tim's Ch Wilson NC 1990-1991; Int S Steph's Epis Ch Erwin NC 1989-1990; R S Matt's Epis Ch Hillsborough NC 1984-1989; Asst S Thos' Ch Whitemarsh Ft Washington PA 1981-1984; Asst S Chris's By-The River Gates Mills OH 1978-1981. jfisher6@nc.rr.com

FISHER, Jill Carmen (ETenn) 1175 Pineville Rd Apt 85, Chattanooga TN 37405 B Bahia Blanca Argentina 1/6/1935 d Cecil Joseph Robinson & Rosina. Cert U of Cambridge 1948; Dioc Sch for Diac TN 1994. D 9/18/1994 Bp Robert Gould Tharp. c 2. D S Ptr's Ch Chattanooga TN 2001-2006; D S Alb's Epis Ch Hixson TN 1999-2001; D S Tim's Ch Signal Mtn TN 1994-1999. jillcfisher@comcast.net

FISHER, John Coale (NY) 8244 Crooked Creek Ln, Edisto Island SC 29438 B New York NY 4/9/1945 s Bernard Fisher & Virginia Bonham. AB Pr 1967; MS Col 1989. D 6/3/1978 Bp Paul Moore Jr P 12/21/1978 Bp Horace W B Donegan. m 7/14/2001 Susan Sage Leigh c 1. Affiliate Ch Of The Heav Rest New York NY 1998-2008; S Jas Ch Upper Montclair NJ 1991-1997; Int S Dav's Ch Kinnelon NJ 1989-1990; Assoc The Ch Of The Epiph New York NY 1986-1989; R Ch Of The H Comm Norwood NJ 1982-1985; R S Andr's Ch Harrington Pk NJ 1982 1985; Asst The Amer Cathd of the H Trin Paris 75008 FR 1980-1982; Assoc Ch Of The Heav Rest New York NY 1978-1980. jcf8244@gmail.com

FISHER, John R(aymond) (SO) Po Box 29064, Columbus OH 43229 B Shreveport LA 10/13/1929 s John Henry Fisher & Hazel Kirk. BFA U of New Mex 1953; MDiv Epis TS of The SW 1964. D 6/9/1964 Bp Frederick P Goddard P 6/1/1965 Bp J Milton Richardson. m 3/21/1991 Mary Alice Bucher c 3. S Jas Epis Ch Columbus OH 1988-1990; R S Steph's Ch Billings MT 1980-1987; S Paul's Epis Ch Lewiston NY 1973-1980; R S Mary's Epis Ch Texarkana TX 1969-1973; R S Paul's Epis Ch Greenville TX 1966-1969; Vic Chr Ch Matagorda TX 1964-1966; Vic S Jn's Epis Ch Palacios TX 1964-1966. Journalism Awd: Top Dio Pub Dio Upper So Carolina 1980; Hon Cn Dio Texas 1964. johnfisher.sq@gmail.com

FISHER, Joy (Ga) 147 SouthSecond Street, Cochran GA 31014 **P Trin Ch Cochran GA 2005-** B Macon GA 2/3/1945 d James Cicero Horne & Sheila. AA Middle Georgia Coll 1964; BA U GA 1966; Med Merc 1978; JD Merc 1982. D 2/5/2005 P 8/7/2005 Bp Henry Irving Louttit. m 2/10/1973 Thomas Wilmore Fisher c 3. attyfisher@aol.com

FISHER, Julie Blake (O) 551 Rockwell Street, Kent OH 44240 **R Chr Epis Ch Kent OH 2006-** B Buffalo NY 4/14/1961 d Richard Edward Fisher & Marilyn Margaret. BA U of Virginia 1983; MDiv VTS 1998. D 2/23/2005 P 9/14/2005 Bp Joe Goodwin Burnett. m 8/14/1982 Jerome 'Kip' Colegrove. Cur Ch Of The H Sprt Bellevue NE 2005-2006. juliefisher@netlink.net

FISHER, Margaret Jo (Spok) 118 E 12th Ave, Spokane WA 99202 **S Andr's Ch Spokane WA 2011-** B Butler PA 10/18/1955 d Peter John Surrey & Patricia. BA Chatham Coll 1977; MDiv Candler TS Emory U 1997. D 6/2/2001 P 10/26/2002 Bp James Edward Waggoner. c 3. P Assoc Cathd Of S Jn The Evang Spokane WA 2008-2011; Gr Ch Ellensburg WA 2002-2007. rev.margaret.fisher@gmail.com

FISHER, Mary Carlton (NCal) 66 E Commercial St, Willits CA 95490 B Brooklyn NY 1/13/1928 d Charles Mackall Fisher & Margaret Graham. BA Mid 1949; JD U MI 1957; MA U CA 1970; MDiv CDSP 1984. D 12/11/1982 Bp William Edwin Swing P 12/27/1990 Bp John Lester Thompson III. P-in-c S Fran In The Redwoods Mssn Willits CA 1991-2006; D Ch Of The Incarn Santa Rosa CA 1988-1991; D S Christophers Ch Anchorage AK 1986-1987; D Gr Cathd San Francisco CA 1984-1986; D The Epis Ch Of S Jn The Evang San Francisco CA 1982-1984.

FISHER, Paige Ford (Mass) 206 Clarendon St, Boston MA 02116 B Nashville TN 10/12/1970 d Fred Ford & Patience. BA U So 1993; MDiv EDS 2004. D 6/26/2004 P 1/8/2005 Bp Peter James Lee. m 8/12/2000 Peter Christopher Fisher c 2. Assoc R Trin Ch In The City Of Boston Boston MA 2004-2011. paigeandpeter@hotmail.com

FISHER, Richard Lingham (WNC) 175 Vinal St, Rockport ME 04856 B Brockton MA 7/4/1947 s Robert Thomas Fisher & Jean Lingham. BA U NC 1975; MDiv Chicago TS 1978; Psyd Illinois Sch Of Profsnl Psychol 1986. D 6/19/1978 P 5/12/1979 Bp William Gillette Weinhauer. m 12/27/1975 Doree Ross Koontz c 1. S Jn's Ch Asheville NC 1978-1982. Auth, "The Intentional Sapling," *Openings Into Mnstry*. APA; Mepa. rlfspyd@midcoast.com

FISHER, Robert William (ECR) PO Box 101, Carmel Valley CA 93924 **S Dunst's Epis Ch Carmel Vlly CA 2010-** B South Laguna CA 10/23/1975 BA Ya 1998; MDiv Ya Berk 2005. D 6/11/2005 Bp Chester Lovelle Talton P 1/14/2006 Bp Joseph Jon Bruno. m 12/31/2004 Sarah Ellen Wood c 1. Assoc R All SS-By-The-Sea Par Santa Barbara CA 2007-2010; S Edm's Par San Marino CA 2005-2007. rob@saintdunstanschurch.org

FISHER, Ronald S(pencer) (Md) 23 N Court St, Westminster MD 21157 **R Ch Of The Ascen Westminster MD 1988-** B Baltimore MD 5/7/1950 BS RPI 1972; MDiv VTS 1975; Cert. in Cong. Dev. SWTS 2006. D 1/8/1983 P 5/26/1983 Bp David Keller Leighton Sr. m 6/12/1976 Rebecca S Willaman c 2. Asst S Thos' Ch Garrison Forest Owings Mills MD 1983-1988. Auth, *When Chld Receive Comm*, Forw Mvmt, 1987. rfisher@ascension-westminster.com

FISHER JR, Russell Ellsworth (FtW) Po Box 192, Santa Anna TX 76878 **P-in-c S Mk's Epis Ch Coleman TX 2004-** B Clairon County PA 5/13/1937 s Russell Edward Ellsworth Fisher & Louise Elizabeth. BS U of Memphis 1959; MA U of Memphis 1966; MDiv Nash 1969; PhD Louisiana Bapt U 1997. D 12/10/1975 P 12/19/1976 Bp Bennett Jones Sims. m 8/5/1972 Louann Ward. Int S Anne's Ch Ft Worth TX 2003-2004; R S Jn's Epis Ch Brownwood TX 1997-2003; Dept Assn Dio Dallas Dallas TX 1993-1997; Excoun Dio Dallas Dallas TX 1993-1994; R S Mary's Epis Ch Texarkana TX 1992-1997; Mssnr Great Plains Epis Cluster Dio Oklahoma Oklahoma City OK 1990-1991; Mssn Coun Dio Oklahoma Oklahoma City OK 1986-1991; Vic S Marg's Ch Lawton OK 1986-1990; Ch Educ Field Team Coordntr Dio Oklahoma Oklahoma City OK 1984-1990; Com Dio Oklahoma Oklahoma City OK 1981-1991; Cmsn Mnstry Accountability Dio Oklahoma Oklahoma City OK 1981-1985; Deptce Dio Oklahoma Oklahoma City OK 1980-1991; R All SS Ch McAlester OK 1979-1986; P-in-c The Epis Ch Of The Adv Madison GA 1977-1979. Auth, "Abortions Aftermath: Need For Healing & Wholeness w Pstr Serv". fr_russ@yahoo.com

FISHER, Sarah Kathleen (Chi) St Peter's Episcopal Church, 621 W Belmont Ave, Chicago IL 60657 **R S Ptr's Epis Ch Chicago IL 2007-** B 6/14/1971 D 12/21/2004 P 6/16/2005 Bp J(ohn) Neil Alexander. Asst Ch Of S Paul And The Redeem Chicago IL 2005-2007; Emm Epis Ch Athens GA 2000-2002. lucysojo@gmail.com

FISHER, Scott Owen (Ak) 1030 2nd Ave, Fairbanks AK 99701 **R S Matt's Epis Ch Fairbanks AK 1991-** B Troy NY 11/16/1948 s Radm John Richard Fisher & Kitson Overmeyer. BA Ken 1970; MDiv Epis TS of The SW 1976. D 6/27/1976 P 3/1/1977 Bp David Rea Cochran. m 10/11/2005 Elisabeth Fisher c 1. Asst To Bp Dio Alaska Fairbanks AK 1979-1991; P-in-c S Matt's Ch Beaver AK 1977-1979; Dio Alaska Fairbanks AK 1976-1991; Asst S Steph's Ch Ft Yukon AK 1976-1977. Auth, "Epis Life," Ikantha. sfisher@mosquitonet.com

FISHER, William Anderson (SanD) 1004 Monterey Vista Way, Encinitas CA 92024 B Buffalo NY 3/2/1971 s John Burgess Fisher & Judith Lucille. BA Br 1994; M. Div. GTS 2004. D 2/7/2004 P 8/25/2004 Bp Henry Irving Louttit. m 4/24/2004 Lenna Beth Nussbaum c 1. Assoc The Epis Ch Of S Andr Encinitas CA 2008-2009; Vic S Lk's Ch Eastchester NY 2004-2008. willfisher@msn.com

FISHER, William Kevin (NY) 347 Davis Ave, Staten Island NY 10310 **S Mary's Castleton Staten Island NY 2010-** B Johnson City TN 4/1/1958 BA U of Maryland 1992; MDiv STUSo 2005. D 6/4/2005 Bp Sylvestre Donato Romero P 7/28/2009 Bp Jerry Alban Lamb. m 12/13/1980 Jane E Phillips c 1. Coop Chr Mnstry Burlington VT 2009-2010; R Ch Of The Gd Shpd Barre VT 2008-2010. rector@stmarysi.com

FISHWICK, Jeffrey Palmer (Va) 1260 River Chase Ln, Charlottesville VA 22901 B Madison WI 2/12/1946 s Marshall William Fishwick & Lucy Farley. BA U of Virginia 1968; MA U Of Delaware Newark 1974; MDiv Yale DS 1976. D 6/19/1976 Bp William Hawley Clark P 3/26/1977 Bp Alexander Doig Stewart. m 7/29/1978 Carol Anne Lichtenberger c 2. P-in-c S Ptr's Epis Ch Purcellville VA 2011; Int S Andr's Ch Longmeadow MA 2009-2011; Int S Thos Ch Lancaster PA 2008-2009; R Chr Epis Ch Charlottesville VA 1995-2008; R S Paul's Epis Ch Summerville SC 1988-1994; R Ch Of S Jas The Less Ashland VA 1982-1987; Asst S Paul's Ch Richmond VA 1979-1982; S Cathr's Sch Richmond VA 1977-1979; Asst Ch Of The Atone Westfield MA 1976-1977. revfish@hotmail.com

FISKE, Thomas Walton (Minn) 123 Linden Avenue, Fairmont MN 56031 **R H Trin Epis Ch Gillette WY 2007-** B Santa Fe NM 5/22/1954 s Eugene William Fiske & Elizebeth Ann. BA Metropltn St Coll of Denver 1981; MDiv Epis TS of The SW 2002. D 6/15/2002 P 12/17/2002 Bp James Louis Jelinek. m 7/12/1981 Mary C Wenstrom c 2. S Mart's Epis Ch Fairmont MN 2004-2007; Dio Minnesota Minneapolis MN 2002-2003. fr.tom@holytrinitywy.org

FITCH, Stuart Grunewald (Los) 585 30th Ave, Santa Cruz CA 95062 **Died 3/19/2010** B Los Angeles CA 5/21/1924 s Stewart Jackson Fitch & Marie Benedicta. BA Stan 1947; MA Stan 1948; MDiv CDSP 1953. D 1/1/1953 P 11/6/1953 Bp Richard S Watson. c 3. Integrity 1992; Ord of S Lk 1992; Sis of the Trsfg 1990. snfitch@sbeglobal.net

FITCH, William Babcock (USC) 6342 Yorkshire Dr, Columbia SC 29209 B Charlotte NC 9/4/1943 s Augustus Fitch & Vida Slemin. USNA; BA U So 1966; STB GTS 1969; MA CUA 1972; MA Salve Regina Coll 1988. D 6/29/1969 P 7/1/1970 Bp John Adams Pinckney. m 8/31/1968 Margaret Ancrum Clarkson c 2. S Thos Ch Eastover SC 1993-1998; Off Of Bsh For ArmdF New York NY 1977-1991; R S Andr's Epis Ch Canton NC 1974-1977; Asst Gr Epis Ch And Kindergarten Camden SC 1970-1971; Assoc S Thad Epis Ch Aiken SC 1969-1970. Auth, *Liturg: Journ of the Litergical Conf*; Auth, *Naval War Coll Revs*. Alcuin Club; No Amer Acad of Liturg.

FITE, Robert Cotton (Chi) 212 Wood Ct, Wilmette IL 60091 B New Rochelle NY 5/6/1938 s Robert Hunter Fite & Mary Josephine. BA Wms 1960; MDiv GTS 1965; Urban Trng Cntr 1968; PhD NWU 1981. D 6/19/1965 Bp Charles Ellsworth Bennison Jr P 1/15/1966 Bp Robert Lionne DeWitt. m 10/14/1989 Diane Hummell c 2. Advoc Hlth Care Oak Brook IL 1979-2003; Assoc S Lk's Ch Evanston IL 1976-2003; Trin Ch Princeton NJ 1973-1976; Cur S Paul's Ch Philadelphia PA 1965-1967. Auth, "The Cong as a Workplace," *Par Nrsng*, Sage Publ, 1999; Auth, *Becoming m*, 1993. cotton.fite@sbcglobal.net

FITTERER, John Angus (Cal) 4580 Klahanie Dr Se, Issaquah WA 98029 B Ellensburg WA 7/1/1922 s Clarence Joseph Fitterer & Violet Claire. BA S Louis U 1945; PHL S Louis U 1947; MA S Louis U 1947; STL Gregorian U 1955; DHum Gregorian U 1971. Rec from Roman Catholic 2/1/1979 as Priest Bp Morris Fairchild Arnold. m 10/20/1990 Karen L Guthrie. Asst To Bp Of California Dio California San Francisco CA 1980-1984; Int Ch Of S Jn The Evang Hingham MA 1979-1980. Auth, "Homer'S Odyssey In Latin Hexameters"; Auth, "Metaphy In Plato'S Republ"; Auth, "Legal Logic For Law Students"; Auth, "Life Care For Seniors". Distinguished Citizen Awd Boys Club Of Amer 1972; Distinguished Civil Serv Medal US-A 1968. kjfitterer@aol.com

FITTS, Ronald Sheldon (Eas) 21103 Striper Run, Rock Hall MD 21661 B Buffalo NY 10/15/1928 s William Hitchborn Fitts & Dorothy May. Fllshp Coll of Preachers; BA Hob 1952; BD EDS 1956; MA Colg 1972. D 6/29/1956 P 6/1/1957 Bp Lauriston L Scaife. m 3/1/1984 Nancy Lee Weber c 3. R Chr Ch Denton MD 1990-1993; Chr Epis Ch Great Choptank Par Cambridge MD 1989-1990; Int S Mary's Ch Portsmouth RI 1989; Int S Ptr's By The Sea Narragansett RI 1988; Assoc Bruton Par Williamsburg VA 1983-1988; Dio Sthrn Virginia Norfolk VA 1983-1988; R S Jas Epis Ch Newport Newport DE 1978-1983; Dio Cntrl New York Syracuse NY 1975-1978; R S Thos Ch Hamilton NY 1971-1978; R S Andr's Ch New Berlin NY 1966-1970; P-in-c S Matt's Ch So New Berlin NY 1966-1970; P-in-c S Jn's Epis Ch Elmira Heights NY 1962-1966; Cur S Jas' Ch Batavia NY 1956-1959. Fell Coll of Preachers Washington DC 1968. rsfitts@verizon.net

FITZGERALD, Joe (Az) 2288 W Silverbell Tree Dr, Tucson AZ 85745 B Los Angeles CA 8/21/1956 s Harold Fitzgerald & Carmel. BA U CA, Los Angeles 1978; MA Washington Theol Un 1986; MAPC Loyola U 1996. Rec from

Roman Catholic 4/30/2011 as Priest Bp Kirk Stevan Smith. m 11/8/2008 Deanna Mitchell. Contrib, "The Sprt in the OT from the Perspective of Liberation Theol," *Sword*, Ord of Carmelites, 1987. Acad of Magical Arts / The Magic Castle 1977-1988; Alpha Sigma Nu hon Soc 1996; Theta Xi Fraternity 1974; Tucson Chapl Assn 2005. Honored Alum Crespi Carmelite HS 2001. joe_fitzgerald@q.com

FITZGERALD III, John Henry (Mich) 1350 Berkshire Rd, Grosse Pointe Park MI 48230 **D S Phil And S Steph Epis Ch Detroit MI 1985-** B Brooklyn NY 10/30/1933 s John William Fitzgerald & Gertrude Sexton. Whitaker TS; BS Ya 1955. D 3/9/1985 Bp Henry Irving Mayson. m 8/10/1958 Beverly Byrne c 3.

FITZGERALD, John Paul (HB) No address on file. B Seattle WA 11/27/1934 s Joseph Paul Fitzgerald & Rosalind Florence. BA U of Washington 1958; BD CDSP 1961. D 10/13/1961 P 12/1/1962 Bp William F Lewis. m 12/26/1961 Carolyn Hope Gilfilen c 1. R S Geo's Epis Ch Warren MI 1970-1972; R S Andr's Epis Ch Washington Crt Hse OH 1964-1965; Asst S Steph's Epis Ch Seattle WA 1961-1964.

FITZGERALD, John William (WNC) 4656 E Shores Dr, Morganton NC 28655 **Died 1/12/2011** B Frankfort IN 1/20/1923 s Francis Michael Fitzgerald & Lena Jane. BA Asbury Coll 1948; MDiv Drew U 1951. D 3/14/1952 P 11/1/1952 Bp Noble C Powell. c 1.

FITZGERALD, Todd R. (Md) 17641 College Road, Saint James MD 21740 **Chapl S Jas Sch St Jas MD 2005-** B Shreveport LA 12/1/1969 s Robert William FitzGerald & Patsy Dianne. BA Texas A&M U 1991; MDiv SWTS 1998. D 6/24/1998 Bp Robert Jefferson Hargrove Jr P 6/23/1999 Bp Claude Edward Payne. m 7/29/1995 Amy McGehee c 2. Chapl S Andrews Epis Sch Austin TX 2000-2005; Asst R S Dav's Ch Austin TX 1998-2000. trfitzgerald@stjames.edu

FITZGERALD, William Thomas (Ga) 3168 Seed Lake Rd, Lakemont GA 30552 B Augusta GA 4/10/1927 s William Thomas Fitzgerald & Martha Wall. BS Cit 1949; MS U GA 1953; BD STUSo 1960. D 6/28/1960 Bp Henry I Louttit P 1/10/1961 Bp William Francis Moses. m 6/14/1952 Martha Simpson c 8. R Chr Ch Frederica St Simons Island GA 1978-1992; Vic S Ign Mssn St Simons Island GA 1978-1992; R Ch Of The Redeem Sarasota FL 1960-1978. wtfitz@earthlink.net

FITZGIBBONS, Elisabeth S(usan) (Mass) 19 Pilgrim Rd, Reading MA 01867 **Asst R The Ch Of Our Redeem Lexington MA 2008-** B Cheyenne WY 8/26/1969 d Kerry Charles Fitzgibbons & E(dith). BA Seattle U 1990; MSW Boston Coll 1996; MA Boston Coll 1996; MDiv CDSP 2006. D 6/24/2006 Bp Vincent Waydell Warner P 1/11/2007 Bp Bavi Rivera. m 9/21/1996 Julien Reinaldo Goulet c 2. Cur Trin Ch Topsfield MA 2006-2008. sabethfitzgibbons@hotmail.com

FITZGIBBONS, Michael John (Spok) 8505 W Hood Ave, Kennewick WA 99336 **Wood Rivers Epis Par Shoshone ID 1970-** B Salt Lake City UT 6/24/1941 s James F Fitzgibbons & Virginia L. BA U of Washington 1964; MDiv CDSP 1970; U of Utah 1972; WA SU 1977; Idaho St U 1978; Lsi #1 & 2 78 79 1980; Fam Ther Trng 1981; Var Trng & Vocational Courses 1993. D 12/21/1970 Bp Norman L Foote P 6/1/1971 Bp William Benjamin Spofford. m 8/24/1968 Pamela L Leonard. Dio Spokane Spokane WA 2004-2009; Asst All SS Ch Richland WA 1995-2002; Dio Spokane Spokane WA 1986-1994; P-in-c S Jn's Ch Un Gap WA 1982-1985; Supply P Dio Spokane Spokane WA 1981-1986; Asst S Mk's Epis Ch Moscow ID 1976-1981; P-in-c H Trin Epis Ch Grangeville ID 1974-1975; Supply P Epis Ch of the Nativ Lewiston ID 1972-1974; Wood Rivers Epis Par Shoshone ID 1970-1972.

FITZHUGH, Mark Lee (CGC) 28 Miracle Strip Pkwy SW, Fort Walton Beach FL 32548 **R S Simon's On The Sound Ft Walton Bch FL 2010-** B Mobile AL 4/25/1961 s William Neale Fitzhugh & Dorothea Louise. BA U of So Alabama 1985; MDiv GTS 2001. D 6/2/2001 Bp Onell Asiselo Soto P 12/4/2001 Bp Henry Nutt Parsley Jr. m 8/5/1995 Cheri Smith c 2. Asst Chr Ch Greenwich CT 2003-2010; R Ch Of The Mssh Heflin AL 2001-2003; Asst Gr Ch Anniston AL 2001-2003. revmarkfitzhugh@gmail.com

FITZPATRICK, Michael Carl (Mich) 24699 Grand River Ave, Detroit MI 48219 B Wayne County MI 11/5/1956 s Carl Lee Fitzpatrick & Rosa M. D 12/16/2010 P 7/14/2011 Bp Wendell Nathaniel Gibbs Jr. mfitzpatrick23@comcast.net

FITZPATRICK, Paul Elliot (Nwk) 216 Cypress Ct, Ramsey NJ 07446 **Mem, COM Dio Newark Newark NJ 2009-; D Chr Ch Hackensack NJ 2006-** B Omaha NE 9/19/1961 s Alfred Fitzpatrick & Shirley. BA St Ptr's Coll 1990; Newark TS 2004. D 11/18/2006 Bp John Palmer Croneberger. m 6/27/1981 Bonnie Vietheer c 3. dcnpaul06@yahoo.com

FITZPATRICK, Robert Joseph (NY) 325 Little Silver Point Rd, Little Silver NJ 07739 **S Anne's Ch Washingtonville NY 2010-** B Newark NJ 11/12/1964 s Robert Emmett Fitzpatrick & Dorothy Marie. BA Rutgers U 1989; MA Rutgers U 1990; MDiv GTS 2010. D 11/14/2009 P 6/19/2010 Bp George Edward Councell. m 7/8/1989 Catherine Mae Hawn c 1. bobfitz64@verizon.net

✠ **FITZPATRICK, Rt Rev Robert LeRoy** (Haw) Office of the Bishop, 229 Queen Emma Sq, Honolulu HI 96813 B Decatur IL 9/20/1958 s Kenneth Eugene Fitzpatrick & Mary. BA DePauw U 1981; MDiv GTS 1986; DMin SWTS 1999. D 6/24/1986 P 5/9/1987 Bp Edward Witker Jones Con 3/10/2007 for Haw. m 5/1/1982 Beatrice Elizondo c 2. P-in-c S Lk's Epis Ch Honolulu HI 2003-2006; Cn Dio Hawaii Honolulu HI 2000-2007; R Gr Epis Ch Ft Wayne IN 1990-2000; Asst R S Ptr's Ch Morristown NJ 1986-1990. DD SWTS 2008; DD GTS 2007. rlfitzpatrick@episcopalhawaii.org

FITZSIMMONS, Daniel V (Be) 16 Allenberry Dr, Wilkes Barre PA 18706 **R S Mart-In-The-Fields Mtn Top PA 2009-** B Hazleton PA 1/4/1947 s Steve Voyvodich & Beatrice Doreen. BA Wilkes Coll 1986; MA Marywood U 1989. D 4/29/2000 P 12/2/2000 Bp Paul Victor Marshall. Asst All SS Epis Ch Lehighton PA 2000-2006; Asst S Jn's Epis Ch Palmerton PA 2000-2006. SCARLET_PIPER@VERIZON.NET

FITZSIMMONS, James (Az) 1741 North Camino Rebecca, Nogales AZ 85621 B Los Angeles CA 3/30/1932 d Charles H Polhemus & Carrie. Stan 1953; AA Contra Costa Coll 1962; Cert U of So Carolina 1975; BA Sch for Deacons 1984. D 6/3/1989 Bp William Edwin Swing. m 4/11/1953 Lee Sherwin Vellom c 1. Serv Ch Of The H Trin Richmond CA 1989-1996. Ord Of Dok 1997; Professed Tertiary Of The Soc Of S Fran 1989. annevellom@theriver.com

FLAGSTAD, Judith Marie (SD) 101 W Prospect Ave Apt 3, Pierre SD 57501 **Assoc Trin Epis Ch Pierre SD 2004-** B Webster SD 12/12/1950 d Alvin Flagstad & Marie. BS Nthrn St U Aberdeen SD 1973; MDiv Vancouver TS 2005. D 11/15/1996 P 10/23/2004 Bp Creighton Leland Robertson. Int Trin Epis Ch Pierre SD 2009-2010. flagstad1@pie.midco.net

FLAHERTY, Jane Frances (SVa) 614 E 7th St, Alton IL 62002 B Alton IL 6/29/1939 d Francis William Flaherty & Julia Genevieve. BS Notre Dame Coll 1961; MA S Louis U 1971; EdD Rutgers-The St U 1978; MDiv GTS 1991. D 6/8/1991 P 2/15/1992 Bp George Phelps Mellick Belshaw. Ecum Off Dio Sthrn Virginia Norfolk VA 1999-2002; R S Chris's Epis Ch Portsmouth VA 1995-2004; Dio Sthrn Virginia Norfolk VA 1992-2002; Asst Trin Ch Moorestown NJ 1991-1995. janeflaherty@sbcglobal.net

FLANAGAN, Carol Cole (WA) St. John's Episcopal Church & School, 3427 Olney Laytonsville Road, Olney MD 20832 **Com on Cn Dio Washington Washington DC 2011-; R S Jn's Ch Olney MD 2008-** B Hartford CT 10/25/1947 d Quintin Perry Cole & Joan Van Steenberg. BA Villa Maria Coll 1983; MDiv VTS 1986. D 6/28/1986 Bp Henry Irving Mayson P 5/28/1987 Bp William George Burrill. m 2/3/1968 William Emmett Flanagan c 2. Int Chr Ch Detroit MI 2007-2008; Cn Dio Washington Washington DC 2003-2007; Judicial Panel/Eccl Crt Dio Ohio Cleveland OH 2000-2003; Resolutns Com Dio Ohio Cleveland OH 2000-2003; Com on Cn, Chair Dio Ohio Cleveland OH 1999-2003; R S Ptr's Epis Ch Lakewood OH 1999-2003; Int S Barth's Ch Baltimore MD 1998-1999; Stndg Cmsn on Const & Cn Exec Coun Appointees New York NY 1997-2000; Trst, Epis Hsng Corp Dio Maryland Baltimore MD 1997-1999; Int S Geo Ch Hampstead MD 1996-1998; Bp's Pstr Dio Maryland Baltimore MD 1995-1996; Gvnr's T/F on Sexual Misconduct Dio Maryland Baltimore MD 1994-1995; Stndg Cmsn on Hlth Exec Coun Appointees New York NY 1991-1997; Dio Maryland Baltimore MD 1991-1993; Vic Ch of the H Evangelists Baltimore MD 1990-1995; Chair Stwdshp Com Dio Maryland Baltimore MD 1990-1993; Trst Bex Columbus OH 1986-2001; Chair Liturg & Mus Cmsn Dio Maryland Baltimore MD 1986-1990; Asst Chr Ch Pittsford NY 1986-1989; Asst H Trin Epis Ch Bowie MD 1986; Dio Maryland Baltimore MD 1985-1988; Dio Maryland Baltimore MD 1985-1988; Com on the Full Participation of Wmn in the Ch Exec Coun Appointees New York NY 1985-1988; T/F on the Washington Off Exec Coun Appointees New York NY 1985-1988. AP 1986; AAM 1987; Consult, Washbhington Off 1986-1986; EPF 1985; EUC 1987; EWC 1977; RCRC 1985. Alice Meynell Literary Awd Villa Maria Coll 1982. ccolef@verizon.net

FLANAGAN, Michael Patrick (USC) 104 Brockman Dr, Mauldin SC 29662 **Dep to GC Dio Upper So Carolina Columbia SC 2010-2013; R H Cross Epis Ch Simpsonville SC 1995-** B Charlotte NC 8/18/1955 s Clifford Flanagan & Pearl. BSIE No Carolina St U 1977; MDiv Nash 1991. D 5/19/1991 P 5/30/1992 Bp Roger John White. m 5/22/1982 Deborah Anne Braun c 2. Dioc Exec Coun Dio Upper So Carolina Columbia SC 2007-2010; S Mich And All Ang' Columbia SC 1991-1994. Auth, *Come to the Wilderness (Mus CD)*, Indep, 2002. BroSA 2006. fflan@charter.net

FLANAGAN, Robert Daniel (NY) 1160 Great Pond Rd, North Andover MA 01845 **Sch Min Brooks Sch Chap No Andover MA 2008-** B Stanford CT 5/2/1963 BA Trin 1985; MDiv VTS 2003. D 3/8/2003 P 9/20/2003 Bp Mark Sean Sisk. m 5/13/1989 Elaine Flanagan c 2. Assoc R S Matt's Ch Bedford NY 2003-2008. Auth, "Growing a Soul," *Bk*, Wine Press Pub, 2008. bflanagan@brooksschool.org

FLANDERS, Alden Beaman (Mass) 27 Valley Hill Dr, Worcester MA 01602 B Cincinnati OH 4/16/1945 s Wilmont Baenziger Flanders & Nancy. BA Hob 1967; MA U of Maine 1969; MDiv EDS 1972; MFA Brandeis U 1973. D 6/24/1972 Bp Robert Rae Spears Jr P 5/1/1973 Bp Albert A Chambers. m 6/17/1968 Birgitte Dyrlov Madsen c 1. R The Ch Of Our Redeem Lexington MA 1986-2003; P-in-c Emm Ch Jaffrey NH 1984-1985; Vic H Cross Epis Ch Weare NH 1977-1984; S Paul's Sch Concord NH 1975-1986; Asst R The Ch

Of The Adv Boston MA 1974-1975. Auth, "There Will Always Be A Goody Glover". ABFLAN2000@AOL.COM

FLANDERS JR, J(ames) William (WA) 3714 Harrison St Nw, Washington DC 20015 B New Haven CT USA 5/2/1933 s James William Flanders & Helen. BA Ya 1957; MDiv VTS 1962. D 9/29/1964 Bp Charles F Hall P 8/1/1966 Bp Paul Moore Jr. m 4/30/2005 Susan Mann c 4. Asst Min S Mk's Ch Washington DC 1966-1967; Asst Chr Epis Ch Winchester VA 1964-1965. Auth, *Fishers of Men*; Auth, *Love is a Verb*; Auth, *Sweet Love Remembered*; Auth, *That Time of Year*; Auth, *To Walk the Sea*. billflanders@earthlink.net

FLANDERS, Susan Mann (WA) Susan Flanders, 3714 Harrison St., NW, Washington DC 20015 B Philadelphia PA 10/4/1943 d Robert Mann & Betty. Wellesley Coll 1963; BA GW 1968; MDiv VTS 1985. D 6/8/1985 P 12/18/1985 Bp John Thomas Walker. m 4/30/2005 J(ames) William Flanders c 3. Stndg Com Dio Washington Washington DC 1999-2003; R S Jn's Ch Chevy Chase MD 1998-2008; P-in-c S Jn's Ch Ft Washington MD 1997-1998; Int Pstr Gr Cathd San Francisco CA 1997; Dioc Coun Dio Washington Washington DC 1994-1996; Assoc R S Mk's Ch Washington DC 1986-1997. Washington Dc Epis Cleric Assn Bd 1998-2002. susanflanders@earthlink.net

FLANIGEN, John Monteith (Ida) Po Box 71027, Tuscaloosa AL 35407 B Warren,OH 7/8/1925 s John Monteith Flanigen & Hannah Jane. BA Oglethorpe U 1950; MDiv SWTS 1957. D 7/26/1957 P 5/24/1958 Bp Thomas N Carruthers. Int S Thos Epis Ch Knoxville TN 1998-2002; Int S Fran' Ch Norris TN 1997-1998; Vic S Jn's Epis Ch Amer Falls ID 1990-1996; Emm Ch Hailey ID 1987-1990; R Gr-Calv Epis Ch Clarkesville GA 1977-1980. johnflaniger@mound.net

FLECK, Timothy R (Lex) St. Martha's Episcopal Church, PO Box 21944, Lexington KY 40522 **Jubilee Off Dio Lexington Lexington KY 2011-; Chair, Justice and Peace Cmsn Dio Lexington Lexington KY 2010-; Ldrshp Team Dio Lexington Lexington KY 2010-; P-in-c St Martha's Epis Ch Lexington KY 2009-** B Columbia City IN 5/26/1964 s Richard Grover Fleck & Joyce Ann. AB Harvard Coll 1986; M.Arch Col 1990; MDiv Chr TS 2008; MDiv Bex 2009. D 6/20/2009 Bp Catherine Elizabeth Maples Waynick P 12/21/2009 Bp Stacy F Sauls. m 2/12/1994 Robert Schmeler. D S Paul's Epis Ch Indianapolis IN 2009; Luth-Epis Campus Mnstry Bd Dio Indianapolis Indianapolis IN 2005-2009. tim@archanglican.org

FLEENER SR, William Joseph (WMich) 5665 S Cherokee Bnd, New Era MI 49446 B Amarillo TX 3/28/1931 s Frank Elwood Fleener & Clara Mae. BA SMU 1951; STM Ya Berk 1954. D 6/2/1954 P 4/2/1955 Bp Charles A Mason. m 10/14/1961 Judith Wieland c 4. Int Pstr H Trin Epis Ch Manistee MI 2008-2009; Int S Jn's Ch Fremont MI 1995-1996; R S Greg's Epis Ch Muskegon MI 1971-1993; Cur Ch Of Our Sav Elmhurst IL 1968-1971; Vic S Paulinus Ch Watseka IL 1964-1968; Vic S Alb's Ch Hubbard TX 1954-1960. Auth, "Var arts," *Color Computer News*, 1982. EWC - Bus Mgr 1994; Int Mnstry Ntwk 1992; Ord Of Julian Of Norwich - Assoc 1995. The Jos Awd EWC, Inc. 2006. bill.fleener@charter.net

FLEENOR, David (Ala) 1 E 29th St, New York NY 10016 **Assoc P Ch Of The Trsfg New York NY 2006-** B Roanoke VA 12/20/1974 s Hubert Fleenor & Dorothy. BA Mssngr Coll 1996; MDiv Ch of God TS 1999; STM GTS 2006. D 6/3/2006 Bp Marc Handley Andrus P 12/18/2006 Bp Henry Nutt Parsley Jr. m 6/30/2000 Heather Marshall-Fleenor. dfleenor@gmail.com

FLEENOR, Ryan C (Va) 865 Madison Ave, New York NY 10021 **Lilly Fell S Jas Ch New York NY 2010-** B Atlanta GA 7/4/1984 s Donald Edward Fleenor & Marguerite Ann. BA U of Virginia 2006; MDiv Ya Berk 2010. D 6/5/2010 Bp Shannon Sherwood Johnston P 1/30/2011 Bp Peter James Lee. ryan.fleenor@gmail.com

FLEETWOOD, Zachary William Maddrey (Eur) 70 Maple Ave, Morristown NJ 07960 B Farmville VA 10/3/1950 s James Milton Fleetwood & Hallie Meredith. BA Guilford Coll 1973; Med U of Virginia 1980; MDiv VTS 1987. D 6/13/1987 P 4/1/1988 Bp Peter James Lee. m 5/12/1973 Donna G Garnett c 1. Dn The Amer Cathd of the H Trin Paris 75008 FR 2003-2011; Cmsn On Planned Giving Dio Newark Newark NJ 2000-2003; Com Dio Newark Newark NJ 1998-2002; R S Ptr's Ch Morristown NJ 1997-2003; Stndg Com Dio Virginia Richmond VA 1995-1997; Eccl Crt Dio Virginia Richmond VA 1992-1997; R Gr Ch The Plains VA 1990-1997; Cmsn On Liturg And Ch Mus Dio Virginia Richmond VA 1990-1995; Asst to R Chr Ch Georgetown Washington DC 1989-1990; Asst to R S Mary's Epis Ch Arlington VA 1987-1989. dean@americancathedral.org

FLEISCHER, Marie Moorefield (NC) 8241 Allyns Landing Way Apt 304, Raleigh NC 27615 B Baltimore MD 4/24/1944 d George McDonald Moorefield & Virginia Cox. BA Wake Forest U 1966; UTS 1967; MDiv Van 1970. D 6/9/1973 Bp Paul Moore Jr P 7/29/1974 Bp Robert Lionne DeWitt. Cn to Ord Dio No Carolina Raleigh NC 2001-2006; Int Trin Ch Portsmouth VA 2000-2001; Int Trin Epis Ch Buffalo NY 1998-1999; Cn/Dep for Mnstry Dio Wstrn New York Tonawanda NY 1992-1996; Int Emm Ch Moorefield WV 1991-1992; Hampshire Hardy Yoke Wardensville WV 1991-1992; Int S Steph's Ch Romney WV 1991-1992; Admin Stff Dio Maryland Baltimore MD 1988-1990; Vic S Andr's Ch Clear Sprg MD 1987-1989; Cur Trin Ch Shepherdstown WV 1985-1987. BP Wm Scarlett Awd Wit mag 1994; Citation Unitarian Universalist Wmn Fed 1975. nnfleischerrm@aol.com

FLEISCHER, Scott Ronald (USC) 1010 Palmetto St, Georgetown SC 29440 **S Jn's Epis Ch Columbia SC 2011-** B Minnesota MN 4/22/1970 s Ronald Stephen Fleischer & Sandra Yvette Pauline. BA California St U 1993; MDiv TESM 2002. D 6/8/2002 P 12/8/2002 Bp John Wadsworth Howe. m 1/18/1997 Victoria L Bernardi c 3. P Assoc/ Vol Ch Of The Gd Shpd York SC 2007-2011; York Place Epis Ch Hm For Chld York SC 2006-2010; Prince Geo Winyah Epis Preschool Georgetown SC 2002-2006; Cur Prince Geo Winyah Epis Ch Georgetown SC 2002-2006; Epis Ch Of The Resurr Longwood FL 1997-2000. srf@stjohnscolumbia.org

FLEISCHMAN, Donald Michael (Mil) 297 N Main St, Richland Center WI 53581 **S Barn Richland Cntr WI 2010-** B Danville KY 1/24/1972 s Donald Ray Fleischman & Willette Tanton. BA Wstrn Michigan U 1995; MAOT Gordon-Conwell Theol Seminry 2000; MAR Gordon-Conwell Theol Seminry 2001; Cert. Angl Stds VTS 2009. D 6/6/2009 P 3/13/2010 Bp Steven Andrew Miller. m 12/30/1992 Gypsy Free Gypsy Free Tobin c 4. donfleischman@gmail.com

FLEMING, Carol Ann Spayd (NI) 70865 Wayne St, Union MI 49130 **P in Charge S Jn Of The Cross Bristol IN 2011-; Chapl Howe Mltry Sch Howe IN 2010-** B Sandusky OH 8/11/1955 d Gary Allen Spayd & Carolyn Sue. BS Bowling Green St U 1979; M.Ed U of Toledo 1988; CAS SWTS 2004. D 3/21/1999 Bp John-David Mercer Schofield P 6/18/2004 Bp Edward Stuart Little II. m 10/14/1978 Charles Walter Fleming. P in Charge S Mk's Epis Ch Wadsworth OH 2008-2010; Assitant Gr Epis Ch Sandusky OH 2007-2008; P in Charge S Andr's By The Lake Epis Ch Michigan City IN 2003-2006; D S Paul's Epis Ch La Porte IN 2001-2002; D No Cntrl Dnry Dio Ohio Cleveland OH 1999-2001. NAAD. SW Dist Elem. Phys. Ed. Tender of the Year SWAHPER 1996; California/Physical Educ Elem Tchr of the Year CAHPER 1995. revcarolfleming@gmail.com

FLEMING, Joan Elizabeth (NJ) 183 Hartley Ave., Princeton NJ 08540 B London UK 8/19/1938 d Arthur Charles Cecil Newman & Wynifred Kate. BA Oxf 1960; MDiv PrTS 1979; ThM PrTS 1991. D 6/14/1986 P 3/21/1987 Bp George Phelps Mellick Belshaw. m 6/2/1962 John Vincent Fleming c 3. Chr Ch New Brunswick NJ 1991-2004; Assoc S Paul's Epis Ch Bound Brook NJ 1986-1991. fleming.joan@gmail.com

FLEMING, John Charles (Mo) 638 Huntwood Ln, Kirkwood MO 63122 B Saint Louis MO 10/8/1938 s Raymond Francis Fleming & Rose Ann. BA Glennon Coll St. Louis MO 1960; Kenrich TS 1964; Med Washington U 1970. Rec from Roman Catholic 3/24/1999 as Priest Bp Hays H. Rockwell. m 1/1/1994 Patricia Ann Hayes c 1. R S Tim's Epis Ch Creve Coeur MO 1999-2010. jfleming@saint-tims.org

FLEMING JR, Peter Wallace (SwFla) 1 Beach Dr SE Apt 2214, Saint Petersburg FL 33701 B Augusta GA 3/9/1930 s Peter Wallace Fleming & Sara Elizabeth. AB U GA 1951; STUSo 1953; MDiv VTS 1954. D 6/24/1954 Bp Middleton S Barnwell P 3/25/1955 Bp Albert R Stuart. m 6/9/1960 Marion Courtney Lucas c 3. S Thos' Epis Ch St Petersburg FL 1976-1994; R S Dav's Epis Ch Lakeland FL 1961-1976; Vic The Epis Ch Of The Annunc Vidalia GA 1955-1958; Vic S Paul's Epis Ch Jesup GA 1954-1955. petflem@gmail.com

FLEMING JR, Raymond Edgar (Los) 484 Cliff Dr Apt 10, Laguna Beach CA 92651 B Worcester MA 4/13/1940 s Raymond Edgar Fleming & Betty. BA MacMurray Coll 1963; MDiv SWTS 1966. D 6/11/1966 P 12/17/1966 Bp Albert A Chambers. m 2/16/1963 Marcia Ruth Myers c 2. R S Mary's Par Laguna Bch CA 1989-2004; R H Faith Par Inglewood CA 1976-1989; R Gr Epis Ch Norwalk CT 1972-1976; Cur Emm Meml Epis Ch Champaign IL 1966-1969. frref@aol.com

FLEMING, William Rupert (Mich) 292 Abbey St, Birmingham MI 48009 B Cleveland OH 8/31/1937 s Raymond Joseph Fleming & Mary Elizabeth. BA Denison U 1959; MDiv Bex 1964. D 6/29/1964 P 1/1/1965 Bp Richard S M Emrich. m 3/26/1960 Rosanna Brew c 3. Chr Ch Detroit MI 2001-2004; Asst Chr Ch Cranbrook Bloomfield Hills MI 1998-2004; Dio Michigan Detroit MI 1986-1987; Asst Chr Ch Dearborn MI 1964-1968. Auth, "Var Profsnl," *Personal arts*.

FLEMISTER, Ernestein Cassell (SwFla) 212 W Idlewild Avenue, Tampa FL 33604 **R S Jas Hse Of Pryr Tampa FL 2009-** B Monrovia Liberia 4/8/1952 d Arthur B Cassell & Cora A. BD Franklin U Colubmus OH 1985; MBA Xavier U 1990; MDiv Bex 2007. D 5/13/2006 Bp Kenneth Lester Price P 6/16/2007 Bp Thomas Edward Breidenthal. Vic Gr Ch Cincinnati OH 2007-2009. ernesteinf@yahoo.com

FLEMMING, Leslie Abel (SO) 1 Kent Dr, Athens OH 45701 **P S Ptr's Ch Gallipolis OH 2008-** B Brooklyn NY 10/4/1943 d Michael Abel & Pauline Dell. BA Carleton Coll 1965; MA U Of Wisconsin Madison WI 1968; PhD U of Wisconsin Madison 1973; MDiv Bex 2008. D 6/23/2007 P 6/28/2008 Bp Thomas Edward Breidenthal. m 6/7/1969 John C Flemming c 3. P Gr Ch Pomeroy OH 2008-2010; D S Alb's Epis Ch Of Bexley Columbus OH

2007-2008. Assc, Comm. of the H Sprt 2003. leslieflemming@columbus.rr.com

FLENTJE, Gregory Laurence (Spr) 4210 Honey Creek Ave Ne, Ada MI 49301 B Quincy IL 4/23/1962 s Laurence Frank Flentje & Donna Maxine. BS W&L 1984; MD U IL 1992; PhD U IL 1994; Cert Br 1999. D 8/24/1992 Bp Peter Hess Beckwith. m 5/29/1993 Janice Marie Reifsteck. D S Mk's Ch Grand Rapids MI 2001; D S Thos Epis Ch Rochester NY 1999-2001; D Ch Of The Redeem Providence RI 1994-1997; D Chap Of S Jn The Div Champaign IL 1992-1994. Integrity; NAAD. glflentje@aol.com

FLES, Jacob C (Me) 2 Dresden Ave, Gardiner ME 04345 **R Chr Ch Gardiner ME 1994-** B Patterson NJ 5/26/1954 s Jacob William Fles & Joan Alice. MA Oral Roberts U 1977; Gordon-Conwell TS 1984; Cert Epis TS of The SW 1990; Cler Ldrshp Inst 1998; PrTS 2000. D 7/6/1990 Bp William Harvey Wolfrum P 1/20/1991 Bp Alpha Mohammed. m 4/7/1985 Rebecca Walker c 3. S Alb's Epis Ch Arlington TX 1992-1994; Gr And S Steph's Epis Ch Colorado Sprg CO 1990-1992. Auth, "Living Unit Grp Manuel," *Campus Life*. rebecca.fles@myfairpoint.net

FLESHER, Hubert Louis (Be) 602 Fairway Vlg, Leeds MA 01053 B Elyria OH 4/30/1933 s O Jay Flesher & Armide Elizabeth. BA Pomona Coll 1954; BD Yale DS 1958; MDiv Yale DS 1963; MA Yale DS 1965. D 5/30/1958 P 12/6/1958 Bp Nelson Marigold Burroughs. m 4/3/1965 Mary J Mosher c 2. Int S Jas' Ch Greenfield MA 1998-1999; Form Int S Mary's Epis Ch Manchester CT 1997-1998; Smith Northampton MA 1990-1992; Dio Bethlehem Bethlehem PA 1971-1990; Instr Biblic Stds EDS Cambridge MA 1963-1965. AAR 1960; Soc Of Exegesis Biblic Lit 1960. Schlrs Hist And Philos Of Sci 1st Intl Conf E Germany/USA 1988; Neh Grant Biblic Archeol 1984; Phi Beta Kappa (Pres 1980-90) Leh 1976; Omicron Delta Kappa 1972; Phi Beta Kappa Pomona Coll 1953. hflesher@comcast.net

FLETCHER, Margaret Ann Laurie (Vt) St. Peter's Episcopal Church, 300 Pleasant St., Bennington VT 05201 **S Thos' Epis Ch Brandon VT 2009-** B Butterworth South Africa 12/14/1943 d Harnish Boyd & Margaret. BA SUNY 1995; MDiv Yale DS 2000. D 2/2/2008 P 4/18/2009 Bp Thomas C Ely. m 3/14/1967 Alan Fletcher c 2. margflet@aol.com

FLETT, Carol (WA) St. Alban's Parish, 3001 Wisconsin Ave NW, Washington DC 20016 **Assoc S Alb's Par Washington DC 2010-** B White Plains NY 11/26/1947 d Harold McCormick & Helen. BA U of Connecticut 1969; Untd TS of the Twin Cities 1985; MDiv EDS 1988; DMin EDS 2000. D 6/23/1988 Bp Robert Marshall Anderson P 1/14/1989 Bp David Elliot Johnson. m 6/14/1969 George S Flett c 2. Interfaith Prog Coordntr Cathd of St Ptr & St Paul Washington DC 2007-2010; R S Barth's Ch Laytonsville MD 2007-2010; P-in-c Par Of S Paul Newton Highlands MA 2005-2007; R S Ptr's Ch Weston MA 1997-2005; R S Mk's Epis Ch Burlington MA 1992-1997; Assoc The Ch Of Our Redeem Lexington MA 1988-1992. Fllshp of the Soc of St. Jn 2000. revflett@yahoo.com

FLEXER, Katharine Grace (ECR) 6581 Camden Ave, San Jose CA 95120 **The Epis Ch In Almaden San Jose CA 2011-** B Bellevue WA 12/4/1971 d James Ralph Flexer & Susan Mary. BA Whitman Coll 1993; MDiv CDSP 1997; Ripon Coll Cuddesdon Oxford GB 1998. D 1/23/2000 Bp Vincent Waydell Warner P 9/9/2000 Bp William Edwin Swing. m 5/21/2005 James Keegan Hinch c 2. Assoc R for Chr Formation S Mich's Ch New York NY 2005-2010; COM Dio California San Francisco CA 2004-2005; Chair, Dept of Yth & YA Dio California San Francisco CA 2003-2005; Assoc R S Clem's Ch Berkeley CA 2002-2005; Dir of Alum & Ch Relatns CDSP Berkeley CA 2000-2002; S Aid's Ch San Francisco CA 2000-2001. kateflexer@yahoo.com

FLICK, Robert Terry (Tex) 1410 Cambridge Dr, Friendswood TX 77546 **Assoc S Steph's Epis Ch Houston TX 2011-; Vic Lord Of The St Epis Mssn Ch Houston TX 2010-** B Cincinnati OH 11/17/1947 BA Duns Scotus Coll Detriot MI 1971; MS Wright St U 1979; MDiv St. Leonard Coll Dayton OH 1981; MBA Our Lady Of The Lake U San Antonio TX 1999. Rec from Roman Catholic 11/19/2003 Bp Don Adger Wimberly. m 10/10/1992 Sarah R Robinson c 1. R S Mich's Ch La Marque TX 2004-2011. kaflick@aol.com

FLIESS, Rexford Albert (Eau) P.O. Box 926, Bayfield WI 54814 **Died 11/7/2009** B Medina OH 1/9/1945 s Manfred Fliess & Ruth Way. BA Davis & Elkins Coll 1966; MDiv SWTS 1979; Cert Ldrshp Acad for New Directions 1995. D 6/9/1979 P 12/19/1979 Bp John Shelby Spong. c 1. rex@fliess.org

FLINN, J Seymour (Del) 4140 Villa Ridge Ct Unit 110, Rapid City SD 57701 B Wilmington DE 10/22/1927 s Lewis Barr Flinn & Elizabeth Winchester. BA Pr 1949; MDiv VTS 1954; STM Yale DS 1975. D 6/20/1954 Bp Arthur R Mc Kinstry P 5/1/1955 Bp John Brooke Mosley. m 7/11/1986 Janet Crosby c 3. Int Pstr S Thos's Par Newark DE 1992-1994; Sr Assoc S Jas Ch New York NY 1987-1992; R S Jn's Epis Ch Troy NY 1978-1987; Assoc Chr Ch Greenwich CT 1970-1978; Ovrs Dept Epis Ch Cntr New York NY 1966-1970; Founding R S Dav's Epis Ch Wilmington DE 1954-1959. Auth, "Should Wmn Be Priests?," 1989; Auth, "Responsible Drinking," 1977; Auth, "Why Care?," 1976. Epis Soc for Mnstry on Aging 1991-1996. seyflinn@rushmore.com

FLINTOM, Jack Glenn (Md) 2030 Marshall Ln, Hayes VA 23072 **Supply Dio Sthrn Virginia Norfolk VA 1998-** B Greensboro NC 9/22/1949 s Albert Flintom & Rachel. AA Truett Mcconnell Jr Coll 1969; BA Merc 1971; MDiv Harvard DS 1977. D 6/25/1977 P 5/18/1978 Bp William Gillette Weinhauer. m 10/31/1981 Marjorie Sembert. Cur S Tim's Ch Catonsville MD 1982-1987; Vic S Andr's Ch Bessemer City NC 1980-1982; Vic Trin Ch Kings Mtn NC 1980-1982; Asst S Lk's Ch Salisbury NC 1978-1979; Gr Ch Morganton NC 1978. mflintom@verizon.net

FLOBERG, John F (ND) Po Box 612, Fort Yates ND 58538 **P-in-c All SS Ch Minot ND 2007-; Ch of the Cross Selfridge ND 2005-; Dio No Dakota Fargo ND 1991-** B Moorhead MN 6/26/1959 s Vincent B A Floberg & Alice M. Cert Luth Bible Inst 1984; BA Concordia Coll 1985; MDiv Bex 1991. D 4/5/1991 P 10/6/1991 Bp Andrew Hedtler Fairfield. m 7/16/1993 Sloane R Floberg c 4. R S Jas Ch Ft Yates ND 1991; R/Cn Mssnr S Lk's Ch Ft Yates ND 1991; Asst Trin Ch Rochester NY 1988-1991. Allen Fellowowship 1990. jsfloberg@msn.com

FLOBERG, Sloane R (ND) 820 West Central Ave, Bismarck ND 58501 **Dio No Dakota Fargo ND 2003-; D S Lk's Ch Ft Yates ND 2003-** B Valley City ND 6/27/1971 BS No Dakota St U 1993. D 6/12/2003 Bp Andrew Hedtler Fairfield. m 7/16/1993 John F Floberg c 3. sloanefloberg@msn.com

FLOCKEN, Robin (CNY) 10 Mill St, Cazenovia NY 13035 **R S Ptr's Epis Ch Cazenovia NY 1988-** B Oxnard CA 2/24/1950 s Walter Ivan Flocken & Norma. BA Rutgers Coll 1972; MDiv GTS 1978. D 6/17/1978 P 2/24/1979 Bp Alexander Doig Stewart. m 8/17/1974 Patricia Smith c 2. Dio Wstrn Massachusetts Springfield MA 1981-1988; R S Jn's Ch Athol MA 1981-1988; Cur Gr Ch Utica NY 1978-1980. rector@stpeterscaz.org

FLOOD, Charles TA (Pa) 19 S 10th St, Philadelphia PA 19107 **S Steph's Ch Philadelphia PA 1988-** B Windsor ON CA 5/9/1944 s Patrick F Flood & Margaret M. BD Wayne 1968. D 6/11/1977 P 6/3/1978 Bp Lyman Cunningham Ogilby. m 11/8/2011 Mark J Yurkanin. Ch Of The H Apos Wynnewood PA 1980-1982; Epis Cmnty Serv Philadelphia PA 1977-1979. Doctor Of Sci In Med (Medsc) Thommas Jefferson U 2003. charlesflood@ststephensphl.org

FLOOR, Marjorie Jacobsen (Alb) 77 Sabbath Day Point Rd, Silver Bay NY 12874 **Vic The Epis Ch Of The Cross Ticonderoga NY 1999-** B Brooklyn NY 3/14/1933 d Trygve Jacobsen & Gladys. BS SUNY 1954; MS Hofstra U 1962; DFA Inchbald Sch of Design London GB 1976; CTh Mercer TS 1990. D 6/17/1989 Bp Orris George Walker Jr P 5/20/1999 Bp Daniel William Herzog. m 4/17/1954 William Howard Floor c 2. D Chr Ch Babylon NY 1989-1995. revfloor@nycap.rr.com

FLORES, Kay Osborn (Wyo) 4700 S Poplar St, Casper WY 82601 **P S Steph's Ch Casper WY 2010-** B Cheyenne WY 3/22/1956 d Lloyd Wiseman Osborn & Janet Claire. AA Laramie City Cmnty Coll 1989; BS U of Wyoming 1991. D 3/13/2010 Bp Bruce Edward Caldwell P 9/29/2010 Bp John Sheridan Smylie. c 3. kaydflores@gmail.com

FLORES, Lisa Christen (WTenn) 142 Plainview St, Memphis TN 38111 **Assoc R for Formation and Servnt Mnstrs Ch Of The H Comm Memphis TN 2011-** B New Orleans LA 8/3/1974 d Barbara Jane. BA Sprg Hill Coll 1996; MDiv GTS 2005. D 6/4/2005 Bp Mark Hollingsworth Jr P 12/11/2005 Bp Samuel Johnson Howard. Assoc R for Formation Chr Ch Grosse Pointe Grosse Pointe Farms MI 2007-2011; Asst R S Ptr's Ch Fernandina Bch FL 2005-2007; Yth Min S Paul's Ch Akron OH 2000-2002. Natl Assn for Epis CE Dir (NAECED) 2008. lflores@holycommunion.org

FLORES, Nydia (NY) 630 Water St Apt 4-C, New York NY 10002 B 12/13/1931 d Pedro Flores & Carlota. Inst Pstr Hispano. D 4/26/1997 Bp Richard Frank Grein. Par D Mision San Pablo E Elmhurst NY 1997-2000.

FLORY, Carol Inez (Fla) No address on file. B Coalmont TN 4/25/1954 d George Theodore Brashears & Hazel Louis. BS Jacksonville U 1993; MDiv STUSo 1998. D 6/13/1999 Bp Stephen Hays Jecko.

FLORY, Phyllis Brannon (WK) 1551 Briargate Dr, Salina KS 67401 **Vic S Jn's Ch Great Bend KS 2011-; Dom Mssy Partnership Rep Dio Wstrn Kansas Hutchinson KS 2010-2012; GC Dep Dio Wstrn Kansas Hutchinson KS 2010-2012; Prov VII Rep Dio Wstrn Kansas Hutchinson KS 2010-2012; Dioc Coun/Stndg Com Dio Wstrn Kansas Hutchinson KS 2008-2012; Vic H Apos Ch Ellsworth KS 2007-** B Dermott AR 10/31/1950 d Phillip Pershing Brannon & Cynthia Lena. BS Friends U 1991; MS Friends U 1993. D 9/1/2007 P 12/13/2008 Bp James Marshall Adams Jr. m 4/20/1985 Michael G Flory. Chrm. Bp Search Com Dio Wstrn Kansas Hutchinson KS 2010. pflory1@cox.net

FLORY, Sheldon (Roch) 6981 State Route 21, Naples NY 14512 **Died 9/9/2010** B New York NY 6/28/1927 s Grant Glenwood Flory & Margaret Floyd. BA Mid 1950; MA Col 1952; STB GTS 1958; Fllshp GTS 1960. D 6/11/1958 P 12/22/1958 Bp Horace W B Donegan. c 3. Auth, "Kiandaga (Laureate Poems)," Sm Poetry Press - Concord, Ca, 2001; Auth, "Birds Of No Amer," Sm Poetry Press - Concord, Ca, 1999; Auth, "Poems (Chapbooks)," *To Heal The Sacr Wound: Poems From Hospice*, Rapio Printing, Victor, Ny, 1996; Auth, "A Winters Journey," Copper Bch Press, Providence, 1979; Auth, "These Faces: Things To Tell Or Ask Your Dead," Sm Poetry Press - Concord Ca; Auth, "Tenochtitean: Alvar Nunez Cabeza De Vaca & Malinche," Sm Poetry Press - Concord, Ca; Auth, "Magnetic No: Poems From The Lake Dist

Scotland & Herbride," Sm Poetry Press - Concord, Ca; Auth, "Wyoming," Sm Poetry Press - Concord Ca. Bd Constance Saltonstall Colony Awards; Bd, Ontario Yates Hospice 1990; CALC 1965; EPF 1972; Naples Arts Ntwk 1990; Poets & Writer 1970-2000. Poet Laureate The Vill And Town Of Naples, Ny Naples NY 2001; Constance Saltonstall Awd For Poetry Ithaca Ny 1999; 1st Prize Arvon Intl Poetry Competition Engl 1990. bflory27@gmail.com

FLOWERS JR, James Byrd (CGC) 922 Conti St, Mobile AL 36604 **R All SS Epis Ch Mobile AL 2004-** B Dothan AL 3/29/1955 D 6/12/2004 P 5/27/2005 Bp Philip Menzie Duncan II. m 7/21/1979 Katharine B Flowers c 3. curate@allsaintsmobile.org

FLOWERS JR, James Edgar (WLa) 946 Ockley Dr, Shreveport LA 71106 **Convoc Dn S Geo's Ch Bossier City LA 2011-** B Shreveport LA 2/23/1955 s James Edgar Flowers & Elizabeth. BS Lousiana St U 1977; MDiv VTS 1983. D 6/23/1983 P 1/1/1984 Bp Maurice Manuel Benitez. m 10/17/2008 Denise Eppler. R S Tim's Ch Alexandria LA 1999-2006; Exec Dio Wstrn Louisiana Alexandria LA 1997-2003; R Chr Memi Ch Mansfield LA 1994-1999; Assoc S Mk's Ch Beaumont TX 1986-1988; Asst to R S Jn The Div Houston TX 1983-1984. jeflowersjr@aol.com

F

FLOYD JR, Charles K(amper) (Miss) 4400 King Road, Meridian MS 39305 **Assoc The Epis Ch Of The Medtr Meridian MS 2007-** B Meridian MS 8/12/1942 s Charles Kamper Floyd & Mabel. BBA U of Mississippi 1964; MDiv STUSo 1967; DMin STUSo 1980; Cert GTS 1992. D 6/24/1967 P 5/1/1968 Bp John M Allin. m 6/1/1996 Helen Whitener c 4. Vic H Trin Ch Crystal Sprg MS 1999-2001; Dio Mississippi Jackson MS 1993-2001; R S Mk's Ch Houston TX 1982-1993; Pres, Stndg Com Dio Mississippi Jackson MS 1980-1983; R S Paul's Ch Columbus MS 1978-1982; R Trin Ch Yazoo City MS 1975-1978; Vic Epis Ch Of The Incarn W Point MS 1971-1975; Cur S Jas Ch Jackson MS 1969-1971; Vic H Trin Ch Crystal Sprg MS 1967-1969. Diplomate, AAPC 2003; Lic Mar & Fam Therapists 2003. cfterry@aol.com

FLOYD, Charles Rhein (CGC) 117 Rusty Gans Dr, Panama City Beach FL 32408 B Minneapolis MN 11/21/1931 s Oliver Reed Floyd & Laura. BA U Pgh 1954; STUSo 1990. D 7/25/1990 P 4/20/1991 Bp Charles Farmer Duvall. m 7/14/1979 Celia Louise Wiley c 2. Mem, Cmsn on Dioc Mssn Dio Cntrl Gulf Coast Pensacola FL 1995-1998; Ecum Off Dio Cntrl Gulf Coast Pensacola FL 1994-1997; Vic S Thos By The Sea Panama City Bch FL 1992-2003; Dioc Cmsn Ecum & Interfaith Rela Dio Cntrl Gulf Coast Pensacola FL 1991-1997; Mem, Dioc Cmsn on Ecum and Interfaith Relatns Dio Cntrl Gulf Coast Pensacola FL 1991-1997; D S Thos By The Sea Panama City Bch FL 1990-1991. Distinguished Mltry Grad US AF 1954.

FLOYD, Michael Hinnant (NwT) Calle San Ignacio N30-50, Quito TX 78786 Ecuador B Kingstree SC 8/5/1946 s Eldra Moore Floyd & Eugenia. BA Trin Hartford CT 1968; BD EDS 1971; MA Claremont Grad U 1977; PhD Claremont Grad U 1982. D 7/31/1971 P 3/29/1973 Bp Frederick Barton Wolf. m 2/1/1975 April Jaeger c 3. Prof OT Epis TS Of The SW Austin TX 1982-2007; Asst S Jn's Ch Ft Worth TX 1981-1982; Prof The ETS At Claremont Claremont CA 1977-1979; Asst S Mk's Epis Ch Upland CA 1972-1979. Auth, "Minor Prophets Part 2," *Forms Of The OT Lit*, Eerdmans, 2000. Angl Assn Of Biblic Schlars 1991; SBL 1976. michaelhfloyd@yahoo.com

FLOYD, Peter M (Mil) N48W31340 Hill St, Hartland WI 53029 **Vic S Anskar's Epis Ch Hartland WI 2010-** B Tullahoma TN 2/1/1975 s Richard Dale Floyd & Melody Sue. BS U of Tennesse 1998; MDiv Nash 2008. D 6/21/2008 P 1/16/2009 Bp John Crawford Bauerschmidt. m 10/3/1998 Jeneen Jensen c 1. Asst Gr Epis Ch Hinsdale IL 2008-2010. pmfloyd@gmail.com

FLOYD, Peter Winslow (Ct) 18 Hidden Lake Rd, Higganum CT 06441 B New York,NY 7/24/1937 s Rolfe Floyd & Frances. BA U of New Hampshire 1961; U CA 1964; STM Ya Berk 1965; Bos 1970. D 6/12/1965 Bp Charles F Hall P 1/6/1966 Bp Harvey D Butterfield. c 4. Dioc Coun Dio Vermont Burlington VT 1994-1996; S Dunst's Epis Mssn Waitsfield VT 1992-2002; Asst Mssnr, Middlesex Area Cluster Mnstry Dio Connecticut Hartford CT 1982-1986; R Ch Of S Mary The Vrgn Chappaqua NY 1976-1979; Vic S Ptr's Mssn Lyndonville VT 1974-1976; S Andr's Epis Ch St Johnsbury VT 1971-1976; Cur S Paul's Ch Concord NH 1965-1968. "Let's Talk Wk monthly columns," *Rutland Herald (Rutland, VT)*. Leaveners (Founding Mem) 1995-1996; Living Stones 1996-2000. peterwfloyd@sbcglobal.net

FLOYD, Theresa Ann (Ore) 4177 Nw Thatcher Rd, Forest Grove OR 97116 B Waukegan IL 4/21/1951 d Norman Gordon & Gisella. AA Coll of the Redwoods 1973; Humboldt St U 1974; Dioc Cntr For The Diacon Eugene OR 1983; Pacific U 1995. D 2/14/1988 Bp Robert Louis Ladehoff. m 9/14/1974 Kenneth King Floyd c 2. Dir Renew Dio Oregon Portland OR 1990-1993; D S Bede's Ch Forest Grove OR 1988-2000; Bursar/Secy Dio Oregon Portland OR 1987-1988. Auth, "Renew Curric For Angl Sprtlty," Dio Ore, 1992.

FLOYD-ARCHIBALD, David Roberts (WTex) 1805 W Alabama St, Houston TX 77098 **S Andr's Epis Ch San Antonio TX 2007-** B Dayton OH 12/14/1960 s Rennie Archibald & Mary Hiltner. BS Jas Madison U 1984; MDiv VTS 1991. D 6/8/1991 Bp Don Adger Wimberly P 12/18/1991 Bp Joseph Thomas Heistand. m 1/18/1998 Robbye P Floyd-Archibald. S Steph's Epis Ch Houston TX 2002-2006; S Fran Ch Heber Sprg AR 1998-2002; Asst All SS Epis Ch Corpus Christi TX 1994-1998; Asst Ch Of The Gd Shpd Corpus Christi TX 1991-1993. davidfa1960@gmail.com

FLY, David Kerrigan (Mo) 4400 Lindell Blvd., Apt. 11-N, St. Louis MO 63108 B Monett MO 6/25/1941 s Jack Kerrigan Fly & Kathryn Mae. BS SW Missouri St U 1963; MDiv Nash 1966. D 12/28/1965 P 8/21/1966 Bp Edward Randolph Welles II. m 6/9/1990 Adrienne Anderson c 5. Gr Ch Kirkwood MO 1981-1998; Loc Ten S Lk's Ch Wamego KS 1979-1980; Dio Kansas Topeka KS 1973-1981; Cn Pstr Gr And H Trin Cathd Kansas City MO 1966-1969. Auth, "An Epis P's Reflections on the Kansas City Riot of 1968," *Missouri Hist Revs*, The St Hist Soc of Missouri, 2006; Auth, "Faces of Faith: Reflections in a Rearview Mirror," Ch Pub, Inc, 2004; Auth, "Faces In The Rearview Mirror," Walsworth, 2002; Auth, "Journey To Jerusalem," 1989. ESMHE 1968-1981. dfly992984@aol.com

FLYNN, Anne Regina (CPa) PO Box 612, Carlisle PA 17013 B 3/2/1956 D 2/12/2005 Bp Michael Whittington Creighton. m 12/14/2009 Patrick Early. anneflynn@aol.com

FLYNN, Bernard Thomas (CFla) 9263 Sw 109th Ln, Ocala FL 34481 B Chicago IL 11/7/1927 s Raymond S Flynn & Eveylin V. BA Villanova U 1950; MS CUA 1954; Cert Int Mnstry Prog 1993. Rec from Roman Catholic 2/21/1974 Bp Charles Thomas Gaskell. m 1/4/1972 Madonna Marie Flynn c 2. P-in-c S Steph's Epis Ch Ocala FL 2000-2010; P Epis Ch Of S Mary Belleview FL 1999-2000; Int S Mk's Epis Ch Glen Ellyn IL 1996-1997; Int Ch Of S Ben Bolingbrook IL 1995-1996; R S Columba Ch Fresno CA 1979-1994; R S Jn's Ch Versailles KY 1975-1979; Asst S Matt's Ch Kenosha WI 1974-1975. Auth, "My God Really Loves Me," Cimarron Press, 1999. berniemadonna@aol.com

FLYNN, Michael Thomas (Los) 4406 El Corazon Ct, Camarillo CA 93012 B Glendale CA 10/31/1940 s James Clarence Flynn & Inez. BA U CA 1963; MDiv STUSo 1966. D 9/10/1966 P 3/11/1967 Bp Francis E I Bloy. m 2/12/1961 Linda Sue McCambridge c 4. Asst All SS Epis Ch Oxnard CA 2000-2005; Assoc P Chr Epis Ch Denver CO 1996-2000; R S Jude's Epis Par Burbank CA 1981-1996; Vic Imm Mssn El Monte CA 1970-1981; Cur S Mk's Par Altadena CA 1966-1968. Auth, *How To Be Gd Without Really Trying*, Chosen, 2004; Auth, *Making Disciples*, FreshWind, 1997; Auth, *The Mustard Seed Bk*, Chosen, 1995; Auth, *Inner Healing*, InterVarsity, 1993; Auth, *H Vulnerability*, Chosen, 1990. mkfln@aol.com

FLYNN, Richard Michael (WLa) 318 Parkway Dr, Natchitoches LA 71457 **Dn, Alexandria Convoc Dio Wstrn Louisiana Alexandria LA 2002-** B Memphis TN 4/4/1944 s Thomas Theodore Flynn & Helen Brown. BA U So 1966; MA U of Memphis 1970; MDiv SWTS 1979. D 6/23/1979 Bp William F Gates Jr P 5/1/1980 Bp William Evan Sanders. m 6/11/1966 Janet P Potts c 3. Dio Wstrn Louisiana Alexandria LA 2003-2004; R Trin Epis Ch Natchitoches LA 1998-2003; Vic S Jn's Ch Mart TN 1994-1998; R S Jas Epis Ch Un City TN 1983-1998; Dio W Tennessee Memphis TN 1983; Vic Chr Ch Brownsville TN 1980-1983; Vic Imm Ch Ripley TN 1980-1983; D-In-Trng St Jas Epis Ch at Knoxville Knoxville TN 1979-1980. 318flynn@bellsouth.net

FODOR, Luke (LI) PO Box 266, Cold Spring Harbor NY 11724 **Asst R S Jn's Ch Cold Sprg Harbor NY 2011-** B Akron OH 10/1/1978 s Frank Fodor & Heidi. BA Moody Bible Institue 1999; MA Dur 2002; MA NYU 2004; MDiv Bex 2011. D 2/6/2011 P 9/10/2011 Bp Lawrence C Provenzano. m 5/22/1999 Willow M Bender c 2. Auth, "The Occasional Theol and Constant Sprtlty of Rowan Williams," *ATR*, ATR, 2012; Auth, "What Can One Person Do?: The Millennium Dvlpmt Goals," *What Can One Person Do?: The Millennium Dvlpmt Goals*, Forw Mvmt, 2009. 2011 The Chas Hefling Prize ATR 2011. fodor33@gmail.com

FOERSTER III, Frederick Henry (CNY) 183 Capn Crosby Rd, Centerville MA 02632 B Saginaw MI 5/30/1945 s Frederick Henry Foerster & Ellen. USNA 1965; BA MI SU 1968; MDiv PDS 1971. D 5/30/1971 P 3/1/1972 Bp Ned Cole. m 1/9/1976 Gail Ellen Manfredi c 3. R Chr Epis Ch Jordan NY 1976-1977; St Pauls Ch Baldwinsville NY 1976-1977; Vic S Ptr's Ch So Windsor CT 1973-1976; Cur Chr Ch Binghamton NY 1971-1973.

FOGELQUIST, Albin Hilding (Spok) 1823 W Dean Ave, Spokane WA 99201 B Spokane WA 11/20/1947 s Albin Hilding Fogelquist & Helen Karen. BS Whitworth U 1969; MA Whitworth U 1969; MDiv Assn Free Luth TS 1972; CDSP 1974; ThD Grad Theol Un 1977; LHD Faith Sem 1989. D 12/19/1990 P 4/4/1991 Bp Vincent Waydell Warner. P-in-c H Trin Epis Ch Spokane WA 1997-2007; Dio Olympia Seattle WA 1994; P-in-c St Ptr's Epis Par Seattle WA 1991-1995; H Trin Ch Seattle WA 1991. Alcuin Club; Associated Parishes; RWF. Hon Alum CDSP 1993.

FOGG JR, Ralph Everett (NY) 4908 Gable Ridge Ln, Holly Springs NC 27540 **Vic S Chris's Epis Ch Garner NC 2010-** B Johnson City NY 1/29/1932 s Ralph Everett Fogg & Geraldine Roche. BA Hob 1954; MDiv GTS 1959; Amer Fndt of Rel & Psych 1969. D 6/10/1959 Bp Malcolm E Peabody P 6/29/1960 Bp Walter M Higley. m 1/6/1979 Ingrid Hotrich c 4. P-in-c S Andr's Epis Ch New Paltz NY 1986-2002; Asst S Andr's Epis Ch New Paltz NY 1970-1986; R Ch Of The Div Love Montrose NY 1962-1969. Auth, "Psych-A Process of Discovery," *Pstr Counslr*, 1970. Diplomate: AAPC 1967. ralphfsy78@aol.com

FOISIE, Stephen Drew (SVa) 4449 N Witchduck Rd, Virginia Beach VA 23455 **Old Donation Ch Virginia Bch VA 2010-** B Bellingham WA 10/3/1977 s Charles August Foisie & Karen Jo. BA Cntrl Washington U 2000; MDiv VTS 2010. D 4/17/2010 P 12/18/2010 Bp Gregory Harold Rickel. drewfoisie@gmail.com

FOLEY, William Edward (NY) 2 Scotch Bonnet Ct, Savannah GA 31411 **Died 9/17/2010** B Buffalo NY 5/3/1927 s George Washington Foley & Marion Gertrude. BS Canisius Coll 1951; NYU 1952; Harv 1953; STB EDS 1956; MDiv EDS 1972; DMin Andover Newton TS 1979. D 6/29/1956 P 6/5/1957 Bp Lauriston L Scaife. c 2. Auth, "Fr Foley's Fabulous Fables of Faith," Vantage Press, 2001; Auth, "Sermons," *Boston Globe / Traveler*, 1967; Auth, "The Seekers (Sermons)," *The Pulpit Journ of Contemporary Preaching*, 1967; Auth, "Sermons," *Congressional Record*, 1963. wefoley@bellsouth.net

FOLSOM, Henry Titus (NH) 62 Durand Rd, Randolph NH 03593 B Orange NJ 6/18/1927 s Henry LLoyd Folsom & Anna May. BA Ya 1950; MDiv Ya Berk 1957. D 6/15/1957 P 12/21/1957 Bp Benjamin M Washburn. m 10/29/1995 Clare Cook c 3. Int S Barn Ch Berlin NH 1988-1991; R Gr Ch Old Saybrook CT 1969-1987; R Chr Ch Pompton Lakes NJ 1965-1969; Vic S Ptr's Ch Washington NJ 1959-1964; Cur S Jas Ch Upper Montclair NJ 1957-1959. *Rendezuous In The Bush*, Trophy Room Books, 1999. ERM (inactive); Episcopalians Untd (inactive). folrandolph@aol.com

✠ **FOLTS, Rt Rev James Edward** (WTex) PO Box 6885, San Antonio TX 78209 **Ret Bp of W Texas Dio W Texas San Antonio TX 2006-** B San Antonio TX 3/11/1940 s Alexander Jonathan Folts & Ethel Elizabeth. BA Trin U San Antonio TX 1962; MDiv VTS 1965. D 7/13/1965 Bp Everett H Jones P 1/25/1966 Bp Richard Earl Dicus Con 2/17/1994 for WTex. m 6/21/1964 Sandra Pauline Johnston c 2. Dio W Texas San Antonio TX 1994-2005; R S Mk's Epis Ch San Antonio TX 1992-1993; R Ch Of The Adv Brownsville TX 1985-1992; R Ch Of The Heav Rest Abilene TX 1979-1985; R S Mk's Ch San Marcos TX 1968-1979; Assoc S Fran Epis Ch Victoria TX 1967-1968; P-in-c S Jas Epis Ch Hebbronville TX 1965-1967. DD U So TS 1994; DD VTS 1994. westtexasviii@yahoo.com

FOLTS, Jonathan Hunter (Ct) 40 Main St, Essex CT 06426 **R S Jn's Epis Ch Essex CT 2004-** B Victoria TX 1/30/1968 s James Edward Folts & Sandra Pauline. BA U of No Texas 1991; MDiv VTS 1996. D 6/11/1996 P 2/14/1997 Bp James Edward Folts. m 11/2/1996 Kimberly Spire c 3. R S Fran Epis Ch Victoria TX 1999-2004; Vic S Eliz's Epis Ch Buda TX 1996-1999; Vic The Ch Of The H Sprt Dripping Sprg TX 1996-1997; Asst Dir Of Homeless Ministers Prog S Barth's Ch New York NY 1990-1991. "Listening And Taking Action," LivCh, 2005; "The Daily Diet," LivCh, 2004. rector@stjohnsessex.org

FOLTS, Kimberly Spire (Ct) 40 Main St, Essex CT 06426 B Durango CO 7/26/1968 BA Dickinson Coll 1990; MDiv VTS 1994. P 5/13/1995 Bp Charlie Fuller McNutt Jr. m 11/2/1996 Jonathan Hunter Folts c 3. DCE S Fran Epis Ch Victoria TX 2000-2004; S Steph's Epis Ch Wimberley TX 1997-1998; Asst S Ptr's Epis Ch Washington NC 1995-1996; All SS' Epis Ch Hershey PA 1994-1995. kfolts@sbcglobal.net

FOLTZ, Marvin Lee (Haw) 1391 Kakae Pl, Wailuku HI 96793 **Bd - Camp Mokule'ia Dio Hawaii Honolulu HI 2000-; R The Par Of Gd Shpd Epis Ch Wailuku HI 1998-** B El Paso TX 3/25/1954 s Carl Lee Foltz & Marilyn Louise. BA SW Bapt U Bolivar MO 1975; MDiv MidWestern Bapt TS 1982; SWTS 1992. D 11/24/1992 P 5/25/1993 Bp William Walter Wiedrich. m 6/20/1987 Cynthia Susann Lietz c 4. Chair - COM Dio Hawaii Honolulu HI 2009-2011; Dioc Coun Dio Hawaii Honolulu HI 1998-2002; Exec Coun Dio Lexington Lexington KY 1994-1998; R Ch Of The Nativ Maysville KY 1993-1998. Faith Action for Cmnty Equity 2008. marvinleefoltz@gmail.com

✠ **FOLWELL, Rt Rev William Hopkins** (CFla) 600 Carolina Village Rd., Apt. 2520, Hendersonville NC 28792 **Ret Bp of CFla Dio Cntrl Florida Orlando FL 1990-** B Port Washington NY 10/26/1924 s Ralph Taylor Folwell & Sara Ewing. BCE Georgia Inst of Tech 1947; LTh SWTS 1952; BD SWTS 1953. D 6/22/1952 P 12/22/1952 Bp Henry I Louttit Con 2/9/1970 for CFla. m 4/22/1949 Christine Cramp c 3. Bp Dio Cntrl Florida Orlando FL 1970-1989; Dep GC Dio Cntrl Florida Orlando FL 1967-1969; Hon Cn Cathd Ch Of S Lk Orlando FL 1966-1990; Chair Dept Mssn & Ch Ext Dio Cntrl Florida Orlando FL 1962-1965; Stndg Com Dio Cntrl Florida Orlando FL 1961-1962; R All SS Ch Of Winter Pk Winter Pk FL 1959-1970; R S Gabriels Ch Titusville FL 1956-1959; Vic S Augustines Ch Metairie LA 1955-1956; P-in-c S Lk The Evang Ch Mulberry FL 1954-1955; Vic S Ptr's Ch Plant City FL 1952-1955. DD SWTS 1970; DD U So TS 1970. folwell@bellsouth.net

FONCREE, Rose Mary Ivas (Miss) 4526 Meadow Hill Road, Jackson MS 39206 B Pascagoula MS 4/6/1942 d Arthur W Ivas & Mamie Drucilla. BA Valdosta St U 1982; MA Valdosta St U 1986. D 1/6/2001 Bp Alfred Clark Marble Jr. c 1.

FONES, Peter Alden (Ore) Episc. Church of St John the Divine, PO Box 1537, Springfield OR 97478 **P-in-c Ch Of S Jn The Div Springfield OR 2006-** B Portland OR 6/11/1950 s Hamilton Smith Fones & Helen Katherine. BEd U of Oregon 2001; Cert NW Hse of Theol Stds 2004; MDiv CDSP 2005. D 4/20/2006 P 10/21/2006 Bp Johncy Itty. m 11/1/1980 Leah Greene c 4. Mem Dioc Coun Dio Oregon Portland OR 2007-2010; Chapl Epis Campus Mnstry Eugene OR 2006-2008; Lay Chapl Epis Campus Mnstry Eugene OR 1996-2004. pafones@comcast.net

FONTAINE, Ann Kristin (Wyo) 1724 Hillcrest Dr, Lander WY 82520 **Int S Cathr Of Alexandria Manzanita OR 2011-; Stndg Com Dio Wyoming Casper WY 2004-** B Portland OR 11/22/1941 d Gustav Charles Haldors & Dorothy Margaret. BA Lewis & Clark Coll 1963; MDiv Harvard DS 1995. D 6/22/1995 Bp Bob Gordon Jones P 1/6/1996 Bp William Harvey Wolfrum. m 3/9/1963 James Heryford Fontaine c 3. Int Ch Of The Trsfg Jackson WY 2001-2003; Int S Jn's Epis Ch Jackson WY 2000-2006; DDO Dio Wyoming Casper WY 1998-2000; Int Shoshone Epis Mssn Ft Washakie WY 1998-1999; Int S Steph's Ch Casper WY 1997-1998; Int S Thos Ch Dubois WY 1996; Cur Trin Ch Lander WY 1995-1996. Auth, "Streams of Mercy: a meditative commentary on the Bible," *Bk*, Auth Hse, 2005; Contrib, "Contrib," *EFM Mentor Manual*, Sewanee: The U So; Contrib, "essays and reporting," *Epis Café*, Epis Café; Auth, "arts," *LivCh*; Contrib, "Green Lent," *http://greenlent.blogspot.com*, Blog; Contrib, "what the tide brings in," *http://seashellseller.blogspot.com*, Blog. Epis Wmn Caucus; Integrity. annfontaine@me.com

F

FONTAINE, H(oward) Douglas (Minn) 3940 Auburn Dr, Minnetonka MN 55305 B Charleston WV 1/20/1931 s Howard Douglas Fontaine & Elizabeth. BA W Virginia U 1958; BD VTS 1959; DD SWTS 1975. D 6/11/1959 P 9/14/1960 Bp Wilburn Camrock Campbell. m 10/23/1954 Jeanne Ellis c 5. Dn Cathd Ch Of S Mk Minneapolis MN 1971-1994; R Chr Epis Ch Tyler TX 1965-1971; Assoc Chr Ch Cathd Houston TX 1961-1962; In-c Trin Ch Shepherdstown WV 1958-1961. jfontaine4@comcast.net

FONVIELLE, Lloyd William (EC) 1243 Columbus Cir, Wilmington NC 28403 **Died 9/9/2011** B Wilmington NC 2/10/1927 s Wayne Alexander Fonvielle & Pearle. CG Jung Inst; BA U NC 1949; BD VTS 1956; ATC 1975. D 6/29/1956 P 2/1/1957 Bp Thomas H Wright. Surdyk Meml Appreciation Awd Lovett Sch 1986.

FOOTE, Beth (Cal) 705 Grand St, Alameda CA 94501 **Assoc Trin Par Menlo Pk CA 2007-** B Oakland CA 5/30/1958 d Richard H Lind & Beth Anne. BA U CA 1980; MDiv CDSP 2006. D 9/15/2007 P 6/14/2008 Bp Marc Handley Andrus. m 9/10/1983 Robert Hale Foote c 3. bafoote@comcast.net

FOOTE, Nancy Burns (Md) 1 Holmes Ave, Baltimore MD 21228 B Baltimore MD 1/30/1936 d Paul Duncan Burns & Dorothy Louise. BA Towson U 1976; MS Loyola Coll 1989. D 6/26/1983 Bp David Keller Leighton Sr. m 8/28/1954 Arthur C Foote c 2. Dn of D Trng Dio Maryland Baltimore MD 1989-2003; D Cathd Of The Incarn Baltimore MD 1987-2000; Archd Dio Maryland Baltimore MD 1986-2003; COM Dio Maryland Baltimore MD 1985-2003; D H Trin Ch Churchville MD 1983-1986. NAAD 1980. n-a-foote@att.net

FOOTE, Roger Lee (SO) 985 Forest Ave, Cincinnati OH 45246 **R Chr Ch - Glendale Cincinnati OH 1991-** B Cincinnati OH 1/12/1948 s Gordon Lee Foote & Esther. BA U Cinc 1970; MDiv VTS 1981. D 6/22/1981 Bp William Grant Black P 12/1/1981 Bp Frank Stanley Cerveny. m 7/5/2003 Ruth Steinert c 3. R All SS Ch Alexandria VA 1984-1991; Assoc R Chr Epis Ch Ponte Vedra Bch FL 1981-1984. Sis Of Trsfg, Ord Of S Lk. phut@fuse.net

FOOTE JR, Sheldon Burnham (Chi) 5733 N Sheridan Rd Apt 16-C, Chicago IL 60660 **Died 5/5/2011** B Princeton NJ 4/29/1920 s Sheldon Burnham Foote & Isabelle. BA NWU 1946; STB GTS 1949. D 6/16/1949 P 12/17/1949 Bp Wallace E Conkling. Phi Beta Kappa. bigfoote23@aol.com

FOOTE, Stephen Williams (Me) 574 Turner Rd, Bremen ME 04551 B Hartford CT 9/16/1942 s Dwight Williams Foote & Helen Ann. BA Bard Coll 1965; STB GTS 1968. D 6/11/1968 Bp Walter H Gray P 3/15/1969 Bp John Henry Esquirol. Dn Cathd Ch Of S Lk Portland ME 1990-2003; Archd Dio Maine Portland ME 1986-1989; Epis Ch Of S Mary The Vrgn Falmouth ME 1969-1986. foote@tidewater.net

FORAKER, Gregory Alan (Az) PO Box 65840, Tucson AZ 85728 **S Phil's In The Hills Tucson AZ 2011-** B Wichita KS 10/8/1960 s John Charles Foraker & Linda Kay. BA U CO 1999; MA Washingto Theol Un 2005; Cert of Angl Stds ETS at Claremont 2010. D 11/21/2010 P 6/25/2011 Bp Kirk Stevan Smith. greg.foraker@gmail.com

FORAKER-THOMPSON, Jane (Nev) P.O. Box 2665, Gardnerville NV 89410 B Alhambra CA 10/23/1937 d Field Thompson & Margaret Hall. BA U CA 1959; MA U CA 1965; PhD Stan 1985; MDiv CDSP 1997. D 1/29/1994 Bp John Stuart Thornton P 4/10/1999 Bp Stewart Clark Zabriskie. c 4. Del to GC Dio Nevada Las Vegas NV 2009; P Ch Of Coventry Cross Minden NV 2007-2008; Prison Mnstry Chair Dio Nevada Las Vegas NV 2002-2008; Soc Justice Coordntr Dio Nevada Las Vegas NV 2002-2008; P Dio Nevada Las Vegas NV 2000-2011; Bd Mem of Rel Allnce of Nevada Dio Nevada Las Vegas NV 2000-2008; P Gr-St Fran Cmnty Ch Lovelock NV 1999-2000; D All SS' Ch San Francisco CA 1995-1997; D S Mich's Cathd Boise ID 1994-1999. Auth, "Numerous arts And Papers On Var Aspects Of Criminal Justice (1971-2000): Soc Justice, Sentencing, Corrections, Alter," *se Vita*. OHC 1997. Who's Who of Amer Cambridge Who's Who 2008; Who's Who in the Wrld Marquis 1996; Vstng Fell at Cntr for Intergroup Stds U of Cape Town, So Afr

1990; Boise St U Alum Awd for Outstanding Fac Boise St U Alum 1989; Intl Leaders of Achievement Cambridge, Engl 1988; Biographical Historiette on Men and Wmn of Achievement and dist Biography Intl , Delhi, India 1987; Intl Who's Who of Profsnl and Bus Wmn Intl Biographical Cntr, Cambridge, Engl 1987; Dictionary of Inernational Biography Cambridge, Engl 1986; Can Stds Resrch Grant Can Govt, Ottawa 1986; Who's Who of Amer Wmn Marquis 1986; Directory of Distinguished Americans 1985; Intl Who's Who in Crime Prevention Cambridge, Engl 1985; Fell at 1985 Seminar Global Security & Arms Control, UC Irvine 1985; Who's Who in Amer Law Marquis 1985; Wrld Who's Who of Wmn Cambridge, Engl 1984; Cmnty Leaders of the Wrld Cambridge, Engl 1984; Who's Who of the Amer W Marquis 1984; Wmn of the Year Awd Soroptomists, Santa Fe 1981. forakerthompson.jane@charter.net

FORBES, Bruce Willard (NY) 109 E 50th St, New York NY 10022 B Allegany NY 10/1/1921 s R Norman Forbes & Jessie. BA U MI 1942; MA Harv 1943; STB GTS 1961. D 6/23/1961 P 2/24/1962 Bp Lauriston L Scaife. Asst S Barth's Ch New York NY 1964-1990; Cur S Lk's Epis Ch Jamestown NY 1961-1964. forbes@stbarts.org

FORBES JR, Charles Alvin (Oly) 4510 123rd Pl NE, Marysville WA 98271 B San Francisco CA 6/23/1926 s Charles Alvin Forbes & Alice Patricia. BA U of Washington 1949; BD Bex 1952. D 6/24/1952 P 6/29/1953 Bp Stephen F Bayne Jr. m 7/1/1955 Carolyn Liddell c 3. Vic S Geo's Ch Seattle WA 1984-1988; S Mary's Ch Lakewood WA 1978-1983; Vic S Phil Ch Marysville WA 1971-1978; R S Eliz's Ch Burien WA 1959-1967; Vic S Jn's Ch Kirkland WA 1954-1957; Vic Ch Of The Redeem Kenmore WA 1954-1955; Vic S Augustines In-The-Woods Epis Par Freeland WA 1952-1954; Vic St Steph's Epis Ch Oak Harbor WA 1952-1954. cforbes1@frontier.com

FORBES, David Reineman (Cal) 22 Delmar St, San Francisco CA 94117 B Palo Alto CA 4/29/1926 s Francis Henry Forbes & Eleanor Hale. BS Stan 1949; MS Stan 1950; MDiv VTS 1953. D 6/28/1953 Bp Henry H Shires P 1/1/1954 Bp Karl M Block. c 3. Int The Epis Ch Of S Jn The Evang San Francisco CA 2003-2004; Assoc Pstr Gr Cathd San Francisco CA 1991-2000; Dio California San Francisco CA 1988-1991; S Paul's Epis Ch Walnut Creek CA 1987-1988; S Matt's Epis Ch San Mateo CA 1985-1987; S Paul's Ch Oakland CA 1975-1985; Vice-Dn Gr Cathd San Francisco CA 1966-1972; Cn Sacrist & Precentor Gr Cathd San Francisco CA 1954-1972; Asst Gr Cathd San Francisco CA 1953-1954. davidrf2001@yahoo.com

FORBES, Elizabeth Faye (Ga) 3321 Wheeler Rd, Augusta GA 30909 B Wilmington DE 12/19/1941 d Stephen Coverdale & Grace. BA Brandywine Coll 1963; BS U of Delaware 1972; BS Med Coll of Georgia 1976. D 3/27/2009 Bp Henry Irving Louttit. faye@medicalparameters.com

FORBES, Mark S (NC) 172 Dairy Farm Rd, Mooresvillle NC 28115 **R S Pat's Mssn Mooresville NC 2008-** B Winston-Salem NC 6/28/1971 s Charles Forbes & Edna. BA U NC 1994; MDiv VTS 2004. D 5/28/2004 Bp Robert Hodges Johnson P 5/8/2005 Bp Robert Marshall Anderson. m 8/4/2001 Kristen T Traulsen c 2. S Marg Of Scotland Par San Juan Capistrano CA 2004-2008. marksforbes@me.com

FORBES, Michael Philip (Minn) 402 31st St Ne Apt 224, Rochester MN 55906 B Brooklyn NY 5/21/1946 s Alfred Michael Forbes & Eleanor Louise. BA S Pius X 1968; MDiv Bex 1974. D 2/5/1975 P 4/26/1976 Bp Philip Frederick McNairy. m 1/16/1971 Louise G Glass c 2. Supply Chr Ch Frontenac MN 1988-2000; P-in-c Ch Of The Mssh Prairie Island Welch MN 1987-1991. Auth, "The Ch Year," 1975; Auth, "Dio AltGld Manual"; Auth, "Amer Indn Sunday Resources & Curric"; Auth, "Lesser Festivals For Mn"; Auth, "85 Unit Cnfrmtn Curric". ADLMC 1984; Grand (Natl) Assoc Chapl 1999; Priory Chapl 1997; Sovereign & Mltry Ord Of The Temple Of Jerusalem 1997. Advncd Stndg Acpe 1975. milou@qwest.net

FORBES, William (Oly) 425 S 10th St, Mount Vernon WA 98274 **Died 9/15/2011** B Philadelphia PA 11/17/1915 s Hugh Copeland Forbes & Mary Josephine. BA U of Pennsylvania 1937; MA U of Pennsylvania 1939; BD EDS 1942. D 7/6/1942 Bp Francis E Taitt P 11/19/1944 Bp John B Bentley. c 5. Hon Cn S Mk'S Cathd Seattle Washington 1966.

FORD, Austin McNeill (At) 569 Cherokee Ave Se, Atlanta GA 30312 B DeKalb Co GA 2/6/1929 s Harold Augustus Ford & Elizabeth Morgan. BA Emory U 1950; BD STUSo 1953. D 6/11/1953 P 12/1/1953 Bp Randolph R Claiborne. Dio Atlanta Atlanta GA 1967-1996; Dir Emmaus Hse Epis Ch Atlanta GA 1967-1996; Vic S Barth's Epis Ch Atlanta GA 1955-1956; Cur S Lk's Epis Ch Atlanta GA 1953-1954.

FORD, Benjamin Pierson (Ind) 8897 Aztec Rd NE, Albuquerque NM 87111 **Died 9/26/2009** B Newark NJ 11/5/1922 s Edwin Shepard Ford & Dorothy Quinby. BA Pr 1948; MDiv GTS 1951. D 12/27/1951 Bp Benjamin M Washburn P 7/9/1952 Bp William Blair Roberts. c 3. benjaminford05@earthlink.net

FORD, Calvin B(erkley) (SVa) 1530 Degrasse Ave, Norfolk VA 23509 **H Trin Prot Epis Ch Onancock VA 2010-** B Baltimore MD 11/24/1952 s Calvin Berrett Ford & Rosemary Margaret. Loyola U 1971; BA U of Maryland 1986; MDiv STUSo 1989. D 6/17/1989 P 5/1/1990 Bp A(lbert) Theodore Eastman. m 11/5/2009 Marian E Fitzsimmons c 3. R Chr and S Lk's Epis Ch Norfolk VA 2007-2010; R Middleham & S Ptr's Par Lusby MD 1991-2006; Asst to R Ch Of The Ascen Westminster MD 1989-1991. captberk@cox.net

FORD, Charles Allan (NY) 205 Stone Rd, West Hurley NY 12491 **Dio New York New York City NY 2008-; Vic S Marg's Ch Staatsburg NY 2008-** B New York NY 3/9/1938 s Charles Ford & Eleanor Gwendolyn. BA CUNY 1962; M. Div Ya Berk 1965; MS Iona Coll 1970; DMin NYTS 2005. D 6/12/1965 P 12/18/1965 Bp Horace W B Donegan. m 6/25/2005 Leslie Goldring. R S Ptr's Epis Ch Peekskill NY 1999-2006; Int S Geo's Epis Ch Antioch CA 1998-1999; Assoc S Paul's Ch Oakland CA 1993-1998; Vic S Steph's In-The-Field Epis Ch San Jose CA 1991-1993; S Cyp's Ch San Francisco CA 1978-1986; Cur S Mk's Ch In The Bowery New York NY 1965-1968. AAPC 2001. frcaford@gmail.com

FORD, Cheri Lynn (NMich) Rr 2 Box 939-A, Newberry MI 49868 B Pontiac MI 11/10/1950 d Stanley Clare Colby & Gloria Jean. Dio No Michigan TS MI; BA Cntrl Michigan U 1972. D 7/11/1993 P 1/1/1994 Bp Thomas Kreider Ray. m 5/22/1971 Steven Eugene Ford. Newberry Mnstrl Assn.

FORD, Denis B (Colo) 3231 Olive St., Jacksonville FL 32207 B Jacksonville FL 10/1/1946 s Thomas Pierce Ford & Shirley June. BA Jacksonville U 1968; MDiv VTS 1972. D 6/18/1972 P 6/13/1973 Bp Edward Hamilton West. m 7/3/2005 JoAnn Tomlin c 1. Vic S Paul's Ch Montrose CO 2009-2011; R Gr Epis Ch Ottawa KS 1999-2006; Dio Wstrn Massachusetts Springfield MA 1986-1998; P-in-c S Paul's Epis Sum Chap Otis MA 1985-1997; R Ch Of The Gd Shpd So Lee MA 1985-1986; R S Geo's Ch Lee MA 1985-1986; R S Barn And All SS Ch Springfield MA 1978-1985; Asst R Pohick Epis Ch Lorton VA 1975-1978; Cur S Andr's Epis Ch Tampa FL 1974-1975; Vic Chr Ch Cedar Key FL 1972-1974. denisbollingard@gmail.com

FORD, Janet Carol (Nev) No address on file. B Ogden UT 3/17/1939 D 5/3/2003 Bp Katharine Jefferts Schori. m 12/28/1967 Don Nelson Ford c 1. danford@moondog.net

FORD, Janice Celeste (WMass) 16 Crestview Dr, Mendon MA 01756 **R Ch Of The Recon Webster MA 2008-** B Albany NY 12/23/1952 d Dominick Ricchiuti & Grace. BA Coll of St Rose 1975; AAS (NSG) Maria Coll 1980; BS SUNY 1986; MS U of New Hampshire 1989; MDiv Andover Newton Theol Sch 2008. D 12/29/2007 P 6/7/2008 Bp Gordon Paul Scruton. m 10/3/1981 Rodney Ford c 1. pastor@reconciliationweb.org

FORD, Joan Butler (SanD) 4351 Ridgeway Dr, San Diego CA 92116 **Cn For Cmncatn Cathd Ch Of S Paul San Diego CA 2002-** B Youngstown OH 10/16/1933 d Joseph Green Butler & Louise Bowe. BA Stan 1975; MA Stan 1976; PhD Stan 1980; MDiv CDSP 1989. D 12/8/1989 P 12/1/1990 Bp William Edwin Swing. m 6/26/1954 Thomas Ford. S Cyp's Ch San Francisco CA 1991-1996; P-in-c S Aid's Ch San Francisco CA 1991; Transitional D Chr Ch Portola Vlly CA 1989-1990. Dio California Cler Assn 1989. Ch Div D. D. (Honoris Causa) CDSP Berkeley Ca 2004. revjbf@cox.net

FORD, JoAnn (Colo) St. John's Episcopal Church, PO Box 563, Ouray CO 81427 B Wichita Falls TX 4/24/1943 d Ronald Earl Tomlin & Ione Marie. Wichita St U 1964; BA Merc 1980; Luther TS 1989; MDiv STUSo 1991. D 6/24/1991 Bp Robert Marshall Anderson P 1/25/1992 Bp Frank Kellogg Allan. m 7/3/2005 Denis B Ford c 2. R S Jn's Epis Ch Ouray CO 2009-2011; P-in-c S Jn's Epis Ch Ouray CO 2006-2009; Cn to the Ordnry Dio Kansas Topeka KS 2002-2006; R Ch Of The Cov Jct City KS 1998-2002; Asst S Pat's Epis Ch Atlanta GA 1993-1998; Asst Chr Ch Norcross GA 1991-1993. jaford1992@hotmail.com

FORD, John Mark (Ala) PO Box 614, Chelsea AL 35043 **R St Catherines Epis Ch Chelsea AL 2007-** B Barnsville OH 2/16/1960 s Nolan Ford & Mildred. BA Samford U 1982; MDiv STUSo 2006. D 6/15/2006 P 12/12/2006 Bp Henry Nutt Parsley Jr. m 5/27/2000 Charlene P Pitts c 4. P-in-c S Alb's Ch Birmingham AL 2006-2007. johnmarkford@gmail.com

FORD, Richard Barlow (Cal) 2165 West Dry Creek Road, Healdsburg CA 95448 B Ontario CA 8/15/1930 s George Burden Ford & Verna Helen. BA Pomona Coll 1952; MDiv Yale DS 1955. D 6/18/1955 P 12/17/1955 Bp Angus Dun. m 8/15/1953 Patricia L Lynas c 3. Int S Tim's Epis Ch Mtn View CA 1992-1993; Int Chr Epis Ch Los Altos CA 1990; Assoc Chr Epis Ch Los Altos CA 1985-1989; Int S Mk's Epis Ch Palo Alto CA 1985; P-in-c S Tim's Epis Ch Mtn View CA 1980; R S Bede's Epis Ch Menlo Pk CA 1971-1980; Trin Par Menlo Pk CA 1971-1980; Assoc S Mk's Epis Ch Santa Clara CA 1967-1971; Assoc & Headmaster, Par Sch S Andr's Ch Saratoga CA 1963-1967; Assoc Trin Cathd San Jose CA 1960-1963; Vic S Barth's Epis Ch Livermore CA 1957-1960; Assoc S Marg's Ch Washington DC 1955-1957. Cont Educ Fell VTS 1970. pford@sonic.net

FORD, Robert Lawrence (Oly) 10637 Woodhaven Ln, Bellevue WA 98004 B Saint Louis MO 11/18/1937 s Samuel Lester Ford & Margaret. U of Missouri 1958; BS Washington U 1961; MDiv Ya Berk 1968. D 10/18/1968 P 6/29/1969 Bp Chilton Powell. m 8/26/1967 Margaret A Hicks c 2. All SS Ch Bellevue WA 1996; Int All SS Ch Seattle WA 1994-1996; Dio Olympia Seattle WA 1993; S Dav Emm Epis Ch Shoreline WA 1988-1993; Int S Matthews Auburn WA 1988; Int S Catherines Ch Enumclaw WA 1986-1987; Assoc S

Paul's Ch Marion OH 1984-1986; S Paul's Ch Marion OH 1974-1979; R All SS Epis Ch Miami OK 1971-1974. NASSAM. lnpford@comcast.net

FORD, Russell Wayne (CGC) Po Box 5853, Gulf Shores AL 36547 B Chicago IL 11/20/1932 s George Watts Ford & Marie Sadelle. BA Lake Forest Coll 1964; MDiv Nash 1967. D 6/17/1967 Bp James Winchester Montgomery P 12/1/1967 Bp Gerald Francis Burrill. m 7/28/1956 Julie Clare Proctor. Vic The Ch Of The H Innoc Hoffman Schaumburg IL 1968-1970; Chapl Of Hse Correction S Leonards Oratory Chicago IL 1967-1968. Auth, "Nashotah Theol Revs". Kairos Prison Mnstry. Annual Awd For Valor Il St Police 1983.

FORD, Stanley Eugene (Spok) 6763 SW Canyon Rd, Portland OR 97225 B Walla Walla WA 5/11/1930 D 10/19/1959 Bp Edward Makin Cross P 4/14/1960 Bp Russell S Hubbard. m 11/19/1950 Joyce Lindstrom c 2.

FORD, Steven E (NMich) Rr 2 Box 939-A, Newberry MI 49868 **Assoc All SS Ch Newberry MI 1992-** B Sault Saint Marie MI 4/12/1949 s Clayton S Ford & Elizabeth C. BS Cntrl Michigan U 1970; JD U MI 1975. D 9/20/1992 P 1/1/1994 Bp Thomas Kreider Ray. m 5/22/1971 Cheri Lynn Colby.

FORD, Steven Richard (Az) 3436 N 43rd Pl, Phoenix AZ 85018 **Assoc S Aug's Epis Ch Tempe AZ 1998-** B Stamford NY 5/8/1953 s Winfred Nathan Ford & Jean Althea. BA Hob 1975; MDiv GTS 1980. D 6/7/1980 Bp Paul Moore Jr P 12/1/1980 Bp Herbert Thompson Jr. m 10/16/1976 Karen Louise Forshee. S Paul's Ch Phoenix AZ 1987-1992; S Barn On The Desert Scottsdale AZ 1980-1987. Auth, "The Place Of Catechesis In The Early Ch"; Auth, "S Lk Journ"; Auth, "Pstr Psychol". CCU, OHC, ECM.

FORDHAM, James Frederick (EC) 1579 Bayview Rd, Bath NC 27808 B Kinston NC 7/30/1932 s James Albert Fordham & Lena. BS E Carolina U 1959; MA VTS 1965. D 6/29/1965 P 2/1/1966 Bp Thomas H Wright. c 2. Com Dio E Carolina Kinston NC 1978-1979; R Gr Epis Ch Plymouth NC 1975-1994; S Lk's/S Anne's Epis Ch Roper NC 1975-1976; P-in-c Ch Of H Cross Kinston NC 1973-1975; R S Jas Epis Ch Belhaven NC 1968-1973; P-in-c S Jas The Fisherman Epis Ch Shallotte NC 1966-1968; P-in-c S Phil's Ch Southport NC 1966-1968. jgfulton2003@yahoo.com

FOREMAN JR, Harold Vandon (Ala) 603 Turrentine Ave., Gadsden AL 35901 **R Ch Of The Resurr Rainbow City AL 2008-** B Gadsden AL 11/22/1952 s Harold Vandon Foreman & Rosemary Lea. BA Birmingham-Sthrn Coll 1975; Fllshp Tubingen U Tubingen DE 1976; MDiv Yale DS 1980; Nash 1981; MA Jacksonville St U 2008. D 5/27/1981 P 12/15/1981 Bp Furman Stough. m 10/14/2006 Heidi Foreman. R Chr Epis Ch Albertville AL 2005-2008; R S Simon Ptr Ch Pell City AL 1985-2005; Cur S Jn's Ch Decatur AL 1981-1985. Fndt Fell Rotary 1976. gweegoo@bellsouth.net

FORESMAN, R Scott (Ia) Po Box 306, Bishop CA 93515 B Oskaloosa IA 10/8/1954 s Gerald Corwin Foresman & Arloene. BD U of Nebraska 1978; MDiv Epis TS In Kentucky 1982. D 5/7/1983 P 11/7/1983 Bp James Daniel Warner. m 9/11/1989 Sheila Marie Foresman c 5. S Tim's Ch Bp CA 2003-2007; S Paul's Ch Coun Bluffs IA 1999-2003; S Mary's Ch Nebraska City NE 1988; Vic S Matt's Ch San Ardo CA 1985-1987; Cur S Lk's Ch Kearney NE 1984-1985; R S Jn's Ch Broken Bow NE 1983-1984. SocMary 2001. foresman.scott@yahoo.com

FORHAN, Carol Lynn (Spok) 9327 E Leavenworth Rd, Leavenworth WA 98826 **D S Jas Epis Ch Cashmere WA 2006-** B Minneapolis MN 4/18/1947 d Howard Ernest Johnson & Sally Ardell. CDSP 2006; DCOTE 2006. D 10/8/2006 Bp James Edward Waggoner. m 11/25/1967 William Edward Forhan c 2. DOK 1994; NorthAmerican Assoc. for the Diac 2006. carolforhan@yahoo.com

FORINASH JR, Joseph Lynn (Colo) PO Box 1026, Eagle CO 81631 **D Epis Ch Of The Trsfg Vail CO 1999-** B Kansas City KS 4/24/1943 s Joseph Lynn Forinash & Mary Leigh. BS USAF Acad Colorado Sprg CO 1965; MA U of Oklahoma 1971; MBA Wichita St U 1971. D 11/6/1999 Bp William Jerry Winterrowd. m 10/7/1989 Kathleen LaNor Bishop c 1.

FORISHA, Martha Lee (CNY) 102 Delaware St, San Antonio TX 78210 **Supply S Andr's Ch Brackettville TX 2011-** B Corpus Christi TX 5/17/1954 d Arthur Stanley Dickinson & Marilyn Ruth. BD Texas Wmn's U-Denton 1976; MDiv Epis TS of The SW 1993. D 6/12/1993 P 10/8/1994 Bp James Monte Stanton. m 8/23/1975 Donnie Forisha c 3. R Trin Epis Ch Seneca Falls NY 2000-2010; Cur Ch Of The Annunc Lewisville TX 1996-2000; Asst Ch Of The Gd Shpd Dallas TX 1995-1996; Ch Of The Gd Shpd Cedar Hill TX 1995; Cur Epis Ch Of The Ascen Dallas TX 1993-1995. mforisha@gmail.com

FORMAN, Bernard Kim (Oly) 3625 24th Pl. W., Apt. 3, Seattle WA 98199 **Assoc Ch Of The Ascen Seattle WA 2000-** B Sheridan WY 11/9/1933 s Percy Raleigh Forman & Lona Audette. BA U of Montana 1956; ThM U of Dallas Dallas 1991. D 6/20/1998 P 6/24/2000 Bp Vincent Waydell Warner. m 12/29/1957 Mary Frances Travis c 3. Assoc P St Ptr's Epis Par Seattle WA 2000-2002; D All SS Ch Seattle WA 1998-2000. Publ Relatns Soc of Amer (Accredited, 1978).

FORNALIK, Barbara Horn (Roch) 1130 Webster Rd, Webster NY 14580 B Jersey City NJ 2/8/1939 d John Howard Horn & Lillian Kiefer. Dplma Katharine Gibbs Sch 1959. D 3/29/2008 Bp Jack Marston McKelvey. m 4/29/1961 Anthony Fornalik c 3. btfrnlK@frontiernet.net

FORNARO, Francis (Mass) 11 Alaska Ave, Bedford MA 01730 **Int Dio Massachusetts Boston MA 2011-** B Boston MA 11/11/1942 s Simone Fornaro & Grace Anastasia. BS Boston St Coll 1964; MS Boston St Coll 1967; MDiv EDS 1996. D 9/8/1996 P 5/17/1997 Bp M(arvil) Thomas Shaw III. m 10/2/2004 Charles A Frates. R S Paul's Epis Ch Bedford MA 1999-2010; Dio Massachusetts Boston MA 1996-1999. ffornaro@aol.com

FORNEA, Stanley Wayne (EC) 2111 Jefferson Davis Hwy Apt603S, Arlington VA 22202 B Bogalusa LA 4/10/1958 ThM Duke; BA SE Louisiana U; DMin Van. D 12/5/2001 P 4/10/2002 Bp Clifton Daniel III. m 5/22/1982 Belinda Diane Tate c 2. forneasw@hotmail.com

FORNEY, John Craig (Los) 4956 Francis Ave., Chino CA 91710 B Long Beach CA 8/4/1942 s Daniel C Forney & Lillian Adell. BA Cal St U Los Angeles 1969; RelD TS at Claremont 1975; cert of 1 year study CDSP 1986; Tchg Cred Mills Coll 1987. D 6/7/1986 Bp William Edwin Swing P 3/1/1987 Bp Rogers Sanders Harris. m 6/11/1966 Eleanor Jai Handcock c 2. S Ambr Par Claremont CA 2004-2005; Dio Alaska Fairbanks AK 1987-1994. jforney170@aol.com

F

FORREST, E(lizabeth) Louise (Mass) 41 Hall Ave, Watertown MA 02472 B Santa Monica CA 10/1/1947 d John Cathcart Forrest & Janet MacKenzie. BA Whittier Coll 1969; MDiv EDS 1980; Cert Rad 1996. D 5/28/1983 P 12/3/1983 Bp Frederick Barton Wolf. m 8/12/2004 Leslie Horst. Asst R The Ch Of Our Redeem Lexington MA 2007-2008; Dir. Rel Educ Gr Ch Newton MA 2002-2004; Assoc Dio Massachusetts Boston MA 1999-2002; Assoc The Cathd Ch Of S Paul Boston MA 1999; Assoc Ch Of S Jn The Evang Boston MA 1997-1999; P-in-c S Dav's Epis Ch Halifax MA 1992-1993; Cler Assoc S Paul's Ch Brookline MA 1989-1991; Cler Assoc S Paul's Ch Natick MA 1984-1986. RevLouise4@aol.com

FORREST OSB, William (FdL) 56500 Abbey Rd, Three Rivers MI 49093 B Marion NC 1/3/1950 s William Gordon Forrest & Rose Cochran. BA S Andr's Presb Coll Laurinburg NC 1972. D 6/18/1992 P 12/1/1992 Bp William L Stevens.

FORREST, William Clifford (Az) 24922 S Lakewood Dr, Sun Lakes AZ 85248 **P S Matt's Ch Chandler AZ 2005-** B Baltimore MD 6/28/1945 s Nelson Forrest & Marguerite. BA Bridgewater Coll 1969; MDiv CDSP 1972. D 6/18/1972 P 6/17/1973 Bp J(ohn) Joseph Meakins Harte. m 6/5/1983 Julia L Hall c 2. Dio Arizona Phoenix AZ 2000-2004; S Chris's Ch Sun City AZ 2000-2004; S Aug's Epis Ch Tempe AZ 1992-2001; S Mary's Epis Ch Tomah WI 1990-1991; R Chr Ch S Paul MN 1984-1990; Gr Ch Tucson AZ 1981-1984; Gr S Paul's Epis Ch Tucson AZ 1981-1983; All SS' Epis Day Sch Phoenix AZ 1979-1981; All SS Epis Ch Torrington WY 1977-1979; R S Alb's Epis Ch Wickenburg AZ 1973-1977; Cur Trin Cathd Phoenix AZ 1972-1973. frbillaz@yahoo.com

FORREST, William Fred (Dal) 3029 Frances Dr, Denison TX 75020 **Asstg P S Steph's Epis Ch Sherman TX 2002-; S Jn's Epis Ch Pottsboro TX 1988-** B Woodbury NJ 3/22/1931 s Fred La Boube Forrest & Maude Robinson. BA Westminster Choir Coll of Rider U 1954; MDiv PDS 1961. D 4/29/1961 P 10/28/1961 Bp Alfred L Banyard. c 3. Dept Of Missions Dallas TX 1984-1987; Ch Of The H Trin Bonham TX 1983-1985; S Jn's Epis Ch Pottsboro TX 1983; S Lk's Ch Denison TX 1978-1982; S Vinc's Cathd Bedford TX 1973-1978; R S Jn's Ch Farmington NM 1969-1973; Vic S Mk's On The Mesa Epis Ch Albuquerque NM 1969-1973; Asst To Dn S Matt's Cathd Dallas TX 1965-1969; P-in-c S Jn's Ch Sewaren NJ 1964-1965; Vic S Marks Ch Carteret NJ 1961-1965. Amer Hymn Soc. WFFORREST@CABLEONE.NET

FORRESTER, Shelley A (Chi) St. Andrew's Church, 1125 Franklin St., Downers Grove IL 60515 **Asst R S Andr's Ch Downers Grove IL 2008-** B Cheyenne WY 11/8/1963 d William H Hubbard & Edwina Miller. AAS Laramie Cnty Cmnty Coll 1987; BA U of Texas 1989; MDiv Epis TS of the SW 2008. D 12/16/2007 Bp Bruce Edward Caldwell P 12/6/2008 Bp Jeffrey Dean Lee. sforrester@saintandrewschurch.net

FORSYTHE, Margaret Ann Kroy (NJ) 687 Donald Dr S, Bridgewater NJ 08807 **D S Fran Ch Dunellen NJ 2010-** B Detroit MI 7/26/1941 d Walter Henry Kroy & Anne Clara. BA U MI 1963; AAS Raritan Vlly Cmnty Coll 1985; AA Raritan Vlly Cmnty Coll 1985. D 10/31/1998 Bp Joe Morris Doss. c 2. D Chr Ch New Brunswick NJ 2005-2006; D S Mart's Ch Bridgewater NJ 1998-2005. DOK; NAAD. revmarge@verizon.net

FORSYTHE, Mary Louise (Neb) 420 Shorewood Ln, Waterloo NE 68069 **D Ch Of The Resurr Omaha NE 1988-** B Sioux City IA 7/16/1933 d Byron Lawrence Sifford & Helene Lucile. BA U of Iowa 1955; MS U of Nebraska 1968; EFM STUSo 1984. D 5/7/1988 Bp James Daniel Warner. c 2.

FORT, David Acrill (USC) Po Box 108, Gaffney SC 29342 B Gaffney SC 5/21/1924 s James Claude Fort & Gladys. BA Wofford Coll 1960; BD STUSo 1961. D 6/23/1961 P 11/1/1962 Bp Clarence Alfred Cole. m 3/31/1956 Margaret Poole c 3. R S Dav's Ch Cheraw SC 1969-1977; R Trin Ch Yazoo City MS 1966-1969; Vic Our Sav Epis Ch Trenton SC 1962-1965; Vic Trin Ch Edgefield SC 1962-1965; Cur S Martins-In-The-Field Columbia SC 1961-1962.

FORTE, Jeanne (NCal) 700 Wellfleet Dr, Vallejo CA 94591 **R S Paul's Epis Ch Benicia CA 2005-** B Victoria BC 10/20/1951 d David Rolston &

Margaret. BA U Of Calgary Calgary Ab CA 1983; MDiv CDSP 1999. Trans from Anglican Church of Canada 7/16/2005 Bp Jerry Alban Lamb. c 2. jeanneforte@sbcglobal.net

FORTI, Nicholas (SVa) 1700 University Ave, Charlottesville VA 22903 **Assoc R S Paul's Memi Charlottesville VA 2010-** B Richmond VA 2/8/1981 s Kenneth Wayne Forti & Avis Donna. BS Radford U 2004; MDiv VTS 2010. D 6/12/2010 P 12/11/2010 Bp Herman Hollerith IV. m 8/2/2008 Eleis M Lester. uva.chaplain@stpaulsmemorialchurch.org

FORTKAMP, Frank Edwin (Md) 1840 Canvasback Lane, Columbus OH 43215 B Columbus OH 10/30/1938 s Herman John Fortknap & Freda. BA Josephinum 1960; MA OH SU 1968; PhD OH SU 1971. Rec from Roman Catholic 5/5/2002 as Priest Bp John Leslie Rabb. m 1/15/1975 Deborah Dawes c 1. R Gr Ch Brunswick MD 2002-2010. dfortkamp@juno.com

FORTNA, Robert Tomson (NY) 333 W 86th St, Apt 807, New York NY 10024 B Lincoln NE 5/5/1930 s Ralph Edward Fortna & Gertrude Tomson. BA Ya 1952; BD CDSP 1955; MA U of Cambridge 1959; ThD UTS 1965. D 10/13/1956 P 4/1/1957 Bp Sumner Walters. m 8/27/1960 Evelyn Nelson Carr c 3. Asst Chr Ch Poughkeepsie NY 1963-1995; Asst S Mary's Manhattanville Epis Ch New York NY 1960-1963; Vic S Mary's Ch Manteca CA 1956-1958; Tutor/Instr CDSP Berkeley CA 1955-1960. Auth, "Scholars Bible: Matt," Polebridge Press, 2005; Auth, "Fourth Gospel & Its Predecessor," Fortress, 1987; Auth, "Gospel of Signs," Cambridge, 1970. SBL 1954; Soc of NT Stds 1968. Annual Prof Albright Archeological Inst Jerusalem 1979; Fllshp Ecum Inst of Advncd Theol Study Jerusalem 1972. fortna@vassar.edu

FORTNER, Marian Dulaney (Miss) 509 W Pine St, Hattiesburg MS 39401 **Title IV Disciplinary Bd Dio Mississippi Jackson MS 2011-2012; Co-Fac of Post Ord Consult Dio Mississippi Jackson MS 2011-; R Trin Ch Hattiesburg MS 2009-** B Tunica MS 6/30/1956 d John William Dulaney & Dorothy Henry. BA U of Mississippi 1978; JD U of Mississippi 1981; MDiv GTS 1996. D 6/22/1996 P 2/15/1997 Bp Alfred Clark Marble Jr. m 6/9/2001 Thomas M Fortner c 1. Assoc R All SS Ch Phoenix AZ 2005-2009; P-in-c S Chris's Ch Jackson MS 2004-2005; Chapl S Andr's Epis Sch Ridgeland MS 1999-2005; Cur S Jas Ch Greenville MS 1996-1999. mfdfortner@gmail.com

FORTUNATO, Susan Boykin (NY) 82 Ehrhardt Rd, Pearl River NY 10965 **R S Steph's Ch Pearl River NY 2001-** B Nacogdoches TX 3/11/1967 d Richard Sellers & Mitylene. Sweet Briar Coll 1987; BA Seton Hall U 1996; MDiv Drew U 1999. D 6/5/1999 Bp John Palmer Croneberger P 12/11/1999 Bp John Shelby Spong. m 5/13/1988 Christopher Fortunato c 1. Asst S Jas Ch Upper Montclair NJ 1999-2001. revsf@aol.com

FORTUNE, Dwight Chapman (Mass) 246 Mount Hope St, North Attleboro MA 02760 B Fitchburg MA 7/29/1927 s John William Fortune & Gladys May. BA Amer Intl Coll 1958; MDiv Ya Berk 1962. D 6/16/1962 P 5/26/1963 Bp William A Lawrence. m 9/12/1953 Anna D Doake c 5. Int S Mart's Ch Pawtucket RI 2000-2002; S Jn The Evang Taunton MA 1978-1989; Int R All SS Epis Ch Attleboro MA 1976-1978; Int S Paul's Ch Malden MA 1975-1976; All SS Epis Ch Attleboro MA 1974-1975; R S Jn's Ch Sharon MA 1965-1974; Cur S Ptr's Ch Beverly MA 1962-1965.

FOSS, Charles Sanford (USC) 9601 Grove Crest Lane, Apt. 1812, Charlotte NC 28262 B Danville VA 10/11/1949 s Robert Todd Foss & Olive Echols. BA Ya 1971; MDiv STUSo 1978; PhD Grad Theol Un Berkeley CA 1989. D 6/3/1978 P 5/23/1979 Bp George Moyer Alexander. m 4/21/1974 Gwendolyn F Friesen c 2. R Ch Of Our Sav Rock Hill SC 1997-2011; Asst S Jas By The Sea La Jolla CA 1988-1997; Asst S Jas Epis Ch Greenville SC 1978-1982. Auth, "Karl Barth & the Word of God in the So," *S Lk's Journ of Theol*, 1985. cgfoss@carolina.rr.com

FOSTER III, Andrew William (NY) 12 W 11th St, New York NY 10011 **R Ch Of The Ascen New York NY 1999-** B Rockville Centre NY 9/29/1944 s Andrew William Foster & Doris Jane. BS Mt Un Coll 1966; STB GTS 1970. D 6/27/1970 P 2/21/1971 Bp William Foreman Creighton. m 5/28/1969 Lynda Garwood c 2. R S Paul's Ch In Nantucket Nantucket MA 1993-1999; Ken Gambier OH 1986-1993; Cur Gr Ch Washington DC 1970-1972. Auth, "Epis Chapl On Campus: Observations Of The Ch'S MHE," 1983. Fllshp Soc Of S Jn The Evang. frandrew@ascensionnyc.org

FOSTER, Craig Arthur (SO) 508 Thistle Dr, Delaware OH 43015 **S Jn's Ch Columbus OH 2007-** B Hastings MI 6/24/1954 s John Arthur Foster & Juliette. BS U Of Iowa Iowa City IA 1977. D 6/23/2007 Bp Thomas Edward Breidenthal. m 8/10/2002 Kathleen Kathleen West. cfos@columbus.rr.com

FOSTER, Guy Roland (NY) 3505 Oaks Way, #408, Pompano Beach FL 33069 B Beckley WV 11/4/1925 s Walter Roland Foster & Dorothy. BA Tusculum Coll 1946; BD UTS 1949; STM GTS 1957; PhD U Of Edinburgh Edinburgh Gb 1963; DD Nash 1974; ThD U Of Glasgow Glasgow Gb 1977. D 6/7/1950 P 12/1/1950 Bp Theodore N Barth. m 9/16/1950 Anna Foster. Dn/Prof of Ch Hist The GTS New York NY 1973-1989; SubDean/Prof of Ch Hist Nash Nashotah WI 1964-1973; SubDean/Prof of Ch Hist Dom And Frgn Mssy Soc-Epis Ch Cntr New York NY 1952-1964; P-in-c S Paul's Ch Athens TN 1950-1952. Auth, "Role Of Presding Bp," Forw Mvmt, 1982; Auth, "Reformation & Revolution," *The Ch Before the Covenants*, Scottish Acad Press, 1975; Auth, "Bp & Presb," S.P.C.K., 1957. guy007@usa.net

FOSTER, Katharine K (SO) 7919 N Coolville Ridge Rd, Athens OH 45701 **P Gr Ch Pomeroy OH 2000-; P S Geo's Ch Clifton Pk NY 2000-; P S Jn's Ripley WV 2000-; Team Chr Ch Point Pleasant WV 1998-** B Akron OH 10/7/1941 d Arthur H Knippenberg & Virginia G. BS Kent St U 1963; MLS Case Wstrn Reserve U 1965; Cert Dio So Diac Sch 1991. D 5/4/1991 Bp William Grant Black P 6/26/2002 Bp David Colin Jones. m 8/1/1970 Theodore S Foster. D Ch Of The Gd Shpd Athens OH 1993-1998.

FOSTER JR, Kenneth Earl (Mil) 1418 Valley Dr, Wisconsin Dells WI 53965 **D H Cross Epis Ch Wisconsin Dells WI 2001-** B Kilbourn (Wisconsin Dells) WI 3/5/1933 s Kenneth Earl Foster & Blanche Constable. BBA U of Wisconsin 1955. D 1/13/2001 Bp Roger John White. m 10/7/1967 Lucille Mae Mitchell c 3.

FOSTER, Malcolm Lysle (LI) 5 Riverside Drive, Apt 8D, New York NY 10023 B Valley NE 8/13/1927 s Edwin Ronald Foster & Frances Irene. SMM UTS 1951; MDiv GTS 1955; BMus U MI 2049. D 6/5/1955 P 12/18/1955 Bp Horace W B Donegan. m 6/16/1956 Marilyn Ford c 2. P-in-c S Andr's Dune Chap Southampton NY 1969-1988; R S Jn's Epis Ch Southampton NY 1966-1988; R S Ptr's Epis Ch Peekskill NY 1959-1966; Cur Ch Of The Resurr New York NY 1955-1959. Pi Kappa Lambda U MI 1949.

FOSTER, Margaret Reidpath (WNY) 1088 Delaware Ave Apt 5a, Buffalo NY 14209 B New York NY 1/31/1930 d James Forsythe Foster & Dorothy Riedpath. AA Cazenovia Jr Coll 1950. D 11/23/1991 Bp David Charles Bowman. c 3. AEHC; Curs, EFM.

FOSTER, Pamela LaMotte (Mass) 19 Warren Point Rd, Wareham MA 02571 B Danville PA 5/26/1941 d William Oscar LaMotte & Mary Elizabeth. BA U CA 1963; MDiv Pittsburgh TS 1984. D 6/2/1984 P 1/12/1985 Bp Alden Moinet Hathaway. m 8/24/1963 Donald Foster c 3. Assoc R Trin Ch In The City Of Boston Boston MA 2000-2008; Sr Assoc Chr Ch Alexandria VA 1995-2000; Asst Calv Ch Pittsburgh PA 1987-1995; Ch Of The Adv Pittsburgh PA 1986-1987; Int R Dio Pittsburgh Monroeville PA 1986-1987; Dio Pittsburgh Monroeville PA 1984-1985. pamfoster00@aol.com

FOSTER, Penelope Hope (WNY) 54 Delaware Rd, Kenmore NY 14217 **D Ch Of The Adv Kenmore NY 2008-** B Lachine Canada 10/26/1947 d Donald Kinna & Dorothy Janet. D 10/18/2008 Bp J Michael Garrison. m 5/24/1969 Ronald Foster c 2. episcopenny@hotmail.com

FOSTER, Randal Arthur (NC) 105 Pettingill Pl, Southern Pines NC 28387 B Asheboro NC 7/17/1956 s Albert Curtis Foster & Virginia Dare. BA U NC 1979; MDiv VTS 1988; MA U NC 1999; DMin GTF 2004. D 6/30/1990 Bp Robert Whitridge Estill P 6/29/1991 Bp Huntington Williams Jr. m 5/21/1994 Roberta Michelle Adams. S Paul's In The Pines Epis Ch Fayetteville NC 2001-2005; Vic All SS Ch Hamlet NC 1993-1999; R Ch Of The Mssh Rockingham NC 1993-1999; Asst S Mary's Epis Ch High Point NC 1991-1993; Asst/Day Sch Chapl Emm Par Epis Ch And Day Sch Sthrn Pines NC 1990-1991. Conf Of S Ben 1999. counselingnc@earthlink.net

FOSTER, Simon (LI) 325 Lattingtown Rd, Locust Valley NY 11560 **R S Jn's Of Lattingtown Locust Vlly NY 2009-; R S Jn's Of Lattingtown Locust Vlly NY 2002-** B 3/29/1963 Cert In Theol Of Southampton U Chichester Theol Coll; BA U Of Kent. Trans from Church Of England 1/1/2006 Bp Orris George Walker Jr. P-in-c S Jn's Of Lattingtown Locust Vlly NY 2006-2009. simon@stjlat.org

FOSTER, Steve Leslie (LI) 100 46th Street, Lindenhurst NY 11757 **P-in-c S Bon Epis Ch Lindenhurst NY 2006-** B Barbados 9/23/1976 s Marcia Alvana. Bachelor of Sci CUNY- Brooklyn Coll 2001; MDiv GTS 2004. D 5/26/2004 P 12/21/2004 Bp Orris George Walker Jr. Cur S Geo's Ch Hempstead NY 2004-2006. stevef22@yahoo.com

FOSTER, Willis Renard (SVa) 228 Halifax St, Petersburg VA 23803 **R S Steph's Ch Petersburg VA 2010-** B Greensboro NC 10/31/1948 s Willis Sampson Foster & Linnie Bernice. BS NC A&T St U 1970; MS Troy St U 1991; MDiv VTS 2010. D 6/12/2010 P 12/18/2010 Bp Herman Hollerith IV. m 6/23/2007 Duanne Hoffler c 4. wrfostersr@gmail.com

FOTCH JR, Charlton Harvey (Cal) 681 S Eliseo Dr, Greenbrae CA 94904 **Asst St Johns Epis Ch Ross CA 1989-** B Buffalo NY 6/25/1945 s Charlton Harvey Fotch & Dolores Mary. BA Baldwin-Wallace Coll 1967; MDiv GTS 1970. D 6/29/1970 P 1/9/1971 Bp Harold B Robinson. Sarasota Dnry Chapl Sarasota FL 1978-1987; R S Mk's Epis Ch Moscow PA 1974-1978; P-in-c S Paul's Epis Ch Stafford NY 1972-1974; Asst S Jas' Ch Batavia NY 1970-1974. Auth, "Growing Pains (Poem)," 1984. fotch@marin.cc.ca.us

FOTINOS, Dennis George (Tex) 248 Birchbark Dr., Mills River NC 28759 B Dayton OH 7/20/1945 s Dennis George Fotinos & Frances Rebecca. BA U of Miami 1967; STB GTS 1971. D 5/31/1971 P 5/27/1972 Bp James Loughlin Duncan. m 5/26/1973 Barbara Hemphill c 2. R Ch Of The Gd Shpd Kingwood TX 1993-2008; R Trin Cathd Pittsburgh PA 1987-1993; R S Tim's Ch Alexandria LA 1983-1987; Epis Ch Of S Ptr's By The Lake Denver NC 1983; Vic S Andr Ch Mt Holly NC 1974-1982; Asst S Mk The Evang Ft Lauderdale FL 1971-1974. CT - Assoc 1980-1993. dgfotinos@gmail.com

FOUGHTY, Donna L (Va) 7414 Heatherfield Ln, Alexandria VA 22315 **P-in-c The Ch Of The Epiph Oak Hill VA 2009-** B Ridgewood NJ 11/11/1953 d Domenica Vincensio Lopez & Clara. BA Ramapo St Coll 1978; EFM 1984; MDiv VTS 1995. D 10/10/1987 Bp Craig Barry Anderson P 6/26/2002 Bp David Colin Jones. m 6/22/1974 Michael Arthur Foughty c 2. Cleric Pohick Epis Ch Lorton VA 2007-2008; Asst Olivet Epis Ch Franconia VA 2005; long term supply S Patricks Ch Falls Ch VA 2005; long term supply All SS Ch Alexandria VA 2004; Int S Marg's Ch Woodbridge VA 2003-2004; Int S Geo's Epis Ch Arlington VA 2002-2003; Assoc S Mk's Ch Alexandria VA 1998-2002; Diocesion Evang Com Dio So Dakota Sioux Falls SD 1990-1992; D Emm Epis Par Rapid City SD 1989-1992. All SS Sis of the Poor 2007; Ord Of S Lk. revmom53@gmail.com

FOUKE, Scherry Vickery (ETenn) 1601 Forest Dr, Morristown TN 37814 **Bp's Com on Inclusivity Dio E Tennessee Knoxville TN 2010-; Stndg Com Dio E Tennessee Knoxville TN 2010-; Trnr, Safeguarding God's People Dio E Tennessee Knoxville TN 2009-; R All SS' Epis Ch Morristown TN 2004-** B Royston GA 10/20/1945 d Paul Vickery & Mae Mccarter. MDiv Candler TS Emory U 1988. D 10/19/1988 P 5/1/1989 Bp William Arthur Beckham. Dioc Conv, Co-Host Dio E Tennessee Knoxville TN 2007; Chapl, All SS' Epis Sch Dio E Tennessee Knoxville TN 2004-2011; Assoc R The Epis Ch Of The Adv Kennett Sq PA 2001-2004; R S Dunstans Ch Blue Bell PA 1995-2001; Middle E Study Grp Dio Pennsylvania Philadelphia PA 1993-2002; Assoc R Ch Of S Mart-In-The-Fields Philadelphia PA 1990-1995; Cur Ch Of The Resurr Greenwood SC 1988-1990. revsvf@gmail.com

FOULKE, Mary Lova (NY) 487 Hudson St, New York NY 10014 **Sr. Assoc The Ch Of S Lk In The Fields New York NY 2002-** B Dayton OH 11/26/1962 d Kenneth Webb Foulke & Madeline Anne. BA Earlham Coll 1980; MDiv UTS 1989; EdD Col 1996. D 5/20/2001 P 1/12/2002 Bp Frederick Houk Borsch. m 1/1/2001 Renee Leslie Hill c 2. All SS Ch Pasadena CA 2002. mfoulke@stlukeinthefields.org

FOUNTAIN, Timothy Logan (SD) 2707 W. 33rd St, Sioux Falls SD 57105 **R Ch Of The Gd Shpd Sioux Falls SD 2004-** B Los Angeles CA 6/13/1958 s Erman Alvan Fountain & Mary Librise. BA USC 1982; MDiv GTS 1987. D 6/27/1987 P 1/23/1988 Bp Oliver Bailey Garver Jr. m 5/26/1990 Melissa Ann Clayman c 2. Vic S Jn Chrys Ch And Sch Rancho Santa Margarita CA 1995-2004; Vic S Alb's Epis Ch Yucaipa CA 1991-1995; Assoc R S Nich Par Encino CA 1989-1991; Cur S Ptr's Par San Pedro CA 1987-1989. Host, "Nthrn Plains Anglicans," http://northernplainsanglicans.blogspot.com, 2007; Auth, "Imperious Control," *Orange Cnty Register*, 2002; Auth, "Deeds Of Evil Men," *Orange Cnty Register*, 2001. Outstanding Sermon Epis Ntwk For Stwdshp 1999; Us Army Achievement Medal Us Army 1982. tfountain@sio.midco.net

FOUT, Jason Andrew (WMich) 591 Sheridan Ave, Bexley OH 43209 **Prof Bex Columbus OH 2009-** B Waukegan IL 3/30/1971 s Glenn Fout & Janice. BA U IL 1992; MTS SWTS 2001; MDiv SWTS 2001; PhD Camb 2010. D 6/16/2001 Bp William Dailey Persell P 12/15/2001 Bp Edward Lewis Lee Jr. m 12/16/1995 Kristen Gurga c 2. Cur S Paul's Epis Ch S Jos MI 2001-2005. jayfout@yahoo.com

FOUTS, Arthur Guy (WA) 12304 Guinevere Rd, Glenn Dale MD 20769 B Ancon PA 4/14/1944 s Ben Salem Fouts & Aura Maria. BA U of Washington 1972; GOE U of Cambridge 1981; DMin SWTS 1998. Trans from Church Of England 11/1/1989 Bp William Grant Black. m 9/4/2003 Carol Van den Houten c 1. P-in-c S Paul's Epis Par Point Of Rocks MD 2001-2011; S Mary Magd Ch Silver Sprg MD 1991-2000; Int S Mk's Ch Warren RI 1990-1991; Int S Pat's Epis Ch Dublin OH 1988-1989. Int Mnstry Ntwk 1987-1998; Natl Assn Of Epis Int Mnstry Spec 1999-2001. rubberduck301@yahoo.com

FOUTS, James Ralph (NC) 19 Little Cove Rd, Sylva NC 28779 **Died 4/15/2011** B Macomb IL 8/8/1929 s Ralph Butler Fouts & Mary May. BS NWU 1951; PhD NWU 1954; MDiv Duke 1984. D 6/27/1985 Bp Robert Whitridge Estill P 6/27/1986 Bp Frank Harris Vest Jr. c 3. Auth, *200 Sci Books/arts*. Soc of S Jn the Evang 1986. Phi Lambda Upsilon (Chem) NWU 1950; Phi Beta Kappa NWU 1950; Who's Who in Amer; Jn J. Abel Awd Amer Soc of Pharmacology & Exp. Therap.

FOWLE, Elizabeth (WMass) 15 Old Hancock Rd., Hancock NH 03449 B Pittsburgh PA 4/14/1942 d Milton Fred Heller & Suzanne. BA Smith 1964; MA S Jos Coll W Hartford CT 1987; MDiv Ya Berk 1993. D 6/12/1993 P 2/2/1994 Bp Arthur Edward Walmsley. m 6/20/1964 Stephen Parker Fowle c 3. Dioc Coun Dio Wstrn Massachusetts Springfield MA 2006-2008; Chair, COM Dio Wstrn Massachusetts Springfield MA 2003-2006; COM Dio Wstrn Massachusetts Springfield MA 2001-2008; R All SS Ch So Hadley MA 2000-2008; Search and Nomin Cmte for Bp Dio Chicago Chicago IL 1997-1998; Assoc R Chr Ch Winnetka IL 1996-2000; Bd. Mem, Cathd Shltr of Chicago Dio Chicago Chicago IL 1995-1998; Cur Chr Ch Winnetka IL 1993-1995. revbets@aol.com

FOWLER, Anne Carroll (Mass) 24 Alveston St, Jamaica Plain MA 02130 **R S Jn's Ch Jamaica Plain MA 1992-** B Portland ME 5/5/1946 d Alexander Robert Fowler & Sully Carroll. BA Rad 1968; MA Bos 1971; PhD Bos 1979; MDiv EDS 1984. D 6/1/1985 Bp John Bowen Coburn P 5/3/1986 Bp David Elliot Johnson. m 1/18/1992 Samuel M Allen c 3. R All SS Ch Stoneham MA 1988-1992; Asst S Dunstans Epis Ch Dover MA 1985-1988. Auth, "What I Could," Pudding Hse Press, 2009; Auth, "Whiskey Stitching," Pudding Hse Press, 2007; Auth, "Sum of Salvage," Pudding Hse Press, 2007; Auth, "Five Islands," Pudding Hse Press, 2002; Auth, "Liz, Wear Those Pearl Earrings," Frank Cat Press, 2002; Ed, "Models For Writing". Abigail Adams Awd Massachusetts Womens'S Political Caucus 2002. annecfowler@mac.com

FOWLER, Arlen Lowery (Okla) 817 Virginia Ln, Ardmore OK 73401 **Vic S Mk's Ch Hugo OK 2002-** B Bartlesville OK 6/10/1928 s Benjamin Henry Fowler & Aleene Emma. BA Oklahoma St U 1952; MDiv PrTS 1957; PhD WA SU 1968. D 11/20/1971 P 3/1/1972 Bp Albert A Chambers. m 11/25/1950 Mary Ritchey c 4. R St Phil's Epis Ch Ardmore OK 1983-1995; Assoc R S Dunst's Ch Tulsa OK 1982-1983; R S Andr's Ch Paris IL 1973-1974; P Trin Ch Guthrie OK 1957-1960. "Facing Auschwitz, A Chr Imperative," iUniverse, 2003; Auth, "The Black Infantry in the W, 1869-1891," U of Oklahoma Press, 1996; "From Blinking Lights to Stdt Rts," *Dialog, Vol l, No. 2*, The U of Tulsa, 1977; "The Black Cavalry in the W," *The Dictionary of Amer Hist*, Chas Scribner' Sons, 1976; "The Black Infantry in the W," *The Dictionary of Amer Hist*, Chas Scribner's Sons, 1976; "Chapl D. Eglington Barr: A Lincoln Yankee," *The Hist mag of the Prot Epis Ch*, 1976; Auth, "The Black Infantry in the W," Greenwood,Publ, 1974. majeralf@sbcglobal.net

F

FOWLER, Connetta (NwT) 430 Dallas St, Big Spring TX 79720 **D The Epis Ch Of S Mary The Vrgn Big Sprg TX 2002-** B Mamou LA 2/11/1943 BS McNeese St U; MS U of Texas. D 10/27/2002 Bp C(harles) Wallis Ohl. revbarbara@suddenlinkmail.com

FOWLER, Daniel Lewis (Oly) 4335 NE Rhodes End Rd, Bainbridge Island WA 98110 **D S Barn Epis Ch Bainbridge Island WA 2008-** B Visalia CA 12/15/1943 s Geroge Fredrick Fowler & Ruth Jane. BS San Jose St Coll 1966; BA Sch for Deacons 1983. D 2/21/1986 Bp Charles Shannon Mallory. m 6/12/1966 Patricia Anne Cameron c 3. The Ch Of The H Sprt Lake Forest IL 1997-2005; Archd Dio El Camino Real Monterey CA 1986-1997. dfowler282@msn.com

FOWLER, Donald E (Me) 15 Locust Ln, Albrightsville PA 18210 B 3/16/1924 Trans from Anglican Church of Canada 5/6/1987 Bp Edward Cole Chalfant. m 6/13/1949 Shirley Fowler c 2. Penobscot Mssn Winn ME 1990-1991; S Aug's Epis Ch Dover Foxcroft ME 1988-1989; Ch Of The Gd Shpd Sussex NJ 1966-1976. fowlers1@ptd.net

FOWLER, Emmet Jack (NAM) 2301 E 18th St, Farmington NM 87401 **Mssnr at Lg Navajoland Area Mssn Farmington NM 2000-** B Indianapolis IN 5/7/1929 s Emmet Grandville Fowler & Nellie Annette. BA Olivet Nazarene U 1951; BD Nazarene TS 1954; MA Nthrn Arizona U 1958; MDiv CDSP 1959; U of Kentucky 1980. D 6/14/1959 P 12/20/1959 Bp Arthur Kinsolving. m 7/1/1964 Anna Mae Begay. All SS Farmington NM 1988-1999; Coordntr Mnstry Dvlpmt Navajoland Area Mssn Farmington NM 1986-1987; Vic S Aug's Shiprock Farmington NM 1982-1987; Vic Ch Of The Gd Shpd Ft Defiance AZ 1959-1964. CBS; Tertiary of the Soc of S Fran 1986.

FOWLER, John Clinton (Az) 417 S Main St, Nazareth PA 18064 **Died 3/19/2011** B Douglas AZ 7/29/1924 s Samuel Holman Fowler & Ruth Moreland. BA U of Arizona 1948; STB GTS 1951. D 6/10/1951 P 12/8/1951 Bp Arthur Kinsolving.

FOWLER, Richard Paul (Cal) C/O 454 Mangels Ave, San Francisco CA 94127 B Philadelphia PA 10/6/1932 s Edwin Harper Fowler & Elsie Viola. W&M 1954; BD VTS 1959. D 6/13/1959 Bp Joseph Gillespie Armstrong P 12/1/1959 Bp Oliver J Hart. m 8/8/1959 Florence Ludlow c 3. The Epis Ch Of S Mary The Vrgn San Francisco CA 1966-1999; Vic H Chld At S Mart Epis Ch Daly City CA 1962-1966; Cur Ch Of Our Sav Jenkintown PA 1959-1960.

FOWLER, Stanley Gordon (Oly) 111 Ne 80th St, Seattle WA 98115 B Los Angeles,CA 3/15/1946 s Gordon Fowler & Olga. BA U CA 1967; MDiv SFTS 1971; MA Santa Clara U 1976. D 6/24/1972 Bp George Richard Millard P 1/1/1973 Bp C Kilmer Myers. m 6/15/1968 Jeanne Fowler c 1. R S Andr's Ch Seattle WA 1982-2004; Vic S Jn The Div Epis Ch Morgan Hill CA 1976-1982; Assoc S Edw The Confessor Epis Ch San Jose CA 1972-1974. REVSTANF@AOL.COM

FOWLER IV, William Young (Tex) Po Box 292, Buda TX 78610 **Trin Ch Galveston TX 2009-** B Broadwater County MT 6/25/1952 s William Young Fowler & Mary Green. BA U of Texas 1974; JD U of Texas 1977; MDiv STUSo 2000. D 6/1/2000 P 2/9/2001 Bp James Edward Folts. m 5/11/2002 Deborah F Fowler. R S Thos Epis Ch Coll Sta TX 2005-2009; Vic S Eliz's Epis Ch Buda TX 2000-2005. wfowler@trinitygalv.org

FOWLKES, Tyrone (Chi) 530 W Fullerton Pkwy, Chicago IL 60614 **Asst Ch Of Our Sav Chicago IL 2008-** B Indianapolis IN 3/18/1970 s Thomas Lee Fowlkes & Rosie Lee. BFA Indiana U 1988; MDiv Chr TS 2000; MAM Columbia Coll Chicago 2008; Cert SWTS 2008. D 6/7/2008 P 12/6/2008 Bp Jeffrey Dean Lee. fcreator2002@yahoo.com

FOX, Carol Rogers (NY) 312 West 22nd Street, New York NY 10011 **Hon Assoc Chr And S Steph's Ch New York NY 2002-** B Roxboro NC 6/1/1941

d Nathaniel Hassell Fox & Vera Virginia. BA Duke 1963; BD Duke 1966; STM UTS 1974; MA UTS 1984; Cert Blanton-Peale Grad Inst 1996; Cert Blanton-Peale Grad Inst 1996; CAS GTS 2001; STM GTS 2002. D 3/16/2002 P 9/21/2002 Bp Mark Sean Sisk. c 1. "Modesty & Mystery," Un Sem Quarterly Revs, 1984; "Liberation to Wholeness," The Chr Hm, 1974; "Male & Female - He Created Them," The Chr Hm, 1974. carolrfox@aol.com

FOX, Cheryl Lynn (Nev) 175 9th Ave # 262, New York NY 10011 **The Ch Of The Epiph And S Simon Brooklyn NY 2010-** B Glendale CA 11/3/1952 d James Howard Haskell & Mazie Delilah Brown. BA USC 1973; MDiv The GTS 2009. D 10/24/2008 P 8/15/2009 Bp Dan Thomas Edwards. m 7/17/1988 Tex L Fox. cheryltexfox@yahoo.com

FOX, David Coblentz (Okla) 2455 Sulphur Creek St, Cody WY 82414 **Assoc Chr Ch Cody WY 2005-** B Wyandotte MI 6/1/1941 s Arthur E Fox & Helen Olivia. BA Heidelberg Coll 1963; BD Bex 1966. D 6/29/1966 Bp Archie H Crowley P 3/4/1967 Bp Richard S M Emrich. m 6/26/1965 Lynn Usher c 3. R S Jn's Epis Ch Tulsa OK 1979-2004; R S Ptr's Ch Tecumseh MI 1973-1979; R Chr Ch Pleasant Lake MI 1967-1973; Cur S Tim's Ch Detroit MI 1966-1967. dcfox@bresnan.net

FOX, Deborah (NC) 2208 Hope St, Raleigh NC 27607 **Epis Campus Mnstry No Carolina St U Raleigh NC 2004-; Dio No Carolina Raleigh NC 2003-** B Crisfield MO 8/1/1949 d Harry E Fox & Dorothy. D 6/24/2000 P 3/24/2001 Bp Clifton Daniel III. Ch Of The Gd Shpd Wilmington NC 2000-2003; Asst S Phil's Ch Southport NC 2000. dfox23@nc.rr.com

FOX, Donald Allan (Cal) 185 Baltimore Way, San Francisco CA 94112 **Asstg Cler S Aid's Ch San Francisco CA 2009-** B Waterloo IA 4/28/1940 s Robert L Fox & Fern Worley. Iowa St Teachers Coll 1960; AB U Chi 1962; DB U Chi DS 1966; Indep Study Gesamteuropaisches Studienwerk, Germany 1968; Cuddesdon Theol Coll, Engl 1969. D 4/4/1970 P 4/21/1971 Bp Ivol I Curtis. Night Min San Francisco Night Mnstry San Francisco CA 1995-2006; R True Sunshine Par San Francisco CA 1986-1995; Canal Min San Rafael Canal Mnstry San Rafael CA 1983-1984; Asst P S Paul's Epis Ch San Rafael CA 1982-1986; Epis Chapl Stanford Cbury Fndt Standford CA 1976-1979; Assoc R S Fran' Epis Ch San Francisco CA 1973-1976; Cur S Thos Ch Medina WA 1972-1973; Cur S Jn's Epis Ch Olympia WA 1970-1972. EPF 1970-1982; Integrity 1980-1982. dfoxsf@sbcglobal.net

FOX III, Frederick Carl (Nwk) 441 Lockhart Mountain Rd Unit 4, Lake George NY 12845 B Poughkeepsie NY 1/19/1936 s Frederick Carl Fox & Ann Theresia. BA Un Coll Schenectady NY 1958; STB Ya Berk 1961; NYU 1981. D 6/10/1961 P 12/16/1961 Bp Horace W B Donegan. m 12/28/1957 Norma F Booth c 3. Dioc Coun Dio Newark Newark NJ 1992-1996; Asian Mnstrs Coun Dio Newark Newark NJ 1990-1996; Comp Dioc Relatnpshp W Hong Kong & Macao Dio Newark Newark NJ 1987-1992; Mnstry To Persons Of Chinese Hertiage Dio Newark Newark NJ 1987-1992; Secy & Treas Dio Newark Newark NJ 1969-1996; R S Paul's Ch No Arlington NJ 1968-1996; Dept Ce Dio Newark Newark NJ 1967-1996; R All SS' Epis Ch Glen Rock NJ 1965-1968; R Ch Of S Mary The Vrgn Ridgefield Pk NJ 1963-1965; Cur Gr Ch Utica NY 1961-1963. AAR; Rel Educ Assn Of The Untd States And Can; SBL.

FOX, Jedediah Wynn (Mont) 6345 Wydown Blvd, Saint Louis MO 63105 **Cur S Mich & S Geo Clayton MO 2009-** B Helena MT 6/2/1982 s John Murphy Fox & Sarah Page. BA Carroll Coll 2006; MDiv The GTS 2009. D 10/5/2008 P 5/31/2009 Bp Charles Franklin Brookhart Jr. m 5/27/2006 Mary Elizabeth Jager. jedediahfox@gmail.com

FOX, Loren Charles (CFla) Tang-Lin, Minden Road 24881 Singapore **Ch Of Our Sav Palm Bay FL 2007-; S Geo's Ch SINGAPORE 2003-** B Hartford CT 1/1/1962 s Calvin Charles Fox & Mildred Louise. BS U Roch 1984; MA Fuller TS 1988; MDiv TESM 1993. D 7/10/1993 Bp John-David Mercer Schofield P 2/1/1994 Bp John Wadsworth Howe. m 7/12/1986 Linda Susan Pan c 2. St Georges Ch Tanglin 2000-2005; Angl Frontier Missions Richmond VA 1997-2000; Trin Ch Vero Bch FL 1993-1997. llfox2@earthlink.net

FOX, Matthew Timothy (Cal) 287 17th St Ste 400, Oakland CA 94612 B Madison WI 12/21/1940 s George T Fox & Beatrice. BA Aquinas Inst Of Philos 1961; MA Aquinas Inst Of Philos 1963; MA Aquinas Inst of Theol 1967; PhD Institut Catholique De Paris 1970. Rec from Roman Catholic 12/1/1994 as Priest Bp William Edwin Swing. Auth, "Creativity: Where The Div And The Human Meet," Tarcher, 2002; Auth, "Original Blessing," Tarcher, 2000; Auth, "One River," *Many Wells: Wisdom Springing From Global Paths*, Tarcher, 2000; Auth, "Sins Of The Sprt," *Blessings Of The Flesh*, Harmony, 1999; Auth, "Confessions: The Making Of A Post-Denominational P," Harper San Francisco, 1996; Auth, "Natural Gr (w Rsheldrake)," Doubleday, 1996; Auth, "The Physics Of Ang," Harper San Francisco, 1996; Auth, "Wrestling w The Prophets: Essays In Creation," Tarcher, 1995; Auth, "Reinvention Of Wk," Harper San Francisco, 1995; Auth, "In The Beginning There Was Joy," Godfield, 1995; Auth, "Sheer Joy:Conversations w Thos Aquinas On Creat," *Sheer Joy:Conversations w Thos Aquinas On Creation Sprtlty*, Tarcher, 1992; Auth, "Creation Sprtlty: Liberating Gifts For Peoples Of Earth," Harper San Francisco, 1991; Auth, "Coming Of Cosmic Chr," Harper & Row, 1988; Auth, "Hildegard Of Bingen'S Bk Of Div Wk," *w Letters & Songs (Edited)*, Bear & Co, 1987; Auth, "Illuminations Of Hildegard Of Bingen," Bear & Co, 1985; Auth, "A Sprtlty Named Compassion," Inner Traditions, 1984; Auth, "Meditations w Meister Eckhart," Inner Traditions, 1982; Auth, "Manifetso For Global Civilization (w Bswimme)," Bear & Co, 1982; Auth, "Wstrn Sprtlty: Hist Roots," *Ecum Routes (Edited)*, Bear & Co, 1981; Auth, "Whee! We," *Wee All The Way Hm*, Inner Traditions, 1981; Auth, "Breakthrough," Image, 1980; Auth, "On Becoming A Mus," *Mystical Bear: Sprtlty Amer Style*, Paulist Press, 1972. Doctor Of Letters (Hon) U Of Cape Breton Sidney Nova Scotia 2002; Courage Of Conscience Awd Peace Abbey Sherborn MA 1995; 10th Anniv Awd New York Open Cntr 1994; Tikkun Natl Ethics Awd Tikkun.

FOX, Richard George (Mil) South 24 West 26835 Apache Pass, Waukesha WI 53188 **D St Mths Epis Ch Waukesha WI 1994-; D St Philips Epis Ch Waukesha WI 1994-** B Michigan City IN 7/7/1943 s Edward Craig Fox & Mildred Alison. BS Wstrn Michigan U 1965; MA Wstrn Michigan U 1967; PhD U of Kansas 1974; Cert Inst for Chr Stuides 1993; Cert Inst for Chr Stuides 1993. D 10/22/1994 Bp Roger John White. m 6/24/1976 Catherine A Close c 2. Assn of Epis Healthcare Chapl; NAAD. rfox7743@wi.rr.com

FOX, Ronald Napoleon (SeFla) 3464 Oak Ave, Miami FL 33133 B Fort Pierce FL 1/13/1944 s Rufus Lapoleon Fox & Iris. BA S Aug's Coll Raleigh NC 1966; MDiv GTS 1969. D 6/18/1969 Bp Henry I Louttit P 12/21/1969 Bp James Loughlin Duncan. m 8/26/1967 Anita Leatherwood c 3. R S Bern De Clairvaux N Miami Bch FL 1996-2010; Asst To Bp For Soc Concerns & Yth Mnstrs Dio SE Florida Miami FL 1992-1996; R Chr Epis Ch Miami FL 1982-1992; S Aug's Coll Raleigh NC 1979-1982; S Tim's Epis Ch Daytona Bch FL 1974-1979; Vic S Mary's Epis Ch Of Deerfiel Deerfield Bch FL 1969-1971; Vic S Matt's Epis Ch Delray Bch FL 1969-1971. Hon Doctor Of Civil Laws S Aug'S Coll Raleigh No Carolina 1993; Mary Mccloud Bethune Awd Bethune Cookman Coll Daytona Florida. ronaldfox13@att.net

FOX, R Steven (U) 136 E 57th St Ste 405, New York NY 10022 B Fort Campbell KY 9/9/1955 s Ralph Fox & Martha T. BA Indiana U 1980; MDiv UTS 1984. D 6/6/1984 Bp Otis Charles. D S Lk's Ch Pk City UT 1984-1985. Auth, "Visions & Voices Of The New Midwest"; Auth, "Crowley On Drugs". EUC, AAR, Cg Jung Fndt.

FOX, Sarah McRae (Mich) 8500 Jackson Square Blvd Apt 5D, Shreveport LA 71115 **Assoc Int R S Mk's Ch Houston TX 2007-** B Ferriday LA 11/25/1939 d Joseph Herman Fox & Dorothy Haynie. LSU 1959; BS S Mary's Dominican 1960; MDiv Epis TS of The SW 1984. D 6/25/1988 Bp Henry Irving Mayson P 2/1/1989 Bp R(aymond) Stewart Wood Jr. c 4. S Mk's Ch Houston TX 2006-2007; Asst S Steph's Epis Ch Houston TX 1996-2006; Int S Michaels In The Hills Toledo OH 1992-1993; COM Dio Michigan Detroit MI 1989-1992; Assoc S Jn's Ch Royal Oak MI 1988-1992; Asst to R S Steph's Epis Ch Houston TX 1984-1987. Michigan Epis Aids Coaltion Bd 89-92; Ord Of S Helena, Associated Parishes, Alb Inst, EPF, Epis Cleric Assn Of Michigan. smcraefox@gmail.com

FOX, Susann (Pa) 76 S Forge Manor Dr, Phoenixville PA 19460 B Hillsboro IL 12/24/1947 d Kenneth Floyd Blankenship & Margaret Ann. BS Estrn Illinois U 1969; MDiv Luth Sch of TS-Philadelphia 1995; Cert Thos Jefferson U 2002; Lic Thos Jefferson U 2006. D 1/6/1988 Bp Allen Lyman Bartlett Jr. m 9/18/1971 Terrence Fox c 1. D/Asst S Giles Ch Upper Darby PA 1992-1995; S Andr's In The Field Ch Philadelphia PA 1991; S Mary 's Ch Elverson PA 1990. Assembly Of Epis Hosp & Chapl; Soc Of Chapl. susann1224@verizon.net

FOX SR, Wesley D (ND) HC 2, Box 176, Garrison ND 58540 B Elbowoods ND 6/21/1940 s Robert L Fox & Naomi R. Ft Lewis Coll 1968; Brigham Young U 1969; Minot St U 1977; MDiv Untd TS 1983. D 6/26/1988 P 5/1/1989 Bp Harold Anthony Hopkins Jr. m 12/27/1959 Yvonne Elizabeth Howard c 1. Vic S Paul's Ch Garrison ND 1995; Dio No Dakota Fargo ND 1989-2005; Vic S Sylvan Ch Dunseith Dunseith ND 1988-1995.

FOXWORTH, George Marion (NCal) 4338 Walali Way, Fair Oaks CA 95628 **Assoc S Mich's Epis Ch Carmichael CA 2006-; S Lk's Ch Woodland CA 2000-** B Sumter SC 8/26/1939 s George Marion Foxworth & Emma Carolin. BS Austin Peay St U 1963; MDiv VTS 1967. D 6/27/1967 P 6/1/1968 Bp Gray Temple. m 3/10/2010 Donita Foxworth c 3. R All SS Memi Sacramento CA 1986-1997; Ch Of The Resurr Pleasant Hill CA 1986; Cn Pstr Gr Cathd San Francisco CA 1980-1986; Chr Ch Greenville SC 1975-1980; P-in-c Ch Of The Gd Shpd Sumter SC 1970-1974; Vic All SS Epis Ch Hampton SC 1967-1970; Vic Ch Of The H Comm Allendale SC 1967-1970. Auth, "hon Friend Cdsp Alum 94," 1998; Auth, "You Are The Body," 1978. OHC 1988. geofox@juno.com

FOXX, Louis Nelson (Mass) 397 Putnam Ave., Cambridge MA 02139 B Boston MA 10/13/1951 s Peace Alexander Foxx & Mildred Jackquline. BA U of Massachusetts 1978; MDiv EDS 1981; Adanced Cert. EDS 2006. D 5/15/1982 Bp John Bowen Coburn P 5/1/1983 Bp John Melville Burgess. m 7/28/1973 Debre Celeste Phifer c 2. R S Barth's Ch Cambridge MA 1988-2008; S Mths Ch Philadelphia PA 1984-1988. Auth, "Jubilee mag". foxxlouis@gmail.com

FRAATZ, William Frederick (RI) 43 Ogden Ave, Warwick RI 02889 B Berwyn IL 4/7/1955 s Charles William Fraatz & May Esther. BA Bethel Coll 1978;

MDiv Ya Berk 1981; STM Ya Berk 1983; Oxf 1987; JD U MN 1993. D 9/24/1981 P 5/30/1982 Bp Robert Marshall Anderson. m 11/27/1993 Janet Bernice Mix c 2. R S Barn Ch Warwick RI 2000-2008; Vic Epis Ch of the H Sprt Phoenix AZ 1996-2000; Assoc All SS Ch Phoenix AZ 1994-1996; S Mary's Basswood Grove Hastings MN 1990-1994; R S Nich Ch Richfield MN 1983-1987; Int S Paul's On-The-Hill Epis Ch St Paul MN 1982-1983; Asst S Paul's Ch Brookfield CT 1981-1982. Ord Of The Coif 1993. travelfraatz@yahoo.com

✠ **FRADE, Rt Rev Leopold** (SeFla) 525 NE 15th St, Miami FL 33132 **Bp of SE Florida Dio SE Florida Miami FL 2000-** B Havana CU 10/10/1943 s Leopoldo Frade & Angela. BD Candler Coll De Marianao 1960; MDiv STUSo 1977; BA Biscayne Coll 1978. D 4/17/1977 P 10/17/1977 Bp James Loughlin Duncan Con 1/25/1984 for Hond. m 12/22/1987 Diana Dillenberger c 2. Trst The GTS New York NY 1995-2000; Bp of Honduras Iglesia Epis San Pablo Apostol San Pedro Sula Cortes HN 1984-2000; Dio Cntrl Florida Orlando FL 1982-1983; P-in-c Hisp Min Gr Ch New Orleans LA 1978-1982; Secy - Hisp Cmsn Dio SE Florida Miami FL 1977-1980; Cur H Cross Epis Ch Miami FL 1977-1978. "Winds of Change," *Memories of Wesley Frensdorg*, 1990. Alum Coun TS U So; Bro of S Greg; Fell Fund Theol Educ. D.D. Florida Cntr for Theol Stds 2006; DD ETSS Los Angeles 2001; DD STUSo 1989; DD GTS 1982. bishopfrade@aol.com

FRAIOLI, Karen Ann (RI) 20 Rhodes Ave, Sharon MA 02067 **S Jn's Epis Ch Westwood MA 2011-** B Oak Park IL 8/2/1946 d Wayland Berger Cedarquist & Lois Kathleen. BA Br 1968; MDiv Harvard DS 1993. D 6/18/1994 P 12/20/1994 Bp George Nelson Hunt III. m 8/17/1968 Edward Fraioli c 2. Vic Ch Of The Epiph Providence RI 1997-2009; Dio Rhode Island Providence RI 1997; Asst Gr Ch In Providence Providence RI 1994-1996. Associated Parishes For Liturg Mssn; ADLMC; Catechesis Of The Gd Shpd. Phi Beta Kappa. kafraioli@earthlink.net

FRALEY, Anne Mckinne (Tenn) 1500 Hickory Ridge Rd, Lebanon TN 37087 B Hartford CT 5/13/1957 d Arthur Dale Wolf & Anne Mckinne. BA Earlham Coll 1979; MDiv Ya Berk 1994. D 12/10/1994 Bp Clarence Nicholas Coleridge P 6/24/1995 Bp David Reed. m 3/24/2006 Kenneth Fraley. P-in-c The Ch Of The Epiph Lebanon TN 2008-2011; Int S Paul's Epis Ch Murfreesboro TN 2007-2008; Int S Jas The Less Madison TN 2006-2007; Mssnr Stem SE Tennessee Episc Mnstry Decherd TN 2003-2005; Int S Jos Of Arimathaea Ch Hendersonville TN 2002-2003; Vic/R The Ch Of The Epiph Lebanon TN 1999-2002; Assoc S Ptr's Epis Ch St Louis MO 1995-1999; Asst Chr Ch Cathd Hartford CT 1994-1995. wolfdance9@gmail.com

FRANCE JR, Andrew Menaris (CPa) 651 Harding Ave, Williamsport PA 17701 B Baltimore MD 10/21/1937 s Andrew Menaris France & Anna Virginia. BA Drew U 1962; BD VTS 1966; DMin Pittsburgh TS 1987. D 6/21/1966 P 6/8/1967 Bp Harry Lee Doll. m 8/12/1972 Dorothy Elizabeth Douglas c 3. R Trin Epis Ch Williamsport PA 1984-2007; R S Thos Ch In The Fields Gibsonia PA 1977-1984; Spec Asst S Marg's Ch Annapolis MD 1976-1977; Mid-Atlantic Career Cntr Inc Washington DC 1973-1977; Asst Ch Of The Gd Shpd Ruxton MD 1967-1969; Asst Min S Anne's Par Annapolis MD 1966-1967. Auth, "Dvlpmt of Alternative Models of Direction for a Growing Par"; Auth, "Personal Plnng Mgmt for Leaders"; Auth, "Whole Life & Vocational Prog Manuals"; Auth, "Participant through Mid Atlantic Trng Cmsn"; Auth, "Whole Life & Vocation Prog Manuals". APC 1973-1990; AAPC 1973-1988; ACPE 1973-1988. Hon Cn of the Cathd Dio Cntrl Pennsylvania 1991. amfrance@comcast.net

FRANCE, Robert Lyle (Miss) 1050 Shady Ln, Tunica MS 38676 **R Ch Of The Epiph Tunica MS 2005-** B Memphis TN 8/21/1947 s Hulbert France & Ruth. BS U of Mississippi 1969; MD U Cinc 1973; BA Trin Bristol GB 2003. Trans from Church Of England 5/1/2005 Bp Duncan Montgomery Gray Jr. m 1/29/1978 Betty France c 2. tunicaepiphany@bellsouth.net

FRANCES, Martha (Tex) 6405 Westward #65, Houston TX 77081 B Dallas TX 6/25/1946 d Clarence M Collins & Frances B. MA U of Houston 1977; MRE U of St. Thos 1985; CAS Epis TS of The SW 1999; MDiv SMU 1999. D 11/30/2000 Bp Claude Edward Payne P 6/29/2001 Bp Leopoldo Jesus Alard. c 4. Ch Of The Incarn Houston TX 2005; Hope Epis Ch Houston TX 2005; Vic Lord Of The St Epis Mssn Ch Houston TX 2000-2005; Pstr Asst S Paul's Ch Houston TX 1999-2000. Ord of S Helena - Assoc 1983. martha.frances@gmail.com

FRANCIS, Desmond Charles (Spr) 2011 Trotter Ln, Bloomington IL 61704 **Chr The King Epis Ch Normal IL 2002-** B Madras IN 8/4/1953 s James Francis & Constance. D. H. M. C. T. Inst of Catering Tech, Chennai. 1974; B.Th So India Biblic Sem, Karnataka St. 1978; M.A.R Asbury TS 1984; M.Div Asbury TS 1986; M.Th Asbury TS 1987; D.Miss Asbury TS 1989. Trans from Church of South India 6/1/1999 Bp Don Adger Wimberly. c 2. S Mary's Epis Ch Middlesboro KY 1999-2001; P S Mary's Epis Ch Middlesboro KY 1995-1999; P S Andr's Ch Lexington KY 1995-1996. Rotary Intl . desritt@aol.com

FRANCIS, Elaine Consuela (VI) PO Box 1148, St Thomas VI 00804 B St Thomas Virgin Islands 3/8/1937 d Ector Roebuck & Ruth L. HS Julian Richman HS 1954. D 6/28/2008 Bp Edward Ambrose Gumbs. m 8/5/1961 Bernard G Francis c 1. ecf@viaccess.net

FRANCIS, Everett Warren (Be) 7028 Upland Ridge Dr, Adamstown MD 21710 B Taylor PA 1/18/1927 s Everett Warren Francis & Agnes Marie R. BA Duke 1946; GTS 1955. D 6/25/1955 P 1/1/1956 Bp Richard S M Emrich. c 5. R S Lk's Ch Scranton PA 1977-1992; Publ Affrs Dir Epis Ch Cntr New York NY 1967-1977; Asst Prog Dir Dio Michigan Detroit MI 1964-1967. Auth, "Medium of Soc Responsibility," *ATR*; Auth, "Whither Soc Involvement," *The Epis*; Auth, "UTO Story," *UTO*. ewfran@edurostream.com

FRANCIS, James Woodcock (Mich) 1404 Joliet Pl, Detroit MI 48207 **Dio Sthrn Ohio Cincinnati OH 1959-** B Hamilton BM 9/18/1928 s Thomas James Francis. BA Wilberforce U 1956; BD Payne Sem 1958; Bex 1959. D 6/24/1959 Bp Henry W Hobson P 12/1/1960 Bp Roger W Blanchard. m 8/30/1956 Audrie Arletha Smith. S Cyp's Epis Ch Detroit MI 1974-1985; Vic S Simon Of Cyrene Epis Ch Cincinnati OH 1962-1971; Cur S Andr's Epis Ch Cincinnati OH 1959-1962.

F

FRANCIS, John Robert (Be) 435 Court St, P.O. Box 1094, Reading PA 19603 **Chair of Benefits Com Dio Pennsylvania Philadelphia PA 2011-; Chr Ch Reading PA 2005-** B Syracuse NY 7/8/1956 s George Shrove Francis & Rosemary. BS Richard Stockton Coll Pomona NJ 1978; MDiv GTS 1986; ThM New Brunswick TS 1991. D 6/14/1986 Bp George Phelps Mellick Belshaw P 12/1/1986 Bp Vincent King Pettit. m 11/17/1979 Erminia Bermudez c 1. R S Paul's Ch Philadelphia PA 1997-2004; Chair of CE Cmsn Dio Pennsylvania Philadelphia PA 1995-1996; Chr Ch Media PA 1990-1997; Vic Trin Epis Old Swedes Ch Swedesboro NJ 1986-1990; Cur S Jn's Ch Salem NJ 1986-1988. Soc Of S Jn The Evang. johnrfrancis@att.net

FRANCIS, MaryJane (Oly) 725 9th Ave., Apt. 2109, Seattle WA 98104 **P Assoc S Paul's Ch Seattle WA 2011-; Convenor & Grant Mgr-Team for Sprtl Formation Dio Olympia Seattle WA 1996-** B New York NY 5/26/1937 d Thomas Francis & Dorothy Packard. BA Wellesley Coll 1958; PhD U MI 1970; MDiv STUSo 1984. D 6/24/1984 Bp William Evan Sanders P 4/24/1985 Bp Girault M Jones. Int Dn-Dioc Sch for Mnstry and Theol Dio Olympia Seattle WA 2002-2004; Bd Mem & Fac - Dio Schl of Mnstry and Theol Dio Olympia Seattle WA 1999-2004; Mentor & Prog Design-Total Mnstry Congregations Dio Olympia Seattle WA 1997-2001; P-in-c Ch Of The Ascen Seattle WA 1997; P doing extended supply, vacation & sabbatical coverage Dio Olympia Seattle WA 1996-2002; Dio. Olympia Rep. - Natl Consult on Sprtl Formation in Congregations Dio Olympia Seattle WA 1996-1997; Mem - Cmsn for Congregations Dio Olympia Seattle WA 1995-2000; Mem - Dioc Coun Dio Olympia Seattle WA 1994-1998; Bd Mem [elected] - Cler Assn of the Dio Olympia Dio Olympia Seattle WA 1994-1997; Mem - Bp's Com on Human Sxlty Dio Olympia Seattle WA 1993-1996; Assoc S Marg's Epis Ch Bellevue WA 1992-1995; Dep-GC Dio Tennessee Nashville TN 1990-1991; Mem - Bd. of Editors, Sewanee Theol Revs The TS at The U So Sewanee TN 1989-1994; Vic S Jn's Epis Ch Mt Juliet TN 1989-1992; Chair - Ch Consultants T/F Dio Tennessee Nashville TN 1987-1990; Dep [elected] - GC Dio Tennessee Nashville TN 1987-1988; Sec'y & Chair - COM Dio Tennessee Nashville TN 1985-1992; Secy - COM Dio Tennessee Nashville TN 1985-1990; Asst Chr Ch Cathd Nashville TN 1984-1987. Auth, "Bk Revs/article on retreat," *Regula*, The Friends of St. Ben; Auth, "Bk Revs," *Sewanee Theol Revs*. Cmnty of S Mary - Sewanee Prov, Assoc 1986. retclergy@comcast.net

FRANCKE, Paul (WVa) St Mark'S Church, 1625 Locust St, Philadelphia PA 19103 B Charleston WV 6/16/1979 s Paul Francke & Georganna. BA U Chi Chicago IL 2003; MDiv VTS Alexandria 2007. D 12/16/2006 P 12/5/2009 Bp William Michie Klusmeyer. Emm Ch Keyser WV 2010-2011; Cur S Mk's Ch Philadelphia PA 2006-2008. paulfrancke@gmail.com

FRANCKS, Robert Christopher (NY) 360 W 21st St, New York NY 10011 B New York NY 12/28/1948 s William Georges Francks & Olive. BA Trin Hartford CT 1970; MDiv GTS 1973. D 6/9/1973 Bp Horace W B Donegan P 12/1/1973 Bp Paul Moore Jr. R Chr Epis Ch Sparkill NY 1976-1981; Cur Gr Ch Newark NJ 1973-1975. robertf33@optonline.net

FRANCOIS, Yvan (Hai) Box 1309, Port-Au-Prince Haiti B 6/18/1943 s Gesner Francois & Flora. Cert; BLitt Coll Of S Pierre IIt 1964; BTh ETSC 1968. D 12/2/1967 P 6/1/1968 Bp Charles Alfred Voegeli. m 11/28/1995 Cecile Delienne. Dio Haiti Ft Lauderdale FL 1967-1999. YVANFRANCOIS13@HOTMAIL.COM

FRANDSEN, Charles Frederick (WMich) 509 Ship St, Saint Joseph MI 49085 B Ord NE 6/4/1921 s John Andrew Frandsen & Muriel Marguerite. BS Creighton U 1949; SWTS 1961. D 5/31/1961 Bp Howard R Brinker P 12/1/1961 Bp Russell T Rauscher. c 4. Vic Ch Of The Medtr Harbert MI 1981-1986; R S Aug Of Cbury Epis Ch Benton Harbor MI 1971-1986; Vic S Dav's Ch Lansing MI 1967-1971; R S Thos' Epis Ch Falls City NE 1961-1967. cfrandsen@sbcgobal.net

FRANK, Anna (Ak) 1578 Bridgewater Dr, Fairbanks AK 99709 **Archd Interior Dio Alaska Fairbanks AK 1990-** B Minto AK 8/28/1939 d Jonathan David & Rosie. D 3/28/1974 Bp William J Gordon Jr P 10/1/1983 Bp George Clinton

Harris. m 11/14/1955 Richard Frank c 4. Dio Alaska Fairbanks AK 1989-2007; Asst S Matt's Epis Ch Fairbanks AK 1984-1989; D S Barn Ch Minto AK 1974-1981. afrank@gci.net

FRANK, Richard Lloyd (U) 13640 N 21st Ave, Phoenix AZ 85029 B Ravenna OH 8/9/1939 s Earle L Frank & Eileen Josephine. Hiram Coll. D 8/9/1987 Bp George Edmonds Bates. m 1/23/1960 Esther Reed c 2. Dio Utah Salt Lake City UT 1990-1996. rlfrank@cox.net

FRANK, Travis Ray (Ark) 14 Haslingden Ln, Bella Vista AR 72715 **S Jn's Epis Ch Helena AR 2005-** B Houston TX 5/12/1958 s Henry Arthur Leon Frank & Francis Jennett. BA Howard Payne U 1985; MDiv SW Bapt TS 1989. D 2/8/1997 Bp Larry Earl Maze. S Andr's Ch Marianna AR 2001-2005; Cur S Theo's Epis Ch Bella Vista AR 1999-2001. chapp489@yahoo.com

FRANK JR, William George (Va) 197 Treetops Ln, Asheville NC 28803 **P Assoc Ret Calv Epis Ch Fletcher NC 2002-** B Chicago IL 5/20/1926 s William George Frank & Helen. BA U of Louisiana 1949; BD VTS 1952; MD GW 1964. D 1/27/1952 P 10/1/1952 Bp Charles Clingman. m 4/16/1977 Melba L Blanchette c 2. Asst Prof Pstr VTS Alexandria VA 1956-1960; S Paul's Ch Bailey's Crossroads Falls Ch VA 1954-1956; R S Paul's Ch Hickman KY 1952-1954. wmfrank197@msn.com

FRANKE, Keely (Minn) 60 Kent St, Saint Paul MN 55102 **Asst R S Jn The Evang S Paul MN 2010-** B Fort Smith AR 9/9/1981 d William Thomas Flocks & Mary Lynn. BA Hamline U 2006; MDiv Luther NW Theo Sem 2010. D 7/23/2009 Bp James Louis Jelinek P 7/29/2010 Bp Brian N Prior. m 6/21/2004 Carsten Franke. keelyfranke@gmail.com

FRANKEN, Robert Anton (Mo) 5290 Waterman Blvd, Unit 3W, Saint Louis MO 63108 **D Chr Ch Cathd S Louis MO 2002-** B S'Gravenange Holland NL 6/24/1950 s John Everret Franken & Ann. BBA U of Texas 1979; MA U of Texas 1980. D 6/1/1984 Bp George Clinton Harris. m 11/4/1995 Nancy T Kinney c 5. Archd Dio Missouri S Louis MO 2005-2007; Exec Dir Thompson Cntr St Louis MO 2001-2003; Chf Admin Off Dio Colorado Denver CO 1998-2001; D Dio Colorado Denver CO 1996-1998; D Ch Of S Jn Chrys Golden CO 1988-1995; D H Sprt Epis Ch Eagle River AK 1986-1987; D S Christophers Ch Anchorage AK 1984-1986. Auth, *Cost Efficient Adaptation of Sharp Portfolio Model for Sm Investors*, 1980. rfranken@strataventure.com

FRANKFURT, Dawn M (Kan) 3750 E Douglas Ave, Wichita KS 67208 **R S Jas Ch Wichita KS 2011-** B Syracuse NY 3/2/1966 d William Wallace Frankfurt & Kristin. BA U of Oklahoma 1988; MDiv Ya Berk 2004. D 9/10/2004 Bp Richard Sui On Chang P 5/5/2005 Bp Frank Neff Powell. Int All SS' Epis Ch Duncan OK 2010-2011; Int St Phil's Epis Ch Ardmore OK 2009-2010; Assoc Trin Ch Staunton VA 2004-2008. motherdawn@stjameswichita.org

FRANKLIN, Ann Hope (Mass) 143 Gillespie Circle, Brevard NC 28712 **T/F For Victims Rts Dio Massachusetts Boston MA 1991-** B Mount Airy NC 12/21/1943 s Robert Benjamin Clinton Franklin & Ida Virginia. MDiv EDS 1986; DMin EDS 1991. D 6/28/1986 Bp Henry Irving Mayson P 9/7/1987 Bp H Coleman McGehee Jr. EDS Cambridge MA 2001-2010; Ch Of The Gd Shpd Watertown MA 1994-2010. ann.h.franklin@gmail.com

FRANKLIN, Arthur Alden (SanD) 4769 Panorama Drive, San Diego CA 92116 **Cn Litur Emer Cathd Ch Of S Paul San Diego CA 1997-** B Spokane WA 7/27/1930 s Arthur Carl Franklin & Catharine Mary. BA Gonzaga U 1952; MDiv SWTS 1955. D 6/18/1955 P 12/21/1955 Bp Russell S Hubbard. Int Cathd Ch Of S Paul San Diego CA 1994-1996; Asst Cathd Ch Of S Paul San Diego CA 1979-1996; Headmaster S Jn's Epis Ch Chula Vista CA 1972-1979; Asst H Trin Epis Par San Diego CA 1970-1979; Vic S Barth's Mssn Pico Rivera CA 1966-1970; Asst All SS Par Los Angeles CA 1964-1966; Vic S Columba's Epis Ch And Chilren's Sch Kent WA 1960-1964; Vic H Trin Epis Ch Wallace ID 1955-1957; Vic S Andr's Epis Ch McCall ID 1955-1957. aldenf@cox.net

FRANKLIN, Cecil Loyd (Colo) 2250 E Columbia Pl, Denver CO 80210 B El Reno OK 8/2/1927 s Marion Clyde Franklin & (Mary) Ellen. BA Phillips U 1947; STB Harvard DS 1950; STM Harvard DS 1951; CDSP 1956; PhD Harv 1961. D 3/13/1957 P 11/1/1957 Bp Joseph Summerville Minnis. m 6/20/1981 Priscilla Ann Wendt c 2. Vic S Andr's Ch Denver CO 1984-1986; R The Ch Of Chr The King (Epis) Arvada CO 1962-1965; Vic The Ch Of Chr The King (Epis) Arvada CO 1960-1962; Cur All SS' Epis Ch Belmont MA 1959-1960; Cur Trin Ch Newton Cntr MA 1958-1959; Asst S Jn's Cathd Denver CO 1957-1958. Auth, "Two arts," *Iliff Revs*. kyncl@aol.com

FRANKLIN JR, Denson N (Ala) 517 Mayfair Cir, Birmingham AL 35209 B Bessemer AL 2/5/1937 s Denson N Franklin & Lottie Mae. BA Birmingham-Sthrn Coll 1958; MDiv Candler TS Emory U 1961; Drew U 1965. D 4/17/1991 P 8/25/1991 Bp Robert Oran Miller. m 11/24/1977 Carolyn Pyburn c 2. Int R S Steph's Epis Ch Birmingham AL 2003-2006; Assoc R S Lk's Epis Ch Birmingham AL 1996-2002; P Assoc S Lk's Epis Ch Birmingham AL 1995; R S Barn' Epis Ch Hartselle AL 1991-1994. densonfranklin@bellsouth.net

FRANKLIN III, Gus Lee (Spr) 6508 Willow Springs Rd, Springfield IL 62712 **P The Cathd Ch Of S Paul Springfield IL 1998-** B Covington KY 1/28/1938 s Gus Lee Franklin & Ruth Marie. BS Estrn Kentucky U 1959; MSEd Indiana U 1960; MA U IL 1964; MDiv Nash 1967. D 6/3/1967 P 12/9/1967 Bp Albert A Chambers. Dioc Coordntr LPMSSC Dio Quincy Peoria IL 1995-1996; R S Andr's Ch Peoria IL 1986-1998; Vic Chr The King Epis Ch Normal IL 1984-1986; Cn The Cathd Ch Of S Paul Springfield IL 1979-1984; Asst The Cathd Ch Of S Paul Springfield IL 1975-1979; Cur The Cathd Ch Of S Paul Springfield IL 1967-1970. CBS 1957; GAS 1957; SSC 1983. R Emer St Andr's, Peoria Dioc of Quincy 2001; Dn Emer Bp KL Ackerman Dioc of Quincy 1998. sscdma@aol.com

FRANKLIN, John Thomas (Mich) 2933 Dunsary Ln, Brighton MI 48114 **R S Steph's Ch Hamburg MI 2007-** B Mt. Sterling IL 4/29/1935 s Lawrence Thomas Franklin & Anna Rose. BA Our Lady Of The Lakes Sem Mundelein IL 1957; STL Gregorian U 1961; MA U IL 1971; PhD U MI 1986. Rec from Roman Catholic 7/1/2006 Bp Wendell Nathaniel Gibbs Jr. m 6/1/1972 Cheryl Cunningham c 2. Co-Auth, "For When I Am Weak, The I Am Strong," *Bk of the same name*, Mercy Coll Press, 1988. OSL the Physcn 2011. Prof Emer U of Detroit Mercy 2011; Distinguished Prof U of Detroit Mercy 1998. jofranklin@comcast.net

FRANKLIN, Kenneth Roderick (RI) 60 Cavalcade Blvd, Warwick RI 02889 B Birmingham AL 10/29/1932 s Ellis Brown Franklin & Emily Rachel. BA Birmingham-Sthrn Coll 1954; STB GTS 1959; STM GTS 1964. D 6/29/1959 P 6/1/1960 Bp Charles C J Carpenter. m 2/7/1981 Diane L Young c 2. R S Mk's Ch Warwick RI 1968-2001; Cur S Paul's Ch Riverside CT 1964-1968; Cur S Lk's Ch Gladstone NJ 1962-1964; Vic S Ptr's Epis Ch Talladega AL 1959-1960. Phi Beta Kappa Birmingham Sthrn Coll. dlkrfrank@cox.net

✠ **FRANKLIN, Rt Rev Ralph William** (WNY) 1064 Brighton Road, Tonawanda NY 14150 **Bp of Wstrn New York Dio Wstrn New York Tonawanda NY 2011-** B Brookhaven MS 1/3/1947 s Ralph Franklin & Dorothy C. BA NWU 1969; MA Harv 1971; PhD Harv 1975. D 3/19/2005 P 9/17/2005 Bp Mark Sean Sisk Con 4/30/2011 for WNY. m 6/19/1971 Carmela Vircillo c 2. S Mk's Ch Philadelphia PA 2010-2011; Assoc R Trin Ch In The City Of Boston Boston MA 2003-2005; The GTS New York NY 1993-1998. rwfranklin@episcopalwny.org

FRANKLIN, Sarah Claire (USC) 7128 Caggy Ln, Fort Mill SC 29707 **R S Paul's Epis Ch Ft Mill SC 2004-** B Athens GA 4/26/1960 d Samuel Jasper Franklin & Glenn. BS Clemson U 1983; MA U GA 1984; MDiv VTS 1994. D 6/4/1994 Bp Huntington Williams Jr P 6/4/1995 Bp Robert Carroll Johnson Jr. Chr Epis Ch Dublin GA 1998-2004; Asst S Mary's Epis Ch High Point NC 1994-1998. revscfranklin@yahoo.com

FRANKLIN-VAUGHN, Robyn (WA) 319 Bryant St Ne, Washington DC 20002 **Chapl How Dio Washington Washington DC 2003-** B Boston MA 1/2/1965 MDiv EDS. D 6/15/2002 P 5/31/2003 Bp M(arvil) Thomas Shaw III. m 10/21/1989 Raymond J Franklin-Vaughn.

FRANKS, L(aurence) Edward Alexander (FdL) 299 Corey St, Boston MA 02132 B Houston TX 7/20/1943 s Verlan Harvey Franks & Adela Louise. BS U CA 1965; MA UWA Washington DC 1966; MLitt U of Cambridge 1972; MDiv CDSP 1980. D 6/13/1981 Bp H Coleman McGehee Jr P 6/30/1982 Bp Henry Irving Mayson. Dio Massachusetts Boston MA 1990-2005; Interfaith Aids Mnstry W Newton MA 1990-2005; Jubilee Mnstry Asst Epis Ch Cntr New York NY 1985-1987; R S Ptr's Epis Ch Sheboygan Falls WI 1983-1985. Auth, "L. Edw Alexander Franks," *An Aid to Wrshp in the H Euch*, 2000; Auth, "L. Edw Alexander Franks," *Meaning & Pattern of the H Euch*, 2000. edwinaloca@hotmail.com

FRANTZ JR, P(hilip) Scott (Colo) 110 Via Vallecito, Manitou Springs CO 80829 B La Junta CO 4/24/1923 s Philip Scott Frantz & Helene. Colorado Sch of Mines 1947; BA Colorado Coll 1949; EDS 1952. D 6/10/1952 Bp Norman B Nash P 12/21/1952 Bp Harold L Bowen. m 5/24/1952 Elizabeth Harnett c 2. S Andr's Ch Manitou Sprg CO 1979-1990; Asst Ch Of The H Sprt Colorado Sprg CO 1977-1979; P-in-c Chap Of The Resurr Limon CO 1976-1979; Chr Ch Lima OH 1960-1976; Vic Ch Of Our Sav Colorado Sprg CO 1953-1955; Vic Ch Of The H Sprt Colorado Sprg CO 1952-1960; Asst Gr And S Steph's Epis Ch Colorado Sprg CO 1952-1960. AAC; AFP; ERM; Kairos Prison Mnstry; Kappa Sigma. bsfrantz@juno.com

FRANTZ-DALE, Heidi Hallett (NH) 247 Pound Road, Madison NH 03849 **Vice Chair Bp Election /Transition Com Dio New Hampshire Concord NH 2011-; R S Andr's-In-The-Vlly Tamworth NH 2004-** B Hartford CT 7/9/1950 d David Herr Frantz & Margaret. BA Swarthmore Coll 1972; Med U of Massachusetts 1973; MDiv EDS 2000. D 6/10/2000 P 12/17/2000 Bp Gordon Paul Scruton. m 9/23/1978 Duane Danroy Dale c 2. Dio Wstrn Massachusetts Springfield MA 2000-2004; Asst R S Jas' Ch Greenfield MA 2000-2004; Vic S Andr's Ch Turners Falls MA 2000-2003. frantzdale@gmail.com

FRANZ, Marcia Wheatley (NMich) 1207 Lakeshore Park Pl, Marquette MI 49855 **Presider,Prchr,Eucharistic Vistor/Prayerchain S Paul's Ch Marquette MI 1986-** B Marquette MI 11/15/1943 d James Randall & Harriet. BA MI SU 1965. D 5/9/2006 P 5/27/2007 Bp James Arthur Kelsey. c 2. Stndg Com Dio Nthrn Michigan Marquette MI 2006-2009.

FRASER, Ann Benton (Miss) St. Paul's Episcopal Church, P.O. Box 1225, Corinth MS 38835 **R S Paul's Epis Ch Corinth MS 2009-** B Baton Rouge 9/19/1980 d James Dudley Benton & Susan Laurel Babers. BA LSU 2002;

MDiv TS 2007. D 12/30/2006 P 8/19/2007 Bp Charles Edward Jenkins III. m 1/3/2004 Andrew Edwin Fraser c 1. Lilly Fell S Jas Ch New York NY 2007-2009. annbfraser@gmail.com

FRASER, R(ichard) Trent (RI) 61 Poplar Street, Newport RI 02840 **R S Jn The Evang Ch Newport RI 2009-** B North Bay ON CA 12/29/1965 s Hugh William Fraser & Lillian Joyce. BA Nipissing U No Bay CA 1987; MDiv Trin-U Tor 1990. D 10/28/1992 P 5/18/1993 Bp Edward Harding MacBurney. P-in-c The Ch Of The Redeem Southfield MI 2001-2009; Dio Pennsylvania Philadelphia PA 2001; Cur S Clements Ch Philadelphia PA 1993-2001. CCU 1993; CBS 1993; GAS 1993; Living Rosary of Our Lady & S. Dominic 1993; Soc of King Chas the Mtyr 1993. richelieu2@hotmail.com

FRASER, Thomas A (Chi) 60 Akenside Rd, Riverside IL 60546 **R S Paul's Par Riverside IL 1975-** B Alexandria VA 4/20/1945 s Thomas Augustus Fraser & Marjorie R. BA No Carolina St U 1967; STB GTS 1972. D 6/17/1972 P 12/1/1972 Bp James Winchester Montgomery. Cur Ch Of The H Comf Kenilworth IL 1973-1975; Cur S Mk's Epis Ch Glen Ellyn IL 1972-1973. Bd Dir Living Ch 1989. parishoffice@stpaulsparish.org

FRASER SR, William Carson (ETenn) 4487 Post Place, #129, Nashville TN 37205 B Nashville TN 12/4/1935 s William C Fraser & Margaret Annie. BA U of Tennessee 1958; STB Ya Berk 1960. D 7/6/1960 Bp Theodore N Barth P 5/1/1961 Bp John Vander Horst. m 12/27/2008 Mary Carl Mason c 3. R S Andr's Ch Harriman TN 1988-1997; Vic S Matt's Ch Dayton TN 1983-1988; S Paul's Epis Ch Chattanooga TN 1983-1988; R Ch Of The Gd Samar Knoxville TN 1978-1983; R S Ann's Ch Nashville TN 1965-1978; P-in-c S Andr's Epis Ch Collierville TN 1961-1965; D S Ptr's Ch Chattanooga TN 1960-1961. carsonfras@comcast.net

FRAZELLE, David C (NC) 304 E Franklin St, Chapel Hill NC 27514 **Assoc for Par Mnstry Chap Of The Cross Chap Hill NC 2004-** B Asheville NC 7/23/1975 s Charles William Frazelle & Donna Ann. BA U So 1997; CEB Institut Catholique De Paris 1999; MDiv VTS 2004. D 6/19/2004 P 6/4/2005 Bp Michael Bruce Curry. m 1/5/2002 Emily Crowder Frazelle c 1. dfrazelle@thechapelofthecross.org

FRAZIER JR, Allie Washington (SVa) 1124 Dryden Lane, Charlottesville VA 22903 B Stanardsville VA 1/23/1931 s Allie Washington Frazier & Virginia. BA U Rich 1956; MDiv VTS 1961; DMin Drew U 1992. D 6/23/1961 Bp Robert Fisher Gibson Jr P 6/13/1962 Bp Frederick D Goodwin. m 6/18/1978 Carolyn Wood Gills c 3. R Johns Memi Epis Ch Farmville VA 1985-1996; Exec Bd; Dn Farmville Convoc Dio Sthrn Virginia Norfolk VA 1983-1985; R Chr Ch Amelia Crt Hse VA 1980-1985; R Emm Epis Ch Powhatan VA 1980-1985; Pac Cure Par Cartersville VA 1980-1985; R S Jas Ch Cartersville VA 1980-1985; Dn Dio Virginia Richmond VA 1970-1972; R Gr Ch Keswick VA 1968-1975; R Emm Ch Staunton VA 1966-1968; Assoc R Chr Ch Epis Savannah GA 1964-1966; R Wicomico Par Ch Wicomico Ch VA 1962-1964. Auth, *Informed Chr Living*, Dissertation - Drew U, 1992; Auth, *Take Care of Your Wrld*, Dio Virginia, Stwdshp Dept., 1970. Coll of Preachers Fllshp Washinton DC 1970. CWGF@NEXET.NET

FRAZIER, John T (EC) 5324 Bluewater Pl, Fayetteville NC 28311 **S Paul's In The Pines Epis Ch Fayetteville NC 2005-** B Nashville TN 5/16/1948 s Evelyn A. MDiv VTS; BS Pk U 1993; MA Webster U 2002. D 6/25/2005 P 4/8/2006 Bp Clifton Daniel III. m 2/14/1980 Veronica Frazier.

FRAZIER, Jonathan Edward (WMo) 516 S Weller Ave, Springfield MO 65802 **GC Dep, C3 Dio W Missouri Kansas City MO 2010-2012; Hisp Mnstry Cmte Dio W Missouri Kansas City MO 2008-; Chapl, Missouri St U Dio W Missouri Kansas City MO 2007-; COM Dio W Missouri Kansas City MO 2006-2014; Asst. R Chr Epis Ch Springfield MO 2004-** B Kansas City MO 3/6/1963 B.A. Rockhurst Jesuit U 1985; M.Div. TS 2004. D 6/5/2004 P 12/6/2004 Bp Barry Robert Howe. m 9/4/1999 Ann Marie Fields c 2. Assessment Revs Cmte Dio W Missouri Kansas City MO 2009-2010; Bp Search and Nomin Cmte Dio W Missouri Kansas City MO 2009-2010; Comp Dio Cmte Dio W Missouri Kansas City MO 2007-2009; Dn, Sthrn Dnry Dio W Missouri Kansas City MO 2007-2009; Dioc Coun Dio W Missouri Kansas City MO 2007-2009; Fin Cmte Dio W Missouri Kansas City MO 2007-2009; GC Dep, Alt Dio W Missouri Kansas City MO 2007-2009; Conv Committees, chair and Mem Dio W Missouri Kansas City MO 2005-2011; Bd Dir, Acad for Lay Educ and Mnstry Dio W Missouri Kansas City MO 2004-2007. jonathan_frazier@yahoo.com

FRAZIER, Joseph William (Los) 42305 North Shore Drive, PO Box 1681, Big Bear Lake CA 92315 **Vic S Columba's Epis Mssn Big Bear Lake CA 2007-** B Lebanon PA 1/14/1937 s Joseph Frazier & Carriella. MDiv Yale DS 1972. D 6/6/1972 Bp Morgan Porteus P 1/13/1973 Bp Anson Phelps Stokes Jr. R S Andr's Par Torrance CA 1991-2006; Ch Of The Incarn San Francisco CA 1989-1990; S Bede's Epis Ch Menlo Pk CA 1982-1989; Trin Par Menlo Pk CA 1980-1981; Cathd Ch Of S Jn Wilmington DE 1976-1980; Dio Bethlehem Bethlehem PA 1974-1976; R Trin And S Phil's Epis Ch Lansford PA 1973-1976. frazierjo@sbcglobal.net

FRAZIER, Mark W (SwVa) P.O. Box 1376, Bristol VA 24203 B Memphis TN 10/20/1961 s William Minor Frazier & Jean. BS U of Tennessee 1983; PhD Van 1989; MDiv STUSo 2001. D 5/26/2001 Bp James Malone Coleman P 12/15/2001 Bp David B(ruce) Joslin. m 7/9/1988 Amy Louise Berkenstock c 4. Emm Epis Ch Bristol VA 2008-2011; S Dav's Ch De Witt NY 2003-2008; Asst S Matt's Ch Pennington NJ 2001-2003. Soc for Biblic Lit 2000-2003. frazimw9@gmail.com

FRAZIER, Raymond Malcom (SwFla) 8017 Fountain Ave, Tampa FL 33615 **D S Chris's Ch TAMPA FL 1993-** B Riverside CA 6/27/1949 s Clarence M Frazier & Geraldine N. BA U of So Florida 1976. D 6/26/1993 Bp Rogers Sanders Harris. m 6/5/1971 Donna Marie Lee c 3. NAAD.

FRAZIER JR, Samuel K.(indley) (NC) 500 N Duke St. #55-202, Durham NC 27701 B High Pt NC 10/14/1936 s Samuel Kindley Frazier & Mabel. BA U NC 1959; STB Ya Berk 1962. D 6/29/1962 P 6/29/1963 Bp Richard Henry Baker. m 5/17/1991 Arthur Johnson c 2. S Andr's Ch Haw River NC 1995-2008; Liturg Asst S Jas' Epis Ch Leesburg VA 1977-1983; Vic S Phil's Ch Chas Town WV 1975-1976; Vic S Phil The Evang Washington DC 1965-1970; Vic Galloway Memi Chap Elkin NC 1962-1965. Auth, "Worthy Of The Nation-The Hist Of The Plnng & Dvlpmt Of Washington Dc," 1977. skfrazier@mc.rr.com

FREARSON, Andrew Richard (At) 3136 Lynnray Dr, Doraville GA 30340 B Birmingham UK 9/22/1957 s George Alfred Frearson & Kathleen Rose. Cert Oxf; BA U of Wolverhampton 1980. Trans from Church Of England 2/27/1997 Bp Frank Kellogg Allan. m 5/30/1992 Lesleigh Henderson Ellinger. Assoc Chr Ch Norcross GA 1997-2004.

FREDENBURGH, John Cole (NY) 182 Ridge Rd, Valley Cottage NY 10989 **Ret Affiliate P S Geo's Epis Ch Dayton OH 2005-** B Hudson NY 3/14/1938 s Edward George Fredenburgh & Gladys Dorothy. BA Hob 1960; MDiv Ya Berk 1964. D 6/10/1964 Bp Walter M Higley P 6/1/1965 Bp Ned Cole. m 12/16/1987 Annette E Rowland c 3. P-in-c All SS Epis Ch Vlly Cottage NY 1998; Chr Ch Adrian MI 1995-1996; Assoc Chr Epis Ch Dayton OH 1984-1987; Nativ Epis Ch Bloomfield Township MI 1974-1984; R S Mk's Ch Canton OH 1968-1974; Cur S Ptr's Epis Ch Lakewood OH 1965-1968; Mssy-In-Charge Gr Epis Ch Whitney Point NY 1964-1965; Mssy-In-Charge S Jn's Ch Marathon NY 1964-1965. jfred840@sbcglobal.net

FREDERIC, Eliot Garrison (Eas) 51 Columbine Ave N, Hampton Bays NY 11946 **Supply P Chr Epis Ch Lynbrook NY 2008-** B Brooklyn NY 4/19/1941 s Eliot Herbert Frederic & Dorothy. BA Adel 1964; STB PDS 1967; STM NYTS 1979. D 6/17/1967 P 12/23/1967 Bp Jonathan Goodhue Sherman. m 9/7/1968 Barbara Cartier c 2. R Chr Ch Denton MD 1996-2004; R Chr Ch Sag Harbor NY 1982-1995; R S Mary's Ch Brooklyn NY 1975-1982; Cur S Steph's Ch Port Washington NY 1970-1975; Cur H Apos And Medtr Philadelphia PA 1967-1970. egnbb@verizon@net

FREDERICK, John Bassett Moore (Ct) 32 Chestnut St, Princeton NJ 08542 **Assoc All SS Ch Princeton NJ 1996-** B New York NY 1/25/1930 s Karl Telford Frederick & Anne. BA Pr 1951; MDiv GTS 1954; PhD U of Birmingham Birmingham GB 1973. D 6/9/1954 Bp Walter H Gray P 4/30/1955 Bp Robert McConnell Hatch. m 1/4/1960 Pamela J Norman c 2. Secy, Liturg Cmsn Dio Connecticut Hartford CT 1971-1974; R S Jn's Ch New Haven CT 1961-1971; Cur S Ptr's Epis Ch Cheshire CT 1954-1956. Auth, "A Royal Amer, a New Jersey Off in the King's Serv During the Revolution," Dog Ear Pub, 2009; Compiler, "Fam Histories 1880-2005," *Turner Fam Assn*, Amer Libr Press, 2005; Auth, "The Future of Liturg Reform," Morehouse-Barlow Press, 1987; Auth, "Lineage Bk Brittish Land Forces," Microform Acad Pub, 1984; Auth, "Lineage Bk of the Brittish Army 1660-1968," Hope Farm Press, 1969. OHC (Assoc) 1956. jf9642@netscape.net

FREDERICK, Sherman Richardson (Nev) 2724 Brienza Way, Las Vegas NV 89117 **Assoc Preist Gr In The Desert Epis Ch Las Vegas NV 1992-** B Bloomington IL 6/19/1951 s Sherman Frederick & Christine Augusta. BS Nthrn Arizona U 1977. D 2/6/1994 P 10/1/1994 Bp Stewart Clark Zabriskie. m 11/13/1971 Christina Louise Secker.

FREDERICK, Warren Charles (WMass) 19 Rydal St, Worcester MA 01602 **S Mich's-On-The-Heights Worcester MA 2004-** B Johnstown PA 4/8/1947 s Morris Frederick & Betty. Trans from Church Of England 9/24/2000 Bp Robert Wilkes Ihloff. c 4. R Ch Of The H Cross Cumberland MD 2000-2004. wfrederick@charter.net

FREDERIKSEN III, Victor (EC) Po Box 7672, Wilmington NC 28406 **Supply P S Mk's Ch Wilmington NC 2007-; R S Paul's Epis Ch Wilmington NC 1998-** B Owosso MI 3/17/1943 s Victor Frederiksen & Elizabeth. BA Capital U 1966; MDiv Bex 1969. D 6/28/1969 P 1/1/1970 Bp Roger W Blanchard. c 2. S Paul's Epis Ch Wilmington NC 1996-2005; R Chr Ch Macon GA 1989-1996; Assoc Chr Ch Charlotte NC 1976-1979; S Jn's Epis Ch Charlotte NC 1976-1979; Epis Soc Of Chr Ch Cincinnati OH 1969-1976; Assoc Epis Soc of Chr Ch Cincinnati OH 1969-1976. Auth, "Mnstry In An Intensive Care Unit"; Auth, "The Approach To Parents Of A Brain Dead Chlid In"; Auth, "Requesting Organ Donation For Transplantation"; Auth, "When A Chld Dies: Helping Parents & Siblings". Aape, AAPC; Amer Assoc. of Mar and Fam Ther; Amer Assoc. Griep Counselors 1980; Amer Assoc. of CPE, Amer Assoc. of Suicideugy. vicfred43@hotmail.com

FREDHOLM, Everett Leonard (Tex) 201 Nicholas Dr, Asheville NC 28806 B Lynn MA 2/18/1943 s Bror Gunnar Folke Fredholm & Lois Katherine. Wentworth Inst of Tech 1961; BA Bob Jones U 1965; MDiv Consrvtv Bapt TS 1969; Epis TS of The SW 1970; U Of Houston 1984. D 11/20/1970 Bp J Milton Richardson P 6/1/1971 Bp Frederick P Goddard. m 12/28/1968 Rebekah Able c 1. S Fran Of Assisi Epis Prairie View TX 2000-2005; S Paul's Epis Ch Freeport TX 1990-1991; Ch Of The Adv Houston TX 1977-1979; Vic S Matt's Ch Henderson TX 1972-1977; Vic S Paul's Ch Kilgore TX 1972-1977; Asst to R Trin Ch Longview TX 1970-1972. Natl Assn Alcosm And Drug Abuse Counselors, Amer Prot Correctional Chapl Assn. efredholm@gmail.com

FREDRICK, Lawrence Edward (EO) 1220 Tasman Dr Spc 1k, Sunnyvale CA 94089 B Joplin MO 9/13/1942 s Cecil Clifford Fredrick & Ruth Arline. BS U of Montana at Billings 1963; MA U of Montana, Missoula 1966; MDiv VTS 1975; Cert Mssn Coll, Santa Clara, CA 1998. D 8/3/1975 P 9/26/1976 Bp William Benjamin Spofford. Serv Trin Cathd San Jose CA 1991-1994. LWRNCFRED@hotmail.com

FREDRICKS, John Raymond (Cal) Po Box 296, San Mateo CA 94401 B Paterson NJ 10/28/1922 s Raymond Fredricks & Anna. BS New Jersey St Teachers Coll 1946; GTS 1949. D 4/23/1949 Bp Robert E Campbell P 12/14/1949 Bp William F Lewis. c 4. Assoc Gd Shpd Epis Ch Belmont CA 1970-2002; Asst S Matt's Epis Ch San Mateo CA 1966-1970; Vic S Edm's Epis Ch Pacifica CA 1958-1966; Asst S Ptr's Epis Ch Redwood City CA 1956-1958; Vic S Mary's Ch Winnemucca NV 1955-1956; Vic S Chris's Epis Ch Boulder City NV 1951-1954; Assoc H Trin Epis Ch Fallon NV 1949-1951; D-in-c S Paul's Ch Virginia City NV 1949-1951. waldenjrf@aol.com

FREDRICKSON, David Andrew (Mass) 74 High St, PO Box 719, Wareham MA 02571 **Chr Ch Par Plymouth MA 2010-** B Colorado Springs CO 6/22/1963 s Robert G Fredrickson & Carol M. BS U CO 1986; MDiv PrTS 1994; STM GTS 1999. D 6/24/2000 P 5/12/2001 Bp Charles Ellsworth Bennison Jr. m 8/25/1997 Johnna Lee Fredrickson c 2. R Ch Of The Gd Shpd Wareham MA 2002-2009; Asst to R Trin Ch Buckingham PA 2000-2002. davidfredrickson@yahoo.com

FREE JR, Horace Dagnall (SC) PO Box 125, Johns Island SC 29457 **Cur S Jn's Epis Par Johns Island SC 2010-** B Bamberg SC 7/28/1964 s Horace Dagnall Free & Lynn M. BA Wofford Coll 1986; MDiv Nash 2010. D 6/2/2010 P 12/4/2010 Bp Mark Joseph Lawrence. m 7/21/1990 Sallie M McCutchen c 2. frfree@stjohnsparish.net

FREEMAN, Bruce Allan (SO) 2944 Erie Ave, Cincinnati OH 45208 **R The Ch of the Redeem Cincinnati OH 2003-** B Boston MA 9/9/1959 s William Horne Freeman & Carol B. BA Ken 1981; MDiv EDS 1986. D 6/24/1987 P 12/1/1987 Bp Robert Marshall Anderson. m 9/3/1983 Dana Jean Dahlgren c 3. R Ch Of The Epiph San Carlos CA 1994-2003; Dio Wstrn Massachusetts Springfield MA 1989-1994; R S Jn's Ch Athol MA 1989-1994; Asst S Chris's Epis Ch Roseville MN 1987-1989. bruce@redeemer-cincy.org

FREEMAN JR, Denson Fred (CGC) 8 Fourth Street, Colorado Springs CO 80906 **R Ch Of Our Sav Colorado Sprg CO 2011-** B Mobile AL 5/6/1969 s Denson Fred Freeman & Mary Eleanor. BA Auburn U Auburn AL 1993; MDiv Epis TS of The SW 2007. D 6/2/2007 P 5/17/2008 Bp Philip Menzie Duncan II. m 5/1/1993 Stephanie P Stephanie Lynn Pitts c 3. Stndg Com Mem Dio Cntrl Gulf Coast Pensacola FL 2010-2011; Fresh Start Fac Dio Cntrl Gulf Coast Pensacola FL 2009-2011; Bd Mem/Mgmt Com Beckwith C&C Fairhope AL 2008-2011; Vic Ch Of The Epiph Crestview FL 2007-2011. densonfreeman@gmail.com

FREEMAN, Diana G(ail) (Dal) 6400 Stonebrook Pkwy, Frisco TX 75034 **P-in-c Ch Of The Gd Shpd Terrell TX 2009-** B Kansas City MO 3/1/1955 d Arlan Curtis Burnham & Ruby Lee Maude. BFA Pacific Luth U 1980; MDiv VTS 1995. D 7/21/2000 P 3/3/2001 Bp Charles Farmer Duvall. m 6/15/1974 Paul Loyd Freeman c 3. S Phil's Epis Ch Frisco TX 2007-2009; R S Lk's Ch Catskill NY 2005-2007; Cur H Nativ Epis Ch Panama City FL 2000-2003; Sem Intern/Dir of Chr Ed S Jn's Ch Ft Washington MD 1993-1997. DOK 2006. dianafreeman@stphilipsfrisco.org

FREEMAN, Leonard W (Minn) 190 Cygnet Pl, Long Lake MN 55356 **GC Alt Dio Minnesota Minneapolis MN 2011-; Int Trin Ch Excelsior MN 2010-** B Lawrence MA 2/5/1943 s Wilbur Milton Freeman & Gertrude Florence. BA NEU 1964; Fllshp NEU 1965; MDiv VTS 1969; Fllshp Coll of Preachers 1972; Fllshp Tem 1975. D 6/21/1969 Bp Anson Phelps Stokes Jr P 1/10/1970 Bp George E Rath. m 11/4/1989 Lindsay Hardin c 6. Bp's Cmmtte Mssn Strtgy Dio Minnesota Minneapolis MN 2007-2008; Trst, Chair Invstmt Com Dio Minnesota Minneapolis MN 2001-2007; R S Mart's By The Lake Epis Minnetonka Bch MN 1998-2009; Planned Giving Com Dio Newark Newark NJ 1996-1998; Dioc Coun Dio Newark Newark NJ 1992-1994; R Chr Ch Short Hills NJ 1991-1998; Dir Cmncatns Cathd of St Ptr & St Paul Washington DC 1987-1991; Dir Cmncatns Par of Trin Ch New York NY 1981-1987; Chair, Cmncatn Com Dio Pennsylvania Philadelphia PA 1976-1979; R S Jas Ch Collegeville PA 1975-1981; Int S Aidans Ch Cheltenham PA 1974-1975; Asst Min S Paul's Ch Montvale NJ 1969-1972. Auth, "Gd Lord Deliver Us," *2011 Lenten Bk*, Forw Mvmt, 2011; Contrib, "Praying Day by Day," *A Year of Meditations*, Forw Mvmt, 2010; Auth, "Hildegard Of Bingen Video Series," Morehouse Pub, 1990; Ed, "Cathd Age," *Cathd Age*, Washington Natl Cathed, 1989; Producer/Host, "Searching TV series," *Searching - 1981-87*, Trin Wall St NYC, 1987; Auth, "Theol Of Hope Moltman Video," Harper & Row, 1986; Producer/Host, "The H Land: A Pilgrimage," *WNYC TV, (PBS, NYC)*, Trin Wall St, NYC, 1984; Ed, "Trin News," *Trin News*, Trin Wall St, NYC, 1981; Auth, "Forw Day By Day Lent," *Forw Day by Day*, Forw Mvmt, 1980; Cont Ed, "Film & Media Critic," *The Epis & EpiscopalLife 1972-85*, Epis Ch USA, 1972; Auth, "Var Aticles In," *Epis; Living Ch; Cathd Age; Epis Life; Trin News*. CEEP 1990-2009; ECom 1972-1990; Epis Grp Hm 1999; Evang Educ Soc 1975-2009. Polly Bond Awd ECom 1990; Polly Bond Awd ECom 1989; Loc Emmy Loc NYC Emmy Com 1984; Loc Emmy Awd Loc NYC TV Emmy Com 1984. landl30@aol.com

FREEMAN, Lindsay Hardin (Minn) 190 Cygnet Pl, Long Lake MN 55356 **Chapt Mem Cathd Ch Of S Mk Minneapolis MN 2011-; Mem, Cmsn on Mssn Strtgy Dio Minnesota Minneapolis MN 2011-; Int Trin Ch Excelsior MN 2010-; Mem, Constitutions and Cn Com Dio Minnesota Minneapolis MN 2008-** B Minneapolis MN 9/21/1954 d Franklin John Hardin & Florence Jane. BS Minnesota St U Mankato 1977; MA EDS 1980; MDiv EDS 1984. D 7/24/1984 Bp Robert Marshall Anderson P 6/9/1985 Bp John Bowen Coburn. m 11/4/1989 Leonard W Freeman c 2. Fndr, EpiscoBuilders Dio Minnesota Minneapolis MN 2008-2010; Bp's Com on Mssn Strtgy Dio Minnesota Minneapolis MN 2008-2009; Asst R S Mart's By The Lake Epis Minnetonka Bch MN 2007-2009; P Assoc S Mart's By The Lake Epis Minnetonka Bch MN 1998-2007; P Assoc Chr Ch Short Hills NJ 1992-1998; Ed, Cmncatn Consult ECF Inc New York NY 1988-2010; Asst R Ch Of S Mart-In-The-Fields Philadelphia PA 1986-1989; Cathd Asst The Cathd Ch Of S Paul Boston MA 1984-1986. Auth, "Gd Lord, Deliver Us: A Lenten Journey," Forw Mvmt/Ch Pub, 2011; Ed, "Wisdom Found: Stories of Wmn Transfigured by Faith," Forw Mvmt, 2011; Auth, "The Scarlet Cord: Conversations w God's Chosen Wmn," O Books, 2010; Ed, "Funding Future Mnstry," ECF, 2010; Contributing Auth, "Praying Day by Day: A Year of Meditations," Forw Mvmt, 2009; Auth, "Tips for Vestries," Forw Mvmt, 2008; Ed, "Doing H Bus: The Best of Vstry Papers," Ch Pub, 2006; Ed, "Mnstry on the Frontier," ECF, 2000; Auth, "Theol Educ: A Changing Blueprint," *Epis Life*, Epis Life, 2000; Contributing Ed, "The Zacchaeus Proj," ECF, 1999; Ed, "The Times and Timeliness of Henry Knox Sherrill," ECF, 1999; Ed, "Involuntary Termination of Cler within The Epis Ch," Epis Ch Foundaiton, 1996; Ed, "The Report and Proposal of the PBp and Exec Coun to the GC," ECUSA; Ed, "Vstry Papers," *2001-2010*, ECF. ECom 1980. Polly Bond Awards (30) ECom (1981-2009) 2009; Awd of Excellence (2) Associated Ch Press 1995; Cox Fllshp Dio Massachusetts 1986; Fllshp No Amer Mnstrl Assn 1980. lhfreeman25@gmail.com

FREEMAN JR, Monroe (NC) 1706 Highlands Vw SE, Smyrna GA 30082 B Chattanooga TN 8/9/1936 s Monroe Freeman & Bessie. BA Cntrl St U 1958; Cert U Dijon 1966; MA Montclair St U 1970; Rutgers-The St U 1977; MDiv GTS 1985. D 6/7/1985 P 4/26/1986 Bp John Shelby Spong. m 12/14/1980 Marjorie Diggs c 2. R S Tit Epis Ch Durham NC 1992-1998; R S Paul's Epis Ch Greenwich NY 1989-1991; R S Steph's Ch Schuylerville NY 1988; R Trin Ch Irvington NJ 1986-1988. Auth, "Resurr Dioc Chr Nwsltr," 1990. Life Mem UBE, OHC. salem439@aol.com

FREEMAN JR, Norman Reid (Los) St. George's Church and Academy, 23801 Avenida de la Carlota, Laguna Hills CA 92653 **R and Headmaster S Geo's Epis Ch Laguna Hills CA 2006-** B Orange NJ 5/2/1952 s Norman Freeman & Jane. BA Juilliard Sch 1974; MA Juilliard Sch 1975; CPE Bellevue Hosp 1995; MDiv GTS 1997. D 5/3/1997 Bp Joe Morris Doss P 11/15/1997 Bp Vincent King Pettit. m 5/14/1983 Lori Anne Lynott c 2. Vic S Mich's U Mssn Island Isla Vista CA 2000-2006; Cur S Paul's Ch Riverside CT 1997-2000; Cur The Ch Of S Uriel The Archangel Sea Girt NJ 1997. Auth, "Barbara Streisand: The Concert," 1994. Grammy Awd, w Ny Philharmonic Acad Of Rcrdng Sciences 1987. norm@jazzministry.org

FREEMAN, Reed H. (Miss) 12614 Muirfield Blvd S, Jacksonville FL 32225 **P-in-c Resurr Epis Ch Jacksonville FL 2011-** B Milton MA 2/6/1940 s Reed Freeman & Elizabeth Harlow. BS MIT 1961; SM MIT 1963; MDiv STUSo 1996; DMin STUSo 2005. D 6/29/1996 P 6/21/1997 Bp Robert Carroll Johnson Jr. m 6/17/1961 Nancy Bruce c 3. Int S Mk's Ch Dalton GA 2010-2011; Int S Paul's Ch Macon GA 2010; Int S Andr's Epis Ch Douglas GA 2009-2010; Int Ch Of The H Comf Tallahassee FL 2007-2009; Int S Andr's Ch Jacksonville FL 2005-2007; R Trin Ch Hattiesburg MS 2001-2004; R S Mk's Epis Ch Huntersville NC 1998-2001; Vic All SS Epis Ch Charlotte NC 1996-1998. padrereedh@aol.com

FREEMAN, Robert Arthur (NH) Po Box 182, Poultney VT 05764 B Lynn MA 10/31/1932 s Robert Billups Freeman & Miriam Snow. BA Br 1957; Med Bridgewater Coll 1963; BD EDS 1969. D 6/26/1969 Bp Robert McConnell Hatch P 1/1/1970 Bp Donald J Campbell. m 6/25/1966 Barbara E Edes. S Jn's Ch Walpole NH 1993-2002; Dio Wstrn Massachusetts Springfield MA 1984-1988; R S Phil's Ch Easthampton MA 1984-1988; P-in-c S Paul's Epis

Sum Chap Otis MA 1978-1984; Ch Of The Gd Shpd So Lee MA 1974-1984; R S Geo's Ch Lee MA 1974-1984; P-in-c Chr Ch Island Pond VT 1971-1974; Dio Wstrn Massachusetts Springfield MA 1969-1970; Intern Dio Wstrn Massachusetts Springfield MA 1969-1970.

FREEMAN, Robert W (Vt) 38 Beaman St # 235, Poultney VT 05764 B London UK 2/17/1931 s William R Freeman & Margaret. U of Vermont 1970; MA Antioch Coll 1988. D 1/28/1973 P 11/1/1973 Bp Harvey D Butterfield. m 9/21/1957 Ivy Allan c 3. Trin Epis Ch Poultney VT 1981-1996; S Paul's Epis Ch Wells VT 1981-1990; Asst Chr Ch Montpelier VT 1973-1980. britsus@aol.com

FREEMAN, Sarah Belle (Colo) 726 W Elati Cir, Littleton CO 80120 **S Paul's Epis Ch Cntrl City CO 2003-; D S Tim's Epis Ch Rangely CO 1996-** B Kermit TX 6/18/1949 d Richard Earl Ward & Rose Joyce. Santa Rosa Jr. Coll 1968; Lic Psych Tech St of California 1968; Colorado NW Cmnty Coll 1985; EFM STUSo 2000; Colorado Chr U 2004. D 8/10/1996 P 4/12/1997 Bp William Jerry Winterrowd. m 8/17/2002 Lyndle Freeman. "Pryr for Erin," Wmn Uncommon Prayers/Morehouse Pub, 2000; "Cheryl's Pryr," Wmn Uncommon Prayers/Morehouse Pub, 2000. sarahcanon9@comcast.net

FREEMAN, Sollace Mitchell (At) 5194 Glenstone Ct, Gainesville GA 30504 B Gainesville FL 10/7/1940 s Sollace Mitchell Freeman & Frances Juhan. BA Cntr Coll 1962; MDiv VTS 1965. D 7/19/1965 P 5/21/1966 Bp Frank A Juhan. m 7/7/1990 Patricia G Viles c 3. Int S Mary And S Martha Ch Buford GA 2006-2007; R S Gabr's Epis Ch Oakwood GA 1999-2006; Assoc Gr Epis Ch Gainesville GA 1990-1999; R S Eliz's Epis Ch Dahlonega GA 1990-1994; Com on Aging Dio Cntrl Gulf Coast Pensacola FL 1984-1988; ExCoun Dio Kentucky Louisville KY 1968-1970; R Gr Ch Paducah KY 1967-1973. mf10740@hotmail.com

FREEMAN, Warren Gray (Mass) 77 Lakeside Trailer Park, Mashpee MA 02649 B Attleboro MA 6/2/1937 s Lawrence Gray Freeman & Irene Marguerite. BA Trin 1959; STB EDS 1963. D 6/22/1963 Bp Anson Phelps Stokes Jr P 6/10/1965 Bp Frederic Cunningham Lawrence. c 3. Asst S Barn Ch Falmouth MA 1994-1998; Asst S Jn's Ch Sandwich MA 1978-1979; Assoc Chr Ch Needham MA 1965-1970; Cur Trin Par Melrose MA 1963-1965.

FREEMAN, William Horne (Mass) 25 Thornton Way Apt 233, Brunswick ME 04011 B Greenfield MA 9/26/1934 s Perrin Newell Freeman & Louise. BA Bow 1956; BD EDS 1959. D 6/13/1959 Bp Robert McConnell Hatch P 12/1/1959 Bp Frederic Cunningham Lawrence. m 8/24/1957 Carol B Brickett c 3. Receiving Disabil Ret 1994-1999; R S Mk's Ch Westford MA 1989-1994; Dio Minnesota Minneapolis MN 1975-1989; R Trin Ch Marshfield Hills MA 1966-1975; SS Mary And Mk Epis Ch Oakes ND 1962-1966; Cur S Steph's Memi Ch Lynn MA 1959-1962.

FREES, Mooydeen Claire (SO) 3826 Portrush Way, Amelia OH 45102 **S Tim's Epis Ch Cincinnati OH 2008-** B Hays Kansas 11/2/1938 d Jack Lloyd Thayer & Orpha. BA SW Coll Winfield KS 1960; RN Jewish Hosp Of Cincinnati 1978; Med Xavier U 1988; MA The Athenaeum of Ohio 1994; Cert Sthrn Ohio Sch For The Diac 1999. D 10/30/1999 Bp Kenneth Lester Price.

FREGEAU, Stephen Alfred (Mass) 7719 SE Sugar Sand Cir, Hobe Sound FL 33455 **Asst S Mary's Epis Ch Stuart FL 2007-** B Boston MA 1/23/1943 s Alfred Isidore Fregeau & Thelma Mae. BA Bos 1969; MA Estrn Nazarene Coll 1983; MDiv EDS 1988. D 6/4/1986 Bp John Bowen Coburn P 7/11/1987 Bp David Elliot Johnson. m 8/29/1965 Patricia Lotti c 2. Assoc S Greg's Ch Boca Raton FL 2005; Assoc S Paul's Ch Delray Bch FL 2004; Assoc S Greg's Ch Boca Raton FL 2001; Int Gr Ch W Palm Bch FL 1999-2000; Jas L Duncan Conf Cntr Delray Bch FL 1998-2007; Dio Massachusetts Boston MA 1992-1994; Vic Trin Epis Ch Rockland MA 1987-1998; Asst All SS Ch Whitman MA 1986-1987. ACPE 1988-2003; Epis Camps & Conf Centers 1998; IACCA 1998. Cert Conf Cntr Profsnl IACCA 2007; Cert Int Mnstry IMN 2005. safregeau@aol.com

FREIRE-SOLORZANO, Luis Hernan (EcuC) Barrio El Tambo Sector Bomba De Aqua, Pelileo 24 Ecuador B Riobamba Chimborazo EC 1/30/1969 s Mecias Freire & Gloria De. Universidad Abjerta De Loja. D 4/16/1994 Bp J Neptali Larrea-Moreno. m 11/1/1990 Maria Isabel Nunez Valencia.

FRELUND, Warren F (Wyo) 1029 W State St, Mason City IA 50401 B Mason City IA 5/12/1943 No Iowa Area Cmnty Coll; U of Iowa. D 5/26/1994 Bp Carl Christopher Epting. m 6/10/1962 Susan Whorley c 3. Dio Wyoming Casper WY 2007-2010; Dio Iowa Des Moines IA 2003-2007. wfrelund@q.com

FRENCH, Alan C (NJ) 15 Old Forge Ln, Berkeley Heights NJ 07922 B New York NY 5/20/1952 s Seth Barton French & Frederica. BA Duke 1975; MDiv GTS 1979; MS NYU 2011. D 6/23/1979 Bp Robert Campbell Witcher Sr P 1/10/1980 Bp Paul Moore Jr. m 2/13/1988 Mary Robinson Parkman c 3. Full Time Gr Epis Ch Rutherford NJ 2008-2009; Int S Jas Ch Long Branch NJ 2007; Int All SS Ch Princeton NJ 2004-2007; Secy Dio Conv Dio New Jersey Trenton NJ 1989-1995; R S Andr's Epis Ch New Providence NJ 1985-2004; Cur S Geo's-By-The-River Rumson NJ 1981-1985; Asst Trin Ch Moorestown NJ 1979-1981. frepark13@gmail.com

FRENCH, Clarke (NC) 200 Hayes Rd, Chapel Hill NC 27517 **R Ch Of The H Fam Chap Hill NC 2011-** B Toronto Canada 10/22/1974 s Donald Lester French & Gale Louise. BA U Tor 1996; MDiv Trin Toronto 1999. Trans from Anglican Church of Canada 10/26/2006 as Priest Bp Gladstone Bailey Adams III. m 7/31/2004 Sally Johnson c 2. R Trin Epis Ch Watertown NY 2006-2011; Int Chr Ch New Brighton Staten Island NY 2005-2006. OGS 2000-2004. clarke.french@gmail.com

FRENCH, James K (Alb) 32 S Union St, Cambridge NY 12816 **R S Lk's Ch Cambridge NY 2010-** B Bath NY 5/23/1957 s Floyd Kenwin French & Nancy Jane. AS Corning Cmnty Coll 1979; BS U of N Alabama 1981; MA Nash 2008; MA Nash 2009. D 5/31/2008 P 1/4/2009 Bp William Howard Love. m 4/20/1985 Virginia M Feger c 2. Asst S Lk's Ch Chatham NY 2008-2010. jim.french.137@gmail.com

FRENCH, Jonathan D (CFla) 2304 SE 12th ST, Ocala FL 34471 **R Gr Epis Ch Of Ocala Ocala FL 2007-** B Los Angeles CA 12/3/1972 s Michael Douglas French & Lisa Lynn. BA U of Florida 1995; MDiv Sewanee 2006. D 5/27/2006 P 12/2/2006 Bp John Wadsworth Howe. m 11/19/2009 Maurica W French c 4. jonathandfrench@gmail.com

FRENCH, Peter Andrew (NJ) 53 University Pl., Princeton NJ 08540 **Chapl Epis Ch at Pr Princeton NJ 2008-** B 10/1/1972 s Michael French & Christine. B.Arts U of Melbourne, Melbourne, Australia 1992; B. Theol Untd Fac of Theol, Melbourne, Australia 1998. Trans from Anglican Church Of Australia 12/24/2008 Bp George Edward Councell. m 2/9/1999 Robyn Whitaker. pfrench@princeton.edu

FRENCH, Richard Clement (Oly) 1013 129th St S, Tacoma WA 98444 B Lynchburg VA 12/8/1932 s C Clement French & Helen Augusta. BA WA SU 1954; Dplma Oxf 1957; Wycliffe Hall 1957; MDiv CDSP 1959; M Ed Gonzaga U 1969. D 6/9/1959 P 2/29/1960 Bp Russell S Hubbard. c 2. Vic S Jos And S Jn Ch Steilacoom WA 1988-1997; Int S Marg's Epis Ch Bellevue WA 1987-1988; Int S Jn's Epis Ch Gig Harbor WA 1985-1986; Asst S Jas Epis Ch Kent WA 1983-1985; All SS Ch Richland WA 1968-1969; Vic S Dunst's Epis Ch Grand Coulee WA 1963-1968. CADO 1985; Curs Mvmt 1979; Pastors Pryr Summit 1995. hon CDSP/ Berkeley, CA 1959; Phi Beta Kappa/ scl WA SU/ Pullman, WA 1954. rcbzfrench@yahoo.com

FRENCH, Sally (NC) 407 E. Seneca St., Manlius NY 13104 B 1/11/1970 d Herbert Alan Johnson & Elizabeth. BA U Tor 1999; MDiv Trin, Toronto TS 2001. Trans from Anglican Church of Canada 11/15/2008 as Priest Bp Gladstone Bailey Adams III. m 7/31/2004 Clarke French c 1. Int Chr Ch Manlius NY 2008-2009; Int S Mk The Evang Syracuse NY 2007-2008. sally.french@gmail.com

FRENCH, William A (NwPa) 42 Oak St, Brookville PA 15825 B Williamson WV 1/2/1933 s Marcellus French & Margrette. BS Indiana U of Pennsylvania; BS Edinboro U 1957. D 11/1/1991 P 12/6/1992 Bp Robert Deane Rowley Jr. m 8/9/1959 Andrea Lynne McManigle. Int P Chr Epis Ch Oil City PA 2001-2003; Int S Jn's Ch Franklin PA 1999-2000; Int Chr Ch Punxsutawney PA 1997-1998; Int Ch Of Our Sav DuBois PA 1996-1997; Int S Lk's Epis Ch Smethport PA 1995-1996; Int Emm Epis Ch Emporium PA 1993-1995; Int S Agnes' Epis Ch S Marys PA 1993-1995. billandandee@alltel.net

FRENS, Mary Jean (WMich) 934 Clubview Dr, Fremont MI 49412 **R S Mk's Ch Newaygo MI 2002-** B Fremont MI 2/22/1949 d Authur J Frens & Geraldyne Lenore. BA Calvin Coll 1971; MA Wstrn Michigan U 1973; MDiv Wstrn TS 1995. D 6/17/2000 P 12/16/2000 Bp Edward Lewis Lee Jr. m 5/20/1980 Richard F String c 2. Assoc S Jn's Ch Fremont MI 2001-2003; D S Jn's Ch Fremont MI 2000-2001. maryfrens@sbcglobal.net

FRENSLEY, James Monroe (Colo) 3506 Armstrong Ave, Dallas TX 75205 B Duncan OK 10/27/1925 s Frank Washington Frensley & Nancy Elizabeth. BFA U of Oklahoma 1950; MDiv STUSo 1961. D 6/20/1961 Bp Charles A Mason P 12/1/1961 Bp J(ohn) Joseph Meakins Harte. Cleric S Jn's Cathd Denver CO 1984-1987; Asst S Mich And All Ang Ch Dallas TX 1976-1983; Assoc S Jas Epis Ch San Francisco CA 1974-1976; P-in-c Ch Of S Mths Dallas TX 1961-1965. jfrens@sbcglobal.com

FRETZ, Kimberly Kifer (Neb) 9302 Blondo St, Omaha NE 68134 **All SS Epis Ch Omaha NE 2011-** B Dallas TX 12/20/1977 d Gregory Glen Kifer & Deborah Ann. BA TCU 1999; MACS Brite DS 2001; MDiv Brite DS 2008. D 2/3/2011 Bp Joe Goodwin Burnett. m 6/19/1999 Eric Allan Fretz c 1. candkfretz@gmail.com

FREW, Randolph Lloyd (NY) 332 Bleecker St #K80, New York NY 10014 B Parsons KS 5/30/1947 s Everett Edward Frew & Alice Elizabeth. BA U of Nevada at Las Vegas 1969; MDiv GTS 1972. D 6/29/1972 P 2/8/1973 Bp Wesley Frensdorff. Epis Ch Cntr New York NY 1992-1994; R Ch Of The H Apos New York NY 1978-1984; Field Educ Supvsr The GTS New York NY 1978-1984; Vstng P S Barth's Ch Ely NV 1976-1978; Vstng P S Jas Epis Ch Eureka NV 1976-1978; S Matt's Ch Las Vegas NV 1973-1978; Asst Chr Ch Las Vegas NV 1973-1974. Auth, *Praying w HIV/AIDS*, Forw Mvmt, 2002. rlfaai@mindspring.com

FREY, Louane Florence Virgilio (NC) 801 Footbridge Pl, Cary NC 27519 **Assoc for Chld's & Yth Mnstry S Steph's Ch Durham NC 2008-** B Jamaica NY 7/16/1945 d Michael Louis Virgilio & Geraldine Margaret. BA Limestone Coll 1967; Cert D Formation Prog 2000. D 10/21/2001 Bp David B(ruce)

Joslin. m 10/25/1970 Robert Alden Frey c 2. Yth Dir All SS Ch Princeton NJ 2006-2007; D S Fran Ch Dunellen NJ 2002-2006; D S Paul's Epis Ch Bound Brook NJ 2000-2002. lfrey716@aol.com

FREY, Matthew Vincent (WTex) 10 Scout Dr, Washington PA 15301 **Asst R S Geo Ch San Antonio TX 2008-** B Leadville CO 4/24/1958 s William Carl Frey. BA U of Nthrn Colorado 1981; MA U of Nthrn Colorado 1989; MDIV TESM 2002. D 6/8/2002 P 12/8/2002 Bp William Jerry Winterrowd. m 6/12/1983 Katharine A White c 4. R Ch Of The Adv Pittsburgh PA 2005-2007; Asst Trin Epis Ch Washington PA 2002-2005. freymv@gmail.com

FREY, Paul Anthony (WTex) 139 Kentucky St, Laredo TX 78041 **Chr Ch Epis Laredo TX 2004-** B Philadelphia PA 3/17/1955 s William Carl Frey & Barbara M. Red Rocks Cmnty Coll 1973; U Of Houston 1980; BA Loretto Heights Coll 1987; MDiv TESM 1992. D 6/20/1992 Bp William Jerry Winterrowd P 12/16/1992 Bp Peter James Lee. m 8/10/1980 Anne R Rooney c 2. R Ch Of The Redeem Eagle Pass TX 1998-2004; Asst Truro Epis Ch Fairfax VA 1992-1998. rooneyfrey@sbcglobal.net

FREY, Peter Martin (CFla) 242 Tophill Rd, San Antonio TX 78209 B Los Alamos NM 8/27/1960 s William Carl Frey & Barbara. AA Royal Coll Of Mus London Gb 1979; MA Bulgarian St Conservatory of Mus 1982. Trans 10/1/1988 Bp William Carl Frey. m 7/7/1984 Gayle Timberlake c 2. All SS Epis Ch Lakeland FL 1994-1995; Dio Cntrl Florida Orlando FL 1992-1994; S Matt's Ch Austin TX 1988-1990.

✠ **FREY, Rt Rev William Carl** (Colo) 23315 Eagle Gap, San Antonio TX 78255 B Waco TX 2/26/1930 s Harry Frederick Frey & Ethel. BA U CO 1952; ThB PDS 1955. D 6/29/1955 P 1/25/1956 Bp Joseph Summerville Minnis Con 11/26/1967 for Gua. m 6/12/1952 Barbara Martin c 5. Asstg Bp of the Rio Grande Dio The Rio Grande Albuquerque NM 2008-2010; Int Chr Epis Ch San Antonio TX 2000-2001; Ret Bp of Colo & Guatemala Dio Colorado Denver CO 1996; Dn/Pres TESM Ambridge PA 1990-1996; Dio Colorado Denver CO 1972-1990; Chair CSR Dio The Rio Grande Albuquerque NM 1960-1962; R Trin On The Hill Epis Ch Los Alamos NM 1958-1962. Auth, "The Dance of Hope," Waterbrook Press, 2003. DD VTS 1997; DD PDS 1970. plusbill@aol.com

FRIAS, Miguel (Chi) 941 W Lawrence Ave, Chicago IL 60640 B 10/5/1949 s Nicolas Frias & Cruz. S Andr's TS Manila Ph; Universidad Autonoma De Santo Domingo Santo Domingo Do; Lca U Cntrl Del Este Do 1977; LST Centro De Estudios Teologicas 1980; MDiv McCormick TS 1985. D 3/1/1981 P 8/1/1982 Bp Telesforo A Isaac. m 9/26/1981 Rosa Frias. Dio Chicago Chicago IL 1989-1991; Ch Of Chr The King Chicago IL 1984-1993; S Marg's Ch Bronx NY 1983-1984; Dio The Dominican Republic (Iglesia Epis Dominicana) Santo Domingo DO 1982-1983. MIGUEL.FRIAS@YMAIL.COM

FRIBOURGH, Cynthia Kaye (Ark) 11123 Bainbridge Dr, Little Rock AR 72212 **D S Mk's Epis Ch Little Rock AR 2010-** B Iowa City IA 1/3/1956 d James Henry Fribourgh & Cairdenia. BA U of Arkansas 1978. D 10/28/2000 Bp Larry Earl Maze. m 10/15/1988 Richard Scott Schreiber. Dio Arkansas Little Rock AR 2003-2008; D S Marg's Epis Ch Little Rock AR 2000-2010. cf.itssm@gmail.com

FRICK, Matthew Martin (Tex) 105 N Grove St, Marshall TX 75670 B Harvey IL 12/31/1980 s Robert Eugene Frick & Mary Cathrine. BA Concordia U 2003; MDiv Nash 2008. D 6/14/2008 Bp Keith Lynn Ackerman. Cur Trin Ch Marshall TX 2008-2011. foolishgalatian@yahoo.com

FRIEDEL, James W (WTex) 11905 E Maple Dr, Claremore OK 74019 **S Ptr's Epis Ch Rockport TX 2008-** B Cuero TX 1/25/1955 s James L Friedel & Helen I. Texas A&M U 1975; BBA SW Texas St U San Marcos 1978; MDiv Epis TS of The SW 1994. D 6/24/1994 P 4/1/1996 Bp James Edward Folts. m 4/19/1980 Christine Steinbach c 3. S Paul's Ch Claremore OK 2002-2008; Dio Oklahoma Oklahoma City OK 2000-2008; Dio Missouri S Louis MO 2000-2002; Asst Emm Epis Ch Webster Groves MO 1997-2000; Asst R S Geo Ch San Antonio TX 1994-1997. jfriedel@att.net

FRIEDMAN, Anna Russell (Ala) PO Box 27, Minter AL 36761 **P-in-c S Paul's (Carlowville) Minter AL 2010-** B Nashville TN 2/25/1983 d Mark Humphreys Kelly & Mary Herbert Weaver. BA Lake Forest Coll 2005; MDiv Van DS 2008; Dplma of Angl Stds The TS at The U So 2010. D 6/5/2010 Bp John Crawford Bauerschmidt. m 5/29/2010 Christopher Friedman. annarussellfriedman@gmail.com

FRIEDMAN, Maurice Lane (WTex) 4934 Lakeway Dr, Brownsville TX 78520 **R Ch Of The Adv Brownsville TX 2009-** B Philadelphia PA 11/9/1952 s Donald Jack Friedman & Joyce Ann. BA Penn 1974; MDiv EDS 1979. D 6/16/1979 Bp Lyman Cunningham Ogilby P 6/15/1980 Bp Albert Ervine Swift. m 12/27/2008 Mary Louise B Ball c 4. Vic Ch Of The H Sprt San Antonio TX 2002-2009; R S Ptr's Epis Ch Rockport TX 1997-2002; Chapl Off Of Bsh For ArmdF New York NY 1988-1997; Int Ch Of The Trsfg No Bergen NJ 1988; Cn Cathd Ch Of The Nativ Bethlehem PA 1985-1986; R Memi Ch Of S Lk Philadelphia PA 1981-1985; Cur S Mk's Ch Philadelphia PA 1979-1981. SSJE 1979-1995. rector@adventbrownsville.org

FRIEDRICH, James Louis (Los) 4685 Taylor Ave Ne, Bainbridge Island WA 98110 **Asst S Barn Epis Ch Bainbridge Island WA 2010-** B Los Angeles CA 7/16/1944 s James K Friedrich & Elaine. BA Stan 1966; MDiv EDS 1969. D 9/13/1969 P 9/17/1970 Bp Francis E I Bloy. m 5/21/2005 Martha Karen Haig. Asst Gr Ch Bainbridge Island WA 2005-2010; Asst Chr Ch Par Ontario CA 1990-1995; Asst S Aug By-The-Sea Par Santa Monica CA 1984-1989; Dio Los Angeles Los Angeles CA 1975-1976; Asst St Johns Pro-Cathd Los Angeles CA 1973-1984. Auth, "A Thin Place: Iona & The Celtic Way," Cathd Films And Video, 1998; Auth, "The Greening Of Faith," Cathd Films And Video, 1994; Auth, "The Electronic Campfire," Cathd Films And Video, 1993; Auth, "The Story Of Anglicanism," Cathd Films And Video, 1988; Auth, "The Story Of The Epis Ch," Cathd Films And Video, 1986. frjimfr@earthlink.net

FRIEDRICH JR, Robert Edmund (Ct) 77 Court St, Suite 1060, Laconia NH 03246 B Pittsburgh PA 5/24/1948 s Robert Edmund Friedrich & Mary Ellen. BA Houghton Coll 1970; MDiv Gordon-Conwell TS 1974; GTS 1986; DMin GCTS 1996. D 6/7/1986 Bp Paul Moore Jr P 10/18/1986 Bp Andrew Frederick Wissemann. m 6/19/1971 Sandra Diane Barton c 2. S Steph's Ch Olean NY 2006-2007; The Ekklesia Inst Inc Las Vegas NV 2006-2007; Int Gr In The Desert Epis Ch Las Vegas NV 2004-2006; Ch Of S Jn By The Sea W Haven W Haven CT 2004; All SS Epis Ch Meriden CT 1999-2002; R Ch Of The Epiph Newport NH 1992-1997; R Ch Of The Incarn Penfield NY 1988-1992; Dio Wstrn Massachusetts Springfield MA 1986-1999; Assoc Ch Of The Atone Westfield MA 1986-1988. Auth, "Discerning Your Cong's Future: Strategic & Sprtl Approach," Alb Inst, Inc, 1996. Ord of S Helena 1984. bobfriedrich@comcast.net

FRIEDRICH, Roger Paul (SVa) 1136 Quintara St, San Francisco CA 94116 B Long Branch NJ 12/19/1937 s Paul A Friedrich & Florence Elizabeth. BS Penn 1959; MDiv VTS 1965. D 1/17/1966 Bp David Shepherd Rose P 1/25/1967 Bp George P Gunn. Cur Chr And Gr Ch Petersburg VA 1966-1968. hillloproger@yahoo.com

FRIEND, Robert Douglas (Va) 4011 College Valley Ct, Richmond VA 23233 B Long Beach CA 7/26/1951 s Sidney George Friend & Janice Lillian. BA U of Virginia 1973; MDiv VTS 1976; DMin VTS 1998. D 5/22/1976 Bp John Alfred Baden P 12/18/1976 Bp David Shepherd Rose. m 8/20/1977 Susan Cole c 1. R All SS Ch Richmond VA 2001-2011; R S Fran Epis Ch Great Falls VA 1987-2001; Assoc S Anne's Par Annapolis MD 1983-1986; Asst Estrn Shore Chap Virginia Bch VA 1976-1983. Auth, "Stndg Between Generations," *Honoring Fr And Mo As They Mature Into Elderhood*, 1998. VBGIRL@HOTMAIL.COM

FRIESE JR, Walter Edward (WLa) 107 Shady Ave., Pineville LA 71360 **R S Tim's Ch Alexandria LA 2006-** B Saint Louis MO 3/19/1947 s Walter Edward Friese & Dorothy Pauline. BS Missouri Bapt Coll 1975; SW Bapt TS 1978; MS Amberton U 1985; TESM 1999. D 6/19/1999 P 3/2/2000 Bp James Monte Stanton. m 11/23/1983 Paulette Dumas. S Tim's Ch Alexandria LA 2007-2009; Dio Wstrn Louisiana Alexandria LA 2004-2006; R All SS Epis Ch Russellville AR 2002-2004; S Jas Epis Ch Texarkana TX 1999-2002; The Epis Ch of the Intsn Carrollton TX 1999; Chr Epis Ch Plano TX 1995-1998. wfriese@suddenlinkmail.net

FRINK, James Phillip (RI) 3a Grouse Trl, Smithfield RI 02917 B Saint Johnsbury VT 1/18/1929 s Clarence Justin Frink & Beatrice Judy. BA U of Vermont 1951; MA Br 1957; MDiv Nash 1959. D 6/20/1959 P 12/19/1959 Bp John S Higgins. m 9/3/1962 Caryl S Swinden c 2. R Trin Ch N Scituate RI 1971-1996; R S Mary's Ch E Providence RI 1962-1971. jpfrink@cox.net

FRISBY, Warren Archer (WNY) 69 Dolphann Dr, Tonawanda NY 14150 B Buffalo NY 6/25/1931 s William Archer Frisby & Elizabeth. AA Inst of Applied Arts & Sciences 1951; BA Daemen Coll 1989; MA Chr The King Sem 1995. D 6/11/1983 Bp Harold B Robinson. m 4/12/1958 Ruth Elaine Buckner c 3.

FRISCH, Floyd Charles (ECR) 2 N Santa Cruz Ave, Los Gatos CA 95030 **Assoc S Andr's Ch Saratoga CA 1981-** B Buffalo NY 12/19/1933 s Floyd Millard Frisch & Pearl Louise. Oxf; BS SUNY 1955; BD Yale DS 1958; JD U of San Francisco 1965. D 4/12/1969 Bp C Kilmer Myers P 2/1/1971 Bp George Richard Millard. m 9/10/1967 Leilani Ann Frisch c 2. P-in-c Chr Ch Alameda CA 1980-1981; P-in-c S Fran Epis Ch San Jose CA 1979-1980; P-in-c S Tim's Epis Ch Mtn View CA 1973-1979; Asst S Edw The Confessor Epis Ch San Jose CA 1969-1971. Auth, *Common Law & Cn Law at the End of the 13th Century*, Oxford Press, 1984. scoots1us@yahoo.com

FRITCH, Charles Oscar (CFla) 324 S Lost Lake Ln, Casselberry FL 32707 B Rock Island IL 9/12/1944 s Leo Joseph Fritch & Alice May. BA S Meinrad Coll 1966; MDiv St. Meinrad TS 1970; MA U of W Florida 1976. Rec from Roman Catholic 5/20/1986 Bp William Hopkins Folwell. m 1/8/1977 Patricia Beninati c 3. S Matt's Epis Ch Orlando FL 1989-2010; Asst Emm Ch Orlando FL 1986-1988. fritchc@gmail.com

FRITSCH, Andrew John (WMo) 3702 Poplar Dr, Joplin MO 64804 B Joplin MO 6/7/1932 s John Andrew Fritsch & Norval Elizabeth. MD S Louis U 1957. Rec from Roman Catholic 4/24/1964 Bp Lemuel Henry Wells. m 7/7/1956 Martha Ann Barratt c 2. D S Steph's Ch Monett MO 1997-2005; D S Phil's Ch Joplin MO 1991-1997. "Panlobular and Centulobular Emphysema," Annals of Internal Med, 1961. NAAD.

FRITSCH, Peter Louis (WMass) 901 Diamond St, Springfield OR 97477 B Redwood City CA 5/26/1953 s Stephen Fritsch & Joyce. BA U Pac 1975; MDiv CDSP 1992. D 6/12/1992 P 1/22/1993 Bp Jerry Alban Lamb. m 12/21/1974 Brenda G Briggs c 3. Dio Wstrn Massachusetts Springfield MA 2002-2003; R S Dav's Ch Feeding Hills MA 2002-2003; R S Paul's On The Plains Epis Ch Lubbock TX 1999-2002; S Aug Of Cbury Rocklin CA 1994-1999; Mssnr Dio Nthrn California Sacramento CA 1992-1999; Dio Nthrn California Sacramento CA 1992-1993. CT; Natl Ntwk Of Epis Cler Assns 1992. plfritsch@ft.newyorklife.com

FRITSCHE, Janet Yvonne (NMich) 122 Hunter Rd, Iron River MI 49935 B Geneseo IL 11/22/1945 d Herman Schwark & Mary. D 3/12/2006 Bp James Arthur Kelsey. m 9/21/1968 Jere Fritsche c 3. j-birds@ironriver.tv

FRITSCHNER, Ann Rumage (WNC) Po Box 2818, Hendersonville NC 28793 B Louisville KY 5/25/1955 d William T Rumage & Eleanor Lockwood. BA Connecticut Coll 1977; Cert Assn Of Fundraising Professionals Alexandria VA 2001. D 11/23/2002 Bp Robert Hodges Johnson. m 9/23/1995 Samuel Hunt Fritschner c 2. Ch of the Advoc Asheville NC 2005-2008; D Ch Of S Jn In The Wilderness Flat Rock NC 2002-2008.

FRITSCHNER, John Breckinridge (Ala) 910 Terrace Acres Circle, Auburn AL 36830 **R H Trin Epis Ch Auburn AL 1995-** B Indianapolis IN 2/27/1951 s Charles Henry Fritschner & Elizabeth Breckinridge. BA U of Kentucky 1973; MA U of Iowa 1978; MDiv STUSo 1985. D 6/1/1985 Bp Addison Hosea P 12/7/1985 Bp Don Adger Wimberly. m 11/23/2009 Nancy Nave c 2. R S Dav's Ch Cheraw SC 1988-1995; Cur Ch Of The Gd Shpd Lexington KY 1985-1988. SSJE 1999. Cranmer Cup ECUSA 2008; Porter Cup ECUSA 1991. john@holytrinitychurch.info

FRITTS, John Clinton (WTex) St Paul's Episcopal Church, PO Box 1148, Brady TX 76825 **R S Paul's Ch Brady TX 2008-** B Tyler TX 3/21/1958 s John William Fritts & Marilyn Anderson. BA Texas A&M U 1981; MDiv Epis TS of the SW 2006. D 3/2/2008 Bp David Mitchell Reed P 9/24/2008 Bp Gary Richard Lillibridge. m 10/28/1983 Lynda A Bergin c 2. frittsjc@gmail.com

FRITTS, Julia Anne (Md) 628 Main St, Stamford CT 06901 B Washington DC 9/26/1956 d Lowell Ross Fritts & Barbara Ann Cullers. BS U of Maryland 1985; MA Traditional Acupuncture Inst 1999; MDiv GTS 2008. D 6/14/2008 Bp John Leslie Rabb P 1/24/2009 Bp Andrew Donnan Smith. c 1. Assoc R S Jn's Ch Stamford CT 2008-2010. jfworldwork@hotmail.com

FRITZ, Janice Vary (CPa) 109 Hope Dr, Boiling Springs PA 17007 **D S Andr's Epis Ch Shippensburg PA 2004-** B Bethlehem PA 6/25/1951 d Samuel Vary. BS Millersville U; MS Shippensburg U 1979. D 6/19/2004 Bp Michael Whittington Creighton. m 9/28/1996 John David Fritz.

FRIZZELL, Judith Ann (Dal) 3009 Maple Ave Apt 210, Dallas TX 75201 **Ch Of The Incarn Dallas TX 2003-** B Navasota TX 8/22/1940 d Arthur James Pauly & Louetta Madelyn. U Of Houston; BA Rice U 1962; Cert Angl TS 1991. D 6/27/1998 Bp James Monte Stanton. m 7/21/1962 Wesley Everett Frizzell c 3.

FRNKA, Virginia H (WTex) 314 W Gayle St, Edna TX 77957 **P Partnr In Mnstry Estrn Convoc Kennedy TX 2010-** B San Antonio TX 9/23/1952 d Edward Wheat Holland & Annie Mae. BA U of Texas 1974; MA Epis Sem of SW 2002; Cert Iona Sch for Mnstry 2010. D 6/10/2010 Bp David Mitchell Reed P 12/12/2010 Bp Gary Richard Lillibridge. c 2. vfrnka@sbcglobal.net

FROCK, Samuel Edward (SeFla) 2210 NE 40th Ct, Lighthouse Point FL 33064 B Uniontown PA 12/18/1924 s Charles Thomas Frock & Mary Cummings. BS USNA 1946; MDiv VTS 1966. D 6/29/1966 Bp James Loughlin Duncan P 12/29/1966 Bp William Loftin Hargrave. m 6/1/1947 Louise Hooper c 2. Chair Ecum Cmsn Dio SE Florida Miami FL 1969-1973; Vic/R Ch Of S Nich Pompano Bch FL 1966-1992. tlfrnedd@aol.com

FROEHLICH, Burt H (SeFla) 406b Coopers Cove Rd, St Augustine FL 32095 **S Chris's By-The-Sea Epis Ch Key Biscayne FL 2008-** B Cincinnati OH 12/8/1950 s Fredrick Louis Froehlich & Margaret Carolyn. BA Morehead St U 1974; MDiv VTS 1978. D 5/27/1978 P 3/1/1979 Bp John Mc Gill Krumm. m 8/14/1993 Sharon E Froehlich c 1. S Thos Flagler Cnty Palm Coast FL 2006-2008; Ch Of The Recon St Aug FL 2001-2006; Ch Of The H Comf Cres City FL 2000-2001; Emm Ch Welaka FL 2000-2001; S Mk's Ch Palatka FL 1999; S Cathr's Ch Jacksonville FL 1998-1999; Gd Samar Epis Ch Orange Pk FL 1990-1991; R S Ptr's Ch Ashtabula OH 1985-1988; S Thos Epis Ch Terrace Pk OH 1983-1985; Asst R S Ptr's Ch Jacksonville FL 1980-1982; Asst & P-in-c S Jas Ch Potomac MD 1978-1980. padreburt@mac.com

FROEHLICH, Meghan Foster (O) Our Saviour, Episcopal, 471 Crosby St., Akron OH 44302 **R Ch Of Our Sav Akron OH 2003-** B Mountain View CA 5/8/1964 d Kenneth Ronald Froehlich & Barbara June. BA Oklahoma St U 1986; MDiv Duke 1997. D 12/12/1999 P 6/11/2000 Bp Robert Hodges Johnson. Ch Of The Gd Shpd Dallas TX 2000-2003; Ch Of The Redeem Shelby NC 1999-2000. "An Incarnational Approach to Eucharistic Participation," *Questions Liturgiques/Stds in Liturg, Vol 81, 3-4*, Peeters, 2000; Auth, "What Defines Cler Compstn: Mssn or Mrkt?," *Questions for 21st Century Ch*, Abingdon, 1999. therevmff@mindspring.com

FROILAND, Paul Vincent (Minn) 12525 Porcupine Ct, Eden Prairie MN 55344 B Minneapolis MN 6/10/1947 s Jack H Froiland & Harriet Ophelia. BA S Olaf Coll 1969; MDiv Nash 1972; MA U MN 1978. D 6/29/1972 P 4/1/1973 Bp Philip Frederick McNairy. m 12/19/1970 Laurel Ann Conlon c 2. Assoc The Epis Par Of S Dav Minnetonka MN 1972-1974. Auth, "Alzheimer's Disease A Case Study"; Auth, *Best Short Stories*; Auth, *Holt Guide to Engl*.

FROLICK, Betty Roberson (NI) 6334 Bennington Dr, Fort Wayne IN 46815 **Assoc R Trin Ch Ft Wayne IN 2002-** B Richmond VA 2/2/1942 d Andrew Hubert Roberson & Elizabeth. BS Ohio U 1964; CTh Whitaker TS 1990; CTh SWTS 1994. D 5/26/1990 Bp William J Gordon Jr P 9/1/1994 Bp R(aymond) Stewart Wood Jr. m 3/14/1964 Peter Frolick c 3. R S Ptr's Epis Ch Hillsdale MI 1994-2001; D Gr Epis Ch Standish MI 1990-1993; D H Fam Epis Ch Midland MI 1990-1993; D S Paul's Epis Ch Gladwin MI 1990-1993. revbettyfw@frontier.com

FROMBERG, Paul D (Cal) 500 De Haro Street, San Francisco CA 94107 **S Greg Of Nyssa Ch San Francisco CA 2004-** B Houston TX 12/21/1960 s Henry Fielding Fromberg & Flora Bess. -- Abilene Chr U 1980; BA Rhodes Coll 1984; MDiv Fuller TS 1987; CTh Epis TS of The SW 1990. D 6/16/1990 Bp Maurice Manuel Benitez P 2/3/1991 Bp William Elwood Sterling. m 7/18/2008 Naurice G Martin. St Andrews Epis Ch Houston TX 2003-2004; Chr Ch Cathd Houston TX 1992-2000; D Chr Ch Cathd Houston TX 1990-1991. Coun of AP 2008. paul@paulfromberg.com

FRONTJES, Richard Andrew (Chi) 910 Normal Rd, DeKalb IL 60115 **Int S Paul's Ch McHenry IL 2011-** B Saginaw Michigan 12/18/1972 s Richard James Frontjes & Leslie Ann. BA Hope Coll 1995; PrTS 1996; MDiv Epis TS of The SW 2006. D 12/18/2005 P 7/22/2006 Bp Edwin Max Leidel Jr. m 7/29/2000 Stacy Ann Walker c 2. P-in-c Mssh-S Barth Epis Ch Chicago IL 2009-2010; R S Matt's Epis Ch Saginaw MI 2006-2009. rfrontjes@yahoo.com

FROST, Gregory Hayden (Los) 18354 Superior St, Northridge CA 91325 **R Epis Ch Of S Andr And S Chas Granada Hills CA 1992-** B Medford MA 12/3/1949 s Charles Edward Frost & Hazel Beatrice. BA NEU 1973; MDiv Candler TS Emory U 1980; Mdr Pepperdine U 2005. D 6/14/1980 P 5/2/1981 Bp Bennett Jones Sims. m 8/27/1976 Janice Mary Nagle. Assoc H Innoc Ch Atlanta GA 1983-1992; Asst S Ptr's Ch Rome GA 1980-1983. ghfrost@gmail.com

FROST, Jeffrey Louis (NCal) 2150 Benton Dr, Redding CA 96003 **R All SS Epis Ch Redding CA 1997-** B San Jose CA 12/22/1957 s Robert Harold Frost & Elizabeth. BA California St U 1983; MDiv CDSP 1987. D 6/26/1987 Bp Charles Shannon Mallory P 5/22/1988 Bp Robert Louis Ladehoff. m 5/22/1982 Ellen Page Douglas c 2. Vic Calv Epis Ch Jerome ID 1994-1997; Vic Trin Ch Buhl ID 1994-1996; Cur Trin Epis Ch Ft Worth TX 1990-1994; Legacy Gd Samar Hosp Portland OR 1987-1990. jlfrost@charter.net

FROST-PHILLIPS, Lisa Ann (NC) 128 Creekview Cir, Carrboro NC 27510 B Atlanta GA 7/4/1967 d Roger Thompson Frost & Maxine. BA U So 1989; MDiv Duke 1996; CAS VTS 1996. D 6/29/1996 Bp J(ames) Gary Gloster P 6/1/1997 Bp Robert Carroll Johnson Jr. m 7/7/1990 James Dickson Phillips. S Matt's Epis Ch Hillsborough NC 2007-2008; Assoc S Lk's Epis Ch Durham NC 1996-2000. Wilkin'S Schlr U So Sewanee TN 1985. frost-phillips@mindspring.com

FROTHINGHAM, Christen Struthers (Mass) 6 Sunset Ave, North Reading MA 01864 B New York NY 5/4/1950 d Alan Michael Frothingham & Sara. Bryn 1970; BA Brandeis U 1978. D 6/5/1993 P 6/12/1994 Bp David Elliot Johnson. m 1/5/1985 William Scott Wheeler c 2. Ch Of Our Sav Brookline MA 1994-2007; D All SS Par Brookline MA 1993-1994. Parsons Club 1994.

FROWE, Jeanne Shelton (Nev) 384 Sunset Dr, Reno NV 89509 B Athens AL 5/28/1922 d Oscar Norman Shelton & George Bell. BA U of Miami 1964. D 6/12/1983 P 12/1/1983 Bp Wesley Frensdorff. m 12/20/1941 Warren John Frowe.

FRUEHWIRTH OJN, Gregory Alan (FdL) 2812 Summit Avenue, Waukesha WI 53188 B Phoenix AZ 9/15/1969 s Gregory Herbert Fruehwirth & Joan Marie. D 1/25/1997 P 8/15/1997 Bp Russell Edward Jacobus. gregory@orderofjulian.org

FRY, Barbara Ransom (RG) 8540 S Southpoint Rd, Empire MI 49630 B Salina KS 10/24/1943 d George Phillip Ransom & Christine Bravender. Wstrn Michigan U; Whitaker TS 1991. D 6/21/1991 Bp Henry Irving Mayson. c 2. Bound Together Inc PONTIAC MI 1998-2005; All SS Epis Ch Pontiac MI 1995; Nativ Cmnty Epis Ch Holly MI 1993-1995; D S Mary's-In-The-Hills Ch Lake Orion MI 1991-1993. Auth, "Homelessness," *Meditations on Homelessness*, 1992. "Vill Warrior" Awd for express Mnstry to Afro-Amer c Pontiac Cmnty 2000; Cy Green Awd for Wk in Afr Amer Cmnty 1999; Dioc Jubilee Off Dio Michigan 1996. hildeesmom@yahoo.com

FRY, Gregory Jay (SwFla) 2925 N 56th St, Phoenix AZ 85018 B Covington KY 2/28/1960 s Ralph Thomas Fry & Melanie Sue. BS Nthrn Kentucky U 1986; MDiv VTS 1990. D 6/17/1990 P 12/23/1990 Bp Don Adger Wimberly. m 6/10/1989 Lisa Dawn Smith c 1. R S Steph's Ch Phoenix AZ 2007-2011; S Edm's Epis Ch Arcadia FL 2006-2007; Assoc R S Marg Of Scotland Epis Ch Sarasota FL 2003-2006; Int The Epis Ch Of S Jas The Less Northfield IL

2003; Assoc R S Bon Ch Sarasota FL 1998-2003; S Jn's Ch Powell WY 1992-1994; Cur Calv Epis Ch Ashland KY 1990-1991; P-in-c S Alb's Ch Morehead KY 1990-1991. xinmetoo@gmail.com

FRY, Lisa Dawn (Az) 7604 Apache Road, Little Rock AR 72205 **Cur S Mk's Epis Ch Little Rock AR 2011-** B York ME 6/18/1959 d Gerald Cameron Smith & Peggy Bridges. BA Colby Coll; MTS VTS 1989. D 6/11/2011 Bp Kirk Stevan Smith. m 6/10/1989 Gregory Jay Fry c 1. frylisad@yahoo.com

FRY III, William Nall (WTenn) 10 N Highland St, Memphis TN 38111 **Asst The Ch Of The Gd Shpd (Epis) Memphis TN 1969-** B Memphis TN 11/9/1931 s William N Fry & Polly. U of Memphis 1953; U of Tennessee 1963. D 3/29/1969 Bp John Vander Horst P 2/1/1994 Bp Alex Dockery Dickson. m 9/22/1955 Catherine Dwyer.

FRYE, Donald Jay (Chi) 2843 Gypsum Cir, Naperville IL 60564 **R S Jas Ch W Dundee IL 2008-** B Akron OH 4/1/1960 BA Mt Vernon Nazarene Coll Mt Vernon OH 1982; MDiv Nazarene TS 1988; SWTS 2005. D 6/18/2005 P 12/17/2005 Bp William Dailey Persell. m 11/20/2010 David L Shallow c 2. Asst Ch Of The H Nativ Clarendon Hills IL 2005-2006. padrefrito@gmail.com

FRYE III, Jacob Wade (ETenn) 332 Essex Dr, Knoxville TN 37922 **D S Andr's Ch Maryville TN 2001-** B Newton NC 2/10/1947 s Jacob Wade Frye & Francis Sue Betty. Georgia St U; U of Maryland. D 12/15/2001 Bp Charles Glenn VonRosenberg. m 6/9/1972 Helen Lucille Barnette. Fllshp of S Jn the Evang 2002. jfrye09@comcast.net

FRYE, Linda Lou (Eau) 21836 Gladestone Ave, Tomah WI 54660 B Carlisle PA 5/8/1948 d Carl Richard Mentzer & Anna Gayle. D 6/29/1995 Bp William Charles Wantland. m 9/27/1997 Lyle Lavern Frye. D S Mary's Epis Ch Tomah WI 1995-2007.

FRYMAN, Kay Kirby (SC) St John's Episcopal Church, 252 S Dargan St, Florence SC 29506 **D S Jn's Ch Florence SC 2007-** B Gastonia NC 1/25/1947 d Millard Frederick Kirby & Mary Olive Martin. BA Columbia Coll 1968; Luth Sem 1984. D 9/8/2007 Bp Edward Lloyd Salmon Jr. m 10/7/2000 Eugene Fryman. kayfryman@aol.com

FUDGE, R(alph) Truman (Me) 32 Ocean St, Belfast ME 04915 B Elmira NY 11/1/1933 s Ralph Ellsworth Fudge & Mary Louise. BA Colg 1955; STB Ya Berk 1968. D 6/20/1968 Bp Ned Cole P 6/21/1969 Bp John S Higgins. m 11/11/1955 Suzanne Reynolds c 2. R S Marg's Ch Belfast ME 1974-1995; Assoc R Chr Ch Westerly RI 1971-1972; Cur Chr Ch Westerly RI 1968-1970. Affirming Anglo-Catholicism 1997-2001; Integrity Inc 2001; NNECA 1973; Par for Liturg and Mssn 1973-2004.

FUENER, Paul Charles (SC) Po Box 674, Georgetown SC 29442 **Prince Geo Winyah Epis Preschool Georgetown SC 2000-** B Lansing MI 3/31/1949 s Thomas William Fuener & Elizabeth Carlisle. BA U MI 1971; JD GW 1976; MDiv TESM 1996. D 6/15/1996 Bp Peter James Lee P 12/28/1996 Bp Alden Moinet Hathaway. m 12/28/1971 Rebecca Roberson McCullough c 2. Asst R S Steph's Ch Sewickley PA 1996-2000.

FUESSEL JR, Paul A (Ia) 525 A Ave Ne, Cedar Rapids IA 52401 B New York NY 2/16/1940 s Paul Arthur Fuessel & Ruby Aileen. BA Benedictine Coll 1974; LTh SWTS 1983. D 6/25/1983 Bp William Edwin Swing P 12/27/1983 Bp James Daniel Warner. m 12/30/1961 Chere Livingston c 3. R Gr Ch Cedar Rapids IA 1999-2009; Chr Ch Collinsville IL 1991-1996; Halifax-Pittsylvania Cure Java VA 1990-1991; Vic Emm Ch Halifax VA 1988-1991; Vic S Paul's Ch Peytonsburg Keeling VA 1988-1991; Dio Sthrn Virginia Norfolk VA 1988-1989; Vic S Aug's Ch De Witt NE 1983-1988; S Chas The Mtyr Beatrice NE 1983-1988. Cmnty of Celebration. paultrtn@peoplestel.net

FUIR, Scott J (WVa) 218 Church St., Lewisburg WV 24901 **R S Jas' Epis Ch Lewisburg WV 2008-** B Philadelphia PA 12/13/1955 s John Eugene Fuir & Alethea Mildred. BA Pr 1979; MDiv STUSo 1996. D 6/1/1996 P 1/18/1997 Bp Joe Morris Doss. m 3/5/1988 JoAnn L Peterson c 3. R S Christophers Epis Ch Oxford PA 2002-2008; Vic S Jn's Epis Ch Maple Shade NJ 1996-2002. frscott1@frontier.com

FULFORD, David Edward (NwPa) 118 Terrace Dr, Edinboro PA 16412 **Vic S Aug Of Cbury Ch Edinboro PA 1995-** B Washington DC 1/19/1959 s George Edward Fulford & Ann Gray. Dioc Sch For Mnstry; BS W&M 1981; PhD Med Coll of Virginia 1985. D 12/2/1995 P 12/1/1996 Bp Robert Deane Rowley Jr. fulford@edinboro.edu

FULGHUM, Charles Benjamin (At) 759 Loridans Dr Ne, Atlanta GA 30342 B Selma NC 7/20/1926 s Charles Benjamin Fulghum & Alice Omega. Candler TS Emory U; BS U NC 1950; MD U NC 1954. D 2/14/1965 Bp Randolph R Claiborne P 5/1/1984 Bp Charles Judson Child Jr. m 4/14/1977 Carole M Carson. S Mart In The Fields Ch Atlanta GA 1991-1995; Asst S Bede's Ch Atlanta GA 1983-1984; Asst Ch Of The Atone Sandy Sprg GA 1970-1982; Asst H Innoc Ch Atlanta GA 1965-1970. Auth, "Sermons That Wk". AAPC.

FULGHUM, Peter Clopper (Md) 13007 Still Meadow Rd, Smithsburg MD 21783 B Washington DC 12/17/1934 s James Hooks Fulghum & Frances. BA Hampden-Sydney Coll 1958; BD Epis TS In Kentucky 1964. D 6/23/1964 P 5/30/1965 Bp William Henry Marmion. m 8/25/1956 Joan F Farmer c 4. S Chris Epis Ch Linthicum Heights MD 1994-1995; All SS Ch Frederick MD 1992-1994; S Matt's Par Oakland MD 1990-1992; Trin Ch Elkton MD 1989-1990; Chr Ch Par Kent Island Stevensville MD 1988-1989; Ch Of S Marks On The Hill Pikesville MD 1987-1988; S Alb's Epis Ch Salisbury MD 1986-1987; Ch Of The H Trin Oxford MD 1985-1986; Emm Ch Cumberland MD 1985; Assoc S Jn's Par Hagerstown MD 1982-1984; Int Dio Easton Easton MD 1981-1996; Int Mnstry Spec Dio Maryland Baltimore MD 1981-1996; Dio Maryland Baltimore MD 1980-1981; Washington Co Mssn Hagerstown MD 1975-1980; Vic S Chris's Ch New Carrollton MD 1972-1974; Vic S Andr The Fisherman Epis Mayo MD 1968-1970; Vic Chr Epis Ch Big Stone Gap VA 1965-1967; Vic All SS Epis Ch Norton VA 1964-1967; Vic S Steph's Ch Norfolk VA 1964-1965.

FULK, Michael Thomas (NI) 909 S. Darling St., Angola IN 46703 **S Mk's Par Howe IN 2010-; P-in-c H Fam Ch Angola IN 2007-** B Fort Wayne IN 9/9/1943 s Clifton Fulk & Bertha. AB Indiana U 1965; MSEd U of St Fran 1968. D 12/15/2007 P 6/27/2008 Bp Edward Stuart Little II. m 11/27/1965 Micaela Diane Bowers c 4. mtfulk@frontier.com

FULKS, William B (Pa) 112 Elite Hts, Hurricane WV 25526 B Huntington WV 2/18/1938 s Fenton Hicks Fulks & Mary Ellen. BA Marshall U 1961; BD Bex 1964. D 6/11/1964 P 12/1/1964 Bp Wilburn Camrock Campbell. m 6/3/1961 Joanne H Fulks c 2. Emm Ch Quakertown PA 1996-2000; R Trin Epis Ch So Boston VA 1990-1996; S Barn Bridgeport WV 1982-1990; Exec Coun Appointees New York NY 1979-1982; S Ptr's Ch Huntington WV 1974-1979; Vic Calv Ch Montgomery WV 1969-1974; Vic Epis Ch of the Trsfg Buckhannon WV 1964-1969.

FULLAM, Everett Leslie (CFla) 19 River Ridge Trl, Ormond Beach FL 32174 B Montpelier VT 7/1/1930 s Rex Alvin Fullam & Mary Frances. BA Gordon Coll 1955; MA Bos 1957; DD Barrington Coll 1984; LHD Gordon Coll 1991. D 6/18/1966 P 6/1/1967 Bp John S Higgins. m 9/27/1952 Ruth A Andresen c 2. S Paul's Ch Darien CT 1972-1990; Min (Mus) S Mk's Epis Ch Riverside RI 1962-1972. Auth, "Fit For God's Presence," Chosen, 1989; Auth, "Thirsting," Oliver Nelson, 1989; Auth, "How To Walk w God," Oliver Nelson, 1987; Auth, "Riding the Wind," Creation Hse, 1986; Auth, "Facets Of The Faith," Chosen, 1982; Auth, "Living The Lord'S Pryr," Chosen, 1980.

FULLER, Betty WL Works (WTex) PO Box 7544, Beaumont TX 77726 **All SS Epis Sch Beaumont TX 2010-; CE Dir S Mk's Ch Beaumont TX 2009-** B North Conway NH 2/1/1951 d David Albert Works & Lucy Robb Winston. AB Sweet Briar Coll 1972; MDiv VTS 1975. D 6/20/1975 Bp Philip Alan Smith P 1/17/1993 Bp Earl Nicholas McArthur Jr. m 5/18/1974 Frank E Fuller c 2. R The Epis Ch Of The Adv Alice TX 1997-2007; Ch Of The Gd Shpd Corpus Christi TX 1996-1997; Supply Dio W Texas San Antonio TX 1996-1997; S Thos And S Mart's Ch Corpus Christi TX 1996-1997; Dio W Texas San Antonio TX 1993-1995; Ch Of The Annunc Luling TX 1989-1994; Asst S Mk's Ch San Marcos TX 1982-1988. Auth, *Food For His Friends*, 1986; Auth, *La Familia de Dios*, 1984; Auth, *The Seedlings (Curric)*, 1981. Bp Elliott Soc 2003. seedlings@aol.com

FULLER, Edward Beaty (At) 1601 Turnberry Ln Se, Marietta GA 30067 B 2/20/1943 D 4/20/2006 Bp J(ohn) Neil Alexander. c 1. ed.fuller@optilogistics.com

FULLER III, Frank E (Tex) 4335 Thomas Ln, Beaumont TX 77706 **R S Mk's Ch Beaumont TX 2007-** B Marshall TX 2/12/1949 s Frank Earl Fuller & Joan. BA U of Texas 1971; MDiv VTS 1974. D 6/18/1974 Bp Scott Field Bailey P 10/15/1975 Bp J Milton Richardson. m 5/18/1974 Betty WL Works c 2. Asst Ch Of The Gd Shpd Corpus Christi TX 1995-2007; Secy Dio W Texas San Antonio TX 1991-2007; R S Mk's Ch San Marcos TX 1980-1995; R S Jas' Epis Ch La Grange TX 1975-1980. Auth, *Foundations for Mature Faith*, Seedlings, 1991; Auth, *Engrafting the Word*, Seedlings, 1986; Auth, *The Passion of S Jas*, 1976. Angl Comm Inst 2007; The Bp Elliott Soc 1993. fef3t@aol.com

FULLER, Glen C (WNY) St Marks Episcopal Church, 61 Payne Ave, North Tonawanda NY 14120 **St Mk Epis Ch No Tonawanda NY 2010-** B 7/24/1946 s Charles Frederick Fuller & Elena. BS SUNY 1968; MA SUNY 1985; MDiv Bex 2004. D 12/20/2003 P 11/20/2004 Bp J Michael Garrison. m 7/4/1970 Babette Mitchell. Ch Of The H Comm Lakeview NY 2006-2010. gcgfuller@verizon.net

FULLER, Jan (SwVa) P.O. Box 9711, Roanoke VA 24020 B Oakland CA 8/6/1956 d James Wayne Fuller & Frances Marion Anderson. BA Hollins Coll 1978; MDiv Ya Berk 1982; DMin Wesley TS 1999. D 2/21/2010 Bp A(rthur) Heath Light P 10/7/2010 Bp Frank Neff Powell. c 1. jfuller@hollins.edu

FULLER, John Paul (Los) 940 Ivywood Dr, Oxnard CA 93030 B El Reno OK 8/8/1929 s Joseph Guy Fuller & Irma Louise. Oklahoma St U 1948; BS USNA 1952; MDiv CDSP 1961. D 9/7/1961 P 3/1/1962 Bp Francis E I Bloy. m 2/11/1994 Jarrell Lynn Hyden c 4. Asst S Columba's Par Camarillo CA 1995-2002; Peace & Justice Com Dio Los Angeles Los Angeles CA 1982-1991; Evang Cmsn Dio Los Angeles Los Angeles CA 1978-1981; Hunger T/F Dio Los Angeles Los Angeles CA 1978-1981; Hisp Cmsn Dio Los Angeles Los Angeles CA 1976-1979; Dio Los Angeles Los Angeles CA 1974-1991; R All SS Epis Ch Oxnard CA 1971-1991; Dn, San Luis Obispo Convoc Dio El Camino Real Monterey CA 1968-1970; R S Steph's Epis Ch San Luis Obispo

CA 1964-1971; Cur All SS-By-The-Sea Par Santa Barbara CA 1961-1963. Auth, "Var arts," *LivCh*, LivCh Fndt. frjonoxnrd@aol.com

FULLER, Lynnette Burley (NJ) 8 Sargent Street, #4, Nutley NJ 07110 B Detroit MI 1/26/1945 d John Wilfred Burley & Edith Jeanne. BA Chatham Coll 1966; MDiv GTS 1980; STM NYTS 1983. D 6/11/1980 P 2/1/1982 Bp Albert Wiencke Van Duzer. m 11/30/1985 Frederick H Fuller c 2. S Mary's Epis Ch Rockport MA 2001; Dio Chicago Chicago IL 1992-2000; S Jn's Ch Fords NJ 1983-1986; Pstr Affiliate S Bern's Ch Bernardsville NJ 1983; Trin Epis Ch Cranford NJ 1981-1982. lynnettefuller@gmail.com

FULLER, Margaret Jane Haas (Nev) 2675 Mineral Dr, Ely NV 89301 **P Chr Ch Pioche NV 2008-** B Park Rapids MN 1/29/1947 d Rudolph Kenneth Haas & Jean Ellen. BS Muhlenberg Coll 1969; MPA Angelo St U 1988; MS Texas Tech U 1992; MDiv Epis TS of The SW 2006. D 10/7/2005 P 7/29/2006 Bp Katharine Jefferts Schori. m 8/7/1970 Phillip Fuller c 1. P S Mary's Ch Winnemucca NV 2006-2007. Intl Conf of Police Chapl 2009; Natl Sheriffs' Assoc -Chapl Com 2009; White Pine Mnstrl Assoc, Ely NV 2009. pegfuller@yahoo.com

FULLER IV, Paul Hamilton (WNC) 205 Waterford Dr, Mills River NC 28759 **Vic Ch of the Advoc Asheville NC 2008-** B Deland FL 2/3/1947 s Paul Hamilton Fuller & Julia. BS Florida St U 1969; MEd Stetson U 1975; PhD U Of Florida 1978; MDiv STUSo 1986. D 6/8/1986 Bp Frank Stanley Cerveny P 12/1/1986 Bp Furman Stough. m 4/25/1981 Lynne Pierce c 1. R Emm Epis Ch Bristol VA 1999-2007; S Mk's Epis Ch Jacksonville FL 1995-1999; S Paul's Epis Ch Wilmington NC 1989-1995; Asst S Andr's Epis Ch Tampa FL 1987-1989; Cur Ch Of The H Comf Montgomery AL 1986-1987. Auth, "Parent Participation In The Sch System Its Relatns To"; Auth, "Parent Self-Concepts & Internal-External Locus Of Control". Ord Of S Lk, Ord S Mary. hamfuller@aol.com

FULLER, Perry Thomas (SeFla) 2012 SW 36th Ave, Delray Beach FL 33445 **Int H Sacr Pembroke Pines FL 2008-** B Scranton PA 8/30/1935 s Perry Fuller & Hannah. BA Maryville Coll 1957; MDiv PrTS 1960; DMin CRDS 1984. D 7/11/2004 Bp Leopold Frade P 1/23/2005 Bp James Hamilton Ottley. m 2/4/1961 Pamela Kittinger c 2. Int H Trin Epis Ch W Palm Bch FL 2007-2008; Int S Matt the Apos Epis Ch Miami FL 2005-2006. stbenedict711@aol.com

FULLER SR, Steven George (Vt) 10 South St # 5101, Bellows Falls VT 05101 **P Assoc Imm Ch Bellows Falls VT 2003-** B Windsor VT 9/8/1959 s George Ellsworth Fuller & Sally Ann. D 11/19/2002 P 6/7/2003 Bp Thomas C Ely. m 7/21/1979 Jean Ann Parrott c 2.

FULLMER, Janet M (EO) 1700 Esther Way, The Dalles OR 97058 **R S Pauls Epis Ch The Dalles OR 2008-** B Canton OH 10/12/1951 BA OH SU 1973; JD Franklin Pierce Law Cntr 1984; MDiv CDSP 2006. D 6/10/2006 P 12/9/2006 Bp Robert John O'Neill. m 11/18/1972 Ronald Fullmer. Asst The Ch Of The Ascen Denver CO 2007-2008. janetfullmer@msn.com

FULTON JR, Charles Britton (Fla) 1580 Murdock Rd, Marietta GA 30062 **P-in-c S Jude's Ch Marietta GA 2007-** B West Palm Beach FL 4/30/1938 s Charles Britton Fulton & Imogene. BS Stetson U 1960; MDiv Ya Berk 1964; ThD Intl Sem 1985. D 6/19/1964 Bp William Loftin Hargrave P 12/21/1964 Bp Henry I Louttit. m 6/15/1974 Judith Brassell DeBolt c 3. Acts 29 Mnstrs Atlanta GA 1993-2000; R S Ptr's Ch Jacksonville FL 1987-1993; R Ch Of The H Sprt Osprey FL 1981-1987; Assoc S Wlfd's Epis Ch Sarasota FL 1978-1980; Assoc S Mary's Ch Wayne PA 1975-1976; Asst Hdmstr Chap Of S Andr Boca Raton FL 1973-1974; R S Andr's Epis Ch Ft Pierce FL 1969-1973; Vic S Mary's Epis Ch Palmetto FL 1966-1969; Cur S Bon Ch Sarasota FL 1964-1966. Auth, "Reflections On The Run". Omicron Delta Kappa; Scabbard And Blade; Sigma Nu. charlesfulton@gmail.net

FULTON III, Charles Newell (NY) 815 2nd Ave, New York NY 10017 B Memphis TN 10/25/1942 s Charles Newell Fulton & Ellenor Christine. BA Auburn U 1965; STB GTS 1968. D 6/16/1968 Bp John Vander Horst P 5/24/1969 Bp William Evan Sanders. m 6/12/1965 Donna Smith c 2. Exec Dir Mssn Fund Epis Ch Cntr New York NY 2008-2009; Dir of Cong Dev Epis Ch Cntr New York NY 2001-2008; Pres ECBF Richmond VA 1987-2008; VP Epis Ch Cntr New York NY 1987-1989; R S Paul's Ch Franklin TN 1972-1987; Cur S Geo's Ch Nashville TN 1968-1969. Auth, "Truth and Hope"; Auth, "Ch Sites & Buildings," *Process Guide for Cong*; Auth, "The Ch for Common Pryr," *The Ch for Common Pryr*; Auth, "Ch for Common Pryr," *Video*. cnfulton3@gmail.com

FULTON, J(ohn) (EC) 307 N Main St, Farmville NC 27828 **long term supply P Trin Ch Scotland Neck NC 2007-; P-in-c Emm Ch Farmville NC 2002-** B Canton OH 5/25/1937 s John T Fulton & Margaret. BS U Of Akron 1972; MDiv VTS 1972. D 5/25/1972 Bp John Harris Burt P 12/1/1972 Bp Furman Stough. c 2. S Thos' Epis Ch Bath NC 1988-1999; R Ch Of The H Fam Chap Hill NC 1980-1988; Assoc Chr Ch Grosse Pointe Grosse Pointe Farms MI 1976-1980; Assoc Ch Of The Nativ Epis Huntsville AL 1975-1976. Auth, "A Short Hist Of S Thos Epis Ch Bath Nc". jgfulton2003@yahoo.com

FULTON, Nancy Jane (WMich) 807 South University, Mt Pleasant MI 48858 **D S Jn's Ch Mt Pleasant MI 2007-** B Escanaba MI 11/19/1948 d Robert Earl Casey & Louise Janet. AA Bay De Noc Cmnty Coll 1969; BA Cntrl Michigan U 1971; MA Cntrl Michigan U 1973. D 9/27/1997 Bp Edward Lewis Lee Jr. m 7/13/1974 Henry Levan Fulton c 1. D S Jn's Epis Ch Alma MI 2005-2006; D S Jn's Ch Mt Pleasant MI 1997-2005. Auth, "Serving the Differently Abled," *Diakoneo*, NAAD, 2006; Auth, "20 columns on Rel Page," *The Morning Sun*, Nwspr Mt. Pleasant, MI, 2006; Auth, "Decorating the Easter Tree," *Preaching Through H Days and Holidays: Sermons*, Morehouse, 2003; Auth, "Journey: Confession and Supplication," *Race and Pryr*, Morehouse, 2003; Auth, "Reflections," *Diakoneo*, No Amer Associaton for the Diac, 2001; Auth, "For Those Who are Abused," *Wmn Uncommon Prayers*, Morehouse Pub, 2000. DOK 1994; NAAD 1995. nfulton@deepthought.org

FULTON, Norman Hamilton (NY) Macaulay Road, Rd #2, Katonah NY 10536 B Tarrytown NY 4/13/1941 s Norman H Fulton & Dorothy. BS SUNY 1987; MA NYTS 1991. D 5/30/1992 Bp Richard Frank Grein. m 10/12/1963 Leslie Ann Pepper c 2.

FULTON, Sharline Alahverde (Pa) 213 Rex Ave, Philadelphia PA 19118 B Ardmore PA 1/8/1934 d Evany J Alahverde & Rose Louise. BA Villanova U 1977; MDiv Luth TS 1982; MA Creighton U 2002. D 6/1/1982 P 6/1/1983 Bp Lyman Cunningham Ogilby. c 2. Ch Of S Mart-In-The-Fields Philadelphia PA 1997; R S Andr's Ch Yardley PA 1990-1997; Int Ch Of The Redeem Springfield PA 1989-1990; Int S Ptr's Ch Philadelphia PA 1987-1989; Ch Of S Asaph Bala Cynwyd PA 1984-1985; Asst Ch Of S Mart-In-The-Fields Philadelphia PA 1982-1984. sharline213@gmail.com

FULTON, William Riggs (Oly) PO Box 12126, Seattle WA 98102 **Vic S Antony Of Egypt Silverdale WA 2008-** B Wichita KS 9/29/1953 s William Skinner Fulton & Jean Margaret. BA Evergreen St Coll 1977; MDiv STUSo 1995. D 6/26/1995 P 1/8/1996 Bp William Edward Smalley. m 7/22/1984 Kathryn Ann Smith c 2. Vic S Andr's Epis Ch Florence OR 1999-2008; R Gr Epis Ch Winfield KS 1995-1999; R Trin Ch Arkansas City KS 1995-1999. billfulton2001@yahoo.com

FUNK, Delmar Gerald (Neb) 3668 - 18th, Columbus NE 68601 B Wichita KS 9/12/1930 s Delmar B Jack Funk & Dorothy Mae. BFA U of Kansas 1959; MDiv Nash 1982. D 6/18/1982 Bp Jackson Earle Gilliam P 12/1/1982 Bp James Daniel Warner. m 6/9/1956 Ruth Boyd c 2. Chr Ch Cntrl City NE 1988-2000; P-in-c S Jn's Ch Albion Columbus NE 1987-1989; P-in-c S Jn's Epis Ch Geff IL 1987-1989; R Gr Ch Par -Epis Columbus NE 1985-2000; Vic Chr Ch Sidney NE 1982-1985; Vic Ch Of The Gd Shpd Bridgeport NE 1982-1985. jayhawker59@verizon.net

FUNK, Jeffrey Lawrence (Be) 46 S Laurel St, Hazleton PA 18201 **R S Jas' Ch Drifton PA 2003-; R S Ptr's Epis Ch Hazleton PA 2003-** B Rockville Centre NY 8/29/1955 s Arthur Andrew Funk & Elizabeth Christine. SUNY 1974; Cert Geo Mercer Jr. Memi TS 1987; BA Adel 1997; SWTS 2000. D 12/15/1986 Bp Robert Campbell Witcher Sr P 9/29/2001 Bp Paul Victor Marshall. R S Mary's Epis Ch Reading PA 2001-2002; S Geo's Ch Hempstead NY 1987-1999. EAM 2005-2008; Episcopalians Untd 1989-1992; Hempstead Nrsry Co-op - Advsry Bd 1991-1999; Long Island D's Gld 1989-2001; NAAD 1989-2001. fatherfunk@verzon.net

FUNK, Nicholas J (RG) 5125 Rock House Rd, Las Cruces NM 88011 **Area Dn Dio The Rio Grande Albuquerque NM 2011-; R S Jas' Epis Ch Mesilla Pk NM 2008-** B St Petersburg FL 2/13/1965 s Floyd Donald Funk & Maxine Irene. BA U So 1987; MDiv STUSo 2005; DMin St Petersburg TS 2009. D 6/18/2005 P 12/17/2005 Bp John Bailey Lipscomb. m 3/25/2001 Laura Funk. P-in-c S Alb's Epis Ch St Pete Bch FL 2006-2007; Assoc R S Jn's Ch Naples FL 2005. nick_funk@alumni.sewanee.edu

FUNK, Peter Van Keuren (NJ) 4825 Province Line Rd, Princeton NJ 08540 **D Trin Ch Princeton NJ 1998-** B Glenridge NJ 5/11/1921 s Wilfred John Funk & Eleanor Macneal. BA Pr 1942. D 10/31/1998 Bp Joe Morris Doss. m 11/25/1942 Mary Estelle Pettit. Auth, "Var arts, 15 Books," *6 Audio Books*; Auth, "My Six Loves: Love and Consequences. Fiction On Story Of Six Orphans," *Film-My Six Loves*; Auth, "It Pays To Enrich Your Word Power, 4 books on words," *Rdr'S Dig*. Tertiary Of The Soc Of S Fran. Distinquisleed Alum Awd Montclair Kimberley Acad 1995; Min Gnrl'S Awd Soc Of St Fran 1985. pvkfunk@aol.com

FUNKHOUSER, David Franklin (Pa) 456 66th St, Oakland CA 94609 B New Market VA 8/1/1945 s Roscoe Garland Funkhouser & Carrie Eleanor. BS Heidelberg Coll 1967; MDiv VTS 1972. D 5/27/1972 P 5/18/1973 Bp Robert Bruce Hall. Ch Of S Jn The Evang Philadelphia PA 1996-2003; P-in-c S Giles Ch Upper Darby PA 1994-1996; The White Mtn Sch Littleton NH 1976-1977; Asst S Dunst's McLean VA 1972-1975. davidfunk801@gmail.com

FUNSTON, A Patrick K (Kan) 4120 Clinton Pkwy, Lawrence KS 66047 **Chapl Bp Seabury Acad Lawr KS 2011-** B San Diego CA 6/11/1983 s C Eric Funston & Evelyn W. BBA U of Missouri 2007; MDiv VTS 2011. D 6/11/2011 Bp Dean Elliott Wolfe. m 8/22/2009 Michael Johanna Knoll. apfunston@gmail.com

FUNSTON, C Eric (O) St. Paul's Episcopal Church, 317 E. Liberty Street, Medina OH 44256 **Trst Dio Ohio Cleveland OH 2009-; R S Paul's Epis Ch Medina OH 2003-** B Las Vegas NV 9/29/1952 s Raymond York Funston &

Betty Jean. BA U CA at San Diego 1974; MBA U of Nevada at Las Vegas 1979; JD California Wstrn Sch of Law 1983; Cert CDSP 1991; DMin SWTS 1998. D 5/8/1990 P 6/21/1991 Bp Stewart Clark Zabriskie. m 4/12/1980 Evelyn W Walther c 2. Dio Kansas Topeka KS 2002; Dio Kansas Topeka KS 2002; Bdgt Com Dio Kansas Topeka KS 1994-1998; Const & Cn Dio Kansas Topeka KS 1993-2003; R S Fran Of Assisi Stilwell KS 1993-2003; Assoc R Chr Ch Las Vegas NV 1991-1993; Dio Nevada Las Vegas NV 1991-1993; Asst Chncllr Dio Nevada Las Vegas NV 1991-1993; D Ch Of The Resurr Pleasant Hill CA 1990-1991; Asst Chncllr Dio Nevada Las Vegas NV 1989-1993; Chncllr Dio Nevada Las Vegas NV 1986-1990; Asst Chncllr Dio Nevada Las Vegas NV 1983-1986. Auth, "One Hour of the Millenium," *Songlines*, 1996; Auth, "Mnstry to the Legal Profession: A Suggested Co-dependency Model," *Journ of Pstr Care*, 1991; Auth, "Made Out of Whole Cloth: A Const Analysis of the Cler Malpractice Concept"," *California Wstrn Law Revs*, 1983. ericfunston@mac.com

FURGERSON, John Arthur (SwVa) 11 Whitmore St, Lexington VA 24450 **Dep GC Dio SW Virginia Roanoke VA 1988-; Alt Dep GC Dio SW Virginia Roanoke VA 1985-** B Louisville KY 1/11/1931 s William Buford Furgerson & Dorothy Gertrude. BS USNA 1953; BS Untd States Naval Postgraduate Sch 1965; MDiv VTS 1976. D 5/22/1976 Bp John Alfred Baden P 2/13/1977 Bp William Henry Marmion. m 6/20/1953 Alice C Crispin c 5. Com Elctns Dio SW Virginia Roanoke VA 1995-1996; Stndg Com Dio SW Virginia Roanoke VA 1990-1993; S Jn's Epis Ch Glasgow VA 1988-1996; Dn Dio SW Virginia Roanoke VA 1986-1988; R Chr Epis Ch Buena Vista VA 1981-1988; Exec Bd Dio SW Virginia Roanoke VA 1977-1980; Asst R R E Lee Memi Ch (Epis) Lexington VA 1976-1981. johnandalice@rockbridge.net

FURLOW III, Charles Marshall (WNC) 3 Creekside Court Park Avenue, Asheville NC 28803 **Died 7/30/2011** B San Francisco CA 1/4/1928 s RAdm Charles Marvin Furlow & Helen Cameron. BS USNA 1952; STB Ya Berk 1959; STM Ya Berk 1965. D 6/11/1959 P 5/1/1960 Bp Thomas N Carruthers. c 2.

FURLOW, Mark D (Lex) 211 Wilderness Cove Ln, Georgetown KY 40324 B Tacoma Park MD 9/19/1978 s Terrance G Furlow & Karen Baker. BA Cntr Coll 2001; MDiv GTS 2006. D 6/10/2006 Bp Stacy F Sauls P 2/3/2007 Bp Peter James Lee. m 12/2/2006 Siobhan Byrns. R Ch Of The H Trin Georgetown KY 2008-2010; Cler Res Chr Ch Alexandria VA 2006-2008. markfurlow@mac.com

FURMAN, James Edmund (Los) 13131 Moorpark St Apt 412, Sherman Oaks CA 91423 B Long Beach CA 5/30/1947 s Alfred C Furman & Elizabeth Lynch. BA Claremont Coll 1969; MA Stan 1970; MDiv CDSP 1973. D 6/23/1973 Bp C Kilmer Myers P 4/1/1974 Bp Robert C Rusack. R S Nich Par Encino CA 1995-2007; R S Ptr's Ch Honolulu HI 1986-1995; S Andr's Ch La Mesa CA 1985-1986; R Sts Ptr And Paul Epis Ch El Centro CA 1980-1985; Assoc Chr Ch Coronado CA 1979-1980; Asst S Mary's Epis Ch Los Angeles CA 1977-1979; Asst S Mk's Par Glendale CA 1973-1977. Auth, "Sand & Stars: A Possibility Bk for CE"; Auth, *Coptic Ch Revs*; Auth, *Homegrown*; Auth, *Living Ch*. Chapl, Can Soc of Sthrn California; CBS; Pres, Inter-Angl Study Prog.

FURNISS III, Robert Hosmer (Minn) 2132 Cameron Dr, Woodbury MN 55125 **St Croix Chapl Assn Stillwater MN 2007-** B Chicago IL 8/26/1958 s Robert Hosmer Furniss & Margaret. BA Ripon Coll Ripon WI 1980; MDiv TS 1988; DMin Luther TS 2004. D 6/18/1988 Bp Frank Tracy Griswold III P 1/6/1989 Bp Robert Marshall Anderson. m 11/5/1983 Jean Marie Diehl c 3. Dio Minnesota Minneapolis MN 2000-2003; Chr Ch S Paul MN 1998-2006; R S Lk's Ch Willmar MN 1991-1998; P-in-c Ch Of The Gd Samar Sauk Cntr MN 1991-1993; Dio Minnesota Minneapolis MN 1991-1992; Asst to R Ch Of The Epiph Epis Plymouth MN 1988-1991. bobfurniss@comcast.net

FURRER, Thomas (Ct) 5 Trout Drive, Granby CT 06035 **R Trin Ch Tariffville CT 2000-** B Ravenna OH 8/10/1950 s George Vincent Furrer & Katherine. BA Wesl 1981; MDiv Ya Berk 1986. D 6/14/1986 Bp Arthur Edward Walmsley P 12/1/1986 Bp William Bradford Hastings. m 10/16/1976 Maryjane Hanson c 3. R S Paul's Epis Ch Shelton CT 1988-2000; Cur Trin Ch Tariffville CT 1986-1988. Auth, "Living Word of The Living God: A Beginner's Guide To Reaing and Understanding The Bible," *Bk*, Winged Lion Press, 2011. Bro of S Andr Bd, Pres Habitat for Humani 1987-2007. Cn - St Mich's Cathd Dio Kaduna, Nigeria 2004; Cn - St Andr's Cathd Dio W. Tanganyika, Tanzania 2002. iamtmfurrer0808@aol.com

FUSELIER, Donald Paul (ECR) 1017 Alameda St, Monterey CA 93940 B Fresno CA 3/26/1946 s Paul Nixon Fuselier & Irene Florence. BA Golden Gate U 1982; BA Sch for Deacons 1984; MPA Golden Gate U 1986. D 6/3/1996 Bp Richard Lester Shimpfky. m 10/29/1990 Margo L Bush c 3. ravchfdon@aol.com

FUSSELL, Stacey Marie (NwPa) 462 Congress St, Bradford PA 16701 **Chair - Exam Chapl Dio NW Pennsylvania Erie PA 2011-; Dioc Strategic Plnng Com Dio NW Pennsylvania Erie PA 2011-; R Ch Of The Ascen Bradford PA 2010-; Dn - NE Dnry Dio NW Pennsylvania Erie PA 2010-** B Jacksonville FL 1/26/1965 d William Rupert Fussell & Joan Marie. AA Houston Cmnty Coll 1993; BA U of St. Thos 1995; MDiv VTS 1998. D 6/20/1998 Bp Claude Edward Payne P 6/20/1999 Bp Leopoldo Jesus Alard. c 2. Exec Bd Dio Texas Houston TX 2008-2009; Vic St. Cathr Of Sienna Missouri City TX 2001-2010; Wrld Mssn Bd Dio Texas Houston TX 1998-2002; Assoc Trin Epis Ch Baytown TX 1998-2001. DOK 1990; VTS Mssy Soc 1995-1998. Harris Awd for Acad Brilliance and Ldrshp VTS Alexandria VA 1998; Tachau Biblic Lang Prize VTS Alexandria VA 1997. motherstacey@gmail.com

G

GABB, James Neil (Neb) 510 S 205th St, Elkhorn NE 68022 **Chapl to the Ret Cler & Families Dio Nebraska Omaha NE 2009-; Int S Jas' Epis Ch Fremont NE 2009-** B Marshall MO 7/30/1943 s James Martin Gabb & Eugenia Kelly. BS U of Missouri 1966; MA U of Missouri 1968; MDiv Phillips TS 1986; CAS SWTS 1986. D 6/14/1986 Bp William Jackson Cox P 2/27/1987 Bp James Daniel Warner. m 5/30/1973 Betsy Shofstall c 2. Chapl to the Ret Cler & Families Dio Nebraska Omaha NE 2009-2010; Pres of the Stndg Com Dio Nebraska Omaha NE 2005-2010; R S Aug's Epis Ch Elkhorn NE 2000-2009; Int Ch Of The H Sprt Bellevue NE 1993-1994; R S Lk's Ch Plattsmouth NE 1992-1993; Asst to Dn Trin Cathd Omaha NE 1988-1991; Cur/Asst Ch Of The H Trin Lincoln NE 1986-1988; Vic Trin Memi Epis Ch Crete NE 1986-1988. fr.jayg@gmail.com

GABEL, Mark Francis (CFla) 5139 Marbella Isle Dr, Orlando FL 32837 B Syracuse NY 9/9/1953 D 12/13/2003 Bp John Wadsworth Howe. m 8/19/1995 Charmaine Kreider. cgabel@cfl.rr.com

GABLE, David Lee (Nwk) 24 Harmony Dr, Pt Jefferson Station NY 11776 B Anniston AL 3/18/1943 s Carl Franklin Gable & Lena Mae. BA Jacksonville St U 1965; MS U of Mississippi 1967; MA/PhD U of Memphis 1977; MDiv VTS 1980. D 6/22/1980 Bp William F Gates Jr P 5/4/1981 Bp William Evan Sanders. R Gr Epis Ch Rutherford NJ 2002-2008; Int S Paul's Epis Ch Chatham NJ 2000-2002; Int Chr Ch Epis Ridley Pk PA 1999-2000; Int Emm Epis Ch Stamford CT 1997-1999; Int S Matt's Epis Ch Louisville KY 1996-1997; Int Ch Of The Gd Shpd S Louis MO 1995-1996; R S Andr's Epis Ch Edwardsville IL 1991-1995; R Chr Ch - Epis Chattanooga TN 1987-1990; R S Andr's Ch Harriman TN 1981-1987; D St Jas Epis Ch at Knoxville Knoxville TN 1980-1981. stamman2@aol.com

GABLE, Stephen Louis (Ind) 1045 E Sassafras Cir, Bloomington IN 47408 B Yonkers NY 2/8/1942 s Harry Louis Gable & Mildred Louise. BA Butler U 1964; MDiv Epis TS of The SW 1967; MA U of St. Thos 1994. D 6/24/1967 P 12/26/1967 Bp John P Craine. m Marcia Brown Bryan c 1. P-in-c Trin Ch Connersville IN 1973-1975; All SS Ch Seymour IN 1967-1969. Soc of Cert Property & Casualty Underwriters. stephen.l.gable@emcins.com

GADDY, Anna Lee (RG) No address on file. B Canyon TX 4/22/1925 d Burt Newlin & Ora Etta. W Texas A&M U. D 2/3/1986 P 8/1/1986 Bp Richard Mitchell Trelease Jr. m 6/13/1975 Randolph Gaddy.

GADSDEN, Carol D (Mass) 403 S 13th St, Philadelphia PA 19147 B Syracuse NY 2/24/1951 d Gordon Sergeant Dinger & Jean Marie. Barnard Coll of Col; BA Keuka Coll 1972; MA Col 1975; EdM Col 1976; MDiv GTS 1985; Radcliffe Seminars Cambridge MA 1997. D 6/8/1985 Bp Paul Moore Jr P 1/1/1986 Bp James Stuart Wetmore. m 10/21/2011 Linda A March c 2. Int S Jn's Ch Bala Cynwyd PA 2008; P-in-c S Lk's And S Marg's Ch Allston MA 2002; Int S Jn's Epis Ch Franklin MA 1992-1995; Vic S Nich-by-the-Sea Hull MA 1990-1992; Epis Soc Serv Ansonia CT 1989; Asst R S Fran Ch Stamford CT 1985-1989. CAROLGADSDEN@GMAIL.COM

GAEDE, Lee A (Chi) 342 Custer Ave. Apt. 2, Evanston IL 60202 **Deacons' Coun Dio Chicago Chicago IL 2011-; D S Giles' Ch Northbrook IL 2011-; 3rd Cler Alt, GC Dio Chicago Chicago IL 2010-; Sprtl Dir, Happ Dio Chicago Chicago IL 2001-** B Waukegan IL 5/23/1947 d Leon Boyd Logsdon & Lorraine. BA Concordia Tchr Coll River Forest IL 1969; JD Washington U 1984; Chicago Deacons Sch 1999. D 2/5/2000 Bp William Dailey Persell. m 6/7/1969 Bruce John Gaede c 1. Millenium Dvlpmt Goals T/F Dio Chicago Chicago IL 2005-2011; COM Dio Chicago Chicago IL 2002-2008; D S Mk's Ch Evanston IL 2000-2010; Deacons' Coun Dio Chicago Chicago IL 2000-2003. Assoc of the CSM 1981; EPF 1995; Epis Publ Plcy Ntwk 1998. The Pro Bono Awd The Missouri Bar Assn 1992. leegaede@aol.com

GAEDE, Sarah Harrell (Ala) 830 Willingham Rd, Florence AL 35630 B Raleigh NC 3/13/1951 d Miller Harrell Peterson & Suzanne. BA Eckerd Coll 1972; MDiv STUSo 1994; DMin SWTS 2005. D 7/25/1995 Bp Henry Irving Louttit P 3/2/1996 Bp John Wadsworth Howe. m 12/5/1981 Henry Frazer Gaede c 1. R S Barth's Epis Ch Florence AL 2003-2009; Supply Chr The King Epis Ch Orlando FL 2002-2003; Cn Cathd Ch Of S Lk Orlando FL 1998-2001; Cur S Mich's Ch Orlando FL 1995-1996. "The Princess in the Pulpit: Preaching Like a Girl," DMin. thesis, 2005. sarahgaede@aol.com

GAESTEL, Robert J (Los) 1100 Avenue 64, Pasadena CA 91105 **Vic Ch Of The Ang Pasadena CA 1983-** B Neptune NJ 6/9/1953 s Herbert Joseph

Gaestel & Helen Elizabeth. BA Chapman U 1975; MDiv CDSP 1979. D 6/23/1979 P 1/12/1980 Bp Robert C Rusack. m 7/9/1977 Tracy Allyn Hurtt c 2. Assoc R S Geo's Par La Can CA 1980-1983; Cur S Mich and All Ang Epis Ch Studio City CA 1979-1980. frbob@lafn.org

GAETZ JR, Theodore Edward (WMass) 419 Southwick Road - Stoney Hill L54, Westfield MA 01085 **Died 10/31/2009** B Schenectady NY 1/22/1929 s Theodore Edward Gaetz & Effie Alma. BS Bos 1951; MDiv PDS 1955. D 6/5/1955 Bp William A Lawrence P 5/25/1956 Bp Malcolm E Peabody. c 4.

GAFFORD, Donna Elizabeth Goodman (At) Po Box 807, Thomaston GA 30286 B Meridian MS 2/21/1957 d William David Goodman & Mildred Elizabeth. BA Valparaiso U 1980; MDiv SWTS 1984. D 6/25/1984 Bp Edward Witker Jones P 4/1/1985 Bp William Evan Sanders. m 11/25/1977 Alexander Thomas Gafford. Mssnr Trin Epis Ch Columbus GA 2003; S Thos Of Cbury Thomaston GA 2000-2003; Trin Epis Ch Columbus GA 1995-1998; Assoc P Trin Ch Epis Pass Chr MS 1993-1994; Chr Ch Cathd Nashville TN 1988; S Dav's Epis Ch Nashville TN 1984-1987.

GAFFORD, Happy Lawton (CFla) 2410 Ridgeside Rd, Apopka FL 32712 B Orlando FL 12/29/1942 d Joseph Benjamin Lawton & Madalyne Beryl. BA Brenau U 1964; Inst for Chr Stds 1990; Diac Trng Sch 1992; CPE 1994; DOCC Trng 1995; CPE 1997. D 11/7/1992 Bp John Wadsworth Howe. m 6/11/1966 George Louis Gafford c 2. D S Mich's Ch Orlando FL 2002-2004; Min of Pstrl Care S Mich's Ch Orlando FL 1997-2002; Gr Ch Stafford Sprg CT 1995-1997; D's Coun Dio Cntrl Florida Orlando FL 1993-1994; S Mich's Ch Orlando FL 1993-1994; Mentor Dio Cntrl Florida Orlando FL 1988-1992. NAAD.

GAFNEY, Wilda Clydette (Pa) 7301 Germantown Ave, Philadelphia PA 19119 B South Hill VA 1/23/1966 d Willie Clyde Gafney & Louvenia Magee. BA Earlham Coll Richmond IN 1987; MDiv How DS 1997; PhD Duke Durham NC 2006. D 6/9/2007 Bp Charles Ellsworth Bennison Jr P 12/15/2007 Bp Franklin Delton Turner. D Trin Epis Ch Ambler PA 2007. wgafney@itsp.edu

GAGE, Bartlett Wright (Ct) 26 Edmond St, Darien CT 06820 **Asst S Andr's Ch Stamford CT 2008-** B Geneva IL 8/3/1935 s Nevin Isaac Gage & Helen Margaret. BA Ya 1957; BD Yale DS 1961; MA U Chi 1968. D 6/10/1989 Bp Arthur Edward Walmsley P 6/1/1990 Bp Clarence Nicholas Coleridge. m 6/2/1961 Faye Cauley c 2. Assoc R S Jn's Ch Stamford CT 1990-2007; Pstr Intern S Mk's Ch New Canaan CT 1989-1990. "Faith, Hope and Stories," *Ben's Press*, Hound of Heaven Pub, 1999; "Faith and More Stories," *Ben's Press*, Hound of Heaven Pub, 1998; "Faith and Stories," *Ben's Press*, Hound of Heaven Pub, 1996. frgage@Yahoo.com

GAHAGAN, Susan Elisabeth (Ga) 1802 Abercorn St, Savannah GA 31401 **D S Paul's Ch Savannah GA 2009-** B Pottsville PA 9/29/1947 d Oscar Henry Welde & Nedra Mae. BSW U of Sthrn Indiana 1999. D 10/28/2009 Bp Henry Irving Louttit. c 2. sgahagan@bellsouth.net

GAHAN III, W(illiam) Patrick (WTex) Saint Stephen's Church, 6000-A FM 3237, Wimberley TX 78676 **S Steph's Epis Ch Wimberley TX 2005-** B Birmingham AL 10/2/1954 s William Patrick Gahan & Lillian Marie. Trin U San Antonio TX; U of Alabama; BS U of Mary Hardin-Baylor 1981; U of Tennessee 1987; MDiv Epis TS of The SW 1994; DMin SWTS 2001. D 4/15/1988 Bp Robert Oran Miller P 10/28/1991 Bp Maurice Manuel Benitez. m 11/26/1975 Marian Kay McLane c 3. S Jas' Ch Indn Hd MD 2001; R S Steph's Ch Beaumont TX 1996-2001; Spck/Usa Sewanee TN 1995-1996; S Steph's Epis Sch Austin TX 1992-1995; Int Chr Epis Ch Tyler TX 1990. Auth, "Foundations of Discipleship," *Bk*, Lulu, 2010; Auth, "Daring to be a Different Ch," *LivCh*, 2007; Auth, "The Seeds of My Faith," *LivCh*, 1997; Auth, "Envisioning a Great Ch Sch," *NAES*, 1996; Auth, "Namelessness and Facelessness: Opportunities for Evil," *New Oxford Revs*, 1994; Auth, "The Secret of Abundant Living," *New Cov*, 1984. Who's Who in Amer Educ 1992; Who's Who So and SW 1988; Stokely Fell 1987. wpgahan@ststeve.org

GAHLER, Robert Edward (NY) 67 Woodmere Rd, Stamford CT 06905 **Trin S Paul's Epis New Rochelle NY 2009-** B Waseca MN 1/15/1948 s James Edward Gahler & Henrietta Mary. BA NWU 1978; MDiv EDS 1982. D 10/31/1982 P 6/1/1983 Bp George Nelson Hunt III. R Epis Ch of Chr the Healer Stamford CT 1986-2006; Asst Cathd Of S Jn Providence RI 1982-1986; Dio Rhode Island Providence RI 1982-1986. EUC, EPF, Assn Of Angl Of Mus. frgahler@optonline.net

GAILLARD, Ann Schwarberg (Alb) 142 Main St, Saranac Lake NY 12983 **The Ch of St Lk The Beloved Physcn Saranac Lake NY 2008-** B Whittier CA 5/26/1960 BA Stan 1982; MA Stan 1983; MDiv GTS 2005. D 6/4/2005 P 12/17/2005 Bp Charles Ellsworth Bennison Jr. m 7/9/1985 Lee Gaillard. Assoc R Chr Ch Media PA 2005-2007. info@stlukessaranaclake.org

GAILLARD IV, Samuel Porcher (SC) 1795 Huntington Dr, Charleston SC 29407 **Epis Ch of the Gd Shpd Charleston SC 2006-** B Charleston SC 3/9/1968 s Samuel Gaillard. BA Hampden-Sydney Coll 1990; MDiv TESM 2004. D 1/24/2004 P 7/24/2004 Bp Edward Lloyd Salmon Jr. m 9/9/1995 Tara Claire Gaillard c 2. Asst S Paul's Epis Ch Conway SC 2004-2006. frshay@bellsouth.net

GAINES, Mary Moore Thompson (Cal) 128 Beaumont Ave, San Francisco CA 94118 B Fort Worth TX 4/23/1931 d James Moore Thompson & Caroline Sherman. BA Vas 1979; MDiv CDSP 1989. D 6/3/1989 P 6/1/1990 Bp William Edwin Swing. m 8/16/1951 George Chilton Gaines c 6. S Jas Epis Ch San Francisco CA 1997-2003; Assoc R S Jas Epis Ch San Francisco CA 1991-1993; P S Jas Epis Ch San Francisco CA 1990-1991; D S Jas Epis Ch San Francisco CA 1989-1990. mmg@sonic.net

GAINES, Winifred B (NCal) 630 Wilhaggin Dr, Sacramento CA 95864 B Sacramento CA 9/13/1928 d Marshal Hale Fisher & Winifred Clare. BS U CA 1950; MDiv CDSP 1978; MA U of San Francisco 1982. D 5/1/1979 P 11/30/1980 Bp John Lester Thompson III. m 2/24/1951 Robert Gaines c 5. Cn Trin Cathd Sacramento CA 1989-2000. Assoc of the Trsfg 1980; Assn of Epis Chapl 1979-1989. Hon DD CDSP Berkeley CA 2000; Hon Cn Trin Cathd Sacramento CA 1984; Phi Beta Kappa U.C. Berkeley 1950. wbgaines@trinitycathedral.org

GAISER, Ted Joseph (Mass) 8 Glenmont Rd, Brighton MA 02135 B Bluffton IN 6/23/1961 s Noel Eugene Gaiser & Grace Bernice. BA Sthrn Connecticut St U 1986; MA Bos 1988; MBA Boston Coll 1994; PhD Boston Coll 2000. D 10/6/2001 Bp M(arvil) Thomas Shaw III. m 6/18/2004 Charles K Hornberger. D The Ch Of Our Redeem Lexington MA 2008-2011; D S Andr's Ch Framingham MA 2001-2004. "A Guide Conducting On-Line Resrch," 2009; "Conducting On-Line Focuse Groups," *The Sage Hand Bk of On-Line Resrch Methods*, 2008; Auth, "Conducting On-Line Focus Groups: A Methodological Discussion," *Soc Sci Computer Revs*, Sage Pub, Inc., 1997. NAAD 1998. Dissertation Fllshp Awd Boston Coll 1996; Fndr's Awd of Merit Soc Sci Computing Assn 1996; Who's Who in Amer Universities and Colleges Sthrn Connecticut St U 1986; hon Soc Mem Tau Pi Sigma 1985. tjgaiser@earthlink.net

GAITHER, Gayle Lee (Spok) 416 E Nelson Rd, Moses Lake WA 98837 **P S Mart's Ch Moses Lake WA 2008-; P S Mart's Ch Moses Lake WA 2007-** B Alamosa CO 5/1/1938 s Lyle Leland Gaither & Virginia Gail. Big Bend Cmnty Coll; Colorado St U 1956; Dioc Cmsn Theol Educ 2006. D 11/19/2006 P 6/9/2007 Bp James Edward Waggoner. m 7/26/1958 Mavis McCormack c 3. glmf58@qosi.net

GALAGAN, John Michael (EpisSanJ) 21105 Carriage Dr, Tehachapi CA 93561 B Milwaukee WI 10/5/1928 s Thomas H Trusty & Kathryn Jane. BA U Pac 1950; MDiv CDSP 1955. D 6/12/1955 P 12/1/1955 Bp Karl M Block. m 3/2/1957 Madeline Bergstrom c 4. S Judes In The Mountains Ch Tehachapi CA 1987-2000; R S Lk's Ch Bakersfield CA 1981-1984; R S Jas Ch Riverton WY 1975-1980; R S Barn Par McMinnville OR 1967-1975; Vic S Jas Epis Ch Tigard OR 1964-1967; Asst S Lk's Epis Ch Vancouver WA 1961-1964; Vic S Dunst's Epis Ch Grand Coulee WA 1958-1961; Vic S Mk's Ch Ritzville WA 1958-1961; Vic Trin Ch Gonzales CA 1956-1958; Vic S Mk's Epis Ch Santa Clara CA 1955-1957. frjohn7@yahoo.com

GALANTOWICZ, Deena McHenry (Fla) 49 Ocean Ct, Saint Augustine FL 32080 B Buffalo NY 8/5/1937 d Charles Eugene McHenry & Beatrice Ethelyn. BS Syr 1958; MDiv GTS 1980; STM GTS 1982. D 6/14/1980 P 12/19/1980 Bp John Shelby Spong. m 8/9/1958 Richard E Galantowicz c 2. Assoc R Trin Epis Ch St Aug FL 1993-2002; R S Steph's Epis Ch Bloomfield CT 1984-1990; Wooster Sch Danbury CT 1982-1984; Int S Lk's Epis Ch Montclair NJ 1982; Asst Min Chr Ch Glen Ridge NJ 1980-1981. Auth, "Sci Article". Ord Julian Of Nowich; Chapl Ord Of S Lk 1994. regdmg@bellsouth.net

GALBRAITH, James MacAlpine (Miss) 2196 Saint James Blvd, Gulfport MS 39507 B Concord NH 4/10/1936 s Hugh Malcolm Galbraith & Marjorie. BS U of Oklahoma 1958; MBA U of Oklahoma 1963; MDiv Nash 1977. D 6/24/1977 Bp Robert Elwin Terwilliger P 1/1/1978 Bp A Donald Davies. m 6/25/1960 Dorothy Daniels c 6. R S Andr's Epis Ch Las Cruces NM 1987-2002; R H Trin Ch Rockwall TX 1981-1986; R S Wm Laud Epis Ch Pittsburg TX 1979-1981; Cur S Dav's Ch Garland TX 1977-1978. OHC 1977. jimg04@bellsouth.net

GALBREATH, Janet Louise (CFla) 01236 Miller Blvd, Fruitland Park FL 34731 **D H Trin Epis Ch Fruitland Pk FL 1995-** B Sewanee TN 6/8/1951 d George Edward Dotsan & Sammie June. Inst for Chr Stds; Lake-Sumter Cmnty Coll. D 11/11/1995 Bp John Wadsworth Howe. m 1/4/1978 Donald Leonard Galbreath c 4.

GALE, John Carl (CPa) Po Box 633, Chambersburg PA 17201 **Died 6/16/2011** B Washington DC 5/31/1925 s John Carl Gale & Violet Lillian. BS U NC 1949; MDiv VTS 1966. D 6/21/1966 P 6/1/1967 Bp Harry Lee Doll. c 2.

GALEANO FRANCO, Gustavo (Hond) 23 Ave C 21 Calle Col Trejo, San Pedro Sula Honduras **Dio Honduras Miami FL 1998-** B 1/15/1970 m 7/5/2003 Keevyn Geraldine Gabourel-Hernandez c 3. reverendogaliano@hotmail.com

GALGANO, Hollis Holder (NY) 311 Huguenot St, New Rochelle NY 10801 **D Trin S Paul's Epis New Rochelle NY 2009-** B Rocky Ford CO 6/28/1955 d Frank S Holder & Greta Griffin. U of Dallas; BA Oral Roberts U 1977. D 5/2/2009 Bp Mark Sean Sisk. m 5/8/1982 Dennis Michael Galgano c 3. hgalgano@aol.com

GALGANOWICZ, Henry C (Pa) Po Box 17719, Philadelphia PA 19135 **R H Innoc S Paul's Ch Philadelphia PA 2001-** B Hamburg DE 12/8/1947 s Joseph Galganowicz & Nina. BA Ken 1969; MDiv Bex 1975. D 6/22/1975 Bp Robert Rae Spears Jr P 3/13/1976 Bp John Mc Gill Krumm. m 7/1/2006 Sandra Galganowicz c 2. Interfaith Off Dio Pennsylvania Philadelphia PA 2003-2006; St Gabr's Ch E Berlin CT 1999-2000; R The Par Of Emm Ch Weston CT 1988-1998; Vic S Paul's Ch Windham CT 1981-1988; Asst Calv Ch Pittsburgh PA 1979-1981; Asst S Alb's Epis Ch Of Bexley Columbus OH 1975-1978. hankcg@aol.com

GALICIA, Kathryn Kitchen (EpisSanJ) 3308 Swallow Dr, Modesto CA 95356 **Exam Chapl Epis Dio San Joaquin Modesto CA 2011-; Epis Dio San Joaquin Modesto CA 2009-; COM, Vice Chair Epis Dio San Joaquin Modesto CA 2008-; P-in-c S Fran' Epis Ch Turlock CA 2008-** B Buffalo NY 3/24/1952 d Denis Kitchen & Norma. AA Las Positas Coll 1992; BA Chapman U 2001; MDiv Mennonite Brethren Biblic Sem 2005. D 6/3/2006 Bp William Edwin Swing P 12/2/2006 Bp Marc Handley Andrus. m 10/6/1979 Alfonso Kitchen Galicia c 1. christgo@earthlink.net

G

GALIPEAU, Steven Arthur (Los) 8805 Azul Drive, West Hills CA 91304 B Summit NJ 11/10/1948 s Arthur Harmars Galipeau & Theresa Louise. BA Boston Coll 1970; MA U of Notre Dame 1972; MDiv CDSP 1977. D 6/18/1977 P 1/14/1979 Bp Robert C Rusack. m 4/22/1984 Linda Holmwood c 2. Assoc S Edm's Par San Marino CA 1978-1982; Vic Gr Epis Ch Glendora CA 1977-1978; Vic S Lk's Mssn Fontana CA 1977-1978. Auth, "Transforming Body & Soul: Therapeutic Wisdom In The Gospel Healing Stories," Fisher King Press, 2011; Auth, "The Journey Of Lk Skywalker: An Analysis Of Mod Myth And Symbol," Open Crt, 2001. C.G. Jung Inst Of Los Angeles 1993; California Assn Of Mar And Fam Therapists 1987; Intl Assn For Analytical Psychol 1993; Natl Assn For The Advancement Of Psychoanalysis 1993-2006. stevengalipeau@earthlink.net

✠ GALLAGHER, Rt Rev Carol Joy (NY) PO Box 95, Cape May Point NJ 08212 **All SS Ch Harrison NY 2009-; Asstg Bp of No Dakota Dio No Dakota Fargo ND 2008-** B San Diego CA 12/24/1955 d Donald K Theobald & Elizabeth Anne. BA Antioch Baltimore MD 1976; MDiv EDS 1989; ThM PrTS 1998; PhD U of Delaware Newark 2004. D 6/17/1989 P 5/12/1990 Bp A(lbert) Theodore Eastman Con 4/6/2002 for SVa. m 5/15/1975 Mark Paul Gallagher c 3. Dio Newark Newark NJ 2005-2008; Bp Suffr Dio Sthrn Virginia Norfolk VA 2003-2005; Dio Sthrn Virginia Norfolk VA 2002-2005; R St Annes Epis Ch Middletown DE 1996-2001; P-in-c Trin Ch Boothwyn PA 1995-1996; Asst S Mart's Ch Radnor PA 1991-1994; Asst Cathd Of The Incarn Baltimore MD 1989-1991; Chapl S Mart's Ch Radnor PA 1989-1991. revcjg@aol.com

GALLAGHER, Daniel Paul (NY) 29 Halcyon Rd, Millbrook NY 12545 B Waverly IA 11/22/1936 s Paul William Gallagher & Genevieve Lucille. BA U of Houston 1966; MDiv GTS 1969. D 6/7/1969 P 12/20/1969 Bp Horace W B Donegan. m 1/10/1981 Merellyn M Gallagher c 2. Dio New York New York City NY 1996-1997; P-in-c S Thos Ch Amenia Un Amenia NY 1991-1996; Assoc Gr Ch Millbrook NY 1988-1991; Supply P Dio New York New York City NY 1971-1988; Dio New York New York City NY 1971-1987; Asst Gr Epis Ch Monroe NY 1970-1971; Asst S Anne's Ch Washingtonville NY 1970-1971; Asst S Paul's Ch Chester NY 1970-1971; Asst S Jas Ch Hyde Pk NY 1969-1970. dgnebttc@aol.com

GALLAGHER, Elvin Ross (Ida) 5605 Randolph Dr, Boise ID 83705 B Grand Junction CO 8/9/1922 s George Albert Gallagher & Annie Florence. BS U of Utah 1951; MDiv CDSP 1954. D 6/14/1954 P 12/21/1954 Bp Richard S Watson. m 8/20/1953 L Margaret Dyche c 4. Emm Epis Ch Placerville ID 1982-2003; All SS Epis Ch Boise ID 1971-1987; Assoc Ch of the H Faith Santa Fe NM 1969-1971; Vic S Jas Ch Tanana AK 1966-1969; Assoc R All SS Ch Phoenix AZ 1960-1966; Vic All SS Ch Salt Lake City UT 1955-1957; Asst-to-Dn Cathd Ch Of S Mk Salt Lake City UT 1954-1955.

GALLAGHER, Gerald J (NY) 8 Somers Dr, Rhinebeck NY 12572 B Flushing NY 9/14/1941 s George Raymond Gallagher & Jessica Ann. BA Cathd Coll of the Immac Concep 1964; STB Gregorian U 1966; STL Gregorian U 1968. Rec from Roman Catholic 5/22/1980 Bp James Stuart Wetmore. m 2/16/1974 Joyce A Kane c 4. R Ch Of The Mssh Rhinebeck NY 1985-2009; P-in-c Ch Of The H Trin Pawling NY 1981-1984; Zion Epis Ch Wappingers Falls NY 1980. gallaghersfolly@yahoo.com

GALLAGHER, John Merrill (Cal) 1363 Filbert St, San Francisco CA 94109 B San Francisco CA 3/18/1929 s Thomas Arthur Gallagher & Merrill Cushing. BA Stan 1951; STB EDS 1965; MA SFTS 1983. D 6/20/1965 Bp James Albert Pike P 2/12/1966 Bp George Richard Millard. m 7/10/1971 Nancy Owens. Asst S Jas Epis Ch San Francisco CA 1984-2010; Dir California Counslg Inst San Francisco CA 1984-1991; Asst S Lk's Ch San Francisco CA 1982-1983; Vic Chr Epis Ch Sei Ko Kai San Francisco CA 1978-1981; Archd Personl Dio California San Francisco CA 1975-1978; Exec Dio California San Francisco CA 1970-1975; Dept Urban Mnstrs Dio California San Francisco CA 1968-1973; Asst The Epis Ch Of S Mary The Vrgn San Francisco CA 1965-1968. nanjohng@earthlink.net

GALLAGHER, Mary Ellen Turner (Ida) 13118 W Picadilly St, Boise ID 83713 **D S Jas Ch Fremont CA 2001-** B Dallas TX 1/1/1950 d Clarence Eugene Turner & Ruth Warren. Steph F. Austin St U 1970; BTh California Sch for Deacons 1994; California St U 2000. D 7/18/1994 Bp William Edwin Swing. m 7/18/1994 Charles Frederick Gallagher. D S Anne's Ch Fremont CA 1996-2000; D S Bede's Epis Ch Menlo Pk CA 1994-1996. Natl St. Steph'S Awd For Mnstry Naad 2001. maryg@ihfa.org

GALLAGHER, Patricia Portley (Ct) 9134 Town Walk Dr, Hamden CT 06518 B Bronx NY 8/23/1946 d Donald Eugene Gallagher & Sylvia. BSN U Of Bridgeport 1976; MA S Jos Coll 1981; MDiv Ya Berk 1989. D 6/9/1990 Bp Arthur Edward Walmsley P 2/1/1991 Bp Jeffery William Rowthorn. m 7/15/1967 James Arthur Portley c 3. P-in-c S Paul's Epis Ch Willimantic CT 2004-2008; P-in-c Chr Ch Waterbury CT 2002-2004; Int S Ptr's Epis Ch Monroe CT 2000-2002; Vic Ch Of S Jn By The Sea W Haven W Haven CT 1991-1998. revpatg@sbcglobal.net

GALLAGHER, Robert (Me) 1640 18th Ave, Apt 2, Seattle WA 98122 **Assoc P for Ascetical and Practical Theol Trin Par Seattle WA 2008-** B Philadelphia PA 10/25/1944 s Thomas A Gallagher & Dorothy. BS Penn 1966; MDiv PDS 1971; MA Goddard Coll 1976. D 11/7/1970 P 5/1/1971 Bp Robert Lionne DeWitt. R Trin Ch Castine ME 2002; Dir CDI The GTS New York NY 1996-1999; Vic S Andr's Ch Trenton NJ 1988-1996; Vic S Mich's Ch Trenton NJ 1988-1991; Congrl Dvlpmt Off Dio Connecticut Hartford CT 1981-1988; Vic S Elis's Ch Philadelphia PA 1975-1981. Auth, "In Your H Sprt: Shaping the Par Through Sprtl Pract," Ascen Press, 2011; Auth, "Fill All Things: The Sprtl Dynamics of the Par Ch," Ascen Press, 2008; Auth, "Power From On High: A Model For Par Life & Mnstry," Ascen Press, 1983; Auth, "Stay In The City," Forw Mvmt, 1981; Auth, "Mnstry Of Laity As Agents Of Instnl Change," Audenshaw Papers, 1978. OA 1983. ragodct@gmail.com

GALLAGHER, Robert Joseph (Mich) 78 Nason St, Maynard MA 01754 B Lowell MA 2/4/1941 s Joseph A Gallagher & Margaret Lillian. BA Merrimack Coll/Maryknoll Sem Coll 1963; M. Ed. Salem St Coll Salem MA 1966; M.A. Salem St Coll Salem MA 1977; M.Div. Weston Jesuit TS 1981; D.Min. Iaps Detroit 1986; J.D. Massachusetts Sch of Law at Andover 1998. D 4/3/1982 Bp Henry Irving Mayson P 4/1/1983 Bp H Coleman McGehee Jr. S Mk's Ch Southborough MA 2001-2004; S Lk's Ch Hudson MA 1998-2000; Ch Of The H Trin Marlborough MA 1995-1997; S Steph The Mtyr Epis Ch E Waterboro ME 1986-1988; Howe Mltry Sch Howe IN 1985-1986; R Trin Ch S Clair Shores MI 1983-1985; S Columba Ch Detroit MI 1982-1983. revdrbob@aol.com

GALLANT III, James Sinclair (SC) 115 Simons St, Charleston SC 29403 **Yth Min Calv Ch Charleston SC 2005-** B Charleston SC 4/23/1949 s James S Gallant & Ruth Washington. ThM Gulf Coast Sem Panama City FL; LHD Med U of So Carolina; Ben Coll 1971. D P 12/14/2005 Bp Edward Lloyd Salmon Jr. m 9/2/1973 Joan G Gallant c 1. Chr Epis Ch Mt Pleasant SC 2008; Yth Min S Andr's Mssn Charleston SC 2005-2006. Dr. of Div Cathd Bible Coll, Myrtle Bch, SC 2001. JGallant@christch.org

GALLEHER, Stephen Cary (Nwk) 6115 Boulevard East, Apt. 2, West New York NJ 07093 B Richmond VA 9/26/1942 s Frank Marion Galleher & Dorothy Elizabeth. BA U of Virginia 1964; U of Edinburgh GB 1967; MDiv VTS 1970. D 6/20/1970 Bp Philip Alan Smith P 1/1/1971 Bp William Henry Marmion. Dio Newark Newark NJ 1982-1985; R Emm Epis Ch (Piedmont Par) Delaplane VA 1975-1982; Asst R S Jn's Ch Lynchburg VA 1971-1975. Auth, *The Voice*, The Dio Newark, 1983. EvangES 1975-1982; Shalem Bd 1977-1982. Rec Video Prod Awds Dio Newark 1983. s.allthatjazz@verizon.net

GALLETLY, David Patrick (WMo) 2812 Amber Wood Pl, Thousand Oaks CA 91362 **R S Patricks Ch And Day Sch Thousand Oaks CA 2002-** B Burbank CA 7/11/1960 s Robert David Galletly & Patricia Morgan. BA U CA 1982; MDiv GTS 1983; MDiv CDSP 1991. D 5/19/1991 Bp John Lester Thompson III P 1/22/1992 Bp Sam Byron Hulsey. m 12/14/1985 Michele Marie Simmons c 1. H Fam Epis Ch Omaha NE 1996-2002; Vic S Aug's Epis Ch Elkhorn NE 1996-1999; Vic Gr Epis Ch Liberty MO 1992-1996; Assoc Ch Of The H Trin Midland TX 1991-1992. frdavid@stpatschurch.org

GALLIAN JR, Paul Vernon (WMo) Po Box 514, Crane MO 65633 **D S Steph's Ch Monett MO 2010-** B Gape Giradeau MO 11/14/1944 s Paul Gallian & Alice. BS U of Missouri 1971; MA U of Missouri 1974. D 12/9/2000 Bp John Wadsworth Howe. m 3/13/1972 Melissa Leake c 1. D Chr Epis Ch Springfield MO 2006-2010; D S Anne's Ch Crystal River FL 2000-2005. gallianp@me.com

GALLIGAN, Joseph Edward (Wyo) Po Box 950, Thermopolis WY 82443 **R H Trin Epis Ch Thermopolis WY 2011-; COM Dio Wyoming Casper WY 1998-** B Hartford CT 6/15/1947 s Edward Joseph Galligan & Marie Louise. BS Montana St U 1974; Certificaton Montana St U 1976; TS 1987; TS 1987; Ldrshp Acad for New Directions XXII 1992; VTS 1998. D 5/23/1984 P 12/12/1984 Bp Jackson Earle Gilliam. m 12/20/1969 Ellen Hand c 1. R S Alb's Ch Worland WY 2004-2009; R H Trin Epis Ch Thermopolis WY 1996-2008; Dio Montana Helena MT 1996; Dioc Mssnr S Andr's Ch Livingston MT

1995-1996; Dioc Mssnr S Jn's Ch Emigrant MT 1995-1996; Stndg Com Dio Montana Helena MT 1994-1996; Eccl Crt Dio Montana Helena MT 1993-1996; Dioc Mssnr Calv Epis Ch Red Lodge MT 1989-1995; Dioc Mssnr S Alb's Epis Ch Laurel MT 1989-1995; Dioc Mssnr S Paul's of the Stillwater Ch Absarokee MT 1989-1995; Vic S Mk's Ch Big Timber MT 1989-1992; Vic S Jn's Ch/Elkhorn Cluster Townsend MT 1984-1989. Wyoming Law Enforcement Chapl Assn 2001. joegalligan@hotmail.com

GALLOWAY, David Alan (At) 845 Edgewater Dr Nw, Atlanta GA 30328 B Atlanta GA 6/30/1954 s Mitchell Olin Galloway & Doris. BA Emory U 1976; MDiv Candler TS Emory U 1979; Emory U 1982; DMin STUSo 1984. D 2/23/1985 P 8/1/1985 Bp Charles Judson Child Jr. m 8/7/1981 Mary Grimes c 2. H Innoc Ch Atlanta GA 2002-2007; Cn Dio Texas Houston TX 1995-2001; Chr Epis Ch Tyler TX 1992-2001; Cathd Of S Phil Atlanta GA 1985-1990. Auth, "Sprtl Direction In Mssn & Mnstry"; Auth, "Journ Pstr Care"; Auth, "Growing Your Ch Through Evang & Outreach"; Auth, "Ldrshp Journ". Assn Cistercian Monstry Of The H Sprt; Cmnty Of The Cross Of Nails, Assn Of S Mary, Soc Of S Jn The Evang, Ch Uniting In Global Mssn. drdavidgalloway@msn.com

GALLOWAY, Richard Kent (USC) 120 Mauldin Rd, Greenville SC 29605 **D Epis Ch Of The Redeem Greenville SC 2010-** B Gainesville FL 11/27/1959 s Kenneth H Galloway & Faye Melinda. BA Col 1982; MDiv The GTS 2010; MA U of So Carolina 2010. D 6/3/2010 Bp W(illiam) Andrew Waldo P 10/29/2011 Bp Terry Allen White. rgalloway@gts.edu

GALLUP, Grant Morris (Chi) Casa Ave Maria, Apartado Rp-10, Managua Nicaragua **Died 11/26/2009** B Stambaugh MI 1/28/1932 s Allan Murray Gallup & Eleanor Else. BA Alma Coll 1954; MDiv SWTS 1959; DePaul U 1970; Fllshp Coll of Preachers 1983; Maryknoll Sum Inst 1987. D 6/20/1959 P 12/1/1959 Bp Charles L Street. Associated Parishes, Witness For Peace, Integrity, Epis Pe. grant73@cablenet.com.ni

GALVIN, Kathleen M (Ore) 2293 NW Mcgarey Dr, McMinnville OR 97128 **R S Barn Par McMinnville OR 2007-** B Saint Paul MN 9/12/1945 d Michael Joseph Galvin & Irene Jean. BS Minnesota St U Mankato 1968; MS Minnesota St U Mankato 1972; Cert SWTS 1994; MDiv Untd TS Of The Twin Cities 1994; DMin SWTS 2005. D 6/29/1994 Bp James Louis Jelinek P 1/7/1995 Bp Sanford Zangwill Kaye Hampton. c 4. R Epis Ch Of The Trsfg Mesa AZ 2002-2006; R S Jn's Epis Ch Mankato MN 1998-2002; Dio Minnesota Minneapolis MN 1995-2002; Vic Ch Of The Mssh Prairie Island Welch MN 1995; D Mazakute Memi S Paul MN 1994-1995. eclectic9559@msn.com

GALVIN, Michael Joseph (Ind) 8304 Coral Bay Ct, Indianapolis IN 46236 **Vic H Fam Epis Ch Fishers IN 2007-** B Madison IN 10/16/1961 BS U Cinc 1984; Med U Cinc 1986; MDiv Chr TS 2004. D 6/18/2005 P 1/29/2006 Bp Catherine Elizabeth Maples Waynick. m 6/28/1986 Rachelle J Galvin c 2. Cur S Fran In The Fields Zionsville IN 2005-2007. mgalvin@comcast.net

GAMBLE, Deborah E (SO) 4234 Hamilton Ave, Cincinnati OH 45223 B Bowling Green OH 1/2/1955 d Carl William Gamble & Virginia Dickman. BS Mia 1977; MS U of Maine 1982; MDiv TESM 1991. D 8/22/1993 P 4/23/1994 Bp Don Adger Wimberly. m 7/27/1991 James Melvin Hazlett c 1. S Phil's Ch Cincinnati OH 2002-2010; D S Andr's Ch Ft Thos KY 1993-1994. revdeb@fuse.net

GAMBLE, Howard Winfield (Mass) Po Box 1049, Kennebunkport ME 04046 **Died 6/18/2010** B Richmond Hill NY 12/7/1929 s Howard Winfield Gamble & Margurite Place. BSME U of Virginia 1952; STM Ya Berk 1962. D 6/23/1962 P 3/1/1963 Bp Duncan Montgomery Gray. c 4.

GAMBLE, John Robert (Be) 1005 Sleepy Hollow Rd FL B Philadelphia PA 5/4/1936 s John Gamble & Lillian. U of Scranton; BSCE U of Pennsylvania 1967. D 9/11/1991 P 9/1/1992 Bp James Michael Mark Dyer. m 10/10/1964 Janette M Harper. P Ch Of The Epiph Glenburn Clarks Summit PA 2000-2001; R S Jas-S Geo Epis Ch Jermyn PA 1996-2000; R S Mart-In-The-Fields Mtn Top PA 1992-1996. jjrg54@embarqmail.com

GAMBLE, Robert David (Ia) ul. Pasieka 24, Poznan 61657 Poland **Dio Iowa Des Moines IA 1974-** B Philadelphia PA 3/9/1937 s Clarence James Gamble & Sarah Merry. BA Harv 1960; MA Harv 1963; BD EDS 1966. D 6/25/1966 Bp Anson Phelps Stokes Jr P 6/1/1967 Bp Wilburn Camrock Campbell. m 5/9/1973 Antonina Spisak c 1. Vic S Paul's Epis Ch Grinnell IA 1974-1979; Asst S Paul's Ch Pawtucket RI 1970-1974; Cur Gr Ch Lawr MA 1966-1970. rdgamble@sylaba.poznan.pl

GAMBLING, Paul (Evans) (SanD) 5079 E 30th Pl, Yuma AZ 85365 **Assoc S Paul's Ch Yuma AZ 1999-** B Tredegar Gwent Wales 2/6/1950 s William Wreyford Gambling & Amelia. BA U Sask 1973; The Coll of Emm and St. Chad 1974; MDiv Hur 1986. Trans from Anglican Church of Canada 5/15/2001 as Priest Bp Gethin Benwil Hughes. m 6/8/1974 Nora Kathleen Marlowe c 2. paulg@hospiceofyuma.com

GAMBRILL, James Howard (Nwk) PO Box 1929, York Beach ME 03910 B Boston MA 10/4/1940 s Howard Gambrill & Mary. BA Ya 1962; MDiv UTS 1965; Bos 1969; JD Rutgers-The St U 1988. D 6/26/1965 P 5/19/1966 Bp John Melville Burgess. m 2/11/1984 Sally Krallman c 4. Affiliate S Geo's Epis Ch York Harbor ME 1993-2002; Dio Newark Newark NJ 1979-1983; Vic Gnrl Dio Newark Newark NJ 1978-1983; R Gr Ch In Providence Providence RI 1974-1978; R S Steph's Memi Ch Lynn MA 1967-1974; Asst S Steph's Memi Ch Lynn MA 1965-1966. Auth, "Bridge Of The Cross," Forw Mvmt, 1982. jgambril@maine.rr.com

GAME, Paul Richard (At) Trinity Episcopal Church, 1130 First Ave, Columbus GA 31901 **R S Pat's Epis Ch Atlanta GA 2010-** B Tampa FL 5/31/1961 s Paul Game & Suzanne Linebaugh. BA Van Nashville TN 1983; JD The U Of Floriday Gainesville FL 1986; MDiv Candler TS Emory U 2007. D 12/21/2006 P 7/17/2007 Bp J(ohn) Neil Alexander. m 5/30/1992 Anne Anne W Zipp c 3. Cur Trin Epis Ch Columbus GA 2007-2010. prgame@gmail.com

GAMMONS JR, Edward Babson (NJ) 7 Oak St, Warren RI 02885 B Cohasset MA 6/30/1934 s Edward Babson Gammons & Betty. BA Harv 1956; BD EDS 1959. D 6/24/1959 Bp Anson Phelps Stokes Jr P 1/3/1960 Bp Leland Stark. m 6/26/1965 Gretchen Greenwood Russell c 3. Assoc S Mich's Ch Bristol RI 2004-2007; R All SS Ch Bay Hd NJ 1988-2000; R S Andr's Ch Yardley PA 1974-1988; Asst Ch Of The Redeem Bryn Mawr PA 1972-1974; Cur S Lk's Epis Ch Montclair NJ 1959-1961. Associated Parishes 1982-1999; Assn of Dioc Liturg & Mus Commissions 1982-1989; OHC 1977. nedgammons@gmail.com

GANDARA-PEREA, Jose R (NY) 15620 Riverside Dr. W, Apt 13I, New York NY 10032 **P-in-c Ch of the Intsn Ch Of The Intsn New York NY 2009-; P-in-c Ch of the Intsn Dio New York New York City NY 2009-** B Mayaguez Puerto Rico 4/15/1964 s Jose R Gandara-Carbonell & Graciela V. BA Universidad Cntrl Bayamon, Puerto Rico 1987; MDiv Seminario Santo Tomas Aquino, Dominican Rep. 1991; STB and STL Universidad Pontificia Salamanca, Spain 1999; Angl Stds GTS 2006. Rec from Roman Catholic 4/18/2009 Bp Mark Sean Sisk. m 7/11/2009 Hugh McPhail Grant. Dir of Field Educ The GTS New York NY 2009-2010. fatherberto@gmail.com

GANDELL, Dahn (Roch) 21 Warwick Dr, Fairport NY 14450 **R S Jn's Epis Ch Honeoye Falls NY 2001-** B New Orleans LA 11/29/1965 d David Franklin Dean & Bette Jo. BS Van 1987; MA U of Mobile 1991; MDiv Yale DS 1995. D 3/4/1998 P 10/31/1998 Bp William George Burrill. m 9/27/1997 David Lee Gandell c 2. D Ch Of The Gd Shpd Webster NY 1998-2001. "Shoveling Snow and Stolen Silver," Living Water/Epis Dio Rochester, 2004. The Polly Bond Awd of Merit ECom 2005. motherdahn@hotmail.com

GANN, Judith Fara Walsman (Okla) 6335 S 72nd East Ave, Tulsa OK 74133 B Kansas City MO 5/30/1951 d John Frederick Walsman & Alice Charlotte. BA U of Missouri 1973. D 6/24/1995 Bp Robert Manning Moody. c 2. Trin Ch Tulsa OK 2000-2006; Asst Dio Oklahoma Oklahoma City OK 1995-2000. jgann@trinitytulsa.org

GANNON, Kathleen Patricia (SeFla) 2014 Alta Meadows Ln Apt 302, Delray Beach FL 33444 **Cur S Paul's Ch Delray Bch FL 2005-** B Oceanside NY 3/12/1953 d John Joseph Gannon & Patricia Ann. BBA Pace U 1980; MDiv VTS 2005. D 4/17/2005 Bp Leopold Frade P 11/6/2005 Bp James Hamilton Ottley. Chap Of S Andr Boca Raton FL 1991-2002. kgannon@vts.edu

GANNON, William Sawyer (Nwk) 11 French Dr, Bedford NH 03110 B Manchester NH 5/30/1936 s Eugene Gannon & Marion. BA Norwich U 1958; STM Epis TS of The SW 1962; MDiv Epis TS of The SW 1962. D 4/1/1962 Bp John E Hines P 10/4/1962 Bp Charles F Hall. m 6/21/1980 Barbara Goldman c 4. S Jas Epis Ch Laconia NH 2004-2005; R S Andr's Ch Harrington Pk NJ 1999-2003; R Chr Ch Glen Ridge NJ 1991-1999; Int Gr Ch Hastings On Hudson NY 1989-1991; St Marys Sch Peekskill NY 1974-1977; R S Andr's Ch Manchester NH 1964-1969; Co-Dir Yth Cmssn Dio New Hampshire Concord NH 1963-1969; Cur All SS Ch Peterborough NH 1962-1964. Auth, *Findings*. Rotary Club 1992-2005. wsgannon@aol.com

GANTER, G David (Vt) 12 Beechwood Lane, Jericho VT 05465 **D S Jas Epis Ch Essex Jct VT 2011-** B Watertown New York USA 9/24/1943 s Charles F Ganter & Florence Wilbur. BS New York St Coll Of Environ Sci And Forestry 1965; MBA Syr 1966; MS Binghamton U 1986. D 11/19/2005 Bp Gladstone Bailey Adams III. m 9/12/1964 Frances Thompson c 2. Asstg D S Matt's Ch Enosburg Falls VT 2006-2011. dave.ganter@myfairpoint.net

GANTER-TOBACK, Gail Sage (NY) 32 Center St, New Paltz NY 12561 **D Ch Of The H Cross Kingston NY 2005-; Dio New York New York City NY 2004-; D Dio New York New York City NY 1994-** B Hartford CT 6/27/1944 d John Humphrey Ganter & Lillian Esther. BS Keuka Coll 1966. D 6/4/1994 Bp Richard Frank Grein. m 8/21/2004 Arnold Toback c 2. D Chr Ch Red Hook NY 1998-2005; D Ch Of The Regeneration Pine Plains NY 1994-1995; S Jas Ch Hyde Pk NY 1985-1994. Assn for Epis Deacons 1994. sagereflections@gmail.com

GANTZ, Jay John (EMich) 10095 E Coldwater Rd, Davison MI 48423 **S Andr's Epis Ch Flint MI 1998-** B Buffalo NY 4/26/1954 s Frank John Gantz & Janet Louise. BA Wadhams Hall Sem Coll 1979; MDiv Cath Theol Un 1988; DMin SWTS 2004. Rec from Roman Catholic 2/1/1998 as Priest Bp Edwin Max Leidel Jr. m 5/3/1997 Patricia Meaz c 3. Dio Estrn Michigan Saginaw MI 2002; Nativ Cmnty Epis Ch Holly MI 1998-2004. "Gr in the Ghetto," *Seabury-Wstrn/No Wstrn U*, 2001. frjjg1@aol.com

GARAB, Arra M (Chi) 8 Evergreen Cir, DeKalb IL 60115 **Died 8/21/2011** B Woodcliff NJ 5/24/1930 s Garaud Garab & Varsenig. BA (w high hon Swarthmore Coll 1951; MA (dist) Col 1952; PhD (dist) Col 1962; SWTS 1970. D 5/23/1970 Bp Gerald Francis Burrill P 3/30/1996 Bp William Walter Wiedrich. c 3. Auth, *Hovanness Toumanian*, T&T, 1971; Auth, *Beyond Byzantium: The Last Phase of Yeats's Career*, NIU Press, 1969; Auth, *Mod Essays (w Russel Nye), 4th ed*, Scott Foresman, 1969; Auth, *A New U*, Nthrn Illinois UP, 1968; Auth, "Var monographs and arts," 1953. Scholars Libr Awd for "Beyond Byzantium" MLA; Hon Alum Nash; Excellence in Tchg Awd Nthrn Illinois U. amgarab@comcast.net

GARAFALO, Robert Christopher (Los) 19988 Promenade Cir, Riverside CA 92508 B New York NY 8/29/1948 BA Oblate TS 1978; MA CUA 1980; MDiv CUA 1981; STL Pontifical Marian U Rome It 1986; Ssl Pontifical Gregorian U 1989; PhD Pontifical Marian U 1993. Rec from Roman Catholic 11/19/2002 Bp Joseph Jon Bruno. m 11/15/1991 Maria Rojas c 5. P S Mich's Epis Ch Riverside CA 2003-2004. "Hist Theol And Symbol: The Cana Narrative In Mod Exegesis," Marianum, 1994; "Through A Glass Darkly: Models Of The Loc Ch Twenty-Five Years After Vatican Ii," Sprtl Life, 1990; "The Fam Of Jesus In Mk'S Gospel," Irish Theol Quarterly, 1989; "Dogma And Consciousness In The Works Of Bern Lonergan," New Blackfriars (London), 1988.

GARBARINO, Harold William (Mass) 2038 Laurel Park Hwy, Laurel Park NC 29739 B Jamaica NY 3/13/1942 s Harold Eugene Garbarino & Dorothy Harragan. BA Hob 1964; MDiv PDS 1967. D 6/17/1967 P 12/23/1967 Bp Jonathan Goodhue Sherman. m 8/6/1967 Ellen Close Cowling c 4. R Ch Of The Gd Shpd Reading MA 1983-2006; R S Jas' Epis Ch Watkins Glen NY 1980-1983; R S Jn's Epis Ch Watkins Glen NY 1980-1983; R S Paul's Ch Montour Falls NY 1980-1983; R Schuyler Cnty Episc Parishes Watkins Glen NY 1980-1983; R Gr Ch Lyons NY 1972-1980; Asst S Lk's Par Darien CT 1970-1972; Cur Epis Ch of The Resurr Williston Pk NY 1967-1970. hgarbarino@mac.com

GARCEAU, John Earle (Alb) 72 Amber Dr, San Francisco CA 94131 B Cohoes NY 8/16/1955 s Alfred Henri Garceau & Martha Lillian. RPI 1976; BS SUNY 1990. D 5/31/1988 Bp David Standish Ball. D Cathd Of All SS Albany NY 1994-1997; D S Steph's Ch Delmar NY 1991-1993; D Ch Of The H Cross Troy NY 1988-1991. NAAD, Curs. jgarceau@jgarceau.com

GARCIA, Christopher (Va) 3116 O St NW, Washington DC 20007 **Asst to the R Chr Ch Georgetown Washington DC 2010-** B Frankfurt, Germany s Charles A Garcia & Barbara C. AB Cor 1981; MBA Cor 1982; JD Cor 1990; LLM The Judge Advoc Gnrl's Sch, US Army 1995; MDiv VTS 2010. D 6/5/2010 P 12/11/2010 Bp Shannon Sherwood Johnston. m 9/15/1990 Cheryl Clarke c 2. christopher@christchurchgeorgetown.org

GARCIA, David Allen (PR) 165 Hoyt St, Brooklyn NY 11217 B Marquette MI 5/14/1944 s Abraham Garbriel Garcia & Barbara Jean. BD Bex; BS Nthrn Michigan U. D 7/15/1969 Bp George R Selway P 1/1/1970 Bp Paul Moore Jr. m 2/1/1970 Migdalia de Jesus Torres. Epis City Mssn Boston MA 1994-1999; S Mk's Ch In The Bowery New York NY 1969-1991. Revson Fell Col 1991. dagecm@lesecm.tiac.net

GARCIA, Hope Jufiar (ECR) Po Box 3994, Salinas CA 93912 B Roseville CA 11/15/1924 d Filoteo Jufiar & Josefina. BTh Dio Ecr Sch For Deacons 1991. D 8/22/1992 Bp Richard Lester Shimpfky.

GARCIA, Louis Fernando (ETenn) 10 Fort Stephenson Pl, Lookout Mountain TN 37350 **D Ch Of The Gd Shpd Lookout Mtn TN 1989-** B Tampa FL 4/8/1926 s Alejandro Garcia Pardo & Carmen Garcia. U of Tennessee; BD Georgia Inst of Tech 1950. D 7/9/1989 Bp William Edwin Swing. m 6/17/1950 Grace Zuue Amat. sllugar@aol.com

GARCIA, Miguel (SeFla) 3574 Nw 12th Ter, Miami FL 33125 **Died 4/24/2010** B Colon CU 7/14/1921 s Rafael Garcia & Josefa. Seminario Evangelico De Teologia Cu 1957. D 8/6/1957 P 2/1/1958 Bp A H Blankingship. c 1.

GARCIA, Ruth Anne (Mont) 801 W Water St, Lewistown MT 59457 B Peoria IL 7/12/1968 d Joseph Charles Garcia & Sharon Joan. NW Coll St. Paul MN; BS Montana St U 1991; MDiv GTS 1998. D 6/20/1998 Bp Charles Jones III P 4/15/1999 Bp Peter James Lee. Trin Par New York NY 2006-2009; S Columba's Ch Washington DC 2002-2005; Dio Montana Helena MT 2002; S Paul's Sch Concord NH 2000-2001; S Tim's Ch Herndon VA 1998-2000. rgarcia@trintywallstreet.org

GARCIA, Sixto Rafael (SeFla) 150 SW 13th Ave, Miami FL 33135 **P-in-c Ch Of The H Comf Miami FL 2009-** B 9/28/1972 s Candido Rafael Garcia & Barbara. Trans from Iglesia Episcopal de Cuba 8/5/2009 Bp Leopold Frade. m 2/10/2003 Anaysa Calderin c 2. priestrafael@yahoo.es

GARCIA, Teodosio R (HB) No address on file. B Echarri ES 7/17/1928 Trin U. Rec from Roman Catholic 8/1/1963 as Deacon Bp Richard Earl Dicus.

GARCIA DE LOS SANTOS, Ramon Antonio (DR) Guarionex #19, Ensanche Quisqueya, La Romana Dominican Republic **Dio The Dominican Republic (Iglesia Epis Dominicana) Santo Domingo DO 1993-** B La Romana DO 12/12/1964 s Leopoldo Garcia & Manuela. U 2 Yrs; Cert Diac Mnstry 1992. D 6/7/1992 P 12/1/1993 Bp Julio Cesar Holguin-Khoury. m 5/24/1992 Iris Margarita Jimenez c 3.

GARCIA-TUIRAN, Carlos Alfredo (SanD) 2660 Hardy Drive, Lemon Grove CA 91945 **S Phil The Apos Epis Ch Lemon Grove CA 2010-; Dio San Diego San Diego CA 2006-; Vic Santa Rosa Del Mar Imperial CA 2005-; Curs Cmnty Sprtl Advsr Dio San Diego San Diego CA 2004-** B Barranquilla CO 5/20/1957 s Christian Garcia-Borrero & Carmen Fausta. U Del Litoral Barranquilla CO 1979; MDiv Pacific Luth TS 1995. D 7/13/1996 P 1/18/1997 Bp Frederick Houk Borsch. m 10/26/1991 Christine Marie LePage c 2. All SS Epis Ch Brawley CA 2006-2009; Hisp Mnstry Comittee Mem Dio San Diego San Diego CA 2003-2004; Vic All SS Epis Ch Brawley CA 2003; Sts Ptr And Paul Epis Ch El Centro CA 2003; Dioc Coun Mem Dio Los Angeles Los Angeles CA 1998-2000; Vic Ch Of The Epiph Los Angeles CA 1997-2002; S Paul's Pomona Pomona CA 1996-2000; Hospice Chapl Dio Los Angeles Los Angeles CA 1996-1999; Hisp Mnstry Chair Dio Los Angeles Los Angeles CA 1992-1994. carlangas1986@yahoo.com

GARDAM, Robert Frederick (Alb) 2a Cass Ct, Ballston Lake NY 12019 B Newcastle IE 5/28/1917 s Maurice George Hart Gardam & Anne Jane Kyle. BA U Tor 1940; LTh U Tor 1942. Trans from Anglican Church of Canada 7/1/1953 as Priest Bp Richard S M Emrich. m 8/7/1945 Shirley Landon c 4. Assoc S Ptr's Ch Plant City FL 1981-1992; R S Lk's Ch Cambridge NY 1966-1981; R Calv Memi Epis Ch Saginaw MI 1954-1959; R S Mary's Ch Detroit MI 1953-1954. rfgpriest@nycap.rr.com

GARDE, Mary (LI) 573 Roanoke Ave, Riverhead NY 11901 **R Gr Ch Riverhead NY 2002-** B Joplin MO 6/12/1951 d Christopher Patrick Garde & Anna Bell. BA Benedictine Coll 1975; MSW-RT Wstrn Michigan U 1986; MDiv Epis TS of the SW 1999. D 6/26/1999 P 1/2/2000 Bp Robert Manning Moody. office@graceriverhead.org

GARDNER, Albutt Lorian (Pa) 600 E. Cathedral Rd., # H-304, Philadelphia PA 19128 **The Ch Of Emm And The Gd Shpd Philadelphia PA 2001-** B Southampton County VA 9/13/1929 s Albutt Lorian Gardner & Ruby Belle. AA Mars Hill Coll 1949; BA U Rich 1951; MDiv Crozer TS 1972; CPE Presb/U Of Pennsylvania Hosp 1983. D 2/28/1965 P 6/5/1965 Bp John Brooke Mosley. c 5. Assoc Trin Ch Gulph Mills King Of Prussia PA 1996-2001; All SS Crescentville Philadelphia PA 1983-1994; Dioc Liturg Com Dio Pennsylvania Philadelphia PA 1975; R S Paul's Ch Elkins Pk PA 1970-1981; R Chr Ch Milford DE 1966-1970; Asst Dn Cathd Ch Of S Jn Wilmington DE 1965-1966. Auth, "Roots In Colonial Virginia: Wm Leonard Joyner & His Descendants," 1992.

GARDNER JR, Alfred Emmett (RG) 500 Chermont Dr, El Paso TX 79912 **Died 7/19/2011** B Henderson TN 8/11/1930 s Alfred Emmett Gardner & Dona Catherine. BS U of Memphis 1953; JD U of Tennessee 1956; Theol Bex 1966; Xavier U 1967; MDiv Rochester Cntr for Theol Stds 1994. D 6/25/1966 Bp Roger W Blanchard P 12/18/1972 Bp Richard Mitchell Trelease Jr. c 5.

GARDNER, Anne Elizabeth (Mass) Phillips Academy, 180 Main Street, Andover MA 01810 B Boston MA 8/2/1960 d Theodore Simmington & Elizabeth. BA Fairfield U 1982; MS U Roch 1988; MDiv Harvard DS 2005. D 6/2/2007 P 1/12/2008 Bp M(arvil) Thomas Shaw III. m 9/29/2006 Beth O'Connor c 2. Assoc S Ptr's Ch Weston MA 2007-2008. hdsannie@yahoo.com

GARDNER, Bruce Norman (Eau) Po Box 637, Hayward WI 54843 B Duluth MN 3/7/1948 s Norman Wilbur Gardner & Beatrice Helen. BA U MN 1981; MA U MN 1983; MDiv Nash 1986. D 9/29/1985 P 5/25/1986 Bp William Charles Wantland. Dio Eau Claire Eau Claire WI 2007-2008; Chr Ch Cathd Eau Claire WI 2005-2007; S Alb's Ch Superior WI 1994-1995; Chr Ch Par La Crosse WI 1992-1993; Chr Ch Chippewa Falls WI 1991-1992; S Simeon's Ch Stanley WI 1991-1992; Int Dio Eau Claire Eau Claire WI 1990-1995; S Alb's Ch Spooner WI 1990-1991; St Stephens Ch Spooner WI 1990-1991; Vic Campus Mnstry Dio W Missouri Kansas City MO 1987-1990; Ch Of The Ascen Hayward WI 1986-2005; S Lk's Ch Spooner WI 1986-2002; Cur S Paul's Epis Ch Flint MI 1986-1987; Sr D Chap Nash Nashotah WI 1985-1986; Asst S Mary's Epis Ch Dousman WI 1985-1986. Assoc Bsg 1999; Csss 1983-1999; Esmhe 1986. canonitchy@gmail.com

GARDNER, Calvin George (SVa) 1405 Bruton Ln, Virginia Beach VA 23451 **All SS Ch Warrenton NC 2004-** B Decatur IL 6/19/1925 s George Corrimer Gardner & Edna May. BA Bob Jones U 1950; MDiv Nthrn Bapt TS 1953. D 4/24/1994 P 11/6/1994 Bp Alden Moinet Hathaway. m 7/20/1951 Naoma Viriginia Lovelady. Asst R Galilee Epis Ch Virginia Bch VA 1996-2002; D Dio Pittsburgh Monroeville PA 1994-1996; Serv S Steph's Ch Sewickley PA 1989-1996. Ord Of S Lk. galileo@1018.com

GARDNER, Carol Hartsfield (WTenn) 1720 Peabody Ave, Memphis TN 38104 B Memphis TN 9/13/1935 d Orville Benton Hartsfield & Juanita Earle. MA U of Memphis 1978; Memphis TS 1999. D 3/4/2000 Bp James Malone Coleman. m 8/13/1971 Lawrence Gale Gardner c 1. Gr - S Lk's Ch Memphis TN 2000-2003. deaconcarol@hotmail.com

GARDNER, Daniel Wayne (EO) 571 Yakima St S, Vale OR 97918 **Loc P - Mnstry Spprt Grp H Trin Vale OR 1995-** B Bend OR 10/10/1939 s Harvey Denson Gardner & Gertrude Margaret. BS Portland St Coll 1962; MS U of Oregon 1971. D 3/9/1995 P 12/1/1995 Bp Rustin Ray Kimsey. m 6/20/1959 Vonna Jean Stewart c 2. dang@fmtc.com

GARDNER, Donald Joseph (Alb) 11 S Union St, Cambridge NY 12816 **Died 8/6/2010** B Gloversville NY 1/22/1925 s Joseph James Gardner & Laura. D 3/10/1962 P 11/20/1962 Bp Horace W B Donegan. c 1. Ord Of S Lk.

GARDNER, Edward Morgan (WNC) 118 Clubwood Ct, Asheville NC 28803 **Mem, Stndg Com Dio Wstrn No Carolina Asheville NC 2010-2014; Dir of Pstr Care S Giles Chap Deerfield Asheville NC 2000-; Dep, GC Dio Wstrn No Carolina Asheville NC 1987-; Dep, GC Dio Wstrn No Carolina Asheville NC 1984-** B Gordonsville VA 4/25/1949 s Edward Berkeley Gardner & Lorraine. BS Appalachian St U 1972; MDiv VTS 1976; Con.Ed. Fell VTS 1989; Cert Luther Sem Ctr for Aging Rel & Sprtlty 2006. D 6/12/1976 P 6/9/1977 Bp William Gillette Weinhauer. m 12/15/2000 Elizabeth Ann Darling c 1. Mem, Exec Coun Dio Wstrn No Carolina Asheville NC 2006-2009; Int Ch Of The Epiph Newton NC 2000; Mem, Stndg Com Dio Wstrn No Carolina Asheville NC 1996-1999; R S Mk's Ch Gastonia NC 1984-1999; Mem, Exec Coun Dio Wstrn No Carolina Asheville NC 1984-1987; Mem, Stndg Com Dio Wstrn No Carolina Asheville NC 1980-1984; R S Jas Ch Black Mtn NC 1979-1984; Dn, Piedmont Dnry Dio Wstrn No Carolina Asheville NC 1978-1979; Mem, Exec Coun Dio Wstrn No Carolina Asheville NC 1977-1979; Vic S Andr's Ch Bessemer City NC 1976-1979; Vic Trin Ch Kings Mtn NC 1976-1979. Star of Merit Medal No Carolina Fire Dept 1997. darling-gardner@charter.net

GARDNER, E(ugene) Clifton (Dal) 6505 Brook Lake Dr., Dallas TX 75248 **R S Jas Ch Dallas TX 2002-** B Champaign IL 6/10/1949 s Malcolm Le Grande Gardner & Lillian Lavergne. OH SU 1970; BS Sthrn Illinois U 1982; MDiv TESM 1986. D 6/15/1986 P 5/24/1987 Bp C(hristopher) FitzSimons Allison. m 1/3/1973 Clarice Ann Gardner c 2. R Epis Ch Of The Gd Shpd San Angelo TX 1993-2002; P-in-c Ch Of The H Fam Moncks Corner SC 1986-1993. clifandgig@sbcglobal.net

GARDNER, H (Ala) 1910 12th Ave. South, Birmingham AL 35205 **R S Mary's-On-The-Highlands Epis Ch Birmingham AL 2002-** B Fairfield AL 10/19/1959 s Harry Gardner & Saidee. BS Auburn U 1982; MDiv VTS 1991. D 5/28/1991 P 12/21/1991 Bp Robert Oran Miller. m 6/27/1992 Irene T Thames c 2. R Chr Ch Macon GA 1998-2002; Asst Calv Ch Memphis TN 1993-1998; Asst Gr Ch Anniston AL 1991-1993. huey@stmarysoth.org

GARDNER, James Edward (CPa) 839 Fraternity Rd, Lewisburg PA 17837 B Philadelphia PA 7/9/1931 s Francis Sidney Gardner & Josephine. BS Carnegie Mellon U 1953; MS Carnegie Mellon U 1954; STB PDS 1961; STM GTS 1963; U of Pennsylvania 1965. D 5/13/1961 P 11/1/1961 Bp Oliver J Hart. m 7/11/1953 Patricia Ruth Treasure c 2. R S Ptr's Epis Ch Livingston NJ 1990-1995; Asst H Apos And Medtr Philadelphia PA 1966-1968. Alb Inst. Fell Ecf; Fell Underwood (Danforth). jgardner@bucknell.edu

GARDNER, Joan Margiotta (ECR) 1970 Cerra Vista Dr, Hollister CA 95023 **Dio El Camino Real Monterey CA 1984-** B Hoboken NJ 8/8/1947 d Eugene Alphonse Margiotta & Theresa Marie. BS California St Polytechnic U 1975; MS W Coast U Los Angeles CA 1977; MDiv CDSP 1984. D 6/10/1984 P 1/19/1985 Bp John Lester Thompson III. S Lk's Ch Hollister CA 1988-2008; R S Lk's Ch Hollister CA 1987-2008; Int S Anselm's Epis Ch Lafayette CA 1985-1986. joan@gardner1.net

GARDNER, John (Cal) 1340 Dolores St, San Francisco CA 94110 B Oakland CA 6/6/1949 s Herbert Gordon Gardner & Alice Agnes. BA San Jose St U 1972; MDiv CDSP 1978. D 5/25/1979 P 11/1/1979 Bp William Arthur Dimmick. Int Ch Of The Nativ San Rafael CA 1989-1990; Asst S Mk's Ch Mt Kisco NY 1984; Cur Gr Ch Newark NJ 1983-1984; Vic Ch Of The Gd Shpd S Ignace MI 1979-1983.

GARDNER, John Burke (SwVa) 117 Autumn Cir, Boones Mill VA 24065 **Co-Chair, Hisp Mnstrs Dio SW Virginia Roanoke VA 2010-; Co-R Trin Epis Ch Rocky Mt VA 2006-** B Abingdon VA 4/3/1973 s Philip Graham Gardner & Betty Lynn. BS W&M 1995; MDiv VTS 2002. D 6/15/2002 P 12/15/2003 Bp Carol Joy Gallagher. m 2/8/2003 Rachel Elizabeth Wenner c 3. Co-Chair, Hisp Mnstrs Dio SW Virginia Roanoke VA 2010; Mem, Exec Bd Dio SW Virginia Roanoke VA 2007-2010; Assoc Chr Ch Whitefish Bay WI 2003-2006. revjohngardner@gmail.com

GARDNER, Mark W (Los) 1031 Lanza Ct, San Marcos CA 92078 B Union City TN 8/16/1956 s Roland Carlos Gardner & Leonore Pauline. U CA 1974; BA California St U 1978; ETSBH 1983; MDiv CDSP 1988. D 6/4/1988 P 12/1/1988 Bp Charles Brinkley Morton. m 7/26/1998 Virginia Gardiner c 4. Vic S Mich's U Mssn Island Isla Vista CA 1991-1999; Cur S Dav's Epis Ch San Diego CA 1988-1991.

GARDNER, Randal B. (SanD) St. James by the Sea, 743 Prospect Street, La Jolla CA 92037 **Trst, Treas CDSP Berkeley CA 2008-; R S Jas By The Sea La Jolla CA 2006-** B Denver CO 8/6/1953 s Robert Belden Gardner & Betty May. BA Seattle Pacific Coll 1975; MDiv CDSP 1984; CTh Ripon Coll Cuddesdon Oxford Gb 1985; DMin VTS 2005. D 6/30/1984 P 10/1/1985 Bp Robert Hume Cochrane. m 6/21/1975 Cathy June Schwind c 2. Dir Epis Cmnty Serv San Diego CA 2006-2009; R Emm Epis Ch Mercer Island WA 1996-2006; Exam Chapl Dio Olympia Seattle WA 1994-1998; Ch Of The Gd Shpd Fed Way WA 1988-1996; Asst R S Barn Epis Ch Bainbridge Island WA 1985-1988. rbgardner@san.rr.com

GARDNER, Van Howard (Md) 89 Murdock Rd, Baltimore MD 21212 B Baltimore MD 11/10/1946 s Edward Elmer Gardner & Annie Ruth. BS Frostburg St U 1968; MS Morgan St U 1973; MDiv VTS 1977. D 5/21/1977 P 11/1/1977 Bp David Keller Leighton Sr. m 10/30/2011 Kathleen K Kelly c 2. Dn Cathd Of The Incarn Baltimore MD 1987-2008; R Ch Of S Marks On The Hill Pikesville MD 1979-1987; Asst Ch Of The Mssh Baltimore MD 1977-1979. Auth, "Sermons That Wk". Natl First Prize For Best Sermon Epis Evang Fndt. vhgardner@comcast.net

GARDNER-SMITH, Fran (NH) 413 Milan Hill Rd, Milan NH 03588 **R S Barn Ch Berlin NH 2008-; Mssnr Dio Nthrn Michigan Marquette MI 2006-** B Worcester MA 2/8/1966 d Francis Gardner & Barbara Emily. ABS Mt Holyoke Coll 1988; MA Mt Holyoke Coll 1990; MDiv VTS 2006. D 3/13/2006 P 10/7/2006 Bp James Arthur Kelsey. m 7/31/2010 David Smith. Dio New Hampshire Concord NH 2008-2010. fbgardner@gmail.com

GARFIELD, Elizabeth Ann (Colo) St Luke's Episcopal Church, 1270 Poplar St, Denver CO 80220 B Minneapolis MN 7/10/1959 d Theodore G Garfield & Mary L. BA Iowa St U 1981. D 11/17/2007 Bp Robert John O'Neill. D S Lk's Ch Denver CO 2007-2010. wibgarfield@hotmail.com

G

GARFIELD, Liston Alphonso (Ala) Po Box 1213, Tuskegee Institute AL 36087 **Dio Alabama Birmingham AL 1994-; R S Andr's Ch Tuskegee Inst AL 1993-** B Saint Thomas VI 4/15/1952 s Franz Garfield & Cassilda. BS Tuskegee Inst 1974; Med Tuskegee Inst 1976; MDiv VTS 1985. D 1/3/1985 P 7/12/1985 Bp Edward Mason Turner. m 11/20/2009 Jacquelyn B Burney c 1. S Geo Mtyr Ch Tortola VG 1985-1993; S Geo Sch Tortola 1985-1993. lgarfield@mailcity.com

GARGIULO, Mariano (Nwk) 384 Hilltop Ave # 7605, Leonia NJ 07605 **R S Jas' Ch Ridgefield NJ 2003-** B Positano Italy 11/20/1954 s Michele Gargiulo & Rosa. BA St. Thos Aquinas Coll 1976; MDiv Immac Concep Sem 1980. Rec from Roman Catholic 11/20/2001 Bp John Palmer Croneberger. m 3/21/2007 William A Borrelli. S Thos Ch Lyndhurst NJ 2001-2003. frmarianog@gmail.com

GARLAND III, John G (USC) 1002 South Main Street, Greenville SC 29611 **R S Andr's Epis Ch Greenville SC 2008-** B Houston TX 9/8/1974 BA Alma Coll 1997; MDiv STUSo 2002. D 6/22/2002 Bp Claude Edward Payne P 6/4/2003 Bp Don Adger Wimberly. Asst to R Trin Epis Ch Marble Falls TX 2006-2008; Asst to R Ch Of The Gd Shpd Tomball TX 2002-2004. trey_garland@alumni.sewanee.edu

GARLAND, Melbourne Charles (NMich) 1117 E Margaret St, Ironwood MI 49938 **Died 12/11/2009** B Bessemer MI 3/8/1929 s Charles Laity Garland & Ruth Ellen. D 5/31/1998 Bp Thomas Kreider Ray.

GARLAND, Philip Owen (Lex) 1060 Argyll Woods, Danville KY 40422 B Benham KY 1/4/1931 s C R Garland & Velma. BA Wofford Coll 1957; Med Rol 1969. D 5/14/1978 Bp Addison Hosea. m 12/26/1960 Mary Lou Burkhart c 2. D S Phil's Ch Harrodsburg KY 1991-1996; D Trin Epis Ch Danville KY 1979-1991. mlgpg@bellsouth.net

GARLICHS, Richard Walbridge (Oly) 900 University St Apt 6G, Seattle WA 98101 B Saint Joseph MO USA 1/24/1923 s Lorren Walbridge Garlichs & Sarah Elizabeth. BS U of Pennsylvania 1943; GTS 1948; MDiv Ya Berk 1949. D 6/22/1949 P 12/22/1949 Bp Robert N Spencer. c 3. Int S Jas Epis Ch Kent WA 1988-1989; Virginia Mason Hosp Seattle WA 1974-1983; Stndg Com Dio Olympia Seattle WA 1974-1977; Dioc Hosp Chapl Dio Olympia Seattle WA 1972-1976; Rgnl Archd Dio Olympia Seattle WA 1969-1972; Stndg Com Dio Olympia Seattle WA 1965-1968; Ch Of The H Cross Redmond WA 1963-1972; S Tim's Epis Ch Chehalis WA 1963-1972; Chair DeptCE Dio Olympia Seattle WA 1958-1960; Vic S Alb's Ch Edmonds WA 1957-1963; Vic S Hilda's - S Pat's Epis Ch Edmonds WA 1957-1963; Vic S Jn's Epis Ch So Bend WA 1953-1957; Vic S Mary's Ch Savannah MO 1949-1953; Vic S Oswald In The Field Skidmore MO 1949-1953; Vic S Paul's Ch Maryville MO 1949-1953. Clincl Pstr Ed. Asst Supvsr, ACPE 1976-1983. rwgwal@gmail.com

GARMA, Joann Marie (La) 3883 Turtle Creek Blvd Apt 1906, Dallas TX 75219 B New Orleans CA 8/11/1942 d Roman Garma & Geihade. BA Centenary Coll 1964; MRE SMU 1967; EdD New Orleans Bapt TS 1984. D 8/22/1982 Bp James Barrow Brown.

GARMAN, Cynthia Anne (Mich) 426 Cottonwood Ln., Saline MI 48176 **P-in-c Ch Of The Resurr Clarkston MI 2010-** B Kingston PA 11/2/1950 d Richard Arnold Garman & Marjorie Jean. BA Prescott Coll 1990; MDiv EDS 1995; BS Wichita St U 2000. D 11/1/2000 P 6/28/2001 Bp William Edward Smalley. c 1. R S Jas' Epis Ch Dexter MI 2006-2010; R S Ptr's Epis Ch Tunkhannock PA 2003-2006; Assoc R S Paul's Ch Kansas City MO 2001-2002; Transitional D S Matt's Epis Ch Newton KS 2000-2001. Assoc of H Cross 2008. cagarman1@aol.com

GARMAN, Gerald Roger (Oly) 11758 Meridian Ave N, Seattle WA 98133 **Gd Samar Epis Ch Sammamish WA 2004-** B Seattle WA 4/22/1938 s Roger Homer Garman & Frances Lillian. BSEE U Of Washington 1962. D 6/26/2004

Bp Sanford Zangwill Kaye Hampton. m 2/1/1963 Sherry Kay Roberts c 3. g.r. garman@att.net

GARMEY, Stephen Squires (NY) 24 W 55th St Apt 7B, New York NY 10019 B Pittsburgh PA 4/24/1933 s Clifford Ronald Garmey & Harriet Louise. BA Harv 1956; MDiv GTS 1959; S Vladimir Russian Orth Sem 1965; Cntr for Intercultural Documentation Cuernavaca MX 1967; MArch Col 1972. D 6/11/1959 P 12/19/1959 Bp Horace W B Donegan. m 8/2/1966 Jane Gibson c 1. Calv and St Geo New York NY 1975-2005; Asst Calv and St Geo New York NY 1971-1974; R S Martha's Ch Bronx NY 1965-1968; S Lk's Cnvnt Av New York NY 1963-1965; Asst Ch Of The Ascen New York NY 1959-1960. Auth, *Gramercy Pk: An Illustrated Hist of a NY Nbrhd*, 1984; Auth, *Rilke Duino Elegies, Transltr*, 1972.

GARNER, Evan D (Ala) 1203 S Lawrence St, Montgomery AL 36104 **S Jn's Ch Decatur AL 2011-; Assoc R S Jn's Ch Montgomery AL 2006-** B Atlanta GA 5/26/1980 s Douglas Garner & Emily. BA Birmingham-Sthrn Coll 2002; BS Birmingham-Sthrn Coll 2002; BA U of Cambridge 2005; VTS 2006. D 5/22/2006 P 12/12/2006 Bp Henry Nutt Parsley Jr. m 9/17/2005 Elizabeth G Garner c 2. evan_d_garner@yahoo.com

G

GARNER, Jeffery (Ala) 150 Sherwood Pl, Pell City AL 35128 **R S Simon Ptr Ch Pell City AL 2007-** B Mobile AL 3/21/1957 s Earl Garner & Audrey. BS Wm Carey U 1979; MS Golden Gate U 2000; MDiv Epis TS of The SW 2005. D 5/25/2005 P 12/13/2005 Bp Henry Nutt Parsley Jr. m 12/30/1977 Angela Louise Garner c 2. R S Phil's Ch Ft Payne AL 2005-2007. stsp_rector@centurytel.net

GARNER, Mary P (Eas) 517 Goldsborough St, Easton MD 21601 **Assoc Chr Ch St Michaels MD 2009-** B Philadelphia PA 3/14/1961 d Frank Putnick & Margaret. St. Jn's Coll; BA St. Jos's U 1999; MDiv EDS 2006. D 6/3/2006 Bp Robert Gaines Johnson P 1/6/2007 Bp John Clark Buchanan. m 6/21/1986 Stephen G Garner c 2. S Ptr's Ch Salisbury MD 2009; Asst To R Ch Of The Epiph Norfolk VA 2006-2008; Norfolk Urban Outreach Mnstry Norfolk VA 2006-2007. thegarnerfamily@aol.com

GARNER, Terry (Mil) 10328 N Stanford Dr, Mequon WI 53097 **D S Jas Epis Ch Milwaukee WI 1986-** B Covington KY 10/5/1955 s Billy Mathew Garner & Wilma Jeanne. AS U of Kentucky 1978; BA U of Wisconsin 1989. D 10/18/1986 Bp Roger John White. m 7/22/1978 Loraine Brewer. NAAD 1987. dcnterry.g@gmail.com

GARNER JR, Thomas Gailor (Eas) 440 Alexian Way Apt #62, Signal Mountain TN 37377 B Nashville TN 8/21/1928 s Thomas Gailor Garner & Fannie Marie. BS Tennessee Tech U 1950; MDiv STUSo 1962. D 6/25/1962 Bp William Evan Sanders P 5/1/1963 Bp John Vander Horst. m 7/29/1960 Caroline Maude Chobot c 2. R Old Trin Ch Ch Creek MD 1987-1993; Int S Paul's Ch Georgetown DE 1986-1987; Supply P S Barn Ch Trion GA 1985-1986; R S Mary's Par Tampa FL 1975-1982; R Ch Of Our Sav Oatlands Hamilton VA 1969-1975; R S Jas' Epis Ch Leesburg VA 1969-1975; R Westover Epis Ch Chas City VA 1964-1969; Vic Ch Of The H Comf Monteagle TN 1963-1964; Vic S Jas Sewanee TN 1963-1964; D-In-Trng S Ptr's Ch Columbia TN 1962-1963. revthomg@aol.com

GARNETT, Sara Kathryn (RG) Po Box 1723, Fort Stockton TX 79735 **Died 3/11/2010** B Oklahoma City OK 4/15/1914 d Charles Hunter Garnett & Mary Ermine. BA Oklahoma St U 1937; LLB Oklahoma City U 1961. D 9/23/1977 P 5/1/1980 Bp Richard Mitchell Trelease Jr.

GARNIER, Maryellen (ECR) 23695 Hutchinson Road, Los Gatos CA 95033 B Minneapolis MN 10/13/1947 d Thomas James Jones & Ellen Catherine. RN S Barn Sch for Nrsng 1970; BS U of Notre Dame 1982; BA Dio El Camino Real Sch for Deacons 1993; MDiv CDSP 2001. D 11/30/1993 P 6/14/2001 Bp Richard Lester Shimpfky. m 4/20/1974 Gary Eldon Garnier c 1. COM Dio El Camino Real Monterey CA 2001-2009; D S Lk's Ch Los Gatos CA 1996-2001; D Ch Of S Jude The Apos Cupertino CA 1993-2001. Excellence in Action El Camino Hosp 2005; Fran Toy Multicultural Awd CDSP 2000; S Steph's Awd Sch for Deacons 1995. maryellengarnier@yahoo.com

GARNO, Arthur Scott (Alb) 5828 State Highway 68, Ogdensburg NY 13669 **S Jn's Ch Ogdensburg NY 2005-** B Gardensburg NY 7/15/1958 s Donald Thomas Garno & Marie June. AAS SUNY 1978. D 6/11/2005 Bp Daniel William Herzog. m 8/11/1979 Tammy Delaney c 2. agarno@homail.com

GARNO, Scott Arthur (Alb) Po Box 537, Unadilla NY 13849 **S Paul's Ch Franklin NY 2011-; R S Matt's Ch Unadilla NY 2006-** B Ogdenburg NY 4/16/1980 s Arthur Scott Garno & Tammy Marie. BA SUNY 2002; MDiv TESM 2006. D 6/10/2006 P 12/16/2006 Bp Daniel William Herzog. m 5/24/2003 Sarah E Garno c 2. ssgarno@yahoo.com

GARNSEY, Elizabeth H (NY) Church of the Heavenly Rest, 2 E 90th St, New York NY 10128 **Assoc Ch Of The Heav Rest New York NY 2008-** B Greeley CO 2/4/1970 BA U CO 1992; MDiv Yale DS 2005. D 3/11/2006 P 9/23/2006 Bp Mark Sean Sisk. Ch Of The Heav Rest New York NY 2007-2008; S Barth's Ch New York NY 2007-2008. ehgarnsey@hotmail.com

GARRAMONE-ROHR, Laurie Marie (Alb) 28 S Market St, Johnstown NY 12095 **S Jn's Ch Johnstown NY 2010-** B Mahopac NY 11/3/1960 d Robert Garramone & Gertrude Ann. BS SUNY 1982; MA U Of Delaware Newark 1986; Mstr of Div St Bern's TS and Mnstry 2011. D 6/21/2003 Bp Daniel William Herzog P 5/12/2007 Bp William Howard Love. m 2/21/1987 Donald F Rohr c 2. Cur S Geo's Ch Clifton Pk NY 2007-2010; Chr Ed Coord. Dio Albany Albany NY 2003-2009. revlmgr@gmail.com

GARRATT, Stephen Richard (Oly) 3512 Ne 189th Pl, Lake Forest Park WA 98155 **R Chr Ch SEATTLE WA 1995-** B Louisville KY 10/12/1951 s Rowland Masters Garratt & Loris Mae. BA U of Washington 1973; MDiv SWTS 1980; MA Seattle U 1992; D Min SWTS 2005. D 7/25/1980 P 7/22/1981 Bp Robert Hume Cochrane. m 7/25/1987 Margaret A Niles c 3. Asst Chr Ch SEATTLE WA 1988-1994; Asst R S Steph's Epis Ch Seattle WA 1983-1988; S Barn Epis Ch Bainbridge Island WA 1980-1983. Auth (D Min. Thesis), "Treas in Earthen Vessels: Contemplative Mnstry in Congrl Settings," 2005; Auth, "Meditation As A Therapeutic: Tool Measuring Effects Of Centering Pryr On Anxiety," 1992. ESMHE 1988-1997; Intl Thos Merton Soc 1997. stephenrgarratt@gmail.com

GARRENTON, Linwood Wilson (Roch) 599 E 7th St Apt 6E, Brooklyn NY 11218 B Portsmouth VA 4/1/1941 s Cecil Wilson Garrenton & Mary Cornelia. BS VPI 1964; MDiv GTS 1970; DMin Bos 1984. D 6/27/1970 Bp William Foreman Creighton P 2/13/1971 Bp Harry Lee Doll. Chair-Soc Mnstry Dio Rochester Rochester NY 1992-1997; Dn Dio Rochester Rochester NY 1983-1989; R Chr Ch Rochester NY 1982-2006; V-Chair Com Cmsn Dio Maryland Baltimore MD 1974-1982; R Ch Of The H Trin Baltimore MD 1972-1982; Cur Mt Calv Ch Baltimore MD 1970-1972. lingarr@verizon.net

GARRETT, David (ETenn) 515 5th St, Newport TN 37821 **R Ch Of The Annunc Newport TN 1998-** B Memphis TN 10/9/1951 s James Eldon Garrett & Edna Angelene. BA SW At Memphis 1973; MDiv STUSo 1977. D 6/26/1977 Bp William F Gates Jr P 4/1/1978 Bp William Evan Sanders. m 6/19/1971 Virginia Ruth Shettlesworth c 1. All SS' Epis Sch Morristown TN 2007; Dio E Tennessee Knoxville TN 1985-1998; Vic Ch Of The Annunc Newport TN 1978-1998; D S Mart Of Tours Epis Ch Chattanooga TN 1977-1978. Auth, "Living Ch". Cmnty Of S Mary, RWF, Me. stillinnewport@etdiocese.net

GARRETT III, Edwin Atlee (Me) 211 Otter Cliff Rd, Bar Harbor ME 04609 B Lansdowne PA 10/19/1923 s Edwin Atlee Garrett & Ethel Pearl. BA Harv 1947; ThB PDS 1950; ThM PDS 1951. D 7/1/1950 Bp Joseph Gillespie Armstrong P 1/6/1951 Bp William P Remington. m 10/11/1952 Margaret Whitaker c 3. Dioc Coun Dio Maine Portland ME 1992-1996; Natl Aids Cltn Dio Maine Portland ME 1987-1988; Hon Asst S Sav's Par Bar Harbor ME 1986-1999; Int S Sav's Par Bar Harbor ME 1984-1985; Trin Ch Castine ME 1976-1977; Trin Ch Castine ME 1975-1976; R S Fran-In-The-Fields Malvern PA 1962-1972; Vic S Andr's Epis Ch Lewisburg PA 1955-1959; Vic Ch Of S Mart-In-The-Fields Philadelphia PA 1950-1955. Contrib, "Var arts," *Bar Harbor Hist Soc Nwsltr*; Contrib, "Wm Massey Huddy," *Journ Co of Mltry Historians*. Gvnr of the Soc of the Colonial Wars in the St of Maine 1996; Pres of the Bar Harbor Hist Soc 1994. Cmnty Serv Awd Natl Soc of the DAR 1997. offercove@gwi.net

GARRETT, G(eorge) Kenneth (Mass) 12 Academy Ave, Fairhaven MA 02719 B Somerville MA 9/2/1929 s George Everett Garrett & Myrtle. BA Tufts U 1953; STB Ya Berk 1957. D 6/22/1957 P 12/21/1957 Bp Anson Phelps Stokes Jr. m 7/26/1958 Mary Chubbuck c 4. R Gr Ch New Bedford MA 1991-1993; Assoc R Gr Ch New Bedford MA 1959-1988; Min in charge S Jas Ch Groveland Groveland MA 1958-1959.

GARRETT, Jane Nuckols (Vt) 206 Fairway Vlg, Leeds MA 01053 B Dover DE 7/16/1935 d David Ellwood Nuckols & Edna Earle. Hartford Sem; BA U Of Delaware Newark 1957; DLitt Mid 1997. D 6/11/1980 P 6/6/1981 Bp Robert Shaw Kerr. S Steph's Ch Middlebury VT 1986-1987; Cur S Steph's Ch Middlebury VT 1980-1983; Dep Gc Dio Vermont Burlington VT 1979-1997. Auth, "Pamphlets On The Amer Revolution," Harv Press, 1965; Auth, "Philadelphia And Baltimore, 1790-1840: A Study Of Intra-Reg Unity," *Maryland Hist mag*, 1960; Auth, "Delaware Coll Lotteries 1815-1845," *Delaware Hist*, 1957. EPF; Integrity. jngarrett1@gmail.com

GARRETT, Kathy Ann (Va) Po Box 8500, Richmond VA 23226 **S Ptr's Ch McKinney TX 2010-** B Bridgeport CT 8/4/1963 d Stephen Robert Rogowski & Dorothy Cecelia. BA W Virginia Wesleyan Coll 1985; MDiv Ya Berk 1993. D 6/12/1993 Bp Arthur Edward Walmsley P 12/1/1993 Bp Jeffery William Rowthorn. m 9/13/1997 Sam Young Garrett. S Steph's Ch Richmond VA 1995-1999; Asst Min S Mk's Ch New Canaan CT 1993-1995.

GARRETT, Mary Ann (La) PO Box 126, Baton Rouge LA 70821 **Assoc R S Jas Epis Ch Baton Rouge LA 2009-** B Grand Saline TX 7/21/1951 d William Jenkins Garrett & Maxine. BA U of Texas 1976; MA U The Incarnate Word 1999; MDiv SWTS 2002. Trans from La Iglesia Anglicana de Mex 4/28/2008 as Priest Bp C(harles) Wallis Ohl. m 6/1/2002 William F Ashby. P S Jn's Epis Ch Odessa TX 2008-2009; P Dio SE Mex 2005-2007; Transitional D Dio SE Mex 2004-2005. mgarrett@stjamesbr.org

GARRETT, Morris Paul (Colo) Po Box 3254, Estes Park CO 80517 **R S Barn Epis Ch Denver CO 2008-** B Denver CO 1/29/1956 s Richard M Garrett & Ruth A. BA Colorado St U 1981; MDiv EDS 1988. D 5/22/1989 Bp William Carl Frey P 6/29/1991 Bp Barbara Clementine Harris. S Barth's Ch Estes Pk

CO 1997-2008; Int Wyman Memi Ch of St Andr Marblehead MA 1995-1997; Int Ch Of The H Trin Marlborough MA 1992-1993. garrett3254@earthlink.net

GARRIGAN, J(oseph) Edward (Pa) PO Box 1681, Doylestown PA 18901 B New York NY 1/1/1947 s Thomas Eugene Garrigan & Jo Ann. BA Wabash Coll 1968; STB GTS 1972; MA Yale DS 1972. D 6/24/1972 Bp Charles Gresham Marmion P 6/29/1973 Bp Charles Alfred Voegeli. m 12/6/1984 Jan Trimbur. R S Paul's Ch Doylestown PA 1979-2004; R Chr Ch Totowa NJ 1974-1979; Cur S Ptr's Ch Springfield MA 1972-1974. rbsmcm@verizon.net

✠ **GARRISON, Rt Rev J Michael** (WNY) 207 Pineneedle Dr, Bradenton FL 34210 **Ret Bp of Wstrn New York Dio SW Florida Sarasota FL 2011-** B Philadelphia PA 4/7/1945 s Jack L Garrison & Rosemary T. BA Pontiff Coll Josephinum 1967; MRE Pontifical Coll Josephinum 1970; DD GTS 1999. Rec from Roman Catholic 4/1/1975 as Priest Bp Wesley Frensdorff Con 4/24/1999 for WNY. m 1/20/1990 Carol Sohanney. Bp of WNY Dio Wstrn New York Tonawanda NY 1999-2011; Rgnl Vic Dio Nevada Las Vegas NV 1980-1999; S Matt's Ch Las Vegas NV 1979-1980; Vic Team Mnstry Cntrl NV Dio Nevada Las Vegas NV 1975-1979; S Mk's Ch Tonopah NV 1975-1978; S Philips-in-the-Desert Hawthorne NV 1975-1978; Asstant R S Paul's Epis Ch Sparks NV 1974-1975. Sis Of Charity Boulder City Nv 1982-1999. jmichaelgarrison@gmail.com

GARRISON, William Brian (CFla) 212 Brevity Ln, DeLand FL 32724 **Dn of the NE Dnry Dio Cntrl Florida Orlando FL 2010-; Dio Bd Dio Cntrl Florida Orlando FL 2010-; Comission on Mnstrs Dio Cntrl Florida Orlando FL 2009-; Vic The Ch Of The H Presence Deland FL 2005-** B 8/1/1973 Asburry (Orlando) 2004; M-Div Nash 2005. D 3/12/2005 Bp Hugo Luis Pina-Lopez P 10/9/2005 Bp John Wadsworth Howe. m 6/28/1997 Susan Cross c 2. iwillybbg@aol.com

GARRISON, William Bruce (Los) 31641 La Novia Ave, San Juan Capistrano CA 92675 **S Mths' Par Whittier CA 2011-; S Marg's Epis Sch San Juan Capo CA 2008-** B Walla Walla WA 11/14/1950 s William Elmer Garrison & Juanita Ruth. BS U of Phoenix 2004; MDiv The ETS At Claremont 2008. D 6/7/2008 P 1/10/2009 Bp Joseph Jon Bruno. m 10/25/1986 Sherry Daniel c 4. S Marg Of Scotland Par San Juan Capistrano CA 2008-2011. BillGarrison3141@yahoo.com

GARRITY, Clelia Pinza (Nev) 3081 Margarita Ave, Pahrump NV 89048 **Chairman, Com on Soc Justice and Mercy Dio Nevada Las Vegas NV 2011-; D Gr In The Desert Epis Ch Las Vegas NV 2010-** B New York, NY 8/29/1941 d Ezio Pinza & Doris Neal. BA Col 1969; MSW Yeshiva U 1972. D 4/10/2010 Bp Dan Thomas Edwards. c 1. garritycpg@gmail.com

GARRITY, Susan E (NH) 97 Halls Mill Rd, Newfields NH 03856 **S Thos Ch Dover NH 2008-** B Salem MA 3/5/1950 BS U of Maine. D 6/14/2003 Bp Douglas Edwin Theuner P 12/20/2003 Bp V Gene Robinson. m 1/30/1976 John Garrity c 2. Asst R S Jn's Ch Portsmouth NH 2003-2007. SEGARRITY03@YAHOO.COM

GARSIDE, Caroline Grubbs (Ct) Po Box 7378, Newburgh NY 12550 B Youngstown OH 2/27/1928 d Richard Holmes Grubbs & Clara Jean. BA Ob 1950. D 12/6/1986 Bp Arthur Edward Walmsley. m 5/5/1951 Richard Garside c 2.

GARTIG, William George (SO) 2146 Cameron Ave Apt 5, Cincinnati OH 45212 B Detroit MI 10/13/1952 s Derry George Gartig & Joanne Esther. BA U of Texas 1974; MDiv Epis TS of The SW 1977; MA Hebr Un Coll 1990; PhD Hebr Un Coll 1994. D 6/30/1977 P 6/1/1978 Bp Roger Howard Cilley. m 4/29/1984 Barbara Evans Rees. Supply P S Lk Ch Cincinnati OH 1995-2000; Int S Phil's Ch Cincinnati OH 1986-1991; Asstg P Trin Ch Covington KY 1982-1984; Vic All SS Epis Ch Hitchcock TX 1977-1980; S Mart's Epis Ch Houston TX 1977. "The Attribution Of The Ibn Ezra Supercommentary Avvat Nefesh To Asher Ben Abraham Crescas Reconsidered.," *Hebr Un Coll Annual*, 1995. Comt. Phi Beta Kappa Comt. gartigwg@episcopal-dso.zzn.com

GARTON, Mary Pamela (CFla) 190 Interlachen Rd, Melbourne FL 32940 B Philadelphia PA 6/17/1955 d George John Haupt & Mary Patricia. BA Cabrini Coll 1978; BS Cabrini Coll 1990. D 12/11/2010 Bp John Wadsworth Howe. m 9/19/1987 Harry Luther Garton c 2. simplelifeinfl@bellsouth.net

GARVIN, Grayson Barry (CFla) 3000 Nw 42nd Ave Apt B401, Coconut Creek FL 33066 B Greenwood SC 8/26/1937 s Grayson Burgess Garvin & Sara Beatrice. BA Lander U 1959; STM GTS 1964. D 6/27/1964 P 6/29/1965 Bp John Adams Pinckney. P-in-c S Jas Epis Ch Leesburg FL 2004-2005; P-in-c S Lk's Epis Ch Merritt Island FL 1998-2003; R S Richard's Ch Winter Pk FL 1989-1998; R S Ptr's Ch Plant City FL 1975-1989; R Epis Ch of the Gd Shpd Charleston SC 1967-1975; P-in-c Epiph Ch Spartanburg SC 1965-1967; Assoc S Matt's Epis Ch Spartanburg SC 1965-1967. Outstanding Young Man Year Awd 1972. graybar45@comcast.net

GARWOOD, David Leigh (Minn) 743 Cheyenne Ln, Mendota Heights MN 55120 **Died 6/6/2010** B Benton IL 8/17/1936 s Thomas Leigh Garwood & Ethel Mae. BA Carleton Coll 1958. D 1/25/1982 Bp Robert Marshall Anderson. c 3. D S Chris's Epis Ch Roseville MN 1999-2005; D S Anne's Epis Ch Sunfish Lake MN 1982-1996. david.garwood@comcast.net

GARWOOD, Martha Jayne (SD) 4640 Sturgis Rd Lot 49, Rapid City SD 57702 **D S Andr's Epis Ch Rapid City SD 2002-** B Deadwood SD 2/16/1953 d Harold W Garwood & Eileen E. BA So Dakota St U 1975. D 6/16/2002 Bp Creighton Leland Robertson. martyj25@rap.midco.net

GARY, Hobart Jude (Ct) 2855 West Commericial Blvd, Apartment 354, Fort Lauderdale FL 33309 B Evanston IL 8/26/1923 s Hobart Jude Gary & Elizabeth Nystrom. BA Carleton Coll 1944; MDiv SWTS 1947. D 6/2/1947 Bp Edwin J Randall P 12/20/1947 Bp Oliver L Loring. m 8/22/1950 Elizabeth Gary c 4. Int S Mart's Epis Ch Pompano Bch FL 1996-1998; Int S Jn's Ch Hollywood FL 1994-1996; Int S Andr's Epis Ch Of Hollywood Dania Bch FL 1992-1994; Int S Anne's Epis Ch Hallandale Bch FL 1992-1994; Volntr All SS Prot Epis Ch Ft Lauderdale FL 1981-1989; R Calv St Geo's Epis Ch Bridgeport CT 1966-1981; R S Jn's Epis Ch Southampton NY 1957-1966; P Ch Of S Fran Of Assisi Levittown NY 1950-1957; Vic S Jas Ch Old Town ME 1950-1957. HJGARY@YAHOO.COM

GARY, Richard Ellis (NY) Po Box 106, Heath MA 01346 B Wichita KS 1/15/1924 s Paul Edmond Gary & Marietta Drummond. BA Phillips U; BD Yale DS. D 4/15/1954 P 12/1/1954 Bp Angus Dun. m 6/13/1954 Dorothy Boykin c 3. Epis Ch Cntr New York NY 1977-1989; Dpt Of Missions Ny Income New York NY 1969-1977; Diocn Msnry & Ch Extntn Socty New York NY 1956-1977; Asst Trin Ch Washington DC 1953-1956. Auth, "Episcopalians & Roman Catholics: Can They Ever Get Together?".

GASKILL JR, Joseph John (EC) 174 Windy Point Rd, Beaufort NC 28516 **Vol (D) S Andr's Ch Morehead City NC 2006-** B New Bern NC 9/29/1942 s John Gaskill & Sophia. BA Wake Forest U 1964; Med Wake Forest U 1965. D 6/3/2006 Bp Clifton Daniel III. m 11/27/1964 Donna Gaskill c 3. dgaskill@ec.rr.com

GASQUET, Mark Cordes (La) 308 Central Ave, Jefferson LA 70121 B Shreveport LA 4/24/1934 s John Benoit Gasquet & Mabel Earl. BA LSU 1958; MDiv PDS 1961; MA Bos 1973; DMin McCormick TS 1979; PhD Somerset U Gb 1992. D 10/5/1961 Bp Girault M Jones P 6/1/1962 Bp Iveson Batchelor Noland. m 8/9/1980 Marylin Hyatt c 2. R The Ch Of The Annunc New Orleans LA 1973-2000; Vic Trin Epis Ch Ball LA 1961-1962. Auth, "Healthy New Orleans Cuisine," 2007; Auth, "Ch-St Relatns In Soviet Bloc," 1973. AAPC, Ord Of The H 1959; Amer Personal & Priv Chefs Assoc. 1996; Bcdac 1993. mgasquet@aol.com

GASTON, Katherine Elizabeth (Neb) 7625 Lafayette Ave, Omaha NE 68114 **Asstg Cler S Peters Epis Sch Kerrville TX 2001-** B Omaha NE 4/8/1918 d William Lewis Anderson & Myrtle Priscilla. BS Nebraska Wesl 1943; Cpt Washington U 1948; EFM STUSo 1987. D 5/7/1988 Bp James Daniel Warner. c 2.

GASTON III, Paul L (O) 2389 Brunswick Lane, Hudson OH 44236 **D Chr Ch Epis Hudson OH 2011-** B Hattiesburg MS 8/23/1943 s Paul Lee Gaston & Ruth Demaris. SMU 1963; BA SE Louisiana U 1965; MA U of Virginia 1966; PhD U of Virginia 1970. D 11/11/1990 Bp William Evan Sanders P 4/10/2010 Bp Mark Hollingsworth Jr. m 6/29/1968 Eileen Margaret Higgins c 1. S Mk's Ch Canton OH 2010-2011; D S Alb's Epis Ch Hixson TN 1990-1993. Prncpl Co-Auth, "Revising Gnrl Educ," AAC&U, 2009; Auth, "Bologna," *Liberal Educ*, 2008; Auth, "Geo Herbert & Angl Hymns," *Jn Donne Journ*, 2006; Auth, "W.D. Snodgrass," E. G. Hall, 1978. pgaston@kent.edu

GAT, Maggie (Nwk) 4230 Cascade Falls Dr, Sarasota FL 34243 **Hisp/Latino Mnstry Cmsn Dio SW Florida Sarasota FL 2008-** B Callao PE 3/14/1940 d John Herrick Moses & Katherine. BA Mt Holyoke Coll 1961; MA Amer Intl Coll 1978; Cert Consulting Psychologists Inc 1989; Drew U 1991; Ya Berk 1993; MDiv Yale DS 1993; Trnr Cert Cntr fo Prevention of Sexual Misconduct , Seattle, WA 1995; Cert Consulting Psychologists Inc 2007; Cert Int Mnstry Ntwk 2007; Cert Epis ChurchSafeguarding Chld 2011. D 6/4/1994 Bp John Shelby Spong P 12/4/1994 Bp Jack Marston McKelvey. c 2. Int S Geo's Epis Ch Bradenton FL 2010-2011; Assoc S Geo's Epis Ch Bradenton FL 2008-2011; Stndg Com Dio Newark Newark NJ 2005-2008; R S Jn's Ch Dover NJ 1999-2008; Bd, Chair last 3 years ACTS/VIM Newark NJ 1999-2005; Int S Jn's Ch Dover NJ 1997-1998; Int S Agnes Ch Little Falls NJ 1996-1997; Sexual Misconduct Prevention and Chld Sfty Trng, Chair from 1999-08 Dio Newark Newark NJ 1995-2008; Wmn Cmsn, Chair last 3 years Dio Newark Newark NJ 1994-2000; Vic Trin Ch Paterson NJ 1994-1996; Hisp Mnstry Cmsn, chair 2000-2005 Dio Newark Newark NJ 1993-2008. Prchr, "Thanksgiving Day: Spreading The Cloth At The Table Of Thanks," *Sermons That Wk 1998*, Morehouse Pub, 1999. revmaggie@aol.com

GATCH JR, Milton McCormick (NY) 105 East 29th Street, New York NY 10016 **P-in-c Chap Of S Jas The Fisherman Wellfleet MA 1980-** B Cincinnati OH 11/22/1932 s Milton Mccormick Gatch & Mary C. BA Hav 1953; U Cinc 1955; BD EDS 1960; MA Ya 1961; PhD Ya 1963. D 6/22/1960 P 6/1/1961 Bp Roger W Blanchard. m 8/25/1956 Ione Georganna White c 3. Cleric Calv and St Geo New York NY 2000-2005; Assoc S Paul And S Jas New Haven CT 1960-1963. Auth, "The Libr of Leander van Ess and the Earliest Amer Collections of Reformation Pamphlets," Bibliographical Soc of Amer, 2007; Auth, "The Yeats Fam and the Bk," Grolier Club, 2000; Auth, "Eschatology and Chr Nurture (collected essays)," Ashgate (Variorum Series), 2000; Auth, "So Precious A Fndt: Libr Of Leander Van Ess," Grolier Club,

1996; Auth, "Anglo-Saxon Stds: The 1st 3 Centuries," G.K. Hall, 1982; Auth, "Preaching & Theol In Anglo-Saxon Engl: Aelfric & Wufstan," U Tor Press, 1977; Auth, "Loyalties & Traditions: Man & His Wrld In Old Engl Lit," Pegasus/Bobbs Merrill, 1971; Auth, "Death: Meaning & Mortality In Chr Thought & Contemporary Culture," Seabury Press, 1969. Fell Medieval Acad of Amer 1998; Fell Soc of Antiquaries of London 1992; Quatercentenary Vstng Fell Emml, Cambridge 1991. mac@miltongatch.us

GATCHELL, Lois Harvey (Okla) 5208 South Atlanta, Tulsa OK 74105 **D S Dunst's Ch Tulsa OK 1977-** B Fort Pierre SD 6/1/1920 d Guy H Harvey & Edythe P. U of So Dakota 1939; BA U of Arizona 1943; U of Oklahoma 1977. D 6/26/1977 Bp Gerald Nicholas McAllister. m 11/27/1942 Donald Gatchell c 2. NAAD. Cert For Outstanding Serv Natl Conf Of Cathd Chars 1983; Awd For Most Innovative Prog Publ Hlth Assn OK 1973. lois-don@compuserve.com

GATELEY, Gail Nicholson (Dal) 200 Shumard Ct, Irving TX 75063 **R Epls Ch Of The Redeem Irving TX 2004-** B San Augustine TX 12/5/1948 d Elton Kincheloe Nicholson & Mary Laverne. BA Austin Coll 1970; MA U of Texas at Arlington 1975; MDiv Epis TS of the SW 1995. D 12/14/1996 P 11/11/1997 Bp James Monte Stanton. m 5/31/1970 Richard Hunt Gateley c 3. Assoc S Anne's Epis Ch Desoto TX 1997-2004. Ord Of S Lk. mthrgail@redeemer-irving.org

GATES, Alan K (RI) 269 Fir St, San Carlos CA 94070 **Ch Of The Epiph San Carlos CA 2011-** B Portland OR 4/8/1975 BA Seattle U 2000; MDiv VTS 2005. D 6/25/2005 P 1/15/2006 Bp Vincent Waydell Warner. m 11/24/2009 Jessica E Gates c 2. Ch Of The H Trin Tiverton RI 2007-2011; Asst S Paul's Ch No Kingstown RI 2005-2007. gatesbox@gmail.com

GATES, Alan McIntosh (O) 2747 Fairmount Blvd, Cleveland Heights OH 44106 **Bexley/Seabury Presidential Search Com Bex Columbus OH 2011-; Bd Dir Bex Columbus OH 2011-; Chair, COM Dio Ohio Cleveland OH 2009-; R S Paul's Epis Ch Cleveland Heights OH 2004-** B Springfield MA 3/25/1958 s J Edward Gates & Marion McIntosh. cert Pushkin Inst, Moscow 1979; BA Mid 1980; Geo 1983; MDiv EDS 1987. D 6/13/1987 Bp Ronald Hayward Haines P 3/26/1988 Bp David Elliot Johnson. m 6/3/1980 Patricia J Harvey c 2. P-in-c The Ch Of The H Sprt Lake Forest IL 2003-2004; Assoc The Ch Of The H Sprt Lake Forest IL 1996-2003; R Trin Epis Ch Ware MA 1990-1996; Cur Ch Of S Jn The Evang Hingham MA 1987-1990. Compass Rose Soc 2005; Epis Preaching Fndt Fac 2008-2008; Teleios Russian Fndtn 1994-2006. amgates@harveynet.net

GATES, Craig Richard Hunter (Miss) 415 Bell Avenue, Greenwood MS 38930 B Detroit MI 10/20/1946 s Richard Eugene Gates & Tina Venet. LSU; BA McNeese St U 1972; MDiv STUSo 1975. D 5/31/1975 Bp Iveson Batchelor Noland P 5/3/1976 Bp James Barrow Brown. m 11/29/1969 Dorothy Helen Crider c 2. Gr Ch Carrollton MS 1997; R Ch Of The Nativ Greenwood MS 1994-2005; R S Phil's Ch Jackson MS 1985-1994; R Trin Ch Crowley LA 1977-1985; Vic S Lk's Ch Jennings LA 1977-1980; Morris Coll Cntr Lafayette LA 1976-1977; Cur Ch Of The Ascen Lafayette LA 1975-1977. Auth, *Hist of the Dio Wstrn Lousiana*, 1985. crhgates@roadrunner.com

GATES, Mary May (Ct) 16 Church St, Waterbury CT 06702 **Chap of All SS W Cornwall CT 2010-; Asst Chr Ch Par Epis Watertown CT 2009-** B Bridgeport CT 12/5/1954 d Charles Joseph May & Edna. BS U of Connecticut 1993; MS U of Connecticut 1996; MDiv Ya Berk 1997. D 6/12/1999 Bp Clarence Nicholas Coleridge P 1/22/2000 Bp Andrew Donnan Smith. m 5/26/1974 Daniel P Gates c 3. Cur S Jn's Epis Par Waterbury CT 1999-2002. mmgates@hughes.net

GATES JR, Robert J (Okla) 1044 Meadow Dr, Bartlesville OK 74006 **Int Gd Shpd Epis Ch Sapulpa OK 2007-** B Ardmore OK 5/31/1945 s Robert Justin Gates & Dorothy Dzelle. BA Oklahoma City U 1968; CSS Epis TS of the SW 1978. D 6/17/1978 P 5/29/1979 Bp Gerald Nicholas McAllister. m 4/26/2008 Georgia L Henry c 2. Vic S Mart's Ch Pryor OK 1987-1994; S Lk's Ch Tulsa OK 1982-1985; Vic S Mk's Epis Ch Weatherford OK 1979-1982; Vic S Paul's Ch Clinton OK 1979-1982; Cur S Matt's Ch Enid OK 1978-1979. frb426@aol.com

GATREL, Larry Gene (Ia) 15471 Highway J46, Numa IA 52544 B Seymour IA 11/10/1933 s Thomas Henry Gatrel & Lena Marie. LTh Epis TS In Kentucky 1977. D 8/6/1977 P 10/1/1978 Bp Walter Cameron Righter. m 7/26/1953 Janice DeVore c 3. S Alb's Ch Sprt Lake IA 1985-1999; P-in-c Trin Ch Carroll IA 1977-1985; Ch Of The H Trin Sac City IA 1977-1982. lgatrel@hotmail.com

GATTA, Julia Milan (Ct) 243 Tennessee Ave, Sewanee TN 37375 **The TS at The U So Sewanee TN 2004-** B New York NY 8/20/1948 d Thomas George O'Brien & Margaret Patricia. BA S Mary's Coll, Notre Dame, IN 1970; MA Cor 1973; PhD Cor 1979; MDiv EDS 1979. D 6/14/1980 Bp Morgan Porteus P 5/30/1981 Bp Arthur Edward Walmsley. m 7/11/1970 John Joseph Gatta c 1. Vic S Paul's Ch Windham CT 1991-2004; Int S Paul's Ch Plainfield CT 1990-1991; Ch Of The Resurr Norwich CT 1986-1990; Ya Berk New Haven CT 1984-1989; Asst P Middlesex Area Cluster Mnstry Higganum CT 1982-1985; Cur S Paul's Epis Ch Willimantic CT 1980-1982. Auth, "The Nearness of God: Par Mnstry as Sprtl Pract," Morehouse, 2010; Auth, "'If You are the s God, Throw Yourself Down': The Temptations of Chr in the Pract of Mnstry," *Sewanee Theol Revs*, 2006; Auth, "Towards Catholicity: More Than We Can Ask or Imagine," *The Angl Cath*, 2001; Auth, "The Mar of the Bride and the Lamb: The Celebrant's Pryr at the Euch," *Sewanee Theol Revs*, 1992; Auth, "The Threefold Rule of Pryr: A Paradigm for Ecum Sprtlty," *Vision: Washington Inst of Ecumenics*, 1987; Auth, "The Pstr Art of the Engl Mystics; rpt. of Three Sprtl Dir for our Time," Wipf & Stock (2004); Cowley, 1986; Auth, "The Cath Feminism of H Mo Ch," *Sewanee Theol Revs*, 1985; Auth, "Julian of Norwich: Theodicy as Pstr Art," *ATR*, 1982. Assoc of SSJE 1978. One of Ten Winners in Best Sermon Competition Epis Evang Fndt 1995. jugatta@sewanee.edu

GATTIS, Larry Russell (Chi) 20326 Harding Ave, Olympia Fields IL 60461 B Harvey IL 1/6/1942 s Thomas Houston Gattis & Modena. Transylvania U 1961; BA Lake Forest Coll 1966; MDiv Nash 1975; Cert Rutgers-The St U 1987; Cert U of Utah 1990; Chicago Sch Of Profsnl Psychol Chicago IL 1995. D 6/14/1975 Bp John P Craine P 12/20/1975 Bp Donald James Davis. m 5/19/1984 Linda Skrzynski. Ch Of The Medtr Chicago IL 1999-2000; S Raphael The Archangel Oak Lawn IL 1998; Santa Teresa de Avila Chicago IL 1998; Ch Of The Gd Shpd Momence IL 1993-1999; S Tim's Ch Griffith IN 1991-1996; Chr Ch Streator IL 1989-1990; Int Dio Chicago Chicago IL 1982-2004; Trin Ch Lincoln IL 1981; R S Paul's Epis Ch Dowagiac MI 1977-1980; Cur Trin Ch Hermitage PA 1975-1977.

GATZA, Mark Francis (Md) Po Box 628, Bel Air MD 21014 **P-in-c Emm Ch Bel Air MD 2009-** B Buffalo,NY 8/7/1955 s James Gatza & Marie Melanie. BA Hampshire Coll 1977; MDiv Ya Berk 1980; ThM S Mary Seminar/U Baltimore MD 1988; DMin SWTS 2003. D 6/12/1982 Bp Arthur Edward Walmsley P 1/25/1983 Bp David Keller Leighton Sr. m 9/5/1981 January Elizabeth Hamill c 2. Stndg Com Dio Maryland Baltimore MD 2001-2002; Eccl Crt Dio Maryland Baltimore MD 1998-2001; COM Dio Maryland Baltimore MD 1993-1999; R Chr Ch Forest Hill MD 1990-2002; Vic H Cross Ch St MD 1990-1993; Asst S Anne's Par Annapolis MD 1987-1990; Dir of Aspirancy Prog Dio Maryland Baltimore MD 1986-2003; Asst to R Ch Of S Paul The Apos Baltimore MD 1985-1987; R S Geo's Ch Perryman MD 1983-1985. Auth, "Another Look at the 1928 Euch," *Living Ch*, 2007; Auth, "Baltimore Declaration Still Has Much To Offer," *Living Ch*, 1996; Forw to, "Joy & Wonder In All God'S Works," Forw Mvmt Press, 1994; Auth, "Another Sunday For Red," *Living Ch*, 1994. mgatza@ang-md.org

GAUMER, Susan Salot (La) 7820 Jeannette St., New Orleans LA 70118 **R S Andr's Epis Ch New Orleans LA 1999-** B Washington DC 4/30/1942 d Nevin Edgar Salot & Helen Balch. BA Mt Holyoke Coll 1964; MA Jn Hopkins U 1965; MDiv STUSo 1993. D 5/23/1993 P 12/4/1993 Bp James Barrow Brown. m 7/17/1965 H Richard Gaumer c 2. Asst S Augustines Ch Metairie LA 1993-1999; Chapl S Mart's Epis Ch Metairie LA 1977-1990. Auth, "From Costly Silence To Sprtl Hlth, Presence:The Journ Of Sprtl Dir'S Intl Volume 6:No 3," *September*, 2000. Epis Dioc Ecamenical and Interreligious Off 1995. Woods Ldrshp Awd U So Sewanee TN 1991. susangaumer@cox.net

GAUSBY, Donald Stephen (NY) 4800 Fillmore Ave, Alexandria VA 22311 **Died 1/19/2011** B Toronto ON CA 6/5/1920 s Harold Stephen Gausby & Margaret Anna. BCA U Tor 1943; LTh U Tor 1947; STB U Tor 1947; MS U Tor 1950. Trans from Anglican Church of Canada 10/1/1953 Bp Al D Beverly. c 2.

GAUVIN, Joseph Henri Armand (NJ) 25 Southwood Drive, Saint Catharine'S L2M 4M5 Canada B Montreal QC CA 6/28/1930 s Pierre Gauvin & Rose. McGill U; LTh Montreal TS. D 5/1/1963 P 3/1/1964 Bp The Bishop Of Montreal. m 11/9/1963 Gloria P Edwards c 1. R Ch of the Gd Shpd Rahway NJ 1968-1993; Cur S Ptr's Ch Spotswood NJ 1967-1968.

GAVENTA, Sarah Kinney (Va) 301 Emmons Dr Apt 5B, Princeton NJ 08540 **Asst Trin Ch Princeton NJ 2009-** B Los Angeles CA 8/1/1977 d Martin Matthew Kinney & Pamela Agnes. BS U Rich 1999; MDiv VTS 2005. D 6/18/2005 P 12/19/2005 Bp Peter James Lee. m 6/8/2007 Matthew R Gaventa c 1. Asst Emm Epis Ch Greenwood VA 2005-2009. sarah.gaventa@gmail.com

GAVIN, Craig Edmonds (Neb) 4321 S 36th St, Lincoln NE 68516 **Bp's Trst Dio Nebraska Omaha NE 2009-; R S Matt's Ch Lincoln NE 2007-** B Chicago IL 6/26/1949 s John Edmonds Gavin & Evelyn Mary. Nebraska Wesl 1971; BS Nebraska Wesl 1991; MDiv Epis TS of The SW 1994. D 5/1/1994 Bp James Edward Krotz P 11/6/1994 Bp Larry Earl Maze. m 5/22/1971 Linda Kay Freeman c 1. R The Epis Ch Of The Nativ Dothan AL 2004-2007; R S Theo's Epis Ch Bella Vista AR 1996-2004; Asst R Chr Epis Ch Little Rock AR 1994-1996. Ord Of S Lk 1996. cgavin@neb.rr.com

GAVIT, Sara Beth (Ak) 2222 E Tudor Rd, Anchorage AK 99507 **S Mary's Ch Anchorage AK 2005-** B Norfolk NE 12/27/1960 d Richard John Gavit & Anne Lois. BA (not complete) U of Alaska; BA - Trans U of Nebraska; MDiv St Jn's U TS 2011. D 6/4/2011 Bp Mark A Lattime. m 4/25/2009 Patricia Kathryn McDaid c 2. SARA_GAVIT@HOTMAIL.COM

GAY, Jean-Ricot Ricot (SeFla) 465 Ne 100th St, Miami Shores FL 33138 B HT 11/19/1957 s Joseph Ricot Gay & Solange. MBA Pacific Wstrn U Los Angeles 1991; MS Nova SE U 1997; MDiv STUSo 2002. D 6/16/2002 P 12/21/2002

Bp Leopold Frade. m 12/27/1988 Marie Rose Dorestant c 2. R Ch Of The Resurr Biscayne Pk FL 2002-2009. ricot41@hotmail.com

GAY, Judith Shumway (Mass) 59 Fenno St, Cambridge MA 02138 **Assoc P S Jas' Epis Ch Cambridge MA 2001-** B New York NY 2/1/1933 d George Alfred Shumway & Orpha Veda. BA Wellesley Coll 1954; MA UTS 1957; PhD U of Cambridge 1980. Trans from Church of the Province of Southern Africa 11/27/2002 Bp M(arvil) Thomas Shaw III. m 6/11/1954 John H Gay c 3. Phi Beta Kappa Wellesley Coll 1954. judyjohngay@comcast.net

GAY, Karen R (La) Episcopal Church of the Holy Communion, P. O. Box 474, Plaquemine LA 70764 **R Ch Of The H Comm Plaquemine LA 2008-; Dioc, Partnr in Mssn Com Mem Dio Louisiana Baton Rouge LA 2008-** B Fort Polk LA 10/20/1957 d James Richards & Mary. BS LSU 1979; Cert Ldrshp Prog for Musicians of Sm Congregations 2000; Dplma Dioc Sch for Mnstry Louisiana 2002. D 1/25/2004 P 8/8/2004 Bp Charles Edward Jenkins III. m 8/16/1980 John Gay c 4. Chapl Trin Epis Ch Baton Rouge LA 2007-2008; Epis HS Baton Rouge LA 2007; Ch Of The Nativ Rosedale LA 2006-2007. Louisiana Epis Cler Assn 2006. motherkaren@trinitybr.org

GAY, Margaret Worcester (CNY) 10051 Florence Hill Rd, Camden NY 13316 B New York NY 12/1/1940 d Maurice Bedell Worcester & Edith. Cor; Loc Formation & Bex; ABS U of Pennsylvania 1962. D 10/7/2006 P 5/30/2007 Bp Gladstone Bailey Adams III. m 4/20/1968 Edward Gay c 2. amygay@twcny.rr.com

GAY, Robert George (SVa) 204 Mill Stream Way, Williamsburg VA 23185 B Oak Park IL 2/19/1944 s George George Gay & Veronica Catherine. BS Loyola U 1966. D 4/24/2010 Bp Herman Hollerith IV. m 12/31/1971 Mary Esther Upperco c 3. rggay@cox.net

GAYLE JR, William Gedge (La) 227 Helios Avenue, Metarie LA 70005 B Lake Charles LA 2/28/1939 s William Gedge Gayle & Shirley. BS Tul 1960; Edinburgh Theol Coll 1962; MDiv STUSo 1963; STM STUSo 1976. D 6/20/1963 Bp Iveson Batchelor Noland P 5/1/1964 Bp Girault M Jones. m 7/25/1990 Susan D Upham c 2. R S Mart's Epis Ch Metairie LA 1976-2004; R S Paul's Ch Albany GA 1970-1976; Cur S Jas Epis Ch Alexandria LA 1966-1970; Cur S Andr's Epis Ch New Orleans LA 1963-1966. Louisiana Epis Cler Assn 1976-2002. Dorothy Porter Serv Awd St Mart's Epis Sch 2005; Alum Serv Awd Sewanee 1994. gayledrycreek@aol.com

GAYLOR, Pamela Elaine (SO) 3149 Indian Ripple Rd, Dayton OH 45440 **COM Dio Sthrn Ohio Cincinnati OH 1999-** B Mariemont OH 2/26/1952 d Clifford Edward Wolf & Flora Julia. BA Morehead St U 1975; MA Mia 1989; MDiv VTS 1995. D 6/24/1995 P 5/4/1996 Bp Herbert Thompson Jr. c 1. Dioc Sprtl Dir - Curs Sec Dio Sthrn Ohio Cincinnati OH 2002-2004; Dio Sthrn Ohio Cincinnati OH 2002; R Chr Ch Xenia OH 2001-2009; R All SS Epis Ch Portsmouth OH 1997-2001; Asst R S Fran Epis Ch Springboro OH 1995-1997. CT 1988. Hon Pi Kappa Lambda Mia Chapt 1987. rector.cecx@att.net

GEARHART, Robert James (Neb) 665 4th St., PO Box 56, Syracuse NE 68446 B Camden NJ 5/21/1938 s Curven Victor Gearhart & Isabelle Amelia. BS S Jos 1970; MDiv Nash 1973. D 6/23/1973 P 12/1/1973 Bp Robert Lionne DeWitt. m 6/17/1960 Wilma M Wilson c 2. Vic S Aug's Ch De Witt NE 1988-2003; R S Chas The Mtyr Beatrice NE 1988-2003; R S Jn's Ch Valentine NE 1978-1988; Vic S Jn's Epis Ch Valentine NE 1978-1988; Vic S Johns Ch Albion NE 1977-1978; Vic S Mk's Ch Creighton NE 1975-1978; Vic S Ptr's Ch Neligh NE 1975-1978; R S Steph's Epis Ch Clifton Heights PA 1973-1975.

GEARING, Charles Edward (At) 6525 Gardenia Way, Stone Mountain GA 30087 **D S Barth's Epis Ch Atlanta GA 2010-** B Charleston WV 12/29/1928 s Raymond Dewey Gearing & Winifred Havergal. BS Georgia Inst of Tech 1952; MS Pur 1964; PhD Pur 1966. D 10/23/1993 Bp Frank Kellogg Allan. m 9/4/1952 Carol Leyh Dodd c 3. D Emory Epis Campus Mnstry Atlanta GA 1993-1999; Stwdshp Consult Epis Ch Cntr New York NY 1991-1996. Auth, "Dioc Gift Plnng Prog," ECF/Morehouse, 2002; Auth, "Funding Future Mnstry," ECF/Morehouse, 2000. Apos in Stwdshp The Epis Ntwk for Stwdshp 2003; Golden Rule Awd Untd Way Atlanta 1994. charles@mailatlanta.net

GEARS, Wallace E (Minn) 3240 Jersey Ave S, Minneapolis MN 55426 **D Dio Minnesota Minneapolis MN 1967-** B Minneapolis MN 11/14/1920 s Charles H Gears & Artie Anna. BA U MN; MA Minneapolis Coll Mus Minneapolis MN 1950. D 12/21/1959 Bp Philip Frederick McNairy. c 2. Auth, "Chr The Lord Is Risen".

GEDDES, R(obert) Douglas (Va) PO Box 86, Hallieford VA 23068 B Wichita KS 8/3/1947 s C(larke) Robert Geddes & Barbara Elizabeth. AAB Columbus Tech Inst Columbus OH 1973; BGS Capital U 1975; MS Untd States Intl U San Diego CA 1980; MDiv STUSo 1997. D 6/14/1997 Bp Frank Harris Vest Jr P 12/13/1997 Bp David Conner Bane Jr. m 8/9/1969 Karen Lynn Read c 1. R Kingston Par Epis Ch Mathews VA 2005-2011; R Cntrl Mecklenburg Cure Boydton VA 1997-2005; R S Jn's Epis Ch Chase City VA 1997-2005; R S Tim's Epis Ch Clarksville VA 1997-2005; R Gr Epis Ch Drakes Branch VA 1997-2000. seddeg47@yahoo.com

GEDRICK III, John Paul (At) 700 Route 22, Pawling NY 12564 B West Point NY 7/28/1968 BA Colg 1990; MA U Chi 1991; MDiv Yale DS 1998. D 6/5/2004 P 2/2/2005 Bp J(ohn) Neil Alexander. jgedrick@trinitypawling.org

GEEN, Russell Glenn (HB) 4 Shad Bush Dr, Columbia MO 65203 B Ironwood MI 5/3/1932 s William Geen & Minnie Jane. BA MI SU 1954; BD Ken 1957; MA U of Wisconsin 1964; PhD U of Wisconsin 1967. D 6/30/1957 Bp Herman R Page P 1/1/1958 Bp Richard Ainslie Kirchhoffer. m 9/9/1960 Barbara June Kimmel c 2. Vic S Barth's Epis Ch Bemidji MN 1959-1963; Cur Trin Ch Indianapolis IN 1957-1959. Auth, "Soc Motivation," Wadsworth, 1995; Auth, "Human Agression," Wadsworth, 1991; Auth, "Human Motivation," Allyn & Bacon, 1984; Auth, "Personality," Mosby, 1976. APA 1967-1996. Fell APA 1986. russellgeen@yahoo.com

GEER, Christine Groves (Md) 23 Briar Patch Rd, Stonington CT 06378 B New York NY 5/1/1935 d Alpheus Montague Geer & Lillian. BA GW 1983; MDiv CDSP 1989; Cert Basic Trng Int Mnstry Ntwk 1992. D 1/21/1990 P 9/1/1990 Bp Stewart Clark Zabriskie. m 7/5/1986 Roy W Cole c 3. P All SS Of The Mtn Epis Chap Crested Butte CO 2002-2003; Supply P Dio Connecticut Hartford CT 1997-2002; R S Marks Pintler Cluster Anaconda MT 1997-1998; Int S Paul's Par Prince Geo's Cnty Brandywine MD 1995-1997; Co-R S Geo's Ch Perryman MD 1994-1995; H Cross Epis Ch Sanford FL 1993-1994; Dio Albany Albany NY 1992-1993; Dio So Carolina Charleston SC 1989-1992; Assoc Pstr S Lk's Epis Ch Las Vegas NV 1989-1990; R The Ch Of The Epiph Eutawville SC 1987-1992; Asst S Fran Ch Greenville SC 1985-1987; Asst Epis Ch Of The Redeem Greenville SC 1984-1985. OHC 1983-2003. Christinegeer12@att.net

GEER, Francis Hartley (NY) Po Box 158, Garrison NY 10524 **R S Phil's Ch Garrison NY 1987-** B Aiea Oahu HI 3/19/1948 s Francis George Geer & Miriam Fraser. BA Rutgers-The St U 1970; MDiv CDSP 1976. D 6/12/1976 Bp Paul Moore Jr P 9/1/1977 Bp Harold Louis Wright. m 9/9/1972 Sarah Davis. New York Spec Account New York NY 1994-2002; S Lk's-Roosevelt Hosp Cntr New York NY 1992-2001; Asst Min Trin Ch In The City Of Boston Boston MA 1984-1987. Auth, "Encyclopedia Of Environ Awareness". ACPE, Fell Coll Of Chapl.

GEERDES, Patricia Seney (WVa) 900 Hillsborough St, Raleigh NC 27603 B Richmond VA 9/2/1938 d John Seymour Seney & Audry Clyde. BA Virginia Commonwealth U 1978; DMin UTS Richmond VA 1983. D 6/11/1983 Bp Robert Bruce Hall P 5/1/1984 Bp David Henry Lewis Jr. m 8/16/1996 Donald Goldstein. Trin Ch Moundsville WV 2002-2009; S Mary's Sch Raleigh NC 1999-2002; S Paul's Ch Key W FL 1996-1999; H Innoc Key W FL 1993-1996; P-in-c S Ptr's Epis Ch Key W FL 1993; Ch Of Our Sav Montpelier VA 1984-1989; Asst Chr Ascen Ch Richmond VA 1983-1984. Phi Kappa Phi.

GEESEY, Barry Stephen (WVa) 3887 Carriage Ln SW, Conyers GA 30094 B Newport RI 4/23/1948 s Marvin Sterling Geesey & Geraldine Lorraine. BA Leh 1970; MDiv Virgina TS 1973; MLS U Pgh 1977. D 6/8/1973 P 3/1/1974 Bp Dean T Stevenson. m 4/7/2006 Richard F Harlan. Assoc Chr Ch Norcross GA 1985-1997; R S Pauls Epis Ch Williamson WV 1981-1985; Int S Mk's Epis Ch S Albans WV 1977-1978; Assoc Ch Of The Gd Shpd Pittsburgh PA 1976-1977; Vic S Andr's Ch Tioga PA 1974-1976; Vic S Jn's Ch Westfield PA 1974-1976; D Dio Cntrl Pennsylvania Harrisburg PA 1973-1974. BGEESEY@COMCAST.NET

GEHLSEN, Thomas J (Ia) 3504 SW Timberline Dr., Ankeny IA 50023 **R S Mart's Ch Perry IA 2008-; Transition Off Dio Iowa Des Moines IA 2004-; R Gr Ch Boone IA 1999-** B Davenport IA 9/5/1946 s William Brent Gehlsen & Andorothy. BA St. Ambr U Davenport IA 1968; MDiv St Thos Univ Sch of Theo St Paul MN 1972; MA U of Iowa 1976; PhD Iowa St U 1998. Rec from Roman Catholic 5/4/1995 as Priest Bp Carl Christopher Epting. m 5/11/1990 Susan K McGirl c 6. S Lk's Ch Des Moines IA 2001-2003; S Anne's By The Fields Ankeny IA 1998-2001; R S Paul's Ch Durant IA 1995-1998. "Day Treatment: Behavioral Disordered Adolescents," *Dissertation*, Iowa St U, 1998. tgehlsen@iowaepiscopal.org

GEHRIG, Stephen James (Oly) 1828 Field Place NE, Renton WA 98059 B Spokane WA 12/19/1951 s James Taylor Gehrig & Mary Janet. BA U of Washington 1974; MDiv CRDS 1979; M.Ed Natl U 2008. D 8/2/1979 P 6/11/1980 Bp Robert Hume Cochrane. R S Marg's Epis Ch Bellevue WA 1988-2005; R Ch Of The H Sprt Vashon WA 1983-1988; Asst S Steph's Epis Ch Longview WA 1979-1983.

GEIB, Lanny Roland (Tex) 5087 Galileo Dr, Colorado Springs CO 80917 B Harrisburg PA 2/12/1942 s Roland Adams Geib & Ruth Naomi. U of Nthrn Colorado; BA VMI 1965; MDiv TESM 1989. D 6/29/1989 Bp C(hristopher) FitzSimons Allison P 6/1/1990 Bp Edward Lloyd Salmon Jr. m 10/27/1975 Thella Price c 2. R S Paul's Ch Katy TX 1999-2004; R S Chris's Ch Killeen TX 1991-1999; D Ch Of The Heav Rest Estill SC 1989-1990; D Ch Of The H Comm Allendale SC 1989-1990.

GEIGER, Clifford Theodore (Me) 2800 Se Fairway W, Stuart FL 34997 B Syracuse NY 1/17/1940 s John Theodore Geiger & Mildred. BA Davis & Elkins Coll 1963; MDiv GTS 1966. D 6/4/1966 P 12/1/1966 Bp Horace W B Donegan. m 9/7/1963 Anne Elizabeth Joyce c 1. S Dav's Epis Ch Kennebunk ME

1968-1985; Cur Epis Ch Of S Mary The Vrgn Falmouth ME 1966-1968. Outstanding Young Men Of Amer 1970. ajgeiger@bellsouth.net

GEIGER, William Linwood (Pgh) 3079 Warren Rd, Indiana PA 15701 **R Chr Epis Ch Indiana PA 1999-** B Darby PA 3/24/1957 s Linwood Townsend Geiger & Glenna Ruth. BA U of Pennsylvania 1979; MDiv TESM 1987. D 6/6/1987 Bp Alden Moinet Hathaway P 4/1/1988 Bp Charles Farmer Duvall. m 10/8/1983 Kathleen Kearney c 2. R Ch Of The Epiph Jacksonville FL 1992-1999; Cur H Cross Ch Pensacola FL 1987-1992. ccrector@earthlink.net

GEISLER, Mark A (Chi) 113 E. Lafayette St., Ottawa IL 61350 **Comm on Yth and Yng Adlt Dio Chicago Chicago IL 2000-** B Waukegan IL 6/25/1963 s John Stuart Geisler & Jane Ekstrand. BA Nthrn Illinois U 1986; MDiv VTS 1994. D 6/18/1994 Bp Frank Tracy Griswold III P 3/25/1995 Bp William Walter Wiedrich. m 4/25/1987 Varsie Ann Garab c 1. Lasalle Cnty Epis Mnstry La Salle IL 2009-2010; Dn of the Rockford Dnry Dio Chicago Chicago IL 2002-2006; Dio Chicago Chicago IL 2002; Dio Chicago Chicago IL 2002; R S Paul's Ch Dekalb IL 2000-2008; Dioc Stwdshp Cmpgn Dio Chicago Chicago IL 2000-2002; Cur Trin Ch Ft Wayne IN 1996-2000; Dioc Coun Dio Chicago Chicago IL 1995-1996; Cur Trin Epis Ch Wheaton IL 1994-1996. frmark@comcast.net

GEISLER, William Fredric (Cal) Po Box 2624, San Anselmo CA 94979 B Cleveland OH 7/29/1935 s Fredric William Geisler & Dorothy Barrows. ABS Harv 1957; MBA Harv 1960; MDiv CDSP 1968. D 6/22/1968 P 1/4/1969 Bp C Kilmer Myers. m 9/16/1967 Barbara Reichmuth c 2. Int S Columba's Ch Inverness CA 2010-2011; Ch Of The H Innoc Corte Madera CA 1998; Serv (non-stipendiary) S Paul's Epis Ch San Rafael CA 1984-1995; Serv (non-stipendiary) St Johns Epis Ch Ross CA 1982-1984; Dio California San Francisco CA 1968-1998; Serv (non-stipendiary) S Fran' Epis Ch San Francisco CA 1968-1982. "Tax Guide for Epis Ministers and Ch," *Ch Pension Fund*, 1998. California Soc of CPA's 1963. wfgcpa@aol.com

GEISLER, William Joseph (Pgh) 1283 Earlford Drive, Pittsburgh PA 15227 **Cn of Formation Dio Pittsburgh Monroeville PA 2011-; R S Ptr's Epis Ch Brentwood Pittsburgh PA 2011-** B Pittsburgh PA 3/1/1956 s William A Geisler & Elizabeth Jane. BA La Roche Coll 1979; MDiv Pontifical Coll 1985; MA Pontifical Coll 1985; DMin Pittsburgh TS 1999. Rec from Roman Catholic 6/1/1997 as Priest Bp Alden Moinet Hathaway. m 10/13/1990 Jennie Elizabeth Korn c 2. S Steph's Epis Ch Mckeesport PA 2003-2010; R S Jas Epis Ch Pittsburgh PA 1998-2003; S Paul's Ch Monongahela PA 1997-1998. PITTSBURGHPRIEST@GMAIL.COM

GEISSLER-O NEIL, Susan Lorraine (Mass) 3350 Hopyard Rd, Pleasanton CA 94588 B Valdosta GA 5/25/1956 d Arthur J Geissler & Ruth Prescott. BA Smith 1978; MDiv Ya Berk 1982. D 6/5/1982 Bp John Bowen Coburn P 9/1/1983 Bp Morgan Porteus. Assoc S Mk's Ch Taunton MA 1989-1996; S Mk's Ch Foxborough MA 1989-1995; S Jn's Epis Ch Westwood MA 1988-1989; The Ch Of Our Redeem Lexington MA 1986-1987; All SS Ch Chelmsford MA 1983-1985.

GEITZ, Elizabeth R (NJ) 431 Twin Lakes Road, Shohola PA 18458 B Clarksville TN 6/8/1953 d Oscar Lane Rankin & Dorothy. BS Van 1974; MAT U of So Carolina 1979; PrTS 1991; MDiv GTS 1993. D 6/12/1993 Bp George Phelps Mellick Belshaw P 12/11/1993 Bp Joe Morris Doss. m 6/8/1974 Michael Meyer Geitz c 2. P Assoc Ch Of The Gd Shpd And S Jn Milford PA 2011; Bd Trst, Vice-Chair The GTS New York NY 2009-2011; Sprtlty Fac Credo Inst Inc. Memphis TN 2005-2011; Dio New Jersey Trenton NJ 2001-2009; Calv Epis Ch Summit NJ 2001-2002; Int S Fran Ch Dunellen NJ 1998-2000; Assoc S Lk's Epis Ch Metuchen NJ 1996-1998; Trin Cathd Trenton NJ 1996; Assoc S Paul's Epis Ch Westfield NJ 1993-1995. Auth, "I Am That Chld," Morehouse Pub, 2012; Ed/Con., "Lifting Wmn Voices," Ch Pub, 2009; Contrib, "All Shall be Well," Ch Pub, 2009; Auth, "Calling Cler," Ch Pub, 2007; Auth, "Fireweed Evang," Ch Pub, 2004; Ed/Con., "Wmn Uncommon Prayers," Morehouse Pub, 2000; Auth, "Soul Satisfaction," Morehouse Pub, 1998; Auth, "Gender & Nicene Creed," Morehouse Pub, 1995; Auth, "Entertaining Ang," Morehouse Publising, 1993. Bd Trst GTS 2009; Distinguished Alum Awd GTS 2007; Polly Bond Awd ECom 2003. egeitz@elizabethgeitz.com

GELDERT, Maurice William (RG) 121 Mescalero Tr, Ruidoso NM 88345 B New Orleans LA 8/27/1944 s Maurice Geldert & Doris. Cert In Rel Stds Rio Grande Sch For Mnstry Tesm; BS U GA 1972; OD Sthrn Coll Of Optometry Memphis TN 1976. D 12/19/2006 P 5/6/2007 Bp Jeffrey Neil Steenson. m 5/30/1992 Mary Geldert c 2. doctor.mwg@gmail.com

GELFER, Miriam Carmel (Mass) 8 Saint Johns Rd, Cambridge MA 02138 **Dn of Stdt and Cmnty Life EDS Cambridge MA 2011-** B Blue Point NY 7/16/1951 d George Washington Gelfer & Genevieve. BS Concord Coll 1975; MA U of Sthrn Mississippi 1976; MA Presb Sch CE 1986; MDiv EDS 1994. D 8/7/1994 Bp Orris George Walker Jr P 3/17/1995 Bp M(arvil) Thomas Shaw III. m 6/25/2005 Lisa M Garcia. R Gr Ch Newton MA 1998-2001; Asst Par Of The Epiph Winchester MA 1994-1998. mgelfer@eds.edu

GELINEAU, Francoise (Mich) P.O. Box 351, Roscommon MI 48653 **P-in-c Ch Of The Gd Shpd Silver City NM 2011-; R S Eliz's Epis Ch Roscommon MI 2007-** B Quebec CA 10/14/1942 d Joseph Campbell Gelineau & Marcelle. BS U of No Texas 1965; MDiv Ya Berk 1990. D 6/18/1983 Bp Wilbur Emory Hogg Jr P 5/1/1991 Bp Steven Charleston. m 10/3/2004 John Cowart c 3. R S Steph's Ch Hamburg MI 2001-2004; R S Ptr's Ch Pittsburg KS 1998-2001; P-in-c Trin Ch Whitehall NY 1994-1996; Int S Jas The Fisherman Kodiak AK 1992-1993; Int S Dav's Ch Wasilla AK 1991-1992; D S Augustines' Epis Ch Homer AK 1990-1991. Ord Of Ascen. frangelineau@gmail.com

GELLER, Margaret (Mass) 4 Key St., Millis MA 02054 B Alexandria VA 1/5/1953 D 6/5/2004 Bp M(arvil) Thomas Shaw III. c 1. MECA 2004; NAAD 2001. maggiegl@comcast.net

GEMIGNANI, Michael Caesar (Tex) 1816 Dublin Dr., League City TX 77573 B Baltimore MD 2/23/1938 s Hugo Gemignani & Dorothy. BA U Roch 1959; MS U of Notre Dame 1964; PhD U of Notre Dame 1965; JD Indiana U 1980. D 10/14/1973 P 1/8/1974 Bp John P Craine. m 5/15/1985 Nilda Borden c 2. Assoc S Mich's Ch La Marque TX 2007-2011; R S Paul's Epis Ch Freeport TX 1993-2007; Asst to R S Chris's Ch League City TX 1989-1991; P-in-c S Johns Epis Ch Brownville ME 1986-1988; Vic S Fran In The Fields Zionsville IN 1974-1979. Auth, "Making Your Ch a Hse of Healing," Judson, 2008; Auth, "Sprtl Formation for Pastors: Tending the Fire Within," Judson, 2002; Auth, "To Know God: Sm Grp Experiences in Sprtl Formation," Judson, 2001. mgmign2@hal-pc.org

GEMINDER, Randolph Jon (LI) 175 Broadway, Amityville NY 11701 **R S Mary's Ch Amityville NY 1975-** B Brooklyn NY 12/12/1947 s John James Geminder & Ruth Eileen. BA S Fran Coll Brooklyn, NY 1968; MDiv GTS 1971. D 6/12/1971 P 12/1/1971 Bp Jonathan Goodhue Sherman. m 6/27/1970 Donna Bourie c 2. Chair, BEC Dio Long Island Garden City NY 1986-1988; Chair, Angl/RC Cmsn Dio Long Island Garden City NY 1983-1985; Secy, Dioc Coun Dio Long Island Garden City NY 1979-1982; Assoc S Geo's Epis Ch Schenectady NY 1973-1975; Cur S Jn's Of Lattingtown Locust Vlly NY 1971-1973. padreone@optonline.net

GENDER III, William Frederick (Ct) PO Box 360, Morris CT 06763 **Died 7/21/2010** B Wilkes-Barre PA 8/9/1928 s William Frederick Gender & Mary Veronica. BA Hob 1954; MDiv PDS 1957. D 6/15/1957 P 12/1/1957 Bp Frederick J Warnecke.

GENEREUX, Patrick Edward (Ia) 621 N 5th St, Burlington IA 52601 **Coordntr, Dioc Disaster Relief & Recovery Dio Iowa Des Moines IA 2008-** B Warren MN 4/5/1947 s Arthur Genereux & Bernice Emily. BS Wm Carey U 1973; MDiv STUSo 1978. D 5/18/1978 P 5/4/1979 Bp George Mosley Murray. m 7/6/1968 Susan Debenham c 2. R Chr Epis Ch Burlington IA 1994-2008; Int Calv Cathd Sioux Falls SD 1992-1994; Dio Colorado Denver CO 1987-1994; Dio So Dakota Sioux Falls SD 1985-1992; Off Of Bsh For ArmdF New York NY 1982-1985; Vic S Anna's Ch Atmore AL 1979-1981; R Trin Epsicopal Ch Atmore AL 1979-1981; Cur Trin Epis Ch Mobile AL 1978-1979. pegenereux@msn.com

GENNETT JR, Paul William (Del) 413 Terra Dr, Newark DE 19702 **R S Thos's Par Newark DE 2008-** B Camden NJ 7/1/1949 s Paul William Gennett & Cora Lydia. BA Grove City Coll 1971; MDiv VTS 1992. D 6/6/1992 P 12/9/1992 Bp Alden Moinet Hathaway. m 7/10/1971 Marilyn Ann Vasey c 2. Assoc S Dav's Ch Wayne PA 2000-2008; R S Mk's Ch Johnstown PA 1996-2000; S Jas Epis Ch Pittsburgh PA 1994-1996; Asst to the R Calv Ch Pittsburgh PA 1992-1994. paulgennett@comcast.net

GENNUSO JR, George (WLa) 500 Edgewood Dr, Pineville LA 71360 **R S Mich's Epis Ch Pineville LA 1998-** B Opelousas LA 12/16/1947 s George Gennuso & Hilda Marie. BS Louisiana Tech U 1970; MDiv Nash 1989. Rec from Roman Catholic 6/1/1989 as Deacon Bp Iveson Batchelor Noland. m 3/5/1973 Grace Maddox c 1. S Mk's Cathd Shreveport LA 1991-1998; Calv Ch Bunkie LA 1989-1991; Vic Trin Epis Ch Ball LA 1989-1991. BroSA 2007; Ord to St. Lk 2008. georgegennuso@hotmail.com

GENTILE, Roger Michael Christopher (NY) 315 W 85th St Apt 2-B, New York NY 10024 B Teaneck NJ 4/26/1950 s Salvatore Peter Gentile & Katherine Bernadette. BA Rutgers-The St U 1976; MDiv GTS 1981. D 6/6/1981 Bp Albert Wiencke Van Duzer P 12/19/1981 Bp Walter Decoster Dennis Jr. The GTS New York NY 2008-2010; Assoc The Ch of S Ign of Antioch New York NY 1981-1982. rogergentile2@verizon.net

GENTLE, Judith Marie (Pgh) 315 Turnpike St, North Andover MA 01845 B Birmingham AL 6/10/1947 BS Auburn U 1970; MDiv Candler TS Emory U 1987; MA U of San Francisco 1992; PhD Boston Coll 2001. D 6/6/1987 P 5/12/1988 Bp Charles Judson Child Jr. m 4/26/2004 Jerry Edward Hardy. Ch Of The Adv Pittsburgh PA 2004; Ch Of The H Trin Marlborough MA 1998-1999; S Lk's Ch Hudson MA 1994-1997; S Bede's Ch Atlanta GA 1987-1990. 2003.

GENTRY, (Bryan) Massey (Tex) 2000 S Maryland Pkwy, Las Vegas NV 89104 B Birmingham AL 7/25/1945 s George Marshal Gentry & Dorys Elizabeth. BA Birmingham-Sthrn Coll 1967; MDiv Chicago TS 1970; MDiv STUSo 1976. D 6/11/1978 P 12/1/1978 Bp Furman Stough. m 12/28/1968 Janeth H Hunt c 1. S Mart's Epis Ch Houston TX 2006-2008; R Chr Ch Las Vegas NV

1997-2006; S Jn's Ch Birmingham AL 1993-1996; Cn To Ordnry Dio Alabama Birmingham AL 1989-1997; The Epis Ch Of S Fran Of Assisi Indn Sprg Vill AL 1986-1988; Dio Alabama Birmingham AL 1982-1996; Trin Ch Wetumpka AL 1978-1986. Angl Consult Intl Cltn On Namibia 1988. padre5000@hotmail.com

GENTRY, Keith A (Ark) 1204 Talihana Drive, North Little Rock AR 72116 **Ch Of The Gd Shpd Forrest City AR 2011-; S Andr's Ch Marianna AR 2010-** B Evansville IN 1/17/1950 s Robert Eugene Gentry & Lois Frances. RT (ARRT) Jn Hopkins Hosp Sch of Radiologic Tech 1971; AB Loyola U Maryland 1976; MDiv GTS 1979. D 6/19/1979 Bp David Keller Leighton Sr P 2/9/1980 Bp Charles Shannon Mallory. c 2. R S Lk's Epis Ch No Little Rock AR 2003-2010; Assoc S Matt's Ch Westerville OH 2000-2003; R S Jas Epis Ch Columbus OH 1992-1997; Assoc S Paul's Epis Ch Modesto CA 1990-1992; Cn Res S Paul's Cathd Peoria IL 1987-1990; R S Lk's Epis Ch Niles OH 1981-1987; Cur Gr Epis Ch Massapequa NY 1979-1981. Co-Auth, "Par Guidelines for use of Seder Meal," *Dioc Nwspr*, Dio Ohio. OSL 1980; P Assoc - All SS Sis of the Poor 1979; SocMary 1985; SocOLW 1985. Theta Alpha Kappa Loyola U Maryland 1976; Rev DJ McGuire Theol Medal Loyola U Maryland 1976. kadfael@comcast.net

GENTY, Marc Daniel (Colo) St Luke's Episcopal Church, 2000 Stover St, Fort Collins CO 80525 **BEC (BOEC) Dio Colorado Denver CO 2008-; D Dio Colorado Denver CO 2008-; Diac Coun Mem Dio Colorado Denver CO 2008-** B Pueblo CO 7/27/1957 s Francois Marie Genty & Susannah Palmer. BS CSU 1980. D 11/17/2007 Bp Robert John O'Neill. m 11/21/1981 Heidi Genty c 3. mgenty@mac.com

GEORGE, Cathy Ann Hagstrom (Mass) Po Box 6, Lincoln MA 01773 B Saint Paul,MN 12/18/1955 d Robert Stanley Hagstrom & Diane Ruth. BA Macalester Coll 1979; MDiv Harvard DS 1984. D 6/4/1986 Bp John Bowen Coburn P 6/1/1987 Bp Roger W Blanchard. m 6/15/1985 Michael S George c 2. Dio Massachusetts Boston MA 2008-2011; P-in-c S Mary's Epis Ch Dorchester MA 2008-2011; R S Anne's In The Fields Epis Ch Lincoln MA 1996-2008; Assoc Trin Ch In The City Of Boston Boston MA 1994-1995; Asst S Jn's Ch Beverly Farms MA 1990-1993; Asst S Paul's Ch Newburyport MA 1989; R Emm Ch Jaffrey NH 1988-1999; Asst All SS' Epis Ch Belmont MA 1987-1988. Billings Prize for Preaching Harvard DS 1984. cathygeorge@ymail.com

GEORGE, C(larence Davis) Dominic (NY) 797 Corbett Ave Apt 3, San Francisco CA 94131 **Assoc S Fran' Epis Ch San Francisco CA 1995-** B Memphis TN 9/18/1942 s Clarence Moore George & Frances Elizabeth. CUNY; U of Memphis; DIT Mercer TS 1974; RN S Lk Sch Nrsng San Francisco CA 1984; BD SUNY 1999. D 6/22/1974 Bp Jonathan Goodhue Sherman. Bro-in-c San Andres Ch Yonkers NY 1978-1979. Professed Soc of S Fran 1967-1999; Professed Tertiary of the Soc of S Fran 1999.

GEORGE, Eldred Hamilton (Chi) 1414 W Lincoln St, Freeport IL 61032 **R Gr Epis Ch Freeport IL 2009-** B Dominican Republic 8/8/1945 m 7/11/1992 Odilia Nanzzi Nanetti Sandoval c 3. P Santa Teresa de Avila Chicago IL 2004-2009; Dio Panama 1992-2004; Dio The Dominican Republic (Iglesia Epis Dominicana) Santo Domingo DO 1975-1977; Dio The Dominican Republic (Iglesia Epis Dominicana) Santo Domingo DO 1972-1973. egrector@aeroinc.net

GEORGE, Erminie A (VI) PO Box 9798 Charlotte Amalie, St. Thomas Virgin Islands 00801 B Tortola VI 12/10/1955 d Henry. AA U of Vrgn Islands 1988; BA U of Vrgn Islands 2005. D 6/14/2008 P 3/5/2011 Bp Edward Ambrose Gumbs. m 6/19/1976 Garfield George c 3. erminie19@yahoo.com

GEORGE JR, Jay Charles (WTex) 7714 Moss Brook Dr, San Antonio TX 78255 **Vic Gr Epis Ch San Antonio TX 2011-** B Boynton Beach FL 3/26/1970 s Jacob C George & Marjorie E. BA Texas Tech U 1992; MDiv TS 2000. D 8/23/2000 P 2/27/2001 Bp James Edward Folts. m 12/18/1993 Jamie Partney c 3. Ch Planter Dio W Texas San Antonio TX 2008-2010; R S Andr's Epis Ch Seguin TX 2003-2008; Asst S Mk's Epis Ch San Antonio TX 2000-2003. revjaygeorge@me.com

GEORGE, Johannes Mark Philip (Tex) 15325 Bellaire Boulevard, Houston TX 77083 **Chr The King Ch Houston TX 2008-** B Freetown SL 10/28/1960 s Philip George & Mariama. BA S Paul's Sem LR 1982; BD S Paul's Sem LR 1985; MA Texas Sthrn U 2001. Rec from Roman Catholic 1/21/2001 as Priest Bp Claude Edward Payne. m 5/22/1999 Betty Momoh c 2. St Lk's Epis Hosp Houston TX 2004; S Jos's Epis Ch Grand Prairie TX 2001-2002. Untd Chapters of Alpha Kappa Delta Intl Sociol 2000. jmpg@att.net

GEORGE, Juan Victor (Del) Trinity Episcopal Church, 1108 N Adams St, Wilmington DE 19801 **Trin Par Wilmington DE 2007-; Vic Santa Rosa Mssn at Gr Ch White Plains NY 1999-** B San Pedro de Macoris DO 5/6/1945 s Jacinto Ismael George & Maria Elisa. BS CUNY 1978; MA Adel 1980. D 6/14/1997 P 12/1/1997 Bp Richard Frank Grein. m 6/3/1973 Joy Mentie Henry c 3. Gr Ch White Plains NY 1998-2005. georgevjtaurus@yahoo.com

GEORGE, Mitzi Gae Shelton (WLa) 1020 Sutherland Rd., Lake Charles LA 70611 **S Andr's Ch Lake Chas LA 1999-** B Onslow County NC 10/10/1957 d James Harvey Shelton & Shirley Ann. BA McNeese St U 1982; MA Loyola U 1993; MPS Loyola U 1993; Ed McNeese St 2001; DM U So 2003. D 1/24/1994 P 5/12/2001 Bp Robert Jefferson Hargrove Jr. m 3/15/1980 Kevin Dale George c 2. S Mich And All Ang Lake Chas LA 1994-1998. NAAD. mothermitzi@hotmail.com

GEORGE JR, Richard Maurice (Az) 7550 N 16th St Apt 6305, Phoenix AZ 85020 **Died 5/5/2010** B Belvidere IL 12/20/1930 s Richard Maurice George & Ada Bernice. BA Gri 1952; MDiv SWTS 1955; Fllshp VTS 1976. D 6/18/1955 Bp Charles L Street P 12/17/1955 Bp William L Essex. c 4. Assoc, OHC 1959. Hon Cn Dio Arizona 2006; Dn Emer, Trin Cathd Dio Arizona 1994. mtgeorge0605@gmail.com

GEORGE, Susanne T (Cal) 60 Brunswick Park, Melrose MA 02176 **D Chr Ch Alameda CA 2011-** B Los Angeles CA 3/14/1946 d Robert Allen Tyler & Frances Jean. BA U CA 1972; MA California St U 1975; BTS Sch for Deacons - Grad Theol Un 2005. D 12/2/2006 Bp Marc Handley Andrus. c 3. D S Cuth's Epis Ch Oakland CA 2006-2010. arbor946@yahoo.com

GEORGE HACKER, Nina (Alb) St Christophers Episcopal Church, PO Box 386, Cobleskill NY 12043 **R St Chris's Epis Ch Cobleskill NY 2009-** B Washington DC 4/1/1954 d Panos Andrew Georgopulo & Mary Evelyn. BA Connecticut Coll 1976; MA Geo 1979; MDiv Lancaster TS 1993; DMin TESM 2011. D 12/15/2008 P 6/24/2009 Bp William Howard Love. m 5/14/1994 Richard Hacker. Phi Beta Kappa 1977. Anne Askew Schlr TESM 2005; Fauth Prize for Acad Excellence Lancaster TS 1993; Georgia Harkness Awd Lancaster TS 1992; Connecticut Stdt Poet Connecticut Poetry Circuit 1977; Chas A. Dana Schlr Connecticut Coll 1974; Marshall Prize for Poetry Connecticut Coll 1973. rectorstchris12043@gmail.com

GEORGI, Geoffrey Mack (NC) Po Box 13, Rougemont NC 27572 B San Bernardino CA 12/10/1948 s Howard Mason Georgi & Mary Alice. Duke; PDS. D 4/27/1974 P 12/1/1974 Bp Albert Wiencke Van Duzer. m 8/26/1972 Sharon Eaton. Yth Min Ch Of The H Fam Chap Hill NC 1974-1979. Auth, "The Source". Chapl Assn.

✠ **GEPERT, Rt Rev Robert R** (WMich) 525 S Burdick St, Apt 4106, Kalamazoo MI 49007 **Bp of Wstrn Michigan Dio Wstrn Michigan Kalamazoo MI 2002-** B Pittsburgh PA 8/24/1948 s Robert Alexander Gepert & LaVerne Catherine. BS Point Pk U Pittsburgh PA 1974; MDiv VTS 1985. D 6/8/1985 P 12/22/1985 Bp John Thomas Walker Con 4/27/2002 for WMich. m 9/13/1997 Anne Labat Lytle c 3. Dn of Trin Cathd, Dio Easton Trin Cathd Easton MD 1996-2002; R St. Mich's S Mich's Epis Ch Bethlehem PA 1988-1996; R St. Paul's, Baden and St. Mary's, Aquasco S Paul's Par Prince Geo's Cnty Brandywine MD 1985-1988. DD VTS 2003. rrgepert@gmail.com

GERARD, Richard Louis (Minn) 716 Main St, Courtland MN 56021 **Died 1/26/2011** B Camden NJ 8/25/1938 s Maurice L Gerard & Mildred F. BA Amer U 1960; MA U of Pennsylvania 1962; GTS 1973. D 9/20/1973 Bp Lloyd Edward Gressle P 3/19/1974 Bp Thomas H Wright. c 2. weaver2@boutwellslanding.com

GERBASI, Virginia Kaye (WA) 4001 Franklin St, Christ Church Parish, Kensington, Kensington MD 20895 **Assit R Chr Ch Par Kensington MD 2007-** B Harrisburg PA 2/21/1964 d John Morse Cook & Virginia Kaye. BA W&M 1986; JD W&M 1989; MDiv Wesley TS 2007. D 6/9/2007 P 1/19/2008 Bp John Chane. m 5/9/1992 Joseph Gerbasi c 1. gingerbasi@mac.com

GERBER, Ronald Dale (Alb) 36 General Torbert Dr, Milford DE 19963 **P-in-c Chr Ch Dover DE 2009-** B Canton OH 4/5/1939 s Dale C Gerber & Mildred F. BA Heidelberg Coll 1961; BD Lancaster TS 1964. Rec from United Church of Christ 1/29/1972. c 3. S Andr's Epis Ch Albany NY 1993-2004; R Gr And H Innoc Albany NY 1977-1993; Cur S Jn's Epis Ch Troy NY 1976-1977; R H Trin Epis Ch Hollidaysburg PA 1972-1976.

GERBRACHT-STAGNARO, Marjorie Ann (WA) 5893 1st St S, Arlington VA 22204 **P-in-c Gr Ch Manchester NH 2011-** B Mineola NY 3/17/1970 d Frederick William Gerbracht & June Carol. BA U So 1992; MDiv GTS 1995. D 6/23/1995 Bp Orris George Walker Jr P 5/1/1996 Bp James Russell Moodey. Assoc R/Day Sch Chapl S Pat's Ch Washington DC 1998-2011; S Pat's Epis Day Sch Washington DC 1998-2011; Epis Soc Of Chr Ch Cincinnati OH 1995-1998. gerbracht@stpatsdc.org

GERDAU, Carlson (Chi) 60 Sutton Place South, Apt 19, New York NY 10022 B New York NY 2/22/1933 s Carl Gerdau & Kathryn. AB Harv 1955; STB GTS 1959. D 6/20/1959 Bp Anson Phelps Stokes Jr P 12/19/1959 Bp Herman R Page. Epis Ch Cntr New York NY 1998-2005; Cn to Ordnry Dio Chicago Chicago IL 1988-1997; Int S Greg's Epis Ch Deerfield IL 1987; Archd Dio Missouri S Louis MO 1979-1986; Trin Epis Ch Houghton MI 1971-1979; Vic S Jn's Ch Munising MI 1965-1971; Vic Ch Of The Ascen Ontonagon MI 1959-1965; S Mk's Ch Ewen MI 1959-1965. cgerdau@episcopalchurch.org

GERDING, Susan Ann (Tex) 836 W. Jones St., Livingston TX 77351 **R S Lk's Ch Livingston TX 2009-** B Oak Park IL 4/24/1957 d Robert Allen Rivenes & Patricia Ann. MA U of Virginia 1978; MLS Rutgers 1979; Cert Iona Sch for Mnstry 2008. D 6/28/2008 Bp Don Adger Wimberly P 1/3/2009 Bp C(harles) Andrew Doyle. m 12/29/1979 Mark S Gerding c 3. susangerding@comcast.net

GERDSEN, Elizabeth Jane (SO) 1219 Amherst Pl, Dayton OH 45406 **Dio Sthrn Ohio Cincinnati OH 2011-** B Cincinnati OH 5/16/1978 d Stephen F Gerdsen & Sally D. BA Mt Holyoke Coll 2000; MDiv EDS 2006. D 5/14/2005 P 6/24/2006 Bp Kenneth Lester Price. m 8/2/2003 Robert R Konkol. P-in-c S Andr's Ch Dayton OH 2006-2011. ejanegerdsen@gmail.com

GERHARD, Ernest J (Neb) 14214 Briggs Cir, Omaha NE 68144 B Omaha NE 3/19/1933 s August H Gerhard & Cornelia E. BA Omaha U 1960. D 8/26/1989 Bp James Daniel Warner. m 9/29/1969 Deanna Pearl McGee c 1. D S Jas' Epis Ch Fremont NE 1989-2000.

GERHARD, Kurt Joseph (WA) Saint Patrick's Episcopal Church, 4700 Whitehaven Pkwy NW, Washington DC 20007 **Dioc Coun Dio Washington Washington DC 2011-; R S Pat's Ch Washington DC 2010-** B Omaha NE 1/1/1973 s Ernest J Gerhard & Deanna Pearl. BS U of Nebraska 1995; MDiv Epis TS of The SW 2000; D.Min VTS 2009. D 5/21/2000 P 12/13/2000 Bp James Edward Krotz. Asst The Ch of the Gd Shpd Austin TX 2003-2010; Chapl S Andrews Epis Sch Austin TX 2001-2010; Asst to R Ch Of The H Trin Lincoln NE 2000-2001. NAES 2001. kurtgerhard@me.com

G

GERHARD, Robert D (SO) 3939 Erie Ave Apt 407, Cincinnati OH 45208 **Died 1/9/2010** B Chicago IL 2/25/1929 s Gilbert Arthur Gerhard & Mary Naomi. BS USMMA 1950; MDiv SWTS 1957. D 6/15/1957 P 11/21/1957 Bp Gerald Francis Burrill. Auth/Ed, *Last Things*, 1975; Contributing Ed, *Epis Fndt of Chicago*, 1962. Assn of St. Greg's Abbey Three Rivers Michigan; Confessor Extraordinary Convert of the Trsfg. Pres Samar Counslg Cntr of Grtr Cincinnati 1990; Pres Epis Healing Mnstry Fndt 1987; Pres Friends of the Groom 1984; Pres UCP of Cincinnati 1981. bgerhard@cccath.org

GERHARDT, Michael Joseph (NJ) 171 Larch Ave., Bogota NJ 07603 B Flushing NY 7/9/1952 s Andreas Gerhardt & Ann. BA St. Johns U 1974; MPA NYU 1980; MDiv Drew U 1997. D 5/31/1997 Bp John Shelby Spong P 12/13/1997 Bp Jack Marston McKelvey. m 10/2/1993 Donna Linley Williams c 2. S Mk's Ch Teaneck NJ 2008-2011; Vic Chr Ch Teaneck NJ 1999-2007; S Paul's Epis Ch Paterson NJ 1997-1998. mikeg52@optonline.net

GERHART JR, John James (CFla) 4315 Longshore Dr, Land O Lakes FL 34639 **H Faith Epis Ch Dunnellon FL 2009-** B Philadelphia PA 1/22/1950 s John James Gerhart & Kathryn Webb. AS Sprg Garden Coll 1972; BS Sprg Garden Coll 1974; MDiv Epis TS In Kentucky 1977. D 5/15/1977 P 5/1/1979 Bp Addison Hosea. Gd Samar Epis Ch Clearwater FL 1992; S Andr's Epis Ch Sprg Hill FL 1991-1992; St Lukes Ch Ellenton FL 1987-1990; Vic S Eliz's Epis Ch Zephyrhills FL 1983-1986; S Steph's Epis Ch Covington KY 1980-1983; Cur S Raphael's Ch Lexington KY 1978-1979; Cur Ch S Mich The Archangel Lexington KY 1977-1978. Soc Of S Jn The Evang. wa3dit@tampabay.rr.com

GERHART, William James (NJ) 2131 Woodbridge Ave, PO Box 1286, Edison NJ 08817 **R S Jas Ch Edison NJ 1978-** B Philadelphia PA 9/22/1950 s David Parker Gerhart & Ruth Hortense. BA La Salle U 1972; MDiv Epis TS In Kentucky 1975. D 5/18/1975 Bp Addison Hosea P 4/10/1976 Bp Albert Wiencke Van Duzer. m 11/26/1977 Karen Lee Bruner c 1. Asst Gr Ch Merchantville NJ 1976-1978. "H Silence," Forw Mvmt; Auth, "An Adv Meditation," *Sharing, LivCh*. Chapl Ord of S Lk, Convenor Cntrl Jersey Chapt 1983-1987.

GERLACH, Aaron Robert (O) 231 North Miami Ave, Sidney OH 45365 **P-in-c S Mk's Ch Sidney OH 2010-** B Mitchell SD 3/10/1974 s Bobby Glen Gerlach & Laura Marie. BS Estrn Illinois 1996; MDiv Bex 2009. D 6/6/2009 Bp Jeffrey Dean Lee P 12/8/2009 Bp Victor Alfonso Scantlebury. revgerlach@gmail.com

GERMAN, Kenneth L (EpisSanJ) 329 Mannel Ave, Shafter CA 93263 B Los Angeles CA 6/29/1930 s Alfred German & Margrethe Sophia. BA California St U Northridge 1962; CDSP 1965. D 6/29/1966 Bp Robert C Rusack P 3/11/1967 Bp Francis E I Bloy. m 12/31/1950 Charlotte Holmes c 5. S Mk's Ch Shafter CA 1997-2002; P S Thos Ch Avenal CA 1994-2006; P S Phil's Ch Coalinga CA 1992-1993; R S Mk's Ch Shafter CA 1989-1991; Epis Dio San Joaquin Modesto CA 1980-1981; S Andr's Epis Ch Mariposa CA 1980-1981; P Chr The King A Jubilee Mnstry Palmdale CA 1971-1979; Dio Los Angeles Los Angeles CA 1966-1968; Vic S Andr's Epis Ch Ojai CA 1966-1967.

GERMINO, Carmen C (Ct) 1205 W Franklin St, Richmond VA 23220 **S Jas' Ch Richmond VA 2011-** B Nashville TN 10/16/1981 d Mark R Germino & Christine B. BA U of So 2004; MDiv Ya Berk 2007; Cert of Angl Stds Ya Berk 2011. D 6/11/2011 Bp Laura Ahrens. carmen.germino@gmail.com

GERNS, Andrew Timothy (Be) 14 Midland Dr, Easton PA 18045 **Pres, Stndg Com Dio Bethlehem Bethlehem PA 2011-; Dioc Renwl Cmsn Dio Bethlehem Bethlehem PA 2009-; Stndg Com Dio Bethlehem Bethlehem PA 2007-; Chair, Evang Cmsn Dio Bethlehem Bethlehem PA 2004-; R Trin Ch Easton PA 2002-** B Washington DC 7/21/1957 s William Henry Gerns & Frances Rebecca. BA Drew U 1979; MDiv GTS 1982; Andover-Newton TS 1989. D 6/12/1982 P 12/18/1982 Bp Arthur Edward Walmsley. m 6/16/1979 Maugarette Louise Wood c 1. GC Dep Dio Bethlehem Bethlehem PA 2004-2007; Dioc Coun Dio Bethlehem Bethlehem PA 2003-2008; Cmsn on the Mnstry Dio Bethlehem Bethlehem PA 2002-2007; Dioc Coun Dio W Virginia Charleston WV 1997-2001; Co-Chair, Hlth T/F Dio W Virginia Charleston WV 1995-2001; Ohio Vlly Epis Cluster Williamstown WV 1994-2001; Dir of Pstr Care S Josephs Hosp Parkersburg WV 1994-2001; R Trin Ch Parkersburg WV 1992-1994; Int S Alb's Ch Danielson CT 1991-1992; Int Ch Of The Resurr Norwich CT 1987-1989; Cmsn on the Mnstry Dio Connecticut Hartford CT 1986-1991; Int Chr Ch Stratford CT 1984-1986; Cur S Paul's Epis Ch Willimantic CT 1982-1984. Columnist, "Occaisional Columnist," *Allentown Morning Call*, Allentown Morning Call, 2002; Columnist, "Rel Columnist," *Parkerburg News and Sentinel*, Parkersburg News & Sentinel, 1996. Assembly Of Epis Healthcare Chapl 1986-2003; ACPE 1986-2002; Assn Of Profsnl Chapl 1994-2003; Intl Critical Incident Stress Fndt 1996. Bd Cert Chapl Assn of Profsnl Chapl 1998; Basic And Advncd Trnr Intl Critical Incident Stress Fndt 1996. rector@trinityeaston.org

GERTH JR, Stephen Shea (NY) Church of Saint Mary the Virgin, 145 West 46th Street, New York NY 10036 **R Ch Of S Mary The Vrgn New York NY 1999-** B Norfolk VA 2/20/1954 s Stephen Shea Gerth & Barbara Ann. BA U of Virginia 1976; AM U Chi 1979; MDiv Nash 1983. D 6/11/1983 Bp Quintin Ebenezer Primo Jr P 12/21/1983 Bp Robert Elwin Terwilliger. R Trin Ch Michigan City IN 1988-1999; Cur S Lk's Ch Baton Rouge LA 1985-1988; Asst Ch Of The Incarn Dallas TX 1983-1985. sgerth@stmvnyc.org

GERVAIS JR, Sidney Joseph (Tex) 1210 E Mesa Park Dr, Round Rock TX 78664 B New Orleans LA 8/9/1927 s Sidney Joseph Gervais & Clarita Hotchkiss. BBA U Of Houston 1951; MDiv VTS 1966. D 6/28/1966 Bp J Milton Richardson P 6/28/1967 Bp Scott Field Bailey. c 4. R S Richard's Of Round Rock Round Rock TX 1978-1992; Vic Dio Texas Houston TX 1978-1986; R Ch Of The Ascen Houston TX 1971-1978; Assoc Trin Ch Houston TX 1968-1971. EvangES 1964-1966. sidgervais@att.net

GESTON, Alejandro Sumadin (Haw) 91-1746 Bond St, Ewa Beach HI 96706 B Bontoc PH 12/11/1938 s Geston Geston & Dorotea. BTh S Andr's TS Manila PH 1967; BA U of The Philippines 1968; MA Fuller TS 1990. D 8/13/1967 P 11/1/1968 Bp Benito C Cabanban. m 1/2/1965 Simeona Madlaay Balabag c 4. S Steph's Ch Wahiawa HI 1993-2000; Dio Hawaii Honolulu HI 1992-1993; S Tim's Ch Aiea HI 1992-1993; St Benedicts Mssn W Covina CA 1989-1992; S Jn's Ch Eleele HI 1979-1989; Ch Of The Resurr Hilo HI 1972-1979. asgeston@gmail.com

GESTWICKI, Ronald Arthur (WNY) 3625 Havenwood Rd, Charlotte NC 28205 **Died 5/18/2010** B Dunkirk NY 1/19/1939 s Ernest Gestwicki & Beatrice. BA SUNY 1960; STM GTS 1964; PhD Syr 1971. D 6/20/1964 Bp Lauriston L Scaife P 3/1/1965 Bp Robert Herbert Mize Jr. c 1. Auth, "A Chld'S Intro To Rel"; Auth, "Santa Claus," *The Tooth Fairy & Other Stories*.

GETCHELL, Philip Armour (ECR) 6524 Hercus Ct, San Jose CA 95119 **Mision Nuestra Sra De Guadalupe San Jose CA 2000-** B Medford OR 1/27/1934 s Bayard McClure Getchell & Myra Gladys. BD CDSP; BA Stan; DD CDSP 1990. D 6/17/1959 P 12/29/1959 Bp James Walmsley Frederic Carman. m 4/23/1960 Claudia Jean Lawson c 3. Dn Trin Cathd San Jose CA 1992-1999; Chair, Dept of Wrld Mssn Dio California San Francisco CA 1983-1987; R S Mk's Par Berkeley CA 1979-1992; Assoc / Int R Trin Epis Cathd Portland OR 1975-1979; Cur S Matt's Epis Ch Portland OR 1959-1960. Auth, "Faces from Prison," *Witness mag*, 1978. DD CDSP. pagetch@comcast.net

GETLEIN, Greta (Ct) 409 Prospect St, New Haven CT 06511 **Ya Berk New Haven CT 2010-** B Derby CT 8/17/1961 d Edward James Getlein & Olive Nancy. BSN Sthrn Connecticut St U 1986; MDiv Ya Berk 2009. D 6/13/2009 P 1/16/2010 Bp John Chane. m 5/23/2009 Wanda Strickland. Cur Chr Ch New Haven CT 2009-2010. greta.getlein@gmail.com

GETTYS, Jeannette Cooper (USC) 308 College Dr., Gaffney SC 29340 **R Ch Of The Incarn Gaffney SC 2008-** B Charlotte NC 7/3/1963 d Thomas Cooper & Jeannette. BA Davidson Coll Davidson NC 1985; MFA U So Carolina Columbia SC 1988; MDiv TS 2006. D 6/4/2006 Bp Samuel Johnson Howard P 12/16/2006 Bp Don Edward Johnson. m 1/22/2011 Miles Gettys III. Assoc Ch of the H Apos Collierville TN 2006-2008. jencoop73@yahoo.com

GETTYS, Laura F (WTenn) 692 Poplar Ave, Memphis TN 38105 **S Mary's Cathd Memphis TN 2011-** B Memphis TN 11/10/1975 D 6/26/2005 P 1/7/2006 Bp Michael Bruce Curry. m 9/2/2000 Joseph C Gettys. S Ptr's Ch Oxford MS 2007-2011; Chr Ch Alexandria VA 2005-2007. lgettys@stmarysmemphis.org

GETZ, Peter Richard Remsen (Dal) 808 Oak Hollow Lane, Rockwall TX 75087 **H Trin Ch Rockwall TX 2006-** B Kerrville TX 12/22/1947 s Henry Bernard Getz & Emily Osborn. BA U of the Incarnate Word 1977; MDiv Epis TS of The SW 1981; Med Trin U San Antonio TX 1990; CTh SWTS 2004. D 6/29/1981 Bp Scott Field Bailey P 10/25/1982 Bp Stanley Fillmore Hauser. m 5/2/1975 Gay Zaumeyer c 2. Dio W Texas San Antonio TX 2000; Dio W Texas San Antonio TX 1999; R Ch Of The H Comf Angleton TX 1998-2005; Dio Texas Houston TX 1996; R S Matt's Ch Henderson TX 1993-1998; Adv Epis Sch Stafford TX 1989-1992; Texas Mltry Inst San Antonio TX 1987-1989; Sprtl Dir Bps Happ Mvmnt Dio W Texas San Antonio TX 1985-1987; Ch Of The Resurr San Antonio TX 1983-1986; Gr Ch Falfurrias

TX 1981-1983; Vic S Jas Epis Ch Hebbronville TX 1981-1983. Auth, "More than I asked for," *Sharing mag*, 1999. Ord of S Lk 1980. prrgetz@hotmail.com

GIACOBBE, Georgia Bates (Ak) 3564 E. Second St. #26, The Dalles OR 97058 B Camden NJ 11/28/1954 d Robert James Bates & Lillian Rebecca. BA S Mary's Coll Of Maryland 1992. D 6/3/2000 Bp Robert Wilkes Ihloff. m 3/10/1980 Peter B Speight. D S Mich And All Ang Ch Haines AK 2003-2011; D Middleham & S Ptr's Par Lusby MD 2000-2003. dngeorgia@gmail.com

GIACOLONE, Anthony Joseph (NY) 21 Weathervane Dr Apt 16, Washingtonville NY 10992 B Brooklyn NY 9/17/1957 s Anthony Giacolone & Lucy. BS SUNY 1999. D 5/16/1998 Bp Richard Frank Grein. likes.living@frontiernet.net

GIACOMA, Claudia Louder (U) 7362 Tall Oaks Dr, Park City UT 84098 **Asst. P S Lk's Ch Pk City UT 2007-** B Park City UT 7/20/1935 d Admiral S Louder & Fanny. BS U of Utah 1972; Cert U of Utah 1996; CAS CDSP 2000; S Mk's Pstr Care Cntr Clincl Pstr Educatio 2001. D 1/11/2001 P 12/8/2007 Bp Carolyn Tanner Irish. m 8/23/1957 J Louis Giacoma. Epis Cmnty Serv Inc Salt Lake City UT 2001-2007; D S Lk's Ch Pk City UT 2001. giacoma@sisna.com

GIANNINI, Robert Edward (Ind) 55 Monument Cir Ste 600, Indianapolis IN 46204 B New York NY 7/8/1940 s Mario Carl Giannini & Elizabeth. BA U So 1964; MDiv GTS 1967; PhD U of St. Andrews 1977; DD GTS 1986. D 6/21/1967 Bp Henry I Louttit P 12/27/1967 Bp James Loughlin Duncan. m 6/12/1965 Josephine Ross. Dn & R Chr Ch Cathd Indianapolis IN 1990-2005; Dn Sch Of Theol The TS at The U So Sewanee TN 1986-1990; Trst The TS at The U So Sewanee TN 1982-1986; Dn Cathd Ch Of S Ptr St Petersburg FL 1981-1986; Dio SW Florida Sarasota FL 1976-1981; Vic S Simons Ch Miami FL 1968-1973; Cur S Bon Ch Sarasota FL 1967-1968. Auth, "arts & Revs". bobg@indy.rr.com

GIANSIRACUSA JR, Michael (Pa) 225 S 3rd St, Philadelphia PA 19106 B Philadelphia, PA 7/2/1968 s Michael Giansiracusa & Caroline. BA La Salle U 1990; MA Villanova U 1993; DMin EDS 2010. D 6/5/2010 Bp Edward Lewis Lee Jr P 1/22/2011 Bp Charles Ellsworth Bennison Jr. m 6/23/2001 Renee Malnak c 1. Epis Cmnty Serv Philadelphia PA 2010-2011. mikegian@earthlink.net

GIARDINA, Denise Diana (WVa) 306 Park Ave, Charleston WV 25302 B Bluefield WV 10/25/1951 B.A. W Virginia Wesleyan Coll 1973; M.Div. VTS 1979. D 6/6/1979 Bp Robert Poland Atkinson. Gr Ch Northfork WV 1979-1980. Auth, "Emily's Ghost," *novel*, W.W. Norton, 2009; Auth, "SS and Villains," *novel*, W.W. Norton, 1998; Auth, "The Unquiet Earth," *novel*, W.W. Norton, 1992; Auth, "Storming Heaven," *novel*, W.W. Norton, 1987; Auth, "Gd King Harry," *novel*, Harper and Row, 1984. Hon doctorate W Virginia Wesleyan Coll 1998.

GIBBES, Joseph A (Ala) 2017 6th Ave N, Birmingham AL 35203 **The Cathd Ch Of The Adv Birmingham AL 2010-** B Columbia SC 9/10/1974 BA Wake Forest U 1996; MDiv Trin Epis Sch 2006. D 7/1/2006 P 1/6/2007 Bp Edward Lloyd Salmon Jr. c 2. S Jn's Epis Par Johns Island SC 2006-2010. frjoe@stjohnsparish.net

GIBBONS, David Austen (Chi) 337 Ridge Rd, Barrington IL 60010 **R S Mk's Barrington Hills IL 2008-** B Westminster UK 6/9/1963 s Kenneth Harry Gibbons & Margaret Ann. MSc U of York, UK 1984; Cert in Theol CDSP 1994; Cert in Theol Ripon Coll, Cuddesdon, UK 1994; MA Oxf 1996; MA Sarum Coll, U of Llampeter 2005. Trans from Church Of England 10/21/2008 Bp Jeffrey Dean Lee. m 3/11/1995 Susan D Jackson c 2. david.gibbons335@comcast.net

GIBBONS, Rowena Gregg (CPa) 64 Mayflower Ln, Mansfield PA 16933 **R S Jas Ch Mansfield PA 2005-** B Wilmington NC 10/13/1962 d Thomas Gregg & Margaret. BA Queens Coll 1984; MDiv STUSo 2003. D 5/24/2003 P 12/1/2003 Bp John Wadsworth Howe. m 12/12/1992 William M Gibbons c 2. Stndg Com-VP Dio Cntrl Pennsylvania Harrisburg PA 2008-2009; Coun of Trst Dio Cntrl Pennsylvania Harrisburg PA 2007-2009; Asst All SS Ch Hilton Hd Island SC 2003-2005. rowena_gibbons@yahoo.com

GIBBS, Charles Philip (Cal) Po Box 29242, San Francisco CA 94129 B Socorro NM 4/28/1951 s Harold Eugene Gibbs & Ruth Lightbourne. BA Pomona Coll 1975; MA U MN 1982; MDiv CDSP 1987. D 6/24/1987 Bp Robert Marshall Anderson P 1/1/1988 Bp William Edwin Swing. m 3/30/1975 Deborah Paul c 2. Ch Of The Nativ San Rafael CA 1999; Dio California San Francisco CA 1996-2006; R Ch Of The Incarn San Francisco CA 1990-1996; Asst S Steph's Par Belvedere CA 1987-1990; San Rafael Canal Mnstry San Rafael CA 1987-1990. Auth, "Reflection on Ezzeddin Nasafi's 'Oh, my friend,'" *Leading From Within -- Poetry That Sustains the Courage to Lead*, Jossey-Bass, 2007; Auth, "Opening the Dream," *Deepening the Amer Dream*, Jossey-Bass, 2005; Co-Auth, *Birth of a Global Cmnty*, Lakeshore Pub, 2004; Auth, "(Chapt)," *Interfaith Dialogue And Peacebuilding*, US Inst Of Peace, 2002; Auth, "A Chr Experience Of Adoration," *Prabuddha Bharata*, Ramakrishna Ord, 2002; Auth, "Interreligious Understanding: A Chr Perspective," *Prabuddha Bharata*, Ramakrishna Ord, 2001. DD CDSP 2004; Distinguished Alum Holland Hall Sch 2003; Cn Of Gr Cathd Bp Of California 2001. charles@uri.org

GIBBS, Dennis Lee (Los) 840 Echo Park Ave, Los Angeles CA 90026 **Chapl Dir Dio Los Angeles Los Angeles CA 2010-** B Nampa, ID 6/10/1954 s Robert Lincoln Gibbs & Evelyn Cleo. Diac Cert BLOY-ETSC 2010. D 5/23/2010 Bp Chester Lovelle Talton. c 2. Dio Los Angeles Los Angeles CA 2007-2010. dennisleegibbs@yahoo.com

GIBBS, James Millard (Chi) 13 Lingfield Court, 60 High St, Birmingham B17 9NE Great Britain (UK) B Chicago IL 4/17/1928 s Frank Cornelius Gibbs & Edna Marion. BSE U MI 1951; BD SWTS 1957; PhD U of Nottingham 1968. D 6/15/1957 Bp Charles L Street P 12/1/1957 Bp Gerald Francis Burrill. m 4/12/1958 Dorothy Anne Hart c 3. Vic S Jn The Evang Lockport IL 1958-1960; Cur Ch Of Our Sav Elmhurst IL 1957-1958. Auth, "Wisdom Power & Wellbeing; The ... Parameters of a ... Biblic Model for Humanity," *Indn Journ of Theol, Vol. 26*, 1977; Auth, "Matt's Use of 'Kingdom,' 'Kingdom of God' and 'Kingdom of Heaven,'" *Bangalore Theol Forum, Vol. 8*, Bangalore Theol Forum, Vol. 8, 1976; Auth, "Jesus as the Wisdom of God: the Normative Man of Hist Moving to Cosmic Chr," *Indn Journ of Theol, Vol. 24*, 1975; Auth, "The Bible in the Ch - A Radical View," *Bangalore Theol Forum, Vol. 6*, Untd Theol Coll, Bangalore, 1974; Auth, "The Gospel Prologues and Their Function," *Studia Evangelica IV*, Akademie Verlag, Berlin, 1968; Auth, "Purpose & Pattern In S Matt'S Use Of Title s Dav," *NT Stds, Vol. 10*, 1964. SBL 1965-1985. JMandDAGibbs@aol.com

G

GIBBS, Lee Wayland (O) 2413 Weymouth Dr, Springfield VA 22151 B Natchitoches LA 3/7/1937 s Norman Brantley Gibbs & Virginia. BA Macalester Coll 1959; STB Harvard DS 1962; ThD Harvard DS 1968. D 6/28/1980 P 11/1/1981 Bp John Harris Burt. m 6/16/1960 Joan Brownlee Lawler c 3. Hon Assoc Chr Ch Shaker Heights OH 1995-2008. Auth, "H Days & Holidays," Forw Mvmt Press, 1995; Ed, "Folger Ed Of The Works Of Richard Hooker," 1993; Co-Ed, "Myth & The Crisis Of Hist Consciousness"; Transltr, "Willam Ames," *Technometry*; Co-Ed, "The Middle Way," *Voices Of Anglicaism*. AAR; Sixteenth Century Stds Soc. ligibbs@csuohio.edu

GIBBS III, Thomas Woodrow (VI) Po Box 1148, St Thomas VI 00804 **Died 7/18/2010** B Chicago IL 1/11/1930 s Thomas Gibbs & Minnie. BA Amh 1951; BD EDS 1958. D 5/26/1958 P 11/1/1958 Bp Albert Ervine Swift. dorian@viaccess.net

✠ **GIBBS JR, Rt Rev Wendell Nathaniel** (Mich) 19594 Renfrew Rd, Detroit MI 48221 **Bp of Michigan Dio Michigan Detroit MI 2000-** B Washington DC 3/21/1954 s Wendell Nathaniel Gibbs & Lillian Pope. S Mary's Sem & U Catonsville MD; BA Towson U 1977; MDiv SWTS 1987. D 6/1/1987 Bp James Winchester Montgomery P 12/12/1987 Bp Frank Tracy Griswold III Con 2/5/2000 for Mich. m 8/19/1989 Karlah A Ambrose. P-in-c Ch Of S Mich And All Ang Cincinnati OH 1997-1998; BEC Dio Sthrn Ohio Cincinnati OH 1994-1999; R S Andr's Epis Ch Cincinnati OH 1993-1999; R Ch of the Gd Shpd Syracuse NY 1991-1993; Paris Cluster Chadwicks NY 1991-1993; R S Geo's Epis Ch Chadwicks NY 1991-1993; R S Mk's Ch Clark Mills NY 1991-1993; CE Cmsn CNY Dio Cntrl New York Syracuse NY 1990-1992; Assoc Gr Ch Utica NY 1989-1991; Cur Emm Epis Ch Rockford IL 1987-1989. Soc of Cath Priests 2010. Hon DD SWTS Evanston IL 2000. bishopwng@comcast.net

GIBSON, Alan Glen (Mich) St Andrew Episcopal Church, 306 N Division St, Ann Arbor MI 48104 **R S Andr's Ch Ann Arbor MI 2008-** B Memphis TN 12/13/1961 s Jess Charles Gibson & Evelyn Susie. BA NWU 1982; MDiv Yale DS 1991. D 6/8/1991 P 12/14/1991 Bp Richard Frank Grein. Trin Ch Rutland VT 2004-2008; R All SS Memi Ch Navesink NJ 1995-2004; Vic Ch Of The H Sprt Tuckerton NJ 1992-1995; Cur The Ch of S Ign of Antioch New York NY 1991-1992. Auth, "The Sunday After 9/11," *The Day Our Wrld Changed: Chld'S Art Of 9/11*, Abrams, 2002. agibson@standrewsaa.org

GIBSON, Barbara Jean (Kan) 701 SW 8th Ave, Topeka KS 66603 **D S Jn's Ch Wichita KS 2011-** B Newton KS 6/26/1945 d Doyle Harold Box & Irene Frances. BS Wichita St U 1967; MD Cntrl Michigan U 1990; Cert Kansas Sch for Mnstry 2010. D 1/8/2011 Bp Dean Elliott Wolfe. c 3. bgibson10@cox.net

GIBSON, Beverly Findley (CGC) 24 Blacklawn St, Mobile AL 36604 **Sub-Dn Chr Ch Cathd Mobile Mobile AL 2005-** B Andalusia AL 5/20/1961 d Grover Waltha Findley & Anne Merle. BA Converse Coll 1983; MA U of Virginia 1985; PhD Auburn U 2000; MDiv GTS 2005. D 6/4/2005 P 5/13/2006 Bp Philip Menzie Duncan II. m 5/31/1987 James Michael Gibson c 2. beverly@christchurchcathedralmobile.com

GIBSON, Charles Gatchell (Ind) 5227 Windridge Dr, Indianapolis IN 46226 **Died 3/24/2010** B Dublin IE 1/31/1918 s John McKeever Gibson & Mary Ann. BA U Coll Dublin; MA U Coll Dublin; Div. Testimonium U Coll Dublin 1943. Trans from Church of Ireland 10/1/1965 as Priest Bp John P Craine. c 3. Hist Soc of Dublin U 1940-1944; Theol Soc of Dublin U 1939-1944.

GIBSON, Earl Dodridge (Az) 114 W Roosevelt St, Phoenix AZ 85003 **Yth Coordntr Prov VIII Tagard OR 2010-; Assoc S Marg Of Scotland Par San Juan Capistrano CA 2010-** B San Gabriel Valley CA 2/6/1971 s John D Gibson. BA California St U 1995; MDiv Claremont TS 2000. D 4/27/2002 Bp Robert Marshall Anderson P 1/11/2003 Bp Joseph Jon Bruno. Assoc S Mk's

Par Glendale CA 2007-2009; Yth Dir Dio Arizona Phoenix AZ 2004-2006; Yth Dir S Jn's Mssn La Verne CA 2002-2004. frearl@hotmail.com

GIBSON, Elizabeth M (Va) 543 Beulah Rd NE, Vienna VA 22180 **Asst R Ch Of The H Comf Vienna VA 2008-** B Baltimore MD 3/29/1971 d Lawrence McGovern & Sally. BA,MA U of Virginia 1993; PhD U of Virginia 2004; MDiv VTS 2008. D 11/16/2008 Bp Shannon Sherwood Johnston P 5/17/2009 Bp Peter James Lee. m 5/25/1997 Miles Gibson c 3. lgibson@holycomforter.com

GIBSON, Emily Stearns (Me) 732 Nottingham Rd, Wilmington DE 19805 **Int Gr Epis Ch Wilmington DE 2010-** B Salem MA 9/25/1953 d William Harry Gibson & Jane Porter. BS U of Sthrn Maine 1975; MDiv EDS 1983; STM GTS 2000. D 5/28/1983 Bp Frederick Barton Wolf P 12/9/1983 Bp John Shelby Spong. m 8/11/1984 David Tallmadge Andrews. Int S Pat's Ch Brewer ME 2008-2010; Int S Brendan's Epis Ch Stonington ME 2006-2008; R S Alb's Ch Syracuse NY 1991-2006; Asst Chr Ch Corning NY 1986-1991; Asst S Paul's Epis Ch Chatham NJ 1983-1986. Soc of S Jn the Evang 1992. gracerector@comcast.net

G

GIBSON, Gregory Hyvestra (VI) C/O Diocese Of Virgin Islands, PO Box 7488, St Thomas VI 00801 B Barbados 3/9/1959 s Eleazar Augustus Gibson & Petrolene Ilene. MA Codrington Coll 2008; BA Codrington Coll 2008. D 6/28/2008 Bp Edward Ambrose Gumbs. m 5/28/1994 Anthia Worrell c 2. marigregs@hotmail.com

GIBSON, John Kenneth (NC) 1520 Canterbury Rd, Raleigh NC 27608 B Roanoke VA 9/22/1958 s Thomas Kenneth Gibson & May Alice. BA U NC 1982; MDiv Ya Berk 1990; DMin SWTS 2004. D 11/10/1990 P 11/16/1991 Bp Huntington Williams Jr. m 8/2/2002 Cindy H McCaw c 1. S Mich's Ch Raleigh NC 2005; R St Elizabeths Epis Ch Apex NC 1999-2005; S Paul's Epis Ch Cary NC 1991-1999. gibson@holymichael.org

GIBSON JR, John Michael (Miss) 11601 Lily Orchard Rd, Moss Point MS 39562 B Bloomington IN 10/28/1946 s John Michael Gibson & Rosemary Mcclure. BA Indiana U 1970; MDiv STUSo 1979. D 5/20/1979 P 2/1/1980 Bp Duncan Montgomery Gray Jr. m 5/20/1972 Joy Robinson c 1. R S Jn's Epis Ch Pascagoula MS 1987-2005; Cn S Andr's Cathd Jackson MS 1983-1987; R Gr Epis Ch Canton MS 1981-1983; Vic S Mary's Ch Enterprise MS 1979-1981; Cur S Paul's Epis Ch Meridian MS 1979-1981; Trin Ch Newton MS 1979-1981. john.m.gibson@gmail.com

GIBSON, John Noel Keith (VI) PO Box 65 Valley, Virgin Gorda VG1150 British Virgin Islands B Reigate England 12/25/1922 s John Gibson & Evelyn. BA U of Cambridge 1944; MA U of Cambridge 1948; BD Lon 1959. Trans from Church in the Province Of The West Indies 4/1/1964 Bp Cedric Earl Mills. m 2/4/1959 Iris Alma Pickering c 3. St Marys Ch 1978-1992. Mem Most Excellent Ord British Empire H.M. Queen Eliz II 1990; Cn Emer 92; Hon Cn 90-92, All SS Cathd St Thos VI.

GIBSON, Kate Snyder (ETenn) 7782 Pine Island Way, West Palm Beach FL 33411 B Philadelphia PA 7/25/1939 d Robert Francis Snyder & Dorothea. Art Students League NYC 1958; Parsons Sch Of Design 1958; Cert Aberdeen TFM GB 1985; Cert Edinburgh Theol Coll 1993. Trans from Scottish Episcopal Church 10/9/2008 Bp Charles Glenn VonRosenberg. c 3. P-in-c S Matt's Ch Dayton TN 2009; for Pstr Care The Epis Ch Of Beth-By-The-Sea Palm Bch FL 2000-2004; Assoc All SS Prot Epis Ch Ft Lauderdale FL 1999-2000. Scottish Assn For Pstr Care And Counselling. revkategib@bellsouth.net

GIBSON III, Owen S (HB) 2926 Maple Springs Blvd, Dallas TX 75235 B Hominy OK 11/21/1937 s Owen S Gibson & Florence Margaret. BA U of Oklahoma 1959; BD Epis TS of The SW 1963. D 6/11/1963 P 6/1/1964 Bp Chilton Powell. Asst Chr Epis Ch Dallas TX 1965-1968; Vic The Epis Ch Of The H Apos Moore OK 1963-1965. Turtle Creek Chorale. owensgibson@aol.com

GIBSON, Robert Burrows (At) 508 High Point North Rd, Macon GA 31210 B Rochester NY 1/25/1943 s Frederick Jay Gibson & Harriette Louise. BA Ohio Wesl 1965; STB Ya Berk 1968; STM Ya Berk 1970; CDSP 1971; Columbia TS 1980; SE Inst for Grp & Fam Ther 1985. D 6/22/1968 P 12/22/1968 Bp George West Barrett. m 7/5/1969 Joy H Hearn c 2. Asst Chr Ch Macon GA 1991-2010; Vic S Jas Ch Macon GA 1974-1990; Asst Trin Ch Branford CT 1969-1970. OHC - Assoc 1970. missjoy2541@yahoo.com

GIBSON, Thomas William (CFla) Po Box 320026, 139 S. Atlantic Avenue, Cocoa Beach FL 32932 **R S Mk's Ch Cocoa FL 1997-** B Elgin IL 3/9/1949 s Stanley Thomas Gibson & Thelma Oline. Cor 1969; MDiv SWTS 1972; BA U of Nthrn Colorado 1972. D 6/8/1991 P 12/15/1991 Bp John Wadsworth Howe. m 5/17/1979 Mary Gail Knox c 1. R Ch Of S Dav's By The Sea Cocoa Bch FL 1993-1997; Asst R S Jn's Ch Melbourne FL 1991-1993. tomgibson2@me.com

GIBSON, Webster S (Va) 111 Stonebrook Rd, Winchester VA 22602 **R Chr Epis Ch Winchester VA 2007-** B Alexandria VA 3/21/1967 s Churchill Jones Gibson & Dorothy. BA U of Virginia; MDiv Epis TS of the SW 1997. D 6/14/1997 P 12/13/1997 Bp Frank Harris Vest Jr. m 7/6/1991 Rebecca N Gibson c 3. Int Bruton Par Williamsburg VA 1997-1999. wbstrgbsn@yahoo.com

GIDDINGS, Monte Carl (Kan) 26755 W 103rd St, Olathe KS 66061 **D S Mich And All Ang Ch Mssn KS 2000-** B Beloit KS 8/15/1950 s Carl Francis Giddings & Mildred Ruth. BS U of Kansas 1972. D 5/26/1999 Bp William Edward Smalley. m 12/23/1972 Jill Huebner c 2. gids@comcast.net

GIDDINGS, Randall Clinton (Ct) 227 Ledges Dr., Laconia NH 03246 **Hon Cur S Jas Epis Ch Laconia NH 1998-** B Carbondale PA 4/27/1921 s Clinton Marion Giddings & Alma. Fllshp EDS; BA Leh 1943; STB EDS 1945; Fllshp Coll of Preachers 1951. D 9/29/1945 P 5/25/1946 Bp Frank W Sterrett. m 9/30/1945 Jean Helen Schoonmaker c 4. Int S Judes Epis Ch Franklin NH 1996-1997; Int Trin Epis Ch Tilton NH 1996-1997; Int The Epis Ch Of S Jn The Bapt Sanbornville NH 1995-1996; Int Ch Of S Jn The Evang Dunbarton NH 1992-1993; Int H Cross Epis Ch Weare NH 1992-1993; Int Chr Ch No Conway NH 1990-1992; Consult Dioc Plnng & Dvlpmt Dio Connecticut Hartford CT 1986; Chair Excoun Cmsn Plnng & Dvlpmt Dio Connecticut Hartford CT 1981-1983; Bd Dir Epis Soc Serv Dio Connecticut Hartford CT 1980-1985; Dio Connecticut Hartford CT 1977; Excoun Dio Connecticut Hartford CT 1976; Chair Outreach Com Dio Connecticut Hartford CT 1973; Excoun Dio Connecticut Hartford CT 1964-1968; R Chr Ch Redding Ridge CT 1958-1986; Excoun; Chmn Bec Dio NW Pennsylvania Erie PA 1953-1958; R S Jn's Ch Franklin PA 1953-1958; Dir Nh Yth Wk Dio New Hampshire Concord NH 1948-1950; P-in-c S Geo's Ch Durham NH 1947-1953; Assoc S Steph's Epis Ch Wilkes Barre PA 1945-1947. gandr@comcast.net

GIEGLER, Carl Esten (Chi) 414 Gaspar Key Ln, Punta Gorda FL 33955 B Oak Park IL 2/11/1939 s Harry Paul Giegler & Eunice Lucille. BA Trin Hartford CT 1961; STB GTS 1964; Med Estrn Illinois U 1970. D 6/11/1964 Bp Walter H Gray P 5/1/1965 Bp Joseph Warren Hutchens. m 6/11/1960 Beverly Pamela Severns c 2. Secy Dio Chicago Chicago IL 1987-1990; Gr Epis Ch New Lenox IL 1976-1991; P-in-c Ch Of S Ben Bolingbrook IL 1975-1976; Dio Chicago Chicago IL 1975-1976; Chair, Coll Wk Dio Springfield Springfield IL 1969-1974; Vic Trin Epis Ch Mattoon IL 1968-1975; Cur S Jn's Ch New Milford CT 1964-1968. BCGIEGLER@JUNO.COM

GIERLACH, David Joseph (Haw) 231 Miloiki Pl, Honolulu HI 96825 **S Eliz's Ch Honolulu HI 2009-** B Binghamton NY 4/8/1957 s Joseph John Gierlach & Jacquelyn Teresa. BA SUNY 1977; MA Maryknoll TS 1981; JD U of Hawaii 1989. D 8/19/2006 Bp Richard Sui On Chang P 5/19/2007 Bp Robert LeRoy Fitzpatrick. m 8/11/2001 Ida Teiti c 3. S Jn's By The Sea Kaneohe HI 2007-2009. gierlach33@aol.com

GIESELER, Gieseler Morgret (Miss) 5927 Couton Dr, Mobile AL 36693 B McClure OH 2/4/1936 RN St. Jos Sch Of Nrsng 1972; BBA U of Memphis 1978; MBA U of Memphis 1979. D 1/6/2001 Bp Alfred Clark Marble Jr. m 8/31/1956 Russell Gieseler c 2. S Jn's Epis Ch Pascagoula MS 2001-2006. mgieseler@mdoc.state.ms.us

GIESELMANN, Robert Kent (Cal) Saint Stephen's Episcopal Church, 3 Bayview Ave, Belvedere CA 94920 **R S Steph's Par Belvedere CA 2010-** B Knoxville TN 9/30/1958 s Paul Ernest Gieselman & Nancy. BS Auburn U 1979; MS Auburn U 1985; JD U of Tennessee 1987; MDiv STUSo 1999. D 6/19/1999 P 2/5/2000 Bp Charles Glenn VonRosenberg. c 2. R Chr Ch Sausalito CA 2005-2010; R S Paul's Par Kent Chestertown MD 2001-2005; Assoc S Lk's Ch Cleveland TN 1999-2001. "The Epis Call to Love," Apcryphile, 2008. robg@ststephenschurch.org

GIFFORD II, Gerald Gerard (Haw) 446 Kawaihae St Apt 119, Honolulu HI 96825 B Columbus OH 5/4/1924 s Gerald Gerard Gifford & Gertrude. BS OH SU 1948; MS EDS 1952; DMin SFTS 1973. D 6/29/1952 P 1/18/1953 Bp Henry W Hobson. m 2/22/1946 Pauline Mohler c 5. R S Eliz's Ch Honolulu HI 1978-1989; S Nich Epis Ch Kapolei HI 1978; S Alb's Chap Honolulu HI 1966-1978; R S Jn's Ch Worthington OH 1957-1966; Vic S Steph's Ch Wahiawa HI 1954-1957; Asst S Barth's Ch New York NY 1952-1954; DCE Trin Ch Columbus OH 1948-1949. HI Epis Cleric Assn. smudge@hawaii.rr.com

GIFFORD, Lance Allen Ball (Md) 1700 South Rd, Baltimore MD 21209 B Baltimore MD 5/30/1944 s Robert Hugh Gifford & Caroline Deloris. BA W&L 1966; STB GTS 1969. D 6/23/1969 Bp David Keller Leighton Sr P 6/22/1970 Bp Harry Lee Doll. m 6/26/1976 Margaret R McCambell c 2. R S Jn's Ch Mt Washington Baltimore MD 1986-2008; Asst S Barth's Ch Baltimore MD 1977-1979; LocTen Ch Of S Kath Of Alexandria Baltimore MD 1976; Asst S Barth's Ch Baltimore MD 1969-1971. Chapl Epis Fac Conf 1978-2000; Maryland Instnl Revs Bd 1987-2003. gif4d@comcast.net

GIFFORD-COLE, Irene Margarete (Minn) 225 Hoylake Rd. W, Qualicum Beach V9k 1k5 Canada B Rosthern Sask. Canada 12/23/1932 d Herman Gerhard Riesen & Marie. BA U of Manitoba 1954; BD U Mb 1955; MA U MN 1972; MDiv LNTS 1990; DMin TESM 2006. D 8/6/1976 Bp Philip Frederick McNairy P 5/1/1989 Bp Robert Marshall Anderson. m 1/4/1998 David Henry Cole c 3. Mssh Epis Ch S Paul MN 1989-1997. the_well@island.net

GILBERT, Carol Beverly (NJ) 34 Mystic Way, Burlington NJ 08016 B Camden NJ 7/6/1946 d Charles Henderson & Mollye S. BS Fsr U Nashville TN 1968. D 6/11/2005 Bp George Edward Councell. c 2. cbgilbertl@comcast.net

GILBERT JR, George Asbury (CGC) 10100 Hillview Dr Apt 432, Pensacola FL 32514 **S Jn The Evang Robertsdale AL 2010-** B Providence RI 10/13/1925 s George Asbury Gilbert & Charlotte Francis. BS U of Rhode Island 1950; Dio California Sch for Mnstry 1978; BTS California Sch for Deacons

1984. D 9/9/1978 Bp C Kilmer Myers P 11/8/1980 Bp William Edwin Swing. m 10/14/1950 Judith Ann Short c 2. Int S Monica's Cantonment FL 2007-2009; Int Ch Of The Epiph Crestview FL 2004-2007; Int S Mary's Epis Ch Milton FL 2001-2003; S Mk's Epis Ch Kimberling City MO 1992-2000; R St Mich & Gr Ch Rumford RI 1986-1991; Ch Of The Mssh Foster RI 1983-1986; Vic Ch Of The Mssh Foster RI 1983-1986; S Steph's Par Belvedere CA 1982-1983; Asst Ch Of The Redeem San Rafael CA 1978-1980. Auth, "Through the Seasons in Meditation, Homily, and Verse," *Bk*, LuLu.Com, 2010. OSL 2008. R Emer St. Mich & Gr Ch 1994. epivicar1@cox.net

GILBERT, Marilynn D (Ct) 28 Windemere Pl, Grosse Pointe Farms MI 48236 B Detroit MI 2/20/1942 d James V Davis & Anne Elizabeth. BS U MI 1965; MDiv SWTS 1994. D 7/11/1998 P 4/5/2003 Bp Edwin Max Leidel Jr. c 3. Asst Chr Epis Ch Norwich CT 2003-2006; Intern and Transitional D S Christophers Epis Ch Grand Blanc MI 1997-2000; Lay Vic All SS Epis Ch Fair Haven MI 1994-1997.

GILBERT, Paul Edward (LI) 1760 Parc Vue Ave, Mount Pleasant SC 29464 B Bay Shore NY 3/15/1944 s Robert Gilbert & Louise. BA Wesl 1966; MDiv VTS 1980. D 6/14/1980 P 12/28/1980 Bp John Shelby Spong. m 9/17/2005 Jeannette Marie Herrmann c 3. R S Jn's Of Lattingtown Locust Vlly NY 1996-2004; R The Par Of S Mary And S Jude NE Harbor ME 1982-1996; Cur Chr Ch Short Hills NJ 1980-1982. Auth, "The Mar Quest," *Mar Preparation*, self, 2010; Auth, "Personally Spkng," *Collected sermons*, self, 1996. Chapl Natl Inst of Soc Sci 1998-2003. paulgilbert65@gmail.com

GILBERT, Shedrick Edward (SeFla) 3368 Nw 51st Ter, Miami FL 33142 **Asst S Agnes Ch Miami FL 1984-** B Miami FL 6/21/1922 s Rufus M Gilbert & Ethel. BS Hampton U 1954. D 3/3/1984 Bp Calvin Onderdonk Schofield Jr. m 1/22/1947 Wilma Jacqueline Wake c 3.

GILBERT, Thomas F (Me) 118 Morrill St, Pittsfield ME 04967 B Valleyfield Quebec 3/27/1951 s Eugene C Gilbert & Norma S. BS U of Maine 1973. D 6/23/2007 Bp Chilton Abbie Richardson Knudsen. m 11/1/1975 Veronica Irizarry c 3. tgilbert@cianbro.com

GILBERT, Trimble (Ak) General Delivery, Arctic Village AK 99722 B Artic Village AK 5/19/1935 s James Gilbert. D 5/19/1974 Bp William J Gordon Jr P 7/6/1975 Bp David Rea Cochran.

GILBERTSEN, George Eugene (Lex) No address on file. B Detroit MI 3/19/1931 s George Eugene Gilbertsen & Marie E. Epis TS In Kentucky; Illinois Coll 1952. D 5/30/1970 Bp William R Moody P 12/1/1970 Bp Jonathan Goodhue Sherman. m 8/28/1954 Carolyn V Baker c 4. Cur S Andr's Ch Oceanside NY 1970-1971.

GILBERTSON, Gary Raymond (WMo) 12301 West 125th Terr, Overland Park KS 66213 B New Ulm,MN 7/21/1938 s Herbert A Gilbertson & Olivene Marie. BS Minnesota St U Mankato 1960; MDiv SWTS 1963; MA No Dakota St U 1971; PhD NCAS 1976. D 6/29/1963 P 5/12/1964 Bp Hamilton Hyde Kellogg. m 5/15/1993 Patricia A Thomas c 3. Int S Matt's Ch Raytown MO 2008-2010; Int S Mich And All Ang Ch Mssn KS 2006-2008; Int S Andr's Ch Kansas City MO 2000-2003; Mssn Strtgy Com Dio W Missouri Kansas City MO 2000-2002; Dioc Misconduct Prevention Trnr Dio Maryland Baltimore MD 1998-2000; Int Memi Ch Baltimore MD 1998-2000; Dioc Misconduct Prevention Trnr Dio Washington Washington DC 1996-1998; Ecum Off Dio Washington Washington DC 1996-1997; Int S Lk's Ch Washington DC 1995-1998; Int Ch Of The Ascen Silver Sprg MD 1994-1995; Off Of Bsh For ArmdF New York NY 1985-1994; Dioc Coun Dio No Dakota Fargo ND 1978-1981; Dep GC 1976, 79, 85 Dio No Dakota Fargo ND 1976-1985; Dioc Coun Dio No Dakota Fargo ND 1974-1976; Pres of Stndg Com Dio No Dakota Fargo ND 1974-1976; Dn Geth Cathd Fargo ND 1973-1985; Chair Dio Assessment Comm & Fin Comm Dio No Dakota Fargo ND 1971-2011; Dioc Coun Dio No Dakota Fargo ND 1970-1972; Vic S Steph's Ch Fargo ND 1969-1971; Dioc Coun Dio Minnesota Minneapolis MN 1967-1969; Cass Lake Camp Bd and Stff Dio Minnesota Minneapolis MN 1964-1969; Vic Samuel Memi Naytahwaush MN 1963-1965. Aircraft Owners and Pilos Assocaion 2000-2012; Amer Socity for Trng and Dvlpmt 1972-1997; Assn for Conflict Resolution 2001-2005; Mltry Oficers Assn of Amer 1985-2012; The Ombudsman Assn 1997-2000. Paul Harris Fell Rotary Intl 2009. gary@garygilbertson.org

GILCHRIST, James Fiveash (Colo) 5478 S Idalia Ct, Centennial CO 80015 **R S Mart In The Fields Aurora CO 2007-** B Brunswick GA 1/5/1950 s Howard Neal Gilchrist & Sarah Eugenia. AA Brunswick Coll 1975; MDiv TS 2006. D 6/10/2006 P 12/9/2006 Bp Robert John O'Neill. m 2/20/1970 Glenna Fabian Gilchrist. Cur/Asstg S Lk's Ch Denver CO 2006-2007. qualconco@aol.com

GILCHRIST, J Edwin (Neb) 124 1st Ave SE, Ronan MT 59864 B Denver CO 12/19/1939 s James Benjamin Gilchrist & Ethel. BS U Denv 1962; MDiv Nash 1967. D 6/5/1967 P 12/1/1967 Bp Joseph Summerville Minnis. m 12/16/1961 June Harding Smith c 2. Supply P Dio Nebraska Omaha NE 1974-1976; Asst Trin Cathd Omaha NE 1972-1974; Asst S Barn On The Desert Scottsdale AZ 1971-1972; Vic S Andr's Epis Ch Ft Lupton CO 1969-1971; Vic Ch Of The H Comf Broomfield CO 1967-1969.

GILCHRIST, John Richard (Ct) Po Box 361, Winter Harbor ME 04693 **P-in-c S Aidans Ch Machias ME 2008-** B Montgomery AL 10/13/1938 s William Clyde Gilchrist & Ann Elizabeth. Westminster Choir Coll of Rider U 1959; BS U of Alabama 1962; MDiv VTS 1967; CG Jung Inst 1976. D 6/10/1967 P 6/1/1968 Bp George Mosley Murray. m 8/27/1982 Gail G Collins c 2. R S Steph's Ch Ridgefield CT 1990-2003; Dio Connecticut Hartford CT 1989-1990; Dio Missouri S Louis MO 1987-1989; R S Dunst's: The Epis Ch at Auburn U Auburn AL 1982-1987; R S Barth's Epis Ch Florence AL 1969-1982; Vic S Paul's Chap Magnolia Sprg AL 1967-1969; Vic S Ptr's Epis Ch Bon Secour AL 1967-1969. Auth, *Evalution of One Cong's Experience w Par Dvlpmt Consultants*. jrgilchrist@yahoo.com

GILDERSLEEVE, Robert Kirk (Be) 435 Center Street, Jim Thorpe PA 18229 **Supply P Calv Ch Tamaqua PA 1993-** B Pittsburgh PA 9/9/1942 s Brunson Kirk Gildersleeve & Jean Lucile. BSed California U of Pennsylvania 1971; MDiv Nash 1976. D 5/29/1976 P 4/1/1978 Bp Robert Bracewell Appleyard. m 5/15/1965 Karen Lynn Lydic c 3. Supply P Dio Bethlehem Bethlehem PA 1993-2005; R Epis Par Of S Mk And S Jn Jim Thorpe PA 1985-1992; Vic S Jos's Ch Port Allegany PA 1978-1984; Vic S Matt's Epis Ch Eldred PA 1978-1984; Nash Nashotah WI 1976-1977. sleeve1@ptd.net

GILES III, James D (CFla) 1049 State Route 949, Dunmor KY 42339 **The Ch Army Usa Branson MO 2005-** B Winter Haven FL 1/21/1960 AS Indn River Cmnty Coll 2000; BD Florida Atlantic U 2002; MDiv TESM 2005. D 5/28/2005 P 11/11/2005 Bp John Wadsworth Howe. m 8/2/1980 Mary C Giles c 2. wherdeego@gmail.com

GILES, Richard Stephen (Pa) 105 Lansdowne Ct, Lansdowne PA 19050 B Birmingham UK 9/5/1940 s Donald Stevens Giles & Gladys Evelyn. BA Newcastle U 1963; MLitt Newcastle U 1988. D 12/1/1965 P 9/1/1996 Bp The Bishop Of Peterborough. m 7/29/1977 Susan Boak c 1. Dn Philadelphia Cathd Philadelphia PA 1999-2008. Auth, *Mk My Word*, Cowley Pub, 2005; Auth, *Creating Uncommon Wrshp*, Liturg Press, 2004; Auth, *Repitching the Tent*, Liturg Press, 2004. Hon.Vstng Fell St Jn's Coll, Durham UK 2007. richardgiles@liturgyworks.org.uk

GILES, Walter Crews (FtW) 1649 Park Ln, Alvarado TX 76009 B Dallas TX 3/21/1960 s Charles Dan Giles & Mildred Harding. U of Texas 1980; Richland Jr Coll Decatur IL 1981; BBA U of No Texas 1983; MDiv Nash 1994. D 12/27/1993 Bp Jack Leo Iker P 7/2/1994 Bp Clarence Cullam Pope Jr. m 1/7/1989 Becky Lynn Gordon. P-in-c S Anth's Ch Alvarado TX 1998; Cur S Michaels By-The-Sea Ch Carlsbad CA 1997-1998; Cur S Jn's Ch Ft Worth TX 1995-1997; Cur All SS' Epis Ch Ft Worth TX 1994-1995. frcregil@sprynet.com

GILES, Walter Edward (CNY) 12914 US Route 11, Adams Center NY 13606 **Dn, Finger Lakes Dist Dio Cntrl New York Syracuse NY 1968-; Dept of CE Dio Cntrl New York Syracuse NY 1966-; Dept of Missioners Dio Cntrl New York Syracuse NY 1957-** B Watertown NY 9/23/1932 s Clarence Frederick Giles & Florence. BA Hob 1954; BD VTS 1957. D 6/22/1957 Bp Malcolm E Peabody P 6/11/1958 Bp Walter M Higley. m 3/3/1978 Patricia Clark c 2. Chr Ch Sackets Harbor NY 1991-1994; S Paul's Ch Brownville NY 1991-1994; Dio Albany Albany NY 1986-1998; Trin Epis Ch Watertown NY 1976-1990; Vic Chr Ch Sackets Harbor NY 1976-1978; Dio Cntrl New York Syracuse NY 1967-1991; R Epis Ch Of SS Ptr And Jn Auburn NY 1966-1976.

GILFEATHER, Gordon Grant (Az) 12990 E Shea Blvd, Scottsdale AZ 85259 **D S Anth On The Desert Scottsdale AZ 2009-** B Great Falls MT 4/24/1938 s Patrick James Gilfeather & Margaret Lenore. BS Montana St Coll 1961; MA WA SU 1970. D 1/24/2009 Bp Kirk Stevan Smith. m 12/18/1971 Susan L Hilliard. g2feather@cox.net

GILFILLIN, William Marion (USC) 1219 Forest Hills Dr, Wilmington NC 28403 B 7/20/1943 BA Furman U; BD STUSo. D 6/29/1969 Bp John Adams Pinckney P 11/26/1973 Bp George Moyer Alexander. S Fran Ch Greenville SC 1987-1992; Ch Of The Gd Shpd Wilmington NC 1980-1984.

GILHOUSEN, Dennis Ray (Kan) 6501 Mapel Dr, Mission KS 66202 B 7/18/1942 BA Kansas Wesl; MS U Pittsburgh Sch Of Publ Hlth; U of Kansas. D 11/27/1977 P 12/8/1978 Bp William Davidson. dennisg@valleyhope.com

GIL JIMENEZ, Ramon Antonio (Iglesia Episcopal Dominicana) Box 764, Dominican Republic Dominican Republic **Dio The Dominican Republic (Iglesia Epis Dominicana) Santo Domingo DO 2010-** B 7/18/1949 s Jose Rafael Gil & Juana Maria. D 2/14/2010 P 2/20/2011 Bp Julio Cesar Holguin-Khoury. c 3.

GILKES, Overton Weldon (Ct) 262 Shelton Ave, New Haven CT 06511 B 10/20/1933 s Christopher Carmel Gilkes & Zulieka Albertha. BA Dur 1956; Codrington Coll 1957; MA Dur 1985. D 12/1/1956 P 12/1/1957 Bp The Bishop Of Barbados. m 4/24/1960 Yvonne Hyacinth Darby c 4. S Andr's Ch New Haven CT 1989-1992; P-in-c S Ptr's Ch Rosedale NY 1985-1987; Asst Gr Epis Ch Plainfield NJ 1983-1985; R Ch Of The H Sprt Brooklyn NY 1980-1983.

GILKEY JR, Sam (Ky) 912 Virginia Ave., St. Cloud FL 34769 **D The Ch Of S Lk And S Ptr S Cloud FL 2004-** B Hopkinsville KY 6/6/1937 s Sam Brown Gilkey & Pauline. Bethel Coll; U of Kentucky. D 6/9/1979 Bp William Hopkins Folwell. m 6/4/1960 Jean Morrow c 2. D S Jn's Ch Morganfield KY 1998-2003; D S Mary's Ch Madisonville KY 1986-1997; D S Jn's Epis Ch Of Kissimme Kissimmee FL 1979-1984. gilkey@embarqmail.com

GILL, Brian William (SC) PO Box 125, Johns Island SC 29457 B Stratford Ontario 8/30/1941 s Frederick John Gill & Catherine Constance. D 9/11/2010 Bp Mark Joseph Lawrence. m 8/29/1964 Marjorie Gill c 2. bgillgroup@aol.com

GILL JR, Charles Henry (Eur) 4210 Colony Club Drive, Catawba Island, Ohio, 43452 OH B Mount Vernon OH 2/6/1936 s Charles Henry Gill & Virginia Aileen. BA Ohio Wesl 1958; BD Ken 1963; MDiv Bex 1972; Clincl Fell Harv 1973; M.Div CRDS 1975; ScD Buxton U 1995; MS Methodist TS In Ohio 2003. D 6/29/1963 P 1/11/1964 Bp William Foreman Creighton. c 3. Dio Sthrn Ohio Cincinnati OH 1982-2002; Emm Epis Ch Geneva 1201 CH 1975-1976; Chapl Hlth Affrs Cathd of St Ptr & St Paul Washington DC 1971-1974; R S Jn's Ch Ft Washington MD 1965-1971; Asst S Jn's Ch Chevy Chase MD 1963-1965. Chas Gill, "The Attack upon the NE Kingdom," Wrld Pub, Vermont, 2003; Chas Gill, *Ch's Role in Healing*, WCC, 1973; Chas Gill, *Tonkin Gulf*, The Amer Friends Serv Com, 1970; Chas Gill, "Hlth for the Americans," *Hlth for the 70s*, Tul, 1969. Dn, The Geneve Consult 1984-1985; ESMA 1976; Wrld Hlth Assembly on Aging 1985. "First" Addictions Treatment Competition St of Maine 1992; Clincl Fell and Fac Harv, Sch of Med 1971; Mem, Acad of Med Acad of Med, Washington, D.C. 1966. gill@swissmail.org

GILL, Cynthia Elizabeth (SeFla) 1400 Riverside Dr, St Mary Magdalene, Coral Springs FL 33071 **S Mary Magd Epis Ch Coral Sprg FL 2004-** B Pampa TX 2/21/1955 d John Maurice Gill & Wanda Louise. BA Trin U 1977; Cert The Drama Studio-London 1981; MDiv Nash 1988. D 6/22/1988 Bp Clarence Cullam Pope Jr P 6/1/1989 Bp Richard Frank Grein. S Mk The Evang Ft Lauderdale FL 2000-2004; S Steph's Ch Coconut Grove Coconut Grove FL 1993-1999; Cur The Ch of S Matt And S Tim New York NY 1988-1993. Cmnty H Sprt. cegill@bellsouth.net

GILL, James Lawrence (Be) PO Box 214, East Winthrop ME 04343 B Newark NJ 4/8/1929 s William John Gill & Anna Marie. BA Leh 1951; STB GTS 1954; STM GTS 1964; MA Ateneo De Manila U 1968; MA Moravian TS 1989. D 6/12/1954 P 12/18/1954 Bp Benjamin M Washburn. c 3. R Trin Ch Easton PA 1968-1991; Vic S Matt's Ch Paramus NJ 1954-1960. meamft2@aol.com

GILL, Jeffrey Shilling (Mass) 29 Central St, Andover MA 01810 **R Par Of Chr Ch Andover MA 2002-** B Muncie IN 5/19/1955 s Harold Leon Gill & Virginia Lucille. Fletcher Sch of Law and Diplomacy (Tufts U); BA Indiana U 1982; MDiv Harvard DS 1985. D 6/11/1988 P 5/20/1989 Bp David Elliot Johnson. m 8/7/1976 Carolyn Shilling c 2. Dn No Shore Deanry Dio Massachusetts Boston MA 1998-2000; R Trin Ch Topsfield MA 1990-2002; Asst R Gr Ch Lawr MA 1988-1990. Bk Reviewer, "A Ch for the Future: So Afr as the Crucible for Anglicanism in a New Century," *ATR*, 2011. Fellows of the ECF 2000; Massachusetts Epis Cler Assn 1988; Phillips Brooks Cler Club of Boston, Pres 1998-2000; Phillips Brooks Cler Club of Boston, Treas 1992-1998. Fell ECF Medford MA 2000. jeffgill5@gmail.com

GILL, John Herbert (LI) 80 La Salle St Apt 21-H, New York NY 10027 B Washington DC 7/29/1933 s W Herbert Gill & Dorothy. BA cl Ya 1954; STB EDS 1958; Patriarchal Sem Istanbul Tr 1959. D 6/14/1958 Bp Angus Dun P 8/1/1959 Bp William Foreman Creighton. Assoc The Ch of S Ign of Antioch New York NY 1993-1996; R The Ch Of The Epiph And S Simon Brooklyn NY 1978-1993; Assoc S Jn's Ch Huntington NY 1976-1978; Assoc The Ch of S Ign of Antioch New York NY 1973-1976; Dir H Trin Epis Ch Inwood New York NY 1972-1973; Asst Ch Of The Intsn New York NY 1968-1972; P-in-c The Ch of S Edw The Mtyr New York NY 1960-1965; Cur S Columba's Ch Washington DC 1959-1960. Auth, "Gerturde Stein: Blood On The Dining Room Floor," Creative Atrs, 1982. Natl Orgnztn Of The Episcopalians For Life 1998. demojr@nyc.rr.com

GILL JR, (John) Nick (SO) 3429 Live Oak Place, Columbus OH 43221 B Chattanooga TN 5/2/1940 s John Nichols Gill & Marie Christine. BA Newberry Coll 1964; MDiv GTS 1967. D 7/10/1967 Bp John Vander Horst P 5/13/1968 Bp William F Gates Jr. m 9/10/1975 Marsha Sykes c 4. Dio Sthrn Ohio Cincinnati OH 1996; S Paul's Ch Columbus OH 1991-1995; R H Trin Epis Ch Oxford OH 1977-1991; R Ch Of The Gd Samar Knoxville TN 1971-1972; R S Johns Ch Old Hickory TN 1968-1972; D S Geo's Ch Nashville TN 1967-1968. JohnGill@columbus.rr.com

GILL, Jule Carlyle (WA) 1509 S Randolph St, Arlington VA 22204 **S Ptr's Ch Lewes DE 2007-** B Baltimore MD 11/11/1945 d William Pinkney Gill & Eleanor. BA Queens Coll 1967; MA Col 1970; MDiv VTS 1976. D 5/22/1976 Bp John Alfred Baden P 4/1/1977 Bp Robert Bruce Hall. Assoc R S Alb's Par Washington DC 1997-2006; R Ch Of S Steph And The Incarn Washington DC 1987-1997; Assoc R S Aug By-The-Sea Par Santa Monica CA 1979-1987; The TS at The U So Sewanee TN 1976-1979; Chapl The U So (Sewanee) Sewanee TN 1976-1979. jcarlylegill@yahoo.com

GILL, Robert Clarence (CPa) 139 N Findlay St, York PA 17402 B Pittston PA 12/27/1927 s Clarence Orville Gill & Ruth Clarice. BS Penn 1953; U MI 1974. D 6/15/1979 Bp Dean T Stevenson. m 4/16/1966 Jean A Lehman c 1. D S Paul's Ch Columbia PA 1998-2000; D The Epis Ch Of S Jn The Bapt York PA 1979-1997.

GILLAND, Carl George (Ind) 7830 E Vawter Park Rd, Syracuse IN 46567 B Carthage OH 11/18/1936 s Byron George Gilland & Lelia Patricia. Black Hill St U 1967; USAF 1975. D 12/4/1993 Bp Francis Campbell Gray. m 6/18/1982 Linda May Hughes. D S Mk's Epis Ch Des Moines IA 1998-1999; Nomin Com Dio Nthrn Indiana So Bend IN 1990-1993; Property Com Dio Nthrn Indiana So Bend IN 1989-1993. Ord Of S Lk.

GILLARD, Gary Laverne (Md) 1811 Lawnview Dr, Frederick MD 21702 B 3/5/1945 D 5/22/1971 P 12/11/1971 Bp Robert Bracewell Appleyard.

GILLEN, Marguerite Webb (Ct) 17 Bernhardt Meadow Ln, Roxbury CT 06783 B Tampa FL 4/28/1936 d William Ralphel Perez & Marguerite. BS Chart Oak St Coll, CT 1991. D 9/17/2005 Bp Andrew Donnan Smith. c 5. The OSL the Physcn 2008. mwg428@sbcglobal.net

GILLESPIE, Ann Hazard (Va) Christ Church, 118 N Washington St, Alexandria VA 22314 **Assoc R Chr Ch Alexandria VA 2007-** B Auburn NY 8/8/1957 d David Marston Gillespie & Joanna Bown. Ya; BA Goddard Coll 2003; MDiv VTS 2007. D 6/9/2007 P 12/17/2007 Bp Joseph Jon Bruno. m 12/29/1984 Jeffrey E Allin c 2. agillespie@ccalex.org

GILLESPIE, David Marston (RI) 2206 N Hollow Rd, Rochester VT 05767 **Asst S Phil's In The Hills Tucson AZ 1992-** B Morristown NJ 3/16/1925 s Samuel Hazard Gillespie & Margaret. BA Ya 1950; MDiv Yale DS 1954. D 6/13/1954 P 12/19/1954 Bp Angus Dun. m 9/1/1951 Joanna Bowen c 2. P-in-c S Lk's Epis Ch E Greenwich RI 1986-1991; Dn Gr Cathd San Francisco CA 1978-1985; ExCoun Dio Newark Newark NJ 1963-1978; R S Paul's Ch Englewood NJ 1962-1978; R S Jame's Ch Skaneateles NY 1957-1962; Asst S Alb's Par Washington DC 1954-1955. Ord of S Jn of Jerusalem 1981. dmjbgillepie@theriver.com

GILLESPIE, Harold Stanley (Az) 501 S. La Posada Cir., Apt. 116, Green Valley AZ 85614 B Rochester MN 11/11/1920 s William Henderson Gillespie & Vivian Virginia. BS U of Iowa 1957; MS Baylor U 1962. D 10/17/1992 Bp Sanford Zangwill Kaye Hampton. m 8/10/1946 C Anne Waterbury c 3. D Epis Ch Of S Fran-In-The-Vlly Green Vlly AZ 1992-2000. gilanne@earthlink.net

GILLESPIE, Patricia Anne (Minn) 4418 Highway 99, Aurora MN 55705 **S Andr's Ch Le Sueur MN 2004-; Trin Epis Ch Hermantown MN 2004-** B Ann Arbor MI 4/2/1950 d Russell Hardy Dean Gillespie & Mary Drusilla. BA Swarthmore Coll 1972; MA St. Johns U 1991; MDiv STUSo 1994. D 9/29/1994 Bp James Louis Jelinek P 4/1/1995 Bp Sanford Zangwill Kaye Hampton. c 3. S Mary's Ch Ely MN 2007-2011; S Paul's Ch Virginia MN 2003-2006; Dio Minnesota Minneapolis MN 1999-2003; Ch Of Our Sav Little Falls MN 1999; S Steph's Epis Ch Paynesville MN 1998; Ch Of The Gd Samar Sauk Cntr MN 1997-1998; Int Emm Epis Ch Alexandria MN 1994-1996. Auth, "Voices From Within: Faith-Life Stories Of Wmn In The Ch," *Hope*, 1994. pat@motherflash.com

GILLESPIE JR, Robert Schaeffer (WA) 14702 W Auburn Rd, Accokeek MD 20607 **P-in-c Chr Ch Wm And Mary Newburg MD 2011-** B Toronto ON CA 3/6/1937 s Robert Schaeffer Gillespie & Helen Louise. BS Tem 1959; STB GTS 1962. D 6/9/1962 Bp Oliver J Hart P 12/15/1962 Bp Joseph Gillespie Armstrong. m 9/26/1964 Charlotte Ann Dalton c 2. P-in-c All Faith Epis Ch Charlotte Hall MD 2008-2009; Vic S Jas Epis Ch Bowie MD 1989-2002; P-in-c S Paul's Epis Ch Hebron MD 1982-1989; R Chr Ch S Jn's Par Accokeek MD 1968-1978; Cur S Lk's Ch Philadelphia PA 1962-1968. RSG3637@gmail.com

GILLETT, Elizabeth Rosa Hamliton (NY) 1213 River Rd, Hamilton NY 13346 B 9/11/1945 d James Anthony Gillett & Monica May. BA Col 1969; MDiv GTS 1983. D 6/26/1983 P 5/8/1984 Bp David Keller Leighton Sr. Epis Soc Mnstrs Baltimore MD 1998-2004; R S Thos Ch Hamilton NY 1988-1998; Cn S Paul's Cathd Syracuse NY 1985-1988; Assoc The Ch Of The Redeem Baltimore MD 1983-1985. Ord Of S Helena 1982. elizabethgillett@frontiernet.net

GILLETT, Richard W (Los) 719 N 67th St, Seattle WA 98103 **Hon Cn Cathd Cntr Of S Paul Cong Los Angeles CA 2000-** B El Paso TX 7/31/1931 s Irvin Walker Gillett & Caroline Hill. BA U So 1952; MDiv Harvard DS 1960; EDS 1974. D 4/14/1960 P 12/1/1960 Bp Frederic Cunningham Lawrence. m 11/18/1960 Anne Bartlett c 3. Vic Imm Mssn El Monte CA 1986-1996; Vic H Fam Mssn No Hollywood CA 1986; Assoc The Epis Ch Pub Co Scranton PA 1980-1986; Dir Par Prog All SS Ch Pasadena CA 1974-1979; Cur Gr Ch Newton MA 1960-1963; Vic S Lk's And S Marg's Ch Allston MA 1960-1963. Auth, "The New Globalization," Pilgrim Press, 2005; Auth, "The Human Enterprise," Leaven Press, 1985. Giant for Justice Cler and Laity Untd for Econ Justice, Los Angeles 2007; Hugh White Awd for worker justice Epis Ntwk for Econ Justice 2003; Hon Cn Cathd Cntr of St. Paul, Dio

Los Angeles 2000; Proctor Fllshp EDS Cambridge MA 1973. dgillseattle@yahoo.com

GILLETTE, Howard Dennis (La) 433 W.21st #10F, New York NY 10011 B Buffalo NY 8/14/1944 s Howard Gillette & Emma. BA SUNY 1966; MS Troy St U-Montgomery AL 1972. D 9/13/2003 Bp Charles Edward Jenkins III. m 4/27/1984 Mary M Gillette. Assn of Form OSI Agents 1977-2012; Assn of Profsnl Chapl 2004-2012; Assn of Ret Customs Agents 1999-2012; Intl Conf of Police Chapl 2005-2012. Bd Cert Chapl Assn of Profsnl Chapl 2004. chaphoward3@aol.com

GILLETTE, Martha Carol (Chi) 154 Timber Ridge Ln, Lake Barrington IL 60010 **P-in-c Ch Of The H Apos Wauconda IL 2007-** B Schenectady NY 9/21/1955 d Gilbert Adams Gillette & Dolores Marie. Colby Coll ME 1975; BA U MN 1978; MS Old Dominion U Norfolk VA 1989; MDiv Epis Divnity Sch Cambridge MA 2007. D 6/9/2007 Bp John Clark Buchanan P 12/15/2007 Bp Victor Alfonso Scantlebury. c 3. Wrshp Assoc S Mich's Ch Barrington IL 2007-2011. marthagillette@att.net

GILLIAM, John Malone (Tenn) 4715 Harding Pike, Nashville TN 37205 **S Geo's Ch Nashville TN 2010-** B Alpine TX 12/30/1967 s Harvey H Gilliam & Helen E. BA U of No Texas 1997; MDiv TESM 2007. Trans from L'Eglise Episcopal au Rwanda 2/3/2009 as Deacon Bp Mark Joseph Lawrence. m 5/25/1996 Mary Sloan c 4. Assoc Ch Of The H Cross Sullivans Island SC 2009-2010. padrejmg@yahoo.com

GILLIATT, Cynthia Ann (Va) 1362 Cumberland Drive, Harrisonburg VA 22801 **Died 8/16/2011** B Saint Louis MO 12/2/1943 d Sidney George Gilliatt & Aline Jesse. BA Duke 1966; MA U MI 1967; PhD U MI 1971; Cert VTS 1988. D 6/18/1988 P 4/4/1989 Bp Peter James Lee. Integrity/Virginia. Phi Kappa Phi; Phi Beta Kappa. gilliaca@jmu.edu

GILLIES, Clara (WNY) 18 N Pearl St, Buffalo NY 14202 **D Ch Of The Ascen Buffalo NY 1983-** B New York NY 6/16/1930 d Frank Lester Boughner & Catherine Pauline. Cmnty Coll Of New York NY. D 6/11/1983 Bp Harold B Robinson. m 11/12/1983 Bruce Nelson Gillies c 4.

GILLISS, Columba (Md) 3200 Baker Cir Unit I209, Adamstown MD 21710 B Washington DC 12/6/1937 d William Weir Gilliss & Ruth. BA GW 1960; MDiv GTS 1975. D 6/14/1975 Bp Paul Moore Jr P 1/30/1977 Bp James Stuart Wetmore. R Gr Ch New Mrkt MD 1990-2002; Ch Of St Jn The Evang Shady Side MD 1987-1989; Team Monticello NY 1985-1986; D-in-c S Ann's Ch For The Deaf New York NY 1977-1983. EPF 1966; EWC 1973; EWHP. cgilliss@erols.com

GILLMAN, Paula Ruth (Minn) 520 N Pokegama Ave, Grand Rapids MN 55744 B International Falls MN 9/25/1951 d Kenneth Swenson & Margarett. D 6/21/2009 P 12/20/2009 Bp James Louis Jelinek. m 7/17/1976 Donald Gillman c 3. Reverend Chr Epis Ch Grand Rapids MN 2009-2011. dgillman@northlc.com

GILLOOLY, Bryan Charles (O) 19636 Scottsdale Blvd, Cleveland OH 44122 B Cleveland OH 8/27/1965 s George Rice Gillooly & Jean. BA Coll of Wooster 1987; Mstr Cleveland St U 1997. D 11/13/1992 Bp James Russell Moodey. m 10/7/1989 Karen E Melech c 2. Asst Dio Ohio Cleveland OH 2002-2005; D S Lk's Ch Cleveland OH 1995-2000. NAAD. bgillooly@sbcglobal.net

GILMAN, James Earl (SwVa) 719 Opie St, Staunton VA 24401 **D Trin Ch Staunton VA 2003-** B Portland OR 7/26/1947 s William Gilman & Florence. BA Seattle Pacific Coll 1969; MDiv Denver Sem 1973; PhD Drew U 1982. D 2/15/2003 Bp Frank Neff Powell. c 2. "Whose God What Rel: Compassion As Normative For Inter-Rel Coop," Journ Of Ecum Stds Vol 40 #3, 2003; "Fidelity Of The Heart: An Ethic Of Chr Virtue," Oxf Press, 2001. jegil3@hotmail.com

GILMAN, Robert Ray (SVa) 2541 Seaview Ave, Virginia Beach VA 23455 B Carlinville IL 10/18/1943 s Ray Edward Gilman & Ruth. BS SUNY 1965; BD/MDiv VTS 1968. D 6/8/1968 Bp Leland Stark P 12/1/1968 Bp Charles F Hall. m 4/22/1972 Barbara W Weidler c 1. Palmer Memi Ch Houston TX 2010-2011; R The Epis Ch Of The Adv Norfolk VA 2001-2009; Off Of Bsh For ArmdF New York NY 1973-2001; Assoc To R Trin Ch Arlington VA 1970-1973; Cur S Mich's Epis Ch Arlington VA 1968-1970. cbgilman@live.com

GILMER, Lyonel Wayman (NC) 2924 Wellesley Trce, Nashville TN 37215 B Rock Hill SC 6/29/1940 s George Barrett Gilmer & Margaret Virginia. MDiv Columbia TS 1962; BA Cit 1962; Supvsr Acpe 1976; SWTS 1981. D 10/29/1981 Bp Quintin Ebenezer Primo Jr P 3/1/1982 Bp James Winchester Montgomery. m 7/16/1976 Mary Strauss c 4. Chr Ch Cathd Nashville TN 2004; S Clare's Ch Matthews NC 1995-1996; Chr Ch Charlotte NC 1994; S Jn's Epis Ch Charlotte NC 1990-1993; Asst R Chr Ch Charlotte NC 1982-1989. Auth, "Care Of Chld In Hospitals". ACPE, Founding Mem Bioethics Resource Grp.

GILMORE, Elizabeth Lameyer (Me) 24 Fairmount St, Portland ME 04103 B Rochester NY 12/6/1935 d William McOuat & Dorothy. BA Smith 1956; MDiv EDS 1980. D 9/16/1981 Bp Morris Fairchild Arnold P 10/27/1982 Bp John Bowen Coburn. m 10/1/1995 Roger Gilmore c 3. R Trin Epis Ch Portland ME 1990-1999; Int Trin Ch Topsfield MA 1989-1990; Int S Mk's Ch Foxborough MA 1987-1988; S Mk's Ch Southborough MA 1981-1987. rgil@maine.rr.com

GILMORE JR, James Madison (SeFla) 2801 Blue Goose Ct, Hendersonville NC 28792 B Jacksonville FL 4/12/1931 s James Madison Gilmore & Marguerite Stella. BA U Of Florida 1953; MDiv STUSo 1956; MS Nova U 1975; DMin Pittsburgh Sem 1986. D 6/29/1956 P 1/7/1957 Bp Henry I Louttit. c 3. R All Souls' Epis Ch Miami Bch FL 1983-1991; R H Cross Epis Ch Miami FL 1965-1983; Vic S Jas The Less Madison TN 1964-1965; Cur All SS Prot Epis Ch Ft Lauderdale FL 1959-1964; Vic S Anne's Ch Crystal River FL 1958-1959; P S Jn's Epis Ch Brooksville FL 1956-1959; Vic S Marg's Ch Inverness FL 1956-1959. jimgilmore72@comcast.net

GILMORE, Janet Green (Tex) 17118 Kiowa River Ln, Houston TX 77095 **Died 12/18/2010** B Galveston TX 6/20/1956 d Burton Green & Laurel. BS LSU Baton Rouge LA 1978; MS Florida St U, Tallahassee, Fl 1979; MDiv Epis TS of The SW 2007. D 6/23/2007 Bp Don Adger Wimberly. c 2. therevjanet@gmail.com

GILMORE, Jerry (Ct) Po Box 309, South Orleans MA 02662 B Wayland MA 6/7/1914 s George William Gilmore & Rena Flanders. BA Harv 1936; MDiv VTS 1948. D 6/4/1948 P 12/1/1948 Bp Angus Dun. m 6/4/1995 Priscilla B Grace c 3. R S Paul And S Jas New Haven CT 1955-1972; R S Paul's Ch Yonkers NY 1951-1955; R All SS Epis Ch Appleton WI 1949-1951; Asst S Jn's Ch Lafayette Sq Washington DC 1948-1949. Auth, *The Bible & The Poor*, WCC. Cntr for Intl Plcy, Washington DC, Bd Mem 1982; Ch and City Conf Founding Mem 1962-1974; EES 1954. Pres Coun of Ch, New Haven, CT New Haven CT 1962; Pres Coun of Ch, Yonkers, NY Yonkers NY 1952; Pres Mnstrl Assn, Appleton, WI Appleton WI 1949. hosanna3@gis.net

GILMORE, Paul Michael (Okla) 6304 Overcourt Mnr, Oklahoma City OK 73132 B Kansas City MO 7/18/1936 s Paul William Gilmore & Gyneth Grace. MDiv Epis TS In Kentucky 1966; BS U of Cntrl Oklahoma 1966. D 6/17/1966 P 12/1/1966 Bp Chilton Powell. m 9/9/1958 Elizabeth McKenzie c 2. R S Dav's Ch Oklahoma City OK 1997-1998; Dio Oklahoma Oklahoma City OK 1988-1997; Vic S Jas Epis Ch Oklahoma City OK 1988-1997; Assoc All Souls Epis Ch Oklahoma City OK 1978-1988; Vic The Epis Ch Of The H Apos Moore OK 1975-1978; R St Phil's Epis Ch Ardmore OK 1968-1976; Vic S Mich And All Ang Ch Lindsay OK 1966-1968; Vic S Tim's Epis Ch Pauls Vlly OK 1966-1968. pgil7@att.net

GILMORE, Teresa Jane (Cal) 1625 8th Ave, Sacramento CA 95818 B Oakland CA 8/14/1953 BA U CA. D 6/21/2003 P 3/6/2004 Bp Jerry Alban Lamb. m 1/4/1992 Richard S Gilmore. S Giles Ch Moraga CA 2010-2011; Alta Bates Summit Med Cntr Berkeley CA 2009-2010; Trin Ch Folsom CA 2005-2009; Dio Nthrn California Sacramento CA 2003-2006. tgilmore1234@yahoo.com

GILPIN, Kathlyn Castiglioni (SwFla) 6418 Glen Abbey Ln, Bradenton FL 34202 **D S Marg Of Scotland Epis Ch Sarasota FL 2006-** B Washington DC 4/19/1948 d Paul Michael Castiglioni & Mary Elizabeth. BA U of So Florida 1969. D 6/18/2005 Bp John Bailey Lipscomb. m 4/6/1975 Joseph Arthur Gilpin c 1. D S Mary Magd Lakewood Ranch FL 2004-2006. kcgilpin@aol.com

GIL RESTREPO, Silvio (Colom) Carrera 6 No 49-85, Piso 2, Bogota Colombia B 11/30/1945 Licenciado en Teologia Universidad Santo Tomas 2000; Gedencia Empresas para Desaddolo Soc Universidad Javeriana 2004. D 2/20/2010 Bp Francisco Jose Duque-Gomez. silviogilr@hotmail.com

GILSDORF, John Walter (EO) 1971 Sw Quinney Ave, Pendleton OR 97801 **D Ch Of The Redeem Pendleton OR 1999-** B Portland OR 12/10/1964 s John William Gilsdorf & Karen. BS Oregon Inst Of Tech 1991. D 9/26/1999 P 5/24/2000 Bp Rustin Ray Kimsey. m 12/12/1992 Kimberly Ann Conover. jkgisdorf@oregontrail.net

GILSON, Anne Elizabeth (WA) 5 Fernwood Cir, Harwich MA 02645 B Warren PA 8/11/1958 d Richard Abbott Gilson & Margaret Lois. BA Chatham Coll 1982; MDiv EDS 1986; MPhil UTS 1991; PhD UTS 1993. D 6/11/2005 P 1/21/2006 Bp John Chane. m 12/30/1995 Judith Anne Davis c 1. Nativ Epis Ch Temple Hills MD 2005-2006; Chr Ch Capitol Hill Washington DC 2000-2004. Auth, "The Battle for Amer's Families: A Feminist Response to the Rel Rt," Pilgrim Press, 1999; Auth, "Eros Breaking Free: Interpreting Sexual Theo-Ethics," Pilgrim Press, 1995; Co-Ed; Co-Auth, "Revolutionary Forgiveness: Feminist Reflections of Nicaragua," Orbis Books, 1987. annegilson2@gmail.com

GILSON, Christine (WMo) Po Box 883, El Dorado KS 67042 **R Trin Epis Ch El Dorado KS 2011-** B Denver CO 9/8/1946 d Edwin Juergen Westermann & Esther Elizabeth. BA Gri 1968; MS U IL 1970; MS Ft Hays St U 1994; MDiv SWTS 2002. D 8/31/2002 P 4/7/2003 Bp James Marshall Adams Jr. m 12/27/1969 Preston Allan Gilson c 1. Dn, Sthrn Dnry Dio W Missouri Kansas City MO 2009-2011; GC Dep 4 Dio W Missouri Kansas City MO 2009-2011; Vic Trin Epis Ch Lebanon MO 2003-2010. chrisgilson@mac.com

GILTINAN, Martha Hughlett (Mass) 311 11th St, Ambridge PA 15003 **TESM Ambridge PA 2010-** B Charleston WV 11/10/1957 d Alexander Smith Giltinan & Allen Carter. BA Wheaton Coll at Norton 1980; ThM Gordon-Conwell TS 1985; MDiv VTS 1988. D 6/11/1988 Bp David Elliot Johnson P 5/1/1989 Bp Roger W Blanchard. Chr Ch So Hamilton MA 2001-2005; R S Andr's Ch

G

Ayer MA 1991-2000; Asst All SS' Epis Ch Belmont MA 1988-1991. mhgiltinan@aol.com

GILTON, Michael R (Dal) 851 Buffalo Springs Dr, Prosper TX 75078 **Vic St Pauls Epis Ch Prosper TX 2011-; Cur S Paul's Ch Bakersfield CA 2005-** B Anaheim CA 8/2/1964 BSChE U of Arkansas 1986; MBA U of Houston 1995; MDiv Fuller TS 2005. D 8/24/2005 P 2/25/2006 Bp John-David Mercer Schofield. m 5/24/1986 Kathleen Powers Gilton c 1. Ch Planter Dio Dallas Dallas TX 2007-2010; Cur S Paul's Ch Bakersfield CA 2005-2007. michael@stpaulsprosper.org

GINGHER, Richard Hammond (O) 4747 Scioto #201, Toledo OH 43615 B Columbus OH 9/15/1930 s Paul Rutter Gingher & Anna Elizabeth. BA Muskingum Coll 1953; ThL Bex 1960; BD Bex 1961. D 9/10/1961 P 6/19/1962 Bp Roger W Blanchard. Supply P Dio Ohio Cleveland OH 1991; Com Alcosm Dio Ohio Cleveland OH 1981-1983; BACAM Dio Ohio Cleveland OH 1979-1981; Rgnl Dioc Chapl Dio Ohio Cleveland OH 1975-1980; Asst Min S Andr's Ch Dayton OH 1961-1963. Gingher Memi Chap Dedication Toledo Mntl Hlth Cntr 1988; Employee of the Year Toledo Mntl Hlth Cntr 1983.

G

GINN JR, Robert Jay (WMass) Oratory Of Saint Francis, Box 300, Templeton MA 01468 B IA 3/14/1946 s P O O & P O. BA U of Nebraska 1968; MDiv Harvard DS 1972. D 6/14/1980 P 2/1/1981 Bp Alexander Doig Stewart. m 12/21/1974 Virginia Thomas Rowland. Vic Chr Ch So Barre MA 1994-1996; Dio Wstrn Massachusetts Springfield MA 1994-1995; Asst All SS Ch Worcester MA 1988-1991; Dio Wstrn Massachusetts Springfield MA 1988-1990; Dio Wstrn Massachusetts Springfield MA 1987-1988; Int S Thos Epis Ch Auburn MA 1987-1988; Dio Wstrn Massachusetts Springfield MA 1987; Int S Jn's Ch Worcester MA 1986-1987; Int Ch Of The Nativ Northborough MA 1985-1986; Cur S Paul's Epis Ch Gardner MA 1980-1984. Auth, "Career Coaching Your Kids," Consulting Psychologists Press, 1997; Auth, "Discovering Your Career Life-Cycle," Rad, 1994; Auth, "The Career Guide," Macmillan Pub Co, 1983; Auth, "The Coll Grad'S Career Guide," Scribner, 1981; Auth, "A Brief Intro To Vocational Testing In A Developmental Co," Harv, 1980. blackslate@comcast.net

GINNEVER, Richard Arthur (Md) 9259 Brush Run, Columbia MD 21045 **R Chr Ch Columbia MD 2001-** B Mineola NY 9/23/1949 s Arthur Robert Ginnever & Mildred Kathleen. AA Nassau Cmnty Coll 1969; BA U of Miami 1971; MDiv Nash 1974. D 3/25/1974 P 12/18/1974 Bp James Loughlin Duncan. m 5/24/1969 Carolyn D Dehler c 4. R Gr Epis Ch Monroe LA 1995-2001; Secy of Dioc Conv Dio Long Island Garden City NY 1994-1995; Chair - Missions Dio Long Island Garden City NY 1985-1995; Dio Long Island Garden City NY 1983-1992; Ch Of Chr The King E Meadow NY 1979-1995; Assoc R Gr Epis Ch Massapequa NY 1976-1979; The Epis Ch Of The Gd Shpd Tequesta FL 1975-1976; Dio SE Florida Miami FL 1974. therector@comcast.net

GINOLFI, Priscilla Grant (CPa) 156 Warren Way, Lancaster PA 17601 B Elizabeth NJ 8/4/1947 d John Edward Havilund & Constance. RN St Lk's Hosp Sch Nrsng; BS Millersville U 1976; MA Millersville U 1994; Cert Sch Chr Stds 2005. D 6/11/2005 Bp Michael Whittington Creighton. m 6/30/1973 Raymond Ginolfi c 2. pghginolfi@yahoo.com

GINSON, Isaias Gonzales (Tex) 1805 W.Alabama st., Houston TX 77098 **Cur S Steph's Epis Ch Houston TX 2011-** B Bacolod City, Philippines 5/24/1965 s Glicerio Ginson & Julieta. Ed.D (cand.) De la Salle U; MSPE U of the Philippines 2000; MDiv Epis TS Of The SW 2010. D 6/19/2010 Bp C(harles) Andrew Doyle P 1/15/2011 Bp Claude Edward Payne. m 5/14/2000 Christie Marie Flores. Cur Ch Of The Gd Shpd Friendswood TX 2010-2011. ISAIASGINSON@YAHOO.COM

GIOVANGELO, Steven Michael (Ind) 337 North Kenyon Street, Indianapolis IN 46219 B Chicago IL 10/26/1947 s Ernest Giovangelo & Rose Dolores. BA U of Albuquerque 1972; MDiv SWTS 1977. D 6/24/1977 P 1/7/1978 Bp James Winchester Montgomery. m 6/11/1905 Gerald J Bedard. R All SS Ch Indianapolis IN 2002-2009; R S Jn's Ch Un City NJ 1996-2002; Asst S Aug By-The-Sea Par Santa Monica CA 1995-1996; Asst S Bede's Epis Ch Los Angeles CA 1993-1996; R S Cross By-The-Sea Ch Hermosa Bch CA 1991-1993; R S Lk's Of The Mountains La Crescenta CA 1987-1991; Assoc R S Patricks Ch And Day Sch Thousand Oaks CA 1985-1987; R H Trin Ch Skokie IL 1979-1985; Cur S Mary's Ch Pk Ridge IL 1977-1979. AGO 1989; Eccl Crt 2006; Int Mnstry Ntwk 1993-1996. sgiovangelo47@gmail.com

GIPSON, Laurence Allan (Tex) 717 Sage Rd, Houston TX 77056 B Memphis TN 10/23/1942 s Winston Mcneal Gibson & Mary Elizabeth. BBA U of Memphis 1964; MDiv Ya Berk 1970; DD Ya Berk 1987. D 7/5/1970 Bp John Vander Horst P 5/15/1971 Bp William F Gates Jr. m 2/4/1964 Mary F Griffith. R S Mart's Epis Ch Houston TX 1994-2008; Alt / Dep Gc Dio Tennessee Nashville TN 1988-1994; Dn The Cathd Ch Of The Adv Birmingham AL 1982-1994; Pres Stndg Com Dio Tennessee Nashville TN 1980-1982; Bec Dio Tennessee Nashville TN 1975-1980; Com Dio Tennessee Nashville TN 1975-1978; R Ch Of The Ascen Knoxville TN 1974-1982; Asst Ch Of The Ascen Knoxville TN 1971-1973; D-In-Trng S Barth's Ch Bristol TN 1970-1971. Hon DD Berk New Haven CT 1987.

GIRALDO OROZCO, German Augusto (Colom) Cra. 6 No. 4985, Bogata BO 99999 Colombia B Santuario 10/12/1963 s Jose Giraldo & Orbilia. D. m 11/30/2004 Libia Marciales. Iglesia Epis En Colombia 2006-2010. padregago@hotmail.com

GIRARD, Jacques Andre (NY) 8 Shore Rd, Staten Island NY 10307 **D S Matt's Ch Paramus NJ 2008-; Chapl Seamens Ch Inst Income New York NY 2001-** B New York NY 7/12/1945 s Georges E Girard & Simone N. D 6/4/1994 Bp Richard Frank Grein. m 1/8/1966 june elizabeth peters c 2. Dio New York New York City NY 1994; D S Andr's Epis Ch Staten Island NY 1994. ladiacre@gmail.com

GIRARDEAU, Charles Michael (At) 1446 Edinburgh Dr, Tucker GA 30084 **Assoc R All SS Epis Ch Atlanta GA 2005-** B Colorado Springs CO 9/21/1954 s Joseph Lang Girardeau & Olive Jane. AA Oxford Coll of Emory U Oxford GA 1974; BA Emory U 1977; MDiv VTS 1982. D 6/12/1982 P 5/29/1983 Bp Bennett Jones Sims. c 1. R S Mary And S Martha Ch Buford GA 1995-2005; Asst for Educ H Innoc Ch Atlanta GA 1991-1995; Asst R H Trin Par Decatur GA 1987-1991; Vic S Jas Ch Cedartown GA 1983-1987; Cur Trin Epis Ch Columbus GA 1982-1983. rockdock@bellsouth.net

GIRARDEAU, Malcolm Douglas (Eas) 211 E Isabella St, Salisbury MD 21801 B Potosi MO 5/12/1937 s Malcolm Douglas Girardeau & Mary Margret. BA Van 1959; BD VTS 1962; DMin VTS 1987. D 6/26/1962 Bp William Evan Sanders P 5/1/1963 Bp John Vander Horst. m 11/27/1981 Ellen Girardeau c 2. Dioc Deploy Off Dio Easton Easton MD 2000-2006; Dio Easton Easton MD 2000; R S Alb's Epis Ch Salisbury MD 1987-2000; Chr Ch S Ptr's Par Easton MD 1987; Ch Of The Epiph Danville VA 1967-1986; Vic S Mary Magd Ch Fayetteville TN 1963-1965; Cur S Ptr's Ch Chattanooga TN 1962-1963. Soc of Cincinnati. mdgirardiau@juno.com

GIRARDIN, Barbara Jeanine (Colo) 2604 S Troy Ct, Aurora CO 80014 B Oakland CA 12/6/1948 d Milutin Krunich & Patricia. D 11/6/1999 Bp William Jerry Winterrowd. m 2/25/1977 Kerry Donald Girardin c 1.

GIRATA, Christopher D (Ala) 3736 Montrose Rd., Birmingham AL 35213 **Assoc R S Lk's Epis Ch Birmingham AL 2008-** B Lakeland FL 4/13/1980 s Daniel J Girata & Anne M. BA Stetson U 2002; MTS Emory U 2004; MDiv VTS 2008. D 12/21/2007 P 6/29/2008 Bp J(ohn) Neil Alexander. m 11/24/2009 Nicole M Roenick c 2. S Lk's Epis Ch Birmingham AL 2004-2006. cgirata@gmail.com

GIROUX, Mark Alan (CNY) 355 Hyde St, Whitney Point NY 13862 B Watertown NY 9/16/1955 s George Elmer Giroux & Mary Ellen. Trin Evang TS; BA Potsdam St Coll 1977; MDiv SWTS 1986. D 6/14/1986 Bp James Winchester Montgomery P 12/27/1986 Bp William Augustus Jones Jr. m 5/29/1976 Paula W Warvel c 2. Dn S Paul's Cathd Syracuse NY 2001-2002; R S Mk's Epis Ch Chenango Bridge NY 1995-2001; R S Lk's Epis Ch Smethport PA 1990-1994; Trin Epis Ch Wheaton IL 1987-1990; Cur S Mart's Ch Ellisville MO 1986-1987. mpgiroux@juno.com

GIRVIN, Calvin Shields (Dal) 4541 County Road 127, Colorado City TX 79512 B Colorado City TX 2/13/1947 s Luke Shields Girvin & Barbara Lynn. BA U of Texas 1969; MA U of Texas 1971; MDiv Nash 1975; DMin SMU 1987. D 6/19/1975 P 12/22/1975 Bp A Donald Davies. m 7/13/1980 Susan Lee Armentrout c 3. S Lk's Epis Ch Stephenville TX 2009-2011; R S Mary's Epis Ch Texarkana TX 2000-2009; S Jn's Epis Ch Pottsboro TX 1998-2000; R S Lk's Ch Denison TX 1989-1997; Bp'S Mssnr Ch Of Our Sav Dallas TX 1987-1988; Dept Of Missions Dallas TX 1987-1988; Supply P Dio Dallas Dallas TX 1986; Assoc The Epis Ch Of The Trsfg Dallas TX 1977-1985; Chr Epis Ch Dallas TX 1975-1977; Cur The Epis Ch Of S Thos The Apos Dallas TX 1975-1977. Aamft; SocMary; Soc Of S Jn The Evang. calvin.girvin@gmail.com

GITANE, ClayOla Hillaker (FtW) 5412 Wales Ave, Fort Worth TX 76133 **Ecclesiastical Crt Dio Ft Worth Ft Worth TX 2011-; W Dnry Cler Rep Dio Ft Worth Ft Worth TX 2010-; P-in-c Chr The King Epis Ch Ft Worth TX 2009-** B Huntsville AL 6/17/1957 d James Woodson Holderman & Ella Margaret. MSSW U of Texas at Arlington 1980; MDiv SMU/Perkins TS 2008; Angl Stds CDSP 2009. D 1/15/2009 P 12/5/2009 Bp Bavi Rivera. c 3. clayola.gitane@gmail.com

GITAU, Samson Njuguna (WTenn) 243 N Mcneil St, Memphis TN 38112 **Chr Ch Sch Forrest City AR 2008-; Chapl Barth Hse Epis Cntr Memphis TN 1998-** B KE 5/25/1951 s Hezron Gitau Njuguna & Gladys Wangari. BD S Paul's Untd Theol Coll Limuru Ke 1980; STM Ya Berk 1985; PhD Bos 1994. Trans from Anglican Church Of Kenya 3/1/1999 Bp James Malone Coleman. m 8/14/1976 Lilian Wairimu Muturi c 6. Chr Epis Ch Forrest City AR 2008-2011; Imm Epis Ch La Grange TN 2008-2010; Dio W Tennessee Memphis TN 1999-2008; Asst R S Jas' Epis Ch Cambridge MA 1996-1998. Auth, "Breaking the Sackles: Contemporary Perspectives in Pauls letters to the Galatians," Auth Hse, 2008; Auth, "Under the Wings: Reflections in the Bk of Ruth," Cader Pub, 2004; Auth, "One Boat One Destiny," Vintage Press, 1999; Auth, "A Comparative Study Of The Transmission," *Actualization And*

Stabilization Of Oral Traditions, Umi Dissertation Serv, 1994; Auth, "Chr Freedom," Uzima Press, Nairobi, 1990. snjgitau@aol.com

GITHITU, James Kimari (Mass) 297 South Union St, Lawrence MA 01843 **S Mk's Ch Dorchester MA 2011-** B Kiambu Kenya 6/24/1940 s John Githitu & Jane. BEd Nairobi U 1977. Trans from Anglican Church Of Kenya 6/26/2008 Bp M(arvil) Thomas Shaw III. m 7/31/1966 Elizabeth Mary Wanjiku c 5. P-in-c S Aug's Ch Lawr MA 2007-2009. jamesgithitu@aol.com

GIVEN, Mark (Ct) 60 Middle Haddam Road, P.O. Box 81, Middle Haddam CT 06456 **S Paul's Epis Ch Dallas TX 2010-** B Winchester MA 11/5/1954 s John F Given & Margaret Louise. BS U of Massachusetts 1980; MDiv Gordon-Conwell TS 1987; GTS 1988. D 6/24/1989 P 1/1/1990 Bp Charles Brinkley Morton. m 1/2/1999 Emily Elizabeth Slichter c 2. R Chr Epis Ch Middle Haddam CT 2001-2009; S Jn The Evang Ch Lansdowne PA 1999-2001; Ch Of The Redeem Bryn Mawr PA 1996-1998; Asst Trin Epis Ch Redlands CA 1991-1996; S Ptr's Epis Ch Del Mar CA 1989-1991; Yth Dir S Jn's Epis Ch Gloucester MA 1986-1988. Soc of S Jn the Evang 1985-2000. MARKEGIVEN@GMAIL.COM

GIVLER, Gary Bruce (SO) 6215 Kenwood Rd, Madeira OH 45243 **Assoc Gr Ch Cincinnati OH 2006-** B Springhill Nova Scotia CA 3/21/1947 s Frank Givler & Lucy. BS Geo Wms Downers Grove IL 1970; Dio SO Diac Sch London OH 1993; MA The Athenaeum of Ohio 2001. D 12/3/1993 Bp Herbert Thompson Jr. m 3/13/1982 Susan Kay May c 2. Assoc S Phil's Ch Cincinnati OH 1997-2006. NAAD. Gary_Givler@cinfin.com

GLANCEY, Bryan Eaton (Eas) 1205 Frederick Ave, Salisbury MD 21801 B Poughkeepsie NY 9/22/1950 s Charles Glancey & Joyce. BA Marist Coll 1972; MDiv GTS 1977. D 6/11/1977 Bp Paul Moore Jr P 12/20/1977 Bp Harold Louis Wright. m 6/6/1970 Barbara Bauer c 1. Ch Of S Paul's By The Sea Ocean City MD 1993-2003; Ch Of The H Comm Lakeview NY 1989-1993; S Steph's Ch Niagara Falls NY 1987-1989; Chr Ch Albion NY 1986-1987; Vic Chr Epis Ch Danville VA 1980-1985; P-in-c Gr Epis Ch Port Jervis NY 1977-1980; Asst Min Ch Of The Gd Shpd And S Jn Milford PA 1977-1978. Auth, *Fam Plan for Ch Stwdshp*. CCN; Curs. frbryan@glancey.net

GLANDON, Clyde Calvin (Okla) 4223 E 84th St, Tulsa OK 74137 B Kansas City KS 4/10/1947 s Clyde Elton Glandon & Virginia Elizabeth. BA U of Kansas 1969; M.Div. EDS 1972; D.Min Phillips TS 1994. D 6/4/1972 Bp Edward Clark Turner P 3/1/1973 Bp Harold B Robinson. m 1/25/1970 Shirley Rohleder c 1. Assoc R Trin Ch Tulsa OK 1985-1995; R S Paul's Epis Ch Harris Hill Williamsville NY 1977-1985; Asst S Jas' Ch Batavia NY 1975-1977; Asst S Paul's Cathd Buffalo NY 1972-1974. "Pstr Counslg as a Pract of Psychoynamic Sprtlty," Journ of Pstr Care, 2000. office@ccetulsa.org

GLANVILLE, Polly Ann (O) 1945 26th Street, Cuyahoga Falls OH 44223 **D - Sr Mnstry S Paul's Ch Akron OH 2002-; Susan Mnstry - Elder Mnstry Dio Ohio Cleveland OH 2001-** B Salem OH 10/24/1943 d George Schmid & Susan. BA OH SU 1965. D 11/8/1996 Bp J Clark Grew II. m 8/27/1966 Richard Glanville c 2. S Phil's Epis Ch Akron OH 1996-2001. NAAD 1996. revgville@aol.com

GLASER, David Charles (Mich) 20500 W OLD US HIGHWAY 12, Chelsea MI 48118 **R S Barn' Ch Chelsea MI 2010-** B Detroit, MI 11/30/1963 s Charles Glaser & Margaret. BBA Estrn Michican U 1985. D 1/30/2010 P 11/20/2010 Bp Wendell Nathaniel Gibbs Jr. Soc of Cath Priests 2011. david@hawkswood.net

GLASER, Geoffrey Scott (ECR) 3631 W Avenida Obregon, Tucson AZ 85746 B Bloomington IL 9/20/1964 s Walter William Glaser & Madeline Gail. BS U of Nthrn Colorado 1985; MA San Jose St U 1991; MDiv CDSP 1997. D 12/16/1998 P 6/16/1999 Bp Richard Lester Shimpfky. S Raphael In The Vlly Mssn Benson AZ 2008-2009; St Agnes RC Ch San Francisco CA 2003-2006; Ch Of The Adv Of Chr The King San Francisco CA 2002; Vic Ch Of S Jos Milpitas CA 1999-2001. dolphinsofthedesert@q.com

GLASGOW, Joseph Rodney (WNC) 300 E Park Ave Unit 2, Charlotte NC 28203 B Litteton NC 8/18/1928 s Joseph Rodney Glasgow & Emily Elizabeth. BS U NC 1951; Nash 1958. D 11/1/1958 P 6/1/1961 Bp Matthew G Henry. Vic S Andr's Ch Bessemer City NC 1961-1964; Vic Ch Of The Trsfg Saluda NC 1958-1961; Vic S Paul's Ch Edneyville NC 1958-1961. jr931@bellsouth.net

GLASGOW, Laurette Alice (Eur) 2 Chaussee De Charleroi, Braine-l'Alleud Belgium 1420 Belgium B Canada 9/4/1950 d Raymond Jean Gauthier & Marie-Anne. BA U of Manitoba 1971; MA Jn Hopkins 1977; Oxf 2007. D 10/20/2007 P 10/11/2008 Bp Pierre W Whalon. m 12/11/1982 Ross Glasgow c 2. All SS Epis Ch Braine-l'Alleud 1420 BE 2008-2009; Pstr Intern The Amer Cathd of the H Trin Paris 75008 FR 2004-2006. glasgola@hotmail.com

GLASS, Fredrick Alfred Livingston (Los) 9210 Whitney Way, Cypress CA 90630 **Died 12/17/2009** B Miami,FL 9/12/1931 s Thomas Alfred Glass & Mary Viola. BS Tuskegee Inst 1952; BS U of Kansas 1969; Cert Indstrl Coll of ArmdF 1978; BD Pacific Luth TS 1996. D 11/1/1993 Bp Chester Lovelle Talton. c 3. CARE Cmsn; Cmsn of Black Mnstrs 1993-2002; Cmsn on Liturg & Mus 1993-2008; COM 1993-1998; Natl Assn of Deacons 1993. fglass@aol.com

GLASS, Rosalee (Me) 38 Chestnut St, Camden ME 04843 **D Ch Of S Thos Camden ME 2005-** B Key West FL 10/1/1943 BA Sthrn Connecticut St U 1966; M Div Bangor TS 2005. D 6/18/2005 Bp Chilton Abbie Richardson Knudsen. m 6/2/1964 Christopher Glass. rosalee.glass@verizon.net

GLASS, Vanessa (Cal) St. Francis of Assisi Episcopal Church, 967 5th Street, Novato CA 94945 **S Fran Of Assisi Ch Novato CA 2011-** B San Francisco CA 11/21/1971 d Ralph Leonard Stickler & Thala Jean. BA California St U 1996; MDiv CDSP 2001. D 6/2/2001 P 12/1/2001 Bp William Edwin Swing. m 11/15/1997 Michael Glass c 2. Gr Cathd San Francisco CA 2007-2011; S Paul's Epis Ch San Rafael CA 2006-2007. vanessaglass@me.com

GLASSER, Joanne Kathleen (Eau) 111 9th St N, La Crosse WI 54601 **D Chr Ch Par La Crosse WI 2008-** B Canada 9/30/1952 d Edwin Henkelman & Edith. BA U of Alberta 1973; MS USC 1979; MBA U of St. Thos 1988; PhD Capella U 2005. D 5/31/2008 Bp Keith Bernard Whitmore. m 12/27/1995 James Glasser. deaconjo@christchurchlacrosse.org

✠ **GLASSPOOL, Rt Rev Mary Douglas** (Los) Episcopal Diocese of Los Angeles, 840 Echo Park Ave, Los Angeles CA 90026 **Bp Suffr of Los Angelies Dio Los Angeles Los Angeles CA 2010-** B Staten Island NY 2/23/1954 d Douglas Murray Glasspool & Ann. BA Dickinson Coll 1976; MDiv EDS 1981; Merrill Fell Harv 2006. D 6/13/1981 Bp Paul Moore Jr P 3/6/1982 Bp Lyman Cunningham Ogilby Con 5/15/2010 for Los. Cn Dio Maryland Baltimore MD 2001-2010; Dep to GC Dio Maryland Baltimore MD 2000-2010; Pres of Stndg Com Dio Maryland Baltimore MD 1995-1998; R S Marg's Ch Annapolis MD 1992-2001; Bd Mem Epis City Mssn Boston MA 1985-1991; R S Lk's And S Marg's Ch Allston MA 1984-1992; Asst S Paul's Ch Philadelphia PA 1981-1984. Contrib, "Remembrance, Witness, and Action: Fuel for the Journey," *Wmn, Sprtlty and Transformative Ldrshp: Where Gr Meets Power*, Skylight Paths, 2011. Epis Cmnty Serv of Maryland 1993-2000; Soc of S Jn the Evang 1982. Lenten Mssnr Memi Ch, Harv 2007; Bp's Awd for Outstanding Ord Mnstry Dio Maryland 1999. mdgsuffagan@ladiocese.org

GLAUDE, Ronald Arthur (Ct) 125 Grand View Ter, Brooklyn CT 06234 B Putnam CT 12/27/1936 s Joseph Alphonse Glaude-LaCharite & Aurore Beatrice. BA U of Connecticut 1974; MDiv EDS 1977. D 6/11/1977 Bp Joseph Warren Hutchens P 5/27/1978 Bp Morgan Porteus. m 6/28/1958 Grace C Carpenter c 3. R Trin Ch Brooklyn CT 1980-2008; Cur S Jn's Ch Stamford CT 1977-1979. CHS. rglaude@charter.net

GLAZIER JR, George H (SO) 174 Desantis Dr, Columbus OH 43214 **R S Steph's Epis Ch And U Columbus OH 2001-** B Huntington WV 2/12/1954 s George Henry Glazier & Charlotte Keoka. BA Marshall U 1976; MDiv VTS 1979; DMin STUSo 2005. D 6/6/1979 P 6/1/1980 Bp Robert Poland Atkinson. m 8/1/1992 Pamela D Hootman c 2. R Gr Ch Chattanooga TN 1995-2001; R Trin Ch Allnce OH 1985-1995; Assoc S Paul's Epis Ch Winston Salem NC 1982-1985; S Matt's Ch Wheeling WV 1979-1982. Soc of S Jn the Evang. glazier.george@gmail.com

GLAZIER II, William Stuart (Ct) 30 Ice House Ln, Mystic CT 06355 B New York NY 2/27/1925 s Philip Alden Glazier & Clare Stennis. BA Trin Hartford CT 1948; MDiv VTS 1956; PhD Hartford Sem 1974. D 6/17/1952 P 12/1/1952 Bp Walter H Gray. m 1/1/2000 Lois Mueller Rimmer c 3. Vic All SS Ch Ivoryton CT 1963-1965; Vic S Paul's Ch Westbrook CT 1963-1965; Asst Gr Epis Ch New York NY 1961-1963; P S Paul's Ch Windham CT 1956-1961; P Trin Epis Ch Collinsville CT 1952-1955. Chapl 100th Infantry Div Assn 1994. william_s_glazier@sbcglobal.net

GLEASON, David Thomas (WA) PO Box 1617, Evergreen CO 80437 B Rochester NY 11/5/1923 s Harold Alan Gleason & Marion Hammond. BA U Roch 1948; LTh SWTS 1952; BD SWTS 1953. D 6/8/1952 P 12/19/1952 Bp Dudley S Stark. m 2/11/1956 Janice Clise c 3. Inter-Faith Chap Inc Silver Sprg MD 1972-1990; Chapl/Instr S Jn's Ch Olney MD 1965-1972; Cur Trin Ch Geneva NY 1954-1956; Vic Gr Ch Scottsville NY 1952-1954; Vic S Andr's Epis Ch Caledonia NY 1952-1954. skypilot10@aol.com

GLEASON, Dorothy Jean (EpisSanJ) Po Box 399, Ambridge PA 15003 B 8/30/1943 Cert California St U; AA Los Angeles Vlly Coll. D 4/9/2000 Bp John-David Mercer Schofield. SAMS Ambridge PA 2002-2003.

GLEASON, Edward Campbell (SwFla) 553 Galleon Dr, Naples FL 34102 **Assoc Trin By The Cove Naples FL 2009-** B New Orleans LA 2/3/1974 s Harvey Gardere Gleason & Mary Frances Mears. BA U of Texas at Austin 1996; JD Loyola U Sch of Law 2000; Mdiv Nash 2008. D 12/29/2007 P 6/29/2008 Bp Charles Edward Jenkins III. m 12/4/2004 Virginia Johnson Gleason c 3. Cur & Chapl S Lk's Ch Baton Rouge LA 2008-2009. egleason@trinitybythecove.com

GLEASON, Edward Stone (Eas) 4000 Cathedral Ave Nw Apt 252b, Washington DC 20016 B Newton MA 7/20/1933 s Gay Gleason & Winifred Nowell. AB Harv 1955; BD VTS 1960; EDS 1967. D 6/18/1960 Bp Anson Phelps Stokes Jr P 4/23/1961 Bp Norman B Nash. m 6/18/1955 Anne Mather Vermilion c 3. R S Paul's Ch Trappe MD 2005-2006; Ed & Dir FMP Cincinnati OH 1995-2005; Dir Dvlmnt VTS Alexandria VA 1987-1995; R S Ptr's Epis Ch Arlington VA 1962-1966; Cur Chr Ch Exeter NH 1960-1962. Auth, "The Pryr Given Life," Ch Pub, 2007; Auth, "Dying We Live," Cowley Pub, 1990; Auth,

"Redeeming Mar," Cowley Pub, 1988. DD VTS Alexandria VA 2000. esgleason@aol.com

GLEAVES, Glen Lee (Mont) 1226 Wildflower Trl, Livingston MT 59047 **Asst S Andr's Ch Livingston MT 2008-; p/t Asst Upper Yellowstone Epis Ch Livingston MT 2008-; P All SS Ch Salt Lake City UT 2003-** B Fairhope AL 2/18/1951 s Donald L Gleaves & Leona Rowena. BA U of So Alabama 1974; MS U of Sthrn Mississippi 1982; MDiv SWTS 1988. D 6/4/1988 P 4/4/1989 Bp Charles Farmer Duvall. c 1. p/t P-in-c H Trin Epis Ch Troy MT 2004-2008; p/t P-in-c S Lk's Ch Libby MT 2004-2008; p/t Asstg P S Paul's Ch Salt Lake City UT 1996-2002; Dio Utah Salt Lake City UT 1993-1996; S Paul's Epis Ch Vernal UT 1990-1992; D-In-Trng S Lk's Epis Ch Mobile AL 1988-1989. glen0218@gmail.com

GLEESON, Terence Patrick (Vt) All Saints Church, 555 Waverley Street, Palo Alto CA 94301 **All SS Epis Ch Palo Alto CA 2011-** B Sydney Australia 1/26/1954 s Terence Peter Gleeson & Marie Cecilia. BTh Cath Inst of Sydney 1980; MSEd U of Wollongong 1987; STM GTS 2002. Rec from Roman Catholic 10/4/2003 Bp Catherine Scimeca Roskam. m 7/1/2011 Dennis L Manalo c 1. R S Steph's Ch Middlebury VT 2005-2011; Asst to R Chr And S Steph's Ch New York NY 2003-2005. tpgleeson@asaints.org

G

GLENDENNING, Audrey Geraldine (SeFla) 3322 Meridian Way N Apt A, Palm Beach Gardens FL 33410 **D Gr Ch W Palm Bch FL 1998-** B Centerville PA 4/26/1927 d Russell Everett Horton & Christine Eleanor. BS Palm Bch Atlantic Coll 1982. D 6/20/1998 Bp Calvin Onderdonk Schofield Jr.

GLENDINNING, David Cross (Me) 108 Marquis Rd, Freeport ME 04032 B Lawrence MA 7/14/1936 s Geoffrey Glendinning & Eve Osgood. BA Dart 1958; BD EDS 1961. D 6/25/1961 Bp Donald J Campbell P 1/6/1962 Bp Oliver L Loring. m 1/24/1982 Dorothy Clapp c 3. P-in-c Chr Ch Biddeford ME 1994-1997; Int S Geo's Epis Ch Sanford ME 1992-1993; Int S Barth's Epis Ch Yarmouth ME 1990-1991; R S Paul's Ch Concord NH 1982-1989; R S Mk's Ch Waterville ME 1969-1982; R S Andr And S Jn Epis Ch SW Harbor ME 1963-1969; Cur Trin Epis Ch Portland ME 1961-1963. dcgx2@marshotel.com

GLENN JR, Charles Leslie (Mass) 1 Robeson St, Boston MA 02130 **Epis Ch Cntr New York NY 1966-** B Cambridge MA 9/20/1938 s Charles Leslie Glenn & Georgiana. none CDSP; none EDS; BA Harv; none U of Tuebingen, Germany; EdD Harv 1972; PhD Bos 1987. D 7/22/1963 P 6/5/1964 Bp John Melville Burgess. m 4/30/1977 Mary Dunning c 5. Asst Ch Of The H Sprt Mattapan MA 1983-1998; S Jn's Ch Jamaica Plain MA 1979-1986; Asst S Jn's S Jas Epis Ch Roxbury MA 1963-1965. Co-Auth w Jan De Groof, "Balancing Freedom, Autonomy, and Accountability in Educ , vol 1-3," Wolf Legal Pub (Netherlands), 2004; Auth, "The Ambiguous Embrace: Govt and Faith-based Schools and Soc Agencies," Princeton U Press, 2000; Auth, "Educating Immigrant Chld," Garland, 1996; Auth, "Educational Freedom In Estrn Europe," Cate Inst Press, 1995; Auth, "Choice Of Schools In Six Nations," US Dept of Educ, 1989; Auth, "Myth Of The Common Schlr," U of Massachusetts Press, 1988; Auth, "200 Bk chapters and arts," Var. Annual Ldrshp Awd Cntr for Publ Justice 2000; Phi Beta Kappa Harvard 1959. glennsed@bu.edu

GLENN, Katherine Merrell (Oly) 1217 S Baltimore St, Tacoma WA 98465 B Daytona Bch FL 5/25/1947 d Robert Alston Merrell & Katherine Lee. Ldrshp Acad for New Directions; Epis TS of The SW 1993. D 6/12/1993 P 12/18/1993 Bp William Jerry Winterrowd. m 1/23/1974 Floyd Wayne Glenn c 2. R S Andr's Epis Ch Tacoma WA 2002-2005; Dir Rgnl Mnstry Dvlpmt Cntr Dio Colorado Denver CO 1995-1998; Vic S Steph The Mtyr Epis Ch Monte Vista CO 1993-2002; Vic S Thos The Apos Epis Ch Alamosa CO 1993-2002. Auth, "Brain Injured Patients in Cmnty: A Chr Response to Suffering," *More Than Survivors*, 1992; Auth, "Insult to Injury: Baptismal Cov Experience," *More than Survivors*, 1992; Auth, *Serv of Naming & Farewell*, 1991; Auth, "Heaven and Hell: Perspectives from Each," *More than Survivors*; Auth, *Serving Healing Abortion*; Auth, "Var arts," *LivCh*. Chapl DOK; New Directions Mnstrs; RWF - Bd Dir, Treas 2002. episkathy@earthlink.net

GLENN, L G (FdL) 1230 Sandpebble Dr., Rockton IL 61072 B Amboy IL 8/14/1953 s Willard Gail Glenn & Carol Mae. Black Hawk Coll; Moody Bible Inst; BA U of the St of New York 1981; MDiv Bethel TS 1989; STM Nash 2001; Psy.D. GTF 2008. D 7/12/1998 P 1/28/1999 Bp Keith Lynn Ackerman. m 8/3/1978 Terri Lynn Sterling c 3. R Ch Of S Mary Of The Snows Eagle River WI 1999-2006; Int S Geo's Ch Macomb IL 1999; D S Ptr's Ch Peoria IL 1998-1999. lawranceg@excite.com

GLENN, Michael Eugene (Okla) 106 E Crawford St, Palestine TX 75801 B Philadelphia PA 4/5/1959 s James Glenn & Ruth. BA Emory U 1981; MDiv Candler TS Emory U 1984; MA Emory U 1991. D 6/27/1992 Bp Maurice Manuel Benitez P 2/2/1993 Bp William Jackson Cox. Gd Shpd Epis Ch Sapulpa OK 2006-2007; R S Phil's Epis Ch Palestine TX 1994-2004; Asst to R Chr Epis Ch Tyler TX 1992-1994. Auth, "Uncovering Oedipus: Freud'S Choice Of The Oedipus Story In The Light Of His Personal Chld Abuse," Umi, 1991; Auth, "His Personal Chld Abuse Issues". Rotary Intl 1995. Paul Harris Fell Rotary 2002. meglenn@flash.net

GLENN, Patricia Foster (Mo) 19424 Highway 54, Louisiana MO 63353 **R Calv Ch Louisiana MO 2007-** B Cedar Rapid IA 11/14/1950 d Fred Wesley Foster & Eileen Marie Kennedy. MercyHospital Sch of Nrsng 1971; BS MacMurray Coll 1977; Epis Sch for Mnstry 2007. D 12/20/2006 P 6/23/2007 Bp George Wayne Smith. m 4/19/1975 Edward Glenn c 3. gfkp@msn.com

GLENNIE, Jannel (Mich) 294 Willoughby Rd, Mason MI 48854 B Grand Rapids MI 3/31/1947 d Harold J Thomas & Virginia W. BA U of Arizona 1980; MDiv SWTS 1988. D 6/25/1988 Bp Henry Irving Mayson P 4/22/1989 Bp R(aymond) Stewart Wood Jr. m 8/12/1967 James William Glennie c 2. Stndg Com Dio Michigan Detroit MI 1997-2000; R S Kath's Ch Williamston MI 1996-2009; Asst All SS Ch E Lansing MI 1994-1996; S Dav's Ch Lansing MI 1989-1990; Cbury MI SU E Lansing MI 1988-1996. Auth, "Confessions Of An Ordnry Mystic," Greenleaf Bk Grp, 2000. Sprtl Dir Intl 2009. jgrev47@yahoo.com

GLICK, Phillip Randall (EC) 184 Watersedge Drive, Kill Devil Hills NC 27948 **R S Andr's By The Sea Nags Hd NC 2010-; Pension Fund Mltry New York NY 2008-** B Burlington WI 12/18/1952 s W Myron Glick & Lucinda Irene. U of Wisconsin 1972; BA Methodist Coll 1982; MDiv STUSo 1986. D 6/24/1986 P 1/10/1987 Bp Brice Sidney Sanders. m 9/11/1976 Barbara Ilse Muldrow c 3. Spec Mobilization Spprt Plan Washington DC 2008-2010; S Dav's Epis Ch Richmond VA 2001-2008; S Thos' Epis Ch Ahoskie NC 1989-2001; Asst S Mary's Ch Kinston NC 1987; R Ch Of The H Innoc Seven Sprg NC 1986-1989. The Bro of S Andr 2011. The Dubose Awd for Serv The TS, The U So 2010. rector@saintandrewsobx.com

GLIDDEN OSB, Charles Aelred (FdL) 56500 Abbey Rd, Three Rivers MI 49093 B Zanesville OH 4/22/1952 s Charles Franklin Glidden & Beatrice June. Mia 1974. D 6/18/1992 P 12/21/1992 Bp William L Stevens. Auth, "Var arts," *Abbey Letter*; Auth, "Abbot Primate, Benedictine," *Encyclopedia of Monasticism*; Auth, "Aelred the Hist," *Erudition in God's Serv*. aelred.glidden@gmail.com

GLIDDEN, Richard Mark (Chi) 49 Larbert Rd # 6490, Southport CT 06890 B 1/12/1943 STB GTS; Cert Inst Rel & Hlth; BA Lawr. D 6/15/1968 Bp James Winchester Montgomery P 12/21/1968 Bp Gerald Francis Burrill. m 8/17/1968 Susan Campbell. Epis Mssn Soc New York NY 1984-1985; Epis Mssn Soc New York NY 1984-1985. AAPC, Aamft. GLIDDEN.MARK@GMAIL.COM

GLOFF, Holly M (NC) 1520 Canterbury Rd, Raleigh NC 27608 **Asst R S Mich's Ch Raleigh NC 2006-** B Norwalk CT 2/5/1955 d Donald Hedin & Kathleen. BA Fairfield U 1977; MDiv VTS 2006. D 6/24/2006 Bp Peter James Lee. m 11/16/1996 Robert Gloff c 2. gloff@holymichael.org

GLOR, Milton Thomas (Ala) 1803 Marie Cir, Sheffield AL 35660 **Died 10/22/2009** B Buffalo NY 6/30/1936 s Leonard Glor & Cleora Chalice. BA U of Alabama- Huntsville 1982; MDiv SWTS 1985. D 5/29/1985 P 12/15/1985 Bp Furman Stough. c 3. frmtg1803@bellsouth.net

GLOSSON HAMMONS, Jamesetta Cheryl (Los) 1508 W 145th St, Compton CA 90220 **Dio Los Angeles Los Angeles CA 2010-** B Chicago Cook Co. IL 7/22/1945 d James Glosson & Martina. AA Compton Coll; BS U of Phoenix 1999; MA Fuller TS 2006. D 12/2/2006 Bp Joseph Jon Bruno. c 3. Episcipal Healthcare Providers Los Angeles CA 2008. jhamo4@msn.com

✠ GLOSTER, Rt Rev J(ames) Gary (NC) 2236 Fernbank Dr, Charlotte NC 28226 **Ret Bp Suffr of No Carolina S Mary Of The Hills Epis Par Blowing Rock NC 2007-; Ret Bp Suffr Dio No Carolina Raleigh NC 2004-** B Hopkinsville KY 6/6/1936 s James K Gloster & Nancy Jane. BA Wabash Coll 1959; MDiv VTS 1962; DMin VTS 1990; DD VTS 1997. D 6/16/1962 P 12/1/1962 Bp John P Craine Con 7/27/1996 for NC. m 6/7/1958 Julia Jayne Huston. Asstg Bp Dio No Carolina Raleigh NC 2004-2007; Suffr Bp of No Carolina Dio No Carolina Raleigh NC 1996-2004; Vic Chap Of Chr The King Charlotte NC 1989-1996; Chr Ch Charlotte NC 1980-1989; R Chr Epis Ch Pulaski VA 1972-1980; Assoc The Ch of the Redeem Cincinnati OH 1968-1971; Vic S Aug's Epis Ch Danville IN 1962-1966. jgarybish@aol.com

GLOVER, Beth Faulk (Nwk) 29 Village Gate Way, Nyack NY 10960 **S Paul's Epis Ch Paterson NJ 2011-** B Richmond VA 5/3/1966 d Bobby Lee Glover & Barbara Marilyn. BA W&M 1988; MDiv UTS 1991; DMin. NYTS 2007; STM GTS 2008. D 6/13/2002 Bp Rufus T Brome P 12/14/2002 Bp John Palmer Croneberger. S Aug's Epis Ch Croton On Hudson NY 2008-2011; Chr Hosp Jersey City NJ 2002-2007. beg9013@nyp.org

GLOVER, Betty M (Kan) Grace Episcopal Trinity Episcopal Church, P.O. Box 490, Winfield KS 67156 **R Trin Ch Arkansas City KS 2007-** B Camp Roberts CA 11/30/1952 d Harold Langford Thralls & Vila Mae. BA New Mex Highlands U 1991; MS U of Kansas 1992; MDiv Candidate VTS 2007. D 2/2/1997 Bp William Edward Smalley P 6/23/2007 Bp Dean Elliott Wolfe. c 2. D Gr Cathd Topeka KS 1997-2002. Intl Conf of Police Chapl. chaplainbetty@sbcglobal.net

GLOVER, Hazel Smith (At) 606 Newnan St, Carrollton GA 30117 **R S Marg's Ch Carrollton GA 2002-** B LaGrange GA 8/30/1952 d Clarence Smith & Martha. MPA Georgia St U 1981; BBA W Georgia Coll 1981; MDiv STUSo 1993. D 6/5/1993 P 12/11/1993 Bp Frank Kellogg Allan. m 11/30/1996 William D Raymond c 3. Assoc R S Cathr's Epis Ch Marietta GA 1996-2002; Gr

Ch Whiteville NC 1996; Vic Ch Of The Trsfg Rome GA 1993-1995; Vic S Jas Ch Cedartown GA 1993-1995. revhazelglover@gmail.com

GLOVER, John Frederick (Va) 14449 S Eastside Hwy, Grottoes VA 24441 B Charleston WV 8/31/1936 s Andrew Frederick Glover & Opal Merle. BA Marshall U 1958; MDiv CRDS 1962. D 3/11/1965 P 8/6/1965 Bp Wilburn Camrock Campbell. m 5/30/1981 Susan Beth Trimble c 2. R Emm Ch Harrisonburg VA 1989-2002; R Chr Ch Austin MN 1981-1989; Stndg Com Dio W Virginia Charleston WV 1976-1981; Eccl Crt Dio W Virginia Charleston WV 1969-1972; R Trin Ch Morgantown WV 1967-1976; R S Paul's Ch Weston WV 1965-1967. jfggro@aol.com

GLOVER, Marsha Bacon (NY) 122 Grandview Ave, White Plains NY 10605 B New York NY 8/6/1947 d Benjamin S Bacon & Marguerite L. BA U of Pennsylvania 1969; Col 1972; JD U of Pennsylvania 1972; MDiv Ya Berk 1994. D 6/11/1994 P 12/1/1994 Bp Richard Frank Grein. c 2. S Barth's Ch In The Highland White Plains NY 2007-2009; R S Ptr's Ch Bronx NY 2001-2007; Chr's Ch Rye NY 1997-2001; Asst S Jas Ch New York NY 1996; Asst Ch Of S Mary The Vrgn Chappaqua NY 1994-1995. mbglover@aol.com

GLOVER, Mary Elizabeth (NwT) 891 Davis Dr, Abilene TX 79605 **P-in-c S Mk's Epis Ch Abilene TX 2011-** B Abilene TX 7/24/1956 d Billy Jack Glover & Bettie Carolyn. BS McMurry U 1978; JD St. Mary's U San Antonio TX 1988; MDiv Epis TS of the SW 2001. D 12/20/2000 P 6/30/2001 Bp C(harles) Wallis Ohl. Assoc R Ch Of The Heav Rest Abilene TX 2006-2010; R Trin Ch Independence MO 2003-2006; Assoc R S Andr's Epis Ch Amarillo TX 2001-2003. maryglover@juno.com

GLUCKOW, Kenneth Allan (NJ) 70 Mount Tabor Way, Ocean Grove NJ 07756 **R Emer S Jas Ch Bradley Bch NJ 2003-** B New York NY 12/29/1931 s Benjamin Gluckow & Pauline. Cert RCA Inst 1957. D 4/19/1969 P 10/1/1969 Bp Alfred L Banyard. m 12/18/1953 Rosemary Matunis. Int The Ch of S Matt And S Tim New York NY 2003-2004; S Andr The Apos Highland Highlands NJ 1977-1978; S Jas Ch Bradley Bch NJ 1973-2002; Asst Trin Ch Asbury Pk NJ 1969-1977. R Emer S Jas Ch Bradley Bch NJ 2003. therevkg@aol.com

GNASSO, Enrico Mario (Los) 10961 Desert Lawn Dr Spc 252, Calimesa CA 92320 **Asstg Gr Mssn Moreno Vlly CA 2001-** B Fort Lee NJ 12/18/1928 s Enrico Raffaele Gnasso & Margaret. BBA Pace Coll 1955; BD SWTS 1964; MS U of Wisconsin 1971; CPA St of Wisconsin 1972. D 6/13/1964 Bp Leland Stark P 12/13/1964 Bp Russell T Rauscher. m 6/25/1955 Edith Marvin Luisa c 3. P-in-c S Mart-In-The-Fields Mssn Twentynine Palms CA 1991-1993; P-in-c S Chris's Ch Trona CA 1987-1991; Int Dio Milwaukee Milwaukee WI 1971-1979; R S Lk's Ch Whitewater WI 1967-1971; Bursar SWTS Evanston IL 1966-1967; P-in-c S Jn's Mssn Hastings NE 1964-1965; Asst S Mk's Epis Pro-Cathd Hastings NE 1964-1965. manpag@dslextreme.com

GOBER, Patricia Derr (Mass) 17 Leroy St, Attleboro MA 02703 B Aberdeen SD 9/24/1942 d John Derr McDowell & Nina Elizabeth. BA U of So Dakota 1965; MDiv Epis TS of The SW 1983. D 6/24/1983 P 1/6/1984 Bp Jackson Earle Gilliam. m 8/23/1975 Wallace Gene Gober c 2. Int Ch Of The Ascen Fall River MA 2005-2008; Cluster Mssnr S Jn The Evang Taunton MA 1994-2005; Cluster Mssnr S Mk's Ch Taunton MA 1994-2005; Co-Mssnr Team Monticello NY 1986-1994; Int S Andr's Ch Anaconda MT 1985-1986; Int The Pintler Cluster of the Epis Ch Deer Lodge MT 1985-1986; Int S Marks Pintler Cluster Anaconda MT 1985; Cur S Jas Ch Bozeman MT 1983-1986. Dio Ma Stndg Com 2000-2001. revrev2@verizon.net

GOBER, Wallace Gene (Mass) 17 Leroy St, Attleboro MA 02703 B Klamath Falls OR 3/4/1939 s Clarence John Gober & Mary Elizabeth. BA Sthrn Oregon Coll 1961; DA U of Oregon 1970; MDiv Epis TS of The SW 1983; MA Iona Coll 1989. D 6/24/1983 P 1/6/1984 Bp Jackson Earle Gilliam. m 8/23/1975 Patricia Derr McDowell c 2. S Jn's/S Steph's Ch Fall River MA 2005-2006; S Dav's Epis Ch Halifax MA 2002-2005; Chr Ch Quincy MA 2000-2002; Chr Ch Waltham MA 1999-2000; All SS Ch Chelmsford MA 1998-1999; Int Dio Massachusetts Boston MA 1996-2000; S Andr's Ch New Bedford MA 1995-1997; S Greg's Epis Ch Woodstock NY 1993-1994; Dioc Int Consult Dio New York New York City NY 1990-1995; Team Monticello NY 1986-1993; Ipc Rep Dioc Coun Dio Massachusetts Boston MA 1986-1987; S Jas Ch Bozeman MT 1983-1986; Asst The Pintler Cluster of the Epis Ch Deer Lodge MT 1983-1986. AAPC. revrevg@earthlink.net

GOCHA, Teresa Payne (NH) 477 Main St, Plymouth NH 03264 **Ch Of The Mssh No Woodstock NH 2003-** B New York NY 7/8/1959 d Edd Payne & Mary Catherine. BA Trin 1981; MDiv GTS 1987. D 6/13/1987 Bp David Elliot Johnson P 6/9/1988 Bp Douglas Edwin Theuner. m 8/18/1990 James Gocha c 3. S Judes Epis Ch Franklin NH 2000-2002; S Steph's Ch Pittsfield NH 1999-2000; Ch Of The H Sprt Plymouth NH 1991; Cur S Paul's Ch Concord NH 1988-1991. tpgocha@yahoo.com

GOCKLEY, Mary Jane (Neb) PO Box 353, Broken Bow NE 68822 **P-in-c S Jn's Ch Broken Bow NE 2010-** B Harrisburg PA 12/10/1936 d Harold Darius Kretzing & Gladys Elizabeth. RN Harrisburg Hosp Sch 1957; BS Albright Coll 1960. D 5/31/2010 P 12/18/2010 Bp Joe Goodwin Burnett. c 4. mjgockley@webtv.net

GODBOLD, Richard Rives (Ind) 829 Wiltshire Dr, Evansville IN 47715 **Alt Dep, GC Dio Indianapolis Indianapolis IN 2010-2013; Exec Coun Dio Indianapolis Indianapolis IN 2008-2012; R S Paul's Epis Ch Evansville IN 2003-; Co Chair Dio The Rio Grande Albuquerque NM 2000-; Dioc Cmsn Dio The Rio Grande Albuquerque NM 1999-** B Montgomery AL 12/7/1949 s John Cooper Godbold & Elizabeth. BA Dart 1972; MDiv EDS 1988; DMin SWTS 2001. D 8/24/1988 Bp William Davidson P 3/19/1989 Bp Terence Kelshaw. m 2/24/1979 Catherine Ann White c 2. Stndg Com Dio Indianapolis Indianapolis IN 2004-2008; COM Chair Dio The Rio Grande Albuquerque NM 2000-2002; COM Dio The Rio Grande Albuquerque NM 1998-2003; Alt Dep, GC Dio The Rio Grande Albuquerque NM 1998-2001; Assoc R Trin On The Hill Epis Ch Los Alamos NM 1997-2003; Exec Com of Dioc Coun Dio The Rio Grande Albuquerque NM 1996-1998; Yth Dir Dio The Rio Grande Albuquerque NM 1994-1997; Asst To Dn S Jn's Cathd Albuquerque NM 1994-1997; Dioc Coun Dio The Rio Grande Albuquerque NM 1993-1998; CE Cmsn Dio The Rio Grande Albuquerque NM 1991-1994; R S Phil's Ch Belen NM 1990-1994; Cur Trin On The Hill Epis Ch Los Alamos NM 1988-1990. rrgecusa@gmail.com

GODDARD, John R (Nev) PO Box 422, Gleneden Beach OR 97388 **Int S Mary's Ch Lakewood WA 2011-; Int S Mary's Ch Lakewood WA 2011-** B Saint Louis MO 1/6/1942 s John Richard Goddard & Jane Ruth. BBA New Mex St U. 1965; MDiv CDSP 1976. D 8/6/1976 P 3/7/1977 Bp Richard Mitchell Trelease Jr. m 11/11/2004 Carol M Mitchie c 2. Int S Marg's Ch Lawr KS 2008-2009; Trin Epis Ch Reno NV 2005-2008; Int All SS Epis Ch Boise ID 2002-2005; S Jas Pullman WA 2001-2002; The Epis Par Of S Dav Minnetonka MN 1992-1996; R Trin Ch Marshfield Hills MA 1987-1992; R S Thos A Becket Ch Roswell NM 1980-1987; S Fran Epis Ch Tyler TX 1978; Asst S Chris's Epis Ch Hobbs NM 1976-1978. jgodd6@gmail.com

GODDARD, Paul Dillon (Chi) 742 Sand Dollar Dr, Sanibel FL 33957 B Lancaster PA 9/23/1938 s Alpheus John Goddard & Margaret Jane. BA U So 1960; STB GTS 1963; LLD S Aug's Coll Raleigh NC 1976. D 6/15/1963 P 12/19/1963 Bp James Winchester Montgomery. S Dunst's Ch Madison WI 1994; Dio Chicago Chicago IL 1973-1988; Vic Gr Epis Ch Galena IL 1972-1988; Asst S Jn's Epis Ch Lancaster PA 1963-1965. pauldillon@worldnet.alt.net

GODDEN, Edward Eastman (Del) 610 Lindsey Rd, Wilmington DE 19809 **Int R The Ch Of The Ascen Claymont DE 2010-** B Norfolk VA 4/19/1953 s Albert Ira Godden & Phyllis Eastman. BS Old Dominion U 1975; MDiv STUSo 1979. D 6/23/1979 P 3/19/1980 Bp C(laude) Charles Vache. c 3. Liturg Off Dio Delaware Wilmington DE 1996; R Imm Ch On The Green New Castle DE 1989-2010; Dioc Coun Dio Easton Easton MD 1985-1989; R Trin Ch Elkton MD 1983-1989; Cur Trin Ch Portsmouth VA 1979-1983. eegodden@gmail.com

GODDERZ, Michael John (Mass) 209 Ashmont Street, Boston MA 02124 **RurD Dio Massachusetts Boston MA 2008-; R The Par Of All SS Ashmont-Dorches Dorchester MA 1998-** B Saint Paul MN 7/3/1952 s Hernando Walter Godderz & Lols Lenore. BA Rutgers-The St U 1974; MDiv Gordon-Conwell TS 1977; MA U Chi 1980. D 6/2/1984 Bp John Bowen Coburn P 6/22/1985 Bp Thomas Kreider Ray. m 6/23/1978 Ruth Martha Foster c 1. Dio Sthrn Virginia Norfolk VA 1997-1998; Chair, Archit Cmsn Dio Sthrn Virginia Norfolk VA 1997-1998; R S Bride's Epis Ch Chesapeake VA 1991-1998; Dioc Coun Dio Vermont Burlington VT 1987-1989; R S Barn Ch Norwich VT 1986-1991; Cur The Ch Of The Adv Boston MA 1984-1986. CCU 1998-2010; GAS 1999; SSC 1994. Phi Beta Kappa 1974. rector@allsaints.net

GODFREY, Samuel Bisland (Miss) Po Box 391, Como MS 38619 **R Chr Epis Ch Vicksburg MS 2011-** B Natchez MS 10/12/1955 s William Edward Godfrey & Irene Bisland. BS SW at Memphis now Rhodes Coll 1977; JD U of Mississippi 1983; MDiv STUSo 1997. D 6/14/1997 P 12/20/1997 Bp Alfred Clark Marble Jr. m 12/29/1981 Patty N Norcross c 1. Vic H Innoc' Epis Ch Como MS 1997-2011. sambgodfrey@hotmail.com

GODFREY, Steven R (Chi) 1095 E Thacker St, Des Plaines IL 60016 **Co-chair of Congregations Cmsn Dio Chicago Chicago IL 2010-; R S Mart's Ch Des Plaines IL 2008-** B 4/15/1967 s Culver Godfrey & Carolyn. BA U of Massachusetts 1993; MDiv EDS 2004. D 6/4/2005 Bp M(arvil) Thomas Shaw III P 1/7/2006 Bp Roy Frederick Cederholm Jr. m 7/2/2004 David M Martin. Mem of Congregations Cmsn Dio Chicago Chicago IL 2009-2010; Assoc R S Geo's Epis Ch York Harbor ME 2006-2008; Dioc Coun Dio Maine Portland ME 2006-2007; Cler In Res Ch Of S Jn The Evang Boston MA 2005-2006. sgodfrey@pobox.com

GODFREY, William Calvin (LI) 102 Thompson Blvd, Greenport NY 11944 B Brooklyn NY 3/10/1927 s George Miller Godfrey & Vinetta Carolyn. BA Ya 1947; MDiv Ya Berk 1950; MA LIU 1979. D 6/24/1950 P 3/10/1951 Bp James P De Wolfe. m 5/31/1975 Irene Lesia Blyznak c 3. Int H Trin Epis Ch Hicksville NY 1993-1994; S Johns Epis Hosp Far Rockaway NY 1985-1992; Stff Cathd Of The Incarn Garden City NY 1951-1954; Asst S Jos's Ch Queens Vill NY 1950-1951. Auth, "Pictoral Hist Cathd Of The Incarn Garden City

Ny," 1971. Amer Coll Of Hlth Care Executives 1979-1992. Theo Roosevelt Awd Nassau-Suffolk Hosp Coun Nassau-Suffolk NY 1970; DSC Dio Long Island 1962. billgodfrey1@verizon.net

GODLEY, Robert James (NY) 4440 E Lady Banks Ln, Murrells Inlet SC 29565 B New York NY 4/24/1941 s Thomas Godley & Mary. BA NYU 1971; MDiv GTS 1976. D 6/12/1976 Bp Paul Moore Jr P 12/1/1976 Bp Harold Louis Wright. m 4/14/1985 Betty Stewart c 2. R S Barn Ch Ardsley NY 1977-2011; Asst Ch Of S Jas The Less Scarsdale NY 1976-1977. bsgardsley@aol.com

GODWIN, Jerry D (Dal) 14115 Hillcrest Rd, Dallas TX 75254 **Bd Archv Epis Ch Cntr New York NY 2010-; R The Epis Ch Of The Trsfg Dallas TX 2000-; R The Epis Ch Of The Trsfg Dallas TX 2000-; Vic The Epis Ch Of The Trsfg Dallas TX 1982-** B Fort Dodge IA 2/5/1944 s John Richard Godwin & Virginia Marie. Westmar Coll 1964; BA Drake U 1966; MDiv SWTS 1972; Coll of Preachers 1976. D 6/18/1972 P 12/20/1972 Bp Walter Cameron Righter. Liturg Consult S Matt's Cathd Dallas TX 1994-2000; Secy Dio Conv Dio Dallas Dallas TX 1985-1989; SCCM Epis Ch Cntr New York NY 1977-1985; Litur Cmsn Dio Iowa Des Moines IA 1976-1979; Vic S Mart's Ch Perry IA 1975-1981; Cur S Tim's Epis Ch W Des Moines IA 1972-1975. Associated Parishes; AAM; ADLMC; Epis Cler Assn. jgodwin@transfiguration.net

GOEKE, Randall Fred (Neb) 87993 482nd Ave, Atkinson NE 68713 **R S Mary's Epis Ch Bassett NE 2006-** B Atkinson NE 3/26/1962 s Roy Goeke & Patricia. BA Westmar Coll 1984; MDiv Iliff TS 1987. D 11/27/2006 P 6/6/2007 Bp Joe Goodwin Burnett. randygoeke@hotmail.com

GOETSCH, Richard William (Ida) 213 E Avenue D, Jerome ID 83338 **supply Trin Ch Gooding ID 1999-; D Calv Epis Ch Jerome ID 1988-** B Oconomowoc WI 1/10/1935 s Elmer Goetsch & Sarah Edwina. D 11/6/1988 Bp David Bell Birney IV. m 7/19/1978 Aileen Amanda Turner c 4. NAAD. rgoetsch35@hotmail.com

GOETZ, Edward Craig (Ct) 504 Saybrook Road, P.O. Box 121, Higganum CT 06441 **H Trin Epis Ch Enfield CT 2007-; Sunday Celebrant Calv Ch Enfield CT 1997-; Asst Gr Ch Broad Brook CT 1997-; Sunday Celebrant S Andr's Epis Ch Enfield CT 1997-; S Jas Epis Ch Higganum CT 1973-; S Jn's Epis Ch Vernon Rock Vernon CT 1972-** B Brooklyn NY 7/23/1947 s Edward A Goetz & Dorothy E. BA Moravian TS 1969; MDiv VTS 1972. D 6/10/1972 Bp Joseph Warren Hutchens P 12/16/1972 Bp Morgan Porteus. m 8/4/1973 Cathleen Louise Connor. No Cntrl Reg Mnstry Enfield CT 1997-2007; Vic S Jas Epis Ch Higganum CT 1973-1974. Auth, *Ya Gotta Wanna: Introducing Tech into Classroom*, NSBA, 1996. Vol of Year Awd Outstanding Cmnty Serv Hartford Courant 1996. ecgoetz@simplybsns.com

GOFF, Nancy Lee (Alb) The Church of the Messiah, 296 Glen Street, Glens Falls NY 12801 **D The Ch Of The Mssh Glens Falls NY 2008-** B Bethesda MD 9/12/1949 d Willard W Crabb & Margaret B. BS SUNY Empire St Coll Albany 2006. D 5/10/2008 Bp William Howard Love. m 8/16/1969 John Goff c 3. DOK 2005. nlgoff@verizon.net

GOFF, Susan Ellyn (Va) 6320 Hanover Ave, Springfield VA 22150 **Dio Virginia Richmond VA 2010-** B Paterson NJ 7/24/1953 d James Henry Goff & Dorothy Ann. BA Rutgers-The St U 1975; MDiv UTS 1980. D 6/14/1980 Bp John Shelby Spong P 5/21/1981 Bp Robert Bruce Hall. m 1/23/1988 Charles Thomas Holliday. VTS Alexandria VA 2002; R S Chris's Ch Springfield VA 1994-2009; R Imm Ch Mechanicsville VA 1986-1994. Auth, "arts," *Epis Tchr*; Auth, "arts," *Virginia Epis*. Hitchcock Prize for Ch Hist UTS New York NY 1980. sgoff@thediocese.net

GOFORTH, Lisa Anne (Okla) 1310 N. Sioux Ave., Claremore OK 74017 **R S Paul's Ch Claremore OK 2009-** B York SC 2/5/1961 D 6/14/2003 Bp Peter James Lee P 12/20/2003 Bp Michael Whittington Creighton. S Andr's Ch Burke VA 2006-2008; The Memi Ch Of The Prince Of Peace Gettysburg PA 2003-2006. goforthla@aol.com

GOFORTH, Thomas Robert (Chi) 1126 W Wolfram St, Chicago IL 60657 B Chicago IL 7/22/1942 s Robert Marvin Goforth & Violette Lucille. BA U of Wisconsin 1964; MDiv Nash 1967. D 6/17/1967 Bp James Winchester Montgomery P 12/1/1967 Bp Gerald Francis Burrill. m 2/22/1971 Jane Dobkin Jacobs c 1. Dio Chicago Chicago IL 1972-1974; St Leonards Hse Chicago IL 1968-1972; Cur Gr Epis Ch Hinsdale IL 1967. "This Wild Life," Newtopia mag, 2005; "Shadow And Light On The Path To Partnership," Newtopia mag, 2004; "Ending The War Between The Genders," Newtopia mag, 2004. TGFORTH@AOL.COM

GOGLIA, Bette Mack (CFla) 9203 Glascow Dr, Fredericksburg VA 22408 B Seattle WA 12/2/1942 d Charles R Plum & Margery W. BA S Leo Coll 1997; MS Stetson U 2000. D 12/9/2000 Bp John Wadsworth Howe. D S Ptr The Fisherman Epis Ch New Smyrna Bch FL 2000-2001.

GOHN, Joseph Murray (WTenn) 295 Buena Vista Pl, Memphis TN 38112 B Memphis TN 7/25/1944 s Henry Ernest Gohn & Naomi Geraldine. BA U of Memphis 1966; MDiv STUSo 1968; MDiv SWTS 1970; PhD NWU 1971. D 6/29/1970 Bp John Vander Horst P 5/1/1971 Bp William Evan Sanders. c 1. P-in-c H Trin Ch Memphis TN 1994; Non-par Dio W Tennessee Memphis TN 1982-1994; D S Ptr's Ch Columbia TN 1970-1982. Auth, "Genesis:," *Genesis: An Etiology Of Hope*, Nu Press, 1972. Jounal Of Wstrn Thought 1973. Pstr Emer Dio Wstrn Tennessee 2002. jmgohn@bellsouth.net

GOING, Virginia Lee (NC) 400 S Boylan Ave, Raleigh NC 27603 **D S Mk's Epis Ch Raleigh NC 1990-** B Roanoke VA 2/6/1942 d Robert Lee Going & Virginia Nadine. Cert D Formation Prog. D 10/4/1987 Bp Robert Whitridge Estill. m 6/30/1990 Thomas R Henderson c 2. D S Johns Epis Ch Wake Forest NC 1987-1990.

GOKEY, Mary Jordheim (ND) 1742 9th St S, Fargo ND 58103 **D Geth Cathd Fargo ND 2002-** B Big Spring TX 6/8/1957 d Robert Phillips Jordheim & Janet Beldon. U of Montana 1976; BS U of No Dakota 1980; MS U of Virginia 1983. D 5/10/2002 Bp Andrew Hedtler Fairfield. m 6/29/1984 Franklyn Guy Gokey c 1.

GOLDACKER, Gary Wray (Mich) 12288 W. Dorado Pl. #101, Littleton CO 80127 **Int S Andr's Ch Burke VA 2011-** B Litchfield IL 9/1/1942 s Carlyle Franzen Goldacker & Florence Marguerite. BA Sthrn Illinois U 1966; MDiv Nash 1969; MA U IL 1972. D 5/24/1969 P 12/2/1969 Bp Albert A Chambers. c 2. Int All SS Epis Ch Las Vegas NV 2010; Int Gd Shpd Epis Ch Wichita KS 2008-2009; Int S Steph's Ch Richmond VA 2004-2005; Int S Paul's Epis Ch Cleveland Heights OH 2002-2004; Int S Clare Of Assisi Epis Ch Ann Arbor MI 2001-2002; Int Chr Ch Detroit MI 1999-2001; Int Ch Of The Trsfg Evergreen CO 1996-1998; Int The Ch Of Chr The King (Epis) Arvada CO 1994-1996; R S Mk's Epis Ch Durango CO 1991-1994; R S Mich's Mssn Anaheim CA 1986-1991; Int S Steph's Epis Ch Orinda CA 1985-1986; Assoc All SS Par Beverly Hills CA 1983-1986; R Trin Ch St Chas MO 1974-1975; Assoc Chr Ch Springfield IL 1970-1974; Cur S Geo's Ch Belleville IL 1969-1970. goldackerg@aol.com

GOLDBERG, Michael William (CFla) 460 38th Sq Sw, Vero Beach FL 32968 **R S Aug Of Cbury Epis Ch Vero Bch FL 1997-** B Lake Forest IL 11/26/1949 s Philip I Goldberg & Edith L. BA St. Johns U 1971; MDiv PDS 1974. D 4/27/1974 P 11/2/1974 Bp Albert Wiencke Van Duzer. c 2. R H Trin Epis Ch Ocean City NJ 1981-1997; R S Mths Ch Hamilton NJ 1976-1981; Cur The Ch Of S Uriel The Archangel Sea Girt NJ 1974-1976. Auth, "Preaching As Image, Story," *Idea*. augcantaur@aol.com

GOLDBLOOM, Ruth Alice (Md) 52 S. Broadway, Frostburg MD 21532 **D S Jn's Ch Frostburg MD 2008-** B Frostburg MD 8/2/1953 d Edward Emmett Boyle & Emily Rachel Miller. BA Frostburg St U 1974; MEd Frostburg St U 1979; MS Frostburg St U 1982. D 7/6/2008 Bp John Leslie Rabb. m 10/24/1992 Donald Scott Goldbloom. rgoldbloom@ang.md.org

GOLDEN JR, John Anthony (Pgh) 5 Devon Ave, Lawrenceville NJ 08648 **Asstg P Trin Ch Princeton NJ 2002-** B Pittsburgh PA 3/29/1937 s John Anthony Golden & Helen Cecilia. AB U Pgh 1959; BD Drew U 1962; MPA U Pgh 1979; GTS 1989. D 11/1/1989 Bp William Davidson P 6/1/1990 Bp Alden Moinet Hathaway. m 12/17/1977 Judith Ann Kunco c 1. S Andr's Epis Ch New Kensington PA 1998-2002; S Paul's Epis Ch Kittanning PA 1996-1997; S Barth's Ch Scottdale PA 1995-1996; S Jas Epis Ch Pittsburgh PA 1993-1994; Ch Of The H Cross Pittsburgh PA 1991-1993.

GOLDEN, Lisa Marie Rotchford (Los) 24352 Via Santa Clara, Mission Viejo CA 92692 B Washington DC 2/13/1963 d Charles Frederick Rotchford & Monica Louise. BS Syr 1984; MDiv VTS 1991. D 4/18/1991 Bp Robert Poland Atkinson P 1/1/1992 Bp Frederick Houk Borsch. m 12/27/1985 Marshall Keith Golden. S Jas' Epis Ch Los Angeles CA 2001-2003; S Wilfrid Of York Epis Ch Huntington Bch CA 1995-1996. revdlisa@mac.com

GOLDEN, Peter PQ (LI) 2115 Albemarle Terrace, Brooklyn NY 11226 B Philadelphia PA 7/18/1944 s Lewis Franklin Golden & Anna Mitchell. BA Allen U 1965; MDiv PDS 1970. D 6/6/1970 Bp Robert Lionne DeWitt P 12/12/1970 Bp Chandler W Sterling. R S Paul's Ch-In-The-Vill Brooklyn NY 1992-2010; Int S Paul's Ch-In-The-Vill Brooklyn NY 1990-2010; Asst S Geo's Ch Brooklyn NY 1990; Int Ch Of The Redeem Merrick NY 1987-1988; Epis Ch Cntr New York NY 1985-1987; to the Ordnry Dio Chicago Chicago IL 1982-1984; R S Clem's Epis Ch Inkster MI 1976-1981. Auth, *arts*. Oblates Mt Calv 1982. Sigma Rho Sigma; Phi Alpha Theta. archgolden@hotmail.com

GOLDFARB, Ronald Allen (Ind) 570 Wheat Field Lane, New Whiteland IN 46184 B Ossining NY 5/12/1946 s Irving Alvin Goldfarb & Clara Concetta. BA SUNY 1990. D 6/24/1997 Bp Edward Witker Jones. m 8/18/1973 Teresa Walker c 3. D All SS Epis Ch Memphis TN 2007-2009; D S Tim's Ch Indianapolis IN 2000-2007; D S Mk's Ch Plainfield IN 1997-2001. NAAD 1998. deaconron@yahoo.com

GOLDMAN, Norman Clifford (Ore) 94416 Langlois Mountain Rd, Langlois OR 97450 **P S Chris's Ch Port Orford OR 2001-** B Phoenix AZ 6/29/1940 BS U CO 1963; MS Arizona St U 1968. D 2/13/2001 P 10/27/2001 Bp Robert Louis Ladehoff. m 6/5/1960 Sharen Kay Earl c 3. purple.honker@verizon.net

GOLDSBOROUGH, Charles Neal (CGC) PO Box 12683, Pensacola FL 32591 **Chr Ch Par Pensacola FL 2006-** B Bethesda MD 10/15/1952 s Charles Wycliffe Goldsborough & Marilyn Louise. BA Old Dominion U 1976; MA Virginia Commonwealth U 1978; MDiv VTS 1981. D 5/31/1981 Bp David Henry Lewis Jr P 5/15/1982 Bp Robert Bruce Hall. m 1/18/1975 Carol Waple c 1. R S Jn's Ch Barrington RI 2006-2008; Dio Rhode Island

Providence RI 2005; Pension Fund Mltry New York NY 2005; Spec Mobilization Spprt Plan Washington DC 2005; Alt, GC Dio Virginia Richmond VA 1994-1997; R S Lk's Ch Alexandria VA 1991-2001; Asst Pohick Epis Ch Lorton VA 1984-1991; S Dav's Ch Aylett VA 1982-1984; R Imm Ch Mechanicsville VA 1981-1984. Auth, "Where is God Amidst the Bombs? A P's Reflections from the Combat Zone," *Bk*, Forw Mvmt, 2008. Bro of S Andr 1984-1991; Ord of St Jn of Jerusalem 2011. revgolds@cox.net

GOLDSMITH III, Robert Sidney (La) 1020 7th St, New Orleans LA 70115 **S Steph's Ch Earleville MD 2011-** B Selma AL 7/18/1953 s Robert Sidney Goldsmith & Isabel Grayson. BA Hampden-Sydney Coll 1975; MDiv EDS 1980. D 9/19/1981 P 9/29/1982 Bp A(rthur) Heath Light. m 5/3/1998 Debra Goldsmith c 2. Assoc R Trin Ch New Orleans LA 1998-2010; S Thos Epis Christiansburg VA 1990-1998; S Mk's Ch Fincastle VA 1985-1990; Asst Par Of The Epiph Winchester MA 1981-1985. LAND Grad; Soc of S Jn the Evang. robogold@aol.com

GOLDSMITH, Rusty (Tex) Saint Luke's Episcopal Church, 3736 Montrose Rd., Birmingham AL 35213 **Int H Apos Ch Birmingham AL 2011-2012; Fin Dept and Trst Dio Alabama Birmingham AL 2009-; P Affiliate S Lk's Epis Ch Birmingham AL 2007-; Invstmt Com Dom And Frgn Mssy Soc-Epis Ch Cntr New York NY 2005-2012** B Selma AL 5/18/1943 s Maurice Goldsmith & Sadie Louise. BA U of Alabama 1965; MDiv STUSo 1981. D 6/6/1981 P 12/15/1981 Bp Furman Stough. m 9/2/1964 Carolyn T Thomas c 3. Int S Andr's By The Sea Epis Ch Destin FL 2010-2011; Vice-R S Mart's Epis Ch Houston TX 2005; Congrl Dvlpmt Dio Texas Houston TX 2003-2004; Adj Fac The TS at The U So Sewanee TN 2001-2003; Regent The U So (Sewanee) Sewanee TN 1989-1995; R S Mary's-On-The-Highlands Epis Ch Birmingham AL 1986-2001; Trst The U So (Sewanee) Sewanee TN 1983-2001; Sub-Dn The Cathd Ch Of The Adv Birmingham AL 1983-1986; Cur Ch Of The Nativ Epis Huntsville AL 1981-1983. Auth, "A Trip No," *Sewanee Revs*, 2008; Auth, "Sum Saturdays," *Sewanee Revs*, 2003; Auth, "arts," *Angl Dig*; Auth, "7 Demopolis-Sermons Tapes," *SPCK*. D. D. The U So 1998. mauricegoldsmith@gmail.com

GOLENSKI, John (Cal) 1360 Montgomery St Apt 1, San Francisco CA 94133 **Assoc S Greg Of Nyssa Ch San Francisco CA 2003-** B New Bedford MA 7/24/1947 BA Boston Coll 1969; Jesuit TS 1977; EdD Harv 1978; Jesuit TS 1980. Rec 6/7/2003 Bp William Edwin Swing. JGOLENSKI@AOL.COM

GOLL JR, Harry Eugene (Mass) 1104 Heatherwood, Yarmouth Port MA 02675 B Beaver PA 5/14/1915 s Harry Ellsworth Goll & Blanche Malissa. BA Washington and Jefferson U 1937; STB Harvard DS 1941; Med U of Massachusetts 1963. D 2/25/1942 Bp Alexander Mann P 10/1/1942 Bp Raymond A Heron. c 3. R S Mk's Ch Southborough MA 1950-1985; Mstr, Sacr Stds Belmont Chap at S Mk's Sch Southborough MA 1950-1955; R S Lk's Ch Hudson MA 1945-1950; Asst to the Dn The Cathd Ch Of S Paul Boston MA 1944-1945. genegoll@aol.com

GOLLER II, Oscar Martin (Dal) 8614 Sikorski Ln, Dallas TX 75228 B St. Louis MO 2/16/1924 s Oscar Martin Goller & Bertha. BS Washington U 1948; Nash 1966. D 12/19/1964 Bp Frederick Warren Putnam P 6/1/1966 Bp Chilton Powell. m 9/28/1946 Gweneth Smith c 1. Supply P S Ptr's By The Lake Ch The Colony TX 1998-2000; Ch Of The Gd Samar Dallas TX 1990-1995; Dept Of Missions Dallas TX 1986-1990; St Albans Epis Ch Richardson TX 1982-1985; R Emm Epis Ch Shawnee OK 1970-1982; Asst To Dn S Paul's Cathd Oklahoma City OK 1967-1970. saxontimes@aol.com

GOLLIHER, Jeffrey Mark (NY) 150 W End Ave Apt 30-M, New York NY 10023 **Vic S Jn's Memi Ch Ellenville NY 2003-** B Elkin NC 5/21/1953 s Bobby Gene Golliher & Evelyn Faye. MA LSU 1975; BA Wake Forest U 1975; PhD SUNY 1989; MDiv GTS 1992. D 6/6/1992 P 1/1/1993 Bp David Charles Bowman. m 5/31/1987 Lynn Rodenberg. Cn Cathd Of St Jn The Div New York NY 1992-2003. Auth, "Moving Through Fear," Tarcher/Penguin, 2011; Auth, "A Deeper Faith," Tarcher/Penguin, 2008. jmgolliher1@earthlink.net

GOLUB, Elizabeth Kress (Nwk) 18 Wittig Ter # 7470, Wayne NJ 07470 **P-in-c Ch Of The H Trin W Orange NJ 2009-** B Hoboken NJ 7/18/1951 BD Seton Hall U 1973; MS Seton Hall U 1977; MDiv GTS 2003. D 5/31/2003 P 1/3/2004 Bp John Palmer Croneberger. m 1/3/1981 David Golub c 3. Assoc S Mich's Epis Ch Wayne NJ 2004-2008. revliz@optonline.net

GOMAN, Jon Gifford (Ore) 2615 Nw Arnold Way, Corvallis OR 97330 B Corvallis OR 11/7/1946 s Edward Gordon Goman & Laverne Marie. BA U Of Puget Sound 1969; U of Cambridge 1970; DMin Claremont TS 1976. D 7/31/1976 P 6/20/1977 Bp Robert Hume Cochrane. m 8/26/1979 Elizabeth M Goman c 3. The Epis Ch Of The Gd Samar Corvallis OR 1985-2003; Chapl S Anselm Cbury Ch Corvallis OR 1982-1984; The ETS At Claremont Claremont CA 1980-1982; P-in-c H Nativ Par Los Angeles CA 1979-1982; S Mich And All Ang Ch Issaquah WA 1977-1978; Dio Olympia Seattle WA 1976-1977; Asst S Ambr Par Claremont CA 1974-1976. Auth, "A Few Comments On BCP". Instr Of The Year Linn-Benton Cmnty Coll 1989; Danforth Fellowow 1969. jon@saintanselmoregon.org

GOMER JR, Richard Henry (CFla) 6400 N Socrum Loop Rd, Lakeland FL 33809 **Pstr Chr The King Ch Lakeland FL 1995-** B Denver CO 11/20/1958 s Richard Henry Gomer & Virginia Sue. U CO 1979; BA San Jose St U 1984; MDiv TESM 1988. D 6/24/1988 Bp Charles Shannon Mallory P 12/1/1988 Bp Frank Tracy Griswold III. m 4/13/1984 Karen Kay Connell c 3. Assoc Ch Of The Apos Fairfax VA 1990-1995; Asst S Mk's Epis Ch Glen Ellyn IL 1988-1990. rick@ctklakeland.com

GOMES, Elizabeth (Kan) 912 N Amidon Ave, Wichita KS 67203 **P in Res S Chris's Epis Ch Wichita KS 2005-; Consult - Congrl Dvlpmt Dio Kansas Topeka KS 1996-** B Pittsfield MA 11/12/1938 d Charles Gomes Jardin & Anna. RN Albany Med Cntr Sch of Nrsng 1961; BS Newton Coll Of The Sacr Heart Newton MA 1971; MDiv EDS 1987; DPL Doctoral Stds SWTS 2005. D 12/20/1990 P 6/1/1991 Bp William Edward Smalley. Mem -Congrl Dvlpmt Cmsn Dio Kansas Topeka KS 1998-2004; Cong Dvlp Dir S Jas Ch Wichita KS 1993-2004; Mem Liturg Arts Cmsn Dio Kansas Topeka KS 1993-2001; Mem Cler/Lay Sexual Abuse/Chld Abuse Prevention Com Dio Kansas Topeka KS 1992-2001; Asst Gd Shpd Epis Ch Wichita KS 1991-1993. Auth, "A Manuel For Surgical Techniques". AAR; S Jn Soc; SBL; Soc Of S Jn The Evang. hayewe@cox.nwt

GOMEZ, Edward (Tex) 2404 Marcus Abrams Blvd, Austin TX 78748 B Miami FL 1/20/1957 s Mario Alberto Gomez & Eva Gisela. BBA U of Miami 1978; MDiv Dominican Sch of Philos & Theol 1987; ThM Dominican Sch of Philos & Theol 1988. Rec from Roman Catholic 12/3/2000 Bp Claude Edward Payne. m 12/24/1991 Cary D Duval c 2. El Buen Samaritano Epis Mssn Austin TX 2003-2010; Palmer Memi Ch Houston TX 2002-2003; S Bede Epis Ch Houston TX 2000-2002. Soc of Biblic Literture 2007. egomez1492@yahoo.com

GOMEZ, Fernando Catalino (Los) 815 S California Ave, Monrovia CA 91016 B Caimanera Oriente CU 2/13/1937 s Antonio Gomez & Vicia Julia. BA Inst Secondary Educ Cu 1956; BTh Matanzas TS 1962. D 6/24/1962 P 2/24/1963 Bp Agueros R Gonzalez. m 8/5/1972 Adela D Diaz-Vallejo. Vic Iglesia Epis De La Magdalena Mssn Glendale CA 1977-2002; Assoc Cong Of S Athan Los Angeles CA 1974-1976; Asst Ch Of The Mssh Santa Ana CA 1970-1971. adelag@earthlink.net

GOMEZ, Luis Enrique (NY) 26 W 84th St, New York NY 10024 **R The Ch of S Matt And S Tim New York NY 2011-** B Gualaceo Ecuador 6/24/1964 s Luis Antonio Gomez & Maria Juana. BS Empire St Coll 2009; MDiv The GTS 2010. D 3/13/2010 P 9/25/2010 Bp Mark Sean Sisk. m 11/15/1996 Carmen Piedad Hajal c 1. rev.luisenriquegomez@hotmail.com

GOMEZ-CARDONA, Rosa Angelica (Hond) C/O Iglesia Episcopal, PO Box 523900, Miami FL 33152 **Dio Honduras Miami FL 1998-** B 6/4/1975

GOMPERTZ, Charles Bates (Cal) Po Box 713, Nicasio CA 94946 B Philadelphia PA 9/13/1935 s John Langdon Gompertz & Margaret. BA U CA 1959; MDiv CDSP 1962. D 6/24/1962 Bp James Albert Pike P 3/16/1963 Bp George Richard Millard. m 7/5/1985 Leslie Ross c 4. Asst St Johns Epis Ch Ross CA 1985-2007; Asst S Steph's Par Belvedere CA 1971-1985; Cur St Johns Epis Ch Ross CA 1962-1965. Auth, *Mend a Broken Heart*, Baytree, 1978; Auth, *Mass of the Gd Earth*, 1969; Producer, *Vince Guaraldi at Gr Cathd*, 1965. S Andr's Soc of San Francisco 1987; San Francisco California Pioneers 1980. chuck@nicasio.org

GONTERMAN, Maynard Carl (Ark) 7008 Flintrock Rd, North Little Rock AR 72116 B Litchfield IL 3/4/1920 s Otto Christopher Gonterman & Bertha Gustavia. D 3/4/2000 Bp Larry Earl Maze. c 3. D S Lk's Epis Ch No Little Rock AR 2000-2007. mrgonterman@sbcglobal.net

GONZALES JR, Ricardo (ECR) 859 Jessica Pl, Nipomo CA 93444 B Los Angeles CA 3/21/1943 s Ricardo Gonzales & Amalia. BS California St U 1956; MS U CA 1976; MDiv Claremont TS 2001. D 6/2/2001 Bp Robert Marshall Anderson P 6/5/2002 Bp Chester Lovelle Talton. m 1/30/1965 Caryl Lokken c 2. S Ptr's Par Santa Maria CA 2007; La Iglesia de Todos Los Santos Nipomo CA 2003-2005; S Thos' Mssn Hacienda Heights CA 2001-2002. rgonzal05@sbcglobal.net

GONZALEZ, Alfredo Pedro (USC) 1115 Marion St, Columbia SC 29201 **Hisp Mssnr Dio Upper So Carolina Columbia SC 2009-** B 10/23/1937 s Dagoberto Gonzalez & Gladys. D 7/26/2007 P 2/2/2008 Bp Dorsey Felix Henderson. m 6/7/1969 Luisa M Pequeno c 2. alflui@yahoo.com

GONZALEZ, Elizabeth Carmody (WA) 8804 Postoak Rd, Potomac MD 20854 **S Andr's Epis Sch Potomac MD 2010-** B Nashville TN 10/30/1974 d Richard Patrick Carmody & Alison Cutter. BS NWU 1997; MDIV CDSP 2010. D 6/5/2010 P 1/22/2011 Bp John Chane. m 5/11/2002 Edward Gonzalez c 1. betsygonz@gmail.com

GONZALEZ, Isabel (U) 4024 Red Hawk Rd, West Valley City UT 84119 **Property Maintenance Dio Utah Salt Lake City UT 2006-** B Mexico 3/10/1963 d Enrique Hernandez & Asuncion. Cmnty Coll of Salt Lake City Salt Lake City UT; San Andres Sem Mex City DF MX; U of Utah. D 6/10/2006 P 2/10/2007 Bp Carolyn Tanner Irish. m 7/3/1999 Sergio Gonzalez c 4. igonzalez@episcopal-ut.org

GONZALEZ, Oscar (Nwk) 28 Ralph Street, Bergenfield NJ 07621 B Los Arabos CU 3/2/1929 s Jose Antonio Gonzalez & Concepcion. BA La

Progresiva Sch of Cuba 1948; CPA U of Havana Havana CU 1952; BTh Matanzas TS 1955. Trans from Iglesia Episcopal de Cuba 9/2/1970 as Priest Bp Leland Stark. m 2/25/1956 Lilliam Ponjuan c 2. P in charge Calv Ch Bayonne NJ 2001-2010; Supply P Dio Newark Newark NJ 1995-2000; Pres Hudson Convoc Dio Newark Newark NJ 1976-1978; R Gr Ch Un City NJ 1970-1994. o.gonzalez2@verizon.net

GONZALEZ AQUDELO, Luis Manano (Colom) Carrera 84 North 50 A-112, Ap 301, Medellin, Antioquia Colombia B Caldas CO 12/30/1958 s Manano Gonzalez & Elvira Agudelo. U Antioquia; BA San Javier 1977. D 5/15/1994 P 11/1/1996 Bp Bernardo Merino-Botero. m 12/15/1990 Ana Maria Hoyos Boile. Iglesia Epis En Colombia 1995-1999.

GONZALEZ DEL SOLAR, Mario Sebastian (Va) 800 Brantley Rd, Richmond VA 23235 **Asst R S Matt's Ch Richmond VA 2004-** B Guatemala City GT 8/10/1948 s Julio Cesar Gonzalez del Gonzalez del Solar & Olive Mary. BA U of Maryland 1973; MA U of Maryland 1978; MDiv VTS 1985; DMin TESM 2005. D 6/8/1985 Bp John Thomas Walker P 5/18/1986 Bp William Hopkins Folwell. m 9/28/1974 Barbara Ann Low c 3. Int Chr Epis Ch Virginia Bch VA 2004; Int S Barth's Ch Richmond VA 2002-2004; R Ch Of The Gd Shpd Richmond VA 1990-2001; Evang Cmsn Dio Cntrl Florida Orlando FL 1988-1990; Assoc R Trin Ch Vero Bch FL 1985-1990. Auth, "Joy in Mnstry (Doctoral Thesis)," TESM, 2005; Auth, "Evang," *Cntrl Florida Epis*. Evang Fllshp in the Angl Comm 1996-2003. gonzalezstmatts@hotmail.com

GONZALEZ-MESA, Gustavo (Ore) 700 Se 7th St, Gresham OR 97080 B 4/20/1939 s Guillermo Gonzalez-Mesa & Piedad. Epis TS of The SW; U Natl Mex Mx. D 6/13/1987 Bp Gordon Taliaferro Charlton P 6/1/1991 Bp Maurice Manuel Benitez. m 8/5/1989 Anne Schoonmaker. Dio Oregon Portland OR 1997-2000; Dio Oklahoma Oklahoma City OK 1994-1997; St Lk's Epis Hosp Houston TX 1989-1993; Asst Vic San Francisco De Asisi Austin TX 1988-1989; Dir The Ch of the Gd Shpd Austin TX 1987-1989.

GONZALEZ-RAMIREZ, Daniel (DR) Apartado 764, Santo Domingo Dominican Republic **Died 8/10/2011** B 3/10/1926 s Jose Guadalupe Gonzalez-Torres & Eulalia. Untd Evangical Cntr Mx 1949. D 7/12/1964 P 11/1/1964 Bp Jose Guadalupe Saucedo. c 4.

GOOCH, Gary Duane (Kan) 117 E Sierra Cir, San Marcos TX 78666 B Avery OK 3/28/1936 s George Francis Gooch & Ruby Viola. BS Oklahoma St U 1957; U of Washington 1959; MS Oklahoma St U 1967; MDiv Nash 1974; CE Fell VTS 1987. D 6/22/1974 P 12/21/1974 Bp Chilton Powell. m 7/3/1963 Donnelle Kay Cooper c 4. Secy, Dioc Conv Dio Kansas Topeka KS 1990-1996; R All SS Epis Cluster Pittsburg KS 1988-1996; COM Dio Kansas Topeka KS 1988-1996; Dioc Coun Dio Kansas Topeka KS 1987-1991; R S Ptr's Ch Pittsburg KS 1987-1988; Chair, Comm on Accountability and Cler Compstn Dio Oklahoma Oklahoma City OK 1984-1987; BEC, Ethics & Moral Theol Dio Oklahoma Oklahoma City OK 1982-1987; Chair, Const & Cn Cmsn Dio Oklahoma Oklahoma City OK 1981-1982; Cmsn on Accountability and Cler Compstn Dio Oklahoma Oklahoma City OK 1980-1987; Pres, NE Oklahoma Cler Dio Oklahoma Oklahoma City OK 1980-1982; COM Dio Oklahoma Oklahoma City OK 1977-1987; Cler Advsr, ECharF Dio Oklahoma Oklahoma City OK 1977-1980; R St Andrews Ch Broken Arrow OK 1976-1987; Cmsn on Renwl & Evang Dio Oklahoma Oklahoma City OK 1976-1981; Cur Gr Ch Muskogee OK 1974-1976. Ord of S Lk. Who's Who in Rel; Who's Who in the Midwest. gary.gooch@centurytel.net

GOOD, Arthur Allen (FdL) 1068 Misty Meadow Circle, De Pere WI 54115 **D S Mk's Ch Sidney OH 1999-; D S Jas Ch Piqua OH 1996-** B Detroit MI 12/31/1928 s Joseph Franklin Good & Lelia Mary. Angl Acad. Trans 1/2/2004 Bp Herbert Thompson Jr. m 2/11/1956 Rose Mary Kerlanoff c 4. S Simeon And S Anna. agood@new.rr.com

GOOD, John McClure (EMich) 7351 Flora Ave, St. Louis MO 63143 B Rochester MN 4/20/1938 s C(larence) Allen Good & Virginia. BA Wms 1960; MA Harv 1961; Washington U 1970; S Louis U 1972. D 6/10/1972 Bp George Leslie Cadigan P 12/17/1972 Bp Robert Herbert Mize Jr. c 4. Int for Par Dvlpmt S Albans Epis Ch Bay City MI 2003-2006; Int R Trin Ch S Clair Shores MI 1999-2001; Int Mssnr Nthrn Miami Vlly Cluster Urbana OH 1997-1999; R S Ptr's Ch Gallipolis OH 1994-1997; Mssy Chapl Dio Arkansas Little Rock AR 1993-1994; R Gr Ch Pine Bluff AR 1987-1993; R S Barn Ch Florissant MO 1976-1987; Vic Trin Ch S Jas MO 1972-1976; Vic S Jas Ch Sullivan MO 1971-1976. Co Auth, "Hmnts In Three Cities," Holt Rinehart & Winston, 1969; Auth, "To Inst A New Govt," Heath, 1969; Auth, "Shaping Of Wstrn Soc," Holt Rinehart & Winston, 1968. revgood@chartermi.net

GOODALE-MIKOSZ, Desiree Ann (Chi) 20913 W Snowberry Ln, Plainfield IL 60544 B Joliet IL 12/17/1946 d William Goodale & Shirley June. BS Elmhurst Coll 1990; MSW UIC Jane Addams Coll of Soc Wk 1994. D 1/19/2008 Bp Victor Alfonso Scantlebury. m 5/20/1989 Gerald Mikosz c 2. NAAD 2008. gjm89dgm@gmail.com

GOODE, Colin (Oly) PO Box 276, Lopez Island WA 98261 B Oldham Lancashire UK 2/3/1937 s George Barton Goode & Agnes Elizabeth. LTh St. Jn's Coll Nottingham GB 1979; BTh U of Nottingham 1979; DMin Fuller TS 1990. Trans from Anglican Church of Canada 9/4/1986 Bp Alden Moinet Hathaway. m 6/29/1968 Moira Hilary Du Toit c 2. Vic Gr Ch Lopez Island WA 2002-2009; R All Ang' Ch New York NY 1993-1999; Substitute Dn Trin Cathd Little Rock AR 1989-1993; Assoc Ch Of The Ascen Pittsburgh PA 1986-1989. Cn Trin Cathd Little Rock AR 1989. colinmoira@hotmail.com

GOODFELLOW, Willa Marie (Ia) 1745 5th St., #8, Coralville IA 52241 B Spokane WA 9/1/1952 d Fred Allison Goodfellow & Mary Frances. BA Reed Coll 1975; Cert U of Utah 1980; MDiv Ya Berk 1981; Cert SWTS 2006. Rec from Roman Catholic 4/4/1971. m 8/10/1996 Helen Lenore Keefe c 1. Mnstry Dvlpmt Dio Iowa Des Moines IA 2003-2010; R S Lk's Ch Ft Madison IA 1997-2005; Untd Campus Mnstry Iowa City IA 1997-1998; Dio Iowa, Cler Fam Com Dio Iowa Des Moines IA 1990-1992; P S Paul's Epis Ch Grinnell IA 1988-1992; Int Trin Ch Muscatine IA 1987-1988; Assoc R S Lk's Ch Minneapolis MN 1981-1982. Auth, "The Easy Yoke," *Daughters of Sarah*, 1989. wgoodfellow@mchsi.com

GOODHEART, Donald P (NC) 1303 Hwy A1A #201, Satellite Beach FL 32937 **Ret Assoc Epis Ch Of The H Apos Satellite Bch FL 2008-** B Denver CO 9/10/1947 s Donald E Goodheart & Allison. BA Stan 1969; MDiv Yale DS 1974. D 6/8/1974 P 2/1/1975 Bp Joseph Warren Hutchens. m 12/21/1973 Ronnie S Segal c 2. Dep to GC Dio No Carolina Raleigh NC 2002-2006; Chairman, Conv Dispatch of Bus Dio No Carolina Raleigh NC 2000-2007; Chairman, Mssy Strtgy Cmsn Dio No Carolina Raleigh NC 2000-2003; R S Paul's Epis Ch Winston Salem NC 1997-2007; Pres, CADO (Cler Assn) Dio Olympia Seattle WA 1995-1996; Ch Of The Epiph Seattle WA 1988-1997; COM Dio Utah Salt Lake City UT 1985-1988; Dep to GC Dio Utah Salt Lake City UT 1984-1989; Dioc Coun Dio Utah Salt Lake City UT 1983-1985; R S Paul's Ch Salt Lake City UT 1980-1988; R S Andr's-In-The-Vlly Tamworth NH 1976-1980; Asst S Jas Epis Ch Farmington CT 1974-1976; Assoc S Jn's Ch New Haven CT 1973-1974. dgoodheart1@gmail.com

GOODING, Ludwick E (Pa) 5910 Cobbs Creek Pkwy, Philadelphia PA 19143 B Bridgetown BB 10/10/1933 s Henry Murray Lampitt & Idalene. Aib U Of Reading Gb 1976; ThD Oxf 1979; STM Oxf 2000. Trans from Church Of England 10/1/1989 Bp Allen Lyman Bartlett Jr. m 4/11/1956 Verna J Eugene. S Phil Memi Ch Philadelphia PA 1989-2002. frjack141@sunbeach.net

GOODISON, Lorna Fay (SeFla) 1400 Riverside Dr, Coral Springs FL 33071 **S Mary Magd Epis Ch Coral Sprg FL 2007-** B Kingston Jamaica WI 8/3/1950 MA Florida Intl U; BSW U of The W Indies; Cert Dioc Sch For CE 2004. D 4/29/2007 Bp Leopold Frade. c 2. lfgoodison@yahoo.com

GOODKIND, Caroline Cox (USC) 231 Cedar Creek Farm Rd, Tuckasegee NC 28783 B Jackson MI 6/16/1945 d Harry Charles Cox & Ellen Athena. BA Duke 1965; MDiv STUSo 2001. D 6/4/2001 Bp Robert Hodges Johnson P 4/6/2002 Bp Michael Bruce Curry. m 12/17/1985 Marcus Jay Goodkind c 2. R S Geo Ch Anderson SC 2004-2010; Asst S Mary's Epis Ch High Point NC 2001-2004. CE Awd For Creativity And Excellence In Bib U So 2001. cgoodkind@frontier.com

GOODLETT, James Calvin (Fla) D 6/12/1977 Bp Frank Stanley Cerveny P 12/1/1977 Bp William Henry Marmion.

GOODMAN, (Herbert) Ray(mond) (Miss) 1202 Antler Dr, Tupelo MS 38804 B El Paso TX 10/31/1932 s Herbert Hatton Goodman & Hattie Mae. BA U of Mississippi 1957; MDiv VTS 1960; JD U of Mississippi 1975. D 6/21/1960 Bp Iveson Batchelor Noland P 5/13/1961 Bp Girault M Jones. m 9/4/1957 Shirley L Lumpkin c 1. Int S Jn's Epis Ch Ocean Sprg MS 1997-1999; Int S Paul's Epis Ch Meridian MS 1996-1997; Int S Jas Ch Greenville MS 1994-1995; R All SS' Epis Ch Tupelo MS 1969-1974; R S Paul's Epis Ch Jesup GA 1966-1969; P S Columba's Winnsboro LA 1961-1965; P S Dav's Ch Rayville LA 1961-1965; Cur Ch Of The Ascen Lafayette LA 1960. Phi Alpha Delta 1975; Pi Kappa Alpha 1956. Who's Who in Amer Law 2012; Who's Who in Amer 2012; Who's Who in Mississippi 1989; Who's Who in Amer Law 1988; Phi Sigma Tau 1957. frhrg@comcast.net

GOODMAN, James M (RG) P.O. Box 1246, Albuquerque NM 87103 **Pres, Stndg Com Dio The Rio Grande Albuquerque NM 2010-; Dn S Jn's Cathd Albuquerque NM 2007-** B Oklahoma City OK 3/11/1958 s Norman Loyal Goodman & Markita Marie. BS U of Oklahoma 1981; MS U of Iowa 1983; MDiv GTS 1991. D 10/25/1991 P 5/7/1992 Bp Don Adger Wimberly. m 8/11/1990 Dawn Melissa Freuchtemeyer c 2. Stndg Com Dio So Carolina Charleston SC 2004-2007; Dioc Coun Dio So Carolina Charleston SC 2000; R Trin Ch Myrtle Bch SC 1999-2007; R Trin Ch Hamilton OH 1994-1999; Chair Compnstn T/F Dio Sthrn Ohio Cincinnati OH 1993-1996; Dio Sthrn Ohio Cincinnati OH 1993-1995; Dioc Coun Dio Sthrn Ohio Cincinnati OH 1992-1996; Dioc Coun Dio Sthrn Ohio Cincinnati OH 1992-1996; Dioc Coun Dio Sthrn Ohio Cincinnati OH 1992-1996; Cn Epis Soc of Chr Ch Cincinnati OH 1991-1994. Cmnty Trsfg. mgood91357@aol.com

GOODMAN, Kevin M (Chi) 509 W Aldine Ave Apt 3D, Chicago IL 60657 **Assoc Dn Cathd Of S Jas Chicago IL 2009-** B New Orleans LA 2/15/1966 s Philip McKean Goodman & Margaret Short. Shaaxi Tchr's U 1987; BA Loyola U 1989; MDiv GTS 2004. D 6/18/2005 P 12/17/2005 Bp William Dailey Persell. m Antonius Pulung-Hartanto. Cur All SS Epis Ch Chicago IL 2006-2009; Asst S Matt's Ch Evanston IL 2004-2006. "San Xia: Three Gorges and The People's Republic of China," Universal Pub, 2000. The Polly Bond Awd of Excellence ECom 2002. therevkevin@me.com

GOODMAN, Timothy Allen (Spr) 9267 HERRIN RD, JOHNSTON CITY IL 62951 **P-in- Charge S Steph's Ch Harrisburg IL 2011-** B Chicago IL 1/8/1938 s Frank C Goodman & Fern. BSB U Of Evansville 1967. D 8/31/1991 Bp Donald James Parsons P 5/31/2008 Bp Peter Hess Beckwith. m 10/19/1963 Carol Michell Funke c 3. Asst P S Jas Epis Ch Marion IL 1991-2011; D/Asst. P Ch Of The Redeem Cairo IL 1991-2008; D/Asst. P S Jas Epis Ch McLeansboro IL 1991-2008; D/Asst. P S Mk's Ch W Frankfort IL 1991-2008; D/Asst. P S Steph's Ch Harrisburg IL 1991-2008. Ord Of S Lk. sowood4@msn.com

GOODNESS, Donald Roy (NY) 47081 Kentwell Place, Potomac Falls VA 20165 **S Jas' Epis Ch Leesburg VA 2001-** B Rochester NY 9/24/1932 s Alfred Louis Goodness & Marion Grace. BA Atlantic Un Coll 1953; BD EDS 1962. D 6/23/1962 Bp Anson Phelps Stokes Jr P 12/23/1962 Bp William A Lawrence. m 9/3/1950 Lorraine Reynolds c 1. R Ch Of The Ascen New York NY 1972-1997; Asst Chr Ch Fitchburg MA 1962-1965. drglrg97@verizon.net

GOODPANKRATZ, Gretchen (WK) Po Box 851, Liberal KS 67905 B Liberal KS 6/21/1937 d Earl Hey Good & Hortense. Cottey Gnrl 1957; BS K SU 1959. D 3/13/1989 Bp William Edwin Swing. c 4. D S Andr's Epis Ch Liberal KS 1989-2000. NAAD, Tertiary Of The Soc Of S Fran.

GOODRICH III, Daniel Hillman (Mich) 39 Hubbard St, Mount Clemens MI 48043 B Highland Park MI 7/26/1933 s Daniel Hillman Goodrich & Harriett. MDiv CDSP; BA U MI. D 6/29/1963 P 12/22/1994 Bp Archie H Crowley. Ed For Nwsltr Dio Michigan Detroit MI 1982-1985; Dioc Mus Cmsn Dio Michigan Detroit MI 1978-1983; Dn Dioc Convoc Dio Michigan Detroit MI 1978-1982; Vic S Edw The Confessor Epis Ch Clinton Township MI 1963-2005; Asst St Paul's Epis Romeo MI 1963-1967.

GOODRICH, Kevin Patrick (ND) 411 2nd Ave Ne, Jamestown ND 58401 **Cn Mssnr Dio No Dakota Fargo ND 2006-; Pstr Gr Epis Ch Jamestown ND 2006-** B Hartford CT 3/10/1979 s Charles Goodrich & Patricia. STB Apage Sem 2002; MDIV Biblic TS 2006; MA Biblic TS 2008; DMIN Nash 2011. Trans from Anglican Church of Tanzania 10/10/2006 Bp Michael Gene Smith. m 6/1/2002 Melissa Ann Mounce. "Plugging into God's Story," Xulon Press, 2007; "Cell Phone Sprtlty," iUniverse, 2005. canongoodrich@aol.com

GOODRIDGE, Robert J (CFla) 4791 Longbow Drive, Titusville FL 32796 **S Gabriels Ch Titusville FL 2009-; H Trin Epis Acad Melbourne FL 2007-** B Youngs Town OH 4/24/1949 s Robert Jenkins Goodridge & Isabel Gantz. BS U of Texas 1975; MDiv U So-TS 2007. D 6/2/2007 P 12/7/2007 Bp John Wadsworth Howe. m 4/8/1989 Kathryn L Goodridge c 2. Chapl H Trin Epis Ch Melbourne FL 2007-2009. rob@robgoodridge.com

GOODWIN III, Frederick Deane (Va) 2301 Wedgewood Ave, Richmond VA 23228 B Norfolk VA 4/26/1944 s Frederick Deane Goodwin & Ruth Evelyn. BA U of Oklahoma 1966; MDiv VTS 1969; Clu 1982. D 6/19/1969 P 5/1/1970 Bp Robert Bruce Hall. m 8/11/1983 Kathryn Kramer. Emm Ch At Brook Hill Richmond VA 1969-1978. kgoodwin54@comcast.net

GOODWIN, Joan Carolyn (Az) No address on file. **D Dio Colorado Denver CO 1994-** B Los Angeles CA 10/9/1939 d Bascom Howard Robison & Velma Irene. BA USC 1961. D 11/7/1992 Bp Joseph Thomas Heistand. m 1/26/1962 Michael Goodwin c 2. NAAD, Dok; Untd Epis Chars.

GOODWIN, Laura Bishop (WMass) St Andrew's Church, 53 N Main St, North Grafton MA 01536 **R S Andr's Ch No Grafton MA 2007-** B Springfield MA 9/9/1953 d Gordon Bishop & Mary Ellen. BS Fitchburg St Coll Fitchburg MA 1977; MDiv Wycliffe Coll Toronto Can 2007. D 6/2/2007 P 12/8/2007 Bp Gordon Paul Scruton. m 8/19/1978 Todd Goodwin c 2. revlaura@comcast.net

GOODWIN, Marilyn Marie (Minn) 27309 County Road 4, Naytahwaush MN 56566 B White Earth MN 6/15/1944 d John Ernest Bellefeuille & Isabelle. D 10/29/2005 P 1/20/2007 Bp James Louis Jelinek. c 2. margood1@localnet.com

GOODWIN, Sarabeth (WA) 1721 Lamont St NW, Washington DC 20010 **Ch Of S Steph And The Incarn Washington DC 2005-** B Phillipi WV 1/25/1949 d Olin Mansell Goodwin & Helen. BA W Virginia U 1970; MA W Virginia U 1973; MDiv VTS 2005. D 6/11/2005 P 1/21/2006 Bp John Chane. m 10/13/1984 John P Racin c 2. sarabeth@attglobal.net

GOOLD, George Charles (Ore) St Stephen's Church, SW Ninth & Hurbert Sts, Newport OR 97365 **D S Steph's Ch Newport OR 2002-; D Dio Oregon Portland OR 1992-** B Portland OR 6/23/1943 s Clifford Henry Goold & Clara Luella. BS Portland St Coll 1968. D 6/29/1992 Bp Robert Louis Ladehoff. georgegoold@charter.net

GOOLSBEE, Arthur Leon (NwT) 602 Meander St., Abilene TX 79602 B Waco TX 2/19/1940 s William Harold Goolsbee & Josephine. BA Baylor U 1967; JD U of Texas Sch of Law 1967. D 10/31/2008 Bp C(harles) Wallis Ohl. m 4/12/1963 Linda Dean c 1. art@artgoolsbee.com

GOOLSBY, Robert Patrick (Tex) 1656 Blalock Rd., Houston TX 77080 **Liturg Cmsn Dio Texas Houston TX 2011-; R S Chris's Ch Houston TX 2008-** B Hollywood FL 6/30/1970 s Elmer Eugene Goolsby & Rose Ann. BA U Of Cntrl Florida 2002; MDiv Epis TS of The SW 2005. D 4/17/2005 Bp Leopold Frade. m 11/27/2005 Karla G Marshall c 2. Stwdshp Cmsn Dio Texas Houston TX 2007-2009; Cur Ch Of The Gd Shpd Kingwood TX 2005-2008. fr.goolsby@gmail.com

GOOLTZ, Janet Reed (Az) 12607 W Westgate Dr, Sun City AZ 85375 **Asstg P Ch Of The Adv Sun City W AZ 2008-** B Baltimore MD 4/21/1937 d Oscar Roy Reed & Garnet Louisiana. BA Vas 1959; MDiv Weston Jesuit TS 1982; DMin GTF 1995. D 6/2/1984 Bp John Bowen Coburn P 5/22/1985 Bp Morris Fairchild Arnold. m 6/13/1959 Robert B Goolltz c 4. Asstg P The Ch Of Our Redeem Lexington MA 2000-2004; Cathdl Chapt Dio Massachusetts Boston MA 1994-1997. Assoc, Ord of Ste Anne 1994. janet.mcw@cox.net

GOONESEKERA, Desmond Joel Peter (Tex) St. Cuthbert Episcopal Church, 17020 - West Rd., Houston TX 77095 **R S Cuth's Epis Ch Houston TX 2000-** B 3/18/1946 s David Justin Goonesekera & Edith Phoebe Theodora. MDiv DS Colombo, Sri Lanka 1968; Ldrshp Acad for New Directions 1980; BA/BS Luth Bible Inst of Seattle 1980. Rec 6/1/1988 as Priest Bp Charles Jones III. m 9/11/1971 Ewena De Mel c 2. R Trin Epis Ch Baytown TX 1995-2000; Asst Gr And S Steph's Epis Ch Colorado Sprg CO 1991-1995; R S Pat's Epis Ch Bigfork MT 1988-1991; Asst P S Lk's Epis Ch Seattle WA 1978-1980. frdesmond@stcuthbert.org

GOORAHOO, Ephraim Basant (LI) 111-16 116th St, South Ozone Park NY 11420 **Supply P Dio Long Island Garden City NY 2008-** B Soesdyke Demerara GY 9/27/1926 s James Edward Goorahoo & Hilda Marion. GOE Codrington Coll 1958; STM NYTS 1977; Cert Blanton-Peale Grad Inst 1984. Trans from Church in the Province Of The West Indies 8/1/1973 Bp Jonathan Goodhue Sherman. m 10/17/1948 Doris Singh. Supply P S Ptr's Ch Rosedale NY 2006-2008; Assoc Trin-St Jn's Ch Hewlett NY 2003-2006; Int Ch Of The Resurr Kew Gardens NY 1998-2002; Int S Mary's Ch Brooklyn NY 1996-1997; Int Ch Of The Resurr E Elmhurst NY 1995-1996; Int All Souls Ch New York NY 1993-1994; R S Barn Epis Ch Brooklyn NY 1989-1991; P-in-c S Lydia's Epis Ch Brooklyn NY 1976-1980; P-in-c S Barn Epis Ch Brooklyn NY 1973-1988; Dio Long Island Garden City NY 1973-1978. ephraimbg@hotmail.com

GORACZKO, Ann Kathleen Reeder (SeFla) 15650 Miami Lakeway N, Miami Lakes FL 33014 B Miami, FL 1/26/1952 d William Almy Reeder & Linda Nester. MSEd, TESOL Florida Intl U 1993; MA Florida Intl U 2003; MDiv Florida Cntr for Theol Stds 2012. D 5/2/2010 Bp Leopold Frade. m 7/9/1978 Anthony Goraczko c 2. annyrbg@gmail.com

GORANSON, Paul Werner (WMass) 130 Sachem Ave., Worcester MA 01606 B Worcester MA 3/2/1940 s Eric Werner Goranson & Katri Emilia. BS Worcester Polytechnic Inst 1962; MDiv GTS 1974. D 6/14/1974 P 1/25/1975 Bp Alexander Doig Stewart. c 1. R Gr Ch Oxford MA 1977-2006; Vic Gr Ch Oxford MA 1975-1976. CCU 1974. pwgoran@charter.net

GORCHOV, Michael Ivan (Alb) 30 William St, Catskill NY 12414 **S Paul's Ch Troy NY 2004-** B Champagne-Urbana IL 5/15/1953 s Maurice Ron Gorchov & Carol Joy. MDiv GTS 2001; BS SUNY 2001. D 6/9/2001 P 12/8/2001 Bp Daniel William Herzog. m 6/23/1971 Marianne C Carey c 3. D S Lk's Ch Catskill NY 2001-2004. mig@michaelgorchov.com

GORDAY, Peter Joseph (WNC) 34 Lullwater Pl Ne, Atlanta GA 30307 B Fall River MA 7/6/1944 s Walter Joseph Gorday & Frances Harmon. BA Dart 1966; MA/PhD Van 1980; ThM Columbia Presb Sem Decatur GA 1995. D 6/29/1974 Bp John Vander Horst P 5/1/1975 Bp William Evan Sanders. m 4/25/1970 Virginia S Gorday c 1. Asst Ch Of The Incarn Highlands NC 2008-2010; Assoc H Innoc Ch Atlanta GA 2001-2002; S Anne's Epis Ch Atlanta GA 1994-1999; Cn Cathd Of S Phil Atlanta GA 1987-1994; Asst S Lk's Epis Ch Atlanta GA 1980-1987; P-in-c S Jas The Less Madison TN 1975-1980. Auth, "Fenelon: A Biography," Paraclete Press, 2012; Ed, "Ancient Chr Commentary On Scripture, NT Ix: Colossians, I-II Thessalonians, I-II Tim, Tit and Philemon," InterVarsity Press, 1999; Auth, "Principals Of Patristic Exegesis," 1983. pgorday@bellsouth.net

GORDON, Billie Mae (Mass) 4301 Pheasant Ln, Middleborough MA 02346 **Int R Ch Of Our Sav Somerset MA 2009-; Ch Of S Jn The Evang Duxbury MA 2007-** B Washington PA 12/12/1941 d William Jesse Dickinson & Ona Mae. AS Massasoit Cmnty Coll 1978; BA Stonehill Coll 1991; MDiv Weston Jesuit TS 1997. D 12/19/1998 P 12/4/1999 Bp M(arvil) Thomas Shaw III. c 1. Int Trin Epis Ch Rockland MA 2007-2009; Asst R and Coordntr of Rel Educ Ch Of The Gd Shpd Waban MA 1999-2005; S Jn The Evang Taunton MA 1999-2005. MA Epis Cleric Assn. biliegordon@verizon.net

GORDON, Constance Leigh (U) 789 White Pine Dr, Tooele UT 84074 **S Paul's Epis Ch Vernal UT 2007-; Cur Dio Utah Salt Lake City UT 2005-** B Colorado Springs, CO 9/8/1964 d Robert Hill & Verna. D 6/11/2005 P 4/19/2006 Bp Carolyn Tanner Irish. m 7/1/1987 James K Gordon c 2. rev.cgordon@gmail.com

GORDON, David Walter (Cal) 130 Avenida Barbera, Sonoma CA 95476 B Oregon City OR 10/30/1927 s John Dawes Gordon & Dorothy. BS OR SU 1948; MDiv CDSP 1952. D 6/23/1951 P 12/21/1951 Bp Benjamin D Dagwell. m 12/29/1974 Ann K Curiale c 4. Assoc Trin Ch Sonoma CA 2002-2007; S Jas' Ch No Salem NY 1989-1990; Stwdshp Off Dio New York New York City NY 1982-1992; Diocn Msnry & Ch Extntn Socty New York NY 1982-1992;

Dpt Of Missions Ny Income New York NY 1982-1992; R Ch Of The Epiph San Carlos CA 1974-1982; R Ch Of The H Trin Richmond CA 1963-1973; Trin Ch Sonoma CA 1963-1973; R S Jas' Epis Ch Coquille OR 1958-1960; Vic S Fran Ch Sweet Hm OR 1952-1958; R S Mart's Ch Lebanon OR 1951-1953. Auth, *A Plan for Stwdshp Educ & Dvlpmt Through the Year*, Morehouse Pub, 1988. dwgor@comcast.net

GORDON JR, Harrington Manly (RI) 108 Columbia Ave, Warwick RI 02888 B Jersey City NJ 7/19/1929 s Harrington Manly Gordon & Ethel Jane. BA Br M.C.L, 1952; BD Nash 1955; MDiv Nash 1956. D 6/24/1955 P 3/24/1956 Bp John S Higgins. m 6/27/1982 Joan Lane. Dn - So Cntrl Dnry Dio Rhode Island Providence RI 1967-1978; R Trin Ch Cranston RI 1960-1994; R S Mk's Ch Warren RI 1957-1960; Cur All SS' Memi Ch Providence RI 1955-1957. Auth, "Dvlpmt, Money," *Plnng Process*, Dio Rhode Island, 1960. NNECA 1986. Honored - Continuous Wk For Exec Com Epis Chars Of Rhode Island; Honored - Continuous Epis Conf Cntr Dio RI Pascoag RI. jalgordon@aol.com

GORDON, Jay Holland (NY) 382 Central Park W Apt 17p, New York NY 10025 B Glen Ridge NJ 1/3/1938 s J Holland Gordon & Dorothy. BA Br 1959; STB GTS 1962; STM 1973. D 6/9/1962 Bp Leland Stark P 12/15/1962 Bp Donald MacAdie. Fndr Dio New York New York City NY 1982-1983; The Ch of S Matt And S Tim New York NY 1973-2003; Cur Par of Trin Ch New York NY 1965-1973; Cur Gr Ch Newark NJ 1962-1965. Soc of S Jn the Theol 1999. Cn of the Dio Bp Sisk 2003; Spec Merit Citation Mayor Jn Lindsay (NYC) New York NY 1972. jh.gordon@verizon.net

GORDON JR, Jim (RG) 311 E Palace Ave, Santa Fe NM 87501 B Pasadena CA 5/9/1951 s James Donald Gordon & Mildred Marie. Dplma DRG Sch for Mnstry; AA Citrus Coll 1972. D 9/18/2010 Bp William Carl Frey. m 10/7/2005 Andrea Shapiro. gjames43@msn.com

GORDON, John Douglas (Los) 1944 FM 1606, Hermleigh TX 79526 B San Jose CA 5/22/1952 s John Albert Gordon & Evelyn Elizabeth. BA U of Redlands 1974; MDiv CDSP 1985. D 6/15/1985 P 1/1/1986 Bp Robert C Rusack. c 3. S Columba's Epis Mssn Big Bear Lake CA 1991-1994; Asst The Par Of S Matt Pacific Palisades CA 1985-1986. DOUG.GORDON@BENTMESA.COM

GORDON, Rodney E (SVa) 701 S Providence Rd, North Chesterfield VA 23236 **P-in-c Ch Of The Gd Shpd Bath Par Mc Kenney VA 2009-** B 4/4/1957 B.Mus. Virginia Commonwelth U 1979; Miv.D. SWTS 1992; Grad Cert in Publ Mgmt Virginia Commonwealth U 2010. D 6/7/1992 P 12/12/1992 Bp Frank Harris Vest Jr. m 8/24/2007 Jennifer Piland c 4. R S Barn Epis Ch Richmond VA 2002; P S Dav's Epis Ch Richmond VA 2000-2001; R S Jn's Ch Hopewell VA 1994; R S Jn's Ch Petersburg VA 1992-1993. fatherrod@hotmail.com

GORDON, Walt (Minn) 834 Marshall Ave, Saint Paul MN 55104 B Montreal QC CA 4/23/1949 s Alec Gordon & Loula. BA Carleton Coll 1971; MDiv CDSP 1976. D 8/6/1976 P 10/30/1977 Bp Philip Frederick McNairy. c 2. P-in-c S Jas Epis Ch Hibbing MN 2000-2006; Hunger Mssnr Par Of The H Trin And S Anskar Minneapolis MN 1985-1988; R Ascen Ch St Paul MN 1982-1985; P-in-c S Paul's Epis Le Cntr MN 1982-1984; R S Andr's Epis Ch Waterville MN 1981-1983; P-in-c H Trin Epis Ch Luverne MN 1976-1978; R S Paul's Ch Pipestone MN 1976-1978. Ed, *(Ed) A Strtgy for Growth in the Epis Ch: Joining Multiculturalism w Evang by the Rt. Rev. Mk MacDonald*, Intercultural Mnstry Dvlpmt, 1994. ECom 1991-1999; ECom 2005; ECom Bd 1997-1998; RCC Chapt Pres 1997-1998; RCC Mem 1991-1998. Fell-in-Res Sewanee 1997; Polly Bond Awards 1990-1996 ECom 1990. revwaltgordon@gmail.com

GORDON, Walter Bernard (WTenn) PO Box 622, Grand Junction TN 38039 **S Jas Bolivar TN 2010-** B Memphis TN 5/10/1951 s Walter G Gordon & Allena H. BS Mississippi St U 1973; AS Auburn U 1984; PhD So Dakota St U 1989. D 9/1/2007 P 12/20/2008 Bp James Marshall Adams Jr. bgordon@nckcn.com

GORDON-BARNES, Janice E (Md) 102 W 39th St Apt 4b, Baltimore MD 21210 B London UK 2/20/1947 d Colin Fraser Gordon & Zena Gertrude. BA NWU 1977; MDiv U Chi 1979; DMin SWTS 1997. D 6/4/1980 Bp James Winchester Montgomery P 2/24/1981 Bp Quintin Ebenezer Primo Jr. m 11/11/2001 William Barnes. Ch Of The H Comf Luthvle Timon MD 1989-2009; S Anne's Par Annapolis MD 1984-1989; Cur S Aug's Epis Ch Wilmette IL 1980-1984. janice.gordonbarnes@yahoo.com

GORDY, Sare (WNY) 371 Delaware Ave, Buffalo NY 14202 B Clearwater FL 7/24/1978 d Robert Gordy & Donna. BA SUNY 2001; MS SUNY 2003; MDiv VTS 2006. D 12/26/2005 P 12/1/2006 Bp J Michael Garrison. Cur Trin Epis Ch Buffalo NY 2006-2009. sgordy@trinitybuffalo.org

GORDY, Zane Wesley (Ct) Po Box 456, Perryville MD 21903 B Milford DE 7/14/1938 s John Phillip Gordy & Eva Houston. BA Bos 1964; MDiv EDS 1969; Advncd CPE 1972. D 6/19/1969 Bp William Henry Mead P 5/2/1970 Bp Paul Moore Jr. Int S Mary's Ch Baltimore MD 1997-1998; S Mary's Epis Ch Woodlawn Baltimore MD 1997-1998; Int Epis Ch Of Chr The King Windsor Mill MD 1996-1997; Int S Mk's Epis Ch Perryville MD 1994-1996; Int S Ptr's Epis Ch Ellicott City MD 1993-1994; Asst P/Mus Dir Trin Epis Ch Hartford CT 1981-1992; Asstg P/Mus Dir S Ptr's Epis Ch Peekskill NY 1975-1980; Assoc R Emm Epis Ch Webster Groves MO 1972-1974. Auth, "Love Your Neighbors Mus"; Auth, "Gd Pstr Musicians Deserve Gd Salaries". Ch Mus Awd Washington Cathd CCM Washington DC 1964. amazane@comcast.net

GORES, Ariail Fischer (Dal) 4229 Tomberra Way, Dallas TX 75220 B New Orleans LA 10/18/1947 D 5/24/2003 Bp James Monte Stanton. c 2.

GORMAN, James Michael (Chi) 5388 W Harvey Rd, Oregon IL 61061 B Dixon IL 7/24/1937 s Leo James Gorman & Ruby Elizabeth. D 12/26/1987 Bp Frank Tracy Griswold III. m 9/19/1959 Jeanne Carole Davis c 3. jgorman53@hotmail.com

GORMAN, W(illiam) Kenneth (NJ) 103 Grove St, N Plainfield NJ 07060 **R H Cross Epis Ch No Plainfield NJ 1997-** B Camden NJ 2/15/1944 s William Rudolph Gorman & Eleanor. BA Ge 1966; MDiv PDS 1969; DMin NYTS 1990. D 4/19/1969 P 10/25/1969 Bp Alfred L Banyard. m 8/1/1992 Cheryl Lynn Barton c 2. R Chr Ch So Amboy NJ 1991-1996; R S Lk the Evang Roselle NJ 1976-1991; R Chr Ch Palmyra NJ 1971-1976; Cur S Mary's Ch Haddon Heights NJ 1969-1971. k-gorman@comcast.net

GORSUCH, John P (Oly) 1811 Douglas Ave, Bellingham WA 98225 B Denver CO 2/1/1932 s John E(lliot) Gorsuch & Freda H(enrietta). BA Wesl 1953; MDiv Yale DS 1956; Cert Shalem Inst for Sprtl Formation 1981. D 6/9/1956 P 12/26/1956 Bp Angus Dun. m 6/5/1955 Beverly Colville c 2. Exec Dir Cntr for Sprtl Dvlpmt Dio Olympia Seattle WA 1985-1990; GC 4x, Chair, Stndg Com, Chair, Exec Coun Dio Olympia Seattle WA 1978-1981; R Ch Of The Epiph Seattle WA 1968-1985; Chair DeptCE, GC Dio Spokane Spokane WA 1965-1968; R S Tim's Epis Ch Yakima WA 1963-1968; Dioc Coun, Del Angl Congr Dio Wstrn Kansas Hutchinson KS 1960-1963; Vic S Jn's Ch Great Bend KS 1959-1963; Assoc S Alb's Par Washington DC 1956-1959. Auth, "An Invitation to the Sprtl Journey," Paulist Press, 1990. jpgorsuch@comcast.net

GORTNER, David Timothy (Chi) 3737 Seminary Road, Alexandria VA 22304 **Dir, Doctor of Mnstry Prog / Prof, Evang & Congrl Ldrshp VTS Alexandria VA 2008-** B Reading PA 2/18/1966 s Robert Vanderbilt Gortner & Aileen Kraekel. BA Wheaton Coll 1988; MA Wake Forest U 1994; MDiv SWTS 1997; PhD U Chi 2004. D 5/8/2003 Bp William Dailey Persell P 11/29/2003 Bp Victor Alfonso Scantlebury. m 10/16/1999 Heather Ann VanDeventer c 2. Multicultural Mnstry T/F Dio California San Francisco CA 2007-2008; Yth & YA Mnstry Cmsn Dio California San Francisco CA 2005-2007; Asstg P S Mk's Par Berkeley CA 2005-2006; Asst. Prof, Pstr Theol / Dir, Cntr for Angl Lrng & Ldrshp CDSP Berkeley CA 2004-2008; Lectr, Practical Theol SWTS Evanston IL 2003-2004; Pstr for YA / Young Fam Mnstrs S Mk's Ch Evanston IL 1999-2004; Congrl Dvlpmt Cmsn Dio Chicago Chicago IL 1998-2001; Cmsn on Campus & YA Mnstry Dio Chicago Chicago IL 1997-2004; Epis Campus Mnstry at NWU Dio Chicago Chicago IL 1997-2004. Auth, "Habits for Effective Ldrshp: Lessons from Beyond the Ecclesia," *ATR*, 2010; Auth, "Looking at Ldrshp Beyond Our Own Horizon," *ATR*, 2009; Auth, "Around One Table," *Around One Table*, CREDO & Coll for Bishops, 2009; Auth, "Transforming Evang," *Transforming Evang*, Ch Pub, 2008; Co-Auth, "Mentoring Cler for effective Ldrshp," *Reflective Pract*, 2007; Co-Auth, "Beyond Wish-Lists For Pstr Ldrshp:Assessing Cler Behavior And Congrl Outcomes To Guide Sem Curric," *Theol Educ*, 2005; Auth, "Varieties Of YA Personal Theologies," U Chi, 2004; Co-Auth, "The Epis Ch Welcomes You? The Challenges Of Evang w Students And YA In Disorganized Rel," *Disorganized Rel (Kujawa, ed.)*, Cowley, 1997. Ntwk of Mnstry Innovators 2007-2008. Conant Grant Rec Epis Ch Cntr (2005, 2010) 2010; Grant Rec EvangES (1996, 2005, 2007) 2007; Fell ECF 1998. dgortner@cdsp.edu

GOSE, R Franklin (SVa) 51 Candlewyck Rd, Portland ME 04102 B Wise VA 3/4/1939 s James Radcliff Gose & Margaret Rebeccah. BA U Rich 1961; UTS 1963; MDiv VTS 1964; MA Leh 1972. D 6/13/1964 Bp Robert Fisher Gibson Jr P 6/1/1965 Bp Samuel B Chilton. m 5/22/2004 Pamela Ann Palamountlin. S Lk's Ch Blackstone VA 2000-2004; S Ambroses Ch Raleigh NC 1995-2000; Vic Trin Ch Fuquay Varina NC 1994-2000; S Alb's Epis Ch Reading PA 1967-1981; Asst Min Ch Of The H Comf Richmond VA 1964-1967. gosewrite@verizon.net

GOSHERT, Mary Linda (Los) 882 Oxford Way, Benicia CA 94510 **Mem, Dioc Coun Dio Los Angeles Los Angeles CA 2004-** B Orange CA 1/4/1944 d Richard Edward Foster & Velma Lorene. BA California St U 1965; MLS California St U 1973; MDiv CDSP 1979. D 6/23/1979 P 2/1/1980 Bp Robert C Rusack. m 6/8/2011 Gene Ekenstam c 2. R S Ambr Par Claremont CA 2006-2011; R S Ptr's Par Santa Maria CA 2001-2006; The Par Ch Of S Lk Long Bch CA 1998-2001; Int Dio Los Angeles Los Angeles CA 1998-2000; S Ambr Par Claremont CA 1998; Stndg Com Dio El Camino Real Monterey CA 1992-1996; R S Jn The Div Epis Ch Morgan Hill CA 1989-1997; Deploy Off Dio Nthrn California Sacramento CA 1982-1989; R S Paul's Epis Ch Benicia CA 1982-1989; Cur Ch Of S Mart Davis CA 1979-1982. Auth, "Var arts Bk Revs Annuals". mlgoshert@aol.com

GOSHGARIAN, Martin John (Mass) 85 Glenwood Rd, Somerville MA 02145 B Boston MA 10/8/1940 s Serop Goshgarian & Ardemis. BA Harv

1962; MDiv VTS 1965. D 6/26/1965 P 5/19/1966 Bp John Melville Burgess. R S Jas Epis Ch Teele Sq Somerville MA 1973-1989; Asst S Cyp's Ch Roxbury MA 1969-1972; Asst S Steph's Memi Ch Lynn MA 1965-1969. margoshmass@verizon.net

GOSHORN, Alice Elizabeth Gill (Ind) 4921 E State Road 252, Franklin IN 46131 **Archd Dio Indianapolis Indianapolis IN 2004-; D S Thos Ch Franklin IN 1997-** B Needham IN 10/4/1941 d Ray Francis Gill & Ruth Crooke. BA Franklin Coll 1963; MA Penn 1965; Chr TS 1997. D 6/24/1997 Bp Edward Witker Jones. m 7/12/1971 Robyn Kent Goshorn c 1. Assn for Epis Deacons 1997. aggoshorn@embarqmail.com

GOSNELL, Linda (USC) 5 Southbridge Ct, Simpsonville SC 29680 **Asst R H Cross Epis Ch Simpsonville SC 2006-** B Spartanburg SC 6/22/1949 d Arnold Talmadge King & Dora Mae. BS Winthrop U 1971; MEd U of So Carolina 1977; MDiv VTS 2005. D 6/11/2005 P 5/24/2006 Bp Dorsey Felix Henderson. m 8/7/1971 Tandy Cleveland Gosnell c 1. Asst S Fran Ch Greenville SC 2005-2006. lindakgos@yahoo.com

GOSS, Alva Joe (CFla) 315 S Mary St, Eustis FL 32726 B McAlpin FL 2/16/1942 s Alva Otis Goss & Dorothy Cornelia. Florida St U; U Of Florida; AA Lake City Cmnty Coll 1967; MDiv TESM 1992. D 6/9/1979 Bp William Hopkins Folwell P 6/1/1992 Bp John Wadsworth Howe. m 11/20/1965 Marlise E Calhoun c 2. Vic/R Ch Of The Adv Dunnellon FL 1992-2008; D S Thos Epis Ch Eustis FL 1979-1992. ajoegoss@yahoo.com

GOSS, Frank Michael (NJ) Po Box 1, Bradley Beach NJ 01/01/7720 **R S Jas Ch Bradley Bch NJ 2004-** B Montclair NJ 10/29/1947 s Frank Arthur Goss & Theresa Marie. BA Seton Hall U 1969; MDiv Seton Hall Univ. Immac Concep Sem. So. Orange NJ 1975. Rec from Roman Catholic 5/17/1997 Bp John Shelby Spong. m 7/1/1995 Roseann M McArdle. R S Lk's Ch Phillipsburg NJ 1998-2004; Asst P S Jas Ch Upper Montclair NJ 1997-1998. randfgoss@optimum.net

GOSS III, James Paul (Cal) 792 Penny Royal Ln, San Rafael CA 94903 B Boston MA 6/12/1951 s James Paul Goss & Alice Cordelia. BA San Francisco St U 1974; BA Epis Dio Sch for Diac 1997; MS Dominican U CA San Rafael CA 2003. D 6/7/1997 Bp William Edwin Swing. D Ch Of The Nativ San Rafael CA 1999-2001; Chr Ch Sausalito CA 1998-2000. Cherokees of California 2004; Marin Amer Indn Assn 2002; Prison Bible Stds 1991-2007; Psi Chi (Psychol hon Soc) 2000. Dr. Robert Skukraft Awd for Inspirational Ldrshp Dominican U 2003. revjpg3@pacbell.net

GOSSARD, Jaclyn Glasgow (Kan) 148 N Fountain St, Wichita KS 67208 B Wichita KS 11/20/1933 d Clayton Buhford Glasgow & Marjorie. K SU; U CO; USC. D 11/1/1984 Bp Richard Frank Grein. m 8/6/1953 Oscar S Gossard c 4. D S Jas Ch Wichita KS 1984-1987. Ord Of S Lk, Dok; Sprtl Dir Intl . gus@infionline.net

GOSSETT JR, Earl Fowler (Ala) 1811 Cedar Crest Rd, Birmingham AL 35214 B Birmingham AL 1/28/1933 s Earl Fowler Gossett & Clara May. BA Birmingham-Sthrn Coll 1954; BD Van 1957; PhD Van 1961. D 5/27/1998 Bp Robert Oran Miller P 12/1/1998 Bp Henry Nutt Parsley Jr. m 7/17/1956 Rhoda Lois Scoates c 1. Int Trin Epis Ch Bessemer AL 2001-2002; S Jn's Ch Birmingham AL 1999-2000. "Angl Essentials," Alabam Dioc Cathecism, 2005; "The Challenge Of The The Orth Theol Of Rowan Williams," The Apos, 2002; "Our Hostiric Connections - Our Common Mssn," The Apos, 2001. AAR; Soc For Chr Ethics. Phi Beta Kappa.

GOSSLING, Nancy (Ct) 25 Chapman Dr, Glastonbury CT 06033 **R S Jas Ch Glastonbury CT 2002-** B Boston MA 2/19/1952 d Albion Keith Eaton & Louise Lambert. BA Wellesley Coll 1974; MDiv Ya Berk 2000. D 6/10/2000 Bp Andrew Donnan Smith P 1/13/2001 Bp James Elliot Curry. m 6/8/1974 Paul Gossling c 2. Cur S Paul's Ch Riverside CT 2000-2002. ngossling@sbcglobal.net

GOTCHER, Vernon Alfred (FtW) 1904 Westcliff Dr, Euless TX 76040 B Little Rock AR 7/21/1932 s Vernon Alfred Gotcher & Irma Sowell. BA U Of Cntrl Arkansas Conway 1954; MDiv STUSo 1957; ThM TCU 1975; PhD Texas Wmn's U-Denton 1984. D 7/3/1957 P 3/19/1958 Bp Robert Raymond Brown. m 6/20/1981 Deanna D Porter c 3. S Alb's Epis Ch Arlington TX 1996-1998; All SS' Epis Ch Ft Worth TX 1993-1995; All SS' Epis Ch Ft Worth TX 1991-1993; R S Steph's Ch Huntsville TX 1988-1991; St Stephens Ch Hurst TX 1969-1979; Vic S Steph's Ch Huntsville TX 1969-1974; Mssnr Dio Dallas Dallas TX 1965-1969; R S Lk's Brinkley AR 1961-1965; Vic Chr Ch Mena AR 1957-1961; R Trin Ch Van Buren AR 1957-1961. Auth, "Concepts Of Personality In Ta Of Berne & Harris As Related To Augustinian Doctor Of Man"; Auth, "Mar/Fam Therapists: Clincal Roles & Ther Outcome Expectations"; Auth, "Mar/Fam Therapists: Clincl Roles & Ther Outcome Expectations". Amer Assn Of Mar And Fam Therapists 1974; Tamft 1978. R Emer St Stpehens Hurst Tx 2004. dvgotch@msn.com

GOTKO, Raymond Morgan (At) 501 Sweet Berry Drive, Mont Eagle TN 37356 B Parris Island SC 10/27/1939 s Raymond Francis Gotko & Kate Lee. BFA U GA 1961; MFA U GA 1963; PhD Florida St U 1972; MDiv STUSo 1990. D 6/5/1999 Bp Onell Asiselo Soto P 12/11/1999 Bp Frank Kellogg Allan. m 9/5/1964 Lynda Rodgers c 2. Assoc R S Jas Epis Ch Marietta GA 2002-2009; R S Andr's Epis Ch Ft Vlly GA 1999-2002. rgotko@gmail.com

GOTT, Amanda Katherine (Ct) 150 Haverford St, Hamden CT 06517 **R Gr And S Ptr's Epis Ch Hamden CT 2009-** B Atlanta GA 7/2/1974 d Walter Edward Gott & Marcia Anne. BA Bard Coll 1996; MDiv Iliff TS 2001; STM GTS 2005. D 6/11/2005 Bp Robert John O'Neill P 12/13/2005 Bp V Gene Robinson. m 6/10/2006 Steven Carpenter c 1. Asst Ch Of The Gd Shpd Nashua NH 2005-2009. Auth, "A Bowl of Figs," *Alive Now. (March/April 2005)*, Upper Room Press, 2005. rectorgasp@gmail.com

GOTT, Jayne C(airns) (Oly) 176 Sunland Dr, Sequim WA 98382 **D S Lk's Ch Sequim WA 2000-** B Independence MO 8/9/1930 d Ferguson Dean Cairns & Fava Ruth. AA Shoreline Cmnty Coll 1982; Cert TS Dio Olympia 1998. D 6/24/2000 Bp Sanford Zangwill Kaye Hampton. m 5/15/1949 Charles Lawrence Gott c 2. D S Andrews Epis Ch Port Angeles WA 2000-2004. NAAD 2000-2006. jlclgott@olypen.com

GOTTARDI-LITTELL, Laura E (Chi) Church of Our Saviour, Chicago IL 60614 **Asst Ch Of Our Sav Chicago IL 2009-** B Morristown NJ 10/13/1969 d Joseph F Littell & Eleanor Jean. Bachelor of Arts Antioch Coll 1982; Mstr of Div Garrett-Evang TS 1996; Cert in Advncd Theol Stds SWTS 2005. D 6/3/2006 P 12/16/2006 Bp William Dailey Persell. m 5/23/1986 Numa Gottardi c 2. Lloyd Mentzer Awd SWTS 2005; Cert of Caring NW Cmnty Hosp 1997; Sprt Awd Luth Gnrl Hosp 1996; ABS Prize Garrett-Evang TS 1994; Hutchinson Fllshp Garrett-Evang TS 1993. numandlaura@comcast.net

GOTTLICH, Samuel Grier (WTex) 5857 Timbergate Dr., Corpus Christi TX 78414 B Corpus Christi TX 9/3/1929 s Samuel Gottlich & Ruth Elizabeth. Del Mar Coll 1951; MDiv VTS 1967; VTS 1980; U So 1988. D 7/12/1967 Bp Everett H Jones P 1/1/1968 Bp Richard Earl Dicus. m 4/14/1952 Diane P Prude c 3. Dir Pstr Serv Guadalupe Vlly Hosp Seguin TX 1990-1996; R S Barth's Ch Corpus Christi TX 1973-1989; R S Andr's Epis Ch Seguin TX 1968-1973; Vic Epiph Epis Ch Raymondville TX 1967-1968; Asst R S Jn's Ch McAllen TX 1967-1968. Auth, "Fr It Hurts-The Subject of Pain," 1999; Auth, "I Jn," *Take You Mary*, 1969. Paul Harris Fell Rotary Intl 1992; Citizen of Year Seguin, Texas 1989. sgottlich@satx.rr.com

GOUGH JR, H(erbert) Frederick (SC) Po Box 804, Darlington SC 29540 **R S Barn Ch Dillon SC 2008-** B Knoxville TN 5/3/1941 s Herbert Frederick Gough & Jessie. BA U Of Chattanooga 1967; MDiv VTS 1972; Cert S Geo's Coll, Jerusalem (Isr.) 1980; Cert US Army War Coll 1990. D 6/25/1972 Bp John Vander Horst P 5/19/1973 Bp William Evan Sanders. m 8/6/1986 Catherine Hill Baker c 1. R S Matt's Epis Ch Darlington SC 1996-2007; R S Barn Ch Dillon SC 1982-1996; Assoc Emm Epis Ch Athens GA 1980-1982; R S Paul's Epis Ch Clinton NC 1976-1980; Vic S Mk's Ch Copperhill TN 1973-1976; D-In-Trng H Trin Ch Memphis TN 1972-1973. Knight Grand Off, Imperial Ord Of The Star Of Ethiopia Crown Coun Of Ethiopia 2000; Sr Chapl Ord Of S Lazarus Of Jerusalem 2000; Knight Grand Cross Ord Of S Stanislas Poland 1994; Sc Medal Merit Sc St Guard 1993. FGOUGH@SC.RR.COM

GOUGH, Karen E (WNY) 315 Oakbrook Dr, Williamsville NY 14221 **Vic Trin Ch Lancaster NY 2006-** B Toronto ON CA 3/30/1952 d James Vernon Stockman & Kathleen Joan. BS U Tor 1975; MA Chr-King Sem E Aurora NY 1989; Cert Sis of Mercy Hosp Buffalo NY 1989; LSS Sis of Charity Hosp Buffalo NY 1990; Sis of Charity Hosp Buffalo NY 1992; Sloan-Kettering Memi Hosp New York NY 1992. D 6/10/1989 Bp David Charles Bowman P 1/31/2004 Bp J Michael Garrison. m 6/8/1974 Kenneth Harold Gough c 2. S Paul's Epis Ch Harris Hill Williamsville NY 2004-2006; Assist. Dir of Pstr Care Epis Ch Hm Buffalo NY 1999-2000; Archd Dio Wstrn New York Tonawanda NY 1993-1996; D S Paul's Epis Ch Harris Hill Williamsville NY 1989-1999. "On Guard Against Greed," *Sermons that Wk, Vol. XIV*, Morehouse Pub, 2006; "The Outcast," *Wmn Uncommon Prayers*, Morehouse Pub, 2000; "Marjorie," *Wmn Uncommon Prayers*, Morehouse Pub, 2000; "September Morning," *Wmn Uncommon Prayers*, Morehouse Pub, 2000. Assembly Of Epis Hlth Care Chapl 1990; ACPE. kareneg@adelphia.net

GOUGH, Lauren A (FtW) 3733 Whitefern Dr., Fort Worth TX 76137 **Asstg P S Mart In The Fields Ch Keller TX 2011-** B Peoria IL 10/26/1944 d Robert William Gough & Naomi Lorene. BA U of No Texas 1967; MDiv EDS 1983; CDSP 2001. D 6/11/1983 Bp Ned Cole P 5/28/1984 Bp O'Kelley Whitaker. R S Paul's Ch Endicott NY 2002-2004; R All SS Epis Ch Watsonville CA 1999-2001; R S Jn's Ch Ft Washington MD 1988-1997; R S Ann's Ch Afton NY 1984-1988; R S Ptr's Ch Bainbridge NY 1984-1988; Cur S Jn's Ch Ithaca NY 1983-1984. Auth, "Calendar of SS," *ABS Online Devotions*, ABS, 2007. EWC 1979; WECA 1988-1997. revlagough@aol.com

GOULD, Glenn Hamilton (USC) 30 Moise Dr, Sumter SC 29150 B Miami FL 2/23/1944 s Raymond F Gould & Leonore. Duke 1963; BA Furman U 1970; MDiv STUSo 1976. Trans 2/23/2004 Bp Michael Bruce Curry. m 4/26/1986 Fran Carson Crawford c 2. S Mk's Epis Ch Huntersville NC 1985-1996; R S Alb's Ch Lexington SC 1984-1985; Vic S Alb's Ch Lexington SC 1978-1983; Epis Ch Of S Simon And S Jude Irmo SC 1978; Dio Upper So Carolina Columbia SC 1976-1978.

GOULD, Jane Soyster (Mass) 19 Nahant Pl, Lynn MA 01902 **P-in-c S Steph's Memi Ch Lynn MA 2000-** B Washington DC 5/19/1956 d Peter Soyster & Eliza Cochran. BA Stan 1978; MA Stan 1979; MDiv EDS 1986. D 6/4/1986 Bp John Bowen Coburn P 5/28/1987 Bp David Elliot Johnson. m 7/10/1982 John Allen Gould c 2. Dio Massachusetts Boston MA 1994-2001; Epis City Mssn Boston MA 1993-1994; Assoc Gr Ch Lawr MA 1991-1994; Asst Par Of The Epiph Winchester MA 1986-1990. Auth, "On Engr And Evang," *Disorganized Rel*, Cowley, 1998; Auth, "Redeeming Imperialism," *Journ Of Wmn Mnstrs*, 1997; Auth, "Weaving The Wrld Together," *Epis Times*, 1996; Auth, "My Sis Struggle To Survive," *Journ Of Wmn Mnstrs*, 1995; Auth, "Cracking Walls And Opening Eyes: Remembering The Washington Four," *Wit*, 1994. ESMHE; EUC; EWC. Barbara C. Harris Awd for Soc Justice Epis City Mssn/ Boston 2008; Cler Renwl Grant Lilly Fndt/Indiana 2005; Kellogg Natl Fllshp Prog WKKellogg Fndt/Michigan 1993. jgould@ststephenslynn.org

GOULD, Jennie Ruth (NH) 32 Templeton Pkwy, Watertown MA 02472 B San Francisco CA 8/8/1963 d Hugh Jay Gould & Ruth Ann. MDiv EDS 1996; PhD Bos 2004. D 6/11/2005 P 12/15/2005 Bp V Gene Robinson. jennie.gould@bmc.org

GOULD, Mary Dolores (Oly) Po Box 1193, Maple Valley WA 98038 B Brunswick GA 11/15/1946 d John William Latham & Irma Elvira. Cert Dioc TS 1990; Cert CPE 1992. D 11/12/1993 Bp Vincent Waydell Warner. m 12/11/1982 Gerald Clark Gould c 2. D S Mk's Cathd Seattle WA 2002-2003; D S Geo Epis Ch Maple Vlly WA 1999-2000; D Gd Samar Epis Ch Sammamish WA 1993-1998. NAAD. margou@sosnet.com

GOULD, Robert Carwyle (NCal) 2528 Clearlake Way, Sacramento CA 95826 **Assoc S Geo's Ch Carmichael CA 2010-** B Vallejo CA 12/18/1919 s Jesse Amasa Gould & Alice Gibbons. BA California St U (Fresno) 1949; BD CDSP 1949. D 6/4/1949 P 12/17/1949 Bp Sumner Walters. m 3/17/1945 Betty Creer Hawkins c 4. Assoc S Matt's Epis Ch Sacramento CA 1982-1986; R S Jn The Evang Ch Chico CA 1961-1966; R S Barn Par McMinnville OR 1960-1961; R S Lk's Epis Ch Merced CA 1954-1960; Vic S Phil's Ch Coalinga CA 1949-1954; Vic S Thos Ch Avenal CA 1949-1954. banjobobg@yahoo.com

GOULDTHORPE JR, Samuel Foster (SVa) Po Box 636, Dahlgren VA 22448 B Casa Nova VA 2/20/1929 s Samuel Foster Gouldthorpe & Edith Allan. BA Bridgewater Coll 1954; MDiv VTS 1957. D 6/7/1957 P 6/14/1958 Bp Frederick D Goodwin. m 6/7/1958 Alice Bruce Payne c 3. R Calv Ch Bath Par Dinwiddie VA 1989-1996; R Ch Of The Gd Shpd Bath Par Mc Kenney VA 1989-1996; Comp Dio Com Dio Sthrn Virginia Norfolk VA 1988-1996; Dioc Pension Com Dio Sthrn Virginia Norfolk VA 1987-1996; Chair, Cmsn on Aging Dio Sthrn Virginia Norfolk VA 1982-1989; R H Trin Prot Epis Ch Onancock VA 1980-1989; R Chr Ch Wm And Mary Newburg MD 1975-1977; R Chr Ch Port Tobacco Paris La Plata MD 1970-1980; Pstr S Mk's Ch Alexandria VA 1965-1970; R S Geo's Ch Pungoteague Accomac VA 1960-1965; S Lk's Historic Shrine Smithfield VA 1960-1965; Asst S Mary's Ch Colonial Bch VA 1957-1958. samandbrucie@verizon.net

GOWEN, Eleanore Louise (Mass) 12 Hobart Ln, Rockland MA 02370 **D S Lk's Epis Ch Scituate MA 1994-** B 7/24/1937 d Thomas W Evans & Grace E. BS Estrn Connecticut St U 1969; MA U of Connecticut 1972; PhD U of Connecticut 1980; DMin EDS 1999. D 5/14/1994 Bp Charles Jones III. Asst S Fran Epis Ch Great Falls MT 1994-1998. egowbos@aol.com

GOWETT, Randall James (EpisSanJ) 1224 E Sample Ave, Fresno CA 93710 **D & Asst To Vic Ch Of The Resurr Clovis Clovis CA 1996-** B Brawley CA 8/11/1951 s Charles Francis Gowett & Dorothy June. San Jose St U; BS U of Phoenix 1991; MDiv TESM 1995. D 6/8/1996 Bp John-David Mercer Schofield. m 10/27/1990 Tamberlin Rachel Spencer.

GOWING, Michael LeVern (Mich) 2696 Indian Trl, Pinckney MI 48169 B Detroit MI 7/6/1937 s Clifford Rife Gowing & Wanda. BA Trin 1959; STB Ya Berk 1963; MA Wayne 1969. D 6/29/1963 Bp Richard S M Emrich P 1/25/1964 Bp Archie H Crowley. Asst S Thos Ch Trenton MI 1964-1967.

GOWLAND, James David (NJ) 11 N Monroe Ave, Wenonah NJ 08090 B Philadelphia PA 10/25/1946 s Edmund Gowland & Mary. D 6/9/2007 Bp George Edward Councell. m 7/2/2007 Janice Gowland c 2. jjgowland@comcast.net

GOWTY, Richard Newton (Tex) No address on file. B Melbourne VIC AU 10/2/1943 s William James Gowty & Nita. Royal Melbourne Inst Of Tech 1963; BTh S Fran Theol Coll 1971. Rec 6/1/1992 as Priest Bp Maurice Manuel Benitez. m 8/4/1972 Margaret Ann Gibson. Assoc R S Dav's Ch Austin TX 1992-1994.

GRAB, Virginia Lee (NY) 74 Montgomery St, Tivoli NY 12583 **Asst Ch Of S Jn The Evang Red Hook NY 2001-** B Los Angeles CA 10/10/1937 d Charles Mattox & Celia. BA U CA 1962; MA Col 1965; MDiv UTS 1991. D 3/18/2000 P 9/16/2000 Bp Richard Frank Grein. c 2. Int Zion Epis Ch Wappingers Falls NY 2005; The Living Pulpit Bronx NY 2001-2005. ggrab@frontiernet.net

GRABHER, Jerald (WMo) 4635 Campbell St, Kansas City MO 64110 B 11/29/1935 D 8/28/2002 Bp Barry Robert Howe.

GRABINSKI, Kenneth Lee (Oly) 5240 46th Ave Sw, Seattle WA 98136 B 7/30/1935 D 7/14/1977 Bp Robert Hume Cochrane. m 8/24/1957 Jane Elizabeth Benson c 3.

GRABNER, John David (Spok) 165 SW Spruce St, Apt 1, Pullman WA 99163 **Supply P Dio Spokane Spokane WA 2003-** B Coeur D'Alene ID 10/7/1940 s Floren Alden Grabner & Ivy Beth. BA U of Washington 1963; MA U of Washington 1971; MDiv PrTS 1974; MA U of Notre Dame 1978; PhD U of Notre Dame 1983. D 4/18/1998 P 10/17/1998 Bp Frank Jeffrey Terry. m 6/21/1975 Sharon Marie Lightle c 2. P Assoc S Mk's Epis Ch Moscow ID 1998-2003. Auth, "All SS' Day," *Homily Serv*, Taylor and Fran Grp, 2010; Auth, "All Souls' Day," *Homily Serv*, Taylor and Fran Grp, 2010; Auth, "There Is No Memory," *Homily Serv*, Taylor and Fran Grp, 2010; Auth, "Reign of Chr-C," *Homily Serv*, Taylor and Fran Grp, 2010; Auth, "What Kind of King?," *Homily Serv*, Taylor and Fran Grp, 2010; Auth, "The Chr Use of the Seder, The Complete Libr of Chr Wrshp," *Libr of Chr Wrshp, vol 2*, Hendrickson Pub, 1995; Auth, "Triduum: Practical Considerations," *Reformed Liturg & Mus*, 1990; Auth, "The Priesthood of the Believing Cmnty," *Sacramental Life*, Ord of S Lk, 1988; Auth, "The Touch of Blessing," *Assembly*, Notre Dame Cntr for Pstr Liturg, 1987; Auth, "Ord and Lay: Them-Us or We?," *Wrshp*, 1980. No Amer Acad of Liturg 1975; Societas Liturgica 1975. fatherralph@msn.com

GRABNER-HEGG, Linnae Marie (ND) 1619 31st Ave S, Fargo ND 58103 B St. Louis Park MN 1/6/1960 d Duwayne Kent Grabner & Barbara Jean. D 5/10/2002 P 5/9/2003 Bp Andrew Hedtler Fairfield. m 10/17/1981 Barry Wayne Hegg c 3. D Geth Cathd Fargo ND 2002-2003. linnaegh@gmail.com

GRACE JR, Harry Tyler (WNY) 36 Parkside Ct, Buffalo NY 14214 **Vic S Mk's Ch Buffalo NY 2004-** B Philadelphia PA 9/17/1941 s Harry T Grace & Anne. BS Penn 1963; MDiv GTS 1970. D 6/27/1970 Bp William Foreman Creighton P 1/1/1971 Bp Stephen F Bayne Jr. m 6/2/1964 Kathryn Cragun c 2. R Ch Of All SS Buffalo NY 1986-2000; Int S Alb Epis Ch Cleveland Heights OH 1986; Assoc S Paul's Epis Ch Cleveland Heights OH 1984-1986; R Calv Epis Ch Jerome ID 1979-1984; R Trin Ch Buhl ID 1979-1984; Assoc Calv Epis Ch Flemington NJ 1977-1978; R Hse Of Pryr Epis Ch Newark NJ 1973-1976; Cur Gr Ch White Plains NY 1970-1973. htg385@gmail.com

GRACE, Holt B (Minn) 215 4th St N, Stillwater MN 55082 **Ch Of The Ascen Stillwater MN 2010-** B Waynesboro VA 6/7/1968 s Holt Buff Grace & Suzanne C. BA U NC 1991; MDiv STUSo 2007. D 12/21/2006 P 8/11/2007 Bp J(ohn) Neil Alexander. m 7/29/1995 Amy L Amy Louise Shmitt c 2. R S Teresa Acworth GA 2007-2010. buffgrace@gmail.com

GRACE SR, James McKay Lykes (Tex) 6167 Olympia Dr, Houston TX 77057 **Cn Chr Ch Cathd Houston TX 2010-** B Houston TX 7/11/1975 s R Randall Grace & Jean Lykes. BA SW U Georgetown TX 1998; MDiv VTS 2005. D 6/11/2005 P 12/12/2005 Bp Don Adger Wimberly. m 1/3/2004 Marla Huseman Grace c 3. Asst Ch Of The Epiph Houston TX 2005-2010; Yth Dir Trin Ch Houston TX 1999-2002. COM 2007. jgrace@christchurchcathedral.org

GRACE, Patricia M. (At) 4753 Scepter Way, Knoxville TN 37912 **Assoc for Chr Ed. & Par Life S Lk's Epis Ch Atlanta GA 2006-** B Trenton NJ 10/1/1955 BA Buc. D 5/29/2004 P 1/8/2005 Bp Charles Glenn VonRosenberg. Cur St Jas Epis Ch at Knoxville Knoxville TN 2004-2006. pat@stmarksdalton.org

GRACELY, Carl Bartlett (Cal) 2225 Pine Knoll Dr Apt 2, Walnut Creek CA 94595 **Died 2/8/2011** B Cincinnati OH 8/29/1909 s William Nast Gracely & Grace Ingles. BA U Cinc 1933. D 4/24/1971 P 10/10/1971 Bp Alfred L Banyard. c 3. Hon Cn Gr Cathdral San Francisco 1989.

GRACEN, Sharon Kay (Ct) 1109 Main St, Branford CT 06405 **R Trin Ch Branford CT 2010-** B Savannah GA 7/4/1951 d Robert W Ballard & Jane Theresa. BD Indiana U 1997; MDiv SWTS 2000. D 6/24/2000 P 6/23/2001 Bp Catherine Elizabeth Maples Waynick. m 2/2/2007 Peter Appleton Schuller c 2. Vic Faith Epis Ch Laguna Niguel CA 2004-2010; The Amer Cathd of the H Trin Paris 75008 FR 2002-2004; Asst Chr Ch Cranbrook Bloomfield Hills MI 2000-2001. "Le Bon Dieu Aussi S'habille en Prada," Presses de la Renaissance, 2007. sgracen@hotmail.com

GRACEY, Colin Beal (Mass) 18 Monmouth Ct, Brookline MA 02446 B Newton MA 5/10/1935 s Ernest James Gracey & Edna. BA Ya 1957; STB Harvard DS 1963; DMin EDS 1984. D 7/22/1963 Bp Anson Phelps Stokes Jr P 5/1/1964 Bp Donald J Campbell. m 6/10/1957 Susan Gracey c 4. Dio Massachusetts Boston MA 1966-2004; Cur Trin Ch Concord MA 1963-1966. Auth, "Gd Genes?: Emerging Values For Sci," *Rel & Soc*. Parson Club, ESMHE, Nacuc.

GRADY, Ann Nadine (Mil) 11 S Church St, Elkhorn WI 53121 B Minot ND 1/25/1951 d Grover Quention Grady & Winifred. BA U of Wisconsin 1974; MDiv Garrett Evang TS 1993; STM Nash 2000. D 7/22/2000 P 7/28/2001 Bp Roger John White. Chr Ch Montpelier VT 2010-2011; S Lk's Luth Ch Sullivan WI 2007-2008; S Jn In The Wilderness Elkhorn WI 2003-2007; P-in-c S Mary's Epis Ch Dousman WI 2001-2003. motherann@core.com

GRADY, Richard Charles (SwFla) 6985 Edgewater Cir, Fort Myers FL 33919 **Assoc R S Lk's Ch Ft Myers FL 2006-** B Rochester NY 7/4/1946 s Sylvester Grady & Lois E. BA Florida Memi Coll 1970; MDiv VTS 1999. D 6/13/1999

P 12/12/1999 Bp Stephen Hays Jecko. m 8/9/1971 Ella Marie Nairn c 2. COM Dio SW Florida Sarasota FL 2005-2011; Assoc R S Hilary's Ch Ft Myers FL 2002-2006; Eccl Crt Dio SW Florida Sarasota FL 2002-2005; Cmsn on Yth Dio Florida Jacksonville FL 1999-2001; Asst R S Mk's Ch Palatka FL 1999-2001; Vic S Mary's Ch Palatka FL 1999-2001. fathergrady@yahoo.com

GRAEBNER, Norman B (NC) Po Box 628, Hillsborough NC 27278 **Historiographed Dio No Carolina Raleigh NC 2007-; R S Matt's Epis Ch Hillsborough NC 1990-** B Ames IA 9/24/1951 s Norman Arthur Graebner & Laura. BA U of Virginia 1973; MDiv Duke 1976; PhD Duke 1984; CAS VTS 1985. D 4/21/1986 Bp Robert Whitridge Estill P 5/3/1987 Bp Frank Harris Vest Jr. m 11/24/2009 Chris A Payne c 1. Asst to R S Ptr's Epis Ch Charlotte NC 1986-1990. "Epis Ch and Race in 19th c. NC," Angl and Epis Hist, 2009. Bd Mem For The HSEC 2000-2006; Secy, HSEC 2006. stmattclergy@embarqmail.com

GRAFE, Robert Frederick (Ore) 8040 Sw Strowbridge Ct, Beaverton OR 97008 B Muscatine IA 4/1/1922 s Paul Frederick Grafe & Minnie Elizabeth. BS OR SU 1948; BD CDSP 1951. D 6/24/1951 P 12/21/1951 Bp Benjamin D Dagwell. c 2. P-in-c S Aug Of Cbury Ch Veronica OR 1992-2005; Int S Fran Of Assisi Epis Wilsonville OR 1991-1992; Asst Gr Memi Portland OR 1987-1991; S Barn Par Portland OR 1952-1987.

GRAFF, Donald T (Pa) 1434 Alcott St, Philadelphia PA 19149 B Pasadena CA 7/29/1944 s Donald Bradger Graff & Frances. BA California Wstrn U 1966; MDiv CDSP 1969. D 9/13/1969 P 3/21/1970 Bp Francis E I Bloy. m 11/16/1985 Betty Ecoff c 2. The Free Ch Of S Jn Philadelphia PA 1984-1990; Dio Pennsylvania Philadelphia PA 1976-1983; The Afr Epis Ch Of S Thos Philadelphia PA 1970-1976; Cur S Jn's Par San Bernardino CA 1969-1970. graff1434@aol.com

GRAHAM IV, Alexander C (Pa) 338 Riverview Ave, Drexel Hill PA 19026 **R Incarn H Sacr Epis Ch Drexel Hill PA 2005-** B Wilmington DE 9/24/1972 s Alexander Coulter Graham & Barbara Ann. BMus U of Delaware Newark 1996; MDiv GTS 2003. D 1/18/2003 P 12/4/2003 Bp Wayne Parker Wright. m 12/22/1995 Heather Lynn Patton-Graham c 1. Asst R The Ch Of The H Trin W Chester PA 2003-2005. acgraham4@yahoo.com

GRAHAM, Carolyn Jane (Kan) 1107 W 27th Ter, Lawrence KS 66046 **D Trin Ch Lawr KS 1993-** B Kansas City MO 10/24/1934 d Robert Israel Farabee & Ruth Eleanor. BS U of Kansas 1970; MA U of Kansas 1976. D 10/27/1993 Bp William Edward Smalley. m 10/31/1975 Hillel Unz. Phi Beta Kappa U of Kansas. cjg@trinitylawrence.org

GRAHAM, Deborah Marie Therese (Ida) 555 37th St, Richmond CA 94805 B Boise ID 9/7/1955 d Franklin Roosevelt Graham & Thelma Ruth. BS U of Idaho 1978; BS Boise St U 1994; MDiv CDSP 2008. D 6/29/2008 Bp Harry Brown Bainbridge III P 10/8/2009 Bp Brian James Thom. m 9/30/2005 Teresa Wood. debbie@listendeeply.org

GRAHAM III, Earnest Newt (SVa) 828 Kings Hwy, Suffolk VA 23432 **S Matt's Epis Ch Chesterfield VA 2010-** B Westminster CA 3/5/1970 s Earnest Newt Graham & Jeanette Elizbeth. Casper Coll 1991; U of Wyoming 1998; MDiv VTS 2001. D 5/24/2001 Bp Bruce Edward Caldwell P 12/29/2001 Bp Peter James Lee. m 8/5/2001 Shirley Elizabeth Smith c 1. S Fran Epis Ch Great Falls VA 2003-2007; Asst To The R/Cler Res Chr Ch Alexandria VA 2001-2003. EARLEYGRAHAM@AOL.COM

GRAHAM, H(arry) James (EMich) 534 Little Lake Dr., Ann Arbor MI 48103 B Springfield IL 8/22/1931 s Harry Pomeroy Graham & Ruth. BA Ken 1952; BD EDS 1957; MA Kent St U 1970. D 2/1/1958 P 9/17/1958 Bp Gordon V Smith. m 9/14/1957 Gail M Moore c 2. COM Dio Estrn Michigan Saginaw MI 1997-2001; Int S Christophers Epis Ch Grand Blanc MI 1991-1992; Int Gr Epis Ch Lapeer MI 1989-1990; COM Dio Michigan Detroit MI 1980-1984; P Trin Ashtabula OH 1967-1970; P S Tim's Epis Ch Perrysburg OH 1963-1967; Asst Trin Ch Concord MA 1960-1963; In-c All SS Epis Ch Storm Lake IA 1957-1960; In-c S Steph's Ch Spencer IA 1957-1960. hjgraham@att.net

GRAHAM, Joanne D (NJ) 30 Foxwood Run, Middletown NJ 07748 **Int S Gabr's Ch Douglassville PA 2010-** B New York NY 11/1/1941 d Charles W Wira & Johanna. BSW Georgian Crt Coll 1990; MDiv GTS 1997. D 5/20/2000 Bp David B(ruce) Joslin P 12/16/2000 Bp Paul Victor Marshall. c 4. S Ptr's Ch Perth Amboy NJ 2008-2009; S Mk's Ch Basking Ridge NJ 2006-2008; Dioc Coun Mem Dio New Jersey Trenton NJ 2005-2008; All SS Epis Ch Lakewood NJ 2005-2006; Intentional Int R H Comf Ch Rahway NJ 2003-2005; Dio New Jersey Trenton NJ 2002-2004; Pstr Eductr of Deacons Dio New Jersey Trenton NJ 2002-2004; Intentional Int R S Jn's Ch Salem NJ 2002-2003; Asst The Epis Ch Of The Medtr Allentown PA 2000-2002. revjoannag@aol.com

GRAHAM, John Kirkland (Tex) 6231 Ella Lee Ln, Houston TX 77057 **Assoc S Mart's Epis Ch Houston TX 1998-** B Shreveport LA 11/26/1937 s Frank Kirkland Graham & Lasca. BS Centenary Coll 1959; MD Tul 1963; MDiv Epis TS of The SW 1994; DMin SWTS 2001. D 6/25/1994 P 1/1/1995 Bp Maurice Manuel Benitez. m 6/4/1960 Patsy Stamps c 1. R Trin Ch Houston TX 1996-1998; S Matt's Ch Austin TX 1994-1996. Auth, "Graham Crackers & Milk," Abringdon, 2003; Auth, "Mold Me & Shape Me," Chosen Books, 1983. Amer Soc Of Plastic & Reconstructive Surgeons. john.k.graham@gmail.com

GRAHAM, John M. (WA) 1041 Wisconsin Ave. NW, Washington DC 20007 **R Gr Ch Washington DC 2004-** B Columbus OH 11/20/1954 s John Earl Graham & Doris. BA Ken 1976; MA U Chi 1977; MDiv VTS 1984. D 6/15/1984 P 12/1/1984 Bp James Winchester Montgomery. m 5/22/1982 Sakena F McWright. R Ch Of The Adv Chicago IL 1986-2004; Vic La Iglesia De Nuestra Senora De Las Americas Chicago IL 1986-2004; Ch Of The Adv Chicago IL 1984-1986; Dio Chicago Chicago IL 1984-1986.

GRAHAM, Julie Ann (Cal) 1104 Mills Ave, Burlingame CA 94010 **Assoc R/Chld S Paul's Epis Ch Burlingame CA 2006-** B Fort Worth TX 11/12/1961 d John B Graham & Deanna J. Texas Tech U 1981; BA U of New Mex 1985; MDiv CDSP 1990. D 6/30/1990 P 6/1/1991 Bp Terence Kelshaw. m 1/1/2001 Thomas Skillings. Coordntr - Yth & YA Mnstrs Dio California San Francisco CA 1995-2003; Assoc S Paul's Epis Ch Walnut Creek CA 1993-1995; CDSP Berkeley CA 1992-1993; Asst S Mths Epis Ch San Ramon CA 1992-1993; Asst S Steph's Epis Ch Orinda CA 1990-1992. Auth, "Yth Mnstry Acad Manual," Diocal, 1997; Auth, "Pstr Care W/Teenagers," *Resources w Yth & YA Mnstrs*, Epis Ch Cntr. Jgraham@stpaulsburlingame.org

GRAHAM JR, Lee (Fla) 1527 Parchment Cv, Tallahassee FL 32308 B Gainesville FL 8/2/1920 s Lee Graham & Marion Carr. BS U of Florida 1942; BD VTS 1948; LLD U of Alabama 1963. D 6/18/1948 Bp Frank A Juhan P 11/1/1948 Bp Edward Hamilton West. m 8/1/1945 Betty Thomas. Assoc R Calv Ch Memphis TN 1983-1991; R S Jn's Epis Ch Tallahassee FL 1964-1983; R S Lk's Epis Ch Birmingham AL 1951-1964; P S Jas' Epis Ch Port S Joe FL 1948-1951. Ed, *Florida Forth*, 1949. Coll of Preachers.

GRAHAM III, Robert Lincoln (Alb) 153 Billings Ave, Ottawa ON K1H 5K8 Canada B New York NY 12/14/1937 s Robert Lincoln Graham & Mary Hudson. BA Col 1960; BTh S Paul U 1989. D 5/24/1990 Bp John Baycroft P 7/1/1991 Bp David Standish Ball. m 10/1/1982 Joan E Leadbeater. Stndg Com Dio Albany Albany NY 1998-2005; R S Jn's Ch Massena NY 1995-2005; R S Phil's Ch Norwood NY 1991-1995; R Trin Ch Gouverneur NY 1991-1995; S Lawr Epis Mnstry Ogdensburg NY 1990-1995. geoghegan@rogers.com

GRAHAM, Suzanne Hope (NY) 279 Piermont Ave, Nyack NY 10960 **Mem, Ecum and Interfaith Cmsn Dio New York New York City NY 2008-** B Teaneck NJ 7/15/1943 M.A. Area Stds Sch of Oriental and Afr Stds, Lon 1974; M.Div. GTS 2006. D 3/11/2006 P 9/23/2006 Bp Mark Sean Sisk. m 12/29/1999 Kelsey Graham c 2. All SS Epis Ch Vlly Cottage NY 2009. shopegraham@verizon.net

GRAHAM, Timothy Harold (At) 4140 Clark St SW, Covington GA 30014 **Stndg Com Dio Atlanta Atlanta GA 2010-2012; Asst Sec Dioc Coun Dio Atlanta Atlanta GA 2008-; R Ch Of The Gd Shpd Covington GA 2000-** B Toccoa GA 12/15/1961 s Carl Harold Graham & Imogene. BBA U GA 1985; MDiv GTS 1996. D 6/8/1996 P 12/14/1996 Bp Frank Kellogg Allan. m 1/30/1999 Deana Kathryn Murphy c 3. Assoc S Mich's Ch Raleigh NC 1998-2000; Asst Emm Epis Ch Athens GA 1996-1998. timothyhgraham@gmail.com

GRAHAM, Wells Newell (CGC) 771 Simon Park Cir, Lawrenceville GA 30045 B Cynthiana KY 10/9/1938 s T Graham & Evelyn. BA Thos More Coll 1960; MDiv Nash 1963. D 6/1/1963 Bp William R Moody P 12/18/1963 Bp William Loftin Hargrave. m 12/28/1985 Mary Ruth Hair c 2. Int S Geo's Epis Ch Griffin GA 2003-2005; Int S Lk's Epis Ch Atlanta GA 2002-2003; Int Emm Epis Ch Athens GA 1999-2000; R S Lk's Epis Ch Mobile AL 1987-1999; Dio SW Florida Sarasota FL 1978-1987; R S Wlfd's Epis Ch Sarasota FL 1968-1977; P S Fran Of Assisi Ch Bushnell FL 1966-1968; P S Jn's Epis Ch Brooksville FL 1964-1968; Cur S Lk's Ch Ft Myers FL 1963-1964. rbxmary@aol.com

GRAHAM JR, William James (Neb) 607 Toluca Ave, Alliance NE 69301 B Oriskany NY 5/4/1945 s William James Graham & Doris Emma. B.Ch.E. Clarkson Coll of Tech 1967; MDiv EDS 1976; MS Chadron St Coll 1982. D 6/11/1977 Bp Lyman Cunningham Ogilby P 12/1/1977 Bp James Daniel Warner. m 12/23/1974 Kathryn Frances Lyon c 1. S Matt's Ch Allnce NE 1997; Vic S Andr's Ch Lincoln NE 1977-1978. "Meeting of Franciscans," *Franciscan Times*, TSSF, 1992. Tertiary of the Soc of S Fran 1974. wjgraham@bbc.net

GRAMBSCH, Mary Frances (NY) 20 Seaman Ave Apt 1k, New York NY 10034 **Zion Ch Dobbs Ferry NY 2011-; Ch Of The Gd Shpd New York NY 2009-; Assoc Par of Trin Ch New York NY 2007-** B New Orleans LA 9/28/1958 d Paul Victor Grambsch & Ada Elizabeth. BA Indiana U 1982; MDiv Ya Berk 1993. D 6/3/1995 P 12/9/1995 Bp Richard Frank Grein. m 3/8/2011 Terri Lucas. Pstr Team Epis Ch Of Our Sav New York NY 1995-2002; Port Mssnr Seamens Ch Inst Income New York NY 1993-2008. Berkeley Grad Soc, No Amer Maritime Mnstrs A 1993. marygrambsch@earthlink.net

GRAMLEY, Thomas S (Roch) 13 Prospect Ave, Canisteo NY 14823 B Hazleton PA 5/20/1944 s Malcolm Eugene Gramley & Edna Mae. BA Moravian Coll 1966; STB Ya Berk 1969; MSW Tul 1972; MHA/MPA NYU 1985. D 1/28/1989 P 12/9/1989 Bp William George Burrill. m 3/14/1975 Sharon Gabb c 3. R Tri-Par Mnstry Hornell NY 2006-2011; R S Jn's Ch Clifton Sprg NY

1999-2006; Int Trin Ch Rochester NY 1998-1999; Int S Mk's And S Jn's Epis Ch Rochester NY 1997; R S Jn's Ch Sodus NY 1991-1995; R S Jn's Ch Sodus NY 1990-1991; Asst Zion Epis Ch Palmyra NY 1989-1990. tsgramley1@yahoo.com

GRANDELL, Peter Frank (Pa) The Church Of The Crucifixion, 620 S 8Th St, Philadelphia PA 19147 **Dio Pennsylvania Philadelphia PA 2010-; Dn - Southwark Dnry Dio Pennsylvania Philadelphia PA 2009-; Ch Of The Crucif Philadelphia PA 2006-** B Brooklyn NY 7/19/1959 s Francis M Grandell & Ruta. BS Wag 1981; MDiv GTS 1995. D 6/3/1995 P 12/1/1995 Bp Richard Frank Grein. Mem Dioc Coun Dio Pennsylvania Philadelphia PA 2008-2011; Chair - Dioc Stwdshp Com Dio Pennsylvania Philadelphia PA 2006-2008; Cathd of St Ptr & St Paul Washington DC 1999-2004; Com on Liturg and Mus Dio Washington Washington DC 1999-2003; Com on Human Sxlty Dio New York New York City NY 1999-2001; S Jn's in the Woods Ch Randolph NY 1996; Asst To The Dn Cathd Ch Of S Paul Burlington VT 1995-1996. Asst Ed, "H Euch and AfterWord," *Hip Hop PB*, Ch Pub, 2006. P Assoc, Shrine of Our Lady of Walsingham 1997; The Ord of S Jn - Dir of Ceremonies, Amer Prio 2000. pgrandell@verizon.net

GRANER, James Frederick (WK) 401 Morris Ave, Larned KS 67550 B Kansas City MO 9/15/1928 s Carl Graner & Marialice. BA U of Missouri 1951; LTh STUSo 1966. D 9/21/1966 P 4/29/1978 Bp George Mosley Murray. m 4/7/1956 Anne LoBianco c 1. Supply P Ch Of The H Nativ Kinsley KS 1994-2006; Vic SS Mary And Martha Of Bethany Larned KS 1970-1994; Vic Ch Of The H Nativ Kinsley KS 1970-1981; Vic S Lk's Ch Scottsboro AL 1966-1970; Vic S Phil's Ch Ft Payne AL 1966-1970. *A Primer for the 21st Century Chr*, Publishamerica, 2006; *Musings of a Country Parson*, Trafford Pub Co, 2005; *Dr Lucifer's Lectures-The Art of Ldrshp and Control 101*, Trafford Pub Co, 2004. Angl Comm Ntwk 2005; FIFNA 1989-2001; SSC 1989. jgraner@sbcglobal.net

GRANFELDT SR, Robert Carl (Pa) 418 Shallowford Circle, Augusta GA 30907 B Detroit MI 6/6/1942 s Robert Charles Granfeldt & Matilda Teresa. BA Wayne 1967; MDiv GTS 1971. D 6/29/1970 Bp Richard S M Emrich P 1/22/1972 Bp Archie H Crowley. m 4/8/1961 Mary Elizabeth Rudick c 3. Calv Ch Glen Riddle PA 2000-2008; Int S Chris's Epis Ch Austin TX 1990-1991; R Emm Ch Quakertown PA 1984-1987; S Geo Mtyr Ch Tortola VG 1981-1984; R S Geo Sch Tortola 1981-1984; Episc. Chapl, Texas Tech Univ Dio NW Texas Lubbock TX 1978-1981; Episc. Chapl, Univ of Massachusetts - Amherst Dio Wstrn Massachusetts Springfield MA 1975-1978; S Helena's Epis Ch Lenox MA 1974-1975; Assoc Trin Par Lenox MA 1974-1975; Asst Min Chr Ch Detroit MI 1971-1973; Asst Min Epis Ch of The Resurr Williston Pk NY 1970-1971. ECAP 2000; ESMHE 1975-1982. frbob@granfeldt.com

GRANGER JR, Charles Irving (Okla) 305 E Douglas Dr, Midwest City OK 73110 B Cleveland OH 7/8/1943 s Charles Irving Granger & Myrtis Georgeanne. BS Ohio U 1965; Cert Bex 1971. D 6/26/1971 P 5/19/1972 Bp John Harris Burt. m 11/29/1986 Marcia L McClain c 3. R Epis Ch Of The Redeem Oklahoma City OK 2004-2006; Chapl S Fran Cmnty Serv Inc. Salina KS 2003-2004; Int All SS Ch S Louis MO 2002-2003; S Ptr's Ch Pittsburg KS 2001-2002; Int Trin Epis Ch Kirksville MO 1999-2001; R Ch Of The Medtr Harbert MI 1997-1999; R S Aug Of Cbury Epis Ch Benton Harbor MI 1997-1999; R S Aug's Ch Kansas City MO 1994-1997; R Epis Ch Of The H Fam Miami Gardens FL 1991-1994; Assoc S Phil's Ch New York NY 1988-1991; Cur S Lk's Epis Ch Bronx NY 1986-1988; Vic Ch Of The Resurr Ecorse MI 1982-1986; Vic Dio Michigan Detroit MI 1980-1981; R S Thos Ch Minneapolis MN 1976-1980; R Mssh-S Barth Epis Ch Chicago IL 1972-1974. cigranger2@sbcgloble.net

GRANGER, Nancy Whittemore (CFla) PMB #260-75 Main Street, Plymouth NH 03264 B Holyoke MA 6/8/1938 d Willis Homans Whittemore & Dorothy Wendell. BEd Plymouth St Coll 1959; Med Bos 1962; MA Springfield Coll Springfield MA 1965; CAS Springfield Coll Springfield MA 1965. D 12/14/2002 Bp John Wadsworth Howe. D H Trin Epis Ch Melbourne FL 2002-2004.

GRANT, Alan Walters (Minn) 4300 W River Pkwy S #327, Minneapolis MN 55406 B Seattle WA 3/1/1944 s Kenneth Grant & Helen Jeanne. BS OR SU 1967; MDiv CDSP 1970. D 6/29/1970 Bp James Walmsley Frederic Carman P 2/21/1971 Bp Hal Raymond Gross. m 8/21/1983 Helen Lovestedt c 2. Chapl Mercy Med Cntr Minneapolis MN 1990-2008; Chapl Chapl Serv Minneapolis MN 1976-1990; Cur Emm Ch Coos Bay OR 1970-1974. Assn Of Profsnl Chapl 1976. revawg@gmail.com

GRANT JR, Blount Hamilton (SeFla) 8500 Bluebonnet Blvd Apt 31, Baton Rouge LA 70810 B Rome GA 8/11/1933 s Blount Hamilton Grant & Lera Graham. U So 1953; BA U GA 1958; MDiv VTS 1962; U of Nottingham 1969. D 6/30/1962 P 6/2/1963 Bp Randolph R Claiborne. Pstr Assoc S Jas Epis Ch Baton Rouge LA 2002-2008; Dio SE Florida Miami FL 1994-2004; Trin Cathd Miami FL 1993-1996; S Fran-In-The-Keys Episcop Big Pine Key FL 1987-1992; Dio SE Florida Miami FL 1980-1984; R S Columba Epis Ch Marathon FL 1976-1993; R S Paul's Epis Ch Newnan GA 1969-1972; Assoc S Anne's Epis Ch Atlanta GA 1965-1968; Vic S Mich And All Ang Ch Stone Mtn GA 1962-1965. blnt@cox.net

GRANT, Elizabeth Wade (NC) 750 Weaver Dairy Rd Apt 176, Chapel Hill NC 27514 B South Bend IN 1/2/1926 d Roderic Paul Wade & Florence. BA Mt Holyoke Coll 1947; U Of Paris-Sorbonne Fr 1948; MA Harv 1951. D 6/17/1989 Bp Robert Whitridge Estill. c 2. Vision Com Dio No Carolina Raleigh NC 1997-1998; Stndg Com Dio No Carolina Raleigh NC 1993-1996; Chapl Duke Epis Cntr Durham NC 1989-2004. Soc Of S Jn The Evang. Durham Sustained Involvement Vol Of The Year No Carolina Gvnr 1995.

GRANT, Hugh McPhail (At) 15620 Riverside Dr. W Apt 13-i, New York NY 10032 **Assoc The Ch Of S Lk In The Fields New York NY 2008-** B Atlanta GA 7/14/1966 s Walter King Grant & Eleanor McPhail. BA Davidson Coll 1988; MSW U GA 1996; MTS Emory U 1997; MDiv The GTS 2008. D 12/21/2007 P 6/29/2008 Bp J(ohn) Neil Alexander. m 7/11/2009 Jose R Gandara-Perea. hughmgrant@gmail.com

GRANT, Joan Louise (Mont) 215 3rd Ave E, Kalispell MT 59901 **R Chr Epis Ch Kalispell MT 2010-** B Columbus OH 5/12/1952 d William Theodore Grant & Beverly D. AB Mia 1974; JD The OH SU Coll of Law 1978; MDiv Bex 2010. D 10/25/2003 P 6/19/2010 Bp Herbert Thompson Jr. c 2. joangrant33@hotmail.com

GRANT, John Alexander (Md) 115 N 2nd St, Oakland MD 21550 **R Emer S Matt's Par Oakland MD 1990-** B Oakland MD 2/27/1923 s William Wallace Grant & Patience Bruce. BD W Virginia U 1950; MDiv PDS 1963; PrTS 1986. D 7/28/1963 P 8/15/1964 Bp Noble C Powell. m 7/1/1950 Jean H Hess c 1. R S Matt's Par Oakland MD 1971-1975; Vic S Jn's Ch Oakland MD 1970-1990; Vic S Andr's Ch Pasadena MD 1964-1970; Cur H Trin Epis Ch Baltimore MD 1963-1964. Auth, "150 Years of Oakland," *Garrett Cnty Hist Soc*, 1999; Auth, "Coxey's 38-Day March," *Journ of the Alleghanies*, 1999; Auth, *Glades Star*. Garrett Cnty Hist Soc 1978. jgrant@mail.gcnet.net

GRANT, Priscilla (Percy) R (O) 2230 Euclid Ave., Cleveland OH 44115 **Cn for Mnstry Dio Ohio Cleveland OH 2007-** B Norwich VT 2/2/1961 d Joseph Lewis Grant & Mary. BA Sweet Briar Coll 1983; MDiv VTS 1992. D 6/11/1992 Bp Daniel Lee Swenson P 12/16/1992 Bp Peter James Lee. m Nan S Hunter. Dio Virginia Richmond VA 1999-2007; St. Steph's and St. Agnes Sch Alexandria VA 1996-1999; Asst S Andr's Ch Burke VA 1992-1995. pgrant@dohio.org

GRANT, Rebecca Ann (Me) 16 Alton Road, Apt 219, Augusta ME 04330 B Portland ME 9/13/1953 d William Gene Bickford & Sally Ann. BS U of Phoenix 2009; Masters U of Phoenix 2011. D 6/20/2009 Bp Stephen Taylor Lane. c 1. rebagrant@gmail.com

GRANT, Richard Ellard (Tex) 1701 Bimini Dr, Orlando FL 32806 **Ret, Asstg Cler Cathd Ch Of S Lk Orlando FL 2002-** B Gallup NM 4/2/1939 s Charles John Grant & Carlotta Violet. BA U of Texas-El Paso 1960; MA U of Texas-El Paso 1971; MDiv VTS 1981. D 6/20/1981 Bp George Nelson Hunt III P 3/22/1982 Bp Roger Howard Cilley. m 12/21/1963 Amy Phillips c 3. R S Thos Ch Wharton TX 1990-2002; R Epis Ch Of The H Sprt Waco TX 1987-1990; R S Paul's Ch Navasota TX 1984-1987; Asst All SS Epis Ch Stafford TX 1981-1984. AAC 1992; Anglicans for Life 1998; Ord of S Lk 1987. dick_amygrant@bellsouth.net

GRANT, Robert McQueen (Chi) 5807 S Dorchester Ave Apt 11-E, Chicago IL 60637 B Evanston IL 11/25/1917 s Frederick Clifton Grant & Helen McQueen. BA NWU 1938; BD UTS 1941; STM Harvard DS 1942; ThD Harvard DS 1944; DD SWTS 1969; DD Glasgow 1979; LHD Kalamazoo Coll 1979; DD CDSP 1992. D 6/3/1942 P 12/1/1942 Bp Henry Knox Sherrill. m 12/21/1940 Margaret Horton c 4. U Chi Chicago IL 1970-1983; P-in-c Ch Of The H Comf Monteagle TN 1944-1947; M-in-c S Jas Ch Groveland Groveland MA 1942-1944. Auth, "Var Books, arts," *Revs in Theol Journ*. DD CDSP 1992; DD Glasgow 1979; LHD Kalamazoo Coll 1979; DD SWTS 1969. rmgrant@midway.uchicago.edu

GRANT, Sandra Marceau (SC) 21 Cottonwood Ln, Hilton Head Island SC 29926 **D All SS Ch Hilton Hd Island SC 2005-** B Washington DC 6/24/1944 BA Harv 1965; PhD U of Connecticut 1971; MBA Ya 1984. D 9/10/2005 Bp Edward Lloyd Salmon Jr. m 5/20/1984 Kerry Grant. sandygrant@roadrunner.com

GRANTZ, Brian Glenn (NI) 117 N Lafayette Blvd, South Bend IN 46601 B Kittanning PA 8/17/1964 s Earl Gene Grantz & Janet Clare. BA Penn 1986; MDiv STUSo 1997. D 12/21/1996 P 6/21/1997 Bp Francis Campbell Gray. m 11/22/1986 Tamisyn Ford c 4. Chr Ch Slidell LA 2006-2008; The Cathd Ch Of S Jas So Bend IN 2006-2008; R S Anne's Epis Ch Warsaw IN 2000-2006; Cur S Anne's Epis Ch Warsaw IN 1997-1999. tamisyn@gmail.com

GRATER, Coval Theodore (Nwk) 2316 Lark Ln, Sarasota FL 34231 B Norristown PA 7/12/1918 s Walter Tyson Grater & Margaret May. U of Pennsylvania 1948; Tem 1956; Pennsylvania Diac Sch 1957. D 10/12/1957 Bp Joseph Gillespie Armstrong P 4/26/1958 Bp William P Roberts. m 6/30/1951 Barbara Singer. Ch Of The Sprt Alexandria VA 1986-1987; Hstr Dio Newark Newark NJ 1979-1983; Assessments & Quotas Com Dio Newark Newark NJ 1972-1981; R S Thos Ch Lyndhurst NJ 1967-1983; Ch of the Redeem Addison NY 1966-1967; Deptartment of Missions Dio Rochester Rochester NY 1964-1966; Reg Yth Advsr Dio Rochester Rochester NY 1963-1965; Vic Ch

Of The Gd Shpd Savona NY 1960-1967; Cur S Jn's Ch Norristown PA 1957-1960. Natl Epis Historians and Archivists 1970; The Angl Soc 1971.

GRATZ JR, L(ouis) Paul (Vt) 116 Morgan St Apt 1, Bennington VT 05201 **Int S Ptr's Epis Ch Bennington VT 2010-; Vic S Mk's-S Lk's Epis Mssn Castleton VT 2009-** B New York NY 6/25/1946 s Louis Paul Gratz & Jean. BA Alleg 1968; MDiv EDS 1971; MA W Virginia U 1976. D 6/25/1971 P 5/20/1972 Bp Harvey D Butterfield. m 6/7/2003 Susan Zouck c 2. Int Slate Vlly Mnstry Poultney VT 2003-2009; Int S Paul's Ch Steubenville OH 2001-2003; Int S Ptr's Epis Ch Butler PA 1999-2000; Assoc Gr Ch Pittsburgh PA 1994-1999; P S Barn Epis Ch Denton TX 1977-1978; P Dio W Virginia Charleston WV 1973-1977. lpgratz1@comcast.net

GRAUER, David Ernst (Chi) 808 S Seminary Ave, Park Ridge IL 60068 **D S Mary's Ch Pk Ridge IL 1989-** B Cincinnati OH 3/17/1927 s Gerhard W Grauer & Marie. BS NWU 1950; DDS U IL 1954; Chicago Deacons Sch 1989. D 12/2/1989 Bp Frank Tracy Griswold III. m 8/2/1952 Joan M Grauer c 2. Auth, *The Dentist & Temporomandibular Joint Disorders*, Clearvue, 1985; Auth, *Journ of the Academy of Gnrl Dentistry*, 1983; Auth, *Dental Journ*, 1980; Auth, *Dental Journ*, 1978. Amer Academy of Orofacial Pain 1993; Amer Academy of Pain Mgmt 2002; Amer Bd Orofacial Pain 1996. Mem Acad Oro-facial Pain; Omicron Kappa Upsilon; Dplma Amer Bd Orofacial Pain. dgrauerdds@aol.com

GRAUMLICH, Nancy Rice (O) 7815 Hedingham Rd, Sylvania OH 43560 **D All SS Epis Ch Toledo OH 1992-** B Toledo OH 8/15/1924 d Claude Bernard Rice & Mabel. BS Bowling Green St U 1947. D 11/13/1992 Bp James Russell Moodey. m 6/14/1947 Albert John Graumlich c 3. 75041.2670@compuserve.com

GRAUNKE, Kristine Helen (WTex) PO Box 68, Hebbronville TX 78361 **Vic S Jas Epis Ch Hebbronville TX 2009-** B Green Bay WI 8/11/1951 d Corbin Benjamen Graunke & Eleanor Pauline. BA U of Wisconsin 1973; MDiv Chicago TS 1978; TESM 1998. D 9/21/1998 Bp Francis Campbell Gray P 3/25/1999 Bp William Walter Wiedrich. m 6/30/1982 C(laude) Patrick Ormos c 1. S Barn-In-The-Dunes Gary IN 2008-2009; S Dav's Epis Ch San Antonio TX 2008-2009; S Andr's By The Lake Epis Ch Michigan City IN 2007; S Barn-In-The-Dunes Gary IN 2005-2007; S Paul's Epis Ch Munster IN 2000-2001; Intern S Anne's Epis Ch Warsaw IN 1999; Intern The Cathd Ch Of S Jas So Bend IN 1999. Assn of Profsnl Chapl 2006; Catechesis Gd Shpd; Epis Chapl Orgnztn 1995. khg.3@juno.com

GRAVATT, J Segar (SVa) 301 49th St, Virginia Beach VA 23451 **Assoc All SS' Epis Ch Virginia Bch VA 1999-** B Richmond VA 6/3/1949 d John Segar Gravatt & Isbell. BA Queens Coll 1971; MS U NC 1972; MDiv UTS Richmond VA 1984; Cert VTS 1985; DMin GTF 1997. D 5/20/1985 Bp C(laude) Charles Vache P 6/24/1999 Bp David Conner Bane Jr. S Aid's Ch Virginia Bch VA 2001-2002; D The Epis Ch Of The Adv Norfolk VA 1997-1999; D S Andr's Ch Norfolk VA 1995-1999; D All SS' Epis Ch Virginia Bch VA 1991-1995; Archd Dio Sthrn Virginia Norfolk VA 1990-1999; D S Paul's Ch Norfolk VA 1986-1991. AAPC 1988; ACPE 1984-2000; Assn of Profsnl Chapl 1988-2006. S Steph's Awd NAAD 1997. jgravatt4@cox.net

GRAVELLE III, Emery Francis (Mich) PO Box 4, Novi MI 48376 **Died 5/23/2011** B Sault Saint Marie MI 5/31/1940 s Emery Francis Gravelle & Edna Elva. BA Estrn Michigan U 1962; STB Ya Berk 1966. D 6/29/1966 Bp Archie H Crowley P 5/1/1967 Bp John Henry Esquirol. c 1. efgravelle@aol.com

GRAVES, Carol Carson (SeFla) 4341 Se Satinleaf Pl, Stuart FL 34997 B Newberry MI 10/10/1951 d Joseph Carson & Darlene. Montana St U; Dioc Sch of SE FL 2006. D 12/17/2006 Bp Leopold Frade. m 11/14/1987 Fielding Graves c 2. DOK 2000. graves@msn.com

GRAVES, Clayton Winn (SwFla) 3114 1/2 Prairie Ave, Miami Beach FL 33140 B Memphis TN 1/22/1928 s Leonard Harrison Graves & Lorraine Winn. BA Florida St U 1954; U So 1961; MDiv Nash 1969; Med Georgia St U 1973. D 7/1/1961 P 12/1/1962 Bp Albert R Stuart. m 2/2/1957 Constance Theodora McDaniel c 3. Vic S Mart's Ch Clewiston FL 1966-1967; Cur H Sprt Epis Ch W Palm Bch FL 1964-1966; Vic S Matt's Epis Ch Fitzgerald GA 1963-1964; D Ch Of The H Sprt Dawson GA 1961-1963; D H Trin Epis Ch Blakely GA 1961-1963.

GRAVES JR, Farrell Dean (Los) 257 Middle Rd, Sayville NY 11782 **S Ann's Ch Sayville NY 2010-** B High Point NC 12/16/1963 s Farrell Dean Graves & Delories Dennis. BA Duke 1986; PhD U CA 2004; MDiv The GTS 2010. D 6/12/2010 Bp Mary Douglas Glasspool P 12/18/2010 Bp Lawrence C Provenzano. fdgraves@hotmail.com

GRAVES, Jon C (Chi) 210 S McHenry Ave, Crystal Lake IL 60014 **S Mary Epis Ch Crystal Lake IL 2009-** B Lansing MI 12/6/1961 s John Richard Graves & Suzanne. BS U of Missouri 1984; MBA Thunderbird Glendale AZ 1986; MDiv Virginia Sem Alexandria VA 2007. D 6/2/2007 Bp Barry Robert Howe P 12/2/2007 Bp Frank Neff Powell. m 6/27/1992 Lisa Beyer Lisa Beyer c 2. Asst S Jn's Ch Roanoke VA 2007-2008. frchip@stmaryepiscopal.org

GRAVES JR, Leonard Roberts (CGC) 1302 E Avery St, Pensacola FL 32503 **chairman of Cmsn on prison Mnstry Dio Cntrl Gulf Coast Pensacola FL 2010-** B Norfolk VA 5/11/1938 s Leonard Roberts Graves & Margaret. BA VMI 1960; MDiv VTS 1963. D 6/20/1963 Bp George P Gunn P 6/27/1964 Bp David Shepherd Rose. m 1/14/1995 Jane Culwell c 3. chairman COM Dio Cntrl Gulf Coast Pensacola FL 2000-2001; Pres of Stndg Com Dio Cntrl Gulf Coast Pensacola FL 2000-2001; chairman Cmsn on Wrld Mssn Dio Cntrl Gulf Coast Pensacola FL 1998-2000; chairman of Cmsn on Yth Dio Cntrl Gulf Coast Pensacola FL 1997-1998; chairman of Cmsn on Educ Dio Cntrl Gulf Coast Pensacola FL 1995-1996; Assoc Chr Ch Par Pensacola FL 1984-2003; R Trin Epis Ch Martinsburg WV 1981-1984; Assoc S Lk's Epis Ch Birmingham AL 1976-1981; Assoc S Paul's Meml Charlottesville VA 1972-1976; R Emm Ch Virginia Bch VA 1965-1972; Asst S Paul's Ch Petersburg VA 1963-1965. GRAVES5924@BELLSOUTH.NET

GRAVES, Lisa Beyer (Chi) 290 Grove St., Crystal Lake IL 60014 **R S Phil's Epis Palatine IL 2009-** B Fort Stll OK 4/3/1967 d Robert Jean Beyer & Marilyn. BA Steph's Coll Columbia MO 1989; MDiv Virginia Sem 2007. D 6/2/2007 Bp Barry Robert Howe P 12/2/2007 Bp Frank Neff Powell. m 6/27/1992 Jon C Graves c 2. Chapl Cbury NW Evanston IL 2009; Asst S Jn's Ch Roanoke VA 2007-2008. revlgraves@gmail.com

GRAVES, Rena B (Pa) 5421 Germantown Ave, Philadelphia PA 19144 B 9/29/1920 D 6/15/1985 Bp Lyman Cunningham Ogilby. deaconrena29@aol.com

GRAVES, Richard W (Ia) 1247 7th Ave N, Fort Dodge IA 50501 **R Ch Of The Gd Shpd Webster City IA 2008-** B Boston MA 4/6/1950 s Harry Graves & Anne Guy. BA Idaho Coll 1972; MDiv CDSP 1976. D 6/17/1978 P 1/1/1979 Bp Robert C Rusack. c 3. R S Mk's Epis Ch Ft Dodge IA 2008; S Paul's Epis Ch Grinnell IA 1994-1996; R S Mk's Par Altadena CA 1985-1994; R S Barn' Epis Ch Los Angeles CA 1981-1985; Asst Min Trin Epis Ch Santa Barbara CA 1979-1981; The Par Ch Of S Lk Long Bch CA 1978-1979. ESMHE. stmarks50501@frontiernet.net

GRAVES, Robert Blice (SO) 3612 Fountain Dr Apt 3, Louisville KY 40218 B Cincinnati OH 4/15/1938 s Robert Edward Graves & Gladys Ruth. BA Bowling Green St U 1965; MDiv TS 1972; Coll of Preachers 1977. D 6/1/1972 Bp Addison Hosea P 12/9/1972 Bp Robert Bracewell Appleyard. c 2. Supply P Dio Kentucky Louisville KY 1985-1989; Asst (P-t) S Jn's Epis Ch Bowling Green OH 1981-1985; Liturg Cmsn Dio Sthrn Ohio Cincinnati OH 1980-1981; Lay Mnsrty Strng Com, criminal justice commsn Dio Sthrn Ohio Cincinnati OH 1978-1981; R Gr Ch Pomeroy OH 1978-1981; Asst S Andr's Ch Downers Grove IL 1976-1978; Dio Pittsburgh Monroeville PA 1972-1976; Asst S Dav's Epis Ch Venetia PA 1972-1976. EvangES 1973-1984.

GRAY, Bruce Alan (Va) 8525 Burgundy Rd, Richmond VA 23235 **Assoc S Andr's Ch Richmond VA 2008-** B Troy NY 5/17/1940 s C Wellington Gray & Dorothy F. Bates Coll 1960; BA Syr 1963; MDiv EDS 1966; DMin VTS 1984. D 6/11/1966 Bp Allen Webster Brown P 12/14/1966 Bp Charles Bowen Persell Jr. m 6/29/1962 Katherine A Lowther c 2. P S Jn's Ch Richmond VA 1997-2007; Trin Ch Fredericksburg VA 1996-1997; Int Ch Of The H Comf Richmond VA 1994-1996; S Paul's Epis Par Point Of Rocks MD 1994; S Alb's Epis Ch Annandale VA 1987-1994; R S Andr's Epis Ch Albany NY 1976-1987; R S Mk's Ch Malone NY 1967-1975; Asst Min S Ptr's Ch Albany NY 1966-1967. Auth, "A Fire Chapl'S Manual," New York St Assn Of Fire Chapl. bag_kag@verizon.net

GRAY, Bruce William (Ind) Episcopal Diocese of Indianapolis, 1100 W 42nd St, Indianapolis IN 46208 **Cn to the Ordnry Dio Indianapolis Indianapolis IN 2009-** B Sacramento CA 1/26/1960 s Wayne David Gray & Elise. BA U CA 1982; MDiv SWTS 1985. D 6/22/1985 P 12/21/1985 Bp Charles Brinkley Morton. m 9/30/2001 Cathy Jean (Testa-Avila) Gray c 4. R S Mths' Par Whittier CA 1998-2009; R The Epis Ch Of The Gd Shpd Hemet CA 1990-1998; Vic S Jn's Ch Washington IN 1987-1990; Cur Chr Ch Coronado CA 1985-1987. brucewgray@yahoo.com

GRAY, Calvin (Colo) 1625 Larimer Street #2501, Denver CO 80202 B Flushing NY 12/30/1934 s Robert Gray & Catherine. BA Barrington Coll 1959; STB NYTS 1963; ThM NYTS 1963; PrTS 1970; Fuller TS 1983; U of Nthrn Colorado 1990. D 6/7/1997 P 9/8/1999 Bp William Jerry Winterrowd. m 10/17/1953 Gloria L Anderson c 3. R S Jas Epis Ch Wheat Ridge CO 2001-2006; Intsn Epis Ch Thornton CO 1999-2001; S Paul's Epis Ch Lakewood CO 1998-1999; S Thos Epis Ch Denver CO 1997-1998. calvingray2@yahoo.com

GRAY, Cathy Jean (Testa-Avila) (Ind) 11120 El Arco Dr, Whittier CA 90604 **Chr Ch Cathd Indianapolis IN 2009-** B Riverside CA 8/10/1952 d Louie Joe Testa & Barbara Jean. BA Loma Linda U 1977; MDiv CDSP 1999. D 6/19/1999 P 1/6/2000 Bp Gethin Benwil Hughes. m 9/30/2001 Bruce William Gray c 4. S Jas' Sch Los Angeles CA 2003-2009; Asst S Edm's Par San Marino CA 2003. CATHYG@CCCINDY.ORG

GRAY, Christopher Neil (SwFla) 513 Nassau St S, Venice FL 34285 **Cn Dio SW Florida Sarasota FL 2010-** B Cincinnati OH 1/31/1949 s Francis Campbell Gray & Jane Elizabeth. BA U of Cntrl Florida 1976; MDiv Nash 1979. D 6/25/1979 P 1/6/1980 Bp William Hopkins Folwell. m 7/8/1978 Paula Klein c 2. R S Mk's Epis Ch Venice FL 1991-2010; R Gr Epis Ch Inc Port Orange FL 1979-1991. two.grays@comcast.net

GRAY, David Dodson (WMass) 4 Linden Sq, Wellesley MA 02482 B Boston MA 1/2/1930 s Clarence Sperry Gray & Marion Fearney. BE Ya 1951; BD

Yale DS 1954; STM Yale DS 1956; Fllshp Ya 1963. D 12/15/1956 Bp John S Higgins P 12/1/1957 Bp Arthur C Lichtenberger. m 7/2/1957 Elizabeth Dodson c 2. Vic S Steph's Ch Westborough MA 1963-1972; Asst/Assoc S Mich & S Geo Clayton MO 1957-1962; DCE Gr Ch In Providence Providence RI 1956-1957. Auth, "I Want to Remember," *A Son's Reflections on His Mo's Alzheimer Journey*, Roundtable Press, 1993; Co-Auth, "Growth & Its Implications for the Future," *Implications for the Future*, Educational Dvlpmt Cntr, 1976; Co-Auth, *Chld of Joy: Raising Your Own Homegrown Christians*, Readers Press, 1975; Co-Auth, *Growth & Its Implications for the Future*, U.S. Gov't Printing Off, 1975. rpol@comcast.net

GRAY, Douglas Alan (SC) 47 Regency Oaks Dr, Summerville SC 29485 **Chr Epis Ch Denver CO 2009-** B Red Bank NJ 11/11/1961 s Russell Houston Gray & Edith Marie. BA U of Maryland 1984; MDiv VTS 1996. D 6/15/1995 Bp Peter James Lee P 1/15/1997 Bp Edward Lloyd Salmon Jr. m 6/13/1987 Patricia Ann Hayes. S Paul's Epis Ch Summerville SC 2003-2009; Asst R S Andr's Ch Mt Pleasant SC 1996-2000. douggray123@gmail.com

G

✠ GRAY JR, Rt Rev Duncan Montgomery (Miss) 3775 Old Canton Rd, Jackson MS 39216 **Ret Bp of Miss Dio Mississippi Jackson MS 1993-** B Canton MS 9/21/1926 s Duncan Montgomery Gray & Isabel Denham. BS Tul 1948; BD STUSo 1953. D 4/8/1953 P 10/28/1953 Bp Duncan Montgomery Gray Con 5/1/1974 for Miss. m 2/9/1948 Ruth Spivey c 4. S Paul's Epis Ch Meridian MS 2002-2004; The TS at The U So Sewanee TN 1991-1997; PBp's Coun of Advice Epis Ch Cntr New York NY 1984-1988; The TS at The U So Sewanee TN 1981-1987; Bp Dio Mississippi Jackson MS 1974-1993; R S Paul's Epis Ch Meridian MS 1965-1974; R S Ptr's Ch Oxford MS 1957-1965; P-in-c H Innoc' Epis Ch Como MS 1957-1960; P-in-c Calv Epis Ch Cleveland MS 1953-1957; P-in-c Gr Ch Rosedale MS 1953-1957. DD U So 1972.

✠ GRAY III, Rt Rev Duncan Montgomery (Miss) PO Box 23107, Jackson MS 39225 **Bp of Mississippi Dio Mississippi Jackson MS 2000-** B Canton MS 9/23/1949 s Duncan Montgomery Gray & Ruth. BA U of Mississippi 1971; MDiv VTS 1975. D 5/31/1975 P 5/27/1976 Bp Duncan Montgomery Gray Jr Con 6/17/2000 for Miss. m 8/21/1974 Kathryn Whittlesey c 2. R S Ptr's Ch Oxford MS 1985-2000; Assoc Ch Of The H Comm Memphis TN 1982-1985; Chapl Trin Ch New Orleans LA 1978-1982; Trin Epis Sch New Orleans LA 1978-1982; Cur S Jas Ch Greenville MS 1975-1978. DD U So Sch of Theological 2001; DD VTS 2001. dmgrayiii@gmail.com

✠ GRAY, Rt Rev Francis Campbell (NI) 3820 Nall Ct, South Bend IN 46614 B Manila PH 6/27/1940 s Francis Campbell Gray & Jane Elizabeth. BA Rol 1966; BD Nash 1969; STM Nash 1979; DD Nash 1987. D 6/20/1969 Bp Henry I Louttit P 12/20/1969 Bp William Loftin Hargrave Con 10/31/1986 for NI. m 2/19/1965 Karen Gray c 3. Asst Bp Dio Virginia Richmond VA 1999-2006; Dio Virginia Richmond VA 1999-2005; Bp Dio Nthrn Indiana So Bend IN 1986-1998; R Emm Ch Orlando FL 1979-1986; R S Jn's Ch Melbourne FL 1974-1979; Cur S Wlfd's Epis Ch Sarasota FL 1969-1970. Auth, *Beloved*, S Aug, 1998; Auth, "Thursday'S C," *Thursday'S Chld*, St Aug, 1994; Auth, "Tithing," *The Heart of the Matter*, Epis Ch Cntr, 1989. Compass Rose Soc - Pres 1999; PBFWR 1990-1993; PBFWR - Chair 1992-1993. Hon Cn Dio Renk, Sudan 2006. karenandfrank@comcast.net

GRAY, Giulianna Cappelletti (La) 4600 Saint Charles Ave, New Orleans PA 70115 B Glendale WV 7/19/1978 d Giulio John Cappelletti & Anne Norton. BSW Xavier U 2000; MSW Tul 2002; MDiv The Prot Epis TS 2008. D 12/29/2007 P 7/6/2008 Bp Charles Edward Jenkins III. m 5/25/2008 Peter Whittlesey Gray c 1. Dio Louisiana Baton Rouge LA 2008-2009; S Geo's Epis Ch New Orleans LA 2008-2009. giuliannagray@gmail.com

GRAY, James Robert (HB) 3001 Wisconsin Ave NW, C/O Diocese Of Washington, Washington DC 20016 B Alexandria KY 1/29/1944 s James William Gray & Maria Flora. BA Kentucky Wesleyan Coll 1966; STB Harvard DS 1969; PhD U Of Edinburgh Edinburgh Gb 1975. D 6/21/1969 Bp Anson Phelps Stokes Jr P 6/1/1970 Bp William Foreman Creighton. m 6/14/1969 Karen Ricketts. Cleric Ch Of The H Comm Washington DC 1976-1978; Asst Min The Ch Of The Epiph Washington DC 1969-1972. Auth, "Mod Process Thought".

GRAY, Katherine Tupper (SVa) 84 Post St, Newport News VA 23601 B Charleston SC 4/29/1945 d William Nicholson Gray & Mary Ramsey. Frederick Coll Frederick MD; STUSo. D 6/6/1998 Bp Frank Harris Vest Jr. D S Mart's Epis Ch Williamsburg VA 2003-2006; R E Lee Memi Ch (Epis) Lexington VA 2000-2003; S Mk's Ch Hampton VA 1998-2000. NAAD, Natl Epis Aids Cltn.

GRAY, Lisa (Mich) 4225 Walden Dr, Ann Arbor MI 48105 **Dio Michigan Detroit MI 2006-; Cn to the Ordnry Dio Michigan Detroit MI 2003-** B Munich Germany 8/2/1962 d Whitmore Gray & Svea Blomquist. BA Ohio Wesl 1984; MDiv CDSP 2003. D 12/18/2004 P 7/2/2005 Bp Wendell Nathaniel Gibbs Jr. m 12/1/2010 Tucker Kim c 3. D Nativ Epis Ch Bloomfield Township MI 2005. lisaannegray@me.com

GRAY, Marie Theresa (FdL) N63W29046 Tail Band Ct, Hartland WI 53029 **S Paul's Ch Plymouth WI 2010-** B Milwaukee WI 7/6/1959 d Howard Leo Heinen & Helen Marie. BS Marq 1981; MDiv Nash 2007. D 4/26/2008 P 11/29/2008 Bp Russell Edward Jacobus. m 5/30/1981 Michael Gray c 3. AEHC-the Assembly of Epis Healthcare Chapl 2007. revmtgray@yahoo.com

GRAY, Michael Fred (Va) 712 Amanda Ct, Culpeper VA 22701 **R S Steph's Epis Ch Culpeper VA 2002-** B Kalamazoo MI 4/2/1947 s James Swain Gray & Florence Louise. BA Stetson U 1970; MDiv Nash 1976; MA U NC 1977. D 5/27/1976 P 5/26/1977 Bp James Loughlin Duncan. m 7/28/1990 Lynn Graham c 3. R Ch Of The Resurr Biscayne Pk FL 1996-2001; Asst R S Mk The Evang Ft Lauderdale FL 1993-1996; Vic S Mich's Ch Miami FL 1990-1993; R Epis Ch Of The H Fam Miami Gardens FL 1980-1990; Asst Dn Trin Cathd Miami FL 1976-1980. mldkjjgray@gmail.com

GRAY, Neil Irvin (Fla) 1002 Neptune Ln, Neptune Beach FL 32266 B Tyrone PA 7/13/1918 s James Edward Gray & Alma Rency. BA U of Virginia 1940; STB GTS 1943; Fllshp Coll of Preachers 1960; Chicago TS 1967. D 2/27/1943 Bp John Raymond Wyatt P 9/29/1943 Bp John T Heistand. c 1. R S Paul's By-The-Sea Epis Ch Jacksonville Bch FL 1970-1985; Cn in Res S Paul's Cathd Peoria IL 1969-1970; Dir, CE S Jn's Ch Larchmont NY 1967-1969; Exec Dir Dio Florida Jacksonville FL 1962-1967; Exec Coun Dio Florida Jacksonville FL 1958-1961; R S Ptr's Ch Fernandina Bch FL 1953-1962; Chapl, US Army Dio Florida Jacksonville FL 1951-1953; P S Jas Ch Macclenny FL 1947-1951; Vic H Trin Epis Ch Hollidaysburg PA 1943-1945. Phi Beta Kappa U. Va 1940. ngray1@bellsouth.net

GRAY, Patrick Terrell (Mass) 140 Mount Vernon St Apt 7, Boston MA 02108 **Chr Ch So Hamilton MA 2009-** B Wilmington DE 7/26/1970 s Terrell Edward Gray & Marjorie Delores. ThD candidate GTS; BA Gordon Coll 1992; MA Gordon-Conwell TS 1997; STM GTS 1998. D 6/2/2001 Bp Barbara Clementine Harris P 6/8/2002 Bp M(arvil) Thomas Shaw III. m 11/21/1992 Naomi Ruth Nyquist c 2. Assoc R The Ch Of The Adv Boston MA 2002-2009; Asstg D All SS Ch W Newbury MA 2001-2002. "Co-Ed of One Lord, One Faith, One Baptism: Stds in Chr Ecclesiality and Ecum in hon of J. Robert Wright," Eerdmans, 2006; "A Meaning Worthy of God: Origen and Scripture in a Pre-Constantinian Age," *One Lord, One Faith, One Baptism*, Eerdmans, 2006; "Cmnty Organizing as Lived Faith," *Why Liberal Ch are Growing*, T&T Clark, 2006; "Eliot the Enigma: An Observation of T. S. Eliot's Thought and Poetry," *ATR*, 2003; "Making Us Make Ourselves: Double Agcy and Its Christological Context in the Thought of Austin Farrer," *The Presence of Transcendence: Thinking 'Sacr' in a Postmodern Age*, Peeters, 2001. frgray@theadvent.org

GRAY, Peter Hanson (Va) 1545 Hunting Ave, Mclean VA 22102 B Indianapolis IN 3/6/1939 s Paul Albert Gray & Jane Sherer. BA Pr 1960; MDiv GTS 1966. D 6/11/1966 P 12/17/1966 Bp John P Craine. S Thos Epis Ch McLean VA 1987-2004; R H Trin Epis Ch Wyoming MI 1973-1976; Asst S Lk's Par Kalamazoo MI 1967-1973; Dir, Yth Outreach S Phil's Ch Indianapolis IN 1966-1967. peterhgray@aol.com

GRAY, Peter Whittlesey (La) 1313 Esplanade Ave, New Orleans LA 70116 **Trin Ch New Orleans LA 2010-** B Memphis TN 8/10/1982 s Duncan Montgomery Gray & Kathryn. BA Millsaps Coll 2004; MTS Venderbilt DS 2006; MDiv The Prot Epis TS 2008. D 6/7/2008 Bp Duncan Montgomery Gray Jr P 12/13/2008 Bp Duncan Montgomery Gray III. m 5/25/2008 Giulianna Cappelletti Giulianna Marie Cappelletti. S Anna's Ch New Orleans LA 2008-2010. revpeterwgray@gmail.com

GRAY, Priscilla Grace-Gloria (Minn) 611 19th St N, Sartell MN 56377 B Flushing NY 9/28/1946 d Nathaniel Richard Sniffin & Ilda. BS U of Maine 1968; Med U of Maine 1972. D 10/25/1987 Bp Robert Marshall Anderson. m 7/21/1973 Warren Roscoe Gray c 4.

GRAY, Roger Scott (Ind) 17468 Riverwalk Way E, Noblesville IN 46062 B Brooklyn NY 5/27/1924 s William Albert Gray & Laura Grace. BA Adel 1949; STB GTS 1954; MRE UTS 1957; DD Epis TS In Kentucky 1978. D 4/19/1952 P 10/18/1952 Bp James P De Wolfe. m 5/31/1952 Mary Theohares c 2. Trst Nca Dio Indianapolis Indianapolis IN 1980-1989; Dn and R Chr Ch Cathd Indianapolis IN 1972-1989; R Gr Epis Ch Trumbull CT 1959-1972; R S Lk's Ch Eastchester NY 1954-1959; Cur S Ann And The H Trin Brooklyn NY 1952-1954.

GRAY, Svea Blomquist (Mich) 306 N Division St, Ann Arbor MI 48104 **D S Andr's Ch Ann Arbor MI 1985-** B Harvey IL 12/13/1935 d Joseph Emmanuel Blomquist & Sara Virginia. BA U MI 1957; PrTS 1958; Whitaker TS 1985. D 6/13/1985 Bp H Coleman McGehee Jr. m 12/13/1958 Whitmore Gray c 4. whitgray@aol.com

GRAY, Thomas Weddle (RG) 108 E Orchard Ln, Carlsbad NM 88220 B Des Moines IA 11/23/1941 s Robert Edward Gray & Honor. BS Iowa St U 1966; MDiv SWTS 1974. D 6/15/1974 P 12/21/1974 Bp Walter Cameron Righter. m 4/28/2001 Jane Shuler Gray c 2. R Gr Ch Carlsbad NM 1997-2007; Chapl St Lk's Epis Hosp Houston TX 1996-1997; R S Mk's Ch Austin TX 1990-1996; R S Jn's Epis Ch Alamogordo NM 1985-1990; R S Thos Of Cbury Epis Ch Albuquerque NM 1982-1984; R Gd Shpd Epis Ch Wichita KS 1976-1982; Vic Trin Ch Carroll IA 1974-1976. OHC 1973. t-gray@mywdo.com

GRAY, Victoria Stephanie (Cal) 116 Bayhurst Dr, Vallejo CA 94591 **D Chr The Lord Epis Ch Pinole CA 2009-** B New York City NY 2/16/1939 d

Victor Gray & Emma Virginia. BS Us Naval Acad Annapolis 1962; MA Bos 1971; PhD U of Maryland 2002; BA Sch for Deacons 2006. D 12/2/2006 Bp Marc Handley Andrus. D S Jas Epis Ch San Francisco CA 2006-2008. vgray54951@aol.com

GRAY, William Lyons (Alb) 801 Fairfield Ct, East Greenbush NY 12061 **Int P S Paul's Epis Ch Greenwich NY 1988-** B Albany NY 8/16/1925 s William John Gray & Ruth Lillian. BA S Bernadine Siena 1950; GTS 1952; MDiv Nash 1956. D 6/6/1954 P 12/1/1954 Bp Frederick Lehrle Barry. c 2. Int P S Lk's Ch Mechanicville NY 1988; P-in-c S Lk's Ch Mechanicville NY 1987; R S Andr's Ch Scotia NY 1962-1987; P-in-c Chr Ch Morristown NY 1959-1962; R S Paul's Ch Waddington NY 1957-1962; Cur S Jn's Ch Massena NY 1954-1957.

GRAYBILL, Richard Martin (NMich) First And Canda St, Ishpeming MI 49849 B 12/8/1943 s Michael Achey Graybill & Carol Wood. BA Albion Coll 1965; JD Wayne 1968. D 5/2/2007 Bp James Arthur Kelsey P 11/4/2007 Bp Rustin Ray Kimsey. c 2. dick.graybill@hotmail.com

GRAY-FOW, Michael John Gregory (Mil) 120 S Ridge St, Whitewater WI 53190 B Wigan Lancashire UK 10/18/1943 s James Gray & Eileen Veronica. Cert U of Nottingham 1967; U of Nottingham 1973; Med U of Nottingham 1978; PhD U of Wisconsin 1985. D 8/17/1991 P 2/20/1992 Bp Roger John White. m 10/29/1983 Tiiu R Rodima c 1. Vic S Lk's Epis Ch Milwaukee WI 1998-2010; Dio Milwaukee Milwaukee WI 1996-1997; Par Dio Milwaukee Milwaukee WI 1992. Auth, "A Problem w Evolution," *JISRS*, A.I. Cuza Univ. Rumania, 2011; Auth, "From Proconsul to S: Sergius Paullus," Classica et Mediaevalia, 2006; Auth, "Neither Vrgn nor Mtyr," Latomus 301, 2006. frmichael@stlukeschurch.com

✠ GRAY-REEVES, Rt Rev Mary (ECR) PO Box 1903, Monterey CA 33410 **Bp of El Camino Real Dio El Camino Real Monterey CA 2007-** B Coral Gables FL 7/5/1962 d James Gray & Florence. AA Miami-Dade Cmnty Coll 1982; BA California St U 1987; BTh Coll S Jn Evang 1994; MDiv Coll S Jn Evang 1994. D 6/11/1994 Bp John Mc Gill Krumm P 1/14/1995 Bp Frederick Houk Borsch. m 12/18/1982 Michael Reeves c 2. Dio SE Florida Miami FL 2005-2007; R S Margarets Epis Ch Miami Lakes FL 1998-2004; Asst S Jas' Par So Pasadena CA 1997-1998; Asst Chr Ch Par Redondo Bch CA 1994-1997. michael-reeves@att.net

GRAYSON, Timothy Holiday (Md) 536 Kinsale Rd, Timonium MD 21093 **Ch Of The Mssh Baltimore MD 2010-** B Wellington New Zealand 1/16/1951 s Peter Court Grayson & Marjorie Joan. BA Victoria U Wellington 1973; MA Victoria U Wellington 1974; MDiv VTS 2007. D 6/16/2007 P 1/5/2008 Bp John Leslie Rabb. m 1/16/1951 Kathleen Kathleen Grau c 2. Asst S Jas' Epis Ch Baltimore MD 2007-2009. tgrayson116@yahoo.com

GREATHOUSE, William Matthew (At) 1816 Harding Road, Paris TN 38242 **R Gr Epis Ch Paris TN 2011-** B Kansas City KS 3/20/1970 s William Mark Greathouse & Janice Kay. BA Trevecca Nazarene U 1995; MDiv Nash 2005. D 6/4/2005 P 4/29/2006 Bp Bertram Nelson Herlong. m 6/13/1992 Laureen Crampsey c 3. R S Paul's Epis Ch Newnan GA 2008-2011; Assoc R/P in Charge S Paul's Epis Ch Murfreesboro TN 2005-2008. matt.greathouse@gmail.com

GREATWOOD, Richard Neil (CFla) 1167 Adair Park Place, Orlando FL 32804 B Olean NY 7/12/1933 s Harry D Greatwood & Dorothy May. BA Colg 1954; MDiv UTS 1957; JD U of Virginia 1960; MA Van 1970; PhD Van 1977. D 11/19/1970 P 5/1/1971 Bp William Hopkins Folwell. m 9/11/1956 Diane Manny. Prof Nash Nashotah WI 1975-1984. rgreatwood@cfl.rr.com

GRECO, John Anthony (LI) 333 E 53rd St Apt 5m, New York NY 10022 **Hon Cathd Of The Incarn Garden City NY 1998-** B Brooklyn NY 4/19/1938 s Joseph Greco & Adeline. BA St. Johns U 1960; MA NYU 1962; MDiv GTS 1967. Rec from Roman Catholic 1/1/1964 Bp Jonathan Goodhue Sherman. Archd of Nassau Cnty Dio Long Island Garden City NY 1984-2004; R Ch of S Jude Wantagh NY 1968-1994. Bp's Cross for Distinguished Dioc Serv Dio Long Island 1992. jag333@verizon.net

GREELEY III, Paul William (USC) 1600 Bulline Street, Daniel Island SC 29492 B Spartanburg SC 12/15/1952 s Paul William Greeley & Mary Leila. BA Wofford Coll 1975; MDiv SWTS 1978; DMin SWTS 2006; MA Prescott Coll 2011. D 6/24/1978 P 6/2/1979 Bp George Moyer Alexander. m 8/16/1975 Sharon Shepherd c 2. R Ch Of The Adv Spartanburg SC 2006-2008; Int Dn Trin Cathd Phoenix AZ 2005-2006; Archd Dio Arizona Phoenix AZ 1998-2006; R S Mk's Epis Ch Mesa AZ 1995-1998; Fndr/Dir The H Innoc Mnstry Chelsea AL 1989-1994; Assoc S Steph's Epis Ch Birmingham AL 1987-1988; Asst R S Lk's Epis Ch Birmingham AL 1982-1987; Vic S Lk's Ch Newberry SC 1980-1982; D-in-trng S Thad Epis Ch Aiken SC 1978-1980. Contrib, *Sundays and Seasons 2001*, Augsburg Press, 2001; Auth, "Creative Fire," *Living Ch*, 1980; Contrib, *Seabury in Memi*, 1978. pwmgreeley@me.com

GREEN, Andrew (SanD) 2004 East Calle Lileta, Palm Springs CA 92262 **S Paul In The Desert Palm Sprg CA 1989-** B Merced CA 9/5/1955 s Marvin Archibald Green & Marie Blanche. California St U; AA Merced Cmnty Coll 1975; BA U of New Mex 1979; MDiv SWTS 1985. D 6/26/1985 Bp Richard Mitchell Trelease Jr P 1/1/1986 Bp Robert Munro Wolterstorff. m 6/18/1977 Susan Croley c 3. Cur S Dunst's Epis Ch San Diego CA 1985-1988. wrector@gmail.com

GREEN III, Anthony Roy (Spok) 1705 5th St, Wenatchee WA 98801 **Supply P S Jn The Bapt Epis Ch Ephrata WA 2007-; Stndg Com Dio Spokane Spokane WA 2005-** B Pittsburg PA 10/3/1953 s Anthony R Green & Dolores M. BA St. Meinrad Coll 1975; BTh St. Aug's (RC) Sem of Toronto 1978; Med Cntrl Washington U 2002. Rec from Roman Catholic 10/23/2005 Bp James Edward Waggoner. m 5/29/1993 Jeannette C Larson c 1. t_roy2@yahoo.com

GREEN, Bruce (WMo) 5229 84th Street, Lubbock TX 79424 **R S Mk's Epis Ch Plainview TX 2002-** B Tuscaloosa AL 9/27/1936 s Benjamin Arthur Green & Alice Bates. BA U So 1958; MDiv VTS 1961. D 6/28/1961 P 2/24/1962 Bp John Vander Horst. m 6/19/1961 Dorothy Cooke c 3. Int S Paul's On The Plains Epis Ch Lubbock TX 1998-2002; R Gr Ch Carthage MO 1990-1998; R S Ptr's Epis Ch Amarillo TX 1977-1990; R Trin Epis Ch Gatlinburg TN 1974-1977; Vic Ch of the H Apos Collierville TN 1968-1969; R S Andr's Ch Marianna AR 1964-1968; P-in-c S Mk's Ch Copperhill TN 1961-1964. bglap@nts-online.net

GREEN, Daniel Currie (NCal) 1557 Trellis Ln, Petaluma CA 94954 **P-in-c St Johns Epis Ch Petaluma CA 2010-** B Riverside CA 12/3/1965 s Alan WilbertCurrie Green & Ellen Kathleen. BA California Inst of Integral Stds 1998; MDiv CDSP 2005. D 6/4/2005 P 12/3/2005 Bp William Edwin Swing. m 8/17/2002 Sarah Tinsley c 1. Assoc R All SS Ch Carmel CA 2005-2010. greenrev@sbcglobal.net

GREEN, David Edward (Cal) 6103 Harwood Ave, Oakland CA 94618 B Adrian MI 6/22/1937 s Edward R A Green & Fannie Amelia. BA Harv 1960; BD CDSP 1963; Grad Theol Un 1965; MLS U CA 1969. D 6/29/1963 P 6/23/1964 Bp Richard S M Emrich. m 6/1/1961 Sharon Weiner c 2. Libr The GTS New York NY 1982-2002; Instr Hebr CDSP Berkeley CA 1962-1965. Transltr, *Many Theol works*. Amer Theol Libr Assn 1967-2002; Country Dance and Song Soc 1988. degreen@post.harvard.edu

GREEN, David Robert (Eas) 623 Cloverfields Dr., Stevensville MD 21666 **R Chr Ch Par Kent Island Stevensville MD 2004-** B Johnstown PA 11/12/1957 s John N Green & Nancy M. BFA Clarion U of Pennsylvania 1979; MDiv TESM 1987; DMin GTF 2000. D 6/6/1987 Bp Alden Moinet Hathaway P 12/1/1987 Bp William Grant Black. m 5/2/1981 Jennifer Lou Rea c 3. R St Christophers Epis Ch Charleston WV 1989-2004; Vic S Andr's Epis Ch Washington Crt Hse OH 1987-1989. frdavid4christ@verizon.net

GREEN, Drury Hamilton (Chi) 971 First St, Batavia IL 60510 B Aurora IL 9/23/1936 s Drury Alfred Green & Christine Catherine. BA Illinois Coll 1962; BD SWTS 1965. D 6/12/1965 Bp James Winchester Montgomery P 12/18/1965 Bp Gerald Francis Burrill. m 12/9/1989 Linda Frances Leudesdorff. R Calv Epis Ch Batavia IL 1998-2000; Co-R Calv Epis Ch Batavia IL 1994-1997; R Calv Epis Ch Batavia IL 1975-1999; Cur Ch Of The H Comf Kenilworth IL 1965-1967. dlf971@sbcglobal.net

GREEN, Elizabeth A (WMass) 66 Highland Ave #C, Short Hills NJ 07078 **S Jn's Epis Ch Sutton MA 2011-** B Pittsburgh PA 9/9/1961 d Charles R Green & Therese M. BA Coll of Wm & Mary 1983; MDiv Drew TS 2007. D 6/7/2008 P 12/20/2008 Bp Mark M Beckwith. c 1. Ch Of The Redeem Morristown NJ 2010-2011; Asst Chr Ch Short Hills NJ 2008-2010. lisagreen2@aol.com

GREEN, Frazier L (Ga) CHURCH OF THE SPIRIT, 5775 BARCLAY DR, ALEXANDRIA VA 22315 **S Athan Ch Brunswick GA 2011-** B Neptune, NJ 12/3/1958 s Frazier Green & Harriet Mitchell. BS U of Florida 1983; Middle Grades Certification Armstrong Atlantic St U 1998; MDiv VTS 2007. D 2/3/2007 P 8/17/2007 Bp Henry Irving Louttit. m 8/16/1986 Victoria L Green c 4. Assoc Pstr Ch Of The Sprt Alexandria VA 2007-2008. grnfraz2@gmail.com

GREEN, G J (Mil) 2030 74th Pl, Kenosha WI 53143 **P in charge S Andr's Ch Kenosha WI 1997-** B Pontiac IL 10/1/1949 s Harry William Green & Louise Elizabeth. Illinois Cntrl Coll; Wartburg Coll 1971; LTh Nash 1986. D 6/14/1986 Bp James Winchester Montgomery P 12/20/1986 Bp William Charles Wantland. m 12/20/1969 Kathleen Lynn Thompson c 2. R S Thos Of Cbury Ch Greendale WI 1991-1997; R Gr Ch Rice Lake WI 1986-1991; Vic S Lukes Ch Ladysmith WI 1986-1991. ggreenjay@aol.com

GREEN, Gretchen Hall (O) 35 Cohasset Dr, Hudson OH 44236 B Waterbury CT 3/15/1940 d Jesse Angell Hall & Louise. Cor; GN Mt Sinai Hosp Sch of Nrsng Cleveland OH 1963; RN Mt Sinai Hosp Sch of Nrsng Cleveland OH 1963; Dio. of Ohio Diac Trng 1996. D 11/8/1996 Bp J Clark Grew II. m 6/13/1964 R Green c 4. D Chr Ch Epis Hudson OH 2002-2005; D Ch Of Our Sav Akron OH 1996-2002. Nurse of Hope Summit Cnty Amer Cancer Soc 1990. ghg2@aol.com

GREEN, J(ames) Allan (Tex) 414 Duck Lake Dr, Lakeway TX 78734 **Died 8/8/2011** B Clovis CA 7/24/1926 s Stanley Earl Green & Kathryn Myrtle. BA U of Texas 1964; MDiv Epis TS of The SW 1976. D 6/8/1976 Bp J Milton Richardson P 6/1/1977 Bp Roger Howard Cilley. c 2. gangreen@sbcglobal.net

GREEN JR, Joseph Nathaniel (SVa) 3826 Wedgefield Ave, Norfolk VA 23502 B Jenkinsville SC 4/15/1926 s Joseph Nathaniel Green & Etta O'Neal. BA S Aug's Coll Raleigh NC 1949; MDiv PDS 1952; STM STUSo 1965; LLD S

Aug's Coll Raleigh NC 1976. D 5/30/1953 Bp John J Gravatt P 4/17/1954 Bp Clarence Alfred Cole. m 6/17/1955 Evelyn G Green. Int S Jas Epis Ch Portsmouth VA 1996-2000; R Gr Ch Norfolk VA 1963-1993; R S Ambroses Ch Raleigh NC 1958-1959; P-in-c Epiph Ch Spartanburg SC 1955-1958; P-in-c S Phil's Epis Ch Greenville SC 1955-1958; Epis Ch Of S Simon And S Jude Irmo SC 1953-1955; M-in-c S Barn Ch Jenkinsville SC 1953-1955. UBE, Natl Pres 1975-1977. DD VTS 1988; Natl Conf of Christians and Jews Honoraryree 1984; DD S Paul's Coll Lawrenceville VA 1984; City Councilman & Vice Mayor Norfolk City Coun 1977. egg910@hotmail.com

GREEN, Kenneth William (Spok) 539 3rd Ave, Havre MT 59501 B Kingman AZ 8/6/1936 s Harold William Green & Ruth Esther. BS Westminster Coll 1972; MDiv VTS 1982. D 6/16/1982 Bp William Benjamin Spofford P 6/18/1983 Bp Robert Whitridge Estill. m 8/30/1967 Carol Gow c 3. Vic S Mary's Bonners Ferry Bonners Ferry ID 2001-2003; R S Mk's Ch Havre MT 1996-2001; Dio Montana Helena MT 1995; Dio Utah Salt Lake City UT 1993-1994; Vic S Jn's Epis Ch Logan UT 1984-1992; Asst H Trin Epis Ch Greensboro NC 1982-1984. nannykenn@yahoo.com

G

GREEN, Kuulei Mobley (ETenn) 1175 Pineville Rd Apt 6, Chattanooga TN 37405 B Washington DC 6/22/1937 d Radford Ellis Mobley & Barbara. BA Hood Coll 1959; MDiv STUSo 1993. D 3/30/1993 Bp John Stuart Thornton P 5/1/1994 Bp Robert Gould Tharp. c 2. S Alb's Epis Ch Hixson TN 2001-2002; S Barn Nrsng Hm Chattanooga TN 1994-2001; D S Steph's Boise ID 1993-1994. Revkmgreen@cableone.net

GREEN, Larry Anthony (Chi) 3450 N Lake Shore Dr Apt 3510, Chicago IL 60657 **D S Chrys's Ch Chicago IL 2005-** B Canton GA 7/22/1952 s Cornelius Green & Jimmie. D 2/5/2005 Bp William Dailey Persell. OAHC 2009. lgreen@winstonandgreen.com

GREEN, Lawrence Joseph (Minn) Saint Pauls Episcopal Church, 265 Lafayette St, Winona MN 55987 **P-in-c S Paul's Ch Winona MN 2004-** B Saint Louis MO 8/3/1941 s Lawrence Delano Green & Rose A. De Andreis Sem 1964; BA S Mary's Sem 1964; MA S Louis U 1967; PhD S Louis U 1982. D 1/15/1994 Bp Sanford Zangwill Kaye Hampton P 12/17/1999 Bp James Louis Jelinek. m 10/7/1989 Sandra Kay Wytske c 6. P-in-c Gr Memi Ch Wabasha MN 2000-2006; P-in-c S Mk's Ch Lake City MN 2000-2004. ljgreen@hbci.com

GREEN, Linda Frances (Chi) 971 First St, Batavia IL 60510 **Chapl Bp Anderson Hse Chicago IL 2009-** B New York NY 4/18/1942 d Alfred Leudesdorff & Frances. BA Augustana Coll 1964; Rutgers-The St U 1967; MS U IL 1968; MDiv SWTS 1991. D 6/15/1991 P 12/21/1991 Bp Frank Tracy Griswold III. m 12/9/1989 Drury Hamilton Green. S Ann's Ch Woodstock IL 2001-2003; Dio Chicago Chicago IL 1998-2001; Co R Calv Epis Ch Batavia IL 1994-1997; P S Paul's Ch La Salle IL 1991-1993. dlf971@sbcglobal.net

GREEN, Mary Emily (Tex) 4626 Cedar St, Bellaire TX 77401 B Shreveport LA 11/15/1944 d Robert Francis Humeston & Beula Beatrice. RN S Lk Sch of Nrsng 1966; BA Stephens Coll 1975; MS U of Missouri 1977; MDiv Epis TS of The SW 1992. D 6/27/1992 Bp Maurice Manuel Benitez P 1/19/1993 Bp William Elwood Sterling. m 9/3/1972 Robert Green c 1. Stff Chapl St Lk's Epis Hosp Houston TX 2004-2011; Chapl Epis TS Of The SW Austin TX 1997-2000; Chr Epis Ch Cedar Pk TX 1995-2003. "Pstr Care of the Dying," *PlainViews-A Pub of Hlth Care Chapl*, 2009; "Chapl Response to Codes," *PlainViews - A Pub of Hlth Care Chapl*, 2008. rev_doc@sbcglobal.net

GREEN, Patricia Anne (WMich) 160 Main St, Somerset MA 02726 B New York NY 6/20/1948 d James Green & Lily Christine. BS U of Pennsylvania 1969; MDiv CDSP 1991. D 6/22/1991 Bp George Nelson Hunt III P 7/1/1992 Bp Rustin Ray Kimsey. m 7/29/2000 Gary Martin. R S Jn's Ch Mt Pleasant MI 2001-2005; Int Dio Nthrn Michigan Marquette MI 1999-2001; So Cntrl Reg Manistique MI 1999-2001; Mnstry Dvlpmt Spec Dio Estrn Oregon The Dalles OR 1992-1995. patriciagreen27@hotmail.com

GREEN, Patricia Lynn (RG) 1678 Tierra Del Rio NW, Albuquerque NM 87107 **St Timothys Luth Ch Albuquerque NM 2003-** B West Point NY 7/12/1948 d Carey Law O'Bryan & Mary Elizabeth. BA U of New Mex 1976; MEd U of Arizona 1979; MDiv Epis TS of the SW 2000. D 6/10/2000 P 12/9/2000 Bp William Jerry Winterrowd. m 4/27/1967 Alfred Laland Green c 2. Samar Counslg Cntr Albuquerque NM 2002-2003; Asst S Matt's Parker CO 2000-2001. pogreen@aol.com

GREEN, Paula Clark (WA) 3001 Orion Ln, Upper Marlboro MD 20774 **P-in-c S Jn's Epis Ch Zion Par Beltsville MD 2008-** B Washington DC 9/7/1962 BA Br. D 6/12/2004 P 1/22/2005 Bp John Chane. m 9/9/1989 Michael Green c 1. Asst S Pat's Ch Washington DC 2004-2007. greenp@stpatsdc.org

GREEN, Randolph Patrick (NC) 343 Dogwood Knl, Boone NC 28607 **S Paul's Epis Ch Wilmington NC 2010-** B Atlanta GA 3/5/1944 s Daniel George Green & Patricia Ruth. BA Georgia St U 1966; BD STUSo 1969. D 6/28/1969 Bp Milton LeGrand Wood P 4/4/1970 Bp Randolph R Claiborne. m 3/30/1985 Nancy H Green c 1. S Andr's By The Sea Nags Hd NC 2008-2010; Int S Tim's Epis Ch Winston Salem NC 2007-2008; Ch Of The Ascen Hickory NC 2005-2007; S Paul's Epis Ch Greenville NC 2004-2005; Dio Wstrn No Carolina Asheville NC 2004; Int S Mich's Ch Raleigh NC 2003-2004; Ch Of The Epiph Eden NC 2001-2003; Asst Min H Innoc Ch Atlanta GA 1969-1982. revrangreen@yahoo.com

GREEN, Richard Lee (Oly) 1428 22nd Ave, Longview WA 98632 **Int S Phil The D Epis Ch Portland OR 2011-** B Angleton TX 2/17/1949 s Thurman Arledge Green & Jimmie Lou. BA cl U of Texas 1977; MDiv CDSP 1991. D 6/8/1991 P 6/6/1992 Bp William Edwin Swing. m 4/6/1991 Kathleen Patton c 1. Resolutns Com - Dioc Conv Dio Olympia Seattle WA 2006-2010; BEC Dio Olympia Seattle WA 2004-2010; R S Steph's Epis Ch Longview WA 2000-2010; Vic S Barn Ch Mt Shasta CA 1997-2000; Co-R S Mk's Ch Yreka CA 1995-2000; Bd Mem Stanford Cbury Fndt Standford CA 1993-1995; Assoc R Chr Ch Portola Vlly CA 1992-1995. Contemplative Outreach 1998. fr.richardgreen@gmail.com

GREEN JR, Roy Donald (EO) 18160 Cottonwood Rd Unit 719, Sunriver OR 97707 **Cn for Circuit Rider Mnstry Dio Estrn Oregon The Dalles OR 2009-** B Orlando FL 1/16/1946 s Roy Donald Green & Sally. BA Florida St U 1968; MDiv VTS 1971; DMin VTS 1984. D 6/29/1971 P 1/18/1972 Bp William Hopkins Folwell. c 2. Cn for Circuit Rider Mnstry Dio Estrn Oregon The Dalles OR 2009; Dio Rhode Island Providence RI 1999-2001; Cn For Chr Formation Dio Rhode Island Providence RI 1998-2001; R Trin Ch Newport RI 1994-1998; R Emm Epis Ch Mercer Island WA 1987-1994; R S Mk's Ch Orchard Pk NY 1978-1987; Assoc Ecum Off Dio Virginia Richmond VA 1975-1978; Asst R, P in C The Falls Ch Epis Falls Ch VA 1973-1978; Cur S Mich's Ch Orlando FL 1971-1973. Auth, "A Model For Spprt Of Lay Mnstry: An Experiment In Bus Ethics," 1984. Assn fo Profsnl Chapl 2011. Awd of Excellence Oregon Hospice Assn 2008. Spiritchaser116@aol.com

GREEN, Tamara Melanie (Cal) 140 Dolores St Apt 103, San Francisco CA 94103 B Butte MT 2/16/1944 d Theodore P Gilbert & Josephine Marie. BA Sch for Deacons 1985. D 6/7/1986 Bp William Edwin Swing. D Ch Of The H Innoc San Francisco CA 1992-1995; D S Ptr's Epis Ch San Francisco CA 1989-1990; D S Andr's Epis Ch San Bruno CA 1986-1988. Tertiary of the Soc of S Fran.

GREEN, William Baillie (Dal) Po Box 2247, Austin TX 78768 **Died 4/19/2011** B Mayfield KY 4/3/1927 s Novella B Green & Eben E. BA Baylor U 1948; BD Louisville Presb TS 1951; STM UTS 1953; PhD U Of Edinburgh Edinburgh Gb 1955; Ya 1962; S Vladimir Orth Sem 1975; DD Epis TS of The SW 1999. D 9/29/1971 P 2/1/1972 Bp J Milton Richardson. c 2. Auth, "Ask, Seek," *Knock*, 1999; Auth, "Seasons Of The Heart," 1994; Auth, "Joy In The Struggle," 1992; Auth, "Sprt & Light," 1976.

GREENALL, Carroll Dean (WMo) 358 Lake Viking Ter, Gallatin MO 64640 **P Chr Ch Epis Boonville MO 1993-; P Chr Ch Lexington MO 1993-; P S Mary's Ch Fayette MO 1993-; P S Phil's Ch Trenton MO 1993-; P Trin Epis Ch Marshall MO 1993-** B Melbourne MO 4/27/1928 s John Greenman & Roberta. Cntrl Bus Coll 1948. D 12/19/1963 Bp Edward Randolph Welles II. m 5/8/1948 Betty L Read. P S Mk's Epis Ch Paw Paw MI 1985-1992; Asst Gr Ch Carthage MO 1966-1969; Asst S Mary's Epis Ch Kansas City MO 1963-1966.

GREENAWAY, Douglas Andrew Gordon (WA) 1116 Lamont St Nw, Washington DC 20010 **Assoc S Paul's Par Washington DC 2008-; Assoc S Paul's Rock Creek Washington DC 2008-** B Bellville ON CA 3/9/1951 s Gordon James Greenaway & Delores Evelyn. BA Carleton U 1974; MArch CUA 1977; MDiv Wesley TS 2000. D 6/10/2000 P 12/10/2000 Bp Ronald Hayward Haines. c 1. Asst R S Alb's Par Washington DC 2000-2007. Auth, "W Germany: Museum Without a Facade Centered on a Massive Drum," *Archit*, Amer Inst of Architects, 1985. daggreenaway@gmail.com

GREENE, Adam S (At) PO Box 400, Salisbury CT 06068 **Epis HS Bellaire TX 2009-** B Princeton NJ 10/27/1964 s Howard Roger Greene & Donna Levy. BA Van 1986; CTM Prog Camb 2008; MDiv Ya Berk 2009. D 12/20/2008 P 6/28/2009 Bp J(ohn) Neil Alexander. m 10/1/1988 Martha G Goodman c 1. mgreene@mggreene.com

GREENE, Dorothy Anne (NY) 27 Willow Ave, Larchmont NY 10538 **P Assoc S Jn's Ch Larchmont NY 1988-** B Mamaroneck NY 1/8/1931 d Harry Olin Baker & Dorothy. BS Col 1968; MA UTS 1986. D 6/13/1987 Bp Paul Moore Jr P 5/15/1988 Bp Lyman Cunningham Ogilby. P-in-c S Andr By The Sea Hyannis Port MA 1989-1990; Supply P S Dav's Epis Ch So Yarmouth MA 1988-1996. Phi Beta Kappa 1968. revdag@webtv.net

GREENE, Edward Rideout (WVa) 19 Valley Rd, Bath ME 04530 **P-in-c S Andr's Ch Readfield ME 2006-** B Bath ME 8/16/1943 s Stanley Warren Greene & Ethel Agda. BA Bow 1965; STM GTS 1968. D 6/8/1968 Bp Leland Stark P 12/21/1968 Bp Frederick Barton Wolf. m 1/21/2010 George O VanHazinga c 2. Nelson Cluster Of Epis Ch Rippon WV 1993-1998; R S Lk's Ch Worcester MA 1987-1993; Dio Wstrn Massachusetts Springfield MA 1981-1993; Assoc Pstr Care Chr Ch Fitchburg MA 1981-1987; Vic S Geo's Epis Ch Sanford ME 1974-1981; P-in-c Chr Ch Biddeford ME 1972-1981; Vic S Jas Ch Old Town ME 1968-1972. Soc Of S Jn The Evang 1997. reverg@gwi.net

GREENE, Elinor Robinson (Pa) 6635 Mccallum St Apt B406, Philadelphia PA 19119 **D Dio Pennsylvania Philadelphia PA 1993-** B Philadelphia PA 7/21/

1952 d George Shaw Greene & Elinor Cooke. BA Hampshire Coll 1977; MA Ya Berk 1982; Pennsylvania Diac Sch 1993. D 10/30/1993 Bp Allen Lyman Bartlett Jr.

GREENE, Everett Henry (RI) 1117 Capella S, Newport RI 02840 **Asstg P S Columba's Chap Middletown RI 2001-** B Providence RI 6/12/1928 s Stephen Henry Greene & Flora Louise. BA Br 1951; MDiv CRDS 1955; MA LIU 1974. D 6/21/1956 P 2/23/1957 Bp Dudley S Stark. m 3/17/1950 Norma C Clow c 3. Asst S Geo's Ch Portsmouth RI 1994-2001; Dioc Coun Dio Rhode Island Providence RI 1986-1990; R Emm Ch Newport RI 1985-1994; Vic S Aug's Ch Kingston RI 1960-1965; R Zion Ch Avon NY 1957-1960; Min in charge Trin Epis Ch Rockland MA 1956-1957. Mltry Chapl Assn 1977. everett.greene3@verizon.net

GREENE JR, Frank Eugene (NH) 5 Nutmeg Cir, Laconia NH 03246 B Boston MA 3/21/1917 s Frank Eugene Greene & Winifred Hollis. BA Harv 1938; STB EDS 1942. D 6/3/1942 P 12/15/1942 Bp Henry Knox Sherrill. m 6/24/1978 Edith Hathaway Leonard c 3. Vic S Mk's Ch Ashland NH 1975-1982; R S Mich's Epis Ch Holliston MA 1962-1964; R The Par Of S Chrys's Quincy MA 1951-1962; R S Jn's Epis Ch Saugus MA 1943-1947; Cur Trin Ch In The City Of Boston Boston MA 1942-1943. Auth, *News from the No Country*, 1999; Auth, *Pieces of the Rock*, 1994; Auth, *Life in the Slow Ln*, 1990; Auth, *Uncle Bob's Camp*, 1983; Auth, "Mid Canyons Deep," *Wrshp II*. Harvard Club of New Hampshire 1975; New Hampshire Soc of Mayflower Descendants 1980; New Hampshire Sons of the Amer Revolution 1982; Pilgrim Jn Howland Soc 1985.

GREENE, George Burkeholder (Alb) 53 West St, Whitesboro NY 13492 B Mohawk NY 12/25/1929 s Arthur Robert Greene & Gladys. BA Indiana Cntrl U 1955; ThB PDS 1958. D 5/31/1958 P 12/6/1958 Bp Frederick Lehrle Barry. m 7/26/1958 Shirley L Wilson c 3. R St Augustines Ch Ilion NY 1968-2001; R Par Of S Jas Ft Edw NY 1958-1968.

GREENE III, Joseph Daniel (At) 1451 Carriage Ridge Dr., Greensboro GA 30642 **R Ch Of The Redeem Greensboro GA 2010-** B Macon GA 8/14/1977 s Joseph Daniel Greene & Kathryn Ann Vk. B.A. The U GA 2002; M.Div GTS 2006. D 12/21/2005 P 8/3/2006 Bp J(ohn) Neil Alexander. m 4/15/2010 Ashley R Greene c 1. Cur S Columba Epis Ch Suwanee GA 2006-2010. frjoegreene@gmail.com

GREENE, Judith (Ct) 5170 Madison Ave, Trumbull CT 06611 B Fairfield CT 9/28/1939 d Gavin Miller Semple & Grace. Chr TS; BA Rad 1961; MA Pur 1968; MDiv GTS 1996. D 6/24/1996 Bp Edward Witker Jones P 1/6/1997 Bp Don Adger Wimberly. c 2. R Chr Ch Trumbull CT 1999-2011; Assoc R Trin Ch Covington KY 1996-1999. judithsemplegreene1@mac.com

GREENE, Lynne Tuthill (SwFla) 1369 Vermeer Drive, Nokomis FL 34275 **D S Mk's Epis Ch Venice FL 1987-** B Newburgh NY 11/7/1924 s Roswell Fish Greene & Dorothy Tuthill. BA Syr 1945; MD Syr 1947. D 9/25/1966 Bp George E Rath. m 4/7/1945 Nora Irene Button c 4. D S Jn's Ch Ithaca NY 1973-1987; D The Ch Of The Annunc Oradell NJ 1966-1973. AMA 1950; Amer Soc of Anesthesiologists 1963. ltgreene@comcast.net

GREENE, Margaret Catharine (Colo) 1300 Washington St, Denver CO 80203 **Faith Formation Coordntr Dio Colorado Denver CO 2008-** B Walnut Creek CA 2/14/1972 d Marshall Demotte Greene & Margaret Wilson. BS U CA, San Diego 1994; MDiv SWTS 2002. D 6/1/2002 P 12/7/2002 Bp William Edwin Swing. m 9/12/2011 Lauren K Robertson. The Ch Of Chr The King (Epis) Arvada CO 2009-2011; St Fran Ch-Dillon Dillon CO 2006-2008; Assoc R S Mk's Epis Ch Palo Alto CA 2002-2006. catiegreene@hotmail.com

GREENE, Michael Paul Thomas (Chi) St Luke's Episcopal Church, 221 W 3rd St, Dixon IL 61021 **R S Lk's Ch Dixon IL 2007-** B Evanston IL 2/11/1974 s Richard William Greene & Gail. BA U of Pennsylvania 2004; BA/MA CRDS 2006; BA/MA Coll of Resurr W Yorkshire GB 2006. D 5/26/2006 P 12/21/2006 Bp Keith Lynn Ackerman. m 7/12/2003 Janet Hope c 1. Cur Gr Epis Ch Galesburg IL 2006-2007. fathermichael@hopegreene.com

GREENE, Patrick James (RI) 55 Main St, N Kingstown RI 02852 **Asst to the R S Paul's Ch No Kingstown RI 2010-** B Providence RI 12/16/1983 s Brian Jerome Greene & Tracy Marie. BA U of Rhode Island 2006; MDiv VTS 2010. D 5/22/2010 P 12/18/2010 Bp Geralyn Wolf. pjgreene@gmail.com

GREENE, Robert B (WTex) 5151 Buffalo Speedway, Apt. 3212, Houston TX 77005 B Morristown NJ 11/7/1925 s Elmer Andrew Greene & Edythe Lucille. BA U So 1946; MDiv VTS 1949. D 8/6/1949 Bp Clinton Simon Quin P 12/1/1950 Bp John E Hines. R Ch Of The Annunc Luling TX 1977-1988; The Resource Cntr Luling TX 1977-1988; Vic S Jn's Epis Ch Bisbee AZ 1974-1976; Vic S Paul's Ch Tombstone AZ 1974-1976; R S Steph's Epis Ch Douglas AZ 1974-1976; Vic S Andr's Epis Ch Sedona AZ 1968-1974; Vic S Thos Of The Vlly Epis Clarkdale AZ 1968-1974; Vic S Mk's Ch Tonopah NV 1966-1968; Vic S Matt's Epis Ch Fairbanks AK 1959-1960; Vic S Tim's Ch Tok AK 1953-1959; Vic S Steph's Ch Liberty TX 1949-1953. natgreene@sbcglobal.net

GREENE, Roger Stewart (SO) 8101 Beechmont Ave, Cincinnati OH 45255 **R S Tim's Epis Ch Cincinnati OH 1993-** B Salt Lake City UT 1/2/1958 s Orrin Edward Greene & Joyce Stewart. BA Stan 1980; MDiv CDSP 1986. D 5/10/1986 Bp Otis Charles P 11/1/1987 Bp Morgan Porteus. m 6/13/1980 Nancy Hopkins c 2. Stff P Trin Ch In The City Of Boston Boston MA 1987-1993. Soc Of S Jn The Evang. roger@sainttimothys.com

GREENE, Timothy Patrick (Cal) 4155 Cesar Chavez St Apt 13, San Francisco CA 94131 B Waterport NY 1/29/1941 s George Patrick Greene & Margaret Ellen. BA Ham 1962; MDiv EDS 1976; Psyd The Wright Inst Berkeley CA 2001. D 12/5/1992 P 12/4/1993 Bp William Edwin Swing. Dio California San Francisco CA 1992-1993. tpgreene@comcast.net

GREENE-MCCREIGHT, Kathryn (Ct) 198 Mckinley Ave, New Haven CT 06515 B Norwalk CT 9/6/1961 d Robert W Greene & Joyce E. BA Wesl 1983; MDiv Yale DS 1988; STM Yale DS 1989; PhD Ya 1994. D 6/8/2002 P 1/25/2003 Bp Andrew Donnan Smith. m 8/4/1984 Matthew Keadle McCreight c 2. Theol-in-Res S Jn's Ch New Haven CT 2002-2010. Auth, "Darkness Is My Only Comp: A Chr Response to Mntl Illness," Brazos Press, 2006; Auth, "Feminist Reconstructions of Chr Doctrine," Oxf Press, 2000; Auth, "Ad Litteram : How Aug, Calvin and Barth Understand the 'Plain Sense' of Genesis 1-3," Ptr Lang, 1999; Co-Ed, "Theol Exegesis: Essays in hon of Brevard Sprg Childs," Eerdmans, 1999; Auth, "Numerous arts and chapters in edited volumes," *Var Pub*, numerous from 1994 though the present, 1994. Chair, Chr Theol and the Bible, Soc of Biblic LiteratureL 2000-2010; Chair, Reformed Theol and the Bible, AAR 1994-2003; Chair, Reformed Theol and the Bible, AAR 1994-2003; Karl Barth Soc of No Amer 1995-2011; Scholarly Engagement w Angl Doctrine 1998-2005; Soc of Angl & Luth Theologians 2001-2005. Pub' Weekly Top Ten in Rel non-Fiction Darkness is my Only Comp 2006; "Choice" Bk Feminist Reconstructions of Chr Doctrine 2000; A "Choice" Bk, 2000 Feminist Reconstructions of Chr Doctrine 2000; Pew Evang Schlr Pew Charitable Trust 1996; Franke Fell in Hmnts Ya Grad Sch of Arts and Sciences 1989; Mstr of Div, cl Yale DS 1988; Evers Schlr Yale DS 1986; Alan MCune Schlr Wesl 1981. greene-mccreight@aya.yale.edu

GREENFIELD, Peter Alan (CPa) 122 Greenview Dr, Lancaster PA 17601 B New York NY 5/29/1933 s Harold Kenneth Greenfield & Judith Karyl. BA Dart 1955; STB PDS 1960. D 5/14/1960 P 12/1/1960 Bp Joseph Gillespie Armstrong. m 8/21/1954 Caroline Patten c 4. P-in-c S Lk's Epis Ch Mt Joy PA 2007-2011; R Bangor Ch Of Churchtown Narvon PA 2003-2007; Cn Cathd Ch Of S Steph Harrisburg PA 1998-2003; R S Jn's Epis Ch Lancaster PA 1983-1995; R S Mk's Epis Ch Lewistown PA 1975-1983; R All SS' Epis Ch Hershey PA 1966-1975; Vic Gd Shpd Ch Hilltown PA 1962-1966; Cur Chr Epis Ch Pottstown PA 1960-1962. Jefferson Awd WGAL 1990; Bro Awd Roundtable of Christians and Jews 1981.

GREENFIELD, William Geddes (EO) 798 Oceanmount Blvd RR8, Gibsons BC V0N 1V8 Canada **Died 10/7/2011** B Hamilton ON CA 8/9/1914 s William Chapman Greenfield & Harriette. BA U Tor 1938; LTh U Tor 1940. D 5/1/1940 Bp The Bishop Of Niagara. c 1.

GREENLAW, William A (NY) 529 West 42nd St. Apt. 4J, New York NY 10036 **R Emer Ch Of The H Apos New York NY 2008-** B Alhambra CA 8/3/1943 s Kenneth Gould Greenlaw & Lois Jane. BA U CA 1965; Drew U TS 1966; MDiv UTS 1968; PhD Duke 1971. D 6/5/1971 Bp Horace W B Donegan P 11/10/1971 Bp Paul Moore Jr. m 2/5/1977 Jane V Veitch. R & Exec Dir, H Apos Soup Kitchen Ch Of The H Apos New York NY 1984-2008; Asst in Par & Proj Dir, H Apos Soup Kitchen Ch Of The H Apos New York NY 1983-1984; Assoc R Chr And S Steph's Ch New York NY 1976-1983; Asst Prof of Chr Ethics The GTS New York NY 1971-1975. The Bp's Cross Dio New York/Bp Mk Sisk 2004; Soc of St. Jn the Theol Dio New York / Bp Mk Sisk 2002. wagrnlaw@verizon.net

GREENLEAF, Richard Edward (NH) 325 Pleasant St, Concord NH 03301 B Winchester MA 5/20/1953 s Malcolm Greenleaf & Ruth. BA U of Massachusetts 1976; TS Gordon-Conwell TS 1984; MDiv Ya Berk 1988. D 2/29/1992 P 11/14/1992 Bp Douglas Edwin Theuner. m 4/19/1980 Jenny Jensen c 1. BDS GS Pres 2005-2007; BDS GS Secy 2003-2004; Berkeley Grad Soc 2002-2007; Dio NH COM 2003-2008; Prov I Epis Sch Chapl Conf 1998. Chas D. Dickey Mstr in Rel & Ethics St. Paul's Sch 2003. rgreenleaf@sps.edu

GREENLEE, Malcolm Blake (Ct) 32 Old Wagon Rd, Wilton CT 06897 B Mercedes TX 8/20/1932 s Walden Gillespie Greenlee & Nelle. GTS; BS Pur 1956; MBA GW 1969. D 6/12/1982 P 4/1/1983 Bp Arthur Edward Walmsley. m 12/7/1953 Dorothy Willard Richmond. Asst Gr Epis Ch Trumbull CT 1990-1998; Asst Ch Of S Thos Bethel CT 1984-1990; Asst S Steph's Ch Ridgefield CT 1982-1984. Auth, "Var arts Bus & Computers". Bd Dir Oratory Little Way.

GREENSHIELDS, Kay Conner (Okla) 405 Roserock Dr, Norman OK 73026 **D S Anselm Cbury Norman OK 2001-** B Oklahoma City OK 2/20/1934 d Herald Albert Conner & Edna Clifford. D Formation Prog; BA U of Oklahoma 1955; Ecole De Normale De Musique 1956. D 7/1/1989 Bp James Russell Moodey. m 7/10/1955 James Bernie Greenshields c 2. D S Jn's Ch Norman OK 1989-2001. Dok; NAAD; Rain Oklahoma. jimnkay@swbell.net

GREENWELL, Gail Elizabeth (Kan) 6630 Nall Ave, Mission KS 66202 **COM, chair Dio Kansas Topeka KS 2009-; R S Mich And All Ang Ch Mssn KS 2008-** B Portland OR 3/25/1955 d Fred Ehman & Barbara Jean. BA U of Oregon 1977; MDiv CDSP 2001. D 5/26/2001 Bp Robert Louis Ladehoff P 12/1/2001 Bp William Edwin Swing. m 1/23/1982 James Greenwell c 2.

Epis Cmnty Serv Bd Dio California San Francisco CA 2005-2008; R Ch Of The Epiph San Carlos CA 2004-2008; Assoc R S Steph's Par Belvedere CA 2001-2004. Pstr Ldrshp Awd Louisville Inst, KY 2008. gail@stmaa.com

GREEN-WITT, Margaret Evelyn Ashmead (SwFla) 2499 Mapleleaf Ct, Spring Hill FL 34606 B Philadelphia PA 2/20/1920 d Robert Huckel Ashmead & Anna Watson. BS SUNY 1984. D 6/29/1991 Bp Rogers Sanders Harris. m 3/5/2000 Kenneth D Witt c 4. D S Jas Epis Ch Leesburg FL 2008-2011; D S Andr's Epis Ch Sprg Hill FL 1991-2007; Proj Dir Soup Kitchen Ch Of The H Apos New York NY 1982-1983; Asst Coordntr Capital Cmpgn The GTS New York NY 1979-1981.

GREENWOOD, April Valeria Trew (Va) Po Box 278, Millers Tavern VA 23115 **Varina Epis Ch Richmond VA 2009-** B Elizabeth City NC 12/5/1955 d I Frederick Trew & Helen. BS Longwood U 1973; Med U of Virginia 1977; MDiv VTS 1983. D 4/28/1984 P 4/1/1985 Bp David Henry Lewis Jr. m 10/13/1984 Daniel R Greenwood. S Andr's Ch Richmond VA 2006-2007; Dio Virginia Richmond VA 2001-2006; S Dav's Ch Aylett VA 1998. Auth, "Coun For Rel In Independant Schools-How To Talk About God"; Auth, "Didache-Here I Stand: What Else Can I Do?". REVAPRIL@VERIZON.NET

GREENWOOD III, Daniel R (SVa) 2910 Stratford Rd, Richmond VA 23225 **Dio Virginia Richmond VA 2009-; R S Paul's Ch Petersburg VA 2009-** B Philadelphia PA 3/8/1954 s Daniel Richard Greenwood & Dorothy Louise. Wms 1974; BA Hav 1976; MDiv VTS 1984. D 4/6/1986 P 5/1/1992 Bp George Nelson Hunt III. m 10/13/1984 April Valeria Trew Greenwood c 2. R S Paul's Epis Ch Miller's Tavern VA 1995-2002; Asst R S Mary's Ch Portsmouth RI 1991-1995. the.revrick@verizon.net

GREENWOOD, Don Robert (SO) 10414 Nw 13th Pl, Vancouver WA 98685 B Orange CA 6/3/1939 s Charles F Greenwood & Kathrine. BA U CA 1961; MDiv STUSo 1967; Cert Int Mnstry Prog 1993. D 6/27/1967 Bp William Evan Sanders P 5/1/1968 Bp William F Gates Jr. m 12/21/1962 Anna Lee Brummett c 3. Vic S Nich Of Myra Epis Ch Hilliard OH 1997-2001; Trin Ch Newark OH 1997; Int All SS Epis Ch Portsmouth OH 1996-1997; Int S Phil's Ch Columbus OH 1994-1995; Int S Ptr's Ch Gallipolis OH 1993-1994; Ch Of The Epiph Nelsonville OH 1993; Whetstone Care Cntr Columbus OH 1990-1992; R Ch Of The Redeem Sayre PA 1983-1990; R Gr Ch In The Mountains Waynesville NC 1978-1983; R S Fran Ch Macon GA 1972-1978; P-in-c S Mary's Ch Enterprise MS 1969-1972; Asst S Paul's Epis Ch Meridian MS 1969-1972; P-in-c Trin Ch Newton MS 1969-1972; Vic Chr Epis Ch Tracy City TN 1968-1969; D-in-Trng S Ptr's Ch Columbia TN 1967-1968. Auth, *S Lk Journ*; Auth, *The Rel Essence & Theol Meaning of Amer Popular Mus*; "Ord and Ret - Freedom to Choose," *Vintage Voice*. greenwood2047@comcast.net

GREENWOOD JR, Eric Sutcliffe (Tenn) 6501 Pennywell Dr, Nashville TN 37205 **R S Dav's Epis Ch Nashville TN 1988-** B Memphis TN 10/6/1948 s Eric Sutcliffe Greenwood & Florence Ruth. BA LSU 1970; MDiv GTS 1973. D 6/24/1973 Bp John Vander Horst P 5/6/1974 Bp William Evan Sanders. m 9/3/1971 Sharon McCormack c 2. Asst to the R Gr & H Trin Epis Ch Richmond VA 1977-1988; Vic S Fran' Ch Norris TN 1974-1977; D S Jn's Epis Cathd Knoxville TN 1973-1974. esgreenwoodjr@gmail.com

GREENWOOD, Harold Lee Hal (Okla) 2201 Nw 18th St, Oklahoma City OK 73107 **Dio Oklahoma Oklahoma City OK 2005-** B Cushing OK 3/6/1949 s Harold Leroy Greenwood & Doris Ellen. BS Oklahoma St U 1971; MDiv GTS 1977. D 6/18/1977 P 1/1/1978 Bp Gerald Nicholas McAllister. m 9/6/1970 Marcia Cozart c 3. Ch Of The H Fam Moncks Corner SC 1981-1982; Assoc R S Jn's Epis Ch Tulsa OK 1979-1981; P-in-c All SS Ch McAlester OK 1977-1979; Trin Ch Eufaula OK 1977-1979. greenwood7@cox.net

GREENWOOD, Mildred Lee Hart (Pa) 30 Glenwood Cir, Aldan PA 19018 **Died 8/19/2011** B Sharon Hill PA 3/11/1931 d George Joseph Hart & Mildred. Widener U; W Chester St Teachers Coll 1950; BA Wheaton Coll 1953; Med Tem 1960; Principals Cert. Villanova U 1976. D 1/27/1990 Bp Allen Lyman Bartlett Jr. c 2. Auth, *Bd Sailing Made Easy*. Athletic Hall of Fame W Chester U 2000; Storzebecker Hall of Fame W Chester U 1996. mgreenw@dccc.edu

GREENWOOD, Susan Anne (Colo) 53 Paradise Rd, Golden CO 80401 **Our Merc Sav Epis Ch Denver CO 2011-** B Bartlesville OK 4/23/1947 BS U of Oklahoma 1969; MA U CO 1994; MDiv GTS 2006. D 6/10/2006 P 12/9/2006 Bp Robert John O'Neill. c 2. Our Merc Sav Epis Ch Denver CO 2009-2010; Assoc R S Lk's Epis Ch Ft Collins CO 2006-2008. revsusangreenwood@gmail.com

GREENWOOD, W(alter) Merritt (O) 2487 E 126th St, Cleveland OH 44120 B Fayetteville NC 2/14/1954 s Walter Greenwood & Mary Logan. BA Ken 1977; MDiv EDS 1981. D 6/27/1981 P 3/1/1982 Bp John Harris Burt. m 8/25/1979 Janette Thomas c 2. S Mich's Epis Ch Brattleboro VT 2009-2011; Int S Andr's Ch Cleveland OH 2006-2009; S Paul's Epis Ch Of E Cleveland Cleveland OH 2000-2004; Assoc Chr Ch Shaker Heights OH 1998-1999; R S Mk's Ch Worcester MA 1992-1997; Dio Wstrn Massachusetts Springfield MA 1991-1998; S Anne's Par Scottsville VA 1986-1991; Cur S Mart's Epis Ch Charlotte NC 1981-1986. mgreen1727@aol.com

GREER, David Jay (WLa) 208 Bruce Ave, Shreveport LA 71105 B Poughkeepsie NY 10/7/1929 s Harry Ross Greer & Marjorie. TESM; BS Wag 1950; MDiv VTS 1955; Fllshp Ldrshp Acad for New Directions 1978; Fllshp VTS 1979; Fllshp Coll of Preachers 1986; Fllshp TS 1986; Fllshp U So 1986; Epis TS of The SW 1987; St Petersburg Acad Russia 1992. D 6/11/1955 Bp Benjamin M Washburn P 1/7/1956 Bp Frederick D Goodwin. m 8/6/1951 Barbara von Broock c 3. Int S Jn's Ch Barrington RI 2005-2006; Int Epis Ch Of The Gd Shpd Lake Chas LA 2003-2004; Int Chr Ch Grosse Pointe Grosse Pointe Farms MI 2001-2002; Chr Ch Nacogdoches TX 2000-2011; Presiding Judge Dio Wstrn Louisiana Alexandria LA 1996-2005; Int S Jn's Epis Ch McLean VA 1995-1996; Int Gr Epis Ch Monroe LA 1994-1995; R S Paul's Epis Ch Shreveport LA 1980-1989; R S Jas' Epis Ch Warrenton VA 1964-1980; R Chr Epis Ch Gordonsville VA 1958-1964; Asst S Paul's Ch Richmond VA 1955-1958. *Var arts & Revs*, 2003. Epis EvangES 1954.

GREER JR, George H (NC) 301 S Circle Dr, Rocky Mount NC 27804 **R S Andr's Ch Rocky Mt NC 2005-** B Owensboro KY 2/4/1961 s George H Greer & Virginia Ann. BA Brescia U 1984; MDiv GTS 2000. D 6/4/2000 P 1/13/2001 Bp Edwin Funsten Gulick Jr. m 1/9/1988 Claire Bennett White c 2. R S Lk's Epis Ch Buffalo WY 2003-2005; Assoc R S Fran In The Fields Harrods Creek KY 2000-2003. rector@saint-andrews-church.org

GREER JR, James Gossett (O) 13710 Shaker Blvd Apt 404, Cleveland OH 44120 **Hon Assoc Chr Ch Shaker Heights OH 2002-** B Dallas TX 12/28/1932 s James Gossett Greer & Lizabeth Kathleen. BA U of No Texas 1955; STB GTS 1958; S Aug's Coll Cbury Gb 1959; STM Nash 1972. D 6/18/1958 P 12/20/1958 Bp J(ohn) Joseph Meakins Harte. m 5/25/1984 Karen A Anderson. S Ptr's Epis Ch Lakewood OH 1987; Int S Jn's Ch Cleveland OH 1986-1996; R S Jas' Epis Ch Of Albion Albion MI 1979-1983; R S Mk's Ch Newaygo MI 1976-1979; R S Thos Epis Ch Plymouth IN 1972-1976; R S Jas' Epis Ch Goshen IN 1968-1972; Vic Ch Of The H Trin So Bend IN 1963-1968; R S Barth's Ch Hempstead TX 1960-1963. Secy'S Awd For Excellence In Chapl Veteran Affrs Washington DC 1996. jkgreer@att.net

GREER III, Rowan Allen (Ct) 72 Cottage St, New Haven CT 06511 B Dayton OH 4/17/1934 s Rowan Allen Greer & Janet Lorraine. BA Ya 1956; STB GTS 1959; MA Ya 1964; PhD Yale DS 1965. D 6/11/1959 P 3/5/1960 Bp Walter H Gray. Cur S Ptr's Epis Ch Charlotte NC 1997-1999; S Thos's Ch New Haven CT 1993-1999; Cur Chr Ch New Haven CT 1961-1964; Cur S Paul's Ch Fairfield CT 1959-1961. Auth, "Chr Hope and Chr Life," Crossroad, 2001; Auth, "Fear of Freedom," Penn St Press, 1989; Auth, "Broken Light & Mended Lives," Penn St Press, 1986; Auth, "The Captain of Our Salvation," JCB Mohr, 1973. DD VTS 2002.

GREGG, Catherine (U) 2235 S. 1400 E Unit 19, Saint George UT 84790 **Dioc Coun Dio Utah Salt Lake City UT 2010-; R Gr Epis Ch St Geo UT 2007-** B Rockledge FL 12/2/1954 d Charles Edward Colletta & Iris Justine. BA California St U Los Angeles 1975; Spec Ed Cred Los Angles Cnty 1976; Certificated Counslr Vineyard TS 1979; TESOL Lifetime Cred Mt San Antonio Coll 1981; DMin Haggard TS 1999. D 1/31/2004 P 8/1/2004 Bp Joseph Jon Bruno. m 4/11/2000 Douglas Hamilton Gregg c 3. Bp Search Com Dio Utah Salt Lake City UT 2009-2010; Liturg/Wrshp Com Dio Utah Salt Lake City UT 2008-2010; Assoc Ch Of Our Sav Par San Gabr CA 2004-2006. Contributing Auth, "The Disease of Ethnocentricity," *IHC Revs*, Intermountain Hlth, 2010; Bk Reviewer, "Revs of," *Presence mag*, Sprtl Dir Intl , 2007; Auth, "Handbook for Sprtl Direction Trng," *Handbook for Sprtl Direction Trng*, CFDM, 2005; Doctoral Candidate, "The Role of Wisdom in the Cure of Souls," *HGST Archv*, HGST, 1999; Monthly Contrib, "Pryr and the Sprtl Life," *DAWN Report*, DAWN Mnstrs, 1989. Iona Cmnty 2009. Wmn of the Year Awd PPAU 2011; Sprt of Cmnty Awd Citizens for Dixie's Future 2010; Wmn of the Year Awd Bus and Profsnl Wmn/UT 2009; Rel Ldr of the Year Awd Washington Cnty Cltn Against Dom Violence 2009. cgregg@gracestgeorge.org

GREGG, Jennifer E (WMass) St Stephen's Episcopal Church, 67 East St, Pittsfield MA 01201 **P Assoc S Steph's Ch Pittsfield MA 2007-** B Easton, MD 10/3/1977 d Alan Tounley Gregg. BS Elmira Coll, Elmira NY 1999; MDiv Berkley DS at Yale 2007. D 6/9/2007 Bp Charles Ellsworth Bennison Jr P 12/15/2007 Bp Franklin Delton Turner. m 8/25/2007 Derek Bodenstab c 1. jgregg@ststephenspittsfield.org

GREGG, Robert Clark (Cal) 659 Salvatierra St, Stanford CA 94305 B Kansas City MO 7/2/1938 s Harris Thompson Gregg & Mary Francis. BA U So 1960; BD EDS 1963; Br 1969; PhD U of Pennsylvania 1974. D 10/28/1963 P 9/1/1964 Bp John S Higgins. m 9/8/1961 Mary Layne Shine c 4. Assoc Chap Of The Cross Chap Hill NC 1978-1987; Co-P-in-c Trin Ch Fuquay Varina NC 1977-1987; Asst Ch Of S Mart-In-The-Fields Philadelphia PA 1969-1970; Assoc Chapl S Geo's Ch Portsmouth RI 1963-1966. Auth, "Consolation Philos"; Auth, "Athan: The Life Of Antony & The Letter To Marcellinus"; Auth, "Jews, Pagans," *& Chr In The Golan*. Hon DD U So 1990. rgregg@stanford.edu

GREGG, Thomas Alexander (SC) 2218 Fernglen Pl, Cary NC 27511 B Laurinburg NC 7/17/1924 s James Maxwell Gregg & Anne-Lynn. BS Davidson Coll 1950; MDiv VTS 1967. P 1/1/1968 Bp Thomas H Wright. m 2/24/1946 Margaret Sax c 3. P in Charge/R S Jas Santee Ch McClellanville SC 1990-1995;

Assoc R S Paul's Epis Ch Conway SC 1977-1978; R S Paul's In The Pines Epis Ch Fayetteville NC 1969-1974. Auth, "Sweetening Relationships," *Why Ch?*, 1967. AAMFT/ AASECT 1967-2003; Licenced Mar Fam Ther 1967-2003. thomasgregg@bellsouth.net

✠ **GREGG, Rt Rev William O** (NC) St. Peter's Episcopal Church, 115 W 7th St, Charlotte NC 28202 B Portsmouth VA 1/1/1951 s Otis Bishop Gregg & Geraldine. BA U Rich 1973; MDiv EDS 1977; MA Boston Coll 1980; MA U of Notre Dame 1990; PhD U of Notre Dame 1993. D 6/4/1977 Bp Robert Bruce Hall P 5/14/1978 Bp John Alfred Baden Con 9/23/2000 for EO. m 5/28/1977 Kathleen E Stark c 1. Bp of EO Dio Estrn Oregon The Dalles OR 2000-2007; Exam Chapl Dio Connecticut Hartford CT 1998-2000; R S Jas Ch New London CT 1997-2000; S Andr's Ch Paris IL 1996; Stndg Com Dio Indianapolis Indianapolis IN 1993-1997; S Geo Epis Ch W Terre Haute IN 1993-1996; Asst S Jn The Evang Ch Elkhart IN 1990-1991; Ch Of The H Trin Kokomo IN 1990; S Mich And All Ang Ch So Bend IN 1988-1989; Int R S Mich And All Ang Ch So Bend IN 1987-1988; R S Thos' Epis Ch Abingdon VA 1982-1987; Cur Ch Of S Jn The Bapt Ivy VA 1978-1979; S Paul's Ch Ivy VA 1978-1979; Cur S Paul's Memi Charlottesville VA 1978-1979; Vic Epis Ch Of Our Sav Midlothian VA 1977-1978. Auth, "Presence of Ch in The Cloud of Unknowing," *Amer Benedictine Revs*, 1992; Auth, "Sacramental Theol in Hooker's Laws: A Structural Perspective," *ATR*, 1991; Auth, *Benedictine Revs 92*. OHC. wgregg@episdionc.org

GREGORIUS, Mary B. (NY) 3 Debbie Ct, Poughkeepsie NY 12601 B Newburgh NY 8/17/1953 d Howard Charles Flemming & Mary Buckbee. Westminster Choir Coll of Rider U 1983; D Formation Prog 1998; BA SUNY 2001; M. Div GTS 2009. D 5/16/1998 Bp Richard Frank Grein P 9/12/2009 Bp Mark Sean Sisk. m 11/6/1983 Harold S Gregorius c 2. Assoc P S Marg's Ch Staatsburg NY 2009-2011; D Chr Ch Poughkeepsie NY 1998-2005. mbgregor@optonline.net

GREGORY, Emma Jean (Nev) 4201 W Washington Ave, Las Vegas NV 89107 B Collinsville AL 4/18/1941 d Samuel Curtis Gregory & Edgie Lee Ford. D 6/10/2007 Bp Jerry Alban Lamb. c 1. imaginem@aol.com

GREGORY, John Chase (NH) 29 Hazen Rd, Whitefield NH 03598 B Johnsonburg PA 4/17/1926 s Jesse Howell Gregory & Esther Ann. BS U IL 1950; MS U Cinc 1952; MDiv EDS 1957. D 6/15/1957 P 12/22/1957 Bp Henry W Hobson. m 6/9/1991 Clara May Ball c 2. S Jas Ch Concord VT 1976-1999; Vic S Mk's Ch Groveton NH 1959-1969; R S Paul's Ch Lancaster NH 1959-1969; Cur S Paul's Epis Ch Dayton OH 1957-1959. OHC, PA 1963.

GREGORY, Leslie Burtner (NwT) 822 Keeler Ave, Dalhart TX 79022 **Supply P Dio NW Texas Lubbock TX 1991-** B Buffalo NY 10/25/1948 d Orville Leslie Burtner & Mildred Nadine. BA U of Kansas 1970; MDiv Epis TS of The SW 1991. D 9/14/1991 Bp William Edward Smalley P 5/1/1992 Bp Sam Byron Hulsey. m 7/31/1988 Alan Bryant Gregory c 1. Exec Com Dio NW Texas Lubbock TX 1995-2000; Chair, Priestly Titles Com Dio NW Texas Lubbock TX 1995; Chair, Sprtl Dvlpmt Com Dio NW Texas Lubbock TX 1994-1996; Missions Com Dio NW Texas Lubbock TX 1992-1994.

GREGORY, Loren Hill (Ct) 40 Halstead Ave, Port Chester NY 10573 **Died 4/27/2010** B Port Chester NY 8/13/1959 d Donald Richard Hill & Lorraine Ebba. AA Green Mtn Coll 1979. D 12/9/2000 Bp Andrew Donnan Smith. c 2. ebbahill@aol.com

GREGORY, Pamela S (RI) 251 Danielson Pike, North Scituate RI 02857 **R Trin Ch N Scituate RI 1998-** B Des Moines IA 7/20/1951 d David Walter Gregory & Berdean Venita. BA Coe Coll 1973; MS Drake U 1978; MDiv SWTS 1986; DMin SWTS 1990. D 5/31/1986 P 12/17/1986 Bp Walter Cameron Righter. m 11/24/2009 Ronald W Tyrrell c 4. Vic S Chad Epis Ch Loves Pk IL 1990-1998; P-in-c Trin Ch Carroll IA 1986-1990. Alb Inst 1997. pamegrego4@aol.com

GREGORY, Phillip Richard (Chi) 2612 Gateshead Dr, Naperville IL 60564 B Aurora IL 7/25/1948 D 2/7/2004 Bp Victor Alfonso Scantlebury. m 12/22/1996 Deborah Humphreys.

GREGORY, Rachael Anne (CFla) 410 Grand Ave, Waukegan IL 60085 **Non-Stipendiary Other Cler Chr Ch Waukegan IL 2010-** B Paoli IN 6/7/1966 d Norman Ralph Gregory & Lois Marie. AA Oxford Coll of Emory U 1987; BA Berry Coll 1989; MDiv The TS at The U So 2010. D 6/5/2010 P 2/12/2011 Bp John Wadsworth Howe. revrachael@gmail.com

GREGORY, Stanley Harold (FdL) 2767 S Via Del Bac, Green Valley AZ 85622 B Johnson City NY 8/3/1917 s Stanley B Gregory & Lula May. BA Gordon Coll 1949; MA U of New Hampshire 1950; VTS 1959. D 4/25/1959 P 11/18/1959 Bp Arnold M Lewis. m 12/13/2003 Barbara Lee Pryor c 2. P Epis Ch Of S Fran-In-The-Vlly Green Vlly AZ 1992-1993; R Ch Of S Jn The Bapt Wausau WI 1965-1981; Assoc Gr Ch Madison WI 1961-1965; R All SS Ch Pratt KS 1959-1961; R S Mk's Ch Pratt KS 1959-1961. Chapl Reserve Off Assn. Meritorious Serv Awd ArmdF 1977; Korean Serv Medal 1958. 19stan17@therim.com

✠ GREIN, Rt Rev Richard Frank (NY) 117 Oenoke Rdg, New Canaan CT 06840 **Ret Bp Dio New York New York City NY 2001-** B Bemidji MN 11/29/1932 s Lester Edward Grein & Lavina. BA Carleton Coll 1955; MDiv Nash 1959; STM Nash 1971. D 6/20/1959 Bp Hamilton Hyde Kellogg P 12/21/1959 Bp Philip Frederick McNairy Con 5/22/1981 for Kan. m 5/28/2004 Anne Frances Connor. Dio New York New York City NY 1994-2001; Ny Income New York NY 1989-1994; Bp Coadj Dio New York New York City NY 1988-1989; Bp Dio Kansas Topeka KS 1981-1988; R S Mich And All Ang Ch Mssn KS 1974-1981; Prof, Pstr Theol Nash Nashotah WI 1973-1974; R The Epis Par Of S Dav Minnetonka MN 1969-1973; Dept of Missions Dio Minnesota Minneapolis MN 1968-1971; Dept of Missions Dio Minnesota Minneapolis MN 1968-1970; Dept of CSR Dio Minnesota Minneapolis MN 1964-1971; R S Matt's Epis Ch Minneapolis MN 1964-1969; Vic H Trin Epis Ch Elk River MN 1959-1963. "On Being A Bp (Contrib)," Ch Hymnal Corp, 1992; Auth, "Angl Theol & Pstr Care (Contrib)," Morehouse Pub, 1985. Bp Visitor, Cmnty of S Mary 1994-2000; Bp Visitor, CHS 1990-2001; Coun, Associated Parishes; OHC 1957-2005. Hon Metropltn of the Ecum Throne Ecum Patriarch; Prelate in Priory in USA Ord of S Jn of Jerusalem. rfg14ny@aol.com

GREISER JR, Ronald (SC) PO Box 14548, Myrtle Beach SC 29587 **R The Epis Ch Of The Resurr Surfside Bch SC 2009-** B Cincinnati OH 9/21/1960 s Ronald Edmond Greiser & Lauren Ann. BS Tennessee Tech U 1985; MDiv VTS 1993. D 6/2/1993 Bp Calvin Onderdonk Schofield Jr P 12/1/1993 Bp Frank Kellogg Allan. m 12/27/1984 Sanna Elizabeth Porcher c 2. R S Jn's Ch Portsmouth VA 1999-2009; Exec Com Dio Atlanta Atlanta GA 1995-1999; Cur Trin Epis Ch Columbus GA 1993-1999. rgreiser@gmail.com

GREISER, Ronald Edmond (WNC) 160 Sunny Ridge Rd, Hendersonville NC 28739 B Cincinnati OH 6/18/1934 s Melvin Rudolph Greiser & Ada Clara. BA U Cinc 1957; MDiv STUSo 1977. D 6/18/1977 Bp William F Gates Jr P 12/19/1977 Bp William Evan Sanders. m 1/29/1986 Rita Oney c 4. S Andr's Epis Ch Panama City FL 1990-1997; R S Jn The Apos Ch Belle Glade FL 1986-1990; Asst H Trin Epis Ch W Palm Bch FL 1981-1986; R S Matt's Epis Ch McMinnville TN 1979-1981; Otey Memi Par Ch Sewanee TN 1977-1978. Ord of S Lk 1982; SocMary 1975. rongreiser@gmail.com

GREMILLION, Dorothy Ann (Tex) 405 South Washington Avenue, Mansfield LA 71052 B Algiers LA 9/1/1942 d Donald Monroe Risinger & Marie Belle. MA Loyola U 1991; MA McNeese St U 1994; MDiv Epis TS of The SW 2000. D 6/3/2000 P 12/9/2000 Bp Robert Jefferson Hargrove Jr. m 12/21/1963 O'Keefe Gremillion Jr c 3. S Lk's Ch Livingston TX 2005-2009; S Andr's Ch Roswell NM 2001-2004; R Chr Memi Ch Mansfield LA 2000-2001. reverendorothy@yahoo.com

GRENNEN, T Kyle (Me) Po Box 115, Springfield Center NY 13468 **R Gr Ch Cherry Vlly NY 2011-; R S Mary's Ch Springfield Cntr NY 2011-; S Paul's Schoharie NY 2008-; Dio Maine Portland ME 2000-** B New Brunswick NJ 6/25/1955 s Raymond F Grennen & Anna. BS Montana St U 1977; MDiv EDS 1988. D 6/11/1988 Bp George Phelps Mellick Belshaw P 2/11/1989 Bp Vincent King Pettit. m 2/11/1983 Vita Sager c 1. S Jn's Ch Johnstown NY 2009-2010; R Ch Of The Gd Shpd Rangeley ME 2002-2007; R Chr Ch Greenville NY 1990-2002; R Trin Ch Rensselaerville Rensselaerville NY 1990-2002; Cur S Ptr's Ch Medford NJ 1988-1990. Contrib, "A Formation Prog for New Monastics," *Visio Divina, A Rdr in Faith and Visual Arts*, LeaderResources, 2009. Anamchairde Celtic Ntwk; Ord Of S Aid. kylegrennen@yahoo.com

GRENZ, Linda L (Del) Leader Resources, Box 302, Leeds MA 01053 **Pub & CEO LeaderResources Leeds MA 2010-** B Eureka SD 4/9/1950 d Milbert Albert Grenz & Frieda. BA Westmar Coll 1972; MTS Harvard DS 1974; MDiv EDS 1977. D 6/9/1976 P 4/25/1977 Bp Morris Fairchild Arnold. m 12/27/1992 Delbert C Glover. R Gd Shpd Epis Ch Silver Sprg MD 2008-2010; Pub & CEO LeaderResources Leeds MA 1994-2008; Adult Ed, Lay Min, Ldrshp Dev Stff Epis Ch Cntr New York NY 1991-1994; Assoc. Coord. Ovrs Dvlpmt Epis Ch Cntr New York NY 1989-1991; Cler Team Ldr S Matt's Ch Jersey City NJ 1989-1991; Assoc Imm Ch On The Green New Castle DE 1984-1987; R S Paul's Ch Camden DE 1977-1984. Auth, "Guide to New Ch's Tchg Series," Cowley, 2000; Auth, "Doubleday Pocket Bible Guide," Doubleday, 1997; Auth, "The Mar Journey," Cowley, 1996; Ed, "I Love to Tell the Story," Cntr for Chr Formation, 1994; Auth, "A Cov of Trust," Forw Mvmt, 1994; Ed, "The Bible's Authority in Today's Wrld," Trin Press, 1993; Ed, Contrib, "In Dialogue w Scripture," Epis Ch Cntr, 1992; Contrib, "Homilies for Chr People," Pueblo Press, 1989. Linda@LeaderResources.org

GRESSLE, Richard Lloyd (NY) 130 1st Ave, Nyack NY 10960 **R Gr Epis Ch Nyack NY 1995-** B Pittsburgh PA 4/3/1945 s Lloyd Edward Gressle & Marguerite Kirkpatrick. BA Hob 1967; MDiv EDS 1971. D 6/10/1971 Bp Lloyd Edward Gressle P 6/1/1972 Bp William Henry Mead. R Ch Of The Gd Shpd Ft Lee NJ 1980-1995; The Germaine Lawr Sch Arlington Heigts MA 1978-1980; Asst Calv Ch Pittsburgh PA 1973-1978. Proctor Fell 1992. rgressle@gracechurchnyack.org

✠ **GREW II, Rt Rev J Clark** (O) One Huntington Avenue, # 304, Boston MA 02116 B New York NY 12/20/1939 s Henry Sturgis Grew & Selina Richards. EDS; BA Harv 1962; MDiv EDS 1978; DD EDS 1997. D 6/18/1978 P 12/20/1978 Bp Morris Fairchild Arnold Con 3/5/1994 for O. m 12/27/1972 Sarah L Loomis c 3. Bp of OH Dio Ohio Cleveland OH 1994-2004; R The Ch Of The

H Sprt Lake Forest IL 1982-1993; R S Jn's Epis Ch Westwood MA 1978-1982. Soc of S Jn the Evang 1985. jcg2@rcn.com

GREWELL, Genevieve Michael (Oly) 1551 Tenth Ave. E, Seattle WA 98102 **Archd Dio Olympia Seattle WA 2009-; D S Jn's Epis Ch Olympia WA 2007-** B Seattle WA 12/4/1946 d John Wilbur Brady & Geraldine Loveland. D 6/24/2000 Bp Sanford Zangwill Kaye Hampton. m 1/7/1983 Gary Eugene Grewell. D S Ben Epis Ch Lacey WA 2003-2009; D S Jn's Epis Ch Olympia WA 2000-2002. ggrewell21@comcast.net

GRIBBLE, Robert Leslie (Tex) 24 N Masonic St, Bellville TX 77418 B Houston TX 1/6/1954 s Joseph Russell Gribble & Lorraine Silvia. BBA U of Texas 1976; MDiv VTS 1979. D 11/27/1979 Bp John E Hines P 12/1/1980 Bp Maurice Manuel Benitez. c 2. R S Mary's Ch Bellville TX 1999-2010; Cleric Trin Ch Galveston TX 1996-1999; R Ch Of The Epiph Houston TX 1989-1996; R S Ptr's Epis Ch Brenham TX 1985-1989; Assoc R S Mart's Epis Ch Houston TX 1979-1985. rlgribble@scbglobal.net

GRIBBON, Robert Troth (Eas) PO Box 1493, Salisbury MD 21802 **R Old Trin Ch Ch Creek MD 2006-; Ch Of The Epiph Forestville MD 1967-** B Plainfield NJ 1/27/1943 s Robert Benjamin Gribbon & Ruth T. BA U of Maryland 1964; STB GTS 1967; DMin Wesley TS 1999. D 5/20/1967 P 12/17/1967 Bp George Alfred Taylor. m 8/28/1965 Nancy Insley c 2. Bp's Asst for Mnstry Dio Delaware Wilmington DE 2001-2006; Deploy Off Dio Easton Easton MD 2000-2001; Int S Paul's Ch Georgetown DE 1999-2001; Int Ch Of The Epiph Forestville MD 1998-1999; R S Paul's Ch Centreville MD 1987-1998; Consult The Alb Inst Herndon VA 1981-1987; Campus Min Untd Coll Mnstrs In Nthrn Va McLean VA 1980; Vic St Matthews Ch Mitchellville MD 1976-1979. Auth, "Developing Faith in YA," The Alb Inst; Auth, "Let's Put YP in Their Place," ECUSA; Auth, "Peacemaking Without Div," The Alb Inst; Auth, "Students," *Ch & Higher Educ*, Judson Press. rtgribbon@aol.com

GRIEB, Anne Katherine (WA) 3737 Seminary Rd, Alexandria VA 22304 **VTS Alexandria VA 1994-** B Chestertown MD 6/3/1949 d Henry Norman Grieb & Lillian Franklin. BA Hollins U 1971; JD CUA 1975; MDiv VTS 1983; PhD Yale DS 1997. D 6/11/1983 P 12/10/1983 Bp John Thomas Walker. Assoc Ch Of S Steph And The Incarn Washington DC 1996; Asst Trin Epis Ch Portland ME 1984-1989. Auth, "The Story of Romans: A Narrative Defense of God's Righteousness," Westminster Jn Knox, 2002. KGrieb@vts.edu

GRIEB, Ray Kline (Neb) 487 Goodrich Rd, Wheatland WY 82201 B Pueblo CO 2/23/1934 s George Frederick Grieb & Lucille Beattie. BA U CO 1957; MDiv Nash 1960. D 6/21/1960 P 12/21/1960 Bp Joseph Summerville Minnis. c 3. Vic S Christophers Ch Cozad NE 1995-2003; R Chr Ch Sidney NE 1987-1992; R S Paul's Epis Ch Dixon WY 1984-1987; St Thos Epis Ch Monte Vista CO 1975-1980; Assoc Cathd Ch Of S Paul Detroit MI 1962-1968; Vic S Ptr's Ch Clearfield UT 1962-1965; Vic S Andr's Ch Cripple Creek CO 1960-1962. raygrieb@yahoo.com

GRIESEL, Bernard Frederick (Cal) 1100 Gough St Apt 6f, San Francisco CA 94109 B Chicago IL 12/13/1933 s Frederick Compton Griesel & Florence Anna. BA U CO 1953; LTh U Tor 1956; STB U Tor 1957; MS San Francisco St U 1979. D 6/24/1957 P 1/1/1958 Bp Joseph Summerville Minnis. P-in-c S Mk's Par Crockett CA 1970; Cur S Mich And All Ang Ch Portland OR 1963-1965; Cur Ch Of The Ascen Pueblo CO 1958-1960; In-charge Trin Ch Trinidad CO 1957-1958. Auth, *Hist of Chld Welf in San Francisco*. bgriesel@aol.com

GRIESER, D Jonathan (Mil) 116 W Washington Ave, Madison WI 53703 **R Gr Ch Madison WI 2009-** B Wauseon OH 4/24/1958 s Dale Edward Grieser & Dorothy Lois. BA Goshen Coll 1981; MDiv Harvard DS 1985; ThD Harvard DS 1993. D 6/11/2005 P 5/10/2006 Bp Dorsey Felix Henderson. m 6/13/1987 Corrie Norman. Assoc R S Jas Epis Ch Greenville SC 2005-2009. djgrieser@gmail.com

GRIESMANN, Donald Andre (NJ) Po Box 7, Pago Pago AS 96799 B Washington DC 6/1/1932 s Otto Griesmann & Muriel. BA Ge 1954; STB PDS 1957; JD Rutgers Sch of Law Camden NJ 1973. D 4/2/1957 P 11/1/1957 Bp Alfred L Banyard. m 5/13/1989 Barbara Ann Griesman. Cn Dio New Jersey Trenton NJ 1967-1970; R S Aug's Ch Camden NJ 1959-1967; Cur Gr Epis Ch Plainfield NJ 1957-1959. Auth, "An Urban Par As Mssn". DGRIESMANN@AOL.COM

GRIESMEYER, Walter Jimmy (Chi) 1468 Elizabeth St, Crete IL 60417 B Plainfield NJ 8/4/1940 s Walter Edward Griesmeyer & Elizabeth Rose. BA Chapman U 1969; BA Chapman U 1970; MDiv SWTS 1974. D 6/15/1974 P 1/4/1975 Bp Robert C Rusack. m 8/3/1974 Cathy Jill Glover. Ch Of The Gd Shpd Momence IL 2001-2005; St Cyprians Ch Chicago IL 1998-2000; All Souls Ch Kaycee WY 1986-1988; Int S Lk's Ch Cleveland OH 1982-1984; S Paul Epis Ch Conneaut OH 1978-1979; Cur S Andr's Ch Longmeadow MA 1976-1978; Cur Trin Epis Ch Orange CA 1974-1975. Natl Assn for the Self-Supporting Active Mnstry; RACA. FRWALL@NETZERO.NET

GRIEVES, Brian Jervis (Haw) 815 2nd Ave, New York NY 10017 **Sr Dir for Mssn Centers and Dir, Advocacy C Epis Ch Cntr New York NY 2008-** B London UK 4/2/1946 s Philip Henry Grieves & Meron. BA U of Hawaii 1968; MDiv CDSP 1972. D 7/29/1972 P 5/6/1973 Bp Edwin Lani Hanchett. m 7/17/2003 Young-Jin Kim. Epis Ch Cntr New York NY 1988-2010; Camp Mokule'Ia Waialua HI 1977-1987; Dir, Camps and Conferences Dio Hawaii Honolulu HI 1977-1987; S Andr's Cathd Honolulu HI 1977-1978; Ch Of The H Nativ Honolulu HI 1973-1977; Assoc S Steph's Ch Wahiawa HI 1972-1973. Ed, "No Outcasts: The Publ Wit of Edmond L Browning," FMP. Hon Doctorate CDSP 2004. grievesbrian@gmail.com

GRIFFIN, Barry Quentin (At) Po Box 169, Morrow GA 30260 **R S Aug Of Cbury Morrow GA 1994-** B Brunswick GA 10/22/1955 s Pleasant Quentin Griffin & Eva. BA Valdosta St U 1977; MA Georgia St U 1982; MDiv GTS 1988. D 6/11/1988 Bp Charles Judson Child Jr P 4/21/1989 Bp Frank Kellogg Allan. Epis Chars Bd Dio Atlanta Atlanta GA 1994-1997; Asst R Emm Epis Ch Athens GA 1990-1994; D S Marg's Ch Carrollton GA 1988-1990. Lilly Fndt Grant 2008; Fullbright Schlrshp For Mus Salzburg Austria 1977. barryqgriffin@earthlink.net

GRIFFIN, Calvin Russell (USC) 200 Tyborne Cir, Columbia SC 29210 **R S Lk's Epis Ch Columbia SC 1994-** B Baltimore MD 6/26/1951 s Russell Calvin Griffin & Elizabeth Mae. BA Morgan St U 1973; MDiv Estrn Bapt TS 1976; S Chas Borromeo Sem 1976. D 10/18/1977 P 2/1/1978 Bp Hunley Agee Elebash. m 9/2/1972 Regina R Rozier c 1. R Ch Of The Gd Shpd Mobile AL 1988-1994; R S Tit Epis Ch Durham NC 1980-1987; R S Mk's Ch Wilmington NC 1977-1980. Cmnty Faith-Mobile Cmnty Orgnztn. Outstndng Young Men Amer 1979; Serv Awd Hd Start 79 New Hanover Cnty; Serv Awd 94 Wilmer Hall Chld Hm Mobile. cgriffin4@live.com

GRIFFIN, Christopher Edward (Chi) 1356 W Jarvis Ave # 1, Chicago IL 60626 **S Mart's Ch Chicago IL 2010-** B Gary IN 10/12/1961 BS MIT 1983; EdM Harv 1993; MA U Chi 1997; MDiv U Chi 1997; CAS SWTS 2002. D 6/15/2002 P 12/21/2002 Bp William Dailey Persell. S Matt's Ch Evanston IL 2002-2010. ECF Fell ECF 2005.

GRIFFIN, Emily Anne (NJ) 300 S Main St, Pennington NJ 08534 **Assoc R S Matt's Ch Pennington NJ 2003-** B Syracuse NY 11/18/1974 MDiv PrTS 2001; MSW Rutgers-The St U 2002; STM GTS 2003. D 6/7/2003 Bp David B(ruce) Joslin P 12/13/2003 Bp George Edward Councell. emilyagriffin@yahoo.com

GRIFFIN, Horace Leeolphus (Chi) 8206 172nd St, Jamaica NY 11432 B Starke FL 4/22/1961 BA Morehouse Coll 1983; MDiv Bos 1988; PhD Van 1995. D 7/12/2005 P 12/17/2005 Bp William Dailey Persell. The GTS New York NY 2005-2009; SWTS Evanston IL 2005. h-griffin@seabury.edu

GRIFFIN, Janet (Spok) 803 Symons St, Richland WA 99354 B Margaretville NY 10/30/1942 d Arnold Maurice Griffin & Elizabeth. BS Syr 1963; MDiv CDSP 1983. D 6/25/1983 P 6/9/1984 Bp William Edwin Swing. R All SS Ch Richland WA 2000-2009; The Epis Ch Of S Mary The Vrgn San Francisco CA 1986-2000; Asst Pstr Gr Cathd San Francisco CA 1983-1986. sulajang@yahoo.com

GRIFFIN, Jon Edward (Spr) 449 State Highway 37, West Frankfort IL 62896 **S Mk's Ch W Frankfort IL 2002-** B Herron IL 4/21/1949 s John Edward Griffin & Georgia. BA Sthrn Illinois U 1971; BS Sthrn Illinois U 1992. D 10/5/2001 P 8/24/2002 Bp Peter Hess Beckwith. m 5/1/1999 Sara Beth Miner. Dio Springfield Springfield IL 2005-2006. jgriffin@marion.quitamlaw.com

GRIFFIN, Mary-Carol Ann (Me) 862 Eagle Lake Rd, Bar Harbor ME 04609 **D Ch Of Our Fr Hulls Cove ME 1999-** B Albuquerque NM 3/10/1950 d Karl Cupples & Ramona Ruiz. D Formation Prog 1998; EFM 1998. D 3/20/1999 Bp Chilton Abbie Richardson Knudsen. m 4/30/1968 Karl Russell Griffin. Ch Of Our Fr Hulls Cove ME 1999-2001. kgriff@adelphia.net

GRIFFIN, Patrick Corrigan (Colo) 127 W Archer Pl, Denver CO 80223 B Dallas TX 1/25/1947 s James B Griffin & Marjorie A. MDiv EDS; BBA TCU. D 8/23/1973 P 2/1/1993 Bp William Harvey Wolfrum. Yth Min S Jn's Epis Ch Boulder CO 1993-1994. AAPC.

GRIFFIN, P Joshua (Cal) 1055 Taylor St, San Francisco CA 94108 **Environ Justice Mssnr Dio California San Francisco CA 2009-** B Providence RI 4/21/1981 BA Dart 2004; MDiv Harvard DS 2009. D 6/5/2010 P 12/4/2010 Bp Marc Handley Andrus. m 7/12/2008 Elizabeth K Harrington. Dio California San Francisco CA 2010-2011. griffonline@alum.dartmouth.org

GRIFFIN, Ronald Wayne (NCal) 3671 F St, Eureka CA 95503 **P Chr Ch Eureka CA 2008-** B Frankfort KY 5/12/1953 s Orville Heath Griffin & Lois Laverne. Cumberland U 1975; MTS Iliff TS 2006. D 1/22/2000 P 8/5/2000 Bp William Jerry Winterrowd. m 7/18/1974 Charlotte Trammell c 2. P S Mart In The Fields Aurora CO 2006-2007; P Epis Ch Of S Jn The Bapt Breckenridge CO 2000-2006. marshillrwg@suddenlink.net

GRIFFIN, Russell Agnew (NJ) 219 Philadelphia Blvd, Sea Girt NJ 08750 **R The Ch Of S Uriel The Archangel Sea Girt NJ 2004-** B Neptune NJ 7/27/1953 s Charles Russell Griffin & Gertrude. BS Norwich U 1976; MDiv Nash 1979; STM Nash 1998. D 6/2/1979 P 12/21/1979 Bp Albert Wiencke Van Duzer. m 4/25/1981 Cynthia Daley c 2. Dio Cntrl Florida Orlando FL 2000-2004; R S Anne's Ch Crystal River FL 1993-2004; Com to elct Bp Dio New Jersey Trenton NJ 1992-1993; Dio New Jersey Trenton NJ 1980-1989; Vic S Mk's At The Crossing Ch Williamstown NJ 1979-1993. OSL 1981; SocMary 2005; SSC 1981. rag53@optonline.net

GRIFFIN, Timothy Lee (Pa) 1946 Welsh Rd, Philadelphia PA 19115 **P-in-c S Andr's In The Field Ch Philadelphia PA 2010-; R Memi Ch Of S Lk Philadelphia PA 2004-** B Keokuk IA 6/25/1957 s Timothy Titus Griffin & Sandra Luan. BA Wstrn Illinois U 1981; JD/MA/PHD U IL 1995; MA Providence Coll 2002; MDiv EDS 2004. D 10/10/2004 P 4/9/2005 Bp Geralyn Wolf. m 11/29/2005 Harriet Kollin c 1. Asst All SS Crescentville Philadelphia PA 2004-2005. frtimgriffin@gmail.com

GRIFFIN JR, William Leonard (Len) (Ark) 40 Cliffdale Dr, Little Rock AR 72223 **D S Mk's Epis Ch Little Rock AR 1998-** B Little Rock AR 3/27/1948 s William Leonard Griffin & Rita Dolores. BS U of Arkansas 1970; MS U of Arkansas 1971; CTh Nash 1983. D 4/7/1984 Bp Charles Thomas Gaskell. m 6/13/1970 Beverly Burton. D S Jn's Ch Fremont MI 1992-1998; D H Cross Epis Ch Wisconsin Dells WI 1983-1992. len.griffin@sbcglobal.net

GRIFFIS SR, Terrell Hathorn (La) 316 Driftwood Dr, Meridian MS 39305 **Assoc The Epis Ch Of The Medtr Meridian MS 2007-** B Sturgis MS 10/3/1932 s Sam B Griffis & Pauline Hathorn. BS Delta St U 1957; MDiv Candler TS Emory U 1970. D 6/1/1974 Bp John M Allin P 5/1/1975 Bp Duncan Montgomery Gray Jr. m 11/29/1957 Marcia Wilson c 2. Vic All SS Epis Ch Ponchatoula LA 1989-1999; Vic S Tim's Ch La Place LA 1987-1999; S Andr's Paradis Luling LA 1987-1989; S Nath's Ch Melville LA 1981-1987; R S Steph's Ch Innis LA 1979-1987; Ch Of The Creator Clinton MS 1979; Vic S Mary's Epis Ch Vicksburg MS 1975-1978. mg01a@bellsouth.net

GRIFFITH, Bernard Macfarren (SeFla) 15100 Sw 141st Ter, Miami FL 33196 B BB 9/13/1942 s Elric Athelston Griffith & Norma. Ford; Cert Erdiston Teachers Coll 1970; BA Codrington Coll 1976; ThM Columbia TS 1985. Trans from Church in the Province Of The West Indies 9/1/1988 Bp Walter Decoster Dennis Jr. m 7/2/1966 Nadine Rosetta Cobham c 3. R Chr Epis Ch Miami FL 1994-2011; R Ch Of S Simon The Cyrenian New Rochelle NY 1988-1994; Chr Ch Oyster Bay NY 1987-1988. plaidy00@yahoo.com

GRIFFITH, Bruce Derby (LI) Po Box 145, Pultneyville NY 14538 B Braham MN 6/14/1944 s Melvin William Griffith & Clela Ione. BA Hamline U 1965; STB U Tor 1968; STM GTS 1969; ThD U Tor 1979. D 6/24/1968 Bp Hamilton Hyde Kellogg P 3/22/1969 Bp Kenneth Daniel Wilson Anand. m 9/9/1967 Mary West. Int Chr Ch Rochester NY 2006-2009; Prof Geo Mercer TS Garden City NY 1988-2000; R Chr Ch Oyster Bay NY 1987-2002; P-in-c Epis Tri-Par Mnstry Dansville NY 1981-1987; Int Chr Epis Ch Hornell NY 1979-1981; R S Mich And All Ang Buffalo NY 1974-1976; Stff P Cathd Ch Of S Mk Minneapolis MN 1969-1971; Cur S Mk's Ch Mendham NJ 1968-1969. Auth, "Yearning: Greg Of Nyssa & The Vision Of God," *Sewanee Theol Revs*, 2000. Angl-RC Natl Consult 1984-1989; Dir Consortium Endowed Epis Parishes 1995-2001; No Amer Reg Comittee 2001; Past Pres Trin Div Assn (Toronto) 1994-2000. R Emer Chr Ch, Oyster Bay 2004. bgriffith1@gmail.com

GRIFFITH, Charles Jefferson (WK) 8631 Beulah Land Dr, Ozark AR 72949 B Little Rock AR 5/27/1937 s Charles Jefferson Griffith & Margaret Dysart. BS U of Arkansas 1959; MDiv VTS 1963; MS Ft Hays St U 1973; CFP Coll for Fin Plnng 1984; BA Arkansas Tech U 2007. D 6/25/1963 P 1/1/1964 Bp Robert Raymond Brown. m 11/3/1989 Renee Hagenau c 3. Int P Epis Ch Of S Jn The Bapt Breckenridge CO 1976-1977; Vic Trin Epis Ch Norton KS 1966-1973; S Lk's Ch Phillipsburg NJ 1966-1967; Vic Chr Ch Mena AR 1964-1965; Vic S Barn Ch Foreman AR 1964-1965. Auth, ",A Shelton Lineage: Five Generations," self, 1993; Auth, ",The Descendants Of Lafayette F Griffith & Cynthia Bradley," self, 1991; Auth, ",A Dysart Lineage: Seven Generations," self, 1986. crjg@centurytel.net

GRIFFITH, David Michael (Los) 821 Valley Crest St, La Canada CA 91011 B Los Angeles CA 5/7/1946 s George Cupp Griffith & Leona Ann. BA Claremont TS; BS USC. D 9/15/1973 P 3/1/1974 Bp Robert C Rusack. m 2/1/1968 Donna Griffith c 1. Asst to R S Andr's Par Fullerton CA 1986-1989; Vic Imm Mssn El Monte CA 1982-1986; Vic S Paul's Mssn Barstow CA 1980-1982; Serv S Columba's Epis Mssn Big Bear Lake CA 1978-1980; S Mths' Par Whittier CA 1973-1977.

GRIFFITH, David W (NY) 1209 Proust Rd, Virginia Beach VA 23454 B Georgetown GY 4/10/1931 s Charles Wellesley Griffith & Lucille Elinor. BA Bp's Coll 1965. Trans from Church in the Province Of The West Indies 12/31/1988 Bp Paul Moore Jr. m 6/2/1956 Mary Ann Griffith. Assoc S Andr's Ch Bronx NY 1991-1998; Assoc Trin Ch Of Morrisania Bronx NY 1980-1991; Asst P S Lk's Epis Ch Bronx NY 1979-1980. dgrif91470@aol.com

GRIFFITH, Gregory Erwin (O) 705 Main St, Coshocton OH 43812 B Akron OH 10/22/1946 s Howard E Griffith & Florence E. BA Hiram Coll 1968; MDiv Andover Newton TS 1976; Shalem Inst Washington DC 1984; DMin Columbia TS 2000. D 6/19/1976 Bp John Harris Burt P 6/26/1977 Bp Philip Alan Smith. R Trin Ch Coshocton OH 2000-2009; Hoosac Sch Hoosick NY 1995-2000; S Ptr's Ch Rome GA 1992-1995; R S Steph's Boise ID 1990-1991; Chair Dio Delaware Wilmington DE 1988-1990; Stwdshp Cmsn Dio Delaware Wilmington DE 1984-1985; Dioc Coun Dio Delaware Wilmington DE 1983-1986; H Trin Ch Wilmington DE 1981-1990; Assoc R Trin Par Wilmington DE 1981-1990; Cur S Jn's Ch Portsmouth NH 1976-1981. Soc of S Marg. Mart Luther King, Jr. Awd Delaware Mart Luther King, Jr. Memi Fndt Delaware 1990. geg12089@yahoo.com

GRIFFITH, Ivan Romito (NY) 2039 Hughes Ave Apt 7, Bronx NY 10457 B 6/11/1934 s George Griffith & Alejandrina. NYTS 1983; Cert Inst Pstrl Hispano 1987. D 11/23/1987 Bp Paul Moore Jr P 11/1/1989 Bp Walter Decoster Dennis Jr. m 5/29/1955 Isdola Douglas. Asst Min Ch Of The Intsn New York NY 1987-2008.

GRIFFITH JR, Norman Early (WTex) 1601 E 19th St, Georgetown TX 78626 B Charlotte NC 11/15/1926 s Norman Early Griffith & Pearl Elizabeth. BS Duke 1947; BD VTS 1968. D 7/30/1968 Bp Everett H Jones P 2/1/1969 Bp Harold Cornelius Gosnell. Vic S Bon Ch Comfort TX 1991-1992; R S Chris's Ch Bandera TX 1991-1992; Assoc R S Jn's Ch McAllen TX 1990-1991; Int Trin Epis Ch Pharr TX 1989-1990; R Emm Epis Ch Lockhart TX 1984-1989; R Emm Epis Ch San Angelo TX 1974-1984; Assoc S Mk's Ch Beaumont TX 1970-1974; D S Jn's Epis Ch Sonora TX 1968-1970. galnorm@verizon.net

GRIFFITH JR, Robert Leon (LI) 36 Cathedral Avenue, Garden City NY 11530 B Lorain OH 11/10/1961 s Robert L Griffith & Judith L. BS Bowling Green St U 1984; Med Kent St U 1994; MDiv GTS 2005. D 6/4/2005 Bp Mark Hollingsworth Jr P 6/3/2006 Bp Arthur Benjamin Williams Jr. Dio Long Island Garden City NY 2008-2011; Ch Pension Fund New York NY 2005-2010. blgriffith@yahoo.com

GRIFFITH, Shawn Lynn (WNC) 3658 Gaston Day School Rd, Gastonia NC 28056 **R S Mk's Ch Gastonia NC 2005-** B Huntington 5/27/1952 s Thomas Martin Griffith & Betty Jo. MA Ball St U; MBA Golden Gate U; MDiv VTS. D 6/10/2000 Bp David Conner Bane Jr P 12/9/2000 Bp Donald Purple Hart. m 12/6/1974 Nellie Roseanne Burns. R All SS Ch So Hill VA 2000-2005. slg@stmarksgastonia.org

GRIFFITHS, Robert Stephen (NJ) 2613 Vista Cove Rd, Saint Augustine FL 32084 **Cn Dio Florida Jacksonville FL 2008-** B Neptune NJ 8/11/1938 s Harold William Griffiths & Lois Marjorie. BA Monmouth U 1960; STB GTS 1963. Trans from Church of the Province of Southern Africa 10/1/1967 Bp Walter H Gray. m 6/26/1965 Diane Harmer c 2. Int San Jose Epis Ch Jacksonville FL 2005-2007; Ch Of The Gd Shpd Jacksonville FL 1999-2003; All SS' Epis Ch Scotch Plains NJ 1997-1999; Int S Lk's Epis Ch Montclair NJ 1995-1997; Trin Educ Fund New York NY 1978-1990; Dir Par of Trin Ch New York NY 1976-1994; Kent Sch Kent CT 1971-1976; R S Andr's Ch Kent CT 1967-1971. ecclescon@aol.com

GRIFO, Lynne A (Ct) D 6/22/1990 Bp Orris George Walker Jr P 4/11/1991 Bp Franklin Delton Turner.

GRIGG, Joel (Alb) 145 Main Street, Massena NY 13662 **R S Jn's Ch Massena NY 2005-** B Coldwater MI 10/16/1959 s Frederick Earl Grigg & Allie E. BS U of Sthrn Mississippi 1987; MPA Auburn U at Montgomery 1993; MDiv TESM 2001. D 12/9/2000 Bp Keith Lynn Ackerman P 6/23/2001 Bp Daniel William Herzog. m 7/29/1978 Carolyn Jean Wyss c 2. S Matt's Ch Unadilla NY 2001-2005.

GRIM, Leland Howard (Minn) 2636 County Road 94, International Falls MN 56649 B 7/15/1943 s Howard Olaf Grim & Adella Emelia. BA No Dakota St U 1965; MS No Dakota St U 1969. D 7/8/2006 Bp James Louis Jelinek. m 9/3/1966 Donna Carol Cann c 2. clgrim57@midco.net

GRIMBALL JR, Richard Barnwell (USC) 101 Brookside Way, Greenville SC 29605 **Sr Chapl Chr Ch Epis Sch Greenville SC 2004-** B Charleston SC 12/3/1965 s Richard Barnwell Grimball & Adele Beatrice. BA Coll of Charleston 1990; MA Clemson U 1995; MDiv STUSo 2002. D 6/8/2002 P 12/14/2002 Bp Robert Hodges Johnson. m 5/22/1993 Donna Paige Martin c 3. Asst to R Trin Epis Ch Asheville NC 2002-2004. grimbalr@cces.org

GRIMES, Daphne Buchanan (Wyo) 16 Thomas The Apostle Rd, Cody WY 82414 B Tulsa OK 4/12/1929 d George Sidney Buchanan & Dorothy Elnora. BFA U of Houston 1952; MA Col 1954; MA Epis TS of The SW 1985. D 8/11/1982 P 11/1/1986 Bp Bob Gordon Jones. Assoc Chr Ch Cody WY 1995-2004; Dir, Thos-Apos Retreat Cntr Dio Wyoming Casper WY 1990-2000; Vic S Andr's Ch Meeteetse WY 1987-1990; D Chr Ch Cody WY 1982-1986. "Journeys in Time and Space," Wordsworth Press, 2006; "Journeys in the Sprt," Wordsworth Press, 2005; Auth, "Though I Walk Through the Vlly," The Print Shop, 1989; Auth, "Journeyings," Wyndham Hall Pr, 1984. Cmnty Celebration - Comp 1987; CHS 2002; Compass Rose Soc - Bd 1998-2006; ECW 1978; EPF; EWC; No Amer Reg Consultants for S Geo's Coll, 2000-2007; Ord of Julian of Norwich - Assoc 1988-2002; Publ Plcy Ntwk. daphneg@tritel.net

GRIMES, Eve Lyn (Colo) 624 W 19th St, Pueblo CO 81003 **D Dio Colorado Denver CO 1992-** B Worthington MN 2/22/1941 d Ralph Jon Mulder & Mildred Genieve. AD U of Sthrn Colorado 1975; Bp's Inst for Diac Formation 1992. D 10/24/1992 Bp William Jerry Winterrowd. c 2. NAAD.

GRIMM, Joan (LI) 124 Jerusalem Ave, Hicksville NY 11801 **R H Trin Epis Ch Hicksville NY 2004-** B Berea OH 9/22/1947 BS Alleg 1969; MDiv EDS 1973; MS U of Arizona 1978; BFA U NC 2000. D 6/16/1973 P 3/5/1977 Bp John Harris Burt. m 7/7/1979 D Ross Fraser. Cn Dio Wstrn Massachusetts Springfield MA 1996-1998; Vic S Paul's Epis Ch Thomasville NC 1994-1996;

Vic S Clem's Epis Ch Clemmons NC 1989-1991; Assoc S Paul's Epis Ch Lakewood CO 1985-1988; Chapl Ken Gambier OH 1974-1976. frasj6@aol.com

GRIMM, Susan (SVa) 24 The Moorings, Clarksville VA 23927 **S Tim's Epis Ch Clarksville VA 2008-; S Jn's Epis Ch Chase City VA 2006-** B Richmond VA 3/10/1953 d Rexdel Elton Grimm & Margaret A S. BA U Rich 1976; JD U Rich 1978; MDiv STUSo 2006. D 6/3/2006 Bp Robert Hodges Johnson P 12/16/2006 Bp John Clark Buchanan. Cntrl Mecklenburg Cure Boydton VA 2006-2008. Comm. of St. Mary (Sthrn) Assoc 2006. susan@susangrimm.com

GRIMSHAW, Gretchen Sanders (Mass) 28 Robbins Rd, Watertown MA 02472 **P-in-c Par Of S Paul Newton Highlands MA 2008-; S Jn's Ch Jamaica Plain MA 2007-** B Cincinnati Ohio 9/30/1959 d James Gradolf & Cynthia. BA Smith 1983; MDiv EDS 2004; ALM Harv 2004. D 6/3/2006 Bp M(arvil) Thomas Shaw III P 1/6/2007 Bp Gayle Elizabeth Harris. "Big Bug Creek," Renaissance Works, 1998. gsgrimshaw@parishofstpaul.org

GRINDON, Carri Patterson (Los) 1014 E. Altadena Dr., Altadena CA 91001 **R S Mk's Par Altadena CA 2009-** B Orange CA 8/27/1960 d Charles Mervin Patterson & Martha Priscilla Jane. BA Occ 1982; MDiv Ya Berk 1992. D 6/24/1995 Bp Chester Lovelle Talton P 1/1/1996 Bp Frederick Houk Borsch. m 10/9/1993 Alfred Joseph Grindon. Asst S Anne's Epis Ch Atlanta GA 2006-2009; Asst S Edw's Epis Ch Lawrenceville GA 2000-2006; Assoc S Columba's Par Camarillo CA 1996-1999; Ch Of Our Sav Par San Gabr CA 1995-1996. carrigd@att.net

GRINDROD, Robert Hamm (Mo) 154 E Palatine Rd, Palatine IL 60067 B Hanover PA 5/18/1951 s James William Grindrod & Nancy Rae. Leh 1971; BA Estrn Nazarene Coll 1974; MDiv GTS 1977; DMin Eden TS 1992. D 6/10/1977 P 12/1/1977 Bp Dean T Stevenson. m 12/31/1993 Michelle K McNamara c 2. Vic S Thos Ch For The Deaf St Louis MO 1980-1993; Epis Deaf Missions Dio Cntrl Pennsylvania Harrisburg PA 1979-1980; Dio Cntrl Pennsylvania Harrisburg PA 1977-1980; Cur The Meml Ch Of The Prince Of Peace Gettysburg PA 1977-1978. Epis Conf Of The Deaf Of The Epis Ch In The USA. ROBERTGRINDROD@SBCGLOBAL.NET

GRINDY, Donald Roy (CNY) 311 Hurlburt Rd, Syracuse NY 13224 **Died 12/28/2010** B Medford MA 7/30/1925 s Roy Melvin Grindy & Gertrude Kincaid. BS Tufts U 1946; Babson Coll 1947; BD EDS 1952. D 6/7/1952 Bp Norman B Nash P 12/21/1952 Bp Charles F Hall. c 2. mcdrgrin@aol.com

GRINER, Robert Tyler (Nwk) 115 Cedar Dr, Newton NJ 07860 **Chr Ch Newton NJ 2003-** B Houston TX 7/27/1958 s Ray Carson Griner & Joanne. BA Drew U 1981; MDiv Yale DS 1985. D 2/19/1986 Bp Arthur Edward Walmsley P 10/4/1986 Bp John Shelby Spong. c 3. R Gr Epis Ch Plainfield NJ 1993-1999; Assoc R S Geo's-By-The-River Rumson NJ 1988-1993; Asst R All SS Ch Millington NJ 1986-1988. Soc Of S Jn The Evang. rgriner@lycos.com

GRINNELL, Janice Louise (RI) 32 Viking Dr, Portsmouth RI 02871 **D S Paul's Ch No Kingstown RI 2010-; COM Dio Rhode Island Providence RI 2009-** B Harrisburg PA 11/11/1947 d Paul Henry Lauver & Jean Catherine. BS Shippensburg U 1969; MBA FD 1973; Rhode Island Sch for Deacons 1991. D 3/16/1991 Bp George Nelson Hunt III. m 7/1/2007 Ann Donnalley c 2. D Trin Ch Newport RI 2008-2010; D S Mich's Ch Bristol RI 1991-2008. Auth, "In Response to the Steps," *In Response to the Steps*, Xlibris, 2009. NAAD 1991. deacjan@aol.com

GRISCOM, Donald Wayne (SwFla) 3324 Chicago Ave, Bradenton FL 34207 B Sellersville PA 1/3/1944 s Russel Rusknian & Helen. D 1/18/2002 Bp John Bailey Lipscomb. m 1/1/1983 Shirley A Griscom.

GRISHAM JR, Lowell Edward (Ark) Po Box 1190, Fayetteville AR 72702 **S Paul's Ch Fayetteville AR 1997-** B Portland OR 6/26/1952 s Lowell Edward Grisham & Jo Ann. BA U of Mississippi 1972; MDiv GTS 1980. D 6/11/1980 P 2/24/1981 Bp Duncan Montgomery Gray Jr. m 6/7/1975 Kathryn McKellar c 1. R S Jn's Epis Ch Ft Smith AR 1992-1997; Curs Com Epis Ch Cntr New York NY 1990-1992; R S Columb's Ch Ridgeland MS 1982-1992; Trin Ch Natchez MS 1980-1982. Presiding Off 1997-2002; Professed OA 1994. lowell@stpaulsfay.org

GRISSOM, Billy Cullen (Colo) 3527 Susan Cir, Wharton TX 77488 B Weatherford TX 4/13/1935 s William Cullen Grissom & Martha Altus. BA Baylor U 1958; MDiv Epis TS of The SW 1961. D 6/1/1961 P 9/1/1962 Bp Frederick P Goddard. m 8/26/1962 Mary Dromgoole c 4. R Ch Of The H Comf Broomfield CO 1987-2002; S Aid's Epis Ch Boulder CO 1984-1987; Vic S Paul's Epis Ch Cntrl City CO 1979-1980; Dio Colorado Denver CO 1978-1984; Epis Ch Of S Ptr And S Mary Denver CO 1978-1979; S Matt's Ch Bellaire TX 1965-1977; Vic Trin Ch Jacksonville TX 1962-1965; Vic Chr Ch Matagorda TX 1961-1962; Vic S Jn's Epis Ch Palacios TX 1961-1962. H Hse of Walsingham. canter1241@aol.com

GRISWOLD, Brendan (WNY) 2165 Via Fuentes, Vero Beach FL 32963 **Died 12/6/2010** B Chicago IL 4/8/1917 BA Pomona Coll 1940; MDiv Ya Berk 1950. D 6/15/1950 Bp Frederick G Budlong P 6/1/1951 Bp Duncan Montgomery Gray. bdwgo8a@prodigy.com

GRISWOLD, Edwin A (O) 9629 W Campana Dr, Sun City AZ 85351 B Defiance OH 10/14/1928 s Rollie Griswold & Millicent. BA Heidelberg Coll 1956; MDiv Untd TS 1959. D 11/21/1960 Bp Robert Lionne DeWitt P 6/29/1961 Bp Richard S M Emrich. m 10/31/1948 Naarah T Corl c 2. R Gr Ch Defiance OH 1984-1990; R S Martha's Ch Detroit MI 1969-1984; Vic S Jn's Ch Clinton MI 1959-1963. Alum Hon Schlrshp Awd (1st Annual) Untd TS 1962. edandna@cox.net

✠ **GRISWOLD III, Most Rev Frank Tracy** (Chi) 151 W Springfield Ave, Philadelphia PA 19118 B Bryn Mawr PA 9/18/1937 s Frank Tracy Griswold & Louisa. AB Harv 1959; GTS 1960; BA Oriel Coll Oxford U. 1962; MA Oxf 1966. D 12/15/1962 Bp Andrew Tsu P 6/23/1963 Bp Joseph Gillespie Armstrong Con 3/2/1985 for Chi. m 11/27/1965 Phoebe Wetzel c 2. PBp of the Epis Ch Epis Ch Cntr New York NY 1998-2006; Bp Dio Chicago Chicago IL 1987-1997; Bp Coadj Dio Chicago Chicago IL 1985-1987; R Ch Of S Mart-In-The-Fields Philadelphia PA 1974-1985; R S Andr's Ch Yardley PA 1967-1974; Cur Ch Of The Redeem Bryn Mawr PA 1963-1967. Auth, "Praying Our Days," Morehouse, 2009; Auth, "Opening Remarks and Closing Reflections," *Waging Recon*, CPC, 2002; Auth, "Called to Another Way," *Where was God on Sept 11?*, Herald Press, 2002; Auth, "Going Hm: An Invitation to Jubilee," Cowley, 2000; Auth, "Chr: The Sovereign Word," *A New Conversation*, CPC, 1999; Auth, "Listening w the Ear of the Heart," *Crosscurrents*, 1998; Auth, "Experiencing Catholicity," *Amer*, 1997; Auth, "The Bp as Presider, Tchr and Person of Pryr," *ATR*, 1995; Auth, "Preaching and the Mnstry of Bishops," *Breaking the Word*, CHC, 1994; Auth, "Towards Catholicity: Naming & Living the Mystery," *Living the Mystery*, DTL, 1993; Auth, "The Mid-day Demon," *Phos*, Trin Inst, 1984; Auth, "Wrshp," *Being God's Fam*, 1982. DD CDSP 2007; DD Bex 2006; DD EDS 2006; Doctor of Hmnts Rikkyo U, Tokyo 2005; DHL Epis TS of the SW 2004; DD Berkeley TS 2002; DD Nashotah TS 2001; DD U So 2001; DD VTS 1999; DD GTS 1985; DD SWTS 1985. ftgriswold@mac.com

GRISWOLD-KUHN, Karl Ernest (Alb) 6 Silvester St, Kinderhook NY 12106 **S Paul's Ch Kinderhook NY 2011-** B Albany NY 10/28/1976 s Ulrich F Kuhn & Kathleen Esther. BA St U of Albany 2007; MDiv Berk of Yale 2011. D 6/4/2011 Bp William Howard Love. m 1/26/2008 Jennifer Griswold. karlkuhn@gmail.com

GROB, Bruce Russell (Fla) 2358 Riverside Ave. #305, Jacksonville FL 32204 B Camden NJ 4/8/1951 BA Drew U 1973; M.Div. Ya Berk 1976; Ph.D. Drew U 1984. D 12/8/2002 P 6/8/2003 Bp Stephen Hays Jecko. m 5/20/1978 Banta Whitner c 1. Fresh Mnstrs Jacksonville FL 1994-2010. BRUCERGROB@GMAIL.COM

GROFF, Addison Keiper (Nwk) 4455 Los Feliz Blvd Apt 101, Los Angeles CA 90027 B Rochester NY 3/22/1919 s Addison Hershey Groff & Rebecca. BA Franklin & Marshall Coll 1941; BD Lancaster TS 1944; GTS 1949. D 7/20/1949 P 6/29/1950 Bp Harold E Sawyer. c 2. Supply P/P Assoc Chr Ch Milford DE 1989-1997; Supply P Dio Easton Easton MD 1989-1997; Supply P Dio Newark Newark NJ 1989-1997; Team Mnstry S Jn The Bapt Epis Ch Milton DE 1989-1997; Supply P S Mary's Ch Bridgeville DE 1989-1997; Team Mnstry S Steph's Ch Harrington DE 1989-1997; Ret/ Supply P Dio Delaware Wilmington DE 1989; S Ptr's Ch Newark NJ 1971-1989; S Agnes And S Paul's Ch E Orange NJ 1953-1971; Cur Trin Ch Hermitage PA 1950-1953; Vic Chr Ch Punxsutawney PA 1949-1950. Angl Soc. addkg@aol.com

GROFF JR, John Weldon (Ala) 12656 N Shoreland Pkwy, Mequon WI 53092 B Atlantic City NJ 3/24/1939 s John Weldon Groff & Tillie. LTh STUSo 1974; Coll of Preachers 1979; U of Notre Dame 1982; U of Notre Dame 1984; Naropa U 1985; U of Notre Dame 1990. D 5/28/1974 P 12/19/1974 Bp Furman Stough. c 2. Int S Fran Ch Menomonee Falls WI 2002-2004; R S Mary's Epis Ch Childersburg AL 1983-1987; Dio TEE Coordntr Dio Alabama Birmingham AL 1978-1981; R Ch Of The Epiph Guntersville AL 1976-1983; Dept of CE Dio Alabama Birmingham AL 1975-1977; Vic S Tim's Epis Ch Athens AL 1974-1976. Auth, "Sebastian," Authorhouse, 2000; Auth, "The Smell of Incense, Sound of Silence," Forw Mvmt Press, 1988; Auth, "The Mystic Journey," Forw Mvmt Press, 1979; Auth, "arts," *Chr New Age Quarterly*; Auth, "arts," *Gnosis*; Auth, "arts," *Inner Directions Journ*; Auth, "arts," *Intuitive Explorations*; Auth, "arts," *LivCh*.

GROFF, Mary E Worobe (Ala) 6141 Sherry Dr, Guntersville AL 35976 B Atlantic City NJ 7/24/1939 d John H Worobe & Dorothy Topping Anderson. EFM STUSo 1980; MSW U of Alabama 1985; ALA Deacons Sch 2004; Audited DMin courses Nash 2009. D 10/30/2004 Bp Marc Handley Andrus. c 2. Amer Assoc. of Pstr Counselors 1986; Natl Assn Soc Worker 1980; No Amer Assoc. for the Diac 2004. +4000 hours of Serv 2011; Presidential Lifetime Vol Awd RSVP 2011. megroff39@yahoo.com

GROH, Clifford Herbert (Mich) No address on file. B Windsor Ontario Canada 9/20/1933 Trans from Anglican Church of Canada 11/30/1967.

GROMAN, Edward Owen (Eas) Po Box 157, Church Creek MD 21622 **Died 1/14/2011** B Philadelphia PA 11/18/1950 s Edward Michael Groman & Wanda

Victoria. Rec from Polish National Catholic Church 3/1/1998 as Priest Bp Martin Gough Townsend. c 2.

GRONEK, Marianna (Mich) St Michael's Episcopal Chuch, 20475 Sunningdale Park, Grosse Pointe Woods MI 48236 B Fort Huron MI 5/23/1959 d William Gronek & Wanda. BFA Rocky Mtn Coll Of Art And Design Denver CO 1994; MDiv SWTS 2006. D 6/10/2006 Bp Robert John O'Neill P 12/9/2006 Bp Wendell Nathaniel Gibbs Jr. Assoc R S Clare Of Assisi Epis Ch Ann Arbor MI 2006-2008; S Mich's Ch Grosse Pointe Woods MI 2006-2008. mgronek@stmichaelsgpw.org

GROSCHNER, Peter Kingston (Mich) 19759 Holiday Rd, Grosse Pointe Woods MI 48236 B Detroit MI 5/23/1938 s Robert K Groschner & Margaret Mary. BA Hillsdale Coll 1960; MDiv PDS 1964. D 6/29/1964 Bp Richard S M Emrich P 2/23/1965 Bp C Kilmer Myers. m 12/6/1980 Kathleen Ann Groschner. P Assoc S Mich's Ch Grosse Pointe Woods MI 1993-2007; R S Tim's Ch Detroit MI 1975-1980; Asst S Steph's Ch Troy MI 1966-1975; Asst S Mich's Ch Grosse Pointe Woods MI 1964-1966. Auth, "Pstr'S Referral Guide".

GROSE, Fayette Powers (O) 310 E Lincoln Way, Lisbon OH 44432 **Ch Of Our Sav Salem OH 2009-** B Youngstown OH 4/25/1933 s James Perry Grose & Arminda Magdeline. BA Duke 1955; BD Bex 1964. D 6/13/1964 P 12/1/1964 Bp Nelson Marigold Burroughs. m 8/8/1980 Phyllis Elaine Coates. H Trin Ch Lisbon OH 1988-1998; R Ch Of Our Sav Salem OH 1980-1987; Ch Of The Redeem Lorain OH 1971-1980; R S Paul's Epis Ch Smithfield NC 1969-1971.

GROSH, Christine Marie (Neb) 7921 N Hazelwood Dr, Lincoln NE 68510 **D S Mk's On The Campus Lincoln NE 1998-; P S Dav Of Wales Epis Ch Lincoln NE 1991-** B North Platte NE 7/12/1953 d George Dean Grosh & Patricia Ann. BA U of Nebraska 1977; EFM 1984; MA Fuller TS 1991. D 5/7/1988 Bp James Daniel Warner. m 4/28/1990 David Ryder Pitts c 2. P S Bede's Epis Ch Los Angeles CA 1989-1991. Amer Assn of Chr Counselors; NAAD.

GROSHART, Nancy Louise (U) 1051 Allen Peak Cir, Ogden UT 84404 **D Ch Of The Gd Shpd Ogden UT 1992-** B Moline IL 8/24/1947 d Joseph R Goran & Margaret M. U of Iowa 1967; BS U of Wyoming 1976. D 11/5/1992 Bp George Edmonds Bates. m 10/5/1977 Jerry Warren Groshart c 2. ngros@comcast.net

GROSJEAN, Lyle Wood (ECR) 3255 Amber Dr, Paso Robles CA 93446 **Chair of the Cmsn of Peace Dio California San Francisco CA 1989-** B Omaha NE 7/20/1933 s Milton O Grosjean & Leora A. BA San Francisco St U 1962; MDiv CDSP 1965. D 6/20/1965 Bp James Albert Pike P 2/1/1966 Bp George Richard Millard. c 2. R S Andr's Epis Ch San Bruno CA 1986-1998; Assoc R S Tim's Ch Danville CA 1983-1986; Vic S Lk's Ch Atascadero CA 1979-1983; Vic S Alb's Epis Ch Brentwood CA 1975-1979; Cur All Souls Par In Berkeley Berkeley CA 1965-1967. l.grosjean@charter.net

GROSKOPH, Elizabeth May (Roch) PO Box 541, Hancock NY 13783 **Vic Gr Epis Ch Whitney Point NY 2002-; Vic S Jn's Ch Marathon NY 2002-** B White Plains NY 5/18/1938 d Frederic Webster May & Lillian Henrietta. BA Wells Coll 1959; MA NYU 1967; Cert GTS 1988; Cert Mercer Hosp Sch of Nrsng 1988. D 5/21/1988 Bp Jose Antonio Ramos P 12/1/1988 Bp William George Burrill. m 7/18/1959 Ralph Gordon Groskoph c 3. Dir, CE Chr Ch Cuba NY 1998-2002; Dir, CE S Andr's Ch Friendship NY 1998-2002; Dir, CE Our Sav Bolivar NY 1988-2002; Dir, CE S Jn's Ch Wellsville NY 1988-2002; Dir, CE S Paul's Ch Angelica NY 1988-2002; Dir, CE S Phil's Ch Belmont NY 1988-2002; Allegany Cnty Epis Mnstry Belfast NY 1988-2001. frliz@proneisp.net

GROSKOPH, Ralph Gordon (Roch) PO Box 541, 211 Somerset Lake Rd, Hancock NY 13783 B Brooklyn NY 9/15/1936 s Ralph Geimer Groskoph & Dorothy Andresen. BA Cor 1958; MBA NYU 1965; Cert GTS 1988; Cert Mercer TS 1988. D 5/21/1988 Bp Jose Antonio Ramos P 12/17/1988 Bp William George Burrill. m 7/18/1959 Elizabeth May c 3. All SS Epis Ch Johnson City NY 2002-2004; Chr Epis Ch Friendship NY 1988-2002; Allegany Cnty Epis Mnstry Belfast NY 1988-2001. fralph@pronetisp.net

GROSS, Daniel La Rue (Eas) 208 E. Campus Ave., Chestertown MD 21620 **Trst Ya Berk New Haven CT 2011-; Chair, COM Dio Easton Easton MD 2011-; R Emm Epis Ch Chestertown MD 2007-** B Denver CO 9/2/1958 s Harvey Seymour Gross & Anna Virginia. BA Col 1980; Dplma Ya Berk 2004; MDiv Yale DS 2004. D 6/12/2004 P 1/4/2005 Bp John Chane. Mem, COM Dio Easton Easton MD 2008-2011; Cur Chr's Ch Rye NY 2004-2007. dlrgross@gmail.com

GROSS, Donald William (CFla) 800 Lake Port Blvd Apt D402, Leesburg FL 34748 **Corpus Christi Epis Ch Okahumpka FL 2008-** B Takoma Park MD 5/8/1936 s William Donald Gross & Pauline Virginia. BS Towson U 1958; STB Pos 1963; U of Birmingham Birmingham GB 1968; DMin S Mary Sem 1981. D 7/20/1963 Bp Noble C Powell P 6/1/1964 Bp Harry Lee Doll. Old Donation Ch Virginia Bch VA 1993-1998; Co-R Ch Of H Apos Virginia Bch VA 1978-1989; Dio Sthrn Virginia Norfolk VA 1977-1978; R Chr Ch Columbia MD 1970-1977. ferdindand143@embarqmail.com

GROSS III, Joseph Owen (Nwk) 173 Killarney Dr, Schenectady NY 12309 **Died 11/28/2010** B Allentown PA 1/28/1930 s Joseph Owen Gross & Flora Mae. PDS; BA Ursinus Coll 1951; BD Lancaster TS 1954. D 6/27/1959 Bp Joseph Gillespie Armstrong P 1/9/1960 Bp Oliver J Hart. CBS; Friends of New Skete Monstry 1994; SocMary.

GROSS, Leonard Scott (WVa) 471 Pythian St, Morgantown WV 26505 B Sutton WV 6/5/1924 s Teddy Otto Gross & Georgia Ethel. BD W Virginia U 1949. D 7/22/1973 P 2/25/1974 Bp Wilburn Camrock Campbell. m 9/25/1955 Louise Moats. Stff Epis Ch of the Trsfg Buckhannon WV 1995-1999; Stff Gr Epis Ch Elkins WV 1995-1999; Stff S Barn Bridgeport WV 1995-1999; Stff S Mths Grafton WV 1995-1999; Vic Emm Ch Keyser WV 1985-1986; Vic Chr Memi Ch Williamstown WV 1982-1985. Kappa Tau Alpha.

GROSS JR, Lester Stephen (Ky) 2604 El Patio Pl Apt 302, Louisville KY 40220 B Wilkes-Barre PA 7/11/1925 s Lester Stephen Gross & Honor Rolf. BA Wilkes Coll 1950; MDiv PDS 1955; DMin Louisville Presb TS 1975. D 6/5/1955 Bp Charles Clingman P 6/5/1956 Bp Charles Gresham Marmion. m 6/5/1946 Irene H Hawkes. Ch Of The Ascen Bardstown KY 1985; S Alb's Epis Ch Fern Creek Louisville KY 1975-1991; Secy, Dio Kentucky Dio Kentucky Louisville KY 1961-1993; Dio Kentucky Louisville KY 1961-1963; Secy of Dioc Conv Dio Kentucky Louisville KY 1956-1993; Trst & Mem, Dioc Coun Dio Kentucky Louisville KY 1956-1963; S Jn's Ch Louisville KY 1955-1963. ligpatio@aol.com

GROSS, Robert Arthur (RG) 10500 Kenworthy Dr., El Paso TX 79924 **P-in-c H Sprt Epis Ch El Paso TX 2008-** B Detroit MI 3/5/1942 s Alan Hamilton Gross & Elizabeth Ann. BA New Mex St U Las Cruces 1965; MMus New Mex St U Las Cruces 1971; MDiv Laud Hall Sem 2004. D 6/7/2008 P 12/6/2008 Bp William Carl Frey. m 8/17/1987 Jessie Louise Harris c 4. Admin All SS Epis Ch El Paso TX 2000-2008. brbob.gross@gmail.com

GROSSMAN, Stacey (Cal) Church of the Nativity, 333 Ellen Drive, San Rafael CA 94903 **Bd Gvnr, Ohlhoff Recovery Prog Dio California San Francisco CA 2011-; GC Dep Dio California San Francisco CA 2010-2013; R Ch Of The Nativ San Rafael CA 1999-** B San Jose CA 10/11/1958 d William Shelton Grossman & Madge. BA Pomona Coll 1980; MBA NYU 1983; MDiv CDSP 1996. D 6/1/1996 P 6/7/1997 Bp William Edwin Swing. Int Fac Mem, Pstr Theol CDSP Berkeley CA 2009; Pres, Stndg Com Dio California San Francisco CA 2007-2008; Stndg Com Dio California San Francisco CA 2005-2009; Receiver, Cler Sexual Misconduct Complaints Dio California San Francisco CA 2004-2008; Coordntr, Cler in Trng Prog Dio California San Francisco CA 2002-2009; Chair, Assessment Appeals Com Dio California San Francisco CA 2001-2004; Chair, Personl Practices Cmsn Dio California San Francisco CA 2001-2003; Asst S Fran' Epis Ch San Francisco CA 1996-1999. Cnvnr and Primary Auth, "Called To Rt Relatns," *Dioc Safe Ch Guidelines*, Dio California, 2008. OHC - Assoc 2002. Pres Stndg Com, Dio California 2008. staceygrossman@comcast.net

GROSSO, Andrew Thomas (Kan) 820 N 5th St, Atchison KS 66002 **R Trin Ch Atchison KS 2008-** B Royal Oak MI 11/11/1967 s Thomas Edward Gross & Sharon Marcella. BA Calvin Coll 1989; MA Wheaton Coll 1996; PhD Marq 2004; MDiv STUSo 2004. D 6/5/2004 Bp Steven Andrew Miller P 1/22/2005 Bp Dean Elliott Wolfe. m 10/17/1998 Diana M P Bauson. Gr Cathd Topeka KS 2004-2008. "Personal Being: Polanyi, Ontology, and Chr Theol," Ptr Lang, 2007; "Trin and Wrshp: the Reception of the Basilian Liturg in BCP (1979)," *Sewanee Theol Revs 47, no. 3*, 2004. rector@trinityks.org

GROSSOEHME, Daniel Huck (O) 1078 Carraway Ln, Milford OH 45150 **P S Thos Epis Ch Terrace Pk OH 2003-** B Cincinnati OH 3/20/1963 s Floyd Grossoehme & JoAnn. BS Indiana U 1985; Cert U Cinc 1989; MDiv VTS 1992; DMin Louisiana Presb TS 2006. D 7/25/1992 Bp Herbert Thompson Jr P 6/1/1993 Bp Arthur Benjamin Williams Jr. m 5/23/1992 Henrietta H Haigh c 1. Assoc Chr Ch Epis Hudson OH 2000-2001; P S Phil's Epis Ch Akron OH 2000. Auth, *Pstr Care of Chld*, Haworth Press, 1999; Auth, *Chld Abuse & Neglect*; Auth, *Chld Abuse & Neglect*. Assembly of Epis Hlth Care Chapl, Pres Elect 1999-2000; Assembly of Epis Hlth Care Chapl, Secy 1977-1999; Assn of Profsnl Chapl 1997; Soc of S Jn the Evang 2006. Bd Cert Chapl Assn of Profsnl Chapl 1997. daniel.grossoehme@cchmc.org

GROSSOEHME, Henrietta H (Lex) 1078 Carraway Ln, Milford OH 45150 **Epis Soc of Chr Ch Cincinnati OH 2011-; Gr Epis Ch Florence KY 2008-** B Toledo OH 1/15/1959 d Lawrence Austin Haigh & Ellen Shannon. BA Indiana U 1982; MDiv VTS 1991. Trans 12/5/2003 Bp J Clark Grew II. m 5/23/1992 Daniel Huck Grossoehme c 1. Epis Ret. Hms. Deupree Hlth Cmnty Cincinnati OH 2006-2008; The Soc of the Transiguration Cincinnati OH 2004-2006; R S Ptr's Ch Akron OH 1996-2002; Chr Ch Shaker Heights OH 1991-1996. EvangES. chaplains@zoomtown.com

GROTZINGER, Terri (Mont) 130 S 6th St E, Missoula MT 59801 **Ch Of The H Sprt Missoula MT 2011-; Vic Gd Shpd Epis Ch Belmont CA 2008-; Ch Of The H Fam Half Moon Bay CA 2000-** B Palo Alto CA 6/17/1957 d Hudson Frederick Grotzinger & Nancy Irene. BS Colorado St U 1980; MDiv CDSP 1993. D 6/5/1993 P 6/1/1994 Bp William Edwin Swing. S Mk's Par Berkeley CA 1994-2000; Transitional D Trin Par Menlo Pk CA 1993-1994. terri.grotzinger@gmail.com

GROUBERT, Gerri Helen (Nev) 3665 Largo Verde Way, Las Vegas NV 89121 **All SS Epis Ch Las Vegas NV 2000-** B Canton OH 12/29/1949 d Gerald Groubert & Dorothy. Kent St U; La Salle U 1976. D 11/8/1998 Bp Stewart Clark Zabriskie.

GROUT III, Earl Leroy (Oly) 6801 30th Ave Ne, Seattle WA 98115 **D S Mk's Cathd Seattle WA 2009-** B Minneapolis MN 3/21/1944 BA Macalester Coll 1966; PhD U of Washington 1974. D 6/28/2003 Bp Vincent Waydell Warner. m 1/25/1967 Nancy Elizabeth Austin c 2. D S Steph's Epis Ch Seattle WA 2003-2009. deaconeg@gmail.com

GROVER III, Charles Lowell (Roch) 1035 Whisper Ridge Drive, Chittenango NY 13037 B Philadelphia PA 8/28/1937 s Charles Lowell Grover & Norma Gilbert. BS Webb Inst 1958; MDiv GTS 1963. D 6/7/1963 Bp Walter M Higley P 6/27/1964 Bp Ned Cole. m 7/19/1958 Joan S Sherman c 4. P Assoc Chr Ch Pittsford NY 2000-2004; Int S Steph's Ch Rochester NY 1998-1999; Int S Steph's Ch Niagara Falls NY 1997-1998; Int S Jas Ch Hyde Pk NY 1995-1997; Int S Paul's Ch Rochester NY 1994-1995; Int Ch Of The H Comm U City MO 1993-1994; Int S Lk's Ch Scranton PA 1991-1993; Cn to the Ordnry Dio W Virginia Charleston WV 1990-1991; Archdn & Admnstrtr Dio Cntrl New York Syracuse NY 1988-1990; Dpty for Prog Dio Cntrl New York Syracuse NY 1971-1986; Mssnry S Matt's Epis Ch Liverpool NY 1968-1971; Mssnry S Andr's Ch Watertown NY 1963-1964. clgrover@twcny.rr.com

GROVES, Barbara T (CNY) 141 Main St, Whitesboro NY 13492 B Rome NY 1/24/1942 d William Thomas & Lucille. BS Empire St Coll 1994; Loc Formation Prog Syracuse NY 2005. D 11/19/2005 Bp Gladstone Bailey Adams III. m 8/7/1965 Thomas Groves c 3. btfgro@aol.com

GRUBB, Daniel Studd (WMich) 4770 W Park Rd, New Era MI 49446 B London UK 4/1/1928 s Norman Percy Grubb & Pauline Evangeline. BA Wheaton Coll 1953; MAT Duke 1957; MA U MI 1963; PhD U MI 1967. D 6/6/1984 P 12/19/1984 Bp Alden Moinet Hathaway. m 6/4/1960 Rosemary Callan c 1. Supply P Dio Wstrn Michigan Kalamazoo MI 1998-2003; Asst S Ptr's By-The-Lake Ch Montague MI 1995-1998; Vic S Mary Epis Ch Red Bank Templeton PA 1990-1995; Vic S Ptr's Epis Ch Blairsville PA 1984-1986. Auth, *Another Gulliver*; Auth, *Cause & Effect: Deductive & Inductive Methods of Argument*. ghh4001@voyager.net

GRUBB, Sarah Ann (Neb) 8800 Holdrege St, Lincoln NE 68505 B Omaha NE 1/16/1949 d Dean Edward Richardson & Edna. D 4/29/2010 Bp Joe Goodwin Burnett. m 1/16/1974 John Grubb c 4. jg64815@alltell.net

GRUBBS, Lucas Michael (Ida) 518 N. 8th St., Boise ID 83702 **Cn Pstr S Mich's Cathd Boise ID 2007-** B Brawley CA 11/10/1979 s Michael Grubbs & Dee. BA U of Idaho Moscow 2001; MDiv Ya Berk 2005; STM Yale DS 2007. D 6/11/2005 Bp James Edward Waggoner P 3/11/2006 Bp James Elliot Curry. m 8/6/2005 Meredith Farmer. Cur Chr Ch New Haven CT 2005-2007. The Soc of Cath Priests 2009. The Hands and Heart of Jesus Awd Dio Idaho 2009. lucas.grubbs@gmail.com

GRUBE, David Quinn (Nev) 777 Sage St., Elko NV 89801 **D S Paul's Epis Ch Elko NV 2008-** B Ashton ID 8/25/1958 s Rulon B Grube & Doris R. BA Idaho St U 1981. D 10/24/2008 P 5/9/2009 Bp Dan Thomas Edwards. sagesven@ctnis.com

GRUBERTH, G Cole (Roch) 12 East Genesee St., Wellsville NY 14895 **P-in-c Allegany Cnty Mnstry Belmont NY 2011-** B Pompton Plains NJ 8/7/1967 s Frederick Gruberth & Lynn. SB MIT 1989; MA Cor Ithaca NY 1997; MDiv GTS 2007. D 6/9/2007 Bp Gladstone Bailey Adams III P 12/15/2007 Bp James Robert Mathes. m 6/7/1989 Corie L Gochicoa c 1. P-in-c Tri-Par Mnstry Hornell NY 2011; Assoc. P-in-c Allegany Cnty Mnstry Belmont NY 2010; Assoc R S Barth's Epis Ch Poway CA 2007-2010. ggruberth@gmail.com

GRUMAN, Stephen Cowles (Ala) 131 Silver Lake Cir, Madison AL 35758 **R St. Matt's Epis Ch Madison AL 2000-** B Birmingham AL 12/20/1949 s Shelton Cowles Gruman & Edna. BA U of Alabama 1987; MDiv Epis TS of The SW 1990. D 4/17/1991 P 10/23/1991 Bp Robert Oran Miller. m 4/20/2006 Gertrude Fowler c 4. R Trin Ch Wetumpka AL 1991-2000. Golf Whisperer, "The Art of The Whisper," *The Golf Whisper*, Self Pub, 2010. Cranmer Cup 2010; Cranmer Cup 2006; Cranmer Cup 2004. steves49andred@hotmail.com

GRUMBINE, Eugene Edmund (Va) 506 Danray Dr, Richmond VA 23227 B Chicago IL 10/26/1925 s Eugene Edmund Grumbine & Mable Harriet. CTh Bex 1960. D 6/28/1960 Bp Frederick D Goodwin P 7/8/1961 Bp Robert Fisher Gibson Jr. m 3/16/1974 Gaynelle Grumbine c 3. Vic Ch of the Incarn Mineral VA 1973-1974; P-in-c S Mart's Epis Ch Henrico VA 1963-1971; Asst S Jas' Ch Richmond VA 1961-1963; Assoc Ch Of The H Comf Vienna VA 1960-1961.

GRUMHAUS, Jennifer Wood (Mass) 23 Loew Cir, Milton MA 02186 B Chicago IL 4/26/1962 d David Dean Grumhaus. BS Boston Coll 1984; MDiv EDS 1990. D 6/16/1990 Bp Frank Tracy Griswold III. Assoc S Mich's Ch Milton MA 1994-2004; Camp S Aug Inc Boston MA 1990-1993. jdaly@epiphanyschool.com

GRUNDY, Elizabeth Anne (Mass) 27 Caswell St, New Bedford MA 02745 **Chr Ch Swansea MA 2003-** B Norwood MA 6/30/1959 d John Robert Grundy & Amy Edna. BA Simmons Coll 1981; MA Sarah Lawr Coll 1991; MDiv Andover Newton TS 1996; CAS GTS 1997. D 6/7/1997 P 5/1/1998 Bp M(arvil) Thomas Shaw III. P-in-c S Andr's Ch New Bedford MA 1997-2003. revelizabethgrundy98@gmail.com

GRUNDY, Sandra Ann (Colo) 9345 Carr St, Westminster CO 80021 B Allentown PA 2/28/1951 d Stephen Joseph Luipersbeck & Helen. BS U of Missouri 1973; MA VTS 1980; MA U of Nthrn Colorado 2007. D 6/14/1985 P 12/22/1985 Bp William Carl Frey. m 6/14/1986 Jimmy Wayne Grundy c 1. Int S Jas Epis Ch Wheat Ridge CO 1994-1995; S Jn's Epis Ch Boulder CO 1993-1999; S Jas Epis Ch Wheat Ridge CO 1993; Int S Martha's Epis Ch Westminster CO 1993. Sprtl Dir Intl . jssgrundy@comcast.net

GRUNFELD, Matthew Theodore (Ala) PO Box 3073, Montgomery AL 36109 **P-in-c All SS Ch Montgomery AL 2011-; Dioc Coun Dio Alabama Birmingham AL 2011-** B Columbus GA 6/19/1981 s David Harold Grunfeld & Carol. BA Emory U 2003; MDiv GTS 2008. D 12/21/2006 P 11/2/2008 Bp J(ohn) Neil Alexander. R Emm Epis Ch Opelika AL 2008-2011; Assoc S Mk's Epis Ch Lagrange GA 2007-2008; D Sem Ch Of The H Trin New York NY 2006-2007. One Montgomery 2011. mtggts@gmail.com

GRUSELL, Katrina Grusell (Md) 5057 Stone Hill Dr, Ellicott City MD 21043 **R The Ch Of The H Apos Halethorpe MD 2001-** B Worcester MA 11/8/1963 d Frank Frederick Grondahl & Sandra Katrina. AS Anna Maria Coll 1984; BA Worcester St Coll 1993; MDiv VTS 1999. D 6/12/1999 Bp John Leslie Rabb P 1/8/2000 Bp Robert Wilkes Ihloff. m 10/20/1984 David C Grusell c 2. Asst R St Martins-In-The-Field Ch Severna Pk MD 1999-2001. mom.kat@verizon.net

GRUSENDORF, William Connor (WTex) 401 W Dry St, San Saba TX 76877 **Vic S Lk's Epis Ch San Saba TX 1981-** B Waco TX 6/23/1931 s Monroe Maurice Grusendorf & Della Mae. BA TCU 1954; MA U of Texas 1967; STUSo 1981. D 6/30/1981 Bp Stanley Fillmore Hauser P 6/23/1982 Bp Scott Field Bailey. m 2/16/1952 Patricia Kay c 2.

GRYGIEL, Janet Carol (Chi) 1415 Temple Cir, Rockford IL 61108 B Woosung IL 6/18/1942 d John Henry Houck & Sadie Viola. D 2/1/2003 Bp William Dailey Persell.

GUAMAN AYALA, Francisco (EcuC) Brasilia Y Buenos Aires, Ambato Ecuador B Sangolqui EC 9/27/1957 s Augusto Ranulfo Guaman Villavicencio & Maria Isabel. BA S Vinc De Paul 1976; U Cntrl 1984. D 12/18/1988 Bp Adrian Delio Caceres-Villavicencio. m 5/28/1987 Maria Dolores Morey Villegas.

GUBACK, Thomas Henry (WMich) 6300 North ManitouTrail, Northport MI 49670 B Passaic NJ 1/1/1937 s Stephen Guback & Margaret Douglas. BA Rutgers-The St U 1958; MS U IL 1959; PhD U IL 1964; MDiv Nash 2000. D 5/27/2000 P 11/25/2000 Bp Edward Lewis Lee Jr. m 6/18/1988 Sylvia Linde c 3. R S Christophers Ch Northport MI 2000-2007. Phi Beta Kappa 1958. meadow49670@lycos.com

GUDGER JR, Gordon B (Tex) 2105 N Josey Ln Apt 218, Carrollton TX 75006 B 12/6/1931 D 6/21/1960 Bp James Parker Clements P 5/25/1961 Bp Frederick P Goddard. m 3/19/1994 Sharon Gudger. All SS Epis Ch Hitchcock TX 1985-1993; Chr The King Epis Ch Humble TX 1979; S Steph's Ch Liberty TX 1972-1985. gordongudger1@yahoo.com

GUENTHER, John Howard (WNY) 88 Cedar Terrace, Hilton NY 14468 B Atlantic City NJ 8/25/1919 s William Frederick Guenther & Anna Bertha. BS Drexel U 1942. D 12/14/1968 Bp George West Barrett P 11/18/1972 Bp Robert Rae Spears Jr. m 6/24/1988 Nancy Louise White. R S Paul's Ch Holley NY 1989-1995; Assoc All SS Angl Ch Rochester NY 1973-1974; D S Mk's And S Jn's Epis Ch Rochester NY 1968-1972. nguenther@rochester.rr.com

GUENTHER, Margaret (WA) 4101 Albemarle St NW Apt 651, Washington DC 20016 **Assoc S Columba's Ch Washington DC 1998-** B Kansas City MO 1/4/1929 d Otto Beltz & Adah. BA U of Kansas 1950; U of Zurich 1950; MA U of Kansas 1953; PhD Harv 1958; MDiv GTS 1983. D 12/5/1983 Bp Paul Moore Jr P 6/24/1984 Bp Walter Decoster Dennis Jr. m 6/11/1956 Jack Donald Guenther c 3. Prof The GTS New York NY 1994-1997; Adj Prof The GTS New York NY 1986-1989; Assoc Ch Of The H Trin New York NY 1983-1997. Auth, "Walking Hm: From Eden to Emmaus," Ch Pub, 2010; Auth, "At Hm in the Wrld," Ch Pub, 2006; Auth, "Just Passing Through," Ch Pub, 2002; Auth, "Notes From A Sojourner," Ch Pub, 2002; Auth, "My Soul In Silence Waits," Cowley Press, 2000; Auth, "H Listening"; Auth, "Toward H Ground"; Auth, "The Pract Of Pryr". Phi Beta Kappa 1949. mbguenther@earthlink.net

GUENTHER, Nancy Louise (WNY) 200 East Center St., Medina NY 14103 **Vic S Jn's Ch Medina NY 2010-** B Framingham, MA 9/23/1939 d Charles White & Louisa. BS SUNY- Brockport 1983; MDiv Colgate Rochester Div 1989. D 4/9/2005 P 10/22/2005 Bp J Michael Garrison. m 6/24/1988 John Howard Guenther c 3. nguenther@rochester.rr.com

GUERNSEY, Jacqueline Louise (CFla) 25510 Belle Alliance, Leesburg FL 34748 **D H Trin Epis Ch Fruitland Pk FL 1999-** B Flint MI 2/9/1932 d Warren M Roberts & Thelma V. BS Estrn Michigan U 1964; MA Estrn Michigan U 1969; Diac Whitaker TS 1989. D 11/25/1989 Bp Henry Irving Mayson. m 12/30/1950 Floyd J Guernsey. D S Fran Epis Ch Grayling MI 1990-2000. NAAD.

GUERNSEY, Justine Marie (Alb) 563 Kenwood Ave, Delmar NY 12054 **D Formation Sch, Asst. Dir Dio Albany Albany NY 2010-; D S Matt's Ch Latham NY 2010-** B Albany NY 4/7/1955 d Gerald Gormley O'Connor & Mary Elizabeth. AS Albany Bus Coll Albany NY 1977; BS SUNY 2000; BBA Sage Coll of Albany 2008. D 3/25/2000 Bp Daniel William Herzog. m 12/28/1979 William Leon Guernsey c 3. D Formation Fac, Fac Mem Dio Albany Albany NY 2007-2010; D Cathd Of All SS Albany NY 2000-2010. jmg1014@aol.com

GUERRA, Eduardo (CPa) Po Box 333, Montoursville PA 17754 **Died 3/15/2011** B Coahuila MX 9/23/1928 s Eduardo Guerra & Evangelina. BD SMU 1953; STM UTS 1955; PhD UTS 1967. D 5/21/1967 Bp Dean T Stevenson P 5/1/1968 Bp Earl M Honaman. c 1. guerraed76@suscom.net

GUERRA-DIAZ, Juan Antonio (Ore) Po Box 1731, Hillsboro OR 97123 **Int Vic S Mich's/San Miguel Newberg OR 2001-; Vic San Pablo Ch Hillsboro OR 2001-** B Santiago Chile 1/26/1943 s Francisco Guerra Reyes & Lidia Diaz. Tecnico Electrico Inacap Santiago Cl 1975; Locutor Locutres De Chile Santiago Cl 1980; Latino Radio Broadcasting Portland OR 1998. D 9/30/2000 P 6/9/2001 Bp Robert Louis Ladehoff. m 6/12/1989 Rilda Olivia Gutierres. Appreciation Kbvm-Fm 88.3 1996; Appreciation Kbvm-Fm 88.3 1994; Appreciation Washington Cnty Cmnty Action Orgnztn 1983. misionsanpablo3@hotmail.com

✠ GUERRERO, Rt Rev Orlando Jesus (Ve) No address on file. **Bp of Venezuela Dio Venezuela Colinas De Bello Monte Caracas 10-42-A VE 2004-** B 3/23/1945 D P Con 1/1/1995 for Ve.

GUERRERO-STAMP, Carmen Bruni (Az) 114 W Roosevelt, Phoenix AZ 85003 B Corpus ChristiTX 12/7/1941 d Louis Bruni & Pricilla. BA Our Lady Of The Lake U San Antonio TX 1972; MS Our Lady Of The Lake U San Antonio TX 1980; MDiv STUSo 1984; DD CDSP 1994. D 6/21/1984 Bp Scott Field Bailey P 1/25/1985 Bp Leopold Frade. c 1. Dio Arizona Phoenix AZ 2005-2006; Jubilee Natl Off Epis Ch Cntr New York NY 1999-2007; Epis Ch Cntr New York NY 1999-2006; St Marys Cnvnt Los Angeles CA 1994; Archd Multicultural Dio Los Angeles Los Angeles CA 1990-1999; Santa Fe Epis Mssn San Antonio TX 1989-1990; Dio W Texas San Antonio TX 1984-1990. carmen@azdiocese.org

GUERRIER, Panel Marc (SwFla) 3950 Estey Ave, Naples FL 34104 B Arcahaie HT 12/26/1957 s Pierre A Moliere & Solange. bachelor 1989; Ceeteh 1989. D 7/30/1989 P 2/14/1990 Bp Luc Anatole Jacques Garnier. m 12/16/1993 Magareth Anesca c 3. Dio Haiti Ft Lauderdale FL 1989-2004. pmguerrier@yahoo.com

GUEVARA RODRIGUEZ, Carlos Eduardo (Colom) No address on file. B Pasca cundinamarca 1/13/1968 s Juan Bautista. D 9/9/2006 Bp Francisco Jose Duque-Gomez. m 4/23/2004 Blanca Janeth Guacheta Sanchez c 3. cmsguevara@yaoot.es

GUIBORD, Gwynne Marlyn (Los) 146 S Beachwood Dr, Los Angeles CA 90004 **Nonstipendiary Asstg St Johns Pro-Cathd Los Angeles CA 2007-** B Flint MI 6/27/1944 D 1/6/2004 Bp Sergio Carranza-Gomez P 1/22/2005 Bp Joseph Jon Bruno. Dio Los Angeles Los Angeles CA 2004-2009; S Thos The Apos Hollywood Los Angeles CA 2004-2005. dr.gguibord@aol.com

GUIDA, Angela Gayle (Az) 2480 Virginia St Apt 4, Berkeley CA 94709 **Asst S Aid's Ch San Francisco CA 2011-** B Tampa, FL 2/24/1950 d Angelo Guida & Violet. BS Amer U 1985; MSW CUA 1988; MTS CDSP 2010. D 11/30/2009 P 6/12/2010 Bp Kirk Stevan Smith. c 2. angeliker@cox.net

GUIDRY, R(obert) (WNC) 869 Daylily Dr, Hayesville NC 28904 B Baton Rouge LA 6/28/1947 s Robert Lucien Guidry & Gwendolyn. BA Centenary Coll 1969; MA Steph F. Austin St U 1973. D 9/6/1997 Bp Robert Hodges Johnson. m 4/25/1987 Georgia Skelton.

GUILE, Frederic Corwith (Alb) 1680 Liebig Rd., Granville NY 12832 B Albany NY 2/21/1927 s George Badger Guile & Gertrude May. BArch RPI 1949; BD Ya 1954. D 6/6/1954 P 12/1/1954 Bp Frederick Lehrle Barry. c 3. R S Dav's Epis Ch E Greenbush NY 1969-1979; Asst S Geo's Ch Clifton Pk NY 1968-1969; R Ch Of The Nativ Star Lake NY 1963-1968; R S Mary's Epis Ch Rockport MA 1962-1963; R S Jn's Ch Johnstown NY 1956-1961. Chapl Emer Integrity, Albany 1979; R Emer Ch of the Nativ, Star Lake-- Hermon 1968. drewsdale@localnet.com

GUILLAUME, Sebastien (Miss) 311 Nw 37th St, Pompano Beach FL 33064 **Dio SE Florida Miami FL 2006-** B HT 10/10/1961 s Michel Guillaume & Velita. BA Law Sch Ht 1992; BA Growol Sem Ht 1994. Rec from Roman Catholic 3/15/2000 as Deacon Bp Calvin Onderdonk Schofield Jr. m 5/20/2001 Clara Metinor c 2. P S Jos's Epis Ch Boynton Bch FL 2002-2006. sebclara20032000@yahoo.com

GUILLAUME-SAM, Sully (LI) 331 Hawthorne St, Brooklyn NY 11225 **Cur S Gabr's Ch Brooklyn NY 2010-** B Haiti 2/29/1968 s Jacksius Guillaume-Sam & Rose Gulna. MA Fordham Univserity; Bachelor Grand Seminaire ND; Dplma in Angl Stds The GTS. Rec from Roman Catholic 6/26/2010 Bp Lawrence C Provenzano. c 1. Epis Cmnty Serv Long Island 1927 Garden City NY 2006-2010. sully.gsam@hotmail.com

GUILLEN, Anthony Anthony (Los) PO Box 512164, Los Angeles CA 90051 **Mssnr for Latino/Hisp Mnstrs Epis Ch Cntr New York NY 2005-** B Richmond TX 4/14/1953 s Jesus Gayton Guillen & Simona. CTh Epis TS of The SW 1990; MA Epis TS of The SW 2000; BS U of Phoenix 2000. D 9/21/1984 P 4/14/1985 Bp Samuel Espinoza-Venegas. m 7/6/1991 Guadelupe Moriel c 3. Exec Coun Mem Dio Los Angeles Los Angeles CA 2000-2006; R All SS Epis Ch Oxnard CA 1993-2005; COM Dio Los Angeles Los Angeles CA 1993-1998; Assoc R S Clem's-By-The-Sea Par San Clemente CA 1990-1992; Dio Wstrn Mex Zapopan Jalisco CP 45150 1984-1987. Auth, "The Epis Ch's Strategic Vision for Reaching Latinos/Hispanics," Off of Latino/Hisp Mnstrs, 2009; Auth, "Crossing the Cultural Divide," *Doing H Bus*, Ch Pub, 2006. Hon Cn Dio Ecuador Cntrl 2007; Hon Cn Dio Puerto Rico 2006. aguillen@episcopalchurch.org

GUINN, Patricia J. (WNY) 2753 Eastwood Rd, East Aurora NY 14052 **Dioc Coun Chautauqua Dnry Dio Wstrn New York Tonawanda NY 2011-; D S Ptr's Ch Westfield NY 2011-** B Buffalo NY 5/17/1944 d Rudolph Odin Liesinger & Patricia Spencer. BA SUNY 1966; MLS SUNY 1967; MSW St Univeristy of New York 1996. D 9/12/1998 Bp David Charles Bowman. m 2/18/1971 Paul Spencer Guinn c 3. D S Aid's Ch Alden NY 2007-2011; D S Simon's Ch Buffalo NY 2002-2007; D Trin Ch Lancaster NY 1999-2001. NAAD 1998-2000. pjguinn@gmail.com

G

GUINTA, Denise Gray (Va) 16 Amiss Ave, Luray VA 22835 **Chr Epis Ch Luray VA 2010-; Chapl @ Univ. of So Florida Dio SW Florida Sarasota FL 2008-** B Graet Falls Va 8/29/1962 MA S Mary-Of-The-Woods Coll. D 5/26/2002 P 6/14/2003 Bp Mark Lawrence Mac Donald. m 3/15/1988 Ronald Guinta c 2. Dio SW Florida Sarasota FL 2007-2009; H Innoc Epis Ch Valrico FL 2006-2007; H Trin Epis Ch In Countryside Clearwater FL 2004-2005; Int S Alfred's Epis Ch Palm Harbor FL 2003-2004. revd@tampabay.rr.com

GUISTOLISE, Kathryn Jean Mazzenga (Chi) 1509 Ridge Ave, Evanston IL 60201 **H Trin Ch Skokie IL 2006-** B Chicago IL 6/25/1948 d Frank Joseph Mazzenga & Betty Helene Livick Mazzenga. Cert SWTS 1995. D 2/3/1996 Bp Frank Tracy Griswold III P 1/6/2005 Bp William Dailey Persell. m 6/9/1985 Philip Sam Guistolise. Par Ministers Coordntr/D S Mk's Ch Evanston IL 1996-2000. Auth, "Var arts". ESMA Chicago; Soc Of S Jn The Evang. The Rev Rbt Dahl Schlrshp. kateguistolise@aol.com

✠ GULICK JR, Rt Rev Edwin Funsten (Va) 425 S 2nd St, Louisville KY 40202 **Ret Bp of Kentucky Dio Virginia Richmond VA 2011-** B Washington DC 7/27/1948 s Edwin Gulick & Nelle. Shalem Inst Washington DC; VTS; BA Lynchburg Coll 1970; MDiv VTS 1973; DD STUSo 1995. D 6/5/1973 Bp William Henry Marmion P 2/9/1974 Bp David Keller Leighton Sr Con 4/17/1994 for Ky. m 8/15/1970 Barbara Lichtfuss c 1. Bp Of Ky Dio Kentucky Louisville KY 1994-2010; R S Steph's Ch Newport News VA 1982-1994; R Gr Ch Elkridge MD 1976-1982; Asst Trin Ch Towson MD 1973-1976. Intl Angl RC Cmsn For Unity And Mssn (Aircum); Scer Angl / RC Dialogue. Hon DD Stuso Sewanee TN 1995; Hon DD VTS 1994. bishoptedgulick@aol.com

GUMBS, Delores Elvida (VI) PO Box 6454, Christiansted, St Croix VI 00823 B St Kitts VI 7/7/1940 d Hubert Adams & Evangeline. RFN The Royal Coll of Nrsng 1963; RN The Royal Coll of Nrsng 1966; NM The Royal Coll of Nrsng 1968. D 6/21/2008 Bp Edward Ambrose Gumbs. c 1. eulie@hotmail.com

✠ GUMBS, Rt Rev Edward Ambrose (VI) P.O. Box 7488, St Thomas VI **Bp of the Vrgn Islands Dio Vrgn Islands St Thos VI VI 2005-** B Stoney Ground Anguilla 5/3/1949 s Edward Alphonso Gumbs & Drucilla Amontine (Brooks). U of Maryland 1980; BA U of the Vrgn Islands 1984; MDiv VTS 1987. D 6/14/1987 P 6/12/1988 Bp E(gbert) Don Taylor Con 6/11/2005 for VI. m 8/7/1999 Phillis Hodge c 2. S Andr's Ch Charlotte Amalie VI VI 1988-2005. DD VTS 2006. bpambrosegumbs@yahoo.com

GUNDERSON, David John (Mont) 313 S Yellowstone St, Livingston MT 59047 **R S Andr's Ch Livingston MT 2004-; Upper Yellowstone Epis Ch Livingston MT 2004-** B Seattle WA 7/23/1952 s John Francis Gunderson & Ellen Eugenia. BA U of Washington 1974; MDiv EDS 1980; MEd Past Counslg U Of Puget Sound 1990. D 7/25/1980 Bp Robert Hume Cochrane P 5/1/1981 Bp Paul Moore Jr. m 1/24/2009 Kory Gunderson c 1. Mssn to Seafarers Seattle WA 2002-2004; Int Ch Of The Ascen Seattle WA 2001-2002; S Hilda's - S Pat's Epis Ch Edmonds WA 1999-2000; S Mary's Ch Lakewood WA 1987-1990; Vic Ch Of Our Sav Monroe WA 1983-1987; Seamens Ch Inst Income New York NY 1980-1983. Auth, "Earth & Sprt". dgmontana@gmail.com

GUNDERSON, Gretchen Anne (Oly) 629 Taft Ave, Raymond WA 98577 **P S Jn's Epis Ch So Bend WA 1992-** B Los Angeles CA 3/14/1943 d Robert Frederick Guethlein & Grace Elizabeth. U CA; U of Washington; WA SU; BA U CA 1964. D 8/29/1992 P 3/1/1993 Bp Vincent Waydell Warner. m 4/9/1976 Karl Darwin Gunderson c 2. geetie@comcast.net

GUNN JR, Clem O (WNC) 914 Rainbow Ln, Hendersonville NC 28791 **Died 7/17/2009** B Pensacola FL 4/25/1922 s Clem Oliver Gunn & Hazel. BA Georgia Inst of Tech 1948; MDiv EDS 1985. Trans from Anglican Church of Canada 4/1/1992 Bp Robert Hodges Johnson. Ord Of S Lk 1997. gunnc@brinet.com

GUNN, Daniel Cube (Be) 180 Riverside Dr., Wilkes Barre PA 18702 **R S Steph's Epis Ch Wilkes Barre PA 2006-** B Union MS 11/11/1973 s David Thomas Gunn & Bobbie Nell. PhD cand Drew U; BS Lee U 1997; MDiv Ch of God TS 1999; MA W Chester U of Pennsylvania 2001; CAS Ya Berk 2002; STM Yale DS 2003. D 4/6/2002 P 10/6/2002 Bp Paul Victor Marshall. m 5/15/1993 Ada Borkowski. Asst to R Chr Ch Bronxville NY 2002-2006. dgunn@ststephenswb.org

GUNN, Reginald Richard (Ga) 688 Covecrest Dr, Tiger GA 30576 B Tifton GA 12/12/1940 s John Samuel Gunn & Helen Louise. BA U GA 1962; MDiv SWTS 1965. D 5/29/1965 P 3/25/1966 Bp Albert R Stuart. m 6/5/1965 Mary Luise Ackerman c 2. R Calv Ch Americus GA 1992-2006; Assoc S Jas Epis Ch Baton Rouge LA 1990-1992; Pres, Stndg Com Dio Georgia Savannah GA 1980-1990; R S Thos Ch Savannah GA 1977-1990; Dep Gnrl Conventions Dio Georgia Savannah GA 1972-1981; Dioc Coun Dio Georgia Savannah GA 1971-1985; R S Patricks Ch Albany GA 1971-1977; R S Andr's Epis Ch Douglas GA 1969-1971; Vic S Lk's Epis Hawkinsville GA 1965-1969; Vic Trin Ch Cochran GA 1965-1969. OHC 1962. gunnvilla@gmail.com

G

GUNN, Scott A (RI) 540 Prospect St, Seekonk MA 02771 **FMP Cincinnati OH 2011-** B Gardner KS 10/28/1967 s Ronald Charles Gunn & Nancy Joann. BA Luther Coll 1990; MA Ya Berk 1992; MDiv Ya Berk 1996; CAS Ya Berk 1996; MA Br 1997. D 2/5/2005 P 9/10/2005 Bp Geralyn Wolf. m 11/24/2009 Sherilyn Pearce. Chr Ch In Lonsdale Lincoln RI 2007-2011; St Mich & Gr Ch Rumford RI 2006-2007; Dioc Coun VP Dio Rhode Island Providence RI 2005-2006. sgunn@forwarddaybyday.com

GUNNESS, Margaret (Mass) 641 Pleasant St, Belmont MA 02478 B Shreveport LA 9/14/1937 d James Theron Brown & Margaret. BA Connecticut Coll 1959; L'Universite de Caen - France/Fulbright Schlr 1960; MDiv EDS 1980. D 6/7/1980 Bp John Bowen Coburn P 2/18/1981 Bp Morris Fairchild Arnold. m 8/17/1962 Peter Gunness c 3. S Mary's Cathd Memphis TN 2001-2002; Calv Ch Memphis TN 1999-2001; R Chr Ch Ridgewood NJ 1991-1999; Stff P Trin Ch In The City Of Boston Boston MA 1987-1990; Chr Ch Cambridge Cambridge MA 1980-1987. pgunness@comcast.net

GUNTER, Matthew Alan (Chi) 22w400 Hackberry Dr, Glen Ellyn IL 60137 **R S Barn' Epis Ch Glen Ellyn IL 2000-** B Warsaw IN 12/20/1957 s Doyle W Gunter & Sue Ann. BA Indiana U 1980; Gordon-Conwell TS 1981; MDiv VTS 1996. D 6/8/1996 Bp John-David Mercer Schofield P 12/21/1996 Bp Frank Tracy Griswold III. m 5/30/1981 Leslie R Renee c 3. Asst S Dav's Ch Glenview IL 1996-1999. Auth, "The Wildness Of God," *Prism mag*, 2001. Jn Hines Preaching Awd Jn Hines Preaching Awd 2001. mattgunter@aol.com

GUNTHORPES, Alexander (LI) 2666 E 22nd St, Brooklyn NY 11235 **Emm Epis Ch Of Sheepshead Bay Brooklyn NY 1990-** B 2/11/1948 s Charles William Gunthorpes & Sarah. LTh Codrington Coll 1975; MS NYTS 1987; DMin Andersonville Bapt Sem 2001. Rec 2/1/1987 as Priest Bp Robert Campbell Witcher Sr. m 6/30/1973 Kathleen Girlette Adassa Parker c 4. Asst Ch Of S Thos Brooklyn NY 1984-1987. agunthorpes@gmail.com

GURNIAK, David Fyodor (Ct) 610a Heritage Villiage, Southbury CT 06488 B Philadelphia PA 10/22/1934 s John F Gurniak & Anna. BS U of Pennsylvania 1956; STB Ya Berk 1959; ThM Yale DS 1959. D 5/16/1959 P 12/1/1959 Bp William P Roberts. m 7/9/1960 Janet G Grayshon. Int S Jn's Ch No Haven CT 1996-1998; S Ptr's Ch Fernandina Bch FL 1991-1996; Chr Epis Ch Dayton OH 1989-1991; Trin Ch Ft Wayne IN 1988-1989; R S Mk's Ch Evanston IL 1984-1988; S Mich's Ch Litchfield CT 1961-1984; Asst H Apos And Medtr Philadelphia PA 1959-1961. gurnct@aol.com

GURRY, Jane Todd (NC) 817 Rosemont Ave, Raleigh NC 27607 B Philadelphia MS 2/26/1932 d Lindsay Ogletree Todd & Sarah Bernice. BA U of Mississippi 1953; MEd U NC 1972; MDiv VTS 1980. D 6/21/1980 Bp Thomas Augustus Fraser Jr P 3/1/1981 Bp Roger W Blanchard. m 7/1/1956 Ellis T Gurry c 3. P For Liturg And Tchg S Ambroses Ch Raleigh NC 2002-2003; S Mk's Epis Ch Raleigh NC 1989-1997; R Ch Of Our Sav Cincinnati OH 1983-1988; Epis Soc Of Chr Ch Cincinnati OH 1980-1984; Asst to R Epis Soc of Chr Ch Cincinnati OH 1980-1983. jegurry@nc.rr.com

GUSHEE, Stephen H (SeFla) 1729 Flagler Manor Circle, West Palm Beach FL 33411 B Detroit MI 7/18/1936 s Edward Tisdale Gushee & Norine. Kent Sch 1954; BA Br 1958; MDiv EDS 1966. D 6/11/1966 Bp Walter H Gray P 2/18/1967 Bp Joseph Warren Hutchens. m 2/9/1996 Mary Coakley c 3. Asst Gr Ch W Palm Bch FL 1995-1996; Sr Assoc The Epis Ch Of Beth-By-The-Sea Palm Bch FL 1991-1994; Dn Chr Ch Cathd Hartford CT 1978-1991; R Trin Ch Newtown CT 1970-1978; Cur S Ptr's Epis Ch Cheshire CT 1966-1970. Bd Amer Friends Epis Dio Jerusalem. Amer Cn S Andr Cathd Aberdeen Scotland 1980. sgushee36@gmail.com

GUSTAFSON II, Karl Edmund (Az) 150 E La Soledad, Green Valley AZ 85614 **All SS Epis Ch Las Vegas NV 2001-** B Denver CO 1/25/1935 s Karl Edmund Gustafson & Ruth Amelia. BA U Denv 1969; Wstrn St Coll of Colorado 1971; Epis TS In Kentucky 1976. D 3/14/1975 P 11/18/1975 Bp Addison Hosea. m 7/30/1955 Nancie A Mitchell c 4. S Andrews Crippled Childrens Clnc Inc Nogales AZ 1994-2000; Epis Ch Of S Fran-In-The-Vlly Green Vlly AZ 1993-2001; S Andr's Epis Ch Nogales AZ 1988-1994; R Ch Of The H Comm Rock Sprg WY 1981-1988; R Gr Ch Ishpeming MI 1979-1981; Vic Adv Ch Cynthiana KY 1975-1979. ECF; RACA. padregus@oldmutt.com

GUSTAFSON, Mary Dannies (WMass) 183 South St, Southbridge MA 01550 **R H Trin Epis Ch Southbridge MA 2004-** B Bethlehem PA 7/18/1946 d Robert Bowen Dannies & Nancy Harper. BA Coll of Wooster 1968; MA U of Kentucky 1972; MFA U of Iowa 1976; MDiv TESM 2000; DMin Luther TS 2007. D 6/9/2001 P 12/17/2001 Bp Robert William Duncan. m 8/17/1974 Ray Everett Gustafson c 4. St Johns Luth Ch Pittsburgh PA 2002-2004; P-in-c S Matt's Epis Ch Homestead PA 2001-2004. Scholarly Achievement Awd ABS 2000; Scholarly Achievement Awd ABS 1997. gustafso1@earthlink.net

GUSTIN, Peter Rochefort (Va) 14899 James Monroe Hwy, Leesburg VA 20176 B Long Beach CA 4/16/1953 s Albert Edwin Gustin & Muriel Jacqueline. BA Coppin St Coll 1979; MDiv VTS 1987; DMin SWTS 2001. D 6/13/1987 P 3/19/1988 Bp Peter James Lee. m 10/22/1977 Debra MacKenzie c 2. Vic Chr Epis Ch Lucketts Leesburg VA 2002-2010; R Cunningham Chap Par Millwood VA 1990-2002; Vic Calv Ch Hanover VA 1987-1990; Asst to R Ch Of S Jas The Less Ashland VA 1987-1990. Auth, "Virginia Sem Journ"; Auth, "Virginia Sem Journ". CERT 2005; ESBVM 1986-1989; VGEC 1998; VOAD 2003. prgustin@gmail.com

GUTHRIE, Donald Angus (Mont) 1801 Selway Dr., Missoula MT 59808 B Dundee Scotland GB 1/18/1931 s Frederick Charles Guthrie & Alison Jean. Westcott Hse Cambridge; BA Oxf 1954; MA Oxf 1958. Trans from Church Of England 10/1/1989. m 1/15/2000 Melissa Harrison c 3. Stndg Com Dio Montana Helena MT 1989-1991; RurD Dio Montana Helena MT 1985-1989; Ecum Off Dio Montana Helena MT 1984-1990; R Ch Of The H Sprt Missoula MT 1979-1993; Dio Montana Helena MT 1977-1979.

GUTHRIE, Emily (WA) 7215 Arthur Dr, Falls Church VA 22046 **S Marg's Ch Washington DC 2010-; D Assoc Chr Ch Capitol Hill Washington DC 1998-** B Bridgeport CT 2/8/1964 d Hugh Delmar Guthrie & Elizabeth Anne. BA Pr 1985; MDiv Yale DS 1995. D 6/12/1999 Bp Ronald Hayward Haines P 1/16/2010 Bp John Chane. m Michael J Lindner. Par Coordntr S Mk's Ch Washington DC 1990-1992; Yth Dir S Mk's Ch Washington DC 1990-1992; Yth Dir S Mk's Ch Washington DC 1989-1992. Cmnty Achievement Awd Capitol Hill Cmnty Fndt 2008. emilyjguthrie@gmail.com

GUTHRIE JR, Harvey Henry (Mich) 1486 Old Telegraph Rd, Fillmore CA 93015 B Santa Paula CA 10/31/1924 s Harvey Henry Guthrie & Emma Leona. BA Missouri Vlly Coll 1944; UTS 1946; STB GTS 1949; STM GTS 1953; ThD GTS 1958. D 6/21/1947 P 11/27/1948 Bp Charles K Gilbert. m 12/29/1945 Doris Mignonette Peyton c 4. Stndg Com Dio Michigan Detroit MI 1989-1995; R S Andr's Ch Ann Arbor MI 1985-1995; Dep GC Dio Massachusetts Boston MA 1973-1982; Prof/Dn EDS Cambridge MA 1958-1985; Fell and Tutor, Instr The GTS New York NY 1950-1958; Vic S Fran Assisi And S Martha White Plains NY 1947-1950. Auth, "Theol as Thanksgiving," *Theol as Thanksgiving*, Seabury Press, 1981; Auth, "Israel's Sacr Songs," *Israel's Sacr Songs*, Seabury Press, 1966; Auth, "God & Hist in the OT," *God & Hist in the OT*, Seabury Press, 1961. Assn of Theol Schools in the US and Can - Presi 1980-1982. DD EDS 1985. harveyguthrie@earthlink.net

GUTHRIE, Suzanne Elizabeth (CNY) St. Aidan's House, 105 Federal Hill Road, Brewster NY 10509 B Hempstead NY 1/30/1951 d James Stanley Guthrie & Lois Jean. BA GW 1973; MTS Oblate TS 1979. Trans 10/22/2003 Bp Mark Sean Sisk. m 10/16/1995 William C Consiglio c 4. Epis Ch At Cornell Ithaca NY 2003-2007; Chr Ch Poughkeepsie NY 2000-2003; CE Mssnr Ch Of The H Cross Kingston NY 1998-2000; Pstr S Anne's Ch Washingtonville NY 1993-1998; Hudson Vlly Mnstrs New Windsor NY 1993-1996; Asst Ch Of S Mart Davis CA 1984-1986. Auth, "Gr's Window: Entering the Seasons of Pryr," Ch Pub, 2008; Auth, "Praying the Hours," Cowley, 2000. Ord of S Ben, Camaldolese Oblate 1983; Res Comp, CHS 2007. ammaguthrie@gmail.com

GUTHRIE, William A (Nwk) 2812 Sequoyah Drive, Haines City FL 33844 B Bartica GY 5/11/1949 s Charles Guthrie & Latchmin. LTh U of The W Indies 1972; DIT Codrington Coll 1974; BA U of The W Indies 1974; DMin VTS 1986. Trans from Church in the Province Of The West Indies 2/1/1980 Bp Robert Bruce Hall. m 6/24/1977 Elizabeth Fiedtkou c 3. Ret Chr Epis Ch E Orange NJ 1993-2011; R S Cyp's Ch San Francisco CA 1989-1990; Vic Trin Epis Ch Charlottesville VA 1980-1988. Auth, "Stwdshp in the Loc Ch," *Unpublished*, Unpub. Diss., VTS, 1986; Auth, "Bartica--Gateway to the Interior of Guyana," *Pub*, Outskirts Press, Inc. NAACP 1985; Natl Geographic Soc 1980; NOEL 1987; UBE 1995. Fllshp Lily Endwmt Grant 2003; Arthur Lichtenberger Awd Trin & St. Phil's Cathd 2001; Bp Allin Fllshp PBp's Off 1987. wguth93700@aol.com

GUTIERREZ, Daniel George Policarpio (RG) 601 Montano Rd. N.W., Albuquerque NM 87107 **Dio The Rio Grande Albuquerque NM 2011-** B Albuquerque NM 10/7/1964 s George Gutierrez & Ramona. MTS St. Norbert's Coll; BA U of New Mex 1987; MPA U of New Mex 1993. D 6/7/2008 Bp William Carl Frey P 12/12/2008 Bp James Robert Mathes. m 2/12/1997 Suzanne Fletcher c 1. S Mich And All Ang Ch Albuquerque NM 2010-2011. dgpgutz@msn.com

GUTIERREZ, Janssen Jose (Fla) 895 Palm Valley Rd, Ponte Vedra FL 32081 **P-in-c San Francisco Del Campo Jacksonville FL 2010-** B Valencia Venezuela 12/29/1972 s Claudio Jose Gutierrez & Maria Petrona Silva. Doctor Chr Counslg / In progress Logos Chr Coll; Pianist Tecnologico de Musica 1995; Computer Engr Universidad Tecnológica del Centro 1998; Bachelor of Theol Logos Chr Coll 2003; Mstr Chr Counslg Logos Chr Coll 2007. D 8/9/2009 P 8/9/2009 Bp Samuel Johnson Howard. m 10/20/1995 Mariely J Coronel c 2. JANSSENG@HOTMAIL.COM

GUTIERREZ, Jorge Martin (Roch) 48 Whitcomb Road, Boxborough MA 01719 B Habana CU 5/17/1947 s Francisco Alberto Gutierrez & Rissett. BA W Virginia U 1969; VTS 1971; MDiv GTS 1973. D 6/7/1973 P 2/25/1974 Bp Wilburn Camrock Campbell. m 7/6/1974 Carolyn Taylor c 1. R Chr Ch Corning NY 1991-2009; Dio Newark, Stndg Com Dio Newark Newark NJ 1990-1991; R S Ptr's Ch Clifton NJ 1981-1991; R Gr Epis Ch Elkins WV 1975-1981; Vic Ch Of The Gd Shpd Elkins WV 1975-1976; Cur The Ch of S Edw The Mtyr New York NY 1973-1975. Bp's Cert of Merit for Outstanding Serv Dio Newark Newark 1987. yoyigutierrez@gmail.com

GUTIERREZ-DUARTE, Edgar Armando (Mass) 32 Franklin Ave, Chelsea MA 02150 **Vic S Lk's/San Lucas Epis Ch Chelsea MA 2007-** B Bogotá, Colombia 12/1/1953 BA Dominican Coll 1986; MA Antioch U 1988; MS Rutgers-The St U 1999; MDiv GTS 2003. D 6/7/2003 P 12/14/2003 Bp John Palmer Croneberger. Assoc R S Paul's Epis Ch Paterson NJ 2003-2007. vicarsanlucas@aol.com

GUTMACHER, Blaine J (Az) Po Box 691, Scottsdale AZ 85252 B Chicago IL 8/13/1922 s Carl Herman Gutmacher & Laura Jean. U of Arizona 1943; CDSP 1966. D 6/22/1966 P 12/23/1966 Bp J(ohn) Joseph Meakins Harte. Asst S Chris's Ch Sun City AZ 1984-1985; Int Ch Of The Epiph Flagstaff AZ 1983-1984; Vic Ch Of The Adv Sun City W AZ 1980-1983; Dio Arizona Phoenix AZ 1980-1983; Stff S Phil's In The Hills Tucson AZ 1968-1980.

GUTWEIN, Martin (NJ) 527 N 2nd St, Camden NJ 08102 **R S Paul's Ch Camden NJ 1980-** B San Diego CA 3/27/1945 s Martin Gutwein & Martha. BA Hob 1967; MA EDS 1969; MDiv EDS 1972. D 6/24/1972 Bp Robert Rae Spears Jr P 12/24/1972 Bp Albert Wiencke Van Duzer. m 5/27/1978 Toni James c 3. R S Wilfrid's Ch Camden NJ 1983-1993; Ch Of Our Sav Camden NJ 1983; Asst Chr Ch New Brunswick NJ 1972-1978. revgutwein@yahoo.com

GUY, Kenneth Gordon (FdL) N11052 Norway Ln, Tomahawk WI 54487 B Auburn NY 1/30/1943 s Kenneth G Guy & Ann B. BA Coll of Wooster 1966; Harvard DS 1969; JD U of Wisconsin 1969; MDiv Nash 1988. D 5/6/1988 P 11/1/1988 Bp Roger John White. m 12/26/1964 Barbara R Riemer c 3. R S Ptr's Ch (S Mary's Chap) Ripon WI 2001-2007; R S Mary's Wautoma Ripon WI 2001; R S Mart's Ch Brown Deer WI 1990-2001; Asst Trin Ch Wauwatosa WI 1988-1990.

GUY, Ronald Alan (WNY) St James Episcopal Church, 405 E Main St, Batavia NY 14020 B Anchorage Alaska 9/16/1952 s James Everett Guy & Alice Louise. MDiv STUSo 2001. D 6/9/2001 P 4/8/2002 Bp James Monte Stanton. m 7/26/1981 Marisa Willis c 2. R S Jas' Ch Batavia NY 2007-2009; S Mk's Epis Ch Lewistown PA 2004-2007; The Epis Ch Of The H Nativ Plano TX 2001-2004.

GUZMAN, Pedro S (NJ) 7709 Piersanti Ct, Pennsauken NJ 08109 **Ch Of S Andr The Apos Camden NJ 2004-** B DO 1/2/1954 s Pedro Antonio Guzman & Luz Graciela. Rec from Roman Catholic 11/1/1996 as Priest Bp David Andres Alvarez-Velazquez. m 8/9/1996 Odeida D Dalmasi c 3. Santa Teresa de Avila Chicago IL 2003-2004. st.andrews4@verizon.net

GWIN JR, Lawrence Prestidge (Tex) Po Box 404, Bay City TX 77404 **Chr Ch Matagorda TX 2004-** B Houston TX 12/23/1959 s Lawrence P Gwin & Rebekah Witherspoon. BA U of Texas 1982; JD U of Mississippi 1985. D 2/3/2002 Bp Leopoldo Jesus Alard P 12/21/2002 Bp Don Adger Wimberly. m 10/2/2004 Roseanne Ritchie-Fusaro. S Thos Ch Wharton TX 2002-2003. hossg@aol.com

GWINN, Thomas Wallace (Alb) PO Box 286, North Stratford NH 03590 B Sioux City IA 4/18/1941 s Ira James Gwinn & H(ope) Winifred. BA Morningside Coll 1963; U of Wisconsin 1964; STB Ya Berk 1968. D 6/22/1968 P 12/20/1968 Bp Gordon V Smith. m 8/12/1967 Edith T Hogan c 5. Dn Dio Albany Albany NY 1991-1997; Dio Alaska Fairbanks AK 1989-1993; R S Mk's Ch Malone NY 1986-2005; Secy Dioc Coun Dio Iowa Des Moines IA 1983-1986; P-in-c S Andr's Epis Ch Waverly IA 1975-1986; P-in-c Trin Ch Emmetsburg IA 1968-1975. twgwinn@yahoo.com

GWYN III, Lewis (CFla) 5855 39th Ln, Vero Beach FL 32966 **D Trin Ch Vero Bch FL 2008-** B Bronxville NY 7/16/1942 s Lewis Ruffner Gwyn & Priscilla Bill. BA U So 1969. D 12/14/2002 Bp John Wadsworth Howe. m 9/1/1968 Clare Gwyn c 2. D S Aug Of Cbury Epis Ch Vero Bch FL 2003-2008. lrgwyn@yahoo.com

GWYN, Roxane Stewart (NC) PO Box 635, Meredith NH 03253 **Trin Ch Fuquay Varina NC 2011-** B Griffin GA 2/5/1953 d Louis John Stewart & Sybil Hartley. BA UNC-Chap Hill 1974; MDiv Duke DS 2007; STM GTS 2010. D 6/19/2010 P 3/8/2011 Bp Michael Bruce Curry. m 6/12/1976 Owen Gwyn c 2. rox6@mac.com

GWYNN, Caron Annette (WA) St. Timothy's Episcopal Church, 3601 Alabama Avenue, S.E., Washington DC 20020 **P-in-c S Tim's Epis Ch Washington DC 2011-** B Washington DC 1/7/1954 d Alverse Monroe Gwynn & Dorothy Jeanne. BS Towson St U 1977; MDiv VTS 2006. D 6/10/2006 P 1/20/2007 Bp John Chane. Int The Ch Of The Ascen Lexington Pk MD 2010-2011; Asst S Marg's Ch Washington DC 2006-2009. setouduc@aol.com

GWYNNE, Geoffrey Carrington (Va) 1484 Bluewater Rd., Harrisonburg VA 22801 **Vic Chr the King Epis Ch Harrisonburg VA 2009-** B Burlingame CA 6/1/1960 s Samuel Carlton Gwynne & Nancy Jane. BA Mia 1982; Cert TESM 1984; U So 1986; MDiv Ya Berk 1988. Trans 1/1/2004 Bp Robert John O'Neill. m 2/10/1990 Karen Newland c 3. Dio Virginia Richmond VA 2004-2009; P-in-c Chr Epis Ch Aspen CO 2003; Vic Ch Of The H Sprt Cherry Hills Vill CO 1995-2002; Chr Epis Ch Denver CO 1989-2002; D-In-Trng Chr Ch Epis Hudson OH 1988-1989. geoff@ctkharrisonburg.org

H

HAACK, Christopher Allyn (Minn) 877 Jessie St, Saint Paul MN 55130 B Rochester MN 12/30/1968 s Kenneth Allyn & Theld Ann. D 12/11/2008 Bp James Louis Jelinek. bennchloe@aol.com

HAAS, Kirk Bayard (WVa) 112 South Walnut St., Morgantown WV 26501 B Bethlehem PA 9/5/1944 s Harold David Haas & Adele Eileen. BA Leh 1966; BS Leh 1967; Gordon-Conwell TS 1976; MDiv EDS 1978; DMin Pittsburgh TS 1996. D 6/10/1978 Bp Morris Fairchild Arnold P 6/7/1979 Bp John Bowen Coburn. m 8/31/1968 Charlotte Bilson c 3. R Trin Ch Morgantown WV 1991-2008; R Ch Of The H Sprt Erie PA 1981-1991; Asst All SS' Epis Ch Belmont MA 1978-1981. kirkhaas@hotmail.com

HAAS, Margaret Ann (Mich) 2923 Roundtree Blvd Apt A2, Ypsilanti MI 48197 B Rochester NY 11/19/1943 d John Walter Haas & Marie Margaret. Estrn Michigan U; S Jn's Prov Sem; SWTS; Whitaker TS; BA Skidmore Coll 1965. D 6/28/1986 Bp Henry Irving Mayson P 9/1/1990 Bp R(aymond) Stewart Wood Jr. Asst Chr Ch Dearborn MI 2003-2006; Supply P Dio Michigan Detroit MI 1996-2003; Asst Ch Of The H Sprt Livonia MI 1991-1996; Par Growth Pstr S Mart Ch Detroit MI 1989-1991; Asst Trin Epis Ch Farmington Hills MI 1986-1989. mhaas@umich.edu

HAAS, Mary Elizabeth (Vt) Po Box 207, Alstead NH 03602 **D Imm Ch Bellows Falls VT 2003-** B Brentwood NH 5/7/1926 d Leroy Lake & Marien. D 6/7/2003 Bp Thomas C Ely. m Charles Haas.

HAAS, Michael James (NI) 2006 E Broadway, Logansport IN 46947 B Kalamazoo MI 8/18/1942 s Terrence Joseph Haas & Jane Eleanor. BA H Cross Sem 1965; MA S Jn Sem 1969; MS U MI 1972; MDiv SWTS 1992. Rec from Roman Catholic 3/1/1992 as Priest Bp Francis Campbell Gray. m 5/28/1971 Mary Ellen Flaherty c 6. Trin Epis Ch Logansport IN 1992-2003. haasmi@fpc.edu

HAASE, Sylvia Anne (Oly) Po Box 208, Vaughn WA 98394 **D - Vol S Hugh Of Lincoln Allyn WA 2002-** B Tacoma WA 3/13/1939 d Henry Haase & Minna. BA Whittier Coll 1962; MA U CO 1966; Universitat Hamburg Hamburg DE 1972. D 11/30/2002 Bp Sanford Zangwill Kaye Hampton.

HABBERFIELD, Jack Richard (Fla) 10790 Old Saint Augustine Rd, Apt 321, Jacksonville FL 32257 B Geneva NY 2/1/1924 s John E Habberfield & Laura B. LTh Epis TS In Kentucky 1966. D 5/28/1966 P 5/27/1967 Bp William R Moody. m 7/26/1947 Shirley Goit c 2. Assoc S Thos Flagler Cnty Palm Coast FL 1996-2006; Ch Of The New Cov Winter Sprg FL 1992-1993; Asst R Ch Of The New Cov Winter Sprg FL 1990-1991; Asst S Jude's Ch Orange City FL 1989-1992; Asst H Trin Epis Ch Fruitland Pk FL 1988-1989; P-in-c Ch Of The H Sprt Dawson GA 1977-1978; P-in-c H Trin Epis Ch Blakely GA 1977-1978; R S Jas Ch Eufaula AL 1972-1977. hjrhsigh@comcast.net

HABECKER, Elizabeth Brewster (Los) Po Box 1584, Rancho Cucamonga CA 91729 **R S Mk's Par Downey CA 2000-** B Montclair NJ 8/31/1941 d Alfred Foster Brewster & Elizabeth Moinette. BA Ohio Nthrn U 1965; MDiv GTS 1977. D 6/11/1977 Bp George E Rath P 12/16/1977 Bp Frederick Barton Wolf. m 4/22/1976 John C Habecker c 3. S Columba's Par Camarillo CA 1999-2000; Dio Los Angeles Los Angeles CA 1997-1999; Vic S Clare Of Assisi Rancho Cucamonga CA 1990-1999; Assoc S Aug By-The-Sea Par Santa Monica CA 1989; R S Paul's Epis Ch Santa Paula CA 1984-1988; Asst S Jn's Meml Ch Ramsey NJ 1983-1984; Assoc Chr Ch Ridgewood NJ 1982-1984; Ch Of The Incarn W Milford NJ 1980-1983; Vic S Ann's Epis Ch Windham Windham ME 1977-1980. revnrev@juno.com

HABECKER II, John C (Nwk) 47 Av Sur #723 Colonia Flor Blanca, Apartado (01) 274, San Salvador CA 000 **P-in-c S Jn's Ch Dover NJ 2008-** B Ancon EC 5/31/1943 s John Christian Habecker & Ann. BA U of Maryland 1975; MDiv GTS 1978. D 10/23/1977 Bp Robert C Rusack P 5/1/1978 Bp Frederick Barton Wolf. m 4/22/1976 Elizabeth Brewster. Exec Coun Appointees New York NY 2005-2008; R S Paul's Epis Ch Santa Paula CA 1984-1987; Int S

Lk's Ch Hope NJ 1984; Vic Ch Of The Incarn W Milford NJ 1980-1984; Vic S Ann's Epis Ch Windham Windham ME 1977-1980. dfmsmission@yahoo.com

HABERKORN, Violet M(arie) (Ind) 5045 W 15th Street, Speedway IN 46224 B Peoria IL 9/23/1954 d Paul Ames Haberkorn & Emma. BSW Illinois St U 1976; MDiv SWTS 1984. D 6/17/1989 Bp Frank Tracy Griswold III P 4/6/1991 Bp Arthur Benjamin Williams Jr. m 10/17/1986 Donald W Kunts. R S Jn's Ch Speedway IN 2000-2004; Pstrl Assoc S Paul's Ch Akron OH 1992-2000; R S Mk's Epis Ch Wadsworth OH 1991-1997. violetpearl@att.net

HABERSANG, Paul Matthew (Vt) 45 Church St, Hartford CT 06103 **Chr Ch Montpelier VT 2011-** B Meriden CT 12/19/1961 s Ralph D Habersang & Susan M. BS Quinnipiac U 1984; MDiv The GTS 2008. D 6/14/2008 P 12/20/2008 Bp Andrew Donnan Smith. c 2. S Jas Ch Glastonbury CT 2008-2011. revpaul123@sbcglobal.net

HABIBY, Samir Jamil (Ga) 24 Sawyers Crossing Rd, Swanzey NH 03446 B Haifa IL 4/18/1933 s Judge Jamil I Habiby & Mary. DD Epis TS In Kentucky; Ibrahim U Eg 1953; BA Phillips U 1955; MDiv CDSP 1958. D 6/29/1958 Bp Henry H Shires P 1/1/1959 Bp James Albert Pike. m 4/8/1972 Kathryn S Ganitch c 5. S Phil's Ch Hinesville Hinesville GA 1995-1998; P-in-c Trin-S Mich's Ch Fairfield CT 1993-1995; Bd Mgrs All SS Ch Ivoryton CT 1992-1995; Int S Paul's Ch Riverside CT 1991-1992; Int S Andr's Ch Meriden CT 1990-1991; S Ptr's Epis Ch Monroe CT 1988-1989; Int Trin Ch Branford CT 1988; Epis Ch Cntr New York NY 1978-1988; Chair Prog Grp Cmncatns Dio Los Angeles Los Angeles CA 1973-1976; R S Anselm Of Cbury Par Garden Grove CA 1970-1978; Fndr/Dir S Anselm's Cross-Cultural Cmnty Ctr Garden Grove CA 1970-1978; R S Marg's Epis Ch So Gate CA 1964-1966; Assoc H Faith Par Inglewood CA 1960-1961; Vic S Lk's Ch Jolon CA 1958-1960; Vic S Matt's Ch San Ardo CA 1958-1960. Auth, "Patient Care Coordntng Team," *An Adj To Htlh Serv*; Auth, "Middle E, Lebanon, Uganda," *Jerusalem For Spec Affrs Updates Dps & Hostage Issues*, Pbfwr/Pub; Auth, "Vol Grp Stds Mnstry To Yth: 4 Part Prog, Mssy Wk Of Dio Jerusalem," *Lebanon & Syria*. Bro Of S Andr; Chapl Ord S Jn Jerusalem. LHD ETSKy 1986; Cn Cesarea Cathd S Geo. padresjh@ne.rr.com

H

HACKBARTH, Michael George (FdL) 108 4th St, Fond Du Lac WI 54935 **D S Paul's Cathd Fond du Lac WI 2005-** B Fond du Lac WI 11/2/1949 s George Hackbarth & Beverly. BA Marian Coll of Fond Du Lac 1990. D 8/27/2005 Bp Russell Edward Jacobus. m 6/17/1972 Debra Lynn Schuchardt c 2. blkhrs22@charter.net

HACKER, Craig A (Me) Po Box 775, Waddington NY 13694 B Albany NY 7/28/1951 MDiv Oblate TS. D 9/7/2002 Bp Daniel William Herzog P 3/23/2003 Bp David John Bena. c 2. Vic S Paul's Ch Waddington NY 2002-2008. chacker@twony.rr.com

HACKETT, Ann R. (At) Po Box 169, Morrow GA 30260 B Paris TN 11/14/1933 d James Rudolf Riley & Wilna Olif. AA Chr Coll For Wmn 1953. D 11/14/1992 Bp Sanford Zangwill Kaye Hampton. c 4. D S Aug Of Cbury Morrow GA 1999-2002; D S Mary's Ch St Paul MN 1993-1997.

HACKETT JR, Charles Dudleigh (At) 1935 Cliff Valley Wayne, Suite 110, Atlanta GA 30309 B Binghamton NY 3/13/1937 s Charles Dudleigh Hackett & Mildred. BA Br 1958; STB Ya Berk 1964; PhD Emory U 1975. D 6/20/1964 P 1/1/1965 Bp Lauriston L Scaife. m 11/19/1960 Sharon A Adams c 2. R S Barth's Epis Ch Atlanta GA 1967-1971; Cur S Jas' Ch Batavia NY 1964-1966. AAMFC.

HACKETT, David Robert (ETenn) 7994 Prince Dr., Ooltewah TN 37363 **Int Chr Ch Epis So Pittsburg TN 2010-** B New Madrid MO 3/11/1941 s James Logan Hackett & Ella Mae. BS U of Tennessee 1967; MDiv STUSo 1970. D 6/28/1970 Bp William Evan Sanders P 5/1/1971 Bp William F Gates Jr. m 9/3/1961 Doris K Kesterson c 4. Int St Jas Epis Ch at Knoxville Knoxville TN 2008-2009; Int S Jas Epis Ch Alexandria LA 2002-2003; R S Tim's Ch Signal Mtn TN 1989-2001; R S Steph's Epis Ch Oak Ridge TN 1985-1989; R H Trin Ch Memphis TN 1978-1985; P-in-c S Chris's Ch Kingsport TN 1974-1978; P-in-c S Thos The Apos Humboldt TN 1971-1974; D Calv Ch Memphis TN 1970-1971. Auth, *Selected Sermons*. Cmnty Cross of Nails. paxhack@aol.com

HACKETT SSJE, Kevin Ralph (Mass) 980 Memorial Dr, Cambridge MA 02138 **S Jn's Chap Cambridge MA 1997-** B Kansas City MO 12/4/1956 s Betty Louise. BS Oral Roberts U 1979; MDiv Duke 1997. D 6/21/1997 Bp Alden Moinet Hathaway P 1/3/1998 Bp M(arvil) Thomas Shaw III. Dioc Mus & Liturg Cmsn Dio Massachusetts Boston MA 1998-2000; Asst S Barth's Ch Cambridge MA 1997-1998. Co-Auth, "A Hymn Tune Psalter," Ch Pub Inc, 1998; Co-Ed, "Come Celebrate!"; Co-Compsr, "Celebration Psalter". Hymn Soc. krhackett@ssje.org

HACKETT, Michael George (La) 3112 Green Acres Rd, Metairie LA 70003 **D S Augustines Ch Metairie LA 2002-** B Decatur IL 3/10/1939 s George Hackett & Bessie. BA NE LSU 1961. D 2/23/2002 Bp Charles Edward Jenkins III. m Janice Ann Dugas Hearly c 2. michael.hackett@cox.net

HACKLER, Wendy Kaye Douglas (WMo) 8564 N. Calle Tioga, Tucson AZ 85704 B Excelsior Sprgs MO 4/17/1952 d Kenneth Harold Douglas & Betty Francis. CPE 1986; W Missouri Sch of Mnstry 1992. D 1/18/1992 Bp John Clark Buchanan. m 9/16/1972 Frederick R Hackler c 1. D Ch Of The Apos Oro Vlly AZ 1998-2004; Ch Of The Gd Shpd Kansas City MO 1992-1993. Arizona Chapl Assn; AEHC; ACPE; NAAD. whackler52@msn.com

HACKLEY, Staley Paxton (Lex) 106 S Maxwell St, Ulysses KS 67880 **Mssnr S Jn's Ch Ulysses KS 2003-** B Amarillo TX 7/6/1933 s Frank Logan Hackley & Abbie Gail. BS W Texas A&M U 1954; ThM SMU 1959. D 3/17/1964 P 7/19/1964 Bp Russell T Rauscher. R Chr Epis Ch Harlan KY 1995-2003; Vic Trin Ch Quanah TX 1988-1995; Vic Gr Ch Vernon TX 1988-1994; Asst Trin Cathd Omaha NE 1963-1965. Oblate Ord Julian Of Norwich. s.hackley@insightbb.com

HACKNEY, Lisa E (O) 2954 Essex Rd, Cleveland Heights OH 44118 **Cmsn for Racial Understanding, Chair Dio Ohio Cleveland OH 2008-; Epis Cmnty Serv, Dvlpmt Coun Mem Dio Ohio Cleveland OH 2007-; Assoc R S Paul's Epis Ch Cleveland Heights OH 2006-** B Omaha NE 4/28/1963 d William Bruce Hackney & Erna Lee. Wayne 1985; BA NE Illinois U 2000; MDiv SWTS 2003. D 6/21/2003 P 12/20/2003 Bp William Dailey Persell. m 5/16/2009 Alan Christopher James c 4. Cur The Ch Of The H Sprt Lake Forest IL 2003-2006. Cantor's Awd Seabury-Wstrn Theol Sem 2003. lhackney@stpauls-church.org

HADAWAY JR, Michael Miller (WVa) PO Box 205, Kingsville MD 21087 **R Trin Ch Morgantown WV 2010-** B Washington DC 4/3/1970 s Michael Miller Hadaway & Vivian Ann. BA Salisbury U MD 1993; MDiv VTS 2000. D 9/9/1999 Bp John H(enry) Smith P 6/10/2000 Bp C(laude) Charles Vache. m 5/20/2000 Elizabeth Leigh Palmer. R S Jn's Ch Kingsville MD 2005-2010; R Varina Epis Ch Richmond VA 2001-2005; Cur Trin Ch Parkersburg WV 2000-2001. hadaway@aol.com

HADDAD, Mary E. (Los) 504 N Camden Dr, Beverly Hills CA 90210 **Dio Los Angeles Los Angeles CA 2011-** B Windsor ON Canada 10/23/1953 d Nicholas Oscar Haddad & Adele Mary. BA U of Windsor 1974; MDiv GTS 2000. D 6/10/2000 P 1/28/2001 Bp Frederick Houk Borsch. All SS Par Beverly Hills CA 2010-2011; Gr Cathd San Francisco CA 2007-2009; All SS Par Beverly Hills CA 1993-1997. maryehaddad@gmail.com

HADDEN, Richard Ray (Ct) 3900 Rose Hill Ave Apt 701-B, Cincinnati OH 45229 B Painesville OH 11/3/1932 s Clyde Chapman Hadden & Florence May. U Cinc 1954; MDiv EDS 1970. D 6/10/1970 Bp John Henry Esquirol P 12/1/1970 Bp Joseph Warren Hutchens. m 11/26/1983 Barbara Zeller c 3. Cur S Paul's Epis Ch Willimantic CT 1970-1973.

HADDIX JR, Theodore Ray (Va) 3825 Indianview Ave, Cincinnati OH 45227 B Parkersburg WV 4/16/1948 s Theodore Ray Haddix & Mary Frances. BA W Virginia U 1974; MDiv VTS 1977; ThM UTS Richmond VA 1979. D 6/8/1977 P 6/1/1978 Bp Robert Poland Atkinson. m 8/14/1976 Cecelia Clark c 2. Abingdon Epis Ch White Marsh VA 1997-2000; Indn Hill Ch Cincinnati OH 1990-1997; Vic Ch Of The Creator Mechanicsville VA 1979-1986; S Thos Epis Ch White Sulphur Sprg WV 1977-1978; Vic S Thos' Ch Richmond VA 1977-1978. AAPC. tedhaddix@yahoo.com

HADDOCK, Gene Moore (La) 1122 W. Chestnut St, Denison TX 75020 B Denison TX 3/3/1938 s Olvis Leon Haddock & Mary E. BS Texas Wesl 1961; MDiv Nash 1964; S Geo's Coll Jerusalem IL 1982. D 6/21/1964 P 12/21/1964 Bp Chandler W Sterling. R S Aug's Ch Baton Rouge LA 1990-1993; Vic Ascen And S Mk Bridgeport TX 1986-1990; Vic S Thos Ch Jacksboro TX 1986-1988; Dio Ft Worth Ft Worth TX 1970-1990; Vic S Simon Of Cyrene Epis Ch Ft Worth TX 1969-1988; Vic S Anth's Ch Alvarado TX 1969-1970; Vic S Alb's Epis Ch Vicksburg MS 1967-1969; Vic S Mary's Ch Vicksburg MS 1967-1969; Vic S Eliz's Mssn Collins MS 1966-1968; Vic S Steph's Ch Columbia MS 1966-1968; Cur S Jn's Ch Butte MT 1964-1966. genemhaddock@aol.com

HADDOX, Jason Monroe (Tex) 80 B Maple Avenue, Morristown NJ 07960 **S Aug Of Cbury Ch Augusta GA 2010-** B Baytown TX 10/1/1969 s Ronald Dennis Haddox & Anna Lee. BA Rice U 1992; MDiv Epis TS of The SW 2000; MA Drew U 2007. D 6/17/2000 Bp Claude Edward Payne P 6/26/2001 Bp Don Adger Wimberly. m 6/4/1994 Shannon L Hobbins. S Ptr's Ch Mt Arlington NJ 2009-2010; Assoc R S Ptr's Ch Morristown NJ 2005-2009; Asst R S Paul's Ch Waco TX 2000-2003. jmhaddox@verizon.net

HADE, Lynn Augustine (CPa) 118 N Cherry St., Lancaster PA 17602 **Assoc S Jas Ch Lancaster PA 2008-** B Ames IA 6/2/1954 d Robert Rezin Augustine & Pauline Louise. BS Iowa St U 1981; MDiv The GTS 2007. D 6/7/2008 P 2/18/2009 Bp Nathan Dwight Baxter. c 2. lynn@stjameslanpa.org

HADEN JR, Robert Lee (NC) 798 Evans Rd., Hendersonville NC 28739 B Greenville SC 6/22/1938 s Robert Lee Haden & Mary Elisa. BA U So 1960; MDiv VTS 1964; STM GTS 1988. D 6/18/1964 P 6/1/1965 Bp Matthew G Henry. m 6/4/1963 Mary Anne Barnes Easterling c 3. Ch Of The Ascen Hickory NC 1995-1996; R S Jn's Epis Ch Charlotte NC 1973-1994; Dir Trin Cathd Columbia SC 1968-1973; P-in-c S Andr's Ch Bessemer City NC 1965-1968; P-in-c Trin Ch Kings Mtn NC 1964-1968. Auth, "Unopened Letters From God," Haden Inst, 2010; Auth, "Souls Labyrinth," Haden Inst, 1994. bob@hadeninstitute.com

HADLER JR, Jacques Bauer (WA) 1736 Columbia Rd NW Apt 201, Washington DC 20009 B Washington DC 12/11/1943 s Jacques Bauer Hadler & Caryl. BA U of Wisconsin 1967; MDiv EDS 1972. D 6/17/1972 P 3/17/1973 Bp William Foreman Creighton. m 6/6/1967 Susan J Johnson c 2. Co-Chair, Com on Racial Recon Dio Washington Washington DC 2002-2008; Chair, COM Dio Washington Washington DC 1996-2000; Dir, Field Educ VTS Alexandria VA 1993-2010; P-in-c S Phil's Epis Ch Laurel MD 1992-1993; P-in-c All Souls Memi Epis Ch Washington DC 1991-1992; R S Paul's Epis Ch Piney Waldorf MD 1979-1991; P-in-c Trin Ch Manassas VA 1979; Dio Sthrn Highlands New York NY 1975-1979; Asst S Matt's Epis Ch Hyattsville MD 1972-1975. Auth, "Two-way Bridge: Tae Cross - Cultural Collancy at Virginia Sem," *Tchg Theol and Rel Vol. 4 No. 2*, Blackwell Pub., 2001; Auth, "Genogram of Cong," *Proceedings of the 24th Biennral Consult of rthe Asseration for Theol Field Edneaton*, 1997. Assn for Theol Field Educ 1995-2009; WECA 1972. Phi Beta Kappa 1966. jhadler@vts.edu

HADLEY, Arthur Clayton (SO) 1500 Shasta, McAllen TX 78504 B Rochester IN 7/8/1938 s Noah Silvanus Hadley & Mary Dela. BA Pur 1960; MDiv Bex 1963; PMD Harv 1970; MA Ball St U 1973; EdD Ball St U 1974. D 6/11/1963 P 12/21/1963 Bp John P Craine. m 6/18/1960 Jane Ellen Keefus c 2. Int St Ptr & St Paul Ch Mssn TX 2011; Int Ch Of The Epiph Kingsville TX 2008-2009; Int S Ptr's Epis Ch Rockport TX 2007-2008; Int S Jas' Epis Ch Goshen IN 2006; S Jn's Ch Worthington OH 1994-2006; Dio Michigan Detroit MI 1993; Dio Missouri S Louis MO 1984-1994; S Mary's Ch Erie PA 1984; Cn To Ordnry Dio NW Pennsylvania Erie PA 1979-1984; Assoc St Johns Epis Ch Lafayette IN 1973-1979; Assoc Trin Ch Ft Wayne IN 1970-1972; P-in-c S Jas Ch New Castle IN 1969-1970; Cur Trin Ch Indianapolis IN 1968-1969; R S Steph's Epis Ch New Harmony IN 1963-1968. Auth, "Resource for Faith-Based Gardens," Alabama Coop.Ext, 2007; Auth, "Yth Wk And Cmnty Dvlpmt". arthur.hadley@gmail.com

HADLEY, Douglas J (Ore) 2261 Hidden Valley Ln, Charlevoix MI 49720 B Seattle WA 9/8/1943 s Wayne Dorman Hadley & Eleanore Maria. BA U of Washington 1965; NYU 1968; PrTS 1968; MDiv GTS 1970; ThM St Vladimir's Sem 2006. D 8/6/1970 P 5/22/1971 Bp Ivol I Curtis. m 3/28/1987 Karen Kassiani Mahoney c 2. Int S Lk's Epis Ch Seattle WA 2000; R S Jas Epis Ch Tigard OR 1994-2000; R S Paul's Epis Ch S Jos MI 1988-1994; R S Matt Ch Tacoma WA 1982-1988; R Emm Ch Hailey ID 1975-1982; R S Thos Epis Ch Sun Vlly ID 1975-1982; Assoc Ch Of The Epiph Seattle WA 1972-1974; Cur S Eliz's Ch Burien WA 1970-1971. symeonnt@yahoo.com

HAFER, Joel Gilbert (WNC) 776 N. Main St., Hendersonville NC 28792 **R S Jas Epis Ch Hendersonville NC 2004-** B Kalamazoo MI 10/31/1957 s Jack Gilbert Hafer & Phyllis Ann. BA Albion Coll 1980; MDiv STUSo 1986. D 6/7/1986 P 2/13/1987 Bp Harry Woolston Shipps. m 4/27/2002 Anne Jackson Hafer c 4. R All SS Ch Florence SC 1996-2004; Stndg Com Dio Georgia Savannah GA 1991; R Chr Epis Ch Dublin GA 1989-1996; Asst S Paul's Ch Albany GA 1986-1989. OHC 1984. joel@stjamesepiscopal.com

HAFFNER, Edward John (WTex) 254 Emerald Ln, Brownsville TX 78520 B Decatur IL 10/16/1925 s Edward John Haffner & Pauline. AA Wentworth Mltry Acad 1946; BA Carroll Coll 1947; MS La Salle U 1952. D 6/11/1955 Bp Everett H Jones P 12/1/1955 Bp Richard Earl Dicus. m 6/11/1947 Jean Lowe. S Paul's Ch Brady TX 1972-1978; R S Alb's Ch Harlingen TX 1965-1969; R S Jn's Epis Ch Brownwood TX 1957-1960; P-in-c Gr Ch Llano TX 1955-1957; P-in-c S Lk's Epis Ch San Saba TX 1955-1957. Outstanding Citizen Awd Brown Cnty 1960.

HAGAN JR, John Ronald (Mich) 11575 Belleville Rd, Belleville MI 48111 **R Trin Ch Belleville MI 1986-** B Columbia MO 1/1/1951 s John Ronald Hagan & Dorothy Hagan. BA U of Kansas 1973; MDiv SWTS 1980. D 6/14/1980 Bp Quintin Ebenezer Primo Jr P 12/13/1980 Bp James Winchester Montgomery. m 5/29/1982 Deborah Ballard c 1. R S Jn's Ch Iron River MI 1983-1986; Vic S Mk's Ch Crystal Falls MI 1983-1986; Cur Trin Epis Ch Wheaton IL 1980-1983. hdebgrace@aol.com

HAGANS, Michele Victoria (WA) 1645 Myrtle St Nw, Washington DC 20012 **Dio Washington Washington DC 2010-; Assoc Gr Epis Ch Silver Sprg MD 2010-; Ch Of The H Comf Washington DC 2007-** B Washignton DC 10/16/1949 d Theodore R Hagans & Delores Day. D 6/9/2007 P 1/19/2008 Bp John Chane. c 3. mvhagans@aol.com

HAGBERG, Joseph Alan (CGC) 9101 Panama City Beach Parkway, Panama City Beach FL 32407 **Ecum Rep Dio Cntrl Gulf Coast Pensacola FL 2010-** B Chicago IL 4/24/1951 s Joseph Memsen Hagberg & Ann Dolores. S Ign' Coll Prep. 1969; BS Loyola U 1973; MDiv GTS 1976. D 5/27/1976 P 11/27/1976 Bp James Winchester Montgomery. Chairman Stwdshp and Planned Giving Cmsn Dio Cntrl Gulf Coast Pensacola FL 2007-2010; R Gr Epis Ch Panama City Bch FL 2007; S Jas' Epis Ch Port S Joe FL 2002-2007; S Mary's Epis Ch Dyersburg TN 2001-2002; Int Ch Of The H Comf Montgomery AL 1999-2001; Int S Steph's Epis Ch Sherman TX 1998-1999; Ch Of The H Cross Dallas TX 1996-1998; R Ch Of S Mich And All Ang Berwyn IL 1983-1996; Cathd Shltr Chicago IL 1981-1983; Cur Ch Of The H Fam Pk Forest IL 1978-1980; Cur S Simons Ch Arlington Heights IL 1976-1978. CCU 1976; Panama City Beaches ChmbrCom 2007; SSC 1981. joealan@knology.net

HAGE, Raymond Joseph (WVa) 2105 Wiltshire Blvd, Huntington WV 25701 **Chr Ch Point Pleasant WV 2004-; River Bend Cluster Point Pleasant WV 2004-** B Huntington WV 11/28/1943 s Raymond Hage & Cathleen Eleanor. U of Kentucky 1963; BBA Marshall U 1966; MA 1967; U of Virginia 1971; MA Wheeling Jesuit U 1997. D 6/14/1997 Bp John H(enry) Smith P 12/20/2003 Bp William Michie Klusmeyer. m 6/27/1964 Susan Lee McCray c 3. S Jn's Ch Huntington WV 1997-2004. rjhage5@gmail.com

HAGEN, Amelia Ann (Me) 39 Highland Ave, Millinocket ME 04462 **Dio Maine Portland ME 2000-** B Winthrop MA 6/30/1939 d Augustine Francis Surprenant & Cecile Anita. BA Bos 1964; MA U CA 1968; MDiv CDSP 2000. D 6/3/2000 P 12/2/2000 Bp William Edwin Swing. c 2. Ch Of The Gd Shpd Rangeley ME 2007-2009; S Andr's Ch Millinocket ME 2006-2007; Chr Ch Sausalito CA 2004-2005; Int H Trin Epis Ch Gillette WY 2002-2004; Int Trin Epis Ch Alpena MI 2001-2002; D All SS' Ch San Francisco CA 2000-2001. Int Mnstry Ntwk; Natl Assn Of Epis Int Mnstry Specialists. motheramelia@mac.com

HAGEN, James Barlow (LI) 21-15 34th Ave apt 14C, Astoria NY 11106 **P-in-c Holyrood Ch New York NY 2009-; Hon Assoc Chr And S Steph's Ch New York NY 1998-** B Akron OH 12/17/1940 s John Ferdinand Hagen & Wilda Brinice. BA Mt Un Coll 1962; STM EDS 1965. D 6/12/1965 Bp Beverley D Tucker P 12/1/1965 Bp Nelson Marigold Burroughs. m 8/26/1967 June Steffensen. R Ch Of The Redeem Astoria NY 1982-1997; Vic S Andr's Ch Brooklyn NY 1968-1982; Asst S Ptr's Ch New York NY 1967-1968; Cur S Paul's Ch Canton OH 1965-1967. jahag2@nyc.rr.com

HAGEN, Maureen Elizabeth (Ore) 3030 Se Bybee Blvd, Portland OR 97202 B Rochester NY 5/30/1956 d William Roy Hagen & Kathleen Frances Claire. BA St. Lawr Canton NY 1978; MIA Col 1983; ABD Col 1985. D 9/18/2004 Bp Johncy Itty. m 6/22/1985 Robie Willard Greene. S Paul's Epis Ch Salem OR 2006-2009; Outreach Coordntr Trin Epis Cathd Portland OR 2005-2006. maureenh@trinity-episcopal.org

HAGENBUCH, Chris Barrett (Spok) 311 South Hall St, Grangeville ID 83530 **Co- Chair of Anti-Racism T/F Dio Spokane Spokane WA 2010-; Vic H Trin Epis Ch Grangeville ID 2005-** B Washington DC 10/3/1963 s Richard Hagenbuch & Joan. DECO of Spokane. D 10/31/2004 P 9/1/2005 Bp James Edward Waggoner. m 10/31/1986 Marcia Kay Hunt c 2. Dioc Coun Dio Spokane Spokane WA 2009-2011; COM Dio Spokane Spokane WA 2007-2010; D H Trin Epis Ch Grangeville ID 2004-2005. cbhholytrinity@hotmail.com

HAGERMAN, Steven William (Md) 1110 Saint Stephens Church Rd, Crownsville MD 21032 **R S Steph's Ch Severn Par Crownsville MD 2004-** B Saint Louis MO 8/4/1951 s Morris Franklin Hagerman & Mary Catherine. Cert Boston Theol Inst; BS Sthrn Illinois U 1975; MDiv CDSP 1982. D 6/19/1982 Bp Quintin Ebenezer Primo Jr P 12/18/1982 Bp James Winchester Montgomery. m 12/29/1973 Bernadette Mary Jaroch c 4. R S Mk's Epis Ch Riverside RI 1995-2004; R S Ptr's Ch Harrisonville MO 1992-1995; Assoc S Barn On The Desert Scottsdale AZ 1991-1992; R S Jas Memi Epis Ch Titusville PA 1986-1991; Assoc Chr Epis Ch Hornell NY 1985-1986; Epis Tri-Par Mnstry Dansville NY 1985-1986; Vic S Ann's Ch For The Deaf New York NY 1983-1984; Cur Ch Of The Adv Chicago IL 1982-1983. Epis Conf of the Deaf 1983; Faith and Sci Exch 2001. swh51us@yahoo.com

HAGGENJOS JR, Clifford R (NCal) 1905 Third Street, Napa CA 94559 **St Johns Epis Ch Roseville CA 2010-** B Evanston IL 6/26/1959 s Clifford Robert Haggenjos & Elizabeth Letitia. BS Marq 1981; JD Marq 1984; MDiv SWTS 2006. D 12/17/2005 P 6/24/2006 Bp Russell Edward Jacobus. m 3/14/1997 Babette F Oliver c 1. Asst S Mary's Epis Ch Napa CA 2006-2010; D S Aug's Epis Ch Wilmette IL 2005-2006. haggenjos@comcast.net

HAGLER, James Robert (ETenn) 933 S. 17th St., Newark NJ 07108 B Knox TN 12/4/1946 s John Brown Hagler & Martha. MLS Geo Peabody Coll for Teachers; BA The TS at The U So; MDiv Trin 1984. D 10/10/1982 Bp William Evan Sanders P 5/14/1983 Bp Lewis Samuel Garnsworthy. rhaglerjr@aol.com

HAGOOD II, M(onroe) Johnson (CFla) 6525 7th Manor, Vero Beach FL 32968 **Asst S Aug Of Cbury Epis Ch Vero Bch FL 2009-** B Durham NC 10/26/1936 s Monroe Johnson Hagood & Ann Heyward. BA Cit 1958; M.Div VTS 1963; MS LIU 1972; MA Pepperdine U 1977. D 7/10/1963 P 2/1/1964 Bp Thomas H Wright. m 9/15/1962 Betty Linton c 3. Int H Faith Epis Ch Port S Lucie FL 2005-2008; R S Ptr's By-The-Sea Swansboro NC 1981-2003; Off Of Bsh For ArmdF New York NY 1964-1982; P S Thos' Epis Ch Bath NC 1963-1964; P Zion Epis Ch Washington NC 1963-1964. johnsonhagood@yahoo.com

HAGUE, Betsy Ann (WA) 4507 Leland St, Chevy Chase MD 20815 B Cleveland OH 7/7/1944 d Joseph Anthony Hague & Virginia Blanch. BSN Geo 1971; MSN U of Maryland 1974; CAS GTS 1993; MDiv Wesley TS 1994. D 6/11/1994 P 12/9/1995 Bp Ronald Hayward Haines. m 11/23/1973 Ralph Weyman Wadeson MD c 3. Pstr Luther Place Memi Ch Washington DC

1995-2001; Pstr N St Vill Washington DC 1995-2001; Asst Chr Ch Prince Geo's Par Rockville MD 1994. betsy.hague@gmail.com

HAGUE, Jane Milliken (WA) 3902 Everett St, Kensington MD 20895 B Houston TX 5/15/1955 d Walter Louis Milliken & Anne Eaton. BS Geo 1977; MTS VTS 1984. D 6/4/2011 Bp John Chane. m 5/30/1981 William Hague c 2. janemhague@verizon.net

HAGUE, Leslie Janette (Va) 1132 N Ivanhoe St, Arlington VA 22205 **R S Mich's Epis Ch Arlington VA 2002-** B Richmond VA 2/17/1967 d Wayne Marshall Hague & Janet Irene. BA W&M 1989; MDiv GTS 1998. D 6/13/1998 Bp Peter James Lee P 4/17/1999 Bp Henry Irving Louttit. S Ptr's Epis Ch Savannah GA 1998-2002. leshague@gmail.com

HAGUE, Loren Virginia (Ga) 2230 Walton Way, Augusta GA 30904 **Asst R The Ch Of The Gd Shpd Augusta GA 2008-** B Charlottesville VA 5/13/1981 d Wayne Marshall Hague & Janet Irene. BA The U GA 2003; MDiv VTS 2008. D 2/9/2008 P 8/28/2008 Bp Henry Irving Louttit. Loren.Hague@gmail.com

HAGUE, Sarah Anne (NH) PO Box 1680, Grantham NH 03753 B Troy NY 10/11/1938 d Howard Samuel Kennedy & Grace Macoun. BA U of Oregon 1968; MA ED U of Oregon 1977; MA U of Oregon 1987; MDiv GTS 1991. D 5/29/1991 Bp Robert Louis Ladehoff P 3/8/1992 Bp Douglas Edwin Theuner. c 4. Int Trin Ch Claremont NH 2002-2004; Assoc R Gr Ch New Bedford MA 1996-2001; Asst R S Thos Ch Hanover NH 1992-1996. haguesally@gmail.com

H

HAGUE, William (WA) 4001 Franklin St, Kensington MD 20895 **R Chr Ch Par Kensington MD 1988-** B Honolulu HI 1/19/1952 s James Duncan Hague & Henriette Catherine. DMin Hartford Sem; BA U of Virginia 1974; MDiv VTS 1980. D 6/28/1980 Bp William Edwin Swing P 7/1/1981 Bp William Benjamin Spofford. m 5/30/1981 Jane Milliken c 2. Asst Chr Ch Georgetown Washington DC 1983-1988; Asst S Jn's Epis Ch Vernon Rock Vernon CT 1982-1983; Asst S Marg's Ch Washington DC 1980-1982. rector@ccpk.org

HAHN, Dorothee Elisabeth (Eur) Fruhling Strasse 1b, Grobenzell 82194 Germany **Asst R, Vic of St. Bon, Augsburg and St. Ja Ch of the Ascen Munich 81545 DE 2006-** B Kiel DE 12/1/1966 d Ferdinand Hahn & Elfriede. Ludwig-Maximilians-Universitat Munich 2004; MA VTS 2005. D 5/7/2005 P 11/26/2005 Bp Pierre W Whalon.

HAHN, William Douglas (At) 2134 Wells Dr, Columbus GA 31906 **R S Thos Epis Ch Columbus GA 1999-; S Clem's Epis Ch Canton GA 1996-** B Lumberton NC 4/24/1952 s William Bryant Hahn & Martha Jean. BA U GA 1974; MDiv Sthrn Bapt TS Louisville KY 1977; DAS Candler TS Emory U 1996. D 6/8/1996 P 12/1/1996 Bp Frank Kellogg Allan. m 8/1/1998 Kaye H Herring c 1. S Geo's Epis Ch Griffin GA 1996-1999. revdhahn@aol.com

HAHNE, Ruth Olive (CFla) 9260-C Sw 61st Way, Boca Raton FL 33428 **D S Mary Magd Epis Ch Coral Sprg FL 1998-** B Maplewood NJ 7/21/1933 d Richard Hahne & Eddie Belle. Dio Sch SE Florida FL; U Of Delaware Newark 1954; BS Med Coll of Virginia 1956. D 9/11/1998 Bp John Lewis Said.

HAHNEMAN, Geoffrey (Ct) 154 Jackman Avenue, Fairfield CT 06825 **R S Jn's Ch Bridgeport CT 2005-** B Houston TX 12/14/1954 s Kenneth William Hahneman & Gloria May. BA Baylor U 1977; MDiv VTS 1980; PhD Oxf 1987. D 6/16/1980 Bp Roger Howard Cilley P 12/19/1980 Bp Frederic Cunningham Lawrence. m 2/14/2003 Lisa DiNunno c 4. Int R S Columba's Chap Middletown RI 2004-2005; Int R Ch Of The H Trin Tiverton RI 2004; Int R S Andr's Ch New London NH 2001-2003; R Trin Ch Portsmouth VA 1995-2000; Cn Cathd Ch Of S Mk Minneapolis MN 1990-1994; R All SS Epis Ch Braine-l'Alleud 1420 BE 1987-1990; Cur The Ch Of The Adv Boston MA 1980-1984. Auth, "The Muratorian Fragment and the Origins of the NT Cn," *The Cn Debate*, Hendrickson Pub, 2002; Auth, "The Muratorian Fragment & The Dvlpmt of the Cn," Oxford Press, 1992; Auth, "More on Redating The Muratorian Fragment," *Studia Patristica*, 1988. Minneapolis Awd Mayor of Minneapolis 1994. ghahneman@gmail.com

HAHNEMAN, Lisa (Ct) 154 Jackman Ave, Fairfield CT 06825 B Washington DC 6/3/1956 d Joseph John DiNunno & Mary Elizabeth. BA CUA 1977; MEd U of Virginia 1978; PhD U of Virginia 1982; MDiv VTS 1999. D 6/10/1999 Bp David Conner Bane Jr P 12/16/1999 Bp Donald Purple Hart. m 2/14/2003 Geoffrey Hahneman. Vic S Ptr's Epis Ch Oxford CT 2005-2009; Assoc S Barn Ch Falmouth MA 2001-2005; Assoc Trin Ch Portsmouth VA 1999-2000. ldhahneman@sbcglobal.net

HAIFLEY, Thomas Leo (Okla) Po Box 10722, Midwest City OK 73140 **Asst All Souls Epis Ch Oklahoma City OK 2007-** B Hanover PA 9/1/1943 s Charles Leo Haifley & Dorothy A. Loyola U; BA Towson U 1975; MDiv Epis TS of The SW 1978. D 7/15/1978 Bp William Jackson Cox P 4/1/1979 Bp Gerald Nicholas McAllister. R S Chris's Ch Midwest City OK 1987-2005; R S Lk's Ch Tulsa OK 1978-1987. AGO 1980.

HAIG, David William (Alb) PO Box 1834, Orleans MA 02653 B Groton MA 3/12/1960 s John Alistair Haig & Mary Haig. BA Queens U 1982; MDiv EDS 2004; MDiv EDS 2004. D 6/10/2006 P 12/17/2006 Bp Daniel William Herzog. m 7/17/1982 Catherine Anne Catherine Ann Christmas c 3. Cmnty of Jesus 1983. dave.hhi@verizon.net

HAIG, Martha Karen (Oly) 4685 Taylor Ave NE, Bainbridge Island WA 98110 **S Thos Ch Medina WA 2010-** B Killeen TX 12/12/1954 d Arthur Norman Haig & Martha Butler. BA U of Washington 1977; MDiv CDSP 2010. D 4/17/2010 P 11/2/2010 Bp Gregory Harold Rickel. m 5/21/2005 James Louis Friedrich c 1. marthakaren@earthlink.net

HAILEY, Victor Curtiss (Md) 3100 Monkton Rd., Monkton MD 21111 **Cur S Jas Ch Monkton MD 2009-** B Lynchburg VA 1/5/1981 s Mark C Hailey & Vicki V. BA St Andr Presb Coll 2003; MDiv The TS at The U So 2009. D 6/11/2009 P 12/11/2009 Bp Frank Neff Powell. vhailey@saintjames.org

HAIN SR, John Walter (NJ) 13 Madison Ave, Flemington NJ 08822 **D Calv Epis Ch Flemington NJ 2006-; Chair, Conv Ballot Com Dio New Jersey Trenton NJ 2005-** B Woodbury NJ 7/27/1950 s Walter Morns Hain & Margaret Joan. AAS Gloucester Coll 1976. D 10/31/1998 Bp Joe Morris Doss. m 11/4/1972 Hope Ann Meiler. Chair, Audit Com Dio New Jersey Trenton NJ 2003; D Ch Of S Jn-In-The-Wilderness Gibbsboro NJ 1998-2005. DEACON. HAIN@GMAIL.NET

HAINES, Denise Lee Games (Nwk) 174 Summit Ave Apt 303, Summit NJ 07901 B Wilmington DE 3/7/1939 d Denbeigh Warren Games & Elizabeth VanKannel. BA U of Delaware Newark 1960; MDiv GTS 1977. D 6/11/1977 P 12/1/1977 Bp John Shelby Spong. S Lk's-Roosevelt Hosp Cntr New York NY 1994-1996; Cabell Huntington Hosp Huntington WV 1989; Archd for Mssn & Urban Mnstry Dio Newark Newark NJ 1983-1989; S Paul's Epis Ch Chatham NJ 1980-1983; P-in-c S Paul's Epis Ch Chatham NJ 1977-1980. Auth, *Journ of Pstr Care*; Auth, *The Chr Century*. Cert Supvsr Assn for Clincl Pstr Educatio 1979. denisehaines3@yahoo.com

HAINES, Harry Jeffrey (WNY) 24 Cobb Ter, Rochester NY 14620 B Philadelphia PA 7/17/1940 s Harry Jepson Haines & Ruth Marie. AAS Monroe Cmnty Coll 1969; BA St. Jn Fisher Coll 1979; MDiv CRDS 1988. D 6/22/1988 P 1/1/1989 Bp William George Burrill. m 4/17/1976 Katherine Anne Fields c 2. Int Gr Ch Lyons NY 2002; R Chr Ch Albion NY 1989-2002; S Geo's Ch Hilton NY 1989.

HAINES, Marlene (Pa) 31 Kleyona Ave, Phoenixville PA 19460 B Troy NY 12/6/1945 d Marvin James Haines & Gloria Blanche. BA SUNY 1970; MS U of Wisconsin 1973; MDiv GTS 1997. D 6/21/1997 Bp Allen Lyman Bartlett Jr P 6/6/1998 Bp Franklin Delton Turner. m 10/8/1977 Thomas C. Wand c 2. Asst Ch Of S Lk And Epiph Philadelphia PA 1997-2011. revmikehaines@gmail.com

HAINES III, Ralph Edward (SVa) 1201 Wickham Ave, Newport News VA 23607 **S Aug's Epis Ch Newport News VA 2004-** B San Francisco CA 9/11/1944 s John L Haines & Winifred. BA U Rich 1967; MDiv Crozer TS 1970. D 12/18/1971 Bp David Shepherd Rose P 12/1/1972 Bp John B Bentley. c 2. Secy of the Dio Dio Sthrn Virginia Norfolk VA 1979-2010; D-in-c S Aug's Epis Ch Newport News VA 1971-1972. Man Of The Year Omega Psi Phi 1984; Outstanding Serv Awd 85 Naacp. fatherned4@hotmail.com

HAINES-MURDOCCO, Sandra Paula (RI) 109 Old Post Rd, Wakefield RI 02879 B Washington DC 12/15/1950 d Samuel Paul Haines & Toni Maravich. BS Towson U 1972; BS Towson U 1976; MA Loyola Coll 1981; MDiv GTS 1988. D 6/18/1988 P 5/20/1989 Bp A(lbert) Theodore Eastman. m 10/18/1997 James Murdocco. Stndg Com Dio Rhode Island Providence RI 2004-2007; COM Dio Rhode Island Providence RI 1995-1999; R Ch Of The Ascen Wakefield RI 1994-2008; Stndg Com Dio Maryland Baltimore MD 1992-1994; S Thos' Ch Garrison Forest Owings Mills MD 1989-1994; Dio Maryland Baltimore MD 1988-1989; D S Thos' Ch Garrison Forest Owings Mills MD 1988-1989. Sphmurdocco@cox.net

HAINLIN, Marion Wendell (SeFla) 33 Wagon Trail, Black Mountain NC 28711 **Died 10/3/2010** B Miami FL 11/3/1927 s Neal Earnest Hainlin & Margaret Elvie. BA U So 1950; STM Ya Berk 1953. D 6/21/1953 P 12/21/1953 Bp Henry I Louttit. c 3.

HAIRSTON, Raleigh Daniel (EC) 3183 Kings Bay Cir, Decatur GA 30034 B Amonate VA 11/15/1934 s Samuel Hardin Hairston & Elsie. BS Bluefield St Coll Bluefield WV 1959; MSW Atlanta U Atlanta GA 1962; MA Bex 1969; MA Case Wstrn Reserve U 1975; DMin CRDS 1978. D 6/24/1970 Bp Thomas Augustus Fraser Jr P 5/9/1971 Bp John Melville Burgess. c 2. R S Mk's Ch Wilmington NC 2001-2004; Chapl S Aug's Coll Raleigh NC 1995-1998; Asst Calv Ch Washington DC 1989-1991; Vic Dio Michigan Detroit MI 1985-1988; Int Ch Of The Trsfg Cleveland OH 1981-1982; R Dio Sthrn Ohio Cincinnati OH 1979-1981. Interdenom Mnstr Assn; Lic Indep Clincl Soc Worker; Prtr Ecum; UBE. DSA S Aug Coll 1998; Who's Who Among Afr Americans Gale Resrch Inc 1996; Who's Who Among Black Americans Gale Resrch Inc 1994. RDANHAIRSTON@HOTMAIL.COM

HAKIEL, Nicholas Edward (Oly) 1014 Wildwood St, Sultan WA 98294 B Leeds UK 3/4/1953 s Zbigniew Symon Hakiel & Olga. BA U Of Lancaster Gb 1975; MA U Of Durham Gb 1976; MA Idaho St U 1991; EDS Idaho St U 1994. D 6/14/1997 P 8/15/1998 Bp John Stuart Thornton. m 11/3/1991 Barbara Larue Robinson. Asst Ch Of Our Sav Monroe WA 1999-2009. nhakiel@aol.com

HALAPUA, Sione (Los) 8614 Foothill Blvd Apt 223, Sunland CA 91040 B Nukualofa To Ga 5/12/1940 s Fine Tengaila & Lesieli Pale. LTh S Jn Coll Nz; CTh S Johns Bapt Coll Fj; BA Claremont Coll 1973. D 9/9/1972 P 3/17/1973 Bp Francis E I Bloy. c 1. S Simon's Par San Fernando CA 1989-1990; S Mk's Par Altadena CA 1975-2000; Ch Of The Ascen Tujunga CA 1975-1987; Cur The Ch Of The Ascen Sierra Madre CA 1974-1975.

HALBROOK, Thomas Robert (Oly) 1805 Graves Ave, Aberdeen WA 98520 B Wauwautosa WI 7/20/1935 s Thomas R Halbrook & Rose. BD U of Missouri-Rolla 1960; MS MI SU 1962; Olympia TS 1980; MDiv CDSP 1986. D 8/3/1982 P 7/22/1986 Bp Robert Hume Cochrane. m 5/7/1960 Ramona Rose c 2. R S Andr's Epis Ch Aberdeen WA 1986-2000; Asst S Marg's Epis Ch Bellevue WA 1982-1985. Auth, "The Viscoelastic Response Of Open Celled Foams," The Boeing Co., 1965. Amer Soc of Civil Engr 1958; Chairman Aberdeen WA Civil Serv Comm. 2000; Chapl For Grp Harbor Com 1988-1992; Chapl Harbors Hm and Hospice 2002; Civil Serv Cmsn 1999; Evergreen Couseling Bd Dir 2000-2003; RWF Bd Dir 1990-1994. trjhalbrook@msn.com

HALE, Douglas John (Mass) 2785 Elysium Ave, Eugene OR 97401 B Portland OR 12/23/1955 s Herbert Howe Hale & Elizabeth Ann. BS U of Oregon 1978; MDiv SFTS 1986; MA Garrett Evang TS 1995. D 2/25/2002 P 8/3/2002 Bp William O Gregg. m 8/11/1990 Patricia Ann Benson c 1. Vic S Dav's Epis Ch Halifax MA 2005-2008; Co-R All SS Ch Whitman MA 2003-2007; Cn Mssnr Dio Estrn Oregon The Dalles OR 2002-2003. Auth, "Sprtlty IN THE Ch OF H SERGIUS AT TEL NESSANA," Garret-Evang TS, 1995; Auth, "Prepared After All," *Mustard-Seed Ch*, Fortress Press, 1990. pdqhale@comcast.net

HALE, Edward Stuart Tracy (Miss) 421 W Minnesota St, Brookhaven MS 39601 **Died 9/28/2009** B Bristol VA 10/24/1921 s Charles Stuart Hale & Virginia Rebecca. BS E Tennessee St U 1948. D 5/23/1951 Bp Edmund P Dandridge P 5/1/1952 Bp Theodore N Barth. c 2.

HALE, George Blodgett Stuart (NC) 2008 Rangecrest Rd, Raleigh NC 27612 B Bristol VA 4/15/1920 s Charles Stuart Hale & Virginia R. U So; U So. D 3/21/1945 P 5/21/1946 Bp James M Maxon. m 9/5/1947 Carolyn Hale. Assoc Ch Of The Nativ Raleigh NC 1992; R S Tim's Ch Raleigh NC 1956-1992; Assoc Gr - S Lk's Ch Memphis TN 1947-1955; Min in charge S Thos Ch Elizabethton TN 1945-1947; D-In-C S Jn's Epis Ch Johnson City TN 1945-1946. Auth, "While I Still Remember," Chap Hill, 1990. BLODGETT41520@AOL.COM

HALE, Linda Mosier (Spok) PO Box 456, Sunnyside WA 98944 B Pendleton OR 5/1/1941 d Ernest Draper Mosier & E Virginia Moore. BS U of Oregon 1963; MEd WA SU 1994. D 11/1/2009 Bp James Edward Waggoner. m 7/13/2006 Jack Hale c 1. halehouse215@embargmail.com

HALE, Patricia Ann (Mass) 2785 Elysium Avenue, Eugene OR 97401 **S Matt's Epis Ch Eugene OR 2011-** B Portland OR 8/23/1970 d Willis Earl Benson & Virginia Diane. BA U of Oregon 1992; MDiv Garrett Evang TS 1996. D 2/25/2002 P 8/3/2002 Bp William O Gregg. m 8/11/1990 Douglas John Hale c 1. S Dav's Epis Ch Halifax MA 2005-2007; R All SS Ch Whitman MA 2003-2011; S Matt's Epis Ch Ontario OR 2003; Cn Dio Estrn Oregon The Dalles OR 2002-2003. revpatti@comcast.net

HALE, William Charles (Mich) 1067 Hubbard St, Detroit MI 48209 **Chr The King Epis Ch Taylor MI 2003-; Dream Cluster Taylor MI 2003-; Co-R S Lk's Epis Ch Allen Pk MI 2003-** B Pottstown PA 4/24/1951 s William Berman Hale & Margaret Eva. BA Indiana U 1973; MA U of Pennsylvania 1975; PhD U of Pennsylvania 1978; MDiv GTS 1989. D 6/24/1989 P 1/1/1990 Bp H Coleman McGehee Jr. m 2/18/1982 Lori Alyson Mendez. Trin Ch Detroit MI 1989-1992. whale@cotl.net

HALE, William Manning (CNY) 59 Frost Hill Road, Box 368, Marlborough NH 03455 **S Fran Chap Marlborough Marlborough NH 2003-** B New York NY 7/12/1925 s Samuel Whitney Hale & Sara Elizabeth. GTS 1954; BA Br 2049. D 6/19/1954 Bp Norman B Nash P 12/18/1954 Bp James R Mallett. m 6/16/1955 Helen Frost c 4. Int Calv Ch Pittsburgh PA 1995-1996; Int S Jn's Ch Cold Sprg Harbor NY 1994-1995; Int Chr Ch Alexandria VA 1992-1993; Dn and R S Paul's Cathd Syracuse NY 1975-1990; The GTS New York NY 1975-1979; Cn Chr Ch Cathd Springfield MA 1970-1975; Trst The GTS New York NY 1967-1973; Pres, Alum Assn The GTS New York NY 1962-1966; Cn Chr Ch Cathd Springfield MA 1956-1957; Chr Ch Cathd Springfield MA 1954-1955. Comp of the Cross of Nails 1983. BillHale368@aol.com

HALEY-RAY, Judith Ray (Pa) No address on file. B Chattanooga TN 10/14/1944 d James Merideth Haley & Corinne Marie. MWC 1964; U NC 1965; BA Villanova U 1988; Sch Of Diac Philadelphia PA 1992; CSD Neumann Coll Aston PA 1996. D 10/17/1992 Bp Franklin Delton Turner. m 6/19/1965 William Allen Ray c 1. D S Gabr's Epis Ch Philadelphia PA 1992-1999. Sprtl Dir Intl 1997. revmommom@comcast.net

HALFORD, Cathrine Nance (Miss) 147 Daniel Lake Blvd, Jackson MS 39212 B Cleveland MS 7/3/1948 d John Walter Nance & Mary Hopson. BS Georgia St U 1975; MEd Georgia St U 1976; EdS Delta St U 1991. D 5/29/2008 Bp Duncan Montgomery Gray III. c 2. chalford48@yahoo.com

HALKETT, Thomas Richmond (Me) PO Box 564, Machias ME 04654 B Bangor ME 2/13/1951 s James E Halkett & Geraldine Ingalls. BA Hampden-Sydney Coll 1973; MDiv Yale DS 1979. D 6/15/1979 P 1/1/1980 Bp Frederick Barton Wolf. m 8/12/2006 Diane Helder c 5. Dio Maine Portland ME 2000-2004; Epis Cmnty Serv Washington Cnty Cherryfield MA 1987-1990; Chr Epis Ch Eastport ME 1986-1987; S Aidans Ch Machias ME 1985-2004; P-in-c Chr Ch New Haven CT 1982-1985; Asst Ch Of The Redeem Bryn Mawr PA 1980-1982. thalkett@maine.edu

HALL, Addison Curtis (Mass) 79 Denton Rd, Wellesley MA 02482 **R S Andr's Ch Wellesley MA 1990-** B Northampton MA 6/16/1947 s Richard Sears Hall & Mary Curtis. BA Mid 1969; MDiv EDS 1974. D 6/8/1974 Bp Harvey D Butterfield P 12/8/1974 Bp Robert Shaw Kerr. m 12/27/1970 Joanna Skinger c 2. R S Steph's Ch Middlebury VT 1978-1990; Cur Cathd Ch Of S Paul Burlington VT 1974-1978. ach@standrewswellesley.org

HALL, Albert Benjamin (WMass) 775 Columbia Northwest, Port Charlotte FL 33952 B Boston MA 7/6/1939 s Raymond Stuart Hall & Mary Elizabeth. BA Br 1961; MDiv EDS 1964; MLS Wesl 1973. D 6/13/1964 P 12/1/1964 Bp Oliver L Loring. m 11/6/1965 Faith Waring c 2. Asst S Paul's Ch Holyoke MA 1964-1966. Auth, "arts Math".

HALL, Allen Keith (Colo) 2226 27th Ave, Greeley CO 80634 B Milwaukee WI 10/16/1924 s Forrest Clarke Hall & Crystal Louise. BA Ripon Coll Ripon WI 1949; MA Middle Tennessee St U 1963; MDiv Nash 1985. D 6/14/1985 P 12/22/1985 Bp William Carl Frey. m 7/5/1947 Mary Lou Ida Becker c 3. Int Trin Ch Greeley CO 1996-1997; Int S Mk's Epis Ch Durango CO 1994-1995; Int S Mk's Epis Ch Durango CO 1990-1991; Vic S Andr's Epis Ch Ft Lupton CO 1985-1990; Vic S Eliz's Epis Ch Brighton CO 1985-1990. Soc of S Fran - Tertiary 1985. alkhallx@comcast.net

HALL, Brian Patrick (ECR) 1324 Redwood Drive, Santa Cruz CA 95060 **Asst Calv Epis Ch Santa Cruz CA 1989-** B London UK 12/29/1935 s Hall Hall & Elsie. BA U Of British Columbia Vancouver Bc CA 1962; BTh Hur 1965; Claremont TS 1969. Trans from Anglican Church of Canada 12/5/1965 Bp David Emrys Richards. m 5/6/1961 Diane Ellis Jones. Auth, "Dvlpmt Of Consciousness"; Auth, "The Wizard Of Maldoone". Dplma AAPC.

HALL, Bruce Turner (WMo) 3331 Wyandotte St, Kansas City MO 64111 **Died 1/5/2011** B San Diego CA 11/9/1961 D 2/7/2004 Bp Barry Robert Howe.

HALL, Caroline J A (ECR) Po Box 6359, Los Osos CA 93412 **Multi-Dioc Disciplinary Bd Dio El Camino Real Monterey CA 2011-; P-in-c S Ben's Par Los Osos CA 2006-** B Woking Surrey England 2/20/1955 d Francis James Addington Hall & Kathleen Mary. ETSBH; BA U of Bradford, Bradford UK 1977; MBA Herriott Watt U 1997; MDiv CDSP 2003; PhD U of Leeds, Leeds UK 2009. D 6/28/2003 P 2/21/2004 Bp Richard Lester Shimpfky. m 6/17/2008 Jill Victoria Denton. Dioc Revs Com, Chair Dio El Camino Real Monterey CA 2009-2011; Conf Educ Resource Team Dio El Camino Real Monterey CA 2009-2010; T/F on Theol of Mar Dio El Camino Real Monterey CA 2009-2010; Lectr The ETS At Claremont Claremont CA 2008-2009; Dioc Coun Dio El Camino Real Monterey CA 2004-2006; Assoc S Lk's Ch Atascadero CA 2004-2006; Dnry Yth Min Dio El Camino Real Monterey CA 2003-2006. Ph D, "Homosexuality as a Site of Angl Identity and Dissent," Leeds U, UK, 2009; Auth, "H and Cath," *LivCh*, 2004; Auth, "For the Love of God," *New Times San Luis Obispo*, 2003. Integrity 1997; Integrity, Pres 2011. Promising Schlr ECF 2005. dentonhall@aol.com

HALL, Charlotte Melissa (Nwk) 80 Maple Ave Apt B, Morristown NJ 07960 **Asst S Ptr's Ch Morristown NJ 2010-** B New York NY 3/2/1953 MS NYU; BA SUNY; M DIv UTS 2003. D 5/31/2003 P 12/7/2003 Bp John Palmer Croneberger. m 3/23/2007 Frances Lapinski c 1. Asst Ch Of The Redeem Morristown NJ 2007-2010; All SS Epis Par Hoboken NJ 2004-2007. ESAUHALL@OPTONLINE.NET

HALL, Daniel Charles (NJ) 114 Willow Dr, North Cape May NJ 08204 **D Ch Of The Adv Cape May NJ 2007-** B Atlantic City NJ 11/13/1936 s Floyd Hall & Mildred. Dplma Philadelphia Coll of Bible 1961; BA Thos Edison St Coll 1981; ThM New Brunswick TS 1995. D 4/13/1985 Bp George Phelps Mellick Belshaw. m 5/4/1963 Barbara Elaine Curvan c 2. D S Barn By The Bay Villas NJ 1985-2007. Assoc, OHC. deacondan85@comcast.net

HALL, Daniel Emerson (Pgh) 408 Greendale Ave, Pittsburgh PA 15218 B Hastings NE 11/10/1969 s David Emerson Hall & Elizabeth. BA Ya 1991; MDiv Ya Berk 1996; MD Ya 1999; MA Duke 2005. D 6/12/1999 Bp Clarence Nicholas Coleridge P 8/7/2002 Bp Robert William Duncan. Assoc Ch Of The H Fam Chap Hill NC 2003-2005; Cn Mssnr For YA Trin Cathd Pittsburgh PA 2001-2002. revdocdan@aya.yale.edu

HALL, David A (Ala) 2753 11th Ave S, Birmingham AL 35205 **Epis Place Bd Dir Dio Alabama Birmingham AL 2011-; Assoc R Epis Ch Of The Ascen Birmingham AL 2008-; Stwdshp Cmsn Dio Alabama Birmingham AL 2005-** B Seattle WA 12/17/1957 s E Eugene Hall & Reba Francis. BA Louisiana Coll 1980; MDiv TS 1992. D 6/6/1992 P 5/15/1993 Bp Alex Dockery Dickson. m 11/25/2008 Phyllis Turnham Hall c 1. Stwdshp Cmsn Dio Alabama Birmingham AL 2005-2007; Dioc Coun Dio Alabama Birmingham AL 2004-2007; R Ch Of The Resurr Rainbow City AL 2002-2007; Assoc R St Thos Epis Ch Huntsville AL 2000-2002; Headmaster H Comf Epis Day Sch Gadsden AL 1999-2000; Chapl St. Geo's Schools Germantown TN

1996-1999; Asst to the R S Geo's Ch Germantown TN 1994-1996; Epis Chapl at the U of Memphis Dio W Tennessee Memphis TN 1992-1994; Asst S Andr's Epis Ch Collierville TN 1992-1994. david.hall@ascensionepiscopal.org

HALL, David Moreland (WMass) 20 Winchester Ave, Auburn MA 01501 **R S Thos Epis Ch Auburn MA 2009-** B Cincinnati OH 3/20/1949 s Harold Hall & Vivian Lee. OH SU 1970; BA Thos More Coll 1976; MDiv EDS 1977. D 6/4/1977 P 3/2/1978 Bp John Mc Gill Krumm. m 8/17/2008 Lisle M Hall c 6. R Chr Ch Montpelier VT 1989-2009; R Chr Epis Ch Clinton MD 1982-1989; R Trin Ch Coshocton OH 1979-1982; Asst S Paul's Epis Ch Dayton OH 1977-1979. plusone49@yahoo.com

HALL, Dianne Costner (Ga) 212 N Jefferson St, Albany GA 31701 B Raleigh NC 4/13/1947 d Robert Lee Costner & Ruth Yates. BA Mars Hill Coll 1969. D 3/25/2009 Bp Henry Irving Louttit. c 3. dhall@habitat.org

HALL, Donna Moody (SeFla) 941 Allendale Rd, West Palm Beach FL 33405 **P H Sprt Epis Ch W Palm Bch FL 2004-** B Fayetteville TN 12/19/1954 d Donald Moody & Betty. BA Middle Tennessee St U 1975; Med U GA 1982; MDiv Epis TS of The SW 2004. D 4/17/2004 P 11/9/2004 Bp Leopold Frade. m 5/28/1977 James H Hall c 2. jdlsb@bellsouth.net

HALL, E Eugene (Spr) 1808 Lakeside Dr Unit A, Champaign IL 61821 B Mansfield LA 6/19/1932 s Alvin Hall & Rose Marie. BA Louisiana Coll 1953; BD Sthrn Bapt TS Louisville KY 1956; MA LSU 1959; PhD LSU 1963. D 11/14/1997 Bp Calvin Onderdonk Schofield Jr P 6/13/1998 Bp John Lewis Said. m 12/27/1955 Reba Frances Hobby c 3. Assoc Emm Meml Epis Ch Champaign IL 2000-2004; S Mk's Ch Palm Bch Gardens FL 1998-1999. *Proclaim the Word: the Bases of Preaching*, Broadman Press, 1983; *Remember to Live*, Broadman Press, 1980. eughall@zworg.com

HALL, Everett (Ore) 11939 NE Davis St Apt 343, Portland OR 97220 B Duluth MN 8/10/1928 s Charles L Hall & Elva S. BA U MN 1951; MDiv Bex 1954. D 6/20/1954 P 3/1/1955 Bp Stephen E Keeler. Assoc Chr Ch Las Vegas NV 1998-2008; Stndg Com Dio Oregon Portland OR 1984-1986; Dioc Liturg Com Dio Oregon Portland OR 1982-1986; Dept of Missions Dio Oregon Portland OR 1980-1990; Dep GC Dio Oregon Portland OR 1979-1988; R S Matt's Epis Ch Portland OR 1974-1992; R S Mary's Ch Woodburn OR 1959-1974. ESMA 1977-1982.

HALL, Gary Richard Richard (Mich) 470 Church Rd, Bloomfield Hills MI 48304 **Chr Ch Cranbrook Bloomfield Hills MI 2010-** B Los Angeles CA 9/22/1949 s Huntz Hall & Leslie. Ya 1968; BA U CA 1972; MDiv EDS 1976; MA U CA 1984; PhD U CA 1989. D 6/19/1976 P 1/15/1977 Bp Robert C Rusack. m 4/17/1978 Kathleen Matheson c 1. Dn & Pres SWTS Evanston IL 2005-2010; Ch Of The Redeem Bryn Mawr PA 2001-2004; Cathd Cntr Of S Paul Cong Los Angeles CA 2001; The ETS At Claremont Claremont CA 1999; The ETS At Claremont Claremont CA 1995; All SS Ch Pasadena CA 1992-2001; R S Geo's Par La Can CA 1989-1990; Vic S Aid's Epis Ch Malibu CA 1983-1989; Ch Of The Epiph Oak Pk CA 1981-1983; Asst Chr Ch Cranbrook Bloomfield Hills MI 1978-1979; Int S Jn The Evang Taunton MA 1977-1978; D Intern Dio Los Angeles Los Angeles CA 1976-1977. Auth, "From Heresy to Sex," *ATR*, 2003. Phi Beta Kappa 1972. Hon Cn Cathd Cntr of St. Paul 2001; ECF Fell 1983. garyhall49@gmail.com

HALL, George E (Ct) 496 F Heritage Vlg, Southbury CT 06488 B Riverton NJ 3/3/1930 s George Ellsworth Hall & Kathryn Cameron. BA U So 1954; GTS 1957; MS Cntrl Connecticut St U 1976. D 4/26/1957 P 11/2/1957 Bp Alfred L Banyard. m 7/7/1987 Beverly D Barras c 3. P-in-c S Mk's Ch Bridgewater CT 1995-2000; Dir Oratory of the Little Way Gaylordsville Dio Connecticut Hartford CT 1992-1995; R S Lk's Ch So Glastonbury CT 1969-1992; R Calv Epis Ch Flemington NJ 1961-1969; R S Jas Ch Bradley Bch NJ 1957-1961. OHC. ghallbev@sbcglobal.net

HALL, James Harold (SVa) 3628 Applewood Ln, Antioch TN 37013 B Brunswick GA 6/20/1928 s James Hall & Clara Belle. Talladega Coll 1947; BA S Aug's Coll Raleigh NC 1950; MDiv Nash 1953; MA U of Montana 1971. D P 12/21/1953 Bp Martin J Bram. m 4/26/1987 Pauline M. R S Cyp's Epis Ch Hampton VA 1987-1996; R Ch Of The H Trin Nashville TN 1982-1987; Ch Of The Redeem Kenmore WA 1982; Vic S Mich And All Ang Ch Tallahassee FL 1974-1979; Vic S Andr's Epis Ch Polson MT 1964-1974; Asst Ch Of The H Sprt Missoula MT 1963-1964; Vic S Tim's Epis Ch Daytona Bch FL 1958-1963; Vic Ch Of S Chris Ft Lauderdale FL 1954-1958; Vic S Andr's Epis Ch Of Hollywood Dania Bch FL 1954-1958; Vic S Phil's Ch Pompano Bch FL 1954-1958; Vic Ch Of S Jn Lake Worth FL 1953-1958; Vic S Cuth's Ch Boynton Bch FL 1953-1958; Vic S Mary's Epis Ch Of Deerfiel Deerfield Bch FL 1953-1958; Vic S Matt's Epis Ch Delray Bch FL 1953-1958.

HALL, John (At) 265 Mail Rd., Exeter RI 02822 B Newport RI 6/22/1936 s Richard Hall & Marguerite. BA Trin Hartford CT 1957; STB Ya Berk 1960; Fllshp EDS 1977. D 6/18/1960 P 12/19/1960 Bp John S Higgins. m 10/2/1965 Mary Bryant Chase c 4. Dio Atlanta Atlanta GA 1998-2001; R All SS Ch Warwick RI 1990-1998; S Aug's Ch Kingston RI 1978-1989; Dio Rhode Island Providence RI 1966-1997; Cur S Jn's Ch Barrington RI 1960-1965. Ed, "Rhode Island Epis News," 1998. Hon Cn S Jn'S Cathd Providence RI 1986. johnhall5@cox.net

HALL, John C N (Az) 955 W Barcelona Dr, Gilbert AZ 85233 **R S Matt's Ch Chandler AZ 1998-** B New York NY 4/10/1958 s Harry William Naulty Hall & Marietta Francis. BA U of Arizona 1981; MDiv VTS 1989; DMin SWTS 2005. D 6/11/1989 Bp Joseph Thomas Heistand P 12/14/1989 Bp Calvin Onderdonk Schofield Jr. m 5/28/1983 Jean E Lindholtz c 4. Dio Arizona Phoenix AZ 1998-2007; Assoc R S Barn On The Desert Scottsdale AZ 1994-1998; Assoc R S Mich And All Ang Ch Mssn KS 1992-1994; S Mary Magd Epis Ch Coral Sprg FL 1989-1992; Yth Min S Phil's In The Hills Tucson AZ 1985-1986. Auth, "What I Would Have Told You," *LivCh*, LivCh Fndt, 2007; Auth, "Strangers and Aliens, Citizens and SS: Multicultural Challenges for Hisp/Latino Mnstry in the Ch," *Doctoral Thesis*, SWTS, 2005; Auth, "Simply Invisible," *LivCh*, LivCh Fndt, 2004; Auth, "When the Ch Lacks Vision," *LivCh*, LivCh Fndt, 2002. jcnhall@gmail.com

HALL, John Liston (Ia) 20 Mcclellan Blvd, Davenport IA 52803 B Elmwood NE 6/20/1937 s Ted Gordon Hall & Margaret Marian. BS U of Nebraska 1958; BD SWTS 1963; MA U of Nebraska 1968; PhD U of Nebraska 1971. D 6/8/1963 P 12/1/1963 Bp Russell T Rauscher. m 8/6/1966 Kay M Huffaker c 3. Dn Trin Cathd Davenport IA 1989-2005; S Jn's Epis Ch Decatur IL 1979-1989; P-in-c S Andr's Ch Lincoln NE 1971-1972; P-in-c H Trin Ch York NE 1966-1967; P-in-c S Andr's Ch Lincoln NE 1966-1967; Asst Chapl S Mk's On The Campus Lincoln NE 1965-1970; Vic S Jos's Ch Mullen NE 1963-1965.

HALL, Jon William (Mo) 15764 Clayton Rd, Ellisville MO 63011 **R S Mart's Ch Ellisville MO 2010-** B Shreveport Louisiana 1/12/1963 Centenary Coll 1986; Profsnl Counslg Asbury TS 2003; CAS GTS 2005. D 6/18/2005 P 12/23/2005 Bp Stacy F Sauls. m 12/27/1987 Colleen William Eastman c 1. S Phil's Ch Harrodsburg KY 2005-2010. 3hallsfamily@gmail.com

HALL, Karen Elizabeth (Mont) PO Box 1309, Bozeman MT 59771 B Cut Bank MT 6/1/1942 d Carl Eric Turnquist & Helen H. Nash; So Dakota St U; BA U CO 1966; MDiv STUSo 1991. D 4/15/1986 P 11/16/1986 Bp Craig Barry Anderson. c 4. R Trin Ch Ennis MT 2007-2011; Supply H Trin Epis Ch Luverne MN 2001; Cn Dio So Dakota Sioux Falls SD 2000-2007; R Trin Epis Ch Watertown SD 1991-2000; Chr Ch Alto Decherd TN 1990-1991; Dio So Dakota Sioux Falls SD 1987-1999; Gr Epis Ch Madison SD 1986. Sis of Mary (Assoc). cl U So 1991. kehall42@gmail.com

HALL, Kenneth (EO) D.

HALL, Laurens Allen (Tex) 2450 River Oaks Blvd, Houston TX 77019 **R S Jn The Div Houston TX 1981-** B San Antonio TX 11/16/1942 s Wilton Earl Hall & Ada Allen. BBA U of Texas 1965; MDiv CDSP 1968; DD CDSP 1995. D 7/24/1968 Bp Everett H Jones P 1/28/1969 Bp Richard Earl Dicus. m 12/30/1968 Bennie Grant c 3. R S Dav's Ch Austin TX 1975-1981; R S Chris's Ch League City TX 1971-1975; Asst R Chr Epis Ch San Antonio TX 1968-1971. DD CDSP 1995. lhall@sjd.org

HALL, Leigh Ellen (Ga) P.O. Box 74, Swainsboro GA 30401 **Dio Georgia Savannah GA 2009-** B Statesboro GA 5/28/1980 d Thomas Talmadge Hall & Ellen Casann. AA E Georgia Coll 2000; BA U GA 2003; MDiv VTS 2009. D 2/7/2009 P 8/27/2009 Bp Henry Irving Louttit. leighellenhall@gmail.com

HALL, Lisbeth Jordan (Mass) 1239 Peterkin Hl, South Woodstock VT 05071 B Philadelphia PA 4/19/1933 d Claus Gustav Jordan & Charlotte Caroline. BA Mt Holyoke Coll 1954; MDiv EDS 1995. D 12/19/1998 P 12/4/1999 Bp M(arvil) Thomas Shaw III. m 11/5/1955 Lyle Gillis Hall c 6. Dio Wstrn Massachusetts Springfield MA 2003; Assoc All SS Par Brookline MA 2002-2003; P-in-c Ch Of S Jn The Evang Boston MA 1999-2002. lamblizhall@gmail.com

HALL JR, Lyle Gillis (Mass) 1239 Peterkin Hill Road, South Woodstock VT 05071 B Ridgway PA 11/2/1929 s Lyle Gillis Hall & Jane Grube. Ya 1952; BS Bos 1975; MDiv EDS 1978. D 6/10/1978 P 12/10/1978 Bp Donald James Davis. m 11/5/1955 Lisbeth Jordan c 6. P-in-c Ch Of S Jn The Evang Boston MA 1999-2002; R S Dunstans Epis Ch Dover MA 1993-1999; Assoc All SS Par Brookline MA 1992-1999; S Dunstans Epis Ch Dover MA 1983-1989; All SS Par Brookline MA 1981-1982; Asst The Ch Of The Adv Boston MA 1979-1980. OHC. lyleghall@gmail.com

HALL, Mark Heathcote (EpisSanJ) 2212 River Dr, Stockton CA 95204 **Chapl Epis Dio San Joaquin Modesto CA 2011-; Dom And Frgn Mssy Soc- Epis Ch Cntr New York NY 2008-; Epis Ch Cntr New York NY 2008-; Cn to the Ordnry Epis Dio San Joaquin Modesto CA 2008-** B Los Angeles CA 10/10/1946 s Kempton Bishop Hall & Emily Stevens. BA U of Hawaii 1969; MDiv EDS 1973; MA U of Maine 1986. D 9/16/1975 P 3/16/1976 Bp Frederick Barton Wolf. m 11/18/1990 Susan Conrad c 2. Epis Ch Of S Anne Stockton CA 2002-2008; H Trin Epis Ch Madera CA 1991-1995; Chair DeptCE Epis Dio San Joaquin Modesto CA 1988-1992; Vic S Alb's Ch Los Banos CA 1987-1990; Vic S Alb's Ch Los Banos CA 1987-1990; Asst S Jas Epis Ch Kent WA 1987; Int S Andr's Ch Millinocket ME 1984-1985; Int S Pat's Ch Brewer ME 1983-1984; S Johns Epis Ch Brownville ME 1982-1983; St Josephs Ch Sebec ME 1982-1983; Int S Alb's Ch Los Banos CA 1982; St Anth Ch Patterson CA 1982; Cn to Bp Epis Dio San Joaquin Modesto CA 1981-1982; Serv St Nich Epis Ch Atwater CA 1980-1982; Serv S Lk's Ch

Caribou ME 1976-1978. Auth, "Bp Mcllvain, The Reluctant Frontiersman," *Ch Hist mag*. krametoc@cell2000.net

HALL, Mavis Ann (Neb) 3214 Davy Jones Dr, Plattsmouth NE 68048 **S Lk's Ch Plattsmouth NE 2003-** B Sioux City IA 11/5/1951 D 5/31/2003 P 11/30/2003 Bp James Edward Krotz. m 7/3/1971 Michael Clifford Hall c 2.

HALL, Michael Gregory (CFla) Shepherd of the Hills, 2540 W Norvell Bryant Hwy, Lecanto FL 34461 **Shpd Of The Hills Epis Ch Lecanto FL 2008-** B Heidleberg Germany 11/28/1958 s Charles Glenwood Hall & Margaret Mary. BBA Fonthonne Coll 1996; MBA/MMA U of Mary 2002. D 6/22/2007 Bp Michael Gene Smith. m 5/9/1987 Linda Ann Liebert-Hall. mhallfm@msn.com

HALL, Patrick Mckenzie (Tex) 915 Saulnier St # B, Houston TX 77019 **Assoc H Sprt Epis Ch Houston TX 2007-; H Sprt Epis Sch Houston TX 2007-** B 5/19/1982 s James Mckenzie Hall & Rosine Wilson. BA U of Texas 2003; MDiv VTS 2007. D 6/23/2007 Bp Don Adger Wimberly. m 1/21/2006 Laura L Tankersley. pmckenziehall@gmail.com

HALL, PaulaClaire (WLa) 361 Cypress Loop, Farmerville LA 71241 **Int S Andr's Epis Ch Mer Rouge LA 2011-** B El Dorado AR 9/20/1945 BS Louisiana Tech U 1967; MBA U of Hawaii 1970; JD UALR Sch of Law 1977; ABD U of Memphis 1989; MDiv Nash 2003. D 6/7/2003 P 3/4/2004 Bp D(avid) Bruce Mac Pherson. Int S Alb's Epis Ch Monroe LA 2010-2011; Stndg Com, Pres Dio Wstrn Louisiana Alexandria LA 2009-2011; Int Chr Memi Ch Mansfield LA 2009-2010; Stndg Com Dio Wstrn Louisiana Alexandria LA 2008-2011; Int Ch Of The Redeem Ruston LA 2008-2009; P-in-c Gr Ch Lake Providence LA 2005-2007; Int S Thos' Ch Monroe LA 2003-2005. "Sprtl Formation column," *Alive*, Dio Wstrn Louisiana. AFP, US Exec Coun 2005. darbonnedarlins@hotmail.com

HALL, Richard Charles (Los) 623 Prospect Ave Unit 7, South Pasadena CA 91030 B Syracuse NY 11/1/1935 s Richard Carlton Hall & Elizabeth Catherine. BA Ham 1957; MDiv GTS 1961; PhD Claremont Coll 1970. D 6/1/1961 Bp Allen Webster Brown P 2/14/1962 Bp Lyman Cunningham Ogilby. c 3. Asst S Paul's Pomona Pomona CA 1985-1991; S Barn Sr Serv Los Angeles CA 1975-2000; Asst S Mk's Epis Ch Upland CA 1975-1983; R S Jn The Bapt Par Corona CA 1970-1975. halldick@hotmail.com

HALL, Richard Hastings (Me) 29 Tarratine Dr, Brunswick ME 04011 B Holyoke MA 6/4/1942 s John Albert Hall & Emma Louise. BA U of Massachusetts 1968; MDiv Ya Berk 1971; STM NYTS 1975; DMin Andover Newton TS 1986. D 6/20/1971 Bp Alexander Doig Stewart P 1/7/1972 Bp Frederick Barton Wolf. m 1/21/1967 Elizabeth Ellen Beacom c 3. R S Phil's Ch Wiscasset ME 1974-2001; Asst S Jn's Ch Bangor ME 1971-1974. dickh@gwi.net

HALL JR, Robert Charles (Va) 132 Lancaster Drive, #828, Irvington VA 22480 **Died 4/13/2011** B Baltimore MD 3/15/1929 s Robert Charles Hall & Marian. BA JHU 1967; STB Ya Berk 1968. D 6/8/1968 Bp Robert Bruce Hall P 12/21/1968 Bp Robert Fisher Gibson Jr. c 4. somerset@va.metrocast.net

HALL, Robert Marshall (Ct) 2 Coles Ct, Norwich CT 06360 B Bronxville NY 12/10/1941 s Robert Marshall Hall & Ruth Pearl. BA Cntrl Coll 1965; MDiv Ya Berk 1969; Med Iona Coll 1980. D 6/12/1971 Bp Jonathan Goodhue Sherman P 2/26/1972 Bp Wilburn Camrock Campbell. m 10/4/1969 Mary Jean Weber. Assoc S Jas Ch Preston CT 2001-2006; S Alb's Ch Danielson CT 1994-1997; Assoc Ch Of The Resurr Norwich CT 1989-1992; Assoc Chr Epis Ch Norwich CT 1984-1989; Assoc Chr Ch Norwalk CT 1978-1979; Int S Paul's Ch Wallingford CT 1977-1978; Int Trin Ch Seymour CT 1976-1977; Vic S Jn's Ch Marlinton WV 1971-1973; Vic S Martins-In-Fields Summersville WV 1971-1973. Elder Ct Soc Of Mayflower Descendants 1985-1995. Elder Of Connecticut Mayflower Descendants. revbobhall@aol.com

HALL, Ryan Ashley (SD) St. Paul's Episcopal Church, 726 6th St, Brookings SD 57006 **R S Paul's Ch Brookings SD 2009-** B Luttrell TN 4/21/1980 s Randy Roy Hall & Donna Hines. No Degree U of Nebraska; BA Carson Newman Coll 2002; MDiv SWTS 2007. D 6/11/2007 P 5/1/2008 Bp Joe Goodwin Burnett. m 1/12/2008 Mary Kyle Hall. Cur S Mk's On The Campus Lincoln NE 2007-2009. Friend (Oblate) of the SSJE 2007; SocMary 2008. ryanashleyhall@hotmail.com

HALL, Samuel Joseph (FdL) 1128 S 35th St, Manitowoc WI 54220 B Manitowoc WI 6/8/1918 D 4/10/1991 Bp William L Stevens. m 4/1/1952 Germaine Hall c 7.

HALL, Samuel Leslie (RG) 1023 Acequia Trl Nw, Albuquerque NM 87107 B San Francisco CA 12/23/1928 s John Leslie Hall & Iris Pauline. BA U CA 1951; BD (M Div.) VTS 1956; S Aug's Coll Cbury Gb 1966. D 6/25/1956 P 2/7/1957 Bp Francis E I Bloy. m 12/23/1976 Leila Tunis c 4. R S Mk's On The Mesa Epis Ch Albuquerque NM 1987-1988; Chair Archit Cmsn Dio Los Angeles Los Angeles CA 1975-1980; R The Par Ch Of S Lk Long Bch CA 1967-1974; R S Steph's Par Whittier CA 1962-1967; Vic S Steph's Par Whittier CA 1959-1961; Cur S Edm's Par San Marino CA 1956-1959. samleehall@earthlink.net

HALL, Sidney J (SVa) 218 Grove Dr, Clemson SC 29631 B Hartsville SC 10/15/1930 s James Robert Hall & Lola Mae. UTS; VTS; BA Baylor U 1955; BD SW Bapt TS 1959. D 11/5/1988 P 3/1/1989 Bp C(laude) Charles Vache. R Chr Ch Amelia Crt Hse VA 1990-1996; R Emm Epis Ch Powhatan VA 1990-1996; R S Jas Ch Cartersville VA 1990-1996; Manakin Epis Ch Midlothian VA 1989-1990; Asst R S Lk's Ch Powhatan VA 1989-1990. peregrine@nctv.com

HALL, Stephen M (Ga) PO Box 69, Clayton GA 30525 **R S Jas Epis Ch Clayton GA 2006-** B Milaukee WI 5/23/1942 s Robert Latham Hall & Jay Lou. BA Lawr 1964; MDiv Nash 1981. D 4/28/1981 Bp William Harvey Wolfrum P 11/1/1981 Bp William Carl Frey. m 8/2/1992 Roxanne Reiter c 6. S Matt's-By-The-Bridge Epis Ch Iowa Falls IA 2000; Ch Of The Gd Shpd Webster City IA 1993-1998; R S Mk's Epis Ch Ft Dodge IA 1990-2006; Cn Theol Calv Cathd Sioux Falls SD 1987-1990; R S Paul's Ch Brookings SD 1981-1987. sandrhall@windstream.net.net

HALL, Tim Stewart (Chi) 146 Court St, Brockton MA 02302 B Indianapolis IN 5/2/1937 s Edwin Albert Hall & Dorothy Irene. BA Hanover Coll 1959; MDiv Nash 1968. D 6/8/1968 Bp John P Craine P 12/28/1968 Bp Harry Lee Doll. m 6/29/1985 Jacqueline Mary Schmitt c 5. Cn for Congrl Dvlpmt Dio Chicago Chicago IL 1996-2001; Ch Of The H Fam Lake Villa IL 1995; COM Dio Cntrl New York Syracuse NY 1984-1993; Stndg Com Dio Cntrl New York Syracuse NY 1984-1991; Calv Ch Syracuse NY 1976-1988; R Ch Of The H Nativ Baltimore MD 1970-1976; Cur Mt Calv Ch Baltimore MD 1968-1970. timstewarthall@gmail.com

HALL, Tod Latham (NH) 140 Muzzy Hill Rd, Milan NH 03588 B Winchester MA 12/25/1941 s Charles F Hall & Constance. Lon 1963; BA Dart 1964; S Jn Coll Gb 1967; BD EDS 1968. D 6/15/1968 P 12/1/1968 Bp Charles F Hall. m 1/30/1976 Patricia Louise Lowry c 3. Dio New Hampshire Concord NH 1996; S Barn Ch Berlin NH 1994-1999; Dio New Hampshire Concord NH 1991-1993; S Lk's Ch Woodsville NH 1986-1991; Vic Ch Of The Epiph Lisbon Lisbon NH 1985-1996; Trin Ch In The City Of Boston Boston MA 1972-1985; Asst S Geo's Epis Ch Dayton OH 1968-1971. barnabas@ncia.net

HALL, V(ernon) Donald (O) 2432 Romar Dr, Hermitage PA 16148 **S Lk's Epis Ch Niles OH 2009-** B Connellsville PA 10/24/1947 s Vernon Hall & Rita Kathryn. BA S Vinc Coll Latrobe PA 1969; MA Mt St. Mary's Sem 1977; MS U Pgh 1982; MPA U Pgh 1983. Rec from Roman Catholic 5/1/1998 as Priest Bp Paul Victor Marshall. m 8/10/1996 Mary Theresa Kyne. S Andr Ch Canfield OH 2003-2008; Int Trin Ch Hermitage PA 1999-2000; Assoc S Gabr's Ch Douglassville PA 1997-1999. NASW. dh3510@msn.com

HALL, Virginia B (Ind) 3436 E. Longview, Bloomington IN 47408 **S Paul's Epis Ch Salinas CA 2003-; Pstr Assoc Ch Of The Resurr Pleasant Hill CA 1992-** B Summit NJ 5/25/1942 d Harold Everett Hall & Virginia Anne. Wells Coll; BA U of New Hampshire 1965; MDiv CDSP 1969; MA Grad Theol Un 1985; Cert Jn F. Kennedy U 1987. D 7/14/1979 P 9/20/1980 Bp Philip Alan Smith. c 2. S Lk's Epis Ch Shelbyville IN 2003-2007; S Mk's-In-The-Vlly Epis Los Olivos CA 2002; Exec Coun Appointees New York NY 1997-2001; Dio Guatemala Guatemala City 1997; Pstr Counslr S Anselm's Epis Ch Lafayette CA 1988-1991; S Paul's Epis Ch Walnut Creek CA 1986-1987; Asst S Thos Ch Dover NH 1979-1980. AAPC, Epis Wmn 1985-1990; DOK 2001. yesvirginia2@yahoo.com

HALLADAY, Richard Allen (Ind) 448 Freeman Ridge Rd, Nashville IN 47448 B Langdon NH 8/30/1932 s Ralph D Halladay & Belle M. BA Natl Coll Kansas City MO 1964; MDiv Epis TS In Kentucky 1967; DMin GTF 1990. D 12/16/1966 P 5/26/1967 Bp William R Moody. m 8/26/1972 Janice Rose c 3. Cn to the Ordnry Dio Indianapolis Indianapolis IN 1997-2001; Vic S Thos Ch Franklin IN 1982-1997; Vic S Lk's Epis Ch Shelbyville IN 1982-1986; R Trin Ch Anderson IN 1970-1972; Assoc R Trin Ch Covington KY 1968-1970; Vic S Pat Ch Somerset KY 1966-1968. Auth, "Formation, Instrn," *Reflection*; Auth, *Sm Congregations - Sm Communities*. rahalladay@att.net

HALLAHAN, T Mark (Los) 3882 Latrobe St, Los Angeles CA 90031 **R S Paul's Pomona Pomona CA 2007-** B Youngstown OH 8/29/1952 D 6/11/2005 Bp Chester Lovelle Talton P 1/14/2006 Bp Joseph Jon Bruno. R S Paul's Pomona Pomona CA 2006-2007; Dio Los Angeles Los Angeles CA 2005-2006; D All SS Par Beverly Hills CA 2003-2005. Soc of Cath Priests 2010; SocMary 2006. frmarkstpauls@yahoo.com

HALLANAN, Sunny No Middle Name (Pa) Chaussee de Charleroi 2, 1420, Braine-l'Alleud PA Belgium **R All SS Epis Ch Braine-l'Alleud 1420 BE 2011-** B Watertown NY 10/24/1958 d George H Hallanan & Alice M. BA Cor 1979; MDiv Ya Berk 1987. D 6/20/1987 Bp O'Kelley Whitaker P 2/27/1988 Bp William George Burrill. c 2. Pres Dio of Pennsylvania Assn Natl Ntwk Of Epis Cler Assn Lynnwood WA 2005-2011; R S Jas Ch Collegeville PA 1995-2011; Evang Consult Dio Rochester Rochester NY 1988-1995; Assoc R S Thos Epis Ch Rochester NY 1987-1995; Yth Coordntr Dio Massachusetts Boston MA 1980-1983; Asst Chapl Epis Chap at MIT Cambridge MA 1979-1983. revsunnyh@gmail.com

HALLAS, Cynthia Johnston (Chi) 3025 Walters Ave, Northbrook IL 60062 **R S Giles' Ch Northbrook IL 2004-** B Lakewood OH 2/10/1954 d Hugh A Johnston & Patricia Lee. B.A. Adrian Coll 1976; M.A. The OH SU 1979; M.Div. SWTS 2000. D 6/9/2000 Bp Michael Whittington Creighton P 1/30/2001 Bp William Dailey Persell. m 9/11/1982 Alvin Jon Hallas c 2. Assoc S Lawr Epis Ch Libertyville IL 2000-2004. rector@saint-giles.org

HALLE, Michael Adderbrooke (Az) 3738 N Old Sabino Canyon Rd, Tucson AZ 85750 B Tucson AZ 12/24/1964 s Michael Carlos Halle & Nancy Adderbrooke. BSBA U of Arizona 1988; MAOM U of Phoenix Tucson AZ 1994. D 1/24/2009 Bp Kirk Stevan Smith. mhalle@aol.com

HALLENBECK, Edwin Forrest (RI) 101 Larchmont Rd, Warwick RI 02886 **Secy, Cmsn on Fin Dio Rhode Island Providence RI 2001-; Mem, Dioc Coun Dio Rhode Island Providence RI 1999-** B Oakland CA 12/20/1926 s Wilbur Chapman Hallenbeck. BA Occ 1951; MA Col 1954; Rhode Island Sch For Deacons 1985. D 7/13/1985 Bp George Nelson Hunt III. m 6/25/1950 Patricia Jean Horrell c 3. D S Lk's Epis Ch E Greenwich RI 1997-2001; D S Barn Ch Warwick RI 1992-1997; D S Eliz's Ch Hope Vlly RI 1987-1991; D S Thos' Alton Wood River Jct RI 1987-1991; D All SS Ch Warwick RI 1985-1987. Auth, "Diakonia-Prophetic Praxis-Agir," Naad, 2002; Auth, "Working Paper Trial Liturg For Celebration Of D Mnstry," Naad, 1996; Auth, "The Ord Of Mnstry-Reflections On Direct Ord," Naad, 1996; Auth, "Personal Mnstry Plnng," Plnng Lab, 1990. Pres NAAD 1991-1993. The Bp Geroge Clinton Awd In Recognition Of Outstanding Serv To Deacons NAAD 2003. teddeacon@aol.com

HALLER BSG, Tobias Stanislas (NY) St James Rectory, 2627 Davidson Ave, Bronx NY 10468 **Stndg Com Dio New York New York City NY 2007-; Vic S Jas Epis Ch Fordham Bronx NY 1999-** B Baltimore MD 9/30/1949 s William Tobias Haller & Mary Louise. BA scl Towson St Coll 1971; MDiv cl GTS 1997. D 6/14/1997 P 12/13/1997 Bp Richard Frank Grein. m 7/29/2011 James Teets. Dioc Trst Dio New York New York City NY 2000-2006; Asst Secy of Conv Dio New York New York City NY 1997-1999; Pstr S Paul's Ch Yonkers NY 1997-1999; Asst Pub Dir Epis Ch Cntr New York NY 1983-1991. Auth, "Reasonable and H," Seabury Books, 2009; Auth, "Defender of His Faith / Henry VII," *Fllshp Papers*, CFEC, 1996; Auth, "St of the Rel Life," BSG, 1991; Auth, "God First: A Tithing Catechism," BSG/TEC, 1990; Ed, "Sermons," *Selected Sermons*, TEC, 1986; Ed, "Var arts," *The Servnt*, BSG, 1983. BSG 1980; Convenor NAECC 2005-2007; Pres CFEC 1988-1994. Off, Most Venerable Ord of St Jn of Jerusalem HM Eliz II 2009; Clem J Whipple, Bp of Newark and J Wilson Sutton Prizes GTS 1997; Polly Bond Awd Epis Cmnctr 1991. bsg@earthlink.net

HALLETT, Timothy Jerome (Spr) 3007 N Ramble Rd W, Bloomington IN 47408 B Fergus Falls MN 11/22/1940 s Leslie William Hallett & Rosa Dell. BA U So 1962; Amer Inst H Land Stds IL 1964; MDiv SWTS 1965; MA U Chi 1973. D 6/24/1965 Bp Hamilton Hyde Kellogg P 3/1/1966 Bp Philip Frederick McNairy. m 8/19/1967 Mary van Eenwyk. R Chap Of S Jn The Div Champaign IL 1976-2011; Asst Gr Epis Ch Hinsdale IL 1974-1976; Cur S Jn's Epis Ch Mankato MN 1965-1968. Auth, "Symbolism Of The Biblic Wrld"; Auth, "Paul The Apos". ESMHE Pres 1976-2003; Interfaith Com for Worker Justice 2001-2005. Mem Ord of St. Jn 2010; Distinguished Ldrshp Awd Off of Campus Mnstrs, The Epis Ch 2006. tjhallett1@comcast.net

HALLISEY, L Ann (NCal) 1711 Westshore St, Davis CA 95616 **CDSP Berkeley CA 2011-** B Los Angeles CA 10/24/1949 d William Bernard Hallisey & Leah Rebecca. BA U CA 1971; MDiv Yale DS 1975; MS California St U 1987; D.Min. CDSP 2005. D 5/1/1983 P 1/6/1984 Bp John Lester Thompson III. m 5/2/1998 Barry Leigh Beisner c 3. S Jn's Epis Ch Oakland CA 2010-2011; Int The Epis Ch Of The Gd Shpd Berkeley CA 2007-2010; Epis Ch Cntr New York NY 2005-2006; ECF Inc New York NY 2001-2005; R Ch Of The Ascen Vallejo CA 1992-2001; Assoc S Paul's Epis Ch Benicia CA 1987-1991; Int Epis Ch Of The Epiph Vacaville CA 1986-1987; Int Trin Ch Sonoma CA 1986-1987; Asst Epis Ch Of The Epiph Vacaville CA 1983-1985. revannie@comcast.net

HALLMARK, Charlotte Anne (Va) PO Box 306, Middleburg VA 20118 **R Emm Ch Middleburg VA 2008-** B Chicago IL 9/27/1945 d John Brennan O'Donoghue & Mildred Leora. BA CUA 1970; MDiv SWTS 1987. D 6/1/1987 Bp James Winchester Montgomery P 12/1/1987 Bp Frank Tracy Griswold III. m 5/21/1977 Nelson Stephen Hallmark c 1. Int S Jn's Ch Roanoke VA 2005-2007; Int Ch Of Our Sav Charlottesville VA 2004-2005; Int S Mart In The Fields Ch Atlanta GA 2003-2004; Int S Mary's-On-The-Highlands Epis Ch Birmingham AL 2001-2002; Int S Ptr's Epis Ch Charlotte NC 1999-2001; Int S Jn's Epis Ch Columbia SC 1998-1999; Int S Mk's Epis Ch Raleigh NC 1997-1998; Int Chr The King Ch Lansing IL 1990-1991; Int Dio Chicago Chicago IL 1987-1989; Cur S Bede's Epis Ch Bensenville IL 1987-1989. steve.hallmark@mindspring.com

HALLOCK JR, Harold Herman (Va) 920 Flordon Dr, Charlottesville VA 22901 B Greenport,NY 3/16/1938 s Harold Herman Hallock & Katharine Dell. BA U of Virginia 1959; MDiv STUSo 1977. D 6/26/1977 Bp William Evan Sanders P 4/30/1978 Bp William F Gates Jr. m 5/13/1961 Virginia Hilton Somerville c 2. R Ch Of Our Sav Charlottesville VA 1981-2004; Asst Ch Of The Gd Shpd Lookout Mtn TN 1977-1981. hhhallock@comcast.net

HALLY SSAP, Jane Eloise (At) 16A Lenox Pointe NE, Atlanta GA 30324 B Boston MA 5/28/1943 d James Thomas Hally & Pauline Mary. AB Vas 1964; MDiv Candler TS Emory U 1982; MSW U GA 2000. D 6/12/1982 P 5/4/1983 Bp Bennett Jones Sims. c 1. Pstr Counslr S Barth's Epis Ch Atlanta GA 1986-1995; D Ch Of The Atone Sandy Sprg GA 1982-1984. Auth, "sermons," *Wmn of the Word*, Susan Smith Pub, 1984. The Soc of S Anna the Prophet 2005. jehally@gmail.com

HALT, David Jason Andrew (Spr) 2153 Crest Rd, Cincinnati OH 45240 **S Matt's Epis Ch Bloomington IL 2010-** B Toledo OH 10/13/1973 s David Walter Halt & Phyllis Deane. BA Sprg Arbor U 1995; M.A.T.S Untd TS 2002; M.Div Bex 2003. D 10/25/2003 Bp Herbert Thompson Jr P 6/19/2004 Bp Kenneth Lester Price. m 5/22/1993 Amy Diane Ray c 2. R S Jas Epis Ch Cincinnati OH 2006-2009; P-in-c H Sprt Epis Ch Cincinnati OH 2004-2006. Congregations of the Comp of the H Sav 2006. fr.halt@gmail.com

HALTER, Karl (WA) 2059 Huntington Ave Apt 1203, Alexandria VA 22303 B Freiburg Germany 2/26/1926 s Karl Halter & Rosa. Bapt TS at Hamburg 1949; Berkeley Bapt TS 1958; Sem Of Old Cathd Ch Bonn DE 1969; VTS 1987. D. Asst The Ch Of The Redeem Beth MD 1982-1992; Asst The Ch Of The Redeem Beth MD 1973-1980; Asst S Mich And All Ang Anniston AL 1971-1972. Bronze Star Us Army 1975.

HALVERSTADT JR, Albert Nast (Colo) 1244 Detroit St, Denver CO 80206 B Cincinnati OH 3/17/1935 s Albert Nast Halverstadt & Jane. BA Ken 1957; MDiv EDS 1975. D 6/14/1975 P 12/1/1977 Bp Lyman Cunningham Ogilby. m 7/8/1988 Susan Weeks c 4. R S Barn Epis Ch Denver CO 1990-2000; Epiph Ch Dulaney Vlly Timonium MD 1977-1986; S Thos' Ch Whitemarsh Ft Washington PA 1975-1977. albertsusan101@aol.com

HALVORSEN, Douglas Carl (NJ) 28 Oakhurst Ln, Mount Laurel NJ 08054 **Evergreens Chap Moorestown NJ 1999-; Asst Trin Ch Moorestown NJ 1999-** B Lexington KY 7/14/1949 s Carl William Halvorsen & Marcella. BA Asbury Coll 1970; MS Rutgers-The St U 1975; MDiv PrTS 1976. D 4/5/1986 Bp George Phelps Mellick Belshaw P 11/16/1986 Bp Vincent King Pettit. m 8/21/1970 Cheryl Grace Pike c 2. Assoc Chr Ch New Brunswick NJ 1995-2002. Auth, "Top Twenty Ways To Beat A Dead Horse," *Open Minds*, 1999; Auth, "From My Perspective, Wall St Journ," *Natl Bus Employment Weekly*, 1998. dhalvorsen@evergreens.org

HAMBLETON, Coralie Voce (NMich) St Paul's Episcopal Church, 201 E Ridge St, Marquette MI 49855 **D S Paul's Ch Marquette MI 2007-** B Marquette MI 12/10/1954 d George Edward Voce & Lottie Isabel. BSW Nthrn Michigan U 1977. D 5/27/2007 Bp James Arthur Kelsey. m 10/27/1990 Patrick Palmer c 3. cvhamblet@hotmail.com

HAMBLIN, Jeffrey Lee (NwPa) 355 S End Ave Apt 25b, New York NY 10280 **Chr Ch Bay Ridge Brooklyn NY 2009-** B Batesville IN 7/14/1953 s David Leroy Hamblin & Opal Pearl. BS Indiana U 1975; MDiv Nash 1980; MS AUC 1990; MD AUC 1992. D 6/11/1980 P 12/20/1980 Bp William Cockburn Russell Sheridan. Ch Of S Mary The Vrgn New York NY 1993-1994; St Philips Epis Ch Waukesha WI 1993-1994; S Jn Ch/Mision San Juan Milwaukee WI 1991-1993; Dio NW Pennsylvania Erie PA 1987-1995; S Mary's Ch Erie PA 1984-1989; Dio NW Pennsylvania Erie PA 1982-1985; S Mk's Ch Erie PA 1981-1989; S Mary's Ch Erie PA 1981-1983; Chr Ch Gary IN 1980-1981. AACAP 1999; AMA 1999; Amer Psych Assn 1999; Bd Trst, Amer U of the Caribbean 1993; Soc of S Barn 1979-1981. Attending Physcian of the Year Kings Cnty Hosp, Brooklyn 2008; Soc WorkerCitizen of the Year Dio NW Pennsylvania. jeffrey.hamblin@nychhc.org

HAMBLIN, Sheldon Neilson (LI) 4301 Avenue D, Brooklyn NY 11203 **Ch Of The Nativ Brooklyn NY 2007-** B Barbados 7/10/1971 MDiv SWTS. D 6/24/2003 P 3/25/2004 Bp Orris George Walker Jr. m 1/22/2010 Lisa M Hamblin c 1. S Aug's Epis Ch Brooklyn NY 2006-2007; Dio Long Island Garden City NY 2003-2005. sheldonhamblin1@mac.com

HAMBY, Daniell C (Pa) 47 W Afton Ave, Yardley PA 19067 **Ecum Off Dio Pennsylvania Philadelphia PA 1999-; R S Andr's Ch Yardley PA 1998-** B Atlanta GA 5/8/1950 s Joseph Carl Hamby & Helen Louise. BA Presb Coll Clinton SC 1973; DMin Columbia TS 1977; MA U of Notre Dame 1990; Cert Ecumencial Inst 1993; Nash 1994; SWTS 1994. D 6/14/1994 P 12/15/1994 Bp Francis Campbell Gray. m 6/16/1973 Virginia Lee Sonnen c 2. Chair, Cler Salaries and Pensions Dio Pennsylvania Philadelphia PA 2008-2011; P-in-c Ch Of The Redeem Andalusia PA 1997-1998; Asst S Andr's Ch Yardley PA 1996-1997; P-in-c All SS Epis Ch Fallsington PA 1995-1996; Gnrl Secy The COCU Princeton NJ 1994-1998. Pres Epis Dioc Ecum and Interriligious Off 2009; Pres of the Philadelphia Theol Inst 1995. Sabbatical Grant EJ Lily Co 2010. daniellhamby@gmail.com

HAMER, Donald Lee (Ct) 240 Kenyon St, Hartford CT 06105 **Prog and Bdgt Com Dio Connecticut Hartford CT 2006-; R Trin Epis Ch Hartford CT 2004-** B Hartford CT 8/9/1950 s Frank Llewellyn Hamer & Marjorie. AB Geo 1972; JD Geo 1977; DAS Ya Berk 2000; MDiv Yale DS 2000. D 6/10/2000 Bp Andrew Donnan Smith P 12/16/2000 Bp James Elliot Curry. m 4/30/1977 Deborah Ann Metzger c 2. Asst S Mary's Epis Ch Manchester CT 2000-2003. dlhquadzilla2@yahoo.com

HAMERSLEY, Andrew C (NJ) 414 East Broad Street, Westfield NJ 07090 **R S Paul's Epis Ch Westfield NJ 2000-** B New York NY 10/8/1953 s Louis Gordon Hamersley & Elsey. U Pac 1973; BA Bos 1975; MS Bos 1979; MDiv EDS 1984. D 3/25/1985 Bp Roger W Blanchard P 4/2/1986 Bp John Bowen

Coburn. m 9/26/1981 Rosamond Hooper-Hamersley c 2. Stndg Com Dio Albany Albany NY 1995-1997; R S Andr's Epis Ch Albany NY 1988-2000; Par Of Chr Ch Andover MA 1985-1988. Soc of S Jn the Evang 1981. Winner of the Best Sermon Competition Epis Evang Fndt 1995. ahamersley@stpaulswestfield.org

HAMES, Patricia (Ct) 330 Hart St, New Britain CT 06052 **R S Mk's Ch New Britain CT 1995-** B Eynesbury Cambs UK 8/11/1945 d Allan Jeffrey Robertson & Daisy Elizabeth. BA U of Maryland 1984; MDiv Ya Berk 1988. D 6/10/1989 Bp Arthur Edward Walmsley P 5/26/1990 Bp Jeffery William Rowthorn. c 2. Chr And Epiph Ch E Haven CT 1994-1995; Dn - Danbury Dnry Dio Connecticut Hartford CT 1992-1994; Trin Ch Newtown CT 1989-1994. prevpat@aol.com

HAMILL, Allardyce Armstrong (CFla) Church of our Saviour, 200 NW 3rd St, Okeechobee FL 34972 B Plainfield NJ 9/10/1931 d John Randolph Armstrong & Myrtle Beatrice. BS Agnes Scott Coll 1953; MLS Florida St U 1978. D 12/1/2007 Bp John Wadsworth Howe. c 2. deche1702@aol.com

HAMILL, January Elizabeth (Md) 703 Peppard Dr, Bel Air MD 21014 B Ann Arbor MI 1/3/1953 d Peter VanVechten Hamill & Margot Joan. St. Jn's Coll Annapolis MD 1973; Cert Universite de Poitiers Tours FR 1973; BA Marlboro Coll 1976; MDiv Ya Berk 1980. D 4/26/1980 P 11/22/1980 Bp David Keller Leighton Sr. m 9/5/1981 Mark Francis Gatza c 2. Cn for Chr Formation Cathd Of The Incarn Baltimore MD 2001-2010; S Jas Ch Monkton MD 1995-2002; Stndg Com Dio Maryland Baltimore MD 1994-1999; Vic H Cross Ch St MD 1990-2001; R Chr Ch Forest Hill MD 1990-1993; Chair, COM Dio Maryland Baltimore MD 1988-1991; Asst St Martins-In-The-Field Ch Severna Pk MD 1984-1990; P in Charge S Jas Ch Irvington Baltimore MD 1983-1984; Chapl, Tchr S Tim's Sch Stevenson MD 1982-1983; Asst Epiph Ch Dulaney Vlly Timonium MD 1980-1982. Soc of Comp of H Cross 1980. Par of H Cross Bp's Awd Outstanding Cong Dio Maryland 1999. jhamill@thecathedral.ang.md.org

HAMILTON, Abigail W (Nwk) 681 Prospect Ave # 7052, West Orange NJ 07052 B Orange NJ 1/13/1941 BA Bryn; MDiv UTS. D 6/8/1974 P 1/5/1977 Bp George E Rath. Ch Of The H Innoc W Orange NJ 1990-2006; S Andr's Ch Newark NJ 1984-1990; Newark Epis Coop For Min & Miss Newark NJ 1979-1983. revabby@aol.com

HAMILTON, Blanche Heywood (Ct) 16 Treadwell Ave, New Milford CT 06776 B Fort Worth TX 8/27/1929 d Milton Scott Heywood & Ruth. BA Texas Wmn's U-Denton 1950; BS Texas Wmn's U-Denton 1950; MDiv UTS 1983. D 6/11/1983 Bp Arthur Edward Walmsley P 2/6/1984 Bp William Bradford Hastings. m 9/4/1950 Bill L Hamilton c 4. Gr Ch Stafford Sprg CT 1992-1994; S Jn's Ch Sandy Hook CT 1989-1991; Int Dio Connecticut Hartford CT 1988-1996; S Jn's Ch Guilford CT 1988-1989; Cur S Jn's Epis Par Waterbury CT 1983-1987. bhamilton5067@charter.net

HAMILTON, David George (Vt) 129 Cumberland Rd, Burlington VT 05408 **COM-Comm on Discernment Dio Vermont Burlington VT 2011-; R All SS' Epis Ch S Burlington VT 2009-** B Fitchburg MA 7/30/1942 s James Hamilton & Ruth Florence. BA Clark U 1964; MDiv EDS 1964; STM Andover Newton TS 1970; DMin Andover Newton TS 1973. D 6/27/1968 Bp Robert McConnell Hatch P 2/2/1969 Bp Charles F Hall. m 8/24/1969 Alida Jane Duddridge c 1. Fletcher Allen Healthcare Burlington VT 1996-2009; Ch Of S Jn The Evang Dunbarton NH 1994-1996; Dn Cntrl Convoc Dio New Hampshire Concord NH 1972-1976; R S Paul's Ch Concord NH 1970-1982; Cur S Paul's Ch Concord NH 1968-1969. dgh8@comcast.net

HAMILTON, David Hendry (Nwk) 75 Summerhill Dr, Manahawkin NJ 08050 B Newark NJ 7/5/1941 s David Hamilton & Mildred. BA Bloomfield Coll 1966; MDiv Ya Berk 1970; DMin Drew U 1975. D 6/13/1970 Bp Leland Stark P 12/19/1970 Bp George E Rath. c 2. R S Paul's Ch In Bergen Jersey City NJ 2000-2007; Trin And S Phil's Cathd Newark NJ 1998-2000; Int Chr Ch Glen Ridge NJ 1995-1997; S Paul's Epis Ch Morris Plains NJ 1970-1996. Hon Cn Trin & S Phil Cathd Dio Nwk.

HAMILTON, Gordon William (USC) 101 Woodside Dr, Gaffney SC 29340 **Chr Epis Ch Lancaster SC 2010-** B Montreal QC CA 10/13/1946 s Robert Penrose Hamilton & Grace Harkness. Edison Jr Coll Asheville-Biltmore Coll; BS U of Lethbridge 1974; MDiv U of Wstrn Ontario 1983. Trans 10/1/1995 Bp Dorsey Felix Henderson. m 5/16/1987 Carol-Lynn Parsons c 3. Chr Ch Greenville SC 2008-2009; R Ch Of The Incarn Gaffney SC 1995-2007. GORLYNN@BELLSOUTH.NET

HAMILTON SR, James Edward (Tex) 13618 Brighton Park Drive, Houston TX 77044 **R S Tim's Epis Ch Houston TX 2004-** B Toledo OH 5/21/1949 s Edward James Culver & Patricia Helene. BA U of Texas 1974; MDiv Epis TS In Kentucky 1979. D 5/13/1979 Bp Addison Hosea P 2/3/1980 Bp Calvin Onderdonk Schofield Jr. m 7/31/1976 Jan Stanuell c 2. Chapl St Lk's Epis Hosp Houston TX 2004; R H Trin Epis Ch Dickinson TX 1985-2003; R S Jn's Epis Ch Marlin TX 1980-1985; Asst S Mk The Evang Ft Lauderdale FL 1979-1980; Chapl S Mk's Epis Sch Ft Lauderdale FL 1979-1980. Auth, "The Liturg Coordntr," *The Liturg Coordntr*, Hymnary Press, 1984. BroSA 1977; CROP 1988; Mnstrl Soc 1985; TCC 1985. Ldrshp Awd for Cmnty Outreach Houston Cltn for the Homeless 1989; Pioneer Awd CROP. jehsr@mac.com

HAMILTON, James Gary (Mich) 1616 Ferris Ave, Royal Oak MI 48067 **R Trin Epis Ch Farmington Hills MI 2010-** B 9/20/1977 s Robert Hamilton & Patricia. BA Hope Coll 1999; MDIV Seabury Wstrn Theol 2008. D 3/7/2009 Bp Mark Sean Sisk P 9/24/2009 Bp Wendell Nathaniel Gibbs Jr. m 7/27/2002 Elizabeth Rogus. Assoc S Jn's Ch Royal Oak MI 2009. jamesgaryhamilton@hotmail.com

HAMILTON, Jamie Lynn (NH) 20 Main St, Exeter NH 03833 **P-in-c Emm Ch Jaffrey NH 1996-** B San Rafael CA 9/13/1955 d James Cahaley Hamilton & Frankie Lorraine. BA Cntrl Washington U 1977; MDiv UTS 1985. D 6/8/1991 P 12/14/1991 Bp Richard Frank Grein. c 2. P Ch Of The Heav Rest New York NY 1992-1995. jhamilton@exeter.edu

HAMILTON, John Marshall (NY) 1 Hudson St., Yonkers NY 10701 **P-in-c S Jn's Ch Getty Sq Yonkers NY 2007-** B Meridan MS 5/22/1962 s Joseph Clay Hamilton & Mary Faye. BA Rhodes Coll 1984; BA Oxf 1989; MPA U of Memphis 1997; MDiv GTS 2004. D 6/5/2004 P 2/5/2005 Bp J(ohn) Neil Alexander. Int Ch Of The Redeem Astoria NY 2006-2007; Cur Gr Ch Newark NJ 2004-2006. jhnmhmltn@yahoo.com

HAMILTON, Lisa B (SwFla) 626 Hibiscus Dr, Venice FL 34285 **Guardian Hospice Venice FL 2009-** B Bloomington IN 3/1/1959 d William Edward Belcher & Edna Maxine. Harlaxton Coll GB 1978; BA DePauw U 1980; MA Indiana U 1983; MA Indiana U 1987; MDiv Ya Berk 1995; STM Ya Berk 1996. D 12/11/1999 Bp Robert William Duncan P 3/17/2001 Bp Andrew Donnan Smith. m 10/13/2007 James Lee Grubbs c 1. Epis Ch Cntr New York NY 2008-2009; Assoc to R Chr Ch Greenwich CT 2000-2004. Auth, "Wisdom from the Middle Ages for Middle-aged Wmn," Morehouse, 2007; Auth, "Prayers to the God of My Life: Psalms for Morning and Evening," Morehouse, 2003; Auth, "For Those We Love and See No Longer: Daily Off for Times of Grief," Paraclete Press, 2001; Auth, "The Gospel According to Fred: A Visit w Mister Rogers," *Chr Century*, 1996; Auth, "One of the Five-Thousand," *Journ of Biblic Storytelling*, 1995; Auth, "Feeding the Five Thousand," *Journ of Narrative Homil*, 1994; Auth, "arts for Chld," *Cobblestone, Cricket, and Humpty Dumpty*, 1987. Pres, Alum Assoc., Berkeley Div. Sch. at Yale 2002; Soc of S Marg 1997. Rel and the Arts Awd Yale DS New Haven CT 1995; Preaching Excellence Conf Preaching Excellence Prog 1994. lisabhamilton@aol.com

HAMILTON, Michael Pollock (WA) 3111 44th St Nw, Washington DC 20016 B Belfast Northern Ireland 1/28/1927 s Hugh Pollock Hamilton & Blanche Rosa. BA U Tor 1951; MDiv VTS 1955. D 6/3/1955 Bp Frederick D Goodwin P 12/1/1955 Bp Henry W Hobson. m 6/13/1981 Eleanore Raven c 2. Int S Jas Ch Potomac MD 1998-1999; Cn Cathd of St Ptr & St Paul Washington DC 1964-1993; Chapl Fac & Stdts Dio Los Angeles Los Angeles CA 1958-1964; Cur Ch Of The Adv Cincinnati OH 1955-1958. Ed, *A Hospice Handbk-New Way to Care for Dying*, Eerdhams, 1986; Ed, *Amer Character & Frgn Plcy*, Eerdhams, 1986; Ed, *To Avoid Catastrophe: A Study in Future Nuclear Plcy*, Eerdhams, 1978; Ed, *Ord of Wmn-Pro & Con*, Morehouse Pub, 1975; Ed, *Chrsmtc Mvmt-Confusion or Blessing?*, Eerdhams, 1974; Ed, *New Genetics & Future of Man*, Eerdhams, 1972; Ed, *This Little Planet*, Scribner's, 1967; Ed, *Vietnam War: Ch Perspective*, Eerdhams, 1967. hamiltonraven18@verizon.net

HAMILTON, Paul Edward Connell (LI) 145-23 19th Ave, Whitestone NY 11357 B Sharon PA 9/30/1945 s Russell Samuel Hamilton & Alice Elizabeth. BA Youngstown St U 1967; Kings Coll London - Lon 1968; MDiv GTS 1971; Chr TS 1978; MS Yeshiva U 1992; LIU 1996. D 7/11/1971 P 3/25/1972 Bp William Crittenden. c 1. S Paul's Ch Coll Point NY 1999-2009; R S Mary's Ch Brooklyn NY 1985-1996; Emm Epis Ch Of Sheepshead Bay Brooklyn NY 1983; Asst S Mart's Ch New York NY 1980-1981; Assoc Ch Of The Intsn New York NY 1976-1979; Asst S Phil's Ch New York NY 1973-1976; Asst All Ang' Ch New York NY 1971-1973. DD Chr Sem 1989; Hon KY Colonel 1974. barndoor349@aol.com

HAMILTON, Pettigrew Verner (Neb) 263 Lake Ridge Rd, Kerrville TX 78028 **Died 5/3/2010** B Spartanburg,SC 12/1/1941 s John Andrew Hamilton & Elizabeth Pettigrew. BA U of So Carolina 1965; MDiv VTS 1969; Advncd CPE 1981. D 6/28/1969 P 1/1/1970 Bp Gray Temple. c 2. padre.pettigrew@gmail.com

HAMILTON, Reid Henry (Mich) 4657 Dexter Ann Arbor Road, Ann Arbor MI 48103 **Cbury Hse Ann Arbor MI 2004-** B Joplin MO 11/19/1956 s Eugene Henry Hamilton & Mary Elizabeth. BA Westminster Coll 1978; JD Van 1981; MDiv Candler TS Emory U 1998. D 6/6/1998 Bp Frank Kellogg Allan P 12/7/1998 Bp John Clark Buchanan. m 6/11/1987 Debra K Garner c 2. S Phil's Epis Ch Akron OH 2004; R Chr Epis Ch Kent OH 2001-2004; Secy Dio W Missouri Kansas City MO 1999-2001; Dio W Missouri Kansas City MO 1999; Asst R S Paul's Ch Kansas City MO 1998-2001. Auth, "Better Get It In Your Soul: What Liturgists Can Learn from Jazz," Ch Pub, 2008. rhhamilt@umich.edu

HAMILTON, Robert Earl (NC) 1200 N Elm St, Greensboro NC 27401 **Asst S Andr's Ch Greensboro NC 1989-** B Olean NY 7/3/1945 s Howard Earl Hamilton & Jane W. BA High Point U 1967; BD VTS 1970; CPE Duke 1976; CPE Delaware St Hosp DE 1977. D 6/29/1970 P 5/1/1971 Bp David Shepherd

Rose. m 7/26/1981 Lynn Hamilton c 3. P-in-c Ch Of The Mssh Mayodan NC 1981-1989; H Trin Ch Wilmington DE 1977; Dio No Carolina Raleigh NC 1975-1976; S Mk's Epis Ch Roxboro NC 1975-1976; S Barn Epis Ch Richmond VA 1973-1975; Asst S Jn's Ch Hampton VA 1970-1973. AEHC 1978; ACPE 1979; Assn for Psychol Type 1989; Cert Chapl Assn Prof Chapl; No Carolina Chapl Assn 1980. Outstanding St Ldr Awd Assn of Profsnl Chapl 1993. bob.hamilton@mosescone.com

HAMILTON, Roger John (CFla) 2499 N Westmoreland Dr, Orlando FL 32804 **R S Mich's Ch Orlando FL 1998-** B Trenton NJ 3/24/1949 s George Hamilton & Marie. BA Trenton St Coll 1971; MDiv PDS 1974. D 4/27/1974 P 11/23/1974 Bp Albert Wiencke Van Duzer. m 4/25/1970 Karen Hoover c 2. R Chr Ch Somers Point NJ 1980-1998; Cur Chr Ch In Woodbury Woodbury NJ 1975-1980; Cur S Ptr's Ch Freehold NJ 1974-1975. OHC, Assoc 1983. Divemaster PADI 1987. rgrhamilton@gmail.com

HAMILTON, Terrell Eugene (EpisSanJ) 401 N Marilyn Ave, Wenatchee WA 98801 B Santa Ana CA 1/26/1945 s Terrell D Hamilton & Mabel Valina. BA California St U 1976; MDiv Fuller TS 1979. D 12/16/1979 P 12/1/1980 Bp Victor Manuel Rivera. m 12/30/1967 Claudia Mary Davis. R S Fran Epis Ch Fair Oaks CA 2002-2004; Chapl Off Of Bsh For ArmdF New York NY 1985-2001; Vic Chr Ch Lemoore CA 1980-1985; Cur S Paul's Epis Ch Visalia CA 1979-1980.

HAMILTON, William Edward (SeFla) 1728 13th Ave N, Lake Worth FL 33460 B Philadelphia PA 12/16/1940 s Frederick Dunham Hamilton & Mildred Marian. LTh Epis TS In Kentucky 1976; VTS 1999. D 5/16/1976 P 12/1/1977 Bp Addison Hosea. m 9/16/1960 Charlotte Massey c 3. Curs Dio SE Florida Miami FL 2001-2002; Vic Ch Of S Jn Lake Worth FL 1988-1991; R S Andr's Ch Lake Worth FL 1986-2005; S Mart's Epis Ch Pompano Bch FL 1984-1986; All SS Ch Cold Sprg KY 1982-1984; S Davids Ch Pikeville KY 1978-1982; Asst Ch S Mich The Archangel Lexington KY 1976-1977. Mssn Cleric of the Year Dio Lexington 1983. weham1@bellsouth.net

HAMILTON, W Michael (Mass) 15 Call St, North Billerica MA 01862 B Boston MA 7/27/1960 s Walter Melbourne Hamilton & Margaret Mary. AS Nthrn Essex Cmnty Coll Haverill MA 1981; BS U Of Rhode Island Kingston RI 1991. D 6/2/2007 Bp M(arvil) Thomas Shaw III. m 7/30/2004 Daniel R Collier c 2. michael.hamilton@comcast.net

HAMLIN, Lonalee Ann (EO) 1712 Sw 17th St, Redmond OR 97756 **Loc D S Alb's Epis Ch Redmond OR 1997-** B Portland OR 8/29/1929 BA OR SU 1962. D 10/31/1996 Bp Rustin Ray Kimsey. laph@bendnet.com

HAMLIN, Richard Lee (SeFla) 14260 Old Cutler Rd, Miami FL 33158 B Rochester NY 2/5/1948 s Roy Charles Hamlin & Florence Elizabeth. BA SUNY 1970; MA SUNY 1972; MDiv EDS 1975. D 6/29/1975 P 4/1/1976 Bp Robert Rae Spears Jr. m 8/21/1976 Stephanie P Pentecost c 3. R S Andr's Epis Ch Palmetto Bay FL 1999-2006; R Ch Of The Resurr Oswego NY 1988-1999; R S Paul's Ch Troy NY 1982-1988; Asst Min S Ptr's Ch Albany NY 1980-1982; Dio Rochester Rochester NY 1975-1980. rlhmiami@aol.com

HAMLIN, W Richard (Mich) 6500 Amwood Dr, Lansing MI 48911 **Bp's Advsry Com for Total Mnstry Dio Michigan Detroit MI 2011-; Stndg Com Dio Michigan Detroit MI 2011-; Bd Trst Bex Columbus OH 2010-; Alt Dep to GC Dio Michigan Detroit MI 2010-; Dn, Capital Dnry Dio Michigan Detroit MI 2010-; Whitaker Inst Advsry Com Dio Michigan Detroit MI 2009-; R S Mich's Epis Ch Lansing MI 2004-** B Syracuse NY 8/24/1946 s Walter Albert Hamlin & Eleanor Ressie. BA Hob 1968; MA U Roch 1971; PhD U Roch 1981; MDiv Bex 1992. D 8/10/1991 P 4/8/1992 Bp William George Burrill. m 6/27/1970 Claudia W Webb c 3. Stndg Com Pres Dio Michigan Detroit MI 2008-2009; Stndg Com Dio Michigan Detroit MI 2005-2009; Chapl Dio Cntrl New York Syracuse NY 2004; Trin Epis Ch Canastota NY 1992-2004; S Jn's Epis Ch Oneida NY 1992-2003. Assoc, SSM 1998; TENS 2000. wrhamlin@juno.com

HAMLYN, Robert Cornelius (NY) 127 Fulton Ave Apt J1, Poughkeepsie NY 12603 **Assoc S Ptr's Epis Ch Peekskill NY 1991-** B Palmer NE 2/17/1929 s Robert P Hamlyn & Helen. BA Laf 1950; STB GTS 1953; MDiv GTS 1968. D 6/13/1953 P 12/19/1953 Bp Benjamin M Washburn. m 1/16/1954 Klara V Raetz c 3. Fdn For Rel & Mntl Hlth Briarcliff Manor NY 1964-1980; Asst to R Gr Epis Ch New York NY 1959-1961. Auth, "Fact Finders Journey to Europe," *Journ of Rel & Hlth*. Dplma AAPC 1968-2006. hamlynr@verizon.net

HAMM, William Chapman (WMich) 920 Walcott St Sw, Wyoming MI 49509 **Dioc Supply P Dio Wstrn Michigan Kalamazoo MI 2004-; Dioc Supply P Dio Wstrn Michigan Kalamazoo MI 2004-** B Hartford CT 8/1/1934 s William Conrad Hamm & Martha Chapman. MDiv Bex 1958; BA MI SU 1962. D 6/29/1962 Bp Robert Lionne DeWitt P 1/26/1963 Bp Archie H Crowley. m 9/3/1955 Deanna M Best c 5. Int P S Phil's Epis Ch Grand Rapids MI 2001-2004; Int P The Epis Ch Of The Epiph So Haven MI 1994-1995; S Lk's Par Kalamazoo MI 1993-1994; Int S Alb's Mssn Muskegon MI 1991-1992; Cathd Par Of Chr The King Portage MI 1991; S Mich's Ch Grand Rapids MI 1987-1990; R Trin Ch Niles MI 1982-1986; Trin Ch Ennis MT 1982; Vic S Paul's Ch Virginia City MT 1977-1982; Vic Chr Ch Sheridan MT 1977-1981; Nativ Cmnty Epis Ch Holly MI 1966-1977; Vic S Mk's Epis Ch Bridgeport MI 1962-1966. chapbill@comcast.net

HAMMATT JR, Edward Augustus (SeFla) 16330 Sw 80th Ave, Miami FL 33157 **D Dio SE Florida Miami FL 1993-** B Baton Rouge LA 4/20/1939 s Edward Augustus Hammatt & Ida Maurie. BS LSU 1963. D 12/20/1993 Bp Calvin Onderdonk Schofield Jr. m 9/6/1975 Judith Drake Jenkins c 2. ehammatt@mhhcpa.com

HAMMETT, Robert Lee (Mass) P.O. Box 224, Oak Bluff MA 02557 B Brooklyn NY 3/29/1929 s John Reynolds Hammett & Margaret Mahin. BA Wesl 1951; MDiv VTS 1954. D 6/9/1954 P 1/1/1955 Bp Walter H Gray. m 9/28/1957 Sarah V Vickery c 3. R S Jn's Ch Newtonville MA 1981-1993; S Geo's Ch Middlebury CT 1975-1981; R Chr Ch Sharon CT 1957-1966.

HAMMON, LeRoy Ralph (Ore) 820 Berwick Ct, Lake Oswego OR 97034 B 10/17/1937 Mdiv Epis TS of the SW 2003. D 6/25/2003 Bp Robert Louis Ladehoff P 1/11/2004 Bp Johncy Itty. m 1/16/1995 Ina L Alumbaugh c 2. Int CBO Dio Oregon Portland OR 2008; Asst P Chr Ch Par Lake Oswego OR 2004-2008. lhammon523@comcast.net

HAMMOND, Blaine Randol (ECR) PO Box 293, Ben Lomond CA 95005 **S Andr's Ch Ben Lomond CA 2009-** B Lincoln NE 10/30/1946 s Blaine Gibson Hammond & Mary Eloise. BA U of Washington 1979; MDiv Iliff TS 1982; CAS CDSP 1988. D 6/11/1988 P 1/28/1989 Bp William Carl Frey. m 9/18/1965 Elizabeth Dianne Forbes c 3. Vic S Ptr's Ch Seaview WA 1996-2008; Cur Chr's Epis Ch Castle Rock CO 1989-1991. Auth, "Donatism For Today," *LivCh*, 2000; Auth, "Peninsula Ch Cntr Celebrates 25 Years Of Joint Mnstry," *The Epis Voice*, 1999; Auth, "Is God Truly Loving?," *The Chr Mnstry*, 1998; Auth, "The Psychol Of Rel In Mnstry (By H Newton Malony)," *The Chr Mnstry*, 1997; Auth, "Hiding In Plain Sight," *The Chr Mnstry*, 1997. blainerh@gmail.com

HAMMOND, Constance Ann (Ore) 4045 S.E. Pine St., Portland OR 97214 **Asst All SS Ch Portland OR 2002-** B Salem OR 6/23/1937 d William Harvey Hammond & Constance Maxine. BS U of Oregon 1959; Med U of Oregon 1962; CAS Harv 1980; MDiv Harvard DS 1985; D Min SFTS 2005. D 6/4/1986 Bp John Bowen Coburn P 5/1/1987 Bp David Elliot Johnson. Int S Andr's Epis Ch Aberdeen WA 2000-2002; Int S Paul's Ch Walla Walla WA 1999-2000; S Steph's Epis Par Portland OR 1990-1998; The Ch Of The Gd Shpd Acton MA 1989-1990; Old No Chr Ch Boston MA 1987-1989; Gr Ch Newton MA 1986-1987. Auth, "Shalom/Salaaw/Peace A Liberation Theol of Hope," 2008. Soc Of S Jn The Evang 1984. Refugee Immigration Mnstry Constance Hammond Awd Refuge Immigration Mnstry, EDS 1996; Billings Prize Harvard DS Cambridge MA 1985; Potter Fllshp U Hosp 1985. revcah@earthlink.net

HAMMOND, D(avid) (Cal) 11 Mesa Ave, Mill Valley CA 94941 **Vol Ch Of The Nativ San Rafael CA 1999-** B Brandon MT CA 12/13/1923 s Stephen Reginald Hammond & Hattie Wilhelmina. BA U CA 1949; BD EDS 1952. D 6/23/1952 P 2/19/1953 Bp Francis E I Bloy. m 8/3/1947 Muriel Albert c 3. Stndg Com Dio California San Francisco CA 1985-1990; Alt Dep GC Dio California San Francisco CA 1979-1982; Elctn Process Com Dio California San Francisco CA 1978-1979; Chair Com Resolutns Dio California San Francisco CA 1975-1989; R Ch Of Our Sav Mill Vlly CA 1957-1989; Vic S Barth's Mssn Pico Rivera CA 1952-1957. murmur1@earthlink.net

HAMMOND, Henry Latane (Md) 6705 Maxalea Rd, Baltimore MD 21239 B Baltimore MD 10/31/1941 s W Hollyday Hammond & Emma Cauthorne. BA Br 1963; MDiv EDS 1967; MA Emory U 1968. D 10/27/1968 P 12/1/1969 Bp Horace W B Donegan. m Leigh Price Hammond c 2. Asst Memi Ch Baltimore MD 1985-1993; Asst S Mich And All Ang Ch Baltimore MD 1980-1985; Asst Ch Of The H Nativ Baltimore MD 1977-1978; S Barn Epis Ch Sykesville MD 1974-1977; R Gr Epis Ch Port Jervis NY 1970-1974; Asst S Mich's Ch New York NY 1969-1970; Vic Trin Ch Richlands VA 1968-1969. henrylhammond@verizon.net

HAMMOND, James Allen (Va) 5856 Old Dominion Ct, Warrenton VA 20187 **Ret P Dio Virginia Richmond VA 2008-** B Baltimore MD 10/5/1944 s William Hollyday Hammond & Emma Cauthorne. BA U of Maryland 1968; MDiv SWTS 1972. D 6/6/1972 P 2/2/1973 Bp David Keller Leighton Sr. m 5/8/1982 Gina Bronkie c 1. P-in-c Chr Epis Ch Brandy Sta VA 1995-2008; R S Paul's Par Kent Chestertown MD 1995; R S Lk's Ch Remington VA 1993-2008; Assoc Epiph Epis Ch Odenton MD 1992-1993; Assoc Epiph Ch Dulaney Vlly Timonium MD 1989-1992; Dn Dio Maryland Baltimore MD 1988-1992; R S Dav's Epis Ch Topeka KS 1986-1988; R H Trin Ch Churchville MD 1981-1986; Assoc Calv Epis Ch Williamsville NY 1978-1981; Asst Ch Of The Mssh Baltimore MD 1972-1973. Auth, "Sine Nomine," *Leaven*, 1993; Auth, "No Longer Immune: A Counslr's Guide to AIDS, Chapt 12," *Amer Assn of Counslg and Dvlpmt*, 1989; Auth, "Strive to Thrive," *LivCh*, 1986; Auth, "Dissolution: Theol, Pragmatism & Morality," *Leaven*, 1983; Auth, "Rel Manifestations," *Hse*, 1978; Auth, "Who Says You Can Teach Ethics," *CRIS Nwsltr*, 1977; Auth, "Early Amer Evang," *Hse*, 1975. Cramer Awd SWTS 1969; Anderson Awd SWTS Evanston IL 1969. hammond.jim@gmail.com

HAMMOND, Jeffrey Benjamin (WTex) 14526 Spaulding Dr, Corpus Christi TX 78410 B Chattanooga TN 8/31/1960 BA U CA; MA Epis TS of The SW 1994; MDiv STUSo 2003. D 6/5/2003 Bp Robert Boyd Hibbs P 1/6/2004 Bp James Edward Folts. m 10/18/1997 Barclay Livingston Hammond c 2. Vic S Andr's Epis Ch Corpus Christi TX 2003-2009. jeff@hammond.net

HAMMOND, Marion Junior (Colo) 9 Chusco Rd, Santa Fe NM 87508 B Gardner KS 8/30/1927 s Marion Everett Hammond & Rose Etta. BA U Denv 1948; MDiv Ya Berk 1951. D 4/7/1951 Bp Austin Pardue P 10/7/1951 Bp Harold L Bowen. m 8/25/1950 Opal Johnson c 5. Sch Bd Dio Colorado Denver CO 1977-1983; R S Thos Epis Ch Denver CO 1963-1988; R S Barn Of The Vlly Cortez CO 1951-1963; Vic S Paul's Ch Mancos CO 1951-1963. maropalhammond@peoplepc.com

HAMMONDS, Joanie (Ala) 755 Plantation Dr, Selma AL 36701 B Mobile AL 10/14/1957 d Frederick Levi Hall & Vivian Viola. D 10/30/2004 Bp Henry Nutt Parsley Jr. m 1/1/1981 James H Hammonds c 2.

HAMNER IV, James Edward (At) 3110-A Ashford Dunwoody Rd Ne, Atlanta GA 30319 **S Mart's Epis Sch Atlanta GA 2000-** B Norfolk VA 12/20/1957 s James Edward Hamner & Joan Gaston. BA W&L 1980; MDiv STUSo 1984; MA Oxf 1989; PhD Oxf 1991. D 6/9/1984 Bp John Thomas Walker P 3/1/1985 Bp James Barrow Brown. m 4/6/2007 Laurie Roberts c 3. Epis HS Baton Rouge LA 1992-2000; S Paul's Ch New Orleans LA 1991-1992; Asst R S Jas Epis Ch Baton Rouge LA 1984-1987. AAR 1992; CAT 1992; SAES Exec Bd 1992-2000; SBL 1992. Presidential Schlr Distinguished Tchr White Hse Cmsn on Presidential Scholars 1997. jhamner@stmartinschool.org

HAMNER, Robert M (SwVa) 4606 Rosecrest Rd, Roanoke VA 24018 B San Antonio TX 7/25/1927 s John Taylor Hamner & Gladys. BA Baylor U 1948; ThM Sthrn Bapt TS Louisville KY 1951; Austin Presb TS 1957. D 11/5/2003 P 5/6/2004 Bp Frank Neff Powell. m 6/2/1959 Donna Sue Meriwether c 2. Pstr Assoc / Asst R S Jn's Ch Roanoke VA 2002-2008. robtham1@cox.net

HAMP, Gary (Mo) 245 Rose Bud Ct, Traverse City MI 49696 B Lansing MI 12/26/1943 s Charles Donald Hamp & Genevieve Arlene. BS Ferris St U 1970; MDiv GTS 1984; STM GTS 1985; PhD SFTU 2003. D 6/30/1984 Bp Henry Irving Mayson P 2/1/1985 Bp Henry Boyd Hucles III. m 12/14/1979 Patricia Powell. Int S Lk's Par Kalamazoo MI 2008-2009; Int S Mk The Evang Ft Lauderdale FL 2005-2008; Int Emm Epis Ch Webster Groves MO 2001-2003; Int S Jas Epis Ch Birmingham MI 2000-2001; Int S Mich & S Geo Clayton MO 1997-2000; Int Gr Epis Ch Port Huron MI 1996-1997; Int Trin Epis Ch Bay City MI 1994-1996; R S Jn's Epis Ch Odessa TX 1990-1994; R Chr Epis Ch Owosso MI 1985-1990; S Lk's Ch Forest Hills NY 1984-1985. gdhamp@gmail.com

HAMPSHIRE, George Jay (WLa) 302 Raiders Rd, Ville Platte LA 70586 **Died 1/25/2010** B Swissvale PA 9/15/1932 s Arch K Hampshire & Nola Mabel. BA Mt Un Coll 1956; BD Lancaster TS 1960; VTS 1963. D 6/29/1963 P 6/1/1964 Bp Richard Henry Baker. c 2.

HAMPSON JR, James Eugene (SC) 903 Hays St, Tallahassee FL 32301 B Shreveport LA 2/2/1937 s James Eugene Hampson & Oretus Amanda. BA U of Oklahoma 1959; BD EDS 1962; Cert 1999. D 6/26/1962 P 5/1/1963 Bp Girault M Jones. m 12/22/1957 Sarah Elizabeth Oden c 3. Assoc R S Jn's Epis Ch Tallahassee FL 2001-2005; Int S Fran Ch Greensboro NC 1999-2000; TESM Ambridge PA 1988-1996; R S Phil's Ch Charleston SC 1987-1999; S Jn's Ch Huntingdon Vlly PA 1977-1987; TESM Ambridge PA 1975-1980; Chr Ch So Hamilton MA 1968-1977. Auth, "Amer Signs Of Hope". jhampson02@comcast.net

HAMPTON, Carol McDonald (Okla) 1414 N Hudson Ave, Oklahoma City OK 73103 B Oklahoma City OK 9/18/1935 d Denzil Vincent McDonald & Mildred Juanita. BA U of Oklahoma 1957; MA U of Oklahoma 1973; PhD U of Oklahoma 1984; CTh Epis TS of The SW 1998; MDiv Phillips TS 1999. D 6/26/1999 P 12/19/1999 Bp Robert Manning Moody. m 2/22/1958 James Wilburn Hampton c 4. Cur S Paul's Cathd Oklahoma City OK 1999-2001. Ed, *First Peoples Theol Journ*. AltGld (Natl) 2007; Indigenous Theol Trng Inst Bd 1999. champton@stpaulsokc.org

HAMPTON, Cynthia Marie (SO) 410 Torrence Ct, Cincinnati OH 45202 B Louisville KY 1/17/1958 d Donald Richard Hampton & Mary Edward. BA Agnes Scott Coll 1980; PhD NWU 1984; MDiv Ya Berk 1996. D 6/29/1996 Bp Herbert Thompson Jr P 4/12/1997 Bp Kenneth Lester Price. Hyde Pk Hlth Cntr Cincinnati OH 2007-2009; Epis Ret Hms Deupree Hlth Cmnty Cincinnati OH 2000-2007; Dio Sthrn Ohio Cincinnati OH 1999; Supply Chap Of The Nativ Cincinnati OH 1998-2000; Ch Of The Adv Cincinnati OH 1997-1998; S Jn's Epis Ch Lancaster OH 1996-1997. Auth, "Pleasure Knowledge & Being: Analysis Of Plato'S Philebus," SUNY Press, 1990. champton@hydeparkhealthcenter.com

HAMPTON, Roger Keith (Los) Po Box 260304, Corpus Christi TX 78426 B Los Angeles CA 5/12/1947 s Gordon F Hampton & Ruth Virginia. Emory U 1967; BA Stan 1970; PSR 1973; Tubingen U Tubingen DE 1973; MDiv CDSP 1975. D 6/21/1975 P 2/1/1976 Bp Robert C Rusack. m 1/25/1981 Nohemi Calvillo c 1. St Dunstans Epis Ch Moreno Vlly CA 1986; S Lk's Mssn Fontana CA 1984-1986; Vic All SS Epis Ch Brawley CA 1982-1983; St Marks Mssn Holtville CA 1982-1983; Vic Ch Of The H Comm Gardena CA 1979-1982; Ch Of Our Sav Par San Gabr CA 1975-1978. Auth, "A Pilgrims Progress". Phi Beta Kappa.

✠ **HAMPTON, Rt Rev Sanford Zangwill Kaye** (Oly) 2211 Cascade Ct, Anacortes WA 98221 B Passaic NJ 4/11/1935 s Sanford Zangwill Kaye & Renee Adel. BS NWU 1956; MDiv SWTS 1966. D 6/11/1966 Bp James Winchester Montgomery P 12/17/1966 Bp Gerald Francis Burrill Con 4/5/1989 for Minn. m 12/18/1953 Marilynn Prage c 4. Asstg Bp Dio Oregon Portland OR 2008-2010; Asstg Bp Dio Olympia Seattle WA 1996-2004; Asstg Bp Dio Olympia Seattle WA 1996-2004; Bp Suffr Dio Minnesota Minneapolis MN 1989-1996; Stndg Com Dio Washington Washington DC 1986-1988; Chair, Dioc Cmsn on Liturg & Mus Dio Washington Washington DC 1985-1988; Adj Fac VTS Alexandria VA 1984-1988; Initiatory Rites T/F Dio Washington Washington DC 1984-1985; Long-R Plnng Com Dio Washington Washington DC 1983-1985; Cler Assn Bd Dio Washington Washington DC 1982-1985; R S Barn Epis Ch Temple Hills MD 1980-1989; R S Ptr's Ch La Grande OR 1977-1980; Vic S Fran Ch Moab UT 1972-1977; R S Jas Epis Ch Midvale UT 1967-1972; Cur The Ch Of S Jn The Evang Flossmoor IL 1966-1967. EPF 2000. DD SWTS Evanston IL 1990. bishop838@comcast.net

HAN, Heewoo Daniel (Va) 4060 Championship Dr, Annandale VA 22003 B Sangjoo S.Korea 12/29/1979 s Valentine S Han & Theresa Kyung-Hae. Wheaton Coll 2002; Yale DS 2007. D 6/16/2007 Bp Peter James Lee P 12/17/2007 Bp David Colin Jones. heewoo.han@allsouls.org

HAN, Valentine S (Va) 4060 Championship Dr, Annandale VA 22003 **H Cross Korean Epis Ch Annandale VA 2000-** B Sachun KR 1/13/1951 s Yee-Sun Han & U-Shun. BA Pusan Natl U Pusan Kr 1976; MDiv S Mich's Sem 1979. Trans from Anglican Church Of Korea 2/1/2000 Bp D L Joseph. m 5/26/1979 Theresa Kyung-Hae Lee c 2. Dio Virginia Richmond VA 1999-2000. valentinehan@gmail.com

HANCHEY, Howard (SVa) 256 Long View Dr, Lancaster VA 22503 **Int R Wicomico Par Ch Wicomico Ch VA 2011-** B Richmond VA 2/17/1941 s Daniel Hemmons Hanchey & Louise. VPI 1961; BA U NC 1963; BD VTS 1967; DMin UTS Richmond VA 1974; CTh S Geo's Coll Jerusalem IL 1991. D 7/10/1967 P 7/10/1968 Bp Robert Fisher Gibson Jr. m 8/17/1963 Anne Ewing Summers c 2. Int R Trin Ch Portsmouth VA 2007-2009; Int R Gr Ch Kilmarnock VA 2005-2006; Int R Old Donation Ch Virginia Bch VA 2003-2004; Arthur Lee Kinsolving Prof Pstr Theol VTS Alexandria VA 1978-2001; R S Andr's Ch Meriden CT 1976-1978; Assoc R Estrn Shore Chap Virginia Bch VA 1972-1976; Asst to Jack Spong S Paul's Ch Richmond VA 1970-1972; R Emm Epis Ch (Piedmont Par) Delaplane VA 1967-1969; Piedmont Ch Madison VA 1967-1969. Auth, "From Survival To Celebration: Ldrshp," Cowley, 1992; Auth, "Ch Growth and the Power of Evang," Cowley, 1990; Auth, "CE Made Easy," Morehouse, 1989; Auth, "Creative CE," Morehouse, 1985; Contrib, "Par Based CPE: A Sampling Of Prog (Homer Bain," Texas Med Cntr, 1974. AAPC - Mem 1972-2000; ACPE - Supvsr 1969; Assn Of Profsnl Chapl - Fell 1972-2000; EvangES 1977. hhanchey@aol.com

HANCKEL, Ellen Jervey (SwVa) 1013 Oakwood Ct, Martinsville VA 24112 B CharlestonSC 7/1/1949 d Richard White Hanckel & Ruth. BA Tul 1971; Med Clemson U 1974; MA U of So Carolina 1982; MDiv STUSo 1995; DMin STUSo 2003. D 6/10/1995 P 5/25/1996 Bp Dorsey Felix Henderson. m 1/25/1997 Robert Allan Scott Derks c 3. R Chr Ch Martinsville VA 2004-2011; Assoc Dio No Carolina Raleigh NC 2004; Assoc S Jn's Epis Ch Charlotte NC 2002-2004; Asst S Mary's Ch Columbia SC 1997-2002; Cur S Dav's Epis Ch Columbia SC 1995-1997. Auth, "For Whom The Bell Tolls," *Sewanee Theol Revs*, 1998. Sis Of S Mary 1997. ehanckel@vzw.blackberry.net

HANCOCK, Arthur B (Eau) 13470 2nd St, Cable WI 54821 **S Andr's Ch Ashland WI 2010-; R Ch Of The Ascen Hayward WI 2005-** B Nashville TN 8/27/1961 s Arthur Stewart Hancock & Charlotte Sutton. MA U So 1984; MDiv VTS 1990. D 7/14/1990 P 5/5/1991 Bp George Lazenby Reynolds Jr. m 8/23/1995 Katherine Leigh Hancock. S Clem's Epis Ch Clemmons NC 1993; S Paul's Ch Franklin TN 1990-1993. art@crosswoods.com

HANCOCK, Bayard (NH) 96 Hogback Rd, Campton NH 03223 B Nutley NJ 3/2/1924 s John Tierbout Hancock & Margery. BA Hob 1949; STM Ya Berk 1952, U of Rhode Island 1960; Fllshp Coll of Preachers 1969. D 6/15/1952 P 12/20/1952 Bp Benjamin M Washburn. m 3/25/1945 Phyllis Riess c 1. Chair Dioc Cmncatns Cmsn Dio New Hampshire Concord NH 1982-1988; Dep Gc Dio New Hampshire Concord NH 1979-1985; Dn Lakes Reg Convoc Dio New Hampshire Concord NH 1974-1976; Dioc Coun Dio New Hampshire Concord NH 1963-1988; Chair Dept Csr Dio New Hampshire Concord NH 1963-1973; Ch Of The H Sprt Plymouth NH 1960-1990; R S Mk's Ch Ashland NH 1960-1964; Vic S Jn The Div Ch Saunderstown RI 1956-1960; Vic Ch Of The Epiph Allendale NJ 1952-1956. Fllshp Coll Of Preachers Washington DC 1969; Phi Beta Kappa. bayardhancocx@cyberportal.net

HANCOCK, Edward James (SC) 1895 Waters Edge Dr, Summerton SC 29148 B Cleveland OH 2/13/1932 s Harold Carr Hancock & Hazel Mae. BS Van 1959. D 9/4/1999 Bp Edward Lloyd Salmon Jr. m 10/10/1959 Frances Furman Jordan. D The Ch Of The Epiph Eutawville SC 2000-2004.

H

HANCOCK, John Julian (Los) 4820 W Slauson Ave Apt 12, Los Angeles CA 90056 **Asstg Min S Bede's Epis Ch Los Angeles CA 1989-** B Aberdeen SD 8/4/1919 s Morris Windfield Hancock & Rae. Menlo Sch & Jr Coll 1939; BA U Pac 1942; Pepperdine U 1971; Loyola U 1972; U CA 1975. D 3/11/1946 P 2/9/1947 Bp Sumner Walters. m 3/15/1979 Dorothy Hancock c 1. Par Of Recon Los Angeles CA 1979-1985; R H Nativ Par Los Angeles CA 1973-1975; Vic All SS Ch Colorado City TX 1969-1970; Vic S Steph's Ch Sweetwater TX 1969-1970; Vic Gd Shpd Epis Ch Susanville CA 1961-1969; Excoun Epis Dio San Joaquin Modesto CA 1957-1961; R Epis Ch Of The Sav Hanford CA 1956-1961; Vic S Alb's Epis Ch Tillamook OR 1947-1956; Cur S Mk's Epis Par Medford OR 1946-1947. "arts Dioc mag; Chr-Ethical Political arts To Newspapers And Politicians; Occasional Nwspr Sermons.," 2003. Pres Susanville Mnstrl Assn 1964.

HANCOCK, Paul Byron (La) 4657 Campos Ln., Winters CA 95694 **Long Term Supply P Gr Epis Ch Wheatland CA 2006-; Headmaster S Johns Epis Sch Roseville CA 2006-; Headmaster St Johns Epis Ch Roseville CA 2006-** B London England 1/24/1951 s Ronald Edward Hancock & Vera. BA U Of Bristol Gb 1971; MA U Of Bristol Gb 1973; Oxf 1975; Ripon Coll Cuddesdon Oxford Gb 1975. Trans from Church Of England 1/1/1980 Bp Scott Field Bailey. m 6/12/1975 Cynthia E Dyer c 2. Vic S Paul's/H Trin New Roads LA 1999-2004; Epis HS Baton Rouge LA 1983-2003; Chapl Texas Mltry Inst San Antonio TX 1980-1983; Asst S Lk's Epis Ch San Antonio TX 1979-1983. p.b. hancock@att.net

HAND, Gary Dean (Los) 69/659 Moo Ban Far Rangsit, Bungyeetho, Thanyaburi, Pathum Thani 12130 Thailand B Inglewood CA 7/12/1942 s Lawrence O Hand & Billie Jean. Near E Sch Archlgy 1962; BA Orlando Childes Pierce Memi TS 1964; BA Wheaton Coll 1964; MDiv GTS 1967; Irish Sch of Ecumenics 1994. D 9/9/1967 P 3/1/1968 Bp Francis E I Bloy. m 7/2/1995 Prasert Tieonieo c 2. R S Mk's Par Van Nuys CA 1988-1995; S Ptr's Par Rialto CA 1976-1988; R Gr Epis Ch Glendora CA 1972-1975; S Aug By-The-Sea Par Santa Monica CA 1970-1972; Asst S Jn's Par San Bernardino CA 1967-1969. "Go Forth: The Ch Moves Into the 21st Century," Pub privately, 1995. OHC, Rialto Mnstry Assn. fathergaryhand@hotmail.com

HANDELSMAN, Barbara Jean (Mich) 210 W Cross St Apt 111, Ypsilanti MI 48197 **Died 5/17/2010** B Detroit MI 5/10/1928 D 6/16/1990 P 7/7/1991 Bp R(aymond) Stewart Wood Jr. c 5. dhandelsman@gmail.com

HANDLEY, Richard John (EC) 52240 Country Acres Dr, Elkhart IN 46514 B Kingston PA 8/17/1934 s Thomas James Handley & Doris. BA Lycoming Coll 1960; MDiv Epis TS In Kentucky 1963; DMin U of Notre Dame 1988. D 6/1/1963 P 12/1/1963 Bp William R Moody. m 9/12/1959 Donna D Handley c 5. Gr Epis Ch Plymouth NC 1996-1998; S Andr's Lawrenceville VA 1993-1996; All SS Epis Ch Fair Haven MI 1993; R Trin Epis Ch Lexington MI 1988-1992; R S Davids Ch Pikeville KY 1987-1988; R S Jas Epis Ch Prestonsburg KY 1987-1988; R S Dav's Epis Ch Elkhart IN 1977-1987; R Emm Ch Callaville FREEMAN VA 1977-1982; S Paul's Ch Richmond IN 1971-1977; R S Paul's Ch Richmond VA 1971-1977; Asst to R Chr Ch Cathd Lexington KY 1967-1971. Sermon Fellows Year Bk 1988. ddhandlee@verizon.net

HANDLOSS, Patricia Diane (Mass) 115 Bayridge Lane, Duxbury MA 02332 B Oakland CA 8/16/1944 d Paul Edward Alfred Handloss & Audrey Jeanne. California St U 1965; BA U CA 1967; S Louis U 1970; MDiv EDS 1976; Fllshp EDS 1993. D 5/22/1977 P 12/1/1978 Bp George Leslie Cadigan. c 3. Assoc Old No Chr Ch Boston MA 2004-2009; Int S Thos Ch Winn ME 2001-2002; R S Paul's Epis Ch Bedford MA 1993-1995; R S Augustines Ch S Louis MO 1987-1993; Asst S Ptr's Epis Ch St Louis MO 1980-1982; Assoc R S Dunstans Epis Ch Dover MA 1978-1979; Asst S Mk's Ch Foxborough MA 1977-1978. Auth, "Var arts". EvangES. assocvicaroldnorth@yahoo.com

HANDS, Donald Raymond (Mil) 6500 N Elm Tree Rd, Milwaukee WI 53217 B New York NY 11/29/1943 s Richard Sidney Hands & Mary Elizabeth. BA Loyola U 1967; MA Col 1970; PhD SUNY 1973; Dplma U of Wisconsin 2011. D 8/20/1977 Bp Harold B Robinson P 6/17/1979 Bp Robert Bracewell Appleyard. m 6/1/2002 Lydia Bishop c 2. S Chris's Ch River Hills WI 2003-2007; Dio Milwaukee Milwaukee WI 1993; Rogers Memi Hosp Oconomowoc WI 1987-1988; St Marys Ch Pittsburgh PA 1980-1982; Pittsburgh Pstr Inst Pittsburgh PA 1977-1980. Auth, *Sprtl Wholeness for Cler/Alb Inst*, 1993; Auth, *20 Pub arts*. AAMFT 1988; ATSA 1998; APA 1993; CCHP 2001. 1st Prize Cath Poetry Soc of Amer 1964. drdonhands@gmail.com

HANDSCHY, Daniel John (Mo) 9373 Garber Rd, Saint Louis MO 63126 **R Ch Of The Adv S Louis MO 1992-** B Walnut Creek CA 4/24/1958 s John Robert Allen Handschy & Pauline Ruth. BA U CO 1980; MDiv Harvard DS 1985. D 6/11/1986 P 1/17/1987 Bp Robert Shaw Kerr. m 6/2/1984 Shelley Palumbo c 2. Ch Of The Redeem Providence RI 1992; Int Ch Of The Redeem Providence RI 1991-1992; Asst All SS Epis Ch Attleboro MA 1986-1991. Phi Beta Kappa. djhandschy@gmail.com

HANDWERK, Larry Wayne (Chi) 9517 Springfield Ave, Evanston IL 60203 **Asst S Elis's Ch Glencoe IL 2009-** B Chambersburg PA 6/2/1941 s Wayne Clydan Handwerk & Dorothy Ann. BS Penn 1963; BA Amer Conservatory of Mus 1965; MDiv Nash 1969; STM GTS 1986; DMin SWTS 1998. D 6/24/1969 Bp Gerald Francis Burrill P 12/21/1969 Bp James Winchester Montgomery. m 4/3/1970 Victoria Lea c 2. Int Chr Ch Elizabethtown KY 2005-2007; Dioc Stff Dio Kentucky Louisville KY 2001-2009; R S Lk's Ch Evanston IL 1983-2002; R Trin Ch Buckingham PA 1981-1983; Dioc Stff Dio Maryland Baltimore MD 1975-1980; R S Ptr's Epis Ch Ellicott City MD 1973-1981; Asst S Barn Epis Ch Temple Hills MD 1971-1973; Cur Ch Of The H Comf Kenilworth IL 1969-1971; All SS Epis Cntr Leitchfield KY 2002. Assoc All SS Sis of the Poor 1975; Assoc of the OHC 1975. lhandwerk@earthlink.net

HANDY, David Allan (Alb) 2919 Maplevale Rd, Chester VA 23831 B Sioux Falls SD 4/20/1955 s Oliver Charles Handy & Betty Lou. BA Wheaton Coll 1977; MA U of Texas 1979; MDiv Ya Berk 1983; PhD UTS Richmond VA 1998. D 6/1/1985 P 12/28/1985 Bp David Standish Ball. m 5/23/1977 Irene Marjorie Dubert c 2. P-in-c S Mart's Epis Ch Henrico VA 1999-2000; S Mths Epis Ch Midlothian VA 1994; Int S Mich's Ch Colonial Heights VA 1992; Int Ch Of The Mssh Fredericksburg VA 1990-1991; P-in-c Trin Ch Watervliet NY 1985-1987; Deans Vic Cathd Of All SS Albany NY 1985. Auth, "The Gentile Pentecost," U Microfilms, 1998; Auth, "Acts 8: 14-25 - Interp," Interp, 1993. Soc of S Jn the Evang - Assoc 1988-1993. fatherruy@yahoo.com

HANEN, Patricia Lida (O) 3785 W 33rd St, Cleveland OH 44109 **R New Life Epis Ch Uniontown OH 2009-; Congrl Dvlpmt Off Dio Ohio Cleveland OH 1998-** B Seattle WA 4/15/1947 d Willis Alton Hanen & Grace Marion. BA Reed Coll 1967; MA Cor 1968; PhD Cor 1974; MDiv EDS 1986. D 6/14/1986 Bp John Thomas Walker P 12/20/1986 Bp William George Burrill. Bp Dep Dio Ohio Cleveland OH 1996-1998; Dio Ohio Cleveland OH 1994-1998; Dio Oh Mssnr Dio Ohio Cleveland OH 1994-1996; R S Mk's Epis Ch Penn Yan NY 1986-1993; Intrn Peace Cmsn Dio Washington Washington DC 1982-1983. Assn For Death Educ And Counslg. Wilson Fellowow; Phi Beta Kappa; Awd For Meritorious Civilian Serv Secy Of Defense. phanen@cometonewlife.org

HANEY, Jack Howard (NH) 2 Leeward Way, Fairhaven MA 02719 B Camden NJ 5/26/1938 s John Hartley Haney & Beulah Mae. BA W Virginia Wesleyan Coll 1962; MDiv Drew U 1966. D 6/10/1989 Bp Paul Moore Jr P 2/24/1990 Bp Frederick Barton Wolf. c 2. Int Epis Ch Of S Mary The Vrgn Falmouth ME 2004-2005; Int Chr Ch Biddeford ME 2002-2003; Ch of theTransfiguration N Conway NH 1992-2002; R Chr Ch No Conway NH 1992-2001; Assoc The Ch Of The H Trin Rittenhouse Philadelphia PA 1989-1992; Adj Prof The GTS New York NY 1987-1989. Ord of H Cross 1995. userhn9650@aol.com

HANEY V, James Paul (NwT) St. Paul's-on-the-Plains, 1510 Avenue X, Lubbock TX 79401 **COM Dio NW Texas Lubbock TX 2009-; R S Paul's On The Plains Epis Ch Lubbock TX 2008-** B Cambridge MA 7/7/1963 s James Paul Haney & Nancy Ruth. BA Texas Tech U 1985; MDiv SWTS 1995. D 6/10/1995 P 12/13/1995 Bp Sam Byron Hulsey. m 11/17/1984 Cynthia R Plummer c 2. Chair, Exam Chapl Dio Kansas Topeka KS 2004-2008; Coun of Trst Dio Kansas Topeka KS 2004-2008; Transition Com for PBp Ecusa / Mssn Personl New York NY 2004-2006; Joint Nomin Com for PBp Ecusa / Mssn Personl New York NY 2003-2006; GC Dep Dio Kansas Topeka KS 1999-2005; Dn, SW Convoc Dio Kansas Topeka KS 1999-2004; R Gd Shpd Epis Ch Wichita KS 1998-2008; Chair, Liturg and Mus Cmsn Dio Kansas Topeka KS 1998-2002; Vic Gr Ch Vernon TX 1995-1998; Vic S Lk's Ch Childress TX 1995-1998; Vic Trin Ch Quanah TX 1995-1998. The Chas T. Mason Awd SWTS 1995; The Seabury-Wstrn Prize SWTS 1995; The Alum Awd In Engl Bible SWTS 1993. haney4@suddenlink.net

HANEY, James Paul (NwT) 4904 14th Street, Lubbock TX 79416 B Pittsburgh PA 11/29/1939 s James Paul Haney & Helen May. BS U Pgh 1961; MDiv EDS 1965; MA W Texas A&M U 1978. D 6/13/1965 Bp Donald J Campbell P 12/17/1965 Bp George Henry Quarterman. m 3/14/1993 Janis Arnold c 3. R S Chris's Epis Ch Lubbock TX 1979-2005; Chapl Dio NW Texas Lubbock TX 1975-1979; P-in-c Epis Ch Of S Geo Canyon TX 1975-1979; Assoc S Jn's Epis Ch Odessa TX 1971-1974; Vic S Mk's Epis Ch Coleman TX 1965-1968. haneys8@cox.net

HANISIAN, James Andrew (SO) 3870 Virginia Ave, Cincinnati OH 45227 B Queens,NY 8/26/1947 s John Hanisian & Jane Elizabeth. BA Hob 1969; MDiv GTS 1972; DMin Untd Sem Dayton OH 1997. D 6/17/1972 P 12/1/1972 Bp Jonathan Goodhue Sherman. m 12/12/2006 Kathleen A Chesson c 3. Prof Bex Columbus OH 2006-2009; Archd Dio Sthrn Ohio Cincinnati OH 2001-2005; R The Ch of the Redeem Cincinnati OH 1979-2001; Vic S Marg's Ch Plainview NY 1977-1978; Dio Long Island Garden City NY 1975-1976; Asst S Mk's Ch Islip NY 1972-1975. "The Cross is the Way of Life," Forw Mvmt, 2000; Auth, "Mnstry of Encouragement," 1996; Auth, "The People of His Pasture," 1984; Auth, "More Than Fine Gold," CDO, 1978. jhanisian@erhinc.com

HANISIAN, Matthew R (SO) 3001 Wisconsin Ave NW, Washington DC 20016 **S Alb's Par Washington DC 2011-** B W Islip NY 4/2/1974 s James Andrew Hanisian & Lauren Ruth. BA Indiana U 1996; MDiv VTS 2010. D 6/13/2009

P 6/11/2011 Bp Thomas Edward Breidenthal. m 9/25/1999 Holly Hanisian c 2. S Paul's Epis Ch Alexandria VA 2010-2011. hanisian@gmail.com

HANKINS, Samuel Scott (Az) 712 N. Wilson, Winslow AZ 86047 **Vic S Paul's Epis Ch Winslow AZ 2010-** B Salina KS 6/10/1951 s Samuel Benjamin Hankins & Vera Aloise. BM Ob Conservatory 1973; MM Ya Sch of Mus 1975; MDiv GTS 1984. D 6/9/1984 Bp Arthur Edward Walmsley P 3/23/1985 Bp William Bradford Hastings. R Chr Epis Ch Norwich CT 2000-2009; P-in-c S Alb's Ch Danielson CT 1998-1999; Vic Ch Of The Resurr Norwich CT 1993-1999; Cur S Jas Ch New London CT 1984-1993. Pi Kappa Lamda 1973. sshankins@yahoo.com

HANKS JR, Alexander Hamilton (WNC) Po Box 8893, Asheville NC 28814 **R Ch Of The Redeem Asheville NC 2000-** B Asheville NC 8/30/1946 s Alexander Hamilton Hanks & Frances Jeanette. BA U NC 1982. D 12/18/1999 P 6/21/2000 Bp Robert Hodges Johnson. m 4/4/1971 Linda Susan Keys c 2. padreahanks@aol.com

HANLEY, Ian David (Los) 59131 Wilcox Ln, Yucca Valley CA 92284 B Isleworth UK 10/12/1946 s Patrick John Hanley & Joan. ThM U Of Oxford Oxford Uk 1998. Trans from Anglican Church in Aotearoa, New Zealand and Polynesia 12/7/2006 Bp Joseph Jon Bruno. m 3/23/1968 Gwenda Joyce Hanley c 2. Dio Los Angeles Los Angeles CA 2006-2008. ian_hl@verizon.net

✠ **HANLEY, Rt Rev Michael J** (Ore) Episcopal Diocese of Oregon, 11800 SW Military Ln, Portland OR 97219 **Bp of Oregon Dio Oregon Portland OR 2010-** B Tulsa OK 11/26/1954 s Eugene Vincent Hanley & Frances O'Connor. BA U of Oklahoma 1976; MDiv SWTS 1981; DMin SWTS 2005. D 6/6/1981 Bp Gerald Nicholas McAllister P 4/15/1982 Bp William Jackson Cox Con 4/10/2010 for Ore. m 12/27/1975 Marla M Martin c 2. R S Chris's Epis Ch Roseville MN 1998-2010; R S Lk's Epis Ch Hastings MN 1990-1998; Assoc R S Tim's Epis Ch Creve Coeur MO 1987-1990; Asst R S Lk's Epis Ch Bartlesville OK 1983-1987; Cur Epis Ch Of The Resurr Oklahoma City OK 1981-1983. Auth, "6 Tips On Sizing Up A Boss," *Epis*, 1988. bishop@episcopaldioceseoregon.org

HANNA JR, Archibald (Ct) 56 Pine Orchard Rd, Branford CT 06405 **Died 6/24/2010** B Worcester MA 9/24/1916 s Archibald Hanna & Rachel. BA Clark U 1939; MA Ya 1946; MS Col 1949; PhD Ya 1951. D 6/13/1961 Bp Walter H Gray. c 3. "A Mirror For The Nation," Gooland, 1985; "Brief Hist Of The Thimle Islands," Archon, 1970; "Jn Buchan," A Bibliography Shoe String, 1953.

HANNA, Bill (Miss) 783 Rosewood Pointe, Madison MS 39110 B Natchez MS 3/13/1952 s Hugh Boyd Hanna & Nona Muriel. BA Millsaps Coll 1974; MA Mississippi St U 1985. D 1/4/2003 Bp Alfred Clark Marble Jr. m 11/26/1977 Jacquelyn Therese Logue c 2. billfromnatchez@yahoo.com

HANNA, Daniel Bassett (Chi) 760 Magazine Street #205, New Orleans LA 70130 B Mishawaka IN 10/24/1935 s Russell Hoover Hanna & Jane Eloise. BA Aurora U 1957; MDiv SWTS 1960; MA NWU 1966; MS Loyola U Chi 1983. D 6/24/1960 P 1/6/1961 Bp Lauriston L Scaife. R S Matt's Ch Buffalo NY 1960-1964.

HANNA, Frederick James (Md) 1 E University Pkwy Unit 810, Baltimore MD 21218 **Died 2/25/2011** B Baltimore MD 12/15/1924 s James Rivers Hanna & Maria Margaretha Carolina. Bex 1956; S Aug's Coll Cbury GB 1964; BS Jn Hopkins U 1969; MDiv Bex 1970. D 7/6/1956 P 4/1/1957 Bp Noble C Powell. Sidney Hollander Awd of dist.

HANNA, Gerald Benson (Oly) 11527 9th Ave Ne, Seattle WA 98125 B San Antonio TX 11/25/1938 s Harvey Edward Hanna & Anna Louise. BA U CO 1960; MFA U MN 1971; MDiv Nash 1986. D 6/14/1986 P 12/1/1986 Bp William Carl Frey. m 12/20/1981 Kay Lynn Kessel c 2. S Dav Emm Epis Ch Shoreline WA 1999-2003; Supply P S Geo Epis Ch Maple Vlly WA 1995-1998; The Cntr For Sprtl Dvlpmt Seattle WA 1991-2003; R S Paul's Epis Ch Steamboat Sprg CO 1988-1991; Dio Colorado Denver CO 1987-1988; S Mk's Ch Craig CO 1986-1987. stdavidemmanuel@clear.net

HANNA, Nancy Wadsworth (NY) 300 E 56th St Apt 27g, New York NY 10022 B Washington DC 1/18/1946 d Arthur Littleford Wadsworth & Betty May. BA Harv 1973; EdM Lesley U 1974; MDiv UTS 1985. D 11/17/1985 Bp Paul Moore Jr P 6/1/1986 Bp Walter Decoster Dennis Jr. m 8/24/1974 Alistair Hanna c 1. Assoc Calv and St Geo New York NY 2004-2010; Assoc S Barth's Ch New York NY 1997-2004; Assoc Chr's Ch Rye NY 1990-1996; Asst S Mary's Ch Of Scarborough Scarborough NY 1985-1989. nancywhanna@yahoo.com

HANNA, Raymond John (NC) Po Box 1043, Mount Airy NC 27030 **R Trin Ch Mt Airy NC 2003-** B Philadelphia PA 2/14/1959 s Raymond Charles Hanna & Joan Margaret. BA U So 1984; MDiv SWTS 1991. D 6/15/1991 P 4/1/1992 Bp Allen Lyman Bartlett Jr. c 2. S Andr's Ch Mt Holly NJ 1999-2002; R Westover Epis Ch Chas City VA 1995-1999; Asst R S Paul's Ch Richmond VA 1993-1995; Cur S Paul's Ch Doylestown PA 1991-1993. rjhanna14@yahoo.com

HANNABASS, Katherine Tootle (NMich) PO Box 357, Mackinac Island MI 49757 B St. Joseph MO 7/7/1929 d William Dameron Tootle & Mildred. Hollins U 1950; MA E Tennessee St U 1980. D 8/12/2001 Bp James Arthur Kelsey. c 5. katherinehannabass@att.net

HANNAHS, John Harvey (Wyo) 201 E South Temple Apt 510, Salt Lake City UT 84111 B Smithfield OH 4/17/1925 s Roscoe Van Hannahs & Myrtle. BA Ohio U 1949; EDS 1952. D 6/19/1952 Bp Henry W Hobson P 1/6/1953 Bp Henry Hean Daniels. m 7/30/1954 Alice Carrington c 3. R Trin Ch Lander WY 1965-1971; R S Paul's Epis Ch Evanston WY 1960-1965; Assoc R S Mk's Epis Ch Venice FL 1959-1960; S Jn's Ch Powell WY 1955-1960; Cur S Lk's Ch Billings MT 1952-1954; S Thos Ch Hardin MT 1952-1954.

HANNIBAL, Preston Belfield (WA) Episcopal Church House, Mount St. Alban, Washington DC 20016 **Cn for Acad and Transition Mnstrs Dio Washington Washington DC 2003-** B New York NY 3/28/1948 s Hamilcar Belfield Hannibal & Netha Ena. BA Westmont Coll 1971; Ridley Hall Cambridge 1972; U of Cambridge 1972; MDiv Bex 1974; St. Edm's Coll, U of Cambridge 1983. D 6/15/1974 P 1/4/1975 Bp Robert C Rusack. m 5/15/1976 La Sandra Jenkins c 3. Sr Chapl and Chair of the Rel Dept. Belmont Chap at S Mk's Sch Southborough MA 1995-2003; Vic Ch Of S Jn The Evang Dunbarton NH 1984-1985; Vic Ch Of S Jn The Evang Dunbarton NH 1981-1983; Asst Chapl and Rel Tchr S Paul's Sch Concord NH 1974-1986. Phi Beta Kappa Alpha of Massachusetts at Harv 1989; Chas D. Dickey Mstr of Rel and Ethics St. Paul's Sch, NH 1980. phannibal@edow.org

HANNIFIN, William J (U) 473 Pioneer Ave, Tooele UT 84074 **Died 9/26/2009** B Eureka UT 8/3/1930 s James Franklin Hannifin & Ella Jane. BA Westminster Coll 1952; LTh GTS 1955. D 6/19/1955 P 12/21/1955 Bp Richard S Watson.

HANNUM, Christopher Cary Lee (At) 2148 Winding Creek Ln Sw, Marietta GA 30064 **Dio Atlanta Atlanta GA 2006-** B Utica NY 4/2/1949 s Ellwood Hannum & Lillian Victoria. BA U So 1971; MDiv SWTS 1976. D 6/22/1976 Bp A Donald Davies P 11/1/1977 Bp James Winchester Montgomery. m 8/14/1976 Kathleen Ann Hannum c 2. H Innoc' Epis Sch Atlanta GA 2000-2005; Int Chapl H Innoc Ch Atlanta GA 2000-2001; H Innoc Ch Atlanta GA 1996-1998; S Mary's Par Tampa FL 1995-1996; S Mary's Par Tampa FL 1986-1995; St Marys Epis Day Sch Tampa FL 1984-1996; Int S Phil's Ch Easthampton MA 1983-1984; R Chr Memi Ch No Brookfield MA 1979-1983; Cur S Aug's Epis Ch Wilmette IL 1977-1979; Cur The Epis Ch Of The H Nativ Plano TX 1976-1977. NAES; Ref. cclhannum@gmail.com

HANNUM, Walter Wink (Los) 627 Leyden Ln. 209, Claremont CA 91711 B West Chester PA 12/30/1925 s T Walter Hannum & Agnes Marion. BS W Chester St Teachers Coll 1950; MDiv PDS 1953; ThM Fuller TS 1975; HD Indn Inst of Missiology Tiruchy IN 1999. D 5/23/1953 Bp Oliver J Hart P 12/1/1953 Bp William J Gordon Jr. m 6/4/1962 Emma Louise Bottle. S Jn's Mssn La Verne CA 2000-2004; Adj Prof TESM Ambridge PA 1990-2000; New Wineskins Mssy Ntwk Ambridge PA 1975-1993; P-in-c S Geo In The Arctic Kotzebue AK 1971-1974; Archd Dio Alaska Fairbanks AK 1969-1971; P-in-c S Thos Ch Point Hope AK 1966-1969; Assoc The Ch Of The H Trin Juneau AK 1964-1966; P-in-c (Archd of the Yukon) S Steph's Ch Ft Yukon AK 1955-1964; P-in-c S Jas Ch Tanana AK 1953-1955. Epis Ch Mssy Cmnty, Fndr and Dir 1974-1994. WLHannum@juno.com

HANSCOM, John David (Ak) CHRIST CHURCH EPISCOPAL, 5101 OMALLEY RD, ANCHORAGE AK 99507 B Indianapolis, IN 9/15/1946 s Howard Edward Hansom & Mary Wilson. Doctoral Stds U of Oklahoma 1977; U So EFM 1984. D 7/25/2007 Bp Mark Lawrence Mac Donald. m 8/26/1967 Roberta Lee Ward c 2. ihs369@msn.com

HANSEL, Robert Raymond (SO) PO Box 217, Little Switzerland NC 28749 **Vic Ch Of The Resurr Little Switzerland NC 2011-; P All SS Ch Hilton Hd Island SC 2008-** B Cincinnati OH 3/7/1936 s Virgil Thomas Hansel & Christina Marie. BA U Cinc 1958; MDiv EDS 1961; DMin SWTS 1999. D 6/12/1961 P 12/24/1961 Bp Roger W Blanchard. m 3/15/1983 Dale Elaine Blue c 6. Int Calv Ch Memphis TN 2002-2004; P-in-c Indn Hill Ch Cincinnati OH 1997-1999; Cn Dio Indianapolis Indianapolis IN 1991-1997; P S Brigid's Mssn Oldenburg IN 1991-1996; Dn & Prog Asst to Bp Dio Sthrn Ohio Cincinnati OH 1978-1988; St. Mk's Sch of Southborough Inc. Southborough MA 1974-1978; Chapl S Geo's Sch Newport RI 1969-1974; R S Lk's Epis Ch Fall River MA 1964-1965; Asst Trin Ch Columbus OH 1961-1964. "All Shall Be Well," *Chapt Contrib*, Ch Pub Inc., 2009; "Free To Be," *Adult/Yth Dialogue*, Seabury; Auth, "Study Guide for," *Faith of the Ch (Ch Tchg Series)*, Seabury; Auth, *Henry Wise Hobson*, Forw Mvmt; Auth, "The Life of St. Aug," *Life of S Aug*, Crowell/Collier; Auth, "Like Fr, Like Son---Like Hell!," *Like Fathter,Like Son---Like Hell!*, Seabury; "Showdown in Seattle," *Showdown in Seattle*, Seabury; Auth, *Vestries in the Epis Ch*, Forw Mvmt. Conf Dio Exec; Credo Proj/Conf Ldr; Deploy Off Ntwk. dalenbob2@yahoo.com

HANSELL, Susan Weir (CFla) 2048 Ryan Way, Winter Haven FL 33884 **COM Dio Cntrl Florida Orlando FL 2002-; D S Paul's Ch Winter Haven FL 2001-** B Troy NY 8/14/1943 d George Moreland Weir & Ruth Evelyn. BS Tufts U 1965; Med U of Virginia 1972; Cert Inst for Chr Stds Florida 2000. D 12/8/2001 Bp John Wadsworth Howe. c 2. Secy - St of the Ch Com - GC Epis

Ch Cntr New York NY 2000-2003; Dio Cntrl Florida Orlando FL 1997-2000. nualamurphy@aol.com

HANSELMAN JR, David Allen (CNY) PO Box 88, Greene NY 13778 **D Zion Epis Ch Greene NY 2011-** B Newark NY 7/28/1969 s David Allen Hanselman & Jean Ann. BA SUNY - Albany 1995; ABD U GA - Athens 2003; MDiv St Bern's TS and Mnstry 2010. D 5/7/2011 Bp Gladstone Bailey Adams III. m 6/26/1993 Sonja Larsen c 2. dhanselm@gmail.com

HANSEN, Alan Whitney (Lex) 1302 Hidden Brook Ln NW, Acworth GA 30101 B Salzburg AT 5/6/1953 s Marcus Whitney Hansen & Patricia Jane. BA VMI 1975; MDiv Epis TS In Kentucky 1982. D 6/5/1982 Bp Charles Gresham Marmion P 12/11/1982 Bp Addison Hosea. m 8/18/1979 Teresa Hughes c 3. Acts 29 Mnstrs Atlanta GA 2002; S Jn's Ch Versailles KY 1991-2002; R & Chapl St Jn's Sch Ch Of The Epiph Jacksonville FL 1986-1991; Asst R S Mk's Epis Ch Jacksonville FL 1983-1986; Cur S Andr's Ch Ft Thos KY 1982-1983. hansen@a29.com

HANSEN, Carl R (ECR) 959 Vista Cerro Dr., Paso Robles CA 93446 B Watsonville CA 12/10/1943 s Raymond Astor Hansen & Lillian Amelia. BS Santa Clara U 1965; MDiv CDSP 1978; DMin CDSP 2002. D 6/24/1978 Bp William Foreman Creighton P 6/1/1979 Bp John Raymond Wyatt. m 1/31/1987 Susan K Hansen c 2. R All SS Ch Carmel CA 1988-2005; R Santa Lucia Chap Big Sur Carmel CA 1988-2005; Dio El Camino Real Monterey CA 1986-1988; R S Jas Ch Paso Robles CA 1980-1986; Asst S Giles Ch Moraga CA 1978-1980. Auth, *Inclusive Evang (thesis)*, CDSP, 2002; Auth, *Friends in Faith*, Sunflower Ink, 1998; Auth, "Friends in Faith," *Monterey Cnty Herald & Scripps-Howard News Serv*. revcarl@charter.net

HANSEN, Janis Lee Harney (Ore) 2430 Sw Crestdale Dr, Portland OR 97225 **D Chr Ch Sheridan MT 2010-; D S Barth's Ch Beaverton OR 1997-** B Elko NV 9/8/1942 d Howard William Harney & June Ferguson. BA U Of SW Louisiana 1964; DA U of Oregon 1978; Oregon Sch Of The Diac 1997. D 10/18/1997 Bp Robert Louis Ladehoff. m 9/27/1969 David Jen Hansen. Enrons Chairman Awd 1999. ubicari@email.msn

HANSEN, Jessica V (Cal) 1532 Burlingame Ave, Burlingame CA 94010 B Stanford CA 5/2/1957 d Heber J Hanson & Barbara Ellen. BA U CA 1979; MA San Francisco St Coll 1989; MDiv CDSP 1990. D 6/3/2000 P 12/2/2000 Bp William Edwin Swing. m 9/27/1980 Robert M Fellows c 1. Assoc R S Matt's Epis Ch San Mateo CA 2000-2002. jvhansen3@gmail.com

HANSEN, Karen Sue (Okla) 310 E. Noble Ave., Guthrie OK 73044 B Oklahoma City OK 2/4/1953 d Marvin Guy Little & Henrietta. BBA U of Cntrl Oklahoma 1993. D 6/21/2003 Bp Robert Manning Moody. m 1/1/2006 Harris Lynn Hansen c 2. lynnandkarenhansen@gmail.com

HANSEN, Knute Coates (Ct) 8 Whitewood Dr, Shelton CT 06484 **D S Paul's Epis Ch Shelton CT 2011-** B New Haven CT 1/10/1939 s Knud Peter Hansen & Emily Calista. BS U MI 1957; MS U Of Bridgeport 1964. D 9/17/2005 Bp Andrew Donnan Smith. m 7/6/1957 Jane Hansen c 3. D Trin Epis Ch Trumbull CT 2008-2011; D Trin Ch Branford CT 2005-2008; Bp/ Dioc Exec Coun and Evang Comm. Dio Connecticut Hartford CT 1990-2003. knute.hansen34@att.net

HANSEN, Michael (Cal) 1055 Taylor St, San Francisco CA 94108 **P Dio California San Francisco CA 1988-** B Saint Paul MN 3/19/1945 s Kenneth Charles Hansen & Lorraine Mary. BA U of St. Thos 1968; MDiv Untd TS 1979. D 6/25/1979 P 12/1/1979 Bp Robert Marshall Anderson. Dio California San Francisco CA 1985-2007; Cn Mssnr Dio California San Francisco CA 1985-1988; S Mart's By The Lake Epis Minnetonka Bch MN 1981-1983; Asst S Jn The Evang S Paul MN 1979-1981. Auth, "Doing A Needs Assessment". michaelkhansen@comcast.net

HANSEN, Michelle Helena (Ct) 125 Parklawn Dr, Waterbury CT 06708 B Oakland CA 2/7/1945 d Estle Miller Hansen & Evelyn May. BA U of Rhode Island 1967; MDiv Ya Berk 1970; STM Ya Berk 1971. D 6/27/1970 Bp John S Higgins P 5/1/1971 Bp Joseph Warren Hutchens. c 3. Middlesex Area Cluster Mnstry Higganum CT 1998-2006; S Ptr's Ch Hamden CT 1978-1983; Dio Kansas Topeka KS 1974-1978; Asst S Jas's Ch W Hartford CT 1972-1974; Asst S Paul's Ch Southington CT 1970-1972. shelhnsn@aya.yale.edu

HANSEN JR, Robert F (ECR) 16 Salisbury Dr Apt 7217, Asheville NC 28803 B Tulsa OK 10/4/1934 s Robert F Hansen & Betty Briscoe. BS U of Oklahoma 1956; MS U of Oklahoma 1958; MDiv Nash 1966. D 6/17/1966 P 12/1/1966 Bp Chilton Powell. m 8/27/1955 Mary C Bryant c 1. Dioc Coun Dio El Camino Real Monterey CA 1980-1985; R S Steph's Ch Gilroy CA 1979-1991; Evang Cmsn Dio Ohio Cleveland OH 1977-1979; Dioc Coun Dio Ohio Cleveland OH 1976-1979; Co-R S Lk's Epis Ch Akron OH 1975-1979; Assoc Ch Of The Redeem Houston TX 1970-1975; Assoc R S Lk's Epis Ch Bartlesville OK 1967-1970; Cur S Andr's Epis Ch Lawton OK 1966-1967. rfh176@gmail.com

HANSEN, Robert John (ECR) 235 Michelle Dr, Campbell CA 95008 **Asstg Cler Ch Of S Jude The Apos Cupertino CA 1983-** B Seaside OR 11/2/1931 s Robert Hansen & Gertrude. BS San Jose St Coll 1960; Dio California Diac Trng Prog 1966; California Sch for Deacons 1972. D 9/10/1966 Bp Richard Ainslie Kirchhoffer P 9/20/1973 Bp George Richard Millard. m 8/20/1955 Sally Blean c 7. Asst S Tim's Epis Ch Mtn View CA 1968-1985. Tau Beta Pi 1958-1960; Tau Delta Phi(Nat. hon Soc) 1960. Graduated scl San Jose St Univerfsity 1960. hansputt@sbcglobal.net

HANSEN, Thomas Parker (NI) 3717 N Washington Rd, Fort Wayne IN 46802 **R Trin Ch Ft Wayne IN 2006-** B Goshen NY 8/7/1951 s Edgar Hansen & Katharine. AA Orange Cnty Cmnty Coll 1973; BA SUNY 1975; MDiv Nash 1978; DMin Fuller TS 2000. D 6/3/1978 Bp Paul Moore Jr P 12/1/1978 Bp William Carl Frey. m 8/2/1981 Nancy Mccammon c 1. R S Lk's Ch Kearney NE 2001-2006; Cn Mssnr Dio Nebraska Omaha NE 1991-2001; Pstr Dvlp S Martha's Epis Ch Papillion NE 1991-2001; R S Jn's Ch Broken Bow NE 1986-1990; R S Steph's Ch Casper WY 1981-1984; Cur S Lk's Epis Ch Ft Collins CO 1978-1981. tnchanse@mac.com

HANSKNECHT, Jeanne Marie (Mich) 306 N Division St, Ann Arbor MI 48104 **Cur/Asst R S Andr's Ch Ann Arbor MI 2010-** B Tawas City MI 9/22/1967 d Harold Porter Sabin & Alberta May. BA MI SU 1990; MA Estrn Michigan U 1994; MDiv Ecum TS 2010. D 12/12/2009 P 7/17/2010 Bp Wendell Nathaniel Gibbs Jr. m 3/17/1990 Blane Hansknecht c 4. jhansknecht@standrewsaa.org

HANSLEY, Mary Belfry (SVa) 6219 Chelsea Crescent, Williamsburg VA 23188 **Ret - Supply Dio Sthrn Virginia Norfolk VA 2005-** B Minneapolis MN 5/14/1944 d Albert Merton Belfry & Marsena Falk. Mt Holyoke Coll 1964; BA NWU 1967; MDiv VTS 1975. D 8/15/1975 P 1/16/1977 Bp Philip Frederick McNairy. m 4/30/1983 Gene B Hansley. Int S Mart's Epis Ch Williamsburg VA 2004-2005; Assoc S Mich's Ch Barrington IL 1998-2003; Int Chr Ch S Paul MN 1997; P-in-c S Pat Minneapolis MN 1994-1996; Int Trin Ch Excelsior MN 1994; Int S Mk's Ch Fairland Silver Sprg MD 1990-1992; Chapl Seabury Resources Washington DC 1988-1990; Assoc Ch Of Our Redeem Aldie VA 1986-1988; Assoc Emm Ch Middleburg VA 1986-1988; Assoc Chapl and Dir of Alum/ae Affrs VTS Alexandria VA 1981-1986; Cn Cathd Ch Of S Mk Minneapolis MN 1977-1981; D Cathd Ch Of S Mk Minneapolis MN 1975-1977. mhansley@cox.net

HANSON III, Aquilla Brown (Fla) 406 Glenridge Rd, Perry FL 32348 **R S Jas Epis Ch Perry FL 2007-** B Columbia SC 3/16/1947 s Earnault Hawkins Williams Hanson & Dorothy. BA Cit 1969; MA Oral Roberts U 1992; MA TS 1992; MDiv VTS 1993. D 6/2/1993 P 12/1/1993 Bp Edward Lloyd Salmon Jr. m 12/30/1994 Dorothy Nola c 1. Int S Mk's Epis Ch Jacksonville FL 2005-2006; Int Trin Epis Ch Baton Rouge LA 2004-2005; R All SS Ch Jackson MS 1999-2004; Ch Of The Adv Sumner MS 1996-1997; Chr Our Lord Epis Ch S Helena Island SC 1994-1996; S Chris's Ch Sumter SC 1993. Masters Thesis, "The Euch, An OT Rite Perfected," *Oral Roberts Grad TS*. aquilla316@comcast.net

HANSON, Bruce Ernest (Roch) 8054 Se 169th Tweedside Loop, The Villages FL 32162 B San Buenaventura CA 4/25/1929 s Paul Ernest Hanson & Lois Evelyn. BA Colorado St Coll 1951; MDiv CRDS 1954; EDS 1956. D 6/21/1956 P 2/23/1957 Bp Dudley S Stark. c 4. Ecum Off Dio Rochester Rochester NY 1985-1991; Assoc Ecum Off Dio Rochester Rochester NY 1981-1985; R S Lk And S Simon Cyrene Rochester NY 1973-1991; R S Mich's Ch Geneseo NY 1969-1973; R Gr Ch No Attleborough MA 1962-1969; Vic Ch Of The Gd Shpd Webster NY 1958-1962; Cur S Mk's And S Jn's Epis Ch Rochester NY 1956-1958.

HANSON, Deborah Ann (Miss) 5400 Old Canton Rd, Jackson MS 39211 B Canada 9/2/1954 d Frederick Randall Ufton & Shirley Anne McInnis. D 1/15/2011 Bp Duncan Montgomery Gray III. m 9/21/1974 Peter Allen Hanson c 3. dhanson5@aol.com

HANSON, Edward Berry (At) 4324 Darwen Ct, Tucker GA 30084 **Died 1/19/2011** B Atlanta GA 9/29/1949 s Edward Berry Hanson & Martha. BA Georgia St U 1976; MDiv STUSo 1981. D 6/13/1981 Bp Charles Judson Child Jr P 5/1/1982 Bp Bennett Jones Sims. m 2/15/2011 Barbara T Russell c 2. bobbyt.russell@yahoo.com

HANSON, Jay D (Minn) 63 Onagon Lake Rd, Grand Marais MN 55604 B Saint James MN 9/28/1937 s Lloyd Willard Hanson & Margaret Elizabeth. BA U MN 1959; MDiv VTS 1962; U of No Dakota 1970. D 6/29/1962 Bp Hamilton Hyde Kellogg P 6/1/1963 Bp Philip Frederick McNairy. m 8/26/1961 Madge Ann Nathe c 4. Int Ch Of The Mssh Rhinebeck NY 2009-2010; Int S Jn In The Wilderness White Bear Lake MN 2002-2003; S Edw The Confessor Wayzata MN 1988-1996; Dio Minnesota Minneapolis MN 1986-2003; Cur The Epis Par Of S Dav Minnetonka MN 1962-1964. jdhanson37@mac.com

HANSON, Norma Halmagyi (Del) 405 Lady Huntingdon Ln, Asheville NC 28803 B Welch WV 1/6/1937 d Anthony Halmagyi & Mildred Evelyn. BA Randolph-Macon Wmn's Coll 1958; MS U of Virginia 1960; MDiv Lancaster TS 1994; Cert VTS 1994; DMin Luth TS at Philadelphia 2004. D 10/8/1994 P 10/14/1995 Bp Cabell Tennis. c 4. Vic Ch Of The Trsfg Saluda NC 2009-2011; R Chr Ch Delaware City DE 2002-2004; D Chr Ch Greenville Wilmington DE 1995. APC 1997-1999; Ord of S Lk 1971-1982. Phi Sigma Univ. of Virginia 1960. rev.drnorma@yahoo.com

HANSON-FOSS, Patricia Jean (Alb) PO Box 237, Au Sable Forks NY 12912 B Canton NY 1/19/1964 D 6/29/2003 Bp David John Bena. c 2.

HANSTINE, Barbara Ann (Alb) 287 Leonard St, Hancock NY 13783 B Middletown NY 11/17/1940 d John Botens & E Belle. BS SUNY 1979; MS SUNY 1982. D 5/27/1989 Bp David Standish Ball. m 10/3/1975 William Hanstine c 3. D St Chris's Epis Ch Cobleskill NY 2002-2009; Fac Dio Albany Albany NY 2000-2002; D Chr Ch Deposit NY 1989-2002; Fam Mnstry Coordntr - Susquehanna Dnry Dio Albany Albany NY 1985-1999. NAAD; Ord Of S Lk. barbarah@hancock.net

HANTEN, Helen Bailey (Minn) 66 E. St. Marie St. #205, Duluth MN 55803 B Caspian MI 3/19/1927 d Carlton Dewey Bailey & Katherine. U of Wisconsin 1948; BS U MN 1966; MS U MN 1975. D 10/25/1987 Bp Robert Marshall Anderson. m 8/20/1949 Paul Thomas Hanten c 3. D S Andr's By The Lake Duluth MN 1987-2001. hhanten@aol.com

HANWAY JR, Donald Grant (Neb) 128 N 13th St Apt #1009, Lincoln NE 68508 B Lincoln NE 12/9/1943 s Donald Grant Hanway & Blanche Elizabeth. BA U of Nebraska 1965; MA U of Nebraska 1967; MDiv VTS 1971; DMin VTS 1997. D 6/17/1971 Bp Robert Patrick Varley P 12/20/1971 Bp Russell T Rauscher. m 5/28/1966 Nadine K Kingman c 3. Secy Dio Nebraska Omaha NE 1998-2004; Exec Cmsn Dio Nebraska Omaha NE 1989-1995; COM Dio Nebraska Omaha NE 1983-1989; R S Mk's On The Campus Lincoln NE 1981-2003; Dio Nebraska Omaha NE 1979-1981; R Chr Ch Epis Beatrice NE 1977-1981; Dio Michigan Detroit MI 1975-1977; Cur S Lk's Par Kalamazoo MI 1975-1977; Ed, The Nebraska Churchman Dio Nebraska Omaha NE 1972-1974; Vic S Eliz's Ch Holdrege NE 1971-1975. Auth, "Words of Life," *Selected Sermons*, iUniverse Bloomington, 2009; Auth, "Her Appearing: A Love Story," iUniverse Bloomington, IN, 2008; Auth, "Theol of Gay and Lesbian Inclusion: Love Letters to the Ch," *Love Letters to the Ch*, Haworth Pstr Press Binghamton NY, 2006. Lincoln Torch Club 1995. Silver Torch Awd Int'l. Assoc. of Torch Clubs 2009; Geo Peek Memi Awd St. Mk's on the Campus 2002; Phi Beta Kappa U of Nebraska- Lincoln 1965. dghanway@hotmail.com

HANYZEWSKI, Andrew J (NI) 303 Merchants Ave, Fort Atkinson WI 53538 **P-in-c S Peters Epis Ch Ft Atkinson WI 2011-; P-in-c S Peters Epis Ch Ft Atkinson WI 2011-; P-in-c S Andr's By The Lake Epis Ch Michigan City IN 2009-; S Fran Ch Chesterton IN 2009-** B Melrose Park IL 8/22/1963 s Daniel Edward Hanyzewski & Ann Carol. M Div. Nash 2009. D 8/23/2008 Bp Keith Bernard Whitmore. m 5/28/2006 Aimee Joelle Whitmore. Mnstry Models Task Grp Dio Nthrn Indiana So Bend IN 2010-2011; Dioc Coun Mem Dio Nthrn Indiana So Bend IN 2009-2011. andyhanyzewski@yahoo.com

HAPP, Howard Jess (Los) 5801 W Crestridge Rd, Apt. B 115, Rancho Palos Verdes CA 90275 **Died 3/27/2011** B Waterloo IA 5/20/1942 s Dale K Happ & Elida. BA Cornell Coll 1965; MA U Chi 1966; BD PrTS 1968; PhD Pr 1974. D 1/30/1973 P 11/4/1973 Bp Robert C Rusack. "Charlie Chaplin's Bp," *AS WE REMEMBER*, Dio Los Angeles, 1996; "Westminster Theol Revs," *Rel PERIODICALS OF THE U.S.*, Greenwood Press, 1986; "Tuchman's View of Hist's Folly," *Theol TODAY*, PrTS, 1986; "Conventions and Crises," *Epis NEWS (Bicentennial Issue)*, Dio Los Angeles, 1985; "The Beauty of the Bible," *Theol TODAY*, PrTS, 1984; "Sexual Issues--Divided Body of Chr," *SPEAK BOLDLY*, St. Jn's Par, Los Angeles, 1978; Auth, "The Incarn and Priesting of Wmn," *LIVING Ch*, Living Ch Fndt, 1976. AAR 1971-1995; Amer Hist Assn, Hist Soc of the Epis 1976-1995; Amer Soc Ch Hist Conf Angl Theol 1976-1995; Conf of Angl Theologians 1979-1981; HSEC 1976-1995; [Dates above uncertain]. Hon Cn Dio Los Angeles 2006. h_happ@yahoo.com

HAPTONSTAHL, Stephen R (Minn) 819 Hamilton Dr, Duluth MN 55811 B Independence IA 12/17/1943 s O R Haptonstahl & Helen P. Knox Coll 1964; U of Nebraska 1969; MDiv EDS 1973. D 6/16/1973 Bp John Harris Burt P 3/1/1975 Bp Robert C Rusack. m 12/31/1977 Thomasina D Dennis c 4. S Paul's Ch Brainerd MN 2006-2008; S Phil's Ch S Paul MN 2004-2005; Trin Epis Ch Hinckley MN 2000-2009; P-in-c S Jas Epis Ch Hibbing MN 1998-1999; S Paul's Ch Brainerd MN 1997-1998; S Andr's Ch Le Sueur MN 1994-1997; S Edw's Ch Duluth MN 1991-1996; S Paul's Epis Ch Of E Cleveland Cleveland OH 1984-1985; Gr Ch Cleveland OH 1982-1983; R S Lk's Ch Cleveland OH 1978-1981; R S Thos' Epis Ch Port Clinton OH 1975-1978; Asst Trin Epis Ch Redlands CA 1973-1975. Auth, "Lay Mnstry Resource Notebook". hapn2stall@aol.com

HARBIN, J Derek (SVa) 424 Washington St, Portsmouth VA 23704 **R S Jn's Ch Portsmouth VA 2011-** B Winston-Salem NC 6/25/1961 s Edgar Finley Harbin & Sally Ann. BS Davidson Coll 1983; MDiv Nash 1988; DMin SWTS 1999. D 5/20/1988 P 11/30/1988 Bp William Gillette Weinhauer. m 9/3/1989 Louise Clifford King c 3. P-in-c S Andr's Ch Bessemer City NC 2008-2011; Founding P / Ch Planter Ch Of The Beloved Charlotte NC 1999-2008; R S Andr Epis Ch Kokomo IN 1992-1999; Asst Gr Ch Asheville NC 1988-1992. Auth, "It'S Not About Us," *Searching For Sacr Space*, Ch Pub, 2002; Auth, "Assuming The Nature Of A Liturg Servent," *Open (The Of Associated Parishes)*, 2000; Auth, "No Mtn Too Steep," S Fran Ch, 1993. St. Geo Epis Awd BSA 1988; Natl DSA Ord of the Arrow, BSA 1983; Eagle Scout BSA 1976. jderekharbin@gmail.com

HARBOLD, Sally L (NC) 221 Union St, Cary NC 27511 **Assoc R S Paul's Epis Ch Cary NC 2000-; Yth & CE Dio No Carolina Raleigh NC 1995-** B Columbus OH 8/25/1952 d Charles Richard Harbold & Mary Ellen. AA Valencia Cmnty Coll 1988; BA U of Cntrl Florida 1989; MDiv Ya Berk 1992; DMin GTF 2005. D 6/20/1992 Bp John Wadsworth Howe P 12/1/1992 Bp William Hopkins Folwell. Int Gr Ch Whiteville NC 1995; The Epis Ch Of The Gd Shpd Lake Wales FL 1992-1994. rector2@stpaulscary.org

HARBORT, Raymond Lewis (Be) 1841 Millard St, Bethlehem PA 18017 B Tarrytown NY 1/14/1944 s Herbert Charles Harbort & Edna Louise. BA Rutgers-The St U 1965; STB GTS 1968. D 6/8/1968 P 12/21/1968 Bp Horace W B Donegan. Trin Par Menlo Pk CA 2002-2003; S Paul's Epis Ch Burlingame CA 2001-2002; Ch Of The Adv Of Chr The King San Francisco CA 1999-2001; S Ptr's Epis Ch Redwood City CA 1999; S Mary's Ch Haledon NJ 1991-1998; R S Anth Of Padua Ch Hackensack NJ 1988-1989; P-in-c S Paul's Ch Chester NY 1975-1977; R Chr Ch Warwick NY 1971-1987; Cur S Ptr's Epis Ch Peekskill NY 1968-1971. rh@rayharbort.com

HARDAWAY IV, John Benjamin (USC) 795 Wilson St, Anderson SC 29621 **Gr Epis Ch Anderson SC 2004-** B Ames IA 2/1/1968 s John Benjamin Hardaway & Mary Lynne Bladon. BA Furman U 1990; MDiv VTS 1995. D 6/10/1995 P 5/26/1996 Bp Dorsey Felix Henderson. m 6/6/1992 Susan Arledge Louttit c 3. R S Paul's Epis Ch Ft Mill SC 1997-2004; Asst S Ptr's Epis Ch Greenville SC 1995-1997. frjack@bellsouth.net

HARDAWAY, Ripp Barton (WTex) 312 S Guenther Ave, New Braunfels TX 78130 **Vic S Jn's Ch New Braunfels TX 2009-** B Midland TX 5/29/1970 s Susan B. BA Texas A&M U 1992; MA Hardin-Simmons U 1998; MDiv The U So (Sewanee) 2003. D 6/10/2003 P 1/6/2004 Bp James Edward Folts. m 8/13/1985 Susan R Susan Renee Carlisle c 2. R S Chris's By The Sea Portland TX 2005-2009; Cur The Ch Of The H Sprt Dripping Sprg TX 2003-2005. ripp@stjohnsnb.com

HARDAWAY, Susan Arledge Louttit (USC) 404 North St, Anderson SC 29621 **P-in-c Ch Of The Epiph Laurens SC 2009-** B Valdosta GA 4/25/1967 d Henry Irving Louttit & Jayne. BA U So 1989; MDiv VTS 1993. D 5/29/1993 Bp Harry Woolston Shipps P 12/1/1993 Bp Peter James Lee. m 6/6/1992 John Benjamin Hardaway c 3. Asst H Trin Par Epis Clemson SC 2005-2009; P-in-c S Mk's Ch Chester SC 2003-2004; Chapl York Place Epis Cluster York SC 2003-2004; Vic S Jas Ch Mooresville NC 1999-2003; Asst S Jas Epis Ch Greenville SC 1995-1997; Asst Trin Ch Manassas VA 1993-1995. epiphany@backroads.net

HARDEN, Rosa Lee (Cal) 15 Riparian Way, Ashevile NC 28778 **Cn for Money & Meaning The Cathd Of All Souls Asheville NC 2011-** B Fulton MS 4/11/1952 d Delmus Harden & Rubye. BS Mississippi Coll 1974; MDiv CDSP 1999. D 5/27/1999 P 3/4/2000 Bp Alfred Clark Marble Jr. m 12/28/1974 Kevin Jones. Ch Of The H Innoc San Francisco CA 2000-2010. rosaleeharden@me.com

HARDENSTINE, Autumn Hecker (Pa) 126 Grist Mill Rd, Schuylkill Haven PA 17963 B Erie PA 10/16/1948 d Joseph L Hecker & Lodeme Shields. BS Edinboro U 1970; Med Edinboro U 1976; MDiv Luth TS 1985; STM Luth TS 1992; DMin Luth TS 1995. D 6/15/1985 P 6/11/1986 Bp Lyman Cunningham Ogilby. c 1. R S Phil's In The Field Oreland PA 1994-2004; Asst S Anne's Ch Abington PA 1987-1990; Asst to R S Paul Ch Exton PA 1985-1987. Auth, "Gifts Of Heart: The Challenge Of Enrichment For The Physically Disabled"; Auth, "Rachel Weeping For Her Chld"; Auth, "Images Of God"; Auth, "The Legacy," *Journ Of Wmn Mnstry*; Auth, "Bk Revs Of Clincl Handbook Of Pstr Counslg," *Journ Of Wmn Mnstry*. Fell Coll Of Chapl 1987; Profsnl Mem Of Assn Of Chapl 1986; Soc Of S Marg 1986. autumnhardenstine@yahoo.com

HARDER, Cheryl Anne (Minn) 10 E Penton Blvd, Duluth MN 55808 **P Trin Epis Ch Hermantown MN 2005-** B 9/5/1956 d Arthur Welsand & Joyce. BS U MN 1986; MS Ed U of Wisconsin 1994. D 10/17/2004 P 7/23/2005 Bp James Louis Jelinek. m 1/12/1985 Edward Harder c 1. harderc@stlouiscountymn.gov

HARDIE JR, John Ford (WTex) 7513 Yorkshire Dr, Corpus Christi TX 78413 **R S Mk's Ch Corpus Christi TX 1999-** B San Antonio TX 11/16/1960 s John Ford Hardie & Hazel Ada. BA Tul 1983; MDiv VTS 1987. D 6/14/1987 P 12/17/1987 Bp John Herbert MacNaughton. m 5/27/1989 Melanie Wood c 3. R S Phil's Ch Uvalde TX 1995-1999; Assoc R All SS Par Beverly Hills CA 1990-1995; S Barth's Ch Corpus Christi TX 1987-1990. jhardie@grandecom.net

HARDIN JR, Hugh Fletcher (Cal) 50 Balboa Ave, San Rafael CA 94901 **Assoc P Chr Ch Sausalito CA 2002-** B Oklahoma City OK 1/24/1928 s Hugh Fletcher Hardin & Hellen Fern. BA U of Oklahoma 1952; BD SMU 1955; UTS 1956. D 12/22/1966 Bp George Richard Millard P 5/16/1967 Bp C Kilmer Myers. m 8/25/1951 Betty Nell Binkley c 4. R S Paul's Epis Ch San Rafael CA 1967-1993. hughstuff@comcast.net

HARDING, Albert (Alb) 16 Locust Ln, Clifton Park NY 12065 **D S Geo's Ch Clifton Pk NY 1967-** B Binghamton NY 9/14/1922 s Albert Henry Harding &

Maude. BA RPI 1949; MS RPI 1973. D 10/1/1967 Bp Allen Webster Brown. m 6/17/1950 Constance Larrabee c 4. Pi Tau Sigma 1948; Tau Beta Pi 1948.

HARDING, Kerith Anne (Ore) 55 Myrtle Ave, Westport CT 06880 **Asst R Chr And H Trin Ch Westport CT 2009-** B New Haven CT 1/23/1975 d James Harding & Diane. BS Vanderbilt 1997; MS Portland St 2005; MDiv Ya Berk 2009. D 5/30/2009 Bp Sanford Zangwill Kaye Hampton P 1/9/2010 Bp Andrew Donnan Smith. m 7/15/2011 Alison Donohue. kerith.harding@gmail.com

HARDING, Leander Samuel (SC) Trinity School For Ministry, 311 Eleventh Street, Ambridge PA 15003 **TESM Ambridge PA 2010-** B New York NY 7/16/1949 s Leander Samuel Harding & Blanche Elizabeth. BA New Coll 1970; MDiv cl Andover Newton TS 1978; PhD Boston Coll 1989. D 12/3/1980 P 5/7/1981 Bp Frederick Barton Wolf. m 7/3/1971 Claudia Esther Bolin c 3. Fox Chap Epis Ch Pittsburgh PA 2008-2009; Asst. Prof of Pstr Theol TESM Ambridge PA 2005-2008; R S Jn's Ch Stamford CT 1989-2005; R Ch Of Our Sav Arlington MA 1984-1989; Int Ch Of The Gd Shpd Houlton ME 1982-1983; S Anne's Ch Mars Hill ME 1981-1984. Auth, "In the Breaking of the Bread," WipfandStock, 2010; Auth, "Reverence for the Heart of the Chld," YTC Press, 2008; Auth, "Why Is Dialogue So Difficult," *Trin Journ*, Trin Sch for Mnstry, 2008; Auth, "Flying Saucers and Christmas," IUinverese Press, 2006; Auth, "What The Ang Say," *Sermons That Wk*, 2002; Auth, "Christmas And Flying Saucers," *Sermons That Wk*, 2001; Auth, "Power And Dignity Of Priesthood," *Sewanee Theol Revs*, 2000; Auth, "What Have We Been Telling Ourselves About The Priesthood," *Sewanee Theol Revs*, 2000; Auth, "Atone And Fam Ther," *ATR*, 1984. ECF Fell 1985-1988; Soc For Ecum Doctrine 1991-2002; VP Mass Epis Cler Assn 1988-1989. lharding@stjohns-stamford.org

HARDING, Leslie Frank (Mich) 15178 Murray Woods Ct, Byron MI 48418 **Int S Andr's Ch Waterford MI 2009-** B Pittsburgh ON CA 7/17/1931 s Charles Leslie Harding & Ethel Jane. BA 1959. Trans from Anglican Church of Canada 12/16/1966 as Priest Bp Richard S M Emrich. m 5/8/1960 Judith A Rodie c 4. Vic S Anne's Epis Ch Walled Lake MI 1972-2001; Vic Ch Of The H Cross Novi MI 1969-2001; Nativ Cmnty Epis Ch Holly MI 1966-1969. Soc of S Jn the Evang (Can) 1956-1966. jharding@chartermi.net

HARDING, Rona Robertine (WA) 22968 Esperanza Drive, Lexington Park MD 20653 **Int S Mk's Epis Ch Durango CO 2011-** B Cleveland OH 11/9/1948 d Talbot Harding & Cecilia Mary. Muskingum Coll 1970; M.Theol. U Of S Andrews Fife Scotland 1973. D 5/7/1977 P 11/18/1977 Bp John Mc Gill Krumm. Int Trin Epis Par Hughesville MD 2009-2011; R The Ch Of The Ascen Lexington Pk MD 1988-2009; Cn Cathd Ch Of S Mk Minneapolis MN 1982-1988; Chapl Untd Campus Mnstrs Oxford OH 1975-1980. rrharding@verizon.net

HARDING, Sahra Megananda (O) 3004 Belvedere Blvd, Omaha NE 68111 **Cur Trin Cathd Cleveland OH 2011-** B Fairfield CA 11/8/1979 d Richard Theodore Harding & Deni Roberta. AA Solano Cmnty Coll 1999; BA U CA, Santa Cruz 2001; MDiv The GTS 2010. D 6/2/2010 P 12/2/2010 Bp Joe Goodwin Burnett. Reverend Dio Nebraska Omaha NE 2010-2011. The Beatitudes Soc 2009. sahraharding@yahoo.com

HARDING, Scott Mitchell (Alb) 25 Bonner Dr, Queensbury NY 12804 **R The Ch Of The Mssh Glens Falls NY 2004-** B Rochester NY 6/26/1971 s Jonathan Mitchell Harding & Sandra Lee. BS U Pgh 1992; MDiv TESM 1997. D 4/25/1998 P 10/31/1998 Bp Robert William Duncan. m 7/14/1990 Kim M MacKeith c 4. Vic Chr Ch Gilbertsville NY 2001-2003; S Thos Memi Epis Ch Oakmont PA 1998-2001. fatherscott@nycap.rr.com

HARDING, Stephen Riker (NY) 1047 Amsterdam Ave, New York NY 10025 B FR 2/6/1957 s John Mason Harding & Margaret. BA Colby Coll 1980; MDiv UTS 1993; STM GTS 1995; Cert Assn of Profsnl Chapl 1997. D 6/23/1995 Bp Orris George Walker Jr P 5/8/1999 Bp Rodney Rae Michel. m 9/18/2004 Storm Kirsten Swain c 1. Dio New York New York City NY 2010-2011; Assoc The Ch of S Ign of Antioch New York NY 2007-2009; The Ch Of The Epiph New York NY 2000-2004; P S Paul's Ch Brooklyn NY 1999-2000. sharding@mindspring.com

HARDMAN, J(ohn) (Chi) 222 Kenilworth Ave., Kenilworth IL 60043 **Assoc R Ch Of The H Comf Kenilworth IL 2008-** B Little Rock AR 11/13/1948 s Louis Atkins Hardman & Florence Emily. BS U of Arkansas 1981; MDiv VTS 1986. D 6/28/1986 P 5/1/1987 Bp Herbert Alcorn Donovan Jr. m 1/24/1970 Elizabeth McCulloch Long c 2. R S Tim's Ch Wilson NC 2002-2008; R S Thos Epis Ch Eustis FL 1992-2002; Vic S Steph's Epis Ch Jacksonville AR 1987-1992; D-in-Trng S Mk's Epis Ch Little Rock AR 1986-1987. jchardman@holycomforter.org

HARDMAN, Louise O'Kelley (Fla) 256 E Church St, Jacksonville FL 32202 B Tallahassee FL 11/6/1941 d Artemas Franklin O'Kelley & Louise Pittman. BA U NC 1961. D 5/23/2010 Bp Samuel Johnson Howard. c 2. hardman.louise@gmail.com

HARDMAN, Richard Joseph (NJ) 3902 Se Fairway W, Stuart FL 34997 B Pittsburgh PA 5/6/1922 s Joseph Hardman & Violet Ivy. BA U Pgh 1947. D 9/16/1949 P 3/18/1950 Bp Austin Pardue. m 6/15/1950 Patricia Gillespie. St Pauls Trust Westfield NJ 1971-1982; Dio New Jersey Trenton NJ 1961; R S Paul's Epis Ch Westfield NJ 1957-1982; Asst Secy Urbn Industrl Ch Wk Ecec Dio Pittsburgh Monroeville PA 1956-1957; R S Steph's Epis Ch Mckeesport PA 1950-1956; Asst Calv Ch Pittsburgh PA 1949-1950. Hon Cn Trin Cathd Trenton NJ 1967. sinstopper@aol.com

HARDMAN, Robert Rankin (Minn) 2338 Como Ave, Saint Paul MN 55108 **P Assoc S Mart's By The Lake Epis Minnetonka Bch MN 2000-** B Framingham MA 12/19/1939 s George D Hardman & Vera Lenore. BA Hob 1962; MDiv VTS 1969; Johnson Inst 1973. D 6/11/1969 Bp John Henry Esquirol P 1/1/1970 Bp Joseph Warren Hutchens. m 8/23/1969 Susan Durand Dukehart c 3. Epis Ch Hm St Paul MN 1989-1999; Dio Oregon Portland OR 1988-1989; R The Epis Ch Of The Gd Samar Corvallis OR 1982-1988; R S Paul's Epis Ch Duluth MN 1976-1982; S Mart's By The Lake Epis Minnetonka Bch MN 1972-1976; Cur Chr Ch Greenwich CT 1969-1972. robrankin3@aol.com

HARDMAN, Samuel Robinson (CGC) 13167 Norris Ln, Foley AL 36535 **Died 2/10/2011** B Zephyr Hills FL 2/26/1925 s Alfred N Hardman & Ann Sergeant. BS U So 1948; MDiv STUSo 1949; MS U of Pennsylvania 1963. D 6/24/1949 Bp John M Walker Jr P 6/1/1950 Bp John J Gravatt. Meritorius Serv Medal 1975; Joint Serv Commendation Medal 1973; Usn Comendation Medal 1949; Phi Delta Kappa. FRSAM@GULFTEL.COM

HARDWICK, Dana (Lex) 2460 Eastway Dr., Lexington KY 40503 B Akron OH 4/7/1942 d Lewis Eugene Hardwick & Mary Emily. BS U of Wisconsin 1967; MDiv Lexington TS 1990; Cert Colorado Cntr For Healing 2000. D 6/17/1990 P 12/22/1990 Bp Don Adger Wimberly. R S Pat Ch Somerset KY 2003-2009; P Chap Of The Nativ Cincinnati OH 1996-1998; Cbury Crt W Carrollton OH 1995-1996; Trin Ch Covington KY 1992-1995. Auth, "Oh Thou Wmn That Bringest Gd Tidings"; Auth, "Men'S Prattle, Wmn Word: The Biblic Mssn Of Kath Bushnell," *Sprtl & Soc Responsibility: Vocational Vision Of Wmn In The Methodist*. Assn Of Epis Healthcare Chapl 1997; Hti 1999; Sdi 1995; Tertiary Of The Soc Of S Fran 1997. danahardwick999@insightbb.com

HARDWICK, Lada Eldredge (NC) 4490 Hanover Ave, Boulder CO 80305 B Chattanooga TN 8/4/1941 d Harold Eldredge & Marinell St Clair. BA E Tennessee St U 1964; MDiv STUSo 1990. D 6/17/1990 Bp William Evan Sanders P 1/13/1993 Bp Robert Gould Tharp. m 9/3/1964 David Hardwick c 2. Primary Pstr All SS Ch Hamlet NC 2002-2004; Sandhills Cluster Hamlet NC 2000-2004; Greenbrier Monroe Epis Mnstry White Sulphur Sprg WV 1996-2000; Vic S Jn's Ch Marlinton WV 1993-1995. ladave64@gmail.com

HARDWICK, Lindy Cornelius (Mo) 1001 Pheasant Hill Drive, Rolla MO 65401 B Saint Louis MO 9/28/1959 d William Edward Cornelius & Mary Virginia. BA DePauw U 1981; MDiv Ya Berk 1986. D 11/22/1986 P 10/1/1987 Bp William Grant Black. m 6/16/1990 Michael Hardwick c 2. Trin Ch S Jas MO 2003-2007; S Mich's Epis Ch O Fallon IL 1996-1999; The Epis Ch Of The Ascen Middletown OH 1991-1996; Int Calv Ch Cincinnati OH 1989-1990; Chap of the H Chld at Chld's Hosp Cincinnati OH 1988-1989; Dio Sthrn Ohio Cincinnati OH 1988; Assoc Min Indn Hill Ch Cincinnati OH 1986-1988. lindy@fidmail.com

HARDWICK, William (Ct) 19 1/2 Murray St, Norwalk CT 06851 **Pstr S Geo's Ch Middlebury CT 2006-** B New York NY 12/27/1945 s Henry Gilbert Hardwick & Josephine Therese. BA Iona Coll 1962; MA U of Notre Dame 1968; CDSP 1992; DMin SWTS 1999. D 6/13/1992 Bp Chester Lovelle Talton P 12/12/1992 Bp George Richard Millard. m 5/25/1991 Marian Stinson c 2. R Gr Epis Ch Norwalk CT 2000-2006; Vic S Richard's Epis Ch Lake Arrowhead CA 1995-2000; Asst S Matt's Epis Ch San Mateo CA 1992-1995. drbill122745@aol.com

HARDY, Cameron Reynolds (NY) 696 Deep Hollow Rd., Millbrook NY 12545 **S Ptr's Ch Millbrook NY 2009-** B Newport RI 2/29/1960 d David Wesley Reynolds & Cecily. AB Bow 1983; MDiv Ya Berk 2009. D 3/7/2009 P 9/12/2009 Bp Mark Sean Sisk. m 7/11/1987 William Hardy c 2. chardy@millbrook.org

HARDY JR, Jerry Edward (Mass) 51 John Ward Ave, Haverhill MA 01830 B 4/13/1939 m 4/26/2004 Judith Marie Gentle. S Steph's Memi Ch Lynn MA 1992-2000; The Epis Ch Of S Ptr And S Paul Marietta GA 1990-1992; H Innoc Ch Atlanta GA 1986-1990.

HARDY, Karen (WNY) 781 Maple Rd., Williamsville NY 14221 **S Simon's Ch Buffalo NY 2010-** B N Adams MA 4/26/1947 d Albert N Hardy & M Eloise. BS Buffalo St Teachers Buffalo NY 1977; MDiv Bex 2005. D 5/28/2005 Bp J Michael Garrison P. c 2. Ch Of All SS Buffalo NY 2007-2009. khardy@roadrunner.net

HARDY, Kim (Mass) 138 W. Plain St., Wayland MA 01778 **P-in-c S Mk's Ch Foxborough MA 2011-; P-in-c S Mk's Ch Foxborough MA 2011-; Celtic Liturg Coordntr All SS Par Brookline MA 2006-; Dio Liturg Com Co-Chair Dio Massachusetts Boston MA 2004-; Dioc Conv Strng Com Dio Massachusetts Boston MA 2001-; Dioc Liturg Com Dio Massachusetts Boston MA 1999-** B Elmira NY 12/5/1958 d Donald Frederick Hardy & Lois Marjorie. BM Ob 1981; MM Ithaca Coll 1983; DAS Ya Berk 1989; MDiv Yale DS 1989; Cler Ldrshp Proj 2005; Cert Cler Ldrshp Inst 2009; Cert Int

Mnstry Ntwk 2011. D 6/17/1989 Bp O'Kelley Whitaker P 12/17/1989 Bp William George Burrill. m 5/28/1988 Frederick Perkins Moser c 2. Int S Ptr's Epis Ch Cambridge MA 2010-2011; Dir of Admin & Liturg, Cler Ldrshp Proj Trin Par New York NY 2006-2010; Dioc Coun Dio Massachusetts Boston MA 2006-2007; Dio Liturg Com Co-Chair Dio Massachusetts Boston MA 2004-2007; R All SS Ch Stoneham MA 1996-2007; Coordntr of the Chld's Choir Emm Ch Boston MA 1994-1995; Dioc Coun Dio Rochester Rochester NY 1992-1993; P-in-c S Lk's Ch Branchport NY 1989-1994. Auth, "Inclusive Lang Hymnal Supplement for the Epis Ch," Self-Pub, 1995. kimhardy138@comcast.net

HARDY, Mary Elizabeth Holsberry (La) Po Box 3654, Durango CO 81302 **Asst S Mary Magd Ch Boulder CO 2009-** B Pensacola FL 11/28/1938 d John Edwin Holsberry & Ethel Elizabeth. Van 1958; Tul 1959; BA Wesleyan Coll 1960; Med Tul 1971; MDiv CDSP 1992. D 6/13/1992 Bp James Barrow Brown P 12/5/1992 Bp William Edwin Swing. c 3. Asst R S Mk's Epis Ch Durango CO 2001; Assoc R Trin Ch New Orleans LA 1993-2001; P-in-c S Mk's Epis Ch Palo Alto CA 1992-1993. Auth, "Preaching Excellence," Cdsp, 1991. Graduated w dist CDSP 1992; Prching Excellence CDSP 1991. mbspirit@frontier.net

HARDY, (Patricia) Joyce (Ark) 2114 Center St, Little Rock AR 72206 **Cler Rep for Prov VII Exec Coun Appointees New York NY 2006-2012** B Pryor OK 8/1/1951 d Omer D Hardy & Reba M. BD U of Arkansas 1973; Med NE St U 1978. D 8/24/1985 Bp William Jackson Cox. Arkansas Dth Penalty Moratorium Cmpgn Little Rock AR 2008-2010; D Chr Epis Ch Little Rock AR 2005-2011; D Chr Epis Ch Little Rock AR 2005-2011; Dio Arkansas Little Rock AR 2001-2007; D Trin Cathd Little Rock AR 2000-2005; S Fran Hse Little Rock AR 1997-1999; Celebration Mnstrs Little Rock AR 1996-2000; S Marg's Epis Ch Little Rock AR 1992-1996; Asst S Paul's Ch Fayetteville AR 1989-1991; Asst S Matt's Ch Sand Sprg OK 1986-1989; Asst S Andr's Ch Grove OK 1985-1986. EPF Bd; EWC; Episcopalians for Global Recon; Exec Coun; NAAD. pjhardy51@comcast.net

HARDY, Stanley P (Mass) Po Box 657, Humarock MA 02047 B Gloucester MA 1/9/1929 s Ralph Theodore Hardy & Viola Frances. BA Bos 1956; STB Ya Berk 1959; MS Emerson Coll 1991. D 6/20/1959 Bp Anson Phelps Stokes Jr P 12/1/1959 Bp William A Lawrence. m 2/3/1973 Jane Laskey. Assoc P Ch Of S Jn The Evang Hingham MA 1993-2000; Assoc P Trin Ch Marshfield Hills MA 1993-2000; Supplement Accounts Boston MA 1975-1976; R S Mk's Epis Ch Fall River MA 1974-1978; Vic The Ch Of S Mary Of The Harbor Provincetown MA 1964-1970; Assoc S Andr's Ch Kansas City MO 1964-1968; Cur S Steph's Memi Ch Lynn MA 1959-1964. www.beykerman@aol.com

HARDY, Velinda Elaine (NC) P.O. Box 86, 4880 Highway 561 East, Tillery NC 27887 **D Calv Ch Tarboro NC 2001-; D S Lk's Ch Tarboro NC 2001-** B Tarboro NC 9/18/1948 d Edwin Beselle Hardy & Ethel Adelle. BA S Aug's Coll Raleigh NC 1970; MA Clark Atlanta U 1972. D 5/19/2001 Bp J(ames) Gary Gloster.

HARE, Ann DuBuisson (NY) 4300 Edson Ave, Bronx NY 10466 **D S Lk's Epis Ch Bronx NY 1998-** B New York NY 12/9/1933 d Elijah Newton Gilliam & Eileyne (Laho) Henry. BA CUNY 1954; MA NYU 1965; MA GTS 1991. D 5/30/1992 Bp Richard Frank Grein. m 2/6/1970 Norman B Hare c 4. D Ch Of The Gd Shpd Wakefield Bronx NY 1992-1998. Auth, "Jewish & Black Dialogue Over The Past 30 Years," 1991. Afr Mnstry Com 2001; Alt Del Prov Syn 1998-2000; Coun Adv Prison Mnstry Natl Ch; Del Prov Syn 2001-2003; Del Prov Syn 1995-1997; E Bronx IPC Chairperson 2008; E Bronx IPC Vice Chair 2004-2008. Lights Awd Bronx Epis Aids Mnstry.

HARE, Delmas (At) 104 Sequoyah Hills Drive, Fletcher NC 28732 **Adjuct Cler The Cathd Of All Souls Asheville NC 2003-** B Baileyton AL 1/8/1934 s Herbert Cleon Hare & Clifford Miranda. BA Berea Coll 1955; BD STUSo 1961; PhD Emory U 1982. D 6/17/1961 P 12/23/1961 Bp Matthew G Henry. m 6/16/1956 Mabel C Herren c 3. P Assoc Ret Calv Epis Ch Fletcher NC 2002-2003; R Gd Shpd Epis Ch Austell GA 1993-1999; Vic St Fran Epis Ch Acworth GA 1990; R Ch Of The Resurr Coll Pk GA 1987-1989; R Emm Ch Staunton VA 1983-1986; Int Assoc Chr Ch Macon GA 1982; R S Jn's Epis Ch Marion NC 1966-1979; Vic S Mary's Ch Morganton NC 1961-1966; Vic S Steph's Epis Ch Morganton NC 1961-1966. dhare@charter.net

HARER, Mark P (CPa) 251 S Derr Dr, Lewisburg PA 17837 **Pres, Disciplinary Bd Dio Cntrl Pennsylvania Harrisburg PA 2011-; R S Andr's Epis Ch Lewisburg PA 2007-** B Williamsport PA 10/25/1950 s Mark Tuttle Harer & Mary Theresa. BA Lycoming Coll 1972; MDiv UTS 1976; DIT Oxf 1977; JD PSU/Dickinson Sch of Law 1992. D 6/29/1980 Bp Dean T Stevenson P 2/8/1981 Bp Charlie Fuller McNutt Jr. m 5/18/1985 Mary Bierman c 1. R Prince Of Peace Epis Ch Dallas PA 2006-2007; R All SS Epis Ch Lehighton PA 1997-2005; R S Jn's Epis Ch Palmerton PA 1997-2005; Asst S Andr's Ch Harrisburg PA 1992-1997; Vic S Jas Ch Mansfield PA 1985-1989; Vic S Andr's Ch Tioga PA 1981-1989; Vic S Jn's Ch Westfield PA 1981-1989; Dio Cntrl Pennsylvania Harrisburg PA 1980-1981. mpharer@ptd.net

HARGETT, William Murray (SC) 1227 Palmetto Peninsula Dr, Mount Pleasant SC 29464 **Died 9/19/2011** B Cleveland OH 7/6/1937 s William Rindfuss Hargett & Genet Marion. BA Rutgers-The St U 1960; STB GTS 1963. D 4/27/1963 P 11/2/1963 Bp Alfred L Banyard. c 4. annbargett@att.net

HARGIS, James Frederick (NCal) 742 El Granada Blvd, Half Moon Bay CA 94019 **Ret Ch Pension Fund New York NY 2003-** B Carthage MO 10/10/1946 s Frederick Funston Hargis & Mary Anne. BA Drury U 1968; MDiv CDSP 1974; MA Grad Theol Un 1975; PhD U CA 1976. D 6/28/1975 Bp George Richard Millard P 2/14/1982 Bp William Edwin Swing. m 6/25/1988 Masumi Ann Hargis c 2. R Gr Epis Ch Fairfield CA 2002-2003; R All SS Ch Kapaa HI 1998-2002; Dioc Coun Dio Hawaii Honolulu HI 1998-2002; P-in-c True Sunshine Par San Francisco CA 1996-1998; Int S Steph's Epis Ch Longview WA 1993-1994; Chapl Off Of Bsh For ArmdF New York NY 1985-1991; R S Andr's Epis Ch Prineville OR 1983-1985; Vic S Alb's Epis Ch Redmond OR 1982-1985; Asst S Tim's Ch Danville CA 1980-1982; Asst S Steph's Epis Ch Orinda CA 1976-1977; The Epis Ch Of S Mary The Vrgn San Francisco CA 1973-1976; S Jn's Epis Ch Oakland CA 1972-1973; St Johns Epis Ch Petaluma CA 1971-1972. "Sleeping w Zeus: Why Cats are better than Men"; Auth, "Visions, Reflections, Wanderings, Thrills of Taneycomo". kahujim@gmail.com

HARGREAVES, Robert Alan (Me) Po Box 964, Jefferson ME 04348 B Providence RI 4/5/1937 s Alan Birtwistle Hargreaves & Virginia Bright. BA GW 1959; MDiv VTS 1962; Postgrad TESM 1990; U of Maine 1996. D 6/9/1962 P 6/1/1963 Bp Robert Fisher Gibson Jr. m 7/31/1965 Frances Richardson Murray c 2. R S Mk's Ch Augusta ME 1983-1993; R Emm Epis Ch Cumberland RI 1973-1983; Dioc Coun Dio Rhode Island Providence RI 1973-1976; Vic S Mths Ch Coventry RI 1969-1973; Vic Ch of the Incarn Mineral VA 1964-1969; R S Jas Epis Ch Louisa VA 1964-1969; Asst Chr Epis Ch Winchester VA 1962-1963. Auth, "From A Parson'S Desk (Weekly Column)," *Cntrl Virginian*, 1964. sabbathrest@juno.com

HARGROVE, Thomas J (Pa) 1628 Prospect St, Ewing NJ 08638 B Fitzgerlad GA 7/9/1951 s Gordon Wendel Hargrove & Virginia Louise. BBA California St U 1989; MDiv Nash 1992. D 11/14/1992 P 3/1/1994 Bp George Nelson Hunt III. m 12/20/2010 Dirk Chrisian Reinken. P-in-c S Phil Memi Ch Philadelphia PA 2009-2010; S Simon The Cyrenian Ch Philadelphia PA 2002-2009; S Mary's Ch E Providence RI 1994-1999; Cur S Steph's Ch Providence RI 1992-1993. OHC (Assoc) 1989.

HARIG, Richard Oliver (O) 3583 Sparrow Pond Cir., Akron OH 44333 B Akron OH 12/19/1924 s William Joseph Harig & Mary Martha. BA Bowling Green St U 1947; BD Bex 1950; S Aug's Coll Cbury GB 1963. D 6/13/1950 P 5/19/1951 Bp Beverley D Tucker. m 6/26/1965 Ruth Murray c 1. Int S Phil's In The Hills Tucson AZ 2001; Int Epis Soc of Chr Ch Cincinnati OH 1998-2000; Int S Dav's Ch Wayne PA 1996; Int S Jn's Of Lattingtown Locust Vlly NY 1995-1996; Int The Ch Of The Redeem Baltimore MD 1993-1995; Int S Barn On The Desert Scottsdale AZ 1991-1992; Int Epis Soc of Chr Ch Cincinnati OH 1990-1991; ExCoun Dio Ohio Cleveland OH 1966-1976; R Ch Of Our Sav Akron OH 1964-1990; Chair Yth Div Dio Ohio Cleveland OH 1960-1962; P-in-c S Mk's Ch Canton OH 1956-1962; Assoc S Paul's Epis Ch Cleveland Heights OH 1952-1956; P-in-c S Jn The Evang Ch Napoleon OH 1951-1952; D-in-c S Jn's Epis Ch Bowling Green OH 1950-1951. richardharig1425@aol.com

HARING, Charlotte (Az) 3942 E Monte Vista Dr, Tucson AZ 85712 B New Milford NJ 6/15/1928 d John Fisher & Jenny. D 10/21/1989 Bp Joseph Thomas Heistand. c 3. Asstg D S Andr's Epis Ch Tucson AZ 1993-2011; Asstg D/Dir Outreach Mnstrs Gr S Paul's Epis Ch Tucson AZ 1990-1993. cjharing@att.net

HARKER, Margaret Ann Griggs (NI) 1364 N Pinebluff Dr, Marion IN 46952 **P-in-c S Paul's Epis Ch Gas City IN 2008-** B Dunkirk NY 10/1/1942 d Robert Francis Griggs & Margaret Robertson. BA MWC 1964; MDiv SWTS 1993. D 4/30/1993 P 11/1/1993 Bp Francis Campbell Gray. m 8/15/1964 Albert C Harker c 4. Chr The King Epis Ch Huntington IN 1993-2004. aharker@indy.rr.com

HARKINS, James Robert (NY) 69 Main St Apt 201, North Adams MA 01247 **Ch Of The Resurr New York NY 2002-** B Watertown SD 9/2/1927 s James Abram Harkins & Mae Lucille. BA U MN 1949; LTh SWTS 1952; BD SWTS 1953; U Madrid Madrid Es 1964. D 6/21/1952 P 12/21/1952 Bp Stephen E Keeler. m 1/2/1967 Dora R Reus-Froylan c 1. French Ch Of S Esprit New York NY 1991-1993; Exec Coun Appointees New York NY 1979-1991; R S Jas Epis Ch Prospect Pk PA 1972-1974; Vic S Alb's Ch Brooklyn NY 1958-1960; Assoc S Andr's Ch Denver CO 1954-1955; Cur Geth Ch Minneapolis MN 1952-1954. SSC, Conf Of The Blessed Sacrame. Hon Cn S Mary Cathd. jrh3789@verizon.net

HARKINS III, J(ohn) William (At) 1703 Grace Ct SE, Smyrna GA 30082 **Cn Assoc. Cathd Of S Phil Atlanta GA 2004-** B Atlanta GA 3/14/1955 s John William Harkins & Myrium Willette. BA Rhodes Coll 1977; MDiv Van 1986; PhD Van 2001. D 6/9/2001 Bp Robert Gould Tharp P 11/12/2002 Bp J(ohn) Neil Alexander. m 9/12/1981 Victoria Joanne Smith c 2. Epis Ch Of The H

Fam Jasper GA 2002-2004; D / Asst R S Jas Epis Ch Marietta GA 2001-2002. Auth, "Psycho Pathology, Sin, and Evil," *A Case Study of the Disconnected Man*, Jounral of Sprtlty and Mntl Hlth, 2008; Auth, "Monday, Tuesday, Wednesday H Week," *Pstr Perspectives on Lectionary*, Feasting on the Word, 2008; Auth, "My Continental Divide," *An Experiential Journey*, Journ for Preachers, 2006. AAMFT Clincl Mem 1997; AAPC Fell 1998. harkinsb@ctsnet.edu

HARLACHER, Richard (CPa) 486 Fencepost Ln, Palmyra PA 17078 B Harrisburg PA 2/7/1940 s William Charles Harlacher & Florence Anna. Pontifical Coll Josephinum 1967. Rec from Roman Catholic 5/27/1976 as Priest Bp Dean T Stevenson. m 12/14/1974 Carol Lynn Frank. R S Paul's Ch Columbia PA 1981-1998; Vic S Andr's Ch Tioga PA 1976-1981; Vic S Jn's Ch Westfield PA 1976-1981; Dio Cntrl Pennsylvania Harrisburg PA 1976-1977. harlacherfamily@aol.com

HARLAN, James Robert (SeFla) 600 Gilpin St, Denver CO 80218 **R The Epis Ch Of Beth-By-The-Sea Palm Bch FL 2011-** B Denver CO 3/17/1966 s Donald Lock Harlan & Kay Louise. BS U CO 1988; MDiv SWTS 1994. D 6/11/1994 P 12/10/1994 Bp William Jerry Winterrowd. m 5/10/1997 Elizabeth June Shaffer c 1. Pres, Epis Camp and Conf Mnstrs of Colorado, Inc. Dio Colorado Denver CO 2010-2011; Mem, Stndg Com Dio Colorado Denver CO 2009-2011; Chair, COM Dio Colorado Denver CO 2005-2009; R The Ch Of The Ascen Denver CO 2002-2011; Chair, Dioc BEC Dio Colorado Denver CO 2002-2004; Command Chapl, US Naval Mobile Construction Battalion ONE Off Of Bsh For ArmdF New York NY 1999-2003; R Epis Ch Of S Jn The Bapt Breckenridge CO 1997-1999; Asst to the R Ch Of S Mich The Archangel Colorado Sprg CO 1994-1997; Yth Dir S Jn's Cathd Denver CO 1988-1991. a031197-cpg@yahoo.com

HARLAND, Mary Frances (Spok) Po Box 1510, Medical Lake WA 99022 **Chapl Correction Cntr Dio Spokane Spokane WA 1995-** B Lakin KS 10/12/1931 d Everett Gareth Wilson & Helen Margaret. BS Idaho St U 1953; Dioc TS Seattle WA 1978; Pacific Luth U 1982. D 3/10/1979 Bp Robert Hume Cochrane P 5/8/1986 Bp Leigh Wallace Jr. m 8/20/1955 Delmar C Harland. Chapl Correction Cntr Dio Olympia Seattle WA 1994-1995; Chapl Dio Spokane Spokane WA 1984-1994. Cert Med Hlth Counslr. WA St Employee of the Year St of WA 1982.

HARMAN, Torrence McClure (Va) 1927 Stuart Ave, Richmond VA 23220 **S Mary's Whitechapel Epis Lancaster VA 2007-** B Richmond VA 12/16/1943 BS Virginia Commonwealth U. D 1/14/2004 P 7/17/2004 Bp Peter James Lee. m 7/27/1985 Julian Weir Harman c 3. Asst S Jas' Ch Richmond VA 2004-2007. priestsmwc@aol.com

HARMON, Elsa Wittmack (Ia) 3131 Fleur Dr Apt 901, Des Moines IA 50321 B Des Moines IA 11/15/1941 d Charles Ewald Wittmack & Elsa Margaret. BS U of Wisconsin 1963. D 1/10/1999 Bp Carl Christopher Epting. m 6/18/1966 Henry Andrew Harmon. D The Cathd Ch Of S Paul Des Moines IA 1998-1999.

HARMON, John (WA) 7005 Piney Branch Rd NW, Washington DC 20012 **Trin Ch Washington DC 2000-** B Cape Palmas LR 11/16/1964 s Henry G Harmon & Annie Klade. BA S Paul's Coll 1988; Lancaster TS 1989; MDiv VTS 1991; ThM UTS 1998. D 6/8/1991 Bp C(laude) Charles Vache P 2/1/1992 Bp Frank Harris Vest Jr. m 10/17/1992 Keeva Patterson c 3. Pres of Stndg Com Dio Sthrn Virginia Norfolk VA 1997-2000; S Steph's Ch Petersburg VA 1993-2000; Asst R Gr Ch Norfolk VA 1991-1993. jharmon@trinitychurchdc.org

HARMON, John Jason (Mass) 535 Mount Hope Ave # 206, Rochester NY 14620 **Died 8/18/2010** B Bridgeport CT 3/13/1921 s John William Harmon & Hortense Jacobs. BA Pr 1942; BD EDS 1950. D 1/28/1950 Bp Norman B Nash P 10/8/1950 Bp Dudley S Stark. c 4. Auth, "Toward a Secular Ecum," *Cross Currents*, 1966; Auth, "The Par: When is it Alive? When Should it Die?," *Cross Currents*, 1965; Auth, "Toward a Theol of the City Ch," *Cross Currents*, 1964; Auth, "The Ch in the City," *Cross Currents*, 1963. jnnk2123@frontiernet.net

HARMON, John Robert (Md) 10128 Camshire Ct Apt B, Saint Ann MO 63074 B Saint Louis MO 2/8/1943 s Robert Edward Harmon & Dorothy Ellen. U of Missouri 1963; BA Drury U 1966; BD CDSP 1969. D 6/24/1969 P 12/1/1969 Bp George Leslie Cadigan. c 3. Dio Maryland Baltimore MD 1996; All Hallows Par So River Davidsonville MD 1992-1996; Chr Epis Ch Bensalem PA 1985-1992; Ch Of Our Sav Jenkintown PA 1984; R Ch Of The Mssh Lower Gwynedd PA 1979-1982; R S Andr's Epis Ch Lewisburg PA 1977-1979; Asst S Paul's Ch Philadelphia PA 1975-1977; Vic S Barn Ch Moberly MO 1969-1975; Vic S Matt's Epis Ch Mex MO 1969-1975.

HARMON, Joseph Albion (Nwk) 205 Halladay Street, Jersey City NJ 07304 **R Chr Epis Ch E Orange NJ 2011-; Eccl Crt/Disciplinary Bd Dio Newark Newark NJ 2008-; Dioc Coun and Strng Com Dio Newark Newark NJ 2007-; P-in-c Ch Of The Incarn Jersey City NJ 2006-; Com on Const and Cn Dio Newark Newark NJ 2006-** B Philadelphia PA 7/15/1953 s Joseph A Harmon & Althea O. BA Cor 1975; MDiv GTS 1978; JD Widener U Sch of Law 2001. D 2/18/1978 Bp Robert Bracewell Appleyard P 8/19/1978 Bp Philip Edward Randolph Elder. c 2. Assoc S Andr's Ch Harrisburg PA 1999-2006; Vic Ch Of The Epiph Chicago IL 1997-1999; R Gr Ch Chicago IL 1994-1996; R Gr Ch White Plains NY 1994-1996; R S Matt's And S Jos's Detroit MI 1989-1994; R S Cyp's Epis Ch Detroit MI 1988-1989; Cn Mssnr Cathd Of All SS Albany NY 1986-1988; Kent Sch Kent CT 1985-1986; Assoc Gr Ch Newark NJ 1982-1985; P-in-c Gr Epis Ch Eliz NJ 1981-1982. Assoc OHC 2006. joseharm@comcast.net

HARMON, Kendall Stuart (SC) 185 Hitching Post Ln, Summerville SC 29483 **Assoc Chr/St Paul's Epis Par Yonges Island SC 2002-; Cn Theol Dio So Carolina Charleston SC 2002-; Dep Gc Dio So Carolina Charleston SC 1997-** B Urbana IL 4/13/1960 s Francis Stuart Harmon & Mary Ann. BA Bow 1982; Regent Coll Vancouver Bc CA 1984; MA Regent Coll Vancouver Bc CA 1987; MDiv TESM 1987; PhD Oxf 1993. D 6/11/1987 Bp George Edward Haynsworth P 6/1/1988 Bp C(hristopher) FitzSimons Allison. m 4/25/1987 Elizabeth Catherine Deenihan. Stndg Com Dio So Carolina Charleston SC 1994-1997; S Paul's Epis Ch Summerville SC 1993-2002; Voc Diac Com Dio So Carolina Charleston SC 1993-1994; Asst to R Ch Of The H Comf Sumter SC 1987-1990. Auth, "Nothingness And Human Destinty," *Pilgrim Guide*; Auth, "He Shall Come Again In Glory," *Rule Of Faith*. AAR; Conf Of Angl Theologians; Mensa; SBL. Phi Beta Kappa. ksharmon@mindspring.com

HARMON, Krista Dawn (NC) 2200 Via Rosa, Palos Verdes Estates CA 90274 B Akron OH 5/8/1975 d Dale Lee Harmon & Susan Marie. BEd U NC at Chap Hill 1999; MDiv CDSP 2008. D 6/28/2008 Bp Alfred Clark Marble Jr P 1/7/2009 Bp Michael Bruce Curry. Assoc S Fran' Par Palos Verdes Estates CA 2008-2010. krista.fregoso@gmail.com

HARMON, R(obert) Dale (NC) 2301 Thousand Oaks Dr, Richmond VA 23294 **Died 10/2/2010** B Gastonia NC 2/5/1939 s Earle Cranston Harmon & Lettie Evelena. BA Lenoir-Rhyne Coll 1962; MDiv STUSo 1965; Med U GA 1970. D 6/24/1965 P 6/13/1966 Bp Matthew G Henry. c 1. Who's Who in Executives and Professionals 1994. rdhnmh@cs.com

HARMON, Robert Dale (Spr) 1119 Oakland Ave, 1119 Oakland Ave, Mount Vernon IL 62864 B Alton IL 10/10/1941 s Dale Harmon & Evelyn. BA U Of Evansville 1968; MDiv SWTS 1971. D 6/19/1971 Bp Gerald Francis Burrill P 12/17/1971 Bp Albert A Chambers. m 9/6/1969 Catherine Ann Schmidt. R Trin Ch Mt Vernon IL 1974-2002; P-in-c S Jn's Epis Ch Decatur IL 1973-1974; Cur S Jn's Epis Ch Decatur IL 1971-1973. Forw In Faith; SSC. harmon@mvn.net

HARMS, Richard Benjamin (Los) 2731 Jody Pl, Escondido CA 92027 B Pasadena CA 7/17/1932 s Herman Benjamin Harms & Gertrude Eileen. BA U of Redlands 1955; MDiv CDSP 1958; DMin Fuller TS 1999. D 6/16/1958 Bp Donald J Campbell P 2/1/1959 Bp Francis E I Bloy. c 4. Cn Mssnr Dio San Diego San Diego CA 1978-1984; All SS Epis Ch Brawley CA 1978; St Marks Mssn Holtville CA 1978; Dio San Diego San Diego CA 1977-1989; S Mk's Par Altadena CA 1969-1972; R Ch Of The Redeem Eagle Pass TX 1966-1968; P-in-c H Trin Carrizo Sprg TX 1966-1968; Cur S Mk's Par Altadena CA 1958-1960. "Paradigms from Lk-Acts for Multicultural Communities," Ptr Lang, 2001. harms.richard@att.net

HARMUTH, Karl Michael (Dal) 9021 Church Rd, Dallas TX 75231 B Pittsburgh PA 4/24/1937 s Joseph Thomas Harmuth & Lucille Helen. BA S Vinc Coll Latrobe PA 1959; MDiv S Vinc Sem Latrobe PA 1963; STM SMU 1974. Rec from Roman Catholic 10/1/1967 Bp Charles A Mason. m 7/15/1965 Marianne Mudrick c 3. R Epis Ch Of The Ascen Dallas TX 1986-1998; R S Andr's Epis Ch Arlington VA 1979-1986; Archd Dio NW Pennsylvania Erie PA 1976-1979; P-in-c H Trin Ch Rockwall TX 1975-1976; Cn To Ordnry Dio Dallas Dallas TX 1973-1976; R All SS Epis Ch Dallas TX 1970-1973; Cur All SS Epis Ch Dallas TX 1967-1970. Cmnty Serv Awd Mha 1986; Awd For Outstanding Serv Untd Way 1986. mmharmuth@prodigy.net

HARNEY, Margaret Ferris (At) 4393 Garmon Rd Nw, Atlanta GA 30327 **Cmsn on Human Trafficking, Chair Dio Atlanta Atlanta GA 2010-; Assoc S Dunst's Epis Ch Atlanta GA 1994-** B Panama PA 4/22/1947 d Raymond Tuttle Ferris & Mary Kate. BA Randolph-Macon Wmn's Coll 1969; Cert U CA 1971; MDiv Candler TS Emory U 1988. D 6/11/1988 Bp Charles Judson Child Jr P 4/8/1989 Bp Frank Kellogg Allan. m 9/20/1969 Thomas Harney c 2. Chapl H Innoc' Epis Sch Atlanta GA 1992-1994; Int S Dunst's Epis Ch Atlanta GA 1990-1992; Asst The Ch Of S Matt Snellville GA 1988-1990. Theta Phi Candler TS 1987. mharney@comporium.net

HARNSBERGER, Charles Edwin Berrien (SD) PO Box 986, Hot Springs SD 57747 B Takoma Park MD 8/16/1932 s Reynolds Trent Harnsberger & Mary Elizabeth. BS VPI 1954; BD VTS 1957. D 6/7/1957 Bp Frederick D Goodwin P 12/1/1957 Bp Conrad Gesner. m 7/9/2009 Margaret Ann Mellspaugh. Serv S Lk's Ch Hot Sprg SD 1992-1997; S Lk's Ch Hot Sprg SD 1974-1986; Dio So Dakota Sioux Falls SD 1966-1992; Vic S Lk's Ch Hot Sprg SD 1958-1965. EPF 2005; OHC 1957.

HARPER, Barbara Anne (ETenn) 1155 Woodlawn Rd, Lenoir City TN 37771 B Memphis TN 8/19/1941 d Paul Brown Hare & Pollyanna. BD U of Florida 1963; EFM 1992; Dio E Tennessee Diac Prog 1994. D 9/18/1994 Bp Robert Gould Tharp. m 9/29/1967 Kenneth Allen Harper c 4. Ch Of The Ascen

Knoxville TN 2002-2004; Dio E Tennessee Knoxville TN 1997-1998. Ch Denominational Leaders Assn; EFM Mentor; NAAD; Ord of S Lk. barbaraharper987@msn.com

HARPER, David Scott (Va) 6107 Franconia Rd, Alexandria VA 22310 **Olivet Epis Ch Franconia VA 2002-** B Harrisburg PA 5/4/1946 s Walter Scott Harper & Ruth Naomi. Bos TS; BA McDaniel Coll 1968; MDiv Gettysburg TS 1972; DMin Gettysburg TS 1984. D 11/9/1996 P 6/14/1997 Bp Michael Whittington Creighton. m 1/11/1997 Donna L Walborn c 7. R S Tim's Ch Bp CA 1999-2002; H Trin Epis Ch Shamokin PA 1997-1999; R S Steph's Ch Mt Carmel PA 1996-1999; Dir Reli Affrs S Jn's Epis Ch Carlisle PA 1990-1996. fr.harper@verizon.net

HARPER, Fletcher (Nwk) 241A Johnson Ave Apt M1, Hackensack NJ 07601 B New York NY 2/16/1963 s Fletcher Moulton Harper & Prudence. BA Pr 1985; MDiv UTS 1991. D 6/13/1991 Bp Richard Frank Grein P 12/21/1992 Bp John Shelby Spong. m 10/10/1992 Jennifer R Rueb c 2. R S Lk's Epis Ch Haworth NJ 1997-2002; R All SS Ch Bergenfield NJ 1994-1996; R S Lk's Epis Ch Haworth NJ 1994-1996; Asst R All SS Ch Bergenfield NJ 1992-1993; Asst R S Lk's Epis Ch Haworth NJ 1992-1993. "Sprt, Stwdshp, Justice and the Earth," *Diversity in the Environ Mvmt*, Yale, 2007; "Ground for Hope," *Eco-Sprt*, Fordham, 2007. revfharper@greenfaith.org

HARPER, Glynn Compton (La) 704 Touro St, New Orleans LA 70116 **Died 1/13/2010** B Shelby County,TX 10/21/1935 s William Bruce Harper & Hattie Francis. BS USNA 1958; MDiv Epis TS of The SW 1977. D 6/3/1978 P 12/8/1978 Bp Victor Manuel Rivera. glynn@glynnharper.com

HARPER, Harry Taylor (WA) 36303 Notley Manor Ln, Chaptico MD 20621 **Int S Paul's Par Prince Geo's Cnty Brandywine MD 2007-; S Alb's Epis Ch Of Bexley Columbus OH 2002-; The Ch Of The Ascen Lexington Pk MD 2002-** B Sydney NSW AU 6/4/1926 s Charles Oswald Harper & Lilias Finlay. Moore Theol Coll, Sydney 1956. Trans from Anglican Church in Aotearoa, New Zealand and Polynesia 3/22/1964 Bp Randolph R Claiborne. m Ramona Harper c 3. Int S Thos Par Croom Upper Marlboro MD 2001-2002; Int Middleham & S Ptr's Par Lusby MD 2000-2002; Asst S Paul's Epis Ch Piney Waldorf MD 2000-2002; R The Ch Of The Redeem Beth MD 1974-1992; R S Geo's Ch Glenn Dale MD 1971-1974; R All SS Ch Oakley Av MD 1968-1971; R S Andr's Ch Leonardtown California MD 1968-1971; R Ch Of The Incarn Atlanta GA 1963-1968.

HARPER, Helen Othelia (Nwk) 784 Columbus Ave Apt 14s, New York NY 10025 B Manhattan NY 7/4/1949 d Evermond Gustaff Haddock & Blanch Dora. MD Vancouver TS 1993. D 6/1/2002 P 5/17/2003 Bp John Palmer Croneberger. Int H Apos And Medtr Philadelphia PA 2007-2008; P-in-c Chr Epis Ch Bensalem PA 2004-2007; P-t Cur S Paul's Ch Englewood NJ 2002-2004; P-t Dir. of Prog (Haven for Families) S Ptr's Ch Clifton NJ 2002-2004. UBE 2008. helen.harper@att.net

HARPER, John Brammer (Ia) 1310 Bristol Dr, Iowa City IA 52245 **Dep GC Dio Iowa Des Moines IA 2003-; D New Song Epis Ch Coralville IA 1995-** B Des Moines IA 3/23/1941 s John Pearsons Harper & Mary Brammer. BA Stan 1962; MBA U of Iowa 1966; U of Iowa 1974. D 9/16/1995 Bp Carl Christopher Epting. COM Dio Iowa Des Moines IA 2004-2006; Dio Iowa Des Moines IA 2002-2004; Dir - Mnstrs Retreat Prog Dio Iowa Des Moines IA 2001-2007. john-harper@uiowa.edu

HARPER, John Harris (Ala) Po Box 31212 - B Florence AL 8/12/1938 s Harry Cleghorn Harper & Mabel Jane. BA Emory U 1960; JD Emory U 1962; MDiv Ya Berk 1980. D 4/26/1982 P 6/18/1983 Bp (George) Paul Reeves. m 12/5/1964 Margaret McCall c 2. Vice Dn The Cathd Ch Of The Adv Birmingham AL 2005-2010; Int Dn The Cathd Ch Of The Adv Birmingham AL 2004-2005; Vice Dn The Cathd Ch Of The Adv Birmingham AL 2000-2004; Int S Andr's Ch Darien GA 1998-1999; Int S Cyp's Ch Darien GA 1998-1999; Int S Andr's Epis Ch Douglas GA 1993-1994; Sum Asst All SS Epis Chap Linville NC 1984-1990; Vic Chr Ch S Marys GA 1984-1988; Vic S Mk's Epis Ch Woodbine GA 1984-1985; Asst S Mk's Ch Brunswick GA 1982-1983. Auth, "Sermons and Words 2000-2010," *Sermons and Words 2000-2010*, 2011; Auth, "Law Course for Customs Off," *Law Course for Customs Off*, Gov Print Off, 1999. Who's Who in Amer Law 1991; Who's Who in Rel 1984; Exceptional Serv Awd Dept of the Treasury 1976; Distinguished Serv Awd 1968. johnharrisharper@gmail.com

HARPER JR, William Rhoderick (SVa) 6829 Cape View Avenue, Norfolk VA 23518 B Birmingham AL 4/19/1931 s William Rhoderick Harper & Sara Francis. BA Birmingham-Sthrn Coll 1958; MDiv TESM 1981. D 12/27/1981 Bp Furman Stough P 6/29/1982 Bp George Edward Haynsworth. m 6/16/1952 Kathleen Lackey. R Chr Ch Waverly VA 1989-1994; Brandon Ch Hopewell VA 1989-1993; S Paul's Epis Ch Kittanning PA 1984-1989; S Matt's Ch (Ft Motte) S Matthews SC 1982-1984. Auth, "Calhoun Times". Compassionate Friends; EvangES, Curs, BSA.

HARPER, William Roland (Oly) 8595 NE Day Road, Bainbridge Island WA 98110 **Vic Gr Ch Bainbridge Island WA 1994-** B Seattle WA 8/8/1958 s Roland William Harper & Carol Loraine. BA U of Washington 1980; PrTS 1983; MDiv GTS 1984. D 6/30/1984 Bp Robert Hume Cochrane P 2/11/1985 Bp James Stuart Wetmore. m 12/29/1979 Carolyn Jean Graves c 2. R Ch Of S Mary The Vrgn Chappaqua NY 1987-1994; Cur S Jn's Ch Larchmont NY 1984-1987. bill@gracehere.org

HARPSTER, Christopher Lee (ETenn) St Paul's Episcopal Church, 161 E Ravine Rd, Kingsport TN 37660 **S Paul's Epis Ch Kingsport TN 2009-; Chapl Dio E Tennessee Knoxville TN 1999-** B Lewistown PA 11/14/1966 s Wilbur Fenton Harpster & Barbara Mae. Gnrl Stds E Tennessee St U 2002. D 12/8/2007 Bp Charles Glenn VonRosenberg. m 11/20/1993 Deborah L Harpster c 3. Gld Of St. Vinc 2008. harpsc@charter.net

HARRELL, Linda J (Ore) 99 Brattle St, Cambridge MA 02138 B Omaha NE 9/11/1946 d Kyle Harrell & Jane Audrey. EDS; BA California St U 1973; MDiv VTS 1978. D 6/17/1978 P 1/1/1979 Bp Robert C Rusack. c 1. Dio Oregon Portland OR 1988-1994; S Fran Ch Sweet Hm OR 1986-1987; Liturg Asst S Matt's Epis Ch Eugene OR 1985-1993; Dio Oregon Portland OR 1980-1984; Assoc S Mary's Epis Ch Eugene OR 1979-1980; CE S Aug By-The-Sea Par Santa Monica CA 1978-1979. ESMHE, EWC, EPF. 3REVLJH@VERIZON.COM

HARRELSON JR, Ernest S (Spok) 915 S 22nd Ave, Yakima WA 98902 **P-in-c S Mich's Epis Ch Yakima WA 2001-** B Trenton NJ 10/7/1945 s Ernest S Harrelson & Isabel. BA Coll of Wooster 1968; MDiv Bex 1971. D 6/26/1971 P 5/20/1972 Bp John Harris Burt. m 11/20/1976 Dorothy M Schirmer c 4. R S Paul's Ch Winona MN 1998-2001; S Jn Hutchinson MN 1995-1998; R Trin Ch Litchfield MN 1994-1998; Supply P Dio El Camino Real Monterey CA 1989-1994; S Mk's Ch Candor NY 1983-1989; R Calv Epis Ch Mc Donough NY 1976-1980; Chr Ch Guilford CT 1976-1980; R S Paul's Ch Oxford NY 1976-1980; R Gr Ch Ravenna OH 1973-1976; Asst S Paul's Ch Maumee OH 1971-1973. ernie.harrelson@ecunet.org

HARRELSON, Larry Eugene (Ida) 3095 W. Ravenhurst St., Meridian ID 83646 **Exam Chapl Dio Idaho Boise ID 2010-; Assoc Ch Of H Nativ Meridian ID 2009-** B McLeansboro IL 4/17/1944 s Willis Murrel Harrelson & Jessie Verla. BS Drury U 1969; MA U of Missouri 1970; MA U of Oklahoma 1973; Epis TS In Kentucky 1976; U. S. Army Chapl Basic Course 1981; DMin Phillips U 1982; U. S. Army Chapl Advncd Course 1984; Command and Gnrl Stff Coll 1989; Lic Soc Worker 1991; Shalem Inst for Sprtl Formation 2001; Sacr Art of Living Cntr 2004. D 6/19/1976 P 12/18/1976 Bp Chilton Powell. m 6/6/1970 Willa R Sommer c 3. COM Dio Idaho Boise ID 2007-2010; Assoc S Steph's Boise ID 2004-2008; Chair, COM Dio Estrn Oregon The Dalles OR 1998-2000; R Epis Ch Of The Trsfg Sis OR 1995-2004; Dioc Coun Dio Spokane Spokane WA 1986-1992; R Epis Ch of the Nativ Lewiston ID 1984-1991; Vic H Trin Epis Ch Wallace ID 1979-1984; Vic S Jn's Epis Ch Woodward OK 1978-1979; Cur S Matt's Ch Enid OK 1976-1977. Auth, "Journ & mag arts," *Var*; Auth, "Nwspr & Nwsltr arts," *Var*. Third Ord, SSF 2001. Paul Harris Fell Rotary Club 2004; Legion of Merit U. S. Army 2003; Meritorious Serv Medallion The Epis Ch 2002; Unit Mnstry Team of the Year U.S. Army 1988. souldoc123@msn.com

HARRES, Elisa P (At) 13479 Spring View Dr, Alpharetta GA 30004 B Philadephia PA 1/31/1957 d William Henry Parker & Martha Ann. Radford Coll; BSW Virginia Commonwealth 1979; MDiv TESM 2003. D 12/14/2002 P 8/9/2003 Bp Robert William Duncan. c 3. Ch Of The Annunc Marietta GA 2009; The Epis Ch Of S Ptr And S Paul Marietta GA 2009; P-in-c Ch Of The Annunc Marietta GA 2008; Int P The Epis Ch Of S Ptr And S Paul Marietta GA 2007; D Chr The King Epis Ch Beaver Falls PA 2003. elisah1957@aol.com

HARRIES, Susan Gratia (NMich) 1111 Bingham Ave, Sault Sainte Marie MI 49783 **Mem, Epis Mnstry Spprt Team Dio Nthrn Michigan Marquette MI 2009-; R S Jas Ch Of Sault S Marie Sault Ste Marie MI 2006-** B Santa Fe NM 4/29/1953 d Harvey Durand & Gratia Antonia. BS U of Arizona 1975. D 11/28/2005 P 5/28/2006 Bp James Arthur Kelsey. m 6/9/1979 Richard Grant Harries c 2. Mem, Epis Mnstry Discernment Team Dio Nthrn Michigan Marquette MI 2008-2009. bmcsharries@yahoo.com

HARRIES, Thomas Dunbar (Minn) 10520 Beard Ave S, Bloomington MN 55431 **Co-Chair Environ Stwdshp Cmsn Dio Minnesota Minneapolis MN 2006-; R Ch Of The H Comm S Ptr MN 2005-** B Saint Paul MN 12/29/1955 s Gilbert Woodward Harries & Beverly Ann. BA S Olaf Coll 1978; MDiv Ya Berk 1983; DMin Untd TS of the Twin Cities 2009. D 12/29/1983 P 7/1/1984 Bp Robert Marshall Anderson. m 6/24/1989 Diannah Robertson c 1. R S Nich Ch Richfield MN 1988-2005; Asst R S Jn The Evang S Paul MN 1984-1988; Dio Minnesota Minneapolis MN 1984. Auth, "Faith and Environ Impace: Congregations Learn About, Celebrate, and Care for Creation," *Congregations*, The Alb Inst, 2011; Auth, "Sprtl Checkins," Action Info; Auth, "The Cell Wall: A Metaphor For Healthy Boundaries," *Congregations*, The Alb Inst. tdh.ltd@q.com

HARRIGAN, Katherine Gunn Lester (CPa) 1105 Old Quaker Rd, Etters PA 17319 **S Paul's Epis Ch Harrisburg PA 2009-; Dio Cntrl Pennsylvania Harrisburg PA 2004-; Dn, Sch of Chr Stds Dio Cntrl Pennsylvania Harrisburg PA 2002-; Eccl Crt Dio Cntrl Pennsylvania Harrisburg PA 2000-; Dept of Cong Develpmnt Dio Cntrl Pennsylvania Harrisburg PA 1999-; Dep GC, chair of deputation Dio Cntrl Pennsylvania Harrisburg PA**

1997-; COM Dio Cntrl Pennsylvania Harrisburg PA 1995-; Com Ecum Affrs Dio Cntrl Pennsylvania Harrisburg PA 1995-; Com Litur & Ch Mus, Chair Dio Cntrl Pennsylvania Harrisburg PA 1993- B New York NY 1/14/1950 d John Milton Lester & Ann Eleanor. Amer U 1970; BS U GA 1972; MA MI SU 1976; MDiv Ya Berk 1989. D 6/10/1989 Bp Paul Moore Jr P 6/10/1990 Bp Jeffery William Rowthorn. m 3/19/2005 Wiliam Alford c 3. Dio Cntrl Pennsylvania Harrisburg PA 1996-2000; VP Cler Assn Dio Cntrl Pennsylvania Harrisburg PA 1996-2000; Dioc Coun Dio Cntrl Pennsylvania Harrisburg PA 1993-1996; R S Mich And All Ang Ch Middletown PA 1992-2007; Bp Com for Chld Advocacy & Fam Life Dio Cntrl Pennsylvania Harrisburg PA 1992-1998; Asst Gr And S Ptr's Epis Ch Hamden CT 1989-1991. Ord of S Helena 1984. Kappa Delta Pi U GA 1972; Phi Kappa Phi U GA 1972. kglharrigan@yahoo.com

HARRIGFELD, Chris L (Cal) 8872 Bronson Dr., Granite Bay CA 95746 B Squirrel ID 4/10/1928 s William Ernest Harrigfeld & Freda Elizabeth. BS U of Idaho Moscow 1950; MD U of Oregon 1960. D 6/3/2000 Bp William Edwin Swing. m 6/24/1968 Bridget Joan Harney c 1. S Matt's Epis Ch San Mateo CA 2000-2004.

HARRIMAN, Barbara June (Nwk) 144 Oldwoods Ct, Mahwah NJ 07430 **COM Dio Newark Newark NJ 2008-** B Philadelphia PA 6/4/1941 d Archie Bonyun Wurster & Jessie May. Orange Coast Coll 1986; Newark TS 2004. D 5/21/2005 Bp John Palmer Croneberger. m 9/26/1959 Allan W Harriman c 3. Treas Dioc AltGld Dio Newark Newark NJ 1999-2007. batta5@verizon.net

HARRINGTON, Debra L (Chi) 1250 Averill Dr, Batavia IL 60510 B Rogers City MI 5/21/1956 d Harold Weise & Mary. Estrn Michigan U. D 2/3/2007 Bp William Dailey Persell. c 2. nippising@aol.com

HARRINGTON, Lynn Beth (NY) 203 Salem Rd, Pound Ridge NY 10576 B White Plains NY 12/20/1943 d Peter Charles Eberhardt & Elizabeth Naomi. BA SUNY 1979; MDiv Yale DS 1983; ThM Maryknoll TS 1991. D 6/4/1983 P 2/5/1984 Bp Paul Moore Jr. m 7/30/1970 Denis Harrington c 3. Conv Plnng Com Dio New York New York City NY 2002-2005; ExCoun Dio New York New York City NY 1996-1997; Conv Credntls Com Dio New York New York City NY 1993-1995; R S Jn's Ch So Salem NY 1988-2011; Asst S Jas' Ch No Salem NY 1985-1988; Asst S Fran Ch Stamford CT 1983-1985. The Soc of S Jn the Theol Bp of New York 1999. stjohnlynn@aol.com

HARRINGTON, Thomas Anthony (Okla) 2961 N 23rd St W, Muskogee OK 74401 **D Gr Ch Muskogee OK 1995-** B Racine WI 6/19/1948 s Gordon Nash Harrington & Mary. BS Tri-St U 1970. D 6/24/1995 Bp Robert Manning Moody. m 9/12/1970 Sheila Kay Rathbun c 1.

HARRIOT, Cameron (Los) 5672 Castle Dr, Huntington Beach CA 92649 B Mamaroneck NY 11/2/1925 s Wesley Ainley Ryan & Helen Marie. BA Occ 1948; CDSP 1951; MS Natl U 1988. D 2/19/1951 P 11/1/1951 Bp Francis E I Bloy. m 11/22/1978 Deborah Lee c 2. Int S Steph's Par Beaumont CA 2001-2004; Int S Jas' Epis Ch Los Angeles CA 1998-1999; Serv S Barth's Mssn Pico Rivera CA 1989-1998; Serv S Wilfrid Of York Epis Ch Huntington Bch CA 1989-1996; Serv S Lk's Par Monrovia CA 1965-1978; P-in-c S Mk's Ch Nenana AK 1952-1956; Cur S Lk's Of The Mountains La Crescenta CA 1951-1952. frcameron@juno.com

HARRIS, Anne Marie (Miss) 705 Rayburn Ave, Ocean Springs MS 39564 **S Jn's Epis Ch Ocean Sprg MS 2009-; Asst Chap Of S Andr Boca Raton FL 2008-** B Inglewood New Zealand 3/30/1953 d Eric Norman Newbold & Eileen. BA Massey U 1973; MA Massey U 1975; Cert Dio SE Florida Dioc Sch 2004; MDiv The Prot Epis TS 2008. D 12/22/2007 P 6/22/2008 Bp Leopold Frade. m 9/4/1976 Marc L Harris c 2. anneandmarc75@hotmail.com

✠ HARRIS, Rt Rev Barbara Clementine (Mass) 11 Atherton Rd., Foxboro MA 02035 **Ret Bp Suffr of Massachusetts Dio Massachusetts Boston MA 2003-** B Philadelphia PA 6/12/1930 d Walter Harris & Beatrice. D 9/29/1979 P 10/18/1980 Bp Lyman Cunningham Ogilby Con 2/11/1989 for Mass. Asstng Bp Dio Washington Washington DC 2003-2007; Suffr Bp Of Mass Dio Massachusetts Boston MA 1989-2002; Int Ch Of The Advoc Philadelphia PA 1988; The Epis Ch Pub Co Scranton PA 1982-1989; P-in-c S Aug Of Hippo Norristown PA 1980-1984; D-Intrn Ch Of The Advoc Philadelphia PA 1979-1980. Auth, "Monthly Column," *Wit*, 1988. Hon DD GTS New York NY 1990; Hon DD Ya 1990; Hon DD Amherst Amherst MA 1989; Hon DD EDS Cambridge NY 1989; Hon DD Trin Hartford CT 1989; Hon STD Hobart and Wm Smith Colleges 1981. bharris26@comcast.net

HARRIS, Barbara L(ucille) (NJ) 111 Sherwood Dr Apt A, Victoria TX 77901 **Vic S Steph's Ch Florence NJ 2002-** B Baltimore MD 10/30/1931 d Samuel Stein & Rose. RN S Hosp Sch Of Nrsng Baltimore MD 1952; BA Glassboro St U 1990; MDiv GTS 1995. D 4/29/1995 P 12/3/1995 Bp Joe Morris Doss. c 3. Assoc Ch Of The Ascen Gloucester City NJ 2005-2008; Vic Trin Epis Old Swedes Ch Swedesboro NJ 1997-2001; S Jn's Ch Eliz NJ 1995-1996. stbarb@juno.com

HARRIS, Carl Berlinger (Md) 1506 Eton Way, Crofton MD 21114 B Baltimore MD 10/20/1929 s Alfred John Harris & Helen Clara. BA Muhlenberg Coll 1952; GTS 1956. D 9/29/1956 Bp Harry Lee Doll P 7/1/1957 Bp Noble C Powell. m 10/5/1967 Tomolyn T Tarayos c 2. Asst P Ch Of The Ascen Westminster MD 1998-1999; R S Steph's Ch Severn Par Crownsville MD 1971-1996; Asst S Anne's Par Annapolis MD 1968-1971; Vic S Andr The Fisherman Epis Mayo MD 1958-1967; Cur S Anne's Par Annapolis MD 1956-1958. tomolyn@aol.com

HARRIS, Carl Burton (Va) 2727 Fairview Ave E Apt 3b, Seattle WA 98102 B Cleveland OH 8/31/1932 s Carle Coville Harris & Myra Anthea. BA Ohio Wesl 1956; MDiv VTS 1961. D 3/3/1962 P 10/1/1962 Bp William Foreman Creighton. m 12/31/1988 Judy Frazier. R S Alb's Epis Ch Annandale VA 1964-1967. harris-rowing@juno.com

HARRIS, Cheryl Jeanne (Neb) 820 Weat 9th Street, Alliance NE 69301 **D S Matt's Ch Allnce NE 1999-** B Alliance NE 10/3/1943 d Richard Leon Edwards & Yvonne Gene. D 12/10/1999 Bp James Edward Krotz. m 12/16/1961 S Todd Harris c 3.

HARRIS III, Daniel Stewart (Mass) 7 Wakefield Rd, Hampton Bays NY 11946 **Int S Mary's Epis Ch Shltr Island NY 2006-** B Paterson NJ 4/22/1942 s Daniel S Harris & Eleanor Jean. BS Babson Coll 1964; Mercer TS 1974. D 6/15/1974 P 12/21/1974 Bp Jonathan Goodhue Sherman. m 11/30/1986 Robin Van Scoy c 6. C&C Bd Dio Massachusetts Boston MA 1992-1995; R Ch Of The H Nativ So Weymouth MA 1991-2004; R Ch Of The Trsfg Freeport NY 1988-1991; Treas Camp Bd Dio Long Island Garden City NY 1986-1991; Assoc R Gr Ch Riverhead NY 1986-1988; Chair Dioc Conv on Misc Bus Dio Long Island Garden City NY 1982-1984; Dn E Suffolk Deanry Dio Long Island Garden City NY 1980-1985; R S Mary's Ch Hampton Bays NY 1978-1985; Chair Yth Mnstrs Com Dio Long Island Garden City NY 1974-1982; Cur S Ptr's by-the-Sea Epis Ch Bay Shore NY 1974-1978. Assn of Traumatic Stress Specialists 1995; Fed of Fire Chapl, 1990; Intl Critical Incident Stress Fndt 1991. firechaplain10@aol.com

HARRIS, Donald Bell (SVa) 121 Jordans Journey, Williamsburg VA 23185 B Boston MA 3/8/1936 s Robert Samuel Harris & Ruth. BA W&M 1957; U of Iowa 1958; Claremont Coll 1960; MDiv CDSP 1964; U CA 1966; U CA 1969. D 1/10/1964 Bp George Richard Millard P 7/11/1964 Bp Robert B Gooden. m 11/28/1964 Faye Ruth Voss c 3. Assoc S Mart's Epis Ch Williamsburg VA 1990-2003; Epis Chapl Wm and Mary Bruton Par Williamsburg VA 1988-1990; Assoc Par of Trin Ch New York NY 1986-1988; Assoc Ch Of The H Comm Charleston SC 1984-1986; Off Of Bsh For ArmdF New York NY 1979-1988; Cur S Lk's Epis Ch Ft Collins CO 1977-1978; Off Of Bsh For ArmdF New York NY 1964-1977. Auth, *That's How the Light Gets In: A Credo of Friendship*, Credo Inst, 1994; Auth, *CREDO: Ministering in the Twilight of the 20th Centry*; Auth, *The Chapl as Fisherman & Shpd*. Bd Inst of Clincal Theology, Regent U 1992-1993; Bd, Regent U Sch of Counslg 1994-2001. Graduated w hon CDSP 1964. dbhcaballero@gmail.com

HARRIS, Edmund Immanuel (Chi) 1336 Pawtucket Ave, Rumford RI 02916 **Asst to the R Ch of the Epiph Rumford RI 2010-** B Virginia Beach VA 11/12/1981 s Robert Lee Etheridge & Laura B. BA U of Virginia 2004; Mstr of Div U Chi 2008; MSTh,Cert. in Angl Stds Ya Berk 2010. D 6/5/2010 Bp Jeffrey Dean Lee P 12/11/2010 Bp David B(ruce) Joslin. EHARRIS1981@GMAIL.COM

HARRIS, Edward George (Pa) 429 Kendal Dr, Kennett Square PA 19348 **Died 3/28/2010** B Boston MA 4/30/1917 s Ulysses Sylvester Harris & Lillian Dennett. BA Harv 1938; MDiv EDS 1941; STM UTS 1942. D 6/11/1941 P 12/21/1941 Bp Henry Knox Sherrill. c 6. Auth, "Prayers for a U," U of Pennsylvania Press, 1961. DD U of Pennsylvania 1961.

HARRIS, Edward Ridgway (Minn) 2225 Crest Ln Sw, Rochester MN 55902 B Rochester NY 11/10/1928 s Edward Harris & Anne Richardson. Trin Hartford CT 1950; BS Col 1956. D 1/17/1977 Bp Philip Frederick McNairy. m 3/7/1964 Emily Van Voorhis Harris c 4. D Calv Ch Rochester MN 1977-1990. jharris@rconnect.com

HARRIS, Gareth Scott (At) Po Box 191708, Atlanta GA 31119 B Athens GA 8/5/1941 s George Elmer Harris & Hazel Janet. BS Georgia Inst of Tech 1965; BD Epis TS of The SW 1970. D 6/28/1970 Bp R(aymond) Stewart Wood Jr P 1/1/1971 Bp Randolph R Claiborne. c 2. Vic S Jas Ch Cedartown GA 1987-1992; Cur H Trin Par Decatur GA 1970-1971. gareth@penres.com

✠ HARRIS, Rt Rev Gayle Elizabeth (Mass) 138 Tremont St, Boston MA 02111 **Bp Suffr of Massachusetts Dio Massachusetts Boston MA 2002-** B Cleveland OH 2/12/1951 d Nelson Arthur Harris & Dorothy Vernon. BA Lewis & Clark Coll 1978; MDiv CDSP 1981; DD CDSP 2001. D 6/19/1981 Bp James Winchester Montgomery P 2/1/1982 Bp John Shelby Spong Con 1/18/2003 for Mass. R S Lk And S Simon Cyrene Rochester NY 1992-2002; P-in-c Ch Of The H Comm Washington DC 1984-1992; Asst To Vic S Phil The Evang Washington DC 1982-1984; Dir Of Pstr Mnstrs Gr Ch Van Vorst Jersey City NJ 1981-1982. shp@diomass.org

HARRIS, Gerald Joaquin (NwPa) 2604 Toucan Ave., McAllen TX 78504 **Int All SS Epis Ch San Benito TX 2008-** B Torreon Coahuila Mexico 8/1/1939 s Leslie Ewart Harris & Rachel. BBA U of Texas 1963; MDiv Bex 1991. D 6/8/1991 P 1/1/1992 Bp David Charles Bowman. m 5/4/1963 Mary Christian Harris c 2. Int St Ptr & St Paul Ch Mssn TX 2011; Supply Preist Dio W Texas San Antonio TX 2005-2011; Dioc Ecum Com Dio NW Pennsylvania Erie PA

2002-2005; Dep to GC Dio NW Pennsylvania Erie PA 2002-2003; Dioc Sch for Mnstry Instr Dio NW Pennsylvania Erie PA 2000-2005; R S Agnes' Epis Ch S Marys PA 2000-2005; Alt Dep to Gnrl Convntion Dio NW Pennsylvania Erie PA 1997-1998; Dn of SE Dnry Dio NW Pennsylvania Erie PA 1996-2005; Spanish Partnership Mssn Com Dio NW Pennsylvania Erie PA 1996-2005; Dioc Bdgt Com Dio NW Pennsylvania Erie PA 1993-2002; COM Dio NW Pennsylvania Erie PA 1993-1998; Gr Epis Ch Ridgway PA 1991-2005. fatherjerry@househeld.com

HARRIS, Henry Gibbard (O) 226 3rd St Se, Massillon OH 44646 **R S Tim's Epis Ch Massillon OH 1989-** B Toledo OH 9/24/1945 s Henry Miller Harris & Janet Juanita. BBA U of Toledo 1967; JD U of Toledo 1970; MDiv VTS 1985. D 6/15/1985 Bp James Russell Moodey P 3/7/1986 Bp John Thomas Walker. m 8/12/1967 Constance Diane Kolby c 2. Assoc All SS' Epis Ch Chevy Chase MD 1985-1989. hgharris@aol.com

HARRIS, Herman (USC) 633 Swallow Rd, Elgin SC 29045 B North Haven CT 10/13/1948 s Gilmore Harris & Elizabeth. BS New Hampshire Coll 1983. D 12/1/1990 Bp Arthur Edward Walmsley. m 10/13/1977 Delmonte Doris Jackson c 4. D S Steph's Epis Ch Ridgeway SC 1994-1996; D Dio Connecticut Hartford CT 1990-1994.

HARRIS, James Kenneth (WMo) 7402 Woodland Meadow Dr, Poplar Bluff MO 63901 **Died 11/30/2010** B Bay AR 4/10/1928 s James Albert Harris & Lena Mae. BA U of Mississippi 1953; Med U of Mississippi 1954; MDiv Epis TS In Kentucky 1977; DD Epis TS In Kentucky 1982. D 5/15/1977 P 12/1/1977 Bp Addison Hosea. c 4.

HARRIS JR, James Raymond (WNC) 111 Bel Air Cir, Daphne AL 36526 **Died 9/7/2011** B Foreman AR 11/16/1927 s James Raymond Harris & Telma Frances. BA LSU 1950; MA LSU 1955; MDiv STUSo 1975. D 4/7/1975 P 10/1/1975 Bp Christoph Keller Jr. c 5.

HARRIS JR, James Wesley (CFla) 44 S Halifax Dr, Ormond Beach FL 32176 **R S Jas Epis Ch Ormond Bch FL 2009-** B TN 4/19/1962 s James Wesley Harris & Talca Nell. BA Sthrn Illinois U 1995; MDiv Aquinas Inst of Theol 1998; Cert SWTS 1998; D.Min SWTS 2011. Trans 3/16/2004 Bp Peter Hess Beckwith. m 12/17/1983 Laural Lee Dearnbarger c 2. Dn Trin Cathd Davenport IA 2006-2009; R Ch Of The Gd Shpd Jacksonville FL 2004-2006; Vic S Thos Epis Ch Glen Carbon IL 1999-2002; Cur S Geo's Ch Belleville IL 1998-1999. frharris@gmail.com

HARRIS, John Carlyle (WA) 3319 Tennyson St NW, Washington DC 20015 B Boston MA 6/28/1930 s Charles Upchurch Harris & Janet Jeffrey. BA Wms 1952; MDiv VTS 1955; MS CUA 1978. D 6/18/1955 P 12/22/1955 Bp Wallace E Conkling. m 6/29/1962 Ruth T Ayers Harris c 3. Dep GC Dio Washington Washington DC 1973-1976; Bd Trst VTS Alexandria VA 1973-1974; Asst to Bp Dio Washington Washington DC 1970-1976; Assoc R S Alb's Par Washington DC 1955-1958. Auth, "Cler & Their Wk," Alb Inst, 1977; Auth, "Pract of Supervision," Dio Washington, 1970; Auth, "Stress, Power & Mnstry," Alb Inst; Auth, *Pstr Care of Pastors*, Journ of Pstr Care; Auth, *Planned Self Appraisal for Ch*. tucker@jacktuck.com

HARRIS, John Edward Crane (Ga) 30 Anderson Ave., Holden MA 01520 B Sarasota FL 1/23/1935 s John Edward Harris & Rebecca. AB Amh 1956; MDiv VTS 1959; ThM Duke 1969; DMin GTF 1989. D 6/29/1959 Bp William Francis Moses P 1/10/1960 Bp Richard Henry Baker. m 5/3/2003 Deborah Johansen Harris c 2. Int The Epis Ch Of S Jn The Bapt Sanbornville NH 2000-2001; R S Andr's Ch Darien GA 1994-1997; R S Cyp's Ch Darien GA 1994-1997; Int Calv Epis Ch Ashland KY 1992-1994; Cmnty Med Cntr Toms River NJ 1990-1992; S Elis's Epis Ch Memphis TN 1989-1990; Memphis Inst Of Med & Rel Memphis TN 1983-1988; Assoc Chr and S Lk's Epis Ch Norfolk VA 1976-1983; R S Lk's Epis Ch Durham NC 1967-1974; Assoc Chr Epis Ch Raleigh NC 1965-1967; Vic S Andr's Ch Rocky Mt NC 1961-1965; Asst S Ptr's Epis Ch Charlotte NC 1959-1961. Auth, "Cumberland Sem Journ," 1989; Auth, "Supervision Biblic Model," *Journ Of Supervision Mnstry*, 1979; Auth, "b Again: Emancipation From The Mo Complex," *from the Negatice Mo Complex*. Amer Assoc. of Pstr Counselors 1986; ACPE 1976; Coll of Pstr Supervision and Psych 1980. Supervisory Certification ACPE 1981; Dplma Aapc 1977. jecharris.harris@gmail.com

HARRIS, John T. (NCal) P.O. Box 1291, Gridley CA 95948 **Vic S Tim's Ch Gridley CA 2011-; Living Stones Coordntr Dio Nthrn California Sacramento CA 2010-** B Oroville CA 3/23/1941 s Glen Russell Harris & Dixie May. BA U CA 1962; JD U CA 1965. D 9/10/2004 P 3/19/2005 Bp Jerry Alban Lamb. m 9/4/1965 Marny Helen Kelleher c 3. Assoc S Tim's Ch Gridley CA 2004-2011. tjohn1@sbcglobal.net

HARRIS, Jonathan Fisher (SwVa) 3286 Avenham Ave Sw, Roanoke VA 24014 **P-in-c Trin Ch Buchanan VA 2004-** B Rochester MN 6/27/1970 s Edward Ridgway Harris & Emily Van Voorhis. BA S Olaf Coll 1993; MDiv Van 2000; Cert SWTS 2004. D 5/8/2004 P 12/4/2004 Bp Frank Neff Powell. m 10/14/2000 Darla Yvonne Schumm c 1. jonathanfharris@msn.com

HARRIS, Julie Nan (WVa) 200 W King St, Martinsburg WV 25401 **BEC Dio W Virginia Charleston WV 2009-; COM - Chair Dio W Virginia Charleston WV 2009-; Stwdshp Cmsn Dio W Virginia Charleston WV 2009-; Trin Epis Ch Martinsburg WV 2006-** B Portland OR 8/24/1951 d Edward John Harris & Nancy Allen. BFA Pacific Luth U 1973; Portland St U 1974; MDiv GTS 1996. D 6/29/1996 Bp Robert Louis Ladehoff P 1/18/1997 Bp J Clark Grew II. Int R S Paul's Ch Canton OH 2004-2006; Congrl Dvlpmt Cmsn Dio Ohio Cleveland OH 2000-2005; Interium P-in-c S Andr's Ch Akron OH 2000-2004; Int P-in Charge S Phil's Epis Ch Akron OH 2000-2004; Dioc Coun Dio Ohio Cleveland OH 1999-2001; Assoc Chr Ch Epis Hudson OH 1999-2000; Assitant to the R S Ptr's Epis Ch Lakewood OH 1996-1998. Int Mnstry Ntwk 2000; Shalem Soc 2011. revjulie2@comcast.net

HARRIS, Ladd Keith (WMich) 5527 N Sierra Ter, Beverly Hills FL 34465 **P-in-c Shpd Of The Hills Epis Ch Lecanto FL 2004-** B Scranton PA 7/21/1941 s Chester H Harris & Dorothy Margaret. BS Mansfield U of Pennsylvania 1963; MD VTS 1966. D 6/18/1966 P 3/1/1967 Bp Frederick J Warnecke. m 6/21/1969 Judith S Scott c 2. R S Mk's Ch Grand Rapids MI 1995-2003; Dio Cntrl New York Syracuse NY 1986-1991; R Gr Ch Baldwinsville NY 1977-1995; R Trin Ch Lowville NY 1970-1977; Cur Chr Ch Reading PA 1966-1970. Curs. jshlkh@aol.com

HARRIS JR, Lawrence (WA) 10450 Lottsford Road, #1218, Mitchellville MD 20721 **Dio Maryland Baltimore MD 1966-** B Baltimore MD 6/18/1940 s Lawrence Reed Harris & Sarah Elizabeth. BA Trin Hartford CT 1962; MDiv VTS 1965. D 6/22/1965 P 6/20/1966 Bp Harry Lee Doll. m 6/29/1968 Susan Marvin Jacob c 1. R S Barn' Ch Leeland Upper Marlboro MD 1976-2011; S Matt's Epis Ch Hyattsville MD 1966-1976. lharris619@verizon.net

H

HARRIS, Lee Marshall (Los) 330 E 16th St, Upland CA 91784 **Chapl-Rel Tchr S Mk's Epis Ch Upland CA 2003-** B Altadena CA 6/23/1948 s E Marshall Harris & Madaly. BS U CA 1969; Diac Cert ETSC/Bloy Hse 2010. D 2/4/2010 Bp Chester Lovelle Talton. c 1. lharris@linkline.com

HARRIS, Lyndon Fitzgerald (NY) 300 Mercer St Apt 22d, New York NY 10003 B Gaffney SC 6/3/1961 s Wallace Harris & Annie Laura. BA Wofford Coll 1983; MDiv STUSo 1990. D 6/9/1990 P 5/18/1991 Bp William Arthur Beckham. m 4/19/1986 Kirsten R Rutherford c 1. Assoc Par of Trin Ch New York NY 2001-2002; Trin Educ Fund New York NY 2001-2002; Gd Shpd Epis Chap Garden City NY 1998-2002; Cur Gr Epis Ch New York NY 1998-2001; Geo Mercer TS Garden City NY 1998-2000; S Hilda's And S Hugh's Sch New York NY 1996-1999; Tutor The GTS New York NY 1996-1999; Int S Paul's Ch Sprg Vlly NY 1996; Stndg Com Dio Upper So Carolina Columbia SC 1993-1994; Assoc R Ch Of The Adv Spartanburg SC 1991-1995; Stwdshp Comm Dio Upper So Carolina Columbia SC 1990-1993; D S Alb's Ch Lexington SC 1990-1991. Auth, "Div Action: An Interview w Jn Polkinghorne:," *Sci And Theol Ed Of Crosscurrents*, 1998; Auth, "Jn Polkinghorne On Natural Theol And Div Action," *Gnrl Sem News*, 1997; Auth, "Recalling Wm Norman Pittenger, 1905-1997," *LivCh*, 1997. AAR; AAR; Assn Of Rel & Intellectual Life; ECF Fllshp 1997-2000; Fell, The Coll Of Preachers, Washington Natl Cathd 1995; Oxford Fndt Fllshp 1998; Soc Of Angl And Luth Theologians. Grant For Trip To E Afr Sem Cmsn On Mssn 1997; Excellence In Biblic Stds (Hebr) ABS 1990. frlyndon@aol.com

HARRIS, Margaret Stilwell (Ia) 1120 45th St, Des Moines IA 50311 B Hollywood CA 8/18/1938 d Leland Stilwell & Elizabeth. BA Drake U 1971. D 4/13/1996 Bp Carl Christopher Epting. m 4/4/1959 John R Harris.

HARRIS, Mark (Del) 207 E Market St, Lewes DE 19958 **Asst S Ptr's Ch Lewes DE 2003-** B Mobile AL 5/21/1940 s Edward Hooper Harris & Anne France. BA Tul 1961; U of Alberta 1964; M.Div. EDS 1967; D. Min. EDS 1995. D 6/10/1967 Bp Leland Stark P 3/6/1968 Bp Francisco Reus-Froylan. c 2. R S Jas Ch Wilmington DE 1995-2000; Partnership Offcr E Asia Pacific & Middle E Epis Ch Cntr New York NY 1991-1994; Coordntr Ovrs Missionaries Dio Delaware Wilmington DE 1987-1991; Coordntr Mnstry Higher Ed. Epis Ch Cntr New York NY 1982-1987; UofDelaware Dio Delaware Wilmington DE 1972-1978; U MI Dio Michigan Detroit MI 1969-1972; Fajardo Dio Puerto Rico S Just PR 1967-1969. Auth, "Challange Of Change," *Angl Comm In Post Mod Era*, Ch Pub Inc, 1998; Ed, "Epis Ch & Its MHE," *Plumbline*, FMP, 1982; Ed, "Plumbline," *Plumbline*, Epis Soc Mnstry Higher Ed., 1978. ESMHE 1972-1990; Epis Urban Caucaus 1996-2000; Global Epis Mssn Ntwk 2000-2006; Integrity 2005; The Consult 2008. Doctor of Hmnts Trin U of Asia 2008. poetmark1940@gmail.com

HARRIS, Mark Hugh (Ore) 385 Doral Place, Pinehurst NC 28374 B Union SC 2/11/1932 s William Ernest Harris & Iris Levonia. BS U CA 1959; DIT Oxf 1964; MDiv Mt Ang Abbey 1976. Trans from Church of the Province of Southern Africa 12/1/1968 Bp C Kilmer Myers. m 12/6/1969 Marilyn Marie Sarty c 3. The Epis Ch Of The Gd Samar Corvallis OR 1973-1979; Asst All SS Ch Carmel CA 1968-1970. Fllshp Assn of Profsnl Chapl 1976-2004. elbosque123@yahoo.com

HARRIS, Marsue (RI) 99 Main St, North Kingstown RI 02852 B Rochester PA 4/27/1940 d John V Harris & Jeanette E. BS Penn 1961; MDiv CDSP 1981. D 6/28/1980 Bp William Edwin Swing P 8/20/1981 Bp George Nelson Hunt III. m 5/19/1985 Ralph C Porter c 2. P-in-c S Geo's Ch Portsmouth RI 2002-2006; Int S Paul's Ch Pawtucket RI 2000-2002; Int S Aug's Ch Kingston RI 1998-2000; S Barn Ch Warwick RI 1995-1997; Dioc Coun Dio Rhode

Island Providence RI 1993-1995; Stndg Com Dio Rhode Island Providence RI 1986-1990; S Ptr's By The Sea Narragansett RI 1986-1988; COM Dio Rhode Island Providence RI 1983-1986; Assoc S Steph's Par Belvedere CA 1980-1982. Auth, "Var 1988-2004," *Rel Columnist*, Providence Journ Bulletin, 2004. marsueharris@earthlink.net

HARRIS, Martha Caldwell (CGC) 79 6th St., Apalachicola FL 32320 **R Trin Ch Apalachicola FL 2005-** B Portsmouth VA 12/16/1952 d Ralph Lawson Caldwell & Mildred Louise. BA U GA 1976; MDiv Candler TS Emory U 1993. D 6/8/1996 P 12/1/1996 Bp Frank Kellogg Allan. m 7/1/1972 Robert Lloyd Harris c 4. Asst R S Chris's Ch Pensacola FL 2003-2005; Assoc R S Simon's On The Sound Ft Walton Bch FL 2000-2003; Asst S Edw's Epis Ch Lawrenceville GA 1997-2000; S Mk's Ch Dalton GA 1997. vicar-trinitychurch@mchsi.com

HARRIS, Melissa (Okla) Post Office Box 451297, Grove OK 74345 **D S Andr's Ch Grove OK 2007-** B Stroud OK 12/4/1933 d William Douglas Anderson & Harriett Ellen. D 6/16/2007 Bp Robert Manning Moody. c 2. NAAD 2008. melissasae@sbcglobal.net

HARRIS, Michael William Henry (SwFla) 24311 Narwhal Lane, Port Charlotte FL 33983 B GY 8/28/1942 s William Harris & Ethel. LTh Codrington Coll 1969; STM NYTS 1977. D 6/1/1970 P 7/1/1970 Bp The Bishop Of Guyana. m 4/3/1972 Beatrice Celestine Peters c 2. S Geo's Epis Ch Bradenton FL 2001-2003; The Epis Ch Of The Gd Shpd Venice FL 2000-2001; Dio Long Island Garden City NY 1998-1999; Chr Ch Cobble Hill Brooklyn NY 1994-1998; R Ch Of S Thos Brooklyn NY 1976-1994. OHC.

HARRIS, Neal Joseph (WMo) 1636 E Grand St, Springfield MO 65804 B Slick OK 3/14/1923 s Neal Joseph Harris & Vivian Madge. BA NE St U 1952; Bex 1955. D 6/26/1955 P 12/1/1955 Bp Chilton Powell. m 6/18/1966 Cecilia Jane Simons. R S Jn's Ch Springfield MO 1979-1985; P Ch Of The Trsfg Mtn Grove MO 1978-1985; Assoc S Jn's Ch Springfield MO 1972-1978; Vic S Jn's Ch Durant OK 1964-1965; Vic S Ptr's Ch Coalgate OK 1964-1965; Vic S Barn Ch Poteau OK 1962-1964; R All SS Ch McAlester OK 1960-1964; Asst S Jn's Epis Ch Tulsa OK 1958-1959; Vic S Ptr's Ch Tulsa OK 1956-1958; Vic S Jas Epis Ch Wagoner OK 1955-1956; Vic S Mart's Ch Pryor OK 1955-1956.

HARRIS, Paula (Mil) St. Luke's Episcopal Church, 4011 Major Ave, Madison WI 53716 **R S Lk's Ch Madison WI 2009-** B Dallas TX 10/28/1964 d Joseph Daniel Harrison & Shelby. BA Wheaton Coll 1986; MTS SWTS 2006. D 6/3/2006 P 12/14/2006 Bp Steven Andrew Miller. m 4/24/2004 Dragutin Cvetkovic c 2. Vic Epis Ch Of The Resurr Mukwonago WI 2006-2009; D S Dunst's Ch Madison WI 2006; Sem S Dunst's Ch Madison WI 2006. Auth, "Being White," *Being White*, InterVarsity Press, 2004; Auth, "Postmodernity is not the Antichrist.," *Postmission*, Paternoster Press, 2002; Auth, "Calling YP to a Mssy Vocation in a Yahoo Wrld.," *Missiology Journ*, Amer Soc of Missiology, 2001; Auth, "Nestorians: Listening to Mssn that Arises from Cmnty and Sprtlty," *Global Missiology for the 21st Century: Reflections from the Iguassu Dialogue*, Wrld Evang Fllshp, 2000. Sprtl Dir Intl 2009. Moss Awd for Acad Achievement SWTS 2006. stlukesmadisonrector@gmail.com

HARRIS JR, Paul Sherwood (Pa) 737 Bradford Aly, Philadelphia PA 19147 B Baltimore MD 11/17/1939 s Paul Sherwood Harris & Grace Naomi. U of Pennsylvania; BA Jn Hopkins U 1961; MDiv PDS 1965. D 6/22/1965 P 6/1/1966 Bp Harry Lee Doll. Assoc S Ptr's Ch Philadelphia PA 1978-1983. johntwopaul@aol.com

HARRIS, Phillip Jay (SO) Po Box 484, Circleville OH 43113 **R S Phil's Ch Circleville OH 2003-** B Point Pleasant WV 5/10/1967 BS U Of Rio Grande 1991; MDiv VTS 2003. D 4/16/2003 Bp Herbert Thompson Jr P 11/1/2003 Bp Kenneth Lester Price. phillippjharris@aol.com

HARRIS, Randall Sellers (Ct) 127-129 Oil Mill Rd, Waterford CT 06385 **Professed Solitary Rel Dio Connecticut Hartford CT 1987-** B Hamilton OH 12/5/1934 s Guy Sellers Harris & Ruth Jeanette. AB Harv 1956; STB Ya Berk 1961. D 6/13/1961 P 3/17/1962 Bp Walter H Gray. c 3. Hartford Dnry Manchester CT 1982-1985; Asst S Jas Ch New London CT 1961-1963.

HARRIS, Robert Charles (Kan) 6649 Nall Dr, Mission KS 66202 **P in Res Gr Epis Ch Ottawa KS 2011-** B Kansas City MO 10/26/1952 s Clifford Andrew Harris & Lucille Charlotte. BBA U of Houston 1975; MBA U of Missouri 1977; MDiv SWTS 2005. D 6/11/2005 P 1/21/2006 Bp Dean Elliott Wolfe. m 11/17/1984 Debra Louise Wear c 5. RHarris740@sbcglobal.net.com

✠ **HARRIS, Rt Rev Rogers Sanders** (SwFla) 5502 Exum Drive, West Columbia SC 29169 B Anderson SC 2/22/1930 s Wilmot Louis Harris & Sarah Sanders. BA U So 1952; BD STUSo 1957; STM STUSo 1969; DMin VTS 1977. D 8/6/1957 P 4/5/1958 Bp Clarence Alfred Cole Con 3/9/1985 for USC. m 3/28/1953 Anne Stewart. Ret Bp SwFla Dio SW Florida Sarasota FL 1997; VP Prov IV Dio SW Florida Sarasota FL 1991-1994; Suffr Bp of USC Dio Upper So Carolina Columbia SC 1985-1989; Dn Spartanburg Deanry Dio Upper So Carolina Columbia SC 1974-1977; Fell Cntr Cont Educ VTS Alexandria VA 1974-1977; Bd Dioc Fndt Dio Upper So Carolina Columbia SC 1973-1977; Chair Div Evang Dio Upper So Carolina Columbia SC 1973-1976; R S Chris's Ch Spartanburg SC 1969-1985; R Ch Of The Gd Shpd Greer SC 1965-1969; P-in-c Ch Of The Gd Shpd Greer SC 1959-1964; P-in-c Ch Of The Ridge Trenton SC 1957-1959; P-in-c S Paul's Ch Batesburg SC 1957-1959. Auth, *The Commitment of Cnfrmtn*, VTS, 1977. OHC Comp 1989. DD U So 1986; DD VTS 1986. rogers795@bellsouth.net

HARRIS, Rory Hartzell Brandybuck (CFla) 827 Tomlinson Ter, Lake Mary FL 32746 **R H Cross Epis Ch Sanford FL 2005-** B Boise ID 10/4/1953 s Thomas Robin Harris & Margaret Mae. Ya Berk; BA Syr 1977; MDiv Melodyland TS 1982; STM Ya Berk 1984. D 1/19/1985 P 7/31/1985 Bp Charles Shannon Mallory. m 4/21/1990 Stacie L LaCava c 4. DE Dnry Exec Com Dio Pennsylvania Philadelphia PA 1998-2001; R S Jas Epis Ch Prospect Pk PA 1997-2005; Chair Evang Com Dio Maryland Baltimore MD 1992-1993; Com on Aging Dio Maryland Baltimore MD 1990-1992; R S Jn's Ch Havre De Gr MD 1988-1997; Com on Aging Dio Maryland Baltimore MD 1988-1989; Yth Dir/ Dir Rel Educ S Jas' Epis Ch Los Angeles CA 1985-1988; S Clem's-By-The-Sea Par San Clemente CA 1985-1987; Cur S Jn's Ch New Haven CT 1983-1985; Yth Min Epis Ch Of The Gd Shpd Salinas CA 1982-1983; Yth Dir/DCE S Jas' Epis Ch Los Angeles CA 1979-1982. Auth, *Sex & Chr Dating*, S Jas Press, 1980. AFP, Fllshp of Wit, Epis Ren. Outstanding Young Men in Amer 1986; Intl Yth in Achievement Awd 1981. frroryholycross@aol.com

HARRIS, Stephen Dirk (CPa) 11791 Dellwood Dr, Waynesboro PA 17268 B Cambridge,MA 11/25/1938 s Samuel Ward Harris & Bernice Howard. BS in Ed. NEU 1963; MDiv VTS 1969; DMin STUSo 1987. D 6/21/1969 Bp Anson Phelps Stokes Jr P 6/21/1970 Bp William Foreman Creighton. m 2/24/1968 Rebecca Caroline Barham c 2. Int Calv Chap Beartown Blue Ridge Summit PA 1990-1991; Int Ch Of The Trsfg Blue Ridge Summit PA 1990-1991; R S Mary's Epis Ch Waynesboro PA 1987-2005; Chr Ch Binghamton NY 1984-1987; Assoc Ch Of The Gd Shpd Raleigh NC 1974-1984; Asst S Matt's Epis Ch Hyattsville MD 1969-1972. Epis Cler Assn Of Cntrl PA 1993; EPF; HSEC 1970; NNECA 1970. sdirkharris@yahoo.com

HARRIS, Suzanne Love (NJ) Box 864, Wilson WY 83014 B Brooklyn NY 5/23/1942 d Hamilton Hamilton Love & Cynthia. Col; Drew U; BA Caldwell Coll 1981; MDiv GTS 1985. D 6/8/1985 P 12/14/1985 Bp John Shelby Spong. m 7/9/1966 George Harris c 3. Assoc Ch of S Jn on the Mtn Bernardsville NJ 1987-1991; S Lk's Epis Ch Montclair NJ 1985-1986. Auth, "Lasting," Ariadne Press, 2000. Ariadne Prize Ariadne Press Rockville MD 2000; Carl Michalson Schlrshp Drew TS Madison NJ 1982. suzanneloveh@cs.com

HARRIS, Terence Manville (SeFla) 5710 Chalyce Ln, Charlotte NC 28270 **Pstr Asst S Jn's Epis Ch Charlotte NC 2004-** B Ada OK 3/19/1934 s Samuel Houston Harris & Katherine. BS LSU 1955; MDiv STUSo 1962. D 6/29/1962 Bp Girault M Jones P 5/11/1963 Bp Iveson Batchelor Noland. m 4/24/1965 Sallie L Lott c 4. R S Jn's Epis Ch Homestead FL 1992-2000; Dio Arkansas Little Rock AR 1992; H Trin Epis Ch Hot Sprg Vill AR 1985-1986; R Ch Of The Gd Shpd Little Rock AR 1974-1991; P-in-c Emm Ch Lake Vill AR 870-2652230or8 1969-1974; P-in-c S Barn Epis Ch Lafayette LA 1969-1974; P-in-c S Paul's Ch McGehee AR 1969-1974; Cur Ch Of The Ascen Lafayette LA 1962-1964. terrymharris@bellsouth.net

HARRIS, Thomas G (Chi) 5749 N Kenmore Ave, Chicago IL 60660 B Hammond IN 12/4/1937 s Henry B Harris & Ethel Mae. BA NWU; MA SWTS. D 4/15/1973 Bp James Winchester Montgomery.

HARRIS, Vincent Powell (WA) 160 U St Nw, Washington DC 20001 **R S Geo's Ch Washington DC 1991-** B Houston TX 11/3/1952 s Toussaint Vincent Harris & Edna Powell. BA Morehouse Coll 1975; MDiv VTS 1979. D 6/5/1979 P 12/18/1979 Bp Frank Stanley Cerveny. m 12/23/1986 Joyce Brown c 3. Chapl Dio Washington Washington DC 1989-1991; Chapl Dio Atlanta Atlanta GA 1983-1988; R S Mich And All Ang Ch Tallahassee FL 1980-1983; Asst H Trin Ch Gainesville FL 1979-1980. Conf of S Ben 1979. vpowellh@verizon.net

HARRIS, Walter M (Haw) 46-328 Kamehameha Hwy, Kaneohe HI 96744 **Vic S Jn's By The Sea Kaneohe HI 1997-** B Henrico County VA 10/4/1938 s Orville S Harris & Elizabeth Ann. BS VPI 1961; MDiv EDS 1974. D 6/10/1974 Bp Paul Moore Jr P 2/1/1975 Bp Morris Fairchild Arnold. m 8/10/1963 Harriet Ann Ropp c 4. S Jn's By The Sea Kaneohe HI 1996-2001; H Innoc' Epis Ch Lahaina HI 1988-1994; Off Of Bsh For ArmdF New York NY 1982-1988; R S Steph's Ch Schenectady NY 1978-1982; Cur The Ch Of The H Sprt Orleans MA 1975-1977. kulikuli.hawaii.ee.com

HARRIS, William Cone (Fla) 873 Enfield Rd, Lexington VA 24450 B Saint Petersburg FL 5/21/1924 s Samuel Henry Harris & Ellen Pauline. MDiv VTS 1965; JD Stetson U 2049. D 6/22/1965 P 3/1/1966 Bp Edward Hamilton West. m 12/3/1995 Virginia Shepard c 4. R Chr Ch Valdosta GA 1999-2001; Asst to R S Jn's Epis Ch Tallahassee FL 1995-1998; Int Calv Ch Indn Rocks Bch FL 1994-1995; S Andr's By The Sea Epis Ch Destin FL 1993; Int Cur S Andr's By The Sea Epis Ch Destin FL 1992-1993; Int All SS Epis Ch Lakeland FL 1988-1989; Int S Mich And All Ang Ch Tallahassee FL 1987-1988; P-in-c The Epis Ch Of The Redeem Avon Pk FL 1978-1979; R Ch Of The H Comf Tallahassee FL 1971-1975; R Emm Epis Ch Alexandria VA 1967-1971; M-in-c Chr Ch Monticello FL 1965-1967; M-in-c S Mary's Epis Ch Madison FL 1965-1967. coneharris@gmail.com

HARRIS, William Henry (NwPa) 940 Route 46, Emporium PA 15834 B Bakerton PA 11/8/1926 s William Henry Harris & Mary. BD EDS. D 6/13/1969 Bp Earl M Honaman P 12/1/1969 Bp Dean T Stevenson. m 12/31/1961 Margaret H Higdon c 1. Supply P S Andr's Ch Clearfield PA 2003-2005; Emm Epis Ch Emporium PA 1974-1992; S Agnes' Epis Ch S Marys PA 1974-1992; P-in-c S Andr's Ch Tioga PA 1969-1976; P-in-c S Jn's Ch Westfield PA 1969-1976. rhysalex@zitomedia.net

HARRIS-BAYFIELD, Maeva-Louise Beckwith Hair (Tex) 20902 Adams Mill Pl, Ashburn VA 20147 B Maui HI 8/3/1934 d Edward Beckwith Hair & Christine Lamb. Mills Coll 1956; Trin Theol Coll, Singapore 1983; MRE S Thos U, Houston, Texas 1988; Penn CPE Residency 1989. D 6/15/1990 Bp Charlie Fuller McNutt Jr P 7/15/1992 Bp William Elwood Sterling. m 8/20/2005 Ralph Wesley Bayfield c 2. St Lk's Epis Hosp Houston TX 1995-1996; Assoc R Trin Ch Galveston TX 1992-1995; D Trin Ch Houston TX 1991-1992; D S Andr's Epis Ch York PA 1990-1991. Auth, "Journ Of Pstr Care". Coll Of Chapl, So Texas Assn Of Chapl, Eva 1990; Epis Hospitalital Chapl Assn 1995.

HARRISON JR, Claude Robert (WA) 6701 Wisconsin Ave, Chevy Chase MD 20815 B Cadiz KY 5/3/1962 s Claude R Harrison & Zelma Marie. BA Wstrn Kentucky U 1983; MDiv Sthrn Bapt TS Louisville KY 1986; PhD Duke 1991; Cert VTS 1992. D 5/30/1992 Bp Huntington Williams Jr P 6/1/1993 Bp Jane Hart Holmes Dixon. m 12/20/1987 Ellen Louise Lyons c 3. VTS Alexandria VA 1993-1994; S Jn's Ch Chevy Chase MD 1992-1995. "Jn Walker: A Man for the Twenty-First Century," Forw Mvmt, 2004; Auth, *ATR*; Auth, *Biblic Archeol*. AABS; Cathd Biblic Assn Soc of Biblicalal Lit. Phi Beta Kappa. mulberryhl@aol.com

✠ **HARRISON, Rt Rev Dena Arnall** (Tex) 3402 Windsor Rd, Austin TX 78703 **Bp Suffr Dio Texas Houston TX 2006-** B Lufkin TX 1/8/1947 d Lloyd Thomas Arnall & Edith Marie. BBA U of Texas 1967; MDiv Epis TS of The SW 1987. D 6/6/1987 Bp Gordon Taliaferro Charlton P 1/8/1988 Bp Anselmo Carral-Solar Con 10/7/2006 for Tex. m 6/10/1967 Larry N Harrison c 2. Archd Dio Texas Houston TX 2003-2006; Cn Ordnry Dio Texas Houston TX 2000-2006; Cn to the Ordnry Dio Texas Houston TX 2000-2003; Stndg Com Dio Texas Houston TX 2000-2001; Dep GC Dio Texas Houston TX 1997-2006; R S Jas The Apos Epis Ch Conroe TX 1997-2000; R S Jas' Epis Ch La Grange TX 1992-1997; Dept CE Dio Texas Houston TX 1987-1995; Asst R All SS Epis Ch Austin TX 1987-1992. DD Sem of the SW 2008. dharrison1009@gmail.com

HARRISON JR, Edward Hendree (SanD) 1114 9th St., Coronado CA 92118 **R Chr Ch Coronado CA 2009-** B Jacksonville FL 6/30/1951 s Edward Hendree Harrison & Laura. BA U So 1975; MDiv Yale DS 1981. D 7/19/1981 P 6/29/1982 Bp Charles Farmer Duvall. m 8/23/1975 Teresa S Sanderson c 2. Trst The TS at The U So Sewanee TN 2002-2008; Dn S Jn's Cathd Jacksonville FL 2001-2008; Trst The TS at The U So Sewanee TN 1996-2000; S Chris's Ch Pensacola FL 1992-2001; Trst The TS at The U So Sewanee TN 1990-1992; R S Paul's By-The-Sea Epis Ch Jacksonville Bch FL 1986-1992; Assoc R Trin Ch Concord MA 1984-1986; Cur S Lk's Epis Ch Mobile AL 1981-1984. tshart2@gmail.com

HARRISON, Elizabeth Arendt (CFla) 215 S Lake Florence Dr, Winter Haven FL 33884 **S Alb's Epis Ch Auburndale FL 2002-** B Orlando FL 5/27/1935 d George Theodore Arendt & Elizabeth May. BA U of So Florida 1966; MA U of So Florida 1978; PhD U of So Florida 1990. D 12/8/2001 Bp John Wadsworth Howe. c 2. revdrbettyh@aol.com

HARRISON JR, Frederick Clarence (SwFla) 19595 Sw 93rd Ln, Dunnellon FL 34432 B South Bend IN 8/20/1922 s Frederick C Harrison & Lora Matilda. VTS 1956; BS Florida Intl U 1975; MDiv VTS 1975; PhD Walden U Minneapolis MN 1979. D 6/24/1956 Bp Richard Henry Baker P 1/12/1957 Bp Edwin A Penick. m 8/15/1973 Lucille Harrison c 4. Assoc S Anne's Ch Crystal River FL 2003-2008; Ch Counslg Cntr Naples FL 1979-1984; R S Andr's Epis Ch Charlotte NC 1958-1960; Chair, Dept of Yth Dio No Carolina Raleigh NC 1957-1960. Auth, "Responsibility: Tthe Moral Substance of Existance"; Auth, "Theory of Dependant Behavior"; Auth, "Dependency-Responsibility-Moralty: A Metapsychological Synthesis"; Auth, "A Metapsychology for Soc Psychol"; Auth, "A Metaspsychology for Dynamic Psychol'". harrison7072@bellsouth.net

HARRISON JR, G Hendree (ETenn) Po Box 326, Athens TN 37371 **P S Paul's Ch Athens TN 2006-** B Atlanta GA 4/15/1975 s G(eorge) Harrison & Carol. BA U So 1997; MDiv STUSo 2003. D 6/7/2003 P 12/18/2003 Bp J(ohn) Neil Alexander. m 6/26/1999 Kristin Jones c 1. S Mk's Ch Dalton GA 2003-2006. hendree@bellsouth.net

HARRISON, Harold Donald (At) 3823 Cherokee Frd, Gainesville GA 30506 **Vic S Anth's Epis Ch Winder GA 2009-** B Atlanta GA 8/1/1935 s Harold Oliver Harrison & Hazel Katherine. BA Emory U 1957; BD STUSo 1960; MA Georgia St U 1974. D 6/13/1960 P 12/21/1960 Bp Randolph R Claiborne. m 9/15/1984 Barbara Young c 2. Assoc Epis Ch Of The H Sprt Cumming GA 2005-2006; Assoc R and Int R Gr Epis Ch Gainesville GA 1998-2003; Dn Dio Atlanta Atlanta GA 1998-2000; R S Jos's Epis Ch McDonough GA 1988-1998; Asst Ch Of The Atone Sandy Sprg GA 1985-1986; Assoc S Bede's Ch Atlanta GA 1978-1985; Assoc Ch Of The Atone Sandy Sprg GA 1973-1978; R S Dunst's Epis Ch Atlanta GA 1965-1969; Vic; R S Marg's Ch Carrollton GA 1960-1965. Omicron Delta Kappa. donrev35@bellsouth.net

HARRISON, James Edward (Chi) 470 Maple St, Winnetka IL 60093 **Cur Chr Ch Winnetka IL 2010-** B Greensburg, PA 4/30/1958 s William Bradley Harrison & Nellie Doreen. MDiv SWTS 2010. D 12/20/2009 P 6/12/2010 Bp S(teven) Todd Ousley. m 11/24/1979 Melissa Melissa Moore c 2. jim@christchurchwinnetka.org

HARRISON, Merle Marie (Colo) 816 Harrison Ave, Canon City CO 81212 B El Dorado KS 1/25/1932 d August Elmer Heitman & Agnes Williams. BA U CO 1953; MLS U of Maryland 1974. D 11/17/2007 Bp Robert John O'Neill. c 3. merleh@bresnan.net

HARRISON, Merritt Raymond (Mass) 12 Remington St Apt 105, Cambridge MA 02138 **Ch Of The Gd Shpd Dedham MA 2005-** B Fort Wayne IN 11/24/1933 s Carlos Evans Harrison & Helen Rose. BA Dart 1957; MDiv McCormick TS 1960. D 12/20/1962 Bp Chandler W Sterling P 4/27/1963 Bp James Winchester Montgomery. m 6/21/1992 Kathleen Marie MacDonald c 3. R S Matt And The Redeem Epis Ch So Boston MA 1999-2002; Int Trin Epis Ch Stoughton MA 1996-1998; Int Chr Ch Somerville MA 1995-1996; R S Jn's Memi Ch Ellenville NY 1966-1968; Asst S Jn's Ch New York NY 1964-1966; Cur Ch Of The H Sprt Missoula MT 1962-1963. merritt105@gmail.com

HARRISON, Ronald Edward (Alb) 24 Summit Ave, Latham NY 12110 B Los Angeles CA 11/29/1946 s William Edward Harrison & Glady Lorraine. BA Biola U 1972; California St U 1975; Cert ETSBH 1977; MDiv CDSP 1979. D 6/23/1979 P 1/13/1980 Bp Robert C Rusack. m 9/14/1968 Pamela Bullard c 5. R S Matt's Ch Latham NY 1991-2009; R Calv Ch Underhill VT 1984-1991; Asst R The Par Of All SS Ashmont-Dorches Dorchester MA 1982-1984; Headmaster S Tim's Epis Ch Apple Vlly CA 1980-1982; Asst Ch Of Our Sav Par San Gabr CA 1979-1980. CBS, NOEL. Phi Alpha Theta; Delta Epsilon Chi. rharris5@nycap.rr.com

HARRISON, Sherridan (WTex) 2431 Michele Jean Way, Santa Clara CA 95050 **Int Ch Of S Jude The Apos Cupertino CA 2011-** B Neosho MO 8/25/1945 d Lawrence Wayne Siegle & Eleanor Lenore. BA Pittsburg St U, Kansas 1965; MA Pittsburg St U, Kasas 1968; CITS Epis TS of The SW 1984. D 5/31/1994 Bp John Herbert MacNaughton P 12/8/1994 Bp James Edward Folts. m 6/20/2003 Lawrence J Harrison c 2. Int All SS Epis Ch Palo Alto CA 2009-2011; Int All SS Epis Ch Corpus Christi TX 2007-2009; Asst S Mk's Epis Ch San Antonio TX 2004-2007; R Chr Ch Epis Laredo TX 1999-2003; Asst R S Barth's Ch Corpus Christi TX 1994-1999. revsherridan@yahoo.com

HARRISON, Susan Wolfe (Ga) 501 E 44th St, Savannah GA 31405 **Died 12/9/2009** B Pittsburgh PA 4/16/1942 d William Lagrange Wolfe & Jeanette. BA Smith 1964. D 9/26/1985 Bp Harry Woolston Shipps. c 2. swh@aol.com

HARRISS, Mary L (Chi) 2338 Country Knolls Ln, Elgin IL 60123 **D Ch Of The Redeem Elgin IL 1991-** B Elgin IL 7/6/1935 d Edward Henry Hoeger & Evelyn Dorothy. Cert Chicago Deacons Sch 1991. D 12/7/1991 Bp Frank Tracy Griswold III. m 11/5/1955 Lucas Edward Harriss c 2. LHarriss@aol.com

HARRISS, Susan Carol (NY) 2 Rectory St, Rye NY 10580 **Co-Chair, Assessment Adjustment Bd Dio New York New York City NY 2009-; R Chr's Ch Rye NY 2000-** B Norfolk VA 7/24/1952 d Ernest Bramwell Harriss & Evangeline Catherine. BA Denison U 1973; MDiv UTS 1977. D 6/2/1979 P 6/9/1980 Bp Paul Moore Jr. m 8/13/1977 Kenneth Ruge c 3. Co-Chair, Assessment Adjustment Bd Dio New York New York City NY 2009; Co-chair, Spec Com on the Assessment Dio New York New York City NY 2009; Vic Cong Of S Sav New York NY 1996-1998; Chapl Cathd Of St Jn The Div New York NY 1992-1995; Theol-In-Res S Mich's Ch New York NY 1989-1991; Assoc R S Jas Ch New York NY 1984-1989; Asst S Mich's Ch New York NY 1983-1984; Diocn Msnry & Ch Extntn Socty New York NY 1980-1983; Dpt Of Missions Ny Income New York NY 1980-1983. Auth, "Jamies Way: Stories For Wrshp & Fam Devotion," Cowley Press, 1991. rector@ccrye.org

HARRITY, Alison Propeck (CFla) 5151 Lake Howell Rd, Winter Park FL 32792 **S Richard's Ch Winter Pk FL 2011-** B Watertown NY 1/22/1973 d David Gordon Propeck & Diana Elizabeth. BA Wm Smith 1995; MDiv CDSP 2000. D 6/14/2000 Bp Calvin Onderdonk Schofield Jr P 12/16/2000 Bp John Lewis Said. m 8/22/1998 Mark C Harrity c 2. Assoc P S Dav's Ch Wayne PA 2004-2011; Asst to R S Greg's Ch Boca Raton FL 2000-2004. apharrity@gmail.com

HARRON II, Frank Martin (WA) 10708 Brewer House Rd, North Bethesda MD 20852 B 3/31/1945 BA Jn Hopkins U 1969; MDiv EDS 1973; MEd Jn Hopkins U 1973. D 4/23/1973 P 1/25/1974 Bp David Keller Leighton Sr. S Barn Ch Wilmington DE 2000-2001; Cn Vic Cathd of St Ptr & St Paul Washington DC 1997-2000; Par of Trin Ch New York NY 1997-2000; R S Ptr's Ch In The Great Vlly Malvern PA 1983-1997; Untd Mnstrs In Higher Ed St. Louis MO 1980-1982; P-in-c S Jn's Ch Ellicott City MD 1979. Auth, *Hlth & Human Values: Making your Own Decisions*, Ya Press, 1992.

HARROP, Stephen Douglas (Tai) 16 W 3rd St, Essington PA 19029 B Sheffield UK 1/23/1948 s Douglas Harrop & Joan. Cert S Johns Coll Of Educ Gb 1974; Edinburgh Theol Coll 1979; U of Manchester 1985; 1990. Trans from Church Of England 10/1/1997. P-in-c Ch Of S Jn The Evang Essington PA 1999-2003; S Jn's Ch Bala Cynwyd PA 1998-1999. Auth, "arts," *Friendship*; Auth, "arts," *S Jn'S Revs*. Indstrl Missions Assn. harropsd@aol.com

HART, Alan (Alb) 120 Waters Rd, Scotia NY 12302 B Schenectady NY 11/29/1946 BA SUNY 1969; MA SUNY 1996. D 6/10/2006 Bp Daniel William Herzog. m 5/22/1994 Mary Carol Hart c 4.

HART, Alvin Van Pelt (NY) 275 W 96th St Apt 27-F, New York NY 10025 **Died 10/29/2009** B Ballinger TX 10/26/1924 s George William Hart & Bertha. BA U of Texas 1944; STB GTS 1947. D 6/24/1947 P 11/1/1948 Bp Clinton Simon Quin.

HART, Curtis Webb (NY) 104 Cty Island Avenue, Bronx NY 10464 B New York NY 2/7/1946 s Frank Frazer Hart & Dorothy. BA Harv 1968; Cert Rutgers-The St U 1972; MDiv UTS 1972. D 6/10/1972 P 1/27/1973 Bp Leland Stark. m 5/16/2009 Stephanie Suzanne St Pierre c 2. P-in-c S Matt's Ch Paramus NJ 2004-2005; P-in-c Ch Of The Gd Shpd - Roosevelt Island Roosevelt Island NY 1999-2001; P-in-c S Geo's Epis Ch Maplewood NJ 1999; P-in-c S Jn's Ch Pleasantville NY 1999; Int S Mary's Ch Haledon NJ 1998; Int S Paul's Ch Sprg Vlly NY 1996; Int S Ptr's Ch Newark NJ 1995-1996; Int Ch Of The H Comm Norwood NJ 1994-1995; Asst S Mk's Ch Brooklyn NY 1973-1975. Auth, "Var," *Profsnl Journ*. Soc for values in Higher Educ 2010-2011. Excellence in Tchg Awd Weill Cornell Med Coll 2005. cuh9001@med.cornell.edu

H

✠ **HART, Rt Rev Donald Purple** (SVa) P.O. Box 461, Peterborough NH 03458 B New York NY 4/22/1937 s Donald Buell Hart & Ann Wentworth. BA Wms 1959; BD EDS 1962. D 6/20/1962 Bp Robert McConnell Hatch P 6/2/1963 Bp William A Lawrence Con 11/30/1986 for Haw. m 9/8/1962 Elizabeth A Howard c 2. Asst Bp of SVa Dio Sthrn Virginia Norfolk VA 1998-2001; Asst Bp Md Dio Maryland Baltimore MD 1997-1998; Int S Mary's Epis Ch Manchester CT 1996-1997; Asst Bp Ct Dio Connecticut Hartford CT 1995-1996; Bp Dio Hawaii Honolulu HI 1986-1995; R Par Of S Jas Ch Keene NH 1983-1986; Chair Fairbanks Chld Protection T/F Dio Alaska Fairbanks AK 1981-1983; Stndg Com Dio Alaska Fairbanks AK 1978-1983; R S Matt's Epis Ch Fairbanks AK 1973-1983; Stff Dio Alaska Fairbanks AK 1969-1973; P-in-c Gd Shpd Huslia AK 1964-1969; Cur Ch Of The Redeem Chestnut Hill MA 1962-1964. donhart@radiusnorth.net

HART, Eleanor E (Be) 108 Quarry View Dr, Morgantown PA 19543 **Int R S Mary's Epis Ch Reading PA 2000-** B Coatsville PA 9/25/1942 d Henry Stanley Espenship & Miriam Darlington. MA Kutztown U; BS Keene St Coll 1966. D 4/22/1989 P 10/1/1994 Bp James Michael Mark Dyer. c 1. P-in-c S Thos Epis Ch Morgantown PA 2002-2011; S Barn Ch Kutztown PA 2001-2002; Assoc S Alb's Epis Ch Reading PA 1998-2008; Int S Anne's Epis Ch Trexlertown PA 1996-1998; P Chr Ch Reading PA 1994-1996; D S Mich's Epis Ch Bethlehem PA 1989-1994. ELLIE@HARTONLINE.NET

HART, Frederick Morgan (WTenn) 78 Ottaray Ct, Brevard NC 28712 B Pittsburgh PA 4/8/1938 s William Frederick Hart & Margaret Bernice. BS W Virginia Wesleyan Coll 1960; CTh Mercer TS 1985; Cert Eger Luth Hm Staten Island NY 1987. D 6/8/1987 P 11/30/1989 Bp Robert Campbell Witcher Sr. m 2/22/1963 Roberta G Gardner c 6. Dioc Coun Mem Dio W Tennessee Memphis TN 2001-2004; R S Jas Epis Ch Un City TN 2000-2004; Hd Sprtl Advsr Curs Dio Long Island Garden City NY 1996-1997; R Gr Ch Riverhead NY 1994-2000; Asst S Thos Ch Farmingdale NY 1987-1994. Bro of S Andr 1987-2000; Ord of S Lk 1990-2000. Walter Wiley Jones Mem AwD BroSA, Prov II 2000. fatherfred@comporium.net

HART JR, George Barrow (Ark) 3802 Hwy 82 W, Crossett AR 71635 B Memphis TN 7/24/1941 s George Barrow Hart & Sarah. BA U So 1963; MDiv STUSo 1972. D 6/25/1972 Bp William F Gates Jr P 5/1/1973 Bp John Vander Horst. m 1/1/1985 Carolyn Hart c 5. Vic Emm Ch Lake Vill AR 870-2652230or8 1997-2005; S Mk's Ch Crossett AR 1991-2004; S Mich's Epis Ch Little Rock AR 1988-1991; Emm Ch Lake Vill AR 870-2652230or8 1988-1989; Vic Chr Ch Brownsville TN 1974-1978; Vic Imm Ch Ripley TN 1973-1978. chart0921@windstream.net

HART, Harry (NJ) 543 Bimini Cay Cir, Vero Beach FL 32966 B Langley Kent UK 6/10/1929 s Harry Hart & Ivy Beatrice. BA Moravian TS 1955; STB PDS 1958. D 4/26/1958 P 11/1/1958 Bp Alfred L Banyard. m 7/12/1976 Mary Jane Hickey. Int H Faith Epis Ch Port S Lucie FL 1997-1998; R Ch Of S Mich The Archangel Wall Township NJ 1972-1992; Dioc Fndt Dio New Jersey Trenton NJ 1972-1980; Secy/Rgstr Dio New Jersey Trenton NJ 1969-1978; Cn Sacrist Trin Cathd Trenton NJ 1967-1972; R S Jn In-The-Wilderness Copake Falls NY 1960-1964; Cur Gr Ch Merchantville NJ 1958-1960. Richard Iii Soc. hhart10120@aol.com

HART, Larry Don (Colo) 8344 W Eastman Pl, Lakewood CO 80227 **The Epis Ch Of S Andr Encinitas CA 2007-** B Bakersfield CA 8/4/1944 s Jessie Herman Hart & Jewell V. AA Bakersfield Cmnty Coll 1967; BS W Texas A&M U 1967; MA Santa Clara U 1974; MA Pepperdine U 1976; MA Fuller TS 1982; DMin Fuller TS 1984. D 6/9/2001 P 12/15/2001 Bp William Jerry Winterrowd. m 6/26/1965 Brenda Sue Buller c 2. Trin Ch Kremmling CO 2006-2007; R H Apos Epis Ch Englewood CO 2001-2005. Auth, "Troubled By Simplistic Notions," *Epis Life*, 2002; Auth, "Confronting Chem Dependency In Your Ch," *Mssn Journ*, 1987; Auth, "The Profsnl Mnstry," *Mssn Journ*, 1986; Auth, "Some Theol Observations On Mnstry," *Restoration Quarterly*, 1984; Auth, "Preaching Without Guile," *Pulpit Dig*, 1980; Auth, "Rollo May And The Experience Of Power," *Journ Of Psychol And Theol*, 1979; Auth, "Brief Hist Of A Minor Restorationist Grp," *Restoration Quarterly*, 1979; Auth, "Mnstrl Trng: What Kind Do We Need?," *Mssn Journ*, 1978. julehart@gmail.com

HART, Lois Ann (Me) 1100 Washington St, Bath ME 04530 **D Gr Epis Ch Bath ME 2008-** B Lewiston ME 9/7/1931 d Gilbert J Young & Anna Marie. D 6/28/2008 Bp Chilton Abbie Richardson Knudsen. c 4. 1hart@gwi.net

HART, Martha Ann (NC) 306 Chowan Trl, Edenton NC 27932 **D Chap Of The Cross Chap Hill NC 1997-** B Sioux City IA 12/30/1933 d Forrest Morten Olson & Miriam. BS U of Iowa 1956. D 1/26/1997 Bp Robert Carroll Johnson Jr. m 6/15/1957 Larry Glen Hart.

HART, Mary Carol (Alb) 120 Waters Rd, Scotia NY 12302 B 10/18/1956 D 6/10/2006 Bp Daniel William Herzog. m 5/22/1994 Alan Hart c 4. alnbljy@aol.com

HART, Robert Lee (Mich) 1471 Bennaville Ave, Birmingham MI 48009 **Int S Jas Epis Ch Birmingham MI 2011-; Cler Ldrshp Proj Dio Michigan Detroit MI 1998-** B Athens TN 11/24/1944 s Frederick Lee Hart & Mary Helen. BA Maryville Coll 1967; BD PrTS 1970; Cert GTS 1971. D 6/12/1971 Bp Leland Stark P 6/25/1972 Bp The Bishop Of Reading. m 6/10/1978 Rebecca Ruth c 2. Int Chr Ch Dearborn MI 2009-2011; P-in-c Chr Ch Detroit MI 2008-2009; R All SS Epis Ch Pontiac MI 1999-2007; Int S Paul's Epis Ch Lansing MI 1997-1999; Int S Andr's Ch Ann Arbor MI 1995-1997; Int S Jn's Epis Ch Saginaw MI 1993-1995; COM Dio SE Florida Miami FL 1992-1993; R S Benedicts Ch Plantation FL 1991-1993; Dn Metro Deanry Dio W Missouri Kansas City MO 1987-1989; Cn Gr And H Trin Cathd Kansas City MO 1983-1991; R Trin Ch Independence MO 1978-1983; Dn Cntrl Deanry Dio W Missouri Kansas City MO 1977-1982; Cn Gr And H Trin Cathd Kansas City MO 1973-1977. bobandbecky@comcast.net

HART, Stephen Anthony (Alb) 49 Killean Park, Albany NY 12205 **R S Mich's Albany NY 2002-** B Lubbock TX 1/6/1954 s Bill B Hart & Beverly June. BA U of Texas 1976; MPA Baylor U 1979; MDiv Nash 1997. D 6/21/1997 P 12/21/1997 Bp Jack Leo Iker. m 4/6/1991 Anna Christina Vaccaro c 4. Vic Our Lady Of The Lake Clifton TX 1999-2002; Cur The Epis Ch Of S Ptr And S Paul Arlington TX 1997-1999. Auth, "Article," *Living Ch*. rev.stevehart@gmail.com

HART, Virginia Frances (Nev) 451 N. Broadway St. Apt. E., Fallon NV 89406 **D H Trin Epis Ch Fallon NV 1996-** B Colusa CA 9/26/1923 d Alvah Thomas Haynes & Ivy Matilda. Butte-Glenn Cmnty Coll; California St U. D 7/19/1986 Bp William Benjamin Spofford. c 5. Ord Of S Lk 1991. hplush@oasisol.com

HART, William Gardner (NY) 414 Haines Rd # 4, Mount Kisco NY 10549 B Madera CA 12/2/1921 s Lucas Perry Hart & Evelyn. BS U CA 1943. D 10/17/1967 Bp Archie H Crowley. m 4/2/1949 Mavis Thomas Davis c 3. D Ch Of S Mary The Vrgn Chappaqua NY 1982-1983; D S Paul's Ch Greenville MI 1980-1981; D Ch Of S Mary The Vrgn Chappaqua NY 1972-1979; Asst S Jn's Epis Ch Alma MI 1967-1970.

HARTE JR, John Joseph Meakin (Az) 1000 Ponderosa Parkway, Flagstaff AZ 86001 B Austin TX 2/12/1945 s John Joseph Meakin Harte & Alice Taylor. BA SMU 1967; STB/MDiv GTS 1970. D 6/18/1970 P 12/21/1970 Bp J(ohn) Joseph Meakins Harte. m 11/5/2005 Susan Brainard c 2. R Ch Of The Epiph Flagstaff AZ 1992-2002; Bd Trst The GTS New York NY 1985-1992; R S Jas Ch Riverton WY 1980-1992; Cur Ch Of The H Cross Dallas TX 1978-1980; P Dio Dallas Dallas TX 1970-1977. Soc of S Jn the Evang Fllshp 1985. jjmhjr@cox.net

HARTE, Susan Brainard (Az) 1000 Ponderosa Parkway, Flagstaff AZ 86001 B Tucson AZ 1/13/1942 d Hollis Harrison Brainard & June Ruth. Wheaton Coll at Norton Mass 1961; BA U of Arizona 1964. D 10/14/2000 Bp Robert Reed Shahan. m 11/5/2005 John Joseph Meakin Harte c 2. D Ch Of The Epiph Flagstaff AZ 2000-2005. DOK 1992; Fllshp of S Jn 2000; Intl Conf of Police Chapl 2010; Intl Critical Incident Stress Fndt 2003. Nominee: Natl Sheriffs' Assn Chapl of the Year Natl Sheriff's Assn 2010; Nominee: Chapl of the Year Natl Sheriff's Assn 2010; Natl Publ Serv Recognition Awd Coconino Cnty Bd Supervisors 2009. sbharte@cox.net

HARTER, Ralph M Peter (Roch) 98 Canfield Rd, Pittsford NY 14534 **Gr Ch Willowdale Geneva NY 2010-** B Auburn NY 3/15/1946 s Donald Robert Harter & Ruth Marion. BA Hob Geneva NY 1968; JD The Cornell Law Sch Ithaca NY 1972; MDiv Bex Sem Rochester NY 2007. D 6/20/2007 P 4/10/2008 Bp Jack Marston McKelvey. m 9/13/1997 Lesile JT Teage c 2. Assoc S Ptr's Epis Ch Henrietta NY 2007-2008. peteharter@rochester.rr.com

HARTJEN JR, Raymond Clifton (Kan) 1015 S. 5th St., Leavenworth KS 66048 B Syracuse NY 9/30/1940 s Raymond Clifton Hartjen & Bertha. BA Furman U 1963; MS No Dakota St U 1977; EdD Ball St U 1985; MDiv Epis TS In

Kentucky 1989; CTh Epis TS of The SW 1989. D 6/23/1989 P 3/7/1990 Bp Edward Witker Jones. m 10/1/1960 Irene Graham Smith c 2. R Trin Ch Atchison KS 1996-2006; R S Jas Ch Vincennes IN 1991-1996; Asst R S Chris's Epis Ch Carmel IN 1989-1991. Auth, *Ethics in Orgnztn Ldrshp*, 1984; Auth, *Human Relatns in the Mltry Enviroment*, 1979. Bro of S Andr.

HARTL, Konrad Palmer (Va) 240 South 3rd Street, Philadelphia PA 19106 B Saint Louis MO 1/9/1943 s Konrad Hartl & Myrtle Palmer. BA Gri 1965; MDiv VTS 1968. D 6/22/1968 Bp George Leslie Cadigan P 6/1/1969 Bp Robert Fisher Gibson Jr. m 8/28/1965 Judith E Edquist c 2. Chr Ch Philadelphia Philadelphia PA 2005-2007; Assoc S Chris's Ch Gladwyne PA 1986-1997; Co-R S Anne's Epis Ch Reston VA 1971-1973; Asst Min S Steph's Ch Richmond VA 1968-1971. Auth, "The Optioned Wk Force," *Advance mag*, 1996. kphartl@aol.com

HARTLEY, Harold Aitken (Mich) 1106 Riverview St, Rogers City MI 49779 **Int R S Paul's Fed Point Hastings FL 2002-** B 8/11/1921 s Herbert Hartley & Ethyl Jane. Whitaker TS. D 6/30/1984 Bp Henry Irving Mayson P 11/1/1985 Bp William J Gordon Jr. m 12/16/1950 Marvella Josephine Cook. Asst Trin Ch S Clair Shores MI 1984-1985. Ord Of S Ben.

HARTLEY, Melissa M (At) 379 Mount Harmony Rd, Bernardsville NJ 07924 B Atlanta GA 10/3/1971 d Charles Larry Hartley & Bonnie Carol. BA U So 1993; MDiv GTS 1998; STM GTS 2005; MPhil Drew U 2010. D 6/6/1998 P 2/20/1999 Bp Frank Kellogg Allan. Int R Ch of S Jn on the Mtn Bernardsville NJ 2009-2011; Assoc R Ch of S Jn on the Mtn Bernardsville NJ 2007-2011; Asst R S Ptr's Ch Morristown NJ 2006-2007; Assoc R H Trin Par Decatur GA 2001-2004; Asst R Gr Epis Ch Gainesville GA 1998-2001. revhartley@yahoo.com

HARTLEY, Robert Henry (NCal) 14530 N Line Post Ln, Tucson AZ 85755 B Seattle WA 8/13/1922 s Charles David Hartley & Marion Elizabeth. BS U CA 1943. D 8/28/1969 Bp J(ohn) Joseph Meakins Harte. m 7/6/1946 Lucille Mae Meyer c 1. D S Barn Ch Mt Shasta CA 1986-1990; Asst Cathd Of S Jn The Evang Spokane WA 1980-1986; Asst All SS Ch Phoenix AZ 1979-1980; Asst Epiph Epis Ch Denver CO 1976-1979; D All SS Ch Phoenix AZ 1969-1976. Ord Of S Lk. robert_hartley@juno.com

HARTLEY, Sherry L (EO) 31535 Union, Box 146, Bonanza OR 97623 B Klamath Falls OR 4/13/1956 d Robert Frank Hartley & Virginia Lee. BS Sthrn Oregon St Coll 1978. D 7/10/1993 Bp Rustin Ray Kimsey. Dio Estrn Oregon The Dalles OR 2000-2009. shartley@eoni.com

HARTLING, David Charles (CFla) 1606 Fort Smith Blvd, Deltona FL 32725 B Northampton MA 6/4/1940 s George Hartling & Madeline. BS Emerson Coll 1965; MDiv STUSo 1974. D 6/14/1974 P 6/14/1975 Bp William Hopkins Folwell. m 5/8/1976 Diana E Ball. R Ch Of The Epiph Kirkwood S Louis MO 1998-2000; Vic S Jude's Ch Orange City FL 1989-1994; Asst Ch Of The Gd Shpd Maitland FL 1987-1988; Asst Ch Of The Gd Shpd Maitland FL 1979-1982; Vic S Nath Ch No Port FL 1977-1978; Asst S Andr's Epis Ch Tampa FL 1976; Asst Ch Of The Gd Shpd Maitland FL 1974-1975. revivalofjoy@aol.com

HARTLING, Gardner J (Lex) No address on file. **D Adv Ch Cynthiana KY 1989-** B Middleboro MA 5/13/1948 s Rennels Gardner Hartling & Pearl May. AS Daytona Bch Cmnty Coll 1976; Lic Epis TS In Kentucky 1988. D 2/5/1989 Bp Don Adger Wimberly. m 10/16/1971 Janet Lee Trowbridge c 1. Acolyte Mstr Adv Ch Cynthiana KY 1984-1988. gjlinc@adelphia.net

HARTMAN, Anthony Eden (EMich) 3458 E Mckinley Rd, Midland MI 48640 B Lakeland FL 4/23/1961 s Paul Taylor Hartman & Anne. BS USMMA 1983; MDiv TESM 1994. D 6/18/1994 Bp John Wadsworth Howe P 1/28/1995 Bp H Coleman McGehee Jr. m 9/29/1990 Sarah Mckoly Woud c 1. D S Jn's Epis Ch Midland MI 1994-1996. tonyhartman@islc.net

HARTMAN, John Franklin (Be) 30 Butler St, Kingston PA 18704 **R Gr Epis Ch Kingston PA 2009-** B Lebanon PA 1/21/1948 s John Franklin Hartman & Geraldine H. Empire St Coll (SUNY); Geo Washington U; New Sch U; York Coll of Pennsylvania; MDiv SWTS 2008. D 6/7/2008 Bp George Edward Councell P 9/29/2009 Bp Paul Victor Marshall. D S Andr's Epis Ch New Providence NJ 2009; Dir of Ch Relatns Seamens Ch Inst Income New York NY 2008-2009. Chas T. Mason Awd/Liturg SWTS 2008. j.franklin.hartman@gmail.com

HARTMAN, Phyllis Colleen (Tex) 1803 Highland Hollow Dr, Conroe TX 77304 **D S Jas The Apos Epis Ch Conroe TX 2009-** B Harrisonburg VA 5/22/1942 d Leroy F Fries & Margaret E. BAS Sam Houston U 1995; Iona Sch of Mnstry 2009. D 2/22/2009 Bp Don Adger Wimberly. m Henry Edmund Hartman c 3. nannypch@mac.com

HARTMAN, Samuel Henry (Eas) 315 S Main St, North East MD 21901 **R S Mary Anne's Epis Ch No E MD 1990-** B Chester PA 6/8/1944 s Adolph J Hartman & Eleanor. BA Bow 1966; STB GTS 1969; DMin Lancaster TS 2003. D 6/28/1969 P 12/28/1969 Bp Frederick Barton Wolf. m 11/26/1977 Judith Ayer c 2. R St Jas Ch 1983-1990; R S Andr's Ch Newcastle ME 1978-1983; Ch Of St Jn Bapt Sebec ME 1972-1978; St Josephs Ch Sebec ME 1972-1978; P-in-c S Jas Ch Old Town ME 1972-1974; Gr Epis Ch Bath ME 1969-1970. judiandsam@verizon.net

HARTNETT, John Godfrey (Nwk) 169 Fairmount Rd, Ridgewood NJ 07450 **R S Eliz's Ch Ridgewood NJ 1993-** B Saint Louis MO 6/29/1951 s Godrey Hartnett & Thelma. BA Harv 1973; MDiv UTS 1987. D 6/13/1987 Bp Paul Moore Jr P 4/23/1988 Bp DM Tutu. m 7/1/2000 Susan Rath. Cathd Chapt Dio Newark Newark NJ 1994-1997; Asst S Jas Ch New York NY 1991-1992; Chair Admin Dio New York New York City NY 1988-1992; Asst Ch Of The Heav Rest New York NY 1987-1991; Dir of Cmncatn S Jas Ch New York NY 1979-1981. jghart@aol.com

HARTNETT, John L (SwFla) 12151 72nd Way, Largo FL 33773 **S Vinc's Epis Ch St Petersburg FL 2008-; Collegial Cn Trin And S Phil's Cathd Newark NJ 2008-** B Carroll IA 8/13/1950 BA U of Iowa 1973; MDiv Nash 1986. D 6/14/1986 Bp James Winchester Montgomery P 12/27/1986 Bp Charles Brinkley Morton. m 8/25/1973 Wendy MacInnes c 2. Dnry Dn Dio SW Florida Sarasota FL 2003-2010; COM Dio SW Florida Sarasota FL 1998-2004; Dioc Coun Dio SW Florida Sarasota FL 1993-1995; R S Giles Ch Pinellas Pk FL 1990-2008; All SS Ch San Diego CA 1986-1990. jlh8131@aol.com

HARTNEY, Michael Elton (Roch) 210 Reading Rd, Watkins Glen NY 14891 **R S Jas' Epis Ch Watkins Glen NY 2006-; R S Jn's Epis Ch Watkins Glen NY 2006-; Vic S Paul's Ch Montour Falls NY 2006-** B Gardner MA 10/25/1948 s Michael Henry Hartney & Juliet Madeline. U So 1968; U of New Hampshire 1970; Ya Berk 1974; MDiv Yale DS 1974; S Geo's Coll Jerusalem IL 1996. D 5/31/1974 P 6/11/1975 Bp Philip Alan Smith. m 10/14/1978 Susan Bradley c 4. S Columba Epis Ch Marathon FL 2002-2004; R S Mths Epis Ch E Aurora NY 1983-2001; R The Ch Of The Gd Shpd Canajoharie NY 1978-1983; Asst Min S Ptr's Ch Albany NY 1976-1978; Asst Min S Thos Ch Hanover NH 1974-1976. Vol of the Year Epis Cmnty Serv of Wstrn New York 1999; Bp's Awd Dio Wstrn New York 1997. michael.hartney@aya.yale.edu

HARTSUFF, Donald Keith (EMich) 8695 North Loxley Drive, Box 275, Higgins Lake MI 48627 B Jackson MI 11/13/1929 s Harry Herbert Hartsuff & Margaret Ellen. Lic VTS 1966. D 6/29/1966 Bp C Kilmer Myers P 4/27/1967 Bp Richard S M Emrich. m 9/4/1948 Gloria Cole. Int The Epis Ch Of The Adv W Bloomfield MI 1993-1994; Int S Thos Ch Trenton MI 1991-1993; R S Jas Ch Detroit MI 1974-1991; R S Andr's Epis Ch Algonac MI 1968-1974; Asst S Columba Ch Detroit MI 1966-1968.

HARTT, Paul Jonathan (Alb) 8 Loudon Hts S, Loudonville NY 12211 **S Ptr's Ch Albany NY 2004-** B Philadelphia PA 12/8/1959 s Walter Fred Hartt & Marilyn Ruth. S Jn Coll Annapolis; U of Pennsylvania; BA NYU 1989; MA S Jn Coll Annapolis 1990; MDiv Ya Berk 1995. D 6/23/1995 Bp Orris George Walker Jr P 2/1/1996 Bp Clarence Nicholas Coleridge. m 3/7/1993 C Jeffrey Hartt c 1. R S Jn's Ch Delhi NY 1998-2004; P-in-c S Ptr's Ch Hobart NY 1998-2004; Cur S Mk's Ch Mystic CT 1995-1998. paulatpeter@yahoo.com

HARTT JR, Walter Fred (NJ) 408 Kingfisher Rd, Tuckerton NJ 08087 B East Orange NJ 5/8/1936 s Walter Fred Hartt & Loretta Bessy. BD Reformed Epis Sem 1960; BA U of Pennsylvania 1963; PDS 1964; MA U of Pennsylvania 1967; ThD GTS 1969; PhD U of Lancaster Lancaster Engl UK 1972. D 6/20/1964 Bp Andrew Tsu P 12/1/1964 Bp Allen J Miller. m 8/27/1957 Marilyn Ruth Harvey c 2. Int Ch Of The H Sprt Tuckerton NJ 2008-2009; S Mary's Epis Ch Pleasantville NJ 2001; R Chr Ch Toms River Toms River NJ 1985-2001; Ch Of The Atone Stratford NJ 1982-1985; Trin Ch Princeton NJ 1982-1983; The GTS New York NY 1976-1982; R S Mk's Epis Ch Perryville MD 1972-1974; Assoc S Ptr's Ch Salisbury MD 1964-1967. "Complete Idiot's Guide to Grandparenting," MacMillian CO, 1998. Cmnty of S Mary; Sprtl Life Cntr. Fell ECF 1969; Fell GTS 1967. 7383mrh@gmail.com

HARTWELL, Edward M. (Tex) 5502-B Buffalo Pass, Austin TX 78745 B Houston TX 6/9/1926 s Arthur Edward Hartwell & Clare. BA SW U Georgetown TX 1950; MDiv VTS 1953; MA U of Texas 1970. D 6/29/1953 Bp Clinton Simon Quin P 7/1/1954 Bp John E Hines. m 6/14/1998 Karen J Bordelon c 5. P-in-c S Geo's Epis Ch Gatesville TX 1983-1988; Chr Ch Sch Temple TX 1979-1981; Asst Chr Epis Ch Temple TX 1979-1981; P-in-c S Jas' Epis Ch La Grange TX 1968-1975; R S Geo's Ch Austin TX 1960-1968; Dce S Mk's Ch Beaumont TX 1956-1960; Vic S Paul's Epis Ch Woodville TX 1955-1957; Vic Chr Ch San Aug TX 1953-1956; Vic Trin Epis Ch Jasper TX 1953-1956. Natl Epis Sch Assn 1957-1961. ehartwell@austin.rr.com

HARTWELL, Michael (Mass) 620 Flick Cir., Thomasville NC 27360 **S Paul's Epis Ch Edenton NC 2002-** B Norwood MA 5/1/1938 s John Ray Hartwell & Shirley. BBA GW 1962; Cert Geo. Mercer TS, Dio of LI 1979. D 1/6/1979 P 8/11/1979 Bp Albert Wiencke Van Duzer. m 6/27/1964 Sandra M MacIvor. R S Ptr's Ch On The Canal Buzzards Bay MA 1985-1986; Vic S Ann's Epis Ch Windham Windham ME 1982-1984; Assoc The Ch Of The H Sprt Orleans MA 1979-1982. theshepherdpartners@hotmail.com

HARTZOG, Dorothy Chatham (Tenn) 211 Chip N Dale Dr., Clarksville TN 37043 **P-in-c Gr Chap Rossview Clarksville TN 2003-; Assoc R Trin Ch Clarksville TN 2003-** B Fort Worth TX 1/26/1947 d Edward Doyle Chatham & Josephine Johnson. BA Carson-Newman Coll 1969; MA So Carolina St U 1979; Luth Theol Sthrn Sem 1992; MDiv VTS 1994. D 6/3/1994 P 1/25/1995 Bp Edward Lloyd Salmon Jr. c 1. Mem Dioc Coun Dio Tennessee Nashville

TN 2006-2010; Supply P Dio Tennessee Nashville TN 2002-2003; Mem, Dioc Coun Dio Delaware Wilmington DE 2001-2002; Prncpl Pstr / Vic S Martha's Epis Ch Bethany Bch DE 1998-2002; P-in-c H Cross Faith Memi Epis Ch Pawleys Island SC 1997-1998; Mgr, St. Eliz Place Camp Baskerville Pawleys Island SC 1996-1998; D S Steph's Epis Ch Charleston SC 1994-1995. revdot@msn.com

HARTZOG, Howard Gallemore (WTex) 109 W Linar Street, Hebbronville TX 78361 B Marlin TX 1/23/1945 s Howard G Hartzog & Anna Paul. AA Victoria Coll Victoria TX. D 4/14/2002 P 2/28/2003 Bp James Edward Folts. m 7/3/1971 Frances Hartzog c 2. Epis Ch Of The Gd Shepard Geo W TX 2009; Vic S Jas Epis Ch Hebbronville TX 2005-2009; Partnr In Mnstry Estrn Convoc Kennedy TX 2003-2005. howdyh@cableone.net

HARVEY, Edwin E (WTex) 868 Porter Rd, Cochran GA 31014 B Dodge City KS 5/13/1930 s John L Harvey & Edna E. BA SW 1952; Drew U 1956; MDiv VTS 1958; STM VTS 1959; ThD Heidelberg Coll 1965. D 6/20/1958 P 6/1/1959 Bp Edward Hamilton West. m 8/15/1956 Mary Meadows c 3. Assoc S Mk's Epis Ch San Antonio TX 1990-1995; R All SS Epis Ch Corpus Christi TX 1981-1990; Assoc S Dav's Ch Austin TX 1976-1981; Asst S Mk's Epis Ch Jacksonville FL 1974-1976; Asst S Paul's Epis Ch Jacksonville FL 1959-1960.

H

HARVEY, Errol Allen (NY) 800 North Miami Ave., Apt. 302, Miami FL 33136 B Grand Rapids MI 8/5/1943 s Fred Donvan Harvey & Elizabeth. BA Aquinas Coll 1965; BD SWTS 1969; MPA NYU 1977; DD Commonwealth U TS 1991. D 6/9/1968 Bp Charles Bennison P 5/25/1969 Bp George E Rath. R S Aug's Ch New York NY 1983-2008; R S Andr's Ch Bronx NY 1972-1983; Diocn Msnry & Ch Extntn Socty New York NY 1972-1976; Dpt Of Missions Ny Income New York NY 1972-1976; R S Mk's Ch Dorchester MA 1970-1972; Cur Trin And S Phil's Cathd Newark NJ 1968-1970. DD Commonwealth Univertsity TS 1991. eahnyc@yahoo.com

HARVEY, Joel (SVa) St Stephen's Church, 1445 Norview Ave, Norfolk VA 23513 B Brooklyn NY 10/26/1938 s Abraham Smolensky & Jennie. BA CUNY 1968; MA Adel 1969; PhD Florida St U 1980; CERT/DCE Mercer TS 1984. D 12/21/1984 P 12/1/1985 Bp Robert Campbell Witcher Sr. m 3/21/1970 Patricia Ann Moore c 3. P-in-c S Steph's Ch Norfolk VA 2007; S Phil And S Jas Ch New Hyde Pk NY 2001-2006; Dir Pstr Care S Jos's Epis Chap Far Rockaway NY 1999-2006; Epis Hlth Serv Bethpage NY 1997-2006; Geo Mercer TS Garden City NY 1994-2000; St Mary's Hosp Bayside NY 1994-1997; Healthcare Chapl New York NY 1993-1994; S Johns Epis Hosp Far Rockaway NY 1984-1986. Cmnty Of S Mary, Ord Of S Lk, Coll Chapl; Psych, Natl Epis Hlth Mnstrs (Bd). fatherjoel@cox.net

HARVEY, Rick E (Ida) 2080 Bodine Ct, Boise ID 83705 **D S Mich's Cathd Boise ID 1997-; D Dio Idaho Boise ID 1983-** B Boise ID 7/19/1949 s Roy Jack Harvey & June Beatrice. BFA Boise St U 1973. D 10/6/1988 Bp David Bell Birney IV. m 8/7/1971 Connie Sue Cooper c 2. Idaho Assn For Pstr Care, NAAD. rharvey@micron.net

HARVEY, Robbin Whitestine (O) 616 Hampton Ridge Dr, Akron OH 44313 B Akron OH 11/25/1934 d Robert Earl Whitestine & Mary T. Dh OH SU 1953. D 11/13/1992 Bp James Russell Moodey P. D Chr Ch Shaker Heights OH 2000-2009; D Chr Ch Epis Hudson OH 1994-1998; D S Paul's Ch Akron OH 1992-1993. deacrobbin@aol.com

HARVEY, Robert William (WA) Episcopal Church of Our Saviour, 1700 Powder Mill Road, Silver Spring MD 20903 **R Ch Of Our Sav Silver Sprg MD 2006-** B Pittsburgh PA 6/7/1964 s William James Nuckels & Roberta Harvey. BA Clearwater Chr Coll Clearwater FL 1986; MDiv Reformed TS 1989; STM STUSo 1998. D 12/17/1994 Bp Robert Oran Miller P 7/1/1995 Bp Charles Lovett Keyser. m 6/16/1990 Anne Turberville Whitaker. R Chr Ch Ansonia CT 1999-2006; Ch Of The Mssh Lower Gwynedd PA 1998-1999; Assoc S Jas Ch Oneonta NY 1997-1998; Cur / Asst Washington Memi Chap Vlly Forge PA 1995-1997. OHC - Assoc 1996. rharvey@episcopalcos.org

HARVEY, Robert William (Az) 8084 W Arching Stone Way, Tucson AZ 85743 **Assoc Ch Of The Apos Oro Vlly AZ 1995-** B Toronto ON CA 1/9/1930 s Francis Harvey & Virginia. Cert U MN 1978; CTh Toronto Dioc Trng Sch 1995. D 6/24/1965 Bp Hamilton Hyde Kellogg P 4/2/1966 Bp Philip Frederick McNairy. c 7. R Gd Shpd Epis Ch Wichita KS 1989-1995; Dn Sw Convoc Dio Kansas Topeka KS 1987-1991; Exec Dir First Step Minneapolis MN 1979-1982; R S Jn The Bapt Epis Ch Minneapolis MN 1970-1982; Vic Emm Epis Ch Alexandria MN 1965-1970. frbobh@q.com

HARVIN, W(infield) Scott (Roch) 677 Vassar Rd, Wayne PA 19087 B Jamaica NY 6/25/1932 s Jacob Roland Harvin & Annabel. BA U of Virginia 1953; MDiv VTS 1957; The Amer Coll 1987; The Amer Coll 1988. D 6/7/1957 Bp Frederick D Goodwin P 12/21/1957 Bp Wilburn Camrock Campbell. m 8/18/1956 Sue S Harvin. The Cov Life Ins Co Oreland PA 1991; Stndg Com Dio Rochester Rochester NY 1975-1979; R Chr Ch Corning NY 1968-1983; Chair Dio Rochester Rochester NY 1968-1972; Excoun Dio W Virginia Charleston WV 1963-1968; Eccl Crt Dio W Virginia Charleston WV 1961-1968; R Trin Epis Ch Martinsburg WV 1961-1968; Asst S Matt's Ch Wheeling WV 1957-1961. sueharvin@earthlink.net

HARWOOD, John Thomas (CPa) 137 3rd St, Renovo PA 17764 **P-in-c Trin Ch Renovo PA 2011-** B Ottumwa IA 2/16/1947 s Arthur Manning Harwood & Nyta Pauline. in the process CDSP; BA Wartburg Coll 1968; PhD U of Nebraska 1977. D 10/31/2010 P 10/19/2011 Bp Nathan Dwight Baxter. m 2/26/1983 Kathryn Grossman c 2. jtharwood@comcast.net

HARY, Barbara Ann (CPa) 20 Heatherland Rd, Middletown PA 17057 **D S Mich And All Ang Ch Middletown PA 1996-** B Bronxville NY 7/21/1931 d Malcolm Garden Packman & Dorothy Muriel. Harrisburg Area Cmnty Coll; Cert Pennsylvania Diac Sch 1991; S Johns Carlisle PA 1996; S Mich & Alll Ang Middletown PA 2000. D 6/14/1991 Bp Charlie Fuller McNutt Jr. m 1/3/1954 Charles Philip Hary. Dio Cntrl Pennsylvania Harrisburg PA 1983-1996. NAAD; Tertiary Of The Soc Of S Fran. barbarahary@juno.com

HASEN, Elizabeth Sorchan (Ky) 409 W 22nd Ave, Spokane WA 99203 B New York NY 11/18/1955 d George Milton Hasen & Charlotte Hunnewell. Bryn 1975; BA Amh 1977; MDiv VTS 1991. D 6/11/1991 P 12/1/1991 Bp Daniel Lee Swenson. Ch Of The Resurr Spokane Vlly WA 2010-2011; S Alb's Epis Ch Fern Creek Louisville KY 1994-2004; Cathd Ch Of S Paul Burlington VT 1991-1994. ehasen@aol.com

HASKELL, Robert Finch (Alb) 9 Long Creek Dr, Burnt Hills NY 12027 **Dio Albany Albany NY 2004-** B Washington,DC 7/29/1942 s Francis Waller Haskell & Mary Delafield. BS Cor 1965; MBA NYU 1972; MDiv EDS 1973. D 6/9/1973 Bp Paul Moore Jr P 2/1/1974 Bp Ned Cole. m 11/7/2011 Margaret J Joggerst c 2. S Jas Ch Oneonta NY 2001-2003; Ch Of The Redemp Southampton PA 1989-2001; R S Andr's Epis Ch Syracuse NY 1975-1988; Cur Trin Memi Ch Binghamton NY 1973-1975. rhaskell2@nycap.rr.com

HASLETT III, William Warner (Pgh) 418 Jerad Ln., Windber PA 15963 B Johnstown PA 10/1/1968 s William Warner Haslett & Louise Christine. BA U Pgh 1990; MDiv TESM 1993. D 6/26/1993 P 6/1/1994 Bp Alden Moinet Hathaway. m 8/21/1993 Tammy Kawchak c 2. S Fran In The Fields Somerset PA 1995-1997; Vic S Ptr's Epis Ch Blairsville PA 1994; Cur S Barn Ch Wilmington DE 1993; Chrmstr S Mk's Ch Johnstown PA 1983-1990. haslett@pitt.edu

HASS, Caroline Vada (WNY) Po Box 161, Alexander NY 14005 B Dalton NY 6/16/1933 d Alfred Henry Kingsley & Frances Phoebe. New Engl Coll 1956; BS Liberty U 1986; EFM Brent Sch E Aurora NY 1996; CPE U Roch 1996; Cont ed. Masters Intl Sch of Div 2005. D 8/7/1999 Bp J Michael Garrison. D S Lk's Epis Ch Attica NY 1999-2005. Auth, "Encounter (poetry)," *Colors of Life*, Intl Libr of Poetry Watermark Press, 2003; Auth, "Beside Still Waters," *Sharing*, Int'l OSL, 2001; Auth, "From the Vlly of The Shadow," *Sharing*, Int'l OSL, 2001. Amer Soc of Clincl Pathologists (Assoc) 1982-1994; Natl Soc for Histotechnology 1973-1994. carolinehass26@live.com

HASSAN, Rosemarie Cohen (Nwk) 954 Ave C, Bayonne NJ 07002 **Assoc Calv Ch Bayonne NJ 2011-; Newark Epis Cler Assn Strng Com Dio Newark Newark NJ 2011-; Trin Ch Bayonne NJ 2011-; Windmill Allnce Inc. Bayonne NJ 2011-** B New York NY 10/25/1953 d Saul Cohen & Bonita Desaro. SUNY 1973; BA Molloy Coll 1977; CUNY 1989; MDiv GTS 1993; Cert GTS 1994; STM GTS 1997; Cert Coaches Trng Inst 2009. D 4/24/1993 P 11/18/1993 Bp Orris George Walker Jr. m 11/10/2001 Judy Piscerchia c 1. Dist 7 Co-Cnvnr Dio Newark Newark NJ 2009-2011; Ch Of The Gd Shpd Ft Lee NJ 2007; Mus and Liturg Cmsn Dio Newark Newark NJ 2005-2007; Hisp Mnstry T/F Dio Newark Newark NJ 2004-2007; Dioc Sprtl Dir for Vocare Dio Newark Newark NJ 2002-2011; Dio Newark Newark NJ 2002; Dist 7 Co-Cnvnr Dio Newark Newark NJ 2001-2003; Wmn Cmsn Dio Newark Newark NJ 2001-2003; Mus and Liturg Cmsn Dio Newark Newark NJ 2000-2003; T/F on Minority Vendors Dio Newark Newark NJ 1999-2001; Camp Com Dio Newark Newark NJ 1999-2000; Ward Herbert Bd Dio Newark Newark NJ 1998-1999; Pstr Counslr at AIDS Resource Cntr S Barn Ch Newark NJ 1997-2001; Wmn Cmsn Dio Newark Newark NJ 1996-2000; Bd Mem The Oasis Newark NJ 1996-2000; Dioc Coun Dio Newark Newark NJ 1996-1998; Vic Trin Epis Ch Kearny NJ 1995-2011; Assoc S Ptr's Ch New York NY 1993-1995. EPF 1993; EWC 1995; Integrity 1990; Ord Of S Helena 1992. trinateerose@gmail.com

HASSE III, Edward Max (Nwk) 4 Woodland Rd, Montvale NJ 07645 **Dep to GC Dio Newark Newark NJ 2000-; Mem, Stndg Com Dio Newark Newark NJ 2000-; R S Paul's Ch Montvale NJ 1996-** B Englewood NJ 9/26/1963 s Edward Max Hasse & Barabara Amelia. BS Ithaca Coll 1985; MDiv VTS 1989. D 6/3/1989 P 12/9/1989 Bp John Shelby Spong. m 8/22/1987 Melissa Blackinton c 2. Alt Dep. to GC Dio Newark Newark NJ 1994-2000; Chair, T/F on Yth Dio Newark Newark NJ 1994-1996; Mem, Yth Mnstry Bd Dio Newark Newark NJ 1991-1999; R Ch Of The H Sprt Verona NJ 1991-1996; Assoc R S Jas Ch Upper Montclair NJ 1989-1991. Integrity; RACA. Cbury Schlr Awd Dio Newark 2000; Bp's Outstanding Serv Awd Dio Newark 1997. edhasse@optonline.net

HASSELBROOK, Audrey Caroline (Nwk) 18 Shepard Pl, Nutley NJ 07110 **Asst S Jas Ch Upper Montclair NJ 2007-** B Kearny NJ 12/12/1957 d Roy Stoeckel & Patricia C. BS Montclair St U 1979; MAT Montclair St U 2001; MDiv GTS 2005. D 6/11/2005 Bp John Palmer Croneberger P 2/25/2006 Bp

Carol Joy Gallagher. m 6/9/1979 James Hasselbrook c 3. Trin And S Phil's Cathd Newark NJ 2005-2006. ahasselbrook@optonline.net

HASSELL, Mariann Barbara (Tenn) 1204 Jackson Dr, Pulaski TN 38478 B Dayton OH 1/1/1941 d Robert Charles Dempsey & Nellie May. MA Franciscan TS 1989. D 1/25/1992 Bp John-David Mercer Schofield P 2/26/2006 Bp Bertram Nelson Herlong. c 4. Assoc The Epis Ch Of The Mssh Pulaski TN 2007-2009; S Mk's Epis Ch French Camp CA 1993-1994; CE & Yth Min S Paul's Epis Ch Modesto CA 1989-1990. therevmary@aol.com

HASSEMER, Donald William (RG) Po Box 747, Medanales NM 87548 B St Louis MO 8/14/1944 s Clarence William Hassemer & Virginia Mae. D 1/5/1981 P 1/8/1982 Bp Richard Mitchell Trelease Jr. m 10/3/1970 Wendy Graef c 3. dhasseme@phs.org

HASSERIES, Robert Alan (Spok) East 360 Springview Drive, Coeur D'Alene ID 83814 B Evansville IN 9/9/1940 s Robert William Hasseries & Ruth. BA U of Arizona 1962; BD CDSP 1964. D 7/3/1965 P 1/1/1966 Bp J(ohn) Joseph Meakins Harte. m 8/28/1964 Kitty Kay Craft c 3. R S Lk's Ch Coeur D Alene ID 1990-2000; Dio Spokane Spokane WA 1984-1990; Vic S Jas Epis Ch Cashmere WA 1981-1990; S Lk's Epis Ch Wenatchee WA 1981-1983; Vic S Cuth's Epis Ch Oakland CA 1975-1981; R Epis Ch Of Our Sav Placerville CA 1969-1975; Cur S Steph's Ch Phoenix AZ 1967-1969; Vic S Paul's Ch Tombstone AZ 1965-1967; Vic S Raphael In The Vlly Mssn Benson AZ 1965-1967. Tertiary Of The Soc Of S Fran.

HASSETT, Miranda Katherine (Mil) 354 Main St, Hopkinton NH 03229 **S Dunst's Ch Madison WI 2011-** B Boston MA 2/4/1975 d Eliot R Smith & Pamela G. BA Indiana U Bloomington 1997; PhD U NC 2004; MDiv EDS 2008. D 6/28/2008 Bp Alfred Clark Marble Jr P 2/6/2009 Bp Michael Bruce Curry. m 12/8/2001 Philip A Hassett c 2. Asst S Andr's Epis Ch Hopkinton NH 2008-2010; Asst for Fam Mnstrs Chr Ch Needham MA 2007-2008. Auth, "Angl Comm in Crisis," *Angl Comm in Crisis*, Pr Press, 2006. miranda@hassetthome.org

HASSETT, Stephen (Cal) 6167 Laird Ave, Oakland CA 94605 **Ch Of The Redeem San Rafael CA 2008-; St Johns Epis Ch Ross CA 2008-** B 5/30/1971 BFA SUNY 1994. D 6/3/2006 Bp William Edwin Swing P 12/2/2006 Bp Marc Handley Andrus. m 4/27/2002 Clancy Drake c 2. Dio California San Francisco CA 2006-2007. steve@stjohnsross.org

HASTIE, Cornelius deWitt (Mass) 24 Castleton St, Jamaica Plain MA 02130 B Spring Lake NJ 1/22/1931 s Frank Bowman Hastie & Cecile Amelie. ABS Harv 1952; MDiv EDS 1956. D 6/9/1956 Bp Angus Dun P 12/7/1956 Bp Anson Phelps Stokes Jr. m 4/18/1981 Linda M Hastie c 2. R S Jn's S Jas Epis Ch Roxbury MA 1996; Serv S Jn's S Jas Epis Ch Roxbury MA 1988-1990; S Jas Educ Cntr Boston MA 1987-1996; Dioc Coun Dio Massachusetts Boston MA 1984-1988; Bd, Epis City Mssn Dio Massachusetts Boston MA 1976-1982; R S Jn's Ch Charlestown (Boston) Charlestown MA 1973-1981; S Jas Pre-Kindergarten Sch Boston MA 1965-1987; S Jn's S Jas Epis Ch Roxbury MA 1956-1965.

HASTINGS, Brian J (Chi) 857 W. Margate Terrace, #1-W, Chicago IL 60640 **Ch Of Our Sav Chicago IL 1998-** B Brantford ON CA 7/23/1954 s James Thomas Hastings & Gertrude Clare. BA U of Wstrn Ontario 1977; MDiv Hur 1980. Rec 3/1/1989 Bp Frank Tracy Griswold III. m Roger Gumm. Ch Of The Ascen Chicago IL 1988-1991. revbriancos@gmail.com

HASTINGS, Donald Louis (RI) 2700 Link Side Dr Apt 4, Cincinnati OH 45245 **Died 1/2/2011** B Washington DC 5/4/1942 s Louis Lantrum Hastings & Louise Virginia. BA Rutgers-The St U 1964; STB GTS 1967. D 6/3/1967 P 12/16/1967 Bp Horace W B Donegan. c 2. hastings37@live.com

HASTINGS, K(empton) (Pa) 2119 Old Welsh Rd, Abington PA 19001 **R S Anne's Ch Abington PA 1994-** B Princeton NJ 10/3/1961 s Howard Kempton Hastings & Lucia Larabee (Brown). BA Hob 1984; MDiv UTS 1989; D. Minn Nash 2015. D 6/10/1989 P 3/31/1990 Bp George Phelps Mellick Belshaw. m 5/6/2000 Pamela Anne Roediger c 2. Int All SS Epis Ch Lakewood NJ 1993-1994; Asst Chr Ch Toms River Toms River NJ 1990-1993; Cur S Jn's Ch Salem NJ 1989-1990. Abington Hosp Pstr Care Com 1994; Bd Emergency Food Bank Dio NJ 1990-1994; Chr Soc Relation Dio NJ 1990-1994; Econ Justice Com Dio PA 1994-1999; Pastors Untd in Pryr, Abington, PA 1999; Resolutns Com Dio NJ 1990-1994; Soc for the Advancement of Chr Faith in Pennsylvania 2004. Alum Awd, Chapin Sch 1998; Phi Beta Kappa 1984. kbhastings@verizon.net

HASTINGS, Mark Wayne (Mich) PO Box 287, Onsted MI 49265 B Ann Arbor MI 11/7/1944 s William Hastings & Alma. BA Siena Heights U 2002. D 10/27/2010 P 5/24/2011 Bp Wendell Nathaniel Gibbs Jr. m 6/11/1966 Susan Hastings c 3. marsue4445@yahoo.com

HASTINGS, Thomas Lewis (Miss) 201 Franklin St, Sardis MS 38666 **Died 3/25/2011** B Louisville KY 1/16/1917 s Thomas Hastings & Anna. DePauw U 1939; BA U of Louisiana 1942; BD GTS 1945. D 6/3/1945 P 12/1/1945 Bp Charles Clingman. Auth, "Ch Of Adv Williamston No Carolina"; Auth, "S Steph'S Ch Batesville Mississippi".

HASWELL JR, Andrew Jordan (Okla) 1107 Hemstead Pl, Oklahoma City OK 73116 B 7/3/1937 s Andrew Jordan Haswell & Margaret Leore. Pr 1959; Ya 1960; LLB Harv 1963. D 10/2/1966 Bp Chilton Powell. m 8/29/1962 Martha Brownlow Martin c 1.

HATCH, Bert Huntington (SO) 3108 Fort St, Edisto Island SC 29438 B Augusta GA 8/17/1931 s James Milo Hatch & Ann Davenport. U GA 1953; BD STUSo 1956. D 6/17/1956 P 3/1/1957 Bp Albert R Stuart. m 6/5/2007 Anne S Hatch c 2. R H Trin Epis Ch Charleston SC 1991-1993; R S Tim's Epis Ch Cincinnati OH 1981-1991; S Clem's Epis Ch Canton GA 1980-1981; Dioc Nwspr Atlanta GA 1978-1981; R S Mk's Ch Dalton GA 1975-1978; R S Tim's Ch Signal Mtn TN 1966-1968; R S Jas Epis Ch Marietta GA 1962-1966; Vic S Fran Ch Menomonee Falls WI 1960-1962; Vic S Mich And All Ang Savannah GA 1958-1960; Vic S Mk's Ch Brunswick GA 1956-1958. Auth, "Forw Day By Day". battendown@aol.com

HATCH, Jessica Ann (U) Po Box 3090, Salt Lake City UT 84110 B New York NY 5/28/1946 d Gilbert Thomas White & Virginia Margaret. BA Seattle U 1968; MDiv GTS 1989. D 6/10/1989 P 1/13/1990 Bp Frederick Houk Borsch. m 4/24/2004 Steven B Kiger. S Mary's Ch Provo UT 2009-2011; Dio Utah Salt Lake City UT 2006-2009; Epis Cmnty Serv Inc Salt Lake City UT 2002-2006; Int All SS Ch Salt Lake City UT 2001-2002; Assoc Dn The GTS New York NY 1999-2001; Asstg Ch Of The Incarn New York NY 1998-2001; Sr Consult Dio New York New York City NY 1998-2001; Pstr Assoc The Ch Of S Lk In The Fields New York NY 1996-1998; Dir Alum & Chrch Relatns The GTS New York NY 1996-1998; Dio Arizona Phoenix AZ 1994-1996; Dn Trin Cathd Phoenix AZ 1994-1995; Co Cnvnr Rgnl Par Dio Arizona Phoenix AZ 1993-1995; Dioc Coun Dio Arizona Phoenix AZ 1993-1995; Gr S Paul's Epis Ch Tucson AZ 1991-1994; Asst R S Mich And All Ang Par Corona Del Mar CA 1989-1991. "Living Boldly," *an eNewsletter*, Epis Dio Utah, 2007; Auth, "Where Do Wmn Find Themselves," *The Epis New Yorker*, Epis Dio NY, 1999. Polly Bond Awd of Excellence ECom 1998. jahatch1@comcast.net

HATCH, Mark Holbrook (WMass) 267 Locust Street, Apt 2K, Florence MA 01062 B Boston MA 9/16/1958 s John Christopher Hatch & Mary Sherrard. BA Dart 1980; MA U of Massachusetts 1987; MDiv Harvard DS 1989. D 3/6/1991 P 11/24/1991 Bp Robert Hodges Johnson. c 2. P-in-c S Phil's Ch Easthampton MA 2009-2010; Int Ch Of The Atone Westfield MA 2007-2009; Int S Jas Ch Great Barrington MA 2006-2007; Int S Paul's Epis Ch Stockbridge MA 2005-2006; Int Cathd Ch Of S Steph Harrisburg PA 2004-2005; Int Dio Caledonia Prince Rupert BC 2003-2004; P-in-c Chr Ch So Barre MA 2003; Assoc S Fran Ch Holden MA 1999-2003; Vic S Andr's Ch No Grafton MA 1993-1996; R Ch Of The H Fam Mills River NC 1991-1992. markhatch108@gmail.com

HATCH, Rebekah Bokros (At) P.O. Box 2574, Decatur GA 30031 **Int US Chapl H Innoc' Epis Sch Atlanta GA 2011-; Asst to the R S Aid's Epis Ch Milton GA 2010-** B Decatur GA 12/1/1976 BA Salem Coll Winston-Salem NC; MDiv VTS 2004. D 6/5/2004 P 1/25/2005 Bp J(ohn) Neil Alexander. m 2/17/2001 Anthony R Hatch c 1. Assoc R Ch Of The Gd Shpd Ruxton MD 2006-2009; Asst Chapl S Paul's Sch Brooklandville MD 2004-2006. revreba@yahoo.com

✠ HATCH, Rt Rev Robert McConnell (WMass) 1855 Plaza Dr Apt 2004, Louisville CO 80027 **Died 7/16/2009** B Brooklyn NY 7/6/1910 s William Henry Paine Hatch & Louise H. BA Harv 1933; MA Col 1935; BD EDS 1939; STD Ya Berk 1951; DD Trin 1951; DLitt Norwich U 1963. D 6/14/1939 P 5/1/1940 Bp Henry Knox Sherrill Con 4/17/1951 for Ct. c 2. Auth, *Major Jn Andre: A Gallant in Spy's Clothing*; Auth, *Major Jn Andre: A Gallant in Spy's Clothing*; Auth, *Thrust for Can: The Amer Attempt on Quebec 1775-1776*. Norwich U Northfolk UT LHD 1963; Trin DD 1951; Berkely DS of Yale STD 1951. wyoangax@msn.com

HATCH, Victoria Theresa (Los) 344 W George St, Banning CA 92220 B Tacoma Park MD 3/26/1947 d William Nagel Hatch & Nancy Constantine. FD 1967; U of Maryland U Coll Europe 1967; BA Amer U 1969; VTS 1975. D 6/5/1975 Bp Robert Bruce Hall P 1/15/1977 Bp Robert C Rusack. Dio Los Angeles Los Angeles CA 2006; S Geo's Ch Riverside CA 2003-2006; P-in-c S Steph's Par Beaumont CA 2000-2001; S Alb's Epis Ch Yucaipa CA 1983-1986; Dep Gc Dio Los Angeles Los Angeles CA 1982-1985; S Agnes Mssn Banning CA 1978-2003; S Cross By-The-Sea Ch Hermosa Bch CA 1977, Dio Los Angeles Los Angeles CA 1976-1977; Asst S Cross By-The-Sea Ch Hermosa Bch CA 1976-1977. Auth, "Our Call"; Auth, "Living Ch". vthatch@pc.net

HATCHER JR, John Harris (Va) Po Box 781, Arnold MD 21012 B Castalian Sprgs TN 8/26/1935 s John Harris Hatcher & Fayola. BA Van 1956; MDiv VTS 1963; MA U of Tennessee 1974. D 6/21/1963 Bp George P Gunn P 5/19/1964 Bp David Shepherd Rose. R S Anne's Epis Ch Reston VA 1987-1998; Chapl Van S Aug's Chap Nashville TN 1971-1987; Vic Ch Of The Gd Samar Knoxville TN 1969-1970; Assoc Calv Epis Ch Williamsville NY 1967-1968; Chapl Bruton Par Williamsburg VA 1963-1967. Auth, "Santayanas Naturalization Of Catholicsm". john21012@yahoo.com

HATCHETT JR, Jefferson Bryan (Ala) Po Box 596, Heflin AL 36264 B Greenville GA 3/25/1929 s Jefferson Hatchett & Louise. BA Emory U 1950; BD UTS 1953. D 2/21/1964 P 6/22/1964 Bp William Henry Marmion. m 4/17/

1982 Meredith Joy Brewer c 3. R Ch Of The Mssh Heflin AL 1996-2001; S Jas Ch Macon GA 1990-1992; Int S Tim's Decatur GA 1989-1990; Cur The Ch Of Our Sav Atlanta GA 1987-1989; R S Paul's Pomona Pomona CA 1970-1972; R Emm Ch Harrisonburg VA 1966-1970; Cur/Asst/Assoc Chr Epis Ch Roanoke VA 1963-1966. Auth, "Stwdshp: A Basic Statement". jbhatchett@bellsouth.net

HATCHETT, Marion Josiah (SC) 92 Carpenter Cir, Sewanee TN 37375 **Died 8/7/2009** B Monroe NC 7/19/1927 s Oliver Howard Hatchett & Myrtle (Harvey). BA Wofford Coll 1947; BD STUSo 1951; STM GTS 1967; ThD GTS 1972. D 6/13/1951 P 6/25/1952 Bp John J Gravatt. c 3. Auth, *A Guide to Pract of Ch Mus*; Auth, *Commentary on Amer PB*; Auth, *Liturg Index for Hymnal 1982*; Auth, *Making of 1st Amer Bk of Common Pryr*; Auth, *Sanctifyng Life Time & Space*. Associated Parishes Coun 1975; NAAL - founding Mem 1975. DD TS 2008; Doctor of Hmnts Wofford Coll, SC 2006; Featured in LivCh as one of fifty "Shapers of the C LivCh 1999; Annual Awd ADLMAC 1997. mhatchet@sewanee.edu

HATFIELD, Adele Dees (Nwk) 221 Boulevard, Mountain Lakes NJ 07046 **Co-R S Ptr's Ch Mtn Lakes NJ 2009-** B Coral Gables FL 5/28/1950 d James Earl Miller & Mary Louise. BS Barton Coll 1972; MDiv VTS 2005. D 6/25/2005 P 1/6/2006 Bp Clifton Daniel III. m 11/11/2006 Charles Jerome Hatfield c 3. Assoc Iona Hope Epis Ch Ft Myers FL 2006-2008; Asst R S Jas Par Wilmington NC 2005-2006. singandchant@yahoo.com

HATFIELD JR, Charles Jerome (Nwk) 221 Boulevard, Mountain Lakes NJ 07046 **Co-R S Ptr's Ch Mtn Lakes NJ 2009-** B Baltimore MD 10/11/1952 s Charles J Hatfield & Doris M. Mgmt VPI 1982; MDiv VTS 2005. D 6/29/2005 P 4/28/2006 Bp Frank Neff Powell. m 11/11/2006 Adele Dees Miller c 2. Assoc R S Monica's Epis Ch Naples FL 2005-2009. chatfd@yahoo.com

HATFIELD, Russell Allen (SwVa) 101 Logan St, Bluefield VA 24605 **Dn of Abingdon Convoc Dio SW Virginia Roanoke VA 2006-2012; R The Tazewell Cnty Cluster Of Epis Parishes Tazewell VA 2001-** B Matewan WV 11/9/1944 s Major Hatfield & Mildred Elizabeth. BA Catawba Coll 1966; Towson U 1971; MS Radford U 1976; STUSo 2000. D 10/25/1997 P 5/17/1998 Bp Frank Neff Powell. m 9/5/1975 Debra Joan Billips c 1. Pres of Stndg Com Dio SW Virginia Roanoke VA 2008-2009; Trst of Funds Dio SW Virginia Roanoke VA 2005-2009; Asst R The Tazewell Cnty Cluster Of Epis Parishes Tazewell VA 1998-2000. fatherruss@yahoo.com

✠ **HATHAWAY, Rt Rev Alden Moinet** (Pgh) 107 Laurens St., Beaufort SC 29902 B Saint Louis MO 8/13/1933 s Earl Burton Hathaway & Margaret. BS Cor 1955; BD EDS 1962. D 6/9/1962 P 12/19/1962 Bp Nelson Marigold Burroughs Con 6/27/1981 for Pgh. m 11/24/2007 Barbara Nesbitt c 3. Bp-In-Res S Jn's Epis Ch Tallahassee FL 1999-2007; Bp of Pittsburgh Dio Pittsburgh Monroeville PA 1983-1997; Bp Coadj of Pittsburgh Dio Pittsburgh Monroeville PA 1981-1983; R S Chris's Ch Springfield VA 1972-1981; Assoc Chr Ch Cranbrook Bloomfield Hills MI 1965-1971; Min in charge Ch Of The H Trin Epis Bellefontaine OH 1962-1965. AAC 1988; Irenaeus Grp 1988; Solar Light for Afr 1978. None: Save that of knowing Jesus Chr and Him crucified. 1974. hathawayvi@gmail.com

HATHAWAY, Dale Caldwell (Haw) 2062 S King St, Honolulu HI 96826 **R S Mary's Epis Ch Honolulu HI 2001-** B Ray AZ 10/4/1950 s Dale Caldwell Hathaway & Helen Marie. BA Colorado Coll 1972; MDiv Nash 1981; MA U of Notre Dame 1986. D 6/2/1982 Bp William Carl Frey P 12/8/1982 Bp Charles Thomas Gaskell. m 8/1/1991 M Bridget Kubley c 5. Pres Stndg Com Dio Hawaii Honolulu HI 2010-2011; R S Andr's By The Lake Epis Ch Michigan City IN 1991-2001; S Ptr's Ch Rensselaer IN 1987-1990; Asst The Cathd Ch Of S Jas So Bend IN 1984-1988; Asst Trin Ch Wauwatosa WI 1982-1984. frdale@hawaiiantel.net

HATT, Blair Martin (LI) 22 Willowick Dr., Asheville NC 28803 B Halifax NS Canada 10/11/1949 s Donald Allen Hatt & Audrey Bernice. BA SUNY 1980; MDiv GTS 1982; MS Yeshiva U 1990. D 6/5/1982 P 12/1/1982 Bp Paul Moore Jr. R Gr Epis Ch Whitestone NY 2004-2009; P-in-c S Cuth's Epis Ch Selden NY 2000-2009; P-in-c S Mk's Epis Ch Medford NY 2000-2009; P-in-c Ch Of S Jn The Bapt Cntr Moriches NY 2000-2004; S Lk The Physcn Miami FL 1999; S Jas Epis Ch S Jas NY 1998; Epis Hlth Serv Bethpage NY 1993-1998; Bp's Dep For Pstr Care Dio Long Island Garden City NY 1991-1998; S Johns Epis Hosp Far Rockaway NY 1991-1993; Dpt Of Missions Ny Income New York NY 1988-1991; S Lk's-Roosevelt Hosp Cntr New York NY 1988-1991; Assoc S Ptr's Ch New York NY 1982-1988. AEHC 1993; Soc Of S Fran 1968-1973. Distinguished Pstr Ldrshp Awd 1995. blairhatt@aol.com

HATZENBUEHLER, Robin Ritter (WTenn) 1544 Carr Ave, Memphis TN 38104 **Chapl Trezevant Epis Hm Memphis TN 2007-** B Memphis TN 3/11/1949 d Louis Vernon Ritter & Gloria Elizabeth. BA Rhodes Coll 1971; MA U of Memphis 1977; MDiv Memphis TS 2004. D 6/18/2005 P 1/7/2006 Bp Don Edward Johnson. m 7/1/1972 Daniel Bruce Hatzenbuehler c 2. Cur Gr - S Lk's Ch Memphis TN 2005-2007. robin@trezevantmanor.org

HAUCK, Barbara Horsley (Minn) 32 W College St, Duluth MN 55812 **D S Paul's Epis Ch Duluth MN 2001-** B Midland MI 1/29/1950 d Lee Herbert Horsley & Fern Fay. D 6/17/2001 Bp James Louis Jelinek. m 12/28/1971 Steven Arthur Hauck. NAAD 2000. barb@stpaulsduluth.org

HAUCK, Mary Ellen (NCal) 2411 Larkspur Ln Apt 15, Sacramento CA 95825 **R S Mich's Epis Ch Carmichael CA 2004-** B Kansas City MO 5/3/1950 d Edward Spencer Rockett & Billie Frances. BA U CA 1972; Cred U CA 1972; MA & Cred U CA 1985; MDiv CDSP 1995. D 5/24/1995 P 11/30/1995 Bp Jerry Alban Lamb. m 3/21/1971 PaUL D Hauck c 3. Pres of Stndg Com Dio Nthrn California Sacramento CA 2004-2006; R S Clem's Ch Rancho Cordova CA 2000-2004; Chair of Chr Formation Com Dio Nthrn California Sacramento CA 1998-2000; Asst S Mich's Epis Ch Carmichael CA 1996-2000; Chapl S Mich's Epis Day Sch Carmichael CA 1996-1997; P-in-c S Lk's Ch Galt CA 1995-1997. Contrib, "Preaching to the Chld of God," *Preaching as Pstr Caring*, Morehouse, 2005. mary.hauck@comcast.net

HAUERT, Robert Harold (Los) 1419 Jorn Ct, Ann Arbor MI 48104 B San Gabriel CA 5/24/1928 s Emil H Hauert & Maria. BA Occ 1953; BD EDS 1959. D 6/22/1959 Bp Francis E I Bloy P 1/16/1960 Bp Donald J Campbell. rohau@hotmail.com

HAUFF, Bradley Sylvan (Fla) 5400 Belle Terre Pkwy, Palm Coast FL 32137 **BEC Dio Florida Jacksonville FL 2010-; R S Thos Flagler Cnty Palm Coast FL 2008-** B Sioux Falls SD 9/4/1963 s Sylvan Racine Hauff & Margaret Kathryn. BA Augustana Coll 1985; Med So Dakota St U 1987; MDiv SWTS 1990; PsyD Minnesota Sch of Profsnl Psychol 2005. D 7/23/1990 Bp Craig Barry Anderson P 10/23/1991 Bp Sanford Zangwill Kaye Hampton. m 4/11/1999 Ruth E Schuette. Bd Trst SWTS Evanston IL 2006-2009; Assoc R Ch Of The Epiph Epis Plymouth MN 2001-2007; Asst S Jn In The Wilderness White Bear Lake MN 1998-2001; Vic Dio Minnesota Minneapolis MN 1996-1998; Asst Ch Of The Epiph Richardson TX 1994-1995; Assoc S Jn The Evang S Paul MN 1991-1994; Vic Dio So Dakota Sioux Falls SD 1990-1991. Auth, "Vine DeLoria's Influence on Native Amer Identity," *First People's Journ of Theol*, Indigenous Theol Trng Inst, 2010; Auth, "Congruence as a Pre-Rogerian Sprtl Construct," *Doctoral dissertation*, Minnesota Sch of Profsnl Psychol, 2005. Lilly Endwmt Sabbatical Schlr Eli Lilly Corp 2007; Markovitz Schlr Amer Schools of Profsnl Psychol 1996. revmoof@aim.com

HAUG, Phillip Russell (Lex) 100 Daisey Dr, Richmond KY 40475 B Merced CA 7/27/1938 s Russell Melvin Haug & Evelyn May. BS U of Nevada at Reno 1960; SMM MIT 1976; MDiv VTS 1990. D 6/2/1990 P 12/1/1990 Bp Peter James Lee. m 5/27/1959 Anna V McMurray c 4. Int Chr Epis Ch Harlan KY 2008-2010; Int S Jn's Ch Versailles KY 2002-2004; Vic Epis Ch of Our Sav Richmond KY 1994-2002; R S Ptr's Port Royal Port Royal VA 1990-1994; R Vauters Ch Champlain VA 1990-1994. SAMS 1977-2000. prhaug@aol.com

HAUGAARD, William P (Chi) 1365 Twin Rivers Blvd, Oviedo FL 32766 B Brooklyn NY 1/19/1929 s William Edward Haugaard & Bess. BA Pr 1951; STB GTS 1954; ThD GTS 1962. D 5/8/1954 Bp Wallace J Gardner P 11/1/1954 Bp Russell S Hubbard. m 5/24/1976 Luisa Collazo. Vice-Pres/Assoc Dn SWTS Evanston IL 1984-1994; Prof SWTS Evanston IL 1979-1982; Epis Sem Of The Caribbean Carolina PR 1963-1977; Fell & Tutor The GTS New York NY 1958-1962; Vic S Jas Epis Ch Brewster WA 1954-1958. Auth, "Reformation In Engl," *Tudor Engl: An Encylopedia*, 2001; Auth, "arts On Miles Coverdale And Richard Hooker," *Hist Handbook Of Major Biblic Interpreters*, 1998; Auth, "Introductions And Commentaries To The Preface And Books Ii, Iii,, The Folger Libr Ed Of The Works Of Richard Hooker," *Vi*, 1993; Auth, "The [Hooker-Travers] Controversy," *The Folger Libr Ed Of The Works Of Richard Hooker*, 1990; Auth, "The Scriptural Hermeneutics Of Richard Hooker: Hist Conte," *This Sacr Hist: Angl Reflections For Jn Booty*, 1990; Auth, "The Bible In The Angl Reformation," *Anglicanism And The Bible*, 1984; Auth, "The Continental Reformation," *A Faithful Ch: Issues In The Hist Of Catechesis*, 1981; Auth, "Eliz & The Engl Reformation," Combridge Univesity Press, 1968. HSEC 1962. The Powel Mills Dawley Memi Lecture GTS 1990; ECF Fllshp ECF 1966; Rockefeller Fndt Rockefeller Doctoral Fllshp In Rel 1960; Phi Beta Kappa Pr 1951; The Daily Princetonian Awd Pr Sudent Govt 1950. whaugaard@cfl.rr.com

HAUGE, Morris John (Oly) 2611 Eastlake Ave E Apt 102, Seattle WA 98102 B Savanna IL 10/7/1937 s Morris Jacobson Hauge & Stella Adeline. U of Washington 1958; BA Pacific Luth U 1961; Luther TS 1963; MDiv SWTS 1964. D 6/29/1964 Bp William F Lewis P 3/13/1965 Bp Ivol I Curtis. m 1/10/2011 Scott D Martin. R S Paul's Ch Seattle WA 1994-2002; Int - DSOMAT Dio Olympia Seattle WA 1993-1994; P-in-c Ch Of The H Sprt Vashon WA 1992-1994; P-in-c All SS Ch Tacoma WA 1990-1992; Int S Geo's Ch Seattle WA 1989-1990; Assoc R S Mary's Epis Ch Eugene OR 1974-1978; Asst Chr Ch Grosse Pointe Grosse Pointe Farms MI 1969-1973; Cur Chr Ch Tacoma WA 1964-1969. mjhauge@comcast.net

HAUGEN, Alice (Ia) 1483 Grand Ave, Iowa City IA 52246 **Asst Gr Ch Cedar Rapids IA 2006-; Assoc P Trin Ch Iowa City IA 2005-** B Nyack NY 7/26/1952 d Paul Dent Bordwell & Charlotte Pluckhahn. BS Br 1973; PhD Br 1977. D 4/30/2005 Bp Alan Scarfe. m 12/26/2002 Thomas Haugen c 2. alice.haugen@gmail.com

HAUGH, William Walter (Az) 10126 S Kraft Dr, Vail AZ 85641 B Bethlehem PA 5/18/1934 s John Harms Haugh & Emilie Lucille. BA U of Arizona 1958; BFT Amer Inst Frgn Trade 1960; MDiv Epis TS of The SW 1981. D 6/13/1981 Bp William Jackson Cox P 5/1/1982 Bp Gerald Nicholas McAllister. m 6/4/1959 Nancy Jane Graver c 2. Chr The King Ch Tucson AZ 2002-2003; R S Lk's Ch Chickasha OK 1985-1992; Cn S Paul's Cathd Oklahoma City OK 1981-1985. fratuc@q.com

HAUGHN, Terry Lee (WMich) 111 W Brighton St, Plainwell MI 49080 **R S Steph's Epis Ch Plainwell MI 2004-** B Jackson MI 3/12/1946 s Charles A Haughn & Anna Mae. Assoc Jackson Cmnty Coll Jackson MI 1972; Cert Whitaker TS 1987; LTh VTS 1991. D 6/27/1987 Bp H Coleman McGehee Jr P 5/18/1991 Bp R(aymond) Stewart Wood Jr. m 1/29/1966 Karen Aileen Goller c 2. P-in-c S Steph's Epis Ch Plainwell MI 2001-2004; R Epis Ch Of The Gd Shpd Allegan MI 1992-2000; Asst R Trin Ch Manassas VA 1991-1992; Asst S Chris's Ch Springfield VA 1988-1991; Asst S Ptr's Ch Tecumseh MI 1987-1988. tkhaughn@charter.net

HAUGHTON, Anson Baldwin (Pa) 306 Paoli Woods, Paoli PA 19301 **Died 2/18/2011** B Philadelphia PA 2/11/1921 s J Paul Haughton & Mary. BS Hav 1942; STB EDS 1949; MS Bryn 1960. D 6/12/1949 Bp William P Remington P 1/1/1953 Bp Oliver J Hart.

HAUSER, Nancy (Pa) 245 Stoughton Cir, Exton PA 19341 **D The Epis Ch Of The Adv Kennett Sq PA 2005-** B Syracuse NY 12/2/1956 d Bruce Tayler & Janet. BS SUNY 1979; MS SUNY 1981; MDiv Luth TS at Philadelphia 2005. D 6/4/2005 Bp Charles Ellsworth Bennison Jr. m 8/4/1979 Edwin Paul Hauser c 4. nth122@verizon.net

HAUTTECOEUR, Mario Alberto (ECR) 95 Stillbreeze Ln, Watsonville CA 95076 **Dio El Camino Real Monterey CA 2004-; El Cristo Rey Watsonville CA 2004-** B Cuba 4/29/1951 Rec from Roman Catholic 9/17/2003 Bp Richard Lester Shimpfky. mariohmacias@hotmail.com

HAVENS, Helen Markley Morris (Tex) 2401 Dryden Rd, Houston TX 77030 B Oak Bluffs MA 7/12/1935 d Walter Markley Morris & Grace Elaine. BA Rice U 1957; MA Indiana U 1960; MDiv EDS 1975. D 4/28/1976 P 4/1/1977 Bp Richard Mitchell Trelease Jr. m 6/1/1957 Adrian Havens. R S Steph's Epis Ch Houston TX 1981-2004; Asst S Fran Ch Houston TX 1976-1981. Cntr For Progressive Chr; EWC, Associated Parishes, Sw Ntwk, Womens Ministers, EWHP, Girls Club Of Houston; Integrity Inc Tx Faith Ntwk Claremont Consult. Outstanding Wmn In Rel Houston; Natl Fell Amer Ldrshp Forum.

HAVERKAMP, Heidi R (Chi) 584 Red Barn Trl, Bolingbrook IL 60490 **Vic Ch Of S Ben Bolingbrook IL 2007-** B Chicago IL 2/25/1976 d Larry Jon Haverkamp & Wenche Nilsen. MDiv U Chi 2006; C.A.T.S. SWTS 2007. D 6/2/2007 Bp William Dailey Persell P 12/15/2007 Bp Victor Alfonso Scantlebury. m 8/30/2008 Adam Michael Frieberg. D S Jn's Epis Ch Chicago IL 2007. heidi_haverkamp@yahoo.com

HAVERLY, Thomas P. (WNY) 5339 S Harper Ave # 3, Chicago IL 60615 **Int R Trin Epis Ch Oshkosh WI 2011-** B Chicago IL 10/22/1953 s Charles Norman Haverly & Ruth Edith. BA Olivet Nazarene Coll 1974; MDiv Nazarene TS 1978; PhD U Of Edinburgh Gb 1983; MLS Syr 1993. D 6/17/1995 P 1/22/1996 Bp David B(ruce) Joslin. m 8/8/2001 Christine Wenderoth c 2. Int R Ch Of Our Sav Elmhurst IL 2009-2011; P in Charge S Paul's Epis Ch Stafford NY 1998-2004; Par Assoc S Lk And S Simon Cyrene Rochester NY 1996-1999. Auth, "You Will Know Them by Their Fruits," *Currents in Theol and Mssn*, Luth TS at Chicago, 2008; Auth, "Info Overloaded: Info Literacy, the Libr and the Sem Curric," *A.T.L.A. Proceedings*, Amer Theol Libr Assn, 2005; Auth, "Cataloging Q(s): a Critical Revs of the Quest for Q and Its Literary Hist," *A.T.L.A. Proceedings*, Amer Theol Libr Assn, 1996. Amer Theol Libr Assn 1992-2008; SBL 1980. thaverly@gmail.com

HAVILAND, Douglas Brant (Ia) 1100 Adams St., Unit 105, Ames IA 50010 B Delhi NY 4/8/1926 BA Bard Coll; STB PDS. D 6/8/1957 Bp David Emrys Richards P 12/14/1957 Bp Frederick Lehrle Barry. m 9/10/1950 Elizabeth Bauer. Coll Field Des Moines IA 1972-1991; Chapl Chapl at Iowa St U Ames IA 1962-1991; R S Andr And S Jn Epis Ch SW Harbor ME 1959-1962; Vic Chr Ch Pottersville NY 1957-1959; Vic S Andr's Ch Brant Lake NY 1957-1959. dougbetty@mchsi.com

HAVILL, Francis Gilmour (Ore) 2552 Ne Rosemary Dr, Bend OR 97701 **Died 3/7/2011** B New York NY 1/25/1915 s Ernest Gilmour Havill & Ivy Ellen. BA Mt Un Coll 1940; BD Drew U 1947. D 6/16/1950 P 10/1/1951 Bp Howard R Brinker. c 4.

HAWES III, Charles Morris (NC) 1848 N Elm St, Greensboro NC 27408 B Chicago IL 1/29/1938 s Charles Morris Hawes & Minnie Moore. BA Trin Hartford CT 1961; STB EDS 1964. D 6/6/1964 P 12/1/1964 Bp Horace W B Donegan. m 5/6/2006 Faith Steverman c 1. Dio No Carolina Raleigh NC 1984-2006; Chapl S Mary's Hse Epis/Angl Campus Greensboro NC 1984-2006; R S Paul's Epis Ch Smithfield NC 1975-1978; Assoc Gr Ch Grand Rapids MI 1973-1975; Vic S Paul's Ch Canaan VT 1971-1973; Vic S Steph's Epis Mssn Colebrook NH 1971-1973; Cur S Paul's Ch Rochester NY 1964-1966. Eugene Rogers, "Mar & Idolatry," *Theol & Sxlty*, Blackwell, 2002; Auth, "As 1 P Sees S Croix Today". St. Jn's Soc, E.D.S. 2006. cjameshawes@aol.com

HAWES, Peter Wortham (USC) 32 Locust Ln, Tryon NC 28782 B Chicago IL 8/10/1941 s Charles Morris Hawes & Mimi Love. BA U NC 1963; MDiv TS 1978. D 6/17/1978 Bp Thomas Augustus Fraser Jr P 5/6/1979 Bp George Mosley Murray. m 6/4/1966 Anna Henry c 3. R Ch Of The Resurr Greenwood SC 2001-2006; Dio W Tennessee Memphis TN 1995-2006; Convenor Dioc Pars Dio W Tennessee Memphis TN 1991-1992; Stndg Com On Cns Dio W Tennessee Memphis TN 1990-1992; Comp Dio Com Dio W Tennessee Memphis TN 1988-1994; Dioc Com Educ Dio W Tennessee Memphis TN 1988-1990; R S Geo's Ch Germantown TN 1986-2001; Chair - Dioc Dept Par Dvlpmt Dio Alabama Birmingham AL 1985-1986; Com Dio Alabama Birmingham AL 1984-1986; Dept Par Dvlpmt Dio Alabama Birmingham AL 1983-1984; R S Paul's Ch Selma AL 1981-1986; Chair - Dioc T/F Wrld Hunger Dio Cntrl Gulf Coast Pensacola FL 1980-1981; Asst Chr Ch Par Pensacola FL 1978-1981. R Emer St. Geo's Ch Germantown TN 2011; Faithful Alum Awd TS Sewanee 2000. pwh810@windstream.net

HAWKES, Daphne Wolcott Parker (NJ) 50 Patton Ave, Princeton NJ 08540 B Paris FR 8/27/1938 d Robert Bogardus Parker & Lorraine Wolcott. BS Penn 1960; MDiv PrTS 1975; Bryn 1985. D 4/26/1975 P 1/29/1977 Bp Albert Wiencke Van Duzer. c 4. Asstg P Trin Ch Princeton NJ 2002; Assoc Trin Ch Princeton NJ 2000; S Andr's Ch Trenton NJ 1998-2001; Assoc S Mich's Ch Trenton NJ 1995-1996; Supply Dio New Jersey Trenton NJ 1986-1998; Asst S Matt's Ch Pennington NJ 1983-1986; Assoc S Mich's Ch Trenton NJ 1981-1982; Trin Ch Princeton NJ 1975-1980. Auth, "Wmn In The Pastorate"; Auth, "Theol Today". dwhawkes@gmail.com

HAWKINS, Charles Thomas (Ky) 3003 Curran Rd, Louisville KY 40205 **R S Mk's Epis Ch Louisville KY 2000-** B Guntersville AL 1/4/1965 s Billy James Hawkins & Charlene Rebecca. BA Samford U 1987; MDiv Sthrn Sem Louisville KY 1990; ThM Duke 1991; PhD Sthrn Sem Louisville KY 1995. D 5/31/1998 P 1/9/1999 Bp Edwin Funsten Gulick Jr. m 8/7/1987 Katherine A Kingren c 2. Cur S Matt's Epis Ch Louisville KY 1998-2000. Auth, "Beyond Anarchy & Tyranny In Rel Epistemology". hawkins@iglou.com

HAWKINS, Deborah J (Cal) 2300 Edison Ave, Sacramento CA 95821 **S Eliz's Epis Ch So San Francisco CA 2010-** B San Mateo CA 7/10/1954 d Robert Wing Wolfe & Maureen Connaught. BS U CA 1976; MDiv CDSP 2009. D 6/13/2009 P 1/12/2010 Bp Barry Leigh Beisner. m 4/15/1978 Daniel W Hawkins c 1. S Matt's Epis Ch Sacramento CA 2009-2010. hawsinsd@cwo.com

HAWKINS JR, Frank Jay (Tex) 1827 Green Gate Dr, Rosenberg TX 77471 B Washington DC 7/18/1945 s Frank Jay Hawkins & Phyllis Georgia. BA St. Mary's U San Antonio TX 1968; MA St. Mary's U San Antonio TX 1972; MDiv VTS 1982; DMin SWTS 2001. D 7/4/1982 P 1/20/1983 Bp Joseph Thomas Heistand. m 9/14/1984 Emma Susan Jean DeBree c 1. All SS Epis Ch Stafford TX 2002-2003; S Mk's Epis Ch Richmond TX 1994-2002; St Lk's Epis Hosp Houston TX 1993-1994; R S Matt's Ch Bellaire TX 1991-1992; Vic Iglesia Epis De San Pablo Phoenix AZ 1982-1989. mt2819@gmail.com

HAWKINS, Gary Altus (WVa) 1803 New Windsor Road, New Windsor MD 21776 B Pauls Valley OK 1/10/1943 s Altus Hawkins & Olive Lorainne. BA U of Oklahoma 1969; MDiv MidWestern Bapt TS 1973. D 6/21/1994 P 1/18/1995 Bp Martin Gough Townsend. c 2. R Chr Ch Fairmont WV 1999-2003; Vic S Phil's Ch Quantico MD 1997-1999; Vic All SS Epis Ch Delmar DE 1995-1999. gh5771@comcast.net

HAWKINS IV, J(ames) Barney (Md) 3737 Seminary Rd, Alexandria VA 22304 **VP for Instnl Advancement and the Associa VTS Alexandria VA 2000-** B Greenville SC 3/2/1949 s James Barney Hawkins & Jertie. BA Furman U 1970; U Of Edinburgh Gb 1972; MDiv Duke 1974; PhD Duke 1981. D 6/30/1979 P 5/3/1980 Bp William Gillette Weinhauer. m 5/24/1975 Linda Wofford c 1. Imm Ch-On-The-Hill Alexandria VA 2006-2008; R The Ch Of The Redeem Baltimore MD 1995-2000; R Ch Of The Ascen Hickory NC 1981-1995; Trin Epis Ch Asheville NC 1979-1981. bhawkins@vts.edu

HAWKINS, Jodene Scaylea (Haw) 203 Kulipuu St, Kihei HI 96753 B Ellensburg WA 6/12/1945 d Joseph Scaylea & Virginia. BA U of Washington 1985; MDiv VTS 1990. D 6/12/1990 P 6/2/1991 Bp Vincent Waydell Warner. m 8/29/1965 Kittredge E Hawkins. S Eliz's Ch Honolulu HI 2004-2009; R St Ptr's Epis Par Seattle WA 1995-2001; S Nich Ch Tahuya WA 1994-1995; Asst R S Paul's Epis Ch Bremerton WA 1991-1994. ECom "Polly Bond" Awd 1994. jodene@hawaii.rr.com

HAWKINS, Linda Wofford (Va) 4801 Ravensworth Rd, Annandale VA 22003 **R S Barn Ch Annandale VA 2001-** B Florence SC 9/4/1950 d Walter Gibson Wofford & Ruby Dell. Salem Coll Winston Salem NC 1970; BA Duke 1972; MDiv Duke 1976; ThM Duke 1979. D 10/28/1984 P 11/1/1986 Bp William Gillette Weinhauer. m 5/24/1975 J(ames) Barney Hawkins c 2. Assoc R Ch Of The Gd Shpd Ruxton MD 1997-2001; Assoc Memi Ch Baltimore MD 1995-1997; P-in-c S Steph's Epis Ch Morganton NC 1992-1995; The Patterson Sch Lenoir NC 1986-1988. stbarnabasrector@vacoxmail.com

HAWKINS, Mary Alice (Spok) 560-F Spengler Road Unit F, Richland WA 99354 **D All SS Ch Richland WA 1999-** B Hamilton OH 11/6/1931 d Ezekiel Wesley Elrod & Mary Clare. BS Un Coll Barbourville KY 1952; MA U of Nthrn Colorado 1960. D 11/13/1999 Bp Leigh Wallace Jr. m 11/8/1958 James Harrison Hawkins c 1. NAAD. jmawahk@bossig.com

HAWKINS, Penelope Elizabeth (Vt) Po Box 492, North Bennington VT 05257 **D S Ptr's Epis Ch Bennington VT 1992-** B Bennington VT 7/15/1941 d Arthur Gates & Ruby Catherine. Bennington Coll. D 9/10/1988 Bp Daniel Lee Swenson. m 9/10/1989 Richard Farraka c 2.

HAWKINS, Thomas Edward (O) 14900 Mark Twain St, Detroit MI 48227 B Kansas City KS 4/8/1960 s George William Hawkins & Shirley Jean. BA U of Kansas 1982; MDiv S Meinrad Sem 1986. Rec from Roman Catholic 9/27/1987 as Deacon Bp Richard Frank Grein. m 5/25/2003 Sianee Hawkins. R S Mk's Ch Canton OH 2009-2010; S Andr's Epis Ch Livonia MI 2008-2009; S Tim's Ch Detroit MI 1999-2008; Ch of the Ascen Kansas City KS 1989-1999. Ch & City; UBE. THEFREEHAWK@YAHOO.COM

HAWLEY, Frank Martin (WTex) 4518 Winlock Dr, San Antonio TX 78228 B San Antonio TX 3/12/1953 s Alfred Dewitt Hawley & Eva Jean. BS Texas A&M U 1976; MDiv VTS 1984. D 6/30/1984 Bp Scott Field Bailey. m 12/21/1978 Patricia Koenigsberger c 2. Epis Ch Of The Gd Shepard Geo W TX 1984-1985.

HAWLEY, Oral Robers (Ak) Po Box 50067, Kivalina AK 99750 B Kotzebue 5/3/1964 s Amos Apugin Hawley & Louise. D 2/5/2002 Bp Mark Lawrence Mac Donald. nananative2002@yahoo.com

HAWORTH, Frederick Francis (NwPa) 341 E Jamestown Rd, Greenville PA 16125 B Sewickley PA 12/23/1923 s Frederick Francis Haworth & Mae Frances. BS U Pgh 1944; MDiv VTS 1947; MS U Pgh 1973; DMin GTF 1989. D 2/1/1947 P 12/23/1947 Bp Harold E Sawyer. m 9/9/1950 Margaret Lydia Sweet c 3. P-in-c Ch Of The Epiph Grove City PA 1983-1985; Vic S Matt's Epis Ch Eldred PA 1971-1979; R Ch Of The Epiph Grove City PA 1964-1969; R S Jos's Ch Port Allegany PA 1958-1964; R Chr Epis Ch Indiana PA 1955-1958; Vic/D Gr Ch Lake City PA 1947-1948. Acad of Cert Soc Workers 1973-2001; Bd Cert Dplma Clincl Soc Wk 1973-2001; Lic Soc Worker 1973-2001. Hon Cn Diocece of NW PA 2010.

HAWS, Howard Eugene (ETenn) 1418 Lonas Dr, Maryville TN 37803 B Knoxville TN 3/4/1931 s Henry N Haws & Rudy. BS U of Tennessee 1953; BD Candler TS Emory U 1960; U So 1966. D 6/29/1966 Bp William Evan Sanders P 1/25/1967 Bp John Vander Horst. m 10/26/1956 Andra T Shelton. S Andr's Ch Maryville TN 1975-1996; R H Trin Ch Memphis TN 1969-1976; P S Thos The Apos Humboldt TN 1966-1969. howarohaws@aol.com

HAWTHORNE, Nanese Arnold (Eas) PO Box 38, Church Hill MD 21623 **Angl Cov Com Dio Easton Easton MD 2011-; COM Dio Easton Easton MD 2010-; Dioc Coun Dio Easton Easton MD 2009-; R S Lukes Ch Ch Hill MD 2006-** B Newport News VA 5/18/1945 d Samuel Arnold & Elsie Elizabeth. BS Missouri Vlly Coll 1968; MDiv VTS 2003. D 1/18/2003 P 12/4/2003 Bp Wayne Parker Wright. c 2. P-in-c Ch Of Our Sav Jenkintown PA 2003-2006. EPF 2002. revnanese@yahoo.com

HAY, Audrey Leona (NMich) 4955 12th Rd, Escanaba MI 49829 **D Dio Nthrn Michigan Marquette MI 1993-** B Escanaba MI 8/8/1929 d Edwin Frank Ettenhofer & Leona Margaret. D 2/21/1993 Bp Thomas Kreider Ray. m 4/19/1952 William Howard Hay c 4.

HAY, Charles Henry (Ga) 1014 Shore Acres Dr, Leesburg FL 34748 B Portland ME 5/14/1934 s Evelyn Doris. BA U of Florida 1956; MDiv STUSo 1959; MA Rol 1970. D 6/28/1959 Bp William Francis Moses P 12/28/1959 Bp Henry I Louttit. m 6/6/1964 Dorothy Herlong c 3. Assoc S Jas Epis Ch Leesburg FL 1999; Dio Georgia Savannah GA 1990-1997; R S Paul's Epis Ch Jesup GA 1985-1990; R S Thos Epis Ch Thomasville GA 1977-1985; R Calv Ch Americus GA 1970-1977; Asst All SS Ch Of Winter Pk Winter Pk FL 1964-1970; Vic S Edw The Confessor Mt Dora FL 1961-1964; Cur S Paul's Ch Winter Haven FL 1959-1961. chayhsd@embarqmail.com

HAY, Daryl Tabor (Tex) 708 N Washington St, La Grange TX 78945 **R S Jas' Epis Ch La Grange TX 2005-** B San Antonio TX 3/2/1971 Bachelor of Arts The U of Texas at Austin 1995; Masters of Div Epis TS of the SW 2003. D 6/21/2003 Bp Don Adger Wimberly P 12/22/2003 Bp Rayford Baines High Jr. m 12/27/1997 Terri R Hay c 3. Asst R Chr Epis Ch Tyler TX 2003-2005. rector@cmaaccess.com

HAY, John Gardner (Spok) 2411 E 35th Ave, Spokane WA 99223 **Assoc Cathd Of S Jn The Evang Spokane WA 2005-; R Emer S Steph's Epis Ch Spokane WA 1991-** B Altoona PA 6/3/1925 s Thomas Reed Hay & Jane. BA Wms 1948; Col 1950; UTS 1951; STB EDS 1954. D 6/17/1954 Bp Joseph Thomas Heistand P 12/1/1954 Bp Henry Hean Daniels. m 6/9/1958 Marcella M Youlden c 4. Int P S Andr's Ch Spokane WA 2002-2004; Int Minster (6 Parishes) Dio Spokane Spokane WA 1992-2001; S Steph's Epis Ch Spokane WA 1968-1990; R St Jas Epis Ch Dillon MT 1959-1967; Vic Chr Ch Sheridan MT 1954-1959; Vic S Paul's Ch Virginia City MT 1954-1959; Vic Trin Ch Ennis MT 1954-1959. Auth, *In The W of Ireland 94, 95, 96*; Auth, *Poetry Anthologies: Emily Dickinson Edgar Allan Poe, Edna S Vinc Millay*. Natl Ch - Supervision and Ldrshp Trng (SALT) 1962-1966; Natl Ch - Town and Country Cmsn 1958-1964.

HAY, Lesley Jean Hamilton (Ala) PO Box 161, Mentone AL 35984 **R S Jos's On-The-Mtn Mentone AL 2010-** B Cardiff UK 5/10/1948 s William Reginald Hay & Mary Constance Dora. Yale DS 2006; Westcott Hse 2007. Trans from Church Of England 1/19/2010 Bp Andrew Donnan Smith. Int Gr And S Ptr's Epis Ch Hamden CT 2008-2010; Asst Chr Ch Bethany CT 2008. lesleyhay@yahoo.co.uk

HAYASHI, Koji (Ida) 2282 Southshore Way, Boise ID 83706 B Engaru cho Hokkaido JP 8/17/1935 s Shinzaburo Hayashi & Sue. Zions Reformed Ch; BD Tokyo Cntrl TS 1964; Toronto Gnrl Hospita; Toronto Can 1967; Queen's Mntl Hosp Toronto Can 1968; Wyc 1968; Appalachian Reg Hosp Harlan KY 1972; Menninger Clnc 1976. m 8/4/1963 Marilee Ann Phelps c 3. Cn S Mich's Cathd Boise ID 1974-1992; Cmsn of Mnstry Dio Idaho Boise ID 1974-1977; St Lukes Med Cntr Boise ID 1973-1992. Auth, "Dvlpmt of a Pstr Care Assn in a Sparsely Populated Area, Coll of Chapl Bulletin," *Spec Ediction on Pstr Care*, Amer Prot Hosp Assn, 1983. ACPE inc. 1973; Collage of Pstr Supervision and Psych Inc. 1998-2008; Coll of Chapl 1972-1992. Diplomate Coll of Pstr Supervision and Psych. Inc 1998; Fell : Coll of Chapl Amer Hosp Chapl's Orgnztn 1983; ACPE Supvsr ACPE. Inc 1982; Actg CPE Supvsr ACPE. Inc 1972; WCC Ecum Schlr WCC 1967; WCC Ecum Schlr WCC / NCC 1967. kojihayashi@yahoo.com

✠ HAYASHI, Rt Rev Scott Byron (U) 2649 E. Chalet Circle, Cottonwood Heights UT 84093 **Bp of Utah Dio Utah Salt Lake City UT 2010-** B Tacoma WA 12/9/1953 s Mitsuru Hayashi & Flora. BSW U of Washington 1977; MDiv Harvard DS 1981; Cert CDSP 1984. D 6/2/1984 P 10/16/1984 Bp Leigh Wallace Jr Con 11/6/2010 for U. m 6/6/1981 Amy P O'Donnell c 3. Cn Dio Chicago Chicago IL 2005-2010; R Chr Ch Portola Vlly CA 1998-2005; R Ch Of The Gd Shpd Ogden UT 1989-1998; Vic S Dunst's Epis Ch Grand Coulee WA 1984-1989; Vic S Jn The Bapt Epis Ch Ephrata WA 1984-1989; St Dunstans Ch Electric City WA 1984-1989. zenichi1209@yahoo.com

HAYCOCK, Randall Hilton (Chi) 1536 Heather Hollow Cir Apt 23, Silver Spring MD 20904 B Chicago IL 2/4/1953 s George Ames Haycock & Ann Marie. MDiv Nash 1982; BA NE Illinois U 1982. D 6/19/1982 Bp Quintin Ebenezer Primo Jr P 12/18/1982 Bp James Winchester Montgomery. m 5/14/1977 Terry S Sanders c 1. Pension Fund Mltry New York NY 2003-2004; The Epis Ch Of The H Trin Belvidere IL 2002-2003; Int All SS Ch Wstrn Sprg IL 2000-2002; R Ch Of The Redeem Elgin IL 1986-2000; Cur Ch Of The H Comf Kenilworth IL 1982-1986. rhhaycock@aol.com

HAYDEN, Andrea Rose-Marie (NJ) 1002 4th Ave, Asbury Park NJ 07712 **S Aug's Epis Ch Asbury Pk NJ 2005-** B Saint Andrew Jama CA 3/14/1958 d George Malachi Hayden & Icill Louise. Illinois Inst of Tech; BS Chicago St U 1987; MDiv SWTS 1998. D 9/19/1998 Bp Herbert Alcorn Donovan Jr P 7/3/1999 Bp William Dailey Persell. S Gabr's Ch Brooklyn NY 2003-2005; Dio Washington Washington DC 2002-2003; S Lk's Ch Washington DC 2002; All Souls Memi Epis Ch Washington DC 1999-2001; Ch Of The H Comf Washington DC 1999; D S Mart's Ch Chicago IL 1998-1999. UBE, EWC. arh314@aol.com

HAYDEN JR, Daniel Frank (Mass) No address on file. B 10/4/1935 D 6/23/1962 Bp Anson Phelps Stokes Jr P 5/23/1963 Bp William A Lawrence.

HAYDEN, John Carleton (WA) 3710 26th St Ne, Washington DC 20018 B Bowling Green KY 12/30/1933 s Otis Rooselvelt Hayden & Gladys. BA Wayne 1955; MA U of Detroit 1962; LTh S Chad Coll Regina SK 1963; PhD How 1972; MDiv The Coll of Emm and St. Chad 1992. Trans from Anglican Church of Canada 8/1/1971 Bp William Foreman Creighton. m 4/8/1972 Jacqueline Green c 2. Dio Washington Washington DC 1994-2002; Epis/Angl Mnstry Washington DC 1993-2002; S Mich And All Ang Adelphi MD 1992-1994; Sis of St Mary Sewanee TN 1989-1992; Dio Tennessee Nashville TN 1987-1992; Assoc Dn The TS at The U So Sewanee TN 1987-1992; R Ch Of The H Comf Washington DC 1982-1986; Long Range Plnng Com Dio Washington Washington DC 1982-1986; Dio Maryland Baltimore MD 1979-1980; Adj Prof Ch Hist VTS Alexandria VA 1978-1987; Interracial T/F Dio Washington Washington DC 1977-1979; Cmnty Action Com and Human Dvlpmt Epis Ch Cntr New York NY 1976-1977; S Geo's Ch Washington DC 1973-1982; P-in-c S Monica's Epis Ch Washington DC 1972-1973; Epis/Angl Mnstry Washington DC 1971-1978; Asst Ch Of The Atone Washington DC 1971-1972. "Absalom Jones Mart Luther King, Jr Alexander Crummell," *Lesser Feasts and Fasts*, Ch Pub, 2006; "The Ch and the Civil Rts Mvmt: Freedom's Matrix," *Afr Amer and Civil Rts: A Reappraisal*, Associated Pub, 1997; Auth, "The Black Ch And The Civil Rts Mvmt|Amer And Civil Rts:The Black Ch And The Civil Rts Mvmt," *Amer And Civil Rts: A R*, Associated, 1997; "From Holly to Turner: Black Bishops in the Amer Succession," *Linkage*, 1988; "Afro-Angl Linkages, 1700-1900: Ethiopia Shall Soon Stretch Out her Hands to God," *Journ of Rel Thought*, 1987; "The Co of Wmn Who Bore the Tidings: Black Epis Mssy Teachers, 1865-1877," *Linkage*, 1984; "Jas Theo Holly (1829-1911) First Afro Amer Epis Bp," *Black Apos: Afro-Amer Cler Confron the Twentieth Century*, GK Hall, 1978; "After the War: The Mssn of the Epis Ch to Blacks, 1865-1877," *Hist mag of the Prot Epis Ch*, 1971. Cmnty of S Mary, Assoc 1992; CBS 1967; GAS 1982; Ord of S Ben, Confracter 1953; Sis of S Jn the Div, P Assoc 1978; UBE 1968. Doctor of Cn Law Emm/S Chad's Coll Saskatoon SK CA 2004; Sesquicentennial Celebration Appreciation H Trin Nashville TN 2002; Distinguished Serv Kanuga Conferences 1992; Absalom Jones Awd UBE 1987. fathercarl30@aol.com

HAYDEN, John Hart (O) 206 S Oval Dr, Chardon OH 44024 B Detroit MI 10/12/1940 s Carl Allen Hayden & Florence Jean. BA U MI 1962; MDiv Ya Berk 1965; STM Yale DS 1974. D 6/29/1965 Bp Richard S M Emrich P 2/1/1966 Bp C Kilmer Myers. R S Lk's Epis Ch Chardon OH 1990-2004; H Fam Epis Ch Midland MI 1984-1990; Assoc Chr Ch Cranbrook Bloomfield Hills MI 1980-1984; Asst S Mich's Ch Grosse Pointe Woods MI 1976-1980; Ch Of The H Sprt Livonia MI 1973-1976; Asst S Lk's Par Darien CT 1969-1973; Asst S Jas Epis Ch Birmingham MI 1965-1969. jharthayden@gmail.com

HAYDEN JR, Louis Harold (FtW) 7193 Neshoba Cir, Germantown TN 38138 B Memphis TN 3/26/1935 s Louis Harold Hayden & Clara Laura. BS U of Memphis 1957; MDiv VTS 1964; STM STUSo 1976. D 6/22/1964 P 3/1/1965 Bp Thomas H Wright. m 2/15/1957 Marie Lemee Bargas c 2. Dio Ft Worth Ft Worth TX 1988-2001; Cn Cathd Ch Of S Ptr St Petersburg FL 1977-1988; Vic S Jn's Ch Versailles KY 1965-1967; P-in-c S Thos' Epis Ch Bath NC 1964-1965.

HAYDEN, Robert Stoddard (SVa) 1101 Sixth Ave, Farmville VA 23901 B Camden ME 4/27/1928 s Ralph Henry Hayden & Ethel Lee. BA Bishops U 1951; MDiv GTS 1954; MA U NC 1975; PhD U GA 1979. D 4/22/1954 P 11/27/1954 Bp Oliver L Loring. m 6/26/1954 Jean M McLachlan c 5. S Andr's Ch Baskerville VA 2001-2002; S Jas Ch Boydton VA 2001-2002; Int Manakin Epis Ch Midlothian VA 1998-2000; Int Epis Ch Of S Paul And S Andr Kenbridge VA 1996-1998; Int Gibson Memi Crewe VA 1996-1998; R S Jn's Epis Ch Charlotte NC 1967-1973; Bp Coun Dio Tennessee Nashville TN 1964-1967; R S Barth's Ch Bristol TN 1961-1967; Cn Pstr Gr And H Trin Cathd Kansas City MO 1958-1961; Vic All SS Epis Ch Skowhegan ME 1955-1958; Vic S Lk's Ch Farmington ME 1955-1958; Ch Of The Incarn New York NY 1954-1955. Auth, *arts Var Geographic Journ*; Auth, *Geographic Journ*. S.Va. Epis Cler Assn. 1990. NASA-ASEE Fac Fllshp 1986; Warren Nystrom Awd Assn of Amer Geographers 1977. rhayden@kinex.net

HAYEK, Hal T (Md) 4 East University Parkway, Baltimore MD 21218 **Dn Cathd Of The Incarn Baltimore MD 2009-** B Cedar Rapids IA 7/3/1962 s Carol George Hayek & Janet Maria. BA Clarke Coll Dubuque IA 1984; MDiv Aquinas Inst of Theol 1991; STM Nash 2000. Rec from Roman Catholic 6/7/2000 Bp Roger John White. m 5/24/1996 Marianne Ley c 3. R S Anne's Ch Winston Salem NC 2002-2009; Asst S Dav's Ch Glenview IL 2000-2001. thedean@cathedral.ang-md.org

HAYES III, Christopher Thomas (Va) 1131 Oaklawn Dr, Culpeper VA 22701 B Warrenton VA 6/29/1936 s Christopher Thomas II Hayes & Elizabeth Barrett. BA VPI 1979; MDiv TESM 1982. D 6/9/1982 Bp David Henry Lewis Jr P 6/4/1983 Bp Robert Bruce Hall. m 12/26/1964 Julie A Olson c 3. P-in-c Little Fork Epis Ch Rixeyville VA 2003-2007; Dn Dio Cntrl New York Syracuse NY 1992-1995; Dio Cntrl New York Syracuse NY 1991; R S Andr's Epis Ch Syracuse NY 1990-2003; Ch of the H Sprt Wylie TX 1987-1990; Supply P Dio Dallas Dallas TX 1986-1987; Asst The Epis Ch Of The Resurr Dallas TX 1984-1986; Bp Comsn On Alcosm Dio Virginia Richmond VA 1982-1984; Vic Little Fork Epis Ch Rixeyville VA 1982-1984; Asst S Steph's Epis Ch Culpeper VA 1982-1984. BroSA 2008; NOEL 1986. ct3njhayes@yahoo.com

HAYES, E Perren (NY) 33165 W Chesapeake St, Lewes DE 19958 B Albany NY 10/10/1930 s E Perren Hayes & Gladys Louise. BA Un Coll New York NY 1952; STB GTS 1955. D 5/29/1955 P 12/3/1955 Bp David Emrys Richards. m 11/16/1968 Gealdine Louise Tower. R S Thos Par Croom Upper Marlboro MD 1998-2001; R Ch Of The Incarn Upper Marlboro MD 1998; R S Marg's Ch Washington DC 1997; Par of St Monica & St Jas Washington DC 1996; Asst S Monica's Epis Ch Washington DC 1996; Asst S Chris's Ch Spartanburg SC 1983-1988; Emm Ch Killingworth CT 1973-1979; Asst Ch Of S Jas The Less Scarsdale NY 1956-1958. Auth, "A Sprtlty For Now"; Auth, "Three Retreats"; Auth, "The Old Way". OHC. kypie@aol.com

HAYES, Valerie Jean (SVa) 3800 Reservoir Rd NW, Washington DC 20007 **D Assoc. All SS Ch Alexandria VA 2009-** B Madison WI 6/20/1965 d Richard Charles Boelkins & Judith Ellen. BBA U GA 1987; MEd U GA 1989; MDiv VTS 2009. D 6/13/2009 P 12/11/2010 Bp Herman Hollerith IV. c 2. vhayes09@gmail.com

HAYES, Vera Evans (EC) 6243 Turtle Hall Dr, Wilmington NC 28409 **D S Jn's Epis Ch Wilmington NC 2000-** B Beaufort County NC 11/16/1926 d Thomas Harold Evans & Mamie. D 2/11/1988 Bp Brice Sidney Sanders. m 5/11/1946 Robert Thomas Hayes. D Ch Of The Gd Shpd Wilmington NC 1992-1995; D S Jn's Epis Ch Wilmington NC 1988-1991.

HAYES JR, Walter LeRoy (SanD) 3663 Princeton Ave, San Diego CA 92117 B Swainsboro GA 6/26/1936 s Walter LeRoy Hayes & Margaret Smith. BS U GA 1960; MDiv GTS 1971. D 9/11/1971 P 3/18/1972 Bp Francis E I Bloy. Asst S Alb's Epis Ch El Cajon CA 1990; S Eliz's Epis Ch San Diego CA 1973-1985; Cur Chr Ch Coronado CA 1971-1973. RoyHayesSD@aol.com

HAYES-MARTIN, Gianetta Marie (O) 1 S El Camino Real, San Mateo CA 94401 **Assoc R S Matt's Epis Ch San Mateo CA 2010-** B Charlotte NC 9/25/1977 d James Benedict Hayes & Claire Marie. BA Xavier U 1999; MA Van 2001; PhD Van 2004; MDiv CDSP 2010. D 6/5/2010 Bp Mark Hollingsworth Jr P 4/9/2011 Bp Marc Handley Andrus. m 8/3/2007 Melville Knox Martin. Cmncatn Dir S Paul's Epis Ch Cleveland Heights OH 2004-2007. ghayes925@yahoo.com

HAYLER, Andrew James (SC) 3202 John Bartram Pl, Mount Pleasant SC 29466 B Nottingham UK 7/24/1966 s Brian Miles Hayler & Janet Sandra. BA Winthrop U 1991; MDiv Nash 2001. D 6/3/2001 P 1/6/2002 Bp Edward Lloyd Salmon Jr. m 8/17/1991 Julie Claire Ivester c 2. Ch Of The Redeem Sarasota FL 2006-2007; S Phil's Ch Charleston SC 2004-2005; S Alb's Ch Kingstree SC 2004; Assoc Gr Ch Charleston SC 2001-2003. AAM. ajayler@gmail.com

HAYMAN, Robert Fleming (Oly) 1102 E Boston St, Seattle WA 98102 B Kittanning PA 12/11/1931 s Firman Knotly Hayman & Catharine Henrietta. BA Pr 1953; MDiv GTS 1956. D 4/28/1956 P 10/27/1956 Bp Alfred L Banyard. m 9/8/1962 Sarah P Pritchard c 2. Asst S Thos Ch Medina WA 2000-2003; R S Lk's Ch San Francisco CA 1983-1988; Archd Dio Olympia Seattle WA 1977-1983; R S Jn's Ch Kirkland WA 1958-1977; Asst Min S Geo's-By-The-River Rumson NJ 1956-1958. Auth, "Var arts," *Living Ch*. Fell Coll of Preachers 1982; A.A. (Hon) Bellevue Cmnty Coll, Bellevue, WA 1973. rshayman@msn.com

HAYNES, Alice Smith (USC) 1852 Gingercake Cir Apt 207, Rock Hill SC 29732 B Boston MA 11/2/1948 d Winfield Davis Smith & Lois Lowery. AA St. Mary's Coll Raleigh NC 1968; BA U of So Carolina 1970; Luth Theol Sthrn Sem 1993; MDiv STUSo 1995. D 8/21/2004 P 2/26/2005 Bp Frank Neff Powell. c 3. S Mths Ch Rock Hill SC 2006-2011; Ch Of The Adv Spartanburg SC 2005-2006; S Jn's Ch Lynchburg VA 2001-2004; Dir. of Chr Ed. and Yth Mnstrs Ch Of The Adv Nashville TN 1997-1998. alicehaynes2.26@gmail.com

HAYNES, Argola Electa (Los) 1979 Newport Ave, Pasadena CA 91103 B San Bernardino CA 5/24/1940 d TA Patterson & Ruth Gladys. BA Pasadena Coll 1962; Med USI U 1989; MDiv CDSP 1998. D 6/15/1998 Bp Chester Lovelle Talton P 5/13/1999 Bp Frederick Houk Borsch. c 1. P-in-c Chr The Gd Shpd Par Los Angeles CA 2008-2010; D Epis Ch Of The Adv Los Angeles CA 2000-2001; Asst S Bede's Epis Ch Los Angeles CA 1998-2007. Auth, "Pryr," *Wmn Uncommon Prayers*, Morehouse Pub, 2000. Delta Kappa Gamma 1980; Delta Sigma Theta Sorority 1973; Phi Delta Kappa 1975-1999. mizrola@aol.com

HAYNES, Elizabeth S (Be) 621 Prices Dr, Cresco PA 18326 B Catavi BO 3/7/1939 d Thoris Layland Stephenson & Marjorie G. Our Lady of Lourds BO 1962; Gr Downs 1963; Cert GTS 1991. D 6/14/1997 P 12/12/1997 Bp Paul Victor Marshall. m 12/14/1963 William Haynes c 3. Trin Epis Ch Mt Pocono PA 2011; Chr Ch Stroudsburg PA 2001-2010; Trin Ch Easton PA 1999-2001; Gr Epis Ch Allentown PA 1999-2000. revbeth@ptd.net

HAYNES, Frank James (EMich) 2518 Woodstock Dr, Port Huron MI 48060 B Ann Arbor MI 7/5/1935 s Frank Jacob Haynes & Effie. BA U of Wstrn Ontario 1958; BTh Hur 1961. D 6/29/1961 Bp Archie H Crowley P 3/1/1962 Bp Robert Lionne DeWitt. m 6/18/1960 Yolanda Mary Petho c 2. Asst Min Chr Ch Detroit MI 1963-1966; Asst S Matt's And S Jos's Detroit MI 1961-1963.

HAYNES, John Connor (NJ) 45 W Broad St, Burlington NJ 08016 **R S Mary's Ch Burlington NJ 1996-** B Decatur IL 8/17/1959 s Harrington Clanahan Haynes & Janet. BA Illinois Coll 1980; MDiv Nash 1986. D 6/14/1986 P 12/1/1986 Bp Donald Maynard Hultstrand. m 6/14/1981 Anita M Haynes c 2. R All SS Ch Morton IL 1986-1995. SSC. frchaynes@verizon.net

HAYNES, Kendall Thomas-Biethan (Oly) PO Box 1652, Renton WA 98057 **Assoc S Andr's Epis Ch Tacoma WA 2011-** B Portland OR 11/7/1975 s Thomas Lanier Haynes & Elisabeth Louise. BA Willamette U 1998; MDiv GTS 2005. D 6/18/2005 Bp William Dailey Persell P 12/21/2005 Bp Johncy Itty. m 8/8/1998 Mindy Paige-Biethan c 2. Rainier Reg Mnstry Co-Cnvnr Dio Olympia Seattle WA 2009-2011; R S Mary's Ch Lakewood WA 2008-2011; Anti Racism Cmsn Co-Chair Dio Chicago Chicago IL 2007-2011; Assoc Ch Of The H Comf Kenilworth IL 2005-2008. Fllshp of St. Alb and St. Sergius 2005. kendallhaynes2011@gmail.com

HAYNES SR, Larry Lee (NY) 34 Point St, New Hamburg NY 12590 **D Ch Of S Nich On The Hudson New Hamburg NY 1992-** B Greenfield OH 6/21/1947 s David Elton Haynes & Lucy. D 5/30/1992 Bp Richard Frank Grein. m 1/20/1967 Michele Elizabeth Relyea.

HAYNES, Peter Davis (Los) 3233 Pacific View Dr, Corona Del Mar CA 92625 **Dn of Orange Cnty Coastal Dnry Dio Los Angeles Los Angeles CA 2003-; R S Mich And All Ang Par Corona Del Mar CA 1988-** B Evanston IL 7/30/1946 s Donald Wayne Haynes & Margaret Pauline. BA U CA 1968; STM EDS 1971; MS U CA 1973. D 3/8/1972 Bp Francis E I Bloy P 7/11/1973 Bp CE Crowther. m 6/30/1985 Frances E Bolles c 1. Assoc R All Souls Par In Berkeley Berkeley CA 1982-1988; Assoc R S Mk's Par Berkeley CA

1982-1988; Field Educ Supvsr CDSP Berkeley CA 1975-1988; Berkeley Cbury Fndt Berkeley CA 1973-1988. Auth, *Plumbline*. ESMHE 1973; GEM 1996. Ph.D. KN 2002. phaynes@stmikescdm.org

HAYNES, Rachel Fowler (NC) Po Box 504, Davidson NC 28036 B Atlanta GA 3/28/1939 d Samuel Hall Fowler & Wilhelmina Gertrude. BA Agnes Scott Coll 1961; MDiv Candler TS Emory U 1979; DMin Columbia TS 1996. D 9/22/1979 Bp Charles Judson Child Jr P 6/1/1980 Bp Bennett Jones Sims. m 3/17/1990 William H Tiemann c 2. Assoc R S Alb's Ch Davidson NC 1998-2002; Int Chr Ch Charlotte NC 1995-1998; S Mart's Epis Ch Charlotte NC 1989-1995; S Jn's Epis Ch Charlotte NC 1987-1989; Ch Of The Cov Atlanta GA 1984; Asst S Barth's Epis Ch Atlanta GA 1980-1981; Dio Atlanta Atlanta GA 1979-1980; D-In-Trng S Lk's Epis Ch Atlanta GA 1979-1980. Auth, "In The Image Of God? Wmn In The Newtestament Period & Beyond"; Auth, "Black & Feminist Perspectives". ACPE 1984-1990.

HAYNES, Ralph Douglas (Ore) Po Box 100, Alvadore OR 97409 **Died 7/25/2010** B Winnipeg MT CA 10/31/1933 s Stanley George Haynes & Muriel Eileen. BA U Tor 1956; BA/LTH U Tor 1959; U Tor 1959; DMin Fuller TS 1986. D 5/1/1959 P 11/1/1959 Bp The Bishop Of Toronto. RD1AB2@Q.COM

HAYNES, Susan (NI) 616 Lincolnway East, Mishawaka IN 46544 **CDI Trnr Dio Nthrn Indiana So Bend IN 2010-; Dep, GC 2012 Dio Nthrn Indiana So Bend IN 2010-; Dioc Coun Dio Nthrn Indiana So Bend IN 2008-; R S Paul's Ch Mishawaka IN 2008-; Dioc Liturg Dio Nthrn Indiana So Bend IN 2005-; Chair, Ethics Com Dio Nthrn Indiana So Bend IN 2004-** B Tampa FL 6/27/1959 d Randolph Leonard Bunton & Karen Joan. BA U So 1981; MA Middle Tennessee St U 1989; MDiv Van 1993. D 12/21/2004 P 6/24/2005 Bp Edward Stuart Little II. m 6/12/1982 Thomas Erskine Haynes c 2. P-in-c The Cathd Ch Of S Jas So Bend IN 2006-2008; Assoc The Cathd Ch Of S Jas So Bend IN 2005-2006. susan.haynes@gmail.com

HAYNES, Thomas Erskine (NI) 515 State St, Culver IN 46511 **Fin Com Dio Nthrn Indiana So Bend IN 2011-; Pstr S Eliz's Epis Ch Culver IN 2010-** B Cedar Key FL 11/27/1960 s John Marshall Haynes & Ann. BA U So 1981; MST Middle Tennessee St U 1992; non-degree Nthrn Indiana TS 2010; D.Min. VTS 2013. D 6/15/2010 P 1/14/2011 Bp Edward Stuart Little II. m 6/12/1982 Susan Bunton c 2. teh.culver@gmail.com

HAYNES, Warren Edward (LI) 429 E 52nd St Apt 27h, New York NY 10022 **Mem Ecum Cmsn Dio New York New York City NY 2005-** B Pensacola FL 1/30/1932 s James Edward Haynes & Mary Evelyn. BA Birmingham-Sthrn Coll 1952; STM Van 1955; Fllshp Coll of Preachers 1966. D 6/29/1955 Bp Theodore N Barth P 3/26/1956 Bp John Vander Horst. m 6/28/1979 Mary Melikian. Asst Ch Of The Trsfg New York NY 2000-2006; R S Mary's Ch Hampton Bays NY 1986-1998; Ch Of The Incarn New York NY 1983-1984; S Ptr's Ch Morristown NJ 1981-1982; Dn Chr Ch Cathd Houston TX 1977-1980; R Calv Ch Memphis TN 1973-1977; R Chr Ch Epis Savannah GA 1967-1973; R S Andr's Ch Maryville TN 1959-1967; R S Mary's Epis Ch Dyersburg TN 1956-1959; Cur S Steph's Epis Ch Oak Ridge TN 1955-1956. warrenhaynes@earthlink.net

HAYNIE, Amy Peden (FtW) 223 S Pearson Ln, Keller TX 76248 **InReach / Recon Coordntr Dio Ft Worth Ft Worth TX 2011-; S Mart In The Fields Ch Keller TX 2011-; Yth Coordntr to Prov VII Dio Ft Worth Ft Worth TX 2010-** B Clovis NM 9/8/1967 d Gary David Peden & Laura Francis. BS Midwestern St U 1991; MDiv Perkins TS 2009. D 5/25/2011 Bp C(harles) Wallis Ohl. m 9/26/1992 David Haynie c 2. amy_david_75077@yahoo.com

✠ HAYNSWORTH, Rt Rev George Edward (SC) One Gadsden Way #14, Charleston SC 29412 **Ret Asst Bp Of SC Dio So Carolina Charleston SC 1991-; Exec Coun Appointees New York NY 1965-** B Sumter SC 10/25/1922 s Joseph Herbert Haynsworth & Katherine Rees. BA Cit 1946; MDiv STUSo 1949; Spanish Lang Sch San Jose Cr 1962; Universidad Iberoamericana Mex City Mx 1967; DD STUSo 1969; Dh Cit 1975. D 6/18/1949 P 5/10/1950 Bp Thomas N Carruthers Con 1/10/1969 for Nic. m 4/6/1948 Sarah Elizabeth Veronee. Asst Dio So Carolina Charleston SC 1985-1990; Epis Ch Cntr New York NY 1980-1985; Natl Coun Of Ch New York NY 1961-1964; Dep Gc Dio Georgia Savannah GA 1958-1967; Chair Deptce Dio Georgia Savannah GA 1958-1960; Archd Of Savannah Dio Georgia Savannah GA 1956-1958; Yth Advsr Dio Georgia Savannah GA 1955-1957; Min In Charge Ch Of The Heav Rest Estill SC 1949-1953; Min In Charge Epis Ch Of The H Trin Ridgeland SC 1949-1953; Min In Charge The Ch Of The Cross Bluffton SC 1949-1953. Bd Soc For Promoting Chr Knowledge.

HAYS, Bret Bowie (Colo) 48 Middle St, Gloucester MA 01930 **R S Jn's Epis Ch Gloucester MA 2011-** B Washington DC 9/20/1981 s Louis B. Hays & Maude Bowie. BA U of Pennsylvania 2004; MDiv VTS 2008. D 6/14/2008 Bp Andrew Donnan Smith P 1/10/2009 Bp Robert John O'Neill. Int The Ch Of Chr The King (Epis) Arvada CO 2011; Cur S Jn's Cathd Denver CO 2008-2011. Auth, "Dual-Use Tech In the Context of the Non-Proliferation Regime," *Hist and Tech*, Taylor & Fran, 2006. bret@sjcathedral.org

HAYS, Donald Lewis (O) 322 Wendy Ln, Waverly OH 45690 **Supply All SS Epis Ch Portsmouth OH 2001-** B Malcolm NE 10/16/1928 s Hobart Glen Hays & Allegra. BA U of Nebraska 1950; STM PDS 1966. D 5/28/1966 Bp William S Thomas P 12/1/1966 Bp Austin Pardue. m 7/3/1951 Barbara Sasse. Supply S Ptr's Ch Gallipolis OH 2000-2001; Supply S Ptr's Ch Gallipolis OH 1997-1998; R S Paul's Epis Ch Put-In-Bay OH 1988-1993; R S Chris's Ch River Hills WI 1980-1988; Chr Epis Ch No Hills Pittsburgh PA 1966-1980. bjdlhays@bvres.org

HAYS, Joseph Spurgeon (At) 666 E College St, Griffin GA 30224 B Gorden GA 11/27/1936 s Joseph Spurgeon Hays & Jewell Agnes. BA Merc 1960; BD SE Bapt TS 1963; MDiv SE Bapt TS 1968; DMin VTS 1982. D 10/23/1988 P 2/1/1989 Bp Don Adger Wimberly. c 2. Ch Of The Epiph Atlanta GA 2000-2003; R S Geo's Epis Ch Griffin GA 1992-2003; Ch Of The Gd Shpd Lexington KY 1989-1991; Dio Lexington Lexington KY 1988-1989.

HAYS, Lloyd Phillip Whistler (Pgh) Po Box 43, Ambridge PA 15003 B Oklahoma City OK 9/6/1950 s Miller Bevan Hays & Barbara Le. BFA SMU 1972; MDiv Fuller TS 1977. D 6/11/1983 Bp Arthur Edward Walmsley P 6/14/1984 Bp William Bradford Hastings. m 9/7/1974 Mary Maggard c 2. P-in-c S Dav's Epis Ch Venetia PA 2008; Assoc Prof TESM Ambridge PA 1991-2006; Assoc R All SS Epis Ch Woodbridge VA 1985-1989; Cur Trin Ch Tariffville CT 1983-1985. Auth, "(Video) Many Crowns: Wrshp In The Loc Ch," *ERM*, 1988; Auth, "(Video) Jesus, Hd Of The Ch," *Epis Radio-Tv Fndt*, 1980. haysp@ymail.com

HAYS, Louis B. (Pgh) 505 Kingsberry Cir, Pittsburgh PA 15234 **Chair, COM Dio Pittsburgh Monroeville PA 2008-; Mem, Com on Const and Cn Dio Pittsburgh Monroeville PA 2008-; R S Paul's Epis Ch Pittsburgh PA 2007-** B Burbank CA 6/2/1945 s Marion C Hays & Carolyn R. BA U of Redlands 1966; JD U CA 1969; MPH Jn Hopkins U 1994; MDiv VTS 1999. D 6/12/1999 Bp John Leslie Rabb P 12/11/1999 Bp Robert Wilkes Ihloff. c 2. R S Andr's Ch Madison CT 2001-2007; Asst R S Jas' Par Lothian MD 1999-2001. lbhays@yahoo.com

HAYS, Miriam Peggy Wall (Ark) 16 Birchwood Dr., Conway AR 72034 B Little Rock AR 9/12/1937 d Harry Boykin Wall & Verna. BA U of Arkansas 1959; MS U of Arkansas 1976; MDiv Ya Berk 1990; CAS Ya Berk 1990. D 6/23/1990 P 1/18/1991 Bp Herbert Alcorn Donovan Jr. c 3. P S Ptr's Ch Conway AR 1999-2000; Dio Arkansas Little Rock AR 1999; Vic S Ptr's Ch Conway AR 1990-1998.

HAYS-SMITH, Melissa Beth (SwVa) Christ Episcopal Church, 1101 Franklin Rd SW, Roanoke VA 24016 **D Chr Epis Ch Roanoke VA 2007-** B Parkersburg WV 8/11/1955 d Samuel Arnold Hays & Mary Powell. BS Virginia Tech 1977; MSW Virginia Commonwealth U 1982; n/a D Formation Prog-- Dio No Carolina 2007. D 10/20/2007 Bp A(rthur) Heath Light. m 6/9/1979 Howard Smith c 2. mhayssmith@aol.com

HAYWARD, Dennis Earl (Vt) 511 Rankinville Rd, Mabou NS B0E1X0 Canada B Newport NH 1/1/1944 s Earl Jessie Hayward & Eleanor Louise. BA Nath Hawthorne Coll 1978; MDiv EDS 1981; Postgraduate Dplma U of Wales 2006. D 5/23/1981 Bp Philip Alan Smith P 1/25/1982 Bp Harold B Robinson. m 6/20/2004 Deborah L'Esperance c 2. R S Lk's Ch S Albans VT 1990-2007; R Ch Of The Ascen Buffalo NY 1984-1990; Cur S Lk's Epis Ch Jamestown NY 1981-1984. Auth, "Encounter the 80's," *Radio Programing*, WJTN, 1982. Soc of S Jn the Evang 1981. celticrector@gmail.com

HAYWARD, Stephen H (WA) Stephen H Hayward, 154 Mills Point Rd, Brooksville ME 04617 B Cleveland OH 3/11/1949 s Joseph Hunter Hayward & Rosemary. BA Van 1971; MDiv CDSP 1974. D 6/22/1974 P 12/14/1974 Bp George Leslie Cadigan. m 6/29/1974 Kathleen Blackwood c 3. Int S Jn's Ch Chevy Chase MD 2008-2010; Int Ch Of The Ascen Gaithersburg MD 2007; R S Ptr's Ch Poolesville MD 1982-2006; Vic Trin Epis Ch Kirksville MO 1978-1982; Asst Calv Ch Columbia MO 1975-1978; Cur Emm Epis Ch Webster Groves MO 1974-1975. WECA 1982. shh@millspoint154.com

HAYWORTH, Joseph Allison (NC) 910 Croyden St, High Point NC 27262 B High Point NC 1/1/1926 s Charles Emerson Hayworth & Myrtle Crystel. BA Duke 1948; BD VTS 1954; MA Col 1964. D 7/15/1954 Bp Richard Henry Baker P 2/1/1955 Bp Edwin A Penick. c 1. Int S Matt's Epis Ch Kernersville NC 1996-1997; Int All SS Ch Greensboro NC 1994-1995; Int Chr Ch Albemarle NC 1991-1992; P-in-c S Eliz Epis Ch King NC 1984-1995; Asst S Barn Ch Irvington on Hudson NY 1962-1964; Asst R S Jas Ch Hyde Pk NY 1958-1960; M-in-c S Thos Epis Ch Sanford NC 1954-1958.

HAZEL, Dorothy Massey (USC) 546 Woodland Hills West, Columbia SC 29210 **Dir of Mnstry Dvlpmt Dio Upper So Carolina Columbia SC 2005-** B Greenville SC 3/20/1960 d John Jasper Massey & Caroline Pinckney. Luth Theol Sthrn Sem; BS Winthrop U 1982. D 12/14/2002 Bp Dorsey Felix Henderson. m 2/5/1983 Tony Charles Hazel c 3. S Mary's Ch Columbia SC 2002-2005. dhazel@edusc.org

HAZEL, James (FtW) 6828 Woodstock Road, Fort Worth TX 76116 **Dio Louisiana Baton Rouge LA 1974-** B Jennings LA 12/27/1948 s Robert Grady Hazel & Betty L. BS LSU 1970; MDiv Epis TS of The SW 1973; Advncd CPE 1979. D 6/24/1973 P 3/1/1974 Bp Iveson Batchelor Noland. m 8/8/1968 Marileen Cole c 2. Trin Epis Ch Ft Worth TX 1987; Baylor All SS Med Cntr Ft Worth TX 1979-1986; Asst Trin Epis Ch Ft Worth TX 1974-1978. jimhazel@mac.com

HAZELETT, Jackson Reiser (Ore) 18989 Ne Marine Dr Slip 4, Portland OR 97230 B Salt Lake City UT 6/12/1926 s Jackson Thomas Biesinger & Blanche Arlie. BA Willamette U 1949; MDiv CDSP 1965. D 6/29/1965 P 1/6/1966 Bp James Walmsley Frederic Carman. m 8/29/2009 Elizabeth Patterson Hazelett c 5. Assoc S Ptr's Ch Litchfield Pk AZ 1996-2011; Assoc S Ptr And Paul Epis Ch Portland OR 1993-1996; Chair Stwdshp Consult Dio Oregon Portland OR 1982-1988; Stndg Com Dio Oregon Portland OR 1981-1984; Stwdshp Consult Dio Oregon Portland OR 1976-1981; Trst Legacy Gd Samar Hosp Portland OR 1973-1979; Deptce Dio Oregon Portland OR 1970-1973; R S Jas Epis Ch Tigard OR 1967-1992; Cur S Mich And All Ang Ch Portland OR 1965-1967. Biblic Archeological Soc, Assn Of S Jn The B. jrbhhaze@gmail.com

HAZELETT, William Howard (CFla) 1666 Parkgate Dr., Kissimmee FL 34746 B Abington PA 2/27/1935 s William Orlando Hazelett & Clarissa Markley. BS Tem 1957; MDiv PDS 1960. D 5/14/1960 Bp Joseph Gillespie Armstrong P 11/24/1960 Bp Benjamin M Washburn. P-in-c Chr Ch Ft Meade FL 1998-2010; R Ch Of Our Sav Palm Bay FL 1990-1997; R S Mk's Epis Ch Haines City FL CA 1987-1990; H Nativ Day Sch Panama City FL 1986-1987; Cur H Nativ Epis Ch Panama City FL 1986-1987; Vic Ch Of The Epiph Crestview FL 1985-1986; Vic S Agatha's Epis Ch Defuniak Sprg FL 1985-1986; Cur S Andr's By The Sea Epis Ch Destin FL 1982-1983; R Ch Of The Epiph Newport NH 1970-1982; Asst S Mk's Par Van Nuys CA 1967-1968; Cur Par Of S Jas Ch Keene NH 1963-1966; Vic S Jn's Ch Walpole NH 1963-1966; Cur S Geo's Par Flushing NY 1961-1963; Cur Cathd Ch Of S Paul Burlington VT 1960-1961. prssngon@aol.com

HAZEN, Alba (Ore) 1317 E 42nd St., Kearney NE 68847 **S Jas' Epis Ch Coquille OR 2009-** B Hancock NY 9/15/1951 s Alba Weaver Hazen & Eva Marguerite. LTh VTS 2001. D 4/21/2001 P 9/29/2001 Bp Paul Victor Marshall. m 9/17/1997 Susan Marcotte Hazen c 3. S Lk's Ch Kearney NE 2006-2007; S Geo's Wm And Mary Vlly Lee MD 2004-2006; S Dav's Par Washington DC 2003-2004; Int S Lk's Ch Trin Par Beth MD 2001-2003. revalbie@gmail.com

HAZEN, Susan Marcotte (Be) St John's Episcopal Church, PO Box 246, Bandon OR 97411 **Int S Jn-By-The-Sea Epis Ch Bandon OR 2009-** B Omaha NE 8/24/1950 d Robert Delphis Marcotte & Barbara Hope. BA Cedar Crest Coll 1996; MDiv VTS 2000. D 4/29/2000 Bp Paul Victor Marshall P 11/12/2000 Bp Peter James Lee. m 9/17/1997 Alba Hazen c 3. Dio Oregon Portland OR 2007-2009; Assoc S Geo's Wm And Mary Vlly Lee MD 2005-2006; Assoc Chr Ch Columbia MD 2002-2004; Asst Pohick Epis Ch Lorton VA 2000-2002. hazenrevs@gmail.com

HAZLETT, Brant Vincent (Spr) 600 N Mulberry St # 674, Mount Carmel IL 62863 **R Ch Of S Jn The Bapt Mt Carmel IL 1997-** B Latrobe PA 8/12/1951 s Paul J Sloan & Ethel I. Indiana U of Pennsylvania 1971; BA S Mary Sem/U 1974; MDiv S Vinc Sem 1978; Cert TESM 1990. Rec from Roman Catholic 5/29/1990 as Priest Bp Alden Moinet Hathaway. m 7/31/1982 Stephanie Hazlett c 5. R Chr Ch Cape Girardeau MO 1992-1997; R The Ch Of The Adv Jeannette PA 1990-1992.

HAZZARD SR, Richard Augustus (CPa) 132 2nd St, Mount Carmel PA 17851 B Lewes DE 4/27/1932 s Augustus Nichols Hazzard & Phyllis Flora. Dioc Sch Of Chr Stds Harrisburg PA 1996. D 11/21/2001 Bp Michael Whittington Creighton. m 3/19/1958 Caroline Martha Fesniak. hapha@verizon.net

HEACOCK, Donald Dee (WLa) 3820 Fairfield Ave Apt 113, Shreveport LA 77104 **Dir, H Cross Chld Placement Agcy, Inc Ch Of The H Cross Shreveport LA 1983-** B Anthony KS 2/21/1934 s Carl Wesley Heacock & Thelma Olive. ThD Slidell Bapt Sem; BA Washburn U 1956; BD UTS 1959; MS Barry Coll 1971. D 6/29/1964 Bp Richard S M Emrich P 1/6/1965 Bp C Kilmer Myers. m 9/4/1953 Margaret Ann Newberry c 2. COM Dio Wstrn Louisiana Alexandria LA 1980-1990; COM Dio Louisiana Baton Rouge LA 1978-1979; Vic S Jn's Ch Clinton MI 1963-1966. domahea@aol.com

HEACOX, Don (RG) PO Box 1863, Deming NM 88031 **Vic S Lk's Epis Ch Deming NM 2010-** B Anderson IN 6/29/1940 s Maynard L Heacox & Joy Darlene. BS USAFA 1962; MS Stanford 1967; Dplma Trin Sch for Mnstry 2009. D 9/19/2009 P 3/30/2010 Bp William Carl Frey. m 4/20/1969 Suzanne M Westley c 3. frheacox@gmail.com

HEAD JR, Edward Marvin (WLa) 504 Tech Dr, Ruston LA 71270 **P-in-c Chr Ch Bastrop LA 2008-** B Bastrop LA 3/22/1942 s Edward M Head & Johnnie. BS NE Louisiana U 1966; MDiv STUSo 1986. D 5/31/1986 P 11/30/1986 Bp Willis Ryan Henton. m 9/5/1964 Mary Nell Drummond c 2. R Ch Of The Redeem Ruston LA 1996-2007; Ch Of The Ascen Lafayette LA 1988-1996; R S Alb's Epis Ch Monroe LA 1986-1988. Ord Of S Mary. emhead@suddenlink.net

HEAD, Paul Anthony (EC) 656 Avenue L, NW, Winter Haven FL 33881 **R S Paul's Ch Winter Haven FL 2011-; Assoc R S Paul's Ch Beaufort NC 2006-** B Miami FL 8/6/1964 s George Head & Alice. BS U Of No Florida Jacksonville FL 2003; MDiv U So 2006. D 6/4/2006 Bp Samuel Johnson Howard P 1/13/2007 Bp Clifton Daniel III. m 7/30/1988 Callie Anthony Johnson c 2. paulstpauls@earthlink.net

HEALD, David Stanley (Me) 8 Pine Ln, Cumberland Foreside ME 04110 B Weymouth MA 8/14/1955 s John Tower Heald & Elizabeth Roelse. BA Amh 1978; MDiv Harvard DS 1982; CAS GTS 1983. D 5/28/1983 P 12/3/1983 Bp Frederick Barton Wolf. m 12/12/1987 Susan Bradbury Curtis c 2. R S Barth's Epis Ch Yarmouth ME 1991-2006; Vic S Dav's Epis Mssn Pepperell MA 1988-1991; Assoc S Andr's Ch Wellesley MA 1983-1988. Soc For Buddhist Chr Stds; Soc Of S Jn The Evang. dhealde@maine.rr.com

HEALEY, Joseph Patrick (NY) 1045 Cook Rd, Grosse Pointe MI 48236 B Scranton PA 2/20/1943 s John Evangelist Healey & Margaret Mary. BA Ph.B. Pontificia U Gregoriana Rome IT 1965; PHL Pontificia U Gregoriana Rome IT 1966; STB CUA 1970; MA CUA 1971; PhD Harv 1981. Rec from Roman Catholic 10/1/1983 as Priest Bp C(laude) Charles Vache. m 9/14/1974 Kathleen Ellen Elizabeth Scaldini c 4. Asst to R S Ptr's Memi Geneva NY 1983-1986. Auth/Contrib, "7 arts," *Anchor Bible Dictionary*; Auth, "Kition Tariffs," *Basor*; Auth, "Macabean Revolt," *New Perspectives in Ancient Judaism*; Auth/Contrib, "Sublimation of the Goddess," *Semeia*; Auth, "Bible and Hist," *Wm & Mary Bulletin*. AAR 1980; Cath Biblic Assn 1973; SBL 1975. jhealey@uls.org

HEALY, Denise Catherine (SwFla) 1502 Paddock Dr, Plant City FL 33566 **D H Innoc Epis Ch Valrico FL 2011-** B Baltimore MD 3/12/1954 d Carmen Curcio & Mary Antionetta. Cert Essex Cmnty Coll 1980; BA Goucher Coll 1983; MSW U of Hawaii 1988; Dio Haw Ministers Trng Prog 1989. D 6/29/1991 Bp Rogers Sanders Harris. D S Cathr's Ch Temple Terrace FL 2007-2008; D H Innoc Epis Ch Valrico FL 1993-2006; D S Ptr's Ch Plant City FL 1991-1993. denisehealy@verizon.net

HEALY, Ruth Tenney (At) 1403 Oakridge Cir, Decatur GA 30033 **Assoc Ch Of The Gd Shpd Covington GA 2009-; Asscoiate S Jn's Coll Pk GA 2002-** B London UK 8/4/1929 d Kent Tenney Healy & Ruth. BA Smith 1951; MA Col 1958; MDiv Candler TS Emory U 1988; GTS 1991. D 6/8/1991 P 1/1/1992 Bp Frank Kellogg Allan. Int S Eliz's Epis Ch Dahlonega GA 2000-2002; Ch Of The Epiph Atlanta GA 1997-2001; P H Innoc Ch Atlanta GA 1991-1995. ACPE; SSAP 2006. rhealy66@aol.com

HEANEY, David Lloyd (SanD) 690 Oxford St, Chula Vista CA 91911 B Chicago IL 12/3/1951 s Lloyd Heaney & Mary Louise. Monmouth Coll 1971; BA SUNY 1973; MDiv Yale DS 1976; MA U of San Diego 1993. D 6/19/1976 P 1/1/1977 Bp Robert C Rusack. m 8/26/1972 Karen Diane Tweddle c 4. Epis Cmnty Serv San Diego CA 1995-1998; R All Souls' Epis Ch San Diego CA 1988-1995; R S Barn Epis Ch Bainbridge Island WA 1983-1987; S Andr's By The Sea Epis Par San Diego CA 1979-1983; Cur S Paul's Epis Ch Tustin CA 1976-1979. Aamft; Ca Assn Mar And Fam Therapists; Natl Soc Fund Raising Exec. dheaney@aol.com

HEARD, Fred (ECR) 2555 Alban Pl, Cambria CA 93428 **R S Paul's Ch Cambria CA 2009-** B Prineville OR 9/9/1940 s Darrell Lee Heard & Wilma Elva. BS Sthrn Oregon U 1963; MS Sthrn Oregon U 1968; MDiv CDSP 2003. D 6/21/2003 Bp Robert Louis Ladehoff P 12/6/2003 Bp Johncy Itty. m 6/11/1966 Adair Elaine Flann c 3. Assoc R Trin Par Menlo Pk CA 2003-2008. retlawfred@charter.net

HEARD, Thomas (CGC) 2201 Dauphin St, Mobile AL 36606 **COM Dio Cntrl Gulf Coast Pensacola FL 2011-; Instr, Sch for Deacons Dio Cntrl Gulf Coast Pensacola FL 2009-; Murray Hse Bd Dir Dio Cntrl Gulf Coast Pensacola FL 2008-; R S Jn's Epis Ch Mobile AL 2007-** B St Louis MO 2/15/1953 s John Thomas Heard & Edith Louise. U of Kansas; MDiv GTS 2007. D 12/20/2006 P 6/29/2007 Bp George Wayne Smith. m 12/11/1983 Cheryl L Wierenga c 1. Cmsn on Fin Dio Cntrl Gulf Coast Pensacola FL 2008-2011; Murray Hse Bd Dir Dio Cntrl Gulf Coast Pensacola FL 2008-2011; Asst Chr Ch Cathd S Louis MO 2007; D Ch Of S Mary The Vrgn New York NY 2006-2007. Soc of Cath Priests 2011. tkheard@att.net

HEARD, Victoria R.T. (Dal) 1630 N Garrett Ave, Diocese of Dallas, Dallas TX 75206 **Cn for Ch Planting Dio Dallas Dallas TX 2006-** B Washington DC 4/3/1956 d Ralph Townsend Heard & Rose. BA U of Virginia 1978; MDiv VTS 1982. D 4/16/1983 Bp David Henry Lewis Jr P 3/17/1984 Bp Robert Bruce Hall. m 7/15/1978 David Ridgely c 3. P-in-c The Epis Ch Of The Resurr Dallas TX 2007-2008; Mssnr For Ch Planting Dio Virginia Richmond VA 1997-2006; P-in-res S Andr's Epis Ch Arlington VA 1997-2000; Int S Geo's Epis Ch Arlington VA 1995-1997; Mssnr S Dav's Ch Ashburn VA 1989-1990; Asst R Pohick Epis Ch Lorton VA 1988-1989; Assoc R S Jas' Epis Ch Leesburg VA 1987-1988; Asst to R S Jas' Epis Ch Leesburg VA 1983-1986. Auth, "Ch Planting In The Of Dio Va," 1998. vheard@episcopal-dallas.org

HEARD, William Hugh (WTex) 415 E Beach St Apt 302, Galveston TX 77550 B Dallas TX 12/30/1935 s Charles Hugh Heard & Nell Gene. BA Texas A&M U 1957; BD Epis TS of The SW 1964. D 6/10/1964 Bp Frederick P Goddard P 6/1/1965 Bp J Milton Richardson. m 9/1/1962 Margot T Terry. R Gr Ch Weslaco TX 1975-1980; Vic Ch Of The Gd Samar Dallas TX 1968-1972; R Chr Ch Jefferson TX 1965-1968; Vic S Paul's Ch Jefferson TX 1965-1968; Asst R S Thos Ch Houston TX 1964-1965. Auth, "Mao'S Legacy-Marxism As A Political Rel".

HEARN, Arnold Withrow (Ark) Po Box 719, Mountain View AR 72560 B Suzhou Jiangsu China 2/22/1926 s Walter Anderson Hearn & Olive Barthenia. BA U of Missouri 1946; MDiv UTS 1949; PhD Col 1961. D 6/12/1965 Bp Oliver L Loring P 3/4/1966 Bp J Milton Richardson. m 3/31/1975 Mary Patricia Davis. Mssn Chapl S Andr's Epis Ch Cherokee Vill AR 1994-2003; R S Andr's Ch Marianna AR 1987-1993; Dn Cntrl Convoc Dio Arkansas Little Rock AR 1982-1986; Vic S Fran Ch Heber Sprg AR 1979-1987; Assoc Prof Epis TS Of The SW Austin TX 1965-1974. "arts & Revs," 2003. AAR 1970; Soc Of Chr Ethics 1962. Phi Beta Kappa 1946. dunstan@mvtel.net

HEARN, George Edmund (Mass) 163 Hickory Ln, Wyomissing PA 19610 **Died 10/25/2011** B Boston MA 8/5/1921 s Ernest Herbert Hearn & Eleanor. EDS 1961. D 6/24/1961 P 12/23/1961 Bp Anson Phelps Stokes Jr. c 2. Ord of S Lk. ebhearn@aol.com

HEARN, Roger Daniel (Va) 2201 Foresthill Rd, Alexandria VA 22307 B Washington DC 10/5/1955 s Roger Vernon Hearn & Marie Smith. BS Babson Coll 1978; MDiv VTS 1988. D 6/18/1988 P 5/10/1989 Bp Elliott Lorenz Sorge. m 10/7/1989 Deirdre Anne Sisk. St. Steph's and St. Agnes Sch Alexandria VA 1992-2004; St Steph Sch Alexandria VA 1990-1992; Cur S Fran Ch Potomac MD 1988-1989.

HEATH, Claudia (U) 14655 S Bay Mare Dr, Tucson AZ 85736 **S Mich's Epis Ch Little Rock AR 2001-** B Memphis TN 2/27/1944 d James Albert Heath & Chole Doris. BA U of Arkansas 1966; MS U of Arkansas 1990. D 11/3/2001 Bp Larry Earl Maze. m 2/2/2002 Jack Hollis. Dir Soc Mnstry S Dav's Epis Page AZ 2003-2006.

HEATH, Glendon Edward (Mich) 19751 Northbrook Dr, Southfield MI 48076 B San Jose CA 11/9/1929 s William Edward Heath & Gladys Markham. BD SFTS 1961; BA San Jose St U 1961; Cert GTS 1962. D 9/23/1962 P 4/1/1963 Bp John S Higgins. m 11/10/1984 Barbara S Schueller c 2. S Matt's And S Jos's Detroit MI 1995-1997; S Steph's Ch Troy MI 1990-1991; S Mich And All Ang Epis Ch Lincoln Pk MI 1988-1990; Dio Michigan Detroit MI 1984-1986; S Geo's Epis Ch Warren MI 1982-1983; R Gr Ch Detroit MI 1979-1981; Dio Rhode Island Providence RI 1975-1978; R S Jas Ch The Par Of N Providence RI 1974-1982; R S Mary's Ch Warwick RI 1968-1974; Vic S Mich's Epis Ch Holliston MA 1964-1968; Cur S Mart's Ch Providence RI 1962-1964. ESCRU 1962-1964. aa8764@wayne.edu

HEATH, Susan Blackburn (USC) 1100 Sumter St, Columbia SC 29201 B Birmingham AL 10/2/1956 d Henry Lewis Heath & Gladys Blackburn. BA Randolph-Macon Wmn's Coll 1979; MDiv VTS 1983. D 12/18/1983 P 12/1/1984 Bp William Arthur Beckham. m 11/28/1992 Benjamin R Smith c 1. Cn Trin Cathd Columbia SC 1984-2004; Dir S Mk's Ch Washington DC 1983-1984. heath@trinitysc.org

HEATHCOCK, Deborah Beth (Oly) 2519 Cliffside Lane NW Apt X104, Gig Harbor WA 98335 **P-in-c S Jn's Epis Ch Gig Harbor WA 2010-** B Birmingham AL 5/14/1953 d James Wilson Heathcock & Genevieve. BA w hon U NC at Wilmington 1992; MDiv CDSP 1999. D 6/12/1999 Bp Clifton Daniel III P 6/24/2000 Bp Vincent Waydell Warner. Int Gr S Paul's Epis Ch Tucson AZ 2009-2010; Int S Geo Epis Ch Maple Vlly WA 2009; Cluster P Komo Kulshan Cluster Mt Vernon WA 2007-2008; P-in-c S Andr's Epis Ch Tacoma WA 2005-2007; Cluster P Komo Kulshan Cluster Mt Vernon WA 2003-2005; Assoc R S Jn's Epis Ch Olympia WA 1999-2003. DBHEATHCOCK@GMAIL.COM

HEATHCOCK, J(ohn) Edwin (Mo) 14485 Brittania Dr, Chesterfield MO 63017 B Detroit MI 12/12/1937 s James Richard Heathcock & Laurel Viola. BS Cntrl Michigan U 1966; MDiv Duke 1970; ThM Duke 1971; PhD Intl Coll Los Angeles CA 1980. D 1/18/1984 P 5/1/1984 Bp Sam Byron Hulsey. m 12/12/1978 Elizabeth Ann Porter c 3. S Lk's Hosp Chesterfield MO 1986-2006; Asst P S Andr's Epis Ch Amarillo TX 1984-1986. "A Parallel Process Seminar for Use in CPE," *The Journ of Pstr Care & Counslg*, v58, no 3, 2004; Auth, "Rel Lang & Pstr Care," *Bulletin of APHA 75*. Amer Assn For Mar and Fam Ther 1975; ACPE 1970; Assn of Profsnl Chapl 1971-2006. Who's Who in the Midwest; Who's Who in Rel. porter.heathcock@charter.net

HEBERT, Francis Noel (NJ) 33 Throckmorton St., Freehold NJ 07728 **R S Ptr's Ch Freehold NJ 1995-** B New Milford CT 11/5/1955 s Jean-Serge Jacques Hebert & Frances Loretta. BA Buc 1977; MLS Wesl 1981; MDiv CDSP 1987. D 6/13/1987 P 12/19/1987 Bp Charles Brinkley Morton. m 10/4/1986 Susan B Hebert c 2. Vic H Trin Epis Ch Wenonah NJ 1988-1995; Cur Chr Ch Coronado CA 1987-1988. fnhrector@aol.com

HECK, John Hathaway (SwVa) 65 Rock Ridge Rd, Callaway VA 24067 **Exec Dir Dio SW Virginia Roanoke VA 1998-; R S Ptr's Epis Ch Callaway VA 1998-** B Hamilton OH 3/3/1959 s David Robert Heck & Ann Bishop. BA U So 1981; MDiv VTS 1989. D 1/26/1991 Bp Girault M Jones P 7/25/1991 Bp Robert Poland Atkinson. m 4/26/1997 Delia Rosenblatt Heck c 2. Assoc Chr Ch Of The Ascen Paradise Vlly AZ 1991-1998; Coordntr of Outreach Mnstry The U So (Sewanee) Sewanee TN 1991. johnhheck@gmail.com

HECKEL, Deborah Lee (FdL) Church of the Holy Apostles, 2937 Freedom Rd, Oneida WI 54155 **D Ch Of The H Apos Oneida WI 2005-** B Green Bay, WI 10/26/1950 d Leland Lambert Powless & Leatrice Joyce. NE WI Tech Coll 2001. D 8/27/2005 Bp Russell Edward Jacobus. m 5/19/1984 Charles Heckel c 2. chhdlh@athenet.net

HECOCK, Georgia Ingalis (Minn) St. Luke's Episcopal Church, P.O. Box 868, Detroit Lakes MN 56502 **Loc P S Lk's Ch Detroit Lakes MN 2008-** B Upland CA 9/10/1941 d John Stewart Ingalls & Margaret Mitchell. BA Gri 1964; MA Estrn Michigan U 1968. D 12/8/2007 Bp Daniel Lee Swenson P 9/13/2008 Bp James Louis Jelinek. m 12/23/1967 Richard Douglas Hecock c 2. ghecock@arvig.net

HECTOR JR, John Robert (WMich) 409 High St, Mineral Point WI 53565 **P-in-c Trin Epis Ch Mineral Point WI 2006-** B Berkeley CA 4/23/1943 s John Robert Hector & Elelya Brackett. BA Claremont Men's Coll 1965; ACPE Cov Hosp, Chicago IL 1972; MDiv SWTS 1973; DMin SWTS 2003. D 5/12/1973 Bp Quintin Ebenezer Primo Jr P 12/8/1973 Bp James Winchester Montgomery. m 8/24/1974 Barbara J Ashby c 3. R Gr Epis Ch Of Ludington Michigan Ludington MI 1987-2006; R S Jas' Epis Ch Of Pentwater Pentwater MI 1987-2006; Dio Milwaukee Milwaukee WI 1986; Vic Trin Epis Ch Mineral Point WI 1977-1987; Vic Trin Epis Ch Platteville WI 1977-1986; Cur Trin Epis Ch Peoria IL 1975-1976; Cur S Andr's Ch Downers Grove IL 1972-1974. Rural Mnstrs Ntwk 1980. Silver Beaver G.R.Ford Coun, B.S.A. 2001; Paul Harris Awd Rotary Intl 2001. frbobandbarbara@gmail.com

HEDELSON, Kenneth Calvin (Ia) Po Box 446, Bridgeport NE 69336 B Burke SD 8/29/1923 s Glen Verlaine Hedelson & Esther Ellen. D 3/25/1965 P 9/1/1965 Bp Russell T Rauscher. c 4. P Ch Of S Thos Algona IA 1975-1985; R S Jn's Ch Shenandoah IA 1969-1975; Vic S Geo's Ch Sidney NE 1967-1969; Vic Ch Of The Gd Shpd Bridgeport NE 1965-1969. chedelson@hamilton.net

HEDEN, Eileen May (WK) 540 W Main St, Valley Center KS 67147 B Willits CA 7/21/1941 d Edwin Frank Heden & Alberta Martha. BA California St U 1975; MS California St U 1983; MDiv CDSP 2001. D 6/30/2001 Bp Robert Louis Ladehoff P 1/20/2002 Bp William Edwin Swing. c 1. Vic H Apos Ch Ellsworth KS 2007; Vic S Mk's Ch Lyons KS 2007; Vic S Thos Ch Garden City KS 2006-2007; Pstr Gd Shpd Luth Ch Liberal KS 2004-2007; R S Andr's Epis Ch Liberal KS 2004-2006; Assoc R S Fran Of Assisi Ch Novato CA 2001-2004. eileenheden721@att.net

HEDGER, John Spencer (Me) 524 Lake Louise Cir Apt 501, Naples FL 34110 B Bay Shore NY 8/15/1931 s F Howard Hedger & Nathalie. BA U of Delaware Newark 1955; STB Ya Berk 1958. D 4/25/1958 P 10/31/1958 Bp Gordon V Smith. m 8/28/1954 Islay Sewall. Vic S Fran By The Sea Blue Hill ME 1990-1993; Int S Dunst's Ch Ellsworth ME 1988-1989; Chr Epis Ch Eastport ME 1982-1985; Vic S Aidans Ch Machias ME 1981-1985; R Chr Epis Ch Clinton IA 1968-1975; Vic S Paul's Epis Ch Grinnell IA 1965-1968; Exec Coun Dio Iowa Des Moines IA 1964-1968; Vic S Mart's Ch Perry IA 1962-1965. AAMFT. jnhedger@aol.com

HEDGES, David Thomas (Chi) 222 Somonauk Street, Sycamore IL 60178 **Bp and Trst Dio Chicago Chicago IL 2011-; Bd Dir Cbury Epis Cntr Dekalb IL 2010-; Dioc Coun Dio Chicago Chicago IL 2010-; R S Ptr's Epis Ch Sycamore IL 2009-** B Modesto CA 5/31/1975 s Tom Lloyd Hedges & Ida Susan. BA San Francisco St U 2002; MDiv SWTS 2005. D 6/4/2005 Bp William Edwin Swing P 12/17/2005 Bp William Dailey Persell. P-in-c S Ptr's Epis Ch Sycamore IL 2007-2009; Cur S Mary Epis Ch Crystal Lake IL 2005-2007. houseofhedges@gmail.com

HEDGES, Merry Helen (Ark) 8201 Hood Rd, Roland AR 72135 B Little Rock AR 12/25/1932 d Samuel Leonard Nevins & Ola Van. AA Mt Vernon Jr Coll 1953; BD U of Arkansas 1955; Memphis TS 1990; Epis TS of The SW 1992. D 1/22/1993 Bp Herbert Alcorn Donovan Jr. m 7/23/1955 Harold Herbert Hedges. D Chr Epis Ch Little Rock AR 1998-2003; D Trin Cathd Little Rock AR 1994-1998; D S Mich's Epis Ch Little Rock AR 1993-1994. NAAD. mhhedges@worldnet.att.net

HEDGES, Robert Boyden (NwT) 6324 Pueblo Pass, San Angelo TX 76901 **Pstrl Asst Emm Epis Ch San Angelo TX 1996-** B Farson IA 2/24/1925 s Walter Raleigh Hedges & Rachael. BA Drake U 1951; MDiv GTS 1955. D 6/13/1955 P 12/13/1955 Bp Gordon V Smith. c 4. Int S Paul's Ch Brady TX 1995-1996; Stwdshp Dio NW Texas Lubbock TX 1982-1992; R Epis Ch Of The Gd Shpd San Angelo TX 1982-1992; Dio Iowa Des Moines IA 1971-1981; S Tim's Epis Ch W Des Moines IA 1956-1982; Cur The Cathd Ch Of S Paul Des Moines IA 1955-1958. Hon Cn Trin Cathd Dio IA Davenport IA 1980. frbhedges@aol.com

HEDGPETH, Martha Holton (NC) 1412 Providence Rd, Charlotte NC 28207 **Assoc R Chr Ch Charlotte NC 1996-** B Greensboro NC 1/17/1953 d James Hedgpeth & Martha. BA Smith 1975; MDiv Yale DS 1982. D 6/5/1982 Bp Paul Moore Jr P 2/10/1983 Bp John Bowen Coburn. Trst Ya Berk New Haven CT 1990-1996; R Gr Ch Newington CT 1989-1996; Assoc R S Andr's Ch Wellesley MA 1984-1989; Asst Calv and St Geo New York NY 1982-1984. hedgpethm@christchurchcharlotte.org

HEDLUND, Arnold Melvin (ECR) PO Box 2131, Salinas CA 93902 **P S Paul's Epis Ch Salinas CA 1992-** B Glendale CA 4/23/1936 s John Gunnar Hedlund & Helga Linnea. AA Los Angeles City Coll 1953; BA Bethany Coll 1957;

MDiv Luth TS 1962; MA San Jose St U 1971. D 12/7/1992 P 4/28/1993 Bp Richard Lester Shimpfky. m 8/4/1957 Janet Eidem Hibbard.

HEDMAN, James Edward (SwFla) 9719 33rd Ave E, Palmetto FL 34221 **Vic S Mary Magd Lakewood Ranch FL 2006-** B St Petersburg FL 6/23/1966 BS U of So Florida 1994; MDiv Epis TS of The SW 2004. D 6/12/2004 Bp Rogers Sanders Harris P 12/21/2004 Bp John Bailey Lipscomb. m 7/3/1993 Amanda Hedman c 3. Asst P Ch Of The Redeem Sarasota FL 2004-2006. jhedman@saintmarymagdalene.org

HEDQUIST, Ann Whitney (Kan) 3205 Sw 33rd Ct, Topeka KS 66614 **D S Phil's Epis Ch Topeka KS 1995-** B Kansas City MO 7/20/1938 d John C Ragland & Georganna Six. Cert Bereavement FAC; EFM STUSo 1990; BA Washburn U 1990. D 5/17/1995 Bp William Edward Smalley. m 1/30/1959 Glenn L Hedquist c 2. Dio Kansas Topeka KS 1981-1996. Ord of S Lk. hedquist1@aol.com

HEERS, Theodore Alfred (Tex) 2754 S Chilton Ave, Tyler TX 75701 B Hornell NY 7/30/1927 s Erwin Heers & Helen Louise. BA U NC 1952; GD STUSo 1958. D 6/18/1958 P 12/1/1958 Bp J(ohn) Joseph Meakins Harte. R S Paul's Ch Kilgore TX 1987-1989; R Trin Ch Marshall TX 1984-1987; Vic S Jn's Epis Ch Carthage TX 1983-1984; R S Thos Ch Wharton TX 1981-1983; R S Andr's Ch Breckenridge TX 1978-1981; Vic S Wm Laud Epis Ch Pittsburg TX 1970-1978; R S Thos Ch Ennis TX 1967-1969; Vic S Wm Laud Epis Ch Pittsburg TX 1962-1967; Cur S Jas Epis Ch Texarkana TX 1958-1962; Vic All SS Ch Atlanta TX 1958-1961. Auth, "How I Overcame My Pride And Became Humble," Self-Pub.

HEETER, Ned J (CPa) 606 Park Hills Dr, Mechanicsburg PA 17055 B Mishawaka IN 5/11/1931 s Delacy J Heeter & Anne Barbara. BA U of Maryland 1957; MDiv Ya Berk 1960. D 6/18/1960 P 12/16/1960 Bp Angus Dun. m 11/3/2011 Barbara Heeter c 3. R S Lk's Epis Ch Mechanicsburg PA 1976-1985; R S Paul's Ch Columbia PA 1966-1976; R S Matt's Epis Ch Sunbury PA 1963-1966. nedheeter@hotmail.com

HEFFNER, John Howard (Be) 119 E Chestnut St, Cleona PA 17042 **D S Jas Ch Schuylkill Haven PA 2001-** B Lebanon PA 1/13/1947 s W Howard Heffner & Marian F. BS Lebanon Vlly Coll 1968; MA Bos 1971; PhD Bos 1976; BA Lebanon Vlly Coll 1987; DAS GTS 2001; MA Lancaster TS 2002. D 10/23/2001 P 10/6/2002 Bp Paul Victor Marshall. c 2. j.h.heffner@comcast.net

HEFFNER, Meredith Tobin (Va) 6744 S Kings Hwy, Alexandria VA 22306 **Assoc R S Mk's Ch Alexandria VA 2008-** B Bermuda 2/15/1963 d Byron Eugene Tobin & Sarah McCollough. BA Smith 1985; MDiv The Prot Epis TS 2008. D 5/24/2008 P 12/14/2008 Bp Peter James Lee. m 9/13/1987 Douglas Heffner c 3. mheffner3@cox.net

HEFFRON, Judith Ann Williams (Los) 4959 Ridgeview St, La Verne CA 91750 **R H Trin Epis Ch Covina CA 1995-** B Burbank CA 9/26/1941 d Sherrell F Williams & Jeanne Elizabeth. BA Westmont Coll 1963; California St U 1968; MDiv Fuller TS 1989. D 6/10/1989 P 1/13/1990 Bp Frederick Houk Borsch. c 1. Int H Trin Epis Ch Covina CA 1993-1994; Assoc S Geo's Par La Can CA 1992-1993; Asst S Cross By-The-Sea Ch Hermosa Bch CA 1990-1992; Asst To P-in-c S Lk's Par Monrovia CA 1989-1990; Dir S Mk's Par Glendale CA 1981-1987. motherjudy@aol.com

HEFLIN, Timothy Royce (La) 3552 Morning Glory Ave, Baton Rouge LA 70808 **Assoc R Trin Epis Ch Baton Rouge LA 2008-** B Jackson MS 11/5/1968 s Barney Royce Heflin & Marjorie Ann. BA Mississippi Coll 1991; MDiv PrTS 1994; Angl Stds Nash 2008. D 5/31/2008 Bp Charles Edward Jenkins III P 12/6/2008 Bp Michael Gene Smith. m 6/4/2011 Alexis Heflin. tim@trinitybr.org

HEFLING JR, Charles (Mass) 1619 Massachusetts Ave, Cambridge MA 02138 B Dennison OH 3/6/1949 s Charles Clifford Hefling & Martha Jane. BA Harv 1971; BD Harvard DS 1974; ThD Harvard DS 1981; PhD Boston Coll 1982. D 6/8/1974 Bp John Melville Burgess P 12/8/1974 Bp Morris Fairchild Arnold. Assoc Trin Ch Topsfield MA 1976-1977; Cur S Steph's Memi Ch Lynn MA 1974-1976. Ed, "Oxford Guide to BCP," Oxf Press, 2006; Ed, "Sic Et Non: Encountering 'Dominus Iesus,'" Orbis Press, 2002; Auth, "Why Doctrines?," Boston Coll, 2000; Ed, "Our Selves Our Souls & Bodies: Sxlty & Household Of God," Cowley Press, 1996. AAR; Amer Theol Soc; Fllshp S Jn; Soc Of Angl & Luth Theologians. Grad Fllshp ECF 1978. hefling@bc.edu

HEFLING, David (Roch) 28 Perry Pl, Canandaigua NY 14424 **S Jn's Ch Canandaigua NY 2010-** B Erie PA 3/26/1955 s Charles Clifford Hefling & Martha Jane. BS Kent St U 1980; MA U Of Akron 1986; EdS Kent St U 1998; MDiv SWTS 2003. D 6/14/2003 P 1/6/2004 Bp J Clark Grew II. m 2/14/2006 Michael Dudley. R The Par Of S Chrys's Quincy MA 2006-2010; S Andr's Ch Akron OH 2005; S Phil's Epis Ch Akron OH 2004-2005; D, P Assoc New Life Epis Ch Uniontown OH 2003-2004. St Julian of Norwich (Oblate) 1994. thathouseakron@aol.com

HEFNER, Judy (WNY) 1307 Ransom Rd, Grand Island NY 14072 **Dio Wstrn New York Tonawanda NY 2002-; Vic S Matt's Ch Buffalo NY 1999-** B Buffalo NY 3/12/1947 d Francis Clarence Hefner & Mary Rix. BA SUNY 1969; MS U of Maryland 1971; MDiv VTS 1996. D 6/8/1996 P 9/6/1997 Bp David Charles Bowman. Dio Cntrl New York Syracuse NY 1997. DOK.

HEFTI, William Joseph (NCal) 24300 Green Valley Rd, Auburn CA 95602 B Minneapolis MN 10/24/1942 s Joseph Hefti & Dolores. AS Rca Inst Of Tech 1970. D 4/13/1985 Bp George Phelps Mellick Belshaw. m 5/30/1970 Linda Joan Holland c 2. heftibl@foothill.net

HEGEDUS, Frank Michael (Los) 318 W Robinson Ave Apt 17, San Diego CA 92103 B Muskegon MI 1/29/1948 s Frank Michael Hegedus & Jennie Frances. BA S Louis U 1971; Vordiplom Theol. U of Munich 1973; MA MI SU 1976; DMin CRDS 1980; MBA U of S Thos S Paul MN 1984. Rec from Roman Catholic 2/1/1987 as Priest Bp Robert Marshall Anderson. The Epis Ch In Almaden San Jose CA 2009-2010; Sts Ptr And Paul Epis Ch El Centro CA 2009; Int S Ptr's Epis Ch Del Mar CA 2008-2009; S Alb's Epis Ch El Cajon CA 2005-2007; S Jn's Ch Plymouth MI 2004-2005; Int Trin Epis Ch Redlands CA 2002-2003; Asstg P S Wilfrid Of York Epis Ch Huntington Bch CA 2001-2002; P-in-c S Fran Mssn Norwalk CA 1998-1999; Asstg P Trin Epis Ch Orange CA 1997-1998; Adv Ch Farmington MN 1988-1996; Int Ch Of The H Cross Dundas MN 1988-1990; Int All SS Ch Northfield MN 1988-1989; S Paul's On-The-Hill Epis Ch St Paul MN 1987-1988. Writer, "Multiple Sermons," *Sermons That Wk*, Epis Ch, 2009; Reviewer, "Bk Revs," *LivCh*, LivCh Fndt, 2008; Writer, "One Prchr's Modest Proposal," *Sunday Stwdshp Insert*, The Ecum Stwdshp Cntr, 2006; Reviewer, "Bk Revs," *LivCh*, LivCh Fndt, 2005; Writer, "Stwdshp During Transition," *ReVisions*, Int Mnstry Ntwk, 2004; Presenter, "The Ret Pstr: An Issue in Int Mnstry," *Annual Conf*, Int Mnstry Ntwk, 2003; Auth, "Coping w Chronic Pain," *Coping w Chronic Pain*, Sis Kenny Inst, 1984; Auth, "Beginning Experience Manual," *Beginning Experience Manual*, Beginning Experience Prog, 1980. Cert Employee Assistance Profsnl 2002; Profsnl Transition Spec 2005; Profsnl in HR 2002. frankhegedus@hotmail.com

HEGG, Camille Sessions (At) 753 College St, Macon GA 31201 B Anniston AL 6/3/1945 d Lewe Sessions & Diana Leone. BA Auburn U 1967; MDiv Candler TS Emory U 1978. D 6/10/1978 Bp Charles Judson Child Jr P 6/1/1979 Bp Bennett Jones Sims. S Paul's Ch Macon GA 2004-2010; R The Ch Of The Redeem MOBILE AL 1996-2004; S Jas Epis Ch Marietta GA 1980-1996; S Dunst's Epis Ch Atlanta GA 1979-1980. Auth, "Wmn Of The Word". Netwk Of Biblic Storytellers; Sthrn Ord Of Storytellers. camillehegg@windstream.net

HEGLUND, Janice N (Cal) 84 San Gabriel Dr, Fairfax CA 94930 **D Chr Ch Sausalito CA 2006-** B Portland OR 5/23/1936 d Robert Eugene Ruedy & Thelma Maxine. OR SU 1957; BA Sch for Deacons 1994. D 6/4/1994 Bp William Edwin Swing. m 1/20/1978 Richard Lee Heglund c 3. D Ch Of Our Sav Mill Vlly CA 1994-2005; Diac Field Ed Ch Of The Nativ San Rafael CA 1992-1994; Sr Wrdn St Johns Epis Ch Ross CA 1980-1992. Auth, "Helping First Responders Withstand Traumatic Experiences," *FBI Law Enforcement Bulletin*, U.S. Dept. of Justice, 2009; InterviewedAuthor, "Cops Best Friend," *Marin Indep Journ*, Marin Indep Journ, 2008; Interviewed, "Jan Heglund Story: Police Chapl," *Wmn in Ldrshp inm Faith*, Roberta Swan, 2003; Auth, "Marin Police Chapl's Time at Ground Zero," *Marin Indep Journ*, Marin IJ, 2002; Auth, "I am a D and Police Chapl," *Mod Profiles of an Ancient Faith*, Epis Dio Calif., 2001; Auth, "What You Do And Think Does Matter," *Marin Indep Journ*, Marin IJ, 1999; Auth, "She Takes Pryr on Patrol," *Marin Indep Journ*, Marin IJ, 1998. Critical Incident Stress Mgmt 1995; Intl Conf of Police Chapl 1995; Marin Cnty Chapl Assn 1995; Marin THETA Alum 2011; Narin Soroptimist 2011; NAAD 1995; W Coast Post Trauma Retreat 2001. Cler of the Year NAMI 2010; Making A Difference for Wmn Awd Soroptimist Intl 2008; Sr Level Rating Intl Conf of Police Chapl 2006. decjanheg@aol.com

HEGNEY, Georgina (CNY) 210 Twin Hills Dr, Syracuse NY 13207 **Intake Off Dio Cntrl New York Syracuse NY 2011-; GC Dep Dio Cntrl New York Syracuse NY 2010-; Fresh Start Fac Dio Cntrl New York Syracuse NY 2009-; Dioc Conv Resolutns Com Dio Cntrl New York Syracuse NY 2008-; COM Mem Dio Cntrl New York Syracuse NY 2007-; R S Jn's Ch Marcellus NY 2007-** B New York NY 6/25/1951 d George Joseph Hegney & Phyllis Eileen. BS SUNY 1973; MDiv Bex 2007. D 6/9/2007 P 12/13/2007 Bp Gladstone Bailey Adams III. c 2. georgina.hegney@gmail.com

HEHR, Randall Keith (SwFla) 906 S Orleans Ave, Tampa FL 33606 **Congrl Dvlpmt Com Dio SW Florida Sarasota FL 2011-; Vic St Johns Epis Ch Tampa FL 2002-** B Saint Petersburg FL 3/16/1952 s Gordon Lee Hehr & Mae. BM Indiana U 1976; MA/MAR Ya Berk 1980. D 6/14/1986 P 5/30/1987 Bp Arthur Edward Walmsley. m 7/30/1977 Pamela J Rogers c 2. Dn of Tampa Dnry Dio SW Florida Sarasota FL 2008-2011; Dn Cathd Ch Of S Ptr St Petersburg FL 1998-2002; R Ch Of The Gd Shpd Dunedin FL 1991-1998; Evang Com Dio SW Florida Sarasota FL 1989-1995; Asst R Ch Of The Ascen Clearwater FL 1988-1991; Asst R S Mk's Ch New Canaan CT 1986-1988; Org/Chrmstr & Asst To The R S Matt's Epis Ch Wilton CT 1978-1986; Asst Org/Chrmstr Cathd Ch Of S Ptr St Petersburg FL 1970-1973. rhehr@stjohnstampa.org

HEICHLER, Katherine (Ct) 1689 Litchfield Tpke # 1, Woodbridge CT 06525 **P-in-c Epis Ch of Chr the Healer Stamford CT 2007-** B 7/6/1958 BFA

NYU. D 6/21/2003 P 2/7/2004 Bp Andrew Donnan Smith. Cur Chr Ch Bethany CT 2003-2007. kateheichler@gmail.com

HEIDECKER, Eric Vaughn (Nev) 14645 Rim Rock Dr, Reno NV 89521 **Navajoland Area Mssn Farmington NM 2010-** B Erie PA 9/18/1957 s Jack Bruce Heidecker & Dorothy V. BA Geneva Coll 1979; MDiv CDSP 1987. D 10/16/1988 P 5/13/1989 Bp Stewart Clark Zabriskie. Dio Nevada Las Vegas NV 1988-2003.

HEIDEL, Harrison (Colo) Calvary Episcopal Church, PO Box 57, Underhill VT 05489 **R S Barn Ch Glenwood Sprg CO 2009-** B St Louis MO 5/12/1951 s Raymond William Harrison Heidel & Orienjo. BSN Lunchburg Coll 1991; MSN Old Dominion U 1995; MDiv EDS 2003; MDiv EDS 2003. Trans from Anglican Church of Canada 2/13/2008 Bp Thomas C Ely. m 5/26/2001 Marcie L Nichols c 2. R Calv Ch Underhill VT 2007-2009; Coop Chr Mnstry Burlington VT 2007-2009. Columnist (Bi-weekly), "The View From The Cntr," *Mtn Gazette*, Brenda Bountin, Mtn Gazette. SSJE 2003. fr.heidel@gmail.com

HEIDT, James Kevin (CNY) St John's Church, 341 Main St, Oneida NY 13421 **S Jn's Epis Ch Oneida NY 2009-** B Suffern NY 4/17/1953 s Herbert Heidt & Dorothy M. BA SUNY 1975; JD Ohio Nthrn U Ada OH 1978. D 7/9/2007 P 12/15/2007 Bp Gladstone Bailey Adams III. m 1/23/1995 Suzanne Heidt c 2. D Gr Ch Utica NY 2007-2010. jimheidt@hotmail.com

HEIDT, John H (FtW) 204 N Rosemont Ave, Dallas TX 75208 **Died 10/23/2009** B Madison,WI 4/5/1932 s Homer George Heidt & Lillian Francis. ABS Ya 1954; MDiv Nash 1957; MLitt Oxf 1967; PhD Oxf 1975; DD Nash 2009. D 12/1/1956 P 6/2/1957 Bp Donald H V Hallock. c 5. 2004; "A Faith For Skeptics," Amer Chrisian Writers & Gracewing, 2004; Auth, "Henry Scott Holland," *New Dictionary of Natl Biography*, Oxford Press, 2004; Auth, "Brian Jones of the Rolling Stones," *LivCh*, LivCh Fndt, 2001; Auth, "The King of Terrors," *Contemporary Revs*, Conteemporary Revs, 2000; Auth, "Cn Law in the Angl Tradition," *Foundations*, Forw in Faith, 1999; Auth, "Believe It or Not," Gracewing, 1994. Benedictine Oblate 1993; Conf of Blessed Sacr 1947; Forw in Faith No Amer 1996; Friends of Our Lady of Walsingham 2005. Cn Theol Dio Ft Worth 2003. fjheidt8914@sbcglobal.net

HEIGHAM JR, Llewellyn Maitland (Mo) 1801 Lasalle St, Saint Louis MO 63104 B Washington DC 9/9/1933 s Llewellyn Maitland Heigham & Naomi Medora. BA U of Maryland 1956; MDiv S Paul TS 1963; STM Drew U 1968; ThM PrTS 1971; DMin STUSo 1983. D 6/24/1974 P 12/1/1974 Bp Arthur Anton Vogel. m 6/12/1961 Ella Jean Dixon c 3. Dio Missouri S Louis MO 1995-1998; Gr Ch Kirkwood MO 1986-1999; S Barn Ch Moberly MO 1980-1986; P-in-c S Mich's Epis Ch Independence MO 1979-1980; Asst Ch Of The Resurr Blue Sprg MO 1974-1979. Lichtenberger Soc. Distinguished Grad Awd St Paul TS 1986. eheigham@sbcglobal.net

HEILIGMAN, Sara (Sally) (CNY) 187 Brookside Ave., Amsterdam NY 12010 B Muskogee OK 12/21/1943 d Robert James Martin & Dorothy Roy. BA The Coll of S Rose 1965; MDiv Bex 1999. D 6/5/1999 Bp William George Burrill P 6/24/2000 Bp Jack Marston McKelvey. m 2/6/1982 Edmund Heiligman c 3. Dio Cntrl New York Syracuse NY 2005-2007; R Gr Ch Cortland NY 2004-2009; R S Jas Ch Pulaski NY 2001-2004; Asst Chr Epis Ch Hornell NY 1999-2004; Asst S Ptr's Ch Dansville NY 1999-2004; Dio Rochester Rochester NY 1999-2001; Epis Tri-Par Mnstry Dansville NY 1999-2001. revsally@nycap.rr.com

HEIN, Charles Gregory (CGC) 533 Woodleaf Ct, Saint Louis MO 63122 **S Jude's Epis Ch Niceville FL 2006-** B Huntington WV 10/27/1955 s Charles H Hein & Mary E. BA Marshall U 1977; MDiv STUSo 1982. D 6/2/1982 P 6/1/1983 Bp Robert Poland Atkinson. c 3. Gr Ch Kirkwood MO 2000-2006; Beckwith C&C Fairhope AL 1996-2000; R S Ptr's Epis Ch Bon Secour AL 1992-1996; H Cross Stateburg Stateburg SC 1984-1992; Asst S Steph's Epis Ch Beckley WV 1982-1984. ghein626@aol.com

HEIN, Charles L (Md) Fountain View, 3200 Baker Circle, Adamstown MD 21710 **Died 6/6/2010** B Glen Burnie MD 7/19/1921 s Ernest Henry Hein & Louise Irene. BA U of Maryland 1942; BD VTS 1944. D 6/16/1944 P 7/20/1945 Bp Noble C Powell. c 3.

HEIN, Stephen Daniel (Md) 29 York Ct, Baltimore MD 21218 **Died 3/11/2010** B Baltimore MD 10/2/1954 s Charles L Hein & Ruth. BS Towson U 1975; MDiv VTS 1980; MS U of Maryland 2000. D 10/11/1980 Bp David Keller Leighton Sr P 5/11/1981 Bp Albert Wiencke Van Duzer.

HEINE JR, AJ (La) 5837 S Robertson St, New Orleans LA 70115 **R S Augustines Ch Metairie LA 2006-** B New Orleans LA 5/27/1964 s William August Jude Heine & Linda Ann. BA Rhodes Coll 1986; MDiv SWTS 2003. D 12/28/2002 P 7/5/2003 Bp Charles Edward Jenkins III. m 10/3/1987 Holly H Hubbard c 2. Assoc R S Jas Epis Ch Baton Rouge LA 2003-2006. ajheine@bellsouth.net

HEINE, Mary Anne Rose (La) 15249 Brandon Dr, Ponchatoula LA 70454 **P-in-c S Paul's Ch Woodville MS 2009-** B New Orleans LA 6/17/1946 d Harold Joseph Heine & Althea Delia. Mallinckrodt Coll 1964; BA U Of Dallas Irving 1972; MRE Notre Dame Sem 1977; MDiv VTS 1992; DMin SWTS 2005. D 6/13/1992 P 2/2/1993 Bp Charles Farmer Duvall. P-in-c S Mich's Ch Baton Rouge LA 2003-2004; R Par Of The Medtr-Redeem McComb MS 2000-2002; Asst R S Ptr's By The Lake Brandon MS 1998-2000; S Jn's Epis Ch Bainbridge GA 1994-1998; S Paul's Epis Ch Daphne AL 1992-1994. Auth, "Var Serv - Pstr Liturg Aids," 1984; Auth, "Var Pieces On Chld'S Liturg," 1977; Auth, "Var Pieces On Chld'S Liturg," 1974. revmah@bellsouth.net

HEINEMANN, Ann E (Ga) 1447 US Highway 19 S #27A, Leesburg GA 31763 **S Fran Ch Camilla GA 2010-** B Albany GA 3/31/1945 d Charles Henry Heinemann & Eloise. Dplma All SS' Epis Sch 1963; BS Valdosta St U 1968; MEd Georgia St U 1976; MDiv TESM 1983. D 6/2/1984 P 1/8/1985 Bp Alden Moinet Hathaway. Int The Epis Ch Of S Jn And S Mk Albany GA 2008-2009; Int Calv Ch Americus GA 2006-2007; R S Steph's Epis Ch Indianola MS 1997-2005; Asst S Thad Epis Ch Aiken SC 1989-1996; Vic S Mk Pittsburgh PA 1986-1988; Dio Pittsburgh Monroeville PA 1984-1986. AnnEH45@bellsouth.net

HEINRICH, Judith Capstaff (Chi) 853 Oak Hill Rd, Barrington IL 60010 **D S Mich's Ch Barrington IL 2003-** B Van Nuys CA 4/19/1939 d Albert Capstaff & Genevieve. D 2/1/2003 Bp William Dailey Persell. m 4/25/1958 William Heinrich c 3. pepjch@aol.com

HEISCHMAN, Daniel R (Ct) 20 Park Ave, #9A, New York NY 10016 **VTS Alexandria VA 2010-; Natl Assoc Of Epis Schools- Epis Ch New York NY 2007-** B Columbus OH 5/1/1951 s Robert Paul Heischman & Mary Jane. BA Coll of Wooster 1973; BA U of Cambridge 1975; STM Yale DS 1976; MA U of Cambridge 1979; DMin PrTS 1987. D 5/29/1976 P 11/30/1976 Bp John Mc Gill Krumm. Chapl Trin Chap Hartford CT 2003-2007; Cathd of St Ptr & St Paul Washington DC 1994-2003; Asst S Alb's Par Washington DC 1994-2003; Ch Of The Incarn New York NY 1986-1987; S Ann And The H Trin Brooklyn NY 1982-1984; Chr's Ch Rye NY 1980-1981; Trin Preschool New York NY 1979-1987; S Paul's Ch Englewood NJ 1976-1979. "Gd Influence," *Tchg the Wisdom of Adulthood*, Ch Pub, 2009. NAES, Bd Directorss, 1994-2000; Rea Treas 1992-1996. Phi Beta Kappa. drh@spiscopalschools.org

HEISTAND JONES, Virginia (Va) 6401 John Tyler Memorial Hwy, Charles City VA 23030 **R Westover Epis Ch Chas City VA 2000-** B Richmond VA 3/12/1962 d Joseph Thomas Heistand & Roberta. BA U of Arizona 1983; MDiv VTS 1991. D 6/15/1991 P 12/18/1991 Bp Joseph Thomas Heistand. m 2/14/1995 Stevens Meredith Jones c 3. Chr Ascen Ch Richmond VA 1996-1997; All SS Ch Richmond VA 1993-1996; Asst Ch Of The Gd Shpd Corpus Christi TX 1991-1993.

HEKEL, Ulis Dean (Mil) 7017 Colony Dr, Madison WI 53717 B Rowley IA 5/30/1938 s Raymond Julius Hekel & Hazel Marian. USNA 1959; BS, EE Pur 1964; MS, EE Pur 1964; U of Hawaii 1972; U of Wisconsin 1991; MDiv SWTS 1993; Advncd CPE 1994. D 4/17/1993 P 5/24/1994 Bp Roger John White. m 11/3/1977 Barbara Ruth English Hekel c 2. Vic Ch Of The Gd Shpd Sun Prairie WI 1999-2004; R S Jn The Div Epis Ch Burlington WI 1994-1998; Chr Ch Epis Madison WI 1993. Auth/Ed, *Natl Emergency Procedures & Mltry Cmncatn& Navigational Procedures*, 1978. uhekel@aol.com

HELFERTY, Scott Hanson (Mass) 57 Hillside Ave, Salt Lake City UT 84103 B Minneapolis MN 7/16/1947 s John Kenneth Helferty & Iryne Hazel. BA S Olaf Coll 1969; MDiv GTS 1973; Westcott Hse Cambridge 1989; Harvard DS/EDS 2000. D 6/2/1973 Bp Hanford Langdon King Jr P 12/8/1973 Bp James Winchester Montgomery. Int S Mary's Ch Provo UT 2004-2006; R Gr Ch New Bedford MA 1994-2003; R S Ptr And Paul Epis Ch Portland OR 1984-1994; Dioc Coun Dio Oregon Portland OR 1981-1984; Chair Radio-TV Com Dio Oregon Portland OR 1980-1982; Sr Asst Trin Epis Cathd Portland OR 1979-1984; Asst R S Chrys's Ch Chicago IL 1976-1979; Cur Ch Of The Ascen Chicago IL 1973-1976. Consulting Ed, "Early Chrsnty," *Calliope*, 2003. SHHelferty@aol.com

HELGESON, Gail M (Oly) PO Box 88550, Lakewood WA 98388 B Albany CA 11/2/1949 d Willis Edmund Pigman & Dorothy Mae. BA U CA 1973; VTS 1983; MDiv Ya Berk 1987. D 6/13/1987 Bp Charles Brinkley Morton P 4/1/1988 Bp David Keller Leighton Sr. m 6/19/1971 Marc Helgeson c 2. S Jos And S Jn Ch Steilacoom WA 2006-2010; Dio Olympia Seattle WA 2004-2005; S Paul's Epis Ch Port Townsend WA 1998-2004; Assoc R S Andr's Ch Jacksonville FL 1994-1996; Assoc R Trin Ch Newport RI 1991-1992; S Ptr's By The Sea Narragansett RI 1991; P-in-c Ch Of The H Trin Tiverton RI 1989-1991; D S Andr's Ch Burke VA 1987-1988. gailmph@aol.com

HELLER, Amy Groves (Dal) 6119 Black Berry Ln, Dallas TX 75248 **Assoc R The Epis Ch Of The Trsfg Dallas TX 2011-; Fac, Stanton Cntr for Mnstry Dio Dallas Dallas TX 2008-** B Roanoke VA 8/24/1967 BA Colg 1989; Cert Ya Berk 1994; MDiv Yale DS 1994. D 1/31/2004 P 10/10/2004 Bp James Monte Stanton. m 11/20/1993 Roy Heller c 2. Mem, Nomin Com Dio Dallas Dallas TX 2006; Chapl to the Sch The Par Epis Sch Dallas TX 2005-2011; Assoc R For Adult Educ S Mich And All Ang Ch Dallas TX 2004-2005. aheller@transfiguration.net

HELLER, Jan (Oly) 1663 Bungalow Way NE, Poulsbo WA 98370 B Altoona PA 9/5/1954 s George Louis Heller & Helen Elizabeth. AB The King's Coll 1977; MDiv PrTS 1981; CAS SWTS 1982; PhD Emory U 1995. D 6/5/1982 P 12/11/1982 Bp Charlie Fuller McNutt Jr. m 6/7/1980 Linda Sue Shaffer c 1.

Asst S Barn Epis Ch Bainbridge Island WA 1998-2010; S Anne's Epis Ch Atlanta GA 1993-1999; R S Paul's Ch Manheim PA 1985-1988; Cn Cathd Ch Of S Steph Harrisburg PA 1984-1985; Int S Mk's Epis Ch Lewistown PA 1983-1984; Dio Cntrl Pennsylvania Harrisburg PA 1982-1983. Ed, "Guide to Profsnl Dvlpmt in Compliance," Aspen Pub Inc., 2001; Auth, "Faithful Living, Faithful Dying," Morehouse Pub, 2000; Ed, "Contingent Future Persons," Kluwer Acad Pub, 1997; Auth, "Human Genome Resrch and the Challenge of Contingent Future Persons," Creighton U Press, 1996. jan.c.heller@gmail.com

HELLER, Richard Charles (WVa) 266 Paw Paw Ln, Saint Marys WV 26170 **P-in-c Chr Meml Ch Williamstown WV 2010-; P-in-c Gr Ch S Marys WV 2010-; P-in-c S Ann's Ch New Martinsville WV 2010-** B Akron OH 10/4/1948 s Newton David Heller & Mary Mildred. BA Mar 1975; MA Wheeling Jesuit U 1996; MDiv Bex 2003. D 10/26/2002 P 6/21/2003 Bp Herbert Thompson Jr. m 4/5/1986 Lisa Ann Davis c 2. Ohio Vlly Epis Cluster Williamstown WV 2003-2008. rcheller@frontiernet.net

HELLMAN, Gary Lee (NY) 224 W 11th St Apt 2, New York NY 10014 B Miami FL 2/19/1944 s Stewart Walton Hellman & Gussie Lee. BA U of Texas 1967; MDiv GTS 1973; Cert Blanton-Peale Grad Inst 1978. D 6/10/1973 Bp A Donald Davies P 12/1/1973 Bp Paul Moore Jr. m 6/28/1966 Rebecca Benett c 1. Asst S Jn's Ch New York NY 1976-1978. AAPC. ghellman@idt.net

HELMER, Ben Edward (Ark) 28 Prospect Ave, Eureka Springs AR 72632 **S Jas Ch Eureka Sprg AR 2009-** B SanduskyOH 12/4/1947 s Ben F Helmer & Marian L. BA MI SU 1969; MDiv GTS 1973. D 3/19/1973 P 9/21/1973 Bp Samuel Joseph Wylie. m 6/9/1973 Margaret Jane Coleman c 2. Epis Ch Cntr New York NY 1999-2005; Cn Mssnr Chr Ch Epis Boonville MO 1993-1999; Cn Mssnr Chr Ch Lexington MO 1993-1999; NE Reg Mnstry Lexington MO 1993-1999; Cn Mssnr S Mary's Ch Fayette MO 1993-1999; Cn Mssnr S Phil's Ch Trenton MO 1993-1999; Cn Mssnr Trin Epis Ch Marshall MO 1993-1999; Epis Ch Of The Incarn Salina KS 1989-1991; New Directions For Ch In Sm Communities Cape Coral FL 1987-1989; Vic S Anne's Ch McPherson KS 1982-1993; Vic Epis Ch Of The Incarn Salina KS 1982-1986; Ascen-On-The-Prairie Epis Ch Colby KS 1981; Dio Wstrn Kansas Hutchinson KS 1980-1993; R S Paul's Epis Ch Goodland KS 1975-1981; P-in-c Gr Epis Ch Menominee MI 1973-1975. "When the Environ Changes, Ch Changes," *not dertmined*, CPG, March, 2009. bhelmer1247@msn.com

HELMER, Richard Edward (Cal) 58 Corte Madera Avenue, Apt. 5, Mill Valley CA 94941 **R Ch Of Our Sav Mill Vlly CA 2006-** B Marinette WI 7/21/1974 s Ben Edward Helmer & Margaret Jane. Bradley U 1994; BMus U NC 1997; NWU 1998; MDiv CDSP 2002. D 6/8/2002 Bp Barry Robert Howe P 12/7/2002 Bp William Edwin Swing. m 6/18/2000 Hiroko Fujita c 2. Vic Chr Epis Ch Sei Ko Kai San Francisco CA 2002-2006. OHC - Assoc 2000. Knights Templar Mnstry Schlrshp Knights Templar California 2001; Excellence in Mnstry Schlrshp CDSP Berkeley California 1999. richard@helmerhome.com

HELMS III, David Clarke (SO) No address on file. B Wilmington DE 2/13/1950 s David C Helms & Jeane Mary. BA Bos 1972; MDiv Yale DS 1977. D 6/18/1977 Bp William Hawley Clark P 12/18/1977 Bp John S Higgins. m 5/30/1981 Pamela Pailes Helms. All SS Ch Cincinnati OH 1986-1988; Dio Delaware Wilmington DE 1983-1986; S Lk's Epis Ch E Greenwich RI 1979-1980; Chr Ch Westerly RI 1977-1978. dch3uk@gmail.com

HELSEL, Verle Eugene (Spok) 23024 102nd Pl W, Edmonds WA 98020 B Carmen OK 11/27/1932 s Herbert Harold Helsel & Florain Sylvia. Cntrl Jr Coll 1953; BS Seattle Pacific Coll 1955; Bp Huston TS 1968; MA Antioch U 1997. D 10/5/1968 Bp Ivol I Curtis. m 12/17/1954 Ingrid Ann Berdahl. D S Alb's Ch Edmonds WA 1992-1998; Asst Cur S Lk's Epis Ch Wenatchee WA 1975-1979; Asst Cur S Lk's Epis Ch Seattle WA 1970-1975; Asst Cur Chr Ch SEATTLE WA 1968-1970.

HELT, Dwight Neil (Okla) 720 Miller Ave, Norman OK 73069 **Stndg Com Dio Oklahoma Oklahoma City OK 2010-; R S Jn's Ch Norman OK 2003-** B Oklahoma City OK 10/4/1953 s Bobby Joe Helt & Lovene Ann. BA Oklahoma St U 1975; MS Oklahoma St U 1983; MDiv Epis TS of The SW 1988. D 6/18/1988 Bp Gerald Nicholas McAllister P 4/22/1989 Bp Robert Manning Moody. m 5/17/1975 Mary Martha Ostrander c 2. Stndg Com Dio Oklahoma Oklahoma City OK 2010; Dep to GC Dio Oklahoma Oklahoma City OK 2002-2010; R All SS' Epis Ch Duncan OK 1992-2003; S Steph's Epis Sch Austin TX 1989-1992; Cur S Jn's Epis Ch Tulsa OK 1988-1989. dhelt@episcopalnorman.org

HEMENWAY, Augustus Lawrence (RI) 175 Lloyd Ave, Providence RI 02906 B Boston MA 9/8/1922 s Lawrence Hemenway & Natalie. BA McGill U 1949; BD CDSP 1952. D 8/9/1952 Bp Karl M Block P 1/1/1953 Bp Henry H Shires. m 10/20/1946 Edith Fitz c 4. Serv Ch Of The Epiph Providence RI 1981-2000; Assoc S Jn's Ch Savannah GA 1978-1981; Dio Rhode Island Providence RI 1972-1978; Chr Ch In Lonsdale Lincoln RI 1961-1978; Chr Ch Providence RI 1961-1978; Iglesia Epis Del Buen Samaritano San Francisco CA 1954-1959; Asst S Paul's Epis Ch Burlingame CA 1952-1954.

HEMENWAY, Henry Jack (Me) Po Box 122, Stonington ME 04681 B Clarence NY 12/10/1926 s Frank Allen Hemenway & Amalia Christina. BA Colg 1950; BD Yale DS 1956. D 6/24/1965 P 10/1/1965 Bp Harvey D Butterfield. m 7/23/1970 Harriet Corning Rawle. Asst Cathd Ch Of S Paul Burlington VT 1965-1968.

HEMINGSON, Celeste A (NH) 340 Main St # 3229, Hopkinton NH 03229 **S Andr's Ch New London NH 2011-** B Chicago IL 2/11/1942 BA Smith 1963; M. Div. EDS 2002. D 7/27/2003 Bp Douglas Edwin Theuner P 2/7/2004 Bp V Gene Robinson. S Mk's Ch Ashland NH 2009-2011; Int S Paul's Ch Concord NH 2007-2009; Cur S Thos Ch Hanover NH 2003-2006. celeste340@aol.com

HEMINGWAY, George Thomson (Ore) PO Box 192, Nehalem OR 97131 **P S Cathr Of Alexandria Epis Ch Manzanita OR 2006-** B Corvallis OR 8/23/1940 s George Danforth Hemingway & Margaret Roberta. BS San Diego St U 1966; MS San Diego St U 1973; DIT ETSBH 1983; DMIN Geo Fox Evang Sem 2005. D 7/16/1984 P 3/25/1985 Bp Charles Brinkley Morton. m 5/25/1968 Jean Ann Potym c 1. Dio Oregon Portland OR 2001-2006; P-in-c S Mich's/San Miguel Newberg OR 2001-2006; Int All SS Ch Vista CA 2000-2001; Cn Dio San Diego San Diego CA 1995-2000; Vic La Iglesia Del Espiritu Santo Mssn Lake Elsinore CA 1989-1995; Asst S Dav's Epis Ch San Diego CA 1984-1985; Asst S Matt's Ch Natl City CA 1983-1986. Auth, *Var arts in Sci Journ (Engl and Spanish)*, 1975. Natl Assn for the Self- Supporting Active Mnstry 1985; Oregon Cler Assn 2001; Var Sci societies 1975. Var Sci hon in US and Mex 1984. ghemingway@nehalemtel.net

HEMINGWAY, William Franklin (EC) 2874 Ida St, Fayetteville NC 28306 **Died 10/30/2010** B Fayetteville NC 3/28/1934 s Dallas Washington Hemingway & Edan Earle. D 2/26/1983 P 11/19/1983 Bp Brice Sidney Sanders. c 3.

HEMMERS, Louis Emanuel (Los) 1634 Crestview Rd, Redlands CA 92374 B Jackson MI 7/17/1932 s Louis Frederic Hemmers & Hollis A. BA U MI 1958; MDiv SWTS 1962. D 6/18/1962 P 12/1/1962 Bp Edward Clark Turner. m 8/23/1958 Joan Olsen c 3. R Trin Epis Ch Redlands CA 1981-2002; R Calv Ch Louisville KY 1974-1981; R S Geo's Ch Belleville IL 1965-1974; Vic S Mk's Ch Blue Rapids KS 1962-1965; Vic S Paul's Ch Marysville KS 1962-1965. Auth, "Seabury Quarterly". R Emer Trin, Redlands, CA 2002; Hon Cn (Cathedrdal Cntr) Dio Los Angeles 1995; Hon Archd (Alton) Dio Springfield (Illinois) 1968. 1lecanon@gmail.com

HEMPHILL, Margaret Ayars (Chi) 53 Loveland Rd, Norwich VT 05055 B San Francisco CA 10/8/1931 d David Preston Ayars & Margaret Jane. BA NWU 1979; MDiv SWTS 1986. D 6/14/1986 Bp James Winchester Montgomery P 12/13/1986 Bp Frank Tracy Griswold III. Asst R S Thos Ch Hanover NH 2001-2003; Assoc P The Epis Ch Of S Jas The Less Northfield IL 1997-1998. "Who'S Who In Amer" 2001. jd.hemp@aol.com

HEMPSTEAD, James Breese (Ind) 512 Woodland Ave, Petoskey MI 49770 B Saginaw MI 1/25/1936 s James Leland Hempstead & Helen Katherine. BA Alma Coll 1958; MDiv VTS 1962; Hurley Med Cntr Flint MI 1976; Ldrshp Acad for New Directions 1985. D 6/29/1962 Bp Robert Lionne DeWitt P 2/8/1963 Bp Richard S M Emrich. m 12/26/1959 Susanne Pomeroy c 2. Stndg Com Dio Indianapolis Indianapolis IN 1991-1997; R S Paul's Epis Ch Evansville IN 1990-1998; Gr Ch Holland MI 1990; Dio Wstrn Michigan Kalamazoo MI 1986-1990; Dn The Par Ch Of Chr The King Portage MI 1986-1989; P-in-c Ch Of The Nativ Boyne City MI 1985-1986; Dn Grand Traverse Deanry Dio Wstrn Michigan Kalamazoo MI 1979-1984; R Emm Ch Petoskey MI 1976-1986; S Barth's Ch Swartz Creek MI 1966-1976; Par Mssn Stff S Paul's Epis Ch Flint MI 1966-1976; Vic Chr The King Epis Ch Taylor MI 1964-1966; Cur S Mich And All Ang Epis Ch Lincoln Pk MI 1962-1966. "A Cong of Otters," *Spitball*, 2007; Auth, "Jim, It's What I Want That Matters!," *Sharing*, 1995. Ord of S Lk. Liberty Bell Awd Emmet Cnty Bar Assn Petoskey MI 1981. 2hempys@charter.net

HENAULT JR, Armand Joseph (Vt) 374 Spring Street, St Johnsbury VT 05819 **D S Andr's Epis Ch St Johnsbury VT 2009-** B Worcester MA 3/25/1953 s Armand Joseph Henault & Amelia A. MEd Harv 1975; MA Norwich U 1996; CAS Dioc Study Prog 1999; Cert of Advncd Study Dio VT Dioc Study Prog 1999. D 1/6/2009 Bp Thomas C Ely. m 6/8/1975 Linda Meyer c 2. ahenault@post.harvard.edu

HENAULT, Rita LaVerne (Okla) 145 Middlebrook Dr, Fayetteville GA 30215 **R The Epis Ch Of The Nativ Fayetteville GA 2007-** B Houston MO 8/18/1955 D 11/30/2002 P 7/24/2003 Bp William Edward Smalley. m 7/21/1975 David Mark Henault c 2. Assoc S Mary's Ch Edmond OK 2003-2007.

HENDERSON, Anna Martin (Chi) 205 W Montgomery Xrd Apt 1204, Savannah GA 31406 B San Francsico CA 4/15/1942 d Thaddeus Philip Martin & Elnora Burgess. BA S Aug's Coll Raleigh NC 1964; MS Rutgers-The St U 1973; MDiv GTS 1991. D 6/8/1991 Bp George Phelps Mellick Belshaw P 5/16/1992 Bp Cornelius Joshua Wilson. m 7/16/1966 Enoch Henderson c 2. Asst R S Edm's Epis Ch Chicago IL 2002-2005; Vic S Anselm's Epis Ch Nashville TN 1996-2001; Dio New Jersey Trenton NJ 1991-1996; D, Bayshore Cluster Mnstry Ch Of S Clem Of Rome Belford NJ 1991-1995; S Andr The Apos Highland Highlands NJ 1991-1995; D, Bayshore Cluster Mnstry S Mary's Ch Keyport NJ 1991-1995.

HENDERSON III, Charles (CNY) 39 E Church St, Adams NY 13605 **R Emm Ch Adams NY 1995-; R Zion Ch Adams NY 1995-** B Lawrence MA 8/13/

1946 s Charles Henderson & Ethel Ann. BA U NC 1971; MDiv Gordon-Conwell TS 1989. Trans from Anglican Church of Canada 9/1/1995 Bp David B(ruce) Joslin. c 2. CHIPMONK@GISCO.NET

HENDERSON, Don Keith (Colo) 2855 Rock Creek Cir Unit 179, Superior CO 80027 B Amarillo TX 6/13/1939 s William David Henderson & Mable Jane. Colorado Sch of Mines 1961; MS Colorado Sch of Mines 1963; MDiv STUSo 1991. D 6/15/1991 Bp William Jerry Winterrowd P 12/22/1991 Bp William Harvey Wolfrum. m 6/23/1990 Patricia Jennings c 1. Chair Coll & Ya Mnstry Cmsn Dio Colorado Denver CO 1994-1996; Chair Com Dio Colorado Denver CO 1992-1994; S Aid's Epis Ch Boulder CO 1991-2004. donkhenderson@msn.com

✠ **HENDERSON, Rt Rev Dorsey Felix** (USC) 1115 Marion St, Columbia SC 29201 B Bainbridge GA 1/17/1939 s Dorsey Felix Henderson & Murlean. BA Stetson U 1961; JD U of Florida Coll of Law 1967; MDiv VTS 1977. D 4/17/1977 P 11/1/1977 Bp James Loughlin Duncan Con 2/3/1995 for USC. Bp of USC Dio Upper So Carolina Columbia SC 1995-2009; Dep GC Dio Fond du Lac Appleton WI 1991-1994; Dn S Paul's Cathd Fond du Lac WI 1990-1994; Curs Sprtl Dir Dio SE Florida Miami FL 1986-1987; R S Benedicts Ch Plantation FL 1981-1989; P-in-c S Benedicts Ch Plantation FL 1980-1981; Cur S Benedicts Ch Plantation FL 1977-1979. Sis of the H Nativ (Assoc) 1990. DD VTS 1996; DD U So at Sewanee 1995; Phi Delta Phi U Coll of Law 1965; US-AR Cmmndtn Medal U.S. Army 1964; Walter C Hayes Awd Stetson U 1960. dusc@aol.com

HENDERSON, Dumont Biglar (Me) 65 Eustis Pkwy., Waterville ME 04901 B Bakersville NC 12/24/1935 s Robert Henderson & Doris Dennis. AB U of Maine 1958. D 6/20/2009 Bp Stephen Taylor Lane. m 9/22/1990 Roxanne Henderson c 4. dhenderson41846@roadrunner.com

HENDERSON JR, George Raymond (Fla) 1430 Forest Marsh Dr, Neptune Beach FL 32266 B Atlanta GA 8/15/1957 s George Raymond Henderson & Betty Ann. BS Auburn U 1981; MDiv STUSo 1988. D 6/6/1988 Bp Furman Stough P 12/1/1988 Bp Robert Oran Miller. m 6/1/1985 Rebecca Jane Mayberry c 1. S Cathr's Ch Jacksonville FL 1992-1997; Cur S Jn's Ch Decatur AL 1988-1992. rayjunone7800@gmail.com

HENDERSON, Harvey George (ND) 801 2nd St N, Wahpeton ND 58075 B Winnipeg MT CA 8/8/1952 s James Walter Henderson & Lillian. McMaster U; BS U of Manitoba 1974; MDiv U of Wstrn Ontario 1982. Trans from Anglican Church of Canada 8/20/1995. m 10/9/1981 Marjorie Elsbeth Peat c 2. Dio No Dakota Fargo ND 1998-2001; Geth Cathd Fargo ND 1998; Geth Cathd Fargo ND 1997; Trin Ch Wahpeton ND 1995-2002. hrvyhenderson@yahoo.com

HENDERSON, Jane Pataky (Chi) 624 Colfax St, Evanston IL 60201 B Bridgeport CT 2/16/1942 d Francis J Pataky & Charlotte. BA Wstrn Coll of Mia in Ohio 1964; UTS 1984. D 2/28/1982 Bp Paul Moore Jr P 10/1/1982 Bp Walter Decoster Dennis Jr. m 11/4/1989 Eugene Yerby Lowe c 1. S Matt's Ch Evanston IL 1997-2011; R S Ptr's Ch Freehold NJ 1991-1994; Ch Of The Heav Rest New York NY 1984-1991; Asst Calv and St Geo New York NY 1980-1984. JPHAKBS@AOL.COM

HENDERSON, L Owen (WMo) 288 Cedar Glen Dr Unit 4B, Camdenton MO 65020 **R S Geo Epis Ch Camdenton MO 2005-** B Quincy FL 8/17/1949 s Dorsey Felix Henderson & Murlean. AA Brevard Cmnty Coll 1970; BA Florida St U 1972; MDiv SW Bapt TS 1976; CAS Nash 1994. D 6/20/1994 P 12/29/1994 Bp Jack Leo Iker. m 10/20/1990 Courtney B Bazar. R All SS Epis Ch Aledo TX 1996-2000; Cur All SS' Epis Ch Ft Worth TX 1994-1996. office@saintge.org

HENDERSON, Mark William (Cal) 795 Buena Vista Ave W Apt 6, San Francisco CA 94117 **Assoc D S Aid's Ch San Francisco CA 2010-** B Laurens IA 3/28/1951 s Lloyd Earl Henderson & Margaret Irene. BA Wayne St Coll 1973; MA Iowa St U 1979; MA U of Iowa 1981; BA Sch for Deacons 2000. D 6/3/2000 Bp William Edwin Swing. c 1. D S Cyp's Ch San Francisco CA 2002-2008; D Ch Of The Adv Of Chr The King San Francisco CA 2000-2002. deaconhenderson@yahoo.com

HENDERSON, Michael Brant (Lex) 381 Bon Haven Rd, Maysville KY 41056 **R Ch Of The Nativ Maysville KY 2006-** B Baton Rouge LA 3/17/1951 s Joseph Poley Henderson & Nina Mae. BA Loyola U 1974; Weston Jesuit TS 1979; CAS Yale DS 2005. D 10/8/2005 Bp Johncy Itty P 5/6/2006 Bp Stacy F Sauls. m 5/20/1984 Emily Henderson c 1. Oblate of the H Cross 2005. hnderson@pacifier.com

HENDERSON, Michael Jack (Fla) 1746 Hillgate Ct, Tallahassee FL 32308 B Canton GA 1/28/1942 s James Jackson Henderson & Evelyn Ruth. BBA Georgia St U 1976; MBA Merc 1986; Bp's Sch For Mnstry 1999. D 12/11/1999 P 6/18/2000 Bp Stephen Hays Jecko. m 6/15/1973 Sterling Archibald c 2. Gr Mssn Ch Tallahassee FL 2000-2007. michael.grace@nettally.com

HENDERSON, Paul Edwin (WNY) 6070 Michigan Rd, Arcade NY 14009 **Died 10/15/2010** B Mitchell SD 6/7/1920 s Fred Savage Henderson & Jane. PDS. D 6/11/1954 P 1/1/1956 Bp Lauriston L Scaife. rtdenmom@aol.com

HENDERSON, Robert Bobo (CGC) 108 Sunrise Dr, Eufaula AL 36027 **Trin Ch Wetumpka AL 2011-** B Memphis TN 7/25/1950 s J W Henderson & Elizabeth B. BBA U of Mississippi 1972; JD U of Mississippi 1974; MDiv Epis TS of The SW 1986. D 6/11/1986 P 5/1/1987 Bp Duncan Montgomery Gray Jr. m 8/29/1970 Charlotte Burt c 3. R S Jas Ch Eufaula AL 1989-2011; Assoc S Paul's Ch Columbus MS 1986-1988. Auth, "The Epis Tchr"; Auth, "Ch Eductr"; Auth, "Living Ch". rector@saintjameseufaula.org

HENDERSON III, Samuel Gott (Me) 134 Park St, Portland ME 04101 B Portland ME 8/5/1941 s Samuel Gott Henderson & Winnifred Jane. STB GTS; BA Ricker; Maine Cntrl Inst 1960. D 6/8/1968 Bp Leland Stark P 12/1/1968 Bp Frederick Barton Wolf. S Ptr's Ch Portland ME 2006; Trin Ch Saco ME 2002-2006; S Alb's Ch Cape Eliz ME 1983-1990; S Pat's Ch Brewer ME 1982-1983; R Chr Ch Norway ME 1971-1979; Asst S Jn's Ch Bangor ME 1968-1971.

HENDERSON, Sterling (Fla) 1746 Hillgate Ct, Tallahassee FL 32308 B Jacksonville FL 12/29/1947 d Millard B Archibald & Julia P. Bp's Sch For Mnstry 1999. D 12/11/1999 P 6/18/2000 Bp Stephen Hays Jecko. m 6/15/1973 Michael Jack Henderson c 2. P-in-c Epis Ch Of The H Sprt Tallahassee FL 2004-2005; Gr Mssn Ch Tallahassee FL 2000-2009. sterling.henderson@comcast.net

HENDERSON, Stuart Hanford (SC) 55 Sunfield Dr, Carolina Shores NC 28467 B Orange NJ 5/4/1934 s Frederick Whitehouse Henderson & Marjorie C. BA U of Virginia 1956; MDiv VTS 1964; Coll of Preachers 1975. D 6/13/1964 Bp Leland Stark P 12/16/1964 Bp Lane W Barton. m 8/15/1956 Beverly Ann Brown c 4. Int R S Steph's Epis Ch Culpeper VA 1993-1994; R Gr Ch Keswick VA 1976-1993; R S Jn's Epis Ch Randolph VT 1970-1976; Assoc R S Lk's Ch Alexandria VA 1966-1970; Vic Ch of Our Sav Sum Lake OR 1964-1966; Vic S Lk's Ch Lakeview OR 1964-1966. shhnc@atmc.net

HENDERSON, Susan Edwards (SwFla) 1301 Longwood Dr, Fort Myers FL 33919 **Ch Of The Epiph Cape Coral FL 2003-** B Jacksonville FL 10/14/1950 D 6/12/1999 Bp John Bailey Lipscomb. m 8/17/1973 Robert Page Henderson c 2. suzrobhendo@aol.com

HENDERSON JR, Theodore Herbert (Pa) 236 Glen Pl, Elkins Park PA 19027 **P-in-c Chr Ch Bridgeport PA 2001-** B Providence RI 3/6/1938 s Theodore Herbert Henderson & Millicent. BS U of Pennsylvania 1960; MDiv PDS 1964; Tem 1970. D 5/23/1964 Bp William S Thomas P 12/19/1964 Bp Austin Pardue. m 1/12/1980 Barbara Ann Henderson c 1. Locten S Paul Memi Philadelphia PA 1983-1987; Trin Epis Ch Ambler PA 1978-1981; Seamens Ch Inst Philadelphia PA 1976-1978; Dio Pennsylvania Philadelphia PA 1975-1976; St Lukes Ch Philadelphia PA 1970-1977; Dce Ch Of Our Sav Jenkintown PA 1967-1968; Gnrl Mssy Dio Pittsburgh Monroeville PA 1964-1967. Csss. Exceptional Persons Citation Pa Jvnl Crt Judges Cmsn. MORESERVICEINC@HOTMAIL.COM

HENDRICK, Elizabeth (Los) 4, rue Henri Duchlne, Paris 75015 France **Cn Pstr The Amer Cathd of the H Trin Paris 75008 FR 2011-** B Biloxi MS 9/1/1950 d Robert Davis Hall & Elizabeth Acheson. BS U of Florida 1976; MBA Rol 1990; MDiv Epis TS of the SW 2008. D 6/7/2008 P 1/10/2009 Bp Joseph Jon Bruno. m 7/9/2009 Robert Keith Riley. Assoc R All SS-By-The-Sea Par Santa Barbara CA 2008-2011. canon@americancathedral.org

HENDRICKS, Jeanne Kay (NY) 48 Frankland Rd., Hopkinton MA 01748 **Died 1/26/2010** B Madison WI 4/9/1938 d Merrel F Rogers & Marion Elizabeth. BA Elmhurst Coll 1960; MS U of Wisconsin 1963; MDiv NYTS 1994. D 6/11/1994 P 12/1/1994 Bp Richard Frank Grein. c 3. jhendrks@hotmail.com

HENDRICKS, Mary D (Neb) 307 Seminole Dr, Mc Cook NE 69001 **R S Alb's Epis Ch McCook NE 2008-** B South Haven MI 8/30/1946 d Ernest L Hendricks & Mary D. BA Hastings Coll 1969; MS U of Nebraska at Kearney 1975; EdS U of Nebraska at Kearney 1977; PhD U of Sthrn Mississippi 1989; Angl Dplma Ya Berk 2006; MDiv Yale DS 2006. D 3/11/2006 P 10/20/2006 Bp Larry Earl Maze. Asst Trin Cathd Little Rock AR 2006-2007. rectorstalbans@ocsmccook.com

HENDRICKS, Rebecca Lanham (EO) Po Box 293, Milton Freewater OR 97862 **S Jas Ch Milton Freewater OR 2006-** B Pendleton Oregon 5/1/1951 BA Whitman Coll 1973. D 6/10/2006 Bp William O Gregg P 7/11/2007 Bp James Edward Waggoner. m 6/9/1973 Scott A Hendricks c 2. fruitvale@hughes.net

HENDRICKS III, Walter Frisby (SeFla) 2303 N.E. Seaview Drive, Jensen Beach FL 34957 **Ecum Off Dio SE Florida Miami FL 2007-; Ecum Off Dio SE Florida Miami FL 2007-; R Elect All SS Epis Ch Jensen Bch FL 2005-** B Malone NY 7/10/1945 s Walter Frisby Hendricks & Ruth. BA E Carolina U 1971; MDiv SWTS 1974. D 6/29/1974 P 2/1/1975 Bp David Shepherd Rose. m 6/28/1980 Jean A Maxwell c 3. Alum Assn VP SWTS Evanston IL 2004-2008; R H Trin Epis Ch W Palm Bch FL 2001-2005; Stndg Com Dio Cntrl New York Syracuse NY 1996-2001; Chapt S Paul's Cathd Syracuse NY 1992-1996; Liturg Com Dio Dio Cntrl New York Syracuse NY 1990-1994; R Chr Ch Binghamton NY 1989-2001; Bd Trst SWTS Evanston IL 1988-1991; Ex Bd Dio Cntrl New York Syracuse NY 1987-1989; Nomntns Com-Bp Coadj Dio Virginia Richmond VA 1983-1984; R S Mart's Epis Ch Henrico VA 1982-1989; Bd Trst SWTS Evanston IL 1979-1982; Vic S Mart's Epis Ch Henrico VA 1978-1981; Trin Ch Portsmouth VA 1974-1978. fatherfrisby@yahoo.com

HENDRICKSON, Patricia (Los) 265 W Sidlee St, Thousand Oaks CA 91360 **S Aug By-The-Sea Par Santa Monica CA 2002-** B New York NY 9/6/1942 BA Thos Edison St Coll 2001; CTh CDSP 2002; BA Sch for Deacons 2003. D 9/8/2002 Bp Chester Lovelle Talton. m 5/9/2004 Kate Lewis c 2. peedeefish@aol.com

HENDRICKSON III, Robert Joseph (Ct) 84 Broadway, New Haven CT 06511 **Chr Ch New Haven CT 2010-** B Chicago IL 8/5/1976 s Robert Joseph Hendrickson & Rene M. Cor 2001; Beijing Frgn Stds U 2003; BA U of Mississippi 2004; MDiv The GTS 2009. D 6/12/2010 Bp Ian Theodore Douglas P 1/15/2011 Bp Laura Ahrens. m 9/8/2001 Karrie C Cummings. rhendrickson@gts.edu

HENDRICKSON, Thomas Jeffrey (SC) 143 Ballard Ln, Santee SC 29142 **R The Ch Of The Epiph Eutawville SC 2011-** B 4/15/1951 BA U Denv 1973; MDiv TESM 2004. D 10/30/2004 Bp Henry William Scriven P 5/8/2005 Bp Robert William Duncan. m 8/11/1973 Theresa Hendrickson c 1. S Lk's Epis Ch Hilton Hd SC 2006-2010; P-in-c Chr The King Epis Ch Beaver Falls PA 2004-2006. tjhendrickson@gmail.com

HENDRICKSON, Thomas Samuel (Va) 3845 Village Views Pl, Glen Allen VA 23059 **Vic Gr Ch Bremo Bluff VA 2008-** B Rochester NY 11/7/1942 s Samuel Carmon Hendrickson & Kathleen May. BS Ottawa U 1965; MDiv GTS 1969; MBA UB 1981; PhD CPU 1992. D 6/21/1969 P 12/1/1969 Bp George West Barrett. m 6/17/1966 Catherine Harding. Int Chr Ch Par Epis Watertown CT 1995-1996; S Ptr's Epis Ch Oxford CT 1993; Int Epis Ch of Chr the Healer Stamford CT 1985-1986; Exec Coun Appointees New York NY 1981-1984; Asst S Paul's Ch Darien CT 1975; Vic St Marys Mssn Spencerport NY 1969-1972. Who's Who 1994; Psych Fell 68-68 Gnrl Theolgical Sem. tom42cathy44@verizon.net

HENERY, Charles Robert (Mil) 20 Oakwood Dr, Delafield WI 53018 **Chapl S Jn's Mltry Acad Delafield WI 2008-; Exam Chapl Dio Milwaukee Milwaukee WI 2005-; P-in-c Ch Of S Jn Chrys Delafield WI 1989-** B Kansas City MO 8/14/1947 s James Albert Henery & Morene Helen. BA U of Kansas 1969; STM GTS 1973; ThD GTS 1996. D 5/24/1973 P 11/30/1973 Bp Philip Alan Smith. m 11/27/1999 Jennifer L Grigsby c 4. Prof Nash Nashotah WI 1983-2008; The GTS New York NY 1979-1982; Assoc S Geo's Epis Ch Schenectady NY 1975-1979; Cur S Paul's Ch Concord NH 1973-1975. Co-Ed, "Sprtl Counsel in the Angl Tradition," Wipf and Stock, 2010; Auth, "The First Hundred Bishops of the Epis Ch," *The Angl: A Journ of Angl Identity*, Angl Soc, 1996; Ed, "A Spkng Life: The Legacy of Jn Keble," Gracewing, 1995; Ed, "Beyond the Horizon: Frontiers for Mssn," Forw Press, 1986. HSEC 1974-1981; HSEC 2007; Soc of St. Mary 1999; LivCh Fndt 2007. crhenery@wi.rr.com

HENKING, Patricia Ellen (NH) 2 Lavender Ct, Merrimack NH 03054 **Vic Faith Epis Ch Merrimack NH 1988-** B Darby PA 10/8/1954 d George Augustine Henking & Betty Lindsey. BS RPI 1976; MDiv GTS 1979; STM GTS 1997. D 6/2/1979 Bp Wilbur Emory Hogg Jr P 12/1/1980 Bp Frederick Barton Wolf. Asst & Chapl S Thos Ch Hanover NH 1986-1988; Asst Epis Ch Of S Mary The Vrgn Falmouth ME 1980-1986. awesme@aol.com

HENLEY, Carol Eileen (Pgh) 1212 Trevanion Ave, Pittsburgh PA 15218 B Kentfield CA 12/17/1945 d Edward Joseph Henley & Eileen Gwendolyn. BA Valparaiso U 1968; MDiv GTS 1982. D 6/5/1982 P 3/18/1983 Bp Albert Wiencke Van Duzer. St Andrews Epis Ch Pittsburgh PA 2005-2007; All SS Epis Ch Verona PA 2000-2003; Int S Thos Ch In The Fields Gibsonia PA 1998-1999; Actg R All SS Epis Ch Verona PA 1997-1998; Assoc R S Paul's Epis Ch Winston Salem NC 1991-1994; Vic S Anne's Ch Winston Salem NC 1988-1990; Assoc R Gr Ch Madison NJ 1987-1988; Asst R Gr Ch Madison NJ 1985-1986; Assoc R All SS Par Beverly Hills CA 1983-1985. cehenagain@yahoo.com

HENLEY, Charles Wilbert (ND) PO Box 524, Valley City ND 58072 B Devils Lake ND 11/28/1928 s Wilbert George Henley & Maude. BD Bex 1957; BA U of No Dakota 1957; Grad Stdt Vlly City St Coll 1969. D 6/11/1957 P 3/1/1958 Bp Richard R Emery. m 7/2/1955 Odella O Johnson c 2. All SS Ch Vlly City ND 1977-1995; R All SS Ch Vlly City ND 1964-1969; Cn Geth Cathd Fargo ND 1960-1963; M-in-c S Ptr And S Jas Ch Grafton ND 1957-1960.

HENLEY JR, Edward Joseph (SwFla) 404 Park Ridge Ave, Temple Terrace FL 33617 **Dn, Tampa Dnry Dio SW Florida Sarasota FL 2011-; Dioc Coun Dio SW Florida Sarasota FL 2010-; R S Mk's Epis Ch Of Tampa Tampa FL 2000-** B East Chicago IN 2/22/1949 s Edward Joseph Henley & Eileen Gwendolyn. BA New Coll of Florida 1972; MDiv GTS 1978. D 6/12/1978 P 3/19/1979 Bp Emerson Paul Haynes. m 11/3/1984 Sheryl Lynn Mason c 5. Vic S Mk's Epis Ch Of Tampa Tampa FL 1997-2000; Int S Jas Hse Of Pryr Tampa FL 1995-1996; Int S Cathr's Ch Temple Terrace FL 1993-1994; Int S Jas Hse Of Pryr Tampa FL 1989-1990; Int S Chad's Ch Tampa FL 1989; USF, Tampa Dio SW Florida Sarasota FL 1981-1987; Asst S Mary's Par Tampa FL 1978-1981. henley404@aol.com

HENLEY, Robert Pinkerton (ETenn) 351 Hardin Ln, Sevierville TN 37862 B Winchester TN 9/3/1946 s Robert Allan Henley & Mary Evelyn. BS Mars Hill Coll 1971; MDiv STUSo 1978; CPE Charlotte Memi Hosp Charlotte NC 1989. D 6/24/1978 Bp William Gillette Weinhauer P 11/2/1979 Bp William J Gordon Jr. m 2/15/1969 Ann Lancaster c 2. Dio E Tennessee Knoxville TN 2002-2011; R S Jos The Carpenter Sevierville TN 2001; Vic S Barth's Epis Ch Mio MI 1996-2001; Vic S Fran Epis Ch Grayling MI 1996-2001; P-in-c S Andr Ch Mt Holly NC 1992-1996; S Thos Ch Dubois WY 1982-1984; Vic S Helen's Epis Ch Laramie WY 1981-1985; M-in-c S Paul's Epis Ch Gladwin MI 1978-1981. ALMACA 1989-1996; Comp Dio Relatns; Dioc Pstr Response Team 2005; EPF 1978; Native Amer Mnstrs 1982. Cler of the Year Crawford Cnty 2001. rob.henley2@gmail.com

HENNAGIN, Bob (SwFla) 5011 Mcgregor Blvd, Fort Myers FL 33901 **R S Hilary's Ch Ft Myers FL 1998-** B Detroit MI 10/22/1957 s Robert Brigham Hennagin & Loretta Smith. BA Albion Coll 1979; MDiv Epis TS of The SW 1992. D 6/20/1992 Bp Donis Dean Patterson P 4/3/1993 Bp James Monte Stanton. m 11/15/1986 Kari G Pharr c 4. Vic All SS Ch Atlanta TX 1994-1998; Cur S Barn Ch Garland TX 1992-1994. "I am a P," *Living Ch*, Living Ch, 2003. bobhennagin@gmail.com

HENNE, Bruce Charles (Minn) 1270 118th Ave NW, Coon Rapids MN 55448 **Vic SS Martha And Mary Epis Ch Eagan MN 2008-** B Jackson MI 8/1/1941 s Charles Thomas Henne & Ruth Margaret. BA MI SU 1964; MA W Georgia Coll 1972; MDiv VTS 1985. D 6/24/1985 P 1/1/1986 Bp Robert Marshall Anderson. m 11/17/1961 Penny K Snyder c 2. R S Lk's Epis Ch Idaho Falls ID 2002-2007; R All SS Epis Ch Boise ID 1999-2002; R S Jn's Ch S Cloud MN 1989-1999; Cathd Ch Of S Mk Minneapolis MN 1985-1989. bch71@comcast.net

HENNESSY, F(rank) Scott (SVa) 132 Blue Ridge Dr, Orange VA 22960 **S Paul's Ch Norfolk VA 2006-** B Pittsburgh PA 7/17/1955 s George Hennessy & Kathleen. BA U of Virginia 1978; MDiv VTS 1986. D 6/11/1986 P 3/19/1987 Bp Peter James Lee. m 8/25/1985 Patricia Anne Hughes. R S Thos Epis Ch Orange VA 1994-2006; Asst Ch Of Our Sav Charlottesville VA 1988-1993; Asst Emm Ch At Brook Hill Richmond VA 1986-1988. fsh7@verizon.net

HENNESSY, J Katherine (Minn) 13946 Echo Park Cir, Burnsville MN 55337 B Dubuque IA 6/8/1952 d Ambrose Schroeder & Ethel Hennessy. BA Mt Mercy Coll; Med Universit of MN; Psyd U of St. Thos. D 3/12/2006 Bp Daniel Swenson P 9/16/2006 Bp Daniel Lee Swenson. P S Jas Ch Marshall MN 2006-2011. jkhennessy@aol.com

HENNIGAR, Richard Addison (WMass) 4 Terrie Ln, Holden MA 01520 **Asstg P S Fran Ch Holden MA 2000-** B Malden MA 4/18/1932 s Joshua Monroe Hennigar & Margaret Jane. BA Trin Hartford CT 1954; MDiv EDS 1957. D 6/22/1957 Bp Anson Phelps Stokes Jr P 1/5/1958 Bp William A Lawrence. m 6/25/1955 Lorraine Bragg c 2. S Fran Ch Holden MA 1998-1999; Worcester Cnty Ecum Coun Worcester MA 1986-1993; Dioc Admin. & Fin Com Dio Wstrn Massachusetts Springfield MA 1982-1990; Dn Cntrl Worcester Deanry Dio Wstrn Massachusetts Springfield MA 1974-1977; Chair Liturg Cmsn Dio Wstrn Massachusetts Springfield MA 1970-1974; R S Jn's Ch Worcester MA 1964-1986; Asst S Steph's Memi Ch Lynn MA 1957-1959. hmakeadifference@aol.com

HENNING, Joel Peter (HB) No address on file. B East Orange NJ 6/12/1939 s Joseph Peter Henning & Patricia Nannette. VTS 1963; LTh SWTS 1966. D 6/11/1966 Bp James Winchester Montgomery P 12/1/1966 Bp Gerald Francis Burrill. m 6/8/1963 Jean Louise Fischer c 2. Cur S Simons Ch Arlington Heights IL 1966-1972.

HENNING, Kristina Louise (FdL) 2010 Memorial Dr Apt 211, Green Bay WI 54303 B Milwaukee WI 12/9/1950 d Roy George Olson & Genevieve Louise. TS; BS U of Wisconsin 1973; MDiv SWTS 2004. D 7/24/2004 P 5/21/2005 Bp Russell Edward Jacobus. c 2. Ch Of The H Apos Oneida WI 2005-2008; Ch of the Ascen Merrill WI 2005-2008. DOK 2002. klohenning@yahoo.com

HENNINGER, Annie (SD) 105 E 12th St, Gregory SD 57533 **Rosebud E Epis Mssn Dio So Dakota Sioux Falls SD 2010-** B Cleveland OH 11/18/1948 d Joseph Francis Sowinski & Maryanne Joan. BA Ursuline Coll 1971; MA St. Jn Sem/TS 1991. D 7/20/2008 P 2/19/2009 Bp James Louis Jelinek. m 5/26/1973 Jay Edgar Henninger c 6. jahenninger@msn.com

HENRICHSEN, Robert Anton (Neb) 3414 S 114th St, Omaha NE 68144 B Harlan IA 5/8/1939 D 8/15/2004 Bp Joe Goodwin Burnett. m 6/27/1980 Sula Grace Metz c 3. rasgh70@cox.net

HENRICK, Joan (Ala) 5789 Tydan Ln, Gadsden AL 35907 **Dioc Coun Dio Alabama Birmingham AL 2010-; R H Comf Ch Gadsden AL 2009-; Cbury Schlr in Cbury, Engl The TS at The U So Sewanee TN 2006-** B Lee County 7/14/1955 d Burmon Robinson & Opal Noles. RN Sylacauga Hosp Sch of Nrsng, Sylacauga, AL 1979; BSN Auburn U Auburn AL 1992; MS Troy St U Phenix City AL 2000; MDiv TS 2007. D 6/9/2007 P 12/11/2007 Bp Henry Nutt Parsley Jr. m 4/21/2007 Richard Henrick c 1. D-in-c/R H Cross-St Chris's Huntsville AL 2007-2009; Cbury Schlr in Cbury, Engl The TS at The U So Sewanee TN 2006; Mssy to Romania The TS at The U So Sewanee TN 2005; Anti-Racism Com for Sem The TS at The U So Sewanee TN 2004-2007; Pstr Care Com for Sem The TS at The U So Sewanee TN 2004-2007; Cmsn on Sprtlty Dio Alabama Birmingham AL 2000-2003; Sr

Wrdn, Eucharistic Min, Yth Min, Pastora Emm Epis Ch Opelika AL 1985-2004. DOK 2003. Inducted as Mem Chi Sigma Iota Counslg and Profsnl hon Soc Intl 2000; Inducted as Mem Sigma Theta Tau hon Soc of Nrsng 1992; Awd Awd for Acad Excellence 1979. hcrector@bellsouth.net

HENRICKSON, Mark (Los) 32A Wingate Street, Avondale, Auckland 0600 New Zealand (Aotearoa) B Wilmington DE 11/28/1955 s Bruce Henrickson & Elaine Mary. BA Trin Hartford CT 1977; MDiv EDS 1980; MSW U of Connecticut 1990; PhD U CA Los Angeles 1996. D 6/14/1980 P 2/13/1981 Bp Morgan Porteus. Dioc Counc Dio Los Angeles Los Angeles CA 1996-1999; S Andr's Epis Ch Ojai CA 1995; S Monica's Ch Hartford CT 1983-1986; Cur Trin Ch Torrington CT 1980-1982. Co-Auth, "Living the dream: Rel in the construction of sexual identity," *Fieldwork in Rel 7 (2)*, 2012; Co-Ed, "Co-Ed," *Soc Wk Field Educ and Supervision across Asia-Pacific*, U of Sydney Press, 2011; Co-Auth, "'Stndg in the fire': Experiences of HIV positive Black Afr migrants and refugees to New Zealand," *Tech Report*, U of Auckland, 2011; Co-Auth, "Lavender Ret: A questionnaire survey of lesbian, gay and bisexual people's accommodation plans for old age," *Intl Journ of Nrsng Pract 16: 589-594*, 2010; Auth, "Civilized unions, civlized Rts: Same-sex relationships in Aotearoa New Zealand," *Journ of Gay and Lesbian Soc Serv 22 (1/2): 40-55*, 2010; Auth, Co-Ed, "Soc Wk Educ and sexual minorities," *Educ for Soc Wk: Voices from the Asia-Pacfic*, Vulgar Press, 2009; Auth, "Sxlty, Rel and authority: Towards reframing estrangement," *Journ of Rel and Sxlty in Soc Wk 28 (1/2) 48-62*, 2009; Co-Auth, "HIV disease," *Chronic Illness & Disabil: Principles for Nrsng Pract*, Elsevier, 2008; Co-Auth, "The Const of lavender families: A LGB perspective," *Journ of Clincal Nrsng 18: 849-856*, 2008; Auth, "Deferring identity and Soc role in lesbian, gay and bisexual New Zealanders," *Soc Wk Educ 27 (2): 53-65*, 2008; Lead Auth, "Lavender Islands: The New Zealand study," *Journ of Homosexuality 53 (4): 223-248*, 2007; Auth, "Lavender faith: Rel and Sprtlty in lesbian, gay and bisexual New Zealanders," *Journ of Rel and Sprtlty in Soc Wk 26 (3): 63-80*, 2007; Auth, "Ko wai ratou? Mng multiple identities in lesbian, gay and bisexual New Zealand Maori," *New Zealand Sociol 21 (2) 251-273*, 2006; Auth, "Lavender parents," *Soc Plcy Journ of New Zealand 26: 68-83*, 2005. m.henrickson@massey.ac.nz

HENRY, Barbara D. (WA) 5333 N Sheridan Rd Apt.8H, Chicago IL 60640 **Assoc Epis Ch Of The Atone Chicago IL 2007-** B Bangor ME 9/28/1934 d Lloyd M Dearborn & Marion. BA Bos 1956; MA Bos 1962; MLS U Pgh 1964; MDiv GTS 1983. D 6/2/1983 P 12/1/1983 Bp John Thomas Walker. Assoc All Souls Memi Epis Ch Washington DC 2004-2007; Ch Of S Steph And The Incarn Washington DC 1999-2002; Par of St Monica & St Jas Washington DC 1991-1994; S Jas Epis Ch Scarborough ME 1991-1994; Asst R S Jn's Ch Georgetown Par Washington DC 1985-1988; Asst R/Urban Res Ch Of S Steph And The Incarn Washington DC 1983-1985. barbarahws@aol.com

HENRY, David Winston (VI) Po Box 6119, Christiansted VI 00823 B Antigua 12/15/1932 s William Aaron Henry & Matilda. London GCE GB; MDiv ETSC 1966. D 6/4/1966 P 6/1/1967 Bp Cedric Earl Mills. m 8/6/1995 Sonia Dolores Spencer c 2. R Epis Ch of the H Cross Kingshill VI VI 1991-2000; Vic S Ptr the Apos Ch Christiansted VI 1972-1980; Asst S Barth's Ch Baltimore MD 1966-1967. dav_and_nia@yahoo.com

HENRY, Dean (NJ) 14 Winding Lane, Southwest Harbor ME 04679 B Louisville KY 6/27/1948 s Robert Norman Henry & Ethelene. BS Pur 1970; MBA Claremont Coll 1984; MDiv GTS 1988. D 6/25/1988 Bp Frederick Houk Borsch P 3/4/1989 Bp George Phelps Mellick Belshaw. m 10/1/1988 Alice Lacey Downs c 2. R Chr Ch Middletown NJ 1990-2010; Asst S Ptr's Ch Perth Amboy NJ 1988-1990. OHC, Assoc 1989. dean1@myfairpoint.net

HENRY, Earl Fitzgerald (SeFla) 4401 W Oakland Park Blvd, Fort Lauderdale FL 33313 **R Ch Of The Atone Lauderdale Lakes FL 1998-** B Belize CA BZ 3/19/1951 s Ezekiel Theodore Henry & Catherine Olivia. DIT Codrington Coll 1978; BA Coll of New Rochelle 1991; Blanton-Peale Grad Inst 1995; MA Audrey Cohen Sch of The Metropltn Coll of New York 1997. Trans from Church in the Province Of The West Indies 11/15/1988 Bp Robert Campbell Witcher Sr. m 7/19/1980 Carmen Higging c 1. R S Barn Epis Ch Brooklyn NY 1992-1998; Supply P Dio Long Island Garden City NY 1990-1992; S Aug's Epis Ch Brooklyn NY 1989-1990. revearlhenry@bellsouth.net

HENRY, George Kenneth Grant (NC) 34 Red Fox Lane, Brevard NC 28712 B Tarboro NC 10/21/1942 s Matthew G Henry & Cornelia Catherine. BA U So 1964; MDiv VTS 1971. D 6/6/1971 Bp Matthew G Henry P 2/19/1972 Bp Randolph R Claiborne. m 11/24/1967 Brantley Bell c 3. R S Mich's Ch Raleigh NC 1997-2002; Dio No Carolina Raleigh NC 1992-2002; Stndg Com Dio No Carolina Raleigh NC 1983-1997; R Ch Of The H Comf Charlotte NC 1980-1997; Liturg Cmsn Dio No Carolina Raleigh NC 1977-1979; R Trin Epis Ch Statesville NC 1975-1980; R Epis Ch of the Gd Shpd Charleston SC 1973-1975; Cur Emm Epis Ch Athens GA 1971-1973. kbhenry@citcom.net

HENRY, James Russell (SwVa) 4647 Prince Trevor Dr, Williamsburg VA 23185 B Athens GA 2/14/1940 s Jones Wesley Henry & Elizabeth Hannah. BA U GA 1962; MDiv VTS 1965; DMin VTS 1987; Med Lynchburg Coll 1997. D 6/26/1965 P 3/17/1966 Bp Randolph R Claiborne. m 6/21/1969 Nancy Ann Sinclair c 1. S Jn's Ch Bedford VA 1997-1998; P-in-c S Jn's Epis Ch Glasgow VA 1996-1998; Assoc R Chr Epis Ch Roanoke VA 1993-1996; P Assoc Chr Epis Ch Roanoke VA 1991-1993; Pstr Counslg Cntr Of Roanoke Vlly Inc Roanoke VA 1991-1993; R S Jn's Ch Bedford VA 1981-1991; Asst S Paul's Epis Ch Alexandria VA 1971-1981; R Ch of the Incarn Mineral VA 1969-1979; Asst Emm Epis Ch Athens GA 1967-1969; R S Jas Epis Ch Louisa VA 1967-1969; Vic Gr-Calv Epis Ch Clarkesville GA 1965-1967; Vic S Jas Epis Ch Clayton GA 1965-1967. Auth, *Death Educ: The Tip of the Iceberg*, 1987; Auth, *Alexandria: a Town in Transition 1800-1900*; Auth, *Ch*. AAPC 1997; Chi Sigma Iota 1997. Lic Profsnl Counslr St of Virginia 2001; Fell AAPC 1998; Natrional Certied Counslr Natl Bd Cert Counselers 1997. thedawsdidit@juno.com

HENRY, John Reeves (Spr) PO Box 255, Carlinville IL 62626 **D Admin S Ptr's Ch Carlinville IL 2011-; D Admin S Paul's Epis Ch Carlinville IL 2010-** B Decatur IL 7/1/1949 s Richard Reeves Henry & Mildred Maxine. BS El Ed U IL 1971; MS Estrn Illinois U 1980; MDiv Nash 2010. D 11/30/2010 Bp Donald James Parsons P 6/29/2011 Bp Daniel H Martins. m 4/14/1973 Sheila Wesley c 6. vicar2b@live.com

HENRY II, John Wilfrid (Alb) P.O. Box 175, Clifton Park NY 12065 B Bay Shore NY 4/14/1955 s John W Henry & Florence T. BA Indiana U 1978; MDiv STUSo 1983. D 6/13/1983 P 1/21/1984 Bp Robert Campbell Witcher Sr. m 6/30/1984 Karen E J Wood c 4. S Andr's Epis Ch Livonia MI 2006-2008; S Geo's Ch Clifton Pk NY 2006-2008; Asst P Ch Of The H Cross Novi MI 2004-2006; Ch Of The Ascen Bradford PA 1998; Dioc Mssnr Dio NW Pennsylvania Erie PA 1996-2002; Chr Epis Ch Tarrytown NY 1991-1995; Dio New York New York City NY 1991-1995; S Jas Ch Brookhaven NY 1988-1991; Cur S Jn's Ch Huntington NY 1983-1985.

HENRY, Karen E J (Mich) P.O. Box 175, Clifton Park NY 12065 **P Adirondack Missions Brant Lake NY 2011-; Assoc S Geo's Ch Clifton Pk NY 2009-** B New York NY 5/23/1950 d John S Wood & Eleanor H. BA SUNY 1981; MDiv UTS 1985; ABD The GTS 1991. D 6/15/1991 Bp Orris George Walker Jr P 2/2/1992 Bp Walter Decoster Dennis Jr. m 6/30/1984 John Wilfrid Henry c 4. P-in-c Ch Of The H Cross Novi MI 2002-2008; R S Lk's Epis Ch Smethport PA 1996-2002; Asst S Barth's Ch In The Highland White Plains NY 1994-1995; P Chr Ch Bronxville NY 1991-1994. Auth, "Change Agt," *Living Ch*, 2001; Auth, "Cathd," *Angl Dig*, 1991. The Ord of S Lk, Chapl 2000. henrevs@hotmail.com

HENRY, Lloyd (LI) 4607 Avenue H, Brooklyn NY 11234 **All SS Ch Richmond Hill NY 2010-** B Belize HN 10/23/1947 s Gerald Anthony Henry & Hortense Elvira. Untd Theol Coll Of The W Indies Kingston Jm; MDiv NYTS 1988; DD NYTS 1991. Trans from Church in the Province Of The West Indies 10/21/1982 Bp Robert Campbell Witcher Sr. m 12/18/1971 Leonie I Felix c 3. S Mk's Ch Brooklyn NY 2005-2008; R S Aug's Epis Ch Brooklyn NY 1981-1998; Asst P S Mk's Ch Brooklyn NY 1978-1981.

HENRY, Richard Arlen (EpisSanJ) 1155 Leavell Park Cir, Lincoln CA 95648 **Assoc S Jas Epis Mssn Lincoln CA 2005-** B Cleveland OH 2/6/1930 s Clifford Clair Henry & Ada Pearl. BA U CA 1952; MDiv CDSP 1961; DMin Jesuit TS 1978. D 6/12/1961 P 12/16/1961 Bp Sumner Walters. m 5/3/1957 Allene M Muhlbach c 3. Assoc Chr Ch Eureka CA 2000-2004; Assoc S Columba Ch Fresno CA 1993-2000; R S Mary's Epis Ch Fresno CA 1965-1993; R S Mths Ch Oakdale CA 1961-1965. OHC, Assoc 1965. allenesib@ssctv.net

HENRY, Richard L(ynn) (Nev) 228 Hillcrest Dr, Henderson NV 89015 B Berkeley CA 12/1/1953 s Robert Lee Henry & Frankie Albert. AGS Clark Cnty Cmnty Coll 1985; CDSP 1989. D 6/27/1988 P 6/11/1989 Bp Stewart Clark Zabriskie. c 3. Vic S Lk's Epis Ch Las Vegas NV 1990; Dio Nevada Las Vegas NV 1989-2003.

HENRY JR, Wayman Wright (USC) 116 Sedgewood Ct, Easley SC 29642 B Greenville SC 11/3/1937 s Wayman Wright Henry & Helen. BA Clemson U 1966; MDiv Erskine Coll 1979; VTS 1981. D 1/27/1981 P 12/1/1981 Bp William Arthur Beckham. m 9/21/1965 Carol Terry c 2. S Geo Ch Anderson SC 2002-2003; All SS Ch Cayce SC 1994-1996; Ch Of The H Comf Sumter SC 1994; All SS Epis Hosp Ft Worth TX 1993-1994; R The Ch Of The Epiph Eutawville SC 1992-1993; Chr/St Paul's Epis Par Yonges Island SC 1991-1992; R Ch Of The Redeem Orangeburg SC 1991; R Ch Of The Incarn Gaffney SC 1982-1991; S Fran Ch Greenville SC 1982; Cur Ch Of The Gd Shpd Greer SC 1981; Cur S Fran Ch Greenville SC 1981.

HENSARLING JR, Larry Reid (CFla) 146 Oak Sq S, Lakeland FL 33813 **Assoc R All SS Epis Ch Lakeland FL 2003-** B Shreveport LA 9/11/1956 s Larry Reid Hensarling & Joan. BS LSU 1978; MA The U of Texas at Austin 1981; MDiv TESM 1992; DMin Reformed TS, Orlando 2010. D 6/6/1992 P 12/5/1992 Bp Robert Jefferson Hargrove Jr. m 6/28/1980 Mary D Cass c 2. R Ch Of The Redeem Memphis TN 1999-2003; Chair Dept Yth Mnstrs Dio So Carolina Charleston SC 1996-1999; R S Paul's Ch Bennettsville SC 1994-1999; Cur S Mths Epis Ch Shreveport LA 1992-1994. rhensarling@teamallsaints.org

HENSEL, Charles Howard (Chi) 8414 Oak Ave, Gary IN 46403 B Bridgeton NJ 10/31/1933 s Howard Baker Hensel & Grace. BA Trin Hartford CT 1954; MDiv Nash 1957. D 12/22/1956 P 2/1/1958 Bp Alfred L Banyard. m 6/4/1960

Sarah Anne Harkness. Int S Tim's Ch Griffith IN 1996-1998; Int Geth Epis Ch Marion IN 1994-1996; Vic S Nich w the H Innoc Ch Elk Grove Vill IL 1982-1993; Int Chr Ch W River MD 1979-1980; R S Jn's Epis Ch Decatur IL 1974-1979; R S Barn-In-The-Dunes Gary IN 1971-1974; Vic H Trin Epis Ch Peoria IL 1960-1964; Vic S Jn's Epis Ch Peoria IL 1960-1964; Cur S Andr Ch Grayslake IL 1959-1960; Cur The Ch Of The Epiph And S Simon Brooklyn NY 1958-1959. henselgary@windspring.com

HENSHAW, Richard Aurel (Roch) 199 Crosman Terr., Rochester NY 14620 B San Francisco CA 11/6/1921 s Aurelius Henshaw & Ruth Adele. BS U CA 1943; BD CDSP 1953; PhD Hebr Un Coll 1966. D 6/28/1953 Bp Henry H Shires P 1/6/1954 Bp Henry W Hobson. m 6/8/1943 Marjorie Robb c 2. The Chap of the Gd Shpd Rochester NY 2003; Bex Columbus OH 1968-1993; R Ch Of Our Sav Cincinnati OH 1958-1960; Cur Epis Soc of Chr Ch Cincinnati OH 1953-1958. Auth, "Priesthood," *Eerdmans Bible Dictionary*, 2000; Auth, "Wmn In Israel Cult," *Eerdmans Bible Dictionary*, 2000; Auth, "Female & Male - The Cultic Personl," Pickwick Press, 1994; Auth, "Which Bible," *Forw Mvmt*, 1991; Auth, "Neo Assyrian Offcl," *Journ Of Amer Oriental Soc*, 1967. Amer Oriental Soc 1943; Astronomical Soc Of The Pacific 1953; SBL 1943-2006. rhenshaw@rochester.rr.com

HENSLEY, Erin S (SwVa) St John's Church, Jefferson St. at Elm Ave., Roanoke VA 24002 **S Jn's Ch Roanoke VA 2007-** B Henderson KY 5/4/1977 d David Robert Seltzer & Mary Beth. BS Guilford Coll 1999; MDiv VTS 2007. D 11/15/2007 P 6/29/2008 Bp Michael Bruce Curry. m 7/10/2004 Samuel Edwin Hensley. Asst S Alb's Par Washington DC 2007-2009. ehensley@stjohnsroanoke.org

HENSLEY JR, Joseph H (NC) 1737 Hillandale Rd, St. Luke'S Episcopal Church, Durham NC 27705 **Asst To The R S Lk's Epis Ch Durham NC 2007-** B Winfield IL 10/18/1973 s Joseph Hillard Hensley & Linda Bratton. BA U NC 1996; MDiv The Prot Epis Sem VA 2007. D 5/19/2007 P 12/19/2007 Bp Michael Bruce Curry. m 11/21/2009 Sarah Spencer White c 5. josephhhensley@gmail.com

HENSLEY, Lane Goodwin (SanD) 47535 State Highway 74, Palm Desert CA 92260 **Disciplinary Bd Dio San Diego San Diego CA 2010-; R S Marg's Epis Ch Palm Desert CA 2010-** B Shreveport LA 2/18/1965 s Edward Randolph Hensley & Dorothy Burnett. AB Duke 1987; MDiv SWTS 2001. D 6/16/2001 P 12/15/2001 Bp William Dailey Persell. m 4/24/1993 Rebecca Ruth Karnes c 2. R Ch Of The Trsfg Palos Pk IL 2003-2010; Cur Chr Ch Winnetka IL 2001-2003; Bd Trst SWTS Evanston IL 1999-2011. lane.hensley@alumni.duke.edu

HENSLEY, Robert Eugene (Mass) PO Box 1197, Vineyard Haven MA 02568 **R Gr Ch Amherst MA 2006-; R Gr Ch Vineyard Haven MA 2006-** B Macomb IL 3/22/1951 s Roland Doyle Hensley & Barbara Jean. BA Wstrn Illinois U 1975; MA Wstrn Illinois U 1977; MDiv SWTS 1983. D 6/11/1983 Bp Quintin Ebenezer Primo Jr P 12/17/1983 Bp James Winchester Montgomery. m 4/20/2007 Michael Ward Helgert. Assoc R S Marg's Ch Washington DC 2002-2006; S Marg's Ch Washington DC 1999-2001; Ch Of The Epiph Forestville MD 1998; Assoc The Epis Ch Of S Thos The Apos Dallas TX 1989-1996; Assoc P Epis Ch Of The Atone Chicago IL 1988-1989; Int S Chris's Epis Ch Oak Pk IL 1987-1988; Asst R Emm Epis Ch Rockford IL 1983-1986. Auth, "Care Team Trng Manual," *Care Team Trng Manual*, AIDS Interfaith Ntwk of No Texas, 1989. Bd Mem Epis Caring Response To Aids 1999-2001; Soc Of S Jn The Evang, Natl Epis Aid. rectoratgracemvy@verizon.net

HENSLEY-ECHOLS, Beth Marie (WA) HQ/A, 22th FSB, 25th ID (L), APO, AE 09347 B Cambridge MD 8/19/1961 d Haliburton Bruce Hensley & Joyce Darlene. BA U of Maryland 1985; MDiv VTS 1989. D 6/10/1989 Bp John Thomas Walker P 9/1/1990 Bp Ronald Hayward Haines. m 11/20/1990 Karl William Echols. CE Asst S Barn' Ch Leeland Upper Marlboro MD 1990-1995; Asst to R Ch Of Our Sav Silver Sprg MD 1989-1990. beth.m.echols@us.army.mil

HENSON, Robert Harry (Tex) 32423 Oxbow Ln, Fulshear TX 77441 B Tulsa OK 10/16/1949 s Earl Marian Henson & Virginia Elizabeth. BBA U of No Texas 1971; MDiv TESM 1985. D 6/13/1985 Bp Maurice Manuel Benitez P 12/13/1985 Bp Anselmo Carral-Solar. m 6/1/1971 Karen L Krusz c 3. Ch Of The H Apos Katy TX 2000-2006; Vic Ch Of The H Apos Katy TX 1994-1998; St Lukes Ch Katy TX 1994; Chr Epis Ch Cedar Pk TX 1990-1994; Vic Chr Epis Ch Cedar Pk TX 1990-1994; Vic All SS Ch Cameron TX 1988-1990; Vic S Thos' Epis Ch Rockdale TX 1988-1990; Assoc Chr Epis Ch Temple TX 1985-1988. ERM; Ord Of S Lk. bob.henson@sbcglobal.net

HENSON, Tula (USC) 335 Tennessee Ave, Sewanee TN 37383 **R S Tim's Ch Columbia SC 2007-** B Piraeus Greece 7/14/1953 MDiv STUSo 2005. D 2/5/2005 P 8/8/2006 Bp Henry Irving Louttit. m 4/2/2005 Walter H Henson c 3. Assoc S Mk's Ch Brunswick GA 2005-2007. nurse0714@aol.com

HENSON, William Patrick (CFla) 1203 66th St NW, Bradenton FL 34209 **Died 10/29/2009** B Bradenton FL 6/27/1932 s Worth Allison Henson & Mable. BS Florida St U 1954; MDiv STUSo 1968. D 6/20/1968 Bp William Loftin Hargrave P 12/23/1968 Bp Albert Ervine Swift. c 3.

HENTHORNE JR, Granville Victor (RI) Po Box 296, Brooksville ME 04617 B Providence RI 11/9/1930 s Granville Victor Henthorne & Jeanie Craig. BA Bos 1952; STB Ya Berk 1955; STM Ya Berk 1967. D 6/24/1955 P 3/24/1956 Bp John S Higgins. m 5/5/1981 Priscilla Tew c 4. Dio Vacancy Consult Dio Rhode Island Providence RI 1977-1980; Dio Ecum ARCC Dio Rhode Island Providence RI 1973-1980; R S Geo And San Jorge Cntrl Falls RI 1973-1980; Int P Dio Rhode Island Providence RI 1972-1973; R Trin Ch Portland CT 1959-1972; R All SS Ch Warwick RI 1955-1959; Asst/Actg Cn Pstr Cathd Of S Jn Providence RI 1955-1956. FVC 1956. DD Logos Hse of Theol Stds, Maine 2007. logos74@juno.com

HENWOOD, Karen Lee (Colo) 5604 E Nichols Pl, Centennial CO 80112 B Colorado Springs CO 7/12/1937 d Joseph Wilhelm Farber & Alice Josephine. BA U of Nthrn Colorado 1960; MA U CO 1972. D 11/10/2001 Bp William Jerry Winterrowd. m 6/27/1963 William A Henwood c 2. D All SS Epis Ch Denver CO 2001-2005. chieftwithinglips@yahoo.com

HENWOOD, William A (Colo) 5604 E Nichols Pl, Centennial CO 80112 **Gd Shpd Epis Ch Centennial CO 1995-** B Kingston JM 12/14/1931 s Charles Frederick Henwood & Myrtle Vinnifred. BS Queens U 1963. D 10/21/1989 Bp Joseph Thomas Heistand. m 6/27/1963 Karen Lee Farber c 3. Dio Indianapolis Indianapolis IN 1993-1995; D S Mk's Ch Plainfield IN 1993-1995; Gr S Paul's Epis Ch Tucson AZ 1989-1993. bahenwood@yahoo.com

HERBST, Alan Arnold (Spr) 102 N State St, Champaign IL 61820 **R Emm Memi Epis Ch Champaign IL 1986-** B Brookings SD 11/11/1953 s Arnold T Herbst & Ellestine Estaline. BA Morningside Coll 1976; MDiv Nash 1979. D 5/31/1979 P 12/1/1979 Bp Walter Cameron Righter. R S Jn's Ch Keokuk IA 1982-1986; Vic S Paul's Ch Durant IA 1979-1982. Soc Of S Jn The Evang. aah@ameritech.net

HERBST, Gary Siegfried (Dal) 8320 Jack Finney Blvd., Greenville TX 75402 **R S Paul's Epis Ch Greenville TX 2002-** B Alexandria VA 5/7/1951 s Grant Allison Herbst & Lila Rae. BA U of Texas 1973; MDiv VTS 1976. D 6/16/1976 P 6/1/1977 Bp Roger Howard Cilley. m 1/11/1986 Sandra Jane Byerly c 3. R S Jn's Ch Ketchikan AK 1986-2002; Trin Epis Ch Jasper TX 1980-1986; Assoc R Ch Of The Epiph Houston TX 1976-1979. "Formation for Vestries: Where Equipping the SS Begins," *Vstry Papers*, ECF, 2007. stpaul1@geusnet.com

HERGENRATHER, Lynda Stevenson (Va) 5904 Mount Eagle Dr Apt 318, Alexandria VA 22303 B Newark NJ 10/9/1948 d Leonard Francis Stevenson & Adelaide Emma. BA Eckerd Coll 1970; MA U of So Florida 1972; MDiv UTS Richmond VA 1979. D 6/23/1979 Bp Robert Bruce Hall P 5/1/1980 Bp David Henry Lewis Jr. Assoc S Lk's Ch Alexandria VA 1989-2004; P-in-c S Lk's Ch Alexandria VA 1981-1983; Asst S Lk's Ch Alexandria VA 1979-1981.

HERKNER JR, Robert Thomas (O) 328 Windsor Ct, Huron OH 44839 B Detroit,MI 6/7/1945 s Robert T Herkner & Vivian I. Amer U of Beirut 1966; BA Hope Coll 1967; MA U MI 1969; MDiv EDS 1973. D 6/30/1973 Bp H Coleman McGehee Jr P 2/17/1974 Bp Frederick Hesley Belden. m 8/8/1987 Kay Ellen Klein c 2. S Paul's Ch Fremont OH 2002-2004; Int Ch Of The Ascen Lakewood OH 2001-2002; R Calv Ch Sandusky OH 1975-2000; Asst Trin Ch Newport RI 1973-1975. Auth, "Paper The Un Mnstry Of Epis Ch". rkherkner@aol.com

HERLIHY, Phyllis Cleo (SwFla) 514 50th St W, Bradenton FL 34209 B Waverly NY 7/30/1927 d Ellsworth Foster Schanbacher & Esther Elvina. D 6/29/1991 Bp Rogers Sanders Harris. c 3. D Chr Ch Bradenton FL 1991-1999. Alfa 2001; Disciples Of Chr Cmnty; Fa Lead Lab I, Ii Supvsr & Coordntr.

HERLOCKER SR, John Robert (Bob) (Ida) 3700 NW Orchard Dr, Terrebonne OR 97760 B Greenville TX 2/11/1935 s James Harry Herlocker & Doyle Williams. U So 1952; BBA U of Texas 1956; MDiv STUSo 1967; Boise St U 1985; CREDO 2003; CREDO 2009. D 7/26/1967 P 4/21/1968 Bp William J Gordon Jr. m 2/28/1959 Peggy Felmet c 5. Cn to Ordnry for Dioc Adm Dio Idaho Boise ID 1990-1996; Archd Dio Idaho Boise ID 1982-1990; Dioc Admin Dio Idaho Boise ID 1979-1982; Dioc Fiscal Off Dio Estrn Oregon The Dalles OR 1974-1979; Vic Epis Ch Of The Trsfg Sis OR 1974-1978; Vic S Alb's Epis Ch Redmond OR 1974-1978; R H Trin Epis Ch Ukiah CA 1972-1974; Vic S Mary's Ch Winnemucca NV 1969-1972; Vic All SS' Epis Ch Anchorage AK 1967-1968. bobnpeg2@gmail.com

HERLOCKER, Thomas D. (Kan) 1704 E 10th Ave, Winfield KS 67156 **D Gr Epis Ch Winfield KS 1988-** B Winfield KS 12/15/1938 s John A Herlocker & Carolan. Stan 1957; BA U of Kansas 1960; JD U of Kansas 1963. D 10/28/1988 Bp Richard Frank Grein. m 6/8/1960 Judith Ann Gildehaus c 3. Dio Kansas Topeka KS 1994-2000. NAAD 1987. therlocker@winfieldlawyers.com

✠ HERLONG, Rt Rev Bertram Nelson (Tenn) 230 Temple Crest Tr, Franklin TN 37069 **Died 10/21/2011** B Lake City FL 10/16/1934 s Benjamin Daniel Herlong & Ava Texana. BA U of Florida 1956; MDiv STUSo 1959; STM STUSo 1970; DMin NYTS 1981. D 6/25/1960 P 3/13/1961 Bp Edward Hamilton West Con 6/26/1993 for Tenn. c 2. DD Nash 2006; DD STUSo 1993; Detroit Assn of Black Orgnztn Awd; Booker T Washington Bro Awd. bishopbert@att.net

HERMAN, Alice McWreath (SO) 345 Ridgedale Dr N, Worthington OH 43085 B McDonald PA 3/1/1937 d Guy A McWreath & Mary E. BA Thiel Coll 1959; MDiv Methodist TS In Ohio 1989. D 11/9/1990 Bp Herbert Thompson Jr. m 4/22/1961 Fred W Herman c 2. D S Andr's Ch Pickerington OH 1990-1992. Coll of Chapl.

HERMAN, Elizabeth Frances (Minn) 615 Vermillion St, Hastings MN 55033 **D S Lk's Epis Ch Hastings MN 2010-** B Monticello MN 1/1/1942 d Emil William Dorf & Elizabeth Ida. D 1/9/2010 Bp James Louis Jelinek. c 1. efh042@embarqmail.com

HERMAN, Michael (EMich) 815 N. Grant St, Bay City MI 49708 B Oxford MI 2/19/1950 BA Wayne 1972; MDiv SWTS 1984; A.D.N No Cntrl Michigan Coll Petoskey MI 2000. D 6/30/1984 Bp Henry Irving Mayson P 2/16/1985 Bp H Coleman McGehee Jr. m 8/3/1985 Janet Hastie. R Trin Epis Ch Bay City MI 2006-2011; S Lk's Epis Ch Rogers City MI 2004-2005; Int S Jas' Epis Ch Cheboygan MI 2000-2001; Trsfg Epis Ch Indn River MI 1992-1998; Vic S Mk's Ch Sidney OH 1988-1991; R S Jn's Epis Ch S Johns MI 1985-1988; S Phil's Epis Ch Rochester MI 1985; St Aug Hse Oxford MI 1984-1985. mherman2597@yahoo.com

HERMANSON, David Harold (Nwk) 154 Kingsley St, Long Branch NJ 07740 B Ransomville NY 5/27/1956 s Clair D Hermanson & Gayle. Loyola U 1984; BA Hav 1986; MDiv GTS 1990. D 6/16/1990 P 1/1/1993 Bp Allen Lyman Bartlett Jr. m 5/29/1982 Lynn M Stefanowicz. S Thos Ch Lyndhurst NJ 2003-2005; Trin Ch Asbury Pk NJ 1993-2003; Mssnr Dio Pennsylvania Philadelphia PA 1990-1993. D.H.HERMANSON@GMAIL.COM

HERMERDING, Joseph R (La) 8833 Goodwood Blvd, Baton Rouge LA 70806 **S Lk's Ch Baton Rouge LA 2009-** B Fridley MN 10/28/1983 s Gregg Jon Hermerding & Constance Edith. BA Wheaton Coll 2006; Gordon-Conwell TS 2007; MDiv Nash 2009. D 10/23/2008 P 5/16/2009 Bp Keith Lynn Ackerman. m 6/3/2006 Ellora Fishback c 1. rhermerding@stlukesbr.org

HERMES, Jed Charland (SC) Po Box 5713, Florence SC 29502 **D All SS Ch Florence SC 1997-** B Trinidad Colombia 3/14/1931 s Jack Charland Hermes & Edyth Nina. BA Ashland U 1957. D 9/14/1997 Bp Edward Lloyd Salmon Jr. m 2/27/1976 Antoinette Sexton.

HERN, George Neal (Dal) 4329 Irvin Simmons Dr, Dallas TX 75229 B Saint Louis MO 1/11/1939 s George Addison Hern & Helen Neal. BA Westminster Coll 1961; MDiv EDS 1964. D 6/21/1964 P 12/1/1964 Bp George Leslie Cadigan. c 2. Asst S Mich And All Ang Ch Dallas TX 2000-2001; S Thos Ch Ennis TX 1998-2000; P Dio Dallas Dallas TX 1998-1999; S Mths' Epis Ch Athens TX 1989-1998; Ch Of The Gd Shpd Dallas TX 1984-1986; P Dio Dallas Dallas TX 1981-1982; Assoc S Lk's Epis Ch Dallas TX 1977-1980; R Ch Of S Mths Dallas TX 1974-1976; Cur Gr Ch Kirkwood MO 1964-1966. nealhern@aol.com

HERNANDEZ, Gustavo (Los) Po Box 893, Downey CA 90241 B Cisneros CO 11/16/1934 s Eleazar Hernandez & Eva. BA Xaverian U 1958; MS Gregorian U 1963; BA Xaverian HS 1963; DMin U of Notre Dame 1988. Rec from Roman Catholic 3/1/1984 as Priest Bp Quintin Ebenezer Primo Jr. c 3. R S Clem's Mssn Huntington Pk CA 1989-1999; Dio Chicago Chicago IL 1985-1988; The Annunc Of Our Lady Gurnee IL 1984-1985; Vic Cristo Rey Chicago IL 1982-1984.

HERNANDEZ, Luis Alfonso (Hond) C/O Iglesia Episcopal, Tegucigalpa Honduras **Dio Honduras Miami FL 1998-** B 9/25/1952 m 4/30/1992 Dulce Duellar.

HERNANDEZ, Robert C (Ind) Apartado Aereo 52, Cartagena Colombia B Barranquilla CO 10/19/1916 s Julio Hernandez & Maria Luisa. BD Pur 1942; MA Epis TS of The SW 1979; MS Iusb 1988. D 12/2/1979 P 8/1/1980 Bp Bernardo Merino-Botero. m 12/17/1943 Helen Louise Douglas. Int S Andr's By The Lake Epis Ch Michigan City IN 1987-1988; Supply P Dio Nthrn Indiana So Bend IN 1986-1987; R Iglesia Epis San Alb Bogota CO 1982-1983. Aacd, Cma.

HERNANDEZ CARRERA, Sergio (Mex) Toltecas Manzana 102 lote 27 col, Distrito Federal Mexico 04300 Mexico **Dio Mex 2007-** B 10/1/1970 s Sergio D Hernandez & Maria Luisa. Rec from Roman Catholic 3/29/2008 Bp Carlos Touche-Porter. kamisama93@hotmail.com

HERNANDEZ MESA, Alejandro Felix (SeFla) 9460 Fontainebleau Blvd Apt 334, Miami FL 33172 **R Iglesia Epis De Todos Los Santos Miami FL 2002-** B CU 6/23/1959 s Emilio J Hernandez & Edivia H. BS U Of Havana Cu 1983; BA Theol Sem Of Matantas 1992. Trans from Iglesia Episcopal de Cuba 12/11/1995 Bp Calvin Onderdonk Schofield Jr. m 3/19/1983 Vilma Gonzales Pasos c 3. H Cross Epis Ch Miami FL 1998-2002; S Faith's Epis Ch Cutler Bay FL 1997-1998. iglesiaepiscopal@bellsouth.net

HERNANDEZ ROJAS, Martin Antonio (Colom) Carrera 6 No 49-85, Piso 2, Bogota Colombia B Convencion NdeS Colombia 3/4/1958 s Luciano Hernandez & Mana del Socorro. Filosofia Seminario Reg Barranguilla 1979; Teologia Seminario Reg 1984; Licenciado Universidad Sto Tomas 1995; Especialista Universidad Sto Tomas 1999. Rec from Roman Catholic 3/22/2009 Bp Francisco Jose Duque-Gomez. m 12/8/1998 Magda Yasmin Gil Delgado c 2. martin-her@hotmail.com

HERNDON, James C (Ida) 1055 Riverton Rd, Blackfoot ID 83221 **D Dio Idaho Boise ID 1988-** B Oklahoma City OK 7/26/1941 s John Charles Herndon & Lucile. BS U Of Idaho Moscow 1963; JD U Of Idaho Moscow 1966. D 4/30/1988 Bp David Bell Birney IV. m 4/19/1974 Tommye Rae Low.

HERON, James (NY) 54 Angela Ct, Beacon NY 12508 B Plainfield NJ 12/4/1941 s Robert Heron & Helen. BA Norwich U 1963; STB PDS 1966; DMin Drew U 1978. D 4/23/1966 P 10/29/1966 Bp Alfred L Banyard. c 2. Dir Diac Formation Prog Dio New York New York City NY 1993-1998; R Trin Ch Fishkill NY 1981-2003; Cur S Mary's Ch Burlington NJ 1966-1968. "Denning's Point," *A Hudson River Hist*, Black Dome Press, 2006; Auth, *Tchg Death & Dying to Late Adolescents*, 1978. jimheron@optonline.net

HERON, Marsha Smith (Cal) 1401 E Dry Creek Rd, Centennial CO 80122 B Eureka KS 8/18/1947 D 12/7/2002 Bp William Edwin Swing. m 4/10/1982 Michael Rex Carney. S Anselm's Epis Ch Lafayette CA 2003-2006.

HERRERA, Lourdes del Carmen (Hond) IMS SAP Dept 215. PO Box 523900, Miami FL 33152 Honduras B 6/1/1972 d Basidio Cessato & Dolores. D 10/22/2009 P 8/28/2010 Bp Lloyd Emmanuel Allen. m 6/11/1993 Heriberto Santos Urrutia c 3. hlourdendelcarmen@yahoo.es

HERRERA, Marisa (Pa) Po Box 336, Oreland PA 19075 B 11/6/1949 MDiv Ya Berk; ABS U CA. D 6/3/1989 P 6/9/1990 Bp John Shelby Spong. S Paul's Ch Elkins Pk PA 1999-2011; Dio Pennsylvania Philadelphia PA 1995-1997; S Dav's Ch Philadelphia PA 1995-1997; S Ptr's Ch Morristown NJ 1990-1993. marisa@stpaulselkinspark.org

HERRERA CHAGNA, Raul (EcuC) Avenue Amazonas #4430, Igl Epis Del Ecuador, Quito Ecuador **Ecuador New York NY 1996-; Vic Iglesia San Lucas Pilahuin Ambato 689 EC 1996-** B Otavalo EC 4/12/1957 s Samuel Herrera & Maria Chagna. Epis TS; Pontifical Cath U of Ecuador 1987; Pontifical Cath U of Ecuador 1989; Epis TS 1995. D 4/17/1994 P 5/1/1997 Bp J Neptali Larrea-Moreno. m 8/16/1991 Zoila Chacon c 5.

HERRICK, Robert Frank (NY) 349 W 21st St, New York NY 10011 B Bethlehem PA 8/3/1942 s Robert Ford Herrick & Elizabeth June. BA Pr 1964; STB GTS 1967; MBA Col 1981. D 6/17/1967 P 3/30/1968 Bp Frederick J Warnecke. Supply P Chr Epis Ch Lynbrook NY 1999-2007; P-in-c S Jn's Ch New Rochelle NY 1985-1987; P-in-c S Andr's Epis Ch Hartsdale NY 1983-1984; Cur Par of Trin Ch New York NY 1969-1974. bherrick@pipeline.com

HERRING, Dianne Lerae (Wyo) PO Box 12, Kaycee WY 82639 B Laramie WY 3/28/1947 d Vernon Richards & Virginia. D 8/18/2007 Bp Vernon Edward Strickland. m 8/12/1972 Gordon Herring c 2. gherring@rtconnect.net

HERRING, John Foster (At) 634 W Peachtree St NW, Atlanta GA 30308 **Assoc R All SS Epis Ch Atlanta GA 2008-** B Livingston NJ 9/15/1969 s Joseph Dahlet Herring & Bonita Lynn. BA Washington Coll 1991; MDiv STUSo 2008. D 12/21/2007 P 10/19/2008 Bp J(ohn) Neil Alexander. m 9/22/2001 Keri Lynne Hachenberg c 3. jherring@allsaintsatlanta.org

HERRING, Joseph Dahlet (At) 5575 N Hillbrooke Trce, Alpharetta GA 30005 B Englewood NJ 2/24/1934 s Joseph Dahlet Herring & Alice Josephine. AB Dart 1955; STB GTS 1960; STM GTS 1971. D 6/11/1960 P 12/17/1960 Bp Leland Stark. m 1/26/1963 Bonita Lynn Bender c 3. Asst Chr Ch Norcross GA 2005-2007; Int S Steph's Ch Ridgefield CT 2003-2005; Int Emm Ch Middleburg VA 2002-2003; Int S Barth's Ch Cherry Hill NJ 2000-2002; Int S Steph's Ch Goldsboro NC 1999-2000; Int S Mich's Ch Bristol RI 1996-1999; Int Gr Ch Madison NJ 1995-1996; R Chr Ch Newton NJ 1983-1995; COM Dio Newark Newark NJ 1970-1982; R S Steph's Ch Millburn NJ 1968-1983; Vic Ch Of The Trsfg Towaco NJ 1963-1968; Asst S Paul's Epis Ch Paterson NJ 1960-1963. Soc of Jn the Bapt 1972. Bp's Outstanding Serv Awd Dio Newark 1987; Polly Bond Awd for Ed Writing ECom 1987; Polly Bond Awd for Ed Writing ECom 1985; Fell 83 Coll of Preachers 1983; Polly Bond Awd for Ed Writing ECom 1983; Americanism Awd Millburn/Short Hills 1983. bonnjoe55@hotmail.com

HERRING JR, Lonnie Lee (Miss) Box 217 House 138 Highway 32, Parchman MS 38738 B El Dorado AR 7/22/1937 s Lonnie Lee Herring & Lottie. BS Delta St U 1982; Dio Mississippi Sch For D MS 1996. D 2/18/1996 Bp Alfred Clark Marble Jr. m 12/12/1976 Lucinda Lee Payne. herringc957@aol.com

HERRING, Virginia Norton (NC) 607 N Greene st, Greensboro NC 27401 **H Trin Epis Ch Greensboro NC 1999-** B Norfolk VA 4/13/1945 d Joseph Herbert Norton & Mildred Beckett. BA U NC 1985; MDiv Duke 1988; STUSo 1988; ThM Duke DS 1999. D 5/28/1988 Bp Frank Harris Vest Jr P 6/1/1989 Bp Robert Whitridge Estill. c 6. R S Anne's Ch Winston Salem NC 1992-1999; Asst to R S Lk's Ch Salisbury NC 1988-1992. virginia@holy-trinity.com

HERRINGTON III, Willet Jeremiah (Mich) 30420 Rush St, Garden City MI 48135 B Bad Axe MI 6/24/1927 s Willet Jeremiah Herrington & Margaret Elsie. BA U MI 1950; MA U MI 1952; Whitaker TS 1970. D 3/18/1967 Bp Archie H Crowley P 4/30/1970 Bp Richard S M Emrich. m 12/21/1957 Joan Elizabeth Olsen. Asst S Andr's Epis Ch Livonia MI 1988-1999; Asst Journey of Faith Epis Ch Detroit MI 1967-1987. Soc Of S Paul.

HERRMANN, H(erbert) W(illiam) (Dal) 623 Ector St, Denton TX 76201 **R S Dav's Ch Denton TX 2006-** B Flushing NY 1/10/1951 s Herbert Herrmann &

Gloria. BS U of Texas-Arlington 1974; MDiv Nash 1989. D 12/28/1988 P 10/23/1989 Bp Clarence Cullam Pope Jr. m 5/21/1977 Ginger Alice Till c 2. R S Jn's Epis Ch Peoria IL 1995-2006; Gr Epis Ch Monroe LA 1993-1995; S Fran Of Assisi Epis Ch Aledo TX 1990-1993; Cur S Mk's Ch Arlington TX 1989-1990. Angl Comm Ntwk 2004; Bro of S Andr 1995; CCU 1989; CBS 2002; SocMary 1992; SSC 1991. fatherherrmann@stdavidsdenton.org

HERRON-PIAZZA, Katharine Ann (O) 11 Alden Rd Apt 2l, Larchmont NY 10538 **Cur S Jn's Ch Larchmont NY 2006-** B Panama CZ 3/15/1972 d Philip Herron & Ann. BA Ohio Wesl 1994; MPA Cleveland St U 1997; MDiv GTS 2006. D 6/3/2006 Bp Mark Hollingsworth Jr P 1/6/2007 Bp J Clark Grew II. m 5/27/2006 Jerome Mario Piazza c 1. kherron@gts.edu

HERSCHEL, Richard James (Eas) 80-B King Street, Norwich NR11PG Great Britain (UK) **Died 10/27/2011** B Philadelphia PA 10/9/1927 s Alf Herschel & Aagot. BS Tem 1953; MDiv PDS 1957; MA Villanova U 1972. D 6/8/1957 P 12/7/1957 Bp Oliver J Hart.

HERSHBELL, Jackson Paul (SwVa) 274 Still House Dr, Lexington VA 24450 B Northampton PA 11/27/1935 s Paul Frank Hershbell & Elizabeth Mae. BA Laf 1955; MA U of Pennsylvania 1956; STB GTS 1963; PhD Harv 1964. D 6/22/1963 P 6/6/1964 Bp Anson Phelps Stokes Jr. m 9/1/1984 Anne Snyder. P-in-c Ascen Ch St Paul MN 1985-2000; Asst P S Chris's Epis Ch Roseville MN 1984-2000; P-in-c H Trin Epis Ch Elk River MN 1972-1980; Cur Ch Of S Jn The Evang Hingham MA 1963-1966. Auth, *Iamblichus on the Mysteries*, Scholars Press, 2003; Auth, *Iamblichus on the Pythagorean Way of Life*, Scholars Press, 1991; Auth, "Numerous Pub in," *Hermes*, Classical Journ, Ancient Soc, Gk and Roman Stds. Amer Philological Assn 1969; Amer Philos Assn 1969. U of Durham 1993; Fllshp Alexander von Humboldt U of Munich Munich Germany 1977; Inst for Resrch in the Hmnts U of of Wisco Madison WI 1969. jhershbell@yahoo.com

HERSHON, Lee Edward (SC) 98 Wentworth St, Charleston SC 29401 B New York City NY 6/27/1944 s Martin Hershon & Betsy. AB Rutgers Coll 1966; DDS U of Maryland 1970; MS Harvard Sch of Dental Med 1974. D 9/11/2010 Bp Mark Joseph Lawrence. m 6/5/1977 Nina Haskins Nina Marcia Haskins c 3. leehershon@yahoo.com

HERTH, Daniel Edwin (Cal) 32 Mallorie Park Drive, The Garden House, Ripon North Yorkshire HG42QF Great Britain (UK) B Cincinnati OH 9/23/1936 s Edwin William Herth & Alva V. BS Xavier U 1958; MDiv CDSP 1983. D 6/25/1983 P 6/1/1984 Bp William Edwin Swing. m 5/18/2002 Sheila Margaret Wolvin c 4. Chr Ch Alameda CA 1986-1998; Asst S Paul's Ch Oakland CA 1983-1986. "Memories and Reflections: Hiroshima and the Trsfg," *The Friends Quarterly*, 'The Friend' Pub Ltd., 2005; "How do we know Jesus?," *The Friends Quarterly*, 'The Friend' Pub Ltd., 2003. danielherthsr@fbtinternet.com

HERVEY JR, Theodore E (Tex) 933 N Fm 1174, Bertram TX 78605 **Wolrd Mssn Chair-Dio Tx Dio Texas Houston TX 2010-; R Epis Ch Of The Epiph Burnet Burnet TX 1994-** B Frankfurt, Germany 7/14/1951 s Theodore E Hervey & Cornelia G. U of Montana 1970; BS Virginia Polytech Inst and St U 1973; MDiv VTS 1976. D 6/7/1976 Bp Harold Cornelius Gosnell P 12/12/1976 Bp Scott Field Bailey. m 4/21/1990 Carol J Hayes c 1. Int S Steph's Epis Ch Wimberley TX 1988; Hisp Mnstry Chair - Dio W Tx Dio W Texas San Antonio TX 1982-1986; R Gr Ch Weslaco TX 1981-1987; Asst S Thos Epis Ch And Sch San Antonio TX 1978-1981; Sp Dir Happ - Dio W Texas Dio W Texas San Antonio TX 1977-1987; Asst All SS Epis Ch Corpus Christi TX 1976-1978. revted.hervey@gmail.com

HERZOG, Carole Regina (Los) 1471 Cloister Dr, La Habra Heights CA 90631 B Montclair NJ 12/12/1943 d Joseph Paul Seborowski & Stephanie Regina. BS Seton Hall U 1965; MA ETSBH 1983. D 6/18/1983 Bp Albert Wiencke Van Duzer P 1/1/1984 Bp Robert C Rusack. m 4/6/1988 William A Herzog. S Steph's Par Whittier CA 1986-1996; Asst S Andr's Par Fullerton CA 1983-1986; S Andr's Par Fullerton CA 1980-1983. wahcrh@verizon.net

✠ **HERZOG, Rt Rev Daniel William** (Alb) 612 S Shore Rd, Delanson NY 12053 B Ogdensburg NY 7/9/1941 s William James Herzog & Mary Katharine. BA S Bonaventure U 1964; Nash 1970; Med St. Lawr Canton NY 1971; DD Nash 1998. D 5/12/1971 Bp Allen Webster Brown P 11/13/1971 Bp Charles Bowen Persell Jr Con 11/29/1997 for Alb. m 2/27/1965 Carol Anne Penfield. Dio Albany Albany NY 2003-2007; Dio Albany Albany NY 1997-2002; R Chr Ch Schenectady NY 1995-1997; Stndg Com Dio Albany Albany NY 1995-1997; Com Dio Albany Albany NY 1990-1996; R Chr Ch Morristown NY 1976-1995; Cur S Jn's Ch Ogdensburg NY 1971-1976. Assn Of The Cmnty Of S Mk - Peekskill, Ny 2001; Benedictine Oblate 1964. bishopdan@princetowncable.com

HERZOG, Kenneth Bernard (Fla) 3545 Olympic Dr, Green Cove Springs FL 32043 **Asst Trin Epis Ch St Aug FL 2009-** B Erlanger KY 5/9/1951 s Bernard Leo Herzog & Rita Marie. MA S Vinc de Paul Sem 1990; MDiv STUSo 1995. D 7/29/1995 Bp John Lewis Said P 1/1/1996 Bp Calvin Onderdonk Schofield Jr. m 5/24/1985 Elizabeth A Kamenski c 1. S Marg's-Hibernia Epis Ch Fleming Island FL 1998-2009; S Mary's Epis Ch Stuart FL 1995-1998. frken@trinityepiscopalparish.org

HESCHLE, John Henry (Chi) 7100 North Ashland Blvd, Chicago IL 60626 **R S Paul's By The Lake Chicago IL 1993-** B Hackensack NJ 6/7/1953 s John Henry Heschle & Dorothy Lucile. BA Hope Coll 1975; MDiv SWTS 1978. D 12/20/1978 P 6/29/1979 Bp James Winchester Montgomery. The Ch Of S Anne Morrison IL 1979-1993; Cur Gr Ch Sterling IL 1979-1982. spbylake@stpaulsbylake.org

HESS, George Robert (HB) 7 Canyon Crest Dr, Victor ID 83455 B Gilmer TX 5/5/1941 s Robert Lankin Hess & Alice Marie. STB Ya Berk; BA Baylor U 1963; Oxf 1964. D 6/13/1967 Bp Walter H Gray P 12/1/1967 Bp Charles A Mason. m 6/3/1967 Martha Webb. Cur S Lk's Epis Ch Dallas TX 1967-1969.

HESS, Howard (ETenn) 8500 Cambridge Woods Ln, Knoxville TN 37923 **R Ch Of The Ascen Knoxville TN 2007-** B Atlantic City NJ 7/31/1944 s Howard Johnson Hess & Alice Mae. MA U Chi 1970; DSW U of Alabama 1981; MDiv Ya Berk 2000. Trans 2/3/2004 Bp Charles Glenn VonRosenberg. m 10/17/1970 Mary McCartt c 2. S Chris's Ch Kingsport TN 2003-2007; Assoc R S Thad Epis Ch Aiken SC 2000-2003. frhoward@knoxvilleascension.org

HESS JR, Joseph Wesley (Pa) 600 E Cathedral Rd Apt B-303, Philadelphia PA 19128 **Died 8/13/2010** B Ridley Township PA 3/31/1921 s Joseph Wesley Hess & Gertrude Letitia. BA W Chester St Coll 1968; STB PDS 1969. D P 2/1/1969 Bp Robert Lionne DeWitt. c 2. frjoehess@netzero.net

HESS III, Raymond Leonard (NCal) 9001 Crowley Way, Elk Grove CA 95624 **R St Marys Ch Elk Grove Sacramento CA 2007-** B Sewickley PA 11/5/1947 s Raymond L Hess & Ruth. BA Stan 1969; MDiv CDSP 1972; DMin Fuller TS 2000. D 6/29/1974 Bp C Kilmer Myers P 2/27/1975 Bp Jackson Earle Gilliam. m 4/1/1978 Deborah Gimbel c 1. Vic Ch of the Gd Shpd Colorado Sprg CO 2001-2007; R S Mk's Epis Ch Santa Clara CA 1994-2001; Vic S Mths Epis Ch San Ramon CA 1984-1994; R Chr Ch Cedar Rapids IA 1980-1984; Assoc All SS Ch Carmel CA 1977-1980; Cur Ch Of The H Sprt Missoula MT 1974-1977. fatherray@frontiernet.net

HESS, Richard Walton (Cal) 601 Torre Malibu, 325 Calle Amapas, Puerto Vallarta Mexico B Stewartstown PA 5/31/1932 s Walton Ernest Hess & Alice Thelma. BA U of Pennsylvania 1955; BD Drew U 1958; VTS 1960. D 11/27/1960 Bp Oliver J Hart P 6/1/1961 Bp Joseph Gillespie Armstrong. m 9/17/1984 Sandra Caole Hess c 3. Int The Ch Of S Jn The Evang Flossmoor IL 1994-1995; Gr Cathd San Francisco CA 1988-1993; Actg Dn Trin Cathd Miami FL 1987-1988; The Epis Ch Of Beth-By-The-Sea Palm Bch FL 1985-1987; R S Dav's Ch Wayne PA 1967-1986; Asst Min S Dav's Ch Wayne PA 1963-1966; Vic S Christophers Epis Ch Oxford PA 1960-1963.

HESSE, Alan Roger (Mass) 409 Common St, Walpole MA 02081 **Barbara C Harris Camp & Conf Ctr Boardmember Dio Massachusetts Boston MA 2011-; Dioc Coun Dio Massachusetts Boston MA 2010-; Dioc. Liturg Com Dio Massachusetts Boston MA 2006-; R Epiph Par Walpole MA 2005-** B Sioux City IA 5/3/1963 s Marvin Wilhelm Hesse & Elizabeth Ann. BA Morningside Coll 1986; MDiv EDS 2001. D 5/25/2001 Bp Steven Charleston P 1/18/2002 Bp Thomas Kreider Ray. m 5/21/2004 T T Orwig c 1. Assoc All SS Ch Worcester MA 2001-2005. Auth, "How Do You See God," *The Angl Dig*, 2002. alhesse@verizon.net

HESSE JR, Rayner Wilson (NY) 64 Columbia Avenue, Hartsdale NY 10530 **Pstr S Jn's Ch New Rochelle NY 1994-** B Baltimore MD 9/16/1955 s Rayner Wilson Hesse & Dorothy Margaret. BA U of Maryland 1976; MDiv UTS 1982; STM GTS 1989; DMin NYTS 2005. D 6/5/1982 P 12/12/1982 Bp Paul Moore Jr. c 1. R S Andr's Epis Ch Hartsdale NY 1984-1994; Asst S Jn's Ch Getty Sq Yonkers NY 1982-1984. Co-Auth, "Cooking w the Movies: Meals on Reels," ABC-Clio, 2010; Auth, "Jewelry Making Through Hist: An Encyclopedia," Greenwood, 2007; Co-Auth, "Cooking w the Bible: Biblic Foods, Feasts & Love," Greenwood, 2006; Co-Auth, "We Thank You God For These: Blessings & Prayers for Fam Pets," Paulist, 2004. mem2ndtry@aol.com

HESSE, William Arthur (Okla) 1805 N Canary Dr, Edmond OK 73034 **D S Mary's Ch Edmond OK 1993-** B Deadwood SD 10/18/1938 s Arthur Hesse & Thelma E. AA El Camino Coll 1964; BA U CA 1966. D 6/26/1993 Bp Robert Manning Moody. m 7/7/1962 Diane B Atchley. Bp Seabury Ch Groton CT 2006-2007.

HESSE SR, William O (Ga) 125 Renee Dr, Kingsland GA 31548 **R King Of Peace Kingsland GA 2011-** B Hackensack NJ 1/29/1964 s Oscar A Hesse & Barbara Anne. AA U of So Carolina 2002; BA U of So Carolina 2003; MDiv TESM 2006. D 11/11/2006 P 5/12/2007 Bp Henry William Scriven. m 3/19/1984 MaryBeth King c 2. S Jas Epis Ch Prospect Pk PA 2007-2011. fatherhesse@yahoo.com

HETHCOCK, William Hoover (Tenn) Po Box 3310, Sewanee TN 37375 B Thomasville NC 3/19/1932 s Hugh Thaddeus Hethcock & Emma Leigh. BA U NC 1954; MDiv GTS 1959; DMin STUSo 1984. D 9/18/1959 P 3/19/1960 Bp Richard Henry Baker. m 7/29/1972 Phebe Anne Carter c 3. Int Bruton Par Williamsburg VA 1999-2000; Prof Homil Emer The TS at The U So Sewanee TN 1997; S Lk's Epis Ch No Little Rock AR 1992; Assoc Prof Homil The TS at The U So Sewanee TN 1985-1996; The U So (Sewanee) Sewanee TN 1979-1997; Epis Soc Of Chr Ch Cincinnati OH 1974-1979; Asst Epis Soc of

Chr Ch Cincinnati OH 1974-1979; Dir Prog Dio No Carolina Raleigh NC 1967-1974; Dir Prog Dio No Carolina Raleigh NC 1967-1974; R S Lk's Epis Ch Durham NC 1960-1966; Cur S Andr's Ch Greensboro NC 1959-1960. Acad of Homilitics 1985-1987. Jess Trotter Vstng Fell VTS 2000. whethcock@bellsouth.net

HETHERINGTON, Robert Gunn (Va) 1500 Westbrook Ct Apt 2133, Richmond VA 23227 B Buffalo NY 5/23/1941 s Arthur Fenton Hetherington & Betty. BA Ya 1963; MDiv EDS 1966. D 6/11/1966 Bp William S Thomas P 12/17/1966 Bp Austin Pardue. m 8/28/1965 Elizabeth Ewing Bell c 3. R S Paul's Ch Richmond VA 1984-2006; R Trin Epis Ch Buffalo NY 1973-1984; Assoc Trin Epis Ch Buffalo NY 1969-1972; Asst S Steph's Ch Sewickley PA 1966-1969. Hon Cn Dio Wstrn New York 1982. rghetherington@gmail.com

HETLER, Gwendolyn Kay (NMich) 3135 County Road 456, Skandia MI 49885 B 3/22/1939 BA Albion Coll 1961; MS Wayne 1973. D 12/17/2000 P 7/1/2001 Bp James Arthur Kelsey. m 6/21/1986 James Livingston. *Beginning Algebra: Once and For All*, Kendall/Hunt, 2000. ghetler@nmu.edu

HETRICK JR, Budd A(lbert) (Ida) 45 Difficult Dr, Idaho City ID 83631 B Nampa ID 5/12/1949 s Budd Albert Hetrick & Sylvia E. D 1/29/1994 Bp John Stuart Thornton. m 7/14/1967 Annette Fields. Acolyte Coordntr & Cmnty Outreach Ch Of H Nativ Meridian ID 2001-2002; D Ch Of H Nativ Meridian ID 2001-2002; D S Mich's Cathd Boise ID 1998-2001; D S Dav's Epis Ch Caldwell ID 1995-1998; Liturg & Adult Educ S Dav's Epis Ch Caldwell ID 1995-1998; Yth & Acolyte Coordntr Trin Epis Ch Pocatello ID 1994-1995. deacon4u@hughes.net

HETZEL, Alan Dorn (WNC) Po Box 442, Highlands NC 28741 **D Ch Of The Incarn Highlands NC 1999-** B Charleston SC 1/26/1933 s Harry Clayton Hetzel & Geraldine. U So 1954; BA U Of Florida 1955. D 12/18/1999 Bp Robert Hodges Johnson. m 11/17/1972 Hazel Crawford. D Trin Epis Ch Asheville NC 2000-2002.

HEUSS, William (Mass) 15 Thimbleberry Rd, South Yarmouth MA 02664 B Evanston IL 1/11/1941 s John Heuss & Elizabeth. BA Wag 1964; MDiv STUSo 1968; DMin Bos 1976. D 6/16/1968 P 12/21/1968 Bp Chilton Powell. R S Dav's Epis Ch So Yarmouth MA 1996-2008; R The Ch Of The Gd Shpd Acton MA 1983-1996; Epis Cler Assoc Dio Massachusetts Boston MA 1974-2008; S Andr's Ch Wellesley MA 1974-1983; Assoc Trin Ch Tulsa OK 1968-1974. Auth, "The Sermon'S Over - Hit The Offertory!," *New Par New Cure*. Assn Of Psychol Type 1988; Enneagram Personality Types Assn 1993. Winner For Best Cartoons Associated Rel Press 1985; Winner For Best Cartoons Associated Rel Press 1984. williamheuss@comcast.net

HEVERLY, Craig Brian (Ore) 925 Se Center St, Portland OR 97202 B Buffalo NY 7/8/1938 s Samuel Bowers Heverly & Ruth Marian. BA Colg 1960; MA Colg 1967; Lon 1976; MDiv Chicago TS 1983. D 6/8/1985 P 5/1/1986 Bp O'Kelley Whitaker. m 6/30/1962 Judy Jo Gehrt c 2. Seven Rivers Cluster Payette ID 1988-1995; Paris Cluster Chadwicks NY 1986-1988; R S Mk's Ch Clark Mills NY 1986-1988; Assoc S Jas' Ch Clinton NY 1985-1988; Dio Cntrl New York Syracuse NY 1985-1986. Synagogy.

HEWETT, Clayton Kennedy (Pa) 510 Augusta Rd, Winslow ME 04901 B Providence RI 6/4/1927 s William Bentamin Hewett & Phylis Arlene. VTS 1958; Urban Trng Cntr 1964. D 6/21/1958 Bp Oliver J Hart P 12/20/1958 Bp William Blair Roberts. R Ch Of S Jas The Less Philadelphia PA 1971-1976; R Calv Epis Ch Hillcrest Wilmington DE 1967-1971; Urban Mssnr Dio Pennsylvania Philadelphia PA 1965-1967; R The Ch Of The Atone Morton PA 1958-1965. OHC 1963-1980; S Richard's Gld - Fndr & Dir 1979. Cn to the Ordnry Dio the Resurr 1978.

HEWITT JR, Arch M(erille) (Mont) 11 Washington Pl, Helena MT 59601 B Huntington WV 11/4/1928 s Archibald Merille Hewitt & Ruth. BA Pr 1951; MDiv VTS 1954. D 6/6/1954 Bp Robert E L Strider P 12/15/1954 Bp Wilburn Camrock Campbell. m 7/13/1953 Gail Veatch c 3. Int S Paul's Epis Ch Grand Forks ND 2002-2003; Int S Fran Ch Rio Rancho NM 2001-2002; Int All SS Ch Minot ND 2000-2001; Int S Paul's Epis Ch Grand Forks ND 1999-2000; Int Geth Cathd Fargo ND 1997-1998; Int S Mich's and All Ang' Ch Fairview MT 1992-1993; Int S Jas Epis Ch Taos NM 1991-1992; Dn S Ptr's Par Helena MT 1981-1990; R S Mk's Ch Houston TX 1973-1981; R S Mk's Epis Ch Casper WY 1966-1973; R Calv Epis Ch Ashland KY 1960-1966; Cur S Paul's Ch Mobile AL 1959-1960; P-in-c S Steph's Ch Romney WV 1954-1958. Auth, *A Sentimental Journey of Preaching*, 1988.

HEWITT, Emily Clark (NY) 96 Rockview St, Jamaica Plain MA 02130 B Baltimore MD 5/26/1944 d John Frank Hewitt & Margaret. BA Cor; MA UTS 1975; JD Harv 1978. Rec 11/1/1977 as Priest Bp Paul Moore Jr. Auth, "Wmn P: Yes Or No?"; Auth, "arts Revs".

HEWITT, Robert Gurnee (Colo) 4119 Lupine St, Colorado Springs CO 80918 B Trenton NJ 11/7/1921 s Charles Conrad Hewitt & Elisabeth. BA Pr 1947; GTS 1951. D 6/20/1951 P 12/23/1951 Bp Wallace J Gardner. m 6/10/1950 Barbara Barton c 3. R Gr And S Steph's Epis Ch Colorado Sprg CO 1968-1986; Bp Coun Dio Nebraska Omaha NE 1956-1968; Dn Trin Cathd Omaha NE 1956-1968; P S Christophers Ch Cozad NE 1955-1956; P H Trin Ch Callaway NE 1953-1956; P S Jn's Ch Broken Bow NE 1953-1956; Asst To Dn Trin Cathd Trenton NJ 1951-1953. robertghewitt@yahoo.com

HEWITT, Susan Miller (Ak) Tower 10, 5A South Horizons, Ap Lei Chau Hong Kong B Concord MA 2/25/1944 d Torsten J Miller & Clara Burgess. BA Wilson Coll 1966; MA U of Alaska 1981; MDiv Bex 1984. D 9/14/1984 P 6/1/1985 Bp George Clinton Harris. m 12/18/1965 Robert Hewitt c 2. Epis Ch of the H Sprt Phoenix AZ 2001-2003; S Paul's Epis Ch Grand Forks ND 2000-2001; St Johns Cathd 0 1993-1998; Chr Ch Anchorage AK 1986-1993; D-in-c Chr Ch Anchorage AK 1984-1985; Dio Alaska Fairbanks AK 1984-1985; R S Fran By The Sea Ch Kenai AK 1984-1985. Rossiter Schlr Bex 1987. ESMHEWITT@MSN.COM

HEYD, Matthew F (NY) 74 Trinity Pl, New York NY 10006 **Trin Par New York NY 2009-** B Greenville NC 11/4/1969 s Peter Foster Heyd & Delores Hahn. BA U NC 1992; MAR Yale DS 1995; STM The GTS 2009. D 3/7/2009 P 9/12/2009 Bp Mark Sean Sisk. m 6/1/1996 Ann Duggan Thornton c 1. Assoc Dir,Trin Grants Prog Par of Trin Ch New York NY 2003-2009. mfheyd@aol.com

HEYDT, C(harles) Read (SwFla) PO Box 691, 380 Gilchrist Ave, Boca Grande FL 33921 B Cleveland OH 8/15/1937 s Richard Gordon Heydt & Anita Mueller. BA Dart 1959; MS NWU 1968; MDiv VTS 1979. D 6/30/1979 P 1/10/1980 Bp William Gillette Weinhauer. c 2. Int S Paul's Ch Albany GA 2003-2005; Int S Jn's Epis Ch Clearwater FL 2001-2003; Int S Mk's Epis Ch Jacksonville FL 1999-2000; Assoc Trin By The Cove Naples FL 1995-1999; Stndg Com Dio Ohio Cleveland OH 1992-1994; R Chr Ch Epis Hudson OH 1984-1995; Asst Trin Ch Toledo OH 1979-1984. Int Mnstry Ntwk 1999. read@me.com

HEYDUK, M Therese (Terri) (NY) 7612 N Eastlake Terr Unit 2N, Chicago IL 60626 B Philadelphia PA 4/29/1952 d Walter Joseph Heyduk & Marie Eleanor. BA Marymount Coll 1981; MDiv GTS 1996. D 6/1/1996 P 12/7/1996 Bp Richard Frank Grein. Int Pstr S Jn The Evang Lockport IL 2010-2011; R S Andr's Ch Brewster NY 2000-2009; Int S Steph's Ch Pearl River NY 1999-2000; Asst R Trin-St Jn's Ch Hewlett NY 1996-1999. mtheyduk@aol.com

HEYES, Andrew (SwFla) 706 W 113th Ave, Tampa FL 33612 **R S Clem Epis Ch Tampa FL 2006-** B United Kingdom 12/11/1961 s George Heyes & Joan. Trans from Church Of England 12/7/2006 Bp John Bailey Lipscomb. aheyes@tampabay.rr.com

HEYING, R Christopher (SwVa) 1695 Perrowville Road, Forest VA 24551 **R S Steph's Epis Ch Forest VA 2004-** B Socorro NM 5/18/1964 s Robert Joseph Heying & Doris Frederika. Midwestern St U; BA U of No Texas 1986; MDiv Nash 1998. D 6/27/1998 P 12/28/1998 Bp Jack Leo Iker. m 9/1/1990 Cynthia Gaye Perkins c 2. Vic Ch Of S Jn The Div Burkburnett TX 2001-2004; Dio Ft Worth Ft Worth TX 2001-2004; Vic S Steph's Epis Ch Wichita Falls TX 2001-2004; Cur Ch Of The Trsfg New York NY 2001; Asst S Paul's Epis Ch Murfreesboro TN 1999-2001; Cur S Jn's Ch Ft Worth TX 1998-1999. rector@ststephensforest.org

HEYVAERT, Bruce Thomas (Wyo) 8320 E Via De La Luna, Scottsdale AZ 85258 **Assoc S Anth On The Desert Scottsdale AZ 2011-** B Torrington CT 9/22/1955 s John C Heyvaert & Ruth Mae. S Mary Coll Winona, Minnesota 1975; Iowa St U Ames, Iowa 1977; BA S Thos Sem Denver, Colorado 1979; MDiv S Thos Sem 1983. Rec from Roman Catholic 9/29/1994 Bp Bob Gordon Jones. m 12/12/1985 Donna Mae Demos. BHEYVAERT@COX.NET

HEYWARD, (Isabel) Carter (Mass) PO Box 449, Cedar Mountain NC 28718 B Charlotte NC 8/22/1945 d Robert Heyward & Mary Ann. BA Randolph-Macon Wmn's Coll 1967; MA Col 1971; MDiv UTS 1973; PhD UTS 1980. D 6/9/1973 Bp Paul Moore Jr P 7/29/1974 Bp Robert Lionne DeWitt. Prof Theol EDS Cambridge MA 1975-2005. Auth, "Keep Your Courage: A Radical Chr Speaks," 2010; Auth, "The Redemp of God, 2nd Ed," *w Preface by Janet L. Surrey, Ph.D.*, 2010; Auth, "Flying Changes: Horses as Sprtl Teachers," 2005; Auth, "God In The Balance: Chr Sprtlty In Timeo Of Terror," 2002; Auth, "Saving Jesus From Those Who Are Rt," 1999; Auth, "Staying Power," 1995; Auth, "When Boundaries Betray Us," 1993; Auth, "Spkng Of Chr," 1989; Auth, "Teachng Our Strength: Erotic As Power & The Love Of God," 1989; Auth, "Revolutionary Forgiveness," 1986; Auth, "God'S Fierce Whimsey," 1985; Auth, "Our Passion For Justice," 1984; Auth, "Redemp Of God: Theol Of Mutual Relatns," 1982; Auth, "A P Forever: Formation of a Wmn and a a Pries," 1975. Distinguished Alum Awd Randolph-Macon Wmn'S Coll Lynchburg VA 2001; Distinguished Alum Awd UTS, NYC 1998; Danforth Fllshp 1977. carterheyward@aol.com

HIATT, Kathleen Mary (Nev) Po Box 146, Pioche NV 89043 **D Chr Ch Pioche NV 1995-** B Pioche NV 12/18/1950 d John Donald Cole & Kathleen Mary. Cosmetology Sch. D 12/7/1995 Bp Stewart Clark Zabriskie. m 11/10/1972 Melvin Lee Hiatt c 3. deke1950@lcturbonet.com

✠ **HIBBS, Rt Rev Robert Boyd** (WTex) 1 Towers Park Ln Apt 1807, San Antonio TX 78209 B Philadelphia PA 4/20/1932 s Robert Alan Hibbs & Hazel Romaine. BA Trin Hartford CT 1954; STB GTS 1957; MA U Tor 1959; DD Epis TS of The SW 1996; DD GTS 1996. D 6/1/1957 Bp William P Roberts P 12/

21/1957 Bp Oliver J Hart Con 1/6/1996 for WTex. m 8/24/1957 Nancy Alexander. Bp Suffr Of W Texas Dio W Texas San Antonio TX 1996-2003; Sr Asst Ch Of The Gd Shpd Corpus Christi TX 1988-1996; R S Barn Epis Ch Fredericksburg TX 1983-1988; Prof Epis TS Of The SW Austin TX 1980-1983; Fac Epis TS Of The SW Austin TX 1972-1975. Phi Beta Kappa. hibbsrb@aol.com

HICKENLOOPER, A(ndrew) Morgan (CGC) Po Box 27120, Panama City FL 32411 B Cincinnati OH 3/30/1946 s Smith Hickenlooper & Virginia. BS Buc 1968; MBA Syr 1970; JD U of Missouri 1980; MDiv Epis TS of The SW 1993. D 6/5/1993 Bp John Clark Buchanan P 12/18/1993 Bp John Forsythe Ashby. m 5/16/1998 Mary Stearns c 3. R Gr Epis Ch Panama City Bch FL 2001-2006; Cn To the Ordnry & Deploy Off Dio Michigan Detroit MI 1995-2001; Dioc Exec. & Deploy Off Dio Wstrn Kansas Hutchinson KS 1993-1995; Vic S Anne's Ch McPherson KS 1993-1995. Beta Gamma Sigma (Bus) 1970; Law Sch hon Soc 1980; Missouri Bar Assn 1980; Trst ETSSw 1996-2000. amhlooper@gmail.com

HICKEY, John D (Mil) 1006 E Lyon St, Milwaukee WI 53202 B South Bend IN 4/23/1951 s Austin J Hickey & Rosemary. BA Marq 1973; JD Marq 1991; MDiv SWTS 2005. D 6/4/2005 P 6/13/2007 Bp Steven Andrew Miller. c 2. S Bon Ch Mequon WI 2007-2010; Asstg P S Chris's Ch River Hills WI 2007. rostovdog@aol.com

HICKEY, Mellie (USC) 331 Fairfield St Se, Aiken SC 29801 **Died 2/18/2011** B Tarboro NC 6/16/1916 d William Thaddeus Hossey & Elizabeth Hanks. BA Mary Baldwin Coll 1937; MDiv VTS 1977. D 6/1/1977 P 5/27/1978 Bp George Moyer Alexander. c 1.

HICKEY-TIERNAN, Joseph John (Oly) 3415 S 45th St Apt G, Tacoma WA 98409 **St Paul's Seattle Dio Olympia Seattle WA 2004-** B Philadelphia PA 4/23/1944 s Arnold George Tiernan & Catherine Elizabeth. BA S Mary's Sem & U 1966; STB S Mary's Sem & U 1968; STL CUA 1971. Rec from Roman Catholic. m 12/29/2001 Deborah Hickey. Stndg Com Pres Dio Olympia Seattle WA 1995-1998; Const & Cns Com Dio Olympia Seattle WA 1994-1995; Draft Com Profsnl Standards Dio Olympia Seattle WA 1992-1995; Draft Com Profsnl Standards Dio Olympia Seattle WA 1992-1995; Draft Com Profsnl Standards Dio Olympia Seattle WA 1992-1995; R S Barn Epis Ch Bainbridge Island WA 1988-2004; Dn Cntr For Diac Dio Oregon Portland OR 1984-1988; Com Dio Olympia Seattle WA 1984-1987; R All SS Ch Portland OR 1981-1988; Cmsn Mssn Dio Oregon Portland OR 1979-1981; Wa Assn Chs T/F On Theol Educ Dio Oregon Portland OR 1978-1981; Wa Assn Chs T/F On Theol Educ Dio Oregon Portland OR 1978-1981; Vic S Hilda's - S Pat's Epis Ch Edmonds WA 1977-1981; S Jn's Epis Ch Olympia WA 1976-1977. Auth, "Coping w A Dissolution Struggle: Survival," Leaven, 1995. josf@comcast.net

HICKMAN, Clare Louise (Mich) 241 S Franklin St, Dearborn MI 48124 B Wembury UK 9/28/1967 d John Hickman & Dorothy Mary. BA Macalester Coll 1989; MA Harvard DS 1992; MDiv SWTS 1998. D 6/27/1998 P 2/10/1999 Bp R(aymond) Stewart Wood Jr. S Lk's Ch Ferndale MI 2002-2006; Asst Chr Ch Dearborn MI 1998-2008. chickpriest@wowway.com

HICKMAN, Donald Royce (Dal) 904 Mission Ave, Athens TX 75751 B Tulsa OK 12/7/1940 s Hugh Samuel Hickman & Nola May. BA U of Tulsa 1969; MDiv VTS 1973. D 6/16/1973 P 12/9/1973 Bp Chilton Powell. m 4/3/1959 Lorena Nell Bounds c 2. R S Mths' Epis Ch Athens TX 1999-2005; Asst P Ch Of The Epiph Flagstaff AZ 1998-1999; Grand Canyon Cmnty Ch Grand Canyon AZ 1997-1998; R Ch Of The Ascen Salida CO 1986-1997; Vic Little Shpd Of The Hills Chap Salida CO 1986-1997; Vic Ch of the H Sprt Rifle CO 1983-1986; Vic S Jn's Epis Ch New Castle CO 1983-1986; R S Paul's Epis Ch Dixon WY 1982-1983; Vic Our Fr's Hse Ft Washakie WY 1979-1982; St Michaels Ch - Ethete Laramie WY 1979-1982; R All SS Epis Ch Miami OK 1975-1979; Cur Trin Ch Tulsa OK 1974-1975; Cur S Jn's Epis Ch Vinita OK 1973-1974; Cur S Mart's Ch Pryor OK 1973-1974. Fed Of Fire Chapl 1994-1997. donandlorena@yahoo.com

HICKOX, Jean Webster (RI) 10 Gershwin Rd, Westerly RI 02891 B Atlanta GA 2/22/1922 d Thomas Webster & Helen. MA Col; BA Florida St U 1944. D 4/12/1985 Bp George Nelson Hunt III. m 3/15/1950 Charles Hickox c 4.

HICKS, Catherine Delbridge (Va) PO Box 399, Port Royal VA 22535 **P-in-c S Ptr's Port Royal Port Royal VA 2010-; Com on the Stwdshp of Creation Dio Virginia Richmond VA 2009-** B Columbus GA 9/20/1954 d Matthew G Delbridge & Lola S. BA Salem Coll 1976; Cert in Aging Stds Med Coll of Virginia/VCU 2001; MSW Virginia Commonwealth U 2001; MDIV VTS 2010; Cert in Sprtl Direction Stds Washington Theol Un 2011. D 6/5/2010 P 12/11/2010 Bp Shannon Sherwood Johnston. m 4/23/1977 Ben Hicks c 3. The hon Soc of Phi Kappa Phi 2001. fredgirl@hotmail.com

HICKS, John Wellborn (CGC) 502 La Rose Dr, Mobile AL 36609 **S Andr's Ch Mobile AL 2004-; Ch Of S Marys-By-The-Sea Coden AL 1996-** B Mobile AL 2/19/1947 s Wellborn Smith Hicks & Dorothy Elolise. BA S Mary 1968; ThM Mt St. Mary's Sem 1973. Rec from Roman Catholic 7/1/1980 as Deacon Bp James Winchester Montgomery. m 9/7/1974 Patricia Lynn Rozanski c 1. Int S Ptr's Ch Jackson AL 1984-1985; Asst Dir Dioc Chld Hm S Mich's Ch Mobile AL 1981-1982; Wilmer Hall Mobile AL 1981-1982; Asst S Paul's By The Lake Chicago IL 1976-1980.

HICKS, Mary Kohn (WMass) 88 Masonic Home Rd, #R404, Charlton MA 01507 **D H Trin Epis Ch Southbridge MA 1998-** B Newberry SC 5/28/1923 d Hal Kohn & Verna Louise. BA Winthrop U 1944. D 10/9/1982 Bp Alexander Doig Stewart. m 2/10/1945 John Hick c 5. D Ch Of The Recon Webster MA 1990-1996; D H Trin Epis Ch Southbridge MA 1982-1990.

HICKS, Paul L. (WVa) 430 Juliana St., Parkersburg WV 26101 **Pastorial Assoc Trin Ch Parkersburg WV 2008-** B Roswell NM 7/6/1963 s Billie Carl Hicks & Vivian Vernette. BS W Virginia U 1985; JD W Virginia U Coll of Law 1997; Cert. in Angl Stds Bex 2007; Cert Bex 2007. D 5/1/2008 Bp William Michie Klusmeyer. m 4/9/1994 Beverly Hicks. phicks@bowlescrice.com

HICKS, Phyllis Branham (SwVa) St Paul's Episcopal Church, 2009 Kenmore Rd, Amherst VA 24521 B Lynchburg, VA 5/3/1947 d Albert Hayes Branham & Annie G. D 9/2/2006 P 12/2/2007 Bp Frank Neff Powell. m 6/26/1965 Roy W Hicks. st.paulsbearmtn@verizon.net

HICKS, Richard William (La) 2507 Portola Ave Apt 20, Livermore CA 94551 B San Francisco CA 1/7/1938 s Richard Hicks & Phyllis R. Nash; BA San Francisco St U 1972; MDiv CDSP 1975. D 6/28/1975 Bp George Richard Millard P 1/1/1976 Bp Clarence Rupert Haden Jr. c 2. S Tim's Epis Ch Chehalis WA 2001-2002; Emm Ch Coos Bay OR 2000-2001; Trin Epis Ch Ashland Ashland OR 1999-2000; Int S Barth's Ch Beaverton OR 1998-1999; S Paul's/H Trin New Roads LA 1995-1998; Dio Wstrn Kansas Hutchinson KS 1993-1995; Trin Epis Ch Norton KS 1990-1991; Vic S Paul's Epis Ch Beloit WI 1989-1995; Ch Of The Epiph Concordia KS 1989-1993; Beloit First Chr Beloit KS 1989; Trin Ch Ennis MT 1983-1986; R S Lk's Ch Auburn CA 1977-1983; Vic Ch Of The Gd Shpd Orland CA 1975-1977; Vic H Trin Epis Ch Willows CA 1975-1977. rwmhicks@juno.com

HICKS, Sally Sue (Colo) Po Box 1590, Granby CO 80446 B Glenrock WY 8/23/1934 d Ira Gilbert Warren & Julia Sloan. BA Regis U 1992. D 11/4/1995 Bp William Jerry Winterrowd. m 8/30/1958 Donovan Hicks c 2. NAAD 1995. Bp's Cross Sprtl Direction Mnstry Bp W.interrowd 2001. deacon@rkymtnhi.com

HICKS, Warren Earl (WMass) 921 Pleasant St, Worcester MA 01602 **Dn of Cntrl & Wstrn Worcester Dnry Dio Wstrn Massachusetts Springfield MA 2008-; R S Lk's Ch Worcester MA 2006-** B Ft Sill OK 4/25/1960 s Sally Sue. AOS Culinary Inst of Amer 1987; BA Metropltn St Coll of Denver 2000; MDiv Epis TS of the SW 2003. D 6/14/2003 P 12/13/2003 Bp William Jerry Winterrowd. m 4/4/1986 Mary H Hicks c 2. Vic San Luis Vlly Epis Mssn Monte Vista CO 2003-2006. fr.warren@gmail.com

HIEBERT, Cornelius A (Dal) 8105 Fair Oaks Xing, Dallas TX 75231 B Wichita KS 3/28/1952 s Franklin Hiebert & Elma Francis. BD Wichita St U 1976; MDiv Nash 1981. D 7/9/1981 Bp Richard Frank Grein P 1/3/1982 Bp Robert Elwin Terwilliger. c 1. The Epis Ch Of The Resurr Dallas TX 1981-1982. Auth, "Living The Gd News," *Sunday Sch Curric*, 1976.

HIERS JR, John Douglas (SwFla) 1004 Woodcrest Ave, Clearwater FL 33756 **R Ch Of The Ascen Clearwater FL 2000-** B 11/5/1953 s John D Hiers & Mary A. BA U of So Florida 1975; MDiv VTS 1978. D 6/14/1978 P 3/17/1979 Bp Emerson Paul Haynes. m 6/21/1975 Brenda D Weekly c 3. Asst Chr Ch Bradenton FL 1983-2000; Asst S Mk's Epis Ch Venice FL 1978-1983. johnh@churchofascension.org

HIERS, Sharon Leigh (At) 1790 Lavista Rd NE, Atlanta GA 30329 **Assoc R for Yth & YA Formation S Barth's Epis Ch Atlanta GA 2009-** B Hampton SC 12/13/1971 d James Alton Hiers & Lucyle Jones. BS Coastal Carolina U 1996; MDiv The U So (Sewanee) 2007. D 2/21/2009 P 9/13/2009 Bp J(ohn) Neil Alexander. m 9/9/2011 Lisa Ann Newton. sharon@stbartsatlanta.org

HIESTER, Ronald Norman (SC) 813 S Parker Dr Apt B, Florence SC 29501 **P in Res All SS Ch Florence SC 2010-** B Reading PA 4/20/1935 s Wellington A Hiester & Mary. BA Moravian TS 1958; BD Moravian TS 1962; MDiv Moravian TS 1964. D 7/25/1964 P 12/16/1964 Bp Wilburn Camrock Campbell. m 6/29/1957 Jane Elizabeth Powell. Pstr Assoc S Jn's Ch Florence SC 2006-2010; R Trin Ch Scotland Neck NC 2000-2006; R S Ptr's Ch Seward AK 1993-1997; R S Geo's Ch Cordova AK 1991-1993; Vic St Bartholomews Ch Oak Hall VA 1989-1991; R S Mk's Epis Ch Perryville MD 1980-1989; R S Ptr's Ch Poolesville MD 1969-1980; Asst to R S Mary Magd Ch Silver Sprg MD 1967-1969; R Gr Epis Ch Elkins WV 1965-1967. rjhiester1737@aol.com

HIGGINBOTHAM, John E (RI) 99 Pierce St, East Greenwich RI 02818 **P S Lk's Epis Ch E Greenwich RI 2011-; D S Lk's Epis Ch E Greenwich RI 2010-** B Providence RI 5/22/1954 s Robert Higginbotham & Dorothy. BA St Meinrad Coll 1982; MDiv EDS 2010. D 1/8/2011 P 10/18/2011 Bp Geralyn Wolf. m 7/25/2004 Linda Succi c 3. johnnyhiggs@yahoo.com

HIGGINBOTHAM SR, Kenneth Day (Los) 4488 Mcintosh Lake Ave, Sarasota FL 34233 **Died 8/5/2010** B Worcester MA 5/1/1928 s Charles Washington Higgonbotham & Olive Mary Elizabeth. BA Trin Hartford CT 1950; STB Ya Berk 1954; STD Ya Berk 1983. D 5/15/1954 Bp William A Lawrence P 11/20/1954 Bp Joseph Gillespie Armstrong. c 2. Hon Cn S Andrews Warri Nigeria; Hon Cn S Paul & S Athan Cathd Cntr Los Angeles CA.

HIGGINBOTHAM, Richard Cann (Chi) 3800 N Lake Shore Dr # 1j, Chicago IL 60613 B Saint Louis MO 7/5/1950 s Richard Cann Higginbotham & Jocelyn. BA Macalester Coll 1972; MA U MN 1973; MA U IL 1978; MDiv SWTS 1994. D 6/18/1994 P 12/17/1994 Bp Frank Tracy Griswold III. Asst Ch Of The Ascen Chicago IL 1996-2008; Asst S Chris's Epis Ch Oak Pk IL 1994-1996. r-higginbotham@neiu.edu

HIGGINBOTHAM, Stuart Craig (At) 2900 Paces Ferry Rd SE Bldg D, Atlanta GA 30339 **St Ben's Epis Ch Smyrna GA 2010-** B 8/2/1979 s Marion Lavon Higginbotham & Teresa LuAnn. BS Lyon Coll 2001; MDiv Columbia TS 2005; Dplma Angl Stds The TS at the U So 2008. D 12/21/2007 P 6/29/2008 Bp J(ohn) Neil Alexander. m 5/31/2003 Lisa RS Lisa Ruth Sites c 1. Dio Atlanta Atlanta GA 2008-2009. stuart@mysaintb.org

HIGGINS, Delia Kimball (NC) 221 Hillcrest Dr, High Point NC 27262 B Simmesport LA 11/28/1938 d Riley Bernard Kimball & Ethel Mae. Wake Forest U; BA High Point U 1983; D's Trng Sch 1989. D 6/17/1989 Bp Robert Whitridge Estill. m 4/27/1957 Lloyd Malcolm Higgins c 4. S Mary's Epis Ch High Point NC. Chapl Ord Of S Lk; NAAD.

HIGGINS, Kent (WVa) St Matthews Episcopal Church, 36 Norwood Rd, Charleston WV 25314 **P in Res S Matt's Ch Charleston WV 2011-** B Oak Hill WV 9/5/1944 s Stanley Carmen Higgins & Jean Kent. Cert Dioc Trng Prog; BS W Virginia U 1972. D 12/16/2006 P 6/16/2007 Bp William Michie Klusmeyer. m 1/27/1972 Gail Vaughan c 2. P-in-c Ascen Epis Ch Hinton WV 2009. revkenthiggins@gmail.com

HIGGINS, Pamela (Cal) 272 W I St, Benicia CA 94510 B Bakersfield CA 7/4/1950 d James W Higgins & Delores F. BA U CA 1972; MLS U CA 1974; JD U of San Francisco 1978; MDiv CDSP 1991. D 6/8/1991 P 6/1/1992 Bp William Edwin Swing. Vic Ch Of The H Trin Richmond CA 2005-2009; Int S Barth's Epis Ch Livermore CA 1995-1996; Assoc Gr Cathd San Francisco CA 1992-1995. M.Div. w dist CDSP 1991.

HIGGINS, Teddy John (USC) 226 Haven Rd, Batesburg SC 29006 **S Paul's Ch Batesburg SC 2005-** B Biloxi MS 3/11/1952 s Preston Higgins & Barbara. BS Clemson U 1983; MA Embry-Riclolle Aeronautical U Daytona FL 1987. D 6/11/2005 P 3/26/2006 Bp Dorsey Felix Henderson. m 6/16/1972 Kimberley Higgins c 5. higginstj@aol.com

HIGGINS, Timothy John (Me) 25 Twilight Ln, Gorham ME 04038 **R S Ann's Epis Ch Windham Windham ME 2007-; Dio Maine Portland ME 2004-** B Lewiston ME 10/3/1959 s Gene Higgins & Claudette. BS S Mich's Coll Winooski VT 1981; MDiv S Mary's Sem Baltimore MD 1987; S Mary's Sem Baltimore MD 1987. Rec from Roman Catholic 10/22/2004 Bp Chilton Abbie Richardson Knudsen. m 5/26/2006 Maureen Higgins c 3. timhiggins@maine.rr.com

HIGGINSON, Paul Howard (NH) 472 Swazey La, Bethlehem NH 03574 **D All SS Epis Ch Littleton NH 2005-; Chapl The White Mtn Sch Littleton NH 2005-** B Waterbury CT 12/24/1945 s Howard Henry Higginson & Edna Elizabeth. BS Cntrl Connecticut St U 1977. D 12/7/1991 Bp Arthur Edward Walmsley. m 10/28/1995 Sheelagh Mary McCord c 2. D S Jn's Ch New Milford CT 1999-2004; D S Paul's Ch Woodbury CT 1994-1999; D S Mk's Chap Storrs CT 1991-1992. NAAD. thehiggys1027@aol.com

HIGGITT, Noel (ECR) 1325 San Mateo Dr, Menlo Park CA 94025 B Liverpool UK 12/25/1938 s Charles Higgett & Emma. BS Liverpool Coll Of Commerce Gb 1963; BA Sch for Deacons 1989; MDiv CDSP 1994. D 6/9/1990 Bp William Edwin Swing P 6/1/1996 Bp Richard Lester Shimpfky. m 5/14/1988 Anne Santana c 2. S Mk's Par Berkeley CA 1994-1995; D S Jas Epis Ch San Francisco CA 1990-1995.

HIGGONS JR, Earl T (NJ) 61 Dinwiddie Drive, Greenwich NJ 08323 B Philadelphia PA 10/4/1929 s Earl Thomas Higgons & Mary Elizabeth. BA Penn 1952; ThM PDS 1955. D 4/30/1955 P 11/5/1955 Bp Alfred L Banyard. m 11/14/1964 Florence Anna Stanley. Cmssnr Nj Div Civil Rts Dio New Jersey Trenton NJ 1981-1987; Stndg Com Dio New Jersey Trenton NJ 1969-1972; Bd Mssns & Csr Dio New Jersey Trenton NJ 1965-1970; Dept Csr Dio New Jersey Trenton NJ 1960-1972; Chair Hisp Cmsn Dio New Jersey Trenton NJ 1959-2000; R S Andr's Epis Ch Bridgeton NJ 1959-1993; Dept Mssns Dio New Jersey Trenton NJ 1959-1972; Vic S Mary's Epis Ch Stone Harbor NJ 1955-1959. Auth, "Hist Of S Andrews," Dio Nj, 1965; Auth, "100 Years Of Prayers," *Sacr & Wrshp*. OGS; Oratory Of The Rural Shpd. Hon Cn Trin Cathd Trenton NJ 1969. canoneth@aol.com

✠ **HIGH JR, Rt Rev Rayford Baines** (Tex) 2695 S Southwest Loop 323, Tyler TX 75701 B Houston TX 1/4/1941 s Rayford Baines High & Helen Elizabeth. BA U So 1963; MDiv ETS 1966. D 6/28/1966 Bp Everett H Jones P 1/6/1967 Bp Richard Earl Dicus Con 10/4/2003 for Tex. m 8/29/1964 Patricia Moseley c 3. Bp Suffr of Texas Dio Texas Houston TX 2003-2011; Cn Dio Texas Houston TX 1998-2003; R S Paul's Ch Waco TX 1981-1998; R S Jn's Ch McAllen TX 1977-1981; R S Fran Epis Ch Victoria TX 1969-1977; Asst S Mk's Epis Ch San Antonio TX 1966-1969. Humanitarian of the Year Waco Conf of Christians and Jews 1997. rhigh@epicenter.org

HIGHLAND, Terrence (Pa) 275 Grace St, Pottstown PA 19464 **R Chr Epis Ch Pottstown PA 2007-** B Chicago IL 11/20/1941 s Irving H Highland & Julia. BA St. Olaf Coll 1963; MDiv STUSo 1989. D 6/11/1989 Bp Arthur Anton Vogel P 12/16/1989 Bp John Wadsworth Howe. m 4/19/1975 Christina Flinn c 3. Gloria Dei Epis Ch Cocoa FL 1991-1993; S Jn's Ch Melbourne FL 1989-1991. redeemcec@aol.com

HIGHSMITH, Jennifer Lynn (Ga) 102 Borrell Blvd, Saint Marys GA 31558 B Pawtucket RI 5/22/1958 d Layton Stewart Risley & Jeanne Virginia. Dio Georgnia; EFM U So. D 9/6/2006 Bp Henry Irving Louttit. c 1. ladyrisley@earthlink.net

HILDEBRAND, Nancy Steakley (WA) St Nicholas Episcopal Church, 14100 Darnestown Rd Ste B, Germantown MD 20874 B Denver CO 7/2/1947 d Joe Earl Steakley & Margaret Fern Hopper. U IL; BA U Chi 1969; U CO 2007; VTS 2007; MDiv Wesley TS 2007. D 6/9/2007 P 1/19/2008 Bp John Chane. m 6/17/1967 Peter Henry Hildebrand c 6. Asst S Nich Epis Ch Germantown MD 2007-2009. nancyhildebrand@verizon.net

HILDEBRANDT, M Lise (WMass) PO Box 1737, Onset MA 02558 B Columbus OH 5/9/1959 d Theodore Ware Hildebrandt & Mary Kathryn. BA U NC 1980; MDiv Ya Berk 1986; MPH Bos 2004. D 11/14/1986 Bp Robert Whitridge Estill P 1/30/1988 Bp Alden Moinet Hathaway. m 8/25/1984 Eric Wefald c 4. Int Ch Of The Gd Shpd Wareham MA 2010; Int S Dunstans Epis Ch Dover MA 2009; P-in-c S Jn's Ch Worcester MA 2005-2009; Int Chr Memi Ch No Brookfield MA 2002-2004; R Chr Ch Rochdale MA 1997-2001; Asst/Assoc R Chr Epis Ch No Hills Pittsburgh PA 1987-1992; D Ch Of The Servnt Wilmington NC 1986-1987. lisehild@yahoo.com

HILDESLEY, Christopher Hugh (NY) 570 Park Ave Apt 6-D, New York NY 10021 B Cambridge UK 7/29/1941 s Paul Francis Glynn Hildesley & Mary. Oxf. D 6/12/1976 Bp Paul Moore Jr P 12/1/1976 Bp Harold Louis Wright. m 1/17/1964 Constance Cunningham Palmer c 3. Ch Of The Heav Rest New York NY 1983-1995; Asst Ch Of The Heav Rest New York NY 1977-1983; Asst The Ch Of The Epiph New York NY 1976-1977. Auth, "Journeying w Julian". Osjj.

HILE, Jeanette Theresa (Nwk) 16 Day Rd, Landing NJ 07850 B Morristown NJ 10/11/1949 d James Hile & Carolyn. Immac Concep Sem; BA Montclair St U 1971; MA Montclair St U 1977. D 12/9/2006 Bp Carol Joy Gallagher. jthile49@yahoo.com

HILEMAN, Mary E(sther) (Okla) St. Augustine Canterbury Center, 519 W. University Avenue, Stillwater OK 74074 **Dep Gen Conv Dio Oklahoma Oklahoma City OK 2009-2012; Vic S Mk's Ch Perry OK 2009-; S Andr's Ch Stillwater OK 1989-; Full-time S Aug Cbury Cntr Stillwater OK 1989-** B Detroit MI 12/27/1945 d William Ralph Hileman & Esther Elizabeth. BS U MI 1967; MS U MI 1969; PhD U MI 1973; MDiv VTS 1989. D 6/17/1989 P 12/16/1989 Bp Robert Manning Moody. Pres. Stndg Comm Dio Oklahoma Oklahoma City OK 2010-2011; Pres. Stndg Comm Dio Oklahoma Oklahoma City OK 2007-2008; Dep Gen Conv Dio Oklahoma Oklahoma City OK 2006-2009; Chair - Dio. Cmsn on Min in Higher Ed Dio Oklahoma Oklahoma City OK 2005-2011; Dep Gen Conv. Dio Oklahoma Oklahoma City OK 2003-2006; Pres. Stndg Comm Dio Oklahoma Oklahoma City OK 2001-2002; First Alt Dep Gen. Conv. Dio Oklahoma Oklahoma City OK 2000-2003; Coordntr-Min in Higher Ed Prov VII Fairfax VA 1997-2004; Dep Gen. Conv. Dio Oklahoma Oklahoma City OK 1997-2000; Reg Dn Dio Oklahoma Oklahoma City OK 1991-1996; Rgnl Dn Dio Oklahoma Oklahoma City OK 1991-1996; half-time Ch Of The Ascen Pawnee OK 1989-1991; Chapl-OK St Univ. (half-time) Dio Oklahoma Oklahoma City OK 1989-1991. Epis Soc for Mnstry in Higher Eucation 1991-2005. mary.hileman@mac.com

HILFIKER, Gerald Milton (WNY) 10085 Pfarner Road, Boston NY 14025 **Archd Dio Wstrn New York Tonawanda NY 2011-; D S Paul's Epis Ch Springville NY 2002-** B Rochester NY 6/5/1942 s Milton George Hilfiker & Florence Mary. BS SUNY 1964; MS Alfred Adler Inst of Chicago 1986. D 9/14/2001 Bp J Michael Garrison. m 8/14/1971 Karen Anne Johnson c 4. ghilfiker1@juno.com

HILGARTNER, Elizabeth (Vt) Po Box 6, Orford NH 03777 **S Barn Ch Norwich VT 2004-** B Baltimore MD 12/7/1957 d Charles Andrew Hilgartner & Carol. BA Harv 1979; MDiv EDS 1986. D 6/11/1979 P 12/1/1986 Bp Robert Shaw Kerr. m 9/16/1979 Ernest Alfred Drown. S Lk's Ch Woodsville NH 2001-2004; Int S Jas Ch Woodstock VT 1999-2000; Int S Thos Ch Hanover NH 1996-1997; The Holderness Sch Plymouth NH 1993-1996; R S Lk's Ch Charlestown NH 1989-1993; R Un Ch Claremont NH 1989-1993; Cur Chr Ch Montpelier VT 1986-1989. Auth, "Cats In Cyberspace," Meisha Merlin Pub, 2000; Auth, "A Necklace Of Fallen Stars"; Auth, "Colors In The Dreamweaver'S Loom"; Auth, "The Feast Of The Trickster"; Auth, "A Murder For Her Majesty". pkp@valley.net

HILL, Barbara Jeanne (Cal) 555 Pierce St Apt 340-E, Albany CA 94706 **D Dio California San Francisco CA 1992-** B La Porte IN 7/7/1942 d Alfred Arthur Finley & Dorothy Edith. BS Indiana U 1964; MDiv CDSP 1990. D 6/6/1992 Bp William Edwin Swing. c 4. D The Epis Ch Of The Gd Shpd Berkeley CA 2007.

HILL, C(harleen) Diane (Ala) 1806 Meadows Dr, Birmingham AL 35235 B Macon GA 8/20/1954 d Willie Cephus Hill & Annie Barnes. Savannah St Coll

1976; BA Ft Vlly St U 1988; MDiv Lexington TS 1994; STUSo 1994. D 6/11/1994 P 5/1/1995 Bp Don Adger Wimberly. S Mk's Ch Birmingham AL 2006-2008; Asst to R S Paul's Ch Henderson KY 1999-2000; Ch Of Our Merc Sav Louisville KY 1996-1999; Ch S Mich The Archangel Lexington KY 1994-1996. dyehill@msn.com

HILL, David Ernest (Minn) 103 West Oxford Street, Duluth MN 55803 **D S Paul's Epis Ch Duluth MN 2006-; D Trin Epis Ch Hermantown MN 2001-** B Bay City TX 4/20/1942 s Ernest Benihart Hill & Ebba Elizabeth. BA Texas Tech U 1972. D 6/17/2001 Bp James Louis Jelinek. m 11/21/1964 Diana Van Dyke c 2. norpoint@gate.net

HILL, Derrick Craig (Ala) 1910 12th Ave S, Birmingham AL 35205 **Asst S Mary's-On-The-Highlands Epis Ch Birmingham AL 2011-** B Birmingham AL 12/20/1966 s Steve Hill & JoAnn Owen. BS Auburn U 1990; MPPM Birmingham Sthrn Coll 1995; MDiv The TS at The U So 2011. D 5/18/2011 Bp Henry Nutt Parsley Jr. m 9/26/1998 Beverly Hurley c 2. derrick@stmarysoth.org

HILL, Donald Benjamin (Roch) 321 E Market St, Jeffersonville IN 47130 **Co-Pstr-in-Charge S Paul's Jeffersonville IN 2011-** B Buffalo NY 5/8/1945 s Donald James Hill & Phyllis Edna. BA SUNY 1967; MDiv Bex 1970; Cert Assn of Profsnl Chapl 1998; Cert Cler Ldrshp Inst 2010. D 6/29/1970 P 1/25/1971 Bp Harold B Robinson. m 10/12/1991 Nancy Woodworth c 2. Asst S Mk's Ch Newark NY 2009-2011; P-in-c S Geo's Ch Hilton NY 2006-2009; R Trin Ch Rochester NY 2000-2009; R Ch Of The Ascen Buffalo NY 1991-1995; R Ch Of The Trsfg Buffalo NY 1991-1995; Ed Dio Wstrn New York Tonawanda NY 1984-1996; R S Mk's Ch Buffalo NY 1982-1991; R All SS Ch Round Lake NY 1979-1980; Asst Dir Ecum Cmncatns Off Dio Albany Albany NY 1976-1980; Assoc Chr Epis Ch Ballston Spa NY 1976-1979; Assoc Ch Of Beth Saratoga Sprg NY 1974-1976; Chapl Doane Stuart Sch Albany NY 1972-1974; Cn Sacrist Cathd Of All SS Albany NY 1970-1972. Assn of Profesional Chapl 1997-2010; ECom 1978-2010. Serv to Mankind Awd SERTOMA, Buffao NY 1987; Citizen of the Year Buffalo News 1984. dbhill321@gmail.com

HILL, Ellen R. (Los) 5066 Berean Ln, Irvine CA 92603 B Akron,OH 7/25/1938 d Milo M Ratkovich & Alice D. BA Ohio Wesl 1960; MDiv Claremont TS 1988; DMin Claremont TS 1997. D 6/25/1988 P 1/21/1989 Bp Frederick Houk Borsch. m 8/27/1960 Lamar Mott Hill c 2. R S Mich and All Ang Epis Ch Studio City CA 1993-2003; Assoc Ch Of The Mssh Santa Ana CA 1988-1992. Auth, "A Prog for Congrl Stwdshp Dvlpmt"; Auth, "Resurr: Renwl & Rebirth in Congregations Experienced Betrayal Pstr Trust". thereverh@yahoo.com

HILL, Gary Hill (Tex) 9541 Highland View Dr., Dallas TX 75238 B Norfolk VA 8/9/1948 s Woodrow Pearson Hill & Beatrice Marjorie. BGS U of SW Louisiana 1982; MDiv Nash 1985. D 6/1/1985 P 11/30/1985 Bp Willis Ryan Henton. m 8/19/1972 Nancy Hunter c 3. R Chr Ch Nacogdoches TX 1997-2010; R Trin Epis Ch Jasper TX 1991-1997; Vic Ch Of The Ascen Epis Springfield MO 1988-1991; Dio W Missouri Kansas City MO 1988-1991; Asst S Paul's Epis Ch Shreveport LA 1985-1987. fr.hill@yahoo.com

HILL III, George Aldrich (SO) 12035 Cooperwood Ln, Cincinnati OH 45242 B Boston MA 6/3/1946 s George Aldrich Hill & Marguerite Alice. BA Indiana U 1971; MDiv Methodist TS 1974; DMin Methodist TS 1987; STM Bos 1998. D 2/12/1978 P 6/1/1978 Bp John Mc Gill Krumm. m 9/1/1974 Amy Edgeworth c 2. Vic S Barn Epis Ch Montgomery OH 1982-2011; S Thos Epis Ch Terrace Pk OH 1978-1982. Intl Conf of Police Chapl; Intl Ord of S Lk the Physcn. gah@fuse.net

HILL, Gordon Carman (Az) 2257 E Becker Ln, Phoenix AZ 85028 B Parishville NY 8/14/1932 s Reuben Ca Hill & Dorothy Alice. BS SUNY 1959; MA Arizona St U 1963. D 1/19/1992 Bp Joseph Thomas Heistand. m 9/9/1956 Nazaly D Hill. SocMary.

HILL III, Harry Hargrove (SVa) Po Box 12683, Pensacola FL 32591 **Chr Ch Par Pensacola FL 2004-** B Lexington VA 10/10/1947 s Harry Hargrove Hill & Ellen Cary. BA W&L 1970; JD W&L 1974; MDiv VTS 1992. Trans 1/9/2004 Bp David Conner Bane Jr. Chr Epis Ch Virginia Bch VA 2003; R S Bride's Epis Ch Chesapeake VA 2000-2003; Gr Epis Ch Goochland VA 1994-2000; Gr Epis Ch Goochland VA 1992-1993; Asst S Fran In The Fields Harrods Creek KY 1992-1993. Soc of S Jn the Evang. hhill@christ-church.net

HILL IV, Harvey (At) 302 West Ave., Cedartown GA 30125 B Atlanta GA 9/7/1965 s Harvey Hill & Sarah. BA Ya 1987; MTS Candler TS 1991; PhD Emory U 1996; EDS 2008. D 12/20/2008 P 6/28/2009 Bp J(ohn) Neil Alexander. m 8/1/1992 Carrie Baker c 2. Vic S Jas Ch Cedartown GA 2009-2011. hhill@berry.edu

HILL, Heather Louise (O) 8911 W Ridgewood Dr, Parma OH 44130 **R All SS Ch Parma OH 2009-** B Hong Kong 6/19/1978 BA Buc 2000; MDiv Harvard DS 2003. D 12/20/2003 P 6/26/2004 Bp Wendell Nathaniel Gibbs Jr. m 1/30/2010 Dustin David Berg. R S Phil's In The Field Oreland PA 2006-2009; Asst S Jn's Ch Plymouth MI 2003-2006. pastorheatherhill@yahoo.com

HILL, H Michael (CGC) 2255 Valle Escondido Dr, Pensacola FL 32526 **Epis Day Sch Of Chr Ch Pensacola FL 2006-; Vic S Cyp's Epis Ch Pensacola FL 2000-** B Mobile AL 5/4/1954 s Larcena. MDiv Notre Dame Sem 1988. Rec from Roman Catholic 6/3/2000 Bp Charles Farmer Duvall. m 6/18/1994 Geneva Hill. S Cyp's Epis Ch Pensacola FL 2004-2007; Day Sch Chapl Chr Ch Par Pensacola FL 2000-2002; Epis Day Sch Of Chr Ch Pensacola FL 2000-2002; Dio Cntrl Gulf Coast Pensacola FL 2000. hm.hill@cox.net

HILL, Jerry Echols (Dal) 1123 Lodema Ln, Duncanville TX 75116 B Texarkana TX 5/19/1937 s Harry Echols Hill & Malva G. BS Sthrn Arkansas U Magnolia 1969; MDiv SWTS 1972; DMin McCormick TS 1978. D 4/10/1972 Bp Theodore H McCrea P 10/18/1972 Bp Quintin Ebenezer Primo Jr. m 4/29/1960 Gloria Herring c 2. Vic S Paul's Epis Ch Waxahachie TX 2000-2004; Ex. Dir Shltr Mnstrs Of Dallas Dallas TX 1998-1999; P-in-c S Paul's Epis Ch Waxahachie TX 1989-1999; Ch Planter Ch Of The Gd Shpd Cedar Hill TX 1981-1989; Urban Mnstrs (Dir.) Dio Dallas Dallas TX 1977-1998; St Philips Ch Dallas TX 1975-1977. ex.jeghill@sbcglobal.net

HILL, J Norman (WTex) 11603 Arrowwood Cir, Houston TX 77063 B San Antonio TX 8/20/1965 s Herbert Wheeler Hill & Josephine Spencer. BBA SW U Georgetown TX 1977; MDiv VTS 1988. D 2/20/1998 Bp James Edward Folts P 10/22/1998 Bp Robert Boyd Hibbs. m 7/17/1993 Holly Baker c 2. Asst S Mk's Epis Ch San Antonio TX 2001; Yth Min Dio W Texas San Antonio TX 2000-2004; Asst R S Alb's Ch Harlingen TX 1998-2000. jhilldwtx@aol.com

HILL, Joel (Vt) 17639 Mason Dixon Rd, Hagerstown MD 21740 B 3/22/1936 D 6/3/2000 Bp Robert Wilkes Ihloff.

HILL SSF, Jude (Cal) 573 Dolores St, San Francisco CA 94110 B Lancaster England 8/16/1957 BA Sul 1993; MA Sul 1995; PhD Uil 2002. D 6/3/2006 Bp William Edwin Swing P 12/2/2006 Bp Marc Handley Andrus. judehillssf@aol.com

HILL, Mary Ann (Chi) 10 S. Cherry St., Freeport IL 61032 **S Dunst's Ch Tulsa OK 2008-** B Alton IL 1/29/1965 d James Thomas Hill & Katharina M. BA U IL 1987; MDiv STUSo 2001. D 6/17/2001 P 5/31/2002 Bp Edward Stuart Little II. R Gr Epis Ch Freeport IL 2002-2008; Cur S Mich And All Ang Ch So Bend IN 2001-2002. Shettle Prize for Liturg Reading Sewanee 2001. maryann@stduntulsa.org

HILL, Nicholas T (Minn) 4 Saint Paul Ave, Duluth MN 55803 B Saint Paul MN 9/3/1938 s Samuel N M Hill & Jean. No Dakota St U 1960; BA Dickinson St U 1961; U of Texas 1962; MDiv Epis TS of The SW 1965; Coll of Preachers 1969. D 7/1/1965 P 2/1/1966 Bp George Theodore Masuda. m 11/11/1989 Sharyn Hill c 2. Supply P S Andr's Ch Moose Lake MN 2001-2004; H Trin Intl Falls MN 1990; R Ch Of The Gd Shpd Windom MN 1987-1990; R H Trin Epis Ch Luverne MN 1987-1990; R S Jn Worthington MN 1987-1990; Dio No Dakota Fargo ND 1985-1986; Dio Minnesota Minneapolis MN 1984-1997; R S Edw's Ch Duluth MN 1978-1983; Asst To R S Jas Ch Wichita KS 1973-1978; Cur S Jn's Epis Ch Tulsa OK 1971-1973; Vic Ch Of Our Sav Langdon ND 1965-1971; Vic S Ptr's Ch Walhalla ND 1965-1971. Auth, "3 Went In A Boat The New Indn". nickhill@charter.net

HILL, Ralph Julian (SD) 1044 N 5th St, Spearfish SD 57783 **R Ch Of All Ang Spearfish SD 1991-** B Greensboro NC 5/5/1945 s Ralph Julian Hill & Mary Louise. GTS; BS No Carolina St U 1967; JD Amer U 1973; MDiv VTS 1986. D 6/11/1986 P 3/1/1987 Bp Peter James Lee. m 8/29/1998 Jane T Ahrendt c 3. Asst to R S Aid's Ch Alexandria VA 1986-1991.

HILL, Renee Leslie (NY) 575 Grand St Apt 1801, New York NY 10002 B Washington DC 8/28/1962 d William E Hill & Betty Jean. BA Bryn 1985; MDiv UTS 1990; PhD UTS 1996. D 6/13/1992 P 12/1/1992 Bp Richard Frank Grein. m 1/1/2001 Mary Lova Foulke c 2. Sr Assoc All SS Ch Pasadena CA 1998-2002; Fac EDS Cambridge MA 1996-1998; Asst P S Mary's Manhattanville Epis Ch New York NY 1993-1996; Asst P Cathd Of St Jn The Div New York NY 1992-1993. Auth, "Beyond Colonial Anglicanism," 1999; Auth, "Who Are We For Each Other? Sex, Sexism & Womanist Theol," *Black Theol: A Documentary Hist Volume 2*, 1995; Auth, "Black Faith And Publ Talk". AAR; UBE. Lace Awd For Sprtl Ldrshp Los Angeles Gay And Lesbian Cntr Los Angeles CA 2000. foulkehill@earthlink.net

HILL, Shawn Nathaniel (Md) 7859 Tick Neck, Pasadena MD 21122 **S Andr's Ch Pasadena MD 2007-** B Baltimore MD 4/15/1964 s J Norman Hill & Gwendolyn. BA Towson U 1987; MDiv VTS 1991; MA St. Marys Sem The Ecum Inst. Of Theol 2007. D 6/15/1991 P 5/2/1992 Bp A(lbert) Theodore Eastman. c 5. Vic H Cross Ch Baltimore MD 1999-2006; Receiving Disabil Ret 1997-2006; R S Andr The Fisherman Epis Mayo MD 1995-1997; Asst to R S Tim's Ch Catonsville MD 1993-1995; Asst to R Ch Of The Ascen Westminster MD 1991-1993. Anglicans For Life 1987. shawnnhill@aol.com

HILL, Susan Elizabeth (NY) 225 W 99th St., New York NY 10025 **S Mich's Ch New York NY 2009-** B Fort Lee VA 7/18/1965 d Robert Paul Hill & Mary Alice. BS Hav 1987; MBA Columbia Bus Sch 1992; MDiv UTS 2008; STM Gnrl Thelological Sem 2009. D 3/7/2009 P 9/12/2009 Bp Mark Sean Sisk. Maxwell Fllshp Auburn Sem 2009. shill@saintmichaelschurch.org

HILL, Vernon Willard (EpisSanJ) PO Box 153, Bakersfield CA 93302 **Asst Gr Epis Ch Bakersfield CA 2008-** B San Diego CA 1/22/1944 s Vernon Willard Hill & Cynthia E. AB San Diego St Coll 1965; RelD TS, Claremont CA 1969.

H

D 11/15/2008 P 5/30/2009 Bp Jerry Alban Lamb. m 6/11/1993 Melinda Watten Berger c 4. vwmshill@hughes.net

HILL-DWYER, Paulette (WNY) No address on file. B Buffalo NY 1/31/1947 d Henry G Adaszak & Eleanor T. BS SUNY 1968; Cert Humber Coll 1981; Cert D'Youville Coll 1985. D 6/13/1987 Bp Harold B Robinson. m 8/24/1968 Dennis Dwyer c 1. Dio Wstrn New York Tonawanda NY 1995.

HILLEGAS, Eric (Mass) Parish of St. Chrysostom, 1 Linden Street, Quincy MA 02170 **Bd Mem Epis City Mssn Boston MA 2011-; P-in-c The Par Of S Chrys's Quincy MA 2010-** B Downy CA 2/6/1973 s Roger Hillegas & Elaine. BA U of Notre Dame 1995; MDiv Gordon-Conwell TS 2004; Cert. in Angl St EDS 2008. D 6/7/2008 Bp M(arvil) Thomas Shaw III. m 8/19/2006 Kendyll Hillegas. Assoc S Mary's Epis Ch Dorchester MA 2008-2010. eric.hillegas@gmail.com

HILLENBRAND, Pamela M (Chi) 412 North Church St, Rockford IL 61103 **R Emm Epis Ch Rockford IL 2007-** B Duluth MN 10/6/1948 d John Douglas Merritt & Althea Bernice. Augsburg Coll 1967; U MN 1969; BA Metropltn St U Twin Cities MN 1988; MA Luther TS 1991. D P 5/21/1989 Bp Francisco Reus-Froylan. m 1/17/2009 Robert Allen Hillenbrand. Stndg Comm Pres Dio Wstrn Michigan Kalamazoo MI 1999-2003; Dio Wstrn Michigan Kalamazoo MI 1999; S Andr's Ch Big Rapids MI 1994-2007; R S Chris's Ch Havelock NC 1991-1994. pamelarockford@aol.com

HILLER, Michael (Cal) 278 Hester Ave, San Francisco CA 94134 **S Mk's Par Berkeley CA 2010-** B Los Angeles CA 5/26/1945 s Carlo O A Hiller & Ruth. BA Concordia Sr Coll Ft Wayne IN 1967; MDiv Concordia 1971. Rec from Evangelical Lutheran Church in America 12/6/2008 Bp Marc Handley Andrus. c 1. priestly@batnet.com

HILLIARD-YNTEMA, Katharine Arnold (At) 737 Woodland Ave SE, Atlanta GA 30316 B Atlanta GA 12/26/1949 d Joseph L Arnold & Marie Rose Pruitt. BS U GA 1971; MD Med Coll of Georgia 1979; EFM Cert U of So Sewanee 2002. D 8/6/2011 Bp J(ohn) Neil Alexander. m 9/20/1986 John Richard Yntema c 1. khilliard@pol.net

HILLMAN, George Evans (FdL) P O Box 215, Sturgeon Bay WI 54235 **Vic Chr the King/H Nativ (Sturgeon Bay) Sturgeon Bay WI 2007-** B Philadelphia PA 5/11/1952 s Evans Hillman & Peggy Marie. BA Lycoming Coll 1974; MDiv Nash 1977. D 6/4/1977 P 12/17/1977 Bp Albert Wiencke Van Duzer. m 4/6/2002 Deborah Hillman. Dn All SS' Cathd Milwaukee WI 1998-2007; R S Jas Epis Ch Milwaukee WI 1988-1998; R S Helena's Ch Willowbrook IL 1982-1988; The Par Of All SS Ashmont-Dorches Dorchester MA 1979-1982; S Mary's Ch Haddon Heights NJ 1977-1978; Dio New Jersey Trenton NJ 1977. GEHDean@aol.com

HILLQUIST, Catherine Rinker (Mo) 121 Riverside St., Arcadia MO 63621 **P-in-c All SS Epis Ch Farmington MO 2009-; Vic S Pauls Epis Ch Ironton MO 2001-** B Washington DC 4/6/1944 d St John Moffett Rinker & Esther Virginia. BS Jas Madison U 1966; CPA California St U 1989; MDiv ETSBH 2000. D 6/24/2000 Bp Chester Lovelle Talton P 1/6/2001 Bp Frederick Houk Borsch. m 12/18/1965 David K Hillquist c 1. chillquist@clergy.net

HILLS, Frances Ann (WMass) St James Church, P.O. Box 114, Great Barrington MA 01230 **Epis Search Com Dio Wstrn Massachusetts Springfield MA 2011-; Vic S Geo's Ch Lee MA 2011-; Vic S Geo's Ch Lee MA 2011-; COM Dio Wstrn Massachusetts Springfield MA 2008-; Const and Cn Com Dio Wstrn Massachusetts Springfield MA 2008-; R S Jas Ch Great Barrington MA 2007-** B Oklahoma City OK 12/29/1948 d Cecil Elmer Hills & Athalee Fern. BS Oklahoma St U 1971; MDiv Epis TS of The SW 1991. D 3/17/1992 P 3/4/1993 Bp Sam Byron Hulsey. Commissionon Mnstry Dio Ohio Cleveland OH 2004-2007; Cmsn to End Racism, Chair Dio Ohio Cleveland OH 2003-2006; Epis Transition Com Dio Ohio Cleveland OH 2003-2004; R S Andr's Epis Ch Elyria OH 1996-2007; Dioc Coun Dio Ohio Cleveland OH 1995-1998; Asst R S Paul's Ch Maumee OH 1993-1996; S Andr's Epis Ch Amarillo TX 1992-1993. revfrancie@verizon.net

HILLS, John Bigelow (WMich) 633-E Bayberry Pointe Drive NW, Grand Rapids MI 49534 B Providence RI 6/7/1928 s Henry Bigelow Hills & Florence Marjorie. BA Ya 1949; MA Ya 1950; MDiv Nash 1959. D 6/14/1958 Bp Charles L Street P 12/22/1958 Bp Horace W B Donegan. m 8/20/2009 Richard Ford c 2. Asst Gr Ch Grand Rapids MI 1998-2002; Int The Epis Ch Of S Jas The Less Northfield IL 1992-1993; Int Chr Ch Winnetka IL 1991-1992; Assoc R S Lk's Par Kalamazoo MI 1989-1991; Deploy Off Dio Wstrn Michigan Kalamazoo MI 1986-1991; R S Jn's Epis Ch Grand Haven MI 1971-1986; R H Trin Epis Ch Manistee MI 1965-1971; Vic S Alb's Epis Ch Ft Wayne IN 1962-1965; DCE Trin Ch Ft Wayne IN 1959-1961. Integrity 2003. hillsjohn@comcast.net

HILLS, Julian Victor (Mil) 3046 N Cambridge Ave, Milwaukee WI 53211 **P-in-c S Simon The Fisherman Epis Ch Port Washington WI 2000-** B London UK 11/9/1953 s Victor Hills & Audrey Alice. BA U Of Durham Gb 1975; Ripon Coll Cuddesdon Oxford Gb 1976; STM McCormick TS 1977; Southward 1984; ThD Harvard DS 1985. D 9/1/1984 Bp George E Rath P 6/1/1985 Bp John Bowen Coburn. m 2/25/1995 Nancy Lynn Hays c 1. S Mk's Ch Milwaukee WI 1999-2000; Asst Emm Ch Boston MA 1984-1985. Auth, "Common Life In The Early Ch," Trin Press, 1998; Auth, "Tradition And Composition In The Epistula Apostolorum," Fortress Press, 1990. Cath Biblic Assn; SBL. julian.hills@marquette.edu

HILLS, Lindsay Marie (Pa) 10 Irving St, Worcester MA 01609 **All SS Ch Worcester MA 2011-** B 2/17/1982 d Barry Laurence Hills & Maria Luisa. BA Bryn 2004; MDiv CDSP 2011. D 6/11/2011 Bp Charles Ellsworth Bennison Jr. m 9/8/2011 Michelle Johnson c 1. lmhills@sbcglobal.net

HILLS, Wesley Bert (SanD) 953 Sealane Dr, Encinitas CA 92024 **R The Epis Ch Of S Andr Encinitas CA 1995-** B Key West FL 9/18/1944 s Kenneth C Hills & Zola Mae. BA San Diego St U 1967; JD Hastings Coll of Law 1971; MDiv CDSP 1990. D 6/9/1990 P 6/1/1991 Bp William Edwin Swing. m 10/13/1985 Terri Ann Newhouse c 4. R Ch Of The Redeem Hermitage PA 1991-1995; Asst S Paul's Ch Oakland CA 1990-1991. frwes08@gmail.com

HILLS JR, William Leroy (SC) 121 Live Oak Dr., Mt. Pleasant SC 29464 B Charleston SC 8/13/1943 s William Leroy Hills & Anna Bernadine. BA U of So Carolina 1966; MS Florida St U 1967; PhD Florida St U 1972; MDiv STUSo 1990. D 6/30/1990 P 6/1/1991 Bp Edward Lloyd Salmon Jr. m 10/14/1967 Elizabeth Kent Swayne. Ch Of The Adv Spartanburg SC 2004-2005; S Marys Epis Ch Mt Pleasant SC 2000-2004; Trin Epis Ch Pinopolis SC 2000; S Matt's Ch (Ft Motte) S Matthews SC 1996-1999; S Paul's Epis Ch Conway SC 1993-1996; Asst S Jn's Ch Florence SC 1990-1993. ROYHILLS@AOL.COM

HILSABECK, Polly Hamilton (NC) 3920 S Roxboro St Apt 184, Durham NC 27713 **S Tit Epis Ch Durham NC 2010-; Supply Dio E Carolina Kinston NC 2006-; Supply Dio No Carolina Raleigh NC 2006-** B Cedar Rapids IA 2/7/1949 d James Hall Hamilton & Wava Trunnell. ACPE; U CA 1969; BS U CA 1971; MDiv CDSP 1985. D 6/15/1985 P 12/21/1985 Bp Robert C Rusack. m 3/21/1970 David Hilsabeck c 2. St Philips Epis Sch Waianae HI 2001-2002; The Par Of Gd Shpd Epis Ch Wailuku HI 2000; Vic S Edm's Epis Ch Pacifica CA 1989-1991; Assoc S Paul's Ch Oakland CA 1986-1989. pollyhilsabeck@yahoo.com

HILTON, Olivia P L (WA) 2938 Bellevue Terrace NW, Washington DC 20016 B Syracuse NY 12/16/1961 d Richard Bonnot Lillich & Meredith Parsons. BA Wellesley Coll 1983; MA U of Hawaii 1988; MDiv Wesley TS 2005. D 6/11/2005 P 1/21/2006 Bp John Chane. m 4/10/1990 Robert Hilton c 2. S Dav's Par Washington DC 2006; D S Dav's Par Washington DC 2005-2006. oliviahilton@hotmail.com

HILTZ, Arnold Aubrey (Pa) 801 Yale Ave Unit 822, Swarthmore PA 19081 **Died 8/31/2009** B Sea View CA 7/31/1924 s Aubrey Claremont Hiltz & Fannie Mae. Prince Of Wales Coll 1946; BS Acadia U 1947; PhD McGill U 1952. D 6/12/1976 P 12/15/1976 Bp Lyman Cunningham Ogilby. c 2. LLD U of Prince Edw Island 2004; Bell Debating Awd Pwc Coll 1943; Gvnr Gnrl'S Silver Medal Pwc Coll 1942. aandmhiltz@aol.com

HILYARD, Jack Lee (Ore) 311 NW 20th Ave, Portland OR 97209 B La Grande OR 2/11/1933 s George Lee Hilyard & Gladys Marie. BA U of Nthrn Colorado 1954; BD CDSP 1959. D 6/17/1959 P 12/18/1959 Bp James Walmsley Frederic Carman. c 2. DRE Dio Oregon Portland OR 1973-1995; Vic S Jas Ch Lincoln City OR 1961-1964; Vic S Steph's Ch Newport OR 1961-1964; Cur S Mich And All Ang Ch Portland OR 1959-1961. Auth, "Becoming Fam," St. Mary's Press. Hon Doctorate CDSP 2008. jhilyard@quest.net

HIMES, John Martin (Tex) 106 N Grove St, Marshall TX 75670 **Trin Ch Marshall TX 2005-** B Eglin AFB FL 6/18/1952 s David Alexander Himes & Merle Dea. AA Cntrl Texas Coll Killeen TX 1991; BS U of Cntrl Texas 1993; MDiv Epis TS of the SW 2002. D 6/22/2002 Bp Claude Edward Payne P 7/24/2003 Bp Don Adger Wimberly. m 6/16/1973 Megan Y Choe. Cur Ch Of The Ascen Houston TX 2002-2005. Auth, "The Fallacy of Conversation," *Nevertheless: A Texas Ch Revs*, 2005; Ed, "The Serv Bk of Common Prayers and Devotions for Use in Cmnty," *The Serv Bk of Common Prayers and Devotions for Use in Cmnty*, The Franciscan Ord of the Div Compassion, 2004. Amer Angl Coun 1997; Comm Partnr Rectors 2008; CBS 2006; Forw in Faith - Wrld (Amer) 1997; The Franciscan Ord of the Div Compassion 1996. rector@trinitychurchmarshall.com

HIMMERICH, Maurice Fred (Mil) 107 Fairview St, Watertown WI 53094 **Int S Alb's Ch Sussex WI 2000-** B Grand Forks ND 10/16/1930 s Fred Himmerich & Florence Lucille. BA Macalester Coll 1956; MA U MN 1960; MDiv Nash 1962; PhD Marq 1985. D 3/16/1962 P 9/15/1962 Bp Donald H V Hallock. c 5. Int Dn All SS' Cathd Milwaukee WI 2007-2008; S Alb's Ch Sussex WI 1999; R S Paul's Ch Watertown WI 1965-1995; Cur S Paul's Epis Ch Beloit WI 1962-1965. Auth, "Entries," *An Epis Dictionary of the Ch*, Ch Pub Inc, 2002; Auth, "arts & Bk Revs," *Living Ch mag*, 1970. Masons. Hon Cn Dio Milwaukee 1998.

HINCAPIE LOAIZA, David Hernan (Colom) Manzana 26 Barrio Simon Bolivar, Armenia-Quindio Columbia Colombia B 10/16/1969 s Nestor Mario Hincapie Ocampo & Nory. Especialista Juan de Castellanos; Licenciado Universidad del Quindio; Filosofo y Teologo Nuestra Senora del Rosario 1989. D 10/14/2006 P 6/6/2007 Bp Francisco Jose Duque-Gomez. m 1/18/1992 Dolly Mariem Guzman Lozano c 2. dahpielo2@hotmail.com

HINCHLIFFE, George Lewis (Fla) PO Box 1238, Live Oak FL 32064 **Mem, Dioc Outreach Cmsn Dio Florida Jacksonville FL 2011-; Asst S Lk's Epis Ch Live Oak FL 2011-** B Tallahassee FL 5/15/1952 s Lewis Hinchliffe & Waunitta Rose. BS Florida St U 1973; MDiv VTS 2011. D 12/5/2010 P 6/19/2011 Bp Samuel Johnson Howard. m 6/10/1972 Mary Ellen Poulos c 2. geohinchliffe@gmail.com

HINDLE, James Manchester (WNC) 703 Carolina Village Rd, CV Care Center, Room 3106, Hendersonville NC 28792 **R Emer Ch Of The Trsfg Bat Cave NC 2001-** B Drexel Hill PA 7/3/1925 s Howard Brooke Hindle & Marion Beach. BA Hob 1950; MDiv GTS 1953; S Aug's Coll Cbury GB 1961; Fllshp VTS 1976. D 5/30/1953 Bp Oliver J Hart P 5/27/1954 Bp Matthew G Henry. m 11/29/1986 Carol B Burch. Secy Dio Wstrn No Carolina Asheville NC 1987-1991; R Ch Of The Trsfg Bat Cave NC 1984-1993; R Ch Of The Trsfg Bat Cave NC 1984-1992; Chr Sch Arden NC 1982-1983; Bethany Sch Cincinnati OH 1972-1982; Assoc R H Trin Epis Ch Greensboro NC 1968-1972; R Ch Of The H Cross Tryon NC 1962-1968; S Andr's Ch Mt Holly NJ 1956-1962; Secy Dio Wstrn No Carolina Asheville NC 1954-1958; P-in-c S Paul's Ch Edneyville NC 1954-1955; P-in-c Ch Of The Trsfg Bat Cave NC 1953-1956. CT, Assoc 1973. jamesmhindle@gmail.com

HINDS, Eric (Cal) 1 S El Camino Real, San Mateo CA 94401 **S Matt's Epis Ch San Mateo CA 2007-** B New York NY 4/12/1958 s Howard Clark Hinds & Patricia Joyce. BS SUNY 1982; MS Syr 1983; MDiv GTS 1994. D 6/11/1994 Bp Richard Frank Grein P 1/1/1995 Bp William Jerry Winterrowd. m 6/23/1984 Anne Read Gilbert c 2. R S Ptr's Ch Mtn Lakes NJ 1998-2007; Asst R S Paul's Epis Ch Westfield NJ 1996-1998; Asst S Barn Ch Irvington on Hudson NY 1994-1996; Dept Of CE Ch Of S Jas The Less Scarsdale NY 1989-1992. ekhinds@episcopalstmatthew.org

HINDS, Gilberto Antonio (LI) 9707 Horace Harding Expy Apt 8L, Corona NY 11368 **P-in-c Ch Of The Resurr Kew Gardens NY 2008-** B Panama R of Panama 8/14/1946 s Evelyn Agustus Hinds & Olive Eugene. BS CUNY 1977; MPH CUNY 1989; MDiv Ya Berk 2001. D 6/24/2003 P 8/6/2004 Bp Orris George Walker Jr. c 1. Asst Ch Of The Redeem Astoria NY 2004-2008. revghinds8509@gmail.com

HINES, Caroline Virginia (NH) 2 Wentworth St, Exeter NH 03833 **Asst Chr Ch Exeter NH 2011-** B Hazard KY 3/16/1953 d James Virgil Hines & Virginia Wade. BA U of Sthrn Mississippi 1975; MA Illinois St U 1977; MDiv GTS 2000. D 6/10/2000 Bp Robert Hodges Johnson P 12/16/2000 Bp Douglas Edwin Theuner. S Geo's Epis Ch York Harbor ME 2009-2010. chines195@gmail.com

HINES, J (ohn) Christopher (Tex) 4603 Pro Ct, College Station TX 77845 B Augusta GA 6/26/1940 s John E Hines & Helen Louise. BA Coll of Wooster 1962; BD CDSP 1968. D 12/29/1968 Bp J Milton Richardson P 12/1/1969 Bp John E Hines. m 10/25/2006 Lisa Stolley Lisa Kathryn Stolley c 2. S Jas' Epis Ch La Grange TX 1989; S Steph's Epis Sch Austin TX 1984-1989; Asst Chr Epis Ch Tyler TX 1968-1970. chrishines40@gmail.com

HINES, John Moore (Ky) 1308 Willow Ave, Louisville KY 40204 **P S Paul's Ch Henderson KY 2011-** B Houston TX 1/12/1945 s John E Hines & Helen Louise. BA Duke 1967; MDiv VTS 1970. D 6/17/1970 P 12/20/1970 Bp John E Hines. m 4/16/1988 Maria Gaillard Partlow c 2. P S Thos Epis Ch Louisville KY 2009-2010; P Calv Ch Louisville KY 2007-2009; P Ch Of The Adv Louisville KY 2004-2006; P S Alb's Epis Ch Fern Creek Louisville KY 2002-2004; P S Ptr's Epis Ch Louisville KY 2001-2002; P S Lk's Ch Anchorage KY 2000-2002; P S Andr's Ch Louisville KY 1977-2000; P S Fran HS Louisville KY 1977-1984; P S Fran Sch (K-8) Goshen KY 1972-1996; P Trin Ch Columbus OH 1970-1972. Auth, *Dull Dinners Into Sacr Feasts*, Forw Mvmt Press, 1984; Auth, *By Water & the H Sprt*, Seabury Press, 1972. john.hines64@yahoo.com

HINES, John S (WNC) 219 Chunns Cove Rd, Asheville NC 28805 B Austin TX 9/21/1949 s John E Hines & Helen Louise. BA Hob 1971; MDiv Epis TS of The SW 1976. D 6/16/1976 P 6/1/1979 Bp John E Hines. Trin Epis Ch Danville KY 2006-2007; Trin Ch Hattiesburg MS 2004-2006; Ch Of The Incarn Highlands NC 2003-2004; Int S Lk's Epis Ch Asheville NC 1991-2003; Ch Of The Gd Shpd Cashiers NC 1982-1990; Asst S Mart's Epis Ch Houston TX 1978-1982; S Steph's Epis Sch Austin TX 1976-1978. Auth, "Life Of Chr". stevehines_1949@msn.com

HINES, Lisa Stolley (Tex) Calvary Episcopal Church, PO Box 721, Bastrop TX 78602 **Calv Epis Ch Bastrop TX 2010-** B New Orleans 9/17/1959 d Carl H Stolley & Marcia Eskridge. BA U So 1981; JD U of Texas 1984; MDiv Epis TS of The SW 2007. D 6/23/2007 Bp Don Adger Wimberly P 1/30/2008 Bp Dena Arnall Harrison. m 10/25/2006 J (ohn) Christopher Hines c 3. Asst S Thos Epis Ch Coll Sta TX 2007-2010; Gd Shpd Epis Sch Austin TX 1997-2005. rector@cecbastrop.org

HINKLE, Daniel Wayne (Be) 234 High St, Atglen PA 19310 **Int Ch Of The Trsfg Braddock Heights MD 2011-** B Trenton NJ 8/31/1953 s George R Hinkle & Lois. BA Trenton St Coll 1977; MDiv STUSo 1981. D 6/6/1981 P 12/1/1981 Bp Albert Wiencke Van Duzer. m 10/30/2004 Barbara Peirce c 3. Int St Paul's Untd Ch of Chr Robesonia PA 2009; Int S Jn The Evang Ch Blackwood NJ 2005-2006; Pleasantville Untd Ch Of Chr Chalfont PA 2003-2004; Int Bethany Evang Luth Ch W Reading PA 2002-2003; Int St Peters Luth Ch New Tripoli PA 2000-2002; R S Barn Ch Kutztown PA 1998-2001; R Trin Ch Upper Marlboro MD 1991-1998; Asst S Ptr's Ch In The Great Vlly Malvern PA 1988-1991; R S Paul's Berlin MD 1983-1988; Cur S Mary's Ch Haddon Heights NJ 1981-1983. Int Mnstry Ntwk 2002. dwh323@msn.com

HINMAN, Allen (Nwk) 149 Pennington Ave, Passaic NJ 07055 B Louisville KY 9/28/1942 s Charles Hinman & Alice. BA Cor 1964; BD UTS 1970; GTS 1971. D 7/5/1970 P 6/1/1971 Bp Leland Stark. m 8/31/1969 MarionI Iris van Gelder. R S Jn's Ch Passaic NJ 1985-2004; P in Charge S Phil's Ch New York NY 1983-1985; Asst Min S Phil's Ch New York NY 1975-1982; P in Charge All Souls Ch New York NY 1974-1975; Asst Min All Souls Ch New York NY 1970-1973. Purple Heart 1967. Bronze Star for Valor US Army 1967; Combat Medic Badge US Army 1967. allenhinman@aol.com

HINO, Moki (Haw) Church of the Holy Apostles, 1407 Kapiolani Street, Hilo HI 96727 **R Ch Of The H Apos Hilo HI 2011-** B Guam 5/21/1965 s Graham Coles Kealamokihana Tewksbury & Leilani Suzanne. BA U of Hawaii 1988; U of Hawaii 1989; MDiv SWTS 2005. D 7/3/2005 P 2/4/2006 Bp Richard Sui On Chang. Chapl S Andr's Priory Sch Honolulu HI 2010-2011; Cn S Andr's Cathd Honolulu HI 2007-2010; Chapl Seabury Hall Makawao HI 2005-2007. the.rev.rhino@gmail.com

HINRICHS, William Roger (Alb) 379 Farm to Market Rd., Clifton Park NY 12065 B Mexico DF MX 5/6/1951 s Guillermo Oliver Hinrichs & Eileen Constance. BA/BS U Denv 1974; MDiv Nash 1978; DMin Drew U 1999. D 6/29/1978 P 4/25/1979 Bp William Carl Frey. m 1/20/1979 Barbara Black c 2. R S Geo's Ch Clifton Pk NY 1991-2008; R S Jn's Ch Massena NY 1987-1991; R S Barn Of The Vlly Cortez CO 1980-1986; Cur Ch Of The Ascen Pueblo CO 1979-1980; D to Bp Dio Colorado Denver CO 1978-1979. Cmnty of S Mary; Fllshp of Merry Christians. williamrhinrichs@aol.com

HINSON, Jerome Andrew (WMo) 5 Averil Ct, Fredericksburg VA 22406 **Off Of Bsh For ArmdF New York NY 1994-** B Sikeston MO 6/25/1963 s Elvis Brown Hinson & Janet Huia. BA Knox Coll 1985; MS U of Missouri 1987; MDiv SWTS 1991; STM Bos 2004. D 6/8/1991 Bp William Augustus Jones Jr P 12/15/1991 Bp John Clark Buchanan. m 5/27/1989 Ruth Ann Clark c 3. Asst R Chr Epis Ch Springfield MO 1991-1994. Mltry Chapl Assn 1996-2003. padrejere@aol.com

HINSON, Michael Bruce (Va) 6033 Queenston St, Springfield VA 22152 **St. Steph's and St. Agnes Sch Alexandria VA 2006-** B Albany Georgia 6/12/1963 s William Bruce Hinson & Nancy Annette. BBA U GA 1987; MA Presb Sch of CE Richmond VA 1990; VTS 2005. D 6/24/2006 P 2/3/2007 Bp Peter James Lee. m 6/26/1993 Jane Steiner c 2. Marshall Garrett Grant St. Steph's & St. Agnes Sch 1995; Marshall Garrett Grant St. Steph's & St. Agnes Sch 1992. mjhinson@cox.net

HINTON, Brad (Del) 2320 Grubb Road, Wilmington DE 19810 **Dep to GC Dio Delaware Wilmington DE 2012; Chair of Priestly Formation Dio Delaware Wilmington DE 2009-; R S Dav's Epis Ch Wilmington DE 2007-** B Mobile AL 4/11/1966 s Robert Dowling Hinton & Irmgard. BS U of Montevallo 1990; MDiv GTS 2000. D 5/20/2000 P 12/5/2000 Bp Henry Nutt Parsley Jr. m Thomas N Wood. Dep to GC Dio Delaware Wilmington DE 2009; VP Dioc Coun Inc Wilmington DE 2004-2007; Assoc R Trin Par Wilmington DE 2002-2007; R S Mich's Epis Ch Fayette AL 2000-2002. Ord of St. Jn 2001-2006. brad.stdavids@verizon.net

HINTON, Gregory Paul (CPa) PO Box 701, Wellsboro PA 16901 **Mem, Stndg Com Dio Cntrl Pennsylvania Harrisburg PA 2011-; Chair, Anti Racism Cmsn Dio Cntrl Pennsylvania Harrisburg PA 2010-; Judge, Ecclesiatical Trial Crt Dio Cntrl Pennsylvania Harrisburg PA 2008-; Exam Chapl in Scripture Dio Cntrl Pennsylvania Harrisburg PA 2000-; Cn R S Paul's Ch Wellsboro PA 1994-** B Yukon FL 8/4/1954 s Stanley Cleveland Hinton & Lorraine Marie. BA Blackburn Coll 1976; MDiv Nash 1979. D 6/9/1979 Bp Quintin Ebenezer Primo Jr P 12/8/1979 Bp James Winchester Montgomery. m 12/27/1992 Susan Elizabeth Oldberg c 3. Pres, Stndg Com Dio Cntrl Pennsylvania Harrisburg PA 2005-2008; Clerk, Dioc Coun Dio Cntrl Pennsylvania Harrisburg PA 1998-2001; Cnvnr of Nthrn Tier Convoc Dio Cntrl Pennsylvania Harrisburg PA 1994-2000; One In Chr Ch Prospect Heights IL 1981-1994; Cur S Paul's Ch Kankakee IL 1979-1981. "Christmas Hope," Wellsboro Gazette, 2008; "Caveat Emptor-The Da Vinci Code," Wellsboro Gazette, 2006; "Maybe Come Easter," Wellsboro Gazette, 2003. Confraterinity of the Blessed Sacr; Soc of S Jn the Evang ,Conf of the Bles. Hon Cn Dio Cntrl PA 2008. frgreg@ptd.net

HINTON, Michael (VI) Box 199, Cruz Bay, Saint John VI 00831 B London UK 6/23/1933 s Ernest Charles Hinton & Ena Kathleen. Kings Coll London - Lon 1956; GOE S Bon Coll/Sem 1957. Rec 6/1/1989 as Priest Bp E(gbert) Don Taylor. m 11/12/1986 Frances Eleanor Sauer.

HINTON, Wesley Walker (SO) 974 Apple Blossom Ln, Milford OH 45150 **Const and Cn Com Dio Sthrn Virginia Norfolk VA 1987-; Strtgy and Plnng Com Dio Sthrn Virginia Norfolk VA 1986-; Exec Bd Dio Sthrn**

Virginia Norfolk VA 1985-; Dn of So Richmond Convoc Dio Sthrn Virginia Norfolk VA 1984- B Orange NJ 2/21/1944 s Walker Hinton & Lucy Elizabeth. BA Kean U 1971; MDiv STUSo 1983. D 9/20/1983 Bp Robert Bruce Hall P 6/9/1984 Bp C(laude) Charles Vache. m 7/26/1969 Marjorie Lee Snyder c 3. Int Assoc S Thos Epis Ch Terrace Pk OH 2009-2010; Int Pstr Assoc. Epis Soc of Chr Ch Cincinnati OH 2008; Int Pstr Assoc. Epis Soc of Chr Ch Cincinnati OH 2004-2006; Assoc R S Thos Epis Ch Terrace Pk OH 1996-2004; Int Epiph Epis Ch Richmond VA 1995-1996; R Ch Of S Jas The Less Ashland VA 1989-1995; Assoc R S Mich's Ch Bon Air VA 1983-1989. Auth, "Sermons That Wk," Morehouse Pub, 2000; Auth, "How Much Is Enough," *Preaching Through The Year Of Lk*, Morehouse Pub, 2000. Caso/ NNECA; Int Mnstry Ntwk; Ord Of S Lk. wwhinton@fuse.net

HINTZ, Mary Louise (Cal) 623 28th Street, Richmond CA 94804 **D (non-stipendiary) All Souls Par In Berkeley Berkeley CA 2006-; Epis Sch For Deacons Berkeley CA 2003-** B Saint Louis MO 5/11/1946 d Walter Lawrence Mueller & Louise Rose. BTS California Sch for Deacons 1994; AA Contra Costa Coll 1994. D 6/3/1995 Bp William Edwin Swing. m 9/24/1966 Gregory Alan Hintz c 1. D Ch Of The H Trin Richmond CA 1995-2005. revmother@hintz.us

HINXMAN, Frederic William (Lex) 5639 Highway #1, Granville Ferry NS B0S 1K0 Canada B Portland ME 5/23/1932 s Leroy St Clair Hinxman & Rachel. Acadia Div Coll; Fell New Engl Insitute; Portland Jr Coll; U of Maine; LTh Epis TS In Kentucky 1973. D 6/1/1974 Bp Addison Hosea P 12/1/1974 Bp Morris Fairchild Arnold. m 8/6/1960 Joanna G Tschamler c 4. Soc of S Jn the Evang, P Assoc 1975. RCMP H Div Chapl Royal Can Mounted Police 2007; Hon Padre Ortona Branch 1994. J.hinxman@ns.sympatico.ca

HIO, William Arthur (Alb) 34 Cypress Dr, Scotia NY 12302 **Died 10/20/2009** B Amsterdam NY 10/13/1928 s William Dygert Hio & Mabel Boulton. BA Un Coll Schenectady NY 1950; STB GTS 1953. D 6/14/1953 P 12/27/1953 Bp Frederick Lehrle Barry. Hon Cn Cathd Of All SS Albany NY 1999. whiol@nycop.rr.com

HIPPLE, Judy Kay (Chi) 4511 Newcastle Rd, Rockford IL 61108 B Dekalb IL 1/7/1943 d Edgar Endsminger Hipple & Florence Mabel. MDiv SWTS 1994. Rec 12/1/1987 Bp James Daniel Warner. Vic S Chad Epis Ch Loves Pk IL 2000-2003; Asst The Epis Ch Of The H Trin Belvidere IL 1995-2000.

HIPPLE, Maureen AtLee (Be) Rr 5 Box 5710, Towanda PA 18848 **R Chr Ch Towanda PA 1998-** B New Orleans LA 7/1/1953 d Frank Goodwin Atlee & Ruth Mary. Miami-Dade Cmnty Coll. D 1/6/1994 P 7/6/1994 Bp James Michael Mark Dyer. m 1/17/1981 Joseph Andrew Hipple c 2. Asst S Ptr's Epis Ch Tunkhannock PA 1994-1995. hipple@christchurchtowanda.org

HIRD, John Francis (Md) 7200 3rd Ave, Sykesville MD 21784 B Boston MA 1/9/1923 s Walter Illingsworth Hird & Helen Louise. USMMA 1944; BS U of Rhode Island 1952; MDiv PDS 1972. D 1/30/1969 P 10/4/1969 Bp Harry Lee Doll. c 3. Serv Dio Delaware Wilmington DE 1999-2002; Pres Interfaith Hsng Dio Delaware Wilmington DE 1994-1999; P S Martha's Epis Ch Bethany Bch DE 1992-2000; Cler Team S Martins-In-The-Fields Selbyville DE 1992-1996; Dio Delaware Wilmington DE 1991-1994; VP Intrfaith Hsng Dio Delaware Wilmington DE 1991-1994; Dio Delaware Wilmington DE 1983; R Trin Ch Waterloo Elkridge MD 1974-1982; Vic S Andr The Fisherman Epis Mayo MD 1970-1974; Asst S Jas' Epis Ch Baltimore MD 1969-1970. Auth, *Bulletin of the Soc of Ord Scientists*; Auth, *Many Tech Journ and Periodicals*; Auth, *The Comm*, Bi Monthly Pub. Amer Soc for Quality 1966; Amer Soc for the Advancement of Sci 1982; Comp OGS 1971; Soc of Ord Scientists (Angl) 1991. Norman Bayliss Awd Beebe Med Cntr 2002; Gvnr's Awd St of Delaware 1997; Hon Alum PDS Philadelphia PA 1971; Fllshp Amer Assn Advancement Sci; Fllshp Amer Soc Quality Control. john.hird@comcast.net

HIRSCHFELD, A(lfred) Robert (WMass) 42 N Eagleville Rd, Storrs Mansfield CT 06268 **R Gr Ch Amherst MA 2001-** B Red Wing MN 1/10/1961 s Robert Clyde Hirschfeld & Marie. BA Dart 1983; GTS 1986; MDiv Ya Berk 1991. D 6/8/1991 P 1/18/1992 Bp Arthur Edward Walmsley. m 9/15/1990 Polly Merritt Ingraham c 3. R S Mk's Chap Storrs CT 1993-2001; Asst Chr Ch New Haven CT 1991-1993. Auth, "Preparing A Mansion For God," Untd Mnstrs, 1998. Soc Of S Jn The Evang. arh@gracechurchamherst.org

HIRSCHMAN, Portia Royall Conn (Md) 11860 Weller Hill Dr, Monrovia MD 21770 **R S Jas Epis Ch Mt Airy MD 2002-** B Plandone NY 5/21/1947 d Robert Henry Conn & Virginia. AAS Pur 1974; BS Pur 1974; MDiv SWTS 1993. D 6/24/1993 P 3/24/1994 Bp Edward Witker Jones. m 6/26/1976 Richard Hirschman c 1. Vic H Fam Epis Ch Fishers IN 1994-2002; Assoc R Ch Of The Nativ Indianapolis IN 1993-1994. revportia1@msn.com

HIRST, Dale Eugene (SVa) 4127 Columbus Ave, Norfolk VA 23504 B Cheyenne WY 3/25/1952 s Ronald E Hirst & Onita C. BS USMA at W Point 1974; MDiv VTS 1984; MS Ed Old Dominion U 1994. D 6/13/1984 Bp Roger Howard Cilley P 2/1/1985 Bp Gordon Taliaferro Charlton. m 6/16/1974 Joyce Robbins c 2. Asst to R Galilee Epis Ch Virginia Bch VA 1986-1993; Asst to R Ch Of The Gd Shpd Friendswood TX 1985; Asst to R Trin Epis Ch Baytown TX 1984. *Whos Who in Amer Educ*, 2004; *Whos Who in Amer Educ*, 2003; *Whos Who in Amer Educ*, 2002. Dehirst@verizon.net

HIRST, Robert Lynn (Kan) Po Box 1859, Wichita KS 67201 **D Gd Shpd Epis Ch Wichita KS 2004-** B Boulder CO 5/9/1947 s LeRoy John Hirst & Betttyjo. Guam Cmnty Coll 1966; BA SW Coll Winfield KS 1969; Wichita St U 1985; Kansas Sch of Mnstry 1999. D 8/15/1999 Bp William Edward Smalley. Epis Soc Serv Inc. Wichita KS 2003-2005; D S Steph's Ch Wichita KS 1999-2004. roberthirst@sbcglobal.net

HIRTE, Silas James (CNY) 519 Betzer Rd Unit C, Delavan WI 53115 **Died 10/7/2011** B Sparta WI 2/10/1920 s Christian H Hirte & Laura Mathilda. BA Gallaudet U 1946. D 5/17/1949 Bp Benjamin F P Ivins P 12/1/1950 Bp William Scarlett. m 10/17/2011 Betty C Hirte c 3.

HITCH, Catherine Elizabeth (Colo) 1320 Arapahoe Street, Golden CO 80401 B Denver CO 9/14/1970 d William Lorton Cook & Nancy Elizabeth. BA Stan 1993; MA U CO 1996; MDiv TESM 2001. D 6/9/2001 P 12/23/2001 Bp William Jerry Winterrowd. m 1/13/2007 Bradley Hitch. Pstr for Adult Formation & Wmn Mnstrs Calv Ch Golden CO 2001-2003. cathy.hitch@calvarygolden.net

HITCH, Kenneth R (Vt) 2 St James Place, Essex Junction VT 05452 **P S Jas Epis Ch Essex Jct VT 2007-** B Columbus OH 5/13/1977 s Thomas Lee Hitch & Ellen Carol. BS OH SU 1999; MDiv GTS 2002. D 10/20/2001 P 6/1/2002 Bp Herbert Thompson Jr. m 1/25/2003 Natalie Kay Hitch c 2. P All SS Ch Cincinnati OH 2002-2007. therevken@yahoo.com

HITCHCOCK JR, H(orace) Gaylord (NY) 1030 Aoloa Place, Apt 206A, Kailua HI 96734 **Asst Ch Of The Resurr New York NY 2009-** B New York NY 3/3/1944 s Horace Gaylord Hitchcock & Elinor. BA Dart 1966; MDiv GTS 1971; STM GTS 1975. D 6/26/1971 P 1/5/1972 Bp John Melville Burgess. Int Pstr S Mk's Ch Honolulu HI 2007-2008; R The Ch of S Ign of Antioch New York NY 1996-2006; Dio Newark Newark NJ 1991-1996; Dept Mssn Dio Newark Newark NJ 1984-1987; R Gr Epis Ch Westwood NJ 1979-1996; Cur S Jn's Ch Norristown PA 1976-1979; Cur Ch Of The Resurr New York NY 1971-1976. Soc of Cath Priests 2009. Bp of Newark, Cbury Schlr Dio Newark 1990; Phi Beta Kappa 1966. frhitch1996@yahoo.com

HITCHCOCK, Jessica Katherine (WA) 21100 Archstone Way Apt 301, Germantown MD 20876 **S Lk's Ch Trin Par Beth MD 2010-** B Atlanta GA 8/15/1979 d Gene Hitchcock & Kathrine. BA Oglethorpe U 2001. D 12/21/2004 P 6/16/2005 Bp J(ohn) Neil Alexander. m 10/19/2007 Allen Pruitt. S Jn's Ch Lafayette Sq Washington DC 2009; Asst To The R For Yth, YA & Evang Ch Of The Ascen Gaithersburg MD 2005-2009. hitchcockpruitt@gmail.com

HITE-SPECK, Nancy Jean (NJ) 201 Meadow Ave, Point Pleasant NJ 08742 **Int S Mths Ch Hamilton NJ 2010-** B Detroit MI 8/18/1942 d Robert Henry Hite & Margaret Adelaide. AA Bennett Coll 1962; BD Pace U 1983; MDiv PrTS 2002; DAS GTS 2003. D 6/12/2004 P 1/23/2005 Bp George Edward Councell. m 8/20/1986 Richard Speck c 2. Int The Epis Ch Of The H Comm Fair Haven NJ 2008-2009; Supply P Dio New Jersey Trenton NJ 2007-2008; Asst S Mk's Ch Basking Ridge NJ 2004-2005. revnhs@bayhead.com

HITT, Mary (RI) 11 Beaufort St, Providence RI 02908 B Garfield UT 12/22/1924 d Arthur Frederick Lyster & Marion Aurilla Morrill. BA MacMurray Coll 1945; MA U IL 1946; BS K SU 1954. D 4/13/1995 Bp Donald Purple Hart. c 4. D S Jn's Ch Cumberland RI 2002-2006; D St Mich & Gr Ch Rumford RI 1999-2002; D Ch Of The Gd Shpd Pawtucket RI 1995-1999; Chair, Environ Mnstry Dio Rhode Island Providence RI 1991-2008. Auth, "Column, E-Column," *Rhode Island Source For Epis News*. NAAD 1992. mlhitt@aol.com

HIXON, Beth Wunderlich (Pa) 1201 Lower State Rd, North Wales PA 19454 **Assoc Ch Of The Redeem Bryn Mawr PA 2010-** B Joliet IL 2/6/1952 d William C Wunderlich & Phyllis Jayn. BD U Of Florida 1974; MA U Of Florida 1980; MDiv GTS 1997. D 6/8/1997 P 1/10/1998 Bp Stephen Hays Jecko. m 9/25/1976 William Seldon Hixon c 1. Asst R Ch Of S Mart-In-The-Fields Philadelphia PA 2002-2010; Asst R S Matt's Ch Maple Glen PA 1997-2001. Phi Kappa Phi Scholastic hon Soc 1974; Sigma Theta Tau Nrsng hon Soc 1974. bhixon@theredeemer.org

HIXSON, Mary L (WK) 19 Deer Creek Tr, Anthony KS 67003 B Anthony KS 9/1/1956 d John Earl Hixson & Mary Suzanne. BS SW Oklahoma St U 1978; Med SW Oklahoma St U 1979. D 11/30/2001 Bp Vernon Edward Strickland P 12/13/2002 Bp James Marshall Adams Jr. D Gr Ch Anth KS 2001-2002. marylake@hotmail.com

HIYAMA, Paul Shoichi (Mich) 734 Peninsula Ct, Ann Arbor MI 48105 B Mukilteo WA 3/9/1924 s Koju Hiyama & Hisa. BA Kalamazoo Coll 1949; New Sch for Soc Resrch 1952; BD U Chi 1956; SWTS 1957. D 6/15/1957 Bp Charles L Street P 12/21/1957 Bp Gerald Francis Burrill. c 3. Int S Jn's Ch Westland MI 1995-1996; R S Andr's Ch Clawson MI 1993-1995; ExCoun Dio Michigan Detroit MI 1981-1984; R S Lk's Ch Shelby Twp MI 1977-1990; Trst Dio Michigan Detroit MI 1975-1978; Asst R Chr Ch Grosse Pointe Grosse Pointe Farms MI 1974-1977; Ecum Cmsn Dio Michigan Detroit MI 1971-1975; BEC Dio Michigan Detroit MI 1966-1975; Cathd Chapt Dio Michigan Detroit MI 1965-1968; Dn Woodward Convoc Dio Michigan Detroit MI 1963-1965; R S Andr's Ch Clawson MI 1959-1974; Cur Ch Of S Paul And The Redeem Chicago IL 1957-1959.

HIZA, Douglas (Minn) 10 Meynal Crescent, South Hackney, London E97AS Great Britain (UK) B Newport News VA 4/18/1938 s Martin William Hiza & Reubena. BA U Rich 1960; BD VTS 1963; BS Minnesota St U Mankato 1972. D 6/22/1963 Bp George P Gunn P 6/1/1964 Bp Conrad Gesner. m 6/9/1979 J Hudson c 2. Dio Minnesota Minneapolis MN 1975-1980; R S Ptr's Ch New Ulm MN 1971-1980; Ch Of The H Comm S Ptr MN 1971-1979; Vic Ch Of Our Most Merc Sav Wagner SD 1965-1969; Vic Ch Of The Gd Shpd Sioux Falls SD 1965-1966; Cur Calv Cathd Sioux Falls SD 1963-1965. Auth, "Sprtl Pain: Our Own And Others,'" 1997; Auth, "Hospice: A New Way To Care"; Auth, "Death & Sxlty". Ellison Nash Awd S Barth'S Hosp 1984.

HIZER, Cynthia Ann (At) 550 Jenkins Rd, Covington GA 30014 **Ch Of The Epiph Atlanta GA 2007-** B Logansport IN 9/12/1950 d Frederick Daniel Hizer & Miriam. BS/MS Indiana U; MDiv Candler TS Emory 2006; CAS The GTS 2007. D 12/21/2006 P 7/8/2007 Bp J(ohn) Neil Alexander. m Margaret Mary Putnam c 1. chizer@mindspring.com

HLASS, Lisa (Ark) 2606 Beach Head Ct, Richmond CA 94804 **S Mich's Epis Ch Little Rock AR 2010-** B Wilmington NC 9/28/1957 d Joseph Hlass & Wanda. BS Arkansas St U 1983; MS Oklahoma St U 1995; MDiv CDSP 2006. D 1/15/2006 P 7/23/2006 Bp Larry Earl Maze. S Alb's Ch Albany CA 2009. lisa@stmichaels-church.net

HO, Edward HC (Mass) 24 Greenleaf St, Malden MA 02148 B HK 1/13/1924 s Wing Shiu Ho & Lin. LTh Untd Theol Coll Of The W Indies Kingston Jm 1953. D 11/27/1988 P 6/1/1989 Bp Don Edward Johnson. m 1/25/1964 Isabel Yat Sum Yeung.

HOAG, David Stewart (NY) 503 North Causeway #102, New Smyrna Beach FL 32169 **Assoc S Paul's Epis Ch New Smyrna Bch FL 2009-** B Newark NJ 2/5/1934 s Robert Chester Hoag & Frances. BA Trin Hartford CT 1955; MDiv EDS 1963; Cert AASECT 1974; Cert AASECT 1977. D 6/8/1963 P 12/14/1963 Bp Oliver L Loring. m 4/24/2004 Susan Morris Hoag. Assoc Gr Epis Ch Inc Port Orange FL 1998-2011; Assoc S Ptr The Fisherman Epis Ch New Smyrna Bch FL 1998-2002; Vic S Jos's Ch Bronx NY 1984-1986; Vic S Jos's Ch Bronx NY 1972-1974; The GTS New York NY 1967-1978; R Par Of Chr The Redeem Pelham NY 1966-1998; Cur Chr's Ch Rye NY 1963-1966. Auth, *arts*. halieus@ucnsb.net

HOARE, Geoffrey Michael St John (At) **R All SS Epis Ch Atlanta GA 1998-** D 4/29/1983 P 4/29/1984 Bp Robert Whitridge Estill.

HOBBS, Bryan Arthur (SeFla) 751 Sw 98th Ter, Pembroke Pines FL 33025 **Archd For Congrl Mnstry Dio SE Florida Miami FL 2003-** B Connellsville PA 4/20/1946 s Kenneth Hobbs & Fay Geneva. BS Marshall U 1968; MDiv STUSo 1975; DMin Fuller TS 1997. D 6/1/1975 P 12/11/1975 Bp James Loughlin Duncan. m 6/1/1968 Annabel Hollandsworth c 2. R H Sacr Pembroke Pines FL 1978-2003; R S Ptr's Epis Ch Key W FL 1975-1978; Assoc S Paul's Ch Key W FL 1975-1976. the Dubose Awd for Serv The TS 2008. dochobbs@bellsouth.net

HOBBS, Edward Craig (Cal) 32 Upson Road, Wellesley MA 02482 B Richmond IN 10/10/1926 s Vernon Daniel Hobbs & Benona Klare. BA U Chi 1946; PhD U Chi 1952. D 11/27/1959 P 5/1/1960 Bp James Albert Pike. m 6/17/1950 Violet V van Ostran c 1. Assoc R S Eliz's Ch Sudbury MA 1982-1988; CDSP Berkeley CA 1959-1981; S Mk's Ch Taunton MA 1994. Auth, "Hermeneutical Cartography," Univ. of California Press, 1990; "Gospel Stds," Angl Theol Rev. Press, 1976; Auth, "Wesley Ord of Common Pryr," Abingdon Press, 1957; "A Stubborn Faith," Sthrn Methodist Univ. Press, 1956; Auth, "Bk of the Judges of Israel," Univ. of Chicago Press, 1950. ehobbs@wellesley.edu

HOBBS, Mercy Gardiner (SD) 405 N Madison Ave, Pierre SD 57501 **Trin Epis Ch Pierre SD 2010-; Ch Of Our Most Merc Sav Wagner SD 1997-** B Teaneck NJ 9/19/1959 d Field Howard Hobbs & Mary Witter. BA Concordia Coll 1982; MDiv SWTS 1995. D 6/9/1995 P 4/14/1996 Bp Creighton Leland Robertson. m 7/1/1995 David Payne Hussey c 1. Asst S Paul's Epis Ch Vermillion SD 2002-2010; Dio So Dakota Sioux Falls SD 1995-2010; P-in-c Ch Of The Blessed Redeem Wagner SD 1995-1998; P-in-c S Mk's Ch Creighton NE 1995-1998; S Paul's Epis Ch Vermillion SD 1995-1998. trinity.dakota2k@midconetwork.com

HOBBS, William Battersby (WMass) 38 Chapin St, Southbridge MA 01550 **Dio Wstrn Massachusetts Springfield MA 1999-; R S Mk's Ch Worcester MA 1999-** B Abington PA 4/3/1952 s Wayne Hobbs & Kathryn Lawrence. BA Nthrn Arizona U 1977; MDiv Bex 1982; VTS 1983. D 5/27/1984 P 12/22/1984 Bp Donald James Davis. m 6/19/1998 Shirley L Tremblay. R H Trin Epis Ch Southbridge MA 1989-1998; S Jn's Ch Athol MA 1989-1997; R S Jn's Ch Kane PA 1986-1989; Asst Ch Of The Ascen Bradford PA 1984-1986; S Jos's Ch Port Allegany PA 1984-1986; Vic S Matt's Epis Ch Eldred PA 1984-1986; Dio NW Pennsylvania Erie PA 1984. lzrwlf2@verizon.net

HOBBS, William Ebert (O) 18 Donlea Dr, Toronto ON M4G 2M2 Canada B Ashton ON Canada 6/23/1924 s Robert Henry Hobbs & Blanche. BA Bps; BD S Jn Coll. Trans from Anglican Church of Canada 2/1/1974 Bp John Harris Burt. c 5. Dio Ohio Cleveland OH 1972-1980. Auth, "Jesus," *Dollars & Sense*; Auth, *The Cov Plan*. Royal Can Legion 1982; Royal Can Mltry Inst 1966; Royal Commonwealth Soc 1980. Can Forces Decoration Dept of Defense Can 1980. ebert.hobbs@rogers.com

HOBBY, Kim Annette (ETenn) Christ Church Episcopal, P.O. Box 347, South Pittsburg TN 37380 **R Chr Ch Epis So Pittsburg TN 2011-** B Fayetteville AR 12/29/1965 d Thomas David Merritt & Diane Annette. B.S.B.A. U of Arkansas 1988; MDiv TS 2008. D 6/7/2008 Bp Larry R Benfield P 1/31/2009 Bp Charles Glenn VonRosenberg. m 1/21/1995 Richard Brentwood Hobby c 2. Asst to the R All SS' Epis Ch Morristown TN 2008-2011. khobby@bgroup.org

HOBDEN, Brian Charles (RG) 3160 Executive Hills Rd, Las Cruces NM 88011 B Battle Sussex UK 9/22/1938 s Cyril Henry Hobden & Winifred Mary. Oak Hill Theol Coll 1966. Trans from Church Of England 5/1/1977. m 4/3/1961 Mary Robotham c 3. R S Jas' Epis Ch Mesilla Pk NM 1998-2007; R S Jn's Ch Portsmouth VA 1987-1998; Brandon Epis Ch Disputanta VA 1976-1987; Chr Ch Waverly VA 1976-1987. stjames@lascruces.com

HOBGOOD, Robert Bryan (EC) 403 S Eastern St, Greenville NC 27858 B Jacksonville FL 11/23/1943 s Robert Maynard Hobgood & Doris Bryan. BA U of Florida 1965; MDiv VTS 1968. D 6/26/1968 P 6/24/1969 Bp Edward Hamilton West. m 7/31/1965 Nancy Packard c 3. Chair, Stndg Com Dio E Carolina Kinston NC 1996-1997; R S Tim's Epis Ch Greenville NC 1990-2006; Chair, Congrl Dvlp. Dio Florida Jacksonville FL 1981-1987; Vic, then R S Fran Of Assisi Epis Ch Tallahassee FL 1977-1990; Assoc R S Jn's Epis Ch Tallahassee FL 1977-1979; R S Jas Epis Ch Perry FL 1973-1977; Vic S Mary's Epis Ch Madison FL 1973-1977; Chapl/Tchr S Mary's Chap Sch Raleigh NC 1970-1973; Assoc. R S Mk's Epis Ch Jacksonville FL 1968-1970. hobgoods@gmail.com

HOBGOOD JR, Walter Palmer (Ga) 1499 S Main St, Moultrie GA 31768 B New Roads LA 7/24/1948 s Walter Palmer Hobgood & Velma Davis. BS LSU 1971; MS LSU 1973. D 2/11/2011 P 9/24/2011 Bp Scott Anson Benhase. m 1/30/1971 Gail Riedie c 3. walter.hobgood@expresspros.com

HOBSON, Carol Gordon (Dal) No address on file. B Sweet Water TX 9/13/1946 d Hershel Gordon & Charlsa Ruth. Ord Cert Cathd Cntr for Cont Educ Dallas TX; Mstr Wk U of Dallas; BA Pacific Luth U 1968. D 11/10/2007 Bp James Monte Stanton. c 4. hobson2040@cs.com

HOBSON JR, George Hull (Eur) 119 Blvd. Du Montparnasse, Paris 75006 France **Cn ot the Bp for Theol Educ Convoc of Amer Ch in Europe Paris FR 2008-** B New York NY 3/19/1940 s George Hull Hobson & Felice Harriman. BA Harv 1962; DIT Oxf 1980; MA Oxf 1982; CTh Oxf 1984; Phd Oxf 1989. D 12/10/1988 Bp Matthew Paul Bigliardi P 6/2/1996 Bp Jeffery William Rowthorn. m 6/13/1971 Victoria Lewis. Cn Theol/ Cannon Pstr The Amer Cathd of the H Trin Paris 75008 FR 1995-2008. "Forgotten Genocides of the 20th Century," Garod Books, UK, 2005; "Rumours of Hope," Piquant Editions, UK, 2004; Auth, "La Guerison Interieure En Rapport Avec La Doctrine Chretienne," 1979. Bp'S Awd For Distinguished Serv Bp Of Convoc Of Amer Ch In Europe 2004; 2nd Prize The Bridport Intl Poetry Competition, UK 1995. george@hobson.fr

HOBSON III, Jennings Wise (Va) Po Box 247, Washington VA 22747 **R Trin Epis Ch Washington VA 1974-** B Fairbanks AK 2/22/1948 s Jennings Wise Hobson & Isobel. BA Trin Hartford CT 1970; MDiv VTS 1973. D 5/26/1973 Bp Robert Bruce Hall P 6/1/1974 Bp John Alfred Baden. m 6/12/1970 Mary H Humphrey. R Trin Epis Ch Washington VA 1974. Loc Citizen Of The Year 1993. jenks333@mac.com

HOBSON, Patricia Shackelford (SO) 1014 Academy Ave, Cincinnati OH 45205 B Middletown OH 11/7/1952 d James Sanford Shackelford & Lois Eleanor. BS U of New Engl 1978; MDiv Bex 1986. D 6/14/1986 P 6/1/1988 Bp William Grant Black. c 1. Vic Chap Of The Nativ Cincinnati OH 1989-1994; Dio Sthrn Ohio Cincinnati OH 1989-1994; Our Sav Ch Mechanicsburg OH 1987-1989; Asst Chr Epis Ch Of Springfield Springfield OH 1986-1987. Ord S Eliz Of Hungary. pshobson@fuse.net

HOBSON, Thomas P (Colo) 1236 S High St, Denver CO 80210 B Paducah TX 6/8/1928 s Benjamin Francis Hobson & Dietta Hortense. BA U of No Texas 1955; BD Nash 1959. D 6/20/1959 Bp Charles A Mason P 12/21/1959 Bp J(ohn) Joseph Meakins Harte. m 9/18/1976 Sally R Roemer c 4. St Catherines Epis Ch Aurora CO 1987-1988; S Thos Epis Ch Denver CO 1981-1988; LocTen S Jn's Epis Ch Bisbee AZ 1966-1967; Vic S Steph's Ch Sierra Vista AZ 1963-1969; Cur All SS' Epis Ch Ft Worth TX 1960-1962; Vic S Barn Ch Garland TX 1959-1960.

HOCH, Helen Elizabeth (Kan) 314 N 3rd St, Burlington KS 66839 **Cn Ix P Calv Ch Yates Cntr KS 2001-; P Gr Ch Chanute KS 2001-** B Kansas City MO 7/11/1950 d Murray Lawrence Houston & Pauline Naomi. BS Ft Hays St U 1972; MS Emporia St U 1975. D 8/16/2000 P 2/17/2001 Bp William Edward Smalley. m 12/20/1974 Stephen Ernest Hoch. hochelen@kans.com

HOCHE-MONG, Raymond (Cal) Box 937, Montara CA 94037 **Chapl Gr Cathd San Francisco CA 1993-** B Cairo EG 5/8/1932 s William Hoche-Mong & Marie Aurore. BA U of Tennessee 1961; MDiv CDSP 1964; ThD Grad Theol Un 1977. D 6/26/1964 Bp William Evan Sanders P 5/1/1965 Bp John Vander Horst. m 11/6/1983 Emily Morrow McCormick c 2. Assoc S Eliz's

Epis Ch So San Francisco CA 1995-1997; S Edm's Epis Ch Pacifica CA 1974-1976; Vic S Clem's Ch Rancho Cordova CA 1968-1971; D-In-Trng S Mary's Cathd Memphis TN 1964-1965. Auth, "The Ch In Politics"; Auth, "Encounters w Early Art"; Auth, "Love, Bribes," *Principles Things Like That.* No Amer Acad Of Liturg. r.hochemong@gmail.com

HOCKENSMITH, David Albert (Pa) PO Box 90, Morgan VT 05853 B Indianapolis IN 4/14/1941 s Harold George Hockensmith & Dorothy Louise. BA Wabash Coll 1963; BD EDS 1966; MA Butler U 1974. D 6/11/1966 P 12/11/1966 Bp John P Craine. m 7/9/1966 Stephanie C Duke. Dn Pennypack Deanry Dio Pennsylvania Philadelphia PA 1986-1992; R S Mk's Ch Philadelphia PA 1981-1999; R S Ptr's Epis Ch Hazleton PA 1975-1981; R S Ptr's Ch Smyrna DE 1971-1975; Asst S Lk's Ch Scranton PA 1968-1971; Cur S Paul's Epis Ch Indianapolis IN 1966-1968.

HOCKER, William (Cal) 6135 Laird Ave, Oakland CA 94605 **Assoc S Greg Of Nyssa Ch San Francisco CA 2007-** B Detroit MI 2/2/1956 s Wilbur Hocker & Mary. BA U MI 1978; MS Wayne 1982; MDiv CDSP 2006. D 6/3/2006 Bp William Edwin Swing P 12/2/2006 Bp Marc Handley Andrus. Sojourn Multifaith Chapl San Francisco CA 2006-2010. howilla@umich.edu

HOCKING, Charles Edward (NC) 632 Hughes Rd, Hampstead NC 28443 B Meriden CT 11/17/1930 s Scovill Deforest Hocking & Alma Cecilia. BS U of Connecticut 1953; STB GTS 1964. D 6/11/1964 Bp Walter H Gray P 3/27/1965 Bp John Henry Esquirol. m Deborah Hocking c 3. R S Paul's Epis Ch Cary NC 1981-1996; R S Ptr's Epis Ch Cheshire CT 1972-1979; R Ch Of The Resurr Norwich CT 1966-1972; Cur Chr Ch Greenwich CT 1964-1966. OHC 1965. g4c2004@yahoo.com

H

HOCKRIDGE, Ann Elizabeth (Pa) PO Box 716, Lyndonville VT 05851 B Norristown PA 6/26/1965 d Ralph Richard Hockridge & Doris May. BA Duke 1987; MDiv EDS 1994. D 6/4/1994 P 6/1/1995 Bp Allen Lyman Bartlett Jr.

HODAPP, Timothy (Minn) 519 Oak Grove St, Minneapolis MN 55403 **Dio Minnesota Minneapolis MN 2011-** B Albert Lea MN 9/25/1958 s Philip Henry Hodapp & Kathleen Mary. BA S Mary U Winona MN 1981; MDiv Mt S Mary's Sem Emmitsburg MD 1984; MA Mt S Mary's Sem Emmitsburg MD 1985. Rec from Roman Catholic 1/7/2010 Bp James Louis Jelinek. m 10/30/2008 Gerard Cashmann Sullivan. S Chris's Epis Ch Roseville MN 2010. revtimothyhodapp@me.com

HODGE SR, Vincent Stafford (Va) Po Box 767, West Point VA 23181 B Little Dix Anguilla BW Indies 5/21/1941 s Herbert Hodge & Esther. Commonwealth Universityf; W&M 1964; ECA Trng Cntr, Brooklyn, NY 1965; W&M 1970; UTS 1971; Sch of CPE 1972. D 5/26/1973 Bp Robert Bruce Hall P 5/18/1974 Bp John Alfred Baden. c 5. Dio Virginia Richmond VA 1994-2008; Calv Ch Hanover VA 1973-2008; Vic Gr Ch Millers Tavern VA 1973-2008; Vic S Paul's Epis Ch W Point VA 1973-1994. Auth, "Apathy in Black Cmnty," *Major Causes & What Ch Ought to Do About It.* Captain ECA 1966; Ch Army. amahlhodge@yahoo.com

HODGE SR, Wayne Carlton (SVa) 114 Cross Ter, Suffolk VA 23434 B Martinsville VA 12/9/1946 s Ernest Lee Hodge & Rebecca. BS Virginia St U 1970; MA Hollins U 1980; MDiv VTS 1989. D 7/25/1989 Bp A(rthur) Heath Light P 6/1/1990 Bp C(laude) Charles Vache. m 5/17/1970 Shirley Brown c 3. Vic S Mk's Ch Suffolk VA 1989-1999. Bread For The Wrld.

HODGES, Corinne U (NI) St. John of the Cross, 601 E. Vista, PO Box 433, Bristol IN 46507 **S Anne's Epis Ch Warsaw IN 2011-** B Flushing NY 7/21/1965 d Chuck Cranford & Heidi. BA Indiana U 1987; MDiv SWTS 2006. D 6/2/2007 Bp William Dailey Persell P 12/15/2007 Bp Cecil Scantlebury. m 6/24/1989 Michael Hodges. P-in-c S Jn Of The Cross Bristol IN 2008-2011; Presb Hm Evanston IL 2007-2008; Assoc S Elis's Ch Glencoe IL 2006-2008. mthcuh@comcast.net

HODGES, David Burton (NC) 2701 Park Rd, Charlotte NC 28209 **S Paul's Epis Ch Winston Salem NC 2009-** B Gastonia NC 12/16/1959 s Ruford Burton Hodges & Jo Morris. BS Samford U 1982; MS U of Alabama 1987; MDiv Epis TS of The SW 1996. D 1/13/1996 P 7/20/1996 Bp Robert Oran Miller. m 11/24/2009 Lisa Paul c 4. R Ch Of The H Comf Charlotte NC 1999-2009; Assoc The Ch of the Gd Shpd Austin TX 1997-1999; Assoc Chr Ch Tuscaloosa AL 1996-1997. davidh@holycomforter-clt.org

HODGES, Michael John (Mass) 73 Court Street, Dedham MA 02026 **R S Paul's Ch Dedham MA 2005-** B Waterville ME 4/26/1966 s Terry Carlton Hodges & Mary Helen. BA Gordon Coll 1988; MDiv PrTS 1992. D 6/2/2001 Bp Barbara Clementine Harris P 6/8/2002 Bp M(arvil) Thomas Shaw III. m 6/20/1987 Laurie Jean Howell c 2. Vic S Paul's Ch Boston MA 2001-2005. revmjh@gmail.com

HODGES-COPPLE, Anne Elliott (NC) 1104 Watts St, Durham NC 27701 **R S Lk's Epis Ch Durham NC 2005-** B Austin TX 4/10/1957 d Richard Huff Hodges & Joan. BA Duke 1979; MDiv PSR 1984. D 9/14/1987 Bp Robert Whitridge Estill P 9/1/1988 Bp Frank Harris Vest Jr. m 10/15/1983 John Norval Hodges Copple c 3. Dio No Carolina Raleigh NC 1992-2005; Chapl Duke Epis Cntr Durham NC 1992-2005; Asst to R S Lk's Epis Ch Durham NC 1987-1992. a.hodgescopple@gmail.com

HODGKINS, Lewis (Spok) 605 Sherman Dr, The Dalles OR 97058 **Assoc S Pauls Epis Ch The Dalles OR 1991-** B Bangor ME 8/27/1927 s Norris Lowell Hodgkins & Gladys Mary. BA Duke 1949; BD STUSo 1952. D 6/24/1952 Bp Edwin A Penick P 4/12/1953 Bp William J Gordon Jr. m 6/24/1955 Barbee F Sherman c 1. Int S Matt's Epis Ch Fairbanks AK 1989-1990; Vic Gr Ch Dayton WA 1976-1989; Vic S Ptr's Ch Pomeroy WA 1976-1989; Assoc All SS' Epis Ch Anchorage AK 1959-1967; Vic S Geo's Ch Cordova AK 1956-1959. barbeehodgkins@gmail.com

HODGKINS, Margaret Steuart Rice (NJ) 583 Cherry Hill Rd, Princeton NJ 08540 **Chair, Planned Giving Com Dio New Jersey Trenton NJ 2010-; Com on Priesthood Dio New Jersey Trenton NJ 2007-; R S Andr's Epis Ch New Providence NJ 2005-** B Fort Campbell KY 8/2/1957 d David Kemper Rice & Alice Steuart Haughton. BA Mid 1979; MDiv UTS 1996. D 6/1/1996 Bp John Shelby Spong P 12/7/1996 Bp Jack Marston McKelvey. m 8/20/1983 Robinson C L Hodgkins c 3. Assoc Chapl Epis Ch at Pr Princeton NJ 2001-2005; Assoc R Trin Ch Princeton NJ 2001-2005; Assoc R Calv Epis Ch Summit NJ 1996-2001. Fell Wilson Coll, Pr 2003. hodgkinsp@gmail.com

HODGKINS, Nelson Bainbridge (NC) 874 Simmons Grove Church Rd, Pilot Mountain NC 27041 **Int P Dio No Carolina Raleigh NC 2008-; S Thos Epis Ch Reidsville NC 2000-** B Lewiston ME 9/7/1932 s Franklin Eugene Hodgkins & Inez Bohsen. AAS Rochester Inst of Tech 1952; BS U of Houston 1953; MDiv VTS 1960; MS No Carolina A&T St U 1980. D 6/13/1960 P 1/23/1961 Bp Thomas H Wright. m 9/16/1988 Nicholas Hodgkins c 2. Part Time Vic S Paul's Ch Salisbury NC 2004-2008; Int Trin Ch Mt Airy NC 2000-2003; Int S Lk's Ch Eden NC 1995-1998; S Paul's Epis Ch Thomasville NC 1994-1995; Int S Chris's Epis Ch High Point NC 1992-1995; Int S Anne's Ch Winston Salem NC 1991-1992; Int Dio No Carolina Raleigh NC 1988-1991; Int S Chris's Epis Ch High Point NC 1985-1988; Int P S Lk's Ch Eden NC 1983-1985; S Andr's Ch Greensboro NC 1977; Indstrl Counslg Serv Greensboro NC 1969-1984; P-in-c S Thos' Epis Ch Bath NC 1965-1967; P-in-c Zion Epis Ch Washington NC 1965-1967; R Gr Ch Whiteville NC 1960-1965; Min in charge S Jas The Fisherman Epis Ch Shallotte NC 1960-1964. Auth, *Influence Mozarabic Rite Liturg Ch of Spain*, 1959. RACA 1967. Paul Harris Fllshp Rotary Intl 1980. hodgkinscounseling@yahoo.com

HODGSON, Gregory Scott (SVa) 11940 Fairlington Lane, Midlothian VA 23113 **R S Mich's Ch Bon Air VA 2006-** B New York NY 11/25/1959 s Lawrence Scott Hodgson & Diane Yvonne. BA SUNY 1981; MDiv STUSo 1984. D 6/23/1984 Bp Henry Boyd Hucles III P 1/19/1985 Bp Robert Campbell Witcher Sr. m 2/17/2001 Sherrill L McKay c 2. Assoc Gr Ch Charleston SC 2002-2006; Dn Dio Massachusetts Boston MA 1996-2002; R Trin Epis Ch Wrentham MA 1990-2002; Cur S Mk's Ch Islip NY 1984-1990. ghodgson@stmichaelsbonair.org

HODSDON, Douglas Graham (Fla) 1461 Challen Ave, Jacksonville FL 32205 **R Ch Of The Gd Shpd Jacksonville FL 2007-** B Boston MA 9/23/1949 s George Morse Hodsdon & Evelyn Katherine. BA U NC 1972; MDiv VTS 1984. D 6/15/1984 Bp C(laude) Charles Vache P 6/1/1985 Bp Robert Whitridge Estill. m 7/7/1973 Mary Gallen c 3. R S Thos Epis Ch Sanford NC 1991-2007; R S Jn's Ch Winnsboro SC 1988-1991; Cur Ch Of The H Comf Charlotte NC 1984-1988. trdgh@me.com

HOEBERMANN, Christine Marie (Mich) 123 L St NE, Auburn WA 98002 B Arlington, WA 2/22/1958 d Gary William Hendrickson & Rae Marie. AA Everett Cmnty Coll. D 6/28/2003 Bp Wendell Nathaniel Gibbs Jr. m 8/20/1994 Jay Robert Hoebermann c 2. with_love@msn.com

HOECKER, Maria J. (WNC) 256 East Main Street, Brevard NC 28712 B Wichita KS 10/29/1962 d Robert Gerald Frey & Janice Marie. BS SW Coll Winfield KS 1984; MDiv STUSo 2005. D 6/29/2005 Bp Dean Elliott Wolfe P 2/4/2006 Bp Granville Porter Taylor. c 2. Assoc R S Phil's Ch Brevard NC 2005-2010. Guest Ed, "Chld and the Kingdom: Educ and Formation," *Sewanee Theol Revs*, Univ. of the So, Sewanee TN, 2005; Auth, "Expectation ~a poem and article.," *Sewanee Theol Revs*, Univ. of the So, Sewanee TN, 2004; Guest Ed, "Chld and the Kingdom: The Theol of Childhood," *Sewanee Theol Revs*, Univ. of So, Sewanee TN, 2004. maria.hoecker@gmail.com

HOECKER, Marsha Hogg (Mass) 188 Center Road, Shirley MA 01464 **P-in-c S Dav's Epis Mssn Pepperell MA 2009-; P-in-c Shirley Pepperell Epis Partnership Pepperell MA 2009-** B Portsmouth VA 4/1/1950 d Frank Wells Hogg & Catherine Anne. Carleton Coll; BS Windham Coll 1978; MDiv EDS 1995. D 4/1/1995 P 10/16/1995 Bp Mary Adelia Rosamond McLeod. m 12/29/1990 Henry Tilden Hoecker c 2. R Trin Chap Shirley MA 2006-2009; Mssnr Middlesex Area Cluster Mnstry Higganum CT 2002-2006; Yth Mnstry Dio Vermont Burlington VT 1998-2002; P-in-c H Trin Epis Ch Swanton VT 1998-2001; Asst S Barn Ch Falmouth MA 1995-1998. mhhoecker@hotmail.com

HOEKSTRA, Robert Bruce (Eau) 909 Summit Ave, Chippewa Falls WI 54729 **P-in-c S Simeon's Ch Stanley WI 2009-** B South Holland IL 11/23/1957 s Thomas Richard Hoekstra & Gay Louise. BA Trin Bible Coll Ellendale ND 1981; None Trin Evang DS 1983; MA Multnomah Biblic Sem 1997; Cert Coll of Preachers 2002; S.T.M. Nash 2010. D 11/7/2002 P 5/8/2003 Bp Keith

Bernard Whitmore. m 9/26/1981 Heidi Lynn Nohr c 4. Stndg Com Dio Eau Claire Eau Claire WI 2007-2009; P-in-c S Lk's Ch Altoona WI 2004-2006. rbh.dmin@gmail.com

HOELTZEL, Geo(rge) Anthony (NY) 721 Warburton Ave, Yonkers NY 10701 **P H Cross Yonkers NY 1996-** B Kansas City MO 4/24/1948 s Orval Roland Hoeltzel & Marjorie Miller. BA U of So Alabama 1969; MDiv GTS 1973. D 6/9/1973 Bp Leland Stark P 12/15/1973 Bp Paul Moore Jr. m 9/15/1969 Susan Sadler c 2. Assoc S Jn's Ch Getty Sq Yonkers NY 1985-1995; R All SS Ch Harrison NY 1977-1985; Asst Gr Epis Ch Nyack NY 1975-1976; Cur S Barth's Ch In The Highland White Plains NY 1973-1975. Fllshp Recon. thoeltzel@gmail.com

HOELZEL III, William Nold (Chi) 3221 Cochiti St NE, Rio Rancho NM 87144 B Chicago IL 2/1/1942 s William Nold Hoelzel & Celeste Aida. BA NWU 1964; BD Nash 1968. D 6/15/1968 Bp James Winchester Montgomery P 12/21/1968 Bp Gerald Francis Burrill. m 8/15/1964 Mary Scott c 3. R S Mary Epis Ch Crystal Lake IL 1976-2007; Vic Gr Epis Ch New Lenox IL 1971-1976; Cur S Matt's Ch Evanston IL 1968-1971. hoelzel@cableone.net

HOEY, Anne (Tex) 5608-A Jim Hogg Ave., Austin TX 78756 B Austin TX 12/20/1938 d Fred Franklin Knight & Elizabeth. Wellesley Coll 1958; BA U of Texas 1960; MDiv Epis TS of The SW 1988. D 6/24/1988 Bp Anselmo Carral-Solar P 5/26/1989 Bp Maurice Manuel Benitez. c 3. Assoc R S Mich's Ch Austin TX 2001-2005; R S Jas' Epis Ch La Grange TX 1997-2000; The Ch of the Gd Shpd Austin TX 1990-1997. ahoey1@att.net

HOEY, Lori Jean (CFla) 901 Clearmont St, Sebastian FL 32958 B W Islip NY 6/20/1965 d Walter Thomas Schneider & Patricia Ann. Cert of Grad Istitute for Chr Stds 2009; BA Grand Canyon U 2010. D 12/12/2009 Bp John Wadsworth Howe. m 8/15/1987 Thomas Hoey c 2. D S Eliz's Epis Ch Sebastian FL 2009-2011. lorijhoey@hotmail.com

HOFER, Christopher David (LI) 1400 Poulson St, Wantagh NY 11793 **Dn, So Nassau Dnry Dio Long Island Garden City NY 2006-; R Ch of S Jude Wantagh NY 2004-** B Jasper IN 1/28/1971 s David Lee Hofer & Katherine Louise. BA Walsh U 1993; MDiv GTS 2002. D 6/8/2002 Bp Arthur Benjamin Williams Jr P 12/11/2002 Bp J Clark Grew II. m 8/12/1995 Kerry M Brady. Assoc Mssnr Epis. Shared Mnstrs Nw Lakewood OH 2002-2004. Blogger, "Vital Post Blog," *Epis Ch Vital Practices Blog*, ECF, 2011; Featured, "Transforming Ch," *Transforming Ch (Wantagh) Documentary*, Epis Ch Cntr, 2011. EUC 2003. fatherhofer@gmail.com

HOFER, Larry John (CPa) 32801 Ocean Reach Dr, Lewes DE 19958 B Toledo OH 9/9/1939 s Harry Hofer & Mary. BA Ken 1961; MDiv Trin Luth Sem 1964; GTS 1987. D 6/12/1987 Bp Charlie Fuller McNutt Jr P 10/21/1987 Bp Dean T Stevenson. m 4/25/1970 Susan Mardel Forker c 2. Assoc S Paul's Ch Georgetown DE 2009-2011; R S Andr's Ch St Coll PA 1994-2008; R S Alb's Epis Ch Reading PA 1990-1994; Asst to R S Andr's Ch Harrisburg PA 1987-1990. SSJE 2000. hofer09@gmail.com

HOFF, Timothy (Ala) 2601 Lakewood Cir, Tuscaloosa AL 35405 B Freeport IL 2/27/1941 s Howard Vincent Hoff & Zillah. BA Tul 1963; JD Tul 1966; LLM Harv 1970. D 7/31/1983 P 2/22/1984 Bp Furman Stough. m 3/21/1987 Virginia Nevill Hoff c 4. Secy of the Dio Dio Alabama Birmingham AL 2006-2009; R S Mich's Epis Ch Fayette AL 2003-2010; Epis Black Belt Mnstry Demopolis AL 2002-2003; Int Trin Ch Demopolis AL 2002-2003; R S Mich's Epis Ch Fayette AL 1988-1996; Int Ch Of The H Comf Montgomery AL 1984-1985; Asst S Paul's Ch Greensboro AL 1983-1984. Auth, "The Interpretive Process," *in Merc Judgments & Contemporary Soc*, Camb Press, 2011; Auth, "(Nell) Harper Lee," *in Yale Biographical Dict. of Amer Law*, Ya Press, 2009; Auth, "Anatomy of a Murder," *Legal Stds Forum*, 2000; Auth, "Marketing Law & Lit," *Journ of the Legal Profession*, 1999; Auth, "Lawyers in the Subjunctive Mood," *Legal Stds Forum*, 1999; Auth, "Amer Monarchists & the Cult of Chas I," *Legal Stds Forum*, 1998; Auth, "Influences on Harper Lee," *Alabama Law Revs*, 1994; Auth, "Jn Tyler Morgan & Sthrn Autonomy," *Gulf Coast Hist Revs*, 1994; Auth, "Limitation of Actions, 2nd ed.," Harrison Pub Co, 1992; Auth, "Commencement Invocation," *Journ of the Legal Profession*, 1986; Auth, "Theol Influences on Wstrn Law," *Alabama Law Revs*, 1985; Auth, "Eleventh Circuit Survey Intro," *Mercer Law Revs*, 1982; Auth, "Error in the Formation of Contracts," *Tulane Law Revs*, 1979; Auth, "Joinder of Parties & Claims:," *Alabama Law Revs*, 1973. CBS 1977; GAS 1977; Sectn on Law & Rel, Assn Am Law Schools 1970; Soc of King Chas the Mtyr 1977. Who's Who in Amer 1992; Phi Beta Kappa 1963. thoff34@me.com

HOFFACKER, Charles Edward Niblett (EMich) 7035 Blair Road NW #341, Washington DC 20012 **S Chris's Ch New Carrollton MD 2010-; S Ptr's Ch Poolesville MD 2008-** B Philadelphia PA 10/16/1953 s Carl Theil Hoffacker & Anne Marjorie. BA St. Jn's Coll Annapolis MD 1975; MDiv Nash 1982; Coll of Preachers 1992; CDI STUSo 1996. D 6/2/1982 Bp William Carl Frey P 12/18/1982 Bp James Winchester Montgomery. c 1. Int S Andr's Ch St Coll PA 2008-2009; Dio Estrn Michigan Saginaw MI 2002-2006; Exam Chapl Dio Estrn Michigan Saginaw MI 1997-2005; Dep GC Dio Estrn Michigan Saginaw MI 1997-2003; Dn Blue Water Convoc Dio Estrn Michigan Saginaw MI 1995-2005; Dn Blue Water Convoc Dio Michigan Detroit MI 1993-1994; R S Paul's Epis Ch Port Huron MI 1992-2006; S Ptr's Ch Akron OH 1986-1992; Int S Jude's Epis Ch Rochelle IL 1985-1986; S Paul's Ch Dekalb IL 1982-1983. Auth, *A Matter of Life and Death: Preaching at Funerals*, Cowley, 2003; Auth, "Var arts, sermons, Revs. columns". Excellence in Mnstry Awd Dio Estrn Michigan 2005. charles.hoffacker@gmail.com

HOFFACKER, Michael Paul Niblett (Pa) PO Box 765, Devon PA 19333 B Washington DC 12/15/1942 s Carl Theil Hoffacker & Anne Marjorie. BA U of Pennyslvania 1964; STB PDS 1967; MS Drexel U 1976. D 6/10/1967 P 2/1/1968 Bp Robert Lionne DeWitt. m 12/2/1967 Antoinette Eugenie Cutaiar. Asst Nevil Meml Ch Of S Geo Ardmore PA 1970-1973. MPNHoffacker@csi.com

HOFFER, Jack Lee (CPa) 830 Washington Avenue, Tyrone PA 16686 **D Trin Epis Ch Tyrone PA 2011-** B Windber PA 8/12/1945 s Maurice Franklin Hoffer & Mary Ellen. BS Penn St U 1973; Cert EFM/Sewanee 2006; Cert Dioc Sch of Chriatian Stds 2007. D 6/9/2007 Bp Nathan Dwight Baxter. jlh1134@verizon.net

HOFFER, Wilma(Willie) Marie (EO) 64849 Casa Ct, Bend OR 97701 B Rockford IL 12/29/1937 d Ronald Wolfe & Lola Esther. Cert CDSP 1991. D 6/20/1991 Bp George Edmonds Bates. m 2/2/1958 Richard Ernest Hoffer c 2. D Trin Ch Bend OR 1998; Dio Utah Salt Lake City UT 1997-1998; D All SS Ch Salt Lake City UT 1994-1998; Pstrl Vis Dio Utah Salt Lake City UT 1992-1998; Epis Cmnty Serv Inc Salt Lake City UT 1992-1996; D S Lk's Ch Pk City UT 1991-1994. rockhaven@empnet.com

HOFFMAN, Arnold R (Spr) 862 Starlight Ct, Herrin IL 62948 B Stillwater MN 8/19/1938 s Milton Hoffman & Lena Mae. BA U of Kansas 1963; MA U of Kansas 1965; PhD MI SU 1970; MDiv Nash 1978; completed class Wk DMin TS 1996. D 6/9/1976 Bp Archie H Crowley P 6/8/1978 Bp William Cockburn Russell Sheridan. m 8/29/1982 Sharon McDonald c 2. Supply Cler S Paul's Epis Ch Sikeston MO 2005-2011; COM, Chair Dio Springfield Springfield IL 1997-1998; Cn Mssnr Dio Springfield Springfield IL 1995-2004; Vic S Marys Ch Columbia MO 1990-1995; Cn Mssnr Dio Missouri S Louis MO 1990-1994; R H Trin Ch Skokie IL 1986-1990; R S Jn's Epis Ch Kewanee IL 1981-1986; Actg Vic Chr The King Epis Ch Huntington IN 1980-1981; R S Paul's Epis Ch Gas City IN 1978-1981. Auth, "Var arts," *Poetry*. Som 1991. ashoffman@charter.net

HOFFMAN, Charles Lance (Ct) 8 Sharon Ln, Old Saybrook CT 06475 **R Gr Ch Old Saybrook CT 1988-** B Chicago IL 3/15/1941 s Peter William Hoffman & Jayne Hanson. BA Trin 1962; BD/MDiv EDS 1968; DMin Andover Newton TS 1979. D 6/15/1968 Bp James Winchester Montgomery P 4/10/1969 Bp Gerald Francis Burrill. m 11/27/1976 Ellendale McCollam c 4. R Ch Of The Mssh Woods Hole MA 1971-1988; Asst Par Of The Epiph Winchester MA 1969-1971; Cur The Par Of S Chrys's Quincy MA 1968-1969. Ord of S Lk 1993. rev.hoffman@sbcglobal.net

HOFFMAN, Donald David (WMo) 2525 Main St Apt 509, Kansas City MO 64108 **Died 12/6/2010** B Sacramento CA 7/10/1920 s Elbert Lyle Hoffman & Jessie L. S Paul Theol & Rockhurst Coll. D 4/25/1983 Bp Arthur Anton Vogel. Bro Of S Andr; Soc Of S Paul. dddon@mymailstation.com

HOFFMAN SR, Earl Dirk (Md) 600 Light St Apt 211, Baltimore MD 21230 B Baltimore MD 1/14/1928 s Charles Philip Hoffman & Maria Antoinette. Priv Tutor ECA Trng 1969. D 3/23/1970 P 9/27/1970 Bp Roger W Blanchard. c 1. R Ch Of The Redemp Baltimore MD 1972-1985; Asst Ch Of The Adv Cincinnati OH 1970-1972.

HOFFMAN JR, Edgar Henry (Hap) (Ark) 7 Rubra Ct, Little Rock AR 72223 B Cheyenne WY 12/14/1934 s Edgar Henry Hoffman & Pearl M. BS U Denv 1956; Cert Epis TS of The SW 1994. D 6/15/1995 P 1/19/1996 Bp Larry Earl Maze. m 5/8/1965 Barbara J Cavan. Vic S Alb's Ch Stuttgart AR 2002-2006; R Gr Ch Pine Bluff AR 2000-2002; Dio Arkansas Little Rock AR 1997-2002; Chapl S Alb's Ch Stuttgart AR 1997-2000; S Steph's Epis Ch Jacksonville AR 1995-2007. haphoffman@gmail.com

HOFFMAN, Ellendale McCollam (Ct) 8 Sharon Ln, Old Saybrook CT 06475 **Assoc Gr Ch Old Saybrook CT 1990-** B Alexandria LA 4/3/1951 d William McCollam & Hope Joffrion. AA Briarcliffe Coll 1971; BA Manhattanville Coll 1973; MDiv EDS 1976; DMin Andover Newton TS 1978. D 6/19/1976 Bp James Barrow Brown P 7/1/1977 Bp John Bowen Coburn. m 11/27/1976 Charles Lance Hoffman c 2. Cler and Fam Enrichment Com Dio Connecticut Hartford CT 1991-1995; Supvsr Pstrl Inst TrngAlco Problems EDS Cambridge MA 1976-1978. CT LMFT 1988; Clincl Mem, Amer Assn for Marital and Fam Ther 1982; Fell, AAPC 1982; MA Lic Clincl Psychol 1979. ellendale@sbcglobal.net

HOFFMAN III, Harry Lee (Md) 405 Gun Rd, Baltimore MD 21227 B Baltimore MD 7/13/1927 s Harry Lee Hoffman & Charlotte Herbert. BA Jn Hopkins U 1951; MDiv VTS 1957. D 7/6/1957 Bp Noble C Powell P 3/26/1958 Bp Harry Lee Doll. m 6/21/1958 Mary P Primrose. Asst S Jn's Ch Ellicott City MD 1986-1988; R S Ptr's Epis Ch Purcellville VA 1969-1986; Asst S Matt's Ch Richmond VA 1963-1969; Vic S Jn's Ch Powell WY 1959-1963. Hon Cn S Ptr Cathd Uganda. hlffman3rd@comcast.net

HOFFMAN, Jeffrey Paul (CNY) 38 Rolling Acres Rd, Pine City NY 14871 B Rochester NY 11/26/1954 s Nels Earl Hugo Hoffman & Ruthe Ilene. MDiv TS

2007. D 6/9/2007 P 12/11/2007 Bp Gladstone Bailey Adams III. m 8/1/1998 Margaret Hinds c 7. Cler-in-Charge S Matt's Epis Ch Horseheads NY 2007-2010. fr.jeff@st-matts.net

HOFFMAN, Lisa A (NJ) PO Box 326, Navesink NJ 07752 **S Barn By The Bay Villas NJ 2011-; S Mary's Epis Ch Stone Harbor NJ 2011-** B Neptune NJ 3/1/1962 d William Howard Itinger & Sheila Loretta. BS Kutztown U 1984; MDiv VTS 2011. D 12/4/2010 P 6/30/2011 Bp George Edward Councell. m 7/27/1985 Jeffrey L Hoffman c 3. lisaannhoffman@aol.com

HOFFMAN, Mary Elizabeth (Ia) 2704 E garfield, Davenport IA 52803 **D Trin Cathd Davenport IA 1995-** B Oklahoma City OK 3/6/1933 d Henry Keith Dickson & Vera Morlan. BD Drake U 1954; MS U of Iowa 1985. D 8/15/1995 Bp Carl Christopher Epting. m 6/6/1953 Larry Gene Hoffman c 2. Cmnty of S Mary. molly36@gmail.com

HOFFMAN, Michael Patrick (Dal) 1912 Fair Oaks Dr, Mission TX 78574 **S Ptr's Ch McKinney TX 2011-; S Clare's Epis Ch Pleasanton CA 2005-** B Biloxi, MS 6/19/1978 s John Charles Hoffman & Barbara Ellen. BA U So 2000; MDiv STUSo 2005. D 6/28/2005 P 1/5/2006 Bp James Edward Folts. c 1. St Ptr & St Paul Ch Mssn TX 2007-2011; S Helena's Epis Ch Boerne TX 2005-2011; S Andr's Epis Ch Seguin TX 2005-2007. michael@stpeterstpaul.org

H

HOFFMAN, Robyn Rene (SVa) 2 BL Jackson Road, Newport RI 02840 B Warren MI 1/22/1967 d Ronald Norman Burns & Hope Culich. BA Rol; MDiv Garrett Evang TS 1993; MA SWTS 1993. D 3/19/2000 Bp William Dailey Persell P 10/28/2000 Bp Victor Alfonso Scantlebury. m 2/14/2000 Roy Everett Hoffman c 1. Supply Cler Dio Virginia Richmond VA 2009-2011; Supply Cler Ch Of Engl London 2007-2008; Asst Old Donation Ch Virginia Bch VA 2005-2007; Asst The Epis Ch Of S Andr Encinitas CA 2002-2003; Mssnr Dio Chicago Chicago IL 2000-2002; Yth Dir Epis Ch Of The Gd Shpd Lake Chas LA 1996-1998. robynhoffman99@msn.com

HOFFMAN, Roy Everett (SVa) 2 BL Jackson Road, Newport RI 02840 B Alexandria VA 7/28/1957 s Charles Calvin Hoffman & Doreen Briten. BS Auburn U 1979; JD U GA 1983; MDiv SWTS 1994; DMin GTF 2008. D 9/24/1994 P 5/12/1995 Bp Robert Gould Tharp. m 2/14/2000 Robyn Rene Burns c 1. Vic Ch Of S Ben Bolingbrook IL 1996-2002; Asst Ch Of The Gd Samar Knoxville TN 1994-1996. Auth, "Jn Wesley's Reflection on the Lord's Pryr," *Fndt Theol*, Victoria Press, 2009. royhoffman99@msn.com

HOFFMAN, William Charles (SVa) 4101 Mingo Trl, Chesapeake VA 23325 B Columbus OH 11/11/1923 s William Frederick Hoffman & Mildred. BA W&M 1948; VTS 1951. D 6/12/1951 P 6/1/1952 Bp George P Gunn. m 6/5/1949 Carmen Fitchett c 1. R S Bride's Epis Ch Chesapeake VA 1954-1988. bigbill234@cox.net

HOFFMANN, Beth Borah (Ct) 216 Ludlow Rd, Manchester CT 06040 **Vic Ch Of The Epiph Durham CT 2008-** B Evansville IN 10/29/1943 d Frank David Borah & Barbara. AA Stephens Coll 1963; BS U Of Bridgeport 1990; Col 1992; Pittsburgh TS 1997; MDiv GTS 2000. D 6/10/2000 Bp Robert William Duncan P 12/27/2000 Bp Andrew Donnan Smith. m 12/19/1963 Lewis Edward Hoffmann c 1. S Mary's Epis Ch Manchester CT 2002-2005; Incarn Cntr Ivoryton CT 2000-2001; Chapl S Jn's Chap Ivoryton CT 2000-2001. beausmom1@cox.net

HOGAN, C (Eau) 510 S Farwell St Ste 3, Eau Claire WI 54701 B Quincy IL 9/20/1943 d Claude M Neahring & Maxine L. BS Eureka Coll 1965; Dio Milwaukee Inst of Chr Stds WI 1990; AAS Madison Area Tech Coll 2001. D 9/8/1990 Bp Roger John White. m 6/28/2008 Patrick M Hogan. D S Andr's Epis Ch Monroe WI 1990-2008. NAAD 1990.

HOGAN, F Faye (Los) 1237 Laguna Ln, San Luis Obispo CA 93035 **Pstr Assoc S Ptr's Par Santa Maria CA 2009-** B Baton Rouge LA 1/15/1932 d Oauthor Benjiman Hogan & Frances. BS Texas Wmn's U-Denton 1953; MA Texas Wmn's U-Denton 1956; EdD USC 1983; MDiv ETS Claremont 1997. D 6/1/1996 P 1/18/1997 Bp Chester Lovelle Talton. Asst S Ben's Par Los Osos CA 2006-2008; S Paul's Epis Ch Ventura CA 2002-2004; Trin Epis Ch Santa Barbara CA 2000-2004. Assn Of Profsnl Chapl - Bd-Cert Chaplai; OHC. fayehogan@earthlink.net

HOGAN, Lucy Lind (WA) 4500 Massachusetts Ave Nw, Washington DC 20016 **Exam Chapl Dio Washington Washington DC 2008-** B Minneapolis MN 12/5/1951 d Wilfred Norman Lind & Margaret Anne. BA Macalester Coll 1973; MDiv VTS 1981; DMin Wesley TS 1987; PhD U of Maryland 1995. D 6/29/1981 P 1/25/1982 Bp Robert Marshall Anderson. m 5/26/1973 Kevin Patrick Hogan c 2. Asst S Lk's Ch Trin Par Beth MD 1989-1995; VTS Alexandria VA 1989-1990; Asst S Lk's Ch Trin Par Beth MD 1983-1984; Asst S Fran Ch Potomac MD 1981-1982. Auth, "The Six Deadly Sins of Preaching," Abingdon Press, 2012; Auth, "Lenten Serv," Abingdon Press, 2009; Ed, "Preaching As A Lang of Hope," Protea Bk Hse, 2007; Auth, "Graceful Speech An Invitatin to Preaching," Westminster Jn Knox Press, 2006; Auth, "Connecting w The Cong: Rhetoric And The Art Of Preaching," Abingdon Press, 1999. Acad Of Homil 1994; Societas Homiletica, Past Pres 1998; WECA 1981. lindhogan@gmail.com

HOGARTH, David Judson (Mass) 33 Willet St, Wollaston MA 02170 B New Haven CT 6/11/1938 s William Oswald Hogarth & Gaylord Moreland. BA Br 1960; MDiv Nash 1964; MA Springfield Coll 1965. D 6/1/1964 Bp William Hampton Brady. c 1. The Ch Of The Adv Boston MA 1965; Cur S Alb's Ch Simsbury CT 1964-1965. Auth, *Model In-Hse Prog to Assist Despairing/Suicidal Inmates/Instnl Res*, IASP, 1975; Auth, *Manual of Suicide Prevention*, Suffolk Cty. Sheriff's Dept, 1973. PB Soc of the Epis Ch 1980. davidh@mit.edu

HOGG, Douglas (EC) 347 South Creek Drive, Osprey FL 34229 B Charleston WV 11/1/1936 s Francis Russell Hogg & Kathleen Marshall. BA Randolph-Macon Coll 1958; BD Epis TS of The SW 1963; U of Tennessee 1968; HGC 1980. D 6/27/1963 P 6/1/1964 Bp David Shepherd Rose. R S Chris's Ch Havelock NC 1965-1967; Asst R Chr And Gr Ch Petersburg VA 1963-1965.

HOGG JR, Paul (Peter) (SVa) 7858 Sunset Dr, Hayes VA 23072 **S Jn's Ch Hampton VA 2011-; Gr Ch The Plains VA 2010-** B Newport News VA 11/25/1946 s Paul Hogg & Dorothy. BA Randolph-Macon Coll 1969; MDiv VTS 1974; DMin VTS 1991. D 6/6/1974 P 12/1/1974 Bp David Shepherd Rose. m 8/10/1968 Toni C Chiesa c 2. Int Chr Epis Ch Raleigh NC 2009-2010; Int Trin Ch Portsmouth VA 2008-2009; S Paul's Ch Richmond VA 2008; R S Aid's Ch Virginia Bch VA 1979-2005; S Dav's Epis Ch Richmond VA 1974-1979; Dio Sthrn Virginia Norfolk VA 1974-1976. Auth, *Empowerment for Mnstry: Developing Lay Pstr Caregivers*, VTS, 1991. phogg123@gmail.com

HOGUE, Kelsey Graham (Neb) 9 W 35th St, Scottsbluff NE 69361 **R S Fran Epis Ch Scottsbluff NE 2006-** B Bedford IN 9/29/1950 s James Lawerence Hogue & Ethel Park. BS U CO 1972; MDiv CDSP 1992. D 6/20/1992 P 12/15/1992 Bp William Jerry Winterrowd. m 7/11/1970 Deborah Lyn Van Horn c 2. Bp Search Com Dio Nebraska Omaha NE 2010-2011; Int S Ptr's Ch Basalt CO 2005-2006; Wstrn Coloorado Dio Colorado Denver CO 2000-2005; Stndg Com-ex oficio Dio Colorado Denver CO 2000-2005; Cn Mssnr - Mtn Reg Dio Colorado Denver CO 1998-2000; mutual Mnstry Coordntr Dio Colorado Denver CO 1996-1999; COM Dio Colorado Denver CO 1993-1996; Vic Cranmer Memi Chap Winter Pk CO 1992-2000; R Epis Ch Of S Jn The Bapt Granby CO 1992-2000; Vic Trin Ch Kremmling CO 1992-1998. Fell Coll of Preachers Natl Cathd Washington DC 2000. kelseyhogue@earthlink.net

HOHENFELDT, Robert John (Mil) 1310 Rawson Ave, South Milwaukee WI 53172 B Marinette WI 7/2/1924 D 8/3/1963 Bp Donald H V Hallock. m 4/19/1952 Dolores Ruth Aubinger c 2.

HOHLT, Allan Hunter (Del) 94 Oak Ridge Rd, Plymouth NH 03264 B Brenham TX 6/14/1932 s Ernest William Hohlt & Sarah Hunter. BBA Texas A&M U 1954; BD CDSP 1966; DHL S Aug's Coll Raleigh NC 1989. D 6/22/1966 Bp J Milton Richardson P 5/30/1967 Bp Scott Field Bailey. m 8/8/1964 Winifred L Lehman c 2. Dn, Cn, & Urban Mssnr Cathd Ch Of S Jn Wilmington DE 1976-1994; R S Paul's Epis Ch Freeport TX 1970-1976; Vic H Cross Epis Ch Sugar Land TX 1966-1967. fernbank2@myfairpoint.net

HOIDRA, Carol A (Ct) 333 East 30th Street, Apt. 6G, New York NY 10016 **Assoc Dir, Mssn Funding Epis Ch Cntr New York NY 2008-** B Warren OH 4/7/1952 d Peter Hoidra & Anna. BA Arcadia U (Form Beaver Coll) 1974; MDiv Ya Berk 2003. D 6/10/2006 P 1/20/2007 Bp Andrew Donnan Smith. P S Mk's Ch New Canaan CT 2007-2008; Cur S Mary's Epis Ch Manchester CT 2006-2007; Dvlpmt Assoc S Barth's Ch New York NY 2004-2006. hoidra@earthlink.net

HOKE, Stuart Hubbard (NY) 536 Fearrington Post, Pittsboro NC 27312 B Memphis TN 7/11/1946 s Wallace Stuart Hoke & Mildred Lou. BA SMU 1968; MDiv EDS 1972; STM GTS 1996; ThD GTS 2000. D 7/1/1972 P 12/16/1972 Bp Chilton Powell. c 2. Chapl Trin Par New York NY 2000-2008; The Ch of S Ign of Antioch New York NY 1996-2000; Int Ch Of The Gd Shpd Ft Lee NJ 1995-1996; R S Fran Ch Houston TX 1991-1995; R S Andr's Epis Ch Amarillo TX 1981-1991; R S Jn's Ch Harrison AR 1976-1981; Asst S Mk's Epis Ch Little Rock AR 1974-1976; Cur S Dunst's Ch Tulsa OK 1972-1974. Auth, "A Generally Obscure Calling: Character Sketch Of Isabel Hapgood," *S Vladimir'S Quarterly*, 2001; Auth, "Broken Fragments: Wm Reed Huntington'S Quest For Unity," *Journ Of Angl/Epis Hist*, 2000. shoke46@gmail.com

HOLBEN, Lawrence Robert (NCal) 701 Lassen Ln, Mount Shasta CA 96067 **P-in-c S Barn Ch Mt Shasta CA 2010-** B Los Angeles CA 9/2/1945 s Gordon W Holben & Margaret F. D 6/12/2010 P 12/12/2010 Bp Barry Leigh Beisner. lholben@gmail.com

HOLBERT, John Russell (La) 1645 Carol Sue Ave, Terrytown LA 70056 **Food Dir S Geo's Epis Ch New Orleans LA 2006-** B Charleston SC 4/20/1945 s John Russell Somerville & Alice. D 10/23/2005 Bp Charles Edward Jenkins III. c 2. john2no@hotmail.com

HOLBROOK JR, Paul Evans (Lex) 308 Madison Pl, Lexington KY 40508 B Ashland KY 4/4/1949 s Paul Evans Holbrook & Frances Vivian. BA Denison U 1971; MDiv Harvard DS 1974; ThM Harvard DS 1976; MA U of Kentucky 1983; PhD U of Kentucky 1988. D 8/15/1975 Bp Addison Hosea. D S Aug's Chap Lexington KY 1996-2003; D Ch S Mich The Archangel Lexington KY 1980-1982; Asst Chapl S Aug's Chap Lexington KY 1979-1980; D Calv Epis Ch Ashland KY 1977-1979. Auth, "Victor Hammer," *Printer & Typographer*,

The Anvil Press, 1981; Auth, "Notes for," *Phenomena of Aratus Soliensus*, King Libr Press, 1975. Comp To Solitary Of Dekoven 1996; Sr Chapl Mltry and Hospitaller, Ord of S Laz 1992; Tertiary of the Soc of S Fran 1978. Mem The Most Venerable Ord of the Hosp of St. Jn of Jerusal 2003; Knight Sovereign Mltry Ord of Temple of Jerusalem 1992. peholbr@yahoo.com

HOLCOMB, Justin Seth (Va) 100 W Jefferson St, Charlottesville VA 22902 B Sarasota FL 9/16/1973 s Danny L Holcomb & Janet Marie. BA SE U (Lakeland, FL) 1994; MA Reformed TS (Orlando, FL) 1997; MA Reformed TS (Orlando, FL) 1997; PhD Emory U 2003. Trans from The Episcopal Church of the Sudan 6/25/2008 Bp Peter James Lee. m 12/1/2006 Lindsey Vardy c 1. Asstg P Chr Epis Ch Charlottesville VA 2008-2009. Co-Auth, "Contemporary Amer Funerals: Personalizing Rel Traditions," *Death and Rel in a Changing Wrld*, M.E. Sharpe, 2005; Auth, "Being Bound to God: Participation and Cov," *Radical Orthodoxy and the Reformed Tradition*, Baker Acad Press, 2005; Auth, "Rel ad Pharmakon," *Hedgehog Revs*, 2004; Auth, "Faith," *Rel and Amer Culture*, ABC-CLIO, 2003. justin@christchurchcville.org

HOLCOMB, Steve A (WNC) 1500 Maltby Rd, Marble NC 28905 B Brunswick GA 8/8/1949 s Henry E Holcomb & Amelia Ida Mae. BA Stetson U 1971; MA Wstrn Carolina U 1992. D 6/29/1983 Bp William Gillette Weinhauer P 7/14/2004 Bp Robert Hodges Johnson. m 9/10/1972 Linda Laine c 2. D Ch Of The Mssh Murphy NC 1983-2000. steveholcomb@email.com

HOLCOMBE, Matthew Paul (Pa) 763 S. Valley Forge Rd, Wayne PA 19087 **Asst R S Dav's Ch Wayne PA 2011-** B Tucson AZ 7/3/1981 s Scott T Holcombe & La Nora. BA Shpd U 2002; MDiv The GTS 2011. D 6/11/2011 Bp Charles Ellsworth Bennison Jr. m 8/31/2002 Alicia Brabitz c 2. mph123@gmail.com

HOLCOMBE, Scott T (CFla) 4146 Millstone Dr, Melbourne FL 32940 **P Ch Of S Dav's By The Sea Cocoa Bch FL 2010-** B Lakeland FL 2/13/1954 s Paul Thorne Holcombe & Marilyn. BA U of So Florida 1975; MDiv STUSo 1978. D 6/18/1978 Bp Emerson Paul Haynes P 6/16/1979 Bp Thomas Augustus Fraser Jr. m 3/16/1974 La Nora Hazelwood c 4. Chr Ch Short Hills NJ 2008-2010; R S Steph's Ch Lakeland FL 2001-2008; R Chr Ch Clarksburg WV 1993-2001; R All Souls' Epis Ch Miami Bch FL 1992-1993; R Chr Epis Ch Kennesaw GA 1985-1992; Asst S Phil's In The Hills Tucson AZ 1981-1985; Asst S Andr's Ch Greensboro NC 1978-1981. revsth@gmail.com

HOLDBROOKE, Charles Henry (LI) 835 Herkimer St, Brooklyn NY 11233 **Epis Hlth Serv Bethpage NY 2008-; Chapl S Jn's Epis Chap Brooklyn NY 2008-** B 6/9/1957 s John B Holdbrooke & Christina. L.Th St. Nich TS 1988; Mstr in Theol Stds SWTS 2002. Trans from Church of the Province of West Africa 11/25/2008 Bp Orris George Walker Jr. m 11/30/1991 Rachel M Thompson c 2. choldbrooke@hotmail.com

HOLDEN, Beth (Tex) 4709 Laurel St, Bellaire TX 77401 **Epis HS Bellaire TX 2008-** B Kansas City MO 12/25/1961 d Edward Hart Green & Susan Morley. BA Wesl 1984; MDiv VTS 1990. D 6/17/1990 P 3/4/1991 Bp Maurice Manuel Benitez. m 6/27/1992 Samuel O Holden c 2. Cn Chr Ch Cathd Houston TX 1995-2001; Asst R S Jn The Div Houston TX 1990-1995. bholden@ehshouston.org

HOLDER, Anthony Brian (SeFla) 2801 N University Dr, Pembroke Pines FL 33024 **R H Sacr Pembroke Pines FL 2011-** B Christ Church BB 1/26/1965 s Anthony Bernard Holder & Audrey. AA Barbados Cmnty Coll 1982; Univ of the W Indies/ Codrington TS 1993; BA (Hons)/MDiv Equiv Univ of the W Indies/ Codrington TS 1993; D Min TESM 2009. Trans from Church in the Province Of The West Indies 3/1/2001 Bp Peter Hess Beckwith. m 8/31/1996 Judith De-Ann Blackman c 2. Pres Pro Tem, Dioc Coun Dio Springfield Springfield IL 2010; Pres, Stndg Com Dio Springfield Springfield IL 2009-2010; Pres, Stndg Com Dio Springfield Springfield IL 2005-2006; Dn, Darrow (Wstrn) Dnry Dio Springfield Springfield IL 2003-2010; Mem, Stndg Com Dio Springfield Springfield IL 2003-2010; Web Mgr Dio Springfield Springfield IL 2002-2010; Vic S Mich's Epis Ch O Fallon IL 2001-2010; Sprtl Dir, Happ Dio Springfield Springfield IL 2001-2005. tonyjudi@comcast.net

HOLDER, Arthur Glenn (Cal) 2400 Ridge Rd, Berkeley CA 94709 B Atlanta GA 9/6/1952 s Charles Glenn Holder & Mary Ruth. BA Duke 1973; MDiv GTS 1976; PhD Duke 1987. D 3/12/1977 P 12/17/1977 Bp William Gillette Weinhauer. m 10/21/1978 Sarah Noble Henry c 1. Prof CDSP Berkeley CA 1986-2007; R Ch Of The H Cross Valle Crucis NC 1978-1985; Asst S Jas Epis Ch Hendersonville NC 1977-1978. Transltr, "The Venerable Bede: On the Song of Songs and Selected Writings," Paulist Press, 2011; Ed, "Chr Sprtlty: The Classics," Routledge, 2009; Ed, "Blackwell Comp to Chr Sprtlty," Blackwell, 2005; Transltr, "Bede: Biblic Miscellany," Liverpool U Press, 1998; Transltr, "Bede: On The Tabernacle," Liverpool U Press, 1994. AAR 1989; Amer Soc Of Ch Hist 1981; Medieval Acad Of Amer 1981; No Amer Patristics Soc 1985; Soc For The Study Of Chr Sprtlty 1996. Assoc OHC 1978; Phi Beta Kappa 1973. aholder@gtu.edu

HOLDER, Charles Richard (Md) PO Box A, 4336 Main Street, Rohrersville MD 21779 **Vic S Lk's Ch Brownsville MD 1987-** B Hagerstown MD 8/25/1943 s Charles West Holder & Helen Lola Beatrice. BA Frostburg St U 1965; MEd Frostburg St U 1969; STUSo 1979. D 7/7/1978 Bp William Jackson Cox P 5/6/1979 Bp David Keller Leighton Sr. m 6/10/1967 Trudie Keller c 2. Vic S Lk's Ch Brownsville MD 1979-1985. Auth, "Stdt Oriented Classroom: Engl Guidebook Grade," *SOC Engl Guidebook Grade 10*, WCBOE, 1969. CBS 1978; SocMary 1978. Nancy S. Grasmick Execllence for Minority Achievement Awd Maryland St Dept of Educ 1999. c.holder@myactv.net

HOLDER, Michael Rawle (SVa) 926 Thomasson Lane, South Hill VA 23970 B 9/14/1944 s Eustace Rawle Holder & Edith Louise. ThD Codrington Coll 1975. Rec 9/1/1987 as Priest Bp C(laude) Charles Vache. So Mecklenburg-Brunswick Cure So Hill VA 1986-1997. OHC.

HOLDER, Timothy Scott (NJ) 212-B Bay Blvd, Seaside Heights NJ 08751 **Assoc Chr Ch Toms River Toms River NJ 2009-** B Elizabethton TN 1/30/1955 s John Bell Holder & Ruth Scott. BA U So 1977; MPA Middle Tennessee St U 1979; MDiv Harvard DS 1997. Trans 10/1/2003 Bp Henry Nutt Parsley Jr. R Historic Ch of Ascen Atlantic City NJ 2007-2009; R Trin Ch Of Morrisania Bronx NY 2002-2007; R Gr Ch Birmingham AL 1998-2002; Gr Epis Ch Dio Alabama Birmingham AL 1997. Auth, "I Ain't Got No Hope, Hip Hop Recon," *Ambassadors for God: Envisioning Recon Rites for the 21st Century, Liturg Stds Five*, Ch Pub, Inc., 2010; Ed and Contrib, "The Hip Hop PB, 2nd ed.: The Remix," *The Hip Hop PB, 2nd ed.: The Remix*, Ch Pub, Inc., 2009; Creator, Writer and Artist, "And the Word Was Hip Hop, a cd," *And the Word Was Hip Hop, a cd*, Ch Pub, Inc., 2007; Ed and Contrib, "The Hip Hop PB," *The Hip Hop PB*, Ch Pub, Inc., 2006. The Amer Soc of the Most Venerable Ord of The Hosp of St. Jn of Jerusalem 2000-2011. Mart Luther King, Jr., Awd Sthrn Chr Ldrshp Conf 2006; First Decade Awd Harvard DS 2005; Human Rts Awd Equality Alabama 2002; Fell, TS The U So, Sewanee 2002. timothyholder@gmx.com

H

HOLDER-JOFFRION, Kerry Elizabeth (Ala) 3009 Barcody Rd Se, Huntsville AL 35802 B Cleveland OH 3/1/1964 d Douglas Arlington Holder & Judith Leigh. BA Furman U 1986; MDiv PrTS 1990. D 11/14/1991 P 6/1/1992 Bp Charles Jones III. m 7/24/1999 Ronald Guy Sibold c 1. Assoc Ch Of The Nativ Epis Huntsville AL 1997-2006; R S Jas Ch Lewistown MT 1995-1997; Dio Montana Helena MT 1993-1995; Ch Of The Incarn Great Falls MT 1991-1992. Auth, "Rediscovering Lost Traditions: A Pstr Guide To The New"; Auth, "Supplemental Texts 89". S Aid. Pbf Dom Initiative Proj 1996. kerryholder@nativity-hsv.com

HOLDING, Suzann Van Sickle (SanD) 2728 6th Ave, San Diego CA 92103 **Cn to the Ordnry Dio San Diego San Diego CA 2009-** B Huntington WV 2/18/1955 d Albert Wilson VanSickle & Zeda Delta. BA DePauw U 1976; MA Amer Grad Sch of Intl Mgmt Glendal 1977; MDiv SWTS 1999. D 6/19/1999 P 12/18/1999 Bp William Dailey Persell. c 2. Stndg Com (Pres.2009) Dio Chicago Chicago IL 2006-2009; R Ch Of Our Sav Elmhurst IL 2003-2009; Assoc R Trin Epis Ch Wheaton IL 1999-2002. sholding@edsd.org

HOLDORPH II, Jedediah Dunning (Ore) 2203 Dollarhide Way, Ashland OR 97520 **R S Mk's Epis Par Medford OR 2005-** B Saginaw MI 5/24/1958 s John Albert Holdorph & Edith Marie. BA U of Arizona 1980; MDiv EDS 1988. D 6/2/1988 Bp Joseph Thomas Heistand P 1/6/1989 Bp William Davidson. m 7/19/1980 Barbara Jeanne Price c 2. R S Lawr Epis Ch Libertyville IL 1993-2005; R Chr Ch Lexington MO 1990-1993; Int S Mk's On The Mesa Epis Ch Albuquerque NM 1988-1990. Auth, "Plnng A Funeral Serv," Morehouse, 1998. jholdorph@jeffnet.org

HOLE, Jeremy G (Fla) 4141 Nw 18th Dr, Gainesville FL 32605 **Asstg P H Trin Ch Gainesville FL 1984-** B Detroit MI 10/14/1937 s Harrison Havilland Hole & Estelle Gallaudet. BA U of Florida 1959; STB EDS 1965. D 9/18/1965 P 4/1/1966 Bp George West Barrett. m 5/3/1986 Myra S Brown. Int S Mich's Ch Gainesville FL 1983-1984; Cur Chr Ch Pittsford NY 1965-1967. HOLE@HOLYTRINITYGNV.ORG

✠ HOLGUIN-KHOURY, Rt Rev Julio Cesar (DR) 7990 15th St E, Sarasota FL 34243 B San Francisco de Macoris DO 7/18/1948 s Julio Holguin & Consuelo. Universidad Autonoma De Santo Domingo Santo Domingo Do 1973; STL S Andrews TS Mex City Mx 1976. D 7/11/1976 P 7/1/1977 Bp Telesforo A Isaac Con 8/16/1991 for DR (Iglesia Episcopal Dominicana). m 4/17/1977 Milagros Hernandez. Vic Iglesia Epis San Andres Santo Domingo DO 1987-1991; Vic Iglesia Epis Jesus Nazareno San Francisco de Macoris Du DO 1979-1987; Serv (Vic, Iglesia Epis San Marcos, Haina) Dio The Dominican Republic (Iglesia Epis Dominicana) 100 Airport AvVenice FL 1976-1979; Iglesia Epis San Marcos Haitiana 1976-1979. iglepidom@codetel.net.do

HOLLAND, Albert Leslie (Del) 1420 S 2nd St, Philadelphia PA 19147 B Baltimore MD 9/26/1950 s Albert Atkinson Holland & Estelle. BS Nthrn Illinois U 1972; MDiv SWTS 1979; U of Texas 1995. D 6/9/1979 Bp Quintin Ebenezer Primo Jr P 12/1/1979 Bp James Winchester Montgomery. m 5/19/2011 James Boaldin c 2. R The Ch Of The Ascen Claymont DE 2006-2010; Ch Of Our Sav Silver Sprg MD 2004-2006; S Andr's Ch Glendale AZ 1999-2004; S Mk's Epis Ch Mesa AZ 1996-1998; H Sprt Epis Ch El Paso TX 1990-1995; Sprtl Advsr Dio The Rio Grande Albuquerque NM 1989-1991; Assoc R S Fran On The Hill El Paso TX 1986-1990; Strtgy Com Dio Chicago Chicago IL 1980-1986; S Greg's Epis Ch Deerfield IL 1979-1986. Phi Sigma Kappa. alh50@verizon.net

HOLLAND, Clayton Theodore (Dal) 517 W Hull St, Denison TX 75020 B Brooklyn MI 4/20/1930 s Claude Elwin Holland & Lillian Irene. BA Estrn Michigan U 1957; MDiv Epis TS In Kentucky 1962. D 6/9/1962 P 12/1/1962 Bp William R Moody. Bp Of ArmdF- Epis Ch Cntr New York NY 1980-1996; R S Thos Epis Ch Sturgis SD 1975-1980; R Gr Ch Cuero TX 1973-1975; P-in-c S Jas Epis Ch Hebbronville TX 1971-1973; P-in-c Trin Epis Ch Edna TX 1969-1971; Cur S Jos's Epis Ch Boynton Bch FL 1967-1969; Cur S Mk's Ch Cocoa FL 1966-1967; Vic Ch Of The H Fam McKinney TX 1963-1966; D S Andr's Ch Lexington KY 1962-1963.

HOLLAND, C Lynn (Va) P.O. Box 1626, Kilmarnock VA 22482 **S Mary's Fleeton Reedville VA 2010-** B Norfolk VA 12/2/1959 d Edwin T Holland & Enid M. BA Hood Coll 1981; JD U Rich 1984; MDiv VTS 2007. D 6/16/2007 Bp Peter James Lee P 12/16/2007 Bp Shannon Sherwood Johnston. Kingston Par Epis Ch Mathews VA 2007-2009. lynnholland@rivnet.net

HOLLAND, David Wesley (Dal) Po Box 292365, Lewisville TX 75029 **Cmsn On Archit Dio Dallas Dallas TX 2005-; Chair Mssn Dept Dio Dallas Dallas TX 1998-** B Denver CO 1/17/1946 s Charles Holland & Mary Esther. BS Missouri St U 1968; MDiv GTS 1971. D 5/25/1971 Bp Stephen F Bayne Jr P 11/28/1971 Bp Theodore H McCrea. c 1. Exec Coun Dio Dallas Dallas TX 1995-1998; R Ch Of The Annunc Lewisville TX 1990-2011; R S Chris's Ch Houston TX 1989-1990; Ch Of The H Comf Angleton TX 1982-1989; Vic S Phil's Epis Ch Sulphur Sprg TX 1979-1982; R S Jas' Epis Ch Fremont NE 1978-1979; Asst Trin Cathd Omaha NE 1973-1978; Cur S Chris's Ch And Sch Ft Worth TX 1971-1973. Tertiary Of The Soc Of S Fran. Hon Cn Trin Cathd Omaha NE 1978. dwholland.home@gmail.com

HOLLAND, Eleanor Lois (Md) 3204 Bayonne Ave, Baltimore MD 21214 **R S Mths' Epis Ch Baltimore MD 2004-** B Atlanta GA 12/28/1948 d Dolphus Bradford Holland & Musette. BS Georgia Sthrn U 1971; MDiv VTS 2001. D 6/9/2001 P 2/7/2002 Bp Jane Hart Holmes Dixon. S Jas' Epis Ch Baltimore MD 2001-2003. reveleanor@verizon.net

HOLLAND, Janet Marie (Cal) 12 Via Las Cruces, Orinda CA 94563 B Avalon CA 11/30/1940 d Robert D Chalmers & Zoe B. BA California St U 1975; Cert California St U 1976; MDiv ETSBH 1992. D 6/13/1992 Bp Chester Lovelle Talton P 1/9/1993 Bp Frederick Houk Borsch. m 7/1/1995 Lawrence Scott Hunter c 3. S Steph's Epis Ch Orinda CA 2006-2011; S Tim's Epis Ch Apple Vlly CA 2004; S Jn's Mssn La Verne CA 1998-2004; S Martha's Epis Ch W Covina CA 1997-1998; Int Gr Epis Ch Glendora CA 1995-1997; Asst S Paul's Epis Ch Tustin CA 1992-1995. mo.jan@comcast.net

HOLLAND, J(ohn) Mark (La) Po Box 126, Baton Rouge LA 70821 **R S Jas Epis Ch Baton Rouge LA 2003-; Cmsn Mnstry Dio Wstrn Louisiana Alexandria LA 2000-; Cmsn Mnstry Dio Wstrn Louisiana Alexandria LA 2000-; Dn Lake Chas Convoc Dio Wstrn Louisiana Alexandria LA 1999-; Dn Lake Chas Convoc Dio Wstrn Louisiana Alexandria LA 1999-; Dn Lake Chas Convoc Dio Wstrn Louisiana Alexandria LA 1999-** B Altus AFB OK 4/18/1958 s William Basil Holland & Donna Lynn. BS Louisiana Tech U 1981; MDiv SWTS 1994. D 6/18/1994 P 12/17/1994 Bp Robert Jefferson Hargrove Jr. m 3/6/1982 Elizabeth Langhorst c 3. Sprtl Dir Happenning Dio Wstrn Louisiana Alexandria LA 1998-1999; Stndg Com Dio Wstrn Louisiana Alexandria LA 1996-1998; Ch Hist Instr Bp Sch For Mnstry Dio Wstrn Louisiana Alexandria LA 1995-2001; Epis Ch Of The Gd Shpd Lake Chas LA 1994-2003. Auth, "A Defense For The Theol Of Dioc Giving," *Alive*, Dio Wstrn Louisiana, 2001. mholland@stjamesbr.org

HOLLAND, John Stewart (HB) No address on file. B Oakland CA 7/25/1934 s Francis Marion Holland & Alice Mckay. BS California Inst of Tech 1956; ThM Dallas TS 1961; STB GTS 1962. D 12/22/1963 Bp William G Wright. m 6/23/1962 Karen Andrea Sibley.

HOLLAND III, Jule Carr (Nwk) 7404 Halifax Rd, Youngsville NC 27596 B Raleigh NC 8/17/1949 s Jule Carr Holland & Winifred Lewis. BA U NC 1972; MDiv GTS 1976. D 6/19/1976 P 5/29/1977 Bp William Gillette Weinhauer. m Diane Tremain c 1. Trst Apos Hse Newark NJ 2006-2011; Stndg Com Dio Newark Newark NJ 2006-2011; Chair, COM Dio Newark Newark NJ 2004-2006; Hse of the Gd Shpd, Trst, VP Dio Newark Newark NJ 2000-2011; Cmsn on Ministery Dio Newark Newark NJ 1997-2006; R Gr Ch Newark NJ 1995-2011; Isaiah Team, Cong. Dev. Dio Newark Newark NJ 1991-1998; Dep to Prov Syn Dio Newark Newark NJ 1988-1996; R S Mk's Ch Mendham NJ 1986-1995; Stwdshp Cmsn, Consult Dio Newark Newark NJ 1983-1994; R S Clem's Ch Hawthorne NJ 1981-1986; Int S Ptr's Epis Ch Livingston NJ 1980-1981; Cur Gr Ch Newark NJ 1977-1980; Asst Gr Ch Asheville NC 1976-1977. Assoc, Cmnty of St. Jn Bapt 1985; Soc of Cath Priests 2009. jcarrholland@aol.com

HOLLAND, Katharine Grace (Ore) 13265 Nw Northrup St, Portland OR 97229 B Pasadena CA 5/20/1950 d Kenneth Alan Schmitt & Catherine. U of Redlands; BA California St U 1976. D 10/1/1994 Bp Robert Louis Ladehoff. m 11/26/1977 Darryl Gene Holland.

HOLLAND, Meghan Carey (Ky) 820 Broadway St, Paducah KY 42001 **Asst Gr Ch Paducah KY 2011-** B York PA 7/31/1984 d James Ryan & Barbara. BS Murray St U 2007; MDiv VTS 2011. D 12/18/2010 P 6/17/2011 Bp Terry Allen White. m 7/26/2008 Tyler Holland. megc.holland@gmail.com

HOLLAND JR, Melford Elias (Pa) 121 Penns Grant Dr, Morrisville PA 19067 B Montgomery WV 12/6/1942 s Melford Elias Holland & Hilda Hazel. BA Wake Forest U 1965; MDiv GTS 1968; U CO 1971; ThM PrTS 1985; DMin PrTS 1993. D 6/11/1968 P 12/18/1968 Bp Wilburn Camrock Campbell. m 9/2/1967 Martha Ann Henkle c 3. Epis Ch Cntr New York NY 1998-2009; Coordntr, Off of Min. Dev. Epis Ch Cntr New York NY 1998-2009; Dio Pennsylvania Philadelphia PA 1984-1990; R S Jas Ch Collegeville PA 1982-1993; Coordntr of Prog Dio Wstrn No Carolina Asheville NC 1976-1981; Assoc Trin Epis Ch Asheville NC 1974-1976; Asst S Thos Epis Ch Denver CO 1971-1973; Vic S Barn Bridgeport WV 1968-1970. budholland126@gmail.com

HOLLAND-SHUEY, Basye (Ala) 3740 Meridian St N, Huntsville AL 35811 **H Cross-St Chris's Huntsville AL 2011-** B Lexington KY 2/23/1947 d James Grover Holland & Dorothy Myers. Doctor of Mnstry The TS at The U So 2010; MDiv Vanderbelt DS 2011. D 5/16/2011 Bp Henry Nutt Parsley Jr. m 5/14/1988 Ralph Allen Shuey. basye@knology.net

HOLLAR, Sarah Darnell (NC) 19107 Southport Drive, Cornelius NC 28031 **GC Dep Dio No Carolina Raleigh NC 2011-; Stndg Com Dio No Carolina Raleigh NC 2011-; R S Mk's Epis Ch Huntersville NC 2005-** B Oklahoma City OK 5/11/1955 BA U NC 1983; MDiv VTS 2003. D 6/14/2003 P 1/18/2004 Bp Michael Bruce Curry. m 4/4/2011 Grover Macon c 2. Dioc Coun Dio No Carolina Raleigh NC 2006-2009; Asst S Lk's Ch Salisbury NC 2003-2005. sarah.hollar@stmarksnc.org

HOLLAWAY, Megan Lane (Va) Grace Episcopal Church, 301 S Main St, Kilmarnock VA 22482 **The Epis Sch of Los Angeles Los Angeles CA 2011-** B Fitchburg MA 12/28/1977 d James Hollaway & Peggy Ann. BSW Virginia Commonwealth U Richmond VA 1999; MS Virginia Commonwealth U Richmond VA 2000; MDiv Ya Berk 2007. D 6/16/2007 Bp Peter James Lee P 12/16/2007 Bp Shannon Sherwood Johnston. Gr Ch Kilmarnock VA 2007-2010.

HOLLEMAN, Virginia Falconer (Dal) 5518 Merrimac Ave, Dallas TX 75206 B Montgomery AL 2/11/1943 d Bradley Foote Prann & Mary Virginina. BA U of Connecticut 1964; MDiv SMU 2001. D 6/9/2001 Bp D(avid) Bruce Mac Pherson P 5/13/2002 Bp James Monte Stanton. m 2/15/2003 William Thomas Holleman c 2. Asst to R The Epis Ch Of The Trsfg Dallas TX 2005-2011; Cur/P Assoc S Ptr's Ch McKinney TX 2001-2005. vfholleman@sbcglobal.net

HOLLENBECK, Jon Nelson (Dal) 2215 Tracey Ann Ln, Killeen TX 76543 **Off Of Bsh For ArmdF New York NY 1996-** B Watertown NY 9/29/1951 s Howard Robert Hollenbeck & Annabelle Wright. BD U of Texas 1975; MDiv Epis TS of The SW 1989. D 6/17/1989 Bp Donis Dean Patterson P 5/1/1990 Bp Scott Field Bailey. m 7/28/1973 Freda Dee Christy c 2. S Lk's Epis Ch Dallas TX 1994-1995; Chr Epis Ch Plano TX 1993-1994; Cur S Chris's Ch Dallas TX 1989-1991.

HOLLENBECK, Scott Warren (Colo) PO Box 1226, Meeker CO 81641 **R S Jas' Epis Ch Meeker CO 2007-** B Chilton WI 5/19/1957 s Warren Hollenbeck & Patricia. BA Lakeland Coll 1979; MDiv Epis TS of The SW 2005. D 6/10/2006 P 12/18/2006 Bp Robert John O'Neill. m 8/9/1980 Dawn Zacher c 1. frscott@nctelecom.net

✠ HOLLERITH IV, Rt Rev Herman (SVa) 600 Talbot Road, Norfolk VA 23505 **Bp of Sthrn Virginia Dio Sthrn Virginia Norfolk VA 2008-** B Baltimore MD 7/13/1955 s Herman Hollerith & Agnes Boxley. BS Denison U 1978; MDiv Ya Berk 1981. D 6/11/1983 Bp Robert Bruce Hall P 12/10/1983 Bp A(rthur) Heath Light Con 2/13/2009 for SVa. m 10/27/1984 Elizabeth S Hollerith c 3. R Bruton Par Williamsburg VA 1999-2008; Prince Geo Winyah Epis Preschool Georgetown SC 1990-1999; Prince Geo Winyah Epis Ch Georgetown SC 1990-1999; Assoc R S Jn's Ch Lynchburg VA 1985-1990; P-in-c Chr Epis Ch Roanoke VA 1983-1985. AAPC; ACPE.

HOLLERITH, Melissa Kaye Zuber (Va) 5503 Toddsbury Rd, Richmond VA 23226 **S Chris's Sch Richmond VA 2003-** B Baton Rouge LA 2/10/1962 d B Rivers Penn & Nancy. BA Tul 1984; Cert Ya Berk 1990; MDiv Ya 1990. D 12/12/1991 P 10/14/1992 Bp Peter James Lee. m 12/31/1988 Randolph Marshall Hollerith c 1. HOLLERITHM@STCVA.ORG

HOLLERITH, Randolph Marshall (Va) 1205 W Franklin St, Richmond VA 23220 **R S Jas' Ch Richmond VA 2000-** B Washington DC 10/10/1963 s Herman Hollerith & Agnes Boxley. BA Denison U 1986; MDiv Ya Berk 1990. D 6/2/1990 P 4/3/1991 Bp Peter James Lee. m 12/31/1988 Melissa Kaye Zuber c 2. R S Ptr's Epis Ch Savannah GA 1995-2000; Asst R S Steph's Ch Richmond VA 1990-1995. Auth, "A Connection Between Rudolf Bultmann & Leo Tolstoy," *Ch Divinty 89-90*, 1990. rhollerith@doers.org

HOLLETT, Robert Titus (LI) 220 Valley Rd, Chestertown MD 21620 B Rockville Center NY 2/15/1923 s Norman Hollett & Elizabeth. BA Hofstra U 1949; MDiv PDS 1954. D 4/24/1954 P 11/13/1954 Bp James P De Wolfe. m 8/29/1953 Patricia Gray c 2. Int Shrewsbury Par Ch Kennedyville MD 1994-1995; P-in-c Chr Ch Worton MD 1992-1999; Int S Steph's Ch Earleville MD 1990-1992; Int Ch Of The H Trin Oxford MD 1989-1990; Int Aug Par Chesapeake City MD 1988-1989; Secy, Cathd Chapt Dio Long Island Garden City

NY 1979-1987; Mem, Cathd Chapt Dio Long Island Garden City NY 1974-1987; Mem, Liturg Cmsn Dio Long Island Garden City NY 1973-1979; R Chr Ch Oyster Bay NY 1968-1987; Mem, Exec Coun Dio Easton Easton MD 1964-1968; R Emm Epis Ch Chestertown MD 1963-1968; Assoc Imm Ch Highlands Wilmington DE 1961-1963. Hon Cn Cathd of the Incarn Garden City NY 1985. pat28@atlanticbb.net

HOLLEY, James Paul (Okla) 7609 Nw Stonegate Dr, Lawton OK 73505 B Washington DC 8/4/1931 s James Easton Holley & Constance Grace. MDiv Trin TS; BS VMI 1953; MS Shippensburg St Coll 1975. D 6/19/1988 Bp Gerald Nicholas McAllister. m 7/3/1960 Sonja Myrie White c 3. Hospice Chapl S Andr's Epis Ch Lawton OK 1988-1995. NAAD 1988; Oblate Ord Of S Ben 1998; Oklahoma Assn For Helathcare Ethics 1998. swhjph@aol.com

HOLLEY, Richard Hedge (SVa) 202 Devils Den Road, Hampton VA 23669 B Fort Sill OK 10/5/1936 s James Easton Holley & Constance Grace. BBA U of Oklahoma 1961; MDiv VTS 1964. D 6/20/1964 Bp Chilton Powell P 12/21/1964 Bp Frederick Warren Putnam. m 11/26/1959 Lois Hammond c 2. Asst S Andr's Epis Ch Newport News VA 1999; Emm Epis Ch Portsmouth VA 1995; Off Of Bsh For ArmdF New York NY 1968-1994; Cur S Jn's Ch Norman OK 1964-1968. holley.rh36@verizon.net

HOLLIDAY, Charles Thomas (Va) 8904 Karver Ln, Annandale VA 22003 B Rocky Mount NC 5/17/1944 s Wilton Otis Holliday & Jessie Laird. BS Jas Madison U 1971; Med Jas Madison U 1976; MDiv VTS 1979. D 6/23/1979 P 5/1/1980 Bp Robert Bruce Hall. m 1/23/1988 Susan Ellyn Goff. S Jas' Epis Ch Warrenton VA 2005-2007; Cunningham Chap Par Millwood VA 2002-2005; S Ptr's Epis Ch Purcellville VA 2000-2002; Int R S Ptr's Epis Ch Purcellville VA 1999; S Anne's Epis Ch Reston VA 1998-1999; Old Donation Ch Virginia Bch VA 1997-1998; S Paul's Ch Bailey's Crossroads Falls Ch VA 1995-1996; Chr Epis Ch Saluda VA 1994-1995; S Thos' Ch Richmond VA 1991; Int S Dav's Epis Ch Richmond VA 1990; Cur S Aid's Ch Alexandria VA 1978-1986. cthseg@aol.com

HOLLIDAY, Frances M (Chi) 5057 W. Devon Ave, Chicago IL 60646 **All SS Epis Ch Chicago IL 2009-; Congregations Cmsn Dio Chicago Chicago IL 2009-** B Chicago IL 4/21/1960 d Robert Patterson Holliday & Stella Rose. BA U IL 1989; M.Div SWTS 2003. D 6/21/2003 P 12/20/2003 Bp William Dailey Persell. m 8/6/2003 Eileen M Flynn. R S Richard's Ch Chicago IL 2005-2009; Cur Chr Ch Waukegan IL 2003-2005. ffholl@aol.com

HOLLIGER, John Charles (O) 941 Fenwick Cir, Wooster OH 44691 B Sandusky OH 12/20/1946 s Herbert Holliger & Ardis. EDS; BA Ob; MDiv Yale DS. D 6/8/1974 Bp Joseph Warren Hutchens P 5/1/1975 Bp Morgan Porteus. m 4/27/1976 Carol Hastings c 2. R S Paul's Ch Marion OH 1997-2004; S Jas Epis Ch Wooster OH 1990-1997; Vic S Geo's Ch Bolton CT 1977-1990; Cur Chr Ch Stratford CT 1974-1977. johnholliger@verizon.net

HOLLINGER, Claudia (EMich) 106 E Elizabeth St, Fenton MI 48430 **D S Paul's Epis Ch Flint MI 2010-** B Jackson MS 12/4/1948 d Claude Otis Monroe & Melvin. D 9/13/2008 Bp S(teven) Todd Ousley. c 1. chollinger2003@yahoo.com

✠ **HOLLINGSWORTH JR, Rt Rev Mark** (O) 2230 Euclid Ave, Cleveland OH 44115 **Bp of Ohio Dio Ohio Cleveland OH 2004-** B Boston MA 4/9/1954 s Mark Hollingsworth & Caroline Jeanes. BA Trin Hartford CT 1976; MDiv CDSP 1981. D 6/27/1981 P 5/27/1982 Bp William Edwin Swing Con 4/17/2004 for O. m 7/30/1988 Susan M Hunt c 4. Archd Dio Massachusetts Boston MA 1994-2004; R S Anne's In The Fields Epis Ch Lincoln MA 1986-1994; Assoc R S Fran In The Fields Harrods Creek KY 1983-1986; Chapl Cathd Sch For Boys San Francisco CA 1981-1983. mh@dohio.org

HOLLINGSWORTH-GRAVES, Judy Lynn (SD) 1508 S Rock Creek Dr # 168, Sioux Falls SD 57103 **D Calv Cathd Sioux Falls SD 2006-** B Tracy MN 7/31/1949 d Leonard R Hollingsworth & Helen. D 12/21/2006 Bp Creighton Leland Robertson. c 4. jlcardinal12@yahoo.com

HOLLIS, Anthony Wolcott Linsley (Md) 712 Murdock Rd, Baltimore MD 21212 **Assoc The Ch Of The Nativ Cedarcroft Baltimore MD 2007-; Assoc Ch Of The H Nativ Baltimore MD 1967-** B Bermuda 4/7/1940 s Francis Carlyle Hollis & Elisabeth Livingston. BA McGill U 1961; MDiv GTS 1964; BA CPE 1970; MA LIU 1976. D 6/22/1964 P 5/17/1965 Bp Harry Lee Doll. m 6/16/1965 Linda Lee Benson c 3. St. Ptr's Angl Ch 0 1997-2001; Sherwood Epis Ch Cockeysville MD 1980-1992; Off Of Bsh For ArmdF New York NY 1967-1979; Vic S Ptr's Ch Lonaconing MD 1966-1967. saintpeter@comcast.net

HOLLIS, Joanna Pauline (ECR) 1500 State St, Santa Barbara CA 93101 **Assoc R Trin Epis Ch Santa Barbara CA 2009-** B Atlantic City NJ 2/16/1975 d Arnold Hollis & Janice Danielle. BA Connecticut Coll 1997; MATFL Monterey Inst of Intl Stds 2001; MDiv CDSP 2009. D 6/6/2009 P 12/10/2009 Bp Mary Gray-Reeves. joanna_p_hollis@yahoo.com

HOLLOWAY, Jonathan Aldrich (Spok) 2502 S Amberwood Ln, Spokane WA 99223 **D Cathd Of S Jn The Evang Spokane WA 1976-** B Seattle WA 2/24/1930 s Jackson Kenneth Holloway & Martha Aldrich. Stan 1949; BA Ob 1952; MD U of Washington 1956. D 10/17/1976 Bp John Raymond Wyatt. c 3. pelicanjon@worldnet.att.net

HOLLOWELL II, J Rhoads (Colo) 11675 Flatiron Dr, Lafayette CO 80026 **GC Coordntr Epis Ch Cntr New York NY 2006-** B Charleston SC 5/28/1961 s Samuel Guilds Hollowell & Alma Joyce. BS Pr 1983. D 11/7/1998 Bp William Jerry Winterrowd. m 7/7/1984 Kim Susan Mavor. D S Mary Magd Ch Boulder CO 1998-2011. rhoads@alumni.princeton.edu

HOLLY, Francis Eugene (Nev) 2481 Anderson Lake Rd # 417, Chimacum WA 98325 B Farmington NM 5/8/1935 s Charles Fredrick Holly & Jessie Elizabeth. BS New Mex St U. 1957; MS Van 1960; PhD U CA 1970. D 4/1/2000 Bp John Stuart Thornton P 9/30/2000 Bp George Nelson Hunt III. m 5/11/1974 Lois Elaine Jaynes c 4. Supply St Steph's Epis Ch Oak Harbor WA 2008-2011; P Gr In The Desert Epis Ch Las Vegas NV 2002-2006. *99 papers, abstracts, etc.*. feholly@olypen.com

HOLLY, William David (Okla) 2011 S Aster Pl, Broken Arrow OK 74012 **S Simeons Epis Hm Tulsa OK 2005-; P S Aid's Epis Ch Tulsa OK 2002-** B Houston TX 12/29/1955 s Earl Amos Holly & Nancy Dee. B.A. Oklahoma St U 1980; M.Div. Epis TS of the SW 1983. D 6/25/1983 P 5/19/1984 Bp Gerald Nicholas McAllister. m 1/24/1997 Marlo Louise Stewart. Vic S Pat's Epis Ch Broken Arrow OK 1995-1996; Dio Oklahoma Oklahoma City OK 1991-1996; Vic, St. Columba Mssn, Tulsa, OK Dio Oklahoma Oklahoma City OK 1991-1995; Cur S Dunst's Ch Tulsa OK 1983-1990. wdholly@cox.net

HOLLYWOOD, Trula Louise (Be) 701 S Main St, Athens PA 18810 B Coudersport PA 3/5/1959 s Samuel Irving Duell & Kathryn. D 8/15/2005 P 8/15/2006 Bp Paul Victor Marshall. c 6. trula@verizon.net

H

HOLM, Marjorie H (NC) 635 Hamilton St., Roanoke Rapids NC 27870 **All SS Ch Roanoke Rapids NC 2007-** B Rochester MN 12/21/1954 d William McClure Hardy & M Gwenivere. D 6/1/1996 Bp Frank Harris Vest Jr P 1/29/2004 Bp Carol Joy Gallagher. m 12/19/1976 Richard P Holm. *Report from Virginia*, St Update Nwsltr of Prison Fllshp Mnstrs, 2003; *Plcy and Procedures Manual*, Chapl Serv of the Ch of Virginia, 1998. VA Coll of Chapl. marjorie.holm@gmail.com

HOLMAN, Emily Clark (NJ) 96 Fairacres Dr, Toms River NJ 08753 **Com on the Diac Dio New Jersey Trenton NJ 2008-; Comp Dio Com Dio New Jersey Trenton NJ 2007-; D Chr Ch Toms River Toms River NJ 2000-** B Deposit NY 3/4/1944 d Yerby Rozelle Holman & Emily Brown. BA Ge 1966; MLS U NC 1971; Cert NJ D Formation Prog 2000. D 10/21/2000 Bp David B(ruce) Joslin. NAAD 2000. deaconemily2000@comcast.net

HOLMAN, John(Jack) Earl (Tex) 2400 Spring Raindrive, #1018, Spring TX 77379 B Joplin MO 8/2/1923 s Jack Earl Holman & Stella Mae. BA Subiaco 1949; MA U of San Francisco 1965. Rec from Roman Catholic 8/1/1971 as Priest Bp Philip Frederick McNairy. m 11/27/1954 June Elaine Jensen c 3. Assoc Ch Of The Gd Shpd Tomball TX 2007-2009; R Chr Ch Albert Lea MN 1972-1975; Asst Trin Ch Excelsior MN 1971-1972. Auth, "Hist Of The Old Cath Ch In Amer". jackholman@juno.com

HOLMAN, J(oseph) Lawrence (Be) RR #1, Box 125A, Towanda PA 18848 **D Chr Ch Towanda PA 2005-; D Dio Bethlehem Bethlehem PA 1989-** B Moberly MO 12/26/1931 s Lawrence Holman & Amy Ogle. BS U of Missouri 1953; MS U IL 1954. D 5/20/1989 Bp James Michael Mark Dyer. m 6/22/1957 Sharon Davis c 2. D Ch Of The Redeem Sayre PA 1989-2005. NAAD 1989. Ord of S Steph NAAD 1995. lholman@epix.net

HOLMAN, Kathryn Daneke (At) 1883 Clinton Dr, Marietta GA 30062 B Bartlesville OK 5/23/1953 BA U GA 1975. D 8/6/2006 Bp J(ohn) Neil Alexander. m 7/12/1975 William Holman c 2. kdh53@comcast.net

HOLMBERG, Sandra A (Minn) 14266 E Fox Lake Rd, Detroit Lakes MN 56501 **Cn Mssnr Dio Minnesota Minneapolis MN 2000-** B Beach ND 7/6/1953 d Wilbur Franzen & Malah. BA Concordia Coll 1974; MDiv Van 1979; MS Minnesota St U Mankato 1990; DMin STUSo 1998. D 2/25/1980 P 8/17/1980 Bp Robert Marshall Anderson. m 6/26/1976 G Bruce Holmberg. Asst to Bp of No Dakota Dio No Dakota Fargo ND 1990-2000; R S Steph's Ch Fargo ND 1985-2000; R S Jn's Ch Moorhead MN 1985-1990; Asst Dio No Dakota Fargo ND 1985-1989; Epis Chapl at Mankato St U Dio Minnesota Minneapolis MN 1980-1983. SAHOLMBERG@AOL.COM

HOLMES, Anna Rilla (USC) 205 Meadowlark Ln, Fountain Inn SC 29644 B Birmingham AL 11/23/1963 d Harold Holmes & Alice. Auburn U 1986; BA Iowa St U 1988; CDSP 1996; MDiv Ya Berk 1998. D 6/5/1999 Bp William Edwin Swing P 12/4/1999 Bp Catherine Scimeca Roskam. m 6/28/1986 Akil Abbas Rangwalla. H Cross Epis Ch Simpsonville SC 2008; P-in-c Trin Ch Abbeville SC 2002-2008; Cur S Mk's Ch Mystic CT 1999-2002. rillaakil@yahoo.com

HOLMES, Carol Bahlke (SC) 3157 Martha Custis Dr, Alexandria VA 22302 B Ridgewood NJ 4/14/1940 d Charles Fiske Bahlke & Elizabeth Virginia. BA Hood Coll 1962; MS Oklahoma St U 1981; MDiv VTS 1987. D 6/6/1987 P 4/1/1988 Bp C(laude) Charles Vache. c 3. Int S Jn's Epis Ch Tappahannock VA 1989-1990; Asst to R S Mich's Epis Ch Arlington VA 1987-1988.

HOLMES, Douglas (USC) PO Box 446, Camden SC 29020 B Los Angeles CA 8/23/1953 s Harry Lloyd Holmes & Alice Yvonne. BS USC 1979; MDiv GTS 1985. D 6/15/1985 P 12/20/1985 Bp Robert C Rusack. m 7/30/1985 Fran R Dobranski c 2. R Gr Epis Ch And Kindergarten Camden SC 2005-2011; Int S

Lk's Ch Salisbury NC 2004-2005; Assoc R S Marg's Epis Ch Waxhaw NC 2002-2004; R S Jn's Ch Cornwall NY 1993-2002; Assoc All SS-By-The-Sea Par Santa Barbara CA 1991-1993; Ch Of The Epiph Oak Pk CA 1985-1991. Auth, *Video Let My People In: Realizing Dream of Inclusive Wrshp*. douglholmes@eathlink.net

HOLMES, Forrest Milton (Ida) 1100 Burnett Dr Unit 416, Nampa ID 83651 B Wapato WA 4/22/1932 s Forrest F Holmes & Cordelia Willene. D 12/13/1968 P 12/1/1969 Bp Norman L Foote. m 3/21/1954 Oudean Holmes. Int S Dav's Epis Ch Caldwell ID 1997-1998; R Gr Epis Ch Nampa ID 1988-1997; Vic S Thos Of Cbury Mammoth Lakes CA 1986-1988; Assoc Trin Epis Ch Pocatello ID 1974-1986; P-in-c S Jn's Epis Ch Amer Falls ID 1969-1974. deanmilt@aol.com

HOLMES, Fran R (NY) 944 Thistlegate Rd, Oak Park CA 91377 B Elmira NY 8/17/1953 d Joseph Dobranski & Veronica F. BA Barnard Coll of Col 1976; GTS 1985; MDiv UTS 1985. D 3/26/1987 Bp Walter Decoster Dennis Jr P 5/1/1988 Bp Reginald Heber Gooden. m 7/30/1985 Douglas Holmes c 1. Asst All SS Par Beverly Hills CA 1987-1988.

HOLMES, George Blake (NC) 2305 River Run Rd, Browns Summit NC 27214 B Norfolk VA 7/5/1918 s George Frederick Holmes & Rosa Warrington. BA W&M 1943; LTh SWTS 1948; Med VPI 1956. D 3/15/1948 Bp William A Brown P 3/15/1949 Bp George P Gunn. m 1/27/1950 Rachael Brugh. H Trin Epis Ch Greensboro NC 1994-2000; Asst R (Ret) S Fran Ch Greensboro NC 1990-1991; All Souls Ch Wadesboro NC 1982-1989; Calv Ch Wadesboro NC 1982-1989; P Dio No Carolina Raleigh NC 1973-1982; R S Paul's Epis Ch Edenton NC 1956-1973; Assoc S Jn's Ch Roanoke VA 1954-1956; R All SS Epis Ch Norton VA 1950-1954. gbhrbh972@aol.com

HOLMES, James Colomb (WA) 5203 Downing Rd, Baltimore MD 21212 B Baton Rouge,LA 8/13/1946 s William Walter Holmes & Halcyon Rhoades. BA Van 1968; BD EDS 1971; MBA GW 1983. D 6/21/1971 P 2/10/1972 Bp Iveson Batchelor Noland. m 8/15/2011 Timothy Sabin. S Thos' Par Washington DC 1992-2003; Dio Washington Washington DC 1979-1999; Assoc S Jn's Ch Lafayette Sq Washington DC 1978-1992; Asst The Ch Of The Adv Boston MA 1973-1976; Cur S Mk's Ch Foxborough MA 1971-1973. Associated Parishes 1992. tim.jim@verizon.net

HOLMES, Jane Victoria Frances (NC) 2540 Bricker Drive, Charlotte NC 28273 **D S Mk's Epis Ch Huntersville NC 2007-; Trin Jubilee Cntr Lewiston ME 2004-** B Bedfont England 3/21/1941 d Ivan Beresford Holmes & Honor. U of Connecticut; AA Broward Cmnty Coll 1990; STUSo 2003. D 6/5/2004 Bp Chilton Abbie Richardson Knudsen. m 8/10/2002 Hartley La Duke c 2. cadbury@bellsouth.net

HOLMES, Joyce (CFla) Post Office Box 368, Avon Park FL 33826 B Detroit MI 2/24/1949 d John Douglas Woolever & Patricia Claire. BA Florida St U 1971; Florida St U 1972; MDiv STUSo 1991. D 6/8/1991 Bp Joseph Thomas Heistand P 1/18/1992 Bp William Edward Smalley. c 2. Vic The Epis Ch Of The Redeem Avon Pk FL 2001-2010; R S Matt's Epis Ch Newton KS 1994-2001; Dioc Coun Dio Kansas Topeka KS 1993-1997; Asst S Steph's Ch Wichita KS 1991-1994. Garnet Key Hon Ldrship-FSU FSU 1971; Pres, Univ. Rel. Coun FSU FSU Rel Comm. 1971; Pres Cbury Club-FSU FSU Epis Chap 1970. joycewholmes@aol.com

HOLMES, Phillip Wilson (WNY) 418 Virginia St, Buffalo NY 14201 **Supply P Dio Wstrn New York Tonawanda NY 1969-** B Jamestown NY 4/28/1937 s Louis Howard Holmes & Sara Gladys. BA Hob 1961; STB GTS 1964. D 6/20/1964 Bp Lauriston L Scaife P 1/30/1965 Bp Dudley B McNeil. Cur Gr Ch Lockport NY 1964-1969. phillipwholmes@yahoo.com

HOLMES, Rebecca Elizabeth (NC) 237 N Canterbury Rd, Charlotte NC 28211 B Des Moines IA 6/13/1941 d William Goodwyn Holmes & Anne Price. BA U of San Francisco 1978; MDiv CDSP 1983. D 12/10/1983 Bp William Edwin Swing P 12/9/1984 Bp Charles Shannon Mallory. Dioc Com on Aging Dio No Carolina Raleigh NC 1994-1996; Dir, Pstr Care for Ret Cmnty Dio No Carolina Raleigh NC 1991-2004; Dio No Carolina Raleigh NC 1991; Assoc S Phil's In The Hills Tucson AZ 1986-1991; Yth Min S Andr's Ch Saratoga CA 1983-1986. bholm1313@aol.com

HOLMES, Stanley Warren (WVa) Po Box 79, Hansford WV 25103 **The New River Epis Mnstry Hansford WV 2007-; Pstr Calv Ch Montgomery WV 1998-** B Montgomery WV 4/7/1952 s Jack Stewart Holmes & Mildred Anne. P 6/1/1998 Bp John H(enry) Smith. m 1/10/1970 Joan Carroll. stanholmes@charter.net

HOLMES, William Henry (SC) 739 Levee Dr, Moncks Corner SC 29461 B Charleston SC 7/28/1946 s Charles Holmes & Virginia. D 9/14/2002 Bp Edward Lloyd Salmon Jr. m 2/5/1982 Nancy Holmes c 3.

HOLMGREN, Stephen Carl (WMich) 2200 Thornapple River Dr SE, MI Grand Rapids 49546 **R Gr Ch Grand Rapids MI 2007-; Cn Theol Dio Louisiana Baton Rouge LA 2000-** B Minneapolis MN 9/12/1956 s Carl August Holmgren & Dorothy May. BA Pacific Luth U 1980; BA Oxf 1982; MDiv Nash 1983; MA Oxf 1988; PhD Oxf 1995. D 5/21/1983 Bp William L Stevens P 4/1/1984 Bp Alex Dockery Dickson. m 6/21/1980 Martha Ellen Betzel c 3. Gr Ch Of W Feliciana S Francisville LA 1998-1999; S Simon The Fisherman Epis Ch Port Washington WI 1997-2000; Assoc Prof Nash Nashotah WI 1992-2000; Asst S Mary's Cathd Memphis TN 1991-1992; R Gr Epis Ch Paris TN 1985-1988; Cur Calv Ch Memphis TN 1983-1985. Auth, "Ethics After Easter - A Volume In The New Ch'S Tchg Series," Cowley Press, 2000. Grad Fllshp ECF 1989; Cleaver & Liddon Scholarships Keble Coll Oxford Engl 1988; Dorothy Given Fell. stephenholmgren@att.net

HOLROYD, David D (Me) 3 Waterford Way Unit 207, Manchester NH 03102 **Assoc Chr Ch Exeter NH 2009-** B Fitchburg MA 7/14/1941 s Franklyn John Holroyd & Ruth. BA Trin Hartford CT 1963; MDiv CDSP 1967; DMin Andover Newton TS 1976. D 6/24/1967 Bp C Kilmer Myers P 6/24/1968 Bp Joseph Summerville Minnis. m 1/24/1970 Lucille V Benoit c 2. Int S Anne's In The Fields Epis Ch Lincoln MA 2008-2009; Int S Jas' Ch Greenfield MA 2006-2008; Int Trin Epis Ch Portland ME 2000-2001; Co-chair Bp Nomntns Com Dio Maine Portland ME 1996-1997; Dep GC Dio Maine Portland ME 1985-2000; GC Dep Dio Maine Portland ME 1985-2000; Stndg Com Pres Dio Maine Portland ME 1983-1990; Dioc Coun Dio Maine Portland ME 1976-1983; R S Geo's Epis Ch York Harbor ME 1973-1999; Assoc Chr Ch Gardiner ME 1968-1973. Outstanding Young Men Amer 1971. dholroyd0219@comcast.net

HOLSAPPLE, Kevin Gurney (CFla) 7208 W Milwe Lane, Crystal Rivet FL 34429 **R S Anne's Ch Crystal River FL 2005-** B Valley Stream NY 1/8/1956 s Donald Calvin Holsapple & Betty Jane. AS U of Maine 1977; BA U of Maine 1979; LTh Montreal TS 1989; MA Bangor TS 2001. Trans from Anglican Church of Canada 2/1/1998. m 3/14/1975 Bobbi J Sweet c 4. R S Jn's Ch Bangor ME 1997-2005. thomistic@embarqmail.com

HOLSTON III, George Wilson (Fla) PO Box 254082, Patrick Afb FL 32925 **Vic S Alb's Epis Ch Chiefland FL 1999-** B Chattanooga TN 12/20/1954 s George Wilson Holston & Ethel Mae. BA Florida Sthrn Coll 1976; MDiv Candler TS Emory U 1978; MS Columbus St U 1994. D 6/22/1980 P 1/11/1981 Bp William Hopkins Folwell. m 5/10/1991 Donna Lynn Mulbarger c 3. Dio Florida Jacksonville FL 1999-2006; Off Of Bsh For ArmdF New York NY 1987-1990; Dio Minnesota Minneapolis MN 1984-1985; P-in-c Trin Epis Ch Pk Rapids MN 1984-1985; S Julian's Epis Ch Douglasville GA 1983-1984; The Epis Ch Of The Gd Shpd Lake Wales FL 1980-1982. ACPE. george.holston@us.army.mil

HOLSTROM, Susan A. (Chi) 737 N Randall Rd, Aurora IL 60506 **R S Dav's Epis Ch Aurora IL 1999-** B Chicago IL 9/15/1947 d Edwin Ridgway Burgess & Fern. BS Nthrn Illinois U 1969; Cert EFM 1991; M. Div. SWTS 1995. D 5/7/1995 P 11/25/1995 Bp Roger John White. m 6/25/1994 Richard Lambert c 1. COM Dio Chicago Chicago IL 2000-2006; Bdgt Com Dio Chicago Chicago IL 1996-1998; Vic Ch Of The Gd Shpd Momence IL 1995-1999; Asst S Paul's Ch Kankakee IL 1995-1998. s_holstrom@yahoo.com

HOLT, Ann Case (NJ) 60 Main St, Clinton NJ 08809 **Assoc Calv Epis Ch Flemington NJ 2007-** B Rahway NJ 6/28/1934 d Clifford Philip Case & Ruth Miriam. BA Mid 1956; MDiv PrTS 1980. D 6/6/1981 Bp Albert Wiencke Van Duzer P 1/9/1982 Bp George Phelps Mellick Belshaw. m 6/29/1957 John C Holt c 3. Assoc S Lk's Ch Gladstone NJ 2002-2006; Stndg Com Dio New Jersey Trenton NJ 2000-2003; Dioc Coun Dio New Jersey Trenton NJ 1997-2000; Chapl Nj Womens Prison Dio New Jersey Trenton NJ 1994-1997; Stndg Com Pres Dio New Jersey Trenton NJ 1994-1996; Stndg Com Dio New Jersey Trenton NJ 1992-1996; Com Dio New Jersey Trenton NJ 1986-2000; R S Thos Ch Alexandria Pittstown NJ 1982-1999; Asst Ch Of The H Sprt Lebanon NJ 1981-1982. ESMA 1981. Winner Epis Best Sermon Competition 1994. ach34@comcast.net

HOLT, Charles Lindley (CFla) 2741 Teak Pl, Lake Mary FL 32746 **R S Ptr's Epis Ch Lake Mary FL 2001-** B Gainesville FL 5/24/1971 s Charles Tutewieler Holt & Sue Lindley. BS U Of Florida 1993; Reformed TS 1996; MDiv SWTS 1997. D 9/6/1997 Bp John Wadsworth Howe P 3/28/1998 Bp J(ames) Gary Gloster. m 8/12/1995 Brooke E Egerton c 3. Asst R S Jn's Epis Ch Charlotte NC 1997-2001. Auth, "A Journey Through The Bible," *Journey Through The Word*, 1999; Auth, "Psalms: A Pilgrim Journey," *Journey Through The Word*, 1996; Auth, "Early Hist: Joshua, Judges & Ruth," *Journey Through The Word*, 1996. revholt@stpeterslakemary.org

HOLT, David Lewis (Mass) 81a Cockle Bay Road, Cockle Bay, Auckland 2014 New Zealand (Aotearoa) B Auckland NZ 11/22/1938 s Alan Douglas Holt & Leila Mary. ScD MIT 1967; MDiv EDS 1978. D 6/10/1978 Bp Morris Fairchild Arnold P 6/1/1979 Bp John Bowen Coburn. m 7/4/1967 Judith Greene c 3. P S Steph's Epis Ch Boston MA 1982-1983; Dioc Coun Mem Dio Massachusetts Boston MA 1981-1984; R Gr Ch Fed E Boston MA 1978-1984. Post-Ord Schlrshp S Jn Coll, Auckland 1996. drsholt@hotmail.com

HOLT, Jane L (Bonnie) (Minn) 224 2nd St N, Cannon Falls MN 55009 **D The Epis Cathd Of Our Merc Sav Faribault MN 1999-** B Cannon Falls MN 3/10/1935 d Carl Algot Verntrom & Louise Adeline. D 10/17/1992 Bp Sanford Zangwill Kaye Hampton. m 2/7/1959 Lavern Holt c 3. D Adv Ch Farmington MN 1992-1999. mcholt@frontiernet.net

HOLT, John Marshall (Pa) 404 Cheswick Pl Apt 110, Bryn Mawr PA 19010 B Waco TX 11/7/1924 s Frank Holt & Frances. BA U of Texas 1947; STB GTS

1950; PhD Van 1958; ASOR 1964. D 6/29/1950 Bp Clinton Simon Quin P 1/19/1951 Bp John E Hines. Cur The Ch Of The Gd Shpd Bryn Mawr PA 1971-1972; Instr Rel Epis TS Of The SW Austin TX 1951-1958; P-in-c Chr Epis Ch Mexia Mexia TX 1951-1952; Min in charge All SS Epis Ch Crockett TX 1950-1951; Min in charge Trin Ch Jacksonville TX 1950-1951. Auth, *Patriarchs of Israel*, Van Press, 1964. Phi Beta Kappa 1947.

HOLT, Joseph (Cal) 2237 Fulton #103, San Francisco CA 94117 **Assoc Ch Of The Incarn San Francisco CA 2009-** B Seagraves TX 3/2/1948 s Joseph Holt Holt & Imogene. BA Texas Tech U 1973; MA Texas Tech U 1978; MA U Of Dallas Dallas 1986; MDiv CDSP 1992. D 6/20/1992 Bp Donis Dean Patterson P 6/6/1993 Bp William Edwin Swing. m 11/23/2009 Paula B Tobin. Ch Of The Epiph San Carlos CA 2004; Asst S Steph's Epis Ch Orinda CA 1998-2003; The Epis Ch Of S Mary The Vrgn San Francisco CA 1997; Int S Cyp's Ch San Francisco CA 1996-1997; D The Epis Ch Of S Jn The Evang San Francisco CA 1992-1996. Auth, "The Communal Aspect Of Scriptural Auth," *Ch Div*, 1990; Auth, "Story-Telling In The Weedy Garden," *Ch Div*, 1988. JOE-PAULA@COMCAST.NET

HOLT, Meredith Louise (Tex) 15415 N Eldridge Pkwy, Cypress TX 77429 **Assoc S Mary's Epis Ch Cypress TX 2010-** B Newport RI 3/28/1985 d Thomas Hugh Holt & Diane Ryan. BA Claremont McKenna Coll 2007; MDiv VTS 2010. D 6/19/2010 P 1/6/2011 Bp C(harles) Andrew Doyle. meredith.holt@gmail.com

HOLT, William Mayes (Tenn) 202 Kimberly Dr, Dickson TN 37055 B Nashville TN 9/12/1939 s J P Montgomery Holt & Grace Marie. Evangel U 1957; Van 1958; Tennessee Tech U 1959; LTh STUSo 1973. D 7/1/1973 Bp William Evan Sanders P 5/25/1974 Bp William F Gates Jr. m 12/31/1966 Patricia Harper c 3. CE Com Dio Tennessee Nashville TN 1990-2004; Dandridge Trust Chair Dio Tennessee Nashville TN 1990-1992; Vacancy Consult Dio Tennessee Nashville TN 1988-1991; Steph Mnstry Trnr/Supvsr Dio Tennessee Nashville TN 1986-1991; Bp and Coun Dio Tennessee Nashville TN 1986-1989; Vic S Jas Ch Dickson TN 1983-2008; Liturg Cmsn Dio Tennessee Nashville TN 1983-1986; Vic S Columba's Epis Ch Bristol TN 1976-1983; Asst Ch Of The Gd Shpd Lookout Mtn TN 1973-1976; Sem-In-Charge S Bern's Ch Gruetli Laager TN 1972-1973. quambonum@bellsouth.net

HOLT III, William Therrel (Az) 270 17th Street Unit 1101, Atlanta GA 30363 **Int R Chr Ch Clermont-Ferrand France Clermont-Ferrand FR 2011-** B San Francisco CA 10/5/1941 s William Therrel Holt & Ellen Heath. BA U of Tennessee 1965; MDiv STUSo 1968. D 6/14/1968 Bp William F Gates Jr P 4/25/1969 Bp John Vander Horst. m 6/2/1979 Diane P Pettigrew c 3. Int R S Alb's Epis Ch Tucson AZ 2009-2011; Int Vic S Mich's Ch Coolidge AZ 2008-2009; R Epis Ch Of S Fran-In-The-Vlly Green Vlly AZ 1993-2007; Assoc R The Epis Ch Of Beth-By-The-Sea Palm Bch FL 1981-1993; Assoc R H Trin Epis Ch W Palm Bch FL 1972-1974; P-in-c Ch Of The Redeem Shelbyville TN 1969-1972. Ord of St. Jn of Jerusalem 2000. wthiii@juno.com

HOLTKAMP, Patrick John (LI) 44-03 Douglaston Parkway, Douglaston NY 11363 **R Zion Ch Douglaston NY 1992-** B Saint Louis MO 12/17/1948 s Ferdinand Holtkamp & Lorene. BA S Fran Coll 1971; MDiv Crosier Hse of Stds 1975; MA Ford 1986. Rec from Roman Catholic 4/1/1988 as Priest Bp Walter Decoster Dennis Jr. m 6/26/1982 Elisabeth A Peters c 2. Asst Ch Of The H Trin New York NY 1988-1992. Auth, *Ch.* No Amer Acad of Liturg 1988. pjholt@aol.com

HOLTMAN, Kimberly Erica (Nwk) 655 W Briar Pl, Apt 1, Chicago IL 60657 B New Brunswick NJ 9/23/1966 d John Walter Haag & Diane. BA U of Virginia 1988; MA SUNY 1992; MDiv GTS 1998. D 6/6/1998 Bp David Charles Bowman P 12/12/1998 Bp Franklin Delton Turner. m 5/30/2004 Eric Holtman. R The Ch Of The Annunc Oradell NJ 2000-2003; Cur Trin-St Jn's Ch Hewlett NY 1999-2000; Cur S Dav's Ch Wayne PA 1998-1999. HP Mongomery Prize; H Land Travel Prize; J Wilson Sutton Prize; Psi Chi; SUNY Presidential Fell; Wm C Winslow Prize. keh2@holtmans.com

HOLTON, Stephen C (At) 84 Broadway, New Haven CT 06511 **Cur Chr Ch New Haven CT 2011-** B Dublin GA 7/8/1973 s Tommy Jackson Holton & Jacqueline Jeanette. BA Emory U 1995; MDiv Ya Berk 2011. D 4/30/2011 Bp Keith Bernard Whitmore. sholton@christchurchnh.org

HOLTON, Steve (NY) 40 Ganung Dr, Ossining NY 10562 **S Jn's Ch Cornwall NY 2011-** B Washington DC 4/11/1960 s David Caryl Holton & Dorothy. BA Hav 1982; MDiv GTS 1988; Cler Ldrshp Proj 2002. D 6/25/1988 Bp Frederick Houk Borsch P 5/1/1989 Bp Richard Frank Grein. m 6/3/1989 Charlotte Bacon c 2. Envoy to Afghanistan Dio New York New York City NY 2002-2003; R S Pauls On The Hill Epis Ch Ossining NY 1992-2011; Cur All SS Ch New York NY 1989-1992. stevecharlotteholton@msn.com

HOLTZ, Frank John (Kan) 106 Naroma Ct, Abilene KS 67410 **D S Jn's Ch Abilene KS 1996-** B Minneapolis KS 4/7/1940 s Harold Bilbee Holtz & Olive Clara. DDS U of Missouri 1965; BA Washburn U 1985. D 3/17/1996 P 11/24/1996 Bp William Edward Smalley. fholtz@classicnet.net

HOLTZEN, Thomas Lee (Mil) 2777 Mission Rd, Nashotah WI 53058 **Prof Nash Nashotah WI 2003-; P-in-c S Paul's Ch Ashippun Oconomowoc WI 2003-** B Aurora NE 12/7/1968 BA U of Nebraska 1992; MA Gordon-Conwell TS 1996; PhD 2002. D 5/10/2003 Bp Russell Edward Jacobus P 11/13/2003 Bp Steven Andrew Miller. m 12/28/1991 Candace Kay Maloley c 4.

HOLZ JR, John Clifford (Ak) Po Box 80074, Fairbanks AK 99708 B New London CT 9/3/1952 s John Clifford Holz & Joanne Beverly. MDiv Estrn Bapt TS; BA San Diego St U; AA SW Cmnty Coll Chula Vista CA. D 3/28/2004 P 10/18/2004 Bp Mark Lawrence Mac Donald. m 8/2/1975 Carol Mary Atkinson c 2. jcholz@att.net

HOLZHALB, Leon Stephen (La) 100 Christwood Blvd, Covington LA 70433 B New Orleans LA 9/2/1940 s Leon Stephen Holzhalb & Irene Lillian. BA U So 1962; STB GTS 1967; DMin PrTS 1997. D 10/7/1967 Bp Iveson Batchelor Noland P 10/1/1968 Bp Girault M Jones. m 10/27/2005 Julie Anne Hopkins c 2. R, Adv Hse Chr Ch Cathd New Orleans LA 1996-2003; R Chr Ch Covington LA 1976-1996; Vic S Alb's Epis Ch Monroe LA 1970-1976; Vic S Pat's Epis Ch W Monroe LA 1970-1974; Cur Ch Of The Ascen Lafayette LA 1968-1970. sholzhalb@christwood.com

HOLZHAMMER, Robert Ernest (Ia) 1 Oaknoll Court, Iowa City IA 52246 B Rock Island IL 11/26/1922 s Edward William Holzhammer & Hester. BS U of Iowa 1949; MDiv VTS 1952; STM STUSo 1971. D 6/24/1952 P 1/21/1953 Bp Gordon V Smith. c 1. Stndg Cmsn Dio Iowa Des Moines IA 1985-1989; Com Dio Iowa Des Moines IA 1978-1981; Chair - Com Dio Iowa Des Moines IA 1972-1975; R Trin Ch Iowa City IA 1962-1990; Dep Gc Dio Iowa Des Moines IA 1958-1967; R S Jn's Epis Ch Dubuque IA 1957-1962. Auth, "Mstr'S Thesis," *Hist Of Mssy Expansion Of Ecusa 1790-1835*, 1971; Auth, "Stwdshp Plan For Par Endowments," 1965. 2nd Lt. Pilot Usaaf 1943-1946; Ch Hist Soc; Delta Sigma Pi 1946-1962; Mason'S Hm Lodge #192; Rotary 1952; U Of Iowa Alum 1949; Virginia Thelogical Sem Alum 1952. Paul Harris Fellowowship 1993; Epis Awd S Geo Cross, Ecusa 1985; Hon Cn Trin Cathd, Davenport, Ia Davenport IA 1977; Stwdshp Plan For Par Endowments 1975; Silver Beaver Awd BSA 1971. bholzhammer@trinity1c.org

HOME JR, George Everette (At) 154 Vinings Dr SE, Rome GA 30161 B San Diego CA 4/22/1914 s George Everette Home & Marjorie McKenzie. BS Wabash Coll 1936; STUSo 1965. D 6/12/1960 P 7/10/1965 Bp Randolph R Claiborne. m 7/23/1939 Jane Lee c 3. Vic Ch Of The Trsfg Rome GA 1979-1985; R S Dunst's Epis Ch Atlanta GA 1969-1979; R Ch Of The Gd Shpd Covington GA 1965-1969; Asst S Ptr's Ch Rome GA 1960-1965.

HOMEYER, Charles Frederick (WMich) 3539 Quiggle Ave Se, Ada MI 49301 B Saint Louis MO 8/12/1944 s August H Homeyer & Ruth M. BA Br 1966; MAT Wesl 1968; MDiv CDSP 1974. D 6/22/1974 P 12/21/1974 Bp George Leslie Cadigan. m 2/17/1968 Sara Hobart c 2. Ch Of The H Cross Kentwood MI 1978-2009; Cur Gr Ch Kirkwood MO 1974-1978. homeyer44@comcast.net

HONAKER, Martha Anne (Ind) 111 Ivy Lane, Sparta NC 28675 B Asheville NC 12/18/1946 d Ernest Elmer Honaker & Selma Vee. MDiv 1983. D 6/2/1984 P 12/18/1984 Bp Alden Moinet Hathaway. R S Steph's Epis Ch New Harmony IN 2002-2010; S Jn's Cathd Albuquerque NM 2001-2002; Assoc H Trin Epis Ch Fayetteville NC 1993-2000; R S Jas Epis Ch Pittsburgh PA 1985-1990; Asst All SS Ch Aliquippa PA 1983-1985. marthahon@gmail.com

HONDERICH, Thomas (Ind) 3941 N Delaware St, Indianapolis IN 46205 B Detroit MI 8/11/1944 s Merrill Eugene Honderich & Helen Elizabeth. BA Albion Coll 1966; BD SWTS 1970. D 5/19/1970 Bp Charles Ellsworth Bennison Jr P 12/1/1970 Bp John P Craine. m 10/18/2011 Gordon Lee Chastain. Affiliate All SS Ch Indianapolis IN 1979; Cur S Paul's Epis Ch Indianapolis IN 1976-1978; S Steph's Elwood IN 1973-1976; Cur Gd Samar Epis Ch Clearwater FL 1971-1972; Trin Ch Indianapolis IN 1970-1972. honderte@msn.com

HONEA JR, Bertrand Needham (FtW) 4701 Harley Ave, Fort Worth TX 76107 **Died 2/13/2011** B Fort Worth TX 5/24/1927 s Bertrand Needham Honea & Mary Louise. BA U of Texas 1950; BD VTS 1953; EdM Harv 1961. D 12/1/1952 P 6/1/1953 Bp Charles A Mason. c 4. bnhjr27@sbcglobal.net

HONEA, Janice Bailey (CFla) 6246 Tremayne Dr, Mount Dora FL 32757 **S Andr's Ch Omaha NE 2004-** B Memphis TN 3/19/1952 BA U of Memphis 1974. D 1/31/2004 Bp Joe Goodwin Burnett. m 5/19/1973 James Edward Honea c 3. janice.honea@jpfinancial.com

HONEYCHURCH, J(ohn) Robert (Cal) 840 Echo Park Ave, Los Angeles CA 90026 **Prof of Ch Ldrshp The ETS At Claremont Claremont CA 2009-; Mssnr for Congrl Vitality Epis Ch Cntr New York NY 2008-** B Butte MT 3/29/1957 s Fred Alexander Honeychurch & Dorothy Anne. BS Montana St U 1979; MDiv SWTS 1984; DMin SWTS 1999. D 6/12/1984 P 12/13/1984 Bp Jackson Earle Gilliam. m 3/10/1985 Sylvia A Sweeney c 1. Adj Fac CDSP Berkeley CA 2002-2007; R S Jas Ch Fremont CA 2001-2008; Vic - Estrn Dnry Dio Idaho Boise ID 1999-2000; Co-R S Lk's Epis Ch Idaho Falls ID 1992-2001; Pstr Assoc H Trin Epis Ch Troy MT 1988-1992; Vic S Lk's Ch Libby MT 1984-1992. bhoneychurch@episcopalchurch.org

HONIG - SMITH, Julie Honig (Ore) 6300 Sw Nicol Rd, Portland OR 97223 **Vic S Bede's Ch Forest Grove OR 2005-** B Saint Louis MO 7/1/1952 d Harry Donald Honig & Ellen Jayne. BSW S Louis U 1974; MS S Louis U 1979; Seattle U TS & Mnstry 1999; MDiv CDSP 2000. D 6/24/2000 Bp Sanford Zangwill Kaye Hampton P 1/13/2001 Bp Vincent Waydell Warner. m 10/22/

1994 Thomas Martin Smith. S Mk's Ch Yreka CA 2004-2005; Vic S Barn Ch Mt Shasta CA 2002-2005; All SS Epis Ch Redding CA 2002-2003; Assoc R S Barn Epis Ch Bainbridge Island WA 2000-2002. AAPC; CHS. reverendmotherj@comcast.net

HONNOLD, Sandra Elizabeth (Haw) PO Box 7063, PMB 295, Ocean View HI 96737 B Oakland CA 5/4/1944 d Ronald Charles Kersh & Edna Pearl. Cosumes River Comm. Coll Placerville CA 1993; BTh Sch for Deacons 1996. D 10/16/1996 Bp Jerry Alban Lamb. m 10/12/1963 Frederic Kelly Honnold c 3. Pstr Asst Trin Ch Sutter Creek CA 1996-2005. No. Amer Assn for the Diac 1993-1996. deaconsandy@aholabroadband.net

HONODEL, Jill (Cal) 285 Kaanapali Dr, Napa CA 94558 **Gr Ch Martinez CA 2004-** B Vallejo,CA 7/14/1966 d Nicholas Joseph Honodel & Carolyn Jean. BA U CA 1989; MDiv Fuller TS 1995; MA CDSP 1996. D 12/4/1998 P 9/25/1999 Bp Jerry Alban Lamb. Asst S Paul's Epis Ch Benicia CA 1998-2002. RVJILL@EARTHLINK.NET

HONSE, Robert Wayne (Kan) 1533 Fountain Dr, Lawrence KS 66047 B 8/5/1943 D 6/11/2005 Bp Dean Elliott Wolfe. c 1. bobhonse@sunflower.com

HOOD, Nancy Elizabeth (Dal) 6883 Lagoon Dr, Grand Prairie TX 75054 **Suppy S Mart's Ch Lancaster TX 2009-** B Washington DC 11/19/1941 d James Edward Hood & Elizabeth Bowen. Longwood U 1960; Dioc TS 1973; TCU 1979; BA U of Texas 1980; Med Ntsu 1983; PhD Texas Wmn's U 1994. D 6/25/1978 Bp Robert Elwin Terwilliger P 5/22/1996 Bp James Monte Stanton. m 4/15/1981 Charles V Smith c 3. Assoc Ch Of The Apos Coppell TX 2004-2009; Ch Of The Gd Shpd Dallas TX 2001-2003; S Paul's Epis Ch Dallas TX 1997-2001; S Jas Ch Dallas TX 1997; Asst S Jas Ch Dallas TX 1978-1980. Dok, Assn Of Wmn In Mnstry 1980-1984. Kappa Delta Pi.

HOOD, Stephen Dale (Ala) 3648 Dabney Drive, Vesatvia Hills AL 35243 **Chair, Dept of Camp McDowell Dio Alabama Birmingham AL 2010-2013; Dioc Coun Dio Alabama Birmingham AL 2008-2012; R Epis Ch Of The Ascen Birmingham AL 2007-** B La Marque TX 11/9/1967 s Charles David Hood & Martha Sue. BA SW Texas St U San Marcos 1995; MDiv STUSo 2002. D 12/27/2001 P 7/7/2002 Bp Charles Edward Jenkins III. m 8/1/1992 Emily U Umfress c 2. Assoc R S Jas Epis Ch Baton Rouge LA 2004-2007; R S Jn's Epis Ch Thibodaux LA 2002-2004; Intern S Fran Of Assisi Epis Ch Ooltewah TN 2001-2002. Sabbath Lv Grant Cntr for Pstr Excellence, Samford U 2012. fathershood@gmail.com

HOOD, William Rienks (La) 1808 Prospect St, Houston TX 77004 **S Paul's Ch New Orleans LA 2006-** B Austin TX 4/13/1956 s Charles Fuller Hood & Antoinette. BA St. Edw's U Austin TX 1979; MDiv Epis TS of The SW 1983; M Theol Studie SMU 1994. D 6/28/1983 Bp Maurice Manuel Benitez P 1/1/1984 Bp Gordon Taliaferro Charlton. m 11/17/2007 Martha Parker c 3. Spec Mobilization Spprt Plan Washington DC 2008-2010; Pension Fund Mltry New York NY 2008-2009; S Paul's Ch New Orleans LA 2003-2004; S Steph's Ch Beaumont TX 2002; R S Jn's Ch La Porte TX 1998-2002; Off Of Bsh For ArmdF New York NY 1986-1998; Cur S Chris's Ch League City TX 1983-1986. hoodwr1@yahoo.com

HOOGERHYDE, Scott Matthew (Nwk) 7 E Main St, Mendham NJ 07945 B Midland MI 11/6/1962 s James Dale Hoogerhyde & Karen Yvonne. BA Estrn Michigan U 1985; UTS 1992; MDiv GTS 1993. D 6/19/1993 P 1/15/1994 Bp R(aymond) Stewart Wood Jr. m 10/10/1993 Lynne Cheryl Einhorn. R S Mk's Ch Mendham NJ 1996-2010; Cur S Paul's Ch Doylestown PA 1993-1996. hoo@nac.net

HOOK, Edward Lindsten (Colo) PO Box 1388, Green Valley AZ 85622 B Oak Park IL 10/9/1933 s Joseph Porter Hook & Esther Merwyn. BA NWU 1956; MDiv VTS 1963. D 6/22/1963 Bp Robert McConnell Hatch P 1/24/1964 Bp William A Lawrence. m 8/20/1955 Barbara B Baldwin c 3. P Epis Ch Of S Fran-In-The-Vlly Green Vlly AZ 2001-2002; R S Dav Of The Hills Epis Ch Woodland Pk CO 1991-1999; Assoc R Gr And S Steph's Epis Ch Colorado Sprg CO 1988-1991; Int Gr And S Steph's Epis Ch Colorado Sprg CO 1986-1987; Supply P Epis Ch Of S Jn The Bapt Breckenridge CO 1971-1975; R All SS Ch Worcester MA 1966-1971; Asst All SS Ch Worcester MA 1963-1965. Auth, *Case Hist of Tentmakers*. NASSAM 1971. behook@aol.com

HOOKE, Ruthanna Brinton (WMass) 3737 Seminary Rd, Alexandria VA 22304 **Asst Prof VTS Alexandria VA 2003-** B Boston MA 4/1/1963 d Richard Harris Hooke & Ruth Brinton. BA Harv 1986; MA Emerson Coll 1993; MDiv Ya Berk 1996; Ph.D. Ya 2007. D 5/16/1998 P 1/30/1999 Bp Arthur Edward Walmsley. c 1. S Paul's Ch Wallingford CT 2000-2003; Presb Ch Of The Epiph Durham CT 1999-2000; Presb Emm Ch Killingworth CT 1999-2000; D S Andr's Ch Northford CT 1998-1999; D S Jas Epis Ch Higganum CT 1998-1999; D S Paul's Ch Westbrook CT 1998-1999. Auth, "I Am Here In This Room," *Homil*, 2002. Acad Of Homil 1998; Amer Acad of Relgion 1997; SBL 2007. rhooke@vts.edu

HOOKER, Alan Bruce (SVa) 6645 Northumberland Hwy, Heathsville VA 22473 **Int S Jas Ch Montross VA 2011-** B Norwalk CT 5/3/1950 s Alexander Boyd Hooker & Alice P. W&L 1969; BA W&M 1972; MDiv VTS 1976; MA U of Connecticut 1986. D 6/12/1976 Bp Joseph Warren Hutchens P 4/2/1977 Bp Morgan Porteus. m 6/1/1974 Cathy Schlenz c 3. R S Geo's Ch Pungoteague Accomac VA 2000-2010; R S Jas' Ch Accomac VA 2000-2010; R S Steph's Epis Ch Culpeper VA 1995-2000; R Cople Par Hague VA 1986-1995; R S Paul's Epis Ch Willimantic CT 1983-1984; R Chr Ch Canaan CT 1978-1983; Cur Chr Ch Cathd Hartford CT 1976-1978. abhook143@hotmail.com

HOOKER, John L (Mass) 139 Union St Unit 18, Westfield MA 01085 B Leesville LA 8/15/1944 s Roy Wall Hooker & Laura Ellie. BA Centenary Coll 1966; MA SMU 1968; Cert Fulbright Schlr Staatliche Fuer Mus 1969; DMA U of Memphis 1978; MDiv EDS 1992. D 6/13/1992 Bp Joseph Thomas Heistand P 3/6/1993 Bp Otis Charles. m 6/7/2004 David Bucchiere. Ascen Memi Ch Ipswich MA 2000-2004; Assoc S Phil's In The Hills Tucson AZ 1998-2000; Prof EDS Cambridge MA 1992-1998; Min of Mus S Phil's In The Hills Tucson AZ 1984-1989; Min of Mus Calv Ch Memphis TN 1976-1984; Min of Mus S Paul's Epis Ch Chattanooga TN 1971-1976. Auth, "Ldr's Guide to Wonder, Love," *& Praise*; Auth, "Hymn Tunes and Harmonies," *Gather*; Ed, *In The Shadows of H Week: Tenebrae*; Auth, "Hymn Tunes and Harmonies, Wonder," *Love and Praise*, Ch Pub Inc; Auth, "Hymn Tunes and Harmonies," *The Hymnal 1982*, Ch Pub Inc; Auth, "Hymn Tunes and Harmonies," *The Presb Hymnal*. AGO; Assn of Angl Mus; ADLMC. revdrhooker@comcast.net

HOOP, Kimberly Ann (WMich) 4155 S Norway St Se, Grand Rapids MI 49546 **D Ch Of The H Cross Kentwood MI 1996-** B Grand Rapids MI 1/21/1955 d Raymond Ernest Hoop & Dorothy Kathryn. BD Amer U 1977; Grand Vlly St U 1996. D 11/16/1996 Bp Edward Lewis Lee Jr. 3rd Ord Francisan; NAAD.

HOOPER, John K (Mich) 42 Cottage Circle, West Lebanon NH 03784 B Cincinnati OH 7/7/1933 s William Davis Hooper & Elizabeth. ACSW Acad of Cert Soc Workers; U of Detroit; U MN; BS U GA 1955; MDiv VTS 1958; Cert St of Michigan 1981; MSW U MI 1981; Bd-Cert Dplma 1983; Clin & Macro Lic St of Michigan 2004. D 6/25/1958 Bp Archie H Crowley P 3/1/1959 Bp Richard S M Emrich. m 8/27/1955 Carolyn Jane Woodhouse c 4. Environ Justice Coordntr Dio Michigan Detroit MI 2001-2005; Environ Justice Coordntr Dio Michigan Detroit MI 2001-2005; R Trin Epis Ch Farmington Hills MI 1970-1981; R S Jn's Ch Howell MI 1965-1970; Vic S Dunst's Epis Ch Davison MI 1960-1965; Asst S Edw The Confessor Epis Ch Clinton Township MI 1958-1960; Asst Trin Ch S Clair Shores MI 1958-1960. DSA Mich. Alco & Addictions Assoc MI 1986. jackbnimb@comcast.net

HOOPER, Larry Donald (SeFla) 401 Duval St, Key West FL 33040 **S Paul's Ch Key W FL 2009-** B Birmingham AL 3/12/1952 s Donald Hooper & Katie Kinzel. AS Palm Bch Jr Coll 1974; BA Florida St U 1986; MDiv VTS 1989. D 6/12/1989 Bp Calvin Onderdonk Schofield Jr P 12/21/1989 Bp Rogers Sanders Harris. m 12/17/1983 Katherine M McVey c 3. Int Chr Ch Rolla MO 2007-2009; S Mart's Ch Ellisville MO 2000-2007; Gr Ch Tampa FL 1996-2000; Dio SW Florida Sarasota FL 1993-1995; Asst R Trin By The Cove Naples FL 1989-1992. frhooperstpauls@aol.com

HOOPER III, Robert Channing (Ct) 10 Cumberland Rd, West Hartford CT 06119 **R S Jas's Ch W Hartford CT 2002-** B Albany NY 10/28/1963 s Robert Hooper & Janet. BA New Engl Coll 1987; MDiv VTS 1995. D 6/10/1995 Bp Clarence Nicholas Coleridge P 1/10/1996 Bp Peter James Lee. m 1/2/1988 Priscilla Long c 3. R Ch Of The Adv Medfield MA 1997-2002; Asst S Fran Epis Ch Great Falls VA 1995-1997. rchooper3@aol.com

HOOPER, Ruth Isabelle (Az) 4440 N Campbell Ave, Tucson AZ 85718 B Stambaugh MI 5/8/1950 d Lloyd James Hooper & Brenda Mary. D 1/29/2011 Bp Kirk Stevan Smith. ruthhooper08@comcast.net

HOOPER-ROSEBROOK, Elizabeth E (Los) 1014 E. Altadena Drive, Altadena CA 91001 **Stndg Committe Dio Los Angeles Los Angeles CA 2009-; Assoc P/Chapl S Mk's Par Altadena CA 1999-** B CA 9/29/1961 d R L Hooper & F. BA Pitzer Coll 1983; MDiv GTS 1987. D 6/27/1987 P 1/16/1988 Bp Oliver Bailey Garver Jr. m 2/29/1992 Thomas Alan Hooper-Rosebrook c 2. Vic S Thos' Mssn Hacienda Heights CA 1993-1999; Assoc R S Columba's Par Camarillo CA 1990-1993; S Lk's Par Monrovia CA 1987-1990. mobetsyhr@gmail.com

HOOPES OHC, David Bryan (LI) Church of St Edward the Martyr, 14 E 109th St, New York NY 10029 B San Antonio TX 6/25/1943 s Harry Crawford Hoopes & Genevieve May. BA Findlay Coll 1966; MDiv Andover Newton TS 1970. Trans from Church in the Province Of The West Indies 2/4/1988 as Priest Bp Robert Campbell Witcher Sr. Int The Ch of S Edw The Mtyr New York NY 2008-2010; Dep to GC Dio Long Island Garden City NY 2000-2003; R S Thos Ch Farmingdale NY 1993-1999; Assoc Gr Ch Brooklyn NY 1987-1993. Chapl Ord of S Lk 1997-1999; EDEIO 2008; Ecum Off- CAROA 2008; Life Professed Ord of H Cross 1977; Pres CAROA 2000-2008. DAVIDBOHC@HCMNET.ORG

HOOVER, Billy Joe (ECR) 15040 Union Ave, San Jose CA 95124 **Died 6/14/2010** B 3/26/1928 s Joseph R Hoover & Wilma G. Bts. D 1/22/1968 P 8/1/1971 Bp George Richard Millard. H Trsfg Aggregate Min.

HOOVER, Gregory T (WMo) 107 Walnut Ln, Branson MO 65616 **R Shpd Of The Hills Branson MO 2010-** B Independence MO 8/14/1968 s Fred Hoover & Bernice. Missouri Sthrn St U 1992; Grad Non Degree Prog Geo Herbert Inst of Pstr Stds 2009; Mstr of Mnstry Providance TS 2010. D 6/5/2010 P 12/8/

2010 Bp Barry Robert Howe. m 10/28/2000 Kristen Matthews c 3. ft. greghoover@gmail.com

HOOVER II, Henry Harrison (Minn) 904 Brenner Ave, Saint Paul MN 55113 B Minneapolis MN 4/21/1931 s Henry Harrison Hoover & Lillian Emma. BA U MN 1952; BD SWTS 1955; DD SWTS 1979. D 6/26/1955 Bp Hamilton Hyde Kellogg P 12/21/1955 Bp Stephen E Keeler. m 2/18/1977 Jean Lancaster c 3. R Chr Ch S Paul MN 1990-1996; Dio Minnesota Minneapolis MN 1984-1990; R S Chris's Epis Ch Roseville MN 1967-1984; Asst Cathd Ch Of S Mk Minneapolis MN 1959-1964; P-in-c Emm Epis Ch Alexandria MN 1955-1959. HenryHoover@aol.com

HOOVER, John Frain (CPa) 99 Willowbrook Blvd, Lewisburg PA 17837 B Philadelphia PA 12/28/1942 s Creighton Wertz Hoover & Marjorie Frain. BS Tem 1963; MDiv GTS 1966; DMin GTF 1995; Cert PSU 1995. D 6/11/1966 P 1/28/1967 Bp Robert Lionne DeWitt. m 9/3/1966 Margaret Barr c 2. Sr Consult for Sm Ch Mnstry Dio Cntrl Pennsylvania Harrisburg PA 2008-2011; P-in-c S Jas Ch Muncy PA 2000-2004; P-in-c S Paul's Ch Lock Haven PA 1988-2000; R Chap Of The Gd Shpd Hawk Run PA 1987-1998; R S Paul's Ch Philipsburg PA 1987-1998; R S Andr's In The Field Ch Philadelphia PA 1966-1987. jfhoover@ptd.net

HOOVER, Joshua Aaron (EMich) 74 Hurstbourne Rd, Rochester NY 14609 **S Jude's Epis Ch Fenton MI 2005-** B Wilmington DE 6/10/1972 BA Alfred U. D 6/1/2002 P 1/11/2003 Bp Jack Marston McKelvey. m 11/23/2009 Allison Womack c 2. Asst Chr Ch Pittsford NY 2002-2005. REVMRJOSH@YAHOO.COM

HOOVER, Judy Verne (Minn) 2020 Orkla Dr, Golden Valley MN 55427 B Minneapolis MN 5/28/1933 d Vernon Earl Hanlon & Bertha Anna. BS U MN 1955; MBA U of St. Thos 1983; Cert SWTS 1991; MDiv Untd TS Minneapolis 1991. D 6/24/1991 P 1/6/1992 Bp Robert Marshall Anderson. m 10/18/2005 Raymond Edward Jorgensen c 4. Dio Minnesota Minneapolis MN 1999-2004; S Edw The Confessor Wayzata MN 1996-1998; Asst Ch Of The Epiph Epis Plymouth MN 1991-1996. "Flames and Faith," *Doing H Bus*, Ch Pub, 2006. Associated Parishes for Liturg and Mnstry 1996; Int Mnstry Ntwk Associated Parishes 1993-1996; Minnesota Epis Cleric Assn 1992. Paul Harris Fell Rotary Inst 2001. frdr@aol.com

HOOVER, Melvin Aubrey (SO) No address on file. B Columbus OH 9/24/1944 s Alfred Benjamin Hoover & Felicia Louise. BS OH SU 1968; CRDS 1972; U Assoc Intrnshp 1976. D 7/3/1971 Bp John Mc Gill Krumm. m 12/18/1970 Rose Edington. Auth, "Living Ecum". Outstanding Ldr Rochester Cmnty 1976. mhoover@uua.org

HOOVER, Richard A (CFla) 209 S Iowa Ave, Lakeland FL 33801 **D All SS Epis Ch Lakeland FL 2011-; Dir of Cmncatn All SS Epis Ch Lakeland FL 2011-** B MO 8/24/1950 s Mario Hoover & Ruth. BA SW Missouri St U 1971. D 12/1/2007 Bp John Wadsworth Howe. m 6/1/1974 Melanie Hoover. rickhoover@tampabay.rr.com

HOOVER-DEMPSEY, Randy (Tenn) 1829 Hudson Rd, Madison TN 37115 **Cur Dio Tennessee Nashville TN 2010-** B Greensboro NC 5/21/1947 s Luther Edgar Dempsey & Merrimon Dempsey. BA U NC 1969; M.Div. Columbia TS 1976; BS Middle Tennessee St U 1982. D 6/10/2006 P 12/16/2006 Bp Bertram Nelson Herlong. m 5/23/1982 Kathleen V Hoover c 4. Cur S Mary Magd Ch Fayetteville TN 2009-2010; Asst S Barth's Ch Bristol TN 2006-2009. randyhd@comcast.net

HOPEWELL, Gloria Grayson (Chi) 939 Hinman Ave, Evanston IL 60202 **P Assoc S Lk's Ch Evanston IL 2010-** B Sandwich IL 10/5/1945 d Raymond H Grandgeorge & Patricia C. BS Nthrn Illinois U 1968; MBA Loyola U 1979; MDiv Chicago TS 1996; DMin Garrett-Evang 2007. D 6/5/2010 P 12/11/2010 Bp Jeffrey Dean Lee. c 2. revhope1@sbcglobal.net

HOPKINS, Christine Carroll (Spr) 102 E Mchenry St, Urbana IL 61801 **D Emm Memi Epis Ch Champaign IL 2000-** B Mayfield KY 4/25/1950 D 6/11/2000 Bp Peter Hess Beckwith. m 6/13/1971 Robert Michael Hopkins c 3.

HOPKINS, Daniel Warren (Colo) 20254 E Maplewood Pl, Aurora CO 80016 **D S Thos Epis Ch Denver CO 2002-** B Nurnberg DE 12/9/1954 s Willie Hopkins & Lula. BA U of Oklahoma 1977; MDiv GTS 1985. D 6/14/1985 P 12/22/1985 Bp William Carl Frey. m 12/6/1973 Sheila D Hopkins. Assoc S Lk's Ch Hot Sprg AR 1993-1996; Dio Colorado Denver CO 1992-1993; R Ch Of The H Redeem Denver CO 1985-1992. Ne Denver Mnstrl Allnce. danhopkins8922@msn.com

HOPKINS, David Lucius (Pa) 7117 Se Birchwood Ln, Stuart FL 34997 B Green Bay WI 7/15/1944 s Lucius Daniel Hopkins & Lucile. BS U of Wisconsin 1968; MDiv GTS 1971. D 6/10/1971 P 12/1/1971 Bp William Hampton Brady. m 6/19/1971 Virginia Lynn Ryan c 4. Cleric Ch Of The Annuniciation Philadelphia PA 1995-2002; Calv Ch Syracuse NY 1990-1994; R S Jn Ch/Mision San Juan Milwaukee WI 1979-1990; Vic All SS Epis Ch Charlotte NC 1976-1977; Dio No Carolina Raleigh NC 1976; Vic S Anth Of Padua Ch Hackensack NJ 1974-1976; Vic St Jas Epis Ch Mosinee WI 1971-1974. GAS, SHN. Vol Healthcare For The Homeless Of Milwaukee 1988; Friends Of The Gathering Dio. Of Milwaukee Meal Prog 1986. dlhphil3@aol.com

✠ HOPKINS JR, Rt Rev Harold Anthony (ND) 15 Piper Rd Apt K211, Scarborough ME 04074 **Ret Bp Of Nd Dio No Dakota Fargo ND 1988-** B Philadelphia PA 4/24/1930 s Harold Anthony Hopkins & Ellen. BA U of Pennsylvania 1952; MDiv GTS 1955; DD GTS 1980. D 5/7/1955 Bp Joseph Gillespie Armstrong P 11/21/1955 Bp Oliver J Hart Con 2/18/1980 for ND. m 6/11/1955 Nancy Myer. Dir - Pstr Dvlpmt Epis Ch Cntr New York NY 1988-1998; Bp Of Nd Dio No Dakota Fargo ND 1980-1988; Vic S Barth's Epis Ch Yarmouth ME 1974-1978; Dio Maine Portland ME 1969-1979; Asst To Bp Of Me Dio Maine Portland ME 1969-1975; R S Sav's Par Bar Harbor ME 1963-1969; R S Andr's Ch Millinocket ME 1957-1963; Cur Par Of Chr The Redeem Pelham NY 1955-1957. Contrib, "Restoring The Soul Of A Ch," Liturg Press, 1995; Auth, "The Interval Between Election And Consecration," 1992; Auth, "Nominees In An Epis Process," 1989. nhop@aol.com

HOPKINS, John Leonard (Alb) 34 Velina Dr, Burnt Hills NY 12027 **S Lk's Ch Mechanicville NY 2010-** B Glens Falls NY 10/14/1946 s John Harold Hopkins & Ruth Elenor. MA SUNY; BA SUNY 1968; MA SUNY 1982; MA St. Bernards TS And Mnstry Albany NY 2001. D 6/2/2002 Bp Daniel William Herzog P 11/30/2002 Bp David John Bena. m 7/30/1977 Cynthia Young c 2. S Lk's Ch Cambridge NY 2008-2009; Asst S Geo's Ch Clifton Pk NY 2002-2007.

HOPKINS, Michael Warren (Roch) 56 Vassar St, Rochester NY 14607 **GC Dep Dio Rochester Rochester NY 2012-; Dn of Rochester Dist Dio Rochester Rochester NY 2011-; Dioc Cmsn on Liturg& Mus Dio Rochester Rochester NY 2005-; R S Lk And S Simon Cyrene Rochester NY 2004-** B Avoca NY 4/26/1961 s William Laverne Hopkins & Patricia Carol. BS Plattsburgh St U 1983; Nash 1985; MDiv SWTS 1988; CUA 1992. D 6/17/1989 Bp Frank Tracy Griswold III P 1/10/1990 Bp Ronald Hayward Haines. m 7/22/2010 John Bradley. SCLM T/F on C056 Dom And Frgn Mssy Soc- Epis Ch Cntr New York NY 2010-2011; P-in-c S Steph's Ch Rochester NY 2007-2008; Dioc Coun Dio Rochester Rochester NY 2006-2010; Bp Search Com Dio Rochester Rochester NY 2006-2008; R S Geo's Ch Glenn Dale MD 2002-2004; Bp Search Com Dio Washington Washington DC 2001-2002; Dio Washington Washington DC 1996; Dioc Coun (Moderator 98-00) Dio Washington Washington DC 1994-2000; Vic S Geo's Ch Glenn Dale MD 1990-2001; Cmsn on Liturg & Mus Dio Washington Washington DC 1989-1996; Assoc Par of St Monica & St Jas Washington DC 1989-1990. Auth, "Paying the Price: A No Amer Perspective," *Rebuilding Comm: Who Pays the Price?*, Monad Press, 2008; Auth, "Reaffirmation of Ord Vows," *Baptism & Mnstry*, Ch Pub, 1994. Associated Parishes 1989-2006; Ch in Metropltn Areas 2006; ECom 1997-1999; EPF 1997; EUC (Bd 09-) 2002; EWC 1998; Integrity (Pres 98-03; Dir Com 96-98) 1985; OA 1994-2002. Pres's Awd Integrity 2006; Polly Bond Awd ECom 1998. mwhopkins@rochester.rr.com

HOPKINS, Terry Robert (Minn) P.O. Box 402, Monticello MN 55362 B Bradford PA 4/26/1947 s Robert George Hopkins & Virginia Lillian. BA Estrn U 1969; MA U of Vermont 1976. D 11/14/1992 Bp Sanford Zangwill Kaye Hampton. m 6/19/1971 Janice Ruth Frank c 2. D S Jn's Ch Of Hassan Rogers MN 1996-1999; D S Mich's All Ang Ch Monticello MN 1994-1996; D S Chris's Epis Ch Roseville MN 1992-1994. terryrhopkins@yahoo.com

HOPKINS, Vivian Louise (Oly) 32820 20th Ave S #61, Federal Way WA 98003 **Coordntr of Epis Relief and Dvlpmt Dio SE Florida Miami FL 2002-; Dir of Outreach Ministies Chr Epis Ch Miami FL 2001-** B Miami FL 9/5/1937 d Joseph Leonard Hopkins & Iva Louise. BS USC 1960; MA California St Polytechnic U 1977; Cert Dio SE Florida Sch for CE 2001. D 9/1/2001 Bp Leopold Frade. c 1. dk_vihop@comcast.net

HOPKINS-GREENE, Nancy (SO) 6255 Stirrup Rd, Cincinnati OH 45244 **Asst Ed FMP Cincinnati OH 2009-; Asst The Ch of the Redeem Cincinnati OH 2004-** B Philadelphia PA 12/18/1957 d Robert Clinton Hopkins & Louise DeFreece. BA Stan 1980; MDiv EDS 1992. D 6/5/1993 Bp David Elliot Johnson P 12/3/1994 Bp Herbert Thompson Jr. m 6/13/1980 Roger Stewart Greene c 2. S Anne Epis Ch W Chester OH 2004; S Tim's Epis Ch Cincinnati OH 1994-2003. hopkinsgreene@cinci.rr.com

HOPNER, Kathryn Ann (Nev) St Paul's Episcopal Church, PO Box 737, Sparks NV 89432 **Assoc P S Paul's Epis Ch Sparks NV 2007-; Assoc Trin Epis Ch Reno NV 2007-** B Denver CO 8/31/1953 d Franklin Paul Hammond & Marilyn June. BA, Soc Sci San Jose St U 1987; MA Educ Chapman U 2000; Masters of Div CDSP 2007. D 6/2/2007 Bp Barry Leigh Beisner P 12/8/2007 Bp Jerry Alban Lamb. m 9/29/1972 Victor Hopner c 2. kathrynhopner@att.net

HOPPE, Robert Donald (FdL) 806 4th St, Algoma WI 54201 **Vic Ch Of S Agnes By The Lake Algoma WI 1992-; Vic Ch Of The Precious Blood Gar Algoma WI 1992-** B Mankato MN 4/5/1961 s Robert Andrew Hoppe & Judith Ann. BS Minnesota St U Mankato 1983; BS Minnesota St U Mankato 1985. D 8/15/1992 Bp William L Stevens P 9/6/1997 Bp Russell Edward Jacobus. Dio Fond du Lac Appleton WI 1992-1995. SocMary 1999.

HOPWOOD, Alfred Joseph (Minn) 1417 Blue Flag Ct, Northfield MN 55057 B New York NY 10/4/1933 s Alexander Ireland Hopwood & Winifred Ione. BS Colorado St U 1956; PhD Colorado St U 1967; MA S Jn's U Collegeville MN 1987. D 6/24/1986 P 12/30/1986 Bp Robert Marshall Anderson. m 6/22/

1955 Lillian Barbara Rugen c 4. Vic SS Martha And Mary Epis Ch Eagan MN 2005-2010; Int Chr Epis Ch Grand Rapids MN 2000-2001; R All SS Ch Northfield MN 1993-1999; Assoc S Jn's Ch S Cloud MN 1986-1993. "Nine Meditations," *Soundings: The mag of the Dio Minnesota*, 1979. frjoe@charter.net

HORINE JR, Robert Baker (Lex) 232 Chenault Rd, Lexington KY 40502 B Lexington KY 7/6/1934 s Robert Baker Horine & Emma Catherine. ABJ U Of Kentucky 1956; MDiv Epis TS In Kentucky 1968; DMin GTF 1986. D 5/25/1968 P 12/15/1968 Bp William R Moody. m 6/27/1985 Rebecca Bailey c 2. R Ch S Mich The Archangel Lexington KY 1976-1985; Cn To Ordnry Dio Lexington Lexington KY 1975-1976; Asst Chr Ch Cathd Lexington KY 1972-1975; R S Steph's Epis Ch Covington KY 1968-1972; Chapl S Aug's Chap Lexington KY 1968-1969. Auth, "Stories, Tales and a Few Sm Lies of a Country Parson," FMP, 2002; Auth, "Lgr Than Life," FMP, 1994; Auth, "January Crt," St Mich's, 1983. Fllshp of St. Jn 2006. Ord Of Merit Dio Lexington 1978. bobandbecky1@insightbb.com

HORLE, Garrison Locke (Colo) 720 Downing St, Denver CO 80218 B Bronxville NY 6/11/1940 s Ariel Frances Horle & Elizabeth. BA U CO 1962; MBA U Denv 1976; MDiv Iliff TS 1996. D 6/7/1997 P 12/6/1997 Bp William Jerry Winterrowd. m 7/8/1966 Carol Enman c 2. Int The Ch Of Chr The King (Epis) Arvada CO 2011; Int Ch Of Our Sav Colorado Sprg CO 2009-2011; Int S Matt's Ch Grand Jct CO 2007-2009; Int S Paul's Epis Ch Lakewood CO 2006-2007; Int S Tim's Epis Ch Centennial CO 2004-2006; R All SS Epis Ch Denver CO 1999-2004; P-in-c S Andr's Ch Cripple Creek CO 1997-1999. horle@msn.com

HORN, Charles Kettler (Miss) 117 Poplar Dr, Brandon MS 39047 B Birmingham AL 4/20/1927 s Joseph Robert Horn & Mildred Kettler. BA U So 1952; VTS 1955; MA Samford U 1977. D 5/19/1956 P 6/8/1957 Bp Robert Fisher Gibson Jr. m 5/4/1996 Jane Ann Childs c 2. Vic H Trin Ch Crystal Sprg MS 1990-1994; Vic S Steph's Ch Hazlehurst MS 1990-1994; Vic The Epis Ch Of The Gd Shpd Terry MS 1988-1994; S Columb's Ch Ridgeland MS 1988-1989; R Gr Ch Birmingham AL 1977-1987; Assoc S Andrews's Epis Ch Birmingham AL 1975-1976; Vic S Andr's Ch Montevallo AL 1965-1970; R S Alb's Ch Birmingham AL 1962-1975; Cur All SS Epis Ch Birmingham AL 1962-1964; R Ch Of The Epiph Guntersville AL 1958-1962; Vic S Lk's Ch Scottsboro AL 1958-1960; Vic S Phil's Ch Ft Payne AL 1958-1960; Cur The Falls Ch Epis Falls Ch VA 1956-1958. AAPC 1992-1994. chasandjanehorn@aol.com

HORN, Eckart (Me) 46 Cliffords St, Portland ME 04102 **Died 11/17/2010** B Rotenborg Fulda 10/4/1961 s Gerhad Horn & Friedhilde. BDiv Kiho Wupperal Germany 1985; MA Bangor TS 1993; MDiv Bangor TS 2007. D 6/9/2007 P 12/15/2007 Bp Chilton Abbie Richardson Knudsen. c 5. eckartfrg@aol.com

HORN, John C (Ia) Christ Episcopal Church, 623 N Fifth St, Burlington IA 52601 **Chair, Resolutns Com Dio Iowa Des Moines IA 2011-; Strategic Plnng Com Dio Iowa Des Moines IA 2010-; R Chr Epis Ch Burlington IA 2009-; Bd Dir of the Epis Corp Dio Iowa Des Moines IA 2009-** B Philadelphia PA 10/18/1952 s William Melchior Horn & Ruth Stackel. BA Ob 1974; PhD Duke 1981; MDiv Seabury-Wstrn Theol Sem. 2007. D 12/16/2006 P 6/16/2007 Bp Alan Scarfe. m 8/1/1975 Raisin Gaiz c 1. Asst S Ptr's Ch Bettendorf IA 2008-2009; Stndg Com Dio Iowa Des Moines IA 1998-2000. fatherjohn@christchurchonline.com

HORN IV, J Robert (SC) 2718 Bees Creek Rd, Ridgeland SC 29936 **Vic Epis Ch Of The H Trin Ridgeland SC 2009-** B Selma AL 10/9/1953 s Joseph Robert Horn & Jean Haden. BA Coll of Charleston 1976; MDiv VTS 1981. D 6/24/1981 Bp Gray Temple P 6/3/1982 Bp C(hristopher) FitzSimons Allison. m 7/9/1977 Martha McGougan Horn c 2. Int Cathd Of S Lk And S Paul Charleston SC 2008-2009; Int Ch Of Our Sav Johns Island SC 2008; Asst S Jas Ch Charleston SC 2004-2008; Ch Of The H Fam Moncks Corner SC 2003-2004; R Trin Epis Ch Pinopolis SC 2000-2004; R S Paul's Ch Foley AL 1995-2000; Asst R Chr Ch Epis Savannah GA 1984-1988; Vic S Mths Epis Ch Summerton SC 1981-1984. Auth, "A Misused Label," *Living Ch.* Bd Dir Victorious Mnstry Through Chr USA; Vmtc-Intl , Pres 1999. Who'S Who In The So And So W. pastorbob@100foldlife.org

HORN, Martha McGougan (SC) 2718 Bees Creek Rd, Ridgeland SC 29936 **D Epis Ch Of The H Trin Ridgeland SC 2010-** B Charleston SC 11/5/1952 d Bruce Allsbrooks McGougan & Lillian Brockington. Assoc Richland Memi Sch of Radiology 1974; MDiv TESM 2010. D 11/4/2010 Bp Mark Joseph Lawrence. m 7/9/1977 J Robert Horn c 2. martha100fl@gmail.com

HORN, Michael John (ND) 1814 E Capitol Ave Apt 346, Bismarck ND 58501 **R S Geo's Epis Ch Bismarck ND 1998-** B Mobridge SD 7/20/1951 s Robert Craig Horn & Dorothy Sutton. BS So Dakota Sch Mines & Tech 1973; MDiv Nash 1977. D 6/30/1977 P 1/18/1978 Bp Walter H Jones. Vic S Barth's Epis Ch Bemidji MN 1991-1998; Dio Minnesota Minneapolis MN 1984-1991; P S Antipas Ch Redby MN 1984-1991; P S Jn-In-The-Wilderness Redlake MN 1984-1991; Vic All SS Epis Ch Greg SD 1977-1983; Dio So Dakota Sioux Falls SD 1977-1983; Ch Of The Incarn Greg SD 1977-1980; S Andr's Ch Greg SD 1977-1980. Land 1987. hornmike@bis-midco.net

HORN, Peter Moya (Ala) 3969 Natchez Dr, Birmingham AL 35243 B Bessemer AL 5/11/1933 s Joseph Robert Horn & Mildred. BA U So 1956; MDiv VTS 1961. D 6/24/1961 P 5/1/1962 Bp Charles C J Carpenter. m 9/13/1956 Patricia Ann Forrester c 4. Assoc R S Steph's Epis Ch Birmingham AL 1988-2004; Assoc R Ch Of The Nativ Epis Huntsville AL 1986-1988; R Trin Epis Ch Bessemer AL 1976-1986; R The Epis Ch of The Redeem Jacksonville FL 1968-1976; Vic Emm Epis Ch Opelika AL 1962-1968; Vic S Matthews In The Pines Seale AL 1962-1968; Cur S Paul's Ch Mobile AL 1961-1962. peterhorn@att.net

HORN, Raisin (Ia) Trinity Church, 320 E College St, Iowa City IA 52240 **Dep to Prov Syn Dio Iowa Des Moines IA 2011-; Asst R Trin Ch Iowa City IA 2008-; Chapl U Of Iowa Chapl Iowa City IA 2007-; GC Dep Dio Iowa Des Moines IA 2003-** B Chicago IL 9/19/1953 d Vincent M Gaiz & Delores. BA Ob 1975; MA Hollins U 1978; MDiv SWTS 2007. D 12/16/2006 P 6/16/2007 Bp Alan Scarfe. m 8/1/1975 John C Horn c 1. rhorn@trinityic.org

HORN, S(tanley) Huston (Los) 334 S Parkwood Ave, Pasadena CA 91107 B Nashville TN 10/7/1930 s Claude Sheetz Horn & Lillian Norton. BA Van 1956; Mercer TS 1966; BD EDS 1969. D 6/28/1969 Bp C Kilmer Myers P 1/20/1970 Bp Robert C Rusack. m 11/30/1957 Polly Lee Carroll c 4. Dio Los Angeles Los Angeles CA 1987-1988; The Caltech Y Pasadena CA 1982-1984; Dir Pstr Mnstrs All SS Ch Pasadena CA 1969-1981. Auth, "The Pioneers," Time/Life Old W Series, 1972. writerev@earthlink.net

HORNADAY, Evelyn W (Ark) 1616 S Spring Street, Little Rock AR 72206 **P All SS Epis Ch Paragould AR 2011-; P Assoc Trin Cathd Little Rock AR 2011-** B Muskogee OK 3/6/1941 d Fredrick Lee Wallace & Evelyn Lucille. BM U of Tulsa 1963; U of Texas 1964; MDiv Epis TS of The SW 2000. D 6/3/2000 P 12/9/2000 Bp Barry Robert Howe. c 1. Int R S Marg's Epis Ch Little Rock AR 2009-2011; Int R All SS Epis Ch Stafford TX 2008-2009; Int R H Cross Epis Ch Sugar Land TX 2007-2008; Int R All SS Epis Ch Russellville AR 2005-2007; Int R S Jn's Epis Ch Helena AR 2003-2005; Vic Ch Of The Ascen Epis Springfield MO 2000-2003. "Death and Dying Done Well," *Reflection on Bioethics and Chr Theol*, U of Texas SW Med Cntr, 2008. Dn Sthrn Dnry, Dio W Missouri 2001. evelyn.hornaday@gmail.com

HORNBECK, Jennifer (Cal) 2325 Union St., San Francisco CA 94123 **The Epis Ch Of S Mary The Vrgn San Francisco CA 2006-** B Berkeley CA 11/4/1976 d Parker Britten Hornbeck & Janel Monique. MDiv Ya Berk; California St U 1998. D 6/2/2001 P 12/1/2001 Bp William Edwin Swing. Asst Trsfg Epis Ch San Mateo CA 2001-2005. jennifer@smvsf.org

HORNBERGER-BROWN, Sharon Lois (Mass) 1d Autumn Dr, Hudson MA 01749 B Pittsburgh PA 6/23/1946 d Ernie Hornberger & Lois Marie. BA Denison U 1967; BD Yale DS 1970; JD Boston Coll 1978. D 6/4/1986 Bp John Bowen Coburn P 9/1/1987 Bp George E Rath. m 5/19/1978 George Dennett Brown. Asst Gr Ch Newton MA 1987-1990; D All SS Ch Chelmsford MA 1986-1987.

HORNE, Lance Cameron (Fla) 3275 Tallavana Trl, Havana FL 32333 B Gulfport Mississippi 4/6/1945 s Roger Bigelow Horne & Helen Leota. BS USNA 1968; MS Untd States Naval Postgraduate Sch 1972; MDiv VTS 2001. D 6/10/2001 P 3/17/2002 Bp Richard Sui On Chang. m 8/19/1989 Elizabeth Turi c 1. S Barth's Ch High Sprg FL 2011; S Paul's Epis Ch Jacksonville FL 2007-2011; S Paul's Epis Ch Quincy FL 2004-2007; D S Geo's Epis Ch Honolulu HI 2001-2004. lhorne@lava.net

HORNE, Martha Johnston (Va) 3737 Seminary Rd, Alexandria VA 22304 B Durham NC 8/14/1948 d Robert Milton Johnston & Martha Josephine. BA Duke 1970; MDiv VTS 1983. D 6/11/1983 P 5/1/1984 Bp Robert Bruce Hall. m 3/30/1969 McDonald Horne c 2. Dn & Pres VTS Alexandria VA 1994-2008; Assoc R Chr Ch Alexandria VA 1985-1986; Asst To Vic S Andr's Ch Burke VA 1983-1985. mmjhorne@gmail.com

HORNER, John Scott (O) 813 West Main St, Elizabeth City NC 27909 B Richmond VA 10/26/1944 s Charlie Edward Horner & Mildred Corr. BS VMI 1967; MDiv Duke 1971; CPE Virginia Commonwealth U 1976. D 6/28/1977 P 10/18/1978 Bp Robert Bruce Hall. m 4/13/1974 Annette Demonde Maddra c 2. R S Jn's Ch Youngstown OH 2000-2009; R S Mary's Epis Ch Ardmore PA 1987-2000; Assoc Chr Ch Reading PA 1981-1987; Asst Ch Of The H Comf Richmond VA 1977-1980. jhorner44@sbcglobal.net

HORNER, Robert Allen (SeFla) 20000 Us 19n, #402, Clearwater FL 33764 **Died 12/19/2009** B Chicago Heights IL 7/12/1923 s Allen Thomas Horner & Helen Orlena. BA U IL 1949; MA U IL 1950. D 5/17/1969 Bp William S Thomas P 12/20/1969 Bp Robert Bracewell Appleyard.

HORNER, Robert William (Tex) 8 Coralvine Ct, The Woodlands TX 77380 **D Trin Epis Ch The Woodlands TX 1987-** B Trenton NJ 6/27/1929 s Lafayette Horner & Edith Swan. BS Rider U 1957; MBA U Pgh 1971; D Formation Prog 1974. D 12/15/1974 Bp James Winchester Montgomery. m 3/5/1951 Jane Lee Milum c 3. D/Asst H Comf Epis Ch Sprg TX 1985-1986; D/Asst Trin Epis Ch The Woodlands TX 1979-1985; D/Asst S Tim's Epis Ch Creve Coeur MO 1978-1979; D/Asst S Simons Ch Arlington Heights IL 1975-1978. deaconbobz@houston.rr.com

HORNER, William McKinley (Miss) 14981 W Verde Ln, Goodyear AZ 85338 B Chicago IL 6/26/1924 s William Mckinley Horner & Margaret Mae. ICS S Jos/Coll Troy St U; Mississippi TS 1997. D 1/4/1997 Bp Alfred Clark Marble Jr. m 2/21/1947 Elvira De Angelis.

HORNING, David J (Mich) 104 Mount Homestake Dr., Leadville CO 80461 **Cler Spnsr - Area HabHum Dio Michigan Detroit MI 1997-** B Detroit MI 7/2/1951 s Walter John Horning & Dorothy Lee. Michigan TS; Wayne; MA CRDS 1989. D 10/18/1979 Bp Henry Irving Mayson P 8/6/1982 Bp H Coleman McGehee Jr. m 10/12/1974 Jane Ann Woodward c 3. Co-Dn Dio Michigan Detroit MI 1996-1999; BEC Dio Michigan Detroit MI 1994-2001; S Andr's Epis Ch Flint MI 1993; S Jas' Epis Ch Dexter MI 1992-2004; Econ Justice Com Dio Michigan Detroit MI 1988; Ch Of The Mssh Detroit MI 1986-1989; Ch Of The Mssh Detroit MI 1982-1984. stjames@ic.net

HORNSBY, James Harmon (Mass) 260 Lake Ave, Fall River MA 02721 **R Emer S Lk's Epis Ch Fall River MA 2003-** B Cambridge MA USA 10/22/1939 s Robert Harmon Hornsby & Gladys Flora. BA Harv 1961; MDiv ETSC 1965; MS Ricssw 1982. D 6/26/1965 Bp Anson Phelps Stokes Jr P 12/26/1965 Bp Francisco Reus-Froylan. m 6/6/1964 Joan Carolyn Rigney c 3. S Lk's Epis Ch Fall River MA 1967-1999. jjhornsby@aol.com

HOROWITZ, Robert Alan (USC) 4 Kingsley Ct, Mauldin SC 29662 **R Epis Ch Of The Redeem Greenvllle SC 2005-** B Queens NY 4/3/1956 s Morton Horowitz & Bernice. BA Oneonta St Coll 1979; MDiv VTS 2001. D 6/10/2001 P 12/9/2001 Bp Stephen Hays Jecko. m 4/4/1982 Stephanie Chrobak c 3. Chr Ch Greenville SC 2002-2005; Asst R S Paul's By-The-Sea Epis Ch Jacksonville Bch FL 2001-2002. bhorowitz@churchoftheredeemer.com

HORST, Diane Elizabeth (NMich) 12769 W Lakeshore Dr, Brimley MI 49715 **D S Jas Ch Of Sault S Marie Sault Ste Marie MI 2006-; COM Dio Nthrn Michigan Marquette MI 2002-** B Detroit MI 4/5/1949 d Duane Horst & Shirley M. I; BS Indiana U 1971. D 5/28/2006 Bp James Arthur Kelsey. c 2. dhorst@jamadots.com

HORTON, Carol J (NJ) 3 Plumstead Ct, Annandale NJ 08801 **R S Thos Ch Alexandria Pittstown NJ 2006-** B Morristown NJ 10/21/1949 d William A Steinberg & Jean Christine. Kean U; BA Westminster Choir Coll of Rider U 1971; MDiv Drew U 1992; CAS GTS 1995. D 6/17/1995 P 12/16/1995 Bp James Michael Mark Dyer. R Susquehanna Country Mnstry New Milford PA 1995-2006. Cmnty of S Jn Bapt, Assoc. dochort@embarqmail.com

HORTON, Cathy Lynne (O) 121 Champion Ln, Chagrin Falls OH 44022 B Columbus OH 2/27/1962 JD Coll Of Law OH SU At Columbus; ThM U Of Kent; BA U MI. Trans from Church Of England 1/22/2004 Bp J Clark Grew II. c 2. Chr Ch Shaker Heights OH 2004-2009.

HORTON, Edward Robert (Cal) 6618 Taylor Dr., Woodridge IL 60517 **Asst S Andr's Ch Downers Grove IL 2001-; Asst S Mary Of The Ang Epis Ch Orlando FL 2000-** B Crawfordsville IN 8/10/1931 s George William Horton & Leah Mae. BA Illinois Coll 1953; MS USN Sch 1960. D 2/25/1969 Bp C Kilmer Myers. m 4/11/1953 Mary Potter c 2. Asst S Jn's Cathd Albuquerque NM 1971-1973; Asst S Barth's Epis Ch Livermore CA 1969-1971. Wycliffe Bible Transltr. ed_horton@wycliffe.org

HORTON, Fred Lane (NC) 2622 Weymoth Rd, Winston Salem NC 27103 B Alexandria VA 2/4/1944 s Fred Lane Horton & Loetta Josephine. BA U NC 1964; BD UTS 1967; PhD Duke 1971; CAS VTS 1985. D 6/11/1985 P 6/1/1986 Bp Frank Harris Vest Jr. m 8/29/1964 Patricia Horton c 2. S Paul's Epis Ch Winston Salem NC 1996-1998; Int S Clem's Epis Ch Clemmons NC 1993-1994; Asst R S Paul's Epis Ch Winston Salem NC 1985-1991. Auth, "The Melchizedek Tradition," Camb Press, 1976. AAR 1970-1990; Amer Schools Of Oriental Resrch 1976; Egypt Exploration Soc 1969; Ord Of S Lk 1987; Phi Beta Kappa 1971; SBL 1968. Prof Emer Wake Forest U 2011; Jn Thos Albritton Prof of Rel Wake Forest U 1991. horton@wfu.edu

HORTON, James Roy (EC) 207 W Franklin St, Williamston NC 27892 **R Ch Of The Adv Williamston NC 1972-** B Baltimore MD 5/9/1942 s Leslie Charles Horton & Marie. BA W&L 1964; MDiv VTS 1967. D 6/20/1967 P 6/6/1968 Bp Harry Lee Doll. m 6/4/1966 Lucy Duncan c 1. Asst Chr Ch New Bern NC 1968-1972; Asst S Thos' Ch Garrison Forest Owings Mills MD 1967-1968. Rec DSA Jaycees 1975. coa@coastalnet.com

HORTON JR, James Taylor (NC) 7413 Hillstone Dr, Benbrook TX 76126 B Fort Worth TX 6/17/1941 s James T Horton & Eleanor. BA Louisiana Coll 1963; MA Van 1966; MDiv Epis TS of The SW 1972; DMin STUSo 1982. D 6/11/1972 P 5/1/1973 Bp John M Allin. m 8/15/1969 Anne Bruce. S Elis Ch Ft Worth TX 2002-2007; S Steph's Epis Ch Erwin NC 1991-1992; Dn S Mary's Cathd Memphis TN 1989-1990; R Emm Epis Ch San Angelo TX 1985-1989; R S Lk's In The Meadow Epis Ch Ft Worth TX 1978-1985; R S Mich's Ch La Marque TX 1975-1978; Cur S Andr's Cathd Jackson MS 1972-1974. frjiminfw@sbcglobal.net

HORTON, Richard Lamar (Nwk) 8730 Beckenham Ln Unit A, Inglewood CA 90305 **Died 8/22/2011** B Augusta GA 9/26/1938 s Albert Jackson Horton & Minnie. BA Texas Coll 1964; MA U of Windsor 1971; D. Min. TS 1991. D 6/7/1970 Bp Richard S M Emrich P 5/1/1971 Bp Archie H Crowley. c 5. pastorhoron2@att.net

HORTON, Sarah Catherine (Vt) 17 Mack Ave, West Lebanon NH 03784 B Bristol UK 2/12/1943 d John William Horton & Olwen Morfydd. BA Oxf 1965; PhD Col 1980. D 6/11/1991 P 12/18/1991 Bp Daniel Lee Swenson. m 6/21/1971 Gunnar Urang c 2. R S Barn Ch Norwich VT 1992-2003; Asst S Mary's In The Mountains Wilmington VT 1991-1992. Auth, "Kindled In The Flame," 1983. sarah.horton@valley.net

HORTUM, John Derek (Va) 1407 N Gaillard St, Alexandria VA 22304 **R The Ch of S Clem Alexandria VA 2000-** B Arlington VA 4/23/1948 s Ernest John Hortum & Eileen. VTS; BA Jn Hopkins U 1971; STB Gregorian U 1975. Rec from Roman Catholic. m 11/30/1985 Leslie Anne Wheeler c 2. Goodwin Hse Incorporated Alexandria VA 1998-2000; Asst to R The Ch of S Clem Alexandria VA 1996-1998. jdhortum@aol.com

HORVATH, Leslie Ferguson (USC) 400 Dupre Dr., Spartanburg SC 29307 B Latta SC 12/12/1960 d William Byron Ferguson & Mary Darling Fenn. BS U of Tennessee 1983; MM U of Kentucky 1988; Cert Dioc Sch For Mnstry 2007. D 1/31/2009 Bp Dorsey Felix Henderson. m 10/22/1983 Gary Horvath c 1. sisterfergie@att.net

HORVATH, Victor John (Vt) 6 South St, Bellows Falls VT 05101 **R Imm Ch Bellows Falls VT 2003-** B Buffalo NY 8/26/1949 s Victor Horvath & Adelaide. U of Bridgeport; BS Manhattan Coll 1971. D 11/19/2002 P 6/7/2003 Bp Thomas C Ely. m 9/23/2000 Arne Andersen. vichorvath@verizon.net

HORWITT, Joan (Ct) Po Box 716, Sandy Hook CT 06482 B Wyncote PA 1/25/1924 d John Oscar Bower & Armorel. Wellesley Coll 1943; BFA Carnegie Mellon U 1946; MDiv Yale DS 1977. D 9/16/1978 P 6/1/1979 Bp Morgan Porteus. c 3. S Jn's Ch Guilford CT 1995-1997; R S Jn's Ch Sandy Hook CT 1982-1989; Cur Chr Ch Ansonia CT 1978-1982.

HOSEA, Beverly Ann (Oly) 1833 13th Ave Apt 304, Seattle WA 98122 **Assoc Emm Epis Ch Mercer Island WA 2008-** B Spokane WA 5/5/1946 d Noel Earl Hosea & Margaret Louise. BA U of Washington 1968; MDiv CDSP 1983. D 6/8/1985 Bp William Edwin Swing P 3/6/1986 Bp Robert Marshall Anderson. c 2. Ch Of Our Sav Monroe WA 2003-2005; S Eliz's Ch Burien WA 2003-2005; The Cmnty Of The Lamb Mercer Island WA 2002-2004; S Matt Ch Tacoma WA 2002; Reg Mssnr Chr Epis Ch Zillah WA 1994-1999; Dio Spokane Spokane WA 1994-1999; Reg Mssnr S Matt's Ch Prosser WA 1994-1999; Chr Ch Duluth MN 1990-1994; Vic S Andr's Ch Le Sueur MN 1990-1994; Dio Minnesota Minneapolis MN 1985-1989; R Trin Epis Ch Pk Rapids MN 1985-1989; S Mk's Ch Houston TX 1985; S Mk's Ch Houston TX 1984-1985. "Var arts," *Dawn Pie*, Cntr for Sprtl Dvlpmt, 2001; Auth, "A People Gathered Around a Mnstry," *Crossroads*, RWF, 1994; "Total Mnstry," *Soundings*, Dio Minnesota, 1990; "Total Mnstry models...in Minnesota," *Crossroads*, RWF, 1989. Curs Sec, Dio Olympia 2007-2009; MN Epis Cler Assn 1985-1994; RWF 1986-1999; Sindicators 1991-1999; Third Ord, Soc of S Fran 1981. bhosea@mac.com

HOSEA, Janice Forney (RG) 7171 Tennyson St NE, Albuquerque NM 87122 **S Chad's Epis Ch Albuquerque NM 2010-; S Jn's Cathd Albuquerque NM 2010-** B Tulsa OK 12/9/1948 d Jene Lysle Forney & Dorothy Rose. BS U of Tulsa 1971; MA S Mary U 1997. D 9/19/2009 P 9/25/2010 Bp William Carl Frey. m 6/25/1983 Bruce James Hosea. hoseajb@flash.net

HOSKINS, Charles L (Ga) 4629 Sylvan Dr, Savannah GA 31405 B 9/14/1931 s Clement Hoskins & Florencia. Mt S Ben Abbey, Trinidad 1961; Lic S Thos U, Rome, Italy 1966; Doctorate Sc.Soc.D 1966. Rec from Roman Catholic 5/1/1970 as Deacon Bp George E Rath. m 4/1/1991 Evalena M Mccound. S Matt's Ch Savannah GA 1975-1996; R Trin Ch Montclair NJ 1970-1975. Auth, "black episcopalians," *SS stepher, Aug, and Matt;150 years of struggle, hardship and success*, chartles l. hoskins, 2005; Auth, "black savannah," *Out of Yamacraw and beyond; discovering black savannah*, Chas l. hoskins, 2002; Auth, "black savannahians," *Yet w a sready beat;biographies of early black savannah*, Chas l. hoskins, 2001; Auth, "black savannahians," *The Trouble They Seen:Profiles in the Life of Jn H. Deveaux1846-1909*, Chas l.hoskins, 1989; Auth, "Black Episcopalians," *Black Episcopalians in Savannah*, Chas L. Hoskins, 1983; Auth, "Afr Amer Epis In Savannah," *Black Episcopalians in Georgia:strife, struggle and salvation*, Chas L. Hoskins, 1980. clh4629@ix.netcom.com

HOSKINS, JoAnn Smith (Fla) 4241 Duval Dr, Jacksonville Beach FL 32250 B Atlanta GA 3/8/1944 AA Florida Cmnty Coll at Jacksonville. D 9/21/2003 Bp Stephen Hays Jecko. m 3/24/1963 Charles Ross Hoskins c 2. D/Dir Of Lay Mnstrs And Newcomers Chr Epis Ch Ponte Vedra Bch FL 1998-2009. johoskins@christepiscopalchurch.org

HOSLER, Carol Smith (Az) PO Box 171, 408 Jamestown Road, Kearny AZ 85237 B Portland OR 7/15/1945 d Harold Fremont Smith & Dorothy Vesta. BA Linfield Coll 1968; MA CRDS 1970. D 8/4/1991 P 2/29/1992 Bp Thomas Kreider Ray. m 12/19/1969 Samuel Odyth Hosler c 2. Dio Arizona Phoenix AZ 1996-2005; Co-Rgnl Mssnr NE Rgnl Par Dio Arizona Phoenix AZ 1994-2005; P/Mnstry Spprt Team Ch Of The Gd Shpd S Ignace MI 1991-1994; Dio Nthrn Michigan Marquette MI 1986-1991; S Jas Ch Burley ID 1976-1986; St Matthews Epis Ch Rupert ID 1976-1986; Chr Ch Delaware City DE 1975-1976; Imm Ch On The Green New Castle DE 1975-1976; S Lk's Ch

Scranton PA 1972-1975; Trin Cathd Phoenix AZ 1970-1972. carol_hosler@msn.com

HOSLER, Samuel Odyth (Az) 168 W Arizona St, Holbrook AZ 86025 B Seligman AZ 9/19/1945 s Odyth Guthrie Hosler & Ada Lucretia. BA U of Arizona 1967; BD Bex 1970. D 6/28/1970 P 6/13/1971 Bp J(ohn) Joseph Meakins Harte. m 12/19/1969 Carol Smith. Reg Mssnr S Paul's Epis Ch Winslow AZ 1995-2006; S Geo's Epis Ch Holbrook AZ 1994-2006; Dio Arizona Phoenix AZ 1994-2005; S Jas Ch Burley ID 1976-1986; St Matthews Epis Ch Rupert ID 1976-1986; Chr Ch Delaware City DE 1975-1976. Associated Parishes; ECom; Land Viii; RWF; Sindicators; Synagogy. carol_hosler@msn.com

HOSTER JR, David William (Tex) 7505 Daugherty St, Austin TX 78757 **Int S Mary's Ch Bellville TX 2010-** B Philadelphia PA 7/22/1947 s David William Hoster & Marilyn. BA Ken 1969; MDiv Yale DS 1973. D 6/11/1973 Bp Scott Field Bailey P 6/1/1974 Bp J Milton Richardson. m 4/8/1973 Terrie Champion c 4. R S Geo's Ch Austin TX 1989-2010; R S Thos Ch Wharton TX 1983-1989; S Steph's Epis Sch Austin TX 1980-1983; Asst Trin Ch Longview TX 1977-1980; Vic H Comf Epis Ch Sprg TX 1974-1977. "Sermons at St. Geo's 2007," Lulu, 2008; "Sermons at St. Geo's 2006," Lulu, 2007; "Continuous Creation," Lulu, 2007. david.w.hoster@gmail.com

HOSTER, Elizabeth M (O) Trinity Episcopal Church, 316 Adams Street, Toledo OH 43604 **COM Dio Ohio Cleveland OH 2009-; Trin Ch Toledo OH 2007-** B Columbus OH 5/26/1965 d George Sheldon Hoster & Nancy Elizabeth. BA Ohio U 1987; MDiv TS 2003. D 9/19/2002 P 6/7/2003 Bp William Michie Klusmeyer. m 11/23/2009 Barbara E Clarke. S Jn's Epis Ch Charleston WV 2003-2007. emhoster@yahoo.com

HOSTETLER, Hugh Steiner (WMich) 313B 15th Ave S, Surfside Bch SC 29575 B Sugarcreek OH 11/13/1922 s Lester Hostetler & Charity. BD UTS 1950; Cert Amer Fndt of Rel & Psych 1957; BA Bethel Coll 2043. D 9/18/1971 P 6/1/1972 Bp Walter C Klein. m 6/7/1952 Harriet Smith. Supply P Trin Ch Three Rivers MI 1999-2001; Supply P S Steph's Epis Ch Plainwell MI 1989-1996; Mem of Exec Coun Dio Wstrn Michigan Kalamazoo MI 1985-1987; R S Paul's Epis Ch Dowagiac MI 1981-1987; Supply P S Paul's Epis Ch Grand Rapids MI 1980; Cn The Cathd Ch Of S Jas So Bend IN 1972-1979. Diplomate Amer Psych Assn; No Amer Angl Soc. hhostetler@sc.rr.com

HOSTETTER, Jane (SeFla) 2303 NE Seaview Dr, Jensen Beach FL 34957 B NJ 3/4/1952 d Frederick G Hostetter & Blanche Belcher. D 12/15/2007 Bp Leopold Frade. janeho@bellsouth.net

HOSTON, Veretta Louise (SanD) 9443 Filago Ct, San Diego CA 92129 B Morgantown WV 5/10/1932 d Clarence Cidney Harris & Isabel. AAS Burlington Cnty Coll 1987; Trenton St Coll 1988; Cntrl Jersey Bible Inst 1992. D 10/31/1998 Bp Joe Morris Doss. c 2. D Gr-S Paul's Ch Mercerville NJ 1998-2005. NAAD 1998. vlhoston1@gmail.com

HOTCHKIS, Gilbert Bruce (Spok) 221 N 35th Ave, Yakima WA 98902 **Died 7/2/2011** B Toronto ON CA 2/15/1918 s Thomas Finlay Hotchkis & Marguerite Mack. BA U Tor 1948; LTh U Tor 1951. Trans from Anglican Church of Canada 9/1/1958 as Priest Bp Hamilton Hyde Kellogg. c 1. AFP 1970.

HOTCHKISS, Thomas S (Tenn) 5501 Franklin Pike, Nashville TN 37220 **R Ch Of The Adv Nashville TN 2001-** B Washington DC 1/22/1960 s George Burton Hotchkiss & Mary Elizabeth. BA Van 1982; MA Fuller TS 1990; MDiv VTS 1993. D 6/22/1993 P 5/14/1994 Bp Alex Dockery Dickson. m 5/10/1986 Marcia Wheat c 2. Cn The Cathd Ch Of The Adv Birmingham AL 1995-2001; S Lk's Epis Ch Birmingham AL 1993-1995; S Lk's Epis Ch Jackson TN 1993-1995; S Jn's Epis Ch Memphis TN 1987-1991. adventrector@comcast.net

HOTRA, Nancy Louise (WMich) 9733 Sterling, Richland MI 49083 **Ecum Relatns Off Dio Wstrn Michigan Kalamazoo MI 2011-** B Bay City MI 3/7/1946 d Robert Pittsley & Doris Mae. BS U MI 1969; Pharmd U MI 1971; MDiv SWTS 1997. D 6/21/1997 P 1/17/1998 Bp Edward Lewis Lee Jr. m 8/26/1972 Nicholas J Hotra c 2. R Ch Of The Resurr Battle Creek MI 1997-2007. nhotra@aol.com

HOTZE, Janice A (Ak) Po Box 91, Haines AK 99827 **Vic S Mich And All Ang Ch Haines AK 1992-** B Berwyn IL 12/16/1948 d Wilfred H Hotze & Elaine E. BA Blackburn Coll 1970; MDiv SWTS 1974; Cert U of Alaska 1994; MA U of Alaska 2004. D 9/15/1980 P 5/1/1981 Bp William Augustus Jones Jr. S Phil's Ch Wrangell AK 1987-1988; Dio Alaska Fairbanks AK 1983-1986; Stephens Coll Coll MO 1981-1982; Calv Ch Columbia MO 1980-1981; Dir Trin Ch S Louis MO 1975-1979; Dir Emm Epis Ch La Grange IL 1975-1976. SocMary 1996. jhotze@wytbear.com

HOUCK III, Ira Chauncey (Be) 107-A Arizona Rd, Fort Huachuca AZ 85613 **P Assoc Gr Ch Pittsburgh PA 2001-; Off Of Bsh For ArmdF New York NY 1992-** B Pittsburgh PA 5/2/1953 s Ira Chauncey Houck & Jeannine. BA U of So Carolina 1975; MDiv VTS 1980; DMin Pittsburgh TS 1991. D 6/14/1980 P 12/1/1980 Bp Robert Bracewell Appleyard. m 5/26/1979 Margaret McKenna c 1. Cn For Mnstrs Cathd Ch Of The Nativ Bethlehem PA 1991-1992; S Ptr's Epis Ch Brentwood Pittsburgh PA 1983-1990; Cur Ch Of The Ascen Pittsburgh PA 1981-1983. Houckmm73@yahoo.com

HOUCK, John Bunn (Chi) 5236 S Cornell Ave, Chicago IL 60615 B Little Rock AR 4/21/1936 s Jesse French Houck & Jane. BS Mississippi St U 1958; TCU 1961; MDiv SWTS 1964; Kirchliche Hochschule Wuppertal DE 1965; MA U Chi 1968; PhD Illinois Inst of Tech 1974. D 6/18/1964 Bp Theodore H McCrea P 2/12/1965 Bp Roderic Norman Coote. m 5/6/1995 Ina Robbins Hamilton c 2. Vic S Geo/S Mths Ch Chicago IL 2004-2011; P-in-c S Geo/S Mths Ch Chicago IL 2001-2004; Asst Ch Of S Paul And The Redeem Chicago IL 1988-1991; Pstr So Cmnty Ch Chicago IL 1975-1976; Campus Min Untd Campus Mnstry Chicago IL 1968-1976; Int Ch Of The Gd Shpd Momence IL 1967-1968; P LocTen Emm Epis Ch La Grange IL 1965-1966. Auth, "Leiblichkeit Und Grenzen In Praktischer Theologie," *Leiblichkeit Als Hauptthema Der Praktische Theologie*, 1997; Auth, "Pstr Psychol -- The Fee For Serv Model & Profsnl Identity, Journ Of Rel And Hlth, Vol. 16, No. 3," *1977*, 1977. AAPC, Fell 1973; APA 1975; Chicago Psychol Assn 1990-1994; Illinois Psychol Assn 1995; Intl Transactional Analysis Assn 1974. johnbhouck@aol.com

HOUCK, Kay Melanie (CNY) 8201 Dexter Pkwy, Baldwinsville NY 13027 B Virginia Beach VA 9/6/1984 d Theodore Scott Houck & Margaret L. BS Florida Sthrn Coll 2006; MDiv Seabury Wstrn 2009. D 8/3/2011 Bp Gladstone Bailey Adams III. kay.houck@gmail.com

HOUGH III, Charles Albert (Dal) 2900 Alemeda St, Fort Worth TX 76108 B Findlay OH 8/1/1954 s Charles Albert Hough & Alice Ruth. BA U of Texas 1976; MDiv Nash 1979. D 6/10/1979 Bp A Donald Davies P 5/31/1980 Bp Robert Elwin Terwilliger. m 8/10/1973 Marilyn Morris c 2. Cn Dio Ft Worth Ft Worth TX 1994-2008; R S Andr's Ch Grand Prairie TX 1989-1993; R Gd Shpd Granbury TX 1982-1989; Ch Of The Redeem Sarasota FL 1981-1982; Ch Of The Epiph Richardson TX 1979-1981. Soc of H Cross 1983. S Geo Awd BSA 1981. cahough@fwepiscopal.org

HOUGH, George Willard (NwPa) 904 Holiday Hills Dr, Hollidaysburg PA 16648 B Williamsport PA 4/1/1938 s Eben Parker Hough & Marian Alice. BA Leh 1960; STB PDS 1963; MA S Fran Coll Loretto PA 1989. D 6/17/1963 Bp Joseph Thomas Heistand P 3/1/1964 Bp William Crittenden. m 8/19/1961 Elizabeth Jean Prater c 5. S Jas Meml Epis Ch Titusville PA 1992-1997; Ch Of The H Cross No E PA 1989-1992; R Gr Ch Waverly NY 1989-1992; R H Trin Epis Ch Hollidaysburg PA 1975-1989; Vic S Mich And All Ang Ch Middletown PA 1973-1975; Asst S Jn's Epis Ch Lancaster PA 1972-1973; Vic Chr Ch Milton PA 1966-1972; St Jas Epis Ch Muncy PA 1966-1972; Vic Ch Of The H Trin Houtzdale PA 1963-1966. Theta Kappa Alpha.

HOUGH, Johnnie Lynne (Miss) 2501 Gulf Ave Apt 2, Gulfport MS 39501 **D S Patricks Epis Ch Long Bch MS 1996-** B Louisville MS 2/28/1938 d John Zachriah Oldham & Lena Pearl. Gulf Coast Jr Coll; Phillips Coll; Wm Carey U; 1985. D 2/18/1996 Bp Alfred Clark Marble Jr. c 2. D S Ptr's By The Sea Gulfport MS 1996-1999. "D As Hosp Chapl," Many Servnt/Cowley, 2004. AEHC. St Steph Awd Naad 2005. lhough@cableone.net

HOUGHTON, Alanson Bigelow (Mass) 43 Blockade Dr, Pawleys Island SC 29585 B Corning NY 8/3/1930 s Amory Houghton & Laura. MBA Harv 1959; GTS 1966; LLD Emerson Coll 1970. D 6/4/1966 P 12/1/1966 Bp Horace W B Donegan. m 6/14/1979 Billie C Fisher. Ch Of The Heav Rest New York NY 1974-1983; R Chr Ch Shaker Heights OH 1969-1974; Cur The Ch Of The Epiph New York NY 1966-1969. Auth, *Be Not Afraid-Words of Hope & Promise*; Auth, *Epis*; Auth, *Living Ch*; Auth, *Partnr in Love-Ingredients For A Deep & Lovely Mar*; Auth, *Priv Choices-Publ Consequences*; Auth, *Readers Dig*.

HOUGHTON, Frederick Lord (EMich) 4138 N Francis Shores Ave, Sanford MI 48657 **S Jn's Epis Ch Midland MI 2003-** B Ionia MI 9/30/1941 s Edwin John Houghton & Katharine. BA Ken 1963; MA MI SU 1967; STB GTS 1969. D 6/11/1969 Bp Charles Ellsworth Bennison Jr P 7/1/1970 Bp The Bishop Of Damaraland. m 9/3/1966 Jean Norma Sawyer c 2. Dn of Formation Stds Dio Estrn Michigan Saginaw MI 1999-2001; Epis Tri Par Cluster Gladwin MI 1996-1999; H Fam Epis Ch Midland MI 1991-1996; Cathd Ch Of S Paul Detroit MI 1989-1991; S Phil And S Steph Epis Ch Detroit MI 1982-1989; R S Paul's Epis Ch Brighton MI 1977-1981; Vic S Ptr's Ch New York NY 1974-1977. LAND.

HOUGHTON, John William (NI) 609 Houghton St., Culver IN 46511 **Assoc Chr Epis Ch Pottstown PA 2008-** B South Bend Indiana 7/24/1953 s Forrest Floyd Houghton & Leta Felicia. AB cl Harv 1975; MA Indiana U 1977; Dplma Ya Berk 1989; M.A.R. s.c.l. Yale DS 1989; MMS U of Notre Dame 1991; PhD U of Notre Dame 1994. D 10/16/2006 Bp Edward Stuart Little II P 5/25/2007 Bp Charles Edward Jenkins III. Co-Auth, "Tolkien, King Alfred and Boethius: Platonist Views of Evil in The Lord of the Rings," *Tolkien Stds*, W Viriginia U, 2005; Auth, "Aug in the Cottage of Lost Play: The Ainulindalë as Asterisk Cosmogony," *Tolkien the Medievalist*, Routledge, 2002; Auth, "St. Bede among the Controversialists: A Survey," *Amer Benedictine Revs*, 1999; Auth, "No Bp, Nò Queen: Queens Regnant and the Ord of Wmn," *Angl and Epis Hist*, 1998; Auth, "The Augustinian Tradition: A Different Voice," *Rel Educ*, 1984. Nelson Burr Prize HSEC 1998; Dorothy A. Given Fllshp ECF 1990; Lansing Hicks Serv Prize Ya Berk 1989. numenor@aya.yale.edu

HOUGHTON, Philip G (WNY) 105 S. Clinton St., Olean NY 14760 B Joliet IL 7/20/1942 s Francis Donald Houghton & Marguerite. BA W Chester St Coll 1965; BD Westminster TS 1971; MDiv Westminster TS 1997. D 11/17/1971 P 5/1/1972 Bp Alexander Doig Stewart. m 4/20/1968 Ann Fairbrother c 3. R S Steph's Ch Olean NY 2008-2011; S Jas Bedford PA 2001-2007; The Ch Of The H Sprt Ocean City MD 2000; R S Paul's Ch Weston WV 1997-2000; R Memi Ch Of The H Nativ Rockledge PA 1989-1997; Asst To R All SS Ch Wynnewood PA 1986-1989; S Geo's Ch Waynesburg PA 1984-1986; S Geo's Epis Ch Sanford ME 1982-1983; Nevil Memi Ch Of S Geo Ardmore PA 1978-1981; S Ptr's Epis Ch Uniontown PA 1977-1978; S Barth's Ch Bristol TN 1975-1977. Auth, "Bk Revs," *Eternity mag*, 1972. Ch Soc 1981; EFAC 1981. puddleglum@aol.com

HOUGHTON, William Clokey (NwT) 27 Painted Canyon Place, The Woodlands TX 77381 B Pasadena CA 5/9/1930 s William Mixer Houghton & Carolyn Clokey. BA U CA, Los Angeles 1955; MDiv CDSP 1958. D 6/2/1958 Bp Francis E I Bloy P 3/15/1959 Bp Lyman Cunningham Ogilby. m 5/14/1966 Candida Baguyos c 2. Int S Barn Epis Ch Houston TX 1999-2009; Dioc Rgstr Dio NW Texas Lubbock TX 1983-1996; Vic All SS Epis Mssn Perryton TX 1980-1996; Vic/R S Ptr's Epis Ch Borger TX 1975-1996; Vic S Paul's Epis Ch Dumas TX 1975-1981. whoughclok@aol.com

HOUGLAND JR, Whayne Miller (NC) 418 W Liberty St, Salisbury NC 28144 **R S Lk's Ch Salisbury NC 2005-** B Owensboro KY 12/29/1962 s Whayne Miller Hougland & Elaine. BA U Of Kentucky 1986; MDiv STUSo 1998. D 6/13/1998 P 12/19/1998 Bp Don Adger Wimberly. m 8/4/1984 Dana L Menges c 2. Cn Evang Chr Ch Cathd Lexington KY 1998-2004. whougland@carolina.rr.com

HOUI-LEE, Samuel Sroun (Oly) 34608 8th Ave Sw, Federal Way WA 98023 B Phnom Penh KH 9/4/1955 s Ock Kim Ly & Lim Vouch. D 6/28/1997 Bp Vincent Waydell Warner P 3/1/1998 Bp Sanford Zangwill Kaye Hampton. m 5/24/1992 Phet Von Gvanith. Dio Olympia Seattle WA 2007-2008; D H Fam of Jesus Epis Ch Tacoma WA 1997-1998.

HOUK, David Stangebye (Dal) 848 Harter Road, Dallas TX 75218 **R S Jn's Epis Ch Dallas TX 2006-** B Ludington MI 5/28/1970 s Charles Frederick Houk & Vicki. BA Wheaton Coll 1992; Wheaton Coll 1998; MDiv TESM 2000. D 6/9/2001 P 12/15/2001 Bp Robert William Duncan. m 9/16/1995 Megan Rebecca Stangebye c 4. Cur/Assoc R Ch Of S Mths Dallas TX 2001-2006; Asst in Mnstry St Andrews Epis Ch Pittsburgh PA 2000-2001. houk@stjohnsepiscopal.org

HOUK, Vickie Lynn (SwVa) PO Box 975, Pulaski VA 24301 **R Chr Epis Ch Pulaski VA 1996-** B Rapid City SD 4/5/1948 d Rodney Lawrence Houk & Lois Ella. BS So Dakota St U 1970; MDiv STUSo 1989. D 7/2/1989 Bp Craig Barry Anderson P 4/19/1990 Bp James Russell Moodey. Int Trin Ch Allnce OH 1995-1996; Int S Paul's Epis Ch Medina OH 1994-1995; Zion Ch Monroeville OH 1993-1994; Cur Gr Epis Ch Sandusky OH 1990-1992; Cur S Michaels In The Hills Toledo OH 1989-1990. vlhouk@comcast.net

HOULE, Michael Anthony (EMich) 4525 Birch Run Rd, Birch Run MI 48415 B Detroit MI 7/6/1935 s Jack Cormier Houle & Thelma Naomi. BA Sacr Heart Sem 1958; MDiv S Jn's Prov Sem 1980; MS Wayne 1980. Rec from Roman Catholic 2/27/1998 as Priest Bp Edwin Max Leidel Jr. m 1/17/1986 Elaine Barbara Detrick. R S Mk's Epis Ch Bridgeport MI 1998-2006.

HOULIK, Michael Andrew (Colo) 2712 Geneva Place, Longmont CO 80503 **R S Mary Magd Ch Boulder CO 1991-** B Wichita KS 4/15/1951 s Anton Frank Houlik & Barbara Landis. BA U of Kansas 1973; MDiv Nash 1978. D 4/25/1978 P 11/1/1978 Bp Edward Clark Turner. m 5/29/1976 Barbara Bailey c 2. Dio Colorado Denver CO 2005-2010; R Ch Of The Gd Samar Gunnison CO 1980-1991; Cur S Jas Ch Wichita KS 1978-1980. mhoulik@gmail.com

HOUPT, Cameron Wheeler (Colo) 10222 W Ida Ave Unit 238, Littleton CO 80127 B Rochester NY 12/31/1943 d Harold F Wheeler & Jean B. BS Syr 1965; MS Mia 1967. D 11/15/2008 Bp Robert John O'Neill. c 3. cammiehoupt@hotmail.com

HOUSE, G(eorge) Markis (NC) 1256 India Hook Rd, Rock Hill SC 29732 B Charleston SC 11/20/1935 s George Washington House & Beulah Ellen Wall. Palmer Charleston SC 1958; Coll of Preachers 1974; BS Charleston Sthrn U 1978; MDiv VTS 1978. D 6/24/1970 P 1/16/1971 Bp Gray Temple. c 2. Curs Secy Dio No Carolina Raleigh NC 1993-1995; R S Andr's Epis Ch Charlotte NC 1988-2000; Curs Secy Dio No Carolina Raleigh NC 1983-1986; Vocational Diac Cmsn Dio No Carolina Raleigh NC 1982-1988; Chr Ch Rocky Mt NC 1978-1988; Dioc Coun Dio No Carolina Raleigh NC 1978-1979; P-in-c Lk Latta S Barn Ch Dillon SC 1971-1975; P-in-c Chr Mullins Ch Of The Adv Marion SC 1970-1975. Who's Who in Colleges of the Untd States Bapt Coll at Charleston, SC 1978; Who's Who in So Carolina: Personalities of the So 1975. markhouse@comporiom.net

HOUSE, Karen Ellen (CFla) PO Box 68, Okahumpka FL 34762 **D Corpus Christi Epis Ch Okahumpka FL 2008-** B Pittsburgh PA 3/4/1950 d Carnot Carlyle Larson & Cleone Ellen. BSEd Ohio U 1972. D 12/13/2008 Bp John Wadsworth Howe. c 2. OSL 2007. khouse34@comcast.net

HOUSER III, Bond (Wyo) 251 Willow Ct, Torrington WY 82240 B Troy OH 7/31/1931 s Bond Houser & Kathryn Louisa. Pr; The Coll of Emm and St. Chad; U Amers; BA Fairfax U 1989; MDiv U Sask 1992. D 2/27/1984 P 5/1/1992 Bp Bob Gordon Jones. m 9/10/1955 Mary Frisbie c 4. Asst S Matt's Epis Cathd Laramie WY 1996-2002; S Barn Epis Ch Saratoga WY 1994-1996; Vic S Jas Ch Rawlins WY 1992-1996; Vic S Mk's Epis Ch Hanna WY 1992-1996.

HOUSER, Lucy Anne Latham (Ore) 11476 SW Riverwoods Rd., Portland OR 97219 **D Gr Memi Portland OR 1995-** B Durham NC 4/28/1939 d Ector Brooks Latham & Grace Evelyn. U of Virginia 1959; BA Whitman Coll 1960; S Geo's Coll Jerusalem IL 1990. D 3/13/1989 Bp Robert Louis Ladehoff. m 9/1/1961 Douglas Guy Houser c 3. Pres - Dioc Ecw Dio Oregon Portland OR 2002-2005; Dioc Coun Dio Oregon Portland OR 1998-2000; Coordntr Dio Oregon Portland OR 1989-2005; D All SS Ch Portland OR 1989-1995. luhou@aol.com

HOUSER III, Richard Truett (Tex) 13131 Fry Rd, Cypress TX 77433 **Dio Texas Houston TX 2011-; S Aid's Ch Cypress TX 2009-** B Corpus Christi TX 6/12/1978 s Richard Truett Houser & Melinda Ann Arnold. BA Texas A&M U 2001; MDiv The U So (Sewanee) 2009. D 6/20/2009 Bp C(harles) Andrew Doyle P 1/12/2010 Bp Rayford Baines High Jr. m 10/28/2006 Patricia Muras. rich_houser@att.net

HOUSTON, Barbara Pearce (EC) 206 North Fairlane Drive, Box 939, Grifton NC 28530 **D S Mary's Ch Kinston NC 1996-** B Louisville KY 8/11/1940 d Edward Clay Pearce & Sue Kathering. Dio Ec Sch For Mnstry; U Of Kentucky Spencerian Coll Murray St Colle. D 8/17/1996 Bp Brice Sidney Sanders. m 12/20/1961 Russell Houston. Ord Julian Of Norwich.

HOUSTON JR, Lawrence Patrick (EC) 2060 Quail Ridge Rd. Apt. F, Greenville NC 27858 B Bellaire OH 8/21/1927 s Lawrence Patrick Houston & Esther Louise. BA Ken 1951; VTS 1973. D 6/24/1960 P 6/24/1961 Bp Lauriston L Scaife. m 8/22/1957 Sandra Smith Tucker. P-in-c Emm Ch Farmville NC 1995-2000; Stndg Com Dio E Carolina Kinston NC 1986-1989; Deaconir Deaconioc Sch For D Dio E Carolina Kinston NC 1985-1987; Excoun Dio E Carolina Kinston NC 1984-1987; Com Dio E Carolina Kinston NC 1981-1985; Com Dio E Carolina Kinston NC 1971-1973; Excoun Dio E Carolina Kinston NC 1968-1975; S Paul's Epis Ch Greenville NC 1965-1992; Asst S Steph's Ch Richmond VA 1961-1965. path@greenvillenc.com

HOVENCAMP, Otis (WNY) 85 Wide Beach Rd, Irving NY 14081 B Bath PA 8/20/1937 s Otis Hovencamp & Lillian Esther. BA Kent St U 1959; MDiv SWTS 1971; DMin Chr TS 1972. D 8/28/1971 P 3/1/1972 Bp John P Craine. m 5/31/1970 Maxine Carrie Van Wagner c 3. Ch Of The Adv Kenmore NY 1999-2001; St Mk Epis Ch No Tonawanda NY 1998-1999; S Pat's Ch Cheektowaga NY 1990-1998; R S Jn's Ch Medina NY 1987-1990; Vic Trin Ch Bryan OH 1977-1987; R All Faith Epis Ch Charlotte Hall MD 1974-1977; Stff Chr Ch Cathd Indianapolis IN 1971-1972. Theta Phi.

HOVERSTOCK, Rolland William (Colo) 1419 Pine St, Boulder CO 80302 **S Jn's Epis Ch Boulder CO 2004-** B Buffalo NY 9/12/1942 s Gerald Musselman Hoverstock & Margueritte. BS U CO 1970; Cert STUSo 1980. D 4/25/1983 P 12/1/1983 Bp William Harvey Wolfrum. m 8/19/1967 Beatrice Black c 3. R Ch Of The Gd Shpd Sioux Falls SD 1987-1991; Asst S Jn's Epis Ch Boulder CO 1983-1987. Ord Of S Jn. rhoverstock@stjohnsboulder.org

HOVEY JR, Frederick Franklin (WNC) 724 Cobblestone Dr, Ormond Beach FL 32174 B Jacksonville FL 10/21/1930 s Frederick Franklin Hovey & Margery. LTh SWTS 1965. D 6/24/1965 Bp James Loughlin Duncan P 12/27/1965 Bp Henry I Louttit. m 6/6/1953 Velva LaVonia Coburn c 2. Int S Jas Epis Ch Ormond Bch FL 2008-2010; Dn Wstrn Deanry Dio Wstrn No Carolina Asheville NC 1973-1978; R Ch Of The Incarn Highlands NC 1972-1978; ExCoun Dio SW Florida Sarasota FL 1970-1972; Chair Dnry Coll Chapl Prog Dio SW Florida Sarasota FL 1969-1972; Asst Ch Of The Redeem Sarasota FL 1968-1972; Vic Gloria Dei Epis Ch Cocoa FL 1965-1968. ffhovey@gmail.com

HOWANSTINE JR, John Edwin (Md) 3090 Broomes Island Road, Port Republic MD 20676 **R Chr Ch Port Republic MD 1985-** B Carlisle PA 10/12/1949 s John Edwin Howanstine & Gloria Louise. BA Florida Presb Coll 1971; MDiv Wstrn TS 1979; Cert SWTS 1980. D 6/14/1980 Bp Quintin Ebenezer Primo Jr P 12/13/1980 Bp James Winchester Montgomery. m 12/30/1977 Catherine Johnson c 2. Assoc R All SS' Epis Ch Chevy Chase MD 1982-1985; Asst to the R S Mk's Ch Evanston IL 1980-1981. Bro Of S Andr. HOWANSTINE@CHESAPEAKE.NET

HOWARD, Anne Sutherland (Los) 950 Dena Way, Santa Barbara CA 93111 **Prchr-in-Res Trin Epis Ch Santa Barbara CA 2006-** B Red Wing MN 12/10/1952 d Carl Everet Sutherland & Jean. BA U CA 1975; MA EDS 1985. D 6/25/1988 P 1/21/1989 Bp Frederick Houk Borsch. m 8/9/1975 Randall Hugh Howard c 1. Assoc R Trin Epis Ch Santa Barbara CA 1998-2006; Mt Calv Retreat Hse Santa Barbara CA 1996-1998; Cn Dio Los Angeles Los Angeles CA 1993-1995; All SS-By-The-Sea Par Santa Barbara CA 1988-1993. Auth, "Claiming the Beatitudes: Nine Stories for a New Generation," Alb, 2009. Core Curric in Preaching Coll of Preachers Washington DC 1999. anne@beatitudessociety.org

HOWARD, Cynthia A (CGC) 2005 Boxwood Ave, Andalusia AL 36421 **R S Mary's Epis Ch Andalusia AL 2011-** B Carthage MO 12/6/1954 d Charles Carter & Gloria. BS Missouri Sthrn St Joplin MO 1976; MA U of Missouri 1978; PhD Cor Ithaca NY 1984; MDiv Epis TS of The SW 2007. D 6/2/2007 P 12/1/2007 Bp Barry Robert Howe. m 12/29/2003 Gerald L Howard c 1. R S Anne's Ch Lees Summit MO 2007-2011. cahoward1229@gmail.com

HOWARD, David Z (SO) 7921 Fairhope Ct, Cincinnati OH 45224 B 9/15/1940 Mstr of Div (M.Div) Degree Pittsburgh TS 1967; Mstr of Educ (M.ED) Degree U Pgh 1968. Trans from Church of the Province of West Africa 12/1/1992 Bp William Grant Black. m 2/20/1971 Albertha Howard c 4. P H Sprt Epis Ch Cincinnati OH 2007-2009; Dio Sthrn Ohio Cincinnati OH 2004-2005; H Sprt Epis Ch Cincinnati OH 1997-2004; Trin Ch Lawrenceburg IN 1995-1996; Dio Sthrn Ohio Cincinnati OH 1992-1994; P Ch Of S Mich And All Ang Cincinnati OH 1991-1993; Asst R/ Mem of Stndg commitee/ Chairman of Com on Educ Dio Liberia 1000 Monrovia 10 Liberia 1981-1989. frhoward9@yahoo.com

HOWARD, Francis Curzon (Ct) 116 Terry's Plain Road, Box 423, Simsbury CT 06070 **Assoc S Andr's Ch Longmeadow MA 2000-; Sum R Trin Sum Chap Kennebunk ME 2000-** B Bedford UK 7/28/1927 s Harry Howard & Eleanor May. Lon; S Aid's TS GB 1957. Trans from Church Of England 9/1/1971 Bp Alexander Doig Stewart. m 9/1/1973 Joyce Russell c 2. R Trin Ch Tariffville CT 1976-1998; Ch Of The Atone Westfield MA 1972-1976. *arts Ch mag*, 2003. Chapl Ord of S Lk 1972-1985. Cn Dio Sokato Nigeria 1986.

HOWARD, Frederick Jordan (LI) 343 Dennis Rd, Honesdale PA 18431 B Houston TX 3/19/1934 s James Aubrey Howard & Mary Almeda. BA U of Texas 1960; BD Epis TS of The SW 1966. D 6/8/1966 Bp J Milton Richardson P 5/31/1967 Bp Scott Field Bailey. c 1. The Ch Of S Lk and S Matt Brooklyn NY 1996-2000; Epis Hlth Serv Bethpage NY 1992-1999; Epis Ch Cntr New York NY 1977-1992; R S Ptr's Epis Ch Amarillo TX 1971-1977; P-in-c S Thos Epis Ch Hereford TX 1968-1971; D-in-c Epis Ch Of The Epiph Burnet Burnet TX 1966-1967; D-In-C Trin Epis Ch Marble Falls TX 1966-1967. ACC; Coc; EPF; Wfs. fhoward34@aol.com

HOWARD III, George Williams (Spr) 1811 Highland Vw, Mount Vernon IL 62864 **Asstg D S Jn's Epis Ch Geff IL 2011-** B Mount Vernon IL 1/7/1935 s George W Howard & Mabel B. BS U IL 1956; JD U IL 1959. D 6/29/2004 Bp Peter Hess Beckwith. m 12/21/1957 Sylvia Lord c 2. Asstg D S Jas Epis Ch McLeansboro IL 2004-2010. gwh@mvn.net

HOWARD, Guy Wesley (Los) 12723 Dilworth St, Norwalk CA 90650 **Died 1/21/2010** B Lawrence KS 1/7/1917 s John Edward Howard & Leona Mae. BA Wichita St U 1947; SWTS 1948. D 12/8/1949 P 6/12/1950 Bp Goodrich R Fenner. CBS; OHC (Assoc) 1995-2001.

HOWARD, Harry Lee (ETenn) 2668 Karenwood Dr, Maryville TN 37804 **S Andr's Ch Maryville TN 2006-** B Dubuque IA 6/2/1945 s Hillard Roscoe Howard & Johanna. BA Tennessee Wesleyan Coll 1967; ThM SMU 1970; MA SMU 1971; PhD U of Tennessee 1980. D 6/18/2005 P 1/21/2006 Bp Charles Glenn VonRosenberg. m 6/24/1966 Nancy Ellen Ketchersid c 1. harry.howard@maryvillecollege.edu

HOWARD, James William (SC) 1170 Watson St, Orangeburg SC 29115 B McClanville SC 1/28/1940 s Leon Mott Howard & Matha Bertha. BA Clatlin Coll 1966. D 9/8/2007 Bp Edward Lloyd Salmon Jr. m 8/31/1963 Barbara Holmes c 4. jwhoward_i@yahoo.com

HOWARD II, Joseph Burton (Tenn) 2458 Center Point Rd, Hendersonville TN 37075 **R S Jos Of Arimathaea Ch Hendersonville TN 2012-; R S Jos Of Arimathaea Ch Hendersonville TN 2012-; P-in-c S Jos Of Arimathaea Ch Hendersonville TN 2010-; Ecum Off Dio Tennessee Nashville TN 2008-; Dio Tennessee Nashville TN 2006-** B Asheville NC 12/22/1980 s Joseph Burton Howard & Mamie Lee Sheila. BA U NC, Asheville 2003; MDiv STUSo 2006. D 6/10/2006 P 12/17/2006 Bp Bertram Nelson Herlong. m 6/3/2006 Anna A Aven c 1. Vic S Fran Ch Nashville TN 2007-2009. Auth, "Emerging Questions," *LivCh*, LivCh Fndt, 2011; Auth, "Reviving the Quadrilateral," *LivCh*, LivCh Fndt, 2009; Co-Auth, "Approaches to Ch, Cmnty and Age: Discussing the Ideas of Stanley Hauerwas," *Aging & Sprtlty*, The Amer Soc on Aging, 2003. jbhoward2@gmail.com

HOWARD, Karin Dreiske (SwVa) 903-A Park Place Drive, Kernersville NC 27284 **S Jn's Ch Roanoke VA 2004-** B Chicago IL 11/8/1937 d John Herman Dreiske & Margaret Louise. Watts Sch of Nrsng 1978; Lic VTS 1990. D 6/2/1990 Bp Peter James Lee P 3/1/1991 Bp A(rthur) Heath Light. m 1/2/1988 William A Lindsay c 6. S Phil's In The Hills Tucson AZ 2000-2001; All SS Epis Ch Atlanta GA 1998-2000; Trin Epis Ch Rocky Mt VA 1993-1998; Asst R S Paul's Epis Ch Lynchburg VA 1990-1993. Comp H Cross. karinhoward@embarqmail.com

HOWARD, Kenneth W(ayne) (WA) 9 Liberty Heights Court, Germantown MD 20874 **Eccl Trial Crt Dio Washington Washington DC 2007-2012; R S Nich Epis Ch Germantown MD 2005-; Founding Vic S Nich Epis Ch Germantown MD 1995-** B Lubbock TX 9/19/1952 s Kenneth Newton Howard & Ann. BS Old Dominion U 1979; MEd Virginia Commonwealth U 1989; MDiv VTS 1993; Vstng Schlr Glastonbury Abbey 2004; Vstng Schlr Camb - Westcott Hse 2005. D 6/5/1993 P 12/12/1993 Bp Frank Harris Vest Jr. m 2/14/1976 Rhee M McWilliams c 3. GC Alt Del (74th Conv) Dio Washington Washington DC 2003-2006; T/F on Human Sxlty Dialogue (Cnvnr) Dio Washington Washington DC 2003-2005; Bp's Rep for Epis-Jewish Dialogue Dio Washington Washington DC 2002-2003; T/F on Mssn Cn Evaltn Dio Washington Washington DC 2002-2003; Bp's Pstr Rep to Chr Ch, Accokeek Dio Washington Washington DC 2001-2002; Dioc Coun (Exec Com) Dio Washington Washington DC 2000-2003; GC Alt Del (73rd Conv) Dio Washington Washington DC 2000-2003; GC Alt Del (72nd Conv) Dio Washington Washington DC 1997-2000; Dioc Coun (Mem) Dio Washington Washington DC 1996-2003; Asst Ch Of The Ascen Gaithersburg MD 1993-1995. Auth, "Paradoxy: Creating Chr Cmnty Beyond Us & Them," Paraclete Press, 2010; Auth, "A New Middle Way: Surviving and Thriving in the Coming Rel Realignment," *ATR*, The Epis Ch, 2010; Auth, "Jewish Chrsnty in the Early Ch," VTS, 1993; Auth, "Power Meetings: Working Effectively in Groups," Ken Howard Assoc, Inc., 1990; Auth, "A Comprehensive Theory of Adult Educ Motivation," *Adult Educ Quarterly*, Sage Pub, 1989; Co-Auth, "Strategic Plnng," *The Bd Effectiveness Trng Series*, Commonwealth of Virginia, 1988; Co-Auth, "Decision Making," *The Bd Effectiveness Trng Series*, Commonwealth of Virginia, 1987; Co-Auth, "Ldrshp," *The Bd Effectiveness Trng Series*, Commonwealth of Virginia, 1987; Co-Auth, "Mgmt Skills," *The Trnr Effectiveness Series*, Commonwealth of Virginia, 1986; Co-Auth, "Presentation Skills," *The Trnr Effectiveness Series*, Commonwealth of Virginia, 1985; Co-Auth, "Design Skills," *The Trnr Effectiveness Series*, Commonwealth of Virginia, 1984; Co-Auth, "Adolescence: Intervention Strategies," Commonwealth of Virginia, 1983. Washington Epis Cler Assn 1993. hon in Ch Hist VTS Alexandria VA 1990. vicofnick@gmail.com

HOWARD, Leonard Rice (Haw) 98-1128 Malualua St, Aiea HI 96701 **D S Andr's Cathd Honolulu HI 1996-** B Detroit MI 2/25/1933 s Wilkie Leonard Howard & Carolyn. BA Albion Coll 1954; MD U MI 1957. D 11/7/1993 Bp Donald Purple Hart. m 6/18/1955 Marilyn Joanne Funk. Ord Of S Lk.

HOWARD, Lois Waser (Lex) 713 Dicksonia Ct, Lexington KY 40517 **D Ch Of The Resurr Jessamine City Nicholasville KY 2008-** B Pottstown PA 11/10/1937 d John Robert Waser & Agnes Jeanette. BS U of Nebraska 1959; MA U MI 1963; MRE PrTS 1968; MRE PrTS 1968; BA Estrn Kentucky U 1987. D 6/26/1999 Bp Don Adger Wimberly. m 2/3/1968 Scott Allen Howard c 2. Min of Chr Formation S Raphael's Ch Lexington KY 2006-2007; Min Of Chr Formation Emm Epis Ch Winchester KY 2003-2005; Min of Chr Formation Presb Ch Of Danville Danville KY 2000-2003; Min of Chr Formation Ch Of The Gd Shpd Lexington KY 1999-2000; Min of Chr Formation Ch Of The Gd Shpd Lexington KY 1994-2000; Min Of Chr Formation Chr Ch Cathd Lexington KY 1988-1994. Writer, "Using Godly Play w Alzheimers," *The Diakonia*, No Amer Assn of Deacons, 2010; Writer, "Using Godly Play w Alzheimers," *The Advoc*, The Epis Dio Lexington, 2009; Writer, "Godly Play w Adults The Advoc," *The Advoc*, The Epis Dio Lexington, 2002. AGO 1986; NAAD 1999. beeperlex@aol.com

HOWARD, Mary Merle (SeFla) 4905 Midtown Ln Apt 2107, Palm Beach Gardens FL 33418 **D Dio SE Florida Miami FL 2003-** B Columbus MS 11/20/1942 BA U GA 1964; MA U GA 1968; Cert Dioc Sch Of Chr Stds 2003. D 7/26/2003 Bp Leopold Frade. c 1. Admin The Epis Ch Of The Gd Shpd Tequesta FL 2001-2004. mimihoward@comcast.net

HOWARD, Noah B (NC) 206 Maryland Ave, Tarboro NC 27886 B Tarboro NC 2/2/1931 s Henry Clay Howard & Ella. Read Under Bp. D 6/12/1976 P 6/18/1977 Bp Thomas Augustus Fraser Jr. m 10/15/1949 Evelyn Ruth Howard. Cluster Mssnr To Yadkin Vlly Cluseter Ch Of The Gd Shpd Cooleemee NC 2001-2004. nbh2231@aol.com

HOWARD, Norman (SwFla) 766 Lake Forest Rd, Clearwater FL 33765 B Fence Houses Durham UK 2/22/1926 s George Henry Howard & Florence Annie. AKC King's Coll, London U 1957; - St. Bon Coll, Warminster, GB 1958; St. Bon Coll,Warminster, GB 1958. Trans from Church Of England 2/1/1969. m 7/28/1959 Sybil Irene Warren. Ch Of The H Cross St Petersburg FL 1995-1997; Int S Cecilia's Ch Tampa FL 1994-1996; Int Vic Ch Of The H Cross St Petersburg FL 1993-1994; Int S Anne Of Gr Epis Ch Seminole FL 1992-1993; Gd Samar Epis Ch Clearwater FL 1975-1992; Trst Bp Gray Inn Dio SW Florida Sarasota FL 1972-1992; Vic S Jn The Div Epis Ch Sun City Cntr FL 1969-1973. nhoward@tampabay.rr.com

✠ HOWARD, Rt Rev Samuel Johnson (Fla) 325 N Market St, Jacksonville FL 32202 **Bp Dio Florida Jacksonville FL 2003-; Bp of Florida Dio Florida Jacksonville FL 2003-** B Lumberton NC 9/8/1951 s Samuel Augustus Howard & Helen. BA Wms 1973; JD Wake Forest U 1976; MDiv VTS 1989. D 6/1/1989 Bp Robert Whitridge Estill P 6/8/1990 Bp Huntington Williams Jr Con 11/1/2003 for Fla. m 6/1/1974 Marie Zaytoun c 2. Trin Educ Fund New York NY 1998-2003; Vic Par of Trin Ch New York NY 1997-2003; R S Jas Ch Charleston SC 1992-1997; Asst R Ch Of The H Comf Charlotte NC 1989-1992. DD U So 2004; DD VTS 2004. MZH2000@AOL.COM

HOWARD, Sylvia Lord (Spr) 1811 Highland Vw, Mount Vernon IL 62864 **D S Jn's Ch Centralia IL 2006-** B Wichita Falls TX 5/17/1936 BS U IL 1958;

MS Sthrn Illinois U 1977. D 6/29/2004 Bp Peter Hess Beckwith. m 12/21/1957 George Williams Howard c 2. D Trin Ch Mt Vernon IL 2004-2006. gwh@mvn.net

HOWARD, Theodore B (Colo) 1419 Pine St., Boulder CO 80302 **Mem, BEC Dio Colorado Denver CO 2010-; Assoc S Jn's Epis Ch Boulder CO 2010-; Mem, Front Range Exec Com Dio Colorado Denver CO 2009-** B Chicago IL 5/25/1942 s John B Howard & Dorothy K. BA Dart 1964; MPA U Pgh 1968; PhD Col 1972; MDiv VTS 2007. D 6/9/2007 P 12/8/2007 Bp Robert John O'Neill. m 6/27/1992 Sallye Sallye Hutman c 5. howardted@msn.com

HOWARD, William A(belard) R(eynolds) (WNY) 16 Oliver Pl, Silver Creek NY 14136 **Died 12/7/2009** B Rochester NY 9/21/1932 s William Abelard Reynolds Howard & Delores Loraine. BA U Roch 1954; STB GTS 1957. D 6/23/1957 P 3/15/1958 Bp Dudley S Stark. warhh32@hotmail.com

HOWARD, William Alexander (Colo) 7168 Burnt Mill Rd, Beulah CO 81023 **Int Vic S Ben Epis Ch La Veta CO 2010-; Int Vic S Thos The Apos Epis Ch Alamosa CO 2010-** B Chattanooga TN 12/13/1939 s William Felix Howard & Alma Blanche. BA Trin U San Antonio TX 1966; MDiv TS 1969; MS U of Tennessee 1979; DMin TS 2008. D 6/10/1969 P 12/10/1969 Bp Harold Cornelius Gosnell. m 12/22/1992 Carla Jackson-Howard c 3. Pstr Ch Of S Ptr The Apos Pueblo CO 2003-2009; Dn - Sangre De Cristo Dio Colorado Denver CO 1993-1998; Int Ch Of S Ptr The Apos Pueblo CO 1993; Parkview Hosp Pueblo CO 1982-2003; Asst P S Andr's Ch La Junta CO 1979-1982; Asst P S Thaddaeus' Epis Ch Chattanooga TN 1976-1979; Vic Epiph Epis Ch Raymondville TX 1969-1971. OHC 1990. veracruz@socolo.net

HOWCOTT, Jeffernell Ophelia Green (Mich) 19320 Santa Rosa Dr, Detroit MI 48221 **D S Jn's Ch Royal Oak MI 2001-** B Dayton OH 8/8/1934 d Samuel Lynch Green & Mary Hatta. BS OH SU 1956; MA U of Detroit 1975; Whitaker TS 1982. D 6/20/1982 Bp H Coleman McGehee Jr. m 5/14/1956 James Fredrick Howcott c 2. Archd Dio Michigan Detroit MI 2001-2008; Asst to Bp for Faith & Wrshp Dio Michigan Detroit MI 1983-1990; Asst All SS Ch Detroit MI 1982-2001. Auth, "Simple Abundance," *Diakoneo*, NAAD, 1999. DOK 2003; Delta Sigma Theta Sorority, Inc. 1953; NAAD 1985; Untd Black Episcopalians 1978; Whitaker TS, Bd Dir 1997-2003. St.Stephens Awd NAAD; Hall of Fame Whitaker TS. revjeffdst@yahoo.com

✠ **HOWE, Rt Rev Barry Robert** (WMo) Po Box 413227, Kansas City MO 64141 B Norristown PA 11/9/1942 s Nathan A Howe & Sarah M. BA Ge 1964; MDiv PDS 1967; DMin STUSo 1989; DD STUSo 2001. D 6/10/1967 P 1/13/1968 Bp Robert Lionne DeWitt Con 3/14/1998 for WMo. m 6/26/1965 Mary Ballard c 2. Bp of W Missouri Dio W Missouri Kansas City MO 1998-2011; Dn St Petersburg Deanry Dio SW Florida Sarasota FL 1988-1994; Dn Cathd Ch Of S Ptr St Petersburg FL 1987-1998; R Chr Ch So Hamilton MA 1983-1987; Par Cmsn Dio Cntrl Florida Orlando FL 1981-1983; R S Richard's Ch Winter Pk FL 1978-1983; Bd Dio Dio Cntrl Florida Orlando FL 1977-1980; Cn Cathd Ch Of S Lk Orlando FL 1973-1978; Assoc S Bon Ch Sarasota FL 1971-1973. DD STUSo Sewanee TN 2001. barryrhowe@gmail.com

HOWE, Gregory Michael (Del) 7 Conway St, Provincetown MA 02657 B New York NY 1/3/1939 s James William Howe & Dorothy Anita. BA Col 1961; STB GTS 1964; Cert S Geo's Coll Jerusalem IL 1980. D 6/6/1964 Bp Horace W B Donegan P 6/5/1965 Bp John Brooke Mosley. m 7/3/1965 Bernice Ann McNulty. COM Dio Delaware Wilmington DE 1986-1990; Stndg Com Dio Delaware Wilmington DE 1981-1985; Dep GC Dio Delaware Wilmington DE 1973-1997; Stndg Com Dio Delaware Wilmington DE 1972-1974; Off Liturg Cmsn Dio Delaware Wilmington DE 1971-1973; Dioc Coun Dio Delaware Wilmington DE 1969-1974; Chr Ch Dover DE 1964-1998. Auth, "Expansive Lang in Cyberspace," *Gleanings*, 2001; Auth, "Death, Appearance, and Reality," *PB for the 21st Century*, 1996; Auth, *Delaware Lawyer*; Auth, *H Land.* greyfriar3636@yahoo.com

HOWE, Heath (NH) 1240 Hinman Ave, Evanston IL 60202 **Yth Dir Ch Of The H Comf Kenilworth IL 2010-** B Helena AK 11/30/1968 d John Hornor Howe & Claudia. Educ Boston Coll 1991; M Div CDSP 2000. D 6/17/2000 P 1/4/2001 Bp William Dailey Persell. m 10/6/2007 David P Jones c 3. S Paul's Ch Concord NH 2004-2005; Asst Trin Memi Ch Binghamton NY 2000-2003. heath.howe@hotmail.com

HOWE, Jeffrey Newman (Lex) 201 Price Rd Apt 216, Lexington KY 40511 **D S Mk's Ch Hazard KY 2010-** B Naysville KY 9/7/1960 s William Frances Howe & Betty Ray Walton. BA Morehead St U 1982; MA Estrn Kentucky St U 1983. D 8/22/2009 Bp Stacy F Sauls. jnhowe@aol.com

✠ **HOWE, Rt Rev John Wadsworth** (CFla) 1017 E Robinson St, Orlando FL 32801 **Bp of Cntrl Florida Dio Cntrl Florida Orlando FL 1989-** B Chicago IL 11/4/1942 s John Wadsworth Howe & Shirley Anita. BA U of Connecticut 1964; MDiv Yale DS 1967; DD Ya 1989; DD STUSo 1990; DD Nash 1991; PhD GTF 2011. D 6/6/1967 Bp Charles F Hall P 6/22/1968 Bp John Henry Esquirol Con 4/15/1989 for CFla. m 9/1/1962 Karen Elvgren c 3. R Truro Epis Ch Fairfax VA 1976-1989; Assoc S Steph's Ch Sewickley PA 1972-1976. Auth, *Our Angl Heritage*; Auth, *Sex: Should We Change the Rules?*; Auth, *Which Way? A Guide for New Ch*; Auth, *Who Swallows Jonah Today?*. Acts 29 Mnstrs 1977; Fllshp of Witness; NOEL, Chairman of th 1989-1993; NOEL, Pres 1985-1989; Sharing of Ministers Abroad 1978. bcf3@aol.com

HOWE, Karen Elvgren (CFla) 5583 Jessamine Ln, Orlando FL 32839 **COM Dio Cntrl Florida Orlando FL 2009-** B Evanston IL 4/27/1938 d Gillette Alexander Elvgren & Janet Cecelia. BA Ohio Wesl 1961; MA U of Connecticut 1964. D 12/18/2004 Bp John Wadsworth Howe. m 9/1/1962 John Wadsworth Howe c 3. D S Mary Of The Ang Epis Ch Orlando FL 2005-2010. *Which Way? A Guide For New Christians*, Morehouse-Barlow, 1973. karenhowe839@aol.com

HOWE JR, Ralph Finch (La) 8965 Bayside Ave, Baton Rouge LA 70806 **Epis HS Baton Rouge LA 2004-** B Baton Rouge LA 5/30/1956 s Ralph Finch Howe & Anne. BA U So 1978; MDiv GTS 1983. D 6/9/1983 Bp James Barrow Brown P 5/24/1984 Bp Robert Campbell Witcher Sr. m 8/14/1981 Suzette Fourrier c 4. Trin Epis Ch Baton Rouge LA 1991-2004; R Trin Ch Crowley LA 1986-1991; Cur S Jas Epis Ch Alexandria LA 1984-1986; D Trin Ch New Orleans LA 1983-1984. ralphhoweehsbr@gmail.com

HOWE, Raymond Jordan (Be) 833 Gillinder Place, Cary NC 27519 B Boston MA 7/28/1939 s Norman Jefferson Howe & Rosaleen Jordan. BA Bates Coll 1961; MDiv VTS 1965; DMin VTS 1987. D 6/26/1965 Bp Anson Phelps Stokes Jr P 6/4/1966 Bp John Melville Burgess. m 8/13/1966 Beverly Ann Nugent c 2. R S Phil's Ch Easthampton MA 2000-2009; R S Ptr's Epis Ch Tunkhannock PA 1978-2000; R Ch Of Our Sav Arlington MA 1967-1978; Cur Chr Ch Quincy MA 1965-1967. Felowship of Way of The Cross (Vice Superior 2007-2009) 2002. rayhowe25@msn.com

HOWE, Timothy John (Tenn) 8534 Forest St, Annandale VA 22003 B Washington DC 8/16/1960 s Joseph Howe & Alice. BA W&M 1983; MDiv TESM 1991. D 12/1/1990 Bp William L Stevens P 10/23/1991 Bp Charles Farmer Duvall. m 1/12/1985 Kim Alyson Moody c 4. Ch Of Our Sav Gallatin TN 2003-2005; R Gr Epis Ch Florence KY 1999-2003; Assoc R S Jas Ch Fairhope AL 1997-1999; Cur S Jas Ch Fairhope AL 1991-1995. fathertim2@cox.net

HOWE, Wendy Salisbury (ECR) 203 Lighthouse Ave, Pacific Grove CA 93950 **COM Dio El Camino Real Monterey CA 2010-; COM Dio El Camino Real Monterey CA 2003-** B Phoenix AZ 9/18/1944 d Grant Angus Salisbury & Phyllis Patrick. Cert Allnce Française 1965; BA MI SU 1967; MDiv CDSP 1997. D 5/18/1997 P 11/20/1997 Bp Richard Lester Shimpfky. m 2/1/1969 Kevin Howe c 4. Int S Geo's Ch Salinas CA 2010-2011; Int Epis Ch Of The Gd Shpd Salinas CA 2009; Int S Lk's Ch Hollister CA 2008-2011; Chapl Epis Sr Communities Walnut Creek CA 2007-2009; Bd, El Camino Cler Orgnztn Dio El Camino Real Monterey CA 2005-2008; COM Dio El Camino Real Monterey CA 2003-2007; Chapl All SS' Epis Day Sch Carmel CA 2001-2007; Asst S Dunst's Epis Ch Carmel Vlly CA 1997-2000. wshowe@comcast.net

HOWELL, Charles Henry (NY) 1446 Colorado Ave Se, Grand Rapids MI 49507 **R Chr Ch New Brighton Staten Island NY 2006-; Cmsn Mnstry Dio Wstrn Michigan Kalamazoo MI 2000-** B La Grange IL 1/20/1962 s Joseph Andrew Howell & Georgia Lee. BA U Chi 1984; MDiv SWTS 1995. D 6/14/1995 P 12/13/1995 Bp Edward Lewis Lee Jr. m 10/1/1988 Elizabeth H Amatruda c 1. Gr Ch Grand Rapids MI 1997-2006; Asst R Gr Ch Grand Rapids MI 1995-1996. Whipple Schlr SWTS Evanston IL 1995; Anderson Schlr SWTS Evanston IL 1994. ehowell96@gmail.com

HOWELL, David Silva (NCal) Po Box 52008, Toa Baja PR 00950 B Sacramento CA 5/2/1958 s Joseph Charles Howell & Gilda Jacqueline. AA Amer River Coll 1978; BS Sacramento St U 1980; Cert. in Mgmt Sonoma St U 1984; CDSP 1993; MDiv TESM 1993. D 6/10/1993 Bp Jerry Alban Lamb P 12/20/1993 Bp David Charles Bowman. m 10/23/1982 Linda Gail Hollingshead c 1. Cathd Of St. Jn The Bapt San Juan PR 1995; Cur H Apos Epis Ch Tonawanda NY 1993-1995. EUC 2003. sac76@live.com

HOWELL, Edward Allen (NCal) 1953 Terry Rd, Santa Rosa CA 95403 **P-in-c Ch Of The Gd Shpd Cloverdale CA 2008-** B Brookings SD 7/26/1938 s Edward Tibertius Howell & Wilda Yvonne. BA U of Oklahoma 1965; MS Bos 1971; MDiv SWTS 1990. D 3/2/1981 P 5/8/1982 Bp Walter H Jones. m 12/28/1963 Terry J Allen c 4. P-in-c Ch Of The Ascen Vallejo CA 2004-2007; Int Ch Of The Incarn Santa Rosa CA 2001-2003; Assoc S Patricks Ch Kenwood CA 2000-2007; Chair Cong Dvlpmt Com Dio Chicago Chicago IL 1996-2000; R S Edw The Mtyr and Chr Epis Ch Joliet IL 1991-2000; Dioc Coun Dio Chicago Chicago IL 1991-1994; Vic S Andr's and Pentecostal Epis Ch Evanston IL 1988-1991; R S Thos Epis Ch Sturgis SD 1983-1987; Vic Ch Of The H Apos Sioux Falls SD 1981-1983; Devlpmt Off Dio So Dakota Sioux Falls SD 1981-1983; Asst Emm Epis Par Rapid City SD 1981-1982. Bro of S Andr, 1976-2000; Chapl Chicago Assembly 1990-1997. edhowell@isonic.net

HOWELL, Joseph Andrew (WMich) 148 Sligh Blvd Ne, Grand Rapids MI 49505 B Scottsville KY 5/10/1929 s Ralph Bunyon Howell & Elizabeth Adeline. BA DePaul U 1951; BD SWTS 1954. D 5/24/1954 Bp Edwin J Randall P 11/30/1954 Bp Dudley B McNeil. m 4/16/1982 Jeanne M Resseguie c 3. Assoc Gr Ch Grand Rapids MI 1997-1999; P-in-c S Jas Epis Mssn Beaver Island MI 1994-1999; BEC Dio Wstrn Michigan Kalamazoo MI 1993-1999; Pstr Assoc Gr Ch Holland MI 1993-1994; R S Mk's Ch Grand Rapids MI

1971-1993; BEC Dio Chicago Chicago IL 1963-1971; R S Aug's Epis Ch Wilmette IL 1962-1971; R All SS Ch Wstrn Sprg IL 1956-1962. DD SWTS, Evanston, IL 1980. jhowell2241@sbcglobal.net

HOWELL, Laura (Be) 44 E Market St, Bethlehem PA 18018 **Trin Ch Bethlehem PA 2001-** B Johnson City NY 6/4/1951 BA SUNY 1972; MA SUNY 1975; CPE Lehigh Vlly Hosp 1993; Cert Oasis Mnstrs 2000. Rec from The Orthodox Church in America 5/6/2001 Bp Paul Victor Marshall. m 8/3/1996 David Howell. spirit@spiritcare.org

HOWELL, Margery E (SVa) 3316 Hyde Cir, Norfolk VA 23513 **D S Chris's Epis Ch Portsmouth VA 2009-** B Pulaski VA 8/30/1949 d Asher Atkins Howell & Frances. D Formation Prog; BS Oklahoma St U 1972. D 6/9/2007 Bp John Clark Buchanan. D S Fran Ch Virginia Bch VA 2007-2009. mehowell@cox.net

HOWELL, Miguelina (Nwk) 451 Van Houten St, Paterson NJ 07501 **Ch Of The Epiph Orange NJ 2010-** B Santo Domingo 2/14/1976 D 9/7/2001 Bp Julio Cesar Holguin-Khoury P 9/13/2002 Bp William Jones Skilton. Epis Ch Cntr New York NY 2008-2009; Dio The Dominican Republic (Iglesia Epis Dominicana) Santo Domingo DO 2003-2008. miguelina_espinal@yahoo.es

HOWELL, Peggy Ann (Mass) Po Box 134, North Billerica MA 01862 **R S Anne's Ch No Billerica MA 1996-** B Hartford CT 4/29/1947 d Salvino Sylvio Yetz & Lora. BA U MI 1969; MDiv Andover Newton TS 1991. D 8/15/1992 P 4/3/1993 Bp Douglas Edwin Theuner. m 11/23/1968 John P Howell c 2. Assoc R S Mart's Ch Providence RI 1992-1996. peggyhowell05@yahoo.com

HOWELL, Robert Lee (Chi) 8400 Vamo Rd Unit 463, Sarasota FL 34231 B Linton IN 7/4/1928 s Willard Lynk Howell & Chloe Margaret. BA MI SU 1950; MDiv VTS 1958; LHD S Aug Coll 1979. D 6/13/1958 Bp Frederick D Goodwin P 6/7/1959 Bp Robert Fisher Gibson Jr. c 2. Adj Cler S Bon Ch Sarasota FL 1992-1999; Pstr / Chair - Com Dio Chicago Chicago IL 1976-1986; R S Chrys's Ch Chicago IL 1967-1990; Stndg Com Dio Wstrn Massachusetts Springfield MA 1966-1967; R Ch Of The Gd Shpd W Springfield MA 1963-1967; Asst S Paul's Epis Ch Alexandria VA 1961-1963. Auth, "Fish For My People"; Auth, "The Fish: A Mnstry Of Love"; Auth, "Lost Mtn Days". Dhl St.Aug Coll 1979.

HOWELL, Robert MacArthur (SO) 69081 Mount Herman Rd, Cambridge OH 43725 **D S Jas Epis Ch Zanesville OH 2007-** B Sumter SC 4/4/1940 s Alfred Wayne Howell & Mildred. DDS Med Coll of Virginia 1965; MS Indiana U 1967; BS U of Nebraska 1990; Dioc Trng Prog 2004. D 12/10/2005 Bp William Michie Klusmeyer. m 11/7/1991 Joan Carol Gibson c 2. Coun of Deacons Dio Sthrn Ohio Cincinnati OH 2010-2011. NAAD 2006; OSL 2008. rmhowell@columbus.rr.com

HOWELL, S(ydney) Caitlin (Va) 495 Melrose Dr, Monticello FL 32344 B Blakely GA 6/25/1941 d Sidney Wilton Howell & Jane Oretha. BS Brenau U 1977; MDiv EDS 1984. D 6/23/1984 Bp Peter James Lee P 3/1/1985 Bp Edward Cole Chalfant. c 2. S Fran Ch Macon GA 2008-2009; R S Paul's Epis Ch Miller's Tavern VA 2002-2006; Gr & H Trin Epis Ch Richmond VA 2001-2002; Ch Of The Gd Shpd Rangeley ME 2001; Downeast Epis Cluster Deer Isle ME 1985-1986; Pstr care Calv Epis Ch Bridgeport CT 1984-1985; Asst to R S Paul's Epis Ch Willimantic CT 1984. sydneycate@yahoo.com

HOWELL, Terry Robert (At) 2135 Zelda Dr Ne, Atlanta GA 30345 B Warner Robins GA 2/12/1961 s Garneff Howell & Linda. ABS U GA 1983; JD U GA 1986. D 8/6/2006 Bp J(ohn) Neil Alexander. m 8/6/1983 Paige Sugden c 2. thowell@fieldshowell.com

HOWELL-BURKE, Undine Jean (Neb) No address on file. B New Orleans LA 4/6/1947 d Roy Hilland Howell & Yvonne Ursula. BA OH SU 1970; MA U of Massachusetts 1972; MDiv CDSP 1976; MD U of Nebraska 1985. P 9/1/1978 Bp C Kilmer Myers. m 6/28/1975 James T Howell-Burke c 2. Ch Of The H Trin Lincoln NE 1992-1993; Ch Of The H Trin Richmond CA 1978-1979.

HOWELLS, Donald Arthur (Be) 1936 Chestnut Hill Road, Mohnton PA 19540 B Robertsdale PA 11/30/1934 s Arthur Howells & Florean. Diac Traning Prog 1970. D 12/19/1970 Bp Frederick J Warnecke. m 2/14/1959 Florence Patricia Gring c 4. Assoc S Gabr's Ch Douglassville PA 1971-2006; Asst S Mary's Epis Ch Reading PA 1971-1973.

HOWLETT, Gail Edward (U) 48 W Broadway Apt 1001-N, Salt Lake City UT 84101 B Terre Haute IN 8/19/1927 s Berton Arthur Howlett & Alice Blackney. BA Indiana St U 1948; STB GTS 1951. D 6/4/1951 P 1/5/1952 Bp Richard Ainslie Kirchhoffer. m 9/3/1956 Phyllis Mira Morris c 4. Angl Consult Dio Utah Salt Lake City UT 1990-1992; Vic S Ptr's Ch Clearfield UT 1979-1990; Chapl Cathd Ch Of S Mk Salt Lake City UT 1967-1979; Chapl Trin Epis Ch Pocatello ID 1959-1967; Vic S Thos Ch Las Vegas NV 1953-1959; Gnrl Mssnr Dio Nevada Las Vegas NV 1953-1954; Vic S Jn's Epis Ch Crawfordsville IN 1953-1954; Cur S Steph's Ch Terre Haute IN 1952-1953. ESMHE, Recovered A 1959-1979; NECAD, Vice Preside 1989-1991; RACA 1986-1992. fredhow@msn.com

HOWLETT, Louise (Del) 350 Noxontown Rd, Middletown DE 19709 B Washington DC 7/16/1961 d William Crossman Howlett & Virginia Ford. BA Pr 1983; MDiv Ya Berk 1988. D 4/25/1990 Bp Arthur Edward Walmsley P 12/5/1990 Bp Cabell Tennis. m 6/15/1990 Gordon Lindsay Brown. Asst St Annes Epis Ch Middletown DE 2005-2009; Chapl S Anne's Epis Sch Middletown DE 2002-2011; Asst St Annes Epis Ch Middletown DE 2002-2003; S Andrews Sch Of Delaware Inc Middletown DE 1990-2002; Assoc Chapl S Andr's Sch Chap Middletown DE 1988-2002. lhowlett61@gmail.com

HOWSER, Carol Louise Jordan (Ore) 192 Harrison St, Ashland OR 97520 B Burns OR 7/24/1939 d Daniel Carrol Jordan & Emma Eva. Cntr for Diac Mnstry; BD U of Oregon 1961. D 1/18/1996 Bp Robert Louis Ladehoff.

HOWZE, Lynn Corpening (CFla) 215 West Park, Lakeland FL 33803 **Asst All SS Epis Ch Lakeland FL 2002-** B Asheville NC 4/11/1946 d Jessie Eugene Corpening & Vera Bush. LTh VTS 1978; BA Eckerd Coll 1989; MDiv VTS 1989. D 6/3/1978 Bp John Alfred Baden P 6/1/1979 Bp Robert Bruce Hall. Dio Cntrl Florida Orlando FL 1997-1999; S Jn's Epis Ch Charleston WV 1981-1982; Ch Of The H Comf Charlotte NC 1978-1980. LHOWZE@TAMPABAY.RR.COM

HOY, Lois (Cal) 36 Dos Posos, Orinda CA 94563 B Seattle WA 11/27/1935 d Gale Edward Wilson & Lois. Stan 1955; BS U of Washington 1957; CDSP 1976. D 6/26/1976 Bp C Kilmer Myers P 6/24/1977 Bp CE Crowther. c 2. R S Giles Ch Moraga CA 1980-1999; P-in-c S Mich And All Ang Concord CA 1979-1980; Assoc S Paul's Ch Oakland CA 1978-1979; Asst S Andr's Ch Saratoga CA 1976-1977; Ch Of The Epiph Seattle WA 1970-1971; S Mk's Cathd Seattle WA 1962-1970. Auth, "Pastoring Wmn in Crises"; Auth, "The Forgotten Faithful"; Auth, "Understanding Islam"; Auth, "Truth," *Justice & Peace*. revdmother@aol.com

HOY, Mary Ann Collins (Me) 6 Old Mast Landing Rd, Freeport ME 04032 B Clifton Forge VA 8/24/1940 d Edward James Collins & Helen Kathryn. BS Syr 1962; MDiv Bangor TS 1999. D 5/22/1999 P 3/25/2000 Bp Chilton Abbie Richardson Knudsen. m 8/9/1969 Robert Hoy c 2. S Andr's Ch Newcastle ME 2001-2010; Dio Maine Portland ME 1999-2001. mahoy@suscom-maine.net

HOYT, Calvin Van Kirk (CPa) 1418 Walnut St, Camp Hill PA 17011 **Hon Cn Cathd Ch Of S Steph Harrisburg PA 1985-** B Reading PA 9/25/1938 s Ralph Charles Hoyt & Josephine. BA Albright Coll 1961; BD STUSo 1964. D 6/20/1964 P 3/27/1965 Bp Frederick J Warnecke. m 12/22/1956 Judith Lorraine Hoyt. R Mt Calv Camp Hill PA 1970-2009; R Chr Ch Susquehanna PA 1964-1970; R S Mk's New Milford PA 1964-1970. mtcp01@telocity.com

HOYT, Timothy Lynn (WNC) Po Box 1138, Saluda NC 28773 B Dobbs Ferry NY 9/12/1942 s Richard Andrews Hoyt & Mary Elizabeth. BA Hanover Coll 1964; MD EDS 1969. D 6/14/1969 P 12/20/1969 Bp Dudley S Stark. Mssnr for Latino Mnstry Dio Wstrn No Carolina Asheville NC 1994-2007; Vic H Cross Epis Ch Portland OR 1988-2007; Mssnr for Latino Mnstry Dio Oregon Portland OR 1980-1994; R S Paul's Ch Holley NY 1974-1980. thoyt@charter.net

HROSTOWSKI, Susan (Miss) No address on file. B 4/19/1958 d Michael Martin Hrostowski & Mary Edith. Mississippi U For Wmn 1976; Jefferson Davis Jr Coll 1977; BA U of Sthrn Mississippi 1979; MDiv VTS 1987. D 5/27/1987 P 5/1/1988 Bp Duncan Montgomery Gray Jr. Assoc R H Trin Epis Ch Fayetteville NC 1989-1990; Cur S Paul's Epis Ch Meridian MS 1987-1989. Golden Rule Awd Outstanding Vol Serv Jc Penney.

HSIEH, Nathaniel Wei-Chung (Eur) 44 Rue Docteur Robert, Chatillon Sur Seine 21400 France B 7/25/1940 s Wen-Hwa Hsieh & Yen-Yu. BTh Chung Tai Theol Coll Tw 1968; Birmingham Bible Inst Gb 1977; S Jn Coll Nottingham Gb 1978. P 9/1/1994 Bp Jeffery William Rowthorn. m 7/22/1968 Su-Yen Wu. Mem of Coun Advice Convoc of Amer Ch in Europe Paris FR 1998-2003; Cn The Amer Cathd of the H Trin Paris 75008 FR 1997-2005. Auth, "Film Voice Of Hope For Question Of Chinese Refugees In Paris"; Auth, "Cassettes Daily Devotions In Mandarin". nhsieh@orange.fr

HU, Kuo-hua (Tai) Chieh Shou Road 5, Kangshan 82018 Taiwan B Anhwei CN 1/5/1934 s Chi-ching Hu & Ting Yu. Tainan Theol Coll Tw 1969. D 6/29/1968 P 6/1/1970 Bp James Chang L Wong. m 3/15/1959 Yuen Mei Huang.

HUB, Michael George (SC) Saint Matthew'S Parish, Saint Matthews SC 29135 **R S Matt's Ch (Ft Motte) S Matthews SC 2003-** B Washington DC 11/8/1949 BS USAF Acad 1973; MA Command and Gnrl Stff Coll 1986; MDiv TESM 2003. D 6/7/2003 P 12/6/2003 Bp Edward Lloyd Salmon Jr. m 6/7/1973 Callie Ann Phillips c 2. stmatthew.parish@earthlink.net

HUBBARD, Austin Flint (ETenn) 2674 Winkler Ave Apt 526, Fort Myers FL 33901 **Died 10/17/2011** B Norwich CT 8/12/1920 s James Lanman Hubbard & Louise Eliot. U of Connecticut 1940; BS USCG Acad New London CT 1943; MS MIT 1951; U of San Francisco 1965; MDiv Epis TS of The SW 1973; DMin Eden TS 1976. D 6/19/1966 Bp James Albert Pike P 6/1/1973 Bp J Milton Richardson. Ecd; Epis Conf Of The Deaf Of The Epis Ch In The USA. Congratulations On Retiring Pres Geo W Bush 1990.

HUBBARD, Carol Murphy (WNC) 260 Kanuga Chapel Dr, Hendersonville NC 28739 **Chairman of Cmsn on Mnstrs Dio Wstrn No Carolina Asheville NC 2011-; Assoc Trin Epis Ch Asheville NC 2005-** B Ann Arbor MI 8/26/1951 d Ralph A. Murphy & Mary Atkins. BA Smith 1973; MDiv Duke DS 1977; STM GTS 2001. D 6/16/2001 Bp Dorsey Felix Henderson P 3/3/2002 Bp Catherine Scimeca Roskam. m 5/27/1978 Stanley B Hubbard c 2. P-in-c

Chr Epis Ch Sparkill NY 2003-2004; Asst The Ch Of The Epiph New York NY 2001-2003. carolhubbard@bellsouth.net

HUBBARD JR, C(harles) Clark (Ga) 227 McDuffie Drive, Richmond Hill GA 31324 **R S Eliz's Epis Ch Richmond Hill GA 2005-** B Montgomery AL 2/12/1952 s Charles Clark Hubbard & Henrietta Hill. BA Jn Hopkins U 1974; MS Auburn U Montgomery 1984; MDiv TESM 2001; DMin TESM 2011. D 12/9/2000 P 6/24/2001 Bp Keith Lynn Ackerman. m 11/6/1992 Emily Irene Cater c 5. Auth, "Integrating the Chrsmtc Experience into Par Wrshp and Mnstry," *DMin Thesis*, self, 2011. hubcc@aol.com

HUBBARD, Colenzo James (WTenn) 604 Saint Paul Ave, Memphis TN 38126 **Emm Ch Memphis TN 2011-; Emm Epis Cntr Memphis TN 1998-** B Brighton AL 2/22/1955 s Dudley Daniel Hubbard & Cynthia Ocia. BS U of Alabama 1977. D 9/30/1986 Bp Robert Oran Miller P 10/1/1987 Bp Furman Stough. m 11/3/2007 LaVerne K Comerie-Hubbard c 2. Ch Of The Redeem Memphis TN 2004-2010; S Paul's Ch Memphis TN 2004-2005; Dio W Tennessee Memphis TN 1989-1997; Chr Ch Fairfield AL 1988-1989. Cook Halle Cmnty Ldrshp Awd Carnival Memphis; Cmncatn Ldrshp Awd Toastmaster Intl . colenzohubbard@bellsouth.net

HUBBARD, Cynthia Plumb (Mass) 45 White Trellis, Plymouth MA 02360 **Cn for Transition and Deploy Dio Massachusetts Boston MA 2006-** B Springfield MA 2/18/1951 d David S Plumb & Faith. BA Smith 1973; EDS 1976; STM McGill U 1978. D 7/30/1977 Bp William Augustus Jones Jr P 2/3/1979 Bp Alexander Doig Stewart. m 5/15/1976 Theodore L Hubbard c 2. Int Ascen Memi Ch Ipswich MA 2004-2006; Int Par Of The Epiph Winchester MA 2003-2004; Int S Mk's Ch Westford MA 2001-2003; Int Asst Par Of The Epiph Winchester MA 2000-2001; P-in-c S Lk's Epis Ch Malden MA 1998-2000; Assoc Trin Ch Topsfield MA 1978-1989. Auth, "The Gift of the Butterfly Weed," *Faith at Wk Journ*, 2000; Auth, "Risk Mgmt," *Crit Iss in K-12 Serv-Lrng*, 1996; Auth, "The Lesson from the Oyster," *Natl Inst for Campus Mnstry Journ*. HAWC Cmnty Awd Help for Abused Wmn and Chld Shltr 1998. cynthiaphubbard@comcast.net

HUBBARD, Francis Appleton (NJ) 5 North Rd, Berkeley Heights NJ 07922 **Int Chr Ch New Brunswick NJ 2011-; Alt Dep, GC Dio New Jersey Trenton NJ 2011-; Chair, Property T/F Dio New Jersey Trenton NJ 2010-; Chair, Loan & Grant Com Dio New Jersey Trenton NJ 2001-** B Boston MA 11/30/1951 s Charles Wells Hubbard & Nathalie. BA Ob 1974; MDiv EDS 1981; D.Min. SWTS 2010. D 5/30/1981 P 5/27/1982 Bp John Bowen Coburn. m 6/24/2000 Elda G Hubbard c 1. Int S Steph's Ch Riverside NJ 2010-2011; Fin and Bdgt Com Dio New Jersey Trenton NJ 2005-2008; Coun Dio New Jersey Trenton NJ 2002-2005; R S Barn Epis Ch Monmouth Jct NJ 1984-2009; Asst All SS' Epis Ch Belmont MA 1981-1984. Auth, "three Liturg dramas," *(included in) Skiturgies*, Ch Pub, 2011. Chapl Ord Of S Lk 2001. therevfah50@hotmail.com

HUBBARD, Henry Winfield (Spok) 17202 97th Pl SW, Apt B104, Vashon WA 98070 B Baker OR 8/20/1917 s Forrest Hubbard & Mary Lucinda. DIT ATC 1964. D 6/29/1964 P 1/19/1965 Bp Russell S Hubbard. R H Trin Epis Ch Gillette WY 1973-1979; P S Fran On The Prairie Ch Wright WY 1973-1979; D S Paul's Ch Cheney WA 1964-1965; S Tim Med Lake WA 1964-1965.

HUBBARD, James Alan (SwVa) 384 Waughs Ferry Rd, Amherst VA 24521 **S Mk's Ch Clifford VA 2006-** B Erie PA 2/9/1942 s Vernon Robert Hubbard & Lucile Marian. BA Lee Coll 1963; BD Fuller TS 1966; MA California St U 1970; PhD U of Tennessee 1976; Cert GTS 1981. D 9/6/1981 Bp William Evan Sanders P 4/25/1982 Bp William F Gates Jr. m 5/20/2000 Mary J Schroder c 3. Int Gr And H Trin Cathd Kansas City MO 2003-2004; Dio Virginia Richmond VA 2002; Vic S Fran Epis Ch Manakin Sabot VA 2002; Int S Jn's Ch Roanoke VA 2000-2002; S Geo's-By-The-River Rumson NJ 2000; Int R S Geo's-By-The-River Rumson NJ 1999-2000; S Lk's Epis Ch Jamestown NY 1999-2000; Int S Paul's Epis Ch Cary NC 1997-1998; Int S Paul's Epis Ch Lynchburg VA 1995-1997; R Trin Epis Ch Pottsville PA 1993-1995; R Trin Ch Easton PA 1991-1993; R S Jn's Ch Canandaigua NY 1986-1991; Vic S Matt's Epis Ch McMinnville TN 1981-1986. Auth, *arts Psychol Behavior*. heypadre@gmail.com

HUBBARD, Lani Marie (ETenn) PO Box 5623, Knoxville TN 37928 B Los Angeles CA 9/26/1944 d Frank R Hubbard & Marjorie R. AS Brigham Young U 1965. D 12/9/2006 Bp Charles Glenn VonRosenberg. lanihubbard@aol.com

HUBBARD, Martha L (Mass) St. Paul's Church, 166 High St., Newburyport MA 01950 **R S Paul's Ch Newburyport MA 2007-** B Poughkeepsie NY 5/6/1964 d William Hart Hubbard & Norma Elain. BA SUNY 1986; MDiv Ya Berk 1993. D 6/12/1993 Bp Richard Frank Grein P 2/12/1994 Bp Robert Scott Denig. m 8/6/1994 Markus Brucher c 2. R Ch of S Aug of Cbury 65189 Wiesbaden DE 2003-2007; R S Mk's Epis Ch Penn Yan NY 1995-2003; Cur Ch Of The Atone Westfield MA 1993-1995; Dio Wstrn Massachusetts Springfield MA 1993-1995. Muehl Preaching Prize Ya- Berk DS New Haven CT; Mersick Preaching Prize Ya- Berk DS New Haven CT. mx3hb@hotmail.com

HUBBARD, Mavourneen Ann (NY) 17 South Ave, Beacon NY 12508 B Buffalo NY 5/28/1952 d Edward J Murphy & Loretta McDonald. BS Suny Plattsburgh 1975. D 5/1/2010 Bp Mark Sean Sisk. m 3/5/1971 James T Hubbard c 2. mavhubbard@msn.com

HUBBARD, Philip Ray (Kan) 8503 W 156th Ter, Overland Park KS 66223 **Dio Kansas Topeka KS 2008-** B Kansas City MO 7/9/1961 s Robert Allen Hubbard & Nadine Ella. BA U of Missouri Kansas City 1983; MA PrTS 1987; MBA U of Connecticut 1992; MDiv CDSP 2008. D 6/7/2008 P 12/6/2008 Bp Dean Elliott Wolfe. m 12/21/1999 Sonya Stokes c 1. pastorpip@stclareschurch.com

HUBBARD, Thomas Beckwith (Los) 621 Mayflower Rd 104, Claremont CA 91711 **Dio Los Angeles Los Angeles CA 2000-** B Cleveland OH 6/24/1938 s Harold Hyde Hubbard & Janet. BA Hiram Coll 1960; MDiv EDS 1964. D 6/13/1964 P 12/18/1964 Bp Nelson Marigold Burroughs. m 5/10/1997 Mary P Pavlak c 2. LocTen S Tim's Epis Ch Apple Vlly CA 1982-1983; Serv All SS Ch Pasadena CA 1979-1999; Epis Dio San Joaquin Modesto CA 1974-1977; Assoc/R S Paul's Ch Bakersfield CA 1974-1977; Consult Par Rnwl Dio Cntrl New York Syracuse NY 1971-1974; Dio Chair Cmsn Dio Cntrl New York Syracuse NY 1967-1969; R Geth Ch Sherrill NY 1966-1974; Cur Trin Ch Elmira NY 1964-1966. Contrib, *Hm Sweet Tax Break*, 1982; Contrib, *Celebration*, 1973. Epis Cleric Assn 1970-1974; Fiduciary Round Table 2000-2004; Fin Plnng Assn 1984-2004. tbhplans@usa.net

HUBBELL, Gilbert Leonard (O) 1094 Clifton Ave # 2, Akron OH 44310 B 5/29/1936 s Leonard Franklin Hubbell & Mae Margaret. BA Bex 1958; BA U of Toledo 1958. D 6/19/1968 P 1/1/1969 Bp John Harris Burt. m 1/21/1999 Diana Lynn Sollberger c 2. Asst S Lk's Epis Ch Akron OH 1982-1984; Brunswick Epis Ch Brunswick OH 1977-1981; Int S Paul's Ch Canton OH 1976; R Trin Ch Coshocton OH 1970-1974; Cur S Ptr's Epis Ch Lakewood OH 1968-1970.

HUBBELL, Sally Hanes (Colo) 7400 Tudor Rd, Colorado Springs CO 80919 **Asst Ch Of S Mich The Archangel Colorado Sprg CO 2009-** B Charlotte NC 4/23/1968 d Andrew Thomas Hanes & Letitia Esteridge. BA Hampshire Coll 1990; MDiv Duke DS 1999; Angl Stds Iliff TS 2009. D 6/6/2009 P 1/9/2010 Bp Robert John O'Neill. m 5/23/1992 David Hubbell c 3. sallyhubbell@me.com

HUBBS, James Dorsey Bashford (SwFla) 1801 Brantley Rd Apt 209, Fort Myers FL 33907 **Died 1/21/2010** B Geneva NY 3/14/1927 s Andrew Dunsmore Hubbs & Marguerite Van Marter. BA Hob 1951; LTh SWTS 1954. D 6/24/1954 P 5/28/1955 Bp Dudley S Stark.

HUBBY III, Turner E(rath) (Tex) PO Box 73, New Baden TX 77870 B Waco TX 6/23/1936 s Turner Erath Hubby & Christine. Texas Tech U 1955; Texas A&M U 1956; BBA Midwestern U 1961; MDiv Epis TS of The SW 1987. D 6/23/1987 Bp Anselmo Carral-Solar P 2/1/1988 Bp Maurice Manuel Benitez. m 11/4/1956 Martha Harris c 4. S Jn's Epis Ch Marlin TX 1987-2002. thubby@att.net

HUBER, Amy Whitcombe (Eau) 234 Avon St, La Crosse WI 54603 B Madison WI 7/3/1951 d Edward Whitcombe & Marie. BS U of Wisconsin 1989. D 6/17/2001 Bp James Louis Jelinek. m 8/18/1990 Steven Huber c 4. awh_51@yahoo.com

HUBER, Donald Marvin (Neb) 1225 Box Butte Ave, Alliance NE 69301 **Bp and Trst Dio Nebraska Omaha NE 2009-; R Calv Ch Hyannis NE 2006-; R S Matt's Ch Allnce NE 2006-** B 3/9/1948 BS SUNY at Buffalo 1970; MDiv Nash 1978. D 6/3/1978 P 3/31/1979 Bp Harold B Robinson. m 6/6/2003 Beth Ann Huber. R S Mary's Epis Ch Gowanda NY 1980-1983; Cur S Ptr's Ch Niagara Falls NY 1978-1980. me.scarecrow@gmail.com

HUBER, Ellen (Ct) 171 Old Tannery Rd # 6468, Monroe CT 06468 **R Chr Ch Easton CT 2004-** B Coatesville PA 6/2/1969 BA Mills Coll. D 6/9/2001 P 12/15/2001 Bp Andrew Donnan Smith. m 8/9/1997 Kurt J Huber c 3. S Lk's Epis Ch New Haven CT 2002-2004.

HUBER, Frank A (Colo) 12295 West Applewood Drive, Lakewood CO 80215 B Erie PA 10/7/1942 s Frank J Huber & Jean M. BA Colg 1964; DVM U of Pennsylvania 1967; MDiv STUSo 1990. D 6/10/1990 P 12/19/1990 Bp David Reed. m 9/7/1969 Lynn Wallerstein. R S Jos's Ch Lakewood CO 2000-2007; R Gr Ch Pine Bluff AR 1994-2000; Chr Epis Ch Bowling Green KY 1990-1994.

HUBER, Kurt J (Ct) 171 Old Tannery Rd, Monroe CT 06468 **R S Ptr's Epis Ch Monroe CT 2002-** B Royal Oak MI 10/31/1971 s Edwin Lawrence Huber & Shirley Ann. BGS U MI 1993; MDiv CDSP 1998. D 6/27/1998 P 1/20/1999 Bp R(aymond) Stewart Wood Jr. m 8/9/1997 Ellen Banks c 4. Asst R Trin Ch Newtown CT 1998-2002. kjhuber@umich.edu

HUBER, Stephen Anthony (Los) 4000 Cathedral Ave NW, Apt 712-B, Washington DC 20016 B Dayton OH 4/11/1951 s Arthur J Huber & Helen. BA Duns Scotus Coll 1973; MDiv Yale DS 1998. Rec from Roman Catholic 1/9/1983 Bp John Bowen Coburn. Cathd of St Ptr & St Paul Washington DC 2006-2010; S Columba's Ch Washington DC 2002-2006; Calv St Geo's Epis Ch Bridgeport CT 2000; Ya Berk New Haven CT 1998-2002. stephenhuberla@gmail.com

HUBERT, Deven Ann (Roch) 66 Little Briggins Circle, Fairport NY 14450 **R S Lk's Ch Fairport NY 2004-** B Tomah WI 8/1/1957 d Richard Dennis Hubert

& Joyce Barbara. BA Stetson U 1978; MDiv Yale DS 1982. D 12/8/1985 P 12/21/1986 Bp Robert Poland Atkinson. c 2. Assoc R Ch Of The H Comf Burlington NC 1999-2004; Cbury Sch Greensboro NC 1996-1999; COM Dio Bethlehem Bethlehem PA 1994-1995; Renwl and Evang Com Dio Bethlehem Bethlehem PA 1992-1995; Assoc P Cathd Ch Of The Nativ Bethlehem PA 1989-1995; Vic S Lk's Ch Wheeling WV 1986-1989. NAES. dhubert@frontiernet.net

HUBERT, Lawrence William (Alb) 970 State St, Schenectady NY 12307 B Schenectady NY 3/25/1947 s Lawrence W Hubert & Marion M. D 5/30/2009 Bp William Howard Love. m 7/18/1981 Jerusha Hubert c 4. jmsnlhubert@nycap.rr.com

HUBINSKY - PHELPS, Sarah E (Los) 2200 Via Rosa, Palos Verdes Estates CA 90274 **R S Fran' Par Palos Verdes Estates CA 2006-** B Potsdam NY 12/25/1970 d Michael Hubinsky & Barbara Ann. BA SUNY Coll at Geneseo 1993; MDiv PSR Berkeley CA 1998. D 6/3/2006 P 1/6/2007 Bp Joseph Jon Bruno. m 10/31/2011 Michael B Phelps. sarah.phelps@stfrancispv.org

HUCK, Beverly Jean (Nwk) 668 Timber Creek Dr, Littleton NC 27850 **Vic S Alb's Ch Littleton NC 2011-** B Dumont NJ 1/8/1952 d Kenneth Fletcher Huck & Rose Marie. BS Montclair St U 1981; MDiv VTS 1984; Isaiah Team 1995; Cler Ldrshp Inst 2005; Credo 2008. D 6/9/1984 P 12/18/1984 Bp John Shelby Spong. m 6/10/1989 William V Magnus c 1. Stndg Com Dio Newark Newark NJ 2004-2009; R The Ch Of The Sav Denville NJ 1992-2009; Dioc Coun Dio Newark Newark NJ 1987-1992; R Trin Epis Ch Kearny NJ 1986-1992; COM Dio Newark Newark NJ 1986-1991; Cur Calv Epis Ch Summit NJ 1984-1986. revbev1@aol.com

HUCKABAY JR, H(arry) Hunter (ETenn) 1706 Glenroy Ave., Chattanooga TN 37405 B Shreveport LA 1/26/1934 s Harry Hunter Huckabay & Katherine. BS LSU 1956; MDiv STUSo 1969; DMin STUSo 1984; DD STUSo 2000. D 6/28/1969 Bp Girault M Jones P 5/1/1970 Bp Iveson Batchelor Noland. m 2/9/1957 Prestine Sue Crosby c 3. R S Paul's Epis Ch Chattanooga TN 1986-2006; COM, Chair Dio Wstrn Louisiana Alexandria LA 1980-1986; R Ch Of The Ascen Lafayette LA 1972-1986; Epis Sch Of Acadiana Inc. Cade LA 1972-1977; Asst R Trin Ch New Orleans LA 1969-1972. thesis, "Lord to Whom Shall We Go?," Univerity of the So, 1984; optime merens, "How the NT speaks to Issues and questions in the Bk of Ecclesiastes," U So, 1969. DD U So 2000; Distinguished Alum STUSo Sewanee TN 1995. hhhjr@aol.com

HUDAK, Bob (EC) St Paul's Church, 401 E. 4th St, Greenville NC 27858 **Chair, Anti-racism Cmsn Dio E Carolina Kinston NC 2007-; R S Paul's Epis Ch Greenville NC 2005-** B Passaic NJ 1/29/1948 s Robert Edward Hudak & Anne. BA CUA 1971; MDiv Washington Theol Un 1983. Rec from Roman Catholic 4/1/1998 as Priest Bp Frank Kellogg Allan. m 11/3/1991 Louise M Moye c 2. S Tim's Epis Ch Greenville NC 2005-2006; R The Epis Ch Of The Nativ Fayetteville GA 2003-2005; Vic The Epis Ch Of The Nativ Fayetteville GA 1998-2002. rector@stpaulsepiscopal.com

HUDAK, Mary Lou (Cal) 66 Saint Stephens Dr., Orinda CA 94563 **Assoc S Steph's Epis Ch Orinda CA 2007-** B Detroit MI 5/10/1962 d Charles Roland Case & Bernice Rose. BA U MN 2004; MDiv CDSP 2008. D 7/26/2007 P 7/8/2008 Bp James Louis Jelinek. m 10/21/1989 James Hudak c 5. mlhudak@comcast.net

HUDDLESTON, Darrell Kent (WMass) 18 Bridle Path Trail, Concord NH 03301 **Wrld Mssn Com Dio Wstrn Massachusetts Springfield MA 2000-** B Caldwell KS 12/2/1941 s Francis Vernon Huddleston & Lela Audrey. BA SW Coll Winfield KS 1964; STB Bos 1968; K SU 1969; DMin Bos 1981; U of Kansas 1988. D 6/20/1998 P 12/2/1998 Bp Gordon Paul Scruton. m 5/23/1964 Helen Bunny Elizabeth Markel c 2. Int R Gr Ch Manchester NH 2010-2011; Co-chair Dioc Revisioning Com Dio Wstrn Massachusetts Springfield MA 2005-2006; Assoc R S Fran Ch Holden MA 2004-2007; Same Sex Blessing T/F Dio Wstrn Massachusetts Springfield MA 2004-2005; P-in-c Ch Of The Gd Shpd Clinton MA 2000-2004; Asst S Fran Ch Holden MA 1998-2000. Auth, "Our Money and Ourselves," *Networking*, TENS, 2007; Auth, "Farm as Ecosystem: Ecological Place of Domesticated Animals," *CARAPHIN*, Caraphin, 1995; Auth, "The Biblic Call to Wholeness: Our Relatns to the Natural Wrld," *Heifer Monographs*, Heifer Proj Intl , 1988; Auth, "Biblic Perspectives on Wrld hungers," *Heifer Monographs*, Heifer Proj Intl , 1983. FVC (Fllshp of the Way of the Cross) 1998. darrellandbunny@comcast.net

HUDDLESTON, Kevin Douglas (Dal) PO Box 12385, Dallas TX 75225 **Assoc for Mssn and Outreach S Mich And All Ang Ch Dallas TX 2008-** B Rockford IL 6/21/1956 s Jack Richard Huddleston & Dorothy Jean. BA Milligan Coll 1977; MDiv Van 1982; Dmin SWTS 2005. D 3/8/1988 P 7/18/1988 Bp Maurice Manuel Benitez. m 9/1/1984 Gayle Lynn Sharpe c 3. R S Barn Epis Ch Fredericksburg TX 1999-2003; Exec Com Coll Cler Dio W Tennessee Memphis TN 1997-1999; Asst Ch Of The H Comm Memphis TN 1996-1999; R Ch Of The Gd Shpd Cedar Hill TX 1994-1996; Assoc S Mich And All Ang Ch Dallas TX 1989-1994; Yth Min S Dav's Ch Austin TX 1988-1989. Auth, "Resources Mnstrs w Yth & YA". revkevdallas@gmail.com

HUDGEN, Calvin Rodney (Mass) 206 Clarendon Street, Boston MA 02116 **Assoc R for Wrshp and Cmncatn Trin Ch In The City Of Boston Boston MA 2008-** B Stuttgart AR 3/27/1962 s Calvin Refus Hudgen & Rubye Estal. BA Rhodes Coll 1984; MDiv EDS 1993. D 6/18/1994 P 7/29/1995 Bp R(aymond) Stewart Wood Jr. m 9/30/1987 William Allen Finley. R Ch Of S Asaph Bala Cynwyd PA 2006-2008; Int Trin Ch Toledo OH 2000-2006; Assoc S Lk's Epis Ch No Little Rock AR 1995-1997. Auth, "Practical Postmodernism For Parishes," *Open*, Associated Parishes, 2001. Coun, Associated Parishes for Liturg & Mssn 2004; Gathering the NeXt Generation 2003. rodsberg@mac.com

HUDSON, Andrew (SeFla) 7538 Granville Dr, Tamarac FL 33321 **Dir Of Evang S Ambr Epis Ch Ft Lauderdale FL 2010-** B Flint MI 4/11/1931 s Edward Joseph Popilek & Helen Lucille. BS Wstrn Michigan U 1952. D 10/14/1986 Bp Calvin Onderdonk Schofield Jr. m 6/25/1954 Bobsie Lou Robbins c 2.

HUDSON, Andrew George (SeFla) 2250 SW 31st Ave, Fort Lauderdale FL 33312 B Athens Greece 12/1/1966 s Peter James Motegue Hudson & Tatiana. BA St Thos U 1992. D 6/5/2010 Bp Leopold Frade. m 3/31/2001 Laura Black c 1. andy1201@bellsouth.net

HUDSON, Betty (NY) 120 John Bratton, Williamsburg VA 23185 **Asst S Andr's Epis Ch Newport News VA 2009-** B Fort Worth TX 9/15/1948 d Jack Dearing Brownfield & Mackey. BA Tul 1970; MBA Simmons Coll 1976; MDiv GTS 1986. D 6/7/1986 Bp Paul Moore Jr P 6/24/1987 Bp Walter Decoster Dennis Jr. m 6/9/1984 John Hudson c 2. Transition R Trin Ch Portsmouth VA 2009; R Gr Ch Hastings On Hudson NY 1991-2007; Int R S Steph's Ch Pearl River NY 1987-1991. Rev.BettyHudson@gmail.com

HUDSON, Daniel Mark (La) 205 N 4th St, Baton Rouge LA 70801 B New Orleans LA 9/18/1957 s Daniel Levern & Susan Morris. BA SE Louisiana U 1979; MBA Tul 1996. D 12/1/2007 Bp Charles Edward Jenkins III. m 3/26/1983 Debra Speed c 1. dmhudson@cox.net

HUDSON, Henry Lee (La) 1424 4th St, New Orleans LA 70130 **R Trin Ch New Orleans LA 2007-** B Birmingham AL 12/10/1951 s William Goode Hudson & Lois. BA Tul 1974; MDiv Nash 1977. D 5/26/1977 P 12/15/1977 Bp Furman Stough. m 5/22/1976 Mary Curtin c 2. Dn and R Trin Cathd Little Rock AR 1996-2007; R S Paul's Epis Ch Meridian MS 1984-1996; R Ch Of The Adv Sumner MS 1980-1984; Cur Ch Of The Nativ Epis Huntsville AL 1977-1980. EPF; Itfs. hhudson@trinitynola.com

HUDSON, Joel Pinkney (At) 1225 N Shore Dr, Roswell GA 30076 B Atlanta GA 2/13/1931 s James Edward Hudson & Louise. BD Clemson U 1953; MDiv VTS 1963. D 6/15/1963 P 12/1/1963 Bp Nelson Marigold Burroughs. m 6/12/1953 Shirley Ann Ford c 4. Int Gr-Calv Epis Ch Clarkesville GA 2003; Chr Ch Norcross GA 1988-2003; Assoc Ch Of The Atone Sandy Sprg GA 1973-1978; Assoc S Eliz's Ch Ridgewood NJ 1969-1971; Assoc H Trin Epis Ch Bowie MD 1967-1969; Asst Min Chr Ch Shaker Heights OH 1963-1967. jhudson1225@yahoo.com

HUDSON, John Richard Keith (Del) 1300 Morris Ave, Villanova PA 19085 **P-in-c S Paul's Ch Chester PA 2011-** B London UK 11/4/1935 s John Charles Hudson & Nora Mary. BA Oxf 1960; GOE Lincoln Theol Inst 1962; MA Oxf 1964; PhD SUNY 1983. Trans from Church Of England 4/1/1984. Int Calv Epis Ch Hillcrest Wilmington DE 2003-2010; P-in-c S Paul's Ch Camden DE 1985-2002; Asst R S Jas Epis Ch Alexandria LA 1984-1985. Auth, "Free To Share Books I And Ii," Ch Info Off Of London, 1973. keith@hudsonid.com

HUDSON, Kimberly Karen (NC) No address on file. B Ft Bragg NC 9/24/1964 d Willie Hudson & Betty L. BA U NC 1986; JD The Dickinson Sch of Law 1990. D 6/29/2002 Bp Michael Bruce Curry.

HUDSON, Linda Ann (Wyo) 860 S 3rd St, Lander WY 82520 B Denver CO 11/24/1950 d John R Shaw & Garnet I. BA U of Nthrn Colorado 1971; MA U of Wyoming 1978. D 8/25/2007 Bp Bruce Edward Caldwell. c 1. lhuson1950@msn.com

HUDSON, Mary Bowen (CFla) 4345 Indian River Dr, Cocoa FL 32927 B Atlanta GA 1/25/1925 d Sylvester C Bowen & Roberta Elizabeth. BA Georgia St U 1960. D 2/20/1988 Bp William Hopkins Folwell. m Joseph A Hudson. Dok.

HUDSON, Michael Vincent (WNC) Po Box 152, Cullowhee NC 28723 **R S Dav's Ch Cullowhee NC 1992-** B Greenville SC 12/17/1950 s Heyward Wayman Hudson & Ruth. BA Furman U 1973; MDiv TESM 1989. D 6/23/1989 Bp C(laude) Charles Vache P 3/1/1990 Bp Frank Harris Vest Jr. m 5/29/1976 Barbara Jane Hardie c 1. Asst R Ch Of The Gd Shpd Norfolk VA 1989-1992. "Songs for the Cycle," Ch Pub Corp, 2004; Auth, "Lrng to Trust," 1990; Auth, "Enter His Gates," 1985. Dove Awd for Song of the Year CMA 1980. stdavids1879@gmail.com

HUDSON, Sonja Snyder (WNC) 2435 Pine Tree Ln, Rocky Mount NC 27804 B Hazelwood NC 6/12/1938 d Jack Harrison Snyder & Robena Howell. AA Mars Hill Coll 1958; BA U NC 1960; Med U NC 1980; MDiv GTS 1990. D 6/23/1990 Bp Huntington Williams Jr P 6/1/1991 Bp Robert Whitridge Estill. S Jn's Ch Asheville NC 2005-2006; S Andr's Ch Rocky Mt NC 2004-2005; Assoc S Jn The Bapt Epis Ch Seattle WA 2000-2003; Int Trin Epis Ch Everett WA 1999-2000; S Cyp's Ch Franklin NC 1993-1998; R S Jn's Epis Ch Franklin NC 1993-1998; S Cyp's Ch Oxford NC 1990-1992; Asst to R S Steph's Ch Oxford NC 1990-1992. rhetthudson@charter.net

HUDSON, Thomas James (Md) St James Episcopal Church, 32 Main Street, Westernport MD 21562 **Com on Sci, Tech, and Faith Exec Coun Appointees New York NY 2009-; Mutual Mnstry Team S Jas Epis Ch Westernport MD 2007-** B Wilmington DE 4/24/1948 Theol Mt S Mary's Sem, Emmitsburg, MD 1977; Dplma in Theol Stds VTS - ICFL 2011. D 12/21/2007 Bp John Leslie Rabb P 6/29/2008 Bp Katharine Jefferts Schori. m 8/25/1979 Judith C Judith A Crocken. stjames.westernport@verizon.net

HUDSON-LOUIS, Holly (ECR) 65 Highway 1, Carmel CA 93923 **All SS' Epis Day Sch Carmel CA 2006-** B San Rafael CA 11/27/1957 d David Hudson & Sabra. BS U CA 1981; MDiv CDSP 1991. D 6/29/1991 P 3/25/1992 Bp Richard Lester Shimpfky. m 5/23/1981 August James Louis c 2. Assoc All SS Ch Carmel CA 2000-2005; Trin Cathd San Jose CA 1997-1999; S Phil's Ch San Jose CA 1991-1995; S Fran Epis Ch San Jose CA 1985-1987. Citation of Excellence-Chld's Mnstry, Trin Cathd Dio El Camino Real 1999. hhudson-louis@asds.org

HUDSPETH, Denise Wardell (SeFla) 208 Nw Avenue H, Belle Glade FL 33430 B Bronx NY 2/20/1953 d Arnold Edward Wardell & Lillian. Cert Diac Sch For Mnstry 1985; AS Palm Bch Cmnty Coll 1986. D 6/29/1989 Bp Calvin Onderdonk Schofield Jr P 6/1/2002 Bp John Lewis Said. m 1/22/1973 William Broughton Hudspeth c 3. S Jn The Apos Ch Belle Glade FL 2002-2006; D H Sprt Epis Ch W Palm Bch FL 1989-2002. Yth Mnstry, CE Mnstry To Elderly, Mnstry In 12 Step Recovery Prog. REVDENISE@BELLSOUTH.NET

HUERTA, Efrain (FtW) 12607 Banchester Ct, Houston TX 77070 **Dir Comp Pension Relatns The CPG New York NY 2002-** B San Martin de las Flores MX 5/19/1937 s Crescencio Huerta & Praxedis. CTh S Andr's Sem Mex City MX 1964; U Mariano Galvez Guatemala City GT 1964; MDiv Epis TS of The SW 1981; DD Epis TS of The SW 2002. D 9/13/1964 P 4/1/1965 Bp Jose Guadalupe Saucedo. m 4/24/1965 Silvia Margoth-Paz. The Cntr For Hisp Mnstrs Austin TX 1993-2001; Dio Ft Worth Ft Worth TX 1983-1993; R San Juan Apostol Ft Worth TX 1982-1993; Dio Dallas Dallas TX 1982; Dio Guatemala Guatemala City 1968-1980. Auth, *Meditaciones Diarias*, Centro Para Ministerios Hispanos, 1998; Auth, *Coments Biblicos*, Centro Para Ministerios Hispanos, 1996; Auth, *Quince Anos*, Centro Para Ministerios Hispanos, 1995; Auth, *Necesidad de un Proceso Administrativo*, Universidad Mariano Galvez, 1978. Amnesty Prog 1987-1993; Hogar Taller de Guatemala 1970-1979. Necesidad de Un Proceso Administrativo Guatemalteco.

HUERTA GARCIA, Oscar (Tex) Chamela 33 A, Tlaquepaque Jalisco 45589 Mexico **Dio Texas Houston TX 2005-** B 12/19/1961 s Daniel HUerta Fierros & Antonia. S Andrews TS Mex City Mx 1988. D 1/22/1989 P 11/1/1989 Bp Samuel Espinoza-Venegas. m 10/30/1981 Maria Del Rosario Arellano c 5. Dio Wstrn Mex Zapopan Jalisco CP 45150 1989-2000. oscar-huerta@sbcglobal.net

HUEY JR, Stewart Marshall (SC) 4416 Betsy Kerrison Pkwy, Johns Island SC 29455 **R Old S Andr's Par Ch Charleston SC 2006-** B Atlanta GA 2/5/1958 s Stewart M Huey & Carol. BA Duke 1980; JD Van 1983; MDiv STUSo 2001. D 6/23/2001 P 1/5/2002 Bp Edward Lloyd Salmon Jr. c 2. Ch Of Our Sav Johns Island SC 2004-2006; Porter-Gaud Sch Charleston SC 2002-2004; Asst R S Jas Ch Charleston SC 2001-2002. Bd Trst U So 2004. marshall_huey@yahoo.com

HUFF, Carolyn Tuttle (Pa) 1015 N Trooper Rd, Eagleville PA 19403 B Iowa City IA 12/29/1965 d Roger L Tuttle & Barbara F. BS NE Missouri St U 1988; MDiv VTS 1998. D 6/6/1998 P 12/19/1998 Bp William Jerry Winterrowd. m 1/25/2003 David B Huff. Assoc Trin Luth Ch Fairview Vill PA 2008-2011; Assoc S Dav's Ch Wayne PA 1999-2004; Asst S Steph's Ch Longmont CO 1998-1999. carolynfromiowa@gmail.com

HUFF, Christopher Mercer (SC) 1612 Dryden Ln, Charleston SC 29407 B Charleston SC 5/4/1956 s William Dekalb Huff & Dorothy Jeanette. BA Coll of Charleston 1978; MDiv TESM 1988. D 6/23/1988 P 5/31/1989 Bp C(hristopher) FitzSimons Allison. m 8/19/1978 Kim Diane Yeager c 2. W Shore Epis Charleston SC 1998-2008; Epis Ch of the Gd Shpd Charleston SC 1993-1998; S Paul's Ch Bennettsville SC 1988-1993.

HUFF, Clark Kern (Tex) 2252 Garden Court, San Marcos TX 78666 B New Orleans LA 2/6/1936 s Joe Hooker Huff & Ethyl Iphigenia. BS U of Texas 1958; MDiv Epis TS of The SW 1994. D 6/17/2000 P 4/18/2001 Bp Claude Edward Payne. m 3/25/1978 Rebecca Smith c 2. Partnr In Mnstry Estrn Convoc Kennedy TX 2005-2006; P-in-c of Trin Cntr Mnstrs S Dav's Ch Austin TX 2002-2005; S Aug's Epis Ch Galveston TX 2000-2008. ckhuff@austin.rr.com

HUFF, Susan Ellen (At) 1031 Eagles Ridge Ct, Lawrenceville GA 30043 B Providence RI 5/26/1949 d Edward Huff & Margaret. D 8/6/2006 Bp J(ohn) Neil Alexander. sue@georgiabenefits.com

HUFFMAN, Charles Howard (Tex) 8124 Greenslope Dr, Austin TX 78759 B Houston TX 1/2/1926 s Ben Mashaw Huffman & Lattie May. BS U of Texas 1949; MDiv Epis TS of The SW 1966; STM Epis TS of The SW 1968. D 6/24/1966 Bp J Milton Richardson P 6/6/1967 Bp Scott Field Bailey. m 3/10/1951 Carolyn Barlow. Int S Mk's Ch New Canaan CT 1995-1996; Int Trin Ch Newtown CT 1994-1995; Int Chr Ch Greenwich CT 1993; R S Matt's Ch Austin TX 1973-1991; Asst S Dav's Ch Austin TX 1966-1971. padrechuck@sbcglobal.net

HUFFMAN, Robert Nelson (SVa) 761 E Northfield Blvd, Murfreesboro TN 37130 B Chicago IL 11/4/1931 s Troy Nelson Huffman & Mary Ellen. BA U of Florida 1953; BD/MDiv SWTS 1958; STM STUSo 1976. D 6/29/1958 Bp William Francis Moses P 12/30/1958 Bp Henry I Louttit. m 5/14/1955 Margaret Elizabeth Page c 1. Exec Bd Dio Sthrn Virginia Norfolk VA 1981-1985; Dn Convoc IV Dio Sthrn Virginia Norfolk VA 1981-1984; R Trin Ch Portsmouth VA 1977-1993; Stndg Com Dio Cntrl Florida Orlando FL 1976-1977; Dio Cntrl Florida Orlando FL 1970-1977; Chair Lakeland Dnry Dio Cntrl Florida Orlando FL 1970-1973; Secy of the Conv Dio Cntrl Florida Orlando FL 1969-1977; R H Trin Epis Ch Bartow FL 1964-1977; Asst S Mary's Epis Ch Daytona Bch FL 1961-1964; P-in-c H Nativ Pahokee FL 1958-1961; Vic S Jn The Apos Ch Belle Glade FL 1958-1961.

HUFFORD, Robert Arthur (SO) 52 Bishopsgate Dr Apt 703, Cincinnati OH 45246 **The Soc of the Transiguration Cincinnati OH 1992-** B Chicago IL 1/26/1944 s Harold Everett Hufford & Barbara Frances. BA Br 1966; McGill U 1966; MDiv Nash 1972. D 6/17/1972 P 12/16/1972 Bp James Winchester Montgomery. R S Steph's Epis Ch Covington KY 1983-1992; R S Alb's Ch Chicago IL 1974-1981; Cur Chr Ch Waukegan IL 1972-1974. CT, Assoc 1989; Csss 2001. rahuffo@msn.com

H

HUFFSTETLER, Joel (ETenn) 3920 Clairmont Dr Ne, Cleveland TN 37312 **R S Lk's Ch Cleveland TN 2003-** B Charlotte NC 11/6/1962 s Joe Raymond Huffstetler & Pansy Rachel. BA Elon U 1985; Emory U 1987; MDiv STUSo 1990. D 5/24/1990 P 3/1/1991 Bp Robert Hodges Johnson. m 11/22/1998 Deborah Ann Williams. Asst R S Paul's Epis Ch Chattanooga TN 1995-2003; S Andr's Epis Ch Canton NC 1990-1995. Auth, "Henry Lee & Banastre Tarleton How Historians Use Their Memoirs"; Auth, "Sthrn Hist". FATHERNASCAR@AOL.COM

HUFT, Jerry Ray (CGC) Po Box 595, Wewahitchka FL 32465 B Beckley WV 9/27/1938 s John Huft & Lyda Mary Ann. BA SE Coll Lakeland FL 1977; MDiv TESM 1980. D 6/22/1980 Bp William Hopkins Folwell P 2/14/1981 Bp Calvin Onderdonk Schofield Jr. m 3/17/1963 Jacqueline Burlingham. S Jas' Epis Ch Port S Joe FL 1984-2000; S Jn The Bapt Epis Ch Wewahitchka FL 1984-2000; Cur S Paul's Ch Delray Bch FL 1980-1983. Bro Of S Andr. jhuft@aol.com

HUGGARD, Linda S (EpisSanJ) 4300 Keith Way, Bakersfield CA 93309 **VP of So Dnry Epis Dio San Joaquin Modesto CA 2011-; Co Chair/ Cmsn on Equality Epis Dio San Joaquin Modesto CA 2009-; Vic All Souls Epis Fllshp Ridgecrest CA 2008-; Vic S Andr's Ch Taft CA 2008-** B Berkeley CA 7/20/1950 d Dewey Enright Huggard & Allison Eugenia. BA Sonoma St U 1995; MDiv CDSP 2005. D 6/2/2007 Bp Marc Handley Andrus P 12/21/2007 Bp Barry Leigh Beisner. c 1. D S Tim's Ch Gridley CA 2007-2008. lhug1950843@cs.com

HUGGINS, Arthur Hoskins (VI) P.O. Box 748, St. Vincent Saint Vincent & the Grenadines B 1/12/1928 s William Alfred Huggins & Annie. Codrington Coll. Trans from Church in the Province Of The West Indies 5/1/1984 Bp Edward Mason Turner. m 7/4/1972 Patricia A Richards c 3. R S Paul's Epis/Angl Ch Frederiksted VI VI 1986-1999; S Geo Mtyr Ch Tortola VG 1984-1985.

HUGHES, A(lan) (Pa) 1408 Sw 20th Ct, Gresham OR 97080 B Llanelli Dyfed South Wales GB 1/28/1934 s Daniel Hughes & Beatrice Ceinwen. BA U of Wales 1954; LTh S Michaels TS 1960; DMin Lancaster TS 1979. Trans from Church in Wales 3/15/1976 Bp Lloyd Edward Gressle. Ch Of The H Cross Cumberland MD 1989-1991; R Ch Of The Redeem Springfield PA 1981-1989; R S Mich's Epis Ch Bethlehem PA 1976-1980. Auth, "Pstr Care Adult Pre-Operative Cardiac Patient," 1979. Ord Of S Lk.

HUGHES, Allen Chaplin (SC) 1248 Calais Dr, Mount Pleasant SC 29464 B Charleston SC 8/19/1967 s William E Hughes & Sarah De. BA U of So Carolina 1989; MDiv STUSo 1996. D 6/4/1996 P 12/15/1996 Bp Edward Lloyd Salmon Jr. Dio So Carolina Charleston SC 1999-2001; S Andr's Ch Mt Pleasant SC 1998; Ch Of The Redeem Orangeburg SC 1996-1998.

HUGHES, Carlye Juanita (NY) 133 Fields Ln, Peekskill NY 10566 **S Peters Ch Peekskill NY 2007-; R S Ptr's Epis Ch Peekskill NY 2007-** B Tulsa OK 10/30/1958 d Robert Hughes & Jackie. BA U of Texas 1998; MDiv VTS 2005. D 3/19/2005 P 9/17/2005 Bp Mark Sean Sisk. m 11/9/2008 David Smedley. P S Jas Ch New York NY 2005-2007. carlyehughes@verizon.net

HUGHES, Frank W. (CPa) 735 Ockley Drive, Shreveport LA 71106 **Int S Tim's Ch Alexandria LA 2009-** B Texarkana TX 2/23/1954 s William Morris Hughes & Mary. BA Hendrix Coll 1975; MDiv SWTS 1979; MA U Chi 1981; PhD NWU 1984. D 1/19/1981 Bp James Winchester Montgomery P 12/5/1981 Bp Quintin Ebenezer Primo Jr. S Paul's Ch New Orleans LA 2009-2011; Int Ch Of The H Cross Shreveport LA 2008-2009; Int S Jn's Epis Ch Decatur IL 2006-2008; Supply P S Jas Ch Magnolia AR 2005-2006; Exec Coun Appointees New York NY 2000-2004; Codrington Coll 1998-2000; R S Mk's Epis Ch Lewistown PA 1991-1997; S Jas Ch Greenridge Aston PA 1990-1991; Asst S Lk's Ch Philadelphia PA 1987-1990; S Fran Ch Greensboro NC 1985-1986; Asst Ch Of The Epiph Chicago IL 1981-1985. Auth, "The Soc

Situations Implied by Rhetoric," *The Thessalonians Debate*, Eerdmans, 2000; Auth, "Thessalonians, First and Second Letters to the," *Dictionary of Biblic Interp*, Abingdon Press, 1999; Auth, "Rhetorical Criticism," *HarperCollins Bible Dictionary*, HarperCollins, 1996; Auth, "Diakonos and Diakonia in Pauline Traditions," *Diac Mnstry: Past, Present, and Future*, NAAD, 1994; Auth, "The Parable of the Rich Man and Lazarus," *Rhetoric and the NT*, Sheffield Acad Press, 1993; Auth, "The Rhetoric of 1 Thessalonians," *The Thessalonian Correspondence*, Peeters, 1990; Auth, "Early Chr Rhetoric and 2 Thessalonians," *JSNTSup 30*, Sheffield Acad Press, 1989; Auth, "Feminism and Early Chr Hist," *ATR*, 1987. Angl Assn of Biblic Scholars, Secy Treas 1994; SBL 1977; Studiorum Novi Testamenti Societas 1996. Fulbright Schlr, U of Göttingen Fulbright-Kommission, Germany 1986. fwhughes54@hotmail.com

✠ HUGHES, Rt Rev Gethin Benwil (SanD) 461 Quail Run Rd, Buellton CA 93427 **Ret Bp Dio San Diego San Diego CA 2005-** B Lampeter Cardiganshire GB 10/1/1942 s Hubert Benjamin William Hughes & Sarah. BA Exeter U - Engl; MDiv SWTS 1967; Oxf 1968. Trans from Church in Wales 2/1/1972 as Priest Bp Francis E I Bloy Con 6/20/1992 for SanD. m 6/22/1968 Lenore Hughes c 1. Bp Of San Diego Dio San Diego San Diego CA 1992-2005; Trst SWTS Evanston IL 1986-2002; Stndg Com Dio Los Angeles Los Angeles CA 1986-1989; R All SS-By-The-Sea Par Santa Barbara CA 1980-1992; Mssnr Dio Los Angeles Los Angeles CA 1975-1980; Vic Prince Of Peace Epis Ch Woodland Hills CA 1973-1975; Asst Cong Of S Athan Los Angeles CA 1969-1972; Asst Epis Chap Of S Fran Los Angeles CA 1969-1972. Hon DD Seabury Wstrn 1993. gethinbhughes@yahoo.com

HUGHES, Harry Alfred (SwFla) 303 Stanwood Ct, Florence AL 35633 **S Anna's Ch Atmore AL 2005-** B Montgomery AL 10/14/1944 s John Cotter Hughes & Kathleen. Div Mt. St. Mary's Seminery 1977; Div S Mary Coll And Sem Leavenworth KS 1977. Rec from Roman Catholic 9/1/1983 as Priest Bp Duncan Montgomery Gray Jr. m 9/10/2005 Nancy Jones Kirby c 2. Int S Paul's Epis Ch Corinth MS 2007-2009; S Anne Of Gr Epis Ch Seminole FL 2000-2003; S Pierre's Epis Ch Gautier MS 1994-1999; The Epis Ch Of The Gd Shpd Columbus MS 1989-1994; R Chap Of The Cross ROLLING FORK MS 1986-1989; Vic S Fran Of Assisi Ch Philadelphia MS 1983-1986; Vic S Matt's Epis Ch Kosciusko MS 1983-1986. frharry442@aol.com

HUGHES, Jennifer Scheper (Mass) 1147 Walnut St, Berkeley CA 94707 **S Greg Of Nyssa Ch San Francisco CA 2003-** B Berkeley CA 12/29/1969 BA U CA. D 6/7/2003 P 6/5/2004 Bp M(arvil) Thomas Shaw III. m 2/3/1995 Santos Roman c 1. The ETS At Claremont Claremont CA 2010; All SS Epis Ch Riverside CA 2007-2010; Chr Ch Hyde Pk MA 2006; Iglesia De San Juan Hyde Pk MA 2006.

HUGHES, John Richard (Lex) 2449 Larkin Rd, Lexington KY 40503 B Milwaukee WI 8/16/1957 s John Richard Hughes & Mary Larkin. BA U of Wisconsin 1979; MDiv Gordon-Conwell TS 1984; CAS Nash 1991. D 6/9/1991 P 1/4/1992 Bp Roger John White. m 6/20/1998 Martha Davis c 2. Ch S Mich The Archangel Lexington KY 1993-1998; Ch Of The Ascen Frankfort KY 1992-1993.

HUGHES, Linda May (Ia) 102 LaMarr Circle, Elizabethtown KY 42701 B Fort Wayne IN 4/11/1943 d Willard Jack Hughes & Mary Patricia. AGS Indiana U 1985; BGS Indiana U 1989; MDiv SWTS 1995. Rec from Roman Catholic 9/1/1982 Bp William Cockburn Russell Sheridan. m 6/18/1982 Carl George Gilland c 7. R S Mart's Ch Perry IA 1999-2008; Vic All SS Ch Syracuse IN 1995-1999. Ord of S Lk 1992-1995; Ord of S Lk 2005. carlinda@bbtel.com

HUGHES, Malcolm Albert (FdL) Saint John's Episcopal Church, 139 South Smalley, Shawano WI 54166 B Liverpool UK 3/20/1933 s William Henry Hughes & Fredericka. BA Bps 1958; LST Bps 1960. Trans from Church Of England 9/1/1985 as Priest Bp Frederick Barton Wolf. m 11/14/2008 Lydia McIntyre c 3. R S Sav's Par Bar Harbor ME 1985-1998. Auth, "A Handbook for Ch Wardens," 1982; Auth, "Hiding Behind a Teacup," 1981. Off, Ord of S Jn of Jerusalem HM Eliz II, Queen of Engl 1982.

HUGHES, Mary London (ECR) 902 California Ave, San Jose CA 95125 **Assoc R Ch Of S Jude The Apos Cupertino CA 2010-; Secy of Conv Dio El Camino Real Monterey CA 2009-; Alt Dep to GC Dio El Camino Real Monterey CA 2008-; COM - Vocations Secy Dio El Camino Real Monterey CA 2008-** B Atlanta GA 8/22/1959 d Matthew Jackson Carswell & Mary London james. BA Brenau U 1981; MDiv CDSP 1996. D 11/18/1996 P 6/3/1997 Bp Richard Lester Shimpfky. m 7/1/2006 Allan Charles Hughes c 3. P Exec S Tim's Epis Ch Mtn View CA 2000-2010; Asst R S Mk's-In-The-Vlly Epis Los Olivos CA 1997-2000; Chr Epis Ch Los Altos CA 1997; Trin Cathd San Jose CA 1997. DOK 1999. maly.c.hughes@gmail.com

HUGHES III, Robert Davis (SO) 335 Tennessee Ave, Sewanee TN 37383 **Norma and Olan Mills Prof of Div The TS at The U So Sewanee TN 2001-; Prof Syst Theol The TS at The U So Sewanee TN 1992-** B Boston MA 2/16/1943 s Robert Davis Hughes & Nancy. BA Ya 1966; BD EDS 1969; MA U of St. Mich's Coll 1974; PhD U of St. Mich's Coll 1980. D 6/28/1969 P 1/11/1970 Bp Roger W Blanchard. m 6/12/1965 Barbara Brunn c 1. GBEC Secy HOB 2000-2009; Asst Prof The TS at The U So Sewanee TN 1980-1984; Vic Ch Of The Epiph Nelsonville OH 1969-1972; Asst Ch Of The Gd Shpd Athens OH 1969-1972. Auth, "Beloved Dust," Continuum, 2008; Auth, "S," *Var arts.* AAR 1999; Assoc, C.S.M. 1980; Soc for the Study of Anglicanism 2003; Soc for the Study of Chr Sprtlty 1999; Soc of Angl and Luth Theologians 1978. Shortlisted, Mich Ramsey Prize Archbp of Cbury 2011; Shrtlisted, Mich Ramsey Prize Archbp of Cbury 2011; des Places-Libermann Awd in Pneumatology Duquesne U 2010; Fellowowship ECF 1972; Phi Beta Kappa 1966. rhughes@sewanee.edu

HUGHES, Rosalind Claire (O) 28920 Turnbridge Rd, Bay Village OH 44140 **Assoc S Andr's Epis Ch Elyria OH 2011-** B Wells UK 2/6/1968 d Alan McNee & Ann. BA Keble Coll 1989; MDiv Bex 2011. D 6/4/2011 Bp Mark Hollingsworth Jr. m 9/7/1991 Gareth David Hughes c 3. rosalindchughes@oh.rr.com

HUGHES II, Theron Rex (WK) 1825 Spring St, Quincy IL 62301 B Casper WY 2/2/1924 s Theron Rex Hughes & DeEtte Marie. BA Knox Coll 1950; MDiv Nash 1953. D 4/27/1953 P 11/4/1953 Bp William L Essex. m 8/30/1954 Anne Agee c 4. P-in-c S Jas Epis Ch Griggsville IL 1989-1992; Beloit First Chr Beloit KS 1984-1989; R Ch Of The Epiph Concordia KS 1982-1989; R S Andr's Ch Kenosha WI 1975-1982; Dioc Coun Dio Nthrn Indiana So Bend IN 1972-1974; NI Dio Quincy Peoria IL 1971-1974; Vic S Tim's Ch Griffith IN 1968-1975; Dep GC Dio Quincy Peoria IL 1961-1967; Chair Cmsn Dio Quincy Peoria IL 1959-1968; Div C&C Dio Quincy Peoria IL 1958-1968; Vic S Andr's Ch Peoria IL 1954-1968; S Jn's Epis Ch Peoria IL 1954-1959; S Steph's Ch Harrisburg IL 1954-1959. SSC 1973. DD Nash Nashotah WI 1992.

HUGHES, Thomas Downs (WNC) 1304 River Ridge Drive, Asheville NC 28803 B Shamokin PA 8/16/1933 s Franklin Edward Hughes & Ora Emma. Maryville Coll 1951; BA Ohio U 1954; BD Ken 1958; MDiv Bex 1972. D 6/1/1958 Bp Henry W Hobson P 12/10/1958 Bp Harry S Kennedy. m 6/12/1961 Margaret A Masters c 2. Asst Trin Epis Ch Asheville NC 1998-2007; P-in-c Ch Of S Mths Asheville NC 1992-1996; Int Chr Ch Cedar Rapids IA 1980; R S Paul's Ch Minneapolis MN 1974-1979; Dn The Epis Cathd Of Our Merc Sav Faribault MN 1970-1974; Asst S Lk's Ch Minneapolis MN 1964-1970; Vic Chr Ch Frontenac MN 1962-1964; R S Mk's Ch Lake City MN 1962-1964; Cn S Andr's Cathd Honolulu HI 1960-1962; Vic Chr Memi Ch Kilauea HI 1958-1960; Vic St Thos Ch Hanalei HI 1958-1960. Auth, "Estate Plnng," *Older Americans Almanac*, Gale Resrch Inc., 1994. tompeghughes@bellsouth.net

HUGHES JR, Thomas Roddy (Eas) 852 Spring Valley Dr, Fredericksburg VA 22405 **Assoc S Geo's Ch Fredericksburg VA 2011-** B Chattanooga TN 1/16/1944 s Thomas Roddy Hughes & Leta. BA U of Tennessee 1968; MDiv STUSo 1975. D 6/15/1975 Bp John Vander Horst P 5/10/1976 Bp William Evan Sanders. m 12/21/1993 Jan Hughes. R Shrewsbury Par Ch Kennedyville MD 1995-2010; St Marys Ch 1992-1994; Asst Chr Epis Ch Charlottesville VA 1987-1990; R Ch Of The Nativ Ft Oglethorpe GA 1980-1986; Trin Epis Ch Fulton KY 1980; S Jn's Ch Mart TN 1976-1980; D-in-Trng S Jn's Epis Cathd Knoxville TN 1975-1976. Harriet Tubman Awd Dio Easton 1998. shrewsburry@dmv.com

HUGHES-HABEL, Deborah Jean (U) 4615 S 3200 W, West Valley City UT 84119 **Cur S Steph's Ch W Vlly City UT 2010-** B Iowa City IA 8/16/1951 d William R Wagner & Wilma Joyce. ASN U of Nebraska 1974; BSA Weber St U 1991; MDiv Epis TS Of The SW 2010. D 6/12/2010 Bp Carolyn Tanner Irish P 5/21/2011 Bp Scott Byron Hayashi. m 6/15/1991 Ronald William Habel c 7. dhugheshabel@gmail.com

HUGHS, Leslie Curtis (LI) 16 Birch Road, Danbury CT 06811 **Assoc S Steph's Ch Ridgefield CT 2009-** B Watertown NY 3/28/1941 s Richard Woodman Hughs & Margaret Jane. BS SUNY 1963; MDiv PDS 1971. D 6/5/1971 Bp Allen Webster Brown P 12/11/1971 Bp Charles Bowen Persell Jr. m 6/17/1967 Linda Hazard c 2. R Chr Ch Manhasset NY 1988-2002; R S Paul's Epis Ch Albany NY 1980-1988; R S Mk's Ch Malone NY 1976-1980; R The Epis Ch Of The Cross Ticonderoga NY 1972-1976; Untd Putnam Ch Putnam Sta NY 1972-1976; Cur Chr Ch Schenectady NY 1971-1972. R Emer S Paul's Ch, Albany, NY 2005. leshughs@gmail.com

HUGUENIN, Robert (Fla) 4224 Coastal Hwy, Crawfordville FL 32327 B New York NY 6/27/1943 D 12/22/2002 P 6/29/2003 Bp Stephen Hays Jecko. m 9/11/1965 Sandra Abbott c 3. Epis Prison Mnstry Clarksdale MS. rhuguenin@aol.com

HUINER, Peter Bruce (Del) 500 Woodlawn Rd, Wilmington DE 19803 B Oak Park IL 8/16/1935 s Bernard P Huiner & Edith. BA Calvin Coll 1957; BD Calvin TS 1962; CAS SWTS 1970. D 5/19/1970 Bp Charles Ellsworth Bennison Jr P 9/29/1970 Bp Gerald Francis Burrill. m 8/13/1960 Tona L Kenbeek c 5. Vic S Barn Ch Wilmington DE 2009-2011; Cn Cathd Ch Of S Jn Wilmington DE 2000-2005; R Gr Epis Ch Wilmington DE 1987-1997; R S Alb's Ch Silver Creek NY 1985-1987; R Ch Of S Jn The Bapt Dunkirk NY 1983-1987; Assoc S Paul's Cathd Buffalo NY 1979-1982; Archd Dio Wstrn New York Tonawanda NY 1975-1982; Dn SWTS Evanston IL 1973-1975; Assoc S Paul's Ch Dekalb IL 1970-1973. phuiner@aol.com

HULBERT, James Edward (NJ) 1620 Mayflower Ct Apt A405, Winter Park FL 32792 B New York NY 2/20/1926 s Jason Holmes Hulbert & Anna Louise.

BA Hob 1949; MDiv GTS 1952. D 6/15/1952 P 12/20/1952 Bp Benjamin M Washburn. Serv Dio New Jersey Trenton NJ 1985-1988; R The Ch Of S Uriel The Archangel Sea Girt NJ 1971-1988; Serv Dio New Jersey Trenton NJ 1970-1973; R H Trin Ch So River NJ 1965-1971; Urban Deptartment Dio Newark Newark NJ 1959-1961; R S Mk's Ch W Orange NJ 1957-1965; DRE Dio Newark Newark NJ 1956-1958; Vic S Lk's Epis Ch Haworth NJ 1952-1957. Ord of H Redeem. DD Nash Nashotah WI 1982; Hon Cn Trin Cathd Trenton NJ 1970.

HULET, Charles Alan (Mich) 1011 Salem Rd, Cherry Hill NJ 08034 **P Assoc S Barth's Ch Cherry Hill NJ 2001-** B Pottsville PA 5/27/1936 s Charles Hulet & Marion Gertrude. BS Tem 1959; MDiv VTS 1962; MA Tem 1967. D 6/16/1962 P 12/21/1962 Bp Oliver J Hart. m 8/30/1958 Lois Geisser c 4. Trin Ch Detroit MI 1999-2000; Dio Michigan Detroit MI 1997; All SS Ch Detroit MI 1996-1997; P-in-c Chr Ch Millville NJ 1987-1990; P-in-c H Trin Ch Pennsauken NJ 1986-1990; Assoc Gr Ch Merchantville NJ 1982-1983; P-in-c H Trin Ch Pennsauken NJ 1968-1982; R Gr Ch And The Incarn Philadelphia PA 1962-1964. Auth, "Mgmt Textbooks". Hultet Awd 1976. cheesteak@email.msn.com

HULET, Jefferson R (NJ) 14 Saint Remy Ct, Newport Coast CA 92657 **Asst S Mich And All Ang Par Corona Del Mar CA 2010-** B Champaign Illinois 6/27/1951 s Richard Earle Hulet & Kathleen Ruth. BS U of San Francisco 1981; CTh Oxf 2002; MSt Oxf 2003; MDiv GTS 2006. D 6/3/2006 P 12/9/2006 Bp George Edward Councell. m 3/21/1987 Deborah Hulet c 1. Pstr Response Team Dio New Jersey Trenton NJ 2007-2009; R S Steph's Ch Riverside NJ 2006-2009; Vic Chr Ch Palmyra NJ 2006-2007; P-in-c Riverfront Epis Team Mnstry Riverside NJ 2006-2007. frjeffhulet@yahoo.com

HULICK, Clement Updike (Alb) 1708 Helderberg Trl, Berne NY 12023 **Died 1/23/2011** B Robbinsville NJ 1/10/1923 s Albert W Hulick & Edna L. BA Hartwick Coll 1946; MS SUNY 1962. D 6/30/1963 Bp Charles Bowen Persell Jr.

HULL, Carol Wharton (SO) 14590 Wilmot Way, Lake Oswego OR 97035 B Providence RI 4/5/1943 d Willard Dee Wharton & Mildred. BA U of Texas 1963; MS Elmira Coll 1969; MDiv Bex 1984. D 6/16/1984 Bp Robert Rae Spears Jr P 12/17/1984 Bp William George Burrill. m 8/10/1963 Tommy A Hull c 2. Bex Columbus OH 1997-2008; R S Geo's Epis Ch Dayton OH 1991-2008; R S Jas Ch Hammondsport NY 1987-1991; P Ch of the Redeem Addison NY 1987; Dn SE Distr Dio Rochester Rochester NY 1986-1991; Vic Ch Of The Gd Shpd Savona NY 1984-1991. carolandtomh@gmail.com

HULL, George Andrew (Chi) 509 Brier St, Kenilworth IL 60043 **Chapl to Ret Cler & Surviving Spouses Dio Chicago Chicago IL 2011-; Pstr Assoc Ch Of The H Comf Kenilworth IL 2007-** B Elmore MN 6/1/1939 s Andrew Woodrow Hull & Naomi. BA Roa 1962; MDiv VTS 1981. D 5/28/1981 Bp A(rthur) Heath Light P 11/29/1981 Bp James Winchester Montgomery. m 8/27/1966 Dorothy Jean Leonard. Trst Epis Chars And Cmnty Serv (Eccs) Chicago IL 2001-2007; R S Mk's Barrington Hills IL 1993-2007; Bd Dir Cathd Shltr Chicago IL 1983-1994; Assoc R S Chrys's Ch Chicago IL 1981-1993; Stdt VTS Alexandria VA 1978-1981. ghull509@yahoo.com

HULL, S (Los) 13025 Bloomfield St., Studio City CA 91604 **Campbell Hall Vlly Vill CA 2010-** B New Orleans LA 1/8/1963 s Frank W Hull & Katherine Powell. BA Claremont Coll 1985; MDiv CDSP 1995. D 6/10/1995 Bp Chester Lovelle Talton P 1/1/1996 Bp Frederick Houk Borsch. m 6/17/1989 Susan Elizabeth Bade c 1. R S Mk's Par Van Nuys CA 1997-2010; S Mich and All Ang Epis Ch Studio City CA 1995-1997. hulln@campbellhall.org

HULL IV, William Franklin (Az) No address on file. B Pittsburgh PA 4/6/1941 s William Franklin Hull & Elva Frances. MDiv UTS; U of Ghana Legon GH Afr; BA Westminster Coll; MED/DED Penn 1970; NYU 1986. D 1/19/1974 P 11/1/1975 Bp John Harris Burt. c 2. S Mk's Epis Ch Jacksonville FL 2005-2006; Dio Eau Claire Eau Claire WI 2003-2004; Asst All SS-By-The-Sea Par Santa Barbara CA 1977-1978. Auth, *Innovations & Tchg Todays Undergraduates*; Auth, *The Chrisitan Coll*. amra227@yahoo.com

HULLAR, Leonard Earl (Tex) 107 E Edgebrook Dr, Houston TX 77034 B Birmingham AL 8/15/1954 s Joseph P Hullar & Barbara C. BA U of Alabama 1975; MA U of Alabama 1976; Cert Iona Sch for Mnstry 2009. D 6/20/2009 Bp C(harles) Andrew Doyle P 1/9/2010 Bp Rayford Baines High Jr. m 6/7/1975 Sharon Loveless c 2. Vic S Barn Epis Ch Houston TX 2008-2010. linkhullar@gmail.com

HULL-RYDE, Norman Arthur (WNC) 2535 Sheffield Dr, Gastonia NC 28054 B New York NY 3/7/1930 s Arthur Hull-Ryde & Kathleen T. Kent Sch; BA U NC 1952. D 12/5/1982 Bp William Gillette Weinhauer. m 9/9/1952 Anne Dewsnap Bergh c 3. D S Mk's Ch Gastonia NC 1983-2005. n952an@aol.com

HULME, Kenneth Edward (Ct) 40 Ashlar Village, Wallingford CT 06492 B Providence RI 12/2/1932 s Raymond Edward Hulme & Gladys Louise. BS Bos 1954; MDiv Ya Berk 1961. D 6/17/1961 P 12/23/1961 Bp John S Higgins. m 5/7/1955 Beverly R Coulthurst c 2. Vic Ch Of S Jn By The Sea W Haven W Haven CT 1989-1990; R S Ptr's Epis Ch Milford CT 1975-1997; Asst R S Paul's Ch Riverside CT 1970-1975; R Ch Of The Ascen Cranston RI 1966-1969; Vic S Mths Ch Coventry RI 1961-1966. kbhulme@ashlarvlg.org

HULME, Steven Edward (Ct) 26 Colony Road, East Lyme CT 06333 B Iowa City IA 3/30/1934 s Edward Stanford Hulme & Helen Landon. BA U of Iowa 1956; MDiv GTS 1959. D 6/10/1959 P 12/16/1959 Bp Gordon V Smith. m 12/31/1960 Mary Kay Sergeant c 2. R S Jn's Epis Ch Niantic CT 1971-1998; Vic S Alb's Ch Davenport IA 1960-1963; Cur Trin Cathd Davenport IA 1959-1960. shulme@snet.net

HULME, Thomas Stanford (Ia) 1617 W Benton St, Iowa City IA 52246 **Assoc P Trin Ch Iowa City IA 1991-** B Burlington IA 2/9/1930 s Edward Stanford Hulme & Helen Landon. BA U of Iowa 1952; STB GTS 1955; MSW U of Iowa 1970. D 6/15/1955 P 12/16/1955 Bp Gordon V Smith. m 6/16/1978 Jean M Marsden c 5. S Lk's Ch Ft Madison IA 1989; S Paul's Epis Ch Grinnell IA 1988; Trin Epis Par Waterloo IA 1988; Trin Ch Muscatine IA 1987; S Paul's Ch Durant IA 1970-2011; DCE Trin Ch Iowa City IA 1968-1971; R Gr Ch Cedar Rapids IA 1959-1968; P-in-c Gr Ch Boone IA 1955-1959. Auth, *Mntl Hlth Consult w Rel Leaders*; Auth, *Networking Through Reg Chld's Hlth Centers*; Auth, *Plnng Fam Enrichment Weekends - A Manual*. Cn Dio Iowa, St. Paul's Cathd, Des Moines, Iowa 2005. thomas-hulme@uiowa.edu

HULS II, Frederick Eugene (Az) 2812 N 69th Pl, Scottsdale AZ 85257 **D S Steph's Ch Phoenix AZ 1993-** B Columbus OH 3/29/1941 s Frederick E Huls & Alice Thelma. BD Nthrn Arizona U 1990. D 6/5/1993 Bp Robert Reed Shahan. m 12/15/1962 Patricia Taylor. Admin Trin Cathd Phoenix AZ 1991-1993. NAAD 1993. Phi Kappa Phi Nthrn Arizona U Flagstaff AZ 1990. fritzhuls@aol.com

HULS, Patricia Taylor (Az) 2310 N 56th St, Phoenix AZ 85008 **D S Steph's Ch Phoenix AZ 2008-** B Lakewood OH 10/25/1941 d Clyde E Taylor & Helen W. BSC The OH SU 1963; BSN Arizona St U 1980. D 1/26/2008 Bp Kirk Stevan Smith. m 12/15/1962 Frederick Eugene Huls c 2. fritz_pat_huls@msn.com

HULSE JR, Granvyl Godfrey (NH) 57 Pleasant St, Colebrook NH 03576 B Seattle WA 1/29/1929 s Granvyl Godfrey Hulse & Mae Areleen. D 6/21/1986 P 1/31/1987 Bp Douglas Edwin Theuner. c 4. P S Paul's Ch Canaan VT 1998-2011; Vic S Steph's Epis Mssn Colebrook NH 1986-1998. Auth, "Hist," *The News & Sentinel*, N&S Pub, 2011; Auth, "Hist," *The Colebrook Hse*, N&S Pub, 2010; Auth, "Hist," *From Paddy Acre to the Stevens Store*, N&S Pub, 2008; Auth, "Hist," *From Pleasant to Parsons*, N&S Pub, 2008; Auth, "Hist," *Let's Eat Out*, N&S Pub, 2002; Auth, "Hist," *A Hist of S Steph's Ch*, N&S Pub, 2000; Auth, "Hist," *Evening Star Lodge No 37*, N&S Pub, 1997. ghulse@ncia.net

✠ HULSEY, Rt Rev Sam Byron (NwT) 801 Hillcrest St, Fort Worth TX 76107 **Ret Bp of NW Texas Dio NW Texas Lubbock TX 1997-** B Fort Worth TX 2/14/1932 s Simeon Hardin Hulsey & Ruth Selby. BA W&L 1953; MDiv VTS 1958; DD VTS 1981; DD STUSo 1985; Epis TS of The SW 1998. D 6/18/1958 P 1/25/1959 Bp J(ohn) Joseph Meakins Harte Con 12/13/1980 for NwT. m 9/21/2002 Isabelle Brown Newberry. Exec Coun Dio NW Texas Lubbock TX 1991-1997; Bp Dio NW Texas Lubbock TX 1980-1997; R Ch Of The H Trin Midland TX 1978-1980; R S Dav's Epis Ch Nashville TN 1973-1978; P-in-c All SS Epis Mssn Perryton TX 1966-1973; R S Matt's Ch Pampa TX 1966-1973; Asst S Mich And All Ang Ch Dallas TX 1963-1966; Cur/Asst S Jn's Epis Ch Corsicana TX 1958-1960. DD TS U So 1985; DD VTS 1981.

HULTMAN, Eugene Bradlee (Mass) 255 N Central Ave, Quincy MA 02170 B Quincy MA 6/21/1949 s Eugene Craft Hultman & Marion Elizabeth. BA U of Massachusetts 1977; MDiv GTS 1985. D 6/1/1985 Bp John Bowen Coburn P 5/9/1986 Bp O'Kelley Whitaker. m 11/28/1992 Pamela Hilton c 4. Dio Massachusetts Boston MA 2002-2006; S Andr's Ch Hanover MA 2000-2006; R Trin Ch Bridgewater MA 1996-2000; Ch Of The Gd Shpd Fairhaven MA 1991-1996; S Steph's Ch Providence RI 1989-1991; Dio Cntrl New York Syracuse NY 1988-1989; Vic Emm Ch E Syracuse NY 1988-1989; Int Gr Ch Utica NY 1987-1988; Cn S Paul's Cathd Syracuse NY 1985-1987. BRADHULTMAN@HOTMAIL.COM

✠ **HULTSTRAND, Rt Rev Donald Maynard** (Spr) 1706 Parkins Mill Rd, Greenville SC 29607 **Bp-in-Res Chr Ch Greenville SC 2005-** B Parkers Prairie MN 4/16/1927 s Aaron Emmanuel Hultstrand & Selma Avendla. BA Macalester Coll 1950; BD Bex 1953; MDiv Bex 1972; DD Nash 1986; DD Bex 2004. D 6/14/1953 Bp Hamilton Hyde Kellogg P 12/19/1953 Bp Stephen E Keeler Con 2/6/1982 for Spr. m 2/18/2006 Lenora Hultstrand c 2. Ch Deploy Bd Dio Springfield Springfield IL 1985-1991; Joint Cmsn on Evang & Renwl Dio Springfield Springfield IL 1985-1988; Joint Cmsn Prog Bdgt & Fin Dio Springfield Springfield IL 1983-1989; Bp Dio Springfield Springfield IL 1982-1991; R Trin Ch Greeley CO 1979-1981; The AFP Lancaster PA 1975-1979; R S Paul's Epis Ch Duluth MN 1969-1975; Assoc S Andr's Ch Kansas City MO 1968-1969; R S Mk's Ch Canton OH 1962-1968; R Gr Memi Ch Wabasha MN 1957-1961; H Trin Epis Ch Luverne MN 1953-1957; S Jn Worthington MN 1953-1957. Auth, *And God Shall Wipe Away All Tears*; Auth, *The Praying Ch*. AFP, Exec Dir 1975-1979. Hon Cn Trin Cathd Cleveland OH 1966. ahultstrand@live.com

HUMBERT, Karen Flynt (WVa) St. John's Episcopal Church, 3000 Washington Blvd, Huntington WV 25705 **S Jn's Ch Huntington WV 2008-** B Radford

VA 7/12/1959 d James Flynt & Linda P. BA E Carolina U 1982; MDiv GTS 2006. D 6/24/2006 P 1/20/2007 Bp Dorsey Felix Henderson. m 1/26/1985 W Lindsley Humbert c 1. S Alb's Ch Lexington SC 2006-2008. mtr.kfh@gmail.com

HUMKE, Richard Herbert (Ky) 200 S Galt Ave, Louisville KY 40206 **ExCoun Dio Kentucky Louisville KY 1963-** B Dubuque IA 7/3/1931 s Frederick Oliver Humke & Martha L. BA U of Iowa 1955; BD VTS 1956. D 6/21/1956 P 12/21/1956 Bp Gordon V Smith. m 8/20/1960 Joan Reed c 2. R S Matt's Epis Ch Louisville KY 1973-1996; Assoc S Fran In The Fields Harrods Creek KY 1968-1973; R Gr Ch Hopkinsville KY 1961-1968; P-in-c Gd Samar Epis Ch Honolulu HI 1958-1961; Cur Trin Cathd Davenport IA 1956-1958. richardhumke@gmail.com

HUMM, Matt (O) 2747 Fairmount Blvd, Cleveland Heights OH 44106 B Akron OH 4/2/1979 s Richard L Humm & Carolyn Sue. BA SE U 2002; MDiv Prot Epicopal Sem in Virginia 2008. D 6/13/2009 P 12/19/2009 Bp Mark Hollingsworth Jr. m 12/15/2001 Charity Ann Bridge c 2. Cler-in-Charge S Alb Epis Ch Cleveland Heights OH 2009-2011; Yth Min S Paul's Epis Ch Cleveland Heights OH 2009-2011. rmhumm@gmail.com

HUMMEL, Marvin Heber (Del) 1 Bristol Ct, Newark DE 19702 **Assoc S Jas Ch Wilmington DE 2004-** B Middleburg PA 11/27/1927 s Heber Harrison Hummel & Vera Ann. BA Otterbein Coll 1949; BD, STM Crozer TS 1953; U of Pennsylvania 1953; Cert. Bex 1954; MA U Of Delaware Newark 1968. D 6/20/1954 Bp Arthur R Mc Kinstry P 5/1/1955 Bp John Brooke Mosley. c 1. P-in-c Ch Of Our Merc Sav Penns Grove NJ 2002-2003; P-in-c S Geo's Ch Pennsville NJ 1999-2001; Ch Of The Nativ New Castle DE 1988; Dio Delaware Wilmington DE 1984-1988; P-in-c Ch Of The Nativ New Castle DE 1978-1988; Vic All SS Epis Ch Delmar DE 1954-1959. Ed/Contrib, "Wellness," Kendall/Hatl, 1991; Auth, "Written Cmncatn," Kendall/Hart, 1988; Columnist, "Newark Post," 1970.

HUMMEL, Thomas Charles (Va) 1200 N Quaker Ln, Alexandria VA 22302 B Middletown CT 4/16/1947 s Reginald Hummel & Beatrice. BA Ups 1969; MDiv Yale DS 1972; Resrch Fell Oxf 1976; MA Van 1976; PhD Van 1981. D 9/10/1972 P 7/25/1973 Bp George E Rath. m 12/28/1968 Ruth Victor. VTS Alexandria VA 2006; VTS Alexandria VA 1991; P-in-c S Anselm's Epis Ch Nashville TN 1974-1975. "Lord Who May Dwell in Your Sanctuary, Who May Abide on your H Hill: A Palestinian Pilgrimage," *They Came and They Saw*, Melisende, London, 2000; "Patterns of the Past Prospects for the Future: The Chr Heritage in the H Land," Melisende, London, 1999; Auth, "Patterns of The Sacr," Scorpion Cavendish, London, 1995; Auth, "Engl Prot Pilgrims of the 19th Century," *The Chr Heritage in the H Land*, Scorpion Cavendish, London, 1995; "The Sacramentality of the H Land," *The Sense of the Sacramential*, SPCK, London, 1995. Conf of Angl Theologicans. Natl Endwmt Fell 1989; Fulbright Fell 1987; Jarvis Fellowshp Yale DS 1972; Fellowshp 76-78 Epis Ch Fndtn. tch@episcopalhighschool.org

HUMMEL, Virginia (Ct) 30 Woodland Street, #6D, Hartford CT 06105 B York PA 4/22/1936 d Richard Mansfield Klussman & Thelma Marie. BA U Of Delaware Newark 1958; MDiv GTS 1994. D 6/4/1994 Bp Jack Marston McKelvey P 12/17/1994 Bp Joe Morris Doss. c 2. P-in-c S Andr's Ch Milford CT 2006-2009; R S Lk's Ch So Glastonbury CT 1999-2006; Cur S Lk's Epis Ch Metuchen NJ 1994-1999. amma860@sbcglobal.net

HUMMELL, Mark William (NY) NYUAD, PO Box 903, New York NY 10276 B Cincinnati OH 7/24/1965 s Mitchell Cowin Hummell & Virginia Rose. BA U of Notre Dame 1987; MS Arizona St U 1999; MDiv Yale DS 2002. D 6/21/2003 P 6/9/2004 Bp Andrew Donnan Smith. Chair, Soc Concerns Cmsn Dio New York New York City NY 2008-2010; Assoc R Ch Of The Ascen New York NY 2007-2010; Dio New York New York City NY 2003-2007; Cathd Of St Jn The Div New York NY 2003. NASW 1988. R. Wm Muehl Awd For Preaching Berkeley Div. At Yale 2002. fatherhummell@gmail.com

HUMPHREY, Barbara Myers (Roch) 5389 County Rd. 36, Honeoye NY 14471 B Rochester NY 9/7/1929 d Ford Albert Myers & Lois Julianna. RN Gnrl Hosp Sch of Nrsng 1950; CRDS 1982. D 11/14/1981 P 5/14/1983 Bp Robert Rae Spears Jr. m 2/24/1950 Paul Humphrey c 3. Mem, Dioc Coun Dio Rochester Rochester NY 2005-2007; Dn, Monroe Dist Dio Rochester Rochester NY 1991-1994; S Mths Epis Ch E Rochester NY 1985-1994; Assoc Ch Of The Gd Shpd Webster NY 1983-1985; Consult Dio Rochester Rochester NY 1981-1999. "Chr be w Me- The Journey of an Icon Writing Workshop," Living Water, 2004. EWC 1976. revrn3@frontiernet.net

HUMPHREY, Christine Ann (Mich) 544 W Iroquois Rd, Pontiac MI 48341 **R S Mary's-In-The-Hills Ch Lake Orion MI 1995-** B Lansing MI 9/19/1946 d Harold E B Humphrey & Dorothea Marie. BA Albion Coll 1968; Bex 1989; S Cyril Methodist Sem 1989. D 12/2/1989 Bp H Coleman McGehee Jr P 4/1/1991 Bp R(aymond) Stewart Wood Jr. Assoc Trin Epis Ch Farmington Hills MI 1993-1994; All SS Epis Ch Pontiac MI 1991-1993. catpriest@aol.com

HUMPHREY, Georgia Lehman (Colo) 15064 Sheridan Ave, Clive IA 50325 B Lancaster PA 3/29/1941 d Joseph A Lehman & Georgiana E. BS Millersville U 1963; Med Arcadia Coll 1983; MDiv SWTS 1993; DMin SWTS 2003. D 6/19/1993 P 4/1/1994 Bp Hays H. Rockwell. m 7/17/2003 Janet M Nelson c 3. Dir of Congrl Dvlpmt and Tchr SWTS Evanston IL 2006-2007; S Barn Epis Ch Denver CO 1996-2006; Min For Mssn & Dir Chr Ch Cathd S Louis MO 1993-1995. Richard Hooker Forum; SCHC 1987. glhumphrey0326@gmail.com

HUMPHREY JR, Howard MacKenzie (O) 6295 Chagrin River Rd, Chagrin Falls OH 44022 **R S Mart's Ch Chagrin Falls OH 2001-** B Edenton NC 7/24/1949 s Howard Mackenzie Humphrey & Emma Marjorie. BS U of Texas 1972; MS U of Texas 1974; MDiv Epis TS of The SW 1983. D 6/25/1983 P 4/1/1984 Bp Gerald Nicholas McAllister. m 6/13/1987 Sharon Armstrong. R S Mich's Epis Ch Arlington VA 1996-2001; R S Dav's Ch Oklahoma City OK 1988-1995; Cur S Jn's Ch Oklahoma City OK 1983-1987. SHN 1990. frhumphrey@roadrunner.com

HUMPHREY, Marian Teresa (WA) 9801 Livingston Rd, Fort Washington MD 20744 **Asst S Jn's Ch Ft Washington MD 2011-** B Hartford CT 7/13/1954 d Patrick James Humphrey & Joan Lynch. BA St Jos Coll 1976; MSW Virginia Commonwealth U 1988; MDiv Wesley TS 2007; Post- Grad Dplma VTS 2010. D 6/4/2011 Bp John Chane. fiesta818@verizon.net

HUMPHREY, Martin Graham (Mass) 401 12th St S Apt 611, Arlington VA 22202 **Died 1/18/2011** B Coventry UK 7/28/1951 s Bruce Edwin Humphrey & Joyce Edna. BA FD 1973; MDiv EDS 1976; Cert San Francisco St U 1979; Cert California St Teachers Coll 1990. D 6/5/1976 Bp George E Rath P 12/18/1976 Bp John Bowen Coburn. Auth, "Bay Area Rapid Transit". martyact@aol.com

HUMPHREY, M(ary) Beth (WA) St Albans School, Mount St Albans, Washington DC 20016 **Groton Sch Groton MA 2010-; Chapl S Jn's Chap Groton MA 2010-** B Hartselle AL 6/4/1956 d Wayne Morrow Humphrey & Sue Maddox. BS U of Alabama 1977; PhD U NC 1982; MDiv STUSo 2003. D 5/20/2003 Bp Marc Handley Andrus P 1/26/2004 Bp A(lbert) Theodore Eastman. m 12/31/2003 Jonathan Hemenway Glazier c 5. S Geo's Epis Ch Arlington VA 2005; Cathd of St Ptr & St Paul Washington DC 2003-2010. bhumphrey@groton.org

HUMPHREY, Nathan J A (WA) St Paul's Church, 2430 K St NW, Washington DC 20037 **Vic S Paul's Par Washington DC 2005-** B Anaheim CA 7/20/1973 s David Gleason Humphrey & Lois Fay. BA St. Jn's Coll Annapolis MD 1994; DAS Ya Berk 1997; MDiv Yale DS 1997; Cert Jn Hopkins U 1999; Westcott Hse Cambridge 2006. D 11/1/2001 Bp John Leslie Rabb P 5/9/2002 Bp Robert Wilkes Ihloff. m 9/4/2004 Anne McCabe Stone c 2. Cur S Jas Ch Monkton MD 2001-2005. Auth, *Gathering The NeXt Generation: Essays on the Formation and Mnstry of GenX Priests*, Morehouse Pub, 2000; Auth, "The Still, Sm Multiple Choice," *Re:Generation Quarterly*, 2000; Auth, "A Bapt Benediction," *Re:Generation Quarterly*, 2000. Gathering The NeXt Generation Core Team 2002; Grad Soc Coun, Ya Berk 2001-2002; Trst, Ya Berk 1995-1997. Thos Phillips Awd for Liturg Excellence Ya Berk 1997; Resrch Fell Yale DS 1997; Harriet Jackson Ely Prize in Theol Ya 1996; Hooker Fllshp in Theol Stds Ya 1996; Palmer Schlrshp for Serv to Berkeley Ya Berk 1995. njahumphrey@gmail.com

HUMPHREY, Shirley Hall Wise (WLa) Po Box 10976, Pensacola FL 32524 **Died 8/30/2010** B Columbus OH 8/28/1922 d Stanley Delano Hintz & Ruth Elizabeth. OH SU 1943; BA LSU 1978; MDiv Epis TS of The SW 1984. D 5/10/1986 Bp Willis Ryan Henton P 3/1/1990 Bp Robert Jefferson Hargrove Jr. c 5. Assoc, Cnvnt of St. Helena's 1951; La Chapl Assn, Wla Cleric Assn, Natl Cler 1990. swhumphrey@cox.net

HUMPHREYS, Eugene L (NC) 3601 Central Ave, Charlotte NC 28205 B Rome GA 4/12/1955 s William P Humphreys & Alice H. D Trng Duke; BA Queens U 1984. D 6/20/2009 Bp Michael Bruce Curry. genehumphreys1@bellsouth.net

HUMPHREYS, Walter Lee (ETenn) 7113 Hampshire Dr, Knoxville TN 37909 B Long Beach CA 1/16/1939 s Cecil Walter Humphreys & Alberta Mae. BA U Roch 1961; STB Ya Berk 1964; PhD UTS 1970. D 6/16/1964 P 1/1/1965 Bp George West Barrett. m 6/22/1963 Laurel Kristine Jensen c 1. Cur Chr Epis Ch Hornell NY 1964-1966. Auth, "Crisis & Story: Intro To OT"; Auth, "Tragedy & Hebr Tradition The Jos Story In Genesis".

HUMPHRIES, Charles E (SeFla) 9127 N.W. First Avenue, Miami Shores FL 33150 **D All Souls' Epis Ch Miami Bch FL 2010-; Treas NEAC Washington DC 2009-** B Newark NJ 10/20/1937 s Charles Humphries & Mary. Cert Dioc Sch for Chr Stds 2003. D 12/16/2005 Bp James Hamilton Ottley. Conf of Blessed Sacr 1979. anglicansmoker@aol.com

HUMPHRIES JR, John Curtis (CNY) 405 Euclid Avenue, Elmira NY 14905 B Alexandria VA 7/29/1932 s John Curtis Humphries & Kathleen Selma. BA Lynchburg Coll 1957; MDiv VTS 1960. D 6/28/1960 Bp Frederick D Goodwin P 1/14/1961 Bp Nelson Marigold Burroughs. c 4. R Trin Ch Elmira NY 1975-1997; Asst S Mk's Ch Mt Kisco NY 1968-1975; Min in charge S Mk's Epis Ch Wadsworth OH 1960-1968. jhum@stny.rr.com

HUNDLEY, Brooks F (WA) 2810 35th St NW, Washington DC 20007 **Cathd of St Ptr & St Paul Washington DC 2005-; S Albans Sch Washington DC 2005-** B New York NY 5/1/1970 s Jay Hundley & Isabel. BA Skidmore Coll

1992; MDiv UTS 2002. D 6/11/2005 P 1/21/2006 Bp John Chane. m 6/20/1998 Courtney Hundley c 2. bhundley@cathedral.org

HUNGATE, Carla Valinda (At) 4318 Windmill Trce, Douglasville GA 30135 **D Gd Shpd Epis Ch Austell GA 2000-** B Montgomery AL 7/20/1954 d Obie T Head & Lavada Sara. EFM STUSo; W Georgia Coll. D 10/28/1995 Bp Frank Kellogg Allan. m 4/2/1973 Robert Benjamin Hungate c 3.

HUNGERFORD, Eric Paul (Tex) 3901 S Panther Creek Dr, The Woodlands TX 77381 **Cur Trin Epis Ch The Woodlands TX 2010-** B Austin TX 4/8/1984 s Donald L Hungerford & Michelle F. BA Austin Coll 2006; MDiv Epis TS Of The SW 2010. D 6/19/2010 Bp C(harles) Andrew Doyle. m 8/5/2006 Shyla C Ray. ehungerford@trinitywoodlands.org

HUNKINS, Claire Morfit (SVa) PO Box 186, Oak Hall VA 23416 **Vic Emm Ch Oak Hall VA 2008-** B New Brunswick NJ 10/16/1950 d Edwin Fiske Morfit & Margaret Edna. BS U of Kentucky 1973; MDiv Bex 2006. D 5/14/2005 Bp Herbert Thompson Jr P 6/24/2006 Bp Kenneth Lester Price. c 5. P-in-c Trin Epis Ch London OH 2006-2008. cmhunkins@yahoo.com

HUNKINS, Orin James (Okla) 3724 Bonaire Pl, Edmond OK 73013 **Emm Epis Ch San Angelo TX 2000-** B Lincoln NE 10/6/1935 s Orin Melven Hunkins & Mary Jane. BA U of Nebraska 1961; MDiv SWTS 1962; MS U of Missouri 1982. D 6/20/1962 P 12/21/1962 Bp Russell T Rauscher. m 5/29/1959 Carol Anderson c 4. Int S Paul's Ch Altus OK 2006-2008; Int S Mary's Ch Edmond OK 2001-2002; R S Andr's Epis Ch Lawton OK 1994-2000; R Trin Ch Arkansas City KS 1986-1993; Asst S Paul's Ch Kansas City KS 1981-1986; Dio Missouri S Louis MO 1979-1980; R S Alb's Epis Ch Fulton MO 1977-1979; S Lk's Ch Kearney NE 1971-1977; R S Thos' Epis Ch Falls City NE 1967-1971; R S Mk's Ch Creighton NE 1962-1967; R S Ptr's Ch Neligh NE 1962-1967. ECom 1991-1994. orinhunkins@mac.com

HUNLEY, Deborah Hentz (SwVa) 1101 Franklin Rd Sw, Roanoke VA 24016 **R Chr Epis Ch Roanoke VA 1991-** B Minneapolis MN 6/16/1952 d Robert Jeremiah Hentz & Zelda Verona. BA Hollins U 1974; MDiv Yale DS 1977. D 5/29/1977 P 12/3/1977 Bp William Henry Marmion. m 4/20/1985 William Johnson Hunley c 1. Assoc R Chr Epis Ch Roanoke VA 1985-1990; Dio SW Virginia Roanoke VA 1980-1981; Asst S Jas Ch Roanoke VA 1977-1978. dhunley@christroanoke.org

HUNN, Meg Buerkel (NC) 412 N East Street, Raleigh NC 27604 **Assoc R Chr Epis Ch Raleigh NC 2010-** B Tupelo MS 12/8/1973 d Jay Allen Buerkel & Susan Elizabeth. BA Mary Baldwin Coll 1996; MDiv GTS 2004. D 6/24/2004 P 1/6/2005 Bp Frank Neff Powell. m 7/27/2009 Michael Carter Buerkel Hunn. Ch Of The Nativ Raleigh NC 2010; Davidson Coll Epis Campus Min Dio No Carolina Raleigh NC 2007-2009; Assoc R S Alb's Ch Davidson NC 2007-2009; Asst P The Ch Of The H Trin Rittenhouse Philadelphia PA 2004-2007. megbuerkel@gmail.com

HUNSINGER, Jimmie Ruth (Fla) 350 Sw Stallion Gln, Lake City FL 32024 **D Dio Florida Jacksonville FL 2001-; D Dio SW Florida Sarasota FL 1990-** B Birmingham AL 8/28/1935 d Houston Henery Coshatt & Frances Elizabeth. BSN U of Vermont 1953; Med Rhode Island Coll 1973. D 6/30/1990 Bp Rogers Sanders Harris. m 4/15/1994 Vern Richard Hunsinger. S Jas' Epis Ch Lake City FL 2000-2011. NAAD 1990. hansinggr8@hughes.net

HUNT, Ashley Stephen (EC) No address on file. B London UK 8/9/1950 s Frederick James Hunt & Margaret Louise. GOE St. Jn's Coll Nottingham Gb 1983. Rec 2/1/1988 as Priest Bp Calvin Onderdonk Schofield Jr. m 8/21/1977 Lyda Bell Timm c 2. R S Thos' Ch Windsor NC 1988-1991; S Mk The Evang Ft Lauderdale FL 1988; Assoc R S Mk The Evang Ft Lauderdale FL 1987-1988.

HUNT SSP, Barnabas John William (SanD) PO Box 34548, San Diego CA 92163 B Sayre PA 1/6/1937 s Clarence Elmer Hunt & Margarite Frances. Clackamas Cmnty Coll; Elmira Coll; Mt Hood Cmnty Coll Gresham OR; Portland St U; BS Penn 1958. D 11/3/1983 P 5/5/1984 Bp Charles Brinkley Morton. Mutual Mnstry Revs Team Dio San Diego San Diego CA 2002-2003; Int S Jn's Ch Indio CA 1988-1989; Int S Jn's Ch Indio CA 1984-1985. Amer Coll of Hlth Care Admin 1975; Conf of Angl Rel Ord of Amer 1972; NECAD 1982; Recovery Ministers 1982; Soc of S Paul 1961; The Most Venerable Ord of the Hosp of St. Jn of Jerusal 2008. Hon Cn S Paul's Cathd San Diego CA 2000; Fell Amer Coll Healthcare Admin Washington DC 1978. anbssp@earthlink.net

HUNT, Donald Aldrich (Mass) 221 Atlantic Ave, Marblehead MA 01945 B Pawtucket RI 7/15/1930 s Gordon Everett Hunt & Helen Curtis. BA Bos 1954; MDiv Ya Berk 1960. D 6/18/1960 P 12/21/1960 Bp Anson Phelps Stokes Jr. m 8/21/1971 Louise A Mohlenhoff c 4. Chapl, ACPE Supvsr Beverly Hosp Beverly MA 1969-1992; R Ch Of Our Sav Middleboro MA 1967-1968; R S Jn's Epis Ch Franklin MA 1962-1967; Cur S Ptr's Ch Beverly MA 1960-1962. LAHDAH@COMCAST.NET

HUNT, Edward Walter (CNY) 1024 12th St. S., Birmingham AL 35205 B West Orange NJ 6/11/1959 s Edward Walter Hunt & Lorraine Frances. BA SUNY 1981; MA U Of Delaware Newark 1984; MDiv GTS 2002. D 6/1/2002 P 12/6/2002 Bp Jack Marston McKelvey. m 3/15/1986 Mary Coleman Joiner c 3. R Zion Ch Rome NY 2004-2011; Cur S Paul's Ch Rochester NY 2002-2004. FRHUNT@BHAM.RR.COM

HUNT III, Ernest Edward (Eur) 3310 Fairmount St Apt 9b, Dallas TX 75201 B Oakland CA 5/23/1934 s Ernest Edward Hunt & Maselia. BA Stan 1956; MDiv Epis TS of The SW 1959; MA Stan 1965; Fllshp Coll of Preachers 1974; Fllshp Epis TS of The SW 1976; DMin PrTS 1980; DD Epis TS of The SW 1997. D 6/21/1959 Bp James Albert Pike P 3/1/1960 Bp George Richard Millard. m 8/23/1958 Elsie Beard c 2. Dn The Amer Cathd of the H Trin Paris 75008 FR 1992-2003; Dn S Matt's Cathd Dallas TX 1988-1992; R The Ch Of The Epiph New York NY 1972-1988; Assoc S Paul's Epis Ch Salinas CA 1963-1966; Trin Ch Gonzales CA 1959-1963. Auth, "Terror on E 7nd. St," *Terror on E 72nd. St*, Publish Amer, 2009; Auth, "Paris On Fire," *Paris On Fire*, Publish Amer, 2008; Auth, "A Death in Dallas," *A Death in Dallas*, Publish Amer, 2007; Auth, "Paris Under Siege," *Paris Under Siege*, Publish Amer, 2006; Auth, "Sermon Struggles," *Sermon Struggles*, Seabury Press, 1982. Cmnty of Cross & Nails 1978; Ord of S Jn of Jerusalem 2000. Par hall named in hon. H Trin, Paris, France 2003; DD Epis TS SW 1997. eeh546@aol.com

✠ **HUNT III, Rt Rev George Nelson** (RI) 1401 Fountain Grove Pkwy #107, Santa Rosa CA 95403 **Ret Bp of Rhode Island S Patricks Ch Kenwood CA 1998-; Ret Bp of RI Dio Rhode Island Providence RI 1995-** B Louisville KY 12/6/1931 s George Nelson Hunt & Jessie M. BA U So 1953; MDiv VTS 1956; DD Ya Berk 1980; DD VTS 1981; DD Br 1991; LHD U of Rhode Island 1996. D 6/13/1956 Bp Charles Gresham Marmion P 12/13/1956 Bp James W Hunter Con 5/3/1980 for RI. m 6/18/1955 Barbara Noel Plamp c 3. Asst Dio New Jersey Trenton NJ 1997-1998; Int Dio Hawaii Honolulu HI 1995-1996; Prog Bdgt & Fin Dio Rhode Island Providence RI 1983-1994; Bp Dio Rhode Island Providence RI 1980-1994; Exec Off Dio California San Francisco CA 1975-1980; Chair COM Dio California San Francisco CA 1971-1975; R S Paul's Epis Ch Salinas CA 1970-1975; R S Anselm's Epis Ch Lafayette CA 1965-1970; R S Alb's Ch Worland WY 1962-1965; Asst S Paul's Ch Oakland CA 1960-1962; Vic H Trin Epis Ch Gillette WY 1956-1960. Bro Awd Natl Conf Of Christians & Jews 1988; Never Again Awd Ri Jewish Fed 1985; Civil Libertarian Of The Year ACLU 1984. gnhuntl@aol.com

H

HUNT, Hazel Bailey (Be) Po Box 86, Towanda PA 18848 B PA 12/9/1943 d Thomas F Bailey & Hazel Ellen. D 10/23/2001 Bp Paul Victor Marshall. m 5/9/1964 Ronald Leroy Hunt c 1. Dn Chr Ch Towanda PA 2001-2005. hazelhunt@sosbbs.com

HUNT, John C (O) 44267 Route 511 East, Oberlin OH 44074 B Louisville KY 9/16/1936 s George Nelson Hunt & Jessie Mae. BA U of Louisiana 1959; BD VTS 1964. D 1/6/1965 Bp Charles Gresham Marmion. m 5/11/1963 Iris Rivera Hunt c 1.

HUNT, John Patrick (NJ) 55 Lake Delaware Drive, Lake Delaware, Delhi NY 13753 **R S Jas Ch Delhi NY 2006-** B Pasadena CA 12/25/1946 s John Quinby Hunt & Virginia. BA Otterbein U 1969; MDiv UTS 1980; Cert Blanton-Peale Grad Inst 1992. D 6/21/1980 Bp John Harris Burt P 6/6/1981 Bp Robert Campbell Witcher Sr. Int S Simeon's By The Sea No Wildwood NJ 2004-2006; S Jn The Evang Ch Blackwood NJ 2001-2004; R Historic Ch of Ascen Atlantic City NJ 1996-2000; Assoc Admin S Geo's Par Flushing NY 1990-1991; R S Phil And S Jas Ch New Hyde Pk NY 1985-1990; S Ptr's Ch Rosedale NY 1984-1985; P H Trin Epis Ch Vlly Stream NY 1982-1983; Cur Ch Of The Trsfg Freeport NY 1980-1982. SSC 1990. frjphunt@delhitel.net

HUNT, Katherine Ann (Ak) 2006 W 31st Ave, Anchorage AK 99517 **Chr Ch Anchorage AK 2006-** B Bellington WA 4/15/1963 d Arthur Bernard Hunt & Jean M. BA U of Alaska. D 12/16/2000 P 6/18/2001 Bp Mark Lawrence Mac Donald. m 6/25/1994 Arthur Franklin Bell c 3. S Mary's Ch Anchorage AK 2001-2004. revkatherine@christchurchanchorage.org

HUNT, Lisa Wynne (Tex) 419 Woodland St, Nashville TN 37206 **R S Steph's Epis Ch Houston TX 2006-** B Pikeville TN 5/6/1959 d Howard Hunt & Frona. BA U of Toledo 1982; MDiv Van 1986; CAS GTS 1987. D 9/19/1987 P 4/16/1988 Bp George Lazenby Reynolds Jr. m 11/18/1989 Bruce S Farrar c 2. S Ann's Ch Nashville TN 1989-2006; The TS at The U So Sewanee TN 1988-1989; The U So (Sewanee) Sewanee TN 1988-1989; Dio Tennessee Nashville TN 1987-1988; Int S Andr's Epis Ch New Johnsonville TN 1987-1988. lhunt@ststephenshouston.org

HUNT, Marshall William (Mass) Po Box 1205, East Harwich MA 02645 B Bristol CT 12/3/1931 s Henry Hunt & Ardena. BA U of New Hampshire 1953; EDS 1956; Med MI SU 1964. D 6/16/1956 P 4/15/1957 Bp Charles F Hall. m 11/24/2001 Victoria Wells c 1. Int S Dav's Epis Ch So Yarmouth MA 2008-2010; Int S Chris's Ch Chatham MA 2001-2003; Asst S Anne's In The Fields Epis Ch Lincoln MA 1998-2001; Int Gr Ch Vineyard Haven MA 1996-1998; Dio Massachusetts Boston MA 1994-1996; Int S Anne's In The Fields Epis Ch Lincoln MA 1994-1995; Int The Ch Of The Epiph Washington DC 1992-1994; Stwdshp Off Dio Massachusetts Boston MA 1978-1988; R S Anne's Ch Lowell MA 1969-1992; Assoc R Gr Ch Detroit MI 1967-1968; Assoc R S Jn's Ch Royal Oak MI 1961-1967; P-in-c S Pat's Epis Ch Madison Heights MI 1961-1967; R S Ptr's Epis Ch Hillsdale MI 1958-1961; Cur Par Of

S Jas Ch Keene NH 1956-1958. Int Mnstry Ntwk 1988; Mem, Marg Coffin PB Soc 2004; Phillips Brooks Cler 1976-1992; Pres, Marg Coffin PB Soc 2005. VWMWHUNT@GMAIL.COM

HUNT, Meredith (WMich) 110 S Clay St, Sturgis MI 49091 **Trst, Whittemore Fndt Dio Wstrn Michigan Kalamazoo MI 2006-; R St Jn's Epis Ch of Sturgis Sturgis MI 2004-** B Philadelphia PA 5/9/1948 d Harry Edwin Hunt & Edythe Joy. BA Swarthmore Coll 1970; MDiv EDS 1974. D 6/8/1974 Bp John Melville Burgess P 6/18/1977 Bp H Coleman McGehee Jr. m 9/19/1970 David Matthew Lillvis c 2. Cn Evang Cathd Ch Of S Paul Detroit MI 1992-2004; Assoc P S Lk's Epis Ch Allen Pk MI 1989-1992; Bp Of ArmdF-Epis Ch Cntr New York NY 1984-1992; Cmsn on Alcosm and Chairperson Dio Michigan Detroit MI 1982-1988; Asst Chr Ch Dearborn MI 1979-1980; Assoc Emm Ch Detroit MI 1977-1978; EDS Cambridge MA 1975-1976; New Ch Plnng Consult Dio Massachusetts Boston MA 1974-1975. Auth, "Healing at Tenebrae," *Sharing mag*, OSL, 2011; Auth, "A Moment w Mary Chester," *Guideposts*, Guideposts mag, 2005. Assn of Profsnl Chapl - Bd Cert 1984; Intl OSL the Physcn 1992; Michigan Assn of Alco and Drug Abuse Counselors - Cert 1984. Acad Fell Epis Sem of the SW 1997. hunt4merry@charter.net

HUNT, Paul Stuart (Pa) 212 S High St, West Chester PA 19382 **The Ch Of The H Trin W Chester PA 2008-** B Gilette WY 12/2/1958 s George Nelson Hunt & Barbara P. BA Providence Coll 1983; MDiv CDSP 1988. D 6/25/1988 P 1/28/1989 Bp George Nelson Hunt III. m 8/6/1983 Jennifer L Osborn c 3. S Dunst's Epis Ch Succasunna NJ 2006-2008; S Jas Ch Upper Montclair NJ 2005-2006; Cn Dio Newark Newark NJ 1999-2005; R S Andr's Epis Ch Lincoln Pk NJ 1991-1999; Asst S Chris's Ch Chatham MA 1988-1991. canonhunt@ecunet.org

HUNT, Teresa Gioia (Mich) 1335 Berryman Avenue, Bethel Park PA 15102 B New York NY 5/28/1946 d Joseph Daniel Gioia & Concetta. BA Manhattanville Coll 1968; MA U MI 1972; MDiv TESM 1988; Ph.D. Duquesne U 2009. D 6/4/1988 Bp Alden Moinet Hathaway P 12/17/1988 Bp Jose Antonio Ramos. c 2. Celebrant and Mentor for Total Mnstry S Pat's Epis Ch Madison Heights MI 2004-2010; Long Term Supply S Mich And All Ang Epis Ch Lincoln Pk MI 2001-2002; R Gr Ch Mt Clemens MI 1997-1999; R S Andr's Epis Ch New Kensington PA 1991-1997; Assoc S Thos Ch Mamaroneck NY 1988-1990. Assn of Profsnl Chapl 2004; Bd Salvation Army Mt. Clemens. MI 1997-1999; Epis Natl Cleric Assn 1988; P.E.O. Intl 1976; SE Michigan Hosp Chapl Assn 2001-2009. Grant Doctoral Resrch Ford Fndt 1973; Fulbright Fllshp Untd States Govt 1968. revdoctghunt@comcast.net

HUNT, Terry Lynn (Nev) 79 Northwood Commons Pl, Chico CA 95973 B Holt MI 1/27/1937 s Ernest Earl Hunt & Virgilene May. BA Alma Coll 1959; BD VTS 1967. D 6/15/1967 Bp Charles Ellsworth Bennison Jr P 7/1/1968 Bp Charles Bennison. m 11/9/1975 Carol J Herring c 4. Caplain U of Nevada, Reno Dio Nevada Las Vegas NV 1989-1990; R S Steph's Epis Ch Reno NV 1987-1989; Stff Trin Ch Toledo OH 1976-1987; Assoc S Michaels In The Hills Toledo OH 1969-1976; Asst S Mk's Ch Grand Rapids MI 1967-1969. Jefferson Awd Amer Inst for Publ Serv 1985. chicobookhawk@att.net

HUNT, Victoria Wells (Mass) Po Box 1205, East Harwich MA 02645 **Chapl to Ret Cler Dio Massachusetts Boston MA 2007-; Supply P Dio Massachusetts Boston MA 2002-** B Cleveland OH 5/5/1938 d Reginald Douglas Wells & Vera Jane. BA Wellesley Coll 1960; MA Andover Newton TS 1970. D 11/26/1977 Bp Morris Fairchild Arnold P 5/5/1979 Bp John Bowen Coburn. m 11/24/2001 Marshall William Hunt. Co-Int P S Dav's Epis Ch So Yarmouth MA 2008-2010; R Trin Epis Ch Weymouth MA 1983-2001; Asst Ch Of S Jn The Evang Duxbury MA 1980-1982; D Gr Ch Newton MA 1977-1979; Lay Asst S Ptr's Ch Weston MA 1973-1976. P Assoc SSM (SSM) 1968; SCHC (SCHC) 1977. VWMWHUNT@GMAIL.COM

HUNT, William Gilbert (Miss) 510 Godsey Rd., Apt. 183, Bristol TN 37620 B Norfolk VA 1/17/1934 s Gilbert Hunt & Mildred Lucile. AA Miami-Dade Cmnty Coll 1966; LTh Nash 1969. D 6/24/1969 P 12/29/1969 Bp James Loughlin Duncan. m 2/23/1952 Myra Kennedy c 3. R Calv Epis Ch Cleveland MS 1990-1994; Vic Gr Ch Rosedale MS 1990-1994; Asst H Cross Epis Ch Sanford FL 1987-1990; Vic S Jude's Ch Orange City FL 1984-1986; Asst All SS Epis Ch Kansas City MO 1980-1984; Dio W Missouri Kansas City MO 1978-1980; Vic S Geo Epis Ch Camdenton MO 1978-1980; Vic Trin Epis Ch Lebanon MO 1978-1980; R H Sacr Pembroke Pines FL 1974-1978; Cn Trin Cathd Miami FL 1972-1974; Cur S Mart's Epis Ch Pompano Bch FL 1969-1972.

HUNTER, Anne Louise (Me) 1593 Buck Mountain Rd., Earlysville VA 22936 B Annapolis MD 4/6/1943 d Gould Hunter & Mary Louise. BA Br 1964; MD SUNY 1974. D 6/24/2006 Bp Chilton Abbie Richardson Knudsen. D Buck Mtn Epis Ch Earlysville VA 2008-2010. NAAD 2006. annehunter@gwi.net

HUNTER, Benjamin Hartz (Spr) 4016 Belle Ave, Davenport IA 52807 B Columbus OH 12/29/1930 s J Keith Hunter & Maude. BA Augustana Coll 1955; Ga STUSo 1959. D 6/20/1959 P 6/1/1960 Bp Francis W Lickfield. m 10/19/2004 Mary Lynn Hunter c 3. Vic Trin Epis Ch Mattoon IL 1966-1968; Cur Emm Memi Epis Ch Champaign IL 1962-1965.

HUNTER, Charles William (Oly) 2800 Utter St, Bellingham WA 98225 B Los Angeles CA 5/6/1927 s John Wary Hunter & Lillian Louise. BA U of Washington 1951; BD CDSP 1957. D 6/24/1957 Bp Stephen F Bayne Jr P 6/24/1958 Bp Frank A Rhea. m 6/14/1952 Evelena M LeCocq. P S Dav's Epis Ch Friday Harbor WA 1991-1993; Int S Mk The Evang Ft Lauderdale FL 1988-1989; S Lk's Epis Ch Cedar Falls IA 1987-1988; Int S Andr's Ch Spokane WA 1986-1987; Ch Of The Trsfg Darrington WA 1985-1986; Emm Ch Orcas Island Eastsound WA 1984; Dio Olympia Seattle WA 1981-1984; Chr Epis Ch Blaine WA 1975-1980; Vic S Anne's Epis Ch Washougal WA 1969-1974; Vic S Jn's Epis Ch So Bend WA 1966-1969; Asst Emm Epis Ch Mercer Island WA 1957-1960; Vic S Marg's Epis Ch Bellevue WA 1957-1960. Alb Inst 1984. huntersgreens@spiritone.com

HUNTER, Colenthia Hill (SO) 8387 Vicksburg Dr, Cincinnati OH 45249 B Madison Wisconsin 2/8/1938 BS Cntrl St U 1960; Med Xavier U 1968; PhD U Cinc 1983. D 5/13/2006 Bp Kenneth Lester Price. m 5/23/1959 Thomas Hunter c 2. cocotomh@aol.com

HUNTER, Elizabeth Lane (Miss) 327 N First St, Rolling Fork MS 39159 **D Chap Of The Cross ROLLING FORK MS 2005-; D Ch of the H Trin Vicksburg MS 2005-** B Greenville MS 2/4/1955 d Afred Lane & Mary. Mississippi St U 1978; Mississippi Sch For Deacons Jackson MS 2004. D 1/15/2005 Bp Duncan Montgomery Gray III. c 1. liz.hunter@4ap.com

HUNTER, Elizabeth Sue (U) 231 E 100 S, Salt Lake City UT 84111 B Berlin NH 5/26/1945 d George Ewing Hunter & Jane Moore. BEd Plymouth St Coll 1967; Med Brigham Young U 1971. D 6/14/2001 Bp Carolyn Tanner Irish. Cathd Ch Of S Mk Salt Lake City UT 2001-2003; D Dio Utah Salt Lake City UT 2001-2003; Epis Cmnty Serv Inc Salt Lake City UT 1999-2003. lhunter@stmarkscathedral-ut.org

HUNTER JR, Herschel Miller (Va) Po Box 37, Ivy VA 22945 **Chr Epis Ch Raleigh NC 2010-** B Gallatin TN 1/8/1954 s Herschel Miller Hunter & Virginia. BA U So 1976; MA U of Alabama 1979; MDiv GTS 1988. D 5/24/1988 P 12/14/1988 Bp Robert Oran Miller. m 8/26/1978 Carol Frances Richardson c 3. R S Paul's Ch Ivy VA 1994-2010; Chapl The Cathd Ch Of The Adv Birmingham AL 1990-1994; Cur Ch Of The H Comf Montgomery AL 1988-1989. mhunter@christchurchraleigh.org

HUNTER, James Wallace (RG) St Mary's Church, 1500 Chelwood Park Blvd NE, Albuquerque NM 87112 **NW Dnry Pstr Dio The Rio Grande Albuquerque NM 2011-; P S Mary's Epis Ch Albuquerque NM 2008-** B Central Islip NY 1/6/1954 s Harold Wallace Hunter & Nadene Denison. BA Tul 1976; MDiv VTS 1984. D 2/9/1985 Bp James Russell Moodey P 8/24/1985 Bp Rogers Sanders Harris. m 6/12/2001 Jeannine Hunter. P-in-c All Faith Epis Ch Charlotte Hall MD 2003-2007; R S Fran Ch Virginia Bch VA 1997-2000; P S Steph's Epis Ch Morganton NC 1996-1997; Pres of Stndg Com Dio Wstrn No Carolina Asheville NC 1995-1996; R Ch Of The Epiph Newton NC 1992-1996; Chapl Off Of Bsh For ArmdF New York NY 1989-1999; Chapl - US Naval Reserve Dio Upper So Carolina Columbia SC 1989-1992; Cur H Trin Par Epis Clemson SC 1985-1989; Cur S Ptr's Ch Mtn Lakes NJ 1984-1985. Auth, *The Battle Hymn of the Republic*, 1991. Polly Bond Awd of Excellence 1992. jhunter@stmarysabq.org

HUNTER II, J Nathaniel (Ak) 322 Cross Way, North Pole AK 99705 B Glasgow VA 8/16/1943 s James N Hunter & Helen Louise. BA S Paul's Coll Lawrenceville VA 1966; BD Bex 1969; MS SUNY 1970. D 6/21/1969 P 12/1/1969 Bp George West Barrett. m 7/22/1972 Sharron Condon. Vic S Jude's Epis Ch No Pole AK 1988-2003; Assoc R S Jude's Epis Ch No Pole AK 1983-1985. Mart Luther King Cmnty Awd NAACP 2002; Man of the Year ChmbrCom No Pole AK 2000; Golden Rule Awd JC Penney 1995; Cmnty Serv Awd ML King Jr 1985. jnhunter@gci.net

HUNTER, Karen (Ida) 204 Courthouse Dr, Salmon ID 83467 **Gr Epis Ch Nampa ID 2007-** B 12/2/1952 BA Concordia Coll; MA U of San Francisco. D 10/19/1997 P 4/10/1998 Bp John Stuart Thornton. Cn Dio Idaho Boise ID 2005-2009; First Presb Ch Salmon ID 1999-2004; Ch Of The Redeem Salmon ID 1997-2007; Ch Of The H Sprt Missoula MT 1988-1993. ESMHE. khunter@idahodiocese.org

HUNTER, Kay Smith (WLa) 401 Washington Ave, Mansfield LA 71052 B Shreveport LA 7/15/1947 d Boardman Hartwell Smith & Mary Alice Bowser. BA Louisiana Tech U 1968; Mstr Louisiana NW St U Natchitoches 1986. D 6/7/2008 Bp D(avid) Bruce Mac Pherson. c 2. kayhunter1@aol.com

HUNTER, Kenneth Eugene (Alb) 29 Walnut St., Oneonta NY 13820 **R S Jas Ch Oneonta NY 2003-** B Kansas City MO 2/2/1952 s Clarence Alexander Hunter & Della Joyce. BA Rgnts U Virginia Bch VA 1984; MDiv GTS 1989. Trans 11/14/2003 Bp Russell Edward Jacobus. m 3/16/1980 Mary Veronica Cote c 5. St Johns Epis Ch Wisconsin Rapids WI 1997-2003; S Andr's Ch Farmers Branch TX 1996-1997; R S Mk's Ch Irving TX 1995-1996; S Jas' Epis Ch Los Angeles CA 1990-1995; Assoc R The Ch Of Ascen And H Trin Cincinnati OH 1989-1990. Auth, "First Things"; Auth, "Chr Challenge"; Auth, "The Evang Cath". sjrector@stny.rr.com

HUNTER, Lawrence Scott (Cal) 12 Via Las Cruces, Orinda CA 94563 **R S Steph's Epis Ch Orinda CA 2004-** B Everett WA 10/16/1947 s William

Hodge Hunter & Doris Ann. BA U of Washington 1974; MDiv CDSP 1992; DMin CDSP 2004. D 6/13/1992 Bp Chester Lovelle Talton P 1/9/1993 Bp Frederick Houk Borsch. m 7/1/1995 Janet Marie Chalmers. R S Jn's Mssn La Verne CA 1995-2004; Asst S Wilfrid Of York Epis Ch Huntington Bch CA 1992-1995. lshunter@comcast.net

HUNTER, Marcia G (Lex) 104 Dellwood Dr, Berea KY 40403 B Saint Paul MN 9/22/1940 d Robin Sawyer Wren Gipple & Doris Loretta. BS U MN 1962; MDiv Untd TS Of The Twin Cities 1992; Nash 1994. D 6/29/1994 Bp James Louis Jelinek P 6/28/1995 Bp Sanford Zangwill Kaye Hampton. c 2. Cn Chr Ch Lexington MO 2005-2008; Chr Ch Cathd Lexington KY 2005-2007; R S Paul's Ch Brookings SD 1997-2004; Cur Ch Of Our Sav Colorado Sprg CO 1994-1997. marciaghunter@gmail.com

HUNTER, Mary Veronica (Alb) 305 Main St, Oneonta NY 13820 B Pennsylvania 8/27/1956 D 5/30/2009 Bp William Howard Love. m 3/16/1980 Kenneth Eugene Hunter c 5. deaconvicky@gmail.com

HUNTER SR, Robert Fulton Boyd (WA) 12213 Rolling Hill Ln, Bowie MD 20715 B Sheffield AL 11/3/1935 s Robert Fulton Boyd Hunter & Ella. BA Fisk U 1956; LTh SWTS 1959. D 7/1/1959 Bp Theodore N Barth P 7/1/1960 Bp John Vander Horst. m 5/16/1959 Dorothea V Gregg c 3. R Ch Of The Atone Washington DC 1975-2003; R S Paul's Epis Ch Atlanta GA 1964-1975; Asst Emm Ch Memphis TN 1959-1960. UBE 1961. robertbhunter35@yahoo.com

HUNTER, S Scott (Mich) The Cathedral Church of St. Paul, 4800 Woodward Ave, Detroit MI 48201 **Comm on Constitutions & Cn Dio Michigan Detroit MI 2010-; Stndg Com Dio Michigan Detroit MI 2010-; Dn Cathd Ch Of S Paul Detroit MI 2007-** B Greenville SC 3/11/1959 s James Lipscomb Hunter & Lulie Hunter. BS Wofford Coll 1981; MDiv SWTS 1988; Cert Coll of Preachers 1995; DMin GTF 2012. D 6/11/1988 P 5/20/1989 Bp William Arthur Beckham. m 8/10/1985 Tina Marie Campbell c 2. Dioc Trst/ V.P. Dio Michigan Detroit MI 2007-2010; Trst's Invstmt & SRI Comms. Dio Michigan Detroit MI 2007-2010; Dioc Coun Off Dio Michigan Detroit MI 2000-2007; COM Dio W Virginia Charleston WV 1998-2000; Peterkin Camp & Conf Bd Dio W Virginia Charleston WV 1998-2000; R Trin Ch Parkersburg WV 1997-2000; Assoc S Mich's Ch Barrington IL 1991-1997; Dn of Dnry Dio Wstrn No Carolina Asheville NC 1990-1991; Asst Calv Epis Ch Fletcher NC 1989-1991; D Ch Of The Ascen (Hagood) Rembert SC 1988-1989; Cur Gr Epis Ch And Kindergarten Camden SC 1988-1989. Anamchara Fllshp (Comp) 2010. 2shunter@sbcglobal.net

HUNTER JR, Victor Edward (Dal) 1115 S. Bryan St., Mesquite TX 75149 B Dallas TX 10/21/1935 s Victor Edward Hunter & Irene. BBA U of No Texas 1958; SMU 1961; VTS 1963; MDiv GTS 1964; Cathd Cntr for Cont Educ Dallas TX 1976. D 8/28/1975 P 10/13/1976 Bp A Donald Davies. m 12/21/1968 Barbara Lee c 1. Exec Coun Dio Dallas Dallas TX 1995-1996; Dept Of Missions Dallas TX 1984-1990; S Mart's Ch Lancaster TX 1977-2001; St Marys Ch Mesquite TX 1975-1977. SocMary; Travel Seminars. dodiddy@tx.rr.com

HUNTER, Walcott Wallace (SwFla) Po Box 646, Kinderhook NY 12106 **S Mart's Epis Ch Hudson FL 2010-; P-in-c S Steph's Ch New Port Richey FL 2010-** B Central Islip NY 4/3/1959 s Harold Wallace Hunter & Nadene. BA Wag 1982; MDiv Nash 1985. D 5/11/1985 P 6/1/1986 Bp William L Stevens. m 5/25/1985 Teri-Lea Gale c 3. R S Paul's Ch Kinderhook NY 1998-2010; Vic Ch of the Ascen Merrill WI 1987-1998; S Barn Epis Ch Tomahawk WI 1987-1998; St Jas Epis Ch Mosinee WI 1987-1998; Dio Fond du Lac Appleton WI 1987-1995; Cur S Thos Ch Medina WA 1985-1987. CBS, Soc Of The H Cro. walcott.hunter@gmail.com

HUNTINGTON, Carol L (Me) 121 Bowery St, Bath ME 04530 **D S Jn's Epis Ch Hamlin PA 2002-** B Natick MA 2/8/1946 d Jonathan Trumbull Huntington & Joan Shirley. BA Hood Coll 1968; MSW Bos Sch of Soc Wk 1973; MDiv Drew U 1991. D 4/6/2002 Bp Paul Victor Marshall. m 2/14/1993 Albert R Ferguson. S Ptr's Ch Clifton NJ 1987-1988; S Jn's Epis Ch Westwood MA 1986-1987; Ch Of The H Sprt Wayland MA 1984-1986; Trin Ch In The City Of Boston Boston MA 1981-1983. authored and presented, "AIDS and Spiruality: Seeking Life in the Midst of Death," *5th Internation AIDS Conf, Montreal Can*, same in abstracts 5th Intl Conf, 1989; co authored, "The Way We Go to Sch the Exclusion of Chld in Boston," Beacon Press, 1970. EUC 1980-1990; Natl Assn of Lay Profefessions in the Epis chur 1990-2002. Carol@CarolHuntington.com

HUNTINGTON, Francis Cleaveland (NY) 11 Rassapeague, Saint James NY 11780 B New York NY 9/20/1931 s Prescott Butler Huntington & Sarah Hopper. BA Harv 1953; STB GTS 1957; ThM PrTS 1961. P 12/1/1957 Bp James P De Wolfe. m 1/8/1966 Patricia Florence Skinner c 2. Seamens Ch Inst Income New York NY 1978-1985; Ch Of The H Trin New York NY 1964-1966; Asst Trin Ch Princeton NJ 1957-1964. Trst, Halo USA 2002. fchunt@optonline.net

HUNTINGTON, Frederic DuBois (Va) 219 Wolfe St, Alexandria VA 22314 B Washington DC 10/28/1946 s E C Huntington & Catherine. BA Colg 1969; MA U of Arizona 1973; MDiv VTS 1979; Lic Dio Ely GB 1989. D 12/27/1979 P 6/28/1980 Bp Anselmo Carral-Solar. m 11/25/1971 Linda Budinger c 3. P-in-c Iglesia Epis San Marcos Alexandria VA 1999-2011; Mssnr Gr Epis Ch Alexandria VA 1995-2008; R Ch Of The H Comf Miami FL 1983-1987; Mssy Exec Coun Appointees New York NY 1979-1983. myrr7379@msn.com

HUNTINGTON, John Hermann (Colo) 5903 Joe Road, Deale MD 20751 B Belgrade YU 6/1/1939 s Morgan Gurdon Huntington & Maria Luisa. BS U of Iowa 1962; MS U of Wisconsin 1965; PhD Br 1968; none CDSP 1997. D 6/21/1997 P 3/25/1998 Bp Richard Lester Shimpfky. m 6/16/1974 Judith Ann Sutherland. S Andr's Ch Cripple Creek CO 2005-2006; Ch Of The H Redeem Denver CO 2003-2004; Dio El Camino Real Monterey CA 2000-2003; Assoc R S Tim's Epis Ch Mtn View CA 2000-2002; P Trin Cathd San Jose CA 1999-2000; D Trin Cathd San Jose CA 1997-1998. johnhdr@comcast.net

HUNTLEY JR, Preston Brooks (USC) 312 Powe St., Cheraw SC 29520 B Bennettsville SC 4/13/1941 s Preston Brooks Huntley & Julia Margaret. BA U So 1963; MDiv VTS 1968. D 6/20/1968 P 6/18/1969 Bp Gray Temple. m 8/14/1965 Lunell B Brasington. R S Jn's Ch Winnsboro SC 1997-2007; R S Steph's Epis Ch No Myrtle Bch SC 1981-1997; R S Paul's Ch Monroe NC 1974-1981; Asst to R S Andr's Ch Mt Pleasant SC 1972-1974; P-in-c Epis Ch Of The H Trin Ridgeland SC 1968-1972; P-in-c The Ch Of The Cross Bluffton SC 1968-1972. nphuntley@bellsouth.net

HUPF, Jeffrey L (RG) 2801 Westwood Rd S, Minnetonka Beach MN 55361 **Assoc S Mart's By The Lake Epis Minnetonka Bch MN 2009-** B Wichita KS 4/2/1970 s Gary Lee Hupf & Deborah Dawn. BBA U of Wisconsin 1992; MDiv Regent Coll Vancouver BC CA 2002. D 9/7/2002 Bp David John Bena P 3/21/2003 Bp Daniel William Herzog. m 1/22/2005 Carmen R Lichtl c 1. S Fran On The Hill El Paso TX 2003-2008; St Marys Cnvnt Greenwich NY 2003; D Zion Ch Morris NY 2002-2003. jeff_hupf@mac.com

HUR, Won-Jae (Cal) 420 S San Pedro St Apt 604, Los Angeles CA 90013 B Seoul Korea 2/18/1975 BA Ob 1996; MDiv EDS 2000; STM Bos 2001. D 7/31/1999 Bp Arthur Benjamin Williams Jr P 12/16/2000 Bp Barbara Clementine Harris. Dio California San Francisco CA 2009-2010; Int S Jas Epis Ch San Francisco CA 2009-2010; Dio Los Angeles Los Angeles CA 2007-2009. huiostheo@gmail.com

HURD JR, Austin Avery (CFla) 102 Fountain Cv, Leesburg FL 34748 **Ret Assoc S Jas Epis Ch Leesburg FL 1998-** B Sewickley PA 5/2/1931 s Austin Avery Hurd & Hannah Mary. LTh Epis TS In Kentucky 1967. D 6/3/1967 Bp William S Thomas P 12/16/1967 Bp Austin Pardue. m 9/1/1953 Mary Nell J Johnstone c 2. R S Thos Memi Epis Ch Oakmont PA 1972-1993; Vic S Fran In The Fields Somerset PA 1967-1972. Cnvnt of Trsfg (P Assoc) 1991. hurd53@aol.com

HURLBURT, Martha Cornue (EO) 801 Jefferson St, Klamath Falls OR 97601 **Assoc S Paul's Ch Klamath Falls OR 2006-** B Bellingham WA 5/20/1944 d Frank Gordon Cornue & Hazel. BA Whitman Coll 1966; Tchg Cred Chico St U 1995. D 6/24/2006 Bp William O Gregg P 11/28/2007 Bp Barry Leigh Beisner. c 3. mhurlbur@tulesd.tulelake.k12.ca.us

HURLEY, Janet (Los) St John the Evangelist Episcoapl Church, PO Box 183, Needles CA 92363 **Vic S Jn The Evang Mssn Needles CA 2002-** B Wakefield UK 6/3/1938 D 6/7/2002 P 12/19/2002 Bp Joseph Jon Bruno.

HURLEY, Thomas James (Neb) 113 N 18th St, Omaha NE 68102 **Dn Trin Cathd Omaha NE 1995-; Dn Trin Cathd Omaha NE 1995-** B Pigeon MI 1/20/1946 s Grover R Hurley & Lois. BS Cntrl Michigan U 1969; MDiv Yale DS 1972. D 6/26/1972 Bp Richard S M Emrich P 9/1/1973 Bp H Coleman McGehee Jr. m 8/9/1969 Diane Yedinak c 1. Ch Of The Resurr Omaha NE 1997; R Chr Epis Ch Yankton SD 1988-1995; R Chr Epis Ch Lead SD 1985-1988; R S Jn's Ch Deadwood SD 1985-1988; P-in-c S Andr's Ch Anaconda MT 1981-1985; R S Marks Pintler Cluster Anaconda MT 1981-1985; R The Pintler Cluster of the Epis Ch Deer Lodge MT 1981-1985; S Jn's Chap Monterey CA 1981; S Matt's Epis Ch Saginaw MI 1978-1979; R Hope - S Jn's Epis Ch Oscoda MI 1976-1978; Cur S Mich's Ch Grosse Pointe Woods MI 1974-1976; Cur S Phil's Epis Ch Rochester MI 1972-1974. ddhurley@cox.net

HURST, Hassell Jacoba (Ga) PO Box 50555, Nashville TN 37205 B Middleboro KY 6/22/1946 s Oliver Hassell Hurst & Jewell. MDiv EDS 1972. D 12/21/1971 P 6/1/1972 Bp Addison Hosea. R S Anne's Ch Tifton GA 1982-2006; S Mk's Epis Ch Woodbine GA 1979; Chr Ch Cathd Lexington KY 1975-1976; Vic S Alb's Ch Morehead KY 1972-1976. HJHDENVER@GMAIL.COM

HURST, Michael W (Dal) 400 S Church St, Paris TX 75460 B Nashville TN 6/22/1961 s Robert Welch Hurst & Bettye Hughes. BA Middle Tennessee St U 2005; MDiv The TS at The U So 2009. D 6/6/2009 P 1/9/2010 Bp John Crawford Bauerschmidt. m 11/29/1980 Gilda H Hurst c 3. Assoc Ch Of The Adv Nashville TN 2009-2011. fathermichael09@gmail.com

HURST, Rodney Shane (RG) 508 W Fox St, Carlsbad NM 88220 **COM Dio The Rio Grande Albuquerque NM 2011-; R Gr Ch Carlsbad NM 2009-** B Vancouver Washington 7/19/1970 s John Aaron Hurst & Shirley Jean. BA NW U 1992; MDiv Nash 2009. D 10/23/2008 P 5/16/2009 Bp Keith Lynn Ackerman. m 4/29/2006 Carolyn M Christel c 1. Third Ord Carmelites (T.OCarm.) 2009. grace.rector@windstream.net

H

HURST, William George (NH) 108 Wecuwa Dr, Fort Myers FL 33912 B Butte MT 7/10/1921 s Percy Cummin Hurst & Dora Swan. BD EDS 1969; DMin Andover Newton TS 1979. D 6/10/1969 P 12/13/1969 Bp Charles F Hall. m 11/16/2007 Mary Lou Wasser c 5. Asst Iona Hope Epis Ch Ft Myers FL 1998-2011; Asstg P S Hilary's Ch Ft Myers FL 1988-1998; Int Ch Of The Trsfg Derry NH 1981-1982; Nevil Memi Ch Of S Geo Ardmore PA 1981-1982; R S Andr's Ch Manchester NH 1969-1977. "One Soldier'S Love Story," Rit Amelia Press, 2004. AAPC 1977-1987; ACPE 1977-1981. wgh21@aol.com

HURTADO, Homero (EcuC) Guallabamba 214, Cuenca Ecuador B Cuenca EC 8/31/1938 s Julio Hurtado Rierra & Clementina Diaz. LTH/LPH Sem Mayor De Quito 1967. Rec from Roman Catholic 6/1/1981 as Priest Bp Adrian Delio Caceres-Villavicencio. m 12/23/1979 Nelly Fabiola Quintamilla c 2. Iglesia de la Reconciliacion Quito EC 1981-1995; Iglesia Epis Del Ecuador Ecuador 1980-2004; Vic Iglesia Huaquilias Huaquilias EC 1980-2004; Iglesia Machala Cuenca EC 1980-2004; Iglesia Sagrada Familia Cuenca EC 1980-2004.

HURTT, Annie Lawrie (Pa) 659 W Johnson St, Philadelphia PA 19144 B Boston MA 12/14/1955 d Spencer Hurtt & Anne. BA Ob 1980; MDiv EDS 1988. D 12/2/1989 P 6/24/1990 Bp Daniel Lee Swenson. Philadelphia Cathd Philadelphia PA 1993-1996; Epis Cmnty Serv Philadelphia PA 1991-1993; The Epis Com Univ Of Pa Philadelphia PA 1989-1991.

HURWITZ, Ellen Sara (Md) 12147 Pleasant Walk Rd, Myersville MD 21773 B Baltimore MD 11/24/1951 d William G Hurwitz & Marilyn Estelle. BA Reed Coll 1976; MDiv EDS 1982. D 6/28/1986 Bp Henry Irving Mayson P 10/1/1987 Bp H Coleman McGehee Jr. Assoc Ch Of The Trsfg Braddock Heights MD 2000-2004; S Johns Shltr For The Homeless Hagerstown MD 1995; Vic S Anne's Epis Ch Smithsburg MD 1992-1995. reveleven@hotmail.com

HUSBAND, John Frederick (Minn) Route 3, Box 309, Detroit Lakes MN 56501 B Rochester MN 2/15/1941 s Ross Twetten Husband & Frances Estelle. BA U MN 1963; BD SWTS 1966. D 6/29/1966 P 3/19/1967 Bp Philip Frederick McNairy. m 6/2/1990 JoAnn Lois Stein-Husband. S Helen's Ch Wadena MN 2004-2007; S Barth's Epis Ch Bemidji MN 2004; S Lk's Ch Detroit Lakes MN 1990-1998; S Andr's By The Lake Duluth MN 1985-1988; Dio Minnesota Minneapolis MN 1974-1990. husband@arvig.net

HUSBY, Mary Eloise Brown (SD) 1504 S Park Ave, Sioux Falls SD 57105 B Sioux Falls SD 8/11/1927 d Roger Sherman Brown & Agnes Augusta. BA Augustana Coll 1951. D 8/23/1984 Bp Craig Barry Anderson. m 12/22/1950 Earl Milton Husby c 2. D Calv Cathd Sioux Falls SD 1986-2011. ESMA.

HUSSEL, Oscar James (Ala) Po Box 281, Mentone AL 35984 **Died 3/16/2010** B Cincinnati OH 7/14/1925 s Oscar Jacob Hussel & Alice. EdD Col 1968. D 6/13/1992 P 10/16/1992 Bp Robert Oran Miller. "Conversations w the Red Giraffe," Vantage Press, Inc., NYC, 2007.

HUSSEY OSB, David Payne (SD) 12 Linden Avenue, Vermillion SD 57069 **Cn to the Ordnry Dio So Dakota Sioux Falls SD 2001-** B Chicago IL 10/9/1945 s Charles William Hussey & Marjorie. BA Geo Wms of Aurora U 1975; MA Webster U 1983; MDiv SWTS 1995. D 12/21/1998 P 10/18/2000 Bp Creighton Leland Robertson. m 7/1/1995 Mercy Gardiner Hobbs c 2. P-in-c Ch Of Our Most Merc Sav Wagner SD 1998-2010; P-in-c Ch Of The Blessed Redeem Wagner SD 1998-2010; Assoc S Paul's Epis Ch Vermillion SD 1998-2010. canondavid.diocese@midconetwork.com

HUSSEY-BYNES, Teddra Renee (SC) 5071 Voorhees Rd, Denmark SC 29042 B Kinston NC 12/25/1954 d Theodore Roosevelt Hussey & Beulah Davis. BS Hampton U 1977; MDiv Duke 2000; CAS VTS 2001. D 1/18/2002 Bp Michael Bruce Curry P 2/22/2003 Bp J(ames) Gary Gloster. c 2. Chr Epis Ch Bensalem PA 2009-2010; D S Cyp's Ch Oxford NC 2002-2007; D S Steph's Ch Oxford NC 2002-2007; S Phil's Chap Denmark SC 2002-2006; Voorhees Coll Denmark SC 2002-2006; The Epis Ch of Oxford Oxford NC 2002. revteddrabynes@yahoo.com

HUSSON, Brenda G (NY) 865 Madison Ave, New York NY 10021 **Dio New York New York City NY 1999-; R S Jas Ch New York NY 1996-** B Syracuse NY 10/30/1954 d George Shaheen Husson & Patricia. BA Beloit Coll 1976; MDiv UTS 1983. D 12/17/1983 Bp O'Kelley Whitaker P 7/15/1984 Bp Ned Cole. m 7/29/1995 Thomas Dickson Faulkner c 1. Int Pstr S Jn's Ch New City NY 1994-1996; Exec Dir Epis EvangES Arlington VA 1993-1996; Int Pstr Gr Ch White Plains NY 1992-1994; Assoc R S Jas Ch New York NY 1988-1992; Assoc R All Ang' Ch New York NY 1983-1987. "Lost Sheep Lost Coins," Restoring Faith; Walker and Co., 2001. DD Berk New Haven CT 1998; Phi Beta Kappa Beloit Coll 1975. bhusson@stjames.org

HUSTON, Jeffrey Clayton (Okla) 1805 NW 56th Ter, Oklahoma City OK 73118 **Cur Dio Oklahoma Oklahoma City OK 2005-; Epis Ch Of Oklahoma Oklahoma City OK 2005-** B Tulsa Ok 1/2/1978 s Paul Edward Huston & Virginia Eileen. BA Drury U 2000; MDiv VTS 2005. D 6/25/2005 P 12/21/2005 Bp Robert Manning Moody. m 10/13/2007 Elisa Anne Davis c 1. padrejeff@gmail.com

HUSTON SR, John A (Oly) 725 9th Ave Apt 1201, Seattle WA 98104 B San Antonio TX 1/15/1924 s Simeon Arthur Huston & Dorothea. BA U MI 1949; BD CDSP 1956. D 6/29/1956 P 6/24/1957 Bp Simeon A Huston. m 9/2/1953 Barbara Bloxom c 3. Cler Bd Mem Chap of S Martha and S Mary of Bethany Seattle WA 1989-1993; S Mk's Cathd Seattle WA 1986-1994; Epis Ch Cntr New York NY 1980-1994; Assoc R S Thos Ch Medina WA 1962-1969; Cur Ch Of The Epiph Seattle WA 1956-1958. Auth, *Refugees: The Pstr Challenge to Anglicans (ACC 1985)*, PBp's Fund of Epis Ch, 1984; "Asian Cmnty Role in Econ Life of Seattle's Intl Dist," City of Seattle, 1975. Hon Cn S Mk's Cathd Seattle WA 1976. johnhuston@comcast.net

HUSTON, Julie Winn (At) 2950 Mt. Wilkinson Pkwy, Unit 817, Atlanta GA 30339 B Atlanta GA 1/20/1942 d Robert Talmadge Winn & Mae Avant. BA Emory U 1963; MDiv Candler TS Emory U 1989. D 6/10/1989 P 3/26/1990 Bp Frank Kellogg Allan. m 9/5/1965 David Huston c 2. Dn No Atlanta Convoc Dio Atlanta Atlanta GA 1991-1999; Assoc S Anne's Epis Ch Atlanta GA 1989-2002. Theta Phi 1989. djhust67@comcast.net

HUSTON, Nancy Williams (Neb) 923 S 33rd St, Omaha NE 68105 B Johnson City TN 9/18/1932 d Charles Williams & Julia. BS Carson-Newman Coll 1954; Med U NC 1976. D 11/8/1985 Bp James Daniel Warner. D Ch Of The H Sprt Bellevue NE 1985-1993. NAAD. n.huston@cox.net

HUTCHENS, Donald E (Ga) 522 Hancock Dr, Americus GA 31709 **R Calv Ch Americus GA 2007-** B Lebanon IN 3/21/1951 BBA Georgia Coll and St U 1978; Masters of DS of Theol 2004. D 6/12/2004 Bp John Leslie Rabb P 12/18/2004 Bp Robert Wilkes Ihloff. m 8/5/1972 Nancy W Hutchens c 3. R Gr Epis Ch Darlington MD 2004-2007. frhutch@hotmail.com

HUTCHENS, Holly Blair (WMo) St Ninians Cottage, Melton, Drumnadrochit SCOTLAND IV63 6UA Great Britain (UK) B Petersburg VA 8/22/1942 d Edward James Hutchens & Charlotte. BA U MI 1964; MA U Chi 1969; MDiv SWTS 1988. D 6/18/1988 P 12/17/1988 Bp Frank Tracy Griswold III. S Aid's Ch Olathe KS 2004; R Ch Of The Resurr Blue Sprg MO 1996-2004; S Mich And All Ang Ch Mssn KS 1995-1996; Int Pstr S Mich And All Ang Ch Mssn KS 1993-1995; Int Trin Ch Lawr KS 1993-1995; S Chris's Epis Ch Wichita KS 1993; Int S Matt's Epis Ch Newton KS 1991-1992; Cur S Jas Ch Wichita KS 1989-1991. hollyhutchens5@optonline.net

HUTCHENS, Marquita (EC) Saint Paul's Episcopal Church, 161 E Ravine Rd, Kingsport TN 37660 **Assoc Chr Ch New Bern NC 2009-** B Purcell OK 8/16/1947 d Gilbert Rupert Hutchens & Helen Joyce Graham. MA U of Oklahoma 1972; MDiv Brite DS 2002; STM Candler TS Emory U 2007. D 6/2/2007 Bp C(harles) Wallis Ohl P 12/16/2007 Bp Charles Glenn VonRosenberg. P's Asst S Paul's Epis Ch Kingsport TN 2007-2009. mlhutchens@gmail.com

HUTCHERSON, Anne V (WMo) 624 W 61st Ter, Kansas City MO 64113 **Assoc R S Andr's Ch Kansas City MO 2007-** B Englewood NJ 9/5/1941 d Konrad Wilhelm Julius Emil Valentin & Phyllis Ivins. BFA Wesleyan Coll 1963; MA U Of So Dakota Vermillion SD 1964; MDiv S Paul TS Kansas City 2006. D 6/2/2007 P 12/1/2007 Bp Barry Robert Howe. m 4/8/1989 Robert M Hutcherson. Biblic Stds S Paul TS 2006; Excellence: Theol and. mtranne@standrewkc.org

HUTCHERSON, Robert M (WMo) 624 West 64th Terrace, Kansas City MO 64113 B Marshall MO 4/26/1944 s Willis Walker Hutcherson & Hattie Eileen. BS U of Missouri 1966; MS Pur 1969; MDiv GTS 1971. D 6/12/1971 Bp John P Craine P 12/18/1971 Bp Albert A Chambers. m 4/8/1989 Anne V Valentin c 1. Stndg Com Dio W Missouri Kansas City MO 1995-1998; Dep Gc Dio W Missouri Kansas City MO 1994; Dioc Coun Dio W Missouri Kansas City MO 1991-1993; Ch Growth Dio W Missouri Kansas City MO 1989-1990; Dioc Coun Dio W Missouri Kansas City MO 1988-1989; Pres Dio W Missouri Kansas City MO 1988-1989; Bec Dio W Missouri Kansas City MO 1985-1992; Chair Litug Cmsn Dio W Missouri Kansas City MO 1984-1993; Dioc Coun Dio W Missouri Kansas City MO 1984-1985; R S Matt's Ch Raytown MO 1983-2008; Dept Mssns Dio W Missouri Kansas City MO 1980-1982; Dioc Coun Dio W Missouri Kansas City MO 1980-1982; Dioc Coun Dio W Missouri Kansas City MO 1980-1982; R S Mary's Epis Ch Kansas City MO 1978-1983; Vic Ch Of The Resurr Blue Sprg MO 1976-1978; Dio W Missouri Kansas City MO 1976-1978; Vic S Mich's Epis Ch Independence MO 1976-1978; P-in-c Chap Of S Jn The Div Champaign IL 1975-1976; The ECF New York NY 1971-1976. Assn Of Dioc Liturg & Mus Com; ESMHE. rhutcherson.stmat@sbcglobal.net

HUTCHESON, Reese Mart (Ark) 2201 Antelope Train, Harker Heights TX 76548 **Off Of Bsh For ArmdF New York NY 1983-** B Camden AR 1/5/1946 s Mart Jasper Hutcheson & Edrie Alberta. BBA Sthrn Arkansas U Magnolia 1968; MDiv STUSo 1971. D 6/24/1971 P 5/23/1972 Bp Christoph Keller Jr. m 8/31/1985 Ingrid Kopp Reynolds c 2. Vic Trin Ch Van Buren AR 1975-1983; Vic S Aug's Ch Ft Smith AR 1975-1982. rhutch146@earthlink.net

HUTCHINGS, Douglas Wayne (LI) 1030 Kayton Ave, San Antonio TX 78210 B Paris TX 7/14/1935 s Horace Grady Hutchings & Mable Lorene. BA Jn Hopkins U 1957; BD VTS 1960; Coll of Preachers 1968. D 6/24/1960 Bp Noble C Powell P 6/1/1961 Bp Harry Lee Doll. S Jas Epis Ch Del Rio TX 2000-2011; R S Paul's Ch Glen Cove NY 1998-2005; Int Gr Epis Ch Massapequa NY 1997-1998; R S Jn's Ch New Milford CT 1995-1997; P-in-c S Mk's Ch So Milwaukee WI 1994-1995; Assoc S Barn On The Desert Scottsdale AZ 1990-1993; Vic S Dunst's Epis Ch Houston TX 1969-1971; Vic Ch

Of The Gd Shpd Tomball TX 1966-1969; Asst S Jn's Par Hagerstown MD 1963-1966; Vic Epiph Ch Dulaney Vlly Timonium MD 1960-1961. Bro Of S Andr. dhutch6341@aol.com

HUTCHINS, Gordon (WMass) 388 Ludlow St, Portland ME 04102 **Asst Trin Epis Ch Portland ME 1996-** B Ancon PA 11/23/1917 s Gordon Hutchins & Kathleen Radcliffe. BA Wms 1939; MDiv GTS 1948. D 3/7/1943 P 10/1/1943 Bp William A Lawrence. m 5/29/1948 Margaret Elen Pierce. R S Paul's Epis Ch Gardner MA 1970-1985; Asst S Jn's Ch Williamstown MA 1943-1944. Epis Cler of Maine; Mltry Chapl Assn.

HUTCHINS, Margaret Smith (EC) 7909 Blue Heron Dr W Apt 2, Wilmington NC 28411 B Flushing NY 1/29/1932 d Matthew Everett Smith & Laurie Helen. BS NWU 1953; MDiv EDS 1981. D 6/13/1981 Bp Arthur Edward Walmsley P 2/27/1982 Bp Clarence Nicholas Coleridge. m 6/16/1953 Walter James Hutchins c 4. Int Ch Of The Gd Shpd Hartford CT 1993-1994; S Alb's Ch Danielson CT 1992-1993; Int S Andr The Apos Rocky Hill CT 1990-1991; Int S Ptr's Epis Ch Cheshire CT 1989-1990; Int Trin Ch Seymour CT 1988-1989; Int S Paul's Ch Wallingford CT 1987-1988; Int S Paul And S Jas New Haven CT 1985-1987; Int S Ptr's Ch So Windsor CT 1984-1985; Int S Mk's Chap Storrs CT 1983-1984; Vic Chr Ch Par Epis Watertown CT 1981-1984; Chr Ch Harwinton CT 1981-1983. Soc For The Increase Of The Mnstry.

HUTCHINS, M(aurice) Gene (RG) Po Box 223, Tyrone NM 88065 **Asst Ch Of The Gd Shpd Silver City NM 1990-** B Cody WY 9/30/1927 s John Wesley Hutchins & Emma Rachel. U of Wyoming 1946; BS U CO 1955; BD Nash 1970. D 12/29/1969 P 6/29/1970 Bp Edwin B Thayer. S Mk's Epis Ch Pecos TX 1991-1994; Dio The Rio Grande Albuquerque NM 1988-1991; S Paul's Epis Ch Vernal UT 1983-1988; Vic Ch Of The H Sprt Randlett UT 1982-1988; S Mk's Ch Craig CO 1976-1978; Vic S Jn's Epis Ch New Castle CO 1975-1976; S Barn Ch Glenwood Sprg CO 1972-1976; Cur Chr Epis Ch Denver CO 1970-1972. frgene@starband.net

HUTCHINSON, Barbara (CPa) 9 Carlton Ave, Port Washington NY 11050 **Asst R S Steph's Ch Port Washington NY 2010-** B Westchester PA 12/11/1954 d James Harvey Smedley & Joyce Reisner. BA Millersville U; MDiv The GTS 2008. D 6/7/2008 P 2/18/2009 Bp Nathan Dwight Baxter. m 1/1/1983 William Hutchinson c 2. Dir of Stwdshp & Congrl Dvlpmt S Jas Ch Lancaster PA 1999-2004. barbara.htchnsn@gmail.com

HUTCHINSON JR, Jay (Del) 350 Noxontown Rd, Middletown DE 19709 **S Andrews Sch Of Delaware Inc Middletown DE 2002-; Assoc Chapl S Andr's Sch Chap Middletown DE 2001-** B Monterey CA 8/14/1962 s John Fuller Hutchinson & Donna Lee. BA Amh 1984; MDiv Harv 2000. D 6/15/2002 P 5/31/2003 Bp M(arvil) Thomas Shaw III. m 8/11/1984 Elizabeth Ann Mather c 1. jhutchinson@standrews-de.org

HUTCHINSON, Ninon N (NY) PO Box 71, Burlingham NY 12722 **S Jn's Epis Ch Monticello NY 1997-** B Princeton NJ 6/15/1952 d Charles Black Hutchinson & Pauline. BA Trenton St Coll 1979; MDiv EDS 1984; MS Yeshiva U 1994. D 6/2/1984 P 6/25/1986 Bp George Phelps Mellick Belshaw. m 11/29/2010 Boman B Bushor. Team Monticello NY 1995; Team Monticello NY 1989-1990; S Jn's Chap Cambridge MA 1987-1988; Asst Gr Epis Ch Eliz NJ 1985-1986; S Andr's Epis Ch New Providence NJ 1984-1985; St Marys Ch Rutherfordton NC 1984. NASW 1992; Samoyed Club Of Amer 1997; Soc of S Jn the Evang 1984; Ther Dogs Intl 1997. Trin Transformational Fell Trin Ch NY, NY 2007. ninontravelemail@gmail.com

HUTCHINSON JR, Robert Henri (Kan) 3533 N Governeour St, Wichita KS 67226 **S Barth's Ch Wichita KS 2006-** B Philadelphia PA 8/1/1932 s Robert Henry Hutchinson & Fannie Isabel. CPE Wesley Med Cntr Wichita KS; BA U of Pennsylvania 1957; STB PDS 1960; W Chester St Coll 1969. D 5/14/1960 Bp Joseph Gillespie Armstrong P 11/26/1960 Bp Oliver J Hart. m 9/10/1955 Alberta L Glunz c 3. Int San Jose Epis Ch Jacksonville FL 1993-1994; Int S Chas Ch S Chas IL 1992-1993; Int S Anskar's Ch Rockford IL 1991-1992; S Steph's Epis Ch No Myrtle Bch SC 1990-1991; Trin Ch Myrtle Bch SC 1990-1991; Int S Jn's Epis Ch Decatur IL 1989-1990; Int Chr Ch Of The Ascen Paradise Vlly AZ 1988-1989; Int Chr Cathd Salina KS 1987-1988; Int Calv Ch Yates Cntr KS 1987; Int S Tim's Ch Iola KS 1987; St Mths Ch Wichita KS 1981-1987; R S Alb's Epis Ch Wichita KS 1972-1975; R S Jas Epis Ch Prospect Pk PA 1964-1972; R Epis Par Of S Mk And S Jn Jim Thorpe PA 1962-1964; Cur S Jn's Ch Norristown PA 1960-1962. rhutchinson5@cox.net

HUTCHISON, Hal T. (ETenn) 309 Quail Dr., Johnson City TN 37601 **R S Jn's Epis Ch Johnson City TN 2007-** B Orange TX 5/10/1950 s Horace Leonard Hutchison & Alice Elizabeth. BA U Denv 1972; MDiv Nash 1980; DMin STUSo 2003. D 6/16/1980 Bp Willis Ryan Henton P 3/18/1981 Bp James Barrow Brown. m 9/1/1984 Sandy Curry c 3. R H Trin Epis Ch Sulphur LA 1997-2006; Chapl Epis Sch Of Acadiana Inc. Cade LA 1995-1997; R S Paul's Ch Edneyville NC 1989-1994; Asst S Ptr's Ch Oxford MS 1987-1989; R Chr Memi Ch Mansfield LA 1985-1987; Vic S Pat's Epis Ch W Monroe LA 1983-1985; Asst S Paul's Ch New Orleans LA 1980-1983. rector@stjohnstn.org

HUTCHISON, Jonathan Schofield (Ind) 4470 Covered Bridge Rd, Nashville IN 47448 B Danville PA 10/26/1951 s Schofield D Hutchison & Edith. BA Ham 1974; MDiv Ya Berk 1981. D 8/6/1981 P 5/19/1982 Bp Richard Mitchell Trelease Jr. m 9/14/1974 Deborah Pender. Vic S Dav's Ch Beanblossom Nashville IN 1991-2009; Coordntr Of Yth Mnstry Dio Indianapolis Indianapolis IN 1986-1993; Asst S Jas Epis Ch Taos NM 1982-1986; Dio The Rio Grande Albuquerque NM 1981-1982. EPF. chesed2@msn.com

HUTCHISON, Sheldon Butt (ECR) 921 Eton Way, Sunnyvale CA 94087 **Asst S Thos Epis Ch Sunnyvale CA 2007-** B Alton IL 1/31/1950 BA U IL 1971; MS U IL 1977; PhD U IL 1980; MDiv CDSP 2003. D 6/28/2003 P 1/31/2004 Bp Richard Lester Shimpfky. m 4/19/1997 Eileen Patricia Phalen c 1. Mssnr Trin Cathd San Jose CA 2003-2007. Cn Mssnr To Silicon Vlly El Camino Real 2003. sheldonhutchison@aol.com

HUTCHSON, Lee Allen (Va) 18256 Oxshire Ct, Montpelier VA 23192 **R S Mart's Epis Ch Henrico VA 2004-** B Creighton NE 11/24/1963 s Richard Lee Hutchson & Ann Louise. U of So Dakota; BA Iowa St U 1987; MDiv Nash 1991. D 12/19/1990 P 7/1/1991 Bp James Edward Krotz. m 9/1/1990 Michelle Magyar-Hutchson c 1. S Paul's Epis Ch Quincy FL 2000-2004; S Matt's Ch Lincoln NE 1991-1994. MAGYARMISH@EARTHLINK.NET

HUTJENS, Dale Henry (FdL) 123 Nob Hill Ln, De Pere WI 54115 **D S Anne's Ch De Pere WI 2003-** B Green Bay WI 11/1/1952 BA St. Norbert Coll 1976. D 8/30/2003 Bp Russell Edward Jacobus. m 5/16/1981 Winifred Elaine Etter c 2.

HUTSON, Blake Robert (Az) 1767 E Deer Hollow Loop, Oro Valley AZ 85737 **Asst to the R S Phil's In The Hills Tucson AZ 2007-** B 9/30/1979 s Carl Thomas Hutson & Carol Hutson. BA Lipscomb U 2001; Mstr of Div PrTS 2004; Mstr of Sacr Theol/Angl Stds TS 2005. D 6/11/2005 P 1/14/2006 Bp George Edward Councell. m 5/17/2003 Christina Hutson. Asst to the R Trin Ch Moorestown NJ 2005-2007. bsewanee1@aol.com

HUTSON, Robert Wayne (WMich) 950 N County Line Rd, Watervliet MI 49098 B Knoxville TN 1/5/1949 s Samuel Luther Hutson & Juanita. BS Michigan Tech U 1972; MA Asbury TS 1977; MDiv Asbury TS 1978. D 6/30/1979 P 3/1/1994 Bp R(aymond) Stewart Wood Jr. m 5/26/1973 Lauren Krugman c 3. S Aug Of Cbury Epis Ch Benton Harbor MI 1999-2004; Ch Of The Medtr Harbert MI 1999-2001; S Mk's Ch Coldwater MI 1998-1999; S Gabr The Archangel Ch Vernon Hills IL 1995-1997; Nthrn Convoc Gaylord MI 1993-1995; S Lk's Epis Ch Rogers City MI 1993-1995. rwaynehutson@earthlink.net

HUTSON, Thomas Milton (ETenn) 3502 Wood Bridge Dr, Nashville TN 37217 B Chattanooga TN 11/29/1929 s William Thurman Hutson & Thelma Lucille. BS U of Chattanooga 1955; STM Ya Berk 1958. D 6/24/1958 Bp John Vander Horst P 3/4/1959 Bp Theodore N Barth. m 8/30/1958 Shirley Crooks. Asst S Paul's Epis Ch Chattanooga TN 1988-1994; R Ch Of The Adv Nashville TN 1979-1987; Asst R Ch Of The Ascen Knoxville TN 1974-1979; R S Paul's Ch Memphis TN 1964-1974; P-in-c Ch Of The Redeem Shelbyville TN 1960-1964; P-in-c S Thos The Apos Humboldt TN 1959-1960. Americans Untd for the Separation of Ch and St; Amnesty Intl ; Friends of S Ben.

HUTTAR BAILEY, Julia Ruth (Mich) 1609 Cambridge Rd, Ann Arbor MI 48104 **P-in-c S Mich And All Ang Epis Ch Lincoln Pk MI 2011-** B Beverly MA 5/3/1961 d Charles Adolph Huttar & Joy Anne. BA Hope Coll 1983; MMus The U MI 1987; MDiv Ecum TS 2011. D 12/11/2010 P 6/11/2011 Bp Wendell Nathaniel Gibbs Jr. c 1. S Clare Of Assisi Epis Ch Ann Arbor MI 1984-2007. juliahuttar@gmail.com

HUTTON III, James Laurence (SVa) 3429 Boyce Court, Norfolk VA 23509 **Assoc S Jn's Ch Hampton VA 2006-** B Raleigh NC 7/10/1952 s James Laurence Hutton & Elizabeth Stimpson. BA U NC 1974; MDiv Duke 1978; Cert VTS 1979. D 6/30/1979 P 6/1/1980 Bp William Gillette Weinhauer. m 7/7/1979 Cindy H Hart c 1. Int S Paul's Ch Norfolk VA 2004-2007; Ctr. For Sprtl Formation Norfolk VA 1988-2009; R S Steph's Ch Norfolk VA 1982-1988; Assoc S Mich's Ch Raleigh NC 1979-1982. jameslhutton@yahoo.com

HUTTON, Linda Arzelia (Tenn) Box 3167, Sewanee TN 37375 **P-in-c S Jas Sewanee TN 2011-; Chr Epis Ch Tracy City TN 2008-** B Eugene OR 10/15/1948 d Arthur Anderson Dorsey & Gladys Arzelia. Estrn Oregon U 1982; BA Kensington U 1990; MBA GTF 1995; DIT STUSo 1995; DMin VTS 2005. D 3/16/1986 Bp Robert Louis Ladehoff P 9/15/1997 Bp Carl Christopher Epting. m 3/29/1981 Peter Michael Hutton. Trin Ch Winchester TN 2001; Int Trin Ch Winchester TN 1999-2000; Prog Dir The TS at The U So Sewanee TN 1996-2006; CE Consult Epis Ch Cntr New York NY 1990-1996; Dio Iowa Des Moines IA 1986-1994; Evang Dio Oregon Portland OR 1977-1996. "DMin," *Praise is What We Do - Initiating Change in the Culture of a Congregration from Scarcity to Abundance*, VTS, 2005; Auth, "Docc 16/20," *Curric*, 1999; Auth, *Ang Unaware*, GTF, 1995; Auth, *The Mnstry of Hosp*, GTF, 1995; Auth, "Outdoor Mnstrs," *Plnng Guide*, 1994. DOK 2002. justlinda@charter.net

HUTTON, Lin Vaught (Va) 119 Caroline St, Orange VA 22960 **R S Thos Epis Ch Orange VA 2007-** B Oakland CA 10/31/1951 d William Joseph Vaught & Marion. BS Florida St U 1973; MA Geo 1982; MDiv STUSo 2004;

DMin TS 2010. D 6/26/2004 Bp Peter James Lee P 1/25/2005 Bp Edward Stuart Little II. Asst To The R S Anne's Epis Ch Warsaw IN 2004-2007. rectorstt@verizon.net

HUXLEY, David B (Mil) 1240 Peninsula Ln, Whitewater WI 53190 **P S Lk's Ch Whitewater WI 2009-** B Detroit MI 10/15/1951 s Frank Huxley & Anne. MDiv Nash 2004. D 6/5/2004 P 12/6/2004 Bp Steven Andrew Miller. m 8/8/1992 Lois N Nelson c 2. S Jn's Epis Ch Vinita OK 2007-2009; P-in-c S Jn The Bapt Portage WI 2004-2007. dehuxrev@sbcglobal.net

HUYCK, Jonathan Taylor (RI) 175 Mathewson St, Providence RI 02903 **R Gr Ch In Providence Providence RI 2010-** B New York City 4/26/1969 BA Br 1991; M.Div. U Chi 1995; S.T.M. GTS 2003. D 3/13/2004 P 9/18/2004 Bp Mark Sean Sisk. m 8/23/2004 Ann D Huyck c 1. Cn The Amer Cathd of the H Trin Paris 75008 FR 2004-2010. johnathanhuyck@gmail.com

HUYNH, Tinh Trang (Va) 3241 Brush Dr, Falls Church VA 22042 **S Patricks Ch Falls Ch VA 1997-** B Hai-Phong VN 5/16/1948 s Luyen Kim Huynh & Thien. BA Dalat U 1971; MDiv VTS 1994. D 6/11/1994 P 12/14/1994 Bp Peter James Lee. m 10/16/1971 Kim-Anh Thi Nguyen c 2. Dio Virginia Richmond VA 1994-1997. STPATS3241@GMAIL.COM

HYATT, David W (Pa) 404 Donna Ln, Phoenixville PA 19460 B Owego NY 2/16/1933 s Howard Elmer Hyatt & Ruth Ella. BA McKendree U 1955; MDiv Tem 1958. D 6/13/1964 Bp Robert Lionne DeWitt P 12/1/1964 Bp Angus Dun. m 8/28/1955 Susan R Rhode c 2. R Trin Ch Gulph Mills King Of Prussia PA 1974-1981; Asst H Apos And Medtr Philadelphia PA 1964-1967. "Rules On Trial Not The Pstr," Philadelphia Inquirer/Knight Ridder, 2004. Legion Of hon Chap Of The Four Chapl 1967. dw4hyatt@aol.com

HYCHE, Jerald Walton (Tex) 1803 Highland Hollow Drive, Conroe TX 77304 **Epis Fndt Bd Mem Dio Texas Houston TX 2011-; R S Jas The Apos Epis Ch Conroe TX 2010-** B Gadsden AL 7/10/1960 s Jesse Walton Hyche. BA U of Alabama 1982; M.Div. VTS 2004. D 6/12/2004 P 4/16/2005 Bp Philip Menzie Duncan II. m 4/26/1985 Colleen M McCaffery c 3. Sprtl Formation Bd Mem Dio Texas Houston TX 2007-2010; Assoc R S Mart's Epis Ch Houston TX 2006-2010; Cmncatn Bd chair Dio Cntrl Gulf Coast Pensacola FL 2005-2006; Cur S Jas Ch Fairhope AL 2004-2006. Writer, "Daily reflections," *Finding God Day by Day*, Forw Mvmt, 2010; Reporter, "News and feature arts," *GC Daily*, Epis News Serv, 2009; Writer, "Daily reflections," *Praying Day by Day*, Forw Mvmt, 2009; Writer, "Dioc Nwspr," *The Texas Epis*, Dio Texas, 2008; Ed, "Dioc Nwspr," *The Coastline*, Dio Cntrl Gulf Coast, 2006. jhyche@stjames-conroe.org

HYDE, John Ernest Authur (SwFla) 4650 Cove Cir Apt 407, Madeira Beach FL 33708 **Assoc S Anne Of Gr Epis Ch Seminole FL 2009-** B Montreal QC CA 1/29/1941 s William Ernest Hyde & Barbara Edith Marie. BTh S Paul U Ottawa On CA 1986. Trans from Anglican Church of Canada 6/20/2000 Bp John Bailey Lipscomb. m 2/2/1963 Katherine Frances Kerr c 3. Assoc S Dunst's Epis Ch Largo FL 2001-2009; R Ch Of The Annunc Holmes Bch FL 2000-2001; Int Gd Samar Epis Ch Clearwater FL 1998-1999; Int Gr Epis Ch And Kindergarten Camden SC 1997-1998; Int S Mary's Epis Ch Bonita Sprg FL 1995-1996. revjhyde@tampabay.rr.com

HYDE, Lillian (Tex) Po Box 580117, Houston TX 77258 **Dio Texas Houston TX 2011-** B Greenville MS 11/20/1950 d George Crozier Wade & Betty Coker. BA Mississippi St U 1972; MDiv Epis TS of The SW 2004. D 5/29/2004 Bp Duncan Montgomery Gray III P 11/30/2004 Bp Don Adger Wimberly. m 12/26/1978 Robert Willis Hyde c 1. R S Geo's Epis Ch Texas City TX 2008-2011; Assoc R Trin Ch Galveston TX 2004-2008. lillian.hyde@comcast.net

HYDE III, Robert Willis (Tex) 208 Seawall Blvd, Galveston TX 77550 **R S Thos The Apos Epis Ch Houston TX 2004-** B Jackson MS 2/19/1947 s Robert Willis Hyde & Rufie. BD U of Mississippi 1970; MDiv Epis TS of The SW 1994. D 6/24/1994 P 12/21/1994 Bp Alfred Clark Marble Jr. m 12/26/1978 Lillian Wade c 3. Gr Epis Ch Georgetown TX 2004; All SS Epis Ch Austin TX 2002-2004; Ch Of The Creator Clinton MS 1998-2002; S Lk's Ch Brandon MS 1994-1998. rwhyde3@aol.com

HYNDMAN, David Lee (NI) 8981 E 5th Ave Apt 101, Gary IN 46403 B Gary IN 4/20/1939 s William Thomas Hyndman & Mary Ann. BA Shimer Coll 1961; BD SWTS 1964. D 5/30/1964 P 12/1/1964 Bp Walter C Klein. R S Augustines Ch Gary IN 1991-2006; Vic All SS Ch Syracuse IN 1966-1991. davhgary@aol.com

HYNSON VIII, Nathaniel (SwFla) 6283 Dartmouth Ave N, Saint Petersburg FL 33710 B Washington DC 8/10/1934 s Nathaniel Thornton Hynson & Priscilla Harriett. BA Duke 1956; MDiv VTS 1964; STUSo 1971; Luther NW TS 1988. D 6/22/1964 P 3/18/1965 Bp Thomas H Wright. m 8/4/1961 Marianna Howell c 3. Cn Dio SW Florida Sarasota FL 1999-2002; Cn Pstr to Cler, active and Ret, to spouses and survivors. Dio SW Florida Sarasota FL 1999-2002; Archd Dio SW Florida Sarasota FL 1993-1998; R Trin By The Cove Naples FL 1988-1993; R S Lk's Epis Ch Rochester MN 1975-1988; R S Anne's Epis Ch Jacksonville NC 1969-1975; P-in-c S Mary's Ch Gatesville NC 1964-1969; P-in-c S Peters Epis Ch Sunbury NC 1964-1969. Auth, "God Parents By Proxy," *LivCh*. nhynson@knology.net

I

IALONGO, Donna M (Chi) 909 Lily Cache Ln., Bolingbrook IL 60440 B Evergreen Park IL 5/27/1947 d Arthur Ialongo & Jane McGrath. BA U IL 1973; MA U IL 1975; PhD Nthrn Illinois U 1979; MDiv SWTS 2009. D 6/6/2009 P 12/5/2009 Bp Jeffrey Dean Lee. c 1. SWTS Evanston IL 2009-2011. donnarnold@rocketmail.com

IBE, Morgan Kelechi (Mo) 2424 Pinon Pl, Edmond OK 73013 **R Dio Oklahoma Oklahoma City OK 2010-** B Nigeria 3/23/1968 s Justice Ibe & Janet. BA Trin Theol Coll Nigeria 1991; BS Imo St U Nigeria 1997; 4 UNITS ST LOUIS U Hosp, ST LOUIS MO 2008. Trans from Church Of Nigeria 5/15/2007 Bp George Wayne Smith. m 2/16/1999 Charity C Ibe c 3. R Trin Ch Hannibal MO 2007-2010; R S Paul's Ch Palmyra MO 2005-2011. Auth, "LORD TEACH US TO PRAY," *GUIDE TO EFFECTIVE Pryr*, SKILL Mk, 2003. ibechidih@yahoo.com

IDEMA III, Henry (WMich) 13562 Redbird Ln, Grand Haven MI 49417 **Asst Gr Ch Holland MI 2008-** B Grand Rapids MI 2/4/1947 s Henry Idema & Jane. BA U MI 1969; MDiv EDS 1975; MA U MI 1981; PhD U Chi 1987. D 6/2/1975 Bp Charles Ellsworth Bennison Jr P 6/1/1976 Bp Charles Bennison. m 12/27/1986 Karen Fennel c 2. S Jn's Epis Ch Grand Haven MI 1987-2008; Assoc R The Ch Of The H Sprt Lake Forest IL 1984-1987; Asst S Mary's Ch Pk Ridge IL 1981-1984; Ch of the H Sprt Belmont MI 1977-1980. Auth, "Before Our Time, A Theory of the Sixties From a Rel, Soc and Psychoanalytic Perspective," U Press of Amer, 1996; Auth, "Freud, Rel and the Roaring Twenties," Rowman & Littlefield, 1990. henryidema3@yahoo.com

IDENDEN, Nancy Louise (Neb) 2053 23rd Ave # 306, Columbus NE 68601 B Belleville NJ 3/9/1958 d John Edward Idenden & Nancy Beard. BA Chatham Coll 1980; MDiv Pittsburgh TS 1991. D 8/1/1992 Bp Alden Moinet Hathaway P 2/6/1993 Bp Roger John White. R Gr Ch Par -Epis Columbus NE 2000-2008; Gr Epis Ch Blair NE 1999-2000; R S Mary's Epis Ch Blair NE 1999-2000; Int S Alb's Ch Sussex WI 1998-1999; Assoc R Gr Ch Madison WI 1992-1997; D The Ch Of The Redeem Pittsburgh PA 1992. Epis Womens Caucus; Intl Assn Of Wmn Ministers. nidenden@comcast.net

IDICULA, Mathew P (Chi) The Church of St Columba of Iona, 1800 Irving Park Rd, Hanover Park IL 60133 **Vic Ch Of S Columba Of Iona Hanover Pk IL 2007-** B Kodukulanji India 9/10/1950 s P M Idicula & Mariamma Mathew. BA Bp Moore Coll 1971; MA Luth TS at Chicago 2004; Doctor of Mnstry Luth TS at Chicago 2009; CPE Dplma The Ch Hm at Montgomery Place 2009. Trans from Church of South India 11/1/2007 Bp William Dailey Persell. m 7/9/1977 Elizabeth P Mathew c 3. Auth, "A Travelogue," *In the Land of Jesus*, ISPCK, Delhi, 2011; Auth, "Bk," *Captive of Culture*, ISPCK, Delhi, 2010. roychicago@hotmail.com

IFILL, Angela Sylvia S (O) 64 Bayley Ave, Yonkers NY 10705 **Epis Ch Cntr New York NY 2004-** B TrinidadWI 10/5/1944 d Henry Smith-Dorian Ifill & Esther. Ford; BA SUNY 1992; MDiv VTS 1995. D 6/23/1995 Bp Orris George Walker Jr P 7/11/1996 Bp Charles Lovett Keyser. c 3. Assoc R S Paul's Epis Ch Cleveland Heights OH 1998-2004; Cn Pstr Trin And S Phil's Cathd Newark NJ 1996-1998; D Trin-St Jn's Ch Hewlett NY 1995-1996. Ord of S Helena 1989-1998. aifill@episcopalchurch.org

IGARASHI, Peter Hiroshi (Pa) 600 E Cathedral Rd # D202, Philadelphia PA 19128 B Sacramento CA 1/11/1923 s Kensaburo Igarashi & Toshi. BA Colby Coll 1944; BD Crozer TS 1946; ThD Harvard DS 1950; Cert VTS 1960. D 6/28/1960 Bp Frederick D Goodwin P 12/1/1960 Bp Frederick J Warnecke. m 6/26/1949 Kimiko K Kato. R S Mk's Ch Waterville ME 1983-1988; Ch Of The Redeem Sayre PA 1983; Trin Ch Bethlehem PA 1983; R Ch Of S Jn The Div Hasbrouck Heights NJ 1981-1983; Vic S Cyp's Epis Ch Hackensack NJ 1981-1983; The TS at The U So Sewanee TN 1966-1981; The U So (Sewanee) Sewanee TN 1966-1981; Vic S Jas-S Geo Epis Ch Jermyn PA 1964-1966; Asst Cathd Ch Of The Nativ Bethlehem PA 1960-1964. peterhigarashi@aol.com

IHFE, Betty (Nev) 2950 Kings Canyon Rd, Carson City NV 89703 **Died 8/5/2010** B Milwaukee Wisconsin 9/15/1933 d Roy Victor Ihfe & Bertha Berniece. BA U of Nevada, Reno, Nevada 1956; MFA U of Utah, Salt Lake, Utah 1979. D 9/14/2003 Bp Katharine Jefferts Schori.

IHIASOTA, Isaac Iheanyichukwu (Nwk) 8283 Effie Drive, Niagara Falls NY 14304 **Cler Dep Dio Wstrn New York Tonawanda NY 2009-; S Steph's Ch Niagara Falls NY 2006-** B Atta-Owerri NG 3/5/1950 s Michael Onyeaguhele Ihiasota & Angelinah Nwanyikwereonye. DIT Trin Umuahia Abia Ng 1976; DIT Lon 1977; BA MI SU 1986; MA MI SU 1988; PhD MI SU 1994. Trans from Church Of Nigeria 8/11/1997 Bp Edward Lewis Lee Jr. m 12/11/1982 Agatha C Duru c 5. Mem of Dicesan Coun Dio Wstrn New York Tonawanda NY 2006-2008; Stwdshp Com Dio Newark Newark NJ 2005; S Dunst's Epis Ch Succasunna NJ 2004-2006; Gr Epis Ch Ft Wayne IN 2001-2003; First Alt Cler Dep Dio Nthrn Indiana So Bend IN 2001-2002; Stndg Com Dio Springfield Springfield IL 2000-2001; Cler Dep Dio Springfield Springfield IL 1999-2001; R S Andr's Ch Carbondale IL 1997-2001; Int Trin Epis Ch Grand

Ledge MI 1991-1997; Int S Mich's Epis Ch Lansing MI 1989-1991; Asstg R S Dav's Ch Lansing MI 1986-1989; Asst Chapl All SS Ch E Lansing MI 1984-1986. Auth, "Mass Media Changing Partisanship & British," 1994; Auth, "Electoral Behavior". Electoral Behavior 1994; Mass Media Changing Partisanship And British; Phd Dissertation MI SU. fatherisaac@roadrunner.com

IHLEFELD, Robert Lee (RG) 508 E 33rd St, Silver City NM 88061 B Davenport IA 7/2/1936 s George Ludwig Ihlefeld & Bessie Evalina. BA Augustana Coll 1960; MDiv PDS 1964; U of Nthrn Iowa 1970; U of Cntrl Florida 1979; STM Nash 1997. D 6/18/1964 P 12/17/1964 Bp Gordon V Smith. m 12/21/1987 Mary Wallace c 4. R Emer Ch Of The Gd Shpd Silver City NM 1988-2008; Dir Edu Gr And S Steph's Epis Ch Colorado Sprg CO 1982-1987; R S Mich's Ch Hays KS 1979-1982; R S Eliz's Ch Russell KS 1979-1980; R Emm Ch Orlando FL 1970-1979. Contrib, *Educ Video for Dio Colorado.* BroSA 1990. maryihlefeld@gmail.com

✠ **IHLOFF, Rt Rev Robert Wilkes** (Md) 292 Brandis Ct, Prince Frederick MD 20678 B New Britain CT 5/19/1941 s Ernest Otto Ihloff & Mildred Arlene. BA Ursinus Coll 1964; MDiv EDS 1967; MA Cntrl Connecticut St U 1971; Boston Gestal And Inst 1978; DMin EDS 1985; U of Cambridge 1992; DD EDS 1996. D 6/13/1967 P 3/30/1968 Bp Walter H Gray Con 10/21/1995 for Md. m 6/11/1966 Nancy V Bailey. Bp Dio Maryland Baltimore MD 1995-2007; R Gr Ch Madison NJ 1987-1995; R S Paul's Ch Natick MA 1976-1987; P-in-c Trin Epis Ch Southport CT 1972-1976; Vic S Geo's Ch Bolton CT 1969-1972; Cur S Mk's Ch New Britain CT 1967-1969. Auth, "Sharing Resources To Bared A Cmnty-Based Ch," *Wit*, 2002; Auth, "Contributions In One Minute Stwdshp Sermens," Morehouse, 1997; Auth, "The Journey Toward Wholeness w S Theresa Of Avila," *Word & Sprt*, 1988; Auth, "Suffering To Grow," *Journ Rel & Hlth*, 1976. Assoc Of The OHC 1976; Fell Coll Of Preachers 1985. DD Virginia TS 1996; Doctor Of Divinny Epis Divinty Sch 1995. rihloff@verizon.net

IJAMS, Carl Phillip (Mass) 38295 S Bogie Ct, Tucson AZ 85739 **Assoc Chr The King Ch Tucson AZ 1994-** B Tombstone AZ 8/24/1928 s Sheldon L Ijams & Jessie Maud. BA U of Arizona 1951; MDiv Ya Berk 1958. D 6/11/1958 Bp Walter H Gray P 12/20/1958 Bp Reginald Heber Gooden. m 6/8/1957 Anne Kibbe. R Trin Ch Newton Cntr MA 1972-1993; R Ch Of The H Nativ So Weymouth MA 1970-1972; R Trin Epis Ch Stoughton MA 1963-1970; Asst Trin Ch Newton Cntr MA 1961-1963. Phillips Brooks Cler Club 1965-1993. cpijams@msn.com

IKENYE, Ndungu John Brown (Chi) 1930 Darrow Ave, Evanston IL 60201 **Exec Coun Appointees New York NY 2006-** B Gakoe-Thika KE 4/16/1954 s Ikenye Charles Mwaura & Wanjiku Hannah. BA Pan Afr Chr Coll Nairobi Ke 1984; MA Intl TS 1986; MA Garrett Evang TS 1989; DMin Garrett Evang TS 1993; PhD NWU 1996. Trans from Anglican Church Of Kenya 6/1/1997 Bp Frank Tracy Griswold III. m 5/9/1981 Njeri Rose Maimba c 3. Prof SWTS Evanston IL 1997-1999; Vic S Andr's and Pentecostal Epis Ch Evanston IL 1993-2006; Assoc Ch Of The Epiph Chicago IL 1990-1993. Auth, "Decolonization Of The Soul," Envoy Graphic @ Print Systems, 2003; Auth, "Afr Chr Counslg," Envoy Graphic @ Print Systems, 2002; Auth, "Bi-Cultural Personality For Mnstrs," *ATR*, 2001; Auth, "Ritual In Cross Cultural Pstr Care & Counsritual In Cross Cultural Pstr Care & Counslg," *Journ Of Supervision*, 1998; Auth, "Trng & Supervision For Mnstry In Kenya," *Journ Of Supervision*, 1992. AAMFC 1996; AAPC 1994; AEHC 1993. dr.njbikenye@gmail.com

ILEFELDT, Willard Garcia (ECR) Hacienda Carmel - 220, Carmel CA 93923 **Died 5/23/2010** B Cooper TX 2/22/1917 s George Herman Ilefeldt & Grace Helen. BD CDSP 1959; BA Occ 1966; Rel. Dr. Claremont TS 1969. P 2/1/1960 Bp Francis E I Bloy. c 2. Auth, "Thoughts While Tending Sheep," 1988; Auth, "Theol Analogies from Sci".

ILES, Robert Harold (Ore) 5495 Greenridge Rd, Castro Valley CA 94552 **Died 12/20/2010** B Peoria IL 4/7/1938 s Harold Arvene Iles & Marian Francis. BA La Sierra U 1960; MDiv VTS 1967. D 9/9/1967 P 3/9/1968 Bp Francis E I Bloy. c 3. Ed, "The Gospel Imperative in the Midst of AIDS," Morehouse Pub, 1990; Auth, "Selecting Computors for Mnstry," 1985. riles@ltoceramics.com

ILLES, Joseph Paul (NI) 56869 Sundown Rd, South Bend IN 46619 **D The Cathd Ch Of S Jas So Bend IN 1992-** B South Bend IN 2/19/1926 s Joseph Illes & Theresa Elizabeth. Diac Sch For Faith & Mnstry 1991. D 10/9/1991 Bp Francis Campbell Gray. m 9/3/1949 Lillian Marie Bakos c 3. Ord Of S Lk, OHC.

ILLINGWORTH, David Paul (Me) 28 Wayne St, Portland ME 04102 B Waterville ME 11/12/1948 s Paul Thomas Illingworth & Phyllis Arline. AB Harvard Coll 1971; Harvard DS 1973; MDiv GTS 1980. D 5/17/1975 P 11/21/1975 Bp Frederick Barton Wolf. Dio Maine Portland ME 2010-2011; Epis Ch Of S Mary The Vrgn Falmouth ME 2010-2011; Cathd Ch Of S Lk Portland ME 2010; S Ann's Epis Ch Windham Windham ME 2005-2006; S Jn's Ch Jamaica Plain MA 1994-2002; S Jn's Ch Jamaica Plain MA 1991-1992; S Jn's Ch Jamaica Plain MA 1986-1988; Vic S Hugh Lincoln ME 1975-1980; Vic S Thos Ch Winn ME 1975-1980. davidi@gwi.net

ILOGU, Edmund Christopher Onyedum (WA) 2355 Weymouth Ln, Crofton MD 21114 B Ihiala NG 4/25/1920 s Ilogu Nwaku & Agnes Ugboego. Prog Advncd Rel Stds; Alcd Lon 1953; STM UTS 1958; MA Col 1959; PhD U Leiden Nl 1974. Rec 8/1/1988 as Priest Bp John Thomas Walker. m 4/25/1946 Elizabeth Chineze Obiago c 3. Int Calv Ch Washington DC 1986-1988. Auth, "Coping w Three Cultures: an Autobiography," Sungai Books, 1999; Auth, "Chrsnty and Igbo Culture," E.J. Brill, 1974; Auth, "W Meets E," C.M.S. London, 1954.

IMARA, Mwalimu (Ind) 4550 Orkney Ln Sw, Atlanta GA 30331 B Halifax NS CA 4/21/1930 s William Dawson Gaines & Blanche Irene. BA Case Wstrn Reserve U 1964; DMin Meadville/Lombard TS 1968. P 9/18/1982 Bp Edward Witker Jones. m 5/14/1960 Harriet Latimore c 3. S Tim's Decatur GA 1994. Auth, "Growing Through Grief," *Hospice Care: Principles and Pract*, Springer, 1983; Auth, "A Theol of Hospice From Encounters w Howard Thurman," *Debate & Understanding*, Bos, 1982; Auth, "Coping w Death," *Encyclopedia Americana*, 1979; Auth, *Dying as the Last Stage of Growth*, Prentice Hall, 1975. AAPC Dplma 1970; Sigma Pi Phi Fraternity 1979. Schlr in Res Fetzer Inst 1997; Tchg Execellence Awd Morehouse Sch of Med Dept of Publich Hlth: Resi 1994; Tchg Exellence Awd Morehouse Sch of Med 1988; Recognition Natl Hospice Orgnztn 1988; Recognition Natl Hospice Orgnztn 1983. mimara@aol.com

IMBODEN, Stanley Franklin (CPa) 315 Dead End Rd, Lititz PA 17543 B Reading PA 6/20/1932 s Livingstone Seltzer Imboden & Margaret Jane. BA Lebanon Vlly Coll 1955; STB Tem 1958; STM Tem 1971; DD Lebanon Vlly Coll 1988. D 6/14/1959 P 12/15/1959 Bp John T Heistand. m 2/11/2006 Sandra Imboden c 2. P-in-c Bangor Ch Of Churchtown Narvon PA 1996-2003; Planned Giving Off Dio Cntrl Pennsylvania Harrisburg PA 1995-1996; S Jas Ch Lancaster PA 1978-1994; R S Andr's Epis Ch York PA 1972-1978; Ch Of The Redemp Southampton PA 1964-1967; Vic Hope Epis Ch Manheim PA 1959-1962; Vic S Paul's Ch Manheim PA 1959-1962. Auth, "War and Peace," *Tidings (Dioc news)*, 1991; Auth, "arts & Poems in Collgt & Ch Pub," *Sunday Sch Times*, 1952. EUC; ood of S AndrewBrotherh 1959-1990. Hon Cn Cathd of St. Steph, Harrisburg PA Harrisburg PA 1982; Hon Alum PDS Philadelphia PA 1959. srvr4c@aol.com

IMMEL, Otto Wigaart (NJ) Po Box 2379, Tybee Island GA 31328 B Reading PA 1/10/1937 s Amos Roland Immel & Loretta. BA Leh 1959. D 4/22/1972 P 10/1/1972 Bp Alfred L Banyard. c 2. R S Thos' Epis Ch Glassboro NJ 1979-1999; Evergreens Chap Moorestown NJ 1974-1979; Cur Trin Cathd Trenton NJ 1972-1974. coimmel@hotmail.com

INAPANTA PAEZ, Lourdes Esther (EcuC) Calle Hernando Sarmiento, N39 - 54 Y Portete, Quito Ecuador **Cntrl Dio Ecuador EC 2000-** B Quito 5/4/1964 d Miguel Inapanta. Programa De Educacion Teologica. D 10/14/2000 Bp J Neptali Larrea-Moreno P 2/11/2006 Bp Orlando Jesus Guerrero. m 8/24/1982 Jose Flores Suarez c 3. Ecuador New York NY 2000-2009.

INCE JR, Edgar Elmer (WTenn) 3749 Kimball Ave, Memphis TN 38111 B Memphis TN 1/15/1927 s Edgar Elmer Ince & Camilla Bell. D 12/21/1962 Bp John Vander Horst P 1/27/2001 Bp James Malone Coleman. m 8/29/1947 Flora Marie Young. D H Trin Ch Memphis TN 1962-1990.

INESON JR, John Henry (Me) 53 High St., Damariscotta ME 04543 **Assoc S Mk's Ch Marco Island FL 2007-** B Rochester NH 6/4/1939 s John Henry Ineson & Mary. BA U of New Hampshire 1961; STB Ya Berk 1964. D 6/4/1964 P 12/16/1964 Bp Charles F Hall. m 12/24/1975 Hannah C Heiselman c 1. Vic S Barn Ch Augusta Augusta ME 1997-2008; R S Andr's Ch Newcastle ME 1984-1995; R Trin Epis Ch Fayetteville NY 1970-1972; R Trin Ch Lowville NY 1967-1970; Cur Chr Ch Binghamton NY 1964-1967. Auth, "The Way Of Life," Japan Pub, 1986. jiai@lincoln.midcoast.com

INGALLS JR, Arthur Bradford (Md) 2929 Level Rd., Churchville MD 21028 **R H Trin Ch Churchville MD 2006-** B San Angelo TX 4/25/1951 s Arthur B Ingalls & Bementa. BA Steph F. Austin St U 1973; MPA Lamar U 1984; MDiv VTS 2004. D 5/22/2004 P 1/22/2005 Bp John Wadsworth Howe. m 1/1/1972 Margaret Eileen Fowler c 2. Asst H Trin Epis Ch Fruitland Pk FL 2005-2006. ingallsb48@aol.com

INGALLS, Clayton Dean (Tenn) 5501 Franklin Pike, Nashville TN 37220 **Emm Epis Ch Kailua HI 2011-** B Atlanta GA 10/23/1979 s Clyde Ingalls & Betty. MDiv TESM; BA Belmont U 2002. D 6/10/2006 P 12/16/2006 Bp Bertram Nelson Herlong. m 12/15/2001 Teresa Lyn Ingalls. Vic S Geo's Epis Ch Honolulu HI 2009-2011; D Ch Of The Adv Nashville TN 2006-2008. clayton@emmanualkailua.com

INGALLS, Jason Travis (Tenn) Ridley Hall, Ridley Hall Rd, Cambridge CB3 9HG Great Britain (UK) B Marshall TX 3/7/1981 s Ricki Gene Ingalls & Terri Lynn. BA Jn Br 2003; MDiv PrTS 2006; ThM Wycliffe Coll, U Tor 2010. D 6/5/2010 P 1/8/2011 Bp John Crawford Bauerschmidt. m 5/19/2001 Monique Harris. St. Matt's Riverdale Angl Ch of Can Toronto ONTARIO 2010-2011. Can Bible Soc Awd for Excellence in the Publ Reading of Scripture Can Bible Soc 2011; The Leonard Griffith Prize for Expository Preaching Wycliffe Coll, U Tor 2010. jasoningalls@gmail.com

INGALLS, Margaret Eileen Fowler (WA) Transfiguration Church, 13925 New Hampshire Ave, Silver Spring MD 20904 **Ch Of The Trsfg Silver Sprg MD 1993-** B Macon GA 10/4/1951 d Waller Fowler & Geneva Waucel. BA

Steph F. Austin St U 1973; MA Auburn U 1979; MDiv VTS 1989. D 6/10/1989 P 3/17/1990 Bp Peter James Lee. m 1/1/1972 Arthur Bradford Ingalls c 2. R H Trin Epis Ch Fruitland Pk FL 1993-2008; Asst Ch Of The H Comf Richmond VA 1989-1993; D Ch Of The H Comf Vienna VA 1989. Amer Friends of Jerusalem 1992; Via Media USA 2004. meg@transfig.org

INGE, F Coleman (CGC) 1117 Williamsburg Drive, Mobile AL 36695 B Mobile AL 10/10/1927 s Herndon N A Inge & Margaret Erwin. BS U of Alabama 1950; MDiv STUSo 1956. D 7/6/1956 Bp Charles C J Carpenter P 2/24/1957 Bp William J Gordon Jr. m 8/1/1986 Jean Peden c 2. Dep to 1994 GC in Indianapolis Dio Cntrl Gulf Coast Pensacola FL 1994-1997; Dep to 1991 GC in Phoenix Dio Cntrl Gulf Coast Pensacola FL 1991-1994; Fin Com Dio Cntrl Gulf Coast Pensacola FL 1991-1994; Stndg Com Dio Cntrl Gulf Coast Pensacola FL 1989-1994; R S Paul's Ch Foley AL 1986-1995; Cmsn on Ch Growth Dio Cntrl Gulf Coast Pensacola FL 1978-1981; Beckwith Lodge Bd Dir Dio Cntrl Gulf Coast Pensacola FL 1975-1978; Chapl Wilmer Hall Mobile AL 1971-1981; Dio Alabama Birmingham AL 1971-1972; Mem of Com to Establish the Dio the Cntrl Gulf Coast Dio Alabama Birmingham AL 1970-1980; Vic S Paul's Ch Mobile AL 1967-1982; Dio Alabama Birmingham AL 1966-1967; R S Lk's Epis Ch Mobile AL 1964-1986; R S Paul's Ch Greensboro AL 1959-1964; R S Wilfrid's Ch Marion AL 1959-1964; P-in-c S Jas Ch Tanana AK 1956-1959. Curs. theinges@bellsouth.net

INGEMAN, Peter Lyle (Ga) 1521 N Patterson St, Valdosta GA 31602 **Chair, Cmsn on Liturg Dio Georgia Savannah GA 1995-** B Chicago IL 7/22/1939 s Milton Joseph Ingeman & Ellen. BA Rutgers-The St U 1960; MA Baylor U 1975; MDiv Nash 1987. D 7/22/1982 Bp (George) Paul Reeves P 6/6/1987 Bp Harry Woolston Shipps. m 6/17/1961 Harriet Plews c 2. R Chr Ch Valdosta GA 2000-2011; R S Fran Of The Islands Epis Ch Savannah GA 1989-2000; Asst Chr Ch Valdosta GA 1987-1989; Dio Georgia Savannah GA 1987-1989; D S Anskar's Epis Ch Hartland WI 1984-1987; D S Aug Of Cbury Ch Augusta GA 1982-1984. OHC. hingeman@bellsouth.net

INGERSOLL, Russell William (WNC) 500 Christ School Rd, Arden NC 28704 B Saint Paul MN 5/20/1938 s Russell Richard Ingersoll & Jeanette M. BA Dart 1960; MDiv VTS 1965. D 6/24/1965 P 1/1/1966 Bp Hamilton Hyde Kellogg. m 12/21/1960 Patricia Ann Podas c 3. Calv Epis Ch Fletcher NC 2002-2004; Chr Sch Arden NC 1993-2004; Headmaster Chr Sch Arden NC 1993-2003; S Marks Sch Of Texas Dallas TX 1989-1993; S Greg HS Tucson AZ 1979-1988; Chatham Hall Chatham VA 1975-1979. Auth, "Role Of Ch Sch"; Ed, "Role Of Chapl In Epis Schools & Coll". Jn Verdery Awd For Serv To Epis Schools Natl Assoc Of Epis Schools 2002. rustyi@zebray.com

INGRAHAM, Doris Williams (SeFla) 15955 Nw 27th Ave, Opa Locka FL 33054 B Hawkinsville GA 11/20/1937 d Albert Odom & Maggie. BD Barry U 1995. D 9/1/2001 Bp Leopold Frade. m 4/30/1983 Tellis Clyde Ingraham.

INGRAM, Charles Owen (Az) 6380 E Printer Udell, Tucson AZ 85710 B Lee County MS 10/23/1929 s Leonard Thaddeus Ingram & Elizabeth. BS U of Memphis 1950; BD SW Sem 1953; MA U of Memphis 1958; PhD U of Arizona 1967; Oxf 1975; U So 1988. D 6/2/1974 Bp J(ohn) Joseph Meakins Harte P. c 1. Chair Campus Mnstry Cmsn Dio Arizona Phoenix AZ 1989-1992; Chapt Trin Cathd Phoenix AZ 1988-1992; CDSP Berkeley CA 1984-1993; Pres Dio Arizona Phoenix AZ 1984-1985; R S Andr's Epis Ch Tucson AZ 1982-1992; Chair Bd Fndt Campus Msntry Dio Arizona Phoenix AZ 1982-1988; Chair Bd Fndt Campus Msntry Dio Arizona Phoenix AZ 1982-1988; Chair Dio Arizona Phoenix AZ 1978-1982; Com Dio Arizona Phoenix AZ 1976-1982; Vic S Andr's Epis Ch Tucson AZ 1975-1981. Cmnty Of S Mary 1988. Who'S Who Rel.

INIESTA-AVILA, Bernardo (Nev) 4201 W Washington Ave, Las Vegas NV 89107 **Dio Nevada Las Vegas NV 2010-** B 4/16/1971 s Victor Iniesta & Esperanza. BA Seminario Conciliar Mex DF; MDiv Pontifical Coll Josephinum 2001. Rec from Roman Catholic 12/7/2008 Bp Dan Thomas Edwards. m 12/7/2007 Delores Cabrera. bini@safenest.org

INMAN, John Wesley (WMich) 135 Old York Road, New Hope PA 18938 B Michigan City IN 8/16/1932 s John Wesley Inman & Alice Marie. BA Denison U 1954; MDiv EDS 1964. D 6/12/1965 P 12/1/1965 Bp Horace W B Donegan. Int S Jn's Ch Norristown PA 2003-2004; Int S Tim's Ch Roxborough Philadelphia PA 2002-2003; Asst S Jn's Ch Norristown PA 1998-2002; Asst S Paul's Ch Doylestown PA 1996-1997; Int S Paul's Epis Ch Grand Rapids MI 1995-1996; Asst Gr Ch Grand Rapids MI 1995; Int S Mk's Ch Grand Rapids MI 1994-1995; R Ch of the H Sprt Belmont MI 1992-1994; R S Lk's Epis Ch Smethport PA 1983-1988; Stff Ch Of The Ascen Chicago IL 1981-1983; Stff Ch Of The Resurr Norwich CT 1980-1981; Stff Chr Ch Cathd Hartford CT 1977-1979; Stff Trin Ch Ft Wayne IN 1972-1977; R H Trin Epis Ch Inwood New York NY 1968-1969; Cur S Alb's Epis Ch Of Bexley Columbus OH 1965-1967. The Ord of Julian of Norwich 1994-1994. jwinman135@comcast.net

INMAN, Virginia Bain (NC) 520 Summit Strett, Winston-Salem NC 27101 **Mssn Implementation Team Dio No Carolina Raleigh NC 2005-; Mssn Implementation Team Dio No Carolina Raleigh NC 2005-** B Lakeland FL 2/6/1972 BS Randolph-Macon Wmn's Coll 1994; MDiv Van 1999; JD Van 1999; CAS VTS 2004. D 6/19/2004 P 1/29/2005 Bp Michael Bruce Curry. m 4/26/2003 Stephen Thomas Inman. Assoc R S Paul's Epis Ch Winston Salem NC 2004-2009. gbain@earthlink.net

INNES, Neil Fraser (WTex) 1702 S Medio River Cir, Sugar Land TX 77478 B New York NY 11/25/1930 s Walter Ingram Innes & Doris. BA Pan Amer U 1976; MDiv Epis TS of The SW 1979. D 6/13/1979 P 12/14/1979 Bp Scott Field Bailey. m 11/7/1953 Mary Christine Kennedy c 3. R S Geo Ch San Antonio TX 1990-1995; R S Mk's Ch Austin TX 1984-1990; R Gr Ch Cuero TX 1981-1984; Asst R All SS Epis Ch Corpus Christi TX 1979-1981. nfimai@windstream.net

INSCOE, Laura D (Va) 2319 E. Broad Street, Richmond VA 23223 **Dioc Disciplinary Bd Dio Virginia Richmond VA 2011-2012; R S Jn's Ch Richmond VA 2009-** B Richmond VA 11/30/1954 d Ernest Herbert Dervishian & Anne. BA, w dist U of Virginia 1977; JD U Rich 1980; MDiv UTS Richmond VA 2001; VTS 2001. D 6/15/2002 P 12/16/2002 Bp Peter James Lee. m 5/1/1993 Walter Ray Inscoe. Bp's T/F Dio Virginia Richmond VA 2010-2011; Reg XII Dn Dio Virginia Richmond VA 2009; Clerk, Eccl Trial Crt Dio Virginia Richmond VA 2008-2010; Dir of Mid-Atlantic Par Traing Prog Dio Virginia Richmond VA 2007-2009; Exec Bd Mem Dio Virginia Richmond VA 2004-2006; Assoc R S Mary's Ch Richmond VA 2002-2009. linscoe@saintjohnsrichmond.org

INSERRA, John Michael (La) 6249 Canal Blvd, New Orleans LA 70124 **Assoc S Paul's Ch New Orleans LA 2010-** B Jamestown, NY 12/11/1979 s Richard Inserra & Dolores. AA Niagara Cnty Comunity Coll 2003; BA Canisius Coll 2006; MDiv Nash 2010. D 6/5/2010 P 12/7/2010 Bp William Howard Love. m 5/27/2006 Sarah E Sarah Walter. jminserra@gmail.com

IRELAND, Clyde Lambert (USC) 2517 Duncan St, Columbia SC 29205 B Columbia SC 3/30/1929 s Clyde Henry Ireland & Hallie Pauline. BA U of So Carolina 1951; MDiv VTS 1954. D 6/10/1954 P 6/6/1955 Bp Clarence Alfred Cole. m 8/1/1955 Betty Jean Crenshaw c 4. P in charge S Thos Ch Eastover SC 1999-2010; Dio Upper So Carolina Columbia SC 1981-1992; Vic S Jn's Ch No Augusta SC 1981-1987; R Calv Epis Ch Richmond TX 1978-1981; Dir - Ch Relatns The TS at The U So Sewanee TN 1976-1978; Assoc S Lk's Epis Ch Birmingham AL 1970-1976; R Epis Ch Of The Redeem Greenville SC 1961-1970; Consult - Chr. Ed. Dir-Camp Gravatt, Youthj Dio Upper So Carolina Columbia SC 1957-1961; Vic H Cross Epis Ch Simpsonville SC 1956-1957; Dio So Carolina Charleston SC 1954-1961; Vic All SS Epis Ch Clinton SC 1954-1957; Vic Ch Of The Epiph Laurens SC 1954-1957; D-in-c S Lk's Ch Newberry SC 1954-1955. clydeireland@aol.com

IRELAND, Joel T (Az) 532 E 1st St, Tucson AZ 85705 B Tucson AZ 12/16/1953 s Alfred Leon Ireland & Ann Lucile. MA OH SU 1977; MDiv GTS 1981; JD U of Arizona 1990. D 6/11/1981 P 12/8/1981 Bp Joseph Thomas Heistand. c 2. Tuller Sch Tucson AZ 2008-2010; Asst Epis Par Of S Mich And All Ang Tucson AZ 1981-1987. Auth, "The Trsfg of the Lemon Test: Ch & St Reign Supreme in Bowen vs Kendrick," *Arizona Law Revs*, 1990; Auth, "Bowen vs Kendrick," *Arizona Law Revs*, 1990. St Bar of Arizona,St Bar of Arizona 1990. jireland@1800theeagle.com

✠ **IRISH, Rt Rev Carolyn Tanner** (U) 1930 South State, Salt Lake City UT 84115 B Salt Lake City UT 4/14/1940 d Obert Clark Tanner & Grace. BA U MI 1962; MLitt Oxf 1968; MDiv VTS 1983. D 6/11/1983 P 1/7/1984 Bp John Thomas Walker Con 5/31/1996 for U. m 6/16/2001 Eugene Frederick Quinn c 4. Bp of U Dio Utah Salt Lake City UT 1996-2010; Dvlpmt Cathd of St Ptr & St Paul Washington DC 1988-1995; Archd Dio Michigan Detroit MI 1986-1988; H Faith Ch Saline MI 1986-1988; Vic H Faith Ch Saline MI 1985-1988; Asst Ch Of The Gd Shpd Burke VA 1984-1985; Asst Min The Ch Of The Epiph Washington DC 1983-1984. Auth, "Love Thy Neighbor: Par Resouces for Faithfulness in Creation". Hon Doctoral Degree VTS 2002; Hon Doctoral Degree CDSP 1999. carolyn.tanner.irish@octanner.com

IRISH, Charles Manning (O) 4324 Janwood Dr, Copley OH 44321 B Lorain OH 7/13/1929 s Warren Baker Irish & Marie Jane. BA Ohio Wesl 1957; BD Bex 1966. D 6/11/1966 P 12/10/1966 Bp Nelson Marigold Burroughs. c 1. Acts 29 Mnstrs Atlanta GA 1986-1992; S Lk's Epis Ch Akron OH 1969-1994; Vic Trin Ch Bryan OH 1966-1969. Auth, *Back to the Upper Room*; Auth, *By My Sprt*; Auth, *Gospel Conspiracy Workbook*. chuckirish7@msn.com

IRISH, Donald Le Roy (DR) 390 Tavernier St, Boulder City NV 89005 **Died 1/28/2011** B Los Angeles CA 1/18/1927 s Raymond Gilbert Irish & Erma. BA U CA 1949; ThM GTS 1952. D 6/23/1952 Bp Francis E I Bloy P 2/1/1953 Bp Donald J Campbell. c 1. SSC, CCU, Epis S. hdirish@embarqmail.com

IRONSIDE, Susan Roberta (NJ) 414 E Broad St, Westfield NJ 07090 **Cur S Paul's Epis Ch Westfield NJ 2010-** B Philadelphia PA 3/14/1971 d Kenneth Ironside & Valerie. Kean U 2000; MDiv The GTS 2010. D 11/14/2009 P 6/19/2010 Bp George Edward Councell. m 1/9/1993 Andrew P Moore c 2. sriironside@gmail.com

IRSCH, Leona Medora (WNY) 108 S Thomas Ave, Edwardsville PA 18704 B Tulsa OK 4/6/1939 d Charles George Irsch & Medora Matilda. BA Valparaiso U 1962; MS U of Maryland 1968; MDiv Bex 1983; DMin Luth TS at Gettysburg 2007. D 9/17/1983 P 5/12/1984 Bp Robert Rae Spears Jr. Int S Mk's Ch

Buffalo NY 1997-1999; Dn Dio Rochester Rochester NY 1988-1990; R Zion Ch Avon NY 1984-1990; Asst Chr Ch Rochester NY 1983-1984. Auth, "A Subject Misunderstood," *LivCh*, 2000. jaiyogin@comcast.net

IRVIN, Cynthia Diane (Colo) 546 N Elm St # 1496, Cortez CO 81321 **D S Barn Of The Vlly Cortez CO 1981-** B Massillon OH 11/27/1943 d Leroy James Miller & Beulah Marie. Prchr Lewis Sch Of Mnstry 1987. D 6/12/1988 Bp William Carl Frey. m 2/7/1970 Vernon Irvin c 4. SHN 1985. Citizens Police Acad Montezuma Police Dept 1998; Cmnty Serice Awd Seventh-Day Adventist Ch 1993; Bellringer Awd Salvation Army 1989. tulipspatc@yahoo.com

IRVIN JR, Harland MacMillan (Tex) 6 S Peak Rd, Austin TX 78746 **Died 6/10/2011** B El Paso Texas 2/23/1927 s Harland MacMillan Irvin & Virginia. BA U So 1950; MDiv VTS 1955; STM VTS 1962. D 7/1/1955 Bp Clinton Simon Quin P 6/22/1956 Bp John E Hines. c 4. Auth, "Epis Schools," *LivCh*, 1964. AFP 1978-1986; Bp's Chapl to Ret Cler and Spouses 2004-2008; BroSA 1969-1998; Epis Curs 1978; Epis Recovery Mnstrs 1957; Ord of S Lk 1970-2002. hirvin@austin.rr.com

IRVIN, Henry (Stuart) (WA) 425 Crowfields Dr, Asheville NC 28803 B Augusta GA 4/8/1932 s Willis Irvin & Willye Stuart. No Carolina St U; U of Pennsylvania; BA U NC 1952; MDiv Candler TS Emory U 1955; CWA VTS 1957; MA Amer U 1972; DMin SFTS 1978. D 12/22/1956 P 6/22/1957 Bp Angus Dun. m 12/28/1957 Georgia K Kennedy c 2. R All SS' Epis Ch Chevy Chase MD 1981-1997; Assoc All SS' Epis Ch Chevy Chase MD 1964-1979; S Geo's Wm And Mary Vlly Lee MD 1956-1957; R St Marys Par St Marys City MD 1956-1957. Mem Emer, Hon. Gen. Coun of Ch Untd for Globa Crystal Cathd Mnstrs 2007; Hon Gnrl Coun of Ch Untd for Global Mssn Crystal Cathd Mnstrs Garden Grove CA 1978.

IRVINE, Peter Bennington (Chi) 2640 Park Drive, Flossmoor IL 60422 **The Ch Of S Jn The Evang Flossmoor IL 2010-** B Chattanooga TN 6/8/1951 s James Bennington Irvine & Susan Chambliss. BA U of Tennessee 1974; JD U of Tennessee 1979; MDiv GTS 2002. D 6/3/2006 Bp Mark Hollingsworth Jr P 12/3/2006 Bp Steven Andrew Miller. m 10/25/2008 Janet Collins. Dekoven Fndt for Ch Wk Racine WI 2008; Precentor Chr Ch Waukegan IL 2007-2010; S Lk's Ch Racine WI 2006-2007; Chapl S Lk's Hosp Racine WI 2006-2007; Assoc The Ch Of The Redeem Pittsburgh PA 2003-2006. Ed, "The Inner Voice: a Hymnic Tribute to Julian of Norwich," Ord of Julian of Norwich, 2008. AGO 2007; The Hymn Soc 2005. pbirvine@yahoo.com

IRVING, Anthony Tuttle (Oly) 5445 Donnelly Dr Se, Olympia WA 98501 **D S Ben Epis Ch Lacey WA 1999-** B Butte MT 12/14/1936 s Irving Guck Irving & Kathryn. BA U of Washington 1963. D 6/26/1999 Bp Vincent Waydell Warner. m 1/8/1982 Leona Rackleff. Auth, "The Road To Self Understanding And Ord," *Diakoneo*, Michaelmass, 2000. tony@justtheirvings.com

IRVING, H(annah) Jocelyn (WA) 118 Division Ave NE, Washington DC 20019 **R Ch Of The Atone Washington DC 2005-** B Paterson NJ 8/27/1951 d Vian Miller & Cecilia. BA WPC 1973; MDiv Drew U 1999. D 6/21/2000 P 2/24/2001 Bp John Palmer Croneberger. c 4. S Lk's Epis Ch Montclair NJ 2000-2005. jocy51@yahoo.com

IRVING, Stanley Herbert (Vt) 5205 Georgia Shore Rd, Saint Albans VT 05478 B Brome QC CA 1/25/1924 s Joseph Irving & Marjorie Elfrida. BA Concordia U 1949; BD McGill U 1953; LTh Montreal Dioc Theol Coll 1953. Trans from Anglican Church of Canada 3/1/1961 as Priest Bp The Bishop Of Montreal. m 5/21/1949 Betty Benoit c 2. Chair Stndg Com Dio Vermont Burlington VT 1976-1977; Chair Dnry Grants Com Dio Vermont Burlington VT 1974-1975; Secy Convoc Dio Vermont Burlington VT 1965-1973; Secy Dioc Coun Dio Vermont Burlington VT 1963-1970; R S Lk's Ch S Albans VT 1961-1989; P-in-c S Barn Ch Norwich VT 1961-1971; Dept Mssn Dio Vermont Burlington VT 1961-1966. ssbb1947@comcast.net

IRWIN, Bruce Foster (LI) 4501 Hedley Way Apt 203, Charlotte NC 28210 **Died 8/15/2009** B Garden City NY 2/16/1931 s Theodore Newman Irwin & Dorothy. BA Hofstra Coll 1956; LTh SWTS 1959; MA SWTS 1970. D 7/4/1959 P 2/27/1960 Bp James P De Wolfe. bfirwin@bellsouth.net

IRWIN, Margaret Bertha (Mil) 6989 Apprentice Pl, Middleton WI 53562 B Madison WI 5/23/1942 d Fred Ehrensperger & Lena Marty. BA U of Wisconsin 1964; MA U of Wisconsin 1968; MDiv CDSP 1986. D 6/29/1986 P 6/6/1987 Bp Charles Shannon Mallory. m 8/29/1964 Joseph Paul Irwin c 3. R All SS Epis Ch Palo Alto CA 1994-2004; Int Ch Of S Jn The Bapt Aptos CA 1993-1994; Int Asst S Thos Epis Ch Sunnyvale CA 1993; Int Trin Cathd San Jose CA 1991-1992; Assoc S Andr's Ch Saratoga CA 1986-1991. AFP 1986-2003; Associated Parishes 1986; EWC 1986; NNECA 2002. Phi Beta Kappa U of Wisconsin-Madison 1964. mirwin@tds.net

IRWIN, Sara Hariett (Mass) 260 Grove St, Medford MA 02155 **P-in-c Chr Ch Waltham MA 2005-** B Erie PA 11/27/1978 d Zachary Tracy Irwin & Monica. BA New Coll of Florida 2000; MDiv, cl GTS 2004. D 6/12/2004 P 1/8/2005 Bp M(arvil) Thomas Shaw III. m 2/15/2003 Noah Hearne Evans c 2. Emm Ch Boston MA 2004-2005. Auth, "The religiophoneme: Liturg and some uses of deconstruction," *the Journ Wrshp*, Liturg Press, 2006; Auth, "My Red Couch," *My Red Couch*, Pilgrim Press, 2005. sara@irwinevans.com

IRWIN, Zachary Tracy (NwPa) 4216 E South Shore Dr, Erie PA 16511 **D S Mary's Ch Erie PA 2000-** B Port Jervis NY 1/10/1947 s William David Irwin & Margaret Evelyn. ABS Ham 1968; MA Jn Hopkins U 1973; PhD Penn 1978. D 6/10/2000 Bp Robert Deane Rowley Jr. m 6/4/1968 Monica Johnson c 1. zti1@psu.edu

ISAAC, Donald Tileston (Mass) 99 Centre Avenue, Rockland MA 02370 **Vic Trin Epis Ch Rockland MA 1997-** B Brockton MA 12/10/1932 s Melville Tileston Isaac & Doris Mae. BA Bos 1954; STB Ya Berk 1957; MA Bos 1974. D 6/22/1957 P 12/21/1957 Bp Anson Phelps Stokes Jr. m 6/19/1954 Patricia Ann Dorr c 3. Trin Epis Ch Rockland MA 1960-1996; Cur S Mk's Ch Westford MA 1957-1960. donisaac@verizon.net

ISAAC III, F(rank) Reid (O) 2181 Ambleside Drive, Apartment 412, Cleveland OH 44106 B Baltimore MD 12/30/1925 s Frank Reid Isaac & Majorie Arthur. BA Drew U 1946; BD Yale DS 1949; Fllshp Coll of Preachers 1982. D 6/18/1955 P 12/17/1955 Bp Angus Dun. S Paul's Epis Ch Cleveland Heights OH 1984-1990; Ch Of The H Trin New York NY 1975-1984; Reg Off Dio New York New York City NY 1971-1973; R S Barn Ch Irvington on Hudson NY 1968-1971; S Columba's Ch Washington DC 1955-1956. Auth, *Fleshing the Word*, St. Paul's Press, 1996; Auth, *Conversations w the Crucified*, Seabury, 1982; Auth, *What is God Doing Today*, Seabury, 1967. reidisaac@msn.com

✠ **ISAAC, Rt Rev Telesforo A** (SwFla) JP 8600, PO Box 02-5284, Miami FL 33102 B DO 1/5/1929 s Simon Alexander Isaac & Violet Alexandria. Epis TS 1958; U Antonoma de Santo Domingo Santo Domingo DO 1970; MDiv ETSC 1971; Universidad Pontificia de Salamanca, España 1988. D 6/11/1958 P 12/14/1958 Bp Charles Alfred Voegeli Con 3/9/1972 for DR (Iglesia Episcopal Dominicana). m 8/30/1961 Juana Maria Rosa-Zorrilla c 3. Int Bp of VI Dio Vrgn Islands St Thos VI VI 2004-2005; Int Dio Vrgn Islands St Thos VI VI 1996-1997; Asst Bp Dio SW Florida Sarasota FL 1991-1996; Exec Coun Appointees New York NY 1987-1991; Bp Dio The Dominican Republic (Iglesia Epis Dominicana) 100 Airport AvVenice FL 1972-1991; Vic Iglesia Epis San Andres Santo Domingo DO 1965-1971. Auth, "Bk," *Comentarios en Domingos de Cuaresma*, CETALC, 2010; Auth, "Bk," *Fe y Práctica de la Espiritualidad Cristiana*, Promociones y Publicidad, Inc., 2002; Auth, "Bk," *La Labor Educativa Iglesia Epis*, Eligio Delgado, Inc., 1972. Hijo Adoptivo Municipio de San Francisco de Macoris 2003; Macorisano Ejemplar Ayuntamiento San Pedro Macoris 1999; Cert of Merit as Distinguished Citizen Ayuntamiento San Pedro de Macoris 1983. ta_isaac@yahoo.com

ISAACS, James Hunter (Miss) 1208 Grandview Drive, Gautier MS 39553 B Lexington KY 3/27/1939 s William Bruce Isaacs & Elinor Faison. BA Transylvania U 1963; MDiv STUSo 1981. D 6/29/1981 Bp Emerson Paul Haynes P 1/1/1982 Bp Furman Stough. m 7/17/1999 Mary McLendon-Isaacs c 2. Vic S Pierre's Epis Ch Gautier MS 2005-2011; Vic S Steph's Ch Columbia MS 1999-2005; S Mk's Ch Prattville AL 1996; S Mich's Epis Ch Birmingham AL 1986-1994; Asst R S Bon Ch Sarasota FL 1981-1985. BroSA 2007. cissymcl@aol.com

ISAACS, James Steele (Md) 114 Claiborne Rd., Edgewater MD 21037 **Asst S Jas Ch Potomac MD 2011-** B 12/22/1976 s James William Isaacs & Amy Partridge. BA Sarah Lawr Coll 1999; MDiv VTS 2002. D 5/18/2002 Bp Charles Lindsay Longest P 11/23/2002 Bp John Bailey Lipscomb. R S Andr The Fisherman Epis Mayo MD 2005-2009; Assoc R S Paul's Ch Naples FL 2002-2005. rev.isaacs@gmail.com

ISHIBASHI, Samuel Wataru (NY) 164 Valley Rd, Princeton NJ 08540 B Seattle WA 10/11/1927 s Henry Shiro Ishibashi & Mary Fujiko. BA U IL 1950; LTh GTS 1955; MS Bank St Coll of Educ 1969. D 6/5/1955 P 12/16/1955 Bp Horace W B Donegan. c 2. Wkr-p Trin Ch Rocky Hill NJ 1975-1989; P-in-c Chr Epis Ch Sparkill NY 1962-1969; Cur S Mk's Ch Mt Kisco NY 1955-1961. samishibashi@yahoo.com

ISHIZAKI, Norman Yukio (Los) 580 Hilgard Ave, Los Angeles CA 90024 B Sacramento CA 10/27/1939 s Yazo Ishizaki & Esther. BA U CA 1962; BD SWTS 1967. D 9/9/1967 P 3/9/1968 Bp Francis E I Bloy. m 9/7/1953 Velda Marie Young c 2. S Alb's Epis Ch Los Angeles CA 1967-2003.

ISHMAN, Martha S. (NwPa) 245 Valley Trails Ln, Franklin PA 16323 **Vic S Jas Memi Epis Ch Titusville PA 2011-; Cn to the Ordnry Dio NW Pennsylvania Erie PA 2007-** B Columbia PA 6/23/1955 d Burton Y Staman & Marjorie Ann. BS Penn 1977; MDiv VTS 1998. D 5/23/1998 P 11/22/1998 Bp Robert Deane Rowley Jr. m 10/18/1980 Dale Alan Ishman c 2. R S Clem's Epis Ch Hermitage PA 1998-2007. mishman@dionwpa.org

ISLEY, Carolyn W (ETenn) 118 Oak Grove Rd, Greeneville TN 37745 **R S Jas Epis Ch of Greeneville Greeneville TN 2005-** B Buckingham County VA 2/27/1944 BA U of Louisville; MDiv Sthrn Bapt TS, Louisville, KY 1984; Angl Stds U So, Sewanee, TN 2003. D 10/29/2003 P 5/14/2005 Bp Charles Glenn VonRosenberg. m 9/29/1962 Walter A Isley c 2. Bp Search Com Dio E Tennessee Knoxville TN 2010-2011. CISLEYRECTOR@ST-JAMES-EPISCOPAL.COM

ISRAEL, Carver Washington (LI) 322 Clearbrook Ave, Lansdowne PA 19050 **S Phil's Ch Brooklyn NY 2007-** B Kingstown VC 1/7/1956 s Claude A Isreal. Codrington Coll 1983; BTh U of The W Indies 1983. Rec 6/1/1991 as Priest

Bp George Phelps Mellick Belshaw. m 7/8/1987 Suzette Munroe c 3. R H Apos And Medtr Philadelphia PA 1997-2007; Emm Ch Memphis TN 1993-1996; Assoc Ch Of Our Sav Camden NJ 1991-1993; Assoc S Wilfrid's Ch Camden NJ 1991-1993; Assoc S Paul's Ch Camden NJ 1991-1992. casa8987@optimum.net

ISRAEL JR, Fielder (Md) 4720 Winterberry Ct, Williamsburg VA 23188 B Washington DC 4/20/1937 s Fielder Israel & Margaret. BA W&L 1964; MDiv VTS 1975; CPE 1983; Cert VTS 1990. D 6/7/1975 Bp William Foreman Creighton P 5/27/1978 Bp Gray Temple. m 8/21/1971 Gretchen Elizabeth Scherer c 2. Fairhaven Sykesville MD 1994-2004; R S Lk's Ch Eden NC 1986-1994; Ch Of The Gd Shpd Columbia SC 1982-1986; Vic Ch Of The Adv Marion SC 1978-1982; Asst Min S Jas Ch Charleston SC 1977-1978; Asst Min S Jn's Ch Chevy Chase MD 1975-1977. gretchen.israel@gmail.com

ISWARIAH, James Chandran (Va) 465 Walnut Ln, King William VA 23086 **S Dav's Ch Aylett VA 2002-** B Madras India 9/20/1950 s David Chandran Iswariah & Sarojini Ruth. BCA U of Madras 1975; MDiv Serampore U IN 1979. Trans from Anglican Church Of Australia 3/1/2000 Bp Peter James Lee. m 9/14/1981 Sheila M Iswariah c 2. jamesiswariah@yahoo.com

✠ ITTY, Rt Rev Johncy (Ore) 10 Avalon Road, Garden City NY 11530 B Bhopal Madhya Pradesh IN 4/10/1963 s John Itty & Annacutty. BA CUNY 1985; MA CUNY 1985; MA Col 1986; MPhil CUNY 1994; PhD CUNY 1994; MDiv NYTS 1994. Trans from Church of South India 12/29/1995 Bp Orris George Walker Jr Con 9/20/2003 for Ore. m 1/10/1990 Jolly Itty c 2. Geo Mercer TS Garden City NY 2009-2010; Bp Dio Oregon Portland OR 2003-2008; Cathd Of The Incarn Garden City NY 1998-2003; Soc Justice Epis Ch Cntr New York NY 1998-2000; Int Ch Of The Nativ Mineola NY 1998; Int S Gabr's Ch Hollis NY 1997-1998; Int S Matt's Ch Woodhaven NY 1996-1998; Assoc P S Matt's Ch Woodhaven NY 1993-1995. ",Bishops Column," *Oregon Epis Ch News*, OECN, 2008; ",Lectionary Reflections," *Wit*, Wit mag, 2005; ",The Global Debt Crisis," *Angl Wrld*, Angl Comm Sec, 1996; Johncy Itty, "The Role Of Political Ldrshp In Political Dvlpmt Of India: A Comparative Case Study," *Political Ldrshp*, CUNY, 1994; ",The Fin Crisis in Perspective," *Sec News*, Untd Nations Sec, 1986; "Operation Bluestar," *Queens Coll, CUNY*, Queens Coll, CUNY, 1985. Pi Sigma Alpha; Whos Who Among Amer Colleges & Universities 1985. dist in Mnstry Awd NYTS 2008; DD GTS 2006; Phi Beta Kappa; Phi Beta Kappa Schlr; PhD Merit Fllshp Schlr; Phi Beta Kappa. johncyi@verizon.net

IVES, Joel (Mass) 23 Monmouth St., Brookline MA 02446 **R Ch Of Our Sav Brookline MA 2007-** B Gloucester MA 5/13/1961 s Frederick Manley Ives & Nancy Perron. BA U Of Hartford 1983; MDiv GTS 1996. D 9/8/1996 P 5/17/1997 Bp M(arvil) Thomas Shaw III. m 8/22/1998 Florence S Slingluff c 3. COM Dio Massachusetts Boston MA 2003-2009; Bp's Search Com Dio Massachusetts Boston MA 2000; R S Paul's Ch In Nantucket Nantucket MA 1999-2006; Cox Fell The Cathd Ch Of S Paul Boston MA 1996-1999. Fllshp Of The Soc Of S Jn The Evang 2002. jmives@gmail.com

IVES, Walter William (FdL) Po Box 88, Iron Belt WI 54536 **Died 1/20/2011** B Lanhin ND 5/6/1923 s George Smith Ives & Katherine. Orange Cnty Cmnty Coll. D 5/31/1998 Bp Thomas Kreider Ray. NAAD.

IVEY, Valerie Ann (Ore) 15240 Nw Courting Hill Dr, Banks OR 97106 **D Trin Epis Cathd Portland OR 1992-** B Kingston Surrey UK 6/29/1934 d William George Pow & Elsie. BA Lon 1955; AMIA Lon 1957; MS Bryn 1962; MS Portland St U 1982. D 6/23/1992 Bp Robert Louis Ladehoff. m 10/10/1964 Dean Benjamin Ivey c 2. NAAD.

IWICK, Richard Edward (Mich) 25755 Kilreigh Ct, Farmington Hills MI 48336 **Supply P S Eliz's Ch Redford MI 2011-; Supply P S Mart Ch Detroit MI 2001-** B Oshkosh WI 3/31/1936 s Edward Walter Iwick & Theresa Klatt. BA Lawr 1958; MST GTS 1961; MS Iowa St U 1976. D 6/18/1961 P 12/22/1961 Bp William Hampton Brady. m 12/15/1996 Diana Rowe Foote c 1. Archd Dio Michigan Detroit MI 1992-1994; R Trin Epis Ch Farmington Hills MI 1983-1999; Assoc R Trin Ch Anderson IN 1980-1983; Supply P Dio Iowa Des Moines IA 1974-1976; R S Alb's Ch Superior WI 1968-1972; Asst S Mk's Ch Milwaukee WI 1965-1968; Vic Chr the King/H Nativ (Sturgeon Bay) Sturgeon Bay WI 1961-1965. Auth, "An Evaltn Of The Ottumwa Yth Dvlpmt Bureau"; Auth, "An Evaltn Of Dubuque Yth Serv".

IZADI, Samira (Dal) 3310 Ivanhoe Lane, Garland TX 75044 **St Pauls Epis Ch Prosper TX 2010-** B Shiraz Iran 7/23/1972 MDiv Perkins TS; MA U of Shiraz. D 6/26/2010 Bp Paul Emil Lambert P 5/12/2011 Bp James Monte Stanton. c 2. samiraizadi@clear.net

IZUTSU, Margaret Widdifield (Mich) 18 Fairview Ave, Arlington MA 02474 B Pontiac MI 2/12/1955 d Charles George Widdifield & Margaret Scarlett. MDiv Harvard DS 1995. D 6/18/1994 Bp R(aymond) Stewart Wood Jr P 6/1/1995 Bp Arthur Edward Walmsley. m 2/6/1983 Merguru Izutsu. Asst - Pstr Care Par Of The Epiph Winchester MA 1995-1996. Auth, "Ao-Tung". Japanese Cntr For The Quality Of Life Stds. Natl Media Awd Mntl Hlth Assn 1980; Marg Augur Schlrshp Awd 73. mizutsu@hds.harvard.edu

J

JABLONSKI, Carol J (WA) 4512 College Ave, College Park MD 20740 **R S Andr's Epis Ch Coll Pk MD 2009-** B Milwaukee WI 7/12/1951 d George Gerard Jablonski & Eleanor Virginia. BA Alleg 1973; MA Pur 1975; PhD Pur 1979; MDiv VTS 2006. D 6/10/2006 Bp John Bailey Lipscomb P 2/4/2007 Bp Michael Bruce Curry. m 3/14/1987 John T Jones. Assoc S Steph's Ch Durham NC 2006-2009. Harris Prize VTS 2006. carolty2@verizon.net

JACKSON, Brad Lee (Va) Po Box 305, Madison VA 22727 **R Piedmont Ch Madison VA 1995-** B Pratt KS 6/26/1953 s Claude Eugene Jackson & Ilya Ruby. BA Phillips U 1976; MA Wichita St U 1983; MDiv VTS 1989. D 6/21/1989 Bp John Forsythe Ashby P 1/25/1990 Bp William Edward Smalley. m 2/25/1984 Jayne E Edwards c 2. R Imm Ch King and Queen Courthouse VA 1992-1995; R S Jn's Ch W Point VA 1992-1995; Asst R S Paul's Ch Leavenworth KS 1989-1992. jacksbjcp@verizon.net

JACKSON, Carl Thomas (Va) 2940 Corries Way, Conneaut OH 44030 B Painesville OH 8/18/1938 s Carl Kelsey Jackson & Pearl Janet. BSME Case Wstrn Reserve U 1961; MDiv VTS 1995; DMin Austin Presb TS 1999. D 11/4/1973 Bp William Crittenden P 12/23/1989 Bp Donald James Davis. m 8/5/1961 Carol Turner c 2. Dn Dio Virginia Richmond VA 2006-2008; R S Paul's Ch Bailey's Crossroads Falls Ch VA 1996-2009; R Epis Ch Of The Mssh Gonzales TX 1995-1996; Adj S Paul's Ch Bailey's Crossroads Falls Ch VA 1992-1995; Int Ch Of The H Sprt Erie PA 1991-1992; Int S Mary's Ch Erie PA 1989-1990; Stff Cathd Of S Paul Erie PA 1987-1991; Com Mssn Strtgy Dio NW Pennsylvania Erie PA 1981-1984; D Gr Ch Lake City PA 1977-1987; Liturg Cmsn Dio NW Pennsylvania Erie PA 1976-1978; D S Steph's Ch Fairview PA 1973-1977. Auth, "Behold," *I Make All Things New: Mssn As Catalyst For Revitalization*, Austin Pres Theo Sem, 1999. Ord Of S Lk 1991. frtom@aol.com

JACKSON, David (SwFla) 2507 Del Prado Blvd S # 5, Cape Coral FL 33904 B 9/2/1946 s David Maurice Jackson & Gertrude. MBChB U of Glasgow GB 1970. D 6/6/2009 Bp Dabney Tyler Smith. m 12/14/1968 Yvette Jackson c 3. djacksonmd@hotmail.com

JACKSON, David Hilton (Haw) 1041 10th Ave., Honolulu HI 96816 **Ch Of The Epiph Honolulu HI 2009-** B Leicester GB 3/18/1962 s Dennis Herbert Jackson & Georgiana. MS Oxf; MDiv PrTS; BA Stan 1984. Trans from Church Of England 10/23/2002 Bp Joseph Jon Bruno. m 2/29/1988 Ariane Elizabeth Hagoor c 1. The ETS At Claremont Claremont CA 2006; Int S Jn's Mssn La Verne CA 2004-2005; Sr Assoc for Par Life All SS Ch Pasadena CA 2003-2004; S Mk's Epis Ch Upland CA 2002-2003. davidhiltonjackson@yahoo.com

JACKSON, Deborah Mitchell (Fla) 5620 Columbia Pl, Jacksonville FL 32210 **Asst R S Paul's By-The-Sea Epis Ch Jacksonville Bch FL 2010-** B Gainesville FL 1/14/1958 d Jerry D Mitchell & Mary I. BA Rol Winter Pk FL 1979; MBA Jacksonville U 1983; MDiv TS 2007. D 5/27/2007 P 12/9/2007 Bp Samuel Johnson Howard. m 9/4/1982 James B Jackson c 3. Cn S Jn's Cathd Jacksonville FL 2007-2010. jack393@bellsouth.net

JACKSON, Eric Michael Colin (Oly) 26291 Pennsylvania Ave NE APT 105, Kingston WA 98346 **Asstg P S Mk's Cathd Seattle WA 2001-** B Grand Prairie Alberta CA 1/24/1933 s Eric Whitcliffe Jackson & Ivy Lydia. LST Bps 1965; MTh McGill U, Can 1966. Trans from Anglican Church of Canada 6/1/1966 Bp Clarence Rupert Haden Jr. m Joanne Reid c 4. Prog Admin Ch Of The Epiph Seattle WA 1974-1987; TACS Sr Trnr Dio Olympia Seattle WA 1974-1987; LTD Trnr Dio Spokane Spokane WA 1972-1974; R S Jas Pullman WA 1972-1974; R S Ptr's Epis Ch Red Bluff CA 1969-1972; Vic S Andr's Of The Redwoods Redway CA 1966-1968. Awd, Mem of the British Empire HM Queen Eliz II 1962; Hon Mem, Natl Press Club of Can Natl Press Club, Ottawa, Can 1962. comprose@earthlink.net

JACKSON JR, Gary Leon (CFla) 500 W Stuart St, Bartow FL 33830 **R H Trin Epis Ch Bartow FL 2011-** B Arkadelphia AR 2/12/1970 s Gary Leon Jackson & Verda Sue. BS Henderson St U 1993; MDiv Nash 2011. D 6/11/2011 Bp Hugo Luis Pina-Lopez. m 1/26/1991 Christina Lee Jackson c 2. rev.garyleon@gmail.com

JACKSON JR, Hillyer Barnett (Okla) 3149 NW 24th St, Oklahoma City OK 73107 **Supply Chr Memi Epis Ch El Reno OK 1999-** B Oklahoma City OK 3/23/1934 s Hillyer Barnett Jackson & Roberta Lovelace. BA U of Oklahoma 1956; MDiv Epis TS of The SW 1959; Jas Mills Fllshp Cambridge GB 1968. D 5/23/1959 P 11/30/1959 Bp Chilton Powell. Alt Dep GC Dio Oklahoma Oklahoma City OK 1991-1997; Chrmn Div of Mnstry Dvlpmt Dio Oklahoma Oklahoma City OK 1991-1996; Chr Memi Epis Ch El Reno OK 1987-1996; Chair - Dioc Liturg Dio Oklahoma Oklahoma City OK 1987-1995; Rgnl Dn OK City OK Dio Oklahoma Oklahoma City OK 1987-1992; R S Jn's Ch Oklahoma City OK 1980-1987; Dep GC Dio Oklahoma Oklahoma City OK 1979-1982; Bd Trst Epis TS Of The SW Austin TX 1977-1982; Stndg Com Dio Oklahoma Oklahoma City OK 1976-1997; Chrmn BEC Dio Oklahoma Oklahoma City OK 1972-1997; R S Matt's Ch Enid OK 1968-1980; Assoc S

Matt's Ch Enid OK 1966-1968; Vic Ch Of The Ascen Pawnee OK 1964-1966; Vic S Mk's Ch Perry OK 1964-1966; Vic S Jas Ch Antlers OK 1959-1964; Vic S Mk's Ch Hugo OK 1959-1964. Angl/RC Cmsn OK 1981. The Bp's Awd The Bp, Dioc. of Oklahoma 1997. fatherb@earthlink.net

JACKSON, Hugo Terrance (At) 4246 Glenforest Way Ne, Roswell GA 30075 **Ch Of The Annunc Marietta GA 2011-** B Toronto Ontario 7/26/1953 MDiv Vancouver TS. m 10/15/1982 Ann Margaret Fischer c 1. S Teresa Acworth GA 2003-2005. hugo@apres.net

JACKSON, Jared Judd (Pgh) 903 Orchard Park Dr., Gibsonia PA 15044 B New Haven CT 7/26/1930 s William Alexander Jackson & Dorothy. BA Harv 1952; BD EDS 1958; ThD UTS 1962. D 6/21/1958 Bp Frederic Cunningham Lawrence P 12/1/1958 Bp Anson Phelps Stokes Jr. m 7/21/1984 Cynthia Irene Bonnett c 4. Asst The Ch Of The Redeem Pittsburgh PA 1997-2004; Dn Of The Trng Prog For Mnstry Dio Pittsburgh Monroeville PA 1978-1981; Chair Of The BEC Dio Pittsburgh Monroeville PA 1970-1977; Asst Gr Epis Ch Westwood NJ 1961-1962; Asst S Matt's Ch Bedford NY 1958-1961. Auth, "Rhetorical Criticism". jaredjudd2000@yahoo.com

JACKSON, Jeffery Rand (At) 69 Mobley Road, PO Box 752, Hamilton GA 31811 **R S Nich Epis Ch Hamilton GA 2008-** B Memphis TN 6/3/1978 s Albert Henry Jackson & Glenda Gail. BA Berry Coll 2000; MDiv VTS 2003. D 2/8/2003 P 8/1/2003 Bp Henry Irving Louttit. m 8/18/2001 Molly Elizabeth Sanders c 4. S Ptr's Epis Ch Savannah GA 2004-2008. fatherjeff@stnicholashamilton.org

JACKSON, Jimmy (NwT) PO Box 3346, Odessa TX 79760 **P-in-c S Jn's Epis Ch Odessa TX 2011-; D S Chris's Epis Ch Lubbock TX 1999-** B Lubbox TX 4/18/1956 s Jimmy Leo Jackson & Lucille Marvin. BSW Texas Tech U 1989; Dplma of Angl Stds Epis TS Of The SW 2011. D 10/29/1999 Bp C(harles) Wallis Ohl P 8/13/2011 Bp James Scott Mayer. m 5/22/1983 Valinda Joan Bradshaw-Jackson c 2. lesval@att.net

JACKSON, J(ohn) Robert (WNY) 2330 Maple Rd Apt. No. 390, Buffalo NY 14221 B Lockport NY 12/31/1913 s William Jackson & Mary Elizabeth. U of Virginia 1937; Delancey DS Buffalo NY 1938. D 3/13/1954 P 4/18/1964 Bp Lauriston L Scaife. c 2. R S Ptr's Ch Westfield NY 1972-1976; R S Mary's Ch Salamanca NY 1964-1969; Cur S Andr's Ch Newfane Burt NY 1956-1964; D-In-C S Paul's Ch Holley NY 1954-1956.

JACKSON, John Teele Pratt (NH) 41 Gore Road, Lancaster NH 03584 **Died 2/8/2011** B Boston MA 12/21/1937 s James Jackson & Sally Pratt. BA Ya 1959; STB Ya Berk 1962. D 6/23/1962 P 11/22/1963 Bp Anson Phelps Stokes Jr. c 3. jtpj@earthlink.net

JACKSON, Julius W D (Pa) 803 Macdade Blvd, Collingdale PA 19023 B Freetown SL 8/22/1949 s Taiwo Jackson & Isabella Sarah. AA Spartanburg Jr Coll 1974; BA Wofford Coll 1976; AA Spartanburg Tech Coll 1982; MDiv VTS 1988; Cert Int Mnstry Ntwk 2012. D 6/11/1988 P 5/1/1989 Bp William Arthur Beckham. m 8/22/1998 Kanku Jackson c 1. Vic S Dismas Epis Mssn At Graterford Philadelphia PA 1995-2011; Vic S Mary's Epis Ch Philadelphia PA 1995-2010; R S Phil's Ch Buffalo NY 1989-1995; D-In-Trng S Lk's Epis Ch Columbia SC 1988-1989. ekundayo1948@msn.com

JACKSON, Kenneth Leroy (Haw) 1801 - 10th Avenue #A, Honolulu HI 96816 **D Dio Hawaii Honolulu HI 1986-** B Sheridan WY 5/7/1934 s Gilbert Mansfield Jackson & Imogene. AA No Wyoming Cmnty Coll 1954; BA Hendrix Coll 1956; MA Col 1960; EdD Col 1967. D 12/14/1986 Bp Donald Purple Hart. Tertiary Of The Soc Of S Fran Professed 1985.

JACKSON, Kimberly Sue (At) 2598 Lavista Rd, Decatur GA 30033 **Dio Atlanta Atlanta GA 2010-** B Elkins WVA 8/25/1984 d Timothy Lamont Jackson & Brenda Sue. BA Furman Univeristy 2006; MDiv Emory U 2009; Angl Stds VTS 2010. D 12/19/2009 Bp J(ohn) Neil Alexander. m 7/1/2010 La Trina Jackson. KIMBERLYSJACKSON@GMAIL.COM

JACKSON, Larry Dean (WVa) 2004 Maxwell Ave, Parkersburg WV 26101 **R Trin Ch Parkersburg WV 2004-; S Matt's Epis Ch Chesterfield VA 1998-** B Parkersburg WV 4/24/1948 s Donald Clarence Jackson & Mildred Anna. BA Glenville St Coll 1970; MDiv TESM 1982. D 6/5/1982 Bp Robert Bracewell Appleyard P 5/17/1983 Bp Alden Moinet Hathaway. m 6/26/1971 Ruby J Keith c 2. Mssnr Chr Ch Wellsburg WV 1998-2004; Mssnr Olde S Jn's Ch Colliers WV 1998-2004; S Thos' Epis Ch Weirton WV 1998-2004; Brooke-Hancock Cluster Wellsburg WV 1997-2004; S Thos' Epis Ch Weirton WV 1990-1997; R Gr Epis Ch Drakes Branch VA 1983-1990; R S Jn's Epis Ch Chase City VA 1983-1990; R S Tim's Epis Ch Clarksville VA 1983-1990; Cur S Thos Ch In The Fields Gibsonia PA 1982-1983. "I Started a Joke...," *Hstgr (NEHA)*, 2003. S Meinrad's Archabbey - Oblate 2003. Who's Who in Amer Ch Ldrshp 1989; Chase City Citizen of the Year ChmbrCom 1986. larry@trinity-church.org

JACKSON, Margaret Joan (NY) 414 Fern Rd, Villas NJ 08251 **Ch Of The Adv Cape May NJ 2000-** B Greenport NY 1/1/1935 d Edward Spaque Copin & Margaret Jane. RN S Jn's Epis Hosp Sch of Nrsng 1955; BS SUNY 1987; MDiv CDSP 1990. D 6/9/1990 P 12/15/1990 Bp Richard Frank Grein. c 3. R S Jn's Epis Ch Kingston NY 1998-2001; Dio New York New York City NY 1997-1998; Dioc Coun Dio New York New York City NY 1993-1996; The Ch Of S Steph Staten Island NY 1990-1996. mjoanj2@verizon.net

JACKSON, Margaret Ruth Brosz (Ia) 2702 17th Ave N, Fort Dodge IA 50501 **P-in-res Trin Ch Emmetsburg IA 2008-** B Parkston SD 10/30/1937 d Oscar Brosz & Ruth. BA Yankton Coll 1958; BA Augustana Coll 1968; MA U of St. Thos 1990; Untd TS Of The Twin Cities 2003. D 6/12/2004 P 1/15/2005 Bp Alan Scarfe. m 1/23/1958 John Philip Jackson c 2. P Assoc Ch Of The Gd Shpd Webster City IA 2005-2008; P Assoc S Mk's Epis Ch Ft Dodge IA 2005-2008. mjack@frontiernet.net

JACKSON, Micah T (Chi) 1207 Cullen Ave, Austin TX 78757 **Asst Prof of Preaching Epis TS Of The SW Austin TX 2008-** B Cleveland Heights OH 6/19/1969 s James Dwight Jackson & Donna. MDiv Meadville/Lombard TS 2002; MTS SWTS 2004; PHD Grad Theol Un 2011. D 6/3/2006 Bp William Dailey Persell P 12/2/2006 Bp Marc Handley Andrus. m 5/19/2002 Laura W Gowdy c 1. S Mk's Par Berkeley CA 2008. mjackson@ssw.edu

JACKSON, Patricia Gladys (Ct) 120 Sigourney St, Hartford CT 06105 B Jamaica WI 3/9/1937 d Ivan Harold Griffiths & Ethel H. BSC Empire St Coll 1991. D 9/15/2007 Bp Andrew Donnan Smith. c 2. jayjay5077@hotmail.com

JACKSON, Paula Marie (SO) 65 E Hollister St, Cincinnati OH 45219 **R Ch Of Our Sav Cincinnati OH 1990-** B Springfield MO 6/14/1952 d Herman Dale Jackson & Frances Marie. BA U of Missouri 1974; MDiv Sthrn Bapt TS Louisville KY 1979; CAS GTS 1985; PhD Sthrn Bapt TS Louisville KY 1985. D 6/30/1985 P 6/30/1986 Bp David Reed. m 8/16/1975 Daniel Marshall Watson c 2. Assoc Epis Soc of Chr Ch Cincinnati OH 1987-1990; Int S Geo's Epis Ch Louisville KY 1986-1987; D Calv Ch Louisville KY 1985-1986. Integrity. pjackson@fuse.net

JACKSON, Paul Phillip (CFla) 1620 Mayflower Ct., A-211, Winter Park FL 32789 **D All SS Ch Of Winter Pk Winter Pk FL 1976-** B Atlanta GA 10/15/1921 s Paul Phillip Jackson & Dora Virginia. BA Emory U 1949. D 6/15/1975 Bp William Hopkins Folwell. m 2/5/1955 Mary Jean Atwood c 2. Asst Chr The King Epis Ch Orlando FL 1975-1976. Chapl Ord of S Lk, Chapl DOK 1986. Chap OSL 1988; Chap DOK 1986.

JACKSON, Peter (Nwk) 130 Bessida St, Bloomfield NJ 07003 B Georgetown Guyana 9/26/1947 PhD U of Bordeaux FR; BA U of Guyana. D 6/3/2006 Bp John Palmer Croneberger. m 1/11/1991 Lorita Jackson c 2. pjackson_69@msn.com

JACKSON, Peter Jonathan Edward (WA) 1 The Green, London N14 7EG Great Britain (UK) B Swansea Wales 8/1/1953 BA Oxf 1974; MA Oxf 1978; PGCE Oxf 1978; Cert Theol St Steph's Hse, Oxf 1980. Trans from Church Of England 12/31/2002 Bp John Chane. Assoc R and Dir of Educ S Pat's Ch Washington DC 2001-2003. Auth, "Ethics," SPCK, 2011; Auth, "Faith Confirmed," SPCK, 1997; Auth, "The People of God," Herga Press, 1991; Auth, "The Ways of God," Herga Press, 1990; Auth, "The Ch of God," Herga Press, 1990. peterjejackson@aol.com

JACKSON, Phillip A (Az) 4015 E Lincoln Dr, Paradise Valley AZ 85253 **R Chr Ch Of The Ascen Paradise Vlly AZ 2007-** B Chicago IL 4/16/1963 s Albert Leverne Jackson & Margaret Ann. BA Amh 1985; JD Ya 1989; MDiv CDSP 1994. D 6/24/1994 Bp Donald Purple Hart P 1/25/1995 Bp Claude Edward Payne. m 4/27/1996 Page Y Underwood. Dio Arizona Phoenix AZ 2007; R Chr Ch Detroit MI 2001-2007; Cn Educ Cathd Ch Of S Paul Detroit MI 1998-2001; Vic Ch Of The Incarn Houston TX 1994-1998. phillipjackson1@mac.com

JACKSON, Reginald Fitzroy (LI) 1695 E 55th St, Brooklyn NY 11234 B Antigua WI 4/21/1949 s Herbert Whitsun Jackson & Ruth Vivian. BBA CUNY 1985; MBA CUNY 1988; Mercer Hosp Sch of Nrsng 2005. D 2/24/2006 Bp Rodney Rae Michel. m 4/13/1987 Sadie C Hines c 2. regjackson@mindspring.com

JACKSON, Rhea Ewing (Ark) PO Box 36, Roland AR 72135 B Little Rock AR 2/14/1941 s Rhea Ewing Jackson & Arline. BA U of Arkansas at Little Rock 1963; BD Epis TS of The SW 1966. D 6/29/1966 P 3/1/1967 Bp Robert Raymond Brown. m 9/1/1964 Virginia Nelson c 2. Int Dn & R Trin Cathd Little Rock AR 2008-2009; Int R S Mk's Epis Ch Little Rock AR 2001-2003; Int Dn & R Trin Cathd Little Rock AR 1994-1995; R S Jn's Epis Ch Helena AR 1972-1974; Asst S Geo's Ch Nashville TN 1969-1972; Vic Emm Ch Lake Vill AR 870-2652230or8 1966-1969; Vic S Paul's Ch McGehee AR 1966-1969. rheajackson.99@comcast.net

JACKSON, Robert Sumner (Mass) 339 S Madison St, Woodstock IL 60098 B New York NY 1/25/1926 s Sumner Allen Jackson & Jean Roy. BA Beloit Coll 1949; Oxf 1954; STB Harvard DS 1956; PhD U MI 1958. D 11/23/1958 P 12/1/1959 Bp Anson Phelps Stokes Jr. m 1/1/1974 Jacqueline Dougan c 4. Robert S. Jackson, "Breakthrough In Econ Well Being For All People," *Journ For Global Transformation*, Landmark Educ Corp., 2001; Robert S. Jackson, "No Amer Gold Stocks," Probus Pub, 1988; Robert S. Jackson, "Gold As Barbaric Relic: Modernist Myth," *Nomos mag*, Nomos mag, 1985; Robert S. Jackson & Sarah Cook, "The Bailly Area," *Porter Cnty Indiana*, Robert Jackson & Assoc, 1974; Robert S. Jackson, "Jn Donne's Chr Vocation," NWU Press, 1970. Non-

Stipendiary Priests Assn Of Chicago 1966. Hon Grad Berk. Date? 1962. robertsumnerjackson@yahoo.com

JACKSON, Rosemary Herrick (WNC) 145 Old Mt Olivet Rd, Zirconia NC 28790 B New York NY 5/28/1947 d Richard Seymour Jackson & Helene Coler. BFA New Sch Parsons Sch of Desnan 1970; MDiv Epis TS of the SW 2001. D 9/14/2003 Bp Rayford Baines High Jr P 5/27/2004 Bp Don Adger Wimberly. The Wm Temple Fndt Galveston TX 2004-2005; Asst Gr Ch Galveston TX 2002-2007; Exec Dir Epis Ch Cntr New York NY 2001-2007. jaxon07@bellsouth.net

JACKSON, Terry Allan (NY) 600 W 246th St Apt 1515, Bronx NY 10471 **S Andr's Ch New York NY 2001-** B Birmingham AL 9/10/1957 s Terry Jackson & Lucy. BA U of Alabama 1979; MDiv GTS 1986. D 5/24/1986 Bp Furman Stough P 11/18/1987 Bp Frank Tracy Griswold III. Supply S Ambr Epis Ch New York NY 1998-1999; Wooster Sch Danbury CT 1994-1997; Asst Ch Of S Mary The Vrgn New York NY 1987-1994. Nasd 1997; Nfa 1997.

JACKSON, Terry Wightman (CFla) 728 Lake Dora Dr, Tavares FL 32778 **Del GC Dio Cntrl Florida Orlando FL 1997-** B Palestine TX 6/19/1939 s Chester Warren Jackson & Vera Ann. BA U of Kansas 1961; MDiv SWTS 1964; MS Florida Inst of Tech 1972; DMin PrTS 1982; Cert Oxf 1985. D 6/11/1964 Bp Edward Randolph Welles II P 12/21/1964 Bp James Loughlin Duncan. m 8/8/1959 Donna Knutson c 4. Dn Leesburg Deanry Dio Cntrl Florida Orlando FL 1995-1999; Dio Cntrl Florida Orlando FL 1984-1992; Stndg Com Dio Cntrl Florida Orlando FL 1976-1980; Chair - COM Dio Cntrl Florida Orlando FL 1974-1979; Chair Prog Com Dio Cntrl Florida Orlando FL 1974-1978; R S Jas Epis Ch Leesburg FL 1973-2004; Chair - COM Dio Cntrl Florida Orlando FL 1973-1980; Plnng Com Dio Cntrl Florida Orlando FL 1972-1974; Dn Melbourne Deanry Dio Cntrl Florida Orlando FL 1972-1973; Com Coll Wk Dio Cntrl Florida Orlando FL 1971-1975; Pres Stndg Com Dio Cntrl Florida Orlando FL 1970-1978; R S Jn's Ch Melbourne FL 1968-1973; Asst R H Trin Epis Ch Melbourne FL 1964-1968. Auth, *Intro to Philos*. Who's Who in Rel 1976. tdubyaj@embarqmail.com

JACKSON, Thomas C (Cal) Christ Episcopal Church, 1700 Santa Clara Avenue, Alameda CA 94501 **Asstg Preist Chr Ch Alameda CA 2011-** B Ayer MA 9/13/1949 s Wallace Renton Jackson & Helen Suitor. U of Maryland 1969; U of Connecticut 1971; MBA U of New Haven 1987; MDiv CDSP 2008. D 6/5/2010 P 12/4/2010 Bp Marc Handley Andrus. m 6/26/2005 Alexander Jonghee Han c 2. Int Admin Ch Of The Epiph San Carlos CA 2011; D S Bede's Epis Ch Menlo Pk CA 2010. Ed, "So the People May Know: A Guide to Water Utility Publ Info Practices," *Bk*, Amer Water Works Assn, Denver, CO, 1993; Ed, "Nuclear Waste Mgmt: The Ocean Alternative," *Bk*, Pergamon Press, New York, NY, 1983; Ed, "Coast Alert: Scientists Speak Out," *Bk*, Friends of the Earth Books, San Francisco, CA, 1981. TCJACKSON@GMAIL.COM

JACKSON, Thomas Lee (Ala) Po Box 4155, Tyler TX 75712 B Detroit MI 8/29/1942 s Clifford Lee Jackson & Mary Esperance. BA Washington U-St. Louis 1964; MDiv VTS 1967; PhD Amer Inst 1988. D 6/29/1967 Bp Richard S M Emrich P 1/6/1968 Bp Archie H Crowley. m 8/2/1997 Patricia Fischer c 3. Dioc Counslr Dio Alabama Birmingham AL 1985-1988; Assoc R S Paul's Ch Englewood NJ 1968-1969; Cur Ch Of The Mssh Detroit MI 1967-1968. Auth, "Me & Us: A Journey Of Self-Discovery," Xlibris, 2003; Auth, "Moments Of Clarity," Xlibris, 2002; Auth, "In Any Given Moment," Xlibris, 2002; Auth, "Moments Of Clarity," *Vol. II*, Xlibris, 2002; Auth, "Life'S Secrets (Parts 1&2)," Ad Hoc Press, 1984; Auth, "Go Back, You Didn't Say May I," Seabury Press & Xlibris, 1974. Journey-ocw@earthlink.net

JACKSON-MCKINNEY, Statha Frances (SwFla) 484 E Shade Dr, Venice FL 34293 **D S Mk's Epis Ch Venice FL 2003-** B Hopewell VA 12/14/1935 D 6/14/2003 Bp John Bailey Lipscomb. m 11/3/1956 Curtis McKinney. sfranmckinney@aol.com

JACOBS, Allston Alexander (Md) 2019 Division St, Baltimore MD 21217 **R Ch Of S Kath Of Alexandria Baltimore MD 2009-** B Antigua 3/9/1948 s Alexander Jacobs & Daisy. Dplma of Theol Codrington Coll 1976; BA Somerset U 1986; MA St. Mary's Sem & U 1990. Trans from Church in the Province Of The West Indies 1/7/2010 as Priest Bp Eugene Sutton. m 8/19/1978 Margo E Margo McCollin c 2. CANONALJ@HOTMAIL.COM

JACOBS, Connie Hartquist (EpisSanJ) PO Box 446, Oakhurst CA 93644 B Austin MN 7/17/1943 d Richard Earl Hartquist & Margaret Jean. BA U CA 1966; Tchg Cert California St U 1968; Cert Dioc Sch for Mnstrs 1979; BTS Sch for Deacons 1985. D 6/25/1979 Bp George West Barrett. m 5/18/2002 Thomas Jacobs. D S Cuth's Epis Ch Oakland CA 2003-2004; Dio California San Francisco CA 1986-1990; D S Aid's Ch San Francisco CA 1981-1983. Auth, *Franciscan*. NAAD. conniehjacobs@yahoo.com

JACOBS, Gregory A (Nwk) 31 Mulberry St., Newark NJ 07102 **Cn for Mnstry Dio Newark Newark NJ 2008-** B Bilwaskarma NG 3/10/1952 s Solomon Napoleon Jacobs & Lynette Gwenelda. BA Pr 1974; JD Col 1977; MDiv Bex 1995. D 6/17/1995 Bp J Clark Grew II P 12/17/1995 Bp Arthur Benjamin Williams Jr. m 9/30/1978 Beverly Faye Canzater c 2. Dio Massachusetts Boston MA 2006-2008; Cn for Mssn & Mnstry Trin Cathd Cleveland OH 2001-2005; Dio Ohio Cleveland OH 1999-2001; Asst to Bp Dio Ohio Cleveland OH 1999-2000; Vic S Phil's Epis Ch Akron OH 1995-1999; S Paul's Ch Akron OH 1995-1998. EPF 2001; EUC 2000; UBE 1991. revjacobs@aol.com

JACOBS, John R(ay) (CFla) 1406 Chesterfield Ct, Eustis FL 32726 **Trin Ch Vero Bch FL 2010-** B Fort Smith AR 12/25/1955 s Harry Martin Jacobs & Joyce. BA U So 1978; JD U of Memphis 1981; MDiv STUSo 2000; DMin STUSo 2006. D 5/27/2000 P 12/9/2000 Bp John Wadsworth Howe. m 5/16/1981 Elizabeth P Pfieffer c 2. R S Thos Epis Ch Eustis FL 2003-2009; Asst S Barn Ch Deland FL 2000-2003. jjacobs@trinityvero.org

JACOBS, Marlene M (Minn) 1917 Logan Ave S, Minneapolis MN 55403 **Dioc Coun Dio Minnesota Minneapolis MN 2009-; R S Paul's Ch Minneapolis MN 2007-** B Harlan IA 11/24/1962 d Gerald Francis Jacobs & Marietta Cecilia. BA U of St. Thos 1987; MS U of Wisconsin 1995; MDiv VTS 2005. D 6/15/2005 Bp James Louis Jelinek P 12/18/2005 Bp Robert R Gepert. Asst to the R S Lk's Par Kalamazoo MI 2005-2007. marle_918@yahoo.com

JACOBS, Mary Lee (WMo) 121 West 48th Street, Suite 1001, Kansas City MO 64112 B Tarry AK 9/24/1947 d Johnie Jacobs & Lillie Bell. BS U of Arkansas 1970; GW 1977; Loyola U 1992; Westcott Hse 2000; MDiv SWTS 2001; Cert Int Mnstry Ntwk Trng 2003. D 6/9/2001 Bp Robert Wilkes Ihloff P 12/22/2001 Bp John Leslie Rabb. m 8/9/1968 Leo Jackson c 2. R All SS Epis Ch Kansas City MO 2003-2008; Anti-Racism T/F Dio Maryland Baltimore MD 2002-2003; Dioc Coun Mem Dio Maryland Baltimore MD 2002-2003; Congrl Dvlpmt:Urban & Suburban Dio W Missouri Kansas City MO 2001-2008; Assoc R S Steph's Ch Severn Par Crownsville MD 2001-2003. mjacobs3@yahoo.com

JACOBS III, Philip Chauncey (Mass) 203 Chapman St, Canton MA 02021 **R Trin Ch Canton MA 1990-; Archv & Libr Bd Dio Massachusetts Boston MA 1988-; Archv & Libr Bd Dio Massachusetts Boston MA 1988-; Peace & Justice Cmsn Dio Massachusetts Boston MA 1987-; Peace & Justice Com Dio Massachusetts Boston MA 1987-** B Newton MA 6/10/1944 s Philip Chauncey Jacobs & Lillian Hermon. BS U of Maine 1966; MDiv Ya Berk 1971; STM Yale DS 1972; ThM Weston TS 1982; Boston Coll 1983; S Deiniol's Libr Hawarden GB 1985. D 11/7/1970 Bp John Melville Burgess P 5/29/1971 Bp Joseph Warren Hutchens. m 8/3/1968 Phebe Elizabeth Allen c 3. Dioc Coun Dio Massachusetts Boston MA 2002-2009; Dioc Coun Dio Massachusetts Boston MA 2002-2009; GC Alt Dep Dio Massachusetts Boston MA 1997; GC Dep Dio Massachusetts Boston MA 1994; Anti-Racism T/F Dio Massachusetts Boston MA 1992-1995; GC Alt Dep Dio Massachusetts Boston MA 1991; Dioc Coun Dio Massachusetts Boston MA 1987-1988; Ch Of The Gd Shpd Fairhaven MA 1982-1990; R S Ptr's Ch On The Canal Buzzards Bay MA 1974-1982; Asst All SS' Epis Ch Belmont MA 1972-1974; Asst Imm S Jas Par Derby CT 1971-1972; Asst Chr Ch New Haven CT 1970-1971. Assoc, Soc of S Jn the Evang 1975; Comp, Oratory of Gd Shpd 2007; Conf of Blessed Sacr 1967; EUC 1993; GAS 1975.

JACOBS, Robert Alexander (NY) 20 Trestle Way, Dayton NJ 08810 **D Ch Of The H Apos New York NY 2010-** B New York NY 9/9/1943 s Randolph Vincent Jacobs & Iona Elaine. Cert Amer Inst of Banking New York NY 1965; BS Manhattan Coll 1972. D 5/30/1992 Bp Richard Frank Grein. m 10/4/1975 Miriam Mary Hendricks c 3. D Cathd Of St Jn The Div New York NY 1997-2010; Mem Exec Coun Appointees New York NY 1993-1995; D S Phil's Ch New York NY 1992-1997. robjac9@bellatlantic.net

JACOBS, William Lockhart (Ia) 13731 Hickman Rd Unit 1405, Urbandale IA 50323 B Dyer TN 3/30/1917 s William Albert Jacobs & Mattie Belle. BA U So 1941; BD VTS 1943. D 9/19/1943 Bp James M Maxon P 6/18/1944 Bp Edmund P Dandridge. m 6/5/1945 Marian Shanley. Dio Iowa Des Moines IA 1976-1994; R The Cathd Ch Of S Paul Des Moines IA 1965-1984; R Chr Ch Springfield IL 1951-1965; R S Paul's Newport AR 1945-1950; Asst S Jn's Epis Cathd Knoxville TN 1943-1945; Chapl Tyson Hse Stdt Fndt Knoxville TN 1943-1945. Hon Cn Dio Springfield 1963. msjrehab@aol.com

JACOBSEN, Leigh Christian (SanD) PO Box 1648, Rancho Santa Fe CA 92067 B 3/29/1938 D 10/18/2005 P 12/11/2005 Bp James Robert Mathes. m 5/28/1977 Roberta Jacobsen c 2. Dio San Diego San Diego CA 2006-2007.

JACOBSEN, Peter Arthur (LI) 21 Dogwood Rd N, Wurtsboro NY 12790 B Buffalo NY 10/4/1930 s James Arthur Jacobsen & Asta Elanore. Juilliard Sch 1949; BS NYU 1951; Cert Merc TS 1961; MA H Name U 1976. D 4/8/1961 P 10/1/1961 Bp James P De Wolfe. R S Geo's Par Flushing NY 1987-1993; R S Paul's Epis Ch Flint MI 1981-1987; S Andr's So Fallsburg Woodbourne NY 1977-1981; R S Jn's Epis Ch Monticello NY 1971-1981; Team Monticello NY 1971-1981; Dpt Of Missions Ny Income New York NY 1971-1977; Diocn Msnry & Ch Extntn Socty New York NY 1971-1976; P-in-c S Jas Ch Callicoon NY 1969-1971; R Ch Of The Redeem Mattituck NY 1965-1968; P-in-c Ch Of The Redeem Mattituck NY 1962-1964; Dept of Bdgt Dio Long Island Garden City NY 1962-1964. Auth, *Machiavellis Mandrake*. SSC. abouna80vasilios@yahoo.com

JACOBSON, Arthur Theodore (Ia) 307 S Dickinson St, Rock Rapids IA 51246 B Quincy MA 9/25/1949 s Harold Edward Jacobson & Agnes. NEU; BS U of Nthrn Iowa; BS U of New Hampshire 1971. D 5/30/1995 Bp Carl Christopher

Epting. m 6/29/1986 Mary Margaret Bowen. Natl Inst Bus & Indstrl Chapl; NAAD. dcnart@rocketmail.com

JACOBSON, Bruce Harvey (NH) 9 Esty Way, Groveland MA 01834 B Erie PA 12/5/1935 s Earl Clarence Jacobson & Mary Elizabeth. BA Ken 1956; LTh SWTS 1959; Fllshp Coll of Preachers 1988. D 6/29/1959 P 3/12/1960 Bp Lauriston L Scaife. m 6/18/1966 Gayle D Dudley c 3. Int Gr Ch Manchester NH 2000-2001; Int S Jn's Ch Beverly Farms MA 1998-1999; R S Jn's Ch Bala Cynwyd PA 1990-1998; R Ch Of The Redeem Bryn Mawr PA 1989; Dn Cathd Ch Of S Paul Burlington VT 1982-1989; Stndg Com Dio Rhode Island Providence RI 1979-1982; R S Paul's Ch Pawtucket RI 1973-1982; R S Paul's Epis Ch Mayville NY 1963-1973; Vic Ch Of The Gd Shpd Irving NY 1960-1963; Vic S Ptr's Ch Forestville NY 1960-1963; Cur Trin Epis Ch Buffalo NY 1959-1969. Auth, *Cathedrals Are More Than Just Buildings*; Auth, *Epis*. brucejacobson@comcast.net

JACOBSON, H(arold) Knute (Mo) 123 S. Ninth Street, Columbia MO 65201 **Calv Ch Columbia MO 2010-** B New Haven CT 9/1/1954 s Harold Karan Jacobson & Merelyn Jean. BD U MI 1976; MDiv Yale DS 1980; ThM PrTS 1981. D 6/20/1982 P 10/1/1986 Bp H Coleman McGehee Jr. m 12/28/1985 Rosemary E Funk c 4. R S Tim Ch Richland MI 2000-2010; R S Matt's Ch Charleston WV 1996-2000; Int S Paul's Epis Ch Shreveport LA 1995-1996; R S Steph's Ch Beaumont TX 1991-1995; Assoc S Jn's Epis Ch Saginaw MI 1986-1991. rosey4kids@jasnetworks.net

JACOBSON, Jeanne Ellen (CPa) 616 Spruce St., Hollidaysburg PA 16648 **H Trin Epis Ch Hollidaysburg PA 2005-** B Tulsa OK 4/21/1954 BA LSU 1975; MDiv SWTS 2004. D 6/12/2004 P 7/23/2005 Bp Andrew Donnan Smith. Trin Epis Ch Tyrone PA 2005-2009. revjj2000@yahoo.com

JACOBSON, Marc R (Pgh) 4604 Crew Hall Ln, Waxhaw NC 28173 **Dio Pittsburgh Monroeville PA 2004-** B Palo Alto CA 3/31/1951 s Ray M Jacobson & Patricia L. BA Gordon Coll 1976; MA TESM 2004. D 6/12/2004 Bp Robert William Duncan P 12/14/2004 Bp Henry William Scriven. m 5/25/1975 Suzanne Mary Jacobson c 3. Trin Cathd Pittsburgh PA 2004. marc_jacobson@sil.org

JACOBSON, Paul Alan (Ct) 1089 Whitney Ave, Hamden CT 06517 B Evanston IL 9/1/1957 s Lowell Victor & Dorothy. BA Blackburn Coll 1979; MAR/MM Yale Div 1983; PhD Grad Theol Un 1997. D 6/13/2009 P 1/27/2010 Bp Andrew Donnan Smith. pajacobson@aol.com

JACOBSON, Stephen Kent (Pa) 13202 SE 91st Court Road, Summerfield FL 34491 B Melrose MA 11/4/1938 s Carl Wesley Jacobson & Alice Gwendolyn. BA Tufts U 1960; MDiv EDS 1966; DMin Estrn Bapt TS 1993. D 6/25/1966 P 2/18/1968 Bp Anson Phelps Stokes Jr. m 3/18/1960 Denise Elizabeth Proctor c 3. Int S Gabr's Epis Ch Marion MA 2008-2009; Int S Mary's Epis Ch Bonita Sprg FL 2003-2004; Int S Jas Epis Ch Port Charlotte FL 2002-2003; Int Chr Ch Whitefish Bay WI 1999-2000; Int Trin By The Cove Naples FL 1999; Int Chr Ch Exeter NH 1998-1999; Int Chr Ch Grosse Pointe Grosse Pointe Farms MI 1997; Asst S Matt's Ch Maple Glen PA 1996-1997; R S Dav's Ch Wayne PA 1984-1997; R S Mary's Epis Ch Manchester CT 1974-1984; Vic S Geo's Ch Middlebury CT 1970-1974; Asst Trin Ch Topsfield MA 1967-1969; Cur S Mk's Ch Foxborough MA 1966-1967. Auth, "SPERANZA," *A Novel*, Self, 2011; Auth, "The Novation," *Epis Life*, 1976; Auth, "Ulster's Bitter Fruit: The Troubles in Ulster," *The Epis*, 1976; Auth, "The Great Manuscript Hoax," *Yankee mag*, 1972. drskjacobson@gmail.com

✠ **JACOBUS, Rt Rev Russell Edward** (FdL) 1051 N. Lynndale Drive, Suite 1B, Appleton WI 54914 **Trst Nash Nashotah WI 2008-; Bp Of Fond du Lac Dio Fond du Lac Appleton WI 1994-** B Milwaukee WI 9/27/1944 s Lester Edward Jacobus & Sarah Louise. BA U of Wisconsin-Milwaukee 1967; MDiv Nash 1970. D 2/21/1970 P 8/22/1970 Bp Donald H V Hallock Con 5/24/1994 for FdL. m 5/25/1968 Jerrie Evrard c 2. Dio Eau Claire Eau Claire WI 2009; Stndg Com Dio Milwaukee Milwaukee WI 1991-1994; Trst Nash Nashotah WI 1990-1998; Sprtl Dir Curs Dio Milwaukee Milwaukee WI 1984-1986; Stndg Com Dio Milwaukee Milwaukee WI 1983-1986; Wrdn of Alum Assn Nash Nashotah WI 1983-1986; Dep Gc Dio Milwaukee Milwaukee WI 1982-1991; Com Dio Milwaukee Milwaukee WI 1982-1986; Com Dio Milwaukee Milwaukee WI 1982-1986; R St Mths Epis Ch Waukesha WI 1980-1994; Exec Bd Dio Milwaukee Milwaukee WI 1977-1980; Vic S Ptr's Ch No Lake WI 1977-1979; R S Anskar's Epis Ch Hartland WI 1974-1980; Asst Trin Ch Wauwatosa WI 1970-1973. Sis Of The H Nativ -- Assoc 1994. DD Nash Sem 1994; P of the Year Dio Milwaukee 1984. rjacobus@att.net

JACQUES, Mary Martha (Mont) 13100 Highway 41 North, Dillon MT 59725 B Tampa FL 12/28/1940 d Adolphus Daniel Jaques & Lillian Russell. U of Tampa 1962; BS U of Missouri 1963; MS Washington U 1967; PhD Washington U 1971; MDiv CDSP 1984. D 6/9/1984 Bp William Edwin Swing P 12/17/1984 Bp Jackson Earle Gilliam. m 4/25/1987 Justin Knox Burgin. R Chr Ch Sheridan MT 1993-1997; Dio Montana Helena MT 1993-1995; The Majestic Mountains Mnstry Dillon MT 1991-1992; Int St Jas Epis Ch Dillon MT 1985-1986; Vic Chr Ch Sheridan MT 1984-1986. Auth, "Pathways, Kdbm Dillon," *Montana*, 1998; Auth, "Reflections, Kdbm Dillon," *Montana*, 1998; Auth, "Outpourings Of Love Images Of Stwdshp," *Natl Ch Video*, 1989. Land. mjacques@mcn.net

JAEGER, George Marvin (Nick) (Ky) 2502 Jefferson St., Paducah KY 42001 **Assoc S Ptr's of the Lakes Gilbertsville KY 2005-** B Washington DC 12/16/1940 s George Marvin Jaeger & Eleanor. BA U of Maryland 1966; MDiv PDS 1968. D 6/29/1968 Bp William Foreman Creighton P 12/29/1968 Bp Leland Stark. m 8/17/1968 Julie Elizabeth Teeple c 5. Dio Kentucky Louisville KY 1995-2004; Dio Kentucky Louisville KY 1991-1993; Dio Kentucky Louisville KY 1990-1992; Dio Kentucky Louisville KY 1989-1990; Gr Ch Paducah KY 1987-2003; Dio Kentucky Louisville KY 1987-1989; Dio Wstrn Michigan Kalamazoo MI 1979-1986; Dn The Par Ch Of Chr The King Portage MI 1979-1986; Dio New Jersey Trenton NJ 1974-1979; R Trin Ch Matawan NJ 1972-1979; Cur S Paul's Epis Ch Chatham NJ 1968-1972. jaeger.nick@gmail.com

JAEGER, Janet (Ct) 1308 Elmwood Rd, Rocky River OH 44116 **Died 10/21/2010** B Milford MA 11/20/1924 d Stewart Bryon Atkinson & Margaret Isabel. BA Tufts U 1946; MS Cntrl Connecticut St U 1968; MA S Jos Coll 1979; MA S Jos Coll 1989. D 12/3/1988 Bp Arthur Edward Walmsley. Hie Hill Cmnty; Sigma Phi Omega; NAAD.

JAEKLE, Charles Roth (WA) 7446 Spring Village Dr Apt 307, Springfield VA 22150 B Bayonne NJ 8/13/1922 s Charles Anthony Jaekle & Martha. BA Doane Coll; Grad U Texas U Pennsylvania; STM Luth TS; BD UTS. D 6/21/1958 Bp James Parker Clements P 3/1/1959 Bp John E Hines. m 11/24/1945 Ann Murden. Pstr Counslg Cntr Richmond VA 1964-1987; Assoc Prof Of Care Epis TS Of The SW Austin TX 1958-1966. Auth, "Pstr Care In Hist Perspective"; Auth, "Ang: Their Mssn & Message"; Auth, "Pilgrimage: Journ Pstr Psychol". CHARLES.JAEKLE@GMAIL.COM

JAENKE, Karen Ann (NJ) 24 Woodland Road, Fairfax CA 94930 B Arlington VA 12/16/1957 d Edwin August Jaenke & Claire Louise. BA Wake Forest U 1980; MDiv PrTS 1986; CAS GTS 1989; PhD California Inst of Integral Stds 2000. D 6/9/1990 Bp George Phelps Mellick Belshaw. Asst to Bp Chr Ch Trenton NJ 1990-1991. Ed, "Earth Dreaming," *Revs: Journ of Consciousness & Transformation*, ReVisionpublishing.org, 2011; Auth, "Dreaming w the Earth," *Revs: Journ of Consciousness & Transformation*, ReVisionpublishing.org, 2011; Auth, "Ed's Essay: Shamanism & the Wounded W," *Revs: Journ of Consciousness & Transformation*, ReVisionpublishing.org, 2010; Ed, "Shamanism and the Wounded W," *Revs: Journ of Consciousness & Transformation*, ReVisionpublishing.org, 2010; Auth, "Earth Dreaming," *Rebearths: Conversations w a Wrld Ensouled*, Wrld Soul Books, 2010; Auth, "Soul & Soullessness," *Revs: Journ of Consciousness & Transformation*, ReVisionpublishing.org, 2009; Auth, "Earth, Dreams, Body," *Revs: Journ of Consciousness & Transformation*, ReVisionpublishing.org, 2008; Auth, "Dreaming w the Ancestors," *Revs: Journ of Consciousness & Transformation*, Heldref, 2006; Auth, "Dreaming the Ritual Onward," *Revs: Journ of Consciousness & Transformation*, Heldref, 2006; Auth, "The Participatory Turn," *Revs: Journ of Consciousness & Transformation*, Heldref, 2004; Auth, "Ode to the Intelligence of Dreams," *Revs: Journ of Consciousness & Transformation*, Heldref, 2004; Auth, "Personal Dreamscape as Ancestral Landscape," *Dissertation*, UMI, 2000; Auth, "Water & Stone: All of Nature Participates in Our Remebering," *Revs: Journ of Consciousness & Transformation*, Heldref, 1998. Assn for the Study of Dreams 1996. Phi Beta Kappa Phi Beta Kappa 1979. dreamhut7@gmail.com

JAGO, Frank Kincaid (NJ) 40 Glenwood Road, Lumberton NJ 08048 **Ins Com Dio New Jersey Trenton NJ 1997-** B Camden NJ 12/10/1937 s Frederick West Jago & Margaret. BA Trin Hartford CT 1960; STB PDS 1963; DMin Drew U 1989. D 4/27/1963 P 11/2/1963 Bp Alfred L Banyard. c 4. Dn - Convoc Dio New Jersey Trenton NJ 1981-1984; R S Andr's Ch Mt Holly NJ 1976-1997; Bd Mssns Dio New Jersey Trenton NJ 1976-1978; Dn Dioc Boys Sum Conf Dio New Jersey Trenton NJ 1974-1980; Bd Rel Educ Dio New Jersey Trenton NJ 1971-1980; S Barn Epis Ch Monmouth Jct NJ 1963-1976; Bd Rel Educ Dio New Jersey Trenton NJ 1963-1965. Longsdorf Awd Unselfish Serv to the Cmnty 1982; So Brunswick Jaycees Outstanding Young Man 1971; So Brunswick Cmnty Outstanding Citizen 1969. f.jago@att.net

JAIKES, Donald William (Mass) 6909 Dr MLK Jr St S #327, Saint Petersburg FL 33705 B Wilkes Barre PA 7/28/1930 s William August Jaikes & Margaret Marie. BS Wilkes Coll 1957; MDiv Bex 1967. D 6/24/1967 P 5/18/1968 Bp Anson Phelps Stokes Jr. m 4/26/1958 Joan Walmsley c 2. S Andr's Epis Ch Sprg Hill FL 1997-2003; R Ch Of The Ascen Fall River MA 1972-1995; Min in charge S Lk's Epis Ch Malden MA 1967-1972; Cur S Paul's Ch Malden MA 1967-1971. djaikes@tampabay.rr.com

JAKOBSEN, Wilma Terry (Los) 420 S Madison Ave Apt 301, Pasadena CA 91101 **Sr Assoc For Liturg Peace And Justice All SS Ch Pasadena CA 2003-** B Cape Town South Africa 10/15/1959 BS U Of Cape Town Cape Town Za 1979; MDiv Fuller TS 1987; STM UTS 1997. Trans from Church of the Province of Southern Africa 6/19/2003. "Lang Matters: Towards And Inclusive Cmnty," Journ For The Study Of Rel, 2001; "Like Water In A Desert: Wmn Ch In So Afr," Dissident Daughters: Feminist Liturgies In Global

Context, 2001; "Ethics In Feminist Theol," Doing Ethics In Context Orbis Books, 1994; "Wmn And Vocation: The 'If' Question," Wmn Hold Up Half The Sky; Cluster Pub Sa, 1991. wjakobsen@allsaints-pas.org

JALLOUF, Georges (Okla) PO Box 210, Cedar St FL 32625 **R S Lk's Ch Tulsa OK 2010-** B Damascus Syria 4/13/1964 s Moussa Jallouf & Jeanette. Mstr of Philos Oriental Franciscan Sem 1987; Mstr of Theol Studium Theologicum Franciscanum 1992; Lic Of Pstr Theol Lateranese U Rome Italy 1995; Angl Study STUSo 2007. Rec from Roman Catholic 4/25/2003 as Priest Bp Pierre W Whalon. Chr Ch Cedar Key FL 2007. JALLOUFGEORGES@GMAIL.COM

JAMBOR, Christopher Noel (FtW) 1805 Malibar Rd, Fort Worth TX 76116 **R All SS' Epis Ch Ft Worth TX 2003-; Par Assoc All SS' Epis Ch Ft Worth TX 1995-** B Cincinnati OH 12/25/1951 s James John Jambor & Louise Irma. BS Trin U 1974; MD U of Kansas 1978; MDiv Nash 1995. D 11/30/1994 P 6/1/1995 Bp Keith Lynn Ackerman. m 4/23/1978 Patricia Ann Braddy c 2. SocMary, CBS. frjambor@yahoo.com

JAMES, Alan Christopher (O) 2230 Euclid Ave, Cleveland OH 44115 **Cn to the Ordnry Dio Ohio Cleveland OH 2005-** B Chula Vista CA 4/30/1967 s Frederick William James & Nyla E. BSFS Geo 1989; MDiv VTS 1996. D 6/8/1996 P 12/15/1996 Bp Gethin Benwil Hughes. m 5/16/2009 Lisa E Hackney c 2. R S Matt's Epis Ch Brecksville OH 1999-2005; Cur S Dunst's Epis Ch San Diego CA 1996-1999. frhoya@roadrunner.com

JAMES, C(harles) Scott (CGC) Po Box 29, Bon Secour AL 36511 B Memphis TN 2/28/1938 s Spencer James & Mary M. BS U of So Carolina 1961; BD VTS 1968. D 6/21/1968 P 1/1/1969 Bp Gray Temple. m 8/12/1967 Sylvia Saunders c 2. R S Ptr's Epis Ch Bon Secour AL 1996-2006; R Trin Ch Winchester TN 1982-1996; R S Phil's Ch Nashville TN 1980-1982; Vic H Cross Epis Ch Simpsonville SC 1974-1980; Asst All SS Ch Florence SC 1972-1974; R S Paul's Ch Bennettsville SC 1969-1972; Cur S Paul's Epis Ch Summerville SC 1968-1969. Chapl Asst, Ord of S Lk. ssjames@bellsouth.net

JAMES, Claudia Jan (Az) 423 N. Beaver St., Flagstaff AZ 86001 **R Ch Of The Epiph Flagstaff AZ 2006-** B Waco TX 6/20/1948 d Thomas Freeman Webb & Martha Ruth. BA U of Texas 1988; MDiv Brite DS 1997. D 6/19/1999 P 6/7/2000 Bp James Monte Stanton. m 9/18/1971 Robert C James c 3. Trin Epis Ch The Woodlands TX 2002-2006; S Jas Ch Dallas TX 1999-2002. Auth, "Journ Of Pstr Care," 1999; Auth, "Power Of Valuing In Brief Pstr Counslg". Intl Soc Theta Phi. janjames@epiphanyaz.org

JAMES, Darryl Farrar (LI) 3312 S Indiana Ave, Chicago IL 60616 **Gr Ch Jamaica NY 2007-** B Bridgeport CT 7/3/1954 s Anthony Francis James & Laurayne. BA How 1976; MDiv Yale DS 1979. D 6/30/1984 Bp Henry Irving Mayson P 2/2/1985 Bp John Melville Burgess. R Mssh-S Barth Epis Ch Chicago IL 1985-2007; S Matt's And S Jos's Detroit MI 1984-1985. frdfjames@aol.com

JAMES, Edmund Ludwig (Okla) 104 W Hanover St, Hoyt OK 74472 **Supply P S Jas Epis Ch Wagoner OK 2011-** B Leuters Hausen DE 10/27/1956 s Edward Ames & Tilli Emma. BA NE St U 1980; M.Div. Phillips TS 2008. D 6/22/2002 Bp Robert Manning Moody P 5/14/2011 Bp Edward Joseph Konieczny. m 8/3/1979 Diana Ruth Shaw c 2. D Trin Ch Eufaula OK 2002-2011. eljames@kuhl65.net

JAMES, Jay Carleton (NC) Po Box 17787, Raleigh NC 27619 **R S Tim's Ch Raleigh NC 1993-** B Houlton ME 7/19/1956 s Carleton Kenneth James & Josephine May. BS U of Maine 1978; MDiv GTS 1985. D 6/8/1985 P 12/14/1985 Bp Frederick Barton Wolf. m 10/22/1988 Elizabeth M Poskel c 2. Cur The Par Of All SS Ashmont-Dorches Dorchester MA 1985-1993. jcjames@nc.rr.com

JAMES, Joseph Emerson (Del) PO Box 163, Milford DE 19963 **Died 7/30/2011** B Cambridge MD 8/19/1929 s Wildai James & Eva Allen. BA U of Maryland 1952; MDiv GTS 1955; Grad Shalem Inst for Sprtl Formation Washington 1988. D 6/1/1955 P 12/17/1955 Bp Allen J Miller. c 3. joej1929@aol.com

JAMES, Marcus Gilbert (Roch) No address on file. B 12/27/1920 Trans from Church in the Province Of The West Indies 1/2/1946 Bp Bartel H Reinheimer.

JAMES, Molly Field (Ct) 258 Beaver Meadow Road, Haddam CT 06438 **Secy of the Dio Dio Connecticut Hartford CT 2011-; Stndg Com Dio Connecticut Hartford CT 2010-; Fin Com Dio Connecticut Hartford CT 2009-; Prog and Bdgt Com Dio Connecticut Hartford CT 2007-** B New Haven CT 1/19/1980 d Eliot Field & Catherine. BA Tufts U 2002; MDiv Ya Berk 2005; PhD U of Exeter 2011. D 6/11/2005 P 12/16/2005 Bp Chilton Abbie Richardson Knudsen. m 6/4/2005 Reade William James c 1. Transition Com Dio Connecticut Hartford CT 2008-2010; Transition Com Dio Connecticut Hartford CT 2007; S Jn's Epis Ch Essex CT 2006-2011. mollyfjames@gmail.com

JAMES, Nancy Carol (WA) 713 E St Ne, Washington DC 20002 **P-in-c Trin Epis Par Hughesville MD 2011-** B Laredo TX 6/28/1954 d Franklin Joseph James & Eve. BA California St U 1981; MDiv VTS 1984; PhD U of Virginia 1997. D 6/22/1985 P 5/1/1986 Bp Peter James Lee. m 1/31/2005 Roger James Nebel c 2. P Gr Ch Washington DC 2008-2011; Int S Thos Par Croom Upper Marlboro MD 2007-2008; Assoc S Jn's Ch Lafayette Sq Washington DC 2000-2009; R Emm Ch Rapidan VA 1991-1997; R Chr Epis Ch Brandy Sta VA 1986-1995; D The Falls Ch Epis Falls Ch VA 1985-1986. Auth, "The Complete Madame Guyon," Paraclete Press, 2011; Auth, "Bastille Witness: The Prison Autobiography of Madame Guyon," U Press, 2011; Auth, "In Your Mercy, Lord, You Called Me," Edwin Mellen Press, 2010; Auth, "The Developing Schism Within the Epis Ch 1960-2010," Edwin Mellen Press, 2010; Auth, "Chas Phil Price," *Blackwell Comp to the Theologians*, Wiley-Blackwell, 2009; Auth, "The Conflict Over the Heresy of," Edwin Mellen Press, 2008; Auth, "The Pure Love of Madame Guyon: The Great Conflict in the Crt of Louis XIV," U Press, 2007; Auth, "Stndg in the Whirlwind," Pilgrim Press, 2005. AAR 1999; Auth's Gld 2005. ncjames@earthlink.net

JAMES JR, Ralph Matthew (WVa) PO Box 401, Union WV 24983 **D All SS Ch Un WV 2007-** B Charleston WV 8/12/1946 s Ralph Matthew James & LaRene Adkins. BA Concord Coll 1968; MS The GW 1971. D 12/15/2007 P 6/14/2008 Bp William Michie Klusmeyer. m 6/8/1968 Renda Renda Rae Pennington c 1. downhill@city.net

JAMES, Robert Arthur (LI) 5 Fig Ct E, Homosassa FL 34446 **S Andr's Epis Ch Sprg Hill FL 2001-** B Chicago IL 6/25/1935 s William Cross James & Martha Pearl. BA Knox Coll 1957; STB GTS 1960; MA Villanova U 1970; MS U of Pennsylvania 1975; EdD U of Pennsylvania 1978. D 6/18/1960 Bp Gerald Francis Burrill P 12/21/1960 Bp Oliver L Loring. c 2. Int S Steph's Epis Ch Ocala FL 2000-2001; Dioc AIDS Cmsn Dio Long Island Garden City NY 1993-1998; R Chr Ch Bay Ridge Brooklyn NY 1991-1998; Chair Human Sxlty Cmsn Dio Pennsylvania Philadelphia PA 1990-1991; CEC Dio Pennsylvania Philadelphia PA 1988-1991; H Trin Ch Lansdale PA 1982-1983; S Mary's Ch Wayne PA 1981-1991; S Clements Ch Philadelphia PA 1978-1979; H Trin Ch Lansdale PA 1975-1976; Int Trin Ch Gulph Mills King Of Prussia PA 1969-1970; Vic S Columba Epis Ch Marathon FL 1964-1968; R H Trin Epis Ch Bartow FL 1963-1964. Auth, *Model for a Long-R Developmental Plan*, U Microfilms, 1978. Bro of S Andr 1994. Ford Fellowowship Admin Ldrshp U of Pennsylvania 1972. notveryrev@aol.com

JAMES, Robin L (U) 660 S 500 E, Salt Lake City UT 84102 **Cur/Precentor Cathd Ch Of S Mk Salt Lake City UT 2003-** B Ottawa KS 5/28/1964 BA U of Kansas 1987; MSEd U of Kansas 1992; MDiv CDSP 2003. D 6/19/2003 P 5/29/2004 Bp Carolyn Tanner Irish. rljames755@stmarkscathedral-ut.org

JAMES, Sally Patricia (NMich) 402 W Fleshiem St, Iron Mountain MI 49801 B Houghton MI 1/13/1937 d Dante Angelo Oradei & Arthenia Mae. Coll S Scholastica Nrsng Duluth MN 1957. D 3/1/1998 Bp Thomas Kreider Ray.

JAMES, Sue Costanzo (EO) 2675 Sw Pumice Ave, Redmond OR 97756 **Died 2/12/2010** B Philadelphia PA 8/18/1921 d Nicholas Costanzo & Rosa Altomare. BS Tem 1942. D 10/31/1996 Bp Rustin Ray Kimsey P 12/16/2001 Bp William O Gregg. suecjames@hotmail.com

JAMES, William Evans (CGC) 1530 University Dr NE Apt 15, Atlanta GA 30306 B Atlanta GA 2/20/1939 s Herman Mack James & Sarah Elizabeth. BA Georgia St U 1961; BD STUSo 1965. D 6/26/1965 P 3/1/1966 Bp Randolph R Claiborne. Vic S Mk's Epis Ch Troy AL 1988-1990; R S Mich's Ch Mobile AL 1979-1988; S Paul's Ch Greensboro AL 1970-1977; Cur S Barth's Epis Ch Atlanta GA 1965-1967.

JAMESON, Elizabeth Butler (Chi) 644 Haven St, Evanston IL 60201 **VP and COO SWTS Evanston IL 2005-** B Michigan 1/23/1968 d Samuel Garland Slaughter & Katherine Slaughter. BA Harv 1990; MDiv SWTS 1997. D 6/26/1997 P 1/24/1998 Bp Richard Sui On Chang. m 9/4/2010 James Jameson c 3. Assoc Ch Of The H Comf Kenilworth IL 1997-2005. ebjameson2@gmail.com

JAMESON, J Parker (Tex) 8 Troon Dr, Lakeway TX 78738 **Assoc R S Lk's On The Lake Epis Ch Austin TX 1998-** B Abilene TX 7/22/1953 s Jay Reese Jameson & Mary Josephine. AB Harv 1975; MDiv Epis TS of the SW 1981; DMin SWTS 2006. D 6/11/1981 P 6/29/1982 Bp Sam Byron Hulsey. m 1/17/1981 Paula W Whitfield c 2. R S Tim's Ch Alexandria LA 1988-1997; Asst R S Lk's Epis Ch San Antonio TX 1983-1988; D/P-in-c S Paul's Epis Ch Dumas TX 1981-1983; Cur S Ptr's Epis Ch Amarillo TX 1981-1983. jpjameson@austin.rr.com

JAMIESON, Sandra C (SwFla) 301 Jasmine Way, Clearwater FL 33756 **D H Trin Epis Ch In Countryside Clearwater FL 2010-** B Warham MA 8/23/1946 d Walter Enos Cornett & Eloise Ann. AS St. Petersburg Jr Coll St. Petersburg FL 1967. D 1/18/2002 Bp John Bailey Lipscomb. m 6/3/1967 Harry Bruce Jamieson. D Gd Samar Epis Ch Clearwater FL 2001-2010. SJAMIE@TAMPABAY.RR.COM

JAMIESON JR, William Stukey (WNC) 15 Macon Ave, Asheville NC 28801 B Jacksonville FL 11/21/1943 s William Stukey Jamieson & Suzannne. BA U of Arizona 1965; MS Georgia St U 1976. D 10/21/1989 Bp Joseph Thomas Heistand. m 9/6/1969 Kennon Barksdale c 2. Chruch of the Advoc Dio Wstrn No Carolina Asheville NC 1997-2001; D The Cathd Of All Souls Asheville NC 1996-1997; D Epis Ch Of The H Sprt Mars Hill NC 1995-1996; Archd Dio Arizona Phoenix AZ 1993-1995. Achievement Awd, Citizen Awd (Both w dist) Arizona St U; Alumnini Awd, w Distiction Georgia St U; Citizen Awd, w Distiction Phoenix Un HS Dist. billjamieson@bellsouth.net

JAMIESON-DRAKE, Victoria Kapp (NC) 304 E Franklin St, Chapel Hill NC 27514 **Assoc for Pstr Mnstry Chap Of The Cross Chap Hill NC 1995-** B

6/24/1957 d John Richard Jamieson & Ruth Alice. Ya Berk; BA Wellesley Coll 1978; MDiv Duke 1985. D 6/24/1986 Bp Frank Harris Vest Jr P 7/2/1987 Bp Robert Whitridge Estill. m 8/8/1981 David Jamieson-Drake c 2. Int S Andrews Ch Durham NC 1995; Vic Ch Of The H Sprt Greensboro NC 1990-1994; Com Dio No Carolina Raleigh NC 1988-1992; Asst to R S Phil's Ch Durham NC 1986-1989. vjd@thechapelofthecross.org

JAMISON, Dale Martin (NMich) 901 Dakota Ave, Gladstone MI 49837 **D Trin Ch Gladstone MI 2010-** B Detroit MI 1/25/1948 s Robert Thomas Jamison & Dolores May. BS Nthrn Michigan U 1971; MA Ferris St U 1988. D 9/12/2010 Bp Thomas Kreider Ray. m 9/5/1970 Susan Schram c 3. dalejamison@charter.net

JAMISON, Dorothy Lockwood (Cal) 850 Cedro Way, Stanford CA 94305 **D Chr Ch Portola Vlly CA 2006-** B Philadelphia PA 2/7/1939 d John Salem Lockwood & Dorothy Tufts. BA DePauw U 1960; BA California Sch for Deacons 1989; Bex 1990; MDiv CDSP 1992. D 6/9/1990 Bp William Edwin Swing. m 3/3/1962 Rex Lindsay Jamison c 2. D Chr Epis Ch Los Altos CA 1998-2003; D Chr Ch Portola Vlly CA 1990-1997. Auth, "New PB, New Mnstrs," *Mod Profiles of an Ancient Faith*, The Epis Dio CA, 2001. Assn of Epis Hosp Chapl 1994-2002. Dn & Trst' Awd The Sch for Deacons, Dio California 2003; Pres's Awd NAAD 1997. dcndede@yahoo.com

JANDA, Mary S (U) 8650 Acorn Ln, Sandy UT 84093 **COM Dio Utah Salt Lake City UT 2010-; Assoc R All SS Ch Salt Lake City UT 2009-; Anti-Racism Com Dio Utah Salt Lake City UT 2007-** B Plymouth IN 3/29/1951 d William Cockburn Russell Sheridan & Rudith Treder. St Mary's Coll 1971; BA Indiana U 1976; Dio Utah - Formation for Mnstry 2007. D 6/9/2007 P 1/26/2008 Bp Carolyn Tanner Irish. m 2/25/1978 James F Janda c 2. Assoc R S Jas Epis Ch Midvale UT 2009-2010. Auth, "Out of the Storm," Outskirts Press, 2006. pastor.maryjanda@gmail.com

JANELLE, Nicole Simonne (Los) St. Michael's University Church, 6586 Picasso Rd., Isla Vista CA 93117 **Vic and Chapl S Mich's U Mssn Island Isla Vista CA 2006-** B Augusta ME 1/27/1978 d Andre Janelle & Suzanne. BA NWU 2000; MDiv UTS 2004; Indep Theol Stds Universidad Biblica Latinoamericana San Jose Costa Rica 2004. D 6/13/2004 P 12/18/2004 Bp Chilton Abbie Richardson Knudsen. Ass. R S Mary's Epis Ch Los Angeles CA 2004-2006. revjanelle@gmail.com

JANESS, Nancy Kingswood (Nev) Po Box 1417, Fallon NV 89407 B Englewood NJ 6/3/1941 d George Gregory Dixon Kingswood & Thelma Palmer. BA U of Nevada at Reno 1999. D 6/28/2003 Bp Katharine Jefferts Schori. m 4/18/1959 William King Janess c 4.

JANEWAY IV, John Livingston (Tenn) 885 Lake Odonnell Rd, Sewanee TN 37375 B Pittsburgh PA 11/22/1942 s Wade Baldwin Janeway & Jane. BA U So 1964; MDiv STUSo 1969. D 6/23/1969 Bp William Evan Sanders P 12/1/1969 Bp William F Gates Jr. m 8/11/1965 Linda Ann Folk c 1. R S Jas Ch Greenville MS 1982-1983; R S Thaddaeus' Epis Ch Chattanooga TN 1972-1982; Trst The TS at The U So Sewanee TN 1972-1980; Vic S Matt's Epis Ch McMinnville TN 1969-1972. Auth, "Sewanee Theol Revs". jjaneway@sewanee.edu

JANG, T Vincent (Cal) 5072 Diamond Heights Blvd, San Francisco CA 94131 **D S Jas Epis Ch San Francisco CA 2011-** B San Francisco CA 7/28/1948 s Yok Wu Jang & Christine Wong. AA City Coll of San Francisco 1969; BA San Francisco St U 1980; BTS Sch for Deacons 2001. D 12/4/2004 Bp William Edwin Swing. D True Sunshine Par San Francisco CA 2004-2011. vjang@earthlink.net

JANIEC, Thomas Daniel (Chi) 342 E Wood St, Palatine IL 60067 B Chicago IL 12/5/1941 s Stephen Janiec & Lorraine. AA/AS Elgin Cmnty Coll 1978; BS Natl Coll of Educ 1984; MDiv SWTS 1998; Cert Inst of Sprtl Comp 2000. D 6/18/1988 P 12/17/1988 Bp Frank Tracy Griswold III. m 7/26/1996 Anne Marie Korecky c 2. R S Phil's Epis Palatine IL 1996-2008; Ch Of The Annunc Bridgeview IL 1988-1996. SocMary 1996; Soc of S Fran 2000-2006. Spec Serv Awd M.E.B.T.C. 2003; Cert of Sprtl Dir 2000; Cert in Advncd Pstr Psychol Stds 1993; Cert of CPE Elmhurst Memi Hosp 1986; Phi Theta Kappa 1977.

JANKOWSKI, John A (Minn) 10174 Bald Eagle Trl, Woodbury MN 55129 **S Jn's Ch S Cloud MN 2009-** B Virginia MN 7/19/1963 s Victor Jankowski & Irene. BA Gustauus Adolphus St Ptr MN 1985; MDiv Untd TS Of The Twin Cities 2007. D 6/14/2007 P 12/20/2007 Bp James Louis Jelinek. m 7/19/1963 Jennifer L Jankowski c 2. The Rev S Mk's Ch Lake City MN 2007-2009. john_jankowski99@msn.com

JANNUCCI, James Francis (Nwk) 74 Oakdene Ave, Cliffside Park NJ 07010 B Perth Amboy NJ 9/16/1929 s Dominick A Jannucci & Julia A. Div Word Sems 1956; Darlington Sem 1960; MDiv Epis TS of The SW 1978. Rec from Roman Catholic 10/1/1978 as Priest Bp John Shelby Spong. m 11/10/1973 Ana M Pacchioni c 2. Trin Ch Cliffside Pk NJ 1979-2001; Stff Of Epis Coop Dio Newark Newark NJ 1978-1979; Resurr Hse Hsng Corp Newark NJ 1978-1979. jfjannucci@yahoo.com

JANSEN, Frederick Bromley (Mich) 1204 Bedford Rd, Grosse Pointe Park MI 48230 **Died 3/17/2011** B New York NY 2/3/1923 s Frederick Bromley Jansen & Bertha Marie. BA Carroll Coll 1944; MDiv Nash 1960; MS Wayne 1967. D 1/26/1946 P 3/26/1947 Bp James P De Wolfe. c 1.

JANSMA, Barbara Treichler (NJ) 501 Green St, Haddon Heights NJ 08035 B Trenton NJ 4/13/1955 d John Howard Treichler & Margaret Loretta. BSN Thos Jefferson U 1977; MSN U of Pennsylvania 1993. D 9/21/2002 Bp David B(ruce) Joslin. m 6/23/2005 Henry Peter Jansma. barbarajansma@yahoo.com

JANSMA, Henry Peter (NJ) 501 Green St, Haddon Heights NJ 08035 **R S Mary's Ch Haddon Heights NJ 2001-** B Passaic NJ 3/8/1957 s Jan Hendriks Jansma & Sjouk Pieters. BA NE Bible Coll Essex Fells NJ 1979; MA Westminster TS 1985; Cert Lincoln Theol Inst 1991; PhD U of Durham Untd Kingdom 1991. Trans from Church Of England 10/1/2001 Bp David B(ruce) Joslin. m 6/23/2005 Barbara Treichler c 2. Angl Pacifist Fllshp 1993; EPF 2001. henry.jansma@gmail.com

JARRELL, Robin Campbell (CPa) 229 Alana Ln, Lewisburg PA 17837 **S Matt's Epis Ch Sunbury PA 2008-** B Augusta GA 2/13/1959 d Robert Henry Jarrell & June Lyda. BA Wellesley Coll 1991; MA Claremont TS 1994; MDiv VTS 2002. D 6/8/2002 P 1/19/2003 Bp Michael Whittington Creighton. m 8/22/1992 Chris James Boyatzis. Chr Ch Milton PA 2002-2008.

JARRETT, Emmett (Ct) Po Box 2185, New London CT 06320 **Died 10/9/2010** B Alexandria LA 2/21/1939 s Emmett Jarrett & Virginia. BA Col 1965; MDiv GTS 1976; Lon 1979. D 6/5/1976 P 12/18/1976 Bp Jonathan Goodhue Sherman. c 2. Auth, "To Heal The Sin-Sick Soul," 1996; Auth, "For The Living Of These Days," 1986; Auth, "God'S Body," Hanging Loose Press, 1975; Auth, "Gk Feet," Crossing Press, 1972; Auth, "Living The Vow Of Non-Violence". EPF; EUC; Third Ord, Soc Of S Fran. stfrancishouse@mindspring.com

JARRETT III, John Jacob (SeFla) 1052 Nw 65th St, Miami FL 33150 **Assoc Ch Of The Incarn Miami FL 2008-** B Miami FL 1/13/1952 s John Jacob Jarrett & Altermeas Maria. BA Florida Intl U 1976; MDiv VTS 1985. D 7/19/1986 P 6/24/1987 Bp Calvin Onderdonk Schofield Jr. P-in-c S Andr's Epis Ch Of Hollywood Dania Bch FL 2003-2008; P-in-c S Anne's Epis Ch Hallandale Bch FL 2003-2007; R S Phil's Epis Ch Grand Rapids MI 1998-2002; Asst S Lk's Ch Washington DC 1987-1997; Dio SE Florida Miami FL 1986-1987; D S Lk's Epis Ch Atlanta GA 1986-1987. jjjacob20032003@yahoo.com

JARRETT, Rondesia (WA) 2306 Jones Ln, Silver Spring MD 20902 **Ch Of The Trsfg Silver Sprg MD 2008-** B Germany 8/23/1978 BA Gonzaga U 2000; MDiv CDSP 2005. D 6/11/2005 P 6/9/2007 Bp James Edward Waggoner. m 7/26/2006 Peter G Schell. Memi Ch Baltimore MD 2007-2008. rev.rodojar@yahoo.com

JARVIS III, F(rank) Washington (Mass) 1241 Adams St Apt 511, Dorchester MA 02124 B Pittsburgh PA 6/24/1939 s Frank Washington Jarvis & Prudence. BA Harv 1961; BD EDS 1964; MA U of Cambridge 1967. D 6/13/1964 Bp Beverley D Tucker P 1/24/1965 Bp Nelson Marigold Burroughs. Assoc The Par Of All SS Ashmont-Dorches Dorchester MA 1998-2004; Assoc The Par Of All SS Ashmont-Dorches Dorchester MA 1976-1996; Cur S Paul's Epis Ch Cleveland Heights OH 1964-1971. Auth, "w Love and Prayers," Godine, 2000; Auth, "Var arts," *Schola Illustris*, Godine, 1995; Auth, "And Still is Ours Today," Seabury, 1980; Auth, "Prophets, Poets," *Priests Kings*, Seabury, 1974; Auth, "Come & Follow," Seabury, 1972. Doctor of Letters (Litt.D.) Mid 2004; Pres Country Day Sch Headmaster's Assn 2001; Doctor of Humane Letters (L.H.D.) Bow 1998; Pres Headmaster's Assn of the U.S. 1993; Chairman Cmsn on Indep Schools NEAS&C 1991. tony.jarvis@roxburylatin.org

JARVIS, Leon Gerald (NMich) 1300 West Ave, Marquette MI 49855 B Detroit MI 4/2/1958 s Darcey Lee Jarvis & Dolores Mary. Nthrn Michigan U 1991. D 7/27/2004 P 1/30/2005 Bp James Arthur Kelsey. m 12/24/1988 Lesa Ann Bozek c 2. ljarvis@mgh.org

JARVIS, Michael Bennett (Okla) 702 County Rd 3420, Pawhuska OK 74056 B Dallas TX 5/21/1935 s Joseph Bennett Jarvis & Helen Agnes. BSF (B.S. Forestry) U of Washington 1959; BD SFTS 1962; CDSP 1984. D 6/29/1984 P 6/1/1985 Bp Robert Hume Cochrane. m 6/25/1961 Mary E Little. Supply P S Thos Ch Pawhuska OK 1999-2002; Vic S Phil Ch Marysville WA 1986-1997; Cur St Steph's Epis Ch Oak Harbor WA 1984-1986. mejarvis.2@juno.com

JASMER, Gerald Bruce (Mont) 3630th Street West, Billings MT 59102 B Miles City MT 10/1/1940 s Paul Jasmer & Florence. BS Montana St U 1966. D 8/15/1990 P 11/15/1997 Bp Charles Jones III. S Lk's Ch Billings MT 1990-2004. jerry_jasmer@nps.gov

JASPER SR, John Weaver (CFla) 1151 Sw Del Rio Blvd, Port Saint Lucie FL 34953 **D Epis Ch Of The Nativ Port S Lucie FL 1998-; D Dio SE Florida Miami FL 1990-** B Lewiston ME 7/18/1933 s Charles Clinton Jasper & Jennette. BS Barry U 1983. D 2/14/1990 Bp Calvin Onderdonk Schofield Jr. m 11/18/1976 Joan Marie Hayes. jjasper202@aol.com

JASPER, Michael Angelo (Okla) 13112 N Rockwell Ave, Oklahoma City OK 73142 **Epis Ch Of The Resurr Oklahoma City OK 2001-** B Kansas City MO 7/26/1951 s William Roderick Jasper & Anna Louise. BA U of Missouri 1975; MDiv Nash 1989. D 5/9/1989 Bp Arthur Anton Vogel P 11/1/1989 Bp John Clark Buchanan. c 2. S Barn' Epis Ch Of Odessa Odessa TX 1996-2001; St Lk's Epis Hosp Houston TX 1995-1996; R Gr Epis Ch Houston TX

1990-1995; Dio W Missouri Kansas City MO 1989-1990; Vic S Lk's Epis Ch Excelsior Sprg MO 1989-1990. majjtj@aol.com

JASTER, Leon Anthony (WLa) 1535 Fife Ct, Dunedin FL 34698 **Asst H Trin Epis Ch In Countryside Clearwater FL 2005-** B Fairview NJ 6/26/1929 s Francis Joseph Jaster & Alice Madeline. BA Loyola U 1952; MA Loyola U 1957; BTh Jesuit TS 1961. Rec from Roman Catholic 2/1/1982 as Priest Bp James Stuart Wetmore. m 5/22/2004 Margaret Ann Everett c 1. Asst Ch Of The Gd Shpd Dunedin FL 2000-2004; Ch Of Our Sav Lake Chas LA 1988-1994; Asst R S Mary's Par Tampa FL 1984-1986; Vic Chr Ch Magnolia NJ 1982-1983. leejaster@hotmail.com

JAY, Lynn Antoinette Duba (Los) 24901 Orchard Village Rd, Santa Clarita CA 91355 B Santa Monica CA 7/21/1941 d Rex Quarnberg Duba & Virginia Brazelton. California St U; ETSBH; BA California St U 1976; MDiv Claremont TS 1982. D 6/19/1982 P 1/22/1983 Bp Robert C Rusack. m 6/22/1963 Herman Jay c 3. Vic S Steph's Epis Ch Santa Clarita CA 1984-2011; Epis Ch Of S Andr And S Chas Granada Hills CA 1982-1984. Assn of Wmn Clerics 1983; Camp Wrightwood Advsry Bd 2000; Los Angeles Cler Assn Bd 2006. Cn Dio Los Angeles 1997. revlynn@ca.rr.com

JAYAWARDENE, Thomas Devashri (Los) 1141 Westmont Rd, Santa Barbara CA 93108 **Asst Trin Epis Ch Santa Barbara CA 2000-** B Dalugama Kelaniya LK 12/15/1946 s John Clarence Perera & Cecilia Pearl. Dss U Internazionale Rome It 1972; STL U Pontifical Rome It 1972; PhD U Of Surrey Guildford Gb 1978. Rec from Roman Catholic 8/25/1986 as Priest Bp William Cockburn Russell Sheridan. m 11/14/1980 Jasmine Monica Fernando.

JAYNES, Larry W. (Neb) 12108 Westover Rd, Omaha NE 68154 B Lawrence KS 2/14/1949 s Wayne Jaynes & Jennie. BBA Washburn U 1971; MDiv Epis TS of The SW 1997. D 6/11/1997 P 12/21/1997 Bp James Edward Krotz. m 1/30/1971 Ruth Louise McKinney Jaynes c 3. Int S Matt's Ch Lincoln NE 2006-2007; Mssnr S Christophers Ch Cozad NE 2002-2004; S Jn's Ch Broken Bow NE 2000-2007; S Pauls Epis Ch Arapahoe NE 2000-2007; S Ptr's In The Vlly Lexington NE 2000-2007; S Eliz's Ch Holdrege NE 1997-2004. revsjaynes@cox.net

JAYNES, Ronald P (Pa) 314 Prince George Street, Williamsburg VA 23185 B Geneva NY 4/9/1941 s Paul Edwin Jaynes & Doris Legerwood. BA IL Wesl 1963; MDiv Nash 1966. D 6/11/1966 Bp James Winchester Montgomery P 12/1/1966 Bp Gerald Francis Burrill. m 1/21/1983 Colleen Farrell. Int Bruton Par Williamsburg VA 2009-2011; Int Chr Ch Coronado CA 2006-2009; Int S Jas By The Sea La Jolla CA 2003-2006; Int Ch Of The Gd Shpd Philadelphia PA 2002-2003; Int S Mary's Epis Ch Ardmore PA 2000-2002; Asst S Paul's Ch Philadelphia PA 1998-2000; R S Cathr's Ch Temple Terrace FL 1994-1998; R S Dav's Epis Ch Wilmington DE 1986-1994; R S Jn's Epis Ch Little Silver NJ 1972-1986; R Prince Of Peace Epis Ch Sterling CO 1969-1972; Cur S Lk's Epis Ch Ft Collins CO 1967-1969; Cur Gr Ch Sterling IL 1966-1967. Int Mnstry Ntwk 1997. ronaldpjaynes@gmail.com

JAYNES, Ruth Louise McKinney (Neb) 1322 S 52nd St, Omaha NE 68106 **S Martha's Epis Ch Papillion NE 2010-; S Ptr's Ch Salisbury MD 2010-; Mssnr S Jn's Ch Broken Bow NE 2002-** B Topeka KS 5/29/1951 d Eugene Lowell McKinney & Leone Ruth. MA Epis TS of The SW; BA U of Wyoming. D 5/31/2002 P 12/1/2002 Bp James Edward Krotz. m 1/30/1971 Larry W. Jaynes. Ch Of The H Sprt Bellevue NE 2008; Dio Nebraska Omaha NE 2004-2010; On Track Mnstry Lexington NE 2002-2004. rjaynes@episcopalne.org

JEAN, MacDonald (Hai) Box 1309, Port-Au-Prince Haiti B Latortuo PR 5/12/1941 s Thomas Jean & Parlera. BA Coll S Pierre PR 1965; STB ETSC 1969; Institut Catholique De Paris 1979; U Of Paris-Sorbonne Fr 1979. D 11/30/1968 Bp Charles Alfred Voegeli P 12/1/1969 Bp John Brooke Mosley. m 12/19/1970 Marie-Gisele Prosper c 1. Dio Haiti Ft Lauderdale FL 1968-1995. Auth, "Theol Reflection On Pryr For Ord Of Bp"; Auth, "Theol Reflection On Voodoo Initiation In Haiti"; Auth, "Procession & Creation In Plato'S Philos," *Prot & Dvlpmnt In Haiti*.

JEANES III, Paul (NJ) 25 Mercer St, Princeton NJ 08540 **R Trin Ch Princeton NJ 2008-** B Louisville KY 1/17/1965 s Paul Jeanes & Betty. BA Wake Forest U 1987; DAS GTS 1997; MA/MDiv Louisville Presb TS 1997. D 6/28/1997 P 1/18/1998 Bp Edwin Funsten Gulick Jr. m 7/8/1995 Christina Barker c 3. R S Jas Ch Pewee Vlly KY 1999-2008; Trin Ch Princeton NJ 1999-2008; Pstr Asst Chr Ch Cathd Louisville KY 1997-1999; Dio Kentucky Louisville KY 1997-1999. jeanesp@trinityprinceton.org

JEAN-JACQUES, Harry Musset (Hai) Boite Postale 1309, Port-Au-Prince Haiti B Hinche HT 1/20/1953 D 12/15/1985 P 10/12/1986 Bp Luc Anatole Jacques Garnier. m 12/30/1980 Martha Rosier.

JEFFERSON, Alyce Lee (La) 1329 Jackson Ave, New Orleans LA 70130 B New Orleans LA 2/8/1949 d Stockton Bennett Jefferson & Vilma Alice. BA U of New Orleans 1971. D 12/27/2008 Bp Charles Edward Jenkins III. c 2. a.l. jefferson@att.net

✠ **JEFFERTS SCHORI, Most Rev Katharine** 815 2nd Ave, New York NY 10017 **PBp Epis Ch Cntr New York NY 2006-** B Pensacola FL 3/26/1954 d Keith Bartlett Jefferts & Elaine. BS Stan 1974; MS OR SU 1977; PhD OR SU 1983; MDiv CDSP 1994. D 5/26/1994 P 11/30/1994 Bp Robert Louis Ladehoff Con 2/24/2001 for Nev. m 9/1/1979 Richard M Schori c 1. Bp of Nevada Dio Nevada Las Vegas NV 2001-2006; The Epis Ch Of The Gd Samar Corvallis OR 1994-2001; Dept CE Dio Oregon Portland OR 1994-2000. Auth, "The Heartbeat of God: Finding the Sacr in the Middle of Everything," Skylight Paths, 2010; Auth, "Gospel in the Global Vill: Seeking God's Dream of Shalom," Morehouse, 2009; Auth, "A Wing and a Pryr: A Message of Faith and Hope," Morehouse Pub, 2007; Auth, "Bldg Bridges/Widening Circles sermon in Preaching Through H Days and Holidays," *Sermons that Wk XI*, Morehouse Pub, 2003; Auth, "Multicultural Issues in Preaching sermon in Preaching Through the Year of Matt," *Sermons that Wk X*, Morehouse Pub, 2001; Auth, "The Nag sermon in Preaching Through the Year of Lk," *Sermons that Wk IX*, Morehouse Pub, 2000; Auth, "Maundy Thursday sermon," *What Makes this Day Different?*, Cowley, 1998; Auth, "Sermon: Preaching as the Art of Sacr Conversation," *Sermons that Wk VI*, Morehouse Pub, 1997; Auth, "Article," *LivCh (March 3, 1996)*, LivCh Fndt, 1996. CHS 1991. DD Huron U 2011; DD Bexley 2010; DD GTS 2009; DD Bex 2008; DD U So 2008; DD VTS 2008; Doctor of Humane Letters Coe Coll 2007; DD ETSS 2007; DD Seabury-Wstrn 2007; DD CDSP 2001; The Preaching Excellence Conf 1993. pboffice@episcopalchurch.org

JEFFERY, Anne-Marie (WA) St. James Episcopal Church, P. O. Box 187, Bowie MD 20719 **S Marg's Ch Washington DC 2010-** B NYC 11/30/1967 d Alfred Edwin Jeffery & Agnes. BA/BS SUNY 1988; MS U of Connecticut 1990; PhD U of Connecticut 1993; MDiv VTS 2004. D 6/12/2004 P 1/22/2005 Bp John Chane. Bowie St Unversity Chapl Dio Washington Washington DC 2007-2010; P-in-c S Jas Epis Ch Bowie MD 2007-2009; Urban Mssnr The Ch Of The Epiph Washington DC 2004-2007. ajeffery04@yahoo.com

JEFFERY, David Luce (Fla) 1843 Seminole Rd, Atlantic Beach FL 32233 B Lansing MI 4/17/1936 s Donald D Jeffery & Constance L. BA Syr 1958; ThM SMU 1973; DMin VTS 1990. D 6/10/1973 P 12/13/1973 Bp A Donald Davies. m 10/4/1980 Priscilla Jeffery c 4. P-in-c S Lk's Epis Ch Jacksonville FL 2005-2007; P-in-c S Paul's By-The-Sea Epis Ch Jacksonville Bch FL 2001-2002; Vic S Geo's Epis Ch Jacksonville FL 1995-1998; S Paul's By-The-Sea Epis Ch Jacksonville Bch FL 1992; Asst All SS Epis Ch Jacksonville FL 1988-1992; R S Paul's Epis Ch Lees Summit MO 1986-1988; Dn Of Convoc Dio Arkansas Little Rock AR 1982-1995; Dio Arkansas Little Rock AR 1982-1986; R S Thos Ch Springdale AR 1982-1986; Vic Gr Ch Vernon TX 1980-1982; Vic Trin Ch Quanah TX 1980-1982; Dio NW Texas Lubbock TX 1980-1981; R S Jos's Epis Ch Grand Prairie TX 1977-1980; Chair -Yth Div; Exec Coun Dio Dallas Dallas TX 1976-1980; Vic S Pat's Ch Bowie TX 1974-1977; Vic Trin Ch Henrietta TX 1974-1977; Assoc Trin Epis Ch Ft Worth TX 1973-1974. Auth, "Trng Lay Hosp Visitors". OHC, Ord Of S Lk. dandpjeffery@aol.com

JEFFERY, V(incent) James (Nev) 1500 Mount Rose St, Reno NV 89509 B Elgin IL 8/3/1933 s Stanley Jeffery & Helen Wilhelmina. BA Ohio Nthrn U 1954; STM Bos 1957; MA OH SU 1961. D 12/21/1965 P 5/9/1972 Bp Nelson Marigold Burroughs. m 4/15/1972 Leslie Simmons c 1. R Trin Epis Ch Reno NV 1973-2005; Cur S Paul's Ch Akron OH 1965-1967. R Emer Trin Epis Ch, Reno 2005; Humanitarian Of The Year Awd Conf Of Christians & Jews 1990. jimandbunny@pyramid.net

JEFFORDS III, Julian (SC) 710 Main Street, Conway SC 29526 **R S Paul's Epis Ch Conway SC 1998-** B Richland County SC 12/10/1966 s Julian Thomas Jeffords & Juanita Ellmore. BA U of So Carolina 1990; MDiv Duke DS 1994; Angl Stds VTS 1995. D 5/28/1995 P 12/3/1997 Bp Edward Lloyd Salmon Jr. Asst Par Ch of St. Helena Beaufort SC 1995-1998. frtripp@sccoast.net

JEFFREY, James Beck (NY) 30 The Circle, East Hampton NY 11937 B Jeanerette LA 5/22/1929 s Neill Pressley Jeffrey & Minnie Meade. BS Tul 1950; STB GTS 1958; MA Amer U 1984. D 6/16/1958 Bp Iveson Batchelor Noland P 5/2/1959 Bp Girault M Jones. S Lk's-Roosevelt Hosp Cntr New York NY 1984-1994; R S Lk's Ch Eastchester NY 1963-1966; Asst Ch Of The Incarn New York NY 1958-1962. AEHC 1968; Assn Profsnl Chapl 1968; ACPE 1969; NECAD 1986; RACA 1986. Mgmt of HIV Disease Del to People's Republic of China 1990. jbjeffrey@optonline.net

JEFFREY, Kathryn Mary (Minn) 29 Nord Circle Rd, North Oaks MN 55127 B Hadley MA 1/14/1956 d Edward Gronostalski & Mary Veronica. BA Br 1977; JD Geo 1980; MDiv Ya Berk 1985; STM Ya Berk 1987. D 6/29/1985 P 3/1/1986 Bp A(rthur) Heath Light. m 5/28/1994 Benjamin W Jeffrey. Dio Minnesota Minneapolis MN 2001-2003; R S Jn The Evang S Paul MN 2000-2001; Int H Cross-St Chris's Huntsville AL 1999-2000; Dir Dio Massachusetts Boston MA 1993-1995; Int Ch Of The Ascen Cranston RI 1991-1992; S Geo's Ch Portsmouth RI 1988-1991; Lead R Dio Cntrl New York Syracuse NY 1987-1988; Utica Area Coop Mnstry Whitesboro NY 1987-1988; Assoc Chr Ch Poughkeepsie NY 1986-1987; Asst S Jn's Epis Ch Niantic CT 1985-1986. "A Mighty Flood," *Epis News*, 1993. Phi Beta Kappa. kathryn.jeffrey@worldnet.att.net

JEKABSONS, Wendie Susan (ETenn) 334 Sourwood Hill Rd, Bristol TN 37620 B Hamilton ON CA 10/23/1942 d Harold Francis Scudds & Helen May.

BA E Tennessee St U 1982; MA U of Tennessee 1990; Cert of Study TS 2001. D 6/30/1985 Bp William Evan Sanders P 6/20/2001 Bp Charles Glenn VonRosenberg. c 3. P-in-c Emm Epis Ch Bristol VA 2007-2008; P-in-c The Sav Epis Ch Newland NC 2001-2003; Mem of Episcopate Com Dio E Tennessee Knoxville TN 1997-1998; Chapl Epis U Mnstry Johnson City TN 1993-2000; Mem of COM Dio E Tennessee Knoxville TN 1993-1998; Mem of Bp and Coun Dio E Tennessee Knoxville TN 1991-1995; D S Columba's Epis Ch Bristol TN 1985. "Called to be a D," *Diakoneo, vol.17 #1*, No Amer Assoc. for the Diac, 1995; "Called to be a D," *E Tennessee Epis*, Dio E Tennessee, 1994. NAAD. wenjek@aol.com

✠ **JELINEK, Rt Rev James Louis** (Minn) 1013 Fosse Court, Nekoosa WI 54457 B Milwaukee WI 5/9/1942 s James Francis Jelinek & Ruth Dorothy. Cert Universite Laval 1963; BA Carthage Coll 1964; Van 1967; STB GTS 1970. D 6/28/1970 Bp John Vander Horst P 1/14/1971 Bp J Milton Richardson Con 10/29/1993 for Minn. m 6/18/1988 Marilyn Kay Wall c 1. Bp of Minnesota Dio Minnesota Minneapolis MN 1993-2010; R S Aid's Ch San Francisco CA 1985-1993; R Ch Of S Mich And All Ang Cincinnati OH 1977-1984; Assoc Ch Of The H Comm Memphis TN 1972-1977; Cur S Barth's Ch Bristol TN 1971-1972. DD GTS 1994. ELIJAH4359@AOL.COM

JELLEMA, Alice Moore (Md) 1401 Carrollton Ave, Ruxton MD 21204 **R Ch Of The Guardian Ang Baltimore MD 1997-** B Buffalo NY 11/11/1956 d Lyman Ira Jellema & Alice Dykema. BA Colby Coll 1978; MDiv GTS 1992. D 6/6/1992 Bp David Charles Bowman P 12/1/1992 Bp Frank Harris Vest Jr. Ch Of The Gd Shpd Ruxton MD 1994-1997; Asst to R Emm Epis Ch Hampton VA 1992-1994.

JELLISON, Frederick Kingston (RI) 75 East Ave, #31, North Providence RI 02911 **Died 10/11/2011** B Bangor ME 11/4/1914 s Hosea E Jellison & Olive I. BA Br 1940; BD EDS 1943; Med Rhode Island Coll 1977. D 9/15/1943 Bp Raymond A Heron P 3/19/1944 Bp Beverley D Tucker. c 6. Chair, "An Anchor of Hope for Rhode Island," *The Hist of Epis Chars of Rhode Island*, 2008. Legend of hon Kiwanis Intl 1997; Max Grant Awd Epis Chars of RI 1985.

JELLISON, Mary L (Wyo) 2601 Main St, Torrington WY 82240 **R All SS Epis Ch Torrington WY 2003-** B Portland OR 3/24/1940 d Howard Bert Hugger & Emily Westlake. BA Lewis & Clark Coll 1963; Fifth Year Wstrn Washington U 1969; Olympia TS 1991; MDiv EDS 2001. D 4/22/1993 Bp Vincent Waydell Warner P 5/26/2001 Bp Robert Wilkes Ihloff. c 3. Asst R S Ptr's Epis Ch Ellicott City MD 2001-2003; D Emm Ch Cumberland MD 1996-2001; D S Paul Epis Ch Bellingham WA 1994-1996. DOK 1986. mljellison@msn.com

JEMMOTT, Brian Anthony Lester (At) 2005 South Columbia Place, Decatur GA 30032 **R Ch Of The H Cross Decatur GA 2006-** B Trinidad W.I. 9/22/1955 s Lester Jemmott & Ena. BA Tougaloo Coll 1982; MDiv SWTS 1993; DMin EDS 2009. Trans from Church in the Province Of The West Indies 5/1/1996 Bp Frank Tracy Griswold III. m 9/5/1987 Michelle Camille Colastic c 2. S Tim's Decatur GA 2004-2006; S Andr's Epis Ch Cincinnati OH 2001-2002; Absalom Jones Stdt Cntr & Chap Atlanta GA 1997-2003; Dio Atlanta Atlanta GA 1997-2001; S Geo/S Mths Ch Chicago IL 1996-1997. Soc Of S Jn The Evang 1992. rector@holy-cross.org

JENCKS, Jeffrey A (CGC) 7979 N 9th Ave, Pensacola FL 32514 B Warwick RI 8/21/1951 s Leo Francis Jencks & Blanche Marie. BA Our Lady Of Providence 1974; MDiv S Mary Sem/U 1978. Rec from Roman Catholic 4/1/1986 as Priest Bp George Nelson Hunt III. m 1/6/1996 Eileen McCarten c 1. R H Cross Ch Pensacola FL 2008; S Jn's Ch Cumberland RI 2007-2008; Spec Mobilization Spprt Plan Washington DC 2005-2006; Pension Fund Mltry New York NY 2003-2004. frjeff@holycrosspensacola.org

JENEVEIN, Richard George (Cal) 100 Bay Pl Apt 1610, Oakland CA 94610 **Died 5/11/2010** B Oakland CA 11/20/1926 s George Antoine Jenevein & Esther Elizabeth. BA S Mary's Coll Moraga CA 1950; STB GTS 1953. D 6/28/1953 Bp Henry H Shires. c 2.

JENKINS, Al W (CFla) 103 W Christina Blvd, Lakeland FL 33813 **R All SS Epis Ch Lakeland FL 1989-** B Milan TN 6/30/1946 s Paul Wellington Jenkins & Allie France. AA Sandhills Cmnty Coll 1969; BS Lambuth U 1976; MDiv STUSo 1979; DMin STUSo 1983. D 6/24/1979 Bp William F Gates Jr P 9/22/1980 Bp Emerson Paul Haynes. m 10/22/1966 Vivian R Rogers c 1. R S Marg's Ch Inverness FL 1986-1989; Assoc S Dunst's Epis Ch Largo FL 1982-1986; R S Jas Epis Ch Port Charlotte FL 1981-1982; Asst Chr Ch Bradenton FL 1980-1981; The U So (Sewanee) Sewanee TN 1979-1980; The TS at The U So Sewanee TN 1976-1979. Auth, "Hist Of Epis Churchwomen In The Dio Tennessee". awjvrj@verizon.net

JENKINS, Arthur Mack (SC) 1872 Camp Rd, Charleston SC 29412 **Sr. Pstr S Jas Ch Charleston SC 1998-** B Ahoskie NC 9/2/1952 s Clyde Wilson Jenkins & Mildred Copeland. BS No Carolina St U 1975; MDiv VTS 1991. D 6/15/1991 Bp Huntington Williams Jr P 6/6/1992 Bp Edward Lloyd Salmon Jr. m 4/3/1976 Marjorie Kay Rogers c 2. Dioc Coun Dio So Carolina Charleston SC 2000-2003; R Chr Ch Fitchburg MA 1993-1998; Dio Wstrn Massachusetts Springfield MA 1993-1998; Asst S Jas Ch Charleston SC 1991-1993. Vts Mssy Soc. ajenkins@saint-james.org

✠ **JENKINS III, Rt Rev Charles Edward** (La) P.O. Box 3000, St. Francisville LA 70775 B Shreveport LA 7/27/1951 s Don Green Jenkins & Helen Baker. BA Louisiana Tech U 1973; MDiv Nash 1976. D 6/17/1976 P 4/13/1977 Bp James Barrow Brown Con 1/31/1998 for La. m 6/28/1975 Charollette Louise Hazel c 2. Bp of La Dio Louisiana Baton Rouge LA 1998-2010; Chair Stndg Com Dio Louisiana Baton Rouge LA 1992-1993; Stndg Com Dio Louisiana Baton Rouge LA 1989-1993; R S Lk's Ch Baton Rouge LA 1985-1997; BEC Dio Ft Worth Ft Worth TX 1982-1985; Bd Trst Nash Nashotah WI 1981-1991; R S Mk's Ch Arlington TX 1979-1985; Chair Div Yth Dio Louisiana Baton Rouge LA 1978-1979; Asst Gr Epis Ch Monroe LA 1977-1979; Asst Chapl S Alb's Chap & Epis U Cntr Baton Rouge LA 1976-1977. CBS 2000. DD The GTS 2011; DD TS U So Sewanee TN 1999; DD Nash Nashotah WI 1992. cjenkins1468@gmail.com

JENKINS, David P (Alb) 517 Lakeside Circle, Pompano Beach FL 33060 B South Weymouth MA 10/3/1935 s Alexander Jenkins & Eva Gladys. BA Br 1958; MDiv GTS 1961; MA U of Rhode Island 1970; EdD SUNY 1976. D 6/17/1961 P 12/23/1961 Bp John S Higgins. Var Int Mnstrys Dio Albany Albany NY 1988-1994; Int S Steph's Ch Delmar NY 1987-1988; Int Chr Ch Greenville NY 1982-1986; Int Trin Ch Rensselaerville Rensselaerville NY 1982-1985; P-in-c S Paul's Ch Bloomville NY 1970-1982; P-in-c S Ptr's Ch Hobart NY 1970-1982; R S Paul's Ch Portsmouth RI 1962-1969. Auth, "Drugs A-Z," 1972. OHC. dpj5458@comcast.net

JENKINS, George Washburn (Ct) 680 Caribou Rd, Enfield ME 04493 B Ridgewood NJ 1/6/1936 s George Washburn Jenkins & Harriet Stanton. BA Rutgers-The St U 1962; MDiv VTS 1965. D 6/12/1965 Bp Leland Stark P 6/18/1966 Bp Gray Temple. m 5/3/1971 Loreli Hanscom c 4. R S Jas Ch Glastonbury CT 1986-2001; Dioc Fndt Dio New Jersey Trenton NJ 1985-1986; Bd Missions Dio New Jersey Trenton NJ 1979-1981; R H Trin Ch So River NJ 1977-1986; Asst Min Ch Of The Redeem Orangeburg SC 1968-1969; P-in-c S Paul's Epis Ch Orangeburg SC 1968-1969. jenkinsgl@midmaine.com

JENKINS JR, Harry O (Ga) 1534 7th St, Slidell LA 70458 **Chr Ch Slidell LA 2011-** B Savannah GA 8/6/1952 s Harry Oliver Jenkins & Marion Bordeaux. BA Armstrong St U 1974; EdS Georgia Sthrn U 1987; MDiv The TS at The U So 2011. D 5/21/2011 Bp Scott Anson Benhase. m 7/6/2011 Regina Brewster c 2. hjenk1@aol.com

JENKINS, Hedley Percy (Nwk) 7100 Sorenson Dr, Boise ID 83709 B Fordingbridge Hamps UK 7/23/1917 s Percy Archibald Jenkins & Ethel Elizabeth. U of Cambridge 1950; MA U of Cambridge 1950; Westcott Hse Cambridge 1952. Trans from Church Of England 10/1/1954 as Priest Bp Herbert Alcorn Donovan Jr. m 10/5/1945 Barbara Jenkins c 1. R Chr Ch Harrison NJ 1958-1968; Asst Calv Epis Ch Summit NJ 1956-1958.

JENKINS, James Leonard (Minn) 8200 Stanley Rd Apt 24, Minneapolis MN 55437 B 3/12/1931 s Jasper Nathan Jenkins & Ethel Johanna. BA Macalester Coll 1952; BD SWTS 1955. D 6/29/1955 Bp Hamilton Hyde Kellogg P 12/21/1955 Bp Stephen E Keeler. c 2. R Trin Ch Excelsior MN 1982-1992; R S Geo's Ch St Louis Pk MN 1969-1975; R S Jas On The Pkwy Minneapolis MN 1964-1969; R S Paul's Ch Virginia MN 1957-1962; Min in charge S Ptr's Epis Ch Kasson MN 1955-1957.

JENKINS, John Stone (La) 708 Forest Point Dr, Brandon MS 39047 B Shreveport LA 7/26/1924 s Robert Eloyd Jenkins & Glena. BA LSU 1947; MA U Chi 1948; BD SWTS 1951; DD SWTS 1973. D 7/15/1951 P 9/1/1952 Bp Girault M Jones. m 1/25/1985 Lynn Biggs c 2. R Trin Ch New Orleans LA 1971-1984; Dn S Andr's Cathd Jackson MS 1967-1971; Asst Hdmstr S Mart's Epis Ch Metairie LA 1954-1962. Auth, "What Think Ye Of Jesus". llbiggs@bellsouth.net

JENKINS, Judith Ann (RG) 601 Montano Rd. N.W., Albuquerque NM 87107 **S Mich And All Ang Ch Albuquerque NM 2011-** B Albuquerque NM 7/10/1942 d CF Ted Boyd & Dorothy J. BS Colorado St U 1967; Tchr Cert Boise St 1980; MAR Denver U 1993; MAR Iliff TS 1993. D 6/7/2008 Bp William Carl Frey. c 2. judithj@all-angels.com

JENKINS, Kathryn E (Va) 3507 Pond Chase Dr, Midlothian VA 23113 **Assoc S Paul's Ch Richmond VA 2007-** B Rochester NY 12/9/1963 d Richard J Eaton & Susanne W. BA Mt Holyoke Coll 1986; M Ed. U of Virginia 1991; MDiv VTS 2002. D 6/15/2002 Bp David Conner Bane Jr P 12/18/2002 Bp Carol Joy Gallagher. m 6/24/1989 Stephen G Jenkins c 3. Ch Of The Redeem Midlothian VA 2002-2007. keej89@hotmail.com

JENKINS, Mark A (NH) St. James Episcopal Church, 44 West St, Keene NH 03431 **R Par Of S Jas Ch Keene NH 2010-** B Greeneville TN 6/15/1958 s Paul Alex Jenkins & Mary Louise. Ohio Wesl 1976; BA Wayne 1982; MDiv STUSo 1985. D 6/29/1985 Bp H Coleman McGehee Jr P 1/1/1986 Bp William J Gordon Jr. m 5/14/1977 Leigh H Harrison c 2. P-in-c S Andr's Ch Clawson MI 2009-2010; Dioc Coun Dio Michigan Detroit MI 2005-2007; COM Dio Michigan Detroit MI 2000-2003; Ed Bd, The Record Dio Michigan Detroit MI 1997-2009; GC Dep / Alt Dio Michigan Detroit MI 1997-2009; Chf Fin Off Dio Michigan Detroit MI 1994-1995; Chapl Epis/Luth Chapl at Wayne Detroit MI 1992-1994; R Journey of Faith Epis Ch Detroit MI 1990-2009; Dioc Coun Dio Michigan Detroit MI 1990-1993; P-in-c S Jn's Epis Ch Caseville MI

1985-1990; P-in-c S Jn's Epis Ch Sandusky MI 1985-1990; P-in-c S Paul's Epis Ch Bad Axe MI 1985-1990; P-in-c The Epis Ch In Huron Cnty Bad Axe MI 1985-1990. rector@stjameskeene.com

JENKINS, Martha L (SVa) 120 Reykin Dr, Richmond VA 23236 B Rutherfordton NC 3/23/1935 d Carl Graham Laughridge & Gladys Wolfe. BA U NC 1956; MDiv VTS 1997. D 6/14/1997 Bp Frank Harris Vest Jr P 12/13/1997 Bp David Conner Bane Jr. m 2/4/1961 Blair Jenkins c 3. Dio Sthrn Virginia Norfolk VA 1997-2010; R S Matt's Epis Ch Chesterfield VA 1997-2010. revmjenkins@aol.com

JENKINS, Michael L (WNC) 5165 Hayes Waters Rd, Morganton NC 28655 **D Gr Ch Morganton NC 2011-** B Asheville NC 10/15/1951 s Grover Mark Jenkins & Anne. U NC 1972. D 12/18/1999 Bp Robert Hodges Johnson. m 8/12/1979 Linda Kay Mitchell. D S Jn's Epis Ch Marion NC 2007-2010; D S Mary's Ch Morganton NC 1999-2007. MICHAELLJENKINS@BELLSOUTH.NET

JENKS, Alan W (WVa) 450 Elm St, Morgantown WV 26501 B Las Vegas NM 3/23/1934 s William Stuart Jenks & Mildred. BA U of New Mex 1956; MDiv CDSP 1959; ThD Harvard DS 1965. D 6/26/1959 Bp C J Kinsolving III P 4/14/1960 Bp Donald J Campbell. m 8/29/1959 Denda Slaughter c 3. Vic S Mich's Ch Kingwood WV 1984; P-in-c S Jos's Ch Durham NC 1966-1968. Auth, "Eating and Drinking in the OT," *Anchor Bible Dictionary*, 1992; Auth, "The Elohist," *Anchor Bible Dictionary*, 1992; Auth, "Theol Presuppositions of Israel's Wisdom Lit," *Horizons in Biblic Theol*, 1985; Auth, *The Elohist and No Israelite Traditions*, Scholars Press, 1977; Auth, *Tchg the OT in Engl Classes*, Indiana U Press, 1973. Cath Biblic Assn 1973-2003. Fulbright Fllshp in Semitic Linguistics Israel and US Governments 1965; B.D. w dist CDSP, Berkeley, CA 1956. drj@mail.wvnet.edu

J

JENKS, Glenn Baylor (Az) 5417 E Milton Dr, Cave Creek AZ 85331 B Wilkinsburg PA 11/23/1944 s Glenn Baylor Jenks & Dorothy McKinley. BA Muskingum Coll 1966; MDiv PDS 1969; JD U of Arizona 1985. D 5/24/1969 Bp William S Thomas P 12/20/1969 Bp Robert Bracewell Appleyard. m 6/4/1966 Nancy Scott c 2. Gd Shpd Of The Hills Cave Creek AZ 2002-2009; S Jn The Bapt Epis Ch Glendale AZ 1996-1998; Vic Ch Of The Resurr Tucson AZ 1979-1984; Epis Par Of S Mich And All Ang Tucson AZ 1979-1984; Gr Ch Tucson AZ 1974-1979; Asst Gr S Paul's Epis Ch Tucson AZ 1974-1979; R All SS Ch Aliquippa PA 1970-1974. frnlaw@msn.com

JENKS, Peter Quick (Me) 200 Main St, Thomaston ME 04861 **R The Epis Ch Of S Jn Bapt Thomaston ME 1992-** B Chicago IL 12/13/1956 s Bruce Jenks & Susan. BA U So 1979; MDiv GTS 1985. D 6/24/1985 Bp Robert Marshall Anderson P 3/22/1986 Bp C(laude) Charles Vache. m 7/18/2004 Emily Ann Jenks c 5. Assoc R S Andr's Epis Ch Newport News VA 1985-1992. peter_jenks@yahoo.com

JENKS, Shepherd Martin (NCal) Pmb 320, 2132-A Central 5e, Albuquerque NM 87106 B Berkeley CA 9/29/1926 s Christopher Martin Jenks & Frances Cecilia. Grad Theol Un; BS USNA 1949; Bts 1984. D 11/12/1981 Bp William Edwin Swing. m 9/9/1982 Nancy Jenks. D Chr Epis Ch Windsor CA 1996-2000; D S Steph's Epis Ch Sebastopol CA 1991-1996; D S Steph's Ch Wahiawa HI 1987-1989; D Dio Hawaii Honolulu HI 1986-1991; D /Asst S Barn Ch San Francisco CA 1985-1987; D /Asst S Barn Ch San Francisco CA 1981-1983. shep@n21mail.com

JENNEKER, Bruce William Bailey (WA) 30 Digtebij Street, Mabille Park, Kulis River, Cape Town 7580 B 11/21/1948 s Gordon Edward Jenneker & Helen Hope. CUA; BA U Coll Wstrn Cape 1969; MDiv EDS 1984. D 1/1/1985 Bp Roger W Blanchard P 6/1/1985 Bp John Thomas Walker. Assoc Trin Ch In The City Of Boston Boston MA 1996-2005; Cn Precentor Cathd of St Ptr & St Paul Washington DC 1992-1996; VTS Alexandria VA 1991. brucej@sgcathedral.co.za

JENNER, Helen McLeroy (NC) 1079 Ridge Dr, Clayton NC 27520 B Savannah GA 9/16/1933 d Hugh Finlay McLeroy & Lillian Azell. BA Wesl 1954; MA NWU 1957; MDiv STUSo 1996. D 6/29/1996 Bp Robert Carroll Johnson Jr. c 3. Dio No Carolina Raleigh NC 1998; Dio No Carolina Raleigh NC 1997; Asst S Barth's Ch Pittsboro NC 1997; S Paul's Epis Ch Smithfield NC 1996-1997.

JENNINGS, Albert Arthur (O) 8667 Shepard Rd # 204, Macedonia OH 44056 **Dn of Mssn Area Dio Ohio Cleveland OH 2009-; R S Tim's Ch Macedonia OH 1988-; Int Consult Dio Ohio Cleveland OH 1987-** B Richmond VA 8/28/1951 s George Wood Jennings & Betty Irma. BS Virginia Commonwealth U 1973; MDiv EDS 1977. D 6/4/1977 Bp Robert Bruce Hall P 5/20/1978 Bp John Alfred Baden. m 8/14/1976 Gay Clark c 2. Stndg Commitee Dio Ohio Cleveland OH 2001-2005; Congrl Developpment Comm. Dio Ohio Cleveland OH 1987-2002; Dio Ohio Cleveland OH 1987-1989; Com Const & Cns Dio Ohio Cleveland OH 1985-1987; DeptCE Dio Ohio Cleveland OH 1983-1986; R Ch Of The Redeem Lorain OH 1980-1988; Dept Cong LIfe Dio Ohio Cleveland OH 1980-1987; Asst Trin Ch Arlington VA 1977-1980. jennings4@roadrunner.com

JENNINGS, Carl Eugene (Ore) 771 14th Ave, Coos Bay OR 97420 B King City MO 3/11/1935 s Carl Francis Jennings & Ruth Maxton. San Antonio Coll 1955; BS Trin U San Antonio TX 1957; MDiv CDSP 1960. D 7/7/1960 Bp Everett H Jones P 1/19/1961 Bp Richard Earl Dicus. m 6/25/1960 Julia Christine Moon c 2. R Emm Ch Coos Bay OR 1995-2000; Archd S Alb's Ch Harlingen TX 1989; Archd Dio W Texas San Antonio TX 1987-1995; Cn Dio W Texas San Antonio TX 1977-1987; Chair Human Rela Cmsn Dio W Texas San Antonio TX 1971-1973; R S Jn's Ch McAllen TX 1968-1977; Chair Dept C&C Dio W Texas San Antonio TX 1965-1970; R S Mk's Ch San Marcos TX 1964-1968; Exec Bd Dio W Texas San Antonio TX 1963-1976; Cur S Mk's Epis Ch San Antonio TX 1960-1964. Contributing Ed, "The Back Page continuous 1977-1994," *Ch News (Dio W Texas)*, 1977; Auth, "Candidates for Mar," Forw Mvmt Press, 1976. gjjennings@charter.net

JENNINGS, Debora (Okla) 924 N Robinson Ave, Oklahoma City OK 73102 **Vic S Basil's Epis Ch Tahlequah OK 2011-; Dio Oklahoma Oklahoma City OK 2009-; Reg Mssnr/Vic Dio Utah Salt Lake City UT 1999-** B Morris IL 7/22/1954 d Kenneth Hendrix & Helen Roberta. Shalem Inst; BS Arizona St U 1990; MDiv CDSP 1993; SWTS 1995. D 6/5/1993 P 12/18/1993 Bp Robert Reed Shahan. c 1. R H Trin Epis Ch Sunnyside WA 2006-2009; Dio Utah Salt Lake City UT 1998-2006; Vic S Jude's Ch Cedar City UT 1998; S Lk's Ch Prescott AZ 1994-1998; Dio Arizona Phoenix AZ 1993-1994. Auth, "Aquinas & Eckhert S & Sinner?". Wmn Of Excellence Awd Aauw. holymama@infowest.com

JENNINGS, Gay Clark (O) 168 Hiram College Dr, Sagamore Hills OH 44067 **Cler Rep - Angl Consultative Coun Exec Coun Appointees New York NY 2010-2016; Exec Coun Mem Exec Coun Appointees New York NY 2006-2012; Assoc Dir Credo Inst Inc. Memphis TN 2003-; GC Dep Dio Ohio Cleveland OH 1991-2012** B Syracuse NY 2/23/1951 d Robert Taylor Clark & Nancy Borthwick. BA Colg 1974; MDiv EDS 1977. D 4/22/1978 P 5/1/1979 Bp Ned Cole. m 8/14/1976 Albert Arthur Jennings c 2. GC Dep Dio Ohio Cleveland OH 1991-2003; Int Cn Pstr Trin Cathd Cleveland OH 1986-1987; Int R S Ptr's Epis Ch Lakewood OH 1985-1986; Asst R S Ptr's Epis Ch Lakewood OH 1980-1985; P Assoc The Ch of S Clem Alexandria VA 1978-1980. Auth, "Kellogg Lectures EDS 92". gjennings51@gmail.com

JENNINGS, James Courtney (HB) 5701 Snead Rd, Richmond VA 23224 B 1/1/1940 D 6/24/1970 Bp William Foreman Creighton.

JENNINGS, Kelly Kathleen (Tex) 1406 Karen Ave, Austin TX 78757 **S Jas' Ch Taylor TX 2006-; Ch Of The Gd Shpd Charlottesville VA 2004-** B Evanston IL 10/8/1968 d Kirk R Hagan & Kendall K. BA U of Kansas 1991; MA Oxf 1994; MDiv Ya Berk 2001. D 1/14/2004 P 7/17/2004 Bp Peter James Lee. m 8/12/2000 Nathan Grady Woodruff. McIlhany Par Charlottesville VA 2004-2005. vicar@stjamestaylor.org

JENNINGS, Mary Kay (SD) Yankton Mission Cluster, 126 N Park NE, Wagner SD 57380 **R S Thos Epis Ch Sturgis SD 2010-; Vic Ch of the H Sprt Wagner SD 2007-; Vic S Phil the D Ch Wagner SD 2007-** B Sioux Falls SD 12/6/1942 d Gordon Neil Reecy & Genevieve Lily. BS DSU 1974; MA U CO 1989; MDiv TS, Sewanee TN 2007. D 4/27/2007 P 12/21/2007 Bp Creighton Leland Robertson. c 1. Dio So Dakota Sioux Falls SD 2007-2009. kay@mizinformation.com

JENNINGS, Nathan Grady (Tex) PO Box 2247, Austin TX 78768 **Assoc Prof of Liturg and Angl Stds Epis TS Of The SW Austin TX 2009-** B Austin TX 8/7/1974 s Marsha Kay. BA U of Texas 1997; MDiv Ya Berk 2001; PhD U of Virginia 2007. D 6/20/2009 P 2/9/2010 Bp C(harles) Andrew Doyle. m 8/12/2000 Kelly Kathleen Jennings c 2. njennings@ssw.edu

JENNINGS, Richard Paul (NMich) 1015 Parnell St, Sault Sainte Marie MI 49783 B Flint MI 12/16/1926 s Richard Jennings & Maybelle. BA U MI 1950; M.Div VTS 1953; MA Cntrl Michigan U 1970. D 6/27/1953 Bp Russell S Hubbard P 1/25/1954 Bp Richard S M Emrich. m 9/18/1948 Lillian Gill c 3. R S Paul's Epis Ch St. Clair MI 1962-1969; R S Andr's Ch New Berlin NY 1960-1962; P S Matt's Ch So New Berlin NY 1960-1962; D & R Chr Epis Ch E Tawas MI 1953-1957.

JENNINGS, Robert Tallmadge (Ky) 2002 High Ridge Rd, Louisville KY 40207 **R S Fran In The Fields Harrods Creek KY 1983-** B Evanston IL 9/27/1949 s William Ellery Jennings & Beverly. BA Cntr Coll 1971; MDiv VTS 1974. D 6/29/1975 Bp William Evan Sanders P 5/1/1976 Bp William F Gates Jr. m 7/15/1972 Mary McCutchan Moore. Assoc S Fran In The Fields Harrods Creek KY 1978-1982; Asst S Mary's Cathd Memphis TN 1975-1978. robinj@stfrancisinthefields.org

JENNINGS III, William Worth (NC) 702 Hillandale Ln, Garner NC 27529 B Wellsboro PA 11/21/1941 s Edwin K Jennings & Ruth. MDiv PDS; BA U Pgh. D 5/26/1973 P 12/1/1973 Bp Robert Bracewell Appleyard. m 7/31/1976 Gaynell Donaldson. Vic S Chris's Epis Ch Garner NC 1986-2008; S Jas Epis Ch Pittsburgh PA 1985; St Georges Ch Pittsburgh PA 1973-1983.

JENNINGS TODD, Margaret Herring (USC) 301 W Liberty St, Winnsboro SC 29180 B Greenwood SC 11/5/1949 d Walter Townes Herring & Wilmer Margaret. BA Columbia Coll 1971; MEd Clemson U 1976; Cert Sch for Mnstry - EDUSC 2007. D 1/31/2009 Bp Dorsey Felix Henderson. m 12/27/2007 William Lane Todd c 1. maggiejenn@aol.com

JENSEN, Andrew (Minn) 4870 Johnson Ave, Saint Paul MN 55110 B Lynn MA 12/30/1927 s Andrew C Jensen & Helene M. BA Harv 1950; STB Ya

Berk 1960. D 6/25/1960 P 12/1/1960 Bp Robert McConnell Hatch. m 10/9/1965 Lura Ann Lawton c 2. Hazelden Cntr City MN 1987-1989; Asst Min S Jn In The Wilderness White Bear Lake MN 1973-1975; R Ch Of The Gd Shpd Fitchburg MA 1960-1965. acjensen@comcast.net

JENSEN, Anne Hislop (Cal) 865 Walavista Ave., Oakland CA 94610 B Fort Sill OK 1/17/1945 d George Kelton Hislop & Virginia. BA Stan 1967; MA Stan 1968; Untd TS 1985; MDiv Ya Berk 1988. D 6/23/1988 Bp Robert Marshall Anderson P 4/8/1989 Bp Clarence Nicholas Coleridge. m 6/22/1968 Douglas Odell Jensen c 3. Chr Ch Alameda CA 2009-2010; S Paul's Ch Oakland CA 2007-2009; Int Trin Par Menlo Pk CA 2005-2007; Int Chr Ch Redding Ridge CT 2003-2005; S Andr's Ch New Haven CT 2003; Int S Andr's Ch Meriden CT 2001-2003; Int S Tim's Ch Fairfield CT 2000-2001; Int Trin Ch Portland CT 1999-2000; P-in-c Ch Of The Gd Shpd Shelton CT 1997; Asst S Jn's Ch Bridgeport CT 1990-1996; Asst S Fran Ch Stamford CT 1989-1990; Asst Chr And H Trin Ch Westport CT 1988-1989. annehj@aol.com

JENSEN, Barbara Ann (NJ) 238 Main St, South River NJ 08882 B York PA 12/22/1944 d Stowell Allen Dickinson & Olive Oldfield. BA U of So Florida 1967; MPA Kean U 1991; D Formation Prog 2002. D 9/21/2002 Bp David B(ruce) Joslin. m 6/10/1972 Robert R Jensen c 2. bjensen238@aol.com

JENSEN, James Michael (CNY) 6 Elizabeth St, Utica NY 13501 **Died 11/14/2009** B Racine WI 11/28/1946 s Marny Norholm Jensen & Joyce Elsie. BA U of Wisconsin 1969; MDiv SWTS 1972. D 5/5/1972 P 11/10/1972 Bp Donald H V Hallock. c 1. jjensen@gracechurchutica.org

JENSEN, Jan Darrel (Tex) 11 Sherwood St, Dayton TX 77535 B Salt Lake City UT 1/13/1953 s Darrel Hilmer Jensen & Florence. Hochschule fuer Musik Vienna 1975; Ohr Somayach 1975; BA U of Utah 1976; MDiv Epis TS of The SW 2002. D 6/22/2002 Bp Claude Edward Payne P 7/16/2004 Bp Don Adger Wimberly. m 6/25/1977 Ruth Ziat c 2. Intercontinental Ch Soc 2010-2011; Intercontinental Ch Soc Warwick 2010-2011; R S Steph's Ch Liberty TX 2004-2008; D/Assoc P Ch Of The Epiph Houston TX 2002-2004. "Lost Legions of Rome," Greystone Productions, 1996. Amer Soc of Composers, Authors, and Pub 1995. jdjensen13@hotmail.com

JENSEN, Jonathon Wesley (Ark) 310 W 17th St, Little Rock AR 72206 **Trin Cathd Little Rock AR 2009-** B Greenville KY 2/18/1971 s Charles Thomas Jensen & Linda Darlene. BA Transylvania U 1993; MDiv VTS 1996. D 6/8/1996 Bp Don Adger Wimberly P 1/11/1997 Bp Ronald Hayward Haines. m 9/14/1996 Natalia Valerievna Tolkacheva. R Trin Ch Lawr KS 2002-2009; Cn Chr Ch Cathd New Orleans LA 1998-2002; Asst S Fran Ch Potomac MD 1996-1998. Ed, "The Catalyst". jwj@trinitylawrence.org

JENSEN, Julia Kooser (Ore) 2020 SW Knollcrest Dr., Portland OR 97225 **D Epis Par Of S Jn The Bapt Portland OR 2007-** B Kansas City MO 10/2/1937 d Parke Herman Kooser & Ruth Hafner. BA Colorado Coll 1959; BA Sch for Deacons 2002. D 6/1/2002 Bp William Edwin Swing. m 7/3/1965 William Charles Jensen c 3. D S Steph's Par Belvedere CA 2005-2006; Dioc Coun Mem Dio California San Francisco CA 2004-2006; D Ch Of The Redeem San Rafael CA 2002-2005. Phi Beta Kappa 1959. juleskj@comcast.net

JENSEN, MaryAnn (NJ) 194 Carter Rd, Princeton NJ 08540 **D All SS Ch Princeton NJ 2004-** B Milwaukee WI 11/24/1936 d Marinus Christian Jensen & Anna Marie. BA Milwaukee-Downer Coll 1958; Dio New Jersey 2000. D 5/8/2001 Bp David B(ruce) Joslin. NAAD; The HSEC 2005; The Natl Epis Historians and Archivists 2005. majensen@newjersey.anglican.org

JENSEN, Patricia Ann (CFla) 9301 Hunters Park Way, Tampa FL 33647 B Tampa FL 4/8/1948 d George Francis LaRue & Betty. BS Florida St U 1971; Inst For Chr Stds 1977. D 6/9/1979 Bp William Hopkins Folwell. m 8/5/1972 Dan Jensen. D S Alb's Epis Ch Auburndale FL 1991-1998; D S Wlfd's Epis Ch Sarasota FL 1979-1980.

JENSON, Constance (WA) 17413 Audrey Road, Cobb Island MD 20625 B Evanston IL 2/18/1945 d Urban Leonard Jenson & Mary Cordelia. BA U Of La Verne CA 1978; MDiv VTS 2001. D 6/9/2001 P 12/14/2001 Bp Jane Hart Holmes Dixon. R Chr Ch Wm And Mary Newburg MD 2001-2011. charmolly@aol.com

JERAULD, Philip Eldredge (Mass) 1 Concord Coach Ln, Litchfield NH 03052 B Barnstable MA 3/18/1926 s Bruce Kempton Jerauld & Jenny Lucile. BA Bos 1949; MDiv CDSP 1954; STM Yale DS 1968; Naval Chapl Sch 1974. D 6/18/1954 P 1/9/1955 Bp William J Gordon Jr. m 6/19/1982 Nancy Jerauld c 2. S Andr's Ch Framingham MA 1985-1991; Int All SS' Epis Ch Belmont MA 1984-1985; Int Gr Epis Ch Medford MA 1983-1984; Off Of Bsh For ArmdF New York NY 1958-1969; Vic S Mary's Ch Anchorage AK 1956-1958; Asst All SS' Epis Ch Anchorage AK 1954-1956. Navy Achvmnt Medal USN; Meritorious Serv Medal USN. philipjerauld@comcast.net

JERGENS, Andrew MacAoidh (SO) 2374 Madison Rd, Cincinnati OH 45208 B Omaha NE 7/16/1935 s Alfred William Rogahn & Edna May. BS Ya 1957; MBA U of Pennsylvania 1962. D 6/2/1973 P 12/22/1973 Bp John Mc Gill Krumm. m 2/21/1977 Linda Busken c 2. Int Chap Of The Nativ Cincinnati OH 1995-1996; Secy of Conv Dio Sthrn Ohio Cincinnati OH 1994-1995; S Thos Epis Ch Terrace Pk OH 1994; Int S Andr's Epis Ch Cincinnati OH 1992-1993; Int Chr Ch - Glendale Cincinnati OH 1990-1991; Assoc The Ch of the Redeem Cincinnati OH 1979-1990; Serv The Ch of the Redeem Cincinnati OH 1973-1977. Assoc, OHC 1980. Spec Recognition Ohio St Senate 2007; Trst Emer Cincinnati Playhouse in the Pk 1975. macaoidh@eos.net

JERNAGAN, Hope Welles (Fla) 4455 Atlantic Blvd, Jacksonville FL 32207 **Jacksonville Epis HS Jacksonville FL 2009-** B Toledo OH 9/8/1981 D 12/21/2007 P 6/21/2008 Bp George Wayne Smith. m 1/18/2008 Luke Jernagan. hopiewelles@gmail.com

JERNAGAN III, Luke (Fla) 400 San Juan Dr, Ponte Vedra Beach FL 32082 **Assoc R Chr Epis Ch Ponte Vedra Bch FL 2008-** B Pensacola FL 9/23/1980 s Louis Jernagan & Betty. BS U of Alabama 2003; MDiv GTS 2006; STM GTS 2008. D 6/3/2006 P 5/12/2007 Bp Philip Menzie Duncan II. m 1/18/2008 Hope Welles Jernagan c 1. Asst Chr Ch Bronxville NY 2007-2008; Asst S Paul's Epis Ch Daphne AL 2006-2007. ljernagan@christepiscopalchurch.org

JEROME, Douglas Darrel (EO) 1332 SW 33rd St, Pendleton OR 97801 B Blackduck MN 12/24/1939 s Frederick Jerome & Phyllis Matilda. STUSo 1998. D 6/16/1999 Bp Rustin Ray Kimsey P 4/3/2002 Bp William O Gregg. m 9/30/1967 Phyllis J Jerome c 2. Prison Mnstry Dio Estrn Oregon The Dalles OR 1999-2003; D Ch Of The Redeem Pendleton OR 1999-2002. dpjerome1@eot.net

JEROME, Joseph (LI) 3956 44th St, Sunnyside NY 11104 **R All SS' Epis Ch Long Island City NY 1997-** B Cazale HT 10/17/1957 s Thelamon Pierre Jerome & Maria Kersulie. BS LIU 1987; MDiv SWTS 1991. D 6/15/1991 P 6/6/1992 Bp Orris George Walker Jr. Int S Gabr's Ch Hollis NY 1996-1997; Int S Bon Epis Ch Lindenhurst NY 1995-1996; Dio Long Island Garden City NY 1991-1993; Cur The Ch Of S Lk and S Matt Brooklyn NY 1991-1993. Alb Inst; Cmnty Bd Two; Kiwanis Intl Sunnyside; Sunnyside ChmbrCom. josephjerome@verizon.net

JERSEY, Jean Staffeld (Vt) RR 1, Box 164, Hartland VT 05048 **P Assoc S Mich's Epis Ch Brattleboro VT 2004-** B Detroit MI 6/17/1931 d John Daniel Staffeld & Muriel Gertrude. Bos 1951; BA Goddard Coll 1984; MDiv EDS 1987. D 6/11/1987 P 12/1/1987 Bp Daniel Lee Swenson. c 4. S Mich's Epis Ch Brattleboro VT 1999-2000; R Chr Ch Bethel VT 1987-1997. "Her Daughters Shall Rise Up: the Wmn Witnessing Cmnty at Lambeth 1988," Off of Wmn in Mssn & Mnstry, 1989. jeansj77@gmail.com

JESSE JR, Henry (Colo) 7787 E Gunnison Pl, Denver CO 80231 B Mill Valley CA 3/21/1924 s Henry Jesse & Maria. BA U CA 1953; MDiv CDSP 1958; M Ed. WA SU 1971. D 9/20/1958 Bp Henry H Shires P 3/1/1959 Bp James Albert Pike. m 8/22/1988 Ann Loomis c 5. Assoc S Jn's Cathd Denver CO 1989-2001; Int Chap Of The H Comf New Orleans LA 1987-1988; Int Chr Ch Bay St Louis MS 1985-1986; Assoc R Chap Of The H Comf New Orleans LA 1983-1985; P-in-c S Andr's Paradis Luling LA 1982-1983; Dioc Coun Dio Olympia Seattle WA 1974-1977; Chair - Coll Wk Dio Olympia Seattle WA 1972-1975; R Chr Ch SEATTLE WA 1971-1979; R S Jas Pullman WA 1969-1971; Secy of the Convoc Dio Nevada Las Vegas NV 1964-1969; Vic S Steph's Epis Ch Reno NV 1962-1964; Assoc Vic S Andr's Ch Saratoga CA 1960-1962. Cmnty of Cross of Nails 1993-2001. Bd Dir Cmnty of the Cross of Nails 2002. holier2005@msn.com

JESSETT, Frederick Edwin (Oly) 21919 Ne 18th St, Sammamish WA 98074 **Dismantelling Racism Trng Team Dio Olympia Seattle WA 2001-** B Wenatchee WA 3/4/1934 s Thomas Edwin Jessett & Louise. BA U of Washington 1956; BD CDSP 1961; MS Applied Sci Montana St U 1968. D 6/7/1961 P 12/11/1961 Bp Conrad Gesner. m 6/25/1960 Kristen Olson c 4. Vic And Overlake Mssnr Gd Samar Epis Ch Sammamish WA 1989-1998; Dep to GC Dio Spokane Spokane WA 1981-1984; Vic S Paul's Ch Cheney WA 1974-1980; Vic S Tim Med Lake WA 1974-1980; Dep to GC Dio So Dakota Sioux Falls SD 1972-1973; Assoc Rosebud Epis Mssn Mssn SD 1969-1973; Chapl to Montana St U Dio Montana Helena MT 1965-1969; Assoc Rosebud Epis Mssn Mssn SD 1963-1965; Vic Trin Epis Ch Mssn SD 1961-1963. Auth, "That's Gr?," *Networking*, Epis Ntwk for Stwdshp, 2010; Auth, "The Prchr's Gift," *Ancient Paths*, Skyler H. Burris, 2007; Auth, "(Three short stories)," *On The Hm Front - So Dakota Stories*, So Dakota Hmnts Coun, 2007; Auth, "Remembering Gr," *Remembering Gr*, FMP, 2006; Auth, "Gr Happens: Who's Rich," *Networking*, Epis Ntwk for Stwdshp, 2003; Auth, "(Three short stories)," *Country Congregations: So Dakota Stories*, So Dakota Humanties Coun, 2002; Auth, "Drummer Loves Dancer," *New Voices III*, Goodfellow Press, 2000; Auth, "Recalling A Long Ago Prank," *Seattle Times*, Seattle Times Inc, 2000; Auth, "Gr Happens monthly column," *Epis Voice, So Dakota Epis ChurchNews and Inland Epis*, Var Dioc Newspapers, 1999; Auth, "The Par Mnstry Of Priests And Deacons," *Liturg Volume 21 #6*, Liturg Conf, 1976; Co-Auth w Kristen O. Jess, "12 Rules For Marital Fighting," *12 Rules for Marital Fighting*, FMP, 1974; Auth, "Chanukah," *Simple Gifts Volume 2*, Liturg Conf, 1974; Auth, "Chanukah," *Liturg Volume 17 #8*, Liturg Conf, 1972; Co-Auth w Kristen O. Jess, "Sioux Farming Today," *The Indn Hist*, The Amer Indn Hist Soc, 1970. ACLU 2002; Amnesty Intl 1981; Cler Assn Of The Dio Olympia 1991; Fllshp Of Merry Christians 1996; Kiwanis Intl 1993; Museum of Hist and Industry 2000; Pacific NW Writers Assn 1998; The Interfaith Allnce 2000. jessett@earthlink.net

JESSUP, Dorothy Margaret Paul (Pa) 278 Friendship Dr, Paoli PA 19301 B Philadelphia PA 9/11/1929 d Samuel Allen Paul & Dorothy Mildred. Luth TS 1987. D 6/20/1987 Bp Allen Lyman Bartlett Jr. c 3. D Ch Of The Gd Samar Paoli PA 1987-1993. Bd Trst Dss Ret Fund Soc. dorothypj@verizon.net

JESSUP, Elaine Anderson (SeFla) 464 NE 16th St, Miami FL 33132 **D Trin Cathd Miami FL 2008-** B Miami FL 8/12/1945 d Perry Anderson & Ethelyn. BS Indiana U 1982; MS Nova SE U 1989; EdS Nova SE U 1994. D 12/22/2007 Bp Leopold Frade. c 4. jessupe@bellsouth.net

JETT, Charles D (Spok) 107 Sea Lavender Ln, Summerville SC 29483 **S Steph's Epis Ch Spokane WA 1999-** B Milledgeville GA 11/17/1938 s William Stark Jett & Estelle Cotton. Coll of Charleston; BA U of So Carolina 1961; BA Sch for Deacons 1994. D 6/3/1995 Bp William Edwin Swing. m 8/15/1959 Margaret Jane Adams c 2. D S Steph's Epis Ch Charleston SC 1997-1999; D Emm Ch Kellogg ID 1996-1999; D H Trin Epis Ch Wallace ID 1996-1999; D S Mich And All Ang Concord CA 1995-1996. ceedeej@gmail.com

JEULAND, Eric Vincent (Ct) 25 Church St, Shelton CT 06484 B Chicago IL 4/1/1981 s Abel Pierre Jeuland & Maretta K. BA U Chi 2003; Angl Dplma Berk 2008; MDiv Yale DS 2008. D 6/12/2010 Bp Ian Theodore Douglas P 6/11/2011 Bp James Elliot Curry. m 6/17/2006 Jane Catherine Eppley. Dio Connecticut Hartford CT 2010-2011; S Paul's Epis Ch Shelton CT 2010. ERIC.JEULAND@GMAIL.COM

JEULAND, Jane Catherine Eppley (Ct) 300 Main St, Wethersfield CT 06109 B New York NY 12/10/1979 d Richard Lee Eppley & Carole Catherine. Bachelor of Liberal Arts Harv 2003; MDiv Ya Berk 2009. D 6/12/2010 P 12/18/2010 Bp Ian Theodore Douglas. m 6/17/2006 Eric Vincent Jeuland. Trin Ch Wethersfield CT 2010-2011. jane.jeuland@gmail.com

JEVNE, Lucretia Ann (NCal) 120 Lorraine Ct, Vacaville CA 95688 **P-in-c S Lk's Mssn Calistoga CA 2007-; Pres, Bd Epis Cmnty Serv Dio Nthrn California Sacramento CA 2006-; Pres, Bd Epis Cmnty Serv Dio Nthrn California Sacramento CA 2006-** B Norwalk CT 8/17/1946 d Henry Marcus Jevne & Helen Henderson. BA Wm Smith 1968; MDiv CDSP 1996. D 8/24/1996 Bp Jeffery William Rowthorn P 6/20/1997 Bp Robert Louis Ladehoff. m 11/20/1996 Walter E Phelps. Trin Ch Sonoma CA 2007; Int R Trin Ch Sonoma CA 2005-2007; Int S Clem's Ch Rancho Cordova CA 2004-2005; Int Gr Epis Ch Fairfield CA 2003-2004; Asst Epis Ch Of The Epiph Vacaville CA 2000-2002; S Alb's Epis Ch Tillamook OR 1996-1999. Assoc Of The Ord Of S Lk 2002; Cler Assn Of Nthrn California 2001-2004; Oregon Cler Assosciation 1997-1998. lajevne@comcast.net

JEW, Cynthia Lynne (Los) 24901 Orchard Village Rd, Santa Clarita CA 91355 **Trin Par Fillmore CA 2011-** B Denver CO 5/30/1960 d James Jew & Dorie. MA U CO 1986; PhD U Denv 1991. D 7/9/2010 P 2/12/2011 Bp Joseph Jon Bruno. c 2. S Steph's Epis Ch Santa Clarita CA 2010-2011. cjew@att.net

JEWELL, E(arle) Barton (WMo) 8100 Wornall Road #21, Kansas City KS 64114 B Chicago IL 1/22/1924 s Earle B Jewell & Elise. BS NWU 1949. D 9/15/1963 Bp Edward Randolph Welles II. m 6/30/1950 Elizabeth Mumford c 2.

JEWELL, Kenneth Arthur (Nev) 777 Sage St., Elko NV 89801 **Com on Ord and Licensing Dio Nevada Las Vegas NV 2011-; Soc Justice and Mercy Com Dio Nevada Las Vegas NV 2011-; Vocational D S Paul's Epis Ch Elko NV 2009-** B Flint MI 2/12/1950 s Kenneth Cameron Jewell & Elizabeth Jeanne. BS U of Wisconsin 1973. D 7/3/2009 Bp Dan Thomas Edwards. m 12/31/2005 Donna Selleck c 3. k9vx@arrl.net

JEWISS, Anthony Harrison (Los) 1290 Kent Street, Brooklyn NY 11222 B Dorking UK 11/22/1939 s Stanley James Frederick Jewiss & Patricia Dorothy. UE Sacr Heart Coll Auckland Nz 1957; ETSBH 1990; BA Pacific Wstrn U Los Angeles 1992; MDiv VTS 1992. D 6/13/1992 Bp Chester Lovelle Talton P 1/9/1993 Bp Frederick Houk Borsch. Epis Ch Cntr New York NY 1999-2008; Epis Ch Cntr New York NY 1999; Chapl To Bp Of Los Dio Los Angeles Los Angeles CA 1992-1999. tonyjewiss@gmail.com

JEWSON, Alfred Joseph (WMo) 2846 E Wildwood Rd, Springfield MO 65804 **Mem of COM Dio W Missouri Kansas City MO 2008-** B Saint Louis MO 12/22/1943 s Lillian Jane. BA Cardinal Glennon Coll 1965; Kenrick-Glennon Sem 1967; MA S Louis U DS S Louis MO 1970. Rec from Roman Catholic 12/3/1994 Bp John Clark Buchanan. m 3/25/1988 Dayna Geddes c 2. Pres, Stndg Com Dio W Missouri Kansas City MO 2004-2008; R Chr Ch Warrensburg MO 2001-2010; Dn, Sthrn Dnry Dio W Missouri Kansas City MO 2000-2001; Vic Ch Of The Gd Shpd Springfield MO 1998-2001; Assoc R S Andr's Ch Kansas City MO 1996-1998. padreal@charter.net

JEWSON, Dayna (WMo) 303 Lawson Dr, Warrensburg MO 64093 **D All SS Epis Ch Kansas City MO 2012-** B Los Angeles CA 5/14/1953 d Roderic Day Geddes & Nancy Alice. RN S Lk's Hosp Sch of Nrsng Webster U 1983; W Missouri Sch for Mnstry 2003. D 2/7/2004 Bp Barry Robert Howe. m 3/25/1988 Alfred Joseph Jewson c 2. D Chr Ch Warrensburg MO 2004-2010. NAAD 2004. daynaccf@charter.net

JILLARD, Christina Liggitt (Oly) St. Margaret's Episcopal Church, 4228 Factoria Blvd SE, Bellevue WA 98006 **R S Marg's Epis Ch Bellevue WA 2008-** B Grove City PA 2/17/1952 d Oliver Eugene Liggitt & Mary Ellen. BA Grove City Coll 1974; MA Ohio U 1976; MLS U Pgh 1977; MDiv GTS 2001. D 6/8/2001 P 12/8/2001 Bp Michael Whittington Creighton. m 6/2/1989 William Richard Jillard c 2. R S Lk's Epis Ch Altoona PA 2001-2008. cjillard@gmail.com

JIM, Rosella A (NAM) Po Box 5854, Farmington NM 87499 **All SS Farmington NM 2005-; San Juan Mssn Farmington NM 2005-** B Farmington NM 8/10/1951 d Allen King John & Elizabeth Grace. AA San Juan Coll 1980; San Juan Coll 1981. D 6/12/2005 Bp Mark Lawrence Mac Donald P 12/13/2005 Bp Rustin Ray Kimsey. m 7/1/1971 Tommy Jim c 4. Navajoland Area Mssn Farmington NM 1981-2005. hooghan@advantas.net

JIMENEZ, Darla Sue (NwT) 908 Sartain Dr, Andrews TX 79714 B Pontiac MI 9/11/1960 d Carl Wayne Wright & Treva Gerildine. D 12/3/2005 P 7/1/2006 Bp C(harles) Wallis Ohl. m 3/23/1996 Jose Jimenez. darla_jimenez@palmertank.net

JIMENEZ, Juan (SeFla) 311 W South St, Anaheim CA 92805 B Camaguey CU 4/19/1945 s Juan A F F Jimenez & Mirta Rafaela. BA K SU 1970; MDiv Epis TS of The SW 1988. D 3/14/1987 Bp James Daniel Warner P 3/1/1988 Bp Anselmo Carral-Solar. m 11/20/1983 Janice Kay Hanway c 2. R Iglesia Epis De Todos Los Santos Miami FL 1997-2001; S Matt's Cathd Dallas TX 1990-1997; Vic San Francisco De Asisi Austin TX 1988-1990. padrejuan@hotmail.com

JIMENEZ-IRIZARRY, Edwin (Ct) Urb. El Vedado, Calle 12 de Octubre #428-A, San Juan PR 00918 B 1/1/1946 s Heriberto Jimenez-Pantoja & Gladys. BA U Inter-Americana 1968; MDiv ETSC 1971; MS Psychol Inst PR 1976. Trans from Province IX 5/11/1981 Bp Clarence Nicholas Coleridge. m 2/16/1980 Celida Jimenez c 4.

JIMENEZ-MESENBRING, Maria Jesus (Oly) 2020 E. Terrace St., Seattle WA 98122 **Spanish Tchr, Dioc TS Dio Olympia Seattle WA 2008-; Spanish Tchr, Dioc TS Dio Olympia Seattle WA 2008-** B Burgos Castilla Spain 11/24/1954 d Rafael Jimenez & Carmen. BA U of Madrid; MDiv NYTS 1992. D 2/20/1999 Bp Calvin Onderdonk Schofield Jr. m 6/1/1991 David Mesenbring c 2. D S Steph's Ch Coconut Grove Coconut Grove FL 2000-2004. mariafromspain@aol.com

JINETE, Alvaro E (Chi) 3241 Calwagner St, Franklin Park IL 60131 B Manati CO 1/21/1951 s Alfredo Jinete & Ramona. MA McCormick TS 1987. Rec from Roman Catholic 4/1/1987 as Deacon Bp James Winchester Montgomery. m 2/23/1985 Erlina Ortega c 2. Dio Chicago Chicago IL 1989-1999; San Pedro Mssn Maywood IL 1987-2006.

JIZMAGIAN, Mary Gibson (Cal) 2570 Chestnut St, San Francisco CA 94123 B Kingston Jamaica West Indies 8/12/1949 d James Davis Gibson & Myrtis Allene. BA Austin Coll 1970; MDiv CDSP 1985. D 6/8/1985 P 6/1/1986 Bp William Edwin Swing. m 1/15/1983 George S Jizmagian c 2. Asst The Epis Ch Of S Mary The Vrgn San Francisco CA 1986; S Jas Epis Ch San Francisco CA 1985-1987. MaryJizmagian@gmail.com

JOBES, Amy Louise Carle (WTenn) 2 Beverly Commons Dr, Beverly MA 01915 **Asst (Ret.) Vol S Ptr's Ch Beverly MA 2004-** B Birmingham AL 12/15/1936 d Howard Holt Carle & Louise. BA St. Jn's Coll Annapolis MD 1959; MS U of Memphis 1984; STUSo 1992. D 11/19/1995 P 6/1/1996 Bp Larry Earl Maze. m 6/3/1961 James W Jobes Jr c 2. Ch Of The H Comm Memphis TN 2001-2002; Mssnr Chapl S Mary's Epis Ch Monticello AR 2000-2002; Dioc Mssnr S Paul's Ch McGehee AR 2000-2002; Mssnr Chapl Ch Of The Gd Shpd Little Rock AR 2000-2001; Dioc Mssnr S Lk's Epis Ch No Little Rock AR 1998-2000; Cur S Lk's Epis Ch No Little Rock AR 1996-1997; Ch Of The H Cross W Memphis AR 1996. ajobes@aristotle.net

JODKO, Juliusz Siegmond (Ct) 954 Lake Ave, Greenwich CT 06831 B Heerlen Netherlands 3/23/1951 s Piotr Jodko & Genevieve Konieczka. BA Leh 1973; MBA U of Scranton 1990; MDiv The GTS 2010. D 6/11/2011 Bp Laura Ahrens. m 6/15/1974 Anne Frost Anne Frost Wiegand c 2. S Barn Epis Ch Greenwich CT 2011. julesjodko@gmail.com

JOFFRION, A(lban) Emile (Ala) 433 Mcclung Ave Se, Huntsville AL 35801 B Laurel MS 3/30/1923 s Felix Alzide Joffrion & Adele Elise. BA Tul 1948; MDiv STUSo 1951; MS Alabama A&M U 1975; U of Notre Dame 1975. D 4/4/1951 P 10/14/1951 Bp Duncan Montgomery Gray. m 8/30/1947 Martha S Sheffey c 5. Dep to GC Dio Alabama Birmingham AL 1967-1982; R Ch Of The Nativ Epis Huntsville AL 1957-1986; P-in-c S Ptr's Ch Oxford MS 1954-1957; P-in-c Ch Of The Ascen Brooksville MS 1951-1954; P-in-c Ch Of The Resurr Starkville MS 1951-1954; P-in-c Epis Ch Of The Incarn W Point MS 1951-1954. Outstanding Alum, S Lk's TS Sewanee TN 1997. aeandmsjoff@comcast.net

JOFFRION JR, Felix Hughes (Ala) 1180 11th Ave S, Birmingham AL 35205 **Pstr Counslr Dio Alabama Birmingham AL 1967-** B Vicksburg MS 10/17/1938 s Felix Joffrion & Kathleen Mary. BA U of Alabama 1961; MDiv VTS 1967; ThM Duke 1971; ThD Candler TS Emory U 1982. D 6/10/1967 P 5/1/1968 Bp George Mosley Murray. m 7/13/1968 Isabelle Constable c 2. Cur All SS Epis Ch Birmingham AL 1969-1971; Asst S Mk's Ch Washington DC 1968-1969. Diplomate AAPC; Lic Profsnl Counslr. fjoffrion@bham.rr.com

JOHANNS, Karen (Mich) 842 Golf Dr Apt 302, Pontiac MI 48341 **COM Dio Michigan Detroit MI 2009-; R All SS Epis Ch Pontiac MI 2008-** B Jersey City NJ 3/22/1959 d Henry Johanns & Blanche. BA Mt Holyoke Coll 2003; MDiv CDSP 2006. D 6/3/2006 Bp William Edwin Swing P 1/26/2007 Bp Jerry Alban Lamb. Assoc Trin Epis Ch Reno NV 2006-2008. karen_johanns@comcast.net

JOHANNSEN, Carole (NY) 8 Pine Road, Bedford Hills NY 10507 B New York NY 4/11/1942 d Christian Fredrick Jepsen & Mary Ann. AA Dn Coll 1961; BA Wstrn Connecticut St U 1983; MDiv Yale DS 1986. Rec from Roman Catholic 5/1/1986 Bp Clarence Nicholas Coleridge. c 2. R S Lk's Ch Katonah NY 1998-2001; Int Trin Epis Ch Hartford CT 1997-1998; Prince Of Peace Luth Ch Brookfield CT 1996-1997; Int S Ptr's Epis Ch Monroe CT 1995-1996; S Matt's Epis Ch Wilton CT 1994; Trin Ch Newtown CT 1993; Exam Chap Dio Connecticut Hartford CT 1992-1997; Asst for CE Chr And H Trin Ch Westport CT 1991-1993; Asst S S Barn Epis Ch Greenwich CT 1990-1991. Ord of S Helena (Assoc) 1991. carolejo@optonline.net

JOHANNSON, Johanna-Karen (NY) 20 Cumming St, New York NY 10034 B Augusta ME 4/13/1950 d Albert Chronquist Johnson & Millicent Geneva. BS SUNY 1984; MDiv GTS 1987. D 6/13/1987 Bp Paul Moore Jr P 1/10/1988 Bp Alexander Doig Stewart. H Trin Epis Ch Inwood New York NY 1997-2011; Vic H Trin Epis Ch Inwood New York NY 1991-1996; The Ch Of The Epiph New York NY 1987-1990. Wmn Helping Wmn Soroptomists's Intl 2002; Cmnty Action Hero Awd Upper Manhattan Fresh Yth Initiatives 2000. abishag51@yahoo.com

JOHANSEN, Paul Charles (SwFla) 504 3rd St Nw, New Philadelphia OH 44663 **Dn Dio Ohio Cleveland OH 2007-; P-in-c Trin Ch New Philadelphia OH 2001-** B Cambridge MA 10/11/1933 s Martin Henry Johansen & Beth Landon. BEd U of Miami 1961; STB Ya Berk 1964; Command and Gnrl Stff Coll 1979; US Army Chapl Cntr and Sch 1989. D 6/24/1964 Bp William Loftin Hargrave P 12/28/1964 Bp James Loughlin Duncan. m 9/7/1991 Barbara J Montgomery c 3. P-in-c S Ptr's Ch Gallipolis OH 1998-2001; R S Steph's Ch New Port Richey FL 1985-1995; R S Mary's Ch Dade City FL 1982-1985; Dioc Coun Dio SW Florida Sarasota FL 1975-1980; R S Bede's Ch St Petersburg FL 1969-1982; Vic S Cathr's Ch Temple Terrace FL 1966-1969; Chapl Dio Florida Jacksonville FL 1965-1991; Cur Cathd Ch Of S Ptr St Petersburg FL 1964-1966. Auth, "The Gift of Ought to Be," *Tampa Bay mag*, 1966. p.johansen@roadrunner.com

JOHANSON, Norman Lee (Neb) 116 S Sunset Pl, Monrovia CA 91016 B Colusa CA 3/26/1944 s Earl Henry Johanson & Anna Belle. D 11/8/1985 Bp James Daniel Warner. m 7/15/1967 Patricia Carol Neville c 3.

JOHANSSEN, John Ralston (SO) 9429 Lighthouse Cut, Thornville OH 43076 B Lafayette IN 3/21/1946 s John Jacob Johanssen & Ruth Margaret. BS OH SU 1970; MA OH SU 1971; JD U of Toledo 1975; MDiv VTS 1990. D 6/9/1990 P 2/23/1991 Bp James Russell Moodey. m 5/12/1984 Pamela Knowlton c 2. Cn Dio Sthrn Ohio Cincinnati OH 2008-2011; R S Alb's Epis Ch Of Bexley Columbus OH 2004-2008; Dio Colorado Denver CO 2001-2003; R Gd Shpd Epis Ch Centennial CO 1996-2003; Ecum Cmsn Dio Eau Claire Eau Claire WI 1991-1996; R Gr Epis Ch Menomonie WI 1991-1996; Asst S Paul's Ch Akron OH 1990-1991. john.johanssen@gmail.com

JOHN, James Howard (Kan) 7603 E Morris St, Wichita KS 67207 B Chanute KS 3/23/1944 s James Howard John & Doris Loneta. BBA Wichita St U 1973. D 4/30/1982 Bp Richard Frank Grein. m 4/14/1966 Marilyn Kay Miller c 2. jimjohn@cox.net

JOHN, Rene R (NJ) 16 Fanning Way, Pennington NJ 08534 **Stndg Com Dio New Jersey Trenton NJ 2008-; Trin Cathd Trenton NJ 2007-** B San Fernando TT 6/17/1960 s George John & Phyllis Pearl. STM GTS; LTh Codrington Coll 1984. Trans from Church in the Province Of The West Indies 1/1/1991 Bp Orris George Walker Jr. m 6/16/1984 Andrea Sandiford c 3. R Ch Of S Thos Brooklyn NY 1994-2006; Assoc R S Paul's Ch Brooklyn NY 1990-1994; S Paul's Ch-In-The-Vill Brooklyn NY 1990-1994. Bro of S Andr 1997. Cler Renwl Sabbatical Lily Endwmt 2005; Pstr of the Year CWU 1999. reneroryjohnz@verizon.net

JOHNS, Ernest William (SwFla) 20024 Behan Ct, Port Charlotte FL 33952 B Sault Saint Marie MI 11/29/1932 s Ernest Wellington Johns & Jean Gladys. BA Wag 1953; STM Drew U 1956, GTS 1960; Coll of Preachers 1966; Coll of Preachers 1971; Coll of Preachers 1987. D 1/15/1960 P 10/12/1960 Bp Charles Francis Boynton. m 6/24/1956 Beverly Ireland c 2. S Edm's Epis Ch Arcadia FL 1993-1995; Evang Com Dio SW Virginia Roanoke VA 1989-1993; R S Steph's Epis Ch Forest VA 1989-1993; BEC Dio Virginia Richmond VA 1987-1989; Bd Sch Chr Stds Dio Cntrl Pennsylvania Harrisburg PA 1983-1987; R The Memi Ch Of The Prince Of Peace Gettysburg PA 1982-1989; COM Dio W Missouri Kansas City MO 1980-1982; R S Jas' Ch Springfield MO 1979-1982; Trst Cathd Of St Jn The Div New York NY 1971-1976; Chr Ch Of Ramapo Suffern NY 1968-1979; Dioc Coun Dio New York New York City NY 1968-1971; R S Andr's Ch Brewster NY 1961-1968. Auth, *Intro to the Epis Ch: Pstr Perspective*. Int Minstry Ntwk 1997-2004. BBJRT@MSN.COM

JOHNS, Leila Margaret (NMich) 416 S 28th St, Escanaba MI 49829 **D S Steph's Ch Escanaba MI 1993-** B Sale VIC AU 7/22/1919 d Henry William Schroeder & Mary Lucy. Cert Melbourne Tchr's Coll 1939. D 2/21/1993 Bp Thomas Kreider Ray. m 7/6/1944 Benjamin Hartley Johns.

JOHNS III, Norman S (Oly) 5787 Lenea Dr Nw, Bremerton WA 98312 B Philadelphia PA 12/24/1944 s Norman S Johns & Marianne. BA U of Maryland 1974; MDiv GTS 1977. D 5/13/1978 Bp William Foreman Creighton P 5/13/1978 Bp John Thomas Walker. m 1/17/1964 Eileen Evelyn Brenner c 2. Dio Olympia Seattle WA 2006; Epis Ch Of The Trsfg Mesa AZ 2002-2006; Vic S Jos And S Jn Ch Steilacoom WA 1998-2006; S Dav Emm Epis Ch Shoreline WA 1993-1994; S Paul's Ch Seattle WA 1992-1993; St Steph's Epis Ch Oak Harbor WA 1991-1992; St Bede Epis Ch Port Orchard WA 1988-1989; S Paul's Epis Ch Bremerton WA 1981-1987; The Epis Ch-King Geo Co King Geo VA 1980-1981; Asst R Ch Of The H Comf Vienna VA 1977-1980. Auth, "Lord Of Morning," *Lord Of Light*. Ord Of S Lk. johns.norman1@gmail.com

JOHNS, Richard Gray (Los) 1199 Marinaside Crescent, Apt. 1701, Vancouver BC V6Z 2Y2 Canada B Seattle WA 6/19/1928 s Ernest Haskell Johns & Mary Opal. BA Whitman Coll 1949; PhD U CA 1952; MDiv CDSP 1955. D 6/12/1955 P 12/17/1955 Bp Karl M Block. c 4. Cmnty Of The Sis Of The Ch 1991-1995; R Gr Ch S Helena CA 1956-1958; Vic S Barth's Epis Ch Livermore CA 1955-1956. Auth, *The Amer's: How Many Worlds?*. rgjohns@shaw.ca

JOHNSON, Alston Boyd (Miss) 140 Devereaux Dr, Madison MS 39110 **The Chap Of The Cross Madison MS 2005-** B Memphis TN 8/8/1968 s Cleveland Eric Johnson & Fay Wade. BA U of Vermont 1991; MDiv STUSo 1998. D 5/27/1998 P 1/1/1999 Bp Alfred Clark Marble Jr. m 7/17/2003 Elizabeth Irwin Jabaley c 2. S Andr's Cathd Jackson MS 2003-2005; Calv Epis Ch Cleveland MS 2002-2003; Cur Ch Of The Nativ Greenwood MS 1999-2002. alstonbj@bellsouth.net

J

JOHNSON JR, Alvin Carl (Chi) 212 Biltmore Dr, N Barrington IL 60010 B Chicago IL 9/26/1953 s Alvin Carl Johnson & Eileen Myrtle. BS U of Tulsa 1975; MDiv SWTS 1979; DMin SWTS 1998. D 6/9/1979 Bp Quintin Ebenezer Primo Jr P 12/1/1979 Bp James Winchester Montgomery. m 1/3/1976 Victoria Arnold c 3. R S Mich's Ch Barrington IL 1990-2010; Ch Of The Incarn Bloomingdale IL 1984-1990; Dio Chicago Chicago IL 1981-1984; Cur S Dav's Ch Glenview IL 1979-1981. Auth, *Ldrshp mag*. ajohnson9@aol.com

JOHNSON, Andrew (Roch) 1957 Five Mile Line Rd., Penfield NY 14526 B Rochester NY 6/19/1938 s Byron Arthur Johnson & Charlotte Adeline. BA U Roch 1962; D Formation Prog Bexley Inst 2008. D 5/2/2009 Bp Prince Grenville Singh. m 11/2/1984 Linda D Linda Cheryl Daggs c 4. lindandy@rochester.rr.com

JOHNSON, Ann Elizabeth Simmons (Az) PO Box 40, 13803 North Watts Lane, Fort Thomas AZ 85536 **D All SS Epis Ch Safford AZ 2002-** B Decatur GA 11/29/1939 d Jesse Donald Simmons & Sara Rowena. BS Auburn U 1962; Florida St U 1965; MA Cntrl Michigan U 1984. D 10/5/2002 Bp Robert Reed Shahan. m 8/25/1962 James Donaldson Johnson c 2. Amer Soc For Clincl Laboratory Scientists 1976. sable@aznex.net

JOHNSON, Ann L (WVa) 1105 Quarrier St, Charleston WV 25301 **Assoc S Jn's Epis Ch Charleston WV 2009-** B Cambridge MA 11/24/1963 BS U of Rhode Island. D 12/22/2001 Bp Wendell Nathaniel Gibbs Jr P 3/21/2003 Bp Chilton Abbie Richardson Knudsen. c 3. R S Phil's Ch Wiscasset ME 2003-2009. alovejoy@suddenlink.net

JOHNSON, Ann Ruth (Az) 701 North Apollo Way, Flagstaff AZ 86001 **Vic Dio Arizona Phoenix AZ 2006-; Vic S Jn's Ch Williams AZ 2006-** B Corsicana TX 3/7/1942 d James R Ruth & Eliza H. BS U of Texas 1965; MA Texas A&M U 1979; Angl TS 1996; CTh Epis TS of The SW 2006. D 7/29/2006 P 2/3/2007 Bp Kirk Stevan Smith. c 3. anajohn@localnet.com

JOHNSON, Arthur Everitt (Miss) 1052 Deer Dr, Bay Saint Louis MS 39520 B San Antonio TX 11/25/1943 s Woodrow Andrew Johnson & Hattie Bee. BS Trin U San Antonio TX 1966; MDiv STUSo 1972; DMin STUSo 1989. D 6/11/1972 Bp Harold Cornelius Gosnell P 12/21/1972 Bp Richard Earl Dicus. m 6/1/1985 Gail H Lee c 2. Chr Ch Bay St Louis MS 1985-2003; S Greg The Great Athens GA 1981-1985; Emm Epis Ch Athens GA 1975-1981; Asst The Ch Of The Gd Shpd Augusta GA 1973-1975. Auth, "Why Bother w Adv," *Angl Dig*, Adv, 1992; Auth, "January Eagerness (poem)," Journ of Sch Theol, 1981; Auth, "Greening of Dr Mart Luther & the Conversion of Chas A Reich," Journ of Sch Theol, 1972. stedefaestii@aol.com

JOHNSON, Barbara Carlton (FdL) 730 Holden Dr, Ashtabula OH 44004 B Rockford IL 6/1/1965 d Richard Carlton & Roma Lucille. BA Marq 1987; MDiv SWTS 1994. D 5/7/1994 P 11/20/1994 Bp Roger John White. m 6/21/1986 Eric Allen Johnson c 2. R S Ptr's Ch Ashtabula OH 2002-2007; R S Ptr's Epis Ch Sheboygan Falls WI 1997-2001; Asst Trin Ch Toledo OH 1994-1996. motherbj@alltel.net

JOHNSON, Brian David (Los) 1000 Hancock Ave Apt 6, West Hollywood CA 90069 B Albany NY 6/4/1960 s Robert Johnson & Mary. RN Memi Sch Nrsng 1980; BS Emml 1984; MA/PhD California Sch of Profsnl Psychol 1989; MDiv CDSP 1992. D 6/27/1992 P 12/20/1992 Bp Gethin Benwil Hughes. Non-stipendiary P Dio Los Angeles Los Angeles CA 2003-2004; Assoc R S Thos The Apos Hollywood Los Angeles CA 2002-2003; P-in-c S Mart's Epis Ch Compton CA 1997-2000; P H Faith Par Inglewood CA 1995-1996; P S Steph's Mssn Menifee CA 1993-1994; D Gr Cathd San Francisco CA 1992-1993. bjohn87242@aol.com

JOHNSON, Broaddus (NY) 2336 Meadow Rdg, Redding CT 06896 **D S Matt's Ch Bedford NY 1992-** B Springfield MA 10/26/1922 s Andrew B Johnson & Mildred Wiley. BA Ya 1948. D 5/30/1992 Bp Richard Frank Grein. m 8/20/1949 Kate deForest Chamberlin c 3.

JOHNSON, Candine Elizabeth (Va) PO Box 158, Tappahannock VA 22560 **Vauters Ch Champlain VA 2011-; S Marg's Sch Tappahannock VA 2004-** B Brooklyn NY 7/26/1953 BS CUNY 1976; Med U of Virginia 1978; PhD U of Virginia 1983; MDiv GTS 2004. D 6/26/2004 P 1/18/2005 Bp Peter James Lee. cjohnson@sms.org

JOHNSON, Charles Lenwood (Va) Po Box 1074, Mathews VA 23109 B Four Oaks NC 7/30/1937 s Ira B Johnson & Cartha Ellen. BA Roa 1962; Cert VTS 1965; Cert VTS 1980. D 6/12/1965 P 6/18/1966 Bp Robert Fisher Gibson Jr. m 7/29/1961 Virginia S Smith c 2. Int All SS Ch Richmond VA 2000-2001; Dioc Mssy Soc Dio Virginia Richmond VA 1999-2008; Stndg Com Dio Virginia Richmond VA 1995-1998; R Kingston Par Epis Ch Mathews VA 1993-1999; R Chr Ch Gardiner ME 1989-1993; Asst to Bp for Mnstry & Cong Dvlpmt Dio Virginia Richmond VA 1980-1989; Asst to Bp for Mnstry & Cong Dvlpmt Dio Virginia Richmond VA 1980-1989; R S Barn Epis Ch Richmond VA 1976-1980; Asst S Matt's Ch Richmond VA 1970-1976; R S Paul's Ch Haymarket VA 1967-1970; Asst, & P-in-c S Thos' Ch Richmond VA 1965-1967. EvangES 1989. gincha@verizon.net

JOHNSON, Christopher Allen (Colo) 45 Woodland Ave, Glen Ridge NJ 07028 **Epis Ch Cntr New York NY 2008-** B Maracaibo VE 5/11/1958 s Robert Morris Johnson & Cynthia Ann. AS Onondaga Cmnty Coll 1978; BS Franciscan U of Steubenville 1980; MDiv Epis TS of The SW 2000. D 6/10/2000 P 12/23/2000 Bp William Jerry Winterrowd. m 5/8/1980 Debra E Eyler c 3. Vic Our Merc Sav Epis Ch Denver CO 2002-2008; Cur Ch Of S Jn Chrys Golden CO 2000-2001. cjohnson@episcopalchurch.org

JOHNSON, Craig (Chi) 877d Kilkenny Dr, Wheaton IL 60187 B Wheaton IL 5/24/1943 s George Rupert Johnson & Chana Frances. BA Shimer Coll 1965; BD Nash 1968. D 6/15/1968 Bp James Winchester Montgomery P 12/21/1968 Bp Gerald Francis Burrill. S Helena's Ch Willowbrook IL 1972-1982; Cur S Mary's Ch Pk Ridge IL 1968-2000. cjohnson@mortonarb.org

JOHNSON, David (NY) 108 Central Ave, Sea Cliff NY 11579 B New York NY 4/20/1926 s John H Johnson & Jessie H. BA Hav 1946; MA Col 1947; LLB Col 1951. D 6/15/1957 P 12/1/1957 Bp Benjamin M Washburn. R S Mart's Ch New York NY 1957-1998.

JOHNSON, David (NMich) 1021 E E St, Iron Mountain MI 49801 B 2/13/1942 D 8/13/2003 P 2/29/2004 Bp James Arthur Kelsey. m 8/15/1964 Mary Richardson c 1.

JOHNSON, David Allen (Va) 1700 Ashwood Blvd, Charlottesville VA 22911 **Assoc Chr Epis Ch Charlottesville VA 2007-** B Newport RI 12/7/1968 s Darold L Johnson & Judy C. BA Oral Roberts U 1991; MDiv Gordon-Conwell TS 2001; STM Nash 2002; DMin TESM 2010. D 9/12/2001 Bp Edward Lloyd Salmon Jr. m 7/21/1990 Stephanie J Mort c 5. Vic Ch Of The Cross Charlottesville VA 2003-2007; Asst S Andr's Ch Mt Pleasant SC 2001-2003; Yth Dir Dio Wyoming Casper WY 1995-1996. davejohnson68@embarqmail.com

JOHNSON, David Hemeter (Miss) 901 Gillespie St, Jackson MS 39202 **Dio Mississippi Jackson MS 2003-; Cn to the Ordnry Dio Mississippi Jackson MS 2001-** B Columbia MS 1/23/1952 s Wilton Jerome Johnson & Frances Leighton. BA U of Mississippi 1975; MDiv STUSo 1987. D 5/30/1987 P 12/3/1987 Bp Duncan Montgomery Gray Jr. m 7/13/1974 Nora Knight c 2. R Ch Of The Resurr Starkville MS 1993-2001; Assoc R S Geo's Ch Nashville TN 1992-1993; Vic S Patricks Epis Ch Long Bch MS 1987-1992; Cur Trin Ch Epis Pass Chr MS 1987-1990. Fell Coll of Preachers 1999. canonjohnson@gmail.com

JOHNSON, Dennis Lee (Wyo) Po Box 3485, Jackson WY 83001 B Chula Vista CA 11/9/1946 s Herbert Hadley Johnson & Elsie Denise. AA Palomar Coll. D 2/3/2000 Bp Bruce Edward Caldwell. m Vicki Jaye Smith c 2. COM Dio Wyoming Casper WY 1996-2006. denjohn1@wyoming.com

JOHNSON, Deon K. (Mich) 200 W Saint Paul St, Brighton MI 48116 **R S Paul's Epis Ch Brighton MI 2006-** B Bridgetown Barbados 11/8/1977 s Henderson Wayne Brathwaite & Verna. B.A. Case Wstrn Reserve U 2000; B.A. Case Wstrn Reserve U 2000; M.Div GTS 2003. D 6/15/2003 Bp J Clark Grew II. Assoc Chr Ch Shaker Heights OH 2003-2006. deonjohnson@gmail.com

JOHNSON, Diana Patricia (U) 1854 Kensington Avenue, Salt Lake City UT 84108 B Syracuse NY 1/16/1943 d William R Maher & Lucille M. BS Utah St U 1975; MDiv CDSP 1994. D 4/30/1994 P 12/8/1994 Bp Stewart Clark Zabriskie. m 4/1/1978 Gerald T Johnson c 1. Cn Pstr Cathd Ch Of S Mk Salt Lake City UT 2003-2009; R S Steph's Ch W Vlly City UT 2000-2003; Int Ch Of The Gd Shpd Ogden UT 1998-2000; Int Ch Of The Gd Shpd Rocky Mt NC 1998; Int S Mich's Ch Raleigh NC 1998; Int S Paul's Ch Louisburg NC 1996-1997; Chapl Duke Epis Cntr Durham NC 1996; Int Gr Ch Whiteville NC 1995-1996; Int S Mths Ch Louisburg NC 1995-1996. revdianaj@msn.com

JOHNSON, Donald Keith (Dal) 2026 Cherrywood Ln, Denton TX 76209 **R S Barn Epis Ch Denton TX 1995-** B Greenville TX 7/7/1957 s Cecil Augusta Johnson & Mary Louise. BS Texas A&M U 1978; MS Texas A&M U 1984; MDiv TS 1988. D 6/18/1988 P 6/18/1989 Bp Donis Dean Patterson. m 4/20/1991 Emanda R Richardson. Vic Ch Of The Epiph Commerce TX 1991-1995; Vic S Phil's Epis Ch Sulphur Sprg TX 1991-1995; Trst The TS at The U So Sewanee TN 1991-1994; Vic All SS Ch Atlanta TX 1990-1991; Cur S Matt's Cathd Dallas TX 1988-1990. rector.stbarn@verizon.net

✠ JOHNSON, Rt Rev Don Edward (WTenn) 692 Poplar Ave, Memphis TN 38105 **Bp of W Tennessee Dio W Tennessee Memphis TN 2001-** B Nashville TN 1/23/1949 s Eldridge Ewing Johnson & Fonda Leigh. BA Van 1972; MDiv SWTS 1976; DMin Grad Theol Un 1988. D 6/20/1976 Bp John Vander Horst P 5/1/1977 Bp William Evan Sanders Con 6/30/2001 for WTenn. m 5/31/1975 Jean Pitt c 2. R The Epis Ch Of The Resurr Franklin TN 1996-2001; R S Jn's Epis Ch Johnson City TN 1986-1996; R Chr Ch - Epis Chattanooga TN 1978-1986; P-in-c Calv Ch Memphis TN 1977-1978; D S Paul's Ch Memphis TN 1976-1977; S Paul's Epis Ch Chattanooga TN 1976-1977. Curs. Hon D.Div. Seabury Wstrn TS Evanston IL 2002; Hon D.Div. S Lk's Sem Sewanee TN. donandjeannie@yahoo.com

JOHNSON, Doris Buchanan (Md) 603 Bellerive Ct, Arnold MD 21012 **R St Martins-In-The-Field Ch Severna Pk MD 2007-** B Miami Beach FL 5/28/1946 d Frank Malone Buchanan & Doris. BA U of Florida 1968; MA U of So Florida 1986; MDiv VTS 1999. D 6/12/1999 P 12/16/1999 Bp John Bailey Lipscomb. m 10/15/2007 NA c 2. Assoc R S Jn's Ch Ellicott City MD 2000-2007; Asst P H Trin Epis Ch In Countryside Clearwater FL 1999-2000. Auth, "Where is God?," *Preaching Through the H Days and Holidays: Sermons that Wk*, Morehouse, 2003. Mem Phi Kappa Phi Hon 1985. dorisjohnson08@comcast.net

JOHNSON, Douglas Peter (WMo) 315 E Partridge Avenue, Independence MO 64055 **Dn Cntrl Dnry Dio W Missouri Kansas City MO 2008-** B Sidney NE 5/13/1951 s Wright Ramsett Johnson & Mary Louise. BA Indiana U 1973; MA Indiana U 1975; MDiv Nash 1982; DMin SWTS 1998. D 4/30/1982 Bp William Cockburn Russell Sheridan P 12/10/1982 Bp William Hopkins Folwell. m 4/27/1991 M Suzanne Blaco c 2. Chair, Epis Transition Comm Dio W Missouri Kansas City MO 2009-2011; Dio W Missouri Kansas City MO 2002; Dio W Missouri Kansas City MO 2001-2002; R S Ptr's Ch Harrisonville MO 2000-2011; St Lk's So Chap Overland Pk KS 1999-2000; Eccl Crt Dio Indianapolis Indianapolis IN 1993-1998; R S Tim's Ch Indianapolis IN 1993-1998; Educ & Conf Cmsn Dio W Missouri Kansas City MO 1984-1993; Vic Chr Ch Lexington MO 1984-1989; Lakeland Dnry Exec Comm Dio Cntrl Florida Orlando FL 1983-1984; Cur The Epis Ch Of The Gd Shpd Lake Wales FL 1982-1984; Chair Clumet Dnry Dio Nthrn Indiana So Bend IN 1977-1979. Auth, *A Time of Transition*, Seabury-Wstrn, 1998. Alb Inst 1982; AFP 1982; AP 1994; RWF 1985. Bp's Shield Awd Dio W Missouri 1992; Bp's Shield Awd Dio W Missouri 1988. dpjmsj@aol.com

JOHNSON, Edwin Daniel (Mass) 1991 Massachusetts Ave, Cambridge MA 02140 **Asst R S Jas' Epis Ch Cambridge MA 2010-** B Boston MA 9/29/1982 s Walter Daniel & Vilma. BA Tufts U 2004; MDiv CDSP 2010. D 6/5/2010 Bp Gayle Elizabeth Harris P 1/8/2011 Bp M(arvil) Thomas Shaw III. edwindjohnson@gmail.com

JOHNSON, Emmanuel W (SC) 20268 Macglashan Ter, Ashburn VA 20147 B Fishtown LR 5/24/1924 s Sie Dabe Johnson & Helena Tode. BS Langston U 1958; MA Roosevelt U 1959; DIP Seth C. Edw Theo Inst Monrovia R.L. 1967. Trans from Church of the Province of West Africa 5/18/1998 Bp Edward Lloyd Salmon Jr. m 11/6/1965 Henrietta Beatrice Johnson c 4. Chapl/Vic S Phil's Chap Denmark SC 1991-2003; Dio Liberia 1000 Monrovia 10 Liberia 1970-1982. H Cross 1988; The Intl Ord of St Lk The Physcn 2005. DSA Cuttington U 2011; Lifetime Educ Awd Liberian Awards 2010; DD (Honoris Causa) Cuttington U Coll Liberia 1984; LLD (Honoris Causa) S Aug's Coll Raleigh NC 1973. info@stdavidsashburn.org

JOHNSON, Frances Kay (Haw) 959 W 41st Street, Houston TX 77018 B Fort Worth TX 11/29/1953 d James Dennis Carter & Rubye Faye. BS TCU 1975; MDiv Bex 1989; PhD Pacifica Grad Inst 2007. D 6/4/1989 Bp William Augustus Jones Jr P 12/18/1989 Bp William George Burrill. m 10/20/1979 Robert A Johnson c 2. S Lk's Epis Ch Honolulu HI 2001-2002; Cvnr Hiv-Aids Com Dio Hawaii Honolulu HI 1998-2001; Cn Pstr S Andr's Cathd Honolulu HI 1997-2001; Cn Pstr Cathd Of S Paul Erie PA 1994-1997; Com Dio NW Pennsylvania Erie PA 1992-1995; Dioc Coun Dio NW Pennsylvania Erie PA 1991-1997; Vic S Mary's Ch Erie PA 1990-1997. fkcjohn@gmail.com

JOHNSON, Franklin Orr (Mont) 355 Francis Way, Jackson WY 83001 B Buffalo NY 4/12/1938 s Philip Thackwell Johnson & Clare. BS Mar 1960; MS U of Wyoming 1963; MDiv VTS 1966. D 6/3/1966 P 12/15/1966 Bp Wilburn Camrock Campbell. m 8/4/1973 Sally Milliken. Int S Fran Of The Tetons Alta WY 2007-2008; All SS Epis Ch Whitefish MT 2001; R Ch Of The Trsfg

Jackson WY 1981-2000; R S Jn's Epis Ch Jackson WY 1981-2000; Assoc S Lk's Epis Ch Birmingham AL 1977-1981; Asst Chr Ch Cathd Lexington KY 1971-1977; Cur S Ptr's Ch Huntington WV 1966-1971. fjsally@aol.com

JOHNSON, Frank T (SanD) 651 Eucalyptus Ave, Vista CA 92084 B Nampa ID 12/9/1939 s Jay Horace Johnson & Olive Elizabeth. BA Pepperdine U 1976; MDiv Nash 1980. D 6/10/1980 P 12/1/1980 Bp Robert Munro Wolterstorff. m 4/2/1960 Cynthia Margo Cruse c 3. All SS Ch Vista CA 1995-1996; Gr Epis Ch Of The Vlly Mssn San Marcos CA 1982-1991; Cur All SS Ch Vista CA 1980-1982; Dio San Diego San Diego CA 1980-1982.

JOHNSON, Frederick Frank (NY) 4833 Europa Dr, Naples FL 34105 B Tulsa OK 4/23/1931 s Forest R Johnson & Laura M. BA U of Oklahoma 1953; MDiv Yale DS 1956. D 5/29/1957 Bp William A Lawrence P 12/1/1957 Bp Robert McConnell Hatch. m 8/27/2005 Joan Cottrell Charles c 3. Diocn Msnry & Ch Extntn Socty New York NY 1994; R S Paul's Ch Sprg Vlly NY 1960-1995; Cur S Jas' Ch Greenfield MA 1958-1960; Cur Trin Ch On The Green New Haven CT 1957-1958. Auth, "Living Ch". meta.johnson@comcast.net

JOHNSON JR, Fred Hoyer (NY) 124 NE 20th Ct, Wilton Manors FL 33305 B Columbus GA 10/31/1943 s Fred Hoyer Johnson & Viola June. Ohio Wesl 1962; BA Ya 1965; U of Paris 1966; MDiv Yale DS 1970. D 6/26/1971 Bp John Harris Burt P 2/1/1973 Bp Joseph Warren Hutchens. Assoc Ch Of The Intsn New York NY 1980-1982. Transltr, "No Souvenirs," *No Souvenirs*, Harper & Row, 1977; Auth, "When the Wrld Is No Longer Flat," *Packer Collgt Alum mag*, Packer Collgt Inst; Auth, "(Article)," *Reflections*, CSEE. Phi Beta Kappa 1965. Vic Emer Ch of the Intsn/New York City 2008; Macquarrie Fell GTF at Oxf 2002. halfsquarehead@yahoo.com

JOHNSON, Gregory Mervin (Haw) PO Box 893788, Mililani HI 96789 **Int Vic S Lk's Epis Ch Honolulu HI 2011-; Int Vic S Steph's Ch Wahiawa HI 2011-** B Stillwater MN 5/7/1951 s Mervin Roy Johnson & Delores Lorraine. BA U of Hawaii 1973; MTS STUSo 1976; D.Min. S Thos Cath Sem 1981; Dplma USAF Chapl Sch 1981; Dplma Acad Instr Sch 1982. D 3/23/1993 P 9/14/1993 Bp Donald Purple Hart. m 6/10/1973 Rebecca Gwynn Boardman c 4. P-in-c S Tim's Ch Aiea HI 2008-2010; P-in-c Gd Samar Epis Ch Honolulu HI 2005-2008; Int Vic H Cross Kahuku HI 2004-2005; Supply P Dio Hawaii Honolulu HI 2003-2004; Int R Ch Of The Epiph Honolulu HI 2001-2002; Assoc R S Mk's Ch Honolulu HI 1996-2000; Int R The Par Of S Clem Honolulu HI 1994-1995; Cur S Geo's Epis Ch Honolulu HI 1986-1993. pilgrimtravel@yahoo.com

JOHNSON JR, H(arold) Vance (WA) 1520 Farsta Ct, Reston VA 20190 B Niles MI 4/2/1938 s Harold Vance Johnson & Shirlee Eleanore. BA U MI 1960; MDiv EDS 1963; MBA Drexel U 1972. D 6/11/1963 Bp Charles Bennison P 12/14/1963 Bp William Foreman Creighton. m 8/7/1975 Mary Gaunt c 3. R S Chris's Ch New Carrollton MD 1966-1970; Asst Min S Jn's Ch Georgetown Par Washington DC 1963-1966. IORDInc@aol.com

JOHNSON JR, Harrel Brown (NC) 210 South Chestnut Street, Henderson NC 27536 B Brunswick GA 8/17/1947 s Harrel Brown Johnson & Doris Kelly. BS U GA 1970. D 6/20/2009 Bp Michael Bruce Curry. m 2/16/1974 Amy Cobb c 2. HBACJOHNSON@EMBARQMAIL.COM

JOHNSON JR, Henry Clarence (CPa) Po Box 1397, State College PA 16804 B Butte MT 3/21/1929 s Henry Clarence Johnson & Goldie Marie. BA Cbury Coll 1951; BD Nash 1957; PhD U IL 1970. D 5/21/1954 P 11/1/1954 Bp William Hampton Brady. m 5/29/1954 Mary Deane Lachicotte. Asst Chapl Chap Of S Jn The Div Champaign IL 1962-1966; Cur Gr Epis Ch Hinsdale IL 1961-1962; Vic H Trin Epis Ch Waupun WI 1954-1957. Auth, "Teachers For The Prairie-The U Of Il & The Schools 1868-1945"; Auth, "Var Monographs On Edu," *Hist & Philos*. nedscholar@aol.com

JOHNSON JR, Henry Poston (Ore) No address on file. B Shreveport LA 11/4/1933 s Henry Poston Johnson & Ruby L. Coll Resurr; BA LSU 1955; Mirfield Coll Gb 1967; Nash 1968. D 6/26/1968 Bp Charles A Mason P 12/1/1968 Bp Theodore H McCrea. S Mths Epis Ch Cave Jct OR 1978-1979; Vic Ch Of The H Cross Burleson TX 1968-1970.

JOHNSON, Herbert Alan (WNC) 245 Laurel Falls Rd, Franklin NC 28734 **Ch Of The Cross Columbia SC 1999-** B Jersey City NJ 1/10/1934 s Harry Oliver Johnson & Magdalena Gertrude. BA Col 1955; LLB New York Law Sch 1960; MA Col 1961; PhD Col 1965; Luth Theol Sthrn Sem 1984. D 9/28/1991 Bp William Arthur Beckham. m 6/4/1983 Jane McCue c 2. Cmsn on Daic Dio Upper So Carolina Columbia SC 1996-2000; Select Cmsn on Const & Cn Dio Upper So Carolina Columbia SC 1995-1999. Ed, *Amer Legal & Const Hist, 2nd Ed*, 2001; Auth, *Wingless Eagle: U.S. Army Aviation through Wrld War I*, 2001; Auth, *Chf Justiceship of Jn Marshall*, 1997. Assembly of Epis Hospitals & Chapl 2000; Coll of Chapl 1989-2008. janeherb@dnet.net

JOHNSON, Horace S (Ct) 3404 Castlebar Cir, Ormond Beach FL 32174 B Jamaica WI 5/11/1941 s David Josiah Johnson & Agatha Agnes. Andover Newton TS; Ya Berk; MBA U Of Hartford 1979. D 6/9/2001 Bp Andrew Donnan Smith P 12/15/2001 Bp James Elliot Curry. m 5/6/1967 Fay Dorothy Clarke. Assoc R Trin Epis Ch Hartford CT 2001-2006. hjohnson151@cfl.rr.com

JOHNSON, Ida Louise (Cal) 535 Joaquin Ave #D, San Leandro CA 94577 B Miami FL 4/8/1948 d Samuel Hensdale Johnson & Dorothy Clarice. S Aug's Coll Raleigh NC 1968; BA San Francisco St U 1991; MDiv CDSP 1994. D 6/4/1994 P 6/3/1995 Bp William Edwin Swing. R S Barth's Ch Pittsboro NC 2001-2004; Vic S Mich And All Ang Epis Ch Charlotte NC 1997-2001; Chapl Dio No Carolina Raleigh NC 1996-1997; Yth Dir Dio Massachusetts Boston MA 1995-1996; Dio California San Francisco CA 1994-1995; D S Cyp's Ch San Francisco CA 1994-1995. UBE. eyeljay@gmail.com

JOHNSON, Ira Joseph (WTenn) 4150 Boeingshire Dr, Memphis TN 38116 B Gastonia NC 2/26/1949 s Ira Gingles Johnson & Lydia. BA Belmont Abbey Coll 1974; MDiv GTS 1977. D 6/25/1977 P 3/1/1978 Bp William Gillette Weinhauer. m 4/25/1993 Linda Johnson c 5. Voorhees Coll Denmark SC 2006-2011; Emm Ch Memphis TN 1999-2004; S Paul's Epis Ch Orangeburg SC 1992-1999; Ch Of The H Cov Baltimore MD 1988-1992; S Steph's Epis Ch Winston Salem NC 1985-1988; S Thos Ch Minneapolis MN 1982-1985; R S Aug's Ch Kansas City MO 1978-1982; S Andr's Ch Dayton OH 1977-1978. ijohnson@voorhess.evu

JOHNSON, James Arthur (WNC) 584 Tarheel West Dr, Murphy NC 28906 **R Ch Of The Mssh Murphy NC 2005-; S Thos' Epis Ch Weirton WV 1998-** B Washington DC 11/22/1947 s Herbert Charles Johnson & Lily Ruth. BA Shorter Coll 1968; MDiv VTS 1975; DMin Drew U 1991; MA Georgia Sch of Profsnl Psychol Atlanta GA 1999. D 5/24/1975 P 4/25/1976 Bp Robert Poland Atkinson. m 8/17/1968 Betty Jean Smith c 2. The Ch Of S Matt Snellville GA 1998-2005; Int The Epis Ch Of The Adv Madison GA 1995-1996; R S Andr's Epis Ch Douglas GA 1991-1993; All SS Ch Bergenfield NJ 1988-1991; S Clem's Ch Hawthorne NJ 1987-1988; S Paul's Ch Englewood NJ 1986-1987; Vic S Gabr's Ch Oak Ridge NJ 1981-1985; St Josephs Ch Newark NJ 1981-1983; Vic S Matt's Ch Chester WV 1979-1981; R S Thos' Epis Ch Weirton WV 1977-1981; Dio W Virginia Charleston WV 1975-1977; Cur S Mk's Epis Ch S Albans WV 1975-1977. Auth, *Dissertation Developing An Outreach Mnstry in Bergenfield New Jersey*, 1991; Auth, *Mnstry From A Minefield*, 1986. AAMFT (Amer Assn for Mar and Fam Ther)(Cl 1998; AAPC (AAPC) (Fell) 1995; Natl Conf of Viet Nam Veterans Ministers 1988; Soc for Post Traumatic Stress Stds 1988. Cross of Gallantry Republic of So Vietnam 1970; Commendation Medal, Viet Nam Cmpgn USAF 1970. efmman@aol.com

JOHNSON, James Baxter (Colo) 1715 Holly Way, Fort Collins CO 80526 B Minneapolis MN 12/21/1936 s Harold Freeman Johnson & Kathryn Anita. BA U CO 1959; MDiv Nash 1962; MA Adams St Coll 1973. D 6/18/1962 P 12/21/1962 Bp Joseph Summerville Minnis. m 10/9/1976 Anne Elizabeth Moorhead c 4. Ch Of The H Nativ Kinsley KS 1999-2000; Dioc Coun Dio Wstrn Kansas Hutchinson KS 1993-1997; R S Corn Epis Ch Dodge City KS 1989-1998; R S Jas' Epis Ch Meeker CO 1986-1989; CDO Dio Colorado Denver CO 1984-1989; Chair Coll Dept Dio Colorado Denver CO 1969-1975; Chairman, Coll Dept Dio Colorado Denver CO 1969-1975; Dio Colorado Denver CO 1969-1973; Cur S Thos Epis Ch Denver CO 1965-1967; Vic Epis Ch Of S Jn The Bapt Granby CO 1963-1965; Vic Trin Ch Kremmling CO 1963-1965; Vic S Andr's Ch Cripple Creek CO 1962-1963. Conf Blessed Sacr; FIFNA; SSC. jandajohnson1@comcast.net

JOHNSON, Jane Margaret (FdL) 898 Midway Rd, Sewanee TN 37375 **R Ch Of The Intsn Stevens Point WI 2011-** B Shenandoah IA 9/13/1966 d Paul Richard Dicks & Carol M. BA U of Wisconsin-Eau Clare 1989; MDiv The TS at The U So 2011. D 12/18/2010 Bp Russell Edward Jacobus. m 8/5/1989 Murray Duane Johnson c 5. mthrjane@gmail.com

JOHNSON, Janet Hill (NJ) 538 Epping Forest Road, Annapolis MD 21401 B Orange NJ 3/7/1939 d Ernest Clayton Johnson & Jean Hill. BA Cor 1961; Cert Harvard-Radcliffe Prog In Bus Admin 1962; MBA Harv 1967; MDiv UTS 1997; CSD GTS 1999. D 6/22/2002 P 12/21/2002 Bp David B(ruce) Joslin. S Geo's Ch Perryman MD 2006-2008; Stff Liaison Dio New Jersey Trenton NJ 2002-2005; Vic Trin Ch Rocky Hill NJ 2002-2005. janethj@verizon.net

JOHNSON, Janis Lynn (Oly) 1541 Vista Loop SW #33-101, Tumwater WA 98512 B Raymond, WA 7/14/1952 d Harold Sigund Johnson & Virginia Vera. BA Seattle Pacific Univ 1974; Fuller TS 2004; M.Div. GTS 2006. D 6/24/2006 Bp Vincent Waydell Warner P 1/6/2007 Bp William O Gregg. P All SS Memi Epis Ch Heppner OR 2006-2009. revjanisjohnson@msn.com

JOHNSON, Jay Emerson (Cal) 632 38th St, Richmond CA 94805 **Prof PSR Berkeley CA 2003-; Assoc The Epis Ch Of The Gd Shpd Berkeley CA 1992-** B Ann Arbor MI 9/27/1961 s James Leonard Johnson & Rosemary. BA Wheaton Coll 1983; MDiv Nash 1988; PhD Grad Theol Un 1998. D 6/18/1988 P 12/17/1988 Bp Frank Tracy Griswold III. Prof CDSP Berkeley CA 1997-1998; Cur S Simons Ch Arlington Heights IL 1988-1991. "Dancing w God: Angl Chrsnty And The Pract Of Hope," Morehouse Pub, 2005. Newhall Resrch Fllshp Grad Theol Un 1996; Bogard Tchg Fllshp CDSP 1995; Ecf Grad Fllshp 1992. jayemersonjohnson@earthlink.net

JOHNSON, Joan Cottrell (Mass) 4833 Europa Dr, Naples FL 34105 B Darby PA 2/24/1927 d William John Charles & Helen Louise. BA Penn 1948; MDiv CDSP 1984. D 12/8/1984 P 12/1/1985 Bp William Edwin Swing. m 8/27/2005

Frederick Frank Johnson c 2. S Paul's Epis Ch Hopkinton MA 1992-1999; Assoc S Andr's Ch Edgartown MA 1988-1991; Assoc R S Thos Epis Ch Sunnyvale CA 1985-1988. johnson4833@comcast.net

JOHNSON, Johan (NY) 521 W 126th St, New York NY 10027 B 8/8/1963 s John Howard Johnson & Faith Carol. BA Clark U 1985; MDiv UTS 1989. D 9/9/1990 P 5/1/1991 Bp Edward Harding MacBurney. m 7/28/2011 Gabriela Johnson c 1. S Mart's Ch New York NY 1999-2005.

JOHNSON, John Brent (Tex) Trinity Episcopal Church, PO Box 777, Anahuac TX 77514 B Houston TX 8/9/1961 s Robert Johnson Lee & Shirley Lee. BA/MPA Lamar U 1993; JD St of Texas Coll of Law 1998; Dplma Iona Sch for Mnstry (Dio TX) 2007. D 6/23/2007 Bp Don Adger Wimberly. c 2. jjohnsontxus@hotmail.com

JOHNSON JR, John Romig (NY) 1020 Tyron Cir, Charleston SC 29414 **Sr Assoc S Steph's Epis Ch Charleston SC 2009-** B Augusta GA 2/17/1935 s John Romig Johnson & Harriet Elizabeth. BA Furman U 1957; MDiv GTS 1960; PhD UTS 1966; CG Jung Inst 1977. D 6/13/1960 P 5/27/1961 Bp Clarence Alfred Cole. m 8/3/1995 Nicole Watts c 3. Assoc Old S Andr's Par Ch Charleston SC 2005-2009; R S Jn's Ch Staten Island NY 1999-2005; Assoc Chr Ch Riverdale Bronx NY 1995-1999; Assoc The Ch Of The Epiph New York NY 1980-1995; Pstr Theol The GTS New York NY 1970-1982; Assoc Prof Of Pstr Theol Ya Berk New Haven CT 1965-1970; P-in-c S Ptr's Ch Great Falls SC 1960-1962. Auth, "Shaping The Mnstry For The 70'S," Ats, 1971; Auth, "Stdt Changes In Pstr Role Perception," *Journ Of Pstr Care*, 1967. AAPC, Diplomate 1977; Intl Assn For Analytical Psychol 1977; New York Assn For Analytical Psychol 1977. jromig@aol.com

JOHNSON, John W (Dal) 302 San Mateo Ct, Irving TX 75062 **Asst S Mk's Ch Irving TX 1986-** B Aitkin MN 4/11/1921 s John Edward Johnson & Adele Marie. GTS; St. Johns U; BA U MN 1947. D 9/13/1975 P 10/28/1976 Bp A Donald Davies. m 10/16/1943 Barbara Jean Gottlich. Cur Ch Of S Mths Dallas TX 1976-1981; Int S Mk's Ch Irving TX 1975-1976. Auth, "Nwspr & mag arts".

JOHNSON, John William (CFla) 116 E 4th St, Brownsville TX 78520 B Valliant OK 8/28/1927 s Richard Lewis Johnson & Leola. BA S Aug's Coll Raleigh NC 1962. D 6/10/1967 Bp Leland Stark.

JOHNSON, Juanita Hanger (Neb) 10761 Izard St, Omaha NE 68114 **D Ch Of The Resurr Omaha NE 1999-** B 7/6/1929 d Saybert Cyrus Hanger & Ione Williams. D 2/22/2004 Bp Joe Goodwin Burnett. m 8/2/1958 George Warren Johnson c 2.

JOHNSON, Julie Anna (Tenn) St Mary Magdalene Church, PO Box 150, Fayetteville TN 37334 **S Mary Magd Ch Fayetteville TN 2011-** B Vallejo CA 11/12/1961 d Norman Keith Hicks & Geraldine. BA Humboldt St U 1984; MDiv U So TS 2008. D 12/17/2007 P 6/30/2008 Bp Edward Stuart Little II. m 4/27/2008 Thomas D Johnson c 3. R S Alb's Epis Ch Hixson TN 2009-2010. motherjulie@smm-episcopal.net

JOHNSON, June (Ga) 519 Parker Ave, Decatur GA 30032 **Int S Jn's Epis Ch Bainbridge GA 2010-** B Albany GA 12/13/1946 d Willard Marion Johnson & Eunice. BMusEd U GA 1968; MDiv Chandler TS 2009. D 2/7/2009 P 8/20/2009 Bp Henry Irving Louttit. m 5/26/1990 Richard K Failing. yourofficemgr@gmail.com

JOHNSON, June B (Oly) 114 20th Ave SE, Olympia WA 98501 **P Assoc S Jn's Epis Ch Olympia WA 2009-** B Chehalis WA 11/12/1947 d Frank Joseph Pakar & Dorothy June. AA Centralia Coll 1991; BA Evergreen St Coll 2002; MDiv CDSP 2007. D 6/28/2008 Bp Bavi Rivera. m 8/12/1978 David Johnson c 2. junij@comcast.net

JOHNSON, Karen Brown (WA) 1 Irish Ct, Gaithersburg MD 20878 B Worcester MA 11/2/1943 d Chester Woodbury Brown & Dorothy Antoinette. BA Bates Coll 1965; MDiv Yale DS 1980. D 5/28/1980 Bp Frederick Barton Wolf P 1/11/1981 Bp Charles F Hall. c 3. Chr Ch Prince Geo's Par Rockville MD 2000-2007; Chr Ch Prince Geo's Par Rockville MD 1996-2000; Cmnty Mnstrs Of Rockville Rockville MD 1994-1995; Chr Epis Sch Rockville MD 1993-2007; Pres Dio Washington Washington DC 1990-1992; R S Anne's Ch Damascus MD 1985-1993; Asst R Ch Of The Ascen Gaithersburg MD 1983-1985; S Cathr's Sch Richmond VA 1980-1983. Winner, Best Sermon Contest 1992. karenebj@aol.com

JOHNSON, Katherine Ann Bradley (NC) 2504 Englewood Ave, Durham NC 27705 B Durham NC 3/22/1950 d David Gilbert Bradley & Gail Soules. BA Ob 1971; U of Texas 1975; JD U NC 1979; MDiv VTS 1982. D 5/31/1992 Bp Robert Whitridge Estill. m 8/21/1981 Jeffrey Hirst Johnson. Dio No Carolina Raleigh NC 1998-2000; Admin Asst Duke Epis Cntr Durham NC 1998-2000; D S Matt's Epis Ch Hillsborough NC 1994-1998; D S Phil's Ch Durham NC 1992-1994. Auth, "The Wide Appeal Of Harry Potter, Novelist," *An On-Line Pub Of Ebsco Pub*, 2000; Auth, "Going For The Gold, Novelist," *An On-Line Pub Of Ebsco Pub*, 2000; Auth, "Reading Sum, Novelist," *An On-Line Pub Of Ebsco Pub*, 2000. EPF 1989; NAAD 1991. jhj.kbj@verizon.net

JOHNSON, Keith (La) 1222 N Dorgenois ST, New Orleans LA 70119 **S Lk's Ch New Orleans LA 2010-** B New Orleans LA 7/31/1961 s Robert Johnson & Minnie. BA U IL 1983; MDiv VTS 2001. D 6/20/2001 Bp Leopold Frade P 12/20/2001 Bp John Lewis Said. m 8/8/1998 Virginia L Bare c 2. Asst H Trin Epis Ch In Countryside Clearwater FL 2008-2010; S Andr's Ch Ben Lomond CA 2003-2008; R S Matt's Epis Ch Delray Bch FL 2001-2003; Asst S Paul's Ch Delray Bch FL 2001-2003. keithj0731@aol.com

JOHNSON, Kenneth William (Mass) 11699 Bennington Woods Rd, Reston VA 20194 B Omaha NE 3/18/1941 s Philip Courdt Johnson & Wilma Ruth. BA DePauw U 1963; BD EDS 1969. D 6/21/1969 Bp Anson Phelps Stokes Jr. Cur S Paul's Ch Holyoke MA 1969-1970.

JOHNSON, Kent William (LI) 4216 67th Street, Woodside NY 11377 B Washington DC 5/14/1949 s Reuben Joseph Johnson & Bernice Marguerite. BA Bow 1971; PhD Br 1976; MDiv GTS 1984. D 1/28/1984 Bp Alexander Doig Stewart P 8/6/1984 Bp Andrew Frederick Wissemann. m 8/21/1982 Rita Karciauskas c 2. P-t Asst Chr Ch Manhasset NY 2008-2009; Dio Long Island Garden City NY 2003-2004; R All SS Ch Bayside NY 2002-2003; R S Mich's Ch Marblehead MA 1998-2002; Vic S Chris's Ch Hampstead NH 1986-1998; Asst S Mich's-On-The-Heights Worcester MA 1984-1986. Colloquium On Violence And Rel 1998-2004; FVC 1988-2002; Soc Of Ord Scientists 1999-2009. kwj0369@yahoo.com

JOHNSON, Kevin Allen (EC) St Peter's Episcopal Church, 101 N Bonner St, Washington NC 27889 **R S Ptr's Epis Ch Washington NC 2007-** B Amarillo TX 10/10/1963 BA U of Texas 1986; MDiv VTS 2003. D 6/17/2003 Bp Robert Boyd Hibbs P 1/6/2004 Bp James Edward Folts. m 12/30/1987 Sandra Lynne Johnson c 2. Asst St Fran Epis Ch San Antonio TX 2003-2007. rector@saintpetersnc.org

JOHNSON, Lee (EpisSanJ) 310 Audubon Dr, Lodi CA 95240 B Saint Louis MO 10/16/1945 d Charles Allen Rossiter & Patricia Lee. BA Florida Bible Coll 1987; Cert In Angl Stds San Joaquin Schools For Mnstry 2006. D 12/16/2006 Bp John-David Mercer Schofield. m 4/20/1996 Robert George Johnson. leenbob2@aol.com

JOHNSON, Lewis Chamberlayne (NY) 3636 Greystone Ave., Apt. 5B, Bronx NY 10463 **Vic Ch Of The Gd Shpd - Roosevelt Island Roosevelt Island NY 2005-; Consult Dio New York New York City NY 1995-** B Bethesda MD 11/17/1947 s Clarence Hazelton Johnson & Mary Gibson. BA Bow 1969; MA U of Massachusetts 1971; MDiv Yale DS 1980; Cert Blanton-Peale Grad Inst 1989. D 6/14/1980 P 1/10/1981 Bp Alexander Doig Stewart. m 1/29/1994 Dorothea E Crites c 1. Asst P S Mich's Ch New York NY 2000-2005; P-in-c Gr Epis Ch Monroe NY 1994-2000; P-in-c S Andr's Ch Walden NY 1986-1991; P-in-c St Fran of Assisi Montgomery NY 1986-1991; Cur All SS Ch Worcester MA 1980-1984. AAPC 1990. lewis_c_johnson@hotmail.com

JOHNSON, Linda Catherine (Ind) IU Episcopal Campus Ministry, PO Box 127, Bloomington IN 47402 **Dn of NW Dnry Dio Indianapolis Indianapolis IN 2011-; Indiana U Dio Indianapolis Indianapolis IN 2007-; COM in Higher Educ Dio Indianapolis Indianapolis IN 1994-** B Thomas WV 10/20/1949 d Theodore Frank Johnson & Wilma Jean. BA Berea Coll 1971; MA Ohio U 1973; MDiv GTS 1994; CSD Ben Inn/Monstry Indianapolis IN 2002; PHD Indiana U 2010. D 7/29/1994 P 2/24/1995 Bp A(rthur) Heath Light. Stndg Com Dio Indianapolis Indianapolis IN 1997-2005; COM Dio Indianapolis Indianapolis IN 1997-1998; Eccl Trial Crt Dio Indianapolis Indianapolis IN 1995-1998; Assoc R & Chapl Trin Epis Ch Bloomington IN 1994-2006; Dir Gr Hse On The Mtn Roanoke VA 1976-1994. "Integrating Indiana's Latino Newcomers: Levinson, Everitt, and Johnson, A Study of St and Cmnty Responses to the New Im," *Cntr for Educ and Soc, Working Paper #1*, Cntr for Educ and Soc, Indidan U, 2007; Auth, *Colonialism in Mod Amer: The Appalachian*; Auth, *The Chr Century*; Auth, *The Mnstry Dvlpmt Journ*; Auth, *Wit*. ESMHE 1995-2003; Pi Lambda Theta 2006; Sprtl Dir Intl 2002. Discipline Based Schlrshp in Educ Assoc Indiana U 2005; Cler Renwl Grant Lilly Endwmt 2000; Ch and Soc Prize for M.Div. Thesis GTS 1994. lijohnso@indiana.edu

JOHNSON, Linda Marie (Oly) Po Box 354, Westport WA 98595 B Seattle WA 7/10/1944 d Walter Paul Dehnert & Marjorie Kathryn. AA Clackamas Cmnty Coll 1991; Total Mnstry Trng Westport WA 1997. D 11/19/1997 Bp Sanford Zangwill Kaye Hampton P 6/27/1998 Bp Vincent Waydell Warner. D S Christophers Epis Ch Westport WA 1997-1998. lindaj_333@hotmail.com

JOHNSON JR, Lloyd Winthrop (NI) 144 Grove Pl, San Antonio IN 78209 **S Ptr's Epis Ch Rockport TX 2000-** B Hartford CT 8/7/1939 s Lloyd Winthrop Johnson & Vera Gertrude. BBA U of Miami 1963; M Div Nash 1966. D 6/29/1966 Bp James Loughlin Duncan P 12/29/1966 Bp William Loftin Hargrave. m 12/28/1967 Jane Gray c 3. R S Alb's Epis Ch Ft Wayne IN 2001-2006; R S Paul's Epis Ch Pekin IL 1984-2001; R S Ptr's Ch Peoria IL 1974-1984; Cur S Greg's Ch Boca Raton FL 1966-1974. BENJACOV@NETSCAPE.NEET

JOHNSON, Lori Elaine (EMich) 315 1/2 N Maple St, Flushing MI 48433 **Trin Epis Ch Flushing MI 2008-** B La Mesa, CA 2/10/1967 d Theodore M Johnson & Joanne Annett. BA California St U 1992; MDiv Epis TS of The SW 2006. D 6/4/2006 Bp James Robert Mathes P 1/5/2007 Bp Gary Richard Lillibridge. Asst S Dav's Epis Ch San Antonio TX 2006-2008. lori_bythesea@yahoo.com

J

JOHNSON JR, Lucius Curtis (Ga) 552 Hunterdale Rd, Evans GA 30809 **P Ch Of The Gd Shpd Swainsboro GA 2011-; P Ch of the Gd Shpd Detroit MI 2009-; D The Ch Of The Gd Shpd Augusta GA 2000-** B Cuthbert GA 10/16/1947 s Lucius Curtis Johnson & Mary Harris. D 2/15/1999 P 11/19/2009 Bp Henry Irving Louttit. m 2/15/1991 Martha Ann Kobs. lcjohnson@knology.net

JOHNSON, Lynn H (NJ) 3 Azalea Dr, Lumberton NJ 08048 **Serv S Jn's Epis Ch Maple Shade NJ 2000-** B Camden NJ 5/9/1945 d Charles B Henderson & Mollye E. ABD Rutgers-The St U; BA Fisk U 1969; MA Rowan U 1979. D 10/21/2000 Bp David B(ruce) Joslin. m 2/15/1969 Vernon L Johnson. Auth, "So . . . You'Re On The Vstry," Ihj, 1998; Auth, "When The Mstr Calls," Ihj, 1998; Auth, "Presenting The AltGld," Ihj Pub, 1997. Upstream Navigator Cmnty Serv Awd Geo Elliot Heardy Memi Fndt 1997; Dedicated Serv Awd Chr The King Ch 1995; Wrld Class Serv Awd Zeta Phi Beta Sorority 1995. ihj@oo.net

JOHNSON, Maeve Maud Vincent (Az) 114 W Roosevelt St., Phoenix AZ 85003 B Phoenix AZ 10/23/1951 d Thomas B Vincent & Frances Daly. BA U of Arizona 1972; MEd Arizona St U 1981. D 10/14/2006 Bp Kirk Stevan Smith. m 2/19/1993 Richardson Stater Richardson c 3. maevev.johnson@gmail.com

JOHNSON, Malinda Margaret (Eichner) (Ct) 9 Arrow Head Rd, Westport CT 06880 B Stamford CT 7/20/1963 d Lambert John Eichner & JoAnn. BA Connecticut Coll 1985; MA Harvard DS 1989. D 6/8/2002 P 12/14/2002 Bp Andrew Donnan Smith. m 6/17/1993 Krister Frederick Johnson c 2. Calv St Geo's Epis Ch Bridgeport CT 2010-2011; Cur S Jn's Epis Par Waterbury CT 2002-2007. mmej@optonline.net

JOHNSON, Marietta (Mont) Po Box 78, Red Lodge MT 59068 B Shreveport LA 6/3/1939 d Thurston Lamar Forehand & Martha. Spec Ed. Montana St U 1961; Mnstry Formation Prog 2001. D 10/31/2001 P 4/13/2002 Bp Charles Lovett Keyser. m 12/22/1962 Joseph E Johnson c 2.

JOHNSON, Marta DV (Md) 140 N Beaver St, York PA 17401 B New York NY 2/22/1951 d Pedro Dove-Vila & Genoveva. BS Pace U 1974; MA S Mary's Sem & U Baltimore MD 1998; MSc Loyola Coll Baltimore MD 2005; MDiv VTS 2008. D 6/14/2008 P 1/10/2009 Bp John Leslie Rabb. m 6/4/1977 Alfred D Johnson c 4. Asst The Epis Ch Of S Jn The Bapt York PA 2008-2010. a.johnson@amborate.com

JOHNSON, Mary Peterson (At) Episcopal Church of the Holy Family, 202 Griffith Road, Jasper GA 30143 B Montreal QC CA 7/16/1955 d David Walter Peterson & Grace Elizabeth. Wheaton Coll; BA U IL 1976; MA U IL 1977; MDiv PrTS 1983; STM GTS 1986. D 6/14/1986 P 1/14/1987 Bp George Phelps Mellick Belshaw. m 6/19/1976 Wayne Paul Johnson c 5. R Epis Ch Of The H Fam Jasper GA 2004-2011; Trin Ch Columbus OH 1999-2001; S Jn's Ch Worthington OH 1998-1999; Assoc S Mk's Epis Ch Columbus OH 1991-1993; Int S Mk's Epis Ch Columbus OH 1989-1990; Chr Ch Cranbrook Bloomfield Hills MI 1988-1989; DCE S Bern's Ch Bernardsville NJ 1986-1987. mjp0619@gmail.com

JOHNSON, Mary Richardson (NMich) 1021 E E St, Iron Mountain MI 49801 B 2/25/1943 D 2/29/2004 Bp James Arthur Kelsey. m 8/15/1964 David Johnson c 2.

JOHNSON, Matthew Ransom (Va) PO Box 32, 6507 Main St., The Plains VA 20198 **Assoc R for Yth and YA S Steph's Ch Richmond VA 2011-** B Atlanta GA 1/6/1978 s (William) Pegram Johnson & Candis. AB W&M 2000; MDiv GTS 2008. D 5/24/2008 P 12/6/2008 Bp Peter James Lee. m 1/5/2008 Katharina Petra Schaefer. Assoc R Gr Ch The Plains VA 2008-2011. ransomrj@gmail.com

JOHNSON, Michaela (Kay) (RI) 1214 Noyes Dr, Silver Spring MD 20910 B New York NY 8/22/1937 d Erwin Memelsdorff & Ilse. BA Swarthmore Coll 1958; MDiv Ya Berk 1987; MS U of Connecticut 1987. D 8/22/1987 P 2/27/1988 Bp Andrew Frederick Wissemann. m 8/20/1960 Richard August Johnson c 4. The Ch Of The Epiph Washington DC 2003; Int The Ch Of The Epiph Washington DC 2002; R Ch Of The Mssh Providence RI 1992-2000; Dio Wstrn Massachusetts Springfield MA 1987-1992; Asst Gr Ch Amherst MA 1987-1992. "No One is Ever Alone," *Sermons that Wk IV*, Forw Mvmt, 1994. Polly Bond Awd ECom 1999. michaela.johnson@starpower.net

JOHNSON, Michael R (ND) 3600 25th St S, Fargo ND 58104 **Dio No Dakota Fargo ND 2011-; P-in-c S Jn's Ch Moorhead MN 2008-; Int Geth Cathd Fargo ND 2006-** B Ada MN 12/16/1948 s Ralph Johnson & Pearl. BA Minnesota St U Moorhead 1970; Ecole Internationale De Mime Marcel Marceau Paris France 1971; Mnstrl PCIM Mableton, GA 1987. D 6/15/2005 P 12/17/2005 Bp Michael Gene Smith. m 6/12/1983 Pamela Cottrell c 1. Ord of S Lk the Physcn 1990. mrjohns@rrv.net

JOHNSON, Mildred Jane (U) 147 N 875 E, Logan UT 84321 B Indianapolis IN 10/28/1921 d Harry Charles Johnson & Jessie. BA Ob 1944; MA Westminster Choir Coll of Rider U 1948; PhD Indiana U 1955. D 5/21/1991 Bp George Edmonds Bates.

JOHNSON, Neil Edward (NwPa) 18 Harrogate Square, Williamsville NY 14221 **Assoc Cler S Paul's Epis Ch Lewiston NY 1997-** B Corning NY 4/29/1942 s Hans John Johnson & Wilma Louise. Syr; AS Corning Cmnty Coll 1964; BS Elmira Coll 1974. D 1/6/1996 P 12/21/1996 Bp Robert Deane Rowley Jr. m 6/28/1980 Dianne Jean Gradl. P-in-c Ch Of The Epiph Niagara Falls NY 1998-2000. neiljo606@aol.com

JOHNSON, Patricia Ann (Ia) 2222 McDonald St, Sioux City IA 51104 **D S Thos' Epis Ch Sioux City IA 1999-** B Sioux City IA 4/22/1953 d Donald E Schomberg & Leona M. BA Briar Cliff U 1986. D 4/24/1999 Bp Carl Christopher Epting. c 2. Auth, "Comp on the Way," *Diakeno*, Michaelmas, 2000; Auth, "The Activist Decade, Essays in Hist," *E.C. Barksdale Lectures*, 1988. Phi Alpha Theta. Hist Schlrshp 1985. PAJ3C@CABLEONE.NET

JOHNSON, Paul Andrew (Va) 5000 Pouncey Tract Rd, Glen Allen VA 23059 **Chr Ch Glen Allen VA 1995-** B Hinsdale IL 7/7/1961 s Alvin Carl Johnson & Eileen M. BA Duke 1983; MDiv Ya Berk 1990. D 6/2/1990 P 4/1/1991 Bp Peter James Lee. m 8/23/1986 Bernadette D Deane c 3. S Paul's Ch Richmond VA 1990-1994. bernbaby@verizon.net

JOHNSON, Ralph Foley (SeFla) 88181 Old Highway, #G41, Islamorada FL 33036 B Aiken SC 11/27/1929 s William Foley Johnson & Mae. BS Newberry Coll 1952; BD STUSo 1958; Med U of Miami 1967; EdD U of Miami 1971. D 6/11/1958 P 3/21/1959 Bp Clarence Alfred Cole. m 12/2/1961 Louise Bradley c 1. S Jas The Fisherman Islamorada FL 1995-1996; Assoc S Paul's Ch Delray Bch FL 1966-1970; Assoc All Souls' Epis Ch Miami Bch FL 1966-1968.

JOHNSON, R Dean (At) 1480 Pineview Ln Nw, Conyers GA 30012 B Amery WI 9/4/1928 s James Johnson & Helene. BA Gustavus Adolphus Coll 1950; STM GTS 1956. D 6/18/1956 Bp Charles L Street P 12/21/1956 Bp Gerald Francis Burrill. m 10/6/1961 Anna Schille. S Simon's Epis Ch Conyers GA 1984-1987; R S Mich's Ch Gainesville FL 1979-1983; R S Ptr's Epis Ch Sycamore IL 1963-1973; Cur S Ptr's Epis Ch Chicago IL 1956-1957. 1st Place Awd For Rel Journalism Georgia Press Assn. deananna@juno.com

JOHNSON SR, Richard E (Me) PO Box 688, Castine ME 04421 B Mount Pleasant TX 11/8/1935 s Ernest Clayton Johnson & Martha Frances. MDiv SMU 1961; PhD Wright Inst 1978. D 4/17/1978 Bp Frederick Barton Wolf P 11/1/1978 Bp Harvey D Butterfield. m 5/24/2000 Christine Talbott c 4. P Aroostook Epis Cluster Caribou ME 1997-2000; P Ch Of The Adv Caribou ME 1997-2000; P S Anne's Ch Mars Hill ME 1997-2000; P S Jn's Ch Presque Isle ME 1997-2000; Assoc S Lk's Ch Caribou ME 1997-2000; P S Paul's Ch Ft Fairfield ME 1997-2000; R S Mary's Epis Ch Inc Lampasas TX 1981-1987; Vic Chr Ch Gardiner ME 1979-1981; Asst S Matt's Epis Ch Hallowell ME 1978-1981. Auth, *A Beautiful Way to Make a Living*; Auth, *Wisdom as Viewed by Older Adults*. Amer Assn of Mar and Fam Ther 1974-2004; AAPC 1973-2004. rejohnson@gwi.net

JOHNSON, Richard E (Mont) 902 Logan St, Helena MT 59601 **S Ptr's Par Helena MT 2011-** B Deer Lodge MT 10/27/1950 s Wilbur Johnson & Frances Jeanne. BA/MT Carroll Coll 1973. D 7/20/1990 Bp Charles Jones III. S Ptr's Par Helena MT 2008-2010; Dio Montana Helena MT 1995-1996; S Ptr's Par Helena MT 1990-1994. rjohnson1950@yahoo.com

✠ **JOHNSON JR, Rt Rev Robert Carroll** (NC) 100 Ashworth Dr, Durham NC 27707 B Columbus GA 7/18/1938 s Robert Carroll Johnson & Mildred Allen. BA Merc 1960; MDiv Yale DS 1964; MA No Carolina St U 1973. D 9/19/1964 Bp Richard Henry Baker P 6/29/1965 Bp Thomas Augustus Fraser Jr Con 5/14/1994 for NC. m 12/27/1959 Connie Nevelle Smith. Bp of NC Dio No Carolina Raleigh NC 1994-2000; R S Lk's Epis Ch Durham NC 1975-1994; P-in-c S Chris's Epis Ch Garner NC 1969-1975; R S Paul's Epis Ch Smithfield NC 1966-1969; Asst S Ptr's Epis Ch Charlotte NC 1964-1966. DD U So TS 1996; DD Ya Berk 1995. conniej1@msn.com

JOHNSON, Robert Gaines (SVa) 1411 25th St, Galveston TX 77550 **Hungars Par Eastville VA 2004-** B Corsicana TX 8/2/1951 s Clyde Edwin Johnson & Ann. MDiv Epis TS of The SW; JD So Texas Coll Of Law Houston TX; BA U of Texas 1975. D 6/17/2000 Bp Claude Edward Payne. m 3/14/1982 Joanie Milligan. S Jn's Ch La Porte TX 2001-2003; D Trin Ch Galveston TX 2000-2001. rg1johnson@aol.com

✠ **JOHNSON, Rt Rev Robert Hodges** (WNC) 18 Woodcrest Rd, Asheville NC 28804 B Jacksonville FL 10/1/1934 s William Weakley Johnson & Edith Marjorie. BSBA U of Florida 1956; MDiv VTS 1963. D 6/24/1963 P 3/26/1964 Bp Edward Hamilton West Con 3/11/1989 for WNC. m 8/25/1962 Julie McMaster c 2. Stndg Cmsn on Structure of the Ch Epis Ch Cntr New York NY 1994-1997; Bd Rgnts The TS at The U So Sewanee TN 1993-1999; Bp Dio Wstrn No Carolina Asheville NC 1989-2004; BEC Epis Ch Cntr New York NY 1988-1991; Pres Alum Coun VTS Alexandria VA 1981-1988; Dep GC Dio Atlanta Atlanta GA 1976-1988; Chair COM Clers Dvlpmt Dio Atlanta Atlanta GA 1976-1983; Chair Stwdshp Dept Dio Atlanta Atlanta GA 1973-1975; R H Innoc Ch Atlanta GA 1972-1989; Cn Pstr S Jn's Cathd Jacksonville FL 1968-1972; P-in-c Ch Of Our Sav Jacksonville FL 1963-1965; P-in-c S Geo's Epis Ch Jacksonville FL 1963-1965. DD U So TS 1990; DD VTS 1990. rhjwnc@aol.com

JOHNSON III, Roberts Poinsett (Ala) 3620 Belle Meade Way, Birmingham AL 35223 **Int Gr Ch Birmingham AL 2006-** B Winnfield LA 8/30/1940 s Roberts Poinsett Johnson & Dee Tannehill. MDiv GTS 1965; BA LSU 1965. D 6/29/1965 Bp Iveson Batchelor Noland P 5/26/1969 Bp Girault M Jones. m

1/4/1970 Barbara Jane Boasberg c 1. Dio Alabama Birmingham AL 1993-2006; R S Alb's Ch Birmingham AL 1987-2006; Asst R S Mary's-On-The-Highlands Epis Ch Birmingham AL 1985-1987; Asst R S Lk's Epis Ch Birmingham AL 1983-1985; S Matt's Epis Sch Houma LA 1978-1983; Cur S Mart's Epis Ch Metairie LA 1971-1978; Yth Dir Dio Louisiana Baton Rouge LA 1971-1974; Vic S Tim's Ch La Place LA 1967-1971; Vic All SS Epis Ch Ponchatoula LA 1966-1971. robandjanine@aol.com

JOHNSON, Ronald Arthur (O) 66 Market St, Onancock VA 23417 **R Adv Epis Ch Westlake OH 2010-** B Longmont CO 10/10/1971 BA Oral Roberts U 1994; MDiv Nash 1998. D 11/7/2002 P 4/15/2003 Bp Keith Bernard Whitmore. m 6/22/2002 Lisa Jo Le Barron c 2. H Trin Prot Epis Ch Onancock VA 2004-2010; P-in-c S Lk's Ch Altoona WI 2003-2004. revrj11@verizon.net

JOHNSON, Ronald Norman (SeFla) 27 Bahama Ave, Key Largo FL 33037 B Tampa FL 10/9/1942 s Norman Miller Johnson & Mildred Amanda. Cit 1962; BA Stetson U 1964; MBA W&M 1971; MDiv STUSo 1977; ThM PrTS 1991. D 6/11/1977 P 12/17/1977 Bp Emerson Paul Haynes. m 8/21/1967 Johnnie Grace Hevener. R S Jas The Fisherman Islamorada FL 2001-2008; S Fran Cmnty Serv Inc. Salina KS 1999-2001; Chapl Off Of Bsh For ArmdF New York NY 1981-1999; R H Innoc Key W FL 1978-1980; R S Ptr's Epis Ch Key W FL 1978-1980; Cur S Hilary's Ch Ft Myers FL 1977-1978. Clincl Mem, Amer Assn For Mar And Fam Ther 1996; Fell, Amer Assn Of Pastorlal Counselors 1993; Mem, Amer Coll Of Healthcare Executives 1999-2002. fr.ronjohnson@gmail.com

JOHNSON, Rudolph (Cal) 5655 Black Ave, Pleasanton CA 94566 B Boulder CO 6/19/1933 s Rudolph Johnson & Bernice. BA U CO 1954; BD Pacific Luth TS 1963; PhD Stan 1974. D 1/13/1981 P 5/13/1981 Bp William Edwin Swing. m 8/19/1958 Marguerite McNair. R S Clem's Ch Berkeley CA 1990-1995; H Cross Epis Ch Castro Vlly CA 1981-1989. rudymargejohnson@comcast.net

JOHNSON, Russell L (SwFla) 13555 Heron Cir, Clearwater FL 33762 B Jamestown NY 8/13/1944 s E Milton Johnson & Gladys Pearl. BS USNA 1967; MDiv STUSo 1982; DMin STUSo 2001. D 6/7/1982 P 12/1/1982 Bp Hunley Agee Elebash. m 8/5/1983 Judith A Shopf c 4. Cathd Ch Of S Ptr St Petersburg FL 2004-2008; Cn Chr Ch Cathd Lexington KY 1999-2004; R Chr Ch Detroit MI 1997-1999; R S Paul's Epis Ch Edenton NC 1991-1997; R Trin Ch Lumberton NC 1988-1991; R Trin Epis Ch Pinopolis SC 1984-1988; Asst to R S Jn's Epis Ch Wilmington NC 1982-1984. "Call, Response, Restoration," *Disciples of Chr in Cmnty*, Sewanee, 2001. priestrjohnson@yahoo.com

JOHNSON, Russell Michael (Haw) 1407 Kapiolani St, Hilo HI 96720 B Chicago IL 1/15/1950 s James Earl Johnson & Lucille Ann. SW Cmnty Coll Chula Vista CA 1982; BA Natl U 1984; MDiv STUSo 1987; Cert SWTS 2002. D 6/6/1987 P 12/21/1987 Bp Donald James Davis. m 11/25/1975 Margo Mahaffey c 3. Congrl Hlth and Growth Com Dio Hawaii Honolulu HI 2005-2010; Ch Of The H Apos Hilo HI 2004-2010; Dio Coun Dio Wyoming Casper WY 2000-2003; S Jn's Ch Green River WY 1996-2004; Ch Of The H Comm Rock Sprg WY 1995-2004; Stndg Committy Dio Wyoming Casper WY 1995-1997; RurD Dio NW Pennsylvania Erie PA 1993-1995; COM Dio NW Pennsylvania Erie PA 1992-1995; Vic S Jos's Ch Port Allegany PA 1987-1995; Vic S Marg's Epis Ch Mt Jewett PA 1987-1995; Vic S Matt's Epis Ch Eldred PA 1987-1995; Tri-Mssn Mnstry Port Allegany PA 1987-1995. garplool1@aol.com

JOHNSON JR, Russell Woodrow (WMo) 100 E Red Bridge Rd, Kansas City MO 64114 **Dioc Coun Dio W Missouri Kansas City MO 1999-; Dioc Coun Dio W Missouri Kansas City MO 1999-; Preaching, Pstr care, Admin, outreach, Educ S Ptr's Epis Ch Kansas City MO 1997-** B Olivia MN 6/6/1951 s Russell Woodrow Johnson & Dorothy. BA Gustavus Adolphus Coll 1973; Untd TS Of The Twin Cities 1981; MDiv SWTS 1982; DMin SWTS 2007. D 6/24/1982 P 12/30/1982 Bp Robert Marshall Anderson. m 12/30/1978 Susan L Laufer c 2. Chairman - Search/Transition/Consecration Com for a new Bp Dio W Missouri Kansas City MO 2009-2011; Pres of Stndg Com Dio W Missouri Kansas City MO 2007-2011; Dn - Metro Dnry Dio W Missouri Kansas City MO 2000-2004; Cnvnr - Wrshp and Sprtlty Cmsn Dio W Missouri Kansas City MO 1998-2008; Dn Dio W Missouri Kansas City MO 1998-2004; Dio W Missouri Kansas City MO 1988-1990; Dio W Missouri Kansas City MO 1987-1993; Preaching, Pstr care, Admin, outreach, Educ S Mary's Ch St Paul MN 1986-1997; Supply P Dio Minnesota Minneapolis MN 1986; Pstr Care, preaching, Admin Chr Ch Albert Lea MN 1985-1986; Dio W Missouri Kansas City MO 1984-1993; Dio W Missouri Kansas City MO 1984-1993; Yth Mnstry, Pstr care, Yth Educ Chr Ch S Paul MN 1982-1985. Auth, "The Search Process for a new Bp," *The Sprt*, Epis Dio W Missouri, 2009. Alb Inst 1982; Angl-Luth Conf 1988-1997; Associated Parishes 1982-2000; Assn Of Dioc Liturg & Mus Com 1985-2000; Epis Cler Assoc. 1988; Rotary Intl 1982-2004. rjstp@planetkc.com

JOHNSON, Ryder Channing (WNY) 19013 N 74th Dr, Glendale AZ 85308 **Non-Stipen S Lk's At The Mtn Phoenix AZ 2007-** B Ithaca NY 6/27/1928 s Elmer Marker Johnson & Amelia Anne. BA Cor 1950; M Div. Ya Berk 1953; STM STUSo 1971; PhD SUNY 1973. D 6/29/1953 Bp Walter M Higley P 6/6/1954 Bp Lauriston L Scaife. m 5/25/1977 Joyce V Dashiell c 4. Assoc R S Andr's Ch Glendale AZ 1996-2005; Asst S Andr's Ch Glendale AZ 1995; Asst Calv Epis Ch Williamsville NY 1967-1968; Vic S Lk's Epis Ch Attica NY 1956-1962; Cur S Jas' Ch Batavia NY 1953-1956. R Channing Johnson, "Where have all the YP Gone," Amazon, 2011; RC Johnson, "A Study Guide to Where have all the YP Gone," Amazon, 2011; Auth, "Cercla Site Assessment Workbook," USDOE, 1994; Auth, "Chemicals From Wood: Plcy Implications Of Fed Subsidy," The MITRE Corp, 1983; Auth, "Workshop," *Workshop Psychol Stress Associated w The Proposed Restart Of 3 Mile Island*, The MITRECorp, 1982; Auth, "Spprt Documents For The Natl Priorities List," USEPA. Amer Chem Soc 1976-1990; Human Factors Soc 1973-1990. Prog Achievement Awd The MITRE Corp 1987. rcjphd@aol.com

JOHNSON, Sandra Parnell (SwFla) 14640 N Cleveland Ave, N Ft Myers FL 33903 **D All Souls Epis Ch No Ft Myers FL 2009-** B Norfolk VA 4/15/1943 d Troy Parnell & Martha A. D 10/10/2009 Bp Dabney Tyler Smith. m 8/21/1962 Emery Johnson c 3. D S Hilary's Ch Ft Myers FL 2009-2011. deaconsandy7431@aol.com

JOHNSON, Sanford Ralph (WMass) 50 Shaker Farm Rd N, Marlborough NH 03455 B Geneva NY 12/26/1949 s Kenneth William Johnson & Elva Amaret. U of Massachusetts 1969; BA U of Maine 1972; MDiv Andover Newton TS 1975. D 9/18/1975 P 4/9/1976 Bp Alexander Doig Stewart. m 6/13/1970 Barbara Bragg c 1. Assoc S Lk's Ch Chester VT 2008; Par Of S Jas Ch Keene NH 2005; P-in-c Ch Of The Epiph Newport NH 2000-2001; Int Par Of S Jas Ch Keene NH 1999-2000; Assoc Gr Ch Amherst MA 1983-1985; Liturg Cmsn Dio Wstrn Massachusetts Springfield MA 1978-1982; Vic S Jn's Ch Ashfield MA 1977-1983; Cur Chr Ch Fitchburg MA 1975-1977; Yth Cmsn Dio Wstrn Massachusetts Springfield MA 1975-1977. sanfordbonnie@hughes.net

JOHNSON, Simeon O (NY) 165 Saint Marks Pl Apt 10H, Staten Island NY 10301 **S Edm's Ch Bronx NY 2009-; Supply P Dio New York New York City NY 2006-** B Freetown 5/5/1956 s Simeon Oyesile Johnson & Olive Lucetta. HTC U of Sierra Leone (MMTC) 1982; CPS Sierra Leone Theol Hall 1987; AA Coll of Staten Island 2005; BA Coll of Staten Island 2006; M.Div GTS 2008. Trans from Lib 3/1/1996 Bp Walter Decoster Dennis Jr. m 8/29/1993 Renate Celiana Denise Spring c 2. Asst All SS Ch Staten Island NY 1996-2001; Chapl Dio New York New York City NY 1995-2001. simeonoj@aol.com

JOHNSON, Stanley Ethan (Pa) 215 Saint Marks Sq, Philadelphia PA 19104 B New York NY 12/26/1928 s Stanley Johnson & Belle. BA Pr 1950; ThB PDS 1954. D 6/5/1954 Bp William P Roberts P 12/11/1954 Bp Oliver J Hart. m 8/23/1952 Sally B Haws. Dn - Nashville Convoc Dio Tennessee Nashville TN 1960-1961. sej215@aol.com

JOHNSON, Stephanie McDyre (NY) 176 Linden St Apt F3, New Haven CT 06511 **Epis Prov Of New Engl Dorset VT 2011-; Yth Dir S Ann's Epis Ch Old Lyme CT 2010-** B Brooklyn, NY 12/27/1964 d Robert T Johnson & Patricia. BA Ford 1980; Grad Dplma U of Stockholm 1990; MDiv Ya Berk 2010. D 3/13/2010 P 9/25/2010 Bp Mark Sean Sisk. m 12/29/1990 Gordon Hinshalwood c 2. stephanie.m.johnson@yale.edu

JOHNSON, Susan Elaine (Eur) Schiesstaettberg 44, Eichstatt AL 49842 Germany **D Ch of the Ascen Munich 81545 DE 2003-** B Bedford UK 10/11/1944 BA Lon 1966; E Angl Mnstrs Trng Course Cambridge Gb 2001. D 5/31/2003 P 11/30/2003 Bp Pierre W Whalon. susanjohnson@ku.eichstaett.de

JOHNSON, Susan Heckel (At) 571 Holt Road, Marietta GA 30068 **Assoc S Cathr's Epis Ch Marietta GA 2008-** B Camp Atterbury IN 7/26/1946 d Charles Clark Heckel & Jacqueline Bowman. BA U of So Carolina 1968; MM Florida St U 1971; MS Florida St U 1990; MDiv STUSo 1997. D 6/8/1997 Bp Stephen Hays Jecko P 12/1/1997 Bp Frank Kellogg Allan. m 12/12/1970 Roy H Johnson c 3. R S Clare's Epis Ch Blairsville GA 2000-2008; Asst H Innoc Ch Atlanta GA 1997-2000. fathersue@bellsouth.net

JOHNSON, Taylor Herbert (Mich) 3837 W 7 Mile Rd, Detroit MI 48221 B Cleveland OH 2/17/1933 s Elgenia Johnson. AA Vorhees Jr. Coll 1959; BA Pace Coll 1971; MDiv ITC Atlanta GA 1973; Ashland TS 1983. D 9/9/1973 Bp Leland Stark P 7/17/1977 Bp Henry Irving Mayson. m 9/8/1962 Beverly King. All SS Ch Detroit MI 1997-2005; Asst R Gr Ch Jamaica NY 1985-1987; Coop Campus Mnstry Youngstown OH 1980-1982; S Phil's Epis Ch Jacksonville FL 1979; Vic S Aug's Epis Ch Youngstown OH 1976-1978; Metropltn Ecum Mnstry Newark NJ 1975-1976; Cur Trin And S Phil's Cathd Newark NJ 1973-1975. Auth, "Ch Life". Life Mem Ord Of S Lk, Bro Of S Andr & UBE; OHC (Assoc).

JOHNSON, Thalia Felice (Mich) 8261 Cypress Way, Dexter MI 48130 **1st Cler Alt. Gen. Conv 2009 Dio Michigan Detroit MI 2009-; 1st Cler Alt. Gen. Conv 2009 Dio Michigan Detroit MI 2009-; Cler Alt 1, Gen. Conv 2012 Dio Michigan Detroit MI 2009-; D Ch Of The Incarn Pittsfield Twp Ann Arbor MI 2008-; Cler Alt 4, Gen. Conv 2006 Dio Michigan Detroit MI 2004-** B Flint MI 7/25/1946 d Donald Robert Johnson & Shirley Roberta. BS MI SU 1968; MA MI SU 1976; Cert Whitaker TS 1987. D 9/10/1987 Bp H Coleman McGehee Jr. D S Mich And All Ang Onsted MI 1991-2005; D Chr

Ch Adrian MI 1987-1991. Cambios Inc 1997-2002; NAACP; NAAD. Awd of St. Steph NAAD 2007. tfjohns@comcast.net

JOHNSON, Theodore Arthur (Nev) P.O. Box 4551, South Lake Tahoe CA 95729 B Madera CA 12/31/1922 s Jordon Edward Johnson & Theodora Idell. AA Ventura Cnty Cmnty Coll 1966. D 1/6/1985 P 7/1/1985 Bp Wesley Frensdorff. m 2/14/1945 Betty Jean Price.

JOHNSON, Theodore William (WA) PO Box 386, Basye VA 22810 B Worcester MA 6/13/1944 s Theodore Titus Johnson & Carol Livingston. BA Franklin & Marshall Coll 1966; UTS 1969; MDiv VTS 1986; DMin SWTS 2000. D 6/11/1986 P 4/11/1987 Bp Peter James Lee. Emm Epis Ch Chestertown MD 2006; Ch Of The Ascen Silver Sprg MD 2003-2004; Pstr All Faith Epis Ch Charlotte Hall MD 2000-2002; S Dav's Epis Ch Richmond VA 1996-2000; Int S Mk's Ch Alexandria VA 1996; Emm Ch Middleburg VA 1994-1996; Int Ch Of S Paul's By The Sea Ocean City MD 1992-1993; Int Meade Memi Epis Ch Alexandria VA 1991-1992; R Emm Epis Ch (Piedmont Par) Delaplane VA 1988-1991; Int S Paul's Epis Ch Prince Frederick MD 1987-1988; Asst-To-R Emm Epis Ch Alexandria VA 1986-1987. theodorewjohnson@msn.com

JOHNSON, Thomas Stanley (NCal) 214 Leafwood Way, Folsom CA 95630 **P-in-c S Mich Ch Alturas CA 2011-** B Minneapolis MN 2/21/1940 s Stanley Nasen Johnson & Muriel Monique. No Pk U; BA U CA Los Angeles 1965; BD Fuller TS 1968; ETSBH 1997. D 12/14/1997 P 6/1/1998 Bp Gethin Benwil Hughes. m 12/12/1986 Susan Noel Ackland c 2. S Jn's Ch Indio CA 2002-2006; Vic Santa Rosa Del Mar Imperial CA 2002-2006; Dio San Diego San Diego CA 2002-2005; Vic S Hugh Of Lincoln Mssn Idyllwild CA 1998-2002. Professed, 3rd Ord, Soc of S Fran 1996. tjohnsonret@gmail.com

JOHNSON OHC, Walter Steve (Los) 1264 N Kings Rd Apt 17, West Hollywood CA 90069 **Mem, Cmsn on Black Mnstry Dio Los Angeles Los Angeles CA 2002-** B Wilmington DE 12/18/1938 s Walter H Johnson & Mary E. D 12/2/2006 Bp Chester Lovelle Talton. c 1. Soc Cath P 2010. holydeacon@hotmail.com

JOHNSON, W(ard) Kendall (ND) 1003 Crescent Ln, Bismarck ND 58501 B Fargo ND 5/17/1931 s Ward Kendall Johnson & Peggy N. BS U of No Dakota 1960; The Coll of Emm and St. Chad 1993. D 6/6/1986 P 10/2/1988 Bp Harold Anthony Hopkins Jr. m 6/23/1956 Anne Whittemore Short. Assoc R S Geo's Epis Ch Bismarck ND 1988-2008.

JOHNSON, Wayne Leonard (Chi) 3706 44th St, Rock Island IL 61201 B Minneapolis MN 1/11/1919 s Walfrid Leonard Johnson & Ruth Isabel. BA Trin Hartford CT 1940; BD SWTS 1945. D 3/23/1945 Bp William Blair Roberts P 12/1/1945 Bp Conrad Gesner. m 6/30/1945 Marie Bonell c 4. Trst Bp & Trsts Dio Springfield Springfield IL 1976-1986; R Ch Of The H Comf Kenilworth IL 1971-1985; Trst SWTS Evanston IL 1965-1981; R Trin Epis Ch Peoria IL 1963-1971; Dep GC Dio Springfield Springfield IL 1958-1969; R S Paul's Epis Ch Pekin IL 1950-1963; Cur S Jn's Epis Ch Decatur IL 1948-1950; P-in-c S Paul's Ch Brookings SD 1946-1948; D-in-c S Lk's Ch Hot Sprg SD 1945-1946. DD SWTS 1971. marpif@qconline.com

JOHNSON, William Alexander (NY) 27 Fox Meadow Rd, Scarsdale NY 10583 B Brooklyn NY 8/20/1931 s Charles Rafael Johansson & Ruth Augusta. BA CUNY 1953; BD Drew U 1956; MA NYU 1957; PhD Col 1959; ThD Lund U 1962. D 12/2/1967 P 3/30/1968 Bp John P Craine. m 6/11/1955 Carol Genevieve Lundquist c 3. Cathd Of St Jn The Div New York NY 1985-2001; P-in-c S Paul's Within the Walls Rome 00184 IT 1975-1976; Ch Of S Jas The Less Scarsdale NY 1970-1974; San Andres Ch Yonkers NY 1967-1970. Auth, *Search for Transcendence*, 1975; Auth, *Philos & The Gospel*, 1971; Auth, *Invitation to Theol*, 1970; Auth, *On Rel*, 1965; Auth, *Nature & the Supernatural*, 1960; Auth, *Philos of Rel of Anders Nygren*, 1960. AAR 1960; Amer Philos Soc 1960. "Who's Who in Amer" 1976; Phi Beta Kappa 1960.

JOHNSON, William Curtis (Oly) 19303 Fremont Ave N, Shoreline WA 98133 B Asbury Park NJ 3/1/1913 s William Curtis Johnson & Laura. Ch Army Trng Coll 1948. D 11/11/1952 P 5/1/1953 Bp Frank A Rhea. c 3. Asst P Ch Of The Ascen Seattle WA 1980-2001; S Andr's Ch Seattle WA 1968-1978; Archd Dio Idaho Boise ID 1958-1967; R All SS Epis Ch Boise ID 1954-1958; Vic S Jas Ch Burley ID 1952-1954; Vic St Matthews Epis Ch Rupert ID 1952-1954.

JOHNSON, William Francis (Chi) 5749 N Kenmore Ave, Chicago IL 60660 **Assoc Epis Ch Of The Atone Chicago IL 1967-** B Schaffer MI 7/4/1935 s Carl Louis Johnson & Cecile Bernadette. BA Elmhurst Coll 1961; MDiv SWTS 1964. D 6/13/1964 Bp James Winchester Montgomery P 12/1/1964 Bp Gerald Francis Burrill. Epis Ch Of The Atone Chicago IL 1964-2004.

JOHNSON, William Gerald (Az) Po Box 30742, Tucson AZ 85751 B Putnam CT 9/25/1939 s William Edward Johnson & Phyllis. AA Bos 1960; BA Bos 1962; STM Ya Berk 1965; MPA U of Arizona 1969. D 6/19/1965 P 2/12/1966 Bp John S Higgins. m 10/23/1988 Barbara Iler. S Raphael In The Vlly Mssn Benson AZ 1998-2007; Vic S Paul's Ch Tombstone AZ 1991-1998; Asst Ch Of S Matt Tucson AZ 1971-1980; Asst Gr S Paul's Epis Ch Tucson AZ 1971-1977; R All Faith Epis Ch Charlotte Hall MD 1968-1970; Cur S Paul's Ch No Kingstown RI 1965-1967. barbillj@me.com

JOHNSON, William Joseph (Roch) No address on file. B Brantford ON CA 2/17/1922 MA Col; BA McGill U. D 6/15/1974 P 5/1/1975 Bp John Harris Burt. Assoc S Mk's Ch Cleveland OH 1974-1982.

JOHNSON III, (William) Pegram (WA) 2004 Floyd Ave, Richmond VA 23220 B Petersburg VA 7/5/1939 s William Pegram Johnson & Nolie. BA W&M 1960; BD VTS 1965; STM STUSo 1970; PhD Emory U 1978. D 9/19/1965 Bp David Shepherd Rose P 6/10/1966 Bp George P Gunn. m 4/16/1977 Candis Veale c 1. S Asaph's Par Ch Bowling Green VA 2004-2010; Vic Chr Ch Accokeek MD 1985-1998; R Chr Ch S Jn's Par Accokeek MD 1985-1998; Asst S Jas Par Wilmington NC 1967-1969; Cur S Steph's Ch Newport News VA 1965-1967. Auth, "The Roads From Bethlehem," 1993. Sewanee Fllshp STUSo Sewanee TN 1998; Woods Fllshp VTS 1996; Fell Coll Of Preachers 1989; Fell For Hist Resrch Mellon. wpjoh3@juno.com

JOHNSON-TAYLOR, Allan B (WA) 4211 Enterprise Rd, Bowie MD 20720 B Bluefields NI 5/10/1961 s Artemus B Johnson & Alice Brunilda. BA U of Maryland 1989; MDiv VTS 1993; ThM PrTS 1999. D 6/12/1993 P 12/16/1993 Bp Peter James Lee. m 5/24/2003 Donna J J Bailey c 1. R Ch Of The Epiph Forestville MD 2007; Assoc S Mich And All Ang Ch Baltimore MD 2002-2004; Int S Phil Memi Ch Philadelphia PA 2002; R S Mich's Ch Yeadon PA 1995-2001; Asst Vic Trin Epis Ch Charlottesville VA 1993-1995. frallaj@msn.com

JOHNSON-TOTH, Louise M (Roch) 243 Genesee Park Blvd, Rochester NY 14619 B Buffalo NY 10/10/1946 d Theodore Roy Johnson & Betty. BA U Roch 1969; MA U Roch 1970; MSW Syr 1978; MDiv Bex 1993. D 6/5/1999 Bp William George Burrill P 5/27/2000 Bp Jack Marston McKelvey. m 5/4/1985 Gregory Martin Toth. R Gr Ch Scottsville NY 2001-2007; Vic S Andr's Epis Ch Caledonia NY 2001-2007; Int Assoc S Mk's And S Jn's Epis Ch Rochester NY 1999-2000. ljohnsontoth@yahoo.com

JOHNSTON, Clifford Ancel (CPa) 3147 Grahamton Rd, Morrisdale PA 16858 **P-in-c Chap Of The Gd Shpd Hawk Run PA 2008-** B Philipsburg PA 3/8/1956 s Clifford A Johnston & Mabel Ruth. BA Franklin & Marshall Coll Lancaster PA 1979. D 6/9/2007 P 12/22/2007 Bp Nathan Dwight Baxter. m 1/31/1987 Rebecca Susan Alberth c 1. EPF 2006; Integrity 2006. cliff@iqnetsys.net

JOHNSTON, David Knight (Mass) 78 Bishop Dr, Framingham MA 01702 B New York NY 11/8/1934 s John Harold Johnston & Lucile. CPE Advncd CPE; BA Colg 1956; MDiv VTS 1961; Coll of Preachers 1973. D 7/6/1961 P 6/29/1962 Bp Noble C Powell. m 4/20/1963 Valerie Anne Springer c 2. S Andr's Ch Framingham MA 1999-2000; S Andr's Ch Methuen MA 1998-1999; S Paul's Ch Peabody MA 1997-1998; S Ptr's Ch Salem MA 1995-1997; Trin Ch Newton Cntr MA 1993-1995; Dio Wstrn Massachusetts Springfield MA 1991-1992; S Steph's Ch Westborough MA 1991-1992; S Jn's Ch Winthrop MA 1989-1991; Ch Of The H Trin Marlborough MA 1988-1989; St Andrews Ch Boston MA 1985-1986; S Lk's And S Marg's Ch Allston MA 1983-1984; Trin Ch Canton MA 1983; S Anne's Ch No Billerica MA 1981-1982; S Paul's Ch Natick MA 1977-1981; Int S Geo's Ch Maynard MA 1976-1977; Int S Paul's Ch Natick MA 1975-1976; Dio Massachusetts Boston MA 1970-1973; Ch Of The H Sprt Wayland MA 1969-1975; The Ch Of The Nativ Cedarcroft Baltimore MD 1965-1969; S Ptr's Ch Lonaconing MD 1963-1965; S Jn's Ch Ellicott City MD 1961-1962. Fell, AAPC 1979; Int Ntwk 1983.

JOHNSTON, Duncan Howard (CPa) 125 N 25th St, Camp Hill PA 17011 **Mt Calv Camp Hill PA 2011-** B Matlock ENGLAND 9/3/1963 s Alan Keith Johnston & Edna Alice. BA (Hons) U Of Hull Hull Gb 1985; MA St. Jn's Coll Nottingham Gb 1993. Trans from Church Of England 8/31/2004 Bp Robert R Gepert. m 7/21/2005 Cindy Johnston c 3. S Jn's Ch Fremont MI 2004-2010. djepisc@sbcglobal.net

JOHNSTON, Edward (NY) Po Box 1502, Millbrook NY 12545 **Vic S Ptr's Ch Millbrook NY 1998-** B Clinton IA 3/8/1938 s Edward Johnston & Dorothy Hazel. BA Gri 1960; GTS 1962; STB EDS 1963; MA Col 1964. D 6/20/1963 P 6/19/1964 Bp Gordon V Smith. m 6/3/1962 Sally Eileen Edgar. Trst Dio New York New York City NY 1991-1993; Chair - Fin Com Dio New York New York City NY 1986-1988; Trst Emer Cathd Of St Jn The Div New York NY 1984-1998; R Chr's Ch Rye NY 1979-1997; Fin Com Dio New York New York City NY 1979-1985; Chair Cler Cont Educ Com Dio Newark Newark NJ 1978-1979; Chair Com Elctn Bp Coadj Dio Newark Newark NJ 1975-1976; Dept Fin Dio Newark Newark NJ 1970-1973; R S Dav's Ch Kinnelon NJ 1967-1979; Cur S Mk's Ch Mt Kisco NY 1964-1967; Asst S Mich's Ch New York NY 1963-1964. Trst Emer Cathd of St. Jn the Div, New York 1998; R Emer Chr's Ch, Rye, New York 1998. novavita.edward@gmail.com

JOHNSTON, Frank Norman (LI) PO Box 566, Onset MA 02558 B New York NY 5/28/1929 s Frank Frederick Johnston & Edith Elsa. BA St. Lawr Canton NY 1952; MDiv St. Lawr Canton NY 1955. D 6/25/1955 P 6/1/1956 Bp Norman B Nash. m 2/23/1952 Muriel Johnston c 5. Int Cathd Ch of All SS St Thos VI VI 1989-1991; Chr Ch Manhasset NY 1988-1989; R Chr Ch Manhasset NY 1967-1986; R S Mk's Ch Foxborough MA 1957-1967; Cur Trin Ch Newton Cntr MA 1955-1957. jonce@zworg.com

JOHNSTON, Hewitt Vinnedge (NJ) 41087 Calla Lily St, Indian Land SC 29707 B Milwaukee WI 7/6/1939 s Milton Urban Johnston & Katherine. BA

J

Hope Coll 1961; LTh SWTS 1964. D 7/26/1964 P 7/25/1965 Bp Charles Bennison. m 8/20/1964 Cynthia Jo Hendricks c 1. S Paul's Epis Ch Bound Brook NJ 1999-2000; Int Ch of S Jn on the Mtn Bernardsville NJ 1998-1999; Int S Lk's Ch Gladstone NJ 1997-1998; Int Ch Of The Ascen Clearwater FL 1996; Int S Anselm Epis Ch Lehigh Acres FL 1995-1996; Dio SW Florida Sarasota FL 1988-1993; R S Mary's Par Tampa FL 1983-1994; R S Geo's Ch Belleville IL 1976-1983; Vic S Paul's Epis Ch Elk Rapids MI 1970-1976; Vic Chr Epis Ch Charlevoix MI 1967-1976; Asst S Lk's Par Kalamazoo MI 1964-1967. hewitt.johnston@gmail.com

JOHNSTON, Laurel A (ECR) 222 Claudius Dr, Aptos CA 95003 **Epis Ch Cntr New York NY 2008-** B Milton MA 9/25/1964 d Thomas Johnston & Margaret. BA U CA 1987; MDiv CDSP 2006. D 6/24/2006 P 4/21/2007 Bp Sylvestre Donato Romero. Ch Of S Jn The Bapt Aptos CA 2006-2008. ljohnston@episcopalchurch.org

JOHNSTON, Lewis Tyra (WMo) 2105 Quail Creek Dr, Lawrence KS 66047 B Minneapolis MN 5/15/1930 s Raymond Franklin Johnston & Ruth. BA U MN 1953; MDiv SWTS 1957; MPA U of Missouri 1982. D 6/24/1957 P 2/1/1958 Bp Hamilton Hyde Kellogg. m 12/27/1952 Virginia Dunn c 3. R S Ptr's Epis Ch Kansas City MO 1989; Chair - Com on Aging Dio W Missouri Kansas City MO 1982-1990; COM Dio W Missouri Kansas City MO 1978-1981; Eccl Crt Dio W Missouri Kansas City MO 1976-1978; Bp's Coun Dio W Missouri Kansas City MO 1966-1972; Assoc R S Andr's Ch Kansas City MO 1964-1969; Vic S Ptr's Epis Ch Kansas City MO 1964-1969; Vic S Edw's Ch Duluth MN 1959-1964; Bp's Coun Dio Minnesota Minneapolis MN 1958-1964; D & P-in-c Geth Ch Appleton MN 1957-1959. Deer Lke Assn 1990; Endacott Soc 1992; ESMA 1979-1989. Citizen of the Year Jackson Cnty 1975. vljohnst@gmail.com

JOHNSTON, Madelynn Kirkpatrick (RG) Po Box 8716, Santa Fe NM 87504 **S Bede's Epis Ch Santa Fe NM 2004-** B Chicago IL 11/13/1945 d James Harold Dunn & Madelynn Leora. D 9/23/1977 Bp Richard Mitchell Trelease Jr. c 3.

JOHNSTON, Mark Wylie (Ala) 105 Delong Rd, Nauvoo AL 35578 **Exec Dir Chap Of The Ascen Nauvoo AL 1990-** B Nashville TN 10/23/1950 s Archie Simpson Johnston & Martha. BA U So 1973; MDiv S Lk TS 1980. D 6/12/1980 P 12/1/1980 Bp Furman Stough. m 8/14/2004 Margaret Wade. Dio Alabama Birmingham AL 1988-1989; S Mths Epis Ch Tuscaloosa AL 1984-1987; S Mich's Epis Ch Fayette AL 1980-1984. Outstanding Young Al Rel Ldr Jaycees.

JOHNSTON, Michael Adair (WMo) 3726 W/ 75th Street, Prairie Village KS 66208 B Kansas City MO 5/26/1946 s Ellis Thomas Johnston & Lucille Milanovitch. BA Colorado Coll 1968; MS U of Glasgow Glasgow GB 1971; MA Ya 1973; PhD Ya 1974; MDiv GTS 1991. D 6/15/1991 Bp Frank Tracy Griswold III P 1/18/1992 Bp William Walter Wiedrich. R Gr Ch Oak Pk IL 1997-2005; Vic Ch Of The Epiph Chicago IL 1996-1997; Assoc S Matt's Ch Evanston IL 1991-1996. Auth, "Praying w Icons," *ATR*, 2000; Auth, "Engaging the Word," *New Ch's Tchg Series*, Cowley Press, 1998; Auth, "Renaissance Sacr Arti," *Angl Theol Art*, 1993. mjohns06@sbcglobal.net

JOHNSTON, Nature Nancy Alice (Colo) 2881 C Rd, Grand Junction CO 81503 **R Ch Of The Nativ Grand Jct CO 2007-** B Miami FL 9/21/1954 d Bovard Tomlinson & Elizabeth. AA Florida St U 1974; BS Florida A&M U 1980; MDiv Ya Berk 2001. D 6/11/2005 P 12/17/2005 Bp Robert John O'Neill. Assoc P All SS Epis Ch Denver CO 2006-2007. naturejohnston@aol.com

JOHNSTON, Paul Martin (Pgh) 2219 Wightman St, Pittsburgh PA 15217 **P/Arts Chapl Trin Cathd Pittsburgh PA 2007-** B Fresno CA 4/22/1957 s Robert Johnston & Madeline. Trin Epis Sch; B.Mus Andr's U Berren Sprg MI 1980. D 6/10/2006 P 1/20/2007 Bp Robert William Duncan. m 6/17/1979 Sharon Sharon Lael Cumbo. pauljohnston777@hotmail.com

JOHNSTON, Philip Gilchrist (Va) 4773 Thornbury Dr, Fairfax VA 22030 B Buhl MN 3/14/1929 s Kenneth Alexander Johnston & Arlyn Grace. BS U of Kentucky 1952; BD/MDiv Epis TS In Kentucky 1958; LIU 1969; VTS 1979. D 6/14/1958 P 9/19/1958 Bp William R Moody. m 5/23/1987 Carol Lindblom c 2. Int S Matt's Epis Ch Sterling VA 1999-2001; Vic Piedmont Ch Madison VA 1983-1995; Int S Andr's Epis Ch Arlington VA 1978-1979; Asst Pohick Epis Ch Lorton VA 1978; Int Ch Of The Gd Shpd Burke VA 1977-1978; Nave Chapl (Mltry) Cathd of St Ptr & St Paul Washington DC 1970-1972; R Chr Epis Ch Harlan KY 1958-1960. Auth, *Var arts*. episcopro@aol.com

JOHNSTON III, Robert Hugh (Dal) 5311 Ridgedale Dr, Dallas TX 75206 **Assting Ch Of The Incarn Dallas TX 2004-** B Wharton TX 2/17/1966 s Robert Hugh Johnston. BS Baylor U; MTS SMU 2005. D 11/15/2003 P 6/3/2004 Bp James Monte Stanton. m 7/15/1989 Robin Lynn Johnston c 2. bjohnston@incarnation.org

JOHNSTON JR, Robert Hugh (WTex) 102 E. Live Oak St., Cuero TX 77954 B Houston TX 11/25/1930 s Robert H Johnston & Meddie. MD Baylor Coll Med; BS Baylor U. D 6/8/2009 P 12/9/2009 Bp Gary Richard Lillibridge. m 8/20/1955 Sara Stuart Sara Aileen Stuart c 4. bobyjohn@aol.com

JOHNSTON, Robert Owen (SVa) 207 Marshall St, Petersburg VA 23803 B Uniontown PA 12/16/1919 s Walter Owen Johnston & Edna Rose. Indiana U of Pennsylvania 1946; MA U Chi 1949; Command and Gnrl Stff Coll 1951; Penn 1951; MDiv VTS 1970. D 6/29/1970 P 4/9/1971 Bp David Shepherd Rose. m 8/19/1952 Josephine Lauretta Rich c 4. Calv Ch Bath Par Dinwiddie VA 1979-1984; Ch Of The Gd Shpd Bath Par Mc Kenney VA 1979-1984; Jackson Field Hm Jarratt VA 1975-1979. rbtjojohn@covad.net

JOHNSTON, Roy Wayne (WLa) 243 Whippoorwill Ln SW, Rome GA 30165 B Lexington KY 6/14/1936 s Roy Bell Johnston & Elsie Mae. BBA U of Miami 1959; BD Lexington TS 1962; MDiv STUSo 1969. D 12/27/1969 P 5/1/1970 Bp George Leslie Cadigan. m 10/27/1978 Mary C Stanfield c 1. Assoc Chr Epis Ch Tyler TX 1999-2001; R Ch Of The Redeem Oak Ridge LA 1990-1999; R S Andr's Epis Ch Mer Rouge LA 1990-1999; R S Thos' Ch Monroe LA 1988-1990; R S Steph's Ch Heathsville VA 1986-1988; Bp's Coun Dio Maryland Baltimore MD 1976-1978; R Emm Ch Cumberland MD 1974-1978; P-in-c S Alb's Epis Ch Fulton MO 1970-1972. miami59@att.net

JOHNSTON, Sally (USC) St. Martin's-In-The-Fields, 5220 Clemson Ave., Columbia SC 29206 **S Martins-In-The-Field Columbia SC 2004-** B Charlotte NC 6/5/1950 d William Johnston & Virginia. BA U NC 1972; MPA California St U 1979; MDiv GTS 2004. D 6/19/2004 P 1/15/2005 Bp Michael Bruce Curry. m 1/28/1980 Harold L Newfield c 2. Assoc Ch Of The H Comf Charlotte NC 2004-2009. svj2007@gmail.com

✠ **JOHNSTON, Rt Rev Shannon Sherwood** (Va) 110 W Franklin St, Richmond VA 23220 **Bp of Virginia Dio Virginia Richmond VA 2007-; Dep Gc Dio Mississippi Jackson MS 2000-; Dep Gc Dio Mississippi Jackson MS 2000-; Dn Dioc Conv Dio Mississippi Jackson MS 1998-; VP Exec Com Dio Mississippi Jackson MS 1997-** B Florence AL 10/20/1958 s Albert Sherwood Johnston & Nancy Kopp. BA U So 1981; MDiv SWTS 1988. D 6/11/1988 P 12/14/1988 Bp Robert Oran Miller Con 5/26/2007 for Va. m 5/20/1995 Ellen G Gammill. R All SS' Epis Ch Tupelo MS 1994-2007; Kairos Prison Mnstry Dio Mississippi Jackson MS 1991-1995; R Ch Of The Adv Sumner MS 1990-1994; Cur S Paul's Ch Selma AL 1988-1990. Omicron Delta Kappa; Phi Beta Kappa; Vstng Stdt Schlr Westcott Hse Theol Coll Camb Engl. sjohnston@thediocese.net

JOHNSTON, Suzanne Elaine (Roch) 1245 Culver Rd., Rochester NY 14609 B Canada 7/1/1959 d William Frank Flockhart & Jean Margaret. BA SUNY Geneseo 1981; MA SUNY Buffalo 1983. D 5/2/2009 Bp Prince Grenville Singh. m 6/4/1983 William Johnston c 3. S Mk's And S Jn's Epis Ch Rochester NY 2009. suzanneejohnston@aol.com

JOHNSTON, William Merrill (FdL) 1010 Congress St, Neenah WI 54956 **Cn to the Ret Cler Dio Fond du Lac Appleton WI 1997-** B Beloit WI 3/14/1935 s Wallace Chester Johnston & Evelyn Leonora. BA Macalester Coll 1957; LTh SWTS 1960; Cert Minneapolis Mha Minneapolis MN 1971; MDiv SWTS 1976. D 6/18/1960 Bp Hamilton Hyde Kellogg P 5/22/1961 Bp Philip Frederick McNairy. m 12/20/1958 Beverly Hogan. Cler Deploy Off Dio Fond du Lac Appleton WI 1997-2010; S Thos Ch Menasha WI 1976-1997; R S Jas On The Pkwy Minneapolis MN 1969-1976. revbevj@new.rr.com

JOHNSTON, Zula Jean (Oly) 8527 46th Ct Ne, Olympia WA 98516 **D S Jos And S Jn Ch Steilacoom WA 2009-** B Pittsburgh PA 7/4/1939 BS No Carolina Cntrl U 1972; MS U CO 1976. D 6/18/2003 Bp Sanford Zangwill Kaye Hampton. D S Ben Epis Ch Lacey WA 2003-2005. Ord of S Lk 1992. thezul@aol.com

JOHNSTONE, Elise Beaumont (Lex) 101 Whitney Path Apt 9, Georgetown KY 40324 **P-in-c Ch Of The H Trin Georgetown KY 2011-; GC Dep Dio Lexington Lexington KY 2011-; Liturg and Mus Co-Chair Dio Lexington Lexington KY 2007-; Mem, Commisson on Mnstry Dio Lexington Lexington KY 2006-** B 3/11/1975 d John Moser Johnstone & Sandra Lee. BA U GA 1997; MDiv GTS 2005. D 6/18/2005 P 1/5/2006 Bp Stacy F Sauls. m 2/10/2007 Ryan Douglas Shrauner c 1. Mem, Commisson on Mnstry Dio Lexington Lexington KY 2006-2009; Mem, Exec Coun Dio Lexington Lexington KY 2006-2009; Assitant To The R Ch Of The Gd Shpd Lexington KY 2005-2011. elisebjohnstone@gmail.com

JOHNSTONE, Mary Boardman McAvoy (Me) 89 Pinckney St, Boston MA 02114 B New York NY 11/30/1935 d Clifford Thomas McAvoy & Frances Chisolm. Smith 1956; BA NWU 1970; Rhode Island Sch for Deacons 1985; MA Ya Berk 1989; Dio So Carolina SC 2000. D 7/13/1985 P 6/24/1989 Bp George Nelson Hunt III. m 6/16/1956 Robert Le Grand Johnstone c 4. Assoc Gr Ch Charleston SC 1998-2003; Eccl Crt Dio Maine Portland ME 1994-1996; Vic S Columba's Epis Ch Boothbay Harbor ME 1994-1996; Int R Emm Ch Newport RI 1994; Eccl Crt Dio Rhode Island Providence RI 1989-1994; Assoc R Trin Ch Newport RI 1989-1994; D Trin Ch Newport RI 1985-1989. mbj@jboats.com

JONES, Alan (Cal) 1100 California St, San Francisco CA 94108 B London UK 3/5/1940 s Edward Augustus Jones & Blanche Hilda. BA U of Nottingham 1963; STB GTS 1965; STM GTS 1968; Fllshp GTS 1968; PhD U of Nottingham 1971; D. Litt U of San Francisco 2008. Trans from Church Of England 3/15/1967 Bp Horace W B Donegan. m 4/18/1999 Virginia Franche c 2. Dn Gr Cathd San Francisco CA 1985-2009; Ascetical Theol The GTS New York NY 1975-1985; Assoc Dir Dio New York New York City NY 1971-1974; Asst

The Ch of S Ign of Antioch New York NY 1967-1968. Auth, "Common Pryr on Common Ground," *Common Pryr on Common Ground*, Morehouse, 2006; Auth, "Reimagining Chrsnty," *Reimagining Chrsnty*, Wiley, 2005; Auth, "Seasons of Gr," *Seasons of Gr*, Wiley, 2003; Auth, "Living the Truth," *Living the Truth*, Cowley, 2001; Auth, "The Soul's Jounrey," *The Soul's Journey*, Cowley, 2001; Auth, "Exploring Sprtl Direction," *Exploring Sprtl Direction*, Cowley, 1992; Auth, "Sacrifice and Delight," *Sacrifice & Delight*, Harper Collins, 1992; Auth, "Passion for Pilgrimage," *Passion for Pilgrimage*, Harper and Row, 1989; Auth, "Soul Making," *Soul Making*, HarperSanFrancsico, 1985; Auth, "Living in the Sprt," *Living in the Sprt*, Seabury, 1982; Auth, "Journey Into Chr," *Journey into Chr*, Cowley, 1977. OBE(Ord of the British Empire) Queen of Engl 2003; Hon Cn-Chartres Cathd Chartres Cathd 2001; Chapl The Venerable Ord of St. Jn 1985. alanj1947@me.com

JONES, Andrew Boyd (Mil) 2920 Pelham Rd, Madison WI 53713 **GC Dep Dio Milwaukee Milwaukee WI 2010-; Dn, W Convoc Dio Milwaukee Milwaukee WI 2009-; Exec Coun Dio Milwaukee Milwaukee WI 2009-; R S Andr's Ch Madison WI 2006-** B Baltimore MD 8/6/1960 s Stanley Boyd Jones & Linda May. BA Juniata Coll 1982; MDiv VTS 2002. D 6/8/2002 Bp John Leslie Rabb P 1/4/2003 Bp Robert Wilkes Ihloff. m 8/13/1983 Suzanne Eileen Brown c 2. Asst R All SS Ch Frederick MD 2002-2006. Bp's Shield Awd Dio Milwaukee 2011. abj@chesapeake.net

JONES, Andrew Lovell (Ct) Po Box 1083, Norwalk CT 06856 B Huntington WV 5/14/1949 s Franklin V Jones & Ruth Campbell. BA Marshall U 1971; MDiv VTS 1974; Certification Mid-Atlantic Trng & Consulting 1977; Certification Mid-Atlantic Trng & Consulting 1978; MBA U of Bridgeport 1990. D 6/10/1974 Bp Robert Poland Atkinson P 2/1/1975 Bp Wilburn Camrock Campbell. m 6/14/2003 Kathleen Crist c 2. Supply P Calv Epis Ch Bridgeport CT 1997-1999; Supply P Calv Epis Ch Bridgeport CT 1986-1987; Supply P S Lk's/S Paul's Ch Bridgeport CT 1986-1987; Trin Epis Ch Southport CT 1981-1984; St Davids Ch 1974-1981; Cur The Memi Ch Of The Gd Shpd Parkersburg WV 1974-1976. Ord of S Vinc 1975-1981. andrew_jones@msn.com

JONES, Angela Louise (Neb) 1555 14Th St, Mitchell NE 69357 B Falls City NE 2/4/1949 d Roy James Wheeler & Deila Mae. D 12/9/2006 Bp Joe Goodwin Burnett. c 2. musicmom2@earthlink.net

JONES, Ann Brewster (NC) 2121 E 8th St, Charlotte NC 28204 **Died 2/28/2010** B Portland OR 12/10/1952 d Howard Richard Jones & Marjean Eleanor. BA U Roch 1974; MDiv VTS 1977; DMin Candler TS Emory U 1992. D 6/25/1977 Bp William Foreman Creighton P 4/8/1978 Bp John Thomas Walker. c 1. Contrib, *PB Manual*. Who's Who in Amer Wmn. abjones2121@hotmail.com

JONES II, Bennett Green (WMass) 569 Main Street, Fitchburg MA 01420 **P-in-c Chr Ch Fitchburg MA 2010-** B Cleveland OH 10/6/1959 s Wayne Summers Jones & Shirley. BA Bowling Green St U 1982; MDiv VTS 1986. D 6/28/1986 Bp James Russell Moodey P 1/12/1987 Bp Furman Stough. m 5/1/1993 Carolyn Gibson c 2. R S Paul's Epis Ch Munster IN 2000-2010; Int Chr Ch Cape Girardeau MO 1999-2000; All SS Epis Ch Farmington MO 1998-1999; Int S Pauls Epis Ch Ironton MO 1998-1999; Dio Maryland Baltimore MD 1997-1998; Supply P Dio Missouri S Louis MO 1997-1998; Supply P Dio Los Angeles Los Angeles CA 1994-1997; Vic Ch Of The Trsfg Lake S Louis MO 1988-1994; Asst R S Paul's Ch Selma AL 1986-1988. benjones@keepingupwith.com

✠ JONES, Rt Rev Bob Gordon (Wyo) 87 Wapiti Estates Drive, PO Box 292, Wapiti WY 82450 B Paragould AR 8/22/1932 s F H Jones & Helen Truman. BBA U of Mississippi 1956; MDiv Epis TS of the SW 1959. D 6/29/1959 P 4/25/1960 Bp Robert Raymond Brown Con 10/31/1977 for Wyo. m 5/22/1993 Mary Page deBordenave c 4. Int Chr Ch Par Pensacola FL 2007-2008; Assoc. Bp (Ret) Chr Ch Cody WY 2002-2011; Exec Coun Appointees New York NY 1996; Chair Bd Casper Yth Crisis Cntr Dio Wyoming Casper WY 1986-1996; Pres WY Coun Chs Dio Wyoming Casper WY 1985-1986; Chair Bd Laramie Yth Crisis Cntr Dio Wyoming Casper WY 1981-1996; Exec Com C14 Dio Wyoming Casper WY 1981-1987; Bp of Wyo Dio Wyoming Casper WY 1977-1997; Dio Wyoming Casper WY 1977-1996; S Christophers Ch Anchorage AK 1975-1977; Vic S Ptr's Ch Seward AK 1974-1975; Vic S Christophers Ch Anchorage AK 1967-1974; Vic S Barth's Ch Palmer AK 1967 1971; P-in-c S Geo In The Arctic Kotzebue AK 1962-1967; Asst Trin Cathd Little Rock AR 1959-1962. Newcomin Soc 1978-1996. Hon DD Epis TS of the SW Austin TX 1978. bobgjones822@yahoo.com

JONES, Bonnie Quantrell (Lex) 1801 Glenhill Dr, Lexington KY 40502 **All SS Epis Ch Richmond KY 2006-; Dio Lexington Lexington KY 2006-** B Detroit MI 4/13/1944 d Arthur Everet Quantrell & Eleanor Marie. BA U MN 1966; MDiv Lexington TS 1996. D 11/30/1996 P 5/31/1997 Bp Don Adger Wimberly. m 7/21/1984 William Jones c 2. St Martha's Epis Ch Lexington KY 2007-2009; S Ptr's Ch Paris KY 1996-2005. Philanthropist of the Year Assoc. of Fundraising Professionals 2007; Bluegrass Bus Hall of Fame JA of the Bluegrass 1999; YWCA Wmn of the Year YWCA of the Bluegrass 1995. bonnie@stmarthaslex.org

JONES, Bradley Tyler (NY) 161 Mansion St., Poughkeepsie NY 12601 B Seattle WA 3/12/1948 s Bradley Tyler Jones & Phyllis Howard. BA Alaska Pacific U 1990; MDiv GTS 2004. D 4/17/2004 P 10/31/2004 Bp Leopold Frade. m 12/12/1972 Mary L Bowditch c 2. Vic S Paul's Ch Poughkeepsie NY 2006-2010; Cur Ch of the Ascen Munich 81545 DE 2004-2006. pastortyler@gmail.com

JONES, Bryan William (Los) 5306 Arbor Road, Long Beach CA 90808 **S Lk's Of The Mountains La Crescenta CA 2009-** B Salt Lake City UT 8/17/1953 s Felton Taylor Jones & Rose. BA U of Utah 1976; MDiv EDS 1979. D 11/6/1978 P 6/1/1979 Bp Otis Charles. m 11/11/2005 Amy Fay Pringle. S Thos Of Cbury Par Long Bch CA 2002-2009; S Aid's Epis Ch Malibu CA 2000-2002; MHA Long Bch CA 1987-1995; R Ch Of The Epiph Los Angeles CA 1982-1987; Int S Steph's Epis Ch Boston MA 1981-1982; Int Chr Ch Swansea MA 1980-1981; Dio Utah Salt Lake City UT 1979-1980; P-in-c S Jn's Epis Ch Logan UT 1979-1980. bryjones@aol.com

JONES, Carolyn Gibson (WMass) 29 Payson St, Fitchburg MA 01420 **Yth Min Chr Ch Fitchburg MA 2011-** B Philadelphia PA 6/15/1949 d Mark Mendelssohn Gibson & Bernice. U Chi; Weston Jesuit TS; BA Beaver Coll 1971; MDiv EDS 1985. D 6/8/1985 Bp Paul Moore Jr P 6/9/1986 Bp Robert Rae Spears Jr. m 5/1/1993 Bennett Green Jones. Cler Alt Dep Dio Nthrn Indiana So Bend IN 2009; Examing Chapl Dio Nthrn Indiana So Bend IN 2007-2010; COM Dio Nthrn Indiana So Bend IN 2004-2009; Wrshp Min S Paul's Epis Ch Munster IN 2003-2010; Assoc For Fam Mnstrs All SS Par Beverly Hills CA 1994-1997; Cn For Educ And Admin Chr Ch Cathd S Louis MO 1991-1994; Asstg P Par of Trin Ch New York NY 1987-1991; Asst Ch Of The H Trin New York NY 1986-1987; Dir - CE S Jas Ch New York NY 1979-1982. Keynoter ECW, Arkansas 2001; Keynoter ECW, Cntrl Gulf Coast 2001; Keynoter ECW, W Texas 2001; Chapl Ecw Trien, Denver 2000; Keynoter Aspiring Wmn Conf, Pgh 1998; Prchr Twa Flight 800 Memi Serv, LA 1996. carolyngjones@keepingupwith.com

JONES JR, Cecil Baron (Miss) 147 Links Dr Apt 42C, Canton MS 39046 B Meridian MS 10/2/1941 s Cecil Baron Jones & Margaret Devane. BA U of Mississippi 1963; MDiv STUSo 1966. D 5/28/1966 P 5/1/1967 Bp John M Allin. c 3. R All SS' Epis Ch Tupelo MS 1980-1992; R Gr Epis Ch Canton MS 1970-1980; The Chap Of The Cross Madison MS 1970-1977; Vic S Eliz's Mssn Collins MS 1968-1970; Vic S Steph's Ch Columbia MS 1968-1970; Vic Ch Of The Redeem Greenville MS 1966-1968; Cur S Jas Ch Greenville MS 1966-1968. jones_cecil@bellsouth.net

✠ JONES III, Rt Rev Charles (Mont) 5407 Kerr Dr, Helena MT 59602 B El Paso TX 9/13/1943 s Charles Irving Jones & Helen Abbott. BS Cit 1965; MBA U NC 1966; S Geo Coll 1976; MDiv STUSo 1977; Ldrshp Acad for New Directions 1982; DD STUSo 1989. D 6/2/1977 Bp David Shepherd Rose P 12/10/1977 Bp David Reed Con 2/8/1986 for Mont. m 6/18/1966 Ashby M Jones c 4. Bp Of Mt Dio Montana Helena MT 1986-2001; Archd Dio Kentucky Louisville KY 1982-1985; Barren River Area Coun Louisville KY 1977-1985; Vic Trin Ch Russellville KY 1977-1985; Coll Chapl Dio Kentucky Louisville KY 1977-1982. Auth, "Mssn Strtgy In The 21st Century"; Auth, "Total Mnstry: A Practical Approach". DD TS U So 1989. bpci@aol.com

JONES, Charles James (CNY) 9 Jutland Road, Binghamton NY 13903 **Chapl to Ret Cler & SurvivingSpouse Dio Cntrl New York Syracuse NY 2005-; Dio Cntrl New York Syracuse NY 1982-** B Niagara Falls NY 2/19/1934 s Theodore Melvin Jones & Dorothy. BS SUNY 1962; MDiv VTS 1967. D 6/17/1967 P 3/9/1968 Bp Lauriston L Scaife. m 8/27/1960 Joan Margaret Jones c 2. Zion Ch Windsor NY 2000-2011; Vic Zion Ch Windsor NY 1999; Chair Educ Mnstry Dept Dio Cntrl New York Syracuse NY 1977-1981; Chair Educ Mnstry Dept Dio Cntrl New York Syracuse NY 1977-1981; R The Ch Of The Gd Shpd Binghamton NY 1974-1999; Secy/Treas Binghamton Distr Dio Cntrl New York Syracuse NY 1974-1982; Asst Gr Epis Ch Elmira NY 1969-1974; Mssy-in-c S Jn's Epis Ch Elmira Heights NY 1967-1969. cjones2@stny.rr.com

JONES, Constance M (SVa) 6214 Monroe Pl, Norfolk VA 23508 **Assoc Gr Ch Yorktown Yorktown VA 2006-** B Plainfield NJ 3/20/1947 d Hugh McCulloch & Patricia. BA Mt Holyoke Coll 1968; MA Duke 1970; PhD Duke 1974; Cert UTS 2002; Cert VTS 2003. D 6/14/2003 P 12/14/2003 Bp Carol Joy Gallagher. c 2. Assoc Chr and S Lk's Epis Ch Norfolk VA 2003-2007. Auth, "She's Leaving Hm: Letting Go as My Daughter Goes to Coll," Andrews McMeel, 2002; co-Auth, "A Goodly Heritage:The Dio Sthrn Virginia 1892-1992," Pictorial Heritage, 1992. Phi Beta Kappa 1974. Prof Emer Tidewater Cmnty Coll 2004; Mem Phi Beta Kappa 1974. wcdjones@infionline.net

JONES, Constance Ruth (Ak) 2241 Sunburst Cir, Anchorage AK 99501 B Tracy MN 11/4/1940 BA Carleton Coll. D 12/16/2000 P 7/22/2001 Bp Mark Lawrence Mac Donald. Assoc R S Mary's Ch Anchorage AK 2001-2007. Graduating Sr Awd For Reading Scripture And Liturg VTS 2001; hon Grad VTS 2001. connie@godsview.org

JONES, Curtis Carl (Ark) 20900 Chenal Pkwy, Little Rock AR 72223 **S Marg's Epis Ch Little Rock AR 2011-** B Little Rock AR 4/8/1950 s Tracy Duncan Jones & Leone Bellingrath. Henderson St Coll; U of Arkansas Little Rock. D

10/28/2000 Bp Larry Earl Maze P 10/9/2010 Bp Larry R Benfield. m 9/28/1996 Mary Price Mary Balch Price c 2. curtisj501@hotmail.com

JONES, DANIEL GWILYM (Be) 315 Calvin St, Dunmore PA 18512 **COM Dio Bethlehem Bethlehem PA 2007-** B Scranton PA 4/23/1932 s Thomas John Jones & Sarah Jane. BS U Of Scranton 1963; MBA Wilkes Coll 1969; EFM STUSo 1996. D 6/14/1997 P 12/13/1997 Bp Paul Victor Marshall. m 6/20/1959 Laura Dovaston DEYKES c 1. Dioc Coun Dio Bethlehem Bethlehem PA 1999-2005; R H Cross Epis Ch Wilkes Barre PA 1998-2010; D Gr Epis Ch Kingston PA 1996-1998. dgjldj@verizon.net

JONES, David Alexander (Md) Po Box 121, Highland MD 20777 B Huntington,NY 8/14/1931 s J Denovan Jones & Jessie H. BA MI SU 1953; BD EDS 1957. D 6/30/1957 Bp Richard S M Emrich P 2/1/1958 Bp Archie H Crowley. m 2/27/1960 Rose Bolt c 4. Dir Of Coll Wk Dio Maryland Baltimore MD 1964-1968; R S Andr's Ch Manchester NH 1961-1964; Min Chr Ch Cranbrook Bloomfield Hills MI 1957-1958.

✠ JONES, Rt Rev David Colin (Va) 4800 Fillmore Ave, Alexandria VA 22311 **Bp Suffr Of VA Dio Virginia Richmond VA 1995-** B Youngstown OH 6/20/1943 s John Henry Jones & Jean. BA W Virginia U 1965; MDiv VTS 1968; Coll of Preachers 1980; DMin VTS 1991; DD VTS 1996. D 6/11/1968 P 12/18/1968 Bp Wilburn Camrock Campbell Con 6/24/1995 for Va. m 6/5/1965 Mary B Biddle c 2. Bd Theol Educ Dio Virginia Richmond VA 1995-1997; Cmsn On Ch Planting Dio Virginia Richmond VA 1991-1994; Chair, Cmsn On Congreg Mssns Dio Virginia Richmond VA 1990-1993; Chair, Dioc Bdgt Com Dio Virginia Richmond VA 1990-1991; Exec Bd Dio Virginia Richmond VA 1988-1991; Dioc Bdgt Com Dio Virginia Richmond VA 1987-1991; Chair E Afr Mnstry Com Dio Virginia Richmond VA 1985-1988; Stndg Com Dio Virginia Richmond VA 1985-1988; Chair, Evang Com Dio Virginia Richmond VA 1983-1986; Com Mssn Outreach & Chs Under Bp Supvsn Dio Virginia Richmond VA 1981-1985; Mentor Field Educ VTS Alexandria VA 1980-1995; R Ch Of The Gd Shpd Burke VA 1978-1995; R S Steph's Epis Ch Beckley WV 1972-1977; Vic S Jas' Epis Ch Lewisburg WV 1968-1972. Paul Harris Fell Rotary 1996. djones@thediocese.net

JONES, David George (ECR) 1061 Garcia Rd, Santa Barbara CA 93103 B Nashville TN 7/21/1931 s George Francis Jones & Elizabeth Wilson. PhD Columbia Pacific U; BA U So 1953; BD STUSo 1957. D 6/24/1957 Bp John Vander Horst P 12/1/1957 Bp Theodore N Barth. Asst Trin Cathd San Jose CA 1991; Asst Ch Of S Jn The Bapt Aptos CA 1972-1990; Serv S Steph The Mtyr Ch Minneapolis MN 1967-1971. Auth, "The Kit For Ch Renwl"; Auth, "Beyond Bravery," *The Courage To Lead.* Presidential Round Table 1990.

JONES, David James (ECR) le bourg, 47120 Loubes-Bernac, Duras 47120 France B Palo Alto CA 5/21/1945 s James Frederick Jones & Annette Victoria. BA San Francisco St U 1967; BD EDS 1970; S Geo's Coll Jerusalem IL 1986. D 6/27/1970 Bp C Kilmer Myers P 5/1/1971 Bp George Richard Millard. m 10/3/1970 Martha Millard. Secy Conv Dio El Camino Real Monterey CA 1987-1997; Stndg Com Dio El Camino Real Monterey CA 1985-1986; R Calv Epis Ch Santa Cruz CA 1981-2001; Chair Dept Yth Mnstrs Dio El Camino Real Monterey CA 1975-1978; Vic S Lk's Ch Hollister CA 1974-1981; Cur All SS Epis Ch Palo Alto CA 1970-1972. davidjjones@free.fr

JONES, David P (NH) 1229 Hinman Avenue, Evanston IL 60202 **Int Dio Chicago Chicago IL 2010-** B Saint Louis MO 3/8/1949 s Howard Gist Jones & Frances. Loyola U 1970; BA Hob 1971; MDiv PDS 1974; S Geo's Coll Jerusalem 1978; DMin Fuller TS 1986. D 6/22/1974 P 12/14/1974 Bp Robert Bracewell Appleyard. m 10/6/2007 Heath Howe c 2. Dvlpmt and PR Off SWTS Evanston IL 2007-2008; R S Paul's Ch Concord NH 1991-2006; Archd Dio Pittsburgh Monroeville PA 1985-1991; R S Jas Epis Ch Pittsburgh PA 1979-1984; Asst Chr Epis Ch No Hills Pittsburgh PA 1974-1979. Soc of S Jn the Evang - Assoc 2001. davidinnh@hotmail.com

JONES, Derek Leslie (Cal) 786 Tunbridge Rd, Danville CA 94526 B London UK 11/13/1939 s Frederick George Thomas Jones & Lucy Ethel. D 10/23/1978 Bp Robert Marshall Anderson. m 4/16/1966 Selena-Jane Lees Verral c 3. Asst The Epis Par Of S Dav Minnetonka MN 1978-1991.

JONES, Donald Avery (Ind) 312 E Lookout Ln, Bloomington IN 47408 B Oak Park IL 12/2/1938 s Avery Carlson Jones & Margaret. BA Beloit Coll 1960; MD CDSP 1963. D 6/15/1963 Bp James Winchester Montgomery P 12/21/1963 Bp Gerald Francis Burrill. m 5/26/1963 Margaret Simpson c 2. R Trin Epis Ch Bloomington IN 2000-2006; R Ch Of The Nativ Indianapolis IN 1987-2000; Cn Res S Paul's Cathd Peoria IL 1979-1987; R Ch Of The H Comm Lake Geneva WI 1971-1979; Cur Emm Epis Ch Rockford IL 1963-1966. donjones4@juno.com

JONES, Dorothy Kovacs (Cal) Po Box 768, Tiburon CA 94920 **Pres, Bd of Trst Epis Sch For Deacons Berkeley CA 2010-** B Lorain OH 3/18/1931 d Louis Kovacs & Sophia Mary. BA Kent St U 1955; BA Sch for Deacons 1990. D 12/8/1990 Bp William Edwin Swing. Archd Dio California San Francisco CA 1999-2007; Vocations Secy Dio California San Francisco CA 1996-2006; Bd Trsts Dioc Sch Dio California San Francisco CA 1991-1993; D S Andr's Epis Ch San Bruno CA 1990-1993; S Steph's Par Belvedere CA 1975-1986. NAAD 1990. dcndort@comcast.net

JONES, Duncan Haywood (NC) PO Box 338, Jackson NC 27845 B Fayetteville NC 6/12/1932 s Duncan Henry Jones & Mary Catherine. BS USNA 1957; MS Untd States Naval Postgraduate Sch 1969. D 5/28/2000 Bp Robert Hodges Johnson. m 5/10/2003 Frances Page c 3. duncanhjones@yahoo.com

JONES JR, Eddie Ellsworth (Fla) 160 Bear Pen Rd, Ponte Vedra Beach FL 32082 B MobileAL 6/25/1947 s Eddie Ellsworth Jones & Mattie Clyde. BS U of W Alabama 1969; MDiv Candler TS Emory U 1972. D 6/11/1989 P 12/1/1989 Bp Frank Stanley Cerveny. m 7/6/1967 Janine McCurley c 1. Vic S Gabriels Epis Ch Jacksonville FL 2005-2008; Int St Fran in the Field Ponte Vedra FL 2004-2005; R Chr Ch Monticello FL 1996-2004; Chapl Off Of Bsh For ArmdF New York NY 1989-1997. eejones72@gmail.com

JONES, Elizabeth Claiborne (At) 221 Upland Rd, Decatur GA 30030 **Dio Atlanta Atlanta GA 2005-** B Durham NC 11/22/1950 d Claiborne Stribling Jones & Annie. Mt Holyoke Coll 1969; BA U NC 1972; MDiv Candler TS Emory U 1978. D 6/10/1978 Bp Charles Judson Child Jr P 6/12/1979 Bp Bennett Jones Sims. R Ch Of The Epiph Atlanta GA 1985-2004; Chair Com Dio Atlanta Atlanta GA 1985-1988; Pres Cler Assn Dio Atlanta Atlanta GA 1981-1983; Chapl/Asst Ch Of The H Comf Atlanta GA 1979-1985; H Innoc Ch Atlanta GA 1979-1985; H Innoc' Epis Sch Atlanta GA 1979-1985; D Epis Ch Of The H Sprt Cumming GA 1978-1979. Auth, "Wmn Of The Word". Sr Preaching Awd. claibby@gmail.com

JONES, Elizabeth Goodyear (Miss) 621 Briarwood Drive, Gulfport MS 39560 **Int S Ptr's By The Sea Gulfport MS 2008-** B Key West FL 6/22/1946 d William Parkhurst Goodyear & Sarah Elizabeth. BA U of Mississippi 1968; MDiv CDSP 1986. D 6/7/1986 P 6/6/1987 Bp William Edwin Swing. m 2/14/1981 David B Jones c 1. R S Jas Ch Greenville MS 2001-2007; Vic S Paul's Epis Ch Corinth MS 1995-2001; Int S Phil's Ch Jackson MS 1994-1995; Non-par Dio Mississippi Jackson MS 1993-1994; Chapl S Andr's Cathd Jackson MS 1991-1993; Vic S Matt's Epis Ch Forest MS 1989-1991; Assoc S Paul's Epis Ch Walnut Creek CA 1986-1988. Hon Fellowowship Sem of the SW Autsin TX 1996. lizgjones1@gmail.com

JONES, Eustan Ulric (LI) 721 E 96th St Apt 2, Brooklyn NY 11236 B Calliaqua St. Vincent 10/20/1941 s Wilfred Cornelius Jones & Gertrude Hope Iona. Dip.Th Codrington Coll 1977. Trans from Church in the Province Of The West Indies 11/1/1993 Bp Orris George Walker Jr. m 10/20/1965 Marilyn S Williams c 3. Stndg Com Dio Long Island Garden City NY 2001-2007; DCOM; Merc Bd Thel Dio Long Island Garden City NY 1998-1999; R Ch Of S Jas The Less Jamaica NY 1994-2007; Asst Gr Ch Jamaica NY 1993-1994. frgaf1941@yahoo.com

JONES, Frederick Lamar (At) 3803 Corinth Dr, Gainesville GA 30506 B Winston-Salem NC 11/24/1947 s Lamar Ramsuer Jones & Anne Poytress. MDiv SWTS 1973; BA U So 1973. D 6/25/1973 P 2/9/1974 Bp Christoph Keller Jr. c 3. Assoc Cathd Of S Phil Atlanta GA 2001-2004; Gr Epis Ch Gainesville GA 1988-2001; R S Paul's Ch Fayetteville AR 1979-1988; Dio Arkansas Little Rock AR 1976-1979; Chapl S Mart's U Cntr Fayetteville AR 1976-1979; Asst Trin Ch Pine Bluff AR 1975-1976; R S Steph's Ch Blytheville AR 1973-1975. cjones867@neo.rr.com

JONES, Gary Durward (Va) 412 Maple Ave, Richmond VA 23226 B Chapel Hill NC 9/4/1958 s Durward Spencer Jones & Nancy Little. BA U NC 1980; MDiv Ya Berk 1985. D 6/23/1985 P 4/1/1986 Bp William Evan Sanders. m 6/6/1981 Cherry H Hill c 3. R Ch Of The H Comm Memphis TN 2001-2005; S Andr's Epis Ch Charlotte NC 2001; Epis. Urban Mnstry Charlotte NC 2000-2001; R Ch Of The Redeem Bryn Mawr PA 1999-2000; R S Ptr's Epis Ch Charlotte NC 1991-1999; R S Eliz's Epis Ch Knoxville TN 1988-1991; Dio E Tennessee Knoxville TN 1987-1989; Cn For Soc Mnstry Dio E Tennessee Knoxville TN 1987-1988; S Jn's Epis Cathd Knoxville TN 1985-1987; D-In-Trng S Steph's Ch Richmond VA 1985-1986. Soc Of S Jn The Evang. gjones@saintstephensrichmond.net

JONES, Gary H (Tex) 3806 Kiamesha Drive, Missouri City TX 77459 **Chapl Dio Texas Houston TX 2007-** B Bellingham WA 7/11/1947 s Howard Harned Jones & Ellen Joyce. BS Pacific Luth U 1970; MDiv CDSP 1975. D 1/6/1979 Bp C Kilmer Myers P 1/12/1980 Bp William Edwin Swing. m 4/30/1992 Lyn V Merrill. Chapl Samar Hlth Serv Corvallis OR 1997-2007; Int Chr The King Ch Houston TX 1997; Int S Steph's Ch Beaumont TX 1995-1996; Int Gr Ch Galveston TX 1989-1990; Assoc S Chris's Ch Houston TX 1986-1989; Vic S Andr's Ch Chelan WA 1980-1986; Vic S Jas Epis Ch Brewster WA 1980-1985; Assoc Chr Ch Portola Vlly CA 1979-1980. Auth, "CPE In A Hosp Setting," Goodsam Pub, 2000. Assoc of Epis Healthcare Chapl 2006-2010; Assn Of Clincl Pstr Educators 1997. garynlyn1811@att.net

JONES, Helen Hammon (Ky) 30 River Hill Rd, Louisville KY 40207 **Pstr Assoc S Matt's Epis Ch Louisville KY 2001-** B Lexington KY 5/23/1934 d Stratton Owen Hammon & Helen Louise. AB Vas 1955; MDiv Louisville Presb TS 1980; Claremont TS 1982; DMin Louisville Presb TS 1994; MFA in Writing Spalding U 2008. D 10/19/1987 Bp David Reed P 10/27/2007 Bp Edwin Funsten Gulick Jr. m 5/24/1987 Thomas Howell Pike c 3. Stndg Com Dio Kentucky Louisville KY 1996-2002; Com for Nomntns of Bp Dio Kentucky Louisville KY 1993-1994; Stndg Com Dio Kentucky Louisville KY

1990-1993. Essayist, "On Waiting," *Waiting and Being*, Fons Vitae, Louisville, 2010. APC (Fell) 1989-2003; AEHC 1983-2003; Soc of S Jn the Evang 1984; Sprtl Dir Intl 1999-2002. The Wayne Oates Awd for Lifetime Achievement in Pstr Care Wayne Oates Inst 2011; Distinguished Alum Awd Louisville Collgt Sch 2006. hhjthp@iglou.com

JONES, Herbert H (Va) 3801 Fauqhier Ave, Richmond VA 23227 **Ch Of Our Sav Montpelier VA 2011-** B Richmond VA 7/6/1955 s John Paul Jones & Elizabeth Adkins. JD W&M - Law 1988; MDiv Un Presb 2011; Angl Stds VTS 2011. D 6/4/2011 Bp Shannon Sherwood Johnston. m 6/27/1981 Anne Coxe Anne Eaton Coxe. herbert.jones57@gmail.com

JONES JR, Hugh Burnett (ETenn) P. O. Box 1884, Anniston AL 36202 **Int S Mich And All Ang Anniston AL 2011-** B Paterson NJ 9/8/1948 s Hugh Burnett Jones & May McCouen. BA Millsaps Coll 1970; MA Middle Tennessee St U 1975; MDiv STUSo 1976; EdD Mississippi St U 1990. D 5/29/1976 P 5/19/1977 Bp Duncan Montgomery Gray Jr. m 4/13/1985 Debra Cordray c 3. Bd Trst The U So (Sewanee) Sewanee TN 2008-2011; Int S Thaddaeus' Epis Ch Chattanooga TN 2007-2011; Bd Trst The U So (Sewanee) Sewanee TN 1996-1999; R S Alb's Epis Ch Hixson TN 1994-2007; R S Mk's Ch Bay City TX 1987-1994; Asst S Mk's Ch Houston TX 1985-1986; Vic S Bernards Ch Okolona MS 1982-1985; Vic Ch Of The Ascen Brooksville MS 1978-1985; Vic Ch Of The Nativ Macon MS 1978-1985; Cur S Jn's Ch Laurel MS 1976-1978. bamhsdad@bellsouth.net

JONES, Irene Clifford (Chi) 8300 Delmar Blvd. Apt 203, St Louis MO 63124 **Died 11/25/2009** B St Louis MO 9/19/1954 d Alfred Clifford Jones & Janet Mercer. BA U of Missouri 1976; MDiv VTS 2003. D 12/27/2002 P 6/6/2003 Bp George Wayne Smith. revirene@gmail.com

JONES, J(ack) Monte (WTex) 1615 S Monroe St, San Angelo TX 76901 B San Angelo TX 7/15/1936 s Arvid Arthur Jones & Christine. BA Sul Ross St U 1961; MA Sul Ross St U 1967; MDiv STUSo 1977. D 6/14/1977 P 6/9/1978 Bp Willis Ryan Henton. m 2/3/1962 Eira Virginia Inabinet c 2. Vic S Jas Epis Ch Ft McKavett TX 1987-1998; R S Jn's Epis Ch Sonora TX 1984-1998; Vic All SS Ch Colorado City TX 1977-1984; St Johns Ch Lubbock TX 1977-1984; Dio NW Texas Lubbock TX 1977-1981. "Biscuits O'Bryan, Texas Storyteller," *Statehouse Press*, 2005; Auth, "More Bull From Biscuits," *Record Stockman Press*, 1992; Auth, "Biscuits O'Bryan's Bk of Beans, Bread & Bull," *Rercord Stockman Press*, 1989. Acad Of Wstrn Artists. Best Cowboy Humorist Acad of Wstrn Artists 2003; Listed in "Who's Who in SW" 1995; VP, Texas Cowboy Poets Assn 1994; Sul Ross St U Distinguished Alum 1994. etnom6391@suddenlink.net

JONES, Jacqueline Sydney (Alb) 8 Byard St, Johnstown NY 12095 **D Asst Trin Ch Gloversville NY 2007-** B Amsterdam NY 8/6/1956 d Richard Edward Blake & Madelyn Nastacie. BA Suc At Potsdam NY 1978; MS Coll Of St Rose Albany NY 1981; Cert Of Pstr Stds St Bern's TS And Mnstry 2007. D 6/9/2007 P 12/2/2007 Bp William Howard Love. m 8/10/1985 Kevin Stewart Jones c 1. jackie@cphny.org

JONES, James Boyd (Cal) 674 Colusa Ave, Berkeley CA 94707 B Detroit MI 10/6/1925 s Paul Ernest Jones & Charlotte Mary. BA U MI 1950; MA U MI 1951; MDiv CDSP 1964. D 6/21/1964 P 12/26/1964 Bp James Albert Pike. c 4. CDSP Berkeley CA 1972-1991; R Ch Of The Incarn San Francisco CA 1965-1970; Cur S Fran' Epis Ch San Francisco CA 1964-1965. Hon DD CDSP. jbjones99@gmail.com

JONES, James Place (SeFla) 8440 S Dixie Hwy Apt 1101, Miami FL 33143 **S Matt the Apos Epis Ch Miami FL 2007-** B Morristown NJ 6/23/1950 s Joseph John Jones & Grace Joy. BA Amer U 1972; MDiv EDS 1976; PhD Bos 1981. D 6/5/1976 P 3/5/1977 Bp George E Rath. m 9/6/1975 Karen Helder c 2. R S Paul's Epis Ch La Porte IN 2002-2007; R S Ptr's Ch Albany NY 2000-2002; R S Marg's Ch Inverness FL 1993-2000; Int S Thos Epis Ch Eustis FL 1991-1992; Dir - Epis Coun Cntr Dio Cntrl Florida Orlando FL 1990-1993; Asst R Truro Epis Ch Fairfax VA 1988-1990; Int Gr Ch Everett MA 1987-1988; Assoc S Ptr's Ch Beverly MA 1985-1987. Auth, "A Lifecycle Approach to Mnstry w The Aging," *Journ of Pstr Care*, 1999; Auth, "Psychol Hm Vstng Serv," *Emergency Psychol*, 1984. jamesjones1454@hotmail.com

JONES III, James W (NJ) Oceanview Towers 30, 510 Ocean Ave., Long Branch NJ 07740 **Assoc S Geo's-By-The-River Rumson NJ 2009-** B Detroit MI 1/23/1943 s James William Jones & Betty. BA Earlham Coll 1964; MDiv EDS 1967; PhD Br 1970; PsyD Rutgers-The St U 1985. D 6/29/1967 Bp Richard S M Emrich P 3/25/1968 Bp John S Higgins. Auth, ",The Blood That Cries Out From the Earth," Oxford U Press, 2008; Auth, ",The Mirror of God," Palgrave, 2003; Auth, ",Rel & Psychol in Transition," Yale U Press, 1996; Auth, ",The Sprt & The Wrld," Hawthorn Press, 1975; Auth, ",Shattered Synthesis," Yale U Press, 1973. AAR. JamWJones3@cs.com

JONES, Jane (Denton) (Los) 457 W 39th St, San Pedro CA 90731 **D S Greg's Par Long Bch CA 2010-** B Columbus OH 7/26/1943 d Sterling Chaney Scott & Mary Jane. BS Otterbein Coll 1966; Cert U CA 1985; EFM U So 2002; ETSBH 2006. D 12/2/2006 Bp Chester Lovelle Talton. m 8/16/2008 John Jones c 5. D S Andr's Par Torrance CA 2006-2008. LA ECW Bd Dir- D 2008; N. Amer Assn of the Diac 2006. buckeyedeacon@aol.com

JONES, Janice Lynn (Tex) 1314 E University Ave, Georgetown TX 78626 **Asst R Gr Epis Ch Georgetown TX 2008-** B Bridgeport CT 2/27/1953 d Edward Baker & Heste Riggott. BS Sthrn Connecticut St U 1971; MS Sthrn Connecticut St U 1974; MDiv Epis TS Of The SW 2008. D 6/28/2008 Bp Don Adger Wimberly P 1/10/2009 Bp C(harles) Andrew Doyle. m 8/23/1986 Richard B Jones c 3. janicejones2@aol.com

JONES, Jeffrey Thomas (Tenn) 1500 Hickory Ridge Rd, Lebanon TN 37087 B Paris KY 9/16/1960 s Roy Jones & Betty Jo. BA Midway Coll 1998; MDiv STUSo 2002. D 6/8/2002 P 6/7/2003 Bp Stacy F Sauls. m 11/19/1996 Loretta Anne Strippelhoff c 2. R The Ch Of The Epiph Lebanon TN 2003-2005; Vic S Phil's Ch Harrodsburg KY 2002-2003. fr.jeff@comcast.net

JONES, Jerry Steven (WK) 1113 Pinehurst St, Hays KS 67601 B Omaha NE 5/14/1939 s Beecher Clifford Jones & Margaret Helen. BA Dana Coll 1962; LTh SWTS 1965. D 6/6/1965 P 12/1/1965 Bp Russell T Rauscher. m 6/1/1990 Susan Andrea Brown c 2. Dn Chr Cathd Salina KS 2006-2010; S Mich's Ch Hays KS 1996-2002; R S Steph's Ch Casper WY 1993-1996; S Pauls Epis Ch Arapahoe NE 1990-1993; S Eliz's Ch Holdrege NE 1989-1993; Vic S Eliz's Ch Russell KS 1989-1993; All SS' Epis Ch Ft Worth TX 1979-1982; Cur S Steph's Ch Wichita KS 1977-1979; R S Matt's Epis Ch Newton KS 1974-1977; Vic S Mk's Ch Gordon NE 1968-1970; Cur All SS Epis Ch Omaha NE 1965-1968. jerjones@eaglecom.net

JONES, Judith Ann (Ga) PO Box 33, 216 Remington Avenue, Thomasville GA 31799 **R S Thos Epis Ch Thomasville GA 2007-** B Chicago IL 1/21/1943 d Jerome Felix Olszewski & Rose Janina. U of Tennessee; BA S Mary Of The Woods Coll Terre Haute IN 1984; MDiv SWTS 1997. D 6/14/1997 P 2/11/1998 Bp Henry Irving Louttit. m 7/18/1987 Robert T Jones c 4. R S Dav's Barneveld NY 2002-2007; S Steph's Ch New Hartford NY 2002-2007; R Gr Ch Sterling IL 2000-2002; Assoc R Emm Epis Ch Rockford IL 1997-2000. Producer/Dir, "Chld and Stwdshp," *Video*, St. Lk's - Atlanta, 1991. revjjones@rose.net

JONES, Judith Anne (Ia) 316 3rd St Ne, Waverly IA 50677 **P-in-c S Andr's Epis Ch Waverly IA 2010-** B Wasim Maharashtra India 7/8/1961 d Donald Douglas Miller & Willa. BA Point Loma Coll 1982; MDiv PrTS 1986; Cert in Angl Stds STUSo 1990; PhD Emory U 1999. D 12/18/2004 P 6/18/2005 Bp Alan Scarfe. m 7/26/1980 Brian Jones c 2. P-in-c Gr Epis Ch Chas City IA 2005-2009. coauthor w/ Edmond F. Desueza, "Conversations w Scripture: Daniel," Ch Pub, 2011. Angl Assn of Biblic Scholars 1998; SBL 1983; The Ch in Metropltn Areas 2005. judith.jones@wartburg.edu

JONES, Judith Gay (Tex) PO Box 28, Pflugerville TX 78691 **Vic S Paul's Epis Ch Pflugerville TX 2009-** B Austin TX 11/3/1947 d John Graham Jones & Wilma Marie Richter. Cert for Mnstry The Iona Sch for Mnstry 2008. D 6/28/2008 Bp Don Adger Wimberly P 1/24/2009 Bp Dena Arnall Harrison. m 12/14/1985 Lewis Jones c 1. jgjones1214@gmail.com

JONES, Kathleen Andrea (Okla) 1901 Skyline Place, Bartlesville OK 74006 **Prov Syn Dio Oklahoma Oklahoma City OK 2010-; Vic S Thos Ch Pawhuska OK 2010-** B Saint Cloud MN 10/15/1945 d William Mathis Wallace & Mary Lee. Cntrl Missouri St U 1963; U of Iowa 1966; AA Kirkwood Cmnty Coll 1990; MDiv STUSo 1997. D 6/12/2000 Bp Carl Christopher Epting P 5/1/2001 Bp Robert Manning Moody. m 8/16/1967 William Jones c 3. R S Matt's Ch Sand Sprg OK 2006-2009; R All SS Epis Ch Miami OK 2005-2006; Bp's Com Dio Nebraska Omaha NE 2004-2005; R S Jas' Epis Ch Fremont NE 2003-2005; Prov Syn Dio Oklahoma Oklahoma City OK 2002-2003; Coun on Missions Dio Oklahoma Oklahoma City OK 2001-2003; Asst S Lk's Epis Ch Bartlesville OK 2000-2003. OSL 1985-1987. bnaokies@cableone.net

JONES, Kenneth Leon (Mass) 62 Hopetown Road, Mt.Pleasant SC 29464 B Charleston SC 8/13/1941 s Leon Gilliam Jones & Estelle Geraldine. BS Coll of Charleston 1963; CTh U of Cambridge 1967; MDiv VTS 1970. D 7/12/1970 Bp Robert Bruce Hall P 6/1/1971 Bp Robert Fisher Gibson Jr. m 6/12/1960 Sandra H Harley c 2. R S Paul's Epis Ch Alexandria VA 1972-1975; Asst Imm Ch-On-The-Hill Alexandria VA 1970-1971. kljones@finsvcs.com

JONES, Kent Trevor (Chi) 3706 W Saint Paul Ave, McHenry IL 60050 B Lansing MI 7/18/1969 s Thomas Carl Jones & J Kaye. D 5/23/2009 Bp Victor Alfonso Scantlebury. m 6/13/1992 Alice Finn c 4. kent.jones@amcore.com

JONES, Leland Bryant (SanD) 25640 E Old Julian Hwy, Ramona CA 92065 **Int S Jn's Ch Fallbrook CA 2011-** B Yuma AZ 12/15/1947 s Bryant Wade Jones & Helen. BA U Pac 1969; MDiv CDSP 1973. D 4/1/1973 P 5/1/1974 Bp J(ohn) Joseph Meakins Harte. m 10/3/1969 Sheila O'Connor c 3. Int S Andr's By The Sea Epis Par San Diego CA 2008-2010; Vic S Mary's In The Vlly Ch Ramona CA 2006-2008; Vic Dio San Diego San Diego CA 2000-2005; Vic S Andr's Epis Ch Irvine CA 1989-2000; R The Epis Ch Of The Gd Shpd Hemet CA 1980-1989; R S Steph's Ch Phoenix AZ 1976-1980; Cur Chr Ch Of The Ascen Paradise Vlly AZ 1973-1976. Fndr Comps In Mnstry, Chapl Ord Of S Lk. lelandbjones47@yahoo.com

JONES, Lynne Elizabeth (SeFla) 206 Pendleton Ave, Palm Beach FL 33480 B Boynton Bch FL 7/9/1955 d Howard Chandler Jones & Ella Irene. AA Palm Bch Jr Coll 1975; BA Florida St U 1977; JD U Of Florida 1980; MDiv GTS

1993. D 6/2/1993 P 12/21/1993 Bp Calvin Onderdonk Schofield Jr. The Epis Ch Of Beth-By-The-Sea Palm Bch FL 2004-2010; R Epis Ch Of S Simon And S Jude Irmo SC 2000-2004; R S Columba Epis Ch Marathon FL 1995-2000; R S Fran-In-The-Keys Episcop Big Pine Key FL 1995-2000; Asst All SS Prot Epis Ch Ft Lauderdale FL 1993-1995. pastorlynnejones@comcast.net

JONES, Margaret W (WTenn) 4757 Walnut Grove Rd, Memphis TN 38117 B Saint Louis MO 7/13/1937 d Claude Ralph Wood & Highland. Memphis TS; BA Hollins U 1959. D 1/22/1994 Bp Alex Dockery Dickson. m 4/21/1979 Frank Aubrey Jones c 2. Calv Ch Memphis TN 1994-1999. Auth, *The Christmas Invitation*.

JONES, Mark Andrew (SeFla) 2707 NW 37th St, Boca Raton FL 33434 **D S Greg's Ch Boca Raton FL 2010-** B Indianapolis IN 5/5/1957 s Norman C Jones & Edith Wilma. BA Indiana U 1979; MPA Indiana U 1981; JD U Chi Law Sch 1989; MDiv Florida Cntr for Theol Stds 2010; Dplma Angl Stds The U So (Sewanee) 2010. D 6/5/2010 P 12/4/2010 Bp Leopold Frade. m 6/6/1981 Diane Marie Dilger c 2. brmarkandrew@bellsouth.net

JONES, Mark Stephen (Ga) 212 N Jefferson St, Albany GA 31701 **Dn of Albany Convoc Dio Georgia Savannah GA 2006-; R S Paul's Ch Albany GA 2005-** B Atlanta GA 3/5/1976 s Eddie Ellsworth Jones. B.S. Florida St U 1999; MDiv VTS 2003. D 6/8/2003 P 12/7/2003 Bp Stephen Hays Jecko. m 2/26/2000 Emily J Jones c 2. Asst. R Ch Of Our Sav Jacksonville FL 2003-2005. mark.jones@stpaulsalbany.org

JONES, Marx Arthur (Chi) 6241 W Washington Ave, Las Vegas NV 89107 **Asst Pstr Chr Epis Ch Ottawa IL 2000-** B Abilene KS 7/29/1926 s Nathan Leroy Jones & Blanche H. ThB PDS; BA Colorado St Coll 1950. D 5/23/1953 Bp Oliver J Hart P 12/1/1953 Bp Shirley Hall Nichols. c 4. R S Anskar's Ch Rockford IL 1977-1985; Vic S Mary Epis Ch Crystal Lake IL 1960-1976; Cur S Mich And All Ang Ch Mssn KS 1958-1960; P-in-c Ch Of The Trsfg Logan KS 1956-1958; P-in-c Trin Epis Ch Norton KS 1956-1958; M-in-c Ch Of The H Nativ Kinsley KS 1953-1956; M-in-c S Jn's Ch Great Bend KS 1953-1956. marxplus@aol.com

JONES, Mary-Frances (Minn) Village Cooperative, 2301 10th St NW #314, Austin MN 55912 **D Chr Ch Austin MN 1996-** B Melrose Park IL 5/26/1931 d James Garrard Jones & Alice. The Coll of Emm and St. Chad; BA U MN 1977; D Formation Prog 1981. D 6/29/1982 Bp Robert Marshall Anderson. RWF. deaconj8@yahoo.com

JONES, Michael (Alb) 785 Forest Ridge Dr, Youngstown OH 44512 B Indianapolis IN 11/11/1947 s James Garrard Jones & Alice. BA NE Illinois St U Chicago IL 1971; MDiv Nash 1976. D 8/6/1976 P 6/1/1977 Bp James Loughlin Duncan. c 3. S Eustace Ch Lake Placid NY 2005-2008; R S Steph's Epis Ch Steubenville OH 1996-2003; S Jas Epis Ch Boardman OH 1982-1996; Asst Chr Epis Ch Warren OH 1980-1982; Asst All SS Prot Epis Ch Ft Lauderdale FL 1979-1980; S Dav's-In-The-Pines Epis Ch Wellington FL 1978-1979; Asst Ch Of The H Redeem Lake Worth FL 1977; Dio SE Florida Miami FL 1976. padremigel@aol.com

JONES, N(elson) Bradley (Alb) 970 State St, Schenectady NY 12307 **R Chr Ch Schenectady NY 1998-** B New Orleans LA 11/27/1957 s Nelson Buckner Jones & Martha. BA U So 1979; MDiv VTS 1991. D 6/9/1991 P 12/18/1991 Bp James Barrow Brown. m 9/29/1984 Mary Helen Barrow c 7. Assoc S Andr's By The Sea Epis Ch Destin FL 1994-1998; Cur Ch Of The Ascen Montgomery AL 1991-1993. Amer Angl Coun; NOEL. revjones@christchurchschenectady.org

JONES, Nikki Lou (NwT) 1400 McCaulley St Apt 31, Sweetwater TX 79556 **D S Steph's Ch Sweetwater TX 2000-** B Stamford TX 7/10/1943 d Thaddeus Casner & Letha. BA Hardin-Simmons U 1965. D 10/29/2000 Bp C(harles) Wallis Ohl. m 8/1/1988 Bernard Wayne Jones. church@camalott.com

JONES, Patricia Loraine (Alb) 1295 Myron St, Schenectady NY 12309 **D S Steph's Ch Schenectady NY 1982-** B Rochester NY 2/8/1936 d Arthur Thomas Smith & Blanche Ely. BA Wm Smith 1957; MDiv Bex 1990. D 12/1/1982 Bp Wilbur Emory Hogg Jr. m 6/12/1958 Christopher Curtiss Jones c 2. patjones99@verizon.net

JONES, Patricia Wayne (WNC) 260 21st Ave Nw, Hickory NC 28601 B Camp Lejeune NC 1/20/1947 D 12/18/1999 Bp Robert Hodges Johnson. m 6/14/1969 David Scott Jones c 3.

JONES, Peter Hoyt (HB) 7571 Greenlake Way Apy B, Boynton Beach FL 33436 B Cleveland OH 7/23/1937 s Eben Hoyt Jones & Alfreda Sarah. BA Ya 1959; STB GTS 1962. D 6/9/1962 Bp Nelson Marigold Burroughs P 12/1/1962 Bp Richard S Watson. m 7/7/1959 Susan Robin Burt. Cur All SS Ch Salt Lake City UT 1962-1966.

JONES, Philip Hill (RG) 810 N Campbell St, El Paso TX 79902 B Dallas TX 10/7/1953 s Joe Hill & Margaret. BA U So 1976; JD Baylor U 1979; MDiv VTS 1989. D 6/27/1989 Bp Maurice Manuel Benitez P 3/15/1990 Bp William Elwood Sterling. m 7/2/1977 Claudia Ramsey Clinton c 4. Pro Cathd Epis Ch Of S Clem El Paso TX 1998-2005; Trin Ch Marshall TX 1991-1998; Asst R S Paul's Ch Waco TX 1989-1991. padreperro@aol.com

JONES, Rebecca Ann (Colo) 1350 Washington St, Denver CO 80203 **Dioc Jubilee Off Dio Colorado Denver CO 2007-** B Cleveland TN 11/6/1958 d Paul Alexander Jones & Viola. BS E Tennessee St U 1980; MA OH SU 1984; MDiv Iliff TS 2007. D 11/15/2008 Bp Robert John O'Neill. killarneyrose@comcast.net

JONES, Richard John (SwVa) Washington Theological Consortium, 487 Michigan Ave. NE, Washington DC 20017 B Washington DC 1/14/1943 s Homer Jones & Alice. BA Ob 1964; MA Jn Hopkins U 1966; MDiv VTS 1972; PhD U Tor 1988. D 6/17/1972 Bp William Foreman Creighton P 12/17/1972 Bp Adrian Delio Caceres-Villavicencio. m 6/3/1972 Jody Williams c 2. Prof VTS Alexandria VA 1988-2009; Asst S Jn's Ch Lynchburg VA 1980-1984; S Mary's Epis Ch Andalusia AL 1978-1980; Vic Ch Of The Epiph Enterprise AL 1975-1980; Cur The Epis Ch Of The Nativ Dothan AL 1975-1978. Auth, "Nairobi Muslims' Concept of Prophethood," *Journ of Muslim Minority Affrs*, 2002; Auth, "How To Talk To Your Muslim Neighbor," *Forw Mvmt*, 1996; Auth, "Wlfd Cantwell Smith & Kenneth Cragg on Islam as a Way of Salvation," *Intl Bulletin of Mssy Resrch*, 1992. Amer Friends of the Epis Ch of Sudan 2005; Amer Soc of Missiology 1985. rjones@vts.edu

JONES, Robert Michael (WNC) PO Box 729, Highlands NC 28741 B Eufala AL 12/31/1942 s William Burns Jones & Margaret Elizabeth. BA U So 1965; MDiv VTS 1969; STM STUSo 1977; DMin Van 1988. D 6/20/1969 P 1/1/1970 Bp Gray Temple. m 6/20/1970 Agnes Elizabeth Abrams c 4. R Ch Of The Incarn Highlands NC 1995-2003; R S Dav's Epis Ch Columbia SC 1987-1995; R S Paul's Ch Bennettsville SC 1985-1987; R Ch Of The H Comf Sumter SC 1974-1982; R S Jude's Epis Ch Walterboro SC 1971-1974. Auth, "One Eye Squinted Flannery O'Connor'S Vision Of Judgement & Gr". mikejones1411@yahoo.com

JONES, Roland Manning (NC) 501 Parkmont Dr, Greensboro NC 27408 B Washington DC 1/30/1932 s Roland Elmer Jones & Rachael. BS U of Maryland 1953; MDiv VTS 1958. D 6/14/1958 P 12/1/1958 Bp Angus Dun. m 12/26/1953 Marcia Wiebe c 3. Field Wk Supvsr Ya Berk New Haven CT 1991-1995; Prog Com Dio Connecticut Hartford CT 1986-1989; Par Supvsr Ya Berk New Haven CT 1985-1990; R S Mk's Ch New Canaan CT 1984-1995; R S Fran Ch Greensboro NC 1974-1984; R Ch Of The Ascen Silver Sprg MD 1967-1974; Field Wk Supvsr VTS Alexandria VA 1959-1973; Vic Chr Ch Accokeek MD 1958-1967; R Chr Ch S Jn's Par Accokeek MD 1958-1967. Auth, *Know Your Par*; Auth, *The Unfreezing of Ascenension*. rjones4098@aol.com

JONES, Ruth Elise (NwT) 3010 - 60th, Lubbock TX 79413 **D S Paul's On The Plains Epis Ch Lubbock TX 1993-** B Newellton LA 1/27/1936 d Robert Wesley Warren & Josephine Lenora. LSU 1955; AAS Clarendon Jr Coll 1981; BA Texas Tech U 1982; Med Texas Tech U 1986. D 10/25/1985 Bp Sam Byron Hulsey. m 11/27/1955 Louis Clinton Jones c 5. The TS at The U So Sewanee TN 1986-1995; D S Chris's Epis Ch Lubbock TX 1985-1993. AEHC; No Amer Assn of Deacons; OHC. rwjones10@earthlink.net

JONES, Samuel Gregory (NC) 1520 Canterbury Rd, Raleigh NC 27608 **August Vic S Mart's In The Field Sum Chap Biddeford Pool ME 2007-; R S Mich's Ch Raleigh NC 2004-** B Charlottesville VA 3/20/1969 s Samuel Shepard Jones & Helen. BA U NC 1991; MDiv GTS 1999. D 4/14/1998 P 6/20/1999 Bp Leopold Frade. m 5/23/1998 Melanie Bartol c 3. Dio Virginia Richmond VA 2002-2004; Assoc R S Jas' Ch Richmond VA 1999-2004; Chapl Catedral Epis El Buen Pstr San Pedro Sula HN 1994-1996. Auth, "On the Priesthood," *ATR*, ATR, 2009; Auth, "Beyond Da Vinci," Seabury, 2004; Auth, "Baxter to Cummins: The Baptismal Regeneration Controversy (1662-1873)," *GTS Thesis*, 1999. Ord of St. Jn 2000. Fac Hist Prize GTS 1999; Sutton Prize for Best Grad Thesis GTS 1999; hon GTS 1999. jones@holymichael.org

JONES, Scott Daniel (Az) 10716 E Medina Ave, Mesa AZ 85209 **R S Mk's Epis Ch Mesa AZ 2009-** B Melbourne FL 3/6/1960 s John William Jones & Constance. BS U of Florida 1982; MDiv Epis TS of The SW 2007. D 1/6/2007 P 7/14/2007 Bp Leopold Frade. m 1/12/1985 Yolanda Irizarry c 2. Assoc R Gd Shpd Of The Hills Cave Creek AZ 2007-2009. frscottaz@gmail.com

JONES, Sidney Ross (Okla) 385 Racquet Club Rd., Asheville NC 28803 B Woodville MS 8/10/1940 s Ben Shaifer Jones & Frances Ernestine. BA Tul 1962; MDiv STUSo 1965; DMin STUSo 1998. D 5/29/1965 Bp Duncan Montgomery Gray P 5/1/1966 Bp John M Allin. m 8/31/1963 Gwin S Sorrells c 3. R Trin Ch Tulsa OK 1992-2000; R S Jas Epis Ch Alexandria LA 1981-1992; R S Paul's Epis Ch Jacksonville FL 1978-1981; Dio Florida Jacksonville FL 1971-1978; Chapl Resurr Chap Tallahassee FL 1971-1978; R S Steph's Epis Ch Indianola MS 1968-1971; Cur S Andr's Cathd Jackson MS 1965-1968. Citizen Of The Year La LA 1988. rossgwin@charter.net

JONES, Stanley Boyd (WVa) 53 Windward Lane, Box 1848, Shepherdstown WV 25443 B Baltimore MD 7/27/1938 s Arthur Boyd Jones & Lillian Aileen. BA Dart 1960; Yale DS 1963. D 6/11/1991 P 6/13/1992 Bp John H(enry) Smith. m 3/9/1980 Judith K Miller c 1. Assoc Trin Ch Shepherdstown WV 1992-2000. Auth, "What'S Driving The Hlth System Change," *Hlth Affrs*, 1997; Auth, "Why Not The Best For The Chronically Ill," *GW Resrch Brief*, 1996; Auth, "Many Will Be Hurt," *Bulletin Of New York Acad Of Med*, 1990;

Auth, "Competition Or Conscience," *Inquiry*, 1987. Fllshp Of Contemplative Pryr 1995. Elected Mem Natl Acad Of Soc Ins 1990; Elected Mem Inst Of Med / Natl Acad Of Sciences 1980; Elected Fell Inst Of Soc, Ethics, & The Life Sciences 1978. stan@stanjudyjones.com

JONES, Stephen Chad (La) 1322 Church Street, Zachary LA 70791 **Vic S Pat's Ch Zachary LA 2008-** B Milton FL 1/24/1976 BA LSU 1999; M.Div. Nash 2003. D 2/1/2003 Bp Clarence Cullam Pope Jr P 8/20/2003 Bp Charles Edward Jenkins III. m 12/12/1998 Kimberley Leigh Jones c 3. Trin Epis Ch Baton Rouge LA 2006-2008; Cn for Mssn and Deploy Dio Louisiana Baton Rouge LA 2005-2007; Dio Louisiana Baton Rouge LA 2005-2006; R S Matt's Ch Bogalusa LA 2003-2005. fatherchad@stpatszachary.org

JONES JR, Stewart Hoyt (Colo) 2421 S Krameria St, Denver CO 80222 B Bethlehem PA 9/20/1940 s Stewart Hoyt Jones & Elizabeth Stahl. BA NWU 1962; None GTS 1963; BD SWTS 1965. D 5/29/1965 Bp William S Thomas P 12/21/1965 Bp Joseph Summerville Minnis. m 8/3/1963 Jean Correy Evans c 2. S Ambr Epis Ch Boulder CO 1974-1980; Asst Chr Epis Ch Denver CO 1968-1969; Cur Ch Of S Phil And S Jas Denver CO 1965-1968. jonesjcsh@msn.com

JONES, Tammy Lynn (Ida) PO Box 324, Rupert ID 83350 B Nampa ID 5/11/1961 d Claude James Bright & Geraldine May. D 10/22/2006 Bp Harry Brown Bainbridge III. m 2/28/1985 Ronald Jones c 2. tjones@pmt.org

JONES, Teresa Crawford (NY) 5 Christopher Ave, Highland NY 12528 **D Ch Of The Ascen And H Trin Highland NY 1999-** B Bend OR 11/14/1949 d Ralph William Crawford & Mary Kathryn. BA Arizona St U 1971. D 5/15/1999 Bp Richard Frank Grein. m 10/28/1988 Geoffrey Albert Jones.

JONES, Theodore Grant (Md) 2604 Halcyon Avenue, Baltimore MD 21214 B Utica NY 10/7/1940 s Emerson Klug Jones & Inza. BArch Cor 1963; MFA Pr 1965; MDiv EDS 1970. D 6/14/1970 P 5/25/1971 Bp Ned Cole. c 1. Int Ch Of The Mssh Baltimore MD 2001-2002; Int The Ch Of The H Apos Halethorpe MD 2001; R Ch Of S Kath Of Alexandria Baltimore MD 1999-2001; Int Chr Ch S Ptr's Par Easton MD 1998-1999; Int S Ptr's Ch Clifton NJ 1997-1998; Int Chr Ch Waukegan IL 1996-1997; R S Barn Epis Ch Portage MI 1995-1996; Int Ch Of The H Comm Washington DC 1993-1994; R S Chris's Ch Springfield VA 1982-1993; R S Steph's Ch New Hartford NY 1975-1982; Asst S Jn's Ch Ithaca NY 1970-1975. Soc of S Marg 1977. Fulbright Schlr Amer Acad Rome Italy 1966. senecaeagl@aol.com

JONES, Thomas A (Neb) 1512 N 160th St, Omaha NE 68118 **R Ch Of The H Sprt Bellevue NE 2008-** B Chicago IL 11/23/1955 s Arthur G Jones & Alma M. BS Sthrn Illinois U 1979; MS Embry Riddle Aeronautical U 1989; MDiv TS 2006. D 9/26/2006 P 3/27/2007 Bp Joe Goodwin Burnett. m 10/30/2006 Sharon Danelczuk c 2. Cur/Assoc S Andr's Ch Omaha NE 2006-2008. jonesfamuk@aol.com

JONES, Thomas Glyndwr (At) 4425 Colchester Ct, Columbus GA 31907 B Caersws Wales GB 8/14/1941 s John Francis Jones & Hilda. Clifton Theol Coll GB 1965. P 9/1/1966 Bp The Bishop of London. m 7/24/1965 Nan Fager c 2. R Trin Epis Ch Columbus GA 1987-2004; R Gr Ch Anniston AL 1973-1987; R Chr Ch Fairfield AL 1969-1973. welshwiz@knology.net

JONES, Tim (WNC) 290 Old Haw Creek Rd, Asheville NC 28805 **D S Jas Epis Ch Hendersonville NC 2010-** B Hendersonville NC 6/16/1969 s Charles Foy Jones & Sharon A. BA Bob Jones U 1991. D 1/23/2010 Bp Granville Porter Taylor. m 6/29/1991 Kerry Medders c 2. pakt@bellsouth.net

JONES, Timothy Kent (Tenn) 1209 Countryside Rd, Nolensville TN 37135 **Sr Assoc R S Geo's Ch Nashville TN 2005-** B Phoenix AZ 8/7/1955 s Francis Byron Jones & Susan LaVergne. MDiv PrTS; STM STUSo; BA Pepperdine U 1976. D 6/23/2001 P 4/21/2002 Bp Bertram Nelson Herlong. m 5/27/1978 Jill Zook c 3. Assoc S Paul's Epis Ch Murfreesboro TN 2002-2005. Auth, "The Art of Pryr," WaterBrook Press, 2005; Auth, "Workday Prayers," Loyola Press, 2000; Auth, "Awake My Soul," Doubleday Image, 1999. tim.jones@stgeorgesnashville.org

JONES OHC, Vern Edward (Cal) 3814 Jefferson Ave, Redwood City CA 94062 **Supply P Dio California San Francisco CA 1992-** B Enid OK 7/19/1927 s Cary Elmer Jones & Agnes Ethel. BA Phillips U 1949; STB GTS 1952; S Aug's Coll Cbury Gb 1960; S Aug's Coll Cbury Gb 1963; Fllshp GTS 1964; Grad Sem Phillips U 1977. D 6/16/1952 P 12/17/1952 Bp Chilton Powell. Dept Of Missions Dio California San Francisco CA 1983-1987; R S Ptr's Epis Ch Redwood City CA 1977-1992; Bd Trst The GTS New York NY 1974-1980; Vic S Steph's Ch Guymon OK 1973-1977; Vic S Jn's Epis Ch Woodward OK 1957-1977; P-in-c S Steph's Ch Guymon OK 1957-1960; Cur & Org/Chrmstr S Jn's Ch Oklahoma City OK 1955-1957; S Jas Ch Antlers OK 1952-1955; Vic S Lk The Beloved Physcn Idabel OK 1952-1955; S Mk's Ch Hugo OK 1952-1955. Auth, "O Come, Let Us Adore Him," *The Vintage Voice*, CPF, 2005; Auth, "A Goodly Heritage," *The Vintage Voice*, CPF, 2003. Assoc OHC 1951; Soc Of King Chas The Mtyr 1951. Ord of St. Laud of Cbury Soc of King Chas the Mtyr 2011. veernedjones@juno.com

JONES JR, Vernon A. (Ala) 6312 Willow Glen Dr, Montgomery AL 36117 B Brunswick County VA 9/19/1924 s Vernon Algie Jones & Harriet Ann. BA Virginia Un U 1945; BD VTS 1948; MDiv VTS 1970. D 4/7/1948 Bp William A Brown P 6/2/1949 Bp George P Gunn. m 5/19/1948 Lillian Clark c 3. S Andr's Ch Tuskegee Inst AL 1957-1990; R S Steph's Ch Petersburg VA 1953-1957; P-in-c S Jas Ch Emporia VA 1949-1953; P-in-c S Thos Ch Freeman VA 1949-1953; Vic Chr Epis Ch Halifax VA 1948-1949.

JONES, Walton Womack (Miss) 308 South Commerce St., Natchez MS 39120 **R Trin Ch Natchez MS 2011-** B Grenada MS 7/23/1978 s Girault W Jones & Sandra P. BS Mississippi St U Starkville MS 2003; MDiv U So 2007. D 6/2/2007 P 1/23/2008 Bp Duncan Montgomery Gray III. m 10/19/2002 Keri D Jones c 2. Assoc S Paul's Epis Ch Meridian MS 2007-2010. wjones@gmail.com

✠ **JONES JR, Rt Rev William Augustus** (Mo) 58 Kendal Dr, Kennett Square PA 19348 B Memphis TN 1/24/1927 s William Augustus Jones & Martha. BA Rhodes Coll 1948; BD Yale DS 1951. D 1/1/1952 P 7/25/1952 Bp Edmund P Dandridge Con 5/3/1975 for Mo. m 8/26/1949 Margaret Loaring-Clark. Bp Dio Missouri S Louis MO 1975-1993; R S Jn's Epis Ch Johnson City TN 1972-1975; Assoc S Lk's Epis Ch Birmingham AL 1965-1966; R S Mk's Epis Ch Lagrange GA 1958-1965; Cur Chr Ch Cathd Nashville TN 1957-1958; P-in-c The Epis Ch Of The Mssh Pulaski TN 1952-1957. DD Rhodes Coll 1986; DD Ya Berk 1975; DD U So TS 1975. magwill1@verizon.net

JONES, William Henry (O) 2651 Cheltenham Rd, Toledo OH 43606 B Tarpon Sprgs FL 6/23/1929 s Holton Arthur Jones & Lotta Mai. BA Ohio Wesl 1951; BD/MA U Chi 1955; VTS 1956; Lic LPCC/SC 1992; Lic Chem Dependency Counslr Supvsr/ US 1997; DMin Ecum TS 1997; Certification CSAT/SC (Intl) 2002; Certification CMAT/SC 2008. D 6/1/1956 Bp Frederick D Goodwin P 6/1/1957 Bp Robert Fisher Gibson Jr. c 4. Toledo Reg Coun Perrysburg OH 1985; Asst Dio Ohio Cleveland OH 1964-1982; R Imm Ch King and Queen Courthouse VA 1959-1964; R S Jn's Ch W Point VA 1959-1964; Cur S Thos' Ch Richmond VA 1956-1959. Auth, *Exploring the Fam Map*, ETS, 1997; Auth, "The Impact of Multiple Counsultants in the Treatment of Addictions," *Please Help Me w This Fam*, Brunner/Mazel, 1994; "Agony Called Unemployment," *Journ of Meth Wmn*, 1988. bjonestmm@tmmohio.org

JONES JR, William Isaac (SVa) 721 W Ellis St, Jefferson City TN 37760 **Died 11/30/2010** B Harrogate TN 2/10/1924 s William Isaac Jones & Ann Rosalie. BA/MA Cincinnati Conservatory of Mus Cincinnati 1950; BD VTS 1967; PhD Florida St U 1973. D 6/27/1967 P 6/1/1968 Bp Edward Hamilton West. c 3. wisaak@aol.com

JONES, William Ogden (SVa) 8137 Brown Rd, Bon Air VA 23235 **Archd Dio Sthrn Virginia Norfolk VA 2008-** B Atlanta GA 7/19/1937 s Benjamin Rhys Jones & Elizabeth. Hendrix Coll; Loc Formation Prog; U of Arkansas; CLU The Amer Coll 1987. D 6/15/1989 Bp C(laude) Charles Vache. m 5/15/1957 Gaye Lynne Shinall c 3. D Ch Of The Redeem Midlothian VA 2002-2007; D Trin Ch Wauwatosa WI 1999-2002; D S Dav's Epis Ch Richmond VA 1993-1996; D Ch Of The Redeem Midlothian VA 1989-1993. "Diokonia," 1991. deaconbill89@aol.com

JONES, William Robert (NY) 6700 Gulf Of Mexico Dr Apt 117, Longboat Key FL 34228 B Irvington NY 5/10/1931 s William Jones & Kathleen. BA Hob 1953; MDiv UTS 1956. D 6/17/1957 P 12/1/1957 Bp Horace W B Donegan. m 9/7/1985 Nancy L Lowden c 3. R S Dav's Ch Highland Mills NY 1967-1968; R S Jn's Arden NY 1967-1968; Asst San Andres Ch Yonkers NY 1957-1959.

JOO, Indon Paul (Chi) 1300 Hallberg Ln, Park Ridge IL 60068 **One In Chr Ch Prospect Heights IL 2000-** B Republic of Korea 8/1/1962 s Keynghoon Joo & Aein. BA Yonsei U 1985; MDiv St. Mich Sem Seoul Korea 1989. Trans from Anglican Church Of Korea 5/29/2001 Bp William Dailey Persell. m 4/8/1989 Youngsook Deborah Lee c 2. "The Lord Shall Reign Forever and Ever," *Exodus Bible Study in Korean*, Maleunoolleem(Korean), 2004. joopdim@sbcglobal.net

JOOS, Heidi L (Minn) 3105 W 40th St, Minneapolis MN 55410 **S Jn The Bapt Epis Ch Minneapolis MN 1998-** B Columbus WI 11/2/1945 d Loyal Wilson Joos & Ethel Mary. BS U of Maryland 1967; MD U MI 1971; MDiv Ya Berk 1980. D 12/11/1993 P 12/11/1993 Bp Charlie Fuller McNutt Jr. S Paul's Epis Ch Harrisburg PA 1993-1996.

JOPLIN, Susan Colley (Okla) 2513 Sw 123rd St, Oklahoma City OK 73170 **S Paul's Cathd Oklahoma City OK 1993-** B Austin TX 3/5/1951 d Thomas Milton Colley & Margaret Jean. BFA U of Oklahoma 1978; MA U of Oklahoma 1982; MDiv Epis TS of The SW 1991. D 6/22/1991 P 1/25/1992 Bp Robert Manning Moody. m 4/28/1996 Larry Ercell Joplin. Dio Oklahoma Oklahoma City OK 2006-2009; Dio Oklahoma Oklahoma City OK 1991-1993. thejoplins@cox.net

JOPLING, Wallace Malcolm (Fla) 416 Salt Wind Court W, S. Ponte Vedra Beach FL 32082 **The Epis Ch of The Redeem Jacksonville FL 2010-** B Lake City FL 10/14/1948 BS Wofford Coll; MDiv STUSo 2005. D 6/5/2005 P 12/11/2005 Bp Samuel Johnson Howard. m 11/24/1973 Marsha S Jopling c 2. R Chr Ch Monticello FL 2005-2010. MALJOP@EMBARQMAIL.COM

JORDAN, Darryl Mark (Dal) 1610 Iroquois Dr, Garland TX 75043 B Dallas TX 1/10/1962 s Glenn Jordan & Susie. BS U of Texas 1985; MDiv SMU 2005. D 1/31/2004 P 8/1/2004 Bp James Monte Stanton. m 11/20/1993 Lisa Shaver c 1. Assoc Chr Epis Ch Dallas TX 2004-2005. darrylmarkjordan@cs.com

JORDAN SR, John Ellwood (Nev) 7560 Splashing Rock Dr., Las Vegas NV 89131 **D S Tim's Epis Ch Henderson NV 2003-** B Dallas TX 1/27/1945 s Ralph Louis Jordan & Ethel May. Estrn New Mex U 1964; Riverside City Coll 1965; Rio Grande Sch For Mnstry 1997. D 2/21/1998 Bp Terence Kelshaw. m 8/5/1965 Carol Marie Hennings c 3. DCE All SS Epis Ch Las Vegas NV 2001-2002; D Chr Ch Las Vegas NV 2000-2001; D H Sprt Epis Ch El Paso TX 1998-2000. jcjor@cox.net

JORDAN JR, John Hartley (SVa) 201-A 54th St, Virginia Beach VA 23451 **Died 4/20/2010** B Saint Louis MO 5/8/1927 s John Hartley Jordan & Elizabeth Garlick. BA VMI 1951; BD VTS 1958; DD VTS 1992. D 6/13/1958 P 5/1/1959 Bp Frederick D Goodwin. c 4. Humanitarian Awd Natl Conf for Cmnty and Justice 2002; First Citizen of VA Bch 91 1991; Sports Hall Fame VMI 1978.

JORDAN, Katherine H (WA) 3156 Gracefield Rd. Apt. 501, Silver Spring MD 20904 B Cleveland OH 7/28/1939 d Lewis Fuller Herron & Gwendolyn Florence. BA Wells Coll 1961; MLS U Pgh 1964; MDiv VTS 1992. D 6/13/1992 Bp Robert Poland Atkinson P 12/16/1992 Bp Peter James Lee. c 1. R S Jn's Epis Ch Zion Par Beltsville MD 1997-2007; Assoc R S Phil's Epis Ch Laurel MD 1994-1997; Asst S Jn's Epis Ch Arlington VA 1992. EWC 1989; WECA 1996. kathyhjordan@gmail.com

JORDAN, (Richard) Alan (Oly) PO Box 830, Bremerton WA 98337 B Whittier CA 8/26/1922 s Frank Everett Jordan & Kathleen. BA Pomona Coll 1949; MDiv CDSP 1963. D 7/1/1963 P 6/7/1964 Bp William F Lewis. m 6/11/1955 Maryann Wolcott c 4. Vic S Hugh Of Lincoln Allyn WA 1978-1988; Vic S Nich Ch Tahuya WA 1978-1988; S Jn's Ch Chehalis WA 1965-1978; Vic Ch Of Our Sav Monroe WA 1963-1965; Cur S Jn's Epis Ch Snohomish WA 1963-1965. Chapl DOK 1975-1988. rajrdn3@comcast.net

J

JOSE, Nancy Lee (WA) 1304 Emerson St NW, Washington DC 20011 **R S Thos' Par Washington DC 2004-** B Washington DC 7/31/1949 d William Jose & Harriett Louise. BS Jas Madison U 1971; MS Towson U 1976; PhD Sthrn Illinois U 1979; MDiv Candler TS Emory U 1991; MA VTS 1998. D 6/20/1998 Bp Calvin Onderdonk Schofield Jr P 1/9/1999 Bp Michael Whittington Creighton. m 7/12/2003 Wayne Floyd. Int R S Jn's Ch Suffolk VA 2003-2004; Assoc R S Paul's Ch Norfolk VA 2001-2003; Cn Pstr Cathd Ch Of S Steph Harrisburg PA 1998-2001. Auth, "Silent Gift Proj; A Method For Sprtl Hlth," *Joy Of Sch Hlth*, 1987; Auth, "Sprtl Hlth, A look At Barriers To its Inclusion In Hlth Educ Curric," *Eta Sigma Gamma*, 1986; Auth, "Death: Fam Adjustment to Loss," *Stress and the Fam Vol 2: Coping w Catastrophe*, Brunner-Mazel Inc., 1983; Auth, "Sexism and Ageism," *Educ in the 80s*, NEA, 1981. Jn Owen Smith Preaching Awd Chandler TS 1991; Patillo Fndt Middle E Schlrshp Chandler TS 1989; Dn Schlr Awd Chandler TS 1988; Elmer T Clark Schlr Awd Sthrn Illinois Univeristy Edwardsville IL 1979. nljose@verizon.net

JOSEPH, Annette Beth (Me) 420 N Main St, Poplar Bluff MO 63901 **R H Cross Epis Ch Poplar Bluff MO 2011-** B Portland ME 4/17/1966 d Frank Phillip Rogers & Catherine Blanche. Bachelor Gnrl Stds U of ME Farmington 2006; MDiv Bangor TS 2010. D 6/19/2010 Bp Stephen Taylor Lane P 1/20/2011 Bp George Wayne Smith. m 10/11/1998 Richard M Joseph c 5. arjoseph7@gmail.com

JOSEPH, Arthur Eric (NY) 450 Convent Ave, New York NY 10031 **R Ch Of The Crucif New York NY 1987-** B 9/5/1940 s John Isaac Joseph & Grace Elizabeth. DIT Codrington Coll 1974. Rec 10/1/1987 as Priest Bp Paul Moore Jr. m 6/21/1967 Omah Icilma c 3. Cmsn of Mnstry Dio New York New York City NY 1990-1997. coc@churchofthecrucifixion.org

JOSEPH, Augustine (EC) 509 Ramsey St, Fayetteville NC 28301 B 11/5/1942 s Lucien Joseph & Adriana. LTh Codrington Coll 1972; BA U of The W Indies 1974. D 6/1/1973 P 6/1/1974 Bp The Bishop Of Trinidad. m 12/22/1966 Barbara Walcott c 1. R S Jos's Epis Ch Fayetteville NC 1991-2007; Voorhees Coll Denmark SC 1988-1991. rector@stjoseph-episcopal.org

JOSEPH, Jean Jeannot (Hai) P.O. Box 1390, Port-Au-Prince Haiti **Dio Haiti Ft Lauderdale FL 1991-** B 9/10/1959 s Alfred Joseph & Lorene. Cert TS 1991. D 9/15/1991 P 4/1/1992 Bp Luc Anatole Jacques Garnier. m 5/22/1997 Aline Joseph.

JOSEPH, Joseph Hyvenson (SeFla) 1840 Lortie Ave # 3, Quebec QC G1E 3X3 Canada **S Phil's Ch Pompano Bch FL 2011-** B Port-Au-Prince Haiti 7/17/1971 D 4/17/2004 P 10/23/2004 Bp Leopold Frade. S Ptr's Epis Ch Key W FL 2004-2007. hyvenson@yahoo.com

JOSEPH, Leo (NCal) 9233 Highway 175, Kelseyville CA 95451 **S Jn's Epis Ch Lakeport CA 2009-** B Brooklyn NY 5/21/1947 s Joseph Francis Brown & Marie Agnes. S Jn Inst Sacr Stds; DD S Thos Coll Montreal Qc S Thos Coll Montre 1974. D 10/23/1996 P 3/1/1997 Bp Jerry Alban Lamb. Chr Ch Eureka CA 2006-2008; S Mich And All Ang Ch Ft Bragg CA 2004-2006; Pstr Assoc S Jn's Epis Ch Lakeport CA 1996-2004. Ord Of S Fran. frleo@yahoo.com

JOSEPH, Pierre Jean (Ve) Calle Tiuna y Callejon, Sta Elena Venezuela Venezuela **Dio Venezuela Colinas De Bello Monte Caracas 10-42-A VE 2007-** B Cabaret Haiti 12/10/1953 s Alias Joseph & Teremise Louis. D 3/30/2007 Bp Orlando Jesus Guerrero. m 2/5/1985 Marie Mimose De Joseph c 2. jeancene@hotmail.com

JOSEPH, Winston B (SeFla) 6501 Sandy Bank Ter, Riviera Beach FL 33407 **R S Patricks Ch W Palm Bch FL 2000-** B 3/23/1947 Trans from Church in the Province Of The West Indies 10/4/2000 Bp Leopold Frade. m 8/24/1974 Moilan Joseph c 1. canonjoe.joseph@gmail.com

✠ **JOSLIN, Rt Rev David B(ruce)** (CNY) 10 Meadow Ridge Rd, Westerly RI 02891 **Bp Asstg Dio Rhode Island Providence RI 2004-** B Collingswood NJ 1/8/1936 s Sheppard Joslin & Elizabeth Anderson. BA Drew U 1958; MDiv Drew U 1961; Cert ETS 1965. D 3/31/1965 Bp Leland Stark P 8/8/1965 Bp George E Rath Con 11/9/1991 for CNY. m 6/15/1958 Kathrine B Brockett c 2. Bp Asstg Dio New Jersey Trenton NJ 2000-2003; Bp Dio Cntrl New York Syracuse NY 1991-2000; R S Steph The Mtyr Ch Minneapolis MN 1987-1991; Dio Rhode Island Providence RI 1979-1982; Dio Rhode Island Providence RI 1978-1982; Dio Rhode Island Providence RI 1975-1978; R Chr Ch Westerly RI 1974-1986; R S Dav's Epis Ch Wilmington DE 1967-1974; Asst S Paul's Ch Montvale NJ 1965-1967. Angl Soc 1982. DD VTS 2004. dbjoslin871@aol.com

JOSLIN, Roger Dale (Ark) 313 Sw F St, Bentonville AR 72712 **Vic All SS Ch Bentonville AR 2006-** B Cleburne TX 6/27/1951 s Hollis Joslin & Lillian. BA U of Texas 1973; MA U of Texas 1976; MDiv Epis TS of The SW 2005. D 5/13/2006 P 12/2/2006 Bp Larry Earl Maze. m 6/10/2007 Cindee Joslin c 2. Ch Planter S Paul's Ch Fayetteville AR 2006-2009. rogerjoslin@sbcglobal.net

JOY, Charles Austin (SVa) 1009 W Princess Anne Rd, Norfolk VA 23507 B Bangor ME 11/19/1944 s Nathan Sargent Joy & Jessie Viola. BA W&M 1966; MDiv VTS 1969; Coll of Preachers 2006. D 6/14/1969 P 5/23/1970 Bp Robert Bruce Hall. m 8/20/1966 Marilyn Allen c 1. R S Andr's Ch Norfolk VA 1982-2007; Assoc S Jas' Ch Richmond VA 1980-1982; D-in-c, R S Mart's Ch Doswell VA 1969-1980; St Martins Par Ruther Glen VA 1969-1980. Auth, "Poems," *Living Ch*; Auth, "Poems," *New Fire*. Soc of S Marg 1988. cajjoy1@aol.com

JOY, Stewart Murray (Ky) 305 S Birchwood Ave, Louisville KY 40206 B Atlantic City NJ 10/8/1922 s Percy Clark Joy & Gladys Marie. BA U of Virginia 1947; VTS 1956. D 6/9/1956 P 12/1/1956 Bp Angus Dun. m 8/19/1950 Ellen Beam. S Mk's Epis Ch Louisville KY 1958-1987; Asst S Paul's Rock Creek Washington DC 1956-1958. Chapl Ord Of S Lk. Paul Harris Awd Rotary.

JOYCE, Thomas Joseph (Chi) 214 Hillside Dr., East Berlin PA 17316 **Assoc S Lk's Epis Ch Mechanicsburg PA 2009-** B Boston MA 3/9/1933 s Martin Joyce & Mary. BA Boston Coll 1955; MA Boston Coll 1959; STL Weston Jesuit TS 1966; PhD Geo 1980. Rec from Roman Catholic 7/1/1987 as Priest Bp Peter James Lee. m 10/7/1989 Margaret Wise. Select Com. for Ord Dio Cntrl Pennsylvania Harrisburg PA 2010-2011; P in Res Hope Epis Ch Manheim PA 2004-2008; Dn Chicago W Dio Chicago Chicago IL 1998-2002; Select Com. for Ord Dio Chicago Chicago IL 1997-2003; R S Jn's Epis Ch Chicago IL 1996-2004; Asst Chr Epis Ch Winchester VA 1989-1995; S Patricks Ch Falls Ch VA 1988-1989. Pdk Tchr Of The Year Awd 1982. jycwise@comcast.net

JOYNER, Thomas Roland (Ala) 100 Church Drive, Auburn AL 36830 **Asst R H Trin Epis Ch Auburn AL 2010-** B Birmingham AL 5/22/1971 s Frank Hilton Joyner & Myra Gayle. BA U of Alabama Tuscaloosa 1995; MA U of Mississippi 2000; MDiv The GTS 2008. D 5/20/2008 P 12/16/2008 Bp Henry Nutt Parsley Jr. Cur Ch Of The H Comf Montgomery AL 2008-2010; Yth Dir S Steph's Epis Ch Huntsville AL 2001-2005. trjoyner@gmail.com

JOYNER JR, William Henry (NC) 309 N Boundary St, Chapel Hill NC 27514 **Archd Dio No Carolina Raleigh NC 2006-; D Chap Of The Cross Chap Hill NC 1998-** B Washington DC 9/21/1946 s William Henry Joyner & Nancy Holland. BS U of Virginia 1968; PhD Harv 1973. D 5/30/1992 Bp Richard Frank Grein. m 12/21/1968 Mary Brenda Payne c 2. Bp's Com on the Diac Dio No Carolina Raleigh NC 1999-2005; D S Ann's Ch Of Morrisania Bronx NY 1997-1998; D S Mk's Ch Mt Kisco NY 1997-1998; COM Dio New York New York City NY 1996-1998; Com on the Diac Dio New York New York City NY 1993-1998; D S Lk's Ch Katonah NY 1992-1996. NAAD 1992. william.joyner@src.org

JOYNER-GIFFIN, Sally Burt (Md) 13736 Catoctin Furnace Rd, Thurmont MD 21788 **R Harriet Chap Catoctin Epis Par Thurmont MD 2006-** B Richmond VA 2/26/1954 d Edward Grey Joyner & Carol SImpkin. BA Lyndon St Coll 1977; M.Ed. Jas Madison U 1979; MDiv STUSo 2005. D 6/11/2005 P 1/25/2006 Bp John Leslie Rabb. m 10/31/1981 John Ellis Giffin c 2. joynesb9@sewanee.edu

JUAREZ, Martin (Cal) 113 Morcroft Ln, Durham NC 27705 **Iglesia El Buen Pstr Durham NC 2009-** B San Luis Potosi Mexico 6/19/1964 Sem Guadalupano Josefino San Luis Potosi Slp 1982; Sem Guadalupano Josefino San Luis Potosi Slp 1990. Rec from Roman Catholic 12/6/2003 Bp William Edwin Swing. m Esperanza Juarez c 3. Dio California San Francisco CA 2006-2009. mtnjuarez@hotmail.com

JUAREZ VILLAMAR, Betty Marlene (EcuL) Coop Esperanza Mz.1 Sl.7, Canton Catarama Ecuador **Litoral Dio Ecuador Guayaquil EQ EC 2007-** B Canton Catarama Ecuador 12/9/1951 d Galo Juarez & Amada. DIT Litoral Sem

Guayaquil Ec. D 7/14/2002 P 4/13/2008 Bp Alfredo Morante-España. m 5/14/1997 Pedro Andaluz c 2.

JUBINSKI, Christopher David (Eas) 302 S. Liberty St., Centreville MD 21617 **R S Paul's Ch Centreville MD 2006-** B Silver City NM 1/8/1964 s James Kenneth Jubinski & Gretchen Hazel. BA S Basil Coll 1986; CUA 1989; MDiv GTS 1998. D 6/20/1998 P 5/29/1999 Bp Charles Ellsworth Bennison Jr. m 8/24/1991 Carol Jones c 3. S Paul's Epis Ch Santa Paula CA 2001-2006; Assoc Chr Ch Alexandria VA 2000-2001; Asst R Chr Ch Epis Ridley Pk PA 1998-2000. cdjubinski@aol.com

JUCHTER, John Perkins (NwPa) 4062 Zimmerman Rd, Erie PA 16510 **Died 5/26/2010** B Schenectady NY 7/22/1936 s Pieter Juchter & Ruth. AA Warren Wilson Coll 1956; BA Guilford Coll 1959; Coll of Preachers 1977. D 10/21/1973 Bp William Crittenden. c 3. juchters@erie.net

JUCHTER, Mark Russell (NwPa) 5321 Cook Ave., Tinker Afb OK 73145 B Erie PA 8/6/1972 s John Perkins Juchter & Annabelle. BS Gannon U 1994; Commissioned Off Trng 2002; MDiv SWTS 2003. D 6/15/2003 P 12/20/2003 Bp Robert Deane Rowley Jr. Int The Par Of S Clem Honolulu HI 2007-2008; Vic S Geo's Epis Ch Honolulu HI 2005-2007; Cur S Jn's Epis Ch Sharon PA 2003-2005. mark@juchter.com

JUDD, Steven William (Minn) 460 Willow Creek Dr, Owatonna MN 55060 **D S Paul's Epis Ch Owatonna MN 1999-** B Saint Paul MN 6/2/1950 s Allen W Judd & Elizabeth C. BA S Olaf Coll 1972. D 1/15/1994 Bp Sanford Zangwill Kaye Hampton. m 1/29/1972 Barbara C Mattlin c 2. D S Ptr's Epis Ch Kasson MN 1994-1999. swjudd@fedins.com

JUDSON, Donald Irving (Chi) 830 North Washington Street, Wheaton IL 60187 B Newark NJ 10/18/1930 s Lemuel Benedict Judson & Helen. BA Amh 1952; BD EDS 1956; MA U Chi 1977; MA U Chi 1989. D 6/21/1956 Bp William A Lawrence P 12/21/1956 Bp Frederick Lehrle Barry. m 7/29/1978 Jean Judson c 2. Chr Ch River Forest IL 1989-2000; Epis Ch Coun U Chi Chicago IL 1975-1978; R S Paul's Ch Fremont OH 1959-1967; Cur S Paul's Epis Ch Albany NY 1956-1958. Auth, "Importance of Awe & Mystery," *LivCh*, 2008; Auth, "Branches of the Vine," *LivCh*, 2002; Auth, "Ch in the Wrld," *The L:iving Ch*; Auth, "Lay Mnstry," *LivCh*; Auth, "Scenario for Ch," *LivCh*. djudson@comcast.net

JUDSON, Horace Douglas (Los) 1065 Lomita Blvd Spc 197, Harbor City CA 90710 B Glendale CA 5/29/1935 s Horace Turpen Judson & Blanche Helfrid. ETSBH; BA U CA 1961. D 9/12/1970 P 3/1/1971 Bp Francis E I Bloy. m 5/28/1966 Kathern L Macklin. Int S Mich The Archangel Par El Segundo CA 1993-1994; S Tim's Par Compton CA 1982-1989; Asst S Fran' Par Palos Verdes Estates CA 1978-1981; Assoc S Jn's Epis Ch Marysville CA 1977-1978; Vic S Mk's Epis Ch French Camp CA 1975-1977; Epis Dio San Joaquin Modesto CA 1972-1977; Vic S Jn's Epis Ch Tulare CA 1972-1975; Asst Ch Of The H Trin and S Ben Alhambra CA 1970-1972. OHC. hdjudson@sbcglobal.net

JULIAN, Mercedes I (RI) Ascension Church, 390 Pontiac Ave, Cranston RI 02910 Panama **P Ch Of The Ascen Cranston RI 2010-; Dio Rhode Island Providence RI 2010-; Iglesia Epis de San Juan Johns Island SC 2005-** B Higuey Dominican Republic 11/29/1949 d Napoleon Julian & Ludis Maria. Universidad Republica Dominicana 1978; Centro De Estudios Teologicos 1982. D 11/30/1988 P 5/1/1990 Bp James Hamilton Ottley. m 1/3/1982 Oscar Olmedo Rivera c 2. S Jn's Epis Par Johns Island SC 2005-2010; Gr Ch New Orleans LA 2004-2005; Vic Centro Buen Pstr San Pedro de Macoris DO 1997-2003; Vic Iglesia Epis San Esteban San Pedro de Macoris DO 1997-2003; Vic Iglesia Epis San Juan El Bautista Santo Domingo DO 1994-1997; Dio The Dominican Republic (Iglesia Epis Dominicana) Santo Domingo DO 1993-2004; Dio Panama 1988-1993; Iglesia Epis Dominicana Dominican Republic 1981-1987. mjulian91@hotmail.com

JULNES-DEHNER, Noel (SO) 3491 Forestoak Court, Cincinnati OH 45208 B Seattle WA 9/13/1951 d Norval Stanley Julnes & Marilyn Gay. BA Eckerd Coll 1973; VTS 1974; MDiv CDSP 1978. D 5/26/1978 P 6/24/1979 Bp John Mc Gill Krumm. m 11/19/1983 Joseph Dehner c 2. Int S Thos Epis Ch Terrace Pk OH 1995-1996; Par Asst The Ch of the Redeem Cincinnati OH 1986-1987; Asst Ed FMP Cincinnati OH 1982-2009; Asst The Ch Of Ascen And H Trin Cincinnati OH 1980-1982. "Y-a-t'il une vie?"; Auth, "The Kharkov Connection"; Auth, "Ukraintsi'"; Auth, "Under Fire: Soviet Wmn Combat Veterans," *WWII*. njulnes@gmail.com

JUNGER, Erich Paul (WA) 13314 Keystone Dr., Woodbridge VA 22193 **Asst P The Angl/Epis Ch Of Chr The King Frankfurt am Main 60323 DE 2011-** B Glendale CA 2/5/1958 s Bill Richard Junger & Florentina Catherine. MS U Of New Haven W Haven CT 1990; PhD Un Inst And U Cincinnati OH 1994; MA Cath Dist. U 2007; Th.D. (Candidate) Golden St TS 2009. Rec from Roman Catholic 7/14/2007 Bp Keith Lynn Ackerman. m 5/26/1984 Mary Ruth Mary Ruth Beaver c 2. R All Faith Epis Ch Charlotte Hall MD 2009-2011; Asst P S Lk's Par Bladensburg MD 2007-2009. scl Cath Dist. U 2007; hon Roll DET hon Soc 2007; mcl GW 1985. ejunger@aol.com

JUNK, Dixie Roberts (Kan) 2701 W 51st Ter, Westwood KS 66205 **Dioc Jubilee Off Dio Kansas Topeka KS 2010-; P-in-c S Paul's Ch Kansas City KS 2010-; Capital Cmpgn Bldg Com Dio Kansas Topeka KS 2008-; Cmsn on Archit & Allied Arts Dio Kansas Topeka KS 2000-** B Hutchinson, KS 8/28/1957 d Dick Chester Roberts & Patsy Lou Fortier. Assoc of Arts Hutchinson Cmnty Coll 1977; Bachelor of Archit K SU 1981; MDiv S Paul TS 2008. D 6/5/2010 P 1/8/2011 Bp Dean Elliott Wolfe. m 8/9/1980 Robert P Junk c 1. dixiejunk@mac.com

JUNKIN, Hays M (NH) Church of Our Saviour, P.O. Box 237, Milford NH 03055 **Int Ch Of Our Sav Milford NH 2011-** B Pittsburgh PA 1/20/1952 s John Maclean Junkin & Margaret. BA Washington and Jefferson U 1975; MDiv VTS 1978. D 6/9/1978 P 12/13/1978 Bp Dean T Stevenson. m 1/25/2008 Sarah Rockwell c 2. Int R Ch Of The H Sprt Plymouth NH 2010-2011; P-in-c S Jas Epis Ch Laconia NH 2005-2008; R S Andr's Epis Ch Hopkinton NH 1987-2005; R S Dav's Epis Ch W Seneca NY 1980-1987; Cur S Jas Ch Lancaster PA 1978-1980. hjunkin@comcast.net

JUPIN, J Michael (SO) 1937 Country Pl, Lancaster OH 43130 B Indianapolis IN 1/27/1942 s John M Jupin & Maxine Elizabeth. BA Br 1964; BD EDS 1967; STM GTS 1986. D 6/24/1967 P 6/15/1968 Bp John P Craine. m 8/24/1982 Barbara Emser c 1. Transitional R S Alb's Epis Ch Of Bexley Columbus OH 2008-2011; Int Chr Ch Clarksburg WV 2006-2007; CREDO II Vocational Fac Credo Inst Inc. Memphis TN 2005-2011; Int Ch Of The Gd Shpd Athens OH 2003-2006; P-in-c Ch Of The Epiph Nelsonville OH 1999-2003; P-in-c S Paul's Epis Ch Logan OH 1999-2003; R S Mk's Epis Ch Columbus OH 1990-1998; R Chr Ch Corning NY 1984-1990; Cn Trin Cathd Cleveland OH 1974-1984; Asst Gr Ch In Providence Providence RI 1973-1974; Asst S Chris's Ch Gladwyne PA 1969-1971; Asst Par Of The Epiph Winchester MA 1967-1969. Healthy Congregations, Inc. Bd Dir 2005; Voyagers - The Ed Friedman Mem. Soc 2001. jjupin@columbus.rr.com

JURADO, Ruben Dario (Nwk) 326 Westervelt Pl, Lodi NJ 07644 **Hisp Min Trin Epis Ch Kearny NJ 2006-** B Manizales Colombia 12/20/1961 s Dario Jurado & Blanca. MDiv Our Lady Of The Rosary 1987. Rec from Roman Catholic 9/16/2006 Bp John Palmer Croneberger. m 6/15/1996 Maria Jurado c 2. rudjusa@gmail.com

JURKOVICH-HUGHES, Jocelynn Lena (NCal) 216 A Street, Davis CA 95616 **Campus Chapl Belfry-Epis & Luth Campus Mnstrs Davis CA 2008-** B Sacramento CA 8/12/1976 d David Dowd Jurkovich & Jacquelynn Lee. BA Goucher Coll 1998; MA U of So Florida 2000; Cert U of So Florida 2001; MDiv Ya Berk 2004. D 6/25/2004 P 12/19/2004 Bp Jerry Alban Lamb. m 7/27/2002 Christopher A Hughes c 2. Assoc R The Epis Ch Of S Andr Encinitas CA 2004-2008. pastor@thebelfry.org

JUSTICE, Simon Charles (Ore) 445 NW Elizabeth Drive, Corvallis OR 97330 **R The Epis Ch Of The Gd Samar Corvallis OR 2006-** B Cheslyn Hay Staffordshire UK 6/6/1966 s Keith Leornard Justice & Norma Irene. BD S Dav's Coll, Lampeter UK 1988; MTh U of Edinburgh Edinburgh UK 1990; Theol Stds Cranmer Hall, U of Durham UK 1992. Trans from Church Of England 1/1/1995 Bp David Standish Ball. m 9/3/1992 Michele Marie Mingo c 3. Stndg Com Dio Oregon Portland OR 2007-2011; Dn of Sunset Convoc Dio Oregon Portland OR 2004; R S Jas Epis Ch Tigard OR 2001-2004; Cn Capitular Cathd Of All SS Albany NY 1998-2001; R S Paul's Ch Troy NY 1995-2001. simon.justice@gmail.com

JUSTIN, Daniel John (Los) 306 S Prospect Ave, Park Ridge IL 60068 **Asst R S Mary's Ch Pk Ridge IL 2009-** B Harvey IL 8/1/1972 s Larned John Justin & Kathleen Ann. BS Missouri Bapt U 1995; MA Lindenwood U 2001; MDiv SFTS San Anselmo 2008. D 6/6/2009 Bp Sergio Carranza-Gomez P 12/11/2009 Bp Jeffrey Dean Lee. danjustin101@yahoo.com

K

KADEL, Andrew Gordon (NY) 440 W. 21st Street, New York NY 10011 **Dir of St. Mk's Libr The GTS New York NY 2003-** B Nampa ID 6/8/1954 s Donald Milburn Kadel & Bernice. BA Ob 1976; MDiv CDSP 1981; MLS Rutgers-The St U 1989. D 7/15/1981 Bp Hanford Langdon King Jr P 2/26/1982 Bp James Daniel Warner. m 5/22/1999 Paula R Schaap c 3. Assoc S Ptr's Ch Port Chester NY 1995-1998; Cur S Mk's Epis Ch Yonkers NY 1989-1995; Asst S Lk's Ch Ewing NJ 1985-1989; Vic Trin Epis Ch Kirksville MO 1983-1985; Asst S Matt's Ch Lincoln NE 1981-1983. Auth, "Mart Niemöller: transformation of an oral text," *Journ of Rel and Theol Info*, 1996; Auth, *Matrology: Bibliography of Writings by Chr Wmn from the 1st to the 15th Centuries*, Continuum, 1995. kadel@gts.edu

KAEHR, Michael Gene (SanD) 9503 La Jolla Farms Rd, La Jolla CA 92037 **Hon Cathd Ch Of S Paul San Diego CA 2009-** B Decatur IN 1/26/1942 s Lores Kaehr & La Vera. BA Heidelberg U 1964; MA U of Wisconsin 1970; MDiv Nash 1983. D 4/16/1983 P 10/15/1983 Bp William L Stevens. m 1/25/1997 Nancy Chester Olmsted. R S Jn's Epis Ch Chula Vista CA 1988-1997; Asst R S Jas By The Sea La Jolla CA 1985-1988; Asst to Dn S Paul's Cathd Fond du Lac WI 1983-1985. SHN. mkarob@san.rr.com

KAESTNER, James Andrew (Mil) N52 W37111 Washington Street, Oconomowoc WI 53066 B Milwaukee WI 8/17/1935 s Arthur Wilhelm Ernst Kaestner & Lillian Alice. BA Carroll Coll 1956; MDiv Nash 1959. D 12/6/1958 P 8/22/1959 Bp Donald H V Hallock. m 5/7/1960 Judith Pallett. Vic S Ptr's Ch No Lake WI 2008-2010; Vic Ch Of The H Comm Lake Geneva WI 2003-2008; Int Zion Epis Ch Oconomowoc WI 2000-2002; P-in-c S Paul's Ch Ashippun Oconomowoc WI 2000-2001; Chapl Nash Nashotah WI 1998-2000; Cn All SS' Cathd Milwaukee WI 1997-1998; ExCoun Dio Milwaukee Milwaukee WI 1989-1997; COM Dio Milwaukee Milwaukee WI 1978-1984; R S Lk's Ch Racine WI 1975-1997; R S Alb's Epis Ch Marshfield WI 1969-1975; P-in-c S Thos Of Cbury Ch Greendale WI 1962-1969; Asst Trin Ch Janesville WI 1960-1961; Asst Zion Epis Ch Oconomowoc WI 1958-1959. OHC 1958; The CSM - P Assoc 1963. 1st Distinguished Alum Nash 2009. jkaestner1@wi.rr.com

KAETON, Elizabeth Marie Conroy (Nwk) 94 Chatham St, Chatham NJ 07928 **P All SS Ch Rehoboth Bch DE 2011-** B Fall River MA 4/21/1949 d John C Souza & Lydia Lima. BS Lesley U 1983; MDiv EDS 1986; U Of Sheffield Gb 1999; D.Min Drew U 2008. D 4/12/1986 P 10/1/1986 Bp Frederick Barton Wolf. m 10/13/1976 Barbara Conroy c 1. R S Paul's Epis Ch Chatham NJ 2002-2011; Assoc Ch Of The Redeem Morristown NJ 1998-2002; Mssnr At The Oasis Dio Newark Newark NJ 1996-2002; The Oasis Newark NJ 1996-2002; Hse Of Pryr Epis Ch Newark NJ 1995-1996; Vic S Barn Ch Newark NJ 1991-1995; Memi Ch Baltimore MD 1987-1989; P-in-c S Dav's Ch Salem NH 1986-1987. Auth, "Two Grooms Revisited," *A Sea Of Stories: The Shaping Power Of Narrative*, Harrington Pk, 2000; Auth, "To Have And To Hold," *Journ Of Lcgm*, 2000; Auth, "The Power Of Pryr," *The Voice*, 2000; Auth, "The Adv Of Desire, Sermons That Wk Vii," *Adv Iii*, Morehouse, 1999; Auth, "Called To Full Humanity: Letters To Lambeth Bishops," *Journ Of Lgcm*, 1998; Auth, "Pstr Care At The End Of Life," *Journ Of Palliative Med*, 1998; Auth, "Lambeth," *The Voice*, 1998; Auth, "Dealing w Grief," *Wit*, 1998; Auth, "Beyond Inclusion Report," *Wit*, 1998; Auth, "Maria'S Chld," *Wit*, 1997. Beyond Inclusion: Just Commitments Natl Coordntng Grp 1998; Coun Of Wmn Mnstrs 2000; Dir Of Prog-Integrity Usa 1999; EWC; Integrity 1976; New Commandment T/F On Recon 2000; Nj Rel Cltn On Reproductive Rts 2000; No Jersey Epis City Mssn Bd 1996; Oasis-Pres, Bd 1996; The Consult 1999; Voice Ed Bd 1992. Awd Of Merit For Spec Achievement In Ch Cmncatn ECom 1999; Resolution Of Gratitude, Lambeth Oasis Bd Dir Newark NJ 1998; 3 Awards Of Excellence In Rel Journalism ECom 1997; Wmn Of Influence Ywca Essex and W Hudson NJ 1995; Awd Of Gratitude Latino/A People Living w Aids Newark NJ 1992. motherkaeton@gmail.com

KAGEY JR, Guy Edison (Alb) RR #3, Box 181, Lost Lake Road, Arlington VT 05250 **P-in-c Par Of S Jas Ft Edw NY 1989-** B Evanston WY 9/25/1918 s Guy Edison Kagey & Mary Langdon. Universal Bible Inst; BA Loyola U 1941; BD McGill U 1950; MA Loyola U 1955; MA Mid 1959; MS Russell Sage Coll 1968; BD/MDiv Montreal TS 1972. D 9/20/1969 Bp Charles Bowen Persell Jr P 11/1/1972 Bp Allen Webster Brown. P-in-c S Steph's Ch Schuylerville NY 1985-1988; R Trin Ch Granville NY 1979-1982; R S Paul's Ch Salem NY 1975-1982; All SS Ch No Granville NY 1973-1982; R Trin Ch Whitehall NY 1971-1975; Asst S Lk's Ch Cambridge NY 1969-1971. Auth, "Wilhelm Vs Bismark"; Auth, "Brain Damage In Chld". ECM, GAS, Ord Of S Ben. Air Intelligence 1942; Combat Flying Citations 1942; Flight Wings 1941.

KAHL, Eric (SwFla) 1142 Coral Way, Coral Gables FL 33134 **R S Mary's Par Tampa FL 2011-** B Sendai JP 1/5/1955 s Donald Kahl & Yayo. BA Florida St U 1977; MDiv CDSP 1994. D 6/10/1984 P 1/6/1985 Bp Frank Stanley Cerveny. m 8/4/1984 Judith Carolyn Carter. S Simons Ch Miami FL 2010; R S Phil's Ch Coral Gables FL 1992-2010; Asst R S Mk's Epis Ch Jacksonville FL 1986-1992; Sprtl Dir Dio Florida Jacksonville FL 1985-1990; S Paul's By-The-Sea Epis Ch Jacksonville Bch FL 1984-1986; Cur S Paul's Epis Ch Jacksonville FL 1984-1986. OHC. ekahle@comcast.net

KAHL JR SSJE, Robert Mathew (NJ) 107 E Tampa Ave, Villas NJ 08251 **S Mich's Ch Grosse Pointe Woods MI 1964-** B Brigham City UT 5/29/1945 s Robert Mathew Kahl & Anna Luella. STB GTS; STM UTS; AA Amer Coll of Switzerland 1966; BA U of Pennsylvania 1968; MPhil U of St. Andrews 1997. D 6/29/1971 P 7/2/1972 Bp Chilton Powell. Ch Of The Adv Cape May NJ 1979-1994; Asst Trin Ch Moorestown NJ 1973-1979; Asst Ch Of The Resurr New York NY 1972-1973. Auth, "Chr & Hisp Communities," Ed. Bibliography, 1990; Auth, "Living Ch"; Ed and Auth, "Chr and Chrsnty," *Intro*; "Numerous Revs," *TLC and ATheology Journ*. Soc Of S Jn The Evang 1974. robertkahl107@comcast.net

KAHLBAUGH, George Ralph (Alb) 6 Winners Cir Apt 323, Albany NY 12205 **Died 10/7/2011** B Chester PA 3/25/1927 s Ralph Kahlbaugh & Dorothy. BA Franklin & Marshall Coll 1950; MDiv PDS 1953. D 5/23/1953 P 12/19/1953 Bp Oliver J Hart. Hon Cn Cathd All SS Cathd Albany NY 1977. kahlbaugh2@aol.com

KAHLE, George Frank (SVa) 16711 Holly Trail Dr, Houston TX 77058 B Pensacola FL 6/20/1919 s George Frank Kahle & Blanche. BD U of Alabama 1947. D 6/6/1979 P 6/1/1980 Bp Robert Poland Atkinson. Asst Gr Ch Galveston TX 1989-1996; Vic Emm Ch Oak Hall VA 1984-1988; Cur S Matt's Ch Charleston WV 1980-1984.

KAHLER, Jerome Evans (Los) 9061 Santa Margarita Rd, Ventura CA 93004 B Los Angeles CA 9/4/1944 s James Elias Kahler & Rosemary. BA Whittier Coll 1966; MDiv Nash 1970. D 8/17/1969 P 7/26/1970 Bp Robert C Rusack. m 6/1/1968 Elizabeth H Henderson c 1. Cmsn on Sch Dio Los Angeles Los Angeles CA 1996-2000; Stndg Com Dio Los Angeles Los Angeles CA 1991-1994; R S Paul's Epis Ch Ventura CA 1988-2010; Dio Los Angeles Los Angeles CA 1983-1988; R S Paul's Epis Ch Santa Paula CA 1979-1984; S Geo's Par La Can CA 1971-1979; Asst S Mich's Mssn Anaheim CA 1970-1971. Cn Dio Los Angeles 2009. jeromekahler@aol.com

KAHN, Paul S. (NY) 552 West End Avenue, New York NY 10024 **D The Ch of S Ign of Antioch New York NY 2008-** B Bethpage NY 3/10/1957 s Sam Kahn & Hazel Ruth. BA Ob 1979; MBA NYU 1985. D 5/5/2007 Bp Mark Sean Sisk. D Ch Of The Gd Shpd New York NY 2007-2008. pskahn@verizon.net

KAIGHN, Reuel Stewart (Be) 145 The Hideout, Lake Ariel PA 18436 B Hartford CT 12/17/1936 s Reuel S Kaighn & Sarah S. BA U of Pennsylvania 1958; MDiv EDS 1964. Trans 12/6/2003 Bp Robert William Duncan. m 1/22/2000 Barbara Brown c 3. Assoc S Jn's Epis Ch Hamlin PA 2002-2004; R All SS Epis Ch Verona PA 1992-2000; R Trin Epis Ch Beaver PA 1984-1991; R S Jn's Epis Ch Montclair NJ 1970-1984; Asst Trin Ch Princeton NJ 1967-1970; Cur S Mk's Ch New Britain CT 1964-1967. rskaighn@echoes.net

KAISCH, Kenneth Burton (Los) 2112 Camino Del Sol, Fullerton CA 92833 B Detroit MI 8/29/1948 s Kenneth R Kaisch & Marjorie Frances. Ken 1969; BA San Francisco St U 1972; MDiv CDSP 1976; MS Utah St U 1982; PhD Utah St U 1986. D 8/15/1976 P 3/1/1977 Bp Otis Charles. m 2/4/2006 Julia LePrevost. P-in-c S Jn's Epis Ch Logan UT 1980-1984; Vic S Fran Ch Moab UT 1977-1980; Ordinand'S Trng Prog Dio Utah Salt Lake City UT 1976-1977. Auth, "Finding God: A Handbook Of Chr Meditation". Phi Kappa Phi 82. KENKAISCH@YAHOO.COM

KAISER, Marcus Adam (SC) PO Box 338, Sumter SC 29151 **Asst R Ch Of The H Comf Sumter SC 2010-** B Orlando FL 1/29/1975 s Wendell Andrew Kaiser & Kathryn Marie. BS U.S. Naval Acad 1998; MDiv Nash 2009. D 5/28/2009 Bp Mark Joseph Lawrence. m 7/3/1999 Kimberly Roberts c 2. mkaiser98@aol.com

KALEMKERIAN, Louise Knar (Ct) 5030 Main St, Trumbull CT 06611 B Detroit MI 12/2/1945 d Arshavir Yeghissian & Bettye Jane. BA Wayne 1968; MA SWTS 1970; CAS GTS 1994; STM GTS 1998. D 6/3/1995 Bp John Shelby Spong P 12/2/1995 Bp Jack Marston McKelvey. m 8/7/1971 Joseph Kalemkerian c 2. Int S Ptr's-Trin Ch Thomaston CT 2009-2011; Asst to the R Chr And H Trin Ch Westport CT 2009; S Andr's Ch Madison CT 2007-2009; S Mary's Ch Of Scarborough Scarborough NY 2004-2005; Par of St Paul's Ch Norwalk Norwalk CT 2004; S Lukes Cmnty Serv Inc. Stamford CT 2003-2007; Emm Epis Ch Stamford CT 1999-2003; Int S Mary's Ch Sparta NJ 1997-1998; Int S Paul's Epis Ch Morris Plains NJ 1996-1997; Asst for Educ Trin And S Phil's Cathd Newark NJ 1995-1996. revlouisek@yahoo.com

KALLENBERG, Richard Arthur (NI) 55805 Oak Manor Pl, Elkhart IN 46514 **Int S Mich And All Ang Ch So Bend IN 2008-** B Anderson IN 5/22/1944 s Herbert August Kallenberg & Helen Elizabeth. BA Hanover Coll 1966; BD Nash 1969. D 6/11/1969 Bp John P Craine P 11/11/1969 Bp Albert Ervine Swift. m 3/31/1970 Kathryn Carol Westlund. R S Jn The Evang Ch Elkhart IN 1987-2008; R Ch Of The Intsn Stevens Point WI 1977-1987; Vic Chr the King/H Nativ (Sturgeon Bay) Sturgeon Bay WI 1970-1977; P Ch Of The H Nativ Jacksonport Sturgeon Bay WI 1970-1977; Dio Fond du Lac Appleton WI 1970-1977; Cur S Mk's Ch Cocoa FL 1969-1970. SHN. Hon Cn The Cathd Ch Of St. Jas 2004. kallenbe@frontier.com

KALLIO, Craig Martin (ETenn) 119 Newell Lane, Oak Ridge TN 37830 **R S Steph's Epis Ch Oak Ridge TN 2000-** B Painesville OH 3/18/1949 s Melvin Evert Kallio & Maxine Jeannette. BA Adrian Coll 1971; MDiv Iliff TS 1983; DMin SWTS 1998. D 6/6/1988 P 10/14/1988 Bp Francis Campbell Gray. m 5/2/1987 Pamela K Nichols. R All SS Ch Wstrn Sprg IL 1991-2000; Cur Trin Ch Ft Wayne IN 1988-1991. Auth, "Greet the Unepected," *The Angl Dig; Adv*, Adv, 2008; Auth, "Baptismal Identity," *The Angl Dig; Easter*, 2008; Auth, "The Poor," *The Angl Dig; Pentecost*, Pentecost, 2008; Auth, "Sunday's Readings," *LivCh*, TLC Fndt, 2007; Auth, "A Faith Worth Living," *The Angl Dig*, Thanksgiving, 2006; Auth, "Discipleship," *The Angl Dig*, Michelmas, 2006. Ord of S Lk 1991. ckallio@bellsouth.net

KALOM, Judith Christine Lilly (At) 190 Eagle Ct, Woodstock GA 30188 B Sturgis MI 11/8/1939 d Harold Lilly & Grace. D 12/19/1990 Bp Don Adger Wimberly. m 8/26/1961 Peter Grant Kalom c 2.

KALUNIAN, Peter J (Oly) 5506 W. 19th Ave., Kennewick WA 99338 **P-in-c H Trin Epis Ch Sunnyside WA 2011-; Dn - Snake River Dnry Dio Spokane Spokane WA 1997-** B Waltham MA 12/4/1942 s John Peter Kalunian & Rose Nevart. BA Parsons Coll Fairfield IA 1967; Med Boston St Coll 1969; EdD Bos 1974; MDiv CDSP 1990. D 6/2/1990 Bp Joseph Thomas Heistand P 12/1/1990 Bp Frank Jeffrey Terry. m 5/9/1976 Kathryn Angela

Bonacci c 2. Ch Of The Resurr Bellevue WA 2004-2008; Dioc Ecum Off Dio Spokane Spokane WA 1998-2001; Stndg Com Dio Spokane Spokane WA 1997-2002; R S Paul's Epis Ch Kennewick WA 1994-2004; COM Dio Spokane Spokane WA 1993-1998; Vic Gr Ch Dayton WA 1990-1994; S Ptr's Ch Pomeroy WA 1990-1994. pkalunian@charter.net

KAMINSKI, Neil Mitchell (CGC) 6650 Avenida Oakleigh, Navarre FL 32566 **R The Epis Ch Of S Fran Of Assisi Indn Sprg Vill AL 2007-** B Montreal QC CA 1/21/1959 s Mitchell M Kaminski & Alice Elizabeth. BA Asbury Coll 1982; MA Sprg Hill Coll 1988; MDiv STUSo 1995. D 5/27/1995 P 1/1/1996 Bp Charles Farmer Duvall. m 8/28/1986 Gwendolyn Rose Smith c 1. Vic St Aug of Cbury Navarre FL 1998-2007; Trin Epis Ch Mobile AL 1995-1998. RECTORSTFRAN@BELLSOUTH.NET

KAMM, Wayne Kenneth (Ia) 1451 Salem Rd., Salem IA 52649 B Dubuque Iowa 7/22/1936 s Kenneth Henry Kamm & Sadie Inez. BA U Of Dubuque 1958; MDiv Garrett Evang TS 1963. D 4/9/1985 P 10/23/1985 Bp Walter Cameron Righter. m 6/2/1990 Mary Louise Farr c 2. Assoc Chr Epis Ch Burlington IA 2000; Dioc Search Com Dio Iowa Des Moines IA 1987-1988; Bd Dir Dio Iowa Des Moines IA 1986-1994; Chair - Com Dio Iowa Des Moines IA 1986-1990; COM Dio Iowa Des Moines IA 1986-1990; R S Mich's Ch Mt Pleasant IA 1985-1999; Vic Ch of the Gd Shpd Detroit MI 1984-1985. Land 1989. rockermacher@yahoo.com

KANE, E Ross (Va) 228 S Pitt St, Alexandria VA 22314 **Asst S Paul's Epis Ch Alexandria VA 2009-** B 11/7/1979 s Robert Edward Kane & Anne Wade. BA U of Virginia 2002; MDiv Duke DS 2009. D 11/14/2009 Bp Shannon Sherwood Johnston P 5/15/2010 Bp David Colin Jones. m 8/25/2006 Elizabeth MD Doughty. e.ross.kane@gmail.com

KANE, Maria Alexandria (NC) 15 Buford Rd, Williamsburg VA 23188 **Com on Human Sxlty Dio Sthrn Virginia Norfolk VA 2011-** B Dallas TX 12/22/1980 d Samuel Kermit Kane & Patricia Anne Lord. BA How 2003; MDiv Duke DS 2006; MA W&M 2008. D 6/19/2010 Bp Michael Bruce Curry P 5/4/2011 Bp Herman Hollerith IV. Cur Hickory Neck Ch Toano VA 2010-2011. Auth, "That Darn Collar," *Fidelia's Sis*, Young Wmn Cler Proj, 2011; Contributing Auth, "Prayers for Chld," *Forty Days of Pryr in hon of 9/11*, Meth Ch, 2011. mariakane3@gmail.com

KANELLAKIS, Theodore (NY) 10 Rawson Ave, Camden ME 04843 B Brooklyn NY 11/30/1943 s Louis Kanellakis & Pauline. Inst of Theol New York NY 1981; BA SUNY 1981. D 6/13/1981 Bp Paul Moore Jr P 1/23/1982 Bp James Stuart Wetmore. m 6/28/1974 Susan Brooks c 3. Int P S Ptr's Ch Rockland ME 2007-2008; Cler Day Com Dio Maine Portland ME 2006-2009; Dioc Coun Dio New York New York City NY 1992-1996; Pstr S Paul's And Trin Par Tivoli NY 1989-2005; P in Charge Ch Of The Regeneration Pine Plains NY 1989-1998; Assoc Ch Of The H Trin New York NY 1982-1989. ttk@roadrunner.com

KANESHIRO, Morimasa (Haw) 385 Oomano Pl, Honolulu HI 96825 **Died 11/22/2009** B Hilo HI 3/27/1925 s Micha Kaneshiro & Uto. BA Drury U 1951; BD SWTS 1956; MS U of Hawaii 1972. D 6/10/1956 Bp Arthur C Lichtenberger P 12/1/1956 Bp Harry S Kennedy. c 4. Treas Hawaii Epis Cleric Assn.

KANESTROM, Glenn Walter (EpisSanJ) 6443 Estelle Ave, Riverbank CA 95367 **R Chr The King Ch Riverbank CA 2002-** B Seattle WA 2/3/1961 s Gilbert Olaf Kanestrom & Priscilla Jane. Syr; BA Seattle Pacific U 1983; MDiv SWTS 1991. D 6/22/1991 Bp O'Kelley Whitaker P 5/12/1992 Bp David B(ruce) Joslin. m 6/14/1986 Jane Ellen Neufelder c 2. S Paul's Epis Ch La Porte IN 1997-2002; Asst To The R Trin Epis Ch Hartford CT 1993-1997; Dio Cntrl New York Syracuse NY 1991-1993; Dioc Intern Trin Memi Ch Binghamton NY 1991-1993. frgwk@yahoo.com

KANGAS, John Gilbert (NMich) 302 E Arch St, Ironwood MI 49938 **P Ch Of The Trsfg Ironwood MI 1999-** B New York NY 4/10/1930 s John Carl Kangas & Tyyne Lydia. Beloit Coll; Nthrn Michigan U. D 11/12/1997 P 5/1/1998 Bp Thomas Kreider Ray. m 8/16/1953 Maj-Britt Nyberg. gilsat@gogebic.net

KANNAIR, Nancy Elizabeth (Mass) 97 Ocean St, Lynn MA 01902 **Died 10/30/2009** B Newton MA 7/10/1935 d Albert Edward & Faith Elizabeth. U Pgh; AS Chandler 1955; MDiv EDS 1987. D 6/11/1988 Bp David Elliot Johnson P 6/1/1989 Bp Edward Cole Chalfant. c 1. nancy@dragonfabrication.com

KANNENBERG, James Gordon (Ia) 605 Avenue E, Fort Madison IA 52627 B Fond du lac WI 12/18/1952 s Vernon Kannenberg & Carol. BS U of Wisconsin 1975; MD U of Wisconsin 1979. D 10/25/2009 Bp Alan Scarfe. m 7/7/1978 Kathy Anderson. jkannenberg@fmchosp.com

KANOUR, Marion Elizabeth (SwVa) 732 S Chestnut Ave, Arlington Heights IL 60005 **R Trin Epis Ch Lynchburg VA 2003-** B Norfolk VA 9/10/1953 d Marion Gunter Kanour & Mildred Knight. BS OR SU 1982; MDiv Ya Berk 1985; CAS VTS 1992. D 6/7/1992 Bp Frank Harris Vest Jr P 12/1/1992 Bp Frank Kellogg Allan. m 9/9/2011 Barbara Heyl. R S Barn Ch Lynchburg VA 2003-2009; Vic The Ch Of The H Innoc Hoffman Schaumburg IL 2001-2003; Asst S Barth's Epis Ch Atlanta GA 1997-2001; Int Emmaus Hse Epis Ch Atlanta GA 1996-1997; Dio Atlanta Atlanta GA 1996; Assoc All SS Epis Ch Atlanta GA 1993-1997; D Emmaus Hse Epis Ch Atlanta GA 1992-1993. Pi Sigma Alpha. MKANOUR@GMAIL.COM

KANYI, Peter (ETenn) 630 Mississippi Ave, Signal Mtn TN 37377 B Londiani 4/9/1946 s Muraya Kanyi & Wangui. BSC Dallas Chr Coll 2000; MAR Emmanual Sch of Rel Johnson City TN 2004; MDiv The Prot Epis TS 2008. D 5/31/2008 P 1/24/2009 Bp Charles Glenn VonRosenberg. m 10/29/2008 Anne Anne Ndia Njeru c 3. D S Tim's Ch Signal Mtn TN 2008-2009. pkanyi@sttimsignal.com

KANZLER JR, Jay Lee (Mo) 20 Southmoor Dr, Clayton MO 63105 **S Ptr's Epis Ch St Louis MO 2004-** B Washington DC 2/19/1961 s Jay L Kanzler & Gail Lynn. BS Maryville U 1988; JD S Louis U 1991; ThM S Louis U 2005. D 12/22/2004 P 9/11/2005 Bp George Wayne Smith. m 6/10/1989 Karen Haesard c 2. jaykanzler@dunnandmiller.com

KAPP, Charl Ann (NwPa) 1731 Warren Rd, Oil City PA 16301 B Oil City PA 12/1/1936 d William Charlton Taylor & Elizabeth Jean. Dioc Sch for Mnstry Titusville PA 1995. D 1/28/1996 Bp Robert Deane Rowley Jr. c 3.

KAPP, John Deane (Az) 2800 W Ina Rd, Tucson AZ 85741 B Phoenix AZ 3/8/1945 s George Harold Kapp & Louise Campbell. BFA Arizona St U 1973; MFA U of Arizona 1977. D 1/23/2010 Bp Kirk Stevan Smith. m 6/16/1973 Martha Sears c 2. eons2io8@comcast.net

KAPPEL, Roger Dale (EC) 1302 N Walnut St, Lumberton NC 28358 **Trin Ch Lumberton NC 2004-; Off Of Bsh For ArmdF New York NY 1997-** B Clinton OK 2/21/1947 s Roy F Kappel & Ruby Lilian. BA Sthrn Nazarene U 1969; MDiv S Paul TS Kansas City MO 1972. D 12/14/1996 P 6/11/1997 Bp Robert Manning Moody. m 9/14/1990 Dollie Marie Moorefield c 2. Our Lady of Walsingham 2009; The Angl Soc 2007. rector@trinitylumberton.net

KAPPS, Charles (Pa) 923 Penn Sylvan Dr, Mohnton PA 19540 B New York NY 2/17/1939 s Charles Albert Kapps & Charlotte. BS U of Pennsylvania 1961; SMM Harv 1963; PhD U of Pennsylvania 1970. D 6/20/1987 P 6/1/1988 Bp Allen Lyman Bartlett Jr. m 7/10/1965 Marcia Moreton. P-in-c All SS Epis Ch Fallsington PA 1996-2007; Assoc Ch Without Walls Gwynedd PA 1995-1996; Int Gr Ch And The Incarn Philadelphia PA 1992-1994; Asst S Mary's Ch Hamilton Vill Philadelphia PA 1987-1992. Auth, "Vax: Programmerovaneye Na Yazikye Assemblyera Y Arkhetektura," Moskva, Radio Y Svyaz, 1991; Auth, "Assembly Lang For The Pdp-11," *Rt-Rsx-Unix 2d Ed*, Prindle, Weber, & Schmidt, 1987; Auth, "Vax Assembly Lang And Archit," Prindle, Weber, & Schmidt, 1985; Auth, "Assembly Lang For The Pdp-11," Prindle, Weber, & Schmidt, 1981; Auth, "Intro To The Theory Of Computing," Chas E. Merrill, 1975. kapps@cis.temple.edu

KAPURCH, Linda Marie (Va) 54 Palamino Ct, Horsham PA 19044 **Asst The Epis Ch Of The Adv Kennett Sq PA 2011-** B Worcester MA 6/7/1950 d Joseph Robert Kapurch & Rita Marie. BA Coll of New Rochelle 1972; MS SUNY 1976; MDiv VTS 2002. Rec from Roman Catholic 4/9/1988 Bp Robert A Gibson. Assoc R S Matt's Ch Maple Glen PA 2006-2011; S Geo's Epis Ch Arlington VA 2005-2006; Asst R S Jas' Epis Ch Leesburg VA 2002-2005. Friends of Cbury Cathd US 2008; Friends of St. Ben 2002. Cbury Schlr Cbury-Cathd Intl Study Canter 2001; Fulbright Awd 1973. lindakapurch@hotmail.com

KARANJA, Daniel Njoroge (Spr) PO BOX 534, BLYTHEWOOD SC 29016 **Off Of Bsh For ArmdF New York NY 1998-** B 1/10/1965 s Joseph Karanja Wabuga & Saraphina Wanjiku. BA E Afr TS 1989; MDiv Bos 1994; DMin Andover Newton TS 1999. D 12/1/1988 P 12/1/1990 Bp The Bishop Of Nairobi. m 7/10/1993 Joyce Muthoni Gitahi c 3. "Female Genital Mutilation In Afr," Xulon Press, 2003. Jonathan Daniels Fllshp EDS Cambridge Ma 1993. daniel.karanja@us.af.mil

KARCHER, David Pirritte (SeFla) 5374 Sw 80th St, Miami FL 33143 **D S Phil's Ch Coral Gables FL 1999-** B Chicago IL 11/5/1933 s Leo Michael Karcher & Lida Mary Elizabeth. Dioc Sch For Mnstry; BA U Chi 1953; JD U of Miami 1961. D 9/29/1986 Bp Calvin Onderdonk Schofield Jr. m 3/4/1955 Joanne Leona Ramer c 3. Assoc Trin Cathd Miami FL 1986-2000. jrkarcher@aol.com

KARDA, Margaret R. (Nwk) 6095 Summerlake Dr, Port Orange FL 32127 B Grand Rapids MN 1/11/1953 d Richard B Reinfeld & Mitzi C. BS Van 1975; MA CUNY 1978; MA GTS 1983; STM GTS 1991. D 6/15/1991 P 1/1/1992 Bp Orris George Walker Jr. m 10/11/1997 William J Karda c 1. Ch Of The Incarn W Milford NJ 1995-2006; Asst S Lk's Ch Forest Hills NY 1991-1995. mreinfeld@aol.com

KARDALEFF, Patricia Ann (Okla) 777 Chosin, Lawton OK 73507 **D S Andr's Epis Ch Lawton OK 2005-** B Tulsa OK 10/11/1940 d Charlie Payne & Lavone. BA Cameron U 1980; BS Cameron U 1981; MLIS U of Oklahoma 1987. D 6/19/2004 Bp Robert Manning Moody. m 6/7/1961 Steven T Kardaleff c 3. pkardalf@aol.com

KAREFA-SMART, Rena Joyce Weller (WA) 4601 N Park Ave Apt 1202, Chevy Chase MD 20815 B Bridgeport CT 3/2/1921 d Sailsman William Weller & Rosa Lee. BEd Cntrl Connecticut St U 1940; MA Drew U 1942; BD Ya Berk 1945; ThD Harvard DS 1976. D 6/11/1988 P 2/1/1989 Bp John Thomas Walker. m 3/27/1948 John Albert Mussulman Karefa-Smart. Ecum & Interfaith Off Dio Washington Washington DC 1991-1996; Asst to R S Aug's Epis Ch Washington DC 1989-1990. Auth, "The Halting Kingdom"; Auth,

K

"Homily Serv"; Auth, "Ecum Encounters". Cntr For Theol And Publ Plcy Coun, Chuches Of Grtr Washington Dc 1983-1996; Metro Washington Dc 85-96 Intl Div Exec Amer Friends Serv Com 92-95. tonkolili@aol.com

KARELIUS, Bradford Lyle (Los) 29602 Via Cebolla, Laguna Niguel CA 92677 B Pasadena CA 6/22/1945 s Lyle Albert Karelius & Linnea Marie. USC 1966; BA Baldwin-Wallace Coll 1967; MDiv PSR 1970. D 5/16/1971 P 12/15/1971 Bp Robert C Rusack. m 10/29/2011 Janice E Breed c 2. R Ch Of The Mssh Santa Ana CA 1981-2011; S Mary's Par Laguna Bch CA 1972-1981. Auth, "The Sprt in the Desert: Pilgrimages to Sacr Sites in the Owns Vlly, CA," Bk Surge, 2009; Auth, "Light and Hope in the Nbrhd," *Amer*, 1999. Hon Cn Cathd Cntr of St. Paul, Los Angeles 2006. karelius@cox.net

KARKER, Arthur Lee (Me) Po Box 277, West Rockport ME 04865 **Assoc S Ptr's Ch Rockland ME 2006-** B Leavittsburg OH 8/11/1947 s Oliver Gould Karker & Louise. BA Estrn Nazarene Coll 1968; MA Bos 1971; MDiv Yale DS 1980. D 10/22/2006 P 5/23/2007 Bp Chilton Abbie Richardson Knudsen. c 2. lkarker@mchinc.org

KARL JR, John Charles (Roch) 995 Park Ave, Rochester NY 14610 B Milwaukee WI 1/5/1942 s John C Karl & Edna. BA NWU 1964; BD CRDS 1967; EDS 1968; STM Bos 1969; MA Sch Pstr Care 1969; DMin CRDS 1974. D 6/22/1968 P 12/1/1969 Bp George West Barrett. m 8/6/1966 Sharon Leith Karl. Samar Pstr Couns Ctr Rochester NY 1974-2003; Asst Ch Of The Ascen Rochester NY 1969-1974. Auth, "Conversations In Many Tongues A Model Of Pstr Consult"; Auth, "Faith & Mnstry: In Light Of The Double Brain"; Auth, "The Presence Of Care In Nrsng". AAPC, Aamft. jkarl2024@frontiernet.net

KARL, Sharon Leith (Roch) 995 Park Ave, Rochester NY 14610 B Washington DC 4/29/1942 d Robert Leary Leith & Frances Elizabeth. BA U Rich 1964; MA CRDS 1966; MDiv Bex 1986. D 6/13/1987 P 6/1/1988 Bp William George Burrill. m 8/6/1966 John Charles Karl. R S Ptr's Epis Ch Henrietta NY 1990-2006; Ch Of The Gd Shpd Webster NY 1987-1990. jkarl995@frontiernet.net

KARNEY JR, George James (Del) 2812 Faulkland Rd, Wilmington DE 19808 B Chicago IL 1/23/1934 s George J Karney & Ella Loretta. BA NWU 1955; MDiv Yale DS 1958. D 6/11/1959 P 3/15/1960 Bp Walter H Gray. m 2/24/1979 Carolyn McDowell. P-in-c S Paul's Ch Chester PA 2002-2007; Stndg Com Dio Delaware Wilmington DE 1995-1999; R S Barn Ch Wilmington DE 1990-2000; Int S Mich's Ch Barrington IL 1988-1990; Int S Anskar's Ch Rockford IL 1985-1986; Cur Chr Ch Waukegan IL 1982-1997; Vic St Gabr's Ch E Berlin CT 1969-1971; R Gr Ch Newington CT 1966-1971; Vic S Jn's Epis Ch Bristol CT 1963-1966; Asst Ch Of The Gd Shpd Hartford CT 1959-1963. cmkgjk@verizon.net

KARPF, Ted (WA) World Health Organization, 20 Avenue Appia, Geneva 27 - 1211 Switzerland B Peekskill NY 9/18/1948 s William Karpf & Joan. ThM Bos 1970; BD Texas Wsleyan U 1974; Cert Boston Theol Inst 1980; Cert Gestalt Inst-Washington 2000. D 6/11/1982 Bp Theodore H McCrea P 10/1/1982 Bp A Donald Davies. c 2. Cn Mssnr for HIV/AIDS Exec Coun Appointees New York NY 2001-2003; Cn Cathd of St Ptr & St Paul Washington DC 1999-2003; Dvlpmt and Deploy Dio Washington Washington DC 1999-2001; R S Lk's Ch Washington DC 1998-1999; Exec Dir NEAC Washington DC 1993-1998; Asst Ch Of The Ascen Gaithersburg MD 1992-1993; Dir of Mnstry The Epis Ch Of S Thos The Apos Dallas TX 1984-1988; Pstr Care and Dvlpmt Chr The King Epis Ch Ft Worth TX 1983-1984; Ed of the Dioc PaperNewspaper Dio Ft Worth Ft Worth TX 1982-1983; Cur S Andr's Ch Grand Prairie TX 1982. Prncpl Ed, "Restoring Hope: Decent Care in the Midst of HIV/AIDS," *Restoring Hope: Decent Care in the Midst of HIV/AIDS*, Palgrave Macmillan, 2008; Auth, "Foreword," *Restoring Hope: Decent Care in the Midst of HIV/AIDS*, WHO EURO Pubblishing, 2007; Auth, "Confessions of an AIDS Activist," Ch Pub Inc, 2006; Auth, "Soul Care and HIV," *AIDS & The Cure Of Souls*, NEAC, 1997; Auth, "AIDS and Pstr Care," *AIDS: The Caregivers Handbook*, St Mart's Press, 1991; Auth, "AIDS and Death," *Gospel Imperative in the Midst of AIDS*, Morehouse, 1989. Secy Gnrl's Awd of Achievement Untd Nations/WHO 2009; Red Ribbon Awd Natl AIDS Partnership 2005; Distringuished Alum Texas Wesl 2003; Minority Achievement Awd USDptHealth&Human Serv 1991; PHS Awd USDptHealth&Human Serv 1990. ted.karpf@gmail.com

KARSHNER, Donald Lee (Del) 250 S 13th St Apt 2d, Philadelphia PA 19107 B Columbus OH 11/16/1926 s Glenn Karshner & Louise. BS OH SU 1950; MA OH SU 1954; MDiv UTS 1957. D 12/22/1960 P 6/24/1961 Bp Roger W Blanchard. c 2. R Ch of St Andrews & St Matthews Wilmington DE 1968-1987; S Andrews and S Matthews Mnstry Wilmington DE 1968-1987; Assoc R Epis Soc of Chr Ch Cincinnati OH 1964-1968.

KARSTEN JR, Charles E(mil) (Me) 16 Hunts Ln, Readfield ME 04355 B New York NY 5/30/1924 s Elizabeth Adeline. BA U So 1945; BA Oxf 1947; Ripon Coll Cuddesdon Oxford GB 1948; Ya Berk 1953; U of Cambridge 1973; MA Oxf 1983. D 5/23/1948 Bp Charles K Gilbert P 12/8/1948 Bp Frank W Sterrett. m 5/29/1948 Daphne Wootton c 2. Stndg Com Dio Maine Portland ME 1976-1982; Cn Cathd Ch Of S Lk Portland ME 1968-1988; R Chr Ch Gardiner ME 1957-1987; Min in charge Olivet Epis Ch Franconia VA 1953-1957; Asst Min Trin Ch On The Green New Haven CT 1951-1953; Asst Min S Steph's Epis Ch Wilkes Barre PA 1948-1951. Hon Cn Dio/Bp of Maine ME 1995; Vstng Schlr Cambridge Engl 1972.

KASEY, Philip Howerton (NJ) 4326 Teall Beach Rd, Geneva NY 14456 **R H Trin Ch So River NJ 2004-** B Philadelphia PA 10/1/1950 s Virginius Fowlkes Kasey & Virginia. BA U NC 1972; MDiv SWTS 1979. D 6/2/1979 Bp Albert Wiencke Van Duzer P 12/7/1979 Bp George Phelps Mellick Belshaw. m 5/26/1979 Polly McWilliams c 2. R S Elis's Ch Glencoe IL 1990-2004; Asst Chr Ch Short Hills NJ 1986-1990; Chapl Kent Sch Kent CT 1981-1986; Cur S Lk's Ch Gladstone NJ 1979-1981. phkasey@comcast.net

KASEY, Polly McWilliams (NJ) 4326 Teall Beach Rd, Geneva NY 14456 B Shreveport LA 11/17/1946 d Martin Cadenhead McWilliams & Lucia Moore. BA U CO 1968; MDiv GTS 1981. D 6/6/1981 Bp Albert Wiencke Van Duzer P 1/21/1982 Bp Arthur Edward Walmsley. m 5/26/1979 Philip Howerton Kasey c 2. Pstr Assoc H Trin Ch So River NJ 2008-2010; Asst S Lk's Ch Gladstone NJ 2007-2008; Gr Ch Pemberton NJ 2006-2007; H Comf Ch Rahway NJ 2005-2006; R S Elis's Ch Glencoe IL 1990-2004; Asst Chr Ch Short Hills NJ 1986-1990; Kent Sch Kent CT 1981-1986; Chapl S Jos's Chap at the Kent Sch Kent CT 1981-1986. pmckasey@comcast.net

KASIO, Joseph Lelit (Nev) INDO. 471894, PO BOX 589-00206, KISERIAN Kenya **S Tim's Epis Ch Henderson NV 2004-** B Kenya 1/19/1941 s Mayiane Kasio & Wamoui. Cert Ch Army Trng Coll; MDiv Trin; LTh Wyc. Trans from Anglican Church Of Kenya 2/19/1997 Bp Stewart Clark Zabriskie. m 1/1/1970 Naomi Wanjiru Kasio. Afr Chr Fllshp Henderson NV 2004-2007. KASEVANGEL@HOTMAIL.COM

KASSEBAUM, John Albert (NY) 53 S Clinton Ave, Hastings On Hudson NY 10706 **D Gr Ch Hastings On Hudson NY 1998-** B New York NY 8/18/1937 s Robert Francis Kassebaum & Ruth Eloise. D 5/16/1998 Bp Richard Frank Grein. m 3/3/1962 Joan Carol Bilyeu c 1. No. Amer Assn for the Diac 1995.

KASWARRA, George Abooki (NY) 23 N Willow St, Montclair NJ 07042 B Fort Portal UG 8/1/1948 s Enock Kaswarra & Evelyn. Makerere U 1983; BD Bp Tucker Theol Coll Mukono Ug 1993; MA PrTS 1996. Trans from Church of the Province of Uganda 12/19/2002 Bp John Palmer Croneberger. m 1/21/1985 Maude Katumwebaze c 4. S Fran Assisi And S Martha White Plains NY 2007-2011; P-in-c Trin Ch Montclair NJ 2001-2007. gkaswarra@aol.com

KATER JR, John (Cal) 2116 Tice Creek Dr #2, Walnut Creek CA 94595 **Fac Emer CDSP Berkeley CA 1990-** B Winchester VA 2/15/1941 s John Luther Kater & Mary Louise. BA Columbia Coll 1962; MDiv GTS 1966; PhD McGill U 1973. D 6/4/1966 P 12/17/1966 Bp Horace W B Donegan. Educ Off Dio Panama 1984-1990; Dio Panama Exec Coun Appointees New York NY 1984-1990; R Chr Ch Poughkeepsie NY 1974-1984; Asst R Chr Ch Poughkeepsie NY 1966-1970. Auth, "Jesus My Mentor," Chalice, 2004; Auth, "Finding Our Way," Cowley, 1991; Auth, "Making Sense of Life," Cowley, 1987; "Christians on the Rt," Seabury, 1982. Hon Cn S Lk's Cathd, Panama Panama City RP 1989. jlkater@aol.com

KATHMANN, Charmaine M (La) St. John's Episcopal Church, 2109 17th Street, Kenner LA 70062 **Outreach; Chld's Art Mnstry; Disaster Mgmt S Jn's Ch Kenner LA 2010-; D Dio Louisiana Baton Rouge LA 2007-** B New Orleans LA 12/8/1955 d Salvador Michael Mouton & Gloria Jean. working toward Mstr's Degree Loyola U Inst for Mnstry - New Orleans, LA; BHS U of New Orleans 1996; BS LSU Hlth Sciences Ctr 2000; 2 yrs Cert Dio Louisiana Sch for Mnstry 2004. D 12/1/2007 Bp Charles Edward Jenkins III. m 5/23/1976 Richard Kathmann c 2. Chld's Art Mnstry; Disaster Recovery Gr Ch New Orleans LA 2007-2010. rfkathmann@aol.com

KATNER, Kirk Vaughan Chris (WNY) 88 Main St S, Perry NY 14530 B Bath NY 4/16/1949 s Theodore J Katner & Eileen M. BA SUNY Geneseo 1970; MA SUNY Geneseo 1971. D 4/25/2009 P 5/2/2010 Bp J Michael Garrison. m 6/20/1970 Anne E Nye c 2. kvkatner@aol.com

KATON, Joanne Catherine (SeFla) 1800 Southwest 92nd Place, Miami FL 33165 B Glendale NY 1/6/1943 d Frank John Nahlik & Josephine. AA Barry Coll 1961; Miami-Dade Cmnty Coll 1970; Dio SE Florida 1991. D 4/5/1992 Bp Calvin Onderdonk Schofield Jr. m 7/30/1971 Robert William Katon c 3. S Andr's Epis Ch Palmetto Bay FL 1996-2006. NACED 1999; NAMI 2000; NAAD 1995; Soc of S Jn's the Div 1995. deaconjoanne@peoplepc.com

KATOR, Mary Lou (Chi) 1121 Lincoln Ave, Rochelle IL 61068 B New Castle IN 12/8/1943 d Walter Joseph Buchman & Gertrude Cecilia. Cath Theol Un; BA Loyola U 1989; MDiv SWTS 1995. D 6/17/1995 P 12/16/1995 Bp Frank Tracy Griswold III. m 8/29/1964 William George Kator c 4. S Ptr's Epis Ch Sycamore IL 2000-2003; S Barn Ch Moberly MO 1996-2000. ml.kator@comcast.net

KAUFFMAN, Bette Jo (WLa) 79 Quail Ridge Dr, Monroe LA 71203 B Washington County IA 5/14/1945 d Henry A Kauffman & Isabelle Ruth. BA U of Iowa 1980; MA U of Pennsylvania 1982; PhD U of Pennsylvania 1992. D 6/7/2008 Bp D(avid) Bruce Mac Pherson. bjkauffman@gmail.com

KAUFMAN, Ivan T (Mass) 39 Concord Ct, Bedford MA 01730 B Detroit MI 11/27/1927 s Ivan Curtis Kaufman & Helen Louise. BA U MI 1951; MA U MI

1952; ASOR 1954; MDiv UTS 1956; ThD Harvard DS 1967. D 6/20/1956 Bp Richard S M Emrich P 6/20/1958 Bp Robert McConnell Hatch. m 1/4/1964 Joan Wheeler c 3. Prof EDS Cambridge MA 1974-1993; Fell/Tutor EDS Cambridge MA 1961-1965; Emm Ch W Roxbury MA 1960-1961; P-in-c S Matt's Epis Ch Lisbon ME 1959-1960; Assoc S Paul's Ch Brunswick ME 1959-1960; Cur Gr Ch Amherst MA 1956-1959. Auth, "Samaria (Ostraca)," *The Anchor Bible Dictionary*, Doubleday, 1992; Auth, *The Psalms and Other Stds on the OT*, Forw Mvmt Press, 1990; Auth, "Samaria Ostraca: Early Witness to Hebr Writing," *Biblic Archeologist*, 1982; Auth, "New Evidence for Hieratic Numerals on Hebr Weights," *Bulletin of the Amer Schools of Oriental Resrch*, 1967; Auth, *Undercut by Joy: The Sun Lectionaries & the Psalms of Lament*. SBL. jkaufmancwv@aol.com

KAUFMAN, Linda Margaret (WA) 701 S Wayne St, Arlington VA 22204 **Ch Of S Steph And The Incarn Washington DC 1998-** B Seattle WA 1/23/1951 d Jerome Jacques Kaufman & Margaret Esther. Gordon-Conwell TS; NWU; BS Geo Mason U 1975; MDiv VTS 1986. D 6/11/1986 P 4/11/1987 Bp Peter James Lee. m 8/1/1998 Liane Gay Rozzell c 2. Ch Of The H Comf Vienna VA 1988-1993; Chapl S Marg's Sch Tappahannock VA 1986-1988. NAES, Soc Of Biblic. Soroptomist: Helping Wmn Awd; Hero Of The Week, Fox Tv. lkaufman@cmtysolutions.org

KAUTZ, Richard Arden (Ind) 111 SW G St, Richmond IN 47374 **R S Paul's Ch Richmond IN 2008-** B Casper WY 6/13/1953 s William Kautz & Dorothy Elaine. BA U of Nthrn Colorado 1978; MDiv Nash 1984. D 6/16/1984 P 12/21/1984 Bp William Carl Frey. m 10/28/2010 William P Strauss c 3. Ch Of The H Redeem Denver CO 2005-2008; The Ch Of Chr The King (Epis) Arvada CO 2004-2005; Trin Ch Greeley CO 1997-2003; R S Mart In The Fields Aurora CO 1992-1997; Assoc St Johns Epis Ch Tampa FL 1990-1992; Asst S Thos Epis Ch Terrace Pk OH 1986-1990; Cur S Aid's Epis Ch Boulder CO 1984-1986. Auth, "A Labyrinth Year; Walking the Seasons of the Ch," Morehouse, 2006. rickkautz@gmail.com

KAVAL, Lura Marie (Md) 8522 Light Moon Way, Laurel MD 20723 B Erie PA 6/14/1962 d Gerald Stephen Kaval & Lura Grice. BS Ohio U 1983; Cert Amer U 1985; MDiv VTS 1998. D 6/13/1998 P 12/19/1998 Bp Robert Wilkes Ihloff. m 7/4/2002 David R Mucci. R - Full Time S Chris Epis Ch Linthicum Heights MD 2002-2011; Prov III Chester Sprg PA 2002-2004; Int Chr Ch Columbia MD 1999-2001; Assoc R S Jas Ch Jackson MS 1998-1999. Md. Epis Cler Asso. (MECA) 2004. motherspice@comcast.net

KAVROS, Peregrine Murphy (NY) 4 West 109th Street Apt 2D, New York NY 10025 B Fowler CA 9/29/1954 d Elbert Thurman Pitcock & Patricia Jean. BA California St U 1979; MS California St U 1980; MBA Notre Dame Coll 1982; MDiv GTS 1990; PhD CUNY 2002; Post Grad CUNY 2005; Post Grad NYU Sch of Med 2011. D 6/8/1991 Bp George Phelps Mellick Belshaw P 12/14/1991 Bp Richard Frank Grein. m 10/6/2007 Harry Emanuel Kavros. S Steph's Ch Armonk NY 2005-2007; Dio New York New York City NY 2005; P-in-c San Andres Ch Yonkers NY 2001-2005; Int S Mary's Ch Mohegan Lake NY 1998-2001; Asst S Mk's Ch Mt Kisco NY 1996-1998; Asst Ch Of The Incarn New York NY 1995-1996; Asst Cathd Of St Jn The Div New York NY 1991-1995. Auth, "Impact of Sprtlty & Religiousness on Outcomes in Patients w ALS," *Neurology*, The Amer Acad of Neurology, 2000; Auth, "Sophia - Div Bearer of Wisdom," *The Living Pulpit*, The Living Pulpit, Inc., 2000; Auth, "Rel, Religiousness, Religiosity," *Encyclopedia of Psychol & Rel*, Springer. pmkavros@managementfocus.org

KAY, Frances Creveling (WLa) 2914 W Prien Lake Rd, Lake Charles LA 70605 **Epis Ch Of The Gd Shpd Lake Chas LA 2003-; Cmsn on Schools, Chair Dio Wstrn Louisiana Alexandria LA 2001-; Bp Noland Epis Day Sch Lake Chas LA 2000-** B Lake Charles LA 2/22/1948 d Donald Mcdonald Creveling & Ellanora. BS LSU 1970; Med McNeese St U 1986; ED SPEC McNeese St U 1990; Graduated Bp Sch 2000. D 3/25/2000 Bp Robert Jefferson Hargrove Jr. c 3. bkay@episcopaldayschool.org

KAYE, Robert Pleaman Skarpmoen (EO) 365 SE Highland Park Dr, College Place WA 99324 B Milwaukee WI 11/18/1937 s Harold Christian Skarpmoen & Ruby Faey. Miami Bible Inst 1960; BS Florida Intl U 1974; MPA Nova U 1977; MDiv STUSo 1988. D 9/17/1988 P 3/1/1989 Bp Calvin Onderdonk Schofield Jr. m 6/18/1983 Diane Reed c 2. Vic S Jas Ch Milton Freewater OR 1991-2002; Asst to R S Greg's Ch Boca Raton FL 1988-1991. "The Fascist Pig Cookbook"; Auth, "Safe Streets Unit vol. 1-3," Law Enforcement Assistance Admin. RPSKDRK@msn.com

KAYLOR, Paul Evans (LI) 193 State Route 36, Highlands NJ 07732 B McCaysville GA 4/2/1930 s Thomas Virgil Kaylor & Maude Ethel. BA Merc 1951; MDiv Yale DS 1954; Mercer TS 1966; Fllshp Harv 1967. D 5/28/1966 P 12/2/1966 Bp Jonathan Goodhue Sherman. Auth, "Sci For Survival"; Auth, "The Early Coll Theory & Pract"; Auth, "Of Publ Issues". paulpekv@aol.com

KAYNOR, Robert Kirk (NC) 82 Kimberly Dr, Durham NC 27707 **S Steph's Ch Durham NC 2005-** B Springfield MA 9/13/1948 s Kenneth Winter Kaynor & Doris Eleanor. BA Trin Hartford CT 1972; MDiv EDS 1976; EdM Harv 1982; CAS Harv 1986. D 6/9/1979 Bp John Bowen Coburn P 5/1/1980 Bp Morris Fairchild Arnold. m 6/17/2001 Sue Smith. R Chr Ch Hyde Pk MA 2001-2005; Assoc S Paul's Epis Ch Bedford MA 1997-1999; Assoc S Dunstans Epis Ch Dover MA 1993-2001; Assoc S Mich's Ch Milton MA 1986-1992; P-in-c Chr Ch Hyde Pk MA 1983-1985; Cur Chr Ch Hyde Pk MA 1979-1982. Auth, "Mapping The Anatomy Of Ethical Arguments In The Divestment Debate," Harvard Grad Sch Of Ed., 1986; Auth, "Ch Case Stds," Harvard Grad Sch Of Ed., 1981; Auth, "Plnng & Decisionmaking Suny-Albany," Harvard Bus Sch, 1980. bkaynor@post.harvard.edu

KAZANJIAN, Rosanna Case (Mass) Po Box 1215, Sonoita AZ 85637 **Affiliate S Phil's In The Hills Tucson AZ 2002-** B Topeka KS 10/27/1934 d Harold C Case & Phyllis. BA Bos 1956; Med Bos 1971; MDiv EDS 1985. D 6/1/1985 Bp John Bowen Coburn P 4/1/1986 Bp Donis Dean Patterson. c 3. Int S Andr's Epis Ch Nogales AZ 2003-2004; S Jn's Ch Jamaica Plain MA 1988-1991; R S Jn's Epis Ch Westwood MA 1988-1991; Assoc R Ch Of The Epiph Richardson TX 1985-1988. rkazanjian@theriver.com

KAZANJIAN JR, Victor Hanford (Mass) Acorns House, Wellesley College, Wellesley MA 02181 B Boston MA 4/11/1959 s Victor Hanford Kazanjian & Rosanna Case. BA Harv 1981; MDiv EDS 1986. D 6/4/1986 Bp John Bowen Coburn P 5/1/1987 Bp Don Edward Johnson. m 8/17/1985 Jennifer Amory. Epis City Mssn Boston MA 1991-1993; Asst to R S Mich's Ch Milton MA 1986-1991; Sem Asst S Ann's Ch Of Morrisania Bronx NY 1984-1985. vkazanjian@wellesley.edu

KE, Jason Chau-sheng (Tai) 37 Jen-Chih St., Nanton City Taiwan B Amoy Fukien CN 10/28/1935 s Fu-liang Ke & Juei-Ian. BTh Tainan TS TW 1965. D 9/17/1970 Bp Edmond Lee Browning P 6/1/1971 Bp James T M Pong. c 2.

KEARLEY, David Arthur (Ala) 154 Morgans Steep Rd, Sewanee TN 37375 B Mobile AL 2/23/1929 s Frank Joseph Kearley & Josephine Ida. BA U of Alabama 1951; MA U of Alabama 1956; MDiv GTS 1958; MLS Peabody Coll 1969. D 6/22/1958 P 6/11/1959 Bp George Mosley Murray. m 8/11/1962 Marion Elizabeth Bourgeois. The TS at The U So Sewanee TN 1982-1994; Asst S Paul's Ch Franklin TN 1973-1982; Vic S Mich's Epis Ch Fayette AL 1969-1973; ExCoun Dio Alabama Birmingham AL 1967-1968; Vic S Barth's Epis Ch Florence AL 1963-1968; Cur Trin Epis Ch Florence AL 1960-1963; Vic Emm Epis Ch Opelika AL 1958-1960; Vic S Steph's Epis Ch Smiths Sta AL 1958-1960. "Article," *Apos (Dio ALA)*; Auth, "Article," *Hist mag*. Cmnty of S Mary, Assoc 1985. dkearley@sewanee.edu

KEARNEY, James A (NY) 4410 1/2 Leeland St, Houston TX 77023 **D Ch Of The Redeem Houston TX 1982-** B Staten Island NY 8/13/1947 s Alton C Kearney & Janet Guacci. Ya Berk; BBA Pace Coll; MDiv PDS. D 6/3/1972 Bp Paul Moore Jr. Asst Bus Admin Ch Of The Redeem Houston TX 1974-1977.

KEATEN, Robert W (Nwk) 45 Long Ridge Rd, Randolph NJ 07869 B Atlanta GA 3/20/1935 s Clarence A Keaten & Nettie Winn. BS Ya 1957; MDiv GTS 2001. D 6/9/2001 P 1/6/2002 Bp John Palmer Croneberger. m 12/28/1961 Sheila Ann Bruning c 2. R S Andr's Epis Ch Lincoln Pk NJ 2002-2007; Assoc (half-time) Ch Of The Gd Shpd Ringwood NJ 2001-2002; Assoc (half-time) S Jn's Epis Ch Boonton NJ 2001-2002. rkeaten@att.net

KEATOR, Marnie Knowles (WMass) PO Box 2037, 1 Carley Lane, South Londonderry VT 05155 **S Andr's Ch Turners Falls MA 2005-** B Greenwich CT 10/7/1941 d James Burbank Knowles & Phoebe Knapp. AAS Bennett Coll 1961; BD U of Connecticut 1989; MDiv EDS 2000. D 5/20/2000 Bp Mary Adelia Rosamond McLeod P 12/2/2000 Bp Arthur Edward Walmsley. m 8/25/1962 Gerrit Keator c 3. Curs Sec Dio Vermont Burlington VT 2002-2004; Curs Sec Dio Vermont Burlington VT 2002-2004; Assoc Zion Ch Manchester Cntr VT 2000-2002; Dioc Coun Dio Vermont Burlington VT 1998-2001; FA Bd Mem Dio Vermont Burlington VT 1996-2000. marnbbf@myfairpoint.net

KEBBA, Elaine Marguerite Bailey (NC) 6003 Quail Ridge Dr, Greensboro NC 27455 B Albuquerque NM 7/31/1948 d Lawrence Robert Bailey & Betty Rose. BS U of Maryland 1970; MS U NC 1972; MDiv VTS 1979. D 6/23/1979 Bp John Thomas Walker P 1/5/1980 Bp Lyman Cunningham Ogilby. m 10/12/1974 Thomas Kebba. Servnt Ldrshp Stff H Trin Epis Ch Greensboro NC 2003-2009; R S Dav's Ch Kinnelon NJ 1990-2002; R S Mary's Ch Haledon NJ 1985-1990; Asst Trin Ch Swarthmore PA 1979-1985. Hon Cn Trin & S Phil Cathd 1993. emkebba@triad.rr.com

KEBLESH JR, Joseph (O) 4617 Crestview Dr, Sylvania OH 43560 **R S Matt's Epis Ch Toledo OH 1992-** B Akron OH 5/19/1945 s Joseph Keblesh & Mary Juanita. BS U of Akron 1978; MBA U of Akron 1980; MDiv VTS 1985. D 6/15/1985 Bp James Russell Moodey P 3/1/1986 Bp William Grant Black. c 4. Exec Coun Dio Lexington Lexington KY 1988-1991; R Emm Epis Ch Winchester KY 1987-1991; Asst Chr Ch Xenia OH 1985-1987; Vic S Andr's Epis Ch Washington Crt Hse OH 1985-1987. Beta Gamma Sigma 1978. jlkeblesh@buckeye-express.com

KECK, Carolyn (SO) 401 Hither Creek Lane, Reynoldsburg OH 43068 B Maquoketa IA 10/6/1951 d Allen L Keck & Phoebe L. AA Cottey Coll 1972; BS Phillips U 1974; MSW U of Kentucky 1990; MDiv. SWTS 2005. D 5/22/2004 P 6/25/2005 Bp Herbert Thompson Jr. Ch Of S Edw Columbus OH 2005-2010. ckeck8622@wowway.com

KEEBLE, George McCullough (WTex) 5673 Grand Lake Circle, Robstown TX 78380 **P-in-c Epis Ch Of The Gd Shepard Geo W TX 2007-** B Corpus Christi TX 12/10/1941 s Walter Donelson Keeble & Louise. BS Texas A&M U 1966; DDS U of Texas 1973; MDiv Epis TS of The SW 1985. D 1/23/1985 Bp Stanley Fillmore Hauser P 8/9/1985 Bp Scott Field Bailey. m 5/19/1962 Mary G Cotrell c 2. R S Ptr's Epis Ch Rockport TX 2003-2007; R S Steph's Epis Ch Wimberley TX 1989-2003; Vic Calv Ch Menard TX 1986-1989; Vic Trin Ch Jct TX 1986-1989; Cur Trin Ch Victoria TX 1985-1986. keeblemac@yahoo.com

KEECH, April Irene (NY) No address on file. B 4/1/1954 Trans from Church Of England 10/1/1991 as Deacon Bp Richard Frank Grein. Chr And S Steph's Ch New York NY 1992-1995.

KEEDY, Susan Shipman (SeFla) 1200 Heron Ave, Miami Springs FL 33166 **All Ang Ch Miami Sprg FL 2002-** B Jackson MS 12/3/1946 d William Smylie Shipman & Juliet Manon. BA California St U 1970; MS Florida Intl U 1997; MDiv Yale DS 2001. D 6/16/2001 Bp John Lewis Said P 12/16/2001 Bp Leopold Frade. c 2. Chap of the Venerable Bede Coral Gables FL 2001-2002. skeedy@mindspring.com

KEEFER, John S (Pa) 124 High St, Sharon Hill PA 19079 B Danville PA 8/15/1946 s Bruce Homer Keefer & Anna Carrie. BA NEU 1969; MDiv Epis TS In Kentucky 1972; ThM Westminster TS 1979; ThD U of Bern Bern CH 1990. D 6/22/1972 Bp Addison Hosea P 6/16/1973 Bp Chandler W Sterling. Emm Ch Philadelphia PA 2003-2009; P-in-c Ch Of The Redeem Andalusia PA 2000-2003; Ch Of Our Sav Jenkintown PA 1998; Ch Of Our Sav Jenkintown PA 1994; The Ch Of The Gd Shpd Bryn Mawr PA 1992-1994; The Ch Of The Gd Shpd Bryn Mawr PA 1978-1979; Asst Trin Epis Ch Ambler PA 1975-1978; Asst S Steph's Ch Philadelphia PA 1974-1975; Cur S Tim's Ch Roxborough Philadelphia PA 1972-1974. Auth, "European Ch - E and W," *Crossroads*, 1993; Auth, "Sin," *Crossroads*, 1993; Auth, "Natl Thanksgiving," *Congressional Record*, 1983; Auth, "Capital Punnishment: A Priestly View," *S Dismas Drummer*, 1979. CCU, Philadelphia Chapt 1972. Notable Americans 1978; "Who's Who in Rel," Second Ed; Listed in "Dictionary of Intl Biography" vo. XV; Listed in "Cmnty Leaders and Noteworthy Americans," 10th an. N/A

KEEHN, Randy (ND) 1208 8th Ave W, Williston ND 58801 B Des Moines IA 7/12/1952 s Robert Paul Keehn & Jeannette. BA Luther Coll 1974. D 1/30/1999 P 10/1/1999 Bp Andrew Hedtler Fairfield. m 4/5/1986 Jo Ann Black Hawk c 2.

KEEL, Robert Donald (Pa) 101 Rocky Rift Farm Rd, Lackawaxen PA 18435 B Syracuse NY 1/20/1931 s Robert Ehle Keel & Mabel Marion. BA SUNY 1955; STB PDS 1958. D 5/31/1958 P 12/13/1958 Bp Frederick Lehrle Barry. m 6/21/1952 Patricia Klahr c 2. Int S Jn's Epis Ch Hamlin PA 1996-1998; R Trin Ch Buckingham PA 1984-1995; R S Jn's Ch Bala Cynwyd PA 1965-1984; R Gr Epis Ch Canton NY 1960-1965; Trin And S Mich's Ch Albany NY 1958-1960. keelack@ltis.net

KEEL, Ronald David (WMo) 416 SW Tucker Rdg, Lees Summit MO 64081 **R Ch Of The Resurr Blue Sprg MO 2005-** B Kansas City MO 11/17/1944 s Charles Keel & Betty. BS U of Missouri 1966; MA Cntrl Michigan U 1980; MDiv Epis TS of The SW 2005. D 6/4/2005 P 12/3/2005 Bp Barry Robert Howe. m 12/30/1995 Victoria Helen Keel c 2. ronald_keel@yahoo.com

KEELER, Charles Bobo (Miss) 925 Stiles St, Clarksdale MS 38614 **S Geo's Epis Ch Clarksdale MS 2000-** B Clarksdale MS 11/12/1936 BS Mississippi St U 1963. D 1/15/2000 Bp Alfred Clark Marble Jr. m 12/21/1960 Margaret Rice c 3. bokeeler@juno.com

KEELER, Donald Franklin (Ia) 121 W Marina Rd, Storm Lake IA 50588 B 6/30/1943 BS Truman Coll Chicago IL 1967; MA U of Kansas 1973. D 12/17/2006 Bp Alan Scarfe. m 9/27/2007 Paula Keeler. dfkandpk@yahoo.com

KEELER, John Dowling (At) 225 Brookhaven Cir, Elberton GA 30635 **All Ang Epis Ch Eatonton GA 2007-** B Bedford VA 2/19/1945 s Peter Fenlon Keeler & Mary Buford. BA Wstrn Carolina U 1975; MA W Carolina U 1976; CTh U So 2006. D 8/6/2006 P 7/1/2007 Bp J(ohn) Neil Alexander. m 12/15/1976 Robyn Vincent c 1. jkeeler@elberton.net

KEEN JR, Charles Ford (Dal) 206 Mansfield Blvd., Sunnyvale TX 75182 B Pueblo CO 2/1/1938 s Charles Ford Keen & Dorothy Jane. BA U CO 1961; BD Nash 1967. D 6/5/1967 P 12/1/1967 Bp Joseph Summerville Minnis. m 5/18/1967 Judith Coatney. Gr Ch Mesquite TX 2003-2007; Vic Gr Ch Mesquite TX 2002; Dio Dallas Dallas TX 1999-2002; Cur H Trin Epis Ch Garland TX 1998-2002; Ch Of The Gd Shpd Cedar Hill TX 1996-1998; S Dav's Ch Garland TX 1995-1996; S Mary's Epis Ch And Sch Irving TX 1993-1995; Vic Ch Of Our Sav Dallas TX 1986-1991; Dept Of Missions Dallas TX 1986; Asst-In-Charge Of Lay Ministers The Epis Ch Of The Resurr Dallas TX 1982-1986; All SS Ch Loveland CO 1970-1981; Chair - Dept Yth Dio Colorado Denver CO 1968-1982; Vic Chap Of The Resurr Limon CO 1967-1970. Assn Chr Therapists. ckfrog@tx.rr.com

KEEN, George Comforted (CFla) 1225 W Granada Blvd, Ormond Beach FL 32174 **Curs Cmsn Sprtl Dir. Dio Cntrl Florida Orlando FL 2011-; Honduras Cmsn Hd Dio Cntrl Florida Orlando FL 2009-; R Ch Of The H Chld Ormond Bch FL 1998-** B Tampa FL 6/29/1945 s Clarence Keen & Joni. AA Seminole Cmnty Coll 1970; BA U Of Cntrl Florida 1972; MDiv SWTS 1979. D 6/25/1979 P 1/6/1980 Bp William Hopkins Folwell. m 2/17/1968 Judy Dee Hopkins. Asst Pstr Epis Ch Of The H Sprt Tallahassee FL 1995-1998; R S Alb's Epis Ch Auburndale FL 1984-1995; Asst H Trin Epis Ch Melbourne FL 1980-1984; Cur S Mk's Ch Cocoa FL 1979-1980; Yth Min All SS Ch Of Winter Pk Winter Pk FL 1974-1976. Alpha Tau Omega Coll Fraternity - Natl Chapl 1988. comforted45@earthlink.net

KEEN, Lois B (Ct) 20 Hudson St, Norwalk CT 06851 **P-in-c Gr Epis Ch Norwalk CT 2006-** B Wendover UT 6/30/1945 d William Paul Thien & Louisa Celestia. BA U of Delaware Newark 1968; MDiv SWTS 1997. D 5/26/1998 P 1/21/1999 Bp Martin Gough Townsend. m 1/31/1981 Walter Keen. P-in-c S Mart's Epis Ch Upper Chichester PA 2005-2006; Int. Asst. to Int. R S Steph's Ch Ridgefield CT 2003-2005; R Chr Ch Milford DE 2000-2003; Cur Cathd Ch Of S Jn Wilmington DE 1998-2000. revlois@optonline.net

KEENAN, John Peter (Vt) 73 Oak St, Newport VT 05855 B Philadelphia PA 10/13/1940 s John Peter Keenan & Mary A. BA S Chas Borromeo Sem 1962; STM S Chas Borromeo Sem 1966; MA U of Pennsylvania 1976; PhD U of Wisconsin 1980. Rec from Roman Catholic 10/21/1988 as Priest Bp Daniel Lee Swenson. m 5/20/1972 Linda Klepinger c 2. P-in-c S Mk's Epis Ch Newport VT 2004-2007; Vic S Nich Epis Ch Scarborough ME 2002-2003; Assoc S Steph's Ch Middlebury VT 1994-1997; Bp's Vic Calv Ch Underhill VT 1991-1993. "Wisdom of Jas: Parallels w Mahayana Buddhism," Newman (Paulist), 2005; "Beside Still Waters: Jews, Christians, & the Way of the Buddha," *(co-Ed)*, Wisdom, 2003; "Gospel of Mk: A Mahayana Reading," Orbis Books, 1995; "How Mstr Mou Removes our Doubts," SUNY Press, 1994; "Meaning of Chr: A Mahayana Theol," Orbis Books, 1989. johnpkeenan@mac.com

KEENE, Christopher Paul (Md) Advent Rectory 1301 S Charles St, Baltimore MD 21230 **Chair - Appeals Com Dio Maryland Baltimore MD 2010-; Mem - COM Dio Maryland Baltimore MD 2009-; Pres - Harbor Reg Dio Maryland Baltimore MD 2009-; Mem - Liturg and Mus Com Dio Maryland Baltimore MD 2007-; Mem - Baltimore Urban Cler Dio Maryland Baltimore MD 2006-; R Ch Of The Adv Baltimore MD 2003-** B Pinckneyville IL 8/20/1966 s Daniel Paul Keene & Donna Dean. BA U Of Baltimore 1993; MDiv GTS 2003. D 6/14/2003 Bp Robert Wilkes Ihloff P 11/30/2003 Bp John Leslie Rabb. Soc of Cath Priests 2009. Best Publ Reading of the Liturg GTS 2003. c_p_k_@msn.com

KEENE, John Edward (Del) 1608 Willow Vale Dr, Fort Worth TX 76134 **Died 5/26/2011** B Hackensack NJ 8/31/1920 s Thomas Edward Keene & Hazel Mary. BS Rutgers-The St U 1950; MS Col 1952. D 6/11/1958 Bp Charles F Hall P 12/13/1958 Bp Anson Phelps Stokes Jr. c 4.

KEENE, Katheryn C (Ct) 237 South St. #39, Shrewsbury MA 01545 B Boston MA 5/3/1954 d John Willis Keene & Abigail McKee. BA Smith 1976; MDiv Yale DS 1980; Advncd CPE 1983. D 6/13/1981 Bp Arthur Edward Walmsley P 2/1/1982 Bp William Bradford Hastings. c 3. All SS Epis Ch Attleboro MA 2007-2008; Trin Ecum Ch Moneta VA 2001-2002; Assoc R S Jn's Ch Lynchburg VA 1998-2000; S Paul's Epis Ch Salem VA 1998-1999; S Jn's Ch W Hartford CT 1997; St Gabr's Ch E Berlin CT 1995-1996; Int S Ptr's Ch So Windsor CT 1991-1992; Int Ch Of The Resurr Norwich CT 1987-1988; Int Dio Connecticut Hartford CT 1986-1987; Int Chr Ch Stratford CT 1985-1986; Int Gr And S Ptr's Epis Ch Hamden CT 1983-1984; S Ptr's Ch Hamden CT 1983-1984; Assoc S Andr's Ch Madison CT 1981-1983. kkeene@ementgroup.com

KEENE, R(uth) Claire (ETenn) 4000 Shaw Ferry Rd, Lenoir City TN 37772 **Mem, COM Dio E Tennessee Knoxville TN 2011-; R Ch Of The Resurr Loudon TN 2007-** B Memphis TN 4/10/1950 d Richard DeArmand Allen & Betty Lou. BA Carson-Newman Coll 1972; MA U CA 1973; MDiv STUSo 2002. D 5/25/2002 P 1/11/2003 Bp Charles Glenn VonRosenberg. m 12/27/1990 Michael Lawrence Keene c 2. Chapl/Mem, Bp Search Com Dio E Tennessee Knoxville TN 2009-2011; P-in-c Ch Of The Resurr Loudon TN 2005-2007; Mem, Chr Formation Com Dio E Tennessee Knoxville TN 2004-2009; Chair, Comp Dio Com Dio E Tennessee Knoxville TN 2004-2006; Asst S Steph's Epis Ch Oak Ridge TN 2002-2005; Mem, Com for Handicap Access Dio E Tennessee Knoxville TN 2002-2004. optime merens STUSo 2002; Urban T. Holmes III Prize for Excellence in Preaching STUSo 2002. keenerc9@yahoo.com

KEENER, Esther Michaella (Pa) P.O. Box 594, 36 Bayview Avenue, Stonington ME 04681 **Assoc Ch Without Walls Gwynedd PA 2003-** B Hartford CT 5/8/1934 d Ashley Nixon Keener & Esther Cecelia. BD Wayne 1979; MDiv EDS 1982. D 6/20/1982 P 5/8/1983 Bp H Coleman McGehee Jr. m 8/4/2000 Leland M DeWoody. Dioc Coun Dio Pennsylvania Philadelphia PA 1988-1989; S Giles Ch Upper Darby PA 1986-1994; Com for Sexual Inclusiveness Dio Pennsylvania Philadelphia PA 1986-1990; Race Rela Com Dio Pennsylvania Philadelphia PA 1986-1990; Congreg Spprt Com Dio Pennsylvania Philadelphia PA 1986-1989; Hisp Com Dio Pennsylvania Philadelphia PA 1986-1988; Trin Ch Detroit MI 1985; Hisp Com Dio Michigan

Detroit MI 1983-1985; Asst Chr Ch Detroit MI 1982-1984. Soc of S Jn the Evang 1987. Wm Dietrich Jr Awd for Urban Mssn in Ch EDS Massachusetts 1982. michaella@southave.com

KEENER JR, Ross Fulton (SVa) 117 Cove Road, Newport News VA 23608 **R Glebe Ch Suffolk VA 1998-** B Birmingham AL 10/18/1932 s Ross Fulton Keener & Beulah Rae. BA U of Alabama 1963; MDiv STUSo 1981. D 9/20/1981 P 4/21/1982 Bp C(laude) Charles Vache. m 10/10/2008 Janet Farson c 3. R S Geo's Epis Ch Newport News VA 1986-1997; Trin Ch Gretna VA 1982-1986; R Emm Epis Ch Chatham VA 1981-1986. rossplus432@cox.net

KEENEY, Albert J (Roch) 4952 Butler Rd, Canandaigua NY 14424 B Chicago Heights IL 2/26/1945 s George William Keeney & Jane Elizabeth. BA Loyola U 1968; MA S Louis U 1970; MDiv Drew U 1990. D 6/2/1990 Bp John Shelby Spong P 12/8/1990 Bp Walter Cameron Righter. m 6/14/1969 Linda Gerbac c 2. Int S Mich's Ch Geneseo NY 2010-2011; Int Trin Ch Rochester NY 2009-2010; Cn Dio Rochester Rochester NY 2008-2009; R S Jn's Ch Canandaigua NY 1994-2008; R S Matt's Ch Paramus NJ 1990-1994. H Cross Mnstry OHC 1990. alkeeney@rochester.rr.com

KEENEY, Randall James (NC) Po Box 1547, Clemmons NC 27012 **S Barn' Ch Greensboro NC 2006-** B Columbus GA 2/20/1959 s James Lee Keeney & Myrtle Francis. ABS Middle Georgia Coll 1978; BBA Georgia Sthrn U 1982; MDiv Nash 1988. D 6/11/1988 P 5/1/1989 Bp Harry Woolston Shipps. c 3. Dio No Carolina Raleigh NC 2003; R S Clem's Epis Ch Clemmons NC 1994-2003; Vic Ch Of The Atone Augusta GA 1992-1994; S Paul's Ch Albany GA 1989-1992; Assoc S Paul's Epis Ch Albany NY 1989-1992; D S Fran Of The Islands Epis Ch Savannah GA 1988-1989. keeney.randall@gmail.com

KEENEY-MULLIGAN, Gail Donnell (Ct) 201 Wintonbury Ave, Bloomfield CT 06002 **Seabury Ret Cmnty Bloomfield CT 2009-** B Laramie WY 5/6/1956 d Allen Keeney & Jean. BSW U of Wyoming 1978; MDiv Bex 1984; DMin NYTS 1994. D 5/6/1984 Bp Robert Rae Spears Jr P 11/19/1984 Bp William George Burrill. c 2. R S Jn's Ch New Milford CT 2002-2009; Vic S Aid's Epis Ch Tulsa OK 1995-2002; Dio Oklahoma Oklahoma City OK 1994-2002; Dio Panama 1991-1994; Asst Chr Ch Poughkeepsie NY 1988-1992; Int S Marg's Ch Staatsburg NY 1987-1988; Assoc S Thos Epis Ch Rochester NY 1984-1986. Auth, "Outstanding Wmn," *Wmn Day*, 1987. EUC 1980. Outstanding Ldrshp New York St Coun of Ch 1987; Wmn of the Year Wmn Day mag 1986. keeneymulligan@snet.net

KEE-REES, Jim L (Okla) 135 Crestmont Ave, Norman OK 73069 **Native Amer Mssnr Dio Oklahoma Oklahoma City OK 2007-; Mssnr H Fam Watonga OK 2007-** B Ada OK 11/12/1966 s James Louis Kee & Barbara Lee. MDiv Sthrn Bapt TS Louisville KY 1994; CPE Emory Cntr for Pstr Serv Atlanta GA 1995; CPE Emory Cntr for Pstr Serv Atlanta GA 1996; STM GTS 2001. D 6/9/2001 Bp Robert Gould Tharp P 1/20/2002 Bp J(ohn) Neil Alexander. m 10/11/1997 Josephine E Rees c 2. Ch Of The Epiph Atlanta GA 2001-2006; Pstr Care & Yth S Jas Epis Ch Marietta GA 1996-2000. jkeerees1@gmail.com

KEESE, Peter Gaines (ETenn) 905 Chateaugay Rd., Knoxville TN 37923 **Vic Chr Ch Rugby TN 2002-** B Chattanooga TN 1/28/1936 s William Shelton Keese & Elsie Louise. BA Harv 1958; STB GTS 1961; ThM Duke 1977. D 6/25/1961 P 5/5/1962 Bp John Vander Horst. m 5/3/1963 Helen Lawrence Vander Horst c 2. Bp Coun Dio E Tennessee Knoxville TN 1999-2001; Bp Coun Dio E Tennessee Knoxville TN 1992-1994; Vic S Jas The Less Madison TN 1966-1971; Chair Div Yth Deptce Dio Tennessee Nashville TN 1966-1970; P-in-c S Anne's Ch Millington TN 1962-1966; Asst S Jn's Epis Cathd Knoxville TN 1961-1962. AAPC; ACPE. Helen Flanders Dunbar Awd ACPE 2009; Obert Kempson Awd SE Reg Assn for Clibical Pstr Educ 2003; No Carolina Ptr G Keese Awd Hospice of No Carolina 1986; No Carolina Med Soc Jn Huske Anderson Awd No Carolina Med Soc 1986. pkeese@knology.net

KEESTER, John Carl (Los) 627 Leyden Ln, Claremont CA 91711 B Kane PA 7/15/1929 s Carl Johnson Keester & Alice Augusta. BA U CA 1952; BD CDSP 1955. D 6/13/1955 P 12/12/1955 Bp Sumner Walters. m 6/2/1950 Lauranne Yust. Asst S Clare Of Assisi Rancho Cucamonga CA 1997-2002; R S Tim's Ch Catonsville MD 1985-1991; R All SS Ch Bakersfield CA 1980-1985; The ETS At Claremont Claremont CA 1974-1980; R S Ambr Par Claremont CA 1966-1980; Vic S Mich's U Mssn Island Isla Vista CA 1961-1965; Cur S Jude's Epis Par Burbank CA 1958-1961.

KEETER, Barbara B(eth) (CFla) 811 N Grandview St, Mount Dora FL 32757 **D Ch Of The Gd Shpd Maitland FL 1989-** B Great Lakes IL 10/8/1953 d Ralph Victor Bartelt & Dorothy A. Inst For Chr Stds 1988; Diac Sch Dio Cntrl Florida 1990. D 10/21/1989 Bp John Wadsworth Howe. bzsark@embarqmail.com

KEGGI, J John (Me) 62 Crest Rd, Wellesley MA 02482 B Riga LV 8/24/1932 s Janis Keggi & Ruta. BS CUNY 1954; MS Ya 1958; PhD Ya 1962. D 2/24/1984 P 8/26/1984 Bp Samuel Espinoza-Venegas. m 8/26/1995 Jeanne D Schork c 3. R S Mk's Ch Augusta ME 1995-2004; Int Trin Ch Bridgewater MA 1994-1995; Int Ch Of The H Sprt Wayland MA 1992-1994; Int All SS Par Brookline MA 1989-1992; Dio Maine Portland ME 1984-2007; Dio Mex 1984-1989. Auth, "As the Vic of Wakefield would have it," *Festschrift for Arthur Peacocke*, 1990; Auth, "Serratamolide, A Metabolite Of Serratia Marcescens|Journ Of Ameriserratamolide, A Metabolite Of Serratia Marcescens," *Journ Of Amer Chem Soc*, 1962. Soc of Ord Scientists 1988. Genesis Awd for Sci and Rel Episcoapl Ntwk for Sci, Tech, & Faith 2005. keggi@prexar.com

KEHRER, William Francis (HB) No address on file. B Detroit MI 4/16/1923 s Charles F Kehrer & Gertrude M. LTh VTS 1965. D 6/29/1965 P 1/1/1966 Bp Richard S M Emrich. m 4/11/1942 Lillian Kehrer. wfkehrer@hotmail.com

KEILL, David (Va) 8212 Pilgrim Ter, Richmond VA 23227 **Vic Chr Ascen Ch Richmond VA 1999-** B Ridgewood NJ 11/3/1965 s James Douglas Keill & Judith Neil. BA Ob 1987; MDiv Yale DS 1993. D 6/5/1993 Bp James Russell Moodey P 6/4/1994 Bp Arthur Benjamin Williams Jr. m 4/21/2001 Cynthia Keill. R S Geo's Ch Pennsville NJ 1995-1999; Asst S Barn Ch Wilmington DE 1994-1995; Ch Of S Jas The Apos New Haven CT 1993-1994; Asst S Jas' Ch New Haven CT 1993-1994. Auth, "The Epis Sun Lectionary Computer Prog". Co-Winner Wm A Muehl Purchasing Prize Berk Berkeley CA 1993. delkil@yahoo.com

KEIM, Robert Lincoln (Cal) 600 Colorado Ave, Palo Alto CA 94306 B Camp Lejune NC 5/8/1964 s Robert Keim & Suzanne. BA NWU 1986; MBA Duke 1991; MDiv Fuller TS 2007; Cert. in Angl Stds CDSP 2008. D 6/6/2009 P 12/5/2009 Bp Marc Handley Andrus. c 1. rkeim11@earthlink.net

KEITH, Briggett J (Nwk) 88 Trinity Pl, Hillsdale NJ 07642 **H Trin Epis Ch Hillsdale NJ 2007-** B Hammond IN 5/13/1950 d Willis Cameron Keith & Jayne I. BA Sweet Briar Coll 1972; MDiv VTS 1991. D 6/15/1991 Bp Peter James Lee P 2/15/1992 Bp Arthur Benjamin Williams Jr. R Ch Of The Epiph Allendale NJ 1996-2006; Asst S Chris's By-The River Gates Mills OH 1991-1996. briggettkeith@yahoo.com

KEITH, George Arthur (SanD) 14905 Lone Oak Trail, Ramona CA 92065 B San Antonio TX 11/21/1942 s Ray Keith & Mary Grace. BS SW Texas St U San Marcos 1964; MPS NYTS 1990. D 6/10/1990 P 12/10/1990 Bp Richard Frank Grein. c 1. R S Jn's Epis Ch Chula Vista CA 1993-2009; Vic Calv and St Geo New York NY 1990-1991; Ch Pension Fund New York NY 1990-1991. Auth, "Shksp, Gk classics, Mod classics," *Adaptation of Classics for Secondary Sch Theatre*; Playwright, "To Be Remembered," *Off Broadway Prod.* Chapl- Ord of the H Temple of Jerusalem; Chula Vista Arts Coun; NAES. keith606@hotmail.com

KEITH JR, John Matthew (Ala) 1208 Fearrington Post, Pittsboro NC 27312 **Assoc Chap Of The Cross Chap Hill NC 2011-** B Canton GA 12/14/1937 s John Matthew Keith & Mildred. BA Duke 1960; STB Harvard DS 1963. D 10/12/1969 P 2/15/1970 Bp George Edward Haynsworth. m 6/6/1969 Rilla Louise Carter c 1. Pres Stndg Com Dio Alabama Birmingham AL 1999-2000; R Gr Epis Ch Mt Meigs AL 1984-2000; St Marys Epis Ch Dadeville AL 1983; R Emm Epis Ch Opelika AL 1977-1982; S Mich's Ch Faunsdale AL 1972-1977; R S Wilfrid's Ch Marion AL 1972-1977. Auth, "True Div in Chr w Four Short Stories," New So Books, 2010; Auth, "Complete Humanity in Jesus," *A Theol Memoir*, New So Books, 2009. EPF 1980. johnrillakeith@knology.net

KEITH III, Stuart Brooks (Colo) Po Box 1591, Edwards CO 81632 **R Epis Ch Of The Trsfg Vail CO 1998-** B Tampa FL 8/19/1964 s Stuart Brooks Keith & Kay. BA U of So Florida 1985; MDiv VTS 1992. D 6/20/1992 Bp John Wadsworth Howe P 1/1/1993 Bp William Jerry Winterrowd. m 5/16/1992 Julie P Papa c 2. Asst Epis Ch Of The Trsfg Vail CO 1995-1996; Ch Of S Jn Chrys Golden CO 1992-1995. Auth, "Who Do You Say That I Am? Facilitating YP'S Encounters w The Gospel," *Resource Bk For Mnstrs w Yth & YA In The Episcop*, Dfms, 1995. 4keiths@centurytel.net

KEITH, Thomas Frederick (WK) 406 Champions Dr, Rockport TX 78382 **Vic Ch Of Our Sav Aransas Pass TX 2002-** B Alger OH 8/26/1935 s Frederick Lewis Keith & Virginia Katherine. BA U of So Florida 1965; BD Epis TS of The SW 1968; Med U of Texas 1977; PhD U of Texas 1987. D 6/12/1968 Bp Frederick P Goddard P 5/1/1969 Bp J Milton Richardson. m 10/19/1985 Adelaide K Thornton c 2. SS Mary And Martha Of Bethany Larned KS 1995-2000; Dio Wstrn Kansas Hutchinson KS 1992-2000; H Apos Ch Ellsworth KS 1990-1995; S Jn's Ch Great Bend KS 1990-1995; Sterling Coll Sterling KS 1987-2000; S Mk's Ch Lyons KS 1985-1990; R S Jn's Ch New Braunfels TX 1978-1984; Vic Trin Epis Ch Marble Falls TX 1968-1978; Vic Epis Ch Of The Epiph Burnet Burnet TX 1968-1974. atkeith406@att.net

KEITH, William Jonathan (ETenn) PO Box 145, Lookout Mountain TN 37350 **Asst R Ch Of The Gd Shpd Lookout Mtn TN 2009-** B Asheville NC 9/4/1978 s William Riley Keith & Lynda Phillips. BA Appalachian St U 2001; MDiv The TS at The U So 2009. D 5/30/2009 Bp Granville Porter Taylor P 1/16/2010 Bp Charles Glenn VonRosenberg. m 5/29/2004 Amanda T Amanda Pauline Thomas c 1. wil@goodshepherdlookout.com

KEITH-LUCAS, Diane Dorothea (Mass) 1 Hilltop Ave, Lexington MA 02421 **R Calv Ch Danvers MA 2007-** B Sewanee TN 8/11/1976 BA Swarthmore Coll 1997; MA Harvard DS 2000; MDiv EDS 2004. D 6/4/2005 P 1/7/2006 Bp M(arvil) Thomas Shaw III. m 8/7/1999 Jacob Matthew Montwieler c 2. Coordntr Of CE Trin Ch Randolph MA 2005-2007. revthea@gmail.com

KEITHLY JR, Thomas Graves (Dal) 1612 Kiltartan Dr, Dallas TX 75228 **Div Of Ecum Concerns Dio Ft Worth Ft Worth TX 1976-** B Saint Louis MO 7/23/1931 s Thomas Graves Keithly & Amy Donnan. BA W&M 1953; BA Oxf 1955; GTS 1956; MA Oxf 1959. D 6/21/1956 P 12/21/1956 Bp Edward Randolph Welles II. m 8/13/1955 Virginia Postles c 3. Seniors Min Ch Of The Incarn Dallas TX 1995-1999; Chair - Cntrl Convoc Dio Dallas Dallas TX 1995-1997; Int Ch Of The Gd Shpd Terrell TX 1993-1995; Dept Of Dioc Ministers Dio Ft Worth Ft Worth TX 1986-1989; Dept Of Dioc Ministers Dio Ft Worth Ft Worth TX 1986-1989; Exec Coun Dio Ft Worth Ft Worth TX 1986-1989; Ch Of The H Cross Paris TX 1985-1994; Dio Ft Worth Ft Worth TX 1984; Fin Com Dio Ft Worth Ft Worth TX 1974-1976; Dn Of The SW Dnry Dio Ft Worth Ft Worth TX 1972-1976; Exec Coun Dio Ft Worth Ft Worth TX 1971-1976; Dept Of Mssn Dio Ft Worth Ft Worth TX 1971-1974; R S Jn's Epis Ch Brownwood TX 1967-1985; Asst To Dn S Matt's Cathd Dallas TX 1959-1967; Com Of Acolytes Dio Dallas Dallas TX 1959-1961; Vic S Chris's Ch And Sch Ft Worth TX 1958-1959; Vic Shpd Of The Hills Branson MO 1956-1958. Cmnty Of S Mary 1961. padreandginny@aol.com

KEIZER, Garret John (Vt) 770 King George Farm Rd, Sutton VT 05867 B Paterson NJ 4/17/1953 s John Andrew Keizer & Joan Alice. BA Montclair St U 1975; MA U of Vermont 1978. D 6/16/1992 P 12/19/1992 Bp Daniel Lee Swenson. m 7/19/1975 Kathleen Barbara Van Haste c 1. Vic Chr Ch Island Pond VT 1992-2003. Auth, "Help: The Original Human Dilemma," Harper Collins, 2004; Auth, "The Enigma of Anger," Jossey-Bass, 2002; Auth, "Dresser of Sycamore Trees," Viking, 1991; Auth, "No Place But Here," Viking, 1988.

KELAHER, Edward Thomas (SC) 534 S Creekside Dr, Murrells Inlet SC 29576 **All SS' Epis Ch Chevy Chase MD 2011-; Dn, Georgetown Dnry Dio So Carolina Charleston SC 2007-** B Bayonne NJ 8/28/1954 s Jerome P Kelaher & Norma. Drew U 1973; BS Buc 1976; JD New York Law Sch 1980. D 9/14/1997 P 3/31/2001 Bp Edward Lloyd Salmon Jr. m 7/16/1977 Patricia A Thompson c 2. R Chr the King Pawleys Island SC 2007-2011; D The Epis Ch Of The Resurr Surfside Bch SC 1997-2001. Bucknell Univ. Humanitarian Awd Buc 1995; Natl Pro Bono Lawyer Awd ABA 1993; S. C. Pro Bono Lawyer Of The Year So Carolina Bar 1992; Cnty Vol Of The Year Sun News (Nwspr) 1992; Citizen Of The Year Surfside Bch, Sc 1992. edkelaher@aol.com

KELBAUGH, Charles Franklin (Pa) 277 Countryside Cir, New Hope PA 18938 B Beaver Falls PA 12/2/1931 s James Franklin Kelbaugh & Elizabeth Pearl. BA Geneva Coll 1953; MDiv PDS 1956. D 6/30/1956 Bp Joseph Gillespie Armstrong P 1/19/1957 Bp Oliver J Hart. m 8/13/1983 Marianne Horne c 5. R Emm Ch Philadelphia PA 1967-1996; Vic Incarn H Sacr Epis Ch Drexel Hill PA 1958-1961; Mssy Asst S Ptr's Ch Philadelphia PA 1956-1957. Bp White PB Soc 1967. kelbaughsmc@comcast.net

KELDERMAN, Kate E (Minn) PO Box 3005, 20 W. High Street, C/O Prince of Peace Church, Gettysburg PA 17325 **R The Memi Ch Of The Prince Of Peace Gettysburg PA 2007-** B Roanoke VA 5/23/1963 d Joseph Thomas Engleby & Jane Engleby. BS U So 1985; MT U of Virginia 1994; MDiv VTS 2004. D 6/26/2004 Bp Peter James Lee P 1/6/2005 Bp James Louis Jelinek. m 5/12/1990 Theodoor Kelderman c 2. Assoc R The Epis Par Of S Dav Minnetonka MN 2004-2007. ktkelderman@mac.com

KELLAM, Patricia Marie (SVa) Po Box 647, Nassawadox VA 23413 **Emm Ch Cape Chas VA 2010-** B Nassawadox VA 8/26/1942 d Harry Milson Kellam & Nannie Bet. BS Virginia Commonwealth U 1979; Med Virginia Commonwealth U 1983; UTS Richmond VA 1985; MDiv STUSo 1991. D 6/1/1991 P 2/2/1992 Bp Charles Farmer Duvall. c 2. S Phil's Ch Quantico MD 2000; Assoc H Trin Prot Epis Ch Onancock VA 1999-2005; Vic S Paul's Ch Vienna MD 1999-2000; Vic Ch Of Our Sav Par San Gabr CA 1995-1996; Dio Cntrl Gulf Coast Pensacola FL 1995-1996; Vic Imm Ch Bay Minette AL 1991-1995; D H Nativ Epis Ch Panama City FL 1991; Coordntr S Andr's Epis Ch Panama City FL 1986-1989. Hampton Roads Chapl Assn 2000-2008; Virginia Chapl Assn 2000-2008. pmkellam@esva.net

KELLAWAY, James L. (Ct) 123 Babbitt Hill Road, Pomfret Center CT 06259 B Amityville NY 7/26/1950 s James Lowell Kellaway & Helen Resch. BA Colg 1972; MDiv EDS 1977. D 6/11/1977 Bp Jonathan Goodhue Sherman P 4/1/1978 Bp Robert Campbell Witcher Sr. m 11/24/1979 Genevieve D Doran c 3. Dioc Disaster Relief Com Dio Connecticut Hartford CT 2011; P-in-c Trin Ch Brooklyn CT 2008-2011; Dn, Hartford Dnry Dio Connecticut Hartford CT 2004-2006; Stwdshp Com Dio Connecticut Hartford CT 1995-2011; Stwdshp Consult Dio Connecticut Hartford CT 1995-2000; Fin Com Dio Connecticut Hartford CT 1991-1992; Fin Com Dio Connecticut Hartford CT 1991-1992; R S Jn's Epis Ch Vernon Rock Vernon CT 1989-2008; Stwdshp Com & Chair Dio W Virginia Charleston WV 1984-1986; R Chr Ch Fairmont WV 1983-1989; Asst Chr Ch Greenwich CT 1977-1983. Poet, "The Moonlight Mowers," *Stars In Our Hearts*, Wrld Poetry Mvmt; Mus & Lyrics, "A Habitat for All Humanity," *The Habitat Songbook*, HabHum; Auth, "The Mystical Mangers," *Unpublished.* Epis Ntwk for Stwdshp 2000-2005. jlkellaway@gmail.com

KELLER, Bruce Anthony (Los) 808 Foothill Blvd, La Canada CA 91011 **D S Geo's Par La Can CA 2007-** B Cleveland OH 9/1/1954 s Frank Keller & Helen Anna. Diac Stds Epis TS 2010. D 2/6/2010 Bp Chester Lovelle Talton. anthony@dancetm.net

KELLER JR, Charles Edward (Nwk) 37 Warren St, Clifton NJ 07013 B Orange NJ 5/10/1932 s Charles Edward Keller & Dorothy. BA Dart 1954; UTS 1959; MA FD 1976. D 5/23/1959 Bp Donald MacAdie P 12/1/1959 Bp Leland Stark. m 3/12/1955 Barbara F Ferguson c 2. S Agnes Ch Little Falls NJ 1962-1996; Cur Chr Ch Glen Ridge NJ 1959-1962.

KELLER III, Christoph (Ark) St. Margaret's Episcopal Church, 20900 Chenal Parkway, Little Rock AR 72207 **Dir Epis Collgt Sch Little Rock AR 2010-; Dir The GTS New York NY 2010-** B El Dorado AR 1/4/1955 s Christoph Keller & Caroline Patience. BA, mcl Amh 1977; Harv 1979; MDiv EDS 1982; ThD GTS 2010. D 6/26/1982 Bp Herbert Alcorn Donovan Jr P 5/28/1983 Bp Christoph Keller Jr. m 4/15/1978 Julie Honeycutt c 2. S Marg's Epis Ch Little Rock AR 1993-1998; Cn Mssnr Dio Arkansas Little Rock AR 1986-1998; Vic Trin Ch Van Buren AR 1983-1990; Vic S Aug's Ch Ft Smith AR 1983-1986; Intern Cur Trin Ch Pine Bluff AR 1982-1983. HSEC 2004. Fell ECF 2003; Hon Cn Dio Arkansas 1998. chriskeller1@mac.com

KELLER JR, David Gardiner Ross (Minn) 31 Alexander Farms Lane, Alexander NC 28701 B New York NY 7/6/1937 s David Gardiner Ross Keller & Elizabeth Sterling. BA Hob 1958; MDiv GTS 1961; EdD NYU 1985. D 6/29/1961 Bp Alfred L Banyard P 1/4/1962 Bp William J Gordon Jr. m 1/4/2003 Emily Wilmer c 4. Steward, Epis Hse of Pryr Dio Minnesota Minneapolis MN 1994-2002; Cn Trin Cathd Phoenix AZ 1991-1994; Dir Dept Of Mnstry Dvlpmt Dio Arizona Phoenix AZ 1982-1995; Cook Chr Trng Sch Tempe AZ 1981-1982; Coordntr Ak Tee Dio Alaska Fairbanks AK 1974-1981; P-in-c S Jas Ch Tanana AK 1969-1972; P-in-c S Geo's Ch Cordova AK 1968-1969; P-in-c S Lk's Ch Shageluk AK 1961-1968. Auth, "Desert Banquet:Wisdom from the Desert Fathers and Mothers," *Trade Bk*, Liturg Press, 2011; Auth, "Come and See: The Transformation of Personal Pryr," *Trade Bk*, Morehouse Pub, 2009; Auth, "Oasis of Wisdom: The Worlds of the Desert Fr and Mothers," *Trade Bk*, Liturg Press, 2005; Auth, "Tchg Life of Jesus," *TEE Course*, Chas Cook TS, 1982; Auth, "Gods Living Word: A Biblic Survey," *TEE Course*, Dio Alaska, 1975. tycoedd@yahoo.com

KELLER, John Speake (O) 20508 Hilliard Blvd, Rocky River OH 44116 B Washington DC 8/29/1950 s Howard Lee Keller & Ann West. BA U Rich 1972; MDiv VTS 1975; MA Presb Sch CE 1976. D 7/27/1975 Bp Samuel B Chilton P 6/5/1976 Bp Charles F Hall. m 7/17/2003 Donald J Jackson. Int Ch Of The Ascen Lakewood OH 2008-2011; Int The Memi Ch Of The Prince Of Peace Gettysburg PA 2005-2007; Int S Jn's Epis Ch Lancaster PA 2004-2005; Assoc R S Ptr's Epis Ch Lakewood OH 2000-2004; Int The Ch Of The Nativ Cedarcroft Baltimore MD 1999-2000; Int S Dav's Ch Baltimore MD 1997-1999; Int Trin Ch Towson MD 1996-1997; Int All SS Ch E Lansing MI 1994-1996; Int Sherwood Epis Ch Cockeysville MD 1993-1994; Assoc R S Thos' Par Washington DC 1989-1992; Assoc S Lk's Ch Gladstone NJ 1984-1986; LocTen Ch Of The H Comm U City MO 1981-1984; LocTen Gr Ch Kirkwood MO 1979-1981; Cur Chr Epis Ch Little Rock AR 1977-1979; Cur S Thos' Ch Richmond VA 1975-1977. Auth, "Weca Nwsltr". jskandpk@aol.com

KELLER SR, Patterson (Oly) Po Box 1808, Cody WY 82414 B Highland Park IL 3/30/1930 s Christoph Keller & Kathryn Morris. BA Trin Hartford CT 1953; MDiv VTS 1956. D 6/21/1956 Bp Allen J Miller P 2/25/1957 Bp William J Gordon Jr. m 6/10/1958 Cornelia Godfrey c 4. R Emm Ch Orcas Island Eastsound WA 1988-1995; R Chr Ch Cody WY 1971-1988; Vic S Andr's Ch Meeteetse WY 1971-1978; Vic Ch Of The Gd Shpd Sundance WY 1963-1971; P-in-c Gd Shpd Huslia AK 1956-1963. patkeller@bresnan.net

KELLER, Susan S (Nwk) 24 Rector St, Newark NJ 07102 **Dn Trin And S Phil's Cathd Newark NJ 2009-** B Detroit MI 1/10/1955 d Thomas J Shannon & Freddie L. BA How 1976; MDiv How 1991; CAS VTS 1992. D 6/13/1992 Bp Ronald Hayward Haines P 1/9/1993 Bp Jane Hart Holmes Dixon. m 7/3/1976 Paul F Keller c 1. R S Mary Magd Ch Silver Sprg MD 2003-2008; S Fran Ch Virginia Bch VA 2000-2003; Dir Prog Dio Sthrn Virginia Norfolk VA 1996-2000; Asst Ch Of Our Sav Silver Sprg MD 1992-1996. EPF, UBE. deanskeller@gmail.com

KELLERMANN, Alan Seth (NCal) 245 S Church St, Grass Valley CA 95945 **R Emm Epis Ch Grass Vlly CA 2009-** B New Orleans LA 8/4/1976 s Alan Scott Kellermann & Carol Brown. BA W&L 1999; MDiv TESM 2006. D 8/19/2006 P 3/24/2007 Bp James Monte Stanton. m 8/8/1998 Tara Dorothy Ferguson c 4. Chf of Stff S Phil's Epis Ch Frisco TX 2008-2009; Cur Ch Of The Epiph Richardson TX 2006-2008. sethntara@yahoo.com

KELLETT, James William (SVa) 11233 Tierrasanta Blvd, #40, San Diego CA 92124 **Asst S Barth's Epis Ch Poway CA 2007-** B Ely NV 8/17/1933 s Ernest William Kellett & Mary Bernice. BA Bos 1955; MDiv Bex 1959. D 6/20/1959 P 12/20/1959 Bp Anson Phelps Stokes Jr. m 4/13/1980 Anne Andrew c 4. Int S Andr's Ch La Mesa CA 2004-2006; Bruton Par Williamsburg VA 2000; Hickory Neck Ch Toano VA 1987-2000; S Paul's Ch Windsor VT

1983-1987; Salisbury Sch Salisbury CT 1975-1983; R S Andr's-In-The-Vlly Tamworth NH 1970-1975; R S Matt's Ch Goffstown NH 1966-1970; P-in-c S Dav's Epis Ch Ft Bridger WY 1963-1966; Vic All SS Epis Ch Wolfeboro NH 1961-1963; Cur S Paul's Ch Boston MA 1959-1961. jwkellett44@aol.com

KELLEY, Barbara A (Pa) 159 Windsor Ave, Southampton PA 18966 **R S Jas Ch Langhorne PA 2008-** B New York NY 11/3/1954 d Arthur Faller Kelley & Dorothy Melvine. BA Lawr 1976; MS U of Wisconsin 1978; MDiv GTS 1980. D 6/7/1980 Bp Robert Campbell Witcher Sr P 12/16/1981 Bp Lyman Cunningham Ogilby. Int Ch Of The H Nativ Wrightstown PA 2006-2008; Int Trin Ch Buckingham PA 2006; Int S Jas Ch Langhorne PA 2004-2006; Int Ch Of The H Sprt Harleysville PA 2001-2004; Int Gd Shpd Ch Hilltown PA 1999-2000; Int Ch Of The Mssh Lower Gwynedd PA 1998-1999; Int Gr Epiph Ch Philadelphia PA 1995-1998; Int S Jas Ch Collegeville PA 1994-1995; Int Ch Of The Incarn Morrisville PA 1992-1993; Int Trin Ch Solebury PA 1991-1992; Int Trin Ch Gulph Mills King Of Prussia PA 1991; Int S Paul's Ch Elkins Pk PA 1990-1991; Int S Mary Anne's Epis Ch No E MD 1989-1990; Int S Nathanaels Ch Philadelphia PA 1989; Int Ch Of The Redemp Southampton PA 1987-1989; Asst Min The Epis Ch Of The Adv Kennett Sq PA 1981-1987; Cur All SS Ch Great Neck NY 1980-1981. revbkelley@aol.com

KELLEY, Brian Scott (Mass) 47 Concord Sq, Boston MA 02118 B Quebec City QC CA 9/20/1928 s Arthur Reading Kelley & Mary. BA Bps 1949; BEd McGill U 1953; MDiv EDS 1957; Cert Harvard DS 1972; EdD Harv 1976. Trans from Anglican Church of Canada 5/15/1963 as Priest Bp Anson Phelps Stokes Jr. m 9/8/1956 Sara Gay Avery c 3. R S Lk's And S Marg's Ch Allston MA 1979-1983; Int Ch Of The Trsfg Derry NH 1977-1978; The Cathd Ch Of S Paul Boston MA 1970-1995; Asst Gr Ch Everett MA 1963-1966; R S Jn's Ch Charlestown (Boston) Charlestown MA 1960-1966. Auth, "Poems," *Peacework*, 1999; Auth, "Poems," *The Boston Poet*, 1997. Clipper Ship Fndt 1985. Mary B Newman Awd Untd Way of Mass Bay 2000; Establishment of the Cn Brian Scott Kelley Awd Soc Action Mnstrs 1993; Citizen of the Year Awd Boston Downtown Crossing Assn 1988. canonkelley@gmail.com

KELLEY, Carlton Franklin (Ind) 132 S 6th St, Richmond IN 47374 B Fort Pierce FL 8/28/1949 s Otis Franklin Kelley & Lydia Ella. BSN U of Maryland 1978; MDiv GTS 1982; Int Mnstry Prog 2000. D 6/29/1982 Bp David Keller Leighton Sr P 2/24/1983 Bp Charlie Fuller McNutt Jr. S Paul's Ch Richmond IN 2001-2004; Supply S Wlfd's Epis Ch Sarasota FL 1998-2006; Dio SW Florida Sarasota FL 1990-1991; S Ptr's Epis Ch Ellicott City MD 1984-1989; Vic S Andr's Epis Ch Glenwood MD 1984-1985; Cur S Jas Ch Lancaster PA 1982-1984. Natl Epis Hlth Mnstrs 2008; Ord of Julian of Norwich 2008; Recovered Alchoholic Cler Assn 2008; Recovery Mnstrs of the Epis Ch 2008.

KELLEY, James Thomas (WVa) 86 New Jersey St, Wheeling WV 26003 **D S Paul's Ch Wheeling WV 2007-; D S Lk's Ch Wheeling WV 2000-** B Wheeling WV 8/6/1945 s William Patrick Kelley & Frieda Mcgrail. D 9/21/2000 Bp C(laude) Charles Vache. m 6/16/1990 Theresa Marie Robson.

KELLEY, John Beverley Leffingwell (Ct) 3432 S.R. 580 Unit 210, Safety Harbor FL 34695 B Miami FL 8/1/1928 s Augustus Beverley Kelley & Joyce Marjorie. BA Washington U 1950; MDiv UTS 1953; Epis TS of The SW 1957; U of Texas, Austin 1957; W&M 1969; Chris Newport U 1973; MS Yeshiva U 1990. D 5/24/1953 Bp William Scarlett P 12/6/1953 Bp Arthur C Lichtenberger. m 8/29/1952 Mary Gwynneth Davies c 4. Vic Calv Epis Ch Bridgeport CT 1985-1992; Yth Dir S Lk's/S Paul's Ch Bridgeport CT 1985-1988; Vic St Pauls Ch Bridgeport CT 1985-1988; Asst Ch Of S Thos Bethel CT 1982-1984; Christchurch Sch Christchurch VA 1973-1980; Asst S Ann's Ch Of Morrisania Bronx NY 1961-1964; R S Paul's Ch Palmyra MO 1953-1956. johnkelley30@gmail.com

KELLEY, Theresa Marie (WVa) 86 New Jersey, Wheeling WV 26003 **P-in-c S Paul's Ch Wheeling WV 2006-; P-in-c S Lk's Ch Wheeling WV 2001-** B Spokane WA 5/19/1957 d Richard George Robson & Helen Josephine. BA W Liberty St Coll 2004. D 11/21/2000 P 6/9/2001 Bp C(laude) Charles Vache. m 6/16/1990 James Thomas Kelley c 2. tmkelley57@verizon.net

KELLINGTON, Brian T (Spr) 411 Washington St, Pekin IL 61554 **Evang and Spritual Enrichment Chair Dio Springfield Springfield IL 2010-; P-in-c All SS Ch Morton IL 2009-; Dn, Nthrn Dnry Dio Springfield Springfield IL 2009-; R S Paul's Epis Ch Pekin IL 2005-** B Medford OR 2/8/1949 s George William Kellington & Mary Edith. BA U of Oregon 1971; MDiv CDSP 1984. D 6/29/1984 Bp Robert Hume Cochrane P 6/1/1985 Bp Matthew Paul Bigliardi. m 7/24/1976 Laurie Ruth Dugnolle. Stwdshp Cmsn Chair Dio Springfield Springfield IL 2006-2010; Vic S Phil's Ch Norwood NY 2001-2005; Sprtl Advsr Curs Sec Dio Albany Albany NY 1994-1998; R Chr Ch Herkimer NY 1988-2001; Dio Oregon Portland OR 1988; Vic S Andr's Ch Cottage Grove OR 1984-1988; Vic S Dav's Ch Drain OR 1984-1988. Natl Epis Curs Com 2001-2003. brian.kellington@gmail.com

KELLINGTON, Laurie Ruth (Spr) 411 Washington St, Pekin IL 61554 **D All SS Ch Morton IL 2009-; D S Paul's Epis Ch Pekin IL 2005-** B Englewood CA 10/24/1955 d Charles Edward Dugnolle & Barbara Joan. BA Utica Coll of Syr 1993; MA St. Jos's Coll, Maine 2006. D 6/9/2001 Bp Daniel William Herzog. m 7/24/1976 Brian T Kellington. D S Phil's Ch Norwood NY 2001-2005; D Chr Ch Herkimer NY 2001. deaconlaurie@gmail.com

KELLOGG, Alicia Sue (Me) 27 Forest Ave, Winthrop ME 04364 **D S Matt's Epis Ch Hallowell ME 2007-** B Marion OH 12/30/1947 d Charles William Kellogg & Doris Evelyn. BA OH SU Columbus OH 1969. D 6/23/2007 Bp Chilton Abbie Richardson Knudsen. c 1. askellogg@hotmail.com

KELLOGG III, Edward Samuel (SanD) 3407 Larga Cir, San Diego CA 92110 B Pasadena CA 2/13/1933 s Edward Samuel Kellogg & Dorothy Emily. BS USNA 1954; BA Sch for Deacons 1984. D 8/5/1984 P 12/1/1990 Bp Charles Brinkley Morton. m 6/26/1954 Margaret Anne Wagner c 3. S Andr's By The Lake Temecula CA 1991; S Barth's Epis Ch Poway CA 1990; D Ch Of The Gd Samar San Diego CA 1987-1989; D Cathd Ch Of S Paul San Diego CA 1984-1986; Sem Asst Ch Of The Ascen Vallejo CA 1981-1984.

KELLOGG WBHS, Richard (WMo) 1016 Highland St, 137 Sequoia St, Branson MO 65616 B Sayre PA 4/18/1948 s Frank Nelson Kellogg & Mary Elizabeth. BA Sam Houston St U 1970; Dplma ETSBH 1982; MA Regis U Denver CO 2000. D 6/14/1988 P 11/17/1991 Bp Leopold Frade. m 6/10/1973 Beth Cs Slater. P Chr Epis Ch Forrest City AR 2010-2011; P Ch Of The H Cross W Memphis AR 2008-2009; R Shpd Of The Hills Branson MO 2002-2006; Ohio Vlly Epis Cluster Williamstown WV 1999-2000; Mssnr for Native Amer Wk Dio Wyoming Casper WY 1995-1998; Mssnr For Native Amer Wk Our Fr's Hse Ft Washakie WY 1995-1998; Missionar for Native Amer Wk Shoshone Epis Mssn Ft Washakie WY 1995-1998; SAMS Ambridge PA 1988-1995. Novc, WBHS. frbear@att.net

KELLUM, Rose Edna (Miss) RR 1 Box 20008, Saint Joseph LA 71366 **D Chr Ch S Jos LA 2004-** B Vicksburg MS 2/2/1957 d Thomas Akers & Jennie. Hinds Cmnty Coll 1981; Cpe Res G.V. (Sonny) Montogmer Va Med Cntr 2002. D 1/6/2001 Bp Alfred Clark Marble Jr. c 3.

KELLY, Arthur James (Pa) 1171 Sandy Ridge Rd, Doylestown PA 18901 **Acad Sub Com of COM Dio Pennsylvania Philadelphia PA 1988-** B Colon Panama 4/11/1931 s Arthur Clinton Kelly & Dorcas Rebecca. BA CUNY-Hunter Coll 1962; MDiv GTS 1966; STM NYTS 1972; PhD NYU 1981. D 6/4/1966 P 12/17/1966 Bp Horace W B Donegan. m 4/20/1996 Imogene Carol Taylor c 4. Dioc Relatnshp Com Dio Pennsylvania Philadelphia PA 1986-1991; Cmsn Racism Dio Pennsylvania Philadelphia PA 1986-1990; Ce Com Dio Pennsylvania Philadelphia PA 1985-1990; Dioc Coun Dio Pennsylvania Philadelphia PA 1985-1990; Soc Concerns Com Dio Pennsylvania Philadelphia PA 1984-1990; Chair Black Cler Dio Pennsylvania Philadelphia PA 1983-1990; R S Aug's Philadelphia PA 1978-1999; Prot Chapl St. Jn's R.C. Boys Hm Dio Long Island Garden City NY 1973-1978; Mssn Dio Long Island Garden City NY 1972-1978; Counsellor Queens Pstr Couns. Serv- Jamaica Fam Co Dio Long Island Garden City NY 1970-1975; R S Steph's Epis Ch Jamaica NY 1969-1978; Exec Committe Queens/Nassau Archdnry Dio Long Island Garden City NY 1969-1971; Cur Ch Of The Intsn New York NY 1966-1969. Auth, "The Response Of The Epis Ch To Soc Change And Soc Issues 1960-1978: How These Changes Have Affected The Life And," 1981. Phi Delta Kappa. Phi Delta Kappa. drarthurjkelly@aol.com

KELLY, Christopher Douglas (SeFla) 110 Selfridge Rd, Gansevoort NY 12831 B Sydney NSW AU 6/22/1941 s Fred Douglas Kelly & Maude Brace. BA Pr 1963; MA Ya 1966; PhD Ya 1968; MDiv EDS 1972; DMin STUSo 1990. D 6/17/1972 Bp Jonathan Goodhue Sherman P 12/21/1972 Bp James Loughlin Duncan. m 5/29/1971 Pamela Caddick c 2. R S Christophers Ch Haverhill FL 1978-2002; Cur S Mart's Epis Ch Pompano Bch FL 1972-1978. ckelly14@aol.com

KELLY III, Colin Purdie (RG) 4 Inca Ln, Los Alamos NM 87544 **Cn Mssnr Dio The Rio Grande Albuquerque NM 2008-; Trin On The Hill Epis Ch Los Alamos NM 1985-** B March AFB Riverside CA 5/6/1940 s Colin P Kelly & Marion Wick. BS USMA At W Point 1963; MDiv PDS 1970; Med LIU 1977; DMin SWTS 2001. D 6/6/1970 P 12/1/1970 Bp Robert Lionne DeWitt. m 6/6/1985 Sue Ellen. R Ch Of S Mich The Archangel Colorado Sprg CO 1983-1985; Off Of Bsh For ArmdF New York NY 1973-1983; P-in-c Gr Ch Dalton MA 1971-1973; Asst to R Trin Ch Moorestown NJ 1970-1972. cpkellyL@aol.com

KELLY III, Francis John (Alb) 585 4th Ave, Troy NY 12182 **Trin Ch Lansingburgh Troy NY 2004-** B Syracuse NY 10/26/1955 s Francis John Kelly & Wilda Marie. BA Houghton Coll 1977; MDiv VTS 1986. D 6/21/1986 P 5/21/1987 Bp O'Kelley Whitaker. m 8/20/1978 Letitia Cosco c 4. S Jn's Epis Ch Troy NY 2001-2004; R Ch Of The Epiph Glenburn Clarks Summit PA 1994-2001; R S Mk's Ch Newark NY 1989-1994; Vic Chr Ch Sackets Harbor NY 1986-1989; Cur Trin Epis Ch Watertown NY 1986-1989. EvangES.

KELLY, James Francis (SwFla) 8549 54th Avenue, Circle East FL 34202 **Died 6/25/2011** B Brooklyn NY 10/30/1941 s James F Kelly & Helen Clare. BA S Alphonsus 1966; MDiv Mt St. Alphonsus 1969. Rec from Roman Catholic 2/1/1989 as Priest Bp James Winchester Montgomery. revjfkelly@verizon.net

KELLY, James L (Nev) 1075 Oxen Rd, Incline Village NV 89451 **D S Pat's Ch Incline Vill NV 2005-** B Granite Falls MN 10/15/1931 s Lester Kelly & Barbara. CDSP; TESM; BS U CA 1954; MBA Harv 1958. D 1/9/2005 P 7/25/

2005 Bp Katharine Jefferts Schori. m 1/31/1953 Lora Kelly c 2. Stndg Com Mem Dio Nevada Las Vegas NV 2005-2011. OSL 1996. duckswoody@hotmail.com

KELLY, Jane Young (SwFla) The Church of the Good Shepherd, 401 W. Henry St., Punta Gorda FL 33950 **D Ch Of The Gd Shpd Punta Gorda FL 2010-** B Youngstown OH 10/5/1946 d Earl Hudson Young & Gladys Margaret. D 6/6/2009 Bp Dabney Tyler Smith. D S Jas Epis Ch Port Charlotte FL 2009-2010. janeyk5@comcast.net

KELLY, Karen Joy (SwVa) 109 Bexley Dr, Lynchburg VA 24502 **R S Ptr's Ch Altavista VA 2010-** B Highland Park MI 6/16/1938 d William Begg Kelly & Agnes Lorena. Bachelor of Arts MI SU 1960; CAS STUSo 2003; MDiv Wstrn TS 2003. D 12/18/2003 Bp Robert R Gepert P 6/29/2004 Bp Frank Neff Powell. c 2. Stndg Com Pres Dio SW Virginia Roanoke VA 2010-2011; R S Ptr's Ch Altavista VA 2003-2010; Chapl Westminster-Cbury Of Lynchburg Lynchburg VA 2003-2010. karenjoykelly@verizon.net

KELLY, Kathleen M (NCal) 3601 College Ave, Sacramento CA 95818 **R The Epis Ch Of The Gd Shpd Hemet CA 2010-** B Alhambra CA 1/27/1951 d Richard Kelly & Mary. BA Ya 1973; JD U CA 1976; MDiv CDSP 2005. D 6/29/2005 P 1/29/2006 Bp Jerry Alban Lamb. Cn Trin Cathd Sacramento CA 2005-2010. kmkelly27@hotmail.com

KELLY, Linda Louise (NwT) 727 W Browning Ave, Pampa TX 79065 **R S Matt's Ch Pampa TX 2005-** B Eads CO 10/17/1953 d William Laverne Kelly & Margaret Louise. BA Nebraska Wesl 1976; MTh SMU 1983; Epis TS of The SW 1986; MEd Texas Tech U 1999. D 9/21/1987 Bp Maurice Manuel Benitez P 1/25/1988 Bp Gordon Taliaferro Charlton. Asst R S Ptr's Epis Ch Kerrville TX 1998-2011; Assoc R S Paul's On The Plains Epis Ch Lubbock TX 1995-1998; R S Paul's Epis Ch Orange TX 1991-1995; Assoc R S Paul's Ch Waco TX 1987-1991. jmtthor@sbcglobal.net

KELLY, Margaret I (Ida) 2115 Rancho Vista Dr, Twin Falls ID 83301 B Wendell ID 12/5/1945 d Ray R Brown & Margaret L. Csi 1991. D 1/28/1995 Bp John Stuart Thornton. m 3/7/1966 Earl A Kelly c 1. Happ For Id; NAAD. mibkelly@empnet.com

KELLY, Meaghan M (NC) 340 S Ridge St, Southern Pines NC 28387 **Asst R Emm Par Epis Ch And Day Sch Sthrn Pines NC 2007-** B South Kingstown RI 12/12/1978 d Thomas William Kelly & Margaret Kilroy. BA Rhode Island Coll Providence RI 2002; MDiv VTS 2007. D 6/13/2007 P 1/5/2008 Bp Geralyn Wolf. m 5/19/2007 Jonathan A Brower.

KELLY, Robert Lyle (HB) 506 S Osprey Dr, Post Falls ID 83854 **Died 9/27/2009** B Cottage Grove OR 11/29/1933 s Henry W Kelly & Jeannette E. BA U of Oregon 1956; BD SWTS 1963. D 6/15/1963 P 12/1/1963 Bp J(ohn) Joseph Meakins Harte.

KELLY, Roger Kevin (WVa) 520 11th St, Huntington WV 25701 **R Trin Ch Huntington WV 2001-** B Valdosta GA 3/9/1967 s Roger William Kelly & Bonnie Jean. BA Valdosta St U 1991; MDiv VTS 1994. D 5/25/1994 P 12/1/1994 Bp Harry Woolston Shipps. m 12/28/1993 Christine Mae Sanders c 2. S Dav's Ch Roswell GA 1998-2001; S Mart In The Fields Ch Atlanta GA 1995-1997; Vic S Lk's Epis Hawkinsville GA 1994-1995; Vic Trin Ch Cochran GA 1994-1995. kevink@wvtrinitychurch.org

KELLY, Sarah Elizabeth (O) 137 N Jackson St, Bluffton OH 45817 B Crestview FL 3/19/1957 d Homer Don Kelly & Margaret Campbell. BA U So 1978; MDiv Duke 1990. D 9/23/1990 Bp Arthur Edward Walmsley P 10/30/1991 Bp Huntington Williams Jr. m 6/12/1988 Raymond Franklin Person c 2. R S Paul's Ch Bellevue OH 1994-1996; Assoc Chap Of The Cross Chap Hill NC 1993; S Barth's Ch Pittsboro NC 1990-1993. Jn Templeton Fndt Awd For Sprtlty And Med Cirriculum In Primary Care (Med Residencies, $15,000).

KELLY, Shannon (Mil) 2188 E. Main Street Apt. #B, Columbus OH 43209 **Prov V Yth Mnstrs Liaison Epis Ch Cntr New York NY 2010-** B Gooding ID 4/5/1973 d Earl Alfred Kelly & Margaret I. Pacific U; BA U of Idaho Moscow 1995; MDiv CDSP 1999. D 11/8/1998 Bp John Stuart Thornton P 10/31/1999 Bp Harry Brown Bainbridge III. m 9/4/1999 Thomas Charles Ferguson c 1. COM Pres Dio Milwaukee Milwaukee WI 2009-2011; Chr Formation T/F Chair Dio Milwaukee Milwaukee WI 2008-2009; COM Pres Dio Milwaukee Milwaukee WI 2006-2009; Chapl S Fran Ch Madison WI 2006-2009; Sr Assoc for Chld, Yth & Families All SS Ch Pasadena CA 2003-2006; Asst R Par Of Chr The Redeem Pelham NY 2001-2003; Asst R for Chld and Yth S Mk's Epis Ch Palo Alto CA 1998-2001. Writer, "Lesson Plans that Wk," *Lesson Plans that Wk*, Epis Ch Cntr, 2011; Contrib, "Act Out! Yth Formation," *Water Camping Module*, Epis Relief and Dvlpmt, 2010. Epis Cams and Conf Centers 2009; NAECED 2009. revshanner@yahoo.com

KELLY, Steven Joseph Patrick (Mich) 791 Westchester Rd, Grosse Pointe Park MI 48230 **R S Jn's Ch Detroit MI 2001-** B Brooklyn NY 5/29/1966 s Joseph Francis Kelly & Sharon Anne. U of Pennsylvania 1988; BA Tem 1991; MDiv Nash 1994. D 5/27/1994 Bp Edward Harding MacBurney P 11/26/1994 Bp Keith Lynn Ackerman. m 11/5/1994 Jennifer C Cook c 4. R S Mary's Ch Charleroi PA 1996-2001; Cur The Ch Of The Gd Shpd Bryn Mawr PA 1994-1996. Angl P's Eucharistic League 1996; Conf of the Blessed 1993; Forw in Faith No Amer 1995; Franciscan Ord of the Div Compassion 1995; GAS 1993; SocMary 1993; SocOLW 1997; SSC 1995. Wrdn Angl Priests Eucharistic League 2002. rector@stjohnsdetroit.org

KELLY, Tracey Elizabeth (Va) 400 Fontaine St, Alexandria VA 22302 **St. Steph's and St. Agnes Sch Alexandria VA 2011-** B Baltimore MD 5/9/1965 d Daniel Nichols & Joyce. BA The GW 1987; MA VPI and St U 1997; MDiv VTS 2011. D 6/4/2011 Bp Shannon Sherwood Johnston. m 10/20/1990 David Graham Kelly c 3. tracey509@gmail.com

KELLY JR, William Arthur (ECR) 18 Oak Island Dr, Santa Rosa CA 95409 B Akron OH 2/1/1928 s William A Kelly & Margaret M. BA Ya 1948; BD Bos 1953; New Coll 1954; STM Ya 1965. D 2/7/2004 Bp Richard Lester Shimpfky P 9/18/2004 Bp George Richard Millard. c 7. P Assoc Trin Cathd San Jose CA 2003-2005; S Phil The Apos Scotts Vlly CA 2007. kellkrest@gmail.com

KELLY JR, William Hathaway (WTenn) 6435 Kirby Oaks Dr, Memphis TN 38119 **Died 4/19/2010** B Memphis TN 4/23/1943 s William Hathaway Kelly & Mary Louise. Georgia Inst of Tech; BS U of Tennessee 1965; MDiv STUSo 1979. D 6/30/1979 Bp William Gillette Weinhauer P 1/19/1980 Bp Furman Stough. holyapostleschurch@hotmail.com

KELM, Mark William (Minn) 109 Lawn Terrace, Golden Valley MN 55416 **Annual Conv Prlmntrn Dio Minnesota Minneapolis MN 2010-; Eccl Crt Dio Minnesota Minneapolis MN 2009-; R S Jn In The Wilderness White Bear Lake MN 2003-** B Red Wing MN 11/18/1970 s William Ernest Kelm & Judith Annette. AAS Inver Hills Cmnty Coll 1992; BS Winona St U 1993; MDiv GTS 1999. D 5/27/1999 P 12/17/1999 Bp James Louis Jelinek. m 12/30/2000 Elizabeth Jane Hyduke c 3. Cn Liturg & Fam Pstr Cathd Ch Of S Mk Minneapolis MN 2000-2003; Asst R S Mart's By The Lake Epis Minnetonka Bch MN 1999-2000. Afr Friends in Need Ntwk 2004; Cmnty of the Cross of Nails 2002. revkelm@comcast.net

KELM, William Ernest (Minn) 1914 Launa Ave, Red Wing MN 55066 **D Chr Ch Red Wing MN 1986-** B Goodhue County MN 2/11/1941 s E H Kelm & Adeline M. Hamline U; Winona St U. D 4/3/1986 Bp Robert Marshall Anderson. m 6/5/1965 Judith Annette Johnson c 2. Asst R S Mart's By The Lake Epis Minnetonka Bch MN 2000-2001.

KELMEREIT, Alan Henry (SwFla) 4554 Springview Cir, Labelle FL 33935 **Vic All Souls Epis Ch No Ft Myers FL 2009-; Dn, Ft Myers Dnry Dio SW Florida Sarasota FL 2009-; Vic The Ch Of The Gd Shpd Labelle FL 2003-** B Paterson NJ 11/6/1942 s Henry Clifton Kelmereit & Margaret Elizabeth. BA Estrn U 1964; MPA Auburn U Montgomery 1973; MDiv TESM 1996. D 6/22/1996 P 12/22/1996 Bp Alden Moinet Hathaway. m 11/17/1967 Deborah Eve Spaeth c 2. R Chr The King Epis Ch Beaver Falls PA 1996-2003. alanhk@embarqmail.com

KELSAY, Terence Eugene (CFla) 1138 Se 7th St, Ocala FL 34471 B Columbia KY 6/24/1932 s Samuel Eugene Kelsay & Hazel Cravens. BA Wstrn Kentucky U 1958; MA Wstrn Kentucky U 1960; MDiv Epis TS In Kentucky 1962. D 6/9/1962 Bp William R Moody P 12/19/1962 Bp George Henry Quarterman. m 9/14/1957 Sarah Dye c 2. S Pat's Ch Ocala FL 1992-1993; S Fran Of Assisi Ch Bushnell FL 1973-1978; Vic Ch Of The Medtr Micanopy FL 1968-1972; Vic S Barn Epis Ch Williston FL 1968-1970; Locten S Marg's Ch Inverness FL 1968-1969; Vic S Alb's Ch Morehead KY 1966-1968; Vic S Jas Ch Monahans TX 1962-1965; Vic S Ptr's Ch Kermit TX 1962-1965. Auth, "On Truth," *Fleet St Poet*; Auth, "From First We Met," *Seabury In Memorium*. Epis Conf Of The Deaf Of The Epis Ch In The USA, Fl Epis Assn Of The Deaf 1980.

KELSEY, Anne (Mo) Po Box 4740, Saint Louis MO 63108 **R Trin Ch S Louis MO 2001-** B Cleveland OH 9/20/1947 d Raymond Turner Kelsey & Barbara. U of Oregon; BA Mills Coll 1971; MDiv CDSP 1989. D 6/22/1989 Bp Robert Louis Ladehoff P 2/14/1990 Bp William Edwin Swing. m 9/30/1995 Brooke Myers c 3. Assoc S Jas Ch Fremont CA 1994-2001; Int S Anne's Ch Fremont CA 1993-1994; Asst All Souls Par In Berkeley Berkeley CA 1989-1993. revannekel@sbcglobal.net

KELSEY, Julie Vietor (Ct) 38 Brocketts Point Rd, Branford CT 06405 **Vic Calv Epis Ch Bridgeport CT 2000-** B New York NY 1/9/1942 d Thomas Frederick Vietor & Carolyn. BA Smith 1963; MS U of Bridgeport 1980; MDiv Ya Berk 1984; MDiv Yale DS 1984. D 6/8/1996 P 1/18/1997 Bp Clarence Nicholas Coleridge. m 5/9/1987 David Hugh Kelsey c 2. R Gr And S Ptr's Epis Ch Hamden CT 2001-2008; Calv Epis Ch Bridgeport CT 2001; Assoc R Trin Epis Ch Southport CT 1996-2000. revjuliek@hotmail.com

KELSEY II, Preston Telford (Ct) Kendal @ Hanover #213, 80 Lyme Rd., Hanover NH 03755 B Montclair NJ 5/30/1936 s Preston Haliday Kelsey & Suzanne. BA Dart 1958; BD CDSP 1961. D 6/25/1961 P 5/7/1962 Bp James Albert Pike. m 5/21/1966 Virginia Rice c 4. Executire Dir BTE Epis Ch Cntr New York NY 1984-1996; R Trsfg Epis Ch San Mateo CA 1973-1984; R S Alb's Ch Albany CA 1966-1973; Cur S Thos Ch Hanover NH 1963-1966; Cur Trsfg Epis Ch San Mateo CA 1961-1962. pt2kelsey@myfairpoint.net

KELSEY, Stephen Martien (NAM) 72 Clementel Dr, Durham CT 06422 B Baltimore MD 8/27/1952 s Arthur Corson Kelsey & Louise Martien. BA Colby Coll 1974; MDiv GTS 1979. D 6/1/1979 Bp Robert Shaw Kerr P 11/1/1979 Bp David Rea Cochran. m 1/14/1984 Kathleen M Barrett c 3. Mssnr Supt Grtr Hartford Reg Mnstry E Hartford CT 2004-2009; Int S Ptr's Epis Ch

Hebron CT 2003-2004; Dir Harvesters Partnership New Haven CT 2003; EDS Cambridge MA 2002; Mssnr Ch Of The Epiph Durham CT 1995-2001; Mssnr Emm Ch Killingworth CT 1995-2001; Mssnr S Andr's Ch Northford CT 1995-2001; Mssnr S Jas Epis Ch Higganum CT 1995-2001; Mssnr S Paul's Ch Westbrook CT 1995-2001; Mssnr Middlesex Area Cluster Mnstry Higganum CT 1994-2001; Mssnr Dio Nthrn Michigan Marquette MI 1993-1994; R Chr Ch Warwick NY 1988-1992; Mssnr Team Monticello NY 1982-1988; Dio Alaska Fairbanks AK 1979-1982; Co-R S Andr's Epis Ch Petersburg AK 1979-1982; Co-R S Phil's Ch Wrangell AK 1979-1982; Outreach Worker S Jn The Bapt Epis Hardwick VT 1974-1976. Design Team, "Lifecycles: Chr Transformation In Cmnty," 2003; Auth, "Celebrating The Mnstry Of All The Baptized At The Welcoming Of," *A PB For The 21st Century: Lit Stds 3*, 1996; Auth, "Mnstry Or Discipleship?," *Mnstry In Daily Life*, 1996; Auth, "Celebrating Baptismal Mnstry At The Welcoming Of New Min," *Baptism & Mnstry*, 1994; Ed Team, "Re-Shaping Mnstry," Jethro, 1990. Leaveners 1997-2004; New Directions/New Directions NE 1976-2004; Roland Allen Forum Of The NE 1996-2003; Sindicators 1985-2003. smkelsey@gmail.com

KELTON, Barbara Smoot (Dal) 719 Pampa Street, Sulphur Springs TX 75482 B Dallas TX 12/9/1946 d Lloyd Smoot & Fay Elise. BA Baylor U 1968; MS Baylor U 1973; STL Angl TS 1986. D 6/14/1986 P 7/8/1987 Bp Donis Dean Patterson. m 4/19/1969 Edward Kelton c 2. Dio Dallas Dallas TX 1996-2005; Chapl S Alb's Collgt Chap -SMU Dallas TX 1996-2005; Asst The Epis Ch Of The Trsfg Dallas TX 1986-1996. CHS. b.kelton@gmail.com

KEM, Robert Andrew (Ia) 538 Nw Scott St, Ankeny IA 50023 **S Anne's By The Fields Ankeny IA 2002-** B Des Moines IA 6/12/1953 s Robert William Kem & Roselyn. BS Simpson Coll 1975; MS Wstrn Illinois U 1980; MDiv SWTS 1985. D 5/17/1985 Bp Walter Cameron Righter P 2/2/1986 Bp Wesley Frensdorff. m 8/9/1975 Debra Rantanen c 2. Stndg Com Dio Nebraska Omaha NE 1997-2001; Bd Trst Dio Nebraska Omaha NE 1992-1995; R S Andr's Ch Omaha NE 1990-2002; Assoc S Barn On The Desert Scottsdale AZ 1985-1990. rector@saechurch.org

KEM, Robert William (Ia) 3013 - 34th Street Place, Des Moines IA 50310 B Davenport IA 5/11/1921 s Daniel Adam Kem & Birdie Jane. BS St. Ambr U Davenport IA 1942; STM EDS 1949; MRE Drake U 1957; Fllshp Coll of Preachers 1962; Fllshp ETS 1963. D 6/29/1949 Bp Elwood L Haines P 5/1/1950 Bp Gordon V Smith. c 1. Vic S Andr's Ch Des Moines IA 1951-1956; Cur The Cathd Ch Of S Paul Des Moines IA 1949-1951. Des Moines Rotary Club 1984; Emer Club S Ambr U 1992. Hon Cn (Lifetime) S Paul'S Cathd Des Moines IA 2000; Hon Cn Trinty Cathd Davenport IA 1974.

KEMEZA, Maureen Dallison (Mass) 17 Munroe Pl., Concord MA 01742 B Scranton PA 6/29/1948 d Donald Merrill Dallison & Marie Agnes. BA Rutgers-The St U 1970; MDiv EDS 1977; PhD Boston Coll 1993. D 6/1/1991 Bp David Elliot Johnson P 5/15/1992 Bp Barbara Clementine Harris. m 9/21/1971 William James Kemeza c 2. Emm Ch Boston MA 2005-2007; R Par Of S Paul Newton Highlands MA 1996-2005; Int Gr Ch Salem MA 1995-1996; Trin Ch Concord MA 1991-1993. Boston Ministers Club; MECA; NNECA; Parson's Club; Phillips Brooks. mkemeza@gmail.com

KEMMERER, Stanley C(ourtright) (Ct) Po Box 2025, Burlington CT 06013 **P-in-c Chr And Epiph Ch E Haven CT 2011-; Assoc Chr Ch Cathd Hartford CT 2006-** B Brooklyn NY 5/31/1943 s Lorenzo Botzen Kemmerer & Edna Louise. AB Mid 1965; Hartford Sem 1967; MDiv CDSP 1969. D 6/24/1969 Bp Harvey D Butterfield P 12/28/1969 Bp Gordon V Smith. m 6/3/2000 Nancy Harwood. P-in-c Chr Ch Par Epis Watertown CT 2009-2010; P-in-c Trin Epis Ch Bristol CT 2007-2009; Assoc Trin Epis Ch Collinsville CT 2002-2006; Supply P Dio Connecticut Hartford CT 1998-2002; Assoc S Andr's Ch Wellesley MA 1996-1997; Assoc Trin Ch Concord MA 1988-1996; Evan Com Dio Iowa Des Moines IA 1972-1978; P S Paul's Ch Durant IA 1969-1978. Assoc Of H Cross 1962. stancour@aol.com

KEMMLER, Richard Sigmund (NY) 1420 Pine Bay Drive, Sarasota FL 34231 **Asst S Marg Of Scotland Epis Ch Sarasota FL 2009-** B Chattanooga TN 11/15/1937 s Richard Grant Kemmler & Viola Lavinia. BS U Of Chattanooga 1965; MA Portland St U 1968; PhD NYU 1972; MDiv GTS 1990. D 1/23/1991 P 9/21/1991 Bp Walter Decoster Dennis Jr. Int Ch Of The Gd Shpd Granite Sprg NY 2003-2004; Int Ch Of The Ascen Staten Island NY 2000-2001; Int S Lk's Ch Forest Hills NY 1998-1999; Int S Ptr's Ch Bronx NY 1996-1998; S Ptr's Ch New York NY 1996-1997; Int Chr Ch New Brighton Staten Island NY 1994-1995; Int Ch Of The Ascen Staten Island NY 1993-1994; Asst Chr Ch Riverdale Bronx NY 1991-1992. rskemmler@msn.com

KEMPF, Barbara Anne (Ind) St Christopher's Episcopal Church, 1402 W Main St, Carmel IN 46032 **Assoc S Chris's Epis Ch Carmel IN 2009-** B Connersville IN 1/11/1959 d Fred Knotts & Ruth Elizabeth. BSN Indiana U 1982; JD Indiana U 1987; MDiv SWTS 2007. D 6/23/2007 P 6/1/2008 Bp Catherine Elizabeth Maples Waynick. m 9/5/1987 Richard Allen Kempf c 3. Assoc Dio Indianapolis Indianapolis IN 2007-2009; Cur S Matt's Ch Indianapolis IN 2007-2009. kempfbarbara@hotmail.com

KEMPF, Victoria Nystrom Tonk (Colo) 2220 Katahdin Dr, Fort Collins CO 80525 B Pittsburgh PA 10/25/1946 d George Verner Nystrom & Lillian. BA Barrington Coll 1969; MDiv SWTS 1986; DMin GTF 2006. D 6/14/1986 Bp James Winchester Montgomery P 12/13/1986 Bp Frank Tracy Griswold III. m 6/6/1987 Joseph Kempf c 2. Int S Paul's Epis Ch Ft Collins CO 2002-2004; Int S Matt's Ch Grand Jct CO 2001-2002; Dep for Cmncatn/Mnstry Dvlpmt Dio SW Florida Sarasota FL 1997-2001; Assoc Ch Of The Gd Shpd Punta Gorda FL 1995-1997; Int S Nich w the H Innoc Ch Elk Grove Vill IL 1994-1995; Int S Lawr Epis Ch Libertyville IL 1991-1993; Int S Edw The Mtyr and Chr Epis Ch Joliet IL 1990-1991; Int Ch Of The H Fam Lake Villa IL 1989-1990; Dio Chicago Chicago IL 1988; Asst Ch Of Our Sav Elmhurst IL 1987-1988; Cur S Richard's Ch Chicago IL 1986-1987. Hon Cn Cathd Ch of St. Ptr Dio SWFla 1999. vjkempf@msn.com

KEMPSELL JR, Howard Frederic (Va) Post Office Box 2360, Centreville VA 20122 **Confessor & Sprtl Dir VTS Alexandria VA 2007-; R S Jn's Ch Centreville VA 1994-** B Morristown NJ 5/20/1954 s Howard Frederic Kempsell & Jane Frances Matilda. Emory U 1974; BA U Rich 1976; MDiv VTS 1980; DMin GTF 1992. D 6/14/1980 Bp John Shelby Spong P 2/15/1981 Bp (George) Paul Reeves. m 6/28/1980 Ann Rodgers Gore c 2. Design Team & Fac - The Art of Sprtl Comp Cathd of St Ptr & St Paul Washington DC 2007-2009; Cler Ldrshp Proj - Class XV Par of Trin Ch New York NY 2002-2006; Cmsn on Congrl Dvlpmt (Percept) Dio Massachusetts Boston MA 1992-1994; R Chr Ch Par Plymouth MA 1990-1994; Secy, Cmsn on Congrl Missions Dio Virginia Richmond VA 1988-2001; Cn for Higher Educ Dio Upper So Carolina Columbia SC 1985-1990; Vic Trin Ch Statesboro GA 1982-1985; Assoc S Paul's Ch Albany GA 1980-1982. Auth, "The Changing Context Of Sprtl Direction: Sprtl Direction In An Age Of Mobility w Var Means Of Rapid Communicati," *The Fellows Yearbook*, GTF, 1992. Assoc, Sis of S Marg 1994. Coordntr for Visits of His Gr, the Archbp of Canterbu Dio Upper SC 1987. revdrhfkjr@aol.com

KEMPSTER, Jane Leon (WNC) 7505 Democracy Blvd Apt 114, Bethesda MD 20817 B Chico CA 5/16/1937 d James Robert McClain & Flora Louisa. BA California St U 1959; MA Wesley TS 1993; DAS VTS 1995. D 10/31/1995 P 6/15/1996 Bp John H(enry) Smith. m 6/30/1957 Norman Roy Kempster c 2. R S Lk's Epis Ch Lincolnton NC 2002-2006; Assoc Nelson Cluster Of Epis Ch Rippon WV 1996-2002. jlkempster@aol.com

KEMPSTER, Patricia Sue (NCal) 9903 Armistead Avenue, Fredericksburg VA 22407 B Albany CA 7/31/1935 d Robert Leroy Mealman & Majorie Florence. BS Geo Mason U 1994; VTS 1996; MDiv CDSP 1997. D 3/26/2000 P 10/28/2000 Bp Jerry Alban Lamb. m 5/22/1982 Thomas Brazell Kempster. Asst R Trin Ch Folsom CA 2001-2005; Asst R Epis Ch Of Our Sav Placerville CA 2000-2001; VTS Alexandria VA 1991-1993; Ch Of The Gd Shpd Burke VA 1988-1991. Natl Cler Assn 2000; Nthrn California Cler Assn 2000. patskemp@inreach.com

KENDALL, Michael Jonah (NC) 403 E Main St, Durham NC 27701 **S Phil's Ch Durham NC 2008-** B Waterbury CT 2/5/1974 s Michael Samuel Kendall & Janet Stewart. BA St. Lawr Canton NY 1996; MDiv GTS 2001. D 3/10/2001 Bp Richard Frank Grein P 9/16/2001 Bp Mark Sean Sisk. m 9/21/2002 Catherine Connelley c 1. All SS Ch Harrison NY 2003-2007; Asst To The R Ch Of The H Trin New York NY 2001-2003. njkendall@optonline.net

KENDALL, Michael Samuel (NY) 1047 Amsterdam Ave, New York NY 10025 B Cincinnati OH 8/9/1940 s Harry C Kendall & Blanche M. BA Earlham Coll 1962; Oxf 1962; Ya 1965; MDiv/STB GTS 1966. D 6/11/1966 Bp Walter H Gray P 12/17/1966 Bp John Henry Esquirol. m 5/25/1985 Anne Davis. Dio New York New York City NY 1994-2008; Diocn Msnry & Ch Extntn Socty New York NY 1984-1994; Dpt Of Missions Ny Income New York NY 1984-1994; R Ch Of S Jas The Less Scarsdale NY 1978-1984; S Jn's Epis Par Waterbury CT 1968-1978. Auth, "Jub Report To Stndg Com Of GC"; Auth, "Trial Baptism Liturg," *Chr Initiation*. EAAM' Cross Epis Asiamerica Ministries 2003; Bp'S Cross Dio New York 2000. amk121@verizon.net

KENDALL-SPERRY, David (SO) St. John Episcopal Church, 700 High St., Worthington OH 43085 **Asst to R S Jn's Ch Worthington OH 2008-** B Iowa 2/14/1955 s G Joe Sperry & Patricia. BA Simpson Coll IA 1977; MDiv Bex 2008. D 6/23/2007 P 6/28/2008 Bp Thomas Edward Breidenthal. m 8/27/1977 Karen Kendall c 3. D S Matt's Ch Westerville OH 2007-2008. BroSA 1989. daveks14@gmail.com

KENDRICK, David Park (Ala) 708 Manor Rd Apt 102, Alexandria VA 22305 **Chr Epis Ch Albertville AL 2009-** B Vero Beach FL 6/10/1961 s Robert Kendrick & Bobbye. BA Wafford Coll 1983; MDiv VTS 2007. D 6/16/2007 Bp Peter James Lee P 12/17/2007 Bp David Colin Jones. m 6/27/1987 Laura M Laura Ruth Moore c 1. The Ch Of The Epiph Oak Hill VA 2008; S Dav's Ch Ashburn VA 2007-2008. davidken27@aol.com

KENDRICK, James Russell (Ala) 3557 Hampshire Drive, Birmingham AL 35223 **R S Steph's Epis Ch Birmingham AL 2007-** B Fort Walton Bch FL 8/2/1960 s Claude James Kendrick & Helen Louise. BA/BS Auburn U 1984; BA Auburn U 1984; MDiv VTS 1995. D 5/27/1995 P 1/28/1996 Bp Charles Farmer Duvall. m 7/11/1987 Robin Rhodes c 2. R S Paul's Epis Ch Newnan

GA 1998-2006; The Epis Ch Of The Nativ Dothan AL 1995-1998. russell@ssechurch.org

KENDRICK, William Barton (NCal) 19 Five Iron Ct, Chico CA 95928 B Saint Louis MO 8/14/1932 s Warren Harold Kendrick & Gertrude Reasor. BS U of Arizona 1954; BD CDSP 1957. D 8/3/1957 P 2/1/1958 Bp William F Lewis. c 3. R S Mich And All Ang Ch Ft Bragg CA 1991-1997; Dio Nthrn California Sacramento CA 1987-1993; H Trin Epis Ch Willows CA 1978-1991; Ch Of The Gd Shpd Orland CA 1978-1983; Ch Of The Incarn Santa Rosa CA 1973-1978; R S Steph's Epis Ch Colusa CA 1965-1973; Vic S Fran Ch Fortuna CA 1960-1965; Vic S Mary's Mssn Ferndale CA 1960-1965; Cur Trin Epis Ch Reno NV 1957-1959. bartsam@comcast.net

KENNA, Jennifer Anne (CNY) 904 Vine St, Liverpool NY 13088 B Pawtucket, RI 4/18/1947 d Henry Penn Krusen & Mildred Saile. BA Syr 1969; Certificate Dioc Formation Prog 2010. D 5/1/2010 P 6/18/2011 Bp Gladstone Bailey Adams III. m 3/4/1972 John Kenna c 3. jkenna@tweny.rr.com

KENNARD, Susan Johnson (Tex) 3000 Ave L, Bay City TX 77414 **R S Mk's Ch Bay City TX 2006-** B Houston TX 5/4/1955 d Joseph Ash Johnson & Joyce. BSN U of Texas 1976; MDiv VTS 2004. D 6/12/2004 P 12/12/2004 Bp Don Adger Wimberly. m 11/18/1977 William Walker Kennard c 1. Asst R S Mk's Ch Beaumont TX 2004-2006. susankennard@sbcglobal.net

KENNEDY, (Arthur) Thomas (Ida) 261 Los Lagos, Twin Falls ID 83301 B Los Angeles,CA 1/22/1926 s Raymond Mc CoRmic Kennedy & Elizabeth June. BA U CA 1950; MDiv CDSP 1970. D 6/27/1970 P 2/6/1971 Bp C Kilmer Myers. Dn of Formation For Mnstry Dio Idaho Boise ID 1991-1997; Dio Idaho Boise ID 1988-1989; S Jn's Epis Ch Amer Falls ID 1982; Pres Mstrl Assn Dio Idaho Boise ID 1981-1985; S Paul's Ch Blackfoot ID 1980-1988; St Augustines Ch Fairfax CA 1976-1980; Asst Min Chr Epis Ch Los Altos CA 1970-1973.

KENNEDY, Dana Forrest (Ct) 299 Wyman Rd, Milbridge ME 04658 B Milbridge ME 11/3/1917 s Chester Alexander Kennedy & Geneva May. BA Husson Coll 1938; BS U of Maine 1941; MDiv EDS 1945. D 11/15/1945 P 5/29/1946 Bp Henry Knox Sherrill. m 4/13/1996 Thelma Russell Small c 1. Structure Com Dio Connecticut Hartford CT 1980-1982; Serv Dio Connecticut Hartford CT 1977-1981; Dn Mid-Fairfield Deanry Dio Connecticut Hartford CT 1976-1980; Stwdshp Trng Dio Connecticut Hartford CT 1976-1977; ExCoun Dio Connecticut Hartford CT 1973-1986; R Chr And H Trin Ch Westport CT 1961-1989; R S Jas Epis Ch At Woonsocket Woonsocket RI 1950-1954; R S Barn And All SS Ch Springfield MA 1947-1950; Cur S Steph's Memi Ch Lynn MA 1945-1947. Auth, *My Very First Golden Bible*, Wstrn Pub Co, Inc., 1991; Auth, *Water Brooks of the Sprt*. Gnrl Soc of Mayflower Descendants 1968; Mason 1940; Rotary 1965; Shrine 1999; Sons of the Amer Revolution 1968. Doctor of Publ Serv Husson Coll 2006. milbridge@msn.com

KENNEDY, David Crichton (SeFla) 7231 Hearth Stone Ave, Boynton Beach FL 33437 **P-in-c The Ch Of The Guardian Ang Lantana FL 2007-** B Floral Park NY 9/29/1937 s Albert Crichton Kennedy & Emma Rose. BA U of Miami 1959; MDiv Nash 1963. D 6/15/1963 Bp James Loughlin Duncan P 12/21/1963 Bp Henry I Louttit. m 5/23/1964 Beverly J Noble c 2. Alum Trst Nash Nashotah WI 1985-1993; Dn of the So Palm Bch Dnry Dio SE Florida Miami FL 1985-1987; R S Cuth's Ch Boynton Bch FL 1969-2003; The Ch Of The Guardian Ang Lantana FL 1966-2003; Cur All SS Epis Ch Lakeland FL 1963-1966. All SS Sis of the Poor P Assoc; CBS; Fllshp of Concerned Churchmen; Forw in Faith; GAS; PB Soc; Shrine of Our Lady of Walsingham; Soc of King Chas the Mtyr; SSC, SocMary. DD Nash Nashotah WI 2002. frdkennedy@aol.com

KENNEDY, David Kittle (Haw) 1 Keahole Place, Apt.3409, Honolulu HI 96825 B Alamosa CO 10/29/1932 s Harry Sherbourne Kennedy & Katharine Jane. BA Trin Hartford CT 1954; MDiv CDSP 1963. D 7/7/1963 P 1/12/1964 Bp Harry S Kennedy. m 11/1/1956 Anna Marie Hemberger c 4. R Trin Ch By The Sea Kihei HI 2007-2008; Asstg P S Andr's Cathd Honolulu HI 2000-2005; Headmaster S Andr's Priory Sch Honolulu HI 1981-1996; R S Tim's Ch Aiea HI 1973-1981. DSC Dio Hawaii 1971. davidk7713@comcast.net

KENNEDY, Ellen Kathleen (Ct) 243 Harbor St, Branford CT 06405 **Vic Trin Epis Ch Trumbull CT 2006-** B Staten Island NY 5/8/1949 D 6/8/2002 P 4/12/2003 Bp Andrew Donnan Smith. m 9/15/1979 John Kennedy c 2. Asst Calv Epis Ch Bridgeport CT 2003-2006. trinitynichols@charter.net

KENNEDY, Gary Grant (Kan) 1900 E Front St, Galena KS 66739 **P S Epis Mary's Ch Inc Galena KS 1999-; P S Steph's Ch Columbus KS 1999-** B Joplin MO 2/22/1940 s Claude Max Kennedy & Catherine Louise. BS Pittsburg St U 1964; MS Pittsburg St U 2003. D 7/20/1999 P 2/15/2000 Bp William Edward Smalley. m 8/6/1960 Carol Rae Means. gcrkennedy@earthlink.net

KENNEDY, Hilda Lee (WVa) Po Box 665, Northfork WV 24868 B Wyoming County WV 1/14/1945 d Ray Mack Baldwin & Eugenia C. BA Concord U 1966; BSW Concord U 1987. D 6/10/2000 Bp C(laude) Charles Vache. Dio W Virginia Charleston WV 2000-2008. hkemh@citlink.net

KENNEDY, Nan (At) 790 Bellhaven Chase Ct, Mableton GA 30126 B Taylor TX 11/24/1953 d William Felix Needham & Virginia Ann. BS U of Texas 1977; MDiv Epis TS of The SW 1992. D 6/13/1992 P 1/16/1993 Bp Robert Manning Moody. m 11/20/1993 Stephen Glen Kennedy. Assoc S Lk's Epis Ch Atlanta GA 2003-2008; All SS Epis Sch Beaumont TX 1998-2002; Assoc R S Steph's Ch Beaumont TX 1998-2001; Holland Hall Sch Tulsa OK 1997-1998; Trin Ch Tulsa OK 1992-1997. kenn7727@bellsouth.net

KENNEDY, Paul Sherbourne (Haw) 691 Kealahou St, Honolulu HI 96825 B Denver CO 7/28/1934 s Harry S Kennedy & Katherine. BA Trin Hartford CT 1957; MDiv CDSP 1963. D 7/7/1963 Bp Harry S Kennedy P 5/1/1964 Bp David Emrys Richards. m 11/15/1963 Rebeca H Hernandez c 3. S Alb's Chap Honolulu HI 1971-2004. papapaul34@mac.com

KENNEDY, Thomas B (Mass) 46 Glen Road, Brookline MA 02445 B New Milford CT 1/11/1942 s Robert George Kennedy & Roberta Marian. BA Claremont (Men's) McKenna Coll 1964; BD EDS 1968. D 6/22/1968 Bp Anson Phelps Stokes Jr P 5/15/1969 Bp John Melville Burgess. m 8/29/1964 Joanna W Warner c 3. Outreach Trin Ch In The City Of Boston Boston MA 2009-2011; P S Paul's Ch Brookline MA 1989-2008; Dn The Cathd Ch Of S Paul Boston MA 1983-1989; Assoc R Trin Ch In The City Of Boston Boston MA 1983-1984; Min in charge Trin Ch In The City Of Boston Boston MA 1981-1982; Min in charge Trin Ch In The City Of Boston Boston MA 1973-1974; Asst Min Trin Ch In The City Of Boston Boston MA 1970-1972; Min to Stdts Trin Ch In The City Of Boston Boston MA 1968-1970. Auth, “Article,” *Jesus Dollars & Sense*. Morris F Arnold Awd, Epis City Mssn. REV.TBK@verizon.net

KENNEDY, Zelda Miller (Los) 2194 Cooley Pl, Pasadena CA 91104 **All SS Ch Pasadena CA 2003-** B Nassau BS 9/1/1947 d Cyril Henry Miller & Mildred Miriam. D 6/4/2000 Bp Robert Carroll Johnson Jr P 4/28/2001 Bp Michael Bruce Curry. S Pat's Mssn Mooresville NC 2000-2003. zkennedy@allsaints-pas.org

KENNEY, Christine Swarts (Okla) 505 Fieldstone Dr, Georgetown TX 78633 B Rushville IN 12/5/1944 BS Butler U 1967; MDiv Epis TS of The SW 2002. D 6/29/2002 P 2/8/2003 Bp Robert Manning Moody. m 6/17/1967 Joseph Kenney c 2. ckenney3@sbcglobal.net

KENNEY, Marguerite (SVa) 800 Little John Ct, Virginia Beach VA 23455 B Cincinnati OH 6/6/1924 d Harvey Jack Shirley & Helen Myrtle. BA U Cinc 1946; MDiv VTS 1977. D 6/25/1977 Bp William Foreman Creighton P 2/27/1978 Bp John Thomas Walker. c 5. Gd Samar Epis Ch Virginia Bch VA 1983-1988; Chr Ch Chaptico MD 1982; S Marg's Ch Woodbridge VA 1980-1981; S Jn's Ch Ft Washington MD 1977-1980. Chapl Ord Of S Lk; Curs.

KENNEY, Nancy Jones (USC) 215 Ascot Dr, Aiken SC 29803 B Columbus OH 4/10/1948 d Charles Prior & Margaret. Regent U Virginia Bch VA; BS U of Tennessee 1970; MDiv TESM 2004. D 11/6/2005 P 5/27/2006 Bp Dorsey Felix Henderson. m 4/22/1976 Patrick J Kenney c 2. S Aug Of Cbury Aiken SC 2005-2008. njk410@hotmail.com

KENNEY, Stacy A (Pgh) 7000 Christopher Wren Dr Apt 314, Wexford PA 15090 B Decatur GA 12/16/1968 d John Joseph Kenney & Wanda White. U of Mississippi 1987; BA Mississippi Coll 2000; MDiv TESM 2007. Trans from Anglican Church Of Kenya 6/15/2007 Bp Robert William Duncan. c 1. skenney@zoominternet.net

KENNINGTON, S(pergeon) (CGC) 1900 Dauphin St, Mobile AL 36606 **Assoc S Paul's Epis Ch Daphne AL 2007-** B Butler AL 9/5/1942 s Spergeon F Kennington & Florence Virginia. BS Troy U-Troy AL 1964; MA U of Alabama 1967; MDiv STUSo 1974. D 6/20/1974 P 5/17/1975 Bp George Mosley Murray. m 12/20/1969 Nancy Butler c 3. S Mary's Epis Ch Milton FL 1977-1983; S Monica's Cantonment FL 1977-1978; Trin Epis Ch Mobile AL 1974-2007. Auth, “Hearing God through the Noise,” Forw Mvmt, 2008; Auth, “From The Day Of Sm Things,” Factor Press, 1996; Auth, “The Epis Ch: A Primer For Inquirers,” Self; Auth, “arts,” *Angl Dig*; Auth, “arts,” *Living Ch*. revsak@gmail.com

KENNY JR, John Roy (Md) 8210 River Crescent Dr, Annapolis MD 21401 **D S Andr's Ch Pasadena MD 1998-; Assoc S Anne's Par Annapolis MD 1998-** B Portland OR 5/8/1922 s John Roy Kenny & Flora Eleanor. BS U CA 1944; SWTS 1972; EFM STUSo 1983. D 9/16/1972 Bp James Winchester Montgomery. m Mary E Glover c 4. Asst S Paul's Epis Ch Bantam CT 1986-1997; Asst S Ann's Epis Ch Old Lyme CT 1978-1986; Asst S Jas' Epis Ch Of Pentwater Pentwater MI 1976-1978; Asst Trin Ch Glen Arm MD 1973-1976; Asst The Epis Ch Of S Jas The Less Northfield IL 1972-1973. jmrk@mindspring.com

KENNY, Susie Fowler (Los) 1020 N. Brand Blvd., Glendale CA 91202 **D S Mk's Par Glendale CA 2008-** B Inglewood CA 2/5/1956 d Luther Herbert Fowler & Gwendolyn S. D 5/25/2008 Bp Chester Lovelle Talton. c 3. deacon@stmarksglendale.org

KENT, Clifford Eugene (NCal) 5555 Montgomery Dr # 62, Santa Rosa CA 95409 **Assoc S Patricks Ch Kenwood CA 1990-; Supply P Dio Nthrn California Sacramento CA 1987-** B Butler County KS 10/11/1920 s Oris Glee

K

Kent & Lucy. BD Pur 1942; Cert Dioc Sch/Mnstrs CA 1980. D 3/25/1982 P 3/19/1984 Bp Charles Shannon Mallory. m 6/24/2006 Virginia Canfield-Kent c 3. Asst P Trin Ch Sonoma CA 1987-1989; Assoc S Andr's Ch Saratoga CA 1982-1986. Auth, "Environ Aspects of Nuclear Power Stations," *ASME Journel*, Int'l Atomic Energy Agcy, 1971; Auth, "Environ Aspects of Nuclear Power Stations," *Intl Atomic Energy Agcy*, 1970. Amer Chem Soc 1943; Amer Inst of Chem Engr 2043-1982. Three USA Patents in High Energy Batteries US Patent Off (1966-1968) 1966. ckent9011@comcast.net

KENT, David Williamson (Kan) 1900 Spyglass Court, Lawrence KS 66047 B Montclair,NJ 6/12/1938 s Frederick Thomas Kent & Helen Jenny. BA U of Wisconsin 1960; MDiv Nash 1963; MEd Bos 1972; MA LIU 1974; Command and Gnrl Stff Coll 1978; US-A War Coll 1984. D 3/9/1963 Bp Robert E Campbell P 9/21/1963 Bp Donald H V Hallock. m 5/8/1965 Orean Harolyn Zeiger c 1. Cn Ordnry Dio Kansas Topeka KS 1992-2002; Asst S Mich And All Ang Ch Mssn KS 1987-1992; Cathd Of St Jn The Div New York NY 1973-1974; Off Of Bsh For ArmdF New York NY 1966-1987; Cur Chr Ch Whitefish Bay WI 1963-1966. CODE 1992; Mltry Chapl Assn 1970; RCMA 1997. Legion of Merit US-A 1987; Phi Beta Kappa 1960. badger@sunflower.com

KENT, Stuart Matthews (Dal) 3216 Lakenheath Pl, Dallas TX 75204 B Westerly RI 6/6/1944 s George L Kent & Edwina M. BA U of Connecticut 1966; STB Ya Berk 1969. D 6/21/1969 P 6/1/1970 Bp John S Higgins. m 6/8/1968 Paula Susuette McNutt. S Dav's Ch Garland TX 2001-2008; S Anne's Epis Ch Desoto TX 1991-1992; St Gabriels Ch De Soto TX 1987-1991; Dio Rhode Island Providence RI 1976; Dio Rhode Island Providence RI 1971-1974; P-in-c S Ptr's And S Andr's Epis Providence RI 1971-1972; Cur S Mary's Ch Portsmouth RI 1969-1971.

KENWORTHY, Stuart Albert (WA) 3116 "O" Street NW, Washington DC 20007 **R Chr Ch Georgetown Washington DC 1991-** B Toledo OH 5/1/1951 s Stuart Albee Kenworthy & Alice Beverly. BD Ohio U 1973; MDiv Bos 1976; DMin Andover Newton TS 1980; GTS 1984. D 6/16/1984 Bp Lyman Cunningham Ogilby P 12/7/1984 Bp Walter Decoster Dennis Jr. m 9/27/1980 Frances P Prescott c 3. Cur S Thos Ch New York NY 1986-1991; Asst Ch Of The Heav Rest New York NY 1984-1986. The Bishops Awd Dio Washington 2007; Iraq Cmpgn Medal US Army 2006; Iraqi Freedom Medal US Army 2006; The Bronze Star Medal US Army 2006; Global War on Terrorism Serv Medal Us Army 2006. stuart@christchurchgeorgetown.org

KENYI, Alex Lodu (ND) 3725 30th St, San Diego CA 92104 **R S Jn's Ch Moorhead MN 2000-** B Juba 11/23/1953 s Ezekiel Keny & Sarah Juan. BA S Paul Untd Theol Coll Limuru Ke 1989; MDiv Nairobi Intl TS Ke 1995. Trans from Church Of England 5/1/1998 Bp Andrew Hedtler Fairfield. m Hellen Juan Simon c 4. Dio No Dakota Fargo ND 2000-2010; Cur S Lk's Ch San Diego CA 1998-2000. Ord Of S Lk.

KENYON, James Howard Benjamin (Alb) 1606 5th St, Rensselaer NY 12144 **Dioc Refugee Coordntr Dio Albany Albany NY 2004-; Asst Gr And H Innoc Albany NY 2002-; Trin Ch Whitehall NY 2001-** B Lake Placid NY 8/11/1925 s Raymond Taylor Kenyon & Hariot Catherine. BA Hob 1947; LTh GTS 1950. D 5/21/1950 P 11/26/1950 Bp Vedder Van Dyck. m 9/28/1957 Grace Leslie. Chr & S Barn Troy NY 1998-2002; Dioc Refugee Coordntr Dio Albany Albany NY 1998-2002; Dioc Refugee Coordntr Dio Albany Albany NY 1989-1997; Dio Albany Albany NY 1981-1988; R S Barth's Ch Brooklyn NY 1980-1988; R S Alb's Ch Superior WI 1979-1980; P-in-c S Mich And All Ang Epis Ch Charlotte NC 1968-1979; Dio No Carolina Raleigh NC 1968-1976; Vic S Ptr's Ch Mt Arlington NJ 1966-1968; P-in-c Chr Epis Ch E Orange NJ 1954-1966; Vic S Jn The Bapt Epis Hardwick VT 1951-1952; S Jn's In The Mountains Stowe VT 1951-1952; Chr Ch Montpelier VT 1950-1951. "(autobiography)," *The Time of My Life*, Troy Bookmakers. DeWitt Clinton Masonic Awd 1995. jhbkp@aol.com

KEOUGH, Christopher John (Mil) 313 Lakeview Drive Apt 2, Hartland WI 53029 B Fort Wayne IN 10/29/1962 s Robert Joseph Keough & Sarah Louise. AA U of Wisconsin 1988; BA U of Wisconsin 1990; MDiv Nash 1993; DMin SWTS 2002. D 5/29/1993 P 11/27/1993 Bp Roger John White. m 10/6/1984 Dawn Marie Miller c 1. St Mths Epis Ch Waukesha WI 2003-2004; R S Barth's Ch Pewaukee WI 1995-2003; Dio Milwaukee Milwaukee WI 1993-1995; Assoc R S Jn Ch/Mision San Juan Milwaukee WI 1993-1995; Assoc R St Mths Epis Ch Waukesha WI 1993-1995. "A Theol Of Evang For The Epis Ch," Dio Milwaukee, 2002. Franciscan 3rd Ord Div Compassion. fr.chris@juno.com

KEPHART, Arthur Keith D'Arcy (FdL) 228 N. Union St., Appleton WI 54911 **Cn S Paul's Cathd Fond du Lac WI 2003-** B Des Moines IA 12/13/1929 s Arthur Milton Kephart & Letha. BFA Drake U 1956; MDiv Nash 1959. D 12/6/1958 P 6/6/1959 Bp Donald H V Hallock. Dn Winnebago Deanry Dio Fond du Lac Appleton WI 1992-1994; R All SS Epis Ch Appleton WI 1981-1994; COM Dio Fond du Lac Appleton WI 1981-1994; COM Dio Milwaukee Milwaukee WI 1977-1981; Dn NW Deanry Dio Milwaukee Milwaukee WI 1973-1979; Trin Ch Baraboo WI 1962-1981; Mus Cmsn Dio Milwaukee Milwaukee WI 1962-1967; Asst Trin Ch Wauwatosa WI 1959-1961; Asst S Andr's Ch Madison WI 1958-1959. SHN 1981. Cn St. Paul's Cathd Found Dulac, WI 2003. keppie@vbe.com

KEPLINGER, Stephen James (Az) 2331 E Adams St, Tucson AZ 85719 **Gr S Paul's Epis Ch Tucson AZ 2010-** B Baltimore MD 8/7/1953 s William Stephen Keplinger & Elizabeth Ann. MDiv CDSP 2001. D 1/18/2001 P 8/4/2001 Bp Carolyn Tanner Irish. m 9/6/1986 Jean Miller. Dio Utah Salt Lake City UT 2001-2010; R S Dav's Epis Page AZ 2001-2010. "TheComeback Kids," *Bk*, Pub's Place, 1989. Polly Bond Awd ECom 2004. rector@gracestpauls.org

KEPPELER, Lisa Leialoha (Pa) 124 S Main Street, Coopersburg PA 18036 **R Emm Ch Quakertown PA 2007-** B Hoolehua HI 5/8/1956 d Richard Keppeler & Gail. BA Lewis & Clark Coll 1978; MDiv GTS 1989; Cert Dio New York Int Mnstry Trng Prog New Yo 2001. D 5/6/1989 P 11/10/1989 Bp David Bell Birney IV. c 2. Gr Epis Ch Monroe NY 2006-2007; P-in-c S Lk's Ch Katonah NY 2001-2004; Sabbatical Pstr S Pauls On The Hill Epis Ch Ossining NY 2001; EFM Coordntr Dio New York New York City NY 2000-2004; Dio New York New York City NY 2000-2001; Diac Formation Bd Dio New York New York City NY 1994-1999; Ch Of The H Comm Mahopac NY 1994-1998; Com Elect Bp Dio New York New York City NY 1994-1996; Asst S Mary's Ch Mohegan Lake NY 1992-1994; Asst S Mk's Ch Mt Kisco NY 1989-1992. lisakkahuna@aol.com

KEPPLER, Mitchell M (Tex) 142 O K Rd, Smithville TX 78957 B New York NY 10/18/1924 BS Trin U 1949; MDiv Epis TS of The SW 1956. D 6/26/1956 Bp John E Hines P 6/1/1957 Bp Frederick P Goddard. m 12/19/1948 Daisy Moravits. H Innoc' Epis Ch Madisonville TX 1987-1989; Dio Texas Houston TX 1980; Ch Of The Resurr Houston TX 1966-1970; Liturg Cmsn Dio Texas Houston TX 1966-1970; St Lukes Ch Katy TX 1963-1980; R S Paul's Ch Navasota TX 1959-1963; Vic S Mary's Epis Ch Cypress TX 1956-1959. Amer Correctional Assn 80-95; Amer Prot Correctional Chapl Assn 1980-1995; Intl Conf Of Police Chapl 1977-1980. keppmida@aol.com

KEPPY, Susan C (WNY) 419 Cherry Ln, Lewiston NY 14092 B Toledo OH 8/11/1953 d Clyde Harrison Cox & Helen Jewell. BS U Cinc 1976; MDiv GTS 1981. D 6/27/1981 Bp John Harris Burt P 2/4/1982 Bp William Davidson. m 1/27/1996 John Keppy. R S Paul's Epis Ch Lewiston NY 1993-2011; Assoc R Trin Epis Ch Buffalo NY 1986-1993; Cur S Dav's Ch Wayne PA 1981-1986. Intl Critical Incident Stress Fndt 2002; Intl Dio Police Chapl 2000. sckeppy@verizon.net

KERBEL, Carol Anne (NJ) 232 Camino De La Sierra, Santa Fe NM 87501 B Waco TX 12/27/1940 d Dee Robert Foster & Anna Doris. BA Texas Tech U 1963; MDiv GTS 1981. D 9/13/1980 Bp Albert Wiencke Van Duzer. m 6/8/1962 Waldemar Kent c 3. Asst Trin Ch Princeton NJ 1992-2001; Nassau Presb Ch Princeton NJ 1983-1992; Epis Urban Wk Com New Brunswick NJ 1981-1983; Chr Ch New Brunswick NJ 1980-1981. NAAD (Past Pres).

KERBEL, Walter Jarrett (Pa) 1418 E 57th St, Chicago IL 60637 **Ch Of S Mart-In-The-Fields Philadelphia PA 2011-** B Fort Worth TX 10/7/1966 s Waldemar Kent Kerbel & Carol Anne. BA NWU 1989; U Chi 1990; MDiv UTS 1992; GTS 1994. D 6/11/1994 Bp Richard Frank Grein P 2/1/1995 Bp Charlie Fuller McNutt Jr. m 10/9/1993 Alison Leslie Boden c 2. Crisis Mnstry of Princeton and Trenton Trenton NJ 2008-2011; S Mary's Ch Pk Ridge IL 2003-2007; Assoc R Ch Of S Paul And The Redeem Chicago IL 1999-2003; Assoc R The Ch Of S Jn The Evang Flossmoor IL 1995-1999; S Edm's Epis Ch Chicago IL 1995-1996; D Intern Chr Memi Epis Ch Danville PA 1994-2002. OHC. jkerbel@stmartinec.org

KERN, David Paul (Nwk) Po Box 1703, North Eastham MA 02651 B Brooklyn NY 9/18/1928 s Samuel Kern & Sabina. BS NYU 1952; MDiv Ya Berk 1956; MA NYU 1966. D 6/3/1956 P 12/1/1956 Bp Horace W B Donegan. m 12/20/1954 Elenor M Tete c 4. Meadowlands Mnstrs Rutherford NJ 1983-1992; Ch Of Our Sav Secaucus NJ 1980-1992; The Gunnery Washington CT 1969-1980; R Ch Of The Div Love Montrose NY 1957-1961; Asst Min S Andr's Ch Beacon NY 1956-1957. Auth, "The Indep Sch Bulletin". Phi Delta Kappa U Ct Chapt.

KERN, Karl Lee (Be) 182 Gable Dr/, Myerstown PA 17067 **R S Alb's Epis Ch Reading PA 2001-** B Lebanon PA 9/5/1949 s Lester Paul Kern & Doris Mae. FBI Natl Acad 1978; AA Harrisburg Cmnty Coll 1978; BS York Coll 1989; MDiv GTS 1994. D 4/23/1994 P 11/27/1994 Bp James Michael Mark Dyer. m 8/10/2002 Karen Cassamassa c 1. Commonwealth Of Pennsylvania Lebanon PA 1997-2001; R S Jas Ch Schuylkill Haven PA 1997-2001; Chr Ch Reading PA 1994-1997. fatherfrog61@comcast.net

KERN, Roy Allen (CPa) 613 Eschol Ridge Rd, Elliottsburg PA 17024 **D S Jn's Epis Ch Carlisle PA 2003-** B Carlisle PA 5/5/1958 D 6/8/2002 Bp Michael Whittington Creighton. m 6/24/1989 Karen Ann Lightner c 2. rak6802@yahoo.com

KERNER, Robert J(oseph) (SVa) Po Box 98, Bracey VA 23919 B Erie PA 1/9/1942 s Jack Joseph Kerner & Bertha Catherine. BA Gannon U 1964; MDiv S Mary Sem & U 1971. Rec from Roman Catholic 12/9/1990 Bp Frank Stanley Cerveny. m 8/22/1980 Sandra B Barbary. R S Andr's Lawrenceville VA 2003-2009; R Epis Ch Of Our Sav Midlothian VA 1998-2003; R S Andr's

K

Epis Ch Douglas GA 1994-1997; Int Ch Of The Epiph Jacksonville FL 1991-1992; Assoc S Ptr's Ch Jacksonville FL 1990-1991. Auth, "The Fr's Blessing," *The HeaLingLine Nwsltr, Sharing mag, New Cov mag*, 1993; Auth, *sev mag Articless*. Ord of S Lk the Physcn 1998. ecos3@juno.com

KERNER, Sandra B (SVa) 405 W Church St, Lawrenceville VA 23868 **R S Lk's Ch Powhatan VA 2011-; Supply P Trin Ch So Hill VA 2007-** B Pittsburgh PA 12/28/1956 d Austin John Barbary & Aurletta A. BS Penn 1978; MDiv UTS Richmond VA 2005; CAS VTS 2005. D 6/4/2005 P 12/3/2005 Bp David Conner Bane Jr. m 8/22/1980 Robert J(oseph) Kerner. Chair, COM: Dioc Formation Dio Sthrn Virginia Norfolk VA 2008-2010; Dn, Convoc VIII Dio Sthrn Virginia Norfolk VA 2007-2010; R S Lk's Ch Blackstone VA 2005-2011; D Trin Ch So Hill VA 2005-2007. Fllshp of Chr the Healer USA; Co-Fndr and Mem 2004; OSL the Physcn 1998. bskerner@aol.com

KERR, Denniston Rupert (SwFla) 5609 N Albany Ave, Tampa FL 33603 B Hanover JM 11/22/1939 s Hartford Alexander Kerr & Sarah Ann. Coll Arts Sci & Tech 1960; Wilson Carlyle Trng Coll 1965; Untd Theol Coll Of The W Indies Kingston Jm 1979. Rec 10/1/1992 as Deacon Bp Rogers Sanders Harris. m 7/23/1966 Clarissa Henry c 1. S Jas Hse Of Pryr Tampa FL 1995-1997; St Jas Ch Tampa FL 1992-2008. cgdkerr@aol.com

KERR, Kyra Anne (RG) P.O. Box 188, Tesuque NM 87574 B Houston TX 7/27/1939 D 6/21/2003 Bp Terence Kelshaw.

KERR, Lauri (CPa) 1435 Scott St, Williamsport PA 17701 **P Gleam Williamsport PA 2009-** B Wellsboro PA 6/2/1970 d Thomas Lane Kerr & Deborah Ann. MDiv VTS; BS Mansfield U of Pennsylvania 1995. D 6/8/2001 P 12/12/2001 Bp Michael Whittington Creighton. P S Paul's Ch Manheim PA 2001-2004. laurikerr@hotmail.com

KERR, Linda L (Pa) 1603 Yardley Commons, Yardley PA 19067 **P-in-c Ch Of The Incarn Morrisville PA 2011-; P-in-c Ch Of The Incarn Morrisville PA 2011-** B Bryn Mawr PA 7/22/1950 d David Alexander Kerr & Ruth Bertha. BA Wm Smith 1972; MA Wheaton Coll 1978; MDiv Yale DS 1985. D 6/21/1986 Bp Lyman Cunningham Ogilby P 5/9/1987 Bp Allen Lyman Bartlett Jr. Chapl CFS The Sch At Ch Farm Exton PA 2011; R S Mart's Ch Radnor PA 2006-2011; Assoc The Ch Of The Redeem Baltimore MD 2000-2005; Chapl S Andew's Sch Boca Raton FL 1991-2000; Asst S Fran-In-The-Fields Malvern PA 1986-1987. Auth, *A Mod Mssy*. revlkerr@comcast.net

KERR, Richard Samuel (Cal) 442 34th Ave, San Francisco CA 94121 B Denver CO 6/25/1938 s John Nisewonger Kerr & Katherine Cornelia. BA Ken 1960; STB GTS 1963. D 6/20/1963 P 2/1/1964 Bp Chandler W Sterling. c 2. Dir of Homeless Prog Trin Ch San Francisco CA 1981-1982; Spalding Rehab Cntr Denver CO 1979; R Ch Of The H Redeem Denver CO 1970-1979; Cur S Thos Epis Ch Denver CO 1968-1970; R The Pintler Cluster of the Epis Ch Deer Lodge MT 1964-1966; Cur Ch Of The H Sprt Missoula MT 1963-1964.

KERR, Robert Anthony (Mich) 23851 Goddard Rd, Taylor MI 48180 **R S Jn's Ch Westland MI 2009-** B Belleville MI 7/6/1963 s Robert Kerr & Helen. B.A. Concordia U 1987; M.A. Estrn Michigan U 1990; Psy.S. The Cntr for Humanistic Stds 1992; Ph.D. The Un Inst and U 1997; M.A. Ashland TS 2002. D 11/18/2004 P 3/18/2005 Bp Wendell Nathaniel Gibbs Jr. Dir of Pstr Care Cbury on the Lake Waterford MI 2007-2009; Commision on Mnstry Dio Michigan Detroit MI 2005-2011; P S Martha's Ch Detroit MI 2005-2007. Auth, "A Psychodynamic Revs of "Stranger at the Gate,"" *Journ of Psychol and Chrsnty*, Chr Assn of Psychol Stds, 1996. GAS 1995; SocMary 1995. Bd Cert Diplomate in Psych Amer Psych Assn 2009. bobbyak_2000@yahoo.com

KERR, Sarah Elizabeth (Tenn) St. George's Episcopal Church, 4715 Harding Rd, Nashville TN 32705 **Assoc R S Geo's Ch Nashville TN 2010-** B Portland ME 12/22/1981 d Scott S Kerr & Meredith Thompson. BA Wheaton Coll 2004; MDiv Duke DS 2008. D 6/6/2009 P 1/15/2010 Bp Dabney Tyler Smith. Asst S Thos' Epis Ch St Petersburg FL 2009-2010. sekerr@gmail.com

KERR JR, Thomas Albert (Del) 111 Canterbury Dr, Wilmington DE 19803 **Ret Dio Delaware Wilmington DE 2002-; Dio New Jersey Trenton NJ 2002-; Dio New Jersey Trenton NJ 2002-** B New York NY 2/5/1938 s Thomas Albert Kerr & Jean. AB Pr 1959; STB GTS 1962. D 4/28/1962 P 10/27/1962 Bp Alfred L Banyard. m 7/24/1965 Janet Spence c 3. R Imm Ch Highlands Wilmington DE 1995-2002; Cn Pstr Cathd Ch Of S Jn Wilmington DE 1985-1995; R Gr Epis Ch Plainfield NJ 1982-1985; Epis Chapl, Rutgers U The Wm Alexander Procter Fndt Trenton NJ 1972-1982; R S Jn's Epis Ch Little Silver NJ 1968-1972; Vic, Ch of Our Sav, Cheesequake NJ Dio New Jersey Trenton NJ 1965-1968; Cur Gr Ch Merchantville NJ 1962-1965. Fell Coll of Preachers 1971. takerrjr@verizon.net

KERR, W(illiam) Verdery (NC) Po Box 6124, Charlotte NC 28207 **Sr Assoc Chr Ch Charlotte NC 1999-** B Fayetteville NC 3/13/1949 s Douglas Hendrie Kerr & Stuart. BA U NC 1972; MDiv VTS 1976. D 6/26/1976 Bp Hunley Agee Elebash P 1/27/1977 Bp Arthur Anton Vogel. m 8/4/1973 Mary Ann O Kerr c 2. R S Thos' Epis Ch Sioux City IA 1992-1999; Chair Stwdshp Com Dio No Carolina Raleigh NC 1990-1991; Chair Hunger Com Dio No Carolina Raleigh NC 1986-1990; R S Thos Epis Ch Reidsville NC 1983-1991; Asst S Steph's Ch Durham NC 1979-1983; Assoc S Paul's Ch Kansas City MO 1976-1979. vmebkerr@aol.com

KERRICK, Michael W (NCal) 2612 Colin Rd, Placerville CA 95667 **Int Trin Ch Folsom CA 2011-** B Santa Cruz CA 1/29/1948 s William Bertram Kerrick & Irma Mason. AA Amer River Coll 1972; BA Csus Sacremento CA 1974; Cert Csus Sacramento 1982; MDiv CDSP 2007. D 6/2/2007 P 1/26/2008 Bp Barry Leigh Beisner. m 6/9/1968 Judy S Kerrick c 1. Asst R Trin Ch Sutter Creek CA 2007-2008. mkerrick@sbcglobal.net

KERSCHEN, Charles Thomas (WK) 520 East Ave S, Lyons KS 67554 **S Mk's Ch Lyons KS 2008-** B Modesto CA 11/11/1957 s James John Kerschen & Mary Sylvia. BA Dominican Sch of Philos & Theol 1997; MAMM Franciscan TS 1999. D 9/1/2007 P 3/15/2008 Bp James Marshall Adams Jr. m 12/28/1999 Karen J Karen Laws c 2. kerschenc@hughes.net

KERSHAW, Thomas Martin (Mass) 71 Norfolk St Apt 1, Hampstead NH 03841 B Fall River MA 11/24/1933 s George Henry Kershaw & Josephine Ashworth. BS NEU 1959; MDiv EDS 1963. D 6/15/1963 P 3/7/1964 Bp Frederick J Warnecke. m 10/29/1992 Joyce Johnstone c 3. Par P S Andr's Ch Methuen MA 1995-1999; Ch Hsng Foxfield Consult Wolfeboro NH 1986-1989; Exec Off Ord Of St Anne Arlington MA 1980-1985; P The Cathd Ch Of S Paul Boston MA 1979-1980; Dio Massachusetts Boston MA 1976-1980; Fin Off Dio Massachusetts Boston MA 1973-1974; Headmaster The Germaine Lawr Sch Arlington Heigts MA 1965-1973; Asst R The Epis Ch Of The Medtr Allentown PA 1963-1965. Hon DD Trin Philippines 1972. tmkershaw@comcast.net

KESHGEGIAN, Flora A. (Pa) 2451 Ridge Rd, Berkeley CA 94709 **CDSP Berkeley CA 2010-** B Brooklyn NY 2/22/1950 d Charles Keshgegian & Asdghig. BA U of Pennsylvania 1969; MDiv PDS 1974; Fllshp EDS 1978; PhD Boston Coll 1992. D 6/15/1974 P 1/29/1977 Bp Lyman Cunningham Ogilby. Asst Prof Systematic Theol Epis TS Of The SW Austin TX 1999-2005; Int Par Of S Paul Newton Highlands MA 1982; Calv Ch Danvers MA 1981; Dio Pennsylvania Philadelphia PA 1974-1978. Auth, "God Reflected: Metaphors for Life," Fortress Press, 2008; Auth, "Time for Hope: Practices for Living in Today's Wrld," Continuum Pub Grp, 2006; Auth, "Finding a Place Past NIght: Armenian Genocidal Memory in Diaspora," *Rel, Violence, Memory, and Place*, Indiana U Press, 2006; Auth, "Coming to Terms: Exploring the Dynamics of Our Differences," *ATR. Vol. 86*, 2004; Auth, "Witnessing Trauma: Dorothee Soelle's Theol of Suffering in a Wrld of Victimization," *The Theol of Dorothee Soelle*, Trin Press Intl , 2003; Auth, "Defining Testimoies: Narrative Remembrances by Armenian Survivors of Genocide," *Proteus: A Journ of Ideas, Vol, 19*, 2002; Auth, "Redeeming Memories: A Theol of Healing and Transformation," Abingdon Press, 2000; Auth, "The Scandal of the Cross: Anselm and His Feminist Critics," *Angl Theol Revs, Vol. 82*, 2000; Auth, "Power to Wound, Power to Mend: Toward a Non-Abusing Theol," *Journ of Rel and Abuse*, 1999. AAR 1985; Authors Gld 2006. Trin Prize Trin Press Intl Fndt 2005; Fllshp Roothbert Fund 1983; Fllshp ECF 1980. fkeshgegian@alumni.upenn.edu

KESLER, Walter Wilson (FtW) 3937 Anewby Way, Fort Worth TX 76133 B Exeter NH 2/19/1942 s Robert Wilson Kesler & Ellen Shaw. BS USNA 1964; MDiv VTS 1979. D 5/24/1979 P 12/5/1979 Bp Philip Alan Smith. c 3. Int S Alb's Epis Ch Arlington TX 2009-2010; Assoc Trin Epis Ch Ft Worth TX 2000-2004; Headmaster Trin Vlly Sch Ft Worth TX 1994-2000; Asst. Headmaster The Holderness Sch Plymouth NH 1979-1994; Vic Trin Ch Meredith NH 1979-1994. keslerw@juno.com

KESSEL-HANNA, Kay Lynn (Oly) 11527 9th Ave NE, Seattle WA 98125 **D S Andr's Ch Seattle WA 2009-** B Blue Earth, MN 12/17/1953 d Ray D Kessel & Doris M. BS Applied Art U of Wisconsin 1978; MA Applied Behavioral Sci Bastyr U 1996; MA Transforming Sprtlty Seattle U TS & Mnstry 2010. D 10/17/2009 Bp Gregory Harold Rickel. m 12/20/1981 Gerald Benson Hanna c 2. kaykhanna@comcast.net

KESSELUS, Ken (Tex) 1301 Church St., Bastrop TX 78602 B Bastrop TX 7/25/1947 s William Richard Kesselus & Kathryn. BA U of Texas 1969; MDiv Epis TS of The SW 1972; Coll of Preachers 1979; Fllshp Epis TS of The SW 1991. D 6/25/1972 Bp Scott Field Bailey P 6/21/1973 Bp J Milton Richardson. m 6/14/1969 Antoinette Bonelli c 2. P-in-c S Chris's Epis Ch Austin TX 2003-2006; R S Paul's Ch Waco TX 2000-2003; Stndg Com Dio Texas Houston TX 1998-2000; Exec Bd Dio Texas Houston TX 1995-1997; Dept Evang Dio Texas Houston TX 1987-1990; Chair Dispatch Bus. Dio Texas Houston TX 1986-2003; Alum Strng Com Epis TS Of The SW Austin TX 1983-1985; R Calv Epis Ch Bastrop TX 1981-2000; Strng Com Epis TS Of The SW Austin TX 1973-1975; Vic/ R S Andr's Epis Ch Pearland TX 1972-1981. Auth, "Jn E Hines: Granite On Fire," Sem of the SW, 1995. Distinguish Alum Awd Sem of the SW 1997; Texas Rural Min Of The Year TX A & M Ext Serv 1991. kesselus@juno.com

KESSLER, Dexter Williamson (SeFla) 4885 Sw Honey Ter, Palm City FL 34990 B West Palm Beach FL 4/14/1943 s Frederick Williamson Kessler & Isabel Fisk. Pres Coll; BA U of W Florida 1971; MDiv VTS 1986. D 6/5/1986 P 12/1/1986 Bp Calvin Onderdonk Schofield Jr. m 11/17/2007 Pamela Miller. R Epis Ch Of The Adv Palm City FL 1988-2008; Asst S Greg's Ch Boca Raton FL 1986-1988. friar1@bellsouth.net

KESSLER, Edward Scharps (Pa) 44 Hinde Street, Sheffield S4 8HJ Great Britain (UK) B Newark NJ 6/10/1926 s Samuel Isadore Kessler & Hortense. BA Pr 1947; MA Chicago Chicago IL 1951; DIT S Chad Coll Gb 1966. D 9/1/1966 Bp The Bishop Of Jarrow P. m 2/17/1955 Elizabeth Allen Goldsmith. Auth, "Practical Chr Radicalism"; Auth, "A Jubilee & Disciples".

KESSLER, Judith Maier (CNY) 17 Elizabeth St, Binghamton NY 13901 **Asstg Cler S Mk's Epis Ch Chenango Bridge NY 2000-** B Syracuse NY 9/1/1939 d Frederick Capron Maier & Charlotte Lucile. BA Buc 1961; Bex 1993. D 6/8/1985 P 5/1/1986 Bp O'Kelley Whitaker. m 8/5/1961 Brian Richard Kessler c 2. Supply P Zion Ch Windsor NY 1989-1994; Asst S Mk's Epis Ch Chenango Bridge NY 1985-1989. judy1@stny.rr.com

KESTER, Martha Ruth (Ia) 1916 Merklin Way, Des Moines IA 50310 **R S Lk's Ch Des Moines IA 2011-; COM Dio Iowa Des Moines IA 2009-** B Englewood NJ 11/16/1967 d Lee Kester & Patricia. BA F&M Lancaster PA 1990; MDiv TESM 2006. D 5/27/2006 Bp John Wadsworth Howe P 12/2/2006 Bp Alan Scarfe. Dioc Conv Registration Chair Dio Iowa Des Moines IA 2011; Pension Fund Mltry New York NY 2010-2011; Spec Mobilization Spprt Plan Washington DC 2010; Asst S Lk's Ch Des Moines IA 2006-2010. mkester9@gmail.com

KETCHAM, William Lowerre (NwT) PO Box 4996, Odessa TX 79760 **Died 10/29/2009** B Bayshore NY 12/11/1930 s Edward Ketcham & Gertrude. MDiv Ya Berk 1955; MA U of No Texas 1975; LHD Sangreal Fndt 1976; BA Stetson U 1982. D 4/16/1955 P 11/5/1955 Bp James P De Wolfe. c 5. boss05030@aol.com

KETTLEWELL, Charles G (Ark) 13456 Victory Gallop Way, Gainesville VA 20155 **P-in-c Meade Memi Par White Post VA 2008-** B Muskingum County OH 6/25/1939 s Samuel Franklin Kettlewell & Emma. CDSP; BA Muskingum Coll 1961; MDiv VTS 1970. D 6/29/1970 P 4/1/1971 Bp David Shepherd Rose. m 9/9/1960 Gail Biery c 3. Int S Ptr's Epis Ch Washington NC 2006-2007; Int S Lukes Ch Ch Hill MD 2005-2006; Int Chr Epis Ch Great Choptank Par Cambridge MD 2003-2005; Int S Phil's Epis Ch Rochester MI 2001-2003; Int S Paul's Ch Naples FL 2000-2001; Int Trsfg Epis Ch Indn River MI 1998-2000; P-in-c Ch Of The Gd Shpd Bluemont VA 1991-1998; R S Jn's Ch Camden AR 1983-1990; Vic S Jas Epis Ch Portsmouth VA 1981-1983; Vic S Mk's Ch Suffolk VA 1978-1980; Dio Sthrn Virginia Norfolk VA 1978; Vic Emm Epis Ch Portsmouth VA 1970-1983. ckwell@aol.com

KETTLEWELL, John Michael (Alb) 110 Monument Dr, Schuylerville NY 12871 **S Steph's Ch Schuylerville NY 2004-** B Chicago IL 7/27/1930 s John Kettlewall & Audrey Genevieve. BA Harv 1952; STB GTS 1955; MA U of Virginia 1969. D 6/18/1955 Bp Charles L Street P 12/15/1955 Bp Horace W B Donegan. m 5/23/1992 Susan Anne Cosby c 2. Gr Ch Stanardsville VA 1969-1990; Blue Ridge Sch Dyke VA 1965-1990; R S Mk's Ch Geneva IL 1960-1965; Asst Ch Of Beth Saratoga Sprg NY 1957-1960; Cur Par of Trin Ch New York NY 1956-1957. Auth, *Issues In Philos and Rel*, 1999; Auth, "Truth, Beauty," *Goodness & Committment*, 1983. kettlewelljohn@hotmail.com

KETTLEWELL, Paula Swaebe (Va) 705 Wilder Dr, Charlottesville VA 22901 B Boston MA 10/6/1934 d Henry Swaebe & Pauline Aloa. U of Virginia; Wheaton Coll; Ya; BA NWU 1956. D 6/14/1980 Bp Arnold M Lewis P 5/1/1981 Bp Robert Bruce Hall. c 2. Assoc R S Paul's Memi Charlottesville VA 1986-2003; Assoc R S Paul's Memi Charlottesville VA 1982-1985. Auth, "Hist Of S Paul Memi Ch". pktlwl@earthlink.net

KEUCHER, Gerald Werner Otto (NY) 1 Pendleton Pl, Staten Island NY 10301 **P-in-c S Mary's Ch Brooklyn NY 2010-** B New Haven CT 8/22/1952 s Werner Gerald Keucher & Martha Elizabeth. BA Indiana U 1973; MA Indiana U 1975; MDiv PrTS 1993; STM Ya Berk 1994. D 1/15/1994 Bp Walter Decoster Dennis Jr P 7/30/1994 Bp E(gbert) Don Taylor. m 7/18/2003 John Howard Walsted. Vic Ch Of The Intsn New York NY 2006-2009; Dep to GC Dio New York New York City NY 2003-2006; Dio New York New York City NY 1995-2009; Cur S Jn's Ch Getty Sq Yonkers NY 1994-1995. Auth, "Humble and Strong," Ch Pub Grp, 2010; Auth, "Remember the Future," Ch Pub Grp, 2006. Phi Beta Kappa Indiana U 1972. jerrykeucher@gmail.com

KEVERN, John Robert (WVa) C/O Trinity Epis Church, PO Box P, Moundsville WV 26041 **S Paul's Within the Walls Rome 00184 IT 2011-** B Dixon IL 10/8/1953 s Walter Lee Kevern & Esther May. Diplome Superieur U of Paris IV 1974; BA U IL 1975; MDiv GTS 1980; PhD U Chi 1996. D 6/14/1980 Bp Quintin Ebenezer Primo Jr P 12/1/1980 Bp James Winchester Montgomery. Prof Bex Columbus OH 1992-2010; S Bon Ch Tinley Pk IL 1990-1992; S Raphael The Archangel Oak Lawn IL 1989; S Fran Epis Ch Chicago IL 1988-1989; Vic S Fran Epis Ch Chicago IL 1986-1988; Cathd Of S Jas Chicago IL 1985; Dio Chicago Chicago IL 1983-1984; Cur S Chris's Epis Ch Oak Pk IL 1980-1982. Auth, "The Trin and Soc Justice," *ATR*, 1997; Auth, "Ecclesiology of the Concordat," *The Angl*, 1996; Auth, "A Future for Angl Cath Theol," *Angl Theoligical Revs*, 1994; Auth, "Form inTragedy: Balthasar as Correlational Theol," *Communio*, 1994. Affirming Catholicism 1998; AAR 1988; ATR 2001. DD The GTS 2004; Fell ECF. jkevern@earthlink.net

KEW, W(illiam) Richard (Tenn) 41 Way Lane, Waterbeach CAMBRIDGE CB25 9NQ Great Britain (UK) **Ridley Hall Cambridge 2009-** B Luton Bedfordshire England 8/28/1945 s William Reginald Kew & Brenda Ennels. LTh London Coll Div Gb 1968; BD Lon 1969. Trans from Church Of England 10/1/1977 Bp John Bowen Coburn. m 7/20/1968 Rosemary Anne Errington. The Epis Ch Of The Resurr Franklin TN 2006-2007; Mem, Bp and Coun Dio Tennessee Nashville TN 2004-2007; Mem, Episcopate Com Dio Tennessee Nashville TN 2004-2006; Ch Of The Apos Nashville TN 2003-2006; Trst, Dandridge Trust Dio Tennessee Nashville TN 2001-2004; Us Angilcan Congr Nashville TN 2000-2002; Mem, 20/20 Taskforce Dom And Frgn Mssy Soc-Epis Ch Cntr New York NY 2000-2001; Mem, COM Dio Tennessee Nashville TN 1997-2004; AFP Orlando FL 1996-1998; Russian Mnstry Ntwk Murfreesboro TN 1995-1999; Spck/Usa Sewanee TN 1985-1995; R All SS Angl Ch Rochester NY 1979-1985; Chr Ch So Hamilton MA 1977-1979; Trst SAMS Ambridge PA 1976-1985. Auth, "Brave New Ch," Morehouse, 2001; Auth, "Toward 2015: A Ch Odyssey," Cowley, 1997; Auth, "Vision Bearers," Morehouse, 1996; Auth, "Venturing Into The New Millennium," Latimer, 1994; Auth, "Starting Over," Abingdon, 1994; Auth, "New Millennium," *New Ch*, Cowley, 1992; Auth, "No Foothold in the Swamp," Zondervan, 1988. Cmnty Of Mary 1986; Wrld Future Soc 1985. Lifetime Trst SAMS 1996. richardkew@aol.com

KEY, Sanford Allen (NY) St. Luke's Church, POB 94, Somers NY 10589 **R S Lk's Ch Somers NY 2007-** B Beaufort SC 8/2/1968 s Jimmy Ray Key & Cheryl Suzanne. BA Cit 1990; MDiv STUSo 1997. D 6/21/1997 P 6/20/1998 Bp Robert Carroll Johnson Jr. m 1/9/1993 Laura Lynn Shumpert c 2. Coll Chapl Bruton Par Williamsburg VA 2001-2007; Cur & Chapl Cathd Of S Lk And S Paul Charleston SC 1998-2001; D Chr Ch Charlotte NC 1997-1998. Auth, *DOCC 16/20*, Sewanee, Univ. of the So, 1999. sakey90@gmail.com

KEYDEL JR, John F (Ct) 20410 Ronsdale Dr, Beverly Hills MI 48025 **Ch Of The Trsfg Palos Pk IL 2010-** B Detroit MI 6/6/1954 s John F Keydel & Jane P. BA Hampshire Coll 1976; MEd Bos 1977; MBA U of Connecticut 1985; MDiv Ya Berk 1995; CAGS SWTS 2003; ABT Adizes Grad Sch 2010. D 6/10/1995 Bp Clarence Nicholas Coleridge P 2/3/1996 Bp R(aymond) Stewart Wood Jr. m 7/24/1976 Margaret Jean Zwick c 2. S Jame's Ch Skaneateles NY 2009-2010; Dio Michigan Detroit MI 1998-2009; R Nativ Epis Ch Bloomfield Township MI 1998-2000; Asst to R S Jas Epis Ch Birmingham MI 1995-1998. Int Mnstry Ntwk 2002. jkeydel@gmail.com

KEYES, Charles Don (NY) 5801 Hampton St, Pittsburgh PA 15206 B Wewoka OK 1/24/1937 s Robert Keyes & Ruth. BA U of Oklahoma 1958; BD SWTS 1961; STM SWTS 1964; MA U Tor 1966; ThD U Tor 1966; PhD Duquesne U 1968. D 6/17/1961 P 12/1/1961 Bp Chilton Powell. m 8/20/1966 Aileen May Johnston. Assoc The Ch of S Ign of Antioch New York NY 2000-2009; Hon Asst Ch Of The Trsfg New York NY 1997-2000; St Andrews Epis Ch Pittsburgh PA 1996-1997; Asst Prof The GTS New York NY 1967-1969; Vic S Steph's Ch Guymon OK 1961-1963. Auth, "Brain Mystery Light And Dark," London: Routledge, 1999. Fndr Julian Casserley Resrch Cntr. Phi Beta Kappa U Of Oklahoma 1958. charlesdonkeyes@aol.com

KEYES, John Irvin (SD) 513 Douglas Ave, Yankton SD 57078 **Chr Epis Ch Yankton SD 2010-** B Sommers Point NJ 8/7/1948 s John Hunter Keyes & Ruth B. BS U of So Dakota 1977. D 12/4/2010 Bp John Thomas Tarrant. m 2/6/1993 Jo Neubauer c 4. john@dakotaphysicians.com

KEYS, Joel Thompson (Tenn) PO Box 24183, Saint Simons Island GA 31522 B Seneca SC 6/27/1947 s Theodore Crawford Keys & Margery Ellen. BA Davidson Coll 1969; MDiv VTS 1973. D 6/14/1973 P 4/27/1974 Bp Gray Temple. m 10/3/1969 Mary Elizabeth Taylor c 2. Asst Chr Ch Frederica St Simons Island GA 2005; R S Geo's Ch Nashville TN 1991-1993; Pres, Stndg Com Dio SW Virginia Roanoke VA 1988-1991; Trst VTS Alexandria VA 1988-1991; Long-R Plnng Dio SW Virginia Roanoke VA 1985-1987; R S Jn's Ch Lynchburg VA 1984-1991; Long Range Plnng Com Dio No Carolina Raleigh NC 1983-1984; CDO Dio No Carolina Raleigh NC 1980-1984; R Trin Epis Ch Statesville NC 1980-1984; COM Co-Chair Dio No Carolina Raleigh NC 1980-1981; COM Dio No Carolina Raleigh NC 1979-1981; APSO Bd Gvnr Dio No Carolina Raleigh NC 1977-1979; Dept Mssn Dio No Carolina Raleigh NC 1976-1984; Assoc Chr Ch Charlotte NC 1976-1980; COM Dio So Carolina Charleston SC 1974-1975; Dept of Missions Dio So Carolina Charleston SC 1974-1975; Vic Chr Ch Denmark SC 1973-1975; Asst Ch Of The Redeem Orangeburg SC 1973-1975; Dept CE Dio So Carolina Charleston SC 1973-1975. Auth, *Letters to the Newly Baptized*, Forw Mvmt, 1995; Auth, "Columns," *GC Daily*, Epis Ch, 1988; Auth, *Our Older Friends*, Fortress Press, 1983. JOELTKEYS@COMCAST.NET

KEYSE, Andrew C. (Ala) 262 Creekside Dr, Florence AL 35630 **Dept of Camp McDowell Dio Alabama Birmingham AL 2009-; Dept of Par Dvlpmt and Evang Dio Alabama Birmingham AL 2008-; R Trin Epis Ch Florence AL 2007-** B Rochester NY 10/13/1969 s Howard Richard Keyse & Mary Jane. BA U So 1992; MDiv TS 2002. D 6/15/2002 P 12/21/2002 Bp William Dailey Persell. m 10/22/1994 Elizabeth JS Stocks c 2. Chair, Liturg and Dioc. Events Dio Chicago Chicago IL 2005-2007; Chair, Liturg and Dioc

K

Events Dio Chicago Chicago IL 2005-2007; Dioc Conv Wrshp Com Dio Chicago Chicago IL 2004-2006; Dioc Conv Wrshp Comm. Dio Chicago Chicago IL 2003-2005; Assoc R Gr Epis Ch Hinsdale IL 2002-2007. akeyse@trinityflorence.org

KEYSE, Howard Richard (Chi) Po Box 146, Huntley IL 60142 B Bucyrus OH 12/31/1939 s Howard W Keyse & Beatrice J. BA OH SU 1971; MDiv Bex 1972. D 6/17/1972 P 5/1/1973 Bp John Harris Burt. m 11/22/2004 Laura E Keyse c 2. R S Ann's Ch Woodstock IL 1993-2001; R S Helena's Ch Willowbrook IL 1990-1993; Int S Ann's Ch Woodstock IL 1988-1990; R S Mich's Ch Barrington IL 1987-1988; R S Jn The Evang Ch Elkhart IN 1981-1986; R Ch Of S Thos Berea OH 1973-1981; Asst S Paul's Ch Canton OH 1972-1973. hlk@att.net

✠ **KEYSER, Rt Rev Charles Lovett** (Fla) 4719 Ivanhoe Rd, Jacksonville FL 32210 **Ret Bp Suffr of ArmdF Dio Florida Jacksonville FL 2007-** B Greenville SC 1/19/1930 s Lovett Keyser & Catherine Jane. BA U So 1951; MDiv STUSo 1954. D 6/24/1954 P 2/15/1955 Bp Frank A Juhan Con 3/24/1990 for Armed Forces and Micr. m 8/6/1955 Christine Crutchfield. Bp Asstg Dio Georgia Savannah GA 2004-2005; Chr Ch Cathd New Orleans LA 2001-2003; Bp Asstg Dio Montana Helena MT 2001-2003; Bp for the ArmdF, VA Hospitals and Fed Prison Epis Ch Cntr New York NY 1990-2000; R S Jas Ch Montross VA 1986-1990; R S Ptr's Ch Oak Grove Montross VA 1986-1989; Off Of Bsh For ArmdF New York NY 1960-1969. DD TS U So Sewanee TN 1993. bshp854@aol.com

KEYSER, Henry Griswold (Cal) 21239 Gary Dr Apt 419 Unit 419, Castro Valley CA 94546 B Ithaca NY 12/15/1925 s Henry Dearborn Keyser & Daisy Le Neta. BS Ithaca Coll 1952; Cert Dioc Inst Sch for D Honolulu HI 1995; BA Sch for Deacons 2001. D 11/20/1999 Bp William Edwin Swing. m 10/11/1977 Carol Helen Conrad c 4. D H Cross Epis Ch Castro Vlly CA 1999-2009. NAAD 1992. Makule E. Akamai Awd Dio Hawaii 1997; Profsnl Agt of the Year Profsnl Ins Agents Assn. 1985; Chairman of the Year Profsnl Ins Agents Assn. 1985; Chairman of the Year Profsnl Ins Agents Assn. 1984. dcnhenry@mail.com

K

KEYSER-MARY, Catherine Iona (Los) 5491 Taylor Way, Felton CA 95018 B Glendale CA 1/11/1942 d Paul A Butz & Mary Catherine. BA Warner Pacific U 1964; MA U of Redlands 1981; MDiv CDSP 1997. D 6/21/1997 Bp Richard Lester Shimpfky P 12/21/1997 Bp Frank Jeffrey Terry. c 1. Chapl The Epis Hm Communities Pasadena CA 2006-2008; Assoc Chr Ch Par Redondo Bch CA 2002-2005; P-in-c Ch Of Our Sav Pasco WA 1997-2000. catherinekeysermary@yahoo.com

KEYWORTH, Gill (Tex) 1215 Ripple Creek Dr, Houston TX 77057 **D Emm Ch Houston TX 2007-** B Thornton Heath UK 1/23/1947 d Ronald Ernest Munday & Joan Kathleen. BS Bradford U Bradford Yorkshire Uk 1969; Iona Texas 2007. D 2/9/2007 Bp Don Adger Wimberly. m 9/4/1971 John Keyworth c 2. deacon@emmanuel-houston.org

KEZAR, Dennis Dean (SwFla) 4030 Manatee Ave W, Bradenton FL 34205 B Webster City IA 9/3/1946 s Roger C Kezar & Donna. BA New Coll of Florida 1967; Oxf 1968; MDiv STUSo 1971; PhD Oxf 1974. D 6/29/1971 P 2/1/1972 Bp William Loftin Hargrave. c 3. Asst S Mary's Par Tampa FL 2011; Chr Ch Bradenton FL 1980-2004; Cathd Ch Of S Ptr St Petersburg FL 1976-1979; Asst Ch Of The Redeem Sarasota FL 1971-1974. kzsand7@aol.com

KHALIL, Adeeb Mikhail (WVa) 127 Brookwood Ln, Beckley WV 25801 B Jerusalem 12/26/1937 s Mikhail Khalil & Nagla. BTh Evang TS Cairo 1971. D 7/1/1970 P 8/1/1972 Bp The Bishop Of Jerusalem. m 7/2/1982 Marcia B Khalil c 2. Vic Ch Of The Redeem Ansted WV 1979-1987; Asst S Andr's Ch Oak Hill WV 1979-1984; S Andr's Ch Mullens WV 1977-2003; Vic All SS Ch Un WV 1975-1979; Vic Ascen Epis Ch Hinton WV 1975-1977.

KHAMIN, Alexei (Nwk) All Saints Episcopal Church, 230 E. 60th St., New York NY 10022 **Exec Coun Appointees New York NY 2007-** B Yaroslavl Russia 12/6/1970 s Sergey A Khamin & Lioudmila V. MDiv St Vladimir's Sem 1998; MPhil Drew U 2001; PhD Drew U 2007. D 6/2/2007 P 12/15/2007 Bp Mark M Beckwith. m Ronald Wei. S Mary's Ch Sparta NJ 2010-2011; Asst All SS Ch New York NY 2007-2009. akhamin@gmail.com

KHOO, Oon-Chor (Tex) 3203 W Alabama St, Houston TX 77098 B Penang MY 1/29/1931 s Cheng-Hoe Khoo & Chin-Poh. BS U of Singapore SG 1955; AMLS U MI 1971; MA Gordon-Conwell TS 1973; MA Bos 1974; CTh Epis TS of The SW 1985; DMin STUSo 1993. D 5/1/1986 Bp William Jackson Cox P 9/1/1988 Bp Gerald Nicholas McAllister. m 12/27/1958 Peck-Lim Tay. P-in-c Ch Of The Ascen Houston TX 2000-2002; Asian Mssnr Chr The King Ch Houston TX 1998-2000; Chr The Redeem Luth Ch Tulsa OK 1998; Ascen Luth Ch Tulsa OK 1995-1997; S Lk's Ch Tulsa OK 1990-1994; Ch Of The H Sprt - Epis Tulsa OK 1986-1987. Ord of S Lk. plockhoo@att.net

KIBLER SR, Bryant Carleton (Lex) 1013 Marco Ln, 607 Highway 1746, Lexington KY 40509 **Dio Lexington Lexington KY 2004-; P-in-c S Tim's Barnes Mtn Irvine KY 1994-** B Stuttgart DE 11/3/1953 s Nelson Frank Kibler & Emilie Maydalene. BA Cit 1976; MAT Cit 1978; MDiv Epis TS In Kentucky 1983. D 6/4/1983 P 12/10/1983 Bp Addison Hosea. Supply S Mk's Ch Hazard KY 1997-2010; Dio Lexington Lexington KY 1983-1997; Vic S Jn's Ch Corbin KY 1983-1994. BKIBLER@DIOLEX.ORG

KIBLINGER, Charles Edward (Va) 3737 Seminary Rd, Alexandria VA 22304 B Independence KS 2/21/1939 s Cleo Russell Kiblinger & Maxine Syble. BA U So 1961; MDiv VTS 1966; MA CUA 1973; Oxf 1980; DD STUSo 1996. D 6/18/1966 P 12/1/1966 Bp Edward Clark Turner. m 6/9/1962 Janet Irene Porter c 1. Dir Of Ldrshp / Mnstry Dvlpmt VTS Alexandria VA 2000-2004; S Jn's Cathd Denver CO 1991-2000; S Jas Ch Jackson MS 1981-1991; Chapl The TS at The U So Sewanee TN 1973-1981; Assoc S Alb's Epis Ch Annandale VA 1967-1973; Cur S Lk's Epis Ch Shawnee KS 1966-1967. Auth, "Preaching From Cathd". Comp Ccn, Fell Shalem Inst; CEEP. cjkiblinger@comcast.net

KIDD, Paul David (At) 161 Long Lake Rd, Hawthorne FL 32640 B Fisher IL 1/9/1936 s Shirley Raymond Kidd & Mable Adeline. BS U of Florida 1959; MDiv SWTS 1976. D 6/6/1976 P 12/12/1976 Bp Frank Stanley Cerveny. m 4/17/1960 Margaret B Bache c 2. Vic S Barth's Ch High Sprg FL 2005-2011; Vic Ch Of The Trsfg Rome GA 1996-2002; Coun For Mnstry Cedartown GA 1996-2002; Vic S Jas Ch Cedartown GA 1996-2002; Vic Ch Of The Nativ Jacksonville FL 1991-1996; Vic S Barn Epis Ch Williston FL 1985-1987; Vic S Alb's Epis Ch Chiefland FL 1978-1987; Vic Chr Ch Cedar Key FL 1978-1984; Asst S Cathr's Ch Jacksonville FL 1976-1978; S Jas Ch Macclenny FL 1976-1978. Bp's Cross Dio Florida 2011. paulkidd1@windstream.net

KIDD, Scott Austin (At) 20 Whisperwood Way, Cleveland GA 30528 **Ch of the Resurr Sautee Nacoochee GA 2006-** B Marietta GA 5/23/1959 s Michael Scott Kidd & Betty Jo. EFM STUSo 1996; BS Excelsior Coll 2001; MDiv Candler TS Emory U 2005. D 10/18/1998 Bp Onell Asiselo Soto P 1/21/2006 Bp J(ohn) Neil Alexander. m 9/15/1984 Patricia Bridges Kidd c 4. Assoc R Chr Ch Macon GA 2006-2007; D S Teresa Acworth GA 1998-2006. NAAD 1998. frscott@windstream.net

KIDD, Stephen Willis (Ark) 310 W 17th St, Little Rock AR 72206 **D-Transitional Trin Cathd Little Rock AR 2010-** B Monroe LA 12/15/1976 s Willis James Kidd & Mary Virginia. BA Nthrn Arizona U 2002; MDiv Epis TS Of The SW 2010. D 6/5/2010 P 5/27/2011 Bp James Monte Stanton. m 10/9/1999 Melanie Kidd c 2. The Epis Ch Of The Trsfg Dallas TX 2003-2007. skidd@trinitylittlerock.org

KIDDER, Ann (Me) Po Box 767, Southwest Harbor ME 04679 **S Pat's Ch Brewer ME 2011-** B Plymouth NH 3/20/1955 d Kent Hartwell Kidder & Lurlyne Vietta. BA U of New Hampshire 1977; MDiv GTS 1993. D 7/22/1993 P 1/1/1994 Bp Douglas Edwin Theuner. m 9/18/1993 Theodore G Fletcher c 2. S Marg's Ch Belfast ME 2008-2009; R S Andr And S Jn Epis Ch SW Harbor ME 1998-2004; Vic Gr Epis Ch Concord NH 1996-1998; Cur Epis Ch Of S Mary The Vrgn Falmouth ME 1993-1995. annkidder@earthlink.net

KIEFER, Lee (EO) 1031 Nw Spruce Ave, Redmond OR 97756 **S Lk's Epis Ch Wenatchee WA 2011-; Mssnr S Alb's Epis Ch Redmond OR 2003-** B Syracuse KS 8/28/1949 s Lee William Kiefer & Neva Fern. K SU 1969; BA Wichita St U 1971; MDiv STUSo 1990. D 5/26/1990 Bp William Edward Smalley P 12/1/1990 Bp Donald Purple Hart. m 1/1/2005 Marcia L Kiefer. Cn Dio Estrn Oregon The Dalles OR 2007-2011; R Ch Of The Epiph Honolulu HI 1992-2002; Inst For Human Serv Inc Honolulu HI 1990-1992; Vic S Matt's Epis Ch Waimanalo HI 1990-1992. leekiefer@gmail.com

KIELDSING SR, William Howard (WVa) 1537 Venice Ct, Kissimmee FL 34746 **Died 7/3/2011** B Wheeling WV 7/10/1918 s William Frank Kieldsing & Hilda Lillian. VTS 1962. D 6/13/1962 P 6/1/1963 Bp Wilburn Camrock Campbell. c 1.

KIENZLE, Edward Charles (Mass) 165 Pleasant St Apt 303, Cambridge MA 02139 **P Assoc S Ptr's Epis Ch Cambridge MA 2009-** B Flushing NY 7/10/1946 s Edward Arthur Vincent Kienzle & Ethel Mary. BS U of Maryland 1970; PhD Boston Coll 1976; MDiv Harvard DS 1995. D 6/5/1996 Bp M(arvil) Thomas Shaw III P 2/1/1997 Bp Roger W Blanchard. m 6/14/1969 Beverly M Mayne c 1. Int S Steph's Ch Cohasset MA 2007-2008; Int Ch Of Our Sav Brookline MA 2005-2006; Int S Andr's Ch Ayer MA 2005; Mem, Audit Com Dio Long Island Garden City NY 2003-2004; Mem, Bd Dir, Epis Chars of Long Island Dio Long Island Garden City NY 2002-2004; R S Geo's Par Flushing NY 2002-2004; Mem, Dioc Coun Dio Massachusetts Boston MA 2000-2002; R Ch Of The Gd Shpd Dedham MA 1999-2002; P-in-c Ch Of The Gd Shpd Dedham MA 1997-1999; Asst Emm Ch W Roxbury MA 1997; D Emm Ch W Roxbury MA 1996-1997. Auth, "Study Guide w Readings for Stiglitz's Econ of the Publ Sector," W.W. Norton & Co, 1989; Auth, "Post-Fisc Distributions of Income: Measuring Progressivity w Application to the Untd States," *Publ Fin Quarterly*, Sage Pub, 1982; Auth, "Measurement of the Progressivity of Publ Expenditures and Net Fiscal Incidence," *Sthrn Econ Journ*, Sthrn Econ Assn, 1981; Auth, "Measurement of Tax Progressivity: Comment," *Amer Econ Revs*, Amer Econ Assn, 1980; Auth, "The Cyclical Response of U.S. Income Inequality: Some New Empirical Results," *Publ Fin Quarterly*, Sage Pub, 1980. Epis Ntwk For Econ Justice 1995-2000.

KIESCHNICK, Frances Hall (Cal) 134 La Goma St, Mill Valley CA 94941 **Trin Par Menlo Pk CA 2008-** B Santa Barbara CA 4/21/1953 d George Johnson Hall & Sarah Griffin. BA Ya 1975; MDiv EDS 1982. D 6/19/1982 P 1/1/

1983 Bp Robert C Rusack. m 6/29/1985 Michael Kieschnick. Asst The Epis Ch Of S Mary The Vrgn San Francisco CA 1998-2003; Trin Par Menlo Pk CA 1994-1995; Trin Par Menlo Pk CA 1989-1994; Asst R S Bede's Epis Ch Menlo Pk CA 1986-1988; All SS Ch Pasadena CA 1982-1986. revfhk@gmail.com

KIESSLING, Donna Jean (Be) 2848 St. Alban's Drive, Sinking Springs PA 19608 **Assoc S Alb's Epis Ch Reading PA 2011-; Stwdshp Cmsn Chairperson Dio Bethlehem Bethlehem PA 2010-** B Neptune City NJ 10/1/1963 d David Mair & Claudia Jane. ABA Ursinus Coll 1987; BBA Ursinus Coll 1993; MDiv Luth Sem at Philadelphia 2006. D 5/17/2006 P 9/9/2007 Bp Paul Victor Marshall. Assoc S Gabr's Ch Douglassville PA 2007-2011. modj@comcast.net

KIKER, Norman Wesley (Okla) 5705 Earl Dr, Shawnee OK 74804 B Shawnee OK 4/22/1947 s James Virgil Kiker & Kathleen Rose. D 7/1/1989 Bp Robert Manning Moody. m 7/20/1968 Claudia Bea Henderson. D Dio Oklahoma Oklahoma City OK 1989-2002.

KILBOURN, Lauren Michelle (NC) 160 W South Orange Ave, South Orange NJ 07079 **Assoc S Paul's Epis Ch Cary NC 2011-; Cur S Andr And H Comm Ch So Orange NJ 2010-** B Decatur GA 1/22/1982 d Lawrence Winford Kilbourn & Deidre Ann. BA Florida Sthrn Coll 2004; MDiv Duke DS 2007; Angl Stds VTS 2010. D 6/19/2010 Bp Michael Bruce Curry. m 10/13/2007 Holly Gaudette. lmkgaudette@gmail.com

KILBOURN, Thomas Lewis (Ct) 51 Paddy Hollow Rd, Bethlehem CT 06751 **Vic S Paul's Epis Ch Bantam CT 1989-** B Torrington CT 4/21/1941 s Norton Ravenscroft Kilbourn & Helen. BA Norwich U 1964; BD Ya Berk 1967; MA Fairfield U 1970. D 6/13/1967 Bp Walter H Gray P 3/1/1968 Bp John Henry Esquirol. m 12/22/1973 Maureen Brown. S Paul's Epis Ch Bantam CT 1991-2006; Int S Paul's Ch Woodbury CT 1986-1987. Tchr Of Year Finalist CT 1991. tmj3@aol.com

KILBOURN-HUEY, Mary Esther (Lex) 310 Edgemont Rd, Maysville KY 41056 **D S Andr's Ch Lexington KY 2011-; COM Dio Lexington Lexington KY 2010-** B Saint Clair Shores MI 9/19/1949 d Robert Chester Kilbourn & Mary Elizabeth. BD U of Kentucky 1981; MS Nthrn Kentucky U 2007. D 7/10/1999 Bp Don Adger Wimberly. m 10/4/1997 Howard Terry Huey c 4. Montessori Sch Bd Dir Ch Of The Nativ Maysville KY 2008-2011; Dio Lexington Lexington KY 1999-2002; D Mgr S Marg's Chap Lexington KY 1999-2002. NAAD 1999. S Steph Recognition NAAD 2001. mekh1949@yahoo.com

KILBY, John Irvine (Ia) 4903 California St Apt 5, Omaha NE 68132 **COM Dio Iowa Des Moines IA 1978-** B Pittsylvania County VA 5/20/1931 s Virginus Claiborne Kilby & Willie Irvine. BA Hampden-Sydney Coll 1953; BD VTS 1959; Cert Creighton U 1997. D 6/27/1959 P 7/2/1960 Bp Clarence Alfred Cole. Stndg Com Dio Iowa Des Moines IA 1986-1989; Dioc Coun Dio Iowa Des Moines IA 1980-1981; R Chr Epis Ch Clinton IA 1976-1994; Chr Ch (Limestone) Peoria IL 1974-1976; Chair Dept Mnstry Dio Quincy Peoria IL 1971-1976; Dio Quincy Peoria IL 1970-1972; Secy Dioc Conv Dio Quincy Peoria IL 1970-1971; Cn Pstr S Paul's Cathd Peoria IL 1969-1976; P-in-c S Andr's Epis Ch Greenville SC 1962-1969.

KILFOYLE, J(ohn) Richard (WMass) 240 Belmont St Apt 103, Worcester MA 01604 B Cambridge MA 6/25/1933 s John Joseph Kilfoyle & Doris Carolyn. BA Emerson Coll 1959; MDiv Ya Berk 1962. D 6/23/1962 P 4/20/1963 Bp Anson Phelps Stokes Jr. R S Jn's Epis Ch Sutton MA 1993-1994; Dio Wstrn Massachusetts Springfield MA 1985-1994; R S Mk's Ch Worcester MA 1985-1990; The Ch Of The Adv Boston MA 1983; S Jn's Ch Jamaica Plain MA 1973-1979; Assoc Old No Chr Ch Boston MA 1972; Ltrgcs Com Dio Massachusetts Boston MA 1965-1972; R S Jn's Epis Ch Lowell MA 1964-1972; Cur Gr Ch New Bedford MA 1962-1964. Soc of S Marg, Soc of S Jn the Evang.

KILGORE, John William (Mo) 320 Union Blvd, Saint Louis MO 63108 B Joplin MO 4/10/1953 BA U of Missouri 1975; MD U of Missouri 1980; Cert GTS 2004. D 3/28/2003 P 3/25/2004 Bp George Wayne Smith. Chr Ch Cathd S Louis MO 2004-2005; S Mich & S Geo Clayton MO 2003-2004. jkilgoremd@aol.com

KILIAN, Joan M (Ga) 9003 Oakfield Dr, Statesboro GA 30461 **R Trin Ch Statesboro GA 2002-** B El Paso TX 12/12/1958 d Joseph Richard Kilian & Jeune Marie. BS Penn 1980; MFA / MFA Savannah Coll of Art & Design 1989; MDiv STUSo 1997. D 5/16/1997 P 12/13/1997 Bp Henry Irving Louttit. Ch Of Our Sav Martinez GA 1997-2002. Woods Ldrshp Awd U So 1995. rector@trinitystatesboro.org

KILLEEN, David Charles (Fla) St. John's Episcopal Church, 211 North Monroe St., Tallahassee FL 32301 **R S Jn's Epis Ch Tallahassee FL 2010-** B Red Bank NJ 1/12/1973 s Charles Lloyd Killeen & Nancy Anne. BA Muhlenberg Coll 1995; MDiv GTS 2004. D 3/13/2004 P 9/18/2004 Bp Mark Sean Sisk. m 12/12/1998 Carol Ann Corcoran c 4. Assoc R S Mk's Epis Ch Jacksonville FL 2007-2010; S Mary's-In-Tuxedo Tuxedo Pk NY 2004-2007; Dir of Cmncatn S Barth's Ch New York NY 1999-2001. OHC 2008. dave.killeen@saint-john.org

KILLIAN, David Allen (Mass) 1789 Beacon St, Brookline MA 02445 **R All SS Par Brookline MA 1992-** B Mondovi WI 8/16/1940 s Alphonse Killian & Helen. Marq 1959; S Ptr's Coll Baltimore MD 1959; BA S Paul's Coll Washington DC 1964; MA New Sch for Soc Resrch 1984; DMin Andover Newton TS 1990. Rec from Roman Catholic 12/17/1988. m 6/23/1984 Barbara Oneil c 2. Stndg Com Dio Massachusetts Boston MA 1995-1999; Ch Of The Gd Shpd Watertown MA 1991; S Mich's Ch Marblehead MA 1990; Int S Dunstans Epis Ch Dover MA 1989-1990. Auth, "Developing The Kinds Of Sm Communities Your Par Needs"; Auth, "Pace". Alb Inst; EPF; Ma Epis Cler Assn. EPF Alb Inst. rector@allsaintsbrookline.org

KILLINGSTAD, Mary Louise (Spok) 502 Hillside Dr, Yakima WA 98903 B Parsons KS 5/21/1933 d Forrest Hatch & Mary A. Yakima Vlly Coll 1980; Heritage Coll Toppenish WA 1987; Cemanahuac Spanish Lang Sch 1990. D 11/1/1980 Bp Leigh Wallace Jr P 7/13/2003 Bp James Edward Waggoner. m 12/31/1952 John A Killinstad. Asst S Mich's Epis Ch Yakima WA 1984-1992; Asst H Trin Epis Ch Sunnyside WA 1980-1983.

KILPATRICK, Alan William (SC) 565 Antebellum Ln, Mount Pleasant SC 29464 B Lanark SC 9/4/1964 s Robert Kilpatrick & Eileen. DIT Birmingham Bible Inst Gb 1994; BA Oak Hill Theol Coll 1996; U of Cambridge 1996. Trans from Church Of England 1/4/2002 Bp Edward Lloyd Salmon Jr. m 6/17/1989 Janet Elizabeth Andrew c 4. Asst S Andr's Ch Mt Pleasant SC 2001-2004. alan@samp.cc

KILPATRICK MADLOCK, Marcía Jean (Ia) 1641 1st Ave Se, Cedar Rapids IA 52402 B Cedar Rapids IA 6/9/1956 D 1/6/2000 Bp Carl Christopher Epting. m 6/3/1995 Darin Richard Lovelace c 4. S Ptr's Epis Ch Cheshire CT 2000; Asst to R Chr Ch Cedar Rapids IA 1999-2001.

KIM, andrew Jung (Los) 13091 Galway St, Garden Grove CA 92844 **P-in-c Ch Of The Resurr Garden Grove CA 2008-** B 2/26/1961 MS Philadelphia Biblic U; DMin Regent U Norfolk VA; CAS STUSo. D 12/13/2004 P 6/18/2005 Bp Leopold Frade. m 11/17/1990 Esther Kim. resurrectiongg@hotmail.com

KIM, John Jong-Kun (Pa) 3204 Ashy Way, Drexel Hill PA 19026 **Chapl Seamens Ch Inst Income New York NY 2008-** B Kea-san KR 7/12/1944 s Moon Bae Kim & Alma. LLB Chung Angl U Kr 1971; Vancouver TS 1994; SFTS 1997. D 4/5/1988 Bp Donald Purple Hart P 2/28/1998 Bp Charles Ellsworth Bennison Jr. m 1/11/1975 Sue Soon Ja Kim c 1. Assoc Philadelphia Cathd Philadelphia PA 2000-2007; Vic S Mart's Korean Ch Philadelphia PA 1998-2007; Dio Pennsylvania Philadelphia PA 1997-2007. jkimpa@hotmail.com

KIM, Jonathan Jang-Ho (WNY) Kumi Box 1039, Kumi Kyungbuk 730-600 Korea (South) B Kwang Ju KR 6/11/1932 s Jae Ie Kim & Soon-Sam. BS Seoul Natl U Seoul Kr 1955; MS Carnegie Mellon U 1961; PhD U of Oklahoma 1965; U Tor 1993. D 6/5/1993 P 5/1/1994 Bp David Charles Bowman. m 10/28/1957 Kun Ai Chu. Assoc S Andr's Ch Buffalo NY 1993-2011. kim4480@chollian.dacom.co.kr

KIM, Richard (Mich) 19983 E Doyle Pl, Grosse Pointe MI 48236 B 6/29/1927 s CS Kim & CS. Command and Gnrl Stff Coll; Dickinson Coll; U So. D 11/2/1973 P 5/1/1974 Bp Furman Stough. m 10/19/1985 Helen Ann Drake c 4. S Jn's Ch Detroit MI 1987-1997; R Trin Epis Ch Lexington MI 1981-1987; The Par Of Gd Shpd Epis Ch Wailuku HI 1977-1980; Prov Iv Hunger Taskforce & Conf Dio Alabama Birmingham AL 1975-1976; Prov Iv Hunger Taskforce & Conf Dio Alabama Birmingham AL 1975-1976; R Gr Ch Sheffield AL 1974-1977. Ord Of S Lk.

KIM, Stephen Yongchul (Los) 43115 62nd St West, Lancaster CA 93536 **Dio Los Angeles Los Angeles CA 2002-** B Inchon KR 1/9/1947 s Myung Hwan Kim & Kyung In. BA Yonsei U 1970; S Nich Sem Seoul KR 1972; Presb TS Seoul KR 1986; DMin SFTS 1988. Trans from Anglican Church Of Korea 2/1/1997 Bp Frederick Houk Borsch. m 11/8/2011 Kyung Ja Ryuk c 2. S Nich Korean Mssn Los Angeles CA 1991-2001. EAM. stephenkim@ladiocese.org

KIM, Yong Gul (Ninian) (LI) 2235 36th St, Astoria NY 11105 B 7/22/1939 s Shin-Duk Kim (Kyung Duk & Yang-Soon Song. Trin Sem; BS In-Ha U 1968; S Michaels Sem 1970. D 3/1/1971 P 9/1/1979 Bp The Bishop Of Seoul. m 9/28/1974 Chung Martha Kang. Trin Ch Great Neck NY 1981-1983; P-in-c St Josephs Epis Korean Ch Great Neck NY 1979-2005.

KIMBALL, Anne Bogardus (Ct) 14890 David Drive, Fort Myers FL 33908 B New Rochelle NY 4/29/1934 d Paul Hurley Bogardus & Elizabeth. BA Vas 1956; MDiv Ya Berk 1986. D 6/14/1986 P 2/7/1987 Bp Arthur Edward Walmsley. m 6/21/1958 Richard A Kimball c 3. Assoc S Mk's Ch New Canaan CT 1997-2000; Assoc Ya Berk New Haven CT 1995-2000; S Lk's Par Darien CT 1986-1994. Doctor of Cn Law Ya Berk 1999. abkrak2@embarqmail.com

KIMBALL JR, George Allen (Mil) 521 Frederick Ct, Oconomowoc WI 53066 B Monroe LA 1/24/1938 s George Allen Kimball & Stephen Aimee. BA Pr 1960; LLB LSU 1965; MDiv Nash 1980; MA Marq 1990. D 6/11/1980 P 3/1/1981 Bp James Barrow Brown. m 8/26/1962 Doris Ruth Dalziel c 2. Mem-Com for Const & Cn Dio Milwaukee Milwaukee WI 1996-2000; Mem- Ecclelsiastical Crt Dio Milwaukee Milwaukee WI 1996-2000; Adj Instr Nash Nashotah WI 1990-1992; Vic S Mary's Epis Ch Dousman WI 1989-2000;

Acad Sub-Dn & Rgstr Nash Nashotah WI 1987-1989; Instr Nash Nashotah WI 1983-1990; P-in-c S Aidans Ch Hartford WI 1981-1982; Tchg Asst Nash Nashotah WI 1980-1983. Grad Fell ECF 1981. kimballdg@charter.net

KIMBALL, Jennifer W (Va) 125 Beverly Rd, Ashland VA 23005 B Urbana IL 11/2/1967 d Linden Warfel & Constance. BA Wheaton Coll 1989; MA CUA 1993; MDiv VTS 2004. D 6/26/2004 P 1/18/2005 Bp Peter James Lee. m 8/3/1991 Sven Layne vanBaars. Dio Sthrn Virginia Norfolk VA 2009; Epis HS Alexandria VA 2007-2008; Cur Ch Of S Jas The Less Ashland VA 2004-2007. jenSJTL@aol.com

KIMBALL, John C (Pa) 202 Park Ave, Collegeville PA 19426 B New London CT 9/30/1929 s Charles Herbert Kimball & Georgiana. BA Daniel Baker Coll 1951; STB Ya Berk 1954. D 6/2/1954 P 6/14/1955 Bp Walter H Gray. m 7/15/1972 Barbara Nielson. Int Emm Ch Philadelphia PA 1997-1999; P-in-c Ch Of S Jn The Evang Philadelphia PA 1989-1996; Assoc S Jas Ch Collegeville PA 1988-1989; Dept Mssns Dio Albany Albany NY 1962-1964; Vic Chr Ch Cuba NY 1961-1965; P-in-c Our Sav Bolivar NY 1961-1965; Vic Gd Shpd Ft Hall ID 1958-1961; BEC Dio Idaho Boise ID 1957-1961; Vic Gr Epis Ch Glenns Ferry ID 1955-1958; Vic S Jas Ch Mtn Hm ID 1955-1958; Cur Ch Of The H Trin Middletown CT 1954-1955. jkimball202@comcast.net

KIMBER, Arthur Frederick (Mass) 71 Saint Joseph Street, Hyannis MA 02601 **Died 6/23/2010** B Boston MA 3/16/1934 s Arthur Frederick Kimber & Emma. BA Fairmont St Coll 1959; MDiv EDS 1962; MPA U of Massachusetts 1978; DMin GTF 1992. D 6/23/1962 P 12/23/1962 Bp Anson Phelps Stokes Jr. c 3. afkimber@comcast.net

KIMBLE, John Raymond (O) 2701 Regency Oaks Blvd, Clearwater FL 33759 B Scranton PA 3/27/1937 s William Philip Kimble & Lenore Florence. BA Leh 1960; MDiv GTS 1963. D 8/6/1963 P 5/22/1964 Bp Frederick J Warnecke. m 6/17/1960 Marilyn Sage Deykes c 2. R All SS Epis Ch Toledo OH 1979-2004; Assoc Trin Ch Toledo OH 1972-1978; R S Mich's Epis Ch Bethlehem PA 1967-1972. johnksaint@aol.com

KIMBLE, Shell Teyssier (WA) 5316 Taylor Rd, Riverdale MD 20737 **S Barn Epis Ch Temple Hills MD 2010-** B Hollywood, FL 12/3/1970 d Wynn Henry Kimble & Sophie Fitzgerald. Masters of Sci Florida St U; BA Florida St U; M Div VTS 2009. D 6/13/2009 P 1/16/2010 Bp John Chane. revshell.kimble@gmail.com

KIMBROUGH, Brendan Lee (Dal) 9845 McCree Rd, Dallas TX 75238 **S Jas Ch Dallas TX 2010-** B Dallas TX 9/10/1964 s Richard Lee Kimbrough & Nancy Lee. BBA U of Mississippi 1991; MDiv Westminster TS 2009. D 6/5/2010 P 5/19/2011 Bp James Monte Stanton. m 4/24/1999 Stephanie Kolwitz c 1. kimbrough@swbell.net

KIMBROUGH, Timothy Edward (Tenn) 435 Patina Circle, Nashville TN 37209 **Chr Ch Cathd Nashville TN 2009-** B Birmingham AL 8/12/1957 s S T Kimbrough & Sarah Ann. BA Duke 1979; MDiv Duke 1983; CAS GTS 1984. D 5/31/1984 P 6/1/1985 Bp Robert Whitridge Estill. c 4. Joint Com on the Philippine Cov Exec Coun Appointees New York NY 2004-2009; Liturg Off Dio No Carolina Raleigh NC 1998-2001; R Ch Of The H Fam Chap Hill NC 1989-2009; Liturg Cmsn Dio No Carolina Raleigh NC 1984-1997; Vic S Dav's Epis Ch Laurinburg NC 1984-1989. "We Will Be God's People," *Kids' Praise*, GBGMusik, 2007; "Canticle H," *Global Praise III*, GBGMusik, 2004; "Jesus, your light again I view," *Songs of Love and Praise*, GBGMusik, 2003; Auth, "Whither Should Our Full Souls Aspire," *A Song for the Wrld*, GBGMusik, 2002; Auth, "Violence," *Preaching Through the Year of Matt*, Morehouse Pub, 2001; Auth, "10, 22, 43, 45, 46," *Global Praise II*, GBGMusik, 2000; Auth, "Peace is My Last Gift," *Global Praise I Resource Bk*, GBGMusik, 1997; Auth, "37, 54, 55," *Global Praise I*, GBGMusik, 1996; Auth, *Theol in Hymns? (translation)*, Kingswood Books: Abingdon Press, 1995; Mus Ed, *A Song for the Poor*, GBGMusik, 1990; Auth, "74, 652, 799, 821, 844," *The Meth Hymnal*, Abingdon Press, 1989. AAM 1989; Chas Wesley Soc 1988; Hymn Soc of the U.S. and Can 1990. priestek@mac.com

KIMES, Nicki Sagendorf (Ct) 134 East Ave, New Canaan CT 06840 B New York NY 8/28/1944 d Forrest Cowles Sagendorf & Nadia Crandall. BA Chart Oak St Coll 2006; MDiv GTS 2006. D 6/10/2006 P 12/16/2006 Bp Andrew Donnan Smith. m 1/28/1967 Russell Kimes c 2. Asst S Paul's Ch Fairfield CT 2006-2010. shortprsn@juno.com

KIMMEY, Jimmye Elizabeth (NY) 928 W Hickory St, Denton TX 76201 **Assoc S Barn Epis Ch Denton TX 1995-** B Houston TX 9/28/1925 d John Albert Kimmey & Mary Elizabeth. BA U of Texas 1948; MA Col 1954; PhM Col 1973; MDiv UTS 1980. D 6/7/1980 Bp Paul Moore Jr P 12/14/1980 Bp Walter Decoster Dennis Jr. Dio New York New York City NY 1994-1995; Diocn Msnry & Ch Extntn Socty New York NY 1983-1994; Dpt Of Missions Ny Income New York NY 1983-1994; Exec for Mnstry Dio New York New York City NY 1983-1991; The Ch Of The Epiph New York NY 1980-1982. jekimmey@yahoo.com

KIMMICK, Donald William (Nwk) 9625 Miranda Dr, Raleigh NC 27617 B Teaneck NJ 9/15/1932 s William Francis Kimmick & Marie Elizabeth. BA Trin Hartford CT 1954; STB Ya Berk 1957; MA Col 1968; EdD Col 1975. D 6/15/1957 P 12/21/1957 Bp Benjamin M Washburn. m 6/23/1956 Genevieve Jardine c 2. Sr Chapl Seamens Ch Inst Income New York NY 1986-1993; Dioc Coun Dio Newark Newark NJ 1984-1986; Stndg Com Dio Newark Newark NJ 1978-1982; COM Dio Newark Newark NJ 1970-1978; Bdgt Com Dio Newark Newark NJ 1963-1970; Ch Of The Gd Shpd Midland Pk NJ 1957-1986. Auth, "Role Playing & Lecture-Discussion Parent Educ"; Auth, "Statement On Ch Mem"; Auth, "Lit Of Evang". AAMFT 1993-2009. donandgene@bellsouth.net

✠ KIMSEY, Rt Rev Rustin Ray (EO) 420 East 11th, The Dalles OR 97058 **Ret Bp of Estrn Oregon Dio Alaska Fairbanks AK 2009-** B Bend OR 6/20/1935 s Lauren Chamness Kimsey & Lois Elena. BS U of Oregon 1957; BD EDS 1960; DD Coll Idaho Nampa ID 1985; DD CDSP 2000. D 6/1/1960 P 12/1/1960 Bp Lane W Barton Con 8/4/1980 for EO. m 12/27/1961 Gretchen Beck Kimsey c 3. ExCoun Dio Estrn Oregon The Dalles OR 1988-1994; Bp Dio Estrn Oregon The Dalles OR 1980-2000; R S Pauls Epis Ch The Dalles OR 1971-1980; ExCoun Dio Estrn Oregon The Dalles OR 1969-1976; R S Steph's Baker City OR 1967-1971; Vic S Alb's Epis Ch Redmond OR 1961-1967. rustin@gorge.net

KIMURA, Gregory William Mitamura (Ak) 9900 Toakee Cir, Eagle River AK 99577 B Saint Paul MN 6/23/1968 s Kerry William Kimura & Betty Jane. BA Marq 1990; MDiv Harvard DS 1993. D 8/21/1993 P 4/1/1994 Bp Steven Charleston. m 7/27/1991 Joy Kimura. H Sprt Epis Ch Eagle River AK 1994-1999. Auth, "Anchorage Daily News". Theta Alpha Kappa; Alpha Sigma Nu. gwkimura@akhf.org

KINARD III, George Oscar (SeFla) 12840 Se Laurel Valley Ln, Hobe Sound FL 33455 B West Palm Beach FL 8/11/1939 s George Oscar Kinard & Sidney. Dioc Sch For Chr Stds; AA Palm Bch Jr. Coll 1959. D 3/24/2007 Bp Leopold Frade. m 12/30/1989 Judith Harden c 3. gojud3@bellsouth.net

KINCAID III, Samuel Thomas (Dal) 3966 McKinney Ave., Dallas TX 75204 **Cur Ch Of The Incarn Dallas TX 2009-** B Dallas TX 9/6/1982 s Samuel Thomas Kincaid & Barbara Williams. MDiv Duke 2009; BBA/BA SMU 2995. D 6/6/2009 P 12/5/2009 Bp James Monte Stanton. m 7/9/2011 Elisabeth Kincaid. tkincaid@incarnation.org

KINDEL JR, William H (Colo) 802 Navajo Avenue, Fort Morgan CO 80701 B Denver CO 2/23/1948 s William Harvey Kindel & Jane Enberg. SB MIT 1970; MS The OH SU 1971; MDiv Epis TS of the SW 2007. D 6/9/2007 P 12/8/2007 Bp Robert John O'Neill. m 10/31/2010 Cynthia Kindel c 3. P-in-c Par Ch Of S Chas The Mtyr Ft Morgan CO 2008-2011; Secy of Conv Dio Colorado Denver CO 2007-2009; Lay Rep, Dioc Coun Dio Massachusetts Boston MA 1991-1997. kindel@alum.mit.edu

KINDLE, Charles Richard (Oly) 902 Barnhart St, Raymond WA 98577 **Died 4/17/2010** B Cut Bank MT 8/29/1920 s William M Kindle & Beatrice. D 8/29/1992 P 3/1/1993 Bp Vincent Waydell Warner.

KING, Allan B (Mass) 222 Sayre Drive, Princeton NJ 08540 B Boston MA 4/4/1936 s Allan Brewster King & Carolyn Louise. BA Harv 1957; JD Harv 1960; MDiv EDS 1967. D 6/24/1967 Bp Anson Phelps Stokes Jr P 10/6/1968 Bp Frederic Cunningham Lawrence. m 12/30/1978 Helen Burke c 1. Asst. P Trin Ch Princeton NJ 2008-2009; Dioc Coun Dio Massachusetts Boston MA 1978-1980; Vic S Alb's Ch Lynn MA 1975-1999; LocTen S Jas Epis Ch Teele Sq Somerville MA 1971-1972; Cur The Ch Of Our Redeem Lexington MA 1968-1969. aking@post.harvard.edu

KING, Benjamin (Mass) School of Theology University of the South, 335 Tennessee Ave., Sewanee TN 37383 **Dir of the Advncd Degrees Prog The TS at The U So Sewanee TN 2010-; Asst Prof of Ch Hist The TS at The U So Sewanee TN 2009-** B Brighton East Sussex UK 12/26/1974 s Roger Wilfrid John King & Carolyn Sylvia. BA U of Cambridge 1996; BA Westcott Hse Cambridge 1999; MA U of Cambridge 2000; ThM Harvard DS 2003; PhD Dur 2007. Trans from Church Of England 1/28/2003 Bp M(arvil) Thomas Shaw III. m 8/1/2009 Leyla Kamalick c 1. Chapl Harvard Radcliffe Ch Cambridge MA 2005-2009; Cur The Ch Of The Adv Boston MA 2002-2005. Auth, "Newman and the Alexandrian Fathers: Shaping Doctrine in Nineteenth-Century Engl," Oxf Press, 2009; Auth, "'In Whose Name I Write: Newmans Two Translations of Athan," *Journ for the Hist of Mod Theol 15:1*, Walter de Gruyter, 2008. AAR 2008. bjking@sewanee.edu

KING JR, Charles Baldwin (Alb) 377 Reynolds Rd, Ft Edward NY 12828 B Schenectady NY 1/3/1943 s Charles Baldwin King & Alma Louise. BA SUNY 1966; MDiv SWTS 1969. D 6/15/1969 Bp Charles Bowen Persell Jr P 12/15/1969 Bp Allen Webster Brown. m 6/12/1965 Alice Templeman c 4. Cathd Of All SS Albany NY 1999-2006; Dio Albany Albany NY 1996-1999; Ch Of The H Cross Warrensburg NY 1994-2006; Chair Cler Compstn Com Dio Albany Albany NY 1986-1993; R Chr Ch Deposit NY 1980-1994; Trin Ch Gouverneur NY 1975-1980; Vic Calv Epis Ch Cairo NY 1970-1975; Vic Gloria Dei Epis Ch Palenville NY 1970-1975; Vic Trin Ch Ashland Webster NY 1970-1975; Vic All SS Ch No Granville NY 1969-1970; Vic Trin Ch Whitehall NY 1969-1970. Forw in Faith 1997; GAS 2011; NOEL; SocMary; SSC 2003. Hon Cn Cathd of All SS, Albany 2001; Bp's Awd Dio Albany Albany NY 1995. frking@aol.com

KING, Charles Malcolm (SD) 15A Church St, New Milford CT 06776 B New York NY 8/15/1943 s Charles Philip King & Margaret. BA Queens Coll 1965;

MA Col 1967; MDiv EDS 2003. D 12/21/2006 P 5/17/2008 Bp Creighton Leland Robertson. m 10/18/1997 Carolyn Ford c 1. Vic Calv Cathd Sioux Falls SD 2008-2010; P-in-c Dio So Dakota Sioux Falls SD 2008-2010. revcharlieking@gmail.com

KING, Darlene Dawn (EMich) 3201 Gratiot Ave, Port Huron MI 48060 B Midland MI 5/6/1936 d Richard Butcher & Reva F. D 12/13/2008 Bp S(teven) Todd Ousley. m 6/13/1953 Robert John King c 4. kingdarlene@att.net

KING JR, Earle Cochran (WNY) 2595 Baseline Rd, Grand Island NY 14072 **Stndg Com Dio Wstrn New York Tonawanda NY 2003-; R S Mart In The Fields Grand Island NY 1987-** B Ellwood City PA 3/11/1950 s Earle Cochran King & Margaret Elizabeth. BA Eastman Sch of Mus 1972; MA U of Oklahoma 1974; MDiv SWTS 1985. D 6/25/1985 Bp Richard Mitchell Trelease Jr P 1/6/1986 Bp Harold B Robinson. m 7/15/1972 Paula Jill Hunsicker c 2. Asst S Jas' Ch Batavia NY 1985-1987. padreking@aol.com

KING, Edward Albert (WMass) PO Box 374, North Adams MA 01247 **R S Jn's Ch No Adams MA 1999-** B Cochrane ON CA 6/8/1940 s Albert King & Dorothy. BA Ryerson Polytech 1962; Michigan TS 1973; MA S Jn's Prov Sem 1988. D 6/30/1979 Bp William J Gordon Jr P 6/28/1985 Bp Henry Irving Mayson. m 10/6/1962 Ann E Moore c 2. R H Trin Epis Ch Southbridge MA 1999-2003; P-in-c Dio Michigan Detroit MI 1996-1999; Dream Cluster Taylor MI 1996-1999; S Lk's Epis Ch Allen Pk MI 1985-1996; Asst S Andr's Epis Ch Livonia MI 1979-1985. stjohnspriest@earthlink.net

KING, Francis Marion Covington (WNC) 140 Saint Marys Church Rd, Morganton NC 28655 **S Mary's Ch Morganton NC 2009-** B Tulledega AL 1/4/1950 s Johnsey King & Marie Covington. BA Mississippi Coll; JD U of Mississippi 1984; MDiv STUSo 2000. D 2/12/2006 P 8/20/2006 Bp Charles Edward Jenkins III. m 8/30/1997 Peggy Walker c 1. Ch Of The H Sprt New Orleans LA 2006-2008. franciskin50@compascable.net

KING JR, Frank Hiram (NI) 904 N Fenton Rd, Marion IN 46952 B Marion IN 9/17/1933 s Frank Hiram King & Freda. BA Franklin Coll 1955. D 9/12/1987 P 3/25/1988 Bp Francis Campbell Gray. m 8/8/1969 Marilyn Jo Campbell c 1. S Andr Epis Ch Kokomo IN 2003-2005; S Paul's Ch Naples FL 2003-2005; S Andr Epis Ch Kokomo IN 1998-2000; S Paul's Epis Ch Gas City IN 1993-1997; Asstg P Geth Epis Ch Marion IN 1987-1993. CBS. Pstr Emer St Andr / Kokomo 2007.

KING, Frank Walter (WNC) 4425 Huntington Dr, Gastonia NC 28056 B Wilmington NC 2/21/1958 s John William King & Mary Ellen. BA U NC 1980; MDiv VTS 1985; DMin SWTS 2001. D 5/1/1985 P 11/1/1985 Bp Brice Sidney Sanders. m 6/13/1981 Jocelyn Ann Prttibone. S Mk's Ch Gastonia NC 2001-2004; R The Epis Ch Of The Epiph So Haven MI 1996-2001; R Chr Epis Ch Hope Mills NC 1986-1994; St Marks Ch Hope Mills NC 1986-1988; Int S Jn's Epis Ch Fayetteville NC 1985-1986. fwking@carolina.rr.com

KING, Gayle (Colo) 12634 Irving Cir, Broomfield CO 80020 B Denver CO 11/11/1932 d Harold Emery Howerton & Jeanette Louise. K SU 1953; Sarah Lawr Coll 1972; MDiv SWTS 1987. D 6/12/1987 P 6/1/1988 Bp Arthur Anton Vogel. m 6/11/1955 William R King c 5. Assoc S Bon Ch Sarasota FL 1992-1998; S Matt's Ch Evanston IL 1987-1992. gaylehking@aol.com

KING, Giovan Venable (Haw) St Christopher Church, PO Box 456, Kailau HI 96734 **R S Chris's Ch Kailua HI 2011-** B Winston Salem NC 12/10/1956 d Joel William Venable & Joann Harbour. AB Dart Hanover NH 1979; MDiv Harvard DS 1983; JD Stanford Law Sch Palo Alto CA 1988; DMin VTS Alexandria VA 2005. D 5/26/2007 P 1/12/2008 Bp Joseph Jon Bruno. m 1/26/1998 Thomas King c 1. Faith Epis Ch Laguna Niguel CA 2010-2011; S Edm's Par San Marino CA 2010; Assoc R S Jas Par Los Angeles CA 2007-2009; Fac, Sum Collegium VTS Alexandria VA 2006-2010. Auth, "Psalms in the Key of Life," *Intl Congrl Journ*, ICF, 2006; Auth, "Preaching: Our Hope for Years to Come," *The Congrl*, NACCC, 2003; Auth, "Courts and Congregationalism," *Stanford Law Revs*, Stanford Law Sch, 1989. Cmsn on Ecum and Interreligious Concerns 2007; Eccl Crt Judge 2008; Friends of Jerusalem 2009. JJ Russell Sermon Awd Natl Assn 2006; La Rochelle Schlr Huguenot Soc for VTS 2004; Natl Playwriting Awd Natl Assn 2003; Billings Preaching Prize Harvard 1983; Phi Beta Kappa Dartmouth 1979. rector@stchristopherkailua.org

KING, Janet Gay Felland (Ida) 678 E 400 N, Rupert ID 83350 **D Dio Idaho Boise ID 1986-** B Ann Arbor MI 5/5/1947 d Robert Marcy Felland & Marjorie Marie Sherman. BD Ball St U 1972; MA U of Arkansas 1976. D 12/20/1986 Bp David Bell Birney IV. m 10/26/1974 Robert Allen King c 1. robking@pmt.com

KING, John Christopher (ECR) 220 W Penn St, Long Beach NY 11561 **Luth-Angl-RC Dialogue, Epis Mem Dio Long Island Garden City NY 2011-; Vic Par Of S Jas Of Jerusalem By The Sea Long Bch NY 2008-** B Columbus MS 11/8/1965 s John Wayne King & Wanda Vernelle. BA Baylor U 1987; MA CDSP 1991; DPhil Oxf 2000. D 6/26/1999 Bp Richard Lester Shimpfky P 1/28/2000 Bp Catherine Scimeca Roskam. Hon Non-Stip Assoc The Ch Of S Lk In The Fields New York NY 2006-2007; Assoc S Barth's Ch New York NY 2004-2005; Dioc Yth Cdntr Dio New York New York City NY 1999-2004. Auth, "Origen on the Song of Songs as the Sprt of Scripture: The Bridegroom's Perfect Mar-Song," Oxf Press, 2005; Auth, "A Love As Fierce As Death: Reclaiming The Song Of Songs For Gay Men and Lesbians," *Take Back the Word*, Pilgrim Press, 2000; Auth, "A Commentary On The Catechism Or Outline Of Faith," *A Faith for Living*, Enoptika Productions, 1994. Fell ECF 1993; Phi Beta Kappa 1987. jchristopherking@mac.com

KING, Jonathan LeRoy (NY) 340 Godwin Ave, Ridgewood NJ 07450 B New York NY 8/20/1929 s Frederic Rhinelander King & Edith Percy. BA Harv 1951; EDS 1953; MDiv GTS 1956; STM NYTS 1975. D 10/18/1956 Bp Horace W B Donegan P 5/9/1957 Bp Charles Francis Boynton. m 5/10/1958 Jacqueline Esmerian c 4. S Barth's Ch In The Highland White Plains NY 1995-1997; Gr Epis Ch Nyack NY 1993-1995; The Ch Of S Jos Of Arimathea White Plains NY 1993; All Ang' Ch New York NY 1991-1993; S Mich's Epis Ch Wayne NJ 1990-1991; All SS' Epis Ch Glen Rock NJ 1988-1990; Trin Ch Irvington NJ 1988; All SS Ch Bergenfield NJ 1986-1988; Cathd Of St Jn The Div New York NY 1974-1986. Angl Soc 1955; Retreat Hse Redeem Nyc 1992. jlking340@aol.com

KING, Joseph Willett (Az) 7735 N Via Laguna Niguel, Tucson AZ 85743 **D Chr The King Ch Tucson AZ 2006-** B Springfield MO 8/26/1934 s Charles B King & Evelyn G. BA SMU 1956; MD U of Texas 1962; EFM STUSo 1996. D 6/22/1996 Bp Robert Manning Moody. m 7/2/1972 Doris Ann Toby c 4. D S Andr's Epis Ch Lawton OK 1998-2000; Lic D S Phil's In The Hills Tucson AZ 1997-2004; Vocational D S Dunst's Ch Tulsa OK 1996-1998. NAAD 2001. jdking@aol.com

KING, Karen G (Mont) PO Box 2168, Lake Charles LA 70602 **R Dio Montana Helena MT 2011-** B Lake Charles LA 10/15/1947 d Jean LaRue King & Alice Mae Judice. BS LSU 1970; MEd LSU 1976; MDiv The GTS 2010. D 12/10/2009 Bp Charles Franklin Brookhart Jr. c 2. karengailking@gmail.com

KING, Karen L (Ind) 3401 Lindel Ln, Indianapolis IN 46268 **Del to GC 2012 Dio Indianapolis Indianapolis IN 2010-; Assoc R for Outreach and Pstr Care Trin Ch Indianapolis IN 2010-; Assoc R for Mssn and Outreach Trin Ch Indianapolis IN 2002-** B Springfield MA 6/7/1953 d Samuel Alexander King & Frances Elizabeth. BA Knoxville Coll 1975; MS U of Tennessee 1977; MDiv Chr TS 2002. D 6/29/2002 P 6/8/2003 Bp Catherine Elizabeth Maples Waynick. c 2. COM Dio Indianapolis Indianapolis IN 2009-2011; Stndg Com Dio Indianapolis Indianapolis IN 2003-2006; Racial Recon T/F Dio Indianapolis Indianapolis IN 2002-2005. kking@trinitychurchindy.org

KING, Kathryn Louise (Nwk) 28 Ralph St, Bergenfield NJ 07621 **S Alb's Ch Oakland NJ 2009-** B Monroe LA 6/23/1961 d W(illiam) Alan King & Audrey Kathryn. BS Elizabethtown Coll 1984; MDiv CDSP 1995. D 6/3/1995 Bp John Shelby Spong P 12/1/1995 Bp Jack Marston McKelvey. c 1. Vic All SS Ch Bergenfield NJ 2003-2009; S Tim's Ch Danville CA 1998-2003; Asst Chr Epis Ch Los Altos CA 1996-1998; Asst S Ptr's Ch Mtn Lakes NJ 1995-1996. KATHRYNLKING@OPTONLINE.NET

KING JR, Kenneth Vernon (EO) 702 Grant Street, Summit MS 39666 B Lexington MS 12/17/1950 s Louise. BS U of Mississippi 1973; Cert of Theol CDSP 2000; MDiv CDSP 2003; 4 Units CPE Med Cntr of San Francisco Mofit/Long Hosp 2005; Advncd Cert in Pstr Care PSR 2005. D 6/4/2005 Bp William Edwin Swing P 11/30/2005 Bp Julio Ernesto Murray Thompson. m 12/17/2009 Barbara Mosley. R Ch Of The Redeem Pendleton OR 2010-2011; Supply P Dio Mississippi Jackson MS 2008-2009; Mssy P Dom And Frgn Mssy Soc- Epis Ch Cntr New York NY 2005-2008; Prov of Bocas del Toro Exec Coun Appointees New York NY 2005-2008. Supply Cler Dio Mississippi 2009; Mssy P Angl Global Relatns 2005. father.kenny@gmail.com

KING, Leslie Anne (NCal) 55 Maria Dr Ste 837, Petaluma CA 94954 **Non-stipendiary Assoc S Patricks Ch Kenwood CA 2008-** B Baltimore MD 2/21/1956 d William Connor King & Virginia Bodell. BA Colby Coll 1978; MA Bos 1986; PhD Bos 1996. D 6/29/1993 P 7/29/1994 Bp Edward Cole Chalfant. m 5/28/1989 Keith Sadko. St Johns Epis Ch Petaluma CA 2009-2010; Vic S Paul's Epis Ch Grinnell IA 1997-2002; Cur Ch Of The H Sprt Sfty Harbor FL 1994-1995. Auth, "Surditas:The Understandings of the Deaf and Deafness in the Writings of Aug, Jerome, and Bede," *Dissertation*, Bos, 1996. rector.episcopal.petaluma@gmail.com

KING, Leyla (ETenn) 1607 W 43rd St, Chattanooga TN 37409 **R Thankful Memi Ch Chattanooga TN 2010-** B Houston TX 1/7/1981 d Joseph A Kamalick & May F. BA Dart 2002, Cert Mld 2004; MDiv Harvard DS 2009. D 10/26/2008 P 9/5/2009 Bp J Michael Garrison. m 8/1/2009 Benjamin King c 1. Asst Dio Massachusetts Boston MA 2008-2009. lkamalick@gmail.com

KING, Margaret Creed (Tenn) 704 Vauxhall Dr, Nashville TN 37221 **S Geo's Ch Nashville TN 2007-; S Jn's Epis Sch Ocean Sprg MS 2004-** B Knoxville TN 12/6/1952 d Albert Creed & Merrillyn. D 5/30/2004 Bp Samuel Johnson Howard P 1/6/2005 Bp Duncan Montgomery Gray III. m 10/18/1986 John C King c 1. S Jn's Epis Ch Ocean Sprg MS 2004-2007. marcia.king@stgeorgesnashville.org

KING, Nancy English (Okla) 1123 E 18th St, Tulsa OK 74120 **Died 7/16/2011** B Lawton OK 4/13/1934 d Exall English & Lucile. BA Bryn 1958. D 7/1/1989 Bp Robert Manning Moody. c 3.

KING, Robert Andrew (Ky) 146 State St Unit 101, Clayton NY 13624 B Homestead PA 10/20/1932 s John Andrew King & Mary Elizabeth. BA Ken

1954; BD Bex 1966. D 6/11/1966 P 10/12/1966 Bp Nelson Marigold Burroughs. m 12/28/1957 Regina Evaul c 2. R S Mary's Ch Madisonville KY 1979-1995; S Barth's Ch Mayfield Vill OH 1971-1979; R Trin Ch New Philadelphia OH 1966-1971. bobking3@earthlink.net

KING, Tom Earl (NC) 419 S Main St, Lexington NC 27292 **R Gr Epis Ch Lexington NC 2004-** B Waco TX 2/8/1948 s Hershel Earl King & Virgie Leona. BA Baylor U 1970; MDiv Sthrn Bapt TS Louisville KY 1973; ThM Sthrn Bapt TS Louisville KY 1978; PhD Sthrn Bapt TS Louisville KY 1982; Cert Epis TS of The SW 1995. D 7/5/1995 Bp Sam Byron Hulsey P 1/1/1996 Bp William Elwood Sterling. m 3/6/1993 Judy Ann Gibson c 4. Int S Paul's Epis Ch Pflugerville TX 2001-2004; Int S Jas' Epis Ch La Grange TX 2001; Vic S Thos' Epis Ch Rockdale TX 1996-1997. Amer Assn for Mar and Fam Ther 1977-2004; AAPC, AAMFT 1975-2004. teking48@gmail.com

KING, W(illiam) Alan (Nwk) 627 Starboard Ave, Edgewater FL 32141 B Glen Ridge NJ 8/7/1932 s William King & Louise. BS Rutgers-The St U 1954; Drew U 1957; MDiv GTS 1958. D 6/14/1958 Bp Benjamin M Washburn P 12/27/1958 Bp Dudley B McNeil. m 5/31/1958 Audrey Maise c 4. Int S Ptr The Fisherman Epis Ch New Smyrna Bch FL 2001-2003; Bd Trst The GTS New York NY 1989-1993; Vic Ch Of The Gd Shpd Sussex NJ 1986-1995; Bps Dep Asian Mnstry Dio Newark Newark NJ 1986-1990; Dioc Coun Dio Newark Newark NJ 1981-1982; Alum Exec Com The GTS New York NY 1976-1988; Chair Cmsn Evan. Dio Newark Newark NJ 1976-1979; R S Mart's Ch Maywood NJ 1964-1986; Vic S Alb's Epis Ch Monroe LA 1960-1964; Vic S Pat's Epis Ch W Monroe LA 1960-1964; Cur S Lk's Par Kalamazoo MI 1958-1960. R Emer St Martins Epis Ch Maywood NJ 1986. alanaudrey32141@peoplepc.com

KING, William Michael (Ala) 905 Castlemaine Drive, Birmingham AL 35226 **Pat-time Cler Transition Off Dio Cntrl Gulf Coast Pensacola FL 2009-; P-in-c Trin Epis Ch Clanton AL 2003-** B Birmingham AL 8/22/1941 s Richard Eugene King & Mary Catherine. BA S Mary Coll, Lebanon KY 1963; MA Notre Dame Sem 1966; Univ. of San Francisco 1968; MSW Tul 1971; STUSo 1987. Rec from Roman Catholic 6/1/1987 as Priest Bp Furman Stough. m 6/7/1969 Patricia A Kaiser c 3. Dep to GC Dio Alabama Birmingham AL 2002-2005; Diac Formation Dir Dio Alabama Birmingham AL 2000-2011; Dep to Bp Dio Alabama Birmingham AL 1998-2007; Ecum Off Dio Alabama Birmingham AL 1995-1998; Pres of the Stndg Com Dio Alabama Birmingham AL 1994-1995; R All SS Epis Ch Birmingham AL 1990-1998; Assoc R S Mary's-On-The-Highlands Epis Ch Birmingham AL 1987-1990. Auth, "Places of Secret Pryr: Pilgrimage In Alabama," Samford U Press, 2004. bp3king@bellsouth.net

KINGDON, Arthur M (Vt) 334 Oak Grove Rd, Vassalboro ME 04989 B Wisconsin Rapids WI 11/20/1943 s Robert Wells Kingdon & Catherine. BA Ob; ThM U Chi 1967; MA U Chi 1970. D 11/6/1980 P 7/16/1981 Bp Frederick Barton Wolf. m 6/14/1966 Linda B Sarasohn c 2. R S Ptr's Epis Ch Bennington VT 1992-2003; R All SS Ch So Hadley MA 1985-1992; Dio Wstrn Massachusetts Springfield MA 1985-1992. akingdon2000@yahoo.com

KINGMAN, Donna Watkins (WMass) 3 Newington Ln, Worcester MA 01609 **D Ch Of The Gd Shpd Clinton MA 2007-** B West Point GA 11/12/1943 d William Alvis Watkins & Florence Evelyn. BS Jacksonville St U 1964; MDiv EDS 1967; MA Assumption Coll 2000. D 10/18/1977 Bp George Theodore Masuda. m 10/14/1967 Perry Alden Kingman c 2. COM Dio Wstrn Massachusetts Springfield MA 1997-2001; D Ch Of The Recon Webster MA 1996-2006; D Aroostook Epis Cluster Caribou ME 1990-1996; Lay Mnstry Com Dio New Hampshire Concord NH 1988-1990; D Chr Ch No Conway NH 1985-1990; D H Trin Intl Falls MN 1977-1985. Intl OSL the Physcn 2008; NAAD 1980. pakecusame@aol.com

KINGMAN, Perry Alden (WMass) 3 Newington Ln, Worcester MA 01609 B Orange NJ 9/23/1941 s Barclay Alden Kingman & Eleanora Balch. BA Wms 1963; MDiv EDS 1966. D 6/11/1966 Bp Leland Stark P 12/16/1966 Bp George E Rath. m 10/14/1967 Donna Watkins c 2. Dioc Coun Dio Wstrn Massachusetts Springfield MA 1998-2003; R Ch Of The Recon Webster MA 1996-2006; Dioc Coun Dio Maine Portland ME 1992-1996; Sr P Aroostook Epis Cluster Caribou ME 1990-1996; Dioc Coun Dio New Hampshire Concord NH 1987-1989; R Chr Ch No Conway NH 1985-1990; P Ch of theTransfiguration N Conway NH 1985-1990; R H Trin Intl Falls MN 1976-1985; P S Ptr's Ch Warroad MN 1976-1985; Dioc Coun Dio No Dakota Fargo ND 1974-1976; R All SS Ch Vlly City ND 1969-1976; P Ch Of The H Trin 1969-1976; P Gr Ch Madison NJ 1966-1969. AAM 2006; RWF 1980-1996. pakecusame@aol.com

KINGSLEY, Myra Jessica (Az) 100 W Roosevelt St, Phoenix AZ 85003 **D Trin Cathd Phoenix AZ 2009-** B New Jersey NJ 1/27/1948 d Judd Kingdon Kinzley & Mina. BSN Arizona St U 1987; MS Arizona St U 1993. D 1/24/2009 Bp Kirk Stevan Smith. m 6/15/1968 Donald Kingsley c 3. myra@azcathedral.org

KINGSLEY MURRAY, Miguel (DR) Dr Zafra# 3, Puerto Plata Dominican Republic **Dio The Dominican Republic (Iglesia Epis Dominicana) Santo Domingo DO 2010-** B 9/29/1946 s Gregorio Kingsley & Elena. D 2/14/2010 Bp Julio Cesar Holguin-Khoury. c 2. mikimu29@hotmail.com

KINGSLIGHT, Kathleen Anne (Oly) 700 Callahan Dr, Bremerton WA 98310 **R S Paul's Epis Ch Bremerton WA 2010-; Dep to GC, Anaheim, CA Dio Wstrn Michigan Kalamazoo MI 2009-; Dep to GC, Columbus, OH Dio Wstrn Michigan Kalamazoo MI 2006-; Alt to GC, Minneapolis, MN Dio Wstrn Michigan Kalamazoo MI 2003-** B Owosso MI 5/20/1952 d Robert Joseph Olance & Therese Marie. MI SU 1972; BA Concordia Luth U 1993; MDiv Epis TS of The SW 1993; Cert Marywood Dominican Cntr Grand Rapids MI 1995; Cler Ldrshp Proj 2005; Cert CISM Inter.Critical Incident Stress 2006; Certificates Spanish Lang Immersion 2007; Cert SWTS 2009. D 8/24/1993 Bp Bob Gordon Jones P 3/17/1994 Bp Edward Lewis Lee Jr. m 7/11/1976 John Victor Koenigsknecht c 2. Alt to GC, Minneapolis, MN Dio Wstrn Michigan Kalamazoo MI 2003-2007; Dioc Chapl to DOK Dio Wstrn Michigan Kalamazoo MI 2000-2007; Mem of Exec Coun Dio Wstrn Michigan Kalamazoo MI 1998-2003; R S Barn Epis Ch Portage MI 1997-2010; Assoc S Tim Ch Richland MI 1993-1997. Performer/Compsr, "Heart of Love," *Audio Rcrdng*, Self Pub, 1989; Compsr/Performer, "De Colores," *Audio Rcrdng*, Self Pub, 1989; Compsr/Performer, "The Light of Christmas," *Audio Rcrdng*, Self Pub, 1988; Compsr/Performer, "He's Shinin,'" *Audio Rcrdng*, Self Pub, 1986; Compsr/Performer, "Let Light Stream Forth," *Audio Rcrdng*, Self Pub, 1979. Oblate Ord Of S Ben 1998. Lily Fndt Grant for Ongoing Renwl of Cler in Active Mnstry Lily Fndt 2006; Mk Jorjorian Preaching Excellence Awd Epis Theo. Sem. of SW 1992; Natl Merit Scholarships 1970. kkingslight@comcast.net

KINGSTON, Louise Lauck (NJ) 85 Westcott Rd, Princeton NJ 08540 B Bryn Mawr PA 5/13/1941 d Peter Lauck & Annette C. BA Vas 1963; MDiv PrTS 1977. D 6/4/1977 Bp Albert Wiencke Van Duzer P 1/14/1978 Bp George Phelps Mellick Belshaw. m 6/22/1963 Michael Kingston c 3. Trin Ch Princeton NJ 1993-2003; Comm On Rel Mnstry Of Princeton Princeton NJ 1978-2001. AEHC 1979-2009; Bd Cert Chapl Assn of Profsnl Chapl 1979-2009. llkingston@gmail.com

KINMAN, Mike (Mo) 6209 Pershing Ave, Saint Louis MO 63130 **Dn Chr Ch Cathd S Louis MO 2009-** B Santa Clara CA 11/15/1968 s Thomas David Kinman & Jacqueline Louise. BJ U of Missouri 1990; MDiv Ya Berk 1996. D 7/27/1996 P 6/24/1997 Bp Hays H. Rockwell. m 6/27/1992 Robin Lynn Blust c 2. Exec Dir Episcopalians for Global Recon Brandon FL 2006-2009; Campus Mnstry Coordntr Dio Missouri S Louis MO 1999-2005; Assoc S Mich & S Geo Clayton MO 1996-1999. Auth, "Sermon for Wrld Mssn Sunday, Matt 17:1-9," *Sermons That Wk*, Epis Ch, 2005; Auth, "An Army of One, A Palm Sunday Sermon," *Get Up Off Your Knees: Preaching the U2 Catalog*, Cowley, 2003; Auth, "A Bp For The 21st Century Ch," *The Catalyst/Gathering The Next Generation*, 2001; Auth, "Who Owns The Ch, A Sermon on Romans 7:13-25 and Jn 2:13-22," *Sermons That Wk VIII*, Morehouse, 1999. Jn Hines Preaching Awd VTS 2008. mkinman@gmail.com

KINMAN, Thomas David (Az) PO Box 40126, Tucson AZ 85717 **D Gr S Paul's Epis Ch Tucson AZ 1997-** B Rugby UK 8/10/1928 s Thomas Hilary Kinman & Ella Attewell. MA Oxf 1954; PhD Oxf 1954. D 2/8/1997 Bp Robert Reed Shahan. m 1/19/1963 Jacqueline Louise Schroedter c 2.

KINNER, Heidi Ellen (Ala) St. Peters Episcopal Cathedral, 511 N. Park Avenue, Helena MT 59601 **Dn S Ptr's Par Helena MT 2011-** B Alamosa CO 10/3/1970 BA Colorado St U 1993; MDiv Nash 2004. D 6/19/2004 Bp Chester Lovelle Talton P 1/22/2005 Bp Joseph Jon Bruno. m 7/21/1994 Scott John Kinner. Cn The Cathd Ch Of The Adv Birmingham AL 2005-2011; D S Mart-In-The-Fields Mssn Twentynine Palms CA 2004-2005. dean@stpeterscathedral.net

KINNETT, Kenneth (WNC) 57 Half Timber Ln, Flat Rock NC 28731 B Atlanta GA 12/25/1934 s Frank Marion Kinnett & Joyce. BA U So 1956; MDiv STUSo 1969. D 6/21/1969 Bp Milton LeGrand Wood P 4/8/1970 Bp Randolph R Claiborne. m 7/7/1956 Loyd N Nichols c 3. Ch Of The Cov Atlanta GA 1982-1985; R S Greg The Great Athens GA 1973-1980; The TS at The U So Sewanee TN 1971-1974; R Ch Of The H Comf Atlanta GA 1970-1973; Vic S Simon's Epis Ch Conyers GA 1970-1971; Cur S Bede's Ch Atlanta GA 1969-1970. AAPC 1988-1990. ken@kinnett.com

KINNEY, Elise (Mass) 193 Clifton St, Malden MA 02148 B New York NY 12/5/1944 d John Irvine Kinney & Alice. BA Transylvania U 1965; MDiv EDS 1981. D 6/4/1983 Bp Paul Moore Jr P 5/12/1984 Bp Vincent King Pettit. m 1/6/1983 JC Woods. S Andr's Ch Of The Deaf Natick MA 1994-1995; Supply P Dio Massachusetts Boston MA 1984-1989; Dre S Jn's Ch Arlington MA 1983-1984. ableacces@aol.com

KINNEY, Eugenia Wood (Cal) 1746 29th Ave, San Francisco CA 94122 B Mount Vernon IL 11/23/1938 d Eugene Wood & Virginia. BA U of Wyoming 1965; MDiv Iliff TS 1982; CAS CDSP 1990. D 6/16/1984 Bp William Carl Frey P 11/25/1990 Bp William Harvey Wolfrum. Ch Of The Incarn San Francisco CA 1992-2005; S Jas Epis Ch San Francisco CA 1988-1989. revgkinney@aol.com

KINNEY, John Mark (Dal) 1751 Evergreen Ave, Juneau AK 99801 B Syracuse NY 6/4/1932 s John Edwards Kinney & Louise. BS U of Texas 1956; MDiv Epis TS of The SW 1958; STM Nash 1967; MLS U of Texas 1968; MA U of Texas 1970. D 5/31/1958 Bp J(ohn) Joseph Meakins Harte P 1/26/1959 Bp William J Gordon Jr. m 4/20/1974 Nina Keeler c 5. Dio Alaska Fairbanks AK 1958-1961. Auth, *numerous (over 20) arts in Hist and Archv Journ.* Fell Soc of Amer Archivists 1973; Distinguished Mltry Grad The U of Texas at Austin 1956. johninak@gci.net

KINNEY, Kathleen (Oly) 716 N 67th St, Seattle WA 98103 B East Cleveland OH 5/9/1944 d Edwin Kramer & Marcelline. BD S Jn Coll 1967; MA U of Notre Dame 1976; MS Pace Coll 1984; MDiv NYTS 1992. D 6/11/1994 P 12/1/1994 Bp Richard Frank Grein. m 4/11/1998 Wray MacKay. All SS Ch Seattle WA 2003-2010; Cn S Mk's Cathd Seattle WA 1995-2001; Assoc S Ptr's Ch New York NY 1994-2002. kkinney@seattleacademy.org

KINNEY, Robert Sturgis (Okla) 2621 Cooper Dr, Seminole OK 74868 B Endicott NY 8/17/1933 s John Edwards Kinney & Louise. BBA U of Texas 1955; MBA U of Texas 1961; MDiv CDSP 1962; STM STUSo 1969; DMin STUSo 1977. D 6/28/1962 Bp Everett H Jones P 12/1/1962 Bp William J Gordon Jr. m 4/26/1958 Emily Fariss c 2. R S Barn Epis Ch Saratoga WY 1980-1985; R S Andr's Epis Ch Amarillo TX 1975-1980; R Ch Of The Epiph Kingsville TX 1968-1975; Vic Ch Of Our Sav Aransas Pass TX 1965-1968; Vic Trin-By-The-Sea Port Aransas TX 1965-1968; Vic S Jn's Ch Allakaket AK 1962-1965.

KINNEY, Stephen W (WTex) 11849 Sterling Panorama Ter, Austin TX 78738 B Houston TX 12/19/1955 s William George Kinney & Patricia. BA U of Texas 1979; MDiv Epis TS of The SW 1984; MA U of Texas 2009; PhD U of Texas 2011. D 6/7/1984 Bp Maurice Manuel Benitez P 1/18/1985 Bp Gordon Taliaferro Charlton. m 6/8/1985 Gwendolyn Carlisle King c 3. Adj Fac Epis TS Of The SW Austin TX 2002-2010; P-in-c of Bethell Serv S Dav's Ch Austin TX 2002-2008; Int S Chris's Ch Killeen TX 2000-2002; R S Barn Epis Ch Fredericksburg TX 1992-1998; Asst S Jn The Div Houston TX 1989-1992; Chapl Epis HS Bellaire TX 1984-1988. Auth, "Sustaining Mar in a Post-Traditional, Postmodern Wrld," *Dissertation*, U of Texas, 2011. swk.kinney@gmail.com

KINSER, David Dixon (Tenn) St Bartholomew's Church, 4800 Belmont Park Ter, Nashville TN 37215 **Asst S Barth's Ch Bristol TN 2007-** B Memphis TN 1/4/1974 s William Clark Kinser & Caroline Dixon. BA U of So Carolina 1996; MDiv TESM 2007. D 6/2/2007 P 3/30/2008 Bp John Crawford Bauerschmidt. m 1/2/1999 Kristin Kiema c 2. Yth Dir S Barth's Ch Bristol TN 1999-2007; S Dav's Epis Ch Venetia PA 1999-2003. dkinser@stbs.net

KINSER III, Prentice (Va) 200-B Beverly Rd, Ashland VA 23005 B Charlottesville VA 8/18/1939 s Prentice Kinser & Gladys. BA Randolph-Macon Coll 1961; MBA U of Virginia 1967; MDiv STUSo 1978; DMin Garrett-Evang TS 1997. D 6/3/1978 Bp John Alfred Baden P 12/9/1978 Bp William Henry Marmion. m 5/13/1961 Mary Ann Honaker c 3. Montross & Washington Par Montross VA 2000-2010; R S Jas Ch Montross VA 2000-2010; R S Ptr's Ch Oak Grove Montross VA 2000-2010; S Geo's Ch Fredericksburg VA 2000; S Jas' Epis Ch Warrenton VA 1981-1993; Asst S Jn's Ch Roanoke VA 1978-1981. Auth, "HAWKSBILL," Ancient Otter Pub, 2011; Auth, "Limitless Living, A Guide...," Ancient Otter Pub, 2007; Auth, "Pstr Hypnotherapy," *INTERLINK*, Natl Bd for Cert Clincl Hypnotherapists, 2005; Auth, "Prophecy, Trance & Transference," *doctoral thesis*, Garrett-Evang Theo. Sem., 1997. Intl Conf Of Police Chapl; Natl Assn Of Cleric Hypnotherapists. drkinser@gmail.com

KINSEY, David Leon (Pgh) 101 Cherry Hill Drive, Presto PA 15142 B Pittsburgh PA 10/30/1937 s Albert Todd Kinsey & Ila Kathryn. BA U Pgh 1963. D 12/10/1977 P 6/3/1998 Bp Robert Bracewell Appleyard. m 2/14/1980 Margaret J Morrison. Int S Paul's Ch Monongahela PA 1998-1999; P S Thos' Epis Ch Canonsburg PA 1978-1994. revdav@comcast.net

KINSEY, Theron Harvey (Cal) 917 Avis Dr, El Cerrito CA 94530 B Albany CA 1/20/1942 s Raymond K Kinsey & Alice Cornelia. BA Sacramento St U 1964; BD CDSP 1969; MA U of Wyoming 1973. D 12/28/1969 P 8/1/1970 Bp George Richard Millard. m 8/29/1964 Kathryn Lee Chandler.

KINSEY, Thomas Burton (SO) 5004 Upton Ave S, Minneapolis MN 55410 B Cleveland OH 10/28/1942 s Harold E Kinsey & Gladys S. BA Heidelberg Coll 1965; MDiv EDS 1972. D 6/17/1972 Bp John Harris Burt P 12/1/1972 Bp John Mc Gill Krumm. Assoc S Steph's Epis Ch And U Columbus OH 1983-1988; R Chr Ch Xenia OH 1980-1983; R S Paul's Ch Bellevue OH 1975-1980; Asst Trin Ch Columbus OH 1972-1976.

KINSOLVING, John Armistead (RG) 107 Washington Ave, Santa Fe NM 87501 B Santa Fe NM 10/30/1936 s Charles James Kinsolving & Mary Virginia. BA U of New Mex 1958; MA U of New Mex 1963; BD CDSP 1964. D 6/7/1965 Bp C J Kinsolving III P 12/7/1965 Bp James W Hunter. m 1/30/1959 Patricia Young c 1. S Bede's Epis Ch Santa Fe NM 1969-1977; R S Paul's Epis Ch Evanston WY 1965-1969. teesandskis@cs.com

KINYON, B(rice) Wayne (USC) 1900 Woodvalley Drive, Columbia SC 29212 **S Thos Ch Eastover SC 2010-; Chapl, Ret Cler, etc. Dio Upper So Carolina Columbia SC 2007-; Bd Trst York Place Epis Ch Hm For Chld York SC 2007-; Bd Trst Finlay Hse Columbia SC 2004-** B Camden NJ 5/3/1936 s Brice Whitman Kinyon & Zilla Lougee. BA Duke 1958; MDiv STUSo 1961. D 7/15/1961 P 2/11/1962 Bp John Vander Horst. m 11/23/1984 Carolyn Jean Templeton c 5. P-in-c Ch Of The Epiph Laurens SC 2006-2009; Chapl So Carolina Epis Hm At Still Hopes W Columbia SC 1999-2006; P-in-c S Paul's Ch Clinton OK 1989-1994; Judge Eccl Crt Dio Oklahoma Oklahoma City OK 1984-1989; Chapl Epis Ch Coun Tulsa OK 1981; R S Jn's Ch Kenner LA 1973-1981; Vic S Tim's Ch La Place LA 1973-1978; P-in-c S Mary's Ch Chattanooga TN 1969-1970; Vic Ch Of The Nativ Ft Oglethorpe GA 1967-1969; P-in-c Chr Ch Brownsville TN 1963-1967; P-in-c Imm Ch Ripley TN 1963-1966; Cur S Paul's Epis Ch Chattanooga TN 1962; Asst Ch Of The Ascen Knoxville TN 1961-1962. Assembly of Epis Healthcare Chapl 1982; Assembly of Epis Healthcare Chapl, Pres 1999-2001; Bd Cert Chapl of Assn of Profsnl Chaplai 1992; Lexington Med Cntr, Chapl Bd 2011; Pres Oklahoma Chapl Assn 1986-1987; S.C. Soc of Chapl 1999. DSA Coll of Chapl 1998. wkinyon@sc.rr.com

KIRBY, Erin Colleen (WNC) 2451 Ridge Rd, Berkeley CA 94709 B Boone NC 1/31/1958 d Jack D Cobb & Eva King. MA Appalachian St U 1995; EdD Appalachian St U 2004; MDiv CDSP 2011. D 12/18/2010 Bp Granville Porter Taylor. c 1. erinkirby@mac.com

KIRBY, H(arry) Scott (Eau) 510 S Farwell St, Eau Claire WI 54701 **P-in-c Gr Ch Rice Lake WI 2005-; Exam Chapl Dio Eau Claire Eau Claire WI 1994-; Liturg Off Dio Eau Claire Eau Claire WI 1992-; Dep Gc Dio Eau Claire Eau Claire WI 1991-** B Richmond VA 5/6/1938 s William Alphus Kirby & Lucielle Viola. BA U Rich 1960; MDiv GTS 1963. D 6/15/1963 Bp Robert Fisher Gibson Jr P 12/20/1963 Bp Lauriston L Scaife. m 6/22/1963 Heather Roberts c 2. Chair, CoM Dio Eau Claire Eau Claire WI 1996-2010; Pres Stndg Com Dio Eau Claire Eau Claire WI 1991-2002; Chr Ch Cathd Eau Claire WI 1989-2005; Dio Wstrn Kansas Hutchinson KS 1989-2005; Eccl Crt Dio Eau Claire Eau Claire WI 1989-1995; Dio Wstrn Kansas Hutchinson KS 1985-1988; Ecum Off Dio Wstrn Kansas Hutchinson KS 1983-1988; Liturg Off Dio Wstrn Kansas Hutchinson KS 1981-1988; Epis Ch Of The Incarn Salina KS 1980-1981; Chr Cathd Salina KS 1979-2005; S Fran Cmnty Serv Inc. Salina KS 1979-1989; R Ch of S Jn on the Mtn Bernardsville NJ 1973-1978. Auth, "arts, Appeal Letters, etc.," *Developmental & Estate Plnng*, St. Fran Acad. Angl Soc 1973; Cmnty of S Jn The Bapt 1973. Bp's Serv Awd Dio Wstrn Kansas 1980. snhkirby@aol.com

KIRBY, Kelly Ellen (O) 179 Pleasant St, Claremont NH 03743 **R S Andr Epis Ch Mentor OH 2007-** B Royal Oak MI 1/11/1977 d Thomas Edmund West & Jeannie Ellen. BS MI SU 1998; MDiv CDSP 2002. D 12/22/2001 P 7/17/2002 Bp Wendell Nathaniel Gibbs Jr. m 1/10/2003 Brian Kirby c 2. R Trin Ch Claremont NH 2004-2007; Asst All SS Epis Ch Pontiac MI 2002-2004. kellytherev@gmail.com

KIRBY, Richard Allen (Neb) No address on file. B 8/23/1929 D 2/24/1955 Bp Howard R Brinker.

KIRBY-COLADONATO, Jeanne Wise (Del) 9703 Cedar Lane, Seaford DE 19973 B Savannah GA 12/19/1939 d Alphonso Joseph Wise & Lucie Dennis. U GA; BA Hood Coll 1983; MDiv VTS 1986. D 6/7/1986 Bp A(lbert) Theodore Eastman P 5/2/1987 Bp Barry Valentine. m 5/28/2006 Joseph P Coladonato. Pres, Stndg Com Dio Delaware Wilmington DE 2004-2008; R S Lk's Epis Ch Seaford DE 1995-2011; Assoc R S Anne's Par Annapolis MD 1994-1995; R S Chris Epis Ch Linthicum Heights MD 1986-1994. Treas Seaford Area Min. jwkirby@comcast.net

KIRCHER, Kathleen L (SwFla) 1741 Winding Oaks Way, Naples FL 34109 B Rochester NY 1/7/1943 d Joseph W Kircher & Ruth M. BA Nazareth Coll 1968; MS Boston Coll 1974; PhD U Roch 1992. D 10/17/2001 P 4/19/2002 Bp John Bailey Lipscomb. Assoc R S Monica's Epis Ch Naples FL 2002-2011. kathy1743@gmail.com

KIRCHHOFFER, Jim (Cal) 1028 3Rd St Apt A, Novato CA 94945 B Mobile AL 1/24/1933 s Richard Ainslie Kirchhoffer & Arlene Leicester. BA Wabash Coll 1955; BD VTS 1958; CFP VTS 1980. D 6/21/1958 P 12/1/1958 Bp Richard Ainslie Kirchhoffer. m 9/16/1978 Elaine Marie Biagini c 3. Vic S Giles Ch Moraga CA 1963-1967; Asst R S Jn's Ch Youngstown OH 1960-1963; Vic Trin Ch Lawrenceburg IN 1958-1960.

KIRCHHOFFER JR, Richard Ainslie (Mont) 306 Lupfer Ave, Whitefish MT 59937 **Died 3/21/2011** B Los Angeles CA 8/5/1919 s Richard Ainslie Kirchhoffer & Arline Leicester. BS U So 1940; BD VTS 1948; Urban Trng Cntr 1969. D 4/27/1948 Bp Richard Ainslie Kirchhoffer P 1/1/1949 Bp Edmund P Dandridge.

KIRCHMIER, Anne Ruth (Va) 104 Berkley St, Ashland VA 23005 **Dn of Reg XI Dio Virginia Richmond VA 2010-; R The Fork Ch Doswell VA 2005-** B Pittsburgh PA 10/10/1965 d Thomas McNeel Kirchmier & Ruth Moyer. BS Westfield St Coll 1987; MDiv SWTS 2001. Trans 11/19/2003 Bp Gordon Paul Scruton. Chr Epis Ch Winchester VA 2003-2005; Asst to the R / Cler Res Chr Ch Alexandria VA 2001-2003. kirchmier@juno.com

KIRCHNER, Laurence Ernest (Eau) 213A W Jefferson St, Oconomowoc WI 53066 B Saint Paul MN 6/15/1953 D 2/16/2003 P 10/1/2003 Bp Keith Bernard

Whitmore. m 10/18/1980 Wanda Marie Jarchow c 2. St Mths Epis Ch Waukesha WI 2003-2004. kirchner@priest.com

KIRK, Jeffrey Malcolm (NJ) 102 Pearlcroft Rd, Cherry Hill NJ 08034 **P-in-c Gr Ch Merchantville NJ 2010-** B Astoria NY 6/26/1946 s Francis Shallus Kirk & Hazel. BS Leh 1968; MBA Kent St U 1971; MDiv EDS 1975; DMin CRDS 1982. D 6/21/1975 Bp John Harris Burt P 12/27/1975 Bp David Shepherd Rose. m 8/29/1981 Betsey L Watson c 2. R Ch Of The Atone Stratford NJ 2000-2010; R S Mary's Ch Haddon Heights NJ 1990-1995; R Epis Ch Of S Mary The Vrgn Falmouth ME 1987-1990; R Ch Of The Ascen Rochester NY 1982-1987; Asst S Paul's Ch Rochester NY 1978-1982; Asst S Jn's Ch Hampton VA 1975-1978. "Intelligent Design," LivCh, 2005; "Baptism," *First Act of Stwdshp*, LivCh, 1985. Beta Gamma Sigma Kent St U 1971; Chi Epsilon Leh 1968. jm125kirk@gmail.com

KIRK, Patricia Lanier (USC) 501 S La Posada Cir Apt 118, Green Valley AZ 85614 **D Epis Ch Of S Fran-In-The-Vlly Green Vlly AZ 2000-** B Decatur AL 9/5/1933 d Charner Ross Lanier & Pearl Elizabeth. U of No Alabama. D 10/14/2000 Bp Robert Reed Shahan. m 5/24/1953 william Leroy Kirk c 3. patkirk2000@cox.net

KIRK, Richard Joseph (Pa) 319 Lea Dr, West Chester PA 19382 B Trenton NJ 8/30/1931 s Richard Alexander Kirk & Jane. BSE Pr 1953; M.Div. GTS 1956; STM Tem 1960; U of Missouri 1965; New Sch for Soc Resrch 1967; DMin Eden TS 1976; Neumann Coll 1993. D 4/28/1956 P 10/28/1956 Bp Alfred L Banyard. m 4/17/1993 Janice M Mogavero. Dn Brandywine Deanry Dio Pennsylvania Philadelphia PA 1994-2000; R The Epis Ch Of The Adv Kennett Sq PA 1979-1996; Dio Missouri S Louis MO 1976-1979; Assoc S Ptr's Epis Ch St Louis MO 1968-1976; Assoc Dce Dio New York New York City NY 1963-1968; R S Mk's Epis Ch Yonkers NY 1958-1963; Vic S Jn's Epis Ch Maple Shade NJ 1956-1958. Auth, "Love Anew," Self-Pub, 1996; Auth, "On The Calling And Care Of Pastors; Orgnztn And Function Of The Bp'S Off - A Behavioral Sci View," *Patterns For Par Dvlpmt*, Crossroads, 1974; Auth, "On Calling & Care Pastors". rjkirkcons@aol.com

K

KIRK, Ruth Lawson (Del) P. O. Box 3510, Greenville, 507 East Buck Road, Wilmington DE 19807 **Dep, GC Dio Delaware Wilmington DE 2011-; Mem, Stndg Com Dio Delaware Wilmington DE 2011-; R Chr Ch Greenville Wilmington DE 2007-** B Newark NJ 10/3/1961 d Peter Raymond Lawson & Mary Helen. BA Indiana U 1983; MDiv VTS 1989. D 6/23/1989 P 5/1/1990 Bp Edward Witker Jones. m 11/24/1990 Richard Joseph Kirk c 2. Dep, GC Dio Delaware Wilmington DE 2011; Alt Dep, GC Dio Delaware Wilmington DE 2008-2011; Mem, Stndg Com Dio Pennsylvania Philadelphia PA 2006-2007; Dep, GC Dio Pennsylvania Philadelphia PA 2004-2006; Dn, Montgomery Dnry Dio Pennsylvania Philadelphia PA 2000-2006; R S Ptr's Ch Glenside PA 1993-2007; Asst S Paul's Ch Philadelphia PA 1989-1993. Contrib, "Meditations," *Walking w God Day by Day*, FMP, 2011; Contrib, "Meditations," *Wisdom found: Stories of Wmn Transfigured by Faith*, FMP, 2011. rkirk@christchurchde.org

KIRK, Virginia Adele (Pa) 354 Heathcliffe Rd, Huntingdon Valley PA 19006 **D Ch Of The Resurr Philadelphia PA 2000-** B Philadelphia PA 1/19/1942 d John Mundell Kirk & Muriel Adele. STUSo 1986; NOD La Salle U 1987. D 12/12/1987 Bp Allen Lyman Bartlett Jr. D The Free Ch Of S Jn Philadelphia PA 1987-1999. NAAD 1987; OA 1985-1995.

KIRKALDY, David (Tex) 612 Duroux Rd, La Marque TX 77568 B Northumberland UK 7/30/1935 s David Kirkaldy & Lilian. BD U of Nottingham 1956; PhD U of Nottingham 1959. D 6/11/2005 Bp Don Adger Wimberly P 12/15/2005 Bp Rayford Baines High Jr. m 8/22/1959 Doris Robinson c 4. dkirkaldy@ghg.net

KIRKHAM II, Hall (Mass) 320 Boston Post Rd, Weston MA 02493 **Asst R S Ptr's Ch Weston MA 2008-** B Cleveland OH 6/12/1964 s Walter Rich Kirkham & Jane Louise. BA Amh 1987; MSc U of Edinburgh 1988; MBA U of Pennsylvania 1994; MDiv EDS 2008. D 6/7/2008 Bp M(arvil) Thomas Shaw III. m 9/13/2003 Marjorie Marie Rose Susan Asfour c 3. Jn Robbins Hart Memi Prize for Excellence in Preaching EDS 2008. hall.kirkham@gmail.com

KIRKHAM JR, Harry Adams (Minn) 822 Baylis St Apt 308, Duluth MN 55811 B Minneapolis MN 4/1/1926 s Harry Adams Kirkham & Madeleine. BA Macalester Coll 1949; BD VTS 1961. D 6/24/1961 Bp Hamilton Hyde Kellogg P 5/26/1962 Bp Philip Frederick McNairy. c 3. Port Rehab Cntr Duluth MN 1978-1982; H Apos Ch Duluth MN 1977-1982; S Marys Hosp Of Superior Superior WI 1977-1978; Vic Trin Epis Ch Hermantown MN 1975-1982; Vic S Edw's Ch Duluth MN 1971-1977; R Ch Of The Gd Shpd Windom MN 1964-1971. RACA.

KIRKING, Kerry Clifton (Spok) 2408 S Browne St, Spokane WA 99203 **P Assoc Cathd Of S Jn The Evang Spokane WA 2001-** B Coeur d'Alene ID 7/5/1946 s Hilbert Clifton Kirking & Mary Evelyn. BA Pacific Luth U 1968; MA Yale DS 1972. D 10/15/1994 Bp Frank Jeffrey Terry P 6/2/2001 Bp James Edward Waggoner. m 7/12/1975 Judith Marie Krell. D Cathd Of S Jn The Evang Spokane WA 1996-2001; D-in-c H Trin Epis Ch Spokane WA 1995-1996; D Cathd Of S Jn The Evang Spokane WA 1994-1995. Affirming Angl Catholicism 1994; CBS 1999. Wolcott Calkins Prize for Preaching Yale DS 1970. frkerry@comcast.net

KIRKLAND, Robert Gaillard (USC) 804 N Congress St., York SC 29745 B Beaufort SC 6/11/1954 s James Stanford Kirkland & Mary Elizabeth. BA U of So Carolina 1999; MDiv TESM 2002. D 5/25/2002 Bp Edward Lloyd Salmon Jr P 12/7/2002 Bp Robert Deane Rowley Jr. m 9/6/1991 Linda Belle Kirkland. Ch Of The Gd Shpd York SC 2006-2011; R S Fran Of Assisi Epis Ch Youngsville PA 2002-2006. frrobertkirkland@gmail.com

KIRKLAND III, William George (At) Po Box 337, Dahlonega GA 30533 B Quitman MS 10/9/1926 s William G Kirkland & Eva. Emory U; EFM U of Alabama; BA U of Alabama 1949. D 10/28/1995 Bp Frank Kellogg Allan. m 2/14/1987 Susanne M Clark. D Ch of the Resurr Sautee Nacoochee GA 1998-2008. Kairos. fallguys@hotmail.com

KIRKLAND, William Matthews (WVa) Po Box 471, Scott Depot WV 25560 **Died 4/19/2011** B Amity GA 12/27/1918 s Julius Robert Kirkland & Maude. BA Merc 1939; BD New Orleans Bapt TS 1945; MA UTS 1948; PhD U of Edinburgh Edinburgh GB 1951. D 6/16/1954 P 12/1/1954 Bp Randolph R Claiborne. c 2. Auth, "Dad's Road to Zestful Living," *Rdr's Dig*, 1990; Auth, "Baron von Hugel and Flannery O'Connor, The Flannery O'Connor Bulletin," *Georgia Coll*, 1989; Auth, "Jn Birch & Heresy at Merc," *Atlanta mag*, 1988; Auth, "A Letter From Dad: Fresh Water From an Old Well," *Chr Sci Monitor*, 1988; Auth, "Flannery O'Connor: The Person & Writer," *E-W Revs*, 1967. dogwalker@citykat.net

KIRKLEY, John Lawrence (Cal) 389 Belmont Street #105, Oakland CA 94610 **R S Jas Epis Ch San Francisco CA 2010-** B Gary IN 4/29/1967 s John Roger Kirkley & Joan Marie. BA Indiana U 1989; MDiv Chicago TS 1993; Cert CDSP 2002. D 6/1/2002 P 12/7/2002 Bp William Edwin Swing. m 9/14/2008 Andrew Russell Aldrich c 1. R The Epis Ch Of S Jn The Evang San Francisco CA 2004-2010; Every Voice Ntwk San Francisco CA 2004; Assoc Ch Of The H Innoc San Francisco CA 2002-2004. "Struggling for Sacramental Equality," Witness mag, 2005; "A Contest Between the Normalcy of Civilization and the Reign of God," Do Justice Series/Louie Crew's Angl Pages, 2005; "Why I Believe In Gay Mar," Pacific Ch News, 2004; "Mod Demoniacs," Do Justice Series/Louie Crew's Angl Pages, 2004. Integrity 2000. john@stjamessf.org

KIRKMAN, John Raymond (WMich) 4713 Rockvalley Dr NE, Grand Rapids MI 49525 B Adrian MI 2/12/1942 s Ernest Robert Kirkman & Kathryn May. BS Wstrn Michigan U 1965; MDiv Bex 1968. D 6/29/1968 Bp Charles Bennison P 12/30/1968 Bp Frederick Barton Wolf. m 7/11/1991 Sherry L Vanderwerf c 2. S Paul's Ch Greenville MI 1994-2007; S Andr's Ch Grand Rapids MI 1985-1990; Assoc S Andr's Ch Grand Rapids MI 1983-1985; R Emm Ch Petoskey MI 1973-1975; R S Jn's Epis Ch Saugus MA 1970-1973; Vic Chr Ch Norway ME 1969-1970; Cur Epis Ch Of S Mary The Vrgn Falmouth ME 1968-1969. jrkirkman@juno.com

KIRK-NORRIS, Barbara H (NwT) PO Box 2949, Big Spring TX 79721 **Exec Coun Dio NW Texas Lubbock TX 2011-; R The Epis Ch Of S Mary The Vrgn Big Sprg TX 2009-** B Knoxville TN 8/15/1967 d Joseph Kirk & Helen. BS Middle Tennessee St U 1990; MS U of Tennessee 1993; MDiv VTS 2004. D 5/29/2004 Bp Charles Glenn VonRosenberg P 1/22/2005 Bp Edwin Funsten Gulick Jr. m 8/15/1967 William Christopher Norris. judicial Crt Dio Kentucky Louisville KY 2006-2007; R Ch Of The Ascen Bardstown KY 2004-2008. Pres (two years) Bardstown Mnstrl Assn 2008. tater5355@hotmail.com

KIRKPATRICK, Daisy (CNY) 741 W 2nd St, Elmira NY 14905 **Par D Gr Epis Ch Elmira NY 2008-** B Northampton MA 12/25/1944 d John Kirkpatrick & Hope Miller. BS Cor 1989; M Div Bex 2003. D 8/21/2003 Bp Gladstone Bailey Adams III. c 2. Intern Chemung Vlly Cluster Elmira NY 2007-2008; Cur Zion Epis Ch Greene NY 2004-2005; D in Charge Shared Epis Mnstry E Carthage NY 2003-2004. Cmnty of the Gospel 2006-2010; Comp of St. Lk 2003-2006. dkirkpatrick1@stny.rr.com

KIRKPATRICK, Frank Gloyd (Ct) 154 Clearfield, Wethersfield CT 06109 **P Assoc Trin Epis Ch Hartford CT 1980-** B Washington DC 8/4/1942 s George Gloyd Kirkpatrick & Amy. BA Trin Hartford CT 1964; MA UTS 1966; PhD Br 1970. D 6/9/1973 P 5/1/1974 Bp Morgan Porteus. m 6/11/1966 Elizabeth Kirkpatrick c 2. Chair - COM Dio Connecticut Hartford CT 1982-1994. authohr, "The Epis Ch in Crisis," *The Epis Ch in Crisis*, Praeger, 2009; Auth, "The Ethics of Cmnty," *The Ethics of Cmnty*, Blackwells, 2001; Auth, "A Moral Ontology for A Theistic Ethics," *Moral Ontology for a Theistic Ethic*, Ashgate, 1996; Auth, "Together Bound," *Together Bound*, Oxford, 1993; Auth, "Cmnty: A Trin of Models," *Cmnty: A Trin of Models*, Georgetown, 1986. AAR 1972; Soc for Philos of Rel 1996. Brownell Prize for Tchg Excellence Trin 2011; Bp's Awd for Distinguished Serv Dio Connecticut 1999; Chas A Dana Resrch Prof Trin 1993; Ellsworth M Tracy Lectureship Trin Hartford CT 1981; Phi Beta Kappa Trin Hartford CT 1963. frank.kirkpatrick@trincoll.edu

KIRKPATRICK, Martha (Me) PO Box 1187, Waldoboro ME 04572 **S Marg's Ch Belfast ME 2009-; Asst Gr Epis Ch Bath ME 2007-** B Portland ME 10/2/1956 d William Kirkpatrick & Priscilla. BA Skidmore Coll 1978; JD GW

1981; MDiv Harvard DS 2007. D 6/9/2007 P 12/15/2007 Bp Chilton Abbie Richardson Knudsen. Dio Maine Portland ME 2007-2009. mgkirkp@midcoast.com

KIRKPATRICK, Rebecca Blair (Oly) 111 NE 80th St, Seattle WA 98115 **Dir Chld & Yth Mnstrs S Andr's Ch Seattle WA 2008-** B Fort Collins CO 12/22/1977 d John B Knezorich & Susan W. BA Mt Holyoke Coll 2001; MDiv Yale DS 2004. D 6/28/2008 Bp Bavi Rivera P 1/17/2009 Bp Gregory Harold Rickel. rckirkpatrick@yahoo.com

KIRKPATRICK JR, Robert Frederick (Lex) 4700 Ky Highway 1194, Stanford KY 40484 B Montgomery AL 5/22/1940 s Robert Frederick Kirkpatrick & Margaret. BA U So 1962; MDiv VTS 1971; DMin STUSo 1981. D 6/11/1971 Bp Furman Stough P 12/5/1971 Bp George Mosley Murray. m 5/2/1974 Priscilla Anne Lee c 6. R Trin Epis Ch Danville KY 1990-2006; R Ch Of The Gd Shpd Covington GA 1979-1990; Asst Ch Of The Ascen Clearwater FL 1976-1979; Vic S Jn The Evang Robertsdale AL 1971-1973; R S Paul's Ch Foley AL 1971-1973. shepherdsrest@windstream.net

KIRKWOOD, Donald Wayne (WNY) 555 E Main St, Batavia NY 14020 **Died 7/7/2010** B Buffalo NY 6/29/1938 s John A Kirkwood & Jessie M. BA Hob 1963; STB GTS 1967. D 6/17/1967 P 12/21/1967 Bp Lauriston L Scaife.

KISNER, Mary Elizabeth (CPa) 712 E 16th St, Berwick PA 18603 **Chr Ch Berwick PA 2010-; R S Paul's Ch Troy PA 1995-** B Detroit MI 7/28/1950 d Walter Joseph Kochan & Alexandria. BS Drexel U 1972; MA U Of Scranton 2003. D 11/3/1994 P 7/12/1995 Bp James Michael Mark Dyer. m 8/3/1974 Francis C Kisner. S Paul's Ch Troy PA 2000-2010. mryksn@aol.com

KISS, Margaret Mary (Mil) 2965 S Delaware Ave #1, Milwaukee MI 53207 **D All SS' Cathd Milwaukee WI 2011-** B Milwaukee WI 1/13/1944 d Louis Giovanni Kiss & Regina Margaret. BA Alverno Coll Milwaukee WI 1966; MSEd Dayton U 1991. D 6/5/2010 Bp Steven Andrew Miller. margex1@netzero.com

KISSAM, Todd William (Eas) 507 N. Pinehurst Ave., Salisbury MD 21801 **R S Ptr's Ch Salisbury MD 2009-** B Glens Falls NY 2/15/1966 s William Allen Kissam & Diane. MDiv Washington Theol Un 1996. Rec from Roman Catholic 12/19/2001 as Priest Bp William Jerry Winterrowd. m 5/28/2004 Heather C Kissam c 1. R Ch Of Our Sav Washington DC 2005-2009; Asst Chr's Epis Ch Castle Rock CO 2002-2004. toddwmkissam@gmail.com

KISSINGER, Debra Jean (Ind) 1100 W. 42nd St., Indianapolis IN 46208 **Dioc Transition Min Dio Indianapolis Indianapolis IN 2009-** B Pottsville PA 10/4/1961 d Kenward Edward Kissinger & Anna Crowsdale. AS Penn 1981; BA La Salle U 1988; MDiv Ya Berk 1992; Cert The Ch Dvlpmt Inst 1996; Cert The Ch Dvlpmt Inst 1997; Cert Cler Ldrshp Proj 2007; Cert Off of Transition Mnstrs 2010; Cert Cler Ldrshp Inst 2012. D 6/13/1992 Bp Allen Lyman Bartlett Jr P 12/12/1992 Bp Richard Frank Grein. c 1. GC Dep Alt Dio Bethlehem Bethlehem PA 2006; Epis Coun for CE Epis Ch Cntr New York NY 2001-2008; Dioc Counc Dio Ohio Cleveland OH 1997-2001; R Gr Epis Ch Willoughby OH 1997-2001; Vic S Ptr's Epis Ch Oxford CT 1993-1997; Sum Camp Chapl Dio Connecticut Hartford CT 1993; Asst S Barn Ch Irvington on Hudson NY 1992-1993. Auth, "Var arts," *AWE Chld's Mnstrs*, www.diobethkids.org; Auth, "Var arts," *Dioc Life*, Dio Bethlehem; Auth, "Var arts," *Epis Life*, ECUSA; Auth, "Var arts," *Epis Tchr*, Virginia Sem; Auth, "Var arts," *Go Forth*, Dio Indianapolis; Auth, "Windows of St. Ptr's," *Windows of St. Ptr's*, St. Ptr's Ch, Oxford, CT. kissinger@indydio.org

KITAGAWA, Chisato (WMass) 5 Hickory Ln, Amherst MA 01002 B Tokyo Japan 7/29/1932 s Chiaki Kitagawa & Sumi. BA Rikkyo Daigaku Jp 1958; BD EDS 1964; MA/PhD U MI 1972. D 6/20/1964 P 1/1/1965 Bp Robert McConnell Hatch. m 6/17/1961 Mary Joan Messinger c 2. Serv H Faith Ch Saline MI 1970-1972; Cur Gr Ch Amherst MA 1964-1967. Auth, "Purpose Expressions In Engl"; Auth, "Case Marking & Causativization"; Auth, "Making Connections w Writing". chisatomary@gmail.com

KITAGAWA, John Elliott (Az) 1700 E Chula Vista Rd, Tucson AZ 85718 **R S Phil's In The Hills Tucson AZ 2001-** B Minneapolis MN 5/10/1950 s Daisuke David Kitagawa & Fujiko. BA Hob 1972; Inter/Met Sem 1977; CPE St. Elizabeths Hosp Washington DC 1977; MDiv UTS 1978; DMin SWTS 2005. D 6/3/1978 P 12/3/1978 Bp Paul Moore Jr. m 7/10/1982 Kathleen A Stack. Dio Maryland Baltimore MD 1998-2004; Cn Ordnry Dio Maryland Baltimore MD 1997-2001; Exec Offcr Dio Maryland Baltimore MD 1991-1997; Cn For Mssn Dvlpmt Dio Maryland Baltimore MD 1984-1988; Excoun Dio Connecticut Hartford CT 1981-1984; Interfaith Coop Mnstrs New Haven CT 1980-1984; Asst Calv and St Geo New York NY 1978-1980; Dio Maryland Baltimore MD 1000. john.kitagawa@stphilipstucson.org

KITAYAMA, Scott D (WTex) 12111 Chevening Ct, San Antonio TX 78231 **Chr Epis Ch San Antonio TX 2008-** B 4/30/1962 s Neho Kitayama & Kay. MDiv Fuller TS 2003; Angl Stds VTS 2006. D 6/24/2006 Bp Don Adger Wimberly P 1/10/2007 Bp Rayford Baines High Jr. m 9/7/2002 Susanna Huans c 2. S Cyp's Ch Lufkin TX 2006-2008; S Jn The Div Houston TX 2002-2005. sdkyama@yahoo.com

KITCH, Anne E (Be) 333 Wyandotte St, Bethlehem PA 18015 **GC Deputation, chair Dio Bethlehem Bethlehem PA 2007-; Stndg Com Dio Bethlehem Bethlehem PA 2004-** B 3/7/1962 d John Ira Kitch & Betsy. BA Carleton Coll 1984; MA U of St. Thos 1993; MDiv GTS 1995. D 6/3/1995 P 12/9/1995 Bp Richard Frank Grein. m 8/6/1988 James H Peck c 2. Cn for Chr Formation Cathd Ch Of The Nativ Bethlehem PA 1999-2008; Asst to R S Ptr's Epis Ch Peekskill NY 1995-1999. Auth, "Stumbling Into the Sacr: Meditations for Lent," Ldr Resources, 2011; Auth, "Adv Morning," *Wisdom Found: Stories of Wmn Transfigured by Faith*, Forw Mvmt, 2011; Auth, "In the Dark Night," *Lifting Wmn Voices: Prayers to Change the Wrld*, Morehouse Pub., 2009; Auth, "What We Do in Lent," Morehouse Pub, 2007; Auth, "Taking The Plunge: Baptism and Parenting," Morehouse Pub., 2006; Auth, "What We Do in Adv," Morehouse Pub., 2006; Auth, "Tending The Hm Fires," *Doing H Bus: The Best of Vstry Papers*, Ch Pub, 2006; Auth, "What We Do in Ch," Morehouse Pub, 2004; Auth, "The Angl Fam PB," Morehouse Pub., 2004; Auth, "Bless This Way," Morehouse Pub, 2003; Auth, "One Little Ch Mouse," Morehouse Pub, 2002; Auth, "Bless This Day," Morehouse Pub, 2000. akitch@diobeth.org

KITCH, Sarah Underhill (Los) 280 Royal Ave, Simi Valley CA 93065 **D S Fran Of Assisi Epis Ch Simi Vlly CA 2010-; Chapl S Patricks Ch And Day Sch Thousand Oaks CA 2009-** B White Plains, NY 11/13/1956 d Charles Matthew Underhill & Julie Foote. No Degree Syr 1976; Sprtl Dir Stillpoint Cntr for Sprtl Direction 2005; Diac Bloy Hse 2010. D 5/23/2010 Bp Chester Lovelle Talton. m 6/21/1980 David John Kitch. trinity.sdo5@sbcglobal.net

KITT, Michael (Chi) 523 Courtland Ave, Park Ridge IL 60068 **D S Mary's Ch Pk Ridge IL 2002-** B Phoenix AZ 10/19/1950 s Carl Norman Kitt & Barbara Ann. BA/BS Roosevelt U 1975. D 2/2/2002 Bp William Dailey Persell. m 10/9/1982 Stephanie Lucille Parke. Dir'S Serv Awd Cmnty Counslg Centers Of Chicago 1994. mkitt@compuserve.com

KITTELSON, Alan Leslie (Vt) 6 Park St, Vergennes VT 05491 **R S Paul's Epis Ch On The Green Vergennes VT 2008-; S Paul's Epis Ch Waxahachie TX 1987-** B Montevideo MN 3/26/1950 s Leslie Gene Kittelson & Rudell Ione. BA S Olaf Coll 1972; U of Oslo Oslo NO 1973; U MN 1975; MDiv EDS 1986. D 6/24/1987 Bp Robert Marshall Anderson P 7/22/1989 Bp Edward Cole Chalfant. Gr Ch Amherst MA 2001-2008; Epis Ch Of The Epiph Wilbraham MA 1998-2006; Asst Gr Ch Amherst MA 1998-2000; S Andr's Ch Newcastle ME 1990-1997. alankittelson@gmail.com

KITTREDGE, Cynthia Briggs (Tex) Seminary of the Southwest, 501 East 32nd Street, Austin TX 78705 **The Ch of the Gd Shpd Austin TX 2000-; Assoc Prof of the NT Epis TS Of The SW Austin TX 1999-** B New York NY 8/12/1957 d Taylor R Briggs & Jane Ann. BA Wms 1979; MDiv Harvard DS 1984; ThM Harvard DS 1989; ThD Harvard DS 1996. D 6/2/1984 Bp John Bowen Coburn P 4/1/1985 Bp Christoph Keller Jr. m 7/12/1981 Frank D Kittredge c 3. Emm Chap Manchester MA 1997-1999; S Jn's Ch Beverly Farms MA 1984-1986. Ed, "The Bible in the Publ Sq," Fortress Press, 2008; Auth, "Conversations w Scripture: The Gospel of Jn," *Angl Assn of Biblic Scholars*, Ch Pub, 2007; Auth, "Intro and Annotation - Hebrews," *New Oxford Annotated Bible*, Oxf Press, 2000; Auth, "Cmnty & Authority," *Cmnty & Authority*, Trin Press, 1999; Auth, "Pauline Texts," *Dictionary of Feminist Theologies*, Westminster/Jn Knox, 1996; Ed, "Hebrews," *Searching the Scriptures*, Crossroad/Continuum, 1994. AAR; Angl Assn Biblic Scholars; ECF; EvangES; Soc of Biblicalal Lit. Chr Faith and Life Grant Louisville Inst 2007; Grant EvangES 2005; Conant Fund Incentive Grant Conant Fund 2004; Conant Fund Sabbatical Grant Conant Fund 2003; Eugene M. Stetson Fllshp ECF 1990. ckittredge@ssw.edu

KITTS, Joseph (Eur) Windyridge, Cottage Lane, Saint Martins, Oswestry, Shropshire SY11 3BL Great Britain (UK) B Saint Helens Lancashire UK 1/5/1927 s Richard Kitts & Catherine. Brasted Kent; Tyndale Hall Bristol Gb. D 5/1/1960 P 5/1/1961 Bp The Bishop Of Liverpool. m 3/26/1949 Freda Jones. Asst Truro Epis Ch Fairfax VA 1976-1994; Gr Ch Henryetta OK 1975-1976; R Ch Of The Redeem Okmulgee OK 1974-1976.

KLAAS III, Anthony Rudolph (La) 4 Yacht Club Dr Apt 36, Daphne AL 36526 B Mobile AL 11/4/1933 s Anthony Rudolph Klaas & Marietta Harriet. BA Georgia Inst of Tech 1956; MBA Pace Coll 1978; MDiv TESM 1983; MA SE Sem Wake Forest NC 1999. D 6/11/1983 Bp William Grant Black P 1/1/1984 Bp James Russell Moodey. m 4/22/1957 Beverly Weigand c 4. S Phil's Ch New Orleans LA 1993-1996; S Mary's Ch Franklin LA 1989-1993; St Georges Ch Pittsburgh PA 1985-1988; S Geo's Ch Waynesburg PA 1984-1988; Assoc S Lk's Epis Ch Akron OH 1983-1984. arudolphklaas@aol.com

KLAM, Warren Peter (Va) 200 Harbor Dr Unit 2803, San Diego CA 92101 B Cambridge MA 12/8/1946 s Najeeb Klam & Louise. Tul 1967; MD LSU 1971; MS U of Texas in Dallas 2004. D 6/16/1978 Bp John Alfred Baden P 6/29/1979 Bp Robert Bruce Hall. Assoc Ch Of The H Cross Dunn Loring VA 1984-1986; Asst S Paul's Rock Creek Washington DC 1980-1984. klamshell@aol.com

KLATT, William Blodgett (NI) 416 N Huron Terrace Dr, Harrisville MI 48740 B Saginaw MI 3/22/1926 s William E Klatt & Gladys. BS U MI 1952; BD CDSP 1957. D 6/30/1957 Bp Richard S M Emrich P 1/1/1958 Bp Archie H Crowley. R S Barn-In-The-Dunes Gary IN 1983-1989; Chap Of The Gd Shpd

K

W Lafayette IN 1967-1983; Mssy-in-charge S Paul's Epis Ch Brighton MI 1957-1960. Epis Syn. sandflea@chartermi.net

KLATTE, Andrew P (Ind) 5437 Basin Park Drive, Indianapolis IN 46239 **D Chr Ch Cathd Indianapolis IN 2008-** B Marion IN 5/12/1957 s Edward Pendleton Klatte & Patricia. BA U NC 1987. D 6/23/2003 Bp Catherine Elizabeth Maples Waynick. m 4/23/1988 Peggy Kathleen Woodhall c 1. D S Mk's Ch Plainfield IN 2003-2008. apklatte@sbcglobal.net

KLEE, George M (Ark) 1516 Willow St., Blytheville AR 72315 B Memphis TN 3/7/1947 s George Edward Klee & Carolyn. BA U of Memphis 1969; MDiv Sthrn Bapt TS Louisville KY 1972; Cert SWTS 1983; STM GTS 1995; ThD GTS 2004. D 2/4/1984 P 10/1/1984 Bp Alex Dockery Dickson. m 5/18/1991 Martha Enoch. S Steph's Ch Blytheville AR 2006-2010; S Geo's Ch Germantown TN 2000-2004; Vic S Paul's Ch Mason TN 1987-1992; Vic Trin Ch Mason TN 1987-1992; Dio W Tennessee Memphis TN 1985-1992; P-intern Chr Ch Brownsville TN 1985-1986; P-intern Imm Ch Ripley TN 1985-1986; Asst S Mary's Cathd Memphis TN 1984. "Celtic Sprtlty," *The Angl*, 1995; Auth, *Lauderdale Cnty Voice*. georgeklee@sbcglobal.net

KLEFFMAN, Todd Aaron (Ind) 5757 Rosslyn Ave, Indianapolis IN 46220 **S Jn's Epis Ch Crawfordsville IN 2005-** B Indianapolis IN 6/20/1963 s Herschell Kleffman & Doris. BA Ball St U 1987; MDiv SWTS 2001. D 6/30/2001 P 1/6/2002 Bp Catherine Elizabeth Maples Waynick. m 3/20/2006 Michael Samuel Scime. S Fran In The Fields Zionsville IN 2001-2005. revtoddkleff@yahoo.com

KLEIN, Craig Alan (NCal) 107 S Curry St, West Plains MO 65775 B Kansas City MO 2/21/1955 s Ralph Ronald Klein & Nancy Elaine. Cert-EFM The U So; BS U of Kansas 1978; MA Indiana U 1985; EdD U of Florida 1992. D 2/4/2006 Bp Jerry Alban Lamb. m 12/24/1989 Marybeth Fitzpatrick. craigklein@missouristate.edu

KLEIN, Everett H. (WMich) 7521 Anthony St, Whitehall MI 49461 **R S Alb's Mssn Muskegon MI 2008-; R S Ptr's By-The-Lake Ch Montague MI 2002-** B New York New York 7/1/1942 s Henry W Klein & Cecelia M H. BS U of Maryland U Coll Europe 1979; MDiv SWTS 2001. D 12/1/2001 Bp Edward Lewis Lee Jr P 9/14/2002 Bp Robert R Gepert. m 2/27/1968 Barbara Carol Caldwell c 1. barbandev@aol.com

KLEIN, John Harvey (SeFla) 3586 Woods Walk Blvd, Lake Worth FL 33467 B Tampa FL 10/23/1933 s Frank Joseph Klein & Helen. BA U Of Florida 1955; MDiv GTS 1962. D 7/3/1962 Bp Henry I Louttit P 1/1/1963 Bp William Loftin Hargrave. m 3/15/1958 Marie J Jordan. Pstr Asst S Dav's-In-The-Pines Epis Ch Wellington FL 2005-2009; R S Margarets Epis Ch Miami Lakes FL 1984-1993; R Trin Epis Ch Natchitoches LA 1974-1980; Vic S Pat's Ch Ocala FL 1969-1974; Asst All SS Prot Epis Ch Ft Lauderdale FL 1964-1969; M-in-c S Lk The Evang Ch Mulberry FL 1962-1964.

KLEIN, John William (Md) 601 Rustic St, Opelika AL 36801 B Eustis FL 12/20/1945 s William G Klein & Virginia May. BD Rol 1968; MDiv PDS 1971; Untd States Chapl Sch 1977. D 6/28/1971 P 1/1/1972 Bp William Hopkins Folwell. m 8/6/1966 Mary Olive. Mt Calv Ch Baltimore MD 2001-2006; Chr Ch Par La Crosse WI 1995-2001; R S Andr's Epis Ch Princess Anne MD 1990-1994; Curs Dio Ohio Cleveland OH 1980-1999; S Paul Epis Ch Norwalk OH 1979-1982; Off Of Bsh For ArmdF New York NY 1977-1990; Chair - Com Dio Cntrl Florida Orlando FL 1973-1975; Fac - D'S Sch Dio Cntrl Florida Orlando FL 1973-1975; Asst Emm Ch Orlando FL 1973-1975; Plnng Cmsn Dio Cntrl Florida Orlando FL 1972-1973.

KLEIN, Susan Webster (Los) 9606 Oakmore Rd, Los Angeles CA 90035 **S Alb's Epis Ch Los Angeles CA 2004-** B Saint Louis MO 6/1/1951 d Louis Edward Klein & Crockett Leslie. BA Wheaton Coll at Norton 1973; MDiv Ya Berk 1977. D 7/30/1977 P 2/5/1978 Bp William Augustus Jones Jr. m 11/28/1981 John Joseph Spano c 1. S Aid's Epis Ch Malibu CA 1990-2004; Assoc S Andr's Epis Ch Irvine CA 1984-1989; Cn Chr Ch Cathd S Louis MO 1977-1984. Auth, "Preaching Through The Year," *Sermons That Wk, Volumes VIII, IX and X*, Morehouse Pub. ESMHE 1984-1989. Bachelor of Arts (Philos) - mcl Wheaton Coll 1973. susanklein51@earthlink.net

KLEIN-LARSEN, Martha Susan (Ct) 25 West St, Danbury CT 06810 **S Jn's Epis Ch Bristol CT 2009-** B 7/8/1955 d John Klein & Margaret Irma. BA Concordia U 1976; MDiv Luth TS at Chicago 1981; PhD Chicago TS 2005. Rec from Evangelical Lutheran Church in America 1/24/2009 Bp Andrew Donnan Smith. c 2. Int S Jas Epis Ch Danbury CT 2009. kleinlarsen@comcast.net

KLEMMT, Pierce Wittfield (Va) 118 N Washington St, Alexandria VA 22314 **R Chr Ch Alexandria VA 1994-** B Cincinnati OH 12/29/1949 s Raymond Maynard Klemmt & Jane Coleman. BA Wabash Coll 1972; MDiv Ya Berk 1976. D 6/9/1976 P 12/12/1976 Bp John Mc Gill Krumm. m 12/29/1976 Mary T Gates c 2. Chr Epis Ch Springfield MO 1986-1993; Trin Epis Ch Troy OH 1980-1986; Asst S Mk's Ch Evanston IL 1976-1980. mtklemmt@verizon.net

KLEVEN, Terence James (Ia) 1334 N. Prairie St., Pella IA 50219 B British Columbia Canada 5/22/1955 BA U Of Calgary Ab CA. Trans from Anglican Church of Canada 7/17/2003 Bp Alan Scarfe. m 7/5/1986 Kathryn Kleven. S Jas Epis Ch Oskaloosa IA 2003-2010; Trin Ch Ottumwa IA 2003-2008. Auth, "Trsfg Of Chr In Lk 9:22-36," *Princeton Theol Revs*, 2001; Auth, "Bk Revs: Wrld Of Ibn Tufayl," *Bulletin Of Middle E Medievalists*, 2000; Auth, "Bk Revs: Alcinous: Handbook Of Platonism," *Mind*, 1999; Auth, "Tam Fontaine'S Account Of Ibn Daud'S The Exalted Faith," *Interpretaion*, 1998; Auth, "Inquiry Into The Fndt Of Law," *Jewish Political Stds Revs*, 1997; Auth, "Bk Revs: Allegory And Philos," *Intl Journ Of Middle Estrn Stds*, 1996; Auth, "Use Of Snr In Agaritic And 2 Samuel V8," *Vetus Testamentum*, 1994. KLEVENT@CENTRAL.EDU

KLEY, Robert William (Los) PO Box 31657, Phoenix AZ 85046 B Denver CO 9/10/1938 s Walter Kley & Elizabeth. BA U Denv 1960; MDiv Nash 1963; MA Gallaudet U 1968; Fllshp USC 1972; MA Pepperdine U 1981. D 7/25/1963 P 2/24/1964 Bp Joseph Summerville Minnis. Assoc All SS Ch Phoenix AZ 2003-2007; Asstg S Paul In The Desert Palm Sprg CA 1998-2002; S Mart-In-The-Fields Mssn Twentynine Palms CA 1996-1998; Asst Gr Cathd San Francisco CA 1990-1994; Vic Trin Epis Par Los Angeles CA 1987-1988; St Edw The Confessors Ch Los Angeles CA 1973-1976; Vic S Edw The Confessor Epis Ch San Jose CA 1972-1976; Vic Trin Epis Par Los Angeles CA 1968-1976; Vic Epis Ch Of S Jn The Bapt Breckenridge CO 1963-1966; Vic Gr Ch Buena Vista CO 1963-1966; Vic S Geo Epis Mssn Leadville CO 1963-1966. Auth, *The Mnstry to the Deaf.* Fell Epis Ch Fllshp 1965. arizona2002@gmail.com

KLICKMAN, John Michael (Dal) 4017 Hedgerow Dr, Plano TX 75024 B Saint Louis MO 1/11/1944 s John Klickman & Marianne. AB Wm Jewell Coll 1965; MDiv VTS 1969; MBA U Of Dallas Dallas 1988. D 6/24/1969 Bp George Leslie Cadigan P 1/6/1970 Bp C J Kinsolving III. c 1. Archd Dio Panama 1986; R Ch Of The Epiph Richardson TX 1981-1985; R S Tim's Epis Ch Lake Jackson TX 1974-1981; Assoc Pro Cathd Epis Ch Of S Clem El Paso TX 1969-1974. Contrib, "Aicpa Item Dvlpmt Workshop," 2009; Reviewer, "Cost Acctg," Prentice Hall, 2002; Reviewer, "Cost Acctg," McGraw-Hill; Auth, "Gnrl Motors Schlr"; Auth, "Album," *Today You Shall Be w Me*. Make A Wish-Audit Com 2009-2011; Ord Of H Cross 1974-2011; SAMS, Bd Trst 1976-1986; St Phil's Epis Sch Bd-Dallas 1981-1986. mike.klickman@verizon.net

KLIMAS, Marcella Louise (CPa) 5095 Woodridge Way, Tucker GA 30084 **Asstg Cler S Pat's Epis Ch Atlanta GA 2002-** B Plainfield NJ 4/5/1948 d Joseph Jacob Klimas & Helen Margaret. Oxf 1969; BA Douglass 1970; MDiv EDS 1981; DMin Columbia TS 1994. D 6/13/1981 Bp William Foreman Creighton P 3/6/1982 Bp Lloyd Edward Gressle. R Ch Of The Trsfg Blue Ridge Summit PA 1986-1990; Assoc R Ch Of The Redemp Southampton PA 1983-1986; Dioc Intern S Lk's Ch Scranton PA 1981-1983. Auth, "Journey Toward The Promised Land". Jonathan Daniels Meml Fllshp 1980. 444mlk@gmail.com

KLINE, Andrew Ferguson (Colo) 5 Brookside Dr, Greenwood Village CO 80121 **S Aug Of Hippo Norristown PA 2010-** B Cheyenne WY 11/16/1956 s Duane Kline & Joanna. BA Dart 1979; MDiv Ya Berk 1983. D 6/29/1983 Bp Bob Gordon Jones P 2/2/1984 Bp William Bradford Hastings. m 4/28/1984 Kathleen Kovner c 4. R Chr Epis Ch Denver CO 2003-2009; S Thos Ch Hanover NH 1994-2003; S Steph's Ch E Haddam CT 1986-1994; S Jas' Ch New Haven CT 1983-1985. AKLINE@ESTREET.COM

KLINE, Harold Emmett (Ida) 3847 N Bayou Ln, Boise ID 83703 B Harrisburg PA 9/5/1923 s Emmett Milton Kline & Esther Mae. BS Leh 1949; MS Leh 1952; CDSP 1963. D 9/5/1963 P 3/12/1964 Bp Francis E I Bloy. m 6/10/1944 Jean K Kline. Assoc Trin Cathd Phoenix AZ 1982-1986; Asst S Steph's Ch Phoenix AZ 1974-1977; R S Andr's Par Torrance CA 1973-1974; R S Steph's Par Los Angeles CA 1965-1973; Cur S Mart-In-The-Fields Par Winnetka CA 1963-1965. Cn Res S Mich's Cathd Boise ID 1991; Hon Cn Trin Cathd Phoenix AZ 1986. hkline@bsu.net

KLINE, John William (NwPa) 825 Matilda Dr, Plano TX 75025 **Assoc The Epis Ch Of The H Nativ Plano TX 1999-** B Ridley Park PA 12/7/1933 s John Reuben Kline & Christine Long. BS W Chester St U 1955; Drew U 1957; MDiv Luth TS at Gettysburg 1959; CTh PDS 1965; STM Luth TS at Gettysburg 1971. D 4/24/1965 Bp Oliver J Hart P 8/24/1965 Bp Harvey D Butterfield. m 6/24/1955 Jane Beeghley c 4. Int Epis Ch Of The Ascen Dallas TX 1998-1999; R Ch Of The Ascen Bradford PA 1983-1997; Dn Dio NW Pennsylvania Erie PA 1983-1997; R S Jn's Epis Ch Sharon PA 1975-1979; R S Matt's Epis Ch Sunbury PA 1968-1974; R S Mary's Ch Williamsport PA 1967-1968; R Chr Ch Bethel VT 1965-1967; R S Jn's Epis Ch Randolph VT 1965-1967. Assoc.,OHC 1965; Chapl, Ord of S Lk 1973. padrejwk@verizon.net

KLINE, Nancy Wade (CFla) St. Barnabas Episcopal Church, 319 W. Wisconsin Ave., Deland FL 32720 **D S Barn Ch Deland FL 2004-** B LaFayette GA 5/2/1947 d Thomas Merrell Wade & Anna May. BA U Of Cntrl Florida 1972; Inst for Chr Stds Sch of Diac Trng, 2004. D 12/18/2004 Bp John Wadsworth Howe. m 11/17/1973 Sims Dubose Kline c 2. nkline@stetson.edu

KLINE, Timothy Eads (WK) 50 Oyster Bay Dr, Graford TX 76449 **Chair, Cio. Com. Dep, GC Dio Wstrn Kansas Hutchinson KS 1998-** B Cincinnati OH 1/15/1942 s Edward Elmer Kline & Reva Louise. BS USAF Acad Colorado

Sprg CO 1964; MA LSU 1972; MDiv VTS 1991. D 12/10/1991 Bp Peter James Lee P 6/1/1992 Bp John Forsythe Ashby. m 7/6/1964 Bonnie Louise Kline c 3. Pres Dio Wstrn Kansas Hutchinson KS 2002-2004; Stndg Com Dio Wstrn Kansas Hutchinson KS 2002-2004; Dn Chr Cathd Salina KS 1999-2006; Dep, GC Dio Wstrn Kansas Hutchinson KS 1999-2006; Chair - COM Dio Wstrn Kansas Hutchinson KS 1993-2006; Dio Oklahoma Oklahoma City OK 1992-1999; Vic S Steph's Ch Guymon OK 1992-1999; Reg Mssnr S Tim's Epis Ch Hugoton KS 1992-1999; P-in-c S Jn's Ch Ulysses KS 1991-1999; D/Asst for Mnstry S Aid's Ch Alexandria VA 1991-1992. Phi Kappa Phi LSU 1972. bklineizoz@gmail.com

KLINE-MORTIMER, Sandra Louise (Md) PO Box 3298, Shepherdstown WV 25443 **S Anne's Epis Ch Smithsburg MD 2005-** B Santa Ana CA 4/4/1957 d George K Harshbarger & Leslie Elouise. BS W Virginia U; MDiv VTS 1989; MS Loyola U 1995. D 7/19/1989 P 6/1/1990 Bp John H(enry) Smith. Asst R Trin Epis Ch Martinsburg WV 1990-1992; D S Steph's Epis Ch Beckley WV 1989-1990. okok1215@aol.com

KLINGELHOFER, Stephan Ernest (Eas) 545 Fey Rd # 21620-, Chestertown MD 21620 **Assoc Shrewsbury Par Ch Kennedyville MD 2000-** B Fond du Lac WI 6/17/1943 s Herbert Ernest Klingelhofer & Mary Katherine. BA Ya 1964; JD Duke 1967; MDiv VTS 1979. D 6/23/1979 P 1/6/1980 Bp John Thomas Walker. m 6/19/1965 Diane Marie Dundas c 1. Del to GC Dio Wstrn Michigan Kalamazoo MI 1991; R S Lk's Par Kalamazoo MI 1988-1992; Adj Fac VTS Alexandria VA 1985-1988; Stndg Com Dio Washington Washington DC 1984-1988; R Gr Ch Washington DC 1982-1988; Dioc Coun Dio Washington Washington DC 1982-1984; Assoc The Ch Of The Epiph Washington DC 1979-1982. sklingel@incl.org

KLINGENSMITH, Roxanne Elizabeth Pearson (Mont) 1715 South Black, Bozeman MT 59715 **S Jas Ch Bozeman MT 2001-** B Duluth MN 10/22/1940 d Vernon Theodore Eugene Pearson & Maxine Elizabeth. BS U MN 1962. D 5/8/1999 Bp Charles Jones III. m 9/27/1990 Laverne Oakley c 1. julianofnorwich@msn.com

KLITZKE, Dale Edward (Eau) 1816 Crestwood Ln, Menomonie WI 54751 **R Gr Epis Ch Menomonie WI 2003-** B Mauston WI 4/19/1947 s Kenneth Rinehold Klitzke & Lucille Johanna. D 9/29/1985 P 8/16/1992 Bp William Charles Wantland. m 7/16/1966 Linda Marion Klitzke c 3. S Mary's Epis Ch Tomah WI 1992-1996; D S Jn's Epis Ch Oxford WI 1985-1992. dale.klitzke@gmail.com

KLITZKE, Paul Kenneth (Haw) PO Box 700501, Kapolei HI 96709 **S Nich Epis Ch Kapolei HI 2010-** B Tomah WI 11/28/1979 s Dale Edward Klitzke & Linda Marion. BAF Viterbo U 2002; MDiv TS 2005. D 2/27/2005 Bp Mark Lawrence Mac Donald. m 8/17/2005 Sarah E Holley c 3. R S Dav's Ch Wasilla AK 2005-2010. paul.klitzke@gmail.com

KLOPFENSTEIN, Timothy David (CGC) 106 Galaxy Ave, Bonaire GA 31005 B Hartsville IN 10/28/1940 s Clarence Christian Klopfenstein & Bernice Caroline. BS Auburn U 1964; MS Untd States Naval Postgraduate Sch 1973; MDiv STUSo 1984; DMin GTF 2000. D 6/4/1984 P 4/1/1985 Bp Charles Farmer Duvall. m 12/18/2007 Hannah M McKinley. Wilmer Hall Mobile AL 2005; R S Jn's Epis Ch Mobile AL 1991-2005; Vic S Anna's Ch Atmore AL 1986-1991; R Trin Epsicopal Ch Atmore AL 1986-1991; H Nativ Day Sch Panama City FL 1985-1986; Headmaster Dio Cntrl Gulf Coast Pensacola FL 1984-1986; Cur H Nativ Epis Ch Panama City FL 1984-1986. timklop@yahoo.com

KLOTS, Stephen Barrett (Ct) 40 Bulls Bridge Rd, South Kent CT 06785 **Chapl S Mich's Chap So Kent CT 1999-; So Kent Sch So Kent CT 1999-** B Tallahassee FL 8/8/1962 s Cornelius Ephraim Klots & Mary Ellen. BA Trin Hartford CT 1984; MDiv Harvard DS 1989; STM Ya Berk 1999. D 6/5/1999 P 6/3/2000 Bp M(arvil) Thomas Shaw III. Auth, *Native Americans & Chrsnty*, 1997; Auth, *Carl Lewis*, 1995; Auth, *Ida Wells-Barnett*, 1994; Auth, *Richard Allen*, 1991. klotss@southkentschool.net

✠ **KLUSMEYER, Rt Rev William Michie** (WVa) 1 Roller Rd, Charleston WV 25314 **Trst The GTS New York NY 2008-; Bp of W Virginia Chap of the Resurr Charleston WV 2001-; Bp of WVa Dio W Virginia Charleston WV 2001-** B Glen Cove NY 11/4/1955 s William Klusmeyer & Mary Elisabeth. BA Illinois Coll 1977; MDiv GTS 1980. D 6/14/1980 Bp Quintin Ebenezer Primo Jr P 12/13/1980 Bp James Winchester Montgomery Con 10/13/2001 for WVa. m 8/13/1977 Marsha H Haertel c 2. Bd, Epis Chars Dio Chicago Chicago IL 1998-2001; Bd - Peoples Resource Cntr Dio Chicago Chicago IL 1998-2001; Stndg Com Dio Chicago Chicago IL 1994-1997; R Trin Epis Ch Wheaton IL 1990-2001; Bd, Cathdral Shltr Dio Chicago Chicago IL 1990-1993; Chair Dioc T/F on Cnfrmtn Dio Chicago Chicago IL 1985-1988; Gr Epis Ch Freeport IL 1980-1990. Sis of Charity - Epis Visitors 2002-2008. DD VTS 2002; DD GTS 2001. mklusmeyer@wvdiocese.org

KLUTTERMAN, David Lee (FdL) 330 McClellan, Wausau WI 54401 **P St Jas Epis Ch Mosinee WI 2009-; R Ch Of S Jn The Bapt Wausau WI 1996-** B Watertown WI 12/30/1955 s Gerald Klutterman & Kathleen. BA U of Wisconsin 1977; MDiv GTS 1980. D 4/12/1980 Bp William Hampton Brady P 11/15/1980 Bp William L Stevens. c 3. S Jas Ch Manitowoc WI 1984-1996; Dio Fond du Lac Appleton WI 1980-1984; S Mths Minocqua WI 1980-1984; Ch Of S Mary Of The Snows Eagle River WI 1980-1981. Auth, "Bringing Chr Hm," Self Pub, 2007; Auth, "A Catechism Curric," LeaderResources, 1995. klutterman@aol.com

KNAPICK, Veronica Helene (Ak) 6816 E. Riverwood Cir, Palmer AK 99645 B Johnson City NY 10/18/1945 d Joseph Knapick & Veronica. BS SUNY 1967; Med U of Montana 1971; MDiv CDSP 1985; Int Mnstry Prog 1993. D 6/30/1985 P 4/29/1986 Bp George Clinton Harris. R S Phil's Ch Wrangell AK 1997-1998; R S Steph's Epis Ch Douglas AZ 1995-1996; Int S Dunst's Ch Tulsa OK 1994-1995; R Ch Of The Gd Shpd Houlton ME 1993-1994; R S Giles Ch Jefferson ME 1989-1992; R S Jude's Epis Ch No Pole AK 1986-1987; D S Mary's Ch Anchorage AK 1985-1986.

KNAPP, Carl Jude (Pa) 584 Fairway Ter, Philadelphia PA 19128 **D S Tim's Ch Roxborough Philadelphia PA 1982-** B Philadelphia PA 8/20/1939 s Carlyle Maurice Knapp & Anne Catherine. BS W Chester St Coll 1961; MS U of Pennsylvania 1968; MA La Salle U 1984. D 6/12/1982 Bp Lyman Cunningham Ogilby. m 7/11/1964 Josephine Ann Costello c 1. Phi Delta Kappa 1976. carl.knapp@verizon.net

KNAPP, Clayton L (WMass) 10 Bittersweet Ln, Wilbraham MA 01095 B Albany NY 12/5/1940 s Alden Leroy Knapp & Harriette Kathryn. BS Siena Coll 1967; MDiv PDS 1971; DMin Andover Newton TS 1993. D 6/5/1971 P 12/14/1971 Bp Allen Webster Brown. m 8/4/1990 Judith Bolam c 2. Vic S Chris's Ch Fairview Chicopee MA 1990-2001; Cn Chr Ch Cathd Springfield MA 1981-1988; Downtown Min Chr Ch Cathd Springfield MA 1979-1981; Legis Liason N Y St Coun Of Ch Syracuse NY 1978; R The Ch Of The Mssh Glens Falls NY 1974-1977; R Chr's Ch Duanesburg NY 1971-1974. AAPC 1989-1998. Coll hon Soc Mem Delta Epsilon Sigma 1967. clayknapp120540@gmail.com

KNAPP, Cynthia Clark (Ct) 43 Twin Oak Ln, Wilton CT 06897 B Columbia MO 6/10/1963 d Ralph Willard Clark & Carolyn Ann. BS Duke 1985; MDiv VTS 1989. D 6/9/1990 Bp Arthur Edward Walmsley P 6/15/1991 Bp Clarence Nicholas Coleridge. m 6/4/1988 Cheston David Knapp. S Barn Epis Ch Greenwich CT 2005-2011; Trin Epis Ch Southport CT 2002-2004; Supply P Dio Connecticut Hartford CT 1998-2004; Asst to R Trin Ch Branford CT 1996-1998; Asst S Sav's Epis Ch Old Greenwich CT 1993-1996; Chr Ch Greenwich CT 1990-1993. cynthiaclarknapp@gmail.com

KNAPP, Donald Hubert (Be) 162 Springhouse Rd, Allentown PA 18104 **Mem, Dioc Peace Cmsn Dio Bethlehem Bethlehem PA 2008-** B Kent OH 10/29/1928 s John Lewis Knapp & Florence Cora. BA S Mary Coll KY 1953; The Athenaeum of Ohio 1957; MDiv PDS 1968. Rec from Roman Catholic 3/1/1968 Bp Robert Lionne DeWitt. m 8/6/1965 Virginia Mary Horak c 3. Mem, Liturg Cmsn Dio Bethlehem Bethlehem PA 2006-2009; Int R S Barn Ch Kutztown PA 2004-2005; Int S Lk's Ch Lebanon PA 2000-2001; Int S Geo's Epis Ch Hellertown PA 1996-2000; Int S Alb's Epis Ch Reading PA 1995-1996; Mem, Dioc Coun Dio Bethlehem Bethlehem PA 1990-1992; Mem, Jubilee Cmsn Dio Bethlehem Bethlehem PA 1975-2009; R Gr Epis Ch Allentown PA 1969-1993. Lehigh Cnty Conf of Ch - Secy 1971-1973; Lehigh Cnty Prison Soc - Fndr and Pres 1970-2006; Pennsylvania Prison Soc 1976-2006. Human Relatns Awd Human Relatns Cmsn Allentown PA 1978. dvknapp@ptd.net

KNAPP, Gretchen Bower (Mont) Po Box 794, Hilger MT 59451 **D S Jas Ch Lewistown MT 1996-** B Worland WY 10/1/1941 d Vernon Earl Bower & Mary Louise. BA U of Wyoming 1964; Montana Mnstry Formation Prog 1996. D 8/10/1996 Bp Charles Jones III. m 10/19/1974 Franklin Theodore Knapp. grknapp@lewistown.net

KNAPP, Kate S (Miss) 1316 N Jefferson St, Jackson MS 39202 B Waltham MA 9/22/1913 d William Chapman Spelman & Elinor. Wells Coll 1933; BA Barnard Coll of Col 1935; MA SWTS 1970. D 8/6/1970 Bp William Hopkins Folwell. m 10/10/1936 Walter Howard Knapp. D Ch Of The H Cross Decatur GA 1993-1994; D S Tim's Ch Aiea HI 1990-1992; Serv S Jn's By The Sea Kaneohe HI 1985-1986; Serv S Andr's Ch Denver CO 1977-1979; Com Dio Colorado Denver CO 1976-1979; Serv Epis Ch Of S Ptr And S Mary Denver CO 1976-1977; Pryr Mnstry Dio Cntrl Florida Orlando FL 1972-1974; Asst The Epis Ch Of S Jn The Bapt Orlando FL 1972-1974; Stff On The Renwl Taskforce Dio Cntrl Florida Orlando FL 1970-1974. Soc Of S Marg. Seabury Convoc Cross 1970.

KNAPP, Raymond Clinton (EpisSanJ) 2145 W Kettleman Lane Apt 108, Lodi CA 95242 **Died 5/3/2010** B Acme WY 8/23/1919 s Melvin R Knapp & Sarah Evelyn. BA Hastings Coll of Law 1942; ThB PDS 1949; ThM PDS 1971. D 8/20/1948 P 8/1/1949 Bp James W Hunter. c 2. Ord of S Lk.

KNAPP, Ronald David (Eas) 11240 Gail Dr, Princess Anne MD 21853 **S Paul's Epis Ch Hebron MD 2008-** B Batavia NY 3/31/1942 s Charles Lloyd Knapp & Virginia Mae. BS SUNY 1964; MDiv Ya Berk 1969. D 6/21/1969 P 1/10/1970 Bp Lauriston L Scaife. m 9/1/1962 Hildreth P Price c 2. R S Andr's Epis Ch Princess Anne MD 1996-2005; P-in-c S Aid's Ch Alden NY 1994-1996; Int S Mk's Epis Ch Le Roy NY 1992-1994; Int S Jn's Ch Medina NY 1990-1992; Vic Ch Of The Redeem Niagara Falls NY 1982-1988; R Ch

Of The Epiph Niagara Falls NY 1972-1990; Asst to R Trin Epis Ch Hamburg NY 1969-1972. frrdknapp@aol.com

KNAUP JR, Daniel Joseph (O) 30615 Shaker Blvd, Pepper Pike OH 44124 **P Dio Ohio Cleveland OH 2009-; Chapl Off Of Bsh For ArmdF New York NY 2009-** B Inglewood CA 1/5/1958 s Daniel Joseph Knaup & Blanche Irene. M.A. The St. Paul Sem Sch of Div (RC); M.Div. The St. Paul Sem Sch of Div (RC); B.A. California Polytechnic St U, San Luis Obispo 1982. Rec from Roman Catholic 6/13/2009 as Priest Bp Mark Hollingsworth Jr. m 7/7/2000 Vicky Jones. SocMary 2010. daniel.joseph.knaup@us.army.mil

KNEBEL, Frank Carson (SanD) 6210 E. Arbor Ave. Apt. 102, Mesa AZ 85206 B Los Angeles CA 11/11/1933 s Henry Carson Knebel & Alice Margarete. BA U Of La Verne La Verne CA 1955; MDiv CDSP 1958; MA California St U 1973. D 6/16/1958 Bp Donald J Campbell P 2/12/1959 Bp Francis E I Bloy. c 2. Headmaster S Jn Chrys Ch And Sch Rancho Santa Margarita CA 1990; Asst and Day Sch Headmaster Chr Ch Coronado CA 1988-1990; Vic Gr Epis Ch Wheatland CA 1966-1968; Vic S Tim's Ch Gridley CA 1966-1968; Vic S Matt's Ch Chandler AZ 1962-1965; Asst H Trin Epis Ch Covina CA 1961-1962; Cur Ch Of The Mssh Santa Ana CA 1958-1959. Auth, "Short Stories," Jack and Jill Mag and Chld Life; Auth, "Vintage Voice for Ch Pension Fund"; Auth, "Lloque Yupanqui," *Lefthander Mag*. fatherknebel@gmail.com

KNEE, Jacob S (Mont) St Stephen's Episcopal Ch, 1241 Crawford Dr, Billings MT 59102 **R S Steph's Ch Billings MT 2007-** B Blackburn UK 8/16/1966 s Anthony Knee & Gillian. BSc London Sch of Econ 1987; MSc London Sch of Econ 1988; BA Ripon Coll, Cuddesdon 1993; MA Ripon Coll, Cuddesdon 1997. Trans from Church Of England 10/19/2007 Bp Charles Franklin Brookhart Jr. m 5/23/1993 Susan Knee c 3. JKNEE@QWESTOFFICE.NET

KNEIPP, Lee Benson (WTenn) Po Box 3874, Pineville LA 71361 B Shreveport LA 2/6/1956 s Leonard Edward Kneipp & Patricia Ann. BA Centenary Coll 1978; MDiv STUSo 1982; MA McNeese St U 1988; PhD Epis TS 1991. D 6/12/1982 P 2/1/1983 Bp Willis Ryan Henton. m 10/18/2003 Melinda Kneipp c 2. Gr - S Lk's Ch Memphis TN 2003-2004; S Alb's Epis Ch Monroe LA 1998-2003; S Mich's Epis Ch Pineville LA 1992-1997; Assoc Ch Of The H Cross Shreveport LA 1990-1992; Gr Epis Ch Monroe LA 1986-1988; S Andr's Ch Lake Chas LA 1986; Ch Of The Ascen Lafayette LA 1982-1983. Auth, "Differences In Comprehension Processes As A Function Of Hemisphericity"; Auth, "Perceptual & Motor Skills"; Auth, "Texan Psychol". Cmnty Of Intsn. Alexander Awd For Resrch In Bio-Psychol Tx Psychol Assn 1991.

KNICKERBOCKER, Driss Richard (NH) 985 Pierpont St., Rahway NJ 07065 **Died 12/13/2009** B Flint,MI 4/16/1939 s Driss Russell Knickerbocker & Marjorie Elizabeth. BA U MI 1963; MDiv EDS 1968; PhD Oxf 1981. D 6/29/1968 Bp Archie H Crowley P 1/26/1969 Bp Charles F Hall. ADLMC; Intl Ntwk; NEAC. drknick@juno.com

KNIGHT, Arthur James (NJ) 3 Blueberry Rd, Shamong NJ 08088 **D S Barth's Ch Cherry Hill NJ 2009-** B Detroit MI 8/21/1942 s Arthur Joseph Knight & Eleanore Theresa. BA U of Texas 1971. D 10/21/2000 Bp David B(ruce) Joslin. m 5/26/1979 Margaret Elizabeth Whitehurst c 1. D Trin Epis Ch Vineland NJ 2004-2009; Co-Chair, Com on the Diac Dio New Jersey Trenton NJ 2002-2005; D Timber Creek Epis Area Mnstry Gloucester City NJ 2000-2004. Assn for Epis Deacons 2000. artknight@comcast.net

KNIGHT, David Edward (Spok) 1221 N Sherwood St, Spokane WA 99201 B Compton CA 4/5/1930 s David John Knight & Elvis. BA Gonzaga U 1953; MDiv CDSP 1958. D 6/17/1958 Bp Edward Makin Cross P 12/1/1958 Bp Russell S Hubbard. m 11/21/1951 Betty E Martinson. All SS Ch Spokane WA 1969-1978; Vic Ch of the H Sprt Spokane Vlly WA 1969-1976; R S Dav's Ch Spokane WA 1961-1966; Vic H Trin Epis Ch Wallace ID 1958-1961. Auth, "Delta Devil Nineteen (Article), Vietnam," *A Time Of War And A Time Of Peace*, 1994; Auth, "Supreme Six (Chapt On Curates)," *The Other Side Of Glory*, Ballantine Books, 1987. City Gate 1997; Dept Of Ce 1963-1966; Dioc. Corp. 1966; Mssn Spokane 1990; New Chr Fllshp, Pres 1973-1976; Our Place 1995; Reserve Off Assn 1995. Air Medal, Signed By Julian Ewell, Major Gnrl Cg Us Army, Ninth Infantry Div 1968; Bronze Star Us Army, Ninth Infantry Div 1968; Silver Star Us Army, Ninth Infantry Div 1968. supremesix@msn.com

KNIGHT, David Hathaway (Va) 6005 S Crestwood Ave, Richmond VA 23226 B Salem MA 8/5/1945 s Edward Vinton Knight & Lois Hathaway. BA U of Massachusetts 1968; VTS 1971. D 6/20/1971 P 12/1/1971 Bp Alexander Doig Stewart. m 7/4/1970 Jean L Knight. S Mich And All Ang Ch Dallas TX 2005-2007; Assoc R S Steph's Ch Richmond VA 1995-2005; Virginia Hm Dio Virginia Richmond VA 1984-2007; Chr Epis Ch Winchester VA 1978-1994; Stwdshp Advsry Serv Dio Wstrn Massachusetts Springfield MA 1976-1977; Bd Admin & Fin Dio Wstrn Massachusetts Springfield MA 1975-1978; Evang Cmsn Dio Wstrn Massachusetts Springfield MA 1974-1977; Ed Bd Dio Wstrn Massachusetts Springfield MA 1973-1975; S Steph's Ch Westborough MA 1972-1978; Cur S Paul's Ch Holyoke MA 1971-1972. JLKDHK@VERIZON.NET

KNIGHT, Frank Lauchlan (NY) 3859 Dogwood Trail, South Whitehall Township, Allentown PA 18103 B New York NY 7/10/1938 s Frank Edward Knight & Grace Anna. BA CUNY 1959; STB PDS 1962. D 6/9/1962 P 12/22/1962 Bp Horace W B Donegan. m 9/16/1967 Noel Berkel c 2. Trst Dio Dio New York New York City NY 1990-1992; R Ch Of The Medtr Bronx NY 1974-2003; Asst All Souls Ch New York NY 1965-1967; Asst The Ch of S Edw The Mtyr New York NY 1962-1963. brassbahlz@gmail.com

KNIGHT IV, Frank Michael (Pa) 803 Montbard Dr, West Chester PA 19382 **P-in-c S Steph's Epis Ch Norwood PA 2007-** B Saratoga Sprgs NY 7/28/1945 s Frank J Knight & Elizabeth. BS Un Coll Schenectady NY 1967; MDiv PDS 1974; Cert Estrn Bapt TS 1981. D 6/15/1974 P 12/21/1974 Bp Jonathan Goodhue Sherman. m 6/17/1967 Karen M Penndorf. Vic Ch Of The Trsfg W Chester PA 1985-2007; Vic S Mary Epis Ch Chester PA 1976-1985; Asst S Giles Ch Upper Darby PA 1975-1976. michaelknight@sstephen.org

KNIGHT, Harold Stanley (Az) 145 N Fraser Dr, Mesa AZ 85203 B Rochester NY 7/26/1912 s Merton Jay Knight & Elizabeth Jane. BA U Roch 1934; MDiv CRDS 1937. D 1/6/1949 P 7/6/1949 Bp Malcolm E Peabody. m 10/30/1971 Edithanne Davis Ball c 2. Hon Cn Dio Arizona Phoenix AZ 1977-1978; R S Mk's Epis Ch Mesa AZ 1957-1977; R The Ch Of The Epiph Rochester NY 1950-1957; P-in-c S Mk's Ch Clark Mills NY 1948-1950; P-in-c S Ptr's Ch Oriskany NY 1948-1950. Man of Year Awd City of Mesa Mesa AZ 1977.

KNIGHT, Hollinshead T (Ore) 7524 SW View Point Ter., Portland OR 97219 **Int The Epis Ch Of S Mary The Vrgn San Francisco CA 2011-; Mssnr S Matt's Epis Ch Portland OR 2010-** B Philadelphia PA 2/18/1934 s R Barclay Knight & Mary Hare. BA Ya 1956; MDiv EDS 1962. D 6/16/1962 Bp Oliver J Hart P 12/19/1962 Bp Norman L Foote. m 7/19/1974 Ann Bishop Morrison c 5. Dio Oregon Portland OR 2008-2010; Int Deploy Off Dio Oregon Portland OR 2008-2010; Secy of Conv Dio Oregon Portland OR 2008-2009; Int S Steph's Epis Par Portland OR 2006-2008; Int S Paul's Epis Ch Salem OR 2004-2005; Int S Jn's Epis Ch Jackson WY 2000-2003; Int Gd Shpd Epis Ch Belmont CA 1999-2000; Int S Matt's Epis Ch San Mateo CA 1997-1999; Int H Chld At S Mart Epis Ch Daly City CA 1996-1997; Pres of Stndg Com Dio Hawaii Honolulu HI 1989-1990; Election Process Com Dio Hawaii Honolulu HI 1986; Dn S Andr's Cathd Honolulu HI 1984-1995; Stndg Com Dio California San Francisco CA 1981-1984; Pres of San Francisco Dnry Dio California San Francisco CA 1980-1982; S Aid's Ch San Francisco CA 1973-1984; Dept of Missions Dio California San Francisco CA 1972-1978; S Lk's Ch San Francisco CA 1964-1969; Vic Gr Epis Ch Glenns Ferry ID 1962-1964; Vic Trin Ch Gooding ID 1962-1964. linknight@comcast.net

KNIGHT, James David (Miss) 982 Glen Oaks Dr, Pass Christian MS 39571 **R S Patricks Epis Ch Long Bch MS 2004-** B Meridian MS 6/25/1958 s Harold Victor Knight & Elizabeth Ann. BS U of Sthrn Mississippi 1981; MDiv SWTS 2002. D 5/26/2002 P 12/14/2002 Bp Duncan Montgomery Gray III. m 9/24/1983 Jennifer Faye Forrester c 3. Cur S Jas Ch Greenville MS 2002-2004. Preaching Awd Seabury Wstrn 2002. revdknight@gmail.com

KNIGHT, Joseph Sturdevant (CGC) 436 Lapsley Street, Selma AL 36701 B Selma,AL 8/29/1932 s Claude Kirkpatrick Knight & Clara Ida. U of Tampa; BS Samford U 1960; BDiv New Orleans Bapt TS 1964; MPA Auburn U 1980. D 8/21/1988 Bp Furman Stough P 5/1/1989 Bp Robert Oran Miller. m 5/5/1973 Anne Falkenber Falkenberry c 3. Vic Trin Ch Apalachicola FL 2000-2004; R Epis Ch Of The Epiph Leeds AL 1990-2000; D S Steph's Epis Ch Birmingham AL 1988-1990. hazenone@bellsouth.net

KNIGHT, Kimberly Adonna (SO) 830 Hedgerow Ln., Cincinnati OH 45246 **Chr Formation Cmsn Dio Sthrn Ohio Cincinnati OH 2009-; Yth Coun Dio Sthrn Ohio Cincinnati OH 2009-; Chapl The Soc of the Transiguration Cincinnati OH 2008-** B Coral Gables FL 3/29/1972 d Donald Laurence Knight & Barbara Carol. BA Florida St U 1994; MS U of Miami 1996; MDiv VTS 2000. D 6/14/2000 P 11/17/2001 Bp Calvin Onderdonk Schofield Jr. Assoc Chapl Epis HS Bellaire TX 2004-2008; Asst R / Sch Chapl S Mk The Evang Ft Lauderdale FL 2001-2004; Asst R S Matt's Ch Chandler AZ 2000-2001; S Thos Epis Par Coral Gables FL 1996-1997. "Ash Wednesday, Psalm 131, Time Out," *Preaching from psalms, oracles, & parables*, Moorhouse Pub, 2004. knight@bethanyschool.org

KNIGHT, Kirkland Wallace (La) 3200 Woodland Ridge Blvd, Baton Rouge LA 70816 **All SS Epis Sch Tyler TX 2007-** B Baton Rouge LA 8/7/1969 s William Vincent Knight & Johnelle. BA LSU 1991; MDiv STUSo 2004. D 6/5/2004 P 5/25/2005 Bp D(avid) Bruce Mac Pherson. m 1/8/1994 Mary Sue Baldridge c 2. Cur S Mk's Cathd Shreveport LA 2004-2007. marysueknight@att.net

KNIGHT, Patricia Cullum (NwT) 1601 S Georgia St, Amarillo TX 79102 B Holdenville OK 12/2/1936 d Clifford Elwood Cullum & Dorris G. BA Texas Tech U 1958; MA Texas Tech U 1968. D 8/28/2010 Bp James Scott Mayer. pknight929@gmail.com

KNIGHT, Peter David (Ct) 106 Pineridge Dr, Westfield MA 01085 **Died 10/10/2009** B Bridgeport,CT 2/13/1940 s Arthur R Knight & Rubye Irene. Dickinson Coll 1960; BA Scarritt Coll 1962; BD Ya Berk 1966. D 6/11/1966 Bp Walter H Gray P 3/1/1967 Bp John Henry Esquirol. c 4. marymamabear@aol.com

KNIGHT, Samuel Theodore (Mich) 28725 Sunset Boulevard West, Lathrup Village MI 48076 B AG 6/4/1939 s Gershom Ebenezer Knight & Patience Octavia. GOE Codrington Coll 1964; BA U of Wstrn Ontario 1971; MA Marygrove Coll 1990; MA Wayne 2009. D 12/1/1963 P 12/1/1964 Bp The Bishop Of Antigua. c 2. P-in-c S Martha's Ch Detroit MI 1999-2002; S Andr's Ch Clawson MI 1998-1999; R Gr Ch Detroit MI 1985-1991; Asst to R S Jas' Epis Ch Baltimore MD 1983-1984. sknite@comcast.net

KNIGHT II, Steve (SanD) 403 Shalimar Drive, Prescott AZ 86303 B Detroit MI 9/19/1933 s Hale Gifford Knight & Mary Louise. BS NWU 1955; STB EDS 1961; Cert Rutgers-The St U 1965. D 6/29/1961 Bp Archie H Crowley P 6/1/1962 Bp Robert Lionne DeWitt. m 9/3/1961 Joanna Velonides c 2. Stff Dio California San Francisco CA 1968-1970; Asst S Jn's Ch Plymouth MI 1965-1968; P-in-c Mariners Ch Detroit MI 1964-1965; Asst S Jn's Ch Detroit MI 1963-1964. Founding Mem RACA 1968. Navy Commendation Medal (2) U.S. Navy 1993; Meritorious Serv Medal U.S. Navy 1992; Navy Commendation Medal U.S. Navy 1991. ezduzit449@cableone.net

KNIGHT, Theolinda Lenore Johnson (Cal) 806 Jones St, Berkeley CA 94710 B New Britain CT 9/17/1936 d Theodore Allen Johnson & Virginia Lorraine. BTh Sch for Deacons 1986. D 6/8/1991 Bp William Edwin Swing. m 1/1/1960 Warren W Knight c 2. D The Epis Ch Of The Gd Shpd Berkeley CA 1998-2000; D S Aug's Ch Oakland CA 1992-1997; D S Paul's Epis Ch Walnut Creek CA 1991-1992. anabba@aol.com

KNIGHT, W(illiam) Allan (NH) 58 Hanson Rd, Chester NH 03036 **Gr Ch Manchester NH 2000-** B Meaford ON CA 11/15/1937 s Charles Frederick Knight & Olive Lillian. BA McMaster U 1959; BD 1962; STM Andover Newton TS 1969. D 1/30/1982 Bp Morris Fairchild Arnold P 3/19/1983 Bp George E Rath. m 9/19/1987 Jane Whitbeck Van Zandt c 6. Int The Epis Ch Of S Andr And S Phil Coventry RI 2002-2003; Int S Andr's By The Sea Little Compton RI 2001-2002; Int Ch Of Our Sav Milford NH 1999-2000; Int S Barn Epis Ch Sykesville MD 1998-1999; Vic H Trin Epis Ch Baltimore MD 1991-1998; S Steph's Ch Fall River MA 1985-1991; All SS Par Brookline MA 1983-1984. EPF 1985; HabHum 1992; NEAC 1985. allan65050@comcast.net

KNISELY, Harry Lee (Ct) 365 Hickory Rd, Carlisle PA 17015 **Assoc P S Paul's Epis Ch Harrisburg PA 2009-; Mem of the Cmsn on Anti Racism Dio Cntrl Pennsylvania Harrisburg PA 2001-** B Hopewell Township PA 7/15/1940 s Harry Knisely & Ada Mae. BA Juniata Coll 1963; Med Shippensburg St Teachers Coll 1965; MDiv Ya Berk 1969. D 6/4/1969 Bp Dean T Stevenson P 12/1/1969 Bp Earl M Honaman. m 5/27/1967 Gail Lohrman c 3. Int S Jn's Ch New Milford CT 1999-2000; Int S Jn's Ch Bridgeport CT 1997-1998; Int Trin Epis Ch Trumbull CT 1996-1997; Int Chr And Epiph Ch E Haven CT 1995-1996; R Chr Epis Ch Burlington IA 1989-1995; R Chr Epis Ch Oil City PA 1981-1989; R Ch Of All SS Buffalo NY 1974-1981; Coordntr Of Prog Dio Estrn Oregon The Dalles OR 1972-1974; R S Mary's Ch Williamsport PA 1969-1972. Auth, "Reverend Doctor Edw R Hardy Jr: P, Tchr, Schlr," *Friend*, 1969. Int Mnstry Ntwk 1995. hknisely@juno.com

KNISELY JR, William Nicholas (Az) 5625 N. Palacio Place, Phoenix AZ 85014 **Dn Trin Cathd Phoenix AZ 2006-** B Harrisburg PA 8/3/1960 s William Nicholas Knisely & Joan Amelia. BA Franklin & Marshall Coll 1982; MS U Of Delaware Newark 1986; MDiv Ya Berk 1991. D 6/8/1991 P 6/1/1992 Bp Cabell Tennis. m 8/28/1982 Karen Kenney McTigue c 1. Dio Arizona Phoenix AZ 2006-2009; R Trin Ch Bethlehem PA 1998-2006; R S Barn Ch Brackenridge PA 1993-1998; Cur S Barn Ch Wilmington DE 1991-1993. Allegheny Vlly HabHum; Sw Pa Ecum Assocs. Sub Chapl Ord Of St. Jn 1995. nick@wnknisely.org

KNOCKEL, Wayne (Mich) 546 W South St, Mason MI 48854 B Dubuque IA 10/9/1969 s Walter William Knockel & Celine Pearl. BA Luther Coll 1987; MA U of Nthrn Iowa 1995; MDiv Trin Luth Sem 2000. Rec from Evangelical Lutheran Church in America 12/20/2006 Bp Wendell Nathaniel Gibbs Jr. Ch Of The H Sprt Livonia MI 2010-2011; S Aug Of Cbury Mason MI 2008-2010. prwayno@yahoo.com

KNOLL-WILLIAMS, Sarah Jacqueline (Kan) 4120 Clinton Pkwy, Lawrence KS 66047 B Topeka KS 8/19/1981 d Steven John Knoll & Marlene Genevieve. BA U of Kansas 2003; MDiv CDSP 2008. D 6/7/2008 P 12/6/2008 Bp Dean Elliott Wolfe. m 6/26/2004 Matthew Austin Knoll-Williams c 1. Bp Seabury Acad Lawr KS 2008-2010. sknollwilliams@gmail.com

KNOTT, Joseph Lee (Ala) 5528 - 11th Court South, Birmingham AL 35222 **P Assoc Gr Ch Birmingham AL 1989-** B Birmingham AL 11/28/1928 s Joseph Z Nutt & Lillian. BA Birmingham-Sthrn Coll 1953; MDiv Van 1955; STUSo 1962; Med U of Montevallo 1988. D 6/1/1962 P 1/1/1963 Bp George Mosley Murray. c 3. R S Andr's Ch Montevallo AL 1982-1988; Assoc S Mths Epis Ch Tuscaloosa AL 1977-1982; R S Jn's Ch Birmingham AL 1965-1972; Vic S Mich's Ch Ozark AL 1962-1965. Auth, *Bible Lessons for Yth*. jknott1128@aol.com

KNOTTS, Harold Wayne (Mich) 26431 W Chicago, Redford MI 48239 B Fort Worth TX 3/27/1939 s R A Knotts & Nettie Pauline. BA Oklahoma City U 1966; MDiv Nash 1975; Command and Gnrl Stff Coll 1987. D 6/28/1975 Bp Frederick Warren Putnam P 1/1/1976 Bp Chilton Powell. m 12/30/1972 Katherine Eve Rose. S Eliz's Ch Redford MI 1997-2002; S Alb's Epis Ch Marshfield WI 1993-1995; Ch Of The Gd Shpd Swainsboro GA 1989-1990; Off Of Bsh For ArmdF New York NY 1983-1989; R S Jn's Ch Durant OK 1979-1982; Vic S Paul's Ch Clinton OK 1977-1979; S Jas Epis Ch Oklahoma City OK 1975-1976.

KNOUSE, Amanda Rue (Md) 5757 Solomons Island Rd., Lothian MD 20711 **Asst R S Jas' Par Lothian MD 2008-; Asst S Mk's Chap Deale Lothian MD 2008-** B Carlisle PA 7/14/1982 d Wilmer Jay Finkenbinder & Robin. BA Juniata Colllege 2004; MDiv The Prot Epis TS 2008. D 6/7/2008 Bp Nathan Dwight Baxter P 2/21/2009 Bp Eugene Sutton. m John R Knouse. amanda@stjameslothian.com

KNOWLES II, Harold Frank (Los) 623 El Centro St, South Pasadena CA 91030 B Chicago IL 1/2/1937 s Harold Edwin Knowles & Maxine Alberta. BA U CA 1958; MDiv CDSP 1961. D 9/7/1961 P 3/1/1962 Bp Francis E I Bloy. S Jas' Par So Pasadena CA 1969-1989; Assoc R S Mk's Par Glendale CA 1967-1969; Cur S Cross By-The-Sea Ch Hermosa Bch CA 1961-1967. Chapl Soc Mayflower Descendants; Ord S Lazarus, Ord S Jn Bapt, Ord S Jn Jerusalem. Who'S Who In Rel; Zeta Psi; Chi Delta Pi.

KNOWLES, James Earl (Okla) 1311 S. Johnston St., Ada OK 74820 **Died 12/12/2010** B Seminole OK 2/7/1938 s Earl Knowles & Martha Lucille. BS E Cntrl U 1960; Cert Alco/Drug Counslr OK 1991. D 7/6/1985 Bp Gerald Nicholas McAllister. c 1. imissioner@att.net

KNOWLES, Jeremy Harrison (NH) 423 North Ln., Bristol RI 02809 **Died 1/4/2011** B Cambridge MA 1/2/1931 s Thomas Harrison Knowles & Elizabeth Gertrude Hubley. BA Harv 1953; MDiv EDS 1956; MS Syr 1976; DMin EDS 1986. D 6/23/1956 Bp Norman B Nash P 12/29/1956 Bp Anson Phelps Stokes Jr. c 3. Auth, "Gloryland From Revelation," *The Bible Today*, 1985; Auth, "The Pract of Dying," *LivCh*, 1981; Auth, "My Par," *The Chapl*, 1971; Auth, "Emergency of the Day," *The Chapl*, 1969. Amer Assn of Variable Star Observers 1949-2003. Dn's List Harvard 1949; Freedom Fndt Awd Freedom Fndt; Valedictorian Marblehead HS Masachusettes; Speech Winner Squadron Off Sch. elfriede@fullchannel.net

K

KNOWLES, Jessica Trout (Md) 106 W Church St, Frederick MD 21701 **Asst to the R All SS Ch Frederick MD 2010-** B Baltimore MD 3/20/1984 d Douglas Palk Knowles & Sarah Elizabeth. BS Towson U 2006; MDiv VTS 2010. D 6/19/2010 Bp John Leslie Rabb P 1/15/2011 Bp Eugene Sutton. jknowles@allsaintsmd.org

KNOWLES, Melody Dawn (Chi) 15 Barnard Ave., Poughkeepsie NY 12601 B Surrey BC Canada 7/15/1969 BA Trin Wstrn U Langley BC CA 1991; MDiv PrTS 1994; PhD PrTS 2001. D 2/7/2004 Bp Victor Alfonso Scantlebury P 12/18/2004 Bp William Dailey Persell. m 6/10/2001 John Allan Knight c 2. "COntesting Texts: Jews and Christians in Conversation about the Bible," Fortress Press, 2007; "Jerusalem Practiced: Jerusalem in the Rel Practices of Yehud and the Diaspora in the Persian Period," Scholars Press, 2006; "The Flexible Rhetoric of Retelling: The Choice of Dav in the Texts of the Psalms," *Cath Biblic Quarterly*, 2005; "The Returns in Ezra as Pilgrimage:," *Journ of Biblic Lit*, 2004. Assn of Angl Biblic Scholars 2002. mknowles@mccormick.edu

KNOWLES, Roberta Gertrude (Tex) 2444 Hickory Oak Blvd, Orlando FL 32817 **Hope Epis Ch Houston TX 2011-** B Nassau Bahamas 4/27/1956 BS Bethune-Cookman Coll 1978; MDiv TESM 2005. D 5/28/2005 Bp John Wadsworth Howe P 2/2/2006 Bp Don Adger Wimberly. c 1. Vic S Phil The Joy Giver Austin TX 2007-2009; Reverend S Jas Epis Ch Houston TX 2005-2007. roberta_knowles@hotmail.com

KNOWLES, Walter Roy (Oly) 11020 Ne 64th St, Kirkland WA 98033 **Assoc All SS' Ch San Francisco CA 2008-** B Seattle WA 4/16/1951 s Harold Eugene Knowles & Joy Virginia. BA Westmont Coll 1972; MDiv U Tor 1977; PhD Grad Theol Un 2009. Trans from Anglican Church of Canada 7/1/1980 Bp Robert Hume Cochrane. m 12/18/1971 Lorelette Meryl Lein c 1. Vic S Lk's Epis Ch Elma WA 1984; Vic S Mk's Epis Ch Montesano WA 1980-1984. No Amer Acad of Liturg 2008; Societas Liturgica 2009. waltk@rainforsoft.com

KNOWLTON, Elizabeth Marie Clemmer (At) 1750 Broadwell Oaks Dr, Alpharetta GA 30004 **Cathd Of S Phil Atlanta GA 2006-** B Atlanta GA 11/18/1968 D 6/5/2004 P 1/9/2005 Bp J(ohn) Neil Alexander. m 6/19/1994 Ronald Knowlton c 4. The Epis Ch Of S Ptr And S Paul Marietta GA 2004-2006. plbcpa@tbc.net

KNOX, David Paul (CFla) 216 Sheridan Ave, Longwood FL 32750 **R Chr Ch Longwood FL 1999-** B Sydney NSW AU 11/7/1959 s David Broughton Knox & Alisa. MDiv Regent Coll Vancouver Bc CA 1990; ThM Moore Theol Coll, Sydney 2000. Trans from Anglican Church Of Australia 9/1/1999. m 8/23/1997 Susan E Livinski c 1. Asst The Falls Ch Epis Falls Ch VA 1996-1999. lakesidegourmet@yahoo.com

KNOX, Floyd Leonard (La) 10587 Birchwood Dr, Baton Rouge LA 70807 B Oak Ridge LA 6/13/1928 s Foster Baron Knox & Celia. BS Sthrn U Baton Rouge LA 1948; MA Col 1951; Col 1955; Boston Coll 1964; CTh Nash 1987.

D 12/19/1984 P 6/27/1987 Bp James Barrow Brown. Asst S Mich's Ch Baton Rouge LA 1987-1997.

KNOX, Jannet Marie (Mont) 59 Mill Creek Rd # 463, Sheridan MT 59749 B Alpena MI 3/22/1930 d Guy Moulds & Gertrude Martha. No Cntrl Coll 1949. D 11/19/1994 Bp Charles Jones III. m 9/20/1953 Bruce Edward Knox c 2.

KNOX, Jeffrey Donald (CNY) 1755 State Route 48, Fulton NY 13069 **Chapl to the Ret Cler and Spouses Dio Cntrl New York Syracuse NY 2001-** B Seneca Falls NY 5/28/1941 s Donald Knox & Norma Vivian. BA U of Tampa 1963; Ya Berk 1966. D 6/4/1966 Bp Walter M Higley P 10/4/1967 Bp Ned Cole. c 2. R All SS Ch Fulton NY 1974-2001; P-in-c Emm Ch Adams NY 1968-1974; P-in-c Zion Ch Adams NY 1968-1974; Asst Headwaters Epis Mssn Boonville NY 1966-1968. Soc of S Marg 1981. jknox12@windstream.net

KNOX, John Michael (WK) 16019 W 80th St, Lenexa KS 66219 B Whittier CA 5/24/1954 s Albert Whitney Knox & Grace Kathryn. BA U of Kansas 1978; MDiv Nash 1981. D 6/11/1981 P 12/1/1981 Bp Richard Frank Grein. m 12/18/1976 Carole Denis Garrett c 1. Off Of Bsh For ArmdF New York NY 1987-1990; R S Lk's Epis Ch Scott City KS 1985-1987; S Andr's Epis Ch Emporia KS 1984-1985; S Jas Ch Wichita KS 1981-1984. SSC.

KNOX, Regina Gilmartin (Me) 143 State St, Portland ME 04101 B Philadelphia PA 2/28/1950 d Eugene J Gilmartin & Marguerite. BA Villanova U 1980; MATS EDS 2004. D 6/19/2010 P 6/25/2011 Bp Stephen Taylor Lane. m 4/28/1984 John B Knox c 1. knoxre@bc.edu

KNOX, Thomas Stephen (Me) 1262 Route 845, Clifton Royal E5S 2B6 Canada **Died 4/17/2010** B Saint John New Brunswick CA 5/4/1924 s John Samuel Knox & Edyth Pearl. BA Bishops U 1950; LST Bishops U 1952; MA Post Grad Theol Coll GB 1978. Trans from Anglican Church of Canada 7/15/1958 as Priest Bp Oliver L Loring. brookhse@nbnet.nb.ca

✠ **KNUDSEN, Rt Rev Chilton Abbie Richardson** (Me) 940 Washington St, Bath ME 04530 **Int Dio Lexington Dio Lexington Lexington KY 2011-; Ret Bp of Maine Dio Maine Portland ME 2008-** B Washington DC 9/29/1946 d William Castle Richardson & Anne Bass. BA Chatham Coll 1968; MDiv SWTS 1980; DD SWTS 1999. D 6/9/1980 Bp James Winchester Montgomery P 2/24/1981 Bp Quintin Ebenezer Primo Jr Con 3/28/1998 for Me. m 5/29/1971 Michael J Knudsen c 1. Bp Dio Maine Portland ME 1998-2008; Instr Theol Diac Prog Dio Chicago Chicago IL 1987-1998; Asst Ch Of Our Sav Elmhurst IL 1986-1987; Ch Of S Ben Bolingbrook IL 1982-1986. Auth, *Pstr Care for Congs in the Aftermath of Sexual Misconduct*; Auth, *Pstr Care for Congregations in the Aftermath of Sexual Misconduct*. EWC 1978; OHC 1979. Maine Wmn Hall of Fame Maine W Hall of Fame 2005; Hon DD SWTS 1999; Outstanding Wmn Ldr YWCA 1991. mainebishop@gmail.com

KNUDSEN, Richard Alan (Mo) 15 Whitney Ln, Union MO 63084 B Saint Louis MO 12/9/1933 s Bertel Knudsen & Elise Marie. BA U So 1957; MA U of Missouri 1959; MDiv EDS 1962; ThM Harvard DS 1972. D 11/11/1973 P 5/11/1974 Bp George Leslie Cadigan. S Jas Ch Sullivan MO 1974-1999; Asst Min Calv Ch Columbia MO 1972-1974.

KNUDSON, James Clarence (Mass) 85 Grozier Rd, Cambridge MA 02138 B Denver CO 11/11/1933 s Clarence Milton Knudson & Frank May Louise. BA U Denv 1956; MDiv EDS 1962; DMin EDS 1992. D 6/23/1962 P 6/1/1963 Bp Anson Phelps Stokes Jr. m 7/11/1964 Esther Louise Isaacs c 2. P-in-c Gr Epis Ch Medford MA 1997-2000; Int S Anne's Ch No Billerica MA 1995-1996; Int Calv Ch Danvers MA 1993-1995; Supply Dio Massachusetts Boston MA 1991-1993; Int Ch Of The Gd Shpd Waban MA 1990-1991; Sprtl Dir Dio Rhode Island Providence RI 1986-1989; Cmssnr Mnstry Dvlpmt Dio Rhode Island Providence RI 1982-1986; Curs Secy Dio Rhode Island Providence RI 1982-1984; Dir Intern in Mnstry Prog Dio Rhode Island Providence RI 1981-1989; EFM Mentor Dio Rhode Island Providence RI 1981-1987; Rdr GOEs Dio Rhode Island Providence RI 1977-1987; Com Lay Mnstry Dio Rhode Island Providence RI 1976-1982; Dioc Coun Dio Rhode Island Providence RI 1975-1978; R All SS Ch Warwick RI 1973-1989; COM Dio Rhode Island Providence RI 1973-1980; DeptCE Dio Rhode Island Providence RI 1971-1981; Com Cont Educ Mnstry Dio Rhode Island Providence RI 1971-1974; Asst S Lk's Epis Ch E Greenwich RI 1967-1973; Asst Chr Ch Waltham MA 1963-1965. Auth, *Var arts & Revs*. Bp Atwood Prize in Hist Epis TS Cambridge MA. trollsang@aol.com

KNUDSON, Kay Francis (Neb) 1304 Wade St, Lexington NE 68850 **P S Ptr's In The Vlly Lexington NE 2005-** B Knox County NE 10/25/1935 s Francis Knudson & Grace. BS U of Nebraska 1957. D 12/13/2004 P 6/13/2005 Bp Joe Goodwin Burnett. m 8/11/1957 Shirley Mae Knudson c 3. frkay@msn.com

KNUDSON, Richard Lewis (Alb) 9 Saint James Pl Apt 207, Oneonta NY 13820 **Vic Ch Of The H Sprt Schenevus NY 2001-** B Newton MA 6/4/1930 s Henry Spurgeon Knudson & Magda Olsen. BS U of Sthrn Maine 1957; MS U of Maine 1960; DEd Bos 1970. D 6/9/2001 Bp Daniel William Herzog P 7/31/2004 Bp David John Bena. m 6/23/1957 Ann Rankin c 2. emgeeone@stny.rr.com

KNUTSEN, James Kenyon (NCal) P.O. Box 3601, Santa Rosa CA 95402 **Asstg Cler Ch Of The Incarn Santa Rosa CA 2007-** B San Rafael CA 6/17/1960 s Martin Knutsen & Elaine Carlotta. BA Stan 1983; MA EDS 1985; Cert No Chas Inst for the Addictions 1985; MDiv EDS 1990. D 6/27/1990 Bp John Lester Thompson III P 4/27/1991 Bp David Bell Birney IV. Sabbatical Assoc Ch Of The Incarn Santa Rosa CA 2009; Int Assoc R Ch Of The Incarn Santa Rosa CA 2007-2008; Novc, SSJE S Jn's Chap Cambridge MA 2004-2006; R S Mich And All Ang Ch Ft Bragg CA 1998-2003; Assoc Trin Ch Sonoma CA 1998; Assoc Gr Ch S Helena CA 1997-1998; Asst Ch Of The Incarn Santa Rosa CA 1994-1996; Int S Lk's Mssn Calistoga CA 1993-1994; Cur Ch Of S Jn The Evang Hingham MA 1990-1993. knujam@yahoo.com

KOCH JR, John Dunbar (CFla) HUSEMann str. #3, Berlin 10435 Germany B Baton Rouge LA 9/8/1977 s John Dunbar Koch & Sally. BA W&L; MDiv TESM 2007. D 6/2/2007 Bp John Wadsworth Howe P. m 9/7/2004 Elizabeth Tucker Elizabeth Tucker. jadykoch@gmail.com

KOCH, William Christian (RG) P.O. Box 1614, Blue Hill ME 04614 B Santa Fe NM 9/13/1933 s Ferdinand Adolph Koch & Kathleen Anne. BA Knox Coll 1955; MDiv CDSP 1958. D 6/28/1958 P 4/1/1959 Bp C J Kinsolving III. m 8/3/1985 Jean Alice Uehlinger Koch. Fllshp Of The Ascen Hse Wellesley MA 1984; R All SS Par Brookline MA 1973-1983; Yth Mssnr, Dir of the Derbish Conf Cntr Dio Pennsylvania Philadelphia PA 1967-1971; Vic Ch Of The Ascen Parkesburg PA 1967-1969; Cur Pro Cathd Epis Ch Of S Clem El Paso TX 1958-1959. Chapl SCHC 1977-1984.

KOCHARHOOK, Kenneth G (Pgh) 4603 1/2 Corday Way, Pittsburgh PA 15224 **Died 5/3/2010** B Pittsburgh PA 3/31/1949 s Peter Paul Kocharhook & Virginia Dolores. BA La Salle U; MDiv Nash 1987. D 6/7/1986 P 12/18/1986 Bp Alden Moinet Hathaway. Interfaith Allnce 1995; Interfaith Care Givers 1994; Ministral Netwk On Aids, Natl Epis Aids, Cltn NECAD 1986; Ord Of S Lk 1990.

KOCHENBURGER, Philip Alan (CFla) 67 CSH Chaplain, Unit 26610 Box 64, APO, AE 09244 **Off Of Bsh For ArmdF New York NY 1999-** B Bergen County NJ 7/11/1962 s John Frederick Kochenburger & Patricia Ann. Assemblies of God TS; BA SE Coll Lakeland FL 1989; MDiv Gordon-Conwell TS 1993. D 12/3/1995 Bp John Wadsworth Howe P 6/2/1996 Bp Hugo Luis Pina-Lopez. m 12/15/1984 Dorothy Elizabeth Horner. S Agnes Ch Sebring FL 1997-1999; Assoc R Gr Epis Ch Of Ocala Ocala FL 1996-1997. Auth, "arts Var Pub"; Auth, "The Blood"; Auth, "The Sound Of His Voice". philip.kochenburger@wur.armed.army.mil

KOCHTITZKY, Rod Kochtitzky (Tenn) The Pastoral Center for Healing, 3605 Hillsboro Pike, Nashville TN 37215 B Nashville TN 8/30/1953 s Otto Morse Kochtitzky & Marjorie Stephenson. BA U So 1975; MDiv GTS 1982; Cert Inst of Imago Relatns Ther 1991; Cert Blanton-Peale Grad Inst 1995; Cert Imago Relationships Intl 1995; Cert Imago Relationships Intl 1996; Cert Imago Relationships Intl 2009. D 6/20/1982 P 4/10/1983 Bp William Evan Sanders. m 2/9/1991 Jane Cazort Hardy. Pstr Counslr S Dav's Epis Ch Nashville TN 2002-2009; P-in-c Dio New York New York City NY 1988-1991; Asst Ch Of S Jas The Less Scarsdale NY 1986-1988; Vic Dio Tennessee Nashville TN 1983-1986; D-In-Trng Dio Tennessee Nashville TN 1982-1983; D Gr Ch Chattanooga TN 1982-1983. Cmnty Of S Mary 1997; Fell Amer Assn Pstr Counselors 1987. Serv Recognition Awd Assoc. of Imago Ther 2002. rod@rodk.net

KOCZKA, Claudia (WNY) 400 Ridge St. PO Box 354, Lewiston NY 14092 **Int S Paul's Epis Ch Lewiston NY 2011-** B Buffalo NY 5/25/1965 d Francis Allen Scheda & Ruth Tekla. BA SUNY Buffalo 1987; MS Canisus Coll 1989; MDiv The GTS 2011. D 4/22/2010 Bp J Michael Garrison. m 4/29/1989 Kevin Koczka c 2. myzoobie@roadrunner.com

KODERA, T(akashi) James (Mass) 212 Old Lancaster Rd, Sudbury MA 01776 **R S Lk's Ch Hudson MA 2003-** B JP 5/19/1945 s Haruo Kodera & Utae Katherine. BA Carleton Coll 1969; Yale DS 1970; MA Col 1972; MPhil Col 1974; PhD Col 1976; EDS 1983. D 6/1/1985 Bp John Bowen Coburn P 5/6/1986 Bp Roger W Blanchard. m 3/27/1995 Nancy S Sabug c 2. P-in-c S Lk's Ch Hudson MA 2000-2003; Asst S Eliz's Ch Sudbury MA 1992-2000; Assoc S Mk's Ch Southborough MA 1988-1991; Asst All SS Par Brookline MA 1985-1988. Auth, "Why Asian Amer Stds Matter: challenges and pPromises in the Undergraduate Curric," *ASIANETWORK Journ*, ASIANetwork, 2008; Auth, "Asian Americans: Where Do They Belong?," *Wit*, The Ch Pub Co., 2004; Auth, "Asians In Amer Soc & Ch: Their Struggles & Calling," *THE JAPAN Chr Revs*, The Chr Lit Soc of Japan, 1996; Auth, "Reshaping of Consceience: Challenges and Promises of Multiculturalism in Amer Educ," *THE JAPAN Chr Revs*, The Chr Lit Soc of Japan, 1994; Auth, "Am I My Sis's Keeper?," *PLUMBLINE: A Journ OF Mnstry IN HIGHER EDUCAITON*, ECUSA, 1992; Auth, "Paradoxes of Being Rel: A Case of Mod Japan," *REKISHI KENKYU*, The Hist Sudy Grp of the Angl Ch of Japan, 1990; Transltr, "The 1979 Bk of Common Pryr," *into Japanese*, ECUSA, 1988; Co-Ed, "DIALOGUE & Allnce: ENCOUNTERS BETWEEN ASIAN & Wstrn CONCEPTIONS OF THE ULTIMATE," Paragon, 1987; Auth, "What Are We To Do?," *PLUMBLINE: A Journ OF MHE*, ECUSA, 1987; Auth, "Uchimura Kanzo & His 'No Ch Chrsnty: Its Origin & Significance in Early Mod Japan," *Rel SUDIES*, Cambridge U Press, 1987; Auth, "Continuity Of Change And

Change In Continuity," *THE DHARMA Wrld*, The Kosei Pub Co., 1984; Auth, "A Vortex Of E & W: Probelems Of Contextualization," *THE Ecum Revs*, WCC, Geneva, 1983; Auth, "The Study Of Rel At Wellesley Coll: Tradition & Change, The Coun On The Study Of Rel Bulletin," *THE Coun O THE STUDY OF Rel BULLETIN*, AAR, 1982; Auth, "Toward And Asianization Of Chrsnty:Demise Or Metamorphosis, Ten Theologians Respond To The Unificaiton Ch," *TEN THEOLOGIANS RESPOND TO THE UNIFICAITON Ch*, The Rose of Sharon Press, 1981; Auth, "DOGEN'S FORMATIVE YEARS IN CHINA," Routledge & Kegan Paul, London, 1980; Auth, "Nichiren And His Nationalistic Eschatology," *Rel Stds*, Cambridge U Press, 1979; Auth, "Images Of The Ideal: Islamic, Buddhist And Confucian," *Sekai Gakusei Shimbun*, 1979. AAR; Assn For Asian Stds; Buddhist-Chr Dialogue; Coun For Asian And Pacific Theol; Intl Assn Buddhist Stds; Soc Of S Jn The Evang. jkodera@wellesley.edu

KOEHLER, Anne E (Nwk) 9 Vose Ave, Apt. 227, South Orange NJ 07079 **P-in-c Chr Ch Glen Ridge NJ 2006-** B Pensacola FL 4/19/1951 BA Duke 1973; MBA NWU 1974; MDiv PrTS 2002; DAS GTS 2003. D 5/31/2003 P 12/13/2003 Bp John Palmer Croneberger. m 6/22/1974 Steven Hubrig Koehler. Int S Thos Ch Alexandria Pittstown NJ 2005-2006; Cur S Lk's Ch Gladstone NJ 2003-2005. aekoehler51@gmail.com

KOEHLER III, Norman Elias (Pgh) 408 Forest Highlands Dr, Pittsburgh PA 15238 **Assoc S Thos Memi Epis Ch Oakmont PA 2007-** B Washington PA 3/3/1934 s Norman Elias Koehler & Elizabeth Mae. BA Grove City Coll 1956; Transltr/Interpreter Defense Lang Inst 1965; MS USC 1969; PhD U Pgh 1973; MA Pittsburgh TS 2002. D 6/15/2002 P 12/13/2006 Bp Robert William Duncan. m 10/13/1956 Virginia Ann Schadt. Int S Paul's Epis Ch Kittanning PA 2008; D The Ch Of The Redeem Pittsburgh PA 2002-2004.

KOEHLER, Robert Brien (La) 8833 Goodwood Blvd, Baton Rouge LA 70806 **R S Lk's Ch Baton Rouge LA 2001-; Trst Nash Nashotah WI 1994-** B Hastings NE 8/26/1950 s Robert Joseph Koehler & Melba Deloris. BA U Of Dallas Irving 1972; U of Wisconsin 1973; MDiv Nash 1976. D 5/1/1976 P 11/1/1976 Bp Charles Thomas Gaskell. m 8/5/1972 Terry Collins c 3. R S Lk's Ch Ft Myers FL 1993-2001; Admin Of The ESA Dio Ft Worth Ft Worth TX 1991-1993; The Esa Mssy Soc Inc. Ft Worth TX 1991-1993; Cn To The Ordnry Dio Ft Worth Ft Worth TX 1989-1991; Exec Secy To The Bp Dio Ft Worth Ft Worth TX 1987-1989; Vic Ch Of The H Cross Burleson TX 1984-1987; R S Raphael's Ch Ft Myers Bch FL 1981-1984; Cur Emm Epis Ch Rockford IL 1978-1981; S Lk's Ch Racine WI 1976-1978; Cur S Lk's Hosp Racine WI 1976-1978. Ancient & Honorable Artillery Co Of Massachusetts 1984; CCU 1976; CBS 1997; Ecm/ESA/Forw In Faith 1977; GAS 1986; Soc Of Colonial Wars 1985; SSC 1978; Sons Of The Amer Revolution 1982. brienkoehler@yahoo.com

KOELLN, Theodore Frank (CFla) 505 Ne 1st Ave, Mulberry FL 33860 **Part Time R S Lk The Evang Ch Mulberry FL 1998-** B Boston MA 12/26/1944 s Theodore Herman Koelln & Geneva Cathleen. BS Dakota St U 1967; MDiv STUSo 1988. D 6/10/1988 P 1/1/1989 Bp Craig Barry Anderson. m 6/19/1999 Patricia N Koelln. R Gd Shpd Decatur AL 2004-2009; S Lk The Evang Ch Mulberry FL 1996-2004; S Paul's Ch Brookings SD 1991-1996; D Chr Epis Ch Milbank SD 1988-1998; D S Mary's Epis Ch Roslyn SD 1988-1998; Dio So Dakota Sioux Falls SD 1988-1991. semikoelln@centurylink.net

KOENIG, Diane L (Chi) 86 Pomeroy Ave # 2, Crystal Lake IL 60014 **D/Pstr S Mary Epis Ch Crystal Lake IL 1998-** B Michigan City IN 2/10/1940 d Lewis Edward Bartholomew & Ann. MA Amer Conservatory of Mus 1964. D 2/7/1998 Bp Herbert Alcorn Donovan Jr. m 5/20/1967 Peter Frederick Koenig. NAAD. dizer@mc.net

KOENIG, John Thomas (NJ) 440 W. 21st St., New York NY 10011 B Fort Wayne IN 6/20/1938 s Melvin Henry Koenig & Doris Lavonne. BA Concordia Sr Coll 1961; BD Concordia TS 1965; ThD UTS 1971. D 6/12/1993 P 12/14/1993 Bp George Phelps Mellick Belshaw. m 6/5/1976 Kathleen J Jameson. Prof The GTS New York NY 1978-2011. Auth, "Soul Banquets," Morehouse Pub, 2007; Auth, "The Feast of the Wrld's Redemp," Trin Press Intl , 2000; Auth, "Rediscovering NT Pryr," HarperCollins; Wipf & Stock, 1992; Auth, "NT Hosp," Fortress Press; Wipf & Stock, 1985; Auth, "Philippians, Philemon," *Augsburg Commentary on the NT*, Augsburg, 1985; Auth, "Jews & Christians in Dialogue: NT Foundations," Westminster, 1979; Auth, "Charismata: God's Gifts," Westminster, 1978. Angl Assn of Biblic Scholars; Soc for Values in Higher Educ; SBL. jkoenig@gts.edu

KOENIGER, Margaret Smithers (Nwk) 574 Ridgewood Rd, Maplewood NJ 07040 B Rhinebeck NY 6/16/1949 d John Abram Smithers & Margaret McClure. AA Pine Manor Jr Coll 1970; BFA U of New Mex 1973; MDiv Drew U 1995. D 6/3/1995 Bp Jack Marston McKelvey P 12/9/1995 Bp John Shelby Spong. m 5/27/1976 John Crawford Koeniger c 3. Serv Dio Newark Newark NJ 2005-2009; Int Dio Newark Newark NJ 2002-2004; S Paul's Epis Ch Chatham NJ 1996-2002; S Paul's Epis Ch Chatham NJ 1995-1996. Alb Inst. revbambi@aol.com

KOEPKE III, John Frederick (SO) 412 Sycamore Street, Cincinnati OH 45202 **Cn to the Ordnry Dio Sthrn Ohio Cincinnati OH 2011-** B Cannonsburg PA 3/27/1953 s John Frederick Koepke & Catherine Ruth. BA Hob 1975; MDiv Yale DS 1979. D 6/9/1979 P 12/8/1979 Bp Robert Bracewell Appleyard. m 6/4/1977 Nanci Ann McCray. Chair - Com Dio Sthrn Ohio Cincinnati OH 2001-2010; Ch Dedploy Bd Epis Ch Cntr New York NY 1998-2006; R S Paul's Epis Ch Dayton OH 1997-2011; R Ch Of Our Sav Silver Sprg MD 1986-1997; Cn For Pstr Dvlpmt Dio Wstrn Michigan Kalamazoo MI 1982-1986; Vic S Steph's Epis Ch Plainwell MI 1982-1985; Asst R Fox Chap Epis Ch Pittsburgh PA 1979-1982. Auth, "Var arts". jkoepke@diosohio.org

KOFFRON-EISEN, Elizabeth Mary (Ia) 945 Applewood Ct #1, Coralville IA 52241 **D Trin Ch Iowa City IA 1996-** B Cedar Rapids IA 11/3/1952 d Marvin Joseph Koffron & Esther Louise. Mt Mercy Coll 1973; BA Coe Coll 1975; EFM 1994. D 1/7/1996 Bp Carl Christopher Epting. m 6/8/1985 Thomas Jay Eisen. D Gr Ch Cedar Rapids IA 1996-1999. Animal Cmncatn Spec; NAAD, ESMA, Steph Mnstry Ldr. teisen211@mchsi.com

KOH, Aidan Youngduk (Los) 4344 Lemp Ave, Studio City CA 91604 **S Jas' Sch Los Angeles CA 2006-** B 3/11/1953 s Basil Changlye Koh & Ruth Boolye. BA Hankook Theol Coll 1981; MDiv Hankook TS 1987; CDSP 1991. D 6/15/1991 P 1/1/1992 Bp Frederick Houk Borsch. m 9/10/1983 Christina Eunkyung Koh c 1. Asst S Jas Par Los Angeles CA 1991-2006.

KOHLBECKER, Eugene Edmund (NI) 600 Franklin Sq, Michigan City IN 46360 B Urbana IL 1/12/1954 s Eugene Edmund Kohlbecker & Billie Lu. BS MacMurray Coll 1975; MS U IL 1977; PhD Indiana U 1986; MDiv STUSo 1992. D 6/20/1992 Bp George Nelson Hunt III P 2/6/1993 Bp Alfred Clark Marble Jr. R Trin Ch Michigan City IN 2000-2006; Assoc Epis Ch Of The Gd Shpd Lake Chas LA 1996-1999; Vic All SS Ch Dequincy LA 1994-1995; S Andr's Ch Lake Chas LA 1994-1995; D-in-c Chr Ch S Jos LA 1993-1994; D-In-C Gr Ch Waterproof LA 1993-1994; Asst Trin Ch Natchez MS 1992-1994. kohlbecker@mac.com

K

KOHLMEIER, Susan Collins (Roch) 1017 Silvercrest Dr, Webster NY 14580 **Zion Epis Ch Palmyra NY 2008-** B Clifton Springs NY 7/3/1956 d John Arden Collins & Ramona Anne. BA St. Jn Fisher Coll 1978; MA St. Bern's Inst Rochester NY 1988; MDiv St. Bern's Inst Rochester NY 1992. D 3/13/1993 P 2/11/1994 Bp William George Burrill. m 10/17/1981 Charles Kohlmeier. S Mths Epis Ch E Rochester NY 2005-2008; Dio Rochester Rochester NY 2002-2005; Asst The Ch Of The Epiph Rochester NY 1994-1995; Asst Ch Of The Gd Shpd Webster NY 1993-1994. chuck13@frontiernet.net

KOHN, George Frederick (ECR) 1220 Funston Ave, Pacific Grove CA 93950 **S Jas' Ch Monterey CA 2001-** B Evanston IL 4/18/1949 s Clyde Frederick Kohn & Doris M. MDiv GTS 1975; MA U of Iowa 1989; BA U of Iowa 1989. D 6/11/1975 P 12/13/1975 Bp Walter Cameron Righter. m 5/18/2002 Molly Jean Lewis. Fin Cmsn Dio El Camino Real Monterey CA 1989-1994; Dio California San Francisco CA 1988-1994; COM Dio El Camino Real Monterey CA 1986-1994; Epis Ch Of The Gd Shpd Salinas CA 1985-1994; Gd Samar Epis Ch Virginia Bch VA 1983-1988; Alcosm Cmsn Dio Iowa Des Moines IA 1980-1986; Trin Ch Muscatine IA 1978-1985; Trin Epis Ch Mobile AL 1978-1985; Dio Cntrl Gulf Coast Pensacola FL 1977-1991; S Mary's Epis Ch Milton FL 1977-1981; S Monica's Cantonment FL 1977-1978; Trin Cathd Davenport IA 1975-1978. gfkohn@redshift.com

KOHN, Mary-Marguerite (Md) 5000 Cedar Ave., Halethorpe MD 21227 **Asst S Ptr's Epis Ch Ellicott City MD 2003-** B Montgomery AL 6/4/1949 d Frank Cowell Kohn & Marguerite Jean. BA Duke 1972; MSW U NC 1976; CDSP 1989; MDiv Duke 1992; CAS EDS 1993. D 6/26/1993 Bp Huntington Williams Jr P 5/24/1994 Bp Don Edward Johnson. Int S Mk's Epis Ch Newport VT 2002-2003; Dio Wstrn Massachusetts Springfield MA 2000-2002; Int S Steph's Ch Pittsfield MA 2000-2002; Stwdshp Cmsn Dio Albany Albany NY 1997-1998; P-in-c S Lk's Ch Mechanicville NY 1996-1999. Fllshp of SSJE 1988. mmkohn@loyola.edu

KOLANOWSKI, Ronald James (Ct) St. James Episcopal Church, 95 Route 2A, Preston CT 06365 **Mem of Wrshp and Liturg Com Dio Connecticut Hartford CT 2011-; Vic S Jas Ch Preston CT 2010-** B Manistee MI 10/8/1957 s Arthur S Kolanowski & Helen. BA CUA 1979; MA Washington Theol Un 2002; MDiv EDS 2006. D 6/9/2007 P 12/15/2007 Bp Andrew Donnan Smith. Cur Trin Epis Ch Hartford CT 2007-2010. ronkol@sbcglobal.net

KOLB, Jerry Warren (WMo) 8256 Outlook Lane, Prairie Village KS 66208 **Chapl to Ret Cler/Surviving Spouses Dio W Missouri Kansas City MO 2008-; Coordntr, Provinces V, VI & VII, Chapl to Ret Cle The CPG New York NY 2002-** B Denver CO 2/13/1936 s Lewis Jackson Kolb & Jean. BS U CO 1958; MDiv SWTS 1968. D 6/11/1968 Bp Joseph Summerville Minnis P 12/4/1968 Bp Edwin B Thayer. m 2/8/1964 Brenda M Morgan c 2. Chapl St Lk's Chap Kansas City MO 1972-1999; Asst R Epiph Epis Ch Denver CO 1971-1972; Cur S Tim's Epis Ch Centennial CO 1968-1970. Auth, "A Randomized, Controlled Trial of the Effects of Remote, Intercessory Pryr on Outcomes in Patients Admitted to the Coronary C," *Archv of Internal Med*, 1999. ACPE 1970; Assn of Profsnl Chapl 1976; Comp Worker Sis of the H Sprt 1979-2008. Bp's Shield Dio W Missouri 1999; Chapl Emer S Lk's Hosp of KC 1999. jerryandbrenda@swbell.net

KOLB, John Clemens (Pa) 321 Fairview Rd, Glenmoore PA 19343 **Died 4/28/2011** B Lynn MA 11/6/1930 s Jacob Clemens Kolb & Esther. BFA U of Pennsylvania 1954; BD EDS 1957. D 6/8/1957 P 12/1/1957 Bp Oliver J Hart. c 2.

KOLB, William A (WTenn) 531 S. Prescott St, Memphis TN 38111 B New York NY 11/8/1937 s Bernard Sherman Kolb & Alice. U of Florida 1958; LTh VTS 1973; Fllshp VTS 1986; Cont Educ/Sabattical Epis TS of The SW 1990; Cert Int Mnstry Prog 2000; U of Memphis 2007; U of Memphis 2008; U of Memphis 2009. D 6/5/1973 Bp William Henry Marmion P 12/15/1973 Bp George Leslie Cadigan. m 12/26/2003 Melinda Shoaf c 4. Regular Supply P Emm Ch Memphis TN 2007-2010; Int R Estrn Shore Chap Virginia Bch VA 2004-2005; Int Accociate Calv Ch Memphis TN 2002-2004; Int R S Jas Ch Jackson MS 2001-2002; Int R Gr - S Lk's Ch Memphis TN 2000-2001; Assoc R Calv Ch Memphis TN 1992-2000; R S Thos Ch Mamaroneck NY 1978-1992; Vic Ch Of The H Apos Barnwell SC 1976-1978; Vic S Alb's Ch Blackville SC 1976-1978; Vic Chr Ch Denmark SC 1976-1977; Cn Chr Ch Cathd S Louis MO 1973-1976. williamkolb2@bellsouth.net

KOLBET, Paul Robert (Oly) 8 Ivy Cir., Wellesley MA 02482 **Assoc R S Paul's Ch Natick MA 2010-** B Reno NV 2/6/1968 s Robert Francis Kolbet & Diana Mae. BA Oral Roberts U 1990; MDiv Ya Berk 1994; STM Yale DS 1995; MA U of Notre Dame 1999; PhD U of Notre Dame 2003. D 6/24/1995 Bp Vincent Waydell Warner P 5/18/1996 Bp Francis Campbell Gray. m 5/24/2003 Devorah Egloff c 1. Asst P S Andr's Ch Wellesley MA 2007; Asst P S Mich And All Ang Ch So Bend IN 1999; Cur S Mich And All Ang Ch So Bend IN 1996-1998. Auth, "Rethinking the Christological Foundations of Reinhold Niebuhrs Chr Realism," *Mod Theol*, Vol. 26 pp 437-65, 2010; Auth, "Aug and the Cure of Souls: Revising a Classical Ideal," *U of Notre Dame Press*, 2010; Auth, "Rethinking Mnstrl Ideals in Light of the Cler Crisis," *Ecclesiology*, Vol. 5 pp 192-211, 2009; Auth, "Torture and Origen's Hermeneutics of Nonviolence," *Journ of the AAR*, Vol. 76 pp. 545-72, 2008; Auth, "Athan, the Psalms, and the Reformation of the Self," *Harvard Theol Revs*, Vol. 99 pp. 85-101, 2006; Auth, "Formal Continuities Between Aug's Early Philos Tchg and Late Homiletical Pract," *Studia Patristica*, Vol. 43 pp. 149-54, 2006. AAR 1995; No Amer Patristic Soc 1995; SBL 1995. kolbet@aya.yale.edu

K

KOLLIN, Harriet (Pa) 3738 W Country Club Rd, Philadelphia PA 19131 **Assoc Ch Of S Mart-In-The-Fields Philadelphia PA 2011-; Mem of Stndg Cmsn on Hlth, GC Dio Pennsylvania Philadelphia PA 2010-; Mem of Anti-racism team Dio Pennsylvania Philadelphia PA 2009-** B Philippines 10/28/1952 BD Trin Of Quezon City Ph 1974; MS U of Pennsylvania 1993; MDiv EDS 2004. D 6/19/2004 P 6/4/2005 Bp Charles Ellsworth Bennison Jr. m 11/29/2005 Timothy Lee Griffin. P-in-c Ch Of S Jn The Evang Philadelphia PA 2004-2011; D Ch Of S Asaph Bala Cynwyd PA 2004. harrietkollin@msn.com

KOLLIN JR, James T. (NJ) 120 Sussex St Apt 1b, Hackensack NJ 07601 **Chapl Seamens Ch Inst Income New York NY 2001-; P S Lk And All SS' Ch Un NJ 2000-** B 9/9/1963 m 11/28/1992 Jet O Kollin c 3. Dio No Cntrl Philippines 1990-1993. JTKollin@aol.com

KOMSTEDT JR, William Andrew (FtW) 1504 Alcaraz Place, The Villages FL 32159 B New York NY 3/18/1928 s William Andrew Komstedt & Estelle. DIT Nyack Coll 1948; BA U of Sthrn Mississippi 1958; Joint Forces Stff Coll 1964; MS U of Sthrn Mississippi 1965; DMin TCU 1984; PhD NW Intl U Ballerup DK 2002. D 12/31/1972 Bp Clarence Edward Hobgood P 9/21/1973 Bp Wilburn Camrock Campbell. m 8/21/1948 Martha Sebolt. Assoc Epis Ch Of S Mary Belleview FL 2003-2008; P-in-c S Fran Of Assisi Ch Bushnell FL 2000-2003; S Geo Epis Ch The Villages FL 1998-1999; Chr Ch Cathd Louisville KY 1997-1999; S Raphael's Ch Lexington KY 1997-1999; S Fran Of Assisi Epis Ch Aledo TX 1992-1999; ExCoun Dio Ft Worth Ft Worth TX 1989-1991; S Fran Of Assisi Epis Ch Aledo TX 1987-1990; Dio Ft Worth Ft Worth TX 1984-1987; The Epis Ch Of The Resurr Dallas TX 1980-1982; Chr The King Epis Ch Ft Worth TX 1980; Cur/Day Sch Chapl All SS' Epis Ch Ft Worth TX 1977-1978. Auth, *Redemptive Side of Anger*, (self-Pub), 1995. Assn for CPE 1981; Assn of Profsnl Chapl 1982; Assy of Epis Hospitals and Chapl 1981; ComT 1981; CBS 1977. Fell Fell of NW Intl U 2002; Bd Cert Chapl Assn of Profsnl Chapl 1981; Listed in "Who's Who in Rel" Marquis Who's Who Pub Bd 1977; Legion of Merit US Govt 1977; Legion of Merit US Govt 1972. wkomstedt463@comcast.net

KONDRATH, William Michael (Mass) 25 Richards Ave, Sharon MA 02067 **Field Educ Dir & Assoc Prof Pstr Theol EDS Cambridge MA 1995-** B Glendale CA 4/16/1948 s Joseph Andrew Kondrath & June Audrey. S Jn's Sem Coll Camarillo CA 1969; BA CUA 1971; MDiv U Tor 1974; MA U Tor 1977; EdM Harv 1983; DMin Andover Newton TS 1987. Rec from Roman Catholic 2/1/1986 as Priest Bp Morris Fairchild Arnold. m 9/11/1982 Christina Emma Robb c 3. R S Mk's Ch Foxborough MA 1989-1995; Asst All SS' Epis Ch Belmont MA 1985-1988. Auth, "Styles Of Mnstrl Ldrshp". bkondrath@eds.edu

✠ KONIECZNY, Rt Rev Edward Joseph (Okla) 924 N. Robinsons, Oklahoma City OK 73102 **Bp of Oklahoma Dio Oklahoma Oklahoma City OK 2007-** B Spokane WA 12/20/1954 s Edwin Theodore Konieczny & Johanna Josephine. AA Long Bch City Coll 1976; BA California St U 1987; MDiv CDSP 1994; DMin SWTS 2001; DD SWTS 2007. D 5/28/1994 Bp John Mc Gill Krumm P 11/30/1994 Bp Claude Edward Payne Con 9/15/2007 for Colo. m 8/17/1978 Debra Lynn Maroney c 2. Alt GC Dep Dio Colorado Denver CO 2006; Ch & Congrl Growth Com Dio Colorado Denver CO 2005-2007; Stndg Com Pres Dio Colorado Denver CO 2005-2007; Fin Com Dio Colorado Denver CO 2003-2011; Secy of Conv Dio Colorado Denver CO 2003-2005; R S Matt's Ch Grand Jct CO 2002-2007; Chair Supervisors and Tellers Dio Texas Houston TX 1996-2002; R Epis Ch Of The H Sprt Waco TX 1996-2002; Asst S Mk's Ch Beaumont TX 1994-1996. DD SWTS 2008. edjk1220@att.net

KONRAD, William Wesley (NY) 9701 Little River Ct, Matthews NC 28105 **Died 11/9/2009** B Newark NJ 3/29/1921 s William Konrad & Sarah Helen. BA Rutgers-The St U 1948; STB GTS 1951. D 5/26/1951 P 12/1/1951 Bp Benjamin M Washburn. c 4. Bro of S Andr 1969; Caribbean Mnstrs 1986; OHC 1934. Human Rts Awd City of White Plains, New York White Plains NY 1972. wwkonrad@carolina.rr.com

KONTOS, George Demetrios (La) 5010 Mancuso Ln, Baton Rouge LA 70809 **Sr S Steph's Ch Innis LA 2004-** B Waycross GA 4/16/1943 s James George Kontos & Anastasia. BA U GA 1965; MDiv GTS 1968; Cert Shalem Inst 1985. D 6/5/1968 P 3/25/1969 Bp Albert R Stuart. m 8/15/1970 Theresa W Wilkerson c 3. R S Jas Epis Ch Baton Rouge LA 1993-2004; R Ch Of The H Comf Tallahassee FL 1975-1992; Cn-In-Res S Jn's Cathd Jacksonville FL 1973-1975; R Chr Epis Ch Dublin GA 1970-1973; Vic Trin Ch Cochran GA 1969-1970; Cur S Paul's Ch Albany GA 1968-1969. Auth, "Deepening The Baptismal Cov," 1987; Auth, "Liturg Families," *Liturg Families: Intergenerational Approach To Chr Formation*, 1985. St. Jas Cntr for Sprtl Formation Trin Ch, NYC 2000. georgekontos@hotmail.com

KOONCE, Kelly Montgomery (Tex) 6625 Whitemarsh Valley Walk, Austin TX 78746 **Assoc R The Ch of the Gd Shpd Austin TX 2007-** B Houston TX 9/28/1969 s Kenneth Terry Koonce & Beverly Ann. BA Drew U 1993; MA Austin Presb TS 1996; MDiv Epis TS of The SW 2002. D 6/22/2002 Bp Claude Edward Payne P 7/6/2003 Bp Don Adger Wimberly. m 1/20/1996 Kimberley C Curry c 1. Asstg P S Steph's Epis Ch Orinda CA 2005-2007; Asst R The Ch of the Gd Shpd Austin TX 2002-2004. oneeyeblue@earthlink.net

KOONZ, Ellsworth Earl (Ind) 5 Kingswood Dr, Eastham MA 02642 B Greenfield MA 8/31/1925 s Earl Robert Koonz & Estella Roanna. BD U MI 1946; STB GTS 1949. D 7/10/1949 Bp Russell S Hubbard P 2/11/1950 Bp Richard S M Emrich. Asst The Ch Of S Mary Of The Harbor Provincetown MA 1989-1996; Asst The Ch Of The H Sprt Orleans MA 1972-1985; Vic Chap Of The Gd Shpd W Lafayette IN 1960-1970; Asst Ch Of The Trsfg New York NY 1954-1955; R Calv Memi Epis Ch Saginaw MI 1952-1954; Cur S Andr's Ch Ann Arbor MI 1949-1952. Massachusetts Recognition Awd AIDS Action Com of Massachusetts.

KOOPERKAMP, William Earl (NY) 521 W 126th St, New York NY 10027 **R S Mary's Manhattanville Epis Ch New York NY 2000-** B Louisville KY 10/25/1956 s Wayne Wheeler Kotkamp & Eileen Elizabeth. BA Hampshire Coll 1979; Lucb U Coll Buckingham Gb 1980; MDiv UTS 1983. D 6/10/1984 P 6/18/1988 Bp David Reed. m 6/27/1980 Elizabeth B Cooper c 3. Asst Min Ch Of The Intsn New York NY 1992-2000. revkooperkamp@aol.com

KOOR, Margaret Platt (SwFla) 4017 Heaton Ter, North Port FL 34286 **Disciplinary Bd Dio SW Florida Sarasota FL 2011-; D S Nath Ch No Port FL 2003-** B Westerly RI 7/27/1944 d Thomas Alfred Platt & Mildred Ester. Jos Lawr Sch of Nrsng 1965. D 6/13/1992 Bp Rogers Sanders Harris. c 3. D S Bon Ch Sarasota FL 1995-2002; D Ch of the Nativ Sarasota FL 1992-1995. Ord of Julian of Norwich - Oblate 1998. mpkoor@comcast.net

KOOSER, Robert Lee (Pgh) 221 S Prospect St, Connellsville PA 15425 B Connellsville PA 9/17/1929 s Harry E Kooser & Della M. BA Waynesburg Coll 1952; MDiv Bos 1957; DAS EDS 1962. D 6/23/1962 Bp Anson Phelps Stokes Jr P 5/1/1963 Bp Roger W Blanchard. m 6/2/1979 Frances Jean Kooser. Vic Trin Ch Connellsville PA 1980-1992; R S Ptr's Epis Ch Brentwood Pittsburgh PA 1973-1975; Cur Trin Ch Newton Cntr MA 1963-1964; Asst All SS Ch Cincinnati OH 1962-1963.

KOPERA, Dorothy Jean (NMich) 214 E Avenue A, Newberry MI 49868 B Croswell MI 6/24/1950 d Arthur Anthony Grubba & Vera Mary. Nthrn Michigan U 1969. D 7/15/1993 P 1/1/1994 Bp Thomas Kreider Ray. m 8/14/1971 Paul Daniel Kopera.

KOPPEL, Mary E (La) 1420 Valmont Street, New Orleans LA 70115 B New Orleans LA 3/22/1977 d Harwood Koppel & Evelyn Elizabeth. BA U So 1999; MDiv SWTS 2002. D 12/27/2001 P 7/3/2002 Bp Charles Edward Jenkins III. m 10/9/2004 Mark A Vicknair c 1. Cn for Yth & YA Mnstry Chr Ch Cathd New Orleans LA 2007-2011; R All SS Ch Kapaa HI 2005-2007; Asst R S Mart's Epis Ch Metairie LA 2002-2005. marykoppel@hotmail.com

KOPREN, Kristin Corinne (NY) Saint Hilda'S And Saint Hugh'S School, 619 W 114th St, New York NY 10025 **S Hilda's And S Hugh's Sch New York NY 2003-** B Orange CA 1/15/1964 d Wayne Allen Kopren & Barbara Lorainne. BA Appalachian St U 1986; MDiv GTS 1997. D 6/14/1997 P 12/13/1997 Bp Richard Frank Grein. m 6/6/1994 Thomas Masterson. Asst The Ch of S Matt And S Tim New York NY 1997-2003. kckopren@aol.com

KORATHU, Anna Maria (Oly) 19229 65th Place Northeast, Seattle WA 98155 B Seattle WA 10/14/1946 d John Kazmere Krasuckl & Clarise Victoria. BA Wstrn Washington U 1991; MDiv CDSP 1997. D 6/28/1997 Bp Vincent Waydell Warner P 12/19/1998 Bp Sanford Zangwill Kaye Hampton. R S Geo's Ch Seattle WA 1999-2011; Asst S Geo's Ch Seattle WA 1997-1999.

KORIENEK, Martha Susan (Los) 530 W Fullerton Pkwy, Chicago IL 60614 **Ch Of Our Sav Chicago IL 2011-** B Elgin Illinois 3/9/1979 d John Paul Korienek & Jane Leslie. BA U IL 2001; Cert Ya Berk 2006; MDiv Yale DS 2006. D 6/3/2006 P 1/6/2007 Bp Joseph Jon Bruno. S Mich And All Ang Par Corona Del Mar CA 2006-2011. martha_korienek@yahoo.com

KORN, Elizabeth Louise (NMich) N2809 River Dr, Wallace MI 49893 B Marinette WI 12/31/1939 d Clifford John Harding & Barbara Elizabeth. D 6/4/2006 Bp James Arthur Kelsey. m 9/20/1997 Paul Herman Korn c 5.

KORTE, Mary Jane (Mass) 5 Oyster Lane, Warren RI 02885 **Int Ch Of The Trsfg Cranston RI 2010-; Consult Dio Rhode Island Providence RI 2008-** B Newport RI 6/8/1956 d James Edwin Bryant & Abbie. DMin CRDS; BS K SU 1984; MDiv EDS 1991; CTh EDS 1992. D 1/27/1996 Bp Morgan Porteus P 1/11/1997 Bp Geralyn Wolf. m 6/5/1976 Timothy Korte c 2. Int S Jn The Div Ch Saunderstown RI 2008-2009; Chr Formation S Lk's Epis Ch E Greenwich RI 2007; R Ch Of The Mssh Woods Hole MA 2002-2006; R (After Pstr) The Par Of Emm Ch Weston CT 2000-2002; Assoc Trin Ch On The Green New Haven CT 1997-2000. Wm Dietrich Memi Prize for Urban Mnstry 1990; Geo F Mercer Memi Schlrshp Awd 1989. mjkorte@cox.net

KOSHNICK, Loxley Jean (Minn) PO Box 868, Detroit Lakes MN 56502 **Total Mnstry D S Lk's Ch Detroit Lakes MN 2008-** B Fond Du Lac WI 10/2/1946 d Arthur H Kaemmer & Jean Taylor. BS Iowa St U 1968. D 9/13/2008 Bp James Louis Jelinek. m 7/5/1969 Robert Arthur Koshnick c 2. loxbobkoshnick@arvig.net

KOSKELA, David Michael (Colo) 5433 South Buckskin Pass, Colorado Springs CO 80917 **R S Raphael Epis Ch Colorado Sprg CO 2000-** B Worcester MA 6/9/1947 s Arne Wilhelm Koskela & Virginia May. None Worcester St Coll 1968; BA U of Texas 1974; Cert Epis TS of The SW 1977; MS Our Lady Of The Lake U San Antonio TX 1979. D 1/24/1987 Bp Brice Sidney Sanders P 12/27/1997 Bp William Jerry Winterrowd. m 6/9/1972 Jane R Robbins c 3. Asst to R Ch Of S Mich The Archangel Colorado Sprg CO 1998-2000; D H Trin Epis Ch Fayetteville NC 1987-1989. ACPE 2006. dmkoskela@earthlink.net

KOSKELA, Robert Norman (Mil) 1260 Deming Way Apt 310, Madison WI 53717 B Evanston IL 4/21/1942 s Elmer Veiko Koskela & Ina Joseph. BA Trin Deerfield IL 1964; MA U of Wisconsin 1967; PhD U of Wisconsin 1973; MS Edgewood Coll 2001. D 7/20/2002 Bp Roger John White P 3/25/2003 Bp Chilton Abbie Richardson Knudsen. m 8/8/1964 Ruth Alma Koskela. Gr Ch Madison WI 2003-2004; S Lk's Ch Madison WI 2003. rkoskela@chorus.net

KOSKELA, Ruth Alma (Mil) 1260 Deming Way Apt 310, Madison WI 53717 B Madison WI 8/1/1942 d Leif Herman Breiby & Doris Evelyn. BA Trin Deerfield IL 1964; MS U of Wisconsin 1975; PhD U of Wisconsin 1985; MS Edgewood Coll 2001. D 7/20/2002 Bp Roger John White P 3/25/2003 Bp Chilton Abbie Richardson Knudsen. m 8/8/1964 Robert Norman Koskela. S Lk's Ch Madison WI 2003.

KOSKI, Hope Gwendlyn Phillips (LI) 4526 Nw 34th Dr, Gainesville FL 32605 **S Jos's Ch Newberry FL 2009-; P-in-c S Alb's Epis Ch Chiefland FL 2007-** B New Haven CT 9/27/1939 d Robert Morgan Phillips & Hope Northam. BA U of Connecticut 1961; SMM UTS 1963; STM Nash 1980. D 5/31/1981 Bp H Coleman McGehee Jr P 3/12/1982 Bp Henry Irving Mayson. c 3. Eucumenical Cmsn Dio Long Island Garden City NY 2005-2006; Dio Long Island Garden City NY 1997-2006; Trst Dio Long Island Garden City NY 1993-1995; Cmsn on Liturg & Mus Dio Long Island Garden City NY 1991-1995; R S Lawr Of Cbury Ch Dix Hills NY 1989-2006; COM Dio Long Island Garden City NY 1989-1996; Asst S Lk's Ch Cleveland OH 1987-1989; Cn Trin Cathd Cleveland OH 1985-1987; Assoc S Matt's And S Jos's Detroit MI 1983-1985; Ch of the Gd Shpd Dearborn MI 1982-1983; St Paul's Epis Romeo MI 1981-1982. AGO 1958; Associated Parishes 1981; Liturg Conf 1981; Long Island Coun of Ch (Pres since 2000) 1989-2006. Dn, Atlantic Dnry Dio Long Island 1999. lhasi@hotmail.com

KOSSLER, Robert Joseph (Cal) 399 San Fernando Way, C/O St Francis Episcopal Church, San Francisco CA 94127 **Ch Of The Adv Of Chr The King San Francisco CA 2003-; S Fran' Epis Ch San Francisco CA 2003-** B Glendale CA 1/4/1958 s Robert Anthony Kossler & Carolann. BS Engr Harvey Mudd Coll 1980; MS Engr Stan 1983; M.Div. CDSP 2004. D 12/6/2003 P 6/5/2004 Bp William Edwin Swing. m 9/10/1983 Carol Kossler c 1. bkossler@sonic.net

KOSTAS, George Agapios (WVa) 133 Riverside Dr, Logan WV 25601 **P H Trin Ch Logan WV 2001-** B Dorothy WV 2/1/1930 s Agapios Kostas & Irene. BS U of Maryland 1952. D 6/9/2001 Bp C(laude) Charles Vache P 6/8/2002 Bp William Michie Klusmeyer. m 5/13/1959 Elizabeth Savas. Hon Degree of Doctor of Hmnts Sthrn W Virginia Comminity and Tech Coll 1998. georgeattrinity@verizon.net

KOSTIC, Elizabeth M (Pa) 2523 E Madison St, Philadelphia PA 19134 B Philadelphia PA 1/20/1949 d John J Roche & Sara W. D 10/23/1999 Bp Charles Ellsworth Bennison Jr. m 10/10/1981 John A Kostic c 2. D Gr Ch And The Incarn Philadelphia PA 2008-2010; D Trin Ch Oxford Philadelphia PA 2004-2008; D Gr Ch And The Incarn Philadelphia PA 2002-2004; D Chr Epis Ch Bensalem PA 1999-2002. tsleek@comcast.net

KOTRC, Ronald Fred (Ia) 5129 N. Tongass Hy, Ketchikan AK 99901 **R Emer S Jn's Ch Ketchikan AK 2010-** B Loup City NE 10/14/1938 s Carl Vincent Kotrc & Nora Louise. BA U of Nebraska 1960; MA U of Washington 1963; PhD U of Washington 1970; MDiv STUSo 1996. D 6/8/1996 Bp Robert Reed Shahan P 12/8/1996 Bp Don Adger Wimberly. m 12/17/2006 Christa Kotrc. S Jn's Ch Ketchikan AK 2004-2010; Trin Cathd Davenport IA 1999-2004; Assoc R S Andr's Ch Ft Thos KY 1996-1999. frkotrc@gmail.com

KOTUBY-AMOCHER, Janice (U) 7486 Union Park Ave, Midvale UT 84047 **COM Dio Utah Salt Lake City UT 2011-; Stndg Com Dio Utah Salt Lake City UT 2011-; Cur S Jas Epis Ch Midvale UT 2010-** B Rahway NJ 3/19/1960 d George Maynard Kotuby & Dorothy Carswell. BS Muhlenberg Coll 1982; MS The Penn 1984; PhD LSU 1989; MDiv CDSP 2010. D 6/12/2010 Bp Carolyn Tanner Irish P 12/18/2010 Bp Scott Byron Hayashi. jan.kotuby@gmail.com

KOULOURIS, Beulah Atkins Cratch (Mass) 12 Sunrise Ave, Plymouth MA 02360 B Plymouth NC 10/26/1937 d Cleveland Atkins Cratch & Beulah Mae. BA Lynchburg Coll 1960; Westminster Choir Coll of Rider U 1968; MA Col 1971; MDiv EDS 1989. D 6/3/1989 P 5/1/1990 Bp Don Edward Johnson. m 4/24/1965 Constantine Peter Koulouris. Chr Ch Epis Harwich Port MA 2006; Wyman Memi Ch of St Andr Marblehead MA 2005-2006; Ch Of Our Sav Somerset MA 2004-2005; Int S Jn's Ch Newtonville MA 2002-2003; Int Ch Of The Gd Shpd Wareham MA 2001-2002; P-in-c S Mk's Epis Ch Fall River MA 1999-2001; Int S Mk's Epis Ch Burlington MA 1997-1999; Gr Ch Salem MA 1996-1997; Int Gr Ch Newton MA 1995-1996; Int P Gr Ch Salem MA 1993-1996; S Ptr's Ch Osterville MA 1993-1995; Asst R S Gabr's Epis Ch Marion MA 1990-1993; Chr Ch Par Plymouth MA 1989-2009; Int S Andr's Ch Wellesley MA 1989-1990; Org/Chrmstr S Mk's Ch Foxborough MA 1988-1989. Sr hon Soc Lynvhburg Coll 1960; Who'S Who Among Amer. Un. Col. bkoulouris@comcast.net

KOUMRIAN, Paul Sprower (RI) PO Box 294, Tiverton RI 02878 B Jamaica NY 4/2/1938 s Moses Koumrian & Dorothy. BA Mid 1959; MDiv GTS 1967; DMin EDS 1984. D 6/17/1967 P 12/21/1967 Bp Jonathan Goodhue Sherman. c 1. R Ch Of The H Trin Tiverton RI 1991-2003; S Mary's Ch Newton Lower Falls MA 1991; S Andr's Ch Ayer MA 1976-1989; Asst S Geo's-By-The-River Rumson NJ 1972-1976; Int Chr Ch Roxbury CT 1969-1972; Cur S Lk's Ch Forest Hills NY 1967-1969. Contrib, *Homily Serv*, 1986. Soc of S Jn the Evang (Fllshp Mem) 1997. grpsk@cox.net

KOUNTZE, Louise (WMich) 13287 Bluff Rd, Traverse City MI 49686 **Gr Epis Ch Traverse City MI 2000-** B Denver CO 8/5/1950 d Harold Kountze & Pricilla. Wheaton Coll at Norton 1971; BA U Denv 1980; MDiv SWTS 1985. D 6/14/1986 Bp James Winchester Montgomery P 12/18/1986 Bp Howard Samuel Meeks. c 4. Gr Epis Ch Traverse City MI 1995-1999; Asst R Gr Epis Ch Traverse City MI 1985-1988. lpk@pentel.net

KOVACH, Gary David (WNC) 19 Old Youngs Cove Rd, Candler NC 28715 **D S Mary's Ch Asheville NC 2002-** B Pittsburgh PA 7/7/1943 s Gasper Kovach & Marion Virginia. D 11/23/2002 Bp Robert Hodges Johnson. m 12/28/1965 Geraldine Valarie Lowe c 2.

KOVIC, Fenton Hubert (Tex) 821 Pam Dr, Tyler TX 75703 B Pittsburgh PA 8/25/1937 s Raymond Kovic & Olive Elizabeth. BS U of No Texas 1960; STM Epis TS In Kentucky 1964. D 6/20/1964 P 12/1/1964 Bp J(ohn) Joseph Meakins Harte. m 12/16/1959 Judith Ann Capps c 2. S Fran Ch Winnsboro TX 1999-2001; S Matt's Ch Henderson TX 1998; Vic-in-charge S Lk's Epis Ch Lindale TX 1994-1999; R Chr Epis Ch Lead SD 1968-1971; Asst Gr S Paul's Epis Ch Tucson AZ 1965-1968. FEJUKO@SBCGLOBAL.NET

KOWALEWSKI, Mark Robert (Los) 841 Kodak Dr., Los Angeles CA 90026 **Dn And R St Johns Pro-Cathd Los Angeles CA 2006-** B Buffalo NY 11/12/1957 s Eugene Leonard Kowalewski & Evelyn Beatrice. SUNY; BA Franciscan U of Steubenville 1981; PhD USC 1990; CAS CDSP 1995. D 6/10/1995 Bp John Mc Gill Krumm P 1/13/1996 Bp Chester Lovelle Talton. Dio Los Angeles Los Angeles CA 1999-2005; S Wilfrid Of York Epis Ch Huntington Bch CA 1995-1999. Auth, "Gays," *Lesbians And Fam Values*, The Pilgrim Press, 1998; Auth, "All Things To All People: The Cath Ch Confronts The Aids Crisis". Assn Of The Sociol Of Rel; Rel Resrch Assn. Cn of the Cathd Cntr of St. Paul Dio Los Angeles 2005. chaplain@ladiocese.org

KOWALEWSKI, Paul James (Los) 112 S Plymouth Blvd, Los Angeles CA 90004 **R S Jas Par Los Angeles CA 2005-; Cn Visionary Dio Cntrl New York Syracuse NY 2002-** B Buffalo NY 11/19/1947 s Eugene Kowalewski & Evelyn. BA Chr The King Sem 1969; MDiv Chr The King Sem 1972; PhD SUNY 1982. Rec from Roman Catholic 6/1/1990 as Priest Bp James Michael Mark Dyer. m 11/4/1978 Karen Marie Sedlak. Dio Cntrl New York Syracuse NY 1999-2005; R S Dav's Ch De Witt NY 1993-2001; R S Mk's Epis Ch Chenango Bridge NY 1990-1993.

KOWALSKI, James August (NY) The Cathedral Church of Saint John the Divine, 1047 Amsterdam Ave, New York NY 10025 **Dn Cathd Of St Jn The Div New York NY 2002-** B Willimantic CT 9/11/1951 s Thaddeus George Kowalski & Sophie. BA Trin Hartford CT 1973; MDiv EDS 1978; DMin Hartford Sem 1991. D 6/10/1978 P 3/24/1979 Bp Morgan Porteus. m 9/4/1976 Anne Kowalski c 2. R S Lk's Par Darien CT 1993-2002; R Ch Of The Gd Shpd Hartford CT 1982-1993; Asst Trin Ch Newtown CT 1978-1982. Chapt Auth, "Committees of Discernment: A Strtgy for a Shared Vision of Philanthropy," *Mapping the New Wrld of Amer Philanthropy*, Wiley, 2007. Amer Ldrshp Forum - Fell 1990-1992; Aspen Inst - Crown Fell 1997-1999; OHC - Assoc 1982; Ord of the Hosp of S Jn of Jerusalem 2002. DD Berk 2003; Pi Gamma Mu Trin 1973; Phi Beta Kappa Trin 1973. kowalski@stjohndivine.org

KOWALSKI, Ronald Chester (SwFla) 2165 NE Coachman Rd, Clearwater FL 33765 **R Gd Samar Epis Ch Clearwater FL 2009-** B Chicago IL 11/12/1946 s Chester James Kowalski & Helen Dopieralski. MDiv Sacr Heart TS 1980. Rec from Roman Catholic 6/6/2009 Bp Dabney Tyler Smith. frk701@gmail.com

KOWALSKI, Vesta Marie (Me) Po Box 598, Mount Desert ME 04660 B Malad City ID 9/1/1939 d Charles Joseph Horejs & Lelia Marjorie. BA San Diego St U 1961; MDiv GTS 1981; STM GTS 1983; PhD Jewish TS 1996. D 6/9/1984 P 12/20/1984 Bp John Shelby Spong. c 1. Int Pstr S Andr And S Jn Epis Ch SW Harbor ME 2004-2006; Int S Fran By The Sea Blue Hill ME 1999-2001; Int S Sav's Par Bar Harbor ME 1998-1999; Int S Andr And S Jn Epis Ch SW Harbor ME 1996-1998; R Par Of S Jas Ch Keene NH 1992-1994; Asst The Ch Of S Lk In The Fields New York NY 1987-1992; Int S Jn's Ch New York NY 1986-1987. SBL 1981-2009. vkowalski@roadrunner.com

KOZAK, Jan (EO) PO Box 214, Madras OR 97741 **Vic S Mk's Epis and Gd Shpd Luth Madras OR 2004-** B Oakland CA 9/4/1947 d Homer Charles Thiele & Patricia Elizabeth. BA U CA 1969. D 5/1/2002 P 4/24/2003 Bp William O Gregg. m 9/8/1979 Albert Allen Kozak. kozaks@dishmail.net

KOZIELEC, Mark A (NH) PO Box 67, Sanbornton NH 03269 **P-in-c Trin Epis Ch Tilton NH 2007-** B NJ 6/25/1958 BA U of New Hampshire 2002; MDiv EDS 2005. D 6/11/2005 P 12/17/2005 Bp V Gene Robinson. m 4/10/2005 Charles J Doyle. Asst P S Andr's Ch Yardley PA 2005-2007. makcjd@metrocast.net

KOZLOWSKI, Matthew William (SeFla) 623 SE Ocean Blvd, Stuart FL 34994 **S Mary's Epis Ch Stuart FL 2011-** B Boston MA 3/5/1983 s John Vincent Kozlowski & Lynne Prescott. BA Trin 2005; MDiv VTS 2011. D 12/21/2010 Bp Leopold Frade. m 6/17/2006 Danielle M Markel c 1. Phi Beta Kappa 2005. St Georges Coll Jerusalem Awd VTS 2011. matthew.koz@gmail.com

KOZUSZEK, Jeffrey Frank (Spr) 512 W Main St, Salem IL 62881 **S Thos Ch Salem IL 2010-** B Pickneyville IL 8/23/1965 s Eugene Frank Kozuszek & Margaret Irene. D 11/30/2010 Bp Donald James Parsons P 6/10/2011 Bp Daniel H Martins. m 12/29/1994 Bonnie Mathis c 2. jbkozuszek@yahoo.com

KRADEL, Adam P (Pa) 311 S Orange St, Media PA 19063 **R Chr Ch Media PA 2009-** B New Martinsville WV 4/21/1973 s Paul Franklin Kradel & Susan Diane. Candler TS Emory U; VTS; BA Bethany Coll 1995; MA U of Wisconsin 2003; PhD U of Wisconsin 2008. D 9/24/1998 P 6/12/1999 Bp John H(enry) Smith. m 7/28/2001 Melissa Quincy Wilcox c 3. Chapl S Fran Hse U Epis Ctr Madison WI 2005-2006; Asst R S Dav's Ch Glenview IL 2002; Asst R S Jn's Epis Ch Charleston WV 1999-2001; D S Mk's Epis Ch Berkeley Sprg WV 1998-1999; Pstr Asst The Amer Cathd of the H Trin Paris 75008 FR 1997-1998. Amer Political Sci Assn. apkradel@gmail.com

KRAEMER, Carl Jeff (ECR) 760 Burchart Dr, ., Prosper TX 75078 B Lake Charles LA 7/7/1946 s Carl Warren Kraemer & Hazel Jana. BA McNeese St U 1969; MDiv Epis TS of The SW 1974. D 7/7/1974 P 7/22/1975 Bp Willis Ryan Henton. m 5/29/1969 Mary Von Oven. R S Dunst's Epis Ch Carmel Vlly CA 1999-2009; Headmaster S Geo's Epis Ch Laguna Hills CA 1993-1999; Assoc R Gr Epis Ch Monroe LA 1989-1993; R S Lk's Ch Mineral Wells TX 1987-1989; Cbury Hse U Pk TX 1982-1983; Chapl/Dir S Alb's Collgt Chap - SMU Dallas TX 1982-1983; Assoc S Lk's Epis Ch San Antonio TX 1976-1981; Cur Ch Of The H Trin Midland TX 1974-1976; Dio NW Texas Lubbock TX 1974-1976. CHS 1984; St. Jn of Jerusalem 2004. La St Bd Educ Louisiana. cjeffkraemer@gmail.com

KRAFT, Carol Joyce (Chi) 124 West Prairie Street, Wheaton IL 60187 **D S Barn' Epis Ch Glen Ellyn IL 1989-** B Jackson MI 12/8/1935 d Lester Christian Kraft & Grace Florence. Mid; BA Wheaton Coll 1957; MA Col 1958; MA U MI 1960; Goethe Inst Munich DE 1978. D 12/2/1989 Bp Frank Tracy Griswold III. "Birthed by the Sprt," Image Pub, 2005. Friend of SSJE 1992; NAAD. kcarolj@aol.com

KRAFT, Harry Bishop (LI) 17117 108th Ave, Jamaica NY 11433 B New York NY 4/3/1931 s Harry George Kraft & Margaret Lucy. BS SUNY 1953; MDiv CDSP 1970. D 12/28/1969 Bp Edwin B Thayer P 6/28/1970 Bp William Hampton Brady. R Ch Of S Jas The Less Jamaica NY 1986-1994; Asst S Barth's Ch Brooklyn NY 1985-1986; Ch Of The Resurr Warwick RI 1980-1984; Vic Calv Epis Ch Roundup MT 1976-1977; R H Trin Epis Ch Madera CA 1973-1975; R S Paul's Epis Ch Winslow AZ 1971-1973; Asst To Dn S Paul's Cathd Fond du Lac WI 1970-1971. Curs 1983; OHC.

KRAMER, Aron M (Minn) 3011 E Superior St, Duluth MN 55812 **Full Time Geth Ch Minneapolis MN 2005-** B Saint Paul MN 8/31/1974 s Michael Raymond Kramer & Mary Victoria. BA U of St. Thos 1997; MDiv CDSP 2000. D 5/25/2000 Bp James Louis Jelinek P 11/30/2000 Bp Daniel Lee Swenson. m 8/3/2000 Sara B McGinley c 2. Asst S Paul's Epis Ch Duluth MN 2000-2005. aronkramer@gmail.com

KRAMER, Charles Edward (NY) 4536 Albany Post Rd, Hyde Park NY 12538 **R S Jas Ch Hyde Pk NY 1997-** B Decatur IL 3/23/1961 s James Thomas Kramer & Susan Marie. Ripon Coll Ripon WI; BA Indiana U 1984; MA Indiana U 1987; MDiv GTS 1990. D 6/9/1990 P 12/15/1990 Bp Richard Frank Grein. m 2/8/1992 Elizabeth Granados c 3. R S Mary's Ch Morganton NC 1995-1997; Asst S Ptr's Epis Ch Peekskill NY 1990-1995. revckramer@gmail.com

KRAMER, (Else) Anne(liese) (Mich) 18301 W 13 Mile Rd Apt A-27, Southfield MI 48076 **Vic S Andr's Ch Clawson MI 1991-** B Duesseldorf DE 8/13/1921 d Otto Markus & Hildegard Leoni. BA/MA Wayne 1967; Michigan TS 1979. D 7/21/1979 Bp Henry Irving Mayson P 3/1/1991 Bp R(aymond) Stewart Wood Jr. m 9/30/1954 Walter Kramer. Auth, "To The New Year (Poem)"; Auth, "Prism Of The Soul," Morehouse Pub; Auth, "Surviving Discrimination And And Persecution (Poem)," *Wmn Uncommon Prayers*, Morehouse Pub. Oblate Ord Julian Of Norwich 1989. eakjn@aol.com

KRAMER, Frederick F(erdinand) (Ia) 1304 S 4th Ave W, Newton IA 50208 B El Paso TX 6/17/1926 s Paul Steven Kramer & Gay Batchelder. BA NWU 1950; MDiv Ya Berk 1953. D 6/13/1953 P 2/20/1954 Bp Stephen E Keeler. m 6/21/1956 Carol A Annette c 2. Exec Com Prov VI Dio Iowa Des Moines IA 1984-1987; Dioc Coun Dio Iowa Des Moines IA 1975-1979; R S Steph's Ch Newton IA 1966-1989; Bd Dir Cmnty Serv Dio Iowa Des Moines IA 1963-1966; Dn NoWstrn Deanry Dio Minnesota Minneapolis MN 1960-1966; Archd for Indn Wk Dio Minnesota Minneapolis MN 1956-1966; Bps Vic for Indn Wk Dio Minnesota Minneapolis MN 1955-1956; H Cross Epis Ch Mart SD 1953-1960; S Phil Naytahwaush MN 1953-1960. Hon Cn St Paul's Cathd Des Moines IA 2005. fckramer@iowatelecom.net

KRAMER, John Barry (WNC) Po Box 187, Green Mountain NC 28740 B Harrisburg PA 5/14/1942 s John Calvin Kramer & Loretta. BA Franklin & Marshall Coll 1964; MDiv PDS 1967. D 6/22/1967 Bp Dean T Stevenson P 12/1/1967 Bp Earl M Honaman. m 1/21/1984 Carolyn E Hackney c 2. Int S Lk's Epis Ch Lincolnton NC 2000-2001; R Ch Of The H Cross Valle Crucis NC 1986-1991; Mssnr To The Deaf Dio No Carolina Raleigh NC 1977-1986; Assoc The Epis Ch Of S Jn The Bapt York PA 1974-1977; R S Mary's Epis Ch Waynesboro PA 1971-1974; R Trin Epis Ch Tyrone PA 1968-1971; Vic S Andr's Ch Tioga PA 1967-1968; Vic S Jas Ch Mansfield PA 1967-1968. Auth, "Coming Down The Mtn," *Sermons That Wk Iv*, Forw Mvmt Publ., 1994; Auth, "New Life In The Par Of S Mary Waynesboro," *New Life mag*, 1971. OHC/ Assoc. 1967. "Chr Serv Awd" Nc Chr Assoc. Of The Deaf 1986. jbarrykramer@mac.com

KRAMER, Linda Jean (SD) 23120 S Rochford Rd, Hill City SD 57745 B Washington DC 10/16/1946 d Harry Thomson & Beverly Mikkelson. BA Colorado Wmn Coll 1968; MDiv VTS 1987. D 6/11/1988 P 12/20/1988 Bp John Thomas Walker. c 3. Asst Emm Epis Par Rapid City SD 2005-2006; Pstr Asst Emm Epis Par Rapid City SD 2002-2005; J2A Grant Position Ch Of Our Sav Silver Sprg MD 2002-2003; Int / Grant Gr Epis Ch Silver Sprg MD 1999-2001; Int Ch Of All Ang Spearfish SD 1999; Int Ch Of All Ang Spearfish SD 1998; Asst Gr Epis Ch Silver Sprg MD 1998; Cn Dio So Dakota Sioux Falls SD 1992-1997; Asst to the R for CE S Jn's Ch Chevy Chase MD 1988-1992. Green Faith Fell GreenFaith.org 2008; Pstr Ldr Study Grant Louisville Inst 2000. lindajkramer@earthlink.net

KRANTZ, Jeffrey Hoyt (LI) 43 Cedar Shore Dr, Massapequa NY 11758 **Ch Of The Adv Westbury NY 1996-** B Columbus OH 2/14/1955 s Albert Rossel Krantz & Barbara Sewel. BA E Carolina U 1978; MDiv GTS 1993. D 7/16/1993 Bp Brice Sidney Sanders P 2/1/1994 Bp Charles Lovett Keyser. m 4/28/1979 SaraLouise Camlin c 1. Geo Mercer TS Garden City NY 1999-2000; S Jn's Of Lattingtown Locust Vlly NY 1994-1996.

KRANTZ, Kristin (Cal) 2222 Cedar St., Berkeley CA 94709 **Assoc R All Souls Par In Berkeley Berkeley CA 2006-** B Louisville KY 12/31/1973 d Michael Nelson & Phyllis. BA Indiana U 1996; MDiv EDS 2006. D 6/3/2006 Bp William Dailey Persell P 12/2/2006 Bp Marc Handley Andrus. m 7/29/2000 Bryan Krantz c 2. kkrantz13@gmail.com

KRANTZ, SaraLouise Camlin (LI) 555Advent Street, Westbury NY 11590 B Hamlet NC 4/26/1944 d Mervin Clement Camlin & Sarah Louise. BSN U NC 1966; MDiv GTS 1990. D 6/16/1990 Bp Brice Sidney Sanders P 1/12/1991 Bp Richard Frank Grein. m 4/28/1979 Jeffrey Hoyt Krantz. Del-Prov Ii Dio Long Island Garden City NY 2003-2006; R Gr Epis Ch Massapequa NY 1999-2007; Bdgt Dio Long Island Garden City NY 1996-2000; R S Bede's Epis Ch Syosset NY 1994-1998; S Andr's Ch Oceanside NY 1993-1994; Asst Ch Of The H Trin New York NY 1990-1993. OHC. slckrantz@aol.com

KRAPF, Richard D (Roch) 15 Granger Street, Canandaigua NY 14424 **Chair, Com on the Diac Dio Rochester Rochester NY 2010-; COM Dio Rochester Rochester NY 2006-; Exec Dir, Gleaners Cmnty Kitchen S Jn's Ch Canandaigua NY 2002-** B Dunmore PA 3/13/1963 s Richard C Krapf & Sarah M. BArch Tem 1990; D Formation Bex 2007. D 3/29/2008 Bp Jack Marston McKelvey. m 8/20/1988 Lisa Browning c 2. rkrapf@rochester.rr.com

KRASINSKI, Joseph Alexander (Ct) 2 Cannondale Dr, Danbury CT 06810 **S Jas Epis Ch Danbury CT 2009-** B Brooklyn NY 1/7/1954 s Thomas James Krasinski & Katherine. BS St. Fran Coll Brooklyn NY 1977; MDiv GTS 1983; DMin Hartford Sem 1989; MS RPI 1993. D 6/5/1982 Bp Paul Moore Jr P 1/1/1983 Bp Arthur Edward Walmsley. m 6/27/2009 James Hughes c 1. S Ptr's-Trin Ch Thomaston CT 1995-2009; Chr Ch Canaan CT 1984-1992; Cur Chr And H Trin Ch Westport CT 1982-1984. joseph@stjamesdanbury.org

KRATOVIL, Mildred Elsie Ida Johanna (Md) 204 West St Apt A4, Williamsburg IA 52361 B Cleveland OH 4/24/1925 d Carl William Dort & Elsie Ida. BA Cleveland Inst of Mus 1951. D 6/17/1989 Bp A(lbert) Theodore Eastman. c 2. D Trin Ch Waterloo Elkridge MD 1991-1995; D Epiph Epis Ch Odenton MD 1989-1990. Cnvnt Of Trsfg Cincinnati; NAAD.

KRAUS, Susan (Ct) 140 W Washington Rd, Washington ME 04574 B Trenton NJ 11/27/1950 d William Stam & Frances Marie. BA Cedar Crest Coll 1972; BA Coll of New Rochelle 1985; MS Coll of New Rochelle 1987; Doctorate Pace U 1993; MDiv GTS 2005. D 3/19/2005 P 9/17/2005 Bp Mark Sean Sisk. m 8/2/1972 Donald C Kraus. Assoc S Giles Ch Jefferson ME 2009-2011; Asst Cler Par of St Paul's Ch Norwalk Norwalk CT 2006-2008; Asst Cler Gr Ch Millbrook NY 2005-2006. skraus@fairpoint.net

KRAUSE, David (Dal) 2022 Saturn Rd, Garland TX 75041 **P-in-c S Dav's Ch Garland TX 2010-; P-in-c Ch Of The H Trin Bonham TX 2009-** B Maryville MO 3/26/1958 s Robert R Krause & Lois. BA U of Iowa 1981; MDiv VTS 1990; MA Texas Tech U 1998. D 6/23/1990 Bp Robert Manning Moody P 12/23/1990 Bp John Forsythe Ashby. c 1. R S Ptr's Ch McKinney TX 2006-2009; Chapl Cbury Epis Campus Mnstry at Texas Tech Lubbock TX 1993-2006; R S Lk's Epis Ch Scott City KS 1990-1993. davidkrause@me.com

KRAUSE, Fredrick Joseph (NJ) 17 Signal Hill Rd, Pine Hill NJ 08021 **Died 2/17/2011** B Brooklyn NY 12/16/1941 s John Raymond Krause & Anne Olivia. Rec from Roman Catholic 6/27/2000 Bp David B(ruce) Joslin. frfredkrause@yahoo.com

KRAUSS, Harry Edward (RI) 126 Taber Ave, Providence RI 02906 **Dn Cathd Of S Jn Providence RI 2005-** B Philadephia PA 8/3/1945 s Harry Edward Krauss & Josephine Verna. BA W&M 1967; MDiv VTS 1977. D 5/21/1977 Bp Robert Bruce Hall P 3/4/1978 Bp Lyman Cunningham Ogilby. m 9/28/2011 John Metcalfe. Vic S Thos Ch New York NY 1997-2005; Chapl of AltGld Dio Pennsylvania Philadelphia PA 1986-1994; R All SS Ch Wynnewood PA 1980-1997; Cur All SS Ch Wynnewood PA 1977-1979. Ord of S Jn of Jerusalem - Chapl 1994; SocMary - Natl Bd 1983; The Burgon Soc - Fell; Uff Savoy Ord of Merit 1999. Hon Cn S Andr Cathd Wstrn Tanganyika 1988. hkrauss@cathedralofstjohn.org

KRAUTTER, Donald Henry (NJ) 14 Rose Ln, Whiting NJ 08759 **D S Steph's Ch Whiting NJ 2005-** B Newark NJ 1/31/1932 s Henry Krautter & Mabel Louise. BBA Ups 1957. D 6/11/2005 Bp George Edward Councell. c 3. dondeacon@aol.com

KREAMER, Martha Hutchison (CGC) Po Box 57, Lillian AL 36549 **Vic Ch Of The Adv Lillian AL 2004-** B Quantico VA 11/4/1944 d Byron Monroe Hutchison & Mary White. BA Van 1966; MDiv STUSo 2001. D 6/2/2001 P 2/24/2002 Bp Philip Menzie Duncan II. m 9/17/1966 Paul Stoddard Kreamer c 1. Stndg Com Dio Cntrl Gulf Coast Pensacola FL 2008-2010; Eccl Crt Dio Cntrl Gulf Coast Pensacola FL 2008-2009; Vic S Mich's Ch Ozark AL 2001-2004. Intl OSL The Physcn 1992. Optime Merens TS, Univ. Of The So Sewanee TN 2001. martha.kreamer@gmail.com

KREFT, Armand John (Mass) 205 Old Main Street, Yarmouth MA 02664 **R S Dav's Epis Ch So Yarmouth MA 2010-** B San Mateo CA 5/9/1948 s Edwin Bartholomew Kreft & Wynifred Cora. BA New Coll of California 1986; CS CDSP 1987. D 6/3/1989 P 6/9/1990 Bp William Edwin Swing. R Ch Of The Ascen Buffalo NY 2007-2010; P-in-c Ch Of The Epiph Seattle WA 2005-2007; Assoc S Paul In The Desert Palm Sprg CA 2002-2004; Asst S Jas Epis Ch San Francisco CA 2001-2002; Dn Trin Cathd San Jose CA 2000-2001; Vic Ch Of The H Innoc San Francisco CA 1993-1999. nqocd@earthlink.net

KREITLER, Peter Gwillim (Los) 16492 El Hito Ct, Pacific Palisades CA 90272 B Middletown CT 7/21/1942 s John Henry Kreitler & Muriel Taylor. BA Br 1966; MDiv VTS 1969. D 6/14/1969 Bp Leland Stark P 4/27/1970 Bp Robert Rae Spears Jr. m 4/20/1985 Catharine Bates Hunt c 3. The Par Of S Matt Pacific Palisades CA 1974-1991; Assoc S Andr's Ch Kansas City MO 1969-1974. "Untd We Stand," Chronicle Books, 2001; Auth, "The Earth's Killer C's," Morning Sun Press, 1995; "Flatiron," AIA Press, 1991; Auth, "Affair Prevention," Macmillan, 1981. pkreitler@aol.com

KREJCI, Richard Scott (Va) 346 Laurel Farms Ln, Urbanna VA 23175 B Cleveland OH 11/8/1941 s Richard Westphal Krejci & Doris Scott. BA Adrian Coll 1964; BD Bex 1967. D 6/29/1967 Bp Archie H Crowley P 4/1/1968 Bp Richard S M Emrich. m 6/8/1966 Faye Diane Borgia c 2. Chr Epis Ch Saluda VA 1995-2004; S Steph's Ch Newport News VA 1994-1995; Int R S Steph's Ch Newport News VA 1993-1994; R S Jas Ch Grosse Ile MI 1982-1993; Assoc S Andr's Epis Ch Livonia MI 1977-1982; P-in-c The Ch Of The Gd Shpd Canajoharie NY 1970-1977; Vic S Pat's Epis Ch Madison Heights MI 1967-1970. Bro Of S Andr. rskrejci@gmail.com

KRELLER, Daniel Ward (Nwk) 56 Sheridan Ave, Ho Ho Kus NJ 07423 **R S Barth's Epis Ch Ho Ho Kus NJ 1984-** B Dallas TX 1/2/1951 s Bert Clark Kreller & Martha Elizabeth. BA Houghton Coll 1972; PrTS 1975; MDiv GTS 1977. D 6/4/1977 Bp Albert Wiencke Van Duzer P 1/28/1978 Bp George Phelps Mellick Belshaw. m 6/30/1973 Janet Thiemsen c 2. R St Jn the Bapt Epis Ch Linden NJ 1979-1984; S Andr's Epis Ch New Providence NJ 1977-1979. kreller@aol.com

KRESS, John Walter (Ia) 446 Elberta Loop, Lillian AL 36549 B Davenport IA 5/1/1936 s John Smith Kress & Genevieve Vivian. Westminster Coll 1956; BA Augustana Coll 1958; MDiv Epis TS of The SW 1961; Loma Linda U 1970; U of Maine 1975. D 6/16/1961 P 12/1/1961 Bp Gordon V Smith. m 8/29/1958 Elizabeth Ann Frank c 4. CE Consult S Jn's Epis Ch Dubuque IA 1978-1980; R S Dunst's Ch Ellsworth ME 1970-1974; Vic Ch Of The Gd Shpd Webster City IA 1961-1963; Vic S Matt's-By-The-Bridge Epis Ch Iowa Falls IA 1961-1963. Pub, "Pub Goals," *The Charlatan*, Charlatan Publictions, 1965. Conservation Awd Goodyear 1976; Commendation Medal Navy 1970. jnbkress@gmail.com

KRESS, Raymond Paul (SwFla) 6530 Manila Palm Way, Apollo Beach FL 33572 B Newark NJ 5/8/1935 s John William Kress & Rose Louise. BA Laf 1959; MDiv GTS 1962; Med Florida Atlantic U 1968. D 6/9/1962 Bp Leland Stark P 12/1/1962 Bp Benjamin M Washburn. m 7/27/1973 Barbara Doyle c 2. Int S Giles Ch Pinellas Pk FL 2009; Int S Geo's Epis Ch Bradenton FL 2005-2006; Chapl Dio SW Florida Sarasota FL 1998-2002; P-in-c S Edm's Epis Ch Arcadia FL 1998-2002; R S Raphael's Ch Ft Myers Bch FL 1984-1998; Asst All SS Ch Tarpon Sprg FL 1982-1984; The Headmaster S Petersburg FL 1970-1977. RAYBARKRESS@AOL.COM

KREUTZER, Michael Alan (SO) 7 Lonsdale Avenue, Dayton OH 45419 **Dn of Dayton Dnry Dio Sthrn Ohio Cincinnati OH 2002-; Instr, Angl Acad Dio Sthrn Ohio Cincinnati OH 1997-; R S Mk's Epis Ch Dayton OH 1996-** B Cincinnati OH 9/16/1949 s Stanley Henry Kreutzer & Helen Marie. SBL; MA The Athenaeum of Ohio 1975; MA The Athenaeum of Ohio 1976; U of San Francisco 1979; Sinclair Cmnty Coll 1983; SWTS 2001; U of Dayton 2004. Rec from Roman Catholic 6/9/1991 as Priest Bp Herbert Thompson Jr. m 1/14/1983 Judith Ann Caspar c 4. COM Dio Sthrn Ohio Cincinnati OH 1997-2000; Supply P Dio Sthrn Ohio Cincinnati OH 1991-1996. SBL 2005. makreutzer@ameritech.net

KREYMER, Donald Neal (FtW) 423 East Calle Bonita, Santa Maria CA 93455 B Sigourney IA 12/29/1922 s Allen Neal Kreymer & Nina Vivia. BA U of Iowa 1947; U of Iowa 1948; MDiv SWTS 1950; Ya 1956; USN Reserves Chapl Advancement Sch 1978. D 7/21/1950 Bp Gordon V Smith P 3/1/1951 Bp Wallace E Conkling. c 3. Int S Ptr's By-The-Sea Epis Ch Morro Bay CA 1994-1995; Ch Of The H Sprt Graham TX 1982-1988; Vic Ch Of The Gd Samar Dallas TX 1981-1982; Dio Los Angeles Los Angeles CA 1980; S Mk's Par Glendale CA 1980; Vic S Fran Of Assisi Epis Ch Simi Vlly CA 1970-1980; LocTen S Paul's Epis Ch Bremerton WA 1969-1970; R Chr Ch Epis Beatrice NE 1959-1963; R S Andr's Epis Ch Emporia KS 1953-1959; Cur S Matt's Ch Evanston IL 1950-1953. Auth, "The Ch Teaches Us". CBS; Pahh Assn SocOLW.

KRICKBAUM, Donald William (SeFla) 1008 Skyline Trail, Harpers Ferry WV 25425 B Tampa FL 9/21/1938 s Ralph Armstrong Krickbaum & Mary Mcbroom. BA U So 1960; STB GTS 1963. D 6/29/1963 Bp William Foreman Creighton P 2/16/1964 Bp David Emrys Richards. m 8/27/1966 Gail Wallace. Dn Trin Cathd Miami FL 1988-2003; Instr Dio SE Florida Miami FL 1987-1990; Chair- Com Dio SE Florida Miami FL 1986-1988; Exec Bd Dio SE Florida Miami FL 1981-1986; Com Dio SE Florida Miami FL 1977-1981; R The Epis Ch Of The Gd Shpd Tequesta FL 1976-1988; R S Paul's Ch Key W FL 1970-1976. dkrickbaum@aol.com

KRIEGER, Frederick Gordon (SO) 5538 Sebastian Place, Halifax B3K 2K6 Canada B Saint Louis MO 1/1/1938 s John Ernest Krieger & Virginia. BA Hob 1960; BD EDS 1963; U Tor 1970. D 6/15/1963 Bp George Leslie Cadigan P 12/1/1963 Bp Roger W Blanchard. m 7/8/1960 Janet Cleghorn Kelley c 3. Cur

Gr Ch Cincinnati OH 1963-1966. DD Atlantic TS 2002; Hon Cn All SS Cathd 1991; Phi Beta Kappa Hob 1960. f-jkrieger@ns.sympatico.ca

KRIEGER, Kristin Sherry (NJ) 318 Elton Ln., Galloway NJ 08205 B Bryn Mawr PA 7/9/1971 D 9/21/2002 Bp David B(ruce) Joslin. c 2.

KRIEGER, Walter Lowell (Be) Fifth & Court, Reading PA 19603 **Assoc S Alb's Epis Ch Reading PA 2010-; Cler Wellness Dio Bethlehem Bethlehem PA 1994-; BEC Dio Bethlehem Bethlehem PA 1985-; Stndg Com Dio Bethlehem Bethlehem PA 1985-** B Shamokin PA 12/20/1939 s Walter Charles Krieger & Ethel B. BA Wheaton Coll 1961; MA Jn Hopkins U 1962; MDiv PDS 1965; U of Pennsylvania 1970. D 5/1/1965 P 11/6/1965 Bp Alfred L Banyard. m 6/17/1961 Judith Lois Friel c 2. Assoc The Epis Ch Of The Medtr Allentown PA 2006-2010; Pres Of The Stndg Com Dio Bethlehem Bethlehem PA 1987-1990; Dep Gc Dio Bethlehem Bethlehem PA 1982-1997; R Chr Ch Reading PA 1979-2003; R S Jas Epis Ch Wooster OH 1973-1979; Min Of Educ Trin Ch Moorestown NJ 1970-1973; Cur Gr Ch Merchantville NJ 1965-1967. Auth, "Var Bk Revs & arts"; Auth, "Acad Of Preachers". walter.krieger@ecunet.org

KRIEGER, William F (SanD) 1550 S 14th Ave, Yuma AZ 85364 B Brooklyn NY 7/8/1950 s Robert William Krieger & Winifred. BS Pur 1972; MS Pur 1974; PhD Pur 1977; MDiv CDSP 2004. D 6/5/2004 Bp William Edwin Swing P 12/11/2004 Bp Kirk Stevan Smith. m 2/16/1971 Paulette Sikes c 3. R S Paul's Ch Yuma AZ 2008; Assoc for Pstr Care All SS Of The Desert Epis Ch Sun City AZ 2007-2008; All SS Of The Desert Epis Ch Sun City AZ 2004-2008; Asst for Pstr Care All SS Of The Desert Epis Ch Sun City AZ 2004-2007. BroSA 2004-2009. Fran Toy Multicultural Awd CDSP 2004. wmfkrieger@yahoo.com

KRISS, Gary W. (Alb) PO Box 26, Cambridge NY 12816 **Vic S Paul's Ch Salem NY 2003-** B Baltimore MD 12/29/1946 s Warren B Kriss & Margaret L. AB Dart 1964; MDiv Yale DS 1972. D 5/28/1972 P 12/29/1972 Bp Harvey D Butterfield. Int Dn S Jn's Cathd Albuquerque NM 2006-2007; Int R S Paul's Ch Troy NY 2001-2002; Dn and Pres Nash Nashotah WI 1992-2001; Dn Cathd Of All SS Albany NY 1984-1991; Cn Precentor Cathd Of All SS Albany NY 1978-1984; Vic S Mk's-S Lk's Epis Mssn Castleton VT 1974-1978; Chapl Cathd Ch Of S Paul Burlington VT 1972-1974. *Var arts*. Cmnty of the Cross of Nails; SocMary. DD Nash 2001. gkriss@nycap.rr.com

KROGMAN, Robert Allen (Chi) 1167 Arbor Ln, Sycamore IL 60178 B Chicago IL 8/10/1930 s Herbert William Krogman & Elsa Marie. BA Trin Hartford CT 1952; MDiv SWTS 1955. D 6/18/1955 Bp Charles L Street P 12/21/1955 Bp Gerald Francis Burrill. m 6/25/1955 Lisbeth Paul c 5. Int S Ptr's Epis Ch Sycamore IL 1992-1995; Dio Chicago Chicago IL 1990-1995; Dep, GC Dio Chicago Chicago IL 1988-1994; COM Dio Chicago Chicago IL 1987-1990; Stndg Com Dio Chicago Chicago IL 1984-1987; Alt Dep, GC Dio Chicago Chicago IL 1982-1997; COM Dio Chicago Chicago IL 1975-1982; Stndg Com Dio Chicago Chicago IL 1975-1978; Dn, Evanston Deanry Dio Chicago Chicago IL 1971-1977; Dn, Evanston Deanry Dio Chicago Chicago IL 1971-1977; Dio Chicago Chicago IL 1969-1972; Dio Chicago Chicago IL 1969-1972; Pres Alum SWTS Evanston IL 1964-1966; The Epis Ch Of S Jas The Less Northfield IL 1957-1992; Cur S Aug's Epis Ch Wilmette IL 1955-1957. Assoc of the OHC 1962. Hon Cn Cathd of St. Jas, Chicago 2003.

KROH, Timothy Edward (Md) 1802 Barclay St, Baltimore MD 21202 **Dio Maryland Baltimore MD 2010-; P-in-c Mision San Pablo Chester PA 2007-** B DuBois PA 1/11/1979 s Edward Clyde Kroh & Patricia Ann. BA Penn 2002; MDiv VTS 2005. D 7/2/2005 Bp John Leslie Rabb P 1/6/2006 Bp Robert Wilkes Ihloff. S Thos' Ch Garrison Forest Owings Mills MD 2011; P-in-c S Paul's Ch Chester PA 2007-2010; Assoc R Emm Ch Baltimore MD 2005-2007. Assoc, Epis Carmel of St. Teresa 2006; P Assoc, Shrine of Our Lady of Walsingham 2006. fatherkroh@yahoo.com

KROLL, Brenda M. (Dal) 1402 Pagosa Trl, Carrollton TX 75007 **D Ch Of The Epiph Richardson TX 2009-; D Ch Of The Annunc Lewisville TX 1998-** B Louisville KY 8/7/1953 d Milton Norris Machost & Gertrude. Epis Sch for Mnstry. D 10/26/1986 Bp Sam Byron Hulsey. m 1/1/1981 Brial F Carpenter c 1. D S Lk's Epis Ch No Little Rock AR 1995-1997; D S Nich' Epis Ch Midland TX 1986-1995. Cleric Of Year Awd Kiwanis.

KROM, Judith Sue (NJ) 410 S Atlantic Ave, Beach Haven NJ 08008 B 1/13/1942 d Benson Arthur Krom & June Valentine. BA Gordon Coll 1963; MA Syr 1965; PhD SUNY-Buffalo 1979. D 5/16/2009 Bp Sylvestre Donato Romero. m 5/14/1976 Bernard Braen c 4. jsk13@comcast.net

KROMHOUT, Linda Adams (CFla) 2104 Golden Arm Rd, Deltona FL 32738 **D All SS Epis Ch Enterprise FL 1992-** B South Bend IN 9/28/1938 d Robert Chandler Adams & Linda. Pur. D 11/7/1992 Bp John Wadsworth Howe. m 6/7/1958 Ysbrand Kromhout c 2. Pi Beta Phi.

KRONZ, Gregory Joseph (SC) 1 Oyster Landing Rd, Hilton Head Island SC 29928 **Dio So Carolina Charleston SC 2005-; R S Lk's Epis Ch Hilton Hd SC 1992-** B Pittsburgh PA 5/8/1957 s Frederick Kronz & Delores Helen. BA U Pgh 1979; MDiv TESM 1985. D 6/8/1985 P 1/17/1986 Bp Alden Moinet Hathaway. m 8/25/1979 Meredith Jean Fraley c 3. Evang Com Dio So Carolina Charleston SC 1994-1998; Assoc R Chr Epis Ch San Antonio TX 1987-1992; Assoc R S Steph's Epis Ch Wilkinsburg PA 1985-1987. "By What Authority," *SCP Nwsltr*, Sprtl Counterfeits Proj, 2003. Outstanding Bus and Profsnl; Outstanding Young Men. greg_kronz@juno.com

KROOHS, Kenneth (NC) 700 Sunset Drive, High Point NC 27262 **R S Chris's Epis Ch High Point NC 1995-** B New York City 7/19/1949 s William Francis Kroohs & Celilia. BS NEU 1972; MRP Cor 1974; MDiv Duke DS 1995; MDiv Duke 1995; Cert VTS 1995. D 6/10/1995 P 6/29/1996 Bp Robert Carroll Johnson Jr. m 9/18/1971 Mary Lawrence c 3. S Paul's Epis Ch Thomasville NC 1995-2002. Auth, "The Barely Ch," *NetResults*, Net Results Inc, 2011. ken@st-christopher.org

KROOHS, Mary (NC) 1700 Queen St, Winston Salem NC 27103 **D S Tim's Epis Ch Winston Salem NC 2009-** B El Paso TX 11/9/1950 d Thomas Adrian Eckert & Jeanne Lucille. BS NEU 1972; No Carolina Diac Prog 1991. D 5/25/1991 Bp Huntington Williams Jr. m 9/18/1971 Kenneth Kroohs c 3. D S Tim's Epis Ch Winston Salem NC 1991-2005. maryjk004@aol.com

✠ **KROTZ, Rt Rev James Edward** (Neb) 3484 520th Road, Rushville NE 69360 B Rushville NE 9/1/1948 s Anton James Krotz & Naomi Bernadine. BA Chadron St Coll 1970; MDiv SWTS 1973. D 6/13/1973 P 12/7/1973 Bp Robert Patrick Varley Con 9/30/1989 for Neb. m 6/13/1970 Phyllis Christine Jungck c 2. Bp Dio Nebraska Omaha NE 1990-2003; Bp Coadj of Neb Dio Nebraska Omaha NE 1989-1990; R S Matt's Ch Lincoln NE 1986-1989; R Ch Of Our Sav No Platte NE 1977-1986; H Trin Ch York NE 1973-1977; Asst S Matt's Ch Lincoln NE 1973-1977; Vic S Andr's Ch Lincoln NE 1973-1976. jekrotz@rushville.net

KRUEGER, Albert Peter (Ore) 1926 W Burnside St Unit 909, Portland OR 97209 **First Nations Mssnr Dio Oregon Portland OR 2011-; S Andr's Ch Portland OR 1999-** B McAllen TX 5/2/1948 s Harold Frederick Krueger & Esther Lera. BA U of Arizona 1976; MDiv CDSP 1980. D 7/22/1980 Bp C Kilmer Myers P 12/1/1981 Bp Leigh Wallace Jr. m 9/4/1976 Katherine Ann Glendening. All SS Ch Hillsboro OR 1988-1995; Assoc S Paul's Epis Ch Salem OR 1984-1988; Assoc S Paul's Ch Walla Walla WA 1980-1984. HEVIRAIN@YAHOO.COM

KRUG, Philip Sinclair (Nwk) 20 Maple Ave, Montvale NJ 07645 B Elwood IN 12/22/1927 s Floyd Philip Krug & Inda. BA U of Chattanooga 1949; MDiv Yale DS 1952; GTS 1953; EDS 1975; Cntr for Creative Living 1995. D 6/6/1953 P 12/13/1953 Bp Norman B Nash. m 6/16/1951 Lee A Albert. Ed Bd 'The Voice' Dio Newark Newark NJ 1985-1993; Chair Adult Educ Com Dio Newark Newark NJ 1980-1981; R S Paul's Ch Montvale NJ 1976-1994; Asst Min Chr Ch Cambridge Cambridge MA 1953-1957. "Contrib," *Race and Pryr*, Morehouse Pub, 2003; Auth, "arts," *The Chr Mnstry*, 1985-1999, 1985. grushnka@optonline.net

KRUGER, Ann Dufford (CFla) 167 Clear Lake Cir, Sanford FL 32773 **Asst H Cross Epis Ch Sanford FL 2009-** B Sewickley PA 5/8/1936 d Clair Otto Dufford & Margaret Elizabeth. U Of Paris Fr 1957; BA Thiel Coll 1958; MDiv TESM 1967. D 12/7/1997 P 6/1/1998 Bp Stephen Hays Jecko. m 6/14/1960 Kurt W Kruger c 1. R S Mk's Ch Fincastle VA 1999-2006; S Andr's Ch Interlachen FL 1998. OSL 1990. revadk@msn.com

KRUGER, Matthew Carl (Mass) 81 Elm St, Concord MA 01742 **Cur Trin Ch Concord MA 2009-** B Concord MA 6/14/1984 s Paul Kruger & Karen. BA Tufts U 2006; MDiv Harvard DS 2009; PhD Boston Coll 2014. D 6/6/2009 Bp M(arvil) Thomas Shaw III. matt.kruger@gmail.com

KRUGER, Susan Marie (Minn) No address on file. B Cedar Rapids IA 12/25/1954 d Amos B Kruger & Lola M. BA Cor 1977; MDiv Ya Berk 1981. D 11/3/1985 P 7/10/1986 Bp Robert Marshall Anderson. D S Mary's Ch St Paul MN 1985-1986.

KRULAK JR, Victor Harold (SanD) 3118 Canon St Apt 4, San Diego CA 92106 **Asst All SS Ch San Diego CA 2005-** B Manila PH 10/13/1937 s Victor Harold Krulak & Amy. AB W&M 1960; MDiv CDSP 1963. D 5/17/1963 P 11/28/1963 Bp Harry S Kennedy. Asst All SS Ch San Diego CA 1990-1994; Off Of Bsh For ArmdF New York NY 1966-1990; Assoc S Ptr's Ch Honolulu HI 1965-1966.

KRULAK, William Morris (Md) 113 W Hughes St, Baltimore MD 21230 B Quantico VA 10/6/1940 s Victor H Krulak & Amy. BS USNA 1962; MS U Roch 1972; MDiv Ya Berk 1991. D 6/15/1991 Bp Peter James Lee P 12/16/1991 Bp Robert Poland Atkinson. m 7/23/2009 Sharon D Krulak c 2. Dioc Coun Dio Maryland Baltimore MD 2000-2002; R S Dav's Ch Baltimore MD 1999-2007; Exec Bd Dio Virginia Richmond VA 1994-1998; R S Jn's Epis Ch Tappahannock VA 1993-1998; Vic Gr Ch Stanardsville VA 1991-1993. bkrulak@comcast.net

KRUMBACH JR, Arthur William (Ark) 2409 Parkview Cir, Conway AR 72034 B Detroit MI 3/15/1930 s Arthur William Krumbach & Harriet Joella. BS Michigan Tech U 1952; MS MI SU 1957; PhD MI SU 1960; MDiv STUSo 1966. D 6/29/1966 P 2/1/1967 Bp Robert Raymond Brown. m 5/5/1956 Suzanne Prabel c 4. Chr Ch Mena AR 1983-1985; St Matthews Ch Clarksville AR 1983-1985; Vic S Ptr's Ch Conway AR 1971-1976; Vic All SS Epis Ch Paragould AR 1966-1971; Vic Calv Epis Ch Osceola AR 1966-1968. Auth, "Ashes," *S Lk Journ*, 1965.

KRUMBHAAR, Andrew Ramsay (CFla) 144 Carretera Chapala-Ajijic Pmb 108, San Antonio Tlaycapan Mexico B New York NY 7/13/1934 s George Douglas Krumbhaar & Catherine. BA Harv 1956; BD Epis TS of The SW 1961. D 4/6/1961 Bp Richard Earl Dicus P 10/9/1961 Bp Everett H Jones. c 4. Asst S Barn Ch Deland FL 1985-1997; Dio Cntrl Florida Orlando FL 1985; R Chr Ch Longwood FL 1976-1984; Asst Ch Of The Gd Shpd Maitland FL 1973-1976; Cur Emm Epis Ch San Angelo TX 1966-1973; R Gr Ch Mesquite TX 1962-1966; R H Comm Epis Ch Yoakum TX 1962-1966; Vic S Matt's Epis Ch Kenedy TX 1961-1962. Phi Alpha Theta Stetson Uninversity DeLand Florida 1992. andrewkbr@yahoo.com

KRUMENACKER JR, Gerald Walter (Dal) 5720 Forest Park Rd, No. 2-406, Dallas TX 75235 B Trenton NJ 4/3/1970 s Gerald Walter Krumenacker & Penelope Lynn. BA So Dakota St U 1992; MDiv SWTS 1996; MBA U of Dallas 2008. D 6/7/1996 P 12/14/1996 Bp James Louis Jelinek. m 1/23/2007 Rosa Victoria Avalos-Cellis c 2. R Chr Epis Ch Dallas TX 2009-2010; Cn Mssnr for Hisp Mnstry S Matt's Cathd Dallas TX 2001-2002; Asst R Ch Of The Ascen Stillwater MN 1999-2001; P-in-c Trin Ch Waseca-Janesville Waseca MN AG 1996-1999; P-in-c Chr Ch Albert Lea MN 1996-1998. gerald.krumenacker@gmail.com

KRUMLAUF, Dennis Skyler (CFla) 4111 Lillian Hall Ln, Orlando FL 32812 **Transitional D Cathd Ch Of S Lk Orlando FL 2011-** B Port Huron MI 2/27/1949 s Edward S Krumlauf & Arlene E. BA Olivet Nazarene U 1973; MDiv Nazarene TS 1979. D 6/11/2011 Bp Hugo Luis Pina-Lopez. m 5/22/1971 Jane Mosshart Krumlauf c 3. travelinchaplain@hotmail.com

KRUMME, Judith Sterner (Mass) 349 Simon Willard Rd, Concord MA 01742 **Ret, P Assoc. and Sprtl Dir Trin Ch Concord MA 2005-** B Pittsburgh PA 11/7/1938 d William C Sterner & Dorothy. BS Mills New York NY 1967; MA Ya Berk 1988. D 6/10/1989 Bp Paul Moore Jr P 3/1/1990 Bp Richard Frank Grein. m 12/27/1963 Robert Darrel Krumme c 2. R Emm Ch Braintree MA 2000-2004; Assoc Trin Ch Concord MA 1993-2000; Pstr Asst Trin Ch Concord MA 1990-1992; Assoc S Jn's Ch Larchmont NY 1989-1990. ACPE; Braintree Interfaith Cler Assn; CHS; Ma Chapl Assn; Match-Up Vol Bd.; Meca; Natl Hospice Assn; Sherrill Hse Bd Mem; Sprtl Dir Intl . judykrumme@earthlink.net

KRUSE, William G (Chi) 1413 Potomac Ct, Geneva IL 60134 **Asst R S Mk's Ch Geneva IL 1997-** B Chicago IL 7/13/1926 s Theodore A Kruse & Margaret M. BA U IL 1975; MA SWTS 1976. D 6/14/1975 Bp Quintin Ebenezer Primo Jr P 12/1/1975 Bp James Winchester Montgomery. m 6/26/1982 Becky Kondiles Morris c 4. Chair Dio Chicago Chicago IL 1981-1985; S Bede's Epis Ch Bensenville IL 1977-1992; Assoc R S Elis's Ch Glencoe IL 1975-1976. Bro Of S Andr 1997; EPF 2002; Ord Of S Lk 1999.

KRUTZ, Charles Dana (La) 527 North Boulevard, Fourth Floor, Baton Rouge LA 70802 **P-in-c S Fran Ch Denham Sprg LA 2007-; Louisiana Interchurch Conf Baton Rouge LA 1992-** B Blytheville AR 10/29/1946 s Charles Krutz & Virginia Lillian. BA SMU 1968; MDiv Ya Berk 1971; DMin VTS 1995. D 6/18/1971 Bp Theodore H McCrea P 12/1/1971 Bp William Paul Barnds. m 11/24/1973 Julie Clark c 2. S Geo's Epis Ch New Orleans LA 2006-2007; Int Chr Ch Slidell LA 2004-2006; Int S Matt's Epis Ch Houma LA 2003-2004; S Mary's Ch New Roads LA 2000; S Greg's Ch Gonzales LA 1999-2003; R S Jas Epis Ch Shreveport LA 1981-1992; Cur S Andr's Epis Ch New Orleans LA 1976-1981; Epis Coll Cntr Hammond LA 1975-1976; Vic All SS Epis Ch Ponchatoula LA 1974-1976; Vic Ch Of The Incarn Amite LA 1974-1976; Asst Chr Epis Ch Dallas TX 1971-1974. Natl Assn Ecum Stff. dankrutz@aol.com

KRYDER, Edward Hemington (WNY) 86 Saint Matthew Road, Lititz PA 17543 **Died 8/27/2011** B Akron OH 8/23/1920 s Ralph Levi Kryder & Pearle Ardys. AB mcl Pr 1942; MDiv cl VTS 1953; Fllshp Salisbury Theol Coll 1972. D 6/14/1953 P 5/8/1954 Bp Lauriston L Scaife. c 6. Auth, "Essentials of Gd Liturg," *Ldrshp for Musicians in Sm Congregations*, LMSCC, 1994. DD VTS 1975. ekryder@dejazzd.com

KRYDER-REID, Thomas Marshall (Ind) 5354 Olympia Dr, Indianapolis IN 46228 B 11/12/1952 s Edward Hemington Kryder. BA Syr; MA U Chi; MDiv VTS. D 5/31/1986 P 12/1/1986 Bp Harold B Robinson. m 8/27/1988 Elizabeth B Reid. S Tim's Ch Indianapolis IN 1999-2000; S Barth's Ch Baltimore MD 1991-1998; S Columba's Ch Washington DC 1986-1991. tkr@trinitychurchindy.org

KUBBE, Anna Leigh (EMich) Diocese of Eastern Michigan, 924 N Niagara St, Saginaw MI 48602 **Dio Estrn Michigan Saginaw MI 2007-** B Detroit MI 9/27/1943 d Leighton Albert Moats & Leora Angela. BA Estrn Michigan U 1980; MA Estrn Michigan U 1988. D 4/18/1998 Bp Edwin Max Leidel Jr. m 8/20/1979 Myron Kubbe c 3. alkubbe@sbcglobal.net

KUBICEK, Kirk Alan (Ct) 3695 Rogers Ave, Ellicott City MD 21043 **R S Ptr's Epis Ch Ellicott City MD 1994-** B Oak Park IL 12/4/1949 s Robert Anthony Kubicek & Patricia Ruth. BA Trin Hartford CT 1972; MDiv GTS 1983. D 6/18/1983 Bp George Nelson Hunt III P 12/1/1983 Bp James Winchester Montgomery. m 11/1/1975 Mallory M H Harris c 3. S Tim's Sch Stevenson MD 2009; R S Ptr's Epis Ch Monroe CT 1989-1994; Ch Of The Gd Shpd Ruxton MD 1985-1989; Chr Ch Winnetka IL 1983-1985. "Living w Money," Epis Media; Auth, *Cler & Money TENS Nwsltr*. Mnstry of Money 1985; TENS 1995. perechief@gmail.com

KUBLER, Barry P(aul) (EC) 194 Saint Brendan Ct, Southport NC 28461 **R S Phil's Ch Southport NC 2004-** B SuffernNY 9/4/1947 s Jack Merle Kubler & Barbara Louise. BS U of So Florida 1976; MDiv VTS 1997. D 6/29/1991 Bp Rogers Sanders Harris P 6/14/1997 Bp John Bailey Lipscomb. m 2/15/1969 Vonceal Arlene Doerr c 2. R S Mart's Epis Ch Hudson FL 1997-2004; D S Ptr's Ch Plant City FL 1991-1994. revkubler@aol.com

KUCIK, Amanda (Va) 10 Ann St Apt 303, Norwalk CT 06854 **Assoc R Ch Of The H Comf Charlotte NC 2011-** B Washington DC 11/29/1979 d George Kucik & Karen. BA U Of Virginia Charlottesville VA 2002; MDiv Ya Berk 2006. D 6/24/2006 P 2/3/2007 Bp Peter James Lee. Assoc R Ch Of The Incarn New York NY 2006-2011. amandak@holycomfortercharlotte.org

KUEHL JR, H(enry) August (RI) 40 Bagy Wrinkle Cv, Warren RI 02885 B Dennison OH 3/25/1923 s Henry August Kuehl & Della Virginia. BA Moravian TS 1944; MDiv PrTS 1946; Fllshp Coll of Preachers 1960. D 6/11/1948 P 12/18/1948 Bp Frank W Sterrett. c 4. Chair - Scholarshp Fund Dio Rhode Island Providence RI 1993-1999; Scholarshp Fund Dio Rhode Island Providence RI 1988-1991; Cmsn Apportnmnt & Rev Chair Dio Rhode Island Providence RI 1988-1990; Cmsn Apportnmnt & Rev Dio Rhode Island Providence RI 1985-1988; Comp Dioc ExCoun Dio Rhode Island Providence RI 1983-1990; ExCoun Dio Rhode Island Providence RI 1983-1985; Dioc Coun Dio Rhode Island Providence RI 1982-1986; Dn E Bay Deanry Dio Rhode Island Providence RI 1980-1984; Chair Com Trans Epispcy Dio Rhode Island Providence RI 1979-1980; Com on Deferred Giving Dio Rhode Island Providence RI 1978-1984; Dept Stwdshp Dio Rhode Island Providence RI 1977-1983; Dept Prom & Publ Chair Dio Rhode Island Providence RI 1977-1982; ExCoun Dio Rhode Island Providence RI 1977-1980; ExCoun Dio Rhode Island Providence RI 1977-1980; Conv Prog Chair Dio Rhode Island Providence RI 1977-1978; Conv Prog Dio Rhode Island Providence RI 1974-1977; Dept Prom & Publ Dio Rhode Island Providence RI 1974-1977; R S Jn's Ch Barrington RI 1973-1988; P-in-c S Lk And S Simon Cyrene Rochester NY 1972-1973; R S Paul's Ch Rochester NY 1964-1969; ExCoun Dio Rochester Rochester NY 1962-1964; Dioc Coun Dio Rochester Rochester NY 1961-1964; R S Barn Ch Irvington on Hudson NY 1955-1964; Del Prov II Syn Dio Bethlehem Bethlehem PA 1954-1955; R Ch Of Our Merc Sav Penns Grove NJ 1951-1955; Dir Yth Div DeptCE Dio Bethlehem Bethlehem PA 1950-1951; R S Mary's Epis Ch Reading PA 1949-1951; Cur S Lk's Ch Scranton PA 1948-1949. Coll of Preachers 1960; EvangES 1964. R Emer St Jn's Epis Ch, Barrington, RI 1992.

KUEHN, Craig Charles (NCal) 2821 Bronzecrest St, Placerville CA 95667 **Dn Dio Nthrn California Sacramento CA 2005-; R Epis Ch Of Our Sav Placerville CA 1999-** B Salt Lake City UT 4/13/1951 s Charles Donald Kuehn & Louise Rita. U of Arizona 1970; U of Utah 1972; BA Westminster Coll 1986; MDiv CDSP 1993. D 12/26/1985 P 9/19/1986 Bp Otis Charles. m 10/7/1972 Suzanne Richardson c 2. Reg Mssnr S Paul's Epis Ch Oroville CA 1997-1999; Reg Mssnr S Steph's Epis Ch Colusa CA 1997-1999; Dio Nthrn California Sacramento CA 1993-1999; Reg Mssnr H Trin Epis Ch Willows CA 1993-1999; Reg Mssnr S Tim's Ch Gridley CA 1993-1999; P S Steph's Ch W Vlly City UT 1986-1990. therev@c-skuehn.net

KUEHN, Jerome Frederick (FdL) 806 4th St, Algoma WI 54201 B Chicago IL 8/1/1947 s William F Kuehn & Grace E. D 7/25/1992 Bp William Charles Wantland. m 8/4/1969 Vicki Florence Lockner. Asst S Jn's Epis Ch Sparta WI 1992-1999.

KUENKLER, Richard Frederick (CNY) 1 W Church St, Elmira NY 14901 B Milwuakee WI 2/2/1935 s Arthur Stefan Kuenkler & Grace Lydia. BA Jn Hopkins U 1956; Cert Peabody Conservatory Of Mus 1958; MDiv UTS 1963. D 6/14/1978 P 11/1/1978 Bp Ned Cole. m 11/7/1992 Natalie B Kuenkler c 1. R Gr Epis Ch Elmira NY 1986-1996; R S Paul's Aurora NY 1970-1986. RICHARD_KUENKLER@HOTMAIL.COM

KUENNETH, John R (Tenn) 538 Hickory Trail Drive, Nashville TN 37209 B Litchfield IL 2/6/1932 s Harold H Kuenneth & Grace L. BA U Denv 1954; MDiv Nash 1957. D 6/24/1957 P 1/6/1958 Bp Joseph Summerville Minnis. m 8/20/1966 Loralee Kay Raymond c 3. Dir, Instnl Mnstrs Dio Tennessee Nashville TN 1987-1993; R S Jas Ch Wichita KS 1971-1984; R S Jas Epis Ch Wheat Ridge CO 1968-1971; R Prince Of Peace Epis Ch Sterling CO 1964-1968. ACPE 1984-1987. Phi Beta Kappa Gamma of Coloado 1954. beadseye@hotmail.com

KUHLMAN, Donald Herms (Mil) 1200 Green Valley Drive, #2, Janesville WI 53546 **D Trin Ch Janesville WI 1998-** B Chicago IL 2/8/1927 s Clarence Bernard Kuhlman & Violet May. BS Beloit Coll 1950. D 5/9/1998 Bp Roger John White.

KUHLMANN, Frederick Jennings (Ct) 15 Highland Rd, Oxford CT 06478 **P Assoc S Paul's Ch Woodbury CT 1993-** B St. Paul MN 4/28/1923 s Frederick Kuhlmann & Ruth R. BS U MN 1944; MDiv VTS 1967; Ya 1974. D 6/13/1967 Bp Walter H Gray P 12/1/1967 Bp John Henry Esquirol. m 4/24/1992 J Charlotte Cummings c 2. Vic S Ptr's Epis Ch Oxford CT 1975-1992; Int S

Mk's Chap Storrs CT 1973-1974; Vic Chr Ch Trumbull CT 1967-1973. frfred@sbcglobal.net

KUHLMANN, Martha Chandler (Cal) 107 Franciscan Dr, Danville CA 94526 **H Cross Epis Ch Castro Vlly CA 2008-** B Boston MA 6/8/1948 d Alan Freeman Peterson & Harriette Isabelle. BA Bates Coll 1970; MDiv CDSP 2002. D 6/1/2002 P 12/7/2002 Bp William Edwin Swing. m 5/27/1977 Ronald Kuhlman c 2. Assoc P S Geo's Epis Ch Antioch CA 2002-2005. mckuhlmann@aol.com

KUHN, Michael Cray (La) Trinity Episcopal School, 1315 Jackson Ave, New Orleans LA 70130 **Trin Ch New Orleans LA 1994-** B Philadelphia PA 12/15/1956 s William Thomas Kuhn & Marion Louise. BA STUSo 1979; MDiv GTS 1982; DMin EDS 1998. Trans 2/26/2004 Bp M(arvil) Thomas Shaw III. m 9/24/1988 Maria Elliott c 2. Emm Ch Boston MA 1990-1994; The Cathd Sch New York NY 1989-1990; Cathd Of St Jn The Div New York NY 1983-1989; The Ch of S Matt And S Tim New York NY 1982-1983. Auth, "Bk Revs," *Books & Rel*. mkuhn@trinitynola.com

KUHN, Philip James (Roch) 25 Wood lane, Maynard MA 01754 B Columbus OH 6/5/1968 s Bernard Kuhn & Geraldine. BA Providence Coll 1990; MDiv Epis TS of The SW 1995. D 12/16/1995 P 6/15/1996 Bp John Stuart Thornton. m 6/22/1991 Marilyn Anne Clarke c 3. R S Lk's Ch Branchport NY 2006-2011; R Tri-Par Mnstry Hornell NY 1998-2005; Vic Chr Ch Shoshone ID 1995-1998; Vic Trin Ch Gooding ID 1995-1998.

KUHN, Thomas Randall (EC) 328 Kelly Ave, Oak Hill WV 25901 B Welch WV 8/28/1939 s James Duane Randall Kuhn & Beatrice Catherine. BA Wofford Coll 1964; BD Epis TS In Kentucky 1967. D 6/12/1967 P 2/1/1968 Bp Wilburn Camrock Campbell. m 10/8/1987 Mary Helen Murphy. S Ptr's Epis Ch Washington NC 1981-1983; R H Trin Ch Logan WV 1976-1981; R Chr Ch Point Pleasant WV 1972-1976; Vic Epis Ch of the Trsfg Buckhannon WV 1969-1972; Vic Mt Zion Epis Ch Hedgesville WV 1967-1969; Vic S Mk's Epis Ch Berkeley Sprg WV 1967-1969.

K

KUHR, Carolyn S. (Mont) 454 1st Avenue East N, Kalistell MT 59901 B Yakima WA 8/10/1946 d James Frederick Leghorn & Phyllis Caroline. BA Cntrl Washington U 1969. D 9/14/1984 Bp Jackson Earle Gilliam P 1/6/1987 Bp Charles Jones III. c 2. Asst Ch Of The H Sprt Missoula MT 2005-2007; R S Pat's Epis Ch Bigfork MT 1997-2005; P-in-c S Mich And All Ang Eureka MT 1993-2002; Dio Montana Helena MT 1993-1996; R H Trin Epis Ch Troy MT 1993-1996; R S Lk's Ch Libby MT 1993-1996; R S Mk's Ch Havre MT 1987-1992; Ch Of The Incarn Great Falls MT 1985-1987. blessyu@bresnan.net

KUHR, Elisabeth Schader (Spok) 2490 Thompson Rd, Cowiche WA 98923 **P Chr Epis Ch Zillah WA 1999-** B Jamaica NY 8/18/1941 d Fredrich Keith Schader & Frances Nell. BS California St Polytechnic U 1964; BA California St Coll, Stani-Laus 1969. D 4/14/1999 Bp Cabell Tennis P 10/16/1999 Bp John Stuart Thornton. c 2.

KUJAWA-HOLBROOK, Sheryl Anne (Los) Claremont School of Theology, 1325 N College Avenue, Claremont CA 91711 **Prof Claremont TS Claremont CA 2009-; Prof of Angl Stds The ETS At Claremont Claremont CA 2009-** B Milwaukee WI 5/30/1956 d Alexis Roman Kujawa & Elaine Bertha. BA Marq 1977; MATS Harvard DS 1979; MA Sarah Lawr Coll 1979; MDiv EDS 1983; PhD Boston Coll 1993; EdD Col 1993; Ed.D UTS 1993; PhD CUNY 1998. D 6/1/1985 P 6/25/1986 Bp John Bowen Coburn. m 11/17/2001 Paul Holbrook c 1. Acad Dn EDS Cambridge MA 2004-2009; Prof EDS Cambridge MA 1998-2009; Prog Dir, Mnstrs w YP Epis Ch Cntr New York NY 1995-1998; Asst Ch Of The Incarn New York NY 1991-1998; Yth Dir Epis Ch Cntr New York NY 1988-1998; Yth Dir Epis Prov Of New Engl Dorset VT 1985-1988; Asst The Cathd Ch Of S Paul Boston MA 1985-1988; Yth Dir Dio Massachusetts Boston MA 1983-1988. Auth, "God Beyond Borders," Alb Inst, 2012; Co-Auth, "b of Water, b of Sprt," Alb Inst, 2010; Auth, "The Heart of A Pstr," Forw Mvmt, 2010; Co-Auth, "Injustice and the Care of Souls," Augsburg Fortress, 2009; Ed, "Seeing God in Each Other," Morehouse, 2006; Co-Ed, "Deeper Joy: Lay Wmn And Vocation in the 20th Century Epis Ch," Ch Pub, 2005; Auth, "By Gr Came the Incarn," Books Just Books, 2004; Auth, "A Hse of Pryr for All Peoples," Alb Inst, 2003; Auth, "Freedom is a Dream," Ch Pub, 2002; Ed, "Disorganized Rel," Cowley, 1998; Auth, "God Works," Morehouse Pub, 1997; Auth, "Handbook For Mnstrs w Younger Adolescents," Epis Ch Cntr, 1996; Auth, "Handbook For Mnstrs w Older Adolescents," Epis Ch Cntr, 1996; Ed, "Resource Bk for Ministeries w Yth and YA," Epis Ch Cntr, 1995. Amer Academiy of Rel 2000; EPF 1998; EUC 1990; EWC 1990; EWHP 1998; HSEC 1993; Soc of S Jn the Evang 1981; Sprtl Dircetors Intl 2005. Chr Ldrshp Fllshp Amer Jewish Com and the Shalom Hartman Inst, Jeruslame, 2010- 2011; Fac Mentoring Awd Claremont TS 2010; Bogert Grant for the Study of Chr Mysticism Soc of Friends 2010; Conant Grant Epis Ch, 2000, 2003, 2005 2008; Adelaide Teague Case Awd EWHP 2006; Resolution Cambridge City Coun 2004; Evang for the 21st Century Grant Epis EvangES, 2000, 2003; Hist Resrch Grant HSEC 2003; Alb Inst Grant 2002; EWHP Travel Grant EWHP 2002; Fllshp Boston Coll, 1981-1984 1984; BTI Urban Educ Grant Boston Theol Inst 1982; Bradley Fisk Fllshp Harvard DS 1979; Ford Fndt Fllshp Sarah Lawr Coll 1978; Alum Educ Grant Marq 1977. skujawa-holbrook@cst.edu

KUKOWSKI, Richard George Paul (WA) 412 Colesville Manor Dr, Silver Spring MD 20904 **Washington Epis Cler Assn Treas Dio Washington Washington DC 2009-; Wrdn of Fllshp of St. Jn Dio Washington Washington DC 2008-; Chapl Cathd of St Ptr & St Paul Washington DC 2006-; Sthrn Afr Partnership Chair Dio Washington Washington DC 2006-** B Winona MN 5/20/1943 s George Lawrence Kukowski & Helen Cecelia. BA S Mary's U MN 1965; STB CUA 1968; MA CUA 1969; CAS GTS 1976. Rec from Roman Catholic 12/21/1975 as Priest Bp George E Rath. m 12/27/1975 Elaine Klein. Planned Giving Chair Dio Washington Washington DC 1996-2002; Dioc Coun Dio Washington Washington DC 1983-1985; Supvsr VTS Alexandria VA 1981-2006; R Ch Of The Trsfg Silver Sprg MD 1979-2006; Vic S Andr's Ch Turners Falls MA 1977-1979; Asst S Jas' Ch Greenfield MA 1977-1979; P-in-c Gr Ch Madison NJ 1976-1977; Yth Dir S Ptr's Ch Morristown NJ 1975-1976. Action In Montgomery 1999; Action In Montgomery, Treas 2005; Fllshp of St Jn 2006; WECA 1979. richk20904@verizon.net

KULP, John Eugene (SwFla) 17 W Vernon Ave Unit 301, Phoenix AZ 85003 B New York NY 11/3/1944 s John Eugene Kulp & Mary Francis. BA Sthrn Illinois U 1968; MDiv Nash 1971; MS California Coast U 2006. D 6/12/1971 P 12/1/1971 Bp Jonathan Goodhue Sherman. m 6/26/1971 Dianne L Bezek. S Paul's Epis Ch Clinton NC 2004; Chr Epis Ch Hope Mills NC 2003-2004; Trin Ch Lumberton NC 2002-2003; S Paul's In The Pines Epis Ch Fayetteville NC 2002; Supply P Dio No Carolina Raleigh NC 2001-2005; Off Of Bsh For ArmdF New York NY 1981-2001; R S Barth's Ch St Petersburg FL 1979-1980; Asst S Dunst's Epis Ch Largo FL 1976-1979; Asst S Lk's Ch Ft Myers FL 1974-1976; Asst S Ptr's by-the-Sea Epis Ch Bay Shore NY 1971-1974. jdkulp@live.com

KUMP, Mary Frances Prioleau (CFla) 1100 Cedar St, Leesburg FL 34748 **Honduran Taskforce Dio Cntrl Florida Orlando FL 1978-** B Fairmont WV 6/29/1926 d Philip Ford Prioleau & Hazel. BFA Tul 1948; U of Virginia 1966; OH SU 1968; MA U of So Florida 1974; EDS U Of Florida 1984. D 5/14/1977 Bp William Hopkins Folwell. DCE S Jas Epis Ch Leesburg FL 1976-1991. CHS.

KUNDINGER, Hazel Doris (CFla) 2404 Fairway Dr, Melbourne FL 32901 **Ch Of Our Sav Palm Bay FL 2005-; Epis Ch of the Blessed Redeem Palm Bay FL 2005-** B Hackensack NJ 5/27/1943 d Salvatore Guisippi Fiorenza & Hazel Annie. Asbury TS; MDiv STUSo; Inst for Chr Stds Florida 1995; AA Brevard Cmnty Coll 1997. D 12/13/1997 P 2/6/2005 Bp John Wadsworth Howe. m 6/3/1976 Robert Kundinger. D H Trin Epis Ch Melbourne FL 1997-2003. DOK; Ord Of S Lk The Physcn - Wrdn, Reg IIII (Pres. 1980.

KUNES JR, Robert Mitchell (Alb) 3928 Pacific Ave, Virginia Beach VA 23451 **Asst Galilee Epis Ch Virginia Bch VA 2010-** B Anderson SC 6/6/1976 s Robert M Kunes & Noel M. BA Coll of Charleston; MDiv Nash 2010. D 6/3/2010 P 12/6/2010 Bp Mark Joseph Lawrence. m 2/2/2002 Julie Bennett c 2. rob@galileechurch.net

KUNHARDT, Daniel Bradish (WMass) 304 Princes Point Rd, Brunswick ME 04011 B Lawrence MA 9/21/1926 s George Edward Kunhardt & Joan Alexandra. BA Bow 1949; MDiv GTS 1952; Cert Springfield Coll Springfield MA 1978. D 6/8/1952 Bp David Emrys Richards P 4/29/1953 Bp Stephen F Bayne Jr. Asst Chr Ch Cathd Springfield MA 1967-1973; Vic Epis Ch Of The Epiph Wilbraham MA 1958-1966; Vic S Mary's Epis Ch Thorndike MA 1958-1959; Vic S Matt Ch Tacoma WA 1954-1955; Cur Chr Ch Tacoma WA 1952-1954.

KUNHARDT III, Philip Bradish (NY) Po Box 33, Waccabuc NY 10597 **Asst S Mk's Ch Mt Kisco NY 1997-** B Morristown NJ 11/15/1951 s Philip Bradish Kunhardt & Katharine. BA Coll of the Atlantic 1977; MDiv EDS 1980. D 6/13/1981 Bp Paul Moore Jr P 4/3/1982 Bp Lyman Cunningham Ogilby. m 10/1/1983 Margaret Sweatt c 4. Asst S Barth's Ch In The Highland White Plains NY 1991-1997; R S Pauls On The Hill Epis Ch Ossining NY 1984-1991; Asst Ch Of Our Sav Jenkintown PA 1981-1984; Ch Of S Asaph Bala Cynwyd PA 1981-1984. Auth, "Looking for Lincoln," Knopf, 2008; Auth, "Pbs-Tv Miniseries," *The Amer Pres*, 2000; Auth, "The Amer Pres," Riverhead, 1999; Auth, "P.T. Barnum: Amer's Greatest Showman," Knopf, 1995; Auth, "Lincoln: An Illustrated Biography," Knopf, 1992; Auth, "Abc-Tv Miniseries," *Lincoln*, 1992. The Century Club 2001. philip@kunhardtproductions.com

KUNICHIKA, Thomas Kazuyoshi (Haw) No address on file. B Lahaina HI 5/13/1936 s Kazuo Kunichika & Kiyoko. BA Ham 1958; BD CDSP 1961. D 6/10/1961 Bp Leland Stark P 12/1/1961 Bp Harry S Kennedy. Hawaii Prep Acad Kamuela HI 1961-1976; Vic S Jas Epis Ch Kamuela HI 1961-1976.

KUNKLE, Owen (RG) 1914 Tijeras Rd, Santa Fe NM 87505 **D S Bede's Epis Ch Santa Fe NM 1985-** B Leavenworth KS 9/24/1940 s George Owen Kunkle & Elizabeth Claire. Harvard DS; BA S Jn's Coll 1962; MA Emory U 1966; LPN NMMCC 1984. D 1/15/1985 Bp Richard Mitchell Trelease Jr. m 10/8/1977 Gail Margaret Williams c 5.

KUNZ JR, Andrew George (Va) 1006 Greenway Ln, Richmond VA 23226 B Rome NY 1/1/1936 s Andrew George Kunz & Leonora Adelaide MacPhail.

BA Colg 1957; Drew U 1959; Drew U 1959; BD EDS 1961. D 6/10/1961 P 12/21/1961 Bp Leland Stark. m 11/27/1992 Claire H Hendry. Exec Bd Mem Dio Virginia Richmond VA 1990-1993; Dn of Richmond Reg Dio Virginia Richmond VA 1984-1988; Vic S Ptr's Epis Ch Richmond VA 1981-1998; Vic Prince of Peace S Louis MO 1980-1981; Stndg Com Mem Dio Missouri S Louis MO 1975-1980; Dio Missouri S Louis MO 1974-1981; Vic Ch Of The Ascen S Louis MO 1971-1980; Gr Epis Ch Rutherford NJ 1968-1974; Assoc R Trin Ch S Louis MO 1964-1965; Cur Gr Epis Ch Rutherford NJ 1961-1964. ckunzfotog@aol.com

KUNZ JR, Carl Norman (Del) Po Box 5856, Wilmington DE 19808 B Philadelphia PA 3/18/1937 s Carl Norman Kunz & Ethel C. BA Hav 1958; MDiv EDS 1961. D 6/17/1961 P 3/1/1962 Bp Oliver J Hart. m 11/25/1961 Carol Ann Heginbothom c 2. S Andrews Sch Of Delaware Inc Middletown DE 1993-2004; Sr Chapl S Andr's Sch Chap Middletown DE 1993-2004; Dio Delaware Wilmington DE 1972-1993; Dioc Del Dio Delaware Wilmington DE 1972-1992; Exec Off Dio Delaware Wilmington DE 1972-1987; R St Annes Epis Ch Middletown DE 1967-1972; Asst S Paul's Ch Newburyport MA 1963-1964; Cur S Dav's Ch Wayne PA 1961-1963. opaku@comcast.net

KUNZ, Phyllis Ann (Minn) 67982 260th Ave, Kasson MN 55944 **D S Lk's Epis Ch Rochester MN 2005-** B Winona MN 2/19/1955 d Thomas Francis Rowan & Lela Irene. LPN Rochester Sch Of Practical Nrsng Rochester MN 1974. D 6/18/2005 Bp James Louis Jelinek. m 7/7/1979 Thomas Leo Kunz c 3. kunz.phyllis@mayo.edu

KUNZ, Richard Andrew (NY) Grace Church, 33 Church St, White Plains NY 10601 **R Gr Ch White Plains NY 2010-** B Philadelphia PA 6/23/1951 s William Richard Kunz & Eleanor Cherry. BS NWU 1972; MDiv PrTS 1979; GTS 1980. D 6/14/1980 P 12/13/1980 Bp Robert Bracewell Appleyard. m 10/17/2009 Barbra Ann McCune c 2. Exec Director, El Hogar Projects, Honduras Exec Coun Appointees New York NY 2004-2010; R All SS Ch Princeton NJ 1993-2004; Vic Emm Ch Pittsburgh PA 1986-1993; Cn Trin Cathd Pittsburgh PA 1981-1986. kunzrichard@gmail.com

KURATKO, Lauren Elizabeth Browder (Va) 8 N Laurel St, Richmond VA 23220 **Gr & H Trin Epis Ch Richmond VA 2008-** B Montgomery AL 8/28/1980 d Larry Fulton Browder & Catherine Hudson. BA Rhodes Coll 2002; MDiv VTS 2005. D 5/25/2005 Bp Marc Handley Andrus P 12/13/2005 Bp Henry Nutt Parsley Jr. m 9/14/2007 Ryan Kuratko. Cbury Epis Campus Mnstry at Texas Tech Lubbock TX 2006-2008; Dio NW Texas Lubbock TX 2006-2008; S Jn's Ch Decatur AL 2005-2006; S Jn's Ch Montgomery AL 2005-2006. lauren.browder@stjohnsdecatur.org

KURATKO, Ryan (Va) P.O. Box 788, Mechanicsville VA 23111 **R Imm Ch Mechanicsville VA 2009-** B Odessa TX 2/6/1981 s Charles Patrick Kuratko & Connye Nall. BA NWU 2003; MDiv VTS 2006. D 12/14/2005 Bp C(harles) Wallis Ohl P 7/23/2006 Bp Charles Wallis Ohl. m 9/14/2007 Lauren Elizabeth Browder Kuratko. Assoc R S Paul's On The Plains Epis Ch Lubbock TX 2006-2008; Bp Geo Quarterman Conf Cntr Lubbock TX 2006. associatestpaul@nts-online.net

KURTZ, James Edward (CFla) 4004 Ann Ave., Sebring FL 33870 **S Agnes Ch Sebring FL 2000-** B Mechanicsburg PA 3/2/1941 s Kenneth Morrell Kurtz & Margaret Ann. U Pgh 1969; AA Valencia Cmnty Coll 1973; BS Florida Sthrn Coll 1976; Cert Inst for Chr Stds 1991; MDiv TESM 2000. D 11/7/1992 P 7/30/2000 Bp John Wadsworth Howe. m 6/30/1980 Mary Jo Shreckengast c 7. jkurtz4004@comcast.net

KURTZ, Kelli Grace (Los) 408 Greenfield Ct, Glendora CA 91740 **Treas for Bd Trst The ETS At Claremont Claremont CA 2009-; Prog Grp on Mssn Congregations Dio Los Angeles Los Angeles CA 2008-; Vic S Jn's Mssn La Verne CA 2007-; Bd Trst The ETS At Claremont Claremont CA 2007-** B Fresno CA 3/4/1964 d Martin Leroy Hickle & Margaret Nadine. BA California St U 1986; MA TS At Claremont 1996. D 11/22/1997 Bp Chester Lovelle Talton P 10/21/2006 Bp Robert Marshall Anderson. m 7/6/1984 Mark Steven Kurtz c 4. Asst All SS Epis Ch Riverside CA 1999-2007; Cur S Mary's Par Laguna Bch CA 1998-1999. Ord Julian Of Norwich 1996-1999. vicar@stjohnslaverne.org

KURTZ, Margaret Eileen (Ida) 3185 E Rivernest Dr, Boise ID 83706 **Assoc S Mich's Cathd Boise ID 1996-** B La Crosse WI 3/15/1942 d William Haig Rowe & Marie Eileen. BD U of Iowa 1976; MA U of Iowa 1979. D 12/22/1996 P 6/29/1997 Bp John Stuart Thornton. m 5/15/1993 Karl Bunning Kurtz c 2. easterm@cableone.net

KURTZ, Robert Guy (Eas) 1 Meadow St, Apt. 120, Berlin MD 21811 B Fort Collins CO 11/16/1920 s Guy Orth Kurtz & Harriette Agnes. BS USMA At W Point 1943; Epis TS In Kentucky 1966. D 12/16/1966 Bp William R Moody P 11/1/1967 Bp E(gbert) Don Taylor. c 2. R S Andr's Epis Ch Princess Anne MD 1975-1984; R Emm Epis Ch Chestertown MD 1972-1975; R All Hallow's Ch Snow Hill MD 1967-1972.

KUSCHEL, Catherine M. (Neb) 713 Church Rd, Grand Island NE 68801 B Milwaukee WI 4/2/1951 d Richard George Schuda & Dolores Marie. BS U of Wisconsin 1973; MS U of Wisconsin 1980; MDiv SWTS 1990; Cert Int Mnstry Prog 1992; Cert Racine Dominican Sprtl Gdnc Trng Prog 2004; MA Doane Coll 2010. D 4/29/1990 P 12/1/1990 Bp Roger John White. m 7/21/1973 Joseph J Kuschel c 1. R S Steph's Ch Grand Island NE 2005-2009; Int S Anskar's Ch Rockford IL 2003-2005; Int Our Saviors Luth Ch Milwaukee WI 2002-2003; Int Chr Ch Whitefish Bay WI 2000-2002; Int Chr Ch Epis Madison WI 1998-2000; Int S Dav Of Wales Ch New Berlin WI 1996-1998; P-in-c Trin Epis Ch Mineral Point WI 1994-1996; Stndg Com Dio Milwaukee Milwaukee WI 1992-1996; Int S Chris's Ch River Hills WI 1992-1994; Cur S Lk's Ch Madison WI 1991-1992. CSM 2004; Ord of Julian of Norwich 1991-1995. Outstanding Stdt Awd Doane Coll 2010; Helen Ledyard Field Prize in Homil SWTS 1990; Henry Benjamin Whipple Schlr SWTS 1990; Chas Palmerson Anderson Schlr SWTS 1989. cmkuschel@yahoo.com

KUSKY, Donna Lee Stewart (EMich) 13685 Block Rd, Birch Run MI 48415 **D S Mk's Epis Ch Bridgeport MI 1992-** B Flint MI 10/4/1942 d Vernon Sheldon Stewart & Olga Sarah. Whitaker TS 1992; AA Mott Cmnty Coll 1993. D 6/13/1992 Bp R(aymond) Stewart Wood Jr. m 2/13/1965 William Paul Kusky c 4.

KWAN, Franco Chan-hong (Cal) 425 Swallowtail Ct, Brisbane CA 94005 **R True Sunshine Par San Francisco CA 1999-** B Canton CN 9/24/1950 s Lok Ping Kwan & Kwok Ming. LLB Chinese Culture U Taipei TW 1976; BD Chung Chi Sem Chinese U of Hong Kong CN 1979; MSW CUNY 1990; DMin NYTS 1993. D 7/25/1979 Bp James T M Pong P 9/21/1980 Bp Pui-Yeung Cheung. c 3. Dioc Coun Dio Long Island Garden City NY 1993-1994; S Geo's Par Flushing NY 1992-1999; Racial Justice Cmsn Dio Long Island Garden City NY 1991-1998; Rep Ecum Wrkng Grp Asian Pacific Amers Dio Long Island Garden City NY 1989-1996; Dio Long Island Garden City NY 1988-1991; Chair Asian Com on Aging Dio Long Island Garden City NY 1987-1996; Cler Advsry Com Chld Abuse & Neglect NY St Dio Long Island Garden City NY 1985-1987; Vic Epis Ch Of Our Sav New York NY 1983-1987. "A Mssy from the E," *Mod Profiles of An Ancient Faith*, Epis Dio California, 2001; Auth, "The Needs of the Chinese Elderly -- Who Should Care for Them," *ACA*, 1990. Citation of Outstanding Contributions to the Flushing Cmnty Lunar New Year Fest Com 1999; Citation of hon Pres of Manhattan, New York 1999; Citation of hon Pres of Queens Borough, New York 1999; Proclamation The City Coun of New York 1999; Citation of hon The Mayor of New York City 1999; Who's Who among Asian Americans Gale Resrch Inc., 1994. francokwan@aol.com

KWIATKOWSKI, Janet Mary Jaworowicz (Mil) 9333 W Goodrich Ave, Milwaukee WI 53224 B Milwaukee WI 3/17/1955 d Jerome Chester Jaworowicz & Helen. BA Alverno Coll 1977; MS Capella U 2003; SWTS 2006. D 12/7/2002 Bp Roger John White P 9/14/2006 Bp Steven Andrew Miller. m 12/15/1979 Dennis A Kwiatkowski c 4. Asstg P S Chris's Ch River Hills WI 2007-2009; S Johns Communities INC Milwaukee WI 2005-2007; D S Chris's Ch River Hills WI 2002-2004. jkwiatkowski@saintjohnsmilw.org

KYGER JR, Paul Scholl (Chi) 2304 Finwick Ct, Kissimmee FL 34743 B Glen Ridge NJ 10/4/1930 s Paul Scholl Kyger & Lola Palmer. BA Wesl 1952; BD SWTS 1955. D 6/18/1955 Bp Charles L Street P 12/21/1955 Bp Gerald Francis Burrill. m 6/26/1954 Marion Elizabeth Stueck c 1. P-in-c S Ambr Ch Chicago Heights IL 1976-1992; R S Richard's Ch Chicago IL 1971-1976; Vic St Cyprians Ch Chicago IL 1956-1963; Cur Gr Ch Oak Pk IL 1955-1956. kissimkid@earthlink.net

KYLE, Michael Raymond (Mo) 1014 N. Summit Dr., Willow Springs MO 65793 **All SS Ch W Plains MO 2008-; Mssnr S Paul's Ch Palmyra MO 1995-; Mssnr Trin Ch Hannibal MO 1995-** B Hamilton OH 2/24/1949 s Franklin Charles Kyle & Patricia Alice. BA Kent St U 1972; MDiv Bex 1975. D 6/2/1976 P 3/1/1977 Bp John Mc Gill Krumm. c 2. Dio W Missouri Kansas City MO 2004-2010; No Convoc Hannibal MO 2004-2010; Mssnr Calv Ch Louisiana MO 1995-2000; Mssnr Gr Ch Clarksville MO 1995-2000; Mssnr S Jn's Ch Prairieville Louisiana MO 1995-2000; P-in-c S Ptr's Epis Ch Bonne Terre MO 1989-1995; P-in-c Trin Ch De Soto MO 1989-1995; R Emm Epis Ch Alexandria MN 1987-1989; S Andr's-In-The-Vlly Tamworth NH 1981-1985; Emm Epis Ch Webster Groves MO 1976-1981; Intern Emm Epis Ch Webster Groves MO 1975-1976. michaelrkyle@aol.com

L

LABARRE, Barbara L (Root) (Okla) 10901 S Yale Ave, Tulsa OK 74137 **D Ch Of The H Sprt - Epis Tulsa OK 1984-** B Newton KS 10/9/1935 d Vincent Clifford Root & Frieda Lavere. U of Oregon; BS K SU 1957; EFM STUSo 1986. D 6/28/1984 Bp William Jackson Cox. m 12/27/1956 Gary C LaBarre c 3. CHS.

LABATT, Walter Bruce (Mo) 520 Coventry Cir, Dexter MI 48130 B Petoskey MI 5/10/1940 s Dee Walter LaBatt & Mary Elizabeth. BA U MI 1962; MDiv SWTS 1991. D 6/23/1990 P 4/1/1991 Bp R(aymond) Stewart Wood Jr. m 9/19/1981 Judith Moyer. Gr Epis Ch Mansfield OH 2004-2006; Int S Simon's On The Sound Ft Walton Bch FL 2003-2004; Int The Epis Ch Of The Nativ

Dothan AL 2002-2003; Untd Evang Luth Ch Of Peace Steeleville IL 2001-2002; No Convoc Hannibal MO 2001; S Gabr's Epis Ch Eastpointe MI 1999-2001; R S Paul's Ch S Louis MO 1994-1999; Vic S Mich's Epis Ch O Fallon IL 1991-1994; D S Dav's Ch Southfield MI 1990-1991. ecinterim@aol.com

LABELLE, Philip N (Colo) 9925 Hoyt Lane, Westminster CO 80021 **S Mk's Ch Southborough MA 2011-** B Mount Clemens MI 11/10/1970 s Russell J LaBelle & Betty J. BA Gordon Coll 1992; MA NEU 1998; MDiv Ya Berk 2004. D 6/19/2004 P 1/23/2005 Bp Gordon Paul Scruton. m 12/29/1995 Melissa T Tobey c 2. R The Ch Of Chr The King (Epis) Arvada CO 2007-2011; Assoc R S Lk's Par Darien CT 2004-2007. pnlabelle@mac.com

LABORDA, Christy Elisa (ECR) Iglesia El Buen Pastor, 1852 Liberty St, Durham NC 27703 **S Steph's Epis Ch Sebastopol CA 2011-** B Wynnwood PA 5/20/1981 d Oscar E Laborda & Suzanne Kerr. BA Bryn 2003; MDiv VTS 2007. D 6/9/2007 Bp Charles Ellsworth Bennison Jr P 12/9/2007 Bp Michael Bruce Curry. Dio El Camino Real Monterey CA 2009-2011; Vic Iglesia El Buen Pstr Durham NC 2007-2009. christylaborda@gmail.com

LABUD, Richard John (CFla) 28097 Se Highway 42, Umatilla FL 32784 **D S Thos Epis Ch Eustis FL 1995-** B Pasadena CA 10/27/1959 s William George Labud & Lillian Marie. Inst for Chr Stds; AA Lake-Sumter Cmnty Coll 1979. D 11/11/1995 Bp John Wadsworth Howe. m 8/4/1979 Lisa Patricia Foisy c 2.

LACEY, John Howard (SwFla) 851 Moonlight Ln, Brooksville FL 34601 B London UK 7/18/1923 s Horace Edgar Lacey & Dorothy Vida. MDiv STUSo 1975. D 6/11/1975 Bp William Loftin Hargrave P 12/22/1975 Bp Emerson Paul Haynes. m 8/5/1996 Ivy Constance Langley c 2. Vic S Jn's Epis Ch Brooksville FL 1979-1988; Vic S Aug's Epis Ch St Petersburg FL 1975-1979. jlacey@innet.com

LACEY, Maryanne (SanD) 3208 Old Heather Rd, San Diego CA 92111 B Brooklyn NY 4/14/1943 d Milton Paul Dudeck & Anne Lee. AA Mesa Cmnty Coll 1986; BA Natl U 1988; DIT ETSBH 1991; MA Stc 1993. D 6/15/1991 Bp Joseph Thomas Heistand P 6/1/1994 Bp Gethin Benwil Hughes. Ch Of The Gd Samar San Diego CA 2005-2006; R S Phil The Apos Epis Ch Lemon Grove CA 1999-2006; Chr Ch Cranbrook Bloomfield Hills MI 1996-1998; All SS Ch Wheatland WY 1995-1996; Cathd Ch Of S Paul San Diego CA 1994-1995; D Cathd Ch Of S Paul San Diego CA 1992-1994; Chapl To Bp Dio San Diego San Diego CA 1992-1994; Epis Cmnty Serv San Diego CA 1991-2003; D S Tim's Ch San Diego CA 1991-1992. malacey@aol.com

LACHARITE, Paul Alfred Lorne (Mass) 25 Revere St Apt 5, Boston MA 02114 **Assoc Old No Chr Ch Boston MA 2011-** B Sherbrooke QC CA 10/29/1946 s Armand Arsen LaCharite & Shirley Elizabeth. BPh S Paul U Ottawa ON CA 1971; BA U of Ottawa 1971; Dip. Ed. McGill U 1973; STM McGill U 1976; MLS U of Rhode Island 1990. Trans from Anglican Church of Canada 9/2/1980 Bp Wilbur Emory Hogg Jr. m 5/22/2006 Robert Bruce Shaw. R S Jas Epis Ch Teele Sq Somerville MA 1990-2005; Libr Weston Jesuit TS Cambridge MA 1987-2008; Libr EDS Cambridge MA 1986-2009; R S Jn's Ch Ogdensburg NY 1980-1983. p.lacharite@verizon.net

LACKEY JR, Boston Mcgee (SVa) 1906 Cumberland Ave, Petersburg VA 23805 **Died 11/16/2010** B Raleigh NC 7/5/1921 s Boston Mcgee Lackey & Janet Lee. BA U NC 1942; BD VTS 1944; STM STUSo 1969; DMin VTS 1989. D 6/25/1944 P 7/5/1945 Bp Robert E Gribbin. c 1. R Emer Chr And Gr Epis Ch Petersburg VA 1991. grammama919@hotmail.com

LACKEY II, Kelley Jud (Kan) 1307 Rural St, Emporia KS 66801 **R S Andr's Epis Ch Emporia KS 2005-** B Parsons KS 5/16/1972 s Kelley Jud Lackey & Kristine Vail. BA U of Missouri 1997; S Paul TS Kansas City MO 2001; MDiv GTS 2003. D 7/22/2003 P 2/14/2004 Bp Barry Robert Howe. m 9/13/2003 Carolyn Jean Luecke c 2. Gr Ch Carthage MO 2003-2005. kjlii@prodigy.net

LACOMBE III, Edgar Arthur (Alb) 150 Lake Street, Rouses Point NY 12979 B Ogdensburg NY 5/24/1951 s Edgar Arthur LaCombe & Winifred Elaine. Potsdam St U; AAS Mater Dei Coll Ogdensburg NY 1975; BS Clarkson U 1977; LTh McGill U 1986. D 6/7/1986 P 12/1/1986 Bp David Standish Ball. m 6/20/1974 Carolyn Beatrice Cogswell c 4. P-in-c S Thos Ch Tupper Lake NY 1989-2003; Int Gr Epis Ch Canton NY 1988-1989; Asst P S Jn's Ch Ogdensburg NY 1986-1989. lacombe@primelink1.net

LACRONE, Frederick Palmer (SeFla) 3059 Casa Rio Ct, Palm Beach Gardens FL 33418 B Kalamazoo MI 11/20/1936 s Fred Austin La Crone & Margaret Louise. BA MI SU 1958; MDiv GTS 1961; DMin So Florida Cntr of Theol Miami FL 1992; MA Florida Atlantic U 2001. D 6/20/1961 P 12/21/1961 Bp Charles Bennison. m 5/21/1994 JoAnn Gooding c 4. R Gr Ch W Palm Bch FL 1981-1998; Rgnl Assoc Evang & Renwl Dio Sthrn Ohio Cincinnati OH 1978-1981; R S Steph's Epis Ch Cincinnati OH 1975-1981; Assoc S Thos Epis Ch Terrace Pk OH 1969-1975; ExCoun Dio Wstrn Michigan Kalamazoo MI 1965-1969; R Gr Epis Ch Of Ludington Michigan Ludington MI 1963-1969; Cur Trin Ch Niles MI 1961-1963. CT 1980. Faith and Rel Awd Bus & Profsnl Wmn Grtr Palm Beaches FL 1996. flacrone@fau.edu

LACROSSE, Diana Parsons (Dal) 2700 Warren Cir, Irving TX 75062 B Del Rio TX 10/22/1939 d Chester Nimitz Parsons & Audrey Gail. BS U of Texas 1961; MS U of Nebraska 1975. D 6/3/2001 Bp James Edward Krotz. m 4/6/2008 Julian Terry LaCrosse c 2. dpchamp1@msn.com

LACY II, Lonnie (Ga) St. Anne's Episcopal Church, P.O. Box 889, Tifton GA 31793 **R S Anne's Ch Tifton GA 2009-** B Valdosta GA 3/3/1980 s James Lacy & Anne. BA Reinhardt Coll Waleska GA 2002; MDiv VTS 2006. D 2/4/2006 P 8/10/2006 Bp Henry Irving Louttit. m 8/7/2004 Jessica Whitmire Lacy c 2. Asst R Trin Ch Statesboro GA 2006-2009. lonnielacy@gmail.com

LACY, Mary C (EC) 107 Louis St, Greenville NC 27858 **GC Dep Dio E Carolina Kinston NC 2011-; Fin Com Dio E Carolina Kinston NC 2008-; Mssn Dvlpmt Dio E Carolina Kinston NC 2008-; Stwdshp Cmsn Dio E Carolina Kinston NC 2008-; R S Tim's Epis Ch Greenville NC 2007-** B Johnstown PA 7/31/1956 d John Knox Deible & Gertrude Ann. BS Indiana U of Pennsylvania 1978; MDiv SWTS 2001. D 6/16/2001 P 12/15/2001 Bp William Dailey Persell. m 2/18/1984 Thomas Scott Lacy c 3. COM Dio Chicago Chicago IL 2003-2007; Conv Plnng Com Dio Chicago Chicago IL 2003-2006; Sprtl Dir Chicago Epis Curs Dio Chicago Chicago IL 2002-2007; Assoc R S Andr's Ch Downers Grove IL 2001-2007. mimilacy@gmail.com

✠ **LADEHOFF, Rt Rev Robert Louis** (Ore) 1330 SW 3rd Ave., Apt. P8, Portland OR 97201 **Ret Bp of Oregon Ascen Par Portland OR 2008-** B Ridgway PA 2/19/1932 s Henry William Ladehoff & Bertha Melius. BA Duke 1954; STB GTS 1957; DMin VTS 1980. D 6/15/1957 Bp Edwin A Penick P 12/18/1957 Bp Richard Henry Baker Con 11/30/1985 for Ore. c 1. Bp Dio Oregon Portland OR 1985-2003; Chair C&C Cntr Plnng Com Dio E Carolina Kinston NC 1982-1985; R S Jn's Epis Ch Fayetteville NC 1974-1985; BEC Dio No Carolina Raleigh NC 1962-1974; Min in charge S Paul's Epis Ch Thomasville NC 1957-1960; Min in charge Chr Ch Walnut Cove NC 1957-1959. roblad@earthlink.net

LAEDLEIN, George Robert (CNY) 201 Granite Rd Apt 340, Guilford CT 06437 B Philadelphia PA 2/14/1924 s Hepburn Christian Laedlein & Florence Emily. BA Trin Hartford CT 1947; ThB PDS 1950; MA Trin Hartford CT 1951; MDiv PDS 1959. D 6/3/1950 Bp William P Remington P 12/21/1950 Bp Noble C Powell. m 6/5/1950 Jean Winifred Zirkman c 5. Int S Geo's Ch Middlebury CT 1989-1991; Pstr Asst Gr Epis Ch Trumbull CT 1985-1997; R S Paul's Ch Owego NY 1978-1984; R Emm Par Epis Ch And Day Sch Sthrn Pines NC 1976-1978; Bd Epis Soc Serv Dio Connecticut Hartford CT 1969-1975; R The Par Of Emm Ch Weston CT 1966-1976; Evang Dio Maryland Baltimore MD 1961-1966; Ldrshp Trng Div DeptCE Dio Maryland Baltimore MD 1958-1966; Dir Sr HS Conf Dio Maryland Baltimore MD 1954-1959; Vic S Chris Epis Ch Linthicum Heights MD 1952-1966; Cur S Dav's Ch Baltimore MD 1950-1952. cve69@juno.com

LAFFLER, Brian Howard (Nwk) 72 Lodi St, Hackensack NJ 07601 **R S Anth Of Padua Ch Hackensack NJ 1990-** B Passaic NJ 9/20/1957 s Howard Laffler & Mary. BA Montclair St U 1980; MDiv GTS 1987. D 6/8/1987 Bp Robert Campbell Witcher Sr P 6/1/1988 Bp David Standish Ball. m 8/12/1979 Patricia Catherine Augenti. Cur S Geo's Epis Ch Schenectady NY 1987-1990. CBS, GAS, SSC.

LA FOLLETTE, Melvin Walker (RG) Po Box 778, Presidio TX 79845 B Evansville IN 9/7/1930 s Melvin Lester La Follette & Genevieve. BA U of Washington 1953; MA U of Iowa 1954; U CA 1957; MDiv/STB Ya Berk 1967; Fllshp ECF 1967. D 7/9/1967 Bp Walter M Higley P 2/1/1968 Bp Ned Cole. m 12/26/1958 Alice Louise Simpson c 2. Big Bend River Mnstry Albuquerque NM 1989-1994; Cn Mssnr Dio The Rio Grande Albuquerque NM 1984-1994; Trans Pecos Reg Epis Mnstry Alpine TX 1984-1989; Vic S Patricks Ch Kenwood CA 1971-1978; Assoc S Fran Epis Ch San Jose CA 1968-1971; Cur Epis Ch Of SS Ptr And Jn Auburn NY 1967-1968. Auth, "The Clever Body," Spenserian Press, San Francisco, 1959; Auth, "Poems And Stories," *Var Periodicals And Anthologies*, 1952. AAR 1976. Texas Rural Min Of The Year Texas A&M/Progressive Farmer mag 1990. padremel@llnet.net

LAFON, Alvin Paul (Los) 2691 Foxglove Loop Se, Albany OR 97322 B Cambridge MA 1/25/1927 s Louis George Lafon & Sophorina Ellen. BA Bos 1951; MDiv CDSP 1954; DIT S Aug's Coll Cbury GB 1965; Cert Coll of Preachers 1969. D 6/14/1954 P 12/21/1954 Bp Richard S Watson. m 12/11/1993 Dorothy Everroad c 3. Asst S Geo's Epis Ch Laguna Hills CA 1987-1998; The Cbury Pasadena CA 1985-1986; Kensington Epis Hm Alhambra CA 1976-1978; Assoc All SS Ch Pasadena CA 1973-1975; R S Mich's-On-The-Heights Worcester MA 1966-1973; R S Mk's Ch Leominster MA 1960-1966; Cur S Steph's Ch Pittsfield MA 1956-1960; Vic S Jn's Epis Ch Logan UT 1954-1956. Auth, *COP Fllshp Paper*; Auth, *Clergical Placement & Career Dvlpmt*; Auth, "Reordering a Ch for a More Meaningful Liturg Wrshp," *The Angl.* alafon@comcast.net

LAFON, Kirk David (ETenn) 950 Episcopal School Way, Knoxville TN 37932 **Assoc St Jas Epis Ch at Knoxville Knoxville TN 2011-; Chapl The Epis Sch Of Knoxville Knoxville TN 2010-** B Staunton VA 7/18/1972 s James David LaFon & Shirley Furr. BA U of Virginia 1994; MTS VTS 1998; MDiv The U So (Sewanee) 2010. D 5/29/2010 P 4/30/2011 Bp Charles Glenn VonRosenberg. m 6/17/1995 Kristan Dawson. lafon@esknoxville.org

LA FOND II, Charles Drummond (NH) 1023 Pleasant Street, Webster NH 03303 **Dio New Hampshire Concord NH 2008-** B Washington DC 8/29/1963 s Charles Drummond LaFond & Anne Margaret. BA U So 1986; MDiv VTS 2001. D 6/23/2001 P 12/29/2001 Bp Peter James Lee. Ch Of The Gd Shpd Nashua NH 2006-2008; Cur Ch Of Our Sav Charlottesville VA 2001-2003. clafond@nhepiscopal.org

LAFONTANT, Fritz Raoul (Hai) Eglise Street Pierre, Mirebalais Haiti B 7/25/1925 s Bores Lafontant & Elizabeth. D 7/10/1949 P 2/1/1950 Bp Charles Alfred Voegeli. m 1/31/1951 Yolande Racster. Dio Haiti Ft Lauderdale FL 1949-1990.

LAGANA, Gaye Lynn (Spok) PO Box 18917, Spokane WA 99228 B Pittsburgh PA 10/28/1943 d Leroy Donald Williard & Marie Katherine. BA Penn 1965; MA Immac Heart Coll 1980. D 6/7/2008 Bp James Edward Waggoner. m 2/18/1995 Stephen Lagana c 4. gayelagana@comcast.net

LAGER, Michael Alan (Ark) 16816 Summit Vista Way, Louisville KY 40245 **R S Jn's Epis Ch Ft Smith AR 2010-** B Saint Paul MN 8/22/1964 s Dennis Jack Lager & Judith Lou. BA Cntrl Bible Coll Springfield MO 1986; MA Assemblies of God TS 1987; MDiv Sthrn Louisville KY 1994; CAS GTS 1996. D 6/22/1996 P 1/18/1997 Bp Edwin Funsten Gulick Jr. m 6/22/1990 Kimberly Dawn Brack c 2. Stndg Com Dio Kentucky Louisville KY 2005-2006; Com Dio Kentucky Louisville KY 2001-2006; R S Thos Epis Ch Louisville KY 2000-2010; Asst R S Matt's Epis Ch Louisville KY 1996-2000. lager64@gmail.com

LAGOS, Hilda Marina (Hond) Municipio de Ojo de Agua, Departamento de el Paraiso, Tegucigalpa, 21105 Honduras **Died 10/14/2011** B 6/20/1954 d Marcelino Gonzolez & Dolores. DIT Seminario Diocesano. D 10/29/2005 Bp Lloyd Emmanuel Allen. m 3/19/1976 Jose Hector Zuniga Sevilla c 7.

LAHEY, Stephen Edmund (Neb) 1935 Sewell St, Lincoln NE 68502 **Assoc S Matt's Ch Lincoln NE 2006-; Assoc S Matt's Ch Lincoln NE 2004-; Assoc S Matt's Ch Lincoln NE 2004-; P Assoc S Matt's Ch Lincoln NE 2004-** B Philadelphia PA 12/2/1960 BA W Chester U of Pennsylvania 1986; MA U of Kansas 1990; PhD U of Connecticut 1997; CAS SWTS 2002. D 12/13/2003 Bp Gladstone Bailey Adams III P 9/21/2004 Bp Joe Goodwin Burnett. m 7/2/1994 Julia McQuillan c 1. Auth, "Jn Wyclif," Oxford Univ. Press, 2009; Auth, "Philos And Politics In The Thought Of Jn Wyclif," Cambridge Univ. Press, 2003; Auth, "Wyclif And Lollardy," The Medieval Theologians/Blackwell, 2001; Auth, "Wm Ockham And Trope Nominalism," Franciscan Stds Vol.55, 1998; Auth, "Wyclif On Rts," Journ Of The Hist Of Ideas Vol.58, 1997. Mem Phi Beta Kappa 2010. slahey3@unl.edu

✠ **LAI, Rt Rev Jung-Hsin** (Tai) 7, Lane 105, Hangchow S. Road Sec. 1, Taipei 10060 Taiwan B Cha-Yi TW 3/3/1948 s Bee-Yi Lai & Chou. MDiv Tainan Theol Coll TW 1975; ThM SE Asia TS 1993. D 3/23/1975 P 4/11/1976 Bp James T M Pong Con 11/25/2000 for Tai. m 9/2/1974 Shu-Ying Lin c 2. Auth, *Video Tape Land of Bible & Jesus*. skhtpe@ms12.hinet.net

LAI, Paul C (LI) 1321 College Point Blvd, College Point NY 11356 B Taiwan 9/21/1976 s Jung-Hsin Lai & Shu-Ying. BS Polytechnic U 1998; MDiv The GTS 2010. D 6/26/2010 P 6/4/2011 Bp Lawrence C Provenzano. m 3/12/2006 Lichia Yang c 2. plai01@yahoo.com

LAI, Peter Pui-Tak (LI) 1000 Washington Ave, Plainview NY 11803 B HK 4/24/1956 s Nelson Sai-Fan Lai & Pauline Po-Shan. BA U Sask 1980; MA U Tor 1986; Off Trng Sch 1995. D 1/15/1984 P 9/1/1985 Bp Pui-Yeung Cheung. m 10/21/2000 Christine M Lai c 1. S Marg's Ch Plainview NY 2004-2010; Chr Ch Worton MD 2001-2004; Off Of Bsh For ArmdF New York NY 1995-1998; Ch Of The Epiph Seattle WA 1994; Dio Olympia Seattle WA 1994; Ch Of The H Apos Seattle WA 1988-1994; Dio Massachusetts Boston MA 1984-1986. chrispeterlai@gmail.com

LAING, Christopher A (Ore) 8275 Sw Canyon Ln, Portland OR 97225 B Minneapolis MN 3/27/1944 s George Laing & Kathryn. Carleton Coll 1963; BA U MN 1966; MA U of Oregon 1968; MDiv Nash 1977. D 6/24/1977 P 2/24/1978 Bp Philip Frederick McNairy. m 9/13/1969 Judy Louise Torvend c 3. Portland Metro Epis Campus Mnstry Portland OR 1998-2006; S Gabr Ch Portland OR 1997-1999; R Ch Of The H Apos S Paul MN 1992-1997; H Trin Intl Falls MN 1991-1992; R S Phil's Ch S Paul MN 1987-1990; R Ch Of The H Comm S Ptr MN 1980-1984; S Andr's Epis Ch Waterville MN 1977-1980. *Revs & arts*, 2003. Conf Ord of S Ben 1977; Epis Ntwk Econ of Justice 1994-2000; EUC 1989-2000. Alumnini of Notable Achievement U MN Minnealopis Minnesota 1994. chris.27@comcast.net

LAINSON, Vinnie Van (Va) 9325 West Street, Manassas VA 20110 **Constitutions and Cn Dio Virginia Richmond VA 2009-2012; Assoc R Trin Ch Manassas VA 2000-** B Hastings NE 10/9/1953 d John Jennings Lainson & Phyllis Anne. BA Hastings Coll 1976; St. Geo's Coll, Jerusalem 1999; MDiv VTS 2000. D 12/7/2000 Bp David Colin Jones P 6/10/2001 Bp Peter James Lee. c 3. Exec Bd/Chair Dio Virginia Richmond VA 2005-2008; Cmsn Wmn/Mssn/Mnstry Dio Virginia Richmond VA 2002-2006. vlainson@trinityepiscopalchurch.org

LAIRD, I Bruce (Colo) 505 4th Street, Ouray CO 81427 B Wichita KS 8/3/1945 s David Golden Laird & Mary Elizabeth. BS K SU 1968; MDiv Epis TS of The SW 1987. D 6/9/1987 Bp Anselmo Carral-Solar P 2/1/1988 Bp Maurice Manuel Benitez. m 6/6/1964 Sherrie Lou Palmer. Mssnr - Wstrn Retion Dio Colorado Denver CO 1998-2002; R S Jn's Epis Ch Ouray CO 1994-2006; P-in-c S Mich's Ch Telluride CO 1994-2000; Vic Chr Epis Ch Mexia Mexia TX 1993-1994; S Ptr's Epis Ch Brenham TX 1989-1993; Asst R S Jas The Apos Epis Ch Conroe TX 1987-1989. bruceblaird@gmail.com

LAIRD, Joseph Headen (Pa) 523 Montgomery Ave, Haverford PA 19041 B Fort Wayne IN 12/7/1919 s Joseph Stanley Laird & Marion Josephine. BA Harv 1942; BD/MDiv VTS 1953. D 5/16/1953 Bp William P Roberts P 12/12/1953 Bp Joseph Gillespie Armstrong. m 1/4/1947 Shirley Jean Eder c 3. Asst Nevil Memi Ch Of S Geo Ardmore PA 1973-1975; Asst Chr Epis Ch Villanova PA 1969-1971; Conf Cntr Dio Pennsylvania Philadelphia PA 1963-1969; Dept CSR Dio Pennsylvania Philadelphia PA 1960-1967; ExCoun Dio Pennsylvania Philadelphia PA 1959-1961; DeptCE Dio Pennsylvania Philadelphia PA 1958-1967; Vic S Mk's Ch Honey Brook PA 1955-1963; Vic S Mary's Ch Warwick RI 1955-1963; Cur Ch Of The Redeem Bryn Mawr PA 1953-1955. Phi Beta Kappa 1942; Iota of Massachusetts Harvard Coll 1942. joseph.laird@verizon.net

LAIRD, Lucinda Rawlings (Ky) 330 N Hubbards Ln, Louisville KY 40207 **Trst & Coun Dio Kentucky Louisville KY 2002-; Com Dio Kentucky Louisville KY 1998-; R S Matt's Epis Ch Louisville KY 1997-** B New York NY 10/24/1952 d Carroll Walton Laird & Barbara Lee. BA Barnard Coll of Col 1979; MDiv GTS 1982. D 6/5/1982 P 12/1/1982 Bp Paul Moore Jr. Stndg Com Dio Newark Newark NJ 1996-1997; Stndg Com On Ecum Relatns Epis Ch Cntr New York NY 1995-2000; Dep Gc Dio Newark Newark NJ 1994-1997; Com Dio Newark Newark NJ 1991-1995; Dioc Coun Dio Newark Newark NJ 1989-1993; S Mk's Ch Teaneck NJ 1986-1997; R S Mk's Ch W Orange NJ 1986-1997; Asst Coll Min Cathd Of St Jn The Div New York NY 1984-1986; Asst Par Of Chr The Redeem Pelham NY 1982-1984. Auth, "Television Show Point Of View," 1991; Auth, "Chld'S Video Tell Me Why God". Ord Of S Helena, Assoc 1982. Bp Outstanding Serv Awd Dio Newark 1996; Hon Lifetime Cn Trin & S Phil'S Cathd. lucinda.laird@insightbb.com

LAIRD, Robert Charles (Minn) 316 E 88th St, New York NY 10128 **Lilly Fell Ch Of The H Trin New York NY 2010-** B Glenwood MN 3/11/1978 s Robert Alexander Laird & Elizabeth Woodward. BA Hamline U 2005; MDiv The GTS 2010. D 7/23/2009 Bp James Louis Jelinek. m 5/24/2008 Angela Beth Merrill. rc.laird@holytrinity-nyc.org

LAKE, Mark William (RG) 2602 S 2nd St, Tucumcari NM 88401 B Sac City IA 8/2/1949 s William John Lake & Anna Jean. BA U of Nthrn Iowa 1971; MDiv Dubuque Theo Sem 1980. D 9/18/2010 Bp William Carl Frey. m 12/27/1969 Beverly Lake c 3. nmgeezer@plateautel.net

LAKE JR, (Orloff) Levin (Chi) 8137 Blue Heron Dr E Apt 105, Wilmington NC 28411 B Chattanooga TN 8/3/1927 s Orloff Levin Lake & Hallie. BA SMU 1949; MDiv SWTS 1952. D 6/20/1952 Bp Charles A Mason P 12/22/1952 Bp Gerald Francis Burrill. m 9/19/2009 Jean Marie Lake c 3. Dn Joliet Deanry Dio Chicago Chicago IL 1988-1990; Search Com Dio Chicago Chicago IL 1983-1984; Nmntns Com Dio Chicago Chicago IL 1980-1986; Com Ecum Affrs Dio Chicago Chicago IL 1970-1976; R S Edw The Mtyr and Chr Epis Ch Joliet IL 1965-1990; Vic Ch Of The H Nativ Clarendon Hills IL 1955-1965; Vic Chr The King Epis Ch Ft Worth TX 1953-1955; Cur All SS' Epis Ch Ft Worth TX 1952-1953. lake-17706@hotmail.com

LAKEMAN, Thomas Edmund (CGC) 127 Oak Bend Ct, Fairhope AL 36532 B Clanton AL 5/17/1928 s Edmund Wulstan Lakeman & Pauline. BA Birmingham-Sthrn Coll 1951; ABT U of Alabama 1954; MDiv Epis TS of The SW 1959. D 6/11/1959 P 2/7/1960 Bp Albert R Stuart. m 8/18/1984 Linda C Lakeman c 6. Vic Imm Ch Bay Minette AL 1978-1980; R S Mich's Ch Mobile AL 1976-1978; Vic S Ptr's Ch Jackson AL 1972-1983; Vic All SS Epis Ch Mobile AL 1968-1976; Vic S Geo's Epis Ch Savannah GA 1961-1964; Vic Chr Epis Ch Cordele GA 1959-1961. Stff Sociol, "Resrch," *How a Cmnty Took Action to Dvlp a Comprehensive Hlth and Rehab Facility*, US Hlth and Rehab, 1972. edlakeman@aol.com

LA LIBERTE, Joan Louise (NY) Po Box 608, Fort Hall ID 83203 **S Jas Ch Callicoon NY 2001-** B Fort Sam Houston TX 10/29/1938 d Clarence Edmond LaLiberte & Louise Isabelle. BS Portland St U 1962; MDiv CDSP 1981. D 8/31/1981 Bp Everett H Jones P 11/1/1982 Bp David Bell Birney IV. S Andr's So Fallsburg Woodbourne NY 2010; Dio Idaho Boise ID 1999; Gd Shpd Ft Hall ID 1992-1999; Dio Idaho Boise ID 1985-1989; R S Jas Ch Payette ID 1982-1985. Natl Fed Press Wmn Awd Top Natl Writing 77; Inter Amer Press Assoc Fllshp To Latin Amer 74. joanlaliberte@gmail.com

LALONDE, Kathryn Nan (Pgh) 100 Great Pl Ne, Albuquerque NM 87113 B 9/17/1946 D 12/19/1992 P 10/19/1993 Bp Alden Moinet Hathaway. m 9/5/2004 Walter J LaLonde. Hope in the Desert Eps Ch Albuquerque NM 2001-2004; S Mk's On The Mesa Epis Ch Albuquerque NM 1993-2000. revkathy@comcast.net

LALOR, Donald Jene (Minn) No address on file. B 6/25/1932 D 5/16/1978 Bp Robert Marshall Anderson.

L

LAM, Connie Miu-Sheung (Cal) 4851 El Grande Pl, El Sobrante CA 94803 **Assoc P Chr Epis Ch Sei Ko Kai San Francisco CA 2011-** B Canton China 7/30/1955 d Yuet Wah Ng & Lai Lung. AS Contra Costa Coll 2002; BA Sch for Deacons 2005. D 6/3/2006 Bp William Edwin Swing P 6/2/2007 Bp Marc Handley Andrus. m 12/13/1981 Santos Lam c 1. Assoc P True Sunshine Par San Francisco CA 2007-2010; Asst Cler S Jas Epis Ch San Francisco CA 2006-2009. clams168@yahoo.com

LAM, Peter (LI) 33 Howard Pl, Waldwick NJ 07463 B HK 6/29/1942 s Chap Wing Lam & Sheh Wha. BA Hong Kong U Hk 1965; LTh UTS Hk 1971; MDiv Queens Coll 1976; MDiv GTS 1983. Trans from Hong Kong Anglican Church 8/9/1996 Bp Orris George Walker Jr. m 11/11/1972 Nancy Wai Ling Lo c 1. Auth, "The Ord Of H Comm w Explanation"; Auth, "Mus For The Morning," *Evening Prayers & H Comm*. fatherpeterlam

LAM, Vivian P (LI) 500 S Country Rd, Bay Shore NY 11706 B Hong Kong 11/3/1977 d Peter Lam & Nancy. BA NYU 1998; MDiv CDSP 2009. D 6/22/2009 Bp James Hamilton Ottley P 1/16/2010 Bp Lawrence C Provenzano. S Ptr's by-the-Sea Epis Ch Bay Shore NY 2009-2011. vivianplam@gmail.com

LA MACCHIA, James Robert (Mass) 25 Marlborough Road, PO Box 9105, Southborough MA 01772 **St. Mk's Sch of Southborough Inc. Southborough MA 2008-** B Brookline MA 2/3/1952 s Robert Anthony La Macchia & Elizabeth Marie. BA U of Massachusetts 1973; MA U of Massachusetts 1976; MA EDS 1990. D 10/15/1994 P 5/25/1995 Bp Douglas Edwin Theuner. Assoc S Chris's Ch Hampstead NH 1995-1998; Dio New Hampshire Concord NH 1994-1995; Asst S Dav's Ch Salem NH 1994-1995. Auth, "The Riches of the Word of God," Polygraphia Ltd., 2001. Contemplative Outreach 1999; NAES 1998; SBL/AAR 1998. cl Soc S Mk's Sch 1998; Phi Beta Kappa U of Mass at Amherst 1973; Commonwealth Schlr St of Massachusetts 1969. jameslamacchia@stmarksschool.org

LAMAZARES, Gabriel (Ore) 1704 NE 43rd Ave, Portland OR 97213 **S Mich And All Ang Ch Portland OR 2010-** B San Juan PR 12/27/1971 s Avelino Lamazares & Sara. BA Boston Coll 1992; MDiv The GTS 2010. D 6/19/2010 Bp Michael Bruce Curry P 1/8/2011 Bp Michael J Hanley. glamazares@gmail.com

L

LAMB, Jan (NC) 3064 Colony Rd Apt D, Durham NC 27705 B Hattiesburg MS 11/2/1951 BA Millsaps Coll 1973; Med U of Texas 1976. D 6/3/2006 Bp Michael Bruce Curry. c 2. janlamb@verizon.net

✠ **LAMB, Rt Rev Jerry Alban** (NCal) 1065 Villita Loop, Las Cruces NM 88007 **Provsnl Bp of San Joaquin Epis Dio San Joaquin Modesto CA 2008-** B Denver CO 9/4/1940 s Dale Morris Lamb & Mary Agnes. BA S Thos Sem 1964; MA S Thos Sem 1966; MA U of Oregon 1973; DD CDSP 1992. Rec from Roman Catholic 3/1/1977 as Deacon Bp Matthew Paul Bigliardi Con 6/9/1991 for NCal. m 8/7/1971 Jane Mary Lamb c 1. Dio Nthrn California Sacramento CA 1991-2006; Asst Dio Oregon Portland OR 1988-1991; Dn Sthrn Conv Dio Oregon Portland OR 1982-1988; R Trin Epis Ch Ashland Ashland OR 1980-1988; Dioc Coun Dio Oregon Portland OR 1979-1981; Asst Emm Ch Coos Bay OR 1978-1980; Asst S Mary's Epis Ch Eugene OR 1977-1978. bishopjal@msn.com

LAMB, Ridenour Newcomb (Ga) 2425 Cherry Laurel Ln., Albany GA 31705 B Albany GA 1/28/1949 d Robert Dixon Newcomb & Muriel Pace. AD/RN U of Nevada 1979; EFM U So 2007. D 6/13/2009 Bp Henry Irving Louttit. m 9/20/1969 Donald Lamb c 3. rlamb@ppmh.org

LAMB, Thomas Jennings (Chi) 503 Macon Dr, Rockford IL 61109 B Norwalk CT 4/4/1937 s Roger Henry Lamb & Dorothy Cathrine. BTh Queens Coll 1984. Trans from Anglican Church of Canada 10/19/1990 Bp Frank Tracy Griswold III. Vic S Bride's Epis Ch Oregon IL 1990-2008. lamb503@comcast.net

LAMB, Trevor Vanderveer (CFla) 316 Ocean Dunes Rd, Daytona Beach FL 32118 B Bayshore NY 3/25/1947 s Trevor Edgar Lamb & June Helen. BA Colg 1968; JD U Of Florida 1971. D 2/4/1976 Bp William Hopkins Folwell. m 2/7/1975 Edith Leah del Sol. D Gr Epis Ch Inc Port Orange FL 1979-1988; D S Mary's Epis Ch Daytona Bch FL 1976-1979.

LAMB, Watson Howard (Miss) 10701 Saint Francis Dr, Philadelphia MS 39350 **D S Fran Of Assisi Ch Philadelphia MS 2011-** B Greenwood MS 7/11/1985 s Henry Darby Lamb & Rebecca Raney. BA Mississippi St U 2007; MDiv The TS at the U So 2011. D 6/4/2011 Bp Duncan Montgomery Gray III. m Maria K I Maria Pigg c 2. whl711@gmail.com

LAMBERT, Gary Paul (Mil) 205 Nichols Rd, Monona WI 53716 **S Matt's Ch Kenosha WI 2011-; S Ptr's Ch W Allis WI 2009-** B Stevens Pt WI 7/3/1948 s Donald Paul Lambert & Aune Ingrid. BA MI SU 1976; MDiv SWTS 1986. D 6/14/1986 Bp James Winchester Montgomery P 12/13/1986 Bp Frank Tracy Griswold III. m 9/22/1973 Jeri S Sharpe c 3. S Edmunds Ch Milwaukee WI 2009-2011; S Aidans Ch Hartford WI 2008-2009; R S Lk's Ch Madison WI 1995-2008; Vic Gr Epis Ch Galena IL 1989-1995; Vic S Paul's Ch Savanna IL 1989-1995; Asst P S Ptr's Epis Ch Sycamore IL 1986-1990; Dio Chicago Chicago IL 1986-1988. 3rd OHC. gplambertpriest@gmail.com

LAMBERT, George A (Me) 259 Essex St. Apt. 3, Bansor ME 04401 **Int R S Jas Ch Old Town ME 2008-** B Springfield MA 6/13/1947 s Arthur Lambert & Evelyn R. M. Div. EDS 1992; R.A. NYU 1997. D 5/30/1992 P 5/1/1993 Bp David Elliot Johnson. m 5/24/1969 Judith Lambert c 2. Int S Geo's Epis Ch Sanford ME 2007-2008; Int Chr Ch Hyde Pk MA 1994-1997; Dio Massachusetts Boston MA 1992-1995; The Cathd Ch Of S Paul Boston MA 1992-1994. geolam1347@aol.com

LAMBERT, John Peck (Oly) 26621 128th Ave South East, Kent WA 98030 B Oklahoma City OK 2/1/1945 s Robinson McMillan Lambert & Page. BA U of Oklahoma 1967; MA U of Oklahoma 1968; MDiv VTS 1971. D 6/29/1971 P 12/18/1971 Bp Chilton Powell. m 1/25/1964 Martha Jean Bates c 3. R S Jas Epis Ch Kent WA 1996-2003; Int Emm Epis Ch Mercer Island WA 1994-1996; R Ch Of The Resurr Bellevue WA 1980-1993; Assoc All SS Epis Ch Kansas City MO 1976-1980; Asst Chr Epis Ch S Jos MO 1973-1976; Cur S Marg's Ch Lawton OK 1971-1973. Ord of S Helena - P Assoc. 1981; Ord of S Lk 1973; WBHS 1976. jlamb59@comcast.net

✠ LAMBERT, Rt Rev Paul Emil (Dal) 1439 Tranquilla Dr., Dallas TX 75218 **Bp Suffr Dio Dallas Dallas TX 2008-; Cn Dio Dallas Dallas TX 2002-** B Reno NV 5/19/1950 s Paul Emil Lambert & Norma Edna. BA San Francisco St U 1972; MDiv Nash 1975. D 6/24/1975 P 6/9/1976 Bp Victor Manuel Rivera Con 7/12/2008 for Dal. m 5/24/1975 Sally Lynne Nicholls c 3. R S Jas Epis Ch Texarkana TX 1987-2002; Assoc The Epis Ch Of The H Nativ Plano TX 1984-1987; R S Jn's Ch Great Bend KS 1981-1984; Asst The Epis Ch Of The Trsfg Dallas TX 1978-1981; Epis Dio San Joaquin Modesto CA 1977-1978; Vic S Andr's Ch Taft CA 1977-1978; S Mths Ch Oakdale CA 1975-1977; Cur S Paul's Epis Ch Modesto CA 1975-1977. Hon DD Nash TS 2009. psl@sbcglobal.net

LAMBERT, Richard Tippin (SwFla) 226 Kings Way, Saint Simons Island GA 31522 B Syracuse NY 9/17/1923 s Robert Stanley Lambert & Sylvia. BA Wms 1947; BD VTS 1950; DD STUSo 1975. D 6/22/1950 P 3/1/1951 Bp Henry W Hobson. Trin By The Cove Naples FL 1959-1979; R S Matt's Epis Ch Fairbanks AK 1955-1959; P S Steph's Ch Ft Yukon AK 1953-1955; Min in charge S Lk's Ch Granville OH 1950-1953. DEBLANGE@AOL.COM

LAMBERT, Robert Ira (Mil) 3200 S Hermon, Milwaukee WI 53207 B Los Angeles CA 3/10/1949 s Fred Alpheus Lambert & Rita Ann. AA Pasadena City Coll 1971; BA California St U 1973; MDiv Nash 1977; MS So Dakota St U 1991. D 11/4/1979 P 2/1/1981 Bp Walter H Jones. m 6/14/1986 Marie Gauthier. Int S Dunst's Ch Madison WI 2008-2010; Int S Lk's Ch Whitewater WI 2006-2008; Int S Andr's Ch Milwaukee WI 2004-2005; Int S Alb's Ch Sussex WI 2002-2004; R S Dav Of Wales Ch New Berlin WI 2000-2002; P-in-c S Pauls Epis Ch Arapahoe NE 1995-1999; P-in-c S Ptr's In The Vlly Lexington NE 1995-1999; P-in-c Chr Ch Chamberlain SD 1979-1983. LAMBERTHOME@YAHOO.COM

LAMBERT, Sally Anne (Ore) 8265 Sw Canyon Ln, Portland OR 97225 **D S Phil The D Epis Ch Portland OR 2002-** B Parsons KS 6/3/1938 d Dale E Foose & Sarah E. EFM STUSo; BA Washburn U 1960; MA Geo Fox U 1965. D 6/18/1983 Bp John Forsythe Ashby. c 2. D S Jas Epis Ch Tigard OR 1987-2002; D Chr Cathd Salina KS 1983-1987. dcnsal@comcast.net

LAMBERT III, William Jay (CFla) 204 N. Lee St., Leesburg FL 34748 **R S Jas Epis Ch Leesburg FL 2007-** B Detroit MI 10/2/1948 s William Jay Lambert & Louise Deputy. BA Rol 1970; MA U GA 1976; MDiv Nash 1981. D 6/29/1981 P 5/1/1982 Bp Emerson Paul Haynes. m 8/23/1969 May Ruth Berryhill c 3. Pres Stndg Com Dio Milwaukee Milwaukee WI 1996-1997; Cler Ldrshp Proj Dio Milwaukee Milwaukee WI 1995-1998; Fin Com Dio Milwaukee Milwaukee WI 1995-1997; R S Bon Ch Mequon WI 1990-2007; R S Ptr's Ch W Allis WI 1983-1990; Asst Calv Ch Indn Rocks Bch FL 1981-1983. stjimmy204@aol.com

LAMBORN, Amy Bentley (Ind) The General Theological Seminary, 440 West 21st Street, New York NY 10011 **Fac The GTS New York NY 2011-** B Dyersburg TN 7/24/1969 d Gordon Kenneth Bentley & Carolyn Sue. BA Un U Jackson TN 1991; MDiv STUSo 1996; PhD UTS (NYC) 2009. D 6/24/1997 Bp Edward Witker Jones. m 5/28/1994 Robert Cole Lamborn. Theol in Res Chr Ch Bronxville NY 2009-2011; R S Mk's Ch Plainfield IN 2000-2004; Cur Chr Ch Cathd Indianapolis IN 1998-2000; Asst Dio Indianapolis Indianapolis IN 1997-1998; Asst S Andr's Epis Ch Greencastle IN 1997-1998. lamborn@gts.edu

LAMBORN, Robert Cole (NY) 5030 Henry Hudson Pkwy E, Bronx NY 10471 **R Chr Ch Riverdale Bronx NY 2004-** B Fort Oglethorpe GA 8/14/1965 s Robert Mabon Lamborn & Elinor Cole. BA U GA 1987; MA Indiana U 1989; MDiv STUSo 1994; DMin VTS 2007. D 6/24/1994 P 3/29/1995 Bp Edward Witker Jones. m 5/28/1994 Amy Bentley c 1. Mem, Stndg Com Dio Indianapolis Indianapolis IN 1997-1999; R S Jn's Epis Ch Crawfordsville IN 1996-2004; Mem, Stewadship Cmsn Dio Indianapolis Indianapolis IN 1995-2000; Mem, Wrshp & Mus Cmsn Dio Indianapolis Indianapolis IN 1995-1997; Precentor Chr Ch Cathd Indianapolis IN 1994-1996. rlamborn1@verizon.net

LAMMING, Sarah Rebecca (Pa) 1801 W Diamond St, Philadelphia PA 19121 **Dio Pennsylvania Philadelphia PA 2011-; S Marg's Ch Annapolis MD 2011-** B Lincoln England 7/12/1977 d John Lamming & Sheila Margaret. BA

Middlesex U 2002; CTM Westcott Hse Cambridge GB 2004; CTM Westcott Hse Cambridge GB 2004. Trans from Church Of England 2/10/2011 Bp Charles Ellsworth Bennison Jr. Asst to the Vic Ch Of The Advoc Philadelphia PA 2010-2011. therevsarah@gmail.com

LAMONTAGNE, G(eorge) Allen (Eas) 111 Acorn Dr., Chestertown MD 21620 **R S Paul's Par Kent Chestertown MD 2006-** B Springfield MA 9/2/1950 s Robert James LaMontagne & Elizabeth. BA Barrington Coll 1975; MDiv Ya Berk 1994. D 6/10/1995 Bp Clarence Nicholas Coleridge P 1/20/1996 Bp Donald Purple Hart. c 2. R S Paul's Epis Ch Put-In-Bay OH 1998-2006; Cur Trin Ch Torrington CT 1995-1998. Berk's Grad Soc 1994. alamodelmarva@verizon.net

LAMPE, Christine Kay (WK) 710 N Main St, Garden City KS 67846 B Hanover KS 2/16/1951 d Alvin LeRoy Lampe & Virginia. BA Marymount Coll 1982; Masters K SU 1991. D 9/1/2007 Bp James Marshall Adams Jr. c 1. clampe1@cox.net

LAMPERT, Richard B (SwFla) 826 Hampton Wood Ct, Sarasota FL 34232 B Washington DC 2/13/1941 s James Lampert & Margery. BA Lawr 1964; MSW Boston Coll 1969; BD EDS 1970; DMin VTS 2000. D 6/14/1970 P 6/1/1971 Bp Ned Cole. m 11/21/1973 Molly Ann Shera c 3. Asst Ch Of The Redeem Sarasota FL 2009-2010; R The Epis Ch Of The Gd Shpd Venice FL 2001-2006; Gr Ch Un City NJ 1996-2001; Evang Cmsn Dio Minnesota Minneapolis MN 1990-1994; R S Jn The Evang S Paul MN 1988-1996; Urban Mssn Com Dio Massachusetts Boston MA 1985-1988; Vic S Steph's Epis Ch Boston MA 1983-1988; R Chr Ch Binghamton NY 1978-1983. Soc of S Jn the Evang 1985. rdmlampert@comcast.net

LANA, Jose Luis (LI) 1474 Bushwick Ave, Brooklyn NY 11207 B Los-Arcos Navarra ES 5/27/1934 s Fausto Lana & Maria Cruz. Irache Philos 1953; Alboldo Theol 1955; Bristol U 1962; GTS 1971; Caribbean Cntr for Advncd Stds 1975; GTS 1979. P Bp Robert Wilkes Ihloff. Dio Long Island Garden City NY 2001-2006; Iglesia Epis Del Buen Samaritano San Francisco CA 1979-1985; Dio California San Francisco CA 1978; Epis Sem Of The Caribbean Carolina PR 1972-1976.

LANCASTER, James Mansell (Miss) 2721 Brumbaugh Rd, Ocean Springs MS 39564 B Greenville MS 11/1/1940 s Archie Bedon Lancaster & Irma Louise. BS Delta St U 1964; MS U of Sthrn Mississippi 1974. D 1/4/2003 Bp Alfred Clark Marble Jr. m 8/5/1977 Emily Williams Lancaster.

LANCASTER, Robert Vaughan (WNY) 537 Cortez St., Sante Fe NM 87501 B Wilmington DE 2/23/1921 s Vaughan Collins Lancaster & Ida Pearl. BA U Of Delaware Newark 1946; MA U Of Delaware Newark 1949; BTh PDS 1955; PhD Syr 1974. D 7/23/1955 Bp John Brooke Mosley P 11/1/1955 Bp Russell S Hubbard. m 6/25/1943 Serena Weggenmann. Exec Coun Dio Wstrn New York Tonawanda NY 1963-1965; R Trin Ch Lancaster NY 1960-1965; Bec Dio Spokane Spokane WA 1958-1960; Vic S Ptr's Ch Pomeroy WA 1955-1960. Auth, "Ella Middleton Tybout:De Writer". Ord Of S Ben. rlanc@backspaces.net

LANCE, Philip J (Los) 1523 Gordon St, Apt 10, Los Angeles CA 90028 B Redlands CA 6/13/1959 s Wayne D Lance & Jessie Louise. BA Wheaton Coll 1981; MDiv GTS 1987. D 6/20/1987 P 1/1/1988 Bp Oliver Bailey Garver Jr. Pueblo Nuevo Epis Ch Los Angeles CA 1993-2001; Dio Los Angeles Los Angeles CA 1987-1992. plance@pueblonuevo.org

LANCTOT, Merv(yn) J (Me) 832 Wicklow St., Winnipeg MB R3T 0H7 Canada B Melfort Sask Canada 6/30/1954 BA Can Nazarene Coll 1991; BTh St. Paul U Ottawa ON CA 1995. Trans from Anglican Church of Canada 8/9/2003 Bp Chilton Abbie Richardson Knudsen. m 4/26/1974 Susan E Lanctot c 2. S Matt's Epis Ch Lisbon ME 2003-2005. lanctotinmaine@aol.com

LANDER, Barbara Temple (ND) 319 S 5th St, Grand Forks ND 58201 B Denver CO 5/24/1928 d Wesley Temple & Ethel M. DSW Stephens Coll 1948; Grad U Denv 1956. D 10/8/1999 Bp Andrew Hedtler Fairfield. c 1. revlander@yahoo.com

LANDER III, James Rollin (Oly) 1101 E Terrace St. #202, Seattle WA 98122 **Vic S Columba's Epis Ch And Chilren's Sch Kent WA 2010-** B Minneapolis MN 11/10/1976 s James Rollin Lander & Donna Kay. BA Emory U 1998; MDiv GTS 2003; MPA U of Washington 2009. D 8/17/2003 P 3/13/2004 Bp J(ohn) Neil Alexander. Assoc R for Chr Formation S Augustines In-The-Woods Epis Par Freeland WA 2007-2009; Assoc R S Alb's Epis Ch Los Angeles CA 2003-2004. jameslander@gmail.com

LANDER, Stephen King (Minn) 5029 Girard Ave S, Minneapolis MN 55419 B Grand Forks ND 1/16/1951 s Edward King Lander & Barbara Temple. MA Antioch/W 1983; PhD Cntr For Psychol Study Albane CA 1993; MDiv SWTS 2002. D 6/15/2002 P 12/17/2002 Bp James Louis Jelinek. m 8/27/2008 Bejamin Dann Lander c 2. S Jn The Bapt Epis Ch Minneapolis MN 2007; Int S Clem's Ch S Paul MN 2005-2006; Int S Matt's Ch St Paul MN 2004; Int S Jn In The Wilderness White Bear Lake MN 2002-2003. sbcm@earthlink.net

LANDERS, Davidson Texada (Ala) 5220 Midway Cir, Tuscaloosa AL 35406 B New Orleans LA 11/23/1943 s Edward Leslie Landers & Mary Vance. BA Louisiana Coll 1966; MDiv STUSo 1970. D 6/22/1970 P 5/1/1971 Bp Iveson Batchelor Noland. c 3. Int S Barth's Epis Ch Florence AL 2002-2003; R S Lk's Ch Scottsboro AL 1998-2001; Ch Of The Adv Nashville TN 1988-1997; R S Andr's Epis Ch Collierville TN 1979-1988; Assoc Gr - S Lk's Ch Memphis TN 1975-1979; R S Phil's Ch New Orleans LA 1973-1975; Cur S Andr's Epis Ch New Orleans LA 1971-1973; Vic S Paul's Ch Winnfield LA 1970-1971. Pres St. Lk's Soc, U So, TS 1970; Pres St. Lk's Soc, U So, TS New Orleans 1969. davidsonlanders@comcast.net

LANDERS JR, Edward Leslie (Tenn) 6536 Jocelyn Hollow Rd, Nashville TN 37205 B Alexandria LA 11/24/1935 s Edward Leslie Landers & Mary Vance. BA Louisiana Coll 1958; MDiv STUSo 1965; DD Van 1969. D 6/24/1965 Bp Iveson Batchelor Noland P 5/1/1966 Bp Girault M Jones. m 6/18/1958 Carolyn Craig c 2. Cov Assn Inc Nashville TN 1994-1995; Chf Admin Dio Tennessee Nashville TN 1991-1993; Dio Tennessee Nashville TN 1986-1993; Asst To Bp Dio Tennessee Nashville TN 1985-1991; Urban & Reg Mnstry Nashville TN 1977-1985; Chr Ch Cathd Nashville TN 1975-1977. Auth, "Plnng Skills For Profsnl Ministers". ESMA, Epis Fam Netwk. Outstanding Cmnty Proj Ford Fndt. elanders2001@comcast.net

LANDERS, Gail Joan (Md) 303 North Main Street, Bel Air MD 21014 B Baltimore MD 12/16/1958 d James Hiriam Robertson & Myrtle Gertrude. AA Essex Cmnty Coll 1977. D 6/6/2009 Bp John Leslie Rabb. m 8/9/1997 Michael Landers c 4. gjlanders@verizon.net

LANDERS, Gregory LeRoy (NY) 2150 Baileys Corner Rd, Wall Township NJ 07719 B Cayonville OR 10/8/1953 s Marvin L Landers & Pauline Frances. BA Portland St U 1980; MDiv GTS 1983; MS CUNY 1985. D 10/24/1984 Bp Paul Moore Jr P 11/23/1985 Bp Walter Decoster Dennis Jr. gregorywyatt@optonline.net

LANDERS, Kay Marie (Cal) 25307 Belhaven St, Hayward CA 94545 **Chair Dio California San Francisco CA 2000-** B Oakland CA 6/13/1935 d Edward Bennet Finley & Leah Catherine. BA San Francisco St U 1979; MA Wheaton Coll 1979; BTh Sch for Deacons 1997. D 6/7/1997 Bp William Edwin Swing. m 6/17/1956 David Leonard Landers c 3. D All SS Epis Ch San Leandro CA 1997-2001. Auth, "Clutched From Cler Reserves," Chapl Today, 2002; Auth, "God'S Fuel," Mavian Holdings Ltd., 1998; Auth, "A Heart For God," Sekand Printing Co, 1994; Auth, "I Wonder What'S Going To Happen?," Wrld Radio Mssy Fllshp, 1991; Auth, "Landscape Of The Poor," Wrld Radio Mssy Fllshp, 1988; Auth, "Catch A Wild Pony," Wrld Radio Mssy Fllshp, 1986; Auth, "Antenna Country," Moody Press, 1972. Assn Profsnl Chapl 1997. Caregiver Of The Year Alameda Cnty Med Cntr 2002. klanders@comcast.net

LANDERS, Sylvia C (Neb) 206 Westridge Drive, Norfolk NE 68701 **D Trin Epis Ch Norfolk NE 1989-** B Minden NE 10/12/1935 d Clarence Andrew Christensen & Hildur. Nebraska St Coll 1955; EFM STUSo 1987. D 8/25/1989 Bp James Daniel Warner. m 9/17/1987 Larry Ray Jones c 3. Liturg Cmsn Dio Nebraska Omaha NE 1996-2006; Exec Cmsn Dio Nebraska Omaha NE 1990-1994; Bp Search Com Dio Nebraska Omaha NE 1989-1990; EFM Mentor Dio Nebraska Omaha NE 1987-1996. NAAD 1989. landers@inebraska.com

LANDIS, Richard Delano (ETenn) 113 Gardner St, Chattanooga TN 37411 B Chattanooga TN 2/16/1926 s Frederick Delano Landis & Ethel. No Carolina St U; BBA U Of Chattanooga 1949. D 7/24/1977 Bp William F Gates Jr P 1/29/1978 Bp William Evan Sanders. m 2/21/1947 Martha May Fraker. Gr Ch Chattanooga TN 1988-2004; Vic S Mk's Ch Copperhill TN 1978-1988. dnmlandis@aol.com

LANDON, Harold Ransom (NY) 90 La Salle St Apt 12-A, New York NY 10027 B Cleveland OH 8/19/1912 s Harry Hill Landon & Mary Louise. BA Denison U 1934; MDiv UTS 1938; MA Col 1968. D 1/20/1944 P 9/1/1944 Bp Beverley D Tucker. Cathd Of St Jn The Div New York NY 1958-1978; DRE Chr Ch Greenville Wilmington DE 1952-1955; R S Paul's Ch Steubenville OH 1946-1952; D S Thos' Epis Ch Port Clinton OH 1943-1946. Auth, "Reinhold Niebuhr Aprophetic Voice In Our Time," *Our Time*, 1963; Auth, "Living Thankfully," 1962.

LANDRETH, Robert Dean (Mass) 7 Mechanic Sq, Marblehead MA 01945 **Assoc Wyman Memi Ch of St Andr Marblehead MA 1999-** B Modesto CA 7/20/1926 s Clifton Gerald Landreth & Zala A. BA San Jose St U 1950; MA San Jose St U 1957. D 6/19/1966 Bp James Albert Pike P 5/28/1981 Bp Charles Shannon Mallory. m 7/8/1950 Jean Emerson Miller. Vic Ch Of The H Sprt Campbell CA 1994-1998; COM Dio El Camino Real Monterey CA 1984-1998; Assoc S Fran Epis Ch San Jose CA 1981-1998. The Bp's Cross Bp Richard Shimpfy 1995. rdlandreth@comcast.net

LANDRITH, Richard Stanley (EO) 123 S G St, Lakeview OR 97630 **diocesean Coun Dio Estrn Oregon The Dalles OR 2005-; P-in-c S Lk's Ch Lakeview OR 2005-** B 1/17/1949 s Richard Landrith & Margaret Jean. Arizona St U; BA U Of Idaho Moscow 1974. D 2/2/1991 Bp James Edward Krotz P 7/12/2005 Bp William O Gregg. m 5/31/1998 Marsha Landrith. rslandrith@gmail.com

LANDRY, Bradley Jackson (Ala) 208 Eustis Ave SE, Huntsville AL 35801 **Asst Ch Of The Nativ Epis Huntsville AL 2010-** B Columbia, MO 4/3/1981 s Larry Jackson Landry & Janine Sue. BA Samford U 2003; MDiv The TS at The U So 2010. D 5/19/2010 Bp Henry Nutt Parsley Jr P 12/7/2010 Bp John

McKee Sloan. m 5/25/2002 Rebecca Elizabeth Lewallen c 2. bradleylandry@gmail.com

LANDRY, Joseph Francis (LI) 1032 Preakness Blvd, Indian Trail NC 28079 **Died 7/31/2010** B Fishers Island NY 12/10/1927 s Alfred Landry & Florence. Ba, Bd, Ma, Pd Cert Psychol. Rec from Roman Catholic 6/1/1972 Bp Charles Waldo MacLean.

LANDRY, Robert Wayne (Me) 42 Spruce St, East Millinocket ME 04430 **D S Andr's Ch Millinocket ME 2005-** B Bangor ME 1/25/1954 s Edgar Norman Landry & Mary June. BD U of Maine 2004; Bangor TS 2005. D 5/22/2005 Bp Chilton Abbie Richardson Knudsen. m 5/14/1977 Catherine Landry c 3. fojc1@myfairpoint.net

LANDWER, Virginia Bess (SeFla) 401 66th Street Ocean, Marathon FL 33050 **S Columba Epis Ch Marathon FL 2000-** B Platterville WI 6/17/1929 D 10/17/2000 Bp Leopold Frade. vlandwer@digitalsail.com

LANE III, Edward Jacob (Ky) PO Box 1282, Radcliff KY 40159 B Jackson MI 8/28/1948 s Jacob E Lane & Mary. AA Baker Coll 1970; Dio Kentucky Sch of Mnstry 2009. D 4/17/2010 Bp Edwin Funsten Gulick Jr. m 5/31/1997 Shirley Lane.

LANE JR, H(oward) Arthur (Mass) Po Box 363, Orleans MA 02653 **Died 2/5/2011** B Boston MA 1/17/1916 s H(oward) A Lane & Grace Prockway. BA Br 1939; MDiv EDS 1955. D 6/24/1955 P 3/1/1956 Bp John S Higgins. Auth, "mag arts". Ecum Cmnty Of Jesus.

LANE, John Charles (Oly) 311 Ridge Dr, Port Townsend WA 98368 **D Dio Olympia Seattle WA 1975-; Stdng Com Dio Spokane Spokane WA 1971-** B Nampa ID 1/2/1938 s Irvin Walter Lane & Priscilla Belle. U of Washington 1958; BA The Coll of Idaho 1961. D 5/14/1972 Bp John Raymond Wyatt. m 12/26/1958 Jacqueline K Gleason c 4. Dir Dioc Corp Dio Spokane Spokane WA 1972-1975. Auth, "Forum For Contemporary Hist"; Auth, "Bank Admin".

LANE, John David (SwVa) 307 Rainbow Dr, Staunton VA 24401 B Princeton NJ 9/24/1944 s Howard Rich Lane & Doris Andrews. BA Amh 1966; MDiv GTS 1972; DMin Drew U 1991. D 6/3/1972 Bp Paul Moore Jr P 12/9/1972 Bp Horace W B Donegan. m 9/4/1971 Elizabeth Bartelink c 3. Ret Trin Ch Staunton VA 1987-2007; R Chap Of The H Comf New Orleans LA 1975-1987; Cur Ch Of The H Comf Charlotte NC 1972-1975. Ed, "Two - Five - Oh," Heritage, 1996; Ed, "Plain Preaching," Heritage, 1996; Ed, "Trin Ch as an Instrument of Serv in the Staunton Area," U of Michigan, 1991. jdlrfd@comcast.net

LANE, Johnny (Ga) Route #4, Leslie Road, Box 1455, Americus GA 31709 **D The Epis Ch Of S Jn And S Mk Albany GA 1999-; D Calv Ch Americus GA 1990-** B Clay Sink FL 11/11/1933 s John Hubert Lane & Pearl Dean. BS U Of Florida 1960. D 11/11/1990 Bp Harry Woolston Shipps. m 12/16/1978 Elizabeth H Lewis c 4.

LANE, Joseph Andrew (Cal) 1048 Susan Way, Novato CA 94947 **Vic Ch Of The Redeem San Rafael CA 2010-** B Pine Bluff AR 4/13/1954 s Ethiel John Lane & Maxine. BA U of Arkansas 1976; MDiv CDSP 1995; DMin SWTS 2011. D 6/3/1995 P 6/1/1996 Bp William Edwin Swing. m 11/4/2008 Jay Edward Framson. P Assoc S Bede's Epis Ch Menlo Pk CA 2008-2010; R Gd Shpd Epis Ch Belmont CA 2000-2008; Assoc R S Bede's Epis Ch Menlo Pk CA 1997-2000; Cur/Asst R S Matt's Epis Ch San Mateo CA 1995-1997. josephlane@pacbell.net

LANE, Keith Cecil (NY) 487 Hudson St, New York NY 10014 B The Bronx NY 3/23/1948 s Cecil Lane & Zelphia. MDiv The GTS; BA The New Sch U 2008. D 3/5/2011 P 9/10/2011 Bp Mark Sean Sisk. m 5/7/1968 Marion Dineen c 2. mlane3@nyc.rr.com

LANE III, Lewis Calvin (CFla) PO Box 95, Franklin LA 70538 **S Mary's Ch Franklin LA 2011-** B Rocky Mount NC 1/29/1980 s Lewis Calvin Lane & Ann Drew. BA U NC 2002; PhD U of Iowa 2010; MTS Nash 2011. D 6/11/2011 Bp Hugo Luis Pina-Lopez. m 7/24/2010 Denise D Kettering-Lane. lcalvinlane@gmail.com

LANE, Nancy Upson (CNY) D 6/11/1983 Bp Ned Cole P 4/10/1984 Bp O'Kelley Whitaker.

LANE, Peter Austin (NH) 35 Long Meadow Drive, East Greenwich RI 02818 **Int S Dav's On The Hill Epis Ch Cranston RI 2011-** B East Providence RI 6/23/1957 s Howard Arthur Lane & Elinor Nancy. BA U of New Hampshire 1982; Cert. in Ethics Kennedy Sch of Ethics at Georgetown U. 1997; MDiv VTS 1998. D 6/13/1998 Bp Philip Alan Smith P 2/27/1999 Bp Douglas Edwin Theuner. m 9/25/1993 Kate Reed c 2. Vic Ch Of Our Sav Monroe WA 2009-2011; COM Dio New Hampshire Concord NH 2002-2007; Vic Trin Ch Hampton NH 2000-2008; Cur Trin Ch Newport RI 1998-2000. "Reaching Out: Pstr Care w The Elderly," Self-Pub, 1997. palane3@cox.net

LANE, Peter Carlson (Chi) 4945 S Dorchester Ave, Chicago IL 60615 **R Ch Of S Paul And The Redeem Chicago IL 2010-** B Oak Park IL 2/21/1977 s Robert Whitman Lane & Patricia Carlson. BA U Chi 1999; MDiv PrTS 2003; STM GTS 2007. D 6/9/2007 Bp Charles Ellsworth Bennison Jr P 12/15/2007 Bp Victor Alfonso Scantlebury. m 7/3/1999 Erin Pfautz c 2. Asst Ch Of S Paul And The Redeem Chicago IL 2007-2010. pcl@sp-r.org

✠ **LANE, Rt Rev Stephen Taylor** (Me) 84 Parsons Rd., Portland ME 04103 **Bp of Maine Dio Maine Portland ME 2008-** B Batavia NY 6/19/1949 s William Taylor Lane & Elizabeth. BA U Roch 1971; MDiv CRDS 1978. D 10/28/1978 P 5/1/1979 Bp Robert Rae Spears Jr Con 5/3/2008 for Me. m 7/10/1976 Gretchen J Farnum c 3. Cn Dio Rochester Rochester NY 2000-2008; R Zion Epis Ch Palmyra NY 1985-2000; Assoc Chr Ch Corning NY 1984-1985; Ch of the Redeem Addison NY 1979-1983; Asst Chr Ch Corning NY 1978-1983. DD Bex 2008; Cler Ldrshp Proj 1995; Rossiter Schlr Bex Rochester NY 1983. slane@episcopalmaine.org

LANE, Steve (WNY) 371 Delaware Ave, Buffalo NY 14202 **D Trin Epis Ch Buffalo NY 2009-** B 8/18/1958 s Warren Wilson Lane & Virginia. BS U of Arizona 1985. D 6/29/2008 Bp J Michael Garrison. m 5/21/1985 Ellyn Zahn c 3. slane.deacon@gmail.com

LANE, Warren Wilson (WNY) 194 Windsor Ave, Buffalo NY 14209 **Died 12/16/2009** B Baltimore MD 10/13/1928 s Emory Wilson Lane & Margaret Sedgewick. BA U Chi 1946; BA U Denv 1949; UTS 1951; BD EDS 1952; PhD PrTS 1969. D 6/19/1952 Bp Lauriston L Scaife P 2/19/1953 Bp Harold L Bowen. c 4. warrenwlane@verizon.net

LANE, Wendy DeFoe (Chi) 1775 W Newport Ct, Lake Forest IL 60045 B Norwalk CT 3/18/1941 d Warner Frederick Defoe & Patricia Margaret. BA Barat Coll 1997; MDiv SWTS 2000. D 12/21/2000 P 6/26/2001 Bp William Dailey Persell. m 7/14/1962 Charles A Lane c 2. Assoc R The Ch Of The H Sprt Lake Forest IL 2004-2010; Assoc R S Simons Ch Arlington Heights IL 2001-2004. wendydefoelane@comcast.net

LANE SR, Wilfred (Ak) Po Box 269, Kotzebue AK 99752 B Pt Hope AK 8/5/1940 s Lennie Lane & Daisy. D 6/29/1975 P 5/5/1976 Bp David Rea Cochran. m 9/1/1965 Vivian S Carter.

LANE, William Benjamin (Be) 614 Loveville Rd., B-1-I, Hockessin DE 19707 **Int Cathd Ch Of S Jn Wilmington DE 2006-** B Baltimore MD 8/12/1938 s William Benjamin Lane & Bessie Genevieve. BA U of Maryland 1960; MDiv VTS 1963. D 7/26/1963 Bp Noble C Powell P 6/11/1964 Bp Harry Lee Doll. m 8/5/1967 Beverly George Butler c 1. Eccl Crt Dio Bethlehem Bethlehem PA 1998-2006; Dn Cathd Ch Of The Nativ Bethlehem PA 1997-2005; Chr Ch Greenville Wilmington DE 1986-1997; Dio Delaware Wilmington DE 1980-1985; S Nich' Epis Ch Newark DE 1975-1980; Vic S Jas' Epis Ch Parkton MD 1968-1975; Asst Ch Of The Mssh Baltimore MD 1963-1967. laneiii@hotmail.com

LANEY, Mary Elizabeth (Pa) 3010 Gowan Ln, Lafayette Hill PA 19444 **Par Assoc S Chris's Ch Gladwyne PA 2005-** B Philadelphia PA 7/12/1941 d William Erskin Selby & Evelyn Elizabeth. BA Tem 1983; MDiv GTS 1986. D 6/21/1986 P 6/29/1987 Bp Allen Lyman Bartlett Jr. m 10/15/1960 Earl William John c 3. GC Dep Dio Pennsylvania Philadelphia PA 2003-2009; Stndg Com Mem Dio Pennsylvania Philadelphia PA 1997-2007; Vic S Gabr's Epis Ch Philadelphia PA 1989-2004; D S Thos' Ch Whitemarsh Ft Washington PA 1986-1989. OHC 1981-2003. revmlaney@aol.com

LANG, Anne Adele (FdL) 1900 Carriage Ln, Appleton WI 54914 **D All SS Epis Ch Appleton WI 2004-** B Milwaukee WI 1/26/1949 d John A Stenz & Dorothy Mary. BS U of Wisconsin 1981; MS U of Wisconsin 1983. D 11/6/2004 Bp Russell Edward Jacobus. c 3.

LANG, Ellen Davis (SD) 111 W 17th St Apt 450, Sioux Falls SD 57104 **Supply P Dio So Dakota Sioux Falls SD 2005-** B Norfolk VA 12/27/1939 d Fredrick Graham Davis & Ellen Inez. BS Jas Madison U 1961; MDiv Ya Berk 1988. D 6/9/1990 P 10/7/1991 Bp Arthur Edward Walmsley. c 2. Vic S Paul's Ch Plainfield CT 1991-2005; Cur Chr Ch Ansonia CT 1990-1991. eidlang@msn.com

LANG, Martha Ellen (Ia) 2101 Nettle Ave, Muscatine IA 52761 **D New Song Epis Ch Coralville IA 2004-** B Bloomfield IA 4/6/1954 d C L Lang & Z Elexene. D 11/22/1999 Bp Carl Christopher Epting. D Trin Ch Muscatine IA 1999-2004. melang54@yahoo.com

LANG, Nicholas Gerard (Ct) 14 France St, Norwalk CT 06851 **R Par of St Paul's Ch Norwalk Norwalk CT 2003-** B Orange NJ 6/15/1948 s Eugene Joseph Lang & Josephine Theresa. Seton Hall U 1970; S Andr's TS Jamaica NY 1973; BS U Of Bridgeport 1988; MS U Of Bridgeport 1989; PhD Cpu San Raphael CA 1997. Rec from Roman Catholic 1/13/1993 as Priest Bp Arthur Edward Walmsley. Par of St Paul's Ch Norwalk Norwalk CT 1993-1999. padrenick@aol.com

LANG, Thomas Andrew (Ore) 2812 Ne Kaster Dr, Hillsboro OR 97124 **D S Gabr Ch Portland OR 2004-** B Patuyent NAS 4/22/1958 s William Lang & Mary. D 9/18/2004 Bp Johncy Itty. m 6/20/1981 Kathy Lynn Lang c 2. tandklang@comcast.net

LANGDELL, Melissa Christina (Los) 144 S. C St, Oxnard CA 93030 **Int P-in-c All SS Epis Ch Oxnard CA 2011-** B London UK 3/25/1981 d Timothy Richard Langdell & Cheri Colby. BA Vassar Colleg 2003; MDiv CDSP 2009. D 6/6/2009 Bp Sergio Carranza-Gomez P 1/9/2010 Bp Chester Lovelle Talton. Cur All SS Epis Ch Riverside CA 2009-2011. Fran Toy Preaching Awd CDSP 2009. revmelissalangdell@gmail.com

LANGDON, Clarence Merle (Chi) 1249 Hedgerow Dr, Grayslake IL 60030 **Mnstry Dvlpmt Dio Chicago Chicago IL 2001-** B Fowler CO 12/13/1936 s Ronald Langdon & Adadah Jesse. BA Colorado St Coll 1959; STB GTS 1962; U Chi 1968; DMin McCormick TS 1985. D 6/18/1962 P 12/1/1962 Bp Joseph Summerville Minnis. m 5/23/2005 Drew Ann Drout c 3. Dn Elgin Deanry Dio Chicago Chicago IL 1990-2001; S Mary's Ch Pk Ridge IL 1976-2001; R Gr Epis Ch Freeport IL 1970-1976; R S Geo/S Mths Ch Chicago IL 1965-1970; Cur Ch Of The Ascen Pueblo CO 1962-1965. clangdon@episcopalchicago.org

LANGDON, David Stetson (Miss) PO Box 40, Parchman MS 38738 B Norfolk NY 2/27/1939 s Walter Crosby Langdon & Ada. STB GTS 1965; DMin Drew U 1977; Cert Assn of Prot Chapl 1985; Cert ACPE 1987; Cert ACPE 1987; Cert Coll of Chapl 1987; STM STUSo 1999; MTS Sprg Hill Coll Moblie 2006; MA Sprg Hill Coll Moblie 2010. D 6/12/1965 P 12/18/1965 Bp Charles Bowen Persell Jr. m 5/26/1990 Louise M Landingham c 4. Ch Of The Nativ Greenwood MS 1999-2003; Vic S Paul's Ch Hollandale MS 1998-2008; S Geo's Epis Ch Clarksdale MS 1996-1998; Dio Mississippi Jackson MS 1994-1995; Asst All SS Epis Ch Lakeland FL 1993-1994; Int S Fran Of Assisi Epis Ch Lake Placid FL 1991-1992; Wm Crane Gray Inn For Old People Davenport FL 1987-1990; R S Mk's Ch Malone NY 1981-1986; Dio Albany Albany NY 1976-1978; Ch Of The Gd Shpd Elizabethtown NY 1966-1981; S Jn's Ch Essex NY 1966-1981; Cur S Steph's Ch Schenectady NY 1965-1967. Auth, "The Episcopate of Theo DuBose Bratton," *Third Bp of Mississippi*, U So, 1999; Auth, *Quality Assurance in Gerontological Chapl*, APC, 1990; Auth, "Sailing & Gerontology," *BGI News*, 1987; Auth, *Cnfrmtn in a Rural Par*, U. Microfilms, 1973. Epis Chapl 1993; OHC 1959. bonequrusher@yahoo.com

LANGE, Charles Edward (WMass) 3939 Rainroper Dr, Bozeman MT 59715 B New York NY 5/2/1931 s Arnold Herman Lange & Dorothy. BA Wms 1953; MDiv EDS 1956; UTS 1961; MA UTS 1961; MA CUNY 1971. D 6/21/1956 P 1/6/1957 Bp William A Lawrence. c 2. S Jn's Ch Larchmont NY 1983-1984; Asst P Par Of Chr The Redeem Pelham NY 1965-1967; Asst R S Jn's Ch Williamstown MA 1956-1958. Grad Fell EDS Cambridge MA 1961. lange71boze@msn.com

LANGENFELD, Robert Joseph (Minn) 615 Vermillion St, Hastings MN 55033 **P S Lk's Epis Ch Hastings MN 2010-** B Hastings MN 5/15/1951 s Frank M Langenfeld & Leona. D 6/24/2009 P 1/9/2010 Bp James Louis Jelinek. rjlangenfeld1951@embargmail.com

LANGE-SOTO, Anna Beatriz (Cal) 1503 E Campbell Ave, Campbell CA 95008 **Vic Dio California San Francisco CA 1998-** B Douglas AZ 4/5/1952 d Harry Burton Lange & Beatriz. BA Stan 1974; MBA Santa Clara U 1989; BTh Dio El Camino Real Sch for Deacons 1995. D 11/20/1993 P 11/18/1997 Bp Richard Lester Shimpfky. m 11/23/2009 Russell L Briggs. P Dio Arizona Phoenix AZ 1998; Campus Min Trin Cathd San Jose CA 1996-1998. Cltn of Epis Latinos 2010; Integrity 1998. St. Steph's Cross Dio of CA Sch for Deacons 1995. ablange@aol.com

LANGFELDT, John Addington (EO) 744 E 20th St, The Dalles OR 97058 B Cedar Rapids IA 8/22/1936 s Lawrence Ralph Langfeldt & Mary Lenore. BA U of Washington 1960; MDiv CDSP 1964. D 6/29/1964 Bp William F Lewis P 3/9/1965 Bp Ivol I Curtis. m 9/5/1985 Harriet G Hume. R Emer S Pauls Epis Ch The Dalles OR 1999; R S Pauls Epis Ch The Dalles OR 1988-1998; Exec Coun Appointees New York NY 1983-1988; Vic S Pat's Ch Incline Vill NV 1972-1983; Vic S Jn's In The Wilderness Ch Glenbrook NV 1972-1980; Chapl S Mk's Chap Salt Lake City UT 1971-1972; Vic Ch Of The Resurr Centerville UT 1967-1971; Cur S Mk's Cathd Seattle WA 1964-1967. Auth, "Arabian Archeol & Epigraphy," 1994; Auth, "Recently Discovered Early Chr Monuments In NE Arabia," *Arabian Archeol & Epigraphy*. ASOR; SBL. abunajn@gmail.com

LANGFORD, Thomas William (Spr) 873 S Park Ave, Springfield IL 62704 **Fin Com Dio Springfield Springfield IL 2011-; COM, Chairman Dio Springfield Springfield IL 2009-; Dn, Sch for Mnstry Dio Springfield Springfield IL 2008-; D Trin Ch Jacksonville IL 1996-** B Pittsburgh PA 11/16/1937 s Thomas William Langford & Anna. Carnegie Inst of Tech 1957; BS U of Pennsylvania 1962; MBA U of Pennsylvania 1964; PhD U of Pennsylvania 1976. D 11/22/1988 Bp Donald Maynard Hultstrand. m 7/24/1980 Elisabeth Lenore Braithwaite c 3. Fin & Admin Dio Springfield Springfield IL 1999-2004; D S Lk's Ch Springfield IL 1993-1996; D Chr Ch Springfield IL 1990-1993; D The Cathd Ch Of S Paul Springfield IL 1988-1990. NAAD 1988. thomas@langfordassoc.com

LANGILLE, David (Minn) Messiah Episcopal Church, 1631 Ford Pkwy, Saint Paul MN 55116 **R S Mart's By The Lake Epis Minnetonka Bch MN 2011-** B Halifax Canada 3/15/1960 s Arnold Franklin Langille & Shirley May. BTS Nova Scotia Coll of Art and Design 1983; MCS Regent Coll 1992; Atlantic TS 2005. D 6/14/2007 P 12/20/2007 Bp James Louis Jelinek. m 3/4/1995 Diane M Langille c 2. Mssh Epis Ch S Paul MN 2007-2011. d.langille@messiahepiscopla.org

LANGLE, Susan (NH) Unit 6, 26 Myrtle St, Claremont NH 03743 **P-in-c Trin Ch Claremont NH 2008-** B N Kingstown RI 5/2/1956 d John Hewitt Langle & Jean Virginia. AB Assumption Coll 1978; JD U of Connecticut 1981; MDiv EDS 2007. D 6/28/2007 P 2/15/2008 Bp V Gene Robinson. skldogwood@gmail.com

LANGLOIS, Donald Harold (Spr) 916 W Loughlin Dr, Chandler AZ 85225 B Rochester NY 11/25/1940 s Harold Lionel Langlois & Eleanor Emma. BA Ken 1962; MDiv GTS 1966; MLS Queens Coll, CUNY 1973. D 6/11/1966 P 1/7/1967 Bp George West Barrett. m 8/28/1965 Ullrike Baudisch c 2. S Aug's Epis Ch Tempe AZ 1991-1992; R Ch Of The H Trin Danville IL 1985-1987; Vic S Lukes Ch Ladysmith WI 1983-1985; R Gr Ch Rice Lake WI 1976-1985; P-T Asst S Geo's Par Flushing NY 1973-1976; Vic Ch of the Redeem Addison NY 1967-1972; Asst Chr Epis Ch Hornell NY 1966-1967. CBS; GAS; SHN (P Assoc); Soc of King Chas the Mtyr; SocMary. Beta Phi Mu Queens Coll, Flushing NY 1973. don.langlois@gmail.com

LANGSTON, John Lee (NJ) 107 E 26th Ave Apt 2, N Wildwood NJ 08260 **D S Simeon's By The Sea No Wildwood NJ 1990-** B Cranford NJ 1/28/1941 s James Richard Langston & Agnes. D 6/9/1990 Bp George Phelps Mellick Belshaw. m 8/28/1965 H Eugenia Maxfield c 3. jelangston1@verizon.net

LANGSTON, Michael Griffith (NC) 203 Denim Dr, Erwin NC 28339 B Philadelphia PA 4/24/1965 s Randall Autrey Langston & Glee Hardwick. PhD Case Wstrn Reserve U; AA Florida St U 1984; BA U of W Florida 1986; MA U of W Florida 1989; MDiv Ya Berk 1990. D 8/6/1991 P 2/1/1992 Bp Rogers Sanders Harris. S Steph's Epis Ch Erwin NC 1999-2002; H Trin Epis Ch W Palm Bch FL 1996-1999; S Paul's Ch Naples FL 1991-1996. Auth, "Mntl Hlth Values Of Ministers".

LANIER, Justin Ray (SO) 232 E Main St, Lebanon OH 45036 **S Pat's Epis Ch Lebanon OH 2010-** B Alexandria LA 2/20/1978 s Ray Dempsey Lanier & Jennifer Marguerite. BA U of Delaware 2001; MDiv CDSP 2010. D 6/12/2010 P 6/11/2011 Bp Thomas Edward Breidenthal. m 3/20/2010 Heather Kirn c 1. justinraylanier@yahoo.com

LANIER, Sidney (NY) 1014-B Creekside Way, Ojai CA 93023 B Brooklyn NY 8/21/1923 s Sidney Lanier & Sarah Ann. U Of Florida; BA Rol 1949; BD EDS 1953. D 7/5/1953 Bp Martin J Bram P 1/1/1954 Bp Henry I Louttit. m 9/6/1966 Jean B Webster c 3. Vic S Clem's Ch New York NY 1962-1965; Asst S Thos Ch New York NY 1958-1962; Actg R Par of Trin Ch New York NY 1957-1958; R S Jn's Ch Christiansted VI 1954-1957; Asst Cathd Ch Of S Ptr St Petersburg FL 1953-1954.

LANIER, Stanley Lin (At) PO Box 637, Waycross GA 31502 B Waycross GA 6/3/1952 s Sidney Leo Lanier & Willie. Grad Theol Un; BA S Andr's Presb Coll 1974; Andover Newton TS 1976; MA Wesley TS 1979; U of Virginia 1985; MDiv GTS 1993. D 6/5/1993 P 12/1/1993 Bp Frank Kellogg Allan. Asst To Bp Dio Atlanta Atlanta GA 1993-1994. slanier@wayxcable.com

LANNING JR, James C. (Chi) 1315 W. Roosevelt Rd., Wheaton IL 60187 **D Trin Epis Ch Wheaton IL 1986-** B Grand Island NE 1/22/1948 s James Clair Lanning & Marian. BA U of Nebraska 1971; JD U of Nebraska 1973; LLM Geo 1976. D 1/25/1984 Bp Robert Marshall Anderson. m 6/7/1969 Nancy Hassell c 2. D S Mths Ch St Paul Pk MN 1985-1986. jimlanning@ameritech.net

LANNON, Nicholas Jewett (Nwk) Grace Church Van Vorst, 39 Erie St., Jersey City NJ 07302 **The Ch Of The Sav Denville NJ 2011-** B Alexandria VA 5/14/1978 s Paul Lannon & Susan. BA The U Of Arizona Tucson AZ 2000; MDiv TESM Ambr PA 2007. D 6/9/2007 Bp James Robert Mathes. m 5/22/2004 Ayala Masayo Solis Ayala Solis c 2. Asst R Gr Ch Van Vorst Jersey City NJ 2007-2011. nicklannon@gmail.com

LANPHERE, Lynette (Ala) 8132 Becker Ln, Leeds AL 35094 **R Epis Ch Of The Epiph Leeds AL 2004-** B Marshalltown IA 4/25/1947 d Guy Richard Lanphere & Helen Edna. BA Briar Cliff U 1969; MS Creighton U 1978; MA Loras Coll 1990; MDiv STUSo 2002. D 6/20/2002 Bp Thomas Kreider Ray P 12/17/2002 Bp Marc Handley Andrus. S Steph's Epis Ch Huntsville AL 2002-2004. rllanphere@windstream.net

LANSFORD, Theron George (NI) 10225 Calverton Pass, Fort Wayne IN 46825 **P-in-c H Fam Ch Angola IN 2005-** B Denton TX 6/13/1931 s Marcus Leslie Lansford & Lucille. BA U of Texas 1957; MA U of Texas 1959; PhD S Johns 1998. D 10/9/1971 P 4/22/1972 Bp Walter C Klein. m 9/1/1959 Mary Elizabeth Lansford. Asst Gr Epis Ch Ft Wayne IN 1995-2005; P-in-c H Fam Ch Angola IN 1974-1980. Auth, "Var Sci Pub". Who'S Who Among Amer Tchrs; Who'S Who In Amer Sci,; Who'S Who In Amer Rel.

LANTER, James Joseph (WVa) HC 69 Box 88, Slatyfork WV 26291 **Cler in Charge S Jn's Ch Marlinton WV 2008-** B Marion IL 9/10/1936 s Joseph John Lanter & Kathryn M. BS Pur 1964; MA DePaul U 1968; PhD CUA 1971; Cert of Wk VTS 2008. D 9/30/2008 P 6/15/2009 Bp William Michie Klusmeyer. m 1/1/1982 Joyce Carolin Lanter c 6. jlanter@netscape.net

LANTZ, F(rederick) William (Nwk) 1115 Black Rush Cir, Mount Pleasant SC 29466 **Pstr Assoc Chr Epis Ch Mt Pleasant SC 2002-** B Quantico VA 8/7/1940 s William Frederick Lantz & Catharine. BS VPI 1963; MDiv GTS 1968. D 6/29/1968 Bp William Foreman Creighton P 6/1/1969 Bp Paul Moore Jr. m 6/11/1966 Llewellyn Ann Murphy c 2. R S Dunst's Epis Ch Succasunna NJ 1997-2001; Asst Estrn Shore Chap Virginia Bch VA 1996-1997; R Chr Epis

Ch Smithfield VA 1990-1996; Chr Ch Charlotte NC 1975-1990; S Chris's Ch Charlotte NC 1975-1990; Asst S Aug's Epis Ch Washington DC 1968-1969. billlantz2@aol.com

LANTZ, John Daron (SC) 1150 E Montague Ave, North Charleston SC 29405 **D S Mk's Epis Ch Charleston SC 2007-** B Carlisle PA 7/16/1922 s Samuel Franklin Lantz & Florence Kathryn. BS Millersville U 1946; MS U Of Bridgeport 1962; MS U Of Bridgeport 1975. D 12/3/1988 Bp Arthur Edward Walmsley. m 4/22/1957 Sidnea Jane Baker c 3. D S Thos Epis Ch No Charleston SC 1995-2006; D Chr Ch Trumbull CT 1988-1994. jdlsid@dycon.com

LANUM, Duncan Jay (RG) 801 E Zia Rd, Santa Fe NM 87505 **Asst P Ch of the H Faith Santa Fe NM 2001-** B Evanston IL 8/9/1938 s Franklin Vincent Lanum & Dorothy. BA Dart 1960; JD NWU 1963; MDiv TESM 1988. D 4/13/1989 P 11/1/1989 Bp Bob Gordon Jones. c 2. R S Clem's Ch Woodlake CA 1990-2000; All Souls Ch Kaycee WY 1989-1990. duncanjaylanum@aol.com

LAPENTA-H, Sarah (Los) 514 W Adams Blvd, Los Angeles CA 90007 **S Jn's Ch Chevy Chase MD 2011-** B Detroit MI 10/3/1974 d Joe Stettenbenz & Cecelia L. BS Pur 1997; MDiv Fuller TS 2008. D 6/12/2010 Bp Diane M Jardine Bruce P 1/8/2011 Bp Mary Douglas Glasspool. m 8/11/1996 Paul Hebblethwaite. St Johns Pro-Cathd Los Angeles CA 2010-2011. slaponta-h@stjohnsnorwood.org

LAPRE, Alfred Charles (Ct) 616 Shamrock Dr, Fredericksburg VA 22407 B Norwich CT 8/4/1932 s Alfred C Lapre & Victoria F. CEU STUSo 1989. D 12/3/1988 Bp Arthur Edward Walmsley. m 5/21/1955 Mary C Boller.

LAQUINTANO, David Lloyd (NJ) 2998 Bay Ave, Ocean City NJ 08226 **R H Trin Epis Ch Ocean City NJ 1999-** B Stroudsburg PA 8/16/1950 s David Laquintano & Irene Evelyn. BA Estrn Bapt Coll 1972; MDiv Estrn Bapt TS 1975; U of Wales 1976. D 6/20/1987 P 11/7/1987 Bp Allen Lyman Bartlett Jr. m 6/3/1972 Christine Laquintano c 3. R Gr Epis Ch Kingston PA 1989-1999; Asst Chr Ch Philadelphia Philadelphia PA 1987-1989. frdavidoc@comcast.net

LARA, Lino (Dal) 5923 Royal Lane, Dallas TX 75230 **Cur S Lk's Epis Ch Dallas TX 2010-** B Hidalgo Mexico 1/29/1965 s Pedro Lara & Silvia Flores. Instituto Teologio de San Mateo 1998. D 6/26/2010 Bp Paul Emil Lambert P 5/28/2011 Bp James Monte Stanton. m 6/12/1996 Juana Rodriguez c 3. linol@peoplepc.com

L

LARCOMBE, David John (Vt) 37 Premo Rd, Roxbury VT 05669 B Exeter UK 8/20/1951 s Raymond James Larcombe & Patricia. BS U Natal Gb 1972; DIT S Paul TS 1974; BTh U Safr 1978. Trans from Church of the Province of Southern Africa 8/28/1984 Bp John Bowen Coburn. m 1/17/2003 Sandra Carrillo c 1. Ch Of The Gd Shpd Barre VT 2004-2007; S Paul's Ch Peabody MA 1996-1997; Int Ch Of Our Sav Arlington MA 1989-1992; R Emm Epis Ch Wakefield MA 1984-1989; Int Trin Par Melrose MA 1981-1982; Assoc R Ascen Memi Ch Ipswich MA 1979-1980.

LAREMORE, Darrell Lee (SeFla) 6003 Back Bay Ln, Austin TX 78739 B New Castle IN 2/12/1942 MA Florida Atlantic U 1971; Florida Atlantic U 1973; MDiv Epis TS of The SW 2003. D 12/16/2003 Bp James Hamilton Ottley P 3/13/2005 Bp Leopold Frade. m 12/15/1989 Karyn Kirsch c 1. S Jn's Epis Ch Austin TX 2004-2005. fatherdarrell@earthlink.net

LAREMORE, Richard Thomas (RI) 76 Norfolk St, Cranston RI 02910 B Albany NY 11/6/1925 s Thomas Henry Laremore & Ellen. BA Br 1951; STM EDS 1954; U of Rhode Island 1980. D 6/20/1954 P 3/5/1955 Bp John S Higgins. m 5/20/1989 Ila Winterbottam c 3. Int Emm Ch Newport RI 1994-1995; Int S Jn The Div Ch Saunderstown RI 1992-1994; Int Ch Of The Mssh Providence RI 1991-1992; Int Trin Epis Ch Whitinsville MA 1990-1991; Int S Alb's Ch No Providence RI 1988-1990; Int S Jn's Ch Cumberland RI 1986-1988; Ch Of The Ascen Cranston RI 1986; Asst S Dav's On The Hill Epis Ch Cranston RI 1984-1985; S Andr's Ch Turners Falls MA 1982-1983; Asst S Jas' Ch Greenfield MA 1982-1983; Int Gr Ch Dalton MA 1981-1982; P-in-c St Mich & Gr Ch Rumford RI 1980-1981; R S Matt's Ch Barrington RI 1959-1979; Asst S Mk's Epis Ch Riverside RI 1954-1956; Min in charge S Matt's Ch Barrington RI 1954-1956. Freedom Fndt Awd 1978. hugly1@aol.com

LARGE, Alexander R (CFla) 3411 Bradley Ln, Chevy Chase MD 20815 **Asst R All SS' Epis Ch Chevy Chase MD 2008-** B Grosse Point MI 5/25/1979 s James Large & Nancy. BA W&L Lexington VA 2002; MDiv TESM 2006. D 5/27/2006 Bp John Wadsworth Howe P 12/9/2006 Bp Robert John O'Neill. m 8/13/2005 Emily A Averitt c 2. Cur Epis Ch Of The Trsfg Vail CO 2006-2008. largea2000@yahoo.com

LARGENT, Lacy (Tex) Po Box 10603, Houston TX 77206 **Sprtl Dir of Dioc AltGld Dio Texas Houston TX 2007-; Bd Secy Camp Allen Navasota TX 2005-; Dio Texas Houston TX 2002-; Camp Allen Navasota TX 2001-** B Fort Smith AR 7/22/1960 d Larry Kennon Largent & Anne Kay. BA U of Arkansas 1982; MSW Washington U 1983; MDiv Epis TS of The SW 1990. D 6/16/1990 Bp Maurice Manuel Benitez P 1/13/1991 Bp Anselmo Carral-Solar. Dn of Cntrl Convoc Dio Texas Houston TX 2002-2006; Bd Mem Camp Allen Navasota TX 1996-2000; Exec Bd Dio Texas Houston TX 1996-1999; Sprtl Dir of Happ Dio Texas Houston TX 1996-1998; R S Paul's Ch Navasota TX 1994-2002; Chair of Dioc Single Adults Dio Texas Houston TX 1991-1998; Asst R Ch Of The Gd Shpd Kingwood TX 1991-1994; Stff Chapl Cullen Memi Chap Houston TX 1990-1991; St Lk's Epis Hosp Houston TX 1990-1991. Hal Brook Perry Distinguished Alum Awd Sem of the SW 2009; Five Outstanding Young Texans Awd Texas Jaycees 2000. camplacy@yahoo.com

LARIBEE JR, Richard (Md) American University of Iraq - Sulaimani, Sulaimani, Iraq, Pittsburgh PA 15206 B Rome NY 6/18/1952 s Richard Alansing Laribee & Eileen Ida. BA The King's Coll Briarcliff Manor NY 1974; Wheaton Coll 1974; ThM Dallas TS 1981; CTh Epis TS of The SW 1997; DMin Fuller TS 1998. D 6/7/1997 P 12/21/1997 Bp William Jerry Winterrowd. m 5/3/1974 Jeanne M Lubenow c 3. R S Mk's Ch Highland MD 2002-2010; R S Andr The Fisherman Epis Mayo MD 1998-2002; The Ch Of Chr The King (Epis) Arvada CO 1997-1998. "From Generation to Generation: Intergenerational Wrshp," *Ch Mus Workshop*, 2006. rlaribee@gmail.com

LARISEY, Frank Edward (SC) 1996 Mcqueen Blvd, Orangeburg SC 29118 **R Ch Of The Redeem Orangeburg SC 2005-** B Charleston SC 6/29/1953 s Walter Earle Larisey & Virginia. BS U So 1977; MDiv VTS 1983; 4 Quarters Cert for Pstr Educ 1999; DMin STUSo 2005. D 7/3/1983 P 5/1/1984 Bp William Evan Sanders. m 1/10/2003 Hope Nye Halford c 2. Assoc R S Andr's In-The-Pines Epis Ch Peachtree City GA 2000-2005; Int H Trin Par Epis Clemson SC 1996; Other Cler Position Dio Atlanta Atlanta GA 1995-1996; R S Jn's Coll Pk GA 1992-1995; Assoc R S Jn's Epis Ch Columbia SC 1987-1992; Vic Dio E Tennessee Knoxville TN 1984-1987; Vic S Columba's Epis Ch Bristol TN 1984-1987; D Dio Tennessee Nashville TN 1983-1984; D S Dav's Epis Ch Nashville TN 1983-1984. Amer Angl Coun 2000; Ntwk of Angl Comm Dioceses and Parishes 2003. redeemeroburg@bellsouth.net

LARIVE, Armand Edward (Spok) 4812 Fremont Ave, Bellingham WA 98229 B Winner SD 3/19/1936 s Armand Ovid Larive & Martha. BA Whitman Coll 1958; BD Bex 1961; MA U of Missouri 1970; PhD Claremont Grad U 1976. D 7/11/1961 P 3/1/1962 Bp Lane W Barton. m 8/30/1959 Ruby D Larive c 2. S Jas Pullman WA 1975-2001; P-in-c H Trin Vale OR 1963-1968; P-in-c S Paul's Epis Ch Nyssa OR 1961-1968. Auth, "After Sunday: A Theol Of Wk," Continuum, 2004. alarive@comcast.net

LARKIN, Gregory Bruce (Los) 1251 Las Posas Rd, Camarillo CA 93010 **R S Columba's Par Camarillo CA 2000-** B Los Angles CA 10/7/1955 s Robert Hale Larkin & Catherine. BA U of Redlands 1977; MDiv GTS 1982. D 6/19/1982 P 2/5/1983 Bp Robert C Rusack. m 5/31/1986 Nancy Louise Trott c 2. R S Thos Of Cbury Par Long Bch CA 1987-2000; S Lk's Of The Mountains La Crescenta CA 1984-1987; Cur & Asst S Mich's Mssn Anaheim CA 1982-1984. Cn Cathd Cntr Of St. Paul Dio Los Angeles 1999. greg.larkin@stcolumbaca.com

LARKIN, Paul G (WA) 9407 Holland Ave, Bethesda MD 20814 **Died 2/18/2011** B Philadelphia PA 2/25/1928 s Joseph Larkin & Josephine. BA La Salle U 1953; STB/STL Gregorian U 1957; MA GW 1968; PhD GW 1973. Rec from Roman Catholic 4/1/1963 as Priest Bp William Foreman Creighton. lark@boo.net

LAROCCA, Lucy Driscoll (Ct) 1109 Main St, Branford CT 06405 **Zion Epis Ch No Branford CT 2011-** B Bristol CT 11/13/1959 d Arthur Joseph Driscoll & Lucy Peckham. AA Albertus Magnus Coll 1979; BFA Paier Coll of Art 1983; MS Sthrn Connecticut St U 1996; MDiv Ya Berk 2008. D 6/4/2008 P 12/20/2008 Bp Andrew Donnan Smith. m 5/30/1987 David LaRocca c 2. Trin Ch On The Green New Haven CT 2010-2011; Cur Trin Ch Branford CT 2008-2010. lucylrock@comcast.net

LAROCHE WILSON, Jill Monica (Pa) 246 Fox Rd, Media PA 19063 B Gardner MA 5/14/1975 d James Herve LaRoche & Diane C. BA Bos 1997; MDiv EDS 2002. D 6/22/2002 P 5/31/2003 Bp Charles Ellsworth Bennison Jr. Asst R S Ptr's Ch In The Great Vlly Malvern PA 2002-2005. jlarowils@gmail.com

LAROM JR, Richard U (NY) Po Box 577, Ivoryton CT 06442 B Bay Shore NY 1/30/1946 s Richard Larom & Pauline. CUNY; BA Cor; STB GTS. D 6/17/1972 P 12/14/1972 Bp Jonathan Goodhue Sherman. m 2/4/1976 Margaret Smith Larom c 2. Exec Dir Seamens Ch Inst Income New York NY 1992-2002; Gr Ch White Plains NY 1985-1992; Exec Coun Appointees New York NY 1980-1985; Cathd Of St Jn The Div New York NY 1977-1978; R S Geo's Ch Astoria NY 1975-1980; Cur Chr Epis Ch Tarrytown NY 1974-1975. Auth, *Seafarer's Handbook*, 1995; Auth, *Commentary on St. Mk*, 1984; Auth, *Pstr*, 1984; Auth, *Practical Guide for Ch Leaders*, 1984. Century Assn; Marine Soc; Pilgrims. Dn's Medal, GTS 2002; Paul Harris Rotary Fellowowship 1991; Ethical Culture Soc Humanitarian Awd 1991; Westchester Human Rts Awd 1991; Hon Cn Ch of Uganda 1991. plarom@incarnationcenter.org

LARRIMORE, Sloane Barker (Cal) 178 Clinton St, Redwood City CA 94062 **R S Ptr's Epis Ch Redwood City CA 1999-** B Miami Beach FL 7/28/1963 s Sloane Barker & Donna. BA U of Oregon 1985; MDiv CDSP 1995. D 6/3/1995 P 6/1/1996 Bp William Edwin Swing. m 5/26/1990 Christopher Paul Thorman c 1. Assoc Pstr Gr Cathd San Francisco CA 1995-1999. cblarrimore@gmail.com

LARSEN, Erik W (Ct) 1335 Asylum Ave., Hartford CT 06002 **Dio Connecticut Hartford CT 2007-** B Hartford CT 7/13/1953 s Erik Eigill Larsen & Margaret. BA Trin Hartford CT 1975; MDiv EDS 1980. D 6/14/1980 P 12/15/1980

Bp Morgan Porteus. m 10/13/1984 Karin Bengtson c 2. Stndg Com Dio Connecticut Hartford CT 1998-2003; R S Alb's Ch Simsbury CT 1994-2006; St Johns Cathd 0 1990-1995; R S Andr's Epis Ch New Preston Marble Dale CT 1983-1990; Cur Ch Of The H Trin Middletown CT 1980-1983. Soc of S Jn the Evang 1980. Hon Cn Chr Ch Cathd 2007. prsnlrsn@aol.com

LARSEN, Gilbert Steward (Ct) 9160 Sw 193rd Cir, Dunnellon FL 34432 **Assoc S Anne's Ch Crystal River FL 2000-** B New York NY 9/4/1943 s Lawrence Bernard Larsen & Astrid Charlotte. BA Hamline U 1965; MDiv GTS 1968. D 6/8/1968 P 12/21/1968 Bp Horace W B Donegan. m 6/22/1968 Judith B Braine c 2. Cler & Fam Enrichment Com Dio Connecticut Hartford CT 1991-1993; R Chr Ch Sharon CT 1983-2000; R Ch Of The H Comm Mahopac NY 1980-1983; Dn Of SW Nassau Dio Long Island Garden City NY 1979-1980; R Chr Epis Ch Lynbrook NY 1972-1980; Liturg Cmsn Dio Long Island Garden City NY 1972-1976; Cur Trin Epis Ch Roslyn NY 1968-1971. SSC 1992-2011. judyngil@bellsouth.net

LARSEN, Peter Michael (LI) PO Box 5068, Southampton NY 11969 **P-in-c S Andr's Dune Chap Southampton NY 1989-; R S Jn's Epis Ch Southampton NY 1989-** B Hackensack NJ 11/15/1948 s Knud Anthon Larsen & Mary Hamlin. BA Wofford Coll 1970; MDiv VTS 1974; Naval Chapl Sch 1984. D 6/5/1974 Bp William Hopkins Folwell P 12/19/1974 Bp Frederick Hesley Belden. m 6/26/1986 Nancy B Slater c 3. R S Jn The Div Ch Saunderstown RI 1983-1989; P-in-c Atone Ch Walterboro SC 1978-1983; R S Jude's Epis Ch Walterboro SC 1978-1983; Asst S Jn's Ch Lafayette Sq Washington DC 1975-1978; Cur S Jn's Ch Barrington RI 1974-1975. *arts in LivCh*. Gd Samar Awd Hospice 2002; Outstanding Achievement Awd Mltry Chapl Assn 2001; Reserve Chapl of the Year Awd Reserve Off Assn 1998; Cmnty Serv Awd So Carolina 1980. larsen@hamptons.com

LARSEN JR, R James (Pa) PO Box 341490, Dayton OH 45434 B Iowa City IA 2/13/1942 s Richard James Larsen & Isabel Mary. BA U of Iowa 1964; STB Ya Berk 1968; MS U of Wisconsin 1982. D 6/20/1968 P 12/21/1968 Bp Gordon V Smith. m 4/19/1974 Donna K Grover c 2. Int S Geo's Epis Ch Dayton OH 2008-2010; R Washington Memi Chap Vlly Forge PA 2001-2007; R S Mary's Epis Ch Bonita Sprg FL 1997-2001; R H Trin Ch Cincinnati OH 1986-1997; S Ambr Epis Ch Ft Lauderdale FL 1982-1986; S Mich's Ch Miami FL 1981-1982; Vic Trin Ch River Falls WI 1978-1979; Vic S Lk's Epis Ch Altoona PA 1974-1978; Chr Ch Cathd Eau Claire WI 1973-1978; S Lk's Ch Altoona WI 1973-1978; P-in-c Trin Ch Winterset IA 1970-1974; P-in-c S Paul Epis Ch Des Moines IA 1968-1974. Kappa Delta Pi; Phi Delta Kappa. rjlarsen1974@gmail.com

LARSON, Frances Jean (Minn) 1010 1st Ave N, Wheaton MN 56296 B Windom MN 11/30/1938 d Edward John Spielman & Gladys. S Barn Hosp Minneapolis MN; LPN Miller Hosp Sch Nrsng S Paul MN 1960; BSW Bemidji St U 1996. D 10/25/1987 Bp Robert Marshall Anderson. m 7/28/1962 Louis I Larson c 2. Oustanding Soc Wk Stdt Bemidi St U 1995; Who'S Who Amer Coll Stdt 96; S Geo Epis Awd 82 Emm Epis Ch.

LARSON, John Milton (Los) 1480 Vista Ln, Pasadena CA 91103 **Asst The Ch Of The Ascen Sierra Madre CA 2002-** B Chicago IL 4/16/1935 s John Clarence Larson & Lillian Marie. BMus NWU 1956; MDiv SWTS 1959. D 6/20/1959 P 12/19/1959 Bp Charles L Street. m 11/27/1970 Barbara Schulz. R S Barn' Par Pasadena CA 1995-2002; Int Chr The Gd Shpd Par Los Angeles CA 1995; Asst S Mk's Par Downey CA 1985-1989; Asst Chr The Gd Shpd Par Los Angeles CA 1977-1984; Asst Chr Ch Las Vegas NV 1974-1975; Asst S Simons Ch Arlington Heights IL 1968-1969; R St Ambr Epis Ch Antigo WI 1966-1968; Cur Emm Epis Ch Rockford IL 1959-1961. OHC 1957. jmlarson@charter.net

LARSON, Laurence (Q) 2424 41st St Apt 48, Moline IL 61265 **Chapl to the Ret Cler Dio Quincy Peoria IL 2001-** B East Chicago IN 3/3/1936 s Roy John Larson & Agnes Marie. BA Illinois Coll 1960; MDiv Nash 1963; DMin GTF 1988. D 6/15/1963 Bp James Winchester Montgomery P 12/21/1963 Bp Gerald Francis Burrill. m 12/30/1961 Betty L Izard c 3. R Trin Epis Ch Peoria IL 1977-2001; Ch Of S Jn The Bapt Lincoln IL 1971-1977; R Trin Ch Lincoln IL 1971-1977; S Jas Ch Old Town ME 1965-1967. CBS 1984. Cn Theol Dio Quincy 1998; Ord of St. Paul Awd Dio Quincy 1995; Phi Beta Kappa ILL Coll 1960. lblarson5@aol.com

LARSON, Lawrence Andrew Adolph (NY) 1 Bayview Ter, New Fairfield CT 06812 B Chicago IL 12/27/1934 s Adolph Gustave Larson & Beverley Julia. BS Indiana U 1957; Drew U 1959; MDiv Bos 1962; MS Bos 1967. D 12/24/1967 P 4/1/1968 Bp Robert McConnell Hatch. m 11/26/1983 Patricia J B Belcher c 2. R S Andr's Ch Brewster NY 1981-1999; R Chr Ch Ansonia CT 1969-1981; Asst S Jas Ch Great Barrington MA 1967-1969. Auth, "Chr Symbolism & The Tragic Point Of View"; Auth, "The Cinematic & The Biblic Points Of View: A New Correlation". Alb Inst Assn Rel & Intellectual Life; Angl Soc, Gld S Raphael. lawren4849@aol.com

LARSON JR, L(awrence) John (Cal) 1835 NW Lantana Dr., Corvallis OR 97330 B Arcadia FL 11/22/1935 s Lawrence John Larson & Kathryn Mabelle. BA U of Florida 1957; Ya 1958; BD SMU 1960. D 1/26/1963 Bp George Richard Millard P 6/10/1963 Bp James Albert Pike. m 2/3/1978 Ellen Brockman. Assoc S Lk's Ch Sequim WA 1999; Com on Environ Dio California San Francisco CA 1992-1997; R Ch Of The Nativ San Rafael CA 1990-1997; R Ch Of The Epiph Flagstaff AZ 1984-1990; Stndg Com Dio Alaska Fairbanks AK 1981-1984; R The Ch Of The H Trin Juneau AK 1977-1984; Dioc Coun Dio Spokane Spokane WA 1972-1977; R S Lk's Ch Coeur D Alene ID 1970-1977; ExCoun Dio California San Francisco CA 1969-1970; Vic S Anne's Ch Fremont CA 1962-1968. ljlarson57@comcast.net

LARSON, Robert Anton (Colo) P.O. Box 563, Ouray CO 81427 B Greeley CO 11/21/1945 s Ralph Anton Larson & Hallie Grace. Engr Colorado Sch of Mines 1968. D 11/14/2009 Bp Robert John O'Neill. m 4/12/1969 Pamela Larson c 2. larsouray@qwestoffice.net

LARSON, Wayne H (Md) 15 East Bishop's Road, Baltimore MD 21218 **Dir of Chapl Serv Fairhaven Sykesville MD 2005-** B Buffalo Center IA 11/28/1954 s Jerome C Larson & Maxine. BS Minnesota St U Mankato 1978; Ch Army Trng Coll 1987; MDiv Hur 2003. D 6/29/2003 P 1/25/2004 Bp Edwin Max Leidel Jr. P-in-c S Jn's Epis Ch S Johns MI 2003-2005; Jubilee Cntr Visitor Dom And Frgn Mssy Soc- Epis Ch Cntr New York NY 1994-1997; New Ch Planting Com Dio Michigan Detroit MI 1991-1994; Dir of Chr Cntr S Paul's Epis Ch Flint MI 1988-2001; Urban Mnstry & Evang Dio Michigan Detroit MI 1988-1991; Bd Mem The Ch Army Usa Branson MO 1987-1990. Ch Army 1987. Vol of Year Escape Mnstrs 2009; Azell Cromwell Awd Chr Cntr 2008; Bp's Awd Dio Estrn Michigan 1998. whllondon@aol.com

LARSON-MILLER, Lizette (Los) 926 Santa Fe Ave, Albany CA 94706 **Assoc S Mk's Par Berkeley CA 2010-; Prof CDSP Berkeley CA 2003-** B Los Angeles CA 1/26/1958 d Robert Harald Larson Nugent & Billie Eileen. BA USC 1978; MA St. Johns U 1982; PhD Grad Theol Un 1992. Rec from Roman Catholic 1/1/1996 Bp Frederick Houk Borsch. m 4/10/1983 Steven Miller c 2. Assoc Ch Of The Adv Of Chr The King San Francisco CA 2003-2010. Auth, "Anointing the Sick," Liturg Press, 2005; Auth, "Medieval Liturg: A Bk of Essays," Garland, 1997. Affirming Catholicism 2005; Intl Angl Liturg Consult 2000; Soc of Cath Priests 2009. Lilly Fac Resrch Grant Eli Lilly 2005; Bp Garner Cler Awd Garner Fund, Dio of LA 2004; SCOM Grant SCOM 2004; Luce Fell Luce 2002. llarson@cdsp.edu

LA RUE, Howard Arlen (Va) 164 W Main St # 72, Searsport ME 04974 B Maud OK 1/3/1930 s William La Rue & Veloura I. VTS 1967. D 6/22/1967 Bp George P Gunn P 5/1/1968 Bp David Shepherd Rose. R Emm Epis Ch Greenwood VA 1969-1995; R H Cross Ch Batesville VA 1969-1995; Epis Ch Of S Paul And S Andr Kenbridge VA 1967-1969; R Gibson Memi Crewe VA 1967-1969.

LASH, Rebecca Henry (NwPa) 501 West 31st Street, Erie PA 16508 **Vic Ch Of The H Sprt Erie PA 2010-** B Greenville SC 8/31/1949 d Daniel Gordon Henry & Eloise Campbell. NWPA Dioc Sch for Mnstry; ADN Villa Maria Coll 1983; BASS Edinboro U of Pennsylvania Edinboro PA 1988. D 11/1/2008 P 6/6/2010 Bp Sean Walter Rowe. m 7/1/2000 David Lash c 4. rhl@zoominternet.net

LASITER JR, Douglas Norman (Tex) 2525 Seagler Rd, Houston TX 77042 **S Mich's Ch La Marque TX 2011-** B Houston TX 8/24/1962 s Douglas Lasiter & Jony. Hist U of Houston 2005; MDiv Epis TS Of The SW 2009. D 6/20/2009 Bp C(harles) Andrew Doyle P 1/5/2010 Bp Rayford Baines High Jr. m 7/16/1988 Robi Norfolk c 2. Assoc/Cur Ch Of The Ascen Houston TX 2009-2011. dnlasiter@comcast.net

LASKE, Holger (Los) Riehler Strasse 7, Koeln 50668 Germany B Hagen DE 1/25/1965 s Heinz Laske & Gisela. Kirchliche Hochschule Wuppertal DE; U Of Bochum Ruhr DE; MDiv Geo-August U DE 1991; MDiv Old Cath Sem Bonn 1996. P 9/24/1998 Bp Frederick Houk Borsch. S Bede's Epis Ch Los Angeles CA 1998-1999. hollakoeln@gmx.de

LASSALLE, David Fredric (SVa) 1526 W 49th St, Norfolk VA 23508 B Greenville PA 9/30/1941 s Fredric William Lassalle & Elizabeth Holden. BA Thiel Coll 1963; STM PDS 1966. D 6/18/1966 P 6/1/1967 Bp William Crittenden. m 7/24/1965 Sherran A Gotjen c 4. Int Ch Of H Apos Virginia Bch VA 1997-2009; Dio Sthrn Virginia Norfolk VA 1997-2009; S Ptr's Epis Ch Norfolk VA 1996-1997; Vic Ch Of The Epiph Grove City PA 1969-1978; Vic S Jn's Ch Kane PA 1966-1969; Vic S Marg's Epis Ch Mt Jewett PA 1966-1969. padre2@verizon.net

LASSEN, Coryl Judith (Cal) 409 Topa Topa Dr, Ojai CA 93023 B San Antonio TX 10/16/1955 d Carl Guenther Lassen & Carol Lee. BA U of Pennsylvania 1977; MDiv EDS 1982. D 4/8/1983 Bp Lyman Cunningham Ogilby P 5/1/1984 Bp George Nelson Hunt III. m 1/22/1983 James Rutherford Lassen-Willems. S Mk's Epis Ch Palo Alto CA 2010-2011; Trsfg Epis Ch San Mateo CA 2009-2010; Stanford Cbury Fndt Standford CA 2008-2009; Trin Par Menlo Pk CA 2008-2009; R S Andr's Epis Ch Ojai CA 1995-2005; Pres Of The Stndg Com Dio Rhode Island Providence RI 1993-1994; Stndg Com Dio Rhode Island Providence RI 1990-1994; Dio Rhode Island Providence RI 1989-1995; Intrnshp Mnstry Prog S Ptr's And S Andr's Epis Providence RI 1989-1995; Vic Calv Ch Providence RI 1985-1995; S Jn's Ch Barrington RI 1983-1985. Auth, "Report On The Condition Of The Cler Cmnty Of The Dio Ri". SCHC. coryl.lassen@sbcglobal.net

LASSITER, Arleigh Walter (Kan) 13060 Metcalf Ave Apt 303, Overland Park KS 66213 **Died 5/11/2010** B Memphis TN 11/20/1920 s Arleigh Walter Lassiter & Nelle. BA U of Kansas City - U Missouri Kansas City 1941; MDiv STUSo 1945. D 6/29/1944 P 5/5/1945 Bp Robert N Spencer. c 3. Kansas City Ecum Ret Cler 1997-2006. Tough Love Awd NCADD 1995. gball1951@aol.com

LASSITER, Richard Bruce (Nev) 1311 Ramona Ln, Boulder City NV 89005 B Lebanon NH 1/11/1946 s Jerry Bruce Lassiter & Bertha May. Ags Ccsn 2000. D 8/28/1996 P 3/1/1997 Bp Stewart Clark Zabriskie. m 7/28/1990 Eleanor Ruth Richardson. P S Chris's Epis Ch Boulder City NV 1997-2000. richardlassiter@juno.com

LATHAM, Betty Craft (ETenn) 628 Magnolia Vale Dr, Chattanooga TN 37419 **R Ch Of The Nativ Ft Oglethorpe GA 1998-** B Memphis TN 11/2/1953 d Henry Craft & Norma. BS Van 1975; MS U of Tennessee 1978; MDiv VTS 1995. D 6/24/1995 P 1/1/1996 Bp Robert Gould Tharp. m 6/7/1975 Luther Cleveland Latham c 1. Dok. CLATHAM10@COMCAST.NET

LATHAM, Donald Conway (LI) 75 Meadow Rue Pl, Ballston Spa NY 12020 **Vic All SS Ch Round Lake NY 2005-** B Rockville Centre NY 12/24/1933 s Walter Arlington Latham & Agnes. BA Hob 1955; MDiv Ya Berk 1958; Adel 1961. D 4/12/1958 P 10/25/1958 Bp James P De Wolfe. m 10/10/1959 Margaret A Thomas c 1. R The Ch Of The Ascen Rockville Cntr NY 1972-1994; Cn to Bp Dio Long Island Garden City NY 1967-1972; Vic All Souls Ch Stony Brook NY 1958-1966. Who's Who Rel 1977; Dictionary Intl Biographies 1970. revdon@nycap.rr.com

LATHROP, Brian Albert (NY) 63 Downing St Apt 4-A, New York NY 10014 B Buffalo NY 8/17/1957 s Calvin Albert Lathrop & Wilma Joyce. BA Canisius Coll 1979; MDiv GTS 1983; Psyd Westchester Inst 1992. D 6/11/1983 P 3/1/1984 Bp Harold B Robinson. Sr Asst Gr Epis Ch New York NY 1987-1993; Tutor The GTS New York NY 1986-1988; S Geo's-By-The-River Rumson NJ 1985-1987; Cur Gr Ch Utica NY 1983-1985. AAPC 1993; Amer Grp Psych Assoc 2000; Natl Assn Advancement Of Psychoanalysis 1993. brianlat@gmail.com

LATHROP, John (Me) 101 Paseo Encantado Ne, Santa Fe NM 87506 B Norwalk CT 7/21/1947 s Alvin Lathrop & Dorothea. BFA Denison U 1969; MDiv Yale DS 1972; ADN U of Maine 1986. D 6/16/1972 P 12/20/1972 Bp John Mc Gill Krumm. m 9/4/2004 Ann Evans Dilworth. Int S Paul's Ch Brunswick ME 1986-1988; The Hunger Ntwk Columbus OH 1980-1984; Dio Sthrn Ohio Cincinnati OH 1979-1980; R Our Sav Ch Mechanicsburg OH 1977-1984; Trin Ch Columbus OH 1972-1976. johnlath@me.com

LATHROP, John Campbell (Los) 1447 Kentwood Lane, Pisgah Forest NC 28768 B Detroit MI 4/21/1931 s Henry Irving Lathrop & Thelma Genevieve. BA U CA 1955; MDiv Epis TS of The SW 1958; PhD Grad Theol Un 1974; Command and Gnrl Stff Coll 1975. D 6/16/1958 P 2/1/1959 Bp Donald J Campbell. m 11/29/1981 Leslie Slagle. R S Tim's Par Compton CA 1991-2000; P-in-c S Dav's Par Los Angeles CA 1990-1991; P-in-c S Jas' Par So Pasadena CA 1989; Ch Of Our Sav Par San Gabr CA 1979-1980; R S Geo's Par La Can CA 1966-1978; R S Tim's Par Compton CA 1960-1966; S Paul's Pomona Pomona CA 1958-1959. Assn of CA Inst of Tech; Sons of the Amer Revolution. R Emer S Tim's Par, Compton CA 2000; Prov Cn All SS Cathd, Kampala, Uganda (Angl) 1993; Legion of Merit U.S. Army 1991; Colonel U.S. Army 1984. jclathrop@aol.com

LATIMER, Boyd Curtis (Okla) 6110 N Pennsylvania Ave, Oklahoma City OK 73112 **Died 12/18/2010** B Petrolla KS 1/3/1929 s Glenn Albert Latimer & Grace Lucille. BA U of Kansas 1950; BD SWTS 1953. D 3/16/1953 P 10/13/1953 Bp Goodrich R Fenner.

LATIMER, Susan J (WVa) 502 Druid Hills Road, Temple Terrace FL 33617 **R S Cathr's Ch Temple Terrace FL 2011-** B Escondido CA 2/18/1960 d James Harold Latimer & Jane. BA Ya 1982; MA USC 1984; MDiv Candler TS Emory U 1992. D 6/6/1992 P 12/12/1992 Bp Frank Kellogg Allan. m 5/9/1992 John B Roberts c 2. R S Jn's Epis Ch Charleston WV 2008-2011; R S Mk's Ch Waterville ME 2001-2008; Asst S Barth's Epis Ch Atlanta GA 1998-2001; Assoc H Trin Par Decatur GA 1994-1998; Asst Emm Epis Ch Athens GA 1992-1993. ACPE; Compass Rose Soc. Theta Pi. latimerdoves@yahoo.com

LATTA, Clyde Arthur (Colo) 1290 Williams St, Denver CO 80218 B Anacortes WA 12/14/1938 s Clyde Hayes Latta & Mildred. BS Montana St U 1962; Tul 1962; U of Montana 1963; STB GTS 1968; DMin Andover Newton TS 1990. D 6/22/1968 Bp John Raymond Wyatt P 12/1/1968 Bp Jackson Earle Gilliam. m 2/18/1982 Alice Jo Hawk c 3. Calv Ch Golden CO 1993-2001; H Apos Epis Ch Englewood CO 1991-1993; Int Gr Epis Ch Medford MA 1989-1990; R St Jas Epis Ch Dillon MT 1983-1985; All SS Ch Portland OR 1982-1983; Evang Com Dio Oregon Portland OR 1982-1983; Asst All SS Ch Portland OR 1979-1981; Exec Coun Dio Idaho Boise ID 1975-1978; R Calv Epis Ch Jerome ID 1973-1978; R Trin Ch Buhl ID 1973-1978; Lindisfame Com Exec Coun Dio Montana Helena MT 1969-1973; Lindisfame Com Exec Coun Dio Montana Helena MT 1969-1973; Vic S Paul's Ch Hamilton MT 1968-1973. Auth, "The Transformative Image Icon," *Symbol & Introject*. Ord Of S Ben.

LATTA, Dennis James (Ind) 2742 S Hickory Corner Rd, Vincennes IN 47591 **Vic S Jn's Ch Washington IN 1994-** B Terre Haute IN 10/29/1948 s Dennis Leroy Latta & Marjorie Roberta. BA Indiana St U 1970; MS Indiana St U 1972; MS Indiana St U 1976. D 6/24/1994 P 2/25/1995 Bp Edward Witker Jones. m 6/20/1976 Mary Kathryn Barekman c 3. dlatta@vincennes.net

✠ **LATTIME, Rt Rev Mark A** (Ak) 1205 Denali Way, Fairbanks AK 99701 **Bp of Alaska Dio Alaska Fairbanks AK 2010-; Dist Dn Dio Rochester Rochester NY 2001-** B Puerto Rico 5/26/1966 s Roy Alan Lattime & Deborah. BA Dickinson Coll 1988; MDiv Bex 1997. D 5/31/1997 P 12/13/1997 Bp William George Burrill Con 9/4/2010 for Ak. m 10/13/1990 Lisa C Cox c 3. R S Mich's Ch Geneseo NY 2000-2010; Asst R E Lee Memi Ch (Epis) Lexington VA 1997-2000. mlattime@gci.net

LAU, Gordon K (Cal) 1003 Azalea Dr, Alameda CA 94502 B Canton Kwangtung CN 4/26/1942 s Baldwin Lau & Yi-So. BS California Bapt U 1973; MDiv CDSP 1976; DMin CDSP 2000; DD CDSP 2007. Trans from Hong Kong Anglican Church 3/18/1980 as Priest Bp Robert Hume Cochrane. m 10/22/1977 Yvonne Man c 2. R Epis Ch Of Our Sav Oakland CA 1985-2008; Vic Ch Of The H Apos Seattle WA 1980-1984; Dio Olympia Seattle WA 1979. "Chinese Bk of Common Pryr (Translation)," Ch Pub, Inc., New York, 2004. DD CDSP 2007. frgordonlau@gmail.com

LAU, Ronald Taylor Christensen (LI) 326 Clinton St, Brooklyn NY 11231 **Area Dn, St Mk's Dnry, Archdnry of Brooklyn Dio Long Island Garden City NY 2007-; R Chr Ch Cobble Hill Brooklyn NY 1999-** B Los Angeles CA 9/6/1947 s Edward John Lau & Robley Ann. B.A. U CA 1970; MDiv GTS 1973; STM GTS 1975; Harv 1982; Cert Col-Bus Sch 1996. D 6/9/1973 Bp Paul Moore Jr P 12/16/1973 Bp Horace W B Donegan. Mem, Bd Fam Consult Serv Dio Long Island Garden City NY 2004-2007; Mem, COM Dio Long Island Garden City NY 2003-2005; Treas Geo Mercer TS Garden City NY 2000-2002; P-in-c Ch Of The Nativ Brooklyn NY 1998-1999; Vic S Jas Epis Ch Fordham Bronx NY 1996-1998; Int S Jas' Epis Ch Hackettstown NJ 1995-1996; Int All SS Epis Par Hoboken NJ 1995; R Epis Par Of S Mich And All Ang Tucson AZ 1988-1995; R Ch Of The H Nativ Bronx NY 1982-1988; Asst S Jn's Ch Norristown PA 1979-1981; Asst S Jos's Ch Queens Vill NY 1976-1977; Asst Ch Of S Mary The Vrgn New York NY 1973-1979. Ed, "The 1979 Bk of Common Pryr and the New Revised Standard Version Bible w the Apocrypha," Oxf Press, 1993; Ed, "The Cath Study Bible," Oxf Press, 1990; Ed, "1981 Epis Ch Annual," Morehouse-Barlow, 1981; Ed, "1980 Epis Ch Annual," Morehouse-Barlow, 1980; Ed, "New Scofied Reference Bibleof Common Pryr," Oxf Press, 1980; Ed, "1979 Epis Ch Annual," Morehouse-Barlow, 1979; Ed, "1978 Epis Ch Annual," Morehouse-Barlow, 1978; Ed, "New Revised Standard Version Study Bible," Oxf Press, 1977; Ed, "1977 Epis Ch Annual," Morehouse-Barlow, 1977; Ed, "1976 Epis Ch Annual," Morehouse-Barlow, 1976; Ed, "1975 Epis Ch Annual," Morehouse-Barlow, 1975; Ed, "1974 Epis Ch Annual," Morehouse-Barlow, 1974. Affirming Catholicism 1999; Angl Soc 1972. rtlau@aol.com

LAUCHER, Bill (Tex) 417 Avenue Of Oaks St, Houston TX 77009 **Vic S Alb's Ch Houston TX 2001-** B Saint Louis MO 9/9/1950 s Richard G Laucher & Jean C. TCU 1969; BA U Of Houston 1973; MDiv VTS 1994. D 6/25/1994 Bp Maurice Manuel Benitez P 1/3/1995 Bp William Elwood Sterling. m 4/5/1974 Cheryl E Cowan c 2. Asst Calv Epis Ch Richmond TX 1994-2001. Bro Of S Andr; Ord Of S Lk. St. Geo Epis Awd Epis Ch And Bsa 2000; 6-Year Serv Recognition SAMS 1989. blaucher@sbcglobal.net

LAUDISIO, Patricia Devin (Colo) 3328 Sentinel Dr, Boulder CO 80301 B Sarasota FL 2/27/1943 d Fletcher Marsh Devin & Mary Agnes. Hollins U; Iliff TS; Loyola U; BS Metropltn St Coll of Denver; OH SU; S Thos Sem; U Of Florida. D 6/18/1994 Bp William Jerry Winterrowd. m 5/26/1969 Antonio L Laudisio c 2. D S Jn's Epis Ch Boulder CO 1994-2008. Colorado Haiti Proj; Contemplative Outreach. patlaudisio@me.com

LAUER, Daniel Donald (WTex) 2006 Pinetree Ln, San Antonio TX 78232 B Duluth MN 3/17/1967 s Donald E Lauer & Mary Lou. MDiv Epis TS of The SW 2002. D 6/4/2002 Bp Robert Boyd Hibbs P 2/28/2003 Bp James Edward Folts. m 11/12/1988 Renae Ann Wilslef c 4. Cur Chr Epis Ch San Antonio TX 2002-2007. danl@cecsa.org

LAUER, Jay Leroy (Fla) 3815 Sw 6th Pl, Gainesville FL 32607 **D Dio Florida Jacksonville FL 1986-; D S Jos's Ch Newberry FL 1986-** B New York NY 11/8/1923 s Julian Laver & Helen. Inst for Chr Stds; San Diego St U. D 6/29/1986 Bp Frank Stanley Cerveny. m 3/8/1950 Barbara Alice Beyer.

LAUGHLIN III, Ledlie I (Pa) 313 Pine St, Philadelphia PA 19106 **R S Ptr's Ch Philadelphia PA 1999-** B New York NY 7/9/1959 s Ledlie Irwin Laughlin & Roxana Dodd. BA Ob 1982; Cert Urasenke Chanoyu Gakuen TS Kyoto JP 1984; MDiv Ya Berk 1987. D 10/9/1988 Bp Paul Moore Jr P 5/6/1989 Bp John Shelby Spong. m 11/7/1987 Sarah Clifford c 2. R Gr Epis Ch Norwalk CT 1993-1999; R S Paul's Ch In Bergen Jersey City NJ 1991-1993; Asst R S Pat's Ch Washington DC 1989-1991; Par Mssnr S Paul's Epis Ch Paterson NJ 1988-1989. laughlin@stpetersphila.org

LAUGHLIN JR, Ledlie Irwin (Eur) 63 Ford Hill Rd, West Cornwall CT 06796 B Princeton NJ 5/18/1930 s Ledlie Irwin Laughlin & Roberta Howe. BA Pr

1952; STB GTS 1955. D 6/19/1955 P 1/1/1956 Bp Benjamin M Washburn. m 4/19/1958 Roxana Dodd c 3. Int Cathd Ch Of S Paul Burlington VT 1996-1997; R S Jas Epis Ch Firenze IA IT 1992-1995; St Jas Ch 1992-1995; Hon Cn The Amer Cathd of the H Trin Paris 75008 FR 1992-1995; Joint Cmsn on AIDS Dio New York New York City NY 1988-1991; Chair, COM Dio New York New York City NY 1988-1990; The Ch Of S Lk In The Fields New York NY 1976-1992; Educ Off Dio New York New York City NY 1971-1972; Adult Educ Div DeptCE ECEC Dio New York New York City NY 1969-1971; Dn Trin And S Phil's Cathd Newark NJ 1963-1969; Assoc Gr Ch Van Vorst Jersey City NJ 1955-1963. irlaughlin@earthlink.net

LAUGHLIN, Ophelia G (NJ) Waterman Avenue, Rumson NJ 07760 **R S Geo's-By-The-River Rumson NJ 2000-** B Princeton NJ 1/8/1959 d James Ben Laughlin & Julia. BA Pr 1981; MS Pace U 1983; MDiv GTS 1993. D 6/12/1993 Bp George Phelps Mellick Belshaw. m 5/3/1996 Eric Pearl c 2. R S Paul's Ch Southington CT 1997-2000; Cur S Geo's-By-The-River Rumson NJ 1993-1997. ophelia@stgeorgesrumson.org

LAUK, Candice Ruth (NMich) 1003 Wickman Dr, Iron Mountain MI 49801 **P H Trin Ch Iron Mtn MI 2004-** B 9/8/1956 D 3/1/1998 Bp Thomas Kreider Ray P 2/29/2004 Bp James Arthur Kelsey. m 5/12/1984 Vincent C Lauk c 2.

LAUN, Gerhard Hermann (Haw) 2010 W San Marcos Blvd Unit 98, San Marcos CA 92078 B Frankfurt-am-Main DE 1/17/1941 s Hermann Laun & Elisabeth Luise. MA U of Frankfurt DE 1967; UU Sch of Alco & Drugs 1987. D 1/11/1970 P 5/22/1971 Bp Chilton Powell. m 11/11/1994 Belquis A Amdamjar c 1. R S Eliz's Ch Honolulu HI 1990-2003; R S Mary's Ch Provo UT 1978-1990; Vic H Fam Watonga OK 1974-1977; Cur S Jas Epis Ch Oklahoma City OK 1971-1974. Auth, *Angl-RC Relatns: the Influence of the Oxford Mvmt on Intl -Ch Relatns*, U of Frankfurt, 1968. glaun@att.net

LAURA, Ronald Samuel (Vt) No address on file. B Boston MA 5/1/1945 D 8/29/1970 Bp Harvey D Butterfield.

LAURINEC, Jennene Lawton (Tex) 308 Cottage Rd., Carthage TX 75633 **Vic S Jn's Epis Ch Carthage TX 2008-** B Craig CO 6/30/1954 d Dean Alton Lawton & Viola Watkins. BBA LeTourneau U 2001. D 6/28/2008 Bp Don Adger Wimberly P 1/10/2009 Bp Rayford Baines High Jr. m 1/29/1977 Steven Laurinec c 3. jennenel@aol.com

LAUSCH, Ronald Robert (CPa) 315 W Sheridan Ave, Annville PA 17003 **R H Trin Epis Ch Shamokin PA 2001-; R S Steph's Ch Mt Carmel PA 2001-** B Lebanon PA 2/13/1950 s Robert Lausch & Helen Esther. Millersville U; Penn; BA Ursinus Coll 1972; Franklin & Marshall Coll 1976; MA Lancaster TS 1976. D 6/15/1990 P 5/22/1991 Bp Charlie Fuller McNutt Jr. Vic Chr Ch Milton PA 1992-2001; Vic St Jas Epis Ch Muncy PA 1992-2001; P S Jn's Epis Ch Lancaster PA 1991-1992. Third Ord, Soc of S Fran 1974.

LAUTENSCHLAGER, Paul John (Colo) 11 W. Madison Street, Colorado Springs CO 80907 **R Ch Of S Mich The Archangel Colorado Sprg CO 2001-** B Kitchener ON CA 5/30/1946 s Kenneth Lautenschlager & Lucile Adeline. BA Mssh Coll 1969; MDiv PDS 1972. D 5/27/1972 P 3/14/1973 Bp Dean T Stevenson. m 12/28/1989 Nancy Jane Schoenbeck c 1. Dio Colorado Denver CO 2007-2010; R Ch Of The Trsfg Palos Pk IL 1992-2001; R S Mk's Ch S Louis MO 1985-1992; Asst R S Tim's Epis Ch Creve Coeur MO 1978-1984; R S Paul's Ch Philipsburg PA 1975-1978; Asst R Cathd Ch Of S Steph Harrisburg PA 1972-1975. paulandnancy@q.com

LAVALLEE, Armand Aime (Ct) 5523 Birchhill Rd, Charlotte NC 28227 **S Mart's Epis Ch Charlotte NC 2000-** B Pawtucket RI 12/16/1934 s Alphonse E LaVallee & Stacia M. BA Ken 1956; MDiv EDS 1959; PhD Harv 1967. D 6/20/1959 P 12/19/1959 Bp John S Higgins. m 4/7/2005 Alison H Freund c 2. Asst S Mart's Epis Ch Charlotte NC 1998; Asst S Jas Epis Ch Danbury CT 1982-1998; Fac Dio Rhode Island Providence RI 1982-1987; Dep GC Dio Rhode Island Providence RI 1973-1979; R S Mk's Epis Ch Riverside RI 1971-1982; R S Thos Ch Greenville RI 1962-1970; Asst S Mk's Epis Ch Riverside RI 1960-1962; Cur S Barn Ch Warwick RI 1959-1960.

LAVALLEE, Donald Alphonse (RI) 1665 Broad St, Cranston RI 02905 B Central Falls RI 12/16/1940 s Alphonse LaVallee & Stacia Marion. BA Br 1962; BD EDS 1965; DMin STUSo 1982; MBA U of Rhode Island 1990. D 6/19/1965 P 2/1/1966 Bp John S Higgins. m 6/30/1991 Terri Idskou c 1. Ch Of The Trsfg Cranston RI 1965-1999. TLIDSKOU2@YAHOO.COM

LAVENGOOD, Henrietta Louise (NJ) 211 Falls Ct, Medford NJ 08055 B Mount Holly NJ 5/28/1954 d Henry Walter Brandt & Margaret. BA Drew U 1976; MDiv UTS 1982; Cert Blanton-Peale Grad Inst 1985; DMin NYTS 2002; Cert Trauma Cntr Boston MA 2004. D 6/7/1986 P 12/11/1986 Bp Paul Moore Jr. m 1/1/2001 Martin Brownlee Lavengood. S Mary's Ch Clementon NJ 2004-2008; Par Of Chr The Redeem Pelham NY 2000-2001; Trin Ch Ft Wayne IN 2000-2001; Int S Jn Of The Cross Bristol IN 1997; Assoc P Par Of Chr The Redeem Pelham NY 1995-1996; S Mk's Ch Mt Kisco NY 1994-1995. AAPC 1988. hlavengood@aol.com

LAVENGOOD, Martin Brownlee (NJ) 211 Falls Ct, Medford NJ 08055 **The Evergreens Moorestown NJ 2009-** B New York NY 8/26/1953 s Russell Wilson Lavengood & Roberta. BA Eisenhower Coll 1976; MA Col 1983; MDiv GTS 1991. D 6/8/1991 P 12/1/1991 Bp Richard Frank Grein. m 1/1/2001 Henrietta Louise Brandt. All SS Ch Syracuse IN 2000-2003; R S Alb's Epis Ch Ft Wayne IN 1998-2000; R S Jas' Epis Ch Goshen IN 1994-1998. Roberta C Rudin Dioc Schlr. frmbl@aol.com

LAVERONI, Alfred Frank (Md) 312 Cigar Loop, Hvre De Grace MD 21078 B New York NY 8/8/1938 s Walter Paul Laveroni & Annette Gloria. BA Hofstra U 1960; MDiv GTS 1963; MS Amer Tech U 1974; DMin Drew U 1983. D 6/15/1963 Bp James P De Wolfe P 12/1/1963 Bp Jonathan Goodhue Sherman. m 6/30/1973 Jean Mohr c 1. Mssn Cltn Taskforce Dio Maryland Baltimore MD 1989-1993; Assoc S Mary's Ch Abingdon MD 1986-2000; LocTen Gr Epis Ch Darlington MD 1985-1986; Assoc Gr Ch Pemberton NJ 1982-1983; Off Of Bsh For ArmdF New York NY 1967-1987. Auth/Ed, “The Seder: Serv Bklet”; Auth, “Personl Effectiveness Trng Manual”; Auth, “Soc Alienation In Jr Enlisted Ranks”; Auth, “Ldrshp In Pluralistic Setting”. alaveroni@aol.com

LAVERY, Patricia Anne (NwPa) PO Box 1714, Hermitage PA 16148 **D Ch Of The Redeem Hermitage PA 2011-** B Pittsburgh PA 12/26/1950 d Charles James Lavery & Irene Constance. BS Ohio U 1972; MA Carlow U 2002. D 12/4/2010 Bp Sean Walter Rowe. c 2. palavery@msn.com

LAVINE, Patricia Iva (Alb) 323 Lakeshore Dr, Norwood NY 13668 **Vic Zion Ch Colton NY 2005-** B Potsdam NY 4/1/1942 d Clarence William Campbell & Harriett Cornelius. D 6/30/2002 Bp Daniel William Herzog. m 6/1/1963 Richard Douglas LaVine c 2. D Zion Ch Colton NY 2004-2005; D S Phil's Ch Norwood NY 2002-2004. pclavine@yahoo.com

LAVOE, John F (CNY) 210 Yoxall Ln, Oriskany NY 13424 B Brooklyn NY 9/29/1946 s George Francis LaVoe & Josephine Bernice. S Josephs Novitiate Valatie NY 1965; St. Edw's U Austin TX 1967; BA Rockhurst Coll, KC MO 1969; MDiv PDS 1972; Licenses FCC-Ham & Gnrl Radiotelephone 1985; Cert Par Dvlpmt Inst 1987; DMin Ecum TS 1999. D 5/15/1972 Bp Ned Cole P 6/20/1973 Bp Lloyd Edward Gressle. m 10/4/1986 Susan D Lavoe c 2. Dio Cntrl New York Syracuse NY 2005-2008; S Geo's Epis Ch Chadwicks NY 1995-2009; S Jn's Ch Whitesboro NY 1995-2009; Epis Mnstry Whitesboro NY 1990-2008; In-charge; then R S Jn's Ch Whitesboro NY 1986-2008; Dio Cntrl New York Syracuse NY 1986-1991; All SS Ch Utica NY 1981-1990; R Emm Ch Adams NY 1975-1981; R Zion Ch Adams NY 1975-1981; Cur Chr Ch Reading PA 1972-1975. Auth, “Multiple Rel Bk Revs,” *Sharing the Pract*, APC Journ, 2011; Auth, “Var arts on Mnstry,” *Sharing the Pract*, APC Journ, 1992; Auth, “6 Selected Sermons,” *LayR Sermons*, Seabury, 1981. Acad of Par Cler 1984; Cbury Way 1991. johnlavoe@juno.com

LAW, Eric Hung-Fat (Los) 351 Sandpiper St, Palm Desert CA 92260 **Kaleidoscope Inst Los Angeles CA 2006-** B HK 1/1/1957 s Kwok-Nam Law & Un-Oi. BS Cor 1978; MDiv EDS 1984. D 6/23/1984 Bp O'Kelley Whitaker P 6/2/1985 Bp Robert C Rusack. Mssnr for Congrl Dvlpmt Dio Los Angeles Los Angeles CA 2000-2006; Dio Los Angeles Los Angeles CA 1984-2005. “El Labo Habitara con el Cardero,” Cathd Cntr Press, LA; Auth, “Finding Intimacy in a Wrld of Fear,” Chalice Press, St Louis; Auth, “,The Wolf Shall Dwell w The Lamb,” Chalice Press, St Louis; Auth, “,Inclusion,” Chalice Press, St Louis; Auth, “,The Bush Was Blazing But Not Consumed:,” Chalice Press, St Louis; Auth, “,Sacr Acts, H Change,” Chalice Press, St Louis; Auth, “,The Word at the Crossings,” Chalice Press, St Louis. ehflaw@aol.com

LAW, Sylvan Watson (ECR) 6803 N 68th Plaza, Apt. 309, Omaha NE 68152 B Miami FL 8/29/1927 s Burt Smith Law & Bernice Elsie. BBA U of Miami 1949; MS VPI 1951; MDiv VTS 1956. D 6/1/1956 P 12/1/1956 Bp Robert Raymond Brown. m 5/29/1948 Evelyn Zavodsky c 3. Vic S Paul's Ch Cambria CA 1981-1989; R Redeem And Hope Epis Ch Delano CA 1979-1981; Dn Chr Cathd Salina KS 1973-1979; Vic Ch of SS Jn & Geo Jct City KS 1970-1973; R Ch Of The Cov Jct City KS 1968-1973; Vic S Jn's Ch Neosho MO 1964-1968; Vic S Nich Ch Noel MO 1964-1968; Vic Ch Of The Redeem Kansas City MO 1959-1964; Vic All SS Epis Ch Russellville AR 1956-1959; Vic S Ptr's Ch Conway AR 1956-1959.

LAWBAUGH, Will Medley (CPa) 112 East Main St, PO Box 206, Lock Haven PA 17745 **R S Paul's Ch Lock Haven PA 2007-** B St Marys MO 8/29/1942 s Emmanuel Sylvester Lawbaugh & Halita Joan. PhD U Of Missour Columbia MO 1972; MA Mt St Marys Sem Emmitsburg MD 1995; MTS VTS 2007. D 6/9/2007 P 12/22/2007 Bp Nathan Dwight Baxter. c 7. wlawbaugh@yahoo.com

LAWLER, Gary Elwyn Andrew (Chi) 401 N Cherry St, Morrison IL 61270 **R The Ch Of S Anne Morrison IL 1997-** B Monroe WI 6/13/1944 s Elwyn William Lawler & Shirlah Mae. BA Elmhurst Coll 1966; MDiv Nash 1989. D 6/17/1989 Bp Frank Tracy Griswold III P 12/1/1989 Bp James Winchester Montgomery. S Greg's Ch Gonzales LA 1991-1997; S Mich's Ch Baton Rouge LA 1991-1997; Cur Ch Of S Mary The Vrgn New York NY 1989-1991. SocMary, La Epis Cleric Assn, Ord Of S Ben. stannemorrison@frontiernet.net

LAWLER, Richard (WNC) Po Box 2680, Blowing Rock NC 28605 **R S Mary Of The Hills Epis Par Blowing Rock NC 1995-** B Chicago IL 3/31/1957 s Joseph Andrew Lawler & Helen May. BA Indiana U 1979; MDiv Nash 1985. D 6/14/1985 P 12/1/1985 Bp William Carl Frey. m 12/22/1984 Elizabeth Duer c 2. R S Raphael Epis Ch Colorado Sprg CO 1987-1995; S Tim's Epis Ch

Centennial CO 1987; Cur S Jos's Ch Lakewood CO 1985-1987. Soc Of S Jn The Evang. lawlerr@bellsouth.net

LAWLER, Steven William (Mo) 47 Aberdeen Pl, Saint Louis MO 63105 **Int R S Steph's Ch Ferguson MO 2001-** B Woodstock IL 10/8/1954 s James David Lawler & Helen Elaine. Tilburg U Tilburg Nl; BS Rockford Coll 1981; MDiv SWTS 1984; STM Ya Berk 1988; MBA Washington U 1997. D 6/16/1984 Bp Quintin Ebenezer Primo Jr P 12/15/1984 Bp James Winchester Montgomery. c 1. Int S Matt's Epis Ch Warson Warson Woods MO 1998-1999; S Mich & S Geo Clayton MO 1988-1998; Holland Hall Sch Tulsa OK 1986-1988. Auth, "Chrsnty & Crisis"; Auth, "The Angl Dig"; Auth, "Thesquare.Com"; Auth, "The St Louis Post-Dispatch"; Auth, "LivCh"; Auth, "The Ch Times"; Auth, "The Alb Inst"; Auth, "Sprtlty And Hlth". Amer Chapl Ord Of S Jn Of Beverley 1990. swl@lawler.org

LAWLOR, Jay R (WMich) Diocese of Western Michigan, 535 S. Burdick Street, Suite 1, Kalamazoo MI 49007 **R S Lk's Par Kalamazoo MI 2009-** B Exeter NH 4/27/1970 s Joseph Thomas Lawlor & Lois Ellen. BA Stonehill Coll 1993; MA U of Connecticut 1995; MDiv EDS 2002. D 6/15/2002 P 5/31/2003 Bp M(arvil) Thomas Shaw III. m 7/20/2002 Angela Kay Dotson c 1. Assoc Ch Of The Nativ Raleigh NC 2008-2009; R S Paul Ch Exton PA 2005-2007; Assoc S Mary's Epis Ch Ardmore PA 2003-2005; Asst Gr Ch New Bedford MA 2002-2003. Contrib, "Reconcilers in a Violent Wrld," *Get Up Off Your Knees: Preaching the U2 Catalog*, Cowley, 2003; Auth, "The Ch and Intl Dvlpmt: Seeking Justice and Peace in Mssn to the Wrld's poor," Universal Pub, 1999. jayrlawlor@yahoo.com

LAWRENCE JR, Albert Sumner (Tex) 14 Sedgewick Pl, The Woodlands TX 77382 B Medford MA 7/21/1936 s Albert Sumner Lawrence & Gladys Hannah. BA U of Maryland 1958; BD EDS 1961; DMin Luther TS 1979. D 9/10/1961 P 12/30/1962 Bp Frederic Cunningham Lawrence. m 4/20/1968 Dawn Bates c 4. R Ch Of The Ascen Houston TX 1979-2000; R S Paul's Ch Winona MN 1971-1979; Assoc S Jas Ch Lancaster PA 1966-1970; Asst Chr Ch Cambridge Cambridge MA 1961-1966. Auth, "The Contentment You Long For," *Winepress Grp*, 2009; Auth, "The Original Christmas Gift," *Selah*, Selah, 2001. EvangES 1971-1979; FOW 1971-1979; Ord Of S Lk 1971-1979. asl36@sbcglobal.net

L

LAWRENCE, Amy (Cal) 2711 Harkness St, Sacramento CA 95818 B Walnut Creek CA 2/10/1964 d Gary Lawrence & Joan. BA U Pac 1986; MDiv UTS 1991. D 6/4/1994 P 6/3/1995 Bp William Edwin Swing. All Souls Par In Berkeley Berkeley CA 2004; Asst S Ptr's Epis Ch Redwood City CA 1995-1998. amy.lawrence1@comcast.net

LAWRENCE, Bruce Bennett (NC) C/O Department Of Religion, Duke University, Durham NC 27706 B Newton NJ 8/14/1941 s Joseph Stagg Lawrence & Emma Frances. BA Pr 1962; BD EDS 1967; PhD Ya 1972. D 6/13/1967 P 12/1/1967 Bp Walter H Gray. m 4/20/1983 Miriam Cooke c 2. Cur S Barth's Ch Pittsboro NC 1972-1974; Cur Ascen Ch New Haven CT 1967-1971. Auth, "Notes From A Distant Flute"; Auth, "Ibn Khaldun & Islamic Ideology".

LAWRENCE, Catherine Abbott (NY) 1415 Pelhamdale Ave, Pelham NY 10803 B San Francisco CA 8/27/1939 d Louis Ramon Moretti & Shirley Lillian. D 5/1/2010 Bp Mark Sean Sisk. c 3. ccamie8@aol.com

LAWRENCE, Charles Kane Cobb (Lex) 101 S. Hanover Ave, Apt 7M, Lexington KY 40502 B Lynn MA 1/20/1917 s William Appleton Lawrence & Hannah Cobb. BA Harv 1938; BD VTS 1941; GTS 1952; STM UTS 1952. D 6/13/1941 Bp William A Lawrence P 5/28/1942 Bp Edwin A Penick. m 6/14/1980 Mildred Terrell c 4. Epis TS Lexington KY 1971-1981; ExCoun Dio Lexington Lexington KY 1959-1965; Chapl (U of K) S Aug's Chap Lexington KY 1958-1962; Coll Wk Cmsn Dio Pennsylvania Philadelphia PA 1953-1958; Vic Chr Ch Biddeford ME 1944-1949; Cur Gr Ch Amherst MA 1943-1944; Cur Trin Epis Ch Columbus GA 1942-1943; Cur Calv Ch Tarboro NC 1941-1942. Hon DD ETSKy Lexington KY 1970.

LAWRENCE, Eric John (Nev) 2306 Paradise Dr Apt 222, Reno NV 89512 B Buffalo WY 4/28/1967 BA U of Nevada at Reno. D 6/21/2003 P 12/24/2003 Bp Katharine Jefferts Schori. m 10/18/2002 Robyn Opoka.

LAWRENCE, Gerard Martin (Mass) 15 Bridge St, Norwell MA 02061 B Long Beach CA 4/24/1936 s Joseph Carter Lawrence & Tillie Amalia. California Inst of Tech 1958; BA U of Washington 1960. D 9/29/1975 Bp Ivol I Curtis P 6/13/1980 Bp Robert Hume Cochrane. m 4/3/1982 Karen Simon c 4. P-in-c Trin Epis Ch Rockland MA 1999-2007; Assoc S Lk's Epis Ch Scituate MA 1997-1998; Assoc S Wilfrid Of York Epis Ch Huntington Bch CA 1986-1996; Assoc Emm Epis Ch Mercer Island WA 1982-1984; Assoc S Marg's Epis Ch Bellevue WA 1975-1982.

LAWRENCE JR, Harry Martin (ETenn) 1800 Lula Lake Rd, Lookout Mountain GA 30750 **Asstg P Chr Ch - Epis Chattanooga TN 1979-** B Chattanooga TN 6/9/1931 s Harry Martin Lawrence & Mildred Carolyn. BS W&L 1953; MD U of Tennessee 1956; MS Mayo Clnc 1967. D 6/25/1978 Bp William F Gates Jr P 6/1/1979 Bp William Evan Sanders. m 12/29/1957 Martha Sue Rice. P-in-c S Mart Of Tours Epis Ch Chattanooga TN 1979-1980. Auth, "Effect Of Corneal Contact Lenses In Rabbits".

LAWRENCE, James Dean (Tex) PO Box 852, League City TX 77574 **Assoc R S Chris's Ch League City TX 2009-** B Houston TX 5/26/1970 s James Alfred Lawrence & Mary Ann. BS Texas A&M U-Coll Sta 1993; MDiv VTS 2009. D 6/20/2009 P 1/28/2010 Bp C(harles) Andrew Doyle. m 11/1/1997 Sarah B Barringer. deanlawre@gmail.com

LAWRENCE, John Arthur (Chi) 712 Mockingbird Lane, Kerrville TX 78028 B Fort Worth TX 5/26/1935 s Kelley Edward Lawrence & Hazel Annette. BA Sewanee: U So 1957; MDiv SWTS 1971. D 6/16/1971 P 12/21/1971 Bp Iveson Batchelor Noland. m 1/9/1987 Waynoka Lee West. R Gr Epis Ch Hinsdale IL 1989-1999; R S Augustines Ch Metairie LA 1979-1989; EFM Mentor The TS at The U So Sewanee TN 1976-1999; R S Thos' Ch Monroe LA 1972-1979; Cur Gr Meml Hammond LA 1971-1972. johnalaw@gmail.com

LAWRENCE, John Elson (WA) 4336 Wordsworth Way, Venice FL 34293 **Int R S Alb's Par Washington DC 2010-** B Brooklyn NY 12/1/1945 s Edward Arthur Lawrence & Gladys Bates. Capital U; BA GW 1967; MDiv GTS 1970. D 6/13/1970 P 12/19/1970 Bp Jonathan Goodhue Sherman. m 5/10/1986 Jeramy Leslie c 3. Int S Pat's Ch Washington DC 2008-2010; S Pat's Epis Day Sch Washington DC 2008-2010; Int Calv Ch Columbia MO 2006-2008; R Trin Ch Newport RI 2000-2006; Cn Ordnry Dio Sthrn Ohio Cincinnati OH 1991-2000; R S Chris's Ch Fairborn OH 1987-1991; R S Ann's Ch Sayville NY 1980-1985; Secy of the Dio and Conv Dio Long Island Garden City NY 1978-2005; Secy of the Dio Dio Long Island Garden City NY 1978-1985; R All SS Ch Bayside NY 1975-1980; Asst R Gr Epis Ch Nyack NY 1971-1975; Cur All SS Ch Great Neck NY 1970-1971. Auth, *Leaven (Ed) (1981-1988)*. Hon Cn Chr Ch Cathd Cincinnati OH 1993. jelawrence1@yahoo.com

✠ LAWRENCE, Rt Rev Mark Joseph (SC) PO Box 20127, Charleston SC 29413 **Bp of SC Dio So Carolina Charleston SC 2008-** B Bakersfield CA 3/19/1950 s Leo Douglas Lawrence & Bertha Ann. BA California St U 1976; MDiv TESM 1980. D 8/2/1980 P 7/18/1981 Bp Victor Manuel Rivera. m 9/8/1973 Allison K Taylor c 5. R S Paul's Ch Bakersfield CA 1997-2007; S Steph's Epis Ch Mckeesport PA 1984-1997; Vic S Mk's Ch Shafter CA 1981-1984; Epis Dio San Joaquin Modesto CA 1981-1982; Ch Of H Fam Fresno CA 1980-1981.

LAWRENCE, Matthew Richard (NCal) 550 Mendocino Ave, Santa Rosa CA 95401 **R Ch Of The Incarn Santa Rosa CA 2003-** B Missoula MT 9/2/1956 s Van Sheerin Lawrence & Dulcie Ann. BA Reed Coll 1980; UTS 1981; MDiv U Chi 1986; MA U Chi 1987; DMin SWTS 2011. D 6/3/1989 Bp David Elliot Johnson P 6/17/1990 Bp Barbara Clementine Harris. m 11/13/1982 Rosa Lynn Thomas c 1. Dep GC Dio Nthrn California Sacramento CA 2008-2011; Stndg Com Dio Nthrn California Sacramento CA 2007-2011; First Alt Dep GC Dio Nthrn California Sacramento CA 2005-2008; First Alt Dep GC Dio Michigan Detroit MI 2002-2003; COM Dio Michigan Detroit MI 1999-2003; Sr Chapl Cbury Hse Ann Arbor MI 1996-2003; Dir Par Mssn S Geo's Ch Milford MI 1995-1996; Int Epis City Mssn Boston MA 1993-1994; R Ch Of Our Sav Arlington MA 1992-1995; Chair, Peace and Justice Cmsn Dio Massachusetts Boston MA 1992-1994; D The Cathd Ch Of S Paul Boston MA 1989-1990. Auth, "Letter to an Alpha Friend," *Living Ch*, 2002; Auth, "It's Time for a New Kind of Reformation," *Living Ch*, 2001; Auth, "How to Create a Successful Cmnty-Based Proj," *Congregations*, 2000; Auth, "Bad Preaching 101," *Living Ch*, 1999; Auth, "Foolish Beatitudes," *Chr Century*, 1993; Auth, "Helping the H Sprt Elect a Bp," *Chr Century*, 1989; Auth, "Urban Job Creation Strategies: An Evaltn," *Cntr for Urban Resrch and Plcy Stds*, U Chi, 1986. Natl hon Soc 1974. Urban Scholars Fllshp U Chi Chicago Illinois 1987. revml@sonic.net

LAWRENCE, Novella E (NY) 20 Laguardia Ave Apt 4f, Staten Island NY 10314 **D S Paul's Ch Darien CT 2000-** B Brooklyn NY 9/20/1937 d Herbert Brown & Pauline. BS SUNY 1995. D 4/26/1997 Bp Richard Frank Grein. Amer Angl Coun 2002; Evang Fllshp Of Angl Comm 1998. lord3287@cs.com

LAWRENCE, Philip Archer (Okla) 32251 S 616 Rd, Grove OK 74344 **Vic S Andr's Ch Grove OK 2011-; Dio Oklahoma Oklahoma City OK 2006-** B Tulsa OK 7/17/1940 s Philip A Lawrence & Evelyn. BA U of Kansas 1964. D 12/21/2001 P 7/20/2002 Bp Robert Manning Moody. m 3/10/1984 Donna Anis Lawrence. frphil@sbcglobal.net

LAWRENCE JR, Raymond Johnson (SwVa) 913 Ash Tree Ln., Niskayuna NY 12309 B Portsmouth VA 6/5/1934 s Raymond Johnson Lawrence & Gertrude. Randolph-Macon Coll 1954; A.B. Bos 1956; U of St. Andrews 1957; Oxf 1958; STM STUSo 1966; Chicago Urban Trng Cntr 1967; DMin NYTS 2000. D 6/22/1962 P 6/1/1963 Bp George P Gunn. m 10/30/1993 Ruth Kuo c 4. Epis Mssn Soc New York NY 1986-1987; Epis Mssn Soc New York NY 1986-1987; Asst Ch Of The Ascen Knoxville TN 1964-1966; Cur S Andr's Epis Ch Newport News VA 1962-1964. Auth, "Sexual Liberation: The Scandal of Christendom," Praeger, 2007; Auth, "The Poisoning Of Eros," Aug Moore Press, 1989; Auth, "Dav The Bubble Boy & The Boundries Of The Human," *Journ Of The AMA*, 1985. AK Rice 1993; Coll of Pstr Supervision and Psych 1990. lawrence@cpsp.org

LAWRENCE, Robert Stratton (SC) 2810 Seabrook Island Road, Johns Island SC 29455 **Exec Dir S Chris C&C Johns Island SC 2010-; Chair - Angl**

Comm Dvlpmt Com Dio So Carolina Charleston SC 2009-; Bd Dir Kanuga Confererences Inc Hendersonville NC 2009- B Rome GA 8/21/1955 s Henry Newman Lawrence & Margaret. BA U NC 1977; MA Tul 1985; MDiv GTS 1990. D 5/19/1990 Bp Frank Harris Vest Jr P 2/25/1991 Bp C(laude) Charles Vache. m 4/28/1979 Carol Howard c 3. Int Assoc R Chr Epis Ch Mt Pleasant SC 2010; Dioc Coun Dio So Carolina Charleston SC 2007-2011; Assoc R S Mich's Epis Ch Charleston SC 2005-2010; P Assoc S Mich's Epis Ch Charleston SC 2002-2005; Chapl Off Of Bsh For ArmdF New York NY 1995-2005; Assoc P S Chris's Ch Pensacola FL 1995-1998; R S Matt's Epis Ch Darlington SC 1993-1995; Cur Trin Ch Portsmouth VA 1990-1993. robert.stratton.lawrence@gmail.com

LAWRENCE, Wade William (Pgh) 6911 Prospect Ave, Pittsburgh PA 15202 **D Chr Epis Ch No Hills Pittsburgh PA 2004-; Trin Cathd Pittsburgh PA 1992-** B Almont MI 5/31/1947 s Wade Hampton Lawrence & Amelia Ruth. BS Wayne 1975; Cert Whitaker TS 1984. D 6/30/1984 Bp Henry Irving Mayson. m 12/23/1967 Ann Alice Caldwell c 3. D S Brendan's Epis Ch Sewickley PA 1990-1992; S Dav's Ch Southfield MI 1989-1990; D S Chris-S Paul Epis Ch Detroit MI 1987-1988; S Dav's Ch Southfield MI 1986-1987; D S Tim's Epis Ch Winston Salem NC 1985-1986. Ord of S Lk 1956-2002. awlpgh@verizon.net

LAWS III, Robert James (NC) 820 College Ave, PO Box 3400, Fredericksburg VA 22401 **S Andr The Fisherman Epis Mayo MD 2010-** B Burlington NC 9/14/1968 s Robert James Laws & Evelyn Sue. BS E Coast Bible Coll Charlotte NC 1990; MRE Duke DS 1994; MDiv TESM 2000. D 6/10/2000 Bp Robert William Duncan P 12/12/2000 Bp Henry Irving Louttit. m 6/6/1992 Kimiko Naito c 1. Asst R/ Cbury Chapl Trin Ch Fredericksburg VA 2007-2010; Int S Paul's Ch Bennettsville SC 2004-2005; Vic S Mary Magd Ch W End NC 2002-2004; Asst S Thos Ch Savannah GA 2000-2002. SocMary 1998. fatherroblaws@yahoo.com

LAWS, Thomas Richard (Nwk) 11 Harvard St, Montclair NJ 07042 B Burlington KS 3/22/1939 s Floyd E Laws & Vesta E. BA U of Kansas 1960; MDiv UTS 1964. D 6/3/1967 P 12/1/1967 Bp Horace W B Donegan. m 10/2/1977 Oneida A Mendez-Laws. S Gabr's Ch Oak Ridge NJ 2000-2011; All SS' Epis Ch Scotch Plains NJ 1999-2000; Chr Ch Belleville NJ 1997-1999; Chr Ch Newton NJ 1997; Ch Of The H Sprt Verona NJ 1997; R San Andres Ch Yonkers NY 1972-1974; Asst Min Ch Of S Mary The Vrgn New York NY 1967-1971. Auth, "The New Professionals". thomaslaws@hotmail.com

LAWSON, Frederick Quinney (U) 4294 Adonis Dr, Salt Lake City UT 84124 **Dn Emer Cathd Ch Of S Mk Salt Lake City UT 2010-** B Dayton OH 5/21/1945 s Frederick Richmond Lawson & Janet Eccles. Hob 1965; BA U of Leicester 1972; GOE Oxf 1975; GOE Oxf 1979. Trans from Church Of England 6/1/1989 Bp George Edmonds Bates. Dn Emer Cathd Ch Of S Mk Salt Lake City UT 2010; Stndg Com - Secy Dio Utah Salt Lake City UT 2002-2005; Cn Cathd Ch Of S Mk Salt Lake City UT 1984-2002. Auth, "Through the Eyes of Many Faiths," *Through the Eyes of Many Faiths 2nd Ed*, Utah Hist Soc, 1992. Fell of Edw King Soc St. Stephens Hse, Oxf Engl 2008; DD Utah St U, Logan, Utah 2007; Doctor of Publ Serv Westminster Coll, Salt Lake City, Utah 2005. rql@xmission.com

LAWSON, Neil-St Barnabas J (EpisSanJ) P.O. Box 7606, Stockton CA 95267 **S Paul's Epis Ch Visalia CA 2009-** B Chicago IL 2/9/1951 s Charles Delbert Lawson & Natalie Soares. BA California St U 1974; MDiv CDSP 1990. D 6/3/1990 P 6/14/1991 Bp John-David Mercer Schofield. m 2/15/1980 Cindy S Zepeda c 4. St Pauls Epis Fllshp Visalia CA 2009-2010; S Ptr's Epis Ch Talladega AL 2006-2008; R Ch Of The Redemp Southampton PA 2002-2006; Chr Ch Lemoore CA 1993-2002; Epis Ch Of The Sav Hanford CA 1991-1992. njlawson@excite.com

LAWSON, Paul David (Los) PO Box 1573, Palm Desert CA 92261 **GC Coordntr Epis Ch Cntr New York NY 1985-** B Davenport IA 8/22/1946 s David George Lawson & Winifred Adella. BA S Mary Coll Moraga CA 1968; MDiv Epis TS of The SW 1979; DMin Claremont TS 1998. Trans 2/24/1980 Bp Lemuel Barnett Shirley. m 8/8/1970 Cristina Collins. S Cross By-The-Sea Ch Hermosa Bch CA 1994-2009; Cathd Cntr Of S Paul Cong Los Angeles CA 1993; Cn for Soc Mnstry Dio Los Angeles Los Angeles CA 1989-1993; S Thos Of Cbury Epis Ch Albuquerque NM 1984-1989; Asst S Mk's On The Mesa Epis Ch Albuquerque NM 1983-1984; Exec Coun Appointees New York NY 1982-1983; Dio Panama 1980-1982. Auth, "Pryr and the Wk of Cler," *Sprtlty,Contemplation & Transformation*, Lantern Books, 2008; Auth, "Old Wine in New Skins," Lantern Books, 2001; Auth, "Change & Contemplation," *The Div Indwelling*, Continuum, 2001; Auth, "Ldrshp & Change Through Contemplation," *The Sewanee Theol Revs Volume 43:3 Pent*, 2000; Auth, "Breaking Free: Freedom and Self-differentiation," *Leaven Volume 28 no 11 June/July*, 1999; Auth, "Systems Theory and Centering Pryr," *Centering Pryr in Daily Life and Minisry*, Continuum, 1998; Auth, "Pstr & Ch Anxiety," *Leaven*, 1997; Auth, "Losing the W a Second Time," *Evang Outlook*, 1991. Miata Club of Sthrn California 1995; No Amer Patristic Soc 1993-2005. Cn Dio Los Angeles 2002; hon Pub Claremont Theol 1998. olot@aol.com

LAWSON, Peter Raymond (Cal) Po Box 563, Valley Ford CA 94972 B New Britain CT 1/3/1929 s Raymond Carl Lawson & Alice Louisa. BA Br 1950; STB Ya Berk 1956; Grad Study Hartford Sem Fndt 1958. D 8/30/1956 P 6/14/1957 Bp Walter H Gray. m 2/14/1981 Danielle Durham c 5. R S Jas Epis Ch San Francisco CA 1985-1997; Dio California San Francisco CA 1982-1985; Int Epis Ch Of Our Sav Oakland CA 1980-1984; Stndg Com Dio Indianapolis Indianapolis IN 1965-1971; Dn Chr Ch Cathd Indianapolis IN 1964-1971; Dir Downtown Mnstry Chr Ch Cathd Indianapolis IN 1962-1963; Cn Trin And S Phil's Cathd Newark NJ 1960-1962; Vic Gr Ch Broad Brook CT 1957-1960; Cur Trin Epis Ch Southport CT 1956-1957. Auth, "JESUS CIRCLES, A Way to Heal Our Wounds, Subvert the Domination System, and Build an Abundant Future," *Bk*, XLIBRIS, 2004. peterlawson@mac.com

LAWSON, Richard T (WTenn) 1720 Peabody Ave, Memphis TN 38104 **R Gr - S Lk's Ch Memphis TN 2010-** B Guntersville AL 3/23/1974 s Richard T Lawson & Mary Elizabeth. BA Auburn U 1997; MDiv GTS 2001; S.T.M. TS 2009. D 6/3/2001 Bp Onell Asiselo Soto P 12/4/2001 Bp Henry Nutt Parsley Jr. m 11/30/2009 Katherine Evans Lawson c 2. Cur S Jn's Ch Decatur AL 2001-2010. Auth, "Greg of Nyssa's Homilies on the Song of Songs: Is the Erotic Left Behind?," *Sewanee Theol Revs*, 2010. richard@gracestlukes.org

LAWSON, Rolfe Adrian (Vt) No address on file. B Albany NY 3/9/1936 D 1/26/1964 Bp Allen Webster Brown P 12/10/1964 Bp Charles Bowen Persell Jr. m 8/23/1958 Patricia Ruth Krieger c 1.

LAWSON, Victor Freeman (WVa) 64 Barley Lane, Charles Town WV 25414 B Washington DC 1/12/1943 s Slater A Maddox & Isabell Holiday. BA S Aug 1964. D 6/27/1970 P 3/7/1971 Bp William Foreman Creighton. m 9/27/1999 Marlene Ola Tyler c 1. Mssnr Gr Epis Ch Middleway WV 1999-2007; Mssnr Nelson Cluster Of Epis Ch Rippon WV 1999-2007; Mssnr S Andr's-On-The-Mt Harpers Ferry WV 1999-2007; Mssnr S Barth's Leetown Kearneysville WV 1999-2007; Mssnr S Jn's Ch Harpers Ferry WV 1999-2007; Mssnr S Phil's Ch Chas Town WV 1999-2007; Mssnr St Johns Epis Ch Rippon WV 1999-2007; R Ch Of Our Sav Washington DC 1976-1999; Cur S Geo's Ch Washington DC 1970-1972. victorf@citlink.net

LAWSON, William Burton (Mass) 2496 Orchid Bay Dr Apt 103, Naples FL 34109 **Died 8/25/2011** B Minneapolis MN 10/14/1930 s Lawrence Burton Lawson & Mabel. BA U MN 1952; MDiv Ya Berk 1955; DD Ya Berk 1979. D 6/26/1955 P 12/21/1955 Bp Stephen E Keeler. c 2. Auth, *Var arts*. WBLGDL@PRODIGY.NET

LAWSON-BECK, David Roswell (NJ) 80 Elm Ave., Rahway NJ 07065 B Hartford CT 3/7/1944 s James M Beck & Florence. D 5/16/2009 Bp Sylvestre Donato Romero. c 3. lawsond44@aol.com

LAWTHERS, Robert (CNY) Po Box 23, Lake Clear NY 12945 **Died 6/23/2011** B Boston MA 12/18/1922 s Robert Joseph Lawthers & Virginia Esther. BA Harv 1948; MS U Chi 1950; MDiv VTS 1959. D 6/20/1959 P 12/19/1959 Bp Angus Dun. melawthers@roadrunner.com

LAWTON, John Keith (Ak) Po Box 530, Palmer AK 99645 B Watertown NY 10/4/1930 s John Stewart Lawton & Edrienne Matilda. BA Hob 1953; BD EDS 1956; MDiv EDS 1967. D 6/29/1956 Bp Walter M Higley P 6/1/1957 Bp Malcolm E Peabody. m 8/23/1952 Jacqueline Joan Stochl c 4. Dio Alaska Fairbanks AK 1976-1978; Asst S Barn' Ch Leeland Upper Marlboro MD 1967-1969; Asst R Par Of The Epiph Winchester MA 1965-1966; P-in-c S Thos Ch Point Hope AK 1959-1965.

LAWYER, Evelyn Virden (Minn) 4539 Keithson Dr, Arden Hills MN 55112 B Shanghai CN 9/29/1939 d Frank Virden & Katherine. EDS; BA Wellesley Coll 1962; Ord D Formation Prog 1984. D 11/4/1984 Bp Robert Marshall Anderson. m 2/1/1964 John Elder Lawyer c 4. Asst Chapl Epis Ch Hm St Paul MN 1993-1999; Refugee Resettlement Coordntr Dio Minnesota Minneapolis MN 1990-1991; D S Matt's Ch St Paul MN 1985-2004; D S Jn's Ch S Cloud MN 1984-1985. NAAD 1985. St. Steph Awd NAAD 2004. lynlaw@comcast.net

LAYCOCK, John Emerson (Mich) 7112 Kauffman Blvd., Presque Isle MI 49777 B Orlando FL 3/30/1945 s Ralph Bradley Laycock & Constance Emerson. BA Denison U 1969; MDiv GTS 1984. D 6/30/1984 Bp Henry Irving Mayson P 4/1/1985 Bp H Coleman McGehee Jr. S Jn's Epis Ch Grand Haven MI 2008-2010; S Mich's Ch Grosse Pointe Woods MI 2006-2008; S Thos Ch Trenton MI 2005-2006; St Paul's Epis Romeo MI 2001-2005; S Jas Ch Grosse Ile MI 1999-2001; Int Gr Epis Ch Southgate MI 1997-1999; Int S Geo's Ch Milford MI 1996-1997; R S Columba Ch Detroit MI 1986-1996; Assoc R Chr Ch Detroit MI 1984-1986. jelaycock741@gmail.com

LAYCOCK JR, R(alph) Bradley (SwVa) 42 E Main St, Salem VA 24153 B Rockledge FL 2/21/1943 s Ralph Bradley Laycock & Constance Emerson. BA Dart 1966; MBA Bowling Green St U 1968; MDiv CRDS 1996; CTh Epis TS of The SW 1999. D 6/7/1999 P 12/18/1999 Bp Robert Jefferson Hargrove Jr. m 3/22/1994 Letitia Lee Smith c 2. Int R S Paul's Epis Ch Salem VA 2006-2011; H Trin Ch Churchville MD 2005-2006; R Aug Par Chesapeake City MD 2000-2005; Int Ch Of The Mssh Lower Gwynedd PA 1999-2000. brad@laycock.us

LAYDEN, Daniel Keith (NI) 11009 Brandy Oak Run, Fort Wayne IN 46845 **R S Alb's Epis Ch Ft Wayne IN 2007-** B . 1/7/1971 BS OH SU; MDiv VTS. D 10/20/2001 P 6/1/2002 Bp Herbert Thompson Jr. c 1. S Paul's Epis Ch Greenville OH 2002-2007; S Mk's Epis Ch Columbus OH 1996-1999. dklayden@gmail.com

LAYER, Karl G. (Pa) 1420 Locust St Apt 36-R, Philadelphia PA 19102 **Died 8/5/2010** B Philadelphia PA 4/23/1940 s Karl G Layer & Ruth Irene. BA Br 1962; BD Nash 1965. D 3/20/1965 P 9/4/1965 Bp Donald H V Hallock. "arts In Var mag," 2003. Ord Of The Hloy Cross 1996; Philosophers Natl hon Soc 1971.

LAYNE, Najah Suzanne (Kan) 631 E. Marlin St., McPherson KS 67460 **D Gr Epis Ch Winfield KS 2003-** B Elmira NY 8/18/1935 d Ernest Donald Balcom & Beatrice Virginia. Potsdam St Teachers Coll 1956; Wichita St U 1976. D 12/19/1993 Bp William Edward Smalley. m 5/23/1979 Robert Patterson Layne. Serv./ D Epis Ch Of S Fran-In-The-Vlly Green Vlly AZ 1998-2000; Serv./ D S Dav's Epis Ch Topeka KS 1993-1997. Mus Hon Soc. robertplane@sbcglobal.net

LAYNE, Robert Patterson (Kan) 1016 Grandview Ave, Newton KS 67114 **P-in-c S Matt's Epis Ch Newton KS 2006-** B Louisville KY 8/28/1933 s Herman Louis Layne & Mary Emily. BA Bellarmine U 1959; MDiv VTS 1968. D 6/18/1968 P 5/20/1969 Bp Charles Gresham Marmion. m 5/23/1979 Najah Suzanne Balcom. R S Dav's Epis Ch Topeka KS 1989-1997; R S Barth's Ch Wichita KS 1981-1989; S Steph's Ch Wichita KS 1970-1979; Vic Trin Epis Ch Fulton KY 1968-1970. fatherbob33@cox.net

LAZARD, Amirold (Hai) PO Box 407139, C/O Lynx Air, Fort Lauderdale FL 33340 **Dio Haiti Ft Lauderdale FL 2002-** B 7/20/1970 D.

LEA, William Howard (Miss) 1 Fair Hope Ln, Savannah GA 31411 **P-in-c S Phil's Ch Hinesville Hinesville GA 2010-** B Greenville MS 3/3/1941 s J C Lea & Winona De Woody. BS Colorado St U 1963; MDiv Nash 1979. D 6/29/1979 P 1/1/1980 Bp William Carl Frey. m 6/29/1989 Ellen Beaver c 4. Assoc S Fran Of The Islands Epis Ch Savannah GA 2006-2009; Int Emm Epis Ch Winchester KY 2004-2006; Int Trin Ch Wauwatosa WI 2002-2004; Int Ch Of The Nativ Epis Huntsville AL 2001-2002; R Ch Of The Redeem Brookhaven MS 1995-2001; Vic S Jn's Ch Leland MS 1992-1995; Vic Ch Of The Redeem Greenville MS 1992-1994; Vic S Paul's Ch Hollandale MS 1992-1994; Int H Innoc' Epis Ch Como MS 1991-1992; Int S Jn's Ch Barrington RI 1988-1990; Int All SS Ch Stoneham MA 1987-1988; Int R All SS Ch Stoneham MA 1986-1987; R S Fran Of Assisi Colorado Sprg CO 1983-1985; Vic Ch of the H Sprt Rifle CO 1979-1982; Vic S Jn's Epis Ch New Castle CO 1979-1982. wmhlea@comcast.net

LEACH, Fredric Francis (Alb) 585 4th Ave, Troy NY 12182 **Vic S Lk's Ch Mechanicville NY 2003-** B Salamanca NY 4/14/1939 s Francis H Leach & Elsie A. BA Alfred U 1962; STB Ya Berk 1967; MDiv Yale DS 1974. D 6/17/1967 P 3/1/1968 Bp Lauriston L Scaife. m 7/20/1963 Diane Handy c 2. Dioc Coun Dio Albany Albany NY 1996-2002; R Trin Ch Lansingburgh Troy NY 1990-2003; S Lawr Epis Mnstry Ogdensburg NY 1985-1990; R Trin Ch Gouverneur NY 1985-1990; R S Andr's Ch La Junta CO 1979-1985; Rep Of Nciw Dio Wstrn New York Tonawanda NY 1972-1979; R Gr Ch Randolph NY 1971-1979; Sprtl Life Com Dio Wstrn New York Tonawanda NY 1970-1979; Cur S Mk's Ch Orchard Pk NY 1967-1971. Auth, "The Epis mag". leach@capital.net

LEACH, JoAnn Zwart (Ore) Po Box 447, Lake Oswego OR 97034 **Assoc R Chr Ch Par Lake Oswego OR 2000-** B Redlands CA 7/4/1950 d Floyd Bertus Zwart & Ann. BA Westmont Coll 1972; Masters U CA 1974; MDiv CDSP 1985. D 6/11/1985 Bp Robert Hume Cochrane P 1/18/1986 Bp Otis Charles. m 12/8/2004 Shannon Paul Leach. Chapl Epis Ch at Pr Princeton NJ 1997-1999; The Wm Alexander Procter Fndt Trenton NJ 1997-1999; Chap of the Epiph Salt Lake City UT 1990-1999; Dio Utah Salt Lake City UT 1990-1997; Cn Cathd Ch Of S Mk Salt Lake City UT 1988-1989; Chapl S Mk's Chap Salt Lake City UT 1985-1988; Rowland Hall/S Mk's Sch Salt Lake Cty UT 1985-1987. CDSP Bd Mem 2002-2008; ESMHE Strng Com 1992-1995; Pres Of ESMHE 1998-2000; Recovery Cmsn 2000. jleach@ccparish.org

LEACH, John Philip (WTenn) 1380 Wolf River Blvd, Collierville TN 38017 **Dep - The GC Dio W Tennessee Memphis TN 2009-; R Ch of the H Apos Collierville TN 2008-; St. Columba Bd Dir Dio W Tennessee Memphis TN 2008-; Stndg Com Dio W Tennessee Memphis TN 2008-** B Helena AR 5/16/1969 s Philip M Leach & Patricia. BBA Millsaps Coll 1991; MDiv VTS 2004. D 6/26/2004 P 1/8/2005 Bp Don Edward Johnson. m 11/28/1998 Lisa Lichterman Leach c 2. Stndg Com Dio W Tennessee Memphis TN 2008-2009; Ch Of The Annunc Cordova TN 2004-2008. john@holyapostlestn.net

LEACH, Marilyn May (Minn) 408 N 5th St, Marshall MN 56258 **P S Jas Ch Marshall MN 2005-** B Norwich CT 3/15/1941 d Earl Leach & Jean. BA U of Hawaii 1963; MA U of Missouri 1964. D 6/12/2005 Bp Daniel Lee Swenson P 12/11/2005 Bp James Louis Jelinek. c 2. mmleach@charter.net

LEACH, Shannon Paul (Ore) Po Box 447, Lake Oswego OR 97034 **R Chr Ch Par Lake Oswego OR 1999-** B Denver CO 11/15/1956 s Doyce Leach & Carolyn. BS Westminster Coll 1979; MDiv CDSP 1985. D 12/22/1984 P 1/18/1986 Bp Otis Charles. m 12/8/2004 JoAnn Zwart c 2. Assoc Trin Ch Princeton NJ 1997-1999; COM Dio Utah Salt Lake City UT 1993-1997; Dep GC Dio Utah Salt Lake City UT 1991-1997; R S Jas Epis Ch Midvale UT 1987-1997; Stndg Com Dio Utah Salt Lake City UT 1986-1989; Rowland Hall/S Mk's Sch Salt Lake Cty UT 1985-1987; Chapl S Marg's Chap Salt Lake City UT 1985-1987; Yth Min All Souls Par In Berkeley Berkeley CA 1984-1985. spleach@ccparish.org

LEACOCK, Robert (Tex) 10311 Crittendon Dr, Dallas TX 75229 **S Andrews Epis Sch Austin TX 2010-** B Gainesville FL 3/17/1979 s Robert Leacock & Rebecca Dowdle. AB Davidson Coll 2001; MDiv Yale DS 2005. D 6/24/2006 P 2/3/2007 Bp James Monte Stanton. m 8/14/2004 Stefanie West c 1. S Mich And All Ang Ch Dallas TX 2006-2010. robertleacock@yahoo.com

LEAHY, John Joseph (CFla) 1007B Kings Way, New Bern NC 28562 B Worcester MA 7/19/1948 s John Joseph Leahy & Anne L. BS Assumption Coll; MDiv GTS 1998. D 6/20/1998 P 6/12/1999 Bp Gordon Paul Scruton. m 4/19/1969 June Ann Lawrences c 2. Pstr S Mary Of The Ang Epis Ch Orlando FL 2006-2010; Pstr S Paul's Epis Ch Gardner MA 2000-2006; Cur/PIC S Mich's-On-The-Heights Worcester MA 1998-2000. frjohnleahy@msn.com

LEANILLO OSB, Rick (SwFla) 5033 9th St, Zephyrhills FL 33542 B Sacramento CA 8/28/1947 s Ricardo Macaraeg Leanillo & Ethel May. AA Pasco-Hernando Cmnty Coll 1975; BA U of So Florida 1977; Cert S Leo Coll 1984. D 1/18/2003 Bp John Bailey Lipscomb. m 8/10/1996 Kimberly Ann Anderson c 5. D S Eliz's Epis Ch Zephyrhills FL 2003-2004. Oblate Ord of S Ben 2005. rickleanillo@hotmail.com

LEANNAH, Scott Robert (Mil) 3734 S. 86th St., Milwaukee WI 53228 **Dep, GC Dio Milwaukee Milwaukee WI 2009-; Vic S Mary's Epis Ch Dousman WI 2003-** B Escondide CA 2/11/1966 s Robert William Leannah & Susan Ann. BA Marq 1988; MDiv St. Fran Sem Milwaukee WI 1993. Rec from Roman Catholic 11/23/2003 Bp Steven Andrew Miller. m 7/29/2006 Virginia Rose Kuemmel. sleannah@earthlink.net

LEARY, Albert Paris (Alb) No address on file. B 1/7/1931 D 6/29/1954 Bp Iveson Batchelor Noland P 1/9/1955 Bp Frederick Lehrle Barry.

LEARY, Charles Randolph (SO) 133 Croskey Boulevard, Medway OH 45341 B Mingo WV 1/21/1930 s William Bryan Leary & Mary Eva. BA Davis & Elkins Coll 1953; MDiv Tem 1957; PDS 1958. D 11/22/1958 P 5/23/1959 Bp William P Roberts. m 12/27/1950 Juanita M Lindsay c 4. Supply Cler S Andr's Ch Dayton OH 1995-2000; Supply P S Jas Ch Piqua OH 1985-2000; Supply P S Mk's Ch Sidney OH 1985-2000; Supply P S Paul's Epis Ch Greenville OH 1985-2000; S Chris's Ch Fairborn OH 1961-1985; Cur S Paul's Epis Ch Dayton OH 1959-1961. Auth, *Mssn Readiness*, CCS, 1990; Auth, *18 Sermons*. Best Sermon Awd - "What is the Question Seven Worlds Corp Lima Ohio 1990. crleary.recordnut@att.net

LEARY, Kevin David (Ct) 15 Rimmon Rd, Woodbridge CT 06525 B New Haven CT 3/21/1944 s David Paul Leary & Cecilia Claire. S Thos Sem Bloomfield CT; U of New Haven. D 12/3/1988 Bp Arthur Edward Walmsley. m 1/27/1968 Carolyn Shutter Grant c 4. NAAD.

LEAS, Bercry Eleanor (Mich) 7051 Wakan Ln., Corryton TN 37721 **Emergency Response Chapl Dio E Tennessee Knoxville TN 2009-; D S Hilary's Ch Ft Myers FL 2008-** B Philadelphia PA 4/1/1945 d Edgar Nile Leas & Mary Alice. BA Estrn Michigan U 1967; MA Estrn Michigan U 1971; Ds Whitaker TS 1990. D 6/23/1990 Bp R(aymond) Stewart Wood Jr. D S Lk's Ch Knoxville TN 2008; D S Jn's Ch Royal Oak MI 1990-2001. DOK 2008; NAAD; OSL. deaconbercry45@gmail.com

LEATHERMAN, Daniel Lee (Haw) 7 Pursuit, Aliso Viejo CA 92656 **Chapl S Alb's Chap Honolulu HI 2005-; Assoc The Epis Ch Of S Andr Encinitas CA 2001-** B Honolulu HI 8/28/1970 s David Lee Leatherman & Karen Jp. BA U of Hawaii 1993; MDiv Epis TS of The SW 1996. D 6/25/1996 Bp George Nelson Hunt III P 1/6/1997 Bp Robert Manning Moody. m 11/17/1996 Charmaine Mee Yin Chong. S Mary And All Ang Sch Aliso Viejo CA 2002-2005; S Marg Of Scotland Par San Juan Capistrano CA 1999-2002; Asst S Jn's Epis Ch Tulsa OK 1996-1999. Epis Armdf Chapl Assn. daniel.leatherman@smaa.org

LEAVITT, Christie Plehn (Nev) 1739 Carita Ave, Henderson NV 89014 **P S Matt's Ch Las Vegas NV 1986-** B Omaha NE 10/24/1949 d Robert Vernon Plehn & Rose Arlene. BA U of Nevada at Las Vegas 1973; MA U of Nevada at Las Vegas 1979. D 4/6/1986 Bp Robert Reed Shahan P 11/23/1986 Bp Stewart Clark Zabriskie. m 5/12/1973 Robert Merrill Leavitt. hippodrag@att.net

LE BARRON, Bruce E(rie) (WK) 3218 White Tail Way, Salina KS 67401 B Jamestown NY 2/9/1930 s Erie Hiram Le Barron & Coralyn Alice. BA SUNY 1951; MDiv Ya Berk 1955. D 5/29/1955 P 11/30/1955 Bp Frederick Lehrle Barry. m 6/30/1956 Lilith A Harding c 3. Chr Cathd Salina KS 1998-2011; R All SS Ch Nevada MO 1986-1992; Asst & Org/Chrmstr S Lk's Par Kalamazoo MI 1980-1986; Asst & Org/Chrmstr S Jn The Evang Ch Elkhart IN 1976-1980; R Chr Ch Bethany CT 1969-1976; Dio New Jersey Trenton NJ 1964-1976; R S Barn Ch Burlington NJ 1962-1964; Chr Chr Ch Magnolia NJ 1959-1962; Vic Ch Of S Jn-In-The-Wilderness Gibbsboro NJ 1959-1962; Cur

S Thos Ch New York NY 1958-1959; All SS Ch New York NY 1955-1957. CBS; GAS; Mem of the SocMary; Oblate of (Benedictine) Blue Cloud Abbey; Oblate of S Gilbert of Sempringham, Engl Ord of Cister; Soc of S Marg. tallcanon@cox.net

LEBATARD, James Henry (Miss) 305 De La Pointe Dr, Gautier MS 39553 **D S Pierre's Epis Ch Gautier MS 2005-** B 11/23/1954 s James Monroe LeBatard & Henrietta. Auburn U; AA Jackson Cnty Jr. Coll Gautier MS 1974; BS U of So Alabama 1976; Med U of So Alabama 1977. D 1/15/2005 Bp Duncan Montgomery Gray III. james-henry@earthlink.net

LEBENS-ENGLUND, Paul J (Spok) 245 E 13th Ave, Spokane WA 99202 **Cn to the Ordnry Dio Spokane Spokane WA 2011-** B Yakima WA 7/13/1974 s James Alexander Englund & Judith Rae. BA Evergreen St Coll 1997; MDiv CDSP 2004. D 6/12/2004 P 1/8/2005 Bp James Edward Waggoner. m 7/24/1999 Erica Ann Ingham c 2. Cn for Congrl Dvlpmt Dio Spokane Spokane WA 2007-2011; re-start Vic H Trin Epis Ch Spokane WA 2007-2009; P Assoc Cathd Of S Jn The Evang Spokane WA 2004-2007. puall@spokanediocese.org

LE BLANC, Frances Andre (Telles) (Md) 204 Monument Rd, Orleans MA 02653 **Chr Ch Forest Hill MD 2004-** B Rio De Janeiro BR 8/3/1953 d Andre Le Blanc & Elvira Viviani Telles. BA New York Inst of Tech 1977; MBA Dart 1981; MDiv GTS 1993. D 6/12/1993 Bp Richard Frank Grein P 5/1/1994 Bp Frank Stanley Cerveny. P-in-c S Ptr's Ch Great Falls SC 2004; Asst The Ch Of The H Sprt Orleans MA 2003; St Gabr Of The Annunc Columbia SC 1999-2001; Dio Upper So Carolina Columbia SC 1999; Stndg Com Dio Upper So Carolina Columbia SC 1998-2003; St Gabr Of The Annunc Columbia SC 1998; Asst R S Jn's Epis Ch Columbia SC 1996-1998; S Hilda's And S Hugh's Sch New York NY 1994-1996; Assoc All SS Ch New York NY 1994-1995; Cur S Thos Ch New York NY 1993-1994. christch@charm.net

LEBLANC, Ronald James (WLa) 100 Newcastle Dr, Lafayette LA 70503 B Lafayette LA 1/12/1938 s Daniel Sidney Leblanc & Ruth Dorithy. Cert RC Dioceses Formation Prog 1980. Rec from Roman Catholic 6/16/1990 Bp Willis Ryan Henton. m 6/21/1987 Janis Lee Marie Boudreaux. Dio Wstrn Louisiana Alexandria LA 2005-2010; Min in charge Ch Of The Incarn Lafayette LA 2000-2002; D The Epis Ch Of The Epiph New Iberia LA 1990-2002. jimmy_leblanc@bellsouth.net

LEBLANC, Tracy Jean (Ore) 15416 Ne 90th St, Vancouver WA 98682 **D S Ptr And Paul Epis Ch Portland OR 2007-** B Greeley CO 7/8/1971 d John Charles Craig & Michelle Alison. Cntr for Diac Mnstry; BA Willamette U 1993; MS Portland St U 1997. D 10/21/2006 Bp Johncy Itty. m 8/21/1993 James LeBlanc c 3. tracy.leblanc@comcast.net

LEBRON, Robert Emmanuel (Mil) 409 E. Court St., Janesville WI 53545 **R Trin Ch Janesville WI 2005-** B New York NY 12/25/1952 s Bernard John Lebron & Rose Nan. AA SUNY 1976; BSW Florida Intl U 1980; Geisinger Med Cntr 1983; MDiv Sthrn Bapt TS 1983; Trin Epis Sch for Min. 2000. D 12/10/1995 Bp C(laude) Charles Vache P 6/15/1996 Bp Brice Sidney Sanders. m 8/20/2005 Robyn Lebron c 2. Coll Chapl, Bd Cert 1986-2000; US Navy Chapl Corp 1985-2005. rockin-robyn@msn.com

LECHE III, Edward Douglas (Oly) 205 Olympic View Dr, Friday Harbor WA 98250 B Longview WA 1/26/1926 s Edward Douglas Leche & Muriel Evelyn. BA Cbury Coll 1951; Cert GTS 1954. D 6/29/1954 P 6/29/1955 Bp Stephen F Bayne Jr. Int Emm Ch Orcas Island Eastsound WA 1995-1996; S Dav's Epis Ch Friday Harbor WA 1967-1988; Vic Gr Ch Lopez Island WA 1967-1983; Vic Emm Ch Orcas Island Eastsound WA 1967-1974; Vic S Chas Angl Par Poulsbo WA 1963-1967; Vic S Paul's Epis Ch Poulsbo WA 1961-1967; Asst S Lk's Epis Ch Vancouver WA 1959-1961; Vic S Jn's Epis Ch So Bend WA 1957-1959; Vic S Ptr's Ch Seaview WA 1957-1959; Cur Chr Ch SEATTLE WA 1955-1957; Cur S Mary's Ch Lakewood WA 1954-1955. Illustrator, "Illustrations," *Ch Facts (Dio Wstrn New York)*, 2003; Illustrator, "Illustrations,The Epis," *Profsnl Additions*, 2003; Illustrator, "Illustrations," *The GC Daily*, 2003; Illustrator, "Illustrations," *The Olympia Churhman*, 2003; Writer, Illustrator, "Illustrations," *The Pig That Loved Potatoes-A Somewhat Whimsical Hist Of The Pig War*, Edw Douglas Leche Iii, 2000; Illustrator, "Illustrations," *The Wild Wrld By Geo And Netty Macginitie*, Longhouse, 1974. mjedl3@rockissand.com

LECLAIR, Arthur Anthony (Colo) 8221 E Fremont Cir, Englewood CO 80112 B Charleroi PA 11/3/1931 s A E LeClair. BA U of Dayton 1956; MA Loyola U 1969. Rec from Roman Catholic 3/1/1974 as Priest Bp William Carl Frey. m 8/22/1970 Joanne Juneau c 2. Gd Shpd Epis Ch Centennial CO 1976-1995; Dio Colorado Denver CO 1975-1976; Cur Trin Ch Greeley CO 1974-1976. Ord Of S Lk. jlleclair43@gmail.com

LECLAIR, Paul Joseph (Mich) 1434 E 13 Mile Rd, Madison Heights MI 48071 **Dn Dio Michigan Detroit MI 2011-; P S Pat's Epis Ch Madison Heights MI 2010-** B Detroit, MI 2/13/1950 s Paul Joseph LeClair & Grace Isabell. U So TS; Whitaker Inst; BA Oakland U 1972; MAT Saginaw Vlly St U 1978. D 2/13/2010 P 11/6/2010 Bp Wendell Nathaniel Gibbs Jr. m 8/26/1972 Elizabeth Hoppin c 3. D S Pat's Epis Ch Madison Heights MI 2010. leclair143@wowway.com

LECLAIRE, Patrick Harry (Nev) 620 W B St, Fallon NV 89406 **P H Trin Epis Ch Fallon NV 2000-** B Minneapolis MN 10/14/1947 s Wallace Fredrick LeClaire & Dorothy Ann. AA Wstrn Nevada Coll 1990. D 12/12/1999 P 7/16/2000 Bp John Stuart Thornton. m 3/11/1968 Loraine Margaret Bailey. patch72@yahoo.com

LECLERC BSG, Charles Edward (NH) 1873 Dover Rd, Epsom NH 03234 **D S Paul's Ch Concord NH 2000-** B Woonsocket RI 5/26/1944 s Laureni Leclerc & Claire. BS Johnson & Wales U 1991. Rec from Roman Catholic 2/1/1988 as Deacon Bp George Nelson Hunt III. D-In-Res Ch Of The Epiph Providence RI 1988-1991. BCEBSG@METROCAST.NET

LECROY, Anne Evelyn (ETenn) 400 N Boone St, Apt As14, Johnson City TN 37604 B Summit New Jersey 1/21/1927 d Arthur Howard Kingsbury & Anne Evelyn. BA Bryn 1947; MA Bryn 1948; PhD U Cinc 1952; PostDoc Duke 1978. Trans 6/6/2001 as Deacon Bp Charles Glenn VonRosenberg. c 3. D S Tim's Epis Ch Kingsport TN 2001-2008; SLC Dio E Tennessee Knoxville TN 1974-1983. *Var arts Chrsnty and Lit*, 2003; *10 Hymn Texts*, Ch Hymnal Corp, 1982; Co-Ed, *Lesser Feasts and Fasts*, Ch Pension Fund, 1980; Contrib, *Bk of Common Pryr*, Ch Pension Fund, 1979. Amer ACPE 1998; Phi Kappa Phi 1968-2000; Third Ord of S Fran (professed) 1990. Wm Fowler Awd in Tchg E Tennessee St U 1992. lecroya@aol.com

LEDBETTER, William (Los) 934 Venezia Ave, Venice CA 90277 **Asst S Thos The Apos Hollywood Los Angeles CA 2010-** B Topeka KS 8/25/1958 s William Henry Ledbetter & Jean Carol. BA U of Kansas 1985; JD Washburn U 1991; MDiv Epis TS of the SW 1995. D 6/3/2006 P 1/6/2007 Bp Joseph Jon Bruno. m 2/26/2000 Barbara Eve Jacobs c 2. Asst Cathd Cntr Of S Paul Cong Los Angeles CA 2009-2010; Int Ch Of The Trsfg Arcadia CA 2008-2009; Cur Chr Ch Par Redondo Bch CA 2006-2008. SSC 2011. williamledbetter@mac.com

LEDERHOUSE, Susan (Me) PO Box 1586, Orleans MA 02653 **P-in-c S Ptr's Ch On The Canal Buzzards Bay MA 2010-** B Richmond VA 3/26/1954 d Peter Mellette & Susan Jackson. BA Hollins Coll 1975; MS U IL 1976; MDiv GTS 2005. D 6/11/2005 Bp John Palmer Croneberger P 12/17/2005 Bp Carol Joy Gallagher. m 8/29/1987 Howard Bruce Lederhouse. Supply P Dio Massachusetts Boston MA 2009-2010; Int The Ch Of The H Sprt Orleans MA 2008-2009; R S Jas Ch Old Town ME 2007-2008; Asst S Mary's Ch Sparta NJ 2005-2006. Beta Phi Mu 1976; Phi Beta Kappa 1975; Phi Beta Kappa. lederhouse@msn.com

LEDERMAN, Maureen Elizabeth (Ct) 124 Midland Dr, Meriden CT 06450 **Assoc. R, Day Sch Chapl, & Chr Ed. Dir S Thos's Ch New Haven CT 2004-** B 1/25/1977 D 6/12/2004 P 1/29/2005 Bp Andrew Donnan Smith. m 7/13/2002 William Paul Lederman. chaplainmo@stthomasday.org

LEDGERWOOD, Mary Jayne (Va) 6715 Georgetown Pike, McLean VA 22101 **Assoc R S Jn's Epis Ch McLean VA 2008-** B Waynesburg PA 10/26/1958 d Edward Peyton Stafford & Betty Jane. MDiv VTS 2001. D 6/23/2001 Bp Peter James Lee P 1/26/2002 Bp John Leslie Rabb. m 5/28/1994 Brian Ledgerwood. R S Andr's Epis Ch Glenwood MD 2004-2008; Assoc R S Jn's Ch Ellicott City MD 2001-2004. mjledgerwood@stjohnsmclean.org

LEDIARD SR, Daniel E (EO) Po Box 681, Virginia City NV 89440 **R S Jn's Ch Hermiston OR 2010-** B Salt Lake City UT 2/12/1947 s Alfred K Lediard & Frances Mae. D 10/6/2006 Bp Katharine Jefferts Schori P 6/3/2007 Bp Jerry Alban Lamb. m 8/30/1969 JoAnne Margerum c 3. danlediard@aol.com

LEDIARD, JoAnne (Nev) 665 E Gladys Ave, Hermiston OR 97838 **P-in-c S Paul's Epis Ch Kennewick WA 2011-** B Seattle WA 2/15/1947 Dio of Nevada; Dplma St. Mk's Hosp Sch of Nrsng 1969. D 8/23/1998 Bp Stewart Clark Zabriskie P 9/16/2001 Bp Katharine Jefferts Schori. m 8/30/1969 Daniel E Lediard c 3. Mssnr Dio Nevada Las Vegas NV 2006-2009. ljlediard@aol.com

LEDYARD, Florence Livingstone (Md) 1021 Bosley Rd, Cockeysville MD 21030 **S Barth's Ch Baltimore MD 2002-** B Detroit,MI 6/23/1950 d William Hendrie Ledyard & Florence Odell. BA Colorado Wmn Coll 1972; MA U 1972; MDiv VTS 1978. D 6/17/1978 Bp William J Gordon Jr P 6/1/1979 Bp H Coleman McGehee Jr. m 11/4/1974 William Canfield III. S Jas Epis Ch Mt Airy MD 2000-2002; Epiph Ch Dulaney Vlly Timonium MD 1983-1996; Asst S Dav's Par Washington DC 1978-1982. fledyard@comcast.net

LEE III, Arthur Randall (SwFla) 7304 Van Lake Dr, Englewood FL 34224 **Mem, Dioc Disciplinary Bd Dio SW Florida Sarasota FL 2011-; Stff, Sch for Mnstry Dvlpmt Dio SW Florida Sarasota FL 2011-; Stff, Fresh Start Dio SW Florida Sarasota FL 2008-** B Minneapolis MN 10/23/1944 s Arthur Randall Lee & Ethelynn. BA San Francisco St U 1966; MDiv CDSP 1969; MLitt Oxf 1976. D 6/28/1969 Bp C Kilmer Myers P 9/26/1971 Bp The Bishop Of Oxford. m 8/10/1974 Rosemary Baldock c 1. R S Dav's Epis Ch Englewood FL 2000-2009; Ch Of The H Sprt Sfty Harbor FL 1985-2000; R S Mk's Ch Starke FL 1982-1985; Asst S Andr's Epis Ch Tampa FL 1977-1982. Auth, "Morphological Diversity Among The Protists," *Proc. Of 4th Intl. Conf. Of Syst. & Evol. Biology*, 1991; Auth, "Bludgeon: A Blunt Instrument For The Analysis Of Contamination In Textual Traditions," *Proc. Conf. Of The Allc*,

1990; Auth, "Cler Families In Crisis," *Families In Transition*, Epis Ch Cntr, 1984. arlee34224@gmail.com

LEE, Betsy Ann (Minn) St. Edward the Confessor, 865 Ferndale Rd. N., Wayzata MN 55391 **Bd Mem Epis Cmnty Serv Inc Minneapolis MN 2010-** B Decorah IA 11/4/1958 d David A Lee & Lorraine M. BA St. Olaf Coll 1980; MDiv Luth TS at Chicago 1990; Cert Estrn Mennonite U 2001. Rec from Evangelical Lutheran Church in America 1/24/2006 Bp Alan Scarfe. m 10/8/2005 Karen J Diekrager. R S Edw The Confessor Wayzata MN 2008-2011; Int Trin Ch Muscatine IA 2006-2008. bannlee42@yahoo.com

LEE, Chen-Cheng (Tai) 4F-1 31 Rueiyuan Rd, Chien-Jin District, Kaohsiung City Taiwan B Taiwan 11/21/1976 s Chien-Wen Lee & Su-Chen. BA Tainan Theol Coll Taiwan 1999; MDiv Tainan TS Taiwan 2002. D 6/11/2004 P 2/19/2005 Bp Jung-Hsin Lai. m 6/26/2004 Hsin-Yi Yeh c 2. tinseng555@yahoo.com.tw

LEE, Daniel Ki Chul (Ga) 623 Caines Rd, Hinesville GA 31313 B South Korea 4/27/1951 s Eu Jin Lee & Nak Sun. Chom Shin Presb Sem; Gnrl Assembly Presb Sem. D 12/7/1997 P 12/18/1998 Bp Henry Irving Louttit. c 2. Dio Georgia Savannah GA 2001-2005.

LEE, Darry Kyong Ho (Los) 5950 Imperial Hwy Apt 47, South Gate CA 90280 B 3/1/1949 s Tai Soon Lee & Ok Cha. AA Los Angeles City Coll 1972; BA U CA 1973; MS San Francisco St U 1975; MDiv CDSP 1979; PhD Case Wstrn Reserve U 1992. D 6/23/1979 P 5/1/1980 Bp Robert C Rusack. m 5/6/1978 Soo Keun Chung. S Jos's Par Buena Pk CA 1999-2000; Calv Ch Cleveland OH 1989-1991; Dio Los Angeles Los Angeles CA 1982-1986; S Andr's Par Torrance CA 1979-1981. Auth, "Falling Egg". dsmiv5@yahoo.com

LEE, David Edward (Va) 2343 Highland Ave, Charlottesville VA 22903 B Harrisburg PA 10/23/1940 s William Edward Lee & Doris Emma. BA Trin 1962; STB EDS 1966. D 6/17/1966 Bp Joseph Thomas Heistand P 4/1/1967 Bp Clarence Rupert Haden Jr. m 11/29/1990 Elizabeth A Courain. Assoc S Paul's Memi Charlottesville VA 1981-1985; R Trin Ch Belleville MI 1972-1979; Asst S Paul's Epis Ch Flint MI 1970-1972; Asst Vic Ch Of S Mart Davis CA 1966-1970. DAVIDLEE567@YAHOO.COM

L

LEE, Donald DeArman (WTex) Po Box 545, Bandera TX 78003 B Corpus Christi TX 11/21/1942 s William Taylor Lee & Christine. BS Texas A&M U 1965; MDiv Epis TS of The SW 1993. D 6/29/1993 P 1/9/1994 Bp John Herbert MacNaughton. m 6/4/1966 Karen Knowlton c 4. Vic Ch Of The Ascen Uvalde TX 2000-2007; Archd Dio W Texas San Antonio TX 1999-2007; Archd S Jn's Cathd Chap San Antonio TX 1999-2007; R S Chris's Ch Bandera TX 1993-1999; Vic S Bon Ch Comfort TX 1993-1995. dleedio@aol.com

✠ LEE JR, Rt Rev Edward Lewis (WMich) 123 Glenwood Rd, Merion Station PA 19066 **Ret Bp of Wstrn Michigan Dio Pennsylvania Philadelphia PA 2000-** B Philadelphia PA 6/30/1934 s Edward Lewis Lee & Adlyn Cecilia. BA Br 1956; MDiv GTS 1959. D 5/9/1959 Bp Oliver J Hart P 11/14/1959 Bp Joseph Gillespie Armstrong Con 10/7/1989 for WMich. m 6/17/1961 Kathryn F Fligg c 1. Dio Wstrn Michigan Kalamazoo MI 1989-2002; Dio Washington Washington DC 1983-1986; R S Jn's Ch Georgetown Par Washington DC 1982-1989; Convoc of Amer Ch in Europe Paris FR 1974-1982; S Jas Epis Ch Firenze IA IT 1973-1982; St Jas Ch 1973-1982; S Ptr's Ch Philadelphia PA 1971-1973; Ch Of The Annuniciation Philadelphia PA 1964-1971; The Ch Of The H Trin Rittenhouse Philadelphia PA 1959-1964. Amnesty Intl , USA 1998; EPF 1967; Sthrn Pvrty Law Cntr 1988. DD The GTS 1990. bpedwardlee@yahoo.com

LEE, Enoch (Tai) No address on file. B Nan-Jing City CN 1/29/1947 s Ru-Shu Lee & Su-Qin. Cheng-Chicago U Taipei Tw 1989; BA TS Of Fu-Jen U Taipei Tw 1998. D 10/28/2000 Bp John Chih-Tsung Chien. m 11/20/1976 Duan-Yi Chao c 2.

LEE, George (Haw) 2468 Lamaku Pl, Honolulu HI 96816 B New Haven CT 7/1/1927 s Wah Fun Lee & Rose. Ya Berk; BA Ya 1950; BD Yale DS 1955. D 9/21/1957 Bp Albert Ervine Swift P 8/14/1958 Bp Robert McConnell Hatch. m 7/19/1980 Grace B Beach. MacCray Cntr Epis Campus Mnstry Honolulu HI 1989-1991; Vic S Phil's Ch Maili Waianae HI 1983-1988; S Lk's Epis Ch Honolulu HI 1978-1979; Dio Hawaii Honolulu HI 1974-1991; Asst S Ptr's Ch Springfield MA 1957-1958. glee52002@yahoo.com

LEE, Hosea Mun-Yong (Nwk) 1600 Parker Ave Apt 3-D, Fort Lee NJ 07024 **Asst Mssnr Ch Of The Gd Shpd Ft Lee NJ 1985-** B Korea 2/6/1929 s Peter In-Soo Lee & Miryum Kyung. SocMary. D 6/8/1985 P 12/1/1985 Bp John Shelby Spong. m 3/15/1953 Martha Hys-Sook Kim.

LEE, Hyacinth Evadne (NY) 50 Guion Pl, 5H, New Rochelle NY 10801 **D Trin S Paul's Epis New Rochelle NY 1992-** B JM 2/14/1941 d Ezekiel Augustus Woodstock & Sylvia Roberta. RN U Hosp W Indies Kingston JM 1965; BA Marymount Manhattan Coll 1979; MS LIU 1992. D 5/30/1992 Bp Richard Frank Grein. c 1. hyacinthlee@verizon.net

LEE JR, James Oliver (Kan) 9030 Markville Dr Apt 2633, Dallas TX 75243 **S Geo's Epis Ch Dallas TX 2010-** B Lackawanna NY 9/5/1953 s Orea. USNA 1975; BA U of Kansas 1978; JD U of Kansas 1982; MA Harvard DS 2002. D 6/5/2004 P 2/5/2005 Bp James Monte Stanton. m 8/30/1980 Kelly G Learned c 2. Assoc R Trin Ch Lawr KS 2006; Cur S Lk's Epis Ch Dallas TX 2005-2006.

✠ LEE, Rt Rev Jeffrey Dean (Chi) 65 E Huron St, Chicago IL 60611 **Bp of Chicago Dio Chicago Chicago IL 2008-** B Sturgis MI 8/6/1957 s Larry Eugene Lee & Bonnie Lee. BA U MI 1979; MDiv Nash 1985. D 4/13/1985 P 11/16/1985 Bp William Cockburn Russell Sheridan Con 2/2/2008 for Chi. m 12/29/1979 Lisa R Rogers c 2. R S Thos Ch Medina WA 2000-2008; R S Chris's Ch River Hills WI 1994-2000; H Fam Epis Ch Fishers IN 1992-1994; New Ch Planter Dio Indianapolis Indianapolis IN 1991-1994; Dio Indianapolis Indianapolis IN 1991-1992; Cn to Ordnry Dio Nthrn Indiana So Bend IN 1987-1991; Cur S Jn The Evang Ch Elkhart IN 1985-1987. Auth, *Opening the PB*, Cowley Press, 1998. Affirming Catholicsm 2001; Associated Parishes 1999; NAAD 1986. leefamilylrl@comcast.net

LEE JR, John E (NMich) Rr 1 Box 586, Newberry MI 49868 **D All SS Ch Newberry MI 1993-; D Dio Nthrn Michigan Marquette MI 1993-** B Jackson MI 4/18/1935 s John E Lee & Leah. BS Cntrl Michigan U 1974. D 9/20/1992 Bp Thomas Kreider Ray. m 4/22/1957 Judith E Artman.

LEE, Judith Mary (WNY) 36 Marion Rd E # 8540, Princeton NJ 08540 **S Jn's Ch Wilson NY 2007-; Asst Manakin Epis Ch Midlothian VA 2005-; Vic S Andr's Ch Newfane Burt NY 2005-** B Antigonish Nova Scotia 11/5/1947 BA USC. D 6/7/2003 Bp David B(ruce) Joslin P 1/17/2004 Bp George Edward Councell. m 7/27/1977 Dale Bruce Haidvogel c 2. Asst Chr Ch New Brunswick NJ 2003-2005.

LEE, Jui-Chiang (U) 163 Tung-Ming Rd., Keelung Taiwan B Taipei Hsien 8/29/1973 s Wen-Jen Lee & Yu-Chiu. D. m 6/23/2001 Shih-Yung Fung c 2. g982005@yahoo.com.tw

LEE, Kirk A (At) 1195 Village Run NE, Atlanta GA 30319 **S Jas Epis Ch Marietta GA 2002-** B 8/30/1954 BS Rockford Coll 1976; MDiv Trin, U Tor 1990. Trans from Anglican Church of Canada 1/1/2001 Bp Robert Gould Tharp.

LEE, Marc DuPlan (Kan) 4515 W Moncrieff Pl, Denver CO 80212 B Poughkeepsie NY 3/7/1951 s Robert Edson Lee & Jeanne Duplan. BA Col 1973; MDiv EDS 1979; Cfre 1998. D 6/2/1979 Bp Paul Moore Jr P 9/29/1980 Bp Walter Decoster Dennis Jr. m 6/24/1978 Elisabeth Joan McDonald c 2. Metropltn Luth Mnstrs Kansas City MO 1998-1999; Dn Gr Cathd Topeka KS 1993-1998; Cn Chancllr & Dir Dvlpmt Gr Cathd San Francisco CA 1986-1993; R S Mary's Ch Mohegan Lake NY 1982-1986; Asst Cathd Of St Jn The Div New York NY 1979-1982. Auth, "Raise Capital Funds Using The Internet"; Ed, "Prairie Poetry On-Line Journ". Assn Of Fundraising Professionals 1987. marc@affinityesources.com

LEE, Margaret Will (Q) 3412 54th St, Moline IL 61265 **All SS Epis Ch Moline IL 2010-** B Saint Louis MO 11/29/1949 d Louis Alvin Will & Betty R. BA Monmouth Coll 1971; MDIV Nash 2009. D 11/16/1996 Bp Keith Lynn Ackerman P 10/16/2010 Bp John Clark Buchanan. m 11/3/1972 Frank William Lee c 2. D H Trin Epis Ch Peoria IL 2005-2008; D S Mk's Epis Ch Peoria IL 2002-2005; D Chr Ch Peoria IL 1996-2002. Amer Chem Soc 1967; NAAD 1998. Monmouth Coll DSA Monmouth Coll 1996. tudeacon@gmail.com

LEE, Matthew Wen-Hui (Tai) 5F No. 7 Kee-King 2nd Road, Kee Lung City 20446 Taiwan B Chang-Hwa TW 8/18/1953 s Kun-York Lee & Tsai-Lien. BS Natl Taiwan Ocean U 1977; MDiv Taiwan Theol Coll & Sem Taipei TW 1986; Cert St. Lk's Theol Educ CTR Atlanta GA 1988; So E Asia Grad Sch of Thoelogy 1993. D 8/17/1986 Bp Pui-Yeung Cheung P 6/1/1988 Bp John Chih-Tsung Chien. m 8/26/1979 Cho-Fang Lin. Del: GC in Philadelphia Dio Taiwan Taipei TW TW 1997; Dir: Mnstry of Liturg Dio Taiwan Taipei TW TW 1995-2001; Mem: H Ord Com Dio Taiwan Taipei TW TW 1995-2001; Mem: Stndg Com Dio Taiwan Taipei TW TW 1995-2001; Del: CCEA Full Conv In Singapore Dio Taiwan Taipei TW TW 1995; Del: EAM Conf in San Francisco Dio Taiwan Taipei TW TW 1993; Del: CCEA Yth Mnstry Conf in Malaysia Dio Taiwan Taipei TW TW 1991; Dir: Mnstry of Educ & Mssn Dio Taiwan Taipei TW TW 1990-1994; D-In-Trng S Lk's Epis Ch Atlanta GA 1987-1988. matthewwhlee@hotmail.com

LEE, Maurice Charles (Spr) 3231 Alton Rd, Atlanta GA 30341 B Sydney NSW AU 3/26/1935 s William Charles Lee & Muriel. ThL Moore Theol Coll, Sydney 1960. Trans from Anglican Church Of Australia 2/1/1992 Bp Edward Lloyd Salmon Jr. m 11/30/1982 Janet Inez Gruen. S Paul's Epis Ch Pekin IL 2002-2003; S Mich's Epis Ch O Fallon IL 1999-2001; R S Barn Ch Havana IL 1994-1999; Asst S Phil's Ch Charleston SC 1992-1994. maujan@basicisp.net

✠ **LEE, Rt Rev Peter James** (Va) 23 Ave George V, Paris 75008 France **Int Dn The Amer Cathd of the H Trin Paris 75008 FR 2012-; Int Dn The GTS New York NY 2010-2012; Int Dn Gr Cathd San Francisco CA 2009-; Ret Bp of Virginia Ya Berk New Haven CT 1998-** B Greenville MS 5/11/1938 s Erling Norman Lee & Marion Lucille. BA W&L 1960; Duke 1964; BD VTS 1967; DD VTS 1984; DD STUSo 1993; DLitt W&L 1999. D 6/29/1967 Bp Edward Hamilton West P 5/8/1968 Bp William Foreman Creighton Con 5/19/1984 for Va. m 8/28/1965 kristina k lee c 2. Int Dn Gr Cathd San Francisco CA 2009-2010; Chapl Cathd of St Ptr & St Paul Washington DC 1994-2000; Chair, Bd Trst VTS Alexandria VA 1993-2009; Dio Virginia Richmond VA 1984-2009; R Chap Of The Cross Chap Hill NC 1971-1984; Asst S Jn's Ch Lafayette Sq Washington DC 1968-1970; D-In-Trng S Jn's Cathd Jacksonville

FL 1967-1968. Auth, "The New Republic". Dupont Awd 1997; DD Stuso 1993; DD VTS 1984; Phi Beta Kappa. lee@gts.edu

LEE, Rhonda Mawhood (NC) 914 Green St, Durham NC 27701 **Assoc R S Phil's Ch Durham NC 2011-** B Montreal Quebec CA 11/2/1966 BA McGill U 1989; MA McGill U 1991; MDiv Louisville Presb TS 2005; PhD Duke 2007. D 6/4/2005 P 12/4/2005 Bp Edwin Funsten Gulick Jr. m 3/18/1997 Wayne E Lee. Vic S Jos's Ch Durham NC 2006-2010; Cler Assoc. Calv Ch Louisville KY 2005-2006. rhonda@stphilipsdurham.org

LEE, Robert B (Vt) 51 Park St., Canaan VT 05903 **P S Paul's Ch Canaan VT 2000-** B Bridgeport CT 12/19/1943 s Jack Lee & Annette. BS U of Vermont 1965; MS U of Vermont 1967. D 10/22/2000 Bp Mary Adelia Rosamond McLeod P 8/4/2001 Bp Thomas C Ely. m 7/1/1967 Rita Bergeron Lee c 3. rebelee@gaw.com

LEE III, Robert Vernon (Fla) 1131 N Laura St, Jacksonville FL 32206 B El Paso TX 1/14/1951 s Robert Vernon Lee & Cynthia. BA Van 1973; U GA 1975; MDiv Ya Berk 1988; DMin NYTS 1992. D 4/30/1988 Bp C(laude) Charles Vache P 5/18/1989 Bp Jeffery William Rowthorn. m 5/18/1985 Mirte De Boer. Chair Asstg Bp Selection Cmsn Dio Florida Jacksonville FL 2001-2002; Asstg Bp'S Cmsn Chair Dio Florida Jacksonville FL 1997-2000; Exec Coun Dio Florida Jacksonville FL 1995-2011; Chair Strategic Plnng Cmsn Dio Florida Jacksonville FL 1992-1995; Chair Cmsn On Environ Dio Florida Jacksonville FL 1991-1995; Bd Dir S Mary's Ch Jacksonville FL 1991-1994; Chair Bdgt Com Dio Florida Jacksonville FL 1990-1992; R Ch Of Our Sav Jacksonville FL 1989-1994; Cur S Jn's Epis Par Waterbury CT 1988-1989. Bk, "Organizing Parishioners for the Protection of the Environ," NYTS, 1992. Compass Rose Soc 1997-2011; Ord of Jn's of Jerusalem 1998-2011. Annual Diversity Awd Jacksonville Bus Journ 2009; "Eagle Awd" Jacksonville Sheriff's Off 2008; Eagle Awd Jacksonville Sheriff's Off 2008; Change Maker of the Year Jacksonville Times-Un 2006; Humanitarian of the Year Rotary 1998. rvl@freshministries.org

LEE, Sang (Dal) 2783 Valwood Pkwy, Farmers Branch TX 75234 B Korea 5/26/1965 s Se G Lee & Moon Gil. Trans from Anglican Church Of Korea 6/27/2008 Bp James Monte Stanton. m 10/24/1992 Eun Joo Lee c 2. augustinel@gmail.com

LEE, Scott Charles (Ct) 300 Main Street, Wethersfield CT 06109 **R Trin Ch Wethersfield CT 2006-** B Meridian MS 9/7/1951 s Charles Louie Lee & Julia Katherine. BA U So 1973; MA Van 1980; MDiv STUSo 1992. D 6/7/1992 P 12/20/1992 Bp William Evan Sanders. Cn Trin Cathd Little Rock AR 2000-2006; R S Mk's Ch Antioch TN 1994-2000; Cur Trin Ch Clarksville TN 1993-1994; Asst for Admin Chr Ch Cathd Nashville TN 1987-1989. Auth, "The Angl Vision of The New Ch's Tchg Series Bk Revs," *Sewanee Theol Revs*, The U So, 1997; Auth, *DOCC Stdt Handbook*, The U So, 1993; Auth, "The Gd News of Jesus Bk Revs," *Sewanee Theol Revs*, The U So, 1993; Auth, "The Pleasure of Her Text Bk Revs," *Sewanee Theol Revs*, The U So, 1992. revsclee@aol.com

LEE, Shirley Lynne (Ak) 1205 Denali Way, Fairbanks AK 99701 B Fairbanks AK 11/26/1959 d Russell T McConnell & Helen A. Paralegal Cert Antioch Law Sch 1980. D 2/13/2010 Bp Rustin Ray Kimsey. m 12/15/1979 Gary D Lee c 6. Yth Coordntr/Cmncatn Dio Alaska Fairbanks AK 2010-2011. shirleylee99@hotmail.com

LEE, Solomon Sang-Woo (Chi) 9227 Cameron Ln, Morton Grove IL 60053 **D One In Chr Ch Prospect Heights IL 1988-** B Kangwha KR 10/28/1929 s Andrew Yoo-Soon Lee & Grace Hae-Ja. Seoul Natl U Seoul Kr 1950; Cert Sch for Deacons 1987. D 12/26/1987 Bp Frank Tracy Griswold III. m 10/7/1958 Chu Nam Maeng c 3. Amer Mnstry Grant Dioc Asia 1988. solomon.lee@att.net

LEE, Stedwart Warren Rubinstein (VI) 261 Mount Pleasant, Frederiksted VI 00840 Virgin Islands (U.S.) B Stone Castle Tabernacle 10/6/1952 s Lawrence Evered Lee & Anne Marie. U of the Vrgn Islands; BA Codrington Theol 1980. Trans from Church in the Province Of The West Indies 9/30/2006 Bp Edward Ambrose Gumbs. m 12/29/1988 Shirlene Williams c 2. s_williamslee@hotmail.com

LEE, Susan Hagood (Mass) 336 Maple St, New Bedford MA 02740 **S Lk's Epis Ch Fall River MA 1988-** B Oakland CA 5/28/1949 d Richard Dozier Lee & Jeanne. BA Br 1971; MDiv Harvard DS 1988; PhD Bos 2003. D 6/25/1988 P 3/4/1989 Bp George Nelson Hunt III. c 2. Dioc Refugee Coordntr Dio Massachusetts Boston MA 1990-1994. "'Rice Plus': Widows and Econ Survival in Rural Cambodia," Routledge, 2006; "Traffic in Wmn," *Blackwell Encyclopedia of Sociol*, Blackwell Pub, 2006; "Female Genital Mutilation," *Blackwell Encyclopedia of Sociol*, Blackwell Pub, 2006; Auth, "Witness to Chr, Witness to Pain," *Sermons Seldom Heard*, Crossroad Pub, 1991; Ed, "Liberal and Persevering: Wmn in the Epis Dio Rhode Island," *Remembering Our SS: The RI Herstory Proj*, 1986. susanlee@bu.edu

LEE, Tambria Elizabeth (NC) 304 E Franklin St, Chapel Hill NC 27514 **Assoc for U Mnstry Chap Of The Cross Chap Hill NC 1993-** B Athens GA 10/21/1962 d Joseph S Lee & M Frances. BA Florida St U 1985; MDiv Yale DS 1988; DMin SWTS 1993. D 6/12/1993 P 5/1/1994 Bp A(lbert) Theodore Eastman. m 11/21/2009 David E Brown. tlee@thechapelofthecross.org

LEE, Terence A (LI) 19610 Woodhull Ave, Hollis NY 11423 **S Gabr's Ch Hollis NY 2010-** B Charleston SC 10/7/1974 s Cynthia Elaine. BS Coll of Charleston 1996; MDiv Nash 2005. D 6/18/2005 P 12/10/2005 Bp Edward Lloyd Salmon Jr. Cn S Jn's Cathd Albuquerque NM 2008-2010; S Paul's Ch Bennettsville SC 2005-2008. talexanderlee@yahoo.com

LEE III, Thomas Carleton (LI) 3000 Galloway Ridge Apt D104, Pittsboro NC 27312 B Niagara Falls NY 5/6/1928 s Harold Carleton Lee & Fanny Louisa. BA Leh 1948; STB GTS 1951; STM GTS 1953. D 5/26/1951 P 5/31/1952 Bp Lauriston L Scaife. m 7/17/1954 Emily Matson. R S Jn's Ch Cold Sprg Harbor NY 1963-1993; Asst Min S Steph's Ch Port Washington NY 1960-1963; R S Phil's Ch Garrison NY 1954-1960; P-in-c S Jn's Epis Ch Ellicottville NY 1953-1954; Vic Gr Ch Randolph NY 1951-1954; Fell and Tutor The GTS New York NY 1951-1953. tceml@netzero.com

LEE, Thomas Moon (Tenn) 510 Mable Mason Cv, La Vergne TN 37086 **H Sprt Ch Nashville TN 2008-** B Seoul KR 8/9/1962 s Young Nam Lee & Myung Gum. BA Han Young U Seoul KR 1986; B. Th Calvin TS Korea 1989; MDiv Ch of God TS 1993; Angl Stds STUSo 2001; DMin Regent U Virginia Bch VA 2002. D 12/16/2001 P 6/23/2002 Bp Bertram Nelson Herlong. m 4/21/1990 Jung Lee c 2. H Sprt Ch Nashville TN 2001-2006. "A Study of the Ch Growth Through Healing Mnstry," Regent U Virginia Bch. thomaslee10@hotmail.com

LEE, Vicki Yvette (Az) No address on file. **Died 6/17/2011** B Fort Dodge IA 7/13/1942 d Riley Ervin Lee & Ina Lotius. D 10/14/2000 Bp Robert Reed Shahan.

LEE, Wan Hong (Ky) PO Box 1054, Elizabethtown KY 42702 B 10/22/1958 s Ho Kwan Lee & Soon Og. Trans from Anglican Church Of Korea 2/1/2009 Bp Edwin Funsten Gulick Jr. m 9/16/1995 Eun Eun Choi c 2. Assoc Chr Ch Elizabethtown KY 2009-2010. frbany@gmail.com

LEE III, William Forrest (Md) Po Box 2188, Mountain Lake Park MD 21550 **Stndg Com Dio Maryland Baltimore MD 2002-; Vic Our Fr's Hse The Log Ch Altamont MD 1992-; Vic S Jn's Ch Oakland MD 1992-; R S Matt's Par Oakland MD 1992-** B Boston MA 4/6/1948 s William Forrest Lee & Natalie. BS Ithaca Coll 1971; MDiv CDSP 1989; DMin SWTS 2004. D 6/25/1989 Bp Rustin Ray Kimsey P 7/1/1990 Bp Bob Gordon Jones. m 6/26/2002 Mary Kathleen Gibbs c 3. Com Dio Wyoming Casper WY 1991-1992; Vic S Barth's Ch Cokeville WY 1989-1992; Vic S Jas Ch Kemmerer WY 1989-1992. mailorders@verizon.net

LEECH JR., John (Oly) 21405 82nd Pl W, Edmonds WA 98026 **R S Alb's Ch Edmonds WA 2007-** M.Div. CDSP 1984; Cert of Pstr Ldrshp Seattle U 2009. D 11/6/2004 P 8/12/2006 Bp Jerry Alban Lamb. Assoc Trin Cathd Sacramento CA 2006-2007; D Trin Cathd Sacramento CA 2005-2006; D S Patricks Ch Kenwood CA 2004-2005. john.leech@yahoo.com

LEECH, William David (ETenn) 8458 Gleason DR Apt 227, Knoxville TN 37919 **Died 5/2/2011** B Ambler PA 9/1/1923 s Charles Sherman Leech & Margaret Owens. BA U of Pennsylvania 1944; MA U of Pennsylvania 1946; BD Drexel U 1952; MDiv PDS 1952. D 4/27/1952 Bp William P Roberts P 11/1/1952 Bp Oliver J Hart. c 2. Phi Beta Kappa.

LEED, Rolf Amundson (WMo) 226 N Main St, Clinton MO 64735 B Honolulu HI 7/24/1941 s Bjarne Olaf Leed & Alice. MDiv Brigham Young U 1964; M.Div. SWTS 1969; Super. CPE Bapt Med Cntr 1983. D 9/13/1969 Bp Francis E I Bloy P 3/14/1970 Bp Norman L Foote. c 3. S Paul's Epis Ch Clinton MO 1994-2006; Dio W Missouri Kansas City MO 1985-1988; S Andr's Ch Kansas City MO 1985; Vic Gr Epis Ch Liberty MO 1984-1986; Vic All SS Ch Pratt KS 1980-1983; Vic Chr Ch Kingman KS 1980-1983; Vic Gr Ch Anth KS 1980-1983; Dio Wstrn Kansas Hutchinson KS 1979-1982; R Emm Ch Kellogg ID 1976-1980; H Trin Epis Ch Wallace ID 1975-1978; Vic S Jas Ch Mtn Hm ID 1969-1976. rleed@lide.com

LEEHAN, James Edward (Ind) 7047 Vuelta Vistoso, Santa Fe NM 87507 B La Moure ND 12/29/1939 s Floyd Leehan & Florence. BA Crosier Hse of Stds 1964; STB Crosier Hse of Stds 1966; MA Case Wstrn Reserve U 1972; MSSA Case Wstrn Reserve U 1975; DMin Ohio Methodist TS 1986. Rec from Roman Catholic 1/6/1981 as Priest Bp John Harris Burt. m 10/22/1994 Melissa J Spurgeon c 3. Pres, Stndg Com The Epis Ch In Navajoland Coun Farmington NM 2006-2007; Trnr, Sexual Misconduct Prevention The Epis Ch In Navajoland Coun Farmington NM 2005-2007; Vic Ch Of The Gd Shpd Ft Defiance AZ 2003-2007; Vic Navajoland Area Mssn Farmington NM 2003-2007; Chair Global Mssn Com Dio Indianapolis Indianapolis IN 2001-2003; Cler Wellnes Com Dio Indianapolis Indianapolis IN 1996-2003; Assoc R Outreach S Paul's Epis Ch Indianapolis IN 1995-2003; Trnr Sexual Misconduct Prevention Dio Indianapolis Indianapolis IN 1994-2003. Auth, "Psychol," *Grp Treatment for adult Survivors of Abuse*, Sage, 1996; Auth, "Sprtlty," *Defiant Hope: Sprtlty for Survivors of Fam Abuse*, Westminster/ Jn Knox, 1993; Auth, "Pstr Care," *Pstr Care for Survivors of Fam Abuse*, Westminster/ Jn Knox, 1989; Auth, "Psychol," *Grown-Up Abused Chld*, Chas AThomas, 1985. jimleehan@msn.com

LEES, David Roy (Mich) 2815 Omar St, Port Huron MI 48060 B Toronto ON CA 12/26/1923 s Harry Lees & Harriette Eliza. BA U of Wstrn Ontario 1949; LTh Hur 1951. Trans from Anglican Church of Canada 11/1/1954. m 9/22/1954 Doris Sullivan c 3. Fin Spprt Com Dio Estrn Michigan Saginaw MI 1975; Gr Epis Ch Port Huron MI 1953-1988. Hon Cn S Paul Cathd Detroit Michigan 1973. lees.roy@gmail.com

LEES, Everett C (Okla) 606 Bellevue Pl #B, Austin TX 78705 **Dio Oklahoma Oklahoma City OK 2011-** B Oklahoma City OK 8/24/1976 s Donald H Lees & M Ann. BBA U of Oklahoma 2000; MDiv Epis TS Of The SW 2009. D 1/16/2009 Bp Edward Joseph Konieczny. m 5/3/2003 Kristin K Lees c 1. S Pat's Epis Ch Broken Arrow OK 2009-2011. everettlees@gmail.com

LEESON, Gary William (Los) 4457 Mont Eagle Pl, Los Angeles CA 90041 B Laurium MI 12/14/1944 s Ralph Milton Leeson & Margalene. BA Drury U 1966, BD Nash 1969. D 2/12/1969 Bp Edward Randolph Welles II P 8/1/1969 Bp Donald H V Hallock. R All SS Par Los Angeles CA 1988-2007; P Ch Of The Epiph Los Angeles CA 1986-1988; Asst Trin Epis Par Los Angeles CA 1984-1986; R S Jas Ch W Bend WI 1972-1979; P S Aidans Ch Hartford WI 1972-1973; Cur Trin Ch Janesville WI 1969-1972. Hon Cn of the Cathd Cntr The Bp of Los Angeles 2007. bleeson8@sbcglobal.net

LEEWIS-KIRK, MJ Dorothy (Chi) 739 Kenwood Ave, Libertyville IL 60048 **D S Lawr Epis Ch Libertyville IL 2011-** B Toronto Canada 2/1/1950 d George Kirk & Dorothy. D 2/1/2003 Bp William Dailey Persell. m 8/27/1971 Keith Gordon Leewis c 3. mjleewis@earthlink.net

LEFEBVRE, Eugene Francis (Pa) 635 Willow Valley Sq Apt H-509, Lancaster PA 17602 B New York NY 5/21/1929 s Francis William Lefebvre & Antoinette Grace. BA Estrn Kentucky U 1952; MDiv Epis TS In Kentucky 1957; MA Villanova U 1971; U of Durham GB 1984. D 6/14/1956 P 6/14/1957 Bp William R Moody. m 6/21/1952 Gladys Engblom c 3. Assoc All SS Ch San Diego CA 1995-2003; R S Tim's Ch Roxborough Philadelphia PA 1960-1991; Vic S Mary's Ch Williamsport PA 1959-1960. Auth, "Sharing," *Chrsnty Today*; Auth, "Chr Today," *Chrsnty Today*; Auth/Ed, *The Healing Message*. CCU 1961-1978; Chapl Healing Pryr Fllshp 1983-2000; ECM 1988; Ord of S Lk 1960.

LEFEVRE, Ann Raynor (Be) 1190 Bianca Dr Ne, Palm Bay FL 32905 **D Ch Of Our Sav Palm Bay FL 2002-** B Portland OR 11/22/1934 d Spencer Winthrop Raynor & Eleanor Louise. AA Brevard Cmnty Coll 1969; BA U Of Cntrl Florida 1971; MA Stetson U 1972; MA Moravian TS 1991. D 5/23/1991 Bp James Michael Mark Dyer. m 12/23/1979 Carl Anthony Lefevre c 4. D S Lk's Ch Lebanon PA 1991-1995. NAAD. annlefevre@juno.com

LEFFLER, Nadine Vesta Haslett (Nev) 154 Sunset Hills Dr, Yerington NV 89447 **Died 1/18/2011** B Roseville CA 2/28/1923 d Clarence William Haslett & Vesta Maud. LPN Wstrn Nevada Coll 1974; Nevada Dio Theol Seminar 1997. D 11/9/1997 P 5/9/1998 Bp Stewart Clark Zabriskie. CAP 2001. navelef@aol.com

LEGER, Don Curtis (WLa) 919 Anthony Ave, Opelousas LA 70570 **S Paul's Ch Abbeville LA 2010-** B Opelousas LA 9/20/1956 s Curtis Leger & Shirley. AS LSU 1980; Bp Sch Mnstry 1997. D 6/24/1998 Bp Robert Jefferson Hargrove Jr. m 6/28/1975 Jeanette Lyons c 2. S Barn Epis Ch Lafayette LA 1999-2007. deaconleger@yahoo.com

LEGGAT, John Russell (RG) Christ Church of the Ascension, 4015 E Lincoln Dr, Paradise Valley AZ 85253 B Lowell MA 1/17/1949 s William Douglas Leggat & Doris Russell. BA Tufts U 1970; MBA U of Connecticut 1977; AA Pheonix First Pastors Coll 2000; MAR Gordon-Connell Theol Sem 2005. Trans from Iglesia Anglicana del Cono Sur de America 3/19/2007 Bp Jeffrey Neil Steenson. m 3/6/1971 Ann Leggat c 3. jrlegg@aol.com

LEGGE, Don Edward (Tex) PO Box 1314, Salado TX 76571 B Paducah TX 8/4/1931 s Edward Eudell Legge & Margaret Gertrue. BArch U of Texas 1954. D 6/19/1999 Bp Claude Edward Payne P 1/5/2000 Bp Leopoldo Jesus Alard. c 2. delegge@embarqmail.com

LEGNANI, Robert Henry (NJ) 158 Warren St, Beverly NJ 08010 **P-in-c S Steph's Ch Riverside NJ 2011-; R S Steph's Epis Ch Beverly NJ 1988-** B Mount Holly NJ 11/6/1946 s Felix August Legnani & Gertrude Elizabeth. BA Ups 1969; MDiv PDS 1974; STM GTS 1980; Cert Coll of Preachers 1991; Cler Ldrshp Inst 2000. D 4/27/1974 P 11/16/1974 Bp Albert Wiencke Van Duzer. m 12/3/1977 Susan Legnani c 2. Cler Wellness Com Dio New Jersey Trenton NJ 1996-1997; Dn Burlington Convoc Dio New Jersey Trenton NJ 1992-1996; Ed Bd Nwspr Dio New Jersey Trenton NJ 1990-2003; Chair of Cmsn of Cler Salaries Dio New Jersey Trenton NJ 1986-1989; Cmsn of Cler Salaries Dio New Jersey Trenton NJ 1981-1989; Vic H Trin Epis Ch Wenonah NJ 1978-1988; Cathdl Maj Chapt Trin Cathd Trenton NJ 1978-1981; Boys Conf Dio New Jersey Trenton NJ 1975-1982; Cur H Cross Epis Ch No Plainfield NJ 1974-1978; St Andrews Ch Plainfield NJ 1974-1978. Auth, "When is it Rt to Close a Ch?," *Living Ch*, 1994; Auth, "Ch News Column," *Beverly Bee*. AABS; HSEC 1974. legnani3@comcast.net

LEHMAN, Katherine Megee (Cal) 504 Cutwater Ln, Foster City CA 94404 **R S Bede's Epis Ch Menlo Pk CA 1990-** B Austin TX 2/7/1946 d Robert Ernest Megee & Nancy Stover. BA Santa Clara U 1970; MDiv CDSP 1982; DMin CDSP 1999. D 6/19/1982 P 6/1/1983 Bp William Edwin Swing. m 6/11/1966 H Clay Lehman c 2. Assoc R S Steph's Par Belvedere CA 1984-1990; Asst R S Steph's Epis Ch Orinda CA 1982-1984. Auth, "Go and Tell the Others," *God's Friends*, St. Greg Nyssa Ch, 1992; Auth, "Arts in the Ch Model," *CDSP DMin thesis*, GTU Libr, 1990; Auth, "Sing & Dance Chld Of God," Hinshaw Mus, 1980. Associated Parishes 1984-1994. CDSP DD Berkeley 2006. klehman@stbedesmenlopark.org

LEHMAN, Susan C (SwVa) 550 E 4th St #U, Cincinnati OH 45202 B Canton OH 6/9/1941 d Thomas Wilson Conner & Katharyn Jane. BA Mia 1963; MA Xavier U 1973; MA U Chi 1984. D 5/28/1977 P 11/30/1977 Bp John Mc Gill Krumm. m 5/5/1974 John Dalzell. Vic Epis Ch Of The Gd Shepard Blue Grass VA 2001-2006; Vic S Andr's Ch Clifton Forge VA 1995-1999; Chapl Sweet Briar Coll Sweet Briar VA 1985-2001; Vic H Sprt Epis Ch Cincinnati OH 1978-1982; Assoc Chr Ch - Glendale Cincinnati OH 1977-1980. SCLEHMAN@FUSE.NET

LEHMANN, Richard B (Alb) 24 Summit Ave, Latham NY 12110 **S Matt's Ch Latham NY 2010-; D Asst S Andr's Ch Scotia NY 2001-** B Jamaica NY 12/4/1954 s Richard Carlton Lehmann & Ruth Joan. BS No Cntrl Coll 1978; Gordon-Conwell TS 1981; Mercer TS 1989. D 6/9/2001 Bp Daniel William Herzog P 11/22/2008 Bp William Howard Love. m 9/18/1982 Christine Aydinian c 2. Ch Of The H Cross Troy NY 2008-2009. fatheralong@gmail.com

LEHRER, Christian Anton (Cal) 800 Pomona St, Crockett CA 94525 **D S Mk's Par Crockett CA 2009-** B Albany NY 9/19/1963 s Vinzenz Franz Lehrer & Joan Kathleen. BA The Coll of St Rose 1986; MA Dominical U 2001; BTS Sch for Deacons Berkeley CA 2007; MTS Jesuit TS at Berkeley 2013. D 6/6/2009 Bp Marc Handley Andrus. clehrer@msn.com

LEIBHART, Linda Dianne (Be) 9406 Chipping Dr, Richmond VA 23237 **Ch of the Redeem Addison NY 2010-; Off Of Bsh For ArmdF New York NY 1989-** B York PA 5/12/1952 d Lamar Levere Leibhart & June Louise. BS Millersville U 1974; MDiv VTS 1980. D 6/13/1980 Bp Dean T Stevenson P 2/1/1981 Bp Charlie Fuller McNutt Jr. S Mths Epis Ch Midlothian VA 1999-2000; S Paul's Ch Troy PA 1985-1989; S Jas Ch Mansfield PA 1982-1985; Dio Cntrl Pennsylvania Harrisburg PA 1980-1984; Asst All SS Ch Hanover PA 1980-1982.

✠ **LEIDEL JR, Rt Rev Edwin Max** (EMich) 430 W Brentwood Ln, Milwaukee WI 53217 **Provsnl Bp of Eau Claire Dio Estrn Michigan Saginaw MI 2007-** B Baltimore MD 10/13/1938 s Edwin Max Leidel & Gertrude Ruth. BS U of Wisconsin 1961; MDiv Nash 1964; DMin STUSo 1990; DD Nash 1997; DD Huron U Coll 2004; Cert in Coaching Cler Ldrshp Inst 2007. D 2/22/1964 P 8/22/1964 Bp Donald H V Hallock Con 9/7/1996 for EMich. m 6/20/1964 Ira Pauline Voigt c 2. Bp Dio Estrn Michigan Saginaw MI 1996-2006; Corner Stone Field Rep Dio Minnesota Minneapolis MN 1994-1996; Prov VI Exec Coun Dio Minnesota Minneapolis MN 1988-1989; R S Chris's Epis Ch Roseville MN 1986-1996; Dn - So Cntrl Deanry Dio Indianapolis Indianapolis IN 1977-1980; R S Tim's Ch Indianapolis IN 1975-1986; P Assoc Chr Ch Whitefish Bay WI 1970-1975; R S Steph's Ch Racine WI 1967-1970; Cur S Lk's Ch Racine WI 1964-1967. Auth, "Awakening Grassroots Sprtlty," iUniverse, 2004; Auth, "Claiming a Distinctive Character for the Ord," Dio Minnesota, 1994; Auth, "Bp, P or D?," Dio Minesota, 1993; Auth, "Perceptions of Minstry Roles in Relatns to Three Primary Functions of Mnstry," Doctoral Disertation, 1990. Ord of Julian of Norwich 2006; Sis of S Mary 1968; The Cmnty of Aiden and Hilda 2002. DD Hur U, London, ON 2004; DD Nash Sem, Nashotah, WI 1998. ed@leidel.us

LEIDER, Jennifer Claire (O) 805 Sycamore Pl, Ann Arbor MI 48104 **S Paul's Ch Oregon OH 2010-; S Paul's Epis Ch Medina OH 2008-** B Charlotte NC 9/16/1982 d Dwight Sinclair Spreng & Frances Roberta. BA/MA Case Wstrn Reserve Unversity 2005; MDiv EDS 2008. D 6/13/2009 P 5/8/2010 Bp Mark Hollingsworth Jr. m 9/2/2006 Stephen George Leider. jennifer.leider@gmail.com

LEIFUR, (Gloria) Teresa (CGC) 1110 E Gadsden St, Pensacola FL 32501 B Pensacola FL 1/27/1945 d Jesse E Brunson & Artie Missie. AA Pensacola St Coll 1978; BA U of W Florida 1988; MDiv Candler TS Emory U 1994. D 5/27/1995 P 1/27/1996 Bp Charles Farmer Duvall. m 4/12/1968 Duane Eugene Leifur c 3. R S Jn's Ch Pensacola FL 2001-2005; Vic Imm Ch Bay Minette AL 1996-2001; Dio Cntrl Gulf Coast Pensacola FL 1995-1996. OSH (Assoc) 1982. tleifur@gmail.com

LEIGH, W Joseph (NJ) 238 Twilight Ave, Keansburg NJ 07734 **P-in-c S Mary's Ch Keyport NJ 2006-** B Denver CO 2/13/1952 s Walter Leigh & Jane Louise. BA Metropltn St Coll of Denver 1974; MDiv SWTS 1978. D 6/29/1978 Bp William Carl Frey P 2/2/1979 Bp Arthur Anton Vogel. m 12/26/1987 Barbara Redepenning. Asst P The Ch Of S Uriel The Archangel Sea Girt NJ 2000-2004; Vic Ch Of S Clem Of Rome Belford NJ 1992-2000; S Mary's Ch Keyport NJ 1992; Int All SS Epis Ch Lakewood NJ 1990-1991; S Jas Memi Ch Eatontown NJ 1985-1990; Gr Ch Merchantville NJ 1983-1984; Cur The Ch Of S Uriel The Archangel Sea Girt NJ 1980-1982; Cur S Phil's Ch Joplin MO 1978-1979. wjleigh52@yahoo.com

LEIGH-KOSER, Charlene M (CPa) 6219 Lincoln Hwy, Wrightsville PA 17368 **P-in-c All SS Ch Selinsgrove PA 2010-** B Lancaster PA 9/17/1949 d Charles C Koser & Esther Johnson. BS Millersville U 1971; MDiv EDS 1977. D 6/10/1977 Bp Dean T Stevenson P 5/1/1978 Bp Roger W Blanchard. c 1. St Marks Luth Ch York PA 2003-2006; S Paul's Epis Ch Harrisburg PA 2001-2002; S Andr's Epis Ch York PA 1986-2008; Asst to R All SS Ch Hanover PA 1986-1988; P-in-c Ch Of The Gd Shpd Webster City IA 1981-1984; Asst Chr Ch Needham MA 1978-1980; D S Ptr's Ch Beverly MA 1977-1978. mothercharlene@aol.com

LEIGH-TAYLOR, Christine Heath (NCal) 4231 Oak Meadow Rd, Placerville CA 95667 **R S Clem's Ch Rancho Cordova CA 2005-** B Los Angeles CA 9/9/1943 d Denys Milner Leigh-Taylor & Charlotte Henriette. BA U CA, Los Angeles 1964; MS California Sch of Profsnl Psychol 1988; MDiv CDSP 2000. D 12/1/2001 P 6/1/2002 Bp William Edwin Swing. m 12/24/1988 David Ollier Weber c 3. Assoc. R For Yth Mnstry S Ambr Epis Ch Foster City CA 2002-2005; Yth Min S Mich And All Ang Ch Ft Bragg CA 2000-2002. Auth, "Bus Ldrshp As A Sprtl Discipline," *The Physcn Exec*, 2000; Auth, "Storytelling In Healthcare Orgnztn," *The Physcn Exec*, 2000. leighta@mcn.org

LEIGHTON, Christopher (Ct) 471 Mansfield Ave, Darien CT 06820 **R S Paul's Ch Darien CT 1998-** B Boston MA 6/4/1954 s Paul Leighton & Susan. BA U of Massachusetts 1976; MDiv TESM 1979. D 9/29/1979 P 3/29/1980 Bp Robert Bracewell Appleyard. m 10/13/1973 Janet Dorman c 4. R S Jas' Epis Ch Cambridge MA 1994-1998; R S Dav's Epis Ch Venetia PA 1985-1994; R All SS Ch Aliquippa PA 1979-1985. Auth, "Withinsight," Poets' Corner Press, 1972. Bro Of S Andrews 1983; Ch Army (Bd Trst) 1999. jdleighton@hotmail.com

✠ LEIGHTON SR, Rt Rev David Keller (Md) 7200 3rd Ave Apt C132, Sykesville MD 21784 B Edgewood PA 6/22/1922 s Frank Kingsley Leighton & Irene Adele. BS NWU 1947; CTh VTS 1955; DD VTS 1969. D 6/25/1955 Bp William S Thomas P 12/17/1955 Bp Austin Pardue Con 11/30/1968 for Md. m 1/18/1945 Carolyn Smith c 3. Ret Bp of Md Dio Maryland Baltimore MD 1985-1986; Bp Dio Maryland Baltimore MD 1972-1985; Exec Com; Trst VTS Alexandria VA 1972-1985; Bd CDO Epis Ch Cntr New York NY 1970-1979; VP Ch Hm & Hosp Dio Maryland Baltimore MD 1969-1985; Bp Coadj of Md Dio Maryland Baltimore MD 1968-1971; Ch Mssn Help Dio Maryland Baltimore MD 1961-1967; R Ch Of The H Nativ Baltimore MD 1959-1963; R St Andrews Epis Ch Pittsburgh PA 1956-1959; Cur Calv Ch Pittsburgh PA 1955-1956. "Tales Told on Obrect Road," *Hst. of Epis. Min. to the Aging*, 2000. Life in the Jesus Cmnty (Vstng Bp) 1983-1986; Oratory of the Gd Shepard (Vstng Bp) 1984-1994. dleighton2@juno.com

LEIGHTON, Jack Lee (Tex) 135 E Circuit Dr, Beaumont TX 77706 B Wichita KS 8/15/1934 s Walter Byron Leighton & Vera. BA Rice U 1957; BD Epis TS of The SW 1962. D 6/20/1962 Bp John E Hines P 6/10/1963 Bp Frederick P Goddard. m 8/28/1968 Deborah Bradt c 1. S Steph's Ch Beaumont TX 1999; R S Geo's Epis Ch Port Arthur TX 1993-1999; Ch Of The Incarn Houston TX 1986-1993; Assoc S Chris's Ch Houston TX 1984; Asst Emm Ch Houston TX 1978-1983; Asst S Mk's Ch Houston TX 1964-1966.

LEIN, Clay Alan (Dal) 10713 Pineview Ln, Frisco TX 75035 **Sr Pstr S Phil's Epis Ch Frisco TX 2002-** B Inglewood CA 9/25/1961 s Larry Maxwell Lein & Erlys. Gordon Conwell TS; SE Missouri St U; BS U of Missouri 1984; MBA Arizona St U 1990; MDiv TESM 1995. D 6/10/1995 Bp Robert Reed Shahan P 1/6/1996 Bp Edward Lloyd Salmon Jr. m 5/21/1983 Jill Elizabeth Lein c 3. Asst Chr Epis Ch Plano TX 1996-2001; No Amer Mssy Scty Charlotte NC 1996; Asst Chr the King Pawleys Island SC 1995-1996. Auth, "Ordnry Faith," Xulon Press. claylein@stphilipsfrisco.org

LEINBACK, Arlo Leroy (SwFla) 920 Tamiami Trl S Apt 258, Venice FL 34285 B Brookings SD 4/6/1918 s Willis Leinback & Laurena. BA U of So Dakota 1942; MA U MN 1950. D 6/24/1957 Bp Hamilton Hyde Kellogg P 5/9/1959 Bp Philip Frederick McNairy. c 3. R S Dav's Epis Ch Englewood FL 1983-1999; Crt Array Dio SW Florida Sarasota FL 1973-1980; Com On Const & Cn Dio SW Florida Sarasota FL 1970-1986; Dept Of CSR Dio SW Florida Sarasota FL 1965-1969; Vic S Dav's Epis Ch Englewood FL 1964-1972; R S Barn-In-The-Dunes Gary IN 1961-1964; Min in charge Ch Of The Redeem Cannon Falls MN 1957-1959; Min in charge S Lk's Epis Ch Hastings MN 1957-1959; Refugee Resettlement Com Dio Minnesota Minneapolis MN 1956-1959.

LEININGER, Austin (NCal) Church Of The Epiphany, 1839 Arroyo Ave., San Carlos CA 94070 B Eugene OR 11/27/1973 s Jack Leininger & Dorothy. BA U CA 2000; MDiv CDSP 2006; MA GTU 2007. D 6/3/2006 Bp William Edwin Swing P 12/2/2006 Bp Marc Handley Andrus. m 8/2/2003 Elizabeth Jane Northrop c 2. Ch Of The Epiph San Carlos CA 2009-2010; Asst Ch Of S Mart Davis CA 2006-2008. austin@chruchofthеepiphany.org

LEIP, Harry Louis (Mo) 600 N Euclid Ave, Saint Louis MO 63108 **ESM - Bd Mem Dio Missouri S Louis MO 2011-; D Trin Ch S Louis MO 2011-** B St Louis MO 6/26/1965 s Harry Louis Leip & Georgia Ann. BS Missouri St U 1987. D 1/29/2011 Bp George Wayne Smith. hleip@hotmail.com

LEISERSON, Joanna (SO) 2218 Oakland Ave, Covington KY 41014 **Epis Soc Of Chr Ch Cincinnati OH 2005-** B Alameda CA 8/31/1949 d David Louis Chin & Betsy Jean. BA U CA 1970; BA U CA 1972; MA U CA 1974; MDiv Gonzaga U 2004. D 7/10/2004 P 1/8/2005 Bp James Edward Waggoner. c 3. Dir Of Educ & Cmncatn S Steph's Epis Ch Spokane WA 2002-2007; Cathd Of S Jn The Evang Spokane WA 1995-2000. jleiserson@cccath.org

LEMA, Julio M (At) 1379 Craighill Ct, Norcross GA 30093 **S Davids Ch Brunswick GA 2007-** B Columbia 5/24/1942 s Julio Lema & Martha. RC Sem Cartagena Columbia 1961; U Of Bolbariana Meddllein Columbia 1967. D 7/10/2007 P 1/10/2008 Bp J(ohn) Neil Alexander. m 6/28/1964 Maria Dora Lema c 3. S Dav's Ch Roswell GA 2007-2010. jlema2405@yahoo.com

LEMAIRE, Michael E (Cal) 2220 Cedar St, Berkeley CA 94709 **On Lok Lifeways Oakland CA 2011-** B Burlington VT 2/28/1966 s Michael Emile Lemaire & Lois Heath. BA Ham 1988; MDiv Jesnit TS 2000; Cert of Angl Stds CDSP 2010. D 6/5/2010 P 12/4/2010 Bp Marc Handley Andrus. m 11/1/2008 Joseph Anthony Delgado. nmeljr66@yahoo.com

LEMARQUAND, Grant Read (Alb) 3 Sands Ave, Ambridge PA 15003 **TESM Ambridge PA 2010-** B Montreal QC CA 12/7/1954 s Henry Gordon LeMarquand & Marjorie Agnes. BA McGill U 1977; STM McGill U 1982; Montreal TS 1983; MA McGill U 1988; ThD U Tor 2002. Trans from Anglican Church of Canada 4/14/1998 Bp Robert William Duncan. m 7/12/1980 Wendy Jane Beraha c 2. Amer Assn Biblic Schlr 1992; Can Soc Biblic Stds 1991; HSEC 1996; SBL 1990. Honorable Mention Nelson Burr Prize In Recognition Of "Essays On The Angl Ch In China 1844-1997 Historic Soc Of The Epis Ch 1999. grantlemarquant@tesm.edu

LEMAY, Anne Rae (NJ) 576 West Ave, Sewaren NJ 07077 B Manchester NH 4/24/1953 d Emile R Lemay & Colette A. Cert Kean U; BA Rutgers-The St U 1975; MLS Rutgers-The St U 1989. D 10/21/2000 Bp David B(ruce) Joslin. m 12/29/2000 Kenneth L Erb c 2. Seamens Ch Inst Income New York NY.

LEMBURG, David Wesley (Miss) 1350 Courthouse Rd, Gulfport MS 39507 B Houston TX 9/15/1974 BA U of Arkansas 2001; MDiv GTS 2004. D 8/27/2004 Bp Larry Earl Maze P 5/29/2005 Bp Duncan Montgomery Gray III. m 8/23/2003 Melanie Dickson c 2. Vic H Trin Ch Crystal Sprg MS 2007-2009; Asst Par Of The Medtr-Redeem McComb MS 2004-2009. davidlemburg@yahoo.com

LEMBURG, Melanie Dickson (Miss) 1909 15th Street, Gulfport MS 39501 **S Ptr's By The Sea Gulfport MS 2009-** B Jackson MS 1/25/1976 d Stephen Andrew Dickson & Debra. BA Rhodes Coll 1998; MDiv GTS 2004. D 5/6/2004 P 12/1/2004 Bp Duncan Montgomery Gray III. m 8/23/2003 David Wesley Lemburg c 2. Par Of The Medtr-Redeem McComb MS 2004-2009. mdlemburg@yahoo.com

LEMERY, Gary Conrad (RI) 45 Bay View Drive North, Jamestown RI 02835 **Epis Chars Pres Dio Rhode Island Providence RI 2008-** B Woonsocket RI 6/5/1949 s Conrad Albert Lemery & Lorraine Joan. BS Roger Wms 1972; MDiv S Mary TS & U 1977; DMin EDS 1992. Rec from Roman Catholic 11/1/1983 as Priest Bp George Nelson Hunt III. R Ch Of The Trsfg Cranston RI 2000-2010; R S Jn The Div Ch Saunderstown RI 1994-2000; Ch Of The Ascen Wakefield RI 1993-1994; S Mk's Epis Ch Riverside RI 1987-1992; Vic S Thos' Alton Wood River Jct RI 1983-1987; Vic S Eliz's Ch Hope Vlly RI 1983-1986; S Jas Epis Ch At Woonsocket Woonsocket RI 1980-1981; Ch Of The Trsfg Cranston RI 1979-1980. glemery@cox.net

LEMLER, James (Ct) Christ Church, 254 E Putnam Ave, Greenwich CT 06830 **Chr Ch Greenwich CT 2007-; Epis Ch Cntr New York NY 2004-** B Mishawaka IN 11/6/1952 s Forrest Lemler & Juanita Carol. BA DePauw U 1973; Oxf 1974; MDiv Nash 1976; DMin Chr TS 1981; Cert Par Dvlpmt Inst New York NY 1985. D 6/11/1976 P 12/1/1976 Bp William Cockburn Russell Sheridan. m 10/23/1976 Sharon Louise Favorite c 5. Dn S Jn The Div Chap Evanston IL 1998-2004; Dn & Pres SWTS Evanston IL 1998-2004; Dep Gc Dio Indianapolis Indianapolis IN 1988-2000; R Trin Ch Indianapolis IN 1981-1998; Bd Metropltn Campus Mnstry Dio Indianapolis Indianapolis IN 1981-1985; Cn Precentor Chr Ch Cathd Indianapolis IN 1977-1980; Urban Strtgy Cmsn Dio Indianapolis Indianapolis IN 1977-1980; Asst To The Dn The Cathd Ch Of S Jas So Bend IN 1976-1977. Auth, "Transforming Congregations," *Ch Pub*, 2008; Auth, "Groundwork I, II, III," *DFMS*, 2007; Auth, "Serving Those In Need," *Jossey-Bass*, 1999; Auth, "Trst Educ & The Congregregational Bd," *Trst Ldrshp Dvlpmt*, 1996; Auth, "Numerous arts, Monographs and Blue Bk Reports". Ord Of S Ben, Confrater 1980. Sagmore Of The Wabash St Of Indiana 1998. jlemler@christchurchgreenwich.org

LEMLEY, Kent Christopher (At) 764 Springlake Ln NW, Atlanta GA 30318 **D H Innoc Ch Atlanta GA 2011-; Cmsn on Higher Educ Dio Atlanta Atlanta GA 2009-; T/F on Sex trafficking Dio Atlanta Atlanta GA 2009-** B Ft Myers FL 10/10/1946 s Kermit Roosevelt Lemley & Ann M. BA Furman U 1968; MBA Georgia St U 1973. D 8/6/2011 Bp J(ohn) Neil Alexander. m 7/15/2000 Karen Kirkpatrick. clemley@att.net

LEMON, Karen Dillenbeck (WK) 20081 Sw 20th Ave, Pratt KS 67124 **P All SS Ch Pratt KS 1999-; P S Mk's Ch Pratt KS 1999-** B New York NY 5/15/1945 d Douglas Dewitt Dillenbeck & Elizabeth Candlyn. K SU 1966; BA Yale

DS 2006. D 6/5/1998 P 3/27/1999 Bp Vernon Edward Strickland. m 8/20/1966 John Lloyd Lemon c 3. P Chr Ch Kingman KS 1999-2002. vicar_karen@yahoo.com

LEMONS, Catherine Clark Longwell (Minn) 12621 Old Columbia Pike, Silver Spring MD 20904 **Trin Ch Anoka MN 2010-** B Raymondville TX 11/14/1947 d Sam James Longwell & Evelyn Clark. BS Texas A&M U - Kingsville 1969; MDiv VTS 2010. D 7/23/2009 Bp James Louis Jelinek P 7/29/2010 Bp Brian N Prior. m 12/29/1974 Richard Meredith Lemons c 3. richncath@aol.com

L'ENFANT, Jamie E (NC) 1902 N Holden Rd, Greensboro NC 27408 **S Clem's Epis Ch Clemmons NC 2009-** B New Orleans LA 11/13/1967 d Howard William L'Enfant & Julia Claire. BA LSU 1989; MDiv Duke 1993; STM GTS 1994. D 11/30/1995 Bp Huntington Williams Jr P 6/1/1996 Bp Robert Carroll Johnson Jr. m 9/21/1996 Christian Lamar Rachal c 1. Asst S Fran Ch Greensboro NC 2007-2009; Cbury Sch Greensboro NC 2003-2007; Asst H Trin Epis Ch Greensboro NC 1998-2003; S Paul's Epis Ch Winston Salem NC 1995-1998; S Paul's Epis Ch Winston Salem NC 1994-1995. Soc Of S Jn The Evang. jlenfant@triad.rr.com

LENNON, Evelyn Cromartie (Minn) 119 Isabel St. E, Saint Paul MN 55107 B Cordova AK 12/19/1952 d George Bradley Lennon & Beatrice. BA U of Texas 1976; MA Untd Sem 1992; MS Augsburg Coll 1994. D 10/14/1995 Bp Sanford Zangwill Kaye Hampton. c 1. elennon@cvt.org

LENNOX, Daniel Duncan (NY) PO Box 293, Bedford NY 10506 **S Matt's Ch Bedford NY 2009-** B St Catharines Ontario 2/20/1980 s Robert Lennox & Barbara. BA McGill U Montreal QC CA 2003; MDiv Ya Berk 2006; STM Bos 2007. D 6/14/2008 Bp Andrew Donnan Smith P 12/14/2008 Bp Peter James Lee. m 8/25/2007 Abigail Lennox c 1. Chr Ch Alexandria VA 2008-2009. dlennox@stmatthewsbedford.org

LENOIR, Robert Scott (Miss) 2005 Lauban Ln, Gautier MS 39553 **Asstg P S Jn's Epis Ch Ocean Sprg MS 2012-; Co-Coordntr of Disaster Relief Team Dio Mississippi Jackson MS 2011-; The Chap Of The Cross Madison MS 2010-** B McComb MS 12/18/1954 s James Otis Lenoir & Elizabeth. BA Millsaps Coll 1977; MDiv STUSo 1988. D 5/25/1988 P 12/25/1988 Bp Duncan Montgomery Gray Jr. m 2/9/1978 Harriett Coleman c 1. S Mary's Ch Lexington MS 2006-2008; Vic S Pierre's Epis Ch Gautier MS 2001-2005; R S Jas Ch Greenville MS 1995-2000; R S Steph's Epis Ch Indianola MS 1990-1995; P-in-c Ch Of The Redeem Greenville MS 1988-1990; Cur S Jas Ch Greenville MS 1988-1990. Cmnty of St. Jos 2010. slenoir1@comcast.net

LENOSKI, Lauren Michelle (Az) 2220 Cedar St, Berkeley CA 94709 B Tucson AZ 9/2/1986 d Michael Douglas Lenoski & Sandra Leticia. BA Arizona St U 2009; MDiv CDSP 2012. D 6/11/2011 Bp Kirk Stevan Smith. lauren.lenoski@gmail.com

LENT, Morris J (SC) 1855 Houghton Dr, Charleston SC 29412 B Boonville MO 9/20/1941 s Morris J Lent & Luella H. BS USMA At W Point 1964; JD U of Virginia 1970; MDiv STUSo 1978. D 6/17/1978 Bp Hunley Agee Elebash P 2/24/1979 Bp Gray Temple. m 9/2/1967 Harriett Lent c 1. Int All SS Ch Hilton Hd Island SC 2001-2003; Chapl Porter-Gaud Sch Charleston SC 1987-2001; R S Jas Ch Charleston SC 1980-1987; Asst S Mich's Epis Ch Charleston SC 1978-1980. Auth, "arts"; Auth, "A Bk, A Rabbit, & Mouth Full Of Fruit," *Journ Of Theol*. moreylent@yahoo.com

LENTEN, John William (NMich) 11 Longyear Dr, Negaunee MI 49866 **S Jn's Ch Negaunee MI 2007-** B Islepeming MI 5/24/1960 s Wilfred Lenten & Marian. BS Nthrn Michigan U 1982. D 9/13/2006 P 4/22/2007 Bp James Arthur Kelsey. m 10/5/1996 Kathy Lynn Binoniemi c 3. jlenten@rangebank.com

LENTZ, Benjamin Lee (Be) 9758 N. Rome Rd., Athens PA 18810 **Long Term Supply Gr Ch Waverly NY 2011-; Long Term Supply Trin Ch Athens PA 2011-** B Paterson NJ 12/9/1950 s Lee R Lentz & Ruth Hannah. BA Bloomfield Coll 1973; MDiv EDS 1976. D 6/5/1976 Bp George E Rath P 12/11/1976 Bp John Shelby Spong. m 8/25/1973 Andrea Ciaburri c 1. Cluster P Emm Ch Elmira NY 2007-2011; R Ch Of The Redeem Sayre PA 1991-2007; R S Ptr's Ch Dartmouth MA 1980-1991; Chr Ch Pompton Lakes NJ 1980; Old No Chr Ch Boston MA 1980; Vic S Gabr's Ch Oak Ridge NJ 1977-1980; St Josephs Ch Newark NJ 1977; Cur Old No Chr Ch Boston MA 1976. novice@localnet.com

LENTZ III, Julian Carr (ECR) 1001 Sleepy Hollow Ln, Plainfield NJ 07060 **Palmer Trin Sch Palmetto Bay FL 2005-** B Maryville TN 3/4/1951 s Julian Carr Lentz & Mary Nell Lee. BA Maryville Coll 1973; MDiv VTS 1977. D 6/22/1977 Bp William Evan Sanders P 4/2/1978 Bp William F Gates Jr. m 11/4/2011 Lisa Van Sickle-Lentz c 4. All SS' Epis Day Sch Carmel CA 1998-2000; S Andr's Ch Saratoga CA 1989-1998; The Bp's Sch La Jolla CA 1983-1989; Cn S Andr's Cathd Jackson MS 1980-1983; R S Paul's Ch Memphis TN 1978-1980; S Paul's Epis Ch Chattanooga TN 1977-1978. llentz@palmertrinty.org

LEO, Agnes Patricia (Haw) 665 Paopua Loop, Kailua HI 96734 B UK 6/5/1940 D 11/19/1995 Bp George Nelson Hunt III. D Emm Epis Ch Kailua HI 1995-2000. Ord Of S Lk.

LEO, Denise Florence (Pa) 400 S Jackson St, Media PA 19063 **D Ch Of S Jn The Evang Essington PA 1997-** B Drexel Hill PA 9/25/1957 d Ralph C Barnhardt & Florence M. MA Cleveland St U 1980; Cert Pennsylvania Diac Sch 1994; Med Widener U 1995. D 9/24/1994 Bp Allen Lyman Bartlett Jr. m 6/4/1988 Stephen Nicholas Leo c 1.

LEO, James Richard (SO) 2121 Alpine Pl Apt 201, Cincinnati OH 45206 B Somers Pt NJ 8/24/1933 s Joseph N Leo & Muriel. BS Buc 1956; STB GTS 1962. D 6/9/1962 Bp Joseph Gillespie Armstrong P 12/15/1962 Bp Andrew Tsu. m 6/23/1962 Patricia Yerkes Elliman c 2. Epis Soc Of Chr Ch Cincinnati OH 1991-1998; Dn Epis Soc of Chr Ch Cincinnati OH 1991-1998; Dn The Amer Cathd of the H Trin Paris 75008 FR 1980-1991; R S Mary's-In-Tuxedo Tuxedo Pk NY 1969-1980; R S Jn's Ch Cornwall NY 1966-1969; Asst S Jn's Ch Larchmont NY 1964-1966; Asst Chr Epis Ch Pottstown PA 1962-1964. Auth, "Bk," *Exits and Entrances*, Xlibris Corp., 2008. jrleo@mac.com

LEO, Jason Elliman (SO) 3780 Clifton Ave, Cincinnati OH 45220 B 1/24/1966 s James Richard Leo. BA Buc; MDiv GTS. D 6/24/1992 Bp John Herbert MacNaughton P 1/6/1993 Bp Earl Nicholas McArthur Jr. c 1. Trin Epis Ch London OH 1998-2000; Dio Sthrn Ohio Cincinnati OH 1994-1999; S Geo Ch San Antonio TX 1992-1994. revleo@aol.com

LEO, John (Be) 295 Brown St, Wilkes Barre PA 18702 **Assoc R H Cross Epis Ch Wilkes Barre PA 2001-; Supply P Dio Bethlehem Bethlehem PA 1997-** B Winooski VT 12/22/1921 s Abraham Leo & Zaraef. BA U of Vermont 1950; BTh Bex 1953; MA California St Polytechnic U 1965; U of Birmingham Birmingham GB 1970; U of Edinburgh GB 1973; Cantess Cbury GB 1980. D 6/11/1953 Bp Vedder Van Dyck P 12/16/1953 Bp William Crittenden. Supply P S Ptr's By-The-Sea Epis Ch Morro Bay CA 1990-1992; P-in-c S Ben's Par Los Osos CA 1986-1987; Supply P Dio El Camino Real Monterey CA 1983-1997; Int S Paul's Ch Cambria CA 1977-1979; Int S Barn Ch Arroyo Grande CA 1969-1970; DeptCe Dio California San Francisco CA 1965-1970; Int S Barn Ch Arroyo Grande CA 1965-1966; Vic Chap Of The Gd Shpd Hawk Run PA 1953-1961.

LEON, Luis (WA) 1525 H St NW, Washington DC 20005 **R S Jn's Ch Lafayette Sq Washington DC 1994-** B Guantanamo CU 10/25/1949 s Luis Francisco Leon & Concepcion Esther. BA U So 1971; MDiv VTS 1977. D 6/22/1977 Bp William Hopkins Folwell P 6/17/1978 Bp Thomas Augustus Fraser Jr. m 6/27/1981 E Lucille Stanton c 2. Adj Fac SWTS Evanston IL 1993-2002; R Trin Par Wilmington DE 1988-1994; R S Paul's Epis Ch Paterson NJ 1982-1988; Dir, Refugee Prog Dio Maryland Baltimore MD 1980-1982; Asst S Ptr's Epis Ch Charlotte NC 1977-1980. DD U So 1999. luis.leon@stjohns-dc.org

LEON, Sadoni (Hai) c/o Diocese of Haiti, Boite Postale 1309 Haiti **Dio Haiti Ft Lauderdale FL 2008-** B 2/18/1976 s Marc Leon & Rose Meliya. D 1/25/2006 P 2/18/2007 Bp Jean Zache Duracin. leonidasscst@gmail.com

LEONARD, H Alan (USC) 254 Crooked Tree Dr, Inman SC 29349 **R S Marg's Epis Ch Boiling Sprg SC 2005-** B Pittsburgh PA 4/18/1964 s Henry Siggins Leonard & Eva Marie. BA Ripon Coll Ripon WI 1986; MSEd Nthrn Illinois U 1993; MDiv CDSP 1996. D 6/15/1996 Bp Frank Tracy Griswold III P 12/15/1996 Bp Charles Jones III. m 6/5/1993 Brenda Heidhoff Killen c 1. Chapl Off Of Bsh For ArmdF New York NY 1999-2005; Asst Ch Of The H Sprt Missoula MT 1996-1998. St Chapl of the Year VFW 2010. fatheralan@bellsouth.net

LEONARD, Sean T (WNY) 23 Potter Ave, Orchard Park NY 14127 B Attleboro MA 8/23/1973 s Thomas Pardon Leonard & Kathie Nan. BS Bridgewater Coll 1995; MDiv VTS 2006. D 6/3/2006 Bp Michael Whittington Creighton P 1/11/2007 Bp Nathan Dwight Baxter. m 8/7/1999 Chrishelle Leonard c 2. R S Mk's Ch Orchard Pk NY 2006-2008; Asst The Epis Ch Of S Jn The Bapt York PA 2006-2008. sleonard873@gmail.com

LEONARD, Thomas Edgar (Az) 11 Avineda de la Herran, Tubac AZ 85646 B Walla Walla WA 9/10/1936 s Edgar Hugh Leonard & Marie Agnes. U of Oregon 1956; BA U of Arizona 1959; MDiv CDSP 1962. D 6/9/1962 Bp Arthur Kinsolving P 12/1/1962 Bp J(ohn) Joseph Meakins Harte. m 12/18/1975 Ines M Pastor c 5. R S Chris's Ch Sun City AZ 1995-2000; R S Barth's Epis Ch Livermore CA 1982-1995; R Trin Ch Canton MA 1978-1982; R Chr The King Ch Tucson AZ 1974-1977; Vic Chr The King Ch Tucson AZ 1966-1973; Vic S Geo's Epis Ch Holbrook AZ 1962-1964. Auth, "Dioc Plcy On Alcosm"; Auth, "In Memoriam; Rebecca". tomtubac@aol.com

LEONCZYK JR, Kenneth (Dal) 84 Howe Street, Apartment 109, New Haven CT 06511 **P Dio Connecticut Hartford CT 2008-** B Marlton NJ 8/12/1977 s Kenneth George Leonczyk & Kathleen Noone. BA U So: Sewanee 2000; Cert.Ang.Stud. Ya Berk 2002; MA Yale DS 2002; JD Yale Law Sch 2009. D 1/31/2004 P 8/14/2004 Bp James Monte Stanton. m 5/30/2009 Ashley Ridgway. Dio Dallas Dallas TX 2005-2006; S Matt's Cathd Dallas TX 2005; The Epis Ch of the Intsn Carrollton TX 2005; H Trin Epis Ch Garland TX 2004-2005. "RLUIPA and Eminent Domain: How a Plain Reading of a Flawed Statute Creates an Absurd Result," *Texas Revs of Law and Politics*, U of Texas- Austin, 2009; "Meditation on the Third Week of Lent," *Gathered About the Throne*, St. Matt's Cathd (Dallas, TX), 2004. Cn of the Cathd St.

Matt's Cathd (Dallas,TX) 2005; Cn of the Cathd Epis Ch of Sudan (Kadugli Nuba Mts. Dio) 2004. kenleonczykjr@gmail.com

LEONETTI, Stephen James (NCal) PO Box 6194, Vacaville CA 95696 B Glendale CA 5/5/1946 s Robert Leonard Leonetti & Margaret Adline. BA U CA 1968; MA Claremont Coll 1974; MDiv GTS 1978. D 6/20/1981 P 1/11/1982 Bp Robert C Rusack. m 11/29/1974 Judith Burgess. Dio No Carolina Raleigh NC 1997-2000; R Epis Ch Of The Epiph Vacaville CA 1995-2011; Dio Oregon Portland OR 1992-1995; R Gr Epis Ch Medford MA 1990-1992; Dio Oregon Portland OR 1988-1990; Ch Of The Resurr Eugene OR 1984-1988; Dio Los Angeles Los Angeles CA 1981-1984. frsjl@pacbell.net

LEON FARINO, Pedro (EcuC) Calle 11ava Y Sedalana, 5250 Guayaquil, Parroquia Guale Canton Ecuador B EC 1/31/1936 D 12/16/1984 Bp Arthur Edward Walmsley P 2/1/1986 Bp Adrian Delio Caceres-Villavicencio. m 2/17/1989 Gloria Bowen Andrade. Litoral Dio Ecuador Guayaquil EQ EC 1991-2008.

LEON-LOZANO, Cristobel Olmedo (EcuC) Casilla 13-05-179, Manta Ecuador **Litoral Dio Ecuador Guayaquil EQ EC 1997-** B Guayaquil EC 7/10/1961 s Pedro Fausto Leon Farino & Teodocia Finlandia Lazon. BA Antonio Ruiz Flores 1995; Sete 4 Years 1997. D 7/14/1996 P 3/1/1998 Bp Alfredo Morante-España. m 2/25/1983 Ita Ofelia Chila Gracia c 3.

LEOPOLD, Robert Kelly (ETenn) 305 W 7th St, Chattanooga TN 37402 **Assoc R S Paul's Epis Ch Chattanooga TN 2011-; Vstry Papers Advsry Bd Mem The ECF New York NY 2011-** B Charleston SC 5/29/1979 s Robert Charles Leopold & Sophie Katherine. BA U of Tennessee 2004; BA U of Tennessee 2005; MDiv VTS 2008. D 5/31/2008 P 1/10/2009 Bp Charles Glenn VonRosenberg. m 10/29/2008 Lisa Leopold. Asst R S Paul's Epis Ch Chattanooga TN 2008-2011. leopold@stpaulschatt.org

LEOVY JR, James Gillmore (Ore) 1 Skyline Dr Apt 3305, Medford OR 97504 B Hermosa Bch CA 5/3/1930 s James Gillmore Leovy & Katherine. BA USC 1952; BD CDSP 1956. D 6/25/1956 Bp Francis E I Bloy P 2/1/1957 Bp Donald J Campbell. m 12/12/1960 Nancy D Grizzle c 1. Int S Mk's Epis Par Medford OR 2004-2005; Int S Geo's Ch Belleville IL 2000-2001; Int S Jn's Ch Detroit MI 1998-2000; P-in-c All SS' Epis Ch Vancouver WA 1995-1998; Dir of Pstr Serv Legacy Gd Samar Hosp Portland OR 1992-1995; Dio Oregon Portland OR 1992-1993; Int S Bede's Ch Forest Grove OR 1992-1993; Assoc S Jas Epis Ch Tigard OR 1976-1992; P in Charge Chr Ch S Helens OR 1973-1976; Instr Of The OT CDSP Berkeley CA 1959-1962. Alb Inst; Int Mnstry Ntwk; Natl Assn Epis Int Mnstry Specialists. nancyleovy@yahoo.com

LEPLEY, Rebecca Ruth Baird (EMich) 539 N William St, Marine City MI 48039 B Monongahela PA 5/9/1945 d Clinton Orth Baird & June Marie. Whitaker TS; BS Indiana U of Pennsylvania 1967; ThM St. Jn's Prov Sem Plymouth MI 1985. D 1/18/1984 Bp William J Gordon Jr P 6/1/1985 Bp H Coleman McGehee Jr. m 6/17/1967 Robert Lepley c 4. S Mk's Epis Ch Marine City MI 1988-2009; Int Gr Ch Mt Clemens MI 1987-1988; Archd Dio Michigan Detroit MI 1986-1992; Asst R S Chris-S Paul Epis Ch Detroit MI 1985-1987; Asst S Mk's Ch Detroit MI 1984-1985.

LEPORE, Daniel Anthony (CFla) 210 S Indian River Dr, Fort Pierce FL 34950 B Roselle Park NJ 8/22/1922 s Donato Anthony Lepore & Pasqualina. BA Mt Un Coll 1951; STUSo 1975. D 11/23/1970 Bp William Hopkins Folwell. m 8/27/1966 Clara Sogaard Christensen c 1. D/Asst S Andr's Epis Ch Ft Pierce FL 1992-2010; Asst Min All SS Epis Ch Jensen Bch FL 1972-1992; Asst H Faith Epis Ch Port S Lucie FL 1970-1972.

LEROUX, Donald Francis (ND) 319 S 5th St, Grand Forks ND 58201 B Salem MA 5/25/1952 s Robert Philip Leroux & Frances Grace. AS Cmnty Coll of the AF 1992. D 6/30/2007 Bp Michael Gene Smith. m 11/23/1974 Mary Atckinson c 4. lerouxmd@msn.com

LEROUX JR, Grant Meade (Ga) 5 Mooregate Square, Atlanta GA 30327 B Flushing NY 8/8/1941 s Grant Meade LeRoux & Louisa Ayers. BA U So 1968; MDiv TESM 1980. D 6/14/1980 P 12/13/1980 Bp Robert Bracewell Appleyard. m 6/22/1968 Claire Croxton. Int Ch Of The Redeem Greensboro GA 2009-2010; Int All SS Ch Warner Robins GA 2006-2007; Int S Steph's Ch Milledgeville GA 2004-2005; Int The Epis Ch Of The Nativ Dothan AL 2003-2004; R Ch Of The H Nativ St Simons Island GA 1987-2003; Asst Trin Cathd Little Rock AR 1983-1987; R Ch Of The Epiph Pittsburgh PA 1980-1981. GRANT@GRANTLEROUX.COM

LE ROY, Melinda Louise Perkins (Ore) PO BOX 750, Manzanita OR 97130 B Albany NY 8/19/1944 d James Eliab Perkins & Anna Frances. BA Col 1969; MA Col 1970; Cert Portland St U 1987. D 1/10/1991 Bp Robert Louis Ladehoff. m 3/17/1990 Joseph Patrick Dominic LeRoy. D S Paul's Par Oregon City OR 2001-2006; D All SS Ch Portland OR 1991-2001. crimsonmanzanita@yahoo.com

LE ROY, Milton R (Va) 463 Ranier Rd, Massanutten VA 22840 **Died 9/16/2010** B McCormick SC 11/7/1922 s Milton Reese LeRoy & Mary Francis. BS Clemson U 1943; MDiv VTS 1950; STM SWTS 1956; Fllshp Epis TS of The SW 1961. D 6/9/1950 P 2/4/1951 Bp A H Blankingship. c 3. Ed, *Curso Cubana Para Escuelas Dominicales*; Ed, *El Pan nuestro*; Auth, *Guide to Par Plnng*; Auth, *La Iglesia y Tu*.

LERUD, Nathanael D (Ore) Trinity Episcopal Cathedral, 147 NW 19th Ave, Portland OR 97209 **Cn For Sprtl Formation Trin Epis Cathd Portland OR 2009-** B Portland OR 7/21/1982 s David Glen LeRud & Claudia Ann. BA Whitman Coll Walla Walla WA 2004; MDiv GTS 2007. D 6/9/2007 Bp James Edward Waggoner P 12/29/2007 Bp Richard Lester Shimpfky. Cur Chr Ch Ridgewood NJ 2007-2009. nlerud@gmail.com

LESCH, Robert Andrew (Minn) 828 5th St Ne, Minneapolis MN 55413 B 12/19/1924 s Arthur C Lesch & Ruth Adeline. BFA U MN 1956. P 6/1/1960 Bp Hamilton Hyde Kellogg. m 10/22/1976 Pam Lescit c 3. P-in-c Ch Of Our Sav Little Falls MN 1983-1994; Serv S Thos Ch Minneapolis MN 1967-1982; M-in-c All SS Epis Indn Mssn Minneapolis MN 1959-1967.

LESESNE JR, Gray (Ind) 55 Monument Circle, Suite 600, Indianapolis IN 46204 **Cn Chr Ch Cathd Indianapolis IN 2008-** B West Columbia SC 4/8/1975 s William Grainger Lesesne & Ellen Craine. BA Presb Coll Clinton SC 1997; MDiv VTS 2001. D 6/15/2001 P 4/17/2002 Bp Dorsey Felix Henderson. R All SS' Epis Ch Glen Rock NJ 2003-2008; Asst R S Barth's Ch No Augusta SC 2001-2003. graylesesne@gmail.com

LESEURE, Laurence James (NY) 530 E 234th St Apt 1F, Bronx NY 10470 B Peoria IL 9/8/1946 s Kenneth James LeSeure & Anna Lee. BA Wabash Coll 1968; MDiv Yale DS 1971; MA Ya 1972; MPhil Ya 1975. D 6/12/1971 P 12/18/1971 Bp Joseph Warren Hutchens. S Steph's Epis Ch Woodlaw Bronx NY 2000-2010; Ch Of The Trsfg New York NY 1999-2000; Vic S Jn's Ch Centralia IL 1997-1998; Vic S Thos Ch Salem IL 1997-1998; Asst Par of Trin Ch New York NY 1979-1983; Asst Ch Of The Trsfg New York NY 1976-1979; Asst Chr Ch New Haven CT 1971-1976. CBS, GAS 1971; Elizabethan Club Of Ya 1970; Phi Beta Kappa 1968. lleseure@aol.com

LESH, Ryan Edwin (NY) 7423 S Broadway, Red Hook NY 12571 **Vic Chr Ch Red Hook NY 2006-** B Greeley CO 11/2/1959 BS Van 1982; MD U Roch 1986; MDiv CDSP 2006. D 3/19/2005 P 9/23/2006 Bp Mark Sean Sisk. rl344@yahoo.com

LESIEUR, Betsy Ann (RI) 200 Heroux Blvd # 2001, Cumberland RI 02864 **D S Paul's Ch Pawtucket RI 2002-** B Pawtucket RI 5/23/1945 d Irving Equi Evans & Elsie Elizabeth. Rhode Island Sch for Deacons. D 7/13/1985 Bp George Nelson Hunt III. c 1. D Chr Ch In Lonsdale Lincoln RI 1999-2000; Cathd Of S Jn Providence RI 1992-2000; Dio Rhode Island Providence RI 1990-1997; Asst Chr Ch In Lonsdale Lincoln RI 1985-1992. DeaconPTC@aol.com

L

LESLIE, Joanne (Los) 1351 Grant St, Santa Monica CA 90405 **D and Cn Pstr St Johns Pro-Cathd Los Angeles CA 2008-** B Ottawa Ontario Canada 6/9/1944 d John Ducan Leslie & Patricia Campbell. BA Reed Coll 1966; ScD Jn Hopkins U 1983; CTh CDSP 2001. D 6/8/2002 Bp Chester Lovelle Talton. c 3. "Wmn, Wk, and Chld Welf in the Third Wrld," Westview Press, 1989; "Food Plcy:Integrating Supply, Distribution, and Consumption," The JHU Press, 1987. jleslie@ucla.edu

LESLIE III, Richard B (ECR) 146 12th St, Pacific Grove CA 93950 **Pres of Stndg Com Dio El Camino Real Monterey CA 2011-; R Ch of S Mary's by the Sea Pacific Grove CA 2000-** B San Jose CA 4/22/1948 s Richard Black Leslie & Dorothea Maria. BA Santa Clara U 1970; MDiv CDSP 1977. D 6/25/1977 Bp C Kilmer Myers P 5/27/1978 Bp William Foreman Creighton. m 5/29/1971 Kathleen Lynn Shoenhard c 5. Pres of Stndg Com Dio California San Francisco CA 1999-2000; Pres of Dioc Coun Dio California San Francisco CA 1990-1991; Dio El Camino Real Monterey CA 1984-1987; Field Educ Supvsr CDSP Berkeley CA 1983-2000; Dio El Camino Real Monterey CA 1982-1984; R S Jas Ch Fremont CA 1981-2000; Assoc R S Mk's Epis Ch Santa Clara CA 1978-1981; Cur S Fran' Epis Ch San Francisco CA 1977-1978. Ralph B Atkinson Awd Monterey Cnty Chapt of the ACLU 2009. rbliii@scualum.com

LESSMANN, Mary T (Dal) 2750 Virginia Pkwy, Ste 104, McKinney TX 75071 **Epis Cmnty Serv Ntwk Dio Dallas Dallas TX 2010-; Assoc Vic St Andrews Ch McKinney TX 2009-** B Corpus Christi TX 2/1/1964 d Donald Eugene Leiser & Corinne K. BBA Texas A&M U-Coll Sta 1986; M Div Perkins TS @ SMU 2009. D 6/6/2009 Bp James Monte Stanton P 2/26/2010 Bp Paul Emil Lambert. m 4/16/1988 William Russell Lessmann c 2. Intern Ch Of The Annunc Lewisville TX 2008-2009; Dir of Educational Prog Ch Of The Incarn Dallas TX 2005-2008; COM Dio Dallas Dallas TX 1997-2003. maryl@standrewsonline.net

LESTER, Elmore William (LI) 1440 Tanglewood Pkwy, Fort Myers FL 33919 B Saint Clair MI 10/4/1932 s Elmore E Lester & Doris Ellen. BA U of Arizona 1955; MDiv Epis TS of The SW 1960. D 9/29/1959 Bp Richard S M Emrich P 12/1/1960 Bp James P De Wolfe. R All SS Ch Brooklyn NY 1965-1993; Vic S Dav's Epis Ch Cambria Heights NY 1963-1965; Vic S Andrews-By-The-Lake Epis Ch Harrisville MI 1959-1960. Auth, "Mr Drum Major". Bronz Star; Hon Cn Cathd Of S Cyp. bill3fish@aol.com

LE SUEUR II, John Thomas (NH) 18 Gaita Dr, Derry NH 03038 **D Faith Epis Ch Merrimack NH 2003-** B New Orleans LA 4/5/1948 s John Thomas LeSueur & Margaret Evans. BS LSU 1970; MS USC 1975; S Steph U S Steph

Nb CA 2001. D 4/14/2002 Bp Chilton Abbie Richardson Knudsen. m 7/14/1974 Susan Dianne Lassey c 2. jtlesueur@comcast.net

LE SUEUR, Susan Dianne Lassey (NH) Po Box 988, Calais ME 04619 **R Ch Of The Trsfg Derry NH 2002-** B El Centro CA 1/11/1949 d Russell Eldon Lassey & Elvira. BA California St U 1986; ETSBH 1988; MA Creighton U 1992; Andover Newton TS 1994; MDiv STUSo 1996. D 6/24/1996 Bp James Edward Krotz P 12/21/1996 Bp Harold Anthony Hopkins Jr. m 7/14/1974 John Thomas Le Sueur c 2. R S Anne's Ch Calais ME 1996-2002. lesueurs@loa.com

LESWING, James Bartholomew (Chi) 1125 Franklin St, Downers Grove IL 60515 **R S Andr's Ch Downers Grove IL 1988-** B Philadelphia PA 8/24/1948 s Herbert Leswing & Gladys Macfarlane. BA Dickinson Coll 1970; MDiv Yale DS 1973. D 6/9/1973 P 12/15/1973 Bp Leland Stark. c 2. Dn Dio Chicago Chicago IL 1997-2003; Chair Com Dioc Loans Dio Newark Newark NJ 1996-1998; R S Ptr's Epis Ch Monroe CT 1979-1988; Cn Cathd Ch Of S Paul Burlington VT 1975-1979; Asst S Paul's Epis Ch Chatham NJ 1973-1975. ADLMC. jleswing@comcast.net

LETHIN, Judith Lynn Wegman (Ak) 3509 Wentworth St, Anchorage AK 99508 **D S Mary's Ch Anchorage AK 2000-** B Boise ID 8/4/1944 d William George Wegman & Rosalind Mirriam. EFM STUSo; BA Albany Law Sch 1986; MA Albany Law Sch 1992; MDiv Vancouver TS 2003. D 2/1/2000 P 2/1/2004 Bp Mark Lawrence Mac Donald. m 10/20/1963 Kris Walter Lethin c 4. jwlethin@alaska.net

LETHIN, Kris Walter (Ak) 3509 Wentworth St, Anchorage AK 99508 **D S Geo In The Arctic Kotzebue AK 2000-; D S Mary's Ch Anchorage AK 2000-** B Glendale CA 8/19/1940 s Clarke Anthony Lethin & Marjorie Susan. EFM STUSo; BBA U of Alaska 1962. D 2/1/2000 Bp Mark Lawrence Mac Donald. m 10/20/1963 Judith Lynn Wegman c 3. kwlethin@alaska.net

LETTENEY, Barbara Ann (Alb) 2450 Main St, Lake Placid NY 12946 **Died 1/27/2011** B Syracuse NY 9/23/1935 d John E Collins & Haze Catherine. D 6/10/2006 Bp Daniel William Herzog. c 6. bletteney@hotmail.com

LEVENSALER, Kurt H (NCal) 60 Danville Oak Pl, Danville CA 94526 **Assoc S Tim's Ch Danville CA 2011-** B Visalia CA 12/27/1973 BA Biola U 1996; DAS Ya Berk 2004; MDiv Yale DS 2004. D 6/20/2004 Bp Jerry Alban Lamb P 1/10/2005 Bp Peter James Lee. m 7/30/2006 Leighanne DeMarzo c 1. Dir of Outreach Mnstrs Trin Epis Cathd Portland OR 2006-2009; Assoc Imm Ch-On-The-Hill Alexandria VA 2006; Lilly Fell Chr Ch Alexandria VA 2004-2006. Wm Palmer Ladd Prize Ya Berk 2003. kurt.levensaler@gmail.com

LEVENSON JR, Russell J (Tex) St Martin's Episcopal Church, 717 Sage Rd, Houston TX 77056 **R S Mart's Epis Ch Houston TX 2007-** B Birmingham AL 1/2/1962 s Russell Jones Levenson & Lynne. DMin Beeson DS; BA Birmingham-Sthrn Coll 1984; MDiv VTS 1992. D 6/13/1992 P 1/6/1993 Bp Robert Oran Miller. m 1/6/1993 Laura N Norton c 3. R Chr Ch Par Pensacola FL 2002-2007; R Ch Of The Ascen Lafayette LA 1997-2002; Assoc S Lk's Epis Ch Birmingham AL 1993-1997; Asst Chapl The TS at The U So Sewanee TN 1992-1993. Auth, "Provoking Thoughts," St. Mart's Ch, 2010; Auth, "Preparing Room," St. Mart's Ch, 2010; Auth, "Var arts," *Angl Dig*; Auth, "Var arts," *Chistianity Today*; Auth, "Var arts," *Decision mag*; Auth, "Var arts," *Epis Life*; Auth, "Var arts," *Sewanee Theol Revs*; Auth, "Var arts," *LivCh*; Auth, "Var Article," *Virginia Sem Journ*. Comm Partnr Fllshp Founding Bd Advisors 2009; Sigma Alpha Epsilon Fraternity 1980. Distinquished Alum of the Year Beeson DS 2011; Pres Stdt's Serv Awd Birmingham-Sthrn Coll 1984. cgallion@stmartinsepiscopal.org

LE VEQUE, James Rulaf (Md) 2728 N Calvert St, Baltimore MD 21218 B Cassopolis MI 5/29/1931 s Paul Newberry LeVeque & Vera. BA U Chi 1952; MDiv Nash 1955; STM Nash 1966; MA Morgan St U 1969; MA Jn Hopkins U 1975; Ed. D Morgan St U 2003. D 2/20/1955 Bp James R Mallett P 3/3/1956 Bp Archie H Crowley. m 9/17/1955 Katharine Tunstall Williams c 5. Int H Cross Ch Baltimore MD 1989-1994; Sprtl Dir-Curs Dio Maryland Baltimore MD 1981-1984; Cur S Mich And All Ang Ch Baltimore MD 1963-1998; Ch Of The Adv Baltimore MD 1960-1961; R H Cross Ch Baltimore MD 1959-1960. kwleveque@verizon.net

LEVERIDGE, Albert L (WTex) Po Box B, Devine TX 78016 **Died 2/28/2010** B Fort Worth,TX 10/21/1933 s Milam S Leveridge & Beverley A. BBA U of No Texas 1954; MDiv SWTS 1977. D 6/12/1980 Bp James Winchester Montgomery P 1/12/1981 Bp Quintin Ebenezer Primo Jr. c 3. Curs; Happ. all@centurytel.net

LEVESCONTE, Suzanne Joy Kreider (SO) 7121 Muirfield Dr, Dublin OH 43017 **Cur S Pat's Epis Ch Dublin OH 2011-** B Ephrata PA 7/11/1955 d Jacob Brackbill Kreider & Anna Hess. BS Mia 1986; MDiv Earlham Sch of Rel 2009; STM The GTS 2011; Angl Dplma The GTS 2011. D 6/29/2011 Bp Thomas Edward Breidenthal. m 7/1/1995 Steven Michael LeVesconte c 2. slevesconte@gts.edu

LEVESQUE, Paul Valmore (RG) RR 1, Box 655, Plainfield VT 05667 **Died 1/2/2010** B Rochester NH 12/1/1935 s Joseph Levesque & Bernice A. BA Oblate TS 1958; ThM Oblate TS 1962; MRE Institut Catholique De Paris 1965; Liturg Inst at Trier 1966. Rec from Roman Catholic 1/1/1993 as Priest Bp Daniel Lee Swenson.

LEVINE, Paul Christopher Herbert (ECR) 720 S 3rd St Apt 5, San Jose CA 95112 B Monmouth IL 1/14/1946 s Hervert Ervin Levin & Pearl Lee. BA U Denv 1968; MDiv Nash 1971. D 12/27/1970 Bp Edwin B Thayer P 7/1/1971 Bp William Hampton Brady. S Mk's Epis Ch Santa Clara CA 1992-1995; R S Fran' Epis Ch Turlock CA 1976-1989; Assoc S Paul's Epis Ch Visalia CA 1974-1976; Asst To Dn S Paul's Cathd Fond du Lac WI 1971-1974. PAUL5757@SBCGLOBAL.NET

LEVY, Sandra Maria (Va) 9107 Donora Dr, Richmond VA 23229 **Assoc S Jn's Ch Richmond VA 2004-** B Louisville KY 9/28/1943 d James Bertrum Miller & Thelma Catherine. BA Indiana U 1970; PhD Indiana U 1974; MDiv VTS 1994. D 6/25/1994 P 1/7/1995 Bp Alden Moinet Hathaway. m 12/18/2010 Paul Achtemeier c 2. R S Mk's Ch Richmond VA 1997-2004; Assoc R E Lee Mcmi Ch (Epis) Lexington VA 1994-1997. Auth, "The Flourishing Life," Cascade Books, 2012; Auth, "Imagination and the Journey of Faith," Wm. B. Eerdmans Pub Co, 2008; Auth, "Suffering and Post-Mod Consciousness," *ATR*, 1998; Auth, "Coleridges Rime of the Ancient Mariner: Theodicy in a New Key," *ATR*, 1996; Auth, "Behavior and Cancer," Jossey-Bass, 1985. AAR 2007; APA 1975; Soc for Biblic Lit 2003; SCNC 1998-2000. sandilevy8@aol.com

LEVY, William Turner (NY) 22121 Lanark St, Canoga Park CA 91304 B Far Rockaway NY 11/3/1922 s Jacob Levy & Florence Agnes. BA CUNY 1942; MA Col 1947; PhD Col 1953. D 6/8/1952 P 6/1/1953 Bp Horace W B Donegan. Cur All Ang' Ch New York NY 1952-1960. Auth, "Wm Barnes: The Man & The Poems"; Auth, "The Chairman"; Auth, "Affectionately," *Ts Eliot*.

LEWALLEN, Jerrilee Parker (Ala) 174 Carpenter Cir, Sewanee TN 37375 **COM Dio Alabama Birmingham AL 2001-** B Fayetteville GA 11/26/1944 d George Morford Parker & Clyde. BA U of Texas 1966; JD Indiana U 1977; MDiv STUSo 1998; DMin TS 2009. D 5/13/1998 Bp Henry Nutt Parsley Jr P 12/1/1998 Bp Robert Oran Miller. m 2/24/1979 Thomas L Lewallen. Otey Memi Par Ch Sewanee TN 2006-2008; S Columba-In-The-Cove Owens Cross Roads AL 2004-2006; D-in-c/ R S Tim's Epis Ch Athens AL 1998-2004. Auth, "Making Your Way to the Pulpit: Hethcock's Homil Goes to the Par," Wipf and Stock, 2011. jerrielewallen@bellsouth.net

LEWELLEN, Donald Stephen (Q) 523 W Glen Ave, Peoria IL 61614 **D S Paul's Cathd Peoria IL 1999-** B Olney IL 9/28/1934 s Stephen Sylvester Lewellen & Bernadine. BS Estrn Illinois U 1956; MS Estrn Illinois U 1962; PhD Clayton U 1981. D 11/1/1986 Bp Donald James Parsons. m 12/27/1970 Janet Kay McClellan c 3. Archd Dio Quincy Peoria IL 1995-1999; D S Jas Epis Ch Lewistown IL 1995-1999; D S Fran Epis Ch Dunlap IL 1994-1995; D S Paul's Cathd Peoria IL 1987-1993. jadonlew@aol.com

LEWELLIS, Vincent Edward (Be) 3235 Clear Stream Dr, Whitehall PA 18052 **Cn Theol Dio Bethlehem Bethlehem PA 1998-** B Girardville PA 5/21/1937 s William Joseph Lewellis & Mary Madeline. BA S Chas Sem Philadelphia PA 1960; STL Gregorian U 1964. Rec from Roman Catholic 11/1/1999 as Priest Bp Paul Victor Marshall. m 5/23/1981 Monica R Rajnic c 3. P-in-c Gr Epis Ch Allentown PA 2001; Cmncatn Min/Ed Dio Bethlehem Bethlehem PA 1986-2010; Cmncatn Min/Ed Dio Bethlehem Bethlehem PA 1986-2010. Co-Auth, "Your Faith You Life: An Invitation to the Epis Ch," Morehouse, 2009; Auth, "Some 150 Columns," *Var Daily Newspapers*, Var Daily Newspapers. ECom 1988. Cn Theol Dio Bethlehem, ECUSA 1998; Dom Prelate/Monsignor Dio Allentown, RC Ch 1977; Chapl To His Holiness/Monsignor Dio Allentown, RC Ch 1971. blewellis@diobeth.org

LEWIS III, Adam (Del) 115 E 90th St Apt 5C, New York NY 10128 B Marianna FL 2/14/1937 s Adam Macnealy Lewis & Lois Ophelia. BA Florida St U 1960; STB Ya Berk 1966; BFA Ya 1972; MFA Ya 1973; DD Ya 1986. D 6/11/1966 P 3/1/1967 Bp Walter H Gray. m 10/21/2011 Thomas Chu c 1. Chr Ch Greenville Wilmington DE 1983-1995; R Trin By The Cove Naples FL 1980-1983; R S Paul's Ch Fairfield CT 1973-1980; Vic Zion Epis Ch No Branford CT 1968-1970; Asst Min S Lk's Par Darien CT 1966-1968. Auth, "Billy Baldwin: The Great Amer Decorator," Rizzoli, 2010; Auth, "The Great Lady Decorators: The Wmn Who Defined Interior Design 1870-1955," Rizzoli, 2010; Auth, "Albert Hadley: The Story of Amer's Preeminent Interior Designer," Rizzoli, 2005; Auth, "Van Day Truex: The Man Who Defined Twentieth Century Taste and Style," Viking, 2001. adamlewisnyc@gmail.com

LEWIS III, Albert Davidson (ETenn) 340 Chamberlain Cove Rd, Kingston TN 37763 B Alexandria LA 12/26/1938 s Albert Davidson Lewis & Louise Hazel. BA Tul 1960; MDiv STUSo 1963. D 6/24/1963 Bp Girault M Jones P 5/1/1964 Bp Iveson Batchelor Noland. m 11/13/1959 Jan H Hendrick c 4. R Ch Of The Resurr Loudon TN 1991-2001; Asst R Ch Of The Gd Shpd Lookout Mtn TN 1986-1991; Vic Ch Of The Ascen Hattiesburg MS 1977-1986; Vic Ch Of The Resurr Starkville MS 1969-1976; R S Paul's Newport AR 1966-1969; Cur Gr Memi Hammond LA 1963-1966. ESMHE. bojanrun@aol.com

LEWIS, Alice LaReign (NMich) 437n County Road 441, Manistique MI 49854 **P S Alb's Ch Manistique MI 1999-** B Corunna MI 11/3/1936 d Ole Elmer

Price & Florence Mildred. D 9/15/1998 P 5/30/1999 Bp Thomas Kreider Ray. m 12/3/1955 Richard J Lewis c 4. adlew@up.net

LEWIS, Allen Lee (SD) 4705 S Wildwood Cir, Sioux Falls SD 57105 B Charlotte NC 7/6/1941 s Harry Lauren Lewis & Jane Bowen. BA Augustana Coll 1980; MDiv STUSo 1983. D 6/29/1983 P 2/23/1984 Bp Conrad Gesner. m 1/28/1963 Brenda Anderson c 4. P-in-c Ch Of S Mary And Our Blessed Redeem Flandreau SD 1988-2006; S Thos Epis Ch Sturgis SD 1988-1989; Dio So Dakota Sioux Falls SD 1987-1995; Cn to the Ordnry Dio So Dakota Sioux Falls SD 1987-1988; Chr Epis Ch Yankton SD 1983-1987. Ord of S Lk. padreallen@aol.com

LEWIS, Barbara (Tex) 1401 Calumet St. unit 312, Houston TX 77004 **R St Andrews Epis Ch Houston TX 2005-** B New York NY 1/11/1947 d Ralph Ferguson Lewis & Thelma Louise. BA Mt Holyoke Coll 1968; MS Col 1975; MDiv GTS 1998. D 10/24/1993 P 5/29/1999 Bp Franklin Delton Turner. m 11/17/2006 Frank A Venutolo c 1. Int Gr Epis Ch Alvin TX 2004-2005; Assoc R S Thos The Apos Epis Ch Houston TX 2000-2004; Assoc R Lord Of The St Epis Mssn Ch Houston TX 1998-2000; D S Andr's Ch Yardley PA 1993-1998. revblewis@yahoo.com

LEWIS, Barbara Ann (Nev) 1511 Cardinal Peak Ln Unit 101, Las Vegas NV 89144 **Mem, Sr Coun Dio Nevada Las Vegas NV 2011-; D Gr In The Desert Epis Ch Las Vegas NV 1997-** B Chicago IL 10/15/1930 d Reginald Carter Waddell & Lillian Eloise. Chicago Teachers Coll 1951; Roosevelt U 1952. D 6/22/1997 Bp Stewart Clark Zabriskie. m 6/13/1975 Douglas Lewis c 2. UBE 2000-2009. babalew@netzero.net

LEWIS, Barbara Jane (Pa) 19115 Avalon Way, Lawrenceville NJ 08648 **P-in-c Ch Of Our Sav Secaucus NJ 2011-** B Abington PA 12/7/1943 d William A Bell & Elizabeth Jane. BA Gwyneed Mercy Coll Gwyneed Vlly PA 1991; MDiv EDS 1995. D 6/10/1995 P 6/1/1996 Bp Allen Lyman Bartlett Jr. c 4. R S Jas Ch Greenridge Aston PA 1997-2010; Assoc S Mary's Ch Sparta NJ 1995-1997. Assoc OHC 1975. revbarb72@gmail.com

LEWIS, Betsey (Ct) 43 Flying Point Rd, Branford CT 06405 **D S Lk's Epis Ch New Haven CT 1991-** B New Haven CT 9/7/1923 d Thornton John Converse & Margaret Enella. BA Smith 1945; MA U Of Delaware Newark 1969. D 12/7/1991 Bp Arthur Edward Walmsley. m 12/4/1948 Kendall Lewis c 3. Auth, "A Guide For Developing A Hospice Orientation Prog". NAAD. Coffin-Forsberg Fellowowship (Ds) Ya New Haven CT.

LEWIS, Catherine Blanc (Roch) 7086 Salmon Creek Rd, Williamson NY 14589 B New York NY 11/6/1939 d William Peters Blanc & Particia Anderson. BA Bryn 1961; MDiv Bex 1984. D 6/8/1985 P 6/1/1986 Bp William George Burrill. m 9/5/1964 Richard B Lewis. Int Ch Of The Ascen Rochester NY 2000; Chr Ch Pittsford NY 1992-1998; Asst to R S Lk's Ch Fairport NY 1991-1992; Asst to R Ch Of The Ascen Rochester NY 1985-1991; Pstr Asst Ch Of The Ascen Rochester NY 1983-1985. LEWISUSA@ROCHESTER.RR.COM

LEWIS, Charles Robert (Alb) 3711 Glen Oaks Manor Dr, Sarasota FL 34232 B Independence MO 12/7/1936 s Robert Theodore Lewis & Emabel. BS U CO 1958; MDiv Nash 1965. D 3/20/1965 P 9/1/1965 Bp Donald H V Hallock. R Chr Ch Epis Hudson NY 1973-1997; Asst Treas Dio W Missouri Kansas City MO 1970-1973; Cn Mssnr Gr And H Trin Cathd Kansas City MO 1970-1973; Vic Trin Epis Ch Marshall MO 1967-1970; Cur Trin Ch Janesville WI 1965-1967. Delta Upsilon; Delta Sigma Phi. LEWISHEDRICK@COMCAST.NET

LEWIS, Cynthia (Ct) NA, NA NM 88312 B El Paso TX d Thomas Fielding Lewis & Sylvia. MDiv VTS 1985. D 6/25/1985 P 5/1/1986 Bp Richard Mitchell Trelease Jr. Int Chr Ch Waterbury CT 1995; Grtr Waterbury Mnstry Middlebury CT 1992-1993; Asst Chr Ch New Haven CT 1989-1991; Vic All SS' Epis Ch E Hartford CT 1986-1989. Auth, "When A Ch Calls A Mus". revcjlewis@gmail.com

LEWIS, Don Willard (Los) 481 Plymouth St, Cambria CA 93428 B Los Angeles CA 2/7/1931 s Willard J(enks) Lewis & Eve Helen. U CA; MDiv CDSP 1981. D 6/20/1981 P 1/11/1982 Bp Robert C Rusack. m 10/6/1956 Huntley C Cockburn. R S Edm's Par San Marino CA 1985-1994; Vic S Marg Of Scotland Par San Juan Capistrano CA 1981-1984. Hon "Wmn P" Wmn Cler Caucus Dio. Of L.A. 1990; DSA So.Calif. Interfaith Taskforce On Cent. Am. 1988. donhunt@charter.net

LEWIS, (Earl) James (Del) 1313 Lee St E Apt 112, Charleston WV 25301 B Baltimore MD 10/1/1935 s Earl Robertson Lewis & Sara. BA W&L 1958; BD VTS 1964. D 6/22/1964 P 5/1/1965 Bp Harry Lee Doll. m 6/14/1958 Judith Graham c 4. Mssnr Dio Delaware Wilmington DE 1995-2001; Dio No Carolina Raleigh NC 1987-1994; Vic Ch Of The Incarn Pittsfield Twp Ann Arbor MI 1985; R S Andr's Ch Ann Arbor MI 1982-1984; R S Jn's Epis Ch Charleston WV 1974-1982; R Trin Epis Ch Martinsburg WV 1968-1974; Cur S Anne's Par Annapolis MD 1964-1968. Auth, *Strike Terror No More (1 Chapt)*, Chalice Press, 2002; Auth, *The Gulf War: Ch & Peacemaking*, No Carolina Coun of Ch, 1997; Auth, *W Virginia Pilgrim*, Seabury Press, 1976. DD VTS 2000. ejlchas@aol.com

LEWIS, Ernest Loran (NCal) 640 Hawthorne Ln, Davis CA 95616 B Fresno CA 12/4/1935 s Harold Levi Lewis & Esther Emily. AB Fresno St U 1958; MB Washington U 1963; Cert Epis Sch for Deacons 2002. D 9/8/2002 Bp Jerry Alban Lamb P 10/1/2011 Bp Barry Leigh Beisner. m 11/23/1964 Mary Ann Fowler c 3. maernie@pacbell.net

LEWIS JR, Giles Floyd (Tex) 786 Glendalyn Ave, Spartanburg SC 29302 B Orlando FL 9/22/1927 s Giles Floyd Lewis & Florence Baldwin. BS Clemson U 1949; MDiv STUSo 1957. D 7/17/1957 P 3/25/1958 Bp Clarence Alfred Cole. m 10/3/1957 Dorothy Jane Tauber c 4. H Cross Trussville AL 2000-2003; Assoc S Jn The Div Houston TX 1972-1990; R S Barth's Ch Bristol TN 1967-1972; Assoc Chr Ch Cathd Lexington KY 1964-1967; Assoc Chr Ch Greenville SC 1963-1964; Min in charge All SS Epis Ch Clinton SC 1957-1960; Min in charge Ch Of The Epiph Laurens SC 1957-1960. gsljtl@gmail.com

LEWIS, Harold Thomas (Pgh) 315 Shady Ave, Pittsburgh PA 15206 **R Calv Ch Pittsburgh PA 1996-** B Brooklyn NY 2/21/1947 s Frank Walston Lewis & Muriel Kathleen. BA McGill U 1967; MDiv Ya Berk 1971; U of Cambridge 1973; Dplma St Geo's Coll Jerusalem 1990; Fllshp Ya Berk 1991; PhD U Of Birmingham Birmingham Gb 1994. D 6/12/1971 Bp Jonathan Goodhue Sherman P 12/21/1971 Bp William Carl Frey. m 2/7/1970 Claudette Richards. Gnrl Bec Dio Pittsburgh Monroeville PA 1996-2000; Int S Mk's Ch Brooklyn NY 1995-1996; Prof Geo Mercer TS Garden City NY 1988-1996; V-Chair Bd Trsts Ya Berk New Haven CT 1986-1991; Tutor The GTS New York NY 1985-1986; Stff Off Blk Mnstrs Epis Ch Cntr New York NY 1983-1994; R S Monica's Epis Ch Washington DC 1973-1982; P-in-c Iglesia Epis Espiritu Santo Tela HN 1971-1972; P-in-c Iglesia Epis Santisima Trinidad La Ceiba At HN 1971-1972. Auth, "A Ch for the Future So Afr as Crucible for Anglicanism in a New Century," Ch Pub Inc, 2007; Auth, "Chr Soc Witness," Cowley Press, 2001; Auth, "Elijah'S Mantle: Pilgrimage," *Politics And Proclamation*, Ch Pub Inc, 2001; Auth, "Yet w A Steady Beat: The Afr Amer Struggle For Recognitionn In The Epis Ch," Trin Press, 1996; Ed/Compsr, "Lift Every Voice & Sing Ii: An Afr-Amer Hymnal," Ch Hymnal Corp, 1993; Auth, "In Season," *Out Of Season: A Collection Of Sermons*, Dfms, 1992; Auth, "arts & Revs". Advsry Coun, Ang Observer to UN 1998; Bd, Hist Soc of Epis Ch 2004-2011; ECF Fellows Forum 2000; UBE 1968. Dn's Cross for Servnt Ldrshp VTS 2009; Doctor of Cn Law Seabury-Wstrn Theol Sem 2001; DD Berk 1991; Hon Cn Dio Bukavu (Congo) 1980. hlewis@calvarypgh.org

LEWIS JR, Howarth Lister (SeFla) 1110 Sand Drift Way, West Palm Beach FL 33411 **Cn for Deacons Dio SE Florida Miami FL 2004-; D-in-c S Geo's Epis Ch Riviera Bch FL 2001-; D Dio SE Florida Miami FL 1992-** B New York NY 6/13/1934 s Howarth Lister Lewis & Edith. BA U of Florida 1957. D 3/23/1992 Bp Calvin Onderdonk Schofield Jr. m 6/8/1957 Dianna Jean Moore c 3. D S Patricks Ch W Palm Bch FL 1998-2001; D H Trin Epis Ch W Palm Bch FL 1992-1998. NAAD. Coll of Fellows Amer Inst Archits 2001; H Smith Awd Amer Inst Archits Palm Bch; Anth Pullara Awd Florida Assn Amer Inst Archits. haplewis@bellsouth.net

LEWIS JR, Irwin Morgan (SVa) 4449 N Witchduck Rd, Virginia Beach VA 23455 **Chr and S Lk's Epis Ch Norfolk VA 2010-** B Bronxville NY 6/25/1952 s Irwin Morgan Lewis & Dorothy Virginia. BA W&M 1974; Med W&M 1975; MDiv VTS 1980. D 5/31/1980 P 3/1/1981 Bp C(laude) Charles Vache. m 8/12/1989 Catherine Midkiff c 1. Cn to the Ordnry Dio Sthrn Virginia Norfolk VA 2003-2010; R Old Donation Ch Virginia Bch VA 1998-2003; Assoc Chr and S Lk's Epis Ch Norfolk VA 1991-1998; R S Mk's Ch Hampton VA 1983-1991; Chair - Spir Cmsn Dio Sthrn Virginia Norfolk VA 1983-1986; Asst Chr and S Lk's Epis Ch Norfolk VA 1980-1983; Cur The Epis Ch Of The Adv Norfolk VA 1980. Auth, "Confirmed To Serve". Soc Of S Jn The Evang. win@diosova.org

LEWIS, Jason D (WMo) 204 Monroe Ave, Belton MO 64012 **St Mary Magd Epis Ch Belton MO 2007-** B Walkins Glen NY 7/30/1978 s William Ansel Lewis & Donna. MDiv Nazarene TS 2004; CAS Geo Herbert Inst For Pstr Stds 2006. D 6/2/2007 P 12/1/2007 Bp Barry Robert Howe. m 12/19/1998 Amy Lynn Yocum c 3. jason@marymag.com

LEWIS, Jeffrey (Ct) Salisbury School, 251 Canaan Rd, Salisbury CT 06068 B Galveston TX 10/26/1965 s John Walter Lewis & Polly Philbrook. BA U of Texas 1989; MDiv Bangor TS 2004. D 11/1/2004 P 6/10/2006 Bp Chilton Abbie Richardson Knudsen. m 5/22/1993 Susan Boyd Geehr-Lewis c 3. S Giles Ch Jefferson ME 2006-2008; Assoc Cler The Epis Ch Of S Jn Bapt Thomaston ME 2005-2006; Cler Intern S Mk's Ch Waterville ME 2004-2005. jlewis@salisburyschool.org

LEWIS JR, Jim (SC) Diocese of South Carolina, PO Box 20127, Charleston SC 29413 **Cn to the Ordnry Dio So Carolina Charleston SC 2009-** B Petersburg VA 10/16/1958 s James Barton Lewis & Emily Jean. BS U So 1981; MS Virginia Tech U 1984; MDiv SWTS 1994. D 5/28/1994 Bp Frank Harris Vest Jr P 12/3/1994 Bp Edward Lloyd Salmon Jr. m 9/3/1988 Elizabeth Toalsen Trimpe c 3. Assoc R The Epis Ch Of The Resurr Surfside Bch SC 2004-2009; R S Jude's Epis Ch Walterboro SC 1994-2004. Amer Angl Coun 1998. jlewis@dioceseofsc.org

LEWIS, John Goddard (WTex) The WorkShop, 2015 NE Loop 410, San Antonio TX 78217 **S Mk's Epis Ch San Antonio TX 2001-** B Beaumont TX

L

6/9/1952 s ZD Lewis & Edith. BA Houston Bapt U 1974; JD U Of Houston 1977; MDiv VTS 1997; D.Phil. U of Oxford 2004. D 6/19/1997 P 11/15/2001 Bp James Edward Folts. m 10/22/1988 Patricia Bridwell. Auth, "Sewanee Theol Revs". AAR 2002; SBL 2002; Sprtl Dir' Intl 2005. jlewis@theworkshop-sa.org

LEWIS, John Walter (Me) 33 Knowlton St, Camden ME 04843 B Gainesville TX 1/30/1937 s Elbert Eugene Lewis & Jennie Earnest. Rice U - Rel Stds; MD High hon U of Texas Med Branch 1967; JD Yale Law Sch 1982. D 6/18/2005 Bp Chilton Abbie Richardson Knudsen. m 2/10/1995 Roberta Laemmle Brown c 4. jlewismdjd@aol.com

LEWIS, Karen C (Roch) 520 S Main St, Geneva NY 14456 **Int Trin Ch Geneva NY 2010-** B Madison WI 7/20/1956 d William Cichowski & Mary. BA Cntrl Michigan U 1978; MDiv SWTS 1995. D 6/8/1996 P 5/31/1997 Bp R(aymond) Stewart Wood Jr. m 10/21/1978 Donald Bruce Lewis c 3. Cn Dio Cntrl New York Syracuse NY 2006-2010; Cn To The Ordnry Dio Estrn Oregon The Dalles OR 2002-2006; Asst To Bp For Chr Formation Dio Michigan Detroit MI 2000-2002; Asst R S Jn's Ch Plymouth MI 1998-2000; All SS Epis Ch Pontiac MI 1996-1998. lewisk720@gmail.com

LEWIS, Kate (Los) PO Box 1094, Kailua HI 96734 B Lodi CA 4/8/1958 BA Loyola Marymount U 1980; MDiv CDSP 2002. D 6/2/2002 P 1/11/2003 Bp Joseph Jon Bruno. m 5/9/2004 Patricia Hendrickson c 1. Vic Emm Epis Ch Kailua HI 2008-2011; S Cross By-The-Sea Ch Hermosa Bch CA 2003-2008; Ucla Med Cntr Los Angeles CA 2002-2003. k8lewis@aol.com

LEWIS, Katherine Twyford (Minn) 519 Oak Grove St, Minneapolis MN 55403 **The Epis Par Of S Dav Minnetonka MN 2009-** B Alexandria VA 7/10/1964 d Earl James Lewis & Judith Louise. BA Denison U 1986; MDiv VTS 1996. D 6/29/1996 Bp Herbert Thompson Jr P 2/15/1997 Bp Kenneth Lester Price. m 5/1/1993 William Lawrence Bulson c 2. Cn Cathd Ch Of S Mk Minneapolis MN 1998-2002; E Cntrl Ohio Area Mnstry Cambridge OH 1997-1998; P Trin Ch Bellaire OH 1997-1998. klewismpls@aol.com

LEWIS, Kenneth Rutherford (Ala) 708 Fairfax Dr, Fairfield AL 35064 B Sheffield AL 7/22/1946 s William Haven Lewis & Eloise Silvia. BA Miles Coll 1976. D 10/30/2004 Bp Henry Nutt Parsley Jr. m 9/29/1985 Peggy Ann Taylor c 4. klewishvac40@msn.com

LEWIS, Kenrick Ewart (Mass) 309 New York Ave, Jersey City NJ 07307 B Belize HN 7/6/1931 s Roland Alexander Lewis & Florrie. BS U of The W Indies 1956; DIT S Ptr Theol Coll 1959; BD EDS 1969; STM Andover Newton TS 1970; STM Bos 1986. D 5/1/1959 P 6/1/1960 Bp The Bishop Of Jamaica. c 3. Trin Ch Bellaire OH 1998-2001; Trin Ch Montclair NJ 1998-2001; New York Spec Account New York NY 1994-2003; S Lk's-Roosevelt Hosp Cntr New York NY 1988-2003; Dpt Of Missions Ny Income New York NY 1988-2000; Diocn Msnry & Ch Extntn Socty New York NY 1988-1993; S Jn's S Jas Epis Ch Roxbury MA 1985-1988. UBE, Massachusetts Cleric Assn. uzziahk@comcast.net

LEWIS, Kristina D (Ct) 91 Church St, Seymour CT 02630 **R Trin Ch Seymour CT 2009-** B Wadesboro NC 12/4/1952 d Joseph Bennett Lewis & Pauline Emilee. BS Coll of Charleston 1987; MS U of Florida 1991; PhD U of Florida 1994; MDiv GTS 2005. D 6/4/2005 P 1/7/2006 Bp Thomas C Ely. c 4. Asst S Mary's Epis Ch Barnstable MA 2005-2009. revdrkris@gmail.com

LEWIS, Laurie Ann (Kan) PO Box 507, El Dorado KS 67042 **S Steph's Ch Wichita KS 2009-** B Denver CO 11/26/1974 d Jewel James Davis & LaVerna Louise. BBA Wichita St U 1998; MDiv VTS 2008. D 6/7/2008 P 12/6/2008 Bp Dean Elliott Wolfe. m 8/19/2000 Thomas Ray Lewis c 2. Cur Trin Epis Ch El Dorado KS 2008-2009. REVDLAURIE@GMAIL.COM

LEWIS, Lawrence Bernard (WMo) 415 Market Street, Osceola MO 64776 B Osceola MO 4/27/1932 s Bernard Reynolds Lewis & Myrtle. BA U of Missouri 1954; MA U of Missouri 1955; U of Paris FR 1961; MDiv Bex 1973. D 6/9/1973 Bp George Leslie Cadigan P 12/19/1973 Bp Arthur Anton Vogel. m 6/20/1964 Ruth Gilman c 3. Dn Nrthrn Deanry Dio W Missouri Kansas City MO 1996-1997; Eccl Crt Dio W Missouri Kansas City MO 1991-1995; Centennial Com Dio W Missouri Kansas City MO 1990-1991; Dioc Coun Dio W Missouri Kansas City MO 1989-1991; Prov VII CE Cmsn Dio W Missouri Kansas City MO 1989-1990; Sprtl Dir Happ Dio W Missouri Kansas City MO 1987-1993; Chair DeptCE & Yth Dio W Missouri Kansas City MO 1986-1991; Vic S Oswald In The Field Skidmore MO 1985-1997; Vic S Paul's Ch Maryville MO 1985-1997; P-in-c S Paul's Epis Ch Clinton MO 1980-1985; R Chr Ch Epis Boonville MO 1973-1979. redhouse@tri-lakes.net

LEWIS JR, Lloyd Alexander (LI) Virginia Theological Seminary, 3737 Seminary Rd, Alexandria VA 22304 **Bd Gvnr St. Steph's and St. Agnes Sch Alexandria VA 2009-; Hon Asst S Paul's Par Washington DC 2000-; Downs Prof of NT VTS Alexandria VA 2000-; Cn Theol Dio Long Island Garden City NY 1991-** B Washington DC 11/12/1947 s Lloyd Alexander Lewis & Alice Christine. AB Trin Hartford CT 1969; MDiv VTS 1972; MA Ya 1975; MPhil Ya 1981; PhD Ya 1985. D 5/27/1972 Bp Robert Bruce Hall P 12/2/1972 Bp Richard Beamon Martin. Adj Biblic Lang The GTS New York NY 1995-2000; Hon Asst Par Of S Jas Of Jerusalem By The Sea Long Bch NY 1993-2000; Dep for Educ Dio Long Island Garden City NY 1991-2000; Dn Geo Mercer TS Garden City NY 1991-2000; Assoc Prof of NT VTS Alexandria VA 1985-1991; Hon Asst S Geo's Ch Washington DC 1978-1991; Asst Prof of New Testamentew Testament VTS Alexandria VA 1978-1985; Hon Asst S Monica's Ch Hartford CT 1974-1978; Cur S Geo's Ch Brooklyn NY 1972-1974. Auth, "Colossians, Philemon," *True to Our Native Land*, Fortress, 2007; Auth, "The Philemon-Paul-Onesimus Triangle," *Stony the Road We Trod*, Fortress, 1991. SBL 1976. DD VTS 1992. LALewis@vts.edu

LEWIS, Mabel Burke (NY) 40 Barton St, Newburgh NY 12550 B Orange NJ 6/24/1940 d C(harles) Pendleton Lewis & Mabel Burke. BA Wheaton Coll at Norton 1962; MDiv UTS 1982. D 12/15/1982 Bp Paul Moore Jr P 1/6/1985 Bp Walter Decoster Dennis Jr. Int S Anne's Ch Washingtonville NY 2003-2009; Vic S Thos Epis Ch New Windsor NY 2003-2009; S Ptr's Epis Ch Peekskill NY 2002; S Peters Ch Peekskill NY 2000-2002; Outreach Chapl And Cur S Ptr's Epis Ch Peekskill NY 2000-2002; R Ch Of The Ascen Greenpoint Brooklyn NY 1995-2000; Consult S Aug's Ch New York NY 1993-1995; S Martha's Ch Bronx NY 1991-1993; Asst To Archd Dio New York New York City NY 1985-1993; Diocn Msnry & Ch Extntn Socty New York NY 1985-1993; Dpt Of Missions Ny Income New York NY 1985-1993; Assoc S Mary's Manhattanville Epis Ch New York NY 1984-1986.

LEWIS, Mark (WA) 4002 53rd street, Bladensburg MD 20710 B Frederick Memorial Hospital 9/7/1959 s Kenneth Eugeen Lewis & JoAnn. AA Frederick Cmnty Coll Frederick MD 1993; BA Mt St. Mary's Sem 1998; MDiv Nash 2001. D 12/9/2000 P 6/21/2001 Bp Keith Lynn Ackerman. m 8/15/1980 Vicky Himes c 1. S Lk's Par Bladensburg MD 2006-2011; S Steph's Ch Whitehall PA 2001-2006. CBS 2001; Soc of King Chas the Mtyr 2005; SocMary 2001. mvjlewis@aol.com

LEWIS, Mark Alan (Nwk) 380 Mountain Rd Apt 304, Union City NJ 07087 B Howell County MO 2/21/1960 s Gary Laurel Lewis & Willie Mae Gifford. BA U So 1982; U of Virginia 1985; MDiv VTS 1990. D 6/2/1990 Bp Peter James Lee P 1/19/1991 Bp Robert Poland Atkinson. m 8/3/2011 K Dennis Winslow. Vic Ch Of Our Sav Secaucus NJ 1994-2010; Asst Chr Ch Ridgewood NJ 1991-1994; Cur S Steph's Epis Ch Culpeper VA 1990-1991. Auth, *Var Literary & Hist Periodicals*. rville2012@gmail.com

LEWIS, Maurine Ann (Mil) 1717 Carl St, Fort Worth TX 76103 B Kansas City MO 11/19/1942 d Richard Nelson Lewis & Helen. BA U of No Texas 1976; MA U of No Texas 1981; MDiv CDSP 1990. D 6/27/1992 P 1/31/1993 Bp Richard Lester Shimpfky. c 3. Stndg Com Dio Milwaukee Milwaukee WI 2000-2008; R S Dunst's Ch Madison WI 1997-2008; COM Dio Kansas Topeka KS 1994-1997; Assoc Gr Cathd Topeka KS 1994-1997; Cur S Phil The Apos Scotts Vlly CA 1992-1994; S Lk's Ch Los Gatos CA 1992-1993. houndmom3@charter.net

LEWIS III, Philip Gregory (Oly) 26533 Fox Hill Dr N, Stanwood WA 98292 B Philadelphia PA 6/4/1932 D 6/25/2005 Bp Vincent Waydell Warner. m 9/1/1978 Laura Elizabeth Simmons. laura.lews23@verizon.net

LEWIS, Philip Martin (Spr) 420 N. Plum St., Havana IN 62644 B Ypsilanti MI 9/16/1955 s Curtis W Lewis & Thelma. BA Hartwick Coll 1978; MDiv Cranmer Theol Hse 2001. D 11/1/2001 P 5/1/2002 Bp Daniel William Herzog. m 6/30/1979 Alison G Groot c 4. S Barn Ch Havana IL 2004-2010; R S Jn's Epis Ch Mt Vernon IN 2003-2004; S Ptr's Ch Albany NY 2001-2002. fr.phil44@gmail.com

LEWIS, Richard Howard (CNY) none, none NY 13442 B Riverside NJ 5/3/1936 s Charles Allison Lewis & Elizabeth Mae. BA Wilmington Coll 1958; MA U MI 1960; BD VTS 1963; MS Rutgers-The St U 1971. D 6/29/1963 Bp Richard S M Emrich P 1/6/1964 Bp Robert Lionne DeWitt. m 6/4/1962 Sarah Vaughan c 2. Headwaters Epis Mssn Boonville NY 1993-2001; R S Mk's Ch Port Leyden NY 1993-2001; R S Paul's Ch Boonville NY 1993-2001; R Trin Ch Boonville NY 1993-2001; R The Epis Ch Of The Cross Ticonderoga NY 1984-1993; R Trin Ch Whitehall NY 1984-1993; Vic S Barn Epis Ch Monmouth Jct NJ 1981-1984; Vic S Barn Ch Kutztown PA 1980-1981; R No Par Epis Ch Frackville PA 1975-1980; P-in-c S Jn The Evang Ch New Brunswick NJ 1970-1975; Asst Cathd Ch Of S Paul Detroit MI 1966-1969; S Thos Ch Trenton MI 1963-1966. sandrlewisho@juno.com

LEWIS, Robert Michael (CFla) 11251 SW Highway 484, Dunnellon FL 34432 B Saint Petersburg FL 11/20/1977 s Billy Dale Lewis & Doreen. AA St Petersburg Coll 1997; BA U of So Florida 2004; MDiv Nash 2007. D 6/2/2007 Bp John Wadsworth Howe P 1/6/2008 Bp Peter Hess Beckwith. m 7/7/2001 Ellen K Biedermann c 1. Vic All SS Ch Morton IL 2007-2009. CBS 2004; GAS 2004; SocMary 2004. adventrector@aol.com

LEWIS, Sarah Elizabeth (Md) 576 Johnsville Rd, Eldersburg MD 21784 **VP for Mssn Epis Mnstrs To The Aging Sykesville MD 2010-** B Tallahassee FL 12/13/1955 d Benjamin Cheever Lewis & Elizabeth Burwell. AA S Mary's Coll 1975; BA U of Virginia 1978; MDiv SWTS 1988. D 6/12/1988 P 12/17/1988 Bp Frank Stanley Cerveny. Dir. of Chapl EMA Fairhaven Sykesville MD 1991-2010; Int H Trin Epis Ch Baltimore MD 1990-1991; Int S Mths' Epis Ch Baltimore MD 1989. lewiss@emaseniorcare.org

LEWIS, Sarah Vaughan (CNY) PO Box 4353, Rome NY 13442 **Long Term Supply P S Dav's Barneveld NY 2010-** B Grayling MI 4/5/1940 U MI 1960;

Asn Med Coll of Virginia 1962; BA Wayne 1968; MA Bex 2000. D 12/6/2003 P 8/7/2004 Bp Gladstone Bailey Adams III. m 6/4/1962 Richard Howard Lewis c 2. P Assoc Gr Ch Utica NY 2009-2010; COM's Ord for Mnstry Team Mem Dio Cntrl New York Syracuse NY 2007-2010; Occasional Sunday Supply Dio Cntrl New York Syracuse NY 2004-2010; Utica-Rome Dist Chapl Dio Cntrl New York Syracuse NY 2004-2010; Pstr Assoc All SS Ch Utica NY 2004-2008; Safe Ch Trnr Dio Cntrl New York Syracuse NY 2004-2008. Soc of S Marg 2003. revdsvl@hotmail.com

LEWIS, Sharon Lynn Gottfried (SwFla) 3773 Wilkinson Rd, Sarasota FL 34233 B Trenton NJ 12/29/1943 d Joseph John Gottfried & Anne Lois. BEd Trenton St Coll 1965; MS Nova U 1984; MDiv STUSo 1993. D 6/26/1993 P 1/8/1994 Bp Rogers Sanders Harris. Ch Of The H Sprt Osprey FL 1995-2009; S Wlfd's Epis Ch Sarasota FL 1993-1994. Dok Curs. pastorsharon@amazinglovehealing.com

LEWIS, Stephen Charles (Okla) 2523 E 24th St, Tulsa OK 74114 B 1/6/1943 D 6/19/2004 Bp Robert Manning Moody. m 6/25/1988 Nancy Starr Lewis. steve@lewisoklaw.com

LEWIS, Theodore Longstreet (WA) 20235 Laurel Hill Way, Germantown MD 20874 **Theol-in-Res All SS' Epis Ch Chevy Chase MD 2005-** B Hempstead NY 11/5/1926 s Edward Dayton Lewis & Margaret Laurita. BA Hav 1949; MIA Harv 1951; MDiv VTS 1964. D 6/27/1964 Bp Paul Moore Jr P 1/25/1965 Bp William Foreman Creighton. c 2. Dio Washington Washington DC 1973-2004; Supply P Dio Washington Washington DC 1973-2001; Cur S Columba's Ch Washington DC 1964-1965. "Vietnam and the Sxlty Issue in the Ch," *Washington Dio Nwspr*, 1999; "Pilgrimage to Boga [Congo]," *Virginia Sem Journ*, 1997; Auth, "To Restore the Ch: Radical Redemp Hist to Now," *(Bk)*, self, 1996; "Cranmer's Journey," *Virginia Sem Journ*, 1990. theodorell@aol.com

LEWIS JR, Theodore Radford (SC) 106 Line St, Charleston SC 29403 **R Calv Ch Charleston SC 1992-** B Galveston TX 7/23/1946 s Theodore Radford Lewis & Carrie. BA U of Houston 1970; MDiv Epis TS of The SW 1982. D 6/22/1982 Bp Maurice Manuel Benitez P 2/2/1983 Bp Gordon Taliaferro Charlton. m 11/29/1968 Martha Delores Fox c 2. Stndg Com Dio So Carolina Charleston SC 1997-2000; Rel Div Mayors Coun on Homelessness/Homeless Dio So Carolina Charleston SC 1994-1996; Chair Prov VII Mssn Proj Area Dio Texas Houston TX 1990-1991; R S Lk The Evang Houston TX 1983-1991; Assoc S Jas Epis Ch Houston TX 1982-1983. OHC 1982. Outstanding Cmnty Serv Chas. Chapt Negro Wmn 2006; Plaque for Cmnty Serv Delta Sigma Theta Sorority 1999; Omega Psi Phi Man of the Year Mu Alpha Chapt 1999; Plaque for Serv as Police Chap Coastal Police Chapl 1996; Assault on Illiteracy Prog Awd Houston Illiteracy Assoc. 1990; Omega Psi Phi Man of the Year Nu Phi Chapt 1990. reverendque@comcast.net

LEWIS, Theodore William (Mass) Po Box 445, Lunenburg MA 01462 B Oneida NY 8/22/1926 s Clifton Sumner Lewis & Gertrude Elizabeth. BA Ham 1950; MDiv GTS 1953; Fllshp EDS 1970; Med U of Maine 1972; EdD Bos 1976. D 6/20/1953 Bp Malcolm E Peabody P 12/21/1953 Bp Walter M Higley. m 6/20/1988 Joann Carrington c 2. Assoc Chr Ch Fitchburg MA 1987-2005; R S Paul's Epis Ch Hopkinton MA 1974-1983; Asst The Ch Of Our Redeem Lexington MA 1972-1974; Vic S Jas Ch Old Town ME 1957-1970; Vic Chr The King Epis Ch Ft Worth TX 1955-1957. Phi Beta Kappa. mal222@gmail.com

LEWIS, Thom (SVa) 2702 W Market St, Greensboro NC 27403 **P-in-c S Chris's Epis Ch Hobbs NM 2009-** B High Point NC 9/5/1946 s William Claude Lewis & Maude. MDiv Savonarola TS S. Rec from Polish National Catholic Church 4/19/2001 Bp David Conner Bane Jr. Int R Gr Ch Carlsbad NM 2008-2009; Calv Ch Bath Par Dinwiddie VA 2003-2008; Asst Ch Of The Epiph Danville VA 2001-2003. thom_lewis2003@yahoo.com

LEWIS, Timothy John (LI) Po Box 264, Wainscott NY 11975 **R S Ann's Epis Ch Bridgehampton NY 2001-** B Carmarthen Wales 10/7/1956 s Elvet Lewis & Jean. BA U of Wales 1977; BTh Salisbury & Wells Theol Coll Sem Gb 1986. Trans from Church Of England 7/24/2001 Bp Orris George Walker Jr. m 7/17/2003 Sandra Gordon Kerr c 1.

LEWIS, Walter England (Nwk) 60 Dryden Rd, Montclair NJ 07043 B Radford VA 10/6/1938 s James Henry Lewis & Alice Elizabeth. BA U of Virginia 1961; MDiv VTS 1964; DMin Drew U 1983. D 6/27/1964 Bp William Foreman Creighton P 1/9/1965 Bp Paul Moore Jr. m 5/16/1964 Barbara Howe c 3. Int S Clem's Ch Hawthorne NJ 2002-2003; P-in-c S Paul's Ch No Arlington NJ 1999-2001; Int Ch Of The Trsfg No Bergen NJ 1988-1990; Dir Restoration Mnstrs Dio Newark Newark NJ 1985-1999; Assoc S Ptr's Ch Essex Fells NJ 1980-1985; R Chr Epis Ch E Orange NJ 1977-1980; Assoc S Jas Ch Upper Montclair NJ 1972-1977; R S Geo's Wm And Mary Vlly Lee MD 1965-1972. "No Room in the Inn," *The Voice (Dioc Nwsltr)*, Dio Newark, 2004; Auth, "Exam Time," *Acts 29 (mag)*, ERM, 1987; Auth, "Help One Another Make Him Known - Equipping the Laity to Share the Gd News," *Drew U D. Min. Thesis*, U Microfilms Internaitonal, 1983. walterlewis@comcast.net

LEWIS, William Benjamin (WA) 14110 Royal Forest Ln, Silver Spring MD 20904 **Vic S Phil The Evang Washington DC 1996-** B Freetown NE SL 6/20/1942 s William Benjamin Lewis & Gladys Marie. BA How 1969; MA How 1972; PhD How 1981; MDiv How 1991. D 6/15/1991 P 5/1/1992 Bp Ronald Hayward Haines. m 11/29/1969 Tabitha Abiola Nelson c 4. S Paul's Rock Creek Washington DC 1991-1996.

LEWIS, William George (CFla) 442 Sanderling Dr, Indialantic FL 32903 **R Emer H Trin Epis Ch Melbourne FL 2007-** B Aliquippa PA 10/4/1929 s Albert Lewis & Ada Martha. Med U Pgh 1954; MDiv PDS 1958. D 6/7/1958 Bp William S Thomas P 12/21/1958 Bp Austin Pardue. m 9/29/1990 Beverly Klaver c 3. R H Trin Epis Ch Melbourne FL 1980-1994; Archd Dio Pittsburgh Monroeville PA 1972-1980; R Chr Epis Ch No Hills Pittsburgh PA 1964-1972; S Geo's Ch Waynesburg PA 1958-1964. bill@lewismere.com

LEWIS-HEADDEN, Margaret Kempe (Oly) P.O. Box 1997, 1036 Golf Course Rd., Friday Harbor WA 98250 **D S Dav's Epis Ch Friday Harbor WA 2009-** B Riverside CA 11/1/1941 d Frank Arthur Kempe & Margaret Douglas. CDSP; Fuller TS; TS-Honolulu; U Of Idaho Moscow; U of Washington; VTS; BS U MN 1965. D 11/11/1983 Bp Edmond Lee Browning. m 8/21/2008 William Perry Headden. Emm Epis Ch Mercer Island WA 2002-2004; Ch Of The Resurr Bellevue WA 2000-2002; S Andr's Ch Seattle WA 1989-1998; D Chr Ch SEATTLE WA 1985-1988; D The Par Of S Clem Honolulu HI 1983-1985. mklewis@centurylink.net

LEY, James Lawrence (Pa) 101 Lydia Ln, West Chester PA 19382 B Philadelphia PA 12/26/1945 D 6/21/2003 Bp Charles Ellsworth Bennison Jr. m 7/1/1989 Frances E Preiksat c 2. Ch Of The Redeem Springfield PA 2003-2004. jley161@comcast.org

LEYBA, E(rnest) Thomas (Az) 2927 N 47th St, Phoenix AZ 85018 B Denver CO 12/13/1927 s Thomas Leyba & Maria Luz. BS Arizona St U 1953; MDiv CDSP 1959; MC Arizona St U 1972. D 6/14/1959 P 12/20/1959 Bp Arthur Kinsolving. m 7/2/1959 Helen Jo Petty c 2. S Lukes Hosp Med Cntr Phoenix AZ 1970-1988; Chapl Dio Arizona Phoenix AZ 1966-1988; Cur Trin Cathd Phoenix AZ 1960-1964. AZ Chapl Assn; Coll of Chapl.

LEYS, Donovan Ivanhoe (LI) 20931 111 Avenue, Queens Village NY 11429 **P and R S Steph's Epis Ch Jamaica NY 2006-** B JM 9/23/1961 s Seymour Ivanhoe Leys & Margaret Agatha. Untd Theol Coll of the W Indies Kingston JM 1985; BA U of The W Indies 1985. Trans from Church in the Province Of The West Indies 5/29/1995 Bp Orris George Walker Jr. m 7/8/2005 Sandra E Legall c 1. The Ch Of The Epiph And S Simon Brooklyn NY 1995-2006; S Aug's Epis Ch Brooklyn NY 1992-1994. leysdi@msn.com

L'HOMME, Robert Arthur (Q) 8501 Timber Ln, Lafayette IN 47905 B Worcester MA 5/2/1941 s Arthur William L'Homme & Georgina Roberta. BA Assumption Coll 1963; MA Assumption Coll 1964; MDiv Nash 1969. D 6/23/1969 Bp Gerald Francis Burrill P 12/20/1969 Bp James Winchester Montgomery. m 4/15/1989 Carol A L'Homme. S Paul's Cathd Peoria IL 1991-2004; R S Paul's Ch Kankakee IL 1972-1991; Cur The Ch Of S Jn The Evang Flossmoor IL 1969-1972. Auth, "Weekly Rel Column," *The Indianapolis News*, 1965. OHC. Casper News Awd. rac.lhomme@insightbb.com

L'HOMMEDIEU, J(ohn) Gary (CFla) 130 N Magnolia Ave, Orlando FL 32801 **Cn Cathd Ch Of S Lk Orlando FL 2002-** B Rockville Centre NY 4/3/1951 s Ronald Richard L'Hommedieu & Audrey Dein. BA Tufts U 1973; MDiv EDS 1979. D 6/2/1979 P 12/1/1979 Bp Paul Moore Jr. m 8/26/1978 Judith S M Myers c 4. Int Ch Of The Redemp Southampton PA 2001-2002; Dio Pennsylvania Philadelphia PA 1997; The Ch Of The Atone Morton PA 1984-1997; R Ch Of The Redeem Rensselaer NY 1981-1984; Asst S Mary's Epis Ch Manchester CT 1979-1981. jgarylh@aol.com

LIAO KING-LING, Samuel (Tai) 1-105-7 Hangchow South Road, Taipei Taiwan B 12/8/1947 s George Liao Yaw-hwang & Wen-farn. Fong-Chia U Commerce 1971; MDiv Tai-Nan TS 1981. D 9/21/1980 P 7/1/1981 Bp Pui-Yeung Cheung. m 3/27/1976 Jing-fang Su c 1.

LIBBEY, Elizabeth Weaver (USC) 1140 Fork Creek Rd, Saluda NC 28773 B Richmond VA 8/23/1947 d Robert Samuel Weaver & Vera. BS Winthrop U 1968; MA U of So Carolina 1974; MDiv VTS 1984. D 6/9/1984 P 5/1/1985 Bp William Arthur Beckham. m 6/17/1984 Robert Edward Libbey c 1. S Fran of Assisi Chapin SC 1986-1999; S Alb's Ch Lexington SC 1984-1986. elizlibbey@aol.com

LIBBEY, Robert Edward (USC) 16 Salisbury Drive #7410, Asheville NC 28803 B Boston MA 12/21/1939 s Robert Chambers Libbey & Thelma Louise. BA U So 1961; MDiv STUSo 1969. D 6/26/1969 P 1/24/1970 Bp Gray Temple. m 6/17/1984 Elizabeth Weaver c 2. Int Ch Of The H Cross Tryon NC 2001-2002; Int S Mk's Ch Gastonia NC 2000-2001; Dn Cntrl Deanry Dio Upper So Carolina Columbia SC 1992-1994; R Epis Ch Of S Simon And S Jude Irmo SC 1979-1999; Ecum Off Dio Upper So Carolina Columbia SC 1979-1987; R Chr Epis Ch Lancaster SC 1973-1979; Asst Par Ch of St. Helena Beaufort SC 1971-1973; D-in-c S Paul's Epis Ch Conway SC 1969-1971; Asst Trin Ch Myrtle Bch SC 1969-1971. revrelibbey@aol.com

LIBBY, Glenn Maurice (Los) 835 W 34th Street 203, Los Angeles CA 90089 **Bd Trst CDSP Berkeley CA 2011-; Dioc Coun Dio Los Angeles Los Angeles CA 2010-; P-in-c S Phil's Par Los Angeles CA 2010-; Chapl The Cbury USC Fndt Inc. Los Angeles CA 1996-** B Waterville ME 9/23/1953 s

Willis Clair Libby & Norma Gordona. BA U of Maine 1974; MA USC 1977; MBA San Diego St U 1987; MDiv Ya Berk 1995; PhD USC 2001. D 6/3/1995 Bp Jack Marston McKelvey P 1/4/1996 Bp John Shelby Spong. P S Phil's Par Los Angeles CA 2008-2010; Assoc St Johns Pro-Cathd Los Angeles CA 2001-2003; Assoc S Phil's Par Los Angeles CA 2001-2002. Ahmanson Fllshp USC Los Angeles CA 2000; LAS Fllshp USC Los Angeles CA 1999; Hooker Fllshp And Muehl Prize For Preaching Yale DS New Haven 1995; Phi Beta Kappa 1974; Phi Kappa Phi 1973. glibby@usc.edu

LIBBY, Richardson Armstrong (Ct) 235 King George Street, Annapolis MD 21401 B Norwalk CT 1/30/1932 s Richardson Armstrong Libby & Josephine Richards. BA Trin Hartford CT 1954; STB GTS 1960. D 6/18/1960 Bp Angus Dun P 12/21/1960 Bp Oliver L Loring. m 6/3/1961 Kathryn Carolyn Blunck c 2. R Trin Ch Branford CT 1988-1997; Chair, Cmncatn Com Dio Connecticut Hartford CT 1976-1981; R Gr Ch Newington CT 1971-1988; R S Jn's Epis Ch Niantic CT 1963-1965; Cur Gr Epis Ch Bath ME 1960-1963. AFP 1978; Soc of King Chas the Mtyr 1987. ra235lby@gmail.com

LIBBY, Robert Meredith Gabler (SeFla) 200 Ocean Lane Dr Apt 408, Key Biscayne FL 33149 B Flushing NY 11/1/1930 s Francis Meredith Libby & Ethel. BA Emory U 1952; MDiv STUSo 1958; STM STUSo 1972. D 6/19/1958 P 1/2/1959 Bp Randolph R Claiborne. m 5/23/1975 Katherine Ball. R S Chris's By-The-Sea Epis Ch Key Biscayne FL 1990-1998; Alt Dep Gc Dio Florida Jacksonville FL 1988-1997; Gd Samar Epis Ch Orange Pk FL 1981-1990; S Andr's Ch Jacksonville FL 1977-1978; S Marg's-Hibernia Epis Ch Fleming Island FL 1977-1978; Jacksonville Epis HS Jacksonville FL 1971-1977; Dep Gc Dio Florida Jacksonville FL 1964-1985; R S Cathr's Ch Jacksonville FL 1960-1967; Cn S Paul's Epis Ch Atlanta GA 1958-1960. Auth, "Coming To Faith," Iuniverse, 2001; Auth, "Gr Happens," 1994; Auth, "The Forgiveness Bk," 1992. frboblibby@aol.com

LIBERATORE, James Vincent (Tex) 2535 Broadway St, Pearland TX 77581 **R S Andr's Epis Ch Pearland TX 1995-** B Philadelphia PA 3/29/1950 s Eugene Kurt Liberatore & Florence. BS Stevens Inst of Tech 1972; MDiv Epis TS of The SW 1985. D 6/14/1985 Bp William Carl Frey P 1/1/1986 Bp Maurice Manuel Benitez. m 6/13/1970 Christine Kuch c 2. Stff Chapl St Lk's Epis Hosp Houston TX 1994-1995; R Trin Epis Ch Baytown TX 1987-1994; Asst to R S Dunst's Epis Ch Houston TX 1985-1987. Alb Inst, Bread for Wrld, Associated Parishes; Exec Bd; Habitat. frjimbo@msn.com

LICARI, Luigi (Cal) Marie Heinekenplein 108, Amsterdam 1072 MK Netherlands B Ilion NY 9/21/1949 s Bennie Licari & H Ruth. St. Bern's Sem Rochester NY; BA St. Jn Fisher Coll 1971; BA Sch for Deacons 1995. D 12/7/1996 Bp William Edwin Swing. m 11/11/2005 Maxie (Masanori) Sakamakie. D S Jn's Ch New York NY 2002-2005; D S Cyp's Ch San Francisco CA 2000-2002; D S Aid's Ch San Francisco CA 1996-2000. NAAD 1995; Oasis/CA 1995. lewis.licari@tdsecurities.com

LIDDELL, Brendan Edwin Alexander (Q) 1113 N Elmwood Ave, Peoria IL 61606 B Atlanta GA 6/27/1927 s Edwin Carey Liddell & Rose Annette. PhD U MI 1961. D 12/23/1995 Bp Keith Lynn Ackerman. m 10/29/1982 Ruthanne Arnold. D S Andr's Ch Peoria IL 1995-2006; D Gr Epis Ch Galesburg IL 1995-2004. Auth, "Kant on the Fndt of Morality," Indiana U Press, 1970. beal1927@aol.com

LIDDLE, Vincent T (Pa) 1226 Cedar Rd, Ambler PA 19002 B Clarks Summit PA 7/4/1933 s Harry F Liddle & Marie I. BA Mary Immac Sem 1957; PhD Inst of Philosophers U in Louvain BE 1966. Rec from Roman Catholic 6/20/1981 as Priest Bp Lyman Cunningham Ogilby. m 7/31/1970 Rosemary I Gannon c 1. Int Vic Resurr Epis Ch Naples FL 2003-2005; Assoc Resurr Epis Ch Naples FL 1998-1999; P Assoc S Matt's Ch Maple Glen PA 1998; R Ch Of The Mssh Lower Gwynedd PA 1981-1998. Auth, "The Personalism of Maurice Nedoncelle," *Philos Stds*, 1966. vincent@liddlefolks.com

LIDDY, Jeffery T (Pa) 922 Main Street, Ste. 406, Lynchburg VA 24504 **Chapl Westminster-Cbury Of Lynchburg Lynchburg VA 2010-** B Fairfield IA 1/11/1952 s Robert John Liddy & Dorothy Jane. BA U of Iowa 1977; MDiv SWTS 1982; Cert S Geo's Coll Jerusalem IL 1997; Cert Coll of Preachers 1999; Cert Sarum Coll Salisbury Gb 2002. D 6/25/1982 P 6/18/1983 Bp Walter Cameron Righter. m 6/16/1984 Naomi J Liddy c 2. Pennypack Dnry Dio Pennsylvania Philadelphia PA 2005-2009; R All SS Ch Philadelphia PA 2004-2009; R S Jn's Epis Ch Naperville IL 1994-2004; Dioc Coun Dio Kansas Topeka KS 1990-1993; R S Jn's Ch Wichita KS 1987-1993; Asst Ch Of The Ascen Clearwater FL 1985-1987; Vic Ch Of The Epiph Centerville IA 1982-1985. Alb Inst 1988-2004; AAPC 1987-2011; Bro Of S Andr 1994-2004; Ord Of S Lk 1987-1993. Seabury-Wstrn Prize Seabury-Wstrn Sem 1982. jliddy@wclynchburg.org

LIEB, James Marcus (ECR) PO Box 293, Ben Lomond CA 95005 B Los Angeles CA 8/7/1946 s Philip W Lieb & Bernice H. BA Epis Sch for Deacons 1985. D 12/3/1988 Bp William Edwin Swing. m 10/2/1971 Catherine Lieb c 3. lieb@sea-teoll.net

LIEBENOW, Robert Ervin (Chi) 8 Laurel Place Dr, Asheville NC 28803 B Chicago IL 6/27/1925 s Emil W Liebenow & Myrtle G. BA Carroll Coll 1946; MDiv Nash 1949. D 6/16/1949 P 12/1/1949 Bp Wallace E Conkling. c 2. R Trin Epis Ch Wheaton IL 1968-1989; P-in-c S Ambr Epis Ch Ft Lauderdale FL 1956-1959; Asst All SS Prot Epis Ch Ft Lauderdale FL 1954-1956; Cur Gr And S Ptr's Ch Baltimore MD 1950-1954; P-in-c S Andr Ch Grayslake IL 1949-1950. bobliebenow@aol.com

LIEBER, William Louis (SanD) 8975 Lawrence Welk Dr Spc 77, Escondido CA 92026 B Detroit MI 10/15/1936 s John M Lieber & Lucia. U of Detroit 1957; Nthrn St U Aberdeen SD 1959; Michigan TS 1970; SWTS 1971. D 6/29/1970 Bp Richard S M Emrich P 1/1/1971 Bp Archie H Crowley. m 2/9/1957 Joy A McWilliams. Vol Assoc Gr Epis Ch Of The Vlly Mssn San Marcos CA 2000-2006; S Chris-S Paul Epis Ch Detroit MI 1977-1999; Dn of the Down River Convoc Dio Michigan Detroit MI 1974-1976; Dio Michigan Detroit MI 1970-1976. lieberja@earthlink.net

LIEBERT-HALL, Linda Ann (CFla) Shepherd of the Hills, 2540 W Norvell Bryant Hwy, Lecanto FL 34461 **D Shpd Of The Hills Epis Ch Lecanto FL 2008-** B Tulsa 10/1/1959 d Robert Francis Liebert & DeLoris Ann. BSBA Washington U; JD/MBA St Louis U 1985. D 6/22/2007 Bp Michael Gene Smith. m 5/9/1987 Michael Gregory Hall. LindaL@dakotamep.com

LIEBLER, John Stephen Baxter (CFla) 2254 6th Avenue SE, Vero Beach FL 32962 **R S Andr's Epis Ch Ft Pierce FL 2002-** B Coral Gables FL 7/25/1954 s John Baxter Liebler & Mary Evelyn. BA U of Notre Dame 1976; MA U of Notre Dame 1977; MDiv STUSo 1981. D 5/31/1981 P 12/1/1981 Bp Calvin Onderdonk Schofield Jr. m 1/8/1983 M Cynthia Schnell c 2. R S Ptr The Fisherman Epis Ch New Smyrna Bch FL 1992-2002; Vic S Ptr The Fisherman Epis Ch New Smyrna Bch FL 1987-1991; Chapl Epis Campus Mnstry At Ucf Orlando FL 1985-1987; Chapl Dio Cntrl Florida Orlando FL 1985; Cur The Epis Ch Of The Gd Shpd Tequesta FL 1981-1984. frjohn@mystandrews.com

LIEF, Richard C (SanD) 3212 Eichenlaub St, San Diego CA 92117 B Providence RI 2/17/1940 s Richard Lief & Jane. BA U of Redlands 1962; MDiv VTS 1965; DMin Claremont TS 1979. D 9/26/1965 P 5/21/1966 Bp John Brooke Mosley. m 6/23/1962 Carolyn A Grover c 2. Cathd Ch Of S Paul San Diego CA 1997-2001; Ch Of The Gd Shpd Bonita CA 1997-1998; Int S Jn's Ch Fallbrook CA 1996; S Barth's Epis Ch Poway CA 1994-1997; The Epis Ch Of S Andr Encinitas CA 1994-1995; S Jas By The Sea La Jolla CA 1991-1998; Chapl Epis Cmnty Servs Dio San Diego San Diego CA 1990-1995; Epis Cmnty Serv San Diego CA 1990-1994; COM Dio San Diego San Diego CA 1986-1995; Bd Dir Dioc Corp Dio San Diego San Diego CA 1986-1989; Dep GC Dio San Diego San Diego CA 1985-1991; Stwdshp Educ Dio San Diego San Diego CA 1982-1989; Soc Concerns Dio San Diego San Diego CA 1982-1985; Bd Dir Ecum Conf Dio San Diego San Diego CA 1981-1982; Dioc Coun Dio San Diego San Diego CA 1980-1982; Chair Fin Com Dio San Diego San Diego CA 1980-1981; Sprtl Dir Curs Dio San Diego San Diego CA 1978-1980; Dioc Coun Dio San Diego San Diego CA 1975-1977; S Dav's Epis Ch San Diego CA 1970-1990; Asst S Fran' Par Palos Verdes Estates CA 1967-1970; Asst Imm Ch Highlands Wilmington DE 1965-1967. Auth, *The Role of the Sprtl Dir in the Curs Mvmt*, 1979. Dir Acad for Sacr Dramatic Arts San Diego CA 1990. rlief@aol.com

LIEFFORT, Robert John (CFla) 807 Tamarind Cir, Barefoot Bay FL 32976 B Green Bay WI 3/11/1945 s Cyril John Lieffort & Florence Katherine. BA S Norbert Coll De Pere WI 1968; MDiv Cath Theol Un 1971; PhD Pacific Wstrn U 1986. Rec from Roman Catholic 6/29/1978 as Priest Bp William Hopkins Folwell. m 7/8/1989 Sandra Brannon. Int Ch Of S Dav's By The Sea Cocoa Bch FL 2008-2010; Receiving Disabil Ret 1999-2010; S Sebastian's By The Sea Melbourne Bch FL 1999; R S Eliz's Epis Ch Sebastian FL 1995-1999; S Chris's Ch Orlando FL 1981-1995; Asst S Barn Ch Deland FL 1978-1979. 3rd Ord Cn Regular of Premontre 1962. rjlieffort@yahoo.com

LIEM, Jennifer E (NCal) PO Box 855, Tahoe City CA 96145 **Exec Dir Noel Porter C&C Tahoe City CA 2009-; Vic S Nich Mssn Tahoe City CA 2009-** B 10/26/1974 d Charles Liem & Clare. BA Ft Lewis Coll 1999; MDiv SWTS 2005. D 6/10/2006 P 12/9/2006 Bp Robert John O'Neill. Assoc R S Lk's Ch Denver CO 2007-2009; Cur S Steph's Ch Longmont CO 2006-2007. revjenni.liem@gmail.com

LIERLE, Deane Kae (Okla) 5037 E Via Montoya Dr, Phoenix AZ 85054 B Quincy IL 9/17/1932 s Alva Lierle & Susie. BA Culver-Stockton Coll 1954; MDiv Lexington TS 1957; DMin Phillips U 1980; Cert CDSP 1988. D 1/2/1988 Bp William Jackson Cox P 6/4/1988 Bp Gerald Nicholas McAllister. m 12/2/1989 Margaret Lawrence c 2. Int All SS Ch Phoenix AZ 1998-2000; R S Lk's Epis Ch Ada OK 1992-1994; Trin Ch Tulsa OK 1988-1992. dklierle@cox.net

LIESKE, Mark Stephen (Los) 81 Seabreeze Dr, Richmond CA 94804 B Santa Monica CA 9/19/1953 s Hans Arthur Lieske & Mary Suzanne. BA Pepperdine U 1978; MDiv CDSP 1981. D 6/20/1981 P 1/1/1982 Bp Robert C Rusack. m 11/11/1989 San San Tin. S Geo's Par La Can CA 1987-1988; Assoc R All SS Par Beverly Hills CA 1983-1987; Asst S Jas Par Los Angeles CA 1981-1983.

LIETZ, Dennis Eugene (Chi) 935 Knollwood Rd, Deerfield IL 60015 **D S Greg's Epis Ch Deerfield IL 1996-** B Hendricks MN 8/14/1934 s Albert Bernard Lietz & Della Iola. BS So Dakota St Coll 1956; MS So Dakota St Coll

1958. D 2/3/1996 Bp Frank Tracy Griswold III. m 9/22/1959 Helen Wiles c 5. delietz@comcast.net

LIEW, Richard (NY) 168 Long Hill Road, Oakland NJ 07436 **Dir of CPE S Jos's Epis Chap Far Rockaway NY 1994-** B Ipoh Perak MY 7/27/1940 s Liew Peng Choon & Hilda. BTh Trin TS Sg 1964; (STM) Drew U 1971; Cert Blanton-Peale Grad Inst 1973; PhD Mellon U 1973; Cert NYU Med Sch 1980; DMin NYTS 2000. D 2/18/1978 Bp Harold Louis Wright P 10/1/1978 Bp Paul Moore Jr. m 1/4/1967 May Chen Chen. Epis Hlth Serv Bethpage NY 1994-2009; Epis Mssn Soc New York NY 1978-1984; Epis Mssn Soc New York NY 1978-1984. Co-Ed, "Pstr Care Of The Mentally Disabled: Advancing The Care Of The Whole Person," Haworth Press, Inc, 1994. Approved Fell, The Intl Coun of Sex Educ & Parenthood of the Amer U 1981; Assn for Grp Psych 1980; Bd Cert Chapl, Assn of Profsnl Chapl 1977; Clincal Mem, Amer Assn for Mar And Fam Ther 1979; CPE Supvsr, ACPE 1981; Diplomate, AAPC 1979; Diplomate, Coll of Pstr Supervision & Psych 1993. Distinguished Serv Coll of Pstr Supervision & Psych 2010; The Rev. Dr. Jacob W. Diller Awd for Excellence & Distinguished Serv in Pstr Care Epis Hlth Serv, Dio Long Island 2010; Outstanding Achievement Epis Heath Serv, Dio Long Island 2006; Intl Clincl Pstr Eductor ACPE 2001; Distinguished Vol Mayor & Coun, Borough of Franklin Lakes, New Jersey 1996. liewr168@verizon.net

LIGGETT JR, James Edgar (NwT) 4000 W Loop 250 N, Midland TX 79707 **Chair of the GC Deputation Dio NW Texas Lubbock TX 2009-2015; R S Nich' Epis Ch Midland TX 2007-** B El Dorado KS 9/28/1949 s James Edgar Liggett & Cordelia. BA U of Houston 1971; MDiv EDS 1977. D 6/18/1977 P 12/20/1977 Bp Gerald Nicholas McAllister. c 1. R The Epis Ch Of S Mary The Vrgn Big Sprg TX 1994-2007; R S Thos Ch Garden City KS 1989-1994; R Gr Epis Ch Winfield KS 1980-1989; Vic S Jude's Ch Wellington KS 1980-1989; Cur Gr Ch Muskogee OK 1977-1980. liggetts@liggetts.org

✠ **LIGHT, Rt Rev A(rthur) Heath** (SwVa) 2524 Wycliffe Ave Sw, Roanoke VA 24014 **Ret Bp of SwVa Dio SW Virginia Roanoke VA 1996-** B Lynchburg VA 7/7/1929 s Alexander Heath Light & Mary Nelson. BA Hampden-Sydney Coll 1951; BD (M. Div) VTS 1954. D 6/11/1954 P 6/24/1955 Bp George P Gunn Con 6/2/1979 for SwVa. m 6/12/1953 Sarah Ann Jones c 4. Bp Dio SW Virginia Roanoke VA 1979-1996; R Chr and S Lk's Epis Ch Norfolk VA 1967-1979; R S Mary's Ch Kinston NC 1964-1967; R Chr Ch Eliz City NC 1958-1964; R Chr Ch Boydton VA 1954-1958; R S Jas Ch Boydton VA 1954-1958; R S Jn's Epis Ch Chase City VA 1954-1958; R S Tim's Epis Ch Clarksville VA 1954-1958. Auth, "God, the Gift, the Giver," Epis Ch Cntr. DD Hampden-Sydney Coll 1987; DD St Paul's Coll 1979; DD VTS 1979.

LIGHTCAP, Torey Lynn (Ia) 406 12th St, Sioux City IA 51105 **R S Thos' Epis Ch Sioux City IA 2009-** B Weatherford OK 7/4/1972 s Leland Lynn Lightcap & Lura Sue. BA Oklahoma Bapt U 1994; MS Oklahoma St U 1996; MDiv Epis TS of The SW 2004. D 6/12/2004 Bp Robert John O'Neill P 1/8/2005 Bp Rayford Baines High Jr. m 1/9/1993 Jacqueline Whitney c 2. P-in-c S Barn Ch Glenwood Sprg CO 2006-2009; Assoc S Jas The Apos Epis Ch Conroe TX 2004-2006. Coll of Pstr Leaders 2006; Gathering of Leaders 2010; Omicron Delta Kappa 1994. Polly Bond Awards for Writing ECom 2007; Polly Bond Awd for Web Design ECom 2004. father.torey@gmail.com

LIGHTFOOT JR, Roy Cecil (SwFla) 1863 75th Ave N, Saint Petersburg FL 33702 **Died 6/26/2010** B Jacksonville FL 3/24/1944 s Roy Lightfoot & Mildred. D 6/14/2003 Bp John Bailey Lipscomb. c 3. roy.sandye@verizon.net

LIGHTSEY, Pamela Sue Willis (Ga) 2700 Pebblewood Dr, Valdosta GA 31602 **D S Paul's Ch Macon GA 2000-** B Jacksonville FL 8/11/1950 d Douglas Fairbanks Willis & Doris Anne. BA Valdosta St U 1972. D 5/28/1989 Bp Harry Woolston Shipps. m 4/8/1977 Johnny Carroll Lightsey c 2.

LIGHTSEY, Richard Brian (NI) 602 W Superior St, Kokomo IN 46901 **R S Andr Epis Ch Kokomo IN 2000-** B Bakersfield CA 7/7/1959 s Otis Howard Lightsey & Rita Marie. AA Bakersfield Cmnty Coll 1980; BS California St U 1982; MDiv Amer Bapt Sem of The W 1989. D 6/8/1996 P 12/18/1996 Bp John-David Mercer Schofield. m 9/16/1989 Deanne Olson c 3. All SS Ch Bakersfield CA 1996-2000. rblightsey@sbcglobal.net

LIGON, Michael Moran (EC) 517 Brandywine Cir, Greenville NC 27858 B Clarksburg WV 12/27/1949 s James Guthrie Ligon & Mary Elizabeth. BS U NC 1972. D 9/22/1988 Bp Brice Sidney Sanders. m 5/8/1971 Lynda Kay Stanley c 2. D S Tim's Ch Wilson NC 1997-2000; D S Tim's Ch Wilson NC 1993-1997; D Dio E Carolina Kinston NC 1988-1993. mligon@greenvillenc.com

LIGON-BORDEN, Betty Lee (Tex) PO Box 961, Hempstead TX 77445 B Greensboro NC 4/13/1945 d John William Ligon & JoAnne P. MA Texas A & M U 1987; MA Rice U 1991; PhD Rice U 1993; Cert Iona Sch of Mnstry 2009. D 6/20/2009 Bp C(harles) Andrew Doyle P 1/30/2010 Bp Dena Arnall Harrison. m 6/4/1994 Gordon Borden c 4. ligonborden@earthlink.net

LIGUORI, Robert David (SwFla) Po Box 1327, Osprey FL 34229 B Walton NY 7/18/1929 s Anthony Liguori & Donata. BA Hartwick Coll 1950; STB Ya Berk 1953. D 6/14/1953 P 12/13/1953 Bp Frederick Lehrle Barry. m 8/5/1951 Joan Muriel Schrang. S Wlfd's Epis Ch Sarasota FL 1990-1994; Asst S Wlfd's Epis Ch Sarasota FL 1984-1988; Ch Of The Sav Syracuse NY 1973-1981; Asst S Paul's Cathd Syracuse NY 1969-1974; Asst S Alb's Ch Syracuse NY 1966-1968; R Emm Ch E Syracuse NY 1958-1966; Cur Epis Ch Of SS Ptr And Jn Auburn NY 1956-1958; R S Lk's Ch Cambridge NY 1955-1956; R S Paul's Ch Salem NY 1955-1956; Cur S Andr's Epis Ch Albany NY 1953-1955. rliguori@comcast.net

LIKOWSKI, James Boyd (Ore) 2818 Lilac St, Longview WA 98632 B Laguna Beach CA 8/17/1925 s James Boyd Likowski & Martha Anne. BA U CA 1949; BD CDSP 1963. D 6/24/1963 P 2/10/1964 Bp James Walmsley Frederic Carman. m 6/26/1948 Kathryn Bixby. Asst Chapl Legacy Gd Samar Hosp Portland OR 1983-1990; R S Aid's Epis Ch Gresham OR 1970-1982; Sr Assoc S Paul's Epis Ch Salem OR 1967-1970; Vic Ch Of The Gd Shpd Prospect OR 1965-1967; Vic S Mart's Ch Shady Cove OR 1965-1967; Cur S Geo's Epis Ch Roseburg OR 1963-1964.

LIKWARTZ, Judy Saima (Ore) Po Box 51447, Casper WY 82605 B Pocatello ID 9/27/1941 d Donald Earl Cox & Saima Irene. BS U of Wyoming 1994; BSW U of Wyoming 1995. D 2/5/2000 Bp Bruce Edward Caldwell. m 5/30/2004 Don J Likwartz c 2. D Ch Of S Andr's In The Pines Pinedale WY 2000-2004. NAAD 2000.

LILES, Allison Sandlin (Ala) 1722 Beirne Ave NE, Huntsville AL 35801 **Assoc St Thos Epis Ch Huntsville AL 2010-** B Decatur AL 2/16/1980 d Steven Marsh Sandlin & Carol Hill. BA Birmingham-Sthrn Coll 2002; MDiv VTS 2006. D 5/25/2006 Bp Marc Handley Andrus P 12/20/2006 Bp Henry Nutt Parsley Jr. m 5/27/2006 Eric James Liles c 2. Asst H Trin Epis Ch Auburn AL 2007-2010; Chapl S Pat's Epis Day Sch Washington DC 2006-2007. allisonliles@gmail.com

LILES, Eric James (Ala) 1722 Beirne Ave NE, Huntsville AL 35801 **Assoc S Jn's Ch Decatur AL 2010-** B Bakersfield CA 8/30/1978 s Jimmy Ray Liles & Dolly. BA Texas A&M U 1999; MDiv VTS 2007. D 5/17/2007 Bp Frank Neff Powell P 12/11/2007 Bp Henry Nutt Parsley Jr. m 5/27/2006 Allison Sandlin. R S Steph's Epis Ch Smiths Sta AL 2007-2010; Yth Dir S Matt's Ch Austin TX 2000-2004. Epis Ntwk for Econ Justice 2007. ericliles@gmail.com

LILES, L. (NY) 120 W 69th St, New York NY 10023 **R Chr And S Steph's Ch New York NY 1998-** B Beebe AR 9/13/1950 d Doyle Liles & Naomi Christeen. BFA Kansas City Art Inst 1975; MDiv Ya Berk 1988; STM Ya Berk 1990. D 6/11/1988 P 3/18/1989 Bp Herbert Alcorn Donovan Jr. Assoc Trin Epis Ch Southport CT 1994-1998; Assoc S Ptr's Epis Ch Cheshire CT 1991-1994; Int Zion Epis Ch No Branford CT 1990-1991; Assoc S Ptr's Epis Ch Cheshire CT 1988-1990. Menil Schlr Yale 1989. liles@csschurch.org

LILLARD SR, Eddie Lee (NJ) 1819 Columbus Ave, Neptune NJ 07753 **D S Thos Epis Ch Red Bank NJ 2004-; D S Aug's Epis Ch Asbury Pk NJ 2000-** B Middleton OH 3/11/1932 s Joseph Dalton & Joycie Mae. D 10/21/2000 Bp David B(ruce) Joslin. m 6/14/1953 Adaline Jordan.

✠ **LILLIBRIDGE, Rt Rev Gary Richard** (WTex) PO Box 6885, San Antonio TX 78209 **Bp Dio W Texas San Antonio TX 2004-** B San Antonio TX 5/2/1956 s Richard B Lillibridge & Carol Day. BS SW Texas St U San Marcos 1978; MDiv VTS 1982. D 6/23/1982 Bp Stanley Fillmore Hauser P 1/5/1983 Bp Scott Field Bailey Con 2/21/2004 for WTex. m 10/12/1985 Catherine DeForest c 3. R S Dav's Epis Ch San Antonio TX 1998-2003; Archd Dio W Texas San Antonio TX 1995-1998; R Ch Of The Adv Brownsville TX 1992-1995; R S Jas Epis Ch Del Rio TX 1988-1992; Asst Ch Of The Gd Shpd Corpus Christi TX 1982-1984. Distinguished Alum Texas St U 2010; DD Sewanee 2006; DD VTS 2004. lillibridges5@yahoo.com

LILLICROPP, Arthur Reginald (NCal) 1607 54th St., Sacramento CA 95819 **Ch Of S Mart Davis CA 2009-; Assoc Trin Cathd Sacramento CA 2007-** B Rockville Center NY 6/7/1947 s Arthur R Lillicropp & Irene. Cert Addictions Counslr; Lic Int Mnstry Prog; BA Laf 1969; MDiv GTS 1974; MS Loyola U 1986; Cert GTS 1998. D 6/8/1974 Bp Paul Moore Jr P 12/1/1974 Bp Harold Louis Wright. S Paul's Epis Ch Oroville CA 2005-2007; S Jas Epis Ch Mt Airy MD 1999-2000; Ch Of The H Cross Cumberland MD 1997-1999; Int S Mk's Ch Highland MD 1996-1997; R S Jn's Ch Mt Washington Baltimore MD 1979-1985; Trin Ch Towson MD 1976-1979; Asst Chr And S Steph's Ch New York NY 1974-1976. AAPC, Coll Of Chaplai; Assn of Profsnl Chapl 2000; Int Mnstry Ntwk. Employee of the year Redding Med Cntr, Redding CA 2004; Who'S Who Rel 1977; Patuxent Pub Un-Sung Hero 89. moralle@comcast.net

LILLIE, Paul Andrew (Haw) 3311 Campbell Avenue, Honolulu HI 96815 **R S Mk's Ch Honolulu HI 2009-** B St Louis MO 3/1/1975 s James Robert Lillie & Nadine Martha. BM Millikin U 1997; ThM Trin Luth Sem 2000; MDiv Bex 2004. D 6/4/2004 P 2/5/2005 Bp J Michael Garrison. m 12/15/2008 Jayson John O'Donnell. Cn S Paul's Cathd Buffalo NY 2006-2008; P Exec Coun Appointees New York NY 2005-2006; D Ecusa / Mssn Personl New York NY 2004-2005. plillie1975@yahoo.com

LILLIS, Rosemary H (Roch) 1222 Sunset Ave, Asbury Park NJ 07712 **Int Trin Ch Asbury Pk NJ 2011-** B Mineola NY 8/6/1950 d Ernest Victor Haines & Angela Gertrude. BS Molloy Coll 1972; ACPE 1989; MDiv UTS 1994; MS Col 1996; Int Crit Incid Stress Mgmt Fndt 2000. D 6/4/1994 Bp John Shelby Spong P 12/17/1994 Bp Jack Marston McKelvey. c 2. P-in-c S Geo's Ch

Hilton NY 2009-2011; S Mk's And S Jn's Epis Ch Rochester NY 2008; Int S Lk's Ch Brockport NY 2007-2008; R S Andr's Ch Harrington Pk NJ 2005-2007; Int S Mths' Epis Ch Baltimore MD 2003-2004; Int The Ch Of The H Apos Halethorpe MD 2000-2001; P-in-c Ch Of The Gd Shpd Ringwood NJ 1994-1996. garden3priest@frontiernet.net

LILLPOPP, Donald Robert (Ct) 7314 Aloe Dr, Spring Hill FL 34607 **Assoc S Andr's Epis Ch Sprg Hill FL 1999-** B Greenfield MA 5/26/1933 s Robert Albert Lillpopp & Catherine Mary. BA U of Massachusetts 1956; STB Ya Berk 1959. D 6/13/1959 Bp William A Lawrence P 12/19/1959 Bp Robert McConnell Hatch. m 1/6/1960 Joanne Cynthia Lye c 3. Int R S Eliz's Epis Ch Zephyrhills FL 2003-2004; S Andr's Epis Ch Sprg Hill FL 1996-1998; S Eliz's Epis Ch Zephyrhills FL 1992-1998; ExCoun Dio Connecticut Hartford CT 1982-1986; R Chr Epis Ch Norwich CT 1980-1998; R Chr Ch Roxbury CT 1973-1980; Asst Trin Ch On The Green New Haven CT 1968-1970; R S Paul's Ch Windsor VT 1966-1968; R Trin Ch Claremont NH 1966-1968; P-in-c S Ann's Ch Sheldon VT 1964-1966; R S Matt's Ch Enosburg Falls VT 1964-1966; Cur Imm Ch Bellows Falls VT 1961-1964; Asst S Mary's Epis Ch Thorndike MA 1959-1960; Asst S Ptr's Ch Springfield MA 1959-1960. padrepopp@aol.com

LILLVIS, David Matthew (Mich) 111 Pleasant St, Sturgis MI 49091 **R under Contract Trin Ch Three Rivers MI 2006-** B Ashtabula OH 8/10/1948 s Matias Elias Lillvis & Irene Jennie. BA Wayne 1970; MDiv EDS 1973; Dplma Henry Ford Hosp Sch of Nrsng 1983. D 6/30/1973 Bp H Coleman McGehee Jr P 4/6/1974 Bp Albert A Chambers. m 9/19/1970 Meredith Hunt c 2. P Ch Of The Resurr Ecorse MI 1995-2004; P in Res S Ptr's Ch Detroit MI 1992-2005; Int S Lk's Ch Shelby Twp MI 1991; Int S Phil And S Steph Epis Ch Detroit MI 1989-1991; Int Trin Ch Detroit MI 1989; R S Eliz's Ch Redford MI 1976-1981; Cur Ch Of S Jn The Evang Hingham MA 1973-1976. dlillvis@me.com

LILLY, Elizabeth Cobb (WNC) 2953 Ninth Tee Dr, Newton NC 28658 **Bd Dir Valle Crucis Conf Cntr Banner Elk NC 2010-; Lifelong Chr Formation Com Dio Wstrn No Carolina Asheville NC 2005-** B Wilson NC 10/22/1956 Bachelor of Arts Meredith Coll 1978; Mstr of Div Andover Newton TS 1985. D 5/29/2004 Bp Robert Hodges Johnson P 1/22/2005 Bp Granville Porter Taylor. m 7/9/1993 Henry Thomas Lilly c 1. R Ch Of The Epiph Newton NC 2007-2011; Assoc Epis Ch Of S Ptr's By The Lake Denver NC 2004-2007. motherbeth@gmail.com

LILLY, Elizabeth Louise (SO) 152 W Weisheimer Rd, Columbus OH 43214 B Chicago IL 1/4/1933 d Robert Bryant Bates & Mary Louise. Mstr Iconographers; BA OH SU 1955; MAR Trin Luth Sem 1978; MDiv Trin Luth Sem 1979; DMin Untd TS Dayton OH 1987. D 6/28/1976 Bp John Mc Gill Krumm P 9/23/1984 Bp William Grant Black. m 6/11/1955 Carter Hayes Lilly c 2. Trin Ch Columbus OH 2002; Dir - Dioc Resource Cntr Dio Sthrn Ohio Cincinnati OH 1996-2002; S Ptr's Epis Ch Delaware OH 1995-1996; Assoc S Jn's Ch Worthington OH 1994-1998; Vic S Paul's Epis Ch Logan OH 1991-1993; Assoc S Jn's Ch Worthington OH 1988-1990; Assoc S Jas Ch Painesville OH 1985-1987; St Johns Hm Cleveland OH 1985-1987; Vic S Dav Vandalia OH 1982-1983; Asst Chr Epis Ch Dayton OH 1980-1982; Asst Trin Ch Columbus OH 1976-1980. Auth, "Speak To Me," *Wmn Uncommon Prayers*, Morehouse Pub, 2000; Auth, "Icons,By Cmsn," 1996; Auth, "It Is Finished: A Faithful Par Closes Itself," *,Dissertation*, UTS Dayton, OH, 1979; Auth, "God'S Sign Lang; The Faith of the Ch in Symbols," Self-Pub, 1978. Oblate: SHN 1970. fathermom1@aol.com

LIM, You-leng Leroy (Los) 12172 9th St, Garden Grove CA 92840 B SG 3/25/1964 s Chin-hoe Lim & Yun-Nee. UTS; BA Pr 1990; MDiv Harvard DS 1995; MBA Harv 2001. D 5/20/1995 Bp Barbara Clementine Harris P 1/13/1996 Bp Frederick Houk Borsch. S Mary's Epis Ch Los Angeles CA 1996-1998. Auth, "Boundary Wars"; Auth, "Our Families Our Values". lenglim@post.harvard.edu

LIMA, Roy Allen (Fla) 259 Duncan Dr, Crawfordville FL 32327 **D Ch Of The Adv Tallahassee FL 2010-** B Jacksonville FL 10/28/1951 s Pasquale J Lima - Deceased & Reitha H. The Angl Inst Live Oak, FL; BS U of Florida Gainesville, FL 1978. D 5/27/2007 Bp Samuel Johnson Howard. m 6/30/1979 Diane Kay Lima c 2. D Mssnr S Teresa Of Avila Crawfordville FL 2008-2010. deacongator1@centurylink.net

LIMBACH, Mary Evelyn (Eau) W4974 Mill St, La Crosse WI 54601 B Evergreen Park IL 11/1/1954 d Casper Robert Limbach & Mary Ursula. S Fran Sch Of Nrsng Peoria IL 1975; Cert So Dakota St U 1985; BD S Jos's Coll Windham ME 1990; MDiv STUSo 1993. D 5/1/1993 Bp Roger John White P 11/1/1993 Bp John Clark Buchanan. c 2. R All SS Ch Nevada MO 1993-1999.

LIMEHOUSE, A Capers Huffman (SC) 3 Rebellion Rd, Charleston SC 29407 B Jacksonville FL 7/27/1949 d Frederick Hoffman & Annelle. Dio Sc Diac Trng Prog; BA Agnes Scott Coll 1971; MFA Georgia St U 1993. D 9/10/2005 Bp Edward Lloyd Salmon Jr. m 10/9/1971 Walter Limehouse c 3. chlime@bellsouth.net

LIMEHOUSE III, Frank F (Ala) 3538 Lenox Rd, Birmingham AL 35213 **Dn The Cathd Ch Of The Adv Birmingham AL 2005-** B Orangeburg SC 7/17/1943 s Frank F Limehouse & Jean. BA Wofford Coll 1966; MDiv VTS 1989. D 6/29/1989 Bp C(hristopher) FitzSimons Allison P 6/1/1990 Bp Edward Lloyd Salmon Jr. m 8/5/1973 Jane Mewborne c 1. R Par Ch of St. Helena Beaufort SC 1995-2005; R S Barth's Epis Ch Hartsville SC 1991-1994; Asst R S Jas Ch Charleston SC 1989-1991.

LIMOZAINE, Bruce John (Ark) 30 Gettysburg N, Cabot AR 72023 **D/P S Steph's Epis Ch Jacksonville AR 2001-** B Washington DC 2/13/1942 s Jean Charles Limozaine & Hanora Veronica. BA Coll of Emporia 1971; MS U of Wisconsin 1975; U Denv 1979. D 4/28/2001 P 12/9/2006 Bp Larry Earl Maze. m 8/4/1996 Shaun Lenee Wilfong c 2. Athena'S hon Soc Coll Of Emporia 1971. brucelimozaine@classicnet.net

LIMPERT JR, Robert Hicks (Alb) PO Box 119, Brant Lake NY 12815 **Hon Cn Cathd Of All SS Albany NY 2002-; P-in-c Adirondack Missions Brant Lake NY 1991-** B Saranac Lake NY 7/27/1945 s Robert Hicks Limpert & Harriet Emily. BA Hob 1967; STB GTS 1970. D 6/13/1970 Bp Allen Webster Brown P 12/19/1970 Bp Charles Bowen Persell Jr. P-in-c Chr Ch Pottersville NY 1991-2003; P-in-c Ch Of The Gd Shpd Brant Lake NY 1991-2003; P-in-c S Andr's Ch Brant Lake NY 1991-2003; P-in-c S Barbara's Ch Brant Lake NY 1991-2003; P-in-c S Chris's Ch Brant Lake NY 1991-2003; P-in-c S Paul's Ch Brant Lake NY 1991-2003; Cn Chancllr Cathd Of All SS Albany NY 1988-1991; Stff S Paul's Ch Brant Lake NY 1970-1988. boblimpert@hotmail.com

LIMPITLAW, John Donald (Ct) 140 Whidah Way, Wellfleet MA 02667 B New York NY 1/4/1935 s Robert Limpitlaw & Olga. BA Trin Hartford CT 1956; MAR Ya Berk 1992. D 6/13/1992 P 12/23/1992 Bp Arthur Edward Walmsley. m 5/21/1960 Susan Elizabeth Glover c 2. Assoc Trin Epis Ch Southport CT 1997-1999; Vic Chr Ch Easton CT 1992-1997. Integrity 2006. Who's Who in Amer. jlimpitlaw@aol.com

LIN, Justin Chun-Min (Tai) 3/F, 262 Chung-Hsiao I Road, Hsin Hsing Dis, Kaohsiung 800 Taiwan B 8/3/1969 s Fu-Chun Lin & Chun Hung. S Jn & S Mary Inst Of Tech; BS Fu-Jen Cath U 1997. D 3/27/1999 P 1/8/2000 Bp John Chih-Tsung Chien. c 2.

LIN, Philip Li-Feng (Tai) 23 Wu-Chuan West Road Sec. 1, Taichung TAIWAN Taiwan **St Jas Epis Ch Taichung W Dist 2006-** B Taipei 7/7/1975 s Zong-Ren Lin & Zhao. Rsb Caulty Of Theologe; BA Fu-Jen Cath U. D 6/11/2005 P 7/22/2006 Bp Jung-Hsin Lai. m 10/9/2004 Yu-Ta Lin c 2.

LIN, Samuel Ying-chiu (Tai) #280 Fuhsing S Rd, Sec 2, C/O Diocese Of Taiwan, Taipei Taiwan B 7/15/1954 s Chhing-chhuan Lin & Chen-chu. BA Natl Cheng-Kung U Tw 1977; MDiv Tainan TS Tw 1983; MPh U Coll Dublin 1990. D 7/10/1983 P 7/1/1984 Bp Pui-Yeung Cheung. m 2/19/1980 Jane Chai-Chen Lee c 1. "Meditation Of Gospel Lesson (Chinese)," Taiwan Epis Ch, 1997. stjohn@mail.stjohn.org.tw

LIN, Shu-hwa (Tai) 1 F #29 Alley 6, Lane 168 Chung-her Rd Taiwan B Taiwan 12/5/1948 d Yun-Peng Lin & Yeh-Chu. MDiv Chinese Evang Sem; BA Fung-Chia U. D 11/21/2009 Bp Jung-Hsin Lai. c 4. peacehui_lin@yahoo.com.tw

LINARES-RIVERA, Ivette (PR) Ext La Milagrosa A-7, Calle 12, Bayamon 00959 Puerto Rico B 1/28/1973 d Noel Linares & Luz Selenia. Mstr in Div S Ptr and S Paul's Epis Sem- Puerto Rico 2002. D 10/13/2002 P 10/5/2003 Bp David Andres Alvarez-Velazquez. m 4/19/2008 Francisco Javier Caceres c 1. ilinares@episcopalpr.org

LINCOLN, Matthew (Ct) 3 Trumbull Pl, North Haven CT 06473 **R S Jn's Ch No Haven CT 1998-** B Saint Louis MO 4/28/1958 s Charles Ranlet Lincoln & Claire. U Chi; BA Earlham Coll 1984; MDiv GTS 1991. D 10/16/1991 P 4/26/1992 Bp Ronald Hayward Haines. m 9/26/1987 Catherine Carr c 2. Dn, New Haven Dnry Dio Connecticut Hartford CT 2000-2006; Chair, Evang Com Dio Massachusetts Boston MA 1996-1998; Cur S Chris's Ch Chatham MA 1995-1998; Cmsn Liturg & Mus Dio Washington Washington DC 1993-1995; Cur S Fran Ch Potomac MD 1991-1995. mlincoln@stjohns-northhaven.org

LINCOLN, Richard Kent (Los) 15114 Archwood St, Van Nuys CA 91405 B Lubbock TX 9/27/1945 s Eldon Elery Lincoln & Helen Irene. BA U Denv 1967; MDiv GTS 1976; MA Natl U 1982. D 6/12/1976 P 12/1/1976 Bp Paul Moore Jr. m 3/28/1970 Catherine Christy. Asst S Simon's Par San Fernando CA 1994-1995; P S Mich and All Ang Epis Ch Studio City CA 1984-1988; Assoc S Mart-In-The-Fields Par Winnetka CA 1983-1984; Assoc S Mk's Par Altadena CA 1983; Chapl The Bp's Sch La Jolla CA 1981-1982; Assoc Chr Ch Coronado CA 1980-1981; Assoc S Barth's Ch New York NY 1977-1978; Assoc S Clem's Ch New York NY 1975-1976.

LINCOLN, Thomas C(larke) (Nwk) 1156 Carolina Cir Sw, Vero Beach FL 32962 B Mount Vernon NY 8/18/1934 s Alan Mawson Lincoln & Elizabeth. BA Wms 1956; MDiv VTS 1966. D 6/11/1966 P 12/14/1966 Bp Leland Stark. m 6/15/1957 Renee Marie Hermos. Int S Thos Ch Lyndhurst NJ 1998-1999; Int S Thos Ch Lyndhurst NJ 1992-1994; Int S Jn's Epis Ch Montclair NJ 1991; Int S Ptr's Ch Mtn Lakes NJ 1990-1991; Ch Of The Epiph Allendale NJ 1989; Vic The Ch Of The Sav Denville NJ 1967-1968. lincolntr@aol.com

LIND, Douglass Theodore (Ct) 17080 Harbour Point Dr Apt 1017, Fort Myers FL 33908 **P Assoc Calv Ch Stonington CT 2009-; supply P S Mary's Epis Ch Manchester CT 2007-2012** B St Paul MN 12/27/1939 s Olaf Milton Lind

& Jennie Teresa. AB Harv 1961; MDiv UTS 1964; Phd SE U 1974; Dmin GTF So Bend IN 1989; ThD GTF So Bend IN 2007. D 6/10/2006 Bp Andrew Donnan Smith P 2/10/2007 Bp James Elliot Curry. m 7/31/1965 Penelope Dougall. P Assoc Ch Of S Mich And All Ang Sanibel FL 2009-2011; Cur S Jas Ch New London CT 2006-2007. dtlsigma@aol.com

LIND, Tracey (O) 80 E. 252nd St., Euclid OH 44132 **Dn Trin Cathd Cleveland OH 2000-** B Columbus OH 5/17/1954 d Stanley W Lind & Winne H. BA U of Toledo 1977; MA U Cinc 1979; MDiv UTS 1987. D 6/13/1987 Bp Paul Moore Jr P 12/10/1987 Bp John Shelby Spong. m 8/12/2010 Emily Ingalls. R S Paul's Epis Ch Paterson NJ 1989-2000; Assoc Chr Ch Ridgewood NJ 1987-1989. "Interrupted By God: Glimpses from the Edge," Pilgrim Press, 2004. Dio Newark Cantenbury Schlrshp Dio Newark Newark NJ 1994; Maxwell Fellowowship Uts New York NY 1987. tlind@dohio.org

LINDAHL-MALLOW, Rosa Vera (SeFla) 2131 SW 23rd Ave, Fort Lauderdale FL 33312 **P Mssnr S Ambr Epis Ch Ft Lauderdale FL 2010-; P Mssnr All SS Prot Epis Ch Ft Lauderdale FL 2005-** B Cali Colombia 12/1/1959 d Gunnar Lindahl & Ann Elliot. BA Loyola U 1983; MDiv STUSo 1987. D 7/16/2005 P 5/12/2006 Bp Leopold Frade. m 7/9/1988 Sherod Earl Mallow c 1. Auth, "Out of Many, One," *ECF Vital Practices*, ECF, 2011. Transformational Mnstrs Fell ECF 2010. rosa@allsaintsfl.org

LINDBERG, Robert Morris (CPa) 91 Gunn Rd, Keene NH 03431 B Waukegan IL 5/28/1950 s Ernest William Lindberg & Sigve. BA Sthrn Illinois U 1975; MS Sthrn Illinois U 1976; Chr Sem/Seminex 1977; MDiv Bex 1986. D 8/6/1986 Bp Richard Mitchell Trelease Jr P 2/7/1987 Bp Harold B Robinson. m 11/14/1987 Maryann L Lacroix c 2. R Chr Ch Berwick PA 2004-2009; R Chr Epis Ch Warren OH 1994-2004; R S Mths Ch Hamilton NJ 1989-1994; Cn S Paul's Cathd Buffalo NY 1986-1989. Distinguished Grad Awd Lake Cnty Coll 1986. rmlindberg@aol.com

LINDELL, John Allen (Mont) 6629 Merryport Ln, Naples FL 34104 B Chicago IL 2/28/1943 s Julian S Lindell & Irvina Florence. BA Parsons Coll Fairfield IA 1964; MDiv Epis TS In Kentucky 1984; DMin GTF 1988. D 12/15/1985 P 6/15/1986 Bp Don Adger Wimberly. m 5/23/1992 A Arlene Kranz. R S Fran Epis Ch Great Falls MT 1997-1999; R S Paul's Ch Ft Benton MT 1997-1999; S Matt's Hse Naples FL 1993-1996; Assoc S Paul's Ch Naples FL 1987-1993; Vic S Tim's Barnes Mtn Irvine KY 1985-1987. Auth, "Sinned Againstness," *Fellows Yearbook of GTF*, 1989. Life Tenured Fell Grad Theological Fndt 1989. aandjlindell@aol.com

LINDELL, Thomas Jay (Az) 4460 N Camino Del Rey, Tucson AZ 85718 **D S Phil's In The Hills Tucson AZ 2000-** B Red Wing MN 7/22/1941 s Carl Raymond Lindell & Florence Eugenia. BS Gustavus Adolphus Coll 1963; PhD U of Iowa 1969; none Westcott Hse, Cambridge, UK 1997; none Wycliffe Hall, Oxford, UK 2000; none Wycliffe Hall, Oxford, UK 2001. D 10/14/2000 Bp Robert Reed Shahan. m 2/25/2000 Marilyn Jean Andekson c 2. Soc of Ord Scientists 2003. tlindell@email.arizona.edu

LINDEMAN, Eileen Cornish (Cal) 830 Mohican Way, Redwood City CA 94062 B Grand Island NE 4/30/1954 d Arthur Maynard Cornish & Dena Lorraine. BS U of Nebraska 1976; MA Creighton U 1994. D 5/28/1995 P 2/11/1996 Bp James Edward Krotz. m 4/2/1976 Mitchell James Lindeman c 3. The Bp's Sch La Jolla CA 1999-2000; Chr Ch Coronado CA 1997-2006; Epis Cmnty Serv San Diego CA 1996-2002; Asst S Mk's On The Campus Lincoln NE 1995-1996. eilindeman@gmail.com

LINDEMAN, Mitchell James (Cal) 815 Portola Road, Portola Valley CA 94028 **R Chr Ch Portola Vlly CA 2006-** B Tacoma WA 6/1/1956 s William Edward Lindeman & Marilyn Barbara. BA U of Nebraska 1980; MDiv Ya Berk 1983. D 6/15/1983 P 12/16/1983 Bp James Daniel Warner. m 4/2/1976 Eileen Cornish c 3. R Chr Ch Coronado CA 1996-2006; R S Matt's Ch Lincoln NE 1990-1996; R S Thos' Epis Ch Falls City NE 1985-1990; Asst All SS Epis Ch Omaha NE 1983-1985. Cath Fllshp Epis Ch 1987. " " 1983; " " 1982; Fund Schlr Fund for Theol Educ 1981. mlinde1066@gmail.com

LINDENBERG, Juliana T (NC) 231 N Church St, Rocky Mount NC 27804 **Asst Ch Of The Gd Shpd Rocky Mt NC 2011-** B Orlando, FL 7/25/1970 d Jimmie Lee Taylor & Vicki Lois. BA The Coll of Wooster 1997; MDiv Candler TS 2001. D 6/26/2010 Bp Don Edward Johnson. m 6/16/2000 David Lindenberg c 2. St Geo's Indep Sch Collierville TN 2010-2011. jlindenberg0725@gmail.com

LINDER, Callie Maebelle (Mich) 2034 S 69th East Pl, Tulsa OK 74112 B Elgin TX 12/31/1923 d Oscar Joseph Linder & Clara Mae. PhD Indiana U 1970; STUSo 1986. D 6/27/1987 Bp H Coleman McGehee Jr.

LINDER, Mark Allen (Ky) 457 Collett Bridge Rd, Alvaton KY 42122 B Little Rock AR 1/15/1945 s Bernard Westbrook Linder & Ellen. BA/BS U of Arkansas 1970; MDiv VTS 1973. D 6/25/1973 Bp Christoph Keller Jr P 4/16/1974 Bp Reginald Heber Gooden. m 12/28/1968 Patricia G Gilliam c 3. Dep GC Dio Kentucky Louisville KY 2000-2007; Pres Stndg Com Dio Kentucky Louisville KY 1996-1998; R Chr Epis Ch Bowling Green KY 1994-2007; Stndg Com Dio Arkansas Little Rock AR 1986-1989; R Trin Ch Pine Bluff AR 1985-1994; Exec Coun Dio Arkansas Little Rock AR 1982-1985; R S Paul's Epis Ch Batesville AR 1977-1985; Assoc Chr Ch Overland Pk KS 1975-1977; P-in-c S Aug's Ch Ft Smith AR 1974-1975; CE Cmsn Dio Arkansas Little Rock AR 1973-1975; Cur S Jn's Epis Ch Ft Smith AR 1973-1975. m.linder@insightbb.com

LINDER, Philip Conrad (At) 25 Otranto Lane, Columbia SC 29209 **S Jn's Ch Versailles KY 2011-** B Flushing NY 6/10/1960 s Conrad Walter Linder & Leona Louise. BS Villanova U 1982; MDiv GTS 1985; DMin Columbia TS 1993; BA The GTF 2006. D 5/20/1985 Bp Robert Campbell Witcher Sr P 12/21/1985 Bp Henry Boyd Hucles III. m 8/14/1982 Ellen Cooper c 3. Dn Trin Cathd Columbia SC 1999-2011; R H Trin Par Decatur GA 1990-1999; S Mart In The Fields Ch Atlanta GA 1987-1990; Asst Gr Epis Ch Massapequa NY 1985-1987. "A P's Journ of Hope - God and 9/11," IUniverse, Inc.; Auth, "H Trust," *LivCh*; Auth, "The Run Within," *LivCh*. Soc of S Jn the Evang 1998-2006. philiplinder3@aol.com

LINDERMAN, Jeanne Marie Herron (Del) 307 Springhouse Ln, Hockessin DE 19707 B Erie PA 11/14/1931 d Robert Leslie Herron & Ella Marie. BS Cor 1953; MDiv Lancaster TS 1981. D 11/14/1981 P 11/6/1982 Bp William Hawley Clark. m 4/24/1954 James S Linderman c 6. Assoc Ch of St Andrews & St Matthews Wilmington DE 1991-1994; S Andrews and S Matthews Mnstry Wilmington DE 1991-1993; Mem, Cler Compstn Bd Dio Delaware Wilmington DE 1991-1992; Pres, Stndg Com Dio Delaware Wilmington DE 1991-1992; Mem, Const. & Cn Com Dio Delaware Wilmington DE 1989-1994; Mem, Geriatric Serv Bd Dio Delaware Wilmington DE 1989-1993; Chr Ch Delaware City DE 1989-1990; Mem, Stndg Com Dio Delaware Wilmington DE 1988-1992; Mem, Stwdshp T/F Dio Delaware Wilmington DE 1984-1986; Mem, Cler Compstn Bd Dio Delaware Wilmington DE 1983-1986; P-in-c Chr Ch Delaware City DE 1982-1987; Dio Delaware Wilmington DE 1982-1986; Mem, Dioc Coun Dio Delaware Wilmington DE 1982-1985; Chair, Human Sxlty T/F Dio Delaware Wilmington DE 1982-1983; Chapl Cathd Ch Of S Jn Wilmington DE 1981-1982. Auth, *Delaware Silversmiths*, Questers, Inc., 1966; Auth, *A Heritage of Delaware Hm*, Wmn of S Andr's, Wilmington, DE, 1964. DECA 1981; ECW 1995; EWC 1980-1992; NNECA 1981; Wmn Witnessing Cmnty at Lambeth 1990. The Meck Awd for Outstnd Min. in Diversity Lancaster TS 2005. linderjs@verizon.net

LINDH-PAYNE, Kristofer Hans (Md) 2216 Pot Spring Rd., Timonium MD 21093 **Assoc R Epiph Ch Dulaney Vlly Timonium MD 2009-** B Baltimore MD 9/23/1977 s Hans E Lindh & Patricia. BA S Mary's Coll of Maryland 1999; MA Loyola Coll Baltimore MD 2003; MDiv SWTS 2009. D 6/13/2009 Bp John Leslie Rabb. m 8/28/2004 Heather Payne. KRISLINDHPAYNE@GMAIL.COM

LINDLEY, Bernie (Ore) 97955 Hallway Rd, PO Box 3190, Harbor OR 97415 **Vic S Tim's Ch Brookings OR 2008-** B Crescent City CA 2/21/1967 s Jim Lindley & Kathrine Doris. BS Willamette U 1989; Dio Oregon, Cntr for the Diac 2006; VTS 2007. D 9/5/2007 Bp Johncy Itty P 6/14/2008 Bp Robert Louis Ladehoff. m 8/13/1988 Paige dePuglia c 2. bernie@sttimothyepiscopal.org

LINDLEY, Susan Shea (Okla) 1202 W Elder Ave, Duncan OK 73533 **Vic Dio Oklahoma Oklahoma City OK 2008-** B San Mateo CA 11/13/1943 d John Egan Shea & Mary G. BSFS Geo 1965; JD U of Texas at Austin 1970; MDiv Phillips TS 2007. D 6/23/2007 Bp Robert Manning Moody P 1/19/2008 Bp Edward Joseph Konieczny. m 4/24/1971 George Lindley c 1. sslindley@cableone.net

LINDQUIST, Mary Dail (Haw) 18 Bradley Ave, Brattleboro VT 05301 **R S Mich's Epis Ch Brattleboro VT 2011-** B Batavia NY 10/21/1968 d Ray Irving Lindquist & Phyllis. BA Br 1991; MDiv PrTS 1995; STM GTS 2000. Trans 2/11/2004 Bp Wayne Parker Wright. m 7/23/2000 Kurt Brian Johnson. Vic Epis Ch On W Kaua'i Eleele HI 2004-2011; Assoc R S Dav's Epis Ch Wilmington DE 2000-2003; Dir of Chr Formation Trin Ch Princeton NJ 1997-1999. mlind@mindspring.com

LINDSAY JR, Spencer Hedden (La) 273 Monarch Dr Apt L-26, Houma LA 70364 B Houma,LA 9/7/1948 s Spencer Hedden Lindsay & Doris. BA Centenary Coll of Louisiana 1970; MDiv SWTS 1973. D 6/25/1973 P 4/1/1974 Bp Iveson Batchelor Noland. m Earl Woodward. Ch Of The H Apos New Orleans LA 1977-1982; Vic S Mary's Ch Baton Rouge LA 1976-2003; Cur S Lk's Ch Baton Rouge LA 1973-1976. Integrity. spencer.lindsay2@gmail.com

LINDSEY, Barrett Kelland (Oly) 2511 E 40th Ave, Spokane WA 99223 B Oklahoma City OK 9/20/1941 s Lucien Dale Lindsey & Dolores Carolyn. BA U of Oklahoma 1963; STB U Tor 1966. D 6/17/1966 Bp Chilton Powell P 1/1/1967 Bp Frederick Warren Putnam. m 6/14/1998 Barbara Jean Helmer. Int S Steph's Epis Ch Spokane WA 1997-1998; Int S Paul's Epis Ch Mt Vernon WA 1995-1997; Dio Olympia Seattle WA 1994; Chr Ch SEATTLE WA 1980-1994; Assoc R Chr Ch Par Lake Oswego OR 1977-1980; Cn Pstr S Andr's Cathd Honolulu HI 1973-1977; Assoc R S Jn's Ch Oklahoma City OK 1970-1973; Vic S Lk The Beloved Physcn Idabel OK 1969-1970; Vic S Mk's Ch Hugo OK 1967-1970; Cur S Paul's Ch Altus OK 1966-1967. Bostonbbl@comcast.net

LINDSEY, Kenneth Lewis (Me) 466 Rockingham St., Berlin NH 03570 B Barre MA 9/29/1924 s Lewis Reno Lindsey & Mattie Evalina. NEU 1945; LTh Epis TS In Kentucky 1963; U of Kentucky 1964; Coll of Preachers 1976. D 6/22/1963 Bp Robert McConnell Hatch P 12/21/1963 Bp Oliver L Loring. m 7/6/1991 Christine Ann Davis c 1. Asst S Barn Ch Berlin NH 1991-1998; Dio Maine Portland ME 1987-1988; Chairman Cltn for Missions Dio Maine Portland ME 1982-1987; Vic S Lk's Ch Farmington ME 1982-1987; P-in-c Chr Epis Ch Eastport ME 1975-1982; Dioc Coun Dio Maine Portland ME 1972-1986; Cler Compstn Rev Com Dio Maine Portland ME 1971-1986; R S Anne's Ch Calais ME 1967-1982; Vic S Thos Ch Winn ME 1963-1967. chrisken@megalink.net

LINDSEY, Richard Carroll (SC) 3001 Meeting St, Hilton Head Island SC 29926 **R All SS Ch Hilton Hd Island SC 2003-** B Baltimore MD 6/24/1949 s Erle Clayton Lindsey & June Audry. BS Towson U 1972; MDiv EDS 1976. D 5/30/1976 P 1/1/1977 Bp David Keller Leighton Sr. m 5/25/1974 Carolyn Floriana c 2. R S Alfred's Epis Ch Palm Harbor FL 1990-2003; R Nativ Epis Ch Bloomfield Township MI 1985-1990; R Chr Ch W River MD 1980-1985; Asst S Jn's Ch Reisterstown MD 1976-1980. saintsrector@hargray.com

LINDSLEY, James Elliott (NY) Maplegarth, Box 881, Millbrook NY 12545 B Morristown NJ 3/17/1930 s James Mcintyre Lindsley & Alice Wharton. BA Bard Coll 1952; STM GTS 1955; DD GTS 2006. D 6/11/1955 P 12/17/1955 Bp Benjamin M Washburn. m 11/19/1960 Barbara N Newberry. Vic Ch Of S Nich On The Hudson New Hamburg NY 2003-2007; S Paul's And Trin Par Tivoli NY 1977-1992; Hstgr Dio New York New York City NY 1973-1975; Diocn Msnry & Ch Extntn Socty New York NY 1970-1992; Dpt Of Missions Ny Income New York NY 1970-1992; P-in-c Chr Ch Harrison NJ 1967-1969; R Chr Ch Corning NY 1966-1967; Hstgr Dio Newark Newark NJ 1963-1966; R S Steph's Ch Millburn NJ 1957-1966; Asst S Jas Ch Upper Montclair NJ 1955-1957. "First Winter," Trst of the Morristown Green; Auth, "S Ptr'S Ch Of Morristown"; Auth, "S Jas' Ch Of New York City"; Auth, "Certainly Splendid Hse"; Auth, "Ch Club Of New York"; Auth, "This Planted Vine". Washington Assn Of New Jersey 1960. jelgarden@aol.com

L

LINDSTROM JR, Donald Fredrick (CGC) 269 Rainbow Falls Road, Franklin NC 28734 B Atlanta GA 7/18/1943 s Donald Fredrick Lindstrom & Elizabeth Haynes. ABJ U GA 1966; MDiv VTS 1969; JD Woodrow Wilson Coll of Law 1977; U of W Florida 1983. D 6/28/1969 Bp Randolph R Claiborne P 3/6/1970 Bp Milton LeGrand Wood. m 12/30/1983 Marcia Pace c 1. Chairman Dio Cntrl Gulf Coast Pensacola FL 2006-2009; Ecum Off Dio Mississippi Jackson MS 2001-2007; Stndg Com Dio Cntrl Gulf Coast Pensacola FL 2001-2002; Ecum Off Dio Cntrl Gulf Coast Pensacola FL 1998-2009; R S Thos Ch Greenville AL 1997-2010; R The Epis Ch Of The Medtr Meridian MS 1991-1997; Vic H Sprt Epis Ch Gulf Shores AL 1988-1991; Asst Chr Ch Par Pensacola FL 1981-1982; Asst S Mart In The Fields Ch Atlanta GA 1975-1978; Vic Gd Shpd Epis Ch Austell GA 1971-1975; Cur Chr Ch Macon GA 1969-1971. Auth, "The Cry for Help," *Radio Broadcast Documentary*, ECUSA, 1968; Auth, "The Autumn Years," *Radio Broadcast Documentary*, ECUSA, 1968. Amer Assn for Mar and Fam Ther: Clincl 1985; Bd for Chld Advocacy Cntr 1999-2009; Chambellan Prov Bailli Chaine des Rotisseurs 1993-2000; Intl Conf of Police Chapl,Mstr Chapl 1991; OHC (Assoc) 1971; Rotary Intl 1997. Outstanding Citizen of the Year Greenville Alabama Jaycees 2005; Ldrshp Atlanta Ldrshp Atlanta 1974; Superior Awd for Gnrl News Associated Press Broadcasters 1963; Superior Awd for News Specials Associated Press Broadcasters 1963. frfredl@gmail.com

LINDSTROM, Justin Alan (Tex) 16511 Wax Mallow Dr, Houston TX 77095 **Vic S Aid's Ch Cypress TX 2002-** B Escondido CA 4/25/1972 s Joel Edward Lindstrom & Jeanne Rae. BA Texas Luth U 1994; MDiv Epis TS of The SW 1999. D 8/28/1999 Bp Claude Edward Payne P 8/29/2000 Bp Leopoldo Jesus Alard. m 6/22/1996 Susan Alison Hiebert c 2. Asst S Mart's Epis Ch Houston TX 1999-2002. revjustin@staidanshouston.org

LINDSTROM, Marjorie Dawson (Nwk) 91 Francisco Ave, Rutherford NJ 07070 **Assoc Gr Ch Newark NJ 2007-** B Hackensack NJ 7/6/1951 d George Robert Dawson & Roberta. BA Ohio Wesl 1973; MA NYU 1977; MDiv GTS 2005. D 6/12/2005 Bp John Palmer Croneberger P 1/21/2006 Bp Carol Joy Gallagher. m 7/20/1974 Michael A Lindstrom c 2. Seamens Ch Inst Income New York NY 2005-2011. revmlindstrom@comcast.net

LINDWRIGHT, Philippa Elin (Minn) 2300 Hamline Ave N, Roseville MN 55113 B Palo Alto CA 5/21/1987 d Thomas Wright Linder & Jennifer Linda. BA Earlham Coll 2008; MDiv EDS 2012. D 6/30/2011 Bp Brian N Prior. pippa.lindwright@gmail.com

LING, James Kai Fe (Tai) 4149 N Kenmore Ave # 28, Chicago IL 60613 B Chen Kang CN 10/12/1924 s Wann Chuen Ling & Liao. Li Phone Arts Coll Cn 1948; BTh Allnce Sem Hk 1957; Tainan TS Tw 1965; ThM Heav People Sem 1975. D 8/24/1965 P 2/1/1966 Bp James Chang L Wong. m 1/1/1962 Ruth Ru Te Chang c 3. Dio Mauritius Phoenix 1974-1978. Auth, "Traveler In The Globe," 2003; Auth, "The Way To Be Happy," 1982.

LING, John Yoh-Han (Tai) Po Box 2984, Asheville NC 28802 **Died 12/24/2010** B 1/30/1921 s Ming-jen Ling & Shui-chin. BS U Nanking Cn 1946; BD Tainan TS Tw 1963; STM VTS 1972. D 3/19/1960 Bp Harry S Kennedy P 9/1/1963 Bp Charles P Gilson. c 3. Auth, "Death-The Door Of Hope". Sem Hill Soc, Aspinwall Tower Soc 1987. Nomin As Represetative To Angl Consultative Coun 2005; Ep Gen'L Conv From Taiwan 1964; New Way Of Life For Chinese Alum Untd Nations Fllshp 1956. dling77055@yahoo.com

LING, Steven (Be) Trinity Episcopal Church, 345 Main St, Portland CT 06480 **P Asst Ch Of The H Trin Middletown CT 2008-; P-in-c Trin Ch Portland CT 2007-** B Lansing MI 6/29/1951 s Clarence Ling & Dorothy. BA Albion Coll 1973; MA MI SU 1978; MDiv Ya Berk 2007. D 3/25/2007 Bp Paul Victor Marshall P 11/10/2007 Bp James Elliot Curry. m 11/2/1985 Thea Katherine White c 2. frsteveling@yahoo.com

LINK, Michael Roger (Nev) 11844 Orense Dr, Las Vegas NV 89138 **Treas Natl Ntwk Of Epis Cler Assn Lynnwood WA 2009-; Asstg Cler All SS Epis Ch Las Vegas NV 2002-** B Davenport IA 2/23/1941 s Floyd Linzy Link & Elizabeth Carolynn. BA U of Iowa 1962; MDiv SWTS 1965. D 6/24/1965 P 1/1/1966 Bp Gordon V Smith. m 9/1/1962 Linda May Nyenhuis c 2. Transitions Off Dio Nevada Las Vegas NV 2004-2011; R S Phil's Epis Ch Rochester MI 1980-2001; Cn for Educ. and Prog. Dvlpmt S Paul's Cathd Peoria IL 1973-1979; R S Lk's Ch Ft Madison IA 1968-1973; Vic S Paul Epis Ch Des Moines IA 1965-1968; Vic Trin Ch Winterset IA 1965-1967. mikelink41@gmail.com

LINLEY, Eliza Mackay (Cal) 210 Lake Court, Aptos CA 95003 **Asstg P Ch Of S Jn The Bapt Aptos CA 2000-** B Sacramento CA 11/23/1952 d James Slauson Linley & Margaret Mackay. BA Smith 1974; MA U CA 1978; MDiv CDSP 1990. D 12/7/1990 P 12/8/1991 Bp William Edwin Swing. m 1/7/1989 David William Richardson. Vstng Chapl CDSP Berkeley CA 1997-1999; Asstg P S Phil The Apos Scotts Vlly CA 1996-2000; Int S Jn's Epis Ch Oakland CA 1995-1996; Asstg P S Alb's Ch Albany CA 1993-1995; S Anselm's Epis Ch Lafayette CA 1992; Yth Min All Souls Par In Berkeley Berkeley CA 1991-1992. Epis Ch in the Visual Arts 2002. ammaeliza@igc.org

LINMAN, Jennifer (NY) 500 E 77th St Apt 1622, New York NY 10162 **P in Charge The Ch Of The Epiph New York NY 2011-** B Harbor City CA 7/21/1975 d Walter F Reddall & Roberta Hofbauer. BA Ya 1997; MDiv GTS 2002. D 6/29/2002 Bp Robert Marshall Anderson P 1/11/2003 Bp Joseph Jon Bruno. m 10/10/2003 Jonathan Linman c 1. Assoc R The Ch Of The Epiph New York NY 2003-2011; Cur Ch Of The Epiph Oak Pk CA 2002-2003. reddall@aol.com

LINN, David (Cal) Po Box 212, Moraga CA 94556 B San Jose CA 1/11/1939 s Ronald Neill Linn & Mildred M. BA California St U 1967; MDiv CDSP 1969. D 6/28/1969 P 10/1/1970 Bp C Kilmer Myers. Supply P Dio California San Francisco CA 1972-1973. Ord Of S Lk 2000. dnl@dnlco.com

LINNENBERG, Daniel M (Roch) 267 Brooklawn Dr, Rochester NY 14618 B Humboldt TN 12/8/1953 s John Herbert Linnenberg & Mary Margaret. BA Bowling Green St U 1976; MAEd Wstrn Kentucky U 1983; MDiv Nash 1987; EdD U Roch 2008. D 11/11/1987 P 5/29/1988 Bp David Reed. m 8/22/1975 Virginia Mary Skinner. R Ch Of The Ascen Rochester NY 2000-2009; Int S Mk's And S Jn's Epis Ch Rochester NY 1999-2000; P-in-c Ch Of The Nativ Boyne City MI 1994-1998; Asst S Paul's Ch Maumee OH 1988-1992; Cur Trin Epis Ch Owensboro KY 1987-1988. DLinnenberg@rochester.rr.com

LINSCOTT, Burton LaFayette (Haw) 1041 10th Ave, Honolulu HI 96816 **Died 1/13/2010** B Bar Harbor ME 6/25/1913 s Lester J Linscott & Elizabeth C. BA Colby Coll 1942; STB GTS 1945; MA U of Hawaii 1960. D 5/1/1945 Bp Richard T Loring Jr P 11/1/1945 Bp Harry S Kennedy. c 1. hardawaybronzeart@yahoo.com

LINSCOTT, John Burton (NC) 830 Durham Rd, Wake Forest NC 27587 **D S Johns Epis Ch Wake Forest NC 2008-** B Kona HI 5/25/1946 s Burton LaFayette Linscott & Genie. D Trng Duke 2007. D 6/14/2008 Bp Michael Bruce Curry. m 12/11/1995 Susan E Weiss c 3. jblinscott@nc.rr.com

LINSCOTT, Stephanie (Tex) 7675 Phoenix Dr, Houston TX 77030 B Baytown TX 12/2/1960 d Stephen Linscott & Judy. BA U of Houston 1989; MDiv Epis TS of The SW 1996. D 12/3/1997 P 10/18/2002 Bp Claude Edward Payne. St Lk's Epis Hosp Houston TX 1998-1999; Trin Ch Houston TX 1997-1999; Trin Ch Galveston TX 1997-1998. revlinscott@juno.com

LINTERIEUR, Antoine (Mil) No address on file. B Two Rivers WI 5/30/1940 s Louis David Lintereur & Marie. BS St. Mary's Coll Sem 1963; BA U of Wisconsin 1969; BA U of Wisconsin 1973; MA U of Wisconsin 1979; Allnce Francaise De Paris Paris Fr 1980. D 6/3/1990 Bp Roger John White. D All SS' Cathd Milwaukee WI 1990-2006.

LINTNER, Richard James (Ia) 6750 School #304, Windsor Heights IA 50324 B Lansing MI 8/16/1926 s Roy Christian Lintner & Gladys F. U of Nthrn Iowa; BA MI SU 1947; BD SWTS 1953; MA U MN 1969. D 6/6/1953 Bp Lewis B Whittemore P 12/20/1953 Bp Dudley B McNeil. m 4/27/1957 Gloria Norwall c 2. S Andr's Ch Chariton IA 1973-1983; Asst S Andr's Epis Ch Monroe WI 1970-1972; Locum tenans Geth Ch Minneapolis MN 1967-1969; R Gr Ch Chanute KS 1964-1967; R S Jas Epis Ch Sonora CA 1959-1964; Cur S Paul's Ch Oakland CA 1956-1959; Cur Chr Ch Winnetka IL 1954-1956; Vic Chr

Epis Ch Charlevoix MI 1953-1954; Vic S Paul's Epis Ch Elk Rapids MI 1953-1954. ESMA. rlintnergsm@gmail.com

LINTON, Adam Stuart (Mass) 204 Monument Rd, Orleans MA 02653 **R The Ch Of The H Sprt Orleans MA 2009-** B San Rafael CA 10/11/1954 s Stuart Linton & Patricia. AA Coll of Marin 1975; DIT S Tikhon Orth TS So Canaan PA 1980; MDiv Gordon-Conwell TS 1990. Rec 10/17/1997 as Priest Bp Frank Tracy Griswold III. m 7/17/1977 Lori A Weaver c 5. R Ch Of The Gd Shpd Ogden UT 2000-2009; R S Lk's Ch Dixon IL 1997-2000. Cler Ldrshp Proj Class XIII. holyspiritorleansrector@verizon.net

LINVILLE, Harriet Burton (ECR) PO Box 1866, Morro Bay CA 93443 B Mount Clemens MI 7/1/1943 d Fitz James Bridges & Margery. BA U MI 1965; MA U MI 1968; CAS CDSP 1981. D 10/20/1982 P 11/1/1983 Bp Rustin Ray Kimsey. c 2. Curs Dio El Camino Real Monterey CA 1997-2006; R S Ptr's By-The-Sea Epis Ch Morro Bay CA 1996-2011; Int Ch Of Our Sav Pasco WA 1993-1995; Int Ch Of The H Sprt Missoula MT 1993; Curs Dio Estrn Oregon The Dalles OR 1987-1992; R S Jn's Ch Hermiston OR 1986-1992; Par Asst The Par Of S Mk The Evang Hood River OR 1986; Par Asst The Par Of S Mk The Evang Hood River OR 1982-1986. Auth, "In Chr There Is No E Or W," *Epis*, 1988. hlinville@charter.net

LINZEL, Claire Benedict (SwFla) 411 Nottinghill Gale St. #805, #1207, Arlington TX 76014 B Akron OH 4/16/1930 d Clarence Edwin Benedict & Rhoda Love. BA Drew U 1951; MS Indiana U 1967; MDiv CDSP 2003. D 6/24/1995 Bp Telesforo A Isaac. m 6/29/1957 August Linzel c 4. D All Souls Par In Berkeley Berkeley CA 2001-2003; D Ch Of The H Sprt Sfty Harbor FL 1996-2000; D Ch Of The Redeem Sarasota FL 1995-1996. Soc of S Fran, Third Ord, Life Professed 1962. clairelinzel@yahoo.com

LIOTTA BSG, Thomas Mark (NY) 629 County Route 12, New Hampton NY 10958 **Dir of Mus S Jas' Ch Goshen NY 2000-** B Troy NY 7/13/1942 s Sylvester Liotta & Mary Decianni. DC Teachers Coll Washington DC. D 5/14/2005 Bp Mark Sean Sisk. tmbsg@aol.com

LIPP, Beth Ann (ND) P.O. Box 1241, Bismarck ND 58502 B New Ulm MN 6/15/1958 d George N Kipp & Janet Ahr. Assoc Bismarch St Coll 1978; BS U of Mary 1998. D 6/8/2007 Bp Michael Gene Smith. m 8/12/1978 Dennis Lipp c 3. blipp@bis.midco.net

LIPPART, Thomas Edward (NMich) 5207 Eleuthra Circle, Vero Beach FL 32967 B Upper Darby PA 2/21/1937 s John Lippart & Mary Frances. BS Michigan Tech U 1959; BD Nash 1965; Cert VTS 1989. D 6/12/1965 Bp Robert Lionne DeWitt P 12/11/1965 Bp Albert Ervine Swift. m 6/17/1961 Margaret Free Lippart c 2. Chapl to Ret Cler + spouses Dio Nthrn Michigan Marquette MI 2003-2011; So Cntrl Reg Manistique MI 1992-1997; Mssnr SoCntrl Reg Dio Nthrn Michigan Marquette MI 1990-1997; Dioc VIM Coun Dio Nthrn Michigan Marquette MI 1978-1979; Stnd Com Dio Nthrn Michigan Marquette MI 1974-1988; S Steph's Ch Escanaba MI 1971-1991; Cmncatns Dio Nthrn Michigan Marquette MI 1971-1985; Nomntns Com Bp Dio Nthrn Michigan Marquette MI 1971-1981; Vic S Jn's Ch Iron River MI 1967-1971; Vic S Mk's Ch Crystal Falls MI 1967-1971; Ch Of Our Sav Jenkintown PA 1965-1967; Asst Ch Of S Asaph Bala Cynwyd PA 1965-1967. "Beryllides - A Discussion," *Journ of Metals*, AIMME, 1962. k8n9392q@comcast.net

LIPPITT, Dudley Hand (Ga) 1704 11th Ave, Albany GA 31707 **D S Paul's Ch Albany GA 1989-** B Pelham GA 9/17/1930 d C W Hand & Mary. Georgia St U 1989. D 5/14/1989 Bp Harry Woolston Shipps. m 8/20/1954 Samuel Brown Lippitt c 4. slippitt@worldnet.att.net

LIPSCOMB III, C(harles) Lloyd (SwVa) 501 V E S Rd Apt B513, Lynchburg VA 24503 B Buffalo NY 8/17/1936 s C(harles) Lloyd Lipscomb & Mary Edith. BA U Roch 1958; MDiv Harvard DS 1961; VTS 1962. D 6/16/1963 P 6/21/1964 Bp William Henry Marmion. m 8/22/1964 Elizabeth Johnston c 3. R S Barn Ch Lynchburg VA 1971-1998; R Trin Epis Ch Lynchburg VA 1971-1998; Vic S Paul's Ch Todd NC 1967-1971; R S Thos' Epis Ch Abingdon VA 1967-1971; Asst S Paul's Epis Ch Winston Salem NC 1964-1967. R Emer S Barn and Trin Ch Lynchburg VA 2001. cllipscomb@ntelos.net

LIPSCOMB III, John W (CFla) 317 S Mary St, Eustis FL 32726 **S Thos Epis Ch Eustis FL 2011-** B Vero Beach FL 11/22/1966 s John William Lipscomb & Karyl Ann Knight. Grad Stds Ashbury TS; BA Johnson U 2002; MDiv Nash 2011. D 6/11/2011 Bp Hugo Luis Pina-Lopez. m 7/18/1987 Karen Hendricksen c 3. jwltres@yahoo.com

LIPSCOMB, R(andall) Steve (Kan) 3324 NW Bent Tree Ln, Topeka KS 66618 **Dn Gr Cathd Topeka KS 2001-** B Cartersville GA 2/1/1951 s Harry Melvin Lipscomb & Sara Nell. AS Georgia St U 1981; BS Kennesaw St U 1987; MDiv STUSo 1991. D 6/8/1991 P 1/1/1992 Bp Frank Kellogg Allan. m 7/22/1976 Robyn Denise Matthews c 1. Ch of the Resurr Sautee Nacoochee GA 1995-2001; Gr-Calv Epis Ch Clarkesville GA 1993-1995; Vic S Mary Magd Ch Columbus GA 1991-1993. Auth, "Proper Prefaces and Offertory Sentences for Years A, B, C," Ch Pub Grp, 2009; Auth, "Adv Sermons," *Sewanee Theol Revs*, The STUSo, 1998. rslipscomb@gracecathedraltopeka.org

LIPSEY, Howard Martin (Chi) 62 Malden Ave, La Grange IL 60525 B Oak Park IL 8/24/1934 s Albert William Lipsey & Margaret. BA U MI 1956; STB Ya Berk 1966. D 6/11/1966 Bp James Winchester Montgomery P 12/16/1966 Bp Gerald Francis Burrill. m 12/16/1961 Glenda Karen Taylor c 2. Vic Gr Ch Pontiac IL 1969-1970; Cur S Greg's Epis Ch Deerfield IL 1967-1969.

LIRO, Judith Reagan (Tex) 4301 N I H 35, Austin TX 78722 **Associaterector S Geo's Ch Austin TX 1984-** B San Antonio TX 12/2/1942 d Edgar Ullyses Green Reagan & Byrne Elaine. BA Colorado Coll 1964; MDiv Epis TS of The SW 1984. D 11/27/1984 Bp Maurice Manuel Benitez P 6/1/1985 Bp Gordon Taliaferro Charlton. m 6/4/1964 Joseph Julian Liro c 2. jliro@swbell.net

LISBY, Gregory C (RI) C/O Church Of The Ascension, 390 Pontiac Ave., Cranston RI 02910 **P-in-c Chr Ch Ridgewood NJ 2010-** B Indianapolis IN 5/8/1979 s Ricky Lisby & Karen. BSW Indiana U 2002; MSW Indiana U 2003; MDiv GTS 2006. D 6/24/2006 P 1/22/2007 Bp Catherine Elizabeth Maples Waynick. m 2/9/2010 Timothy Hinton Burger. R Ch Of The Ascen Cranston RI 2008-2010; Assoc S Mart's Ch Providence RI 2006-2008. glisby@gmail.com

LISLE, John (SwFla) 759 Norsota Way, Sarasota FL 34242 **Died 8/3/2009** B Philadelphia PA 1/24/1913 s John Lisle & Helen Willard. BS Leh 1935. D 6/19/1980 Bp Emerson Paul Haynes. m 1/22/1972 Hettie Joe Paull c 3.

LISTER, Craig Joseph (NC) 1731 Wilkins Dr, Sanford NC 27330 **R S Thos Epis Ch Sanford NC 2009-** B Camp Roberts CA 1/4/1953 s Herbert Earl Lister & Phyllis Jane. BA Amh 1975; MDiv EDS 1978. D 6/17/1978 Bp Quintin Ebenezer Primo Jr P 12/16/1978 Bp James Winchester Montgomery. m 11/25/1978 Nancy O O'Neil c 2. R S Mk's Ch Southborough MA 1998-2009; R S Dunst's Epis Ch Carmel Vlly CA 1991-1998; R S Thos Epis Ch Sanford NC 1984-1990; Asst S Jn's Chap Monterey CA 1981-1984; Cur Ch Of The H Comf Kenilworth IL 1978-1981. Fr. Michal Judge Awd Mass. Corps of Fire Chapl 2006. frcraig@charter.net

✠ **LITTLE II, Rt Rev Edward Stuart** (NI) 117 N Lafayette Blvd, South Bend IN 46601 **Bp of NI Dio Nthrn Indiana So Bend IN 2000-** B New York NY 1/29/1947 s Stuart Little & Bessie. BA USC 1968; MDiv SWTS 1971. D 6/19/1971 Bp Gerald Francis Burrill P 12/18/1971 Bp James Winchester Montgomery Con 3/18/2000 for NI. m 3/22/1968 Sylvia Gardner c 2. Chair Dioc Vision/Structure Com Epis Dio San Joaquin Modesto CA 1994-1997; Stndg Cmsn Evang Epis Dio San Joaquin Modesto CA 1989-1992; R All SS Ch Bakersfield CA 1986-2000; R S Jos's Par Buena Pk CA 1975-1986; Asst S Mich's Mssn Anaheim CA 1973-1975; Cur S Matt's Ch Evanston IL 1971-1973. Auth, "Bk," *Joy in Disguise: Meeting Jesus in the Dark Times*, Morehouse, 2009; Auth, "Bk," *Ears to Hear: Recognizing and Responding to God's Call*, Morehouse, 2003; Auth, "arts," *Journey Through Word*; Auth, "arts," *Living Ch*. Phi Beta Kappa 1967. DD SWTS 2000. bishop@ednin.org

LITTLE, Geoffery A (Ct) 358 Lenox Street, New Haven CT 06513 B Springfield MA 7/10/1960 s Derek Ralph Little & Dawn Thornton. BA Bow 1982; MDiv TESM 1992; ThM Fuller TS 2004. D 6/13/1992 Bp Arthur Edward Walmsley P 3/1/1993 Bp Jeffery William Rowthorn. c 2. Ch Mssn Soc Usa Inc New Haven CT 1998-2000; P-in-c S Jas' Ch New Haven CT 1994-2010; Ovrs Mnstrs Study Ctr New Haven CT 1992-1998; Asst R S Jn's Ch New Haven CT 1992-1994; SAMS Ambridge PA 1988-1992. Auth, "Discerning Your Mssy Call". geoff.little@cms-usa.org

LITTLE, Harry Robert (CNY) Po Box 396, Copenhagen NY 13626 B Brooklyn NY 9/7/1927 s Harry Little & Arabella Silvey. Long Island Dioc TS 1962. D 4/28/1962 P 12/21/1962 Bp James P De Wolfe. m 6/30/1951 Ruth Marion Conroy c 4. R Gr Ch Carthage NY 1980-1990; R Gr Ch Copenhagen NY 1980-1989; Cur Trin Ch Northport NY 1969-1980; P-in-c S Mk's Epis Ch Medford NY 1962-1969. New York St Assn Of Fire Chapl. hhrrl197@aol.com

LITTLE JR, I(chabod) Mayo (NC) 929 Mocksville Ave, Salisbury NC 28144 B Robersonville NC 10/24/1928 s Ichabod Mayo Little & Ethel. BS No Carolina St U 1951; VTS 1960. D 6/13/1960 P 1/30/1961 Bp Thomas H Wright. m 7/28/1962 Elizabeth Hill c 2. R S Lk's Ch Salisbury NC 1982-1993; R Calv Ch Tarboro NC 1972-1982; Assoc S Paul's Epis Ch Winston Salem NC 1968-1972; R S Andr's Ch Morehead City NC 1962-1968; Asst S Jas Par Wilmington NC 1960-1962. littlei@bellsouth.net

LITTLEFIELD, Jeffrey B (Ore) St. John the Baptist, 6300 SW Nicol Road, Portland OR 97223 **R S Barth's Ch Beaverton OR 2011-** B Salt Lake City UT 6/29/1966 s Diane Louise. Seattle U STM; BA Willamette U 1988; MDiv CDSP 2004. D 6/26/2004 Bp Vincent Waydell Warner P 12/4/2004 Bp William Edwin Swing. Assoc R Epis Par Of S Jn The Bapt Portland OR 2007-2011; Assoc R S Steph's Epis Ch Orinda CA 2004-2007. frjefflittlefield@gmail.com

LITTLEJOHN, Lucrecia Miranda (Tex) 8330 New World, San Antonio TX 78239 **Cn Pstr Chr Ch Cathd Houston TX 2002-** B Panama PA 10/22/1950 d Jose Miranda & Ana Maria. Cert Colegio Felix Olivares PA 1969; BA U of Texas 1994; MDiv STUSo 1997. D 6/24/1997 Bp Robert Boyd Hibbs P 2/1/1998 Bp James Edward Folts. m 7/31/1973 Iain P Littlejohn. Santa Fe Epis Mssn San Antonio TX 1997-2002. luchyl@christchurchcathedral.org

LITTLEJOHN, N. Richard (Alb) 14757 State Highway 37, Massena NY 13662 B Massena NY 12/4/1949 BS Clarkson U 1972; Cert St. Lawr Lewis B.O.C.E.S. 1988; Cert Dn Sch Trin Ch Postdam Ny 3yrs Ord 2003. D 6/28/2003 Bp Daniel William Herzog. m 5/10/1986 Catherine Jane LaFouce c 2. rrll@twinriversfcu.net

LITTLEPAGE, Dorothella Michel (At) 74 S Common St, Lynn MA 01902 B Huntsville AL 8/12/1984 d Willie T Littlepage & Harriett S. BS and BA Spelman Coll 2006; MDiv VTS 2011. D 12/18/2010 P 6/26/2011 Bp J(ohn) Neil Alexander. DMLITTLEPAGE@GMAIL.COM

LITTLETON, William Harvey (Ga) PO Box 20633, Saint Simons Island GA 31522 B Macon GA 8/14/1928 s George Leonard Littleton & Virginia. BA Emory U 1948; BD Candler TS Emory U 1951; PhD U Of Edinburgh Edinburgh Gb 1956; STM STUSo 1960. D 6/12/1960 P 12/1/1960 Bp Randolph R Claiborne. m 6/22/1951 Patricia Hammond c 3. Int S Patricks Ch Albany GA 1992-1993; Res Int P Chr Ch Epis Savannah GA 1990-1992; R S Andr's Epis Ch Douglas GA 1981-1990; Exec Bd Dio Texas Houston TX 1977-1980; Liturg Cmsn Dio Texas Houston TX 1977-1980; R S Paul's Ch Waco TX 1976-1981; BEC Dio Texas Houston TX 1974-1980; Mem of The Bd Dio Texas Houston TX 1974-1977; Cn Pstr Chr Ch Cathd Houston TX 1973-1976; R S Mk's Ch Beaumont TX 1966-1968; Dn of Convoc Dio Georgia Savannah GA 1963-1968; R H Trin Par Decatur GA 1963-1966; Exec Bd Dio Atlanta Atlanta GA 1961-1966; R S Steph's Ch Milledgeville GA 1961-1963; Asst S Lk's Epis Ch Atlanta GA 1960-1961; Asst To Chapl The TS at The U So Sewanee TN 1959-1960. Auth, "Gd Morning Forever," 1966.

LITTMAN, Valentine John (Eur) 10 Rue Moliere, Florensac 34510 France B Lockport NY 5/11/1948 s Walter John Littman & Rose Gertude. MDiv S Jn Vianney Sem 1973; MS Loyola U 1981. Rec from Roman Catholic 10/1/1980 Bp James Winchester Montgomery. m 12/2/1978 Linda Korolewski. H Trin Ch Skokie IL 1990-1991; Int S Alb's Ch Chicago IL 1988-1989; Dio Chicago Chicago IL 1981-1986; Asst Cathd Of S Jas Chicago IL 1980-1991. Employee Assistance Professionals Assn; NASW. mail@petitjardin.com

LITTRELL, James H (Pa) 213 E Cliveden St, Philadelphia PA 19119 **R S Mary's Ch Hamilton Vill Philadelphia PA 1997-** B Lexington VA 7/31/1943 s Ira Robert Littrell & Mary Geneva. BA Davidson Coll 1965; PDS 1970. D 6/6/1970 P 5/1/1971 Bp Robert Lionne DeWitt. m 10/12/1979 LM Skypala c 1. H Apos And Medtr Philadelphia PA 1980-1991; Hobart And Wm Smith Colleges Geneva NY 1977-1978; Trin Epis Ch Buffalo NY 1973-1977; DCE Ch Of S Mart-In-The-Fields Philadelphia PA 1968-1972. Int Mnstry Ntwk. Citizenship Awd Natl Coun Of Christians & Jews 1995. jhlittrell@aol.com

LITWINSKI, Tony (Haw) Mauritiusplatz 1, Wiesbaden MI D65183 Germany **R Ch of S Aug of Cbury 65189 Wiesbaden DE 2010-** B Highland Park MI 7/23/1947 s Harry Adam Litwinski & Dorothy Marie. BA Sacr Heart Sem Coll Detroit MI 1969; STB Pontifical Gregorian U Rome It 1972; STL Pontifical Gregorian U Rome It 1976; ABD Westphalian Wilhelm Universty 1980; MBA City U of Seattle 1988. Rec from Roman Catholic 6/2/2001 as Priest Bp William Edwin Swing. m 4/19/1986 Jana L Johnsen. Cathd Bd Dio Hawaii Honolulu HI 2009-2010; Planned Giving Cmsn Dio Hawaii Honolulu HI 2008-2010; Asst Treas Dio Hawaii Honolulu HI 2005-2008; R S Jas Epis Ch Kamuela HI 2003-2010; Dioc Coun Dio Hawaii Honolulu HI 2003-2008; Cn Bursar Gr Cathd San Francisco CA 2001-2002; Personl Cmsn Dio California San Francisco CA 1997-2002; Fin Com Dio California San Francisco CA 1996-2002. tony.litwinski@gmail.com

LITZENBERGER, Caroline Jae (Ore) 3624 Ne Holman St, Portland OR 97211 **S Matt's Epis Ch Portland OR 2011-** B Tacoma WA 11/2/1942 BS U of Washington 1964; MA Portland St U 1989; PhD U of Cambridge 1993; CTh CDSP 2003. D 5/10/2003 Bp Robert Louis Ladehoff P 1/3/2004 Bp Johncy Itty. Dio Oregon Portland OR 2010; S Anne's Epis Ch Washougal WA 2010; Asst Epis Par Of S Jn The Bapt Portland OR 2003-2004; S Mich And All Ang Ch Portland OR 2003-2004. "Communal Ritual Concealed Belief: Layers Of Response To The Regulation Of Ritual In Reformation Engl," Camb Press, 2004; "Defining The Ch Of Engl: Rel Change In The 1570s," Schlr Press, 1998; "Loc Responses To Rel Changes: Evidence From Gloucestershire Wills," 16th Century Journ Pub, 1998; "The Engl Reformation And The Laity," Camb Press, 1997. litzenbergerc@pdx.edu

LITZENBURG JR, Thomas Vernon (SwVa) 316 Jefferson St, Lexington VA 24450 B Baltimore MD 10/18/1933 s Thomas Vernon Litzenburg & Charlotte Lee. BA W&L 1957; BD Yale DS 1961; MA Pr 1963; PhD Pr 1965. P 5/1/1963 Bp William Henry Marmion. m 8/21/1976 Jayne Dolton c 3. Hon Asst Trin Ch Swarthmore PA 1962-1964. Auth, "Intellctl Honesty & Rel Commitment". tlitzenb@wlu.edu

LIU, Ting-hua (Tai) I-105-7 Hang Chou South Road, Silo Taiwan B 3/31/1939 s Pu-Ching Liu & Kuei. MDiv Tainan Theol Coll Tw; BD Tainan Theol Coll Tw 1966. D 5/21/1967 P 11/30/1967 Bp James Chang L Wong. m 1/16/1967 Su-tsu Li. Auth, "Angl Chant In Chinese". lthmike@ksts.seed.net.tw

LIVELY, James William (CFla) 11610 Chantilly Ct, Clermont FL 34711 **R S Mths Epis Ch Clermont FL 2006-** B Indianapolis IN 12/27/1962 s Daniel William Lively & Elizabeth Ann. BA U Of Cntrl Florida 1997; MDiv STUSo 2002. D 6/8/2002 P 12/7/2002 Bp John Wadsworth Howe. m 11/16/1996 Tracy B Bartlett c 2. Chr Ch Grosse Pointe Grosse Pointe Farms MI 2003-2006; Asst S Jas Epis Ch Ormond Bch FL 2002-2003. jwlively@gmail.com

LIVERMORE, Charles Whittier (ETenn) 7604 Windwood Dr, Powell TN 37849 **Trin Epis Ch Gatlinburg TN 1999-** B Rochester MN 5/25/1949 s George Robertson Livermore & Nancy. BA Westminster Coll 1971; MDiv VTS 1978. D 7/2/1978 Bp William Evan Sanders P 5/1/1979 Bp William F Gates Jr. m 6/17/1978 Diane Debra Smith. Ch Of The Gd Shpd Knoxville TN 1983-1987; P-in-c S Mary Magd Ch Fayetteville TN 1979-1985; D St Jas Epis Ch at Knoxville Knoxville TN 1978-1979. charleslivermore@charter.net

LIVERPOOL, Herman Oswald (Fla) 3405 Nw 48th Ave, # JJ413, Lauderdale Lakes FL 33319 B GY 2/12/1925 s Joseph Nathaniel Liverpool & Hilda Beatrice. Codrington Coll; BA U of The W Indies 1977; MBTh IBIS 1985. Trans from Church in the Province Of The West Indies 11/1/1983. m 6/1/1953 Lucielle Joycelyn Cleaver c 3. P-in-c S Cyp's St Aug FL 1983-1995. "Play," *Ruth and Naomi*, 2008; Auth, "Play," *The Prodigal Son*, 2007; Auth, *A Second Collection of Poems*, 2000; Auth, "The Days Last Ride," *Melodies of the Soul by the Natl Libr of Poetry*, 1998; Auth, "An Immigrants Dilemma," *Passages of Light by the Natl Libr of Poetry*, 1997; Auth, *Collection of Poems*. Bro of S Andrews 2000; Fndr of Friends of S Cyp; Intl Soc of Poets 2000; Vicars Landing -A Ret Cmnty 1988-1991. Hon DD IBIS 1986.

LIVINGOOD, Randel Eugene (SanD) 814 Ne Clyde Place, Grants Pass OR 97526 B North Hollywood CA 8/8/1957 s Max Eugene Livingood & Theresa Louise. BS Lee U 1989; MDiv Ch of God TS 1992; DMin Columbia TS 1996. D 9/21/2000 P 3/4/2001 Bp Gethin Benwil Hughes. m 11/4/1978 Nancy Strong. Cur S Lk's Ch Grants Pass OR 2006-2010. frrandel@mac.com

LIVINGSTON, Diane Howard (Miss) 37 Sheffield Place, Brevard NC 28712 **D S Ptr's By The Sea Gulfport MS 2007-; D The Epis Ch Of The Gd Shpd Columbus MS 2003-** B Vicksburg MS 12/29/1949 d Ernest E Howard & Joy Gamlen. BA SMU 1972; MA Mississippi Coll 1977. D 1/4/2003 Bp Alfred Clark Marble Jr. m 8/26/1977 William Vernon Livingston c 3. D S Alb's Ch Hickory NC 2010-2011; Chapl Coast Epis Schools Inc Long Bch MS 2008-2011; D Chr Ch Bay St Louis MS 2006-2007; D Ch Of The Resurr Starkville MS 2004-2006. Pike Cnty Citizen of the Year Enterprise Journ 1987. rector_bill@bellsouth.net

LIVINGSTON, James (NMich) 3135 County Road 456, Skandia MI 49885 B 10/21/1940 D 12/17/2000 P 7/1/2001 Bp James Arthur Kelsey. m 6/21/1986 Gwendolyn Kay Hetler. jlivings@nmu.edu

LIVINGSTON, James (WA) 31641 La Novia Ave, San Juan Capistrano CA 92675 **S Marg Of Scotland Par San Juan Capistrano CA 2011-** B Montgomery AL 1/4/1976 s Lee Malton Livingston & Martha P. BA U of Florida 1998; BS/MS Florida Coll of Integrated Med 2005; MDiv VTS 2011. D 6/4/2011 Bp John Chane. m 11/4/2011 Joanne J McCall c 1. S Marg's Epis Sch San Juan Capo CA 2011. jameslvin@gmail.com

LIVINGSTON, Leon Arnold (RG) Po Box 1296, Mesilla Park NM 88047 B Ranger TX 11/6/1928 s Carl B Livingston & Lillian Irene. BS New Mex St U. 1957. D 12/2/1984 P 6/1/1985 Bp Richard Mitchell Trelease Jr. m 6/5/1954 Margaret Jane Smith.

LIVINGSTON, Philip Irving Conant (EpisSanJ) 341 Arthur Ave, Aptos CA 95003 B San Jose CA 6/28/1931 s Frank Chester Livingston & Jessie Pearl. BA Ripon Coll Ripon WI 1954; MDiv Nash 1957. D 1/29/1957 P 8/17/1957 Bp William Hampton Brady. m 9/2/1973 Kateri Alice Picou. Vic Ch Of S Mary Of The Snows Eagle River WI 1970-1972; Vic Ch Of The H Apos Oneida WI 1967-1969; Cn To Bp Dio Fond du Lac Appleton WI 1960-1972; Vic S Bon Plymouth WI 1958-1960; R S Paul's Ch Plymouth WI 1958-1960; Cur S Andr's Ch Baltimore MD 1957-1958. Auth, "Brethren In Unity," Par Press, Fond Du Lac, Wi, 1963. piclivingston@sbcglobal.net

LIVINGSTON, William Vernon (Miss) 37 Sheffield Place, Brevard NC 28712 **Fac Mem Credo Inst Inc. Memphis TN 2011-; Mem of Pstr Response Team Dio Wstrn No Carolina Asheville NC 2011-; Epis Relief & Dvlpmt Journey Partnr Mem Ecusa / Mssn Personl New York NY 2010-; Epis Relief & Dvlpmt Partnr in Repsonse Mem Ecusa / Mssn Personl New York NY 2010-** B Vicksburg MS 1/21/1951 s Edward Floyd Livingston & Marjorie Louise. BA Mississippi St U 1973; Med Delta St U 1975; MDiv Epis TS of The SW 1999. D 3/13/1999 Bp C(harles) Wallis Ohl P 10/2/1999 Bp Alfred Clark Marble Jr. m 8/26/1977 Diane Howard Guider c 3. Int S Alb's Ch Hickory NC 2009-2011; Chair of Stndg Com Dio Mississippi Jackson MS 2008-2009; Mem of Stndg Com Dio Mississippi Jackson MS 2006-2008; Vice-Pres of Exec Com Dio Mississippi Jackson MS 2005-2006; Mem of Alum Strng Com Epis TS Of The SW Austin TX 2004-2009; Mem of Exec Com Dio Mississippi Jackson MS 2003-2005; R Ch Of The Resurr Starkville MS 2002-2006; All S's Sch Trst Dio Mississippi Jackson MS 2000-2011; R Chr Epis Ch Vicksburg MS 1999-2002; Stdt Body Pres and Mem of the Trst Epis TS Of The SW Austin TX 1998-1999. co-Auth, "Attendee Help Seeking Behavior after Hurricane Katrina in Mississippi and Louisiana," *Intl Journ of Emergency Mntl Hlth*, 2011; Auth, "From Honeymoon to Disillusionment to Reconstruction: Recognizing Healthy and Unhealthy Coping Mechanisms," *Disaster Sprtl Care: Practical Cler Responses to Cmnty, Reg and Natl Tragedy*, SkyLight Paths, 2008. Paul Harris Fell Paul Harris Fell 1992; DSA

Natl Coun of Cmnty Mntl Hlth Centers 1989; Pike Cnty Boss of the Year Bus and Profsnl Wmn 1987. rector_bill@bellsouth.net

LIZ LOPEZ, Ramon A (PR) PO Box 6814, Elizabeth NJ 07202 **Dio Puerto Rico S Just PR 2009-** B Tambori Domincan Republic 9/10/1954 s Juan Liz & Gregoria. CAS San Pedro Y San Pablo Sem Trujillo Allo Puerto Rico; MDiv Word Educ Serv Inc. San Juan PR. m 12/4/1993 Jacqueline Liz c 2. Vic Gr Epis Ch Eliz NJ 2004-2009; Dio Puerto Rico S Just PR 1997-2004.

LJUNGGREN, M Lorraine (NC) 5400 Crestview Rd, Raleigh NC 27609 **1st Alt Dep to GC Dio No Carolina Raleigh NC 2011-2014; Pres, Stndg Com Dio No Carolina Raleigh NC 2011-2012; R S Mk's Epis Ch Raleigh NC 1999-** B Columbia SC 5/26/1949 d Robert Clarence Ljunggren & Margaret Elizabeth. AA Palm Bch Cmnty Coll 1969; BA Florida St U 1971; MDiv STUSo 1991. D 5/25/1991 Bp Calvin Onderdonk Schofield Jr P 1/4/1992 Bp Robert Hodges Johnson. m 11/17/2009 James Stanley Melnyk c 1. R S Jn's Epis Ch Marion NC 1992-1999; Chapl Kanuga Confererences Inc Hendersonville NC 1991. Assn of Dioc Liturg & Mus Commissions; EPF; Epis Publ Plcy Ntwk; Interfaith Allnce for Justice. Woods Ldrshp Awd U So Sewanee TN 1989. lorraine.ljunggren@stmarks-ral.org

LJUNGGREN, Timothy Merle (Mont) 62 Greenway Dr, Goshen IN 46526 **Ch Of The Incarn Great Falls MT 2004-** B Tucson AZ 11/26/1957 s Philip Gustaf Ljunggren & Cecelia Kathryn. BA SUNY 1991; MDiv Bex 1994. D 6/3/1994 P 4/24/1995 Bp Andrew Hedtler Fairfield. m 6/9/1990 Jane Lesley MacDonald c 4. S Jn Of The Cross Bristol IN 1997-2004; Trin Ch Wauwatosa WI 1994-1997. timandjane@juno.com

LLERENA FIALLOS, Angel Polivio (EcuC) Apartado 89, Guaranda, Provincia De Bolivar Ecuador **Vic Cntrl Dio Ecuador EC 1990-** B Godranda EC 12/28/1967 s Manuel Llerena & Isabel. Coll; Sem (3 Yrs). D 5/1/1990 Bp Adrian Delio Caceres-Villavicencio. m 3/12/1981 Maritza Esthela Martinez Dovilar.

LLOYD II, Arthur Selden (Mil) 1104 Mound St Apt A, Madison WI 53715 B Osaka JP 12/5/1927 s James Hubard Lloyd & Louisa Barton. BA U of Virginia 1950; BD VTS 1956; STM Yale DS 1968; MS U of Wisconsin 1974. D 6/1/1956 Bp Frederick D Goodwin P 12/19/1956 Bp Henry W Hobson. m 9/24/1960 Susan Ellsworth Scherr c 2. Dio Milwaukee Milwaukee WI 1988-1993; Com MHE Dio Milwaukee Milwaukee WI 1968-1977; Chapl S Fran Ch Madison WI 1968-1977; S Fran Hse U Epis Ctr Madison WI 1968-1977; Prov Vic Dio Milwaukee Milwaukee WI 1968-1976; Dept Coll Wk Dio Milwaukee Milwaukee WI 1968-1970; Brazil Comp Dioc Com Dio Indianapolis Indianapolis IN 1961-1967; Dept Coll Wk Dio Indianapolis Indianapolis IN 1961-1964; Asst The Ch of the Redeem Cincinnati OH 1956-1961. Auth, "Freire," *Conscientization & Adult Educ*. Epis Ntwk for Econ Justice 1996; EUC 1980. Phi Beta Kappa. aslloyd@mailbag.com

LLOYD, Dennis (Pa) 615 - 6th Avenue South, Nashville TN 37203 **Ch Of The H Apos Wynnewood PA 2008-** B Everett WA 7/30/1954 s Calvin Carl Lloyd & Barbara. BA U of Washington 1977; MDiv Nash 1980. D 8/6/1981 P 6/22/1982 Bp Robert Hume Cochrane. m 6/17/1995 Pamela Satterfield c 3. P-in-c Ch Of The H Trin Nashville TN 1991-2008; Asst S Simon's On The Sound Ft Walton Bch FL 1983-1988; Cur S Andrews Epis Ch Port Angeles WA 1981-1983. holytrinity@ourchurch.com

LLOYD, Donald Wallace (Colo) 1200 Dominican Drive, Madison MS 39110 **Died 10/17/2010** B Randolph WI 2/4/1912 s Lewis Lloyd & Blanche B. DD Nash 1962. D 5/24/1937 P 1/24/1938 Bp Ernest M Stires. DD Nash 1962.

LLOYD, Elizabeth Anne (Chi) 322 Farragut St, Park Forest IL 60466 **D Ch Of The H Fam Pk Forest IL 2002-** B Duluth MN 11/30/1937 d Bruce Charles Potter & Margaret Mackay. BA U MN 1959. D 2/2/2002 Bp William Dailey Persell. m 2/23/1963 George Stephen Lloyd c 2. AED (Assn for Epis Deacons) 2001. elizabeth_lloyd@comcast.net

LLOYD, James Edward (NJ) Apdo Postal 803, La Cristsina 50-5, Ajijic CHIAPAS 45920 Mexico B Portland OR 2/19/1939 s Cleo James Lloyd & Dorothy Grace. BS Portland St U 1963; BD Nash 1966. D 6/22/1966 Bp James Walmsley Frederic Carman P 12/1/1966 Bp Hal Raymond Gross. c 1. Timber Creek Epis Area Mnstry Gloucester City NJ 1997; Liturg Cmsn Dio Pennsylvania Philadelphia PA 1984; S Barn Ch Burlington NJ 1980-1994; Assoc Ch Of S Lk And Epiph Philadelphia PA 1977-1980; Cur S Clements Ch Philadelphia PA 1974-1977; Ch Of The Epiph Lake Oswego OR 1973-1974; Dioc Coun Dio Oregon Portland OR 1972-1973; Asst The Epis Ch Of The Gd Samar Corvallis OR 1972-1973; Chair On The Dioc Ecum Com Dio Oregon Portland OR 1971-1973; Liturg Cmsn Dio Oregon Portland OR 1970-1973; Vic S Chris's Ch Port Orford OR 1966-1971; Vic S Jn-By-The-Sea Epis Ch Bandon OR 1966-1971. Chapl Fndr & Patriots Of Amer; CBS, GAS, Epis Actor'S Gld, Chapl Mltry Ord Crusades. Human Awd Philadelphia 1979. jelajijic@yahoo.com

LLOYD, John Janney (NY) 115 Iroquois Rd, Yonkers NY 10710 **P-in-c Ch Of S Jas The Less Jamaica NY 2002-** B Wakayama JP 4/10/1920 s James Edward Lloyd & Louisa. BA U of Virginia 1941; MDiv VTS 1947; MA Harv 1954. D 2/1/1947 Bp Henry St George Tucker P 8/9/1947 Bp Frederick D Goodwin. m 12/19/1953 Elisabeth Chaplin c 5. Vic S Jos's Ch Bronx NY 1998-2000; Int All SS Epis Ch Vlly Cottage NY 1995-1997; Int S Jas' Ch No Salem NY 1992-1994; S Andr's Epis Ch Hartsdale NY 1986-1991; R Calv Ch Tamaqua PA 1983-1986; R S Jas' Ch Drifton PA 1983-1986; No Lackawanna Vlly Par Olyphant PA 1980-1983; Assoc All SS Ch Worcester MA 1973-1980; R S Andr's Ch Belmont MA 1968-1973. jjlyonkers@aol.com

LLOYD, Kevin Michael (RI) 67 Mount Hope Ave, Jamestown RI 02835 **Mem of Cmsn on Congrl Dvlpmt Dio Rhode Island Providence RI 2010-; Secy of Conv Dio Rhode Island Providence RI 2009-; R S Matt's Par Of Jamestown Jamestown RI 2006-** B Urbana IL 3/22/1971 s Harry Davidson Lloyd & Susan Moore. BA Wake Forest U 1993; MDiv VTS 2001. D 6/4/2001 P 11/24/2002 Bp Robert Hodges Johnson. m 1/7/2000 Julia A McLaughlin c 2. Asst R Ch Of The Ascen Hickory NC 2002-2006. The Harris Awd VTS 2001; cl Wake Forest U 1993. revlloyd22@verizon.net

LLOYD, Lucia Kendall (Va) PO Box 158, Tappahannock VA 22560 **R S Steph's Ch Heathsville VA 2008-** B Philadelphia PA 6/20/1968 d Wallace Crane Kendall & Susan Jean. BA Davidson Coll 1990; MA Yale DS 1994; MA Mid 1995; MDiv VTS 2005. D 6/18/2005 P 12/19/2005 Bp Peter James Lee. m 6/29/1996 Marshall Lloyd c 2. Asst R S Thos' Ch Richmond VA 2005-2008. lucialloyd@verizon.net

LLOYD, Margaret (Mass) 4 Berkeley Street, Cambridge MA 02138 **Dio Massachusetts Boston MA 2008-** B Bryn Mawr PA 2/2/1953 d Joseph Neff Ewing & Margaret. Wheaton Coll 1972; BA Br 1975; Andover Newton TS 1989; MDiv EDS 1996. D 6/5/1996 Bp M(arvil) Thomas Shaw III P 2/8/1997 Bp Arthur Edward Walmsley. m 1/1/2011 Katherine Hancock Ragsdale c 3. Chr Ch Par Plymouth MA 2002-2008; Int Chr Ch Needham MA 2001; Assoc Chr Ch Needham MA 1996-2000. EWC 1995; Massachusetts Cler Assn 1996; Philips Brooks Club 2000; Recently Ord Cler, Co-Cnvnr 1998-2009. mallyl@diomass.org

LLOYD, Robert Baldwin (SwVa) 3204 Mathews Ln., Blacksburg VA 24060 B Nojiri Japan 8/1/1926 s James Hubard Lloyd & Louisa Barton. BA U of Virginia 1951; BD VTS 1954; DD Epis TS In Kentucky 1982; DD VTS 1983. D 6/4/1954 P 6/1/1955 Bp Robert Fisher Gibson Jr. m 6/5/1954 Mary Ellen West c 3. P-in-c S Paul's Mssn Amherst VA 1990-2007; Exec Bd Dio SW Virginia Roanoke VA 1990-1992; Exec Bd Dio SW Virginia Roanoke VA 1984-1986; EAM Knoxville TN 1969-1991; Supply Emm Chap Blacksburg VA 1954-1997; M-in-c Ch of the Incarn Mineral VA 1954-1958. Auth, "Poems, Var"; Auth, "Coun Sthrn Moutains In Transition"; Auth, "The Need For Phase-Out Of Strip Mining"; Auth, "Quarterly"; Auth, "Art 1"; Auth, "Plumblines"; Auth, "Admidst Devstatn & Desprtn Appalachians Celebrate Lifes Wholeness"; Auth, "Tn Churchman"; Auth, "Redemp Denied: An Appalachian Rdr"; Auth, "Remembrance"; Auth, "The Return"; Auth, "What Is A Mo?"; Auth, "Alas," *Oh Desecrated Mountains*. roidob@yahoo.com

LLOYD III, Samuel Thames (WA) 290 Beacon Street #5, Boston MA 02116 **P-in-c Trin Ch In The City Of Boston Boston MA 2011-** B Brookhaven MS 6/24/1950 s Samuel Thames Lloyd & Marie Anne. BA U of Mississippi 1971; MA Geo 1975; PhD U of Virginia 1981; MDiv VTS 1981. D 6/24/1981 P 4/1/1982 Bp Duncan Montgomery Gray Jr. m 7/3/1976 Marguerite Cooper McCain c 2. Dn Cathd of St Ptr & St Paul Washington DC 2005-2011; R Trin Ch In The City Of Boston Boston MA 1993-2005; Chapl The U So (Sewanee) Sewanee TN 1988-1993; R Ch Of S Paul And The Redeem Chicago IL 1984-1988; S Paul's Memi Charlottesville VA 1981-1984. Auth, ""Gd News for Castaways: Thoughts of a U Chapl,"EvangES Nwsltr," 1992; Auth, "Var Revs,Journ of Rel, Virginia Sem Journ, Sewanee Theol Revs". Ord of S Jn 2008. DD VTS 2006; DD VTS 2003; DD Laf 2000; DD U So TS 1999; DD U So 1996. stlloyd3@gmail.com

LLOYD, Sharon (Vt) 386South St, Middlebury VT 05753 B Cincinnati OH 11/19/1946 d Dale Edwin Lloyd & Adelaide Elizabeth. MDiv GTS; BA U of Maryland 1970; VTS 1974. D 2/10/1979 P 11/1/1979 Bp Morgan Porteus. m 7/25/1986 Arthur St Leger Grindon c 1. Vic S Paul's Epis Ch Wells VT 1991-1993; Asst S Steph's Ch Middlebury VT 1987-1990; Assoc Chr And S Steph's Ch New York NY 1984-1987; Fell The GTS New York NY 1982-1986; Co-R S Andr's Epis Ch Lincoln Pk NJ 1981-1982; S Jn's Ch Stamford CT 1979-1981. Auth, "Var arts". SGRINDON@GMAIL.COM

LLUMIGUANO AREVALO, Nancy (EcuC) Sarmiento, Quito Ecuador B Guarando Bolivar 10/26/1977 d Jose Jenacio Llumiguano & Maria. m 12/25/2004 Mauro Armijos c 1. Ecuador New York NY 2006-2009. nancymlla@latinmail.com

LO, Peter Kwan Ho (Los) 133 E Graves Ave, Monterey Park CA 91755 **R S Gabr's Par Monterey Pk CA 2007-** B Hong Kong 10/24/1954 s Cheung Ming Lo & Yuk Ying. BD Chung Chi Coll 1984; MBA Sterling U 1991; LLB Lon 1999. Trans from Church Of England 12/5/2007 Bp Joseph Jon Bruno. m 8/30/1982 Mei Chung Lau c 2. peterkwanholo@hotmail.com

LOBBAN, Andrew David (WTex) PO Box 6885, San Antonio TX 78209 **Dio W Texas San Antonio TX 2011-** B Palo Alto CA 9/5/1975 s Peter Edward Lobban & Nina Clara. SB M.I.T. 1997; MA U CA 1999; MDiv Sem of the SW 2011. D 6/29/2011 Bp David Mitchell Reed. m 6/12/1999 Olga Olga Barbara Dubois c 2. lobban.andrew@gmail.com

L

LOBDELL, Gary Thomas (Oly) 17320 Red Hawk Ct, Mount Vernon WA 98274 B Spokane WA 3/4/1953 s Harry Richard Lobdell & Dolores Jean. BS WA SU 1975; MS WA SU 1978; MA Seattle U 1993; MDiv CDSP 2004. D 6/26/2004 Bp Vincent Waydell Warner P 1/8/2005 Bp Charles Franklin Brookhart Jr. m 7/12/1975 Carrie Powers c 2. Assoc S Aid's Epis Ch Camano Island WA 2008-2011; R Ch Of The H Fam Mills River NC 2005-2007; Asst Ch Of The H Sprt Missoula MT 2004-2005. gtlobdell@hotmail.com

LOBELL, John James (Md) 4990 Dorsey Hall Dr Unit C4, Ellicott City MD 21042 **Died 7/26/2010** B Baltimore MD 12/12/1923 s James Vincent Lobell & Lillian May. BA St. Jn's Coll Annapolis MD 1949; BD VTS 1964. D 6/22/1964 P 5/26/1965 Bp Harry Lee Doll. c 4. "An Ignatian Sprtl Pract," *Faith At Wk*, 2007; "Examen," *Faith At Wk*, 2006. johnlobell@comcast.net

LOBS, Donna Burkard (CFla) 336 Oak Estates Dr, Orlando FL 32806 B Abingdon PA 12/2/1942 d Frank Burkard & Lillian Ellen. BS E Stroudsburg U 1964. D 12/26/1987 Bp Frank Tracy Griswold III. m 3/21/1964 George Richard Lobs c 3. D Cathd Ch Of S Lk Orlando FL 1994-2002; D S Mk's Ch Geneva IL 1987-1993. Mourners Path Facility 1999; NAAD 1989; Steph Mnstry 1998. dlobs42@aol.com

LOBS III, George Richard (CFla) 128 Legacy Dr, Advance NC 27006 **Int Trin Ch Vero Bch FL 2008-** B Philadelphia PA 11/15/1942 s George Richard Lobs. BS E Stroudsburg U; MDiv PDS; DMin Trin-Deerfield. D 5/25/1968 P 4/20/1969 Bp Frederick J Warnecke. m 3/21/1964 Donna Burkard Lobs. S Mk's Ch Geneva IL 1979-1993; S Steph's Epis Ch Mckeesport PA 1973-1979. Auth, "arts". deanlobs1@yahoo.com

LOBSINGER, Eric John (Mo) 2430 K St NW, Washington DC 20037 B Belleville IL 8/30/1978 s Stephen John Lobsinger & Fusayo. AB Washington U 2000; JD Washington U 2003; LLM Kyushu U 2004; LLD Kyushu U 2007. D 5/13/2010 Bp George Wayne Smith. ejlobsinger@yahoo.com

LOCH, C Louanne (Fla) Holy Trinity Episcopal Church, 100 NE 1st St, Gainesville FL 32601 **BEC Dio Florida Jacksonville FL 2010-; H Trin Ch Gainesville FL 2007-** B Charleston SC 4/18/1962 d Louis Vernon Mabry & Frances Elizabeth. BS Mississippi Coll 1983; Mississippi Coll 1991; MDiv VTS 1995; U of Phoenix 2003; Cert U of Notre Dame 2006. D 6/17/1995 Bp Alfred Clark Marble Jr P 2/1/1996 Bp Robert Wilkes Ihloff. m 11/21/1998 Walter Eric Loch. Chair, Conv Nomin Com Dio Florida Jacksonville FL 2010; R S Jn's Epis Ch Fayetteville NC 2003-2007; S Mths' Epis Ch Baltimore MD 1999-2003; Com on Evang Dio Maryland Baltimore MD 1997-2003; Cmsn on Const and Cn Dio Maryland Baltimore MD 1996-2000; Asst S Thos' Ch Garrison Forest Owings Mills MD 1995-1999; Bp Com on Chr/Jewish Relatns Dio Maryland Baltimore MD 1995-1997; Bp Com on Chr/Jewish Relatns Dio Maryland Baltimore MD 1995-1997; Curs Dio Mississippi Jackson MS 1990; Curs Dio Mississippi Jackson MS 1990. Curs 1990; Soc S Aid and Hilda 1995. louloch424@hotmail.com

LOCH, Jerry Lynn (Chi) 446 Somonauk St, Sycamore IL 60178 B Bloomington IL 11/16/1945 s Harold Weiler Loch & Florence. Eureka Coll 1965; NE Missouri St U 1966; S Lk Hosp Sch Nrsng 1968; S Jn Hosp Sch Anesthesiology 1970; BS Chicago St U 1974; BA Chicago St U 1981; MS Columbia Pacific U 1983; Cert Shalem Inst Washington DC 1984; PhD Emory U 1986; Chicago Deacons Sch 1989. D 12/2/1989 Bp Frank Tracy Griswold III. m 9/18/1977 Kay Lynn Hintzeche c 3.

LOCHNER, Charles Nugent (NJ) 2106 5th Ave, Spring Lake NJ 07762 B Utica NY 11/14/1944 s Walter Joseph Lochner & Kathryn Julia. BA La Salette Sem Ipswitch MA 1967; MA CUA 1971; MRE S Thos U Houston TX 1973; MS Iona Coll,New Rocelle,NY 1985. Rec from Roman Catholic 5/17/1997 Bp John Shelby Spong. m 6/7/1980 Jeanie Masone c 5. R S Ptr's Ch Spotswood NJ 2001-2008; Int Gr Ch Van Vorst Jersey City NJ 2000-2001; Ch Of The Atone Tenafly NJ 1997-2000. Compsr, "Winter In My Life," JC Enterprises, 1986; Compsr, "Just One Man," JC Enterprises, 1986; Contributer, "Being Human in the Face of Death," IBS Press. candjlochner@aol.com

LOCK, John Mason (RG) 6400 N Pennsylvania Ave, Nichols Hills OK 73116 **Cur All Souls Epis Ch Oklahoma City OK 2008-** B Alburquerque NM 1/19/1982 s William Joseph Lock & Judith Marie. BA U of Delaware 2003; M.Div. TESM 2008. D 6/7/2008 Bp William Carl Frey P 5/9/2009 Bp Edward Joseph Konieczny. m 6/10/2006 Bonnie J Wilson c 2. manny4twins@yahoo.com

LOCKARD, Robert Noel (Ala) 1912 Canyon Rd, Birmingham AL 35216 B Saint Petersburg FL 11/13/1928 s DV Lockard & Margaret G. BA U So 1952; BD STUSo 1955. D 6/16/1955 P 2/1/1956 Bp Frank A Juhan. m 4/25/1958 Mary Louise Smith. R Epis Ch Of The Ascen Birmingham AL 1972-2000; R S Thad Epis Ch Aiken SC 1966-1968; R S Paul's Ch Columbus MS 1964-1966; Vic S Paul's Ch Memphis TN 1960-1964; Assoc Chr Ch Greenville SC 1958-1960; M-in-c H Trin Epis Ch Pensacola FL 1955-1958; M-in-c S Monica's Cantonment FL 1955-1958. Bronze Star w Combat.

LOCKE, Carol Ann (Los) 61 Painter St Apt 1, Pasadena CA 91103 B Buffalo NY 1/9/1947 d William Held & Catherine. BS SUNY 1968; MA Luth TS at Phila 1970. D 1/18/2003 Bp John Bailey Lipscomb. c 3. D All SS Par Los Angeles CA 2006-2008; Dir Of Yth Mnstrs S Hilary's Ch Ft Myers FL 2003-2004. caroll62001@yahoo.com

LOCKE, Kay (Nwk) 15 Norwood Ave, Summit NJ 07901 B Raleigh NC 9/27/1937 d William Henry Newell & Nell Bernard. AB Duke 1959; MDiv Drew U 1995. D 11/1/2003 P 5/15/2004 Bp John Palmer Croneberger. c 2. Assn of Epis Healthcare Chapl 1999. Kay.Locke@atlantichealth.org

LOCKE, Ralph Donald (CNY) 11 Orange St, Marcellus NY 13108 **Vic Gr Ch Willowdale Geneva NY 2001-** B Geneva NY 2/1/1931 s Dayton O Locke & Mary. BA SUNY 1987; MDiv Bex 1992. D 6/13/1992 P 1/2/1993 Bp William George Burrill. m 2/19/1955 Nancy Arlene Wright. Vic S Jn's Ch Marcellus NY 1993-2001; D Gr Ch Willowdale Geneva NY 1992-1993. Grand Chap New York Masonic Lodge 1994.

LOCKE, William Russell (RI) 63 Pidge Avenue, Pawtucket RI 02860 **Dioc Coun Dio Rhode Island Providence RI 2010-; GC Dep Dio Rhode Island Providence RI 2006-; R S Paul's Ch Pawtucket RI 2002-** B Erie PA 7/23/1953 s Clarence Edwin Locke & Joan Elizabeth. U II. 1973; BA U of Massachusetts 1981; MDiv EDS 1986. D 12/27/1993 P 7/9/1994 Bp George Nelson Hunt III. m 8/23/1980 Ethel R Cooke c 2. Stndg Com Dio Rhode Island Providence RI 2006-2010; R Ch Of The Gd Shpd Pawtucket RI 1994-2002. Soc Of Cath Priests 2009; Soc of S Marg 1977. frbill@cox.net

LOCKETT, Donna Alcorn (CGC) 102 Shadow Ln, Troy AL 36079 **Ch Of The Epiph Enterprise AL 2008-** B Brookville PA 7/19/1941 D 7/26/2003 P 6/26/2004 Bp Philip Menzie Duncan II. m 4/21/1962 Thomas Walter Lockett c 2. S Jas Ch Eufaula AL 2004-2005; S Mk's Epis Ch Troy AL 2003. dalockett@bellsouth.net

LOCKETT, Harold John (At) 586 Lynn Valley Rd SW, Atlanta GA 30311 **R S Tim's Decatur GA 2006-** B Houston TX 7/15/1954 s Richard Benjamin Lockett & Doris Lillian. BBA U of Texas 1981; MDiv CH Mason TS 1984; DMin CH Mason TS 2002; Angl Stds VTS 2004. D 4/30/2005 P 11/6/2005 Bp J(ohn) Neil Alexander. m 12/21/1985 Carol P Marsh c 2. Dio Atlanta Atlanta GA 2005-2010. cpml@bellsouth.net

LOCKETT, Russell Goodsell (WVa) 230 Wood St. Apt. 312, Sistersville WV 26175 B Hartford CT 7/14/1941 s Eugene Murray Lockett & Bernice Louise. BA Cntrl Connecticut St U 1970; MDiv Bex 1973. D 5/24/1975 P 1/5/1977 Bp Robert Poland Atkinson. c 2. S Steph's Epis Ch Steubenville OH 1988; Ch Consult/ Supply S Steph's Epis Ch Steubenville OH 1984-1985; Gr Ch S Marys WV 1979-1980; Supply Chr Ch Pearisburg VA 1978-1979; Cur Chr Ch Bluefield WV 1977-1978. RGLockett@yahoo.com

LOCKHART, Arthur John (At) 211 NW Craigmont Drive, Lee's Summit MO 64081 B Houston TX 8/13/1925 s Guy Ardell Lockhart & Angelina Lucy. Rice U 1944; BA U So 1949; STB GTS 1952; STM STUSo 1969. D 6/20/1952 Bp Clinton Simon Quin P 7/3/1953 Bp John E Hines. m 5/31/1952 Sally Bangs c 2. Assoc Gr-Calv Epis Ch Clarkesville GA 1988-1992; Assoc S Clare's Epis Ch Blairsville GA 1988-1992; Vic S Jas Epis Ch Clayton GA 1984-1987; Cn Pstr Cathd Of S Phil Atlanta GA 1978-1984; Eccl Crt Dio W Missouri Kansas City MO 1976-1978; Chair - Com for Med Problems Dio W Missouri Kansas City MO 1974-1976; St Lk's So Chap Overland Pk KS 1967-1978; Asst Trin Ch Princeton NJ 1964-1967; R S Mths' Epis Ch Athens TX 1958-1964; Cur St Andrews Epis Ch Houston TX 1956-1958; D-in-c, P-in-c S Jas' Epis Ch La Grange TX 1952-1956. Auth, *Contrib, Westminster Dictionary of Ch Hist*, The Westminster Press. aslockrt@sbcglobal.net

LOCKHART SR, Ronald Wayne (Pa) 687 Sugartown Rd, PO Box 1330, Malvern PA 19355 B Van Buren AR 12/12/1931 s William Othello Lockhart & Reba Elizabeth. BS U of Tulsa 1956; MDiv Crozer TS 1962; U of Pennsylvania 1964; EDS 1966. D 6/11/1966 Bp Robert Lionne DeWitt P 10/1/1966 Bp Albert Ervine Swift. m 7/12/1969 Sandra Lockhart c 1. Chr Ch Media PA 1997-1998; R Ch Of The Redeem Springfield PA 1968-1970; Cur S Paul's Ch Philadelphia PA 1966-1968. padreron1@verizon.net

LOCKLEY, Linda Sue (SwFla) No address on file. B New Castle PA 9/5/1955 d Robert E Lockley & Joanne Marie. BA Eckerd Coll; AA Manatee Cmnty Coll. D 6/20/1993 Bp Rogers Sanders Harris. m 4/5/1975 Wayne Stanley Buckner c 3.

LOCKWOOD, Edgar (Mass) 36 Place Rd, Falmouth MA 02540 **Died 10/10/2009** B Greenwich,CT 8/9/1920 s Edgar Lockwood & Elizabeth Detwiller. BA Ya 1942; LLB U of Virginia 1948; BD VTS 1960; Cert Corcoran Sch of Art 1971. D 6/13/1960 P 3/9/1961 Bp Walter H Gray. m 5/12/1990 Claire Cohen c 3. Auth, *So Afr's Moment of Truth*, Friendship Press, Inc., 1988. edgarlockwood@verizon.net

LOCKWOOD II, Frank Robert (Alb) 14 Spencer Blvd, Coxsackie NY 12051 B Cornwall NY 4/14/1968 s Frank Robert Lockwood & Susan Anne Otlowski. AA Herkimer Cnty Cmnty Coll 1991. D 5/10/2008 Bp William Howard Love. m 9/6/1997 Joanne Charlene Burke c 2. kevanus@yahoo.com

LOCKWOOD, Marcia Miller (ECR) PO Box 345, Rancho del Robledo, Carmel Valley, CA 93924 **Assoc S Dunst's Epis Ch Carmel Vlly CA 2008-** B Kalamazoo MI. 9/14/1936 d Rudel Charles Miller & Elizabeth. BS NWU 1958; MDiv CDSP 1983. D 12/27/1987 P 6/29/1988 Bp Donald Purple Hart. m 6/21/1958 George S Lockwood c 4. Trst CDSP Berkeley CA 1997-2001; Assoc Ch of S Mary's by the Sea Pacific Grove CA 1992-2008; Cn S Andr's Cathd Honolulu HI 1988-1991. RevMLockwood@gmail.com

LODDER, Herbert Kingsley (Md) 130 W Seminary Ave, Lutherville MD 21093 B Syracuse NY 8/8/1933 s Clifford Kingsley Lodder & Eleanor Seeley. BA Duke 1955; MDiv VTS 1958; MA GW 1967; MPA U of Baltimore 1980; MS Loyola Coll 1986. D 6/16/1958 Bp Malcolm E Peabody P 11/21/1959 Bp Walter M Higley. m 2/2/1980 Frances Pinter c 5. Assoc R Ch Of The H Comf Luthvle Timon MD 1994-2000; Vic Ch Of The Resurr Baltimore MD 1982-1992; Assoc R S Jn's Ch Ellicott City MD 1973-1974; Asst to the R S Andr's Epis Ch Arlington VA 1962-1972; Mssy S Andr's Ch Watertown NY 1958-1962. ESCRU 1968-1972. Outstanding Serv Awd MD Drug Abuse Admin 1984. lodder@jhmi.edu

LODWICK, James Nicholas (NY) 925 W Washington St, South Bend IN 46601 B Cincinnati OH 10/22/1938 s Edward Donald Lodwick & Virginia Foy. BA Ya 1960; BD EDS 1963; MA U of Notre Dame 1994. D 6/9/1968 Bp Roger W Blanchard P 12/13/1968 Bp Russell T Rauscher. Int S Jas' Epis Ch Goshen IN 1999-2000; Int S Alb's Epis Ch Ft Wayne IN 1998; Assoc S Mich And All Ang Ch So Bend IN 1991-1997; Assoc S Jas Ch New York NY 1984-1991; The Ch of S Matt And S Tim New York NY 1979-1984; R The Ch of S Edw The Mtyr New York NY 1976-1979; Dpt Of Missions Ny Income New York NY 1969-1977; Cur The Ch of S Edw The Mtyr New York NY 1969-1972; Diocn Msnry & Ch Extntn Socty New York NY 1968-1976. CBS 1972. jaimenick@aol.com

LOEFFLER, George C (Be) 46 Wessnersville Rd, Kempton PA 19529 **D Dio Bethlehem Bethlehem PA 2011-; Chapl to the Ordnry Dio Bethlehem Bethlehem PA 1996-** B Orange NJ 5/4/1931 s George Joseph Loeffler & Ethel Pauline. BA Leh 1953. D 11/18/1967 Bp Leland Stark. m 7/4/1955 Barbara Knaebel Bowen c 2. canong@hughes.net

LOESCHER, Candyce Jean (Ky) St Mary's Episcopal Church, 163 N Main St, Madisonville KY 42431 **Pres, Stndg Com Dio Kentucky Louisville KY 2011-; Dn, Four Rivers Dnry Dio Kentucky Louisville KY 2010-; Co Chair, Mssn Funding Dio Kentucky Louisville KY 2008-; R S Mary's Ch Madisonville KY 2007-** B St Louis MO 5/9/1949 d Gene Roland McKee & Dorothy Thompson. BFA Memphis Coll of Art 1979; MDiv VTS 2007. D 12/21/2006 Bp J(ohn) Neil Alexander P 9/29/2007 Bp Edwin Funsten Gulick Jr. m 9/5/1987 Warren Loescher. cloescher@gmail.com

LOEWE, Richard (Los) 1907 W West Wind, Santa Ana CA 92704 B Chicago IL 9/3/1913 s Sidney Loewe & Olga. ETSBH; JD Loyola U; NWU. D 9/12/1970 Bp Francis E I Bloy P 3/1/1971 Bp Victor Manuel Rivera. m 8/2/1947 Lois Mohan. Assoc S Steph's Par Whittier CA 1970-1974.

LOFFHAGEN, Tracie L (EMich) 543 Michigan Ave, Marysville MI 48040 **Dio Estrn Michigan Saginaw MI 2010-; R All SS Epis Ch Marysville MI 2004-** B Bistroff Moselle France 9/15/1962 d Wayman Sole & Patricia. BA U of Wstrn Ontario 1984; MDiv Hur 2004. Trans from Anglican Church of Canada 11/15/2004 as Deacon Bp Edwin Max Leidel Jr. c 2. Gr Epis Ch Port Huron MI 2006. TLOFFHAGEN@COMCAST.NET

LOFGREN, Claire (NY) PO Box 477-66, 2172 Saw Mill River Road, White Plains NY 10607 **Vic S Paul's Ch Sprg Vlly NY 2010-** B Oakland CA 12/9/1954 d Edward Joseph Lofgren & Lenore. BA U CA 1976; Teach. Cert. Mills Coll 1985; MDiv CDSP 1989; CTh U of Durham GB 1989; STM STUSo 1995. Trans from Church Of England 1/8/1993 Bp Bertram Nelson Herlong. Int The Ch Of S Jos Of Arimathea White Plains NY 2008-2009; Assoc EDS Cambridge MA 1999-2003; Soc Of St Marg Roxbury MA 1998-2003; AssociateRector S Jn's Epis Ch Charleston WV 1995-1998; Assoc Otey Memi Par Ch Sewanee TN 1994-1995. Auth, "Sprtl Formation For Priesthood," *Sewanee Theol Revs*, U So, 1996. Convenor, SOSc No Amer Chapters 1998-2007; Epis Ch Ntwk on Sci Tech and Faith 1993; Soc of Ord Scientists (SOSc) 1991; Sprtl Dir Intl 1994-2006. revclofgren@yahoo.com

LOFMAN, Donald Stig (NY) 12 Depot St, Middletown NY 10940 **D Ch Of The Resurr Hopewell Jct NY 2001-** B Alexandria VA 7/4/1944 D 4/14/1973 Bp James Winchester Montgomery. c 1.

LOFTON SR, William Carter (NC) 17701 Snug Harbor Rd, Charlotte NC 28278 **Died 5/29/2010** B Charlotte NC 9/10/1938 s Thomas Stark Lofton & Helen. BS Belmont Abbey Coll 1961; DDS Loyola U 1965; Cert D Formation Prog 1992. D 5/31/1992 Bp Robert Whitridge Estill. c 5. Unsung Hero Ldrshp Charlotte. carterl@holycomforter-clt.org

LOGAN, Christie Larson (Oly) No address on file. **S Hugh Of Lincoln Allyn WA 2003-** B Philadelphia PA 10/30/1942 D 11/30/2002 P 6/10/2003 Bp Sanford Zangwill Kaye Hampton. c 3. christie1042@peoplepc.com

LOGAN, Jeffery Allen (FtW) Psc 817 Box 43, Fpo AE 09622 **Off Of Bsh For ArmdF New York NY 2000-** B Fort Riley KS 11/18/1956 s Robert Logan & Jeanne. BA DePauw U 1978; MDiv Epis TS of The SW 1983. D 8/14/1983 P 6/24/1984 Bp A Donald Davies. m 9/4/1993 Anne Elizabeth Good. R S Paul's Epis Ch Gainesville TX 1996-2000; R S Lk's Ch Mineral Wells TX 1989-1994; Vic Our Lady Of The Lake Clifton TX 1986-1989; Dio Ft Worth Ft Worth TX 1985-1989; R S Mk's Ch Bridgeport CT 1985-1986; Cur S Tim's Ch Ft Worth TX 1983-1985. CCU; ESA; Mltry Chapl Assn; SSC. Who'S Who In Rel 1987. jamlogan@yahoo.com

LOGAN JR, John A. (Tex) 2808 Sunset Blvd, Houston TX 77005 **Cn Emer Chr Ch Cathd Houston TX 2000-; Secy Dio Texas Houston TX 1986-** B La Grange TX 8/4/1928 s John Alexander Logan & Juanita Raye. BA U of Texas 1948; JD U of Texas 1950; MDiv VTS 1953; MA U of Virginia 1979. D 7/2/1953 P 7/1/1954 Bp John E Hines. Dio Texas Houston TX 1996-1997; Stndg Com Dio Texas Houston TX 1994-1997; St Lk's Epis Hosp Houston TX 1980-1981; S Jas' Epis Ch La Grange TX 1980; Chr Ch Cathd Houston TX 1979-1996; Asst The Ch of the Gd Shpd Austin TX 1965-1977; Asst The Ch of the Gd Shpd Austin TX 1953-1955. Auth, "Dowered w Gifts," 1989. logan5311@sbcglobal.net

LOGAN, Linda Marie (CNY) 405 N Madison Ave, Pierre SD 57501 **Trin Ch Boonville NY 2009-** B Honolulu HI 1/11/1951 d John Alexander Logan & Norma Jeanne. BA Idaho St U 1972; MA Van 1974; MDiv CDSP 1997. D 1/12/1997 P 7/12/1997 Bp John Stuart Thornton. Headwaters Epis Mssn Boonville NY 2003-2009; Cntrl Dn Dio So Dakota Sioux Falls SD 2000-2003; Dioc Yth Coun Dio So Dakota Sioux Falls SD 1998-2000; Assoc R Trin Epis Ch Pierre SD 1997-1998; Dio E Tennessee Knoxville TN 1986-1990. Ed, "The E Tennessee Epis," Associated Ch Press, 1990. Epis Cmnctr; Pierre/Ft Pierre Min. Rel Jrnlst Of The Year Tennessee Assn Of Ch Tennessee 1990; Honorable Mention For Great Excellence The E Tennessee Epis Associated Ch Press E Tennessee 1990; Polly Bond Awd ECom 1987. revlogan@frontiernet.net

LOGAN, Michael Dennis (Alb) St Mark's Church, 32 Elm St, Malone NY 12953 **S Mk's Ch Malone NY 2008-** B Ogdensburg NY 6/9/1955 s Earl Charles Logan & Marjorie Iva. D 6/11/2005 Bp Daniel William Herzog. c 3. mlongan@twcny.rr.com

LOGAN JR, Thomas (WA) 5700 Trinity Prep Ln, Winter Park FL 32792 **Died 4/23/2011** B Philadelphia PA 3/30/1949 s Thomas W S Logan & Hermione Clark. BA Westminster Choir Coll of Rider U 1973; MA PrTS 1975; MDiv GTS 1980. D 6/20/1981 P 7/1/1983 Bp Lyman Cunningham Ogilby. tlogan3049@aol.com

LOGAN SR, Thomas W S (Pa) 46 Lincoln Ave, Yeadon PA 19050 B Philadelphia PA 3/19/1912 s John Richard Logan & Mary Haribson. BA Linc 1935; STB GTS 1938; STM PDS 1941; Cert Oxf 1976; LLD Durham Durham NC 1981; LHD S Aug's Coll Raleigh NC 1982; DD Virginia Sem Lynchburg VA 1987; ThD GTS 1994; ThD PDS 1995. D 6/13/1938 P 6/5/1939 Bp Francis E Taitt. m 9/3/1938 Hermione Clark Hill c 1. The Afr Epis Ch Of S Thos Philadelphia PA 2000-2002; Int Hse Of Pryr Philadelphia PA 1999-2000; Int Ch Of The Annuniciation Philadelphia PA 1993-1995; Intrim The Afr Epis Ch Of S Thos Philadelphia PA 1988-1990; S Simon The Cyrenian Ch Philadelphia PA 1982-1983; Int S Simon The Cyrenian Ch Philadelphia PA 1981-1982; Calv Epis Ch Nthrn Liberty Philadelphia PA 1945-1984. Auth, *Philadelphia Tribune*; Contrib, *Voices of Experience*. Black Episcopalians Life Mem 1950; Frontiers Intl Life 1942; IBPOE of the Wrld 1950; Life Mem of Alpha Phi Alpha 1933; NAACP Life 1940; Natl Champlain 1950; Pres. of NationalChurch Workers Conf 1951-1961; Pres of Hampton U Mionistrie's Conf, Hampto 1961-2009; Un of Black Epis Life Mem. Mart Luther King Awd 2002; UBE 1984; Raftus Awd 1977; S Aug Awd St. Paul Coll 1977; Cler Awd of Phila. PA Dio Penna Awd 1968; Johnson Smith U Awd 1967; Linc Awd 1965; DeMolay Consistory Awd 1962. drthomas@w.s.logansr

LOGAN, William Stevenson (Mich) 1514 Chateaufort Pl, Detroit MI 48207 B Detroit MI 3/10/1920 s William Stevenson Logan & Evelyn Lucille. BS U of Pennsylvania 1941; MA Chrysler Inst of Engr Detroit MI 1943; BD EDS 1951; MA U MI 1980. D 6/30/1951 Bp Richard S M Emrich P 12/30/1951 Bp Russell S Hubbard. m 12/1/1951 Mary Adelaide Siddall c 3. Actg Dn Cathd Ch Of S Paul Detroit MI 1993-1995; Exec VP Cathd Fndt Cathd Ch Of S Paul Detroit MI 1985-1992; CODE Strng Com Dio Michigan Detroit MI 1980-1983; Archd Dio Michigan Detroit MI 1973-1985; Pres MI Cmsn UMHE Dio Michigan Detroit MI 1970-2002; VP Michigan Coun Chairman Dio Michigan Detroit MI 1969-1971; Exec Dir Dept Prog Dio Michigan Detroit MI 1963-1973; Chair Dept CSR Dio Michigan Detroit MI 1960-1963; Chair Dept CSR Dio Michigan Detroit MI 1960-1963; R S Mart Ch Detroit MI 1952-1963; Asst Chr Ch Detroit MI 1951-1952. CODE. Hon Cn S Paul Cathd Detroit MI 1968. logan1514@aol.com

LOGAN, Yvonne Luree (NY) 1185 Park Ave Apt 12j, New York NY 10128 B Los Angeles CA 11/11/1960 d Samuel Logan & Mary. BA Ucla Los Angeles CA 1983; MS London Sch Of Econ London Engl 1991; MDiv UTS 2004. D 3/11/2006 P 9/23/2006 Bp Mark Sean Sisk. m 9/30/1994 Martin Luree Sankey c 2. yllogan@nyc.rr.com

LOGSDON, Tami Davis (NwT) 4207 Emil Ave, Amarillo TX 79106 **D S Andr's Epis Ch Amarillo TX 1999-** B Amarillo TX 7/31/1957 d Max Johnson & Sandra Beth. Amarillo Coll; TCU; W Texas A&M U. D 10/29/1999 Bp C(harles) Wallis Ohl.

LOGUE, Frank (Ga) 111 Clinton Ct, Saint Marys GA 31558 **Dio Georgia Savannah GA 2010-** B Montgomery AL 5/21/1963 s Thomas Odum Logue & Judy Sullivan. BA Georgia Sthrn U 1984; MDiv VTS 2000. D 2/5/2000 P 8/26/2000 Bp Henry Irving Louttit. m 9/7/1985 Victoria S Steele c 1. King Of Peace Kingsland GA 2008-2010. flogue@gaepiscopal.org

LOGUE, Mary Ann Willson (Ct) 173 Livingston St, New Haven CT 06511 B Clinton MA 1/26/1927 d Edward Talpey Willson & Ruth Hawley. BA Smith 1948; MDiv Ya Berk 1985. D 6/13/1987 Bp Arthur Edward Walmsley P 3/18/1988 Bp Clarence Nicholas Coleridge. m 6/10/1950 Frank Logue. Assoc Chr Ch New Haven CT 1998-2002; Assoc P Ch of the H Sprt W Haven CT 1996-1998; Assoc S Jn's Epis Par Waterbury CT 1990-1994; Asst Chr Ch Stratford CT 1987-1990. Ord Of S Helena 1995. fmalogue@cs.com

LOHMANN, John J (Mich) 296 Ackerson Lake Dr., Jackson MI 49201 **P S Andr's Epis Ch Livonia MI 2009-** B Detroit MI 8/18/1933 s Peter Lohmann & Elisabeth. BA U So 1959; M. Div STUSo 1962; MBA Ohio U 1982. D 6/29/1962 Bp Hamilton Hyde Kellogg P 1/1/1963 Bp William R Moody. c 3. Int S Andr's Epis Ch Valparaiso IN 2007-2008; Yoked Par S Jn's Ch Clinton MI 2004-2007; R S Ptr's Ch Tecumseh MI 1998-2007; S Thos Ch Houston TX 1996-1997; R The Epis Ch Of The Adv W Bloomfield MI 1969-1976; Yoked Par Ch Of Our Sav Gallatin TN 1964-1968; Yoked Par S Jos Of Arimathaea Ch Hendersonville TN 1964-1968; Cur Chr Ch Cathd Lexington KY 1962-1964. Mensa. Phi Beta Kappa; Who'S Who In Sci & Engr; Phi Beta Kappa. jjlohmann@voyager.net

LOHSE, Dana (Wyo) Po Box 291, Kaycee WY 82639 B Buffalo WY 6/18/1930 d Daniel Irving Anderson & Eva May. BA U of Wyoming 1971. D 7/11/1997 Bp William Harvey Wolfrum P 6/1/1998 Bp Bruce Edward Caldwell. m 11/24/1952 Glen Raymond Lohse.

LOKEY, Michael Paul (Eas) 29618 Polks Rd, Princess Anne MD 21853 **S Paul's Marion Sta Crisfield MD 2005-** B Yakima WA 7/13/1946 D 9/15/2001 Bp Martin Gough Townsend P 10/2/2002 Bp Charles Lindsay Longest. m 6/22/1973 Viola Mae Wagner c 3.

LOLCAMA, Terri (Oly) 10630 Gravelly Lake Dr SW, Lakewood WA 98499 B Yakima WA 1/22/1941 d Edward B Goeckner & Helen D. D 10/17/2009 Bp Gregory Harold Rickel. m 12/18/1960 Robert C Lolcama c 2. elpio@aol.com

LOLK, Otto Lothar Manfred (Pa) 30866 Buttonwood Dr, Lewes DE 19958 B Bremen Germany 5/28/1936 s Otto Alfred Lolk & Elsie Carolyn. BA Montclair St U 1969; MDiv GTS 1973; PhD Iona Coll 1979; MA Blanton-Peale Grad Inst 1985. D 6/9/1973 Bp Leland Stark P 12/16/1973 Bp George E Rath. c 3. All SS Ch Rhawnhurst Philadelphia PA 1985-2008; R S Ptr's Epis Ch Livingston NJ 1981-1985; R Ch Of S Mary The Vrgn Ridgefield Pk NJ 1975-1981; Asst R S Paul's Epis Ch Paterson NJ 1973-1975. Ord Of S Jn The Bapt - Menham, NJ 1970.

LOMAS, Bruce Alan (Mass) 3 Gould St, Melrose MA 02176 **R Trin Par Melrose MA 2001-** B Providence RI 2/15/1952 s Herbert Harold Lomas & Dorothy. BA Rhode Island Coll 1989; MDiv VTS 1992. D 6/20/1992 Bp George Nelson Hunt III P 1/1/1993 Bp Edward Lewis Lee Jr. m 6/2/1973 Jane Shafer c 2. S Barn Ch Wilmington DE 1998-2001; The Par of S Mich's Auburn ME 1995-1998; Gr Ch Grand Rapids MI 1992-1995. bjlomas6273@mac.com

LOMBARDO, Janet Marie Vogt (NH) 67 Ridge Rd, Concord NH 03301 **Ch Of S Jn The Evang Dunbarton NH 2011-** B Park Ridge NJ 1/22/1959 d Victor Werner Vogt & Marie Cecelia. VTS; BA Rutgers-The St U 1981; Med Rutgers-The St U 1983; MDiv EDS 1997. D 2/15/1998 P 12/1/1998 Bp Douglas Edwin Theuner. m 8/6/1983 Mark Anthony Lombardo c 2. S Andr's Ch New London NH 2008-2011; Cur Trin Epis Ch Tilton NH 1998-2005.

LONDON, Gary Loo (Los) 122 S California Ave, Monrovia CA 91016 **R S Lk's Par Monrovia CA 1995-** B Burley ID 1/1/1940 s Loo London & Maycelle. MDiv SWTS 1991. D 6/15/1991 P 1/1/1992 Bp Frederick Houk Borsch. Trin Par Fillmore CA 1993-1995; S Bede's Epis Ch Los Angeles CA 1991-1992. 2gahre@att.net

LONE, Jose Francisco (Hond) Barrio de Jesus, Atima, Santa Barbara 21105 Honduras **Dio Honduras Miami FL 2006-; Iglesia Epis Hondurena San Pedro Sula 2006-** B Copan Honduras 5/23/1973 s Francisco Menendez & Amelia. ThD Programa Diocesano Educ Teologica 2003. D 10/28/2005 Bp Lloyd Emmanuel Allen. m 8/9/2002 Cori Vanessa Vanessa Sanchez Irias c 2. lonejose5@yahoo.com

LONERGAN, Kathleen Guthrie (Mass) 25 Central Street, Andover MA 01810 **Asst R Par Of Chr Ch Andover MA 2011-; Disciplinary Com Mem Dio Massachusetts Boston MA 2010-; Conv Strng Com Dio Massachusetts Boston MA 2009-** B New York NY 10/5/1979 d Michael Lonergan & Roxana. BA Tufts U 2001; MDiv Harvard Div 2005; Dipl. in Angl Stds The GTS 2008. D 6/6/2009 Bp M(arvil) Thomas Shaw III. Conv Strng Com Dio Massachusetts Boston MA 2009-2011. kitlonergan@gmail.com

LONERGAN, Robert Thomas (Ore) 601 Taylor St, Myrtle Creek OR 97457 **Vic Ch Of The Ascen Riddle OR 1992-; Vic Ch Of The H Sprt Sutherlin OR 1992-** B Aberdeen WA 8/23/1935 s Robert H Lonergan & Angeline. Oregon Sch Of Rel; BA Linfield Coll 1963; MA Linfield Coll 1972; U So 1992. D 1/27/1984 Bp Matthew Paul Bigliardi P 8/25/1992 Bp Robert Louis Ladehoff. m 9/23/1961 Loris C Townsend. llonergan@charter.net

LONERGAN, Wallace Gunn (Ida) 812 E Linden St, Caldwell ID 83605 **Bd Dir Epis Fndt Dio Idaho Boise ID 1997-; Assoc S Dav's Epis Ch Caldwell ID 1997-** B Potlatch ID 3/18/1928 s Willis Gerald Lonergan & Lois. AA Lower Columbia Coll 1948; BA The Coll of Idaho 1950; MBA U Chi 1955; PhD U Chi 1960. D 2/23/1997 P 11/13/1997 Bp John Stuart Thornton. m 2/17/2007 Luise Coldwell Keenahan. Auth, "Mnstry & Higher Educ," *Advance*; Auth, "Ldrshp Trng & Its Role in Ch," *Ch Educ Finding*. Vstng Schlr Intl Angl Exch Prog Rikkyo U Tokyo Japan. wlonergon@collegeofidaho.edu

LONERGAN JR, W(illis) Gerald (Oly) 6114 E Evergreen Blvd, Vancouver WA 98661 B Nampa ID 3/24/1924 s Willis Gerald Lonergan & Lois. BA U of Washington 1949; Cert CDSP 1951; MA U of Detroit 1975. D 6/29/1951 P 11/1/1952 Bp Stephen F Bayne Jr. m 6/26/1948 Geraldine Evelyn Burnham. All SS Epis Ch Pontiac MI 1983-1989; Exec Asst to Bp Dio Michigan Detroit MI 1974-1983; ExCoun Dio Michigan Detroit MI 1973-1984; Secy Dioc Conv Dio Michigan Detroit MI 1973-1984; S Lk's Epis Ch Vancouver WA 1972-1989; Assoc Dir Dept Prog Dio Michigan Detroit MI 1966-1973; Chair DeptCE Dio Spokane Spokane WA 1961-1964; R S Steph's Epis Ch Spokane WA 1961-1964; Vic Epis Ch Of The Redeem Republic WA 1956-1961; Vic S Jn's Epis Ch Colville WA 1956-1961; Vic S Matthews Auburn WA 1954-1956; Asst S Lk's Epis Ch Vancouver WA 1951-1954. Assn of Rel and Applied Behavioral Sci; CODE. willisl@pacifier.com

LONG, Beth Louise (At) 165 Meredith Ridge Rd, Athens GA 30605 **R S Greg The Great Athens GA 2006-** B Nicosia CY 6/7/1952 d Melvin Eugene Long & L Jeanne. BA U Tor 1974; MA U of St. Mich's Coll 1980; Spec Stds U So 1989; Spec Stds VTS 1990. D 6/15/1991 P 1/11/1992 Bp Ronald Hayward Haines. c 3. R Trin Ch Lakeville CT 1999-2006; Vic S Jn's Ch Ashfield MA 1992-1999; Dre S Dunst's Epis Ch Beth MD 1991-1992. Human Relatns Cmsn Ashfield Ma. rector@stgregoryathens.org

LONG, betty ann (WMass) Trinity Episcopal Church, 440 Main Street, Shrewsbury MA 01545 **P-in charge Trin Epis Ch Shrewsbury MA 2007-** B Vintondale PA 10/27/1946 d Albert Magil Gongloff & Sue. BS Rhode Island Coll 1969; MDiv EDS 1985. D 6/1/1985 P 6/14/1986 Bp John Bowen Coburn. m 1/21/1967 William J Long c 2. Int R S Cyp's Epis Ch Hampton VA 2005-2007; Assoc R Ch Of The Epiph Norfolk VA 2005; Int R S Steph's Ch Newport News VA 2002-2005; Assoc R S Jn's Ch Hampton VA 2001-2002; Assoc R Hickory Neck Ch Toano VA 1998-1999; Vic S Simon's-By-The-Sea Virginia Bch VA 1994-1995; Assoc R S Mart's Epis Ch Williamsburg VA 1990-1994; Asst R The Ch Of The Gd Shpd Acton MA 1985-1989. Int Mnstry Int Mnstry Ntwk 2002. bnblong@townisp.com

LONG, Cynthia Andrew (NCal) 7041 Verdure Way, Elk Grove CA 95758 **D S Matt's Epis Ch Sacramento CA 2007-** B Vallejo CA 6/2/1954 d William N Andrew & Patricia M. RN S Lk Sch Of Nrsng 1979; BD H Name U 2002; BA Sch for Deacons 2007. D 6/9/2007 Bp Barry Leigh Beisner. m 7/1/1979 Mark Long c 2. cindylongrn@surewest.net

LONG, Eric Christopher (CGC) 4109 Wynford Cir, Pensacola FL 32504 **R S Chris's Ch Pensacola FL 2007-** B Milton FL 11/8/1971 s John Andrew Long & Edna Ruth. BA U of Memphis 1993; MDiv Nazarene TS 1996; CAS STUSo 1999. D 6/26/1999 P 1/15/2000 Bp Barry Robert Howe. m 12/25/1993 Shelley Renae Henderson c 2. Founding P St Mary Magd Epis Ch Belton MO 2002-2007; Assoc S Anne's Ch Lees Summit MO 1999-2001. eric@scpen.org

LONG, Gail Ann (SVa) 2441 Tuxedo Pl, Albany GA 31707 B Fort Benning GA 5/11/1944 d Jay Mason Warner & Elizabeth Ann. BS U CO 1968; MS California St U 1981; MDiv TESM 2000. D 9/23/2000 P 5/22/2001 Bp Dorsey Felix Henderson. R S Geo's Epis Ch Newport News VA 2005-2010; Coordntr - Cbury Way Dio Upper So Carolina Columbia SC 2004-2005; Int R Gr Epis Ch Anderson SC 2002-2004; Asst To The R S Chris's Ch Spartanburg SC 2000-2002. Auth, "Personal Sprtlty And BCP," *Crosswalk*, Dio Upper So Carolina, 1999. Cbury Way 2000; Christians For Biblic Equality 1998. galong05@att.net

LONG, James Garfield (Ore) 1226 6th Ave S, Edmonds WA 98020 B Bremerton WA 9/18/1909 s James Garfield Long & Sarah Johannah. BA U of Washington 1935; Harv 1943; CDSP 1954; Ya 1961. D 6/29/1954 P 6/29/1955 Bp Stephen F Bayne Jr. m 7/6/1968 Nancy T Tomlinson c 2. Fin Off Dio Oregon Portland OR 1977-1986; Dio Hawaii Honolulu HI 1971-1976; Waikiki Chap Honolulu HI 1970-1972; Cn Pstr S Andr's Cathd Honolulu HI 1963-1966; Vic S Geo's Ch Seattle WA 1956-1963; Asst R S Steph's Epis Ch Seattle WA 1954-1956. Ed, *Cartoon Catechism*, 1967; Ed, *Olympia Churchman*, 1966. Coun of Dioc Executives 1966-1986. Four Clio Awards Intl Broadcasting 1967; PBp's Awd for Best Dioc Nwspr; DSA Dio Hawaii Hawaii; Bp's Cross Dio Hawaii Olympia; Bp's Cross Dio Olympia Hawaii.

LONG II, John Michael (Neb) 1615 Brent Blvd, Lincoln NE 68506 B Lincoln NE 2/13/1961 s John Long & Marilyn. U of Nebraska 1994. D 8/1/2004 Bp Joe Goodwin Burnett. m 4/25/1998 Mary Long Road c 2.

LONG OSB, Lewis Harvey (Az) 28 W Pasadena Ave, Phoenix AZ 85013 B Denver MO 3/29/1931 s Lewis Harvey Long & Lavina Maye. BA U of Missouri 1951; STB GTS 1957. D 6/21/1957 P 12/21/1957 Bp Edward Clark Turner. Assoc R All SS Ch Phoenix AZ 1995-2000; S Mary's Epis Ch Phoenix AZ 1959-1993; R S Jn's Ch Abilene KS 1957-1959. Ord of S Ben. 329lewishlong@cox.net

LONG, Michael Richardson (Chi) Amargura 2, San Miguel De Allende, San Miguel de Allende Guanajuato 37700 Mexico **St Pauls Angl/Epis Ch Laredo TX 1997-** B Fort Worth TX 6/30/1947 s Oscar Symms Long & Marydee. BA Texas A&M U 1969; MA Texas A&M U 1972; MDiv SWTS 1975; DMin SWTS 1996. D 6/14/1975 Bp Quintin Ebenezer Primo Jr P 12/13/1975 Bp James Winchester Montgomery. m 9/9/1967 Cheri Dena Read. S Dav's Epis Ch Aurora IL 1987-1997; Int S Chad Epis Ch Loves Pk IL 1984-1985; Exec Coun Appointees New York NY 1982-1985; Gr Epis Ch Freeport IL 1976-1981; Cur S Giles' Ch Northbrook IL 1975-1976; S Paul's Ch Laredo TX. Auth, "Hemingway'S Attitude Toward Masculinity As Reflected"; Auth, "Which Works Wk? Lit & Preaching". Cmnty Of S Mary. rector@stpauls.org.mx

LONG, Paul Robert (NwPa) 130 Olde Pine Trl, Lexington SC 29072 **Died 8/10/2011** B Philadelphia PA 8/21/1924 s Elmer Christian Long & Velma Ida. BA GW 1949; MA GW 1950; MDiv VTS 1954; Cert Rutgers-The St U 1964. D 6/9/1954 P 12/15/1954 Bp John T Heistand. c 3.

LONG, Robert Carl (WMo) 4301 Madison Ave Apt 218, Kansas City MO 64111 **D Dio W Missouri Kansas City MO 1986-** B Chicago IL 10/30/1927 s Carl Elijah Long & D Irene. BA U of Kansas 1949; MD U of Kansas 1953. D 12/20/1986 Bp John Forsythe Ashby. m 9/2/1950 Ellen O Patterson c 4.

LONG, Robert Harold (USC) 205 Greengate Ln, Spartanburg SC 29307 **Died 2/22/2011** B Washington DC 1/6/1944 s James Edward Long & Grace. BS Lynchburg Coll 1967; MDiv VTS 1979. D 5/27/1979 Bp William Henry Marmion P 12/19/1979 Bp Brice Sidney Sanders. Soc Of S Jn The Evang. frlong21@charter.net

LONG, Shirley Dube (WNC) Po Box 72, Deep Gap NC 28618 **D Par Of The H Comm Glendale Sprg NC 1999-** B Miami FL 12/19/1944 d Raymond Francis Dube & Margaret Kathleen. BS Florida St U 1966; MA Appalachian St U 1969. D 12/18/1999 Bp Robert Hodges Johnson. m 4/8/1980 Donald Finley Long.

LONG, Thomas Mcmillen (Colo) 4155 E Jewell Ave Ste 1117, Denver CO 80222 **Assoc The Ch Of The Ascen Denver CO 2002-** B Denver CO 3/31/1949 s Lawrence Alexander Long & Elizabeth. BA U Denv 1972; MDiv VTS 1975. D 1/5/1975 P 9/1/1975 Bp William Carl Frey. m 6/22/1994 Elizabeth B Beardall c 1. Assoc S Tim's Epis Ch Centennial CO 1995-2001; Chr Epis Ch Denver CO 1984-1988; R S Barth's Ch Estes Pk CO 1978-1984; Cur Ch Of The Ascen Pueblo CO 1975-1978. AAPC. tlong2109@aol.com

LONGACRE, Tracy Elizabeth (Cal) 2323 Magnolia St Ste 11, Oakland CA 94607 B Tarrytown NY 3/17/1962 d Jay Kennard Longacre & A Suzanne. BA U Chi 1983; MBA Golden Gate U 1990; MLa Naropa U 1999; BA Sch for Deacons 2004; DMin U Of Creation Sprtlty Oakland CA 2006. D 12/4/2004 Bp William Edwin Swing. tel@telphoto.com

LONGBOTTOM, Robert John David (Alb) 120 N Hall St, Visalia CA 93291 **GC Alt Dio Albany Albany NY 2012; R S Jn's Ch Ogdensburg NY 2005-** B Techachapi CA 10/15/1974 s David Charles Longbottom & Kendal Ann. BA U CA 1997; MDiv TESM 2002. D 2/16/2002 P 9/21/2002 Bp John-David Mercer Schofield. m 4/2/2005 Amee M Thompson. GC Alt Dio Albany Albany NY 2009; Dioc Coun Mem Dio Albany Albany NY 2008-2010; Asst S Paul's Epis Ch Visalia CA 2002-2005. Pi Sigma Alpha 1997. robertlongbottom@hotmail.com

LONGE, Neal Patrick (Alb) 58 Reber St, Colonie NY 12205 **Cur S Mich's Albany NY 2010-** B Albany NY 2/22/1979 s Patrick Blaise Longe & Sherry Lynn. BM SUNY Coll at Potsdam 2001; AAS Fulton-Montgomery Cmnty Coll 2006; MA S Mary's Sem & U 2006; Dplma in Angl Stds TESM 2010. D 5/30/2009 P 6/30/2010 Bp William Howard Love. m 11/27/2004 Lisa Verville c 2. D Intern Chr Ch Schenectady NY 2009-2010. fatherneal@gmail.com

LONGERO, Ronald Delbert (WK) 5310 Stahl Rd, San Antonio TX 78247 B Carson City NV 9/29/1955 s Delbert Gene Longero & Barbara Jean. BS U of Nevada at Reno 1978; MDiv Nash 1990. D 12/30/1989 P 7/1/1990 Bp William L Stevens. m 12/26/1977 Marjorie Tremain c 3. S Jn's Mltry Sch Salina KS 2004-2008; Texas Mltry Inst San Antonio TX 2002-2004; S Marg's Epis Ch San Antonio TX 1997-2002; The Epis Ch Of The Adv Alice TX 1994-1996; S Nich' Epis Ch Midland TX 1991-1994; Cur S Mich And All Ang' Ch Denver CO 1990-1991. padrerdl@juno.com

✠ **LONGEST, Rt Rev Charles Lindsay** (Md) 7200 3rd Ave., C-035, Sykesville MD 21784 **Ret Bp Suffr of Md Dio Maryland Baltimore MD 1998-** B Catonsville MD 5/7/1933 s George Edward Longest & Mamie Jeannette. BA U of Maryland 1956; STB Ya Berk 1959; DD Ya Berk 1989. D 6/26/1959 Bp Noble C Powell P 4/5/1960 Bp Harry Lee Doll Con 10/14/1989 for Md. m 6/9/1956 Barbara H Hildebrandt. Asstg Bp Dio Easton Easton MD 2001-2003; Bp Suffr of Md Dio Maryland Baltimore MD 1989-1997; R Ch Of The H Cross Cumberland MD 1973-1989; Chair Dioc Com Mssn Dio Maryland Baltimore MD 1972-1983; Vic Epis Ch Of Chr The King Windsor Mill MD 1963-1973; Asst S Barth's Ch Baltimore MD 1960-1973; Asst H Trin Epis Ch Baltimore MD 1959-1960. ASSP 1962; OHC 1962. DD Berk 1989. 848longest@msn.com

LONGHI, Anthony Peter (Chi) 403 E Diggins St, Harvard IL 60033 B New Rochelle NY 6/4/1947 s Peter Longhi & Concetta Mary. BA Concordia Coll 1980; MDiv TESM 1985. D 1/26/1985 P 7/27/1985 Bp Alden Moinet Hathaway. m 5/7/2011 Julie Babenko-Longhi c 1. S Jn's Epis Ch Mt Prospect IL 2002-2003; R S Paul's Ch McHenry IL 1993-2002; P-in-c Ch of SS Thos and Lk Patton PA 1985-1993; S Thos Ch No Cambria PA 1985-1993. Auth, *The Cord*. stpaulrector@aol.com

LONGNECKER, Nelson Charles (La) Po Box 483, Hunt TX 78024 B Houston TX 5/28/1928 s Nelson Davis Longnecker & Alice Golaz. BS U Of Houston 1953; Epis TS of The SW 1956; BA Tul 1969. D 6/25/1956 Bp Frederick P Goddard P 6/29/1957 Bp James Parker Clements. m 4/18/1998 Sylvia P Chavez c 4. P-in-c Ch Of The Ascen Donaldsonville LA 1975-1979; Ch Of The H Comm Plaquemine LA 1968-1994; Int Ch Of The Ascen Donaldsonville LA 1968-1969; Asst Dce Trin Ch New Orleans LA 1961-1965; Cur S Jas Epis Ch Baton Rouge LA 1959-1961; Vic S Jn's Epis Ch Palacios TX 1956-1959. La Archits Assn Cert Appreciation 1985; La Archits Assn Cert Appreciation 1980; Natl Chapl Mcroa 1976; Amer Inst Archit Sch Medal And Cert Of Merit 1969. nelson@longnecker.org

LONGO, John Alphonsus (Haw) 9901 N Oracle Rd, Apt 8103, Tuscon AZ 97062 B Brooklyn NY 12/18/1936 s John Alphonsous Longo & Margaret. BA USC 1980; S Jn Coll Gb 1981; MDiv TESM 1983. D 12/9/1986 Bp Robert Hume Cochrane P 10/1/1987 Bp Robert Louis Ladehoff. m 5/8/1993 Barbara Dailey c 2. S Mary's Epis Ch Honolulu HI 1995-1999; Dio Oregon Portland OR 1991-1995; S Jn's Epis Ch Toledo OR 1989-1991; S Lk's Ch Grants Pass OR 1988-1989; D-In-Trng Ch Of The Trsfg Darrington WA 1986-1987. vicarlango@gmail.com

LONGSTAFF, Thomas Richmond Willis (Me) 39 Pleasant St, Waterville ME 04901 B Nashua NH 10/9/1935 s William Longstaff & Evelene Helen. MDiv Bangor TS 1964; BA U of Maine 1964; PhD Col 1973; Postdoc Hebr Un Coll, Jerusalem 1974; MA Colby Coll 1984. D 3/3/1974 P 7/1/1974 Bp Frederick Barton Wolf. m 8/17/1969 Cynthia Curtis c 5. Co-Auth, "Excavations at Sepphoris," *Excavations at Sepphoris*, Brill, 2006; Auth, "A Synopsis Of Mk (Cd)," Trin Press Intl , 2002; Auth, "One Gospel From Two; Mk'S Use Of Matt And Lk," Trin Press Intl , 2002; Auth, "What Are Those Wmn Doing At The Tomb Of Jesus?," *A Feminist Comp To Matt*, Sheffield Acad Press, 2001; Auth, "Palynology And Cultural Process," *Archeol In The Galilee*, Scholars Press, 1997; Auth, "Computer Rcrdng, Analysis, And Interp," *The Oxford Encyclopedia Of Archeol In The Near E*, 1997; Auth, "Abba, God, H Sprt, Most High, Image Of God, +More," *Harper'S Bible Dictionary*, 1996; Auth, "Synoptic Abstract: Vol. Xv Of The Computer Bible," Biblic Resrch Assoc, 1978; Auth, "Evidence Of Conflation In Mk?," Scholars Press, 1977. Amer Schools Of Oriental Resrch 1978; Assn Of Angl Biblic Scholars; Cath Biblic Assn Of Amer; Israel Exploration Soc 1978; Maine Archeol Assn; SBL 1965; Studiorum Novi Testamentum Societas. Fell Woodrow Wilson Fndt 1964. tlongst@colby.edu

LONGSTRETH, William Morris (Pa) 1146 Handview Circle, Pottstown PA 19464 B Philadelphia PA 4/30/1933 s William Church Longstreth & Laura Lloyd. BA Hav 1959; STM PDS 1963; MA Villanova U 1970. D 6/8/1963 P 12/1/1963 Bp Joseph Gillespie Armstrong. m 6/25/1960 Barbara Caroline Heylmun. Int Chr Ch Bridgeport PA 1970-1978; DCE S Mary's Epis Ch Ardmore PA 1966-1969; Cur S Lk And S Simon Cyrene Rochester NY 1963-1966. Auth, "De-Liberation".

LONGWOOD, K(athleen) Casey Mary (Ore) 280 W Exeter St, Gladstone OR 97027 **Died 7/8/2010** B San Francisco CA 3/10/1955 d William John Long & Dona Mary Scannell. BA Monterey Inst of Intl Stds 1977; MDiv CDSP 1983; Cert Priory Sprtlty Cntr Lacey WA 2003; MA Chapman U 2007. D 11/6/1983 P 10/5/1984 Bp Charles Shannon Mallory. Ord of S Ben Camaldolese 1996. Navy Achievement Medal US Navy 1995; Navy Commendation Medal (2 Awards) US Navy 1994. caseylongwood@comcast.net

LONTO, Michael Joseph (WNY) 99 Wildwood Av, Salamanca NY 14779 **Vic S Jn's Epis Ch Ellicottville NY 2009-; R S Mary's Ch Salamanca NY 2007-** B New York NY 6/21/1956 s Francis Michael Lonto & Elizabeth Mercedes. BS St. Johns U 1978; MDIV TESM 2006. D 7/29/2006 Bp Robert William Duncan P 3/18/2007 Bp John-David Mercer Schofield. m 7/26/1986 Christine Petersen c 4. S Mary Epis Ch Red Bank Templeton PA 2006-2007; S Mich's Wayne Township Freeport PA 2006-2007; S Paul's Epis Ch Kittanning PA 2006-2007. mlonto@yahoo.com

LOOKER, Jennifer Elizabeth (CPa) 241 Sherman Ave Apt 3, New Haven CT 06511 **Archd S Jn's Epis Ch Lancaster PA 2006-** B Washington DC 9/17/1979 d Peter Looker & Vicki. BS Shippensburg U 2001; MDiv Ya Berk 2005. D 6/11/2005 P 10/4/2006 Bp Michael Whittington Creighton. m 12/17/2005 Craig Fenn c 3. jenlooker@hotmail.com

LOOMIS, De Witt Herbert (Va) 517 Plum St, Petersburg VA 23803 **S Lk's Epis Ch Akron OH 2003-** B Denison TX 10/6/1930 s De Witt Herbert Loomis & Kathryn. BA U of Virginia 1957; STM PDS 1965. D 6/26/1965 P 1/26/1966 Bp William Foreman Creighton. m 9/9/1961 Dorothy Elaine Ward. R Chr Ascen Ch Richmond VA 1984-1995; Varina Epis Ch Richmond VA

L

1984-1995; P-in-c Ch Of The Sav Syracuse NY 1983-1984; S Mk The Evang Syracuse NY 1983-1984; Dio Cntrl New York Syracuse NY 1980-1983; R S Ann's Ch Afton NY 1975-1983; R S Ptr's Ch Bainbridge NY 1975-1983; R Chr Ch Durham Par Nanjemoy MD 1966-1970. dewloomis@hotmail.com

LOOMIS, Julia Dorsey Reed (SVa) 416 Court St, Portsmouth VA 23704 B Portsmouth VA 8/9/1945 d Robert Murdaugh Reed & Anna Crump. BA Randolph-Macon Wmn's Coll 1967; Fulbright Cert Georg August U Goettingen Germany 1968; MA Br 1969; MDiv Ya Berk 1992. D 6/7/1992 P 1/5/1993 Bp Frank Harris Vest Jr. m 6/14/1969 David Eugene Loomis c 3. Assoc S Andr's Ch Norfolk VA 2005-2007; Int Ch Of The Gd Shpd Norfolk VA 2002-2004; Assoc S Thos Epis Ch Chesapeake VA 1999-2002; Int Bruton Par Williamsburg VA 1996-1999; D Emm Ch Virginia Bch VA 1992-1996. Auth, "Wisdom Calls at the Threshold," *Faith at Wk*, 2006; Auth, "Who is Chr for Us Today," *Reflections*, Yale DS, 1992. EPF 2000. Julia A. Archibold High Schlrshp Prize Berkeley/Yale DS 1992; Downes Prize for Publ Reading of Scripture Berkeley/Yale DS 1992; Phi Beta Kappa Randolph-Macon Wmn's Coll 1967. loomis.loomisdj@verizon.net

LOOP, Richard Bruce (Ore) 36489 Florence Ct., Astoria OR 97103 **R Gr Epis Ch Astoria OR 2002-** B Okmulgee OK 7/27/1945 s Alfred Bruce Loop & Ruth. U of Washington 1967; BS San Jose St Coll 1969; MS U CA 1971; MDiv Epis TS of The SW 1998. D 6/25/1995 P 12/16/1995 Bp John Stuart Thornton. m 8/3/2001 Marilyn Louise Moller. Mem of Bd Trst Dio Oregon Portland OR 2007-2010; Mem of Stndg Com Dio Oregon Portland OR 2004-2007; Vic Mtn Rivers Epis Cmnty Idaho Falls ID 1995-2002; Vic S Mk's Epis Ch Idaho Falls ID 1995-2002; Vic S Paul's Ch Blackfoot ID 1995-2002. rloop@pacifier.com

LOOR CEDENO, Mariana (EcuL) 22 Ava & 3er Callejon P, Bahia De Caraquez Ecuador **Litoral Dio Ecuador Guayaquil EQ EC 2004-** B 1/8/1956 d Vicente Loor & Jacinta. DIT Litoral Sem Guayaquil Ec. D 3/22/1998 P 7/14/2002 Bp Alfredo Morante-España. m 10/12/1996 Narciso Cevallos c 4.

LOPER, Jerald Dale (Minn) 1524 Country Club Rd, Albert Lea MN 56007 **Asst Chr Ch Albert Lea MN 1981-** B Albert Lea MN 7/13/1931 s Dale Mckinley Loper & Hattie Viola. D 12/14/1981 Bp Robert Marshall Anderson. m 7/27/1963 Elizabeth Plummer c 2.

LOPEZ, Abel Ernesto (Los) 2396 Mohawk St Unit 7, Pasadena CA 91107 **Sr Assoc All SS Ch Pasadena CA 2001-** B CUBA 7/4/1969 s Reinaldo Lopez & Adis. Set Matanzas Cu; MDiv Epis TS of The SW 2000. D 6/11/2005 P 1/14/2006 Bp Joseph Jon Bruno. m 4/22/2006 May Ling Garcia c 2. alopez@allsaints-pas.org

LOPEZ, Bienvenido Taveras (DR) Iglesia Episcopal Divina Providencia, Calle Marcos Del Rosario #39 Republica Dominicana Dominican Republic **Dio The Dominican Republic (Iglesia Epis Dominicana) Santo Domingo DO 2008-** B Republica Dominicana 12/3/1967 s Ramon Lopez & Leonida. Licenciado En Teologia Centro de Estudios Teologicos; Licenciado En Pedagogia Dominicana O & M 2004. D 2/4/2007 P 2/10/2008 Bp Julio Holguin. m 11/25/2001 Benigna Aria c 2. bienvenidol3@yahoo.com

LOPEZ JR, Eddie (Be) 35 South Franklin St, Wilkesbarre PA 18704 **D S Steph's Epis Ch Wilkes Barre PA 2011-; D S Steph's Epis Ch Wilkes Barre PA 2011-** B New York 7/18/1960 s Eddie A Lopez & Juanita G. BS Nyack Coll 1983; MDiv NYTS 1989; STM UTS 1990. D 6/24/2011 Bp Paul Victor Marshall. m 9/29/2007 Rosanna Rosado. elopez60@aol.com

LOPEZ, Mary Alice (SwFla) 504 Columbia Dr, Tampa FL 33606 **D S Mk's Epis Ch Of Tampa Tampa FL 2003-** B Tampa FL 7/29/1951 BA Salem Coll Winston-Salem NC. D 6/14/2003 Bp John Bailey Lipscomb. m 7/11/1974 Victor Manuel Lopez c 3. mary.a.lopez@att.net

LOPEZ, Oscar Obdulio (Hond) 12 Calle, 10-11 Avenue Bo Cabanas, San Pedro Honduras **Dio Honduras Miami FL 1989-; Vic Iglesia Epis San Andres San Pedro Sula HN 1989-; Vic Iglesia Epis San Lucas San Pedro Sula HN 1989-** B San Pedro Sula Cortes HN 7/31/1951 s Maria. D 1/6/1989 P 1/25/1995 Bp Leopold Frade. m 5/11/1990 Marta Isabel Colindres c 1.

LOPEZ, Pedro Nel (Chi) 31 Washington Blvd Apt 101, Mundelein IL 60060 **S Ptr's Ch Pasadena TX 2011-** B Colombia 3/13/1968 BA Universidad San Buenaventura Bogota CO. Rec from Roman Catholic 11/22/2003 Bp Victor Alfonso Scantlebury. m 8/31/2002 Estela Lopez c 2. Ch Of The Redeem Elgin IL 2006-2011; S Mich's Ch Barrington IL 2004-2006; Santa Teresa de Avila Chicago IL 2004. pedronel@sbcglobal.net

LOPEZ JR, Ram (WTex) 1247 Vista Del Juez, San Antonio TX 78216 **R S Geo Ch San Antonio TX 2004-** B Corpus Christi TX 2/21/1964 s Ramiro Eduardo Lopez & Juanita Hernandez. Del Mar Coll 1985; BA SW Texas St U San Marcos 1988; MDiv STUSo 1995. D 6/29/1995 Bp James Edward Folts P 1/25/1996 Bp Robert Boyd Hibbs. m 5/25/1991 Kendra M Morgan c 2. Ch Planter Dio W Texas San Antonio TX 2003-2004; Vic St Ptr & St Paul Ch Mssn TX 2002-2003; Asst R S Jn's Ch McAllen TX 1998-2002; Asst R S Alb's Ch Harlingen TX 1995-1998. rlopez@saintgeorgechurch.org

LOPEZ, Sunny Potter (Chi) 3115 W Jerome St, Chicago IL 60645 **Assoc Gr Ch Chicago IL 2008-; Bethany Methodist Corp Chicago IL 2000-** B Ottowa IL 12/28/1949 d Harry Fowler Potter & Laverne Dee. BA Mundelein Coll 1982; MDiv Garrett Evang TS 1987; DMin Chicago TS 1997. D 12/7/1991 Bp Frank Tracy Griswold III. m 9/30/1978 Frank Lopez c 2. D Cathd Of S Jas Chicago IL 1994-2006. Apc (Assn Of Profsnl Chapl) 1999; EPF 1991; For (Fllshp Of Recon) 1999; No Amer Assn Of The Diac 1991; The Natl Assn Of Female Executives 2000. S Steph's Awd For Peace And Justice Mnstry No Amer Assn Of The Diac 2001. slopezbethany@yahoo.com

LOPEZ-CHAVERRA, Hector (SwFla) Episc Ch St. Francis, P.O. Box 9332, Tampa FL 33674 **Vic S Fran Ch Tampa FL 2002-** B Aguagas Colombia 6/10/1937 s Antonio Ise Lopez & Ines. Bachelor & Sem Stds; Bachelor Sem Chr P 1971. D 6/30/1973 P 8/4/1974 Bp Adrian Delio Caceres-Villavicencio. m 5/19/1974 Olga S Lopez c 2. Iglesia Epis Del Ecuador Ecuador 1984-1987; Iglesia Epis En Colombia 1980-1993. hlchpresbiters@yahoo.com

LORA, Juan Bernardo (Ct) 16 Paul St, Danbury CT 06810 B 3/27/1925 s Jose Manuel Lora & Mercedes Ereminda. Santo Tomas De Aquino Sem 1950. Rec from Roman Catholic 12/1/1979 as Priest Bp Paul Moore Jr. m 6/29/1968 Nildya Amelia Frias. Trin Par So Norwalk CT 1989-1992; Vic Iglesia Betania Norwalk CT 1987-1993; Holyrood Ch New York NY 1981.

LORD, David Charles (CFla) 3760 8th Lane, Vero Beach FL 32960 **Died 8/27/2009** B Danbury CT 11/14/1926 s Charles Augustus Lord & Virginia Hazel. BS Benjamin Franklin U 1948; MA Benjamin Franklin U 1949; DIT EDS 1962. D 6/16/1962 P 12/22/1962 Bp William Foreman Creighton. c 2. Auth, *Journey Through the Word-Bible Reading Fllshp*, 2009. Ord Of S Lk, Bible Reading Fllshp, AFP. Hon Cn Dio Cntrl Florida 1999. canonlord@gmail.com

LORD, James Raymond (Ky) 3001 Myrshine Dr, Pensacola FL 32506 B Dublin GA 11/8/1934 s James Leonard Lord & Susie Elizabeth. BA, scl Presb Coll Clinton SC 1956; BD PrTS 1961; ThM Duke 1964; PhD Duke 1968. D 12/26/1972 P 4/29/1973 Bp Hanford Langdon King Jr. GC Dep Dio Kentucky Louisville KY 1994-1997; Dio Kentucky Louisville KY 1993-1994; Stndg Com Dio Kentucky Louisville KY 1992-1994; Stndg Com Dio Kentucky Louisville KY 1992-1994; R Trin Epis Ch Owensboro KY 1991-1997; GC Dep Dio Kentucky Louisville KY 1988-1991; Stndg Com Dio Kentucky Louisville KY 1988-1990; Trst and Coun Dio Kentucky Louisville KY 1987-1994; R S Lk's Ch Anchorage KY 1986-1991; Stndg Com Dio Kentucky Louisville KY 1982-1984; R Gr Ch Hopkinsville KY 1978-1986; Trst and Coun Dio Kentucky Louisville KY 1977-1980; Vic S Mart's-In-The-Fields Mayfield KY 1975-1978; Vic S Ptr's of the Lakes Gilbertsville KY 1974-1978. Auth, "Bk Revs," *Newman Stds Journ*, 2006; Transltr, "Jesus (by Hans Conzelmann)," Fortress Press, 1973. Cath Biblic Assn 1972. raymondlord@bellsouth.net

LORD, Mary George (Okla) 815 N 427, Pryor OK 74361 **D S Ptr's Ch Tulsa OK 2007-** B Erie PA 1/18/1948 d Ralph George & Marie. Gannon U 1966. D 6/24/2006 Bp Robert Manning Moody. m 5/30/1987 Charles David Lord c 3. fessiemom@upperspace.net

LORD, Philip Warren (WNY) 5013 Van Buren Rd, Dunkirk NY 14048 B Philadelphia PA 1/13/1940 s John Arthur Lord & Edna Payne. BA Hob 1963; MDiv GTS 1966; CLU The Amer Coll Bryn Mawr PA 1987; ChFC The Amer Coll Bryn Mawr PA 1988. D 6/11/1966 Bp Leland Stark P 12/7/1966 Bp John Henry Esquirol. m 10/8/1966 Susan Staiger c 1. Supply P S Paul's Epis Ch Angola NY 2001-2010; Supply P S Alb's Ch Silver Creek NY 1994-1996; R Ch Of S Jn The Bapt Dunkirk NY 1973-1982; Asst Gr Ch Lockport NY 1971-1973; Cur S Steph's Ch Providence RI 1968-1970; Cur S Jn's Ch Stamford CT 1966-1968. Ord of S Ben - S Greg's Abbey, Three Rivers, 1959; Sis of the H Nativ - P Assoc 1969.

LORD, Richard Anthony (Va) 543 Beulah Road Northeast, Vienna VA 22180 **R Ch Of The H Comf Vienna VA 1994-** B Washington DC 1/27/1953 s David Charles Lord & Julie. BA CUA 1976; MDiv VTS 1981; STM Ya Berk 1992. D 6/20/1981 P 12/20/1981 Bp John Thomas Walker. m 11/26/1976 Deborah Ann Greene c 3. R Chr And Epiph Ch E Haven CT 1989-1994; R S Mart's Epis Ch Monroeville PA 1984-1989; Ch Of The Apos Fairfax VA 1981-1984. Hon Cn Schlr Chr Ch Hartford CT 1992. rlord3@verizon.net

LORD, Robert Charles (CFla) 1312 Bridgeport Drive, Winter Park FL 32789 **All SS Ch Of Winter Pk Winter Pk FL 2006-** B Washington DC 1/27/1953 s David Charles Lord & Julie. BA Florida Atlantic U 1977; MDiv Nash 1980; DMin Fuller TS 2002. D 6/22/1980 P 1/26/1981 Bp Calvin Onderdonk Schofield Jr. m 6/14/1975 Nancy Haynes c 2. Dep GC Dio Kansas Topeka KS 2000-2006; Dio Kansas Topeka KS 2000-2003; R S Mich And All Ang Ch Mssn KS 1996-2006; Dep GC Dio Colorado Denver CO 1994-2000; R Trin Ch Greeley CO 1988-1996; R S Mich's Ch Colonial Heights VA 1984-1988; Assoc Ch Of The Apos Fairfax VA 1982-1983; Assoc S Dav's Epis Ch Lakeland FL 1981-1982; Asst S Mk The Evang Ft Lauderdale FL 1980-1981. OHC. frrobl@allsaintswp.com

LORD-WILKINSON, Randall A (WA) Church of the Ascension, 205 S Summit Ave, Gaithersburg MD 20877 **Ch Of The Ascen Gaithersburg MD 2007-** B Charleston WV 10/22/1955 s Paul Roy Wilkinson & Eunice Marie. BA W Virginia U 1978; MDiv Harvard DS 1982. D 5/28/1983 Bp John Bowen Coburn P 5/19/1984 Bp Roger W Blanchard. m 1/1/1994 Cynthia Lord-Wilkinson c 2. R S Paul's Epis Ch Bremerton WA 1995-2007; R S Ptr's Ch Salem MA

1985-1995; S Andr's Ch Framingham MA 1983-1985. mystagogic@gmail.com

LORENSON, Ruth Lorraine (LI) 9 Warton Pl, Garden City NY 11530 B Brooklyn NY 1/26/1937 d David John Green & Lenora. RN Med Cntr Jersey City NJ 1957; BS Coll of New Jersey 1958; Mercer Cnty Cmnty Coll 1976. Trans from Anglican Church of Canada 6/13/1990. m 6/21/1958 Leslie Lorenson. Soc Of S Fran. lbcove@optonline.net

LORENZ, Constance (LI) 87-45 108th Street, Richmond Hill NY 11418 **D S Paul's Ch Great Neck NY 2010-** B Brooklyn NY 9/6/1949 d Richard Theodore Hille & Helen Frances. Cert Mercer TS 1997. D 6/28/1997 Bp Orris George Walker Jr. m 10/9/1971 Leslie Lorenz c 2. D Cathd Of The Incarn Garden City NY 2005-2007; D Ch Of S Alb The Mtyr S Albans NY 2001-2005; D Gr Ch Jamaica NY 2000-2001; D Zion Ch Douglaston NY 1997-2000. dea_con@juno.com

LORENZ, Howard Roberts (Pa) 741 Farmview Ln, Gap PA 17527 B Norristown PA 12/15/1932 s Edward Alexander Lorenz & Katherine Meredith. BA Maryville Coll 1955; MDiv PDS 1958; MA W Chester St Coll 1982. D 5/10/1958 P 11/29/1958 Bp Oliver J Hart. m 12/27/1958 Joan McNaughton c 3. S Jn's Ch Gap PA 1971-1997; Vic Ch Of The Ascen Parkesburg PA 1969-1972; R S Lk's Ch Philadelphia PA 1958-1969. Auth, *Our Fr & God.* Bible and Coomon Pryr Soc of the Epis Ch 1968-2007; Ord of S Lk 1991-2001; The Hymn Soc in the Untd States and Can 1980. jlhr2@comcast.net

LORENZE, James Dennis (Eau) 2304 Country Club Ln, Eau Claire WI 54701 **D Chr Ch Cathd Eau Claire WI 1998-** B Freeport IL 8/29/1942 s Leo Herman Lorenze & Clara. Coll Med Tech. D 4/18/1998 Bp William Charles Wantland. m 4/9/1983 Debra Helen Becker c 2. lorenzes@charter.net

LORING III, Richard Tuttle (Mass) 114 Badger Ter, Bedford MA 01730 **Int S Mk's Ch Westford MA 2008-; Libr Archv Bd Dio Massachusetts Boston MA 1992-; Libr & Archv Bd Dio Massachusetts Boston MA 1982-; Marg Coffin PBS Dio Massachusetts Boston MA 1982-** B Boston MA 10/23/1929 s Richard T Loring & Helen. BA Harv 1951; STB GTS 1957; ThD GTS 1968. D 6/22/1957 Bp Anson Phelps Stokes Jr P 1/25/1958 Bp Oliver L Loring. Int S Paul's Ch Boston MA 2007-2008; Int S Jn's Ch Charlestown (Boston) Charlestown MA 2003-2004; Int Gr Ch Norwood MA 2001-2003; Int Gr Epis Ch Medford MA 2000-2001; Int Emm Ch Braintree MA 1999-2000; Int Asst S Andr's Ch Framingham MA 1998-1999; Int Gr Ch Newton MA 1998; Long-Term Supply P S Mich's Epis Ch Holliston MA 1996-1998; Long-Term Supply P Ch Of The Ascen Fall River MA 1995-1996; Assessment Revs Com Dio Massachusetts Boston MA 1994-2004; Assmnt Rev Com Dio Massachusetts Boston MA 1994-2004; Stndg Com Dio Massachusetts Boston MA 1975-1984; Dioc Coun Dio Massachusetts Boston MA 1972-1975; Com Exam for Ord Dio Massachusetts Boston MA 1971-1975; S Lk's/San Lucas Epis Ch Chelsea MA 1968-1995; Asst Gr Epis Ch Elmira NY 1963-1967; Asst S Jn's Of Lattingtown Locust Vlly NY 1959-1963; Asst The Par Of All SS Ashmont-Dorches Dorchester MA 1957-1959. Auth, "S Lk's Epis Ch in Chelsea Massachusetts 150 Years 1841-1991," privately printed - Chelsea, MA, 1991. Cler Club of Boston 1969-1990; Parsons Club Cambridge 1969-2010. Nash Fllshp Dio MA 1977.

LORING, William Delano (Ct) 15 Pleasant Drive, Danbury CT 06811 **Assoc S Paul's Ch Brookfield CT 2002-** B Saint Petersburg FL 5/17/1937 s Henry Delano Loring & Lydia Whitford. BA Jn Hopkins U 1958; Drew U 1965; MDiv PDS 1965; GTS 1969; MS Wstrn Connecticut St U 1987. D 12/18/1965 P 6/18/1966 Bp Alfred L Banyard. m 7/1/2004 Diane Amison c 2. Exec Coun Dio Connecticut Hartford CT 2000-2001; P-in-c Chr Ch Waterbury CT 1999-2001; Chr Ch Trumbull CT 1999; Int Imm S Jas Par Derby CT 1998-1999; Chr Ch Patterson NY 1990-1997; Fin Com Dio Connecticut Hartford CT 1988; Exec Coun Dio Connecticut Hartford CT 1983-1986; P-in-c S Lk's Epis Ch New Haven CT 1982-1983; Secy of the Liturg Com Dio Connecticut Hartford CT 1976-1988; Evang Com Dio Connecticut Hartford CT 1976-1981; Fin Com Dio Connecticut Hartford CT 1974-1983; Vic S Jn's Ch Sandy Hook CT 1972-1982; P-in-c S Jas Ch Callicoon NY 1971-1972; Asst (Non-stipendiary) S Jos's Ch Queens Vill NY 1968-1969; S Andr The Apos Highland Highlands NJ 1965-1967. "Boone Porter: An Appreciation," *The Angl*, 1999; "What's Wrong w the New Confessions," *Living Ch*, 1971; Auth, "The Beatific Vision of Thos Aquinas," *ATR*, 1969. Angl Soc 1962; CCU 1972; Ord of S Ben, S Greg Abbey, Confrator 1970. frbill@jhu.edu

LOSCH, Richard Rorex (Ala) Po Box 1560, Livingston AL 35470 **P-in-c S Alb's Ch Livingston AL 1994-** B Boston MA 12/26/1933 s Paul Kenneth Losch & Helen Margaret. BA Ya 1956; MDiv Ya Berk 1959; MEd No Carolina St U 1989. D 6/11/1959 Bp Walter H Gray P 3/15/1960 Bp John Henry Esquirol. R S Jas' Ch Livingston AL 1994-2003; Asst S Tim's Ch Raleigh NC 1986-1989; Asst S Mich's Ch Marblehead MA 1970-1986; Asst. Headmaster The Tower Sch Marblehead MA 1969-1981; Yth Dir Dio Connecticut Hartford CT 1964-1966; R S Jn's Ch Sandy Hook CT 1961-1966; Cur Trin Ch Torrington CT 1959-1961. Auth, "All the People in the Bible," Eerdmans, 2008; Auth, "The Uttermost Part of the Earth," Eerdmans, 2005; Auth, "The Many Faces of Faith," Eerdmans, 2001. LitD (Hon.) U of W Alabama 2009; Kappa Mu Epsilon (Mathematics) U of W Alabama 1998; Phi Kappa Phi No Carolina St U 1989. loschr@bellsouth.net

LOUA, Cece A-S (Mich) 20060 Canterbury Rd, Detroit MI 48221 **All SS Ch Detroit MI 2010-** B Republic of Guinea 10/28/1962 s Kpeliwolo Loua & Mami. BA Pontifical Gregorian U 1991; BA Universite Jesuite de Paris Paris FR 1998; ThM Universite Jesuite de Paris Paris FR 2000; MA Wayne 2005. Rec from Roman Catholic 7/6/2006 Bp Wendell Nathaniel Gibbs Jr. c 2. Asst Cathd Ch Of S Paul Detroit MI 2006-2010. aloua@edomi.org

LOUD JR, Johnson D (Minn) 740 Shane Park Cir Apt 2, Prescott WI 54021 **Ch Of The Mssh Prairie Island Welch MN 1997-** B Red Lake MN 2/27/1942 s Johnson Duwayne Loud & Clemence Ann. BS St. Cloud St U 1965; MDiv CDSP 1997. D 6/27/1987 Bp Edmond Lee Browning P 5/1/1988 Bp Robert Marshall Anderson. m 10/2/1965 Lavonne Ellen Lyons c 2. Int S Antipas Ch Redby MN 1997-1998. johnsonloudjr@aol.com

LOUDEN, Molly O'Neill (Ct) 37 Gin Still Ln, West Hartford CT 06107 B Toledo OH 4/9/1943 d Richard Albert O'Neill & Vera Grace. AA U of Florida 1962; BS Florida Sthrn Coll 1967; MDiv Ya Berk 1983; DMin GTF 2003. D 9/16/1984 Bp Arthur Edward Walmsley P 4/27/1985 Bp Clarence Nicholas Coleridge. m 8/11/1962 Bruce Louden c 3. Cur S Andr's Ch Meriden CT 1984-1988; S Mk's Ch New Britain CT 1983-1984. molouden@comcast.net

LOUDENSLAGER, Samuel Charles (Ark) 20000 Hwy 300-Spur, Bigelow AR 72016 B Ardmore OK 3/23/1955 s Charles Edward Loudenslager & Dorothy. BA U of Memphis 1980; MS New Mex St U. 1983. D 11/23/2002 Bp Larry Earl Maze. m 2/12/1983 Teresa Contreras. NAAD 2001. sam.loudenslager@gmail.com

LOUGHRAN JR, Eugene James (SwFla) 633 Coquina Court, Fort Myers FL 33908 B Salem NJ 10/20/1940 s Eugene James Loughran & Grace Anna. BA Hob 1962; MDiv PDS 1965. D 5/1/1965 P 11/6/1965 Bp Alfred L Banyard. m 8/25/1963 Elizabeth Arnold. R S Jn The Div Epis Ch Sun City Cntr FL 1983-1999; R S Paul's Ch Mt Vernon OH 1974-1983; R S Barn Ch Brackenridge PA 1969-1974; R S Paul's Ch Monongahela PA 1967-1969; Cur Calv Epis Ch Flemington NJ 1965-1967. ELIZGENELOU@HOTMAIL.COM

LOUGHREN, James Patrick (Alb) 4879 Lake Shore Dr, Bolton Landing NY 12814 **Dn Dio Albany Albany NY 2005-; R Ch Of S Sacrement Bolton Landing NY 2004-** B Potsdam NY 10/13/1955 B.A. St. Lawr 1981; PreTheology Stds Wadhams Hall Sem 1987; M.Div. St. Jn's Sem Boston 1991; M.A. Systematic Theol St. Jn's Sem Boston 1991. Rec from Roman Catholic 4/16/2003 Bp Daniel William Herzog. m 1/1/2005 Laurie A McKenna c 1. joshua1v9@nycap.rr.com

LOUIS, Richard M (Nwk) 2395 Quill Ct, Mahwah NJ 07430 B Brooklyn NY 7/6/1933 s Mortimer Louis & Olga Florence. BA Colg 1955; MDiv EDS 1959. D 6/11/1959 P 12/19/1959 Bp Horace W B Donegan. m 11/5/1966 M Kristan Bertelsen c 2. Assoc Chr Ch Ridgewood NJ 2002; R S Jn's Memi Ch Ramsey NJ 1978-2000; R S Mk's Ch Teaneck NJ 1971-1978; Cur Chr Ch Hackensack NJ 1970-1971. Cbury Schlr Dio Newark 1988. klouis1@optimum.net

LOUISE SSM, Sister Catherine (Mass) 17 Louisburg Sq, Boston MA 02108 B New York NY 4/4/1916 d Edward N Perkins & Kate C. Brearly Sch; BA Bryn 1938; MA Col 1941. D 11/1/1978 Bp Morris Fairchild Arnold P 12/1/1979 Bp John Bowen Coburn.

LOUTREL, William Frederic (Ct) 1090 Ridge Rd, Hamden CT 06517 B Newton MA 6/5/1951 s Louis F Loutrel & Dora L. BS RPI 1973; MDiv GTS 1978. D 6/10/1978 P 3/17/1979 Bp Morgan Porteus. m 7/24/2004 Thomas M Fynan. R S Jn's Ch E Hartford CT 1984-1989; Chr Ch Cathd Indianapolis IN 1980-1984; Cn Dio Indianapolis Indianapolis IN 1980-1984; Cur S Mich's Ch Naugatuck CT 1978-1980. wloutrel@snet.net

✠ LOUTTIT, Rt Rev Henry Irving (Ga) 611 E Bay St, Savannah GA 31401 **Ret Bp of Georgia The TS at The U So Sewanee TN 2000-** B West Palm Beach FL 6/13/1938 s Henry I Louttit & Amy Moss. BA U So 1960; BD VTS 1963. D 6/11/1963 Bp Henry I Louttit P 4/25/1964 Bp Albert R Stuart Con 1/21/1995 for Ga. m 6/14/1962 Jayne Northway c 1. Bp Of Ga Dio Georgia Savannah GA 1995-2010; Trst VTS Alexandria VA 1984-1989; Dio Georgia Savannah GA 1982-1994; Ap Coun Dio Georgia Savannah GA 1975; R Chr Ch Valdosta GA 1967-1994; D-In-C Trin Ch Statesboro GA 1963-1964. ADLMC; RWF; S Alb & S Sergius. DD STUSo Sewanee TN 1996; DD VTS Alexandria VA 1993; Phi Beta Kappa. diocesega@att.net

LOVE, Leon Lewis (CNY) 5 Gail Dr, Waverly NY 14892 B Elmira NY 2/28/1938 s Clarence L Love & Cecilia R. BS Mansfield U of Pennsylvania 1969; MDiv Bex 1972. D 5/27/1972 P 3/17/1973 Bp Dean T Stevenson. m 8/27/1984 Ann Mair Love c 2. Vic Chr Ch Wellsburg NY 1998-2003; Vic Emm Ch Elmira NY 1998-2003; Vic Gr Ch Waverly NY 1998-2003; Vic S Jn's Epis Ch Elmira Heights NY 1998-2003; Chemung Vlly Cluster Elmira NY 1996-2003; R S Jn's Ch Wilson NY 1989-1991; St Mk Epis Ch No Tonawanda NY 1987-1989; Chr Enrichment Cntr Flint MI 1978-1981; R S Matt's Epis Ch Sunbury PA 1977-1978; S Mary's Ch Williamsport PA 1972-1977. llove1938@yahoo.com

LOVE, Sean David (RG) 7480 No. 1 Rd., Richmond BC V7C1T-6 Canada B Vancouver Canada 6/9/1965 D 7/30/2005 Bp Jeffrey Neil Steenson P 11/10/

2007 Bp William Carl Frey. m 7/17/2003 Penelope J Love c 3. seanandpenny@shaw.ca

✠ LOVE, Rt Rev William Howard (Alb) PO Box 211, Lake Luzerne NY 12846 **Bp of Albany Dio Albany Albany NY 2007-; Bp of Albany Dio Albany Albany NY 2006-** B Dallas TX 8/14/1957 s James Herbert Love & Frances Lee. BA SW Texas St U San Marcos 1980; MS SUNY 1988; MDiv Nash 1991. D 6/22/1991 P 3/1/1992 Bp David Standish Ball Con 9/16/2006 for Alb. m 10/22/1983 Karen Elizabeth Novak. R S Mary's Ch Lake Luzerne NY 1992-2006; Dn'S Vic Cathd Of All SS Albany NY 1991-1992. BISHOPLOVE@ALBANYDIOCESE.ORG

LOVEKIN, A(rthur) Adams (RG) PO Box 756, Cedar Crest NM 87008 **Assoc (Ret) S Jn's Cathd Albuquerque NM 2004-** B Boston,MA 11/6/1928 s Osgood Stevens Lovekin & Marion O. BA Stan 1951; BD CDSP 1954; STM STUSo 1962; PhD Fuller TS 1975. D 6/12/1954 P 12/19/1954 Bp Arthur Kinsolving. m 6/18/1977 Ann Lewis c 8. Fndr Vic Ch Of The H Cross Edgewood NM 1995-1998; Samar Counslg Cntr Albuquerque NM 1987-1991; Clincl Psychol S Jn's Cathd Albuquerque NM 1976-1986; Asst S Paul's Pomona Pomona CA 1973-1974; Fndr Vic S Jn's Mssn La Verne CA 1962-1969; Assoc S Lk's Par Monrovia CA 1960-1962; Fndr Vic S Dav's Epis Page AZ 1959-1960; Vic S Jn's Ch Williams AZ 1956-1960; Asst Gr S Paul's Epis Ch Tucson AZ 1954-1955. Auth, "Glossolalia: Behavioral Sci Perspective on Spkng in Tongues," Oxf Press, 1985. AAPC 1978-2003; Amer Bd Profsnl Psychol 1986-2003; APA 1973-2003; APA, Div 36: The Psycholog 1980-2003; Commision of Mnstry 1978-1985; Cmsn of Mnstry 1991-1997. Diplomate AAPC 1990; Diplomate Amer Bd Profsnl Psychol 1986. aalovekin@yahoo.com

LOVELACE, David Wayne (CPa) 140 N Beaver St, York PA 17401 **Dep to GC Dio Cntrl Pennsylvania Harrisburg PA 2000-; R The Epis Ch Of S Jn The Bapt York PA 1996-** B Richmond VA 10/21/1948 s Ray Lancaster Lovelace & Charlotte. AA Ferrum Coll 1968; BA Emory & Henry Coll 1970; MDiv VTS 1976; MST Columbia TS 1990. D 5/22/1976 Bp John Alfred Baden P 3/19/1977 Bp Hunley Agee Elebash. m 7/8/1989 Elaine Hencley c 3. Stndg Com Pres Dio Atlanta Atlanta GA 1995-1996; R S Paul's Epis Ch Newnan GA 1982-1996; Asst Ch Of The Gd Shpd Rocky Mt NC 1979-1982; S Jas Epis Ch Belhaven NC 1976-1979. Auth, "Min to the Poor," *Congressional Record*. revdwl@aol.com

LOVELADY, Eldwin M (Nev) 3700 14th Ave SE, Unit 3, Olympia WA 98501 **Assoc P S Mary's Ch Lakewood WA 2011-; Multicultural Mnstry Cmsn Dio Olympia Seattle WA 2009-** B Morrilton AR 9/5/1945 s Earnest William Lovelady & Louise Edna. AAS USAF 1986; BS Pk Coll Parkville MO 1989; MDiv STUSo 1993. D 5/29/1993 Bp Frank Jeffrey Terry P 12/4/1993 Bp David Charles Bowman. m 8/1/1974 Deborah Beard c 4. Int R S Lk's Epis Ch Vancouver WA 2010-2011; Multicultural Mnstry Off Dio Nevada Las Vegas NV 2008-2009; R All SS Epis Ch Las Vegas NV 2004-2009; R S Ptr's Ch Westfield NY 1998-2004; Liturg Cmsn Dio Wstrn New York Tonawanda NY 1993-1998; Cur S Lk's Epis Ch Jamestown NY 1993-1998. Cmnty of S Mary 1992. eldwin@lovelady.org

LOVETT, G David (ETenn) PO Box 10944, Knoxville TN 37939 **Asst S Steph's Epis Ch Oak Ridge TN 2011-** B Knox County TN 6/15/1948 s Raymond Lovett & Mildred Leona. BS U of Tennessee 1970; MDiv SE Bapt Sem 1980; DMin Garrett-Evang 1996. D 5/29/2010 P 5/28/2010 Bp Charles Glenn VonRosenberg. m 2/8/1991 Anne E Anne Jerrine Elkins Turner c 2. Transitional D Ch Of The Gd Shpd Knoxville TN 2010-2011. gdavid@pastoral-counseling.net

LOVING, John H (NwT) 8009 Ladera Verde, Austin TX 78739 B Richmond VA 10/28/1938 s Harnish Phillips Loving & Elizabeth. Cbury Coll; BA U Rich 1961; MDiv GTS 1967; S Geo's Coll Jerusalem IL 1985. D 6/22/1967 P 5/23/1968 Bp George P Gunn. m 6/24/1967 Nancy W Ward c 2. Asst The Ch of the Gd Shpd Austin TX 2008-2009; Stndg Com Dio NW Texas Lubbock TX 1999-2000; Long-R Plnng & Structure Dio NW Texas Lubbock TX 1994-1997; Trst Epis TS Of The SW Austin TX 1993-1996; R Emm Epis Ch San Angelo TX 1990-2003; R Gr Epis Ch Ponca City OK 1983-1990; R Johns Memi Epis Ch Farmville VA 1969-1983; Cur Ch Of The Ascen Norfolk VA 1967-1969. Auth, "Adv IV: The Visitation," *LivCh*, 1997. nloving4@austin.rr.com

LOW, James Robert (Ct) 60 Shadagee Rd Unit 22, Saco ME 04072 B Beverly MA 1/28/1939 s James W Low & Nettie. BA Harv 1960; MA Wesl 1966; BD EDS 1969. D 6/21/1969 Bp Anson Phelps Stokes Jr P 5/6/1970 Bp John Melville Burgess. m 3/18/1972 Linda Carol Nutter c 3. Mssnr Calv Ch Enfield CT 1998-2004; Mssnr Gr Ch Broad Brook CT 1998-2004; Mssnr H Trin Epis Ch Enfield CT 1998-2004; No Cntrl Reg Mnstry Enfield CT 1998-2004; Mssnr S Andr's Epis Ch Enfield CT 1998-2004; COM Dio Massachusetts Boston MA 1990-1998; R Epiph Par Walpole MA 1987-1998; Falmouth Coun on Aging Dio Massachusetts Boston MA 1983-1987; Dio Massachusetts Boston MA 1978-1984; Dio Massachusetts Boston MA 1978-1981; Dio Massachusetts Boston MA 1978-1981; Dioc Coun Dio Massachusetts Boston MA 1977-1982; Assoc R S Barn Ch Falmouth MA 1972-1987; Asst R All SS Ch Chelmsford MA 1969-1972. "Rev Jim Low Day" Town of Falmouth Falmouth MA 1987. jlow6@maine.rr.com

LOW, Melvin Leslie (Ia) No address on file. B Everett MA 2/15/1938 s Melvin Leslie Low & Jean Lavinia. BA Gordon Coll 1972; MDiv Nash 1975; U of Notre Dame 1979. D 4/22/1975 Bp Charles Thomas Gaskell P 11/15/1975 Bp Alexander Doig Stewart. Vic Trin Ch Emmetsburg IA 1997-2007; Vic Ch Of S Thos Algona IA 1997-2006; R Gr Ch Cedar Rapids IA 1983-1986; R S Mk's Ch Waupaca WI 1978-1983; R S Paul's Ch Windsor VT 1976-1978; Dio Wstrn Massachusetts Springfield MA 1975-1976; Asst Trin Epis Ch Ware MA 1975-1976. Soc of S Jn the Evang. m@imonmail.com

LOW, Raymond Albert (Mass) 5 Buttonwood Rd, Marshfield MA 02050 **R Emer S Lk's Epis Ch Scituate MA 2003-** B Melbourne VIC AU 3/25/1931 s Roy Albert Low & Mavis Maude. ThL Ridley Coll Melbourne AU 1957; BA Estrn Nazarene Coll 1972; Med Boston St Coll 1982; MA Estrn Nazarene Coll 1987. Trans from Anglican Church Of Australia 6/1/1963 as Priest Bp Anson Phelps Stokes Jr. m 11/7/1959 Joan Elizabeth Looker c 3. S Jn's Epis Ch Saugus MA 2000-2002; Dn Dio Massachusetts Boston MA 1999-2002; R S Lk's Epis Ch Scituate MA 1963-2002; Cur S Paul's Ch Boston MA 1961-1963. Search for Justice and Equality in Palestine/Israel - Pres 1992-2002. Scituate Citizen of the Year Awd ChmbrCom Scituate MA 1993. looklow5@gmail.com

LOW, Salin Miller (Ct) PO Box 27, Pine Meadow CT 06061 **R S Jn's Ch Pine Meadow CT 1993-** B Norman OK 9/20/1949 d Edward Walter Miller & Julia Wheeler. W&M 1969; BBA U of Oklahoma 1971; MBA U of Tulsa 1984; MDiv VTS 1990. D 6/23/1990 Bp Robert Manning Moody P 5/3/1991 Bp Allen Lyman Bartlett Jr. m 1/19/1997 William Harrison Low. Fin Cmte, Planned Giv Cmte Dio Connecticut Hartford CT 1996-1997; Stwdshp Cmte Dio Pennsylvania Philadelphia PA 1992-1993; Asst Chr Ch Philadelphia Philadelphia PA 1990-1993. salin@revslow.net

LOW, William Harrison (Ct) 12 Meadowview Ct, Canton CT 06019 **P-t Chapl S Mich's Chap So Kent CT 1996-** B Hyannis MA 2/18/1928 s Alfred Leslie Low & Lillian Mertis. Oxford Sch of Bus Admin Cambridge MA 1949; Ya Berk 1965; STM Yale DS 1974. D 6/12/1965 Bp Charles F Hall P 12/1/1965 Bp Donald J Campbell. m 1/19/1997 Salin Miller c 2. Assoc S Paul's Epis Ch Bantam CT 2000-2007; ExCoun Dio Connecticut Hartford CT 1980-1993; R S Alb's Ch Simsbury CT 1978-1993; All SS Chap Hartford CT 1966-1978; All SS' Epis Ch E Hartford CT 1966-1978; Dept Mssns Dio Connecticut Hartford CT 1966-1978; P-in-c S Mk's Ch Ashland NH 1965-1966; P-in-c Trin Ch Meredith NH 1965-1966. william@revslow.net

LOWE, Edward Charles (Ga) PO Box 168, Saint Marys GA 31558 **Chr Ch S Marys GA 2009-; S Matt's Epis Ch Rockwood MI 2005-** B Aurora IL 4/25/1951 s Clifford Lowe & Helen. Pstr/Evang Moody Bible Inst 1973; MA Moody Bible Inst 1996; DMin TESM 2006. D 6/2/2007 P 12/15/2007 Bp John Wadsworth Howe. m 4/20/1974 Catherine Lowe c 3. Asst S Barn Ch Deland FL 2007-2009; S Ptr's Epis Ch Lake Mary FL 2005-2007. ed@edplanet.com

LOWE JR, Eugene Yerby (NY) 624 Colfax St, Evanston IL 60201 B Staten Island NY 8/18/1949 s Eugene Yerby Lowe & Miriam Victory. BA Pr 1971; MDiv UTS 1978; MA UTS 1982; PhD UTS 1987. D 6/3/1978 P 12/1/1978 Bp Paul Moore Jr. m 11/4/1989 Jane Pataky Henderson. Asst Calv and St Geo New York NY 1978-1983.

LOWE, Harold Chapin (Dal) 2212 Saint Andrews, McKinney TX 75070 B Wichita KS 8/25/1950 s Harold Ward Lowe & Eris Lynette. BD U of Kansas 1973; MA Pepperdine U 1980. D 11/27/1983 P 6/1/1984 Bp Leonardo Romero-Rivera. m 5/3/1974 Norma Herrera-Camargo c 2. Auth, "Journ Of Indstrl Engr". NAAD. Ralph Jas Awd 1984; Fulbright Schlr 1973. momish@tx.rr.com

LOWE JR, J(ohn) Fletcher (Del) 1600 Westbrook Avenue Apt 27, Richmond VA 23227 **P-in-res S Paul's Ch Richmond VA 1997-** B Greenville SC 3/11/1932 s J(ohn) Fletcher Lowe & Marie Oliver. BA W&L 1954; MDiv GTS 1959. D 6/20/1959 P 7/16/1960 Bp Clarence Alfred Cole. m 6/27/1959 Mary Frances Adamson c 3. Int R Emm Epis Ch Geneva 1201 CH 2000; Int Ch of the Ascen Munich 81545 DE 1996-1997; Cmsn on Lay Mnstry Dio Virginia Richmond VA 1995-2002; Int S Jn's Ch Richmond VA 1994-1996; P-in-c S Jas Epis Ch Firenze IA IT 1994; GC - Alternative Dep Dio Delaware Wilmington DE 1988-1991; Comp Dio Cmsn (Dio Pretoria, SA) Dio Delaware Wilmington DE 1987-1990; Dioc Coun Dio Delaware Wilmington DE 1987-1990; Dioc T/F on Cler/Lay Profsnl Compstn Dio Delaware Wilmington DE 1987-1990; R Imm Ch Highlands Wilmington DE 1985-1993; Stndg Committe, Pres Dio Virginia Richmond VA 1983-1985; Stndg Committe Dio Virginia Richmond VA 1981-1985; Human Needs Com Dio Virginia Richmond VA 1981-1984; Exec Bd Dio Virginia Richmond VA 1978-1980; GC, Alt Dep Dio Virginia Richmond VA 1976-1985; Exec Bd Dio Virginia Richmond VA 1973-1975; R Ch Of The H Comf Richmond VA 1970-1985; Litgurical Cmsn, Organizer/Chair Dio Virginia Richmond VA 1967-1976; Chr Soc Relatns Com, Chair Dio SW Virginia Roanoke VA 1965-1967; Liturg Cmsn, Organizer/Chair Dio SW Virginia Roanoke VA 1965-1967; Virginia Coun of Ch, Exec Com Dio SW Virginia Roanoke VA 1965-1967; Exec Bd Dio SW

Virginia Roanoke VA 1964-1967; Vic S Barn Ch Lynchburg VA 1963-1967; Vic Ch Of The Ascen Seneca SC 1959-1963. Auth, "Baptism:the Event and the Adventure," LeaderResources, 2006; Co-Ed, "Mnstry in Daily Life: A Guide to Living the Baptismal Cov," The Epis Ch Cntr, 1996; Auth, "Wrshp and the Mnstry of the Baptized," *As We Gather to Pray*, Epis Ch Cntr, 1996; "Miscelaneous arts in Natl, Dioc, Loc and Ecum Pub on Liturg, Soc Justice and the Mnstry of t"; Auth, "Selected Sermons 1978-1990," The Epis Ch Cntr. Cntr for Baptismal Living, Bd Mem 1998-2006; Epis Partnr for Faithfulness in Daily Life, Cnvnr 2006. R Emer Ch of the H Comf, Richmond, VA 2009; Distinguished Alum Awd GTS 2007; Commendation Virginia St Senate and Hse of Delegates 2004; Commonwealth Awd, Interfaith advocacy and Relatns Coun for Amer's First Freedom 2003; Hon Cn S Ptr's Cathd, Dio Bukedi, Uganda Tororo Uganda 1982; Virginia Citizenship Awd Anti-Defamation League, Virginia Chapt 1976; All-Amer (lacrosse) Washington & Lee U Lexington VA 1954; ODK - Ldrshp Soc Washington & Lee U Lexington VA 1954. jflowe@aol.com

LOWE, John Leon (Ind) 200 Glennes Ln Apt 205, Dunedin FL 34698 B Indianapolis IN 12/12/1928 s Russel James Lowe & Ethel Jane. BA Pasadena Coll 1954; BD Butler U 1957; MA Butler U 1969. D 6/30/1957 P 1/4/1958 Bp John P Craine. m 2/5/1950 Patricia Ann Hoover c 3. Assoc Ch Of The Ascen Clearwater FL 1998-2007; Vic S Jn's Ch Speedway IN 1959-1965; Vic S Mich's Ch Noblesville IN 1957-1959. Intl Soc of Theta Phi 1957; Pres Indiana Acad of Rel 1976.

LOWE, Lori Marleen (At) 1130 Wilmette Ave, Wilmette IL 60091 **Transitional R S Aug's Epis Ch Wilmette IL 2011-** B Atlanta GA 3/12/1947 d Billy Felix Lowe & Marion Beryl. W Georgia Coll 1966; BA Georgia St U 1969; MDiv Candler TS Emory U 1983. D 6/7/1986 P 12/21/1988 Bp Charles Judson Child Jr. m 1/8/2000 William Pearman McLemore c 3. Int S Marg's Ch Annapolis MD 2009-2010; Dir, Discerning Young Vocations Experience (DYVE) Dio Atlanta Atlanta GA 1999-2009; R S Mk's Epis Ch Lagrange GA 1995-2009; Int S Thos Epis Ch Columbus GA 1994-1995; S Bede's Ch Atlanta GA 1991-1994; Chr Ch Norcross GA 1987-1991; Asst S Barth's Epis Ch Atlanta GA 1986-1987. Auth, "Wmn Of The Word". Cmnty Of S Mary. Omicron Delta Kappa Ldrshp Soc. lorilowe@mindspring.com

LOWE, Steve (Chi) 2009 Regency Ct, Geneva IL 60134 **D S Mk's Ch Geneva IL 2005-** B Joplin MO 9/28/1947 s Billy Gene Lowe & Ardeth. BD U of Arkansas 1970; MS Arizona St U 1971. D 2/5/2005 Bp William Dailey Persell. m 7/18/1969 Lela Williams c 2. DeaconSteve@theloweclan.net

LOWE, Walter James (At) 1647 N Rock Springs Rd NE, Atlanta GA 30324 B Madison WI 7/23/1940 s James T Lowe & Lois Belle. BA DePauw U 1962; BTh U of Louvain 1963; BD Yale DS 1967; PhD Ya 1972. D 6/24/1967 Bp John P Craine. m 6/30/1979 Barbara DeConcini. Auth, "Mystery & The Unconscious: A Study In The Thought Of Paul Ricoent"; Auth, "Evil & The Unconscious"; Auth, "Theol & Difference: The Wound Of Reason". Conf Angl Theol.

LOWERY, Donald Andrew (NC) 210 S Chestnut St, Henderson NC 27536 **Old St. Jn's Com Dio No Carolina Raleigh NC 2005-; R The Ch Of The H Innoc Henderson NC 2005-** B Burlington VT 11/3/1956 s Andrew Lowery & Carolyn Virginia. BA Lee Coll 1979; MA Loyola Coll 1984; MDiv VTS 1987. D 6/20/1987 Bp A(lbert) Theodore Eastman P 4/23/1988 Bp William Gillette Weinhauer. E Reg P Search Com Dio No Carolina Raleigh NC 2009-2010; Sprtl Dir For Happ Dio Upper So Carolina Columbia SC 2002-2005; Sprtl Dir For Happ Dio Upper So Carolina Columbia SC 2002-2005; Sprtl Dir For Curs Dio Upper So Carolina Columbia SC 2001-2005; Cmsn On Racism Dio Upper So Carolina Columbia SC 1997-2000; Com St Of Ch Dio Upper So Carolina Columbia SC 1994-1995; VP Cathd Coll Bd Dio Upper So Carolina Columbia SC 1992-1995; R Ch Of The Gd Shpd York SC 1991-2005; Asst S Mk's Ch Gastonia NC 1987-1991. Soc Of King Chas The Mtyr 2007. Henry Richardson Awd York Place, The Epis Chld'S Hm 2004. donaldlowery@hotmail.com

LOWERY, Hermon Lee (Ala) 931 7th Ave Nw, Alabaster AL 35007 **Ch of the H Sprt Alabaster AL 2002-** B Repton AL 10/6/1955 s Bill George Lowery & Frances. MDiv STUSo 1990. D 6/2/1990 P 4/27/1991 Bp Charles Farmer Duvall. m 11/23/2009 Linda D Davison c 2. Vic Ch Of The Resurr Centerville UT 1995-2002; Dio Utah Salt Lake City UT 1995-2002; S Paul's Ch Mobile AL 1990-1995; Dio Cntrl Gulf Coast Pensacola FL 1990. hleelowery@charter.net

LOWERY JR, James Lincoln (Mass) 8 Mccurdy Rd, Old Lyme CT 06371 **Died 2/14/2010** B Utica NY 7/28/1932 s James Lincoln Lowery & Mary. BA Harv 1954; MDiv VTS 1959. D 6/13/1959 Bp Malcolm E Peabody P 6/4/1960 Bp Walter M Higley. c 1. "Bi-Vocationals," Infinity Pub, 2006; Auth, "The Return of Dual Role Cler," 1997; Auth, "Sm Congregations & Their Cler," Morehouse-Barlow, 1970; Auth, "Case Hist of Tentmakers," Morehouse-Barlow, 1970; Auth, "Peers, Tents & Owls," Morehouse-Barlow, 1970. ACC; Rel Resrch Assn. Harvard Prize Schlr Harv 1950.

LOWREY, Edward Sager (NwPa) Box 54, 107 Harvey Road, Foxburg PA 16036 B Warren PA 7/16/1938 s Edward Charles Lowrey & Emma. BA U of Wstrn Ontario 1960; LTh Huron Angl Sem London On CA 1962; ThM Pittsburgh TS 1975. D 6/29/1962 Bp William Crittenden P 12/21/1963 Bp Winfred Hamlin Ziegler. m 9/14/1963 Melanie Lowrey. Bec Dio NW Pennsylvania Erie PA 1991-1993; Ch Of Our Fr Foxburg PA 1989-2001; R Trin Ch S Clair Shores MI 1980-1982; P S Aid's Ch Michigan Cntr MI 1979-1980; Dn Sw Convoc Dio Michigan Detroit MI 1977-1979; S Paul's Epis Ch Jackson MI 1976-1979; R S Matt's Epis Ch Homestead PA 1972-1975; R Trin Epis Ch Beaver PA 1966-1972; Cur S Jn's Ch Bangor ME 1964-1966; Vic Ch Of Our Fr Foxburg PA 1962-1964. elowrey@csonline.net

LOWREY III, Pierce Lang (At) 3830 Randall Farm Rd, Atlanta GA 30339 **St Ben's Epis Ch Smyrna GA 2010-; The GTS New York NY 2010-** B Austin TX 12/1/1953 s Pierce Lowrey & Rosemari. MDiv Candler TS Emory U; Georgia Inst of Tech; BA Georgia St U. D 9/29/2004 Bp J(ohn) Neil Alexander P 4/3/2005 Bp Frank Kellogg Allan. m 11/12/1988 Julie Marie Seymour c 4. Dio Atlanta Atlanta GA 2010; Dio Atlanta Atlanta GA 2006-2009; S Anne's Epis Ch Atlanta GA 2005-2006. plangiii@msn.com

LOWRY, David Busch (LI) Po Box 51777, New Orleans LA 70151 **Actg Dn Geo Mercer TS Garden City NY 2010-; Dn No Shore Dnry Dio Long Island Garden City NY 2006-; R Chr Ch Manhasset NY 2004-** B Boston MA 8/4/1946 s David F Lowry & Helen B. BA Ham 1968; MDiv/STM GTS 1975; MA, PhD Indiana U 1988. D 1/15/1972 Bp Joseph Warren Hutchens P 7/1/1972 Bp Charles Alfred Voegeli. m 8/29/1970 Mary Coleman c 1. Dir Desmond Tutu Cntr The GTS New York NY 2009-2010; VP Trst of the Estate belonging to the Dio Long Island Dio Long Island Garden City NY 2007-2010; Dn Chr Ch Cathd New Orleans LA 1986-1990; Cn-In-Res Cathd Of The Incarn Garden City NY 1980-1986; R Ch Of The Nativ Indianapolis IN 1978-1980; Asst Chr Ch Manhasset NY 1974-1976. dlowry36@aol.com

LOWRY, Linda Louise (CFla) 4836 Big Oaks Lane, Orlando FL 32806 B Columbus OH 1/1/1952 d James Henry Hodges & Emma. BA Ohio Dominican Coll 1976; MA U of Nthrn Colorado 1982; MA U of Nthrn Colorado 1986; MDiv STUSo 1988; DMin STUSo 2000. D 6/18/1988 P 6/12/1989 Bp Duncan Montgomery Gray Jr. m 9/5/1970 James Richard Lowry. Dn, Angl Inst Dio Florida Jacksonville FL 2004; Instr, Angl Inst Dio Florida Jacksonville FL 2002-2004; R S Jas Epis Ch Perry FL 1999-2006; R S Jas Epis Ch Port Gibson MS 1998-1999; Vic S Matthews Ch Mayo FL 1998-1999; R S Thos Epis Ch Diamondhead MS 1992-1996; Asst S Jn's Epis Ch Ocean Sprg MS 1990-1992; Cur S Jas Ch Jackson MS 1988-1990. Auth, "Journey In Faith-Catecumenate For The Epis Ch," *Doctoral Thesis*, 2000; Auth, "Unexpected Answers," *Journ of Chr Healing*, Intl OSL the Physican, 1989; Auth, "Taking The Time," *Journ of Chr Healing*, IInternational OSL the Physcn, 1988. Amer Assn Chr Coun; Amnesty Intl ; Curs; Life Professed Franciscan Ord Of Div Compassion. Fell in Res, TS U So 2002; Fell In Res, TS U So Sewanee TN 2001; Meritorius Serv Medal Second Awd USAF 1995; Meritorious Serv Medal Second Awd USAF 1995; Meritorious Serv Medal USAF 1985; Joint Serv Commendation Medal USAF 1983; Ldrshp Awd DAR 1976; Phi Beta Kappa Natl hon Soc 1974; Natl Defense Serv Medal USAF 1974. lllowry@aol.com

LOW-SKINNER, Debra Lee (LI) 137 Redding Rd Apt C, Campbell CA 95008 **Int R S Barth's Epis Ch Livermore CA 2010-** B San Francisco CA 10/8/1952 d Donald Fee Lee & Ida Maud. BS U of San Francisco 1974; MS Santa Clara U 1991; MDiv CDSP 1997; Cert Int Mnstry Prog 2002. D 6/21/1997 P 12/27/1997 Bp Richard Lester Shimpfky. m 4/24/1993 Donald Joseph Skinner. P in Res Epis Ch Of S Mk The Evang No Bellmore NY 2009-2010; Int Gr Epis Ch Massapequa NY 2009; R Chr Ch Garden City NY 2003-2009; P in Charge S Mart's Epis Ch New Bedford MA 2000-2003; Cur All SS Ch Carmel CA 1998-2000; Assoc Vic Ch Of The H Sprt Campbell CA 1997-1998. EWC 1997; OSL the Physcn 1999; OHC 1997; Soc of Wmn Engr 1979-2003. revdeb76@msn.com

LOYA, Craig William (Kan) 835 SW Polk, Topeka KS 66612 **Cn to the Ordnry Dio Kansas Topeka KS 2011-** B North Platte NE 4/5/1977 s Ernesto Loya & JaNelle K. BA Hastings Coll 1999; Dplma in Angl Stds Ya Berk 2002; MDiv Yale DS 2002. D 10/11/2002 P 5/3/2003 Bp Creighton Leland Robertson. m 8/14/2004 Melissa Tubbs c 1. Campus Mssnr Dio Kansas Topeka KS 2007-2009; P-in-c Ch Of The Gd Shpd Fairhaven MA 2006-2007; P-in-c S Mart's Epis Ch New Bedford MA 2006-2007; Int Asst R Gr Ch New Bedford MA 2004-2005; Vic Rosebud Epis Mssn Mssn SD 2002-2004. craigloya@gmail.com

LOYD, Janet Ellen (Oly) PO Box 55, Darrington WA 98241 B Pasadena CA 3/19/1957 d Everil Edgar Loyd & Vesta Lee. MA Claremont Grad U; BA Pomona Coll 1979. D 2/15/2011 Bp Gregory Harold Rickel.

LUAL, Anderia Arok (Az) Diocese of Arizona, 114 W Roosevelt St, Phoenix AZ 85003 **Vic Dio Arizona Phoenix AZ 2008-** B 1/1/1956 s Lual Ajang Arok & Deng Mayan. MTS Iliff TS 2006. Trans from The Episcopal Church of the Sudan 9/4/2008 Bp Kirk Stevan Smith. P Dio Colorado Denver CO 2002-2007. lualarok2000@yahoo.com

LUBELFELD, Nicholas Paul Needham (Va) 4460 Edan Mae Ct, Annandale VA 22003 B Detroit MI 4/12/1950 s Prof Jerzy Lubelfeld & Joan Hawley. BA U MI 1972; Th Dip U Of Durham Engl 1976; M Div VTS 1978. D 6/17/1978

Bp William J Gordon Jr P 6/3/1979 Bp H Coleman McGehee Jr. m 5/22/1978 Elizabeth Cardenas c 3. Pstr Assoc Ch Of Our Redeem Aldie VA 2007-2009; Assoc The Falls Ch Epis Falls Ch VA 1994-2007; R Trin Ch Arlington VA 1986-1993; S Paul's Epis Ch Lansing MI 1978-1986. Auth, "I can't get the update to Wk". nlubelfeld@thefallschurch.org

LUCAS, Albert (HB) 4440 Meadow Creek Cir, Sarasota FL 34233 B Philadelphia PA 6/26/1924 s Albert Hawley Lucas & Frances Wharton. PDS 1951. D 6/2/1951 Bp William P Remington P 12/1/1951 Bp Lane W Barton. m 6/26/1948 Alison Lucas. St Fran Hosp Hartford CT 1975-1977; R S Anne's Epis Ch Smithsburg MD 1966-1967; R S Jn's Par Hagerstown MD 1962-1967; R Trin Ch Bend OR 1959-1962; R S Steph's Epis Ch Orinda CA 1955-1959; R S Andr's Epis Ch Prineville OR 1951-1955. Cert Chapl Coll Of Chapl (Amer Prot Hosp Assn). 1st Citizens Awd Jr ChmbrCom Prineville OR 1953. dankeinga@comcast.net

LUCAS, Alison Carey Carpenter (ECR) 19315 Vineyard Ln, Saratoga CA 95070 **D S Phil's Ch San Jose CA 1992-** B Wilmington DE 8/14/1925 d Allan Wallace Carpenter & Edith. AA Centenary Coll 1946; BS U of Pennsylvania 1948; MS U of Hartford 1979; MA S Mary Coll Moraga CA 1980; BA Sch for Deacons 1991. D 12/2/1991 Bp Richard Lester Shimpfky. c 3. Rel Educ Consult Dio Maryland Baltimore MD 1964-1969. Auth, "Fam Life & Sex Educ," *Curric*, Simsbury, Conn., Publ Schools, 1968. Ord of S Lk 1990. Distinguished Alum Awd Centenary Coll Hackettstown NJ 2002. acl222@aol.com

LUCAS, Jeremy Pierce (Ala) 18616 NE 109th Ave, Battle Ground WA 98604 **Ch Of The H Sprt Episco Battle Ground WA 2011-** B Birmingham AL 9/10/1971 BA U of Alabama; M Div GTS 2004. D 6/5/2004 P 12/2/2004 Bp Henry Nutt Parsley Jr. Exec Coun Appointees New York NY 2008-2011; D-in-c S Tim's Epis Ch Athens AL 2004-2008. jlucas71@gmail.com

LUCAS, Kimberly Danielle (NC) 111 Turtleback Crossing Dr, Chapel Hill NC 27516 B Fayetteville NC 1/9/1970 d D D Lucas & Marian Ella. BS Wake Forest U 1992; MDiv UTS 1995. D 6/29/1996 Bp Robert Carroll Johnson Jr P 4/19/1997 Bp Ronald Hayward Haines. m 11/19/2009 Mark D Retherford c 4. S Ambroses Ch Raleigh NC 2001-2005; Chr Epis Ch No Hills Pittsburgh PA 1999-2001; Asst S Lk's Ch Trin Par Beth MD 1996-1999. kymlucas@yahoo.com

LUCAS, Mary Louise (Mass) 136 Bay Street #501, Hamilton L8P 3H8 Canada B Toronto ON CA 6/20/1948 d Harry William Lucas & Mary Evelyn. BA York U 1970; MDiv Harvard DS 1975. Rec 6/1/1987 as Priest Bp David Elliot Johnson. R S Jn's Ch Winthrop MA 1987-1990; Asst Ch Of S Jn The Evang Boston MA 1982-1985.

LUCAS, Rigal (Hai) Box 1309, Port-Au-Prince Haiti **Dio Haiti Ft Lauderdale FL 1992-** B Maissade HT 8/1/1961 s Odver Lucas & Aneclea. Cert Sem Of Theol Montrouis 1992. D 12/1/1992 Bp Luc Anatole Jacques Garnier P 9/1/1993 Bp Jean Zache Duracin. m 12/28/1995 Sherline Desarmes c 1.

LUCAS, Thomas Stewart (Md) 1303 President St, Annapolis MD 21403 **Assoc R S Marg's Ch Annapolis MD 2007-** B Macon GA 5/18/1976 s David Grice Lucas & Mary Jane. BS U GA 1998; MDiv VTS 2001. D 6/9/2001 Bp Robert Gould Tharp P 1/5/2002 Bp John Leslie Rabb. m 5/19/2001 Douglas Campbell. Assoc R Memi Ch Baltimore MD 2001-2007. Stewart@st-margarets.org

LUCAS, Wanda Beth (Ga) 524 Suncrest Blvd, Savannah GA 31410 **D S Fran Of The Islands Epis Ch Savannah GA 1995-** B Guthrie OK 1/5/1938 d Carl A Parrish & Opal. BS Oklahoma St U 1960; CPE 1996. D 12/12/1995 Bp Henry Irving Louttit. m 12/21/1958 Michael Arthur Lucas c 5. ACPE.

LUCE, John Burroughs (NY) 1047 Amsterdam Ave, New York NY 10025 B Boston MA 10/25/1930 s William Burroughs Luce & Catherine Collins. BA Harv 1952; MDiv Nash 1955; Fllshp EDS 1983. D 11/27/1954 P 6/1/1955 Bp Donald H V Hallock. Receiving Disabil Ret 1992-1995; Cn Cathd Of St Jn The Div New York NY 1986-1992; Urban Off Dio New York New York City NY 1983-1985; S Ann's Ch Of Morrisania Bronx NY 1976-1982; Diocn Msnry & Ch Extntn Socty New York NY 1973-1986; Dpt Of Missions Ny Income New York NY 1973-1986; P-in-c Gr Ch Van Vorst Jersey City NJ 1962-1965; Cur Ch Of The Intsn New York NY 1961-1962; Assoc P The Ch of S Edw The Mtyr New York NY 1955-1961; Asst S Jas Epis Ch Milwaukee WI 1954-1955.

LUCENT, Robert Brian (SanD) 629 Judson St, Escondido CA 92027 **Trin Ch Escondido CA 1995-** B Paterson NJ 11/3/1927 s Santos Bellint Lucent & Margaret Marie. BA Hob 1948; BD SWTS 1952. D 6/29/1951 Bp William Blair Roberts P 2/5/1952 Bp Conrad Gesner. m 1/10/1952 Moina MacPherson Ware c 2. Ch Of H Fam Fresno CA 1976-1992; Epis Dio San Joaquin Modesto CA 1976-1982; Vic All SS Epis Ch Omaha NE 1965-1972; Vic S Paul's Epis Ch Grinnell IA 1965-1972; P-in-c Dio Louisiana Baton Rouge LA 1957-1958; Dio So Dakota Sioux Falls SD 1952-1956; S Matt's Epis Ch Rapid City SD 1952-1956; Asst Rosebud Epis Mssn Mssn SD 1951-1952.

LUCEY, David James (RI) 399 Hope St., Bristol RI 02809 **R S Mich's Ch Bristol RI 2009-** B Nansemond County VA 4/25/1957 s Dennis Colbert Lucey & Grace Elizabeth. BA Hampden-Sydney Coll 1979; MBA Wake Forest U 1981; MDiv GTS 1999. D 2/6/1999 P 9/11/1999 Bp Richard Frank Grein. m 4/25/1987 Katherine Vivian Harmer c 5. Assoc R The Ch Of The H Sprt Lake Forest IL 2005-2009; The Par Of S Mary And S Jude NE Harbor ME 2002-2005; Asst Min S Matt's Ch Bedford NY 1999-2002. Omicron Delta Epsilon 1979; Phi Aplha theta 1979; Soc of the Pilgrims 2002. rector@fullchannel.net

LUCHS, Lewis Richard (Chi) 6417 81st St, Cabin John MD 20818 B Portsmouth OH 10/18/1935 s Fred Emil Luchs & Evelyn Mae. BA Beloit Coll 1957; MD SWTS 1961. D 6/24/1961 Bp Charles L Street P 12/1/1961 Bp Gerald Francis Burrill. m 7/13/1963 Susan Jean Robertson. Cur Emm Epis Ch Rockford IL 1961-1963.

LUCK, Diana Nelson (Dal) 6912 Merrilee Ln, Dallas TX 75214 **Mem, COM Dio Dallas Dallas TX 2000-; Asst S Matt's Cathd Dallas TX 1996-** B Holland MI 5/8/1939 d Lewis Marvin Nelson & Lola Marie. Lic in Mnstry Angl TS 1995; U of Texas in Arlington 1996. D 6/29/1996 Bp James Monte Stanton. m 5/30/1987 George Edmund Luck c 3. Archd Dio Dallas Dallas TX 2000-2010; Mem, COM Dio Dallas Dallas TX 2000-2004. dgluck@flash.net

LUCK JR, George Edmund (Dal) 6912 Merrilee Ln, Dallas TX 75214 B Houston TX 5/12/1933 s George Edmund Luck & Allene. Daniel Baker Coll 1953; BA U of No Texas 1955; MDiv PDS 1958; Nash 1967. D 6/18/1958 P 12/20/1958 Bp J(ohn) Joseph Meakins Harte. m 5/30/1987 Diana Nelson Luck c 3. Int Dn S Matt's Cathd Dallas TX 2001-2002; Cn S Matt's Cathd Dallas TX 1999; Pres Stndg Com Dio Dallas Dallas TX 1994-1995; Stndg Com Dio Dallas Dallas TX 1992-1995; COM Dio Dallas Dallas TX 1990-1996; R H Trin Ch Rockwall TX 1987-1999; R S Chris's Ch And Sch Ft Worth TX 1978-1987; ExCoun Dio Dallas Dallas TX 1974-1978; Assoc S Jn's Epis Ch Dallas TX 1969-1978; R S Wm Laud Epis Ch Pittsburg TX 1967-1969; Vic Ch Of Our Merc Sav Kaufman TX 1958-1962; P-in-c S Thos Ch Ennis TX 1958-1959. OHC 1952. dgluck@flash.net

LUCK, G(eorge) Thomas (CNY) 310 Montgomery St., Syracuse NY 13202 **S Paul's Cathd Syracuse NY 2004-** B Philadelphia PA 9/24/1955 s George Edmund Luck & Jane Amantha. Cntrl Coll 1977; BA Austin Coll 1978; MDiv Nash 1981; Cler Ldrshp Inst 2001; ALM Harv 2008. D 6/20/1981 P 5/31/1982 Bp A Donald Davies. m 5/25/1996 Jane Walters c 3. R Epis Ch Of S Mary The Vrgn Falmouth ME 1991-2004; R The Ch Of The Redeem Rochester NH 1986-1991; Cur S Jn's Ch Portsmouth NH 1983-1986; Cur Ch Of The Epiph Richardson TX 1981-1983. EPF; Epis Publ Plcy Ntwk; Episcopalians for Global Recon. gtluck@saintpaulscathedral.org

LUCK, Jane (CNY) 409 Sedgwick Drive, Syracuse NY 13203 B Flint MI 7/16/1955 d Russell Walters & Anita. Cert Champlain Coll 1978; U of Sthrn Maine 2002. D 3/23/2002 Bp Chilton Abbie Richardson Knudsen. m 5/25/1996 G(eorge) Thomas Luck c 3. Dio Cntrl New York Syracuse NY 2005-2006; Epis Ch Of S Mary The Vrgn Falmouth ME 2002-2005. JTluck@msn.com

LUCKENBACH, David Andrew (Tex) 6001 Moon St Ne Apt 3421, Albuquerque NM 87111 **Chr Epis Ch Tyler TX 2009-** B Limestone ME 10/11/1968 s Carl Albert Luckenbach & Carolyn Ann. BA Texas A&M U 1991; MDiv STUSo 1998. D 6/24/1998 Bp Robert Boyd Hibbs P 2/5/1999 Bp James Edward Folts. m 5/5/1999 Silvia Luckenbach c 3. S Mk's On The Mesa Epis Ch Albuquerque NM 2002-2009; S Lk's Epis Ch San Antonio TX 2000-2002; Ch Of The Adv Brownsville TX 1998-2000. DALUCKENBACH91@YAHOO.COM

LUCKETT JR, David Stafford (Miss) 4241 Otterlake Cove, Niceville FL 32578 B Alexandria LA 10/25/1933 s David Stafford Luckett & Anna Mary. BS LSU 1958; MDiv Bex 1962; Med Mississippi Coll 1985. D 6/16/1962 P 12/22/1962 Bp John P Craine. m 6/15/1958 Janice Elaine Cronan c 3. Assoc S Andr's By The Sea Epis Ch Destin FL 2011; Int S Andr's By The Sea Epis Ch Destin FL 2009; Int S Andr's Cathd Jackson MS 2005-2007; Int Trin Ch Apalachicola FL 2004-2005; Int Ch Of The Epiph Crestview FL 2000-2004; All SS' Epis Sch Vicksburg MS 1984-1999; R S Paul's Epis Ch Meridian MS 1974-1984; Vic S Tim's Ch Indianapolis IN 1971-1972; Cur S Lk's Ch Baton Rouge LA 1969-1971; R S Jas Ch New Castle IN 1965-1969; Vic S Jn's Ch Washington IN 1962-1965. jdluckett@jam.rr.com

LUCKEY, Marion Isabelle Aiken (NMich) 1531 Vardon Rd, Munising MI 49862 **P S Jn's Ch Munising MI 1991-; D Dio Nthrn Michigan Marquette MI 1990-** B Newark NJ 12/11/1940 d Raymond Ellsworth Aiken & Margaret Etta. MI SU; Wstrn Michigan U; BA Cntr Coll 1962; MA Nthrn Michigan U 1967. D 6/3/1990 P 1/6/1991 Bp Thomas Kreider Ray. m 8/1/1964 Thomas Hannan Luckey. tmluckey@ecunet.org

LUCKEY III, Thomas Hannan (NMich) E9430 E. Munising Ave. #2, Munising MI 49862 **D S Jn's Ch Munising MI 1996-** B Louisville KY 7/7/1939 s Thomas Hannan Luckey & Justine. BS Manchester Coll 1961; MA Nthrn Michigan U 1967; Cert Cntrl Michigan U 1970. D 9/8/1996 Bp Thomas Kreider Ray. m 8/1/1964 Marion Isabelle Aiken c 2. D S Jn's Ch Munising MI 1996-2007. tluckey@chartermi.net

LUCKRITZ, Denzil John (Mass) 421 Wianno Ave., Osterville MA 02655 **R S Ptr's Ch Osterville MA 2010-** B Clinton IA 11/1/1954 s John Vernon Luckritz & Lila Mae. BA U of Nthrn Colorado 1976; MDiv SWTS 1989. D 6/8/

1989 Bp William Carl Frey P 12/1/1989 Bp Frank Tracy Griswold III. m 8/6/1977 Lisa Speer c 2. R S Jn The Evang Lockport IL 1990-2010; Asst R The Epis Ch Of S Jas The Less Northfield IL 1989-1990; Dir of Oprtns SWTS Evanston IL 1988-1991. denzil_luckritz@comcast.net

LUDBROOK, Helen Christine (Mo) 1422 Lawnwood Dr, Des Peres MO 63131 B Brisbane Queensland AU 1/14/1942 d Arthur Alfred Prowse & Marjorie Eleanor. Eden TS; U Of So Australia Au 1964; MDiv STUSo 1984. D 6/15/1984 P 3/25/1985 Bp William Augustus Jones Jr. m 1/17/1964 Philip Albert Ludbrook c 3. Assoc R S Mart's Ch Ellisville MO 1991-2007; Asst S Mart's Ch Ellisville MO 1987-1990; Asst S Tim's Epis Ch Creve Coeur MO 1984-1987. helenludbrook@att.net

LUDDEN, Carol Parnell (Oly) 4516 Latona Ave Ne, Seattle WA 98105 B Manchester NH 5/12/1943 d Thomas Olin Parnell & Manon Ellen. BA SUNY; MDiv GTS 1983. D 1/25/1984 P 8/1/1984 Bp Robert Hume Cochrane. m 3/28/1970 James Ludden. Auth, "Pike Mrkt: An Assessment"; Auth, "The Mrkt Notebook".

LUECKENHOFF, James Joseph (WLa) 1518 Griffith St, Lake Charles LA 70601 **Supply Dio Wstrn Louisiana Alexandria LA 1999-** B Jefferson City MO 8/14/1939 s Arthur Henry Lueckenhoff & Eleanor Agnes. BA CUA 1970. Rec from Roman Catholic 9/1/1999 as Priest Bp Robert Jefferson Hargrove Jr. m 10/2/1987 Linda Guillory. Trin Epis Ch Deridder LA 2006-2011; Epis Ch Of The Gd Shpd Lake Chas LA 2002-2011. luk_home@bellsouth.net

LUECKERT, Diana Rowe (NCal) 4800 Olive Oak Way, Carmichael CA 95608 **P-in-c S Paul's Epis Ch Sacramento CA 2002-; Asst S Fran Epis Ch Fair Oaks CA 2000-** B Oakland CA 5/20/1933 d Ralph Cornish Rowe & Mary Rebecca. AA Coll of Marin 1969; BD California St U 1976; Cert Olympia TS 1987. D 12/3/1991 P 6/1/1992 Bp Vincent Waydell Warner. m 8/3/1976 Drury Waller Wood. P S Christophers Epis Ch Westport WA 1992-2000.

LUEDDE, Christopher S (Roch) 31 Kitty Hawk Dr, Pittsford NY 14534 B Saint Louis MO 5/25/1951 s Fullerton Woods Luedde & Jeanne Louise. BA Kansas U 1973; MDiv Pittsburgh TS 1976. D 8/19/1976 Bp Robert Bracewell Appleyard P 3/12/1977 Bp Lloyd Edward Gressle. m 1/6/1973 Susan Marie Knowlton c 2. R S Thos Epis Ch Rochester NY 1996-2009; R S Paul's Ch Maumee OH 1987-1996; Int Trin Ch Toledo OH 1985-1987; Vic S Mk's Epis Ch Bridgeport MI 1978-1985; Asst Trin Epis Ch Carbondale PA 1976-1978. Oxford Roundtable affiliate of Oxf, Eng. 2008; Oxford Roundtable affiliate of Oxf, Eng. 2007; Who'S Who In Rel 92-93; El Shaddai Biblic Stds Lld; Jas H Brooks Bible Prize Westminster Coll. csluedde@gmail.com

LUENEBURG, Roxine Elizabeth (NMich) 2701 1st Ave S Apt 114, Escanaba MI 49829 B Philomath OR 8/21/1924 d David Ecker & Naomi Orica. D 5/18/1997 Bp Thomas Kreider Ray.

LUETHE, Robin Lewis (Oly) 789 Highway 603, Chehalir WA 98532 B Bremerton WA 4/15/1940 s Alfred Lewis Luethe & Olivia Lucy. BA Whitman Coll 1962; MDiv GTS 1965. D 6/29/1965 P 3/30/1966 Bp Ivol I Curtis. m 12/27/1968 Lois Mae Drummond c 3. S Anne's Epis Ch Washougal WA 1991-1998; S Tim's Epis Ch Chehalis WA 1972-1989; Cur S Lk's Epis Ch Vancouver WA 1965-1969. Auth, "arts," *Living Ch*. r.l.luethe@gmail.com

LUFKIN, Alison Connor (Colo) PO Box 1305, Leadville CO 80461 **S Geo Epis Mssn Leadville CO 2004-** B Elmhust IL 4/5/1963 BA Wheaton Coll. D 7/19/2003 P 9/20/2005 Bp William Jerry Winterrowd. m 9/7/1985 George Schild Lufkin c 2.

LUFKIN, George Schild (Colo) PO Box 243, Leadville CO 80461 B Tucson AZ 9/23/1963 s George Robert Lufkin & Carolyn C. BA Wheaton Coll 1985; MBA Pace U 1989; No Degree Colgate-Rochester Div 1990. D 1/16/2005 Bp Robert John O'Neill P 7/20/2005 Bp William Jerry Winterrowd. m 9/7/1985 Alison Connor c 2. georgelufkin@live.com

LUGER, Virginia M (ND) 821 N 4th St Apt 3, Bismarck ND 58501 **D S Lk's Ch Ft Yates ND 1996-** B Milwaukee WI 1/18/1928 d Ezra A Langdon & Lauretta. Cert Jamestown Coll 1949; AA Stndg Rock Cmnty Coll 1976; BS U of Mary 1989. D 11/22/1996 Bp Andrew Hedtler Fairfield. m 5/22/1948 Ferdinand Luger c 4. Auth, "No Dakota Veterans Cemetery: A Haven Of Peace," *No Dakota Rea/Rtc*. Tribune Goodwill Awd The Bismarck Tribune 2003; Nominee, Golden Rule Awd J.C. Penney 2000. virginialuger@aol.com

LUI, David Suikwei (Cal) 1011 Harrison St # 202, Oakland CA 94607 **R Ch Of The Incarn San Francisco CA 2003-** B China 2/7/1944 CDSP. D 6/7/2003 P 12/6/2003 Bp William Edwin Swing. m 12/9/1967 Selina Kwan c 2. revdavidlui@gmail.com

LUJAN, Mary Royes (EO) Po Box 25, Hood River OR 97031 B Summerville OR 4/8/1968 d George Edwin Royes & Valerie Fae. BS Estrn Oregon U 1996; MDiv VTS 2001. D 6/5/2001 P 6/5/2002 Bp William O Gregg. m 10/20/2007 Ken Michael Lujan. R The Par Of S Mk The Evang Hood River OR 2003-2008; Palmer Memi Ch Houston TX 2001-2002. oregonmary@gorge.net

LUKAS, Arlene (WNC) 416 N Haywood St, Waynesville NC 28786 **Gr Ch In The Mountains Waynesville NC 2008-** B Chicago IL 11/18/1949 d Lawrence Lukaszewicz & Gertrude. MA Roosevelt U 1981; MDiv Starr King Sch For The Mnstry 1993; DAS VTS 2001. D 6/23/2001 Bp Michael Bruce Curry P 3/16/2002 Bp Robert Hodges Johnson. S Aug's Epis Ch Wilmette IL 2004-2008; T To R S Phil's Ch Brevard NC 2001-2004. arlenelukas@hotmail.com

LUKAS, Randy (Alb) PO Box 114, Columbiaville NY 12050 B Queens NY 1/23/1957 s Edgar A Lukas & Gloria Gladys. BA Queens Coll, CUNY 1986. D 6/5/2010 Bp William Howard Love. m 10/11/1987 Carol Anne Springer c 2. brolrandolph@gmail.com

LUKENS JR, Alexander Macomb (Colo) 1380 S Madison St, Cortez CO 81321 B Helena MT 5/11/1938 s Alexander Macomb Lukens & Julia Parks. U of Heidelberg 1959; Ya 1960; BD CDSP 1964; Dine Coll, Shiprock, NM 2006. D 6/11/1964 Bp Joseph Summerville Minnis P 3/1/1965 Bp Charles F Hall. Asst S Barn Epis Ch Denver CO 1970-1973; Asst Gr Ch Manchester NH 1964-1965. "Thought on the Sacr and the Demonic," *Navajo Stds Conf*, 2009. ACPE 1973. amljrart@fone.net

LUKENS, Ann Pierson (Oly) 2543 - 103rd Avenue Southeast, Bellevue WA 98004 **R S Mich And All Ang Ch Issaquah WA 2000-** B Harrisonburg VA 6/16/1946 d Earl H Pierson & Mary Lyons. BA Br 1971; MDiv Seattle U 1993. D 11/12/1993 P 7/9/1994 Bp Vincent Waydell Warner. m 7/8/1967 Terence P Lukens c 3. S Thos Ch Medina WA 1994-2000; D Dio Olympia Seattle WA 1993-1994. lukens3290@aol.com

LULEY, William Tracy (Mo) 1101 Sulphur Spring Rd, Manchester MO 63021 **R S Lk's Epis Ch Manchester MO 1996-** B Lynwood CA 12/8/1953 s Charles Luley & Adelaide. BBA Wstrn Michigan U 1977; MDiv Nash 1983. D 5/13/1983 Bp William Cockburn Russell Sheridan P 11/25/1983 Bp Charles Bennison. m 5/22/1982 Mary Demler c 3. Vic Ch Of The Ascen Epis Springfield MO 1992-1996; R Trin Epis Par Waterloo IA 1988-1992; R S Andr's Ch Big Rapids MI 1985-1988; Cur Emm Ch Petoskey MI 1983-1985. billndfan77@att.net

LUMBARD, Carolyn Mary (Roch) 326 Frederick Douglas St, Rochester NY 14608 B Durham NC 9/12/1945 d Arthur L Dunsmore & Doris C. Duke 1965; BA Ups 1969; MDiv VTS 1990. D 6/2/1990 P 12/1/1990 Bp John Shelby Spong. m 6/25/1988 Thomas Lumbard c 2. Dio Rochester Rochester NY 2000-2007; Cn Dio Rochester Rochester NY 1999; S Alb's Ch Oakland NJ 1997-2000; Vic Chr Ch Belleville NJ 1992-1997; Assoc S Paul's Epis Ch Morris Plains NJ 1990-1992. carolyn.lumbard@yahoo.com

LUMLEY, Dale Allen (WK) 906 W Wheat Ave, Ulysses KS 67880 **S Jn's Ch Ulysses KS 2010-; Vic Ch Of The Epiph Concordia KS 2007-** B New York NY 3/25/1947 s Thomas Robert Lumley & Julia Eva. BA GW 1983; MDiv VTS 1990. Trans from Anglican Church of Canada 12/1/1994 Bp Orris George Walker Jr. m 1/12/1985 Miriam M Roland. Dio Wstrn Kansas Hutchinson KS 2007-2010; H Trin Epis Ch Madera CA 1998-2005; All SS Ch Brooklyn NY 1994-1997. frdalelumley@hotmail.com

LUMPKIN, Michael Robertson (SC) 316 W. Carolina Avenue, Summerville SC 29483 **R S Paul's Epis Ch Summerville SC 1995-** B Pittsburgh PA 4/11/1951 s William Wallace Lumpkin & Dallas. BA U So 1973; MDiv VTS 1982. D 6/12/1982 P 5/14/1983 Bp William Arthur Beckham. m 5/25/1980 Ellen Bennett c 2. R S Chris's Ch Spartanburg SC 1985-1995; S Thad Epis Ch Aiken SC 1982-1985. mike@stpaulssummerville.org

LUNA JR, Eulalio Gallardo (WTex) 234 W Mariposa Dr, San Antonio TX 78212 B San Antonio TX 4/28/1942 s Eulalio Gallardo Luna & Eva. BA Trin U San Antonio TX 1965; MDiv Epis TS of The SW 1977. D 6/20/1977 P 1/29/1978 Bp Scott Field Bailey. m 6/7/1968 Mary Grace Ramirez c 3. R All SS Epis Ch San Benito TX 1987-2002; R Chr Ch Epis Laredo TX 1982-1987; R All SS Epis Ch San Benito TX 1978-1982; Texas Mltry Inst San Antonio TX 1977-1978. Intl Ord Of S Lk The Physcn 1984.

LUND, Joseph Walter (WA) 70381 Placerville Rd, Rancho Mirage CA 92270 **Asst S Marg's Epis Ch Palm Desert CA 2006-** B Minot ND 9/13/1946 s John Vernon Lund & Marie A. BA/BS U of Akron 1968; JD Geo 1973; MDiv VTS 1991; DMin SWTS 1998. D 6/15/1991 Bp Ronald Hayward Haines P 12/20/1991 Bp James Winchester Montgomery. R S Dav's Par Washington DC 1996-2003; Assoc Chr Ch Par Kensington MD 1991-1996. SKCM 1990. Mem of the Bd Epis Comm. Serv 2007; Co-Chair Epis Peace Cmsn Washington DC 1998. PadreLund@DC.RR.com

LUND, Judith Ann (Ark) 8280 Spanker Ridge Dr, Bentonville AR 72712 B Minneapolis MN 7/18/1940 d Elmer Leonard Kommerstad & Anna Elizabeth. MA Luther TS 1998; CTh Epis TS of The SW 2004. D 12/4/2004 P 6/11/2005 Bp Larry Earl Maze. m 4/22/1961 William V Lund c 2. jk-lund@cox.net

LUND, Virginia U Sapienza (Mil) 1101 Greenough Dr W, Apt. E-6, Missoula MT 59802 B Detroit MI 6/7/1938 d Paul Sapienza & Giovanina. Whitaker TS 1984; MA EDS 1985. D 12/21/1985 P 12/5/1987 Bp H Coleman McGehee Jr. c 2. Chapl S Fran Ch Madison WI 1991-2003; Asst Chapl S Fran Ch Madison WI 1988-1990; Cur S Gabr's Epis Ch Eastpointe MI 1987-1988. Auth, "Revolutionary Forgiveness: Feminists Reflections on Nicaragua," 1986. EWC 1990. vulund@bresnan.net

LUNDBERG III, Nelson John (Alb) 36 Plaza Avenue, Governor's Sq, Rensselaer NY 12144 B Albany NY 7/29/1941 s Nelson John Lundberg & Geraldine Madeline. STB GTS; BA Marist Coll. D 6/3/1967 Bp Allen Webster Brown P 12/2/1967 Bp Charles Bowen Persell Jr. H Name Boyntonville

Hoosick Falls NY 1992-2005; P-in-c Chr's Ch Duanesburg NY 1977-1979; P-in-c S Bon Ch Guilderland NY 1970-1979; Cur Chr Ch Epis Hudson NY 1968-1970; Cur S Paul's Ch Troy NY 1967-1968.

LUNDBERG, Richard Evard (Chi) 515 W George St, Arlington Heights IL 60005 **Chair Cler Com Dio Chicago Chicago IL 1970-** B Mishawaka IN 4/23/1925 s Gustave Evard Lundberg & Blanche Marie. BA Yankton Coll 1949; STB GTS 1959. D 5/26/1951 P 12/8/1951 Bp Wallace E Conkling. c 4. R S Simons Ch Arlington Heights IL 1975-1990; Stndg Com Dio Chicago Chicago IL 1974-1990; Pres Epis Cooprtv Dio Chicago Chicago IL 1969-1971; R S Paul's Par Riverside IL 1968-1975; Dn Denver Deanry Dio Colorado Denver CO 1965-1968; Trst Dio Colorado Denver CO 1960-1966; Chair Div Yth Dio Colorado Denver CO 1958-1966; Coll Wk Div DeptCE Dio Colorado Denver CO 1958-1964; R H Apos Epis Ch Englewood CO 1957-1968; Vic S Tim's Epis Ch Rangely CO 1956-1957; Ch Of The H Trin Price UT 1954-1957; S Eliz's Ch Whiterocks UT 1954-1957; P-in-c Ch Of The H Sprt Randlett UT 1953-1954; Vic S Paul's Epis Ch Vernal UT 1953-1954; Vic S Paul's Ch Dekalb IL 1951-1953. Sprtl Dir, Grad Sums GTS New York NY 1987. rel515@hotmail.com

LUNDEAN, David (Spok) 325 S 5th St Trlr 14, Sunnyside WA 98944 **Died 8/10/2009** B Milwaukee WI 8/3/1932 s David Ira Lundean & Helen Elzina. BS U of Wisconsin 1968; Nash 1984. D 5/21/1972 Bp John Raymond Wyatt P 9/16/1984 Bp Leigh Wallace Jr. c 3. SSC 1998. revdave@charter.net

LUNDELIUS, Heulette Carolyn (Lynn) Sparks (WA) 5801 Nicholson Lane, #1923, Rockville MD 20852 B Bryan TX 1/3/1931 d William McCann Sparks & Heulette. AA Stephens Coll 1950; BS TCU 1983; Lic Angl TS 1984; Grad Stds U So 1995. D 11/24/1984 Bp A Donald Davies P 11/20/1991 Bp Ronald Hayward Haines. c 2. P-in-c Gr Epis Ch Silver Sprg MD 2004-2005; R S Mary Magd Ch Silver Sprg MD 1999-2002; P-in-c S Andr's Epis Ch Coll Pk MD 1997-1999; P-in-c Gd Shpd Epis Ch Silver Sprg MD 1996-1997; Assoc S Mary Magd Ch Silver Sprg MD 1993-1996; Asst Gr Ch Washington DC 1990-1993; Sch Chapl The Epis Ch Of The Trsfg Dallas TX 1987-1990; Assoc Chr The King Epis Ch Ft Worth TX 1985-1986. The OSL 2001. CAROLYN.LUNDELIUS@MYGAIT.COM

LUNDEN, Michael Carl (NY) 118 S Church St, Goshen NY 10924 **R S Jas' Ch Goshen NY 2000-** B Tampa FL 8/6/1962 s Jean Lunden. BS Suc Buffalo 1985; Cert S Hyacinth Coll & Sem Granby MA 1990; MDiv GTS 1997. D 6/14/1997 P 12/13/1997 Bp Richard Frank Grein. m 11/1/2011 Sharon R Lunden c 2. P-in-c Ch Of The Ascen And H Trin Highland NY 1997-2000. Bro Of S Greg. mlunden@hvc.rr.com

LUNDGREN, Linda Lou (Minn) 8 3rd St, Proctor MN 55810 B Teaneck NJ 11/13/1954 d Harold Carl Newman & Violet Harriet. D 11/21/1993 P 6/18/1994 Bp Sanford Zangwill Kaye Hampton. m 7/14/1973 Robert John Lundgren. jaylundgren@yahoo.com

LUNDGREN, Richard John (Chi) 13129 Lake Mary Dr., Plainfield IL 60585 **Assoc R S Edw The Mtyr and Chr Epis Ch Joliet IL 2007-** B Chicago 5/15/1964 s Norman O Lundgren & Carol J. BA Villanova U 1987; MDiv Cath Theol Un 1994; Angl Stds SWTS 2007. Rec from Roman Catholic 6/7/2007 Bp Victor Alfonso Scantlebury. m 10/21/2006 Robert F Davis. rlundgren@secec.net

LUNDIN, George Edward (Miss) 705 Southern Ave, Hattiesburg MS 39401 B Chicago IL 5/7/1942 s George Walter Lundin & Evelyn Mary. BA Ohio Wesl 1964; MS/MPA/PHD U Pgh 1973; MDiv STUSo 1982. D 6/20/1982 Bp H Coleman McGehee Jr P 5/1/1983 Bp James Barrow Brown. m 2/2/2008 Fonda Lundin c 2. Chap Of The Cross ROLLING FORK MS 2008-2011; S Paul's Ch Woodville MS 2001-2008; Vic S Eliz's Mssn Collins MS 1987-1997; S Lk's Ch New Orleans LA 1984-1987; Trin Ch New Orleans LA 1982-1984. Auth, “Ms Philological Assn”; Auth, “Contemporary Rel Ideas”. Ford Fllshp; Woodrow Wilson Fell. gelundin@gmail.com

LUNDQUIST, Robert (WNC) 419 Turnpike Rd, Mills River NC 28759 **Ch Of The H Fam Mills River NC 2009-** B Washington DC 1/4/1956 s Donald Edwin Lundquist & Patricia. BA The Coll of Wm & Mary 1978; MDiv SWTS 1985. D 6/28/1985 P 5/11/1986 Bp William Evan Sanders. m 12/31/1983 Pamela Mumby c 1. P-in-c S Paul's Epis Ch Ft Collins CO 2005-2008; R S Gabr The Archangel Epis Ch Cherry Hills Vill CO 1998-2004; Evang Off Dio Sthrn Virginia Norfolk VA 1995-1998; Vic & R Gd Samar Epis Ch Virginia Bch VA 1989-1998; Asst Trin Ch Manassas VA 1986-1989; D Ch Of The Gd Shpd Lookout Mtn TN 1985-1986. rector@ourholyfamily.org

LUNNUM, Lindsay S (NY) 50 Orchard Ave, Providence RI 02906 **S Barn Ch Irvington on Hudson NY 2010-** B Bellevue WA 3/12/1977 d Ronald K Lunnum & Linda Sue. BA Seattle Pacific U 1999; MDiv Ya Berk 2008. D 3/15/2008 P 9/20/2008 Bp Mark Sean Sisk. m 11/24/2009 James A McGeveran c 2. Asst S Mart's Ch Providence RI 2008-2010. rev.lindsay.lunnum@gmail.com

LUNTSFORD, Sharon Lorene (ND) Po Box 18, Alexander ND 58831 B Watford City ND 8/18/1940 d Leonard Norman Anderson & Selma Henrietta. Minot St U 1958; Jamestown Coll 1959. D 1/29/1994 Bp John Stuart Thornton P 12/18/2009 Bp Michael Gene Smith. c 1. angel@ruggedwest.com

LUONI, Richard Byron (SC) 200 Bucksley Ln Unit 306, Daniel Island SC 29492 **S Geo's Epis Ch Summerville SC 2008-** B Parkelsburg WV 5/26/1963 s Billy Luoni & Naomi. BS Concord U 1988; MDiv SFTS 2005. D 12/3/2005 P 6/3/2006 Bp William Edwin Swing. m 5/28/1996 Renee Luoni. Dio California San Francisco CA 2006. rickluoni@gmail.com

LUPFER JR, William B (Ore) 574 S Sheldon Rd, Plymouth MI 48170 **Trin Epis Cathd Portland OR 2003-; S Jn The Evang Ch Milwaukie OR 2000-** B Berwyn IL 4/21/1961 s William Lupfer & Virginia. U Of Lancaster Lancaster Gb 1982; BA U CO 1983; MDiv Ya Berk 1987; DMin SWTS 2003. D 6/12/1993 P 5/14/1994 Bp A(lbert) Theodore Eastman. m 8/4/1990 Kimiko K Koga c 2. R S Jn's Ch Plymouth MI 1997-2003; Assoc Ch Of The H Comf Kenilworth IL 1993-1997. Psychol Stds And Cler Consult Prog 1999. Lilian Claus Schlr Yale Berkeley 1985. oyabaka@comcast.net

LUPTON JR, Jim (Ark) 241 Riverview St., Belhaven NC 27810 **P-in-c S Geo Epis Ch Engelhard NC 1997-** B Washington NC 9/20/1931 s James Harold Lupton & Grace. BA Duke 1954; MArch U of Pennsylvania 1960; MDiv Epis TS of The SW 1985. D 1/18/1986 Bp Stanley Fillmore Hauser P 7/1/1986 Bp Scott Field Bailey. c 3. Chair, Ecum Cmsn Dio E Carolina Kinston NC 1999-2003; Vic S Alb's Ch Stuttgart AR 1989-1997; R Gr Ch Weslaco TX 1988-1989; S Peters Epis Sch Kerrville TX 1986-1988; S Ptr's Epis Ch Kerrville TX 1986-1988. jlupton2002@yahoo.com

LUSIGNAN, Louise Jennet (WA) 4630 Chesapeake St NW, Washington DC 20016 **Assoc R for Pstr Mnstrs S Jn's Epis Ch McLean VA 2000-** B Berkeley CA 10/4/1943 d Francis Thomas Cornish & Louise Henriette. MAT Antioch U New Engl 1967; MLS U of Wstrn Ontario 1971; MDiv VTS 1988. D 6/11/1988 Bp John Thomas Walker P 1/5/1989 Bp Ronald Hayward Haines. m 8/10/1974 Michael Reeves Lusignan. S Columba's Ch Washington DC 1988-2000. llusignan@stjohnsmclean.org

LUSK JR, Karl K (Ky) 236 Ridgeview Dr, New Haven KY 40051 **Co-chair, Dioc Bdgt Com Dio Kentucky Louisville KY 2010-; R Ch Of The Ascen Bardstown KY 2009-; Chair, Dept. for Mssn and Evang Dio Kentucky Louisville KY 2009-; Dioc Disaster Coordntr Dio Kentucky Louisville KY 2007-** B Lexington KY 11/26/1945 s Karl Kriener Lusk & Ruby Plummer. BS Iowa St U 1967; AT Sthrn Illinois U 1968; MAR Louisville Prebyterian TS 2007. D 4/14/2007 P 10/27/2007 Bp Edwin Funsten Gulick Jr. m 2/20/1982 Anne T Thompson c 2. Trst and Coun Dio Kentucky Louisville KY 2010-2011; Chair, Dept. for Mssn and Evang Dio Kentucky Louisville KY 2009-2011; Vic S Thos Ch Campbellsville KY 2007-2009. karllusk@bellsouth.net

LUSK, William Earl (WMo) 4301 Madison Ave., #210, Kansas City MO 64111 B Rochester PA 8/26/1926 s Earl Graham Lusk & Alice Pauline. BS Estrn Nazarene Coll 1949; MA Bos 1950; BD SWTS 1956. D 6/21/1956 P 12/21/1956 Bp Edward Randolph Welles II. c 3. R S Ptr's Ch Harrisonville MO 1983-1991; Dio W Missouri Kansas City MO 1979-1985; Del Prov VII Syn Dio W Missouri Kansas City MO 1960-1972; R Calv Epis Ch Sedalia MO 1959-1983; Vic S Geo Epis Ch Camdenton MO 1956-1959; R Trin Epis Ch Lebanon MO 1956-1959. Auth, *Visions MO Bishops or Readings in Hist of Dio*, Privately, 1997. david@davidluskgallery.com

LUTAS, Donald McKenzie (Mich) 6114 28th St, Detroit MI 48210 **R S Cyp's Epis Ch Detroit MI 1991-** B Saint Thomas Jamaica WI 4/7/1955 s Walter Mordecai Lutas & Nettie Icilda. Untd Theol Coll of the W Indies Kingston JA 1978; BA U of The W Indies 1978; STM GTS 1984; MLS U of Detroit 1995; DMin GTF 2002. Trans from Church in the Province Of The West Indies 7/1/1987 Bp C(laude) Charles Vache. m 10/15/2007 Belinda Delanco Whitney c 1. Vic S Jas Epis Ch Portsmouth VA 1986-1991. rector2191@scypriansdet.org

LUTES, Kathleen Monson (SD) 2224 Cedar Dr, Rapid City SD 57702 **R S Andr's Epis Ch Rapid City SD 2004-** B Minneapolis MN 8/16/1957 d Juel Adrian Monson & Patricia Mary. BS U MN 1979; MA The Coll of St. Cathr 1986; MDiv Epis TS of The SW 2002. D 6/15/2002 P 4/23/2003 Bp James Louis Jelinek. m 11/24/1984 Richard Kyle Lutes c 2. D S Jn's Ch Of Hassan Rogers MN 2003; S Mart's By The Lake Epis Minnetonka Bch MN 2002-2003. kathymonsonlutes@gmail.com

LUTHER, Carol Luther (Cal) St Paul's Episcopal School, 46 Montecito Ave., Oakland CA 94610 **Vol Ch Of The Nativ San Rafael CA 2007-; S Paul's Day Sch Of Oakland Oakland CA 2007-** B Berkeley CA 8/25/1950 d John Peebles Macmeeken & Mary Swanberg. BA Scripps Coll 1972; MDiv CDSP 1997. D 6/5/1999 P 11/20/1999 Bp William Edwin Swing. m 11/25/1973 Jay W Luther c 1. Ch Of The Redeem San Rafael CA 2004-2007; Assoc & Sch Chapl S Paul's Ch Oakland CA 1999-2004; S Paul's Day Sch Of Oakland Oakland CA 1999-2004. cluther@well.com

LUTHRINGER, George Francis (Los) 232 Shady Hills Ct, Simi Valley CA 93065 B Springfield IL 5/30/1934 s Marshall Sampsell Luthringer & Martha Eleanore. BS MIT 1957; MS MIT 1957; BD CDSP 1966. D 6/25/1966 P 12/31/1966 Bp Roger W Blanchard. m 10/2/1982 Ann Pentecost. S Fran Of Assisi Epis Ch Simi Vlly CA 1992-1995. Auth, “Considering Abortion? Clarifying What You Believe,” *Educational Series No. 9*, Rel Cltn for Abortion Rts, 1992; Auth, “The Ethics of Ordnry Time,” *Nutrition in Clincl Pract*, Amer Soc for Parenteral and Enteral Nutrition, 1991. Rep to Dioc Coun 2001-2006. gufel34@gmail.com

LUTTRELL, John Sidney (LI) 295 Old Kings Hwy, Downingtown PA 19335 B Norman OK 11/6/1943 s John Morter Luttrell & Josephine. BA Ya 1965; STB GTS 1968; PhD Hebr Un Coll 1977. D 5/28/1968 P 12/18/1968 Bp Chilton Powell. m 6/1/1968 Rosemary M Perkins. Chairman, COM Dio Long Island Garden City NY 1996-2002; R S Lk's Ch Sea Cliff NY 1987-2008; P-in-c Chr Memi Epis Ch El Reno OK 1986-1987; Headmaster S Jn's Ch Oklahoma City OK 1982-1986; Chapl Casady Sch Oklahoma City OK 1980-1982; Cur S Lk's Ch Tulsa OK 1968-1969. SBL 1968-1982. The Fndr's Medallion Hebr Un Coll 2008; Henry Knox Sherrill Fllshp Ya 1965. john@luttrell.org

LUTZ, Randall Robert (RG) 2365 Brother Abdon Way, Santa Fe NM 87505 **S Bede's Epis Ch Santa Fe NM 2006-** B Danville PA 6/17/1958 s Robert William Lutz & Margaret Ethel. TESM; BA Bloomsburg U of Pennsylvania 1980; Cert The Sch for Mnstry 2007. D 10/21/2006 Bp Jeffrey Neil Steenson P 11/10/2007 Bp William Carl Frey. rlutz@santafeopera.org

LUTZ, Richard Herbert (LI) Cashelmara 40, 23200 Lake Road, Bay Village OH 44140 B New York NY 4/13/1937 s Stephen Lutz & Amelia Martha. BA,cl Adel 1958; STB GTS 1961. D 4/8/1961 P 10/28/1961 Bp James P De Wolfe. R S Geo's Ch Hempstead NY 1987-1997; R S Matt's Ch Woodhaven NY 1965-1986; Cur & Headmaster All SS Ch San Diego CA 1963-1965; Cur S Matt's Ch Woodhaven NY 1961-1963. Mem of GAS; P Assoc Our Lade of Walsingham; SSC; Trst at Nassau Cnty Hist Soc. RLUTZC@AOL.COM

LUTZ, R(uth) Jeanne (Eric) (RG) 1330 Renoir Ct., Las Cruces NM 88007 **Pstr Peace Luth Ch Las Cruces NM 2003-** B Indianapolis IN 3/18/1947 d Robert Allen McAllister & Ruth. BA U of Texas 1970; MA New Mex St U. 1972; DMin Austin Presb TS 2008. D 2/29/1988 P 9/21/1988 Bp William Davidson. m 12/27/1969 William Lutz c 2. Int Pstr S Jn's Cathd Albuquerque NM 2003; Assoc R S Andr's Epis Ch Las Cruces NM 1997-2003; Asstg Cler S Andr's Epis Ch Las Cruces NM 1991-1997; Asstg Cler S Mary's Epis Ch Albuquerque NM 1989-1991. Auth, "Benediction," *LivCh*, 1996; Auth, "All Sung Out, Except Grandma," *LivCh*, 1993. DOK 1972; Intl Ord of S Lk the Physcn 2001; Soc of St. Ben 2003. Wmn of Faith City of Las Cruces / CareSource Cmnty Mnstrs, Inc. Dona Ana Cnty NM 2003. padrecita@peacelutheranlc.com

LUTZ, William Charles (CNY) 1465 W Water St, Elmira NY 14905 **R Trin Ch Elmira NY 1999-** B Plainfield NJ 3/20/1952 s Charles William Lutz & Marjorie Julia. BA Heidelberg Coll 1974; MDiv GTS 1978; DMin Bangor TS 1997. D 6/3/1978 P 12/2/1978 Bp Albert Wiencke Van Duzer. m 6/17/1978 Heather Anne Conelley c 3. Stndg Com Dio New Hampshire Concord NH 1995-1999; Chair Cler Dvlpmt Com Dio New Hampshire Concord NH 1993-1995; Stwdshp Com Dio New Hampshire Concord NH 1992-1994; Evang Com Dio New Hampshire Concord NH 1988-1991; R Ch Of Our Sav Milford NH 1987-1999; Yth Com Dio New Hampshire Concord NH 1987-1989; Dio Wstrn Massachusetts Springfield MA 1984-1987; Vic S Chris's Ch Fairview Chicopee MA 1984-1987; Chapl Belmont Chap at S Mk's Sch Southborough MA 1982-1984; St. Mk's Sch of Southborough Inc. Southborough MA 1982-1984; Asst S Andr's Ch Turners Falls MA 1979-1982; Asst S Jas' Ch Greenfield MA 1979-1982; Asst Gr Ch Merchantville NJ 1978-1979. OHC 1975. brsebastian@juno.com

LWEBUGA-MUKASA, Katherine N (WNY) 168 Schimwood Ct, Getzville NY 14068 **D S Phil's Ch Buffalo NY 1989-** B Northampton MA 7/5/1947 d Thomas P Nagle & Marion E. BA Smith 1969; MA San Diego St U 1974; MS Sthrn Connecticut St U 1979. D 12/2/1989 Bp Arthur Edward Walmsley. m 5/29/1970 Jamson S Lwebuga-Mukasa.

LYCETT, Horace Abbott (Colo) 1223 Center St, Goodland KS 67735 **P-in-c S Paul's Epis Ch Goodland KS 2004-** B Baltimore MA 5/11/1933 s Isaac Cate Lycett & Caroline. BA Colorado St Coll 1956; MDiv Nash 1963. D 6/29/1959 P 2/2/1960 Bp Joseph Summerville Minnis. m 7/4/1980 Mary Read c 3. Dio Colorado Denver CO 1999-2002; R All SS Epis Ch Denver CO 1971-1999; Vic S Paul's Epis Ch Ft Collins CO 1964-1968; Vic S Mk's Ch Craig CO 1959-1964; Vic S Paul's Epis Ch Steamboat Sprg CO 1959-1964. Auth, "Var arts," *LivCh*, 1979. FLIC 2000; Sis Of Charity 1950. lycett@nilenet.com

LYGA, Robert Michael (Minn) N36457 State Road 93/121, Independence WI 54747 **Supply P S Barn Ch Clear Lake WI 2000-; S Phil's Ch Eau Claire WI 2000-** B Independence WI 8/10/1938 s Marcel Joseph Lyga & Helen. BS U of Wisconsin 1961; MD Nash 1968. D 6/24/1968 P 4/14/1969 Bp Hamilton Hyde Kellogg. R H Trin Intl Falls MN 1992-2000; Vic S Ptr's Ch Warroad MN 1992-2000; S Matt's Epis Ch Minneapolis MN 1969-1992. robtmlyga@tcc.coop

LYLE, Patsy Rushworth (La) 19344 Links Ct, Baton Rouge LA 70810 **D S Jas Epis Ch Baton Rouge LA 2005-** B Baton Rouge LA 10/18/1934 d Locksley Clyde Rushworth & Nell Elizabeth. BS LSU 1956. D 12/19/1986 Bp Charles Edward Jenkins III. m 9/8/1956 John Donald Clyde c 2. Sprtl Dir Dio Louisiana Baton Rouge LA 1994-2005; D Epis Ch Of The H Sprt In Baton Rouge Baton Rouge LA 1994-2005; Chair Dio Louisiana Baton Rouge LA 1988-1992; D S Marg's Epis Ch Baton Rouge LA 1986-1994. NAAD 1979; Sprtl Dir Intl 1994. pat@lylebr.com

LYLE, Randall Robert (Ia) 2350 Glass Rd NE, Cedar Rapids IA 52402 **Asst Chr Ch Cedar Rapids IA 2010-** B Scottsbluff NE 8/30/1952 s Robert Donovan Childs & JoDeen Kathryn. BA Loretto Heights Coll 1977; MDiv SWTS 1982; PhD Iowa St U 1992. D 6/2/1982 Bp William Harvey Wolfrum P 12/29/1982 Bp Walter Cameron Righter. m 6/4/1977 Karla Kay Flentje c 3. St Fran Epis Ch San Antonio TX 2001-2003; R Gr Ch Boone IA 1989-1993; Ch Of The Gd Shpd Webster City IA 1989-1992; Exec Coun Appointees New York NY 1984-1989; Cur S Andr's Ch Des Moines IA 1982-1984. "Neurofeedback Treatment of Type 1 Diabetes: Perceptions of Quality of Life and Stabilization of Insulin Treatment.," *Journ of Neurotherapy*, Haworth, 2006; "Client Experiance of Gender in Therapeutic Re;ationships: An Interpretive Ethnography.," *Fam Process*, Blackwell, 2001; "QUalitative Resrch in Fam Ther.," *Journ of Mar and Fam Ther*, AAMFT, 2001; "Life Cycle Dvlpmt: Divorce and the Hisp Fam," *Fam Ther w Hispanics*, Allyn & Bacon, 2000; "The Narrative Ethics and the Ethics of Narrative: The Implications of Ricoeur's Narrative Model for Fam Ther," *The Journ of Systemic Therapies*, 2000. rlyle@randallrlylephd.com

LYLE, William Edward (SO) 1547 Stratford Dr, Kent OH 44240 **Int Supply Chr Epis Ch Kent OH 2000-** B Mount Hope WV 6/8/1926 s Ernest R Lyle & Margie Lorraine. BA Kent St U 1950; MA U MI 1952; BD Bex 1961. D 6/29/1961 Bp Archie H Crowley P 12/1/1961 Bp Richard S M Emrich. m 5/6/2009 Phyllis Robbins c 4. Int S Paul's Epis Ch Logan OH 1988-1989; Int Ch Of The Epiph Nelsonville OH 1985-1991; R S Paul's Epis Ch Of E Cleveland Cleveland OH 1982-1984; R Gr Ch Ravenna OH 1976-1981; Assoc S Mart's Ch Chagrin Falls OH 1967-1968; R S Lk's Ch Cleveland OH 1963-1966; Asst Min All SS Epis Ch Pontiac MI 1961-1963. bblyle2@gmail.com

LYLES, Robert Hallie (Va) 4800 Fillmore Ave Apt 1153, Alexandria VA 22311 **Died 3/26/2011** B Alexandria VA 3/18/1931 s Hallie C Lyles & Ethel M. BA Randolph-Macon Coll 1954; MDiv VTS 1957. D 6/7/1957 Bp Frederick D Goodwin P 5/1/1958 Bp Robert Fisher Gibson Jr. c 2.

LYMAN, Rebecca (Cal) 115 Sheridan Way, Woodside CA 94062 B Marshall MI 10/21/1954 d Howard Arthur Lyman & Janyce Venora. BA Wstrn Michigan U 1976; MA CUA 1979; PhD Oxf 1983. D 6/5/1993 P 6/1/1994 Bp William Edwin Swing. m 7/27/1985 Andrew Phillip Bridges c 2. Samuel Garret Prof of Ch Hist CDSP Berkeley CA 1994-2005. "Natural Resources: Tradition without Orthodoxy," *ATR*, 2002; "Early Chr Traditions," Cowley Pub, 1999; Auth, "Christology and Cosmology," Oxf Press, 1993. jrlyman@aol.com

LYNBERG, Terry Ellsworth (Los) PO Box 33344, San Diego CA 92163 B Los Angeles CA 9/19/1938 s Ellsworth John Lynberg & Mary Elizabeth. BA USC 1961; STB ETS, Cambridge 1964; MA California St U 1993; EdD USC 2003. D 9/10/1964 P 3/1/1965 Bp Francis E I Bloy. Assoc Epis Cmnty Serv San Diego CA 1997-1998; R Ch Of The H Trin and S Ben Alhambra CA 1991-1994; Int S Andr's Par Torrance CA 1989-1990; Dio Los Angeles Los Angeles CA 1971-1989; Assoc All Souls' Epis Ch San Diego CA 1970-1971; Vic S Dav's Epis Ch San Diego CA 1968-1970; Asst All SS Ch Pasadena CA 1964-1968. Auth, "A Study of Navy Coll Prog," NCPACE, 2003; Auth, "Plcy & Procedures Manual for Mssn Congregations," Dio L.A., 1981; Ed, "Dioc Structures & Boundaries Study," Dio L.A., 1980. Cn Dio Los Angeles 2010; Mem Blue Key hon Soc, USC 1960. TELynberg@aol.com

LYNCH JR, Bobby (WNC) Po Box 561, Rutherfordton NC 28139 **D S Gabr's Ch Rutherfordton NC 1980-** B Rutherfordton NC 2/11/1940 s Thurman Lynch & Lillie M. D 5/29/1975 Bp William Gillette Weinhauer. m 3/9/1963 Helen Edgerton c 3.

LYNCH, Daniel Luke (WVa) 123 Hidden Valley Ests, Scott Depot WV 25560 B Mullens WV 9/27/1930 s Daniel Luke Lynch & Ruth. BA U of Virginia 1957; MDiv VTS 1991. D 6/11/1991 P 6/1/1992 Bp John H(enry) Smith. m 10/10/1983 Pamela Susan Kelsey. Vic S Jas Ch Charleston WV 1991-2002.

LYNCH, Gwynn (SanD) 13319 Fallen Leaf Rd, Poway CA 92064 **Vic S Mary's In The Vlly Ch Ramona CA 2010-; Safeguarding God's People Trnr Dio San Diego San Diego CA 2006-; Safeguarding God's People Trng Coordntr Dio San Diego San Diego CA 2006-** B St. Louis MO 3/8/1961 d David Dillon Lynch & Judith Anton. MDiv Claremont TS; BS California St U 1983. D 6/11/2005 P 12/11/2005 Bp James Robert Mathes. m 5/4/1985 Frank Peter Freund c 3. Dioc Coun Mem Dio San Diego San Diego CA 2007-2010; All Souls' Epis Ch San Diego CA 2005-2010. gmfreund@cox.net

LYNCH, John J (SVa) 4109 Big Bethel Rd, Tabb VA 23693 **R Chr The King Epis Ch Tabb VA 2010-** B Mt. Airy NC 4/2/1982 s Larry G Lynch & Celeste. PhD (in Progess) Trin TS; BA Wake Forest U 2002; Dplma Th. Universidad Catolica De Honduras 2003; MA Trin TS 2009. D 10/28/2005 Bp Lloyd Emmanuel Allen. m 11/14/2003 Cecilia Lynch c 1. D and Mssnr Iglesia Epis de la Epifania San Pedro Sula HN 2006-2007; Dio Honduras Miami FL 2005-2009; Iglesia Epis Hondurena San Pedro Sula 2005-2009; D Catedral Epis El Buen Pstr San Pedro Sula HN 2005-2006. Auth, "The Creeds: A Study for Individuals and Groups," CreateSpace/ Kindle Digital Pub, 2011; Ed and Contrib, "The

L

Irish arts of Rel," CreateSpace/ Kindle Digital Pub, 2011; Transltr, "Orden para la celebración de la Santa Comunión del Libro de Oración Común de la Iglesia de Inglaterra (1662)," CreateSpace/ Kindle Digital Pub, 2009; Ed and Contrib, "Natl Apostasy and the Case of Cath Subscription Considered w an Essay on the Life of the Reverend Jn Keble," CreateSpace/ Kindle Digital Pub, 2009; Ed and Contrib, "Comments on Certain Passages of The Thirty-Nine arts," CreateSpace/ Kindle Digital Pub, 2009; Auth, "Los Santos en el cuerpo de la Iglesia," Forw Mvmt, 2008; Auth, "Devoción Mariana en la Iglesia," Forw Mvmt, 2008; Contrib, "Educación cristiana o formación catequética," IX Prov of the Epis Ch, 2007. ctkrector@aol.com

LYNCH, Ronald J (CPa) 118 E Fleming Ave, Lewistown PA 17044 B Lewistown PA 8/21/1935 s Robert Lee Lynch & Jeanette M. BS Shippensburg U 1964; MDiv VTS 1967; MS Shippensburg U 1973; Mississippi St Police Acad Grad 1984. D 6/29/1967 Bp Earl M Honaman P 1/8/1968 Bp Dean T Stevenson. P-in-c S Mk's Epis Ch Lewistown PA 2001-2004; P-in-c S Mk's Epis Ch Lewistown PA 1998-1999; Stndg Com Dio Cntrl Pennsylvania Harrisburg PA 1996-1999; Vic H Trin Epis Ch Hollidaysburg PA 1990-1997; Trin Epis Ch Tyrone PA 1990-1997; R S Jn's Epis Ch Huntingdon PA 1986-1990; S Geo's Epis Ch Clarksdale MS 1983-1984; Epis Hm Shippensburg PA 1982-1983; Vic S Andr's Epis Ch Shippensburg PA 1969-1983; Cur The Epis Ch Of S Jn The Bapt York PA 1967-1969. Common Ground Awd Shippensburg U 1982; Who'S Who In Rel 1977. exarch@acsworld.com

LYNCH, Suzanne Mchugh Stryker (WMo) 1342 S Ventura Ave, Springfield MO 65804 **D S Jas' Ch Springfield MO 1994-** B Omaha NE 6/1/1949 d Hird Stryker & Suzanne Goodrich. AAS Monticello Jr Coll 1969. D 1/25/1994 Bp John Clark Buchanan. c 2. S Jn's Ch Springfield MO 1995-2006.

LYNN, Connor (Los) Po Box 7795, Stockton CA 95267 B Taft CA 7/22/1931 s Bedford Lynn & Winnie. BA Stan 1952; BD CDSP 1956; DD CDSP 1973. D 6/17/1956 Bp Sumner Walters P 12/22/1956 Bp Robert E Campbell. Par Of S Mary In Palms Los Angeles CA 1990-2003; Exec Coun Appointees New York NY 1985-1989; R Epis Ch Of S Anne Stockton CA 1983-1985. Ord of S Ben - Oblate; OHC 1963; UBE. connorlynn@msn.com

LYNN, Jacqueline Goler (Chi) 316 S Butterfield Rd, Libertyville IL 60048 **Cathd Of S Jas Chicago IL 2009-** B Atlanta GA 6/29/1948 d Benjamin Goler & Martha. BA U of Wisconsin 1971; U IL 1983. D 2/2/2002 Bp William Dailey Persell. c 2. epfnational@ameritech.net

LYNN, Robert Newton (NI) 120 Hemlock St, Park Forest IL 60466 B Brunswick GA 7/7/1936 s William Matthew Lynn & Ollie Kate. BA Merc 1962; MDiv Candler TS Emory U 1969; Cert SWTS 1987. D 12/26/1987 P 7/1/1988 Bp Frank Tracy Griswold III. S Barn-In-The-Dunes Gary IN 1993-2001; Dio Nthrn Indiana So Bend IN 1989-1992; Assoc The Epis Ch Of S Jas The Less Northfield IL 1988-1989; S Aug's Epis Ch Wilmette IL 1988. cplail@bellsouth.net

LYNN, Suzanne Marie (EMich) 2937 Wicklow Dr., Saginaw MI 48603 B Saginaw MI 11/13/1940 D 11/24/2001 Bp Edwin Max Leidel Jr. m 5/22/2004 James Ronald Sorenson c 2. S Jn's Epis Ch Saginaw MI 2002-2004.

LYON IV, James Fraser (USC) 1512 Blanding St, Columbia SC 29201 **R Ch Of The Gd Shpd Columbia SC 1991-** B Cheraw SC 7/14/1956 s James Fraser Lyon & Marcine Agnes. BA Winthrop U 1978; MA Winthrop U 1980; MDiv SWTS 1983; EdD U of So Carolina 2003. D 6/11/1983 P 5/12/1984 Bp William Arthur Beckham. m 6/14/1980 Sallie L Leslie c 2. R Ch Of The Gd Shpd York SC 1986-1991; Asst S Martins-In-The-Field Columbia SC 1983-1986. Angl Euch League 1992; SocMary 1992. Phi Alpha Theta. jlyon@mindspring.com

LYON, Lauren Jean (WMo) 4448 Pennsylvania Ave, Kansas City MO 64111 **S Mary's Epis Ch Kansas City MO 2005-; Assoc S Matt's Ch Raytown MO 2000-; D Gr And H Trin Cathd Kansas City MO 1994-** B Des Moines IA 8/20/1954 d Ivan Crackler & Marilyn. BA U CA 1986; MDiv Ya Berk 1994. D 6/4/1994 P 12/3/1994 Bp John Clark Buchanan. m 8/15/1993 Nelson McGee. S Fran Acad Inc. Salina KS 2004-2005; S Andr's Ch Kansas City MO 1999-2000; S Ptr's Ch Harrisonville MO 1997-1999; Gr Ch Carthage MO 1995-1996. justonelyon@yahoo.com

LYON, Walter Donald (CFla) 1628 Bent Oaks Blvd, DeLand FL 32724 **P-in-c Ch Of The H Sprt Apopka FL 2011-; Chapl to the Ret Dio Cntrl Florida Orlando FL 2011-** B Newport RI 1/13/1947 s Walter Kenneth Lyon & Ruth Carolyn. BS U of Massachusetts 1971; MA U of Iowa 1972; MDiv Bex 1980. D 6/7/1980 Bp Morris Fairchild Arnold P 5/23/1981 Bp Robert Shaw Kerr. m 9/9/1967 Karen L Olson c 2. R S Barn Ch Deland FL 1995-2011; R S Steph's Epis Ch Wilkes Barre PA 1988-1995; R S Mk's Ch Newark NY 1984-1988; Vic Calv Ch Underhill VT 1980-1984. Ord of S Ben 1995; Ord of S Lk 1996. donlyon@bellsouth.net

LYON, William D(arrow) (Md) 10 Albano Ct, Palmyra VA 22963 B Chicago IL 9/3/1936 s William Thorncroft Lyon & Jessie Mary. BS U IL 1958; PhD U of Wisconsin 1967; MDiv VTS 1988. D 6/11/1988 Bp Robert Manning Moody P 4/8/1989 Bp Arthur Benjamin Williams Jr. m 6/15/1958 Judith H Hess c 3. Int S Matt's Epis Ch Lisbon ME 2000-2003; R S Mary's Ch Baltimore MD 1991-1999; Assoc. R Chr Epis Ch Huron OH 1988-1990. wdlyon@embarqmail.com

LYONS JR, James Hershel (Nev) All Saint's Episcopal Church, 4201 W Washington Ave, Las Vegas NV 89107 **P-in-c S Chris's Epis Ch Boulder City NV 2010-; Assoc All SS Epis Ch Las Vegas NV 2006-** B Ft Sill Lawton OK 3/31/1964 s James Hershel Lyons & Naomi Joan. Rec from Roman Catholic 12/9/2007 Bp Jerry Alban Lamb. james.lyonsjr@yahoo.com

LYONS, Leroy A 1208 Prospect Ave, Plainfield NJ 07060 B 1/18/1938 s Wilfred Lyons & Louisa. Rutgers-The St U; GOE Codrington Coll 1964; LTh Hur 1969; STB GTS 1970; STM GTS 1971. Trans 2/24/1971 Bp Alfred L Banyard. m 8/26/1990 Michelle Graham c 3. R S Mk's Ch Plainfield NJ 1971-2010.

LYONS, Lorraine M (Alb) 1154 Hedgewood Ln, Niskayuna NY 12309 **S Mk's Ch Hoosick Falls NY 2007-** B Baltimore MD 10/25/1957 d Roger E Beam & Joanna. BS U Of Delaware Newark 1979; MDiv St. Bern's Inst Rochester NY 2000. D 6/11/2000 P 12/16/2000 Bp Daniel William Herzog. m 7/11/1981 James Patrick Lyons c 2. Assoc R S Steph's Ch Schenectady NY 2000-2003. lmlyons@nycap.rr.com

LYTLE III, Guy Fitch (Tex) 335 Tennessee Ave, Sewanee TN 37383 **Died 7/15/2011** B Birmingham AL 10/14/1944 s Guy Fitch Lytle & Nelle. BA Pr 1966; MA Pr 1969; Oxf 1970; PhD Pr 1976. D 10/30/1986 Bp Gordon Taliaferro Charlton P 10/15/1987 Bp William Edwin Swing. c 2. Auth, "Theol Educ For The Future," CDSP, 1989; Auth, "Reform & Authority In Medieval & Reformation Ch," CUA Press, 1981; Auth, "Lambeth Conferences Past & Present," Forw Mvmt Press, 1969. Hon Doctorate In Div Nash Nashotah WI 1995; Marshall Schlr Oxf Oxford Engl 1967. glytle@sewanee.edu

LYTLE, Ronald Dale (Wyo) 1222 Rosewood Ln, Powell WY 82435 B Donnelly ID 3/23/1935 s Donald Earl Lytle & Evelyn Elizabeth. BS U of Wyoming 1961. D 3/2/1988 P 9/14/1988 Bp Charles Jones III. m 6/12/1960 Kathryn Dale Doto c 4. S Jn's Ch Powell WY 2002-2007; Mnstry Dvlp - Reg 1 Dio Wyoming Casper WY 1999-2007; S Andr's Ch Basin WY 1999-2007; S Andr's Ch Meeteetse WY 1999-2007; R Gr Ch Rice Lake WI 1991-1999; Asst S Lk's Ch Billings MT 1988-1991. rlytle@bresnan.net

M

MAAS, Benjamin Wells (Ky) 1374 S Brook St, Louisville KY 40208 **S Andr's Ch Louisville KY 2004-** B Williamsburg VA 11/18/1974 BA U of Virginia 1997; MDiv VTS 2003. D 5/17/2003 P 12/6/2003 Bp Edwin Funsten Gulick Jr. m 6/1/2002 Anna Hope Martin. S Jas Ch Pewee Vlly KY 2003-2004. benmaas@earthlink.net

MAAS, Jan Alfred (NY) 406 Sackett St, Brooklyn NY 11231 B Syracuse NY 12/30/1940 s Alfred Maas & Catherine. BM U of Wisconsin 1963; MDiv GTS 1973; MLS SUNY 1994. D 6/9/1973 P 12/9/1973 Bp Horace W B Donegan. m 6/23/1973 Georgia Louise Shepherd c 1. Dioc Coun Dio New York New York City NY 1986-1989; R Ch Of The Ascen And H Trin Highland NY 1984-1993; Ed - Epis New Yorker Dio New York New York City NY 1975-1984; P-in-c Ch Of The Incarn New York NY 1974-1975; Asst Ch Of The Incarn New York NY 1973-1974. CHS 1985. janmaas@mindspring.com

MACARTHUR III, Robert Stuart (Mo) 334 Maple Ridge Road, Center Sandwich NH 03227 B Detroit MI 10/9/1942 s Robert Stuart MacArthur & Elizabeth Mower. BA Dart 1964; STB Ya Berk 1967. D 6/10/1967 Bp Leland Stark P 1/6/1968 Bp Charles F Hall. m 6/11/1966 Marguerite Ann Eastman. Cur S Thos Ch Hanover NH 1967-1969. Auth, "Glory Hallelu". bobmacarthur@cyberpine.net

MACAULEY, John Spencer (Kan) 3018 W 29th Terrace, Lawrence KS 66047 B Wichita KS 8/22/1928 s John Simeon Macauley & Orma Vivian. BA Wichita St U 1950; BD EDS 1953; PhD U of Cambridge 1965. D 6/13/1953 P 12/11/1953 Bp Goodrich R Fenner. m 10/20/1967 Frances E Garner-Long c 2. R Trin Ch Lawr KS 1988-1993; Asst R Trin Ch Lawr KS 1982-1988; Dio Kansas Topeka KS 1977-1978; Kansas Sch Of Rel Lawr KS 1965-1977; R Gr Epis Ch Winfield KS 1956-1961; Vic S Mk's Ch Blue Rapids KS 1953-1956; Vic S Paul's Ch Marysville KS 1953-1956. Auth, "Var entries," *New Dictionary of Natl Biography*, Oxf Press, 2004; Ed, "Autobiography of Thos Secker," *Archbp of Cbury*, Univer of Kansas, 1988; Auth, "Richard Mountague, Cn of Windsor," *Soc of Friends of S Geo's*, 1964. Eccl Hist Soc (UK) 1968; HSEC 1965-2002. johnsmacauley@sunflower.com

MACAULEY JR, Robert Conover (Vt) 175 Hills Point Road, Charlotte VT 05445 B New York NY 11/23/1966 s Robert Conover Macauley & Alma Jane. BA Wheaton Coll 1988; MS Oxf 1989; MDiv Ya Berk 1993; STM Ya Berk 1994; MD Ya 1995. D 6/10/1995 Bp Clarence Nicholas Coleridge P 9/29/1996 Bp Robert Wilkes Ihloff. m 1/1/2001 Pamela Burton-Macauley. P-in-c S Paul's Epis Ch On The Green Vergennes VT 2002-2006; Asst P Ch Of The H Apos New York NY 2000-2001; Asst P Par of St Paul's Ch Norwalk Norwalk

CT 1998-1999; Asst P Memi Ch Baltimore MD 1995-1998. revdoc@aya.yale.edu

MACBETH, Andrew Jeffrey (WTenn) 1640 Harbert Ave, Memphis TN 38104 **Int Chr Ch Grosse Pointe Grosse Pointe Farms MI 2010-; Bd Trst VTS Alexandria VA 1998-2012** B Chester PA 6/22/1949 s Andrew Kaye MacBeth & Lois Ann. BA Randolph-Macon Coll 1971; MDiv EDS 1975; DMin VTS 2000. D 6/11/1975 P 1/6/1976 Bp Emerson Paul Haynes. m 6/7/1969 Sybil Jane Prouse c 2. Stndg Com Dio W Tennessee Memphis TN 2008-2010; Stndg Committtee Dio W Tennessee Memphis TN 2008-2010; R Calv Ch Memphis TN 2004-2011; Chair COM Dio Sthrn Virginia Norfolk VA 2003-2004; Stndg Com Dio Sthrn Virginia Norfolk VA 1999-2001; Stndg Com Dio Sthrn Virginia Norfolk VA 1998-2000; Chair Evang Cmsn Dio Sthrn Virginia Norfolk VA 1994-1998; Chair CE Dept Dio Sthrn Virginia Norfolk VA 1994-1996; Chair DeptCE Dio Sthrn Virginia Norfolk VA 1992-1994; R Estrn Shore Chap Virginia Bch VA 1988-2004; Chair Stwdshp Cmsn Dio Ohio Cleveland OH 1986-1988; Stwdshp Cmsn Dio Ohio Cleveland OH 1986-1988; Chair, Par Educ Div Dio Ohio Cleveland OH 1984-1986; Plnng Cmsn Dio Ohio Cleveland OH 1982-1985; R S Jas Ch Painesville OH 1981-1988; Assoc Chr Ch Shaker Heights OH 1978-1981; Asst Trin By The Cove Naples FL 1975-1978. Auth, "Praying in Black and White: A Hands-on Pract for Men," *Bk*, Paraclete, 2011; Auth, "Dearly Beloved: Navigating Your Ch Wedding," *Bk*, Seabury, 2007; Auth, "Envisioning Your Life in the Third Age," *doctoral thesis*, 2000. andrewmacbeth1@gmail.com

✠ MACBURNEY, Rt Rev Edward Harding (Q) 25159 Valley Drive, Pleasant Valley IA 52767 **Ret Bp of Quincy Dio Quincy Peoria IL 1994-** B Albany NY 10/30/1927 s Alfred Cadwell MacBurney & Florence Marion. BA Dart 1949; STB Ya Berk 1952; Oxf 1953; DHum S Ambr U 1987; DD Nash 1988. D 5/22/1952 Bp Charles F Hall P 12/21/1952 Bp E Wynn Con 1/19/1988 for Q. m 2/20/1965 Anne Grubb c 3. Trst Nash Nashotah WI 1991-1993; Bp Dio Quincy Peoria IL 1988-1994; Dn Trin Cathd Davenport IA 1973-1987; Pres Stndg Com Dio New Hampshire Concord NH 1972-1973; Stndg Com Dio New Hampshire Concord NH 1970-1971; CDSP Berkeley CA 1964-1970; R S Thos Ch Hanover NH 1963-1973; Asst S Thos Ch Hanover NH 1953-1957. SSC 1995. Reg Panel White Hse Fllshp 1976; Hon DD Nash Nashotah WI; Hon Doctor of Hmnts St. Ambr U.

MACCOLL, Craig (Colo) 5876 E Kettle Pl, Centennial CO 80112 **R Gd Shpd Epis Ch Centennial CO 2005-** B Pasadena CA 5/23/1952 s Eugene Kimbark MacColl & Leeanne. BA U Chi 1974; MA U Chi 1976; Cert Oxf 1980; MDiv Nash 1981. D 6/22/1981 P 12/21/1981 Bp James Winchester Montgomery. m 2/2/1985 Ann Hiestand c 2. Int S Fran Of Assisi Epis Wilsonville OR 2004-2011; R Ch Of Recon San Antonio TX 1997-2001; Vic S Gabr Ch Portland OR 1985-1987; Cur S Mich's Ch Barrington IL 1981-1983. AAPC 1990-2008. cmaccoll@gshep.org

MACCOLLAM, Joel Allan (Alb) 240 Belflora Way, Oceanside CA 92057 B Albany NY 12/19/1946 s Allan MacCollam & Jacqueline. BA Ham 1968; Col 1969; MDiv GTS 1972. D 6/3/1972 P 12/15/1972 Bp Allen Webster Brown. m 5/3/1975 Jann Marie Scherer c 2. Evang Cmsn Dio Los Angeles Los Angeles CA 1978-1979; Assoc S Mk's Par Glendale CA 1978-1979; R S Steph's Ch Schuylerville NY 1974-1978; LocTen S Jas Ch Oneonta NY 1973-1974; Cur S Jn's Epis Ch Troy NY 1972-1973. Auth, *Carnival of Souls*, Seabury, 1980; Auth, *The Way Doctrine*, Intervarsity, 1980; Auth, *The Weekend That Never Ends*, Seabury, 1979. Hon LLD California Grad TS 1987. joel@wer-us.org

MACCONNELL, James Stuart (Wyo) 403 15th St #1, Dallas Center IA 50063 B Kingston NY 9/10/1930 s Eugene Pairo MacConnel & Maren Alice. DC Natl Coll of Chiropractic Lombard IL 1958; MDiv SWTS 1973. D 5/12/1973 Bp Quintin Ebenezer Primo Jr P 12/8/1973 Bp James Winchester Montgomery. m 6/21/1959 Carolyn June Peters c 3. Ch Of The Resurr W Chicago IL 1994-1995; P S Clare's Epis Ch Pleasanton CA 1990-1994; Assoc S Jos's Ch Lakewood CO 1988-1989; R Ch Of S Thos Rawlins WY 1986-1987; Int P Dio Milwaukee Milwaukee WI 1984-1986; Assoc S Mich's Epis Ch Racine WI 1982-1983; Dio Milwaukee Milwaukee WI 1981-1982; Vic S Laurence Epis Ch Effingham IL 1975-1980; Cur S Matt's Ch Evanston IL 1973-1974. Auth, *Living Ch*; Auth, *Mar & Fam Counslg*. EME, Natl Presenting Cler Couple 1978-1988; Seabury Fell Mnstry 1979. C.MACCONNELL@MCHSI.COM

MACDONALD, Daniel Kent (Mass) 1250 Spear St, South Burlington VT 05403 **Transitional D All SS' Epis Ch S Burlington VT 2010-** B Boston MA 10/20/1981 s Bradley Arthur MacDonald & Barbara Struck. BA Carleton Coll 2004; MDiv Ya Berk 2008. D 6/5/2010 Bp Gayle Elizabeth Harris P 1/8/2011 Bp M(arvil) Thomas Shaw III. m 5/31/2008 Laura Sponseller c 1. dkentmacdonald@gmail.com

MACDONALD, David Roberts (WA) 253 Glen Ave, Sea Cliff NY 11579 **R S Lk's Ch Sea Cliff NY 2011-** B Ancon Canal Zone Panama 3/15/1954 s Malcolm Richard MacDonald & Francis. BA California St Polytechnic U 1976; Nash 1985; MDiv SWTS 1987; MA U of Wales 2004; PhD GTF Oxford GB 2007. D 8/22/1987 P 4/1/1988 Bp Reginald Heber Gooden. m 10/30/1999 Betty Wood c 3. R Chr Ch Durham Par Nanjemoy MD 2004-2011; R S Lk's Ch Denison TX 2002-2003; R S Paul's Epis/Angl Ch Frederiksted VI VI 1999-2002; Asst R S Paul's Epis Ch Shreveport LA 1997-1999; Cathd Stff Cathd Of S Jn The Evang Spokane WA 1996-1997; Trst, Dioc Invstmt Trust Epis Dio San Joaquin Modesto CA 1994-1996; Vic S Mart Of Tours Epis Ch Fresno CA 1994-1996; Co-Chair, Evang & Renwl Cmsn Epis Dio San Joaquin Modesto CA 1990-1991; Co-Chair, Evang & Renwl Cmsn Epis Dio San Joaquin Modesto CA 1990-1991; Active Duty Army Off Of Bsh For ArmdF New York NY 1990-1991; Vic Chr Ch Lemoore CA 1988-1990; Cur S Geo's Epis Ch Laguna Hills CA 1987-1988. Auth, "Padre - E.C. Crosse & The Devonshire Epitaph," Cloverdale Books, 2007; Auth, "The Transit of the Angl Mind to the Maryland Colony," Cloverdale Books, 2007; Auth, "Theol and Certainty," *LivCh (Feb. 6)*, LivCh Fndt, 2005. O.St.J. The Ord of S Jn 2008; Fell Angus Dunn Fndt 2004. padremacdonald@hotmail.com

MACDONALD, Gilbert John (EMich) 331 West Mill Street, Oscoda MI 48750 B Halifax NS CA 9/2/1928 s Fredwick Raymond Currie MacDonald & Mary Kathleen. BA U Of King's Coll Halifax Ns CA 1949; BBA Ns Bus Coll CA 1951; BD S Chad CA 1954. m 6/17/1954 Rosemarie Kathleen Mosig c 4. Hope - S Jn's Epis Ch Oscoda MI 1985-1992; R S Jas Ch Marshall MN 1964-1966; Co-R All SS Epis Indn Mssn Minneapolis MN 1960-1964; R Chr Epis Ch Grand Rapids MN 1960-1964.

MACDONALD, Heyward Hunter (Md) 2551 Summit Ridge Trail, Charlottesville VA 22911 B Richmond VA 12/21/1940 s Donald Grant Macdonald & Anne Middleton. BS U of Virginia 1964; MBA U NC 1965; MDiv VTS 1973; DMin VTS 1990. D 5/26/1973 P 5/18/1974 Bp Robert Bruce Hall. m 8/22/1970 Sandra Macdonald c 2. R S Jas Ch Monkton MD 1981-2003; R Westover Epis Ch Chas City VA 1975-1981; Cur Chr Epis Ch Luray VA 1973-1975. Auth, "Stwdshp Theol and Pract: A Process For Leaders of Congregations," *http://www.lulu.com/content/455137*, Lulu Web Pub, 2006; Auth, "Pearl of Great Price, Oral Hist of a Fam during WWII," *http://www.lulu.com/content/467721*, Lulu Web Pub, 2006; Auth, "Calling of Vstry As Servnt of the People of God," *Forw Mvmt*, Forw Mvmt, 2001; Auth, "Return to VietNam," *https://sites.google.com/site/vietnamreturn/*, self Pub, 2001; Auth, "Theol and Mar: A Theol Primer for Cler and Others Who Seek a Deeper Meaning for Mar," *VTS Doctoral Dissertation*, unpub, 1990. Bishops' Awd for Ord Mnstry Bp of Maryland 2003. 2551@embarqmail.com

MACDONALD, Jean A (Vt) 240 Greenpoint Ln, Lyndonville VT 05851 **R S Andr's Epis Ch St Johnsbury VT 2008-** B Malden MA 8/29/1952 d Roderick Hugh MacDonald & Virginia Alys. BS U of New Hampshire 1974; MA EDS 1994. D 12/12/1997 P 6/26/1998 Bp Mary Adelia Rosamond McLeod. m 2/7/2011 Meg Alison Powden c 2. Asst S Andr's Epis Ch St Johnsbury VT 1997-2000. jeanmac829@hughes.net

MACDONALD, John Gray (NY) 11036 N 28th Dr Apt 312, Phoenix AZ 85029 B Warren PA 11/3/1917 s Earle Vincent MacDonald & Lucy. BA U of Wstrn Ontario 1958; STB Hur 1960. D 5/22/1959 P 5/1/1960 Bp William Crittenden. m 11/16/1944 Susie Elnora Estes c 3. R S Steph's Ch Armonk NY 1980-1987; R Ch Of Our Sav DuBois PA 1976-1980; R S Jas Memi Epis Ch Titusville PA 1962-1976; Vic Gr Ch Lake City PA 1960-1962.

MACDONALD, Linda Jean (Mich) 1780 Nemoke Trl, Haslett MI 48840 **Archd Dio Michigan Detroit MI 2005-; D Asst S Kath's Ch Williamston MI 1995-** B Grand Rapids MI 6/13/1942 d Lee James MacDonald & Margaret Lucile. BS Wstrn Michigan U 1964; MA MI SU 1970; Whitaker TS 1994. D 6/11/1994 Bp R(aymond) Stewart Wood Jr. ljmacdon@aol.com

✠ MAC DONALD, Rt Rev Mark Lawrence (Ak) 2228 Penrose Ln., Fairbanks AK 99709 B Duluth MN 1/15/1954 s Adrian Blake MacDonald & Sue Nell. BA Scholastica Toronto Toronto On CA 1975; MDiv U Tor 1978. D 2/1/1979 P 8/1/1979 Bp Robert Marshall Anderson Con 9/13/1997 for Ak. m 11/11/1989 Virginia Miracle c 3. Bp Of Alaska Dio Alaska Fairbanks AK 1997-2007; Dio Minnesota Minneapolis MN 1993-1997; Vic S Antipas Ch Redby MN 1993-1997; Vic S Jn-In-The-Wilderness Redlake MN 1993-1997; Vic Ch Of The Gd Shpd Ft Defiance AZ 1989-1993; Reg Vic Navajoland Area Mssn Farmington NM 1989-1993; R S Steph's Epis Par Portland OR 1984-1989; Vic S Jn's Epis Ch Oxford WI 1981-1984; Vic S Mary's Epis Ch Tomah WI 1981-1984; S Paul's Epis Ch Duluth MN 1979-1981. Associated Parishes; ACPE; Tertiary Of The Soc Of S Fran. mmacdonald@gci.net

MACDONALD, Susan Savage (publish instead of Jean as middle name) (WVa) P.O. Box 308, Shepherdstown WV 25443 **P-in-c Gr Epis Ch Middleway WV 2010-; Assoc Trin Ch Shepherdstown WV 2007-** B Ithaca NY 7/18/1953 d John Addison Savage & Victoria. Luth TS at Gettysburg; BMus Virginia Commonwealth U/Sch of the Arts 1979; MA The GW 1982; JD Penn St-Dickinson Sch of Law 1997. D 12/15/2007 P 6/14/2008 Bp William Michie Klusmeyer. m 2/21/1992 Randolph MacDonald c 1. sjm5002003@yahoo.com

MACDONALD, Terrence Cameron (O) 207 Weed St, New Canaan CT 06840 B 5/17/1938 s Cameron H MacDonald & Helen G. U MI 1960; BA U of Toledo 1961; BD Bex 1964. D 6/13/1964 P 3/1/1965 Bp Nelson Marigold Burroughs. m 8/10/1968 Jean Turley. Asst S Matt's Ch Bedford NY 1970-1977; Cur S Paul's Ch Akron OH 1964-1967.

MACDONALD, Walter Young (Mich) 2796 Page Ave, Ann Arbor MI 48104 B Boston MA 6/10/1941 s Herman Alban MacDonald & Marion Sarah. BA Davidson Coll 1964; MDiv EDS 1969; MS U MI 1971; Spec Degree Cntr For Humanistic Stds 1981. D 6/10/1969 Bp Robert Bruce Hall P 5/1/1970 Bp Archie H Crowley.

MACDONELL, Alexander (Alex) Harrison (Nwk) 2727 Spruce St, Union NJ 07083 **Chapl for Ret Cler Dio Newark Newark NJ 2009-** B Savannah GA 10/20/1927 s Alexander Radcliffe MacDonell & Kathryn. BA Col 1950; MDiv VTS 1968. D 5/25/1968 Bp William S Thomas P 12/21/1968 Bp Robert Bracewell Appleyard. m 8/19/1950 Clare Lewis c 4. Chapl for Ret Cler Dio Newark Newark NJ 1996-1998; R and Dir, Joint Mnstry All SS Ch Bergenfield NJ 1992-1993; R S Lk's Epis Ch Haworth NJ 1980-1993; R S Steph's Epis Ch Wilkinsburg PA 1971-1980; R Chr Ch Brownsville PA 1969-1971. Cbury Schlrshp Dio Newark 1985. alexmacd@earthlink.net

MACDOUGALL, Matthew Bradstock (NwPa) 343 E Main St, Youngsville PA 16371 **P-in-c S Fran Of Assisi Epis Ch Youngsville PA 2009-** B Lancaster PA 2/8/1981 s Malcolm P MacDougall & Linda B. Lic in Theo VTS 2009. D 6/13/2009 Bp Nathan Dwight Baxter P 2/20/2010 Bp Sean Walter Rowe. REVMATTMAC@GMAIL.COM

MACDOWELL, Barry S (Ind) 138 S 18th St, Richmond IN 47374 **D Dio Indianapolis Indianapolis IN 1993-** B Lansing MI 7/29/1945 s George Oliver MacDowell & Ortha Louise. BA MI SU 1969; MA U MI 1969. D 6/24/1993 Bp Edward Witker Jones. m 5/6/1969 Carolyn Kay Garlock c 3. bmacdowel@insightbb.com

MACDUFFIE OSB, Bruce Lincoln (ND) 836 5th Ave. West, Dickinson ND 58601 **P The Ch Of The Epiph Sherburne NY 2010-** B Newburyport MA 5/22/1936 s William Lincoln MacDuffie & Bertha Margaret. BA Blackburn Coll 1959; Med Bos 1969; MDiv SWTS 1984; DMin SWTS 1998. D 5/8/1985 P 11/30/1985 Bp Harold Anthony Hopkins Jr. m 6/10/1975 Gloria Lee Tuttle c 4. R S Paul's Ch Oxford NY 2002-2005; Vic The Ch Of The Epiph Sherburne NY 2001-2005; R S Thos Ch Hamilton NY 1999-2002; Calv Epis Ch Mc Donough NY 1997-1999; Prncpl, New Cler Acad Dio Cntrl New York Syracuse NY 1996-2003; Emm Ch Norwich NY 1994-1999; R S Paul's Ch Oxford NY 1994-1999; R The Ch Of The Epiph Sherburne NY 1994-1999; R S Jas' Epis Ch Dalhart TX 1991-1994; Dio Minnesota Minneapolis MN 1988-1991; Rgnl Vic Dio No Dakota Fargo ND 1985-1988. "Comparing Study Bibles," *Dio No Dakota web site*, Dio No Dakota, 2006. Associated Parishes 1982-2002; St. Greg's Abbey 1982. blmacduffie@frontier.com

MACEK, Kathryn Ellen (EO) PO Box 1001, La Grande OR 97850 **Int S Ptr's Ch La Grande OR 2011-** B Adams MA 10/2/1946 d Robert Michael Macek & Jacqueline Agnes. BMus Mt St. Mary's Coll 1968; MDiv CDSP 2010. D 4/30/2011 Bp Bavi Rivera. m 9/5/1981 Thorman F Hulse c 2. kathrynmacek@aol.com

MACEO JR, J(ames) Robert (Dal) 9348 Creel Creek Dr, Dallas TX 75228 **Died 10/1/2009** B Fort Worth TX 12/29/1929 s Jaime Roberto Maceo & Elsie Elizabeth. STUSo; BA SMU 1953; STB PDS 1956. D 6/20/1956 P 12/22/1956 Bp J(ohn) Joseph Meakins Harte. c 4. Fell Coll of Preachers 1982.

MAC EWEN, Suzanne Marie (Wyo) Po Box 137, Evanston WY 82931 **D S Paul's Epis Ch Evanston WY 2011-** B Chicago IL 5/1/1941 d Francis William Stedman & Agnes Sarah. Andover Newton TS; Missouri Wstrn St U. D 8/14/2003 Bp Bruce Edward Caldwell. smac@vcn.com

MACEY, Michael Carter (Tex) 9410 Moss Farm Ln, Dallas TX 75243 **R Emer Trin Ch Longview TX 1998-** B Rochester MN 5/2/1939 s Harry Buford Macey & Virginia. BA SW At Memphis 1961; BD VTS 1964; DMin GTF 1991. D 7/17/1964 Bp Frederick P Goddard P 6/19/1965 Bp J Milton Richardson. m 6/10/1961 Martha Nichols. P-in-c S Jn's Epis Ch Carthage TX 1998-2008; R Trin Ch Longview TX 1973-1997; R Chr Ch Nacogdoches TX 1967-1973; Vic Chr Ch San Aug TX 1964-1967; Vic S Jn's Epis Ch Cntr TX 1964-1967. Auth, "A Stone Dropped In A Pool," *Sermons Of Jas Richardson*, 2000; Ed, "Patchwork Pathways," 1997; Ed, "Mirrors Into Windows"; Ed, "Mercy Centered"; Ed, "Adv Alphabet Of Prayers". Cmnty Of Hope 1998. mace5701@yahoo.com

MACFARLANE, Robert John (Chi) 3724 Farr Ave, Fairfax VA 22030 B Sioux City IA 11/7/1931 s Robert Alexander Macfarlane & Esther Elizabeth. BS Iowa St U 1954; MA U of Iowa 1958; STB GTS 1968. D 6/22/1968 P 12/19/1968 Bp Gordon V Smith. m 6/25/1971 Maria Keith c 1. R S Barn' Epis Ch Glen Ellyn IL 1979-1998; Asst Trin Cathd Davenport IA 1974-1978; P-in-c All SS Epis Ch Storm Lake IA 1968-1974. Auth, "An Angl Response To The Encyclical," *Ecum Trends*, 1996. EPF 1991. iowabobinva@yahoo.com

MACFIE JR, Thomas Earle (Tenn) 117 Carruthers Rd, Sewanee TN 37375 **The TS at The U So Sewanee TN 2006-** B Greenville SC 3/14/1958 s Thomas Earle Macfie & Ellen. BA U So 1980; MDiv STUSo 1989. D 5/19/1989 P 12/16/1989 Bp William Gillette Weinhauer. m 3/21/1987 Pamela Lee Royston. R Otey Memi Par Ch Sewanee TN 1997-2006; R S Barn Ch Tullahoma TN 1989-1997. Auth, "Looking For Enchanted Place," *Sewanee Theol Revs*, 1998. Participant, Natl Cler Renwl Prog. tmacfie@sewanee.edu

MACGILL, Martha Nell (Md) 2007 Clipper Park Rd, Unit 122, Baltimore MD 21211 **Memi Ch Baltimore MD 2000-** B Alexandria VA 2/19/1958 d Winfield Scott Macgill & Anna Virginia. BA Davidson Coll 1980; JD U of Virginia 1984; LLM NYU 1986; MDiv VTS 1995. D 6/3/1995 P 1/1/1996 Bp Peter James Lee. m 6/13/1981 Richard Bryan Kelleher c 2. S Steph's Ch Richmond VA 1996-1997. inja44@verizon.net

MACGILL III, William D (WVa) 5909 cedar landing rd, Wilmington NC 28409 B Newport News VA 10/27/1944 s William Daniel MacGill & Eloise. BA Hampden-Sydney Coll 1967. D 6/14/1997 P 6/13/1998 Bp John H(enry) Smith. m 4/4/1986 Sybil Joan Owen. Vic S Jn's Ch Marlinton WV 2000-2006; P S Thos Epis Ch White Sulphur Sprg WV 1998-2001; P Ch Of The Incarn Ronceverte WV 1998-2000. wdmacgill@bellsouth.net

MACGOWAN JR, Kenneth Arbuthnot (Colo) 3440 S Jefferson St Apt 1136, Falls Church VA 22041 B Quincy FL 4/17/1924 s Kenneth Arbuthnot MacGowan & Mary Lou. BS U So 1947; MA Mex City Coll Mex City Mx 1948; JD Harv 1951; MDiv VTS 1984. D 6/23/1984 Bp Peter James Lee P 5/22/1985 Bp David Henry Lewis Jr. m 2/18/1950 Virginia S Pendill. Cn Mssnr Dio Colorado Denver CO 1994-1996; COLM Dio Virginia Richmond VA 1988-1990; Vic & R Trin Ch Manassas VA 1986-1990; Int S Paul's Ch Haymarket VA 1985-1986; Asst Vic All SS Epis Ch Woodbridge VA 1984-1985. Auth, "arts, Wrshp, The Word," *& The Wrld*; Auth, "arts," *Acts 29*. Aac; ERM. Phi Beta Kappa; Phi Beta Kappa. kmacgowan@aol.com

MACGREGOR, Laird Stanley (WK) 322 S Ash St, Mcpherson KS 67460 **Dio Wstrn Kansas Hutchinson KS 2006-; Vic S Anne's Ch McPherson KS 2006-** B Medicine Lodge KS 5/5/1966 s John MacGregor & Barbara. BS U of Kansas 1988; MDiv U So 2006. D 5/9/2006 P 11/25/2006 Bp James Marshall Adams Jr. lstanmac@yahoo.com

MACINNIS, Elyn Gregg Cheney (NY) B21 Jiu Xian Qiao Road, Beijing 10001 China B New York NY 10/17/1951 d Richard Eugene Cheney & Betty Lee. BA Kirkland Coll 1973; MDiv Harvard DS 1977. D 2/14/1993 Bp KH Ting P 8/1/1993 Bp William George Burrill. m 12/30/1974 Peter P MacInnis c 2. Exec Coun Appointees New York NY 1994-2010. Auth, "Powers," *Principalities & People*.

MACINTIRE, Morgan Montelepre (WLa) 9325 West St., Manassas VA 20110 **Dio Wstrn Louisiana Alexandria LA 2011-** B Shreveport LA 7/13/1982 d John Montelepre & Elizabeth Luke. BA Rhodes Coll 2004; MDiv VTS 2008. D 6/7/2008 Bp D(avid) Bruce Mac Pherson P 8/8/2009 Bp David Colin Jones. m 6/4/2005 Angus Alan MacIntire c 1. S Jas Epis Ch Shreveport LA 2010-2011; Asst Trin Ch Manassas VA 2008-2010; Secy of Cmncatn S Mk's Cathd Shreveport LA 2004-2005. morgan_mac_4@hotmail.com

MACINTOSH, Neil K (Kan) Charismead, 11A Browns Road, The Oaks, NSW 2570 Australia B Newtown VIC AU 12/11/1935 s Alexander Keith Macintosh & Evelyn Elizabeth. ThL Moore Theol Coll, Sydney 1961; BD Lon 1963; THS Australia Coll of Theol 1967; AA Libr Assoc of Australia 1976; MA Macquarie U 1977. Trans from Anglican Church Of Australia 4/1/1989 as Priest Bp Gerald Nicholas McAllister. m 8/14/1965 Denise Ve Waddy c 3. Angl Dio the Bahamas and the Turks and Caicos Islands 1997-2000; St. Monica's Angl Ch 1997-2000; R S Paul's Epis Ch Coffeyville KS 1989-1997. Auth, "Richard Johnson," *Blackwell Dict. of Evang Biography*, Blackwell, 1995; Auth, "Mary Johnson," *Australian Dict. of Evang Biography*, Evang Hist Assoc., 1994; Auth, "Richard Johnson," *Australian Dict. of Evang Biography*, Evang Hist Assoc., 1994; Auth, "Richard Johnson, Chapl to the Colony of New So Wales," Libr of Australian Hist, 1978. kingsdale42@yahoo.com

MACK, Alan E (Oly) 12527 Roosevelt Way NE APT 202, Seattle WA 98125 B 7/18/1940 A.B. Harv 1962; M.Div. Ya Berk 1967. D 8/10/1967 Bp Ivol I Curtis P 2/10/1968 Bp Donald H V Hallock. Sch of Mnstry and Theol Dio Olympia Seattle WA 2008-2010; P-in-c St Ptr's Epis Par Seattle WA 2005-2007; Int Pstr S Mk's Cathd Seattle WA 2004; Vic All SS Ch Seattle WA 1973-1979; St. Tim's and St. Greg's S Jn's Ch Kirkland WA 1969-1973; Cur Chr Ch Whitefish Bay WI 1967-1969. Ed, "Icons: The Fascination and the Reality," Riverside Bk Co, Inc., 1995; Ed, "St. Spiridon's Cathd: A Century in Seattley of," St. Spiridon Cathd Press, 1995. fathermack@gmail.com

MACK, Arthur Robert (Mich) 13 Dover Ln., Hendersonville NC 28739 B Watertown NY 8/13/1942 s Arthur Edison Mack & Sarah Ethel. BS USMA at W Point 1964; MDiv GTS 1971. D 5/5/1971 Bp Clarence Edward Hobgood P 2/27/1972 Bp Chilton Powell. m 2/12/1983 Susan G Goldsmith c 4. R S Jn's Ch Westland MI 1998-2008; R Trin Ch Lancaster NY 1989-1997; R The Ch Of The Epiph Sherburne NY 1981-1989; S Paul's Cathd Syracuse NY 1980; S Ptr's Epis Ch Cazenovia NY 1980; Trin Ch Lowville NY 1980; Int R Trin Ch Lowville NY 1979-1980; Off Of Bsh For ArmdF New York NY 1973-1979; Cur S Paul's Cathd Syracuse NY 1971-1973. Ord of S Lk 1974; OHC 1970. mackar4264@yahoo.com

MACK, Ross Julian (NI) Po Box 462, Valparaiso IN 46384 B Lansing MI 4/7/1949 s Walter N Mack & June. BA Hope Coll 1971; MDiv Nash 1974; BSME Valparaiso U 1986. D 4/19/1974 P 11/2/1974 Bp Charles Thomas Gaskell. m 7/31/1971 Patricia Machiela Mack c 1. R S Andr's Epis Ch Valparaiso IN 1977-1984; Asst Trin Ch Wauwatosa WI 1974-1976.

MACKAY III, Donald (Oly) 14405 116th Place NE, Kirkland WA 98034 B Billings MT 9/25/1940 s Donald Mackay & Virginia. BA Trin Hartford CT 1962; MDiv VTS 1965. D 6/24/1965 P 12/28/1965 Bp Chandler W Sterling. m 7/11/1964 Rosemary Irene Jefferson c 5. R S Jn's Ch Kirkland WA 1990-2005; R S Lk's Ch Billings MT 1967-1990. Auth, "Chr's Own Forever," Self Pub - St. Jn'S Ch, 2002. Chapl Ord Of S Lk 1989-1994. drmackay@comcast.net

MACKAY, Wray (Oly) 716 N 67th St, Seattle WA 98103 B Boston MA 9/15/1929 s Woodbury Eshorne MacKay & Catharine Wray. MIT 1949; BS Harv 1951; STB GTS 1955; STM GTS 1959. D 6/19/1954 Bp Norman B Nash P 12/19/1954 Bp Horace W B Donegan. m 4/11/1998 Kathleen Kramer c 3. Assoc All SS Ch Seattle WA 2005-2010; Assoc S Paul's Ch Seattle WA 1998-2004; Dio Olympia Seattle WA 1997; Int Trin Par Seattle WA 1996-1997; Vic and R S Ptr's Ch New York NY 1980-1995; Dir Wrld Hunger Year Inc New York NY 1976-1980; Prof Pstr Theol The GTS New York NY 1971-1976; Vic S Andr's Ch Bronx NY 1960-1971; R S Mk's Ch Plainfield IN 1958-1960; Asst S Ptr's Ch New York NY 1954-1958. wray.mackay@comcast.net

MACKE, Elizabeth Ann (Ind) PO Box 127, Rockport IN 47635 **Dio Indianapolis Indianapolis IN 2010-** B St Louis MO 7/29/1964 d James Paul Macke & Barbara Joan. BS Sprg Hill Coll 1985; PhD Emory U 1993; MDiv STUSo 2001. D 6/9/2001 Bp Robert Gould Tharp P 12/22/2001 Bp J(ohn) Neil Alexander. m 5/11/2011 Mark D. Sellars c 1. R S Paul's Ch Henderson KY 2007-2010; S Mary's Epis Ch Middlesboro KY 2003-2007; Sr Asst to the R S Dav's Ch Roswell GA 2002-2003; Cur S Geo's Epis Ch Griffin GA 2001-2002. Amer Sociol Assn 2000. bethamacke@gmail.com

MACKENDRICK, Gary Winfred (Ore) 1904 Elm St Ste 3, Forest Grove OR 97116 B Dublin TX 7/18/1945 s Elby Winfred Kendrick & Daphnae Faye. CEU U of Oregon; BA W Texas A&M U 1967; MDiv Iliff TS 1971; MA Gonzaga U 1977. D 10/16/1977 P 2/19/1978 Bp John Raymond Wyatt. m 10/1/1999 Janet Elaine Sabbe c 3. Vic / Int S Andr's Ch Portland OR 1984-1985; Pstr Counslr Ch Of The Epiph Lake Oswego OR 1983-1985; Pstr Counslr Epis Par Of S Jn The Bapt Portland OR 1983-1985; Gr Epis Ch Astoria OR 1979-1983; S Steph's Epis Ch Spokane WA 1978-1979. Auth, *Etchings*; Auth, *Jewish & Hellenistic Background Churchr Ch*; Auth, *The Sons of S Mich*. Coll of Chapl. The Mich Lambert, Ph.D., Awd for Clincl Excellence 2003. gwk1515@verizon.net

MACKENZIE JR, Albert Harold (SO) 37 Abbey Ln, Washington NC 27889 **Supply P Emm Ch Farmville NC 2008-** B Gallipolis OH 11/17/1928 s Albert Harold MacKenzie & Martha Elizabeth. BFA Ohio U 1959; MDiv VTS 1962. D 6/17/1962 Bp Roger W Blanchard P 1/5/1963 Bp Samuel B Chilton. m 8/5/1951 Dorothy Barfield. P-in-c Zion Epis Ch Washington NC 1998-2002; Supply P S Jas Epis Ch Belhaven NC 1995-1998; Gr Ch Pomeroy OH 1977-1978; R S Ptr's Ch Gallipolis OH 1964-1992; Asst Gr Epis Ch Alexandria VA 1962-1964. Rotarian of the Year 1995; Outstanding Serv Awd BB/S 1988; Fireman of the Year 1988. DOTALMAC@GOTRICOUNTY.COM

MACKENZIE, A(lexander) James (NCal) 16897 Placer Oaks Rd, Los Gatos CA 95032 B Anchorage AK 12/18/1946 s William MacKenzie & Margaret Lowry. BA/BS U of Montana 1969; Olympia TS 1982; MDiv Nash 1992. D 6/24/1988 Bp Robert Hume Cochrane P 1/18/1992 Bp Rustin Ray Kimsey. c 3. R Chr Ch Eureka CA 2002-2005; R Ch Of The Redeem Pendleton OR 1992-2002; Pres Stndg Com Dio Estrn Oregon The Dalles OR 1992-1998; Asst St Philips Epis Ch Waukesha WI 1989-1991; Asst S Andr's Epis Ch Tacoma WA 1988-1989. Ka Papa (Ha Cmnty Of Ch); NAAD; RWF. tartan18@gmail.com

MACKENZIE, David Cameron (Pgh) 310 Academy Ave, Sewickley PA 15143 **Died 9/3/2009** B Los Angeles CA 9/19/1941 s Dewitt Clinton MacKenzie & Anne. BA Ya 1966; MDiv TESM 1979. Trans 1/13/2004 Bp David Conner Bane Jr. c 4. Auth, "Still m, Still Sober," Intervarsity Press, 1991.

MACKENZIE, Jonathan (NH) 52 Brick Kiln Rd, Chelmsford MA 01824 **Sacramentalist S Mk's Ch Westford MA 2011-** B Ticonderoga NY 9/27/1938 s Harry Kingsley MacKenzie & Kate. BA Un Coll Schenectady NY 1960; MDiv GTS 1967. D 6/3/1967 P 12/21/1967 Bp Allen Webster Brown. m 6/3/2000 Carol Eastman c 4. Asst All SS Ch W Newbury MA 2007-2010; R S Jas Epis Ch Laconia NH 1994-2004; S Lk's Ch Mechanicville NY 1988-1994; Trin Epis Ch Mechanicville NY 1988-1991; Trin Ch Boonville NY 1987-1988; R Chr Ch Coxsackie NY 1982-1988; R S Lk's Ch Mechanicville NY 1982-1988; S Lk's Ch Catskill NY 1982-1987; R S Lk's Epis Ch Smethport PA 1978-1982; Vic Ch Of The Gd Samar Mc Keesport PA 1976-1978; S Jn's Epis Ch Troy NY 1975-1976; R Chr Ch Walton NY 1970-1974; Cur Chr Ch Cooperstown NY 1967-1970. jonmknz@gmail.com

MACKENZIE, Joshua Tayloe (EC) 2047 Rivershore Rd, Elizabeth City NC 27909 **Died 2/3/2010** B Washington NC 11/25/1930 s Robert Preston MacKenzie & Athalia Cotten. VTS 1961. D 6/21/1961 P 2/1/1962 Bp Thomas H Wright. c 2. bjmack@inteliport.com

MACKENZIE, Katharine Helen (Los) 948 W Sierra Nevada Way, Orange CA 92865 **Asst Ch Of The Mssh Santa Ana CA 2000-** B Los Angeles CA 2/8/1957 d John Edwin Snope & Elizabeth Rose. BA California St U 1979; JD Loyola U 1982; MDiv ETSBH 1997. D 6/14/1997 Bp Chester Lovelle Talton P 1/1/1998 Bp Frederick Houk Borsch. m 6/4/1977 Robert Stanley MacKenzie. S Aug By-The-Sea Par Santa Monica CA 1997-2000.

MACKENZIE, Lester Vivian (Los) 1031 Bienveneda Ave, Pacific Palisades CA 90272 **Emerging Mnstrs The Par Of S Matt Pacific Palisades CA 2009-; Mem COM Dio Los Angeles Los Angeles CA 2008-** B South Africa 10/9/1974 s Ernest Hoff & Charmaine. LTh VTS 2007. D 6/9/2007 P 1/12/2008 Bp Joseph Jon Bruno. m 3/4/2004 Angela Angela Lamb c 3. Cur St Johns Pro-Cathd Los Angeles CA 2007-2009. lvmackenzie@stmatthews.com

MACKENZIE, Mary Catherine (Oly) 16060 Ne 28th St, Bellevue WA 98008 **YA Mssnr Chr Ch SEATTLE WA 2009-; Cmsn for Liturg and the Arts Dio Olympia Seattle WA 2008-** B Seattle WA 11/20/1957 d William James MacKenzie & Nancy Marie. BSE U of Washington 1979; MSE U of Washington 1985; MDiv SWTS 2005. D 6/25/2005 P 1/14/2006 Bp Vincent Waydell Warner. m 4/28/1979 Wesley S Ono c 2. Cur Trin Epis Ch Everett WA 2006-2007; Cur Emm Epis Ch Mercer Island WA 2005-2006. Cler Assn of the Dio Olympia 2005. rev.marymack@gmail.com

MACKENZIE, Ross (WNY) 11819 Eastkent Sq, Richmond VA 23238 B Edinburgh Scotland GB 8/26/1927 s Donald Ross Mackenzie & Edith Agnes. MA U of Edinburgh GB 1949; BD U of Edinburgh GB 1952; PhD U of Edinburgh GB 1962; Licentiat Lund U 1964. D P 9/19/1998 Bp David Charles Bowman. m 7/14/1951 Flora Margaret Duncan c 3. Assoc S Lk's Epis Ch Jamestown NY 2000-2006; Int S Paul's Epis Ch Mayville NY 1998-1999. Doctor of Humane Letters Shenandoah U, Winchester VA 1997.

MACKENZIE, Vanessa Mildred (Los) 1739 Buckingham Rd, Los Angeles CA 90019 **R Epis Ch Of The Adv Los Angeles CA 2000-** B Johannesburg ZA 8/29/1959 Trans from Church of the Province of Southern Africa 12/1/2000 Bp Chester Lovelle Talton. m 1/3/2004 Eugenio Ayala-Porfil. revvmack1@aol.com

MACKENZIE, Vincent Victor (Cal) 110 Bella Vista Ave, Belvedere CA 94920 B Peoria IL 7/4/1929 s Victor MacKenzie & Alma Maria. BS Bradley U 1953; JD U IL 1954; S Geo's Coll Jerusalem IL 1991; BA Sch for Deacons 1992. D 12/4/1993 Bp William Edwin Swing P. m 9/15/1956 Carolyn Elaine Good c 3. Bread For The Wrld.

MACKEY, George Rudolph (Los) 801 Haslam Dr, Santa Maria CA 93454 B Casper WY 4/26/1929 s George Rudolph Mackey & Esther May. BS U of Nebraska 1958; MDiv CDSP 1966. D 6/13/1966 P 12/19/1966 Bp James W Hunter. m 12/18/1977 Judith P Young. R S Ptr's Par Santa Maria CA 1985-1999; Vic S Jas' Epis Ch Coquille OR 1981-1985; Vic S Mk's Ch Myrtle Point OR 1981-1985; Vic S Paul's Epis Mssn Powers OR 1981-1985; P S Paul's Epis Ch Salem OR 1977-1981; Ch Of The H Comm Rock Sprg WY 1969-1977; Vic Chr Epis Ch Glenrock WY 1966-1969. rev.mackey@hotmail.com

MACKEY, Guy L (RG) 312 N. Orchard Ave., Farmington NM 87401 **S Jn's Ch Farmington NM 2009-** B Suffern NY 10/18/1972 s M(artha) LaVanne. BS Chadwick U 1993; MDiv Cranmer Theol Hse 1998. D 9/15/1999 P 3/18/2000 Bp Robert Jefferson Hargrove Jr. m 12/20/1997 Cheryl L Chandler c 2. Chr Memi Ch Mansfield LA 2001-2009; Cur Gr Epis Ch Monroe LA 1999-2001. rector@saintjohnschurch.info

MACKEY, Jeffrey Allen (Fla) 500 Grove Street, Melrose FL 32666 **Chair, BEC Dio Florida Jacksonville FL 2009-; R Trin Epis Ch Melrose FL 2008-** B Kingston NY 7/12/1952 s Allen W Mackey & Vivian. BS Nyack Coll 1974; MDiv Macon Bapt TS 1978; DMin GTF 1990; Cert GTS 1993; ThD Evangel Chr U 2011; PhD Trin TS 2011. D 2/22/1993 P 9/14/1993 Bp David B(ruce) Joslin. m 12/18/1971 M(artha) LaVanne Webster c 3. R S Mk's Ch Orchard Pk NY 2007-2008; Acad Dn TESM Ambridge PA 2005-2007; R S Jn's Epis Ch Kingston NY 2002-2003; Ass't VP & Dn Nyack Coll Nyack NY 2000-2005; Vic Leonidas Polk Memi Epis Mssn Leesville LA 1996-1997; R Trin Epis Ch Deridder LA 1996-1997; Assoc. R Gr Ch Utica NY 1993-1996; Vic Gr Ch Utica NY 1991-1992. Auth, "But I Repeat Myself," The Wilson Press, 2011; Auth, "Chr's Centripetal Cross -2nd ed," The Wilson Press, 2011; Auth, "The Four Fold Gospel," The Wilson Press, 2010; Auth, "Take Your Chants," GROVEPUBLISHING, 2010; Auth, "A Hidden Surprise," iUniverse, 2008; Auth, "Hidden Mirth: The Gr Behind the Goodness," Pleasant Word, 2005; Auth, "And Jesus Everything: Conversations w A.B. Simpson," Blackfriar Books, 2000; Auth, "Prophet of Justice, Prophet of Life," Ch Pub, Inc., 1996; Auth, "Where Love & People Are," Wyndham Hall Press, 1990; Auth, "A Wrshp Manifesto," Brentwood Chr Press, 1989; Auth, "Chr's Centripetal Cross," Brentwood Chr Press, 1989; Auth, "Indicatives & Imperatives," Brentwood Chr Press, 1987. SBL 2001. DD GTF 2005; D.Litt. Evang Coll & Sem 2004; D.H.L. S Paul TS 2001; S.L.D. Ridgedale TS 1975. vicarsgrove@windstream.net

MACKEY, Judith P (Los) 801 Haslam Dr, Santa Maria CA 93454 **D Dio Los Angeles Los Angeles CA 1999-** B Wilkinsburg PA 2/2/1942 d Charles Edward Young & Lois Margaret. U Pac 1963; BA Chapman U 1991; Chapman U 1994. D 2/21/1986 Bp Robert Louis Ladehoff. m 12/18/1977 George Rudolph

Mackey c 1. D S Ptr's Par Santa Maria CA 1986-1999. CHS; Integrity; NAAD. judithmackey@juno.com

MACKEY, Peter David (Mich) 614 Company St, Adrian MI 49221 B Pottsville PA 8/15/1940 s Sheldon Elias Mackey & Marie Louise. BA Ursinus Coll 1962; BD Lancaster TS 1965. D 6/24/1974 P 10/25/1974 Bp Dean T Stevenson. c 1. R Chr Ch Adrian MI 1998-2002; S Jn's Epis Ch Bowling Green OH 1993-1996; R S Andr's Epis Ch York PA 1985-1993; R S Jas Bedford PA 1974-1985.

MACKIE, Robert Allan (Mass) 16 Park Ave, Somerville MA 02144 B Washington DC 1/9/1933 s James Andrew Mackie & Helen Victoria. BA NYU 1963; MDiv VTS 1966. D 6/4/1966 Bp Horace W B Donegan P 6/9/1967 Bp Randolph R Claiborne. m 1/19/1957 Myrna Inez Shaw c 2. R S Andr's Ch Hanover MA 1974-1990; R S Jn's Ch Winthrop MA 1967-1974; Asst S Bede's Ch Atlanta GA 1966-1967. samcat19@comcast.net

MACKILLOP, Alan Bruce (SanD) 73 Windward Ln, Manchester NH 03104 B Cambridge MA 2/11/1936 s Kenneth MacKillop & Mildred. BA Willamette U 1958; MDiv GTS 1970. D 4/8/1961 P 10/1/1961 Bp James P De Wolfe. m 6/9/1958 Erica Dorothy Hudson c 2. P-in-c S Andr's Ch Ayer MA 2005-2009; R S Andr's Ch La Mesa CA 1979-1999; R Ch Of The H Comm Mahopac NY 1971-1979; Cur Ch Of The Resurr New York NY 1967-1971; R Gr Epis Ch Port Jervis NY 1964-1967; Cur S Jn's Ch New York NY 1961-1964. Cltn for the Abolition of the Death Penalty, NH 2010; Cmnty of S Mary 1977; Mart Luther King Jr. Cltn, NH 2010; NAACP 1961; OHC 1962; Our Lady of Walsingham 1991. amackillop@comcast.net

MACKNIGHT, Jeffrey Brooks (WA) 5450 Massachusetts Ave, Bethesda MD 20816 **R S Dunst's Epis Ch Beth MD 1999-** B Saint Louis MO 4/30/1959 s Frank Barnett MacKnight & Barbara Penelope. BS Nebraska Wesl 1981; MDiv VTS 1984. D 6/15/1984 P 12/1/1984 Bp James Daniel Warner. m 10/10/1987 Leslie H Hay c 2. R S Phil's Epis Ch Laurel MD 1993-1999; R S Greg's Epis Ch Parsippany NJ 1988-1993; Asst Ch Of The Atone Tenafly NJ 1986-1988; Cur S Matt's Ch Lincoln NE 1984-1986. Ed, "Leaven," *Journ of NNECA*, NNECA, 1998. Lilly Endwmt Pstr Renwl Grant Lilly Endwmt 2006. jbmacknight@verizon.net

MACKOV, Elwyn Joseph (WVa) 118 Five Point Ave, Martinsburg WV 25404 **S Phil's Ch Chas Town WV 2008-** B Brooklyn NY 7/13/1940 s Joseph M Mackov & Emma. MDiv GTS; BA Moravian TS 1965; STB GTS 1968. D 6/15/1968 P 12/21/1968 Bp Jonathan Goodhue Sherman. m 6/24/1995 Janette S Crews. Emm Ch Keyser WV 1999-2006; H Trin Ch Logan WV 1997-2000; S Pauls Epis Ch Williamson WV 1997-2000; Sthrn Appalachian Cluster Williamson WV 1996-1999; Nelson Cluster Of Epis Ch Rippon WV 1995-1996; R All Souls Meml Epis Ch Washington DC 1974-1988; R Emm Epis Ch Great River NY 1970-1974; Cur All SS Ch Bayside NY 1968-1970. JMACKOV@TRIAD.RR.COM

MACLEAN, Burton Allan (Ct) 446 Deerfield Road, Box 255, Pomfret CT 06258 **Died 1/12/2011** B Geneva NY 4/13/1916 s Charles Chalmers MacLean & Elizabeth. BA Ya 1938; BD Yale DS 1942. D 8/13/1959 P 2/20/1960 Bp Harry S Kennedy. c 8. Ed, *Hymnal for Colleges & Schools*. burtonm860@aol.com

MACLEAN, Peter Duncan (LI) P.O. Box 848, Colchester VT 05446 B New York NY 9/6/1930 s Charles Waldo MacLean & Grace Elizabeth. BA Trin Hartford CT 1952; MDiv GTS 1955. D 4/16/1955 P 11/5/1955 Bp James P De Wolfe. m 10/3/1970 Margaret Ellen Mayer. R S Lk's Ch Alburgh VT 2002-2004; Int Chr Ch Sag Harbor NY 1994-1996; S Mary's Epis Ch Shltr Island NY 1976-1993; Dio Long Island Garden City NY 1976-1977; Ch Of The Mssh Mayodan NC 1974-1977; Asst Trin Ch Northport NY 1973-1974; R S Jas Epis Ch S Jas NY 1967-1970; R S Ann's Ch Sayville NY 1960-1964; R Trin Epis Ch Lewiston ME 1957-1960; Min in charge Ch Of The Ascen Greenpoint Brooklyn NY 1955-1957. kintyre@myfairpoint.net

MACLEOD III, Norman M (Vt) 2 Church St, Woodstock VT 05091 **R S Jas Ch Woodstock VT 2011-; S Jn's Epis Par Waterbury CT 2010-** B Southington CT 10/3/1947 s Norman Murray MacLeod & Helen Lenore. BA Clark U 1970; MA Adel 1981; MDiv Ya Berk 1989. D 7/1/1989 P 2/4/1990 Bp George Nelson Hunt III. m 9/18/1982 Elizabeth C MacLeod c 3. Int Par Of S Jas Ch Keene NH 2008-2010; R Chr Ch Guilford CT 1997-2008; Vic S Aug's Ch Kingston RI 1991-1997; Gr Ch In Providence Providence RI 1989-1991. nmacleod03@gmail.com

MACLIN, Charles Waite (Me) Po Box 1259, Portland ME 04104 B Winston-Salem NC 12/14/1934 s Henry Maclin & Lucy Persons. BA Guilford Coll 1956; BD VTS 1959; Cp Fllshp 1970. D 6/21/1959 P 12/13/1959 Bp Richard Henry Baker. m 6/2/1979 Christine Anderson c 2. Dn Reg Dio Virginia Richmond VA 1976-1978; R Chr Epis Ch Winchester VA 1974-1978; Excoun Dio Maryland Baltimore MD 1971-1973; Dept Chr Trng Dio Maryland Baltimore MD 1968-1974; Chair Yth Com & Mem Deptce Dio Maryland Baltimore MD 1968-1971; Assoc R The Ch Of The Redeem Baltimore MD 1967-1974; R S Jos's Ch Durham NC 1962-1966; Min In Charge S Paul's Epis Ch Cary NC 1959-1962; Min In Charge Trin Ch Fuquay Varina NC 1959-1962. Me Pstr Counselors Assn. waite8@gwi.net

MACMILLAN, William McGregor (Colo) 2224 Georgetown Dr, Denton TX 76201 **Died 6/23/2011** B Detroit MI 3/10/1929 s Alexander Romeyn MacMillan & Margaret. BA U MI 1951; BD SWTS 1961; Med K SU 1967. D 8/6/1961 P 2/22/1962 Bp Edward Clark Turner. c 5. ann.macmillan@unt.edu

MACNABB, Anne St. Clair Coghill (Va) 20370 Marguritte Sq, Sterling VA 20165 **Asst R S Matt's Epis Ch Sterling VA 2008-** B Fairfax VA 5/26/1970 BA Mary Baldwin Coll 1992; MDiv VTS 2004. D 6/26/2004 P 1/10/2005 Bp Peter James Lee. c 2. S Dunst's McLean VA 2007-2008; S Thos Epis Ch McLean VA 2004-2007. ascmacnabb@aol.com

MACNALLY, Janet Lee (Minn) 11801 Owatonna St, Blaine MN 55449 **D S Chris's Epis Ch Roseville MN 2007-** B St Paul MN 8/17/1950 BS U MN Duluth MN 1972. D 6/28/2007 Bp James Louis Jelinek. m 9/8/1973 William MacNally c 2. moachmac@aol.com

✠ **MACNAUGHTON, Rt Rev John Herbert** (WTex) 7 Queens Gate, San Antonio TX 78218 **Ret Bp of WTex Dio W Texas San Antonio TX 1996-** B Duluth MN 11/19/1929 s Herbert Ross MacNaughton & Jennie Grant. BA U MN 1951; MDiv Bex 1954; DD STUSo 1985; DD Bex 2003. D 6/20/1954 P 2/28/1955 Bp Stephen E Keeler Con 2/6/1986 for WTex. m 6/25/1954 Shirley Ross c 5. co-adjuter/Dioc Dio W Texas San Antonio TX 1986-1995; Chr Epis Ch San Antonio TX 1975-1986; R S Steph The Mtyr Ch Minneapolis MN 1972-1975; R Trin Ch Excelsior MN 1967-1972; Dn The Epis Cathd Of Our Merc Sav Faribault MN 1958-1968; D-in-c H Trin Intl Falls MN 1954-1958; D-in-c S Ptr's Ch Warroad MN 1954-1958. Auth, *More Blessed to Give*, CPG, 1983; Auth, *Stwdshp Myths & Methods*, Seabury Press, 1975. Apos in Stwdshp The Epis Ntwk in Stwdshp 2006. jhm-srm@sbcglobal.net

MACNEICE, (Alan) (Haw) 29Eo Street 178, Commond Choy Chom, Phnom Penh Cambodia B Drogheda County Louth IE 1/7/1934 s Herbert MacNeice & Evelyn. Trin-Dublin Ie; U Coll Dublin; U Coll Dublin. Trans from Church Of England 12/27/1983 Bp John Shelby Spong. St Thos Ch Hanalei HI 1999-2006; Stndg Com Dio Hawaii Honolulu HI 1999-2003; Dep Gc Dio Hawaii Honolulu HI 1997-2003; Cmncatns Chair Dio Hawaii Honolulu HI 1995-1999; Co Chair Bp Search Com Dio Hawaii Honolulu HI 1995-1996; Dioc Coun Dio Hawaii Honolulu HI 1994-1998; R Chr Meml Ch Kilauea HI 1993-2006; Int S Steph's Ch Millburn NJ 1991-1992; Int Chr Ch Glen Ridge NJ 1990-1991; Asstg S Bern's Ch Bernardsville NJ 1987-1989; S Alb's Ch Oakland NJ 1984-1986; S Barth's Epis Ch Ho Ho Kus NJ 1983-1984; Supply P Dio Newark Newark NJ 1981-1983. Auth, "The Forgotten Country," *Garden Island*, 2002; Auth, "P Visits Cambodia," 2000; Auth, "Bp Spong In Hawai'i," *The Voice*, 1987; Auth, "An Int P Speaks," *The Voice*, 1986. donor@online.com.kh

MACORT, John (Ct) 1170 Main St, Brewster MA 02631 B Philadelphia PA 11/13/1937 s John Macort & Louise. BA Hav 1960; MDiv EDS 1963; MA La Salle U 1971. D 6/8/1963 P 12/14/1963 Bp Joseph Gillespie Armstrong. m 5/1/1965 Sally-Jean Wakeman c 3. R S Andr's Ch Madison CT 1982-1998; Wooster Sch Danbury CT 1980-1982; Assoc The Epis Ch Of Beth-By-The-Sea Palm Bch FL 1973-1980; Assoc Trin Epis Ch Ambler PA 1969-1973; Assoc S Thos' Ch Whitemarsh Ft Washington PA 1963-1968. Auth, *A Reasonable Cov*, Audubon Press, 1995; Auth, *An Outline of Ceremonies for the Euch Liturg-co Auth w Jn A. Schultz*, Trin Press, 1972.

MACPHAIL, Alexander Douglas (Va) 335 Eagle St., Woodstock VA 22664 **R Emm Ch Woodstock VA 2008-; R S Andr's Ch Mt Jackson VA 2008-** B Harrisonburg VA 11/2/1974 s Ralph Cordiner MacPhail & Alice Alene. BA Bridgewater Coll 1997; MDiv VTS 2002. D 6/15/2002 P 12/16/2002 Bp Peter James Lee. m 5/24/2003 Karin L Chambers c 2. Chr Epis Ch Gordonsville VA 2004-2007; Cur Aquia Ch Stafford VA 2002-2004. CSB 2008; SocMary 2008. adm0963@gmail.com

MACPHAIL, Karin L (Va) 335 Eagle Street, Woodstock VA 22664 **P-in-c Cunningham Chap Par Millwood VA 2010-** B Poughkeepsie NY 10/10/1972 d Charles Weldon Chambers & Susan Glenn. BA U of Texas 1994; MDiv VTS 2004. D 6/26/2004 P 1/18/2005 Bp Peter James Lee. m 5/24/2003 Alexander Douglas MacPhail c 2. Assoc R & Chapl S Paul's Meml Charlottesville VA 2004-2005. karinmacphail@hotmail.com

✠ MAC PHERSON, Rt Rev D(avid) Bruce (WLa) PO Box 2031, Alexandria LA 71309 **Bp of Wstrn Louisiana Dio Wstrn Louisiana Alexandria LA 2002-** B Winnipeg Manitoba Canada 7/24/1940 s Kenneth Bruce Mac Pherson & Rose Velma. Cypress Coll Cypress CA 1974; DIT ETSBH 1978; Claremont TS 1979. D 2/17/1980 P 9/20/1980 Bp Robert C Rusack Con 10/9/1999 for Dal. m 7/25/1958 Susan D Hegele c 2. Bp Suffr of Dal Dio Dallas Dallas TX 1999-2002; Bd Epis TS Of The SW Austin TX 1993-2007; Dio Dallas Dallas TX 1993-2002; Cn to Ordnry/Exec Off Dio Dallas Dallas TX 1993-1999; Dio Los Angeles Los Angeles CA 1989-1993; Cn to Ordnry/Exec Off Dio Los Angeles Los Angeles CA 1988-1993; S Jn's Mssn La Verne CA 1981-1988. BroSA 1967. DD U So, Sewanee 2003; Hon Cn Cathd Cntr of S Paul Cong of S Athan 1993. dbm3wla@aol.com

MACQUEEN, Karen Brenna (Los) 23730 Gold Nugget Ave, Diamond Bar CA 91765 **Assoc R S Paul's Pomona Pomona CA 2004-** B Welland Ontario

Canada 7/19/1945 D 12/13/2003 P 6/12/2004 Bp Joseph Jon Bruno. karenmacq@aol.com

MACSWAIN, Robert Carroll (EC) University Of The South School Of Theology, 335 Tennessee Ave., Sewanee TN 37383 **Asst Prof of Theol and Chr Ethics The TS at The U So Sewanee TN 2010-** B Hampton VA 12/8/1969 s Travis Rivers MacSwain & Joyce Gaino. BA Liberty U 1992; MDiv PrTS 1995; ThM U of Edinburgh 1996; Postgrad Dplma VTS 2000; PhD U of St. Andrews 2010. D 6/30/2001 Bp The Archbishop Of Canterbury P 2/2/2002 Bp Clifton Daniel III. Instr of Theol and Chr Ethics The TS at The U So Sewanee TN 2009-2010; Sum Int P S Paul's Ch Beaufort NC 2004; Asst to the R S Mary's Ch Kinston NC 2001-2004. Co-Ed, "The Cambridge Comp to C. S. Lewis (co-edited w Mich Ward)," Camb Press, 2010; Co-Ed, "The Truth-Seeking Heart: Austin Farrer and His Writings (co-edited w Ann Loades)," Cbury Press, 2006; Co-Ed, "Grammar and Gr: Reformulations of Aquinas and Wittgenstein (co-edited w Jeffrey Stout)," SCM Press, 2004. robert.macswain@sewanee.edu

MACVEAN-BROWN, Shannon Lynn (Mich) 8850 Woodward Ave, Detroit MI 48202 **R S Matt's And S Jos's Detroit MI 2006-** B Detroit MI 3/14/1967 d Paul Ronald Spann & Jacqueline Graves. BFA Kendall Coll of Art And Design 1989; MDiv SWTS 2005. D 12/18/2004 P 7/2/2005 Bp Wendell Nathaniel Gibbs Jr. m 10/24/1992 Phillip MacVean c 1. Cur Ch Of The Resurr Ecorse MI 2005-2006; S Matt's And S Jos's Detroit MI 2005. macveanbrown@aol.com

MACWHINNIE II, Anthony Eugene (CGC) 20408 First Ave, Panama City Beach FL 32413 **St Aug of Cbury Navarre FL 2010-** B Pensacola FL 11/24/1969 s Anthony E MacWhinnie & Susan S. BS U of W Florida 1993; MDiv Epis TS Of The SW 2008. D 6/7/2008 P 5/2/2009 Bp Philip Menzie Duncan II. m 8/10/1991 Jane P Jane Elizabeth Philen c 1. D S Thos By The Sea Panama City Bch FL 2008-2010. sthomasepisc@knology.net

MACY, Ralph E. (NC) 3714 Luther Court, 3714 Luther Court, Burington NC 27215 B El Reno OK 11/18/1926 s Shields Semans Macy & Cora Myrtle. BS U of Oklahoma 1946; MDiv EDS 1950; Med Bos 1973. D 6/10/1950 P 12/21/1950 Bp Thomas Casady. m 6/24/1950 Mary Parks c 3. Int R The Ch Of The H Innoc Henderson NC 1997-1998; Int R S Mk's Epis Ch Roxboro NC 1993-1994; Int R S Johns Epis Ch Wake Forest NC 1989-1991; Int R Ch Of The H Fam Chap Hill NC 1988-1989; Sr Assoc Gr Ch In Providence Providence RI 1983-1988; R Ch Of Our Sav Arlington MA 1979-1983; Int R Ch Of Our Sav Boston MA 1978-1979; Int R S Paul's Ch Brookline MA 1976-1978; Assoc Gr Ch Salem MA 1976-1977; Assoc Pastl Inst Trng Alco Problems Cambridge MA 1975-1978; Int R Ch Of The H Sprt Wayland MA 1975-1976; Dir Cont. Educ. EDS Cambridge MA 1973-1983; Int The Ch Of Our Redeem Lexington MA 1973-1974; Brd. Ecam. Chapl Dio NW Texas Lubbock TX 1963-1969; Epis Chapl Texas Tech Cbury Epis Campus Mnstry at Texas Tech Lubbock TX 1959-1970; Asst R S Paul's On The Plains Epis Ch Lubbock TX 1959-1961; Vic S Paul's Ch Clinton OK 1953-1955; Vic S Paul's Ch Altus OK 1952-1959; R Gd Shpd Epis Ch Sapulpa OK 1950-1952. Auth, "The Int Pstr (Monograph)," Alb Inst, 1977. Int Mnstry Ntwk 1975-1995. remacy@att.net

MADDEN, Allan Robert (WK) Po Box 75249, Houston TX 77234 B Galveston TX 5/17/1926 s Hugh Logon Madden & Ruth Emily. BA Baylor U 1951; MDiv Epis TS of The SW 1963. D 6/19/1963 P 6/26/1964 Bp Frederick P Goddard. m 6/3/1988 Marolyn I Madden. Supply P Dio Texas Houston TX 1991-1999; Supply P Dio Texas Houston TX 1983-1985; Beloit First Chr Beloit KS 1981-1982; Dio Wstrn Kansas Hutchinson KS 1981-1982; S Andr's Ch Hays Hays KS 1981-1982; Dio Wstrn Kansas Hutchinson KS 1976-1981; Yth Advsr Dio Wstrn Kansas Hutchinson KS 1976-1981; S Anne's Ch McPherson KS 1976-1981; S Mk's Ch Lyons KS 1976-1978; Gr Epis Ch Hutchinson KS 1976; Supply P Chr Epis Ch Forrest City AR 1974-1975; Chapl Retreat Singers Trin Cathd Little Rock AR 1970-1972; Vic Chr Ch Mena AR 1965-1967; Vic S Barn Ch Foreman AR 1965-1967; Cur S Geo's Epis Ch Port Arthur TX 1964-1965; Min in charge S Paul's Ch Navasota TX 1963-1964. armadden4@gmail.com

MADDEN, John Erwin (LI) Po Box 602, Center Moriches NY 11934 **Supply P S Cuth's Epis Ch Selden NY 2003-** B New York NY 4/9/1937 s James Joseph Madden & Lilly May. BA CUNY 1959; MDiv Nash 1962; GTS 1963; S Vladimir Russian Orth Acad 1966. D 4/28/1962 P 12/1/1962 Bp James P De Wolfe. m 6/28/1992 Gail R Murphy. Ch Of S Jn The Bapt Cntr Moriches NY 1980-1997; R S Thos Of Cbury Ch Smithtown NY 1970-1980; R Chr Ch Cobble Hill Brooklyn NY 1967-1970; P-in-c S Gabr's Ch Brooklyn NY 1962-1964; P-in-c S Lydia's Epis Ch Brooklyn NY 1962-1964. OKEANOS@OPTONLINE.NET

MADDEN, John Langston (Lex) Box 2198, Lexington KY 40522 **R S Hubert's Ch Lexington KY 1988-** B Laurens SC 3/9/1934 s Charles Clyde Madden & Emmie. BS/MS Clemson U 1958; PhD K SU 1968. D 3/19/1976 P 12/1/1976 Bp Addison Hosea. m 6/8/1956 Jane Matthews. P-in-c S Andr's Ch Lexington KY 1979-1987; R Ch S Mich The Archangel Lexington KY 1976-1979; P-in-c S Mk's Ch Hazard KY 1976-1977.

MADDON, Ernest Clinton (Okla) 1823 Sunset Park Ter, Ardmore OK 73401 **St Phil's Epis Ch Ardmore OK 1996-** B Okmulgee OK 2/27/1947 s Norman L Maddon & Dorothy. BA Cntrl St U 1972; MDiv Epis TS of The SW 1994. D 6/25/1994 P 12/17/1994 Bp Robert Manning Moody. m 12/21/1968 Paula JaNeal Nation c 2. Int St Phil's Epis Ch Ardmore OK 1995-1996; St Phil's Epis Ch Ardmore OK 1994-1995. EMADDON@CABLEONE.NET

MADDOX JR, H(ubert) Carter (At) 200 Rocky Branch Rd, Clarkesville GA 30523 **S Tit Epis Ch Durham NC 2008-** B Rochelle GA 6/2/1935 s Hubert Carter Maddox & Thelma. Merc 1955; BS Georgia SW St U 1974; MS Georgia Med Coll Augusta GA 1975; MDiv Nash 1988. D 6/11/1988 P 3/18/1989 Bp Harry Woolston Shipps. Vic S Clare's Epis Ch Blairsville GA 1992-2000; Vic S Thos Aquinas Mssn Baxley GA 1988-1992. Ord Of S Lk. mbuhler@bellsouth.net

MADDOX III, William Edward (NC) 5718 Catskill Court, Durham NC 27713 B Bryn Mawr PA 1/31/1944 s William Edward Maddox & Dorothy. BA U of Maryland 1967; PDS 1970; Tem 1972. D 6/6/1970 P 12/1/1970 Bp Robert Lionne DeWitt. m 1/15/1977 Cleopatra Crawley c 1. Chapl S Aug's Coll Raleigh NC 2008-2010; R S Tit Epis Ch Durham NC 2002-2008; R S Phil's Epis Ch Jacksonville FL 2000-2001; Chapl Off Of Bsh For ArmdF New York NY 1980-1999; R S Marg's Ch Trotwood OH 1976-1979; P-in-c S Mary's Epis Ch Philadelphia PA 1974-1976; P-in-c S Mary Epis Ch Chester PA 1970-1972. Metropltn Untd Ch Dayton; UBE. WEMADDOX33PHA@AOL.COM

MADDUX, Carole Frauman (At) 9695 Hillside Dr, Roswell GA 30076 **D The Ch Of Our Sav Atlanta GA 2008-; D Dio Atlanta Atlanta GA 2007-** B Waycross GA 6/6/1959 d Walter William Frauman & Sally Annette. BA Georgia St U 1991; MS Merc 1994. D 8/6/2006 Bp J(ohn) Neil Alexander. m 12/31/1988 Delane Paul Maddux c 2. "A D's Word and Voice are as Important as Her Example," *Pathways*, Dio Atlanta, 2006. DOK 1999-2006; NAAD 2006. dcmaddux@bellsouth.net

MADDUX, Donald Jess (Oly) 706 West Birch Street, Shelton WA 98584 **Hisp Mnstry S Jn's Epis Ch Olympia WA 2003-2015** B Longview WA 8/27/1938 s Delbert Edward Maddux & Daisy Leona. BS OR SU 1960; MDiv GTS 1964. D 6/29/1964 Bp William F Lewis P 6/5/1965 Bp Ivol I Curtis. m 12/30/1968 Carolyn Laura Freelin c 1. P in Charge S Jn's Epis Ch Olympia WA 2008-2009; Int S Paul's Epis Ch Bremerton WA 2007-2008; Int S Barn Epis Ch Bainbridge Island WA 2006-2007; Dio Rep Hisp Mnstry Ntwk Prov VIII Dio Olympia Seattle WA 1997-2002; Dio Olympia Seattle WA 1990-1992; R S Germains Epis Ch Hoodsport WA 1976-1992; S Hugh Of Lincoln Allyn WA 1975-1977; S Nich Ch Tahuya WA 1975-1977; R The Ch Of S Dav Of Wales Shelton WA 1970-2002; Cur Ch Of The Ascen Seattle WA 1964-1966. Auth, "arts," *Angl Dig*; Auth, "arts," *Crossroads*; Auth, "arts," *Living Ch*. Intl Pres for RWF 1990-1995. padredon@hctc.com

MADDY, Marta Tuff (Minn) 3104 Greysolon Rd, Duluth MN 55812 **P-in-c S Jn's Ch Eveleth MN 2007-; P-in-c S Jas Epis Ch Hibbing MN 2006-** B Minneapolis MN 8/30/1955 BA Carleton Coll 1977; MDiv GTS 2005. D 6/15/2005 P 12/15/2005 Bp James Louis Jelinek. m 8/16/1980 Michael Merle Maddy c 3. Asst S Paul's Epis Ch Duluth MN 2005-2006. mtmaddy@hotmail.com

MADER, Carol Ann (Mich) 6092 Beechwood Drive, Haslett MI 48840 **P-in-c S Jas' Epis Ch Dexter MI 2010-** B Detroit MI 2/12/1957 d Ivan John Mader & Doris Elma. BA Albion Coll 1979; MA Butler U 1982; MDiv Chr TS 1986; CAS SWTS 1987. D 6/24/1987 P 2/1/1988 Bp Edward Witker Jones. c 2. P-in-c S Aug Of Cbury Mason MI 2001-2008; Int S Matt's Ch Indianapolis IN 1997-2000; All SS Ch Seymour IN 1990-1994; Asst R S Paul's Epis Ch Indianapolis IN 1987-1990. Phi Beta Kappa 1979. revcm2010@gmail.com

MADISON, David Andrew (FtW) 5005 Dexter Ave, Fort Worth TX 76107 **All SS' Epis Sch Of Ft Worth Ft Worth TX 2007-** B Baton Rouge LA 9/1/1974 BA Austin Coll 1996; JD Baylor U 1999; MDiv Nash 2004. D 3/13/2004 P 9/14/2004 Bp Jack Leo Iker. Cur All SS' Epis Ch Ft Worth TX 2004-2007. CBS 2001; SocMary 2001. davidmadison@aseschool.org

MADISSON LOPEZ, Vaike Marika (Hond) Km. 119 Crr al Norte, Jugo de Cane, Siguatepeque 21105 Honduras **Dio Honduras Miami FL 2006-; Iglesia Epis Hondurena San Pedro Sula 2006-** B Puerto Cortes Honduras 11/21/1959 d Arnold Friedrich Madisson & Maria Elena. Diocesano Educ. Programa Teologica 2007. D 10/28/2005 P 11/23/2007 Bp Lloyd Emmanuel Allen. m 4/28/1979 Hildebrando Molina c 4. vaikemm@yahoo.com.mx

MADRID, Hector Orlando (Hond) Apartado Postal 30, Siguatepeque, Comayagua Honduras **Vic Iglesia Epis S Juan Apostol Siguatepeque HN 1992-; Vic Iglesia Epis San Bartolome Apostol Siguatepeque MD HN 1992-; Vic Iglesia Epis San Matias Apostol Comayagua HN 1992-; Vic Iglesia Epis Santiago Apostol Siguatepeque Co HN 1992-; Vic Mision Epis Siguatepeque HN 1992-; Vic Mision Epis Siguatepeque HN 1992-; Vic Proteccion Santa Lucia San Pedro Sula Co HN 1992-; Dio Honduras Miami FL 1989-** B Concepcion Norte HN 9/26/1958 s Napoleon Madrid Rapalo & Juliana. D 1/6/1989 P 3/1/1995 Bp Leopold Frade. m 3/14/1980 Reina Isabel Lopez.

M

MADSEN, David Lloyd (WMich) 16 W 3rd St, Essington PA 19029 **P in Charge Ch Of S Jn The Evang Essington PA 2009-** B La Junta CO 10/24/1951 s Robert F Madsen & Betty Joyce. MSM Cornerstone U 2002; BS Cornerstone U 2004; MDiv The GTS 2008; DMin NYTS 2012. D 6/9/2008 Bp Robert Alexander Gepert Jr P 12/21/2008 Bp Robert R Gepert. m 8/28/1973 Naomi M Cochrane c 2. Sum Prog Mgr Ch Of The H Apos New York NY 2008. dmadsenhouse@gmail.com

MADSON, Peter G (CFla) 509 Derby Dr, Altamonte Springs FL 32714 B Lexington KY 2/12/1937 s George Ralph Madson & Jane Agnes. BA Oglethorpe U 1959; STB GTS 1962. D 7/3/1962 Bp Henry I Louttit P 1/1/1963 Bp James Loughlin Duncan. c 2. Epis Ch Of The Resurr Longwood FL 1987-1993; Cur Chr Ch Longwood FL 1980-1985; Vic S Fran Of Assisi Ch Bushnell FL 1972-1973; Asst Gr Epis Ch Of Ocala Ocala FL 1968-1969; Vic S Marg's Ch Inverness FL 1967-1968; Vic Ch Of The H Cross Valle Crucis NC 1966-1967; Vic S Mary Of The Hills Epis Par Blowing Rock NC 1966-1967; Cur S Andr's Epis Ch Tampa FL 1964-1966; Vic S Jas Epis Ch Port Charlotte FL 1963-1964; Cur S Mk's Epis Ch Venice FL 1962-1963. pmadson@mindspring.com

MAESEN, William August (Chi) Po Box 4380, Chicago IL 60680 B Albertson NY 5/18/1939 s August Maesen & Wilhelmina. BA/BSB Oklahoma City U 1961; LLB LaSalle Ext U 1965; MA Indiana St U 1968; PhD U IL 1979; MI SU 1981; SWTS 1985; BA Sthrn California U for Profsnl Stds 2004. D 12/2/1989 Bp Frank Tracy Griswold III. m 11/21/1989 Carolee Patton c 3. D Chr Ch Joliet IL 1989-1992; Bp Coun Dio Wstrn Michigan Kalamazoo MI 1979-1981. Auth, "Fraud in Mntl Hlth Pract," *Admin & Plcy in Mntl Hlth*, 1991. DSA St of Illinois 2001; "Who's Who in Rel". wmaesen@aol.com

MAFLA SILVA, Daniel Antonio (Colom) No address on file. B Cali Valle Colombia 11/14/1979 s Guillermo Antonio Mafla & Amelia. Dplma eu Teologia Seminario Teologia Bautista; Universidad Bautista. D 2/20/2010 Bp Francisco Jose Duque-Gomez. m 7/29/2000 Luz Erika Varela Cardona c 1. danielantonio_maflasilva@yahoo.es

MAGALA, Joy Christine (Los) 8341 De Soto Ave, Canoga Park CA 91304 **S Mk's Par Van Nuys CA 2005-** B Mulago Uganda 11/3/1953 d Ignatius L Kyegimbo & Ekiria N. Trans from Church of the Province of Uganda 5/26/2005. m 1/22/1983 Samuel E Magala c 5. magala-j@sbcglobal.net

MAGDALENE, Deborah (Ga) 2321 Lumpkin Rd, Augusta GA 30906 B Los Angeles CA 5/18/1952 d James Gladney Rogers & Nancy Bejach. BA Humboldt St U 1989; MA Humboldt St U 1991; MDiv The GTS 2009. D 2/7/2009 P 9/5/2009 Bp Henry Irving Louttit. deborah.magdalene@gmail.com

MAGEE JR, Albert Joseph (Tenn) 2936 Fernbrook Ln, Nashville TN 37214 B Salem NJ 4/17/1922 s Albert Joseph Magee & Agnes Cecilia. BS Duquesne U 1949. D 8/21/1965 Bp William Evan Sanders. m 7/15/1950 Okalena Gwyn Magee c 2. All SS Of The Desert Epis Ch Sun City AZ 1994-1995; Dio Tennessee Nashville TN 1987-1995; S Phil's Ch Nashville TN 1965-2000. Bro of S Andr 1998-2003; Steph Mnstry Ldr 1987-2003. ajmagee1@juno.com

MAGEE, Frederick Hugh (Spok) 17 North Street, ST. ANDREWS - KY16 9PW Great Britain (UK) B London UK 8/23/1933 s John Gillespie Magee & Faith. BA Ya 1956; Westcott Hse Cambridge 1959. D 12/20/1959 Bp William Derrick Lindsay Greer P 12/18/1960 Bp Kenneth Ramsey. m 10/14/1989 Yvonne Houston Massey c 3. Cmncatn Off Dio Spokane Spokane WA 2003-2005; Vic S Jas Epis Ch Cashmere WA 1991-2003; Vol P Trin Ch San Francisco CA 1987-1991; P-in-c S Jn's Epis Ch Donora PA 1963-1964. Auth, "How do we Know the Course is from Jesus?," *Miracle Worker*, UK Miracle Ntwk, 2011; Auth, "An Upgrader's Guide," CreateSpace, 2010; Auth, "Is 'A Course in Miracles' Chr?," *Miracle Worker*, UK Miracle Ntwk, 2007; Auth, "Let's Not Wrshp Jesus," *Miracle Worker*, UK Miracle Ntwk, 2006; Auth, "Terrorism," *Miracles Monthly*, Cmnty Miracles Cntr, 2005; Auth, "Heaven," *Insight*, Insight Fndt for ACIM, 1998; Auth, "A Personal Testimony," *Miracles Monthly*, Cmnty Miracles Cntr, 1998; Auth, "Which Jesus?," *Insight*, Insight Fndt for ACIM, 1997; Auth, "Salvation," *Insight*, Insight Fndt for ACIM, 1996; Auth, "Atone Without Sacrifice," *Insight*, Insight Fndt for ACIM, 1994; Auth, "Giving Christmas New Meaning," *Insight*, Insight Fndt for ACIM, 1993; Auth, "Jesus and the Euch," *C.M.C. Nwsltr*, California Miracles Cntr, 1990. Hon Cn Cathd Ch of St. Paul, Dundee 2008. hugh@twomagees.plus.com

MAGEE, Harold Alfred (Colo) 1425 Pitchfork Rd, Montrose CO 81401 B Montrose CO 2/13/1925 s Robert Bruce Magee & Mildred Josephene. BA Wstrn St Coll of Colorado 1950; MA Wstrn St Coll of Colorado 1951; BD CDSP 1954. D 6/20/1954 P 12/21/1954 Bp Harold L Bowen. m 9/21/1978 Pamela Alice Magee c 3. P-in-c All SS Epis Ch Brawley CA 1996-2003; P S Phil's Preaching Sta Parker AZ 1991-1993; S Paul's Ch Montrose CO 1976-1990; Asst Trin Ch Bridgewater MA 1968-1976; Vic S Mk's Ch Warwick RI 1963-1964; Vic Calv Ch Providence RI 1961-1963; Vic S Jas Epis Ch Wheat Ridge CO 1957-1961; Cn S Jn's Cathd Denver CO 1956-1957; Vic All SS Ch Loveland CO 1954-1956; Vic S Andr's Epis Ch Ft Lupton CO 1954-1956. hamandpam@bresnan.net

MAGERS, James Hugh (WTex) 4934 Lakeway Dr, Brownsville TX 78520 B Abilene TX 12/8/1940 s Hugh Thomas Magers & Hazel. BA Texas A&M U 1963; BD VTS 1968. D 5/18/1968 Bp Samuel B Chilton P 12/18/1968 Bp George Henry Quarterman. m 6/1/1963 Joan Hill c 2. S Dav's Epis Ch San Antonio TX 2004; Ch Of The Adv Brownsville TX 2002-2003; S Lk's Epis Ch San Antonio TX 2001-2002; S Andr's Ft Worth TX 2000-2001; Int R S Andr's Ft Worth TX 1997-2000; Dir Stwdshp Epis Ch Cntr New York NY 1993-1996; Dept Of Missions Dallas TX 1986-1992; Cn To Ordnry Dio W Texas San Antonio TX 1982-1985; R Ch Of The Redeem Eagle Pass TX 1977-1982; S Jn's Epis Ch Odessa TX 1975-1977; Vic S Jas' Epis Ch Dalhart TX 1969-1975; Vic S Paul's Epis Ch Dumas TX 1969-1975; R Gr Ch Vernon TX 1968-1969; Cur S Lk's Ch Childress TX 1968-1969; R Trin Ch Quanah TX 1968-1969. Auth, "Mssn Statements"; Auth, "Action Plans"; Auth, "Par Narrative". Epis Ntwk For Stwdshp; EvangES. laquintacostanoda@verizon.net

MAGIE, William Walter (Ia) 301 S 2nd St, Polk City IA 50226 B Albia IA 1/6/1947 s Wilfred Albert Magie & Kathryn E. AA Centerville Cmnty Coll 1969; BA Acadia U 1972; EFM 1993. D 3/17/1993 Bp Carl Christopher Epting. m 2/26/1966 Francis Jane DeMoss c 2. wwmagie@aol.com

MAGILL, Elizabeth Anne (Tex) 301 E 8th St, Austin TX 78701 B Washington DC 4/18/1984 d John Pierson Magill & Susan Aheron. BA Coll of Wm & Mary 2006; MDiv Ya Berk 2009. D 6/6/2009 Bp Peter James Lee P 12/6/2009 Bp Shannon Sherwood Johnston. Assoc S Dav's Ch Austin TX 2009-2011. eamagille@gmail.com

MAGILL, Peter George (CFla) 8310 Crosswicks Dr, Orlando FL 32819 **R H Fam Ch Orlando FL 1997-** B Montreal QC CA 4/23/1949 s Donald Burland Magill & Dorothea Aline. BTh McGill U 1973; MDiv Hur 1975. Trans from Anglican Church of Canada 11/1/1982 Bp Frank Stanley Cerveny. m 1/13/1973 Jane M Hudson c 3. R S Steph's Ch Norfolk VA 1989-1997; R S Lk's Epis Ch Jackson TN 1986-1989; Assoc - Rel Eductr San Jose Epis Ch Jacksonville FL 1982-1986. H Cross 1973. pgmagill@gmail.com

MAGILL, William Hafer (Colo) 1115 Gretchen Ct, Venice FL 34293 **Died 1/26/2011** B Muskogee OK 2/24/1919 s Julian Chaulcer Magill & Hazel. BA Texas A&M U 1940; Oxf 1959; Nash 1965; STM Shelbourne U Dublin IE 1995; PhD Shelbourne U Dublin IE 2000. D 9/14/1960 P 3/25/1961 Bp Edward Randolph Welles II. c 3. Hon Medal DAR 1978; 5 Air Medals 1945; 2 Distinguished Flying Crosses USMC 1943; Who's Who Amer Bus & Profsnl Persons 94. billplus@comcast.net

MAGLIULA OHC, Robert James (NY) Mariya uMama we Themba Monastery, PO Box 6013, Grahamstown 6141 South Africa B Brooklyn NY 11/7/1949 s Amadio Joseph Magliula & Lucy Frances. BA CUNY 1972; MPS Pratt Inst 1976; ATR AATA 1977; MDiv UTS 1982. D 6/5/1982 P 1/9/1983 Bp Paul Moore Jr. R The Epis Ch Of Chr The King Stone Ridge NY 1989-2006; Chapl Epis Mssn Soc New York NY 1983-1989; Chapl Epis Mssn Soc New York NY 1983-1989; Assoc S Mary's Manhattanville Epis Ch New York NY 1982-1983. robert@umaria.co.za

✠ **MAGNESS, Rt Rev James Beattie** (SVa) Office of the Bishop Suffragan for the Armed Forces and Federal Ministries, 110 Maryland Ave. NE, Ste. 203, Washington DC 20002 **Bp Suffr of Fed Mnstrs Epis Ch Cntr New York NY 2010-** B Saint Petersburg FL 10/21/1946 s Jack Magness & Rose Mary. BS Wstrn Carolina U 1974; MDiv Epis TS of The SW 1977; CPE 1981; DMin Gordon-Conwell TS 1999. D 6/25/1977 P 5/20/1978 Bp William Gillette Weinhauer Con 6/19/2010 for Armed Forces and Micr. m 6/27/1970 Carolyn Ann Hall. Cn for Mssn Dio Sthrn Virginia Norfolk VA 2009-2010; R Int Galilee Epis Ch Virginia Bch VA 2007-2009; Cn to the Ordnry Dio Kentucky Louisville KY 2004-2007; Navy Chapl Off Of Bsh For ArmdF New York NY 1980-2003; Vic S Paul's Ch Edneyville NC 1977-1980; Dce Ch Of S Jn In The Wilderness Flat Rock NC 1977-1979. Auth, "Forms & Rituals Of Pstr Care," *The Navy Chapl*. ACPE. jmagness@episcopalchurch.org

MAGNUS, Elsie Linda (ND) PO Box 604, Walhalla ND 58282 B Langdon ND 6/18/1948 d Merle Francis Blair & Mary Budge Belanus. BS U of No Dakota 1968. D 6/30/2007 Bp Michael Gene Smith. m 6/17/1967 Bruce Magnus c 3. elsiemagnus@gmail.com

MAGNUS, Robert Frederick (Be) 507 Green Acres Dr, Mars Hill NC 28754 B Orange NJ 1/4/1934 s Robert Frederick Magnus & Cora Margaret. BA Pr 1955; STM NYTS 1981. D 4/19/1969 P 10/1/1969 Bp Alfred L Banyard. m 8/28/1954 Pat Seaman. Adj Cleric Epis Ch Of The H Sprt Mars Hill NC 1997-2001; R Trin Ch Athens PA 1986-1989; Int Chr Ch New Brunswick NJ 1986; R The Epis Ch Of The H Comm Fair Haven NJ 1973-1981; Cur S Lk's Ch Gladstone NJ 1969-1972. bobandpat4@gmail.com

MAGNUSON, George Peter (Colo) 2015 Glenarm Pl, Denver CO 80205 B Chicago IL 10/8/1934 s Raymond A Magnuson & Astrid. AA No Pk Coll 1954; BA U of Minneapolis 1956; BD No Pk TS Chicago IL 1960; MA McCormick TS 1966; DMin McCormick TS 1973. D 6/9/2007 P 12/8/2007 Bp Robert John O'Neill. m 5/31/1998 Carrie Doehring c 5. GMagnuson@Comcast.net

MAGOON, George Arthur (NC) 5299 S Ventura Way, Centennial CO 80015 B Littleton NH 5/15/1924 s John Alanson Magoon & Ina. BA Dart 1949; Med Springfield Coll Springfield MA 1950; Ya Berk 1957. D 6/10/1957 P 12/21/

M

1957 Bp Charles F Hall. m 12/30/1949 Joanne M Moore c 6. H Trin Ch Townsville NC 1984-1989; S Jn's Ch Henderson NC 1984-1989; S Jas Epis Ch Hendersonville NC 1983-1993; S Mths Ch Louisburg NC 1977-1985; S Jas Ch Kittrell NC 1974-1989; R S Paul's Ch Louisburg NC 1974-1982; Dio No Carolina Raleigh NC 1974-1976; Asst S Paul's Cathd Syracuse NY 1965-1968; P-in-c Ivie Memi Ch of the Mssh Bethlehem Bethlehem NH 1961-1965; Ch Of The Epiph Lisbon Lisbon NH 1957-1961; Vic S Lk's Ch Woodsville NH 1957-1961.

MAGUIRE III, Bernard Leonard (Pa) 224 Flourtown Rd, Plymouth Meeting PA 19462 B Wilmington DE 1/31/1945 s Bernard L Maguire & Elizabeth. BA Trin 1967; MDiv EDS 1972. D 6/3/1972 Bp William Henry Mead P 6/1/1973 Bp Frederick Hesley Belden. Washington Memi Chap Vlly Forge PA 2002-2004; R Calv Ch Conshohocken PA 1978-2002; H Apos And Medtr Philadelphia PA 1976-1978; Ch Of The Trsfg Cranston RI 1972-1976.

MAGUIRE, W(illiam) Francis Bossence (SanD) 950 Eton Ct, Chula Vista CA 91913 B Belfast N Ireland 4/6/1930 s Charles Wesley Maguire & Ada Hogben. BA Trin-Dublin Ireland 1950; DT DS, Trin-Dublin Ireland 1951; ThM PrTS 1952. Trans from Church of Ireland 1/1/1958 as Priest Bp Francis E I Bloy. m 11/10/1963 Joanne Petree c 2. Asstg S Andr's Ch La Mesa CA 1997-1999; Stndg Com Dio San Diego San Diego CA 1989-1992; Dioc Coun Dio San Diego San Diego CA 1985-1991; Curs Sec Dio San Diego San Diego CA 1981-1996; Dep GC Dio San Diego San Diego CA 1979-1988; GC Dep Dio San Diego San Diego CA 1979-1988; Stndg Com Dio San Diego San Diego CA 1978-1982; COM Dio San Diego San Diego CA 1974-1980; Ch Of The Gd Shpd Bonita CA 1961-1997; Assoc S Dav's Par Los Angeles CA 1957-1958; Vic Gr Ch Randolph NY 1955-1956; P-in-c S Jn's Epis Ch Ellicottville NY 1955-1956. "Recon," *St. Paul's Printer*, 2007; Auth, "Love of Horses," *Wstrn Times*, 2002; Auth, "sev arts," *Chr Ranchman*, 2000; Auth, "The Bone Structure of the Bible," *The Line Rider*, 1999; Auth, *Chr Ireland Mnstrs Nwsltr*, 1989; Auth, *The Chairismata & Ch Life*, 1974; Auth, *New Cov.*

MAHAFFEY, Glenn G (Me) 11 White St., Rockland ME 04841 **R S Ptr's Ch Rockland ME 2008-** B Birmingham AL 11/2/1956 s Joseph Harr Mahaffey & Joyous. BA Wstrn St U 1978; MDiv SWTS 1985. D 6/14/1985 Bp William Carl Frey P 12/14/1985 Bp William Harvey Wolfrum. m 4/23/2000 Naomi Miner-Mahaffey c 2. Emm Ch Norwich NY 2000-2008; Chenango Cluster Norwich NY 1997-2000; R Ch Of Our Sav No Platte NE 1989-1997; Asst R Ch Of The Ascen Pueblo CO 1987-1989; Dio Colorado Denver CO 1987; Vic Epis Ch Of S Jn The Bapt Granby CO 1985-1987; Vic Trin Ch Kremmling CO 1985-1987. frglenn@midcoast.com

MAHAN, Charles Earl Earl (WTex) 2208 Arthur Ave, Edinburg TX 78539 **P-in-c S Jn's Ch Wichita KS 2011-** B Tomball TX 4/3/1966 s Charles Lemm Mahan & Joann. BA Concordia U 1989; MDiv Luth Sem Prog in the SW 1993. Rec from Evangelical Lutheran Church in America 2/13/2006 Bp Gary Richard Lillibridge. m 6/13/1993 Shannon E Rowcliffe c 2. R S Matt's Ch Edinburg TX 2006-2011. Bp Elliott Soc 2007; Intl OSL 2007. earlmahan@gmail.com

MAHAN, James Loyd (Okla) 2812 Shiloh Ln, Altus OK 73521 **Died 11/28/2009** B Quinlan OK 11/6/1929 s James Edwin Mahan & Elizabeth Maria. BS NE Oklahoma A&M Coll 1951; MS Texas A&M U 1953; BD Epis TS of The SW 1959. D 8/6/1959 Bp Richard Earl Dicus P 2/1/1960 Bp Everett H Jones. ECM, EPF, RWF, ESA, ERM. esaok@intplsrv.net

MAHEDY JR, William Peter (SanD) 4164 Mount Herbert Ave, San Diego CA 92117 **Died 7/20/2011** B San Diego CA 6/30/1936 s William Peter Mahedy & Loretta Marie. BA Villanova U 1959; MA Augustinian Coll 1963; MA Villanova U 1966; MA Chapman U 1974. Rec from Roman Catholic 6/13/1976 as Priest Bp Robert C Rusack. m 7/25/2011 Carol A. Mahedy c 2. Auth, "The Reason Why," Radix Press, 2008; Auth, "Our Common Life," Radix Press, 2007; Auth, "Out of the Night: The Sprtl Journey of Vietnam Vets," Ballantine in 86 & Radix Press, 2006; Auth, "A Generation Alone: Xers Making a Place in the Wrld (co-Auth)," Intervarsity Press, 1994; Auth, "Starting on Monday: Chr Living in the Workplace (co-Auth)," Ballantine Books, 1987; Auth, "Rt Here, Rt Now: Sprtl Exercises for Busy Christians (co-Auth)," Ballantine Books, 1985; Auth, "It Don't Mean Nothin': The Vietnam Experience," *The Chr Century*, 1983; Auth, "We've Got To Get Out of This Place," *The Chr Century*, 1979. wmahedy@san.rr.com

MAHER JR, John Francis (Az) 13382 W Desert Rock Dr, Surprise AZ 85374 **Vic Dio Arizona Phoenix AZ 2005-** B Philadephia PA 6/17/1952 s John Francis Maher & Barbara Ann. BA Kutztown U 1974; MDiv GTS 1979; DMin Fuller TS 1992. D 6/16/1979 P 5/28/1980 Bp Lyman Cunningham Ogilby. m 2/14/1975 Carol Diane Madden c 2. S Mary 's Ch Elverson PA 1981-2005; Cur S Mk's Ch Philadelphia PA 1979-1981. john@popaz.org

MAHER, Joseph Anthony (CFla) 5997 Heron Pond Dr, Port Orange FL 32128 B Philadelphia PA 3/13/1929 s Patrick Maher & Margaret. BA Villanova U 1952; MA CUA 1956; PhD NYU 1971. Rec from Roman Catholic 4/1/1981 as Priest Bp William Hopkins Folwell. m 7/1/1978 Catherine M McNamee. COM Dio Cntrl Florida Orlando FL 1996-1998; R Ch Of The H Chld Ormond Bch FL 1983-1997; Gr Epis Ch Of Ocala Ocala FL 1981-1983. Auth, "Stations of the Cross for the Elderly," Liquori Pub, 1978. Alb Inst; ESMA. joecatherinemaher@cfl.rr.com

MAHLAU, Franklin Andrew (Mass) PO Box 56, South Orleans MA 02662 B New York NY 12/4/1933 s Reynold Joseph Mahlau & Edna. Field Arty OCS 1954; Cmncatn & Electronics Course 1959; BA Hob 1961; Field Arty Career Course 1962; Command and Gnrl Stff Coll 1963; MDiv GTS 1965. D 6/12/1965 P 12/18/1965 Bp Horace W B Donegan. c 5. P-in-c S Jn's Ch Charlestown (Boston) Charlestown MA 1991-1996; S Andr's Ch New Bedford MA 1990-1991; Int Chr Ch Needham MA 1987-1988; Trin Epis Ch Rockland MA 1986-1987; Gr Ch No Attleborough MA 1986; Int The Ch Of The Adv Boston MA 1985-1986; S Jas Ch Hyde Pk NY 1965-1985. Auth, *Var Pub (Rel & Secular)*. Artillery Off 1954-1965; Chapl Corps 1971-1975; US Army Colonel, Ret. 1950-1976. R Emer St. Jas' Ch Hyde Pk, NY 1983; Phi Beta Kappa 1965.

MAHON, Laurence Franklin (EO) 8501 Ne Wilson Creek Rd, Ashwood OR 97711 **D S Mk's Epis and Gd Shpd Luth Madras OR 2002-** B Walla Walla WA 5/15/1931 s Kenneth Gardener Bentley & Doris Sible. Portland St U. D 5/1/2002 Bp William O Gregg. m 7/2/1950 Patricia Marie Billings c 2. mahon@madras.net

MAHONEY, James Michael (Ida) 1912 Delmar St, Boise ID 83713 **Supply S Steph's Boise ID 1968-** B Salmon ID 3/17/1936 s James Elmer Mahoney & Marian. Idaho St U 1958; Boise St U 1970. D 12/13/1968 P 12/21/1969 Bp Norman L Foote. m 6/6/1957 Jennie Louise Ross c 2. jmmahon3@gmail.com

MAHOOD, Sharon M. (Ia) 5720 Urbandale Ave., Des Moines IA 50310 **R S Andr's Ch Des Moines IA 2004-** B Springfield MO 10/9/1945 d George Mahood & Janet Marie. BA U of Kansas 1967; MA U MN 1969; PhD U of Kansas 1971; MDiv GTS 1989. D 6/4/1989 Bp Lyman Cunningham Ogilby P 1/1/1990 Bp Carl Christopher Epting. Cn Admin Dio Iowa Des Moines IA 2001-2003; R S Anne's Epis Ch Sunfish Lake MN 1998-2001; R S Ptr's Ch Bettendorf IA 1991-1998; P-in-c The Cathd Ch Of S Paul Des Moines IA 1989-1991. smahood@ishsi.com

MAHURIN, Shanda M (SwFla) 1021 Greenturf Rd., Spring Hill FL 34608 **S Andr's Epis Ch Sprg Hill FL 2005-** B Jersey City NJ 5/22/1950 d Joseph Herman Heiser & Victoria Mulford. BA Goucher Coll 1972; MDiv PrTS 1976. D 8/6/1985 P 4/6/1986 Bp William Grant Black. m 10/19/1997 Randy Mahurin c 3. S Mk's Ch Marco Island FL 2001-2005; S Ptr's Par Ch New Kent VA 1997-1998; Assoc R S Paul's Ch Richmond VA 1987-1996; Asst R S Andr's Ch Dayton OH 1985-1987. Auth, *Counselors in Perplexity; Comp in Joy*, self-Pub, 1986. Alb Inst 2004; Phi Beta Kappa 1972; TENS 2004. Wailes Prize in NT Stds Princeton TS 1975. shandam7@earthlink.net

M

MAIER, Andrea R (Oly) 14138 Knaus Rd, Lake Oswego OR 97034 B 8/8/1955 d Raymond Harold Maier & Miriam Rae. Portland St U; BA U of Washington 1984; MDiv GTS 1996. D 6/8/1996 P 1/18/1997 Bp Frederick Houk Borsch. S Andr's Epis Ch Ojai CA 2007-2010; Dio Olympia Seattle WA 2005; R S Lk's Epis Ch Vancouver WA 2002-2004; Assoc R S Barth's Ch New York NY 1998-2001; Asst to R Ch Of Our Sav Silver Sprg MD 1996-1998; Dio Los Angeles Los Angeles CA 1988-1993. andmaier@yahoo.com

MAIER, Beth Ann (Vt) 1924 Blake St A, Berkeley CA 94704 B Oak Ridge TN 4/1/1949 d Robert V Maier & Evelyn. BA Swarthmone Coll 1970; MD Case Wstrn Reserve Sch of Med 1975. D 1/6/2009 Bp Thomas C Ely. m 5/31/1975 Robert Finucane c 3. kidmd@hotmail.com

MAIL, Mary J(ean) (Mil) 509 East University, Bloomington IN 47401 **R S Mk's Ch Beaver Dam WI 1999-** B Buffalo NY 2/14/1952 d John Robert Mail & Mary Elenor. BA IL Wesl 1974; MDiv CDSP 1981; MA Indiana U 1982. D 6/24/1981 P 3/17/1982 Bp Edward Witker Jones. Int S Paul's Epis Ch Greenville OH 1987-1988; Assoc Trin Epis Ch Bloomington IN 1984-1999; Cn To The Ordnry Dio Indianapolis Indianapolis IN 1984-1987; Asst Trin Epis Ch Bloomington IN 1981-1983; DRE S Mk's Par Berkeley CA 1979-1981. mjmail0252@sbcglobal.net

MAINWARING, Simon (SanD) Christchurch School, 49 Seahorse Ln, Christchurch VA 23031 **S Andr's By The Sea Epis Par San Diego CA 2010-** B Manchester, UK 6/27/1974 s Rodney Philip Mainwaring & Myfanwy. BA Oxtford 1996; BA Westcott Hse 2002; MA Oxf 2003; CTh Westcott Hse 2003; ThM Harv 2004; MA Westcott Hse 2006. Trans from Church Of England 7/23/2007 Bp Marc Handley Andrus. m 9/24/2005 Monica B Burns c 3. Christchurch Sch Christchurch VA 2007-2010. simonicamainwaring@gmail.com

MAIOCCO III, Joseph F (SwFla) 500 Park Shore Dr, Naples FL 34103 **R S Jn's Ch Naples FL 2008-** B Beaufort SC 4/3/1958 s Joseph Francis Maiocco & Barbara. BSW W Virginia U 1980; MDiv TESM 1984. D 6/2/1984 P 12/1/1984 Bp Alden Moinet Hathaway. m 9/20/1980 Janet Beth Merlack. Adv Epis Ch Westlake OH 1999-2008; S Barn Ch Bay Vill OH 1991-1993; Off Of Bsh For ArmdF New York NY 1987-1991; Dio Pittsburgh Monroeville PA 1984-1987. jfm4358@gmail.com

MAITREJEAN, J Patrick (Cal) 1549 Circulo Jacona, Rio Rico AZ 85648 B Nogales,AZ 8/24/1941 s John Clement Maitrejean & Viola Sigrid. BA U of Arizona 1964; STM ETSC 1969; Grad Theol Un 1981. D 6/10/1969 P 6/4/1970 Bp David Reed. m 11/7/1987 Barbara Cariker. Vic Chr The Lord Epis

Ch Pinole CA 1981-2005; Iglesia Epis En Colombia 1969-1979. frpat@mac.com

MAJKRZAK, Albert Walter (Chi) 1222 Carpenter Street, Madison WI 53704 B East Orange NJ 1/5/1944 s Joseph John Majkrzak & Sophie. MDiv Epis TS In Kentucky 1979; BS SUNY 1979. D 5/13/1979 Bp Addison Hosea P 12/16/1979 Bp Victor Manuel Rivera. m 10/22/1966 Karen V Pressler c 3. R Chr Ch Waukegan IL 1997-2005; R Chr Ch Ansonia CT 1988-1997; Evang Off Dio Milwaukee Milwaukee WI 1986-1988; R S Mk's Ch So Milwaukee WI 1981-1988; Ch Of The Resurr Clovis Clovis CA 1980-1981. awm1222@sbcglobal.net

MAJOR, John Charles (Be) 220 Montgomery Ave, West Pittston PA 18643 **Dioc Coun Dio Bethlehem Bethlehem PA 2010-; R Prince Of Peace Epis Ch Dallas PA 2009-; R Trin Epis Ch W Pittston PA 2001-** B Williamsport PA 7/11/1960 s Joseph Eugene Major & Mary Martha. BA Mansfield U of Pennsylvania 1982; U of Scranton 1983; MDiv Chr The King Sem 1987. Rec from Roman Catholic 12/18/1999 as Priest Bp Paul Victor Marshall. m 7/27/1996 Sandra Lynn Valli. Int S Jas-S Geo Epis Ch Jermyn PA 2000-2001. jmajor711@msn.com

MAJOR, J(oseph) Kenneth (SeFla) 1835 Nw 54th St, Miami FL 33142 B Miami FL 1/4/1936 s Joseph Wakefield Major & Alice Rebecca. BA S Aug 1959; DIT Mercer TS 1968. D 6/29/1968 Bp Richard Beamon Martin P 1/25/1969 Bp James Loughlin Duncan. m 2/14/1980 Betty Major c 1. Dn Dio SE Florida Miami FL 1980-1983; Trst Trin Cathd Miami FL 1980-1983; Ch Of The Incarn Miami FL 1969-2008; Assoc Ch Of The Incarn Miami FL 1968-1969. Auth, "Gensis Of A Par"; Auth, "What Can Be Salvaged ?".

MAJOR, Philip Stephen (Wyo) 10 Saint Marks Rd, Burlington MA 01803 **Assoc for Multi-Generational Mnstrs S Mk's Epis Ch Burlington MA 2010-** B Summit NJ 8/11/1961 s Russell Gordon Major & Flora Hoelting. BA Ob 1984; BMed Oberlin Conservatory 1984; MDiv Boston Univ Sch Of Theo 2010. D 7/22/2010 P 1/25/2011 Bp V Gene Robinson. m 5/2/1987 Nancy A Bronder c 2. S Andr's Ch New London NH 2002-2009. philipsmajor@gmail.com

MAJOR, Richard John Charles (NY) 347 Davis Ave, Staten Island NY 10310 B Auckland New Zealand 10/23/1963 Trans from Church Of England 9/25/2003 Bp Mark Sean Sisk. m 1/11/1997 Kristen Louise Fresonke c 1. S Mary's Castleton Staten Island NY 2002-2007.

MAKES GOOD, Daniel Harry (SD) Po Box 28, Wanblee SD 57577 B Allen SD 7/17/1937 s Antione Makes Good & Olive. D 6/29/1975 Bp Walter H Jones P 4/26/1980 Bp Harold Anthony Hopkins Jr. m 10/4/1960 Mercy Broken Rope. Dio No Dakota Fargo ND 1982-1985.

MAKI, Steven Edward (Mass) PO Box 51003, Boston MA 02205 **Ecclesia Mnstrs Boston MA 2008-** B Leominster MA 1/6/1976 s Richard Alan Maki & Donna Jean. MDiv EDS 2003; Bachelor of Psychol, Sociol Concordia Coll 2008. Trans from Anglican Church of Canada 11/20/2009 as Priest Bp M(arvil) Thomas Shaw III. makibostonusa@yahoo.com

MAKOWSKI, Chester Joseph (Tex) 1410 Jack Johnson Blvd., Galveston TX 77550 **Vic S Aug's Epis Ch Galveston TX 2010-** B El Paso TX 4/3/1963 s Chester Karol Makowski & Wanda. BA U of St Thos 1984; JD U of Houston 1991; Cert Iona Sch for Mnstry 2009. D 6/20/2009 P 1/21/2010 Bp C(harles) Andrew Doyle. m 6/28/2003 Mary Wolter c 2. chester.makowski@roystonlaw.com

MALCOLM, Frieda Louise (Eas) 1006 Beaglin Park Dr., Salisbury MD 21804 **Dn, Sthrn Convoc Dio Easton Easton MD 2008-; R S Alb's Epis Ch Salisbury MD 2001-** B Miami FL 1/14/1954 d John Lowrie Malcolm & Janet May. ABS Smith 1975; MS SUNY-Albany 1979; MDiv STUSo 1987. D 6/21/1987 Bp James Barrow Brown P 6/15/1988 Bp George Phelps Mellick Belshaw. c 1. Pres, Stndg Com Dio Easton Easton MD 2008-2009; VP, Dioc Coun Dio Easton Easton MD 2003-2005; Asst Trin Ch Towson MD 1995-2001; Int Trin Ch Moundsville WV 1994-1995; Exec Dir Highland Educational Proj Dio W Virginia Charleston WV 1991-1993; Vic Gr Ch Northfork WV 1990-1993; Vic S Lk's Epis Ch Welch WV 1990-1993; The Sthrn Cluster Logan WV 1990-1993; Int Chr Ch Middletown NJ 1990; Chapl Trenton Area Campus Mnstry Lawrenceville NJ 1988-1989; Asst S Matt's Ch Pennington NJ 1987-1990. DuBose Awd for Serv U So 2005. pastormalc@comcast.net

MALCOLM, Kenneth A (Tex) 4909 Norman Trl, Austin TX 78749 **Asstg Fac Epis TS Of The SW Austin TX 2011-** B Ft Smith AK 9/21/1963 s Douglas McDonald Malcolm & Jo-Sue. BA Austin Coll 1986; MA Texas Tech U Lubbock TX 1991; MDiv Epis TS of The SW 2007. D 6/16/2007 Bp Peter James Lee P 12/21/2007 Bp Dena Arnall Harrison. m 6/13/1999 Elizabeth Pfautz c 2. Assoc R S Dav's Ch Austin TX 2008-2011; Prog Dir Dio Virginia Richmond VA 2000-2004. "Death's Reflection of Life: Italian Hagiographical Representations of Death in the 11th, 12th, and 13th Centuries," Texas Tech U Press, 1991; "Death and Soc: the 11th and 12th Centuries," *26th Intl Congr of Medieval Stds*, Kalamazoo, 1990. kmalcolmtx@gmail.com

MALCOLM, Patricia Ann (Del) PO Box 1374, Dover DE 19903 **D Chr Ch Dover DE 2009-** B Yonkers NY 7/4/1951 d William A Webb & Addie D. BA Delaware St U 1998. D 12/5/2009 Bp Wayne Parker Wright. m 6/30/1973 Walter R Malcolm c 3. pwmalcolm3@yahoo.com

MALDONADO-MERCADO, Roberto (Los) 13691 Gavina Ave Unit 557, Sylmar CA 91342 **R S Simon's Par San Fernando CA 2000-** B Manati PR 9/20/1959 s Roberto Maldonado-Rodriguez & Sara D. BA U of Puerto Rico 1982; Seminario Evangelico de Puerto Rico PR 1984; MDiv Estrn Bapt TS 1987; CAS Epis TS of The SW 1988. D 10/29/1988 Bp Franklin Delton Turner P 11/1/1989 Bp Allen Lyman Bartlett Jr. c 1. Vic Los Tres Santos Reyes Catonsville MD 1996-1999; S Andr's Epis Ch Ft Pierce FL 1994-1996; Dio Pennsylvania Philadelphia PA 1988-1991. padreroberto88@hotmail.com

MALE JR, Henry Alfred (Be) 80 Kal Shore Rd, Norway ME 04268 B Atlantic City NJ 4/24/1930 s Henry Alfred Male & Adelaide Martha. BA Hob 1952; LTh GTS 1955; Fllshp Coll of Preachers 1970; DMin Wartburg TS 1982. D 4/30/1955 P 11/5/1955 Bp Alfred L Banyard. m 6/23/1951 Ellen Wright c 3. P-in-c S Barn Ch Rumford ME 1994-2006; R Ch Of The Epiph Glenburn Clarks Summit PA 1967-1993; R S Mary's Ch Keyport NJ 1956-1967. Auth, "Conversion to Ecum," *Ecumical Trends*, 1993. No Amer Acad of Ecuminists 1985-1986. Hon Cn Nativ Cathd, Bethlehem Bethehem 1985. malebox@roadrunner.com

MALERI, Karen D (Me) 112 Randolph Avenue, Milton MA 02186 **S Mich's Ch Milton MA 2010-** B Guantanamo Bay Cuba 6/13/1953 d Robert Bronaugh & Mitzi. MDiv EDS 2001. D 11/6/2004 P 5/14/2005 Bp Chilton Abbie Richardson Knudsen. c 2. Havenwood-Heritage Heights Concord NH 2004-2008. soulstice53@gmail.com

MALETTA, Gregory David Magnon (WA) 9707 Old Georgetown Rd Apt 2222, Bethesda MD 20814 **Died 12/20/2010** B IT 3/15/1912 s Lawrence Maletta & Anna. BA Tufts U 1943; MS Simmons Coll 1948; MDiv Bos 1956; EDS 1957. D 6/22/1957 Bp Anson Phelps Stokes Jr P 2/1/1958 Bp Frederic Cunningham Lawrence. Auth, "A Creative Mnstry to Older Person in the Dio WDC," 1964; Auth, "Var arts," *Living Ch*. CSMAYMD@AOL.COM

MALIA, Linda Merle (WNY) 209 Columbus Ave, Buffalo NY 14220 **Assoc S Simon's Ch Buffalo NY 2003-** B St. Catherine's Ontario CA 5/2/1952 d Ronald Frederick Jeffery & Isabella Rose. ThD U Tor; BA SUNY 1994; MA CRDS 1998. D 6/22/2002 P 11/15/2003 Bp J Michael Garrison. m 8/8/1981 William Malia. S Jude's Ch Buffalo NY 2008-2010. revpeaches@yahoo.com

MALIAMAN, Irene Egmalis (Haw) ECIM, 911 N Marine Corps Dr, Tamuning GU 96913 Guam **Dio Micronesia Tumon Bay GU GU 2009-; P The Epis Ch of S Jn the Div Tamuning GU 2009-** B Philippines 11/28/1963 d Valentin Egmalis & Catherine. ThB St Andr's TS 1987; MDiv St Andr's TS 2002. Trans from Episcopal Church in the Philippines 5/1/2011 Bp Robert LeRoy Fitzpatrick. m 6/8/1991 Alfred Maliaman c 1. Dio Nthrn Luzon 1992-1993; Dio Cntrl Philippines 1988-1990. irene1128@gmail.com

MALIN, Katherine Murphy (Mass) 147 Concord Rd, Lincoln MA 01773 B Greenwich CT 6/15/1964 d Randall Malin & Lucinda. BA Ya 1987; MDiv GTS 2006. D 3/11/2006 P 9/23/2006 Bp Mark Sean Sisk. m 5/4/1996 Bruce E Smith c 3. Cur Chr Ch Bronxville NY 2006-2009. katemalin@gmail.com

MALIONEK, Thomas Vincent (Alb) 3 Chevy Chase Cir, Chevy Chase MD 20815 **Assoc All SS' Epis Ch Chevy Chase MD 2009-** B Newburyport MA 7/18/1954 s Vincent Ignatius Malionek & Stasia. BA U of Virginia 1976; MA U of Virginia 1978; MA/Min Nash 2009. D 12/12/2009 P 12/18/2010 Bp William Howard Love. m 2/8/1986 Judith Webb Judith Gail Webb c 2. tommaliokek@verizon.net

MALLARY JR, R(aymond) DeWitt (NY) 80 Lyme Rd #161, Hanover NH 03755 B Springfield MA 10/31/1926 s Raymond DeWitt Mallary & Gertrude Slater. BA Dart 1948; STB GTS 1951. D 6/10/1951 P 12/9/1951 Bp Horace W B Donegan. m 9/4/1994 Vera Gould c 3. R All SS Ch New York NY 1960-1991; Vic Trin Ch Fishkill NY 1953-1956; Asst Cathd Ch Of S Paul Burlington VT 1951-1952. DD AIC (not Epis affiliated) 1973; Phi Beta Kappa Dart 1948. dmallary@wildblue.net

MALLIN, Caroll Sue Driftmeyer (SeFla) 1150 Stanford Dr, Coral Gables FL 33146 B Indianapolis IN 1/3/1933 d Edgar George Henry Driftmeyer & Helen Lucille. MS Barry U; BA Florida Intl U. D 12/15/1981 Bp Calvin Onderdonk Schofield Jr. c 2.

MALLON, Beth Kohlmeyer (Ore) PO Box 445, Wilsonville OR 97070 **Archd Dio Oregon Portland OR 2011-; D S Fran Of Assisi Epis Wilsonville OR 2007-** B Oakland CA 2/13/1959 BA Oregon Coll of Educ 1982; MBA U of Nebraska 1989; BA Sch for Deacons 2004. D 9/11/2004 Bp Jerry Alban Lamb. m 7/19/1980 Kevin Frederick Mallon c 2. D Gr Epis Ch Fairfield CA 2004-2007. b.mallon@frontier.com

MALLONEE, Anne F (NY) 200 Rector Pl Apt 41A, New York NY 10280 **Trst Ya Berk New Haven CT 2005-; Vic Par of Trin Ch New York NY 2004-** B Wichita KS 1/15/1958 d Robert Eugene Mallonee & Barbara. BA U of Kansas 1979; MDiv Ya Berk 1986. D 6/7/1986 Bp Paul Moore Jr P 1/10/1987 Bp Richard Frank Grein. m 4/6/2002 Anthony C Furnivall. Int Chr Ch Cathd Hartford CT 2002-2004; Cn / Subdean Cathd Ch Of S Mk Minneapolis MN 1997-2002; Assoc Chr Ch Overland Pk KS 1990-1996; Chapl Cbury At

Kansas U Lawr KS 1986-1991; Dio Kansas Topeka KS 1986-1991. Hon Cn S Mk's Cathd Minneapolis MN 2002. annefm@earthlink.net

✠ **MALLORY, Rt Rev Charles Shannon** (ECR) 44059 Chamonix Ct., Palm Desert CA 92260 B Dallas TX 9/9/1936 s William Lee Mallory & Hazelle. BA U CA 1958; MDiv GTS 1961; STD GTS 1970; MA Rhodes U Grahamstown ZA 1971. Trans from Church of the Province of Central Africa 1/15/1979 Con 12/31/1972 for Diocese Of Botswana. m 1/21/2010 Martha Burton Mallory c 5. Asst Bp Dio Oklahoma Oklahoma City OK 2000-2004; Asst Bp Dio Oklahoma Oklahoma City OK 1992-1994; Dioc Bp Dio El Camino Real Monterey CA 1980-1990; Asst Bp of LI Dio Long Island Garden City NY 1979-1980; Bp Dio Botswana New York NY 1972-1978. stmallory@dc.rr.com

MALLORY, Richard Deaver (Ct) 455 Hope St Apt 3-D, Stamford CT 06906 **S Thos Of The Vlly Epis Clarkdale AZ 2010-** B Anniston AL 8/8/1943 s James Davis Mallory & Lena. BA Wake Forest U 1965; BD UTS 1971; Cert Blanton-Peale Grad Inst 1974; DMin Andover Newton TS 1978; Cert Inst of Core Energetics New York NY 2001. D 6/5/1971 Bp Horace W B Donegan P 12/1/1976 Bp Paul Moore Jr. c 1. Epis Ch of Chr the Healer Stamford CT 2005-2006; Int Trin Epis Ch Southport CT 2004-2005; Int S Barn Epis Ch Greenwich CT 2002-2003; Int Gr Epis Ch Norwalk CT 1999-2000; Int All Ang' Ch New York NY 1979-1980. rdmallory@aol.com

MALLORY, Steven Michael (Okla) 1808 Cedar Ln, Ponca City OK 74604 **D Gr Epis Ch Ponca City OK 1996-** B Ponca City OK 8/28/1952 s Ira Ellis Mallory & Bette Charlene. AA No Oklahoma Coll Tonkawa OK 1972; BA Oklahoma St U 1980; MS Oklahoma St U 1982. D 6/22/1996 Bp Robert Manning Moody. m 6/13/1987 Vicki Lynn DeShazer. Chr Motorcycle Assn; Lic Profsnl Counslr; Police Chapl; Vietnam Veterans Of Amer; Ymca. esteban@poncacity.net

MALLOW, Sherod Earl (SeFla) 2131 Sw 23rd Ave, Fort Lauderdale FL 33312 **R All SS Prot Epis Ch Ft Lauderdale FL 1999-** B Selma AL 12/27/1945 s Edwin Earl Mallow & Juanita Derryberry. BS Troy St U-Troy AL 1972; MDiv STUSo 1986; DMin SWTS 1999. D 11/19/1986 Bp Furman Stough P 5/1/1987 Bp Robert Oran Miller. m 7/9/1988 Rosa Vera Lindahl c 1. Assoc All SS Prot Epis Ch Ft Lauderdale FL 1997-1998; R S Elis's Epis Ch Memphis TN 1991-1996; R S Barn' Epis Ch Hartselle AL 1989-1991; Mssnr Dio Alabama Birmingham AL 1989-1990; R H Cross-St Chris's Huntsville AL 1987-1988; Mssnr Trin Epis Ch Florence AL 1986-1987. sherodmallow@me.com

MALLOY, Nancy L (Mil) 320 Broad St, Lake Geneva WI 53147 **R Ch Of The H Comm Lake Geneva WI 2008-** B Chicago IL 5/23/1947 d Erwin David Malloy & Hattie. BA Wstrn Illinois U 1988; MDiv SWTS 1992. D 6/10/2000 P 1/6/2001 Bp William Jerry Winterrowd. c 1. Emm Epis Ch Athens GA 2007-2008; P Par Ch Of S Chas The Mtyr Ft Morgan CO 2001-2007; S Aid's Epis Ch Boulder CO 2001; Calv Ch Rochester MN 1998-2000. malloynancy@msn.com

MALLOY, Patrick Leo (Be) 1013 W Linden St Apt 13, Allentown PA 18102 **The GTS New York NY 2009-** B Cumberland MD 6/30/1956 s Leo F Malloy & Joella R. BA La Salle U 1978; MA Tem 1980; MA U of Notre Dame 1985; PhD U of Notre Dame 1991. Rec from Roman Catholic 6/29/2001 as Deacon Bp Paul Victor Marshall. P-in-c Gr Epis Ch Allentown PA 2002-2011. Auth, "Celebrating the Euch," Ch Pub, 2007. malloy@rcn.com

MALM, Robert Hiller (Va) 3601 Russell Rd, Alexandria VA 22305 **R Gr Epis Ch Alexandria VA 1989-** B New Bedford MA 9/17/1951 s Robert Malm & Nancy. BA U NC 1974; MDiv Ya Berk 1977. D 6/18/1977 P 6/17/1978 Bp Thomas Augustus Fraser Jr. m 6/5/1982 Leslie E Clement c 4. R Chr Ch Portsmouth NH 1983-1989; Asst The Ch Of The Adv Boston MA 1980-1983; Blue Ridge Sch Dyke VA 1979-1980; S Mary's Epis Ch High Point NC 1979; Asst S Mary's Epis Ch High Point NC 1977-1979. Soc Of S Jn The Evang - Assoc. rector@gracealex.org

MALONE, Bonnie Jordan (Oly) 24219 Witte Rd SE, Maple Valley WA 98038 **S Geo Epis Ch Maple Vlly WA 2010-** B Stanford CA 4/7/1973 BS Creighton U. D 6/6/2003 P 12/6/2003 Bp Barry Robert Howe. m 9/2/1995 Carl Malone c 2. Assoc R Calv Ch Memphis TN 2004-2009; Dio W Missouri Kansas City MO 2004. bmalone@calvaryjc.org

MALONE JR, Elmer Taylor (NC) 308 Wilcox St., Warrenton NC 27589 **Chair, Historic Properties Cmsn Dio No Carolina Raleigh NC 2005-** B WilsonNC 12/18/1943 s Elmer Taylor Malone & Mildred Blanche. BS Campbell U 1967; MA U NC 1975; No Carolina Diac Prog 1991; So Carolina Read for H Ord 1998. D 6/1/1991 Bp Robert Whitridge Estill P 6/13/1998 Bp Edward Lloyd Salmon Jr. c 2. Supply P S Jn's Ch Henderson NC 2006-2009; Asst S Tim's Ch Raleigh NC 2004-2005; Chap Of The Gd Shpd Ridgeway NC 2004; P-in-c S Jn's Ch Battleboro NC 2000-2001; Secy of the Dio Dio No Carolina Raleigh NC 1992-2001; D Chap Of The Cross Chap Hill NC 1991-1995. Compiler, "Bp Cheshire's Confirmations, Vol. I, 1912-1915," Literary Lantern Press, 2011; Auth, "Malone's New Hist Map of Georgia," Literary Lantern Press, 2005; Auth, "Malone's New Literary Map of Georgia," Literary Lantern Press, 2002; Auth, "Malone's New Literary Map of Florida," Literary Lantern Press, 2001; Auth, "Malone's New Literary Map of NC," Literary Lantern Press, 1990; Auth, "The View from Wrightsville Bch," Literary Lantern Press, 1988; Co-Auth, "Literary NC: A Hist Survey," NC Div Cultural Resources, 1986; Auth, "U NC in Edwin W. Fuller's 1873 Novel Sea-Gift," *No Carolina Hist Revs*, NC Div Cultural Resources, 1976; Auth, "The Tapestry Maker," Blair, 1972. ECom 1993-2003. Cratis Williams Prize NC Folklore Soc 1979; Smithwick Awd NC Soc of Cnty and Loc Historians 1977. etmalonejr@aol.com

MALONE, Michael James (Dal) Po Box 1352, Warsaw VA 22572 **S Jn's Ch Warsaw VA 2001-** B Hamburg NY 10/4/1955 s Frank William Malone & Irene Margaret. U of Virginia 1975; LTh Nash 1993. D 5/18/1993 Bp Edward Harding MacBurney P 4/25/1994 Bp James Winchester Montgomery. Com Mus & Liturg Dio Dallas Dallas TX 2000-2001; ExCoun Dio Dallas Dallas TX 1999-2001; Wstrn Convoc Chair Dio Dallas Dallas TX 1999-2001; Com Addiction & Recovery Dio Dallas Dallas TX 1998-2001; R S Mk's Ch Irving TX 1997-2001; Dio SW Virginia Roanoke VA 1996-1997; P-in-c S Jn's Ch Petersburg VA 1994-1997; P-in-res Emm Ch At Brook Hill Richmond VA 1993-1997. The Soc of King Chas the Mtyr 2005. stjohns@sylvaninfo.net

MALONE, Michael Taylor (SC) 1413 Seneca Trl., Hartsville SC 29550 B Roxboro NC 2/5/1937 s Wilmer Ellis Malone & Alice. AB Duke 1959; MDiv VTS 1962; PhD Duke 1970. D 6/27/1962 P 1/16/1963 Bp Thomas H Wright. m 10/7/1978 Ann Huntley c 3. Cn Dio So Carolina Charleston SC 1990-2003; Deptce Dio So Carolina Charleston SC 1981-1982; R S Barth's Epis Ch Hartsville SC 1976-1990; Com Dio So Carolina Charleston SC 1976-1982; Com Dio So Carolina Charleston SC 1976-1982; Asst Adv Ch Of The Adv Spartanburg SC 1972-1976; Asst All SS Epis Ch Jacksonville FL 1965-1967; R S Thos' Epis Ch Ahoskie NC 1962-1965. Auth, "arts". Cranmer Cup Soc 2000-2010; Porter Cup Soc 1992-2010. Cranmer Cup Co-Captain Cranmer Cup Soc 2004; Porter Cup Exec. Dir Porter Cup Soc 2004; Co- Rec Porter Cup Trophy Porter Cup Soc 2002. mmalone37@bellsouth.net

MALONE, Timothy Joseph (WA) 2609 N Glebe Rd, Arlington VA 22207 **Asst to the R S Mary's Epis Ch Arlington VA 2009-** B Washington DC 6/12/1960 s David Michael Malone & Anita Whims. BA DeSales U 1983; MA GW 1996; MDiv VTS 2009. D 6/13/2009 P 1/16/2010 Bp John Chane. m 6/28/1992 Leslie Odonovich c 1. tim.malone@stmarysarlington.org

MALONE, Trawin E (NC) 211 N Elam Ave, Greensboro NC 27403 **Cn for Reg Mnstry Dio No Carolina Raleigh NC 2008-** B Fayetteville AR 12/24/1951 s Theodore Ernest Malone & Frances Lorraine. BGS U of Texas 1980; M.Div Epis TS of The SW 1983; M.Ed U of Texas 1992; D.Min SWTS 2004. D 6/11/1983 Bp Robert Elwin Terwilliger P 6/5/1984 Bp Donis Dean Patterson. m 8/26/1995 Melissa R Rein. Stwdshp Cmsn Dio Atlanta Atlanta GA 2006-2008; Congrl Dvlpmt Cmsn Dio Atlanta Atlanta GA 2005-2008; R Ch Of The Atone Sandy Sprg GA 2002-2008; Eccl Crt Dio Louisiana Baton Rouge LA 1999-2002; Asst R S Mart's Epis Ch Metairie LA 1999-2002; Chapl S Mart's Epis Sch Metairie LA 1993-1999; Chr Formation S Mart's Epis Ch Metairie LA 1993-1998; R Ch Of The Gd Shpd Terrell TX 1991-1993; Asst The Epis Ch Of The Trsfg Dallas TX 1985-1991; Yth Cmsn Dio Dallas Dallas TX 1984-1987; Cur S Jas Ch Dallas TX 1983-1985. temrec@gmail.com

MALONEY, Linda Mitchell (Vt) Po Box 294, Enosburg Falls VT 05450 B Houston TX 4/10/1939 d David Bruce Mitchell & Alta Marguerite. BA S Louis U 1963; PhD S Louis U 1968; MA U of So Carolina 1981; MA S Louis U 1983; ThD U of Tuebingen 1990; DAS GTS 2001. D 10/15/2002 P 4/23/2003 Bp James Louis Jelinek. c 3. Int Calv Ch Underhill VT 2009-2011; P-in-partnership S Matt's Ch Enosburg Falls VT 2005-2009. "Proclamation Easter," Fortress Press, 2003; "All That God Had Done w Them: The Narration Of The Mighty Works Of God In The Acts Of The Apos," Ptr Lang, 1995; "The Captain From Connecticut," NEU Press, 1984. LMMALONEY@CSBSJU.EDU

MALONEY, Raymond Burgess (NCal) 517 White Birch Ln, Windsor CA 95492 B Southbridge MA 9/29/1935 s Philip Harold Maloney & Helena Mary. MDiv S Jn RC Sem 1963; MA Assumption Coll 1976; CAGS Rhode Island Coll 1987. Rec from Roman Catholic 6/1/1992 as Priest Bp George Nelson Hunt III. m 7/27/1985 Anna Marie Lause. Asst S Geo And San Jorge Cntrl Falls RI 1992-1994. Ord of S Lk. rayburgess@aol.com

MALONEY, Sean Patrick Henry (WTex) 622 Airline Rd, Corpus Christi TX 78412 **Assoc S Barth's Ch Corpus Christi TX 2008-** B Gary IN 11/26/1974 s James Patrick Henry Maloney & Darlene Kay. MDiv STUSo 2008. D 12/15/2007 P 6/25/2008 Bp Edward Stuart Little II. m 6/20/1998 Jessica Maloney. frseanmaloney@gmail.com

MALOTTKE, William Neill (Spr) 300 W Market St, Mc Leansboro IL 62859 **Pres - Stndg Com Dio Springfield Springfield IL 1989-; Stndg Com Dio Springfield Springfield IL 1987-; Pres - Stndg Com Dio Springfield Springfield IL 1985-; Pres - Stndg Com Dio Springfield Springfield IL 1980-** B Oak Park IL 3/23/1934 s Clarence William Frederick Malottke & Charlotte Sophia. BA Illinois Coll 1955; MA Ya 1956; BD SWTS 1959. D 6/11/1959 P 6/24/1960 Bp Charles A Clough. m 4/23/1960 Carla Cave c 2. Dir: Div of Admin and Fin Dio Springfield Springfield IL 1985-1989; Stndg Com Dio Springfield Springfield IL 1982-1989; Dir: Div of Mssn and Wrshp

Dio Springfield Springfield IL 1981-1985; Stndg Com Dio Springfield Springfield IL 1976-1980; R Trin Ch Jacksonville IL 1970-1996; S Jn's Epis Ch Charlotte MI 1965-1970; Cn Precentor Cathd Of S Jas Chicago IL 1962-1965; S Jas Epis Ch McLeansboro IL 1959-1962; Trin Ch Mt Vernon IL 1959-1962. Auth, *(Compsr) An Ord for Compline*, 1976. R Emer Trin Ch Jacksonville IL 1996; LHD Illinois Coll 1979; Phi Beta Kappa 1955.

MALSEED, Caroline Frey (Be) 4032 Deborah Dr., Juneau AK 99801 B Auburn NY 3/23/1950 d James Slack Malseed & Elizabeth. BA Hiram Coll 1972; MA Cor 1977; MDiv Bex 1980. D 2/1/1981 P 5/1/1982 Bp Robert Rae Spears Jr. m 1/3/1987 Robert Francis Bruschi. S Brendan's Epis Ch Juneau AK 2004; P-in-c S Ptr's Ch Washington NJ 1992-1998; Dio Pennsylvania Philadelphia PA 1992-1993; Asst R Calv Epis Ch Summit NJ 1989-1991; R Chr Ch Bethel VT 1985-1986; Asst R S Eliz's Ch Ridgewood NJ 1983-1984; Pstr'S Asst S Mk's And S Jn's Epis Ch Rochester NY 1982-1983; Ch Of The Gd Shpd Webster NY 1980-1981. mayflower1950@hotmail.com

MALTBIE, Colin S (Minn) 1533 8 1/2 Ave SE, Rochester MN 55904 **S Lk's Epis Ch Rochester MN 2011-** B Bloomington IN 8/15/1979 s Daniel Jay Maltbie & Karen Marie. BA San Francisco St U 2001; MA U of St Thos 2005; MDiv VTS 2011. D 7/29/2010 P 6/30/2011 Bp Brian N Prior. m 10/24/2011 Aurora M Kubach c 2. cmaltbie@gmail.com

MALTBY, Leslie Howard (USC) 714 Gibson Forest Dr, Lexington SC 29072 **R S Alb's Ch Lexington SC 2002-** B Miami FL 11/1/1956 s Leslie Arthur Maltby & Emily Ann. AA Miami-Dade Cmnty Coll 1976; BA Florida Intl U 1979; MDiv GTS 1987. D 6/6/1987 P 12/1/1987 Bp Calvin Onderdonk Schofield Jr. R All Souls' Epis Ch Miami Bch FL 1994-2002; R S Jn The Apos Ch Belle Glade FL 1991-1994; Cur S Mart's Epis Ch Pompano Bch FL 1987-1991. hmaltby@sc.rr.com

MANASTERSKI, Myron Julian (CFla) 2901 Sw 91st St # 2907, Ocala FL 34476 B Sewickley PA 1/15/1956 s Chester Myron Manasterski & Olga Stephanie. BA Washington and Jefferson U 1978; Med Duquesne U 1981; MDiv TESM 1986; AA Inst of Pstr Stds, Chicago 1991; MS U Pgh 1994. D 6/7/1986 Bp Alden Moinet Hathaway P 7/22/1987 Bp Clarence Cullam Pope Jr. m 8/23/1986 Marianne Simashkevich. Gr Epis Ch Of Ocala Ocala FL 2003-2006; S Alb's Epis Ch Murrysville PA 1999-2002; S Jn's Epis Ch Memphis TN 1995-1999; Int Trin Epis Ch Beaver PA 1991-1992; Cur Dio Ft Worth Ft Worth TX 1986-1989; S Andr's Ft Worth TX 1986-1989. mmanaster@aol.com

MANCHESTER, Sean (RI) 19 Trinity Pkwy, Providence RI 02908 **St Fran Epis Ch Coventry RI 2011-; Dio Rhode Island Providence RI 2000-** B Los Angeles CA 7/18/1954 s Arthur Manchester & Marlene. EDS; BA Providence Coll 1978; MDiv Andover Newton TS 1984; MSW Smith 1994. D 7/13/1985 P 4/19/1986 Bp George Nelson Hunt III. m 6/7/1991 Michelle Roth. S Aug's Ch Kingston RI 1998-1999; S Thos Of Cbury Epis Ch Albuquerque NM 1988-1991; Cur S Mich's Ch Bristol RI 1985-1987. sabmanchester@yahoo.com

MANDELL, Cuthbert Heneage (Va) 2010 Schooner Dr, Stafford VA 22554 B Lake Charles LA 11/26/1948 s Cuthbert Bradley Mandell & Ernestine Sims. BA LSU 1970; JD LSU 1973; MDiv VTS 1994. D 6/11/1994 Bp James Barrow Brown P 6/1/1995 Bp John H(enry) Smith. m 12/21/1974 Rebecca Snodgrass c 3. R Aquia Ch Stafford VA 2001-2011; R Ch Of The Gd Shpd Wareham MA 1997-2001; Vic Emm Ch Moorefield WV 1994-1997; S Steph's Ch Romney WV 1994. rector@aquiachurch.com

MANDERBACH, Aaron (Ct) 1207 Meadow Rdg, Redding CT 06896 B Philadelphia PA 10/4/1912 s Edward Oscar Becker & Freida Nash. BA Tem 1934; BD Ya Berk 1937; DD Ya 1974. D 5/24/1937 P 12/15/1937 Bp Francis E Taitt. m 6/29/1968 Judith M Marin c 4. Int Trin Ch Lakeville CT 1995-1996; Int S Andr's Ch Kent CT 1992-1993; Int Trin Ch Lakeville CT 1985-1986; Int Chr Ch Canaan CT 1983-1984; Int Chr Ch Sharon CT 1982-1983; R S Steph's Ch Ridgefield CT 1947-1950; Vic S Faith Ch Havertown PA 1945-1947; Vic Trin Ch Boothwyn PA 1940-1945; Asst H Apos And Medtr Philadelphia PA 1937-1940. Grad Soc Of Berk 1937.

MANDEVILLE, Kathleen Corbiere (NY) Po Box 450, Tivoli NY 12583 B Amarillo TX 7/31/1954 d Howard Churchill Mandeville & Georgia Ann. BA Bard Coll 1976; MDiv EDS 1983. D 6/4/1983 P 4/1/1984 Bp Paul Moore Jr. R S Clem's Ch New York NY 1992-1993; Vic S Clem's Ch New York NY 1986-1992; Cur S Clem's Ch New York NY 1983-1984. KMANDEVILLE@WEBJOGGER.NET

MANDRELL, H Dean (Ak) Po Box 3529, Palmer AK 99645 **S Barth's Ch Palmer AK 2001-** B Lyons KS 10/6/1937 s Morgan Henry Mandrell & Ruth Margaret. BA SW Coll 1963. D 12/7/1975 Bp Matthew Paul Bigliardi P 2/10/2002 Bp Mark Lawrence Mac Donald. m 5/27/1960 Carol Mason. dekeman01@gci.net

MANGELS III, John Frederick (NCal) 6725 Hillglen Way, Fair Oaks CA 95628 **R S Geo's Ch Carmichael CA 1994-** B Livermore CA 5/31/1952 s John Frederick Mangels & Jeanne. BA U CA 1975; MDiv CDSP 1979. D 4/7/1983 P 1/1/1984 Bp John Lester Thompson III. m 7/26/1980 Anne Catherine Schellenbach. S Andr's In The Highlands Mssn Antelope CA 2007-2008; P-in-c S Mich Ch Alturas CA 1993-1994; Vic Gd Shpd Epis Ch Susanville CA 1987-1994; Vic S Andr's Ch Meeteetse WY 1984-1987. Auth, "Living Ch". New Directions; Nthrn Ca NNECA; Soc Of S Fran. jmangels@quiknet.com

MANGRUM, John Fuller (SeFla) 6152 Verde Trl. N. Med:A-2, Boca Raton FL 33433 **Died 3/18/2010** B Grand Rapids MI 5/22/1922 s Melvin Fuller Mangrum & Mary Dennison. LLD El Shaddi; BA Wstrn Michigan U 1943; MDiv Ya Berk 1949; Albion Coll 1951; Nash 1973; LHD U of Tampa 1974; U of Florida 1977; STD Geneva Coll 1979. D 6/26/1949 P 1/6/1950 Bp Lewis B Whittemore. CHS. DSA Alum Ferris Coll 1980.

MANGUM, Frank Burnett (Tex) 14041 Horseshoe Cir, Waco TX 76712 B Natchez MS 10/12/1932 s Frank Foster Mangum & Billie. BA Millsaps Coll 1954; MDiv STUSo 1957; STM STUSo 1965; Chr Ch Coll, GB 1978; Coll of Preachers 1981; U of Durham GB 1991. D 7/3/1957 P 3/17/1958 Bp Robert Raymond Brown. m 6/6/1966 Dorothea Caskey. R Chr Ch Nacogdoches TX 1993-1996; R S Paul's Ch Houston TX 1983-1993; St Lk's Epis Hosp Houston TX 1979-1983; R Ch Of The H Comf Angleton TX 1969-1979; R S Andr's Ch Rogers AR 1968-1969; Assoc S Paul's Ch Waco TX 1961-1968; Min in charge S Lk's Epis Ch No Little Rock AR 1957-1960. DuBose Awd STUSo 2005. Delta25@Grandecom.net

MANIACI, Maria Kathleen (NMich) No address on file. **D Trin Ch Gladstone MI 1997-** B Elkhart IN 2/4/1946 d George Daniel Maniaci & Louella Ruth. D 6/1/1997 Bp Thomas Kreider Ray. c 3. NAAD 1999. deaconmaria@gmail.com

MANION, James Edward (Del) 20 Olive Ave, Rehoboth Beach DE 19971 B Masury OH 8/31/1937 s Joseph Robert Manion & Rose. BA Huntington Coll Huntington IN 1963; MA U Of Kentucky 1964; MDiv Epis TS In Kentucky 1969. D 5/24/1969 P 11/1/1969 Bp William R Moody. m 8/25/1962 Betty Jayne Byrne. All SS Ch Rehoboth Bch DE 1981-1999; R Trin Ch Upper Marlboro MD 1976-1980; Assoc Emm Par Epis Ch And Day Sch Sthrn Pines NC 1974-1976; R S Phil's Ch Laurel DE 1970-1974; Asst Ch Of The Gd Shpd Lexington KY 1969-1970.

MANLEY JR, Derrill Byrne (NwT) 1615 S Carpenter Ln, Cottonwood AZ 86326 **Vic S Thos Of The Vlly Epis Clarkdale AZ 1998-** B Phoenix,AR 10/9/1951 s Derrill Byrne Manley & Inez. California Wstrn U 1970; BA U of Arizona 1973; MDiv EDS 1977; PhD Texas Tech U 1986. D 6/18/1977 Bp Joseph Thomas Heistand P 10/1/1978 Bp Willis Ryan Henton. m 8/11/1973 Cynthia A Smith c 3. S Thos Of The Vlly Epis Clarkdale AZ 1997-2004; S Matt's Ch Austin TX 1986-1988; R Ch Of The H Trin Midland TX 1978-1982. DERKMANLEY@YAHOO.COM

MANLEY, Wendy T (Cal) 1090 Brookfield Rd., Berlin VT 05602 B Summit NJ 3/19/1939 d John W Taylor & Norma L. U of Connecticut; BA Madonna U 1990; MDiv Ya Berk 1993. D 6/19/1993 Bp R(aymond) Stewart Wood Jr P 3/1/1994 Bp Gethin Benwil Hughes. m 6/18/1960 Robert G Manley c 2. Supply P Dio Indianapolis Indianapolis IN 2002-2003; S Jn's Epis Ch Oakland CA 1998-2000; Ch Of The Gd Shpd Cloverdale CA 1996; Pstr'S Asst Ch Of The Gd Samar San Diego CA 1993-1994. revwendy@voyager.net

MANN, Alice B (Mass) 51 Leroy Ave, Haverhill MA 01835 B Philadelphia PA 2/26/1949 d Edward F Mann & Mary. BA U of Pennsylvania 1970; MDiv PDS 1974; MA Temple Gb 1995. D 6/15/1974 P 1/1/1977 Bp Lyman Cunningham Ogilby. m 7/11/2009 Thomas Grannemann. The Alb Inst Herndon VA 1995-2010; Int Trin Ch Asbury Pk NJ 1991-1993; Vic S Andr's Ch Trenton NJ 1988-1991; S Mich's Ch Trenton NJ 1988-1991; Vic S Jn The Evang Yalesville CT 1981-1988; Vic S Gabr's Epis Ch Philadelphia PA 1980-1981; Assoc Ch Of Our Sav Jenkintown PA 1974-1979; Ch Of S Asaph Bala Cynwyd PA 1974-1979. Auth, "Raising The Roof," The Alb Inst, 2002; Auth, "Can Our Ch Live?," The Alb Inst, 2001; Auth, "The In-Between Ch," The Alb Inst, 2000; Auth, "Cler Ldrshp In Sm Cmntys," Ascen Press, 1985; Auth, "Incorporation Of New Members In Epis Ch," Ascen Press, 1983. am1111@comcast.net

MANN, Carl Douglas (Ia) 507 9th St, Spirit Lake IA 51360 **R S Alb's Ch Sprt Lake IA 2006-** B Cedar Rapids IA 12/29/1957 s Thomas Homer Mann & Helen Louise. BA Luther Coll 1980; MDiv Nash 2006. D 12/3/2005 P 6/10/2006 Bp Alan Scarfe. m 11/27/1982 Jane Roberts c 2. revrhino@qwestoffice.net

MANN, Charles Henry (SwFla) 5900 N Lockwood Ridge Road, Sarasota FL 34243 **R Ch of the Nativ Sarasota FL 2004-** B Winter Haven FL 1/11/1954 s Earl Clark Mann & Frances Marie. BA U of So Florida 1977; Masters TESM 1998. D 6/6/1998 Bp John Wadsworth Howe P 12/1/1998 Bp John Bailey Lipscomb. m 12/17/1977 Debra J McAllister c 4. Assoc R S Jn's Ch Naples FL 1998-2004. mannch@aol.com

MANN, Clifton Aynesworth (NwT) 2401 Parker St, Amarillo TX 79109 **Died 7/15/2011** B Waco TX 1/29/1945 s Thomas Clifton Mann & Nancy Milling. BA Ya 1967; JD U of Texas 1970; MDiv Epis TS of The SW 1979. D 6/14/1979 Bp Scott Field Bailey P 2/1/1980 Bp Stanley Fillmore Hauser. cmann@standrewsamarillo.org

MANN, Frederick Earl (WMo) 333 Se Canterbury Ln, Lees Summit MO 64063 B Lakeland FL 11/30/1950 s Earl Clark Mann & Frances Marie. AA Polk Jr Coll Winter Haven FL 1970; BA U of Florida 1972; MDiv Nash 1978.

M

Trans 2/2/2004 Bp Edward Stuart Little II. m 10/10/1981 Denise Dama c 2. R S Andr's Ch Kansas City MO 2004-2011; Dn The Cathd Ch Of S Jas So Bend IN 1993-2003; COM Dio Nthrn Indiana So Bend IN 1993-1996; Stndg Com Dio Cntrl Florida Orlando FL 1989-1992; R H Cross Epis Ch Sanford FL 1986-1992; Dioc Bd Dio Cntrl Florida Orlando FL 1986-1988; Dn Inst Chr Stds Dio Cntrl Florida Orlando FL 1983-1986; R S Mths Epis Ch Clermont FL 1982-1986; Asst Emm Ch Orlando FL 1980-1982; Assoc Chr Epis Ch Springfield MO 1978-1980. Auth, "Bible Rdr Fllshp Series: 1, 2," *3 Jn and Jude*, BRF, 1985. Alum Assn of Nash - Wrdn 1998-2004; Ord of S Lk - Chapl 1987; OHC 1975; SHN 1977. frfmann@gmail.com

MANN III, H(arold) Vance (WNC) 15 Creekside View Dr, Asheville NC 28804 **R S Thos Epis Ch Burnsville NC 2008-** B Miami FL 10/22/1941 s Harold Vance Mann & Ella Lois. BA Randolph-Macon Coll 1964; MDiv STUSo 1977. D 6/5/1977 Bp William Henry Marmion P 5/4/1978 Bp James Barrow Brown. m 7/4/2007 Margaret Mann c 2. Int Trin Epis Ch Watertown NY 2005-2006; Int S Jn's Epis Ch Midland MI 2004-2005; Dn Dio Sthrn Virginia Norfolk VA 2000-2004; R S Paul's Epis Ch Suffolk VA 1993-2004; Dn Reg I Dio Virginia Richmond VA 1988-1992; R S Steph's Epis Ch Culpeper VA 1984-1993; R S Anne's Par Scottsville VA 1980-1984; Asst S Mk's Cathd Shreveport LA 1978-1980; Cur S Augustines Ch Metairie LA 1977-1978. hvancem@gmail.com

MANN, Henry R (SanD) 7981 Hemingway Ave, San Diego CA 92120 **Asst S Dunst's Epis Ch San Diego CA 2003-** B Jacksonville FL 11/16/1932 s Walter Marvin Mann & Ruth Ethel. BA San Diego St Coll 1958; JD U of San Diego 1967; DIT ETSBH 1987; MA TS at Claremont 1988. D 6/13/1987 P 12/19/1987 Bp Charles Brinkley Morton. m 7/17/1954 Shirley June Batt c 3. Dio San Diego San Diego CA 1998-1999; Asst to Bp Dio San Diego San Diego CA 1993-1999; Vic S Columba's Epis Ch Santee CA 1989-1995; Asst to R S Dunst's Epis Ch San Diego CA 1987-1989. hrmann@prodigy.org

MANN, Jo Roberts (NwT) 2401 Parker St, Amarillo TX 79109 **R S Andr's Epis Ch Amarillo TX 2011-** B Wichita Falls TX 7/11/1945 d William Dan Roberts & Eleanor. Rice U; U of St. Thos; BS U of Texas 1967; MDiv Epis TS of The SW 1985. D 4/22/1985 Bp Gordon Taliaferro Charlton P 12/1/1985 Bp Maurice Manuel Benitez. c 3. Assoc S Andr's Epis Ch Amarillo TX 2002-2011; Assoc R S Steph's Ch Lubbock TX 1994-2002; Chapl Dio NW Texas Lubbock TX 1990-1994; Assoc R S Paul's On The Plains Epis Ch Lubbock TX 1988-1990; Assoc R S Mich's Ch Austin TX 1985-1988. jmann@standrewsamarillo.org

MANN, Kenneth Walker (NY) 32 Tallman Ave, Nyack NY 10960 B Nyack NY 8/22/1914 s Arthur Hungerford Mann & Ethel Livingston. BA Pr 1937; STB GTS 1942; MS U MI 1950; PhD U MI 1956. D 6/8/1941 P 5/31/1942 Bp William T Manning. Dir of Pstrl Servs Epis Ch Cntr New York NY 1965-1970; Psych Counlr Cathd Of St Jn The Div New York NY 1952-1958; Asst P S Andr's Ch Ann Arbor MI 1951-1952; Asst P Dio Los Angeles Los Angeles CA 1946-1949; Dioc Dir of Yth Wk and CE All SS Par Beverly Hills CA 1945-1947; P S Steph's Ch Pearl River NY 1942-1943; P All SS Epis Ch Vlly Cottage NY 1941-1943. Auth, *Deadline for Survival: A Survey of Moral Issues in Sci & Med*, Seabury Press, 1970; Auth, *On Pills & Needles*, ECC, 1969. Acad of Rel & Mntl Hlth 1954-1959; Amer Assn for the Advancement of Sci 1970-2003; AAPC 1945-2003; APA 1956; Assembly of Epis Hosp & Chapl; Natl Space Soc; Planetary Soc; US Power Squadron. Fell Am. Assoc. for the Advancement of Sci 1970; Presidency Adoption Inst, LA 1964; Assoc Natl Chapl Untd States Power Squadrons 1956.

MANN, Louise (Mass) 8399 Breeding Rd, Edmonton KY 42129 B Philadelphia PA 7/26/1941 d Edward Francis Mann & Mary Rosalie. BS Chestnut Hill Coll Philadelphia PA 1963; M Ed Tem 1968; MA Chr TS 1974; MDiv EDS 1984. D 6/24/1984 Bp Edward Witker Jones P 10/18/1985 Bp John Bowen Coburn. m 12/19/1964 Robert Joseph Bela c 3. The Ch Of The H Name Swampscott MA 1996-2004; Assoc R Chr Ch Exeter NH 1989-1996; Asst R S Andr's Ch New London NH 1986-1989; S Jn's Epis Ch Westwood MA 1985-1986. Auth, "Listening for the Sacr in the Faith Cmnty," Dio Massachusetts, 1994. No Amer Mnstrl Fell 1984.

MANN, Mary Anne (Ct) No address on file. B Trenton NJ 2/6/1944 d Edward Francis Mann & Mary Rosalie. BS Philadelphia Coll Of Art 1972; MA Goddard Coll 1983; MDiv GTS 1984; PhD NEU 1998. D 6/16/1984 Bp Lyman Cunningham Ogilby P 5/1/1985 Bp William Bradford Hastings. Vic S Jn's Ch Guilford CT 1984-1988; Consult/Instr Dio Pennsylvania Philadelphia PA 1976-1980. Auth, "Conformed To Chr," *Structures & Standards In Par Dvlpmt*. mannm@ninds.nih.gov

MANNING, Deacon Jeanette (SO) 164 Community Dr, Dayton OH 45404 B Aberdeen SD 5/9/1943 D 6/12/2004 Bp Kenneth Lester Price. m 6/12/1971 Lawrence Ray Manning c 4.

MANNING, Gary Briton (Mil) 1717 Church St., Wauwatosa WI 53213 **R Trin Ch Wauwatosa WI 2004-** B Jacksonville FL 3/7/1959 BA Lee U. D 6/9/2002 Bp Stephen Hays Jecko P 12/14/2002 Bp Carol Joy Gallagher. m 2/27/1988 Tabitha Leah Manning c 1. Assoc Chr and S Lk's Epis Ch Norfolk VA 2002-2004. gmanning@trinitywauwatosa.org

MANNING, Gene Bentley (Tenn) 2806 Wimbledon Rd, Nashville TN 37215 **Asst R Chr Ch Cathd Nashville TN 2008-** B Chattanooga TN 11/6/1955 d James Edward Bentley & Ethel Gene. BS U of Tennessee 1977; MEd Van 1991; MDiv STUSo 2001. D 6/23/2001 P 4/21/2002 Bp Bertram Nelson Herlong. m 4/14/1978 James P Manning c 3. Assoc R S Geo's Ch Nashville TN 2002-2007; S Phil's Ch Nashville TN 2001. gmanning@christcathedral.org

MANNING, James D (Md) 3121 Walbrook Ave # 6936, Baltimore MD 21216 B Washington DC 9/27/1937 BA California St U; MDiv CDSP. D 6/3/1972 Bp George Richard Millard P 12/6/1972 Bp James Walmsley Frederic Carman. S Ptr's Ch Rosedale NY 2008-2009; S Gabr's Ch Hollis NY 2006-2008; S Phil's Ch Brooklyn NY 2004-2005; R Ch Of S Mary The Vrgn Baltimore MD 1994-2003; Asst R Chr Ch New Brighton Staten Island NY 1990-1994; R S Phil's Ch Buffalo NY 1982-1987; R S Augustines Ch Gary IN 1978-1982; Vic S Aug And S Mart Ch Boston MA 1974-1978; Vic S Phil The D Epis Ch Portland OR 1972-1974; Dio Oregon Portland OR 1972-1973.

MANNING, Jean Louise (NMich) 1344 M-64, Ontonagon MI 49953 B Ontonagon MI 5/16/1957 d William Edwards Burgess & Ellen Mary. D 4/1/1990 P 10/7/2000 Bp Thomas Kreider Ray. m 8/16/1975 Charles Edwin Manning. Assoc Ch Of The Ascen Ontonagon MI 1990-2008.

MANNING, Ronald Francis (CFla) 510 Gardendale Cir SE, Palm Bay FL 32909 B Hayes Clarendon JM 3/1/1933 s Solomon Francis Manning & Muriel Eugenie. Jamaica Sch of Agriculture 1954; Inst for Chr Stuides 1983. D 9/21/1983 Bp William Hopkins Folwell P 9/30/1990 Bp John Wadsworth Howe. m 8/17/1955 Leila Joyce Monica Halstead c 4. Assoc S Thos Flagler Cnty Palm Coast FL 2000-2003; R S Tim's Epis Ch Daytona Bch FL 1990-1999; D Cathd Ch Of S Lk Orlando FL 1983-1990.

MANNING, Shannon Rogers (Miss) 5335 Suffolk Dr, Jackson MS 39211 **Assoc R S Jas Ch Jackson MS 2007-** B Jackson MS 12/28/1974 d William Ehrmon Rogers & Yvonne Barbara. BA Millsaps Coll 1997; MDiv GTS 2001. D 6/16/2001 Bp Alfred Clark Marble Jr P 12/16/2001 Bp Duncan Montgomery Gray Jr. m 7/29/2000 Richard J Manning c 2. S Jas Ch Jackson MS 2005; Dio Mississippi Jackson MS 2002-2005; S Jn's Epis Ch Ocean Sprg MS 2001-2002. smanning@stjamesjackson.org

MANNING, Slaven Lawrence (Dal) PO BOX 1208, Grapevine TX 76099 **Int Assoc R S Steph's Epis Ch Hurst TX 2008-** B 12/29/1959 BA U of No Texas 1982; M.Div. Nash 1985. D 12/21/1985 P 4/21/1987 Bp Donis Dean Patterson. S Alb's Ch Davenport IA 1990-1994; Ch Of The Gd Shpd Dallas TX 1987-1990; S Lk's Ch Denison TX 1985-1986. fr.manning@gmail.com

MANNING-LEW, Sharon Janine (NY) 522 Washington St, Peekskill NY 10566 B New York NY 8/10/1952 d Clarence Theodore Manning & Sharon. BS Nyack Coll Nyack NY 2003; MDiv GTS 2007. D 3/10/2007 Bp Mark Sean Sisk. m 11/24/1988 Shang Lew c 1. smanninglew@gts.edu

MANNISTO, Virginia Lee (NMich) N4354 Black Creek Rd, Chatham MI 49816 **R S Jn's Ch Munising MI 1991-** B 8/17/1950 d Robert Clair Denewton Tarrant & Letitia Marie. Cntrl Michigan U 1969; Nthrn Michigan U 2002. D 6/3/1990 P 1/1/1991 Bp Thomas Kreider Ray. m 3/4/2006 Charles H Mannisto c 2. Dio Nthrn Michigan Marquette MI 2005-2007; P S Jn's Ch Munising MI 1991-2008; Dio Nthrn Michigan Marquette MI 1991-2002.

MANNSCHRECK, Mary Lou Cowherd (SwVa) St Luke's Episcopal Church, 801 S Osage Ave, Bartlesville OK 74003 **S Paul's Ch Todd NC 2010-** B Wetumka OK 6/24/1943 d Leonard Harold Cowherd & Christine. BS Oklahoma St U 1965; Med Contral St U Edmond OK 1978; MDiv Epis TS of The SW 2007. D 6/23/2007 Bp Robert Manning Moody P 12/8/2007 Bp Edward Joseph Konieczny. c 1. Cur S Lk's Epis Ch Bartlesville OK 2007-2009. maryloumanns@gmail.com

MANOLA, John Edwin (NJ) 10 Colony Blvd Apt 553, Wilmington DE 19802 B 12/17/1917

MANSELLA, Thomas G (Va) 3705 S George Mason Dr, Apt 2105-S, Falls Church VA 22041 B Buenos Aires AR 11/15/1944 s Adolfo B Mansilla & Petrona. Dio Paraguay Asunción Py; Instituto Biblico Buenos Aires AR 1970; Dio Argentina Buenos Aires AR 1971. Rec 3/1/1989 as Priest Bp Peter James Lee. m 12/2/1972 Elizabeth Gonzalez c 3. Epis Ch Cntr New York NY 2005-2009; Translation Serv Coordntr Epis Ch Cntr New York NY 2005-2009; S Mich's Epis Ch Arlington VA 1997-2004; Vic Iglesia Epis San Marcos Alexandria VA 1994-1997; La Iglesia De Cristo Rey Arlington VA 1989-1999; Mssnr Dio Virginia Richmond VA 1987-1989. Auth, "Anglicanism And Ecum," *Panama*, 1986. TMANSELLA@TGMX.US

MANSFIELD, Charles Kirk (Vt) 157 Parker Hill Rd, Bellows Falls VT 05101 **D Imm Ch Bellows Falls VT 2003-** B Norwalk CT 1/9/1924 s Charles Mansfield & Ethel. Norwalk Cmnty Coll Norwalk CT. D 6/7/2003 Bp Thomas C Ely. m 11/14/1953 Gloria Carol Mansfield c 4.

MANSFIELD, Gregory James Edward (SeFla) St. Bernard de Clairvaux Episcopal Church, 16711 West Dixie Highway, North Miami Beach FL 33160 **P-in-c S Bern De Clairvaux N Miami Bch FL 2010-; Asst The Ch Of The Guardian Ang Lantana FL 2007-** B Martinsville IN 11/8/1957 s Jerry George Mansfield & Marcia Lee. BA Huntington Coll 1980; EdM Harv 1986; DMin GTF 1990. D 6/24/1986 P 3/1/1987 Bp Edward Witker Jones. R S

Andr's Ch Kansas City MO 1996-2000; Cn To Ordnry Dio W Missouri Kansas City MO 1993-1995; Assoc R S Paul's Ch Kansas City MO 1988-1993; Cur Gr Ch Muncie IN 1986-1988. Co-Auth, "Let's Go: Greece," St. Mart's Press; Co-Auth, "Let's Go: Italy," St. Mart's Press. Soc of Cath Priests 2010. gregorymansfield@aol.com

MANSFIELD, Mary Robb (Vt) 32 Wood Rd, North Middlesex VT 05682 B Brattleboro VT 12/3/1940 d Hermon Frederick Robb & Bertha Boyd. BA U of Vermont 1977; MS Syr 1983; MDiv CRDS 1994. D 7/16/1994 P 6/5/1995 Bp David B(ruce) Joslin. m 6/24/1962 Richard Henry Mansfield c 3. R S Jn's In The Mountains Stowe VT 1999-2008; Chemung Vlly Cluster Elmira NY 1996-1997; S Jn's Epis Ch Elmira Heights NY 1995-1997; Cur S Paul's Ch Owego NY 1994-1996. revmrm@pshift.com

MANSFIELD JR, Richard Huntington (Ct) 41 Gatewood, Avon CT 06001 **Dn Chr Ch Cathd Hartford CT 2004-; COM Dio Connecticut Hartford CT 1983-** B Mount Vernon NY 5/25/1937 s Richard Huntington Mansfield & Marjory Myles. BA Rol 1960; STM Ya Berk 1963. D 12/27/1965 Bp Horace W B Donegan P 6/10/1966 Bp Charles Francis Boynton. m 6/4/1960 Sharon Kelley c 4. Dn Chr Ch Cathd Hartford CT 1997-2002; Stndg Com Dio Connecticut Hartford CT 1997-2001; Exec Coun Dio Connecticut Hartford CT 1986-1991; Cn Chr Ch Cathd Hartford CT 1982-1991; Dn Bex Columbus OH 1977-1982; R H Trin Epis Ch Oxford OH 1970-1977; Cur S Matt's Ch Bedford NY 1966-1970. Auth, "Holding Cbury Accountable," *Wit*, 1987; Auth, "Footwashing," *Epis*, 1986; Auth, "Sem Educ," *Living Ch*, 1982; Auth, "Wmn as Agents of God," *Wit*, 1982. SIM. DD Ya 1979. tvrmansfield@aol.com

MANSFIELD, Victor Claibourne (WNC) PO Box 187, Fletcher NC 28732 **R Calv Epis Ch Fletcher NC 2000-** B Raleigh NC 10/25/1955 s Raymond MacDonald Mansfield & Jessie Utley. BA Methodist Coll 1977; MDiv VTS 1982. D 6/7/1982 Bp Hunley Agee Elebash P 6/18/1983 Bp Robert Whitridge Estill. c 2. R S Thos' Epis Ch Abingdon VA 1989-2000; Asst H Trin Epis Ch Greensboro NC 1986-1989; Asst S Ptr's Epis Ch Charlotte NC 1982-1986. vcmansfield@gmail.com

MANSON, Anne Leslie Yount (Va) The Prestwould, 612 West Franklin St. #12C, Richmond VA 23220 B Richmond VA 10/13/1944 d Robert Stanley Yount & Eva Church. AB W&M 1967; MDiv UTS Richmond VA 1985; Cert VTS 1986. D 6/11/1986 P 3/30/1987 Bp Peter James Lee. c 1. R Cunningham Chap Par Millwood VA 2006-2010; Vic Ch of the Incarn Mineral VA 1998-2006; Exec Bd Dio Virginia Richmond VA 1996-1998; Pres Dio Virginia Richmond VA 1990-1991; Pres Dio Virginia Richmond VA 1989-1990; Ch Of The Creator Mechanicsville VA 1988-1997; Int Gr Epis Ch Goochland VA 1988; D S Mary's Ch Richmond VA 1986-1987. Kappa Delta Pi At Wm & Mary 1966. Walter D Moore Fllshp For Grad Stds UTS Virginia 1985; W T Thompson Schlr 1983. tpeaglesnest@gmail.com

MANSON, Malcolm (Cal) 35 Keyes Avenue, San Francisco CA 94129 **Archd for Schools Dio California San Francisco CA 2000-** B Melton Mowbray UK 5/31/1938 s James Milne Manson & Williamina. BA Oxf 1961; MA Oxf 1964. D 6/25/1977 Bp C Kilmer Myers P 6/27/1978 Bp William Foreman Creighton. m 4/11/1982 Snowden Johnston Scofield. The Epis Ch Of S Mary The Vrgn San Francisco CA 2000-2002; Sch Hd Gr Cathd San Francisco CA 1990-1999; Cn Epis Par Of S Jn The Bapt Portland OR 1986-1990; Assoc St Johns Epis Ch Ross CA 1977-1982. tallmalc@gmail.com

MANSUR, Richard Winthrop (Ga) 3914 Beacon Square Dr, Holiday FL 34691 **Assoc S Steph's Ch New Port Richey FL 1990-** B Haverhill MA 5/28/1924 s John Percival Mansur & Marion Esther. BA Stetson U 1947; EdM Bos 1950; MDiv VTS 1963; US-A Chapl Sch 1967; US-A Chapl Sch 1971. D 5/30/1963 P 12/7/1963 Bp Arnold M Lewis. c 2. Asst to R Chr Ch Frederica St Simons Island GA 1983-1986; Off Of Bsh For ArmdF New York NY 1967-1969; Vic S Jn's Ch Ulysses KS 1965-1967; R S Thos Ch Garden City KS 1965-1967; Vic S Lk's Epis Ch Scott City KS 1963-1965.

MANTELL, Denise (Del) 2400 Pennington Drive, Wilmington DE 19810 B New York NY 5/17/1946 d Lawrence Albert Pariseau & Andree Marie Louise. BA CUNY 1978; MDiv GTS 1982. D 4/25/1985 P 11/10/1985 Bp Paul Moore Jr. c 2. R Trin Ch Matawan NJ 1999-2008; R Ch Of Our Merc Sav Penns Grove NJ 1988-1999; Assoc S Paul's Epis Ch Morris Plains NJ 1985-1988; Asst All SS Ch Staten Island NY 1985. Ord Of S Jn The Bapt. dpmantell@aol.com

MANTILLA-BENITEZ, Haydee (EcuC) Avenue Libertad Parada 8, Esmeralda Ecuador B Guayaquil EC 10/16/1948 d Luis Mantilla & Teresa. Sem 1989. D 12/18/1988 P 5/1/1990 Bp Adrian Delio Caceres-Villavicencio. Ecuador New York NY 1993-2010. HAYDEEMANTILLA@GMAIL.COM

MANUEL, Joseph (LI) 3907 61st St, Woodside NY 11377 **S Paul's Ch Woodside NY 2002-** B Vellore India 4/16/1953 Trans from Church of South India 12/11/2002 Bp Orris George Walker Jr. m 10/11/1982 Agnes Shanthakumari Manuel c 1. ANANDSEKARJMANUEL1@GMAIL.COM

MANUEL, Linda Eve (SC) 297 Lantana Cir, Georgetown SC 29440 B Pittsburgh PA 5/4/1944 d Max Homer Hofmann & Marian Virginia. BA GW 1966; MDiv TESM 1997. D 6/21/1997 Bp Alden Moinet Hathaway P 12/1/1997 Bp Robert William Duncan. m 2/26/1966 Joseph Robert Manuel. Int S Andr's Epis Ch New Kensington PA 2002-2006; S Mk's Ch Johnstown PA 2000-2001; P-in-c S Jn's Epis Ch Donora PA 1997-2000; Dio Pittsburgh Monroeville PA 1997-1998.

MANZANARES RODRIGUEZ, Zoila Morena (Ind) 6613 El Paso Dr, Indianapolis IN 46214 **Cn Chr Ch Cathd Indianapolis IN 2007-** B El Salvador CA 4/25/1960 d Roberto Rodriguez & Bertha Manzanares. Inst Of Tech Centro Americano Engr 1984; MDiv Epis TS of The SW 1994. D 6/24/1995 Bp Oliver Bailey Garver Jr P 1/1/1996 Bp Frederick Houk Borsch. m 11/6/2009 Robin E Cole. Trin Epis Par Los Angeles CA 2003-2005; Pueblo Nuevo Epis Ch Los Angeles CA 2001-2003; H Faith Par Inglewood CA 1995-1998. mariposa1007@gmail.com

MANZELLA, Evelyn Nancy (O) 127 W. North Street, Wooster OH 44691 **R S Jas Epis Ch Wooster OH 1998-** B Perth Amboy NJ 10/13/1960 d Carmen Michael Manzella & Irene Nancy. BA SUNY 1982; BA SUNY 1986; MDiv GTS 1992. D 6/6/1992 P 12/1/1992 Bp David Charles Bowman. R H Trin Epis Ch Swanton VT 1994-1998; Cur Gr Ch Lockport NY 1992-1994; R S Jn's Ch Wilson NY 1992-1994. evelynm@sssnet.com

MANZO, Peter Thomas (NJ) 69 Penn Rd, Voorhees NJ 08043 **R S Barth's Ch Cherry Hill NJ 2002-; Rules of Ord & Dispatch of Bus Dio New Jersey Trenton NJ 1999-** B Bayonne NJ 2/16/1947 s Valentine Salvatore Manzo & Rita. AB Geo 1968; MBA Col 1972; JD Cor 1972; Angl Stds GTS 1999. Rec from Roman Catholic 11/18/1998 as Deacon Bp Joe Morris Doss. m 3/25/1989 Joan U Manzo c 3. Cur S Lk's Ch Gladstone NJ 1999-2002; D Gr Epis Ch Plainfield NJ 1998-1999. Auth, "Why we're Getting Thrown Out," *LivCh*, 2005. manzorev@gmail.com

MAPPLEBECKPALMER, Richard Warwick (Cal) 472 Dale Rd, Martinez CA 94553 B 3/22/1932 s Richard Harold Palmer & Frances. BA Corpus Christi Coll Cambridge 1956; Gce Ripon Coll Cuddesdon 1958; MA Corpus Christi Coll Cambridge 1960. Rec 6/1/1988 as Priest Bp William Edwin Swing. m 4/29/1973 Lindzi Mapplebeck. Gr Inst For Rel Lrng Berkeley CA 1994-2004; S Clem's Ch Berkeley CA 1988-1989. richardw@mapplebeckpalmer.com

MARANVILLE, Irvin Walter (Vt) 6809 23rd Ave W, Bradenton FL 34209 **D Dio Vermont Burlington VT 1986-** B Wallingford VT 12/17/1928 s Stephen Jay Maranville & Madeline Mary. AS Champlain Coll 1972. D 10/19/1986 Bp Robert Shaw Kerr. m 9/5/1951 Joyce Margaret Mee c 3.

MARANVILLE, Joyce Margaret (Vt) 6809 23rd Ave W, Bradenton FL 34209 **D Dio Vermont Burlington VT 1986-** B London UK 8/26/1931 d Arthur William Mee & Rosamond May. Pryor Bus Acad. D 10/19/1986 Bp Robert Shaw Kerr. m 9/5/1951 Irvin Walter Maranville c 4. imaranvill@aol.com

✠ MARBLE JR, Rt Rev Alfred Clark (NC) 1901 W Market St, Greensboro NC 27403 **Ret Bp Of Mississippi Dio Mississippi Jackson MS 2003-** B Oneonta NY 4/4/1936 s Alfred Clark Marble & Charlotte Elizabeth. BA U of Mississippi 1958; U Of Edinburgh GB 1965; BD STUSo 1967. D 6/22/1967 P 5/1/1968 Bp John M Allin Con 6/15/1991 for Miss. m 1/5/1974 Diene Harper c 2. Bp Of Miss Dio Mississippi Jackson MS 1993-2003; Dio Mississippi Jackson MS 1991-2003; Bp Coadj Dio Mississippi Jackson MS 1991-1993; Stff Asst To Bp Dio E Carolina Kinston NC 1984-1991; Dio E Carolina Kinston NC 1983-1991; The Epis Ch Of The Medtr Meridian MS 1978-1983; S Ptr's Ch Oxford MS 1972-1978; Ch Of The Nativ Oxford MS 1971-1978; Vic H Cross Epis Ch Olive Branch MS 1969-1971; Vic S Timothys Epis Ch Southaven MS 1969-1971; Cur S Jas Ch Jackson MS 1967-1969. chip.marble@episdionc.org

MARCANTONIO, John (Nwk) 39 Johnson Rd, West Orange NJ 07052 B Elizabeth NJ 2/8/1951 s Henry Louis Marcantonio & Carmela Sally. MA Pontifical Coll Josephinum 1983; MS Ford 1989; Dplma Angl Stds The GTS 2010. Rec from Roman Catholic 11/13/2010 as Priest Bp Mark M Beckwith. m 1/3/2008 Kimberly Gunning c 1. rounmidnit@msn.com

MARCH, Bette Ann (Wyo) 34 Thomas The Apostle Rd, Cody WY 82414 B Bozeman MT 7/21/1940 d Clifford Philip Mockel & Jessie Amanda. California St U; AD Ln Cmnty Coll 1978; BD St. Jos's Coll No Windham ME 1982. D 10/16/2004 Bp Bruce Edward Caldwell. m 3/1/1994 Everett Alan March c 2. D Chr Ch Cody WY 2004. everbmarch@msn.com

MARCHAND, R Richard (NY) 1 Kingsley Ave, Staten Island NY 10314 **R Ch Of The Ascen Staten Island NY 2010-** B Seattle WA 2/11/1959 s Frederick James Marchand & Patricia Anne. BA Whitman Coll 1982; MDiv GTS 2008; Cert Academia de Espanol Guatemala 2009. D 1/26/2008 P 8/6/2008 Bp Bavi Rivera. Assoc The Ch of S Matt And S Tim New York NY 2008-2010; D The Ch Of S Lk In The Fields New York NY 2008; Assoc P The Ch of S Matt And S Tim New York NY 2008; D The Ch of S Matt And S Tim New York NY 2008. Soc of Cath Priests 2009-2010. rector@ascensionsi.org

MARCHL III, William Henry (NC) 719 S 1st St, Smithfield NC 27577 B Pittsburgh PA 6/16/1964 s William Henry Marchl & Mary Anne. BA Ken 1986; MDiv Ya Berk 1992. D 1/3/1993 P 7/8/1993 Bp Alden Moinet Hathaway. m 8/3/1991 Laura Lynne Dilts c 1. R S Paul's Epis Ch Smithfield NC 2003-2006; P Cur S Steph's Ch Durham NC 1998-2002; Trin Ch Coshocton OH 1995-1998; P The Ch Of The Adv Jeannette PA 1993-1995; Calv Ch Pittsburgh PA 1993-1994; S Barth's Ch Scottdale PA 1993-1994. Auth, "arts,"

Living Ch. SocMary. Jn Crowe Ransom Poetry Prize; Phi Beta Kappa. bill. marchl@yahoo.com

MARCIALES ARENAS, Alberto Camilo (Colom) Carrera 6 No 49-85, Piso 2, Bogota Colombia B Cucuta Norte de Santander Colombia 9/22/1942 s Luis Alberto Marciales Arenas & Isabel. BA Colegio La Salle 1962; Lic Supervision Educativa Universidad de Pamplona 1993; Especialista en Gestion Eductiva Universidad de Pamplona 1999. D 12/13/2008 P 3/22/2009 Bp Francisco Jose Duque-Gomez. m 8/13/1966 Marleny Blanca Leal de Marciales c 4. p.albertomarciales@hot.mail

MARCOUX, Stephen Kent (Md) 1607 Grace Church Rd, Silver Spring MD 20910 **D Ch Of S Steph And The Incarn Washington DC 1998-** B Los Angeles CA 12/8/1961 s Harvey Lee Marcoux & Mary Ursula. BS U of New Orleans 1986; MDiv Ya Berk 1997; CAS Ya Berk 1997; MA Ya 1997. D 5/30/1998 Bp Charles Edward Jenkins III P 10/7/1999 Bp Ronald Hayward Haines. Gr Epis Ch Silver Sprg MD 2008-2010. KENTMARCOUX@GMAIL.COM

MARCURE, Johanna (CNY) 209 E Main St, Waterville NY 13480 **Gr Epis Ch Waterville NY 2010-** B Ft Jackson SC 11/19/1962 d Richard William Marcure & Anne Williams. BA U of Massachusetts 1994; MDiv Andover Newton TS 2009. D 3/21/2009 P 3/13/2010 Bp Gordon Paul Scruton. m Richard Tabor c 3. jojomal19@aol.com

MARCUSSEN, Bjorn Birkholm (SanD) 2933 B St Apt 3, San Diego CA 92102 **R S Phil The Apos Epis Ch Lemon Grove CA 2001-** B Copenhagen DK 11/21/1942 s Tage Birkholm Marcussen & Hildeborg. MA Copenhagen Sem Copenhagen Dk 1972; MS Royal Danish Grad Sch Of Educ Copenhagen Dk 1974. Rec from Polish National Catholic Church 2/1/2000 as Priest Bp Gethin Benwil Hughes. Dio San Diego San Diego CA 2001-2005; Vic S Eliz's Epis Ch San Diego CA 2000-2001. saintphiliplgl@aol.com

MAREE, Donna L (Pa) 702 Willow Brook Dr NE, Warren OH 44483 **Trin Memi Ch Philadelphia PA 2011-** B Pittsfield MA 9/16/1955 d Ruth M. BS Smith 1997; MDiv EDS 2000. D 10/26/2002 P 6/21/2003 Bp Herbert Thompson Jr. m 5/14/2006 Charles E Carr c 3. R Chr Epis Ch Warren OH 2009-2011; Trin Epis Ch Buffalo NY 2003-2006; Indn Hill Ch Cincinnati OH 2002-2003. dlmaree@smith.alumnae.net

MAREK, Joseph J (Tenn) 204-A Courthouse Dr., Salmon ID 83467 **Vic Ch Of The Redeem Salmon ID 2009-** B Milwaukee WI 10/18/1936 s Joseph James Marek & Sophia Kathleen. St. Bonaventure Minor Sem 1954; BA Wisconsin Inst 1960; LLB La Salle Ext U Sch of Law 1966. D 2/14/2004 P 9/12/2004 Bp Bertram Nelson Herlong. m 10/26/1957 Penny Lee Wade c 2. Vic S Andr's Epis Ch New Johnsonville TN 2003-2006. invictus@centurytel.net

MARGERUM, Michael (Nev) 11205 Carlsbad Rd, Reno NV 89506 B Seattle WA 3/17/1948 s Richard Margerum & Barbara. BS OR SU 1971; BS Golden Gate U 1973. D 12/7/1985 Bp William Benjamin Spofford. m 10/11/1976 Donna Painter. Hospice.

MARGOS, John Emlen (Pa) 8401 Harris Ave Apt 2c, Parkville MD 19064 **Died 9/19/2010** B Philadelphia PA 4/5/1926 s John Margos & Emily. BS Tem 1954; PDS 1957. D 11/1/1957 P 11/1/1957 Bp Alfred L Banyard. c 2.

MARGRAVE, Thomas Edmund Clare (NY) 29 William St, Cortland NY 13045 B Washington DC 1/16/1945 s Oliver Wendell Margrave & Lella. BS USMA At W Point 1968; MA Syr 1973; DAS Ya Berk 1993; MDiv Yale DS 1993. D 8/21/1993 P 9/14/1994 Bp David B(ruce) Joslin. m 5/25/1975 Marianne Krieger c 3. Mem, Prog Com, Mid-Hudson Reg Dio New York New York City NY 2005-2011; Mem, Bd and Com for Campus Mnstry Dio New York New York City NY 2004-2011; R S Jn's Ch Cornwall NY 2004-2011; Mem, Advsry Bd, Epis Chars Dio New York New York City NY 2004-2008; Mem, Exec Com, Mid-Hudson Reg Dio New York New York City NY 2004-2007; Mem, Bd for the Fndt of the Dio Dio Cntrl New York Syracuse NY 2003-2004; Mem, Campus Mnstry Com Dio Cntrl New York Syracuse NY 2001-2004; Chair, Justice, Peace and Integrity of Creation Com Dio Cntrl New York Syracuse NY 1999-2004; R Gr Ch Cortland NY 1999-2004; Curs Sec Lead Sprtl Advsr Dio Cntrl New York Syracuse NY 1994-1996; Cluster Team Vic Emm Ch Norwich NY 1993-1999. Alb Inst 1993; Associated Parishes 1993-2005; Soc of Cath Priests, NA 2008. tecmargrave@twcny.rr.com

MARICONDA, Thomas Nicholas (Ct) 36 Main St, Newtown CT 06470 B 6/9/1952 s Salvatore Mariconda & Mary Rose. BA Estrn Connecticut St U 1976. D 9/10/2011 Bp Laura Ahrens. m 11/18/2008 Walter M Dembowski. thomas.mariconda@att.net

MARIN, Carlos Heli (CFla) 438 Magpie Ct, Kissimmee FL 34759 **P H Faith Ch Saline MI 2006-; Vic S Chris's Ch Orlando FL 2006-** B Calarca-Q-Colombia 12/1/1952 s Hernando Marin & Belarmina. Educ U Quindio Armenia-Colombia 1977; BA Dio Armenia Armenia-Colombia 1980; MA(TS) Asbury TS 2011. Rec from Roman Catholic 5/28/2005 Bp John Wadsworth Howe. m 10/18/1974 Esperanza Baquero c 3. profmarin_73@msn.com

MARINCO, Judith Ann (Mich) 1434 E 13 Mile Rd, Madison Heights MI 48071 **D S Pat's Epis Ch Madison Heights MI 2010-** B Flint MI 5/26/1950 d Frank Edwin Diehl & Doris Marion. Assoc Ferris St U 1972. D 11/6/2010 Bp Wendell Nathaniel Gibbs Jr. m 8/15/1970 Vincent Michael Marinco c 2. mikejudymarinco@att.net

MARINCO, Vincent Michael (Mich) 1434 E 13 Mile Rd, Madison Heights MI 48071 **Reverend D S Pat's Epis Ch Madison Heights MI 2010-** B Detroit MI 1/15/1948 s Vincent Marinco & Betty Jane C. BS Ferris St U 1972. D 2/13/2010 P 11/6/2010 Bp Wendell Nathaniel Gibbs Jr. m 8/15/1970 Judith Ann Diehl c 2. mikejudymarinco@att.net

MARINO, Matthew Anthony (Az) 114 W Roosevelt St, Phoenix AZ 85003 **Youthministryapprentice.com Dio Arizona Phoenix AZ 2010-; D St Judes Epis Ch Phoenix AZ 2008-; Yth & YA Dio Arizona Phoenix AZ 2007-** B Phoeniz AZ 6/12/1964 s Marty Marino & Dorothy. MDiv in progress Fuller TS; BA Grand Canyon 1987; MEd Arizona St U 2005. D 7/17/2011 Bp Kirk Stevan Smith. m 2/18/1989 Kari Phillips c 2. mattmarino@mac.com

MARIS, Margo Elaine (Ore) 13201 Se Blackberry Cir, Portland OR 97236 B Portland OR 11/9/1942 d Earl Thomas Maris & Clarice Beulah. BA Willamette U 1964; MA GW 1967; Lewis & Clark Coll 1967; MDiv CDSP 1978; Portland St U 1978. D 1/22/1978 Bp David Ritchie Thornberry P 1/1/1979 Bp Bob Gordon Jones. m 11/27/1983 John C Pearce c 1. Dio Minnesota Minneapolis MN 1999-2003; Int All SS Ch Portland OR 1995-1996; Cn To Ordnry Dio Minnesota Minneapolis MN 1987-1994; Int S Andr's Epis Ch Minneapolis MN 1985-1987; Int S Chris's Epis Ch Roseville MN 1985-1987; R H Trin Epis Ch Elk River MN 1980-1984; Asst S Matt's Epis Cathd Laramie WY 1978-1980. Contrib, "Breach Of Trust:"; Auth, "Sexual Exploitation By Hlth Care Professionals & Cler 94"; Auth, "Healing The Wounds Of The Ch"; Auth, "Victim/Survivor". marisa@involved.com

MARKEVITCH, Diane Mary (Mil) 370 Kase St., Platteville WI 53818 **3/4 Time Trin Epis Ch Platteville WI 2006-** B Green Bay WI 6/12/1947 d Joseph Frank Buresh & Marquarite Frances. BBA U of Wisconsin 1984; MDiv SWTS 1999; Cert Sprtl Direction 2006. D 4/24/1999 P 10/24/1999 Bp Roger John White. m 7/3/1971 Ronald G Markevitch c 1. R H Cross Epis Ch Wisconsin Dells WI 1999-2006; Cur S Dunst's Ch Madison WI 1999-2001. dmarkevitch@centurytel.net

MARKHAM, Eva Melba Roberts (Ky) 1411 E Breckinridge St, Louisville KY 40204 **Ch Of The Adv Louisville KY 2009-; D Resurr Ch Louisville KY 1997-** B Madisonville KY 8/14/1951 d Samuel Leon Roberts & Mayme Nell. BA U of Louisiville 1969; MS U Of Evansville 1980; EdD U of Louisville 2000. D 4/29/1989 Bp David Reed. m 4/11/1996 Kim L Wadlington c 2.

MARKHAM, Ian Stephen (Va) 3737 Seminary Rd, Alexandria VA 22304 **Dn & Pres VTS Alexandria VA 2007-** B Crediton Devon UK 9/19/1962 s Stephen Keith Markham & Beryl Evelyn. BD Lon 1985; MLitt U of Cambridge 1989; PhD U Of Exeter 1995. D 6/9/2007 Bp Andrew Donnan Smith P 12/11/2007 Bp Peter James Lee. m 7/4/1987 Lesley P Markham c 1. Auth, "Liturg Life Principles," Ch Pub, 2009; Ed, "A Wrld Rel Rdr - Third Ed," Wiley-Blackwell, 2009; Auth, "Understanding Chr Doctrine," Wiley-Blackwell, 2008; Auth, "Do Morals Matter," Wiley-Blackwell, 2007. IMarkham@vts.edu

MARKHAM, Richard Benedict (NY) Ss5 Saint Paul Avenue, Staten Island NY 10304 B Staten Island NY 8/14/1939 s Eugene Markham & Marjorie. BA Wag 1962; GTS 1968; MDiv Nash 1973. D 6/16/1973 Bp Charles Waldo MacLean P 12/1/1973 Bp Paul Moore Jr. S Mary's Castleton Staten Island NY 2000-2009; Assoc S Paul's Ch Staten Island NY 1990-2002; Sum Supply P Chr Ch New Brighton Staten Island NY 1983-1985; Asst S Mary's Castleton Staten Island NY 1982-1990; Sum Supply P S Alb's Epis Ch Staten Island NY 1982-1983; Asst Ch Of S Mary The Vrgn New York NY 1977-1982; P-in-c The Ch Of S Steph Staten Island NY 1976-1977; Sum Supply P S Jn's Ch Staten Island NY 1974-1976; Cur Ch Of The Ascen Staten Island NY 1973-1976. Soc Of S Jn The Evang.

MARKIE, Patrick Gregory (Minn) 770 Parkview Ave, Saint Paul MN 55117 B Saint Paul MN 1/19/1947 s Cecil Markie & Florence. D 6/29/2006 Bp James Louis Jelinek. m 2/14/1975 Roxanna Alford c 1. patnrox75@aol.com

MARKLE, Ann (ETenn) 1076 Sparta Hwy, Crossville TN 38572 **Cnvnr, Sprtl Dir' Grp Dio E Tennessee Knoxville TN 2008-; Pensions Com Dio E Tennessee Knoxville TN 2008-; Dioc Chapl, DOK Dio E Tennessee Knoxville TN 2003-; R S Raphael's Epis Ch Crossville TN 2002-** B Terre Haute IN 6/12/1952 d Richard Theodore Markle & Mary Elizabeth. BS Indiana St U 1976; MS Indiana St U 1979; MS SUNY 1989; MDiv Ya Berk 1999; Certification Haden Inst 2007. D 6/26/1999 P 1/8/2000 Bp J Michael Garrison. Bp & Coun Dio E Tennessee Knoxville TN 2003-2006; Asst Calv Epis Ch Williamsville NY 1999-2002. Auth, "Bldg a Labyrinth," *E Tennessee Epis*, 2009; Auth, "When Recon Is Impossible," *Bulletin of the Worker Sis/Brothers of the H Sprt*, 2004. Gvrng Bd (Interfaith) Ntwk Of Rel Communities 1999-2001. E Williams Muehl Prize In Preaching Berkley DS New Haven CT 1999. ann.markle@aya.yale.edu

MARKLEY, Thomas Hicks (Va) 1937 W. 5th St., Port Angeles WA 98363 B Staunton VA 12/28/1933 s Russell W Markley & Elvira. BA U Rich 1950; MDiv STUSo 1972; DMin STUSo 1985. D 6/19/1972 Bp David Shepherd Rose P 12/1/1972 Bp John B Bentley. m 12/28/1975 Yvonne Rice c 3. R S Jn's Ch Richmond VA 1981-1996; Gd Samar Epis Ch Virginia Bch VA

1978-1981; Dio Sthrn Virginia Norfolk VA 1974-1977; P Chr Epis Ch Danville VA 1972-1974; Cur Ch Of The Epiph Danville VA 1972-1974. vontom@olypen.com

MARKS, Sharla J (FtW) 2431 St Gregory St, Arlington TX 76013 **Exec Coun Dio Ft Worth Ft Worth TX 2011-; UTA Campus Mnstry S Alb's Epis Ch Arlington TX 2011-; Commision on Mnstry Dio Ft Worth Ft Worth TX 2010-; D S Alb's Epis Ch Arlington TX 2009-** B Oklahoma City OK 6/7/1946 d Eugene Truitt & Virginia Grace. BS Texa Wmn's U 1968; MUP Texas A&M U-Coll Sta 1977; Lic Angl TS 2002. D 1/6/2001 Bp Jack Leo Iker. m 7/27/1967 Constant Roberts Marks c 2. deacon.sharla@sbcglobal.net

MARKS, S Patricia (Ga) 814 W Alden Ave, Valdosta GA 31602 **D Chr Ch Valdosta GA 2003-** B New York City 8/16/1943 d LeRoy Smith & Mary. BA Douglass Coll 1965; PhD MI SU 1970. D 11/22/2003 Bp Henry Irving Louttit. m 11/30/1968 Dennis Marks. "The 'Arry Ballads," McFarland Pub Co., 2006; "Sarah Bernhardt's First Amer Tour," McFarland Pub Co., 2003; "Bicycles, Bangs, and Bloomers: The New Wmn in the Popular Press," U Press of Kentucky, 1990; "The Smiling Muse: Victoriana in the Comic Press," Associated U Presses, 1985; "Amer Literary and Drama Revs," G.K. Hall, 1984. No Amer Assoc. for the Diac 2003. spmarks@bellsouth.net

MARKS SR, W(illiam) Parker (USC) 400 Herringbone Run, Easley SC 29642 B Tarboro NC 12/10/1930 s William Ezra Marks & Margaret Elizabeth. BS E Carolina U 1955; MDiv VTS 1960. D 6/18/1960 Bp Richard Henry Baker P 12/20/1960 Bp Thomas Augustus Fraser Jr. m 5/27/1956 Mary Jo Goodwin c 1. R S Mich's Epis Ch Easley SC 1991-2002; All SS' Epis Ch Concord NC 1962-1974; P-in-c S Andrews Ch Durham NC 1960-1962. Auth, "The Golden Doorstop," Meadowbrook Pub, 1977.

MARLIN, John Henry (Okla) Po Box 21594, Oklahoma City OK 73156 **Vic Emer S Edw Chap Oklahoma City OK 2008-** B Muskogee OK 8/10/1939 s John Marlin & W Augusta. BA Oklahoma City U 1961; MDiv VTS 1963; MA GW 1967; Med Marymount U 1987. D 6/25/1966 P 5/1/1967 Bp William Foreman Creighton. All Souls Epis Ch Oklahoma City OK 1988-2008; Casady Sch Oklahoma City OK 1988-2008; S Edw Chap Oklahoma City OK 1988-2001; R Meade Memi Epis Ch Alexandria VA 1972-1977; St Steph Sch Alexandria VA 1969-1988; Asst Min The Ch Of The Epiph Washington DC 1966-1969. Vic Emer Casady Sch 2008. marlinj@mac.com

MARLOW, Douglas J (CNY) 220 Colorado Ave, Watertown NY 13601 **Dir of Mus Trin Epis Ch Watertown NY 2008-; Shared Mnstry Of Nny Watertown NY 2007-** B Malone NY 3/28/1951 s Walter Leon Marlow & Blanche Lucy. Wadhams Hall Sem Ogdensburg NY 1971; Mater Dei Diac Formation Ogdensburg NY 1991. Rec from Roman Catholic 10/4/2006 Bp Gladstone Bailey Adams III. m 5/12/1979 Barbara L Clark c 5. No Country Epis Dist Watertown NY 2008-2010. deacondoug@juno.com

MARONDE, James A (Los) 8013 Lindley Ave, Reseda CA 91335 B 11/27/1949 M.Div. GTS 1978; Ph.D. Wm Lyon U 1987. D 6/17/1978 P 1/20/1979 Bp Robert C Rusack. m 7/18/2003 Denise Peters. P-in-c S Nich Par Encino CA 2005-2010; R S Mart-In-The-Fields Par Winnetka CA 1985-1995; Assoc S Alb's Epis Ch Los Angeles CA 1978-1985. JAMESMARONDE@YMAIL.COM

MARONEY, Gordon Earle (Ark) 766 1/2 W Washington St, Camden AR 71701 B 8/14/1948 s Gordon E Maroney & Myrtle Vesta. BS Sthrn St Coll Magnolia AR 1972; Med Sthrn St Coll Magnolia AR 1979. D 12/3/2004 P 7/15/2005 Bp Larry Earl Maze. gmaroney@cablelynx.com

MARQUAND, Betty Harlina (Colo) 1521 Windsor Way Unit 8, Racine WI 53406 B Oak Creek CO 2/15/1926 d Isaac Charles Farley & Flora. AA Colorado Wmn Coll 1944; BA U CO 1946; MDiv Nash 1985. D 1/22/1985 Bp William Carl Frey. c 2. D All SS Ch Tybee Island GA 1988-1989; D S Matt's Ch Kenosha WI 1985-1987.

MARQUES, Barbara Bressler (Va) 7411 Moss Side Ave, Richmond VA 23227 **Dio Virginia Richmond VA 2010-** B Chicago IL 6/18/1949 d Bernard Bressler & Elizabeth Burgess. MDiv Uniersity Of The So TS At Sewanee 2007. D 6/16/2007 P 12/18/2007 Bp Peter James Lee. c 2. S Ptr's Epis Ch Richmond VA 2007-2010. barbara.dogsma@gmail.com

MARQUESS, Judith Ann (Vt) 212 Woodhaven Dr # 5d, White River Junction VT 05001 **D S Paul's Epis Ch White River Jct VT 2002-** B Rockville Center NY 2/9/1937 d Douglas Leitch & Grace. BA CUNY 1958. D 9/21/2002 Bp David B(ruce) Joslin. c 2. judithmarquess@aol.com

MARQUEZ, Juan I (DR) 9 Corthell Street, Albany NY 12205 **Dio The Dominican Republic (Iglesia Epis Dominicana) Santo Domingo DO 2009-** B San Pedro de Macoris Dom Republic 1/15/1947 s Rafael R Diaz & Ana Maria. BA Inst Advncd Stds DO 1971; MDiv ETSC 1976. D 5/1/1977 P 6/4/1978 Bp Telesforo A Isaac. m 6/15/2011 Carmen Luisa De Jesus Guaba c 3. Epis Ch Cntr New York NY 2001-2008; Intl Partnership Off Epis Ch Cntr New York NY 2001-2008; Chr Epis Ch Ballston Spa NY 1994; S Jn's Ch Cohoes NY 1993; S Mary's Ch Lake Luzerne NY 1991-1992; P Dpt Of Missions Ny Income New York NY 1986-1988; Mision San Juan Bautista Bronx NY 1986-1988; Dio Rochester Rochester NY 1982-1985; Assoc Holyrood Ch New York NY 1981-1982; Dio The Dominican Republic (Iglesia Epis Dominicana) Santo Domingo DO 1977-1981. marquezji@yahoo.com

MARQUIS JR, James Fredrick (ETenn) 7006 Genoa Dr, Chattanooga TN 37421 **Supply P S Matt's Ch Dayton TN 2004-** B New York NY 4/3/1930 s James F Marquis & Thelma. BA Tusculum Coll 1951; MDiv STUSo 1972. D 6/25/1972 Bp William Evan Sanders P 7/21/1972 Bp John Vander Horst. m 2/23/1952 Emma Shipley. Chapl Dio E Tennessee Knoxville TN 1994-1995; R S Mart Of Tours Epis Ch Chattanooga TN 1984-1997; S Paul's Epis Ch Murfreesboro TN 1975-1984; Vic S Andr's Epis Ch New Johnsonville TN 1972-1975. Who'S Who In Rel 1975; Outstanding Young Men Of Amer 1965. jfmarquis@aol.com

MARR JR OSB, Andrew (Chi) 56500 Abbey Rd, Three Rivers MI 49093 B Detroit MI 3/16/1947 s Robert Barie Marr & Dorothy Eileen. BA Kalamazoo Coll 1969; Untd TS Of Thc Twin Citics 1970; MDiv Nash 1972. D 5/24/1988 P 11/29/1988 Bp Frank Tracy Griswold III. Auth, "Creatures We Dream of Knowing," *Story of Our Life Together*, iUniverse, 2011; Auth, "Tools for Peace," iUniverse, 2007; Auth, "b in the Darkest Time of Year," iUniverse, 2004; Auth, "Violence And The Kingdom Of God," *ATR*, 1998. andrewosb@juno.com

MARR, Jon Aidan (RG) 906-B Old Las Vegas Hwy, Santa Fe NM 87505 B Denver CO 8/7/1933 s John Hutton Stark & Helen Margaret. BA U CO 1956; BD Nash 1959; Urban Trng Cntr 1968; Fllshp Coll of Preachers 1972. D 6/29/1959 P 2/2/1960 Bp Joseph Summerville Minnis. R & Abbot S Andr's Ch Denver CO 1969-1984; Vic S Barth's Ch Estes Pk CO 1959-1968. "Men Athirst For God," Familian/OHF, 1984. OHF. braemarr@aol.com

MARRAN, Pauline Matte (NY) 80 Lyme Rd Apt 219, Hanover NH 03755 B Detroit MI 7/11/1923 d Joseph Matte & Beulah. Cert Detroit Commercial Coll Detroit MI 1943; Cert Fndt for Admin Reearch 1962; EFM STUSo 1994. D 5/30/1992 Bp Richard Frank Grein. m 9/13/1981 Robert John Marran. D S Thos Ch Hanover NH 2000-2007; D Ch Of The Gd Shpd Granite Sprg NY 1992-2000. NAAD 1992. dyr219@gmail.com

MARRETT, Michael McFarlene (WA) 1902 C St Ne # 48232, Washington DC 20002 B Greenwich Town Saint Andrew Jamaica West Indies 10/7/1935 s Kenneth Louis Marrett & Ivy McFarlane. AMIET British Inst of Engr Tech 1958; MDiv GTS 1969; STM GTS 1970; BA Ford 1974; PhD NYU 1980; MS Sthrn Connecticut St U 1982. D 3/26/1961 P 3/25/1962 Bp The Bishop Of Jamaica. m 1/30/1984 Margery Mugford. Dio Washington Washington DC 1998-1999; S Mich And All Ang Adelphi MD 1995-1997; R S Monica's Epis Ch Washington DC 1984-1986; R S Lk's Epis Ch New Haven CT 1974-1981; R Ch Of S Jas The Less Jamaica NY 1972-1973; R S Mk's Ch Brooklyn NY 1970-1971. Auth, *The Lambeth Conferences & Wmn Priests*, The Exposition Press, 1981. Amer Psych Assn; ACPE; Assn of Profsnl Chapl Diplomate; CBS; OHC. Hon Cn Dio Akoko, Nigeria, W Afr 1984; STD Estrn Amer U 1981; Phi Delta Kappa 1976.

MARRONE, Michael J (Mass) 410 Washington St, Duxbury MA 02332 B New York NY 9/21/1943 s Dominick Marrone & Catherine. BA Pace Coll; MDiv EDS 1974. D 6/8/1974 Bp Paul Moore Jr P 5/1/1975 Bp Frederick Barton Wolf. m 8/1/1970 Catherine Ann Zittel. R Ch Of S Jn The Evang Duxbury MA 1987-2005; Renwl & Evang Com Dio Massachusetts Boston MA 1987-1988; Chair - Ctte Admission Of Parishes & Missions Dio Massachusetts Boston MA 1985-1986; Liturg Cmsn Dio Massachusetts Boston MA 1984-1987; R S Mk's Ch Westford MA 1977-1987; Chr Ch Gardiner ME 1974-1977.

MARSDEN, Richard Conlon (SwFla) 222 S Palm Ave, Sarasota FL 34236 **Assoc R Ch Of The Redeem Sarasota FL 2007-** B Bridgeport CT 1/30/1952 s Richard Platt Marsden & Eileen Marie. BA Norwich U 1974; MRE Gordon-Conwell TS 1986; MDiv TESM 1990. D 9/7/1990 Bp Rogers Sanders Harris P 4/24/1991 Bp Edward Harding MacBurney. m 12/27/1975 Gail Frances Egerton. Asst Ch Of The Redeem Sarasota FL 1996-2006; Asst Chr Ch Bradenton FL 1990-1996. rmarsden@redeemersarasota.org

MARSH, Abigail (Colo) 6931 E Girard Ave, Denver CO 80224 **D S Thos Epis Ch Denver CO 2002-** B Denver CO 9/13/1947 d Mordecai Lewis Marsh & Helene. AA Monticello Coll Godfrey IL 1967; BA U Denv 1969; Cert Colorado D Sch Denver CO 2001. D 11/10/2001 Bp William Jerry Winterrowd. abbymarsh@comcast.net

MARSH, Caryl Ann (U) 829 E 400 S Apt 110, Salt Lake City UT 84102 B Bromley Kent UK 4/25/1938 d Godfrey Herbert Rose & Irene Kathleen. Inst For Bankers London 1958; BA San Jose St U 1974; MDiv CDSP 1977. D 6/25/1977 Bp C Kilmer Myers P 6/25/1978 Bp John Raymond Wyatt. HOD St Of Ch Com Dio Spokane Spokane WA 1991-1994; R S Paul's Ch Salt Lake City UT 1989-2004; Dep Gc Dio Spokane Spokane WA 1985-1998; Dir Of Chr Growth & Dvlpmt Dio Spokane Spokane WA 1985-1989; Del Prov Syn Dio Spokane Spokane WA 1984-1997; Prov YA Prog Coordntr Dio Spokane Spokane WA 1984-1989; Vic S Paul's Ch Cheney WA 1980-1985; S Tim Med Lake WA 1980-1985; All SS Ch Richland WA 1977-1980. carylmarsh@xmission.com

MARSH IV, Charles Wallace (At) St. James' Episc Church, 161 Church St. N.E., Marietta GA 30060 **S Jas Epis Ch Marietta GA 2009-** B Nashville TN

8/4/1978 s Charles Wallace Marsh & Jean Ewing. BA U So 2001; MDiv Ya Berk 2007. D 2/3/2007 P 8/11/2007 Bp Henry Irving Louttit. m 6/1/2010 Margaret Ann Benton Marsh. Assoc R S Paul's Ch Albany GA 2007-2009. wallace.marsh@stpaulsalbany.org

MARSH, Donald Heber (NH) Po Box 365, York ME 03909 **Died 12/4/2009** B Torrington CT 11/13/1922 s Heber Augustus Marsh & Beatrice Belle. BA U of Connecticut 1948; STB Ya Berk 1951. D 5/27/1951 P 11/1/1951 Bp Charles F Hall. PBS. Citizen of the Year Rochester ChmbrCom 1982; DSA Rochester Jaycees 1973; Ditinguished Serv Awd Rochester Chapt, Elks 1972.

MARSH, Elizabeth (Mass) 368 Kings Hwy W, 358 Farwood Rd, Haddonfield NJ 08033 B New York NY 9/9/1948 d James Bailey Marsh & Elizabeth. BA U of New Hampshire 1973; MDiv Andover Newton TS 1981. D 6/29/1981 P 10/1/1982 Bp Frederick Barton Wolf. m 11/24/1979 Michael Joseph Feicht. Vic S Dav's Epis Ch Halifax MA 1984-1990; Int S Paul's Epis Ch Hopkinton MA 1983-1984.

MARSH, Gayle Mardene (Minn) 1644 Cohansey St, Saint Paul MN 55117 **P-in-c All SS Ch Northfield MN 2006-** B Grove City PA 8/13/1957 d Dean Elmer Marsh & Margaret Ann. A.D.N New Mex St U. 1977; BSN New Mex St U. 1985; MDiv Fuller TS 1988; CAS VTS 1989; Cert Christos Cntr for Sprtl Direction 2004. D 8/2/1989 P 8/22/1990 Bp Terence Kelshaw. m Robyn Schmidt. Ch Of The H Cross Dundas MN 2008-2009; Sr Assoc S Chris's Epis Ch Roseville MN 1998-2006; P-in-c Shpd Of The Prairie Eden Prairie MN 1993-1998; R H Trin Epis Ch Elk River MN 1991-1993; S Brendan's Ch Horizon City TX 1989-1991. thankfulliving@comcast.net

MARSH, Karl Edwin (Neb) 1873 S Cherry Blossom Ln, Suttons Bay MI 49682 B Battle Creek MI 7/8/1934 s William Edward Marsh & Mildred Scott. BA U MI 1956; MDiv SWTS 1959; MA Ball St U 1974. D 6/20/1959 Bp Benjamin M Washburn P 12/23/1959 Bp Francis W Lickfield. m 1/17/1959 Barbara L Wood. S Mk's Epis Pro-Cathd Hastings NE 1976-1998; R S Jas Ch Piqua OH 1967-1974; Vic S Steph's Epis Ch Hobart IN 1964-1967; Vic S Mich's Ch Noblesville IN 1961-1964; Cur Gr Ch Grand Rapids MI 1959-1961. Auth, *Instructed Euch*, Little Farms Pub, 1974; Auth, *Our Whole Being*, Little Farms Pub, 1974. Natl Certied Counslr Natl Bd Cert Counselors; Cert Clincl Mntl Hlth Counslr Natl Bd Cert Counselors. BLMARSH@HOTMAIL.COM

MARSH, Keith A (Pa) Church of the Messiah, PO Box 127, Gwynedd PA 19436 **R Ch Of The Mssh Lower Gwynedd PA 2005-** B Camp Atterbury IN 6/11/1952 s Charles Elmer Marsh & Renee. BS Indiana U 1974; MDiv VTS 1991. D 6/22/1991 P 3/21/1992 Bp George Nelson Hunt III. m 10/9/1982 Deborah Ann Barlas c 2. Dn Chr Ch Cathd Louisville KY 1996-2005; S Matt's Epis Ch Louisville KY 1991-1996. rector@messiahgwynedd.org

MARSH, Michael Killingsworth (WTex) 343 N. Getty, Uvalde TX 78801 **Discernment Com, Mem Dio W Texas San Antonio TX 2009-; Exam Chapl Dio W Texas San Antonio TX 2006-; R S Phil's Ch Uvalde TX 2005-** B Killeen TX 4/12/1960 s Byron Drake Marsh & Janice Jean. BS U of Texas 1982; JD Texas Tech U 1985; MDiv TS 2003. D 6/12/2003 Bp Robert Boyd Hibbs P 1/6/2004 Bp James Edward Folts. m 9/1/1995 Cynthia Ann Marsh c 2. Asst R S Ptr's Epis Ch Kerrville TX 2003-2005. marshmk@gmail.com

MARSH, Ralph Olin (At) 405 W Cloverhurst Ave, Athens GA 30606 **Died 6/7/2010** B Leslie GA 6/14/1926 s Joseph Ellis Moses & Frances Belle. BA Emory U 1949; LTh STUSo 1965; DHN Pfeiffer Coll Misenheimer 1976. D 6/26/1965 P 3/1/1966 Bp Randolph R Claiborne. c 2.

MARSH JR, Robert Francis (Fla) 2462 C H Arnold Rd, Saint Augustine FL 32092 B Jacksonville FL 12/30/1945 s Robert Francis Marsh & Thelma Ruth. BBA Georgia St U 1976; MDiv STUSo 1982. D 6/13/1982 P 12/18/1982 Bp Frank Stanley Cerveny. m 7/25/1968 Diane Nulf c 3. P-in-c Ch Of The Recon St Aug FL 2006-2007; Chapl Jacksonville Epis HS Jacksonville FL 2002-2011; River Reg Cn Dio Florida Jacksonville FL 1997-2002; R S Mk's Ch Palatka FL 1992-2002; P-iu-Charge S Mary's Ch Palatka FL 1992-2002; Int S Cathr's Ch Jacksonville FL 1991-1992; Cn S Jn's Cathd Jacksonville FL 1991; R S Jas Epis Ch Perry FL 1986-1989; Asst S Ptr's Ch Jacksonville FL 1984-1986; Asst Ch Of The H Comf Tallahassee FL 1982-1984. Ed, "Jeshua," *Jeshua*. GC Cler 4 Dio Florida 2006; GC Cler 3 Dio Florida 2003; GC Cler 4 Dio Florida 2000; Pres Conlee Hse Batterd Wmn Shltr Bd 1999; Pres Stndg Com 1994; Chair Div Of Yth Mnstrs 1990; Chair Substance Abuse Com 1982. frbobmarsh@gmail.com

MARSHALL, Carol Phillips (USC) Christ Episcopal Church, PO Box 488, Lancaster SC 29721 **Ch Of The Ascen Seneca SC 2009-; Ch Of The H Sprt Greensboro NC 2006-** B Orangeburg SC 3/4/1950 d Ernest Vance Morris & Carolyn Ackerman. Erskine Coll; BA - French U of So Carolina-Columbia 1972; MDiv TS - Sewanee 1999. D 6/12/1999 P 10/4/2006 Bp Dorsey Felix Henderson. m 6/2/2007 Donald Bruce Marshall c 2. Chr Epis Ch Lancaster SC 2006-2009. cmpusc72@aol.com

MARSHALL, David Allen (Oly) P.O. Box 33029, Seattle WA 98133 **R S Dunst's Ch w the Henry Memi Chap Shoreline WA 2009-** B San Francisco CA 6/3/1961 BS California St U 1985; Masters VTS 2003. D 6/28/2003 P 1/17/2004 Bp Vincent Waydell Warner. m 6/18/1983 Alice Joan Wilson c 5. S Dunst-The Highlands Shoreline WA 2008-2009; Gd Samar Epis Ch Sammamish WA 2006-2008; Asst S Steph's Epis Ch Seattle WA 2003-2006. david@revmarshall.com

MARSHALL, David J (SanD) Grace Episcopal Church, 1020 Rose Ranch Road, San Marcos CA 92069 **R Gr Epis Ch Of The Vlly Mssn San Marcos CA 2008-** B Tacoma WA 4/26/1969 s John Marshall & Nancy. BA S Mart's U 1991; MDiv CDSP 2007. D 6/9/2007 P 6/7/2008 Bp James Edward Waggoner. m 5/21/1995 Christina R Marshall c 4. Cur S Lk's Ch Coeur D Alene ID 2007-2008. revdavidmarshall@verizon.net

MARSHALL III, Elliott Wallace (Chi) 710 Crab Tree Lane, Bartlett IL 60103 B Salisbury MD 11/28/1943 s Elliott Wallace Marshall & Winifred Crockett. BA Randolph-Macon Coll 1965; MDiv The Epis TS in Kentucky 1971; D.Min. Candidate STUSo 1977; Cantess Cbury GB 1978; Coll of Preachers 1985; S Geo's Coll Jerusalem IL 1992. D 5/29/1971 P 12/19/1971 Bp Addison Hosea. m 10/8/2011 Pu Nam c 3. R Ch Of The Incarn Bloomingdale IL 1997-2003; Dioc Coun of Easton Dio Easton Easton MD 1993-1996; R Trin Ch Elkton MD 1990-1995; Dn, Baton Rouge Dnry Dio Louisiana Baton Rouge LA 1983-1989; R S Fran Ch Denham Sprg LA 1982-1989; R Chr Epis Ch Eastville VA 1977-1982; Dn, Estrn Shore Convoc Dio Sthrn Virginia Norfolk VA 1977-1982; R Emm Ch Cape Chas VA 1977-1982; R Hungars Par Eastville VA 1977-1982; R Chr Epis Ch Buena Vista VA 1975-1977; Asst R Chr Epis Ch Charlottesville VA 1972-1974; Vic Adv Ch Cynthiana KY 1971-1972. wallmarsh@aol.com

MARSHALL, (Gordon) Kelly (O) 65 S Kanawha St, Buckhannon WV 26201 **R S Jas Epis Ch Boardman OH 2004-** B Kittanning PA 2/19/1951 s Percy J Marshall & Betty Marie. BA Bob Jones U 1972; MA Slippery Rock U 1982; ThM Duquesne U 1985. D 6/7/1986 P 12/1/1986 Bp Alden Moinet Hathaway. m 8/6/1980 Kathleen S Anderson c 2. Mahoning Vlly Shared Mnstry Boardman OH 2003-2007; Area Mssnr Epis Ch of the Trsfg Buckhannon WV 1996-2003; Area Mssnr Gr Epis Ch Elkins WV 1996-2003; Area Mssnr S Barn Bridgeport WV 1996-2003; Area Mssnr S Mths Grafton WV 1996-2003; The No Cntrl Cluster Elkins WV 1996-2003; Int S Matt's Ch Charleston WV 1995-1996; Chr Ch Greensburg PA 1993-1994; P-in-c All Souls Ch No Versailles PA 1991-1994; Calv Ch Pittsburgh PA 1986-1991. Auth, "Pstr Response To The Aids Crisis". gkm1919@zoominternet.net

MARSHALL III, Howard R (NJ) 6313 Wyndam Rd, Pennsauken NJ 08109 B Camden NJ 10/13/1948 s Howard R Marshall & Jeanette M. BA Glassboro St U 1981; MDiv Nash 1984. D 6/2/1984 Bp George Phelps Mellick Belshaw P 12/1/1984 Bp Vincent King Pettit. m 2/22/1969 Christina R Green. Trin Ch Moorestown NJ 1984-1985.

M

MARSHALL, John Anthony (WNY) 7145 Fieldcrest Dr, Lockport NY 14094 **S Mich And All Ang Buffalo NY 2009-** B Buffalo NY 12/7/1953 s Clyde Marshall & Jean Louise. BA Wadhams Hall Sem Coll 1976; MDiv Chr The King Sem 1980. Rec from Roman Catholic 6/1/1997 as Priest Bp Paul Victor Marshall. m 6/25/1994 Mary Rita Schlau c 4. R Chr Ch Lockport NY 1999-2009; R The Epis Ch Of S Clem And S Ptr Wilkes Barre PA 1997-1999. ACPE 1993-1999; Coll of Chapl 1993-1999; Natl Coll of Cath Chapl 1990-1993. japmarshall@yahoo.com

MARSHALL, John H (NwT) Po Box 2741, Big Spring TX 79721 **D The Epis Ch Of S Mary The Vrgn Big Sprg TX 2002-** B 6/17/1946 D 10/27/2002 Bp C(harles) Wallis Ohl. jmarshall51@suddenlink.net

MARSHALL, Lewis Edwin (LI) 176 Dean St, Brooklyn NY 11217 **All SS Ch Staten Island NY 2009-** B Nashville AR 7/23/1957 s Emmett Asbury Marshall & Nina Loren. BA S Jos Sem Coll 1979; MDiv GTS 1992. D 6/13/1992 Bp James Barrow Brown P 12/1/1992 Bp Orris George Walker Jr. S Ann And The H Trin Brooklyn NY 1993-1995. lejmarshall@gmail.com

MARSHALL, Lynda Youll (Va) 1866 Patrick Henry Dr, Arlington VA 22205 **Asst Pohick Epis Ch Lorton VA 2009-** B Solihull, UK 11/15/1952 d Cyril Thomas Youll & Doreen Mary. BA De Montfort U 1974; MDiv Wycliffe 2001. Trans from Anglican Church of Canada 12/14/2009 Bp Shannon Sherwood Johnston. m 4/5/2008 Paul Marshall c 1. lyoullmarshall@verizon.net

MARSHALL, Margaret (ETenn) 7109 Cheshire Dr, Knoxville TN 37919 B Chattanooga TN 2/27/1952 d Christopher Williams Caldwell & Joanne Shields. D 5/31/1997 Bp Robert Gould Tharp. S Ptr's Ch Chattanooga TN 1999-2002; Ch Of The Gd Samar Knoxville TN 1997-1999. revmcm@comcast.net

MARSHALL, McAlister Crutchfield (Va) 2316 E Grace St # 8011, Richmond VA 23223 B Cleveland OH 6/19/1929 s McAlister Marshall & Isabel. BA U of Virginia 1954; BD Bex 1957; STM STUSo 1971; DMin Van 1979. D 6/10/1957 Bp Frederick D Goodwin P 5/31/1958 Bp Robert Fisher Gibson Jr. m 11/26/1951 Doris Atkins c 2. P-in-c S Asaph's Par Ch Bowling Green VA 1992-2001; Assoc Emm Ch At Brook Hill Richmond VA 1991-2002; S Jn's Ch Richmond VA 1986-1990; Imm Ch Mechanicsville VA 1984-1985; Emm Ch At Brook Hill Richmond VA 1979; Dn Dio Virginia Richmond VA 1978-1979; Chair Dio Virginia Richmond VA 1972-1975; R Trin Ch Manassas VA 1967-1978; R Ch Of S Jas The Less Ashland VA 1960-1967; Ch Of The H Comf Richmond VA 1957-1960. Auth, "Hymns," *Hymn Soc of Amer.*

✠ **MARSHALL, Rt Rev Paul Victor** (Be) 333 Wyandotte St, Bethlehem PA 18015 **Bp Of Bethlehem Dio Bethlehem Bethlehem PA 1996-** B New York NY 7/25/1947 s Victor William Marshall & Frances Mary Augusta. BA Concordia Coll 1969; MDiv Concordia St. Louis MO 1973; ThD GTS 1982; DD GTS 1996; DCnL Epis Sem Lexinton 1999. D 2/4/1978 P 6/10/1978 Bp William Hampton Brady Con 6/29/1996 for Be. m 5/31/1969 Diana Hilty c 2. Ch Of S Jas The Apos New Haven CT 1991-1993; Assoc Prof Ya Berk New Haven CT 1989-1996; Cmsn On Life & Human Hlth Dio Long Island Garden City NY 1986-1988; R Chr Ch Babylon NY 1982-1989. Auth, "Messages in the Mall," CPG; Auth, "One, Cath and Apostolic," CPG; Auth, "Same-Sex Blessisng: Stories & RItes," CPG; Auth, "The Bp is Coming," CPG; Auth, "Angl Liturg In Amer," CPG; Auth, "The Voice Of A Stranger," CPG; Auth, "Preaching For The Ch Today," CPG. Amer Psychoanalytic Assn 2007; No Amer Acad Of Liturg 1982; Societas Liturgica 1979. bpoffice@diobeth.org

MARSHALL, Richard G. (Ala) 6944 Cypress Spring Ct, St Augustine FL 32086 B Detroit MI 7/29/1928 s Richard William Marshall & Hazel Lenora. BS Lawr Tech U 1961; MDiv Epis TS of the SW 1981. D 6/12/1981 P 12/15/1981 Bp Furman Stough. c 5. Int S Steph's Epis Ch Huntsville AL 1998-1999; P-in-c H Cross-St Chris's Huntsville AL 1994-1998; R S Andr's Epis Ch Sylacauga AL 1981-1990. Auth, "My Journey w Jesus and Jo," *My Journey w Jesus and Jo and Poems by Jo*, Brushpanther Press/lulu.com, 2008; Auth, "Pryr: The Begining Of The Journey," *The Cross*, BroSA, 1981. mel_and_rich@bellsouth.net

MARSHALL, Robert (RI) 191 County Rd, Barrington RI 02806 **R S Jn's Ch Barrington RI 2010-** B Wilson, NC 6/19/1969 s Thomas Marshall & Elizabeth. BS Barton Coll 1992; MDiv VTS 2006. D 6/3/2006 P 12/9/2006 Bp Michael Bruce Curry. Asst S Jn's Ch Lynchburg VA 2006-2010. bertmarshall@yahoo.com

MARSHALL JR, William Shattuck (Be) 12 Holiday Ct, Kingston PA 18704 B New York NY 12/19/1942 s William Shattuck Marshall & Marjorie. BS SUNY 1965; Med U Pgh 1968; MS Adams St Coll 1987; Cert Mercer TS 1989. D 6/17/1989 Bp Orris George Walker Jr P 6/24/2000 Bp Paul Victor Marshall. m 5/5/1968 Madeline(div) Barbara Pascarella c 2. The Epis Ch Of S Clem And S Ptr Wilkes Barre PA 2002-2010; Chair Dioc Recovery Cmsn Dio Bethlehem Bethlehem PA 2000-2006; Dio Bethlehem Bethlehem PA 2000-2002; Asst Dio Bethlehem Bethlehem PA 1999-2000; S Jn's Epis Ch Palmerton PA 1999-2000; Ds Advsry Com Dio Bethlehem Bethlehem PA 1991-1995; D Ch Of The Resurr E Elmhurst NY 1991-1993; COM Dio Bethlehem Bethlehem PA 1989-1995; Asst Ch Of Chr The King E Meadow NY 1989-1991; Chair Bps Com Dio Long Island Garden City NY 1985-1998. Auth, *Recovery is More than Words*, 1993; "Mir: The Magic of Medjugorje," *The Deakones*, 1990. NASW 1981; NAAD 1989-2000; Recovery Mnstrs of the Epis Ch 1983. wsmsscnp@verizon.net

MARSTON, Robert Dandridge (SVa) 45 Main St, Newport News VA 23601 **R S Andr's Epis Ch Newport News VA 1993-** B Washington DC 10/25/1952 s Robert Quarles Marston & Ann Carter. BA U of Virginia 1975; MDiv VTS 1979; DMin STUSo 1988. D 6/23/1979 Bp Robert Bruce Hall P 5/1/1980 Bp David Henry Lewis Jr. m 8/19/1978 Maria Seara Barros c 2. Com Of Lay Ministers Dio Virginia Richmond VA 1986-1989; Supvsr Of Field Wk VTS Alexandria VA 1986-1987; R S Thos Epis Ch Orange VA 1985-1993; S Fran Ch Greensboro NC 1982-1985; Mssnr Dio Virginia Richmond VA 1980-1982; Asst Little Fork Epis Ch Rixeyville VA 1979-1982; Asst S Steph's Epis Ch Culpeper VA 1979-1982. Auth, "Experiencing The Presence Of God During Times Of Need: A Case Study". Bro Of S Andr OHC. Outstanding Young Men Amer 1986; Who'S Who Young Amer 90.

MARTA, Dale Charles (Mo) 112 N Ray Ave, Maryville MO 64468 B Rochester PA 8/26/1956 s Thomas Joseph Marta & Martha Anne. BA Penn 1978; MDiv VTS 1982. D 6/5/1982 Bp Albert Wiencke Van Duzer P 6/1/1983 Bp Charles Farmer Duvall. m 8/23/1980 Janet Kay Mullin c 3. Off Of Bsh For ArmdF New York NY 1995-1999; R S Mart's By The Lake Epis Minnetonka Bch MN 1990-1995; R Ch Of The Gd Shpd Pitman NJ 1987-1990; Trin By The Cove Naples FL 1983-1987; Chr Ch Par Pensacola FL 1982-1983. dmarta@kc.rr.com

MARTENS, Ann F (Va) 3050 N Military Rd, Arlington VA 22207 **Asst R S Ptr's Epis Ch Arlington VA 2006-** B Roanoke VA 9/2/1953 BA U Rich; MA Webster U; MDiv VTS 2005. D 6/18/2005 Bp Peter James Lee P 12/21/2005 Bp David Colin Jones. Asst Trin Ch Arlington VA 2005-2006. AFMARTENS@VERIZON.NET

MARTIN, Alison Jane (WNY) 160 Kieffer Ave, Depew NY 14043 **P-in-c S Pat's Ch Cheektowaga NY 2011-** B Buffalo NY 8/10/1953 d John Stewart Martin & Helen Jane. Buffalo Gnrl Hosp Sch of Nrsng 1980; BS SUNY 1991; MDiv Bex 1994. D 6/11/1994 P 12/17/1994 Bp David Charles Bowman. S Aid's Ch Alden NY 2009-2010; R Trin Ch Lancaster NY 1999-2003; Dio Wstrn New York Tonawanda NY 1995-1998; S Jn's Ch Wilson NY 1994-1999. ajmartin53@gmail.com

MARTIN, Andrea Brooke (WA) 4700 Whitehaven Pkwy NW, Washington DC 20007 **Assoc R S Pat's Ch Washington DC 2008-** B Kincheloe AFB MI 9/1/1975 d Randall Brooks Bowlby & Cassandra Jean. BA U of Notre Dame 1998; MDiv Ya Berk 2002. D 6/7/2003 P 6/5/2004 Bp M(arvil) Thomas Shaw III. m 1/8/2005 Christopher Scott Martin. Chr And H Trin Ch Westport CT 2004-2007; Chr Ch Alexandria VA 2003-2004. andreabowlby04@yahoo.com

MARTIN, Barbara J (SwFla) 230 Dent Dr, Naples FL 34112 **D Resurr Epis Ch Naples FL 1999-** B Mount Vernon NY 7/7/1926 d George Leslie Finer & Bessie. D 6/13/1998 Bp John Bailey Lipscomb. c 5. D S Paul's Ch Naples FL 1998-1999. ojmartin26@earthlink.net

MARTIN, Chad Travis (Tex) 4900 Jackwood St, Houston TX 77096 **Dir of Fam Mnstrs S Thos Ch Houston TX 2009-** B Springfield MO 2/29/1976 s Howard Martin & Carolyn. BM U of Mary Hardin-Baylor 1999; MM SW Missouri St 2001; MDiv VTS 2009. D 6/20/2009 Bp C(harles) Andrew Doyle P 1/8/2010 Bp Rayford Baines High Jr. m 6/2/2007 Cinnamon Hill. martin.chad@stes.org

MARTIN, Charles Percy (Pgh) 220 Columbia St, Johnstown PA 15905 B Detroit MI 1/31/1930 s Percy C Martin & Mildred F. BA U Pgh 1952; BD Bex 1955. D 6/25/1955 Bp William S Thomas P 12/17/1955 Bp Austin Pardue. m 6/16/1956 Mary E Balch. R S Mk's Ch Johnstown PA 1978-1995; R All SS Epis Ch Verona PA 1962-1978; R Emm Ch Pittsburgh PA 1961-1962; Secy Of Conv Dio Pittsburgh Monroeville PA 1960-1995.

MARTIN, Christopher (Cal) 1123 Court St, San Rafael CA 94901 **R S Paul's Epis Ch San Rafael CA 2004-** B Wilmington DE 8/19/1968 s Peter Bulkeley Martin & Victoria Howard. BA Ya 1990; MDiv Ya Berk 1996. D 6/22/1996 Bp Vincent Waydell Warner P 2/1/1997 Bp Andrew Donnan Smith. m 11/9/2009 Chloe Drake c 2. Assoc R All SS Par Beverly Hills CA 1999-2004; Asst Chr Ch Cathd Hartford CT 1997-1999. *Gathering the NeXt Generation*, Morehouse, 2000. Soc of S Jn the Evang 1995. christopherhmartin@comcast.net

MARTIN, Christopher S (Fla) PO Box 330500, Atlantic Beach FL 32233 B Decatur IL 4/1/1942 s Percy Lee Martin & Barbara Alice. BA Concordia Sr Coll 1964; MDiv Concordia TS 1968; MA Webster U 1970. D 6/10/1984 P 1/6/1985 Bp Frank Stanley Cerveny. m 1/18/1992 Sandra L Langston c 4. Dep - 2009 GC Dio Florida Jacksonville FL 2008-2011; S Mary's Epis Ch Green Cove Sprg FL 1984-2007. christophersmartin@comcast.net

MARTIN, Clyde Albert (SO) 1600 N Breiel Blvd, Middletown OH 45042 B Painesville OH 5/4/1933 s Walter Martin & Lydia Irene. OH SU; Diac Sch Dio Sthrn Ohio 1994. D 11/11/1994 Bp Herbert Thompson Jr. m 6/14/1955 Mary Carolyn Priest c 2. D The Epis Ch Of The Ascen Middletown OH 1994-2007. clydemarymartin@aol.com

MARTIN, Derrick Antonio (SeFla) 17 Fernhill Ave, Buffalo NY 14215 B 4/26/1944 s Solomon Martin & Madlyn Louise. Untd Theol Coll Of The W Indies Kingston Jm 1971; Lic U of The W Indies 1971; BA U of The W Indies 1975; STM GTS 1980; DMin Estrn Bapt TS 1996. D 6/1/1971 P 7/1/1972 Bp The Bishop Of Jamaica. m 2/14/2009 Jean Alexander-Martin c 2. S Kevin's Epis Ch Opa Locka FL 2003-2005; St. Monica's Angl Ch 2002-2003; Angl Dio the Bahamas and the Turks and Caicos Islands 2001; S Phil's Ch Buffalo NY 1998-2000; R Calv Epis Ch Nthrn Liberty Philadelphia PA 1986-1998. Bro Of S Andr. revdam_1986@hotmail.com

MARTIN, Donald Graham (WK) 1715 W 5th St, Colby KS 67701 **P-in-c S Paul's Epis Ch Goodland KS 2011-; Dioc Coun Dio Wstrn Kansas Hutchinson KS 2010-; P in charge S Fran Epis Ch Goodland KS 1995-; P-in-c S Lk's Epis Ch Scott City KS 1995-; Vic Ascen-On-The-Prairie Epis Ch Colby KS 1991-** B Saint Louis MO 4/16/1946 s William Graham Martin & Winifred. BA Trin 1968; Chicago TS 1973. D 12/19/1986 P 7/22/1992 Bp John Forsythe Ashby. m 4/6/1991 Evelyn Irene Schritter c 4. Cmsn on the Mnstry Dio Wstrn Kansas Hutchinson KS 2009-2011; Stndg Com Dio Wstrn Kansas Hutchinson KS 2002-2005; Dioc Coun Dio Wstrn Kansas Hutchinson KS 1996-1998; D S Paul's Epis Ch Goodland KS 1986-1991. Phi Beta Kappa 1968. evelynmartin04@hotmail.com

MARTIN JR, Edward E (NJ) 1281 Venezia Ave, Vineland NJ 08361 B Wilmington DE 6/23/1942 s Edward Evan Martin & Margaret Elizabeth. BA Widener U 1964; MDiv VTS 1971; MA Webster U 1977; DMin VTS 1987. D 6/10/1971 P 1/15/1972 Bp William Henry Mead. m 5/29/1965 Christianna Radcliffe Martin c 3. R S Andr's Epis Ch Bridgeton NJ 1994-2003; R Gr Epis Ch Rutherford NJ 1982-1994; R S Barth's Epis Ch Ho Ho Kus NJ 1977-1982; Off Of Bsh For ArmdF New York NY 1975-1977; Pres,De Epis Cler Assn Dio Delaware Wilmington DE 1971-1975; Vic S Jn The Bapt Epis Ch Milton DE 1971-1975. Contrib, ",Sprtl Healing," *Psychol Today*, 1989; Auth, ",Trng Laity In Visitation w The Aging," *DMin Dissertation*, VTS, 1987. Letter of Appreciation Bp: Dio New Jersey 2003; Certificates of Spec Congressional Recognition Congr of the Untd States 2003; Letters of Appreciation Congr of the Untd States: Hse of Representatives 2003; Letter of Appreciation Gvnr: St of New Jersey 2003; Cert of Appreciation Gvnr: St of New York 2003; Letters of Apprerciation Off of the Mayor: City of New York 2003; Cert of Appreciation Par of Trin Ch, New York City 2003; Letter of Appreciation The White Hse, Washington, D.C. 2003; Letters of Appreciation Untd States Senate 2003; Remington Cup VTS 1971. emcm52965@comcast.net

MARTIN, George H(arvey) (Minn) 12305 Chinchilla Ct W, Rosemount MN 55068 B Toledo OH 8/24/1942 s John Denman Martin & Gretchen. BA Hob 1964; BD Bex 1967; DMin VTS 1990. D 6/17/1967 Bp Nelson Marigold Burroughs P 2/1/1968 Bp John Harris Burt. m 3/28/1964 Caroline Jones c 4. Int S Marg's Epis Ch Palm Desert CA 2009-2010; Int S Mk's Barrington Hills IL 2007-2008; Int S Barth's Epis Ch Poway CA 2005-2006; Int Chr Ch Red Wing MN 2004-2005; Int Chr Ch Par La Crosse WI 2002; Int S Andr's Epis Ch Amarillo TX 2000-2001; Chair Bex Columbus OH 1990-1994; Vic SS Martha And Mary Epis Ch Eagan MN 1987-2000; Bd Trst Bex Columbus OH 1986-1989; R S Lk's Ch Minneapolis MN 1975-1986; Cur All SS Epis Ch Omaha NE 1972-1975; Asst Ch Of The H Trin Lincoln NE 1969-1972; Cur S Jn's Epis Ch Cuyahoga Falls OH 1967-1969. Auth, "Door-To-Door Ministy," Ch Ad Proj, 2002; Auth, "Rt Start: Birthing New Congregations In The New Millenium," Ch Ad Proj, 2000; Auth, "Advert Loc Ch: Handbook For Prom," Ch Ad Proj, 1999; Auth, "From Disciple To Apos," Ch Ad Proj, 1996. Intl Assn Police Chapl 1996. geoinmn@frontier.net

MARTIN, Hallock (SeFla) 5042 El Claro N, West Palm Beach FL 33415 **R H Sprt Epis Ch W Palm Bch FL 1993-** B Charleston SC 10/15/1950 s Franklin Martin & Margaret. Cntr Coll 1971; BS U of Tennessee 1976; MDiv STUSo 1988. D 6/11/1988 P 3/1/1989 Bp Harry Woolston Shipps. m 6/9/1974 Lydia Jay c 3. Vic S Lk's Epis Hawkinsville GA 1989-1993; Trin Ch Cochran GA 1988-1993. frhallock@bellsouth.net

MARTIN, Irene Elizabeth (Oly) PO Box 83, Skamokawa WA 98647 **P S Jas Epis Ch Cathlamet WA 1992-** B Southsea UK 7/8/1946 d Harold Bennell & Evelyn. BA York U 1969; B U Tor 1970; MLS U of British Columbia Vancouver BC CA 1975. D 1/25/1992 P 8/14/1992 Bp Vincent Waydell Warner. m 4/25/1973 Kent Oliver Martin. Auth, "Bch Heaven," *Hist of Wahkiakum Cnty*, WA SU Press, 1997; Auth, *Legacy & Testament: The Story of the Columbia River Gillnetters*, WA SU Press, 1994. RWF. Govenor Heritage Awd Washington Gvnr 2000; Jas Castles Awd Cntr for Columbia River Hist 1998.

MARTIN, James Mitchell (WVa) 177 Edison Dr, Huntington WV 25705 B Huntington WV 10/13/1928 s Adam Martin & Vera Melville. BS Georgia Inst of Tech 1951. D 6/11/1971 P 2/1/1972 Bp Wilburn Camrock Campbell. m 9/13/1971 Dorothy Jane Fuller.

MARTIN JR, John Charles (Md) 610 Brookfield Ave, Cumberland MD 21502 B Cumberland MD 4/1/1950 s John Charles Martin & Dorothy Mae. BS U of Maryland 1972. D 6/6/2009 Bp John Leslie Rabb. m 11/20/1987 Donna Jean Hampe c 2. johncharlesmartin-jr@hotmail.com

MARTIN, John Gayle (Pa) 8114 Heacock Ln, Wyncote PA 19095 B Bessemer AL 1/18/1941 s John Davis Martin & Marjorie Louise. BA Birmingham-Sthrn Coll 1962; MDiv STUSo 1967; Cert Pstr Trng Inst Philadelphia PA 1993. D 6/10/1967 P 5/4/1968 Bp George Mosley Murray. m 6/23/1967 Robin Pierce. Int R Memi Ch Of The H Nativ Rockledge PA 2004-2006; Int Ch Of The Redeem Springfield PA 2003-2004; Int S Jn's Ch Bala Cynwyd PA 2001-2003; Int H Innoc S Paul's Ch Philadelphia PA 1999-2001; R Chr Ch And S Mich's Philadelphia PA 1982-1998; R S Alb's Ch Birmingham AL 1975-1982; R Ch Of The Epiph Guntersville AL 1971-1975; Asst S Jas Par Wilmington NC 1969-1971; Vic S Mary's Epis Ch Andalusia AL 1967-1969; Vic S Thos Ch Greenville AL 1967-1969. AAPC. revmarts@verizon.net

MARTIN, Kathleen A (NY) 900 W End Ave, New York NY 10025 B Saint Petersburg FL 11/8/1949 d Edward Townsend Martin & Sheila Wolff. D 6/14/1997 P 12/1/1997 Bp Richard Frank Grein.

MARTIN, Kenneth Earl (Fla) 125 Holly View, Holly Lake Ranch TX 75765 **P S Mary's Ch Palatka FL 2008-** B Dalhart TX 12/7/1948 s Wayland Earl Martin & Earlene Joyce. Seward Jr Coll 1970; BBA W Texas A&M U 1972; MDiv Epis TS of The SW 1978. D 6/10/1978 P 6/9/1979 Bp Willis Ryan Henton. m 6/7/1969 Vicki Jean Dysart c 4. R S Paul's Fed Point Hastings FL 2003-2006; Asstg P S Lk's Epis Ch No Little Rock AR 1999-2002; Chair - Stew Cmsn Dio Arkansas Little Rock AR 1994-1996; S Steph's Epis Ch Jacksonville AR 1993-1999; Dir Of The Handicap Camp Dio Arkansas Little Rock AR 1993-1998; Chair - Dept Christn Ed Dio Arkansas Little Rock AR 1993-1994; Dn Of The NE Convoc Dio Arkansas Little Rock AR 1990-1993; R Ch Of The Gd Shpd Forrest City AR 1987-1993; S Andr's Paradis Luling LA 1986-1987; Vic S Tim's Ch La Place LA 1984-1987; Dept Of Missions Dallas TX 1984; Secy Dio NW Texas Lubbock TX 1982-1983; Vic S Phil's Epis Ch Sulphur Sprg TX 1982-1983; Cur S Dav's Ch Garland TX 1981-1982; S Lk's Epis Ch Levelland TX 1981; Dio NW Texas Lubbock TX 1978-1981; Vic The Epis Ch Of The Gd Shpd Brownfield TX 1978-1981; Dio Arkansas Little Rock AR 1000. kenmartin@aol.com

MARTIN, Kevin E (Dal) 10936 Ridgemeadow Dr, Dallas TX 75218 **Dn S Matt's Cathd Dallas TX 2005-** B Cleveland OH 8/30/1946 s Glen E Martin & Clarissa P. BA U of No Texas 1968; MDiv Ya Berk 1971; Advncd CPE 1978. D 6/17/1971 P 12/19/1971 Bp Theodore H McCrea. m 6/13/1964 Sharon D Smith c 2. Cn for Cong Dev Dio Cntrl Florida Orlando FL 2004-2006; Chr Epis Ch Plano TX 2003-2005; Vital Ch Mnstry Plano TX 2003-2005; Dio Texas Houston TX 1998-2002; Acts 29 Mnstrs Atlanta GA 1990-1993; R S Lk's Epis Ch Seattle WA 1984-1990; R S Matt's Ch Westerville OH 1979-1984; R Emm Epis Ch Stamford CT 1973-1977; Cur S Matt's Epis Ch Wilton CT 1971-1973. Auth, "5 Keys for Ch Leaders," *Bk*, Ch Pub, 2007; Auth, "The Myth of the 200 Barrier," *Bk*, Abingdon, 2005; Auth, "Stwdshp and Giving," TENS, 2003; Contrib, "2020," *2020 Report*, The Epis Ch, 2002; Contributing Auth, "Chr Ch, Denver," *Inner City Parishes*, Abingdon, 1992; Auth, "Mssn and Evang," *New Wineskins for Global Mssn*, ECMS, 1992; Auth, "Preaching to the Bereaved," *Coll of Preachers Nwsltr*, Coll of Preachers, 1985; Contributing Auth, "Authentic Preaching," *Coll of Preachers Nwsltr*, Coll of Preachers, 1984. 2020 Taskforce 2000-2003; ERM 1985-1993; Ldrshp Ntwk Ed Bd 1993-1999. canonkevin@sbcglobal.net

MARTIN, Lydia Adriana Peter (Md) 10800 Greenpoint Rd, Lavale MD 21502 B Kortgene The Netherlands 1/18/1941 BS U of No Dakota 1964; BA Frostburg U Frostburg MD 1976; MS Frostburg St U 1983; Cert Sthrn California Sensory Integration Tests 1983. D 6/2/2007 Bp John Leslie Rabb. m 1/24/1964 James Oscar Martin c 4. jomlapm@mindspring.com

MARTIN, Lyle Fay (Neb) 906 Main St, Gregory SD 57533 **P Trin Epis Ch Winner SD 2001-** B Erwin SD 3/26/1926 s Joseph Martin & Hannah. D 11/18/1988 P 10/20/1990 Bp Craig Barry Anderson. m 6/25/2007 Moyra L Mason c 3. P Chr Ch Sidney NE 1990-2001; D S Jas Epis Ch Belle Fourche SD 1988-1990. Homeless Awd Min Assoc 1997. winner@hamilton.net

MARTIN, Mary J (NY) 900 W End Ave Apt 10-C, New York NY 10025 B Saint Petersburg FL 11/8/1949 d Edward Townsend Martin & Sheila Eileen. BA Hollins U; MDiv UTS; MA UTS; PhD UTS. D 6/1/1996 P 12/7/1996 Bp Richard Frank Grein.

MARTIN, Nadine Brown (Az) 7750 E Oakwood Cir, Tucson AZ 85750 B Atlanta GA 2/3/1939 d Robert Dewitt Brown & Florine Agnes. BA Georgia St U 1978. D 10/14/2006 Bp Kirk Stevan Smith. m 7/26/1987 William Jeffrey Martin c 2.

MARTIN, Paul Dexter (WLa) 275 Southfield Road, Shreveport LA 71105 **Commision on Mnstry Dio Wstrn Louisiana Alexandria LA 2010-; Trst, U So Dio Wstrn Louisiana Alexandria LA 2006-; Co-chair, Evang Cmsn Dio Wstrn Louisiana Alexandria LA 2000-; Dioc Sprtl Dir, Curs Dio Wstrn Louisiana Alexandria LA 1998-; Asst R S Paul's Epis Ch Shreveport LA 1997-** B Cincinnati OH 6/2/1950 s Francis Thomas Martin & Mary. BA Wabash Coll 1972; MDiv STUSo 1975. D 6/14/1975 P 6/27/1976 Bp John P Craine. m 11/25/1978 Christine Anne Melloy c 3. Dioc Coun Dio Wstrn Louisiana Alexandria LA 2006-2011; Trst, U So Dio No Carolina Raleigh NC 1996-1999; Dir of Happ Dio No Carolina Raleigh NC 1992-1999; Dioc Yth Cmsn Dio No Carolina Raleigh NC 1991-1999; R S Jn's Epis Ch Minden LA 1990-1994; Asst R S Jn's Epis Ch Charlotte NC 1980-1989. frpaul@stpauls-shreveport.org

MARTIN, Rex L (Wyo) PO Box 64, Hartville WY 82215 **Vol Ch Of Our Sav Hartville WY 2006-** B 12/6/1956 s Sherman L Martin & Daylene R. EFM The U So TS 2005. D 7/22/2006 P 1/6/2007 Bp Bruce Edward Caldwell. m 6/26/1982 Rhonda Owens c 2. martin@champmail.com

✠ MARTIN, Rt Rev Richard Beamon (LI) 1388 Union St, Brooklyn NY 11213 **Ret Bp Suffr Of Li Dio Long Island Garden City NY 1974-** B Peak SC 2/23/1913 s Benjamin Butler Martin & Viola. BA Allen U 1937; BD VTS 1942; LHD STUSo 1975; LHD UTS 1975; LHD Voorhees Coll 1975; LLD S Paul's Coll Lawrenceville VA 1979. D 6/8/1942 P 2/1/1943 Bp Albert S Thomas Con 2/2/1967 for LI. Epis Ch Cntr New York NY 1974-1980; Bp Dio Long Island Garden City NY 1967-1974; Stndg Com Dio Long Island Garden City NY 1965-1967; R S Phil's Ch Brooklyn NY 1963-1965; Archd Dio Sthrn Virginia Norfolk VA 1951-1962; R Gr Ch Norfolk VA 1944-1962; Min In Charge Ch Of The Gd Shpd Sumter SC 1942-1944. DD VTS 1968; DD Stuso 1967; DD Allen U 1955. FORSKIP@VERIZON.NET

MARTIN, Richard Cornish (WA) 4915 Carlton Crossing Dr, Durham NC 27713 **Asst S Tim's Ch Raleigh NC 2009-** B Philadelphia PA 10/15/1936 s Leon Freeman Martin & Virginia Lorette. BA Penn 1958; MDiv VTS 1961; DMin How 1988. D 6/15/1961 P 1/13/1962 Bp John T Heistand. Asst S Thos Ch New York NY 2004-2006; Int Gr Ch Pittsburgh PA 2002-2003; Int S Mk's Epis Ch Charleston SC 2000-2001; Int The Ch Of The Adv Boston MA 1996-1999; R S Paul's Par Washington DC 1989-1996; R S Geo's Ch Washington DC 1973-1989; COM Dio Washington Washington DC 1967-1981; Assoc S Paul's Par Washington DC 1966-1973; Asst S Andr's Ch St Coll PA 1961-1966. Auth, "SocMary," *Stds & Commentaries Volumes I & II*; Columnist, "The Angl Dig," *The Angl Dig*; Ed, "St. Geo's Par," *The Dragon*. Angl Intl Liturg Consult 1984-2004; CBS; Gld of AllSouls; SocMary 1964; SSC 1967. rcornish@mindspring.com

MARTIN JR, Robert Carruthers (NwPa) 7935 Slate Ridge Blvd, Reynoldsburg OH 43068 **Died 1/11/2011** B Cleveland OH 1/16/1921 s Robert Carruthers Martin & Gertrude Estelle. BA Harv 1942; EDS 1950. D 6/6/1951 P 12/16/1951 Bp Henry W Hobson. c 5. Distinguished Flying Cross U.S.A.A.F. 1944. rcm392576@aol.com

MARTIN JR, Robert James (SwFla) 9727 Bay Colony Dr, Riverview FL 33578 B Philadelphia PA 6/2/1936 s Robert James Martin & Anna Jane. BS VMI

1960; MDiv UTS Richmond VA 1965; ThM PrTS 1976; DMin STUSo 1993. D 11/1/1994 Bp Rogers Sanders Harris P 5/24/1995 Bp Telesforo A Isaac. m 6/23/1963 Betsy Priscillia Payne. Asst to R S Ptr's Ch Plant City FL 2005-2008; Gr Ch Tampa FL 2004-2005; S Mary's Ch Dade City FL 2003-2004; S Ptr's Ch Plant City FL 2002-2003; R All Ang By The Sea Longboat Key FL 2000-2004; Asst to R St Johns Epis Ch Tampa FL 1995-2000. robert@martinfamilymail.com

MARTIN, Robin Pierce (Pa) 8114 Heacock Ln, Wyncote PA 19095 **R Ch Of The Adv Hatboro PA 1987-** B Mobile AL 3/5/1947 d Arvin Pierce & Barbara Hortense. BA U of Alabama 1978; MDiv Luth TS at Philadelphia 1984. D 6/28/1984 Bp Furman Stough P 4/25/1985 Bp Lyman Cunningham Ogilby. m 6/23/1967 John Gayle Martin c 2. S Mary's Epis Ch Ardmore PA 1984-1987. rectoradventhatboro@gmail.com

MARTIN, Sean (RG) 518 N Alameda Blvd, Las Cruces NM 88005 B Vancouver Canada 4/22/1969 s Calvin Martin & Judith. MDiv U Tor. D 6/19/2004 P 3/6/2005 Bp Terence Kelshaw. m 10/10/1998 Natalie Anne Martin c 1. P S Andr's Epis Ch Las Cruces NM 2005-2006. seanmartin@zianet.com

MARTIN, Terry L (NJ) 220 Fairview Ave, Hammonton NJ 08037 **R S Steph's Ch Waretown NJ 2010-** B San Luis Obispo CA 2/16/1954 s Gladwyn Paul Martin & Anna Laurie. AA U of Wisconsin 1984; BS U of Wisconsin 1987; MDiv Nash 1990. D 12/30/1989 P 7/25/1990 Bp William L Stevens. m 6/19/1976 Cheryl A Calletta c 1. Epis Ch Cntr New York NY 2008-2009; Epis Ch Cntr New York NY 2008-2009; Vic Ch Of The H Sprt Tuckerton NJ 2005-2008; Ch Of S Mary's By The Sea Point Pleasant Bch NJ 2003-2005; S Chris's Ch Spartanburg SC 2001-2002; S Jas Ch Paso Robles CA 1993-2000; Asst To Dn S Paul's Cathd Fond du Lac WI 1990-1993. terrymartin1@hotmail.com

MARTIN, William C (Tenn) 5633 Knob Rd, Nashville TN 37209 **Vic Gr Ch Sprg Hill TN 2007-** B Clarksville TN 9/13/1956 s Maurice Milton Martin & Julia Graden. BS U of Alabama 1978; MA U of Alabama 1979; MDiv Mid-Amer Bapt TS 1984; DMin Sthrn Bapt TS 1992; MLis Tevecca Nazarene U 2002; TESM 2006. D 6/10/2006 Bp Bertram Nelson Herlong P 12/16/2006 Bp William Evan Sanders. m 5/15/2004 Julia Lindner c 5. Mem, Cmsn on Chr Formation Dio Tennessee Nashville TN 2007-2009; P-in-c Ch Of The Apos Nashville TN 2006-2007. docmartin56@gmail.com

MARTIN, William Henderson (RG) PO Box 640161, El Paso TX 79904 B Sonora TX 5/7/1924 s John Allen Martin & Willie Henderson. BA McMurry U 1949; BA U of No Texas 1954; MA U of No Texas 1955; MDiv GTS 1965. D 5/7/1965 P 11/13/1965 Bp C J Kinsolving III. m 12/21/1946 Joan Herndon. St Pauls Ch 1983; H Sprt Epis Ch El Paso TX 1969-1982; Asst Cathd Of St Jn The Div New York NY 1967-1969; Vic S Mary's Ch Lovington NM 1965-1967. Auth, *The Organ Concerti of GF Handel*, 1955. OGS 1965. wmartin@elp.rr.com

MARTIN, William Jeffrey (Az) 7750 E Oakwood Cir, Tucson AZ 85750 B Washington DC 4/26/1932 s William Mckinley Martin & Cora. BA U of Nebraska 1957; MS U of Utah 1963; PhD U of Utah 1965. D 10/14/2006 Bp Kirk Stevan Smith. m 7/26/1987 Nadine Brown c 2. NEAC 1993-1995. wjmartin426@q.com

MARTIN, William Lamb (Be) 4 West End Avenue, Westboro MA 01581 **R S Brigid's Ch Nazareth PA 2011-** B South Kingstown RI 3/7/1948 s Frederick Martin & Emma Mae. BA U of Rhode Island 1970; MDiv Ya Berk 1973. D 6/16/1973 P 12/21/1973 Bp Frederick Hesley Belden. m 8/6/1977 Gloria Hull. R S Steph's Ch Westborough MA 2002-2010; R S Steph's Epis Ch Clifton Heights PA 1995-2002; R S Lk's Ch Hope NJ 1990-1995; R Cunningham Chap Par Millwood VA 1986-1989; R All SS Ch Chelmsford MA 1982-1986; R S Paul's Ch Windsor VT 1979-1982; Vic Trin Milton VT 1976-1979; Asst S Paul's Ch Plainfield CT 1975-1976; Cur S Thos Ch Greenville RI 1973-1975. frbilmrtn@aol.com

MARTIN, William Richardson (Va) 29 Willway Ave, Richmond VA 23226 B Danville VA 10/12/1930 s Jesse Shackleford Martin & Ila Ann. Oklahoma St U 1951; BA W&M 1953; MDiv VTS 1962. D 6/9/1962 Bp Robert Fisher Gibson Jr P 6/1/1963 Bp Samuel B Chilton. m 6/15/1985 Patti Barnes c 3. R Chr Epis Ch Saluda VA 1989-1994; Int S Paul's Ch Norfolk VA 1981-1982; R S Anne's Par Scottsville VA 1962-1965; R S Steph Esmont Scottsville VA 1962-1965. Auth, *For Redemp Press One (Cartoon Bk)*, Forw Mvmt, 1994; Auth, *Numerous arts*, Epis Pub Hse, Cincinnati. Sigma Pi Fraternity 1951-1953. bmartin456@aol.com

MARTIN, William Thomas (At) 3207 Pristine View, Williamsburg VA 23188 B Hannibal MO 12/3/1942 s Junius Jeffries Martin & Dorothy Whitman. BA Culver-Stockton Coll 1966; M.Div. Andover Newton TS 1970. D 12/27/1969 Bp George Leslie Cadigan P 7/15/1970 Bp Leland Stark. m 8/24/1968 Virginia Griffin c 2. Int S Clare's Epis Ch Blairsville GA 2008-2009; R Ch Of The Ascen Cartersville GA 1994-2007; R All Hallows Ch Wyncote PA 1980-1994; Asst Ch Of The Redeem Bryn Mawr PA 1975-1980; Vic S Lk and S Jn's Caruthersville MO 1972-1975; Cur S Thos Ch Dover NH 1970-1972. Assoc of H Cross Monstry 1973; Ecum Oblate Mt Sav Monstry 1983. frtommartin@me.com

MARTIN, William V (Okla) PO Box 1153, Pryor OK 74362 **Dio Oklahoma Oklahoma City OK 2009-; Vic S Mart's Ch Pryor OK 2009-** B Tulsa OK 7/20/1944 s William Mcfadden Martin & Lottie Louise. BA Pr 1966; MBA SMU 1972; MDiv SWTS 1996. D 6/15/1996 P 12/1/1996 Bp Larry Earl Maze. m 6/25/1966 Carole W Wilson c 2. Dio Colorado Denver CO 2006-2009; All SS' Epis Sch Vicksburg MS 2000-2006; S Marg's Epis Ch Little Rock AR 1998-2000; Trin Cathd Little Rock AR 1996-1998. wvmartin@aol.com

MARTIN-COFFEY, Nancee Lea (Fla) 2015 Glenarm Pl, Denver CO 80205 **Stndg Com Dio Florida Jacksonville FL 2010-; R S Geo's Epis Ch Jacksonville FL 2010-; BEC Dio Florida Jacksonville FL 2009-; Bd Trst The U So (Sewanee) Sewanee TN 2006-** B Jacksonville FL 5/24/1952 d Walter King Martin & Pansy Lee. BA U Of Florida 1974; MA U of No Florida 1976; MDiv TS 2000; DMin TS 2008. D 6/10/2000 P 1/13/2001 Bp William Jerry Winterrowd. m 6/12/1976 Michael Thomas Coffey c 4. BEC Dio Florida Jacksonville FL 2009-2010; P-in-c S Mich's Ch Gainesville FL 2009-2010; Campus Mnstry Coop, Chairperson Dio Florida Jacksonville FL 2008-2010; Chapl Ch Of The Incarn Gainesville FL 2007-2010; Global Recon Cmsn (MDGs), Chairperson Dio Florida Jacksonville FL 2007-2010; Assoc S Jn's Epis Ch Boulder CO 2002-2007; Cur S Andr's Ch Denver CO 2000-2002. Bk reviewer, "Sprtl Dir's Intl ," *Presence mag*, SDI, 2009; Contrib, "Lifting Wmn Voices: Prayers to Change the Wrld," *Bk*, Morehouse, 2009; Contrib, "Wmn at the Well," *Bk*, Judson Press, 2003. Amer Soc For Psychoprophal In Obst 1982-1987; Natl Cert Counselors 1996. Griffin Schlr Stuso 2000; Preaching in Excellence Prog Washington D.C. 1999. nmartincoffey@gmail.com

MARTINDALE, James Lawrence (NMich) 14 Stonegate Hts, Marquette MI 49855 **S Jn's Ch Negaunee MI 2006-** B Green Bay WI 4/14/1937 s James Lawrence Martindale & Mary V. BS Nthrn Michigan U 1967. D 9/13/2006 P 4/22/2007 Bp James Arthur Kelsey. m 11/30/1963 Kathleen D Jaakola c 3.

MARTINDALE, Richard James (At) 213 Orchard Road, Clarksville TN 37042 **R Trin Epis Ch Columbus GA 2005-** B South Bend IN 7/28/1957 s Donald Eugene Martindale & Shirley Mae. U of Nebraska; BA Jn Hopkins U 1979; MDiv VTS 1995. D 6/3/1995 P 12/1/1995 Bp Brice Sidney Sanders. m 10/22/1983 Jenny Lucas c 2. Vic S Jn's Mssn Hastings NE 1998-2005; Dn S Mk's Epis Pro-Cathd Hastings NE 1998-2005; Cur S Jn's Ch Decatur AL 1995-1998. fatherrich@charter.net

MARTINER, John William (Del) 1786 Tarpon Bay Dr S Apt 202, Naples FL 34119 **Adj Cler S Chris's Ch Chatham MA 2010-; Adj Cler S Monica's Epis Ch Naples FL 2009-** B New Haven CT 9/27/1940 s John James Martiner & Genevieve Louise. BS Cntrl Connecticut St U 1962; MDiv Ya Berk 1965; DMin Hartford Sem 1986. D 6/1/1965 Bp Walter H Gray P 4/1/1966 Bp John Henry Esquirol. m 6/19/1965 Elizabeth Ellen Bywater c 2. Assoc S Mary's Epis Ch Bonita Sprg FL 2009; Transition Consult Dio Delaware Wilmington DE 2002-2006; Bp Search Com Dio Delaware Wilmington DE 1998; Trst Ya Berk New Haven CT 1997-2003; R Chr Ch Greenville Wilmington DE 1995-2006; S Thos Epis Ch Rochester NY 1983-1995; Exec Coun Dio Connecticut Hartford CT 1978-1980; R Gr Epis Ch Trumbull CT 1973-1983; Exec Coun Dio Rhode Island Providence RI 1971-1974; Vic Emm Epis Ch Cumberland RI 1968-1972; Cur S Paul's Ch Wallingford CT 1965-1968; Dio Delaware Wilmington DE 1000. Auth, "The Chr Funeral," 1991; Auth, "Ltrgy-A Vehicle For Soc Mnstry," 1986. Fvc. Kappa Delta Pi 1961. tarpon1786@aol.com

MARTINEZ, Gregorio Bernardo (NwT) 907 Adams Ave, Odessa TX 79761 **Vic Iglesia Epis de Santa Maria Midland TX 2001-; Dio NW Texas Lubbock TX 1995-; Hisp Mnstry Dio NW Texas Lubbock TX 1994-** B Carazo Carazo NI 3/22/1946 s Simeon Jesus Martinez & Enriqueta Carmen. Loyola U 1970; Universidad Nacional De Nicara Managua Ni 1973; CTh Epis TS of The SW 1994. D 10/30/1994 P 5/20/1995 Bp Sam Byron Hulsey. m 9/6/1969 Lylliam Urbina Madriz c 2. Vic San Miguel Arcangel Odessa TX 1999; Hisp Mnstry S Jn's Epis Ch Odessa TX 1994-1995. laotzu@nwol.net

MARTINEZ, Heather Ann (Chi) 36w975 Highland Ave, Elgin IL 60123 **Cur S Hugh Of Lincoln Epis Ch Elgin IL 2006-** B Chicago IL 10/19/1975 d Jorge Martinez & Margaret. BA No Cntrl Coll 1997; MDiv VTS Alexandria VA 2006. D 6/3/2006 Bp William Dailey Persell.

MARTINEZ, José (Ct) 155 Wyllys St, Hartford CT 06106 **CMPC Cmncatn Mssn Pub Co. Dio Connecticut Hartford CT 2011-; Prog & Bdgt Com Dio Connecticut Hartford CT 2011-; Asst Ch Of The Gd Shpd Hartford CT 2003-** B Guatemala 11/5/1961 s Cupertina Martinez. BS Carlos Martinez Duran Coll 1988; MDiv GTS 2006; M.Div. GTS 2006; BS SUNY 2006. D 6/9/2007 P 12/15/2007 Bp Andrew Donnan Smith. m 1/30/2008 Herminia Pixcar Barrios c 3. APLM (Assoc Parishes for Liturg & Mnstry 2007. josemg@cox.net

MARTINEZ, Kim Renee (RG) Po Box 1434, Santa Cruz NM 87567 B Denver CO 9/28/1953 The Sch For Mnstry; BA San Francisco St U 1980; MA U of New Mex 1984. D 6/21/2003 P 10/2/2004 Bp Terence Kelshaw. m 5/31/1996 Joseph A Martinez.

MARTINEZ, Lucy Anne Roberts (At) 539 Wagner Way Ne, Kennesaw GA 30144 B Knoxville TN 9/21/1941 d John Harrison Roberts & Juanita Janice.

King Coll 1962; Indiana St U 1983; Chicago Deacons Sch 1991. D 12/7/1991 Bp Frank Tracy Griswold III. m 7/22/1961 Inocencio Martinez c 3. S Clem's Epis Ch Canton GA 1997-2004; D S Mary Epis Ch Crystal Lake IL 1991-1995. EFM Mentor; NAAD; SHN 1977. deakonmex@bellsouth.net

MARTINEZ AMENGUAL, Margarita (Hond) Diocese of Honduras, Imc Sap #215, Miami FL 33152 **Dio Honduras Miami FL 2006-** B Puerto Cortes 10/4/1948 d Arnaldo Martinez & Juana. Programa Dioc. De Ed. Teol.; Profa Educ. Media. Universidad Pedagogica. D 10/28/2005 Bp Lloyd Emmanuel Allen. c 2. maggie_martin31@yahoo.com

MARTINEZ AMENGUAL, Roberto Aaron (Hond) Residencial Girasoles, II Etapa No. 1807, Tegucigalpa, MDC 21105 Honduras **Dio Honduras Miami FL 2006-; Iglesia Epis San Pablo Apostol San Pedro Sula Cortes HN 2006-** B Puerto Cortes, Cortes 7/1/1954 s Arnaldo Martinez Mindieta & Juana. D 10/29/2005 Bp Lloyd Emmanuel Allen. m 2/11/1984 Bienvenida Rodriguez c 3. romamartin54@yahoo.com

MARTINEZ-JANTZ, Jeanie (Va) 6509 Sydenstricker Rd, Burke VA 22015 **Cmsn on Chr Formation Dio Virginia Richmond VA 2011-; Asst R S Andr's Ch Burke VA 2009-** B Shawnee OK 8/11/1956 d Gene Willis Jantz & Frances. BA No Carolina St U 1983; MDiv The Prot Epis TS 2007. D 4/29/2007 P 1/5/2008 Bp Leopold Frade. m 3/1/1986 Carlos Felipe Martinez c 2. SBL 2005. rev.jeanie@gmail.com

MARTINEZ-MORALES, Roberto (Los) 1011 S Verdugo Rd, Glendale CA 91205 **Iglesia Epis De La Magdalena Mssn Glendale CA 2006-** B Mexico Distrito Federal 5/27/1971 s Roberto Martinez Resendiz & Maria Elena. Cetis 1998; BD Seminario de San Andres 2000. D 12/17/1999 P 7/1/2000 Bp Sergio Carranza-Gomez. m 12/27/1996 Yanci Guerrero c 2. Dio Mex 1999-2006. padretacho@earthlink.net

MARTINEZ RAPALO, Arturo (Hond) IMS SAP Dept 215. PO BOX 523900, Miami FL 33152 Honduras B 11/5/1953 s Ramon Martinez Amaya & Serapia R. D 3/11/2007 Bp Lloyd Emmanuel Allen. m 3/11/1977 Miranda Trinidad Azucena Fernandez c 5. arturoepiscopal@hotmail.com

MARTINEZ-RAPALO, Ramon (Hond) No address on file. **Dio Honduras Miami FL 1998-** B 12/8/1947 m 4/5/1998 Miriam Suyapa-Ochoa c 3.

MARTINEZ TORO, Jorge De Jesus (Colom) Carrera 80 #53a-78, Medellin, Antioquia Colombia **Iglesia Epis En Colombia 1995-** B 12/21/1955 s Jorge Emilio & Lucia. BA Sem S Jose 1969; BA Inst S Carlos 1971. P 1/1/1996 Bp Bernardo Merino-Botero. m 11/27/1999 Esmeralda Cardona.

MARTIN FUMERO, Emilio (DR) Mansana C-1 Sagana Perpida, Santo Domingo Dominican Republic **Dio The Dominican Republic (Iglesia Epis Dominicana) Santo Domingo DO 2011-** B Cuba 12/17/1951 s Juan E Martin-Farrey & Ana. Trans from Iglesia Episcopal de Cuba 8/1/2011 Bp Julio Cesar Holguin-Khoury. m 12/12/2005 Maria Gonzalez Paso c 3. emiliomartinf@gmail.com

MARTINHAUK, Jeff (Los) Chaplain Services/Dell Childrens Hospital, 4900 Mueller Blvd, Austin TX 78723 B Bethesda MD 7/15/1970 s Donald Benjamin Hauk & Judy Kay. BBA SMU 1992; MDiv Epis TS Of The SW 2009. D 3/12/2011 Bp Diane M Jardine Bruce. c 2. Integrity USA 2006. jmartinhauk@yahoo.com

MARTINICHIO, John Robert (CNY) 89 Fairview Ave, Binghamton NY 13904 **S Paul's Ch Endicott NY 2011-; P-in-c S Paul's Ch Endicott NY 2011-; Dioc Bd Vice Chair Dio Cntrl New York Syracuse NY 2010-; COM Chair Dio Cntrl New York Syracuse NY 2009-; Dn of the Binghamton Distict Dio Cntrl New York Syracuse NY 2007-** B Binghamton NY 11/10/1958 s John Charles Martinichio & Joanne Mary. AA SUNY 1979; BA Wadhams Hall Sem Coll 1981; BA Wadhams Hall Sem Coll 1981; MDiv Chr The King Sem 1985; M. Div. Chr the King Sem 1985; AAS Simmons Sch of Mortuary Sci 1993; AAS Simmons Sch of Mortuary Sci 1993. Rec from Roman Catholic 10/19/2002 as Priest Bp Gladstone Bailey Adams III. m 9/4/1993 Barbara Anne Petrella c 2. Dioc Bd Vice Chair Dio Cntrl New York Syracuse NY 2010-2011; Coordntr Safe Ch Mnstry Dio Cntrl New York Syracuse NY 2005-2011; Co-Chair Pstr Response Team Dio Cntrl New York Syracuse NY 2004-2011; P-in-c Chr Ch Binghamton NY 2002-2011. johnrobert58@aol.com

MARTINO, Rose Marie (LI) 612 Forest Ave, Massapequa NY 11758 **The Ch Of The Ascen Rockville Cntr NY 2008-; D Cathd Of The Incarn Garden City NY 2000-** B New York NY 7/24/1941 d Frederick Adam Fery & Marie. BS SUNY 1994; Mercer TS 1998. D 6/10/1998 Bp Orris George Walker Jr. c 3. Asst Chr Ch Oyster Bay NY 1998-2000. Auth, "D In The Stock Mrkt Wrld," *Wmn Uncommon Prayers*, Morehouse Pub, 2000; Auth, "The Space Between (Poem)," *Natl Libr Of Poetry*, 1994. NAAD 1994. rmm022@optonline.net

MARTIN-RHODES, Lilla Rebecca (LI) 1405 Bushwick Ave, Brooklyn NY 11207 B JM 9/27/1939 d Rudolphus Harker & Rosetta. BA CUNY 1978; MA CUNY 1978; Mercer TS 1994. D 6/15/1994 Bp Orris George Walker Jr. m 9/28/1985 Eugene Rhodes c 3.

✠ **MARTINS, Rt Rev Daniel H** (Spr) 821 S 2nd St, Springfield IL 62704 **Bp of Springfield Dio Springfield Springfield IL 2011-** B Rio de Janeiro BR 9/7/1951 s Elson Solano Martins & Elizabeth. BA Westmont Coll 1973; MA U CA 1975; MDiv Nash 1989. D 6/18/1989 Bp Robert Louis Ladehoff P 12/20/1989 Bp James Barrow Brown Con 3/19/2011 for Spr. m 8/27/1972 Brenda Fay Ormsbee c 3. Exm Chapl Dio Nthrn Indiana So Bend IN 2008-2011; R S Anne's Epis Ch Warsaw IN 2007-2011; Exm Chapl Epis Dio San Joaquin Modesto CA 1999-2007; R S Jn's Epis Ch Stockton CA 1994-2007; Secy of Conv Epis Dio San Joaquin Modesto CA 1994-1998; Vic S Marg's Epis Ch Baton Rouge LA 1991-1994; Cur S Lk's Ch Baton Rouge LA 1989-1991. DD Nash 2011. dmartins1951@gmail.com

MARTZ, Jeannie (Los) 3107 Pepperwood Ct, Fullerton CA 92835 **R Trin Epis Ch Orange CA 2007-** B Evanston IL 12/31/1950 d John Alexander McLaren & Valerie Jean. BA McGill U 1972; MDiv Ya Berk 1990. D 6/9/1990 P 3/16/1991 Bp James Russell Moodey. c 2. Dio SE Florida Miami FL 2007; Assoc R S Mk's Ch Palm Bch Gardens FL 1995-2007; Assoc R S Mart's Ch Chagrin Falls OH 1990-1995. jeannie@trinityorange.org

MARTZ, Stephen (Chi) 947 Oxford Rd, Glen Ellyn IL 60137 **Ch Of Our Sav Elmhurst IL 2011-** B Washington DC 9/24/1951 s Buford Bryant Martz & Naomi Lois. BA U of Maryland 1976; MDiv Cath Theol U 1988; DMin Chicago TS 1995; Dplma CG Jung Inst 2007. D 6/18/1994 P 12/17/1994 Bp Frank Tracy Griswold III. m 6/17/1989 Carla Amato c 2. Vic S Nich w the H Innoc Ch Elk Grove Vill IL 1995-2011; S Hilary's Ch Prospect Hts IL 1995. "Remembering Fr. Paul Murray," *The Washington Blade*, 2009; "In Your Dreams," *Luth Wmn Today*, 2008. Serv to Ch Cmnty Assn of Chicago Priests 1986. 1bread1body@sbcglobal.net

MARX, Jeffery Wayne (WTenn) 484 Riding Brook Way, Collierville TN 38017 **R S Andr's Epis Ch Collierville TN 2001-** B Chicago IL 4/29/1956 s Francis Ronald Marx & Barbara Jean. BA S Meinrad Coll 1977; MA Cath U of Louvain 1983; MA Cath U of Louvain 1984; MS U of Tennessee 1993. Rec from Roman Catholic 3/1/1999 Bp James Malone Coleman. m 7/9/1993 Ann D Dooley c 3. Cn S Mary's Cathd Memphis TN 1999-2001. Auth, "Fundamentalism, A Cath Response," *Verbum*, 1983. Rotary 2001. PTA Lifetime Achievement Shelby Cnty Sch System 2011; Serv To Yth Natl Conf Of Christians & Jews 1990. jeff@standrewscollierville.org

MASADA, Jennifer Ann (Ia) 912 20th Ave, Coralville IA 52241 **P New Song Epis Ch Coralville IA 2010-** B Kimball NE 5/24/1965 d Teruo Masada & Rita Fern Petersen. BM U of Nebraska Omaha 1988; PhD U of Iowa 1993. D 7/26/2009 Bp Alan Scarfe. m 4/23/1994 Kirk Corey c 2. jennifer-masada@uiowa.edu

MASILLEM, Benedict Baguyos (Ak) 1265 Norman St Unit 12, Anchorage AK 99504 **S Christophers Ch Anchorage AK 2008-; D S Mary's Ch Anchorage AK 2002-** B San Fernando La Union PH 2/9/1970 s Jacinto Kis-Ing Masillem & Lorenza Baguyos. BTh St. Andr's TS Quezon City Ph 1992. Trans from Episcopal Church in the Philippines 9/20/1999 Bp Mark Lawrence Mac Donald. Dio Alaska Fairbanks AK 2001-2004; Filipino Mnstry Mssnr S Christophers Ch Anchorage AK 2001-2002. benz5m@gmail.com

MASON, Alan Newell (Ct) 211 Senexet Rd, Woodstock CT 06281 B Pawtucket RI 3/8/1938 s Lyman R Mason & Rubina. BS U of Rhode Island 1960; MDiv Ya Berk 1963; MPA U Cinc 1970. D 6/22/1963 P 5/1/1964 Bp John S Higgins. m 1/29/2000 Susan M Mason c 2. S Phil's Epis Ch Putnam CT 1991-2004; Inner City Mssy Cathd Of S Jn Providence RI 1963-1968. revalanmason@yahoo.com

MASON, Alice Joan Magnuson (WNC) 106 Lanterns Wick Trl, Sylva NC 28779 **D S Dav's Ch Cullowhee NC 1993-** B Grand Rapids MI 8/5/1934 d Albert E Mason & Edna E. U So; Wayne; AA Grand Rapids Cmnty Coll 1954. D 4/13/1985 Bp William Gillette Weinhauer. c 4. D S Cyp's Ch Franklin NC 1985-1991.

MASON, Bruce (Ct) PO Box 443, Litchfield CT 06759 B Brockton MA 1/26/1936 s Harry Mason & Mildred Josephine. BS Springfield Coll Springfield MA 1958; MSW U of Connecticut 1969; Cert Sthrn Connecticut St U 1981. D 12/1/1990 Bp Arthur Edward Walmsley. m 2/5/1966 Sandra Burrows c 3. D Trin Ch Torrington CT 1995-2008; D S Mich's Ch Litchfield CT 1990-1995. bruce_mason@sbcglobal.net

MASON, Bruce Edmund (Alb) PO Box 211, Lake Luzerne NY 12846 B Evanston IL 6/17/1971 s David Edmund Mason & Margaret Krasberg. BA Ham Clinton NY 1993; MA GW Washington DC 1997; BTh Wycliffe Hall of Oxf 2007. D 6/9/2007 P 12/22/2007 Bp William Howard Love. m 12/23/1995 Shay Sizer c 2. R S Mary's Ch Lake Luzerne NY 2007-2011; Asst Truro Epis Ch Fairfax VA 1997-2000. revbmason@stmarysluzerne.org

MASON JR, Charles Thurston (Ind) 224 N Alden Rd, Muncie IN 47304 B Springfield OH 2/8/1939 s Charles Thurston Mason & Josephine Martin. BA Ob 1962; STB PDS 1966. D 6/11/1966 Bp Robert Lionne DeWitt P 2/4/1967 Bp George Alfred Taylor. m 6/6/1970 Lynne Short c 2. R Gr Ch Muncie IN 1984-2002; R S Paul's Ch Lock Haven PA 1976-1984; S Alb's Epis Ch Salisbury MD 1970-1976. ctm0457@aol.com

MASON, Christopher Perry (SwVa) 128 Laurel Mountain Estates Drive, Todd NC 28684 **Exec Bd Mem Dio SW Virginia Roanoke VA 2008-; R Chr Epis Ch Marion VA 2007-** B Savannah GA 11/5/1949 s Cecil Herbert Mason & Lorraine. BA U So 1971; MDiv STUSo 1974; MA E Carolina U 1992; EdD

California Coast U 2006. D 6/7/1974 Bp (George) Paul Reeves P 1/1/1975 Bp Robert C Rusack. m 4/27/1993 Jeanette C Cawl c 3. Vic St Patricks Ch Pooler GA 2002-2005; R S Steph's Ch Goldsboro NC 1986-1992; Assoc S Jas Par Wilmington NC 1982-1986; Chapl Chr Sch Arden NC 1977-1982; Vic S Phil's Ch Hinesville Hinesville GA 1975-1977; Cur All SS-By-The-Sea Par Santa Barbara CA 1974-1975. "Crossing Into Manhood: A Men's Stds Curric," Cambria Press: Youngstown, NY, 2007. cpmason1105@skybest.com

MASON, David Raymond (O) 2277 N Saint James Pkwy, Cleveland Heights OH 44106 B Hagerstown MD 11/6/1936 s Edwin L'Huillier Mason & Camilla Schindel. BA W Virginia U 1959; STB GTS 1962; MA U Chi 1969; PhD U Chi 1973. D 6/13/1962 P 12/19/1962 Bp Wilburn Camrock Campbell. m 6/29/1963 Margaret Curtis. Assoc S Paul's Epis Ch Cleveland Heights OH 1978-2008; Vic All SS Ch Charleston WV 1962-1966. Auth, "A Christology Of Universal Redemptive Love," *Dialog*, 2002; Auth, "Time & Providence," 1982; Auth, "Can God Be Both Perfect & Free?," *Rel Stds*, 1982; Auth, "Can We Speculate On How God Acts ,," *Journ Of Rel*, 1977. AAR 1971; Metaphysical Soc Of Amer 1977; Soc For The Study Of Process Philosophies 1972. Grail Fac Fell JCU 1979. dmason@jcu.edu

MASON, Jack M (Eas) 114 S Harrison St, Easton MD 21601 B Wilmington NC 1/27/1943 s Jack Malleroyal Mason & Lilly Belle. BS E Carolina U 1965; Med Towson U 1972. D 5/2/2004 P 10/8/2011 Bp James Joseph Shand. m 8/7/1965 Frances G H Harriss c 2. maharra@goeaston.net

MASON, Joel Clark (NY) 39 Morton Pl, Chappaqua NY 10514 **R Ch Of S Mary The Vrgn Chappaqua NY 1996-** B Chattanooga TN 1/11/1955 s Joel Casto Mason & Sarah Elizabeth. Iliff TS 1978; MDiv Duke 1981; STUSo 1984; DMin Drew U 2005. D 7/1/1984 Bp William F Gates Jr P 3/3/1985 Bp William Evan Sanders. m 5/14/1981 Mary Jo Provenza c 1. R Chr Epis Ch Oil City PA 1990-1996; S Mk's Ch Dalton GA 1987-1990; Dio E Tennessee Knoxville TN 1985-1987; P-in-c S Thos Ch Elizabethton TN 1985-1987; S Jn's Epis Cathd Knoxville TN 1984-1985. Auth, "Virtual Sprtl Formation: A Journey Without Steps," VDM Verlag, 2008. Graduation w dist Drew U 2005; Paul Harris Fell Rotary 2001. joelmason@mac.com

MASON, John Skain (HB) Rr 2 Box 542b, Inwood WV 25428 B Springfield OH 2/9/1936 s Charles Thurston Mason & Josephine Martin. BA DePauw U 1958; STB PDS 1963. D 6/8/1963 Bp Joseph Gillespie Armstrong P 5/1/1964 Bp John Brooke Mosley. c 3. S Andr The Fisherman Epis Mayo MD 1988-1989; Ch Of The Gd Shpd Greer SC 1987-1988; S Patricks Ch Falls Ch VA 1985; S Ptr's Epis Ch Arlington VA 1978; Chr Ch Alexandria VA 1976-1977; Vic S Matt's Epis Ch Sterling VA 1974-1976; S Paul's Epis Ch Piney Waldorf MD 1966-1968; Assoc R S Alb's Epis Ch McCook NE 1965-1966; Cur Calv Epis Ch Hillcrest Wilmington DE 1963-1965. skainmason@verizon.net

MASON, Judith Ann (Chi) 5445 N Sheridan Rd Apt 2404, Chicago IL 60640 B Auburn NY 9/20/1949 d Edward Mason & Evelyn. BA DePaul U 1999. D 2/2/2003 Bp William Dailey Persell.

MASON, Keith Wentworth (WMass) 130 Highland Ave, Leominster MA 01453 B Tangier NS Canada 5/28/1927 s James Edgar Mason & Myrtle Victoria. LTh U of King's Coll Halifax N.S. Can 1951; VTS 1980. Trans from Anglican Church of Canada 9/1/1966 Bp Robert McConnell Hatch. m 5/1/1953 Maureen Drope c 5. R S Mk's Ch Leominster MA 1966-1994; Dio Wstrn Massachusetts Springfield MA 1966-1993; LocTen S Andr's Ch Longmeadow MA 1965-1966. "Search for Tomorrow," Axiom Press, 2009.

MASON, Lawrence Walker (SVa) 2355 Brookwood Rd, Richmond VA 23235 B Ashland VA 2/9/1933 s Albert Journey Mason & Blanche West. BA U Rich 1957; VTS 1960. D 6/28/1960 P 6/25/1961 Bp Frederick D Goodwin. R Manakin Epis Ch Midlothian VA 1967-1998; R S Lk's Ch Powhatan VA 1967-1998; R Cople Par Hague VA 1960-1964.

MASON, Lisa P (WTex) 1300 Wiltshire Ave, San Antonio TX 78209 **Asst R S Dav's Epis Ch San Antonio TX 2009-** B Corpus Christi TX 8/16/1964 d John Jay Pichinson & Eloise Jackson. BA SMU 1984; MDiv Epis TS Of The SW 2009. D 5/27/2009 Bp Gary Richard Lillibridge P 12/3/2009 Bp David Mitchell Reed. m 12/21/1984 Kirk B Mason c 2. masonlisap@sbcglobal.net

MASON, Marilyn Joyce Smith (Los) PO Box 40594, Downey CA 90239 B Bristol RI 3/31/1935 d Lowell Irving Smith & Mary Shirley. BEd Rhode Island Coll 1956; MA CDSP 1958; MA U of Nevada at Las Vegas 1972. D 6/8/1996 P 1/1/1997 Bp Chester Lovelle Talton. c 2. S Ptr's Par Rialto CA 2005-2007; S Lk's Mssn Fontana CA 1999-2007; S Clare Of Assisi Rancho Cucamonga CA 1999-2000. revnrev2@juno.com

MASON, Phil C (Colo) 280 Peregrine Dr, San Marcos TX 78666 B Fort Worth TX 9/10/1940 s Sidney Caldwell Mason & Katherine. MDiv Epis TS of the SW 1996. D 6/7/1997 P 12/1/1997 Bp William Jerry Winterrowd. m 9/22/1989 Susan Emory c 3. S Laurence's Epis Mssn Conifer CO 2003-2009; R S Matt's Parker CO 1999-2002; Cur S Matt's Parker CO 1997-1998. phil@philandsusan.net

MASON, Samuel Albert (WMo) 409 W. 144th st., Independence MO 64050 **Stndg Committe Dio W Missouri Kansas City MO 2010-; R Trin Ch Independence MO 2006-; Coll Mnstry (Chair) Dio W Missouri Kansas City MO 2005-** B Emporia KS 7/25/1967 s Gary Mack Mason & Sarah Virginia. BD U of Kansas 1995; MDiv Epis TS of The SW 2001. D 3/17/2001 P 9/30/2001 Bp William Edward Smalley. m 11/10/2005 Susan Mason c 1. Bp Transitional Com Dio W Missouri Kansas City MO 2010-2011; Coll Mnstry (Chair) Dio W Missouri Kansas City MO 2005-2011; Childrens Educ committe Dio Kansas Topeka KS 2004-2005; P-in-c S Paul's Ch Kansas City KS 2003-2005; P Ch Of The Gd Shpd Kansas City MO 2002-2003; Cur Gd Shpd Epis Ch Wichita KS 2001-2002. thesam99@hotmail.com

MASON OJN, Samuel Alison (NC) 1182 Fearrington Post, Pittsboro NC 27312 B Mobile AL 8/19/1944 s Philip Minor Mason & Emma Alison. BA U So 1966; MDiv VTS 1973; DMin Drew U 1999. D 6/6/1973 P 12/1/1973 Bp Furman Stough. m 6/5/1978 Joyce Granade c 2. COM Dio No Carolina Raleigh NC 1991-1994; R S Steph's Ch Durham NC 1990-2003; R S Jn's Epis Ch Mobile AL 1983-1990; R S Mths Epis Ch Tuscaloosa AL 1977-1983; R S Lk's Ch Scottsboro AL 1973-1977. Oblate of Ord of Julian of Norwich 2005. wcolwor@aol.com

MASON, Victoria Anne (Tex) St David's Church, 304 E 7th St, Austin TX 78701 **Cn for Multicultural Mnstrs Dio Texas Houston TX 2009-** B Seattle WA 9/19/1948 d Gerald William Mason & Barbara Lou. BA The U of Texas at Austin 1970; MS Universtiy of Wisconsin Stout Menomenie 1974; Cert Iona Sch for Mnstry Dio of Texas 2007. D 2/9/2007 Bp Don Adger Wimberly. m 2/14/1976 Roy D Larsen c 2. D S Dav's Ch Austin TX 2007-2009. NAAD 2005. victoria.m@stdave.org

MASQUELETTE, Elizabeth Simmons (Tex) 2204 Welch St, Houston TX 77019 B Austin TX 12/12/1927 d David Andrew Simmoins & Elizabeth Feild. Hollins U 1945; BA U of Texas 1948; MA U of St. Thos 1976; MDiv Epis TS of The SW 1978. D 12/5/1978 P 6/8/1979 Bp J Milton Richardson. m 3/17/1948 Phillip Abbott Masquelette. Assoc S Fran Ch Houston TX 1996-1998; Chr The King Ch Houston TX 1982-1996; Asst Ch Of The Epiph Houston TX 1978-1981. Auth, "Adv Recollections," Speedy, 2000; Auth, "Adventures of BoffinBear: A Chld's Story for Adults," Speedy, 1999; Auth, "Back to the Beginning," *Wmn Journ*, Brigid's Place, 1999. Ord of S Helena.

MASSENBURG, Barbara Jean (Ak) P.O. Box 841, 7962 North Tongass Highway, Ward Cove AK 99928 **Asst P S Jn's Ch Ketchikan AK 2005-** B Akron OH 1/23/1936 d Verne E Winans & Olive K. BA Hiram Coll 1958; Wstrn Reserve U 1959. D 10/15/2000 Bp Frederick Warren Putnam P 11/30/2005 Bp Mark William McDonald. c 1. D S Jn's Ch Ketchikan AK 2000-2002. bjmass@aptalaska.net

MASSENBURG, Raymond Douglas (Chi) 4945 S Dorchester Ave, Chicago IL 60615 **Asst R Ch Of S Paul And The Redeem Chicago IL 2010-** B Chicago, IL 5/20/1967 s Willie Massenburg & Sheila. MBA Pur 1992; PhD U IL 2006; MDiv SWTS 2010. D 6/5/2010 P 12/19/2010 Bp Jeffrey Dean Lee. m 7/3/2002 Yvonne Massenburg c 2. rrmasse234@gmail.com

MASSEY, Hoyt B (SwFla) Po Box 2161, Franklin NC 28744 B Saint Petersberg FL 8/6/1927 s Hoyt Virgil Massey & Mary Ione. BS Florida St U 1952; LTh STUSo 1965. D 6/24/1965 P 12/1/1965 Bp Henry I Louttit. m 9/15/1951 Glennie Buntyn. Int S Paul's Chap Magnolia Sprg AL 1995-2000; Int S Agnes Epis Ch Franklin NC 1993-1994; Archd Dio SW Florida Sarasota FL 1979-1990; P-in-c All Ang By The Sea Longboat Key FL 1979-1980; R St Johns Epis Ch Tampa FL 1968-1978; Vic S Chris's Ch Orlando FL 1967-1968; Cur S Mich's Ch Orlando FL 1965-1967. mbgmbg@dnet.net

MASSEY, Nigel John (NY) 111 E 60th St Penthouse, New York NY 10022 **R French Ch Of S Esprit New York NY 1994-** B 8/8/1960 s John Massey & Margaret Ann. BA U Of Birmingham Gb 1981; MA Oxf 1987; CertTheol Oxf 1987; DipIsl Selly Oak Coll Birmingham Gb 1990. Trans from Church Of England 5/14/1996 Bp Walter Decoster Dennis Jr. m John Blair Wyker. Hugenot Soc Of Amer 1994; S Georges Soc 1996. nijabe@msn.com

MASSIE JR, James S (WNY) Po Box 822, Olcott NY 14126 B Evanston IL 6/20/1942 s James S Massie & Hope Keck. AA U MN 1963; BA Minnesota St U Mankato 1965; MDiv SWTS 1968. D 6/24/1968 P 3/14/1969 Bp Hamilton Hyde Kellogg. m 9/15/1964 Kathleen May Salisbury c 2. Int The Epis Ch Of The Gd Shpd Buffalo NY 2008-2009; R Gr Ch Lockport NY 1990-1998; R S Steph's Ch Grand Island NE 1983-1990; R Ch Of The Cov Jct City KS 1974-1983; Vic Ch of SS Jn & Geo Jct City KS 1974-1983; Asst S Lk's Ch Minneapolis MN 1970-1974; Cur S Paul's Epis Ch Duluth MN 1968-1970. jkmassie@roadrunner.com

MASSIE IV, Robert Kinloch (Mass) 140 Sycamore St, Somerville MA 02145 **Assoc S Jas' Epis Ch Cambridge MA 1998-** B New York NY 8/17/1956 s Robert K Massie & Suzanne. BA Pr 1978; MDiv Ya Berk 1982; DBA Harv 1989. D 6/2/1982 P 4/20/1983 Bp Paul Moore Jr. m 11/20/1982 Anne E Tate c 1. P-in-c Chr Ch Somerville MA 1986-1988; P-in-c Chr Ch Cambridge Cambridge MA 1985-1988; Asst & Chapl Gr Epis Ch New York NY 1982-1984. Auth, "A Song in the Night," *A Memoir of Resilience*, Doubleday, 2012; Auth, "Loosing Bonds: US & So Afr In Apartheid Years," Doubleday, 1998; Auth, "From Prophets To Profits," *Manhattan Inc*, 1985; Co-Ed, "The Big Bus Rdr," Pilgrim Press, 1980; Auth, "Setting Their Lives In Motion," *Ny Times Sunday mag*, 1979; Auth, "The Constant Shadow". Joan Bavaria Awd Ceres 2009;

M

Damyanova Awd Tufts U 2008; Sr Fulbright Awd Untd States Govt 1993; Henry Luve Ethics Fllshp Harv Cambridge MA 1987. massie@ceres.org

MASSON, Thomas Howard Forsythe (Mich) 15061 Ford Rd Apt 319, Dearborn MI 48126 B Windsor ON CA 7/31/1926 s George Yule Masson & Alice Eastwick. Hur 1950; BA Wayne 1952; MA Wayne 1969. Trans from Anglican Church of Canada 9/1/1956. m 7/8/1950 Christine Elizabeth Brown. Int S Tim's Ch Detroit MI 1970-1974; Vic S Jn's Epis Ch Tulare CA 1963-1964; Vic S Geo's Epis Ch Honolulu HI 1960-1962; Vic H Innoc' Epis Ch Lahaina HI 1959-1960; Asst Cur Chr Ch Grosse Pointe Grosse Pointe Farms MI 1956-1959. Ed, *Universitas*. gtmasson@earthlink.com

MASTER II, George O (Pa) 6838 Woodland Avenue, Philadelphia PA 19142 **Dioc Coun Mem Dio Pennsylvania Philadelphia PA 2010-; Int Vic S Dismas Epis Mssn At Graterford Philadelphia PA 2009-; Pstr S Jas (Old Swedes) Ch of Kingsessing Philadelphia PA 2009-** B Lake Placid NY 10/12/1947 s Henry Buck Master & Florence Buzby. Colorado Sch of Mines 1966; BS U of Massachusetts 1977; MDiv Ya Berk 1987. D 10/24/1987 Bp Walter Decoster Dennis Jr P 4/23/1988 Bp Vincent King Pettit. m 10/15/2011 Doris Cain. Pstr S Aug's Philadelphia PA 2003-2009; Pstr S Aug's Philadelphia PA 2000-2003; Int S Paul's Ch Chester PA 1998-2000; Asst Vic S Dismas Epis Mssn At Graterford Philadelphia PA 1995-2009; P-in-c S Mart's Epis Ch Upper Chichester PA 1995-1998; Int Vic S Dismas Epis Mssn At Graterford Philadelphia PA 1994-1995; Int Vic S Mary's Epis Ch Philadelphia PA 1994-1995; S Mk's Ch Honey Brook PA 1994; Asst Min The Epis Ch Of The Adv Kennett Sq PA 1991-1994; Cur S Mary's Ch Haddon Heights NJ 1987-1991. revgm@me.com

MASTERMAN, Brenda Patricia (SeFla) 3259 Perimeter Dr, Lake Worth FL 33467 B Huntington WV 3/17/1946 BA Palm Bch Atlantic U. D 9/1/2001 Bp Leopold Frade. c 2.

MASTERMAN, Frederick James (SeFla) 15170 N Rugged Lark Dr, Tucson AZ 85739 B Niagara Falls NY 12/25/1937 s Frederick James Masterman & Marion Margaret. BA SUNY 1959; STB GTS 1963. D 6/15/1963 P 5/23/1964 Bp Lauriston L Scaife. m 12/23/2004 Becky Ann Deminski c 2. Assoc S Greg's Ch Boca Raton FL 2001-2005; Cn Dio SE Florida Miami FL 1988-2001; R Ch Of The Ascen Miami FL 1975-1988; R S Steph's Ch Niagara Falls NY 1971-1975; Vic S Andr's Ch Newfane Burt NY 1967-1971; Vic S Jn's Ch Wilson NY 1967-1971; Cur S Mths Epis Ch E Aurora NY 1963-1966. Auth, "arts," *Ch Hist mag*. masterman1225@yahoo.com

MASTERMAN, Patricia Dinan (NwT) 2700 W 16th Ave Apt 272, Amarillo TX 79102 B Amarillo TX 11/4/1927 d Wilfrid Irving Dinan & Frances Catherine. BA Colorado Coll 1949. D 10/25/1985 Bp Sam Byron Hulsey. c 2. Archd S Andr's Epis Ch Amarillo TX 1993-1999; Stff All SS' Epis Ch Ft Worth TX 1988-1993; Ed Dio NW Texas Lubbock TX 1972-1988. pmdeacon@swbell.net

MASTERS, Ralph Leeper (Tex) 459 Medina Dr, Highland Village TX 75077 **Asst Ch Of The Annunc Lewisville TX 2003-** B Saint Joseph MO 1/26/1929 s Ralph Lynn Masters & Juanita. BS U of Texas 1955; STM Epis TS of The SW 1958. D 6/1/1958 Bp James Parker Clements P 6/1/1959 Bp John E Hines. P-in-c S Mart's Epis Ch Copperas Cove TX 1992-2001; R S Mary's Epis Ch Inc Lampasas TX 1988-1992; R S Mich And All Ang Lake Chas LA 1966-1987; Vic Chr Ch Matagorda TX 1958-1961; Vic S Jn's Epis Ch Palacios TX 1958-1961. mastersp@verizon.net

MASTERSON, Elizabeth Rust (Del) 229 Cheltenham Rd, Newark DE 19711 **R S Nich' Epis Ch Newark DE 2006-** B Milford DE 9/30/1946 d Manford Charles Rust & Virginia Anderson. BA Randolph-Macon Wmn's Coll 1968; MA NWU 1970; MA U of Delaware 1983; MDiv GTS 2006. D 6/8/2006 P 12/12/2006 Bp Wayne Parker Wright. m 6/23/1984 Fred Masterson c 2. Gd Shpd Epis Ch Newark DE 2009-2010. Assoc - Epis Carmel of St. Teresa 2008; Assoc - OSH 1984. ermasterson@gmail.com

MATARAZZO, Laura Rice (Nwk) 10 Doe Hollow Lane, Belvidere NJ 07823 **S Lk's Ch Hope NJ 2011-; S Mary's Ch Belvidere NJ 2011-** B Cleveland OH 5/17/1951 d Norman Stanley Rice & Betty Marie. BA U So 1973; MDiv Drew U 2001. D 4/13/2002 Bp John Palmer Croneberger P 10/19/2002 Bp Rufus T Brome. m 6/1/1973 Robert Joseph Matarazzo c 4. Calv Epis Ch Summit NJ 2002-2008. revlrm@gmail.com

MATHAUER, Margaret Ann (Vt) 7 Holy Cross Rd, Colchester VT 05446 **D All SS' Epis Ch S Burlington VT 1991-** B Cincinnati OH 1/29/1943 d Paul George Mathauer & Otillia Rose. BS Bowling Green St U 1965; Med Bowling Green St U 1967; Cert U of Vermont 1973; Med Trin 1979. D 7/30/1991 Bp Daniel Lee Swenson. c 4.

MATHENY, Clint Michael (CFla) 130 N Magnolia Ave, Orlando FL 32801 B Memphis TN 1/31/1950 s Clint William & Hermina Mcpherson. D 12/9/2006 Bp John Wadsworth Howe. m 5/26/1984 Linda Napier c 1. mathenym@bellsouth.net

MATHER, H(oward) Lester (EpisSanJ) 1120 30th Street, Port Townsend WA 98368 **Died 5/12/2010** B Langhorne PA 11/10/1911 s Howard Mitchell Mather & Augusta Jacoby. BA Cumberland U 1937; ThB PDS 1942; MDiv PDS 1971. D 6/7/1941 P 6/1/1942 Bp Francis E Taitt. c 1.

MATHER, Jean (Pa) 59 W Tulpehocken St, Philadelphia PA 19144 **Bd Mem, Epis Cmnty Serv Dio Pennsylvania Philadelphia PA 2010-; Hstgr Dio Pennsylvania Philadelphia PA 2010-; R Chr Ch And S Mich's Philadelphia PA 1999-** B Evergreen Park IL 9/23/1946 d James Mather & Vanda. BA U Chi 1969; MPhil Ya 1972; PhD Ya 1975; MDiv SWTS 1995. D 6/17/1995 P 12/16/1995 Bp Frank Tracy Griswold III. Asst Cathd Of S Jas Chicago IL 1998-1999; Int Assoc Ch Of S Paul And The Redeem Chicago IL 1995-1998. Lloyd Mentzer Ch Hist Awd SWTS Evanston IL 1995; Mahlen Norris Gilbert Acad Awd SWTS Evanston IL 1995; Engl Bible Acad Awd Seabury-Wstrn Theol Semianry Evanston IL 1994; H N Moss Acad Awd SWTS Evanston IL 1994; M.Phil "w dist" Ya 1972; B.A. "Gnrl hon" U Chi 1969. jmatherphila@juno.com

MATHER, John L. (Az) PO Box 16252, Phoenix AZ 85011 **D Trin Cathd Phoenix AZ 2004-** B Philadelpha PA 10/17/1952 s James Increase Mather & Catherine Elizabeth. Masters Certtificate Rutgers-The St U; BS Tem. D 10/9/2004 Bp Robert Reed Shahan. c 2. john@cathedralhealthservices.org

MATHER-HEMPLER, Portia (ECR) 5981 Chesbro Ave, San Jose CA 95123 **Contemplative Cntr of Silicon Vlly Saratoga CA 2011-; Mem, Stwdshp Cmsn Dio El Camino Real Monterey CA 2005-** B Port Townsend WA 6/10/1949 d H(oward) Lester Mather & Portia. BA U of Oregon 1972; Ripon Coll Cuddesdon Oxford GB 1983; MDiv CDSP 1984; DASD SFTS 2008. D 6/29/1984 Bp David Rea Cochran P 6/7/1985 Bp Charles Shannon Mallory. m 10/6/1990 James Paul Hempler c 2. Supply P S Fran Epis Ch San Jose CA 2011; Supply P The Epis Ch In Almaden San Jose CA 2009; Assoc R S Andr's Ch Saratoga CA 1991-2006; Mem, CE Cmsn Dio Olympia Seattle WA 1987-1990; Assoc R S Jn's Epis Ch Olympia WA 1987-1990; Mem,Yth Cmsn Dio El Camino Real Monterey CA 1985-1987; Assoc All SS Epis Ch Palo Alto CA 1984-1987. Auth, "How to Call People to Tchg Mnstry of the Ch," *AWARE*, The Epis Ch, 1979. NNECA 1988; Sprtl Dir Intl 1998. revpmh7@yahoo.com

✠ **MATHES, Rt Rev James Robert** (SanD) 2628 6th Ave, San Diego CA 92103 **Bp of San Diego Dio San Diego San Diego CA 2005-** B Dallas TX 8/18/1959 s George Curtis Mathes & Elaine Millikan. BA U So 1982; MDiv VTS 1991. D 6/22/1991 Bp William Evan Sanders P 3/22/1992 Bp Philip Alan Smith Con 3/5/2005 for SanD. m 8/15/1981 Teresa S Sutton c 2. Dio Chicago Chicago IL 2001-2005; R The Epis Ch Of S Jas The Less Northfield IL 1994-2001; Asst Min All SS' Epis Ch Belmont MA 1991-1994. Phi Beta Kappa 1981. bishopmathes@edsd.org

M

MATHESON, Jennings (Ct) 74 South St # 809, Litchfield CT 06759 **R S Mich's Ch Litchfield CT 1997-** B Greensboro NC 2/14/1950 d Kenneth Christan Matheson & Frances Elizabeth. BA Sweet Briar Coll 1972; MDiv GTS 1983. D 3/22/1984 Bp Walter Decoster Dennis Jr P 12/1/1984 Bp Paul Moore Jr. m 6/24/1989 Robert Clements c 1. Dio Wstrn Massachusetts Springfield MA 1990-1997; Trin Epis Ch Southport CT 1984-1989; Hosp Chapl Ch Of The Incarn New York NY 1983-1984. office@stmichaels-litchfield.org

MATHEUS, Rob (SO) 6300 Kinver Edge Way, Columbus OH 43213 B Pueblo CO 3/11/1953 s Robert Louis Matheus & Charlotte. BA Coe Coll 1975; MDiv SWTS 1979. D 6/23/1979 P 1/19/1980 Bp Walter Cameron Righter. m 6/14/2003 Donna George. S Alb's Epis Ch Of Bexley Columbus OH 2004-2010; Vic Ch Of The Gd Samar Amelia OH 2001-2004; Adv Ch Cynthiana KY 2000-2001; S Raphael's Ch Lexington KY 1987-2000; R S Paul's Epis Ch Greenville OH 1981-1987; Cur S Andr's Ch Des Moines IA 1979-1981. newdaylight53@gmail.com

MATHEW, Cherian (ND) 304 NW 22 Avenue, Cape Coral FL 33993 B Kerala India 5/17/1941 D 11/17/1990 P 6/21/1991 Bp Andrew Hedtler Fairfield. CM1741@GMAIL.COM

MATHEWS, David Michael (Tenn) 2002 Wisteria Pl, Birmingham AL 35216 **Died 10/16/2010** B Tuscaloosa AL 11/25/1938 s Ormand Verner Mathews & Charlotte. Florida St U 1958; USC 1961; U of Memphis 1968; LTh STUSo 1975. D 6/29/1975 Bp William F Gates Jr P 4/1/1976 Bp William Evan Sanders. c 3.

MATHEWS, Keith Elizabeth (SO) 662 N 600 E, Firth ID 83236 B Charleston WV 9/26/1948 d Robert Norvell Mathews & Elizabeth Jane. BA W Virginia U 1970; Bex 1972; MDiv CDSP 1974; VTS 1992; Sabbatical Dio Chr Ch NZ 1997. D 10/4/1975 Bp Wilburn Camrock Campbell P 1/5/1977 Bp Robert Poland Atkinson. m 6/15/1974 James Patrick Roeder. R S Mary's Epis Ch Hillsboro OH 1999-2004; R S Mk's Ch Lake City MN 1998-1999; R S Jn's Epis Ch New Castle CO 1992-1998; R S Barn Ch Glenwood Sprg CO 1992-1997; R Trin Ch Scotland Neck NC 1988-1992; R S Thos' Epis Ch Syracuse NY 1983-1988; Int Dio Cntrl New York Syracuse NY 1981-1983; Asst Trin Epis Ch Watertown NY 1981-1982; Vic S Ann's Ch New Martinsville WV 1977-1981; D S Matt's Ch Charleston WV 1975-1976. OHC 1970; SMOTJ 1998. Rossiter Fllshp Bex Rochester NY 1988; Rossiter Fllshp Bex Rochester NY 1985; Phi Beta Kappa W Virginia U W Virginia 1970. keithandjim@q.com

MATHEWS, Koshy (Pa) 103 Potters Pond Dr, Phoenixville PA 19460 **S Ptr's Ch Phoenixville PA 2006-** B Tiruvalla Kerala India 4/14/1948 s P C Mathews

& Annamma. BS U Of Kerala Kottayam IN 1970; MDiv PrTS 1977; Med Harv 1981; DMin EDS 2000. D 6/2/2001 Bp Barbara Clementine Harris P 6/8/2002 Bp M(arvil) Thomas Shaw III. m 5/28/1977 Susan Koshy c 4. The Par Of S Chrys's Quincy MA 2005; Epiph Par Walpole MA 2004-2005; Chr Ch Needham MA 2001-2004; Assoc R Chr Epis Ch Sheffield MA 2001-2004; Dioc Intern S Ptr's Ch Weston MA 2000-2001. koshy.mathews@gmail.com

MATHEWS, Miriam Atwell (Md) 3433 Manor Ln, Ellicott City MD 21042 **D S Jn's Ch Ellicott City MD 2002-** B Howard County MD 2/2/1943 d Richard Nelson Atwell & Ethel Mae. Cert Maryland Bankers Sch 1979; Rutgers-The St U 1987; EFM STUSo 1996. D 6/14/1997 Bp Charles Lindsay Longest.

MATHEWS, Ranjit K (Mass) 7 Pond St, Randolph MA 02368 **Assoc The Par Ch Of S Lk Long Bch CA 2011-; Epis Ch Cntr New York NY 2010-** B Brighton MA 1/23/1979 s Koshy Mathews & Susan. BA The GW 2001; MDiv UTS 2005. D 6/3/2006 Bp M(arvil) Thomas Shaw III P 1/6/2007 Bp Gayle Elizabeth Harris. m 8/12/2006 Johanna Jacob Kurwilla. Exec Coun Appointees New York NY 2011; Epis Ch Cntr New York NY 2010-2011; Asst S Mich's Ch Milton MA 2006-2009. ranjit.mathews@gmail.com

MATHEWS JR, Thomas Etienne (Nwk) 5 Surrey Ln, Madison NJ 07940 **R S Lk's Ch Phillipsburg NJ 2007-** B Newark NJ 3/9/1974 BS Trenton St Coll; MDiv EDS 2003. D 6/7/2003 P 12/6/2003 Bp John Palmer Croneberger. m 9/12/1998 Tanya Ann Zygmunt c 2. Cur Gr Ch Madison NJ 2003-2007. tem2001@juno.com

MATHEWSON, Kathryn Carroll (ETenn) 2135 Fairmount Rd W, Signal Mountain TN 37377 B Buffalo NY 6/18/1944 d Kenneth Frederic Carroll & Jean Holbrook. BA Sweet Briar Coll 1966; MDiv Aquinas Inst of Theol 1996; CAS SWTS 1997. D 7/29/1996 P 7/29/1997 Bp Peter Hess Beckwith. m 10/12/1968 David Mathewson Jr c 2. Assoc R S Tim's Ch Signal Mtn TN 2003-2011; Asst R Epis Ch Of The Redeem Greenville SC 1998-2003; P-in-c S Thos Epis Ch Glen Carbon IL 1997-1998. kmathewson@sttimsignal.com

MATHIESON, James West (SVa) 183 Grove Park Cir, Danville VA 24541 B Winthrop MA 2/18/1938 s David Alexander Gray Mathieson & Ruth St Helen. BA Lynchburg Coll 1960; MDiv STUSo 1966. D 6/24/1966 Bp George P Gunn P 6/9/1967 Bp David Shepherd Rose. m 8/1/1959 Joan Ownby c 3. R Ch Of The Epiph Danville VA 1993-2004; R S Andr's Ch Rocky Mt NC 1975-1993; R Emm Epis Ch Chatham VA 1969-1975; Asst R S Mich's Ch Bon Air VA 1966-1969.

MATHIS, Judith S (CFla) 86 Dianne Dr., Ormond Beach FL 32176 B Cincinnati OH 7/28/1941 BA U of Miami 1963; MS Syr 1981. D 12/13/2003 Bp John Wadsworth Howe. m 4/16/1964 Horace Mathis c 2. S Jas Epis Ch Ormond Bch FL 2007-2008. judymat@bellsouth.net

MATIJASIC, Ernest G (O) 401 W Shoreline Dr #253, Sandusky OH 44870 B Pittsburgh PA 4/19/1952 s Ernest Matijascic & Mary. SWTS; BA Penn 1973; MDiv VTS 1978. D 6/3/1978 Bp Robert Bracewell Appleyard P 12/31/1978 Bp William Henry Marmion. c 3. R Gr Epis Ch Sandusky OH 1989-2009; R Trin Epis Ch So Boston VA 1984-1989; P-in-c S Marg's Epis Ch Waxhaw NC 1983-1984; Asst Ch Of The H Comf Charlotte NC 1981-1984; Asst S Paul's Epis Ch Lynchburg VA 1978-1981. erniesailor@sbcglobal.net

MATIS, Glenn Marshall (Pa) 45 Latham Ct, Doylestown PA 18901 **Intake Off Dio Pennsylvania Philadelphia PA 2011-** B Bryn Mawr PA 4/13/1947 s Arthur Paul Matis & C Grace. BME/BMC Shenandoah U 1969; MA Glassboro St U 1974; MDiv EDS 1976; MS Marywood U 1981; DD Providence Sch of Div 2010. D 6/12/1976 P 5/21/1977 Bp Lyman Cunningham Ogilby. m 8/16/1975 Patricia Marshall Coates. R Ch Of The Resurr Philadelphia PA 1989-2006; Ch Of The H Nativ Wrightstown PA 1980-1989; Dio Pennsylvania Philadelphia PA 1978-1979; Ch Of The Redeem Springfield PA 1976-1978. Auth, "The Impact of Dual-Career Marriages on the Priesthood & Ch," *Leaven*, 1990; Auth, *Leaven 90*. gmatis@verizon.net

MATISSE, Jacqueline Edith (SO) 232 E Main St, Lebanon OH 45036 **R S Pat's Epis Ch Lebanon OH 1991-** B New Orleans LA 12/1/1948 d Albert Palmer Matisse & Nancy Eleanor. BA Albion Coll 1970; MA St. Jn's Prov Sem Plymouth MI 1984; MDiv VTS 1988. D 6/25/1988 Bp Henry Irving Mayson P 1/14/1989 Bp H Coleman McGehee Jr. Dir Camping Progs Dio Sthrn Ohio Cincinnati OH 1991-1994; Chr Ch - Glendale Cincinnati OH 1988-1991. jmatisse@yahoo.com

MATLACK, David Russell (NY) Po Box 703, Southwest Harbor ME 04679 B Philadelphia PA 5/25/1922 s David Johnson Matlack & Elizabeth Emily. MBA CUNY 1975; SB Harv 2044; MDiv EDS 2049. D 6/23/1949 Bp Oliver J Hart P 1/1/1950 Bp Joseph Gillespie Armstrong. m 7/22/1950 Margery A Anderson c 3. R S Barn Ch Irvington on Hudson NY 1964-1968; R S Mich's Epis Ch Arlington VA 1956-1964; R S Mk's Epis Ch Penn Yan NY 1950-1956. Auth, "Cost Effectivness Of Spinal Cord Injury Cntr Treatment," Natl Paraplegia Fndt, 1974. margedavematlack@verizon.net

MATOTT, Michele Louise (RI) 80 Fisher Road Unit 90, Cumberland RI 02864 B Albany NY 1/28/1958 d Ellsworth W Matott & Jean L. BS Muskingum Coll 1980; MDiv UTS 1986; DMin SWTS 2008. D 11/22/1992 P 9/1/1993 Bp George Nelson Hunt III. m 6/20/1981 Thomas P Lang c 4. Int Chr Epis Ch Norwich CT 2011; S Alb's Ch Danielson CT 2008-2010; R S Thos Ch Greenville RI 1995-1996; S Eliz's Hm Providence RI 1993-1996; DCE Gr Ch In Providence Providence RI 1992-1995. paschalmys@aol.com

MATSON, David John (Me) 3 Mclellan St Apt 1, Brunswick ME 04011 **Dio Maine Portland ME 1998-** B Worcester MA 11/22/1961 s Arthur B Matson & Nancy Claire. BA Bates Coll 1983; MDiv EDS 1998; MDiv VTS 1998. D 8/15/1998 Bp Chilton Abbie Richardson Knudsen P 6/5/1999 Bp Gordon Paul Scruton. m 6/23/2011 Jessica Gorton. S Nich Epis Ch Scarborough ME 2004-2008; Int S Ptr's Epis Ch Londonderry NH 2002-2004; Int Ch Of The Gd Shpd Rangeley ME 2001-2002; Dio Wstrn Massachusetts Springfield MA 1998-2001; Asst S Steph's Ch Westborough MA 1998-2001. DVD_MATSON@YAHOO.COM

MATTEI, Raul Herminio (NJ) 836 Berkeley Ave, Trenton NJ 08618 B 11/22/1922 s Geronimo C Mattei & Carmen M. BA Puerto Rico Polytech Inst 1953; BD STUSo 1957; STM STUSo 1976. D 6/24/1957 P 12/1/1957 Bp Albert Ervine Swift. Chair - Hisp Cmsn Dio New Jersey Trenton NJ 1979-1985; Chair - Urban Cmsn Dio New Jersey Trenton NJ 1978-1981; S Mich's Ch Trenton NJ 1977-1988; S Fran Of Assisi Ch Philadelphia MS 1977; S Matt's Epis Ch Kosciusko MS 1977; Vic S Paul's Epis Ch Corinth MS 1968-1976; P-in-c S Mary's Ch Vicksburg MS 1967-1968. Auth, "Passover Poems," 1967; Auth, "Devocionario Epis"; Auth, "Poems & arts In Var Pub;".

MATTER, Janice Louise (Me) 5 Boynton Ln, Billerica MA 01821 **D Ascen Memi Ch Ipswich MA 2003-** B Altoona PA 9/14/1941 D 4/26/2003 Bp Chilton Abbie Richardson Knudsen. c 3.

MATTERS, Richard Bruce (ECR) 181 S Corinth Ave, Lodi CA 95242 **R All SS Ch Carmel CA 2007-** B Spokane WA 12/9/1950 s Clyde Burns Matters & Anna Ruth. BA Whitworth U 1973; MDiv GTS 1984; STM GTS 1991. D 6/11/1985 Bp Robert Hume Cochrane P 6/1/1986 Bp William Gillette Weinhauer. m 5/20/1972 Andrea K Kilpatrick c 3. R S Jn The Bapt Lodi CA 1993-2007; Assoc R Trin Epis Ch Everett WA 1987-1993; Asst Trin Epis Ch Asheville NC 1985-1987. rickmatters@gmail.com

MATTHEW, John Clifford (Ida) No address on file. B Anderson IN 6/7/1927 s Mark Neil Matthew & Mary Bertha. BA Hanover Coll 1951; MDiv Louisville Presb TS 1954; DD Albertson Coll 1977; Med Albertson Coll 1991. D 11/20/1994 P 5/28/1995 Bp John Stuart Thornton. m 1/20/1991 Judy Aileen McKay. DD Albertson Coll Caldwell ID 1977. jmatthew@micron.net

MATTHEW, Stephen Albert (Ak) 2457 Loomis Dr, North Pole AK 99705 B Rapids Fish Camp AK 7/31/1931 s Julius Matthew & Cora. D 6/18/1997 Bp Terrence Buckle P 2/13/2000 Bp Mark Lawrence Mac Donald. m 3/9/1960 Valerie Koskela c 4. Asst S Matt's Epis Ch Fairbanks AK 1999-2000.

MATTHEWS, Alan Montague Basil (EpisSanJ) 4236 25th St Apt 8, San Francisco CA 94114 B London UK 9/27/1937 s Hanibal Chin Matthews & Winifred Caroline. Trans from Church Of England 2/19/2009 Bp Jerry Alban Lamb. m 4/22/2006 Cheryl Parker. Int Epis Dio San Joaquin Modesto CA 2009. basil.m@earthlink.net

MATTHEWS JR, A(llen) Russel (WTex) Po Box 348, Luling TX 78648 B Stephenville TX 9/13/1935 s Allen Russel Matthews & Lelia Virginia. SW U Georgetown TX 1956; BA U of Houston 1959; MDiv Epis TS of The SW 1977. D 6/21/1977 P 1/15/1978 Bp Scott Field Bailey. m 5/23/1956 Jane Rogers c 3. Mem, Exec Bd Dio W Texas San Antonio TX 1996-1998; Mem, Stndg Com Dio W Texas San Antonio TX 1992-1995; R Trin Ch Victoria TX 1988-2000; Dio W Texas San Antonio TX 1981-1988; Trst of the Ch Corp Dio W Texas San Antonio TX 1980-1981; Vic S Marg's Epis Ch San Antonio TX 1979-1984; S Fran By The Lake Canyon Lake TX 1979-1981; M-in-c H Trin Carrizo Sprg TX 1977-1979. matthewsrussel@gmail.com

MATTHEWS, Daniel Paul (NY) 1047 Amsterdam Ave, New York NY 10025 B Chicago,IL 1/14/1933 s Robert John Lewis Matthews & Martha Dickson. BA Rol 1955; BD CDSP 1959; Fllshp Coll of Preachers 1972. D 6/29/1959 Bp John Vander Horst P 2/1/1960 Bp Theodore N Barth. m 10/4/1960 Diane Kendrick Vigeant c 3. R Par of Trin Ch New York NY 1987-2004; R S Lk's Epis Ch Atlanta GA 1980-1987; R S Jn's Epis Cathd Knoxville TN 1972-1980; R S Dav's Epis Ch Nashville TN 1965-1972; Asst Ch Of The H Comm Memphis TN 1961-1965; Min in charge Ch Of The H Comf Monteagle TN 1959-1961; Min in charge S Jas Sewanee TN 1959-1961. OBE Ord of the British Empire/British Embassy, Washington D.C. 2006; DD U So TS/ Sewanee, TN 1992; DD GTS/ New York, NY 1987; LHD Rol/ Winter Pk, FL 1986; DD CDSP/ Berkeley, CA 1984. cstevenson@stjohndivine.org

MATTHEWS JR, Daniel Paul (At) 435 Peachtree St, Atlanta GA 30308 **R S Lk's Epis Ch Atlanta GA 2003-** B Memphis TN 12/20/1961 s Daniel Paul Matthews & Diane. BS U So 1984; MDiv VTS 1989. D 6/18/1989 P 5/20/1990 Bp William Evan Sanders. m 8/15/1987 Sarah B Barnes c 2. R S Paul's Epis Ch Kingsport TN 1996-2003; Assoc S Mk's Epis Ch Jacksonville FL 1993-1996; Assoc S Paul's Epis Ch Chattanooga TN 1989-1992. dan@stlukesatlanta.org

MATTHEWS, Donald William (CNY) 375 W Clinton St, Elmira NY 14901 **R Gr Epis Ch Elmira NY 1997-** B Pittsburgh PA 12/25/1960 s Donald Hankey Matthews & Marilyn Ann. BS Ashland U 1983; MDiv Bex 1991. D 6/15/1991 P 1/1/1992 Bp James Russell Moodey. m 7/2/1983 Margaret Ruth Ronk c 2.

Dio Cntrl New York Syracuse NY 2005; Cluster P/Vic Chr Epis Ch Geneva OH 1991-1997; The Cluster Of Ch In Ne Oh Ashtabula OH 1991-1997; Cluster P/Vic Trin Ashtabula OH 1991-1997. Associated Parishes; Assn Ord Oblates Of Sacr Heart Of Jesus; OHC. frdon@stny.rr.com

MATTHEWS, Emily Anne (Miss) 230 W Monticello St, Brookhaven MS 39601 **R Ch Of The Redeem Brookhaven MS 2010-** B 10/12/1951 d Jamie Franklin Matthews & Mary Ellen. BA SW U 1973; MA U of Texas 1975; MS U of Texas 1991; Cert Mnstry Acad Iona Sch 2005. D 6/24/2006 Bp Don Adger Wimberly P 2/17/2007 Bp Claude Edward Payne. m 1/24/1987 Randolph Raynolds. revannie79@cableone.net

✠ **MATTHEWS, Rt Rev Frank Clayton** (Va) PO Box 12686, New Bern NC 28561 **Bp Off of Pstr Dvlpmt Epis Ch Cntr New York NY 1998-** B Raleigh NC 12/31/1947 s Walter Forrest Matthews & Ellinore Geraldine. BA Hampden-Sydney Coll 1970; MDiv VTS 1973. D 6/23/1973 Bp Thomas Augustus Fraser Jr P 4/3/1974 Bp Bennett Jones Sims Con 9/11/1993 for Va. m 6/7/1969 Martha H Matthews. Cn Dio Virginia Richmond VA 1987-1993; R Emm Ch At Brook Hill Richmond VA 1980-1987; Asst Chr Ch New Bern NC 1976-1979; H Innoc Ch Atlanta GA 1973-1976. Auth, "Formulat," *Formulations & Discussions*. DD VTS 1993; Ldrshp Atlanta Awd 1975. cmatthews@episcopalchurch.org

MATTHEWS III, James Houston (WNC) 2232 Water Oak Ln, Gastonia NC 28056 B Gastonia NC 1/1/1947 s James Houston Matthews & Annabelle. BA Belmont Abbey Coll 1974; MDiv GTS 1977. D 6/25/1977 Bp William Gillette Weinhauer P 5/2/1978 Bp James Barrow Brown. m 5/29/1972 Sharon Rose c 3. Stndg Comm. Pres Dio Wstrn No Carolina Asheville NC 2001-2005; R All SS' Epis Ch Gastonia NC 1991-2005; R All SS Ch Cayce SC 1986-1991; R Ch Of The Epiph Opelousas LA 1980-1986; Cur Ch Of The Ascen Lafayette LA 1977-1980. srm704@aol.com

MATTHEWS, Joyce Mary (Mich) 37906 Glengrove Dr, Farmington Hills MI 48331 **Chr Ch Cranbrook Bloomfield Hills MI 2005-** B Detroit MI 2/19/1947 d Gunzie Beard & Gertrude Mary. BS U MI 1974; MS U MI 1976; MDiv SWTS 2005. D 12/18/2004 P 7/2/2005 Bp Wendell Nathaniel Gibbs Jr. m 7/28/1973 Lauriant S Matthews c 2. joyce.matthews@seabury.edu

MATTHEWS, Kevin B (NC) 625 Candlewood Drive, Greensboro NC 27703 **Dio No Carolina Raleigh NC 2006-; Chapl S Mary's Hse Epis/Angl Campus Greensboro NC 2006-** B Baltimore MD 9/29/1956 s Robert Eugene Matthews & LaMoyne (Mason) Matthews. BA U of Maryland 1978; MDiv VTS 1984; ABD Duke 2004. D 5/9/1984 Bp A(lbert) Theodore Eastman P 3/3/1985 Bp David Keller Leighton Sr. St Elizabeths Epis Ch Apex NC 2005-2006; Chap Of Chr The King Charlotte NC 1996; Assoc S Tit Epis Ch Durham NC 1993-2000; Int S Mich And All Ang Adelphi MD 1992; Vic S Phil The Evang Washington DC 1988-1991; Asst to Bp of Maryland Dio Maryland Baltimore MD 1987-1988; P-in-c Cathd Of The Incarn Baltimore MD 1987; Asst to Dn Cathd Of The Incarn Baltimore MD 1985-1987; Dio Maryland Baltimore MD 1984-1987; Asst S Phil's Ch Annapolis MD 1984-1985. kevinbr@earthlink.net

MATTHEWS, Malcolm John (Md) Po Box 91, Pocomoke City MD 21851 B Salisbury MD 12/27/1930 s Malcolm George Matthews & Thera. AA Marion Mltry Inst 1949; BA U NC 1951; MDiv GTS 1960. D 6/18/1960 P 12/21/1960 Bp Allen J Miller. Assoc S Dav's Ch Baltimore MD 1968-1997.

MATTHEWS, Mary Theresa (RI) Woodson Dr 2721, 2721 Woodson Dr, Mckinney TX 75070 **P-in-c S Wm Laud Epis Ch Pittsburg TX 2009-** B Scranton PA 5/15/1952 d Thomas Joseph Gelbride & Mary Margaret. BTh U Of Scranton 1994; MDiv Ya Berk 1999. D 4/17/1999 P 10/23/1999 Bp Paul Victor Marshall. c 2. S Ann's-By-The-Sea Block Island RI 2005-2006; S Mk's Epis Ch Moscow PA 1999-2002. therevterry@aol.com

MATTHEWS, Richard Logan (Minn) 8895 Bradford Pl, Eden Prairie MN 55347 B Rochester NH 4/3/1946 s Elton Lynn Matthews & Virginia. BS U of Massachusetts 1970; MS U of Pennsylvania 1980; MBA Indiana U 1989. D 5/16/1986 P 12/16/1986 Bp William Cockburn Russell Sheridan. m 8/23/1969 Jacqueline Ann LeBeau c 2. H Trin Epis Ch Elk River MN 2006-2008; Trin Ch Anoka MN 2006-2008; R S Paul's Ch Minneapolis MN 1993-2004; Asst R S Lk's Ch Baton Rouge LA 1991-1993; R H Fam Ch Angola IN 1987-1991; Assoc Trin Ch Ft Wayne IN 1986-1987. rmatthews@earthlink.net

MATTIA, Joan Marie (Va) 622 Worchester Street, Herndon VA 20170 **Adj Fac VTS Alexandria VA 2008-** B Clearfield PA 1/25/1953 d Earl Edward Plubell & Irene Delia. BA Geo Mason U 1985; MDiv VTS 1988; PhD U of Birmingham Birmingham GB 2007. D 6/18/1988 P 3/15/1989 Bp Peter James Lee. m 1/21/1978 Lou Mattia c 1. St Johns Mortgage Recovery CDC Passaic NJ 2008-2009; The Leads Fndt Herndon VA 2008-2009; S Peters-In-The-Woods Epis Ch Fairfax Sta VA 2007; Exec Coun Appointees New York NY 1999-2002; Co-R S Mich's Ch Gainesville FL 1991-1999; S Marg's Ch Woodbridge VA 1991; Assoc Trin Ch Arlington VA 1989-1990; Asst S Jas' Epis Ch Leesburg VA 1988-1989. PhD dissertation, "Walking the Rift: Idealism and Imperialism in E Afr, 1890-1911," *PhD dissertation*, U of Birmingham, 2007. joaniematt@hotmail.com

MATTIA JR, Lou (Va) 622 Worchester St, Herndon VA 20170 **Ch Of The Gd Shpd Bluemont VA 2011-; Chr Epis Ch Lucketts Leesburg VA 2010-** B Washington DC 5/29/1952 s Louis Joseph Mattia & Irene. BSc Pur 1974; MDiv VTS 1988; Post-grad Certificat GW 2007. D 6/18/1988 P 3/15/1989 Bp Peter James Lee. m 1/21/1978 Joan Marie Plubell. Assoc R Ch Of The H Comf Vienna VA 2003-2008; Exec Coun Appointees New York NY 1999-2002; Co-R S Mich's Ch Gainesville FL 1991-1999; S Marg's Ch Woodbridge VA 1989-1991; Asst S Jas' Epis Ch Leesburg VA 1988-1989. "Conversation w Sanji," Publish Amer, 2005. louismattia@hotmail.com

MATTILA, Daniel E (Ct) 104 Walnut Tree Hill Rd, Sandy Hook CT 06482 **Supply Dio Connecticut Hartford CT 2006-** B Santa Clara CA 12/21/1968 s William Richard Mattila & Gloria Mae. BA Hamline U 1991; Dplma in Angl Stds Ya Berk 1994; MDiv Yale DS 1994; MSW U of Connecticut 1997. D 9/29/1994 P 3/31/1995 Bp James Louis Jelinek. P-in-c S Jn's Ch Sandy Hook CT 2001-2006; Assoc S Jas Epis Ch Danbury CT 1999-2001; P-in-c Calv St Geo's Epis Ch Bridgeport CT 1996-1999; Asst S Jn's Ch Bridgeport CT 1994-1996. Auth, "Chapt: Schema Focused Ther For Depression," *Comparative Treatments For Depression*, Springer, 2002. Who'S Who In Amer 2003; Founding Fell Acad Of Cognitive Ther 2000; Phi Beta Kappa 1991. mattila@aya.yale.edu

MATTLIN, Margaret Baker (Minn) 2085 Buford Ave, Saint Paul MN 55108 B Saint Paul MN 11/28/1945 d Harold Carl & Mary. BA Hamline U 1967; MLS Hamline U 1988. D 8/14/1996 Bp Sanford Zangwill Kaye Hampton. D Ch Of The Ascen Stillwater MN 1997-1999.

MATTSON, Sherry R (Ind) 11974 State Highway M26, Eagle Harbor MI 49950 B Detroit MI 2/11/1949 d Raymond Lionel Mattson & Ella Anne. BA Simmons Coll 1971; MDiv Epis TS of The SW 1979; Sprtl Dir Haden Inst 2009. D 6/16/1979 P 5/31/1980 Bp H Coleman McGehee Jr. m 9/6/1993 Richard Thorp Draper c 2. Dep to GC Dio Indianapolis Indianapolis IN 2003-2006; P-in-c All SS Ch Seymour IN 2000-2003; Int S Dav's Ch Beanblossom Nashville IN 2000; P All SS Ch Seymour IN 1991-1997; Chapl Dio Sthrn Virginia Norfolk VA 1988-1998; R S Dav's Ch Cullowhee NC 1981-1988; Chapl Oakland U Rochester MI 1979-1981; Cur S Steph's Ch Troy MI 1979-1980. Mayor'S Cmsn On Human Relatns Madison In 1999-2003. sherry_mattson@yahoo.com

MATYLEWICZ, Stephen Jerome (Be) 116 Riverview Ln, Jermyn PA 18433 B Scranton PA 6/4/1934 s Stephen Matylewicz & Genevieve. Dioc Prog. D 6/2/1977 P 10/28/1978 Bp Lloyd Edward Gressle. m 1/18/1968 Maureen Wayman. R Chr Ch Forest City PA 1993-2004; R Trin Epis Ch Carbondale PA 1993-2004; Asst Ch Of The Epiph Glenburn Clarks Summit PA 1985-1994. dduck73@hotmail.com

MAUAI, Brandon Lee (ND) 500 S Main Ave, Sioux Falls SD 57104 **Yth Dir Dio So Dakota Sioux Falls SD 2011-** B Fort Yates ND 11/1/1984 s Benedict R Mauai & Karen L. D 6/9/2007 Bp Michael Gene Smith. m 11/17/2007 Angela Goodhouse c 4. brandon.mauai@gmail.com

MAUGER, K(arl) Frederick (Be) 1019 Maple St, Spring Brook Township PA 18444 B Milton PA 1/27/1923 s Wilbur Harry Mauger & Blanche Marguerite. BS Buc 1953; MS Buc 1956; EdD Penn 1965. D 3/10/1984 P 10/28/1984 Bp James Michael Mark Dyer. c 3. R S Jn's Epis Ch Hamlin PA 1985-1990. Silver Eagles. frfred01@comcast.net

MAUGHAN III, M(atthew) Webster (O) 1226 Waverly Rd, Sandusky OH 44870 B Richmond VA 4/9/1946 s Matthew Maughan & Myra Elizabeth. U of Virginia 1967; Jas Madison U 1968; BS Virginia Commonwealth U 1973; Med Virginia Commonwealth U 1975; MDiv GTS 1986. D 6/7/1986 P 5/28/1987 Bp C(laude) Charles Vache. m 3/19/1967 Joy C Clark c 2. S Paul's Epis Ch Put-In-Bay OH 2008-2010; Assoc R Gr Epis Ch Sandusky OH 2002-2006; R S Jn's Ch Suffolk VA 1988-2002; R Glebe Ch Suffolk VA 1988-1998; Asst to the R Emm Epis Ch Hampton VA 1986-1988. mwmaughan@gmail.com

MAULDEN, Kristina Ann (Okla) 501 S Cincinnati Ave, Tulsa OK 74103 **Asst to R Trin Ch Tulsa OK 2007-** B Mount Clemens MI 1/2/1967 d Zachariah Gustav Gardlund & Sharon Leona. BS U MI 1989; U of Texas 1992; MDiv TESM 1995. Trans 9/2/2003 Bp John Wadsworth Howe. m 11/29/1996 Anthony Wayne Maulden c 2. Vic H Fam Epis Ch Fishers IN 2003-2006; Asst Epis Ch Of The Resurr Longwood FL 1999-2003. kmaulden@trinitytulsa.org

MAUMUS, Priscilla Guderian (La) Christ Church Cathedral, 2219 St. Charles Ave., New Orleans LA 70115 **D Chr Ch Cathd New Orleans LA 2010-; Archd Dio Louisiana Baton Rouge LA 2010-** B New Orleans LA 12/1/1947 d Emmett Charles Guderian & Gwendolyn B. BA Newcomb Coll 1969; MA Tul 1981. D 12/1/2007 Bp Charles Edward Jenkins III. m 1/20/1973 Craig Maumus c 1. D S Mart's Epis Ch Metairie LA 2008-2010. Assn of Epis Deacons 2006. pmaumus@cox.net

MAUNEY, J(ames) Patrick (RI) P.O Box 1236, Sagamore Beach MA 02562 B ParisTN 12/7/1942 s James Buford Mauney & Eleanor Caroline. BA Duke 1965; MDiv EDS 1972. D 6/17/1972 P 12/17/1972 Bp Frederick Hesley Belden. m 3/19/1966 Mardi J Jacobsen c 1. Dir of Angl & Global Relatns Epis Ch Cntr New York NY 1991-2005; Dep - Angl Relatns Epis Ch Cntr New York NY 1989-1991; Coordntr of Ovrs Mnstrs Epis Ch Cntr New York NY 1982-1987; Exec Coun Appointees New York NY 1977-1982; Asst S Mart's

Ch Providence RI 1975-1977; Cur S Paul's Ch No Kingstown RI 1972-1975. DD EDS 2005; Hon Cn Dio DR 1993. pinetops236@earthlink.net

MAURAIS, Robert Irwin (CFla) 175 Groveland Rd, Mount Dora FL 32757 B Davenport IA 7/5/1931 s Robert Wilfred Maurais & Plooma Madge. BS NWU 1955; MDiv SWTS 1958. D 6/14/1958 Bp Charles L Street P 12/20/1958 Bp Gerald Francis Burrill. m 6/20/1953 Lois N Erickson c 4. Int P-in-c S Edw The Confessor Mt Dora FL 2008-2009; Stndg Com, Pres Dio Cntrl Florida Orlando FL 1993-1996; Stndg Com Dio Cntrl Florida Orlando FL 1984-1986; Curs Cmsn Dio Cntrl Florida Orlando FL 1983-1985; Dn, Ocala/Leesburg Dnry Dio Cntrl Florida Orlando FL 1980-1984; R S Edw The Confessor Mt Dora FL 1979-1996; Asst Ecum Off Dio Cntrl Florida Orlando FL 1979-1981; Asst.Ecum Off Dio Cntrl Florida Orlando FL 1979-1981; Chair Com Ecum Rel Dio SW Florida Sarasota FL 1973-1979; Chair Com Ecum Rel Dio SW Florida Sarasota FL 1973-1979; Asst Ch Of The Redeem Sarasota FL 1972-1978; Chair Com Schs Dio SW Florida Sarasota FL 1969-1971; Asst S Thos' Epis Ch St Petersburg FL 1968-1971; Cn Eductr Cathd Ch Of S Lk Orlando FL 1967-1968; LocTen S Aug's Epis Ch St Petersburg FL 1965-1966; Asst. Headmaster Berkeley Preparatory Sch Tampa FL 1961-1967; Asst St Johns Epis Ch Tampa FL 1961-1965; Cur S Andr's Epis Ch Tampa FL 1960-1961; Cur Trin Epis Ch Wheaton IL 1958-1959. revrob175@embarqmail.com

MAURER, David Stuart (Los) 211 Calle Potranca, San Clemente CA 92672 **Co-Vic S Clare Of Assisi Rancho Cucamonga CA 2008-** B Los Angeles CA 3/23/1951 s Arthur Stuart Maurer & Betty Ann. BS California St U 1974; Cert Childrens Hosp Sch Of Physical Ther 1980; MDiv TESM 2007. D 6/9/2007 P 1/12/2008 Bp Joseph Jon Bruno. m 6/5/1976 Karen Diane Maurer c 2. dmaurer29@cox.net

MAURER, Karen Diane (Los) 777 N. Acacia Ave., Rialto CA 92376 **Full Time S Clare Of Assisi Rancho Cucamonga CA 2011-; Full Time S Ptr's Par Rialto CA 2007-** B Downey CA 8/13/1954 d John Wesley Stang & Patricia Ann. BA USC 1976; MDiv TESM 2007. D 6/9/2007 P 1/12/2008 Bp Joseph Jon Bruno. m 6/5/1976 David Stuart Maurer c 2. kdmaurer@cox.net

MAWHINNEY, William Robert (Mass) 85 Greenwood Ln., Waltham MA 02451 **Died 4/21/2011** B Newton MA 5/7/1935 s Harry Mawhinney & Anna Elizabeth. BA Bos 1957; BD EDS 1960; MA Framingham St Coll 1975. D 6/27/1960 Bp Anson Phelps Stokes Jr P 12/20/1960 Bp Frederic Cunningham Lawrence. c 3. Ord Of S Anne. Norman B Nash Fllshp. wmrm@comcast.net

MAXFIELD, Christian D (Mil) 519 S Michigan St, Prairie Du Chien WI 53821 **R H Trin Epis Ch Prairie Du Chien WI 2010-** B Illnois 4/30/1979 s Donald David Maxfield & Kathryn Anne. MDiv Nash 2007. D 6/30/2007 P 1/5/2008 Bp Keith Lynn Ackerman. m 9/16/2003 Kate L Rische. Yth, YA and Fam Mnstry S Paul's Cathd Peoria IL 2007-2010. ckmaxfield@mac.com

MAXSON, J(ohn) Hollis (Haw) 447 Kawaihae St, Honolulu HI 96825 B Oceanside CA 3/14/1929 s Elmer Cyril Maxson & Lulu Mina. BA U of Hawaii 1958; BD CDSP 1961. D 6/4/1961 Bp George Richard Millard P 12/16/1961 Bp Harry S Kennedy. m 5/2/1953 Ethel Moosun Chung c 3. Ch Of The H Nativ Honolulu HI 1983-1989; Asst S Chris's Ch Kailua HI 1964-1969; Vic H Innoc' Epis Ch Lahaina HI 1961-1964.

MAXWELL, Anne Mears (La) 259 W Hickory St, Ponchatoula LA 70454 **Assoc Chr Ch Covington LA 2009-** B Spartenburg SC 7/26/1965 d George Motier Maxwell. D 6/7/2003 P 1/11/2004 Bp J(ohn) Neil Alexander. m 5/20/2003 William Ryan Hussey c 1. P-in-c All SS Epis Ch Ponchatoula LA 2009; H Trin Par Decatur GA 2004-2007; S Dunst's Epis Ch Atlanta GA 2003-2004. maxwell@htparish.com

MAXWELL, Barbara Jean (O) 120 Charles Ct, Elyria OH 44035 **Chapl S Jos's Epis Chap Far Rockaway NY 2000-** B Newport VT 9/7/1944 d Roger Maxwell & Marietta. BS Cleveland St U 1984; MA JCU 1994; BA Cleveland St U 2003. D 11/13/2004 Bp Mark Hollingsworth Jr. c 2. barmaxwell@windstorm.net

MAXWELL, Elizabeth Gail (NY) 225 W. 99th St., New York NY 10025 **S Mich's Ch New York NY 2011-; Int R S Mich's Ch New York NY 2011-** B Madison WI 9/19/1956 d Robert Sidney Maxwell & Margaret Honore. BA Duke 1977; MDiv PrTS 1982. D 6/11/1983 P 12/16/1983 Bp John Shelby Spong. c 1. Assoc R/Prog Dir Ch Of The H Apos New York NY 1989-2011; R S Matt's Ch Paramus NJ 1983-1989. lizmaxwell@mindspring.com

MAXWELL JR, George Motier (At) 920 Memorial Dr SE Unit 30, Atlanta GA 30316 **Vic Cathd Of S Phil Atlanta GA 2005-** B Columbia SC 12/28/1956 s George Motier Maxwell & Virginia. BA U NC 1979; JD Duke 1982; MDiv Candler TS Emory U 2004. D 2/26/2005 P 8/20/2005 Bp J(ohn) Neil Alexander. m 6/15/1999 Sally R Weaver c 3. gmaxwell@stphilipscathedral.org

MAXWELL, George Motier (Ga) 115 E Gordon St, Savannah GA 31401 B Augusta GA 9/11/1930 s Grover Cleveland Maxwell & Corrie Ann. VTS; BS VMI 1951; MDiv VTS 1961. D 6/26/1961 P 6/26/1962 Bp Clarence Alfred Cole. m 7/9/1954 Virginia Towill c 3. Sprtl Dir Dio Georgia Savannah GA 1991-2001; R Chr Ch Epis Savannah GA 1973-1990; R Ch Of The H Comf Sumter SC 1967-1973; Asst Ch Of The Redeem Sarasota FL 1966-1968; R S Chris's Ch Spartanburg SC 1961-1966. DD VTS 1989. gmax1@comcast.net

MAXWELL, James Henry (Mich) 281 W Drayton St, Ferndale MI 48220 B Yonkers NY 1/25/1939 s Frank Donald Maxwell & Mary Letitia. BA Col 1960; MDiv VTS 1964. D 6/6/1964 P 12/19/1964 Bp Horace W B Donegan. m 8/28/1965 Martha Eloise May c 3. Stndg Com, Pres Dio Michigan Detroit MI 2001-2002; Total Mnstry Mssnr Dio Michigan Detroit MI 1996-2004; R S Marg's Ch Hazel Pk MI 1996-2004; GC Dep. Dio Michigan Detroit MI 1996-2002; Mssnr Dio Michigan Detroit MI 1996-2000; Asst Deploy Off Dio Michigan Detroit MI 1994; Chair, Urban Affrs Dio Michigan Detroit MI 1982-1991; R S Lk's Ch Ferndale MI 1979-2004; R Ch Of The Gd Shpd And S Jn Milford PA 1973-1979; R Ch Of S Jn The Evang Philadelphia PA 1967-1973; Cur Trin Ch Covington KY 1964-1967. Epis Peace Fllshp (EPF) 1968; EvangES (EES) 1965; Fran Scott Key Soc of VA Sem 2009; Soc for Increase of Mnstry (SIM) 1965. - So Oakland Shltr (SOS) 2008; Human Serv Profsnl Cmnty Serv of Oakland 1989. jimmardi@wowway.com

MAXWELL, Kevin Burns (Cal) 2 Meadow Park Circle, Belmont CA 94002 B Yakima WA 1/26/1941 s J Alex Maxwell & Mary. BA Gonzaga U 1964; MA Gonzaga U 1966; DIT Kachebere Sem 1971; STM Jesuit TS 1973; MA Rice U 1978; PhD Rice U 1983. Rec from Roman Catholic 12/1/1990 as Priest Bp William Edwin Swing. m 7/16/1988 Josephine L Murphy. Schlr-in-res Trsfg Epis Ch San Mateo CA 1990-2002. "Oral Dynamics of Bagobo Culture," *Tambara Journ*, Ateneo de Davao U, 1986; "Bemba Myth and Ritual: The Impact of Literacy on an Oral Culture," *Amer U Stds*, Ptr Lang, 1983. kmaxwell@ndnu.edu

MAXWELL, Richard Anderson (Ct) Grace Episcopal Church, 55 New Park Ave, Hartford CT 06106 **Gr Epis Ch Hartford CT 2004-** B Midland MI 4/11/1954 s Martin Alec Maxwell & Mary Ruth. BA Stan 1977; MDiv UTS 1994; STM GTS 1998. D 2/6/1999 P 9/11/1999 Bp Richard Frank Grein. m 1/31/2007 F Paul Kline. Asst Min Ch Of The Incarn New York NY 2000-2004. rmaxwell42@comcast.net

MAXWELL, Sally Dawn (Minn) St David's Episcopal Church, 304 E 7th St, Austin TX 78701 **S Paul's Epis Ch Duluth MN 2010-** B Duluth MN 9/10/1953 d Clinton Maxwell & Lillian. BS Coll of St Scholastica 1978; MA Coll of St Scholastica 1990; Dipl. in Angl Stds Epis TS of the SW 2008; MDiv U of MN Untd TS 2008. D 7/26/2007 P 7/8/2008 Bp James Louis Jelinek. m 12/1/1985 Dean Gies c 3. S Andr's By The Lake Duluth MN 2010. sallymax2002@yahoo.com

MAXWELL, William Ferguson (U) 515 Van Buren St, Port Townsend WA 98368 **Non-stip Asst S Paul's Epis Ch Port Townsend WA 1990-** B Philadelphia PA 9/18/1925 s William Ferguson Maxwell & Bessie Annie. BA SMU 1946; MDiv SWTS 1947; Fllshp SWTS 1949; Fllshp Coll of Preachers 1958. D 3/25/1947 Bp Harry Tunis Moore P 9/21/1949 Bp Charles A Mason. m 7/2/1977 Sue Barnhardt c 3. Vic Gr Ch Bainbridge Island WA 1992-1993; Dn Cathd Ch Of S Mk Salt Lake City UT 1978-1990; R S Jn's Epis Ch Tulsa OK 1972-1978; Dn Cathd Of S Jas Chicago IL 1964-1972; R S Jas Ch Bozeman MT 1961-1964; R S Chris's Epis Ch Oak Pk IL 1954-1961; Vic S Lk's Epis Ch Stephenville TX 1949-1950; D-in-c S Matt's Ch Comanche TX 1947-1948. Auth, "Poetry," *Paying Attention*; Co-Auth, "Manual," *Sxlty: A Div Gift*; Auth, "Use Guide," *The Bible for Today's Ch*. Trng & Consulting Serv - Dio Olympia 1990-2008. Dn Emer St. Mk's Cathd, Salt Lake City 1990; DD Seabury-Wstrn 1968. 3max8@olympus.net

MAY, Amanda Gwyn (SanD) 2101 Bridgeway, Unit D, Sausalito CA 94965 **Int R Chr Ch Sausalito CA 2010-** B San Diego CA 10/8/1950 d George Williams Rutherford & Anna Gwyn Foster. BA Stan 1971; MS Lon 1973; Bethel Coll 1991; MDiv CDSP 1993. D 6/5/1993 P 12/21/1993 Bp Gethin Benwil Hughes. c 2. Asst S Dunst's Epis Ch San Diego CA 2006-2007; Exec Dir/CEO Epis Cmnty Serv San Diego CA 1994-2006; Asst The Epis Ch Of S Andr Encinitas CA 1994. "Animating Illustrations," *Fake News - Homil (Dec)*, Cmncatn Resources Inc, 2005; "A Table in the Wilderness," *Preaching as Prophetic Calling: Sermons That Wk XII*, Morehouse Pub, 2004; Auth, "The End Times," *Preaching Through the Year of Mk: Sermons That Wk VIII*, Morehouse Pub, 1999. amandamay438@gmail.com

MAY JR, Boyd Hickman (SVa) No address on file. B Pittsburgh PA 5/22/1932 s Boyd H May & Helen. BA; BS; MDiv; MD. D 6/7/1973 P 12/23/1973 Bp David Shepherd Rose. m 6/9/1956 Patricia S May c 1. Asst Chr and S Lk's Epis Ch Norfolk VA 1974-1982.

MAY, Charles Scott (At) 3530 Piedmont Rd Ne Apt 9f, Atlanta GA 30305 **Cler Assoc All SS Epis Ch Atlanta GA 2001-** B Little Rock AR 3/4/1931 s Guy Noel May & Louise. BA W&L 1953; BD STUSo 1957. D 6/29/1957 P 3/17/1958 Bp Robert Raymond Brown. R S Jas Epis Ch Marietta GA 1973-1996; Assoc Trin Cathd Columbia SC 1972-1973; Asst Trin Cathd Columbia SC 1966-1971; R S Paul's Newport AR 1958-1966; Cur Chr Epis Ch Little Rock AR 1957-1958. cscottmay@gmail.com

MAY, David Hickman (Va) 916 Hedgelawn Dr, Richmond VA 23235 **R Gr Ch Kilmarnock VA 2006-** B Tacoma WA 2/21/1959 s Boyd Hickman May & Patricia Nan. BA U of Tennessee 1981; MFA Virginia Commonwealth U 1987; MDiv STUSo 1993. D 6/12/1993 P 12/1/1993 Bp Peter James Lee. m

2/4/1989 Emily S Smith c 2. R S Andr's Ch Richmond VA 1996-2006; Asst Ch Of Our Sav Charlottesville VA 1993-1996.

MAY JR, Frederick Barnett (NJ) 916 Lagoon Ln., Mantoloking NJ 08738 B New York NY 12/15/1948 D 10/21/2000 Bp David B(ruce) Joslin. m 11/9/1991 Kathleen Dunn c 2. fredmay@comcast.net

MAY JR, James Bowen (Va) 16178 Williams Pl, King George VA 22485 **S Paul's Owens King Geo VA 2004-; S Ptr's Epis Ch Sheridan WY 1998-** B Orlando FL 2/4/1954 s James Bowen May & Janice. BS Florida St U 1976; MA Jacksonville U 1981; MDiv SWTS 1991. D 2/27/1993 P 8/1/1993 Bp Bob Gordon Jones. m 8/9/1980 Katherine A Allison c 1. R S Jas' Ch Indn Hd MD 1997-2004; Vic S Barth's Ch Cokeville WY 1993-1997; Vic S Jas Ch Kemmerer WY 1993-1997; Yth Min S Ptr's Epis Ch Sheridan WY 1991-1993. jkmay1@verizon.net

MAY IV, Lynde Eliot (Mil) 5222 S Russell St, # 27, Tampa FL 33611 **Asstg P Cathd Ch Of S Ptr St Petersburg FL 2007-** B Bridgeport CT 6/12/1933 s Lynde Eliot May & Florence. BS Ya 1955; MDiv Ya Berk 1958; MEd Rhode Island Coll 1970. D 6/7/1958 P 3/7/1959 Bp John S Higgins. m 1/31/1959 Diane Carole Alexander c 3. Asst P S Jn The Div Epis Ch Sun City Cntr FL 2000-2001; Int Cathd Ch Of S Ptr St Petersburg FL 1998-2000; Int S Eliz's Epis Ch Zephyrhills FL 1996-1998; Int S Mary's Par Tampa FL 1994-1996; R S Lk's Ch Madison WI 1983-1994; R Ch Of S Jn Chrys Delafield WI 1978-1983; S Jn's Mltry Acad Delafield WI 1978-1981; U Sch Milwaukee Milwaukee WI 1976-1978; S Andrews Sch Barrington RI 1965-1976; R S Mk's Ch Warren RI 1960-1965; Cur Chr Ch Westerly RI 1958-1960. lemfour@aol.com

MAY, Maureen May (Neb) The Oaks, 2015 County Road R, Fremont NE 68025 **D S Jas' Epis Ch Fremont NE 1993-** B Nottingham GB 5/28/1939 d Clifford Albert Moon & Irene May. CPE; EFM STUSo 1992. D 10/30/1993 Bp James Edward Krotz. m 1/24/1960 Ronald Gail May c 1. deaconmmay@yahoo.com

MAY, Oscar Worth (Lex) 8410 Pheasant Dr, Florence KY 41042 B Grifton NC 2/22/1913 s Oscar Wooten May & Nancy Eloise. BA U of Virginia 1933; BD VTS 1937; DD Epis TS In Kentucky 1985. D 5/14/1937 P 12/1/1937 Bp Thomas C Darst. m 9/22/1993 Hazel E Jordre c 4. Ecum Off Dio Lexington Lexington KY 1973-1979; R Trin Ch Covington KY 1959-1979; R S Steph's Epis Ch Beckley WV 1949-1959; R Johns Memi Epis Ch Farmville VA 1942-1949; R Chr Ch Xenia OH 1939-1942; R S Paul's Epis Ch Clinton NC 1938-1939.

MAY, Philip Walter (WTex) 700 S Upper Broadway St, Corpus Christi TX 78401 **Ch Of The Gd Shpd Corpus Christi TX 2010-** B Ontario Canada 11/29/1957 s Sidney Francis May & Elaine Elizabeth. BA U of Wstrn Ontario 1980; MA U of Wstrn Ontario 1982; MDiv Trin 1989. Trans from Anglican Church of Canada 10/27/2010 Bp Gary Richard Lillibridge. c 2. pmay@cotgs.org

MAY, Richard Ernest (Va) Po Box 155, Campton NH 03223 B Evanston IL 7/9/1946 s Ernest V May & Gladys Irene. BS U Of Delaware Newark 1969; MDiv VTS 1979; MA Norwich U 1989. D 5/24/1979 Bp William Hawley Clark P 6/1/1980 Bp Philip Alan Smith. m 12/28/1968 Barbara Anne Nesbitt c 2. S Ptr's Epis Ch Bridgton ME 1996-1998; H Trin Epis Ch Swanton VT 1993-1994; R S Mary's Epis Par Northfield VT 1983-1987; Bruton Par Williamsburg VA 1982-1983; Dio Sthrn Virginia Norfolk VA 1982-1983; Asst Ch Of The Gd Shpd Nashua NH 1979-1982.

MAY, Richard Leslie (SVa) 349 Archers Mead, Williamsburg VA 23185 B Omaha NE 3/4/1934 s Edgar Wylie May & Mary Yvonne. BA U of Nebraska 1956; JD Creighton U 1962; MDiv Bex 1967; DMin NYTS 1982; STM GTS 1986. D 6/24/1967 P 12/21/1967 Bp Russell T Rauscher. c 2. R Bruton Par Williamsburg VA 1987-1996; Trin Educ Fund New York NY 1978-1987; Exec Asst Par of Trin Ch New York NY 1977-1979; R Ch Of The Epiph Jacksonville FL 1969-1977; R S Jn's Ch Valentine NE 1967-1969; P S Jn's Epis Ch Valentine NE 1967-1969.

MAY, Thomas Richard (NJ) 65 W Front St, Red Bank NJ 07701 B Camden NJ 12/15/1947 s Clayton E May & Olga P. BA Shelton Coll 1970; MDiv Reformed Epis Sem 1973. D 6/1/2010 P 12/3/2010 Bp George Edward Councell. m 5/23/1970 Mary Grace Hawks c 1. fredmay@comcast.net

MAYBERRY, Richard Earl (Ct) 16 Southport Woods Drive, Southport CT 06890 **Asst S Matt's Epis Ch Wilton CT 2010-** B Delano CA 9/26/1945 s Theodore Stephen Mayberry & Elsie Johanna. BS U of Oregon 1967; MDiv GTS 1971. D 6/20/1971 P 1/6/1972 Bp Charles Alfred Voegeli. R S Fran Ch Stamford CT 1978-2007; Asst S Mk's Ch Mt Kisco NY 1971-1978. illustrator, *P's Handbook*, Morehouse-Barlow, 1983; illustrator, *A Manual for Acolytes*, Morehouse-Barlow, 1981. Assn of Angl Mus. R Emer St Fran Ch, Stamford CT 2007. rem9c@optonline.net

MAYBIN, Maxine Roberta (Colo) 915 Yuma St Apt 124, Colorado Springs CO 80909 **D S Raphael Epis Ch Colorado Sprg CO 1992-** B Boston MA 5/17/1923 d Mack Robert Maybin & Eva Jane. BS DePaul U 1979; Bp's Inst for Diac Formation 1992. D 10/24/1992 Bp William Jerry Winterrowd. c 4. Auth, "Significance of Slow Ventricular Tachycardi and Slow Ventricular Couplets during Ambulatory ECG Monitoring," *Amer Journ of Cardiology*, 1979. Chi Eta Phi, Iota Eta Chapt - Colorado Sprg, CO 1991; Ord of the DOK 1989; Sigma Theta Tau, Inc. - Natl hon Soc of Nrsng - Gam 1980.

MAYCOCK, Roma Walker (Va) 3256 Reades Way, Williamsburg VA 23185 B Des Moines IA 6/28/1936 d Howard Free Walker & Ardus Lucille. BS Iowa St U 1958; MDiv VTS 1983. D 6/11/1983 Bp Robert Bruce Hall P 5/12/1984 Bp David Henry Lewis Jr. m 6/21/1958 Paul Dean Maycock c 5. R S Steph's Ch Catlett VA 1985-2005; R Gr Ch Casanova VA 1985-1990; Asst S Aid's Ch Alexandria VA 1983-1985. rm_walker@cox.net

MAYER, Charles David (NY) 141 E 35th St, New York NY 10016 B Oceanside NY 7/23/1955 s Charles William Mayer & Mary Emily. BA Ob 1977; MDiv Harvard DS 1982; Cert Blanton-Peale Grad Inst 1992; Cert Blanton-Peale Grad Inst 1992; Cert Blanton-Peale Grad Inst 1994. D 6/1/1996 P 12/7/1996 Bp Richard Frank Grein. m 1/25/1986 Claudia Powell Ream. Assoc Ch Of The Incarn New York NY 1996-1998. Contrib, "One-Parent," *One-Chld Families*, Amer Inst For Resrch, 1980. Amer Assn Pstr Coun; Assn Clin Mem Amer Grp Psychther Assn; Assn Mem Amer Assn Of Mar & Fam Ther. cmayer723@aol.com

✠ **MAYER, Rt Rev James Scott** (NwT) 1802 Broadway, Lubbock TX 79401 **Chap of the Trsfg Lubbock TX 2009-; Bp of NW Texas Dio NW Texas Lubbock TX 2009-** B Dallas TX 9/23/1955 s James Pettigrew Mayer & Mary Elizabeth. BBA Texas Tech U 1977; MDiv Epis TS of The SW 1992. D 6/20/1992 Bp Donis Dean Patterson P 3/25/1993 Bp James Monte Stanton Con 3/21/2009 for NwT. m 2/4/1978 Katherine K Kistenmacher c 2. Ch Of The Heav Rest Abilene TX 1994-2009; Asst S Jas Epis Ch Texarkana TX 1992-1994. D.D. U So 2011; D.D. Sem of the SW 2010. bishopmayer@nwtdiocese.org

MAYER, Linda Margaret (Spok) PO Box 1226, Chelan WA 98816 **D S Andr's Ch Chelan WA 2010-** B 1/14/1943 d Gardner Thompson & Vera. D 6/13/2009 Bp James Edward Waggoner. m 6/15/1974 Rudolph Mayer c 3. rflmmayer@msn.com

MAYER JR, Nicholas Max (WTex) Po Box 1265, Castroville TX 78009 **H Trin Carrizo Sprg TX 2005-** B Little Rock AR 10/2/1933 s Nicholas Max Mayer & Omie Alma. USNA 1957; BA U of Arkansas 1960; BD VTS 1967. D 6/14/1967 P 4/4/1968 Bp George Henry Quarterman. c 2. R S Phil's Ch Uvalde TX 1971-1994; Ch Of The Ascen Uvalde TX 1971-1991; P-in-c S Mk's Epis Ch Coleman TX 1968-1970; Cur Ch Of The Heav Rest Abilene TX 1967-1971.

MAYER, Peter Woodrich (Md) 1601 Pleasant Plains Rd, Annapolis MD 21409 **R S Marg's Ch Annapolis MD 2010-** B Keene NH 9/6/1969 s Douglas Mayer & Susan. BA Providence Coll 1992; MDiv VTS 2001. D 6/9/2001 Bp Daniel William Herzog P 1/19/2002 Bp A(lbert) Theodore Eastman. m 7/9/2005 Allison H Henry c 2. Cmsn on Cong Dvlpmt Dio Rhode Island Providence RI 2008-2010; R Emm Epis Ch Cumberland RI 2005-2010; Asst S Jn's Ch Lafayette Sq Washington DC 2001-2005. 77harp@gmail.com

MAYER, Philip (Dal) 4809 S Colony Blvd, The Colony TX 75056 B Saginaw MI 2/9/1982 s Paul Duane Mayer & Anna Ileen. BA SE Coll Lakeland FL 2004; MDiv Nash 2008. D 5/31/2008 Bp John Wadsworth Howe P 12/6/2008 Bp James Monte Stanton. m 4/23/2005 Melissa Mary Ward. Vic S Ptr's By The Lake Ch The Colony TX 2008-2011. melissamary@gmail.com

MAYER, Robert James (ECR) 20920 Mcclellan Rd, Cupertino CA 95014 B Lynn MA 8/31/1932 s Max Mayer & Joanne. MIT 1950; Harv 1952; BA Brandeis U 1957; CDSP 1969. D 4/5/1966 P 7/26/1971 Bp George Richard Millard. m 4/12/1958 Joanna Conway March c 4. H Chld Epis Ch San Jose CA 1989; Chair Dept Mssns Dio El Camino Real Monterey CA 1985-1986; Chair Dept Mssns Dio El Camino Real Monterey CA 1981-1982. rjmayer2@aol.com

MAYER, Sandra Crow (CGC) 5158 Border Dr N, Mobile AL 36608 **R S Jn's Ch Monroeville AL 2009-** B 7/7/1941 U of So Alabama; U So. D 7/21/2000 P 2/4/2001 Bp Charles Farmer Duvall. Trin Epsicopal Ch Atmore AL 2001-2008; The Ch Of The Redeem MOBILE AL 2000-2001; Wilmer Hall Mobile AL 1991-2000. newengl@frontiernet.net

MAYERS, Thomas Wycliffe Oswald (Mich) 3837 W. 7 Mile Rd., Detroit MI 48221 **R S Mk's Ch Dorchester MA 1991-** B GY 12/20/1955 s Charles William Mayers & Caroline Matilda. CTh Centro De Estudios Teologicas 1984; M. Ed Cambridge Coll 1993; DMin EDS 1998. Trans from Church in the Province Of The West Indies 8/2/1995 Bp Don Edward Johnson. m 12/27/1984 Altagaracia Paulino Sanchez c 3. All SS Ch Detroit MI 2008-2010; S Mk's Ch Dorchester MA 1995-2007; Asst P S Mk's Ch Brooklyn NY 1990-1991; Asst P S Simeon's Ch Bronx NY 1989-1990; Asst P S Ann's Ch Of Morrisania Bronx NY 1988-1989; Asst P Ch Of S Thos Brooklyn NY 1987-1988. revtwom@yahoo.com

MAYFIELD, Donna Jeanne (O) 515 N Chillicothe Rd, Aurora OH 44202 B Houston TX 6/20/1948 d Donald Frederick Wakeman & Doris Evelyn. TCU; BD St. Edw's U Austin TX 1985; MDiv Epis TS of The SW 1986. D 6/24/1986 Bp Maurice Manuel Benitez P 5/1/1987 Bp Gordon Taliaferro Charlton. c 3. S Paul's Epis Ch Cleveland Heights OH 2004; R S Jn's Epis Ch Cuyahoga Falls OH 1999-2004; S Mart's Ch Chagrin Falls OH 1996-1999; S Chris's Epis Ch Austin TX 1992-1993; Asst S Dav's Ch Austin TX 1986-1988. Auth, "Old Liberty and the Cross," *LivCh*, 2003; Auth, "Just Call Me Donna,"

LivCh, 1987; Auth, "New Frontiers' Wmn In The Ord Mnstry Ap Bulletin," 1986; Auth, "Open". dmayfield@vnaohio.org

MAYFIELD JR, Ellis Oglesby (ETenn) 144 Sister Christabel Rd, Sewanee TN 37375 B Fort Meade MD 1/7/1952 s Ellis Oglesby Mayfield & Susan Ballantyne. BS U So 1973; MDiv SWTS 1979. D 8/6/1979 Bp Richard Mitchell Trelease Jr P 5/16/1980 Bp William Evan Sanders. c 4. Athletic Dir S Andr's Chap S Andrews TN 1997-1999; Chapl S Andr's-Sewanee Sch Sewanee TN 1995-1999; R Ch Of The Gd Samar Knoxville TN 1979-1995. emayfield@sasweb.org

MAYFIELD JR, Judson Townes (EC) Rr 1 Box 84-A, Bath NC 27808 B Calvary GA 12/22/1930 s Judson Townes Mayfield & Marjorie Zena. BBA U GA; MA Duke 1953; BD STUSo 1962. D 6/27/1962 P 4/1/1963 Bp Edward Hamilton West. m 12/16/1950 Dorothy Turner. Dio E Carolina Kinston NC 1990-1992; Zion Epis Ch Washington NC 1984-1989; R S Jas Epis Ch Belhaven NC 1982-1988; Middle Mssn In Macon Dio Georgia Savannah GA 1980-1981; Middle Georgia Dioc Mssn Macon GA 1980-1981; Ch Of The Trin Swainsboro GA 1979-1980; Vic Epis Ch Of S Mary Magd Louisville GA 1976-1980; Vic Gr Epis Ch Sandersville GA 1976-1980; Vic Ch Of The Gd Shpd Swainsboro GA 1969-1976; R S Mary's Ch Jacksonville FL 1964-1969; Vic Ch Of The Ascen Carrabelle FL 1962-1964. Auth, "S Lk Journ". smo1006@ecu.edu

MAYHALL, Monna S (Tenn) 1509 Jaybee Ct, Franklin TN 37064 **S Paul's Ch Franklin TN 2005-** B Alabama 3/31/1963 D 10/1/2005 Bp Stephen Hays Jecko P 4/15/2007 Bp James Monte Stanton. m 4/9/1988 Douglas Mayhall c 1. moomayhall@att.net

MAYHOOD, Gary William (LI) No address on file. B New York NY 10/23/1947 s Alexander Mayhood & Evelyn. BA Pacific Luth U 1969. D 12/21/1974 P 6/28/1975 Bp Jonathan Goodhue Sherman. Clerk Dio Long Island Garden City NY 1975-1976; Cur S Marg's Fresh Meadows NY 1974-1975.

MAYNARD, Beth Harper (Mass) 29 Mill St # 1, Beverly MA 01915 B Nashville TN 10/18/1962 d Robert Preston Maynard & Jane. BA Amh 1984; MDiv Bos 1993; Cert SWTS 1994. D 6/4/1994 Bp David Elliot Johnson P 6/10/1995 Bp John H(enry) Smith. m 4/19/1986 Mark Christopher Dirksen. R Ch Of The Gd Shpd Fairhaven MA 2000-2004; P in charge Ch Of The Gd Shpd Fairhaven MA 1997-2000; Asst S Gabr's Epis Ch Marion MA 1997-2000; Asst Trin Ch Huntington WV 1994-1997. Ed, "Get Up Off Your Knees: Preaching the U2 Catalog," Cowley, 2003; Auth, "How to Evangelize a GenXer (NOT)," Forw Mvmt, 2001; Contrib, "The Bread of Life," Morehouse Pub, 2000; Auth, "Meditations for Lay Eucharistic Ministers," Morehouse Pub, 1999. Phi Beta Kappa 1984. bmaynard@gmail.com

MAYNARD, Dennis Roy (SanD) 49 Via Del Rossi, Rancho Mirage CA 92270 B Arkansas City KS 7/4/1945 s Hue Roy Maynard & Roxie Ola. AA Arkansas City Cmnty Coll 1964; BA Westmar Coll 1966; MDiv SWTS 1969; DMin SWTS 2001. D 6/21/1969 P 12/1/1969 Bp Chilton Powell. m 8/13/1983 Nancy Major c 4. R S Jas By The Sea La Jolla CA 1997-2003; Vice R S Mart's Epis Ch Houston TX 1995-1997; R Chr Ch Greenville SC 1980-1995; R Ch Of The Epiph Richardson TX 1972-1980; Cur Gr Ch Muskogee OK 1969-1970. Auth, "The Magnolia Series," *The Changing Magnolia*, Dionysus, 2011; Auth, "When Sheep Attack," *When Sheep Attack*, Dionysus, 2011; Auth, "The Magnolia Series," *The Magnolia At Sunrise*, Dionysus, 2010; Auth, "The Magnolia Series," *The Sweet Smell of Magnolia*, Dionysus, 2009; Auth, "The Magnolia Series," *The Pink Magnolia*, Dionysus, 2008; Auth, "The Magnolia Series," *Pruning the Magnolia*, Dionysus, 2007; Auth, "The Magnolia Series," *When the Magnolia Blooms*, Dionysus, 2006; Auth, "The Magnolia Series," *Behind the Magnolia Tree*, Dionysus, 2005; Auth, "Forgive and Get Your Life Back," *Forgive and Get Your Life Back*, Dionysus, 2003; Auth, "Forgiven, Healed, Restored," *Forgiven, Healed and Restored*, Dionysus, 1997; Auth, "The Money Bk," *The Money Bk*, Dionysis, 1997; Auth, "Those Episkopols," *These Episkopols*, Dionysus, 1997; Frequent Contrib, "Angl Dig," *Angl Dig*. episkopols@aol.com

MAYNARD, Jane F (Oly) 6732 N Parkside Ln, Tacoma WA 98407 **R Chr Ch Tacoma WA 2010-** B Southbridge MA 3/9/1954 d Paul Emil Maynard & Rita Frances. BA U of Pennsylvania 1975; MA U IL 1979; MDiv CDSP 1992; MA Claremont TS 1998; PhD Claremont TS 2001. D 1/12/1992 P 7/26/1992 Bp John Stuart Thornton. m 12/29/2001 James Treyens c 3. P-in-c S Thos Ch Medina WA 2008-2009; P-in-c Ch Of The Epiph Seattle WA 2007-2008; P-in-c Gd Samar Epis Ch Sammamish WA 2004-2006; Dn, DSOMAT Dio Olympia Seattle WA 2004; Ass Pfr PastoralTheology &Dir of Field Ed. CDSP Berkeley CA 2001-2003; Asstg P All SS' Ch San Francisco CA 1998-2001; Dir of Field Educ CDSP Berkeley CA 1995-2000; Asstg P S Mk's Epis Ch Upland CA 1995. Co-Ed, "Pstr Bearings: Lived Rel and Pstr Theol," Lexington Books, 2010; Auth, "Transfiguring Loss: Julian of Norwich as a Guide for Survivors of Traumatic Grief," The Pilgrim Press, 2006; Auth, "Reflection," *New Westminster Dictionary of Chr Sprtlty*, Westminster Jn Knox, 2005; Auth, "Purgatory:Place or Process? Wmn Views on Purgatory in 14-15th Century Britain," *Stds in Sprtlty*, 2002; Auth, "Finding Rel and Sprtl Meaning in AIDS Related Multiple Loss: The Contributions of Showings to a Constructive Theol," *Wmn Chr Mystics Speak to Our Times*, Sheed & Ward, 2001. scl U of Pennsylvania 1975; Phi Beta Kappa U of Pennsylvania 1975. jmaynardm@gmail.com

MAYNARD, Joan Pearson (SO) 2661 Haverford Rd, Columbus OH 43220 **D S Mk's Epis Ch Columbus OH 1995-** B Austin TX 9/25/1940 d Forest Simms Pearson & Jennie Marie. BA Baylor U 1962; BSW Wright St U 1981; MS U Of Dayton 1984; MA Luth TS 1992. D 1/23/1993 Bp Herbert Thompson Jr. m 1/6/1962 Robert Howell Maynard c 1.

MAYO, H(arold) Jonathan (Be) 240 State Road 65, River Falls WI 54022 **R S Geo's Epis Ch Hellertown PA 2010-** B Carbondale PA 2/25/1953 s Arthur Beavan Mayo & Harriet E. BA Wilkes Coll 1975; MDiv St. Vladimir's Orth Sem 1980. Rec from Greek Orthodox 3/14/2004 Bp Keith Bernard Whitmore. c 2. P-in-c Ch Of S Thos And S Jn New Richmond WI 2004-2010. hjmayo@yahoo.com

MAYOM, Abraham Mabior (SD) No address on file. **Ch Of The H Apos Sioux Falls SD 2005-** B Sudan 1/1/1977 s Dhuka G Mayom & Achiek Akech. D 11/6/2005 P 5/7/2006 Bp Creighton Leland Robertson. m 8/28/2004 Elizabeth Akuol Agok c 1.

MAYOR, Robert Michael (U) 1710 Foothill Dr, Salt Lake City UT 84108 **Consult, Stwdshp Dvlpmt Dio Utah Salt Lake City UT 2008-; Alt Dep, GC Dio Utah Salt Lake City UT 2007-; Dioc Fin Com Dio Utah Salt Lake City UT 2006-; Sum Camp Chapl, Camp Tuttle Dio Utah Salt Lake City UT 2004-; Consult, Congrl Dvlpmt Dio Utah Salt Lake City UT 2003-; Exam Chapl Dio Utah Salt Lake City UT 2003-; R All SS Ch Salt Lake City UT 2002-** B Lexington Park MD 1/1/1966 s Robert Edward Mayor & Kathleen Moore. BA San Diego St U 1995; MDiv SWTS 1996; Cert SWTS 2006. D 6/8/1996 P 12/21/1996 Bp Gethin Benwil Hughes. m 8/3/2005 Liana Lee Bigham c 1. Chair, Dioc Mssn T/F Dio Utah Salt Lake City UT 2009-2010; Plnng Com for Reg Preaching Conf Dio Utah Salt Lake City UT 2005; Exec Com, Dioc Coun Dio Utah Salt Lake City UT 2004-2006; Chair, Mssn Resource Team Dio Utah Salt Lake City UT 2003-2008; Consult, Congrl Dvlpmt Dio Maryland Baltimore MD 2000-2003; Sum Camp Chapl, Bp Claggett Cntr Dio Maryland Baltimore MD 2000-2002; Asst S Thos Epis Ch Towson MD 2000-2002; Chair, Dioc Conv Plnng Com Dio Maryland Baltimore MD 2000; Co-Chair, Plnng Com for Natl YA Conf Dio Maryland Baltimore MD 1999-2001; R S Steph's Ch Severn Par Crownsville MD 1998-2002; Chair, Evang Com Dio Maryland Baltimore MD 1997-2000; Nave Chapl Cathd of St Ptr & St Paul Washington DC 1997-1999; All SS Ch Rehoboth Bch DE 1997-1998; Asst R S Thos Epis Ch Towson MD 1996-1998. Auth, "Liberal or Conservative: Labels Miss the Whole Picture," *Salt Lake Tribune*, Nwspr Agcy Corp, 2008; Auth, "Angl Power - It's About Power Not Sex," *Salt Lake Tribune*, Nwspr Agcy Corp, 2007; Contrib, "Responding w Integrity to an Unjust War," *The Dioc Dialogue*, Epis Dio Utah, 2002. Polly Bond Awd of Merit ECom 2004; Mahlon Norris Gilbert Awd SWTS 1996. lmjmayor@gmail.com

MAYORGA-GONZALEZ, Mary (Ct) 3 Oakwood Ave., Lawrence MA 01841 B 9/3/1939 d Anasis Mayorga & Clementino. U Of Costa Rica Cr 1978; MA Epis TS of The SW 1986; MDiv EDS 1989. D 5/30/1992 P 1/23/1993 Bp David Elliot Johnson. m 4/2/1978 Armando Gonzalez. Dio Massachusetts Boston MA 1994-2000; Hisp Congregations P S Lk's/San Lucas Epis Ch Chelsea MA 1992-2007; Cltn For Hisp Mnstrs Pepperell MA 1992-1994. mary@openscope.net

MAYPOLE, Sara Chandler (Va) 6988 Woodchuck Hill Rd, Fayetteville NY 13066 B Topeka KS 11/15/1941 d John Edgar Chandler & Bertha Madelaine. BFA U of Kansas 1963; MDiv EDS 1979; DMin Fuller TS 1996. D 6/2/1979 Bp Paul Moore Jr P 4/13/1980 Bp Horace W B Donegan. m 5/3/2003 Thomas A Maypole. Int S Barth's Ch Estes Pk CO 2008-2009; Adj Prof of Pstr Theol VTS Alexandria VA 1993-2003; R S Marg's Ch Woodbridge VA 1991-2003; Evang and Renwl Cmsn Dio Connecticut Hartford CT 1989-1990; Advsry Bd Dio Connecticut Hartford CT 1988-1991; R S Ptr's Ch So Windsor CT 1985-1991; Assoc Chr Ch Greenville Wilmington DE 1983-1985; S Paul's Epis Ch Pittsburgh PA 1979-1983. Auth, *Overcoming Resistance to Renwl*; Auth, *Who Will Cast the 1st Stone*. smaypole@twcny.rr.com

MAYRER, Jane Goodhue (Md) 2010 Sulgrave Ave, Baltimore MD 21209 **Cathd Of The Incarn Baltimore MD 2001-** B Pueblo CO 4/21/1947 BA Stamford U 1969; JD U of Alabama 1976. D 6/2/2001 Bp Robert Wilkes Ihloff. m 1/6/1996 Andrew Mayrer c 1. janemayrer@comcast.net

MAYS-STOCK, Barbara L (RI) 50 Charles St, Cranston RI 02920 B Newport RI 4/19/1954 d Judson Harper Mays & Anna. Andover Newton TS; BA Providence Coll 1977; Rhode Island Sch for Deacons 1994. D 3/20/1994 Bp George Nelson Hunt III. m 3/4/1978 Roger William Stock c 1. D Cathd Of S Jn Providence RI 2006-2011; COM Dio Rhode Island Providence RI 2006-2009; D Ch Of The Ascen Cranston RI 2000-2008; D Cathd Of S Jn Providence RI 1994-1999. bmaysstock@cox.net

✠ MAZE, Rt Rev Larry Earl (Ark) 102 Midland St, Little Rock AR 72205 **Ret Bp of Arkansas Dio Arkansas Little Rock AR 2006-** B Havre MT 9/13/1943 s Archie Maze & Goldie. BS No Montana Coll 1968; MS Montana St U 1969; MDiv Epis TS of The SW 1972. D 6/25/1972 P 1/17/1973 Bp Jackson Earle

Gilliam Con 6/11/1994 for Ark. m 8/31/1981 Beth Daniels c 4. Dio Arkansas Little Rock AR 1994-2006; Bp of Ark Dio Arkansas Little Rock AR 1993-2006; Ch Of The Nativ Greenwood MS 1988-1994; R All SS Ch Jackson MS 1981-1988; S Jas Epis Ch Port Gibson MS 1977-1981; Asst Ch Of The H Sprt Missoula MT 1972-1974. DD TS U So 1995; DD Epis TS of the SW 1994. lemaze@sbcglobal.net

MAZGAJ, Marian Stanislaus (WVa) PO Box 206, Valley Grove WV 26060 **Asst S Matt's Ch Wheeling WV 1997-** B Gaj PL 12/8/1923 s Joseph Alexander Mazgaj & Josephine. MA U of Cracow PL 1951; STD U of Cracow PL 1954; JCL CUA 1958; JCD CUA 1970; MA Duquesne U 1972. Rec from Roman Catholic 10/1/1981 as Priest Bp Robert Poland Atkinson. m 6/27/1972 Mildred Juanita Ankrom c 2. R S Paul's Ch Weston WV 1986-1995; R S Steph's Epis Ch Steubenville OH 1983-1986; Vic S Mich's Ch Kingwood WV 1982-1983; Asst Trin Ch Morgantown WV 1981-1983. Auth, *Vstng Hm in Poland After 33 Years & Wrld War II True Stories*, McClain, 1993; Auth, *Communist Govt of Poland as Affecting Rts of the Ch from 1944-1960*, CUA, 1970; Auth, "Numerous arts," *Herald Star*, 1961; Auth, "Numerous arts," *Charleston Gazette*; Auth, "Numerous arts," *Other Pub*; Auth, "Numerous arts," *The Franciscan Monthly*; Auth, "Numerous arts," *The Intelligencer*; Auth, "Numerous arts," *The Steubenville Register*; Auth, "Numerous arts," *Wheeling News Register*.

MAZINGO, Stephen C (EC) 519 Greeridge Rd, Snow Hill NC 28580 **Dom And Frgn Mssy Soc- Epis Ch Cntr New York NY 2008-; S Jas Par Wilmington NC 2008-** B Jacksonville NC 10/17/1981 s Larry Stephen Mazingo & Carol Lynn. BA Appalachian St U NC 2004; MDiv VTS 2007. D 6/9/2007 P 12/8/2007 Bp Clifton Daniel III. Exec Coun Appointees New York NY 2007-2008. mazingomission@gmail.com

MAZUJIAN, Harry (NJ) 44 Broad St, Flemington NJ 08822 **R Calv Epis Ch Flemington NJ 1998-** B East Orange NJ 5/8/1953 s Irvand Mazujian & Valerie. BA Drew U 1975; MDiv GTS 1988. D 6/6/1988 Bp Robert Campbell Witcher Sr P 12/10/1988 Bp Orris George Walker Jr. m 8/4/1979 Ruth Polasik c 3. R St Jn the Bapt Epis Ch Linden NJ 1992-1998; Vic S Mk's Ch Hammonton NJ 1990-1992; Asst S Mary Anne's Epis Ch No E MD 1988-1990. Ord Of H Cross. harry.mazujian@calvary-episcopal.net

MAZZA, Joseph (Fla) 1737 Mayview Rd, Jacksonville FL 32210 B Long Island NY 6/26/1940 s Thomas Mazza & Frances Elizabeth. D 6/13/2009 Bp Thomas Edward Breidenthal. m 12/31/1993 Carol A Mazza c 2. joe.mazza@att.net

MAZZA, Joseph Edward (FdL) 4569 Glidden Dr, Sturgeon Bay WI 54235 B Naperville IL 2/6/1929 s Joseph NMN Mazza & Ethel Mae. VTS; BA Ripon Coll Ripon WI 1951; MDiv SWTS 1954. D 6/19/1954 P 12/20/1954 Bp Gerald Francis Burrill. m 9/7/1957 Susan Dietrich c 5. Vic S Lk's Sis Bay WI 1999-2004; Int Chr the King/H Nativ (Sturgeon Bay) Sturgeon Bay WI 1995-1996; Dn Evanston Deanry Dio Chicago Chicago IL 1991-1992; R S Aug's Epis Ch Wilmette IL 1971-1992; R S Paul's Epis Ch Beloit WI 1962-1971; Cn Cathd Of S Jas Chicago IL 1956-1961; Vic The Annunc Of Our Lady Gurnee IL 1954-1956. Conf of St. Greg's Abbey 1952; Fllshp of St. Jn (SSJE) 1993. jmazza000@gmail.com

MAZZACANO, Leslie G (NJ) 379 Huntington Drive, Delran NJ 08075 **D Trin Ch Moorestown NJ 2002-** B Philadelphia PA 5/23/1952 d Robert Wallace Otterstein & Mary Magdalene. AA Pierce Jr Coll 1971. D 10/31/1998 Bp Joe Morris Doss. m 10/6/1979 John Karl Mazzacano. D Gr Ch Pemberton NJ 1998-2001. deaconleslie@yahoo.com

MAZZARELLA, Virginia Teresa (Roch) 327 Mendon Center Rd, Pittsford NY 14534 B Jackson Hgts NY 7/17/1958 d Anthony Joseph Mazzarella & Justine Marie. BA Dickinson Coll 1979; Med Duquesne U 1983; MDiv Pittsburgh TS 1990. D 6/2/1990 P 12/13/1990 Bp Alden Moinet Hathaway. m 7/23/1999 Charles A Ennis c 8. Joint Pastorate S Mths Epis Ch E Rochester NY 2008-2009; S Jn's Ch Canandaigua NY 2006-2008; Gr Ch Lyons NY 2005-2006; S Mk's Ch Newark NY 2003-2004; Int S Lk's Ch Branchport NY 2002-2003; S Jn's Ch Canandaigua NY 2002; S Geo's Ch Hilton NY 2001-2002; R Gr Ch Scottsville NY 1999-2000; R S Andr's Epis Ch Caledonia NY 1999-2000; S Thos Epis Ch Rochester NY 1995-1998; Asst P S Mich's Ch Geneseo NY 1994-1996; Vic Trin Ch Freeport PA 1992-1993; Vic Ch Of The H Innoc Leechburg PA 1991-1993. Larry G Nagel Memi Prize In Pstr Care Pittsburgh TS Pittsburgh PA; Sylvester S Marvin Fellowowship Pittsburgh TS Pittsburgh PA; Thos Jamison Schlrshp Pittsburgh TS Pittsburgh PA. mamazzarella@gmail.com

MCADAMS, James Lee (Ala) 3775 Crosshaven Dr, AL Birmingham 35223 **Asst R S Steph's Epis Ch Birmingham AL 2008-** B Birmingham AL 7/29/1971 s Stanley Luis McAdams & Helen Graham. BBA Faulkner U 2004; MDiv STUSo 2008. D 5/24/2008 Bp John McKee Sloan P 12/16/2008 Bp Henry Nutt Parsley Jr. m 7/27/1991 Kimberly Carter c 3. jamiemc@ssechurch.org

MCADAMS, Kathleen A (Mass) PO Box 51003, Boston MA 02205 **Alum Coun CDSP Berkeley CA 2009-; Jubilee Mnstry Advsry Com Dom And Frgn Mssy Soc- Epis Ch Cntr New York NY 2009-; Vision Team Ldr - Dom Pvrty Working Grp Dom And Frgn Mssy Soc- Epis Ch Cntr New York NY 2008-; Ecclesia Mnstrs Boston MA 2006-** B Washington DC 11/18/1965 d Merton F McAdams & Bette. AA Arapahoe Cmnty Coll 1985; BA Metropltn St Coll of Denver 1987; MDiv CDSP 2000. D 12/2/2000 P 6/2/2001 Bp William Edwin Swing. m 12/15/2006 Ellen M Grund. Asst/Actg R All SS Epis Ch Palo Alto CA 2001-2005; D / Eucharistic Min - Rite I S Lk's Ch San Francisco CA 2000-2001; Tchg Asst - Pstr Care CDSP Berkeley CA 1999; Asst to the Pres - Oasis/California (LGBT Mnstry) Dio California San Francisco CA 1998-2001; Sem S Tim's Ch Danville CA 1998-2000; Founding Chairperson - T/F on Homelessness CDSP Berkeley CA 1998-1999; St Yth Proj Coordntr w Larkin St Yth Cntr All SS' Ch San Francisco CA 1997. revkathymcadams@yahoo.com

MCAFEE JR, Ernest Wyatt (Dal) 1106 Richland Oaks Drive, Richardson TX 75081 **Int Chr Epis Ch Dallas TX 2010-** B Memphis TN 9/9/1938 s Ernest Wyatt McAfee & Ila Mae. BA Van 1960; MBA Pepperdine U 1980; MDiv Epis TS of The SW 1985; DMin Drew U 1992. D 6/19/1985 Bp Scott Field Bailey P 12/19/1985 Bp Stanley Fillmore Hauser. m 6/4/1960 Diana Duff. R S Barn Ch Garland TX 1998-2005; S Richard's Of Round Rock Round Rock TX 1997-1998; S Lk's Epis Ch Belton TX 1990-1997; D Trin-By-The-Sea Port Aransas TX 1985-1990. Auth, "Generations," Forw Mvmt Press, 1997. erniemcafee@yahoo.com

MCAFOOS JR, Louis Garfield (NJ) 700 S Park Dr, Westmont NJ 08108 **Died 12/6/2010** B Philadelphia PA 9/13/1918 s Louis Garfield McAfoos & Irma Barbara. BA U of Pennsylvania 1940; MD Hahnemann Med 1943. D 6/2/1979 P 12/5/1979 Bp Albert Wiencke Van Duzer.

MCALEER, Ruth Bresnahan (Kan) 8700 Metcalf Ave Apt 102, Shawnee Mission KS 66212 B Newburyport MA 8/18/1931 d Thomas Lawrence Bresnahan & Catharine Elizabeth. Brigham Hosp Sch of Nrsng Boston MA 1954; BA Barat Coll 1976; MA Webster U 1978; SWTS 1991; CPE Residency St. Lk's Med Cntr Milwaukee Wisconsin 1992. D 6/20/1992 P 12/19/1992 Bp Frank Tracy Griswold III. c 3. Chr Ch Overland Pk KS 2001-2003; Eccles. Crt Dio Kansas Topeka KS 1998-2005; Dn Dio Kansas Topeka KS 1998-2003; Dn NE Convoc Dio Kansas Topeka KS 1998-2003; R Gr Epis Ch Ottawa KS 1996-1999; Asst S Steph's Ch Troy MI 1994-1995; Asst Trin Ch Highland Pk IL 1992-1993. "Daily Meditations," *Forw day by Day*, Forw Day By Day, 2004. Coll Chapl 1993-1997; Soc of S Jn the Evang 1993. thom.mcaleer@gmail.com

MCALLEN, Robert (WTex) 1112 S Westgate Dr, Weslaco TX 78596 **Vic Epiph Epis Ch Raymondville TX 2003-** B Brownsville TX 10/1/1934 s Argyle A McAllen & Margaret. BS Rice U 1956; Studied under Cn 9 Prog 2005. D 8/30/2006 P 3/25/2007 Bp Gary Richard Lillibridge. m 12/29/1959 Margaret L Looney c 3. Bro S Andr. robmcallen@aol.com

✠ MCALLISTER, Rt Rev Gerald Nicholas (Okla) 507 Bluffestates, San Antonio TX 78216 **Ret Bp of Oklahoma Dio Oklahoma Oklahoma City OK 1989-** B San Antonio TX 2/16/1923 s Walter Williams McAllister & Leonora Elizabeth. VTS 1951. D 9/30/1953 P 9/24/1954 Bp Everett H Jones Con 4/15/1977 for Okla. m 10/2/1953 Helen Black. Chapl to Cler/Fams Dio W Texas San Antonio TX 1991-1993; Bp-in-Res Epis TS Of The SW Austin TX 1991-1993; Bp Dio Oklahoma Oklahoma City OK 1977-1988; R S Dav's Epis Ch San Antonio TX 1970-1977; Cn to the Ordnry Dio W Texas San Antonio TX 1963-1970; P-in-c S Fran Epis Ch Victoria TX 1958-1963; D Epiph Epis Ch Raymondville TX 1953-1954. Auth, "What We Learned From What You Said"; Auth, "This Fragile Earth Our Is Hm". DD ETSS; DD VTS Alexandria VA. bpgnmca@aol.com

MCALLISTER, Loring William (Minn) 16368 Swede Hill Dr S, Afton MN 55001 B Winnemucca Nevada 6/27/1937 s Glendon William McAllister & Isabel Trenchard. BA GW 1960; MA U of Kansas 1966; PhD U of Kansas 1968. m 4/29/1967 Lucy Jean Remple. D S Mary's Basswood Grove Hastings MN 1982-2001; D S Lk's Epis Ch Hastings MN 1975-1982. loringmcallister@earthlink.net

MCALPINE, James Paul (Mass) 102 Manchester Rd, Newton Highlands MA 02461 B Torrington CT 7/16/1931 s John McAlpine & Julia May. BA Trin 1953; BD EDS 1956; MA New Sch for Soc Resrch 1973. D 12/22/1956 Bp Archie H Crowley P 10/1/1957 Bp Walter H Gray. m 7/17/1954 Sally Ann Larsen c 4. R Gr Ch Newton MA 1984-1994; Ch of theTransfiguration N Conway NH 1983-1984; R Chr Ch No Conway NH 1975-1984; R St Mich & Gr Ch Rumford RI 1959-1963; P-in-c All SS Ch Ivoryton CT 1957-1959. jimsal502@comcast.net

MCALPINE, Thomas Hale (FdL) 215 Houston St, Ripon WI 54971 **R S Ptr's Ch (S Mary's Chap) Ripon WI 2007-** B Stockton CA 10/10/1950 s Arthur C McAlpine & Joy W. BA U CA 1971; MA Fuller TS 1976; PhD Yale DS 1984. D 5/22/2004 Bp Sergio Carranza-Gomez P 11/27/2004 Bp Joseph Jon Bruno. m 12/30/1978 Elvice S Strong c 1. R S Jas Ch Manitowoc WI 2006-2007; Dio Los Angeles Los Angeles CA 2004-2006; Assoc S Jn's Par San Bernardino CA 2004-2006. "Facing The Powers," Wipf & Stock, 2002; "By Word Wk & Wonder," Wipf & Stock, 2002; "Sleep Div And Human In The OT," Sheffield Acad Press, 1986. thomas.mcalpine.grd.rels@aya.yale.edu

✠ **MCARTHUR JR, Rt Rev Earl Nicholas** (WTex) Po Box 734, Wimberley TX 78676 **Curs Sprtl Dir Dio W Texas San Antonio TX 1986-** B Houston TX 1/1/1925 s Earl Nicholas McArthur & Nanabelle. BA Rice U 1948; MDiv VTS 1963; DD VTS 1988; DD STUSo 1990. D 7/10/1963 Bp Everett H Jones P 1/18/1964 Bp Richard Earl Dicus Con 1/6/1988 for WTex. Ret Bp Suffr Of Wtex Dio W Texas San Antonio TX 1994-2002; Bp Dio W Texas San Antonio TX 1988-1993; R S Steph's Epis Ch Wimberley TX 1981-1987; Curs Sprtl Dir Dio W Texas San Antonio TX 1980-1982; R All SS Epis Ch Corpus Christi TX 1967-1981; Assoc H Sprt Epis Ch Houston TX 1965-1967; R Ch Of The Annunc Luling TX 1963-1965. eandsmca48@txwinet.com

MCASKILL, Arthur Donald (Mass) 180 Pleasant Street, South Yarmouth MA 02664 **Died 1/17/2011** B Boston MA 1/7/1932 s Howard A McAskill & Lillian May. BA/BS Suffolk U 1957; BD Bex 1966. D 6/25/1966 P 5/1/1967 Bp Anson Phelps Stokes Jr.

MCAULAY, Roderick Neil (NCal) 7803 Stefenoni Ct, Sebastopol CA 95472 **Chairman, COM Dio Nthrn California Sacramento CA 2010-** B Sacramento CA 3/16/1944 s John Roderick McAulay & Edith Joyce. BA Occ 1966; JD Stan 1969; MDiv CDSP 1999. D 6/26/1999 Bp Vincent Waydell Warner P 1/5/2000 Bp Richard Lester Shimpfky. m 7/25/1970 Mary MacDonald c 1. R S Steph's Epis Ch Sebastopol CA 2001-2010; Assoc All SS Epis Ch Palo Alto CA 1999-2001. sunriser@sonic.net

MCBEATH, Susan A(udrey) (Ind) 13088 Tarkington Commons, Carmel IN 46033 **D S Chris's Epis Ch Carmel IN 1995-** B Madison WI 12/26/1939 d Ivor Charles McBeath & Lida Windemuth. BS U of Wisconsin 1961; MS U of Wisconsin 1962; MA Chr TS 1987. D 6/23/1995 Bp Edward Witker Jones. c 1. NAAD. smcbeath@indy.net

MCBRIDE, Bill (WLa) 9105 Colonial Gdns, Shreveport LA 71106 **Mem, Cmsn on Yth and YA Mnstry Dio Wstrn Louisiana Alexandria LA 2008-; Mem, Ed Bd ALIVE Dio Wstrn Louisiana Alexandria LA 2008-; R S Mths Epis Ch Shreveport LA 2007-** B Meridian MS 10/7/1950 s William Anderson McBride & Diana Elizabeth. BA Rhodes Coll 1972; MA NW St U 1979; PhD Van 1989; Angl TS 2005. D 6/4/2005 P 5/17/2006 Bp D(avid) Bruce Mac Pherson. m 8/6/1978 Cheryl Wisenbaker c 1. Mem, Cmsn on Yth and YA Mnstry Dio Wstrn Louisiana Alexandria LA 2008-2011; Cur S Tim's Ch Alexandria LA 2005-2007. SBL 1996. fatherbill176@gmail.com

MCBRIDE, David Patrick (Cal) 12572 Foster Rd, Los Alamitos CA 90720 B Shreveport LA 3/22/1927 s Jackson Robert McBride & Mary Edwards. BA U of Texas 1947; MDiv VTS 1950; MA SUNY 1971. D 7/10/1950 P 3/24/1951 Bp Clinton Simon Quin. m 3/31/1974 Nancy Jeanette Rodgers c 3. Bp Of ArmdF- Epis Ch Cntr New York NY 1968-1987; R H Trin Epis Ch Dickinson TX 1954-1955; Min in charge H Trin Epis Ch Dickinson TX 1951-1953; Min In Charge S Mich's Ch La Marque TX 1950-1951. (affiliation: Bp of ArmdF; Six Mltry hon US Navy; Assorted Veterans Affrs (VA) hospitals. dmcbride42@verizon.net

MCBRIDE, Gordon Kay (Az) 2120 E. Hampton St., Tucson AZ 85719 **Died 7/10/2010** B Heber UT 8/30/1941 s Frederick Gordon McBride & Hazel Alvira. BA Westminster Coll 1965; MA U of Oregon 1966; PhD U Cinc 1976; Cert SWTS 1983. D 5/16/1983 P 4/27/1984 Bp Otis Charles. c 4. Auth, "The Vic of Bisbee," 2009; Auth, "The Ghost of Midsummer Common," 2008; Auth, "Flying to Tombstones," publishAmerica, 2003; Auth, "Elizabethan Frgn Plcy in Microcasm: The Portuguese Pretender," *Albion*, 1970; Auth, "Once Again: The Case of Richard Hunne," *Albion*, 1966. EPF 1985. Cn Dio Arizona 2006. mcbride1@dakotacom.net

MCBRIDE, Robert Green (Dal) 3460 Forest Lane, Dallas TX 75234 B Laurel MS 6/13/1937 s Lester Gilmore McBride & Erna Lee. BA U Of Florida 1961; MDiv Duke 1964; Cert Nash 1987. D 6/29/1987 P 11/19/1987 Bp William Hopkins Folwell. m 12/29/2007 Deborah Price c 5. R Ch Of The Gd Shpd Terrell TX 1995-2007; R S Mths Epis Ch Clermont FL 1990-1995; R The Epis Ch Of The Redeem Avon Pk FL 1987-1990. frbobgstx@yahoo.com

MCBRIDE, Ronald Winton (Cal) 34043 Calle Mora, Cathedral City CA 92234 **Assoc S Ptr's Epis Ch San Francisco CA 1999-** B Ashland OH 6/7/1925 s Charles Augustus McBride & Blanche Arlene. BA Wheaton Coll 1949; The Biblic Sem New York NY 1952; STB Ya Berk 1954. D 12/23/1954 Bp Horace W B Donegan P 6/24/1955 Bp Charles Francis Boynton. c 5. Assoc S Paul In The Desert Palm Sprg CA 2001-2005; Chapl Dio California San Francisco CA 1996-1998; Admin Dio California San Francisco CA 1989-1990; Vstng Instr CDSP Berkeley CA 1970-1983; Vic Ch Of The Trsfg Towaco NJ 1961-1963; R S Paul's And Resurr Ch Wood Ridge NJ 1957-1961; Asst Min Calv and St Geo New York NY 1954-1957. Auth, "Cottage To Cathd: A Narrative Of The Tawain Epis Ch," Richard T Corsce.

MCBRYDE, Greer Kroening (CFla) 1155 C.R. 753 South, Webster FL 33597 B Greenville SC 2/27/1945 d Walter Herbert Kroening & Margaret Greer. AA Valencia Cmnty Coll 1981; Inst for Chr Stds Florida 1996; MDiv Asbury TS 2004. D 11/23/1996 P 1/15/2005 Bp John Wadsworth Howe. m 8/21/1963 Clyde McBryde c 2. Assoc R Ch Of The Mssh Winter Garden FL 2005-2011; D All SS Ch Of Winter Pk Winter Pk FL 2002-2004; D Emm Ch Orlando FL 1996-2001. Auth, "THrough The Vlly of the Shadow of Death," *Through the Vlly of the Shadow of Death*, self-Pub, 2010. Ord of S Lk 1997. gkmcbryde@aol.com

MCCABE III, Charles Peyton (WMich) 325 West Center, Hastings MI 49058 B Charleston WV 10/16/1953 s Charles Peyton McCabe & Lois. BA Marshall U; MDiv VTS 1987. D 9/20/1987 Bp William Franklin Carr P 5/1/1988 Bp Robert Poland Atkinson. m 12/29/1973 Frankie Winfree c 1. Chair - Estrn Dnry Dio Wstrn Michigan Kalamazoo MI 1993-2002; Dio Wstrn Michigan Kalamazoo MI 1992-2007; R Emm Ch Hastings MI 1990-2007; Assoc R The Memi Ch Of The Gd Shpd Parkersburg WV 1987-1989. MAC. CHARLIE123@YAHOO.COM

MCCABE, Paul Charles (At) 1785 Benningfield Dr Sw, Marietta GA 30064 **Sprtl Dir Dio Atlanta Atlanta GA 2007-; Sprtl Dir Dio Atlanta Atlanta GA 2007-** B Atlanta GA 6/16/1969 s Patrick John McCabe & Vera Maud. BS Georgia St U 1993; MDiv U So 2007. D 12/21/2006 P 6/30/2007 Bp J(ohn) Neil Alexander. m 1/20/2006 Adrian W McCabe c 1. Cur S Edw's Epis Ch Lawrenceville GA 2007-2009. revpaul@dofaya.org

MCCAFFREY, Susan Maureen (CFla) 4110 S Ridgewood Ave, Port Orange FL 32127 **D Gr Epis Ch Inc Port Orange FL 2011-** B Philadelphia PA 11/5/1944 d Amerigo Michael Cristella & Helen Peter. LGPN Estrn Voc. Tech. Sch; Montgomery Cnty Cmnty Coll 1988; Stds Diac Inst of Chr Stds 2011. D 12/11/2010 Bp John Wadsworth Howe. m 5/19/2001 William McCaffrey c 2. mm4ever@embarqmail.com

MCCAGG, Lauriston Hazard (Ore) 6705 Ne 255th St, Battle Ground WA 98604 B New York NY 1/23/1934 s Edward King McCagg & Rosalind. BA Ya 1955; MDiv Epis TS In Kentucky 1969. D 5/24/1969 Bp William R Moody P 5/1/1970 Bp Christoph Keller Jr. c 1. P Ch Of The Gd Shpd Sandy OR 1992-1994; Int Chr Ch Par Lake Oswego OR 1990-1991; P S Jas Epis Ch Cathlamet WA 1989-1992; Assoc S Mich And All Ang Ch Portland OR 1987-1994; Bd Trst Dio Oregon Portland OR 1985-1991; S Aid's Epis Ch Gresham OR 1985-1987; Dept Mssns Dio Oregon Portland OR 1983-1987; Dn Convoc Dio Oregon Portland OR 1983-1984; Vic Ch Of Chr The King On The Santiam Stayton OR 1980-1982; Dio Oregon Portland OR 1980; S Edw's Ch Silverton OR 1979-1984; H Cross Epis Ch Portland OR 1978; Dir Bps Happ Mvmnt Dio W Texas San Antonio TX 1976-1978; S Andr's Ch Port Isabel TX 1974-1978; All SS Epis Ch San Benito TX 1974-1977; Assoc S Mk's Epis Ch Little Rock AR 1971-1973; Asst To Dn Trin Cathd Little Rock AR 1969-1971. Auth, "Happ In The Dio Wtex". elhazard@easystreet.net

MCCALEB, Douglas William (SeFla) 464 NE 16th Street, Miami FL 33132 **Dn Trin Cathd Miami FL 2006-; Com Dio Virginia Richmond VA 1990-** B Burbank CA 5/16/1949 s Sidney Briscoe McCaleb & Rose. BA U CA 1971; MDiv GTS 1987. D 6/13/1987 P 4/24/1988 Bp Peter James Lee. R Chr Epis Ch Winchester VA 1995-2005; Asst S Jn's Ch Lafayette Sq Washington DC 1993-1994; Assoc S Jn's Epis Ch McLean VA 1987-1992. Auth, "Va Epis (1990-1992)". christch@shentel.net

MCCALL, Chad (Tex) 5203 Rico Cv, Austin TX 78731 B Chicago IL 8/26/1971 s Charles W McCall & Jacqueline T. BA Davidson Coll 1993; MBA Georgia Tech 1995; MDiv Duke DS 2005. D 6/18/2011 Bp C(harles) Andrew Doyle. m 7/24/1999 Rhone R McCall c 2. chadmccall@me.com

MCCALL JR, John (Kosho) (Me) 300 Page St, San Francisco CA 94102 B Rochester IN 5/24/1948 s Jack Keith McCall & Mildred Alyce. BA U of Maine 1970; MDiv GTS 1976. D 3/25/1975 P 1/31/1976 Bp Frederick Barton Wolf. Gr Cathd San Francisco CA 1990-1991; Asst Chr Ch Portola Vlly CA 1988-1989; Int S Ann's Epis Ch Windham Windham ME 1985-1986; Deploy Off Dio Maine Portland ME 1983-1985; Dio Maine Portland ME 1979-1984; Asst To Bp Of Me Dio Maine Portland ME 1979-1983; S Giles Ch Jefferson ME 1976-1978; Asst Cathd Ch Of S Lk Portland ME 1975-1976. koshosfzc@gmail.com

MCCALL, Ramelle Lorenzo (Md) 730 Bestgate Rd, Annapolis MD 21401 **D S Phil's Ch Annapolis MD 2011-** B Baltimore MD 5/13/1981 s Leroy McCall & Benita. BS Stevenson U 2003; MDiv Wake Forest DS 2006; Angl Stds VTS 2011. D 6/4/2011 Bp Eugene Sutton. MCCARL3@GMAIL.COM

MCCALL, Richard David (LI) 5117 N Chatham Dr, Bloomington IN 47404 B Baltimore MD 4/27/1947 s Henry David McCall & Olivia Genevieve. BA McDaniel Coll 1968; MA Indiana U 1972; MDiv Nash 1979; PhD Grad Theol Un 1998. D 5/31/1979 P 1/26/1980 Bp Edward Witker Jones. m 12/17/1983 Terry Meacham c 2. Provost S Jn's Chap Cambridge MA 2005-2010; Int Par Of The Mssh Auburndale MA 2004-2005; Prof EDS Cambridge MA 1999-2010; Dn CDSP Berkeley CA 1998-1999; Int All Souls Par In Berkeley Berkeley CA 1996-1997; Lectr CDSP Berkeley CA 1994-1997; R S Paul's Ch Glen Cove NY 1986-1994; Cn Cathd Of The Incarn Garden City NY 1981-1986; Asst R S Steph's Ch Terre Haute IN 1979-1981. Auth, "Angl Wrshp in No Amer," *Encyclopedia of Rel in Amer*, CQ Press, 2010; "Do This: Liturg as Performance," Univ. of Notre Dame Press, 2007; Auth, "Imagining the Other: Aesthetic Thology," *Rel and the Arts*, 2006; Auth, "Drama and Wrshp," *New Dictionary of Liturg and Wrshp*, 2003; Auth, "The Shape of the Eucharistic Pryr," *Wrshp*, 2000; Auth, "In My Beginning is My End: The Future Shape of Liturg," *ATR*, 1999; Auth, "Performing Drama. Liturg, and

M

Being-as-Event," *Doxology*, 1998; Auth, "Enacting Presidenct, Diaconia, and Ch," *Open*, 1997; Auth, "Theopoetics: The Acts of God in the Act of Liturg," *Wrshp*, 1997; Auth, "Anamnesis or Mimesis," *Ecclesia Oran*, 1996. IALC 2003; No Amer Acad of Liturg 1997; Societas Liturgica 2002. Fell ECF 1996. trmccall@bluemarble.net

MCCALL, Terry (Mass) 5117 N Chatham Dr, Bloomington IN 47404 B South Bend IN 3/1/1950 d Justin Ruckle Meacham & Mary Ellis. BS U of Maryland 1971; MS Indiana U 1976; MDiv SWTS 1984; PhD OH SU 1995. D 6/25/1984 Bp Edward Witker Jones P 12/29/1984 Bp William Grant Black. m 12/17/1983 Richard David McCall c 1. Int R S Paul's Ch Brookline MA 2008-2009; S Jas' Epis Ch Cambridge MA 2007-2008; S Andr's Ch Framingham MA 2005-2007; Trin Ch Concord MA 2001-2003; The Ch Of Our Redeem Lexington MA 2000-2005; Int Dio Massachusetts Boston MA 2000-2003; R Epis Ch Of S Ptr And S Mary Denver CO 1997-1999; Assoc P Epis Ch Of The Ascen Dallas TX 1995-1996; Epis Mnstry To The Oh St U Columbus OH 1990-1992; Epis Chapl S Steph's Epis Ch And U Columbus OH 1990-1992; P-in-c S Paul's Ch Columbus OH 1989-1990; Assoc R S Mk's Epis Ch Columbus OH 1986-1989; R Our Sav Ch Mechanicsburg OH 1984-1986. trmccall@bluemarble.net

MCCALLUM, Bruce Allan (FdL) PO Box 561, Waupaca WI 54981 B Chicago IL 1/28/1942 s Robert Allan & Fernella. U IL; Amer Coll 1967. D 5/7/2011 Bp Russell Edward Jacobus. m 12/28/1963 Karen Dennis c 3. deaconbruce@higent.com

MCCALLUM, Lynn Chiles (O) 2268 Robinwood Ave, Toledo OH 43620 **Died 5/3/2010** B Scotts Bluff NE 8/30/1942 s Mark McCallum & Delores. BA U of Nebraska 1964; MDiv VTS 1967. D 6/11/1967 Bp Russell T Rauscher P 1/1/1968 Bp Samuel B Chilton. lynn.mccallum@nemsys.com

MCCANDLESS, Richard Lawrence (O) 1106 Bell Ridge Rd., Akron OH 44303 B Savannah GA 1/29/1946 s Edward Richard Wilson McCandless & Sara. BS MI SU 1966; MS MI SU 1967; MDiv VTS 1970; DMin Lancaster TS 1984. D 6/20/1970 P 5/19/1971 Bp Philip Alan Smith. m 9/10/1966 Patricia Johnson c 3. R S Paul's Ch Akron OH 1992-2006; Chair of BACAM, Commisssion on Mnstry, Ecum Com Dio Ohio Cleveland OH 1992-2004; Dn & R Cathd Ch Of S Steph Harrisburg PA 1985-1992; Pres, St. Steph's Epis Sch Cathd Ch Of S Steph Harrisburg PA 1985-1992; Chair of BACAM, Chair of COM, Ecum Com Dio Cntrl Pennsylvania Harrisburg PA 1985-1992; Prov COMs Strng Com Prov III Chester Sprg PA 1982-1985; Chair of BACAM, Chair of COM Dio NW Pennsylvania Erie PA 1979-1985; R S Jn's Epis Ch Sharon PA 1979-1985; Chair of BACAM, COM, Secy of Stndg Com, Chair of Dept of Educ Dio Easton Easton MD 1975-1980; R S Mk's Epis Ch Perryville MD 1974-1979; Assoc R All SS Ch Richmond VA 1972-1974; Cur S Jas' Epis Ch Leesburg VA 1970-1972. Co-Auth, "Only Love Can Make It Easy," Twenty Third Pub, 1988; Auth, "More than 30 arts and Revs," *Journ, mag, websites*. Reality Ther Assn 1990-1998; Rel Educ Assn 1972-1992. Natl Sci Fndt Grad Fllshp MI SU 1966; Tau Beta Pi MI SU 1966; BS mcl in 3 years MI SU 1966. mccandlessr@sbcglobal.net

MCCANDLESS, Richard W. (Kan) 3028 Washington Ave, Parsons KS 67357 B Mitchell SD 11/23/1932 s Richard William McCandless & Mildred St Clare. BA U of No Dakota 1954; STB EDS 1962. D 6/16/1962 Bp George Leslie Cadigan P 12/21/1962 Bp Gordon V Smith. m 4/25/1985 Jean Sivils. H Trin. Reg Mnstry Parsons KS 1994-2001; Vic Calv Ch Yates Cntr KS 1993-2003; R Gr Ch Chanute KS 1993-2003; Vic S Tim's Ch Iola KS 1993-2003; Dn Dio Kansas Topeka KS 1984-2003; S Jn's Ch Parsons KS 1983-1994; R Trin Epis Ch El Dorado KS 1971-1983; Cn Gr Cathd Topeka KS 1967-1971. r_mccandless@sbcglobal.net

MCCANN, Christopher Richard (O) 16267 Oakhill Rd, Cleveland Heights OH 44112 **P-in-c S Lk's Epis Ch Chardon OH 2006-** B Windsor Nova Scotia 6/26/1963 s R McCann & Beverley. BA U Of King's Coll Halifax Ns CA; MDiv Atlantic TS 1998. Trans from Anglican Church of Canada 6/5/2006 Bp Mark Hollingsworth Jr. 062663@sbcglobal.net

MCCANN, John Harrison (WMo) 1492 Hemlock Ct, Liberty MO 64068 **Archd Dio W Missouri Kansas City MO 1989-; Cn Dio W Missouri Kansas City MO 1985-** B Fort Sam Houston TX 5/24/1945 s Willis Harrison McCann & Catherine. BA U of Kansas 1967; MDiv VTS 1971. D 6/11/1971 Bp Edward Randolph Welles II P 12/17/1971 Bp Arthur Anton Vogel. m 3/5/1993 Susan Griffen. Assoc S Paul's Ch Kansas City MO 1973-1985; Cur Chr Epis Ch Springfield MO 1971-1973. vespers393@kc.rr.com

MCCANN, Michael Louis (HB) 804 E Juneau Ave, Milwaukee WI 53202 B Bay City MI 5/31/1943 s Wilfred R McCann & Geraldine. BS Cntrl Michigan U 1966; Epis TS In Kentucky 1972. D 6/1/1972 Bp Addison Hosea P 12/1/1972 Bp A Donald Davies. m 8/3/1974 Rita R Podoski. S Lk's Epis Ch Milwaukee WI 1973-1974; S Jn's Ch Ft Worth TX 1972-1973.

MCCANN, Michael Wayne (At) 975 Longstreet Cir, Gainesville GA 30501 **P Assoc Gr Epis Ch Gainesville GA 2006-** B Kansas City MO 3/8/1947 s Wayne Melvin McCann & Elinor Blanche. BA Hav 1968; BD Harvard DS 1971. D 6/26/1971 P 4/1/1972 Bp John Melville Burgess. m 7/17/1987 Candace Lighton c 4. Gr Epis Ch Gainesville GA 1980-1987; R Trin Ch Hampton NH 1974-1980; The Par Of S Chrys's Quincy MA 1971-1974. mccannicals@gmail.com

MCCANN, Robert Emmett (Cal) 4023 Canyon Rd, Lafayette CA 94549 B Chicago IL 2/18/1931 s Peter Francis McCann & Mary Agnes. BA Glennon Coll St. Louis MO 1953; MDiv Kenrick-Glennon Sem 1957; Med Washington U 1966. Rec from Roman Catholic 10/1/1976 as Priest Bp C Kilmer Myers. m 12/15/1967 Sylvia Grigul c 2. S Matt's Epis Ch San Mateo CA 2005-2007; Ch Of Our Sav Mill Vlly CA 2002-2007; Int S Giles Ch Moraga CA 1999-2000; Int S Clem's Ch Berkeley CA 1995-1996; Dir Planned Giving Dio California San Francisco CA 1991-1997; S Jn's Epis Ch Oakland CA 1976-1991. Auth, "Congrl Guide To Planned Giving," 1997. Allin Fllshp Ecum Institue Geneva Switzerland; Procter Fellowowship "Anglicanism, Globalism And Ecum" EDS Cambridge MA. robmccann1@gmail.com

MCCANN, Sandra Briggs (At) PO Box 264, Dodoma Tanzania **Exec Coun Appointees New York NY 2004-** B Washington PA 3/22/1944 d David Briggs & Harriett. BS Maryville Coll 1966; MD Tem Sch of Med 1970; MDiv VTS 2003. D 10/17/2004 P 7/3/2005 Bp J(ohn) Neil Alexander. m 4/15/1972 Martin P McCann c 2. mccanns@mindspring.com

MCCANN, Susan Griffen (WMo) 1492 Hemlock Ct, Liberty MO 64068 **R Gr Epis Ch Liberty MO 1996-** B New York NY 4/12/1943 d Richard Daniel Griffen & Sara Catherine. BA Mt Holyoke Coll 1964; MS U of Kansas 1986; MDiv Epis TS of The SW 1996. D 6/8/1996 P 12/14/1996 Bp John Clark Buchanan. m 3/5/1993 John Harrison McCann. AAMFT; ACSW; LMCSW; NASW. mothermccann@prodigy.net

MCCARD, John Fleming (At) 3110 Ashford Dunwoody Rd Ne, Atlanta GA 30319 **S Mart In The Fields Ch Atlanta GA 2004-** B Tampa FL 4/25/1965 s Ray Harold McCard & Rosalyn Sandra. BA Ob 1988; MDiv GTS 1992; STM Nash 2003; DMin VTS 2007. D 7/25/1992 P 6/6/1993 Bp Herbert Thompson Jr. m 6/15/1991 Cynthia Ann King c 3. R S Mk's Ch Marco Island FL 1998-2004; S Mk's Epis Ch San Antonio TX 1997-1998; Asst R S Paul's Epis Ch Dayton OH 1992-1996. jfmccard@yahoo.com

MCCARLEY, Melanie Leigh Smith (WVa) Zion Church, 221 E. Washington St., Charles Town WV 25414 **COM Dio W Virginia Charleston WV 2011-; Comp Dio Com Dio W Virginia Charleston WV 2011-; Prov III VP Prov III Chester Sprg PA 2009-; Dn of Estrn Dnry Dio W Virginia Charleston WV 2004-; Dioc Coun Dio W Virginia Charleston WV 2004-; R Zion Epis Ch Chas Town WV 2001-** B Falls Church VA 10/22/1966 d Terry Lawrence Smith & Rita Gay. Ya Berk; BA MWC 1988; MDiv VTS 1991. D 6/13/1992 Bp Robert Poland Atkinson P 8/1/1993 Bp Edward Witker Jones. m 11/9/1991 Philip Earl McCarley. Vic Emm Ch Rapidan VA 1998-2001; Vic S Steph's Elwood IN 1994-1997; Assoc H Fam Epis Ch Fishers IN 1992-1994. RECTOR@ZIONEPISCOPAL.NET

MCCARROLL SSG, Connie Jo (SO) 4381 S.Rangeline Rd., West Milton OH 45383 B Dayton OH 5/18/1946 d Lawrence McCarroll & Thelma Rosie. BS Wright St U 1968; MS Wright St U 1970; DO MI SU 1976; DSO Sch for the Diac 1995. D 10/28/1995 Bp Herbert Thompson Jr. D Ch Of The Gd Shpd Athens OH 2009-2011; D S Geo's Epis Ch Dayton OH 1995-2010. Living Water Awd Kettering Med Cntr/ Adventist Hosp Systems 2004. conniejodo@cs.com

MCCARROLL, Sandra Kim (Nev) 1806 Hilton Head Dr, Boulder City NV 89005 B American Falls 1/22/1937 d Max Yost. BA U Chi 1961; MA Un Coll Schenectady NY 1968. D 4/10/2005 P 10/15/2005 Bp Katharine Jefferts Schori. m 9/12/1959 Bruce McCarroll c 1. P S Chris's Epis Ch Boulder City NV 2005-2010. skym@cox.net

MCCARRON, Charles Francis (LI) 11 Violet Ave, Mineola NY 11501 **Epis Cmnty Serv Long Island 1927 Garden City NY 2007-** B The Bronx NY 11/11/1955 BA Ford 1978; MDiv Maryknoll TS 1985; MA St. Bonaventure U 1989; JD CUNY 1994; DAS GTS 2001. Rec from Roman Catholic 6/3/2002 Bp Orris George Walker Jr. Dio Long Island Garden City NY 2010-2011; P-in-c Ch Of The Resurr Kew Gardens NY 2003-2007. "Anth Of Padua," Franciscan Inst Pub, 1994; "Lawr Of Brindisi," Franciscan Inst Pub, 1989; "Franciscan Spirituals And Capuchin Reform," Franciscan Inst Pub, 1987. chairlief@aol.com

MCCART, Thomas K (Roch) 152 DartmouthSt, Rochester NY 14607 B Oklahoma City OK 12/17/1948 s Virgil McCart & Dorethea. BA SW Oklahoma St U 1971; MA U of New Mex 1974; MDiv CDSP 1978; Fllshp Oxf 1981; MA Van 1993; PhD Van 1994. D 9/15/1978 P 5/24/1979 Bp Richard Mitchell Trelease Jr. Assoc R S Paul's Ch Rochester NY 2002-2011; Int The Par Of S Clem Honolulu HI 2000-2001; R S Mk's Epis Ch Upland CA 1996-2000; Cn Precentor Chr Ch Cathd Indianapolis IN 1990-1996; Dio Tennessee Nashville TN 1989; Chr Ch Cathd Nashville TN 1987-1988; Cur Trin Epis Ch Ft Worth TX 1981-1985; Dio The Rio Grande Albuquerque NM 1978-1980; Asst S Fran On The Hill El Paso TX 1978-1980. Auth, "Matter & Manner of Praise," Scaarecrow Press, 1998. AAM 1975; Assn of Dioc Liturg & Mus Comm 1979-2000. Fllshp ECF 1988. tmccart2@rochester.rr.com

MCCARTHY, Bartlett Anderson (Dal) 7335 Inwood Rd, Dallas TX 75209 B Refusio TX 9/29/1943 s Richard McCarthy & Jane. BD U MN 1966; MDiv

GTS 1970. D 6/29/1970 Bp Hamilton Hyde Kellogg P 6/10/1971 Bp The Bishop Of Tokyo. m 10/3/1987 Kalita Beck. S Mich And All Ang Ch Dallas TX 1984-1987; Breck Sch Minneapolis MN 1980-1983; Assoc S Mart's By The Lake Epis Minnetonka Bch MN 1976-1979; R S Ptr's Ch Cass Lake MN 1971-1974; Asst Ch Of The H Trin New York NY 1968-1970. andymcc@sbcglobal.netm

MCCARTHY, Jean Elizabeth Rinner (Ia) 2906 39th St, Des Moines IA 50310 **R S Mk's Epis Ch Des Moines IA 2001-** B Mount Pleasant IA 5/31/1943 d Donald L Rinner & Vaughn Belle. BA U of Iowa 1965; MA St. Johns U 1988; MDiv SWTS 2000. D 5/27/2000 P 2/24/2001 Bp Carl Christopher Epting. m 8/29/1964 Michael Lynn McCarthy c 2. D The Cathd Ch Of S Paul Des Moines IA 2000-2001; Dir Of Chr Formation The Cathd Ch Of S Paul Des Moines IA 1996-1998. mikeandjeanmcc@msn.com

MCCARTHY, Jerome (SwFla) 444 Palm Tree Dr, Bradenton FL 34210 B Cork IE 2/7/1944 s Patrick McCarthy & Helen. BS Natl of Ireland U 1967; BD Lon 1971; MA U Of Hull Gb 1973; Hde Natl of Ireland U 1978; DMin Pittsburgh TS 1985. Trans from Anglican Church of Canada 10/1/1988. m 12/28/1985 Charline Elizabeth Iles. Chapl Sarasota Dnry Chapl Sarasota FL 1988-1992. Auth, "Eden & Other Reservations". ESMHE, Fllshp Recon. bookmonk@hotmail.com

MCCARTHY, Marty (NC) 4205 Quail Hunt Lane, Charlotte NC 28226 B Washington DC 10/8/1952 s Maurice Francis McCarthy & Barbara. BA Emory & Henry Coll 1974; MDiv VTS 1978. D 6/3/1978 P 6/4/1979 Bp John Alfred Baden. m 11/23/2009 Cindy L Morris c 2. R S Jn's Epis Ch Charlotte NC 1995-2008; Dn Dio Virginia Richmond VA 1988-1991; R Epiph Epis Ch Richmond VA 1982-1995; Asst S Dunst's McLean VA 1978-1982. mfm108@aol.com

MCCARTHY, Melissa Jane (Los) 5450 Churchwood Dr, Oak Park CA 91377 **Dn, Dnry 1 Dio Los Angeles Los Angeles CA 2011-; Vic Ch Of The Epiph Oak Pk CA 2009-** B Bakersfield CA 7/16/1972 d Michael McCarthy & Linda. BA U CA 1998; MDiv CDSP 2005. D 6/11/2005 Bp Chester Lovelle Talton P 1/14/2006 Bp Joseph Jon Bruno. P-in-c Ch Of The Epiph Oak Pk CA 2008-2009; Assoc Ch Of The Epiph Oak Pk CA 2006-2008. melissajmccarthy@gmail.com

MCCARTHY, Nancy Horton (SeFla) 474 SW 29th Ave, Delray Beach FL 33445 **Assoc S Greg's Ch Boca Raton FL 2009-** B Newark NJ 1/9/1934 d Leonard Mead Horton & Gladys Marie. BA Ob 1956; MDiv VTS 1988. D 10/4/1982 P 11/30/1988 Bp Calvin Onderdonk Schofield Jr. c 1. S Mary's Epis Ch Of Deerfiel Deerfield Bch FL 1999; Assoc S Greg's Ch Boca Raton FL 1988-1999; Asst S Jn's Ch Hollywood FL 1982-1985. Ord of Julian of Norwich 1984. Phi Beta Kappa Ob 1956. revnancy474@comcast.net

MCCARTHY, William Robert (Ore) 5060 SW Philomath Blvd, PMB 165, Corvallis OR 97333 **R Emer The Epis Ch Of The Gd Samar Corvallis OR 2006-** B Tacoma WA 11/17/1941 s Denward Sylvester McCarthy & Florence Elizabeth. BS OR SU 1966; U Cinc 1970; MDiv Nash 1975. D 6/14/1975 Bp Quintin Ebenezer Primo Jr P 12/13/1975 Bp James Winchester Montgomery. m 4/22/1962 Bernice Bigler c 2. Stndg Com Dio Oregon Portland OR 1993-1997; Samar Hlth Serv Corvallis OR 1989-2006; R The Epis Ch Of The Gd Samar Corvallis OR 1989-2006; R Chr Ch Waukegan IL 1981-1989; Curs Off/Sprtl Dir Dio Chicago Chicago IL 1977-1985; One In Chr Ch Prospect Heights IL 1977-1981; S Mich's Ch Barrington IL 1975-1977. Assn For Psychol Type. Who'S Who In Healthcare Marquis 2002; Who'S Who In Rel Marquis. liammacplus@comcast.net

MCCARTY, Barnum C (Fla) 4531 Sussex Ave Unit 5, Jacksonville FL 32210 B Jacksonville FL 4/10/1930 s Harvey Pierce McCarty & Nellie Mae. BA Ccollege of Arts and Sci, U So 1954; MDiv STUSo 1956; DD STUSo 1993. D 6/20/1956 P 4/15/1957 Bp Edward Hamilton West. m 8/6/1956 Betty Ann Roberts c 3. Int S Jn's Cathd Jacksonville FL 1999-2000; Int S Ptr's Ch Fernandina Bch FL 1996-1997; Int S Thos' Epis Ch St Petersburg FL 1995-1996; R S Mk's Epis Ch Jacksonville FL 1971-1995; R S Andr's Epis Ch Panama City FL 1962-1971; R Trin Ch Apalachicola FL 1956-1959. barnummc@aol.com

MCCARTY, Marjorie McDonall (EC) 100 E Sherwood Dr, Havelock NC 28532 B New York NY 9/18/1939 d Bertrand John McDonall & Mildred Suydam. BA La Roche Coll 1979; MDiv Pittsburgh TS 1982. D 6/5/1982 P 12/1/1982 Bp Robert Bracewell Appleyard. c 4. R S Chris's Ch Havelock NC 1996-2008; P-in-res Ware Epis Ch Gloucester VA 1988-1996; Dio Pittsburgh Monroeville PA 1982-1988.

MCCARTY, Mary Sharon (WA) 13301 Baden Westwood Rd, Brandywine MD 20613 **R S Mary's Aquasco Brandywine MD 1997-** B Three Rivers MI 9/4/1951 d John Daniel McCarty & Virginia Elizabeth. BS U CA 1979; MDiv CDSP 1987. D 6/13/1987 Bp Charles Brinkley Morton P 12/1/1988 Bp John Thomas Walker. m 6/23/1984 Jeffrey Samuel Buyer. Chr Ch W River MD 2010-2011; Ch Of Middleham Lusby MD 2007-2008; R S Paul's Par Prince Geo's Cnty Brandywine MD 1997-2006; Queen Anne Sch Upper Marlboro MD 1995-1997; Asst R S Paul's Epis Ch Piney Waldorf MD 1988-1995.

MCCARTY, Patricia Gayle (WTenn) 1720 Peabody Ave., Memphis TN 38104 **Cur Gr - S Lk's Ch Memphis TN 2009-** B Memphis TN 10/15/1958 d Thomas R McCarty & Billie Jean. BA U of Tennessee 1980; JD Cecil C. Humphrey Sch of Law 1983; MDiv Epis TS Of The SW 2009. D 6/7/2009 P 1/16/2010 Bp Don Edward Johnson. mccgayle@sbcglobal.net

MCCARTY, Steven Lynn (Md) Saint Andrew's Episcopal Church, 22 Cumberland St, PO Box 189, Clear Spring MD 21722 **Vic S Andr's Ch Clear Sprg MD 2011-** B Hagerstown MD 6/16/1959 s Roger K McCartry & Marlene. Current Stdt Nash; AA Hagerstown Cmnty Coll 1980; BS Frostburg St U 1990; Cert U So TS 2006. D 6/10/2006 Bp Robert Wilkes Ihloff P 6/12/2011 Bp Eugene Sutton. m 11/8/1981 Melanie Mummert c 2. BroSA 2000; The CBS 2008. revmccarty@gmail.com

MCCASKILL, James Calvin (Va) 3439 Payne St, Falls Church VA 22041 **R S Paul's Ch Bailey's Crossroads Falls Ch VA 2009-** B Charlotte NC 1/13/1973 s John Calvin McCaskill & Frances Clement. BA Wheaton Coll 1995; MA U Of Leeds Gb 2002. D 6/15/2002 P 1/3/2003 Bp Robert William Duncan. Asst S Paul's Epis Ch Pittsburgh PA 2002-2004; Dio Pittsburgh Monroeville PA 2002; Cathd Chapt Trin Cathd Pittsburgh PA 2002. james@mccaskill.info

MCCASLIN, H Kenneth (Pa) P.O. Box 86, Ardmore PA 19003 B Augusta ME 5/6/1955 s Henry Hinton McCaslin & Jacqueline Ann. BSBM U of Phoenix 2004; MAR Luth TS 2009. D 6/14/2008 Bp Edward Lewis Lee Jr. m 6/26/1982 Cheryl Rene Covert c 2. HkenM@me.com

MCCASLIN, Robert Allan (Ark) 209 Park Dr, West Memphis AR 72301 **D in Charge Ch Of The H Cross W Memphis AR 2009-; R Ch Of The H Cross W Memphis AR 2009-; R Ch Of The H Cross W Memphis AR 2009-** B Deerfield IL 5/29/1954 s William Robert Mc Caslin & Nora May. HR Profsnl Certification Soc for HR Managment 2001; CPE Certification U of Arkansas Med Cntr 2007; Upward Bound Off of Congrl Dvlpmt, The Epis Ch 2008; MDiv The TS at The U So 2009. D 3/21/2009 Bp Larry Earl Maze P 9/27/2009 Bp Larry R Benfield. m 11/26/2005 Patricia Pan Adams c 2. Soc for HR Mgmt 1986-2006. CE Prize for Creativity & Excellence in Biblic Stds TS, Sewanee, TN 2009; Shettle Prize for Excellence in Liturg Reading TS, Sewanee, TN 2009. rallanmcc@gmail.com

MCCAUGHAN, Patricia Susanne (Los) 1554 N. Shelley Avenue, Upland CA 91786 **St Fran Epis Mssn Outreach Cntr San Bernardino CA 2011-; Assoc P S Geo's Epis Ch Laguna Hills CA 2010-; Correspondent Epis News Serv New York NY 2004-; Cmncatn Profsnl Dio Los Angeles Los Angeles CA 1999-** B Detroit MI 5/25/1953 d Donald Raymond McCaughan & Madge. BA Wayne 1975; MS Col 1983; MDiv GTS 1997. D 6/21/1997 P 5/31/1998 Bp R(aymond) Stewart Wood Jr. m 5/30/1998 Keith Akio Yamamoto. Assoc R S Geo's Epis Ch Laguna Hills CA 2007-2008; Asst R S Mary's Par Laguna Bch CA 2002-2007; P-in-c S Fran Of Assisi Par San Bernardino CA 1999-2002; Transitional D Cathd Ch Of S Paul Detroit MI 1997-1999; D-in-c S Martha's Ch Detroit MI 1997-1999; Dio Michigan Detroit MI 1997-1998. patmkeithy@aol.com

MCCAULEY, Claud Ward (SwVa) 612 W Franklin St, Richmond VA 23220 B Roanoke VA 2/22/1928 s John Wiley McCauley & Elizabeth Summers. BA Hampden-Sydney Coll 1952; MDiv VTS 1955. D 6/3/1955 Bp Frederick D Goodwin P 6/23/1962 Bp Robert Fisher Gibson Jr. m 9/9/1962 Jane Gaunt c 2. Vic Gr Ch Bremo Bluff VA 2001-2007; Chair-Stwdshp Com Dio SW Virginia Roanoke VA 1996-2000; Dioc Exec Bd Dio SW Virginia Roanoke VA 1996-1999; Vic S Lk's Ch Hot Sprg VA 1995; R Gr Ch Radford VA 1993-1995; All SS Ch Richmond VA 1977-1993; Exec Bd Dio SW Virginia Roanoke VA 1973-1975; Pres (1971)-Stndg Com Dio SW Virginia Roanoke VA 1969-1971; R Chr Ch Blacksburg VA 1964-1976; R Epis Ch Of Our Sav Midlothian VA 1956-1963. Ord Of S Lk 1978.

MCCAULEY, Margaret Hudley (Los) 4215 W 61st St, Los Angeles CA 90043 **D H Nativ Par Los Angeles CA 2007-** B Chicago IL 8/19/1943 d General William Hudley & Cynthia. BA California St U LA 1965; MA California St U 1979; CTh ETS At Claremont CA 2006. D 12/2/2006 Bp Joseph Jon Bruno. m 7/3/1965 Ronald Lee McCauley c 2. DOK 2006. margaret.mccauley@sbcglobal.com

MCCAULEY, Shana (Ore) 1550 Diablo Rd, Danville CA 94526 **S Edw's Ch Silverton OR 2009-** B San Antonio, TX 10/19/1978 d David Lee Price & Myong Cha. BA U Of Washington Seattle WA 2000; MDiv SWTS 2006. D 6/24/2006 Bp Vincent Waydell Warner P 12/2/2006 Bp Marc Handley Andrus. m 12/1/2009 Ryan S McCauley c 1. Assoc S Tim's Ch Danville CA 2006-2008. tyrtal@yahoo.com

MCCAULLEY, Barbara Marie (Ia) 620 Briarstone Dr Apt 28, Mason City IA 50401 **Gr Epis Ch Chas City IA 2010-** B Mason City IA 4/9/1952 d Dale Chris McCaulley & Edna Beryl. BA U of Iowa 1975; MDiv U of Dubuque 1980. D 10/16/2002 Bp George Elden Packard P 5/24/2003 Bp Alan Scarfe. c 1. mccaulbm@mercyhealth.com

MCCAULLEY, Esau Daniel (Alb) 101 Yoshihara, Chatan Japan 904-0105 Japan **All Soul's Epis Ch 2010-** B Huntsville AL 10/28/1979 s Esau McCaulley & Laurie Ann. BA The TS at The U So 2002; MDiv Gordon Conwell Sem

M

2005. D 5/4/2006 Bp David John Bena P 11/11/2006 Bp John Clark Buchanan. m 12/19/2004 Mandy Amanda Waters c 2. Asst S Jn's Ch Portsmouth VA 2008. esaumccaulley@gmail.com

MCCAUSLAND, John Lesher (NH) 457 Reservoir Dr, Weare NH 03281 B Chicago IL 11/10/1939 s John Woods McCausland & Clara Rebecca. BA Harvard Coll 1961; LLB Harvard Law Sch 1964; MDiv Nash 1983. D 6/11/1983 Bp Quintin Ebenezer Primo Jr P 12/17/1983 Bp James Winchester Montgomery. m 6/15/1965 Anne Wiebolt Darrow c 2. Vic H Cross Epis Ch Weare NH 1997-2011; R S Matt's Ch Evanston IL 1992-1997; R S Chas Ch S Chas IL 1985-1992; Cur S Mich's Ch Barrington IL 1983-1984. Chapl SCHC 1998-2002; EPF 1998; Fllshp of St. Jn 1984. holyx@qsinet.net

MCCAW, Mary Ann (Oly) 6 Lincoln Rd, Wellesley MA 02481 B New York NY 6/3/1948 d Frank Cizek & Agatha. BA Bard Coll 1971; MDiv EDS 1974; CTh Seattle U Inst For Ecum Stds 1994. D 7/9/1994 P 1/16/1995 Bp Vincent Waydell Warner. m 2/1/1976 Robert I McCaw. ACPE.

MCCLAIN, Marion Roy (Sam) (FtW) 3650 Chicora Ct Apt 330, Fort Worth TX 76116 B Paris TX 4/27/1938 s Roy McClain & Elizabeth. BS Texas A&M U at Commerce 1960; MS Texas A&M U at Commerce 1963; MTh SWTS 1979; DMin Austin Presb 1984. D 6/24/1977 P 12/1/1977 Bp Robert Elwin Terwilliger. m 8/20/1960 Anndrea Dinse c 1. R S Lk's Epis Ch Stephenville TX 1978-2009; Cur The Epis Ch Of The H Nativ Plano TX 1977-1978. marionmcclain@sbcglobal.net

MCCLAIN, Mikel (Ore) 7875 SW Alden St, Portland OR 97223 B Houston TX 2/10/1948 s Glen McClain & Edna Olga. BA U Of Houston 1974; MDiv Epis TS of The SW 1977. D 9/23/1977 P 5/1/1978 Bp Richard Mitchell Trelease Jr. m 1/14/2006 Marilyn Mills Walkey c 3. S Barn Ch Bonanza OR 2003-2004; S Paul's Ch Klamath Falls OR 2003-2004; Dio Arizona Phoenix AZ 1989-2008; Gd Shpd Of The Hills Cave Creek AZ 1988-2003; R Ch Of The Epiph Houston TX 1986-1988; R Ch Of The Resurr Austin TX 1983-1986; Stwdshp & Evang Departments Dio Texas Houston TX 1978-1988; Assoc R Trin Epis Ch Baytown TX 1978-1983; Assoc R All SS Epis Ch El Paso TX 1977-1978. Ord Of S Lk. mikel_mcc@msn.com

MCCLAIN, Rebecca Lee Kennedy (Oly) Saint Mark's Cathedral, 1245 10th Ave. E., Seattle WA 98102 **Cn Mssnr S Mk's Cathd Seattle WA 2008-** B Lakeland FL 11/9/1947 d Fred Kennedy & Mildred Marlene. Baylor U; BA Trin U 1969; MA Epis TS of The SW 1977; MDiv Epis TS of The SW 1985. D 8/29/1985 Bp Anselmo Carral-Solar P 4/1/1986 Bp Gordon Taliaferro Charlton. c 3. Exec Dir Godly Play Fndt Ch Of Our Sav Par San Gabr CA 2007-2009; Exec Dir CDO Epis Ch Cntr New York NY 2005-2007; Dn Trin Cathd Phoenix AZ 1995-2005; Cn to the Ordnry Dio Arizona Phoenix AZ 1989-2004; Hosp Chapl St Lk's Epis Hosp Houston TX 1987-1988; CE Ch Of The Epiph Houston TX 1986-1987; Chr Formation and Liturg Ch Of The Resurr Austin TX 1985-1986. Auth, *Mssn Statements*. Wmn of Year YWCA 1994. rebeccalmc@aol.com

MCCLAIN, William Allen (NCal) 6825 Sterchi Ln, Montague CA 96064 B Colorado Springs CO 8/20/1927 s Raymond McClain & Belle Jay. BA DePauw U 1951; MDiv CDSP 1966. D 6/19/1966 Bp James Albert Pike P 1/21/1967 Bp C Kilmer Myers. m 11/10/1951 Sally Nugent. P S Barn Ch Mt Shasta CA 1990-1997; Cur Chr Ch Portola Vlly CA 1966-1970. wilsal@snowcrest.net

MCCLANAHAN JR, L (Tenn) A-17-2 Eastlake Residence, Tmn Serdang Perdana, Seri Kembangan Selangor 43300 Malaysia B West Warrick RI 4/18/1935 s Loren B McClanahan & Dorothy. BA S Meinrad Coll; STB CUA 1963; MRE Loyola U 1973; DMin Wstrn TS 1982. Rec from Roman Catholic 6/1/1974 as Priest Bp William Jackson Cox. c 2. Ch Of The Redeem Shelbyville TN 2001; R S Paul's Epis Ch Flint MI 1989-2000; Dio Ohio Cleveland OH 1984-1988; S Paul's Ch Canton OH 1977-1989; S Jn's Par Hagerstown MD 1974-1977. Auth, "Let Those Who Have Ears". Ord of St. Jn of Jerusalem 2005; SSC 1998. frkieran@hotmail.com

MCCLEAREN, Anne Addison (WNC) 1 School Rd, Asheville NC 28806 **Clerin-Charge St Georges Epis Ch Asheville NC 2010-** B Augusta GA 1/21/1957 d Harber Addison & Margery Hovey. BA U of So Carolina 1979; MDiv The GTS 2010. D 5/23/2010 Bp Granville Porter Taylor. c 2. amcclearen@gmail.com

MCCLEERY III, William Acton (SO) St Paul Episcopal Church, PO Box 736, Logan OH 43138 **Vic Ch Of The Epiph Nelsonville OH 2008-; Vic S Paul's Epis Ch Logan OH 2008-** B Lancaster OH 2/2/1945 s William Acton McCleery & Esther Charlene. BA The OH SU 1967; MDiv PrTS 1970; Cert. in Ang. Stds Bex 2007. D 2/2/2008 Bp Kenneth Lester Price P 12/5/2008 Bp Thomas Edward Breidenthal. mccleery.8@osu.edu

MCCLELLAN, Robert Farrell (NMich) Po Box 841, Saint Helena CA 94574 B Chicago IL 6/6/1934 s Robert Farrell McClellan & Katherine. BA MI SU 1956; BD CDSP 1959; PhD MI SU 1964. D 6/28/1959 Bp Richard S M Emrich P 7/1/1961 Bp Archie H Crowley. m 6/23/1956 Sara F Greer c 4. Vic S Annes Ch Dewitt MI 1962-1964; Vic S Geo's Ch Cordova AK 1959-1960. Auth, "The Heathen Chinese," OH SU, 1966; Auth, "Amer Image of China," MI SU, 1964. trr@sonic.net

MCCLELLAN, Thomas Lee (Pa) Po Box 642, Lafayette Hill PA 19444 **R S Mary's At The Cathd Philadelphia PA 1978-** B Wilmington DE 2/9/1942 s William McClellan & Mary. BA Muhlenberg Coll 1965; MDiv EDS 1970; U of Cambridge 1974; S Geo's Coll Jerusalem IL 1976. D 6/6/1970 P 3/6/1971 Bp Robert Lionne DeWitt. Assoc Chapl S Andrews Sch Of Delaware Inc Middletown DE 1976-1977; Assoc S Dav's Ch Wayne PA 1974-1976; Pstr Asst The Epis Ch Of The Adv Kennett Sq PA 1970-1972. *arts*, 2003. Bp White Par Libr Assn 2004; Bp White PB Soc 2001.

MCCLELLAND, Carol Jean (EO) 12019 SE 15th St, Vancouver WA 98683 **D S Mk's Epis and Gd Shpd Luth Madras OR 1998-** B Portland OR 11/25/1937 d Sherman Smith & Lilly Suzanna. U of Washington; BS OR SU 1959; Med Portland St U 1982. D 10/11/1998 Bp Rustin Ray Kimsey. m 9/13/1958 Douglas McClelland. Steph Mnstry. dandcmcclelland@hotmail.com

MCCLENAGHAN, Malcolm Eugene (NCal) 2020 Brady Ln, Roseville CA 95747 B Lancaster OH 9/9/1923 s Donald S McClenaghan & Frances. BA No Cntrl Coll 1945; MDiv Evang TS 1947. D 12/6/1950 Bp Nelson Marigold Burroughs P 6/12/1951 Bp Beverley D Tucker. m 6/5/1949 Elaine Carolyn Helm c 1. Int Ch Of The Ascen Vallejo CA 1992-1993; Archd Dio Nthrn California Sacramento CA 1984-1990; R S Matt's Ch Kenosha WI 1972-1984; R S Paul's Epis Ch Modesto CA 1965-1972; Dn Trin Cathd Sacramento CA 1959-1965; R S Jas Ch Of Sault S Marie Sault Ste Marie MI 1957-1959; Cn Gr And H Trin Cathd Kansas City MO 1955-1957. Appreciation Citation Natl Conferenced Of Christians & Jews 1983. mem4u@surewest.net

MCCLOGHRIE, K(athleen) Lesley (NY) 11 Stirrup Trl, Pawling NY 12564 **Vic Ch Of The H Trin Pawling NY 2003-** B Gateshead County Durham UK 12/8/1947 d Raymond Grey & Margaret. BA U of Manchester 1969; MDiv CDSP 1999. D 11/20/1999 P 6/3/2000 Bp William Edwin Swing. m 7/24/1969 Keith McCloghrie c 3. Assoc R Gr Ch Middletown NY 2000-2003; Chld's Mnstrs Coordntr S Bede's Epis Ch Menlo Pk CA 1999-2000. klmccloghrie@gmail.com

MCCLOSKEY JR, Robert Johnson (SeFla) Po Box 1691, West Jefferson NC 28694 **Assoc S Mary Of The Hills Epis Par Blowing Rock NC 2008-** B York PA 7/9/1942 s Robert Johnson McCloskey & Janet Louise. BA Stetson U 1963; STB GTS 1967. D 6/24/1967 Bp Anson Phelps Stokes Jr P 6/1/1968 Bp Frederic Cunningham Lawrence. m 6/15/1968 Kathleen Anne Fran Winson c 3. Assoc S Paul's Ch Wilkesboro NC 2008-2009; Assoc Ch Of The Incarn Miami FL 2002-2006; Chair-Ecum Cmsn Dio SE Florida Miami FL 1993-1999; R S Steph's Ch Coconut Grove Coconut Grove FL 1989-1999; Chair-Ecum Cmsn Dio Long Island Garden City NY 1985-1989; Chair-Dioc.Liturg Com Dio Long Island Garden City NY 1983-1987; R S Ptr's by-the-Sea Epis Ch Bay Shore NY 1982-1989; R S Mary Of The Hills Epis Par Blowing Rock NC 1976-1982; Chair-Dioc.Liturg & Mus Ctte Dio Wstrn No Carolina Asheville NC 1976-1981; R S Mk's Ch Westford MA 1972-1976; Chair-Dioc.Liturg & Mus Ctte Dio Massachusetts Boston MA 1969-1975; R S Jas Epis Ch Teele Sq Somerville MA 1969-1972; Cur Gr Epis Ch Medford MA 1967-1969. Auth, *Brit Composing for ICET Texts*. ADLMC, Associat 1968-2000; Cmnty Chr Serv Agcy Natl Conf Christia 1989-1993; EDEO 1974-1996; Epis Soc for Cultural Racial Unity [ESCRU] 1963-1972; Epis Soc to MHE [ESMHE] 1970-1972; Grtr Miami Rel Leaders 1989-2000; HOPE Inc 1989-1991; No Carolina ARC Cmsn 1976-1982; No Carolina Bapt Epis Dialogue 1976-1981. hisbobness@skybest.com

MCCLOUD, Christine McCloud (Nwk) No address on file. B Newark NJ 10/26/1961 d Stanley McCloud & Inez F. D 6/3/2006 Bp John Palmer Croneberger. c 2. clmccloud@tpcsinc.org

MCCLOUD, Linda (Mont) PO Box 81362, Billings MT 59108 **Vic Dio Montana Helena MT 2008-** B Topmost KY 12/29/1946 d Everett McCloud & Bonnie. BBA Belmont U 1985; MDiv STUSo 2005. D 2/5/2005 P 8/5/2005 Bp Henry Irving Louttit. lxxmccloud@yahoo.com

MCCLOUGH, Jeffrey David (Chi) 3801 Central Ave, Western Springs IL 60558 B Chicago IL 2/22/1941 s William Joseph McClough & Myrtice A. BA Ripon Coll Ripon WI 1963; MDiv SWTS 1966; MA SWTS 1969. D 6/11/1966 Bp James Winchester Montgomery P 12/17/1966 Bp Gerald Francis Burrill. m 6/29/1985 Caroline McClough c 2. Counslg Mnstrs Glenview IL 1988-1997; Dio Chicago Chicago IL 1986-1987; Pstr Counslr S Dav's Ch Glenview IL 1981-1986; Com Dio Chicago Chicago IL 1977-1980; Pstr Counslr Gr Ch Chicago IL 1969-1980; Assoc Trin Ch Chicago IL 1968-1969; Cur Cathd Of S Jas Chicago IL 1966-1968. carolinejeffrey@comcast.net

MCCLOY, Randolph McKellar (WTenn) 42 S Goodlett St, Memphis TN 38117 B Memphis TN 3/22/1936 s Elise Donelson. MD U of Tennessee Med Sch 1961; MS U MN 1966; MAR Memphis TS 2010. D 11/21/2009 Bp Don Edward Johnson. m 1/1/1979 Linda Kay McCloy c 3. rmmccloy@comcast.net

MCCLURE, Maurice Alden (Ind) 5941 Broadway St, Indianapolis IN 46220 B Hamilton OH 9/29/1933 s Morris B McClure & Lucia Dawson. BA Butler U 1956; U MI 1959; BD SWTS 1963. D 6/11/1963 P 12/21/1963 Bp John P Craine. m 9/14/1991 Rosalind K Hendricks c 4. Trin Ch Anderson IN 1972-1998; P-in-c S Lk's Epis Ch Cannelton IN 1968-1972; Asst R Gr Ch

Muncie IN 1966-1968; Vic S Jn's Epis Ch Mt Vernon IN 1963-1966. Ord of S Ben 1972. arozandal@aol.com

MCCLURE, Robert Coke (Lex) PO Box 858, Harlan KY 40831 **P-in-c Chr Epis Ch Harlan KY 2010-; Dio Lexington Lexington KY 2010-; P-in-c S Mk's Ch Hazard KY 2010-** B Berkeley CA 11/22/1954 s Frank Edward McClure & Augusta Clemens. BA Dart 1976; MDiv Princeton Sem 1980; CAS CDSP 2010. D 2/11/2010 P 8/12/2010 Bp Brian James Thom. m Tamara K Selves c 5. Auth, "Lessons for Revolutionaries," *Viewpoint*, PrTS, 1977. Friar Club Alum Awd PrTS 1980. rcoke.mcclure@yahoo.com

MCCLURE JR, William James (EMich) 232 North 'E' Street, Cheboygan MI 49721 **R S Jas' Epis Ch Cheboygan MI 2001-** B Clare MI 6/4/1959 s William James McClure & Shirley Elaine. BS Cntrl Michigan U 1982; MDiv VTS 2001. D 7/22/2001 P 7/23/2002 Bp Edwin Max Leidel Jr. m 6/10/2006 Deborah D McClure c 1. wmcclurejr@charter.net

MCCOID, Dean Bailey (ECR) 25 Oakmore Dr, San Jose CA 95127 B Vallejo CA 11/27/1925 s Chester Bailey McCoid & Virginia. BA Dickinson Coll 1950. D 1/30/1965 Bp George Richard Millard. m 6/27/1953 Carolyn Anne Watts c 3. Dio El Camino Real Monterey CA 1982-1999; Asst S Phil's Ch San Jose CA 1965-1982. dmccoid@sbcglobal.net

MCCOMAS, Scot Alexander (Nwk) 4 Madison Ave, Madison NJ 07940 **Cur Gr Ch Madison NJ 2010-** B Dallas TX 10/27/1966 s Frederic March McComas & Mary Cox. BA SMU 1991; MDiv Harvard DS 1999; STM GTS 2003. D 1/10/2004 Bp Leopold Frade P 8/27/2004 Bp Michael Bruce Curry. Asst S Ptr's Epis Ch Charlotte NC 2003-2009. scot.mccomas@yahoo.com

MCCONCHIE, Leann Patricia (WNY) 119 Royal Pkwy E, Williamsville NY 14221 **D The Epis Ch Of The Gd Shpd Buffalo NY 2007-** B Detroit MI 2/20/1955 BS U of Detroit Mercy 1978. D 5/6/2004 Bp J Michael Garrison. m 10/17/1981 William Edward McConchie c 1. Cn S Paul's Cathd Buffalo NY 2004-2007. leann.mcconchie@stpaulscathedral.org

MCCONE, Susan Jonal (Ct) 80 Green Hill Rd, Washington CT 06793 **P-in-c S Jn's Ch Washington CT 2010-** B Minneapolis MN 2/20/1949 d John Nicholas McCone & Alyce Cecelia Magdalene. BA Smith 1971; JD Col 1974; MDiv Yale DS 1998; Angl Certif. Ya Berk 1999. D 6/8/2002 P 1/11/2003 Bp Andrew Donnan Smith. m 10/24/1982 Robert Paul Wessely. Dir of Dvlpmt Epis Ch Cntr New York NY 2009-2011; P-in-c Chr Ch Par Epis Watertown CT 2008-2009; Mssn Funding Coordntr Epis Ch Cntr New York NY 2007-2009; Dio Connecticut Hartford CT 2005-2006; P-in-c S Jn's Epis Ch Bristol CT 2005-2006; Chr Ch Poughkeepsie NY 2003-2005; Cur Chr Ch New Haven CT 2002-2003. Auth, "Holiness of Beauty," *AAM Journ*, 2002. Affirming Angl Catholicism Exec Bd 1999; Assoc, CHS, New York 2000; Bd Dir, Amer Friends of Angl Cntr in Rome 2005. sjmccone@aol.com

M

MCCONKEY, David Benton (Alb) 18 Park Lane, Swindon SN1 5EL Great Britain (UK) B Salina KS 7/9/1953 s Howard Benton McConkey & Grace Marie. BA Kansas Wesl 1975; MusM Ya 1977; MDiv Ya Berk 1979; PhD GTF 2008. D 10/28/1983 P 7/1/1984 Bp John Forsythe Ashby. Vstng Adj Instr Nash Nashotah WI 1994; Trst Dio Albany Albany NY 1989-1993; Cn Capitular Cathd Of All SS Albany NY 1988-1993; R Ch Of The H Cross Warrensburg NY 1986-1994; Cur & Org-Chm S Lk's Ch Anchorage KY 1984-1986; D Chr Cathd Salina KS 1983-1984. AGO, Hymn Soc Amer, Epis Sy; SSC 1987. Evelyn Light Fell Soc for the Maintenance of the Faith 2006. frdbmcconkey@yahoo.co.uk

MCCONNELL, Dorsey Winter Marsden (Mass) 381 Hammond St, Chestnut HIll MA 02467 **R Ch Of The Redeem Chestnut Hill MA 2004-** B Omaha NE 11/19/1953 s John Paul McConnell & Sally. BA Ya 1975; MDiv GTS 1983. D 6/4/1983 P 12/1/1983 Bp Paul Moore Jr. m 6/8/1980 Elizabeth Jane Marsden c 1. R S Alb's Ch Edmonds WA 1995-2004; R The Ch Of The Epiph New York NY 1989-1995; Chapl Epis Ch At Yale New Haven CT 1985-1989; Cur S Thos Ch New York NY 1983-1985. Auth, "Apos of Joy," Blue Moon Press, New Haven, 1989. Fulbright Schlr 1975. dorsey.mcconnell@yahoo.com

MCCONNELL, Gary Dee (Ark) 2119 Stagecoach Village, Little Rock AR 72210 B Ada OK 9/23/1939 s O'Dee Francis McConnell & Geraldine. AA Coll City Long Bch 1960; BA Lexington Bapt Coll 1969; MDiv Epis TS In Kentucky 1970; DMin GTF 1989. D 6/17/1970 Bp Robert Raymond Brown P 12/19/1970 Bp Christoph Keller Jr. m 5/29/1959 Donna Fite c 3. R Trin Par Ch Epis Searcy AR 1977-2006; S Steph's Epis Ch Jacksonville AR 1971-1977; Cur S Lk's Epis Ch No Little Rock AR 1970-1971. Auth, *As Tentative As Flight*, GTF, 1989. donnaquilts@gmail.com

MCCONNELL JR, James B (CFla) 2916 Palm Dr, Punta Gorda FL 33950 **Vic S Ann's Epis Ch Wauchula FL 2006-** B New Orleans LA 11/20/1942 s James Bert McConnell & Joyce Evelyn. Loyola U; BS S Mary Dominican 1977; MDiv STUSo 1986. D 6/14/1986 P 12/20/1986 Bp Willis Ryan Henton. m 9/4/1965 Carolyn Louise Cochran c 2. R H Trin Epis Ch Gillette WY 2004-2006; P-in-c S Barn' Epis Ch Hartselle AL 2002-2004; R Ch Of The Resurr Rainbow City AL 2000-2001; R The Epis Ch Of The Redeem Avon Pk FL 1996-2000; R All SS Epis Ch Enterprise FL 1993-1995; R S Paul's Ch Woodville MS 1990-1993; Assoc Trin Ch Natchez MS 1988-1990; Vic S Andr's Ch Lake Chas LA 1987-1988; Cur S Thos' Ch Monroe LA 1986-1987. padrejim86@hotmail.com

MCCONNELL, Joyce (Oly) 965 Winslow Way E Unit 403, Bainbridge Island WA 98110 **Vic Dio Olympia Seattle WA 2000-** B Grantham Lincolnshire England 12/26/1919 d William Westcott Cragg & Harriet. Cert SFTS; Imperial Serv Coll Engl 1943; TS Dio Olympia 1971. D 6/24/2000 P 1/13/2001 Bp Vincent Waydell Warner. c 3. Asstg P S Barn Epis Ch Bainbridge Island WA 2006-2010; Vic Faith Ch Kingston WA 2000-2005. "The Peace of Lord"; "Var Treas Newsletters," Dio Olympia. Soc of the Comp of the H Cross 1980. Cn S Mk's Cathd, Dio Olympia 1991.

MCCONNELL, Ronald Douglas (RG) 12120 Copper Ave Ne, Albuquerque NM 87123 **Died 5/23/2011** B Fort Worth TX 2/2/1932 s Elbert Egbert McConnell & Maude Elizabeth. BS Florida St U 1953; BD SW Bapt TS 1956; ThM Chr TS 1961; PhD U Of Glasgow Gb 1968. D 8/6/1975 P 4/1/1976 Bp Richard Mitchell Trelease Jr. Auth, "Forgiveness". Who'S Who Rel.

MCCONNELL, Theodore Alan (Alb) 106 East Farm Woods Ln, Fort Ann NY 12827 B Burlington IA 2/23/1938 s John McConnell & Helen. BA Gri 1960; STB Yale DS 1963; STM Yale DS 1968; MS Concordia Coll 2000; MA Concordia Coll 2004; PhD Concordia Coll 2005. D 6/26/1965 Bp John Melville Burgess P 4/17/1966 Bp Robert Fisher Gibson Jr. m 11/28/1981 Mary Cochran. R Ch Of The H Cross Warrensburg NY 1983-1984; Ed Dir M-B Co Dio Massachusetts Boston MA 1980-1984; Seabury Press- Epis Ch Cntr New York NY 1976-1977; Asst Chr Ch Cambridge Cambridge MA 1966-1968; Cur S Ptr's Epis Ch Arlington VA 1965-1966. Auth, "The Great Fleeceman and Other Stories," Inkwater, 2011; Auth, "Finding a Pstr," Harper, 1986; Auth, "Ch on the Wrong Road," Regnery Gateway, 1986; Auth, "The Shattered Self," Pilgrim Press, 1971.

MCCONNELL, Theodore Howard (EC) Kingston Parish, P.O. Box 471, Mathews VA 23109 **Kingston Par Epis Ch Mathews VA 2011-** B Pontiac MI 12/4/1947 s Howard Buckles McConnell & Althea Rosemond. BA Alma Coll 1970; MA Cntrl Michigan U 1974; MDiv VTS 1985. D 1/24/1981 Bp William J Gordon Jr P 7/27/1985 Bp Emerson Paul Haynes. m 8/16/1969 Anita Marie Manhart c 3. Calv Ch Tarboro NC 2010-2011; S Lk's Ch Tarboro NC 2010-2011; R S Paul's Epis Ch Wilmington NC 2007-2010; Dn S Paul's Cathd Fond du Lac WI 2003-2007; R Chr Epis Ch Gordonsville VA 1997-2003; R S Mart's Epis Ch Henrico VA 1990-1997; Asst Ch Of The Redeem Sarasota FL 1985-1990; Asst S Jn's Epis Ch Alma MI 1981-1982. avepadre@gmail.com

MCCONNEY, J Anne (Neb) 413 S 78th St Apt 8, Omaha NE 68114 **Dir/ Ed Of Pub All SS Epis Ch Omaha NE 2002-** B Omaha NE 6/23/1932 d Lawrence Howard McConney & Fern. Cottey Coll 1951; BA U of Nebraska 1954; MA U of Nebraska 1978; MDiv Ya Berk 1984. Trans from Anglican Church of Canada 4/1/1992 Bp James Edward Krotz. Dio The Rio Grande Albuquerque NM 1995-1996; Ed Dio The Rio Grande Albuquerque NM 1994-1996; H Trin Epis Ch - Mssn Raton NM 1994-1995; Vic Trin Memi Epis Ch Crete NE 1993-2001; Dio Nebraska Omaha NE 1992-2000; Vic S Aug's Epis Ch Elkhorn NE 1992-1993; St Augustines Of Cbury Epis Mssn Elkhorn NE 1992-1993; Ed Dio Nebraska Omaha NE 1991-1993. Auth, "Pilgrim Songs," *Episocpal Life*, 2000; Auth, "Our December Hearts," Morehouse, 1999; Auth, "Lesser Observances," *Epis Life*, 1994. ECom 1994. Multiple Polly Bond Awards ECom 1994. jamcconney@aol.com

MCCOOK, Carla Benae (Mil) 2320 River Hill Ct, Waukesha WI 53129 **Bp's Asst for Chr Formation Dio Milwaukee Milwaukee WI 2011-** B Saint Petersburg FL 1/1/1973 d Charles Benjamin Manning & Shelia Vonna. BA Flagler Coll 1995; MDiv VTS 2004. D 5/22/2004 Bp John Wadsworth Howe P 11/30/2004 Bp Frank Neff Powell. m 4/23/1994 Shane P McCook c 3. R S Thos Of Cbury Ch Greendale WI 2006-2011; Asst R S Paul's Epis Ch Salem VA 2004-2006. revcarla@gmail.com

MCCORMICK, Brendan P (Ct) 5 Sea Ln, Old Saybrook CT 06475 **Vic All SS Ch Ivoryton CT 2008-; R S Paul's Ch Wallingford CT 1989-** B Chicago IL 4/22/1943 s William Paul McCormick & Irene Elizabeth. STL S Anselmo 1971; MA Providence Coll 1978. Rec from Roman Catholic 10/1/1983 as Priest Bp Arthur Edward Walmsley. m 6/11/1977 Rosemary McDermott c 1. S Paul's Ch Wallingford CT 1988-2007; Asst R S Mk's Ch New Britain CT 1983-1988. bpmccormick@snet.net

MCCORMICK, John Haden (SC) 142 Church St, Charleston SC 29401 **R S Phil's Ch Charleston SC 1997-** B Jacksonville FL 3/28/1946 s John Townsend McCormick & Jean Haden. BA Pr 1968; Harv 1979; MDiv TESM 1997. D 3/19/1997 P 9/20/1997 Bp Edward Lloyd Salmon Jr. m 10/19/1968 Lynn Fant c 1. Pres Dio So Carolina Charleston SC 2004-2008; Dioc Coun Dio So Carolina Charleston SC 2002-2005; Grp Hlth Ins Dio So Carolina Charleston SC 2001-2011. Cler Soc Of So Carolina 1998. hadenmccormick@mac.com

MCCORMICK, Matthew Wright (SC) St. Philip's Church, 142 Church Street, Charleston SC 29401 **P Ch Of The H Cross Sullivans Island SC 2008-; Assoc S Phil's Ch Charleston SC 2008-** B Hickory NC 4/9/1978 s John Haden McCormick & Lynn. BA Coll of Charleston 2001; MDiv TESM 2007. D 12/1/2007 Bp Edward Lloyd Salmon Jr P 6/1/2008 Bp Mark Joseph

Lawrence. m 9/18/2004 Lisa Christian Lisa Christian. mmccormick@stphilipschurchsc.org

MCCORMICK, Phyllis Ann (SwFla) 2850 Countrybrook Dr Apt 13, Apt. 13, Palm Harbor FL 34684 **D S Chris's Ch TAMPA FL 1998-** B Brooklyn NY 10/24/1938 d Frank McCormick & Teresa. BA Marymount Manhattan Coll 1960; JD New York Law Sch 1982. D 6/13/1998 Bp John Bailey Lipscomb. D H Trin Epis Ch In Countryside Clearwater FL 1999-2005.

MCCORMICK, Reid Tate (CGC) 210 Church St, Greenville AL 36037 **S Thos Ch Greenville AL 2011-** B Jacksonville FL 5/22/1957 s John Townsend McCormick & Jean. BS Auburn U 1979; MDiv STUSo 1997. D 6/8/1997 Bp Stephen Hays Jecko P 12/1/1997 Bp Robert Hodges Johnson. m 1/23/1982 Jacqueline J Micheli c 2. R Emm Ch Orlando FL 2000-2002; Assoc All SS Ch Of Winter Pk Winter Pk FL 1998-1999; Asst Ch Of The Ascen Hickory NC 1997-1998. rmccormick5@cfl.rr.com

MCCORMICK, Thomas Ray (Del) PO Box 1478, Bethany Beach DE 19930 B Lewistown, PA 5/2/1938 s Ray Thompson & Margaret Mae. Mstr of Ed (Spec Ed) Shippensburg St Coll; AB Hlth & Physical Ed Lenoir Rhyne Coll 1960. D 12/5/2009 Bp Wayne Parker Wright. m 8/4/1956 Susanne R McCormick c 3. mccormick5O@aol.com

MCCOWN, William Russell (Ala) 3816 Cromwell Dr, Birmingham AL 35243 **Ch Pension Fund New York NY 2009-** B Hunstville, AL 7/18/1962 s James Robert McCown & Jeanne Luther. D 6/1/2004 P 12/2/2004 Bp Henry Nutt Parsley Jr. m 9/25/1993 Laura Reynolds c 2. S Mary's-On-The-Highlands Epis Ch Birmingham AL 2004-2009. rusty@stmarysoth.org

MCCOY OHC, Adam Dunbar (NY) Holy Cross Monastery, PO Box 99, West Park NY 12493 B Chicago IL 12/19/1946 s Duncan Redfield McCoy & Morna Jane. BA MI SU 1969; MA Cor 1972; PhD Cor 1973; MDiv CDSP 1979. D 5/31/1979 P 12/29/1979 Bp Wesley Frensdorff. R The Ch of S Edw The Mtyr New York NY 2001-2008; Dn, Dnry 9 Dio Los Angeles Los Angeles CA 1998-2001; R S Mich's Mssn Anaheim CA 1992-2001; Comm. on Mnstry Dio Los Angeles Los Angeles CA 1986-1990. Auth, "H Cross: A Century of Angl Monasticism," Morehouse-Barlow, 1987. OHC 1973. Phi Beta Kappa MI SU 1969. amccoy0322@aol.com

MCCOY, David Ormsby (SO) 12345 Raintree Avenue, Pickerington OH 43147 **Retirees and Spouses/Partnr and Surviving Spouses Dio Sthrn Ohio Cincinnati OH 1999-** B Portsmouth OH 8/30/1938 s Walter Edward McCoy & Thelma Maxine. AB Ken 1960; STB GTS 1964. D 6/13/1964 P 12/19/1964 Bp Roger W Blanchard. m 4/30/2011 Christine Knisely c 2. Assoc S Andr's Ch Pickerington OH 1998-2011; Dn Angl Acad Dio Sthrn Ohio Cincinnati OH 1994-1998; Ohio Coun Of Ch Columbus OH 1988-1994; Ch Of S Edw Columbus OH 1988; R S Steph's Epis Ch And U Columbus OH 1978-1987; Ch Of The Gd Shpd Athens OH 1977-1978; Assoc S Steph's Epis Ch And U Columbus OH 1973-1978; R Chr Ch Xenia OH 1967-1971; Asst S Steph's Epis Ch And U Columbus OH 1964-1967. davidomccoy@yahoo.com

MCCOY, Elaine (O) 3785 W 33rd St, Cleveland OH 44109 **Epis Westside Shared Minstry Lakewood OH 2006-** B Newark NJ 12/16/1945 d Francis Xavier Langan & Sarah June. BA Leh 1981; PhD U Of Adelaide Au 1987; MDiv EDS 2005. D 6/14/2005 P 1/12/2006 Bp Mark Hollingsworth Jr. c 4. Gr Epis Ch Sandusky OH 2009-2010; S Andr's Epis Ch Elyria OH 2007-2009; Epis. Shared Mnstrs Nw Lakewood OH 2006. mccoyhanen@sbcglobal.net

MCCOY, Frances Jean (SwVa) 1001 Virginia Ave NW, Norton VA 24273 B Connellsville PA 4/18/1943 d Francis Montfort McCoy & Barbara Jean. BA Antioch Coll 1966; MA Marshall U 1968; MDiv VTS 1985. D 6/5/1985 Bp Robert Poland Atkinson P 12/1/1985 Bp William Franklin Carr. All SS Epis Ch Norton VA 1990-2008; S Mk's Ch St Paul VA 1990-2008; Coordntr Of Prog & Educ Dio W Virginia Charleston WV 1987-1990; Emm Ch Moorefield WV 1985-1987. Auth, "Lets Begin Here". EvangES. fjmccoy@verizon.net

MCCOY, Robert Martin (Md) 375 Benfield Rd, Severna Park MD 21146 **D S Mart's-In-The-Field Day Sch Severna Pk MD 2011-** B Washington DC 3/3/1942 s David Evans McCoy & Elizabeth. D 6/2/2007 Bp John Leslie Rabb. m 4/8/1988 Jean K McCoy c 4. D S Jas' Par Lothian MD 2007-2011; D S Mk's Chap Deale Lothian MD 2007-2011. bob21403@gmail.com

MCCOY, W(illiam) Keith (NJ) 312 Copperfield Ln, Metuchen NJ 08840 **D S Jn's Ch Somerville NJ 2002-; Chair Com On Diac Dio New Jersey Trenton NJ 1994-** B Cambridge MA 1/17/1954 s William Charles McCoy & Irene. BA Harv 1976; MLS Drexel U 1978. D 4/13/1985 Bp Matthew Paul Bigliardi. D Gr Epis Ch Plainfield NJ 1987-2002; D Chr Ch New Brunswick NJ 1985-1987; D All SS Ch Highland Pk NJ 1985-1986. Auth, "Mssn At Harvard Lawn"; Auth, "D As Para-Cleric". Kiwanian Of The Year; S Steph'S Awd Naad. kmccoy1@optonline.net

MCCRACKEN-BENNETT, Rick (SO) 9019 Johnstown Alexandria Rd, Johnstown OH 43031 **All SS Epis Ch New Albany OH 2000-** B Bucyrus OH 8/8/1949 s Richard John Bennett & Patricia Anne. BA U of Findlay 1971; MDiv S Meinrad TS 1976; DMin SWTS 2002. Rec from Roman Catholic 12/21/1989 as Priest Bp William Grant Black. m 11/1/1980 Nancy Sue McCracken-Bennett c 2. Dio Sthrn Ohio Cincinnati OH 1997-1999; Nthrn Miami Vlly Cluster Urbana OH 1997; Vic Ch Of The H Trin Epis Bellefontaine OH 1994-1997; Vic Ch Of The Epiph Urbana OH 1992-1997; Vic Our Sav Ch Mechanicsburg OH 1990-1996. mccrackenbennett@gmail.com

MCCREARY, E(rnest) Cannon (USC) 8530 Geer Hwy, Cleveland SC 29635 B Cynthiana KY 8/5/1926 s Ernest Abercrombie McCreary & Marie. BA U So 1950; MDiv VTS 1953. D 6/28/1953 Bp John J Gravatt P 5/10/1954 Bp Clarence Alfred Cole. m 1/10/1957 Ethel W Wright c 4. Vic S Andr's Epis Ch Greenville SC 1984-1988; Asst Chr Ch Greenville SC 1971-1984; Cur S Steph's Epis Ch Ridgeway SC 1969-1971; Chapl Dio Upper So Carolina Columbia SC 1963-1978; Vic S Lk's Ch Newberry SC 1957-1961; Vic Trin Ch Abbeville SC 1953-1957. cannonmcc@bellsouth.net

MCCREATH, Amy Ebeling (Mass) 23 Gilbert St, Waltham MA 02453 **Ch Of The Gd Shpd Watertown MA 2010-** B Kettering OH 8/8/1965 d Harry Guion Ebeling & Martha. BA Pr 1987; MA U of Wisconsin 1991; MDiv SWTS 1998. D 4/23/1998 P 12/18/1998 Bp Roger John White. m 3/20/1993 Brian K McCreath c 2. Dio Massachusetts Boston MA 2001-2010; S Chris's Ch River Hills WI 1998-2001. Coun of APLM 2000. abmccreath@comcast.net

MCCRUM, Lewis Lamb (NJ) 415 Washington St, Toms River NJ 08753 **D Chr Ch Toms River Toms River NJ 1990-** B Newark NJ 12/28/1942 s William H McCrum & Virginia L. BA Pratt Inst 1965. D 6/9/1990 Bp George Phelps Mellick Belshaw. m 6/26/1965 Mary Jane Delisa c 2.

MCCUE, Allan Homer (Mass) 12 Regwill Ave, Wenham MA 01984 B Topeka KS 3/20/1931 s Howard Franklin McCue & Blanche Adeline. BA Antioch Coll 1953; BD EDS 1956. D 6/24/1956 Bp Edward Clark Turner P 12/26/1956 Bp Henry W Hobson. m 9/22/1956 Cynthia Hyde Bryant c 3. Int S Chris's Ch Chatham MA 2002-2003; Int Chr Ch So Hamilton MA 1994-1997; Int S Mary's Epis Ch Rockport MA 1992-1994; S Ptr's Ch Beverly MA 1966-1992; Vic H Sprt Epis Ch Cincinnati OH 1958-1965; Asst Gr Ch Cincinnati OH 1956-1958. Cmsn Wider Mssn Dio Massachussetts 1992-2005; Jubilee Fund Dio Massachussetts 2000-2008; Mass. Schlrshp Africans Studying in Amer Co-Chair 2001; Rep to Global Epis Mssn 1998-1999. homerica@comcast.net

MCCUE, Michael Edlow (WMass) PO Box 270448, Susanville CA 96127 **P-in-c Gd Shpd Epis Ch Susanville CA 2011-; P-in-c H Sprt Mssn Lake Almanor CA 2010-** B Oakland CA 3/22/1949 s Patrick Edlow McCue & Virginia Anna. BA San Jose St U 1973; MDiv CDSP 1980. D 11/8/1980 Bp Charles Shannon Mallory P 1/10/1982 Bp John Raymond Wyatt. m 9/17/1977 Maureen Walsh c 2. Dio Wstrn Massachusetts Springfield MA 2002-2004; R S Mk's Ch Adams MA 2002-2004; S Mich's Ch Yeadon PA 2001-2002; R S Jn's Epis Ch Honeoye Falls NY 1996-2000; R Zion Ch Avon NY 1996-2000; Cur S Barn Ch Arroyo Grande CA 1980-1981. Amer Correctional Chapl Assn 1982; EPF 1971; HSEC 1980. michael.mccue@cdcr.ca.gov

MCCULLOCH, Kent Thomas (Oly) 10630 Gravelly Lake Dr Sw, Lakewood WA 98499 B Portland OR 5/8/1946 s John Robert McCulloch & Elizabeth Jane. BA California St U 1970; MDiv CDSP 1976. D 7/25/1976 Bp Hal Raymond Gross P 8/1/1977 Bp Matthew Paul Bigliardi. c 2. Dioc Coun Dio Olympia Seattle WA 1993-1996; Curs Dio Olympia Seattle WA 1986-1992; R S Mary's Ch Lakewood WA 1985-2007; S Andr's Ch Portland OR 1980-1984; S Barth's Ch Beaverton OR 1979-1980; Chr Ch Par Lake Oswego OR 1976-1979. Auth, "Living Ch". kenttmcculloch@gmail.com

MCCULLOUGH, Brian Duncan (SanD) 332 N Massachusetts St, Winfield KS 67156 B Wichita KS 11/12/1945 s Fredrick Bertram McCullough & Jacquelyn Ann. BA U of Missouri 1968; MDiv GTS 1971; MA Kean U 1985. D 6/12/1971 P 11/26/1971 Bp George Leslie Cadigan. m 7/30/1986 Kimberlin A Fowler c 4. Vic All SS Epis Ch Brawley CA 1991-1992; Gr Ch Middletown NY 1990-1991; Gr Epis Ch Winfield KS 1978-1980; Ch Of The Redeem Houston TX 1976-1978. Psi Chi hon Soc 1982. Psi Chi Natl Psychol Hon Soc 1982. gracewinfield@sbcglobal.net

MCCULLOUGH, Mary (Pa) 708 S. Bethlehem Pike, Ambler PA 19002 **Assoc R Trin Epis Ch Ambler PA 2008-** B Abington PA 10/16/1953 d Walter Grummun & Margaret. 2 years Luth TS; MS Neumann Coll 2003; MDiv GTS 2008. D 6/14/2008 P 1/10/2009 Bp Edward Lewis Lee Jr. m 4/3/1976 David McCullough c 2. Ch Sch Coordntr All Hallows Ch Wyncote PA 2000-2005. mary@trinityambler.com

MCCUNE, Henry Ralph (Dal) 11560 Drummond Dr, Dallas TX 75228 B Birmingham AL 1/23/1939 s John Chambers McCune & Caroline. BA Baylor U 1960; MDiv SW Bapt TS 1965. D 8/26/1979 P 8/1/1980 Bp A Donald Davies. m 8/5/1973 Janice Jeffrey c 2. R H Trin Epis Ch Garland TX 1981-2001; Chapl S Matt's Cathd Dallas TX 1980-1981; Dio Dallas Dallas TX 1979-1980; The Epis Ch Of The Resurr Dallas TX 1979. henryralph@hotmail.com

MCCURDY III, Alexander (Pa) 613 Maplewood Avenue, Wayne PA 19087 B Philadelphia PA 3/20/1939 s Alexander McCurdy & Flora Bruce. BA Wesl 1961; BD EDS 1964; MA Wayne 1973; CG Jung Inst 1977; PhD Un Inst & U Cincinnati OH 1986. D 6/11/1964 Bp Walter H Gray P 3/1/1965 Bp John Henry Esquirol. m 11/16/1992 Patricia Tyson Peterson c 2. H Apos And Medtr Philadelphia PA 1979-1980; Asst S Paul's Ch Philadelphia PA 1965-1969; Cur Trin Epis Ch Southport CT 1964-1965. Auth, "Establishing &

Maintaining the Analytical Structure," *Jungian Analysis*, Open Crt Press, 1982. alexandermccurdy3@verizon.net

MCCURRY MILLIKEN, Cathleen Ann (Mil) 1734 Fairhaven Dr., Cedarburg WI 53012 **D S Jas Ch W Bend WI 2009-** B Richland WA 9/16/1963 d John Wesely McCurry & Anna Mary Shields. AB Duke 1985; AM Duke 1989. D 6/2/2007 Bp Steven Andrew Miller. m 6/20/1987 Charles Kenneth Milliken c 2. cmilliken@wi.rr.com

MCCURTAIN, Glad Robinson (SwFla) 261 1st Ave SW, Largo FL 33770 **S Jn's Epis Ch Clearwater FL 2003-** B Pensacola FL 8/5/1947 d Grover C Robinson & Fauntleroy. BA U of W Florida 1969; MDiv SWTS 2003. D 6/24/1995 Bp Telesforo A Isaac P 6/14/2003 Bp John Bailey Lipscomb. m 9/7/1968 James Hume McCurtain c 4. JPIC Off Cathd Ch Of S Ptr St Petersburg FL 1998-2000; D H Trin Epis Ch In Countryside Clearwater FL 1995-1998. gladmccurtain@tampabay.rr.com

MCCUSKER III, Thomas Bernard (Va) 8225 Carrleigh Pkwy, Springfield VA 22152 B Boston MA 3/8/1946 s Thomas Bernard McCusker & Harriett Francis. MA Duquesne U; BA Ashland U 1969; MDiv VTS 1978. D 6/3/1978 Bp Robert Bracewell Appleyard P 4/1/1979 Bp Charles F Hall. Goodwin Hse Incorporated Alexandria VA 2004-2005; Ch Of The Resurr Alexandria VA 2004; Int S Lk's Ch Alexandria VA 2001-2003; Int S Barn Ch Annandale VA 2000-2001; Int S Paul's Epis Ch Alexandria VA 1998-1999; Ch Of The Gd Shpd Burke VA 1979-1997. thomasb3@aol.com

MCDADE, Shelley Dee (NY) 12 W 11th St, New York NY 10011 **Assoc R Ch Of The Ascen New York NY 2010-** B Wilmington DE 8/4/1961 d William F McDade & Lucille F. BA Ashland Coll 1983; MDiv The GTS 2010. D 3/13/2010 P 9/25/2010 Bp Mark Sean Sisk. sdmcdade@aol.com

MCDANIEL, Elna Irene (Eau) 408 W Nott St, Tomah WI 54660 **S Jn's Epis Ch Oxford WI 2003-; D S Mary's Epis Ch Tomah WI 2002-** B 2/1/1943 D 11/23/2002 Bp Keith Bernard Whitmore. m 9/9/1960 Kenneth Richard McDaniel c 5.

MCDANIEL, Judith Maxwell (Oly) 3737 Seminary Rd, Alexandria VA 22304 **Prof Homil VTS Alexandria VA 1990-** B Oklahoma City OK 12/21/1940 d Don Earl Maxwell & Martha May. BA U of Texas 1961; U of Washington 1971; MDiv GTS 1985; PhD U of Washington 1994. D 6/12/1978 P 6/30/1984 Bp Robert Hume Cochrane. m 6/7/1961 Jackson Lee McDaniel c 2. Cathd Chapt Dio Olympia Seattle WA 1987-1990; Chairman, COM Dio Olympia Seattle WA 1987-1990; R S Jn's Epis Ch Gig Harbor WA 1987-1990; Bd & Fac, TS Dio Olympia Seattle WA 1986-1990; Mem, COM Dio Olympia Seattle WA 1985-1990; Assoc R S Jn's Epis Ch Olympia WA 1985-1986; Treas, Cler Assn Dio Olympia Seattle WA 1982-1983; Mem, COM Dio Olympia Seattle WA 1979-1983; Assoc S Mk's Cathd Seattle WA 1979-1983; D S Barn Epis Ch Bainbridge Island WA 1978-1979. Auth, "Gr in Motion: the Intersection of Wmn Ord and VTS," RiverPlace Cmncatn, 2011; Auth, "Homiletical Perspective: Day of Pentecost, Trin Sunday, Proper 3, Year B," *Feasting on the Word*, Westminster Jn Knox Press, 2009; Auth, "The Interpreter of Dreams: Preaching to Effect Change," Hervormde Teologiese Stds 62(4), 2006; Auth, "A Change of Character," *Sermons from Preaching Excellence Prog, Vol. XV*, Bk Masters, Inc., 2006; Auth, "Redescribing Reality as Scriptural Sabbath," *Preaching as Prophetic Calling: Sermons that Wk XII*, Morehouse Pub, 2004; Auth, "Remember," Virginia Sem Journ, 2003; Auth, "The Place of the Bible in the Virginia Sem Curric: Homil," *Tchg the Bibile in the New Millennium*, ATR, 2002; Ed, "Preaching Gr in the Human Condition," 2001; Auth, "A Votive For The Preaching Of The Gospel," *Sermons That Wk X*, Morehouse Pub, 2001; Auth, "He Came To Proclaim A Message," *Preaching Mk: The Recovery Of A Narrative Voice*, Chalice Press, 1999; Auth, "The Prchr As Theol And Tchr," *Preaching Through The Year Of Mk: Sermons That Wk Viii*, Morehouse Pub, 1999; Auth, "Rhetoric Reconsidered: Preaching As Persuasion," Sewanee Theol Revs, 1998; Auth, "Let Every Heart Prepare Him Room," *The Living Pulpit*, 1997; Auth, "Disciples And Discipline," *Virginia Sem Journ*, 1996; Auth, "What You See Is What You Get," *Sermons That Wk V*, FMP, 1995. Acad Of Homil 1990; CHS; Societas Homiletica 1993. Howard Chandler Robbins Prof Of Homil VTS 2002; Treas Societas Homiletica 1999; Pres Societas Homiletica 1997; Exec Bd Societas Homiletica 1995; Chair COM/Dio Olympia 1987. jmcdaniel@vts.edu

MC DARBY, Mark Daniel (Alb) 8 Summit St, Philmont NY 12565 B Hudson NY 1/1/1960 s Raymond Allen McDarby & Esther Shirley. D 6/10/2006 Bp Daniel William Herzog. m 8/11/2006 Catherine Marie Ebert c 2. deacondarby@berk.com

MCDERMOT, Joanna (NwPa) 19556 E Cole Rd, Meadville PA 16335 B Athens GA 2/20/1936 d John Hulon Mote & Mary. Duquesne U; Franciscan U of Steubenville; BS Linc 1957. D 1/23/1999 Bp Robert Deane Rowley Jr. m 12/27/1961 Richard Frederick McDermot.

MCDERMOTT, James Patrick (LI) 1709 Rue Saint Patrick Apt 504, Montreal QC H3K 3G9 Canada B New York NY 3/11/1948 s Roland P McDermott & Mary V. BA SUNY 1970; MS SUNY 1983; Cert Mercer TS 1989. P 6/1/1990 Bp Orris George Walker Jr. m 3/22/1969 Veronica A De Santis. P Asst S Anselm's Ch Shoreham NY 1990-2004; Asst Ch of S Jude Wantagh NY 1989-1990. jmcdermott@montreal.anglican.ca

MCDERMOTT, Jane Leslie (O) 2918 Kirkhaven Dr, Youngstown OH 44511 **Extended Supply S Aug's Epis Ch Youngstown OH 2008-** B Buffalo NY 11/24/1946 d Raymond Leslie McDermott & Ida Rosamond. Case Wstrn Reserve U 1967; BA U Of Akron 1970; MDiv SWTS 1978. D 6/24/1978 P 2/24/1979 Bp John Harris Burt. R S Andr Ch Canfield OH 1991-2001; Int S Andr Ch Canfield OH 1989-1991; Int S Steph's Ch E Liverpool OH 1988-1989; R Trin Ch New Philadelphia OH 1983-1988; St. Jn's Hm/ girls Dio Ohio Cleveland OH 1982; Int S Tim's Ch Macedonia OH 1979-1982; Asst Ch Of The Trsfg Cleveland OH 1978-1979. Auth, "Var arts". jlmcdermott46@gmail.com

MCDERMOTT, John Roy (Md) 4493 Barberry Ct, Concord CA 94521 **Asstg P S Jn's Epis Ch Clayton CA 2011-** B Pueblo CO 7/5/1937 s Roy Edward McDermott & Beatrice Leola. AB cl Harv 1959; MDiv CDSP 1962; STM UTS 1965. D 6/24/1962 Bp James Albert Pike P 6/8/1963 Bp George Richard Millard. m 5/27/1961 Laurel Lee Seikel c 3. Asstg P Memi Ch Baltimore MD 1976-2005; Asstg P All SS Ch Baldwin NY 1964-1965; Cur S Fran Epis Ch San Jose CA 1962-1964. johrelmcd@sbcglobal.net

MCDERMOTT, Matthew (Cal) 580 Colorado Ave, Palo Alto CA 94306 **R S Mk's Epis Ch Palo Alto CA 1995-** B Lorain OH 7/2/1957 s William Francis McDermott & Dorothea Agnes. AA Lorain Cnty Cmnty Coll 1977; BA San Francisco St U 1982; MDiv CDSP 1987. D 6/6/1987 P 6/4/1988 Bp William Edwin Swing. m 11/5/1983 Lee Anne Vosti c 3. Asst to R Trin Par Menlo Pk CA 1989-1995; Asst to R S Steph's Epis Ch Orinda CA 1987-1989. matt@saint-marks.com

MCDERMOTT, Nelda Grace (Ark) 1204 Hunter St, Conway AR 72032 **D S Ptr's Ch Conway AR 2001-** B Blue Springs MS 10/4/1937 d Wilburn Lyons & Grace Gertrude. MS Blue Mtn Coll 1961; MS U Of Cntrl Arkansas Conway 1984; D Formation Prog 2001. D 11/3/2001 Bp Larry Earl Maze. m 6/4/1961 Cecil Wade McDermott.

MCDONALD, Carol Dawn (CFla) 1457 Barn Owl Loop, Sanford FL 32773 B Canada 7/16/1958 d John Cameron McDonald & Reba Minnie. BTh The Coll of Emm & St. Chad 1995; DMin GTF 2009; MDiv The Coll of Emm & St. Chad 2009. Trans from Anglican Church of Canada 3/31/2010 Bp John Wadsworth Howe. m 4/24/1998 Neville Crichlow. dpreacherdawn@cfl.rr.com

MCDONALD, Catherine Jane Walter (Minn) 9671 Clark Cir, Eden Prairie MN 55347 **Dio Minnesota Minneapolis MN 1990-** B Conde SD 10/6/1938 d Barton Ray Walter & Eunice Marie. BS Nthrn St U Aberdeen SD 1962; MDiv Untd TS of the Twin Cities 1977. D 6/24/1977 P 4/1/1978 Bp Philip Frederick McNairy. m 12/27/1961 John Edward McDonald c 2. jmcdonld@pressenter.com

MCDONALD, Durstan R (Tex) 811 E 46th St, Austin TX 78751 **Int Dn The Amer Cathd of the H Trin Paris 75008 FR 2003-** B New York NY 1/23/1937 s Douglas Ray McDonald & Carolyn Louise. BA Trin Hartford CT 1958; STB PDS 1963; PhD U of Pennsylvania 1968; DD Hob 1979; DHL Epis TS of the SW 2004. D 6/9/1963 P 12/13/1963 Bp Joseph Gillespie Armstrong. m 6/14/1958 Ruth J Jones c 5. Epis TS Of The SW Austin TX 1984-2002; Dn Chr Chap Austin TX 1983-2002; Trin Educ Fund New York NY 1978-1983; Hobart And Wm Smith Colleges Geneva NY 1967-1977. Auth, "W N Pittenger: A Bibliography"; Auth, "Macrina: Fourth Cappadocian?"; Ed, "The Myth," *Truth Of God Incarnate*. Hon Doctor of Humane Letters ETSS 2004; Hon DD Hob Geneva NY 1979. dmcdonald10@austin.rr.com

MCDONALD, James D (Ark) 511 Coley Dr, Mountain Home AR 72653 **S Andr's Ch Mtn Hm AR 2009-** B Pocahontas AR 9/13/1958 s Charles Paul McDonald & Lois Lee King. BA U of Arkansas 1980; MS U of Arkansas 1998; MDiv The U So (Sewanee) 2009. D 3/21/2009 Bp Larry Earl Maze P 9/23/2009 Bp Larry R Benfield. m 12/27/1978 Catherine L Catherine Marie Linder c 3. jdmcdonald@prodigy.net

MCDONALD, James Ross (Alb) 1937 The Plz, Schenectady NY 12309 **Stndg Com Dio Albany Albany NY 1996-; R S Steph's Ch Schenectady NY 1989-** B El Paso TX 7/13/1955 s William McDonald & Julie. BA Ken 1977; MS U Chi 1983; MDiv McCormick TS 1985; DMin PrTS 1996. D 6/15/1985 Bp James Russell Moodey P 4/4/1986 Bp Donald Maynard Hultstrand. m 2/20/2011 Lisa Westman c 2. Vic S Lk's Ch Springfield IL 1987-1989; S Jn's Epis Ch Decatur IL 1985-1989. Auth, "Understanding How Ch Members Reflect Theol On Daily Life Experiences," 1997. james.ross.mcd@gmail.com

MCDONALD, James Roy (NY) PO Box 161897, Austin TX 78716 B Brownwood TX 10/11/1942 s Jimmy McDonald & Helen. BA TCU 1965; STB Ya Berk 1968; MA Col 1973; PhD NYU 1980. D 6/1/1968 Bp Charles A Mason P 2/1/1969 Bp William Elwood Sterling. m 6/5/1999 Mary Guerrero. Pstr Counslr S Ann And The H Trin Brooklyn NY 1976-1979; Instr The GTS New York NY 1971-1975; Asst Calv and St Geo New York NY 1968-1969. "Enterprise Risk Mgmt and Improved Shareholder Value," *Perspectives in Bus*, St. Edw's U, 2006; "Decision Point: Mng Career Change in a Changing Wrld," CareerLynz Intl , 1994. mcdonald@orgstrategies.net

MCDONALD, James Wallace (EpisSanJ) 627 Goshen Ave, Clovis CA 93611 **St Bartholomews Ch Burney CA 1969-; Dio Nthrn California Sacramento CA 1968-** B Myrtle Bch SC 10/11/1943 s James Joseph McDonald & Edna Ruth. BA California St U 1965; MDiv SWTS 1968; MS California St U 1977; MPA California St U 1989. D 6/29/1968 P 1/25/1969 Bp Clarence Rupert Haden Jr. m 2/2/1974 Cheryl Susanne Spurgeon. Assoc R S Columba Ch Fresno CA 1972-1974; Vic S Mich's Ch Anderson CA 1969-1972; Cur Ch Of The Incarn Santa Rosa CA 1968-1969. Who'S Who In Rel; Who'S Who In The Wrld; Phi Kappa Phi. jameswmcdonald@yahoo.com

MCDONALD, Janet Strain (Va) Po Box 233, Free Union VA 22940 **Serving Mssn Dio Haiti Ft Lauderdale FL 2007-; Serving Mssn Dio Haiti Ft Lauderdale FL 2007-** B Birmingham AL 12/31/1957 d John T Strain & Juanelle D. BA Emory U 1980; MA U of Virginia 1987; MDiv STUSo 1998. D 6/19/1999 Bp Peter James Lee P 5/23/2000 Bp David Colin Jones. m 8/16/1980 Jay Adams McDonald c 2. Dio Virginia Richmond VA 2001-2007; S Geo's Ch Stanley VA 2001; Intern Cur S Jas Sewanee TN 1999-2000. "Art and Sprt," *Designing and Tchg a Sem course in Theol on the Arts*, Arts: The Arts in Rel on Theol Stds, 2002; Auth, "Albemarle Country, Virginia Furniture 1750-1850," *mag Antiques*, 1998; Auth, "Alabama Quilts," 1980. mcdonsrun@aol.com

MCDONALD, Karen Loretta (WMich) 89513 Shorelane Dr, Lawton MI 49065 B Buchanan MI 10/21/1939 RN Bronson Sch of Nrsng. D 4/4/2001 Bp Edward Lewis Lee Jr. m 6/25/1960 James McDonald c 3.

MCDONALD, Lauren Miller (SVa) Hickory Neck Episcopal Church, 8300 Richmond Rd., Toano VA 23168 **Assoc R Hickory Neck Ch Toano VA 2008-** B East Point GA 7/28/1969 d Edwin Graham McDonald & Page Mettee. BA U So 1991; MDiv SWTS 2008. D 2/1/2008 Bp John Clark Buchanan P 8/23/2008 Bp O'Kelley Whitaker. lmcdonald@hickoryneck.org

MCDONALD, Mark William (WLa) 106 McIntosh Bluff Rd, Fairhope AL 36532 **P in Charge Imm Ch Bay Minette AL 2011-; P in Charge Trin Episcopal Ch Atmore AL 2011-** B Monroe LA 10/9/1966 s William Franklin McDonald & Shirley. BBA U of Louisiana 1990; MBA U of So Alabama 1992; MDiv STUSo 2000. D 6/3/2000 P 2/17/2001 Bp Charles Farmer Duvall. m 6/4/1994 Joni Angelea Gammill c 4. R The Epis Ch Of The Epiph New Iberia LA 2002-2009; Cur S Lk's Epis Ch Mobile AL 2000-2001. mwmcdonald@me.com

MCDONALD III, Norval Harrison (Md) 309 Royal Oak Dr, Bel Air MD 21015 B Baltimore MD 11/2/1957 s Norval Harrison McDonald & Bettie Jane. BA Loyola Coll 1979; MDiv Ya Berk 1982; MDiv VTS 1985. D 9/13/1984 P 5/1/1985 Bp David Keller Leighton Sr. m 8/18/1979 Janice Lynn Klemming. Int Ch Of The Redemp Baltimore MD 2000-2002; Deer Creek Par Darlington MD 1986-1993; R Gr Epis Ch Darlington MD 1986-1993; Cur Emm Ch Bel Air MD 1984-1986. Assn Of Profsnl Chapl 1999. nickmcd57@gmail.com

MCDONALD, William Kenneth (Mich) 421 East Ellen Street, Fenton MI 48430 B Sedgwick CO 7/28/1941 s Beaty Leroy McDonald & Irene. BA U of Iowa 1963; MDiv cl Drew U 1967; U of Edinburgh GB 1967. D 1/9/1970 Bp Richard S M Emrich P 5/27/1970 Bp Archie H Crowley. c 2. P-in-c Ch Of The Resurr Clarkston MI 1997-2003; P-in-c S Paul's Epis Ch Corunna MI 1986-1991. mcdonald@tir.com

MCDONNELL, Brian K (Md) 8 Loveton Farms Ct, Sparks MD 21152 B Trenton NJ 8/27/1953 s William J McDonnell & Edith M. BS Sprg Garden Coll 1975; EFM STUSo 2004. D 6/5/2004 Bp Robert Wilkes Ihloff. m 4/24/2000 Ashley Hughlett c 1. S Thos' Ch Garrison Forest Owings Mills MD. bmcdonnell@stthomaschurch.us

MCDONNELL III, Richard P (Ga) 8 Barnacle Rd, Hilton Head Island SC 29928 B New York NY 9/22/1945 s Edward Gerard McDonnell & Josephine Helen. BA Belknap Coll 1971; BS SUNY 1974; MA LIU 1976; MDiv UTS 1977; MA + M Phil NYU 1979; MA S Mk's TS So Un KY 1983; D. Min Grad Theol Fund 1992. Trans from Anglican Church of Canada 5/1/1984 Bp (George) Paul Reeves. m 8/7/1972 Maureen Christine Madden c 5. S Fran Of The Islands Epis Ch Savannah GA 2006-2009; Vic The Epis Ch Of The Annunc Vidalia GA 1984-1986. Auth, "The Dr. Peeples Files"; Auth, "Cranmer On Euch," *The Angl*; Auth, "The Momophysite Position In Christological Controversies," *The Angl*. Amer Hist Soc; Angl Soc; Bible And Common PB Soc Of The Epis Soc; Ch Hist Soc; Hilton Hd Island Hist Soc, VP 1997; Skcm. Cn Theol Anglica Bp of the So W 1991; Hon Cn S Andrews Cathd Atlanta GA 1990. moebird@roadrunner.com

MCDOUGALL, Robert Franklin (Mich) 641 Michigan Avenue, Apt 304, Frankfort MI 49635 B Ypsilanti MI 6/21/1929 s Arthur Franklin McDougall & Beulah Maude. BA Estrn Michigan U 1951; MDiv Ya Berk 1956; Ldrshp Acad for New Directions 1975. D 6/23/1956 P 12/23/1956 Bp Dudley B McNeil. m 6/21/1953 Dorothy M Rowe c 2. Exec Coun Dio Michigan Detroit MI 1986-1990; Dn of the SW Convoc Dio Michigan Detroit MI 1981-1986; Alt Dep GC Dio Michigan Detroit MI 1979-1982; R S Paul's Epis Ch Jackson MI 1978-1989; Pres of the Stndg Com Dio Michigan Detroit MI 1977-1978; Pres of the Bd Dioc Paper Dio Michigan Detroit MI 1976-1982; Dir of Cmncatn No Dio Michigan Detroit MI 1976-1978; Stndg Com Dio Michigan Detroit MI 1974-1978; S Eliz's Epis Ch Roscommon MI 1974-1978; Bd Dir for the MI Coun of Ch Dio Michigan Detroit MI 1974-1977; Nthrn Convoc Dio Michigan Detroit MI 1974-1976; Dn McCoskry Convoc Dio Michigan Detroit MI 1971-1973; Trst Assn Dio Wstrn Michigan Kalamazoo MI 1966-1969; Chair on the Dept of CE Dio Wstrn Michigan Kalamazoo MI 1965-1969; Secy Dio Wstrn Michigan Kalamazoo MI 1963-1964; R S Jas' Epis Ch Of Albion Albion MI 1961-1969; Vic S Mk's Epis Ch Paw Paw MI 1957-1960; Cur S Paul's Ch Muskegon MI 1956-1957. dougall@chartermi.net

MCDOUGLE, Jane M (Cal) 173 Sierra Vista Ave Apt 21, Mountain View CA 94043 **S Bede's Epis Ch Menlo Pk CA 2005-** B Exeter England 1/4/1957 BEd Homerton Coll Cambridge Gb 1979; DMA Stan 1989; MDiv CDSP 2005. D 6/4/2005 P 12/3/2005 Bp William Edwin Swing. c 1. jmcdougle@stbedesmenlopark.org

MCDOWELL, Artie Samuel (RG) Po Box 5505, Clovis NM 88102 B Montgomery AL 5/5/1929 s Artie McDowell & Metta Adella. Dio The Rio Grande Instrn; BBA U of Memphis 1951; Mstr'S In Elem Educ Estrn New Mex U 1977. D 1/26/1983 Bp Richard Mitchell Trelease Jr P 9/5/1990 Bp Terence Kelshaw. m 7/30/1966 Susan A McDowell c 2. artiensue@juno.com

MCDOWELL, Eugene C (Mass) 14 Fair St, Nantucket MA 02554 **R S Paul's Ch In Nantucket Nantucket MA 2008-** B Spartanburg SC 10/9/1949 s Lester Earle McDowell & Estelle. BA Wofford Coll 1971; MDiv Yale DS 1976; Drew U 1982; ThD Bos 2002. D 2/16/1986 P 8/1/1986 Bp William Gillette Weinhauer. m 1/30/1983 Mary C Wanucha c 1. Int S Paul's Ch Riverside CT 2007-2008; Ch Of The Redeem Shelby NC 1990-2007; Assoc The Cathd Of All Souls Asheville NC 1987-1990. Auth, "Patristic Thought To Contemporary Theol...," Bos, 2002; Auth, "An Incarnational Approach To Eucharistic . . .," Peeters Press, 2000; Auth, "Aug & Tu Wei-Ming," Appalachian, 1991; Auth, "Thoughts On The Notion Of Trust"; Auth, "Participation"; Auth, "Comparison Of Transformation"; Auth, "Contributions Of Richard Hooker And His Retrieval Of Gk". emcdowell@bellsouth.net

MCDOWELL, Harold Clayton (LI) 27 Private Rd, Medford NY 11763 B Brooklyn NY 11/23/1927 s Harold Frances McDowell & Gudrun Alice. BA Adams St Coll; CTh Mercer TS. D 9/27/1969 P 5/16/1970 Bp Jonathan Goodhue Sherman. m 12/7/1947 Kathryn Louise Burkhardt. Int Chr Ch Bellport NY 1993-1994; Mssn Dio Long Island Garden City NY 1978-1979; Stwdshp Dio Long Island Garden City NY 1975-1976; S Pat's Ch Deer Pk NY 1970-1992; Asst S Cuth's Epis Ch Selden NY 1969-1970. padremac@optonline.net

MCDOWELL, (James) Lynn (SwFla) 2808 Valley Park Dr., Little Rock AR 72212 B Tullahoma TN 11/1/1942 s Carl Collins McDowell & Mary Evelyn. BA Van 1964; MDiv TS 1978. D 6/24/1978 Bp William Evan Sanders P 5/6/1979 Bp William F Gates Jr. m 2/25/1967 Susan T Templeton c 1. Stwdshp Chair Dio SW Florida Sarasota FL 1998-2000; R S Alb's Epis Ch St Pete Bch FL 1994-2004; Cn to the Ordnry Dio Arkansas Little Rock AR 1987-1994; Chair Dept Stwdshp Dio Arkansas Little Rock AR 1985-1986; R Gr Ch Pine Bluff AR 1982-1986; R The Epis Ch Of The Mssh Pulaski TN 1979-1982; D S Geo's Ch Germantown TN 1978-1979. CODE 1987-1994; FD Maurice Soc 1983-1990. jlmstm22@sbcglobal.net

MCDOWELL, James Ralph (SVa) 31 Mill Cove Rd, Brevard NC 28712 B Pitcairn PA 8/4/1923 s James Dudley McDowell & Lucille Oneta. BA Randolph-Macon Coll 1949; MDiv SWTS 1953. D 6/20/1953 Bp Austin Pardue P 12/1/1953 Bp Oliver J Hart. Dio Sthrn Virginia Norfolk VA 1982-1988; Int S Paul's Epis Ch Lynchburg VA 1981-1982; Int S Thad Epis Ch Aiken SC 1980-1981; Int The Ch Of The Gd Shpd Augusta GA 1979-1980; Chr Ch Reading PA 1978-1979; Int Ch Of The Gd Shpd Norfolk VA 1978; The Woodward Acad Coll Pk GA 1972-1976. jrmedowell@citcom.net

MCDOWELL JR, John Sidebotham (Va) 176 E Pomfret St, Carlisle PA 17013 **R Ch Of The Trsfg Blue Ridge Summit PA 2010-** B Wellesboro PA 9/16/1942 s John Sidebotham McDowell & Josephine. AA Hershey Jr Coll Hershey PA 1962; BA Dickinson Coll 1964; MDiv VTS 1971. D 6/11/1971 Bp Dean T Stevenson P 6/1/1972 Bp Thomas Augustus Fraser Jr. m 5/16/1970 Harriet Graham Riddle c 4. Int All SS' Epis Ch Hershey PA 2007-2008; R Ch Of S Jas The Less Ashland VA 1996-2005; Chair - Dept Of Missions Dio Cntrl Pennsylvania Harrisburg PA 1982-1995; Chair - Sch of Chr Stds Dio Cntrl Pennsylvania Harrisburg PA 1982-1995; GC Dep Dio Cntrl Pennsylvania Harrisburg PA 1982-1995; Pres - Cler Assoc. Dio Cntrl Pennsylvania Harrisburg PA 1980-1981; R The Memi Ch Of The Prince Of Peace Gettysburg PA 1973-1982; Cur Emm Par Epis Ch And Day Sch Sthrn Pines NC 1971-1973. john.mcdowell@comcast.net

MCDOWELL, Joseph Lee (CFla) 116 Jamaica Dr, Cocoa Beach FL 32931 B Washington DC 7/4/1939 s Ridgely Lee McDowell & Marguerite Pauline. BA U of Virginia 1961; MDiv Gordon-Conwell TS 1970; EDS 1971. D 6/26/1971 P 2/1/1972 Bp William Foreman Creighton. m 9/10/1965 Helen C Yagerhofer c 5. Int R Gloria Dei Epis Ch Cocoa FL 2004-2005; Assoc Gloria Dei Epis Ch Cocoa FL 1996-2001; Exec Bd Dio SE Florida Miami FL 1991-1994; R S Jas The Fisherman Islamorada FL 1990-1994; R S Paul's Ch Winona MN

M

1980-1990; R All SS Ch Oakley Av MD 1971-1980. helencmcdowell@bellsouth.net

MCDOWELL JR, Malcolm Hume (CPa) 10 Marion Rd., Harwich MA 02645 B Flushing NY 7/9/1940 s Malcolm Hume McDowell & Helen Lenora. BA Washington and Jefferson U 1962; MDiv GTS 1965; MA S Jos Coll W Hartford CT 1980; PhD Washington and Jefferson U (Hon) 2000. D 6/14/1965 Bp Walter H Gray P 12/18/1965 Bp John Henry Esquirol. m 7/3/1965 Kathleen Elsie Otto c 2. Dep Gc Dio Cntrl Pennsylvania Harrisburg PA 1994-2000; Dn/R Cathd Ch Of S Steph Harrisburg PA 1993-2004; Dep Gc Dio Connecticut Hartford CT 1985-1991; R S Mk's Ch New Britain CT 1982-1993; R S Paul's Epis Ch Willimantic CT 1975-1982; Assoc / Team Mnstry S Jas Ch Glastonbury CT 1968-1975; Vic Gr Ch Broad Brook CT 1966-1968; Cur Chr Ch Cathd Hartford CT 1965-1966. Ch & City Conf 1968; EUC 1972; Sojourners 1975; The Liturg Conf 1965. Baccalaureate Address W&J 2000; Ch Ecum Awd New Britain Area 1994; Outstanding Serv Awd Washington & Jefferson U Connecticut 1975; DSA Glastonbury Jaycees 1970. kathmac608@comcast.net

MCDOWELL, Todd S. (Mo) Grace Episcopal Church, 514 E Argonne Dr, Kirkwood MO 63122 **Dioc Coun Dio Missouri S Louis MO 2010-; chair-DHP Com Dio Missouri S Louis MO 2010-; R Gr Ch Kirkwood MO 2009-** B Evansville IN 4/10/1962 s Jerry McDowell & Sonja G. BBA Fontbonne U; MDiv SWTS 2000. D 6/11/2000 Bp Peter Hess Beckwith P 12/16/2000 Bp John Bailey Lipscomb. m 8/27/1994 Sabine Sagawe c 2. S Ptr's Epis Ch St Louis MO 2008-2009; Int R The Angl/Epis Ch Of Chr The King Frankfurt am Main 60323 DE 2007-2008; Coun of Advice Convoc of Amer Ch in Europe Paris FR 2006-2008; Alt to GC Convoc of Amer Ch in Europe Paris FR 2006; Cn Vic The Amer Cathd of the H Trin Paris 75008 FR 2005-2007; chair - Cler Compstn Com Dio SW Florida Sarasota FL 2003-2005; Dioc Coun Dio SW Florida Sarasota FL 2001-2005; Assoc R Trin By The Cove Naples FL 2000-2005. tsmcdowell@gmail.com

MCDOWELL-FLEMING, David Howard (CGC) 3560 Briar Cliff Dr, Pensacola FL 32505 B Melbourne VIC AU 11/8/1944 s Arthur Miller Fleming & Margaret Willis. DIT Melbourne Coll of Div 1972; MDiv Duke 1976; CAS GTS 1987; PhD Logos Grad Sch 2004. D 7/22/1987 P 5/1/1988 Bp Charles Farmer Duvall. c 2. R S Monica's Cantonment FL 1991-2007; Int S Jn's Epis Ch Mobile AL 1990-1991; Cur All SS Epis Ch Mobile AL 1987-1990. "The Deconstruction Of A Dio," Logos, 2004. aususadm@cox.net

MCDUFFIE, John Stouffer (WA) 5320 Westpath Way, Bethesda MD 20816 **R Chr Ch Prince Geo's Par Rockville MD 1998-** B Morrison IL 5/21/1950 s James Henry McDuffie & Mary Elizabeth. S Jn's Coll 1970; BA Bos 1972; MSW U NC 1974; MDiv VTS 1987. D 6/6/1987 Bp C(laude) Charles Vache P 4/16/1988 Bp James Russell Moodey. m 6/8/1996 Mary Stuart Addis c 3. R S Dunst's Epis Ch Beth MD 1989-1998; Cur S Paul's Ch Akron OH 1987-1989. Auth, "What The Thunder Said," *Rel & Intellectual Life*, 1998. jmcduffie@cecrockville.org

MCDUFFIE JR, William Richard (Lex) 166 Market St, Lexington KY 40507 B Brownfield TX 10/22/1929 s William Richard McDuffie & Maurine Elizabeth. BA U of Texas 1950; Med W Texas A&M U 1955; MDiv Epis TS of The SW 1960. D 6/13/1960 P 12/1/1960 Bp George Henry Quarterman. m 2/1/1964 Nancy Barbara Kennedy. Chr Ch Cathd Lexington KY 1977-1994; Cbury Sch Accokeek MD 1967-1977; Cur S Jn's Ch Georgetown Par Washington DC 1967-1968; R Gr Epis Ch Alvin TX 1965-1967; Vic S Mk's Epis Ch Coleman TX 1960-1965; Vic Trin Ch Albany TX 1960-1965. N.MCDUFFIE@INSIGHTBB.COM

MCELLIGOTT, Ann Elizabeth Proctor (Haw) 12705 SE River Road, Apt 404E, Portland OR 97222 **P Assoc, Ret S Jn The Evang Ch Milwaukie OR 2008-** B Boise ID 9/9/1947 d Charles Robert Proctor & Ruth Irene. BA Metropltn St U Twin Cities MN 1981; MDiv GTS 1984; PhD NYU 1995. D 6/11/1984 P 12/1/1984 Bp Robert Marshall Anderson. m 2/24/1979 Thomas James McElligott c 1. Dn S Andr's Cathd Honolulu HI 2002-2007; St Johns Coll 1995-2002; Bd Trst The GTS New York NY 1992-1995; Stndg Com Dio Indianapolis Indianapolis IN 1992-1994; Dioc Liturg & Mus Cmsn Dio Indianapolis Indianapolis IN 1989-1995; Assoc R S Paul's Epis Ch Indianapolis IN 1988-1995; Tutor The GTS New York NY 1985-1987; Assoc Ch Of The H Apos New York NY 1985-1986; Assoc Ch Of The Heav Rest New York NY 1984-1985. Auth, "Evang And The Catechumenal Process," Cowley, 1998; Auth, "The Catechumenal Process: A Journey Of Initiation," *Journ Of The Liturg Conf*, 1993; Auth, "The Catechumenal Process," Ch Hymnal, 1990. No Amer Assn Catechumenate. Hon Doctorate of Div GTS 2002. annepmc@gmail.com

MCELLIGOTT, Thomas James (Minn) 12705 SE River Rd Apt 404E, Portland OR 97222 B Sioux Falls SD 6/8/1919 s William James McElligott & Audencia Bee. D 12/19/1949 P 10/1/1950 Bp Stephen E Keeler. m 2/24/1979 Ann Elizabeth Proctor McElligott c 3. Int S Mk's Ch Mendham NJ 1985-1986; Int Trin Cathd Easton MD 1983-1984; Int S Mary's Ch Brooklyn NY 1982-1983; Mgr - EFM Prog The TS at The U So Sewanee TN 1981-1982; Emm Epis Ch Alexandria MN 1979-1981; Relig. Ed. Coord / Off For Rel Ed. Epis Ch Cntr New York NY 1971-1979; Serv Dio Minnesota Minneapolis MN 1962-1979; Dep Gc Dio No Dakota Fargo ND 1958-1961; Serv Dio No Dakota Fargo ND 1953-1962; P-in-c Chr Ch Frontenac MN 1951-1953; R S Mk's Ch Lake City MN 1951-1953; Vic Emm Ch Rushford MN 1949-1951; Cur S Paul's Ch Winona MN 1949-1951; Vic Trin S Chas MN 1949-1951. Auth, "A Resource For Congregregational Action". DD Seabury Wstrn TS 1992. annepmc@gmail.com

MCELRATH, James Devoe (WNC) No address on file. B 2/27/1935 s Wiley Sigsbee McElrath & Ruth Lucile. BS Wstrn Carolina U 1956; MA U NC 1959. D 12/9/1995 Bp Robert Hodges Johnson. m 8/4/1956 Nancy Evans Trogdon c 2. Franciscan Assn.

MCELROY, Catherine DeLellis (NY) 191 Larch Ave, Teaneck NJ 07666 B Wilmington DE 4/26/1935 d Vincent Anthony DeLellis & Josephine. BA U Of Delaware Newark 1960; S Cecilia Conservatory 1963; MDiv UTS 1985. D 6/3/1978 Bp Paul Moore Jr P 1/1/1979 Bp Richard Beamon Martin. Pstr Asst Ch Of The Intsn New York NY 1975-1979.

MCELROY, Gary Austin (O) 8437 Eaton Dr, Chagrin Falls OH 44023 B Denver CO 11/17/1937 s Louis Albert McElroy & Victoria Gladys. BS Col 1961; MDiv GTS 1964; STM Ya Berk 1969; Cert Ya 1970; Fllshp Oxf 1973; MS U IL 1976. D 4/4/1964 P 10/1/1964 Bp Walter C Klein. m 5/30/1964 Elizabeth M Noble c 3. Ch Of The Epiph Cleveland OH 1997; S Mk's Ch Cleveland OH 1985-1986; Chr Ch Shaker Heights OH 1982-1983; Chapl Chap Of S Jn The Div Champaign IL 1970-1975; R S Andr's Ch Northford CT 1969-1970; Cur Gr Ch White Plains NY 1967-1969; Asst S Jn's Ch New Haven CT 1966-1967; Cur S Jn The Evang Ch Elkhart IN 1964-1966. Auth, "Jas De Koven & The Wi Election Of 1874". ESMHE, AAPC, EPF. Fell AAPC 1978. padremac@yahoo.com

MCELROY, Jamie (SwFla) 140 4th Street North, Saint Petersburg FL 33701 **Coun of Deacons Dio SW Florida Sarasota FL 2011-; Cn Cathd Ch Of S Ptr St Petersburg FL 2010-; Cler Events Plnng Com Dio SW Florida Sarasota FL 2010-** B Washington DC 8/11/1973 s James Harold McElroy & Sally Coltrin. BA Ya 1995; MDiv CDSP 2008. D 12/5/2009 P 6/5/2010 Bp Marc Handley Andrus. m 7/27/1996 Peyton Craig Peyton Craig c 2. S Bede's Epis Ch Menlo Pk CA 2009-2010. jmcelroy@spcathedral.com

MCELWAIN, David Marc (EC) 3594 Stampede Ranch, Cheyenne WY 82007 B Newcastle PA 8/5/1955 s Harry Allen McElwain & Viola Janell. BS Arizona St U Tempe AZ 1977; MDiv Cntrl Bapt TS 1986; Cert CDSP 2008. D 6/9/2007 P 2/9/2008 Bp Clifton Daniel III. m 6/1/1985 Linda Pauline Raker c 7. mcpadre@hotmail.com

MCELYEA, Grover Cleveland (Dal) 6033 Melody Ln Apt 349, Dallas TX 75231 B LeFlore OK 3/13/1923 s Grover McElyea & Jewel. BA Ohio Wesl 1947; LTh SWTS 1950. D 6/29/1950 P 12/30/1950 Bp Charles A Mason. c 4. Vic S Justin's Canton TX 1989-1996; P-in-c S Jas' Epis Ch Kemp TX 1985-1995; Dept Of Missions Dallas TX 1984-1989; Ch Of Our Merc Sav Kaufman TX 1982-1983; R S Lk's Epis Ch Dallas TX 1967-1979; Chair Deptce Dio Dallas Dallas TX 1967-1970; R S Alb's Epis Ch Waco TX 1962-1967; Secy Bec Dio Dallas Dallas TX 1959-1961; Dept Mssns Dio Dallas Dallas TX 1956-1958; Assoc S Mich And All Ang Ch Dallas TX 1952-1962; Vic S Phil's Epis Ch Sulphur Sprg TX 1950-1952; Vic Trin NE Texas Epis Ch Mt Pleasant TX 1950-1952. frmac2@tx.rr.com

MCEWEN, Michael Thomas (Okla) 514 Big Rock Rd, PO Box 338, Medicine Park OK 73557 B Vienna Austria 1/25/1948 s Carl Cecil McEwen & Lois. BS U of Cntrl Oklahoma 1975; MA U of Oklahoma 1976; BA Oklahoma City U 1981; MDiv VTS 1988; DMin Phillips TS 1999. D 5/7/1988 P 11/9/1988 Bp Brice Sidney Sanders. m 11/22/1968 Vycke Collins c 2. Assoc S Andr's Epis Ch Lawton OK 2008-2010; P-in-c S Dav's Ch Oklahoma City OK 2001-2005; Assoc S Mary's Ch Edmond OK 1999; S Mk's Epis Ch Weatherford OK 1997-1999; St Gregorys U Shawnee OK 1995-1999; P-in-c S Tim's Epis Ch Pauls Vlly OK 1995-1997; P-in-c S Ptr's Ch Coalgate OK 1992-1995; R Emm Epis Ch Shawnee OK 1989-1992; Asst R S Jn's Epis Ch Fayetteville NC 1988-1989. Auth, "Combat Stress: What Congregations nedd to Know," *www.tec-Chapl.org/CombatStressPPT_3-1.htm*, The Epis Ch, 2008; Auth, "Wmn in the Bible," *www.episcopalchurch.org/41685_81935_ENG_HTM.htm*, The Epis Ch, 2007; Auth, "Seven Pearls of Sprtlty," FMP, 2002; Auth, "God, Creation, Freedom, and Evil," *Living Ch*, 2001; Auth, "101 Favorite Bible Stories," FMP, 2000. Amer Benedictine Acad 1989; Oblate Ord of S Ben 1989. The DSM Bp Suggragan for Fed Chaplaincies, The Epis Ch 2008. michael.mcewen@us.army.mil

MCFADDEN, Grafton Ridout (Fla) 5302 Fleet Landing Blvd, Atlantic Beach FL 32233 B Coronado CA 9/27/1928 s Archibald George William McFadden & Anna Maria. BS USNA 1951; BS Usnpgs 1964; MDiv VTS 1977. D 6/8/1977 P 4/1/1978 Bp Robert Poland Atkinson. m 6/2/1951 Elesa Evelyn Konigsberg. R S Mk's Ch Starke FL 1991-1993; S Anne's Epis Ch Keystone Heights FL 1989-1992; Assoc Of Pstr Care Ch Of The Gd Shpd Jacksonville FL 1988-1990; Assoc R Gd Samar Epis Ch Orange Pk FL 1986-1987; Assoc R S Mary's Ch Baltimore MD 1982-1984; Asst S Tim's Ch Catonsville MD 1980-1982; R S Jn Wheeling WV 1977-1979.

MCFARLAND, Earl Everett (RG) 8960 Stetson Pl, Las Cruces NM 88011 B Omaha NE 4/16/1934 s Earl Everett McFarland & Isabelle Mae. BA California St U 1960; MA California St U 1965; TESM 2001. D 7/28/2001 Bp Terence Kelshaw. m 5/28/1970 Joy Elizabeth Shuford c 4. D S Andr's Epis Ch Las Cruces NM 2001-2003.

MCFARLANE, Robert Bruce (Mass) 21 Euclid Ave, Lynn MA 01904 B Lynn MA 4/30/1934 s John M McFarlane & Matilda Christine. BA Tufts U 1955; MDiv Ya Berk 1958; Med Tufts U 1968. D 6/21/1958 Bp Frederic Cunningham Lawrence P 1/4/1959 Bp Henry Knox Sherrill. m 8/18/1985 Susan Eileen Barry c 4. Asst S Mk's Ch Southborough MA 1966-1970; R Ch Of The H Trin Marlborough MA 1960-1966; Asst The Cathd Ch Of S Paul Boston MA 1958-1960.

MCGARRY, Susan Ellen (Mich) 2565 Carmel St, Ann Arbor MI 48104 **R S Aid's Ch Ann Arbor MI 1990-** B New Haven CT 3/25/1953 d John Joseph McGarry & Jean Rathburn. BA Ob 1974; MDiv EDS 1978. D 6/24/1978 P 3/1/1979 Bp John Harris Burt. c 2. S Andr's Ch Ann Arbor MI 1978-1984. smcgarry@umich.edu

MCGARRY-LAWRENCE, Marla Terese (Ore) 11229 NE Prescott St., Portland OR 97220 **D S Matt's Epis Ch Portland OR 2010-** B Merced CA 8/28/1952 d Russell Carl McGarry & Doris Evelyn. Cert Cntr for Diac Mnstry 1994; BA Marylhurst U 1998. D 9/29/1994 Bp Robert Louis Ladehoff. m 9/18/1971 Gary L Lawrence c 2. D S Mich And All Ang Ch Portland OR 2002-2010. mmcgarrylawrence@gmail.com

MCGARVEY, Philip Peter (Md) No address on file. B Philadelphia PA 2/17/1944 s John Philip McGarvey & Betty Virginia. BA Dickinson Coll 1966; STB Ya Berk 1969. D 6/23/1969 Bp Harry Lee Doll P 12/1/1969 Bp John Henry Esquirol. c 1. Asst Min S Lk's Epis Ch New Haven CT 1969-1970.

MCGAVRAN, Frederick Jaeger (SO) 3550 Shaw Ave, Cincinnati OH 45208 B Columbus, OH 4/24/1943 s James Holt McGavran & Marion Jaeger. BA Ken 1965; JD Harvard Law Sch 1972; N/A Sch for Diac Mnstry 2010. D 6/12/2010 Bp Thomas Edward Breidenthal. m 1/5/1980 Elizabeth Dolwig c 2. Auth, "The Butterfly Collector," *The Butterfly Collector*, Black Lawr Press, 2009. The Literary Club of Cincinnati 1996. fmcgavran@fuse.net

MCGEE JR, Hubert (Ind) 1609 Rivershore Rd, Elizabeth City NC 27909 B Fort Lauderdale FL 10/5/1928 s Hubert McGee & Jean. U NC; AA San Mateo Jr Coll 1950; BS E Carolina U 1956. D 6/24/1987 P 3/5/1988 Bp Edward Witker Jones. m 7/1/1950 Beverly Clark c 3. P-in-c S Mary's Ch Gatesville NC 2002-2004; P-in-c Chr Ch Eliz City NC 1998-2002; Vic S Lk's Epis Ch Cannelton IN 1988-2000. humcgee@yahoo.com

MCGEE, Kyle M (Ct) 11133 Town Walk Dr, Hamden CT 06518 B Columbus OH 2/23/1942 s Lawrence A McGee & Dorothy Anne. BA DePauw U 1963; MDiv Yale DS 1967. D 6/17/1967 P 12/17/1967 Bp Roger W Blanchard. c 2. P-in-c S Jn The Evang Yalesville CT 2000-2005; Int S Ptr's Epis Ch Oxford CT 1997-2000; Int S Mk's Ch Bridgeport CT 1993-1994; R S Paul And S Jas New Haven CT 1987-1991; Urban Mssn Off Dio Connecticut Hartford CT 1981-1987; Asst Min Ch Of S Steph And The Incarn Washington DC 1969-1972; Asst Min and Campus Min Chr Epis Ch Dayton OH 1967-1969. kylemcgee@snet.net

MCGEE, Robert Rector (NC) Box 7204, Winston-Salem NC 27109 **Dio No Carolina Raleigh NC 1985-; Chapl Winston-Salem Area Colleges Mnstry Winston Salem NC 1985-** B Roanoke VA 7/18/1950 s Robert Lee McGee & Martha Frost. BA Furman U 1972; MDiv STUSo 1976. D 6/23/1976 P 5/1/1977 Bp George Moyer Alexander. m 5/17/1975 Byah RD McGee. S Tim's Epis Ch Winston Salem NC 2010-2011; Int S Matt's Epis Ch Kernersville NC 1993-1994; Asst Chr Epis Ch Raleigh NC 1980-1985; Vic Ch Of The Incarn Gaffney SC 1977-1979; Cur Gr Epis Ch And Kindergarten Camden SC 1976-1977. OHC. MCGEEBOB@WFU.EDU

MC GEE, Vern Wesley (Spok) 1000 E. Craig Ave, Ellensburg WA 98926 **R Gr Ch Ellensburg WA 2009-** B Spokane WA 8/1/1939 s George Wesley Mc Gee & Lela Margaret. MA U of Washington 1968; PhD U of Texas 1986; MDiv The GTS 2008. D 6/7/2008 P 12/13/2008 Bp James Edward Waggoner. mcvern@gmail.com

MCGEE, William Earl (ETenn) 3404-A Taft Hwy, Signal Mountain TN 37377 B Knoxville TN 10/30/1948 s George Carlton McGee & Elinor Hope. BS U of Tennessee 1970; MA U of Tennessee 1976; EdD U of Tennessee 1982. D 6/16/2001 Bp Charles Glenn VonRosenberg. m 6/16/1973 Roslyn Meriwether Vanstone.

MCGEE-STREET, Eleanor Lee (Ct) 35 Killdeer Rd, Hamden CT 06517 B Baltimore MD 8/24/1943 d John Joseph Hofmann & Eleanor Lee. MS CUA; BA U of Maryland; MA Ya. D 10/27/1974 Bp William Foreman Creighton P 9/7/1975 Bp George West Barrett. m 7/30/2000 Claude Parke Street. Prof Ya Berk New Haven CT 1987-1997; R S Paul And S Jas New Haven CT 1987-1991; Clncl Soc Wkr Epis Soc Serv Dio Connecticut Hartford CT 1982-1987. Auth, "Wrestling w The Patriarchs; Retrieving Wmn Voices In Preaching," Abingdon Press, 1996; Auth, "Wmn & Preaching Mnstry," *Yale DS Journ*, 1983; Auth, "The Rite To Be Female/Male". Wmn Of The Year Awd Amer U Washington DC. leemcgee@aya.yale.edu

✠ MCGEHEE JR, Rt Rev H Coleman (Mich) 1496 Ashover Dr, Bloomfield Hills MI 48304 **Ret Bp Of Mich Dio Michigan Detroit MI 1990-** B Richmond VA 7/7/1923 s Harry Coleman McGehee & Annie Lee. BS VPI 1947; JD U Rich 1949; MDiv VTS 1957; DD VTS 1973. D 6/7/1957 P 6/22/1958 Bp Frederick D Goodwin Con 10/7/1971 for Mich. m 2/1/1946 June Stewart. Bp Of Mich Dio Michigan Detroit MI 1973-1990; Dio Michigan Detroit MI 1971-1989; Bp Coadj Of Mich Dio Michigan Detroit MI 1971-1973; R Imm Ch-On-The-Hill Alexandria VA 1960-1971; Vic S Jn's Epis Ch Arlington VA 1957-1960. Mart Luther King Awd Detroit 1995; Mart Luther King Awd U Ch Of Chr 1995; Bro Awd Ame Ch 1993; Ina Jayne Awd Naacp Detroit 1993; Sprt Of Detroit Awd 1989; EPF 1988; Honoree Of The Year ACLU Detroit 1984; Phil Hart Medal Michigan Wmn Stds Assoc. 1984; Feminist Of The Year Awd Detroit Now 1978; DD VTS 1973; Jn Nevin Sayre Awd Naacp Detroit.

MCGEHEE, J(ames) Pittman (Tex) 1105 Milford St, Houston TX 77006 B Fort Smith AR 9/22/1943 s Jarrett Bryan McGehee & Mary Ruth. BS Oklahoma St U 1966; MDiv VTS 1969; CG Jung Inst 1996. D 6/21/1969 Bp Chilton Powell P 12/29/1969 Bp Robert Rae Spears Jr. m 8/29/1964 Bobby Jo Lasater c 2. Dn Chr Ch Cathd Houston TX 1980-1991; R Chr Epis Ch Tyler TX 1978-1980; Chair, Dept of CE Dio Kentucky Louisville KY 1976-1978; Assoc S Fran In The Fields Harrods Creek KY 1973-1978; Assoc S Paul's Ch Kansas City MO 1969-1973. Auth, "The Invisible Ch," Praeger, 2008; Auth, "The Paradox of Love," Bright Sky Press; Auth, "Raising Lazarus," Amazon; Auth, "Words Made Flesh," Amazon; Auth, "Herbie". DD Epis TS of the SW 1988.

MCGEHEE, Lionel Eby (NY) 225 W 99th St, New York NY 10025 B Delhi LA 4/3/1964 s Thomas Harry McGehee & Lynda Jane. BA NE Louisiana U 1988; MDiv SWTS 1993. D 6/12/1993 Bp Robert Jefferson Hargrove Jr P 5/1/1994 Bp Roger W Blanchard. Asst R S Mich's Ch New York NY 1997-2000; Asst Par Of Chr Ch Andover MA 1993-1997. w99.nyc@mci2000.com

MCGILL, James Calvin (Tex) 8214 Cayton St, Houston TX 77061 **Chr Ch Cathd Houston TX 2005-; Dioc Hisp Cmsn Dio Texas Houston TX 1991-** B Dallas TX 11/2/1950 s Charlie Alexander McGill & Virgina Rhodes. BS USMA at W Point 1973; MDiv STUSo 1991. D 6/29/1991 Bp Terence Kelshaw P 12/4/1992 Bp William Elwood Sterling. m 7/21/1973 Elizabeth Rose Fleming c 2. Dioc Liturg Cmsn Dio Texas Houston TX 1996-1999; R S Paul's Ch Houston TX 1994-2004; Assoc R S Ptr's Ch Pasadena TX 1991-1994. iakwbos01@gmail.com

MCGILL JR, William James (CPa) Po Box 682, Cornwall PA 17016 **P-in-c S Jas Ch Lancaster PA 1994-** B Saint Louis MO 3/25/1936 s William James McGill & Ethel. PhD Harv; MA Harv; BA Trin Hartford CT. D 4/28/1973 P 6/1/1974 Bp Robert Bracewell Appleyard. m 6/18/1960 Ellen Buck. Int S Andr's Epis Ch York PA 1993-1994; Int S Thos Ch Lancaster PA 1989-1990; Int S Paul's Ch Manheim PA 1988-1989; P-in-c S Geo's Ch Waynesburg PA 1975-1983. Auth, "Geo Herbert," *R.S. Thos And The Argument w God*, 2003; Auth, "arts," *Rock Sprg Chronicles*, Fithian, 1999; Auth, "Maria Theresa," 1972; Ed, "Spitball". wjmcgill@earthlink.net

MCGIMPSEY, Ralph Gregory (Mich) 8207 Nice Way, Sarasota FL 34238 **Asst S Bon Ch Sarasota FL 1999-** B Cleveland OH 3/15/1937 s John Earle McGimpsey & Muriel Naomi. BA Mia 1959; MDiv Bex 1964. D 6/13/1964 P 12/18/1964 Bp Nelson Marigold Burroughs. m 4/22/1961 Katherine Charlotte Hanau c 2. Cn Provost Cathd Ch Of S Paul Detroit MI 1989-1999; Cathd Chapt Dio Michigan Detroit MI 1985-1999; R S Paul's Epis Ch Brighton MI 1967-1973; Asst Min S Jn's Epis Ch Saginaw MI 1964-1967. rgmcg59@aol.com

MCGINLEY, Charles Richard (Md) 18024 Sand Wedge Dr, Hagerstown MD 21740 **Asstg P S Mk's Ch Lappans Boonsboro MD 1988-** B Hagerstown MD 5/19/1926 s Edward William McGinley & Frances Elizabeth. AA Hagerstown Jr Coll 1948; BS Bos 1949; MDiv VTS 1957. D 6/7/1957 Bp Frederick D Goodwin P 5/25/1958 Bp Robert Fisher Gibson Jr. m 8/24/1950 Katherine Lorraine Morgan c 3. S Mk's Ch Lappans Boonsboro MD 1973-1987; S Paul's Ch Sharpsburg MD 1973-1980; R S Matt's Epis Ch Newton KS 1968-1973; Assoc S Edw The Confessor Epis Ch San Jose CA 1965-1968; R Emm Ch Virginia Bch VA 1959-1965; Assoc S Steph's Ch Richmond VA 1957-1959. frmac21740@aol.com

MCGINN, John Edward (Mass) 159 Main St, Sandwich MA 02563 **R S Jn's Ch Sandwich MA 1995-** B Hartford CT 7/4/1947 s John Edward McGinn & Josephine. BA U of Connecticut 1969; MDiv EDS 1980. D 6/14/1980 P 12/1/1980 Bp Morgan Porteus. m 11/15/1969 Marion G Garrison c 2. R S Paul's Ch Southington CT 1982-1995; Asst Chr Chr Ch Westerly RI 1980-1982. mcginnm@comcast.net

MCGINNIS JR, John Milton (SwFla) 1102 SE 14th Ter, Cape Coral FL 33990 B Shelbyville KY 1/7/1938 s John Milton McGinnis & Dorothy Wright. BA Peabody Coll 1960; MA Peabody Coll 1962; MDiv TS 1966. D 6/24/1966 Bp John Vander Horst P 3/17/1967 Bp William F Gates Jr. m 8/7/1976 Catherine Mary Delahanty c 3. R Ch Of The Epiph Cape Coral FL 1977-2001; Asst S Wlfd's Epis Ch Sarasota FL 1973-1976; Asst Ch Of The H Comm Memphis TN 1972-1973; R The Epis Ch Of The Mssh Pulaski TN 1967-1972; D-in-trng

S Mary's Cathd Memphis TN 1966-1967. R Emer Ch of the Epiph 2005. johnslaptoppad@embarqmail.com

MCGINNIS, Richard H(arry) (Fla) 1312 Wisconsin St., Apt. 137, Hudson WI 54016 B Philadelphia PA 3/5/1929 s Robert Flowers McGinnis & Frances Teste. BA Seattle Pacific Coll 1951; GTS 1954. D 6/29/1954 P 6/29/1955 Bp Stephen F Bayne Jr. m 6/30/1956 Phyllis Good c 3. Assoc S Dav's Ch Jacksonville FL 1984-1994; R Trin Epis Ch Watertown SD 1978-1984; R Trin Epis Ch Winner SD 1967-1978; Vic Chr Ch Anvik AK 1961-1967; Cur Trin Par Seattle WA 1957-1961; Vic Ch Of The Redeem Kenmore WA 1954-1957. Auth, "Mar Mnstry," *Mar Mnstry Trng Outline*, Self, 1993; Auth, "Mar Mnstry," *Mar Mnistry Pstr's Manual*, Self, 1992. AAC 1999; Curs 1971; Forw In Faith N. A. 1997; Kairos 1990; Mar Savers 1996; Ord Of S Lk 1986. Lifetime Achievment Mar Savers 2001. mcginnisrichard@yahoo.com

MCGINNIS, Willard Simpers (Be) 3440 S Jefferson St Apt 1007, Falls Church VA 22041 **Died 9/19/2009** B Chestertown MD 3/31/1931 s William Robert McGinnis & Reba. Ya; BA Washington Coll 1954; MDiv Tem 1957. D 6/14/1958 P 12/13/1958 Bp Angus Dun. c 3. mcginnis30@aol.com

MCGLANNAN, Dorian Legge (Mich) 1035 Andover Dr, Northville MI 48167 **R S Jn's Ch Plymouth MI 2005-** B Baltimore MD 2/7/1952 d Francis McGlannan & Joan. Bos 1971; BA S Olaf Coll 1975; S Mary's Sem 1982; MDiv GTS 1984. D 11/18/1985 P 11/1/1986 Bp A(lbert) Theodore Eastman. m 8/25/1990 Joseph A Cospito c 3. R Ch Of The Gd Shpd Fed Way WA 1997-2005; Natl Excoun Epf Epis Ch Cntr New York NY 1990-1992; Assoc R Ch Of The Epiph Seattle WA 1989-1997; Int S Paul's Epis Ch Prince Frederick MD 1988-1989; Asst Ch Of The Mssh Baltimore MD 1985-1988. dmcglannan5@gmail.com

MCGLASHON JR, Hugh (CFla) PO Box 3303, Haines City FL 33845 B Rochester NY 10/8/1932 s Hugh McGlashon & Rosalind. BS U of So Dakota 1961; MDiv PDS 1973; ThM NBTS 1986. D 4/26/1975 P 11/1/1975 Bp Albert Wiencke Van Duzer. m 3/27/1954 Lois Ross c 3. Chapl Chap Of S Mary & S Martha Bp Gray Inn Davenport FL 2000-2006; R S Mk's Epis Ch Haines City FL CA 1991-1998; R S Paul's Ch Key W FL 1988-1990; Int All SS Ch Bay Hd NJ 1987-1988; R Ch Of The H Sprt Lebanon NJ 1980-1987; R Chr Ch Palmyra NJ 1976-1980; Cur S Andr's Ch Mt Holly NJ 1975-1976; Liaison of Yth Wk and Inter-Dioc Relation Dio Haiti Ft Lauderdale FL 1968-1987. hughlois@tampabay.rr.com

MCGLAUGHON JR, Hugh King (EC) 75 Stone Ridge Way, Apt 3F, Fairfield CT 06824 B Rocky Mount NC 3/17/1952 s Hugh King McGlaughon & Jane Benthall. BA U NC 1973; JD U NC 1976; MDiv GTS 1989. D 6/10/1989 Bp Brice Sidney Sanders P 12/1/1989 Bp Walter Cameron Righter. m 12/28/1975 Susan Carey McFarland. H Fam Epis Ch Fishers IN 1994; Dio E Carolina Kinston NC 1991-1993; Gr Ch Newark NJ 1990-1991.

MCGLYNN, J(ohn) Douglas (SC) 2777 Mission Rd, Nashotah WI 53058 B Kansas City MO 10/1/1939 s Patrick S McGlynn & Jessie May. BA Missouri Vlly Coll 1960; U Chi 1961; MDiv GTS 1963; DMin Asbury TS 1988. D 4/16/1963 P 10/17/1963 Bp Edward Randolph Welles II. m 6/10/1961 Ana Mateu c 2. Dep. GC Dio Pittsburgh Monroeville PA 2004-2006; Nash Nashotah WI 2003-2005; R Ch Of The Ascen Pittsburgh PA 1990-2003; Int S Mart's Epis Ch Monroeville PA 1989-1990; Fac TESM Ambridge PA 1988-1990; R S Mary's Epis Ch Honolulu HI 1979-1988; R S Jn's Ch Ulysses KS 1974-1979; R S Jas' Ch Springfield MO 1969-1974; R S Ptr's Ch Harrisonville MO 1965-1968; Cur All SS Epis Ch Kansas City MO 1963-1965. Bd SAMS 1990. Cn Theol Dio Jos, Nigeria 2004. dmcglynn@nashotah.edu

MCGOVERN, Gerald Hugh (HB) 2600 Lake Michigan Dr Nw, Grand Rapids MI 49504 B Granite City IL 7/24/1933 s Hugh Alvin McGovern & Wilma J. BS Sthrn Illinois U 1955; BS SWTS 1958. D 6/24/1958 P 6/11/1959 Bp Charles A Clough. m 9/5/1953 Betty Lou Stubblefield c 3. Vic S Jn's Ch Centralia IL 2002; Vic S Anne's Epis Ch Warsaw IN 1963-1967; S S Thos Ch Salem IL 1958-1962.

MCGOWAN, Carole Jean (RG) 425 University Blvd NE, Albuquerque NM 87106 **Cn for Ecum Affrs Dio The Rio Grande Albuquerque NM 2011-; Exam Chapl Dio The Rio Grande Albuquerque NM 2009-; GC Dep Dio The Rio Grande Albuquerque NM 2009-; COM Dio The Rio Grande Albuquerque NM 2008-; Bd Mem New Mex Conf of Ch Bernalillo NM 2006-; R S Thos Of Cbury Epis Ch Albuquerque NM 1990-** B Buffalo NY 10/25/1946 d William A McGowan & Lou. BA Vas 1968; MA Ya 1972; MDiv Nash 1979. D 6/14/1980 Bp Morgan Porteus P 3/25/1981 Bp Arthur Edward Walmsley. COM Dio The Rio Grande Albuquerque NM 2008-2011; Cn Liturg Dio The Rio Grande Albuquerque NM 2006-2011; GC Alt Dep Dio The Rio Grande Albuquerque NM 2000-2009; Dioc Coun Dio The Rio Grande Albuquerque NM 1996-2000; SCSD, Chair Epis Ch Cntr New York NY 1994-1997; GBEC Epis Ch Cntr New York NY 1991-1997; SCSD, Co-Chair Epis Ch Cntr New York NY 1991-1993; Fin Com Dio The Rio Grande Albuquerque NM 1991-1992; Exam Chapl Dio The Rio Grande Albuquerque NM 1990-1992; P-in-c S Ptr's Epis Ch Bloomfield NY 1989-1990; Int R S Mk's Ch Newark NY 1988-1989; Int Assoc S Thos Epis Ch Rochester NY 1987; Dir Epis Ch Rela Crds/Bex/Crozer Bex Columbus OH 1984-1990; Asst The Ch of the Redeem Cincinnati OH 1980-1984; Asst to the Bishops Dio Connecticut Hartford CT 1980. Polly Bond Awd ECom 1997. mcgowannm@comcast.net

MCGOWAN, Diane Darby (Minn) 5029 2nd Ave S, Minneapolis MN 55419 **D S Phil's Ch S Paul MN 2003-; D S Thos Ch Minneapolis MN 2003-** B Rhinebeck NY 1/22/1948 d Robert Raymond Plass & Elizabeth Shippen. U Denv 1968; EFM U of So 1989; MBA U of St. Thos 1991. D 5/18/2003 Bp James Louis Jelinek. m 9/12/1991 Mitchell Bruce Pearlstein c 4. smarl@aol.com

MCGOWEN, Willetta Hulett (Ga) 900 Gloucester St, Brunswick GA 31520 B Brunswick GA 2/5/1951 d William Hulett & Margaret B. D 6/15/2009 Bp Henry Irving Louttit. m 10/6/1984 Mitchell McGowen c 3. wmcgowen54@yahoo.com

MCGRADY, Jacqueline Ann (Mass) PO Box 2847, Nantucket MA 02584 B Falmouth MA 11/13/1964 d John Francis McGrady & Patricia Frances. BA Amh 1987; MDiv Harvard DS 1990; GTS 1991. D 5/30/1992 P 5/29/1993 Bp David Elliot Johnson. m 12/10/1994 Peter Swenson c 2. R S Mk's Epis Ch Burlington MA 1999-2005; Asst Ch Of The Gd Shpd Nashua NH 1993-1999; Asst S Phil's Ch Garrison NY 1992-1993. mcgradyja@comcast.net

MCGRATH, Victoria (Nwk) 113 Center Ave, Chatham NJ 07928 **R All SS Ch Millington NJ 2002-; St. Mart's Hse Fund Bd - Pres, Vice-Pres Dio Newark Newark NJ 2002-** B New York NY 8/27/1956 d Abbot Montague Geer & Barbara. BA Wells Coll 1978; MA Col 1987; MDiv Drew U 1994. D 6/4/1994 Bp Jack Marston McKelvey P 12/4/1994 Bp John Shelby Spong. m 8/23/1980 John Byram McGrath c 2. Dioc Bdgt and Fin Com Dio Newark Newark NJ 2009-2011; Vice-Pres, Dioc Coun; Cnvnr, Strng Com; Co-Chair, Equipping Action Team Dio Newark Newark NJ 2008-2011; Cler Peer Coach Dio Newark Newark NJ 2008-2010; COM Formation Liason for Previously Ord Dio Newark Newark NJ 2005-2010; Co-Chair, Bp's Search/Nomin Com Dio Newark Newark NJ 2005-2007; Dio Newark Newark NJ 2002; Int All SS' Epis Ch Glen Rock NJ 1999-2002; COM, Screening Co-Chair; Educ Chair Dio Newark Newark NJ 1996-2004; Yth Mnstrs Bd Dio Newark Newark NJ 1996-2003; Min for Recently Ord Cler Grp Dio Newark Newark NJ 1995-1998; Recently Ord Cler Mentor Dio Newark Newark NJ 1995-1998; Asst R Chr Ch Short Hills NJ 1994-1999; Dioc Nomin Com Dio Newark Newark NJ 1994-1995. Cmnty of S Mary - Assoc 1976-2005; Cmnty of St. Jn Bapt - Assoc 2005. allsaints_rector@verizon.net

MCGRAW, Jean Quarterman (Lex) PO Box 109, Ashland KY 41105 **D Calv Epis Ch Ashland KY 2011-; Dir of Cert Prog in Chr Formation Epis TS Of The SW Austin TX 2011-** B Charleston SC 9/10/1946 d Charles Homer Quarterman & Delilah Floyd. BS Coll of Charleston 1967; MDiv Epis TS Of The SW 2010. D 6/5/2011 Bp Stacy F Sauls. m 4/30/1967 Stanley Earle McGraw c 3. Stdt Bd Rep Epis TS Of The SW Austin TX 2010-2011; Dir of Chr Ed Old S Andr's Par Ch Charleston SC 2005-2007. jean.mcgraw@alum.ssw.edu

MCGRAW, Stanley Earle (At) 14704 Great Willow Dr, Austin TX 78728 **P-in-c S Jas Epis Ch Prestonsburg KY 2010-; Hon Cn Dio Atlanta Atlanta GA 1979-** B Spartanburg SC 5/18/1942 s Ray McGraw & Willie Lee. BA Wofford Coll 1964; MDiv VTS 1969. D 6/23/1969 P 1/1/1970 Bp Gray Temple. m 4/30/1967 Jean Quarterman c 3. Int S Fran Par Temple TX 2007-2010; Asst Old S Andr's Par Ch Charleston SC 2004-2007; P-in-c Chr Epis Ch Sparta NC 1999-2003; R S Jn's Coll Pk GA 1995-1997; Chairperson of Evang Com Dio Atlanta Atlanta GA 1984-1986; Vic Ch Of The H Comf Atlanta GA 1983-1995; Assoc R Emmaus Hse Epis Ch Atlanta GA 1980-1983; Instnl Chapl Dio Atlanta Atlanta GA 1979-1981; Chapl to DOK Dio Atlanta Atlanta GA 1977-1979; Dn of Convoc Dio Atlanta Atlanta GA 1973-1975; R Ch Of The Epiph Atlanta GA 1971-1979; Asst R Par Ch of St. Helena Beaufort SC 1969-1971. Mntl Hlth Wk Awd Fulton Cnty 1993; Mntl Hlth Wk Commendation 93 Dekalb Cnty. sem1942@gmx.com

MCGRAW, Tara L (SwFla) 1611 Murex Ln, Naples FL 34102 **R S Paul's Ch Naples FL 2009-; Const & Cn Com Dio SW Florida Sarasota FL 2005-** B Coral Gables FL 7/21/1957 BBA U of Miami 1977; JD U of Miami 1981; MDiv VTS 2005. D 6/18/2005 P 12/21/2005 Bp John Bailey Lipscomb. m 4/29/2000 John Patrick McGraw. P-in-c S Paul's Ch Naples FL 2007-2009; Vic Resurr Epis Ch Naples FL 2005-2007; Assoc S Paul's Ch Naples FL 2005-2007. frtara@saintpaulsnaples.org

MCGREEVY, Brian Kenneth (SC) PorterGaud School, 300 Albemarle Rd, Charleston SC 29407 **Porter-Gaud Sch Charleston SC 2007-; S Phil's Ch Charleston SC 2007-** B Atlanta GA 3/9/1957 s Martin Kenneth McGreevy & Amy Jones. BA Furman U 1978; JD Emory U 1981. D 9/8/2007 Bp Edward Lloyd Salmon Jr. m 4/9/1983 Jane Jane Hollis Whitney c 4. brian.mcgreevy@portergaud.edu

MCGREEVY, Molly Paine (Ct) 503 Old Long Ridge Rd, Stamford CT 06903 B New York NY 6/11/1936 d Hugh Eustis Paine & Helen Clarehue. BA Vas 1958; MDiv GTS 1986. D 6/10/1989 Bp Paul Moore Jr P 12/1/1989 Bp Walter Decoster Dennis Jr. m 5/21/1976 Earl Warren Hindman c 3. Assoc S Fran Ch

Stamford CT 1996-2003; Tutor The GTS New York NY 1989-1996; The Ch Of S Lk In The Fields New York NY 1989-1995.

MCGREGOR, Patricia Cox (SeFla) PO Box 399, Ambridge PA 15003 **SAMS Ambridge PA 2008-** B Denver CO 8/21/1959 d Gerry White Cox & Audrey R. DMin Gordon Conwell TS; BS Ursinus Coll 1981; MAR Trin Evang DS 1990. Trans from Anglican Church Of Kenya 8/1/2008 Bp Leopold Frade. m 7/27/1985 Todd A McGregor c 2. Global Teams Forest City NC 1988-2003. patsytodd@yahoo.com

MCGUGAN, Terence David (Mil) 4701 Erie St, Racine WI 53402 **R S Mich's Epis Ch Racine WI 1995-** B Boston MA 2/6/1964 s Arthur David McGugan & Janet. AA Emory U 1984; BA Emory U 1986; MDiv GTS 1992. D 5/28/1992 P 12/1/1992 Bp Harry Woolston Shipps. m 5/15/2010 JoEllen M McGugan c 2. Assoc S Mart In The Fields Ch Atlanta GA 1993-1995; Vic S Fran Ch Camilla GA 1992-1993; Vic The Epis Ch Of S Jn And S Mk Albany GA 1992-1993. tmcgugan@stmichaelsracine.org

MCGUINNESS, David (NC) 4330 Pin Oak Dr, Durham NC 27707 **R S Steph's Epis Ch Erwin NC 2003-** B Dublin IE 6/11/1943 s Ignatius McGuinness & Sarah. MDiv S Kieran's Coll Kilkenny Ie 1973. Trans from Church of Ireland 9/7/2002 Bp Michael Bruce Curry. m 11/29/1998 Madlyn Ferraro.

MCGUIRE, Malcolm (Pa) 1300 Lombard St Apt 711, Philadelphia PA 19147 **P-in-c Ch Of The Crucif Philadelphia PA 2002-** B Plattsburg NY 5/3/1935 s Ritchie Quincy McGuire & Lillian. BA New York Sch of Mus 1964; MDiv PDS 1970; STM PDS 1973; EdD Tem 1984; Med Tem 1991. D 6/6/1970 P 12/19/1970 Bp Horace W B Donegan. Dio Pennsylvania Philadelphia PA 1988-2000; R S Alb's Ch Roxborough Philadelphia PA 1987-1994; P-in-c Ch Of The Crucif Philadelphia PA 1975-1979; Asst S Mk's Ch Philadelphia PA 1971-1974; Cur Ch Of S Lk And Epiph Philadelphia PA 1970-1971. Ed, "Coll Tem 84". Alumnini Serv Awd Tem 1984.

MCGUIRE, Mark Alan (WMo) 908 SW Hackney Ct, Lees Summit MO 64081 **R S Paul's Epis Ch Lees Summit MO 2002-** B Warrensburg MO 11/14/1951 s Harry Edward McGuire & Beverly Ann. BS Cntrl Missouri St U 1974; MDiv STUSo 2002. D 6/8/2002 P 12/7/2002 Bp Barry Robert Howe. m 9/1/1984 Donna Jean Reinheimer. mmcguire8@kc.rr.com

MCGURK, Brian William (Mass) 625 Main St, Chatham MA 02633 **R S Chris's Ch Chatham MA 2003-** B Waterbury CT 5/21/1956 s Francis Anthony McGurk & Shirley Catherine. Doctorate Sthrn California U of Hlth Sciences 1982; BA Trin 1990; MDiv Ya Berk 1992. D 6/13/1992 Bp Arthur Edward Walmsley P 12/20/1992 Bp Clarence Nicholas Coleridge. m 4/24/1981 Patricia Ann Brucato c 3. R S Ptr's Par Ch New Kent VA 1998-2003; Asst R S Mary's Ch Richmond VA 1994-1998; Cur S Matt's Epis Ch Wilton CT 1992-1993. brianmcgurk1@verizon.net

MCHALE, Stephen David (Oly) 399 Gregory Lane, Pleasant Hill CA 94523 **Ch Of The Resurr Pleasant Hill CA 2008-** B Rome Italy 7/23/1973 s John Patrick McHale & Laurie Jackson. BA Whitman Coll 1996; MDiv CDSP 2008. D 6/28/2008 Bp Bavi Rivera. m 7/24/2004 Holly C McHale-Larsen c 2. mchalesd@gmail.com

MCHENRY, Richard Earl (FtW) 1010 Willowcreek Rd, Cleburne TX 76033 **Pres Eccl Trail Crt Dio Ft Worth Ft Worth TX 2005-** B Tucson AZ 4/2/1932 s Alfred Earl McHenry & Mary Virginia. BA Missouri Vlly Coll 1954; MDiv McCormick TS 1959. D 5/20/1967 Bp Robert Rae Spears Jr P 10/1/1967 Bp Edward Randolph Welles II. Nomin Com For Bp Coadj Dio Ft Worth Ft Worth TX 1992-1994; R Ch Of The H Comf Cleburne TX 1991-2004; Cmnty Ministers Dio Ft Worth Ft Worth TX 1989-1993; Exec Coun Dio Ft Worth Ft Worth TX 1989-1990; All SS' Epis Ch Ft Worth TX 1984-1991; R Gr Ch Carthage MO 1976-1983; Liturg Cmsn Dio W Missouri Kansas City MO 1969-2004; Asst Gr Ch Carthage MO 1967-1975. CCU, NOEL, Fllshp S Alb & S Sergius, Epis Syn Amer, SSC. R Emer. 1padre@sbcglobal.net

MCHUGH, Brian Harker Orrock Angell (Az) 519 W Taylor St SPC 374, Santa Maria CA 93458 **Assoc S Ben's Par Los Osos CA 2008-** B Montreal QC CA 7/7/1946 s James McHugh & Madge Scott. BA York U 1967; MDiv GTS 1973. Trans from Anglican Church of Canada 12/15/1982 Bp William Grant Black. P-in-c Dio Arizona Phoenix AZ 2006-2008; La Misión Epis Santiago Apóstol [La MESA] Dover Plains NY 1996-2005; P-in-c S Thos Ch Amenia Un Amenia NY 1996-2005; Exec Dir The Oasis Newark NJ 1995; R S Ptr's And S Andr's Epis Providence RI 1986-1995; Int S Anne's In The Fields Epis Ch Lincoln MA 1985-1986; R S Steph's Epis Ch Cincinnati OH 1982-1984. OHC 1967-1982. orrock1946@gmail.com

MCHUGH III, John Michael (NJ) 324 Rio Grande Blvd Nw, Albuquerque NM 87104 B Trenton NJ 1/17/1948 s John M McHugh & Dorothy. BA Glassboro St U 1969; MDiv EDS 1975. D 4/26/1975 Bp Albert Wiencke Van Duzer P 1/1/1976 Bp Morris Fairchild Arnold. Stff S Mk's On The Mesa Epis Ch Albuquerque NM 1981-1988; Asst S Mk's On The Mesa Epis Ch Albuquerque NM 1977-1978.

MCILHINEY, David Brown (NH) 701 E High St Apt 211, Charlottesville VA 22902 **Chapl Blue Ridge Sch Dyke VA 2010-** B Gainesville FL 3/3/1942 s William Gamble McIlhiney & Zelda. BA Harv 1964; BD UTS 1968; PhD Pr 1977. D 6/8/1968 P 12/21/1968 Bp Horace W B Donegan. Chapl S Paul's Memi Charlottesville VA 2004-2009; R Trin Ch Claremont NH 1986-2001; Chapl S Thos Ch Hanover NH 1973-1977. Auth, "A Gentleman in Every Slum," Pickwick, 1988. david@mcilhiney.net

MCILMOYL, William Joseph (NCal) 1314 Spring St, Saint Helena CA 94574 **R Gr Ch S Helena CA 1993-** B Troy NY 10/22/1949 s Sherman William McImoyl & Charlotte Louise. BA Hob 1972; MDiv SWTS 1988. D 6/22/1988 P 12/21/1988 Bp William Hopkins Folwell. m 6/8/1985 Sandra Swetnam c 2. Asst S Jas Epis Ch Ormond Bch FL 1988-1993. frmac@grace-episcopal.org

MCILROY, Ellen LaFleur (Cal) 5555 Montgomery Dr Apt 59, Santa Rosa CA 95409 B Tokyo JP 3/13/1931 d James Garfield McIlroy & Gwynneth. BA Bryn 1952; PhD Syr 1963; Grad Theol Un 1976. D 6/24/1972 P 1/16/1977 Bp C Kilmer Myers. Assoc Ch Of The Epiph San Carlos CA 1985-1987; Chair, Com on the Ord of Wmn Dio California San Francisco CA 1974-1976; Assoc S Jas Ch Oakland CA 1974-1976; Asst S Aid's Ch San Francisco CA 1972-1974; Com on Sxlty Dio California San Francisco CA 1972-1973. emcilro935@earthlink.net

MCILVAIN, Jean Christine (Pgh) 5622 Alan St, Aliquippa PA 15001 **D Chr Epis Ch No Hills Pittsburgh PA 2003-** B Beaver Falls PA 10/20/1946 d Robert Grey McIlvain & Vivian Jean. BS Clarion U of Pennsylvania 1968. D 12/5/1998 Bp Robert William Duncan. D Prince Of Peace Epis Ch Aliquippa PA 1998-2003.

MCILVEEN, Richard William (Me) 26 Concord St, Portland ME 04103 B 9/20/1947 s William Wright McIlveen & Margaret Jane. BA Penn 1969; MDiv GTS 1973. D 5/27/1973 Bp William Crittenden P 1/1/1974 Bp James Stuart Wetmore. m 12/31/1975 Anna Maria Parker. Vic S Barth's Epis Ch Yarmouth ME 1979-1981; Int S Ann's Epis Ch Windham Windham ME 1976-1977; S Jn's Ch Presque Isle ME 1976; Vic For S Ann'S Ch For The Deaf Dio New York New York City NY 1974-1975.

MCINERNEY, Joseph Lee (Cal) PO Box 426797, San Francisco CA 94142 B San Jose CA 8/29/1944 s Joseph Robert McInereny & Norma Jane. Stan; U Of Leeds Gb; U of Pennsylvania. D 1/12/1970 P 1/13/1971 Bp George Richard Millard. P-in-c Chr Ch Creswell NC 1974-1975; P-in-c S Andr's Ch Columbia NC 1974-1975; P-in-c S Geo Epis Ch Engelhard NC 1974-1975.

MCINNIS JR, Clifton Jeter (Miss) Po Box 24, Vicksburg MS 39181 B Meridian MS 9/11/1927 s Clifton Jeter McInnis & Carrie. BA Delta St U 1953; BD VTS 1956. D 6/11/1956 P 12/1/1956 Bp Duncan Montgomery Gray. m 5/26/1953 Frances Erwin c 4. R Ch of the H Trin Vicksburg MS 1969-1992; Vic Ch Of The Resurr Starkville MS 1962-1969; P-in-c Calv Epis Ch Cleveland MS 1960-1962; P-in-c Gr Ch Rosedale MS 1960-1962; M-in-c S Paul's Ch Woodville MS 1956-1960.

MCINNIS, Victor Erwin (Miss) Po Box 63, Lexington MS 39095 **Off Of Bsh For ArmdF New York NY 1997-** B Centerville MS 8/8/1957 s Clifton Jeter McInnis & Francis Percy. BS U of Sthrn Mississippi 1987; MDiv STUSo 1991. D 6/3/1991 Bp Duncan Montgomery Gray Jr P 8/1/1992 Bp Alfred Clark Marble Jr. D Gr Ch Carrollton MS 1991-1997; D S Mary's Ch Lexington MS 1991-1994.

MCINTIRE, Rhonda Gail Smith (SanD) 17 Camino Redondo, Placitas NM 87043 B Pampa TX 1/29/1950 d James Harold Smith & Glorine June. BA Valparaiso U 1972; MDiv Epis TS of The SW 1996. D 6/22/1996 Bp Claude Edward Payne P 6/4/1997 Bp Terence Kelshaw. m 6/10/1978 Timothy Regis McIntire c 1. San Gabr the Archangel Epis Ch Corrales NM 2009-2010; S Andr's By The Sea Epis Par San Diego CA 2004-2008; Vic S Jn's Epis Ch Chula Vista CA 2003-2004; Cn S Jn's Cathd Albuquerque NM 1996-2002. rhonda.mcintire@q.com

MCINTOSH, David Kevin (Ct) 220 Prospect St, Torrington CT 06790 **Asstg P Trin Ch Torrington CT 2010-** B Coral Gables, FL 7/29/1964 s Donald W McIntosh & Patricia M. BS Duke 1986; MD U of Miami 1991; MDiv The GTS 2010. D 6/12/2010 Bp Ian Theodore Douglas P 1/22/2011 Bp James Elliot Curry. m 2/4/2006 Charles Daniel Barr. Connecticut Epis Cler Assn 2010; Soc of Cath Priests 2009. dmcintosh@gts.edu

MCINTOSH, Justin Michael (Va) 4332 Leeds Manor Road, Markham VA 22643 **R Epis Ch Of Leeds Par Markham VA 2011-; Asst S Thos Epis Ch McLean VA 2009-** B Alexandria VA 5/30/1983 s Dennis Francis McIntosh & Susan Hume. Bachelor of Arts The W&M 2005; Dplma of Angl Stds Ya Berk 2009; Mstr of Div Yale DS 2009. D 11/14/2009 Bp Shannon Sherwood Johnston P 5/15/2010 Bp David Colin Jones. m 6/28/2008 Elena Tsiaperas McIntosh. jmac53083@gmail.com

MCINTOSH, Kendra Lea (Nwk) 26 W 84th St, New York NY 10024 B Shawnee Mission KS 9/9/1964 D 6/14/2003 P 1/28/2004 Bp James Edward Waggoner. S Thos Ch Lyndhurst NJ 2007-2010; S Jas Ch New York NY 2003-2005. ceroland@yahoo.com

MCINTOSH, Mark Allen (Chi) 65 E Huron St, Chicago IL 60611 B Evanston IL 2/2/1960 s Gilbert Blodgett McIntosh & Katherine Ann. BA Ya 1982; BA Oxf 1985; MDiv GTS 1986. D 6/14/1986 Bp James Winchester Montgomery P 12/1/1986 Bp Frank Tracy Griswold III. m 8/10/1985 Elizabeth Anne Nagle. Cathd Of S Jas Chicago IL 1986-1989. mark.mcintosh@durham.uc.uk

MCINTOSH, Randy Eugene (WK) 138 S 8th St, Salina KS 67401 **Vic Epis Ch Of The Incarn Salina KS 2008-; Chr Cathd Salina KS 2007-** B Salina KS 12/17/1953 s Wendell Eugene McIntosh & Lillian Mae. D 9/1/2007 P 2/14/2009 Bp James Marshall Adams Jr. Dio Wstrn Kansas Hutchinson KS 2006-2007; Sexton Chr Cathd Salina KS 1998-2004. randymcintosh@christcathedral.net

MCINTOSH, Wayne S (SD) Trinity Episcopal Church, 500 14th Ave NW, Watertown SD 57201 B Winnipeg Manitoba 9/4/1961 s George McIntosh & Henrietta. BA U of Manitoba, Winnipeg Manitoba 1987; MDiv Dioc TS, Montreal Can 1991; BTh McGill U, Quebec 1991. Trans from Anglican Church of Canada 2/1/2008 Bp Creighton Leland Robertson. m 9/18/1982 Lorraine G McIntosh c 4. R Trin Epis Ch Watertown SD 2008. wsmci@hotmail.com

MCINTYRE, Calvin Carney (NY) 4401 Matilda Ave, Bronx NY 10470 **R Ch Of The Gd Shpd Wakefield Bronx NY 2000-** B Saint Ann Jamaica 2/19/1951 s Herbert Constantine McIntyre & Mary Elizabeth. Cert Ch Teachers Coll, Jamaica W.I. 1973; Dplma Untd Theol Coll of the W Indies Kingston JM 1980; LTh Trin 1987; Dplma Blanton Peale Grad of Hlth & Rel, NY 1992; BA Coll of New Rochelle, NY 1992; MDiv Trin 2000. Trans from Church in the Province Of The West Indies 3/5/1992 as Deacon Bp Orris George Walker Jr. m 9/19/1981 Camille Dawn Glasgow. Vic Ch Of The Gd Shpd Wakefield Bronx NY 1998-2000; Asst S Paul's Ch-In-The-Vill Brooklyn NY 1997-1998; Asst Ch Of SS Steph And Mart Brooklyn NY 1995; P-in-c Ch Of The Redeem Brooklyn NY 1993-1994; Asst Ch Of S Thos Brooklyn NY 1990-1993. St. Geo's Soc of New York 2009.

MCINTYRE III, Charles Ernest (NwT) 2429 Santa Cruz Ln, Odessa TX 79763 **Int Team R S Mk's Epis Ch Pecos TX 1994-** B Sparrows Pt MD 3/5/1924 s Charles Ernest McIntyre & Grace Olivia. BA Loyola U 1950; MDiv STUSo 1975. D 11/25/1956 Bp C J Kinsolving III P 6/11/1975 Bp Willis Ryan Henton. m 8/12/1944 Margaret Townsend. Chair Mssn Cmsn Dio NW Texas Lubbock TX 1986-1988; Assoc S Jn's Epis Ch Odessa TX 1981-1992; Assoc S Jn's Epis Ch Odessa TX 1981-1992; Trin Epis Ch Marble Falls TX 1979-1981; Dio NW Texas Lubbock TX 1975-1979; Gr Ch Vernon TX 1975-1979; Trin Ch Quanah TX 1975-1979; Com Mssn Dio NW Texas Lubbock TX 1975-1978; Asst S Jn's Epis Ch Odessa TX 1964-1972; Asst S Alb's Ch El Paso TX 1956-1964. Bd PACT.

MCINTYRE, John George (Md) 326 Pintail Dr, Havre De Grace MD 21078 B Baltimore MD 9/11/1939 s Charles E McIntyre & Grace O. BS Loyola U 1961; BD Bex 1964. D 9/19/1964 P 6/22/1965 Bp Harry Lee Doll. m 8/26/1972 Linda G Wenderoth. R H Trin Ch Churchville MD 1997-2004; R S Mary's Epis Ch Pocomoke City MD 1990-1997; R S Jn's Epis Ch Bellefonte PA 1986-1990; Dio Wstrn Massachusetts Springfield MA 1983-1986; R Trin Epis Ch Shrewsbury MA 1983-1986; R S Andr's Ch Manchester NH 1978-1983; Chr Ch Chaptico MD 1974-1977; R Ch Of The Guardian Ang Baltimore MD 1972-1974; P Chr Ch Worton MD 1968-1971; R S Steph's Ch Earleville MD 1968-1971; Cur Ch Of The Ascen Westminster MD 1964-1966. frmac@htrinitychurchville.org

MCINTYRE, Moni (Pgh) 4601 5th Ave #825, Pittsburgh PA 15213 **P-in-c Ch Of The H Cross Pittsburgh PA 2002-** B Detroit MI 2/12/1948 d Angus James McIntyre & Cathryn Agnes. BA U of Detroit Mercy 1970; MA Estrn Michigan U 1972; MA U of Windsor 1979; MDiv SS Cyril & Methodius Sem 1983; PhD U of St. Mich's Coll 1990. Rec from Roman Catholic 2/3/1998 Bp Robert William Duncan. Co-Ed, "Light Burdens Heavy Blessings," Franciscan, 2000; Co-Ed, "Readings in Ecology & Feminist Theol," Sheed & Ward, 1995; Auth, "On Choosing the Gd in the Face of Genocide," *Genocide Forum*, 1995; Auth, "Sin, Evil and Death in the New Age," *The Way*, 1993; Auth, "Soc Ethics and the Return to Cosmology," Ptr Lang, 1992; Auth, "Chr Soc Ethics and Hlth Care," *The Way*, 1992; Auth, "The Image of God in Rel Autobiography," *Grail*, 1991. AAR 1989; Soc of Chr Ethics 1989. mmcin@aol.com

MCJILTON, Sheila N (WA) St Philip's Church, 522 Main St, Laurel MD 20707 **R S Phil's Epis Ch Laurel MD 2007-** B Kingsport TN 11/5/1953 d Tolbert William Nelson & Anne. Mars Hill Coll; BA Salisbury St U 1976; MDiv VTS 1999. D 5/23/1999 P 12/11/1999 Bp Martin Gough Townsend. c 1. Int R S Dav's Epis Ch Wilmington DE 2006-2007; P-in-c S Paul's Ch Centreville MD 2003-2006; Asst R Chr Ch Par Kent Island Stevensville MD 1999-2003. Auth, "Reflection on Genesis 22:1-14 (poem)," *VTS Journ*, 1998; Auth, "Ash Wednesday," *ATR Sprg 2000 Vol82 No2*; Auth, "Who Sleep on H Stones," *ATR Winter 2000 Volume 82 No 1*; Auth, "Leavetaking," *VTS Journ August 2000*. Exec Com on Status of Wmn. mcjilton@verizon.net

MCKAIG, Byron James (Los) Mount Mesa, Box 1572, Lake Isabella CA 93240 B Los Angeles CA 3/4/1935 s James William McKaig & Elvira Elizabeth. BA U CA 1957; BD CDSP 1966. D 9/9/1967 P 3/1/1968 Bp Francis E I Bloy. m 6/30/1984 Gladys Dean Erickson c 3. Asst S Lk's Ch Bakersfield CA 1990-1997; Asst S Ptr's Epis Ch Kernville CA 1984-1989; Assoc R S Marg's Epis Ch So Gate CA 1972-1974; Assoc R S Paul's Pomona Pomona CA 1968-1971; Asst Imm Mssn El Monte CA 1967-1968.

MCKAY, Judy Aileen (Ida) 3120 S Bown Way, #201, Boise ID 83706 B Oakland CA 12/14/1941 d Stanley Robert McKay & Jean. BA U CA 1963; MDiv SFTS 1977. D 11/20/1994 P 5/25/1995 Bp John Stuart Thornton. m 1/20/1991 John Clifford Matthew. Co-Auth, "CE in the Sm Ch," Judson Press, 1988. Assoc. of Presb Ch Educators 1977. jamck2@cableone.net

MCKAY IV, Robert (NwPa) 1267 Treasure Lk, Du Bois PA 15801 B Cincinnati OH 8/30/1942 s Robert McKay & Dorothy. BA Hob 1964; MDiv PDS 1967. D 4/22/1967 P 10/28/1967 Bp Alfred L Banyard. m 7/21/1985 Gail Probasco c 2. R Ch Of Our Sav DuBois PA 2001-2009; R Chr Epis Ch E Tawas MI 1995-2001; R Hope - S Jn's Epis Ch Oscoda MI 1995-2001; R Lakeshore Epis Area Parishes Oscoda MI 1995-2001; R S Andrews-By-The-Lake Epis Ch Harrisville MI 1995-2001; R Chr Ch Bordentown NJ 1974-1983; Asst Min S Lk's Epis Ch Metuchen NJ 1967-1969. frbob@clearnet.net

MCKAY, William Martin (RG) PO Box 117, Serafina NM 87569 **D S Paul's/Peace Ch Las Vegas NM 2006-** B Hartford CT 7/17/1935 s Kenneth Michael McKay & Evelyn Mae. Basic Chr Stud TESM 2006. D 10/21/2006 Bp Jeffrey Neil Steenson. m 9/18/1978 Elizabeth Quay c 5. w_mckay@plateaunet.net

MCKEACHIE, William Noble (SC) 126 Coming St, Charleston SC 29403 B New York NY 4/6/1943 s William Eugene McKeachie & Anne Amelia. BA U So 1966; MDiv/STB U of Trin 1970. Trans from Anglican Church of Canada 8/1/1981 as Priest Bp David Keller Leighton Sr. m 1/10/1982 Elisabeth Gray c 4. Dn of SC Cathd Of S Lk And S Paul Charleston SC 1995-2009; Dio Coun Dio Maryland Baltimore MD 1988-1992; S Paul's Par Baltimore MD 1982-1995. Auth, *Co. Baltimore Declaration*, 1991; Auth, *Response*, 1975; Auth, *Var Bk chapters/essays*. Sis of the Love of God. Fllshp, Ecu. Cntr, Germany 1973; Fllshp, Ecu. Inst./S. Serge 1972; Phi Beta Kappa 1966; Woodrow Wilson Fell 1966. elisabeth.avery@gmail.com

MCKEAN, Deborah Adams (Me) PO Box 137, Cushing ME 04563 B Memphis TN 4/19/1939 d Thomas Adams & Marie Louise. BA Mt Holyoke Coll 1960; MLS U Of Rhode Island Kingston RI 1972. D 6/23/2007 Bp Chilton Abbie Richardson Knudsen. m 7/1/1961 Philip McKean c 2. D The Epis Ch Of S Jn Bapt Thomaston ME 2006-2011. deborah_mckean@msn.com

MCKEAN JR, William Roulston (Pa) 29 Walters Rd, Glen Mills PA 19342 **Died 4/4/2010** B Philadelphia PA 2/8/1929 s William Roulston McKean & Margaret L. BA Trin 1951; MDiv PDS 1956. D 5/12/1956 P 11/1/1956 Bp Oliver J Hart.

MCKEE, Christianne Louise (Spok) 1909 W. Clearview Dr., Ellensburg WA 98926 B Fort Worth TX 6/10/1953 d Marvin Marshall McKee & Christianne Louise. BA U of Dallas Dallas 1976; MDiv Nash 1987. D 6/13/1987 P 6/12/1988 Bp Donis Dean Patterson. c 1. Chair, Wrshp Com for Dioc Conv Dio Spokane Spokane WA 2011; Int H Trin Epis Ch Sunnyside WA 2010-2011; Assoc The Epis Ch Of S Thos The Apos Dallas TX 1997-2009; Dioc Cmsn on HIV/AIDS Dio Dallas Dallas TX 1994-1995; Int S Barn Epis Ch Denton TX 1994-1995; Com for the Consecration of a Bp Dio Dallas Dallas TX 1993; Vic All SS Ch Allen TX 1991-1994; Liturg and Mus Cmsn Dio Dallas Dallas TX 1989-1991; Asst Epis Ch Of The Ascen Dallas TX 1989-1991; Cur S Barn Epis Ch Denton TX 1987-1989. EWC 1989; Integrity 1990. christianne.mckee@yahoo.com

MCKEE II, Daniel Deupree (Ark) 500 Hazelton Dr., Madison MS 39110 B Vicksburg MS 5/16/1945 s William Wells McKee & Helen. BA Millsaps Coll 1967; ETS 1970; MDiv STUSo 1971; DMin STUSo 1991. D 6/20/1971 P 5/27/1972 Bp John M Allin. m 2/24/1973 Diane Tolbert c 2. Stndg Com Dio Arkansas Little Rock AR 2006-2009; Trin Cathd Little Rock AR 2004-2010; S Steph's Epis Ch Huntsville AL 2003-2004; Ch Of The Nativ Epis Huntsville AL 2002-2003; Dio Arkansas Little Rock AR 1995-2002; ExCoun Dio Arkansas Little Rock AR 1983-1993; R S Paul's Newport AR 1982-1995; S Matt's Epis Ch Kosciusko MS 1978-1979; Vic Imm Jackson MS 1977-1982; Vic S Mary's Ch Lexington MS 1977-1982; Vic S Chris's Ch Jackson MS 1974-1977; Vic All SS Ch Inverness MS 1971-1974; Vic S Thos Ch Belzoni MS 1971-1974. Auth, *Laborers in the Vineyard*. dmckee@arkansas.anglican.org

MCKEE, Elizabeth Shepherd (NC) 408 Woodlawn Ave, Greensboro NC 27401 **D Dio No Carolina Raleigh NC 1993-** B Luebo ZR 1/22/1953 d Charles Theodore McKee & Anne Candlish. BA Florida St U 1974; MS U NC 1977; D Formation Prog 1993. D 6/6/1993 Bp Robert Whitridge Estill. m 1/15/1994 Raymond Joseph Huger.

MCKEE, Helen Louise (SVa) 405 Avondale Dr., Danville VA 24541 **P-in-c Trin Ch Gretna VA 2011-; Asst Chr Epis Ch Danville VA 2008-; R S Steph's Epis Ch Longview WA 2007-; Ch Of The Epiph Danville VA 2006-** B San Francisco 1/8/1936 d August Ross Kesser & Alpha Marie. BS U CA, Los Angeles 1960; MDiv VTS 2006. D 6/24/2006 Bp Vincent Waydell Warner P 2/18/2007 Bp Bavi Rivera. c 4. DOK 1998. hlkmckee@hotmail.com

MCKEE, Lewis Kavanaugh (WTenn) 57 Wychewood Dr, Memphis TN 38117 **Asst Cler Calv Ch Memphis TN 2002-** B Memphis TN 2/1/1921 s William Lytle McKee & Marion Baskervill. D 5/4/1980 Bp William F Gates Jr P 5/1/1981 Bp William Evan Sanders. m 8/6/1943 Heloise M McKee. Asst R S Jn's

M

Epis Ch Memphis TN 1986-1988; D Ch Of The H Comm Memphis TN 1980-1986.

MCKEE, Martha Marcella (NJ) 11 Exeter Ct, East Windsor NJ 08520 **P-in-c Ch Of The H Sprt Tuckerton NJ 2009-** B Houston TX 1/14/1953 d Robert James McKee & Clara Ethel. BS U of Texas 1973; MPA U of Missouri-Kansas City 1978; MDiv GTS 2003. D 6/7/2003 Bp David B(ruce) Joslin P 12/13/2003 Bp George Edward Councell. m 6/22/1985 James Lee Olander. Evergreens Chap Moorestown NJ 2003-2009. marthamckee@comcast.net

MCKEE, Michael Dale (Los) 815 Emerald Bay, Laguna Beach CA 92651 B 1/2/1946 D 12/1/1972 P 4/1/1973 Bp Robert C Rusack. m 8/25/1967 Cynthia McKee c 2.

MCKEE, Stephen Lee (Okla) 501 S Cincinnati Ave, Tulsa OK 74103 **R Trin Ch Tulsa OK 2001-** B Mount Vernon IL 10/6/1950 s Charles Glenard McKee & Mary Elizabeth. BS Van 1973; BTh Chichester Theol Coll 1981. D 5/8/1982 P 2/19/1983 Bp (George) Paul Reeves. m 10/2/1982 Lindsey L Parr c 1. R Ch Of The H Comm U City MO 1994-2001; R S Ptr's Epis Ch Kansas City MO 1990-1994; Chapl Assoc S Paul's Ch Kansas City MO 1986-1990; Asst S Paul's Ch Albany GA 1982-1985; Asst S Paul's Ch Augusta GA 1981-1982. smckee@trinitytulsa.org

MCKEEVER, Anne Dryden (NCal) 2620 Capitol Ave., Sacramento CA 95816 **Trin Cathd Sacramento CA 2010-** B Klamath Falls OR 4/14/1952 d Harold L Dryden & June. AB U CA 1974; MDiv CDSP 2009. D 6/13/2009 P 12/12/2009 Bp Barry Leigh Beisner. m 6/12/1976 Casey McKeever c 2. amckeever@wavecable.com

MCKELLAR, John Lorne (Ore) Corrie, 105 A Clay, Crockerton, Warminster AL BA128AG GB Great Britain (UK) B Rothesay Bute Scotland GB 8/7/1919 s John McKellar & Margaret Duncan. Rothesay Acad 1936; Salisbury TS 1972. Trans from Church Of England 11/1/1974. m 10/13/1945 Betty Rosemary Steadman c 1. S Andr's Ch Cottage Grove OR 1982-1984; S Dav's Ch Drain OR 1982-1984; R Glebe Ch Suffolk VA 1978-1979; R S Jn's Ch Suffolk VA 1978-1979; R Chr Ch Amelia Crt Hse VA 1974-1978; R Emm Epis Ch Powhatan VA 1974-1978; Pac Cure Par Cartersville VA 1974-1978; R S Jas Ch Cartersville VA 1974-1978.

✠ **MCKELVEY, Rt Rev Jack Marston** (Roch) 8 Grove St, Rochester NY 14605 B Wilmington DE 10/8/1941 s George McKelvey & Dorothy. BA U of Delaware Newark 1963; MDiv VTS 1966; DD VTS 1992. D 9/17/1966 Bp John Brooke Mosley P 5/13/1967 Bp Richard Henry Baker Con 4/20/1991 for Nwk. m 8/29/1964 Linda Alice Boardman c 4. Chair, PB Transition Comm Epis Ch Cntr New York NY 2004-2006; Bp of Roch Dio Rochester Rochester NY 1999-2008; Bp Suffr Dio Newark Newark NJ 1991-1999; R S Paul's Ch Englewood NJ 1979-1991; Vic H Trin Ch Wilmington DE 1970-1979. Auth, "Cir Dancing w God - A Tool for Congrl Dvlpmt," 2007; Auth, "Old Swedes Ch-A Photographic Tour," 1974; Auth, "Adult Educ Curric on Teachable Moments"; Auth/Ed, "Inter-Met: Bold Experiment in Theol Educ," Alb Inst. Sigma Phi Epsilon Citation Sigma Phi Epsilon Fraternity 2010; DD VirginiaTheological Semmary 1992. bpjackm@aol.com

MCKENNA, Cynthia Ann (Okla) P.O. Box 187, Boerne TX 78006 B Roswell NM 4/20/1961 d Boyd George McKenna & Erminia. U of New Mex 1982; BS Texas Tech U 1986; MEd Texas Tech U 1989; MDiv Epis TS of the SW 1996; MA St. Mary's U 2003. D 8/26/1996 Bp Sam Byron Hulsey P 3/2/1997 Bp Robert Manning Moody. Chapl All SS Chap Tulsa OK 1998-2002; Holland Hall Sch Tulsa OK 1998-2002; Assoc S Dunst's Ch Tulsa OK 1996-1998. cynthiamckennalpc@gmail.com

MCKENNA, Keith (NY) 429 Lakeshore Drive, Putnam Valley NY 10579 **D S Aug's Epis Ch Croton On Hudson NY 2007-** B Poughkeepsie NY 8/22/1934 s Jefferson Hamilton McKenna & Rae Scott. BA Pace Coll 1956; MS Pace U 1983; Marymount Manhattan Coll 1997; NYTS 1999. D 5/15/1999 Bp Richard Frank Grein. m 9/18/1959 Ann Therese Danehy c 2. D S Ptr's Epis Ch Peekskill NY 2002-2007; D All SS Ch Harrison NY 2000-2001; D S Mary's Ch Mohegan Lake NY 1999-2000. Amer Fed of Teachers 1967. kmckenna34@aol.com

MCKENNA, Warren Henry (Mass) Box 203, Roadtown, Tortola British Virgin Islands **Died 3/3/2011** B Providence RI 1/14/1918 s Walter H McKenna & Henrietta. BA Wesl 1940; BD EDS 1943. D 3/3/1943 P 9/1/1943 Bp James D Perry.

MCKENNEY, Mary Lou R (ECR) 5265 Starr Way, Royal Oaks CA 95076 **Fin Com Dio El Camino Real Monterey CA 2002-** B 3/8/1949 MDiv Vancouver TS 1999. Trans from Province IX 12/1/2002 Bp Richard Lester Shimpfky. m 10/26/1986 John A McKenney. R All SS Epis Ch Watsonville CA 2002-2010. revmckenney@yahoo.com

MCKENNEY, Walter (Ct) 38 Clover Dr, West Hartford CT 06110 B Albany GA 4/16/1934 s Elijah McKenney & Jennie. Cert Hartford Sem 1982; Capital Cmnty Coll 1996. D 10/23/1999 Bp Clarence Nicholas Coleridge. m 5/12/1962 Ida Anita Turner. NAAD. dconmck@aol.com

MCKENZIE, Bryan Keith (FtW) 2117 Ruea St, Grand Prairie TX 75050 B Gastonia NC 5/13/1957 s Thomas Euclid McKenzie & Francis. BA Baylor U 1981; MDiv SWTS 1986. D 7/12/1986 P 8/1/1987 Bp Clarence Cullam Pope Jr. Dio Ft Worth Ft Worth TX 1986-1990. Soc H Trin.

MCKENZIE, Jennifer Gaines (Va) Christ Church, 118 N Washington St, Alexandria VA 22314 **Ch Of The Gd Shpd Burke VA 2010-** B Escambia County FL 5/24/1963 d Robert Pendleton Gaines & Doris. BA Auburn U 1988; Cert Bloy Hse 1993; MDiv VTS 2004. D 6/26/2004 Bp Peter James Lee P 1/6/2005 Bp Charles Lovett Keyser. m 3/26/1988 Kenneth Alan McKenzie c 3. Assoc R Chr Ch Alexandria VA 2007-2009; Asst R S Dav's Par Washington DC 2004-2007. "Benedictine Sprtlty In The Par," *Congregations*, Alb Inst, 2004. jennifermckenzie@verizon.net

MCKENZIE JR, William Bruce (Ore) 1873 Sw High St, Portland OR 97201 B Bellingham WA 10/20/1931 s William Bruce McKenzie & Mary Emaline. BA Seattle Pacific U 1957; BA S Edw's Coll Seattle WA 1959; MDiv S Thos Sem Seattle WA 1963; MA U of San Francisco 1973; PhD Stan 1979. Rec from Roman Catholic 8/1/1973 as Priest Bp James Walmsley Frederic Carman. m 8/10/1969 Darlene Ann Schroedl c 3. S Barth's Ch Beaverton OR 1982-1998; Vic Ch Of The Resurr Eugene OR 1978-1982; Dio Oregon Portland OR 1976-1979; Asst Trin Epis Cathd Portland OR 1973-1976. damckenzie@comcast.net

MCKENZIE-HAYWARD, Renee Eugenia (Pa) 814 N 41st St, Philadelphia PA 19104 B Chester PA 6/7/1955 d Grover McKenzie & Sara Elizabeth. BS U of Pennsylvania 1976; MDiv Estrn Bapt TS 1992; MA Tem 1995; DAS GTS 2001; PhD Tem 2005. D 6/2/2001 P 12/8/2001 Bp David B(ruce) Joslin. m 3/16/1985 Isaac Hayward c 2. R Calv Epis Ch Nthrn Liberty Philadelphia PA 2003-2011; Assoc Gr Ch In Haddonfield Haddonfield NJ 2001-2003. "A Womanist Soc Ontology," Dissertation Tem, 2005; "A Womanist Experience Of God". renee177@comcast.net

MCKEON JR, Richard R (NY) Church of the Messiah, PO Box 248, Rhinebeck NY 12572 **R Ch Of The Mssh Rhinebeck NY 2010-** B Bronxville NY 5/26/1955 s Richard R McKeon & Shirley Anne. BA Mid 1977; Coll of the Resurr 1984; STM Ya Berk 1985. D 6/8/1985 P 12/14/1985 Bp Horace W B Donegan. Asst to Suffr Bp Dio New York New York City NY 1996-2010; P-in-c Zion Ch Dobbs Ferry NY 1988-2010; Cur S Jn's Ch Getty Sq Yonkers NY 1985-1988. SocOLW. CORGIRM@AOL.COM

MCKEOWN, James (Colo) 820 12th St., Boulder CO 80302 **Died 9/2/2010** B Oakland CA 9/3/1921 s Laurie Baker Crisp & Dorothy. BA U So 1943; BD STUSo 1945; MA Drew U 1946. D 3/18/1945 Bp John D Wing P 6/1/1946 Bp Henry I Louttit. c 4. mckeown@earthlink.net

MCKIM, Laurie J (WMo) 507 RATHERVUE PL, AUSTIN TX 78705 **D S Matt's Ch Raytown MO 2004-** B Independence MO 7/8/1956 d Kim McKim & Barbara. BS U of Missouri 1993. D 7/24/2004 Bp Barry Robert Howe. c 3. servantmin708@earthlink.net

MCKINLEY, Ellen Bacon (Ct) No address on file. B Milwaukee WI 6/9/1929 d Edward Alsked Bacon & Lorraine. BA Bryn 1951; MDiv Ya Berk 1976; STM GTS 1979; PhD UTS 1988. D 12/18/1980 P 7/9/1981 Bp Arthur Edward Walmsley. Assoc All SS Ch Princeton NJ 1992-1997; Cathd Chapt Dio New Jersey Trenton NJ 1992-1996; Int Trin Ch Princeton NJ 1990-1991; Trst Donations & Bequests Dio Connecticut Hartford CT 1988-1991; Com Mar & Human Sxlty Dio Connecticut Hartford CT 1988-1990; Epis Elctn Com Dio Connecticut Hartford CT 1986-1987; Asst S Sav's Epis Ch Old Greenwich CT 1982-1990; Cur S Paul's Ch Riverside CT 1981. EWC.

MCKINLEY, Mele Senitila Tuineau (Ore) 1817 E Alsea Hwy, Waldport OR 97394 B Fonoifua TO 1/7/1956 d Viliami Latai Mulinui Tuineau & Lesioli Fangaipulotu. Oregon Cntr for the Diac 1993. D 12/18/1993 Bp Robert Louis Ladehoff. m 6/2/1978 David Leroy McKinley c 2. Auth, "Leipua Of Love".

MCKINNEY, Barbara Jean (Ia) 1435 Park Ave, Des Moines IA 50315 **D The Cathd Ch Of S Paul Des Moines IA 1997-** B Des Moines IA 10/25/1935 d Fred F Anderson & Emily E. BS S Fran Coll Loretto PA; Cert Sprtl Direction; U of Iowa; RN Iowa Luth Hosp Sch Nrsng 1957; Cert Hlth Mnstry 1986; CPE Iowa Luth Hosp Sch Nrsng 1986. D 12/5/1993 Bp Carl Christopher Epting. m 8/20/1960 John F McKinney c 4. Ord Of S Lk.

MCKINNEY, Catherine R (SVa) 3352 Hickory Ln, Port Huron MI 48060 B Memphis TN 12/5/1954 d Max Albert Reese & Barbara Catherine. BS U of Tennessee 1984; MDiv VTS 2001. D 3/23/2003 P 10/26/2003 Bp Edwin Max Leidel Jr. m 3/21/1976 William Daniel McKinney. S Barn Epis Ch Richmond VA 2009-2011; S Andr's Ch Norfolk VA 2007-2009; All SS Ch So Hill VA 2006-2007; Geth Ch Proctorsville VT 2005; D All SS Epis Ch Marysville MI 2003-2004; D S Andr's Epis Ch Algonac MI 2003-2004. CRM2002@AOL.COM

MCKINNEY, Chantal Bianca (NC) 242 Flintshire Rd., Winston-Salem NC 27104 **Dn of Winston-Salem Convoc Dio No Carolina Raleigh NC 2009-; Assoc R S Paul's Epis Ch Winston Salem NC 2008-** B High Point NC 8/8/1977 d Robert William Dennis & Evelyn Ruth. BS Appalachian St U 1998; MDiv VTS 2002; D.Min. Chicago TS 2009. D 6/22/2002 Bp Michael Bruce Curry P 4/26/2003 Bp J(ames) Gary Gloster. m 11/11/2009 Bryson J McKinney c 3. Asst R S Mary's Epis Ch High Point NC 2004-2008; Assoc R S Fran Ch Greensboro NC 2002-2004. mckinney.ws@gmail.com

MCKINNEY, Douglas Walton (Los) 401 S Detroit St Apt 311, Los Angeles CA 90036 B Portland OR 2/20/1948 s John Walton McKinney & Doris Grace. CDSP; BA Lewis & Clark Coll 1970; MDiv SFTS 1973; California Inst of Integral Stds 1989. D 3/2/1981 P 5/21/1982 Bp William Edwin Swing. Int S Jos's Par Buena Pk CA 2008; Ch Of The Ascen Tujunga CA 2006-2007; Int All SS Epis Ch Oxnard CA 2005-2006; Int Ch Of The Ascen Tujunga CA 2003-2004; S Fran Mssn Norwalk CA 2000-2002; The Epis Ch Of S Jn The Evang San Francisco CA 1991-1993; Sprtl Dir S Jas Epis Ch San Francisco CA 1989-1999; Int S Cyp's Ch San Francisco CA 1986-1988; S Paul's Epis Ch Walnut Creek CA 1982-1986; Ch Of The Gd Samar San Francisco CA 1981-1982; Cur/D Iglesia Epis Del Buen Samaritano San Francisco CA 1981-1982. California Ass'N Of Mar And Fam Therapists 1999; Camaldolese Benedictine Ord 1995. doug.w.mckinney@gmail.com

MCKINNON, Michael John (Mass) 9 Svenson Ave, Worcester MA 01607 B New Haven CT 7/16/1968 s James J McKinnon & Ernestine Adelade. BA Cntrl Connecticut St U 1991; MDiv Ya Berk 1994; Nash 1997. Trans from Anglican Church of Canada 10/1/1998 Bp Keith Lynn Ackerman. m 5/22/1993 Christine M McKinnon c 1. Ch Of The H Trin Marlborough MA 2004-2007; S Andr's Ch Peoria IL 1998-2004.

MCKINNON, Stanley Allen (Ark) PO Box 767, Siloam Springs AR 72761 **Vic Gr Ch Siloam Sprg AR 2008-** B Carroltan MO 3/28/1959 s Ronald Jack McKinnon & Geraldine Weltha. BA Texas Tech U 1983; MDiv Asbury TS 1987; STM Ya New Haven CT 1989. D 12/3/2006 Bp Larry Earl Maze P 6/9/2007 Bp Larry R Benfield. m 5/15/1983 Laurie B Freeman c 2. stan@gracesiloam.org

MCKNIGHT, James F (Cal) 801 S Plymouth Ct Unit 817, Chicago IL 60605 **Asstg P Gr Ch Chicago IL 2011-** B Chicago IL 6/1/1941 s James Frederick McKnight & Vivian Mary. BS DePaul U 1964; MDiv CDSP 1999. D 6/5/1999 P 11/20/1999 Bp William Edwin Swing. c 2. Assoc R Chr Epis Ch Los Altos CA 2000-2010; D S Jas Epis Ch San Francisco CA 1999. fatherjim1@gmail.com

MCKNIGHT, Leta Jeannette Zimmer (Vt) 20 South, Box 434, Lyndonville VT 05851 B Utica NY 9/28/1930 d Homer Rozelle Zimmer & Genieve Maude. Bangor TS. D 6/9/1981 P 2/1/1982 Bp Robert Shaw Kerr. m 9/3/1950 Alfred Forest McKnight. S Ptr's Mssn Lyndonville VT 1985-1995.

MCKONE-SWEET, Mark (Mass) 41 Shirley Rd, Needham Heights MA 02494 **Co-Pres BOD, Mass Epis Cler Assn Dio Massachusetts Boston MA 2010-; Stndg Com Dio Massachusetts Boston MA 2010-; R S Dunstans Epis Ch Dover MA 2009-; BOD, Mass Epis Cler Assocation Dio Massachusetts Boston MA 2008-** B Cambridge MA 6/16/1969 s Frank R Sweet & Elizabeth Wood. BA Wheaton Coll at Norton 1992; MBA NEU Boston MA 2002; MDiv EDS 2007. D 6/2/2007 P 1/12/2008 Bp M(arvil) Thomas Shaw III. m 6/7/2003 Kathleen McKone c 2. Cur S Paul's Ch Natick MA 2007-2009; Yth Min Par Of S Paul Newton Highlands MA 1997-1999. mark-mc-s@comcast.net

MCLACHLAN, Devin Shepard (Mass) 1900 Commonwealth Ave, Auburndale MA 02466 **Trst EDS Cambridge MA 2007-** B Chicago IL 12/23/1973 s Donald James McLachlan & Cynthia. BA Harv 1996; MDiv EDS 2002. D 6/12/2004 Bp M(arvil) Thomas Shaw III P 1/8/2005 Bp Gayle Elizabeth Harris. m 6/10/2006 Iza Riana Hussain. Par Of The Mssh Auburndale MA 2007-2011; S Mk's Cathd Seattle WA 2004. revmcdev@gmail.com

MCLAIN III, Paul KIng (Ark) 310 W 17th St, Little Rock AR 72206 **Mem, Bd Trst Dio Arkansas Little Rock AR 2011-; Cn/Assoc P Trin Cathd Little Rock AR 2010-** B Jackson MS 12/13/1960 s Paul King McLain & Marilyn Amanda. BBA U of Mississippi 1982; MALA S Jn's Coll Santa Fe NM 2004; Dplma in Ang. St. Ya Berk 2007; MDiv Yale DS 2007. D 6/7/2008 P 12/6/2008 Bp Dean Elliott Wolfe. m 11/9/2002 Ruth L Laws. Mem, COM Dio Kansas Topeka KS 2009-2010; D Trin Ch Lawr KS 2008. Ya Berk Grad Soc 2007. St. Geo's Coll Awd Ya Berk 2007. pmclain@trinitylittlerock.org

MCLAREN, Beth Ann (WMich) 230 North Kalamazoo Mall, #402, Kalamazoo MI 49007 B Coatesville PA 9/14/1956 d Samuel Reed Calhoun & Doris Jean. BA Taylor U Upland IN 1978; MDiv Ya Berk 1983; Epiph Certification Prog 2006. D 6/9/1984 P 2/2/1985 Bp Arthur Edward Walmsley. m 5/20/1978 James Thomas McLaren c 3. Assoc R S Lk's Par Kalamazoo MI 2007-2010; S Lk's Par Kalamazoo MI 2005; S Thos Epis Ch Battle Creek MI 2003; Asst R S Andr's Ch Meriden CT 1991-1995; Int Sr Mssnr Grtr Hartford Reg Mnstry E Hartford CT 1991; R S Jas Ch Hartford CT 1986-1990; Cur S Mk's Ch Mystic CT 1984-1986. AssociateRector@StLukesKalamazoo.org

MCLAREN, Christopher Todd (RG) 6730 Green Valley Rd NW, Albuquerque NM 87107 **R S Mk's On The Mesa Epis Ch Albuquerque NM 2011-** B Lynwood CA 3/19/1967 s Bruce Russell McLaren & Jean Marie. BS Willamette U 1989; MDiv Epis TS of The SW 2000. D 6/10/2000 Bp Robert Louis Ladehoff P 1/26/2001 Bp Charles Edward Jenkins III. m 12/31/1993 Maren Cole c 3. Assoc R S Mich And All Ang Ch Albuquerque NM 2006-2011; R S Geo's Epis Ch New Orleans LA 2004-2006; Asst. for Yth Mnstry Dio Louisiana Baton Rouge LA 2003-2005; Assoc R S Geo's Epis Ch New Orleans LA 2000-2004. christopher@stmarksonthemesa.org

MCLAUGHLIN, Eleanor Lee (NH) 38 Nekal Ln, Randolph NH 03593 B Boston MA 1/4/1935 d Sidney James Katz & Virginia Lee. BA Wellesley Coll 1957; MA Rad 1958; PhD Harv 1968. D 2/2/1980 P 5/8/1981 Bp John Bowen Coburn. m 1/2/2010 Elizabeth Hess c 2. R S Barn Ch Berlin NH 2001-2008; Vic Chr Ch So Barre MA 1996-2001; Dio Wstrn Massachusetts Springfield MA 1995-2001; Int S Paul's Epis Ch Stockbridge MA 1995-1996; S Ptr's Ch Springfield MA 1994-1995; Gr Ch Amherst MA 1991-1994; Int S Paul's Ch Dedham MA 1987-1988; Asst S Ptr's Epis Ch Cambridge MA 1985-1986; Mem, Liturg Cmsn Dio Massachusetts Boston MA 1981-1987; Asst Ch Of S Jn The Evang Boston MA 1981-1983; Chair, Cmsn on Wmn & Mnstry Dio Massachusetts Boston MA 1974-1980. Auth, "Feminist Christologies: Re-Dressing the Tradition," *Reconstructing the Chr Symbol, ed. M. Stevens*, Paulist Press, 1993; Auth, "Priestly Sprtlty," *ATR:66,1984*, Ascen Press, 1984; Auth, "Anglo-Catholicism And The Wmn Mvmt," *Essays Cath & Radical, eds. Leech,Williams*, London, 1984; Auth, "Wmn Of Sprt"; Auth, "Nashotah Revs"; Auth, "Chr My Mo: Feminine Naming & Metaphor In Medieveal Sprirituality"; Auth, "Priestly Sprirituality". Allnce For Theol Ethics & Ritual (Water) 1985-1993; Boston Ministers Club 1983-1989; Cath Fllshp Of Epis Ch 1982-1990; Cntr For Progressive Chrsnty 2000-2002; The Soc of Cath Priests 2010. Resrch Awd Cmsn On Lay Mnstry, Epis Ch 1975; Kent Fell Soc For Rel In Higher Educ 1958; Phi Beta Kappa Wellesley Coll 1956. revmches@ncia.net

MCLAUGHLIN, John Norris (Mass) 402 Paradise Rd, Unit M1C, Swampscott MA 01907 B Bridgewater MA 7/23/1924 s Everett Norris McLaughlin & Ellen Frances. BS NEU 1945; BD EDS 1949. D 6/8/1949 P 12/10/1949 Bp Norman B Nash. m 10/1/1949 Louise Phyllis Ray c 3. Vic The Ch Of S Mary Of The Harbor Provincetown MA 1979-1987; R S Paul's Ch Newburyport MA 1970-1978; P S Ptr's Ch Dartmouth MA 1959-1963; R Calv Ch Enfield CT 1955-1959; R Trin Epis Ch Weymouth MA 1950-1955; Min In Charge S Jn's Epis Ch Franklin MA 1949-1950.

MCLAUGHLIN, Marlys Jean (Az) 10926 W Topaz Dr, Sun City AZ 85351 B Anoka MN 12/2/1928 d Calvin Edward Reynolds & Georgena Joslin. U So; EFM 1994. D 2/8/1997 Bp Robert Reed Shahan. m 8/15/1946 Jack Dwane. D S Chris's Ch Sun City AZ 1997-2009. jackmarlys825@cs.com

MCLEAN JR, James Rayford (Ark) PO Box 524, Leland MI 49654 B Natchitoches LA 7/17/1941 s James Rayford McLean & Evelyn Frances. BS Sthrn St Coll 1963; Theol Coll Gb 1967; BD TS 1968; D.Min. TS 2008. D 6/18/1968 P 12/1/1968 Bp Robert Raymond Brown. m 5/4/1999 Ellen M McLean c 2. S Paul's Epis Ch Batesville AR 1990-1998; Cn Mssnr Dio Arkansas Little Rock AR 1985-1990; S Ptr's Ch Conway AR 1985-1990; H Trin Epis Ch Hot Sprg Vill AR 1983-2006; R S Lk's Ch Hot Sprg AR 1976-1985; Dio Arkansas Little Rock AR 1972-1976; Asst Chr Epis Ch Charlottesville VA 1971-1972; Vic S Andr's Ch Mtn Hm AR 1968-1971; Com Dio Arkansas Little Rock AR 1947-1974. ellenjim37@suddenlink.net

MCLEAN, Jean Medding (Wyo) 9405 Campstool Rd, Cheyenne WY 82007 **S Andr's Ch Basin WY 2004-** B Greensboro NC 2/17/1945 D 3/7/2004 Bp Vernon Edward Strickland P 9/14/2004 Bp Bruce Edward Caldwell. m 7/12/1977 Paul Dickens Mclean c 2. suejayblue@aol.com

MCLEAN, Richard (WTex) 3821 Sandia Dr, Plano TX 75023 B Woolsey GA 10/30/1935 s Oliver Thomas McLean & Ella Mae. BA Merc 1958; MDiv Sthrn Bapt TS Louisville KY 1964; MA Rice U 1986; CTh Epis TS of The SW 1989. D 6/23/1989 Bp Earl Nicholas McArthur Jr P 1/1/1990 Bp John Herbert MacNaughton. m 6/8/1956 Gayle Laverne Milton. S Eliz's Epis Ch Buda TX 1994-1996; The Ch Of The H Sprt Dripping Sprg TX 1994-1996; Vic S Mich's Epis Ch San Antonio TX 1989-1993; Dio W Texas San Antonio TX 1989. RICHARD.MCLEAN@QMACSMSO.COM

MCLEAN III, William Donald (SwFla) Po Box 15709, Sarasota FL 34277 **Assoc All Ang By The Sea Longboat Key FL 2007-; Com on Healing Dio SW Florida Sarasota FL 1986-** B Camden NJ 5/15/1936 s William Donald McLean & Alice Elizabeth. BA Beloit Coll 1958; MDiv SWTS 1961; Lic Int Mnstry Prog 2000. D 6/24/1961 Bp Charles L Street P 12/24/1961 Bp Gerald Francis Burrill. c 3. Int S Mary's Par Tampa FL 2002-2005; S Thos' Epis Ch St Petersburg FL 2000-2007; The Ch Of The Gd Shpd Labelle FL 1994-2001; Asst S Wlfd's Epis Ch Sarasota FL 1991-1993; S Bon Ch Sarasota FL 1986-1991; Epis Chars Bd Dio Chicago Chicago IL 1984-1986; R S Mich's Ch Barrington IL 1974-1986; R Ch Of The Medtr Chicago IL 1970-1974; Vic S Mich's Epis Ch Racine WI 1963-1970. Auth, *What Is the 5th Step?*. Cmnty of S Mary 1965; Soc of S Jn the Evang 1960. wdmclean3@comcast.net

MCLEESTER, John Hoyt (NJ) 1200 Brickyard Rd, Chipley FL 32428 B Ridgefield Park NJ 2/14/1918 s John Edward McLeester & Florence Elizabeth. BA Thos Edison St Coll 1980; MDiv Epis TS In Kentucky 1982. D 5/26/1973 Bp Addison Hosea P 6/24/1974 Bp Thomas Augustus Fraser Jr. m 3/18/1991 Barbara Farrior c 3. P-in-c Trin Epis Ch Kingman AZ 1997-2000; P-in-c Chr The King Epis Ch Santa Rosa Bch FL 1986-1990; P in Res S Ann's Epis Ch Wauchula FL 1982-1986; S Barn Epis Ch Monmouth Jct NJ 1976-1981; R Ch Of The Adv Enfield NC 1973-1976. Ord of S Lk 1976. mcleesterj@yahoo.com

MCLELLAN, Brenda Jean (Mont) 1977 SW Palm City Rd Apt G, Stuart FL 34994 B New Haven CT 1/15/1943 d Richard Percy McLellan & Edith Beatirce. BA Carroll Coll at Helena 1981; MDiv The Coll of Emm and St. Chad 1990. D 8/5/1989 P 6/3/1990 Bp Charles Jones III. c 5. Dioc Coun Dio Montana Helena MT 1996-1998; COM Dio Montana Helena MT 1994-2007; Dio Montana Helena MT 1993-1994; P-in-c Ch Of The Nativ/Elkhorn Cluster Helena MT 1990-2009; P-in-c S Jn's Ch/Elkhorn Cluster Townsend MT 1990-2009. Rugg Prize For Cmnty Relatns 1990; 8th Metropltn of Rupertsland Prize for Liturg Coll of Emm & S Chad Saskatoon Can 1989; Outstanding Sr Schlr Carroll Coll Helena MT 1981. brendamac7@gmail.com

MCLEMORE, Ann Rossington (SwFla) 8679 Piper Ln, Largo FL 33777 **S Giles Ch Pinellas Pk FL 2009-; S Jn's Epis Ch St Jas City FL 2009-** B St Louis MO 7/30/1952 d Donald William Hutton & Mary Elizabeth. BA Trin U 1974; Lic The Angl TS 2000. Trans from La Iglesia Anglicana de Mex 1/20/2004 as Priest Bp John Bailey Lipscomb. m 10/3/1981 Charles W McLemore. Person of the Year Ft. Myers FL News-Express Nwspr 2005. mclemore.a@gmail.com

MCLEMORE, William Pearman (At) 1130 Wilmette Ave, Wilmette IL 60091 B West Point NY 10/14/1937 s Ephraim Hester McLemore & Edith Adeline. BA Florida St U 1962; BD VTS 1965. D 6/22/1965 P 4/1/1966 Bp Edward Hamilton West. m 1/8/2000 Lori Marleen Lowe c 3. Archv and Hstgr Dio Atlanta Atlanta GA 2002-2009; R S Steph's Epis Ch Smiths Sta AL 1986-2000; Dio Alabama Birmingham AL 1986-1992; R H Trin Epis Ch Auburn AL 1974-1986; R S Paul's Epis Ch Jesup GA 1969-1973; Assoc Chr Ch Par Pensacola FL 1968-1969; Vic Chr Ch Cedar Key FL 1965-1968. Auth, "A Gift of Laughter," *Tribute to Rainbow Vill, Atlanta, GA*, The Brack Grp, Tucker, GA, 2007; Auth, "The Ch Year in Cartoons," St Steph's, Phenix City, AL, 1989; Auth, "Cartoons by Bill McLemore," H Trin, Auburn, AL, 1984; Auth, "An Introdcution to NT Gk," The Auth, 1977. RWF 1966-1986. wmclemore@earthlink.net

MCLEOD, Harrison Marvin (USC) Christ Church, 10 N Church St, Greenville SC 29601 **R Chr Ch Greenville SC 2008-** B 10/31/1960 s Henry Marvin McLeod & Mary Adelia Rosamond. BS U of Alabama 1983; MDiv Epis TS of the SW 1993. D 6/5/1993 P 12/11/1993 Bp Robert Oran Miller. m 8/5/1989 Jennifer B Byers c 2. R Chr Epis Ch Tyler TX 2002-2008; R Gd Shpd Decatur AL 1997-2002; Asst All SS Epis Ch Birmingham AL 1993-1997. tylermcleod@sbcglobal.net

MCLEOD III, Henry Marvin (Vt) 301 Georgetown Cir, Charleston WV 25314 B Mobile AL 1/7/1937 s Henry Marvin McLeod & Margaret Josephine. BA U of Alabama 1959; JD Cumberland Sch of Law 1966; MDiv STUSo 1979. D 5/20/1979 P 12/17/1979 Bp Furman Stough. m 11/25/1970 Mary Adelia Rosamond McLeod c 6. R S Jas Epis Ch Essex Jct VT 1994-2000; Co-R S Jn's Epis Ch Charleston WV 1983-1993; S Tim's Epis Ch Athens AL 1979-1983. Juris Doctor, mcl Cumberland Sch of Law 1966. hmmcleod@suddenlink.net

MCLEOD, James Wallace (ECR) 34400A Mission Blvd Apt 1109, Union City CA 94587 B San Francisco CA 1/28/1934 s John Osbourne McLeod & Ivy Bernice. BA San Francisco St U 1957; MDiv CDSP 1960; DMin VTS 1977; Fllshp Coll of Preachers 1983; Fllshp S Geo's Coll Jerusalem IL 1983. D 6/26/1960 P 5/27/1961 Bp James Albert Pike. m 6/25/1960 Frankie Phillips c 4. Trin Cathd San Jose CA 2001; Int S Fran Epis Ch San Jose CA 1999-2000; R All SS Epis Ch Palo Alto CA 1996-2010; Cn to Ordnry Dio El Camino Real Monterey CA 1993-1996; CDSP Berkeley CA 1989-1992; Dio El Camino Real Monterey CA 1980-1992; R All SS Epis Ch Palo Alto CA 1970-1993; Vic S Tim's Ch Danville CA 1967-1970; Assoc Trin Par Menlo Pk CA 1966-1967; Vic S Clem's Ch Rancho Cordova CA 1963-1966; Cur Trin Par Menlo Pk CA 1960-1963. Auth, *A P Looks at the Diac*, 1983. mcleodjames3@gmail.com

✠ **MCLEOD, Rt Rev Mary Adelia Rosamond** (Vt) 301 Georgetown Cir, Charleston WV 25314 B Birmingham AL 9/27/1938 d Edward Powell Rosamond & Mary Adelia. LTh TS 1980. D 6/11/1980 P 12/1/1980 Bp Furman Stough Con 11/1/1993 for Vt. m 11/25/1970 Henry Marvin McLeod c 6. Bp Dio Vermont Burlington VT 1993-2000; Archd So Reg Dio W Virginia Charleston WV 1988-1991; R S Jn's Epis Ch Charleston WV 1983-1993; S Tim's Epis Ch Athens AL 1980-1983. Contrib, "A Voice Of Our Own," 1996. DD U of Charleston 1996; DD EDS 1994; LHD Smith 1994. vtbishop3@suddenlink.net

MCLEOD, Robert Boutell (CFla) PO Box 446, 6661 N. Placita Alta Reposa, Tucson AZ 85750 B Oxnard,CA 10/11/1954 s John Hugh McLeod & Suzette. BA Pitzer Coll 1976; MA NWU 1978; MDiv VTS 1986. D 6/11/1986 Bp Peter James Lee P 5/3/1987 Bp C(hristopher) FitzSimons Allison. m 12/23/1980 Nancy Carol Spruill c 5. R Chr The King Epis Ch Orlando FL 1996-2001; Asst S Alb's Epis Ch Wickenburg AZ 1993-1996; R Par Ch Of S Chas The Mtyr Ft Morgan CO 1989-1992; Chr the King Pawleys Island SC 1987-1988; D S Mart's Ch Doswell VA 1986-1987; The Fork Ch Doswell VA 1986-1987. Auth, "Everything You Know is Wrong: The Case for a New Reformation," Fenestra Books, 2005. mcleodr@cox.net

MCLEON IV, Richard Alexander (WTex) 507 Dundee St, Victoria TX 77904 **Partnr In Mnstry Estrn Convoc Kennedy TX 2010-; Cler Asst, Estrn Convoc Partnr in Mnstry Dio W Texas San Antonio TX 2009-** B Dallas TX 12/1/1962 s Richard A McLeon & Sandra June. BS Texas A & M U 1985; MBA Sul Ross St U 1998; Cert Iona Sch of Mnstry 2010. D 6/2/2010 Bp David Mitchell Reed P 12/12/2010 Bp Gary Richard Lillibridge. m 12/10/1988 Patricia H Hurley c 2. rpmcleon@suddenlink.net

MCLOUGHLIN, Jose Antonio (Okla) 924 N Robinson Ave, Oklahoma City OK 73102 **Cn to the Ordnry Dio Oklahoma Oklahoma City OK 2008-** B San Juan PUERTO RICO 5/21/1969 s William Alexander McLoughlin & Caridad Maria. BA U of Cntrl Florida 1993; MDiv VTS 2005. D 6/18/2005 P 12/18/2005 Bp Peter James Lee. m 6/26/1993 Laurel L McFall c 2. Assoc R/Sch Chapl S Steph's Ch Coconut Grove Coconut Grove FL 2006-2008; Asst R Chr Epis Ch Winchester VA 2005-2006. canonjose@epiok.org

MCLUEN, Roy Emery (CGC) 2215 E 6th St, Lehigh Acres FL 33972 B Oakland CA 3/6/1945 s Ramon Lloyd McLuen & Mildred Elsie. BS Iowa St U 1968; MA/DMA U of Iowa 1973; MDiv STUSo 1988. D 5/1/1990 P 2/1/1991 Bp Carl Christopher Epting. m 5/18/1968 Kathy Hofmockel c 3. R S Andr's Epis Ch Panama City FL 2002-2010; S Anselm Epis Ch Lehigh Acres FL 1997-2002; S Mk's Ch Maquoketa IA 1991-1997; D S Tim's Epis Ch W Des Moines IA 1990-1991. Auth, "Var Mus arts". Ord Of S Lk. rkmcluen2@gmail.com

MCMAHAN, Larry Wayne (CGC) 3902 E Jamie Ln, Bloomington IN 47401 B Lafayette IN 9/4/1947 s Donald McMahan & Violet Ruth. BA DePauw U 1969; MDiv Yale DS 1972; CPE Emory U 1990. D 7/1/1972 Bp John P Craine P 1/25/1973 Bp William Hopkins Folwell. Int S Jn's Ch Monroeville AL 2007-2008; S Mich's Ch Ozark AL 2006; Int S Simon's On The Sound Ft Walton Bch FL 2003-2004; R S Lk's Ch Marianna FL 2002-2003; Dio Cntrl Gulf Coast Pensacola FL 1994-2004; Cmsn On Sprtl Growth Dio Cntrl Gulf Coast Pensacola FL 1994-2000; R S Matt's Ch Mobile AL 1993-2001; Assoc R S Mich And All Ang Ch Stone Mtn GA 1984-1988; Cmsn On Evang & Renwl Dio Indianapolis Indianapolis IN 1979-1984; R S Mk's Ch Plainfield IN 1978-1983; P-in-c S Mary's Epis Ch Martinsville IN 1978-1982; P-in-c Gr Epis Ch Menominee MI 1975-1976; Cmsn On Yth Dio Cntrl Florida Orlando FL 1973-1975; Cur Trin Ch Vero Bch FL 1972-1975. "Lyrics to Choir Anthem," *O Epiph Star*, St. Jas Mus Pub., 2003; "Severla Poems in Anthology," *Carry Onward*, self-Pub, 1998.

MCMAHON JR, Charles Windle (Cal) 1570 Guerrero St, San Francisco CA 94110 **Died 7/18/2009** B Lancaster PA 10/8/1932 s Charles Windle McMahon & Ruth Baird. BA Kalamazoo Coll 1958; MDiv CDSP 1963. D 6/29/1963 Bp Richard S M Emrich P 3/14/1964 Bp Archie H Crowley. c 3. AEHC; Coll Of Chapl.

MCMAHON, George Ian Robertson (NC) 1 Fulbrooke Road, Newnham, Cambridge CB2 2PH Great Britain (UK) B Indianapolis IN 2/5/1923 s John Robertson McMahon & Henrietta Elizabeth. BA Monmouth U 1944; BA U NC 1944; MA U NC 1950; STB GTS 1952; BLitt Oxf 1961; PhD Birmingham 1973. D 6/18/1952 P 2/1/1953 Bp Edwin A Penick. m 5/19/1961 Jennifer Roy Petty. D & P-in-c Chr Ch Milton PA 1952-1957; D & P-in-c S Lk's Epis Ch Yanceyville NC 1952-1957; D & P-in-c S Mk's Epis Ch Roxboro NC 1952-1957. Auth, "The Scottish Courts Of High Cmsn". Ecclectic Hist Soc; Scottish Ch Hist Soc.

MCMANIS, Dennis Ray (SwFla) 12606 Rockrose Glen, Lakewood Ranch FL 34202 **Archd, Cn for Mssn and Outreach, Dn Sch for Dio SW Florida Sarasota FL 2008-** B Salina KS 4/20/1949 s Ray Chester McManis & Erma. D 1/18/2002 Bp John Bailey Lipscomb. m 7/3/1969 Linda E Mason c 2. Dir Off of Disaster Response Dio Louisiana Baton Rouge LA 2005-2007; Archd Dio SW Florida Sarasota FL 2004-2005; D Calv Ch Indn Rocks Bch FL 2002-2005. Epis Cmnty Serv in Amer 2008; Episcopalians for Global Recon 2011. dmcmanis@episcopalswfl.org

MCMANUS, Bridget (CNY) 531 Cumberland Ave, Syracuse NY 13210 **S Jas Ch Pulaski NY 2005-** B Syracuse NY 7/6/1971 D 12/18/2002 Bp Victor Alfonso Scantlebury P 6/28/2003 Bp William Dailey Persell. m 8/22/1998 William Bradley Hunt c 2. All SS Epis Ch Chicago IL 2000-2003.

MCMANUS, Mary Christie (Cal) 215 10th Ave, San Francisco CA 94118 B Saint Louis MO 8/27/1948 d Donnell Robert Kuntz & Patricia Maria. BA U CA 1970; BEd Cntrl Washington U 1976; MBA Estrn Washington U 1985; BA Sch for Deacons 1995. D 12/7/1996 Bp William Edwin Swing. m Patricia Lynn Ross. D S Jas Epis Ch San Francisco CA 1996-2000.

MCMANUS, Michael J (SeFla) 3395 Burns Rd, Palm Beach Gardens FL 33410 **S Mk's Ch Palm Bch Gardens FL 2011-** B West Palm Beach FL 11/3/1954 s John B McManus & Virginia I. BA St Vinc De Paul Sem 1977; MDiv St Vinc De Paul Sem 1981; Dplma of Angl Stds VTS 2009. Rec from Roman Catholic 12/20/2008 Bp Leopold Frade. m 7/28/1984 Cathleen W Wise c 2. S Geo's Epis Ch Riviera Bch FL 2009. mcmanusattorney@gmail.com

MCMEEKIN, Dorothy Nadine (Oly) 6612 Olympic Hwy, Aberdeen WA 98520 **Chr Ed S Mk's Epis Ch Montesano WA 1980-** B Cowles NE 12/9/1922 d

Frank Clifton Thomas & Ivy Lillian. D 3/15/1999 Bp Sanford Zangwill Kaye Hampton. m 5/28/1970 John Oliver McMeekin.

MCMICHAEL JR, Ralph Nelson (Mo) 1210 Locust St, Saint Louis MO 63103 **Int S Mich's Epis Ch O Fallon IL 2011-; Instr S Mary the Vrgn Ch Nashotah WI 1988-** B Frankfurt DE 1/5/1956 s Ralph Nelson McMichael & Marinell. CUA; BA Los Angeles Trade Tech Coll 1978; MDiv Nash 1981. D 6/13/1981 P 6/5/1982 Bp Willis Ryan Henton. m 8/2/1986 Susan Jan Davidson c 3. Cn Dio Missouri S Louis MO 2005-2010; S Mich & S Geo Clayton MO 2001-2005; Nash Nashotah WI 1988-2001; Cur S Mk's Ch Arlington TX 1987-1988; Stff S Tim's Ch Ft Worth TX 1985-1987; Asst Ch Of The Ascen Lafayette LA 1981-1982. Auth, "ATR". Naal. frankfurt1956@yahoo.com

MCMILLAN, Bruce Dodson (Miss) Po Box 596, Holly Springs MS 38635 **Dn - Nthrn Convoc Dio Mississippi Jackson MS 2008-; P Assoc S Ptr's Ch Oxford MS 2001-; R Chr Ch Holly Sprg MS 1995-; Stndg Com, Exec Com, Fin Com Dio Mississippi Jackson MS 1995-** B Jackson TN 9/22/1954 s William Leon McMillan & Kathleen Mignon. BA U So 1976; MDiv Epis TS of the SW 1988. D 6/4/1988 P 5/20/1989 Bp Alex Dockery Dickson. Exec Coun Dio Mississippi Jackson MS 1998-2002; Trst The U So (Sewanee) Sewanee TN 1996-2008; Vic Calv Ch Ripley MS 1995-2000; Fin Coun, Exec Com Dio W Tennessee Memphis TN 1994-1995; Assoc R Ch Of The H Comm Memphis TN 1992-1995; The TS at The U So Sewanee TN 1990-1996; R Gr Epis Ch Paris TN 1990-1992; D-In-Trng Gr Epis Ch Paris TN 1988-1989; Cur Dio W Tennessee Memphis TN 1988. CBS 1987. millan01@bellsouth.net

MCMILLAN, John Nixon (Alb) 4531 Ethel St, Okemos MI 48864 B Sault Ste. Marie Ontario Canada 7/17/1948 s Hugh McMillan & Mary. BA Wilfrid Laurier U 1985; MA U of Iowa 1991; PhD U of Iowa 1997; MDiv Yale DS 2004. D 12/20/2003 P 6/26/2004 Bp Wendell Nathaniel Gibbs Jr. m 6/19/1976 Barbara A McMillan. Trin Epis Ch Grand Ledge MI 2008-2009; Gr Ch Grand Rapids MI 2006-2007; All SS Epis Ch Pontiac MI 2004-2006; All SS Ch E Lansing MI 1994-2002. mcmill31@msn.com

MCMILLAN, Robert Cates (WNC) 69 Newdale Church Rd, Burnsville NC 28714 B Alamo TN 6/1/1922 s James Neal McMillan & Gladys Marie. BA Cntrl Coll 1944; MDiv Yale DS 1946; Menninger Clnc 1957; MA Bos 1962; Med W&M 1967; PhD California Wstrn U 1980. D 6/23/1984 P 11/14/1984 Bp William Gillette Weinhauer. m 6/3/1946 Elizabeth Munson. P-in-c The Sav Epis Ch Newland NC 1992-1994; Asst S Lk's Ch Boone NC 1984-1986.

MCMILLIN, Andrea McMillin (Oly) 1600 Knox Ave, Bellingham WA 98225 **Chr Epis Ch Blaine WA 2009-; Dio Olympia Seattle WA 2008-** B Little Rock AR 11/2/1966 d AT McMillin & D Stoddard. BA Hendrix Coll 1989; MDiv Ya Berk 1994. D 11/16/1996 P 5/1/1997 Bp Larry Earl Maze. m 6/12/1994 J S Stockburger. S Thos Ch Springdale AR 1998-1999; Trin Cathd Little Rock AR 1996-1998. akmcmillin@gmail.com

MCMULLEN, Andrew L (Haw) 1317 Queen Emma St, Honolulu HI 96813 **S Ptr's Ch Honolulu HI 2011-; Dio Colorado Denver CO 2010-** B Kansas City MO 6/5/1964 s Larry Leroy McMullen & Marilyn. BA U CO 1986; JD U of Missouri 1990; MDiv Epis TS of The SW 2006. D 6/3/2006 Bp Barry Robert Howe P 12/21/2006 Bp William Jones Skilton. m 8/10/1991 Yvete E Siv c 4. R Ch Of The Ascen Pueblo CO 2009-2011; Assoc R Trin By The Cove Naples FL 2006-2009. yvettem259@aol.com

MCMURREN, Jay Junior (Ore) 578 23rd St Ne, Salem OR 97301 B Portland OR 3/7/1928 s Jess Everett McMurren & Eva Almeda. BBA U of Oregon 1952; BD VTS 1968. D 6/26/1968 P 1/6/1969 Bp James Walmsley Frederic Carman. m 12/8/2004 Margaret Hewett Morse c 2. Assoc S Paul's Epis Ch Salem OR 1993-1997; Stndg Com Dio Oregon Portland OR 1982-1985; Stwdshp Cmsn Dio Oregon Portland OR 1980-1989; R Gr Memi Portland OR 1973-1993; Vic S Matt's Epis Ch Eugene OR 1968-1973.

MCMURREN, Margaret Hewett (Ore) 1525 Glen Creek Rd Nw, Salem OR 97304 **Vic The Epis Ch Of The Prince Of Peace Salem OR 1993-** B Portland OR 3/31/1947 d William Bovelle Morse & Jean Patricia. BA Geo Mason U 1974; Theolgical Stds CDSP 1978. D 12/29/1992 P 6/29/1993 Bp Robert Louis Ladehoff. m 12/8/2004 Jay Junior McMurren c 3. The Epis Ch Of The Prince Of Peace Salem OR 1993. themcmurrens@comcast.net

MCMURTRY, Herbert Charles (Ak) 217 Swinomish Dr, La Conner WA 98257 B Guysborough NS CA 11/30/1931 s Percy Boyd McMurtry & Mary Phynetta. BA Un Coll Barbourville KY 1954; BD CDSP 1957; MA Reed Coll 1971; DMin Jesuit TS 1982. D 6/24/1957 Bp Stephen F Bayne Jr P 6/24/1958 Bp Frank A Rhea. m 8/23/1998 Nichola Young c 2. R The Ch Of The H Trin Juneau AK 1992-1994; R S Jas The Fisherman Kodiak AK 1986-1992; Exec Coun Appointees New York NY 1984-1986; P-in-c The Epis Ch of S Jn the Div Tamuning GU 1983-1986; Dio Micronesia Tumon Bay GU GU 1983; R S Jn The Evang Ch Milwaukie OR 1978-1983; P-in-c H Cross Epis Ch Portland OR 1976-1978; Asst Chr Ch Par Lake Oswego OR 1972-1976; Asst All SS Ch Portland OR 1968-1972; Asst Emm Epis Ch Mercer Island WA 1964-1966; Vic Ch Of The Resurr Bellevue WA 1960-1964; Vic S Marg's Epis Ch Bellevue WA 1960-1964; Vic Ch Of The H Sprt Vashon WA 1957-1960; Asst S Lk's Ch Tacoma WA 1957-1960.

MCNAB, (Charles) Bruce (Colo) 536 W North St, Aspen CO 81611 B Texarkana AR 9/3/1945 s Charles Ray McNab & Audrey. BA Austin Coll 1967; MA Pr 1969; MDiv GTS 1972. D 4/10/1972 Bp Theodore H McCrea P 11/11/1972 Bp Stephen F Bayne Jr. m 6/14/1992 Joan T Patterson c 4. R Chr Epis Ch Aspen CO 2004-2011; R S Jn's Epis Ch Midland MI 1997-2003; Dio Colorado Denver CO 1995-1996; R Chr Epis Ch Denver CO 1985-1994; R S Andr's Epis Ch Panama City FL 1977-1985; Cur S Paul's Epis Ch Lakewood CO 1974-1977; Assoc All SS Ch Princeton NJ 1972-1973. Auth, "Let Your Light Shine," *Let Your Light Shine*, Xlibris, 2010; Co-Ed, "Ord & Innovation In The Middle Ages," Pr Press, 1977; Auth, "Obligations of the Ch in Engl Soc: Mltry Arrays of the Cler, 1369-1418," *Ord & Innovation in the Middle Ages*, Pr Press, 1977. Fell ECF 1973; Fell Woodrow Wilson Natl Fllshp Fndt 1967. cbrucemcnab@gmail.com

MCNAB, Joan T (Colo) 536 W North St, Aspen CO 81611 B Lincoln NE 7/28/1935 d William Gustav Tempel & Ruth Tempel. BA OH SU 1957; MDiv Iliff TS 1991. D 12/15/1991 Bp William Harvey Wolfrum. m 6/14/1992 (Charles) Bruce McNab c 3. D S Jn's Epis Ch Midland MI 1997-2000; Pstr Care Assoc Chr Epis Ch Denver CO 1991-1994. NAAD. joanmcnab@yahoo.com

MCNABB JR, Edward Timberlake (SC) Po Box 279, Mount Pleasant SC 29465 B Chicago IL 3/9/1951 s Edward McNabb & Diane. BA U So 1973; MDiv VTS 1978. D 6/25/1978 Bp William Evan Sanders P 5/19/1979 Bp William F Gates Jr. m 11/20/1982 Annetta Beauchamp. R Chr Epis Ch Mt Pleasant SC 1998-2010; R Trin Epis Ch Pinopolis SC 1989-1998; R Ch Of The Adv Sumner MS 1985-1989; P Gr - S Lk's Ch Memphis TN 1978-1985. Auth, "Contemporary Chr Record (In The Voice Of One Comm)," 1993; Auth, "Contemporary Chr Record (Take To The Wing)," 1987; Auth, "Contemporary Chr Record (Walker Of The Way)," 1982. Naras. tmcnabb@bellsouth.net

MCNAIR, David Miller (WNC) The Episcopal Church of the Holy Spirit, PO Box 956, Mars Hill NC 28754 **Epis Ch Of The H Sprt Mars Hill NC 2010-** B Portsmouth VA 7/1/1965 s Donald Russell McNair & Joyce Miller. BA Wake Forest U 1988; MDiv Sthrn Bapt TS Louisville KY 1993; Angl Stds U So TS 2008. D 6/8/2008 P 12/14/2008 Bp Granville Porter Taylor. m 10/5/1996 Cynthia Lynn Michie c 2. Asst S Jas Ch Black Mtn NC 1996-2008; Dio Wstrn No Carolina Asheville NC 1996-2007. rector@holyspiritwnc.org

MCNAIR, Kent Stevens (NCal) 2200 Country Club Dr., Cameron Park CA 95682 **R Faith Epis Ch Cameron Pk CA 1992-** B Los Angeles CA 6/23/1949 s Edward McNair & Ann Stevens. BA Tem 1979; MDiv Reformed Epis TS Philadelphia PA 1980; ThM PrTS 1981; DMin Fuller TS 1996. D 9/29/1981 Bp Edward McNair P 4/19/1982 Bp John Lester Thompson III. c 2. Archd Dio Nthrn California Sacramento CA 1987-1992; Cn Trin Cathd Sacramento CA 1984-1987; Cur Trin Cathd Sacramento CA 1981-1984. kent@faithec.org

MCNAIRY, Philip Edward (Minn) 2287 Bevans Cir, Red Wing MN 55066 B Cincinnati OH 3/6/1937 s Philip Frederick McNairy & Cary Elizabeth. BS Trin Hartford CT 1960; MDiv VTS 1970. D 6/29/1970 Bp Hamilton Hyde Kellogg P 2/14/1971 Bp Philip Frederick McNairy. m 12/14/1976 Mary L Kettner c 3. Dioc Coun Dio Minnesota Minneapolis MN 1997-2003; R Chr Ch Red Wing MN 1995-2003; Stndg Com Dio Olympia Seattle WA 1991-1993; R S Steph's Epis Ch Longview WA 1988-1993; R Gr Epis Ch Sandusky OH 1984-1988; Dioc Coun Dio Ohio Cleveland OH 1982-1988; R Trin Ch Allnce OH 1979-1984; R Ch Of The Gd Shpd Athens OH 1973-1978; Asst S Matt's Ch Bedford NY 1970-1973. Paul Harris Fell Rotary Club 2002. philmcnairy@hotmail.com

MCNAMARA, Beth Cooper (Md) 8015 Rider Ave, Towson MD 21204 B Washington DC 5/29/1949 d Wesley Burt Cooper & Helen Elizabeth. BA Ohio Wesl 1971; MLa Jn Hopkins U 1974; MDiv VTS 1986. D 6/7/1986 P 4/1/1987 Bp A(lbert) Theodore Eastman. m 6/10/1970 David King McNamara c 1. S Paul's Epis Par Point Of Rocks MD 1990-1993; Asst Ch Of The Resurr Baltimore MD 1987-1990; Asst S Jas' Epis Ch Parkton MD 1986-1987.

MCNAMARA, Joseph Francis (CPa) Po Box 474, Mansfield PA 16933 **S Andr's Ch Tioga PA 1991-** B Baltimore MD 11/2/1946 s Frank Joseph McNamara & Mary Joan. BA King's Coll Wilkes-Barre PA 1973; MA Maywood Coll 1975; PhD Un Grad Sch 1979; MDiv VTS 1984. D 6/8/1984 P 5/1/1985 Bp Charlie Fuller McNutt Jr. m 4/1/1978 Ann Margaret Foster c 1. Visitin P S Jn's Ch Westfield PA 2001; S Jas Ch Mansfield PA 1985-1990. Amer Academy Of Forensic Examiners 1997; Amer Bd Psychol Specialties, Diplomate 1997; APA 1980; Pennsylvania Psychol Assn 2001. Distinguished Tchg Awd (Tchr Of The Year) Pa Coll Of Tech At Penn St 1991.

MCNAMEE III, James Joseph (Md) 910 Fell St # 1, Baltimore MD 21231 **S Paul's Par Baltimore MD 2002-** B Baltimore MD 4/29/1935 s James Joseph McNamee & Dorothy Virginia. Geo 1955; U Of Paris Fr 1956; BA Jn Hopkins U 1957; MA Jn Hopkins U 1960; U of Liege 1961; STB GTS 1964. D 6/22/1964 Bp Noble C Powell P 6/19/1965 Bp Harry Lee Doll. Dioc Coun Dio Maryland Baltimore MD 1991-1994; S Lk's Ch Annapolis MD 1982-2000; Exec Coun Epis Ch Cntr New York NY 1975-1981; Cn The Amer Cathd of the H Trin Paris 75008 FR 1966-1970; Cur S Tim's Ch Catonsville MD 1964-1966. Ecum Campus Mnstry - Pres 1998; ESMHE 1988; ESMA 1983;

Natl Coun Of Ch, EFM - Chair 1997-1998; Untd Mnstrs In Educ - Chair 2000. Fullbright Schlrshp U Of Liege Belgium 1960; Fellowowship JHU 1959.

MCNAUGHTON, Bonnie Eleanor (ND) 817 7th St NE, Devils Lke ND 58301 B Minneapolis MN 9/26/1942 d Thomas McNaughton & Gardys Evelyn. D 6/22/2007 Bp Michael Gene Smith. c 2. bonton@gondtc.com

MCNAUGHTON, Margaret (WA) 720 Upland Pl, Alexandria VA 22314 **Assoc Dn For Cmnty Life, Ethnic Mnstrs and Adm VTS Alexandria VA 1995-** B Detroit MI d J McNaughton & C. Colorado St U 1974; BS MI SU 1976; MDiv VTS 1982; Andover Newton TS 1986; DMin Wesley TS 1999. D 6/20/1982 Bp H Coleman McGehee Jr P 6/10/1983 Bp Morgan Porteus. m 4/23/1988 Russell Carlton Ayers. Assoc R S Alb's Par Washington DC 1986-1995; Assoc R S Mk's Ch Foxborough MA 1982-1985. Auth, "A View From The Other Side: Life In Cmnty For Spouses Of Seminarians," *Dmin Thesis*. Alb Inst Resrch Fell. mgtmcnaughton@gmail.com

MCNAUL, Robert Guthrie (Nev) 1909 Camino Mirada, North Las Vegas NV 89031 B Denver CO 4/19/1942 s James Franklin McNaul & Sara Burch. BA U Denv 1965; MDiv CDSP 1968; Moore Theol Coll, Sydney, Australia 1971; Seattle U 1982. D 7/25/1968 Bp Joseph Summerville Minnis P 2/1/1969 Bp Edwin B Thayer. m 12/28/2002 Nancy Nancy Jane Rock c 1. Vic S Phil Amarillo TX 1988-1991; Int All SS Ch Tacoma WA 1986-1988; Asst Emm Epis Ch Mercer Island WA 1984-1985; Asst S Eliz's Ch Burien WA 1983-1984; Asst S Jn's Ch Kirkland WA 1982-1983; Int S Paul's Epis Ch Mt Vernon WA 1981-1982; R Ch Of Our Sav Pasco WA 1972-1980; Cur Epiph Epis Ch Denver CO 1968-1970. rgmcnaul@cox.net

MCNEELEY, David Fielden (Hai) 566 Standish Rd, Teaneck NJ 07666 **P S Thos Ch New York NY 2001-** B Knoxville TN 12/23/1950 s Samuel Gene McNeeley & Madeline Johnson. BA U So 1972; MPHTM Tul 1978; MD Tul 1978; Cert GTS 1987; S Paul's Sem Haiti 1987. D 6/12/1988 P 12/14/1988 Bp Luc Anatole Jacques Garnier. m 12/13/1985 Marise Bayard c 3. Mssy Exec Coun Appointees New York NY 1999-2004; Numerous Com positions Dio Haiti Ft Lauderdale FL 1982-1996. Auth, "numerous," *Over 70 Pub in Profsnl Journ*. Numerous Profsnl Med societies; Soc of S Marg 1974. DD (Hon) U So TS 1996; Outstanding Alum Tulane Sch of Publ Hlth & Tropical Med 1986. dfmcneeley@aol.com

MCNEER, Charles Conrad (Kan) 490 Court St., Abingdon VA 24210 B Huntington WV 6/6/1934 s Henry Porter McNeer & Ruth. BA Duke 1956; MDiv VTS 1963; Fllshp Menninger Clnc 1973; MS U of Kansas 1990. D 6/23/1963 P 5/2/1964 Bp William Henry Marmion. m 6/9/1956 Majorie Bowen. Ch Of St Thos Holton KS 1973-1977; Dio Kansas Topeka KS 1973-1977; S Phil's Epis Ch Topeka KS 1973-1977; P-in-c S Thos Holton Topeka KS 1972-2000; Vic S Mk's Ch St Paul VA 1966-1968. NASW 1990. cmcneer2@gmail.com

MCNELLIS, Kathleene Kernan (RG) 6200 Coors NW, Albuquerque NM 87120 **Cn Dio The Rio Grande Albuquerque NM 2011-; S Chris's Epis Ch El Paso TX 2007-** B Camden NJ 10/10/1944 d William Kernan & Caroline Ruth. Ball St U 1964; BA U of Texas 1968; Oxf 1998. D 8/24/1986 Bp Richard Mitchell Trelease Jr P 5/23/2000 Bp Terence Kelshaw. m 1/22/1966 Robert Emmet McNellis c 2. Vic S Fran On The Hill El Paso TX 2009-2011; P-in-c All SS Epis Ch El Paso TX 2008-2010; Vic S Brendan's Ch Horizon City TX 2002-2007; P-in-c S Lk's Epis Ch Anth NM 2000-2001; Chapl Pro Cathd Epis Ch Of S Clem El Paso TX 1991-2000; D S Chris's Epis Ch El Paso TX 1988-1991. woobusa@yahoo.com

MCNIEL, Donna (EpisSanJ) 7308 Pechora Dr, Rio Rancho NM 87144 **Exec Dir New Mex Conf of Ch Bernalillo NM 2011-** B Belen NM 12/10/1971 BA Austin Coll 1994; MDiv Louisville Presb TS 1999; Cert of Angl Stds STUSo 2002; DMin EDS 2008. D 6/7/2003 P 12/6/2003 Bp Barry Robert Howe. Assoc S Thos's Par Newark DE 2004-2007; Vic S Jn's Ch Neosho MO 2003-2004; Chapl Dio W Missouri Kansas City MO 2001-2004. dlmcnl@gmail.com

MCNISH, Jill L (Nwk) 31 Elston Rd, Upper Montclair NJ 07043 **S Steph's Epis Ch Clifton Heights PA 2011-** B Kearny NJ 1/22/1952 d Howard Norris McNish & Margaret Lois. BA U of Virginia 1973; JD Rutgers-The St U 1976; MDiv UTS 1997; PhD UTS 2002. D 5/31/1997 Bp Jack Marston McKelvey P 12/11/1997 Bp John Shelby Spong. c 2. S Steph's Ch Waretown NJ 2009-2010; Trin Epis Old Swedes Ch Swedesboro NJ 2007-2008; S Mary's Ch Sparta NJ 2004; Int S Greg's Epis Ch Parsippany NJ 2002-2003; Int Gr Ch Un City NJ 2001-2002; S Mk's Ch W Orange NJ 1999-2000; Ch Of The H Trin W Orange NJ 1998; S Lk's Epis Ch Montclair NJ 1997-1998. "Transforming Shame," Haworth Press, 2004; Auth, "Uses of Theories of Depth psychologyin Ord Mnstry and the Instnl Ch," *Journ of Pstr Care and Counslg*, 2002; Auth, "The Passionate Aggression in Creation and the Human Psyche," *Koinonia Fall*, 2000; Auth, "Viewing the Veil: The Sprtlty of Depression, Voice, September," *p8*, 1999; Auth, "Pstr Care Implications," *Lectionary Homil*. AAR; SBL, Psychol and the Bible Steeri. Hudnut Awd for Preaching UN Sem 1997; ECom Awd. mcnishrev@aol.com

MCNULTY, Lynne Herrick (Roch) 28 Gillette St, Rochester NY 14619 **D S Steph's Ch Rochester NY 1986-** B Buffalo NY 7/25/1948 d Roy Sanford Herrick & Yvonne Olga. BA Keuka Coll 1970; MA St. Bern's Sem Rochester NY 1987. D 6/28/1986 Bp William George Burrill. m 3/11/1972 Brian Joseph McNulty c 2.

✠ MCNUTT JR, Rt Rev Charlie Fuller (CPa) 5225 Wilson Ln Apt 2137, Mechanicsburg PA 17055 **Ret Bp of Cntrl Pennsylvania Dio Cntrl Pennsylvania Harrisburg PA 1996-** B Charleston WV 2/27/1931 s Charlie Fuller McNutt & Mary Eastman. BA W&L 1953; MDiv VTS 1956; MS Florida St U 1970. D 6/11/1956 P 12/19/1956 Bp Wilburn Camrock Campbell Con 11/8/1980 for CPa. m 3/3/1962 Alice Turnbull c 3. Chf Operating Off Epis Ch Cntr New York NY 1995-1997; Dio Cntrl Pennsylvania Harrisburg PA 1995; Co-Chair, PA Conf. of Inter-Ch. Coop. Dio Cntrl Pennsylvania Harrisburg PA 1986-1990; Bp Coadj Dio Cntrl Pennsylvania Harrisburg PA 1980-1982; Mem, Bd Trst VTS Alexandria VA 1976-1980; R Trin Epis Ch Martinsburg WV 1974-1980; Cn, Archd Dio Florida Jacksonville FL 1972-1974; Dir Consult Plnng Dio Florida Jacksonville FL 1970-1974; Consult Plnng Dio Florida Jacksonville FL 1968-1970; R S Lk's Epis Ch Jacksonville FL 1962-1968; Asst S Jn's Epis Ch Tallahassee FL 1960-1962; Vic Chr Memi Ch Williamstown WV 1956-1960; Trin Ch Parkersburg WV 1956-1960. Auth, "Is PPBS Feasible in Epis Dio?," *Thesis for MS Degree in Urban and Reg Plnng*, Florida St U, 1970. Doctor of Divnity Lebanon Vlly Coll of Pennsylvania 1996; Doctor of Dvinity VTS 1981. efmcn@ezonline.com

MCNUTT, Robin Lee (Neb) 3020 Belvedere Blvd, Omaha NE 68111 B Omaha NE 3/1/1951 d Robert B McNutt & Gloria Birkner. D 8/15/2004 Bp Joe Goodwin Burnett. c 2. robin@cor.omhcoxmail.com

MCPARTLIN, Julie (Alb) 33 Hubbell Ln, Lake George NY 12845 **R S Jas' Epis Ch Lake Geo NY 1998-** B New York NY 1/9/1948 d Robert Edward Henry & Hester Homer. BA Connecticut Coll 1969; MDiv GTS 1996. D 5/25/1996 P 11/30/1996 Bp David Standish Ball. m 6/28/1969 Kenneth J McPartlin c 2. P-in-c S Jas' Epis Ch Lake Geo NY 1996-1998. revjuls@aol.com

MCPEAK, Helen Crain Laverty (Nev) 2037 Pinion Springs Dr., Henderson NV 89074 **Epis Ch of the Epiph Henderson NV 2005-** B Oakland CA 11/16/1965 d Ross Mackinnon Laverty & Dorothy. BS U CA 1988; MDiv CDSP 1997. D 5/30/1997 P 12/13/1997 Bp Jerry Alban Lamb. m 8/10/1991 Robert Adams McPeak c 2. Trin Ch Sonoma CA 2002-2004; Dio Nthrn California Sacramento CA 2002-2003; Asst R S Patricks Ch Kenwood CA 1997-2000. helen@mcpeak.org

MCPHAIL, Donald Stewart (SC) 22 Saint Augustine Dr., Charleston SC 29407 B Montreal QC CA 7/22/1933 s Melville McPhail & Gladys. BA Concordia U 1959; Cr Mirfield Yorks Gb 1961; MDiv GTS 1962; MDiv GTS 1962. D 4/28/1962 P 12/21/1962 Bp James P De Wolfe. m 4/26/1969 Randall Redington c 3. COM Dio So Carolina Charleston SC 1992-2005; Exam Chapl Dio So Carolina Charleston SC 1992-2005; Gr Ch Charleston SC 1992-2005; Assoc S Lk's Epis Ch Hilton Hd SC 1991; Stndg Com Dio Colorado Denver CO 1986-2005; Dn S Jn's Cathd Denver CO 1981-1991; S Ptr's by-the-Sea Epis Ch Bay Shore NY 1963-1981; Cur The Ch Of The Ascen Rockville Cntr NY 1962-1963. EvangES. dsm17@comcast.net

MCPHERSON, Benjamin Carroll (Tex) 1603 Watchhill Rd, Austin TX 78703 **Died 4/28/2011** B Hallsville TX 9/26/1909 s Malcolm Allison McPherson & Kittie Lou. Epis TS of The SW; BA U of Texas 1948. D 12/3/1970 Bp J Milton Richardson P 12/13/1971 Bp Scott Field Bailey.

MCPHERSON, Clair W (NY) 1234 Midland Ave #5E, Bronxville NY 10708 **Assoc Prof of Ascetical Theol The GTS New York NY 2011-** B (unknown) 12/18/1949 s Walter McPherson & Bonnie Lee. PhD Washington U 1979; MDiv GTS 1982. D 6/19/1982 Bp Quintin Ebenezer Primo Jr P 12/12/1982 Bp James Winchester Montgomery. m 4/10/1971 Connie Leip c 3. Assoc P Ch Of The Trsfg New York NY 2006-2011; R Trin S Paul's Epis New Rochelle NY 1989-2005; Adj Prof SWTS Evanston IL 1985-1989; R S Lk's Ch Dixon IL 1984-1989; Asst Cathd Of S Jas Chicago IL 1982-1984. Auth, "Gr at this Time," *Gr at this Time*, Morehouse Pub, 1999; Auth, "Keeping Silence," *Sprtlty & Hist of Anglo-Saxon Engl*, 1998; Auth, "Understanding Faith," *Understanding Faith*, Morehouse Pub, 1997; Auth, "The Sea A Desert," *Amer Benedictine Revs*, 1985. Conf Angl Theol 1985; Medieval Acad Amer 1985; Soc for the Study of Chr Sprtlty 2011. mcpherson@gts.edu

MCPHERSON, Phebe Lewald (Md) 214 Wardour Dr, Annapolis MD 21401 **Stndg Com Dio Maryland Baltimore MD 1997-; Epiph Epis Ch Odenton MD 1988-** B Richmond VA 8/1/1950 d James Henry Lewald & Ella May. BA Goucher Coll 1972; MDiv SWTS 1975; DMin VTS 2006. D 2/13/1977 P 12/3/1977 Bp David Keller Leighton Sr. m 6/21/1997 William Bruce McPherson c 1. Comission on Ch in Sm Communities Epis Ch Cntr New York NY 1988-1994; Dep Gc Dio Maryland Baltimore MD 1982-1994; Memi Ch Baltimore MD 1979-1987; Dio Maryland Baltimore MD 1979; Assoc S Barth's Ch Baltimore MD 1977-1979. Bp'S Awd Dio Maryland 2006. phebemcpherson@gmail.com

MCPHERSON, Thomas Dale (SwFla) 6 Post Pointe Cir, Valdosta GA 31602 **D Chr Ch S Marys GA 1996-** B Marshall MI 3/6/1941 s Allen Leroy McPherson & Marion Ruth. BS MI SU 1964; MA Cntrl Michigan U 1974. D 5/25/1994 Bp Harry Woolston Shipps. m 6/20/1964 Carolyn Somers c 2.

MCPHERSON, William Bruce (Md) 214 Wardour Drive, Annapolis MD 21401 **S Jn's Ch Georgetown Par Washington DC 2011-** B Cleveland OH 5/4/1940 s William Bruce McPherson & Margaret Stevenson. BA Trin 1962; MBA Loyola U 1973; MDiv GTS 1991. D 3/10/1992 P 1/1/1993 Bp A(lbert) Theodore Eastman. m 6/21/1997 Phebe Lewald c 3. Gr Epis Ch Silver Sprg MD 2009-2011; Int R S Andr's Epis Ch Coll Pk MD 2008-2009; H Trin Epis Ch Bowie MD 2006-2008; S Jn's Ch Ellicott City MD 2004-2006; Cathd of St Ptr & St Paul Washington DC 2004; Int S Steph's Ch Severn Par Crownsville MD 2002-2003; S Ptr's Epis Ch Arlington VA 2001-2002; Ch Of The Gd Shpd Ruxton MD 1999-2001; All SS Epis Par Sunderland MD 1998-1999. wbmcp@verizon.net

MCQUADE JR, Frederick Carleton (Alb) 2 Village Dr Apt A, Delmar NY 12054 **Vic Cathd Of All SS Albany NY 1998-** B Albany NY 5/15/1933 s Frederick Carleton McQuade & Elizabeth May. BA Siena Coll 1954; GTS 1957. D 5/30/1957 P 11/1/1957 Bp Frederick Lehrle Barry. m 5/22/1996 Jane B Van Dusen c 3. R S Lk's Ch Catskill NY 1989-1997; Int S Paul's Epis Ch Albany NY 1988-1989; S Geo's Epis Ch Schenectady NY 1979-1988; R S Jn's Epis Ch Troy NY 1969-1977; R S Eustace Ch Lake Placid NY 1965-1969; R Chr Ch Middletown NJ 1960-1965; The Ch Of The Mssh Glens Falls NY 1957-1960.

MCQUADE, Lynne Dawson (NY) 900 Palmer Rd Apt 7-L, Bronxville NY 10708 B Yonkers NY 7/25/1941 d Alan Russell Dawson & Margaret Victoria. RN S Lk's Hosp. Sch. of Nrsng 1962; BA Marymount Manhattan Coll 1973; MPH Col Sch of Publ Hlth 1974; MDiv GTS 1982. D 6/5/1982 Bp Paul Moore Jr P 4/10/1983 Bp William Evan Sanders. m 5/11/1991 Joseph T McQuade. Supply S Mk's Epis Ch Yonkers NY 2008-2010; Int S Jn's Ch So Salem NY 2008; Assoc Par Of Chr The Redeem Pelham NY 1997-1999; Assoc S Barth's Ch In The Highland White Plains NY 1995-1997; Assoc S Andr's Epis Ch Hartsdale NY 1991-1995; Cur Chr Ch Bronxville NY 1986-1990; Assoc S Paul's Ch Franklin TN 1983-1986; S Barn Nrsng Hm Chattanooga TN 1982-1983. Assn Bro of S Greg - Assoc 1996; Cmnty of S Mary - Assoc 1987. Sigma Theta Tau Natl Nrsng hon Soc 1977. revldm@optonline.net

MCQUEEN, Dale Lee (Oly) 400 E 1st St, Aberdeen WA 98520 **R S Andr's Epis Ch Aberdeen WA 2002-** B Seattle WA 8/5/1945 s Avery Daniel McQueen & Dorothy Lucille. BS City U of Seattle 1996; MDiv SWTS 1999. D 6/26/1999 Bp Sanford Zangwill Kaye Hampton P 1/8/2000 Bp Bruce Edward Caldwell. m 10/19/1985 Carol Joyce Leonard. R All SS Epis Ch Torrington WY 1999-2002. CAROLDALE@STANDREWSGH.COMCASTBIZ.NET

MCQUEEN, Duncan Robert (WMass) 10 Eaton Ln, Pittsfield MA 01201 B Mineola NY 3/13/1929 s William Lutz McQueen & Helen Louise. BA Muskingum Coll 1950; ThM GTS 1954; MDiv GTS 1965. D 4/24/1954 P 11/1/1954 Bp James P De Wolfe. c 4. Dio Wstrn Massachusetts Springfield MA 1981-1996; R Trin Par Lenox MA 1981-1996; R S Matt's Ch Worcester MA 1975-1980; R S Mary's Ch Warwick RI 1956-1968; Asst S Mart's Ch Providence RI 1954-1956. dmcqueen@nycap.rr.com

MCQUEEN II, James Douglas (FdL) 1011 N. 7th St., Sheboygan WI 53081 **Cur All SS Elkhart Lake Sheboygan WI 2008-; Cur Gr Epis Ch Sheboygan WI 2008-** B Peoria IL 4/22/1983 s James D McQueen & Norma E. BS Eureka Coll Eureka IL 2006; MDiv Nash 2008. D 12/8/2007 P 6/14/2008 Bp Keith Lynn Ackerman. m 6/3/2010 Sarah L McQueen. jmcqueen@gracesheboggan.com

MCQUEEN, Paul Dennis (CFla) 322 King Street, Oviedo FL 32765 **Epis Ch Of The Resurr Longwood FL 2009-** B Oakland IL 9/15/1945 s Hubert F McQueen & Glenna R. BS Florida St U 1968; MDiv Nash 1981. D 6/21/1981 P 1/17/1982 Bp William Hopkins Folwell. m 6/29/1968 Roberta Rose Mourant c 3. Cbury Retreat And Conf Cntr Oviedo FL 1990-2009; R Gloria Dei Epis Ch Cocoa FL 1982-1990; Asst Trin Ch Vero Bch FL 1981-1982. Episcopl Campus & Conf Centers, Inc. 1990; IACCA 1991. frpaulmcqueen@gmail.com

MCQUEEN III, William Northington (Ga) 609 S. Main St., Moultrie GA 31768 **R S Jn's Ch Moultrie GA 2009-** B Enterprise AL 7/22/1971 s William Northington McQueen & Mary Ann Malone. BIE Georgia Inst of Tech 1994; MBA Georgia Sthrn U 2002; MDiv U So TS 2007. D 6/8/2007 P 12/12/2007 Bp Henry Irving Louttit. m 9/17/1994 Robyn F Robyn Leigh Ford c 2. Cur All SS Epis Ch Thomasville GA 2007-2009. cranmerian@gmail.com

MCQUIN, Randall Lee (Kan) 3141 Fairview Park Dr Ste 250, Falls Church VA 22042 B Medicine Lodge KS 7/31/1951 s Robert Lee McQuin & Beverly Jean. BA U of Kansas 1973; JD U of Kansas 1976; MDiv Yale DS 1979. D 6/16/1979 Bp Edward Clark Turner P 12/1/1979 Bp William Davidson. R S Paul's Ch Manhattan KS 1984-1987; S Lk's Epis Ch Scott City KS 1979-1984. Auth, "Angl Dig". randall.mcquin@axa-advisors.com

MCRAE, Marcia Owens (Ga) 511 E Broughton St, Bainbridge GA 39817 B San Antonio TX 10/27/1948 d Robert N Owens & Charlotte P. BA Valdosta St Coll 1970; The TS at The U So 2011. D 8/20/2010 P 4/16/2011 Bp Scott Anson Benhase. m 12/19/1970 John Henry McRae c 1. ciga2@bellsouth.net

MCREE, Timothy Patrick (WNC) 274 Sunset Hts, Canton NC 28716 **R S Andr's Epis Ch Canton NC 1995-** B Hickory NC 4/15/1955 s George Clifford McRee & Barbara Ann. AA Caldwell Cmnty Coll and Tech Inst 1977; BS Appalachian St U 1980; MDiv STUSo 1992. D 6/6/1992 P 1/1/1993 Bp Don Edward Johnson. m 8/14/1976 Beverly Adams c 2. Asst R Gr Ch Asheville NC 1992-1995; Gr Ch Asheville NC 1992-1995. mail@standrewscanton.org

MC REYNOLDS, James Craig (NJ) 2 Elwyn Road Ext., Portsmouth NH 03801 B Lynwood,CA 2/13/1948 s Chester Cornell McReynolds & Jean Chaffin. BA U CA 1971; Leningrad St U 1972; New Coll, Oxf 1973; S Vladimir's Orth TS Crestwood NY 1981; MDiv cl GTS 1987. D 6/13/1987 P 1/10/1988 Bp Paul Moore Jr. The Epis Ch Of The H Comm Fair Haven NJ 1992-2008; The Teleios Fndt Shrewsbury NJ 1992-2008; Int S Pauls On The Hill Epis Ch Ossining NY 1991-1992; Pstrl Assoc Par of Trin Ch New York NY 1988-1991; Trin Par New York NY 1988-1990; Manhattan Plaza Assoc New York NY 1987-1988; Epis Mssn Soc New York NY 1987; Epis Mssn Soc New York NY 1987; Asst Verger Trin Par New York NY 1985-1988. Auth, "Chr Is Risen! 1000 Years Of Russian Orth Chrsnty," Forw Mvmt, 1987. SSF 1978-1981. Metropltn's Cross Russian Orth Dio Odessa & Kherson Odessa Ukraine 1988. jcmcr@aol.com

MCSPADDEN, Christine Tully Trainor (Cal) 1990 8th Ave, San Francisco CA 94116 **Cn Gr Cathd San Francisco CA 2010-; Bd Dir FMP Cincinnati OH 2008-** B Charlottesville VA 1/15/1964 d Frederick Marshall Trainor & Constance Louise. BA U of Virginia 1986; MDiv Ya Berk 1995. D 6/8/1996 Bp Clarence Nicholas Coleridge P 12/7/1996 Bp Richard Frank Grein. m 8/19/1989 David Ford McSpadden. S Lk's Ch San Francisco CA 2004-2008; S Barth's Ch New York NY 1996-1999. "The Art Of Reading Scripture Preaching Scripture Faithfully In A Post-Christiandom Ch," Pub By Eerdmans, 2003. christinem@gracecathedral.org

MCSWAIN, William David (Alb) 30 N Ferry St, Schenectady NY 12305 **P-in-c Chr Ch Denmark SC 2008-** B Lakeland FL 11/5/1946 s William Belk McSwain & Carolyn. BA U NC; DMin UTS 1976. D 10/4/1986 Bp William Arthur Beckham P 2/1/1987 Bp Rogers Sanders Harris. m 6/2/1984 Janet Louise McDuffee c 1. R S Geo's Epis Ch Schenectady NY 1999-2007; S Anna's Ch New Orleans LA 1995-1999; R Ch Of The Intsn Stevens Point WI 1991-1995; Vic Ch Of The Cross Columbia SC 1988-1990; Ch Of The Gd Shpd Columbia SC 1987-1988; D S Martins-In-The-Field Columbia SC 1986-1987. ACPE. anglocat@mac.com

MCTERNAN, Vaughan Durkee (Colo) 3330 Springridge Cir, Colorado Springs CO 80906 **Ch Of The Ascen Pueblo CO 2010-** B Denver CO 7/22/1950 BA Trin 1973; MDiv Berk 1978; PhD Denver U And Iliff TS 1998. D 7/17/2004 P 1/25/2005 Bp Steven Andrew Miller. m 3/26/1977 Kevin McTernan c 1. P-in-c S Dav Of The Hills Epis Ch Woodland Pk CO 2006-2010. mcternav@gmail.com

MCVEY, A(rthur) William (Kan) 9218 Cherokee Pl, Leawood KS 66206 **S Matt's Ch Raytown MO 2010-** B Hamilton ON CA 1/16/1942 s James McVey & Margaret. BD St. Aug's Scarboro ON CA; MA Wilfrid Laurier U. Trans from Anglican Church of Canada 2/13/1979 Bp Edward Clark Turner. m 4/5/1975 Linda Myers c 3. R Calv Epis Ch Sedalia MO 2003-2010. *Value Proposition Marketing*, Woods and Waters, 2000. lmcvey@sprintmail.com

MCVEY, James Brian (Ia) 4403 High Ct, Davenport IA 52804 **S Alb's Ch Davenport IA 2006-** B Charleston, WV 12/10/1967 s George Innis McVey & Janis Ann. St. Anne/Wycliffe Hall; BA Hampden-Sydney Coll 1990; U Of Dallas Inst Of Phil. Stds 1992; MDiv TESM 2006. D 12/17/2005 Bp Alan Scarfe P. m 9/29/2003 Karen E Phillips c 7. S Steph's Ch E Liverpool OH 2005-2006. bkmcvey@mchsi.com

MCWHORTER, Elizabeth S (NY) St Mary Church, PO Box 637, Tuxedo Park NY 10987 **R S Mary's-In-Tuxedo Tuxedo Pk NY 2007-** B Tampa FL 1/31/1949 d Ernest Winn Stephenson & Elizabeth Boyd. BS Auburn U 1970; Candler TS Emory U 1984; MDiv U of St. Thos 1987. D 6/6/1987 P 5/16/1988 Bp Charles Judson Child Jr. m 11/27/1970 James B McWhorter c 2. Epis Cler Assn Dio Washington Washington DC 1998-2007; Epis Caring Response To Aids Dio Washington Washington DC 1997-2000; Stwdshp Cmsn Dio Washington Washington DC 1996-1998; R S Pat's Ch Washington DC 1995-2007; Int S Peters-In-The-Woods Epis Ch Fairfax Sta VA 1995; Int S Jn's Epis Ch McLean VA 1993-1995; Dioc Rep Prov Vii Ce Cmsn Dio Texas Houston TX 1990-1993; S Fran Ch Houston TX 1987-1993; Asst S Mich's Ch Austin TX 1987-1993. SCHC - Chapl 1996-1999. bmcwhorter@stmarysintuxedo.org

MCWHORTER, Shirley R (Mich) St Thomas Episcopal Church, 2441 Nichols Drive, Trenton MI 48183 **Vic S Thos Ch Trenton MI 2007-** B Middlesex UK 3/12/1949 d Dennis C T Rolph & Christina. AA Brevard Cmnty Coll 1993; BA U of Cntrl Florida 1995; MDiv STUSo 1999. D 6/19/1999 Bp John Wadsworth Howe P 12/18/1999 Bp Clifton Daniel III. m 9/20/1969 Gary L McWhorter c 4. Dio Sthrn Ohio Cincinnati OH 2006-2007; Vic S Nich Of Myra Epis Ch Hilliard OH 2002-2006; Dir, Par Fam Mnstrs, Assoc R S Ptr's Epis Ch Washington NC 1999-2000. Ord of S Lk; Phi Kappa Phi. revshirley@att.net

MCWHORTER, Stephen Dexter (Va) 136 Serenity Ln, St Simons Island GA 31522 **Int Chr Ch Frederica St Simons Island GA 2010-** B Charleston WV 4/23/1941 s Joseph Clinton McWhorter & Joan Cottrell. BA W Virginia U 1963; MDiv EDS 1967. D 6/12/1967 P 12/20/1967 Bp Wilburn Camrock

Campbell. Int S Thos Epis Ch Birmingham AL 2007-2008; Int Epis Ch Of The Ascen Birmingham AL 2006; R S Dav's Ch Ashburn VA 1992-2005; Dio Virginia Richmond VA 1990-1992; Robert Shuller Mnstrs Orange CA 1987-1988; R S Paul's Epis Ch Walnut Creek CA 1978-1987; R The Ch Of The Redeem Pittsburgh PA 1970-1977. stephendex.1@netzero.net

MCWILLIAMS JR, Milton Elias (Tex) 214 Edgewood Dr, Fredericksburg TX 78624 B Okmulgee OK 9/7/1920 s Milton Elias McWilliams & Christine Emma. BA U of Oklahoma 1942; BD CDSP 1949; PSR 1949. D 10/25/1949 P 4/29/1950 Bp Thomas Casady. c 2. DLC Dio Texas Houston TX 1976-1986; Dn Dio Texas Houston TX 1963-1986; R S Mk's Ch Bay City TX 1962-1986; DeptCE Dio Texas Houston TX 1958-1972; Assoc S Fran Ch Houston TX 1958-1962; Vic Epis Ch Of The Redeem Oklahoma City OK 1951-1953; Vic S Jas Epis Ch Oklahoma City OK 1949-1958; Vic S Mary's Ch Edmond OK 1949-1958.

MEACHAM, Carlyle Haynes (Vt) Po Box 115, Washburn IL 61570 B Dickinson Center NY 1/13/1926 s Leon Samuel Meacham & Hazel May. BA Atlantic Un Coll 1949; STB Harvard DS 1953; STM Harvard DS 1954; Cert Sea 1965. D 5/29/1965 P 11/20/1965 Bp Albert A Chambers. m 1/3/1981 Donna O'Dell c 2. R S Mart's Epis Ch Fairlee VT 1988-1991; S Paul's Epis Ch Pekin IL 1984; Int Trin Ch Lincoln IL 1981-1982; All SS Ch Morton IL 1979.

MEACHEN, Jerome Webster (Ct) 20 W Canal St Apt 423, Winooski VT 05404 B Oklahoma City OK 2/26/1930 s Jerome Wilson Meachen & Mildred Lena. BA Ob 1951; MS UTS 1953. D 12/6/1967 Bp William Loftin Hargrave. m 6/25/1952 Marielouise Emery Meachen c 5. Asst S Paul's Ch Darien CT 1986-1990; Pstr's Asst S Paul's Ch Riverside CT 1983-1986; Pstr's Asst Chr Ch Epis Savannah GA 1974-1983; Pstr's Asst Ch Of The Redeem Sarasota FL 1966-1974. Auth, *The Hymnal 1982*. AAM.

MEAD, Alan Champ (CPa) 25 Hadley Ave Apt 3, Dayton OH 45419 **Int S Paul's Epis Ch Dayton OH 2011-** B Utica NY 10/10/1945 s Warren P Mead & Evelyn. BA Utica Coll 1975; MDiv EDS 1979. D 6/9/1979 Bp John Bowen Coburn P 1/30/1980 Bp Harold B Robinson. m 8/17/1968 Patricia Ann Willmot c 2. S Paul's Epis Ch Indianapolis IN 2009-2011; Int S Jn's Ch Richmond VA 2008-2009; S Paul's Memi Charlottesville VA 2006-2008; Int Ch Of The Epiph Glenburn Clarks Summit PA 2005-2006; Chr Ch Reading PA 2004; R Chr Ch Berwick PA 1995-2004; R Emm Ch W Roxbury MA 1989-1995; Co-Vic Ch Of The H Nativ Seekonk MA 1987-1989; S Mk's Epis Ch Riverside RI 1983-1987; R S Andr's Ch New Berlin NY 1981-1983; R S Matt's Ch So New Berlin NY 1981-1983; Cur S Lk's Epis Ch Jamestown NY 1979-1981. alan45@mac.com

MEAD, Andrew Craig (NY) 1 W 53rd St, New York NY 10019 **R S Thos Ch New York NY 1996-** B Rochester NY 12/8/1946 s Gaylord Persons Mead & Margery Elizabeth. BA DePauw U 1968; BD Yale DS 1971; MLitt Oxf 1974. D 6/11/1971 Bp John P Craine P 12/18/1971 Bp Joseph Warren Hutchens. m 1/1/1972 Nancy Anne Hoxsie c 2. R The Ch Of The Adv Boston MA 1985-1996; R The Ch Of The Gd Shpd Bryn Mawr PA 1978-1985; Cur The Par Of All SS Ashmont-Dorches Dorchester MA 1975-1978; Cur S Paul's Ch Wallingford CT 1973-1975. DD Nash 2002. amead@saintthomaschurch.org

MEAD, Carol Lynn (Miss) 105 Montgomery Hl, Starkville MS 39759 **Chapl/ Cur Ch Of The Resurr Starkville MS 2009-** B Harvey IL 3/10/1955 d George Carroll Mead & Lorraine H. BA Mississippi U for Wmn 1977; MDiv Ya Berk 2009. D 5/30/2009 Bp Joe Goodwin Burnett P 12/2/2009 Bp Duncan Montgomery Gray III. THENEWMEAD@YAHOO.COM

MEAD, Loren Benjamin (WA) 3440 S Jefferson St Apt 1478, Falls Church VA 22041 **Assoc S Alb's Par Washington DC 1994-** B Florence SC 2/17/1930 s Walter Mead & Dorothy Smith. MA U of So Carolina 1951; BA U So 1951; M. Div. VTS 1955. D 6/20/1955 P 6/21/1956 Bp Thomas N Carruthers. m 8/25/1951 Polly M Mellette c 4. The Alb Inst Herndon VA 1974-1992; R Ch Of The H Fam Chap Hill NC 1957-1969; R Trin Epis Ch Pinopolis SC 1955-1957. Co-Auth (w Billie Alb), "Creating the Future Together," Alb Inst, 2008; Auth, "A Change of Pastors," Alb Inst, 2005; Auth, "Fin Meltdown in the Mainline?," Alb Inst, 1998; Auth, "Five Challenges for the Future Ch," Alb Inst, 1996; Auth, "Transforming the Cong for the Future," Alb Inst, 1993; Auth, "The Once & Future Ch," Alb Inst, 1991; Auth, "New Hope for Congregations," Seabury Press, 1972; Auth, "The Whole Truth"; Auth, "More Than Numbers"; Auth, "Critical Moment". Acad Par Cler 1970; Int Pstr Ntwk 1975. The Bp's Awd Bp of Dio Washington 2005; Henry Knox Sherrill Awd ECF 1999; DD Ya Berk 1987; DD VTS 1985; DD U So 1984. lorenbmead@gmail.com

MEAD, Matthew Hoxsie (NY) 37 Granite Springs Rd, Granite Springs NY 10527 **Ch Of The Gd Shpd Granite Sprg NY 2009-** B Boston MA 8/10/1976 s Andrew Craig Mead. D 3/13/2004 P 9/18/2004 Bp Mark Sean Sisk. m 6/5/2004 Nicole D Mead c 2. Cur for Liturg & Educ Ch Of S Mary The Vrgn New York NY 2004-2009. mead@goodshepherdny.org

MEADE, Elizabeth Gordon (Chi) 406 Peck Rd, Geneva IL 60134 **D S Chas Ch S Chas IL 2004-** B Quicy MA 12/30/1952 Skidmore Coll. D 2/2/2002 Bp William Dailey Persell. m 5/16/1981 Gary Lawrence Meade c 2. galameade@aol.com

MEADE, Gary Meade (WTenn) St. Mary's Episcopal Church, 108 N. King Ave., Dyersburg TN 38024 **R S Mary's Epis Ch Dyersburg TN 2007-** B Albuquerque NM 8/20/1961 s Thomas Everett Meade & Caroline Thornton. BA Rice U 1983; JD U of New Mex 1995; MDiv TESM 2001. D 7/28/2001 P 2/23/2002 Bp Terence Kelshaw. c 2. Int R S Mary's Epis Ch Albuquerque NM 2007; Asst to the Dn S Jn's Cathd Albuquerque NM 2001-2006. gmeade@mac.com

MEADE, Jean Alden McCurdy (La) 1314 Jackson Ave, New Orleans LA 70130 **Mt Olivet Epis Ch New Orleans LA 2002-** B San Antonio TX 11/15/1943 d Marion Wallace McCurdy & Anne Ayers. BA Agnes Scott Coll 1964; MA Duke 1965; MA Notre Dame Sem 1988; MA Tul 1998; PhD Tul 2000. D 7/5/2001 P 1/19/2002 Bp Charles Edward Jenkins III. m 6/15/1996 Louis Roy Koerner c 4. S Phil's Ch New Orleans LA 2001-2002. Alamo Chapt, D.A.R.; Ord Of St. Lazarus Of Jerusalem 2001; S.M.O.T.J (Knights Templar) 2000; Texas Mayflower Soc. meadejean@gmail.com

MEADERS JR, Calvin Judson (Miss) 200 E Academy St., Canton MS 39046 **R Gr Epis Ch Canton MS 1995-** B Newton MS 5/9/1947 s Calvin Judson Meaders & Minnie Louise. AA Clarke Memi 1967; BA Mississippi Coll 1969; MDiv New Orleans Bapt TS 1980; Med Mississippi St U 1983; Cert STUSo 1989. D 5/26/1989 P 12/1/1989 Bp Duncan Montgomery Gray Jr. m 12/18/1979 Nancy Jane Dixon c 2. Chap Of The Cross ROLLING FORK MS 1989-1995. jmeaders@bellsouth.net

MEADOWCROFT, Jeffrey Whittaker (USC) 225 W Main St, Laurens SC 29360 **Int S Jn's Epis Ch Congaree Hopkins SC 2006-** B New York NY 8/6/1940 s Ralph Sadler Meadowcroft & Doris. BA U of So Carolina 1962; MDiv VTS 1967; MSW U MI 1981. D 6/22/1967 Bp Gray Temple P 7/1/1968 Bp Archie H Crowley. c 2. R Ch Of The Epiph Laurens SC 1995-2005; Chr Ch Pittsford NY 1989-1995; R Chr Ch Rochester NY 1989-1995; R S Mk's Epis Ch Chenango Bridge NY 1984-1989; The Epis Ch Of The Adv W Bloomfield MI 1977-1980; Vic S Pat's Epis Ch Madison Heights MI 1971-1977; Cur All SS Ch E Lansing MI 1969-1970; D The Ch Of The Cross Bluffton SC 1967-1969. jmeadowcroft@gmail.com

MEADOWS JR, Richard Dean (SVa) 1000 Bethune Dr, Orlando FL 32805 **The Epis Ch Of S Jn The Bapt Orlando FL 2011-** B Buffalo NY 10/31/1957 s Richard Meadows & Mary Louise. MDiv Virginia Un U 2005; Angl Stds VTS 2010. D 6/18/2011 Bp Herman Hollerith IV. m 12/24/1998 Linda Mose Meadows c 4. rdmeadowsjr@hotmail.com

MEAIRS, Babs Marie (SanD) 11650 Calle Paracho, San Diego CA 92128 B Palo Alto CA 3/17/1950 d Laddin Melbert Meairs & Beverlee Elaine. BA U CA at Davis 1972; MDiv CDSP 1979; MA TCU 1988. D 10/14/1979 Bp A Donald Davies P 12/1/1993 Bp William Edwin Swing. m 2/26/1994 Edward L Busch. Epis Ch Cntr New York NY 2007-2010; Chapl Off Of Bsh For ArmdF New York NY 1994-2007; Asst S Chris's Ch And Sch Ft Worth TX 1990-1991; Chapl All SS' Epis Ch Ft Worth TX 1984-1989; Asst Trin Epis Ch Ft Worth TX 1979-1983. meairs@sbc.global.net

MEANS, Carl (Wyo) 300 Mt. Arter Loop, Lander WY 82520 **Shoshone Epis Mssn Ft Washakie WY 1999-** B Hetzel WV 7/22/1937 s Obie Tisdel Means & Mary Magdalene. D 6/30/1990 P 1/18/1991 Bp Terence Kelshaw. m 9/26/2007 Linda R Wilson c 4. Reg Mssnr Dio Wyoming Casper WY 1999-2008; Non-par Dio The Rio Grande Albuquerque NM 1990-1999; Dio The Rio Grande Albuquerque NM 1990. ctommymeans@gmail.com

MEANS, Jacqueline Alline (SwFla) 710 Buchanan St, Plainfield IN 46168 B PeorialL 8/26/1936 d Theodore Ehringer & Minnette. Chr TS. D 4/6/1974 Bp John P Craine P 1/1/1977 Bp Donald James Davis. m 3/31/2001 William D Lyons. S Geo Epis Ch W Terre Haute IN 2002-2004; Epis Ch Cntr New York NY 1998-2006; S Mk's Ch Plainfield IN 1991-1998; R S Mk's Ch Plainfield IN 1986-1990; Dio Indianapolis Indianapolis IN 1977-1990. Auth, "Wrld Bk Encyclopedia". ACPE, Acca, In Chapl Assn, Ord Of Ascen. Who'S Who Of Wmn In Rel. preacherlady@centurylink.net

MEARS, Curtis Franklin (Ga) 153 Circle K Rd, Douglas GA 31535 **R S Andr's Epis Ch Douglas GA 2010-** B Plainview TX 9/25/1962 s Garland Lane Mears & Lavona Pearl. B of ME Georgia Inst of Tech 1985; MDiv Nash 1996. D 12/20/1997 P 6/1/1998 Bp Henry Irving Louttit. m 8/26/2000 Bonnie B Mears. Assoc S Jn's Ch Savannah GA 2006-2010; Asst Chr Ch Frederica St Simons Island GA 2002-2007; Vic S Barn Epis Ch Valdosta GA 2001-2002; Cur Chr Ch Frederica St Simons Island GA 1999-2000; Assoc R S Aug Of Cbury Ch Augusta GA 1998-1999. rectorsaintandrews@windstream.net

MEARS JR, Preston Kennard (NH) 15101 Candy Hill Rd, Upper Marlboro MD 20772 B East Orange NJ 6/27/1940 s Preston Kennard Mears & Marion. BA Hav 1962; BD EDS 1966; MPA NEU 1985. D 6/11/1966 P 12/18/1966 Bp Leland Stark. m 1/12/1963 Laurie Kruger c 3. Assoc S Jas Epis Ch Bowie MD 2006-2008; R Ch Of The Trsfg Derry NH 1970-1974; Cur S Ptr's Ch Morristown NJ 1966-1970. prestonmears@earthlink.net

MEASE, Carole Ann (CPa) 359 Schoolhouse Rd, Middletown PA 17057 B Lebanon PA 3/18/1948 d William Tobias Mease & Dorothy Mae. BA Lebanon Vlly Coll 1971; AA Harrisburg Area Cmnty Coll 1981; Cert Harrisburg Hosp.

M

Sch Of Nurse Anesthesia 1986. D 6/6/2000 Bp Michael Whittington Creighton.

MEAUX, Amy Dafler (Lex) 320 W Main St, Danville KY 40422 **Trin Epis Ch Danville KY 2011-** B Beaufort SC 11/16/1974 d Richard J Dafler & Christy L. BA Louisiana Scholars' Coll Natchitoches LA 1997; MDiv Epis TS of The SW 2002. D 12/28/2001 P 7/10/2002 Bp Charles Edward Jenkins III. m 7/24/1999 Jared Morgan Meaux c 2. S Mich And All Ang Ch Dallas TX 2004-2011; Asst R Trin Ch New Orleans LA 2002-2004. adaflermeaux@gmail.com

MEBANE JR, Willie Henry (O) 2230 Euclid Ave, Cleveland OH 44115 **Cur Trin Cathd Cleveland OH 2009-** B Durham NC 10/16/1952 s Willie Henry Mebane & Carrie Elizabeth M. BA The Univesity of No Carolina at Chap Hill 1975; MDiv Ya Berk 2006. D 6/13/2009 P 1/16/2010 Bp Andrew Donnan Smith. m 12/25/1973 Ilona P Walton Mebane c 2. wmebane@dohio.org

MECK III, Daniel Stoddart (Md) 5620 Greenspring Avenue, Baltimore MD 21209 **Asst S Paul's Par Baltimore MD 2008-; July Vic S Mart's In The Field Sum Chap Biddeford Pool ME 2007-; Chapl S Paul's Sch Brooklandville MD 2007-** B Harve de Grace MD 6/30/1964 s Daniel Stoddart Meck & Patsie. BS U of Maryland 1986; MDiv VTS 2000. D 6/10/2000 Bp John Leslie Rabb P 12/9/2000 Bp Robert Wilkes Ihloff. m 9/8/1990 Kelly J Jordan c 3. Assoc S Dav's Ch Baltimore MD 2000-2007. dmeck@stpailsschool.org

MECK, Nancy E (SVa) 13530 Heathbrook Rd, Midlothian VA 23112 **Assoc R Ch Of The Redeem Midlothian VA 2007-** B Fairmont WV 11/7/1954 d William Leslie Meck & Helen Estella. D 6/3/2000 Bp Barry Robert Howe P 2/6/2001 Bp Peter James Lee. Assoc R S Steph's Ch Richmond VA 2000-2005. nancyemeck@aol.com

MECKLING, Judith B (Pa) 730 S Highland Ave, Merion Station PA 19066 **Vic All Souls Ch For The Deaf Philadelphia PA 2007-; Dio Pennsylvania Philadelphia PA 2007-** B Philadelphia PA 5/6/1952 d Gustav Charles Meckling & Jane. BA Estrn U 1974; MS Cor 1979; MDiv GTS 1985. D 6/8/1985 Bp O'Kelley Whitaker P 3/17/1986 Bp Robert Louis Ladehoff. Legacy Gd Samar Hosp Portland OR 1990-1996; Chr Ch Par Lake Oswego OR 1985-1988. Assn Of Profsnl Chapl; Cler Fam Ntwk; Sprtl Dir Intl . jamie25@comcast.net

MEDELA, Jean Milor (Hai) c/o Diocese of Haiti, Boite Postale 1309 Haiti **Dio Haiti Ft Lauderdale FL 2008-** B 2/20/1978 s Jean Victor Medela & Ulysse. D 1/25/2006 P 2/18/2007 Bp Jean Zache Duracin. m 6/19/2008 Mona J P Jean Pierre c 1. milor1013@yahoo.fr

MEDINA, Ernesto R (Neb) 16611 Castelar St, Omaha NE 68130 **S Martha's Epis Ch Papillion NE 2009-** B San Diego CA 10/26/1960 s Ernest Medina & Maria Del Socorro. BA U CA 1984; MDiv CDSP 1988. D 6/4/1988 P 12/10/1988 Bp Charles Brinkley Morton. m 4/24/1992 Susan J Powers c 2. Trin Cathd Omaha NE 2007-2009; Mssnr Ce Dio Los Angeles Los Angeles CA 1995-2007; Int S Edm's Par San Marino CA 1994-1995; Asst To R S Mk's Epis Ch Upland CA 1990-1994; Cur Trin Ch Escondido CA 1988-1990. Co-Ed, "Awake My Soul," Epis Ch Cntr, 2000. Pres ADLMC 1997. ermedina60@cox.net

MEDINA, Felix (PR) Po Box 2156, Bridgeport CT 06608 B 4/1/1937 s Ramon Medina & Filomena. Harvard DS; MDiv Epis Sem, Puerto Rico 1963. D 6/22/1963 P 12/21/1963 Bp Albert Ervine Swift. m 10/12/1963 Victoria M Cruz c 4. S Lk's/S Paul's Ch Bridgeport CT 1993-2002; The Ch of S Matt And S Tim New York NY 1987-1988.

MEDINA MEJIA, Jorge Reynaldo (Hond) Col Episcopal Tegucigalpa, Bloque 23, San Pedro Sula Honduras **Dio Honduras Miami FL 2006-; Iglesia Epis Hondurena San Pedro Sula 2006-** B Tegucigalpa F.M. 4/18/1960 s Emilio Medina & Eercilia. DIT Programa Diocesano Educacion Teologica 2002. D 10/28/2005 Bp Lloyd Emmanuel Allen. m 5/16/1981 Iris Esther Esther Avila Medina c 4. jorger_medina@hotmail.com

MEDLEY, James W (SVa) PO Box 58, South Hill VA 23970 **Assoc Estrn Shore Chap Virginia Bch VA 2010-** B Richmond VA 8/1/1963 s Wayland Medley & Jo Anne. BA Virginia Commonwealth U 2002; MDiv Epis TS of the SW 2008. D 2/1/2008 P 8/1/2008 Bp John Clark Buchanan. m 11/22/1985 Frances Neblett c 2. R All SS Ch So Hill VA 2008-2010. jwmntx@yahoo.com

MEECH, Michelle M (EO) 2451 Ridge Rd, Berkeley CA 94709 **CDSP Berkeley CA 2010-; Asst S Alb's Ch Albany CA 2010-** B Youngstown, OH 4/6/1968 d David Michael Meech & Judith Helen. BA Indiana U of PA 1990; MDiv CDSP 2010. D 4/13/2010 P 10/14/2010 Bp Bavi Rivera. mmmeech@gmail.com

MEEKS, Edward Gettys (USC) 405 S. Chapel Street, Baltimore MD 21231 B Atlanta GA 5/5/1952 s William Dennis Meeks & Carrie Waters. BA U of So Carolina 1974; DIT Coll of the Resurr 1978. D 8/23/1978 P 7/11/1979 Bp George Moyer Alexander. P Assoc Ch Of The Gd Shpd York SC 2003-2005; P-in-c Ch Of The Nativ Un SC 2002-2005; P-in-c S Ptr's Ch Great Falls SC 1999-2002; R S Mary's Ch Asheville NC 1983-1998; R Chr/St Paul's Epis Par Yonges Island SC 1979-1983; R Trin Ch Edisto Island SC 1979-1983; Asst Ch Of The Gd Shpd Columbia SC 1978-1979. Phi Beta Kappa 1974. egmeeks@aol.com

MEENGS, John Richard (WMich) 622 Lawndale Ct, Holland MI 49423 **D All SS Ch Saugatuck MI 2002-** B Chicago IL 2/19/1938 s John Henry Meengs & Ada Johanna. AA Worsham Coll 1960; Cert STUSo 2001. D 6/15/2002 Bp Edward Lewis Lee Jr. m 8/11/1984 Rose Marie Nyhof c 1. BroSA 1998; Fllshp of St. Jn 1998. jrmeengs@triton.net

MEGEATH, Sally Holme (Colo) 343 Canyon St, Lander WY 82520 B Denver CO 11/13/1943 d James Holme & Mary. Metropltn St Coll of Denver 1990. D 5/7/2005 Bp Bruce Edward Caldwell. m 4/23/1988 Joe D Megeath c 3.

MEGGINSON JR, Marshall Elliot (HB) 5689 Utrecht Rd, Baltimore MD 21206 B New York NY 7/2/1933 s Marshall Elliot Megginson & Mildred Louise. BA U of Maryland 1958; BD Epis TS of The SW 1963. D 6/17/1963 Bp Frederick P Goddard P 5/1/1964 Bp John E Hines. m 8/15/1959 Louise Kricker. Cur Chr Ch Winnetka IL 1966-1969.

MEGINNISS, David Hamilton (Ala) 2407 Glendale Gdns, Tuscaloosa AL 35401 **R Chr Ch Tuscaloosa AL 2005-** B Dothan Al 12/17/1954 s Benjamin Andrews Meginiss & Annette. MA U of Alabama 1977; JD U of Alabama 1980; MDiv STUSo 2001. D 5/31/2001 Bp Henry Nutt Parsley Jr P 12/4/2001 Bp Onell Asiselo Soto. m 11/24/2009 Barbara Osborne c 1. R Trin Ch Wetumpka AL 2001-2005. dmeginniss@hotmail.com

MEGLATHERY, Paul E. (NwPa) 65 Whitefield Ave., Apt 212, Ocean Grove NJ 07756 B Philadelphia,PA 10/29/1937 s James Pryor Meglathery & Jean Isabel. BA Tem 1962; MDiv PDS 1965; MSW Rutgers-The St U 1972. D 6/12/1965 Bp Robert Lionne DeWitt P 12/18/1965 Bp Alfred L Banyard. m 9/24/1983 Kathe Lee Romond c 4. R Emm Epis Ch Emporium PA 1999-2002; Vic S Jos's Ch Port Allegany PA 1997-2002; Vic S Jas Memi Ch Eatontown NJ 1991-1997; S Jas Ch Bradley Bch NJ 1985; Assoc S Jas Ch Long Branch NJ 1982-1983; Trin Ch Asbury Pk NJ 1975-1981; Ch of the Ascen Bloomfield NJ 1970-1973; R S Lk's Ch Ewing NJ 1967-1970; Cur Chr Ch Bordentown NJ 1965-1967. Contemplative Outreach 1992. meglap2006@yahoo.com

MEHEUX, Sybil Adlyn (CFla) 543 Corporation St, Holly Hill FL 32117 B Westmoreland Jama CA 6/16/1933 d Linford Austin Stone & Iva Lillian. Bethlehem Tchr Trng Coll Associations 1954; BA U of The W Indies 1974; Med CUNY 1984. D 6/6/1998 Bp John Wadsworth Howe. m 6/16/1962 Montrose Augustus Meheux. D Gr Epis Ch Inc Port Orange FL 1998-2000. meheuxs@cookman.edu

MEIER, Kermit Irwin (Ore) 1209 Fleet Landing Blvd, Atlantic Beach FL 32233 B Brainerd MN 1/28/1918 s Fred Henry Meier & Helen Marie. Muskegon Jr Coll Muskegon MI 1938; BA Albion Coll 1940; STB Bex 1943. D 6/22/1971 P 1/1/1973 Bp James Walmsley Frederic Carman. m 8/12/1944 Marian Elizabeth Liddell.

MEIKLE SSF, Janice May Wilkins (ECR) 1914 Mcbain Ave, San Jose CA 95125 B Woonsocket RI 4/2/1942 d Woodrow W Wilkins & Myrtle G. BEd Rhode Island Coll 1963; MDiv PSR 1991. D 6/29/1991 P 6/1/1992 Bp Richard Lester Shimpfky. m 7/20/1963 Robert Jack Meikle c 3. P-in-c Dio Oregon Portland OR 2002; Vic S Steph's In-The-Field Epis Ch San Jose CA 1994-2001; Asst to R S Fran Epis Ch San Jose CA 1991-1994; DRE S Phil's Ch San Jose CA 1989-1990. EWC, Amnesty Intl ; Tertiary of the Soc of S Fran. rjmeikle@yahoo.com

MEIN, P(eter) Simon (Del) P.O. Box 13, Odessa DE 19730 **Assoc All SS Ch Rehoboth Bch DE 1999-** B Eastwood Nottinghamshire UK 1/5/1927 s John Boddy Mein & Edith Gwendolyn. GOE Kelham Theol Coll 1952; BA U of Nottingham 1955; MA U of Nottingham 1959. Trans from Church Of England 5/18/1972 as Priest Bp William Henry Mead. m 5/29/1971 Nancy Ann McCleery. Dioc Coun Dio Delaware Wilmington DE 1997-2000; Assoc S Martha's Epis Ch Bethany Bch DE 1992-1998; Assoc S Martins-In-The-Fields Selbyville DE 1992-1998; Stndg Com Dio Delaware Wilmington DE 1975-1989; S Andrews Sch Of Delaware Inc Middletown DE 1971-1992. "Blog arts," *SimonSurmises*, Simon Mein, 2006; Auth, "Revs," *Living Ch*, 1975; Auth, "Art Blessing," *Dictionary of Chr Theol*, SCM Press, 1957; Auth, "Revs," *Theol*, 1957. Assoc. Ord of S Helena 1975. Hon Cn Dio Delaware Wilmington DE 1989; Exam Chapl to Bp of Delaware Delaware 1981. nsmein@earthlink.net

MEISS, Marion (Be) 46 S. Laurel St., Hazleton PA 18201 B Hazelton PA 1/26/1943 d Joseph Tolerico & Rose Plesh. D 9/29/2007 Bp Paul Victor Marshall. m 6/13/1964 Albert George Meiss c 2. mice@epix.net

MEISTER, Deborah Anne (NJ) 3001 Wisconsin Ave. NW, Washington DC 20016 **S Alb's Par Washington DC 2011-; R S Alb's Par Washington DC 2011-; R Chr Ch New Brunswick NJ 2006-** B New York NY 6/17/1968 d Robert Alan Meister & Margaret Ann. BA Harv 1990; PhD U CA 1999; MDiv Ya Berk 2002. D 6/23/2002 Bp Joseph Jon Bruno P 12/14/2002 Bp Marc Handley Andrus. Assoc R S Lk's Epis Ch Birmingham AL 2002-2006. dmeister@aya.yale.edu

MEISTER, Stephen George (Roch) 400 S Main St, Newark NY 14513 B Lansing MI 7/27/1946 s Orley George Meister & Freda Elaine. BSMET Rochester Inst of Tech 1996. D 3/29/2008 Bp Jack Marston McKelvey. m 11/22/1968 Jo Ann Pilling c 3. SGM13374@aol.com

M

MEISTER BOOK, Nancy D (Az) 6322 N Calle Del Caballo, Tucson AZ 85718 B Lincoln NE 1/6/1942 d Ralph E Deeds & Martha A. D 1/23/2010 Bp Kirk Stevan Smith. m 5/1/2010 James B Book c 3. nancymeister@comcast.net

MEJIA, Jairo (ECR) 12149 Saddle Road, Carmel Valley CA 93924 B Aguadas Caldas CO 1/29/1922 s Jesus Mejia & Margarita. Seminario Conciliar de Medellin 1944; Lic Universidad & Javeriana 1945; Lic Collegio Pio Latino Americano 1946; MA Santa Clara U 1976. Rec from Roman Catholic 9/1/1985 as Deacon Bp Charles Shannon Mallory. m 9/2/1970 Geraldine Rose Fischer c 1. Vic S Paul's Epis Ch Salinas CA 1988-1994. Auth, *Paso a Paso con la Biblia*, Ed CLIE, Barcelona, Spain, 1994; Auth, *Curso de Liturgia*, Edit Bedout,, Medellin, Colombia, 1962; Auth, *Tratado de la Divina Gracia*, Edit. Bedout, Medellin, Colombia, 1960. jmejia@mbay.net

MEJIA, Jose Arnaldo (Hond) Calle Principal, La Estrada HN Honduras **Dio Honduras Miami FL 2005-** B Ajuterique Comavagua 2/28/1950 s Gregoria. BA Instituto Immaculado 1970; Seminario Nuestra Senora Sumapa 1974; Seminario Teologicia Salazar 1976; Universidad Ibamisionera 1985. Rec from Roman Catholic 9/20/2003 Bp Lloyd Emmanuel Allen. m 10/2/2002 Dilia Dinora Herrera c 2.

MEJIA, Nelson Yovany (Hond) Roatan Islas De La Bahia, Apartado 193, Roatan, Coxen Hole Honduras **Dio Honduras Miami FL 2006-; Iglesia Epis Hondurena San Pedro Sula 2006-** B Siguatepeque Comyagua 4/14/1972 s Miguel Angel Mejia & Leila Oddi. DIT Programa Diocesano De Educaccion 2003; DIT Universidad Biblica Latinoamericana 2005. D 10/29/2005 Bp Lloyd Emmanuel Allen. m 1/19/2002 Kara Ann Thompson de Mejia c 2. nelsonkara@123.hn

MEJIA ESPINOSA, Jose Vincente (EcuC) Avenue La Castellana 40-06, Zona 8, Guatemala City 01008 Guatemala B Fredonia Ant CO 1/2/1932 s Vincente Mejia Echeverri & Bernice. BA Sem Conciliar De Medellin 1955; BTh Sem Conciliar De Medellin 1959. Rec from Roman Catholic 1/1/1988 as Priest Bp Armando Roman Guerra Soria. m 1/7/1980 Maria Teresa Catalina Louys. Iglesia Epis Del Ecuador Ecuador 1996-2001; Dio Guatemala Guatemala City 1987-1996. Auth, "Tugurianos Y Oligarquias 70 Las Siete Palabras". MOSODELA@HOTMAIL.COM

MELBERGER, MaryJo McConnell (Pa) 261 Tulip Tree Ct, Blue Bell PA 19422 **Assoc Ch Of The Mssh Lower Gwynedd PA 2010-** B Philadelphia PA 12/4/1943 d Joseph McConnell & Marion Elizabeth. BS Elizabethtown Coll 1965; DAS GTS 1991; MDiv Luth TS 1992. D 6/13/1992 P 5/22/1993 Bp Allen Lyman Bartlett Jr. m 12/26/1964 Kenneth E Melberger c 3. Int Ch Of The H Apos Wynnewood PA 2006-2008; Assoc R S Thos' Ch Whitemarsh Ft Washington PA 2003-2006; R S Jn's Ch Bala Cynwyd PA 1999-2001; Asst Ch Of The H Comm Memphis TN 1995-1999; Cler Ldrshp Proj Cordova TN 1994-1995; Asst The Ch Of The H Trin Rittenhouse Philadelphia PA 1992-1994. Alb Inst; OHC 1991. revmjmelb@comcast.net

MELCHER, John Robert (Mich) 2441 Nichols St, Trenton MI 48183 B Minneapolis MN 7/10/1950 s Robert Russell Melcher & Lorraine Yvonne. BA S Louis U 1973; MA S Louis U 1975; MDiv U Tor 1981; GTS 1990. Trans from Anglican Church of Canada 5/1/1990 Bp Robert Marshall Anderson. m 2/15/1986 Elizabeth Ann McNamara c 1. R S Thos Ch Trenton MI 1998-2006; R S Paul's Epis Ch Mayville NY 1993-1998; Assoc R All SS' Epis Ch Chevy Chase MD 1990-1993; DCE & Dvlpmt S Mart's By The Lake Epis Minnetonka Bch MN 1987-1989. Auth, "Testimony Usa Senate: Hlth Care Crisis On Rosebud Reserv". Soc Jof Esus. jmelcher@ymail.com

MELCHER JR, Louis Chester (NC) 2503 E Yacht Dr, Oak Island NC 28465 **Died 9/5/2011** B Clarksville TN 6/5/1929 s Louis Chester Melcher & Mary. BA U of So Carolina 1951; VTS 1954. D 6/1/1954 P 6/17/1955 Bp Clarence Alfred Cole. c 3. lcm3@earthlink.net

MELCHIONNA, Elizabeth Marie (SwVa) PO Box 2533, Davidson NC 28036 **COM Dio No Carolina Raleigh NC 2011-; Israel-Palestine T/F Dio No Carolina Raleigh NC 2011-; Bp's Com on Accessibility Dio No Carolina Raleigh NC 2010-; Com on MHE Dio No Carolina Raleigh NC 2009-; Assoc R S Alb's Ch Davidson NC 2009-** B Roanoke VA 3/15/1980 d Olin Richard Melchionna & Elizabeth Snead. BA Davidson Coll Davidson NC 2002; MDiv Ya Berk 2006; MDiv Yale DS 2006; Cert Yale Inst of Sacr Mus 2006. D 6/4/2006 P 8/23/2007 Bp Frank Neff Powell. Asst S Mary's Epis Ch Arlington VA 2007-2009. Fllshp of S Jn (SSJE) 2007. elizabeth.melchionna@aya.yale.edu

MELENDEZ, Michael Paul (Mass) 138 Tremont St, Boston MA 02111 B Wichita Falls TX 10/29/1952 s Carlos S Melendez & Alice Marian. MSW Bos 1983; PhD Case Wstrn Reserve U 2007. D 6/5/2010 Bp Gayle Elizabeth Harris. melendez@simmons.edu

MELIN, Marilyn Joyce (Chi) 702 N Division St, Harvard IL 60033 B Chicago IL 7/20/1944 d Marshall Mattison & Marion. BA Mundelein Coll 1978; MDiv SWTS 1985. D 2/10/1985 Bp James Winchester Montgomery P 9/1/1985 Bp Frank Tracy Griswold III. c 2. S Mary Epis Ch Crystal Lake IL 2008-2009; S Leonards Oratory Chicago IL 1987-1990; S Aug's Epis Ch Wilmette IL 1985-1988; S Lawr Epis Ch Libertyville IL 1985. marilynmelin@yahoo.com

MELLISH, Roy W (La) PO Box 1825, Morgan City LA 70381 B Santiago Chile 3/24/1941 s John Whyle Mellish & Violet Florence. Cert ETSC 1971; S Geo's Coll Jerusalem IL 1998; Oxf 2003; Durham Ecum Conf 2005. D 8/7/1971 P 2/12/1972 Bp Reginald Heber Gooden. c 1. R Trin Epis Ch Morgan City LA 1993-2008; R S Steph's Ch Innis LA 1990-1993; Ch Of The Epiph Houston TX 1989-1990; Exec Coun Appointees New York NY 1976-1987; St Georges Ch 1972-1976; Dio Panama 1971-1976. Tertiary of the Soc of S Fran 1979. roymellish@teche.net

MELLO, Iris Elaine (RI) 88 Albert Ave, Cranston RI 02905 **D S Mary's Ch Warwick RI 2007-; D Ch Of The Trsfg Cranston RI 1985-** B East Providence RI 7/3/1939 d William Douglas Morton & Edith May. BS Roger Wms 1990; MS U of Rhode Island 1993. D 7/13/1985 Bp George Nelson Hunt III. m 10/12/1957 Charles Edward Mello c 4.

MELLO, Jeffrey William (Mass) 130 Aspinwall Ave, Brookline MA 02446 **Dn Dio Massachusetts Boston MA 2011-; R S Paul's Ch Brookline MA 2009-** B Warwick RI 4/29/1968 s Charles Edward Mello & Iris Elaine. BA Rhode Island Coll Providnce RI 1991; MSW Simmons Coll Boston MA 2000; MDiv EDS 2007. D 6/2/2007 P 1/12/2008 Bp M(arvil) Thomas Shaw III. m 12/12/2004 Paul Daigneault c 1. Adjuct Fac EDS Cambridge MA 2010-2011; Dioc Coun Exec Com Dio Massachusetts Boston MA 2009-2011; Assoc R Chr Ch Cambridge Cambridge MA 2007-2009; Dioc Coun Rep Dio Massachusetts Boston MA 2007-2009. EPF 2007. jmello@stpaulsbrookline.org

MELLO-MAKI, Christine Helene (NMich) 470 North Us 141, Crystal Falls MI 49920 **D S Mk's Ch Crystal Falls MI 1997-** B Royal Oak MI 9/14/1938 d Manuel Chester Mello & Eleanor Ruth. Adb Suomi Coll 1958; A.D.N Jc Mott Jr Coll 1979; BD Lake Superior St U 1986. D 6/22/1997 Bp Thomas Kreider Ray. m 9/5/1959 Warren William Maki. makifarm@up.net

MELLON, Robert Edward (Pa) 5008 Central Ave, Ocean City NJ 08226 B Philadelphia PA 11/12/1941 s Joseph J Mellon & Elizabeth A. Dioc COLM; Cert Pennsylvania Diac Sch 1996. D 9/26/1996 Bp Franklin Delton Turner. m 9/5/1999 Gail V Mellon. S Jas Ch Collegeville PA 1996-2006. deacrem@verizon.net

MELLOTT, Emily Alice (Chi) 105 W Maple St, Lombard IL 60148 **R Calv Ch Lombard IL 2008-** B Chicago IL 11/18/1973 AB Bryn 1995; MDiv CDSP 2005. D 6/18/2005 Bp William Dailey Persell P 1/21/2006 Bp Victor Alfonso Scantlebury. Asst to the R S Ptr's Epis Ch St Louis MO 2005-2008. emellott@calvarylombard.org

MELNYK, James Stanley (NC) 5400 Crestview Rd, Raleigh NC 27609 **P-in-c S Paul's Epis Ch Smithfield NC 2010-; COM Dio No Carolina Raleigh NC 2004-** B Mount Vernon NY 6/27/1955 s Walter Melnyk & Rita. BA U of So Carolina 1977; MDiv STUSo 1989. D 6/10/1989 P 5/19/1990 Bp William Arthur Beckham. m 11/17/2009 M Lorraine Ljunggren c 1. Int Ch Of The H Fam Chap Hill NC 2009-2010; Dio Pennsylvania Philadelphia PA 2005; Asst & Co-Pstr S Mk's Epis Ch Raleigh NC 2000-2009; Int S Lk's Epis Ch Durham NC 1999-2000; P-in-c The Cathd Of All Souls Asheville NC 1997-1998; P-in-c The Cathd Of All Souls Asheville NC 1997-1998; Cn The Cathd Of All Souls Asheville NC 1991-1999; Assoc The Cathd Of All Souls Asheville NC 1991-1997; Assoc The Cathd Of All Souls Asheville NC 1991-1997; P-in-c S Andr's Epis Ch Greenville SC 1990-1991; Asst Chr Ch Greenville SC 1989-1991. Interfaith Allnce for Justice 1995-1998. jmelnyk.stpauls@nc.rr.com

MELTON, Brent Alan (EC) 210 Ellington St, Fayetteville NC 28305 **R Chr Ch Eliz City NC 2007-** B Wilmington NC 2/9/1975 s Norman Harrison Melton & Margarete. BS Coll of Charleston 1999; MDiv STUSo 2005. D 6/25/2005 P 4/8/2006 Bp Clifton Daniel III. m 5/21/2005 Kathryn U Underwood c 1. Asst Min S Jn's Epis Ch Fayetteville NC 2005-2007. revbmelton@gmail.com

MELTON, Heather L (Colo) 76 Chester Ave, Garden City NY 11530 **R Chr Ch Garden City NY 2011-** B Washington Court House OH 7/25/1978 d Thomas Payton & Julie. BS Kent St U 2001; MDiv CDSP 2008; MA Grad Theol Un 2009. D 5/31/2008 P 1/10/2009 Bp Robert John O'Neill. m 1/30/2010 James K Melton. Cur S Ambr Epis Ch Boulder CO 2008-2011; Dir of Yth & YA Mnstrs S Jn's Epis Ch Boulder CO 2000-2005. revhmelton@gmail.com

MELTON, Jonathan Randall (WTex) 427 Turner Ave, Boerne TX 78006 **S Chris's By The Sea Portland TX 2009-** B Austin TX 11/18/1980 s M(ark) Randall Melton & Karen Lee. Indiana U At So Bend IN 2001; BA Wheaton Coll 2003; MDiv Duke 2007. D 12/21/2006 P 9/18/2007 Bp Edward Stuart Little II. m 12/31/2005 Rebekah Lyn Baker c 2. Asst To The R S Helena's Epis Ch Boerne TX 2007-2009. the.jmelton@gmail.com

MELTON, M(ark) Randall (WTex) 721 St. Louis Street, P.O. Box 139, Gonzales TX 78629 **BEC Dio W Texas San Antonio TX 2010-; Dn on NE Cler Dio W Texas San Antonio TX 2010-; R Epis Ch Of The Mssh Gonzales TX 2008-** B Dallas TX 8/11/1953 s Jack Rawson Melton & Anna Jo. BS E Texas St U 1976; MDiv Epis TS of The SW 1983. D 6/11/1983 Bp Robert Elwin Terwilliger P 5/9/1984 Bp Donis Dean Patterson. m 1/5/1978 Karen Lee Bowser c 3. R S Mich And All Ang Ch So Bend IN 1999-2008; Dio Dallas Dallas TX 1996-1999; COM Dio Dallas Dallas TX 1995-1998; All SS Ch Allen TX 1994-1996; Asst P and Sch Chapl S Jn's Epis Ch Dallas TX

1988-1994; R S Mths' Epis Ch Athens TX 1986-1988; Asst P Epis Ch Of The Redeem Irving TX 1984-1986; D Chr Epis Ch Dallas TX 1983-1984. soulman4jc@gmail.com

MENAUL, Marjorie Ann (CPa) 125 E Main St, Bloomsburg PA 17815 **R S Paul's Ch Bloomsburg PA 1995-** B Columbus OH 6/10/1947 d Robert Foresman Menaul & Marilyn. BA U MI 1969; MA U CA 1971; MA U Chi 1986; MDiv Nash 1989. D 6/17/1989 Bp Frank Tracy Griswold III P 1/6/1990 Bp R(aymond) Stewart Wood Jr. Asst S Andr's Ch Ann Arbor MI 1989-1995. "Ascen of the Lord," *The Abingdon Wmn Preaching Annual*, Abingdon, 2002; "I Samuel 1 & 2," *Interp*, UTS, 2001. Epis Cler Assn of Cntrl PA 1998; EWC 1995. Cn St, Steph's Cathd, Harrisburg 2008. mmenaul@aol.com

MENDELSOHN, Randall Paul (Mich) 8440 Jonfred Ct, Cincinnati OH 45231 **Died 8/24/2011** B Waterbury CT 11/30/1928 s Abraham Randall Mendelsohn & Mary. BA U of Connecticut 1952; BD Bex 1955; MA Nthrn Michigan U 1973. D 6/14/1955 Bp Walter H Gray P 12/20/1955 Bp William J Gordon Jr. c 5. HTCHURCH@EOS.NET

MENDENHALL, Elborn E (Kan) 2477 SW Brookhaven Ln, Topeka KS 66614 B Garden City KS 12/9/1928 s Lester Layson Mendenhall & Bessie. BS K SU 1951; MS Harv 1953; STB GTS 1959; K SU 1974. D 4/25/1959 P 2/12/1960 Bp Arnold M Lewis. m 7/20/1972 Burney Bailey c 3. Int Calv Ch Yates Cntr KS 1987-1988; Int S Tim's Ch Iola KS 1987-1988; Vic S Mk's Ch Blue Rapids KS 1983-1986; Vic S Lk's Ch Wamego KS 1972-1976; Vic S Mk's Ch Blue Rapids KS 1970-1980; Vic H Innoc' Epis Ch Como MS 1966-1970; Vic H Cross Epis Ch Olive Branch MS 1966-1967; Vic S Timothys Epis Ch Southaven MS 1966-1967; R H Trin Ch Cincinnati OH 1961-1965; Cur Gr Ch Utica NY 1959-1961. CT 1963; Ord S Ben 1959; Ord of S Lk 1983. alspace@cox.net

MENDEZ, Noe (Dal) The Holy Nativity Episcopal Church, 2200 18th St, Plano TX 75074 **The Epis Ch Of The H Nativ Plano TX 2010-** B Oaxaca Mexico 8/21/1962 s Felipe Mendez & Fidelfa. Escuela Normal de Maestros, Mesico 1982; MDiv Instititulo Teologico San Mateo, Dallas TX 2006. D 11/10/2007 Bp James Monte Stanton P 6/3/2009 Bp Paul Emil Lambert. m 1/27/1984 Maria Perez c 5. noemendez@att.net

MENDEZ, Richard (U) Box 630016, Randlett UT 84063 **R Ch Of The H Sprt Randlett UT 1995-; Dio Utah Salt Lake City UT 1995-** B Pocatello ID 2/27/1948 s Magdaleno Silba Mendez & Aluina Cecilia. Idaho St U 1972; AAS Haskell Indiana Jr Coll 1974; Cert SWTS 1989. D 3/30/1990 P 11/30/1990 Bp Bob Gordon Jones. m 4/8/1975 Josephine Ann Mendez c 3. Dio Wyoming Casper WY 1992-1994; Vic Our Fr's Hse Ft Washakie WY 1991-1995; Shoshone Epis Mssn Ft Washakie WY 1990-1991. hsec@ubtanet.com

MENDEZ, Troy Douglas (Los) Saint Margaret's Episcopal Church, 47535 Highway 74, Palm Desert CA 92260 **Assoc R S Marg's Epis Ch Palm Desert CA 2011-** B Houston TX 8/31/1972 s Roy Jose Mendez & Sandra Schultz. BBA U of Notre Dame 1994; MDiv VTS 2009. D 6/6/2009 P 1/9/2010 Bp Sergio Carranza-Gomez. Cur Ch Of Our Sav Par San Gabr CA 2009-2011. troy90048@yahoo.com

MENDEZ-COLON, Ana Rosa (PR) Urb. Venus Gardens Calle Peliux 1770, San Juan PR 00926 **Dio Puerto Rico S Just PR 2007-** B Puerto Rico 8/1/1954 d Enrique Mendez & Dolores. D 5/1/2005 P 8/27/2006 Bp David Andres Alvarez-Velazquez. m 10/18/1985 Sixto Rodriguez Rios c 3. rvda.mendez@gmail.com

MENDOZA, Loretta (Mil) 2708 Red Fawn Ct, Racine WI 53406 **Wheaton Franciscan Heatlhcare All SS Racine WI 2011-** B Edinburg TX 9/8/1952 d Benito Muniz Juarez & Irene Garcia. Cert Milwaukee Area Tech Coll 1982; Cert St. Fran Sem Milwaukee WI 1992; LTH/MDIV SWTS 2002. D 4/6/2002 Bp Roger John White P 3/25/2003 Bp Chilton Abbie Richardson Knudsen. m 5/22/1971 Gilbert Mendoza c 1. All SS Med Cntr Racine WI 2003-2008; Asst S Jas Epis Ch Milwaukee WI 2003. lmendoza@wirr.com

MENDOZA CEDENO, Eduardo (EcuL) CASILLA 11497, Guayaquil 00000 Ecuador B 10/12/1957 D 2/2/1986 Bp Adrian Delio Caceres-Villavicencio P 6/7/1992 Bp Martiniano Garcia-Montiel. Litoral Dio Ecuador Guayaquil EQ EC 1991-1993.

MENDOZA MARMOLEJOS, Milquella Rosanna (DR) Iglesia San Felipe Apostol, M-C #1 Barrio Invi, Sabana Perdida Dominican Republic **Dio The Dominican Republic (Iglesia Epis Dominicana) Santo Domingo DO 2007-** B 3/11/1969 D 2/12/2006 Bp Julio Cesar Holguin-Khoury. c 2. milquella_mendoza@yahoo.com

MENDOZA QUIROZ, Hugo Eligio (EcuL) Calle #19, #208, Calderon Ecuador **Litoral Dio Ecuador Guayaquil EQ EC 2006-** B Calderon Ecuador 5/24/1942 D 3/22/1998 P 4/13/2008 Bp Alfredo Morante-España. m 11/19/1976 Edita Parraga c 5.

MENGER, James Andrew (Ga) 3521 Nassau Dr, Augusta GA 30909 **S Mary's Ch Augusta GA 2002-; Asst R The Ch Of The Gd Shpd Augusta GA 2001-** B Augusta GA 12/19/1950 s Earl Marion Menger & Betty Walden. STUSo; MA Clemson U 1975; Med U of So Carolina 1983; Cert Camb 1988; DMin GTF 1989. D 2/3/2001 P 8/23/2001 Bp Henry Irving Louttit. m 2/6/1982 Glenda Boswell. Amer Acad Of Bereavement 2000. Fell GTF 1989. andymenger@goodshepherd-augusta.net

MENJIVAR, Nicholas (NC) Po Box 218, Durham NC 27702 B SV 12/22/1942 s Francisco Menjivar & Maria Elisa. BA S Jos Sem 1969; MA S Jos Sem 1973. Rec from Roman Catholic 4/14/1996 Bp Frederick Houk Borsch. m 8/11/1994 Maria Gladys Rivera c 2. Iglesia El Buen Pstr Durham NC 2000-2007; Vic Hisp Mssn S Phil's Ch Durham NC 1998-2000; Dio No Carolina Raleigh NC 1998-1999; Dio Los Angeles Los Angeles CA 1997-1998; All SS Epis Ch Oxnard CA 1996-1997.

MENNELL, John A (Nwk) 75 S Fullerton Ave, Montclair NJ 07042 **R S Lk's Epis Ch Montclair NJ 2006-** B Santa Monica CA 1/4/1965 s Robert Lee Mennell & Antoinette Yarrow. BA U of Notre Dame 1987; MDiv GTS 2005. D 5/14/2005 P 11/26/2005 Bp Herbert Thompson Jr. m Sonia E Waters c 3. Assoc P S Mich's Ch New York NY 2005-2006. jmennell@saintmichaelschurch.org

MENSAH, Albert (Chi) 424 S Harvey Ave, Oak Park IL 60302 B 9/27/1934 D 1/20/1963 Bp Gerald Francis Burrill. m 6/11/1964 Catherine A Mensah.

MENZI, Donald Wilder (Mich) 5 E 10th St, New York NY 10003 B Ypsilanti MI 12/19/1937 s Leonard W Menzi & Margaret. BD Bex 1936; BA Ob 1960; CUNY 1969; PhD NYU 1978. D 6/29/1963 Bp Richard S M Emrich P 2/1/1964 Bp Roger W Blanchard. m 11/28/1958 Mattea Fagin c 3. Asst Min Calv Ch Cincinnati OH 1963-1966. Hud Fell Cuny-Hunter; Levi A Olin Fell Hebr Un Coll. dmenzi@earthlink.net

MEPHAM, Clifford Andrew (Tex) 690 Mason Headley Rd Apt 401, Lexington KY 40504 B Pittsburgh PA 6/24/1924 s Harry Mepham & Elizabeth. BS U Pgh 1945; MD Col 1948; STB GTS 1952; Oxf 1963. D 4/16/1952 Bp Lauriston L Scaife P 10/1/1952 Bp William Crittenden. m 7/1/1971 Florence Thomas. Vic S Fran Of Assisi Epis Prairie View TX 1983-1989; S Michaels Ch Groves TX 1980-1983; R S Thos Ch Wharton TX 1972-1980; Vic Ch Of The H Trin Houtzdale PA 1952-1958.

MERCER JR, Charles Spencer (Md) Saint Bartholomew's Church, 4711 Edmondson Ave, Baltimore MD 21229 **Asst S Barth's Ch Baltimore MD 2011-** B Baltimore MD 5/13/1952 s Charles S Mercer & Anna Mae. Rec from Roman Catholic 5/25/2006 as Deacon Bp Robert Wilkes Ihloff. m 3/11/2005 Karen Fairrow. cmer311@verizon.net

MERCER, Emmanuel A (USC) 489 Fort Hill Circle, Fort Washington PA 19034 **S Paul's Ch Philadelphia PA 2011-; Trin Cathd Columbia SC 2005-** B Sekondi Ghana 6/11/1971 s James Mercer & Georgina. LTh St. Nich TS 1998; MDiv Candler TS Emory U 2004; STM Yale DS 2005; MA VTS 2009. Trans from Church of the Province of West Africa 4/18/2006 Bp Dorsey Felix Henderson. m 6/14/2003 Monique Disere Glivens c 2. atomercer11@gmail.com

MERCER JR, Roy Calvin (CFla) 4932 Willowbrook Cir, Winter Haven FL 33884 B Wyandotte MI 8/18/1934 s Roy Calvin Mercer & Ruth. BA Ob 1956; BD VTS 1962; Med U Of Florida 1971; PhD U Of Florida 1975. D 6/9/1962 P 12/1/1962 Bp Nelson Marigold Burroughs. m 6/7/1958 Wilma Marie McCamey c 2. Assoc Chapl Ch Of The Incarn Gainesville FL 1964-1968; Assoc Chr Ch Lima OH 1962-1964. Phi Delta Kappa; Phi Kappa Phi; Kappa Delta Pi.

MERCER, Thomas Robert (NY) Po Box A, Granite Springs NY 10527 B Liverpool UK 9/7/1941 s Joseph Albin Mercer & Georgina. BA Oxf 1963; MA Oxf 1966; U Of Leeds Gb 1967. Trans from Church of the Province of West Africa 1/1/1982. S Paul's Ch Morrisania Bronx NY 2003-2006; R Ch Of The Gd Shpd Granite Sprg NY 1996-2003; R S Jas Epis Ch Fordham Bronx NY 1991-1995; Vic All SS Epis Ch Skowhegan ME 1987-1991; Asst The Ch Of The Atone Morton PA 1986-1987.

MERCHANT, John Edward (At) 474 Sunset Dr., Asheville NC 28804 B Harrisonburg VA 10/15/1946 s John Preston Merchant & Nellie Virginia. BA U So 1968; MDiv VTS 1973. D 6/7/1973 P 2/25/1974 Bp Wilburn Camrock Campbell. c 2. S Geo's Epis Sch Milner GA 2000-2003; H Innoc' Epis Sch Atlanta GA 1998-2000; Gr-S Lk's Epis Sch Memphis TN 1991-1998; S Jas Sch St Jas MD 1985-1991; S Mk's Epis Sch Ft Lauderdale FL 1982-1985; Jacksonville Epis HS Jacksonville FL 1978-1982; Vic S Andr's in the Vill Ch Barboursville WV 1975-1978; Asst S Matt's Ch Wheeling WV 1973-1975. Gvrng Bd NAES 1985-1991. Ruth Jenkins Awd for Exemplary Serv Nat. Assoc. of Epis Schools 2000. merchant.je@gmail.com

MERCHANT, Patricia Laura (SO) 6000 Drake Rd, Cincinnati OH 45243 B Monterey CA 7/2/1947 d Charles Lincoln Merchant & Aileen Gladys. BS Jas Madison U 1969; MDiv VTS 1974. D 5/24/1974 Bp John Alfred Baden P 1/1/1977 Bp Robert Bruce Hall. m 10/10/1987 Louis Squyres. The Ch Of Ascen And H Trin Cincinnati OH 2007-2009; R Indn Hill Ch Cincinnati OH 2000-2008; Int Chr Ch Cathd S Louis MO 1998-2000; The Epis Ch Of The Nativ Fayetteville GA 1991-1998; Dio Atlanta Atlanta GA 1990-1998; S Lk's Epis Ch Atlanta GA 1985-1990; Emm Ch Virginia Bch VA 1982; Asst S Paul's Ch Richmond VA 1977-1980; Asst Imm Ch-On-The-Hill Alexandria VA 1974-1977. pat.merchant@aol.com

MERCHANT II, Wilmot T (SC) 801 11th Avenue North, North Myrtle Beach SC 29582 **R S Steph's Epis Ch No Myrtle Bch SC 2002-** B Gbarnga Bong County LR 12/28/1961 s Wilmot T Merchant & Martha M. BA Cuttington U Coll 1986; Cert S Geo's Coll Jerusalem IL 1987; MDiv EDS 1992; ThM Weston Jesuit TS 1993; DMin Drew U 2000. Trans from Church of the Province of West Africa 4/20/2000 Bp Edward W Neufville II. m 12/23/1989 Eugenia C Merchant. Asst S Steph's Epis Ch No Myrtle Bch SC 2000-2001; P-in-c Trin Ch Of Morrisania Bronx NY 1996-1999; Assoc S Paul's Epis Ch Paterson NJ 1993-1995; Asst S Barth's Ch Cambridge MA 1991-1992. wtmerchant2@aol.com

MERCURE, Martha Jones (At) 3800 Sherbrook Ct, College Park GA 30349 **Died 2/2/2010** B Atlanta GA 4/11/1950 d Dana Lafayette Jones & Mary Paige. BD Nell Hodgson Woodruff Sch Nrsng Atlanta GA 1973; MDiv Candler TS Emory U 1992. D 6/6/1992 P 12/1/1992 Bp Frank Kellogg Allan. c 4.

MEREDITH, Carol Ann (Colo) 316 Oakland St, Aurora CO 80010 **R S Steph's Epis Ch Aurora CO 2009-** B Manchester UK 5/15/1948 d Colin Gurth Parker & Lillian Flora. Kedron Pk Teachers Coll 1968; BS Friends U 1991; MA Friends U 1994; MDiv SWTS 2004. D 2/13/1992 Bp William Edward Smalley P 1/17/2004 Bp Dean Elliott Wolfe. m 2/6/1970 Howard W Meredith c 2. Int S Andr's Ch Denver CO 2007-2009; Assoc Gd Shpd Epis Ch Wichita KS 2005-2007; P-in-c S Andr's Ch Derby KS 2004-2007; Cur S Jn's Ch Wichita KS 2004-2005. camrev1@yahoo.com

MERFY, Florence Martha (Nev) 1515 Shasta Dr Apt 1510, Davis CA 95616 B Union OR 2/21/1922 d Victor Cornwall Morgan & Florence Martha. BA Reed Coll 1943; Med U of Nevada at Las Vegas 1978. D 11/1/1987 Bp Stewart Clark Zabriskie. c 3. D All SS Epis Ch Las Vegas NV 1987-1997. SHN.

✠ MERINO-BOTERO, Rt Rev Bernardo (Colom) Carrera 17 #96-41 Apt 201, Bogota Colombia **Ret Bp of Colombia Dio Colombia Bogota CO 2002-** B Venecia Antioquia CO 5/13/1930 s Cristobal Merino & Sofia. Mss Sem Colom. D 3/1/1955 P 10/1/1955 Bp Thomas H Wright Con 6/29/1979 for Colom. m 4/1/1971 Josefina Zuleta. Bp of Colombia Dio Colombia Bogota CO 1979-2002; Dio Colombia Bogota CO 1979-2001; Iglesia Epis En Colombia 1975-2002; Archd of Colombia Dio Colombia Bogota CO 1975-1979; Chair on the Stndg Com Dio Colombia Bogota CO 1975-1978. Auth, *Biography of Bp Builes*; Auth, *El Mensajero*. Javerianos. bmobispo@hotmail.com

MEROLA SR, Carl Robert (CFla) 705 Victory Lane, Hendersonville NC 28739 **S Matt's Epis Ch Sterling VA 2001-** B Wilkinsburg PA 2/4/1935 s Domenic N Merola & Lucy Matilda. BSME Carnegie Mellon U 1960; MBA U Pgh 1968; EFM STUSo 1983. D 3/16/1984 Bp William Hopkins Folwell. m 4/13/1957 Jeanne Lynn Brown c 5. crmerola@bellsouth.net

MEROLA JR, Carl Robert (Va) 402 Valencia Cir, Oviedo FL 32765 **S Matt's Epis Ch Sterling VA 2001-** B Pittsburgh PA 9/28/1958 s Carl Robert Merola & Jean Lynn. BA Kings Coll 1980; MDiv Trin Evang DS Deerfield IL 1985. D 5/14/1986 P 12/1/1986 Bp William Hopkins Folwell. m 6/14/1986 Linda Anne Larson. S Jas Epis Ch Ormond Bch FL 1996-2001; S Eliz's Epis Ch Sebastian FL 1988-1994; Cur S Andr's Epis Ch Ft Pierce FL 1986-1988.

MERONEY, Anne Elrod (At) 4919-B Rivoli Dr, Macon GA 31210 B Henderson NC 1/9/1943 d Joseph Edgar Elrod & Florence Perry. BA Georgia St U 1974; JD Woodrow Wilson Coll of Law 1977; MDiv Candler TS Emory U 2002. D 6/8/2002 P 1/5/2003 Bp J(ohn) Neil Alexander. c 2. Chr Ch Macon GA 2004-2005; Asst R S Anne's Epis Ch Atlanta GA 2002-2004. anne.meroney@cox.net

MERRELL, Robin Nicholas (Cal) 3886 Balcom Rd, San Jose CA 95148 B Spokane WA 4/6/1937 s Merton Howard Merrell & Carmen Frances. BA U Of Idaho Moscow 1959; BD CDSP 1964; MA Santa Clara U 1986. D 6/20/1964 P 12/19/1964 Bp J(ohn) Joseph Meakins Harte. c 1. Asstg Mision Nuestra Sra De Guadalupe San Jose CA 1998-2000; S Phil's Ch San Jose CA 1988-1998; Indn Epis Mnstry San Francisco CA 1976-1981; Dio California San Francisco CA 1973-1976; R S Mk's Ch KING CITY CA 1969-1973; Vic S Dav's Epis Page AZ 1964-1966; Vic S Jn's Ch Williams AZ 1964-1966. Auth, "Hometowns"; Auth, "A Mem Of The Fam". klausmerrell@hotmail.com

MERRILL, George Richard (Md) 9046 Quail Run Rd, Saint Michaels MD 21663 B Staten Island NY 10/17/1934 s Elliott Irving Merrill & Irma. BA Hob 1956; STB Ya Berk 1960; Amer Fndt of Rel & Psych 1965. D 6/11/1960 P 12/1/1960 Bp Horace W B Donegan. m 12/10/1983 Josephine Merrill c 2. Asst Ch Of The Resurr Baltimore MD 1974-1976; Asst S Steph's Epis Ch Bloomfield CT 1966-1973; Assoc All Ang' Ch New York NY 1962-1965; Cur S Jn's Ch W Hartford CT 1960-1962. Auth, "Anxiety: Friend Or Foe". AAPC; ACPE. jomerrill@atlanticbb.net

MERRILL, Ralph Edwin (Ct) 517 Pequot Ave, New London CT 06320 B Thompsonville CT 4/10/1932 s Albert Fraser Merrill & Hazel Charlotte. BA Trin Hartford CT 1953; STB GTS 1956. D 6/14/1956 P 6/14/1957 Bp Walter H Gray. m 6/28/1958 Audrey Neal c 3. COM Dio Connecticut Hartford CT 1979-1986; R S Jas Ch New London CT 1974-1995; Archd Dio Connecticut Hartford CT 1961-1973; Cur S Mk's Ch New Britain CT 1956-1960.

MERRILL, Richard Hull (ECR) 1755 W Ridgeview Circle, Palm Springs CA 92264 **Asstg S Paul In The Desert Palm Sprg CA 1997-** B Seattle WA 10/2/1929 s Elmer Leslie Merrill & Inez Isabel. BA U CA 1951; JD U CA 1956; MDiv VTS 1971. D 6/26/1971 Bp C Kilmer Myers P 12/20/1971 Bp George Richard Millard. c 4. Vic S Paul's Ch Cambria CA 1990-1994; Assoc The Epis Ch In Almaden San Jose CA 1987-1988; Dio El Camino Real Monterey CA 1987; Vic S Lk's Ch Hollister CA 1981-1986; Assoc S Geo's Ch Salinas CA 1979-1981; R S Ptr's Epis Ch Red Bluff CA 1972-1978; Cur S Paul's Ch Oakland CA 1971-1972.

MERRILL JR, Robert Clifford (Tex) PO Box 961, Hempstead TX 77445 **R S Barth's Ch Hempstead TX 2006-** B Brooklyn NY 4/23/1958 s Robert Clifford Merrill & Phyllis S. BS U of Virginia 1980; PhD U of Notre Dame 1983. D 6/28/2008 Bp Don Adger Wimberly P 1/24/2009 Bp Rayford Baines High Jr. m 11/26/1983 Carmen Sepulveda c 1. vicar@stbartshempstead.org

MERRILL, Russell Walter (EMich) 262 Raleigh Pl, Lennon MI 48449 **D S Paul's Epis Ch Corunna MI 1984-** B Owosso MI 11/7/1944 s Russell Franklin Merrill & Margaret Maxine. Cert Whitaker TS. D 6/25/1983 Bp William J Gordon Jr P 12/21/2003 Bp Edwin Max Leidel Jr. m 1/20/1968 Jennifer Lynn Alexander.

MERRIMAN, Michael Walter (Minn) 2012 Stain Glass Dr, Plano TX 75075 **Asst The Epis Ch Of The Trsfg Dallas TX 2004-** B Austin TX 2/26/1939 s Walter William Merriman & Jane. BA U of Texas 1963; STB GTS 1966. D 6/15/1966 Bp Charles A Mason P 12/1/1966 Bp William Paul Barnds. m 1/21/1967 Charlotte Ann Stillwagon. Prncpl St. Mk's Coll, Townsville Australia, Dio N. Queensland St Marks Coll 1997-2004; P-in-c Geth Ch Minneapolis MN 1994-1997; Vstng Lectr CDSP Berkeley CA 1984-1987; Chair Of The Liturg Cmsn Dio California San Francisco CA 1983-1989; Precentor and Vice Dn Gr Cathd San Francisco CA 1982-1992; R Camp Crucis Forth Worth TX 1978-1979; R Gd Shpd Granbury TX 1976-1982; Int Dio Dallas Dallas TX 1976-1978; Int S Andr's Ch Grand Prairie TX 1976; Chair Of The Yth Div Dio Dallas Dallas TX 1969-1974; R S Barn Ch Garland TX 1967-1974. Auth, "The Rite Light," *The Rite Stuff*, Ch Pub, 2008; Auth, "The Baptismal Mystery & The Catechumenate," Ch Pub, 1989; Auth, "Our Living Wrshp," Ch Pub. Associated Parishes 1976. m_c_merriman@hotmail.com

MERRIN, Susan (Louise) (Mont) D 8/18/1990 Bp Charles Jones III P 10/15/2005 Bp Charles Franklin Brookhart Jr.

MERRITT, Claudia L Wolfe (Va) 3401 Hawthorne Avenue, Richmond VA 23222 B Los Angeles CA 11/29/1947 d Harold Wolfe & Miriam. BA Carnegie Mellon U 1970; MBA Van 1972; MDiv PrTS 1976. D 8/20/1977 Bp Henry Irving Mayson P 4/8/1978 Bp H Coleman McGehee Jr. m 11/2/2002 Craig Merritt c 4. Assoc S Steph's Ch Richmond VA 2008-2010; S Paul's Epis Ch Miller's Tavern VA 2006-2007; S Andr's Ch Richmond VA 2006; S Ptr's Port Royal Port Royal VA 2003-2005; Int S Jn's Ch W Point VA 2002-2003; Ch Of The H Comf Richmond VA 1996-2001; S Lk's Epis Ch Durham NC 1993-1995; S Thos Epis Ch Reidsville NC 1992-1993; Int S Jn's Ch Bala Cynwyd PA 1989-1990; Asst Ch Of S Mart-In-The-Fields Philadelphia PA 1987-1989; Chr Ch And S Mich's Philadelphia PA 1986-1987; Stwdshp Off Dio Pennsylvania Philadelphia PA 1982-1987; Asst S Thos' Ch Whitemarsh Ft Washington PA 1980-1981; Vic H Faith Ch Saline MI 1977-1979; H Faith Ch Saline MI 1977-1979. merrittclaudia@gmail.com

MERRITT, Frederick Deen (Neb) 238 King St, Chadron NE 69337 B 6/8/1934 D 5/7/1988 Bp James Daniel Warner.

MERRITT, Robert E (CFla) 864 Summerfield Dr, Lakeland FL 33803 B Saint Petersburg FL 11/8/1940 s Edward P Merritt & Mae. BS Florida St U 1965; MDiv STUSo 1975. D 6/17/1975 P 2/1/1976 Bp William Hopkins Folwell. m 12/27/2008 Barbara G Merrit c 3. All SS Epis Ch Lakeland FL 1997; Asst S Steph's Ch Lakeland FL 1984-1990; S Lk The Evang Ch Mulberry FL 1980; Asst R S Dav's Epis Ch Lakeland FL 1975-1980.

MERROW, Andrew T P (Va) 2609 North Glebe Road, Arlington VA 22207 **R S Mary's Epis Ch Arlington VA 1985-** B Alexandria VA 12/21/1954 s Edward Leith Merrow & Helen. BA U of Vermont 1976; MDiv VTS 1981. D 6/7/1981 Bp Robert Bruce Hall P 3/12/1982 Bp David Henry Lewis Jr. m 9/27/2008 Cameron Merrow c 2. VTS Alexandria VA 1994; VTS Alexandria VA 1993; VTS Alexandria VA 1990-1992; Assoc R Chr Ch Alexandria VA 1981-1985. Cn St. Mathrews Cathd 2006. merrowa@aol.com

MERTZ, Mary Ann (Pa) 116 Lancaster Pike, Oxford PA 19363 **R S Christophers Epis Ch Oxford PA 2011-** B Louisville KY 10/7/1951 d Thomas Elmer Brown & Martha Veronica. BA Bellarmine U 1972; Mstr Theol Stds St Meinrad TS 1994; Doctor of Mnstry Louisville Presb TS 2006; Dplma Angl Stds GTS 2009. D 6/19/2009 P 12/21/2009 Bp Edwin Funsten Gulick Jr. m 11/21/1975 Kenneth Louis Mertz c 1. Chapl The Epis Acad Newtown Sq PA 2009-2011. Ntwk of Biblic Storytellers, Intl 2011. Doctorate w dist Louisville Presb Sem 2006. mrymsing@bellsouth.net

MERZ, John (LI) 36 Cathedral Ave, Garden City NY 11530 **Chapl S Matt's Ch Pennington NJ 2005-** B Brooklyn NY 9/16/1965 s Joseph G Merz & Mary L. BA CUNY 1994; MDiv Yale DS 2004. D 3/13/2004 P 9/18/2004 Bp Mark Sean Sisk. m 8/10/2010 Tara L Anderson. Dio New York New York City NY 2005-2010. MAILTOMERZ@GMAIL.COM

MESA, Prospero Eugenio (La) 3104 Verna St, Metairie LA 70003 B Havana CU 1/12/1928 s Prospero Eloy Mesa & Ana Maria. BS U of Havana 1947; MA U of Havana 1954; STB UTS Mantanzas CU 1964; EdD U of Havana 1965. Trans from Iglesia Episcopal de Cuba 12/1/1981. m 4/23/1966 Raquel C Chavez c 3. Assoc S Jn's Ch Kenner LA 1987-1992; S Mart's Epis Sch Metairie LA 1987-1992; Ch Of The H Sprt New Orleans LA 1986-1987; Gr Ch New Orleans LA 1984-1985; Epis Refugee Servs Dio Louisiana Baton Rouge LA 1981-1983; Exec Coun Appointees New York NY 1964-1981. prosperomesa@bellsouth.net

MESENBRING, David (Oly) 1245 10th Ave E, Seattle WA 98102 **Sr Assoc S Mk's Cathd Seattle WA 2006-** B Des Moines IA 3/15/1951 s Victor Hugo Mesenbring & June Elizabeth. BA Kalamazoo Coll 1973; MA U Chi DS 1975. Rec from Evangelical Lutheran Church in America 7/24/2011 as Priest Bp Gregory Harold Rickel. m 6/1/1991 Maria Jesus Jimenez Madrazo c 2. dmesenbring@saintmarks.org

MESERVEY, Norman Rix (WNC) 84 Church St, Franklin NC 28734 B Elmira NY 7/12/1937 s Norman Baldwin Meservey & Lydia Eleanor. BA Syr 1960; MA Syr 1963; MDiv EDS 1977. D 6/19/1977 Bp Frederic Cunningham Lawrence P 1/15/1978 Bp Roger W Blanchard. m 4/22/1995 Lorie Smith. R S Agnes Epis Ch Franklin NC 1994-2002; P-in-c Ch Of The Redeem Andalusia PA 1990-1994; Asst Trin Ch Oxford Philadelphia PA 1986; R S Alb's Ch Philadelphia PA 1983-1985; S Alb's Ch Roxborough Philadelphia PA 1983-1985; R All SS Ch Whitman MA 1978-1983; Asst The Cathd Ch Of S Paul Boston MA 1977-1978. Auth, "Be Not Afraid"; Auth, "Setting Rite Ii"; Auth, "Benedic," *Anima Mea*. frmeserveyatstagnes@juno.com

MESLER JR, Raymond Clyde (NY) 7470 W Glenbrook Rd Apt 313, Milwaukee WI 53223 B Bolivar NY 8/20/1927 s Raymond Clyde (Sr) Mesler & Marion Edna. BMAS U of No Texas 1949; MDiv UTS 1984; STM UTS 1985. D 1/27/1985 Bp Albert Wiencke Van Duzer P 2/19/1986 Bp Otis Charles. c 2. Asst P St Mths Epis Ch Waukesha WI 1997-1999; P S Simon's Ch Staten Island NY 1986-1990; Asst to R Chr And S Steph's Ch New York NY 1985-1986. FRMESLER@AOL.COM

MESLEY, Gordon Warwick (WMo) 2021 S Hummel Dr, Independence MO 64055 B Kansas City MO 3/18/1929 s George Mesley & Blanche. Graceland Coll Lamoni IA 1948; BA U of Nthrn Iowa 1952. D 2/13/1999 Bp Barry Robert Howe. m 8/26/1995 Evelyn Ruth Allen. egmesley@aol.com

MESSENGER, Ray Stillson (CNY) 420 Woodside Way, Moravia NY 13118 B Auburn NY 10/22/1937 s Robert Watson Messenger & Katherine Morse. BS Worcester Polytechnic Inst 1962; MBA U Roch 1970; Bex 1988. D 6/22/1988 P 1/21/1989 Bp William George Burrill. m 9/27/1961 Susan Geer Rogers c 4. V-Chair Dioc Bd Dio Cntrl New York Syracuse NY 1993-1995; R S Jas' Ch Clinton NY 1991-2001; Asst S Jame's Ch Skaneateles NY 1988-1991. Pi Tau Sigma Hon Mechanical Engr Fraternity 1962. buzznsue2@yahoo.com

MESSENGER, William Glen (Mass) 84 Lexington St, Belmont MA 02478 B Fairborn OH 6/16/1960 s William Wilson Messenger & Gwendolyn. BS Case Wstrn Reserve U 1982; MBA Harv 1988; MDiv Bos 1997; DMin Gordon-Conwell TS 2007. D 6/6/1998 P 5/29/1999 Bp M(arvil) Thomas Shaw III. m 9/14/1991 Kimberly Mae Pope c 2. Ch Planter Dio Massachusetts Boston MA 2004-2008; Bus Ldrshp & Sprtlty Ntwk S Tim's Epis Ch Mtn View CA 2002-2003; Asst R All SS' Epis Ch Belmont MA 1998-2001. wmessenger@mba1988.hbs.edu

MESSENGER-HARRIS, Beverly Ann (CNY) 124 W Hamilton Ave, Sherrill NY 13461 B Buffalo NY 4/29/1947 d James Henry Messenger & Eleanor Damaris. BA Wm Smith 1972; MDiv Bex 1975. D 6/16/1975 P 1/1/1977 Bp Ned Cole. m 5/21/1976 James Harris. Oneida Area Epis Consortium Oneida NY 1987-1991; St Andrews Epis Ch Rome NY 1986-1987; Int Chr Ch Manlius NY 1985-1986; R Geth Ch Sherrill NY 1984-1991; Int S Geo's Ch Utica NY 1984-1985; Asst Gr Ch Utica NY 1982-1984; R Geth Ch Sherrill NY 1977-1981; In-charge Zion Ch Rome NY 1975-1977. bmessengerharris@aol.com

MESSER, Charles Wilson (Pa) PO Box 452, Glen Riddle PA 19037 **R Calv Ch Glen Riddle PA 2009-** B Lake Wales Fl 1/13/1971 s David Clifton Messer & Gale Peggy. AA Polk Cmnty Coll 1993; BA Trevecca Nazarene U 1997; MDiv Nazarene TS 2001; CAS STUSo 2002. D 6/7/2003 P 12/6/2003 Bp Barry Robert Howe. m 10/7/1995 Kimberly Rae Estep c 1. Assoc The Ch Of The Redeem Baltimore MD 2005-2009; Asst St Mary Magd Epis Ch Belton MO 2003-2004. frbigman@gmail.com

MESSER, Julia Weatherly (SVa) 5181 Princess Anne Rd, Virginia Beach VA 23462 **Emm Ch Virginia Bch VA 2010-** B Columbia SC 12/29/1983 d Jakob Messer & Betsy Willson. BA Mary Baldwin Coll 2006; MDiv VTS 2010. D 6/12/2010 P 12/18/2010 Bp Herman Hollerith IV. assistant@emmanuelvb.org

MESSERSMITH, Daphne Killhour (CPa) 159 S 2nd St, Newport PA 17074 **R Ch of the Nativ-St Steph Newport PA 2005-** B York PA 4/4/1950 d William Gherky Killhour & Josephine Quarrier. BA Washington U 1972; CAS GTS 1994. D 6/12/1981 Bp Dean T Stevenson P 6/18/1994 Bp Charlie Fuller McNutt Jr. m 12/27/2003 Merton E Messersmith c 3. Cn Pstr Cathd Ch Of S Steph Harrisburg PA 2001-2005; R Calv Chap Beartown Blue Ridge Summit PA 1997-2001; R Ch Of The Trsfg Blue Ridge Summit PA 1997-2001; Int S Lk's Ch Lebanon PA 1996-1997; Asst Chaplin The Epis Acad Newtown Sq PA 1991-1993; D Asst S Jn's Epis Ch Lancaster PA 1990-1991; D S Andr's Epis Ch York PA 1981-1983. daphne@pa.net

MESSERSMITH, Merton E (CPa) 909 Alison Ave, Mechanicsburg PA 17055 B Harrisburg PA 4/14/1947 s Herbert J Messersmith & Lois. BA Hob 1969; MDiv PDS 1972. D 5/27/1972 P 4/1/1973 Bp Dean T Stevenson. c 2. R S Lk's Epis Ch Mechanicsburg PA 1998-2008; Dio Cntrl Pennsylvania Harrisburg PA 1984-1998; Chapl Dio Pennsylvania Philadelphia PA 1984-1998; R S Paul's Ch Newport KY 1980-1984; S Paul's Ch Louisville KY 1980-1983; Ch Of The Trsfg Blue Ridge Summit PA 1976-1980. rectorstlk@pa.net

MESSIER, Daniel J (Az) 1275 N. Abrego Dr., Green Valley AZ 85614 **R Epis Ch Of S Fran-In-The-Vlly Green Vlly AZ 2011-** B Claremont NH 10/16/1953 s Victor Messier & Gilberte. BA S Mich's Coll Colchester VT 1975; MA CUA 1978. Rec from Roman Catholic 2/6/1994 as Priest Bp Edward Lloyd Salmon Jr. m 11/24/2006 Phyllis J Osgood c 3. R S Mk's Epis Ch Charleston SC 2002-2011; R S Thos Epis Ch No Charleston SC 1996-2001; Gr Ch Charleston SC 1994-1996. djmessier@comcast.net

MESSINA JR, Michael Frank (CFla) 94 Pecan Run, Ocala FL 34472 **R S Pat's Ch Ocala FL 1996-** B Duluth MN 3/18/1943 s Michael Frank Messina & Ann Marie. AA Duluth Area Vocational 1970; Cert Prchr Lewis Sch Of Mnstry 1984. D 8/5/1987 P 8/24/1988 Bp Richard Mitchell Trelease Jr. m 11/21/1973 Sandra Kay Flyckt c 4. Asstg P S Anne's Ch Crystal River FL 1993-1996; S Anne's Ch Crystal River FL 1992; Vic Ch Of The Adv Dunnellon FL 1990-1992; S Marg's Ch Inverness FL 1989-1990; D Jordana De Fe Rgnl Mnstry Dio The Rio Grande Albuquerque NM 1987-1989. Chapl For Ord Of S Lk. stpatsepis@aol.com

MESTETH, Rhonda (SD) PO Box 855, Pine Ridge SD 57770 B Pine Ridge SD 6/26/1938 d Peter Rouillard & Sophie. MS Black Hill St U. D 6/16/2002 P 10/28/2004 Bp Creighton Leland Robertson. m 6/29/1963 Robert Eugene Mesteth.

MESTRE JR, José Wilfredo (Ct) 2340 North Ave Apt. 7D, Bridgeport CT 06614 B Manati PR 8/1/1951 s Jose W Mestre & Delia. NW Chr Coll Eugene OR 1972; Inter Amer U of Puerto Rico 1978; Fairfield U 1993; Auburn TS 1997; GTS 2006. D 12/9/2000 Bp Andrew Donnan Smith. D Calv St Geo's Epis Ch Bridgeport CT 2007-2010; D S Lk's/S Paul's Ch Bridgeport CT 2003-2007; D Chr Ch Ansonia CT 2003; D Calv Epis Ch Bridgeport CT 2000-2002. Auth, "Poesia (Poems)," *TERTULIA*, Ediciones del Chorro, 1990; Auth, "Una Poeta Sacerdotal," *TERTULIA*, Ediciones del Chorro, 1988; Auth, "Mujer de Vanguardia: Elena Vigo," *TERTULIA*, Ediciones del Chorro, 1987. Deaconjosew@aol.com

METCALF, Michael Patrick (Dal) 1629 Jasmine Ln, Plano TX 75074 B Tulsa OK 3/21/1950 s Frederick Milton Metcalf & Thelma Pearl. BA U Of Dallas Irving 1973; MDiv Nash 1982; MA Amberton U 1998. D 6/26/1982 Bp A Donald Davies P 4/1/1983 Bp Robert Elwin Terwilliger. c 2. R Ch Of The Epiph Richardson TX 1990-2002; S Jn's Epis Ch Corsicana TX 1986-1990; R S Dunst's Ch Mineola TX 1984-1986; Cur The Epis Ch Of The H Nativ Plano TX 1982-1984. Associated Parishes; Assn Sprtl Ethical Rel Values Counslg; NNECA, Dallas Epis Cleric Assn.

METCALFE, Steven Todd (WNY) 20 Milton St, Williamsville NY 14221 B Dayton OH 2/17/1950 s Watson Blake Metcalfe & Janet Mckinney. BA U Cinc 1979; MDiv EDS 1983. D 6/11/1983 P 1/6/1984 Bp William Grant Black. c 1. R Calv Epis Ch Williamsville NY 1993-2010; R The Epis Ch Of The Gd Shpd Buffalo NY 1987-1993; Asst. R Chr Ch - Glendale Cincinnati OH 1983-1987; Epis Soc of Chr Ch Cincinnati OH 1983-1987. stm21@juno.com

METHENY JR, Lloyd Erwin (NCal) 11070 Hirschfeld Way #66, Rancho Cordova CA 95670 B Kimball NE 2/10/1927 s Lloyd Erwin Metheny & Eva. BA U of Nebraska 1950; ThB PDS 1954. D 4/22/1954 P 12/21/1954 Bp Howard R Brinker. Vic S Clem's Ch Rancho Cordova CA 1980-1989; BEC Dio Nebraska Omaha NE 1963-1972; LocTen S Tim's Ch Scottsbluff NE 1961-1962; P-in-c Ch Of The Gd Shpd Bridgeport NE 1955-1959; R Ch Of The H Apos Mitchell NE 1954-1980. Omicron Delta Kappa; Theta Chi.

METHVEN, Susanne B (Okla) 3108 E 51st St Apt 87, Tulsa OK 74105 **Assoc R S Jn's Epis Ch Tulsa OK 2007-** B Halton England 3/5/1957 d Alexander George Methven & Ingeborg Andrea Susanne. BA Hollins U 1978; MBA Harv 1980; MS U of Nevada at Las Vegas 2003; MDiv Epis TS of The SW 2007. D 10/6/2006 Bp Katharine Jefferts Schori P 7/21/2007 Bp Robert Manning Moody. Auth, *If only I had known: avoiding common mistakes in couple Ther*, WWNorton, 2005. sbmethven@hotmail.com

METHVIN, Thomas Gregory (Dal) 3966 McKinney Ave, Dallas TX 75204 **R Ch Of The Incarn Dallas TX 2008-** B Starkville MS 9/6/1965 BA Louisiana Coll 1987; MDiv New Orleans Bapt TS 2003. Trans from L'Eglise Episcopal au Rwanda 11/17/2008 Bp James Monte Stanton. m 9/3/1994 Steffanie Haskins c 2. Min Of Discipleship Chr Epis Ch Plano TX 2004-2006.

METIVIER, Catherine A (Okla) 4708 NW 75th St, Oklahoma City OK 73132 B Tulsa OK 5/17/1954 BS U of Texas 1978; DDS U of Texas 1985; MDiv VTS

2005. D 6/25/2005 P 12/21/2005 Bp Robert Manning Moody. c 2. Vic Dio Oklahoma Oklahoma City OK 2005-2009. CAMetivier@aol.com

METTLER, Garrett Minarik (Los) 15757 Saint Timothy Rd, Apple Valley CA 92307 B Goleta CA 2/17/1975 BS California St Polytechnic U. D 6/22/2002 Bp Richard Lester Shimpfky P 1/11/2003 Bp Joseph Jon Bruno. m 1/10/1998 Rebecca Lynn Starrick c 1. R S Tim's Epis Ch Apple Vlly CA 2005-2011; S Geo's Acad Laguna Hills CA 2002-2004; Assoc S Geo's Epis Ch Laguna Hills CA 2002-2004. GMETTLER@ALUMNI.CALPOLY.EDU

METZ, Susanna (ETenn) 335 Tennessee Ave, Sewanee TN 37383 B Philadelphia PA 5/15/1950 d Albert George Metz & Elizabeth Marie. BA Immaculata U 1972; MA W Chester St Coll 1982; BA Immaculata U 1983; MDiv STUSo 1996; DMin STUSo 2003. D 12/7/1996 P 6/28/1997 Bp Robert Gould Tharp. The TS at The U So Sewanee TN 2001-2011; Cntr For Mnstry In Sm Ch Memphis TN 1998-2001; S Jn The Bapt Sewanee TN 1996-1998. "You Will Lead Me by the Rt Road," *Sewanee Theol Revs*, TS, Sewanee, 2005; Ed, *Tuesday Morning: Mnstry and Liturg Preaching Journ*, TS, Sewanee. smetz@sewanee.edu

METZGER, Carl Edgar (Pa) 100 E Lehigh Ave, Philadelphia PA 19125 B Lavelle PA 8/28/1939 s Othneil Carl Metzger & Dorothy Louise. BA U Pgh 1961; MA Villanova U 1984. D 6/11/1983 P 12/1/1986 Bp Lyman Cunningham Ogilby. c 1. S Alb's Ch Roxborough Philadelphia PA 1995-2005; Epis Hosp Philadelphia PA 1987-2000; Vic S Lk's Ch Philadelphia PA 1986-1987; The Ch Of The H Trin Rittenhouse Philadelphia PA 1983-1987. carl@gkmetzger.com

METZGER, Curtis (NH) PO Box 1541, Concord NH 03302 **R S Steph's Ch Pittsfield NH 2006-** B 10/21/1957 s J Hayes Metzger & Katherine. Bachelor of Arts U of New Hampshire 1983; Mstr of Div Trin, Univ. of Toronto 1986. Trans from Anglican Church of Canada 1/17/2007 Bp V Gene Robinson. curtismetzger@yahoo.com

METZGER, James Poore (Mo) 3402 Sawgrass Ln, Cincinnati OH 45209 B Cincinnati OH 7/28/1934 s Ralph Dennis Metzger & Katharine. BA Ohio Wesl 1956; MA VTS 1963; Fllshp Coll of Preachers 1971; Amer. Assoc. of MFT U.Cincinnati, Dept of Psych, Fam. Ther Inst. 1983; MO18 Lic Marr.& Fam. Ther 2005. D 6/15/1963 P 12/1/1963 Bp Roger W Blanchard. m 8/26/1961 Hope H Hainer c 3. R S Ptr's Epis Ch St Louis MO 1989-1997; R Indn Hill Ch Cincinnati OH 1973-1989; R Ch Of The Incarn Penfield NY 1966-1973; Asst Ch Of S Edw Columbus OH 1963-1965. City of Cincinnati, Comm. Problem Oriented Policing Cincinnati and Comm. Prob. Oriented Policing CPOP 2005; ,Fell Coll of Preachers 1971. revjmetz@aol.com

METZGER, Mary Jean Birmingham (NJ) No address on file. **Pstr Assoc Trin Ch Princeton NJ 1998-** B Beverly MA 4/15/1929 d John Carney Birmingham & Grace Margaret. MDiv PrTS; ThM PrTS; BA Emerson Coll 1950; MA USC 1950; CAS GTS 1998. D 5/9/1998 P 12/1/1998 Bp Joe Morris Doss. m 10/29/1955 Howard Martin Metzger. AEHC.

METZLER, Carolyn Walburn (Me) 5 Old Hatchery Rd # 4493, West Enfield ME 04493 B Chicago IL 10/5/1955 BA Hope Coll. D 6/14/2003 P 3/13/2004 Bp Chilton Abbie Richardson Knudsen. m 6/2/1984 Eric Metzler c 2. Dio Maine Portland ME 2004-2009. Honorable Mention Polly Bond Awd For Cmncatn 2003. ewmetzler@yahoo.com

METZLER, Martha Grace (Nwk) 40 E 94th St Apt 6A, New York NY 10128 **P-in-c Ch Of The H Innoc W Orange NJ 2010-; S Jas Ch New York NY 2010-** B Monroe LA 5/20/1950 d George Martin Sallwasser & Eleanor Jean. MDiv Bex 1984. D 6/23/1984 P 5/31/1985 Bp O'Kelley Whitaker. m 7/15/1977 Paul Arthur Metzler c 2. Assoc R of Pstr Care and Mew Mem Incorporati S Jas Ch New York NY 2005-2010; Cn S Paul's Cathd Syracuse NY 1991-2003; Syracuse Area Interreligious Coun Syracuse NY 1988-1991; Assoc R Gr Ch Baldwinsville NY 1985-1987; Int S Mk's Ch Clark Mills NY 1984-1985; Paris Cluster Chadwicks NY 1984. m.metzler.chi@gmail.com

METZLER, Paul Arthur (CNY) 40 E 94th Street, Apartment 6A, New York NY 10128 **Assoc Ch Of The Trsfg New York NY 2007-** B Brooklyn NY 11/15/1944 s Arthur Albert Metzler & Edna Irma. AA Concordia Jr Coll 1964; BA Concordia Sr Coll 1966; MDiv Concordia TS 1970; STM Concordia TS 1971; DMin Concordia TS 1992; Dio Angl Stds 1995. D 6/17/1995 P 5/16/1996 Bp David B(ruce) Joslin. m 7/15/1977 Martha Grace Sallwasser c 2. Cathd Precentor S Paul's Cathd Syracuse NY 1996-1999. AAPC; Assn for Death Educ & Counslg; Clincl Mem AAMFT; Coun of Hospice Professionals. pmetzler@twcny.rr.com

MEUSCHKE, Marty O (Ga) 145 River Ridge Loop, Hortense GA 31543 B Washington DC 2/23/1945 s Jack L Meuschke & Verda Jean. D 4/24/2007 Bp Henry Irving Louttit. m 5/13/1973 Paula Ahrens c 2. martymeuschke@gmail.com

MEYER, Alan King (Az) 5909 SW Karla Ct, Portland OR 97239 B San Francisco CA 1/4/1952 s Donald Duncan Meyer & Eleanor King. BA U of Arizona 1979; U of Arizona 1979; MDiv CDSP 1983. D 6/11/1983 P 11/1/1984 Bp Joseph Thomas Heistand. m 12/29/1977 Ann Meyer. S Jn's Epis Ch Bisbee AZ 1985-1988; S Paul's Ch Tombstone AZ 1985-1988; Assoc R S Paul's Epis Ch Salem OR 1983-1984. ACPE. Phi Alpha Theta 1972; Www Vigil Ord Of Teh Arrow 1972; Alpha Phi Omega B.S.A. 1970. m2ga@msn.com

MEYER, Erika K (NY) 240 E. 31st St., New York NY 10016 **Ch Of The Gd Shpd New York NY 2009-** B New York NY 11/19/1963 d John Paul Meyer & Kathleen Ardath. BA U MI 1988; MDiv CDSP 1994. D 6/18/1994 P 2/1/1995 Bp R(aymond) Stewart Wood Jr. c 1. S Barn Of The Vlly Cortez CO 2002-2009; Int Gr Ch Waterford NY 2000-2001; Dio Utah Salt Lake City UT 1996-1998; Assoc Thumb Epis Area Mnstry Dio Estrn Michigan Saginaw MI 1994-1995; Thumb Epis Area Mnstry Deford MI 1994-1995. erikakmeyer@cs.com

MEYER, John A (LI) 423 Falcon Ridge Drive, Sheridan WY 82801 **Int S Ptr's Epis Ch Sheridan WY 2010-** B Brooklyn NY 6/5/1939 s John Edward Meyer & Mildred. Mercer TS 1978. D 6/23/1979 P 12/22/1980 Bp Robert Campbell Witcher Sr. m 8/26/1962 Deanne Keys c 4. Asst S Ptr's Epis Ch Sheridan WY 2003-2010; Int S Lk's Epis Ch Buffalo WY 2002-2003; R S Marg's Ch Plainview NY 1982-2002; Cur H Trin Epis Ch Vlly Stream NY 1979-1982. jdmeyer@brebnan.net

MEYER, John Paul (Mich) 1353 Labrosse St, Detroit MI 48226 B Minneapolis MN 12/17/1935 s Ernest Emerius Meyer & Ellen Amelia. BA U MN 1957; BD UTS 1960; GTS 1962. D 11/9/1960 P 5/1/1961 Bp Horace W B Donegan. m 6/25/1960 Kathleen Ardath Bowlin c 1. S Ptr's Ch Detroit MI 1981-2002; Ch Of The Mssh Detroit MI 1978-1979; R S Anne's In The Field Madison OH 1972-1977; R Trin Ashtabula OH 1972-1977; Asst S Paul's/Trin Chap Alton IL 1964-1967; Asst All SS Ch Brooklyn NY 1962-1964; Cur S Ptr's Epis Ch Lakewood OH 1960-1962. jmeyer@provide.net

MEYER, Mark David (Colo) 1118 Barr Ave, Canon City CO 81212 **R Chr Ch Cn City CO 1998-** B Elmhurst IL 1/28/1954 s Morgan Marion Meyer & Carol Ruth. BA Colorado Coll 1976; MDiv Epis TS of The SW 1979. D 11/30/1979 P 5/30/1980 Bp William Carl Frey. Gr Epis Ch Blair NE 1992-1998; R S Mary's Epis Ch Blair NE 1992-1998; S Mk's Epis Ch Plainview TX 1983-1992; Cur S Jos's Ch Lakewood CO 1980-1983; Cur Epiph Epis Ch Denver CO 1979-1980. markdmeyer@msn.com

MEYER, Nancy Ruth (Chi) St Peter's Episcopal Church, 621 W Belmont Ave, Chicago IL 60657 **D S Ptr's Epis Ch Chicago IL 2008-** B Elmhurst IL 5/11/1946 d Walter William Meyer & Ruth Maude. BSN U of Washington 1970; MSN Wayne 1979; Dioc Sch for D Formation & Trng, Chicago, IL 2007. D 1/19/2008 Bp Victor Alfonso Scantlebury. nrmeyer@ameritech.net

MEYER, Richard Joseph (Ore) 326 Se Davis St, Mcminnville OR 97128 **S Barn Par McMinnville OR 1999-** B Portland OR 7/2/1947 D 10/2/1999 Bp Robert Louis Ladehoff. m 4/22/1970 Susan Margaret Meyer c 4. richard.meyer1@comcast.net

MEYER, Robert Bruce (FdL) PO Box 184, Tremont IL 61568 **Cn S Paul's Cathd Peoria IL 2001-** B Toledo OH 3/2/1935 s Walter Dimsdale Meyer & Vera. BA Ob 1957; PhD Duke 1961; STB GTS 1971. D 4/16/1971 P 10/15/1971 Bp Francis W Lickfield. m 2/3/1962 Robin Witwer c 2. Vic Ch Of The H Nativ Jacksonport Sturgeon Bay WI 1989-1995; Dio Fond du Lac Appleton WI 1989-1995; Vic S Epis Olaf's Ch Amherst WI 1984-1989; R S Mk's Ch Waupaca WI 1984-1989; Liturg Cmsn Dio Fond du Lac Appleton WI 1984-1985; Vic Chr Ch Lexington MO 1981-1984; Dio W Missouri Kansas City MO 1981-1984; Dio Quincy Peoria IL 1971-1981; S Jas Epis Ch Lewistown IL 1971-1981; S Ptr's Ch Peoria IL 1971-1974. Cn Honoris Causis Cathd Ch of S Paul (Dio Quincy)/Peoria Springfield IL 2001; Bp's Awd of Ord S Paul Dio Quincy Peoria IL 1978; Phi Beta Kappa Duke 1961; Sigma Xi Duke 1960; Phi Lambda Upsilon Duke 1959. frrbmeyer@comcast.net

MEYER, Wendel William (Mass) 24 Masconomo St, Manchester MA 01944 B Evanston IL 5/5/1949 s Wendel Noell Meyer & Marion. BA U So 1971; MDiv GTS 1978; STM GTS 1980; PhD U of Cambridge 1986. D 6/18/1978 Bp William Evan Sanders P 5/27/1979 Bp Robert Bracewell Appleyard. m 1/1/1995 Ann W Wevling c 2. R S Jn's Ch Beverly Farms MA 1999-2009; R S Ptr's Ch Philadelphia PA 1989-1997; Cn S Paul's Cathd Buffalo NY 1986-1989; Cur Chr Ch New Haven CT 1979-1982. Auth, *Var arts*. wmeyer@maine.rr.com

MEYERS, David Craig (WMich) Church Of The Holy Spirit, 1200 Post Dr NE, Belmont MI 49306 **Vic Ch of the H Sprt Belmont MI 2008-** B Muskegon MI 6/4/1953 s Eugene James Meyers & Arlene Helen. BA MI SU 1976; MA MI SU 1977; MA U Of Detroit 1979; EdD Wstrn Michigan U 2001. D 5/3/1986 Bp Howard Samuel Meeks P 1/22/2011 Bp Robert R Gepert. m 10/7/1978 Merry Kim Brand c 2. D S Jn the Apos Epis Ch Ionia MI 2008-2009; D S Paul's Ch Greenville MI 1986-2008. MEYERS_DAVID@SBCGLOBAL.NET

MEYERS, Frederick W (Rick) (Colo) 420 Cantril St, Castle Rock CO 80104 **R Chr's Epis Ch Castle Rock CO 1991-** B Sturgis MI 9/30/1946 s Ralph Charles Meyers & Coral May. BA MI SU 1970; MA MI SU 1970; MDiv Iliff TS 1978; STM Nash 1980; DMin GTF 1991. D 6/29/1979 P 5/28/1980 Bp William Carl Frey. m 12/23/1966 Rita K Werner c 2. Exec Coun Dio Colorado Denver CO 1992-1996; Asst S Barn Epis Ch Denver CO 1990-1991; Asst S Thos Epis Ch Denver CO 1988-1989; EDEO Dio Colorado Denver CO

1984-1987; Vic S Matt's Parker CO 1980-1988; Asst Chapl Ch Of S Jn Chrys Delafield WI 1979-1980. meyerheim@msn.com

MEYERS, Michael William (Az) 300 N Constitution Dr, Tucson AZ 85748 B 5/10/1943 D 10/5/2002 Bp Robert Reed Shahan. m 9/27/1966 Patricia Lane c 2.

MEYERS, Ruth (Chi) Church Divinity School Of The Pacific, 2451 Ridge Rd, Berkeley CA 94709 **Hodges-Haynes Prof of Liturg CDSP Berkeley CA 2009-** B Passaic NJ 1/1/1957 d Richard Thomas Meyers & Dorothy Elizabeth. Cardinal Stritch U; BS Syr 1977; MDiv SWTS 1985; MA U of Notre Dame 1989; PhD U of Notre Dame 1992. D 6/5/1985 Bp Otis Charles P 4/13/1986 Bp William Gillette Weinhauer. m 6/10/1989 Daniel L Britton c 1. GC Dep Dio Chicago Chicago IL 2006-2009; Adj Fac SWTS Evanston IL 1995-2009; Int Trin Epis Ch Marshall MI 1993; Rep Of Prov V Syn Dio Wstrn Michigan Kalamazoo MI 1992-1995; Dio Wstrn Michigan Kalamazoo MI 1992-1994; Dioc Liturg Dio Wstrn Michigan Kalamazoo MI 1991-1998; Pstr Care Com Dio Wstrn Michigan Kalamazoo MI 1991-1995; Consulting Team Dio Wstrn Michigan Kalamazoo MI 1990-1991; Int S Paul's Epis Ch S Jos MI 1987-1988; Asst R Ch Of The Ascen Hickory NC 1985-1986. Auth, "Steph, D and Mtyr; Nativ of Jn the Bapt; Thos, Apos; Mary Magd, Apos; Barth, Apost," *New Proclamation Commentary on Feasts, H Days, and Other Celebrations*, Fortress, 2007; Auth, "Fresh Thoughts on Cnfrmtn," *ATR*, 2006; Auth, "Rites of Initiation," *The Oxford Guide to BCP Worldwide*, Oxf Press, 2006; Auth, "The Promise and Perils of Liturg Change," *ATR*, 2004; Auth, "Baptism 4: Angl; Baptismal Vows, Renwl of; Ord of Wmn," *New Westminster Dictionary of Liturg and Wrshp*, Westminster Jn Knox, 2002; Auth, "Journeys of Faith," *The Conviction of Things Not Seen*, Brazos Press, 2002; Ed and Contrib, "Gleanings: Essays on Expansive Lang w Prayers for Var Occasions," Ch Pub, 2001; Auth, "The Gift of Authority: New Steps in Angl/RC Relatns," *Ecum Trends*, 2001; Auth, "By Water and the H Sprt: Baptism and Cnfrmtn in Anglicanism," *Engaging the Sprt*, Ch Pub, 2001; Auth, "Cont the Reformation," Ch Pub, 1997; Ed, "A PB for the 21st Century," Ch Hymnal, 1996; Ed and Contrib, "Chld at the Table," Ch Hymnal, 1995; Ed, "Baptism and Mnstry," Ch Hymnal, 1994; Ed and Contrib, "How Shall We Pray?," Ch Hymnal, 1994. Associated Parishes Coun 1996. rmeyers@cdsp.edu

MEZACAPA, Nicklas A (Minn) 111 3rd Ave SW, Rochester MN 55902 **R Calv Ch Rochester MN 1986-** B Cleveland OH 2/5/1949 s Anthony John Mezacapa & Helen. BA Heidelberg Coll 1971; MDiv Bex 1981. D 6/27/1981 Bp John Harris Burt P 1/3/1982 Bp Charles Bennison. m 7/25/1970 Edna Suzanne Tremayne c 2. R S Johns Ch Cedar Rapids IA 1984-1986; Asst S Lk's Par Kalamazoo MI 1981-1984. Auth, *A10 Spprt Grp*; Auth, *Angl Dig*; Auth, *Living Ch*. father-nick@calvary-rochester.org

M

MICHAEL, Mark Aaron (Alb) 69 Fair St., Cooperstown NY 13326 **R Chr Ch Cooperstown NY 2009-** B Hagerstown MD 6/19/1978 s Dennis Mark Michael & Jo Anne. BA Duke 2000; BTh Oxf 2003. D 4/8/2006 Bp John Leslie Rabb P 10/14/2006 Bp Robert Wilkes Ihloff. m 7/2/2005 Allison Joy Zbicz. R S Paul's Ch Sharpsburg MD 2007-2009; Asst Chapl S Jas Sch St Jas MD 2006-2009. CBS 2003; SocMary 2003. frmamichael@gmail.com

MICHAELS, Glen Francis (Alb) Po Box 242, Essex NY 12936 **P Assoc, Vol Trin Ch Plattsburgh NY 2004-** B Chicago IL 8/8/1955 s Russell Norton Merbach & Elaine Helen. U Chi 1974; BA CUA 1978; JD Ya 1982; MDiv CDSP 1992. D 12/5/1992 P 12/1/1993 Bp William Edwin Swing. m 7/9/1994 Lorelei Rodgers c 3. R S Jn's Ch Essex NY 1996-2000; R Ch Of The Gd Shpd Houlton ME 1994-1996; D S Paul's Ch Oakland CA 1993. glen.michaels@ecunet.org

MICHAELS, Laurie Jane (Chi) 647 Dundee Ave, Barrington IL 60010 **Bp Anderson Hse Chicago IL 2010-; D S Mich's Ch Barrington IL 2010-** B Detroit MI 4/26/1953 d Waldo I Parks & Margaret Kucher. BS Geo 1974; AD HLTH Mgmnt St. Marys Coll 1979; AD Nrsng St. Mary's Coll 1981; Nat'l U Grad Sch Nurse Prog 1996; Dio Chicago Deacons Sch 2009. D 2/6/2010 Bp Jeffrey Dean Lee. m 8/17/1974 Gregory H Michaels c 2. travelaurie@hotmail.com

MICHAELSON, Peter (RI) 2 Gaspee Point Dr, Warwick RI 02888 B Milwaukee WI 7/16/1942 s Stanley Day Michaelson & Elizabeth. Diplomate Defense Languate Inst 1962; BA cl U of Utah 1967; BD EDS 1970; DMin SWTS 1998. D 6/24/1970 Bp Richard S Watson P 3/1/1971 Bp Lyman Cunningham Ogilby. m 9/3/1965 Wanda Stine c 2. Int S Mk's Ch Warwick RI 2008-2009; Ecum Off Dio Rhode Island Providence RI 1995-2000; R St Mich & Gr Ch Rumford RI 1993-2000; Stff to Bp of Idaho Dio Idaho Boise ID 1992-1993; Ecum Off Dio Idaho Boise ID 1986-1993; Prog Dir of Yth Camps Dio Idaho Boise ID 1985-1988; Dioc Coun Dio Idaho Boise ID 1983-1986; Prog Dir of Yth Camps Dio Idaho Boise ID 1979-1982; Vic Ch Of H Nativ Meridian ID 1978-1992; Assoc S Andr's Ch Framingham MA 1970-1978. Auth, "Settling the Homeless," *Living Ch*; Auth, "Conflict in the Ch," *Living Ch*. Cler Assn. of RI - Epis 2006; EPF 1968; OSL 1976; Urban Caucus 1976-1995. peter.michaelson@ecunet.org

MICHAUD, Bruce Alan (EMich) 2090 Wyndham Ln, Alpena MI 49707 **Pres of Stndg Com Dio Estrn Michigan Saginaw MI 2010-; R Trin Epis Ch Alpena MI 2002-** B Alpena MI 12/27/1947 s Gene E Michaud & Betty E. BA MI SU 1969; MDiv VTS 1972. D 6/26/1972 Bp Richard S M Emrich P 9/20/1973 Bp H Coleman McGehee Jr. m 10/11/2002 Margaret L Michaud c 2. R S Paul's Ch Louisville KY 1985-2002; R S Albans Epis Ch Bay City MI 1981-1985; R S Andr's Epis Ch Algonac MI 1974-1981; Asst Gr Epis Ch Port Huron MI 1972-1974. Gospel & Our Culture Ntwk 1990. bruce_michaud@charter.net

MICHAUD, David Norman (Eas) St Andrews Church, 30513 Washington St, Princess Anne MD 21853 **R S Andr's Epis Ch Princess Anne MD 2007-** B Lynn MA 5/24/1963 s Norman Henry Michaud & Patricia Ann. ABS U CA 1985; MDiv GTS 2007. D 6/2/2007 P 12/21/2007 Bp James Joseph Shand. m 6/13/1987 Kelli Lankford c 2. davidmichaud07@gmail.com

MICHAUD, Eleanor Jean (Eau) 6059 167th St, Chippewa Falls WI 54729 B Chicago IL 1/10/1939 D 2/19/2005 P 8/20/2005 Bp Keith Bernard Whitmore. m 11/14/1970 Ronald Michaud c 2. ronmichaud@att.net

MICHAUD, Jean Fruitho (Hai) c/o Diocese of Haiti, Boite Postale 1309 Haiti **Dio Haiti Ft Lauderdale FL 2008-** B 6/6/1976 s Michaud Elie Fruitho. D 1/25/2006 P 2/18/2007 Bp Jean Zache Duracin. michaudfruitho@yahoo.fr

✠ MICHEL, Rt Rev Rodney Rae (LI) 1 Christian St Apt 36, Philadelphia PA 19147 **Ret Bp Suffr of Long Island Dio Long Island Garden City NY 2007-** B Petersburg NE 2/7/1943 s Marion R Michel & Phyllis Y. Nebraska Wesl 1963; BS U of Nebraska 1965; BD SWTS 1970. D 6/21/1970 P 12/1/1970 Bp Russell T Rauscher Con 4/12/1997 for LI. Dio Pennsylvania Philadelphia PA 2009-2011; Suffr Bp of Long Island Dio Long Island Garden City NY 1997-2007; R, Chair, Stndg Com S Ptr's by-the-Sea Epis Ch Bay Shore NY 1991-1997; Cn Pstr Cathd Of The Incarn Garden City NY 1987-1991; R S Paul's Epis Ch Grand Forks ND 1982-1987; Chair, COM Dio Nebraska Omaha NE 1979-1981; R S Fran Epis Ch Scottsbluff NE 1972-1982; Mem, COM, Stndg Com Dio Nebraska Omaha NE 1972-1979; Vic S Mk's Ch Gordon NE 1970-1972; Vic S Mary's Ch: Holly Rushville NE 1970-1972. Epis Visitor: Bro of S Greg 1997; Ord of S Lk 1975; SHN 1995; SocMary 1970. DD SWTS Evanston IL. rodmitre@aol.com

MICHELFELDER, Susan Rebecca (SO) 2301 Hoyt Ave, Everett WA 98201 **Int Chr Ch Middletown NJ 2010-** B Toledo OH 9/1/1951 d George Frederick Michelfelder & Dorothy Maxine. BA Capital U 1980; MA Luth TS at Chicago 1987; MDiv CDSP 1999. D 6/19/1999 Bp Kenneth Lester Price P 3/25/2000 Bp Clarence Wallace Hayes. P-in-c Trin Epis Ch Everett WA 2009-2010; P-in-c Ch Of The Epiph Seattle WA 2008-2009; Int S Ptr's Epis Ch Delaware OH 2005-2007; R S Ptr's Ch Gallipolis OH 2001-2005; R Dio Panama 1999-2001; D Dio Sthrn Ohio Cincinnati OH 1999. Associated Parishes. srmohsrm@mac.com

MICHELL, Neal Michell (Dal) 1630 N Garrett Ave, Dallas TX 75206 **Cn Dio Dallas Dallas TX 2008-; Cn to the Ordnry Dio Dallas Dallas TX 2001-** B Dallas TX 2/16/1953 s James Eldon Michell & Jimmie Lorene. BA U of Texas 1976; JD U of Houston 1979; MDiv STUSo 1986; DMin Fuller TS 2003. D 6/13/1986 Bp Stanley Fillmore Hauser P 12/13/1986 Bp John Herbert MacNaughton. m 8/5/1978 Varita Bean c 4. S Lk's Epis Ch Dallas TX 2007-2008; R S Jn's Ch New Braunfels TX 1998-2001; Ch Of The Redeem Memphis TN 1992-1998; R S Tim's Ch Indianapolis IN 1992-1998; R S Barn Epis Ch Fredericksburg TX 1988-1991; R H Trin Carrizo Sprg TX 1986-1988; Vic S Tim's Ch Cotulla TX 1986-1988. Auth, "Happy Talk," *LivCh*, 2008; Auth, "Beyond Bus as Usual: Vstry Ldrshp Dvlpmt," Ch Pub, 2007; Auth, "We Should Submit," *LivCh*, 2006; Auth, "How to Hit the Ground Running: A Quick Start Guide to Congregations w New Ldrshp," Ch Pub, 2005; Auth, "The Ntwk--An Ancient Pract Revisited," *LivCh*, 2004; Auth, "Congrl Development According to Yogi," *LivCh*, 2003; Auth, "Relating to a Postmodern Generation," *LivCh*, 2001; Auth, "Beyond the Four Sprtl Laws," *Journ of Frgn Missions*, 1999; Auth, "Things I Didn't Learn in Sem," *LivCh*, 1997; Auth, "Psalms, Hymns, & Sprtl Songs," *Acts 29*, 1991. Ord of S Lk. Who's Who Among Executives SE Executives Ass'n 1997; Dwight Gk Medal U So, Sch of Theol 1986. nmichell@edod.org

MICHELS, Sandra B (Ind) 1525 Mulberry St, Zionsville IN 46077 B San Bernardino CA 10/17/1945 d Raymond Eugene Michels & Donna. BA CUNY 1969; MDiv GTS 1975. D 6/26/1975 Bp A Donald Davies P 4/25/1977 Bp Richard Mitchell Trelease Jr. Asst S Jn's Ch New York NY 2009-2011; S Fran In The Fields Zionsville IN 1986-2009; Assoc S Mart's Ch Ellisville MO 1979-1986; Dio The Rio Grande Albuquerque NM 1978-1979; S Clem's Epis Par Sch El Paso TX 1975-1978. sbmichels@aol.com

MICHIE, Michael Williams (Dal) 8701 Tiercels Dr, Mckinney TX 75070 **St Andrews Ch McKinney TX 2008-** B Mineral Wells TX 9/18/1968 s Joe Allen Michie & Juliana. BA U of Texas 1990; MPA SW Texas St U San Marcos 1992; MA Oral Roberts U 1993; CTh Epis TS of The SW 1998. D 11/1/1999 P 11/2/2000 Bp Claude Edward Payne. m 8/10/1991 Laurie L Carter c 3. Dio Dallas Dallas TX 2004-2007; Chr The King Ch Houston TX 2003; S Barn Ch Austin TX 2000-2002; Asst R S Richard's Of Round Rock Round Rock TX 1999-2000. revmichie@tx.rr.com

MICHNO, Dennis Glen (Eau) 34615 County Highway J, Bayfield WI 54814 **P in charge Chr Ch Bayfield WI 1996-** B Chicago IL 5/15/1947 s Thaddeus Frank Michno & Jeanne Geneveve. BS St. Johns U, Collegeville 1969; Juilliard Sch 1971; MDiv GTS 1977; STM GTS 1983. D 5/19/1977 P 11/19/1977 Bp Harold Louis Wright. R Trin Epis Ch Stoughton MA 1991-1995; Asst The Ch Of The H Sprt Orleans MA 1988-1991; Asst S Dav's Epis Ch So Yarmouth MA 1987-1988; Cathd Of St Jn The Div New York NY 1979-1981; Cur All SS Ch New York NY 1977-1984. Auth, *A P's Handbook*, 1983; Auth, *A Manual for Acolytes*, 1981. Assn of Angl Mus; CHS. Bp's Cross Paul Moore, New York 1981. dennis@ncis.net

MICKELSON, Margaret Belle (Ak) PO Box 849, Cordova AK 99574 **S Geo's Ch Cordova AK 2009-** B Lima OH 12/4/1947 d George A Heffner & Mary Jane Steiner. BA Mia 1970; MS U MI 1972; MDiv CDSP 2007. D 12/4/2006 P 6/12/2007 Bp Mark Lawrence Mac Donald. c 1. bellemickelson@gmail.com

MIDDLETON IV, A(rthur) Pierce (WMass) 7200 3rd Ave, Sykesville MD 21784 **Died 10/18/2009** B Berwyn MD 1/4/1916 s Arthur Middleton & Pamela M. MA U of Edinburgh GB 1937; MA Harv 1938; PhD Harv 1947. D 1/6/1949 Bp William A Brown P 12/23/1951 Bp George P Gunn. c 5. Auth, *Angl Maryland*, The Downing Co, 1992; Auth, *New Wine in Old Skins*, 1988; Auth, *Amiable Dwellings: The Epis Ch of W MA*, 1976. Angl Soc 1953; Chapl for The Ord of S Jn 1991; HSEC 1978. Chapl Ord Ord of S Jn of Jerusalem (a British Royal Ord) 1991. apmiddleton@comcast.net

MIDDLETON, Elizabeth Blackford (WNY) 1302 Devonshire Way, Palm Beach Gardens FL 33418 B Brooklyn NY 7/11/1925 d Benjamin Blackford & Elizabeth C. BS Col 1948; RN Presb Hosp 1948; MA U CO 1968. D 6/11/1988 Bp David Charles Bowman. m 9/25/1948 Elliot Middleton c 4. Dio Wstrn New York Tonawanda NY 1988-1999; D Dio Wstrn New York Tonawanda NY 1988-1999.

MIDDLETON, Mark Leslie (Chi) 3238 Park Pl, Evanston IL 60201 **Supply P Ch Of The Gd Shpd Momence IL 2008-; Vic St Cyprians Ch Chicago IL 2000-** B Champaign IL 6/2/1949 s Glenn Robert Middleton & Lois Virginia. BA NWU 1972; MDiv SWTS 1976; MBA U Chi 1981. D 5/8/1976 Bp Quintin Ebenezer Primo Jr P 11/1/1976 Bp James Winchester Montgomery. Ch Of The H Apos Wauconda IL 1978-1980; Vic St Philips Epis Ch Waukesha WI 1978-1980; The Ch Of S Jn The Evang Flossmoor IL 1976-1978. Natl Assn For The Self- Supporting Active Mnstry. H B Whipple Schlr 76; Anderson Schlr; Kramer Prize Theol 75 SWTS. ZMLM07@YAHOO.COM

MIDDLETON III, Richard Temple (Miss) 944 Royal Oak Dr, Jackson MS 39209 **R S Mk's Ch Jackson MS 2003-** B Jackson MS 1/17/1942 s Richard Temple Middleton & Johnie. BS Linc 1963; Med Linc 1965; EdD U of Sthrn Mississippi 1972; Fell in Res. TS 1993. D 7/3/1993 Bp Duncan Montgomery Gray Jr P 2/27/1994 Bp Alfred Clark Marble Jr. m 8/10/1968 Brenda Marie Wolfe c 2. Vic S Mary's Ch Vicksburg MS 1993-2003. Auth, "Afr Americans & Dry Bones," *The Boule Journ*, 2008; Auth, "Stop The Foolishness, Hit The Books," *Close Up mag*, 1999; Auth, "Remember These Things," *The Boule Journ*, Sigma Pi Phi Fraternity, 1998; Auth, "A Recent Miss. Crt Decision Affects Educ & Wmn Rts," *Negro Educational Revs*, 1979. Exec Coun Epis Ch 1988. rtmiii@aol.com

MIDDLETON, Tracie Gail (Tex) 700 E. Ash Ln., Apt. 13304, Euless TX 76039 B Dallas TX 3/15/1976 d Russel Brian Middleton & Virginia Stegman. BA Austin Coll 1998; Iona Sch for Mnstry, Dio Texas 2009; MA Lamar U 2011. D 2/22/2009 Bp Don Adger Wimberly. D S Jn's Epis Ch Silsbee TX 2009-2011. tracie.g.middleton@gmail.com

MIDENCE VALDES, Jose Francisco (Hond) Comercio, Tela Honduras **Dio Honduras Miami FL 1989-** B Tegucigalpa DC HN 9/15/1965 s Alfonso Midence Aguilar & Alba Adela. Santa Maria Sem 1989. D 1/6/1989 Bp Leopold Frade. m 2/6/2004 Veronica Pereira-Lara c 5. jfmiden@yahoo.com

MIDWOOD JR, John Earle (Pa) 300 North Lawrence, Philadelphia PA 19106 **Epis Cmnty Serv Philadelphia PA 2000-** B Trenton NJ 9/21/1946 s John Earle Midwood & Isabel. BS Tem 1971; MDiv EDS 1974; DMin SWTS 2000. D 6/15/1974 P 1/31/1975 Bp Lyman Cunningham Ogilby. m 9/12/1969 Faith Ann Bustard c 1. Archd Dio Pennsylvania Philadelphia PA 1989-2000; Ch Of S Jn The Evang Philadelphia PA 1984-1989; Asst Chr Ch Philadelphia Philadelphia PA 1978-1984. johnmi@ecs1870.org

MIDYETTE III, Charles Thomas (EC) 401 E 4th St, Greenville NC 27858 B 11/28/1940 s Charles Thomas Midyette & Margert. LLD S Paul's Coll Lawrenceville VA; BA U So 1963; BD VTS 1966; DD VTS 2003. D 6/29/1966 P 1/6/1967 Bp Thomas H Wright. m 11/23/1979 Margaret Herrman c 1. R S Paul's Epis Ch Greenville NC 1994-2004; R S Phil's Ch Durham NC 1978-1994; R S Paul's Ch Beaufort NC 1971-1978; R S Paul's Epis Ch Clinton NC 1968-1971; Asst S Steph's Ch Goldsboro NC 1966-1968. Auth, "Sermons From S Phil'S: Selections 1912-1994," 2001; Auth, "Hunger Notes"; Auth, "Jub". tmidyette@earthlink.net

MIDZALKOWSKI, Sarah Frances (Mich) 765 Grove Street, East Lansing MI 48823 **Cbury MI SU E Lansing MI 2007-; Trin Ch Fredericksburg VA 2004-** B Gainesville Florida 12/20/1970 d Joseph Harold Midzalkowski & Sally Ann. BA U of Florida 1992; MDiv VTS 2004. D 3/13/2004 P 9/18/2004 Bp Mark Sean Sisk. smgogator@gmail.com

MIEDKE, Warren Giles (Tex) 13131 Fry Rd, Cypress TX 77433 **D S Aid's Ch Cypress TX 2011-** B Algona IA 12/31/1938 s Ralph Miedke & Mary. Iona Sch. D 6/18/2011 Bp C(harles) Andrew Doyle. m 6/25/1960 Marilyn J Miedke c 2. WGMMJM@SBCGLOBAL.NET

MIESCHER III, Walter Henry (Kan) 2630 N Ridgewood Ct, Wichita KS 67220 **D S Barth's Ch Wichita KS 1999-** B Portland OR 10/8/1945 s Walter Miescher & Francis. BS Nthrn Arizona U 1976; EFM STUSo 1989; Kansas Sch of Mnstry 1999. D 10/6/1999 Bp William Edward Smalley. m 7/21/1990 Cheryl Lee Gunter c 2. NAAD. wtim9999999@sbcglobal.net

MIHALYI, David Richard (CNY) 472 Washington St, Geneva NY 14456 **R S Paul's Ch Waterloo NY 1981-** B Lowville NY 6/7/1950 s Charles Richard Mihalyi & Helen Marie. BS SUNY 1972; MDiv CRDS 1977. D 9/17/1977 P 6/17/1979 Bp Ned Cole. m 12/10/2001 Marylee Burnell. Dio Cntrl New York Syracuse NY 1989-1991; Vic Gr Ch Willowdale Geneva NY 1982-1985; Assoc All SS Angl Ch Rochester NY 1979-1980. episcopalchurch@rochester.rr.com

MIKAYA, Henry C (WMich) Box 1315, Gabrone Botswana B Kasunqu MW 11/11/1940 s Henock Mikaya & Doris. Cert S Cyp Theol Coll 1970; S Jn Sem 1971; Cert Coll Ascen 1975; MBA Mecy Coll 1983; MDiv Drew U 1992; MA Trin 1994. Trans 9/1/1990 Bp John Shelby Spong. m 11/26/1966 Mary Veronica Kalonga. Exec Coun Appointees New York NY 1999-2002; H Trin Epis Ch Wyoming MI 1996-1999; R Epis Ch Of SS Jn Paul And S Clem Mt Vernon NY 1992-1996; Chr Epis Ch E Orange NJ 1990-1991. Newark Cler Assn. holytrinity@juno.com

MIKEL, Joseph F (Oly) 411 W Grove St Apt 4, Shelton WA 98584 B Spokane WA 10/12/1948 s Wallace Stanley Mikel & Janet Field. Grays Harbor Cc 1968; Seattle Cmnty Coll 1968; BA U of Washington 1971; MDiv GTS 1974. D 7/15/1974 P 7/26/1975 Bp Ivol I Curtis. m 10/5/1969 Peggy Martha Humbert. Ch Of The Ascen Seattle WA 1983; S Paul's Ch Walla Walla WA 1977-1979; S Steph's Epis Ch Longview WA 1974-1977. Soc Of S Jn The Evang. JOSEPHMIKEL@AOL.COM

MIKOL, Robert Walter (WTex) 3023 Washington St, Bethlehem PA 18020 **Off Of Bsh For ArmdF New York NY 1989-** B Yonkers NY 6/8/1944 s Walter John Mikol & Mary Ann. BA S Mary 1966; S Jn Hm Mssn Sem 1967; MDiv S Fran Sem 1970; GTS 1973; CPE 1978; Cert Rio Grande Vlly Police Acad 1982. Rec from Roman Catholic 9/1/1973 Bp Harold Cornelius Gosnell. m 5/6/1971 Eileen Ann McCabe c 2. Int Chr Ch Budd Lake NJ 2002; Int The Epis Ch Of S Clem And S Ptr Wilkes Barre PA 2000-2002; S Andr's Ch Port Isabel TX 1978-1981; R Emm Epis Ch Lockhart TX 1976-1977; Asst S Lk's Epis Ch San Antonio TX 1974-1976. ACPE; Intl Assn Trauma Counslr. heartlight1@msn.com

MIKOWSKI, Willa Soule (CFla) 184 Groveland Rd, Mount Dora FL 32757 **Died 3/18/2011** B Lansing MI 10/16/1925 d Harold G Smith & Bertha Elizabeth. AA NW Michigan Coll 1979; MDiv SWTS 1982. D 6/5/1982 Bp Charles Bennison P 12/18/1982 Bp Walter Cameron Righter. c 3. Auth, "Basic Histologic Techniques," 1975. Natl Registery Of Histotechnology 1962. Barbara S. Spillan Awd Michigan Soc Of Histology 1973; Lifetime Mem Michigan Soc Of Histology. LHFLYNN@CHARTER.NET

MILAM, David Ross (Mass) 108 Lakeside Ave, Lakeville MA 02347 **R Ch Of Our Sav Middleboro MA 2004-** B El Paso TX 9/19/1960 s Earl Eugene Milam & Brenda Kay. BS U of Maine 1988; MDiv STUSo 2001. D 6/9/2001 Bp Robert Jefferson Hargrove Jr P 2/17/2002 Bp Geralyn Wolf. m 8/13/1983 Ruth Louise Buckley c 3. Cur Trin Ch Newport RI 2001-2004. milamdr9@verizon.net

MILAM, Thomas Richerson (SwVa) 715 Forest Hills Dr, Wilmington NC 28403 B Winchester VA 12/29/1965 s John H Milam & Louise K. BA W Virginia U 1988; MDiv Ya Berk 1993; MD U of Virginia 1998. D 6/12/1993 P 12/15/1993 Bp Peter James Lee. m 6/17/1995 Noelle Valley c 4. S Jas Par Wilmington NC 2010; S Jas Par Wilmington NC 2008-2009; Asst S Jas Par Wilmington NC 2002; Chr Epis Ch Charlottesville VA 1994; S Paul's Meml Charlottesville VA 1993-1994. nomilam@aol.com

MILAN JR, Jesse (Kan) 7103 Waverly Ave, Kansas City KS 66109 B Depue OK 3/3/1928 s Clarence Winston Milan & Willie Mae. BS U of Kansas 1953; MS U of Kansas 1954; EDS Emporia St U 1969; Hon EDD Baker U 2000. D 6/3/2006 Bp Dean Elliott Wolfe. m 6/13/1954 Alversa Brewster c 4. Dr of Educ Baker U 2001. jmilan@myexcel.com

MILANO, Mary Lucille (Chi) 8765 W Higgins Rd, Chicago IL 60631 **S Alb's Ch Chicago IL 2004-** B Chicago IL 10/29/1952 d Daniel Louise Milano & Catharine. BA Mundelein Coll 1973; MDiv McCormick TS 1977; JD Nthrn Illinois U 1978; DMin GTF 1994; U of Leicester 2002. D 6/11/2000 Bp Peter Hess Beckwith P 7/30/2002 Bp Victor Alfonso Scantlebury. c 1. Asst Cathd Of S Jas Chicago IL 2002-2003; Evang Luth Ch in Amer Chicago IL 2001-2003; Asstg D S Andr's Ch Paris IL 2000-2001. Auth, "Hunger No More - Intl ," Bread For The Wrld Inst, 2003; Auth, "Peace Is In Our Hands: Bldg A Vocabulary Of Peace Through Th," *Law Related Educ*, Illinois St Bar Assn, 2002;

Auth, “The Forcible Transfer Of Palestinians To Gaza,” *The Globe*, Illinois St Bar Assn, 2002; Auth, “A Primer On Impeachment,” Illinois St Bar Assn, 1998; Auth, “Ethical Issues And The Internet,” Illinois St Bar Assn, 1998; Auth, “Practicing Law Across St Boundaries,” *The Globe*, Illinois St Bar Assn, 1998; Auth, “Mortgage Foreclosure,” *Basic Real Estate Pract*, Iicle, 1988. ABA 1978; Assn For Practical And Profsnl Ethics 1993; Coll Theol Soc 1991; Illinois St Bar Assn 1978; Intl Bar Assn 1995; Italian Amer Political Cltn Of Illinois 1999; Justinian Soc Of Lawyers 1978; Ord Of The Easter Star - Grand Chapt Of Illinois 1977. Judith Shanahan Memi Ldrshp And Serv Awd S Mary Of The Woods Coll 2001; DSA For Career Achievement And Publ Serv Nthrn Illinois U Coll Of Law Alum Assn 1998; DSA Illinois St Bar Assn 1990; Ldrshp Awd GSA, Chicago Dist Coun 1988; Mem And Vice Chair City Of Chicago Bd Ethics 1987; Anna L And Jas Nelson Raymond Fell NWU Coll Of Law 1977; Fell Soc For Values In Higher Educ 1975; Fell Danforth Fndt 1973. mary_milano@elca.org

MILES, Frank William (Colo) 1175 Vine St Apt 207, Denver CO 80206 B Springfield OH 1/16/1936 s William Mckinley Miles & Barbara. BS USMA At W Point 1958; MDiv Nash 1968; Marq 1971; NW St U 1972; EdD U Denv 1980; PrTS 1982. D 7/25/1968 Bp Joseph Summerville Minnis P 1/25/1969 Bp Edwin B Thayer. m 6/17/1984 Kathryn Rhodes c 1. Asst S Barn Epis Ch Denver CO 1996-1998; R Intsn Epis Ch Thornton CO 1982-1987; Vic S Mart In The Fields Aurora CO 1978-1982; Asst Chr Epis Ch Denver CO 1975-1978; Vic S Paul’s Epis Ch Steamboat Sprg CO 1969-1970; Vic S Mk’s Ch Craig CO 1968-1970; Vic S Jas’ Epis Ch Meeker CO 1968-1969. Auth, “Stages Human Dvlpmt”. Mltry Chapl, Assn Assn Of Chr Therapists. Air Medal W/Oak Leaf Cluster; Meritorious Serv Medal,; Bronze Star,.

MILES, Glenworth Dalmane (LI) 2714 Lurting Ave, Bronx NY 10469 **S Geo’s Ch Brooklyn NY 2002-** B Manchester JM 10/15/1960 s Arthur Featherstone Miles & Sylvia Beatrice. AA Queensborough Cmnty Coll 1983; BA CUNY 1988; MDiv GTS 1991; DMin Drew U 2001. D 6/8/1991 P 12/14/1991 Bp Richard Frank Grein. P-in-c S Martha’s Ch Bronx NY 1995-2001; Vic Gr Ch (W Farms) Bronx NY 1992-2001; D S Lk’s Epis Ch Bronx NY 1991-1992. OHC 1979; The BroSA 2004. Balm in Gilead HIV/AIDS Awd The Balm in Gilead 2006; Cmnty Serv Awd Lion’s Club of New York 2005; Medal for exceptional Pstr care to the people of God The Soc of St Jn the Evang and Theol, Dio 2000. drglenmiles@aol.com

M

MILES, James B (HB) 11386 Links Dr, Reston VA 20190 B Holden MA 12/1/1937 s James Donald Miles & Mary Lydia. BA Dart 1959; MA Rhode Island Coll 1967. D 5/22/1976 Bp John Alfred Baden P 6/11/1977 Bp Robert Benjamin Hall. m 12/23/1961 Joan Earlene Bovaird c 2. S Anne’s Epis Ch Reston VA 1976-1980.

MILES, John (Q) Po Box 31, Warsaw IL 62379 B Indianapolis IN 6/23/1926 s Arthur Miles & Ida Pearl. BS Illinois St U 1949; GTS 1957. D 6/22/1957 P 12/21/1957 Bp Angus Dun. Vic S Paul’s Ch Warsaw IL 1989-1997; Vic Chr The King Epis Ch Huntington IN 1981-1984; Vic S Lk’s Epis Ch Shelbyville IN 1970-1981; R S Mary’s Ch Williamsport PA 1960-1967; Cur Trin Ch Washington DC 1957-1958.

MILES JR, John Pickett (SVa) 268 Mill Stream Way, Williamsburg VA 23185 B Rochester NY 6/22/1942 s John Pickett Miles & Alice E C. BA U NC 1966; MDiv VTS 1969. D 6/24/1969 P 6/1/1970 Bp Thomas Augustus Fraser Jr. m 6/12/1965 Helen K Knight c 2. R S Mart’s Epis Ch Williamsburg VA 1975-2004; Asst H Trin Par Epis Clemson SC 1971-1975; Asst Calv Ch Tarboro NC 1969-1971. john.pickett.miles@gmail.com

MILES, Kristin Kaulbach (Ct) 661 Old Post Rd, Fairfield CT 06824 **S Paul’s Ch Fairfield CT 2011-** B Washington DC 6/9/1972 d Allan Edward Kaulbach & Linda Coleman. BA Wellesley Coll 1994; MDiv Harvard DS 2000. D 6/11/2011 Bp Laura Ahrens. m 7/17/1999 Christopher Miles c 3. kaulbach@optonline.net

MILES, Richard Alan Knox (Los) 634 Parkway Blvd, Reidsville NC 27320 **Supply P Dio Los Angeles Los Angeles CA 2006-** B Sanger CA 8/3/1950 BA Fresno Pacific U 1972; MDiv PrTS 1977; DMin SFTS 1997. D 4/23/2005 Bp Chester Lovelle Talton P 1/14/2006 Bp Joseph Jon Bruno. m 7/3/1976 Daun Knox c 3. P-in-c S Thos Of Cbury Par Long Bch CA 2010; D S Fran’ Par Palos Verdes Estates CA 2005. Soc of Cath Priests 2011; The Ord of St. Lazarus 1990. mileslanding@gmail.com

MILES JR, Richard Frederick (Neb) 372 N Main St, Valentine NE 69201 B Omaha NE 5/16/1940 s Richard Frederick Miles & Ruth Elaine. BA U of Nebraska 1962; BD SWTS 1965. D 6/9/1965 P 12/1/1965 Bp Russell T Rauscher. m 12/26/1989 Gloria E Bockman. S Jn’s Ch Valentine NE 1988-1998; S Jn’s Epis Ch Valentine NE 1988-1991; R Gr Epis Ch Chadron NE 1970-1988; R S Lk’s Ch Plattsmouth NE 1965-1970. skipmiles@hotmail.com

MILES, Thomas Dee (Kan) 1308 Overlook Dr, Manhattan KS 66503 **Coun of Trst Dio Kansas Topeka KS 2011-; R S Paul’s Ch Manhattan KS 2002-** B Omaha NE 4/3/1947 s Richard Frederick Miles & Ruth Elaine. BA U of Nebraska at Kearney 1970; MDiv STUSo 1976. D 6/28/1976 P 12/1/1976 Bp William Davidson. m 6/1/1968 Susan J Moates c 1. P-in-c S Tim’s Ch Scottsbluff NE 1994-2002; R Ch Of The H Apos Mitchell NE 1992-2002; Assoc All SS Epis Ch Omaha NE 1990-1992; S Eliz’s Ch Holdrege NE 1978-1988; P-in-c S Aug’s Ch Meade KS 1977-1978; P-in-c S Tim’s Epis Ch Hugoton KS 1977-1978; Dio Wstrn Kansas Hutchinson KS 1976. tommiles@kansas.net

MILHOAN, Charles Everett (Az) 4102 W Union Hills Dr, Glendale AZ 85308 **Cnvnr - Wrld Mssn-Comp Dio Prog Grp Dio Arizona Phoenix AZ 2010-; Dioc Coun Dio Arizona Phoenix AZ 2009-; D S Jn The Bapt Epis Ch Glendale AZ 2009-** B Amarillo TX 12/15/1950 s George Milhoan & Ruth. D 1/24/2009 Bp Kirk Stevan Smith. m 7/30/1977 Stacy Milhoan c 2. chuck@milhoan.net

MILHOLEN, Linda Scott (WMo) Po Box 519, Bolivar MO 65613 **D Ch Of The Trsfg Mtn Grove MO 2010-; D S Alb’s In The Ozarks Ch Bolivar MO 2002-** B Hot Springs AR 9/6/1946 d Cleberne Dale Scott & Opal. BS Georgia Inst of Tech 1970; MD Emory U 1974. D 7/6/1996 Bp Don Adger Wimberly. m 6/4/1964 Garland Milholen. D Epis Ch of Our Sav Richmond KY 1996-2001.

MILHOLLAND, Nancy Elizabeth (Mass) 58 Stanford Heights Ave, San Francisco CA 94127 B New York NY 6/23/1959 d Harry Carter Milholland & Helen Esther. BA Dart 1983; MDiv SWTS 1992. D 5/30/1992 Bp David Elliot Johnson P 2/27/1993 Bp R(aymond) Stewart Wood Jr. Gr Ch Millbrook NY 1995-1996; Assoc S Jn’s Epis Ch Saginaw MI 1992-1995. Auth, “The First 9 Weeks,” *Brooklyn Bridge*, 1999. thurible@aol.com

MILIAN, Mario Emilio (SeFla) 5690 N Kendall Dr, Coral Gables FL 33156 **R S Thos Epis Par Coral Gables FL 2011-** B CU 11/19/1976 s Mario Miguel Milian & Ana Maria. BIS Arizona St U 2005; MDiv CDSP 2009. D 7/15/2000 Bp Leopold Frade P 2/10/2001 Bp Robert Reed Shahan. m 7/11/1996 Julie Alvelo. P-in-c S Thos Epis Par Coral Gables FL 2011; Assoc S Thos Epis Par Coral Gables FL 2008-2011; R All SS Epis Ch Oxnard CA 2006-2008; Dio Arizona Phoenix AZ 2000-2006; Asst S Matt’s Ch Chandler AZ 2000-2006. mariomilian@hotmail.com

MILIEN, Jean Baptiste Smith (SeFla) 6744 North Miami Ave, Miami FL 33150 **St Pauls Et Les Martyrs Miami FL 2008-; P Ch Of S Paul The Apos Miami FL 2007-** B Gressier Port-au-Prince HT 3/15/1959 s Ecclesiaste Estalien Milien & Zulema. BA Centro de Estudios Teologicos 1986. D 10/26/1986 P 12/20/1987 Bp Telesforo A Isaac. m 12/22/1991 Marivel Natura Natera c 3. Dio The Dominican Republic (Iglesia Epis Dominicana) Santo Domingo DO 1986-1998. fmiliena@yahoo.com

MILLAR, Charles Wendell (Mich) 14818 Oakes Rd, Perry MI 48872 B Lansing MI 6/10/1933 s Charles Evro Millar & Pamelia. BA Albion Coll 1955; BD Yale DS 1958; MA MI SU 1975. D 6/28/1958 P 7/18/1959 Bp Richard S M Emrich. m 6/18/1955 Susan Pirnie c 4. R Trin Epis Ch Flushing MI 1960-1966. cwmillar@tds.net

MILLAR, John Dunne (Az) 7245 E Manzanita Dr, Scottsdale AZ 85258 B Detroit MI 10/2/1940 s James Nixon Millar & America. BS Geo Mason U 1974; MBA Loyola U 1978; MDiv VTS 1985. D 6/22/1985 P 4/1/1986 Bp Peter James Lee. c 1. Dio Arizona Phoenix AZ 2006; S Aug’s Epis Ch Tempe AZ 2002-2006; Trin Epis Ch El Dorado KS 1999-2002; Ch Of S Phil And S Jas Denver CO 1992-1995; R Chr Epis Ch Ballston Spa NY 1988-1992; Cur The Ch Of The Mssh Glens Falls NY 1987-1988; Asst Chr Epis Ch Winchester VA 1985-1987.

✠ MILLARD, Rt Rev George Richard (Cal) 501 Portola Rd # 8107, Portola Valley CA 94028 B Dunsmuir CA 10/2/1914 s George Ellis Millard & Constance. DD CDSP; STM PSR; MA Santa Clara U; BA U CA 1935; BD EDS 1938. D 7/6/1938 Bp Archie W N Porter P 6/1/1939 Bp Henry Knox Sherrill Con 2/2/1960 for Cal. Ret Bp of Europe Convoc of Amer Ch in Europe Paris FR 1980-2001; Assoc Chr Epis Ch Los Altos CA 1980-2000; Asstg Bp of California Dio California San Francisco CA 1980-2000; Epis Ch Cntr New York NY 1977-1978; Trst The CPG New York NY 1969-1979; Bp Dio California San Francisco CA 1960-1976; R Chr Ch Alameda CA 1951-1960; R S Jas Epis Ch Danbury CT 1941-1951; Cur S Jn’s Epis Par Waterbury CT 1939-1941; Cur S Jas Ch New York NY 1938-1939. grichard.millard@gmail.com

MILLARD, Michael Wayne (WLa) 908 Rutherford St, Shreveport LA 71104 **R Chr Memi Ch Mansfield LA 2010-** B Little Rock AR 2/16/1968 s I Leighton Millard & Sherrill Lou. BA U of Dallas 1990; MDiv Nash 2008. D 6/7/2008 P 3/7/2009 Bp D(avid) Bruce Mac Pherson. m 4/23/1994 Samantha D Deviney c 3. Cur S Mk’s Cathd Shreveport LA 2008-2010. sacerdotal451@gmail.com

MILLARD, Patricia (Ore) 6916 SW 53rd Ave, Portland OR 97219 **Dn, Metro E Convoc Dio Oregon Portland OR 2009-; Rep, Dioc Coun Dio Oregon Portland OR 2009-; Mem, Cmsn to End Racism Dio Oregon Portland OR 2008-; Vic H Cross Epis Ch Portland OR 2008-** B Mexico City Mexico 12/13/1962 d William Steagall & Consuelo. BA Trin U San Antonio TX 1985; MDiv Epis TS of The SW 2004. D 6/11/2004 Bp Joseph Jon Bruno P 1/14/2006 Bp Frank Tracy Griswold III. m 9/23/1989 Jerry Millard c 2. S Wilfrid Of York Epis Ch Huntington Bch CA 2005-2007. pvmillard@gmail.com

MILLER, Alan Clayborne (Fla) 1637 Nw 19th Cir, Gainesville FL 32605 B Birmingham AL 2/5/1949 s Albert David Miller & Eleanor Lee. BA Emory U 1971; MA U Of Florida 1981; PhD U Of Florida 1984; MDiv STUSo 1992. D 6/20/1992 P 12/20/1992 Bp John Wadsworth Howe. m 10/23/1976 Sheila

Maureen Flemming c 2. Serv S Fran Of Assisi Epis Ch Lake Placid FL 1992-1998. Auth, "A Handbook For Wilderness Counslr"; Auth, "Gender Constancy In Pre-Sch Chld". APA. alancmiller1976@gmail.com

MILLER, Alfred Franklin (EO) 665 E Gladys Ave, Hermiston OR 97838 B Portland OR 9/15/1959 s Charles Robert Miller & Doreen Kay. BS OR SU 1983; MDiv Ya Berk 1990. D 6/30/1990 Bp Rustin Ray Kimsey P 1/1/1991 Bp David Charles Bowman. m 8/21/1982 Michelle Leslie Yost c 2. S Lk's Epis Ch Vancouver WA 2000-2001; S Jn's Ch Hermiston OR 1999-2000; Dio Estrn Oregon The Dalles OR 1993-1998; Cur S Lk's Epis Ch Jamestown NY 1990-1993.

MILLER, Ann C (Ct) 99 Timberwood Rd, West Hartford CT 06117 **Int Asst S Jn's Ch W Hartford CT 2008-** B Saint LouisMO 11/29/1947 d William Hamill Charles & Ann Stoughton. BA Smith 1969; MDiv VTS 1989. D 6/10/1989 P 12/10/1989 Bp Arthur Edward Walmsley. m 11/9/1996 Barry William Miller. S Ann's Epis Ch Old Lyme CT 2009-2010; Int Trin Epis Ch Williamsport PA 2007-2008; Emm Ch Covington VA 2006-2007; Calv Epis Ch Santa Cruz CA 2005-2006; Dio El Camino Real Monterey CA 2005; Int Epis Ch Cntr New York NY 2004-2005; Int Cathd Of The Incarn Garden City NY 2003; Dio Wstrn Massachusetts Springfield MA 2002-2003; Int Trin Par Lenox MA 2002-2003; Int S Jas Ch New London CT 2000-2001; Int S Jn's Ch W Hartford CT 1999-2000; Deploy Off Dio Connecticut Hartford CT 1995-1999; S Jas's Ch W Hartford CT 1993-2001; Chapl Trin Chap Hartford CT 1991-1995; Ya Berk New Haven CT 1989-1991; Epis Ch At Yale New Haven CT 1989-1991. Auth of one Chapt, "Renewing Denominational Linkages," *Temporary Shepherds*, Alb Inst, 1998. Soc for the Increase of Mnstry Exec Com 1993-2003. RevsMiller@aol.com

MILLER, Anthony Glenn (Los) 350 S Madison Ave Apt 207, Pasadena CA 91101 B Los Angeles CA 9/24/1959 s Isaac Nimrod Miller & Lillian Lois. BA USC 1984; MDiv GTS 1988; STM Yale DS 1995; STM Ya 1995; EdM Harv 1996. D 6/25/1988 P 1/21/1989 Bp Frederick Houk Borsch. P S Barn' Par Pasadena CA 2002-2011; P S Aug And S Mart Ch Boston MA 1999-2001; Assoc S Ptr's Epis Ch Cambridge MA 1995-1998; Dio Long Island Garden City NY 1988-1992. agm@post.harvard.edu

MILLER, Arthur Burton (ECR) 2050 California St Apt 20, Mountain View CA 94040 B Des Moines IA 1/22/1922 s Howard Wilson Miller & Amy Angeline. BA Whitworth U 1949; BEd Whitworth U 1950; MA U of Oregon 1962; PhD U of Oregon 1964. D 12/14/1988 P 6/1/1989 Bp Charles Shannon Mallory. m 9/11/1942 Lucy Minerva Smith. D Trin Cathd San Jose CA 1988-2001.

MILLER, A Scott (Oly) 211 Calle del Verano, Palm Desert CA 92260 B Los Angeles CA 1/27/1945 s Alden Herbert Miller & Agnes Evelyn. BA USC 1966; ETSBH 1985; MA Claremont TS 1986; MA TS at Claremont 1986. D 6/22/1986 Bp Robert C Rusack P 1/24/1987 Bp Oliver Bailey Garver Jr. m 4/1/2000 Lorraine Ann McMurdie c 1. S Lk's Epis Ch Vancouver WA 2000-2002; S Andr's Ch Seattle WA 1997; S Steph's Epis Ch Seattle WA 1989-1997; Asst R All SS Par Beverly Hills CA 1986-1989. ascottmiller@earthlink.net

MILLER, Barbara Crouse (Me) 223 Lakes At Litchfield Dr, Pawleys Island SC 29585 B Medford MA 5/4/1935 d Mahlon Dale Crouse & Doris Mabel. RN New Engl Dss Hosp 1956; Dio Conneticut Diocanate Prog CT 1991. D 12/7/1991 Bp Arthur Edward Walmsley. m 9/8/1956 John Preston Miller c 4. D S Andr's Ch Readfield ME 1996-1998; D S Steph's Ch E Haddam CT 1991-1995.

MILLER, Barry William (Ct) 99 Timberwood Rd, West Hartford CT 06117 B Monessen PA 3/15/1939 s Charles William Miller & Olga Virginia. BS Penn 1961; MDiv GTS 1966. D 6/14/1966 Bp Ned Cole P 6/13/1967 Bp Walter M Higley. m 11/9/1996 Ann C Charles c 2. R E Lee Memi Ch (Epis) Lexington VA 2006; S Phil The Apos Scotts Vlly CA 2004-2006; Trin Ch Fishkill NY 2003-2004; Seabury Ret Cmnty Bloomfield CT 2001-2003; Vic S Steph's Epis Ch Bloomfield CT 1998-2003; Chr Ch Waterbury CT 1997-1998; Chr Ch Avon CT 1997; S Jas Epis Ch Danbury CT 1995-1997; S Steph's Ch Ridgefield CT 1994-1995; S Andr's Ch New Haven CT 1993; All SS Epis Ch Meriden CT 1992-1993; S Andr's Ch Meriden CT 1990-1991; Cur Zion Ch Rome NY 1966-1967. Contrib, "Being an "After Pstr,"" *Transitional Mnstry*, Ch Pub, 2009. revsmiller@gmail.com

MILLER, Charlene Ida (Tex) 5305 N. Wood Ln., Longview TX 75605 B Phillipsburg NJ 8/20/1955 d Charles Robert Dupont & Marie Joan. BS Trenton St Coll 1977; MDiv Moravian TS 1983; Med Kutztown U 1996. D 5/6/1984 P 4/28/1985 Bp James Michael Mark Dyer. m 5/7/1983 John Martin Miller c 3. Asst All SS Ch Phoenix AZ 2001-2004; All SS' Epis Sch Vicksburg MS 1996-2001; R S Barn Ch Kutztown PA 1989-1996; Int S Jas-S Geo Epis Ch Jermyn PA 1988-1989; R S Mk's Epis Ch Moscow PA 1985-1988; D Trin Ch Easton PA 1984-1985. cmiller01cm@yahoo.com

MILLER, Charles Bernard (SVa) 302 Brittania Dr., Williamsburg VA 23185 B Winston Salem NC 9/8/1947 LLB No Carolina Cntrl U. D 6/15/2002 P 1/28/2003 Bp David Conner Bane Jr. m 6/15/2002 Barbara Pitts. Int S Barn' Ch Greensboro NC 2005-2006.

MILLER, Clark Stewart (NI) 319 7th St, Logansport IN 46947 **D Trin Epis Ch Logansport IN 2010-** B Logansport IN 10/10/1955 s Theodore Franklin Miller & Eunice Rose. BS Indiana St U 1978; MS Indiana St U 1983. D 12/20/2009 P 7/9/2010 Bp Edward Stuart Little II. m 6/2/1984 Debra Miller c 4. miller@lcsc.k12.in.us

MILLER, David Dallas (Dal) 1700 N Westmoreland Rd, Desoto TX 75115 **Cur S Anne's Epis Ch Desoto TX 2010-; D S Anne's Epis Ch Desoto TX 2010-** B Salisbury MD 8/24/1978 s Paul Miller & Joanne. BAS Dallas Bapt U 2004; MDiv Perkins TS 2010. D 6/26/2010 Bp Paul Emil Lambert. m 8/29/2009 Keeley Chorn. daviddallasmiller@yahoo.com

MILLER, David Walton (Los) 1037 16th St Apt 1, Santa Monica CA 90403 B San Bernardino CA 10/23/1950 s Donald Barrett Miller & Patricia Lorene. BA U CA Santa Barbara 1973; MDiv VTS 1977. D 6/25/1977 Bp C Kilmer Myers P 6/25/1978 Bp William Foreman Creighton. m 8/4/1979 Sarah Rodgers c 3. R The Par Of S Matt Pacific Palisades CA 1993-2008; R Ch Of The Epiph San Carlos CA 1983-1993; Assoc R S Jas Par Los Angeles CA 1979-1983; Gr Cathd San Francisco CA 1977-1979. Honoray Cn of the Cathd Cntr of St. Paul Dio Los Angeles 2006. dwmiller23@earthlink.net

MILLER, Donald Peter (Mass) 21 Harley St, Dorchester MA 02124 **Asst Mssnr S Mk's Ch Taunton MA 1995-** B Boston MA 5/4/1929 s John Miller & Alice. BA Suffolk U 1959; MDiv STUSo 1962. D 6/23/1962 Bp Anson Phelps Stokes Jr P 6/1/1963 Bp John Melville Burgess. m 6/20/1970 Ann Wells Weston. Asst Mssnr S Jn The Evang Taunton MA 1995-2003; Trin Epis Ch Rockland MA 1989-1992; Emm Epis Ch Wakefield MA 1981-1983; Supplement Accounts Boston MA 1975-1976; All SS Ch Whitman MA 1972-1977; Asst S Ptr's Ch Weston MA 1966-1967; Asst S Barth's Ch In The Highland White Plains NY 1963-1966; Cur Emm Ch Braintree MA 1962-1963.

MILLER, Donald Stewart (Cal) 45602 State Highway 14, Stevenson WA 98648 B Seattle WA 6/10/1932 s Atwill Deloss Miller & Helen. BA Whitman Coll 1954; MDiv GTS 1957; DMin Claremont TS 1985. D 9/28/1957 Bp Stephen F Bayne Jr P 6/1/1958 Bp Frank A Rhea. m 12/29/1962 Judith Ann Yoder c 2. R S Matt's Epis Ch San Mateo CA 1986-1997; Dioc Coun Dio California San Francisco CA 1984-1987; R Ch Of Our Sav Par San Gabr CA 1975-1985; Excoun Dio Olympia Seattle WA 1974-1977; R Trin Epis Ch Everett WA 1970-1975; Excoun Dio Olympia Seattle WA 1967-1970; R S Andr's Epis Ch Aberdeen WA 1964-1970; Vic Ch Of The H Sprt Vashon WA 1960-1964; Cur Ch Of The Ascen Seattle WA 1957-1960. Auth, "Pehlivan: Turkish Sport, Islamic Sprt," *Intl Revs*, 1998; Auth, "Reformation Of The Liturg Year," Claremont, 1986; Auth, "A Pilgrim'S Progress"; Auth, "arts," *Angl Dig*; Auth, "arts," *Pulpit Dig*. dsmiller1492@earthlink.net

MILLER, Don Dalzell (ETenn) 8226 Arbor Ct, Fort Myers FL 33908 **Died 6/5/2011** B Menomonie WI 4/8/1913 s Don Studebaker Miller & Alice Love. BA Wayne 1934; MA Wayne 1936; PhD U MI 1941. D 6/29/1958 Bp John Vander Horst P 3/21/1959 Bp Theodore N Barth. Auth, "Math Journ Resrch Papers," 2003. Ord Of S Ben. SIXFIVE65@WORLDNET.ATT.NET

MILLER JR, Edward Oehler (Va) 6715 Georgetown Pike, Mclean VA 22101 **Stndg Com Pres Dio Virginia Richmond VA 2010-; Chair, Bd Gvnr Christchurch Sch Christchurch VA 2009-; Stndg Com Dio Virginia Richmond VA 2009-; Bd Gvnr Christchurch Sch Christchurch VA 2004-; R S Jn's Epis Ch McLean VA 1996-** B New York NY 11/16/1948 s Edward Oehler Miller & Ann Lackman. AB cl Harvard Coll 1970; MDiv EDS 1973. D 6/10/1973 Bp John Harris Burt P 2/24/1974 Bp The Bishop Of Quebec. m 10/28/1978 Virginia H W Miller c 2. Stndg Com Vice-Pres Dio Massachusetts Boston MA 2004-2005; Com on Corp Responsibility Exec Coun Appointees New York NY 2003-2009; COM Dio Virginia Richmond VA 1999-2009; Vice- Pres Stndg Com Dio Massachusetts Boston MA 1994-1995; Co-Chair, Nomin Com for a Bp Coadj Dio Massachusetts Boston MA 1993-1994; Stndg Comittee Dio Massachusetts Boston MA 1992-1995; Chair COM Dio Massachusetts Boston MA 1986-1990; R All SS' Epis Ch Belmont MA 1984-1996; Asst Min Trin Ch In The City Of Boston Boston MA 1976-1984; P-in-c Quebec Labrador Fndt Inc Ipswich MA 1975-1976; Chapl The Choate Sch Wallingford CT 1974-1975; Calv and St Geo New York NY 1973. reveom@aol.com

MILLER JR, Edwin Lee (Okla) 3300 N Vermont Ave, Oklahoma City OK 73112 B Houstonia MO 7/1/1937 s Edwin Lee Miller & Frances Marion. BA U of Texas 1965; MDiv Epis TS of The SW 1968; MA U of Oklahoma 1993. D 7/3/1968 Bp Frederick P Goddard P 5/1/1969 Bp J Milton Richardson. m 2/16/1990 Rita A Crockett. Int S Dav's Ch Oklahoma City OK 2000-2002; Asst S Mary's Ch Edmond OK 1986-2002; Int Trin Ch Guthrie OK 1985; Int Epis Ch Of The Resurr Oklahoma City OK 1984-1985; Int S Matt's Ch Enid OK 1982-1983; R S Alb's Ch Houston TX 1969-1974; Asst S Mart's Epis Ch Houston TX 1968-1969. Auth, "Attachment Failure and Trauma," *Psychosynthesis and Healing Trauma*, Assoc for Advancement of Psychosynthesis, 2011; Auth, "Psychosynthesis and a Chr Sprtl Philos," *Psychosynthesis and Sprtlty*, Assoc for Advancement of Psychosynthesis, 2008. speople@sbcglobal.net

MILLER, Elizabeth M (Be) 1426 Wynnewood Dr, Bethlehem PA 18017 **S Mk's Ch Augusta ME 2007-; Trin Ch Bethlehem PA 2003-** B St. Louis MO

M

11/30/1954 D 5/31/2003 Bp Paul Victor Marshall. m 5/26/1990 Terry Miller. liz@trinitybeth.org

MILLER, Elizabeth Sleeper (Me) 286 Lincoln St, South Portland ME 04106 B Doylestown PA 12/13/1944 d William Allen Sleeper & Mary Elise. BA U of Sthrn Maine 1972; MDiv Bangor TS 2002. D 6/1/2002 P 12/8/2002 Bp Chilton Abbie Richardson Knudsen. m 11/22/1961 Robert Thomas Miller. S Mk's Ch Augusta ME 2004-2011; S Matt's Epis Ch Hallowell ME 2004-2005; Cur Epis Ch Of S Mary The Vrgn Falmouth ME 2002-2004. emiller13@juno.com

MILLER, Eric Lee (SO) 321 Worthington Ave., Cincinnati OH 45215 **R The Ch Of Ascen And H Trin Cincinnati OH 2010-** B Parkersburg WV 8/9/1977 s Mark Albert Miller & Margaret Lynn. BA W Virginia U 2000; MDiv VTS 2003. D 9/19/2002 P 6/7/2003 Bp William Michie Klusmeyer. m 5/11/2002 Rosemary R Rutledge c 2. S Steph's Epis Ch Beckley WV 2005-2010; S Jn's Ch Huntington WV 2003-2005. emiller479@hotmail.com

MILLER JR, Ernest Charles (NY) 611 Broadway Rm 520, New York NY 10012 B Norwalk CT 8/25/1956 s Ernest Charles Miller & Edith Grosvenor. BA Franklin & Marshall Coll 1978; MA U MI 1979; MDiv Nash 1982; PhD Oxf 1990. D 6/26/1982 Bp A Donald Davies P 5/1/1983 Bp Robert Elwin Terwilliger. m 7/25/1987 Judith F Masheder c 1. R Ch Of The Trsfg New York NY 2000-2005; S Paul's Ch Watertown WI 1997-2000; S Anskar's Epis Ch Hartland WI 1997; Prof S Mary the Vrgn Ch Nashotah WI 1996-2000; S Simon The Fisherman Epis Ch Port Washington WI 1996; Nash Nashotah WI 1995-2000; Cur S Andr's Ch Farmers Branch TX 1982-1984. Auth, "Toward A Fuller Vision: Orthodoxy & The Angl Experience"; Auth, "Praying The Euch". Sub Chapl The Most Vunerable Ord Of The Hospitals Of St Jn Of Judea 2000. ECHARLESMILLER@BTINTERNET.COM

MILLER, Fred (CPa) 112 Robin Rd, Hershey PA 17033 **S Lk's Epis Ch Altoona PA 2011-** B Wilmington DE 10/8/1950 s John Pearson Miller & Emma Jane. BA Glassboro St U 1972; PDS 1974; MDiv EDS 1975; Cert SWTS 2001. D 4/26/1975 P 10/25/1975 Bp Albert Wiencke Van Duzer. m 5/19/1973 Kristine Lynn Kiebler c 3. S Jas Ch Wichita KS 2010-2011; Pres - Stndg Com Dio Cntrl Pennsylvania Harrisburg PA 2002-2005; COM Dio Cntrl Pennsylvania Harrisburg PA 1991-1997; Chair - Liturg & Ch Mus Cmsn Dio Cntrl Pennsylvania Harrisburg PA 1991-1996; Dioc Coun Dio Cntrl Pennsylvania Harrisburg PA 1990-1996; Dio Cntrl Pennsylvania Harrisburg PA 1990; R All SS' Epis Ch Hershey PA 1989-2008; Chr Ch Somers Point NJ 1989-2008; Dep Prov II Syn Dio Cntrl Pennsylvania Harrisburg PA 1983-1989; R Gr Ch Pemberton NJ 1981-1989; Vic Trin Epis Old Swedes Ch Swedesboro NJ 1977-1981; Cur S Paul's Epis Ch Westfield NJ 1975-1977. Epis Cler Assn 1987. fred_miller@verizon.net

MILLER, Isaac J (Pa) 18th & Diamond, Philadelphia PA 19121 B Raleigh NC 2/23/1943 s Houser Alexander Miller & Ida Louise. BA Morehouse Coll 1964; MDiv EDS 1968. D 9/13/1975 Bp Joseph Warren Hutchens P 5/1/1976 Bp Morgan Porteus. m 7/11/1970 Rose S Sallee c 1. Dio Pennsylvania Philadelphia PA 1991-2009; R Ch Of The Advoc Philadelphia PA 1989-1990; Assoc The Afr Epis Ch Of S Thos Philadelphia PA 1986-1989; R S Tim's Decatur GA 1982-1985; Asst R S Paul And S Jas New Haven CT 1975-1978.

MILLER, James Barrett (NCal) 550 Seagaze Dr, #10, Oceanside CA 92054 B San Bernardino CA 3/30/1949 s Donald Barret Miller & Patricia Lorene. BA U CA, Santa Barbara 1971; MDiv VTS 1974; PhD Fuller TS 1982. D 6/10/1974 Bp Robert Poland Atkinson P 5/24/1975 Bp Wilburn Camrock Campbell. c 3. COM Dio Nthrn California Sacramento CA 1981-1987; Alum/ae Exec Com VTS Alexandria VA 1981-1984; R H Trin Ch NEVADA CITY CA 1980-1989; Asst S Jn's Epis Ch Charleston WV 1975-1977; Chapl to Marshall U Trin Ch Huntington WV 1974-1975. Auth, "The First Bk of Homilies and the Doctrine of H Scripture," *Angl and Epis Hist*, 1997; Auth, "The Struggle of Memory Against Forgetting," *Hist mag PECUSA*, 1984; "Scripture in the Engl Reformation 1526-1553," U Microfilms Intl , 1982; Auth, "The Theol of Wm Sparrow," *Hist mag PECUSA*, 1977. jbarrettmiller@aol.com

MILLER, James Lower (NY) 126 Goldens Bridge Rd, Katonah NY 10536 B Concordia KS 7/16/1927 s Charles Henry Miller & Ruth Elizabeth. BA U of Maryland 1956; BD EDS 1959; STM Andover Newton TS 1969. D 6/20/1959 P 12/19/1959 Bp Angus Dun. m 5/14/1960 Marcia Nan Allen c 1. P-in-c Chr And S Steph's Ch New York NY 1965-1968; Asst S Aug's Ch New York NY 1961-1963; Asst S Paul And S Jas New Haven CT 1960-1961; Asst All Souls Memi Epis Ch Washington DC 1959-1960.

MILLER, Janice Mary Howard (NI) 2117 E Jefferson Blvd, South Bend IN 46617 **D The Cathd Ch Of S Jas So Bend IN 1998-** B Honeoye Falls NY 7/31/1939 d Raymond Arthur Howard & Nina Ruth. Gordon Coll; U Roch; BA No Pk U 1963; MS NWU 1964; Dio Cntrl Florida Inst Chr Stds 1990. D 12/14/1991 Bp John Wadsworth Howe. m 7/10/1975 Richard Roy Miller c 3. D H Cross Epis Ch Sanford FL 1991-1993. Intl Osl-Physcn.

MILLER, Jean Louise (EC) 9191 Daly Rd., Cincinnati OH 45231 B Hershey PA 6/23/1950 d John Yeagly Groff & Bertha Elizabeth. Assoc Tem 1970. D 6/14/2008 Bp Thomas Edward Breidenthal. m 1/20/1973 Gary Lee Miller c 2. mentalfloss@cinci.rr.com

MILLER, Jeffrey Scott (SC) 1109 Craven St, Beaufort SC 29902 **Par Ch of St. Helena Beaufort SC 1999-; Dept Of Yth Mnstry Dio So Carolina Charleston SC 1997-** B Pittsburgh PA 8/26/1969 s Robert James Miller & Patricia. BA Indiana U of Pennsylvania 1991; MDiv VTS 1994. D 6/25/1994 P 1/15/1995 Bp Alden Moinet Hathaway. m 7/29/1995 Kristin Lynne Frazier. S Dav's Ch Cheraw SC 1996-1999; Asst R S Jas Ch Charleston SC 1994-1996. Evangengelical Fllshp In Angl Comm, Fllshp Of Witness; Sead. Pi Sigma Alpha; Pi Gamma Mu; Phi Alpha Theta. miller@islc.net

MILLER, Jerry Lee (WMo) 515 E Division St, Springfield MO 65803 **R S Jn's Ch Springfield MO 2003-** B Columbus IN 6/27/1945 s Arnold Francis Miller & Marjorie Bernice. BA Indiana U 1972; MDiv Nash 1975. Trans 2/5/2004 Bp Mark Sean Sisk. m 11/27/1996 Elizabeth Potter. Zion Epis Ch Wappingers Falls NY 1998-2003; Vic All SS Epis Ch Farmington MO 1988-1997; Vic S Pauls Epis Ch Ironton MO 1988-1997; Asst S Andr's Ch Stillwater OK 1986-1988; All SS' Epis Ch Duncan OK 1981-1985; Ch Of S Jn The Bapt Lincoln IL 1978-1981; Trin Ch Lincoln IL 1978-1981; Cur S Mich And All Ang Ch Mssn KS 1975-1978. jmi5815231@aol.com

MILLER, Jo (Ore) P.O. Box 413, Bandon OR 97411 **Vic S Jn-By-The-Sea Epis Ch Bandon OR 2007-** B Medford OR 4/13/1949 d Cyrus Scott Hamilton & Frances. BS Sthrn Oregon 1971; MDiv CDSP 2005. D 10/8/2005 P 6/28/2006 Bp Johncy Itty. m 5/29/1969 Teddy Charles Miller c 2. Dio Oregon Portland OR 2008-2009. jamandt@oregonfcu.com

MILLER, Joel Prescott (ECR) 160 Robideaux Rd, Aptos CA 95003 **R Calv Epis Ch Santa Cruz CA 2006-** B Glendale CA 11/22/1948 s Steven Whitney Miller & Patricia. BS California St Polytechnic U 1970; MDiv Fuller TS 1975; W-TESOL Wm Carey U 1985. D 6/13/1998 P 1/16/1999 Bp John-David Mercer Schofield. m 4/2/1983 Maria Christina Hagard c 4. R S Fran' Epis Ch Turlock CA 2000-2006; Asst to R S Paul's Epis Ch Modesto CA 1998-2000. "Riding the Fence Lines," BWD Pub, 2003. miller5252@sbcglobal.net

MILLER, Joe Ted (Okla) 2732 Walnut Rd, Norman OK 73072 B Ponca City OK 1/16/1941 s Ted Roosevelt Miller & Mary Helen. MA CUA 1964; STM GTS 1973; DMin McCormick TS 1980. Rec from Roman Catholic 7/1/1973 as Priest Bp James Stuart Wetmore. m 5/28/1973 Estelle Karl c 4. S Jn's Ch Norman OK 1981-2003; R S Elis's Epis Ch Memphis TN 1974-1981; Asst S Jn's Ch Larchmont NY 1973-1974. millhouse@cox.net

MILLER, John Clement (CGC) 5644 Buerger Ln, Fairhope AL 36532 **Vic S Jn The Evang Robertsdale AL 1989-** B Saint Louis IL 1/6/1933 s Clement John Miller & Carolyn Amelia. BS U of Alabama 1959; U So 1989. D 7/25/1989 P 2/1/1990 Bp Charles Farmer Duvall. m 12/28/1953 Marcia Jan Morrisette. S Jn The Evang Robertsdale AL 1996-2004.

MILLER, John Edward (Alb) 7 Pooles Hill Rd # 12, Ancram NY 12502 **Calv Epis Ch Cairo NY 1998-; P-in-c Gloria Dei Epis Ch Palenville NY 1998-** B Batavia NY 11/3/1948 s Frank A Miller & Phyllis C. BA SUNY 1970; MDiv PDS 1974. D 12/22/1973 Bp Allen Webster Brown P 9/14/1974 Bp Wilbur Emory Hogg Jr. m 12/30/1972 Kathie F Miller. P-in-c Calv Epis Ch Cairo NY 1986-1997; P-in-c S Mk's Epis Ch Philmont NY 1986-1997; R S Lk's Ch Willmar MN 1982-1984; R S Jn's Ch Moorhead MN 1980-1982; Vic Ch Of The Nativ Star Lake NY 1974-1978. jemiller@taconic.net

MILLER, John Edward (Va) 10329 Cherokee Road, Richmond VA 23235 **R S Mary's Ch Richmond VA 1981-** B Richmond VA 5/17/1948 s John Broughton Miller & Marion Jeanette. BA W&L 1970; MDiv UTS Richmond VA 1974; ThM UTS Richmond VA 1977; PhD UTS Richmond VA 1982. D 12/12/1981 P 6/25/1982 Bp Robert Bruce Hall. m 11/18/2007 Lisa Fisher c 1. Auth, *Ch Renwl Groups*, Virginia Epis; Auth, *EFM Curric Year 4*, The U So; Auth, *The Relevance of Process Theol*, Virginia Epis. jmiller@stmarysgoochland.org

MILLER, John Leonard (NY) 23 Cedar Ln, Princeton NJ 08540 B Philadelphia PA 7/23/1928 s Harry Miller & Dora. STB Harvard DS; STM Harvard DS; ThD Harvard DS; Fllshp Harv; DIT U of St. Andrews; MA Ya. D 6/15/1974 P 12/1/1974 Bp Jonathan Goodhue Sherman.

MILLER JR, John M (Ct) 1 North St, Roxbury CT 06783 B Pensacola FL 4/16/1943 s John Meredith Miller & Jane Elizabeth. BA Duke 1965; MDiv GTS 1968; VTS 1979; MS Bryn 1984. D 6/29/1968 Bp William Foreman Creighton P 1/4/1969 Bp Jonathan Goodhue Sherman. m 10/5/1968 Adele Maslen c 1. Chr Ch Roxbury CT 2001-2008; S Mk's Ch Westford MA 1996-2001; Int S Thos' Ch Whitemarsh Ft Washington PA 1994-1996; Int S Anne's Ch Abington PA 1992-1994; Int Chr Epis Ch Villanova PA 1991-1992; Int Ch Of The H Nativ Wrightstown PA 1989-1991; Vic Chr Ch Bridgeport PA 1986-1989; S Ptr's Ch Glenside PA 1984-1986; Repersentative The GTS New York NY 1977-1982; Com On Ch Status Dio Virginia Richmond VA 1977-1978; R Ch Of The H Comf Vienna VA 1976-1982; Liturg Cmsn Dio Long Island Garden City NY 1974-1975; Vic S Jas Ch Brookhaven NY 1972-1975; Cur Ch Of The Trsfg Freeport NY 1968-1970. jmmiller43@earthlink.net

MILLER, John Preston (Me) 223 Lakes At Litchfield Dr, Pawleys Island SC 29585 B Cambridge MA 2/15/1933 s John Sterling Miller & Marguerite. BA U of Massachusetts 1954; STM EDS 1957. D 6/1/1957 P 12/1/1957 Bp William A Lawrence. m 9/8/1956 Barbara Crouse c 4. P-in-c S Andr's Ch Readfield

ME 1996-1998; Int Chr And Epiph Ch E Haven CT 1995; Int Ch of the H Sprt W Haven CT 1994-1995; R Ch Of The H Trin Middletown CT 1981-1995; Exec Bd Alum Assn EDS Cambridge MA 1980-1983; Prov I Middletown CT 1980-1982; Stndg Com Dio Maine Portland ME 1970-1977; R S Jn's Ch Bangor ME 1967-1981; R H Trin Epis Ch Southbridge MA 1959-1967; Asst S Paul's Ch Holyoke MA 1957-1959. Auth, "Selected Sermons". Angl Soc. jmiller155@sc.rr.com

MILLER, John Sloan (La) 205 North 4th Street, Baton Rouge LA 70801 **Assoc R/Asst Hd of Sch S Jas Epis Ch Baton Rouge LA 2006-** B Lake Charles LA 10/20/1963 s Joseph Thomas Miller & Mary Joyce. BS McNeese St U 1987; MDiv STUSo 2004. D 6/5/2004 P 4/2/2005 Bp D(avid) Bruce Mac Pherson. m 9/19/1987 Celene Cassa Milburn c 3. Cur S Jas Epis Ch Alexandria LA 2004-2006. jsloanmiller@cox.net

MILLER, Joseph Potter (Los) 2242 W 234th St, Torrance CA 90501 B 7/29/1924 D 9/12/1970 Bp Francis E I Bloy P 3/27/1971 Bp Victor Manuel Rivera.

MILLER, Judith Joelynn (Walker) (Oly) PO Box 1782, Westport WA 98595 **D S Christophers Epis Ch Westport WA 1997-** B Shelton WA 3/27/1952 d Edward Vernon Partlow & Gertrude Sophia. RN NYU 1993; BD S Mart's Coll Lacey WA 2000; MS Gonzaga U 2004. D 11/19/1997 Bp Sanford Zangwill Kaye Hampton. m 6/26/1971 Ronald James Miller c 1. jmiller@olynet.com

MILLER JR, Kenneth C (Mil) 3906 W Mequon Rd, Mequon WI 53092 **R S Bon Ch Mequon WI 2010-** B Bristol TN 5/2/1973 s Kenneth Miller & Betty J. BA King Coll 1995; MDiv VTS 2005. D 6/18/2005 Bp Charles Glenn VonRosenberg P 1/21/2006 Bp Dean Elliott Wolfe. m 12/15/1995 Tania Marie Sholes c 3. R S Paul's Epis Ch Smithfield NC 2007-2010; Asst. R S Jas Ch Wichita KS 2005-2007. FRKENNYMILLER@GMAIL.COM

MILLER, Kurt David (Ga) 3665 Bermuda Cir, Augusta GA 30909 **Vic Ch Of The Atone Augusta GA 2010-** B Newark NJ 1/12/1938 s Kenneth Smith Miller & Florence Gertrude. AAS New York Inst of Tech 1973; BT New York Inst of Tech 1978; MS Bos 1981; MDiv Erskine TS 1996; DMin Erskine TS 2001. D 3/12/1986 Bp Harry Woolston Shipps P 6/1/1997 Bp Henry Irving Louttit. c 1. Vic Ch Of The Atone Augusta GA 1998-2007; Respite P S Aug Of Cbury Ch Augusta GA 1997-1998; D Ch Of The Atone Augusta GA 1994-1997; D S Alb's Epis Ch Augusta GA 1986-1994. Auth, "Disseration," *Bldg the Body of Chr Through the Love of God in a Sm Grp Fllshp*, Erskine TS, 2001. mill1702@bellsouth.net

MILLER, Laura Jean (Alb) 41 Gardiner Pl, Walton NY 13856 B Fairbanks AK 8/21/1954 d Robert William Bolten & Beverly Ann. D 5/10/2008 Bp William Howard Love. m 3/25/1984 Lawrence Miller c 1. RevLMiller@yahoo.com

MILLER, Laurence Henry (Be) 31 Tecumseh Pass, Millsboro DE 19966 B Minneapolis MN 12/29/1936 s Henry Charles Miller & Josephine. BA Wesl 1958; MA Indiana U 1959; BD VTS 1962. D 9/15/1962 P 6/1/1963 Bp John Brooke Mosley. m 8/24/1957 Patricia Walls. R S Ptr's Epis Ch Hazleton PA 1997-2001; Reg Mssnr S Phil's Ch Quantico MD 1995-1997; W Wicomico Cnty Cluster Quantico MD 1995-1997; Gr Epiph Ch Philadelphia PA 1986-1995; Ch Of The Epiph Philadelphia PA 1986-1991; S Dav's Ch Salem NH 1970-1986; Asst Ch Of The Gd Shpd Nashua NH 1965-1970; Dio Delaware Wilmington DE 1962-1965; D S Jn The Bapt Epis Ch Milton DE 1962-1965. mill2a@aol.com

MILLER, Leewin Glen (SwFla) 4279 70th St Cir E, Palmetto FL 34221 B Detroit MI 10/14/1940 s Leslie Allen Miller & Agnes Gertrude. BS U of No Alabama 1966; MDiv Epis TS In Kentucky 1980. D 5/11/1980 P 6/1/1981 Bp Addison Hosea. m 9/1/1962 Yoniece Perry c 2. R S Mary's Epis Ch Palmetto FL 1996-2009; Dn Columbus E Deanry Dio Sthrn Ohio Cincinnati OH 1993-1996; Dn, Columbus E Dnry Dio Sthrn Ohio Cincinnati OH 1993-1996; Ch Of S Edw Columbus OH 1989-1995; Evang/Renwl Cmsn Dio Sthrn Ohio Cincinnati OH 1985-1989; Com Profsnl Dev Dio Sthrn Ohio Cincinnati OH 1984-1990; Com Profsnl Dev Dio Sthrn Ohio Cincinnati OH 1984-1990; R Gr Ch Pomeroy OH 1983-1989; Vic S Jn's Ch Corbin KY 1980-1983. Auth, "Publ in the Loc Ch"; Auth, "40 Days!"; Auth, "Inside The Husk"; Auth, "Awesome Power Of Habit"; Auth, "Awareness, the Missing Ingredient"; Auth, "Natl Syndicated Radio/Tv Prog"; Auth, "There Is More Than Just One Way To Say I Love You," *Natl Psa Proj For Epis Ch.* Host Natl Syndicated Radio/Tv Prog; Natl Psa Proj For Epis Ch. frleemiller@yahoo.com

MILLER, Leon William (Az) 5126 East Emelita Circle, Meza AZ 85206 **Died 12/28/2009** B Winner SD 6/22/1920 s Clarence Marshall Miller & Winfred. BS U CA 1942. D 5/26/1990 Bp Craig Barry Anderson. c 3. El Riad Shrine 1953; Masonic Lodge 1953; Scottish Rite 1953. leonmill2000@yahoo.com

MILLER JR, Louis Oleman (Ga) 106 Ovid Dr, Dublin GA 31021 **Dn Dio Georgia Savannah GA 2007-; Dn Cntrl Convoc Dio Georgia Savannah GA 2007-; R Chr Epis Ch Dublin GA 2005-** B Portsmouth VA 7/18/1940 s Louis Oleman Miller & Mary Virginia. BA U of So Carolina 1970; MDiv STUSo 2005. D 5/28/2005 Bp Granville Porter Taylor P 12/9/2005 Bp Henry Irving Louttit. m 12/27/1974 Mary Anne Gillespie c 3. Ord of S Vinc Acolytes 1979. revlouis.miller@gmail.com

MILLER, Luther Deck (WA) 3815 Jenifer St Nw, Washington DC 20015 B Fort McPherson GA 7/27/1922 s Luther Deck Miller & Cornelia. BA GW 1947; MDiv VTS 1950. D 6/9/1950 P 12/1/1950 Bp Angus Dun. m 9/1/2002 Barbara Miller. R S Dav's Par Washington DC 1964-1994; R S Jas' Par Lothian MD 1956-1964; Asst All SS Ch Frederick MD 1953-1956; Asst All Souls Memi Epis Ch Washington DC 1950-1953.

MILLER, Marion Renee (Tenn) Po Box 1903, Monterey CA 93942 B Denver CO 1/20/1953 d Bruce David Anderson & Barbara Lee. BA NE Illinois U 1975; MDiv SWTS 1984. D 6/24/1984 P 3/1/1985 Bp Joseph Thomas Heistand. c 1. S Andr's Ch Marianna AR 2006-2009; Explorefaithorg Memphis TN 2003-2010; Credo Inst Inc. Memphis TN 2002-2005; Calv Ch Memphis TN 2002-2004; Cn To Ordnry & Exec Off Dio El Camino Real Monterey CA 1997-1999; Dio Idaho Boise ID 1988-1997; Dir Of The Diac Formation Dio Idaho Boise ID 1988-1990; Vic Ch Of The H Sprt Bullhead City AZ 1986-1988; Rural Dir Of Bp'S Sch Mnstry Dio Arizona Phoenix AZ 1986-1988; Vic Trin Epis Ch Kingman AZ 1985-1988; Assoc R Ch Of The Epiph Flagstaff AZ 1985; S Jn The Bapt Epis Ch Glendale AZ 1984-1985. Oblate Ascen Priority Ord Of S Ben. thedesertspirit@yahoo.com

MILLER, Mark Joseph (Oly) 913 2nd St, Snohomish WA 98290 **R S Jn's Epis Ch Snohomish WA 1997-** B Minneapolis MN 6/30/1951 s Robert August Miller & Betty Jean. BA Pacific Luth U 1975; MDiv Nash 1979; St. Petersburg Theol Acad RU 1993. D 7/21/1979 P 7/8/1980 Bp Robert Hume Cochrane. m 4/16/1994 Julie Wilkenson c 1. R S Ptr's Ch Huntington WV 1996-1997; P-in-c Ch Of The H Apos Bellevue WA 1994-1995; Ecum Off Dio Olympia Seattle WA 1989-1993; Cur S Paul's Ch Seattle WA 1987-1993; Vic S Jos And S Jn Ch Steilacoom WA 1981-1987; Asst S Andrews Epis Ch Port Angeles WA 1979-1981. Angl Soc 1997. medwriter1@comcast.net

MILLER JR, Merrill Cushing (WNC) 250 Miller Dr, Brevard NC 28712 B Raleigh NC 7/8/1929 s Merrill Cushing Miller & Hallie Erdine. BA U So 1951; MDiv PDS 1956; SMU 1961; Texas Med Cntr Inst Of Rel 1961. D 6/24/1956 Bp Edwin A Penick P 1/5/1957 Bp Richard Henry Baker. m 7/11/1964 Joyce A Anderson c 3. Secy Dio Wstrn No Carolina Asheville NC 1996-1998; Com Dio Wstrn No Carolina Asheville NC 1987-1988; Stndg Com Dio Wstrn No Carolina Asheville NC 1979-1983; R S Phil's Ch Brevard NC 1976-1996; All SS Epis Ch Charlotte NC 1969-1976; Dio No Carolina Raleigh NC 1965-1976; R S Barth's Ch Pittsboro NC 1956-1959. Apha Coll Of Chapl 1966-1974; Mem Of Assembly Of Epis Chapl 1966-1974. mcjam@comporium.net

MILLER, Monroe Richard (NI) 17716 Downing Dr, Lowell IN 46356 **P-in-c Chr The King Epis Ch Huntington IN 2005-; Supply S Andr's By The Lake Epis Ch Michigan City IN 2002-; COM Dio Nthrn Indiana So Bend IN 1991-** B Portland OR 11/26/1945 s Monroe Marchbank Miller & Alismarie. BS Ferris St U 1969. D 1/4/1989 Bp Francis Campbell Gray P 4/28/2002 Bp Edward Stuart Little II. m 8/23/1969 Cynthia Louise Bird. D S Andr's Epis Ch Valparaiso IN 1989-2002. NAAD 1989-2003. mrichard.miller@att.net

MILLER, Nancy Fay (RI) 82 Rockmeadow Rd, Westwood MA 02090 **COM Dio Rhode Island Providence RI 1995-** B Boston MA 4/3/1938 d Ralph Francis Fay & Vera Isabel. Wheelock Coll 1958; BA Simmons Coll 1988; Rhode Island Sch for Deacons 1995. D 6/24/1995 Bp J Clark Grew II. m 2/22/1958 Richard Watson Miller c 4. Dn Ch Of The Gd Shpd Pawtucket RI 1999-2000; Exec Dir Dio Rhode Island Providence RI 1996-2000; D S Mart's Ch Providence RI 1995-1999. Friends Of The Fllshp; NAAD; SCHC. millerpacem@cs.com

MILLER, Patricia L (WMo) 17212 East 44th Street Court, Independence MO 64055 **Vic S Mich's Epis Ch Independence MO 1999-** B Emory University GA 6/4/1950 d Harold Blaine Miller & Sarah Elizabeth. RN Georgia Bapt Hosp Sch of Nrsng Atlanta GA 1971; BSN Med Coll of Georgia 1978; MSN Med Coll of Georgia 1979; MDiv Epis TS of The SW 1996; DMin St. Paul's TS Kansas City MO 2005. D 6/7/1997 P 12/7/1997 Bp William Jerry Winterrowd. Assoc S Ambr Epis Ch Boulder CO 1997-1999. ppdb86amo@prodigy.net

MILLER, Patrick J. (Tex) 3514 Corondo Ct., Houston TX 77005 **R S Mk's Ch Houston TX 2008-** B Gulfport MI 12/21/1966 s Felix Perryman Miller & Nan Bruce. BA Austin Coll 1990; MDiv Epis TS of the SW 2000. D 6/17/2000 Bp Claude Edward Payne P 6/27/2001 Bp Don Adger Wimberly. m 11/20/1999 Allison S Standish c 2. Cn for Chr Formation Chr Ch Cathd Houston TX 2003-2008; S Mk's Epis Sch Houston TX 2003-2008; Asst R S Richard's Of Round Rock Round Rock TX 2000-2003. Camp Allen Bd 2005; Dn, E Harris Convoc 2008; Stndg Com 2006-2009. revpjm@att.net

MILLER, Paul Bernard (CNY) 829 Hamlin Dr, S Daytona FL 32119 **Died 2/7/2010** B Watertown NY 12/9/1917 s Jacob Walter Miller & Mabel Sarah. BA Hob 1940; BD VTS 1949; MDiv VTS 1970. D 6/27/1949 Bp Malcolm E Peabody P 1/1/1950 Bp Walter M Higley. c 3. Assn Chapl. Combat Infantry Medal; Bronze Star.

MILLER, Richard Allan (Pa) 1521 Ashby Rd, Paoli PA 19301 B Philadelphia PA 5/4/1941 s Charles Ross Miller & Mary. BA Witt 1963; MDiv PDS 1966; STM GTS 1968; SFTS 1976. D 6/11/1966 Bp Robert Lionne DeWitt P 12/21/1966 Bp Jonathan Goodhue Sherman. m 8/21/1965 Linda Webber c 3. Pa Dioc Coun Dio Pennsylvania Philadelphia PA 1981-1984; S Fran-In-The-Fields

Malvern PA 1979-1999; Assoc All SS' Epis Ch Chevy Chase MD 1970-1979; Asst Hdmstr Par Sch Gr Epis Ch Massapequa NY 1968-1970; Cur Adv Ch Of The Adv Westbury NY 1966-1968. richamiller@verizon.net

MILLER, Richard Sevier (Ida) 1312 Wisconsin St Apt 232, Apt 232, Hudson WI 54016 B Milwaukee WI 1/5/1927 s George Benjamin Miller & Inez Fitzhugh. BA Carroll Coll 1950; GTS 1953; Cert No Dakota St U 1972. D 5/17/1953 P 11/30/1953 Bp William J Gordon Jr. m 5/30/1953 Anita Eells c 6. P S Phil's Challis ID 1993-2008; Int S Lk's Epis Ch Idaho Falls ID 1990-1992; Vic S Paul's Indn Mssn Sioux City IA 1981-1986; Dio So Dakota Sioux Falls SD 1974-1981; Geth Epis Ch Sisseton SD 1972-1981; P-in-c S Jas Epis Ch Sisseton SD 1971-1981; P-in-c S Lk's Sta Sisseton SD 1971-1981; P-in-c S Mary's Epis Ch Sisseton SD 1971-1981; Trin Ch Wahpeton ND 1969-1971; Vic Chr Ch Chamberlain SD 1961-1969; R Trin Ch Baraboo WI 1956-1961; Min in charge S Jn's Ch Allakaket AK 1953-1956. Auth, "Power of the Higher One in AA's 12 Steps," 1987. dick.anita@att.net

MILLER, R(obert) Cameron (WNY) Trinity Church, 371 Delaware Ave, Buffalo NY 14202 **R Trin Epis Ch Buffalo NY 1999-** B Muncie IN 12/5/1953 s Robert Grant Miller & Virginia. BA Skidmore Coll 1976; MDiv EDS 1980; Coll of Preachers 1989. D 6/24/1980 P 3/21/1981 Bp Edward Witker Jones. m 6/12/1982 M Kathryn Weeks c 4. R S Steph's Epis Ch And U Columbus OH 1989-1999; R S Matt's Ch Indianapolis IN 1982-1989; Asst St Johns Epis Ch Lafayette IN 1980-1982. cammiller@trinitybuffalo.org

MILLER, Robert McGregor (Pa) 2039 Serendipity Way, Schwenksville PA 19473 **P-in-c Trin Ch Gulph Mills King Of Prussia PA 2008-** B Honolulu HI 10/27/1948 s Frank Dickson Miller & Margaret. BS USMA At W Point 1972; MS USAF Inst Of Tech Wright-Pater 1980; MDiv VTS 1995. D 6/10/1995 P 12/16/1995 Bp Frank Harris Vest Jr. m 6/9/1972 Linda Sue Boyd c 2. Int S Alb's Ch Roxborough Philadelphia PA 2006-2008; Int S Ptr's Ch Phoenixville PA 2003-2006; R Ch Of The Mssh Lower Gwynedd PA 1999-2003; R The Epis Ch Of The Adv Norfolk VA 1995-1999. frbobmiller@gmail.com

MILLER, Robert William (Minn) 11030 Batello Dr, Venice FL 34292 **The Epis Ch Of The Gd Shpd Venice FL 2008-** B San Francisco CA 4/27/1942 s Gerald Koford Miller & Betty Jean. U CA 1964; BA San Francisco St U 1967; MDiv Nash 1971. D 6/27/1970 P 2/28/1971 Bp C Kilmer Myers. m 8/18/1975 Margaret Anne Ehlen. P-in-c Trin Ch Litchfield MN 2002-2008; Hisp Mssnr Chr Ch Albert Lea MN 1999-2000; Dio Minnesota Minneapolis MN 1997-1998; P-in-c La Mision El Santo Nino Jesus S Paul MN 1997-1998; P-in-c S Matt's Epis Ch Minneapolis MN 1993-1997; R S Jas On The Pkwy Minneapolis MN 1990-1993; AIDS T/F Dio Iowa Des Moines IA 1989-1990; Asst S Jn's By The Campus Ames IA 1988-1989; Exec Coun Appointees New York NY 1979-1988; Dioc Ecum Off Dio Honduras Miami FL 1975-1987; Asst S Paul's Ch Oakland CA 1974-1976. Auth, *w Eyes Wide Open*, LN Press, 1998; Auth, *Hm is Where the Heart Wants to Be*, LN Press, 1993; Auth, *A Time of Hope*, Morehouse, 1979; Auth, *A Gift of Time*, Morehouse, 1977; Auth, *Chld's Liturgies*, Paulist Press, 1976. CT 1971; Immac Heart Cmnty 1975. rw2miller@comcast.net

MILLER, Roger Edward (CFla) 11620 Claymont Circle, Windermere FL 34786 B Albany NY 12/11/1936 s Edward Norman Miller & Arlie Mabel. BS Worcester Polytechnic Inst 1959; MS Florida Inst of Tech 1969; MDiv SWTS 1976. D 6/29/1976 P 1/13/1977 Bp William Hopkins Folwell. m 12/8/1962 Rita E Walton c 3. R S Geo Epis Ch The Villages FL 1998-2006; Stndg Com Dio Cntrl Florida Orlando FL 1991-1994; Curs Cmsn Dio Cntrl Florida Orlando FL 1986-1988; R Chr Ch Longwood FL 1985-1998; Evang Cmsn Dio Cntrl Florida Orlando FL 1983-1986; Dioc Bd Dio Cntrl Florida Orlando FL 1980-1983; Hondurasg Cmsn Dio Cntrl Florida Orlando FL 1978-1985; R S Marg's Ch Inverness FL 1978-1985; Cur Trin Ch Vero Bch FL 1976-1978. heyrog@gmail.com

MILLER, Ronald Homer (Md) 830 W 40th St. Apt 860, Baltimore MD 21211 **Int Ch Of S Mary The Vrgn Baltimore MD 2010-** B Butler PA 6/18/1936 s Walter Homer Miller & Marion Elizabeth. BA Ya 1960; STB GTS 1964; STM GTS 1968; PhD Ford 1972. D 6/19/1964 Bp George P Gunn P 5/1/1965 Bp David Shepherd Rose. m 5/20/1961 Mary Hotchkiss c 1. Int Ch Of The Adv Baltimore MD 2000-2003; Asst S Jas' Epis Ch Baltimore MD 1999-2000; Dio Maryland Baltimore MD 1998-2002; Assoc R S Jas' Epis Ch Baltimore MD 1991-1997; Assoc for Ord Mnstry Dio Maryland Baltimore MD 1990-1994; Assoc R S Barth's Ch Baltimore MD 1989-1990; Dio Pittsburgh Monroeville PA 1987; Dio Maryland Baltimore MD 1978-1982; BOEC Dio Pittsburgh Monroeville PA 1977-1986; R S Alb's Epis Ch Murrysville PA 1977-1986; BEC Dio Maryland Baltimore MD 1975-1977; Assoc S Barth's Ch Baltimore MD 1974-1977; Liturg Cmsn Dio Maryland Baltimore MD 1972-1977; Asst Par of Trin Ch New York NY 1971-1972; Asst Zion Epis Ch Wappingers Falls NY 1967-1968; Cur Ch Of The Epiph Danville VA 1964-1965. Auth, "An Instructed Euch," *OPEN*, 1978; Auth, "A Study Guide for the H Euch PBCP," Morehouse Pub, 1977; Auth, "Liturg Materials in the Acts of Jn," *Studia Patristica XIII*, 1971. ADLMC 1973-1989; Ord of S Helena 1978; RACA 1986; Societas Liturgica 1972. ronmiller1@verizon.net

MILLER, Stephen Arthur (WNC) Po Box 177, Glendale Springs NC 28629 **R Par Of The H Comm Glendale Sprg NC 1999-** B Saline MI 5/17/1947 s Harold Albert Miller & Delores Margaret. BA MI SU 1969; MDiv STUSo 1982. D 6/7/1982 Bp Hunley Agee Elebash P 12/18/1982 Bp William Evan Sanders. m 12/28/1968 Susan Robison c 1. S Barn Ch Dillon SC 1996-1998; Int The Ch Of The Cross Bluffton SC 1996; S Thos Ch Savannah GA 1995; S Mk's Epis Ch Charleston SC 1993-1994; R S Jude's Epis Ch Walterboro SC 1984-1993; Atone Ch Walterboro SC 1984-1988; Trst The TS at The U So Sewanee TN 1983-1984; Cur S Mary's Ch Kinston NC 1982-1984. smpriest@skybest.com

✠ **MILLER, Rt Rev Steven Andrew** (Mil) 804 E Juneau Ave, Milwaukee WI 53202 **Bp of Milwaukee Dio Milwaukee Milwaukee WI 2003-** B Detroit MI 9/30/1957 s Ben Andrew Miller & Doris Ann. BA MI SU 1979; MDiv GTS 1984; DD GTS 2004. D 6/30/1984 Bp Henry Irving Mayson P 12/30/1984 Bp H Coleman McGehee Jr Con 10/18/2003 for Mil. m 2/4/1989 Cynthia Celeste Presley. Pres of the Stndg Com Dio Virginia Richmond VA 2002-2003; Dn Reg XV Dio Virginia Richmond VA 1999-2003; R S Alb's Epis Ch Annandale VA 1996-2003; Ecum Cmsn Dio Virginia Richmond VA 1994-1996; Ecum Cmsn Dio Virginia Richmond VA 1994-1996; R Chr Epis Ch Gordonsville VA 1990-1996; Vic Chr Ch Epis Boonville MO 1986-1990; Dio W Missouri Kansas City MO 1986-1990; Vic S Mary's Ch Fayette MO 1986-1990; Cur Chr Epis Ch S Jos MO 1984-1986. Cdl Trainers 2001-2011. Receiving Bp's Shield Dio W Missouri MT 1988. bishop11@diomil.org

MILLER, Susan Heilmann (ECR) 25020 Pine Hills Dr, Carmel CA 93923 B Yuba City CA 1/13/1945 d Paul Clay Heilmann & Helen Christine. BA Stan 1966; MS Col 1969; MA Stan 1973; PhD Stan 1976; MDiv CDSP 2003. D 6/28/2003 P 1/10/2004 Bp Richard Lester Shimpfky. m 6/24/1967 Allen C Miller. S Mths Ch Seaside CA 2003-2008. Preaching & Theol subscription to Interp for excelle CDSP 2003; Preaching Excellence ECF 2003.

MILLER, Thomas Paul (NY) 165 Christopher St Apt 5W, New York NY 10014 **Cathd Of St Jn The Div New York NY 2003-** B West Reading PA 8/13/1949 s Joseph Louis Miller & Shirley Jane. BA U Pgh 1971; MDiv UTS 1989; STM GTS 1998. D 6/9/1990 P 12/15/1990 Bp Richard Frank Grein. S Greg's Epis Ch Woodstock NY 1994-1995; S Mich's Ch New York NY 1990-1994. CHS, Assoc of 1991; SSJE, Fllshp of 2002. stgreg@ulster.net

MILLER, Todd Lawrence (Mass) 12 Ridge Ave., Newton MA 02459 **R Trin Ch Newton Cntr MA 2006-** B Racine WI 8/8/1969 s David Max Miller & Marilyn Jane. BA S Olaf Coll 1991; MDiv VTS 2004. D 6/19/2004 P 1/22/2005 Bp Joseph Jon Bruno. m 11/26/1999 Ashley Paige Duggan c 2. Par Of Chr Ch Andover MA 2004-2006; S Paul's Epis Ch Ventura CA 1999-2002. toddmiller@trinitynewton.org

MILLER, Valerie Ann (Be) 2227 NW 79th Ave, Doral FL 33122 B Opalika AL 10/9/1978 d John McQueen Miller & Sue R. AA Edison Cmnty Coll Ft Myers FL 2001; BFA Florida Atlantic U 2003; MDiv EDS 2008. D 6/16/2007 P 4/19/2008 Bp Leopold Frade. Exec Coun Appointees New York NY 2008-2009. revvalmiller@yahoo.com

MILLER, Victoria C (Ct) 350 Sound Beach Ave, Old Greenwich CT 06870 **R S Sav's Epis Ch Old Greenwich CT 2002-** B Philadelphia PA 11/9/1953 d Sidney Lincoln Miller & Jean Eleanor. BA Smith 1975; MBA Harv 1979; MDiv GTS 1990; ThD GTS 1998. D 6/9/1990 P 12/15/1990 Bp Richard Frank Grein. Asst to R S Steph's Ch Ridgefield CT 1998-2002; Dir The CPG New York NY 1994-1998; Assoc P Chr And S Steph's Ch New York NY 1990-1998; Ch Pension Fund New York NY 1990-1998. Auth, "The Lambeth arts: Doctrinal Dvlpmt And Conflict In The Sixteenth Century Engl," *Latimer Hse Stds*, Latimer Hse, 1994; Auth, "Wm Wake And The Reunion Of Christians," *Angl & Epis Hist*, 1993; Auth, "Ecclesiology, Scripture, & Tradition In The Dublin Agreed Statement," *Harvard Theol Revs*, 1993. VICTORIASTSAV@SNET.NET

MILLER, William Bruce (Haw) PO Box 1745, Lihue HI 96766 **R S Mich And All Ang Ch Lihue HI 2006-** B 1/16/1959 BS Abilene Chr Univ 1981; MDiv McCormick TS 1986; CITS Epis TS of the SW 1991. D 10/2/1989 Bp Maurice Manuel Benitez P 4/3/1990 Bp Anselmo Carral-Solar. m 4/6/1991 Leslie Johnson. R Trin Ch Houston TX 1999-2006; R S Jas Ch Austin TX 1991-1998; P S Jn The Div Houston TX 1989-1991; S Jn The Div Houston TX 1986-1989. Auth, ",The Gospel According to Sam," Seabury Books, 2005. fatherbill@stmichaels-kauai.org

MILLER, William Charles (SC) Association of Theological Schools, 10 Summit Park Drive, Pittsburgh PA 15275 **Asstg P Ch Of The Nativ Crafton PA 2006-** B Minneapolis MN 10/26/1947 s Robert Charles Miller & Cleithra Mae. AB Indiana Wesl 1968; MLS Kent St U 1974; PhD Kent St U 1983; MARS Cntrl Bapt TS 1988; MBA Mid Amer Nazarene U 1997; STM Nash 2001. D 12/7/2006 P 6/30/2007 Bp Keith Lynn Ackerman. m 7/25/1969 Brenda Barnes c 2. The CBS 2004. miller@ats.edu

MILLER, William Robert (CPa) 182 Dew Drop Rd Apt G, York PA 17402 B Anniston AL 2/8/1959 s William R Miller & Joyce. BA Eckerd Coll 1982; MA Hollins U 1983; PhD SUNY 1989. D 6/11/2005 Bp Michael Whittington Creighton. c 1.

MILLER IV, Woodford D (CFla) 2508 Creekside Dr., Fort Piece FL 34981 **S Paul's Epis Ch New Smyrna Bch FL 2010-** B 7/25/1969 s Woodford D Miller & Josephine. AA Polk Cmnty Coll 1994; BA U of So Florida 1995; MDiv TESM 2007. D 6/2/2007 P 12/9/2007 Bp John Wadsworth Howe. m 6/20/2007 Sindy R Miller c 2. Asst R/Acad Chapl S Andr's Epis Ch Ft Pierce FL 2007-2010. dmiller139@gmail.com

MILLER, W Terry (Fla) 25928 Kilreigh Dr, Farmington Hills MI 48336 B Jacksonville FL 10/8/1978 s William Terry Miller & Holly Bothfeld. BA U So 2001; MDiv Virginia Thelogical Sem 2005; STM Luth TS at Gettysburg 2012. D 6/5/2005 P 12/11/2005 Bp Samuel Johnson Howard. m 1/14/2006 Lauren Edith Caywood. Assoc Chr Ch Cranbrook Bloomfield Hills MI 2005-2009. millersoak@hotmail.com

MILLER, Wylie Wayne (Dal) 13739 Spring Grove Ave, Dallas TX 75240 **Vic Ch Of Our Sav Dallas TX 2008-** B Hutchinson KS 12/18/1951 s Chester Wayne Miller & Allene Margarette. BA Pk Coll Parkville MO 1976; MDiv Duke 1993; VTS 1994; MBA U of Phoenix 2010. D 6/5/1995 P 6/1/1996 Bp Robert Carroll Johnson Jr. m 11/18/1987 Patricia Joan Griffin c 3. R S Chris's Ch Dallas TX 2003-2006; R Ch Of The H Cross Paris TX 2000-2003; R Trin Ch Mt Airy NC 1997-2000. wyliemiller@yahoo.com

MILLER-COULTER, William John (WA) 241 Hungry Hollow Rd # 28, Spring Valley CA 10977 **Died 5/6/2010** B Philadelphia PA 6/17/1915 s William Dory Coulter & Jane Scott. MS Tem 1946. D 10/29/1950 P 4/25/1951 Bp Angus Dun. c 4.

MILLER-MUTIA, Sylvia Jean (Cal) 500 De Haro St, San Francisco CA 94107 **Yth and Fam Min S Greg Of Nyssa Ch San Francisco CA 2010-** B Fort Collins CO 2/10/1976 d Mark L Miller & Anne W. BFA U of Utah 1997; MA PSR 2002; CAS CDSP 2009; CTS CDSP 2010. D 6/5/2010 P 12/4/2010 Bp Marc Handley Andrus. m 1/5/2002 Donnel Mutia c 3. S Steph's Par Belvedere CA 2003-2010. sylvia.miller.mutia@gmail.com

MILLETTE, Carol Leslie (RI) 19 Midway Dr, Warwick RI 02886 B Pawtucket RI 1/27/1942 d Harold Johnson Haigh & Gertrude M. Rhode Island Sch For Deacons. D 4/5/1986 Bp George Nelson Hunt III. D S Lk's Ch Pawtucket RI 2011. clmillette@verizon.net

MILLICAN JR, Ford Jefferson (La) 3919 Morris Pl, Jefferson LA 70121 **S Mart's Epis Sch Metairie LA 2006-** B Baton Rouge LA 10/24/1967 s Ford Jefferson Millican & Jacquelyn Ann. BA LSU 1990; MDiv Epis TS of The SW 1999. D 2/28/1999 P 9/7/1999 Bp Charles Edward Jenkins III. m 8/7/1993 Lisa Gayle Ebeyer c 2. Dio Louisiana Baton Rouge LA 1999-2005; Chapl Ch Of The H Sprt New Orleans LA 1999.

MILLIEN, Jean Elie (Hai) Boite Postale 15331, Petionville Haiti B Gressier Port-au-Prince HT 2/19/1934 s Joseph Moliere Millien & Dormela. MDiv ETSC 1964; Dl Eld 1968. D 5/14/1964 Bp Charles Alfred Voegeli P 12/1/1964 Bp James Loughlin Duncan. m 9/6/1966 Marie-Mona Anglade c 2. Dio Haiti Ft Lauderdale FL 1996-1998; S Jn's Ch Stamford CT 1992-1996; Vic-In-Charge Ascen Ch New Haven CT 1991-1992; Dio Connecticut Hartford CT 1991-1992; Asst S Andr's Epis Ch Palmetto Bay FL 1989-1991; Dio Haiti Ft Lauderdale FL 1964-1987.

MILLIEN, Wilner (PR) PO Box 4916, Carolina PR 00984 Puerto Rico B 8/3/1934 D 6/22/1963 Bp Albert Ervine Swift P 12/22/1963 Bp Charles Alfred Voegeli. m 6/30/1964 Raymonde Delienn.

MILLIGAN, Donald Arthur (Mass) 222 Bowdoin St, Winthrop MA 02152 B Charleston SC 7/19/1943 s Walter Milligan & Ruth. BA Hob 1970; MDiv GTS 1973. D 6/9/1973 P 12/15/1973 Bp John Melville Burgess. m 2/9/1985 Kathleen Milligan c 3. R S Jn's Ch Winthrop MA 1991-2008; R St Jn the Bapt Epis Ch Linden NJ 1984-1991; S Barn-In-The-Dunes Gary IN 1978-1983; R S Jn's Ch Sharon MA 1974-1978; Cur Gr Ch Lawr MA 1973-1974. OHC, Ord Of S Anne.

MILLIGAN, Kathleen Sue (Ia) 3714 Pennsylvania Ave Apt. I-86, Dubuque IA 52002 **R S Jn's Epis Ch Dubuque IA 2006-; Chair- COM Dio Iowa Des Moines IA 2004-** B Des Moines IA 7/3/1949 d James Michael Milligan & Lura Thelma. BA Morningside Coll 1971; MDiv Garrett Evang TS 1981. D 4/18/1986 P 11/1/1986 Bp Walter Cameron Righter. Pres- Stndg Com Dio Iowa Des Moines IA 2001-2002; R S Alb's Ch Davenport IA 1996-2006; Vic Trin Ch Emmetsburg IA 1987-1996; Ch Of S Thos Algona IA 1986-1996. Ed, "Iowa Epis," 1988. ksmillig@netins.net

MILLIGAN, Keith Louis (WLa) 11517 South La Hwy #335, Abbeville LA 70510 **Died 4/13/2010** B Lafayette LA 12/31/1951 s Lynn Louis Milligan & Rita Mae. BA NE Louisiana U 1973; MDiv STUSo 1980. D 6/16/1980 P 12/19/1980 Bp Willis Ryan Henton. m 4/19/2010 Jennifer Meaux Milligan c 2. stpaulabbe@aol.com

MILLIGAN, Michael B (U) 28 Ridgeview Drive, Bountiful UT 84010 **Ret P Cathd Ch Of S Mk Salt Lake City UT 2008-** B Atlanta GA 5/22/1942 s Horace Franklin Milligan & Louise Burnley. Oxford Coll of Emory U 1962; BA W Georgia Univ. 1967; MDiv STUSo 1970; Georgia St Univ. 1980. D 6/27/1970 Bp Randolph R Claiborne P 3/6/1971 Bp Milton LeGrand Wood. m 11/6/1982 Katherine Clark January c 3. R Ch Of The Resurr Centerville UT 2004-2007; P-in-c S Paul's/Peace Ch Las Vegas NM 1998-2000; Vic Epis Ch Of The H Fam Santa Fe NM 1996-2004; Int S Bede's Epis Ch Santa Fe NM 1993-1994; Int The Epis Ch Of S Ptr And S Paul Marietta GA 1992-1993; P-in-c Gr-Calv Epis Ch Clarkesville GA 1991-1992; R S Julian's Epis Ch Douglasville GA 1985-1989; Chapl Coordntr Of Pstr Care All SS Epis Ch Atlanta GA 1981-1984; Chair Long-R Plnng T/F Dio Atlanta Atlanta GA 1974-1975; Dn, SW Atlanta Convoc Dio Atlanta Atlanta GA 1974-1975; R S Cathr's Epis Ch Marietta GA 1973-1976; R S Paul's Ch Macon GA 1970-1973. Ed, "Ed," *S Lk's Journ of Theol*, TS, Univ of So, 1970; Assoc. Ed, "Assoc. Ed," *S Lk Journ Theol*, TS, Univ of So, 1969. Woods Ldrshp Awd TS, Univ of So 1968. mbmilligan@gmail.com

MILLIKEN, Jean Louise (Va) 3732 N Oakland St, Arlington VA 22207 B Pittsburgh PA 2/23/1943 d Clyde Robert Moore & Lois Kathryn. BA Westminster Coll 1965; MDiv Candler TS Emory U 1978; DMin Wesley TS 1992. D 6/10/1978 Bp Charles Judson Child Jr P 12/6/1980 Bp Bennett Jones Sims. m 11/6/1965 William Milliken c 2. Assoc Chr Ch Alexandria VA 2006-2009; Pstr Assoc Cathd of St Ptr & St Paul Washington DC 2002-2006; Int S Ptr's Epis Ch Arlington VA 2001-2002; S Andr's Epis Ch Arlington VA 1987-1988; Ch Of The Resurr Alexandria VA 1984-1985; Chapl S Lk's Epis Ch Atlanta GA 1980-1983; D S Tim's Decatur GA 1979-1980. Auth, "Faith At Wk mag," 1992; Auth, "Power And Mnstry". Advncd Clinician Imago Relation Ther; AAPC. jlomill@aol.com

✠ **MILLIKEN, Rt Rev Michael Pierce** (WK) 2 Hyde Park Dr, Hutchinson KS 67502 **Dio Wstrn Kansas Hutchinson KS 2000-; R Gr Epis Ch Hutchinson KS 1998-** B Lexington KY 3/13/1947 s Jack Pierce Milliken & Pauline. BA U of Kentucky 1970; MDiv Epis TS In Kentucky 1973; MA Xavier U 1992. D 5/26/1973 P 11/30/1973 Bp Addison Hosea Con 2/19/2011 for WK. m 8/2/1969 Kathleen Smith c 1. Chair, Dept of Mnstry Dio Lexington Lexington KY 1986-1998; R Gr Epis Ch Florence KY 1977-1998; Vic S Matthews Ch Lexington KY 1973-1977. Soc of S Marg. bishop.wks@sbcglobal.net

MILLNER JR, Bollin Madison (Va) 8 N Laurel St, Richmond VA 23220 **R Gr & H Trin Epis Ch Richmond VA 2003-** B Richmond VA 8/3/1954 s Bollin Madison Millner & Shirley May. BA U Rich 1976; MA VTS 1979; Spec Stdt Duke 1983. D 4/15/1984 P 4/21/1985 Bp Robert Whitridge Estill. m 7/24/1976 Katherine A Kelly c 2. Stndg Com Dio Virginia Richmond VA 2000-2003; New Congrl Dvlpmt Dio Virginia Richmond VA 1998-2000; Ch Of The Gd Shpd Rocky Mt NC 1992-2003; Asst Deploy Off Dio Virginia Richmond VA 1989-1991; Imm Ch King and Queen Courthouse VA 1986-1992; R S Jn's Ch W Point VA 1986-1991; S Steph's Ch Durham NC 1984-1986. Phi Beta Kappa. bmillner2@gmail.com

MILLOTT, Diane Lynn (SwFla) 6710 Matt Pledger Ct, Fort Myers FL 33917 **D S Jn's Epis Ch St Jas City FL 2006-** B Muskegon MI 10/20/1945 d Frances Werschen & Alice. BBA U of No Florida 1976; MA U of So Florida 1994. D 6/18/2005 Bp John Bailey Lipscomb. m 10/23/1988 Robert Thomas Millott c 2. n07smith@aol.com

MILLOTT, Donna Evans (SwFla) No address on file. B Cleveland OH 11/3/1947 d Lester C Evans & Frances Ione. Kent St U. D 6/29/1991 Bp Rogers Sanders Harris. c 3. D S Hilary's Ch Ft Myers FL 1991-2011.

MILLOTT, Robert Thomas (SwFla) 6710 Matt Pledger Ct, North Fort Myers FL 33917 B Cleveland OH 12/31/1944 BS U of So Florida. D 6/14/2003 Bp John Bailey Lipscomb. m 10/23/1988 Diane Lynn Diane Lynn Werschen. D S Lk's Ch Ft Myers FL 2005-2011; D Lamb Of God Epis Ch Ft Myers FL 2003-2005. bach02@earthlink.net

MILLS JR, Arthur Donald (SO) 2696 Cedarbrook Way, Beavercreek OH 45431 **D S Andr's Ch Dayton OH 2008-** B Ft Chaffee AR 3/9/1958 s Arthur Donald Mills & Dorothy Mae. BS W Virginia Wesleyan Coll 1979; MS AF Inst of Tech 1983. D 6/14/2008 Bp Thomas Edward Breidenthal. c 1. amillsjr@woh.rr.com

MILLS, Byron Keith (Az) 596 W. Ord Mountain Rd, Globe AZ 85501 **Curs Sec Sprtl Dir Dio Arizona Phoenix AZ 2011-; R S Jn The Bapt Globe AZ 2002-** B Globe AZ 3/31/1952 s Von Coen Mills & Elwanda. BA U of Phoenix 1988. D 10/27/2001 P 11/9/2002 Bp Robert Reed Shahan. m 9/27/1972 Rayla Alene Beason c 4. D S Jn The Bapt Globe AZ 2001-2002. bkmills@hotmail.com

MILLS, Carol Ann Gillis (Tex) 2107 Olympic Dr, League City TX 77573 B Chicago IL 7/3/1944 d Donald Eugene Gillis & Annie Catherine. U MI; BS Estrn Michigan U 1967; MLS Texas Wmn's U 1973; BA California Sch for Deacons 1984. D 6/8/1985 Bp William Edwin Swing. m 4/17/1971 Joseph Milton Mills c 1. D S Paul's Ch Houston TX 1997-2009; D Chr Epis Ch Plano TX 1985-1988. carol_ann_mills@yahoo.com

MILLS, David Knight (SO) 172 Clark Point Rd # 696, Southwest Harbor ME 04679 B Evanston IL 10/17/1930 s Ellsworth Luther Mills & Mary Louise. BA Wms 1952; MDiv VTS 1957. D 6/8/1957 Bp William A Lawrence P 12/1/1957 Bp Richard S M Emrich. m 6/16/1956 Audrey Sands c 2. R Ch Of Our Sav Cincinnati OH 1960-1972; Cur All SS Epis Ch Pontiac MI 1957-1960. Auth, *The Sea Around Us ME Coast Guide*. amills3@earthlink.net

MILLS III, Edward James (ETenn) 2104 Lamont St, Kingsport TN 37664 **R S Paul's Epis Ch Kingsport TN 2005-** B Charleston WV 11/9/1954 s Edward

James Mills & Betty Berry. BA W Virginia Wesleyan Coll 1977; MDiv VTS 1980. D 6/15/1980 P 6/1/1981 Bp Robert Poland Atkinson. m 8/21/1976 Karen Lee Boyd. Asst Ch Of The Gd Samar Knoxville TN 2001-2004; S Thos' Epis Ch Abingdon VA 2000-2001; All SS' Epis Ch Morristown TN 1999-2000; Emm Epis Ch Bristol VA 1998-1999; S Thos Epis Ch Knoxville TN 1997-1998; S Jn's Epis Ch Johnson City TN 1996-1997; S Paul's Epis Ch Kingsport TN 1994-1996; S Andr's in the Vill Ch Barboursville WV 1985-1994; Vic S Mk's Epis Ch Berkeley Sprg WV 1982-1984; Asst S Mk's Epis Ch S Albans WV 1981-1982; D Chr Ch Clarksburg WV 1980-1981. "An Unexpectal Yet Brdden Journey," Intergrity Monograph. eretess@hotmail.com

MILLS, Eric Christopher (FdL) 347 Libal St, De Pere WI 54115 **R S Anne's Ch De Pere WI 2010-** B Milwaukee WI 6/17/1960 s Gerald M Mills & Elayne C. BA U of Texas 1989; MDiv Nash 1998. D 6/27/1998 P 1/22/1999 Bp Jack Leo Iker. m 10/11/1985 Susan G Moore c 3. Assoc R Chr Ch Bradenton FL 2007-2010; Chapl Off Of Bsh For ArmdF New York NY 2001-2007; Cur S Vinc's Cathd Bedford TX 1998-2001. abbamills@gmail.com

MILLS, Frederick Raymond (Pa) 31 Parkington Cir, East Syracuse NY 13057 B Lynn MA 6/20/1928 s Ernest Lyman Mills & Laura Roe. BA Bos 1954; STB Bos 1960; CAS EDS 1963. D 8/11/1963 P 12/21/1963 Bp Frederic Cunningham Lawrence. m 4/3/1972 Amalia Diane Sarkus c 4. Int Chr Ch Manlius NY 1999-2000; R Trin Ch Camden NY 1991-1997; R Trin Epis Ch Ambler PA 1983-1991; R S Thos' Epis Ch Syracuse NY 1973-1982; P-in-c S Paul's Ch Chittenango NY 1968-1973; P-in-c Trin Epis Ch Canastota NY 1968-1973; Chr Ch Par Lake Oswego OR 1964-1968; The Ch Of Our Redeem Lexington MA 1963-1964. fmills@twcny.rr.com

MILLS, Fred Thomas (Ky) 685 West Dr, Madisonville KY 42431 **D Dio Kentucky Louisville KY 1987-** B Salisbury NC 10/2/1927 s Fred Lee Mills & Hazzie Elizabeth. BS Bowling Green Coll of Commerce 1949. D 6/14/1987 Bp David Reed. m 8/31/1950 Barbara Ann Tucker c 4. NAAD. tmills5@earthlink.net

MILLS, Joe Dan (USC) 952 Hawthorne Lane Ext, Rock Hill SC 29730 **P Asscociate/ Vol Ch Of The Gd Shpd York SC 2009-** B Charlotte NC 6/14/1923 s Charles Hewlings Clark Mills & Eliza. BA U NC 1947; MA U of Wisconsin 1951; PhD U of Wisconsin 1954; MDiv SWTS 1959. D 6/28/1959 P 1/28/1960 Bp Richard S M Emrich. c 4. Asst Ch Of Our Sav Rock Hill SC 1974-1992; Asst S Paul's Ch Seattle WA 1969-1971; R S Steph's Epis Ch Cincinnati OH 1961-1968; Assoc Chr Ch Dearborn MI 1959-1961. Auth, "Dictionary of Educ, 3rd Ed," McGraw-Hill, 1973. CT 1962; S Greg: Abbey, Three Rivers, MI 1964. joemills@comporium.net

MILLS, John Gladstone (NY) 48 Morris Ave, Cold Spring NY 10516 B Marlette MI 3/16/1920 s John Gladstone Mills & Allie Gladys. BA U CA 1941; MA U CA 1943; STB GTS 1949; ABD Ford 1980. D 5/21/1949 Bp James P De Wolfe P 12/15/1949 Bp Donald J Campbell. m 2/14/1950 Margaret Tellor c 1. Asst Chr Ch Of Ramapo Suffern NY 1993-2000; R S Mary's Ch Cold Sprg NY 1961-1992; R S Lk's Ch Whitewater WI 1957-1960; Asst S Mary's Ch Mohegan Lake NY 1956-1957; R Chr Ch Par Ontario CA 1950-1956. Auth, *Ecum Journ*, 1979; Auth, *Cistercian Sprtlty Today*, 1977; Auth, "Hist of Chr Ch, Ontario," *Chr Ch Par, Ontario*, 1956; Auth, *Third Hour: Helene Iswolsky*. Affiliate for Graymoor Franciscan Friars 1990; Fllshp SS Alb & Sergius 1970; MATT TALB Retreat Mvmt 1986; Pax Christi USA. Silver Medal French Govt France 1941; Min des Affaires Etrangeres French Lit Dept., UCLA; DeWitt Clinton Awd Masonic Ord.

MILLS, John McQueen (LI) 1110 W. Ivanhoe Blvd Apt 14, Orlando FL 32804 **Died 9/30/2011** B New York NY 11/2/1923 s Allison Curtis Mills & Louisa Adams. BA U of Virginia 1949; STB Ya Berk 1952. D 5/1/1952 P 11/11/1952 Bp Frederick Lehrle Barry.

MILLS III, Joseph Edmund (LI) 1118 9th St Apt 9, Santa Monica CA 90403 B Brooklyn NY 11/15/1941 s Joseph Edmund Mills & Dorothy. BA Hob 1963; STB GTS 1966. D 6/16/1966 Bp Jonathan Goodhue Sherman P 12/1/1966 Bp Robert C Rusack. Cur S Aug By-The-Sea Par Santa Monica CA 1966-1968. exorcis@aol.com

MILLS JR, Joseph Milton (Tex) 205 Hillcrest Dr, Alvin TX 77511 **D Gr Epis Ch Alvin TX 2009-** B Dallas TX 9/1/1945 s Joseph Milton Mills & Odessa Mary. BS U of Texas 1967; MS LSU 1970; PhD The Australian Natl U 1977; BA California Sch for Deacons 1984. D 6/8/1985 Bp William Edwin Swing. m 4/17/1971 Carol Ann Gillis Mills c 3. D S Paul's Ch Houston TX 1997-2008; D S Chris's Ch League City TX 1990-1997; D Chr Epis Ch Plano TX 1985-1990. k5jmm@arrl.net

MILLS, Joy Anna Marie (Pa) 2103 Quail Ridge Dr, Paoli PA 19301 B Darby PA 9/19/1942 d Arthur Gunnar Carlson & Margaret Helen. Trans Vas 1962; BA Br 1964; MDiv EDS 1986; Fell AAPC 1988; MA Boston Coll 1988. D 6/13/1987 Bp David Elliot Johnson P 4/16/1988 Bp Allen Lyman Bartlett Jr. m 11/6/2004 Arthur C Benedict c 3. Pstr Assoc S Dav's Ch Wayne PA 1990-1992; Ch Of S Asaph Bala Cynwyd PA 1987-1990; Ch Of Our Sav Jenkintown PA 1987-1989. Auth, "My Living into His Dying," *Journeys: Essays from the Heart of Pstr Counslg*, Amer Assn of Pstr Counslg, 2008; Auth, "Living into Dying," *Journ of Pstr Care and Counslg*, Journ of Pstr Care Pub, Inc., 2003; co-Auth, "God's Sweet Surprises: Ang, Mentors, Friends May Fllshp Serv," *CWU*, CWU, 1999; Auth, "Lighting, Troubling, Raising, and Widening: Re-Imagining Revival/Decade Impressions," *Journ of Wmn Ministires*, Epsicopal Ch Pub Co., 1998; Auth, "Fourth Wrld Conf on Wmn," *Equal wRites*, RC Wmn Ord Conf, 1996; Auth, "Biblic Stories of Wmn: Death Dealing or Life Giving?," *The Renfrew Perspective*, The Renfrew Fndt, 1996. AAPC 1992; Wmn of Faith 1990-1995. joymills@verizon.net

MILLS, Keith Alan (La) 8440 East Co Road 200 North, Indianapolis IN 46234 **Died 4/27/2011** B South Haven MI 10/12/1936 s Charles Mills & Mildred. BA Lamar U 1963; Med LSU 1971; MDiv Bex 1973; EdD LSU 1975. D 6/21/1966 P 6/20/1967 Bp J Milton Richardson.

MILLS III, Ladson Frazier (SC) 3114 Mayfair Ln, Johns Island SC 29455 B Rock Hill SC 7/12/1951 s Ladson Frazier Mills & Doris. BA Cit 1973; MDiv STUSo 1980; DMin GTF 1999. D 6/14/1980 P 12/1/1980 Bp Gray Temple. c 2. R Chr Ch Frederica St Simons Island GA 2006-2011; Ch Of The Ascen Knoxville TN 1997-2006; R Trin Ch Myrtle Bch SC 1991-1997; Trst The TS at The U So Sewanee TN 1984-1988; Dio So Carolina Charleston SC 1984; Ch Of Our Sav Johns Island SC 1981-1991; S Jn's Epis Par Johns Island SC 1980. Auth, "It'S Christmas". pmills73@aol.com

MILLS, Nancy Thompson (Ga) PO Box 3136, Thomasville GA 31799 B Philadelphia PA 2/24/1944 d Frederic Charles Thompson & Mary Ruth Steet. Grad Degree Prog The TS at The U So 2004. D 6/10/2003 P 12/20/2003 Bp Henry Irving Louttit. m 11/15/1980 Luther Rice Mills. nmills@rose.net

MILLS, Stephen Howard (ECR) 6884 Burnside Dr, San Jose CA 95120 B South Weymouth MA 12/16/1946 s William Barrett Mills & Marjorie Clara. BA Claremont Coll 1970; JD U Pac 1976; MDiv CDSP 1984. D 6/10/1984 P 12/21/1984 Bp John Lester Thompson III. m 6/16/1990 Eleanor Wakefield c 1. Presiding Judge, Eccl Crt Dio El Camino Real Monterey CA 2008-2009; Bp Search Com Dio El Camino Real Monterey CA 2007; R The Epis Ch In Almaden San Jose CA 2002-2009; Dioc Coun Dio Nthrn California Sacramento CA 1986-1987; Vic H Fam Epis Ch Rohnert Pk CA 1984-2002. Auth, "Ins Fires Stwdshp Tool," *Journ Of Theol Ethics*, 1998. St Bar Of California 1976; Usta 1995. Write In Candidate For Pope RC Ch 2005. stephenmills09@gmail.com

MILLS, Susan Patricia (SO) 1060 Salem Ave, Dayton OH 45406 B Hazard KY 9/13/1939 d James Richard Mills & Mildred. BA Indiana U 1961; MA Indiana U 1966; MDiv GTS 1976. D 6/12/1976 Bp Paul Moore Jr P 3/5/1977 Bp James Stuart Wetmore. R S Andr's Ch Dayton OH 2000-2006; Liturg & Mus Cmsn Dio Indianapolis Indianapolis IN 1989-2000; R S Paul's Jeffersonville IN 1989-2000; Liturg Off Dio Delaware Wilmington DE 1984-1989; Dio Delaware Wilmington DE 1983-1989; Hosp Chapl S Jn's Ch New York NY 1983-1989; Vic S Steph's Ch Harrington DE 1983-1989; S Marg's Ch Bronx NY 1982-1983; Asst S Jn's Ch New York NY 1976-1979. Ord Of S Helena. susanm45406@gmail.com

MILLSAP, William Richard (Nev) PO Box 2246, Reno NV 89505 **Assoc R Trin Epis Ch Reno NV 2010-** B Oakland CA 7/31/1957 s Russel Donald Millsap & Carolyn Joyce. BA U of Nevada, Reno 1980; MA U of Nevada, Reno 1983. D 1/31/2006 P 7/31/2006 Bp Katharine Jefferts Schori. c 2. rmtrinity@gmail.com

MILLS-CURRAN, Lorraine Marie (RI) 7 Kimball Rd, Westborough MA 01581 **D for Brazilian Mnstry, Concord River Dnry Dio Massachusetts Boston MA 2010-; D S Andr's Ch Framingham MA 2007-** B Inglewood CA 1/7/1956 d Charles Roger Mills & Ruth Marie. BA U CA 1978; JD U CA 1982; MDiv Weston Jesuit TS 2001. D 8/24/1988 Bp William Davidson. m 8/27/1977 William Charles Mills-Curran c 3. D S Paul's Ch Natick MA 2001-2006; Yth Mnstry Coordntr Dio Rhode Island Providence RI 1992-1994; D S Paul's Ch No Kingstown RI 1990-1998. DOK; Natl Gld: Catchesis of the Gd Shpd. Phi Beta Kappa. lmcii@aol.com

MILLS-POWELL, Mark Oliver Mclay (Eur) No address on file. B 6/22/1955 s Neil Mclay Mills & Rosamond Mary. BA U Of Durham Gb 1978; MDiv VTS 1982. Rec 10/1/1988 as Priest Bp John Thomas Walker. m 8/21/1981 Dana Sedgwick Powell c 2. Old Fields Chap Hughesville MD 1988-1994. Auth, "Praying In The Shadow Of The Bomb". Soc Of S Fran.

MILNER JR, Raymond Joseph (SanD) 200 E 22nd St Apt 32, Roswell NM 88201 B Williston ND 11/9/1930 No Dakota U Grand Forks ND 1952. D 1/9/2007 Bp Jeffrey Neil Steenson. m 8/2/1954 Mary Martha Milner c 2.

MILTENBERGER, (George Kerr) Gordon (Dal) 10 Oak Village Rd, Greenville TX 75402 **Gr Ch Mesquite TX 2002-** B Saint Louis MO 5/18/1928 s George Kerr Miltenberger & Dorothy Zelle. BA Harv 1950; STB Ya Berk 1953; STM Ya Berk 1958. D 6/20/1953 P 12/21/1953 Bp Charles A Mason. m 2/23/1957 Dolores Shepherd c 2. R All SS Epis Ch Dallas TX 1973-1990; R Ch Of The H Comf Cleburne TX 1967-1973; P-in-c S Paul's Ch Westbrook CT 1956-1958; Vic S Lk's Epis Ch Stephenville TX 1954-1956; Cur S Matt's Cathd Dallas TX 1953-1954. MILTENBERGERFAMILY@GEUSNET.COM

MINARIK JR, Harry J (ETenn) 69 Hickory Trail, Norris TN 37828 **R S Fran' Ch Norris TN 2009-; R S Fran' Ch Norris TN 2009-; P-in -charge S Fran' Ch Norris TN 2007-; P-in-c S Fran' Ch Norris TN 2007-; D S Fran'**

Ch Norris TN 2006- B Atlanta GA 4/23/1949 s Harry J Minarik & Jaqueline V. BA E Tennessee St U 2003; MDiv TS 2006; MDiv U So 2006. D 5/27/2006 P 1/6/2007 Bp Charles Glenn VonRosenberg. m 10/29/2008 Sonya Minarik c 3. volmins@yahoo.com

MINDRUM, Alice Anderson (Ct) 60 Range Rd, Southport CT 06890 B Aurora IL 6/20/1949 d Gene Wilson Anderson & Marjorie Jean. BA U of Iowa 1972; MA Ya Berk 1994. D 6/8/2002 P 12/14/2002 Bp Andrew Donnan Smith. m 8/22/1970 Thomas Leigh Mindrum c 3. P-in-c Calv St Geo's Epis Ch Bridgeport CT 2009-2011; S Paul's Ch Fairfield CT 2007; Chr Ch Bethany CT 2006-2009; Chr Ch Ansonia CT 2006; Gr Epis Ch Norwalk CT 2006. aamindrum@gmail.com

MINER, Daniel Frederick (Az) 843 S Longmore Apt 1053, Mesa AZ 85202 **Died 7/28/2011** B Mineola NY 1/17/1941 s Thomas Daniel Miner & Hellen. BA Mid 1962; STB GTS 1965; STM GTS 1970; S Geo's Coll Jerusalem IL 1971. D 6/19/1965 P 12/1/1965 Bp Jonathan Goodhue Sherman. c 1.

MINER, Darren Ryan (Cal) 1750 29th Ave, San Francisco CA 94122 **Assoc Ch Of The Incarn San Francisco CA 2011-** B Salinas, CA 7/7/1959 s Ronald Francis Miner & Wilma Jean. BA U CA 1980; CPhil U CA 1983; MDiv CDSP 2006; MA Grad Theol Un 2006. D 6/5/2010 P 12/4/2010 Bp Marc Handley Andrus. m 7/28/2008 Mathew Chacko. Assoc Ch Of The Incarn San Francisco CA 2010-2011; D Ch Of The Incarn San Francisco CA 2010. Angl Assn of Biblic Scholars 2007; AP 2010; Integrity USA 1992; Soc of Cath Priests 2010. Trabert-Graebner Gk Scriptural Schlr's Awd CDSP 2005. darren.miner@comcast.net

MINER II, James Stevens (SO) 276 North Ardmore Road, Columbus OH 43209 B Columbus OH 6/24/1942 s Ralph Willis Miner & Phyllis Elisabethe. BA Ya 1964; BD Epis TS of The SW 1967. D 6/17/1967 P 12/16/1967 Bp Nelson Marigold Burroughs. m 6/5/1965 Elizabeth Wells Wilbur c 2. Assoc S Alb's Epis Ch Of Bexley Columbus OH 1999-2002; Int S Lk's Ch Granville OH 1997-1998; Int S Paul's Epis Ch Dayton OH 1996-1997; R Trin Ch Columbus OH 1986-1995; Exec Asst to Bp Dio Ohio Cleveland OH 1980-1986; R S Paul's Epis Ch Medina OH 1975-1980; Assoc S Jn's Ch Youngstown OH 1969-1975; Cur Gr Epis Ch Sandusky OH 1967-1969. jsminer@juno.com

MINER, Malcolm Hubbard (Haw) 2211 Pane Road, Koloa HI 96756 **Assoc R S Mich And All Ang Ch Lihue HI 1989-** B Holyoke MA 11/15/1920 s Harold Edson Miner & Blanche Barton. Bangor TS 1943; BA U of Maine 1946; Ya Berk 1949. D 12/10/1949 P 6/17/1950 Bp William A Lawrence. m 5/28/1989 Imogene Hagensen c 3. Assoc All SS' Epis Ch Anchorage AK 1975-1988; P-in-c S Barth's Ch Palmer AK 1973-1975; Untd Way Of Anchorage Anchorage AK 1969-1987; Asst S Barn Ch Warwick RI 1968-1969; Vic S Mths Ch Seaside CA 1963-1968; R All SS' Epis Ch Anchorage AK 1956-1962; R S Andr's Ch Oakland CA 1952-1956; Vic Chr Ch So Barre MA 1949-1951; Vic Chr Memi Ch No Brookfield MA 1949-1951. Auth, "Your Touch Can Heal," Faith Ridge, 1992; Auth, "Healing & The Abundant Life," Morehouse-Barlow, 1979; Auth, "Healing is for Real," Morehouse-Barlow Co., 1972. malcolm.miner@gmail.com

MINER, Robert Johnston (Ct) 15 Morningside Ter, Wallingford CT 06492 **Int S Jn's Epis Par Waterbury CT 2011-** B Westerly RI 4/1/1939 s John R Miner & Lila C. BA Leh 1961; STB Ya Berk 1964; Cert Trin-Dublin IE 1989. D 6/20/1964 P 3/27/1965 Bp John S Higgins. m 8/22/1964 Gladys L Tilley c 2. Int S Ann's Epis Ch Old Lyme CT 2010-2011; Int Trin Ch Branford CT 2009-2010; Int S Paul's Ch Wallingford CT 2007-2009; Vic All SS Ch Ivoryton CT 2006-2007; Int S Ptr's Epis Ch Bennington VT 2003-2005; Int Trin Chap Hartford CT 2003; Assoc Grtr Hartford Reg Mnstry E Hartford CT 2002-2003; R S Sav's Epis Ch Old Greenwich CT 1974-2000; R Imm S Jas Par Derby CT 1966-1974; Asst Chr Ch In Lonsdale Lincoln RI 1964-1966. EDEO (Pres: 1998-2002) 1980-2006; EPGM (Treas 2003- Cnvnr 2007-2008) 2002-2011. canonminer@aol.com

MINER-PEARSON, Anne (Minn) 15601 Island Road, Burnsville MN 55306 B Kansas City MO 6/13/1941 d Paul V Miner & Dorothy M. Untd TS of the Twin Cities; BS U of Kansas 1963; MDiv SWTS 1983; DMin SWTS 1995. D 6/29/1983 P 1/18/1984 Bp Robert Marshall Anderson. m 5/22/1983 Daniel V Pearson. Ch Of The Nativ Burnsville MN 2004-2007; Dio Minnesota Minneapolis MN 1998-2003; R All Souls' Epis Ch San Diego CA 1996-1998; Int S Mary's Ch St Paul MN 1984-1986; Asst S Clem's Ch S Paul MN 1983-1984. Auth, "Sermon," *Abingdon Wmn Preaching Annual Year A*, Abingdon Press; Auth, *Essays & Interviews on Wmn Sprtlty*; Auth, *Mar & Sprtlty: Revisiting the Mar Cov*; Auth, "Sacr Strands," *Sermons by Minnsota Wmn*; Auth, *The Spiral Path*. anneminer-pearson@comcast.net

MINERVA SR, Royal Edward (Fla) 2541 Lang Ave, Orange Park FL 32073 B New York NY 3/5/1930 s Dominic Thomas Minerva & Emma Elizabeth. Dio Florida Sch Of Mnstry; BA Jones Coll Jacksonville FL 1979. D 12/8/2002 Bp Samuel Johnson Howard. m 6/20/1952 Mildred Minerva c 1. rminer6@aol.com

MINGLEDORFF, Paschal Schirm (Ga) 9541 Whitfield Ave, Savannah GA 31406 **Respite P S Ptr's Epis Ch Savannah GA 2001-** B Savannah GA 3/29/1935 d William Philip Schirm & Doris. S Mary's Jr Coll Raleigh NC 1953; U GA 1954; Armstrong Atlantic St Coll 1978; Cert STUSo 1992; STUSo 2000. D 4/18/1995 P 12/18/1999 Bp Henry Irving Louttit. m 7/11/1960 Frederick William Mingledorff c 3. D S Fran Of The Islands Epis Ch Savannah GA 1998-1999; D S Thos Ch Savannah GA 1995-1998. psming@aol.com

MINICH, Henry Nichols Faulconer (SeFla) 3115 Dundee Rd, Earlysville VA 22936 B West Chester PA 2/18/1931 s Ralph P Minich & Margaret F. BA U of Virginia 1953; MDiv VTS 1958; STM STUSo 1968; JD U of Miami 1976. D 5/10/1958 Bp Oliver J Hart P 11/15/1958 Bp Angus Dun. m 8/30/1975 Helen D Morris c 3. Int S Anne's Par Scottsville VA 2004-2005; Chr Epis Ch Charlottesville VA 1999-2000; Assoc R S Anne's Par Scottsville VA 1998-2001; Int Trin Epis Ch Charlottesville VA 1995-1996; Com Const & Cns Dio SE Florida Miami FL 1990-1994; Dn Dio SE Florida Miami FL 1983-1994; Mem, Comm. on Const & Cn Dio SE Florida Miami FL 1973-1984; Chap of the Venerable Bede Coral Gables FL 1970-1994; Mem, SLC Dio SE Florida Miami FL 1970-1985; Vic H Sacr Pembroke Pines FL 1961-1964. *Var arts in Bioethics*, 2003. CBS; GAS; Oblate Ord of S Ben. Hon Cn Trin Cathd Miami FL 1991; "Who's Who in Rel" 1974; VP's Awd for Serv U of Miami. nm2n@virginia.edu

MINICH, Mason Faulconer (Va) 5055 Seminary Rd Apt 1319, Alexandria VA 22311 B West Chester PA 2/21/1938 s Ralph P Minich & Margaret Elizabeth. BA U of Virginia 1963; SWTS 1964; MDiv VTS 1966; Dplma Universita Italania per Stranieri Perugia IT 1972; Dplma Universidad de Valencia Valencia ES 1974. D 6/11/1966 Bp Robert Fisher Gibson Jr P 4/5/1967 Bp Robert Bruce Hall. Vic Ch of the Incarn Mineral VA 1970-1971; Vic S Jas Epis Ch Louisa VA 1970-1971; Cur S Dunst's McLean VA 1966-1967. masonminich@yahoo.com

MINIFIE, Charles Jackson (NY) 23 Sherman Dr, Hilton Head Island SC 29928 **P All SS Ch Hilton Hd Island SC 2005-** B Providence RI 4/1/1941 s Benjamin Minifie & Frances Turner. BA Trin Hartford CT 1963; MDiv EDS 1966. D 6/4/1966 P 12/17/1966 Bp Horace W B Donegan. m 5/30/2009 Justina Lasley c 4. R Chr Ch Bronxville NY 1995-2003; Int Calv Epis Ch Summit NJ 1993-1994; Int S Lk's Par Darien CT 1992-1993; Cathd of St Ptr & St Paul Washington DC 1983-1991; The Hartford Sem Fndt Hartford CT 1979-1980; R Trin Ch Newport RI 1973-1978; Assoc Trin Epis Cathd Portland OR 1969-1973; Asst S Thos Ch New York NY 1966-1969. Auth, "Wm Reed Huntington & Ch Unity," *Hist mag*. Ord of S Jn 1989. chad@hargray.com

MINIFIE, Thomas Richardson (Oly) 1311 Bonneville Ave Apt C, Snohomish WA 98290 B Corpus Christi TX 10/1/1944 s Benjamin Minifie & Frances Turner. BA Mt Un Coll 1967; MDiv PDS 1971. D 6/5/1971 P 12/18/1971 Bp Horace W B Donegan. m 1/23/1976 Jennifer Reed. S Phil Ch Marysville WA 1997-2004; Asst S Jn's Ch Kirkland WA 1994-1997; R S Paul's Ch Malden MA 1991-1994; Assoc R S Lk's Epis Ch Seattle WA 1985-1991; R S Lk's Ch Marietta OH 1980-1985; Assoc S Paul's Ch Dedham MA 1974-1980.

MINISTER, Marshall Vincent (Neb) 7214 S 183rd St, Omaha NE 68136 **Died 3/21/2010** B Rawlins WY 10/28/1923 s Howard Leslie Minister & Amy Gertrude. BA U of Nthrn Colorado 1947; MDiv SWTS 1950. D 3/25/1950 P 9/29/1950 Bp Harold L Bowen. c 4. Auth, "The Enormities of Rome," *Inc.*, Vantage Press, 2002; Auth, "NE 3 Cathedrals," *Cathd Age*; Auth, "The Punishment of Wickedness & Vice," *Cathd Age & Chr Challenge*; Auth, "Rome Must Disavow Leo," *Epis*. Hon Cn Trin Cathd Omaha NE 1993; Phi Alpha Theta Hon Hist Fraternity 1947.

MINNICH-LOCKEY, Laura Karen (Va) 79 Laurel St, Harrisonburg VA 22801 **Dio Virginia Richmond VA 2001-** B Stuttgart Germany 5/17/1962 d Lawrence Edgar Minnich & Jeanne Smith. BS SW Texas St U San Marcos 1984; Med SW Texas St U San Marcos 1988; BS VTS 1993. D 6/6/1993 Bp Earl Nicholas McArthur Jr P 12/6/1993 Bp Steven Charleston. m 6/6/1992 Russell Garrett Lockey c 3. S Fran Of Assisi Ch Philadelphia MS 1997-2001; Asst The Epis Ch Of The Medtr Meridian MS 1996-1997; Int The Ch Of The H Trin Juneau AK 1994-1995. Auth, "Context Effect & Its Effect on Memory," ERIC.

MINNICK, Margaret (Ct) 381 Main St Box 187, Middletown CT 06457 **Ch Of The H Trin Middletown CT 1995-** B Weymouth MA 11/4/1950 d Wallace Robison Houghton & Elizabeth Crocker. BA U of Massachusetts 1973; MDiv Bex 1978. D 3/19/1982 P 11/1/1982 Bp Lloyd Edward Gressle. m 6/16/1979 David Warren Minnick. S Mk's Ch New Canaan CT 1985-1995; Asst S Fran Ch Greensboro NC 1983-1985; S Lk's Ch Lebanon PA 1982-1983. MAGGIEMIN@AOL.COM

MINNIS, Joseph Abell (FdL) PO Box 486, Boulder Junction WI 54512 B Joliet IL 7/31/1935 s Joseph Summerville Minnis & Mary Katherine. U CO 1959; Nash 1962. D 6/18/1962 P 12/21/1962 Bp Joseph Summerville Minnis. m 9/1/1957 Sue Ann Donaldson c 4. Int S Anne's Ch De Pere WI 1997-1999; Vic S Jn's Ch Shawano WI 1991-1997; Vic S Jn's Epis Ch New London WI 1991-1997; Dio Fond du Lac Appleton WI 1991-1995; Emm Ch Rushford MN 1989-1991; Trst Dio Colorado Denver CO 1969-1972; Vic Ch Of S Jn Chrys Golden CO 1964-1965; Vic Ch Of The H Comf Broomfield CO 1962-1967. Auth, "A Fam's Journey to Christmas". jsminnis@newnorth.net

MINNIS, William Harrison (Colo) 6394 S Grape Ct, Littleton CO 80121 B Joliet IL 7/11/1937 s Joseph Summerville Minnis & Mary Katherine. BA U CO 1961; BD Nash 1964. P 12/1/1964 Bp Joseph Summerville Minnis. m 6/10/1972 Martine Minnis c 1. Ch Of The H Redeem Denver CO 1997-2001; S Mich And All Ang' Ch Denver CO 1986-1997; Vic S Andr's Ch Manitou Sprg CO 1964-1967. bcirm@aol.com

MINNIX, George Myers (NI) 2008 Raintree Dr Apt 4, Elkhart IN 46514 B Elkhart IN 4/22/1939 s Lloyd Zinn Minnix & Marietta Helen. BA W&M 1961; MDiv Nash 1964. D 1/25/1964 P 7/25/1964 Bp Walter C Klein. S Chris's Ch Crown Point IN 1996-2001; S Mk's Par Howe IN 1974-1986; Howe Mltry Sch Howe IN 1969-1986; Vic H Fam Ch Angola IN 1964-1969. gmamen@earthlink.net

MINOR, Albert Neely (ETenn) 7006 Brickton Way, Knoxville TN 37919 **Assoc St Jas Epis Ch at Knoxville Knoxville TN 2006-** B Jennings LA 3/6/1930 s Stephen Duncan Minor & Alberta. BA U So 1952; GTS 1955; STB GTS 1967; MS U of Tennessee 1979. D 6/20/1955 Bp George Mosley Murray P 12/18/1955 Bp Randolph R Claiborne. m 7/29/1955 Carroll Tuthill c 4. Int S Andr's Ch Harriman TN 1997-1998; Int Ch Of The Gd Samar Knoxville TN 1995-1996; Int S Fran' Ch Norris TN 1994-1995; Chair Dioc Ecum Cmsn Dio E Tennessee Knoxville TN 1984-1986; S Mich And All Ang Knoxville TN 1964-1994; Tyson Hse Stdt Fndt Knoxville TN 1964-1994; Vic/R S Andr's Epis Ch Ft Vlly GA 1955-1958. Auth, "A Tie w The Little People," *Living Ch*; Auth, "Moving Toward Cath Unity," *Plumbline*. EDEO; ESMHE. "Al Minor Day" City of Knoxville 1994. aminor@worlnet.att.net

MINOR, Cheryl Vasil (Mass) 65 Common Street, Belmont MA 02478 **Co-R All SS' Epis Ch Belmont MA 1997-** B Concord MA 8/13/1963 d Thomas Vasil & Nancy Susan. BA Bos 1985; MDiv VTS 1991. D 6/1/1991 P 2/15/1992 Bp David Elliot Johnson. m 6/28/1986 Paul Lawrence Minor c 2. Assoc Gr Epis Ch New York NY 1993-1997; D S Lk's Ch Philadelphia PA 1991-1992. revcminor@aol.com

MINOR, Paul Lawrence (Mass) 65 Common St., Belmont MA 02478 **Co-R All SS' Epis Ch Belmont MA 1997-** B Baltimore MD 12/21/1962 s Frederick Stevenson & Elizabeth. BA Bos 1985; MDiv VTS 1991; MA Northcentral U 2011. D 6/1/1991 P 2/15/1992 Bp David Elliot Johnson. m 6/28/1986 Cheryl Vasil c 2. Assoc Gr Epis Ch New York NY 1993-1997; Cur S Lk's Ch Philadelphia PA 1991-1993. revminor@aol.com

MINSHEW, James Keener (SeFla) Po Box 1596, Port Salerno FL 34992 B Hartford AL 12/5/1942 s Monroe Minshew & Eunice Katherine. BS Florida St U 1965; MDiv STUSo 1983. D 6/16/1983 P 12/21/1983 Bp Calvin Onderdonk Schofield Jr. m 6/28/2003 Janice Glorioso c 4. R S Lk's Epis Ch Port Salerno FL 1985-2008; Cur S Andr's Epis Ch Palmetto Bay FL 1983-1985. ERM; RACA. jshew@gate.net

MINSHEW, Nancy Elizabeth (CFla) 3735 Us Highway 17 92 N, Davenport FL 33837 **D Asst Chap Of S Mary & S Martha Bp Gray Inn Davenport FL 2002-; D S Mk's Epis Ch Haines City FL CA 1999-** B Baltimore MD 12/28/1952 d Steven Willis Walker & Laura Alberta. D 1/16/1999 Bp John Wadsworth Howe. m 8/26/1993 Ronald Eugene Minshew.

MINTER, Larry Clifton (Ky) 5409 Hickory Hill Rd, Louisville KY 40214 **Int St Johns Epis Ch Lafayette IN 2011-** B Hugo OK 3/21/1954 s Clifton Bullard Minter & Kathleen Susan. BA Oklahoma Bapt U 1976; SW Bapt TS 1979; MDiv Sthrn Bapt TS Louisville KY 1981; Cert SWTS 1988; Louisville Presb TS 2005; Cler Ldrshp Inst 2008; Kentuckiana Pstr Counselling Consortium 2008. D 5/31/1988 P 4/1/1989 Bp David Reed. m 9/1/1980 Jane Ann Bostain c 1. Int Ch Of The Ascen Frankfort KY 2008-2011; S Ptr's Epis Ch Louisville KY 2004-2008; The Epis Ch Of The Mssh Pulaski TN 2003-2004; S Columba-In-The-Cove Owens Cross Roads AL 1999-2003; Vic All SS Ch Un WV 1996-1999; R S Jas' Epis Ch Lewisburg WV 1991-1999; S Lk's Ch Anchorage KY 1988-1991. AAPC 2006. larryminter@comcast.net

MINTER, Michael William (FdL) 314 Bellevue Rd, Highland NY 12528 B Louisville KY 7/1/1946 s Sheriden Minter & Ruby. BA NWU 1968; MDiv Nash 1973; MA U of Wisconsin 1976; PhD Ford 1981; PhD Hofstra U 1985. D 5/31/1973 P 12/21/1973 Bp Charles Gresham Marmion. Asst Ch Of The H Apos Oneida WI 1975-1976; Dio Fond du Lac Appleton WI 1974-1976; Vic S Jn's Ch Shawano WI 1974-1975; Vic S Jn's Epis Ch New London WI 1974-1975; Dio Kentucky Louisville KY 1973. mintmann@optimum.net

MINTER, Russell Deane (Tex) 364 Beckett Point Rd, Port Townsend WA 98368 B Santa Monica CA 9/11/1926 s Bruce Charles Minter & Norah Minnie. BA U CA 1949; MA U CA 1951; MA U CA 1952; BD CDSP 1963. D 9/5/1963 P 3/6/1964 Bp Francis E I Bloy. m 11/11/2000 Elizabeth Minter c 2. R Chr Ch Eagle Lake TX 1989-1998; Cullen Memi Chap Houston TX 1979-1983; Cur S Aug By-The-Sea Par Santa Monica CA 1963-1966. minterr@olympus.net

MINTON, Anne Mansfield (Mass) 35 Riverwalk Way Unit 303, Lowell MA 01854 B Rochester NY 7/9/1941 d Leo Thomas Minton & Helen Mansfield. BA Coll of New Rochelle 1962; MA CUA 1968; PhD NYU 1979; MA Andover Newton TS 1995. D 6/24/1993 P 1/7/1994 Bp Douglas Edwin Theuner. m 6/20/2004 Janice Mary Luti. Emm Ch Braintree MA 2004-2005; S Matt And The Redeem Epis Ch So Boston MA 2003; R Chr Ch Somerville MA 1996-2000; Int Gr Epis Ch Concord NH 1994-1995; All SS Epis Ch Attleboro MA 1993-1994. amminton@comcast.net

MINTURN, Benjamin Bradshaw (WA) PO Box 488, Hendersonville NC 28793 B Chicago IL 3/7/1929 s Benjamin Earl Minturn & Jeanette Isabella. BA Trin 1951; BD VTS 1954; MDiv VTS 1965. D 6/4/1954 Bp Robert Fisher Gibson Jr P 11/1/1954 Bp Goodrich R Fenner. m 4/3/1976 Lynda B Minturn c 3. The Chesapeake Fndt Washington DC 1969-1971; R Ch Of The Ascen Silver Sprg MD 1957-1964; Vic S Mart-In-The-Fields Edwardsville KS 1954-1956. bbminturn@hotmail.com

MINTURN, Sterling Majors (NY) 5555 N Sheridan Rd Apt 607, Chicago IL 60640 **Assoc Epis Ch Of The Atone Chicago IL 2005-** B Slidell LA 9/5/1933 s Sterling Baber Minturn & Maree Majors. BS NW St U 1956; MDiv GTS 1962. D 6/27/1962 Bp Iveson Batchelor Noland P 5/4/1963 Bp Girault M Jones. Assoc S Geo's Epis Ch Maplewood NJ 2003-2004; Assoc P All SS Ch Orange NJ 1992-2002; Assoc P S Jn's Ch New York NY 1969-1992; Cur Par of Trin Ch New York NY 1964-1968; Asst Min S Clem's Ch New York NY 1962-1963. sterling07079@yahoo.com

MINTZ, Elsa H (Pa) 7 Saint Andrews Ln, Glenmoore PA 19343 **R S Andr's Epis Ch Glenmoore PA 1995-** B Baltimore MD 10/13/1956 d Robert William Hale & Joan. AB Ken 1978; MDiv EDS 1982; MS Loyola U 1993. D 10/12/1982 Bp David Keller Leighton Sr P 9/14/1983 Bp Charlie Fuller McNutt Jr. c 1. Asst Cathd Of The Incarn Baltimore MD 1992-1993; Assoc S Jn's Ch Roanoke VA 1986-1991; Cn Cathd Ch Of S Steph Harrisburg PA 1982-1986. ehalemintz@comcast.net

MINX, Patricia Ann (Kan) 105 S Indian Wells Dr, Olathe KS 66061 B La Crosse WI 8/22/1946 d William Jacob Volk & Helen Lillian. BA Avila Coll 1978; MA Loyola U 1988. D 9/27/2003 Bp William Edward Smalley. m 9/2/1995 Francis B Minx.

MIONSKE, Wayne Allan Robert (FdL) 4535 N 92nd St Apt P203, Wauwatosa WI 53225 B Chicago IL 6/21/1937 s Carl August Herman Mionske & Viola Bertha Wilhelmina. MDiv Luth TS at Chicago 1963; MSEd U of Wisconsin 1969; Cert Nash 1982. D 4/2/1982 P 8/6/1982 Bp Charles Thomas Gaskell. Supply P S Nich Epis Ch Racine WI 2000-2006; Vic H Trin Epis Ch Waupun WI 1985-1998; Dio Fond du Lac Appleton WI 1985-1991; S Andr's Ch Kenosha WI 1982-1985; Dio Milwaukee Milwaukee WI 1982. Assoc, Ord of Julian of Norwich 2006. wmionske1@wi.rr.com

MIRACLE, David Robert (LI) 3322 E. Whittaker Ave., Cudahy WI 53110 **P-in-c S Nich Epis Ch Racine WI 2005-** B Neenah WI 3/10/1943 s Robert John Miracle & Virginia Fern. U of Wisconsin; MDiv Nash 1991. D 12/1/1990 P 7/1/1991 Bp William L Stevens. c 1. Chapl S Jn's Mltry Acad Delafield WI 2001-2002; Dio Long Island Garden City NY 2000-2001; All SS Ch Brooklyn NY 1998-2000; Vic Ch Of S Mary Of The Snows Eagle River WI 1991-1998; Dio Fond du Lac Appleton WI 1991-1995. frmiracle99@yahoo.com

MIRATE, Galen Alderman (Ga) Post Office Box 925, Moultrie GA 31776 **Vic S Marg Of Scotland Epis Ch Moultrie GA 2007-** B Charleston SC 8/7/1955 d Hugh Dorsey Alderman & Annabel. STUSo; BS/BA Emory U 1977; JD U GA 1981. D 2/4/2006 P 8/7/2006 Bp Henry Irving Louttit. m 7/11/1992 Donald Mirate c 1. galenm@bellsouth.net

MIRON, Jane Elizabeth (CPa) 2525 Lititz Pike, Lancaster PA 17601 B Lancaster PA 12/31/1949 d Earl Wert & Anna. BS Millersville U 1971. D 2/12/2005 Bp Michael Whittington Creighton. m 9/8/1973 David Miron c 2.

MISKELLEY, Audrey Lyn (Lex) 416 Dudley Rd, Lexington KY 40502 B Independence MO 10/27/1959 BA Columbus St U 1989; MA U of Tennessee 1991; MDiv VTS 2005. D 6/18/2005 Bp Charles Glenn VonRosenberg P 1/19/2006 Bp Stacy F Sauls. m 10/24/1993 Charles Miskelley c 3. Cn Evang Chr Ch Cathd Lexington KY 2005-2011. miskelley1@gmail.com

MISNER, Mary Jane Brain (Mil) N1639 Six Corners Rd, Walworth WI 53184 B Waukeegan IL 7/1/1936 d Theodore Horatio Brain & Mildred Mary. RN S Lk Hosp Sch Nrsng 1957; U of Wisconsin 1976; Nash 1989. D 10/21/1989 Bp Roger John White. m 10/5/1957 Daniel Wayne Misner c 4. D & Dir'S Asst S Jn In The Wilderness Elkhorn WI 2001-2002; D & Dir'S Asst S Lk's Ch Whitewater WI 1992-2001; Asst Ch Of The H Comm Lake Geneva WI 1989-1992. Cmnty Of S Mary; Ord Of S Lk. mbmisner@mia.net

MISSNER, Heath McDonell (Chi) 470 Maple St, Winnetka IL 60093 B New York NY 7/5/1944 d Alexander Angus McDonell & Patricia Hallswell. BA Wellsley Coll 1966; MA NWU 1967. D 2/6/2010 Bp Jeffrey Dean Lee. c 4. hfisk@aol.com

MITCHEL III, Glen Henry (Hank) (Los) 1072 Casitas Pass Road #317, Carpinteria CA 93014 B Los Angeles CA 7/31/1951 s Glen Henry Mitchel & Cynthia. BA U Pac 1973; MDiv CDSP 1977. D 6/15/1991 P 1/11/1992 Bp Frederick Houk Borsch. m 10/5/1991 Maricela Mercado c 1. Assoc Trin Epis Ch Santa Barbara CA 2009; Vic Ch Of The Epiph Oak Pk CA 1994-2008; Asst S Mart-In-The-Fields Par Winnetka CA 1991-1994. hank.mitchel@gmail.com

MITCHELL JR, Charles Albert (Los) 111 S 6th St, Burbank CA 91501 **R S Jude's Epis Par Burbank CA 1997-** B Tacoma WA 8/9/1944 s Charles

Albert Mitchell & Florence Mary. BA U Of Puget Sound 1966; STB ATC 1969. D 12/19/1969 P 12/21/1970 Bp Jackson Earle Gilliam. m 5/10/1969 Bernice Seiko Shikaze. Ch Of The Gd Shpd Reedley CA 1994-1997; S Jas Epis Cathd Fresno CA 1989-1994; Ch Of The Ascen Forsyth MT 1974-1989; R Emm Ch Miles City MT 1974-1989; Vic S Lk's Ch Libby MT 1969-1974; Vic S Mich And All Ang Eureka MT 1969-1974.

MITCHELL, Dawn-Victoria (Mo) 3206 Pleasant St, Hannibal MO 63401 **R Trin Ch Hannibal MO 2010-** B Melrose MA 3/14/1972 d Richard Scott Mitchell & Linda Carol. BS W Virginia Wesleyan Coll 1994; MDiv S Paul TS Kansas City MO 1998; CAS SWTS 2000. D 6/3/2000 P 12/5/2000 Bp Barry Robert Howe. Assoc R Calv Ch Columbia MO 2000-2006. ESMHE 2001-2004. revdvm@juno.com

MITCHELL, Hugh Fraley (Ct) No address on file. B Charlotte NC 1/1/1930 D 6/11/1959 Bp Walter H Gray P 1/12/1960 Bp John Henry Esquirol.

MITCHELL, Irvin Sharp (Az) 16818 N Burns Dr, Sun City AZ 85351 B West Chester PA 4/15/1934 s Walter Mitchell & Carol Mae. BA Indiana U of Pennsylvania 1966; MDiv VTS 1969; DMin TCU 1984. D 7/12/1969 P 5/1/1970 Bp J(ohn) Joseph Meakins Harte. m 5/9/1953 Loretta S Starr c 2. Asstg P All SS Ch Phoenix AZ 2000; Int Chr Ch Of The Ascen Paradise Vlly AZ 1999-2002; Stndg Com Dio Arizona Phoenix AZ 1990-1993; Fin Commitee Dio Arizona Phoenix AZ 1988-1994; Cler Strng Com Dio Arizona Phoenix AZ 1988-1992; Chair On Invstmt Com Dio Arizona Phoenix AZ 1987-1994; R All SS Of The Desert Epis Ch Sun City AZ 1986-1996; Chair On Cler Compstn & Personl Practices Dio Arizona Phoenix AZ 1986-1994; R S Paul's Epis Ch Gainesville TX 1983-1986; Exec Coun Dio Ft Worth Ft Worth TX 1979-1983; R S Alb's Epis Ch Arlington TX 1978-1983; Chair On The Dioc Conv Stndg Com Dio Ft Worth Ft Worth TX 1976-1980; Asst S Andr's Ft Worth TX 1972-1978; Asst S Barn On The Desert Scottsdale AZ 1969-1972. Auth, "Mnstry To Transients & St People In Downtown Setting"; Auth, "Using Bk Of Common Pryr For Priv & Fam Devotions". Mssy & Chapl Ord Of S Lk, Fllshp Fire Dept Chapl. St Chapl Profsnl Finetiguteds Of Az 2004. irvmitchell@cox.net

MITCHELL III, James Franklin (WTex) 1164 Vista Bonita, New Braunfels TX 78130 B Breckenridge TX 7/4/1932 s Harvey Owen Mitchell & Mary Elizabeth. BS U Of Houston 1970; MDiv Epis TS of The SW 1973; DMin Drew U 1993. D 6/20/1973 Bp Scott Field Bailey P 6/18/1974 Bp J Milton Richardson. m 5/4/1957 Mary M von der Goltz. Bd Trsts Epis TS Of The SW Austin TX 1993-1997; R St Fran Epis Ch San Antonio TX 1982-1997; Prov Vii Rgnl Coordntr Evang Dio W Texas San Antonio TX 1980-1998; Assoc S Mk's Ch Beaumont TX 1976-1982; All SS Ch Cameron TX 1973-1976; Vic S Thos' Epis Ch Rockdale TX 1973-1976. mvandjfm@aol.com

MITCHELL, John Patrick (NJ) PO Box 261, Cape May NJ 08204 **Com on Resolutns Dio New Jersey Trenton NJ 2011-; Stndg Cmsn on Const and Cn Dio New Jersey Trenton NJ 2010-; R Ch Of The Adv Cape May NJ 2008-** B Muncie IN 12/27/1945 s Omer Merl Mitchell & Euva Blanche. BA Ya 1967; JD Indiana U 1970; MPhil Drew U 2001; CAS GTS 2002; PhD Drew U 2007. D 5/31/2003 Bp John Palmer Croneberger P 12/13/2003 Bp Rufus T Brome. m 8/17/1968 Dorothy T Thompson c 3. Stndg Cmsn on Const and Cn Dio Newark Newark NJ 2005-2008; Int Gr Epis Ch Westwood NJ 2005-2008; Assoc Ch Of The Mssh Chester NJ 2003-2005. fr.jpmitchell@gmail.com

MITCHELL, John Stephen (Vt) 372 Canterbury Rd, Manchester Center VT 05255 **R Zion Ch Manchester Cntr VT 1995-** B Wellesley MA 7/29/1948 s Charles Raynes Mitchell & Eltress. BA Berkshire Chr Coll 1982; MDiv Ya Berk 1985. D 8/24/1985 Bp Alexander Doig Stewart P 6/14/1986 Bp Andrew Frederick Wissemann. m 6/7/2009 Jane Uva c 3. S Lk's Ch Farmington ME 1988-1995; Asst S Jn's Ch Naples FL 1987-1988; Par Of S Jas Ch Keene NH 1985-1987. JOHN_S_MITCHELL@HOTMAIL.COM

MITCHELL, Judith N (RI) 24 Hart St, Providence RI 02906 **R S Matt's Ch Barrington RI 2002-** B Providence RI 6/12/1942 d Raymond Francis Naughton & Mary Rita. BA Rhode Island Coll 1966; MA Br 1967; PhD U of Connecticut 1981. D 6/26/1993 P 12/1/1993 Bp George Nelson Hunt III. m 2/10/1965 Raymond E Mitchell c 3. juthnami@aol.com

MITCHELL, Karin Rasmussen (NJ) 125 Orchard Ave, Hightstown NJ 08520 **S Dav's Ch Cranbury NJ 2005-** B Teaneck NJ 4/27/1955 d Carl Arthur Rasmussen & Mabel Adele. BA Rutgers-The St U 1977; MS Rutgers-The St U 1985; MDiv PrTS 2001; Cert GTS 2002. D 6/22/2002 P 12/21/2002 Bp David B(ruce) Joslin. m 10/20/1979 David Frank Mitchell c 3. S Fran Ch Dunellen NJ 2003-2005; Assoc The Ch Of The H Innoc Bch Haven NJ 2002-2003. Womens Epis Caucus 1992. karmitchell@aol.com

MITCHELL, Katherine Nicholson (Mass) 15 Durant Rd., Wellesley MA 02482 **D Trin Ch Randolph MA 2011-** B Washington NC 12/24/1945 d John Lawrence Nicholson & Katherine Hicks. MA Emml 1995; DMin Andover Newton TS 2003. D 6/5/2004 Bp M(arvil) Thomas Shaw III. m 6/22/1974 Albert Phillips Mitchell c 3. AAPC 1995-2010; AEHC 1996; Assn of Profsnl Chapl 2001. Dennis Thompson Schlrshp 2008; Partnr in Excellence 2008; Dennis Thompson Schlrshp Brigham and Wmn Hosp 2004; Partnr's In Excellence Brigham and Wmn Hosp 2002. knmitchell1@msn.com

MITCHELL, Leonel L (NI) 1711 Hoover Avenue, South Bend IN 46615 B New York NY 7/23/1930 s Leonel Edgar William Mitchell & Doris Abbott. BA Trin Hartford CT 1951; STB Ya Berk 1954; STM GTS 1956; ThD GTS 1964. D 6/13/1954 P 12/19/1954 Bp Horace W B Donegan. m 12/19/1953 Beverly Mills c 2. Lectr in Ch Hist & Liturg SWTS Evanston IL 1978-2005; Prof of Liturg SWTS Evanston IL 1978-1995; Cn The Cathd Ch Of S Jas So Bend IN 1972-1978; Lectr in Liturg The GTS New York NY 1968-1969; R S Lk's Ch Beacon NY 1964-1971; R Chr Ch Warwick NY 1959-1964; R S Jn In-The-Wilderness Copake Falls NY 1956-1959; Cur Chr Ch Riverdale Bronx NY 1954-1956. Auth, *Pstr and Occasional Off*, Cowley Press, 1998; Auth, *Lent, H Week, Easter and the Great 50 Days*, Cowley Press, 1996; Auth, *Initiation & the Ch*, Pstr Press, 1991; Auth, *Plnng the Ch Year*, Morehouse Pub, 1991; Auth, *Praying Shapes Believing*, Winston/Morehouse, 1991; Auth, *The Meaning of Ritual*, Paulist/Morehouse, 1988; Auth, *Liturg CHANGE: HOW MUCH DO WE NEED?*, Seabury Press, 1975. Associated Parishes 1964; Intl Angl Liiturgical ConsultationC 1983-1995; No Amer Acad of Liturg 1973; Societas Liturgica 1977. D.D. Ya Berk 1991; Hon Cn S Jas Cathd So Bend IN 1978. leonelmitchell@att.net

MITCHELL, Lisa Sauber (NJ) 380 Sycamore Ave, Shrewsbury NJ 07702 **R Chr Ch Epis Shrewsbury NJ 1997-** B Bartlesville OK 8/1/1957 d Charles Abraham Sauber & Josella Bertha. BS Oklahoma St U 1979; MA Fuller TS 1987; STM Nash 1988. D 9/16/1989 Bp Oliver Bailey Garver Jr P 3/24/1990 Bp Frederick Houk Borsch. c 2. Dioc Coun Dio Oklahoma Oklahoma City OK 1995; R S Jn's Epis Ch Vinita OK 1991-1997; Assoc R S Jos's Par Buena Pk CA 1989-1990; DCE S Paul's Ch Milwaukee WI 1988. "Sermons That Wk". lisa.mitchell2@verizon.net

MITCHELL JR, Louis Livingston (WA) 5904 Mount Eagle Dr Apt 218, Alexandria VA 22303 B Bronxville NY 3/12/1930 s Louis Livingston Mitchell & Mary Gage. BA Col 1953; MDiv VTS 1958. D 6/11/1958 P 12/1/1958 Bp Horace W B Donegan. m 10/18/1968 Anne Talifarro c 5. Gr Ch Washington DC 1978-1979; Asst S Tim's Epis Ch Daytona Bch FL 1963-1964; Cur S Lk's Epis Ch Birmingham AL 1960-1963; Vic Ch Of The H Comm Mahopac NY 1958-1960. lmitchell@pacthg.org

MITCHELL, Marilyn Dean (NC) 90 Worcester Rd Unit 12, Washington Depot CT 06794 **D La Iglesia de la Sagrada Familia Newton Grove NC 2010-** B McPherson KS 3/19/1937 d Albert Leroy Dean & Adeline Ruth Taylor. BA U of Connecticut 1974; MLS Emporia St U 1983; MDiv Yale DS 1994. D 9/17/2005 Bp Andrew Donnan Smith. c 3. D S Jn's Ch New Milford CT 2005-2009; D S Jn's Epis Par Waterbury CT 2005. Soc of S Jn Evang 1992. Robert Watson Schlr Yale DS 1992. mdmitchell19@gmail.com

MITCHELL, Patricia Rhonda (NY) 732 Scarsdale Rd, Tuckahoe NY 10707 **Cn for Chr Formation Dio New York New York City NY 2005-** B Bronx NY 12/11/1949 d Lewis Matthew Sobers & Muriel Dorothy. BA Mt Holyoke Coll 1970; MS Col 1974; M Phil Col 1977; MDiv Ya Berk 2002. D 3/16/2002 P 9/21/2002 Bp Mark Sean Sisk. c 1. Assoc R S Barth's Ch New York NY 2002-2005. Berk Grad Soc Coun 2006. prsmitchell@gmail.com

MITCHELL, Peter Alan (SC) Po Box 2079, Mount Pleasant SC 29465 B Fowler KS 11/12/1965 s Bruce Alan Mitchell & Lenore Clara. BA Oral Roberts U 1990; MDiv VTS 1993. D 5/22/1993 P 3/1/1994 Bp Martin Gough Townsend. m 12/20/1987 Amy Kathleen Butler. H Trin Epis Ch Charleston SC 2003-2008; Rivertown Epis Mt Pleasant SC 1997-2001; Ch Of The H Cross Sullivans Island SC 1993-2003. No Amer Mssy Soc. rivertownchurch@awod.com

MITCHELL, Raymond Scott (Chi) 1200 E Barringer St, Philadelphia PA 19119 B Morton PA 11/6/1918 s Howard Mitchell & Edna Beatrice. BS Cheyney St Coll Cheyney PA 1942; ThB PDS 1949. D 6/25/1949 P 12/1/1949 Bp William P Remington. m 6/29/1946 Mildred S Johnson c 2. S Edm's Epis Ch Chicago IL 1970-1985; R S Phil's Ch Richmond VA 1961-1970; Vic S Aug Of Hippo Norristown PA 1957-1961.

MITCHELL JR, R(ichard) Cope (Neb) 2777 Mission Rd, Nashotah WI 53058 B Chickasha OK 9/2/1951 s Richard Cope Mitchell & Sara Lois. BA Wheaton Coll 1975; Cert Wesley TS 1979; MDiv Gordon-Conwell TS 1980; CAS Nash 1985; Nash 2000. D 6/15/1985 P 5/3/1986 Bp Gerald Nicholas McAllister. m 3/8/1981 Suzan Wall c 4. Pension Fund Mltry New York NY 2003-2004; S Fran Epis Ch Scottsbluff NE 2002-2003; P-in-c S Paul's Ch Watertown WI 2000-2002; S Aidans Ch Hartford WI 2000; Gr Ch Cortland NY 1996-2000; R S Anne's Ch Millington TN 1992-1996; Dio Colorado Denver CO 1990-1992; R S Jas' Epis Ch Meeker CO 1989-1991; Stndg Com Dio Colorado Denver CO 1988-1992; Vic S Tim's Epis Ch Rangely CO 1987-1992; Cur Epis Ch Of The Resurr Oklahoma City OK 1985-1987. copemitchell@msn.com

MITCHELL, R(obert) James (Kan) Via Roma, Wichita KS 67230 **Asst S Steph's Ch Wichita KS 2006-** B Grand Rapids MI 9/16/1930 s Waldemar B Mitchell & Margaret L. BA MI SU 1952; ThM Bex 1963. D 6/11/1963 Bp Charles Ellsworth Bennison Jr P 12/1/1963 Bp Charles Bennison. m 8/24/1990 Judith Thompson Leith c 6. P-in-c S Alb's Epis Ch Wichita KS 2002-2005; P

Mssnr S Jas Ch Wichita KS 1997-2002; Asst Min S Paul's Ch Rochester NY 1966-1969; Vic S Dav's Ch Lansing MI 1963-1966. jmitchell22@cox.net

MITCHELL, Sadie Stridiron (Pa) 3600 Conshohocken Ave Apt 508, Philadelphia PA 19131 **Assoc The Afr Epis Ch Of S Thos Philadelphia PA 1990-; Deptce Dio Pennsylvania Philadelphia PA 1983-** B Philadelphia PA 1/4/1922 d Joseph Alphonso Stridiron & Lucinda Gertrude. BS Tem 1942; MS U of Pennsylvania 1968; EdD Nova U 1978; MDiv Philadelphia Luth TS 1984; MDiv Philadelphia Luth TS 1990. D 6/20/1987 Bp Lyman Cunningham Ogilby P 5/31/1988 Bp Allen Lyman Bartlett Jr. m 8/19/1946 Charles T Mitchell. P S Mk's Ch Philadelphia PA 1988-1990; Chapl Com Dio Pennsylvania Philadelphia PA 1987-1999; Chair Stwdshp Cmsn Dio Pennsylvania Philadelphia PA 1969-1971. Philadelphia Theol Inst 1981-2006; SBL; UBE 1969. Hon Bd Mem Epis Cmnty Serv. sadiesmitchell@aol.com

MITCHELL, Stephanie R (Okla) 809 W Cedar Ave, Duncan OK 73533 **Dio Oklahoma Oklahoma City OK 2010-; S Lk's Epis Ch Bartlesville OK 2010-** B Texarkana TX 10/10/1977 d Alan David Mitchell & Helen Jane. BA U of Oklahoma 1999; MDiv EDS 2010. D 1/16/2010 P 7/31/2010 Bp Edward Joseph Konieczny. m 6/24/2006 Richard A Jenkins. srmitchell.2010@gmail.com

MITCHELL, Thomas James (WNY) 7145 Fieldcrest Drive, Lockport NY 14094 **Cler Rep. to Dioc Coun Dio Wstrn New York Tonawanda NY 2009-** B Buffalo NY 6/21/1947 s Thomas Clarence Mitchell & Marion Jane. Grad Study Cath U; BA St Jn Vianney Sem 1969; MA St Jn Vianney Sem 1974; Assoc Trocaire Coll 1989. D 6/2/2009 P 12/12/2009 Bp J Michael Garrison. c 1. thomasjmitchell@roadrunner.com

MITCHELL, Tim (Ky) 901 Baxter Ave, Louisville KY 40204 **Mem, Bd Trst Ch Pension Fund New York NY 2009-; Ch Of The Adv Louisville KY 2008-** B Louisville KY 5/28/1959 s Joseph William Mitchell & Mary Catherine. BA U of Notre Dame 1981; U of Salamanca 1982; MS Geo 1984; MDiv Mundelein Sem 1992; DMin PSR 2005. Rec from Roman Catholic 6/1/2002 as Priest Bp William Edwin Swing. "The Ovrs List," *Bk, co-Auth*, Augsburg Pub Hse, 1985. Phi Beta Kappa Phi Beta Kappa Arts and Sciences hon Socity 1981. rectoradvent@aol.com

MITCHELL, Winifred L (Minn) 3821 Elk Ln, Pueblo CO 81005 **R Ch Of S Ptr The Apos Pueblo CO 2011-** B Denver CO 8/6/1947 d Arthur Lee Mitchell & Dorothy Fields. BA U CO Boulder CO 1970; MA U CO Boulder CO 1975; PhD U CO Boulder CO 1986; MDiv Epis TS of The SW 2007. D 6/14/2007 P 12/20/2007 Bp James Louis Jelinek. m 5/25/1974 Paul F Brown c 2. Dn, Reg 4 Dio Minnesota Minneapolis MN 2009-2011; Exam Chapl Dio Minnesota Minneapolis MN 2009-2011; Mentor for Mnstry Team H Trin Epis Ch Luverne MN 2009-2011; COM Dio Minnesota Minneapolis MN 2008-2011; P-in-c S Mart's Epis Ch Fairmont MN 2007-2011. Anthropologist, "The Aymara," *The Encyclopedia of Men and Wmn*, Human Relatns Area Files Press, 2004; Anthropologist, "Wmn Age Hierarchies and the Prestige of Suffering," *Wmn among Wmn*, U IL Press, 1998; Anthropologist, "Pragmatic Literacy and Empowerment," *Anthropology and Educ Quarterly 25:3*, Amer Anthropological Assn, 1994; Anthropologist, "Lighting Sickness," *Natural Hist 102 (11)*, Amer Museum of Natural Hist, 1993. Amer Anthropological Assn 1979-2004. Jonathan M. Daniels Fllshp EDS and Daniels Fndt 2006; Fulbright Schlrshp Fulbright Cmsn 1983; Inter-Amer Fndt Fllshp Inter-Amer Fndt 1983. revwinnie@gmail.com

MITCHENER, Gary Asher (O) 2213 Edgewood Rd, Cleveland Heights OH 44118 B Saint Louis MO 2/21/1939 s Paul Edward Mitchener & Elaine. BA Pacific U 1960; BD EDS 1966; ThM Harvard DS 1986. D 6/25/1966 P 1/8/1967 Bp George Leslie Cadigan. m 10/10/1987 Judith C Claghorn c 2. Pstr S Alb Epis Ch Cleveland Heights OH 2007-2009; Int Ch Of The Epiph Euclid OH 2000-2002; Cn Trin Cathd Cleveland OH 1992-2000; R Ch Of The Gd Shpd Fitchburg MA 1986-1992; Dio Wstrn Massachusetts Springfield MA 1986-1992; Assoc R S Thos Ch Hanover NH 1977-1985; Vic S Lk's Ch Woodsville NH 1971-1974; Cur Calv Ch Columbia MO 1966-1969. Natl Sci Fndt Grad Fllshp 1970. loosecanon1@hotmail.com

MITCHICAN, Jonathan A (Pa) 1000 Burmont RD, Drexel Hill PA 19026 **R The Ch Of The H Comf Drexel Hill PA 2008-** B 1/9/1980 MDiv Ya Berk 2006. D 6/3/2006 P 12/16/2006 Bp James Joseph Shand. m 5/21/2005 Gina Sue Mitchican c 1. Assoc R S Ptr's Ch Salisbury MD 2006-2008. father_jonathan@verizon.net

MITHEN III, Thomas Scott (Ga) 516 E Broughton St, Bainbridge GA 39817 B Greenville AL 1/23/1954 s Thomas Scott Mithen & Isabel Dunklin. BS Troy St U 1977. D 10/21/2009 Bp Henry Irving Louttit. m 8/13/1977 Naomi Elliott c 2. smithen@mchsi.com

MITMAN, John Louis (Ct) 31 Steep Hollow Ln # 6107, West Hartford CT 06107 **Planned Giving Com Dio Connecticut Hartford CT 1997-; Ways & Means Dio Iowa Des Moines IA 1986-** B Washington DC 10/30/1940 s Louis Charles Mitman & Dorcas Hannah. BA Randolph-Macon Coll 1962; STB Ya Berk 1965. D 6/12/1965 Bp Charles F Hall P 12/11/1965 Bp Harvey D Butterfield. m 6/9/1962 Ruth Hemingway c 2. Bp Search Com Dio Connecticut Hartford CT 1992-2001; R S Jas's Ch W Hartford CT 1990-2001; Coll Wk Com Dio Iowa Des Moines IA 1985-2001; R The Cathd Ch Of S Paul Des Moines IA 1985-1990; Dioc Com Dio Michigan Detroit MI 1984-2001; Pres, Stndg Com Dio Michigan Detroit MI 1982-1983; Stndg Com Dio Michigan Detroit MI 1979-1981; Cbury MI SU E Lansing MI 1974-1985; Cur S Thos Ch Hanover NH 1965-1972; Soc For The Increase Of Mnstry W Hartford CT 2001. Auth, "Premarital Counslg: A Practical Manual for Cler & Lay Counselors," Seabury Press, 1981. OHC 1962. mitmangroup@snet.net

MIX, Lucas John (Az) 715 N Park Ave, Tucson AZ 85719 **Dio Arizona Phoenix AZ 2009-** B Seattle WA 8/1/1975 s William Dale Mix & Susan Swan. BA/BS U of Washington 1997; PhD Harv 2004; MDiv CDSP 2007. D 6/30/2007 Bp Bavi Rivera P 1/6/2008 Bp Gregory Harold Rickel. Dio Arizona Phoenix AZ 2008-2009; Ch of the Apos Seattle WA 2007-2008. "Life in Space: Astrobiology for Everyone," Harv Press, 2009. lucas@frible.org

MIZIRL, Sandra Lee (Tex) 2011 Moses Creek Ct, College Station TX 77845 **Coll Coordntr Prov VII Fairfax VA 2009-** B Oklahoma City OK 8/2/1947 d George Lee McMahan & Mary Lou. BA U of Oklahoma 1979; MDiv STUSo 1998. D 6/20/1998 Bp Claude Edward Payne P 6/21/1999 Bp Leopoldo Jesus Alard. m 5/22/1970 Larry Alan Mizirl c 1. Dn-Cntrl Convoc Dio Texas Houston TX 2006-2008; Vstng Com The TS at The U So Sewanee TN 2004-2010; co-Fac transitional deacons Dio Texas Houston TX 2002-2008; Div of Liturg-Chair Dio Texas Houston TX 2002-2007; Div of Wrshp-Chair Dio Texas Houston TX 2002-2007; Trin Epis Ch The Woodlands TX 1998-1999. Auth, "Coll Pilgrimage," *The Diolog*, Dio Texas, 2011; Auth, "Angl Sprtlty," *Texas Epis*, Dio Texas, 2008; Auth, "Front-Line Of Life," *From The Mtn*, U So, 2000. Griffin Fllshp U So 1998; Woods Ldrshp Awd U So Sewanee TN 1995. smizirl@episcopalcollegeministry.org

MKHIZE, Danana Elliot (La) 1222 N Dorgenois St, New Orleans LA 70119 B 8/30/1938 s Difile Theophilus MKhize & Annie Maida. Afts Fed TS 1968; BA U Of So Afr Za 1968; DIT U Of Birmingham Gb 1973; DMin Claremont TS 1983. Trans from Church of the Province of Southern Africa 7/29/1985 Bp Robert C Rusack. m 1/1/1968 Ruth Buyisiwe Dladla. R S Lk's Ch New Orleans LA 1996-1999; R S Mart's Epis Ch Compton CA 1989-1996; Vic S Mart's Epis Ch Compton CA 1985-1989; P-in-c S Mart's Epis Ch Compton CA 1982-1984. doyei200@gmail.com

MOBLEY, James E (SO) 955 Matthews Dr, Cincinnati OH 45215 B Chattanooga TN 7/30/1930 s John A Mobley & Janie. Morristown N&I Coll; Mt St. Mary's Sem 1978. D 1/26/1975 Bp John Mc Gill Krumm. m 12/25/1954 Sharon Faye Walton c 2. Grtr Cincinnati Chapl.

MOCK, James Anson (WLa) 4304 W 2nd # 23, Plainview TX 79072 B Pawhuska,OK 11/23/1926 s Jennings Anson Mock & Helen. BS U of Oklahoma 1950; BD Epis TS of The SW 1956. D 6/29/1956 P 1/5/1957 Bp Chilton Powell. c 3. S Phil's Boyce LA 1989-1991; H Comf Ch Ball LA 1982-1991; R Calv Ch Bunkie LA 1982-1989; Vic Trin Epis Ch Ball LA 1982-1989; R S Mk's Epis Ch Plainview TX 1961-1982; Cur S Andr's Epis Ch Amarillo TX 1959-1961; Vic All SS Epis Ch Miami OK 1956-1958. Natl Epis Historians Assn. jim@panhandlepopcorn.com

MOCKRIDGE III, Oscar Alling (Nwk) 358 Stiles Ct, West Orange NJ 07052 B Newark NJ 4/11/1937 s Oscar Alling Mockridge & Georgie. BA Pr 1959; MDiv ETS 1965; MPA NYU 1975. D 6/12/1965 Bp Leland Stark P 12/18/1965 Bp George E Rath. m 9/7/1963 Anne H Mockridge c 1. Pstr Assoc Gr Ch Madison NJ 2000-2004; Coordntng Consult Dio Newark Newark NJ 1972-1974; R The Ch Of The Annunc Oradell NJ 1970-1972; R Trin Ch Irvington NJ 1967-1970; Cur S Ptr's Ch Mtn Lakes NJ 1965-1967. mockridge@msn.com

MOCZYDLOWSKI, Ann Louise Hare (WA) 10120 Brock Dr, Silver Spring MD 20903 **R S Mary Magd Ch Silver Sprg MD 2010-** B Reading PA 10/19/1953 d Clyde Charles Hare & Rose Olga. D 6/9/2000 Bp Michael Whittington Creighton P 2/25/2001 Bp Jane Hart Holmes Dixon. m 6/8/1985 William Wesley Moczydlowski c 2. Ch Of Our Sav Silver Sprg MD 2005; Asst Gr Epis Ch Silver Sprg MD 2000-2004. annwellspring@gmail.com

MODESITT, Lori Jane (Wyo) 1357 Loomis St, Wheatland WY 82201 **Mnstry Dvlp Dio Wyoming Casper WY 2011-; P All SS Ch Wheatland WY 2002-** B Rock Island IL 1/23/1954 d Francis Odendahl & Lola. D 2/7/2002 P 9/21/2002 Bp Bruce Edward Caldwell. m 7/19/1980 Walter Lee Modesitt. modesitt@btinet.net

MOEHL, Thomas Joseph (Ore) 12360 Summit Loop SE, Turner OR 97392 **Vic Ch Of Chr The King On The Santiam Stayton OR 2001-** B Klamath Falls OR 5/10/1949 BS Lewis & Clark Coll 1971; MBA OR SU 1981. D 6/16/2001 P 12/21/2001 Bp Robert Louis Ladehoff. m 3/20/1971 Linda K Kindred c 3.

MOELLER, Linda Lee Breitung (NJ) 13 Blossom Dr, Ewing NJ 08638 **S Steph's Ch Florence NJ 2006-; Dio New Jersey Trenton NJ 2002-** B Port Jefferson NY 9/15/1950 d York Louis Breitung & Liria Lee. BA Barry U 1991; MDiv/STM GTS 1995. D 6/4/1988 P 6/24/1994 Bp Calvin Onderdonk Schofield Jr. m 12/31/1987 Harold Carl Moeller. Asst S Lk's Epis Ch Metuchen NJ 1999-2003; Assoc P Par of Trin Ch New York NY 1995-1997; Assoc P Ch Of The Heav Rest New York NY 1994-1995; D/Asst Chr And S

Steph's Ch New York NY 1993-1994; D/Asst S Mary Magd Epis Ch Coral Sprg FL 1988-1992. Auth, *Baptism: Inclusion or Exclusion*; Auth, *Cnfrmtn: Sacramental Rite or Rite of Discipline and Politics*; Auth, *Investiture of PBp: New Way to Gather*. Assn of Angl Mus 2000; No Amer Acad of Liturg; Societas Liturgica. lindagts@comcast.net

MOERMOND, Curtis Roghair (Ia) 6625 Preston Terrace Ct SW, Apt 3, Cedar Rapids IA 52404 **Gr Ch Cedar Rapids IA 2009-** B O'Brien County IA 7/5/1941 AA S Paul's Coll Concordia MO 1963; BS Concordia Teachers Coll Seward NE 1965; BD Concordia TS 1969; MDiv Concordia TS 1973; DMin Concordia TS 1988. D 12/18/2004 P 6/25/2005 Bp Alan Scarfe. c 4. Int S Thos' Epis Ch Sioux City IA 2005-2008. moermond41@aol.com

MOFFAT JR, Alexander Douglas (FtW) 2100 Santa Fe St Apt 910, Wichita Falls TX 76309 B 3/1/1933 D 6/10/1958 P 12/13/1958 Bp Richard S Watson.

MOHN, Michael Collver (Va) 1527 Senseny Rd, Winchester VA 22602 B Detroit MI 4/19/1938 s Frederick Thomas Mohn & Inez. BA Stetson U 1961; MDiv VTS 1970; S Geo's Coll Jerusalem IL 1981; S Geo's Coll Jerusalem 1993. D 6/6/1970 P 1/1/1971 Bp Robert Lionne DeWitt. m 5/24/1969 Janice Lynn Baker c 1. R Meade Memi Par White Post VA 2005-2007; Emm Epis Ch (Piedmont Par) Delaplane VA 1999-2003; S Jas' Epis Ch Leesburg VA 1998-1999; H Land Com Dio Virginia Richmond VA 1988-1996; Yth Com Dio Virginia Richmond VA 1985-1994; S Pauls On The Hill Epis Ch Ossining NY 1984-2003; S Paul's On-The-Hill Winchester VA 1984-1998; Int S Jas' Epis Ch Leesburg VA 1984-1985; Ch Of The Ascen Hickory NC 1982-1984; Vic S Mary's Ch Morganton NC 1978-1982; Vic S Paul's Epis Ch Morganton NC 1978-1982; Assoc R S Bon Ch Sarasota FL 1974-1978; Vic S Mart's Epis Ch Williamsburg VA 1972-1974; Asst Chr Ch Philadelphia Philadelphia PA 1970-1972. Comt, Evang Educ Sch; Ord of the Sis of the Resurection 1978.

MOHRINGER, J(ohn) Wapshing (Ind) The Four Winds 2880w 250n, Lebanon IN 46052 B Haarlem NL 6/27/1926 s William Frederick Mohringer & Thona. BA Millikin U 1957; BD Chr TS 1960. D 1/9/1960 P 7/1/1960 Bp John P Craine. m 5/18/1955 Johanna A van Dongen. Worker P-in-c S Steph's Elwood IN 1967-1973; Cn Theol S Paul's Cathd Oklahoma City OK 1966-1971; Cur S Jn's Epis Ch Tulsa OK 1965-1966; Asst To Dn S Paul's Cathd Oklahoma City OK 1962-1965; Vic S Ptr's Ch Lebanon IN 1960-1962. Amer Indn Med Soc; Ny Acad Of Sciences.

MOISE, Joseph (LI) 1227 Pacific St, Brooklyn NY 11216 **R S Barth's Ch Brooklyn NY 1989-** B 12/2/1939 s Montesquieu Moise & Leraisse. Coll Of S Pierre Ht 1963; ETSC 1968. D 12/2/1967 P 6/1/1968 Bp Charles Alfred Voegeli. S Barth's Ch Brooklyn NY 1984-2005; Dio The Dominican Republic (Iglesia Epis Dominicana) Santo Domingo DO 1976-1983; Vic Cathd Ch of All SS St Thos VI VI 1975-1976.

MOJALLALI, Darius A (Alb) 13 High Street, Delhigh NY 13753 **R S Jn's Ch Delhi NY 2011-; R S Ptr's Ch Hobart NY 2011-** B Boston MA 12/26/1952 s Rahim Mojallali & Roselle Theodora. BA Connecticut Coll 1975; MDiv PrTS 1981; Angl Stds GTS 1982. D 6/18/1983 P 12/21/1983 Bp Wilbur Emory Hogg Jr. m 9/3/1999 Stephanie Lewis c 4. P-in-c S Dav's Ch Feeding Hills MA 2008-2011; R S Steph's Ch Delmar NY 1988-2008; R S Paul's Ch Salem NY 1983-1988; R S Paul's Epis Ch Greenwich NY 1983-1988. dmojo26@me.com

MOLE, James Frederick (Pa) 10 E 3rd St, Waynesboro PA 17268 **P Assoc S Mary's Epis Ch Waynesboro PA 1999-** B Princeton WV 4/14/1924 s Frederick Arthur Mole & Edith Hill. BS Concord U 1950; M Div PDS 1961; Cert U of Pennsylvania 1965; M Ed Tem 1973. D 5/13/1961 P 11/18/1961 Bp Oliver J Hart. c 2. Dn Fairmount Deanry Dio Pennsylvania Philadelphia PA 1972-1980; S Nathanaels Ch Philadelphia PA 1961-1989. Cerrtificate of Appreciation for Devoted Serv Archdiocesan Sr Citizens Coun Philadelphia PA 1987.

MOLEGODA, Niranjani Shariya (Mo) 217 Adams St, Jefferson City MO 65101 **R Gr Ch Jefferson City MO 2007-** B Colombo LK 5/21/1958 d William Molegoda & Seelawathi Navaratnam. BA Agnes Scott Coll 1981; MS U Of Colombo Lk 1984; MDiv Ya Berk 1993. D 9/8/1996 P 5/1/1997 Bp M(arvil) Thomas Shaw III. Int S Jas' Epis Ch Cambridge MA 2006-2007; P-in-c The Ch Of S Mary Of The Harbor Provincetown MA 2003-2006; Assoc R Chr Ch Cambridge Cambridge MA 1999-2003; S Anne's In The Fields Epis Ch Lincoln MA 1999; Soc Of St Marg Roxbury MA 1998. shariyam@hotmail.com

MOLINE, Mark Edwin (Az) 2000 Shepherds Lane, Prescott AZ 86301 **R S Lk's Ch Prescott AZ 2007-** B Lawrence KS 3/25/1945 s Harold Alvin Moline & Dollie Viola. BS Amer U 1976; MDiv Candler TS Emory U 1998. D 6/26/1999 Bp Richard Lester Shimpfky P 2/5/2000 Bp Frank Kellogg Allan. m 7/8/1966 Judith Ann Schertz c 2. Vic Dio Atlanta Atlanta GA 2003-2006; R Gd Shpd Epis Ch Austell GA 2001-2003; Assoc S Teresa Acworth GA 1999-2000. markemoline@gmail.com

MOLITORS, Elizabeth Anne (Chi) 393 N Main St, Glen Ellyn IL 60137 **Assoc R S Mk's Epis Ch Glen Ellyn IL 2009-** B Toledo OH 6/27/1962 d Thomas Joseph Molitors & Lois Ruth Strater. BA Mia 1983; MBA DePaul U 1998; MDiv SWTS 2009. D 6/6/2009 P 12/5/2009 Bp Jeffrey Dean Lee. c 1. emolitors@yahoo.com

MOLLARD, Elizabeth McCarter (CPa) 235 N Spruce St, Elizabethtown PA 17022 B Providence RI 6/21/1941 d Edward McCarter & Cynthia. BA U of New Hampshire 1962; MA U of Missouri 1981; MDiv VTS 2002. D 6/8/2002 P 1/4/2003 Bp Michael Whittington Creighton. m 12/7/1963 Francois R Mollard c 3. R S Lk's Epis Ch Mt Joy PA 2002-2008. bmollard@embarqmail.com

MOLLEGEN, Glenis Gralton (Ct) 49 Millstone Rd, Glastonbury CT 06033 B Alexandria VA 11/4/1938 d Raymond Martin Gralton & Glenis Anderson. BA Wellesley Coll 1961; MA Col 1969; MA UTS 1969; Br 1974; EDS 1982. D 6/11/1983 P 3/5/1984 Bp Arthur Edward Walmsley. m 2/16/1962 Albert Theodore Mollegen. P-in-c Imm S Jas Par Derby CT 2003-2004; Supply Imm S Jas Par Derby CT 2003; Int S Jas Ch Glastonbury CT 2000-2002; Assoc P Gr Ch Newington CT 1999-2001; Chpl Dio Stff dur Trnstn Dio Connecticut Hartford CT 1999-2000; R S Paul's Epis Ch Willimantic CT 1985-1998; Cur S Jn's Epis Ch Niantic CT 1983-1985; Consult Adult Mnstrs S Mk's Ch Mystic CT 1976-1980. revmullegen@aol.com

MOLLER, Nels D (Ida) 902 E Lakeview Ln, Spokane WA 99208 B Rupert ID 11/14/1936 s Nels Andrew Moller & Deloris Louise. BS U of Idaho Moscow 1960; Cert U CA 1972; EFM STUSo 1992. D 1/29/1994 P 8/7/1994 Bp John Stuart Thornton. m 3/23/1985 Patricia Jeane Burns c 4. S Jas Ch Burley ID 1994-2006; St Matthews Epis Ch Rupert ID 1994-2006. nmoller36@msn.com

MOLLISON, Carol Suzanne (Okla) 308 Sierra Vista Ct, Altus OK 73521 **D S Paul's Ch Altus OK 2004-** B 10/28/1943 d Malcom Mollison & Dorothy Jo. BA U of Oklahoma 1965; MA U of Oklahoma 1967; JD U of Oklahoma 1974. D 6/19/2004 Bp Robert Manning Moody. suzannemollison@oscn.net

MOLNAR, Peter A (NJ) 505 N Atlantic Ave E, Stratford NJ 08084 B Staten Island NY 8/30/1938 s Ludwig Stephen Molnar & Emma Caroline. BA Wag 1960; MDiv Ya Berk 1963; Luth TS 1964; DD E Nebraska Coll 1974; MA Glassboro St U 1974. D 6/11/1963 P 12/1/1963 Bp Horace W B Donegan. m 12/30/1995 Janet L White c 3. Trin Epis Ch Stratford NJ 1999-2010; Int Ch Of The Gd Shpd Pitman NJ 1998-1999; Vic S Mary's Ch Clementon NJ 1969-1998; Vic Ch Of The Atone Stratford NJ 1969-1973; Vic S Andr The Apos Highland Highlands NJ 1967-1969; Cur S Paul's Ch Poughkeepsie NY 1963-1964. F&AM 1963. Outstanding Vol Centers and Corrections New Jersey 1984; DD Estrn Nebraska Coll Nebraska 1974; Patron Chapl of the Four Chapl; Citizen of the Year New Jersey Psychol Soc New Jersey. janawhite@comcast.net

MOLONY, Roberta Diane (Chi) 2009 Boehme St, Lockport IL 60441 **D S Jn The Evang Lockport IL 2001-** B Chicago IL 12/8/1941 d Fred Ignatius Pachol & Violet Irene. D 2/3/2001 Bp William Dailey Persell. m 10/30/1993 William J Molony c 4. bbmolony@juno.com

MOMBERG, Thomas A (Md) 2205 Bear Den Road, Frederick MD 21701 **R All SS Ch Frederick MD 2008-** B Cincinnati OH 2/1/1949 s Robert Arthur Momberg & Elizabeth Katherine. BA Br 1971; MDiv GTS 1986. D 6/14/1986 P 12/13/1986 Bp Frank Tracy Griswold III. m 11/13/2004 Eyleen Hamner Farmer c 2. Assoc R Ch Of The H Comm Memphis TN 2002-2008; P-in-c S Thos Ch Somerville TN 2001-2002; Chapl Bp Spencer Place Inc Kansas City MO 2000-2001; R Trin Ch Lawr KS 1995-2000; R S Mk's Ch Erie PA 1990-1995; Assoc R S Paul's Epis Ch Pittsburgh PA 1988-1990; Cur Gr Ch Oak Pk IL 1986-1988. Cler Ldrshp Proj 1996. fathermom1949@gmail.com

MONAGIN, Mary Edythe Watson (Mich) 603 West Vermont, Royal Oak MI 48067 **D S Andr's Ch Clawson MI 1992-** B Flint MI 12/14/1928 d Arley Watson & Ileth. MS Wayne 1975; Whitaker TS 1992. D 6/13/1992 Bp R(aymond) Stewart Wood Jr. m 7/22/1955 Robert Monagin c 4.

MONAHAN, Anne Duval (WA) 404 S Lee St, Alexandria VA 22314 **Assoc S Paul's Epis Ch Alexandria VA 2006-** B Schenectady NY 7/12/1938 d Armand Joseph Duval & Magdalene Mary. BS Syr 1959; MDiv VTS 1982. D 6/9/1982 P 5/27/1983 Bp David Henry Lewis Jr. m 9/9/1961 William J Monahan c 3. Int S Martha's Epis Ch Bethany Bch DE 2002-2004; Dio Delaware Wilmington DE 2000-2004; Int S Aid's Ch Alexandria VA 1997-1999; Int S Mk's Ch Alexandria VA 1996-1997; Int S Alb's Epis Ch Annandale VA 1993-1996; The Ch Of The Redeem Beth MD 1992-1993; Int All SS Ch Alexandria VA 1991-1992; Stndg Com Dio Washington Washington DC 1990-1993; Int S Mary Magd Ch Silver Sprg MD 1989-1991; St Marys Par St Marys City MD 1987-1989; Int S Fran Ch Potomac MD 1986-1987; Dep, GC Dio Washington Washington DC 1985-1988; Moderator, Exec Com Dio Washington Washington DC 1984-1986; Dioc Coun Dio Washington Washington DC 1983-1987; Assoc S Dav's Par Washington DC 1983-1986; Cur The Ch of S Clem Alexandria VA 1982-1983. EPF 1982-1992; Fllshp of S Jn 1999; Int Ntwk 1986. sojourneranne@hotmail.com

MONASTIERE, Sally Melczer (Los) 1335 North Hills Drive, Upland CA 91784 B Phoenix AZ 2/25/1946 BA Scripps Coll 1967; MA Claremont Coll 1970; MDiv CDSP 2001. D 10/12/2002 P 5/3/2003 Bp Joseph Jon Bruno. The Epis Hm Communities Pasadena CA 2005-2011; Asst Trin Epis Ch Orange CA 2003-2005. monastiere@verizon.net

MONETTE, Ruth Alta (Los) 104-5990 E Blvd, Vancouver BC V6M3V4 Canada B Des Plaines IL 2/7/1977 d William Allen Monette & Elizabeth Ht. BA Wm Smith 1999; MDiv EDS 2004. D 6/11/2005 Bp Chester Lovelle

Talton P 1/14/2006 Bp Joseph Jon Bruno. Cbury Westwood Fndt Los Angeles CA 2005-2006; H Faith Par Inglewood CA 2005-2006. ruthmonette@gmail.com

MONGE SANTIAGO, Juan Angel (PR) Urb. Rafael Bermudez 2nd St. K-6, Fajardo PR 00738 Puerto Rico **Dio Puerto Rico S Just PR 2006-** B Fajardo Puerto Rico 9/27/1963 s Juan Monge Solis & Binicia. BBA Universidad Interamericana 2000; MBA Universidad Interamericana 2002; MDiv Seminario San Pedro Y San Pablo 2006. D 8/27/2006 P 2/11/2007 Bp David Andres Alvarez-Velazquez. m 3/2/1990 Maribel Vazquez c 2. Dio Puerto Rico S Just PR 2005-2006. juanmonge@iepanglicom.org

MONICA, Ted Jay (Fla) 6661 Man O War Trail, Tallahassee FL 32309 **R Ch Of The H Comf Tallahassee FL 2009-** B Watertown NY 3/24/1959 s Oliver John Monica & Rosemarie. BA Wadhams Hall Sem Coll 1982; MDiv Chr The King Sem 1986. Rec from Roman Catholic 4/8/1998 as Priest Bp Daniel William Herzog. m 8/12/1996 Teri A Teri Hunter c 4. R S Jn's Ch Johnstown NY 2002-2009; R Ch Of The Gd Shpd Elizabethtown NY 1998-2002. billsbeliever@yahoo.com

MONICA, Teri A (Fla) 28 S Market St, Johnstown NY 12095 **Ch Of The H Comf Tallahassee FL 2011-; S Jn's Epis Ch Tallahassee FL 2011-; Ch Of The Ascen Carrabelle FL 2009-** B Plattsburgh NY 3/1/1958 d Walter D Hunter & Carol A. BA SUNY 1985; MA SUNY 2001; MA St Bern's Sch Of Mnstry And Theol Albany NY 2007. D 6/9/2007 P 12/8/2007 Bp William Howard Love. m 8/12/1996 Ted Jay Monica. S Teresa Of Avila Crawfordville FL 2009-2010; Asst S Jn's Ch Johnstown NY 2007-2009. tmonica3769@yahoo.com

MONK, Arthur Jameson (Ct) 18 Crosby Commons Rd, Shelton CT 06484 **Pstr Assoc Trin Ch Seymour CT 1982-** B Fall River MA 12/1/1918 s Evan Monk & Sarah. BS NYU 1942; MDiv Ya Berk 1949. D 6/17/1949 P 12/20/1949 Bp Frederick G Budlong. m 6/12/1948 Mary Oliver Quackenbos c 3. Int Chr Ch Ansonia CT 1987-1988; Int S Mich's Ch Naugatuck CT 1985-1987; Int Ch of our Sav Plainville CT 1984-1985; Int Ascen Ch New Haven CT 1983-1984; Int Ch of the H Sprt W Haven CT 1982-1983; Archd Dio Connecticut Hartford CT 1973-1981; R Chr Ch Stratford CT 1962-1973; R Trin Epis Ch Bristol CT 1951-1962. Bp's Awd for Distinguished Serv to Ch and Communit Dio Connecticut 1995. amonk@msn.com

M

MONK, Edward R (Dal) Saint John's Church (Episcopal), 101 N. 14th Street, Corsicana TX 75110 **R S Jn's Epis Ch Corsicana TX 2003-** B Dallas TX 9/22/1972 s J D Monk & Betty Jo. BA Baylor U 1995; MDiv Nash 1999. D 11/29/1998 P 5/29/1999 Bp Keith Lynn Ackerman. m 7/1/1995 Virginia N Newberry c 3. Yth Off Dio Quincy Peoria IL 2000-2003; Cn S Paul's Cathd Peoria IL 1999-2003; D Trin Ch Wauwatosa WI 1998. "So You're Called to be a Bp," Dovetracts, Inc, 2006. CCU 1999; CBS 1995; GAS 2005; Soc of King Chas the Mtyr 2007; SSC 1999. Hon Dioc Cn Dio Quincy 2003. frmonk@stjohnscorsicana.com

MONNAT, Thomas Leonard (Pa) 213 Earlington Road, Havertown PA 19083 B Syracuse NY 10/4/1948 s Leonard Stephen Monnat & Florence Winifred. BA Villanova U 1970; MDiv GTS 1978. D 6/14/1978 P 10/1/1979 Bp Lyman Cunningham Ogilby. m 6/21/1997 Nancy Monnat c 3. P in charge The Ch Of The Atone Morton PA 1998-2007; All SS Ch Wynnewood PA 1995-1998; R Geth Ch Minneapolis MN 1983-1994; S Steph The Mtyr Ch Minneapolis MN 1979-1982; Asst S Nich Ch Richfield MN 1978-1979. tomm12@verizon.net

MONNOT, Elizabeth Lockwood (NCal) 1225 41st Avenue, Sacramento CA 95922 **Co-R All SS Memi Sacramento CA 2006-** B Waterbury CT 5/5/1967 d Robert Coit Hawley & Isabel Lockwood. BA Ob 1989; ALM Harv 1997; MDiv CDSP 2002. D 6/22/2002 P 1/25/2003 Bp Richard Lester Shimpfky. m 9/28/2002 Michael Monnot c 3. Asst R Gr Ch S Helena CA 2002-2005. betseymonnot@comcast.net

MONNOT, Michael (NCal) 1225 41st Ave, Sacramento CA 95822 **Co-R All SS Memi Sacramento CA 2006-** B Burlingane CA 10/8/1961 s John Monnot & Constance. BA U CA 1985; MDiv CDSP 2002. D 12/4/2004 P 6/4/2005 Bp William Edwin Swing. m 9/28/2002 Elizabeth Lockwood Hawley c 1. Asst S Patricks Ch Kenwood CA 2005-2006. michaelmonnot@comcast.net

MONREAL, Anthony A (EpisSanJ) 9323 South Westlawn, Fresno CA 93706 **S Andr's Ch Taft CA 2000-** B Dos Palos CA 8/21/1959 s Anthony G Monreal & Guillermina. BA S Jn Sem Coll Camarillo CA 1983; MDiv Pontifical Coll Josephinum 1988; MS Natl U 1993; EdD GTF 2005. Rec from Roman Catholic 6/1/1994 as Priest Bp John-David Mercer Schofield. m 6/20/1992 Linda Carey. P S Jas Epis Cathd Fresno CA 1994-1999; D Our Lady of Guadalupe Fresno CA 1993-1994. amonreal@nhufoundation.org

MONROE, George Wesley (Chi) 2866 Vacherie Ln, Dallas TX 75227 B Texarkana TX 3/4/1940 s John J Monroe & Bernadine S. BA Baylor U 1962; MDiv Nash 1968. D 6/26/1968 Bp Charles A Mason P 12/28/1968 Bp William Paul Barnds. Assoc To Exec Dir Bp Anderson Hse Chicago IL 1993-2002; Exec Dir Dio Chicago Chicago IL 1984-1993; R Chr Ch Portsmouth NH 1976-1981; Vic S Barn' Epis Ch Glen Ellyn IL 1973-1976; Asst Ch Of The Ascen Chicago IL 1971-1973; Cur S Lk's Ch Evanston IL 1969-1971; Cur S Jn's Ch Ft Worth TX 1968-1969. Novel, "A Perfect Gift," Lulu Press, 2010. monroegeorge@sbcglobal.net

MONROE, Virginia Hill (WNC) Po Box 32, Cashiers NC 28717 **R Ch Of The Gd Shpd Cashiers NC 2002-** B Gadsden AL 3/24/1943 d James Blackburn Hill & Leola. RN U of Alabama 1964; MDiv STUSo 1994; DMin STUSo 2005. D 5/21/1994 P 12/3/1994 Bp Robert Oran Miller. c 1. Chr Ch Greenville SC 1999-2002; S Steph's Epis Ch Birmingham AL 1997-1999; Asst Ch Of The Nativ Epis Huntsville AL 1994-1996. vjmonroe@frontier.com

MONROE - LOES, Brenda Frances (At) 242 Valley St, Clayton GA 30525 **P-in-c S Jn's W Point GA 2010-** B Chicago Heights IL 5/23/1962 d Martin Stafford Monroe & Carol Barbara. BS Pur 1984; MDiv Epis TS of The SW 1998. D 11/23/1998 Bp Herbert Alcorn Donovan Jr P 1/15/2000 Bp Ronald Hayward Haines. m 2/26/2011 Joseph H. Loes. R S Jas Epis Ch Clayton GA 2001-2005; Asst R S Jn's Ch Olney MD 1999-2000. revbrenda@gmail.com

MONSON, Donald William (Az) 5624 N 12th St, Phoenix AZ 85014 B Alhambra CA 12/10/1934 s Donald Corliss Monson & Margaret Katherine. BS USC 1957; MDiv GTS 1965. D 6/26/1965 Bp William Foreman Creighton P 1/8/1966 Bp Paul Moore Jr. Assoc All SS Ch Phoenix AZ 1996-2010; Hstgr & Rgstr Dio Arizona Phoenix AZ 1983-1998; R Epis Ch of the H Sprt Phoenix AZ 1981-1995; Chairman of the COM Dio Arizona Phoenix AZ 1979-1982; Dioc Coun Dio Arizona Phoenix AZ 1974-1977; R S Mich's Ch Coolidge AZ 1970-1981; Cur S Paul's Par Washington DC 1965-1970. donaldmons@aol.com

MONSON, Scott B (Minn) 304 7th Pl Nw, Austin MN 55912 B St Peter MN 11/5/1956 s Karl Sanford Monson & Bernice Karen. BA Gustavus Adolphus Coll 1986; MA Minnesota St U Mankato 1989; MDiv SWTS 2001. D 10/15/2002 P 4/23/2003 Bp James Louis Jelinek. R Chr Ch Austin MN 2003-2009. Seabury-Wstrn Awd SWTS 2001. rector@christchurchaustin.com

MONSOUR, John Vincent (SwFla) 6616 Cimarron Cir, Anchorage AK 99504 B Pawtucket RI 11/18/1947 s George Paul Monsour & Eleanor Marie. CG Jung Inst; Washington Sch of Psych; BA Providence Coll 1969; MA Washington Theol Un 1974; DMin Andover Newton TS 1977. Rec from Roman Catholic 10/4/1995 as Priest Bp Rogers Sanders Harris. m 8/29/2009 Betty Monsour. Dio SW Florida Sarasota FL 2004-2008; Assoc All SS Ch Tarpon Sprg FL 2000-2004; Int S Cathr's Ch Temple Terrace FL 1998-1999; Assoc S Mk's Epis Ch Of Tampa Tampa FL 1994-1996. Fell, Amer Assoc. Pstr Counselors (AAPC) 1998. drjohnvmonsour@yahoo.com

MONTAGNO, Karen Anita Brown (Mass) 536 Main St # 2, Medford MA 02155 **Dir Congrl Resources and Trng Dio Massachusetts Boston MA 2010-** B Portsmouth VA 8/18/1955 d George Walter Brown & Willie Mae. BSW OH SU 1977; MA OH SU 1979; MDiv VTS 1995. D 6/24/1995 P 5/4/1996 Bp Herbert Thompson Jr. m 6/21/1980 Thomas Montagno c 3. Int S Cyp's Ch Roxbury MA 2010-2011; Assoc Chr Ch Cambridge Cambridge MA 1999; Dn of Students & Cmnty Life EDS Cambridge MA 1996-2009; Asst Dio Sthrn Ohio Cincinnati OH 1995-1996; Cur S Matt's Ch Westerville OH 1995-1996. Auth, *Called by Jesus*; Auth, *Epis Curric for Yth*, Morehouse Pub; Auth, *Peace and Justice*; Auth, *Sprtlty*. Soc of S Jn the Evang 1994; UBE, Massachusetts Chapt, Chapl 2000. ,Polly Bond Awd ECom 2004. kmontagno2003@yahoo.com

MONTAGUE, Cynthia Russell (ECR) 17574 Winding Creek Rd, Salinas CA 93908 **Jail Chapl Dio El Camino Real Monterey CA 2002-** B Washington DC 7/18/1953 d Homer Ross Montague & Lillian Dorothy. BA Brandeis U 1975; MDiv Andover Newton TS 1986. D 5/4/2002 Bp Richard Lester Shimpfky. m 3/25/1974 Marilyn Jeanne Westerkamp c 2. D Assoc Trin Ch Gonzales CA 2002. Integrity USA 1977. Jonathan Edwards Soc Andover Newton TS 1986. 39cmont27@sbcglobal.net

MONTAGUE, Eugene Bryan (NC) 624 Deacon Ridge St, Wake Forest NC 27587 B Santa Ana CA 10/27/1928 s William Bryan Montague & Gladys. BA Cntrl Washington U 1950; MA U of Texas 1952; PhD U of Texas 1957; Cert EDS 1967. D 6/29/1967 Bp Archie H Crowley P 6/1/1968 Bp Richard S M Emrich. m 1/1/1950 Barbara Winslow Holliday c 4. Int S Paul's Epis Ch Brighton MI 1991-1992; Asst Min Cathd Ch Of S Paul Detroit MI 1967-1968. Auth, "Four Worlds Of Writing," Harper&Row, 1985; Auth, "Poetry And A Principle," Lippincott, 1973; Auth, "Guide To Amer Engl," Prentice-Hall, 1972; Auth, "The Experience Of Lit," Prentice -Hall, 1966; Auth, "Collequium," Little Brown, 1962. montague28@aol.com

MONTALTO, Alfred Patrick (NY) 3001 58th Ave S Apt 301, Saint Petersburg FL 33712 B Poughkeepsie NY 9/9/1943 s Alfred Donald Montalto & Helen Frances. BA Marist Coll 1966; MA Marist Coll 1966; MDiv Ya Berk 1969; MSTh Ya Berk 1977. D 6/7/1969 P 12/20/1969 Bp Horace W B Donegan. The Ch Of S Steph Staten Island NY 2000-2001; S Barth's Ch In The Highland White Plains NY 1997-1998; Ch Of The Gd Shpd Wakefield Bronx NY 1986-1997; P-in-c S Andr's Ch Bronx NY 1985-1986; All SS Ch Harrison NY 1971-1976. NYPD Citizen of the Year; "Who's Who in Rel". theduchy@gmail.com

MONTANARI, Albert Ubaldo (WNY) 135 Old Lyme Dr Apt 4, Williamsville NY 14221 B Rochester NY 10/4/1926 s Joseph Montanari & Anna. BS

Buffalo St Coll 1958; MDiv Pittsburgh TS 1965. D 6/3/1978 Bp Harold B Robinson P 10/1/1978 Bp Philip Frederick McNairy. m 4/28/1947 Mary Morabito c 1. Asst H Apos Epis Ch Tonawanda NY 1990-1996; R S Pat's Ch Cheektowaga NY 1986-1989; Vic S Pat's Ch Cheektowaga NY 1981-1985; Cur H Apos Epis Ch Tonawanda NY 1978-1981. skypilot71@verizon.net

MONTES, Alejandro Sixto (Tex) 10426 Towne Oak Ln, Sugar Land TX 77478 **Vic San Mateo Epis Ch Bellaire TX 1993-; S Matt's Ch Bellaire TX 1989-** B Lima PE 3/29/1944 s Miguel Montes & Teresa. Cert Cntrl Amer TS GT 1978; Lic Cntrl Amer TS GT 2000. D 6/24/1989 Bp Maurice Manuel Benitez P 2/5/1990 Bp Anselmo Carral-Solar. m 8/6/1966 Laura Vela c 3. iglesiasanmateo@sbc.global.net

MONTES, Alex G. Montes (Tex) 10333 Eagles Mtn, Waco TX 76712 B 12/22/1967 s Alejandro Sixto Montes & Laura. MDiv VTS 2005. D 6/11/2005 P 12/13/2005 Bp Don Adger Wimberly. m 7/20/2005 Hong Duc T Tran c 3. S Paul's Ch Waco TX 2005-2008; Ch Of The Redeem Houston TX 1994-1998. amontes1@hot.rr.com

MONTES, Elizabeth (Neb) 1604 N Jefferson St, Lexington NE 68850 **Trin Ch Victoria TX 2011-** B El Paso TX 3/11/1960 d Gregorio Rubio & Evangelina. U of Texas 1982; U of New Mex 1983; AAS El Paso Cmnty Coll El Paso TX 1987; BS U of Phoenix 1997; MDiv STUSo 2002. D 7/27/2002 Bp Terence Kelshaw P 7/26/2003 Bp Don Adger Wimberly. m 6/4/1988 Joel Montes c 4. S Christophers Ch Cozad NE 2010-2011; Dio Nebraska Omaha NE 2007-2010; On Track Mnstry Lexington NE 2006; S Steph's Ch Beaumont TX 2004-2005; P-in-c S Geo's Epis Ch Port Arthur TX 2003-2004. DOK 2005. pastorelex@gmail.com

MONTES, Gesner Roger (Hai) Box 1309, Port-Au-Prince Haiti B Aux Cayes HT 10/3/1939 s Leogene Montes & Mervelie. BA Coll Of S Pierre Ht 1964; STB ETSC 1969. D 12/14/1969 Bp John Brooke Mosley P 12/1/1970 Bp Paul Axtell Kellogg. m 5/8/1971 Rigaud Marie Juliette. Dio Haiti Ft Lauderdale FL 1969-2004.

MONTGOMERY, Bruce (NJ) 1310 Tullo Rd, Martinsville NJ 08836 **R S Mart's Ch Bridgewater NJ 1982-** B Toledo OH 10/31/1950 s Charles Raymond Montgomery & Mona Jane. BA Albion Coll 1972; PrTS 1975; MDiv GTS 1977. D 6/11/1977 Bp Jonathan Goodhue Sherman P 5/30/1978 Bp Robert Campbell Witcher Sr. m 12/18/1976 Lani Lynn Mueller. Asst S Anne's Ch Abington PA 1977-1982. bmont1310@aol.com

MONTGOMERY, Catharine Whittaker (SwVa) 2231 Timberlake Dr, Lynchburg VA 24502 **P-in-c Gr Memi Ch Lynchburg VA 2006-** B Durham NC 8/16/1944 d William West Whittaker & Catherine. BA Randolph-Macon Wmn's Coll 1994; Cert VTS 1998. D 5/22/1999 P 1/22/2000 Bp Frank Neff Powell. m 3/16/1963 John Robert Montgomery c 2. Assoc S Paul's Epis Ch Lynchburg VA 1999-2006; Educational Consortium Dio SW Virginia Roanoke VA 1999. Omicron Delta Kappa 1993; Psi Chi 1993. Phi Beta Kappa Randolph-Macon Wmn'S Coll 1994. gracememorialcathy@yahoo.com

MONTGOMERY, Ellen M (WNY) 41 Saint Georges Sq, Buffalo NY 14222 B Buffalo NY 9/3/1929 d Arthur George Maddigan & Lillian. GTS; BA SUNY 1981; MDiv U Tor--Trin 1985. D 6/22/1985 P 4/1/1986 Bp Harold B Robinson. m 3/31/1951 H Ernest Montgomery c 3. Dio Wstrn New York Tonawanda NY 1991-1992; Mssn Counslr Trin Epis Ch Buffalo NY 1989-1999; Asst S Mk's Ch Orchard Pk NY 1985-1986. Capture a Heart Awd Homespace, Inc. 2004; Vision Awd Canaan Hse 2003. ellenmont1@verizon.net

MONTGOMERY, Ian (FdL) 26 Gaskill Rd, Chester VT 05143 B London UK 12/11/1944 s Hector Montgomery & Anne. LLB U of St. Andrews 1966; Fca Inst For Chart Accountants 1969; CTh Oxf 1975; DMin STUSo 2002. Trans from Church Of England 8/1/1979 as Priest Bp Alexander Doig Stewart. m 10/9/1976 Polly Cooper c 2. R S Thos Ch Menasha WI 1997-2009; R S Barth's Ch Bristol TN 1992-1997; R S Phil's Ch New Orleans LA 1983-1992; Dio Wstrn Massachusetts Springfield MA 1978-1983. FRIANM@AOL.COM

MONTGOMERY, Ian Bruce (ECR) 175 9th Avenue, New York NY 10011 B Bremerhaven Germany 11/23/1966 s Richard Millar Montgomery & Diana. U of S Andrews 1988; BA U Pgh 1991; MDiv GTS 1998. D 6/13/1998 Bp Robert Gould Tharp P 12/19/1998 Bp George Phelps Mellick Belshaw. m 3/31/2005 Diane France Vasiliki Eliopoulos c 4. All SS Epis Ch Palo Alto CA 2005-2008; Cn Pstr The Amer Cathd of the H Trin Paris 75008 FR 2000-2001; Secy/Treas Dio New Jersey Trenton NJ 1998-2000; Cur S Geo's-By-The-River Rumson NJ 1998-2000. Fllshp of S Jn (SSJE) 2005. ibmontgomery@gmail.com

✠ MONTGOMERY, Rt Rev James Winchester (Chi) 260 S Reynolds St Apt 1010, Alexandria VA 22304 B Chicago IL 5/29/1921 s James Edward Montgomery & Evelyn Lee. BA NWU 1943; STB GTS 1949; STD GTS 1963; DD Nash 1963; DD SWTS 1969; LLD Shimer Coll 1969; LHD Iowa Wesleyan Coll 1974. D 6/18/1949 P 12/17/1949 Bp Wallace E Conkling Con 9/29/1962 for Chi. Ret Bp of Chi Dio Chicago Chicago IL 1987; Trst The CPG New York NY 1975-1988; SCL Dio Chicago Chicago IL 1970-1976; Serv SWTS Evanston IL 1965-1988; Bp Coadj Dio Chicago Chicago IL 1965-1971; Trst The GTS New York NY 1964-1982; Serv Nash Nashotah WI 1962-1988; Bp Dio Chicago Chicago IL 1962-1965; Trst The GTS New York NY 1961-1962; Stndg Com Dio Chicago Chicago IL 1960-1962; Cathd Chapt Dio Chicago Chicago IL 1959-1962; ExCoun, Dn So Deanry Dio Chicago Chicago IL 1954-1962; R The Ch Of S Jn The Evang Flossmoor IL 1951-1962; Cur S Lk's Ch Evanston IL 1949-1951. Phi Beta Kappa 1943.

MONTGOMERY, Jennifer Born (Va) 4000 Lorcom Ln, Arlington VA 22207 **R S Andr's Epis Ch Arlington VA 2009-** B Atlanta GA 6/27/1954 d Robert Eugene Born & Ethel Elizabeth. BA Shorter Coll 1988; MDiv VTS 1998. D 6/13/1998 P 4/20/1999 Bp Peter James Lee. m 2/10/2001 Joseph E Glaze c 3. R S Jas' Ch Clinton NY 2002-2009; Asstg Vic Chr Ch Glen Allen VA 1998-2002. jenny_glaze@hotmail.com

MONTGOMERY, John Alford (Lex) BOX 57 8, Tyne Valley, Pei C0B 2C0 Canada B Mount Holly NJ 1/20/1936 D 6/1/1974 Bp Addison Hosea. m 7/14/1962 Carol Tabler c 4.

MONTGOMERY, John Fletcher (USC) 2827 Wheat St, Columbia SC 29205 **R S Jn's Epis Ch Columbia SC 1999-** B 7/17/1964 BA Furman U; MDiv VTS. D 6/18/1994 P 1/7/1995 Bp John Wadsworth Howe. All SS Epis Ch Enterprise FL 1996-1999; Ch Of The Redeem Bryn Mawr PA 1994-1996; Trin Ch Vero Bch FL 1989-1991. jfm@stjohnscolumbia.org

MONTIEL, Robert Michael (WTenn) 103 S Poplar St, Paris TN 38242 B Gadsden AL 4/13/1951 s Gonzalo Fitch Montiel & Voncile Roena. BS Georgia Inst of Tech 1973; JD U of Alabama 1976; MDiv STUSo 1991. D 6/1/1991 P 1/1/1992 Bp Charles Farmer Duvall. m 12/30/1978 Cynthia Gay Steadman c 3. R Gr Epis Ch Paris TN 2000-2006; R Chr The King Epis Ch Normal IL 1994-2000; Trin Epsicopal Ch Atmore AL 1991-1994; D-In-Trng S Anna's Ch Atmore AL 1991-1992. Tertiary Of The Soc Of S Fran.

MONTILEAUX, Charles Thomas (SD) Po Box 246, Kyle SD 57752 B Porcupine SD 2/27/1960 s Francis Willard Montileaux & Barbara Jean. Rio Salado Cmnty Coll; BA U Of Dubuque 1983; MA U Of Dubuque 1985; MDiv U Of Dubuque 1987. D 6/22/1986 P 6/1/1987 Bp Craig Barry Anderson. m 7/14/1979 Gloria Jean George c 2. Dio So Dakota Sioux Falls SD 1987-1989.

MONTJOY IV, Gid (Md) 411 Penwood Dr, Edgewater MD 21037 B Paris TX 11/9/1944 s William Hemingway Montjoy & Estelle. BBA U of Mississippi 1966; Cert of Completion Mississippi Coll 1970; MDiv TESM 1983; DMin STUSo 1989. D 6/23/1984 P 1/18/1985 Bp Duncan Montgomery Gray Jr. m 5/17/2002 Cynthia Jenkins c 3. Eccl Crt Dio Maryland Baltimore MD 2005-2008; Dio Maryland Baltimore MD 1999; Assoc S Anne's Par Annapolis MD 1995-2010; R H Trin Epis Ch Auburn AL 1987-1995; Vic S Mk's Ch Raymond MS 1985-1987; Vic Ch Of The Creator Clinton MS 1984-1987. Auth, "Chr in the Wrld," *CE in the Dio Alabama*, Dio Alabama, 1993; Auth, "Starting a New Cong in the Epis Ch," *Starting a New Cong in the Epis Ch*, D. Minn Proj, 1989; Auth, "What One needs to Know About Conservatorship and Guardianships in Chancery Crt," *What One Needs to Know About the Crt System in Mississippi*, Mississippi Bar Assn, 1978. gcmontjoy@verizon.net

MONTOOTH, Cynthia Hooton (SwFla) 15 Knob Hill Circle, Decatur GA 30030 B Hollister CA 8/15/1942 d Wade Hooton & Alice Ethel. BA The Curtis Inst of Mus 1961; Lic Sch for Diac Formation Ellenton FL 2004. D 6/12/2004 Bp John Bailey Lipscomb. m 1/18/1974 Gene Montooth c 4. D Assoc S Hilary's Ch Ft Myers FL 2004-2008. chmontooth@earthlink.com

MONTOYA CARPIO, S Leonardo (EcuC) Apartado #17-01-3108, Quito Ecuador B Loja EC 5/15/1949 s Filoteo Montoya & Maria. Salamanca U 1978; Lic Cntrl U 1985; Cuenca U 1988. D 2/7/1982 P 3/1/1983 Bp Adrian Delio Caceres-Villavicencio. m 8/1/1987 Clara Ordonez. Ecuador New York NY 2005-2009. Auth, "Pensamiento Latinoamericano Xaverian U, La Legitima Defensa De La Persona," *Doctoral Thesis*, 1988. Apd. SLMONTOYACARPIO@HOTMAIL.COM

MONTROSE, Richard Sterling (LI) 712 Franklin St, Westbury NY 11590 B Orange NJ 8/13/1927 s Levi Tappington Montrose & Marie Louise. BS LIU 1958; Cert Mercer TS 1995. D 10/18/1997 Bp Rodney Rae Michel. m 1/22/1956 Florence Hilda Brown.

MONZON-MOLINA, Eduardo (Hond) Apartado 2598, San Pedro Honduras B Guatemala City GT 9/9/1943 s Francisco Monzon-Castro & Estela. San Carlos U Gt 1966; EDS 1968; MDiv ETSC 1969. D 5/31/1969 P 12/1/1969 Bp William Carl Frey. m 5/2/1970 Hilda Perez-Tabarini. Cn Catedral Epis El Buen Pstr San Pedro Sula HN 2000-2007; SAMS Ambridge PA 1989-2007; Dio Guatemala Guatemala City 1969-1980. Auth, "Crisis Confrontation," *Crisis Preparedness*. SAMS. Vstg Fell Austin Sem 1979. emonzon@hotmail.com

MOODY, John Wallace (NY) 42 W 9th St Apt 18, New York NY 10011 B Glenside PA 11/16/1926 s Harold Wellington Moody & Lulu Grace. BA Un Coll Schenectady NY 1950; MDiv EDS 1953; MA NYU 1969. D 6/6/1953 P 12/20/1953 Bp Henry W Hobson. Assoc Pstr Mnstrs Par of Trin Ch New York NY 1988-1991; The Vill Nrsng Hm New York NY 1987-1988; S Jn In-The-Wilderness Copake Falls NY 1986-1987; Manhattan Plaza Assoc New York NY 1983-1987; R S Pauls On The Hill Epis Ch Ossining NY 1976-1983; Dir Cntr Forum Ch Of S Paul The Apos Baltimore MD 1974-1976; Asst Cmnty & Cultural Affrs Par of Trin Ch New York NY 1968-1974; Vic Ch Of S Edw Columbus OH 1954-1965; Cur S Alb's Epis Ch Of Bexley Columbus OH 1953-1954. Artist, *Gallery Exhibitions*, 2009; Auth, "Mnstry to the Aging,"

Alb Inst, 1982; Auth, "Liturg and the Arts," *Cath Wrld*, 1962; Auth, "Recent Article in a Climate of Change," *Chr Century*, 1960. Epis Ch and the Visual Arts 2002. Prog Awd to Trin Ch Arts & Bus Coun of NYC New York NY 1973. Johnmoody@nyc.rr.com

✠ **MOODY, Rt Rev Robert Manning** (Okla) 4001 Oxford Way, Norman OK 73072 B Baltimore MD 7/23/1939 s Irving Wright Moody & Ann Elizabeth. BA Rice U 1962; U of Texas 1963; MDiv VTS 1966; S Geo's Coll Jerusalem IL 1981. D 6/21/1966 P 5/29/1967 Bp J Milton Richardson Con 2/6/1988 for Okla. m 4/19/1968 Beryl Lance Baty c 4. Dio Oklahoma Oklahoma City OK 1988-2007; Trst Epis TS Of The SW Austin TX 1988-1992; Trst VTS Alexandria VA 1982-1987; R Gr Epis Ch Alexandria VA 1975-1987; R S Jas Ch Riverton WY 1970-1975; Asst S Jn The Div Houston TX 1968-1970. EvangES 1975-1987. Distinguished Alum St. Jn's Sch, Houston, Texas 2010; Distinguished Alumus Rice U 2005; DD VTS Alexandria VA 1988. lancemoody@cox.net

MOODY, Thomas Edward (At) 802 John Alden Rd, Stone Mountain GA 30083 **Died 8/3/2010** B Atlanta GA 2/6/1941 s Wallace Edward Moody & Mary Lucia. BA U GA 1964; LTh STUSo 1967; BD STUSo 1970; MDiv STUSo 1971. D 6/24/1967 Bp Randolph R Claiborne P 6/1/1968 Bp R(aymond) Stewart Wood Jr. tmoody1790@aol.com

MOON, Abigail White (Ga) 211 N Monroe St, Tallahassee FL 32301 **S Jn's Epis Ch Tallahassee FL 2011-** B Columbia GA 4/7/1975 d Lawrence Kermit White & Signe Ann. BA U of So 1997; MDiv The U So (Sewanee) 2011. D 2/11/2011 P 9/6/2011 Bp Scott Anson Benhase. m 8/4/2007 Robert A Moon. The Ch Of The Gd Shpd Augusta GA 2005-2008. abigailmoon@gmail.com

MOON, Anthony (Okla) 2401 N. Westminster Road, Arcadia OK 73007 **D S Mary's Ch Edmond OK 1997-** B Blackwell OK 6/14/1952 s Sylvester F Moon & Mary Catherine. B.A. Cntrl St U 1975; M.Ed. Cntrl St U 1979; Ph.D. U of Oklahoma 1995; Dioc D Formation Prog 1997. D 6/21/1997 Bp Robert Manning Moody. m 4/5/1985 Marian Jean Schaper c 3. "Coming to Terms w Being Lost," *Sermons That Wk (Series)*, Morehouse Pub, 2004. tonymoon@airosurf.com

MOON, Catherine Joy (Cal) The Curate's House, 7 Walton Village, Liverpool AL L4 6TJ Great Britain (UK) B London UK 10/16/1948 d George Alum Moon & Eileen Olive. Royal Acad of Mus London GB 1972; BA Sch for Deacons 1984; Cert GTS 1985. D 6/9/1984 P 6/8/1985 Bp William Edwin Swing. cmoon@fish.co.uk

MOON JR, Don Pardee (Chi) 438 N Sheridan Rd # A500, Waukegan IL 60085 **Pstr Asst Chr Ch Waukegan IL 1985-** B Manila PH 2/8/1936 s Don Pardee Moon & Sibyl Peaslee. BS Cor 1957; MS NYU 1958; BD Nash 1965. D 6/12/1965 Bp James Winchester Montgomery P 12/1/1965 Bp Gerald Francis Burrill. m 1/18/1985 Joanne Martha Armstrong. Shimer Coll Chicago IL 1995-2003; Chr Ch Waukegan IL 1992-2003; R The Ch Of S Anne Morrison IL 1965-1969. djmoon137@comcast.net

MOON, James Fred (WMo) 43 Old Mill Ln, South Greenfield MO 65752 **P-in-c S Thos a'Becket Epis Ch Cassville MO 2003-** B Springfield MO 7/18/1933 s William Adderley Moon & Gladys. BA Drury U 1955; MDiv Sea 1958. D 5/31/1958 P 12/18/1958 Bp Edward Randolph Welles II. m 5/12/1979 Cheryl A Calvin c 5. S Steph's Ch Monett MO 1992-1996; Dio W Missouri Kansas City MO 1964-1994; R Chr Ch Warrensburg MO 1958-1963. ESMHE 1988. Bp's Shield 1997; Bp's Shield 1969. cjturnback@hotmail.com

MOON, Mary Louise (Oly) 927 S Sheridan Ave, Tacoma WA 98405 **D S Catherines Ch Enumclaw WA 2002-** B Town of Broom NY 4/20/1935 d Mahlon Wilbur Holmes & Catherine. BS Cor 1956. D 6/29/2002 Bp Vincent Waydell Warner.

MOON, Richard Warren (Neb) Po Box 1012, West Plains MO 65775 **Const & Cannons Dio W Missouri Kansas City MO 1993-** B Richmond Hgts MO 1/30/1954 s William Adderly Moon & Virginia Lee. BA Colorado Coll 1976; MA U Chi 1977; JD U CO 1980; MDiv Nash 1991. D 6/11/1991 P 12/1/1991 Bp John Clark Buchanan. m 6/2/1979 Constance Marie Feese c 2. Chr Ch Epis Beatrice NE 2006-2010; Stndg Com Dio W Missouri Kansas City MO 1995; Eccl Crt Dio W Missouri Kansas City MO 1994-1995; R All SS Ch W Plains MO 1993-2006; Assoc To R Gr Ch Carthage MO 1991-1993. moonpeople25@yahoo.com

MOON, Robert Michael (Los) 1294 Westlyn Pl, Pasadena CA 91104 B Santa Monica CA 4/4/1962 BA NWU 1984; JD SW U Sch Of Law Los Angeles CA 1988; MDiv GTS 2003. D 6/14/2003 P 1/24/2004 Bp Joseph Jon Bruno. S Richard's Epis Ch Lake Arrowhead CA 2005-2008; The Ch Of The Ascen Sierra Madre CA 2003-2005. saintrichards9@earthlink.net

MOONEY, Michelle Puzin (Mil) 2633 N Hackett Ave Apt A, Milwaukee WI 53211 **D S Mk's Ch Milwaukee WI 2001-** B Wichita Falls TX 10/15/1942 d Lucien Alexandre Puzin & Andre Jaune. BS U of Texas 1964; MS U of Wisconsin 1980. D 4/21/2001 Bp Roger John White. m 12/7/1991 Richard F Mooney c 3. m_mooney@core.com

MOONEY, Noreen O'Connor (LI) 1 Berard Blvd, Oakdale NY 11769 B Bronx NY 6/22/1940 d Hugh J O'Connor & Elizabeth Ann. BA Col 1968; MDiv GTS 1983. D 12/10/1983 Bp Robert Campbell Witcher Sr P 2/18/1989 Bp Orris George Walker Jr. S Paul's Ch Oxford NY 2001; Chenango Cluster Norwich NY 2000; S Jas Ch Brookhaven NY 1991-1995; Dio Long Island Garden City NY 1987-1991; St Jas Ch Sag Harbor NY 1986-1987; S Johns Epis Hosp Far Rockaway NY 1985-1986; Asst All SS Ch Great Neck NY 1983-1985.

MOORE, Albert Lee (NC) 8705 Gleneagles Dr, Raleigh NC 27613 **D Chr Epis Ch Raleigh NC 1998-** B Philadelphia PA 1/21/1937 s Albert Lee Moore & Harriet M. CUNY; MDiv Shaw DS 1994. D 12/20/1997 Bp Robert Carroll Johnson Jr. m 6/17/1972 Ernstein Saint Claire Wright c 1. amoore@christchurch-raleigh.org

MOORE, Allison (Nwk) 1576 Palisade Ave, Fort Lee NJ 07024 **R Ch Of The Gd Shpd Ft Lee NJ 1996-** B Pasadena CA 2/26/1957 d James Dale Moore & Lois Claire. BA Simmons Coll 1978; MS Ya 1980; MA Harvard DS 1984; PhD Bos 1989. D 6/8/1991 P 12/14/1991 Bp Richard Frank Grein. c 3. Int H Cross Epis Ch No Plainfield NJ 1995-1996; Cur Gr Ch White Plains NY 1991-1994. Allison M. Moore, "Cler Moms: Survival GUide to balancing Fam and Cong," Seabury, 2008. Families of Cler Untd in Spprt 2004; Soc for Values in Higher Educ 1981. allimoore@mac.com

MOORE, Andy J (NJ) 229 Goldsmith Ave, Newark NJ 07112 **Anti-Racism Commision Trin Cathd Trenton NJ 2010-; Cathd Chapt Trin Cathd Trenton NJ 2010-; R S Eliz's Ch Eliz NJ 2008-** B Trinidad & Tobago 9/21/1963 BA Codrington Coll 1993. Trans from Church in the Province Of The West Indies 11/3/2003 Bp George Edward Councell. m 8/5/1995 Natalie Roberts c 2. Dir Seamens Ch Inst Income New York NY 2003-2008. fatherandy@verizon.net

MOORE, Anne Elizabeth Olive (Ore) 630 B St, Silverton OR 97381 **COM Dio Oregon Portland OR 2011-; S Hilda's Ch Monmouth OR 2008-; The Epis Ch Of The Prince Of Peace Salem OR 2005-** B Indianapolis IN 8/14/1950 d George S Olive & Sally Anne. BA Pur 1972; MS Portland St U 1996; MDiv CDSP 2005. D 10/8/2005 P 6/28/2006 Bp Johncy Itty. m 9/2/1980 James R Moore c 3. Dioc Coun Dio Oregon Portland OR 2008-2010. anneolivemoore@gmail.com

MOORE, Bridget Dorothea (Oly) 11 Opal Ln, Sequim WA 98382 **Assoc (Ret) S Lk's Ch Sequim WA 1999-** B London UK 7/2/1927 d Henry James Byrne & Aileen Minnie. BA Chr Brothers U 1985; Sem 1991; CPE Mckinnon Hosp Sioux Falls SD 1992; U So 1998. D 11/8/1992 Bp Craig Barry Anderson P 7/10/1996 Bp Creighton Leland Robertson. m 8/16/1967 Donald Clark Moore. Vic Gr Epis Ch Madison SD 1996-1999; Vic S Steph's Ch De Smet SD 1996-1999; D S Paul's Ch Brookings SD 1992-1996. NAAD.

MOORE JR, Charles Nottingham (Mass) 12800 Nightingale Drive, Chester VA 23836 **P-in-c Merchants Hope Epis Ch Prince Geo Hopewell VA 2010-** B Hopewell VA 1/12/1944 s Charles Burney Moore & Edwina. BS W&M 1966; Med W&M 1969; MDiv Gordon-Conwell TS 1973; DMin Andover Newton TS 1974. D 6/9/1976 P 6/1/1985 Bp John Bowen Coburn. m 5/25/2002 Deborah Jean Moore c 2. Int S Jn's Epis Ch Saugus MA 2009; R S Lk's Epis Ch Malden MA 2000-2009; Int S Jn's Epis Ch Gloucester MA 1994-1996; Assoc S Jn's Epis Ch Gloucester MA 1983-1986. APA. charles.n.moore@comcast.net

MOORE, Charles Owen (Pa) 4631 Ossabaw Way, Naples FL 34119 **Pres Dio Chicago Chicago IL 1979-** B Hamilton OH 6/21/1932 s Buford Owen Moore & Gladys Frances. BA Ob 1954; MDiv GTS 1958. D 6/11/1958 P 12/22/1958 Bp Horace W B Donegan. c 3. COM Dio Pennsylvania Philadelphia PA 1987-1992; R S Mk's Ch Philadelphia PA 1981-1995; Stndg Com Dio Chicago Chicago IL 1976-1979; Chair Dio Chicago Chicago IL 1968-1981; R S Giles' Ch Northbrook IL 1966-1981; Asst Ch Of The Resurr New York NY 1963-1966; Cur Ch Of The Resurr New York NY 1959-1962; Cur S Jas Ch New York NY 1958-1959. Phi Beta Kappa. comoore@comcast.net

MOORE, Charlotte Elizabeth (Eas) 200 Bohemia Ave Apt 2, Chesapeake City MD 21915 B JacksonvilleFL 9/8/1943 d Charles Bowen Moore & Beatrice. BA Coll of Notre Dame 1994; MDiv VTS 2001. D 6/8/2001 P 1/23/2003 Bp Michael Whittington Creighton. Chr Ch Denton MD 2006-2007; Vic Gr Ch Stanardsville VA 2004-2006; S Steph's Ch Severn Par Crownsville MD 2003-2004; S Edw's Epis Ch Lancaster PA 2001-2003. moorecharlottee@yahoo.com

MOORE, Cheryl Patricia (U) 2378 East 1700 South Street, Salt Lake City UT 84108 B Cambridge MA 8/23/1946 d Jesse Molen Moore & Mary Sarkis. BA San Francisco St U 1974; MDiv EDS 1983. D 5/10/1986 Bp Otis Charles P 2/2/1987 Bp George Edmonds Bates. m 6/10/1989 Daniel Lee Andrus c 1. S Jas Epis Ch Midvale UT 2005; Cathd Ch Of S Mk Salt Lake City UT 1990-2001; Dio Utah Salt Lake City UT 1989-2005; All SS Ch Salt Lake City UT 1988-1989. revcpm@qwest.net

MOORE, Christopher Chamberlin (Pa) 20274 Beaver Dam Rd, Harbeson DE 19951 **Sprtl / Vocational Credo Inst Inc. Memphis TN 2008-; Assoc All SS Ch Rehoboth Bch DE 2006-** B Summit NJ 6/5/1943 s John Frederick Chamberlin Moore & Joanna Louise. BA Muhlenberg Coll 1965; MA Drew U 1968; MDiv Andover Newton TS 1975. D 4/27/1974 P 12/21/1974 Bp Albert Wiencke Van Duzer. m 10/14/1978 Janice Elaine Klinger c 2. Deploy Dio Delaware Wilmington DE 2007-2008; R The Ch Of The H Comf Drexel Hill

M

PA 1994-2006; Cmncatn, Deploy, Asst to the Bp Dio New Jersey Trenton NJ 1990-1994; R S Andr's Ch New Bedford MA 1984-1990; Deploy, Cmncatn Dio San Diego San Diego CA 1981; Asst S Lk's Ch San Diego CA 1980-1984; S Alb's Epis Ch El Cajon CA 1979-1981; Asst Gr Ch Merchantville NJ 1974-1977. Auth, "Solitude: A Neglected Path to God," Cowley Press, 2001; Auth, "Opening the Cler Parachute," Abingdon Press, 1995; Auth, "What I Really Want To Do," CBP (Chalice), 1989; Auth, "Rel Column, 2002-2006," *The Pennsylvania Epis*. Soc of the Cincinnati 1994. Emmy Awd for Rel Broadcasting Natl Assn of Television Arts and Sciences, San Diego 1981. ccmsoulman@aol.com

MOORE, Clifford Allan (Wyo) P.O. Box 1086, #3 Valley Dr., Sundance WY 82729 **Int S Lk's Epis Ch Buffalo WY 2010-; Dioc Coun Mem Dio Wyoming Casper WY 2004-** B Concord CA 5/1/1936 s Walter Marshall Moore & Edna Marie. BA Chapman U 1958; MDiv SWTS 1997. D 6/11/1997 Bp Jerry Alban Lamb P 12/11/1997 Bp Bruce Edward Caldwell. m 4/14/1957 K J Cooper c 4. Mnstry Dvlp - SE Wy Dio Wyoming Casper WY 2000-2008; All SS Ch Wheatland WY 1997-1999; Ch Of Our Sav Hartville WY 1997-1999. Knights hon Soc 1958. cliffm@rangeweb.net

MOORE III, Clint (Chi) 3304 Park Pl, Evanston IL 60201 B Corpus Christi TX 11/3/1950 s Clint Moore & Elinor Glynn. BA U So 1972; MDiv SWTS 1992. D 6/13/1992 Bp James Barrow Brown P 12/1/1992 Bp Frank Tracy Griswold III. m 4/3/1988 Jane Peters Nelson c 2. Asst Trin Ch Highland Pk IL 1993-1995; Advoc Hlth Care Oak Brook IL 1993-1994. Bd Cert Chapl Assn Profsnl Chapl. jmoore@enteract.com

MOORE, Courtland Manning (FtW) 2341 Monticello Cir, Plano TX 75075 **P-in-c Ch Of The Annunc Lewisville TX 2011-; Dioc Transition Min Dio Ft Worth Ft Worth TX 2010-** B Tulsa OK 2/22/1929 s Courtland Manning Moore & Mary Elizabeth. BA U of Oklahoma 1950; MDiv CDSP 1953; DMin SWTS 2000. D 6/21/1953 P 12/1/1953 Bp Chilton Powell. m 10/10/1959 Barbara Williams. Cn Dio Ft Worth Ft Worth TX 2009; R S Alb's Epis Ch Arlington TX 1983-1994; Cn Dio Dallas Dallas TX 1971-1983; R S Mk's Ch Irving TX 1965-1971; R All SS Epis Ch Aledo TX 1962-1965; Vic S Dav's Ch Oklahoma City OK 1955-1962; Vic S Mk's Ch Seminole OK 1953-1955. Hon Cn Dio Dallas 2002. courtmoore@verizon.net

MOORE, David C. (Oly) 8992 Kula Highway, Kula HI 96790 **Int S Jn's Epis Ch Kula HI 2010-** B Denver CO 10/28/1947 s Glenn Ezra Moore & Margaret Payne. BA New Coll of Florida 1970; U of Edinburgh GB 1972; MDiv STUSo 1975; DMin U So & Van 1987. D 6/11/1975 P 12/27/1975 Bp Emerson Paul Haynes. m 7/31/1976 Sarah Tippett c 4. S Marg's Epis Ch Bellevue WA 2005; S Alb's Chap Honolulu HI 2002-2005; The TS at The U So Sewanee TN 1996-2002; The U So (Sewanee) Sewanee TN 1996-2002; Dio Michigan Detroit MI 1994-1996; R S Jn's Ch Royal Oak MI 1992-1996; Bp's Cn for Educ & Prog Dio Utah Salt Lake City UT 1988-1992; Dio Estrn Oregon The Dalles OR 1981-1988; R S Ptr's Ch La Grande OR 1981-1988; Dio SW Florida Sarasota FL 1976-1979; S Bon Ch Sarasota FL 1975-1981. davidcmoore@earthlink.net

MOORE, Delrece Lorraine (Colo) 3665 Overton St, Colorado Springs CO 80910 B 10/1/1945 D 11/13/2004 Bp Robert John O'Neill. m 9/30/1979 Luther Moore.

MOORE, Diane Marquart (WLa) 211 Celeste Dr, New Iberia LA 70560 B Franklinton LA 5/18/1935 d Harold O'Neal Marquart & Dorothy Alice. LSU 1954; U Of SW Louisiana 1990; Bp's Sch Of Dio Wstrn Louisiana LA 2000. D 11/30/1999 Bp Robert Jefferson Hargrove Jr. c 2. Archd Dio Wstrn Louisiana Alexandria LA 2001-2005; D The Epis Ch Of The Epiph New Iberia LA 2001-2005; COM Dio Wstrn Louisiana Alexandria LA 1998-2005; Long-R Plnng Dio Wstrn Louisiana Alexandria LA 1998-1999; Trst Epis TS Of The SW Austin TX 1997-2005. Auth, "Avery Island," Acadian Hse, 2001; Auth, "Mart'S Quest," Blue Heron Publ, 1995; Auth, "Live Oak Gardens," Acadian Hse, 1993; Auth, "Their Adventurous Will: Profiles Of Memorable Louisiana Wmn," USL Acadiana Press, 1984; Auth, "Iran: In A Persian Mrkt," Type Co., 1980; Auth, "25 other books to date". Assoc., St. Mary's Cnvnt, Sewanee 2007; Healthy Kids Advsry Bd 1999; Lifetime Mem Of Lafayatte Publ Libr 2000; Lifetime Mem Of The GSA 2000; No Amer Soc Of Deacons 2000. Emmett Broussard Awd For Outreach Mnstrl Allnce Of Iberia Par 2002; Inspirational Poetry: Deep So Writer'S Conf 1967. deacondmoore@aol.com

MOORE, Dominic Clarke (Lex) 533 E Main St, Lexington KY 40508 **Cur Ch Of The Gd Shpd Lexington KY 2011-** B Woodruff SC 6/24/1983 s Lewis Seaton Moore & Rosemary Ann. BA Hob 2005; MDiv CDSP 2011. D 6/18/2011 Bp Prince Grenville Singh. m 7/13/2004 Jesse W Moore. DOMINICCMORE@GMAIL.COM

MOORE, Donald Ernest (Eas) 3946 Rock Branch Rd, North Garden VA 22959 B 7/1/1947 D 6/15/1988 P 11/20/1988 Bp Daniel Lee Swenson. m 8/29/1970 Margaret Moore. Ch Of The Gd Shpd Charlottesville VA 1994-1998; Gr Ch Red Hill Va No Garden VA 1994-1998; S Paul's Berlin MD 1989-1992.

MOORE III, Edward F. (Tex) 13515 King Cir, Cypress TX 77429 B Saint Louis MO 3/15/1927 s Edward Fitzroy Moore & Helen Louise. BA DrakeUniversity 1951; MDiv Drake U 1963; M Ed U of Missouri 1967; Cert U of Missouri 1968. D 5/5/1990 P 12/15/1990 Bp William Augustus Jones Jr. m 6/6/1952 Patricia Ann Perkins c 3. P-in-c S Alb's Epis Ch Fulton MO 1994-1999; Asst P Calv Ch Columbia MO 1991-1994. emoore012@comcast.net

MOORE, Helen M (Ct) 24 Goodwin Circle, Hartford CT 06105 B Chattanooga TN 10/3/1942 d Frank Lubbock Miller & Jane Anne. PhD Bos; BSW Regis 1982; M.Ed Harv 1984; MDiv Harvard DS 1987. D 5/30/1992 Bp David Elliot Johnson P 2/21/1993 Bp John Mc Gill Krumm. m 11/3/1973 Thomas Moore c 5. R S Paul's Ch Richmond VA 2006-2007; R Trin Epis Ch Southport CT 2003-2004; R S Lk's Par Darien CT 2002-2003; Dn Cathd Of S Jas Chicago IL 1999-2001; R S Hubert's Epis Ch Mentor OH 1997-1999; Assoc R Trin Ch In The City Of Boston Boston MA 1992-1997. revhmm@aol.com

MOORE, James Raymond (Haw) 911 N Marine Corps Dr, Tamuning GU 96913 Guam B St Paul MN 4/7/1942 s Samuel Moore & Florence. BA Augsburg 1966; MA U of Guam 1970. D 1/15/2009 Bp George Elden Packard. c 3. jamesm@guam.net

MOORE, James Wesley (WMo) 18151 Dearborn St, Stilwell KS 66085 **D The Epis Ch of S Jn the Div Tamuning GU 2009-; D S Andr's Ch Kansas City MO 1995-** B Osawatomie KS 2/17/1939 s Wesley Harold Moore & Calista Alma. Bethany Coll; DDS U of Missouri 1964; Cert Med Residency 1966. D 2/3/1996 Bp John Clark Buchanan. m 7/23/1960 Patricia Elaine Peterson c 3. Chapl Intl Ord of S Lk Physcn.

MOORE, Joseph I (NJ) 1 Water St, Pennsville NJ 08070 B Philadelphia PA 8/7/1942 s Clarence J Moore & Anna May. BA Ken 1964; MBA U of Pennsylvania 1966; MDiv SWTS 1975. D 6/14/1975 Bp Quintin Ebenezer Primo Jr P 12/13/1975 Bp James Winchester Montgomery. m 2/5/1966 Sharon P Moore. R S Geo's Ch Pennsville NJ 2001-2005; Int S Thos' Epis Ch Glassboro NJ 1999-2001; Int S Jn The Evang Ch Lansdowne PA 1997-1999; R Trin Epis Ch Ambler PA 1993-1996; R Incarn H Sacr Epis Ch Drexel Hill PA 1977-1993; Cur Chr Ch Waukegan IL 1975-1977. josephimoore@verizon.net

MOORE, Judith Ann (O) 7125 North Hills Blvd NE, Albuquerque NM 87109 B East Cleveland OH 4/23/1944 d Herbert Lloyd Moore & Alzada. BA Muskingum Coll 1966; MA Kent St U 1974; MDiv CRDS 1984. D 6/30/1984 P 2/1/1986 Bp James Russell Moodey. Epis Shared Minist Of Nwohio Sherwood OH 1988-1997; Vic Trin Ch Bryan OH 1988-1993; Int S Tim's Ch Macedonia OH 1987-1988; Gr Epis Ch Willoughby OH 1985-1987. REVJAM423@netscape.com

MOORE, Julia Gibert (Miss) 208 S Leflore Ave, Cleveland MS 38732 B Cleveland MS 1/13/1938 BA U of Mississippi 1958; Med Delta St U 1982; EdD Delta St U 1984. D 4/29/2000 Bp Alfred Clark Marble Jr P 12/21/2000 Bp Duncan Montgomery Gray III. m 4/19/1958 Dana Moore c 1.

MOORE, K J (Wyo) PO Box 246, Sundance WY 82729 **P Ch Of The Gd Shpd Sundance WY 2009-** B Yreka CA 1/30/1938 d Arnold Murl Cooper & Muriel May Brown Cooper. D 8/7/2008 P 2/14/2009 Bp Bruce Edward Caldwell. m 4/14/1957 Clifford Allan Moore c 4. Assoc - CHS 2001; DOK 1990. kjamoor@gmail.com

MOORE, Linda Turman (NCal) 155-A Derek Dr, Susanville CA 96130 B Ross CA 7/6/1941 d Hobart Delancey Turman & Frances Newlon. BA Ob 1963; MA Amer U 1973; MS U of Maryland 1991; MDiv VTS 1993. D 6/12/1993 Bp Ronald Hayward Haines P 3/1/1994 Bp Edward Cole Chalfant. c 2. Dio Nthrn California Sacramento CA 1997-2009; Gd Shpd Epis Ch Susanville CA 1996-2009; Asst Trin Epis Ch Lewiston ME 1993-1995. moorelt@sonic.net

MOORE, Lynda Foster (WNC) 138 Murdock Ave, Asheville NC 28801 B Spartanburg SC 3/8/1939 d Hugh Moses Foster & Edith. BA MWC 1961; MA Appalachian St U 1971; Shalem Inst for Sprtl Formation 1987; MDiv VTS 1992. D 6/6/1992 P 12/12/1992 Bp Frank Kellogg Allan. m 7/9/2009 Dianna Gardner c 1. R Ch Of The Mssh Murphy NC 2001-2003; Assoc Ch Of The H Cross Tryon NC 1995-2001; Int Epis Ch Of The H Sprt Cumming GA 1994-1995; Asst Epis Ch Of The H Sprt Cumming GA 1992-1993. mvpx2@bellsouth.net

MOORE, Margaret Jo (NCal) 516 Clayton Ave, El Cerrito CA 94530 **Assoc Ch Of The Incarn Santa Rosa CA 1996-** B Santa Monica CA 7/26/1945 d Russell Clark Moore & Dorothy Virginia. RN S Lk's Sch Of Nrsng 1966; BA California Sch for Deacons 1989; MDiv CDSP 1994. D 7/13/1994 P 1/19/1995 Bp Jerry Alban Lamb. m 6/27/1993 Ed Kahn c 2. S Patricks Ch Kenwood CA 1994-1995. roundpeg@sprintmail.com

MOORE, Mark Ross (Ct) 85 Viscount Dr Unit 12c, Milford CT 06460 **P-in-c S Jn's Ch Sandy Hook CT 2008-** B New Haven CT 6/8/1949 s Luther Franklin Moore & Marjorie Ross. Alleg; BA Sthrn Connecticut St U 1973; Med Bos 1977; MDiv EDS 1985; CSD Cntr for Rel Dvlpmt Cambridge MA 1986; JD Quinnipiac U 2004. D 6/4/1986 Bp John Bowen Coburn P 5/16/1987 Bp Douglas Edwin Theuner. c 1. R Gr Epis Ch Trumbull CT 1999-2007; Int S Ptr's Epis Ch Milford CT 1998-1999; Int S Fran Ch Holden MA 1997-1998; Int Gr Ch No Attleborough MA 1996-1997; R Chr Ch In Lonsdale Lincoln RI 1992-1995; R S Jn The Evang Taunton MA 1988-1992; Cur S Jn's Ch Portsmouth NH 1986-1988. ACPE 1986; Soc of S Jn the Evang 1984. Outstanding Ldrshp Awd MA Assoc. for Retarded Citizens 1991. attmrmoore@aol.com

MOORE, Mark T (Mil) ST PAUL'S EPISCOPAL CHURCH, 413 S 2ND ST, WATERTOWN WI 53094 **R S Paul's Ch Watertown WI 2006-** B 4/29/1952 s Thomas Moore & Joyce. BS Cardinal Stritch U 1990; MDiv SWTS 2005; MTS SWTS 2007. D 6/3/2006 P 12/9/2006 Bp William Dailey Persell. m 4/19/1975 Mary A Moore c 2. t.mark.m@gmail.com

MOORE, M(ary) Diane (Colo) 7796 S Harrison Cir, Centennial CO 80122 **D Dio Colorado Denver CO 2002-** B Saint Joseph MO 11/4/1942 d Charles Marshall White & Thelma Leola. BA U of Kansas 1964; Cert NW Missouri St U Maryville MO 1965; Bp Inst Diac Formation 1992; MA Regis U Denver CO 1992; CSD S Thos Sem Denver CO 1993. D 10/24/1992 Bp William Jerry Winterrowd. m 6/4/1966 Arthur Howard Moore c 3. Asst S Matt's Parker CO 2000-2001; Coordntr Of Vol - Gc Dio Colorado Denver CO 1998-2000; Dio Colorado Denver CO 1996-2000; Adm Liaison Com Dio Colorado Denver CO 1994-1998; Gd Shpd Epis Ch Centennial CO 1993. Auth, "Journey Into The Cross," *Mary'S Hope*, 2002; Auth, "Healing For Wounded Souls," *Mary'S Hope*, 2002; Auth, "Lament And Transitions," *Wmn Uncommon Prayers*, Morehouse Pub, 2000; Auth, "Eastering And Sprt Stroke," *Wmn Uncommon Prayers*, Morehouse Pub, 2000; Auth, "Pistachio Chld," *Wmn Uncommon Prayers*, Morehouse Pub, 2000; Auth, "Collect The Silence," *Prisms Of The Soul*, Morehouse, 1996. NAAD 1992; Sprtl Directory Intl 1996. deacondi@ecentral.com

MOORE, Mary Navarre (ETenn) 715 E Brow Rd, Lookout Mountain TN 37350 B Chattanooga TN 12/31/1949 d Carl Albert Navarre & Laura Evelyn. BA Emory U 1971; CPA St Of Tennessee 1981; MDiv Candler TS Emory U 2000. D 1/23/1999 Bp Robert Gould Tharp P 2/3/2001 Bp Charles Glenn VonRosenberg. m 9/30/1995 Walter Theodore Moore c 1. Asst Ch Of The Gd Shpd Lookout Mtn TN 2001-2007.

MOORE, Melvin Leon (Va) 115 Plantation Dr, Locust Grove VA 22508 B Oklahoma City OK 1/1/1938 s Ovie Moore & Lucille. BS U of Oklahoma 1962; MEA GW 1969; MDiv VTS 1995. D 11/27/1995 Bp Frank Clayton Matthews P 6/13/1996 Bp Peter James Lee. m 9/4/1981 Nancy G Guthrie. Vic Emm Ch Rapidan VA 2002-2005; Asst R S Matt's Ch Richmond VA 1995-2002. leeatstm@aol.com

MOORE, Michael D. (Fla) D 6/12/2005 P 2/26/2006 Bp J(ohn) Neil Alexander.

MOORE, Michael Osborn (NH) 7321 Brad St, Falls Church VA 22042 **P Assoc S Lk's Ch Alexandria VA 2008-** B Detroit MI 5/5/1935 s Edward Young Moore & Mary Bethune. BA Colg 1958; MDiv VTS 1965. D 6/12/1965 Bp Beverley D Tucker P 2/24/1966 Bp Nelson Marigold Burroughs. m 6/20/1959 Patricia Luanne Hill. S Dunst's Epis Ch Beth MD 1998-1999; S Steph's Epis Ch Espanola NM 1997-2001; S Jn's Ch Chevy Chase MD 1997-1998; Ch Of The Gd Shpd Burke VA 1995-1997; S Bede's Epis Ch Santa Fe NM 1995-1997; S Chris's Ch Springfield VA 1992-1994; S Steph's Epis Ch Espanola NM 1991-1995; All Hallows Par So River Davidsonville MD 1991-1992; S Geo's Ch Washington DC 1990-1991; S Paul's/Peace Ch Las Vegas NM 1989-1991; Trin Ch Manassas VA 1988-1990; S Paul's Rock Creek Washington DC 1987-1988; S Lk's Ch Alexandria VA 1986-1987; S Steph's Epis Ch Espanola NM 1985-1988; S Andr's Epis Ch Hopkinton NH 1985-1986; Trin On The Hill Epis Ch Los Alamos NM 1983-1984; S Paul's/Peace Ch Las Vegas NM 1976-1979; S Patricks Ch Falls Ch VA 1970-1985.

MOORE, Michael Stanley (RG) 4615 Baybrook Dr, Pensacola FL 32514 B Grass Creek WY 10/24/1930 s Stanley Moore & Bee. BA Rice 1952; MA Rice 1953; PhD Rice 1956. D 8/6/1975 P 6/10/1976 Bp Richard Mitchell Trelease Jr. m 6/5/1954 Joan Marks. Asst S Jn's Ch Pensacola FL 2002-2006; Asst S Jerome's Epis Ch Chama NM 1997-2002; Asst S Steph's Epis Ch Espanola NM 1997-2002; Int S Bede's Epis Ch Santa Fe NM 1995-1997; Asst S Jerome's Epis Ch Chama NM 1987-1995; Asst S Steph's Epis Ch Espanola NM 1987-1995; Asst Trin On The Hill Epis Ch Los Alamos NM 1983-1985; P-in-c S Paul's/Peace Ch Las Vegas NM 1976-1979. mikenjo@cox.net

MOORE, Muriel Elizabeth (WNC) 355 Red Oak Trl, Boone NC 28607 **Ch Of The H Cross Valle Crucis NC 1993-** B Montreal QC CA 2/27/1934 d Robert Alfred Tedstone & Edna Isabella. Appalachian St U; BA Sir Geo Wms Montreal QC CA 1953. D 12/18/1999 Bp Robert Hodges Johnson. m 7/31/1981 James Grant Moore c 3. DOK; Ord of S Lk; OHC. murielmoore@skybest.com

MOORE, Nancy L (Me) 4 Charles Street, Milo ME 04463 **P in Charge S Aug's Epis Ch Dover Foxcroft ME 2001-; Vic S Johns Epis Ch Brownville ME 2001-** B Brunswick ME 8/5/1967 d George L Moore & Ada B. BA Mid 1989; MDiv Bos 2000. D 6/23/2001 P 1/19/2002 Bp Chilton Abbie Richardson Knudsen. Pstr Excellence Coordntr Dio Maine Portland ME 2003-2007; Vic Ch Of The Mssh Dexter ME 2002-2005; Exec Dir Trin Epis Ch Lewiston ME 2001-2003. nlmoore67@gmail.com

MOORE, Orral Margarite (Neb) 714 N 129th Plz, Omaha NE 68154 **D All SS Epis Ch Omaha NE 1996-** B Newark NJ 4/16/1933 d Nicholas Jaymoore & Orral May. D 5/31/1996 Bp James Edward Krotz.

MOORE, Pamela Andrea (NCal) Po Box 4791, Santa Rosa CA 95402 **D Ch Of The Incarn Santa Rosa CA 2001-; D S Andr's In The Redwoods Monte Rio CA 2001-** B San Diego CA 1/9/1951 d Charles Moore & Camilla. BA Sch for Deacons; MA CUNY 1990. D 9/16/2001 Bp Jerry Alban Lamb.

MOORE, Patricia Craig (USC) 1014 Laurens St, 6045 Lakeshore Drive, Columbia SC 29206 B Columbia SC 3/8/1947 d Charles Justice Craig & Juanita Bennett. Luth Theol Sthrn Sem; BA U of So Carolina 1969; MDiv STUSo 1995. D 6/10/1995 P 5/14/1996 Bp Dorsey Felix Henderson. m 8/9/1969 Caleb Moore c 3. Int S Steph's Epis Ch Ridgeway SC 2002-2003; Cn Pstr Trin Cathd Columbia SC 1996-2000; D S Jn's Epis Ch Columbia SC 1995-1996. Trst U So 1996. pcmalanuk@gmail.com

MOORE, Patricia Elaine (NCal) 1354 Yulupa Ave Apt A, Santa Rosa CA 95405 **Chapl The Bp's Ranch Healdsburg CA 2009-** B New Orleans LA 12/5/1941 d Daniel Seguin Moore & Helen B. BA Mid 1963; MS NWU 1964; MA Claremont TS 1981; PhD U of New Mex 2000. D 11/19/1982 P 6/28/1986 Bp Charles Brinkley Morton. m 12/30/1967 Richard L Backman c 2. S Andr's In The Redwoods Monte Rio CA 2002; Ch Of The Incarn Santa Rosa CA 2000-2007; Asstg P S Bede's Epis Ch Santa Fe NM 1996-1999; All Souls' Epis Ch San Diego CA 1989-1993; Epis Cmnty Serv San Diego CA 1989-1990; Dio San Diego San Diego CA 1985-1988; D S Dav's Epis Ch San Diego CA 1982-1985. patmas41@mac.com

MOORE, Paul R (Tex) 2800 Trimmier Rd, Killeen TX 76542 **S Chris's Ch Killeen TX 2000-** B Quito EC 3/28/1957 s Bruce Robinson Moore & Joyce Eloise. Taylor U Upland IN; MIA Intl Trng Sch 1985; Seminario Ecuatoriano de Teologia Epis EC 1991. D 5/19/1990 Bp Adrian Delio Caceres-Villavicencio P 11/16/1991 Bp J Neptali Larrea-Moreno. m 6/3/1978 Karisse Ann Cone c 3. R Gr Ch Weslaco TX 1992-2000. Auth, "Fruits of the Sprt in Practical Life/Frutos del Espíritu en la Vida Práctica," *Fruits of the Sprt in Practical Life/Frutos del Espíritu en la Vida Práctica*, Stillpoint by the Sea, San Antonio, TX, 2008. harrishawker@live.com

MOORE, Peter Childress (SC) 71 Broad St., Charleston SC 29401 **Discipleship S Mich's Epis Ch Charleston SC 2008-** B Mount Vernon NY 6/22/1936 s Oscar F Moore & Mary-Adair. BA Ya 1958; MA Oxf 1960; BD EDS 1961; DMin Fuller TS 1989. D 6/10/1961 Bp William S Thomas P 12/1/1961 Bp Austin Pardue. m 12/7/1968 Sandra C Moore c 3. Dn TESM Ambridge PA 1995-2004; Focus Greenwich CT 1963-1983. Ed, "Can A Bp Be Wrong? 10 Scholars Challenge Jn Shelby Spong," Morehouse Pub, 1998; Auth, "A Ch To Believe In," Latimer, 1992; Auth, "One Lord, One Faith," *A Step Further, Journey in discipleship*, Nelson&Latimer, Advantage, 1992; Auth, "Disarming The Secular Gods," Inter Varsity Press, 1990. Angl Relief and Dvlpmt Fund 2005-2011. DD Nash 2003. petermoore1@comcast.net

MOORE JR, Ralph Murray (Me) 191 West Meadow Rd., Rockland ME 04841 B Los Angeles CA 5/15/1936 s Ralph Murray Moore & Frankie Vyvyan. BA Stan 1957; MDiv UTS 1961; DMin EDS 1995. D 12/21/1972 P 5/9/1973 Bp Robert Lionne DeWitt. m 11/30/1985 Bridget Gallagher Buck c 3. R S Ptr's Ch Rockland ME 1996-2007; Actg Dn of Students and Cmnty Life EDS Cambridge MA 1995-1996; P-in-c All SS Ch Stoneham MA 1992-1995; El Buen Pstr, San Jose Dio Costa Rica New York NY 1987-1990; Mssy Exec Coun Appointees New York NY 1986-1991; Vic, St. Mk's, Bluefields Dio Nicaragua Managua 1986-1987; Asst Ch Of S Mart-In-The-Fields Philadelphia PA 1984-1986; P-in-c S Mary's Ch Hamilton Vill Philadelphia PA 1976; Assoc S Mary's Ch Hamilton Vill Philadelphia PA 1973-1983. Auth, *The Jesus Deck*, US Game Systems, 1973; Auth, *In Celebration*, Untd Ch Press, 1970; Auth, *Breakout*, Friendship Press, 1968. revrafa@gmail.com

MOORE, Richard Wayne (La) 4500 Lake Borgne Ave, Metairie LA 70006 B Washington DC 11/8/1947 s Harry Christopher Moore & Lois Ann. AA Florida Jr Coll 1973; BA U of No Florida 1974; MDiv VTS 1977; MS Valdosta St U 1984. D 6/12/1977 P 12/1/1977 Bp Frank Stanley Cerveny. m 6/29/1996 Karen Rowlett c 3. R S Phil's Ch New Orleans LA 1997-2003; Trin Epis Ch Baton Rouge LA 1993-1997; S Mart's Epis Sch Metairie LA 1990-1993; R Trin Ch Statesboro GA 1988-1990; Dio Georgia Savannah GA 1986-1988; Asst R Chr Ch Valdosta GA 1984-1986; Vic S Paul's On-The-Hill Winchester VA 1979-1984; Chr Epis Ch Winchester VA 1979-1980; Asst R Ch Of The H Comf Tallahassee FL 1977-1979.

MOORE, Robert Allen (Minn) 19 Lea Road, Whittle-le-Woods, Chorley, Lancs PR6-7PF Great Britain (UK) B San Jose CA 9/11/1932 s Byron Allen Moore & Rosamond Jessie. BA U Pac 1954; Lon 1955; STB Bos 1958; STM Bos 1959. D 2/10/1963 Bp Hamilton Hyde Kellogg P 6/1/1963 Bp Philip Frederick McNairy. m 3/17/2006 Roger Stubbings c 1. Stwdshp Consult Dio Minnesota Minneapolis MN 1979-1980; Reg Dn Dio Minnesota Minneapolis MN 1977-1978; R Trin Ch Anoka MN 1971-1980; P-in-c Emm Ch Adams NY 1964-1968; P-in-c Zion Ch Adams NY 1964-1968; Cur S Jn In The Wilderness White Bear Lake MN 1963-1964; S Jn In The Wilderness White Bear Lake MN 1957-1962. eroomar91@talktalk.net

MOORE, Robert Byron (Cal) 4230 Langland St, Cincinnati OH 45223 B Cleveland OH 3/31/1937 s Robert Edward Moore & Margaret Evelyn. Assoc in Arts El Camino Coll 1964; BS California St U, Long Bch, CA 1967; none California St U, Hayward, CA 1969; MDiv CDSP 1977. D 11/25/1978 P 11/3/1979 Bp C Kilmer Myers. m 2/16/1979 Bavi Rivera c 3. Ch Of The H Trin

M

Richmond CA 2003-2004; S Anselm's Epis Ch Lafayette CA 1992-1997; Dio El Camino Real Monterey CA 1986-1992; St Johns Epis Ch Ross CA 1979-2003. rbyronmoore@gmail.com

MOORE, Robert Joseph (Tex) 3285 Park Falls Ct., League City TX 77573 **Assoc Ch Of The Gd Shpd Friendswood TX 2005-** B Galveston,TX 7/11/1950 s Darwin David Moore & Jane Penny. BA U So 1972; MDiv Epis TS of The SW 1975; DMin STUSo 1993. D 6/17/1975 Bp Scott Field Bailey P 6/17/1976 Bp J Milton Richardson. m 6/18/1983 Nancy Elizabeth Southan c 2. R S Barth's Ch Hempstead TX 1996-2005; Int R S Barth's Ch Hempstead TX 1995-1996; Vic Ch Of The Resurr Houston TX 1984-1995; Assoc S Chris's Ch Houston TX 1979-1984; Vic S Fran Of Assisi Epis Prairie View TX 1975-1979; Vic S Paul's Ch Katy TX 1975-1977. Auth, *Narrative Hist of the Black Epis Ch in the Dio Texas*, 1993. bobmooreleague@comcast.net

MOORE JR, Robert Raymond (SwVa) 110 Clinton Avenue, Big Stone Gap VA 24219 **Vic Chr Epis Ch Big Stone Gap VA 1993-** B Toronto ON CA 4/14/1948 s Robert Raymond Moore & Ellenor Fyfe. Rhodes Coll; BS U of Tennessee 1970; MS U of Memphis 1974. D 10/20/1993 P 6/1/1994 Bp A(rthur) Heath Light. m 12/16/1972 Harriet Carol Ingram.

MOORE, Robin Adair (Oly) Po Box 584, Grapeview WA 98546 B Bend OR 10/14/1938 d Charles Edward Boardman & Frances Annie. Willamette U; BA U of Washington 1962; MA Portland St U 1972; MDiv EDS 1985; ThM Weston Jesuit TS 1985. D 6/15/1985 P 5/24/1986 Bp Herbert Alcorn Donovan Jr. m 4/12/1969 Richard Roy Moore c 2. Dio Olympia Seattle WA 1994-2002; S Hugh Of Lincoln Allyn WA 1988-1999; Vic S Nich Ch Tahuya WA 1988-1993; S Mk's Epis Ch Jonesboro AR 1986-1988; Dio Arkansas Little Rock AR 1985-1986. Cath Fllshp; Living Stones; RWF. robinm@hughes.net

MOORE, Rodney Allen (Colo) 221 S Salem Ct, Aurora CO 80012 B Stromsburg NE 6/4/1942 s Kenneth Kinney Moore & Pauline Esther. BS U of Nebraska 1963; MEd U of Nebraska 1970; MDiv Nash 1975; DMin SWTS 2003. D 5/30/1975 Bp Robert Patrick Varley P 12/1/1975 Bp George Theodore Masuda. m 8/19/1967 Mary Helen Bucknell c 2. Vic Ch Of The H Comf Broomfield CO 2007-2010; Chair on the Yth Cmsn Dio Colorado Denver CO 1989-1992; Bd the Trin Ranch Dio Nebraska Omaha NE 1987-1994; R S Steph's Epis Ch Aurora CO 1986-2006; Pres of the Stndg Com Dio Nebraska Omaha NE 1986-1987; Stndg Com Dio Nebraska Omaha NE 1985-1987; Pres of the Holdredge Mnstrl Assn Dio Nebraska Omaha NE 1985-1986; Dept of Mssn Dio Nebraska Omaha NE 1983-1984; Alt Dep GC Dio Nebraska Omaha NE 1982-1985; Eccl Crt Dio Nebraska Omaha NE 1982-1984; Pres of the Holdredge Mnstrl Assn Dio Nebraska Omaha NE 1982-1983; Plnng Strtgy Cmsn Dio Nebraska Omaha NE 1981-1983; Vice-Chair on the Exec Coun Dio Nebraska Omaha NE 1981-1983; Chair Yth Cmsn Dio Nebraska Omaha NE 1980-1987; Chair Yth Cmsn Dio Nebraska Omaha NE 1980-1987; Chair Yth Cmsn Dio Nebraska Omaha NE 1980-1987; Dio Nebraska Omaha NE 1980-1986; R S Alb's Epis Ch McCook NE 1979-1986; Liturg Cmsn Dio Nebraska Omaha NE 1978-1984; Cmsn on Ch Growth Dio Nebraska Omaha NE 1978-1980; R S Barn Ch Omaha NE 1978-1979; Exec Coun Dio Nebraska Omaha NE 1977-1983; Vic S Eliz's Ch Holdrege NE 1975-1978. maryhmoore@aol.com

MOORE, Rudolph A (Pa) 479 Upper Gulph Rd, Radnor PA 19087 **Treas The Widows Corp Philadelphia PA 1996-; The Ch Fndt Dio Pennsylvania Philadelphia PA 1993-** B Philadelphia PA 7/8/1936 s John Moore & Josephine A. BS U of Pennsylvania 1958; MDiv EDS 1962; EdM W Chester St Coll 1969; MBA U of Pennsylvania 1981; DMin Luth TS in Philadelphia 2004. D 6/17/1962 P 12/21/1962 Bp Oliver J Hart. m 7/8/1972 Honour Howe. Dvlpmt Off S Paul's Ch Philadelphia PA 2007-2008; Dvlpmt Off Dio Pennsylvania Philadelphia PA 2006-2007; Sr Assoc S Dav's Ch Wayne PA 1983-2005; Int S Paul Ch Exton PA 1981; P-in-c Memi Ch Of S Lk Philadelphia PA 1980-1981; Dioc Coun Dio Pennsylvania Philadelphia PA 1975-1980; R All SS Ch Collingdale PA 1972-1980; DCE S Mart's Ch Radnor PA 1970-1972; Asst S Andr's Epis Ch Glenmoore PA 1964-1965; Asst S Ptr's Ch Philadelphia PA 1962-1963. rudym@diopa.org

MOORE, Stephen Edward (Oly) 8509 196th St Sw, Edmonds WA 98026 **Vic All SS Ch Bellevue WA 1997-** B Tacoma WA 3/23/1946 s Edward Chauncey Moore & Jean Theresa. BA WA SU 1973; MA WA SU 1974; JD U of Washington 1977; Dioc TS (Olympia) 1979; U So 1996. D 6/27/1992 P 6/12/1993 Bp Vincent Waydell Warner. m 2/14/1970 Deanna Leslie Dunn c 2. Int S Jn The Bapt Epis Ch Seattle WA 1995-1996; Assoc Trin Par Seattle WA 1993-1995. Auth, "Ch Words: Origin & Meaning," Forw Mvmt Press, 1996. Angl Soc 1992; Cler Assn Of The Dio Olympia 1992. semoore@nwlink.com

MOORE, Theodore Edward (NJ) 17 Cray Ter., Fanwood NJ 07023 B Florence SC 1/5/1936 s Theodore Harrison Moore & Catherine Whittington. BS Morehouse Coll 1957; MBA Ford 1972. D 6/11/2005 Bp George Edward Councell. m 6/2/2007 Karen Frances Oliver c 3. tmoorel2@comcast.net

MOORE, Thomas Daniel (Alb) 2034 Essex Dr, 2034 Essex Dr, Holiday FL 34691 B Jacksonville FL 3/7/1945 s James Rudolph Moore & Mary Alice. BA Eckerd Coll 1994; MDiv TESM 1998. D 6/6/1998 Bp John Wadsworth Howe P 12/1/1998 Bp Hugo Luis Pina-Lopez. m 11/14/1981 Patricia Marie McQuiston c 4. Trin Ch Gouverneur NY 2002-2007; Chr Ch Morristown NY 2002-2004; Cleric Dio Albany Albany NY 2002; H Faith Epis Ch Port S Lucie FL 1998-2002.

MOORE JR, Tillman Marion (Ak) 2316 Via Carrillo, Palos Verdes Estates CA 90274 B Amarillo TX 7/18/1927 s Tillman Marion Moore & Velma. BS Iowa St U 1949; MD Washington U 1953. D 6/21/1967 P 8/1/1968 Bp William J Gordon Jr. m 12/22/1950 Shirley Louise Mayer. Asst S Fran' Par Palos Verdes Estates CA 1970-1988; Asst S Thos' Mssn Hacienda Heights CA 1967-1970. Auth, "Ak Churchmen". Natl Assn For The Self- Supporting Active Mnstry, Fllshp S Jas Of Jerusalem, Fllshp S Alb & S Sergius.

MOORE, Vassilia Shelton (SwFla) 100 NE Loop 410 Ste 1075, San Antonio TX 78216 B New York NY 7/6/1941 d Wilson Addison Shelton & Vassilia. BS Col 1966; MDiv STUSo 1991. D 6/13/1992 Bp Rogers Sanders Harris P 1/1/1993 Bp David Reed. Asst Chr Epis Ch Bowling Green KY 1992-1993. S Mary Cnvnt.

MOORE JR, William Henry (Spr) 141 Candlewood Dr, Wallace NC 28466 **Archd Dio Springfield Springfield IL 1992-** B Natchez MS 4/29/1926 s William Moore & Hazel. Epis Dio Sthrn Ohio 1990; Methodist TS 1990. D 11/9/1990 Bp Herbert Thompson Jr P 6/29/2002 Bp Peter Hess Beckwith. m 6/29/1981 Jacqueline Osteen. D-In-C S Jn's Ch Columbus OH 1990-1992. Auth, "Mystagouge"; Auth, "Links-Stwdshp"; Auth, "Linked To The Body Of Chr". Hon Cn Cathd Ch of St. Paul 2004; S Steph Awd Naad 2000; One O'clock Awd No Texas U 1978; Outstanding Cadet Awd Gulf Coast Mltry Acad 1942. wmoore2900@aol.com

MOORE JR, W Taylor (Miss) St. Peter's Church, 113 South 9th St., Oxford MS 38655 **R S Ptr's Ch Oxford MS 2001-** B Bluefield WV 2/2/1949 s Walter Taylor Moore & Betty Ruth. Phillips Exeter Acad 1967; BA Duke 1971; MDiv UTS 1974; DMin SWTS 2000. D 10/23/1977 P 5/7/1978 Bp David Keller Leighton Sr. m 7/22/1978 Nancy Deane c 2. R S Chris's By-The River Gates Mills OH 1990-2001; R Chr Epis Ch Spotsylvania VA 1983-1990; Asst R Trin Ch Towson MD 1979-1982; Gr Ch Elkridge MD 1978-1979. prologos49@gmail.com

MOOREHEAD, Constance Fay Peek (Oly) 3030 S Findlay St, Seattle WA 98108 **D S Clem's Epis Ch Seattle WA 1997-** B Des Moines IA 7/26/1926 d Charles Henry Peek & Ethel. Drake U; Seattle U 1957; Dio Olympia Dioc TS 1997. D 6/28/1997 Bp Vincent Waydell Warner. c 2. Anti-racism Com Chair 2003; Dep 2006; EUC Bd Mem 2003. cmoorehead3@comcast.net

M

MOOREHEAD, Kate Bingham (Fla) 240 N Belmont St, Wichita KS 67208 **Dn S Jn's Cathd Jacksonville FL 2009-** B New Haven CT 9/10/1970 d Timothy Woodbridge Bingham & Susan Adams. D 6/14/1997 P 2/1/1998 Bp Clarence Nicholas Coleridge. m 8/13/1994 James D Moorehead c 3. R S Jas Ch Wichita KS 2003-2009; R S Marg's Epis Ch Boiling Sprg SC 1999-2003; S Jn's Ch W Hartford CT 1997-1999. deanmoorehead@jaxcathedral.org

MOORER, Dawson Delayne (O) 281 E 244th St Apt D5, Euclid OH 44123 B Tulsa OK 6/21/1954 s Darwin Eugene Moorer & Margaret Marie. Baylor U 1973; BA NWU 1976; MS U of Texas 1980; MDiv SWTS 1989. D 6/17/1989 P 12/1/1989 Bp Frank Tracy Griswold III. m 6/21/1980 Sheila Elizabeth Divorced c 1. P-in-c Calv Ch Sandusky OH 2002-2004; P-in-c No Cntrl Epis Shared Mnstry Port Clinton OH 2002-2004; P-in-c S Thos' Epis Ch Port Clinton OH 2002-2004; P-in-c Zion Ch Monroeville OH 2002-2004; Mssn In Charge S Paul Epis Ch Norwalk OH 2001-2004; Int R S Andr's Ch Cleveland OH 2001-2002; R Ch Of The Epiph Euclid OH 1998-2000; Int R S Jas Epis Ch Wooster OH 1996-1997; Int R Chr Ch Oberlin OH 1995-1996; Int R S Mk's Ch Cleveland OH 1993-1994; Assoc; Int R The Epis Ch Of S Jas The Less Northfield IL 1991-1992; Asst To Dn Cathd Of S Jas Chicago IL 1989-1991. SBL. ddm1954@gmail.com

MOORHEAD, William S J (Ia) PO Box 27, Iowa City IA 52244 **Assoc Trin Ch Iowa City IA 1989-** B Fort Wayne IN 1/27/1942 s Donald Samuel Moorhead & Ruth Armeda. AB Harv 1963; MDiv Nash 1966; MA U of Iowa 1999. D 3/5/1966 P 9/10/1966 Bp Donald H V Hallock. m 5/9/1971 Wendy Ann Nurnberg c 2. Int Chapl, Univ of Iowa Dio Iowa Des Moines IA 1990-1992; R S Jas Epis Ch Oskaloosa IA 1980-1989; R Chr Ch Cntrl City NE 1977-1980; P-in-c S Christophers Ch Cozad NE 1976-1977; Vic S Pauls Epis Ch Arapahoe NE 1973-1977; Cur S Jas Ch Wichita KS 1971-1973; Cur Chr Ch Par La Crosse WI 1971; Vic S Barth's Ch Pewaukee WI 1966-1968. moorhead.w@gmail.com

MOOTE, Kimberly Ann (NMich) E9494 Maple St, Munising MI 49862 **D S Jn's Ch Munising MI 1996-** B Kremling CO 10/20/1957 d Edward Buchman & Janelle. D 3/6/1996 Bp Thomas Kreider Ray. m 7/15/1978 Gordon Moote c 3.

MOQUETE, Clemencia Rafaela (NY) 821 Central Trinity Avenue, Bronx NY 10456 B DO 11/23/1952 d Rafael Moquete & Gladys. D 6/8/1991 P 12/1/1991 Bp Richard Frank Grein. Mid Hudson Catskill Rural and Migrant Min Poughkeepsie NY 1998; Hisp Mnstry New York NY 1992-1995.

MORALES, Carlton Owen (NC) Po Box 21011, Greensboro NC 27420 **Dio No Carolina Raleigh NC 1966-** B JM 2/1/1928 s Henry Morales & Zerita. BA Guilford Coll; S Ptr's Theol Coll, JM 1958; S Geo's Coll Jerusalem IL 1978;

Duke 1982; VTS 1988. D 6/1/1957 P 6/14/1958 Bp The Bishop Of Jamaica. m 12/1/1948 Louise Lamb c 3. Ch Of The Redeem Greensboro NC 1966-1999. Soc Of S Jn The Evang. carlton.morales@mosescone.com

MORALES, Evelyn Ruth (NC) 2009 Hickswood Rd, High Point NC 27265 B San Diego CA 10/3/1942 d Raoul Morales & Belia. BA U CA 1969; Med U NC 1973. D 6/3/2006 Bp Michael Bruce Curry. c 3. evermore11@aol.com

MORALES JR, Frank Russell (NY) 3115 S High St, Arlington VA 22202 B New York NY 1/2/1949 s Frank Morales & Betty. D 9/5/1976 Bp Paul Moore Jr P 3/1/1977 Bp Harold Louis Wright. m 6/14/1971 Leslie Ruth Donaldson. Trin Ch Of Morrisania Bronx NY 1993; S Ann's Ch Of Morrisania Bronx NY 1980-1982; Chr Ch Poughkeepsie NY 1976-1979.

MORALES, Loyda Esther (NY) 7516 Amboy Road, Staten Island NY 10307 **Vic The Ch Of S Steph Staten Island NY 2005-** B San Juan PUERTO RICO 9/24/1960 d Roberto Morales & Irma. BA U of Puerto Rico 1984; Mstr in Arts U of Puerto Rico 1992; Mstr in Div GTS 2005. D 3/19/2005 P 9/17/2005 Bp Mark Sean Sisk. loymor@hotmail.com

MORALES, Roberto (Va) 347 Chiquita Ct, Kissimmee FL 34758 B 5/11/1933 m 1/3/1958 Irma Rodriguez c 4. San Jose Ch Arlington VA 1991-2000; S Ann's Ch Of Morrisania Bronx NY 1986-1990; Dio Puerto Rico S Just PR 1977-1979. curra44@aol.com

MORALES GAVIRIA, Jose Ricardo (Colom) Barrio Las Delicias, El Bagne, Antioquia Colombia B Libano Talima CO 4/30/1942 s Jose Ricardo Morales-Sanchez & Soledad. D 2/11/1986 P 1/1/1987 Bp Bernardo Merino-Botero. Iglesia Epis En Colombia 1987-2007.

MORAN, John Jay (Mont) 2415 Hauser Blvd, Helena MT 59601 **S Ptr's Par Helena MT 1999-** B Fort Meade SD 3/31/1939 D 10/23/1999 Bp Charles Jones III. m 3/24/1961 Sharon Kay O'Neill c 2. jjmoran39@bresnan.net

MORAN, Robert John (LI) 700 Shore Road Apt. 5Z, Long Beach NY 11561 **Assoc S Jn's Epis Ch Ft Hamilton Brooklyn NY 1987-** B New York NY 5/29/1945 s John Robert Moran & Catherine Ann. Cathd Coll of the Immac Concep 1965; BA Niagara U 1967; MDiv, MA Niagara U 1971; MD SUNY 1977. Rec from Roman Catholic 12/1/1987 as Priest Bp Robert Campbell Witcher Sr. m 6/26/1981 Ann Catherine McNeal c 3. Supply P S Phil's Ch Brooklyn NY 2007-2009; Supply P Dio Long Island Garden City NY 2000-2004; Assoc S Jn's Ch Brooklyn NY 1987-2003.

M

✠ MORANTE-ESPAÑA, Rt Rev Alfredo (EcuC) Ulloa 213 Y Carrion, Box 17-0-353-A, Quito Ecuador **Bp Of Ecuador Litoral Dio Ecuador Guayaquil EQ EC 1994-; Bp of Ecuador Litoral Litoral Dio Ecuador Guayaquil EQ EC 1986-** B Vinces Los Rios EC 9/27/1946 s Vicente Morante & Dolores. Theol Seminario Alianza Guayaquil 1971. D 5/18/1975 P 6/1/1976 Bp Adrian Delio Caceres-Villavicencio Con 10/1/1994 for Central Ecu. m 8/15/1977 Olga De Jesus Arevalo. Bp Iglesia Cristo Rey Guayaquil EC 1994-2000; Vic Iglesia Santiago Apostolo Enrique Drouet Peninsula EC 1988-1994; Vic Iglesia Sagrada Familia Cuenca EC 1975-1988; Iglesia Epis Del Ecuador Ecuador 1975-1985. BISHOPMORANTES@HOTMAIL.COM

MORCK, Christopher Robert (EcuC) 815 2nd Ave, New York NY 10017 **Dom And Frgn Mssy Soc- Epis Ch Cntr New York NY 2009-; Exec Coun Appointees New York NY 2009-** B Huntingdon PA 3/17/1975 s Robert Raymond Morck & Patricia Mary Kelly. BA Wheaton Coll 1997; MA/MA Boston Coll 2006. D 5/30/2009 Bp Wilfrido Ramos-Orench P 10/2/2010 Bp Luis Fernando Ruiz Restrepo. m 6/1/1997 Patricia Jean Ohnsorg c 2. morck1@gmail.com

MORE, James Edward (Ida) 645 Liberty Ln, Emmett ID 83617 B Denver CO 12/2/1924 s James Earl More & Helen L. BA U of Wyoming 1965; BD VTS 1968. D 6/19/1968 P 12/1/1968 Bp James W Hunter. m 9/6/1947 Harriet Loine Lowe. R S Mary's Ch Emmett ID 1981-1986; Assoc S Jas Ch Payette ID 1975-1981; Assoc Vic S Andr's Epis Ch Sedona AZ 1972-1975; P-in-c S Dav's Epis Page AZ 1972-1975; Vic Chr Ch - Epis Newcastle WY 1970-1972; Vic S Jn The Bapt Ch Glendo WY 1969-1970; R All SS Ch Wheatland WY 1968-1970.

MOREAU, Joseph Raoul (LI) 15524 90th Ave, Jamaica NY 11432 B Gorman Commune HT 4/15/1922 s Dorcius Moreau & Marie. Epis TS 1948. D 7/1/1948 P 7/1/1949 Bp Charles Alfred Voegeli. m 7/4/1950 Marie Therese Simone Simpson.

MOREAU, Walter Jerome (NJ) 211 Willow Valley Sq # D-319, Lancaster PA 17602 B Indiana PA 9/19/1926 s Walter Jerome Moreau & Ruth Marie. BA Hob 1947; STB GTS 1950. D 4/15/1950 P 10/14/1950 Bp Austin Pardue. c 1. R S Mary's Ch Haddon Heights NJ 1975-1988; Dn Nthrn Convoc Dio New Jersey Trenton NJ 1974-1975; Pres Nthrn Cler Dio New Jersey Trenton NJ 1966-1967; Dio New Jersey Trenton NJ 1963; Dept Mus Dio New Jersey Trenton NJ 1960-1961; R S Lk the Evang Roselle NJ 1959-1975; Stff Cathd Ch Of S Mk Minneapolis MN 1956-1959; R The Ch Of The Adv Jeannette PA 1951-1956; P-in-c S Barn Ch Brackenridge PA 1950-1951. walt319@verizon.net

MOREHOUS, Amy Hodges (ETenn) 800 S. Northshore Dr., Knoxville TN 37919 **D Ch Of The Ascen Knoxville TN 2010-** B Knoxville TN 5/24/1972 d Nancy Osborne. BA U of Tennessee 1994. D 12/9/2006 Bp Charles Glenn VonRosenberg. m 3/11/1997 David Morehous c 1. Dio E Tennessee Knoxville TN 2001-2004. amorehous@gmail.com

MOREHOUSE JR, M(erritt) Dutton (FdL) 1920 Green Tree Road, Washington Island WI 54246 B Evanston IL 7/17/1936 s M(erritt) Dutton Morehouse & Louise. BA Ya 1959; Cert Whitaker TS 1994. D 6/11/1994 Bp R(aymond) Stewart Wood Jr. m 7/23/1973 Joyce Louise Clasen. D S Lk's Sis Bay WI 2000-2011; Archd Dio Michigan Detroit MI 1998-2000; D Chr Ch Cranbrook Bloomfield Hills MI 1996-2000. Ed/Writer, "Diakoneo (Journ)," *Diakoneo*, Assn for Epis Deacons. dutton@washingtonisle.com

MOREHOUSE, Rebecca (Cal) 21 Sonora Way, Corte Madera CA 94925 **Vol Ch Of The Nativ San Rafael CA 2005-; Epis Sch For Deacons Berkeley CA 2005-** B Laconia NH 8/2/1945 d Stephen Winship & Frances Norinne. BA Smith 1967; BA Sch for Deacons 2004. D 12/4/2004 Bp William Edwin Swing. m 8/30/1969 Richard K Morehouse c 2. rebeccamorehouse@earthlink.net

MOREHOUSE, Timothy Lawrence (NY) 122 Indiana St, Maplewood NJ 07040 B Ames IA 2/19/1963 s Lawrence Glen Morehouse & Georgia Ann. BA Harv 1985; MDiv PrTS 1991; MA Harv 1995; STM GTS 2001. D 6/22/2002 P 5/31/2003 Bp Charles Ellsworth Bennison Jr. Asst Ch Of The H Apos New York NY 2002-2007.

MORELL, Ellen Jones (Ky) 8110 Saint Andrews Church Rd, Louisville KY 40258 **S Ptr's Epis Ch Louisville KY 2009-** B Indianapolis IN 9/3/1942 BS Indiana U 1964; MDiv Chr TS 2002. D 6/28/2003 P 2/8/2004 Bp Catherine Elizabeth Maples Waynick. Dio Indianapolis Indianapolis IN 2008-2009; Ch Of The Nativ Indianapolis IN 2003-2008. motherellen@ymail.com

MORELLO, Anthony James (EpisSanJ) 3242 Carver Rd, Modesto CA 95350 B Brooklyn NY 12/31/1950 s Ralph Morello & Maria. ThB Sthrn Chr U Montgomery AL 1989; MDiv S Andr's Sem 1994; PhD GTS 1998. Rec 7/1/1998 as Priest Bp Chester Lovelle Talton. m 1/5/2004 Audrey D Morello c 2. Vic S Dunstans Epis Ch Modesto CA 1999-2005; P-in-c S Lk's Mssn Fontana CA 1998-1999. anthonyjmorello@yahoo.com

MORENO, Juan Severo (LI) 155 3rd Ave, Brentwood NY 11717 **Chr Ch Brentwood NY 2008-** B Choeo CO 5/15/1960 s Luciano Moreno & Gnacia. Pontifical Bolivarian U Of Theol Rome It. D 6/11/1994 P 12/1/1994 Bp George Phelps Mellick Belshaw. m 10/30/1989 Ana Moreno. Epis Hlth Serv Bethpage NY 1995-1998; S Ptr's Ch Perth Amboy NJ 1993-1994. JUANSMORENO@MSN.COM

MORETZ, Matthew John (NY) 1 Rectory St, Rye NY 10580 **Cur Chr's Ch Rye NY 2007-** B Augusta GA 5/23/1979 s John Douglas Moretz & Susan Paige. BA Davidson Coll 2001; MDiv GTS 2006. D 2/4/2006 P 8/9/2006 Bp Henry Irving Louttit. m 6/15/2002 Melanie Wadkins. D S Barth's Ch New York NY 2006; Cur S Paul's Ch Yonkers NY 2006. Producer, "Fr Matt Presents," *Fr Matt Presents*, YouTube, 2006. mjmoretz@gmail.com

MOREY, Gordon Howell (Mil) N4111 Pine St, Brodhead WI 53520 B Providence RI 2/6/1942 s Earl Levi Morey & Florence. BS Florida St U 1965; MDiv STUSo 1969. D 3/8/1970 P 6/27/1971 Bp James Loughlin Duncan. m 6/6/1964 Carol Morey. Asst S Lk's Epis Ch Milwaukee WI 1981-1988; Gr Ch Madison WI 1978-1980; R S Mary Magd Epis Ch Coral Sprg FL 1974-1978; Asst All SS Prot Epis Ch Ft Lauderdale FL 1970-1974.

MORFORD, Norman Lewis (Ind) PO Box 55085, Indianapolis IN 46205 **R S Tim's Ch Indianapolis IN 2001-; R S Tim's Ch Indianapolis IN 2001-** B Fort Wayne IN 12/12/1934 s Elbert S Morford & Harriet. BA DePauw U 1956; BD SMU 1960. D 10/14/1973 P 5/1/1974 Bp John P Craine. m 12/19/1958 Pamela P Patterson c 3. Int Trin Ch Anderson IN 1998-2000; Int S Andr's Epis Ch Greencastle IN 1997; Int S Ptr's Ch Lebanon IN 1994-1995; Int S Tim's Ch Indianapolis IN 1992-1993; Int S Matt's Ch Indianapolis IN 1987-1991; Int S Fran In The Fields Zionsville IN 1986-1987; Int Gr Ch Muncie IN 1983-1984; P-in-c Trin Ch Connersville IN 1977-1978; Assoc S Phil's Ch Indianapolis IN 1973-1975. pmorford@ivpvi.edu

MORGAN, Barbara Jean (Alb) 24 Silver St Apt G8, Great Barrington MA 01230 B Newark NJ 12/30/1938 d Harry Wadsworth Morgan & Myra Meta. U of Delaware Newark 1958; BS Lesley U 1978; Med NEU 1981; MDiv EDS 1988. D 2/16/1991 P 10/1/1992 Bp R(aymond) Stewart Wood Jr. S Jn In-The-Wilderness Copake Falls NY 1998-2007; Cred Com Chair Dio Estrn Michigan Saginaw MI 1994-1997; Assoc R Trin Epis Ch Alpena MI 1992-1998; COM Dio Michigan Detroit MI 1992-1993; D S Andr's Ch Ann Arbor MI 1991-1992. Soc of S Jn the Evang 1978. BJMORGAN@TACONIC.NET

MORGAN, Daniel (Ct) 489 Mansfield Ave, Darien CT 06820 B Royal Oak MI 7/16/1965 s Frank Marshall Morgan & Mildred Francis. BA Gordon Coll 1987; MDiv TESM 1993. D 6/12/1993 Bp Arthur Edward Walmsley P 1/1/1994 Bp Harry Woolston Shipps. m 1/30/2008 Kristin Hagan c 3. S Paul's Ch Darien CT 1999-2010; Chr Ch Epis Savannah GA 1993-1999. REVDANIELCMORGAN@GMAIL.COM

MORGAN, David Forbes (Colo) 740 Clarkson St, Denver CO 80218 B Toronto ON CA 8/3/1930 s Forbes Alexander Morgan & Ruth. BA/THB/MDIV Rocky Mtn Coll/Coll of the Rockies CO; DLitt Tem; DC U of the Natural Healing Arts 1954; ThB Rocky Mtn Coll 1958; MDiv Coll of the Rockies 1968. D 1/6/

1982 Bp William Carl Frey P 11/22/1982 Bp William Harvey Wolfrum. m 9/7/1956 Delores M Storhaug. Cn S Jn's Cathd Denver CO 1982-1995. Auth, *Chr Centered Mnstrs; A Response to God's Call*; Auth, *Songs w A Message*. Contemplation Outreach LTD Intl ; OGS; Ord of Chr Centered Ministers; Ord of S Lk. Who's Who in Hlth; Alpha; Who's Who in the Wrld; Who's Who in Rel. occming@earthlink.net

MORGAN, Diane Elizabeth (Mich) 25710 Beech Ct, Redford MI 48239 **Chapl Dio Michigan Detroit MI 2008-** B Detroit MI 10/21/1940 d Anthony Charles Santon & Dorothy Agnes. BS Wayne 1973; MDiv Bex 1990. D 6/23/1990 P 6/15/1991 Bp R(aymond) Stewart Wood Jr. m 8/30/2011 Karen White c 3. Vic Nativ Epis Ch Bloomfield Township MI 2009-2011; Gr Epis Ch Southgate MI 2004-2005; R S Mart Ch Detroit MI 1991-1997. Auth, "Reiki and Hosp Chapl," *Reiki Intl* , Reiki Intl , 2001. Assembly of Epis Hlth Care Chapl 1996; Bd Cert - Assn of Profsnl Chapl 1995; Cert Thanatologist- ADEC 2006. revdmorgan@gmail.com

MORGAN, Dwight Dexter (SeFla) 2201 S.W. 25th Street, Coconut Grove FL 33133 B Corn Island NI 4/7/1954 s Winston Morgan & Justina. BA Instituto Nacional 1974; Casa San Miguel 1978; Miami Dioc TS 1999. D 5/14/1978 Bp George Edward Haynsworth P 6/1/1999 Bp Calvin Onderdonk Schofield Jr. c 1. Ch Of The H Comf Miami FL 2002-2009; S Bern De Clairvaux N Miami Bch FL 2001. revdmorgan7@yahoo.com

MORGAN III, Edward (Va) 220 Warehams Pt, Williamsburg VA 23185 B Richmond VA 11/18/1924 s Frederic Hamilton Morgan & Edna Ernestine. BME U of Virginia 1948; MDiv VTS 1955; Cert Inst for Pstr Psych 1975; DMin How 1981. D 6/3/1955 P 6/25/1956 Bp Frederick D Goodwin. m 6/24/1949 Margaret R Bryan c 4. Assoc S Mart's Epis Ch Williamsburg VA 1994-2001; Dio Sthrn Virginia Norfolk VA 1994-1997; COM Dio Sthrn Virginia Norfolk VA 1994-1996; Int S Patricks Ch Falls Ch VA 1993-1994; Prof VTS Alexandria VA 1981-1993; Dio Sthrn Virginia Norfolk VA 1981-1984; Secy Of Stndg Com Dio Virginia Richmond VA 1981-1984; Dio Sthrn Virginia Norfolk VA 1977-1984; Dio Sthrn Virginia Norfolk VA 1977-1981; Dn Of Mt Vernon Reg Dio Virginia Richmond VA 1977-1981; VTS Alexandria VA 1967-1981; Chair Of Wrld Affrs Com Dio Virginia Richmond VA 1965-1967; Exec Coun Dio Virginia Richmond VA 1963-1967; R S Lk's Ch Alexandria VA 1960-1981; Racial Study Cmsn Dio Virginia Richmond VA 1959-1960; D Cople Par Hague VA 1955-1956. Ed Bd, "Pilgrimage," 1982; Contributing Auth, "A PB Manual"; Contributing Auth, "The Force Of The Feminine". EvangES 1977-1984. e3morgan@widomaker.com

MORGAN, Edward James (Colo) 5952 E Irish Pl, Centennial CO 80112 B Indianapolis IN 5/5/1944 s James Randolph Morgan & Mary. BA Pur 1966; MDiv Nash 1983. D 6/4/1983 Bp William Carl Frey P 12/14/1983 Bp William Harvey Wolfrum. m 12/30/1967 Sara K Elsbury c 2. Cn Dio Colorado Denver CO 2001-2004; R S Mk's Epis Ch Little Rock AR 1996-2001; R S Barth's Ch Estes Pk CO 1985-1996; Cur S Jos's Ch Lakewood CO 1983-1985. ejmorgan@aol.com

MORGAN, E F Michael (Pa) 313 Main Street, Hulmeville PA 19047 **P-in-c Gr Epis Ch Hulmeville PA 2010-** B Shreveport LA 4/8/1943 s Elmer Francis Morgan & Alice. BA U of Pennsylvania 1964; MA Ob 1966; STB PDS 1970; Ph.D Ohio U 1990; M.Ed Ohio U 1996. D 6/6/1970 P 5/1/1971 Bp Robert Lionne DeWitt. c 2. R S Jn's Ch Bala Cynwyd PA 2003-2007; R Ch Of The Gd Shpd Athens OH 1979-2002; Asst Ch Of The Redeem Chestnut Hill MA 1972-1979. Auth, "Faithful Living: Faithful Dying," Morehouse, 2000. EvangES 1998. Res Fell U So, Sewanee 2007; Cmnty Serv Awd Chld's Rts Coun 2006; Merrill Fllshp Harvard DS 2001; Fellowowship Coll of Preachers Washington DC 1990. efmorgan@frognet.net

MORGAN, Elaine Ludlum (Nev) 402 W Robinson St, Carson City NV 89703 B Los Angeles CA 5/21/1929 d William Francis Ludlum & Helen Katharine. TS Dio Olympia; Claremont Coll 1949; BA Pomona Coll 1949; MA USC 1953. D 6/30/1984 Bp Robert Hume Cochrane. m 4/8/1949 Robert Norman Morgan c 2. Ch Of Coventry Cross Minden NV 1999-2009; D Dio Nevada Las Vegas NV 1996-2011; D S Ptr's Epis Ch Carson City NV 1990-1995; D All SS' Epis Ch Vancouver WA 1984-1990. Auth, "Coventry Cross Cuisine," Morris Pub, 1998; Auth, "Rel arts," Nevada Appeal Nwspr,Carson City, 1996; Auth, "In The Kitchen w Wmn Of St. Mk'S," *Coventry Crossings (1997-2000)*, Ptr Geddes Press, 1962; Auth, "Pipes Of Pan," Pasadena Cmnty Coll Press, 1947. Carson City Mnstrl Assn; NAAD; Vlly Chr Fllshp (Gardnerville). Phi Beta Kappa Pomona Coll 1949; Pi Lambda Theta Pomona C Ollege Chapt 1948. norgancrownsnest@aol.com

MORGAN, George Gale (CGC) Po Box 6251, Gulf Breeze FL 32563 **Vic S Cyp's Epis Ch Pensacola FL 1995-** B Buffalo NY 9/13/1930 s William George Morgan & Mary Kate. U So; AAS SUNY 1950; BA Oklahoma City U 1958. D 8/19/1995 Bp Charles Farmer Duvall P 2/1/1996 Bp John Forsythe Ashby. m 9/7/1957 Janyth Waynelle Wallace c 3. S Fran Of Assisi Gulf Breeze FL 2000-2002; S Cyp's Epis Ch Pensacola FL 1996-2000. S Mary Cmnty. gmorganpax@aol.com

MORGAN III, Harold Edgar (USC) 204 Derby Ln, Clinton SC 29325 **All SS Epis Ch Clinton SC 2006-** B Wilmington DE 9/2/1948 s Harold Edgar Morgan & Martha Jean. BA Cit 1970; MDiv STUSo 1977. D 6/11/1977 P 3/5/1978 Bp George Moyer Alexander. m 4/28/1973 Mamie Elizabeth Wilson. R Ch Of The Gd Shpd Galax VA 2000-2006; Int Ch Of The Resurr Greenwood SC 1998-2000; CE Asst Chr Ch Greenville SC 1996-1997; Chapl Chr Ch Greenville SC 1984-1995; Vic S Barth's Ch Cokeville WY 1979-1984; Vic S Jas Ch Kemmerer WY 1979-1984; Asst S Chris's Ch Spartanburg SC 1977-1979. allsaintsclinton@earthlink.net

MORGAN, Heather M. (Mo) 4603 John Garry Drive, Suites #5 & 6, Columbia MO 65203 B LaGrange IL 4/25/1964 d William B McCain & Susan E. BA Duke 1986; MDiv SWTS 1994. D 6/18/1994 Bp Robert Jefferson Hargrove Jr P 12/17/1994 Bp Frank Tracy Griswold III. m 8/1/2009 Rex A Morgan. Columbia Hope Ch Columbia MO 2009-2011; Dio Missouri S Louis MO 2007-2009; Ch Of The H Sprt Greensboro NC 2002-2007; Cbury Sch Greensboro NC 1999-2001; Asst R Chr Epis Ch Springfield MO 1996-1999; S Greg's Epis Ch Deerfield IL 1994-1996. heathermccainmorgan@gmail.com

MORGAN, James Charles (Tex) 235 Royal Oaks St, Huntsville TX 77320 **S Steph's Ch Huntsville TX 1994-** B Massillon OH 6/26/1943 s James Charles Morgan & Grace Elizabeth. BA Steph F. Austin St U 1965; BD/MDiv VTS 1969. D 7/1/1969 P 5/1/1970 Bp J Milton Richardson. St Ptr The Fisherman Trin TX 1999-2002; R S Mary's Ch W Columbia TX 1971-1993; Vic S Mk's Epis Ch Richmond TX 1971-1974; S Mk's Ch Houston TX 1971; St Lukes Ch Rusk TX 1969-1971; M-in-c Trin Ch Jacksonville TX 1969-1971. jmorgan_huntsville@yahoo.com

MORGAN JR, James Hanly (WVa) 520 11th Ave., Huntington WV 25701 B Huntington WV 12/5/1937 s James Hanly Morgan & MaryAnn. BS W Virginia U 1959. D 9/29/2008 Bp William Michie Klusmeyer. m 3/25/1961 Elizabeth Morgan c 4. jmorgan60@aol.com

MORGAN, James Patrick (RG) Po Box 91, Stockholm ME 04783 B Las Cruces NM 11/27/1946 s Jesse Patrick Morgan & Martha. BA U of New Mex 1969; MBA Clc 1974; MDiv CDSP 1980; MA Sru 1993. D 8/6/1980 P 5/4/1981 Bp Richard Mitchell Trelease Jr. m 8/2/2005 Sonja Morgan c 6. Trin Luth Ch Stockholm ME 1997-2008; Int Gr Ch Carlsbad NM 1996-1997; Off Of Bsh For ArmdF New York NY 1983-1996; Locten S Mich And All Ang Ch Albuquerque NM 1982-1983; Dio The Rio Grande Albuquerque NM 1980-1981. Commendation, 3rd Awd USN 1996; Sea Serv Ribbon USN 1984; Achievement Medal Combat Viet Nam Untd States Navey 1971.

MORGAN, Kimberly Ann (Nev) 305 N Minnesota St, Carson City NV 89703 B Washington DC 10/1/1956 d Richard Linn Morgan & Barbara Capet. BA U of Nevada 1977; JD U of Oklahoma 1980; CTS CDSP 2008. D 7/25/2009 P 2/13/2010 Bp Dan Thomas Edwards. m 12/28/1985 John Slider. kamorgan@pyramid.net

MORGAN, LaVerne (Mich) 3880 Loton Dr, Fort Gratiot MI 48059 B Watfoord Ontario Canada 5/3/1922 s Frederick Joseph Morgan & Martha Jane. LTh Hur 1947. D 5/1/1944 P 6/1/1947 Bp The Bishop Of Huron. m 9/1/1944 Ruth Mountain c 3. S Mich's Epis Ch Lansing MI 1968-1984; R Gr Ch Mt Clemens MI 1966-1967; Vic H Fam Epis Ch Midland MI 1959-1964; Asst S Jn's Epis Ch Midland MI 1956-1959; Vic S Jn The Bapt Epis Ch Ephrata WA 1954-1956; Vic S Mart's Ch Moses Lake WA 1954-1956; R S Mk's Epis Ch Marine City MI 1950-1954.

MORGAN, Mamie Elizabeth (USC) 204 Derby Lane, Clinton SC 29325 **R S Lk's Ch Newberry SC 2007-** B Greenville SC 9/30/1953 d Paul Kenneth Wilson & Alma Ruth. BA U of So Carolina 1974; MDiv STUSo 1979. D 11/1/1980 P 11/1/1981 Bp Bob Gordon Jones. m 4/28/1973 Harold Edgar Morgan. Int Chr Ch Blacksburg VA 2005-2007; R Chr Ch Bluefield WV 2000-2005; Int S Thad Epis Ch Aiken SC 1999-2000; Epis Ch Of The Redeem Greenville SC 1998; S Jn's Ch Winnsboro SC 1995-1997; Epiph Ch Spartanburg SC 1987-1989; Asst S Barth's Ch Cokeville WY 1980-1984; Asst S Jas Ch Kemmerer WY 1980-1984. Int Ministers Ntwk 1997; Prof Trng In Int Mnstry. Woods Ldrshp Awd U So 1976. ohmysol99@yahoo.com

MORGAN, Marilyn Kay (Ark) 1475 Stone Crest Dr, Conway AR 72034 **D S Lk's Epis Ch No Little Rock AR 2008-** B Conway AR 3/22/1947 d Friedman Morgan & Mary Aline. BSE U Of Cntrl Arkansas 1970; MSE U Of Cntrl Arkansas 1976. D 5/5/2007 Bp Larry R Benfield. D S Ptr's Ch Conway AR 2007-2008. kay_sfct@yahoo.com

MORGAN, Michael (Mont) West 3817 Fort Wright Drive 1-204, Spokane WA 99204 B San Francisco CA 3/6/1949 s Alfred C Morgan & Hazel Bell. BA Uscd 1971; MDiv EDS 1975. D 8/2/1975 P 9/1/1976 Bp Wesley Frensdorff. Dio Montana Helena MT 1993-1995; Bd Trst Dio Montana Helena MT 1980-1981; S Andr's Ch Livingston MT 1979-1992; S Jn's Ch Emigrant MT 1979-1992; Advsr Of The Yth Cmsn Dio Nevada Las Vegas NV 1975-1979; Cur S Steph's Epis Ch Reno NV 1975-1979.

MORGAN, Michele Helen (Minn) 3154 Ulysses St NE, Minneapolis MN 55418 **Transitional R S Jn The Bapt Epis Ch Minneapolis MN 2011-** B Calgary 6/24/1963 BA The Coll of St. Cathr 1986; MDiv GTS 2004. D 6/10/2004 P 12/16/2004 Bp James Louis Jelinek. m Michelle Vail Dibblee. Int P S Jas On The Pkwy Minneapolis MN 2009-2011; Int P S Jn's Ch S Cloud MN

2009; Int Chld/Yth S Jn The Bapt Epis Ch Minneapolis MN 2008; Assoc Ch Of The Ascen Stillwater MN 2004-2007. revmichelemorgan@gmail.com

MORGAN, Pamela Sturch (Ark) 1410 E Walnut St., Rogers AR 72756 **R S Thos Ch Springdale AR 2009-** B Little Rock AR 8/25/1955 d Calvin Wayne Sturch & Sibyl Janice. BA St. Mary-Of-The-Woods Coll 1999; MDiv STUSo 2001. D 2/22/2001 P 9/15/2001 Bp Larry Earl Maze. m 9/24/1973 Kevin Ryan Morgan c 3. S Andr's Ch Mtn Hm AR 2003-2008; S Mk's Epis Ch Little Rock AR 2001-2003. pam@stthomasspringdale.org

MORGAN, Philip (Va) 17476 Hawthorne Ave, Culpeper VA 22701 **Bd Trst Mem Howe Mltry Sch Howe IN 2011-; Vic Emm Ch Rapidan VA 2006-** B Swansea Wales 10/22/1951 s Haydn Granville Morgan & Edith Maud. B.Sc. Lon 1975; BD U of Wales 1978; MBA Columbia Sthrn U 2009. Trans from Church in Wales 9/18/1985 Bp William Cockburn Russell Sheridan. m 9/14/1974 Carol Lynne Burrows c 3. Chapl Blue Ridge Sch Dyke VA 2004-2010; R Little Fork Epis Ch Rixeyville VA 2000-2003; Chapl All SS Chap Howe IN 1986-2000; R S Mk's Par Howe IN 1986-2000; Chapl Howe Mltry Sch Howe IN 1985-2000; Vic H Fam Ch Angola IN 1985-1986; Cur S Jn The Evang Ch Elkhart IN 1984-1985. Auth, "Another Walk w Me," LuluPress, 2010; Auth, "Walk Again w Me," LuluPress, 2009; Auth, "Walk Awhile w Me," LuluPress, 2008; Auth, "The First b," *LivCh*, The Ch-in-Wales; Auth, "What is Pryr," *The Welsh Churchman*, The Ch-in-Wales; Auth, "Chr Initiation," *The Welsh Churchman*, The Ch-in-Wales. Lifetime Assoc St. Mary's Ch, Swansea, Wales St. Mary's, Swansea, Wales 1984. padre4u@hotmail.com

MORGAN, Ralph Baier (Tex) 304 E Stockbridge St, Eagle Lake TX 77434 **R Chr Ch Eagle Lake TX 2009-** B Houston TX 5/12/1958 s Ralph Morgan & Dealva. BA Houston Bapt U 1983; MDiv Epis TS of the SW 2006. D 6/24/2006 Bp Don Adger Wimberly P 1/11/2007 Bp Dena Arnall Harrison. m 5/12/2001 Terri S Silver c 2. Asst S Dunst's Epis Ch Houston TX 2006-2009; Yth Dir Ch Of The H Apos Katy TX 1992-2003; Dn Adv Epis Sch Stafford TX 1991-1996; Yth Dir Ch Of The H Sprt 1985-1989; Yth Dir S Jn The Div Houston TX 1984-1986. fr.ralphmorgan@gmail.com

MORGAN, Randall Carl (SC) St Jude's Episcopal Church, 907 Wichman St, Walterboro SC 29488 B Parkersburg WV 10/10/1948 s Douglas Davidson Morgan & Ruth Rebecca. BA Glenville St Coll 1979; MDiv VTS 1985. D 6/5/1985 Bp Robert Poland Atkinson P 12/1/1985 Bp William Franklin Carr. R S Jude's Epis Ch Walterboro SC 2005-2011; P S Paul's Ch Athens TN 2001-2005; Vic Ch Of The Gd Shpd Greer SC 1988-2001; S Fran Ch Potomac MD 1987-1988; Olde S Jn's Ch Colliers WV 1985-1986. rm101048@yahoo.com

MORGAN III, Ray Reid (Tex) 29 Castleberry St., Lampasas TX 76550 **R S Mary's Epis Ch Inc Lampasas TX 2008-** B Gadsden AL 2/15/1955 s Ray Reid Morgan & Flora Mae. BS Texas A&M U 1979; MDiv Epis TS of The SW 2005. D 12/9/2005 P 6/10/2006 Bp Barry Robert Howe. m 5/31/1980 Marie Wilson c 3. Dio W Missouri Kansas City MO 2006-2008. Asssociate OHC 1997. reid_morgan@sbcglobal.net

MORGAN V, Richard (RI) 19 Castle Way, Westerly RI 02891 **P-in-c S Eliz's Ch Hope Vlly RI 2008-** B Hartford CT 8/6/1941 s Richard Morgan & Avice Marie. BA Dart 1963; MDiv EDS 1970. D 12/21/1972 Bp Morgan Porteus P 6/29/1973 Bp Matthew G Henry. m 2/15/1974 Betty Griffith c 2. Vic S Mths Ch Coventry RI 1993-2007; Assoc Chr Ch Westerly RI 1985-1993; Emm Ch Woodstock VA 1983-1985; S Andr's Ch Mt Jackson VA 1983-1985; Trin Ch Spruce Pine NC 1973-1983. Bro Way Cross 1975. The Ord Of S Geo Rhode Island St Coun of Ch/ Providence, RI 2000. castleway19@cox.net

MORGAN, Ruth Margaret (RG) 8017 Krim Dr. NE, Albuquerque NM 87109 **Asst to the R Hope in the Desert Eps Ch Albuquerque NM 2011-** B Racine WI 1/30/1954 d John George Murphy & Iola Jean. BA Coll of Santa Fe 2000; MA Webster U 2003; Chr Mnstry Trin Sch for Mnstry 2009. D 9/19/2009 P 9/25/2010 Bp William Carl Frey. m 9/13/1997 Felix Morgan c 4. P-in-c S Fran Ch Rio Rancho NM 2010-2011; D S Fran Ch Rio Rancho NM 2009-2010; Admin Asst to the R S Fran Ch Rio Rancho NM 2006-2009. ruthmmorgan@aol.com

MORGAN, S(tanhope) Neale (Va) PO Box 506, Shepherdstown WV 25443 **Died 4/30/2010** B Buffalo NY 7/2/1928 s Dwight Cadogan Morgan & Josephine. BA Col 1950; MDiv Ya Berk 1953. D 6/20/1953 Bp Austin Pardue P 12/1/1953 Bp William S Thomas. c 2. Auth, "A Peek at & A Pryr for the Dominican Epis Ch," Priv, 1965; Auth, "Sm Revelation Down at the Corner (film strip)," Natl Coun of Ch, 1965. revneal@intrepid.net

MORGAN, Walter Craig (ETenn) 3475 Edgewood Cir Nw, Cleveland TN 37312 B Monroe LA 9/1/1936 s Gordon Lea Morgan & Mary Louise. BS Tul 1959; MDiv Nash 1979; Cert Mid Atlantic Assn 1982. D 5/10/1979 P 11/14/1979 Bp James Barrow Brown. m 6/25/1960 Janet Mahaffey. Ch Of The Adv Louisville KY 2002; Com Chair Dio E Tennessee Knoxville TN 1995-1999; Com Dio E Tennessee Knoxville TN 1993-1994; B&C Dio E Tennessee Knoxville TN 1991-1993; Design Team Plnng & Structure Dio E Tennessee Knoxville TN 1991-1992; R S Lk's Ch Cleveland TN 1989-2002; Design Team Par Act Consult Trng Dio Wstrn Louisiana Alexandria LA 1986-1987; Dep Gc Dio Wstrn Louisiana Alexandria LA 1985-1988; Dispatch Bus Dio Wstrn Louisiana Alexandria LA 1984-1988; Par Growth Consult Dio Wstrn Louisiana Alexandria LA 1984-1988; Chair Camp Hardtner Cmsn Dio Wstrn Louisiana Alexandria LA 1983-1988; Cdo Dio Wstrn Louisiana Alexandria LA 1982-1988; Cn Ordnry Dio Wstrn Louisiana Alexandria LA 1981-1988; Chair Sum Camping Cmsn Dio Wstrn Louisiana Alexandria LA 1979-1984; R Gr Ch Lake Providence LA 1979-1981. jmmwcm@aol.com

MORGAN-HIGGINS, Stanley Ethelbert (Nwk) 3828 Leprechaun Ct, Decatur GA 30034 B Panama PA 11/13/1938 s Clifford Augustus Morgan & Edna Lucetta. BA RP U Panama; MD ETSC 1975. D 10/31/1976 P 8/26/1979 Bp Lemuel Barnett Shirley. m 5/27/1989 Cecily A Morgan c 2. Receiving Disabil Ret 2002-2003; R Ch Of The H Comm Paterson NJ 1991-2002; P-in-c S Agnes And S Paul's Ch E Orange NJ 1990-1991; P-in-c S Cyp's Epis Ch Hackensack NJ 1990-1991; St Marys & St Margarets Ch 1982-1988; St Stephens Mssn 1982-1988; Chr Ch By The Sea 1979-1981; Dio Panama 1976-1989.

MORICAL, Robin Elizabeth (CFla) 1631 Ford Pkwy, Saint Paul MN 55116 **Assoc Ch of the Incarn Oviedo FL 2010-** B Riverside CA 9/17/1964 d Layton Davis Coombs & Naomi Gaylene. BA U MN 1992; MDiv Nash 2008. D 5/31/2008 Bp John Hornor Howe P 5/30/2009 Bp John Wadsworth Howe. m 6/24/1989 James Harold Morical c 3. D Assoc Mssh Epis Ch S Paul MN 2009-2010. rmorical@gmail.com

MORIN, Geoffrey S (Pa) 841 Shenton Road, West Chester PA 19380 B Methuen MA 8/25/1965 s Rudolph G Morin & Elizabeth. BA Duke 1987; MDiv Ya Berk 1994. D 6/11/1994 Bp Clarence Nicholas Coleridge P 4/1/1995 Bp R(aymond) Stewart Wood Jr. c 1. Assoc Ch Of The Gd Samar Paoli PA 1997-2006; Chr Ch Grosse Pointe Grosse Pointe Farms MI 1994-1997. Geof.Morin@gmail.com

MORISSEAU, Robert Edward Lee (NY) 502 Forest Gln, Pompton Plains NJ 07444 B Saint Louis MO 12/3/1932 s Clarence Engene Morisseau & Corinne. BA Missouri Vlly Coll 1954; MDiv EDS 1957. D 6/15/1957 P 12/21/1957 Bp Arthur C Lichtenberger. m 6/25/1960 Caroline Dalton Byars c 3. Chapl Cathd Of St Jn The Div New York NY 1995-1998; R S Jn's Ch New City NY 1969-1994; R S Jn's Epis Ch Oneida NY 1962-1969; Asst S Ptr's Epis Ch St Louis MO 1957-1962. remorisseau@gmail.com

MORITZ III, B(ernard) Eugene (SwVa) 4022 Fauquier Ave, Richmond VA 23227 B Natchez MS 3/26/1941 s Joseph Samuel Moritz & Jane Stewart. BA Mississippi St U 1963; MDiv Nash 1973; STM STUSo 1983. D 6/11/1973 P 5/19/1974 Bp John M Allin. m 3/14/1964 Jeanelle Lowe c 2. Ascen Epis Ch Amherst VA 1999-2006; Supply P Dio Alabama Birmingham AL 1988-1999; Dio Alabama Birmingham AL 1988-1998; Our Sav Birmingham AL 1986-1988; Assoc R Ch Of The Nativ Epis Huntsville AL 1984-1986; Asst S Paul's Ch Fayetteville AR 1981-1984; Vic Ch Of The Redeem Brookhaven MS 1977-1981; Vic All SS Ch Inverness MS 1974-1977; Vic S Thos Ch Belzoni MS 1974-1977; Cur S Paul's Ch Columbus MS 1973-1974. Cmnty of S Mary, P Assoc 1979. bemoritz@hotmail.com

MORIYAMA, Jerome Tomokazu (WA) Rossbrin Cove, Schull, Co. Cork Ireland B Tokyo 9/18/1943 s Tomokiyo Moriyama & Yoshie. BA Keio U Tokyo 1968; MA Keio U Tokyo 1970; MDiv EDS 1975; MA Lon SOAS 1979; PhD Lon SOAS 1984. D 6/7/1975 P 5/20/1976 Bp William Foreman Creighton. m 12/1/1973 Ann Mary Gamwell c 2. Exec Coun Appointees New York NY 1975-1985. Daniel O'Connor and others, "Part 2: Perspectives 8. Bldg a Hmgrown Ch Jerome T Moriyama," *Three Centuries of Mssn -The Untd Sciety for the Propogation of the Gospel 1701-2000*, USPG and Continuum Intl Pub Grp, 2000. moriyama@eircom.net

MORLAN, Lyn K (EpisSanJ) 2803 Stratford Dr, San Ramon CA 94583 **R Epis Ch Of S Anne Stockton CA 2010-** B Sacramento CA 8/12/1951 BS California St U. D 6/5/2004 P 12/4/2004 Bp William Edwin Swing. m 8/28/1971 David L Morlan c 2. P-in-c Epis Ch Of S Anne Stockton CA 2010; Yth Min S Barth's Epis Ch Livermore CA 2004-2008. davidmorlan@comcast.net

MORLEY, Anthony J (Minn) 825 Summit Ave #806, Minneapolis MN 55403 B Geneva CH 1/17/1930 s Felix Muskett Morley & Isabel. BA Hav 1951; U of Vienna 1952; MDiv EDS 1955. D 6/18/1955 Bp Angus Dun P 12/8/1955 Bp Horace W B Donegan. m 3/11/1978 Ruth Olson c 4. Dir of Resrch Dio Missouri S Louis MO 1965-1968; R Trin Ch S Louis MO 1958-1965; Fell and Tutor The GTS New York NY 1955-1958. Auth, "A Legis Guide to Sch Fin," *Civil Rts Dig*, 1972; "anonymous editorials, signed opinion pieces," *Minneapolis Star Tribune*. ajm.tony@gmail.com

MORLEY JR, Christopher (ETenn) 601 Market St, Chattanooga TN 37402 **Died 6/16/2011** B New York NY 12/5/1916 s Christopher Morley & Helen Fairchild. BA Cor 1938; STB GTS 1949; MDiv GTS 1986. D 5/21/1949 P 12/1/1949 Bp James P De Wolfe. Auth, "Yashiro Of Japan". Oblate Somc 1959.

MORLEY, Richard Matthew (NJ) 140 S Finley Ave, Basking Ridge NJ 07920 **R S Mk's Ch Basking Ridge NJ 2009-; Vic S Ptr's Ch Lonaconing MD 2002-** B Wilmington DE 7/29/1974 s Richard Everett Morley & Sarah Maureen. BA/BS S Jos's U Philadelphia PA 1996; MDiv Candler TS Emory U 2002. D 6/8/2002 Bp John Leslie Rabb P 12/15/2002 Bp Robert Wilkes Ihloff. m 6/24/2000 Karen Renee Childs c 2. Dio Maryland Baltimore MD 2002-2009. rmcmorley@me.com

MORLEY, William Harris (NC) 3454 Rugby Rd, Durham NC 27707 **P Assoc Chap Of The Cross Chap Hill NC 2002-** B Columbus OH 3/15/1951 s Buel Morley & Dorothy Jean. TCU 1970; BA U of Kansas 1973; MDiv Nash 1978; DMin GTF 1991; MBA GTF 1991. D 6/17/1978 Bp Quintin Ebenezer Primo Jr P 12/16/1978 Bp James Winchester Montgomery. m 5/24/2003 Arlene Jayne Diosegy c 2. R S Tim's Epis Ch W Des Moines IA 1983-1991; Vic S Paul's Ch McHenry IL 1979-1983; Cur S Jn's Epis Ch Naperville IL 1978-1979. Auth, "Exec Coaching:An Annotated Bibliography," Cntr For Creative Ldrshp, 2000. OHC 1979. whmorley@gmail.com

MORNARD, Jean Elisabeth (Minn) 440 W 21st St, New York NY 10011 B Duluth MN 9/12/1955 d John David Messer & Jo Ann. Dplma CIDEF U Catholique de l'Ouest 1976; BA U MN 1983; MDiv The GTS 2012. D 6/30/2011 Bp Brian N Prior. m 6/27/1987 Michael Francis Mornard. JMORNARD@GTS.EDU

MORONEY, Kevin John (Pa) 536 Conestoga Rd., Villanova PA 19085 **Chr Epis Ch Villanova PA 2009-** B Summit NJ 10/27/1961 s Robert Thomas Moroney & Joyce Florence. BS Vlly Forge Chr Coll 1986; MDiv GTS 1992; MLS Rutgers U 2000; PhD Milltown Inst of Theol and Philos 2008. D 6/13/1992 P 2/1/1993 Bp George Phelps Mellick Belshaw. m 8/24/2006 Rose Elizabeth Curran c 2. Assoc R S Dav's Ch Wayne PA 2005-2009; S Jas Sch St Jas MD 1998-2000; All SS Epis Ch Lakewood NJ 1994-1998; Asst Pstr S Lk's Epis Ch Metuchen NJ 1992-1994. Auth, "Imperfect, w Peace," *LivCh*, 2009; Auth, "Some Results of a Survey of the BCP 2004," *Ch of Ireland Gazette*, 2005; Auth, "Rebirth, Renwl, Revs," *Search*, 2004; Auth, "Angl Catholicism in the Dio Dublin," *Search*, 2002. OHC. kjmcoi@yahoo.com

MORONTA VASQUEZ, Buddelov Adolfo (DR) C/O Episcopal Church In Dominican Republic, Box 764, Santo Domingo Dominican Republic **Dio The Dominican Republic (Iglesia Epis Dominicana) Santo Domingo DO 2010-** B Republica Dominicana 8/27/1970 s Adolfo Simon Moronta & Octavia Maria. BA Hotel Admin UNIBE 1993; BA Philos PUCMM 1998; BA Theol CET 2008; MA Liturg VTS 2012. D 2/14/2010 P 2/20/2011 Bp Julio Cesar Holguin-Khoury. adolfomoronta27@hotmail.com

MORPETH, Robert Park (Ala) 521 20th St N, Birmingham AL 35203 **Dio Alabama Birmingham AL 1997-; Dep for Fin & Admin Dio Alabama Birmingham AL 1997-** B Columbus GA 8/9/1951 s James E Morpeth & Julia. BS Columbus 1974; MDiv STUSo 1978. D 6/10/1978 Bp Charles Judson Child Jr P 5/1/1979 Bp Bennett Jones Sims. m 1/29/1994 Susan J Jones. Epis Black Belt Mnstry Demopolis AL 1990-1997; Assoc S Thos Epis Ch Columbus GA 1988-1990; Int S Mary Magd Ch Columbus GA 1986-1988; Asst S Mk's Epis Ch Jacksonville FL 1981-1983; Chr Ch Macon GA 1979-1981. rmorpeth@dioala.org

MORRETT, John Joseph (SO) 2970 Saint Johns Ave, Jacksonville FL 32205 **Died 10/14/2011** B Springfield OH 9/21/1916 s George Daniel Morrett & Mary Cecilia. BS OH SU 1939; STM EDS 1947. D 6/19/1947 Bp Henry W Hobson P 6/1/1948 Bp Lloyd Rutherford Craighill. c 3. Auth, "SS I Have Known And Known About.," Infinity Pub.Com, 2003; Auth, "Soldier P Kanok Bannasan Thailand," Omf Pub, 1993; Auth, "We Lived To Tell". Coll Of Admin Scioneas OH SU 1955; Bp'S Distinguish Serv Cross Dio Honolulu 1954; Dioc Honary Soc Serv Dio Honolulu 1954; Man / Fr Of The Year Jr Chambers Of Commerce 1952. pow_survivor@webtv.net

MORRIGAN, Cedar Abrielynne (Minn) 309 13th St Sw, Little Falls MN 56345 B 3/22/1957 AA Anoka-Ramsey Cmnty Coll 1977; BS St. Cloud St U 1981. D 4/1/2002 Bp Frederick Warren Putnam P 10/6/2002 Bp Daniel Lee Swenson. c 1. cmorrigan@earthlink.net

MORRIGAN, Johanna V(irginia) S(tella) (Minn) 309 13th St Sw, Little Falls MN 56345 **D Ch Of Our Sav Little Falls MN 2002-** B Minneapolis MN 6/5/1945 d John M Richmond & Ruby V. Macalester Coll; BS U MN 1969; MA St. Cloud St U 1991. D 10/6/2002 Bp Daniel Lee Swenson. spinster2@fallsnet.org

MORRILL, Bonnie (Dal) 5314 Somerset Dr., Rowlett TX 75089 B Greeley CO 6/23/1946 d John Manville Weber & Laura. BA Sch for Deacons 1999. D 5/22/1999 Bp Richard Lester Shimpfky. m 6/10/1966 Charles Clifford Morrill c 3. H Trin Ch Rockwall TX 2003-2004; D Epis Ch Of The Gd Shpd Salinas CA 1999-2003. Epis Conf of the Deaf of the Epis Ch in the 1985; Ord of S Lk 1999. abcmorrill@aol.com

MORRIS, Alfred Edward (Pa) 505 E Catherine St, Chambersburg PA 17201 B Philadelphia PA 10/15/1934 s Alfred Edward Morris & Viola Mae. BS Tem 1957; BS CRDS 1961. Trans from Anglican Church of Canada 1/22/1991 Bp Allen Lyman Bartlett Jr. c 3. R Ch Of S Jn The Evang Essington PA 1991-1993.

MORRIS, Alfred John (Ct) 9201 Sw 192nd Court Rd, Dunnellon FL 34432 B Pawtucket RI 4/7/1925 s Charles William Morris & Charlotte Anne. BA Barrington Coll 1959; Gordon-Conwell TS 1961; California Bapt U 1963; CDSP 1966. D 9/10/1966 P 3/11/1967 Bp Francis E I Bloy. m 12/22/1956 Dorothy Krautter c 3. R Ch Of The Gd Shpd Shelton CT 1970-1988; Assoc S Paul's Ch Pawtucket RI 1968-1970; Assoc S Paul's Pomona Pomona CA 1966-1968.

MORRIS, Bonnie F (WNY) 20 Milton Street, Williamsville NY 14221 **Asst R Calv Epis Ch Williamsville NY 2011-** B Oklahoma City OK 8/20/1961 d William Scofield Flanigen & Mary Kinman. Bex Sem; BA St Mary's Coll of Maryland 1983; MBA U at Buffalo 2001; M. Div Chr the King Sem 2011. D 12/20/2008 Bp J Michael Garrison. m 5/27/1989 Timothy Patrick Morris c 2. bjmorris@yahoo.com

MORRIS, Cecelia Gilman (Oly) Po Box 268, Tracyton WA 98393 **S Paul's Epis Ch Bremerton WA 2002-** B Wellsville NY 9/14/1949 D 6/29/2002 Bp Vincent Waydell Warner. m 1/16/1988 Henry Minard Morris c 2. deaconcece@comcast.net

MORRIS, Charles Hamilton (Mo) 900 Weatherstone Dr, Saint Charles MO 63304 **Asstg Cler Ch Of The Trsfg Lake S Louis MO 2000-** B Kerrville TX 2/28/1932 s Otho Anderson Morris & Ethel Mae. AA Schreiner Coll 1952; BA U of Texas 1954; MDiv VTS 1957; DMin VTS 1980. D 7/15/1957 Bp Everett H Jones P 2/28/1958 Bp Richard Earl Dicus. m 8/10/1957 Janet Orth c 3. Asstg P Ch Of The Gd Shpd S Louis MO 1997-1999; Stndg Com (Pres., '95) Dio Missouri S Louis MO 1992-1995; Dioc Coun Dio Missouri S Louis MO 1989-1990; S Andr's Ch S Louis MO 1972-1996; Vic St Fran Ch S Louis MO 1966-1979; Asst S Mich & S Geo Clayton MO 1965-1966; Asst S Mart's Epis Ch Houston TX 1962-1965; R Calv Ch Menard TX 1959-1962; P-in-c S Jas Epis Ch Ft McKavett TX 1959-1962; Vic S Jas Ch Hallettsville TX 1957-1959; Vic Trin Epis Ch Edna TX 1957-1959. charlijani@aol.com

MORRIS, Charles Henry (Be) 24 Forsythia Dr, Harwich MA 02645 B West Chester PA 3/20/1941 s Charles H Morris & Miriam. BS W Chester St Coll 1963; MDiv PDS 1969. D 6/7/1969 Bp Chandler W Sterling P 12/13/1969 Bp Robert Lionne DeWitt. m 8/24/1963 Wilma Jean Richards c 2. R Trin Epis Ch Pottsville PA 1995-2005; Assoc S Mary's Epis Ch Barnstable MA 1989-1995; R S Paul's Ch Coll Point NY 1978-1989; Cur Ch Of The Adv Westbury NY 1969-1975. NAES 1980-1984. Cn Pstr Dio Bethlehem Bethlehem 1999. revcanonm@comcast.net

MORRIS, Clayton L (Cal) 815 2nd Ave, New York NY 10017 B EugeneOR 6/23/1946 s Joseph William Morris & Betty Fern. BA Willamette U 1968; MDiv CDSP 1971; MA Grad Theol Un 1971; PhD Grad Theol Un 1986. D 6/22/1971 Bp James Walmsley Frederic Carman P 1/2/1972 Bp C Kilmer Myers. m 12/30/1968 Mary S Pacquer c 2. Ltrgics Off Epis Ch Cntr New York NY 1991-2009; Assoc P/Min S Mk's Epis Ch Palo Alto CA 1986-1991; Ch Of The H Trin Richmond CA 1986; All Souls Par In Berkeley Berkeley CA 1982-1985; Lectr in Mus CDSP Berkeley CA 1982-1984; Org/Chrmstr S Paul's Ch Oakland CA 1979-1980; R S Mk's Ch KING CITY CA 1974-1979; Assoc Min S Andr's Ch Saratoga CA 1971-1974. Auth, "The PB in Cyberspace," *Oxford Guide to BCP*, Oxf Press, 2006; Auth, "H Hosp," *H Hosp: Wrshp and the Baptismal Cov*, Ch Pub Inc, 2005; Auth, "The Future of Liturg Text," *A PB for the 21st Century*, Ch Pub Inc, 1996; Ed, "As we gather to pray," *As We Gather to Pray: An Epis Guide to Wrshp*, Ch Pub Inc, 1996; Auth, "Incarn into Culture," *The Chant of Life*, Ch Pub Inc. Associated Parishes Coun 1991; Assn Angl Musicians 1980; ADLMC 1978-2002; Consult on Common Texts 1991-2009; Intrenational Angl Liturg Consultaion 1992-2009; NAAL 1997. claymorris815@gmail.com

MORRIS, Danielle DuBois (CFla) 444 Covey Cv, Winter Park FL 32789 **S Mich's Ch Orlando FL 2007-; D All SS Ch Of Winter Pk Winter Pk FL 2000-** B 8/25/1947 AA Andr Jr Coll 1968; BA Rol 1972; Cert U Of Cntrl Florida 1999. D 12/11/1999 P 5/19/2007 Bp John Wadsworth Howe. m 1/6/1977 Charles A Morris. Auth, "Adventures Unlimited," *Walking The Mourner'S Path Workbook*. Amer Acad Of Bereavement. therevdanielle@cs.com

MORRIS, David John (Pa) 449 Newgate Ct Apt B2, Andalusia PA 19020 B Plainfield NJ 12/16/1958 s Raymond Harold Morris & Helen. BA Tem 1990; MDiv GTS 1994. D 11/12/1994 P 12/2/1995 Bp Allen Lyman Bartlett Jr. m 11/25/2008 Douglas Scott Cline. Tem Hosp Philadelphia PA 2000-2005; All SS Ch Rhawnhurst Philadelphia PA 1999-2006; R All SS Crescentville Philadelphia PA 1999-2006; Vic Ch Of The Gd Shpd Ringwood NJ 1997-1999; Dio Newark Newark NJ 1997-1999; Assoc S Andr's In The Field Ch Philadelphia PA 1994-1997. Episc. Cmnty Serv--Chapl Adv Comm. Phil PA 2001-2005; NEHM 2005. morrisd@email.chop.edu

MORRIS, David Wayne (NY) 15 Pine St, Lake Peekskill NY 10537 **D Ch Of The H Comm Mahopac NY 2007-** B Ossining NY 12/27/1951 s Edward Morris & Ruth Lois. BA Franklin Pierce Coll 1975; AA Franklin Pierce Coll 1982; MS Pace U 1988. D 6/4/1994 Bp Richard Frank Grein. m 11/27/1976 Charlotte Patricia Avallone c 1. D S Ptr's Epis Ch Peekskill NY 1994-2007.

MORRIS, Donald Richard (Vt) 280 Round Rd, Bristol VT 05443 B Schenectady NY 4/26/1930 s Ernest Alfred Morris & Carmen Wilmetta. BA Harv 1951; MA Harv 1957. D 6/24/1978 P 3/1/1979 Bp John Thomas Walker. m 6/2/1984 May Foster Bowers Gregg c 2. Cn Pstr Ch of Our Sav Killington VT 1995; R S Paul's Epis Ch On The Green Vergennes VT 1991-1995; Chr/St Paul's Epis Par Yonges Island SC 1984-1991; R Trin Ch Edisto Island SC 1984-1990; R Ch Of The H Comm Washington DC 1979-1984. DMORRIS1@GMAVT.NET

MORRIS, Gale Davis (Mass) 164 Newtown Rd # 2025, Acton MA 01720 **Ch Of The Adv Medfield MA 2011-; The Ch Of The Adv Boston MA 2011-; R The Ch Of The Gd Shpd Acton MA 1998-** B Pasadena CA 9/7/1946 d Richard David Davis & Dorothy Gale. Scripps Coll 1966; BS U of San Francisco 1983; MDiv CDSP 1989; DMin SWTS 1998. D 6/24/1989 P 6/1/1990 Bp Charles Shannon Mallory. c 4. S Andr's Ch Milwaukee WI 1995-1998; R S Paul's Ch Milwaukee WI 1994-1998; Cn Cathd Ch Of S Mk Minneapolis MN 1991-1994; Assoc S Fran Epis Ch San Jose CA 1989-1991. rectorgale@aol.com

MORRIS, Gregg Allen (Md) St. John's Episcopal Church, 9120 Frederick Rd., Ellicott City MD 21042 **S Jn's Ch Ellicott City MD 2011-** B Peoria IL 1/14/1963 s Jack Lee Morris & Gladys Jane. BA Taylor U 1986; MA Azusa Pacific U 1994; MDiv VTS 2011. D 6/4/2011 Bp Eugene Sutton. m 12/30/1995 Laura Olsen Laura Diane Olsen c 2. Ch Of Our Sav Par San Gabr CA 1994-1997. gmorris@stjohnsec.org

MORRIS, Hunter Mason (WTex) 7307 Tanbark Cv, Austin TX 78759 **Died 12/22/2010** B San Angelo TX 4/23/1933 s Gilbert Marvin Morris & Doris Elizabeth. BA U of Texas 1955; CTh Epis TS of The SW 1960. D 7/8/1960 P 3/1/1962 Bp John E Hines. Auth, "Bicentennial Nwsltr Epis Ch"; Auth, "Who'S Who In Rel". Outstanding Serv Awd Texas Law Enforcement Fndt.

MORRIS, James Edgar (Pa) 203 Devon Dr, Exton PA 19341 **Int All SS Ch Rhawnhurst Philadelphia PA 2011-** B Bryn Mawr PA 10/20/1933 s Edgar Dunbar Morris & Helen. BA Ursinus Coll 1956; MDiv Epis TS of The SW 1963; AA PC Amer Fndt of Rel & Psych 1967; Fllshp VTS 1996; Cert Oxf 1998; Cert Oxf 1998; DMin VTS 2000. D 6/8/1963 P 12/1/1963 Bp Joseph Gillespie Armstrong. m 9/10/1966 Shirley Joan Clark c 2. Int Ch Of Our Sav Jenkintown PA 2006-2010; Int The Ch Of The Ascen Claymont DE 2004-2005; Int S Martha's Epis Ch Bethany Bch DE 2002-2003; P-in-c S Mart's Epis Ch Fairlee VT 2002-2003; S Paul Ch Exton PA 1982-2003; Actg R Ch Of The Redemp Southampton PA 1981-1982; Hospice Com Dio Pennsylvania Philadelphia PA 1980-1983; Chr Epis Ch Villanova PA 1979-1981; Asst Min S Mary's Epis Ch Ardmore PA 1967-1969; Stff Dept Mssns Dio New York New York City NY 1966-1967. Auth, "Hlth & Med In The Angl Tradition," *Journ Of Chr Healing*, 1984; Auth, "Bridging Renwl: A Cmnty Bldg Process That Celebrates Diversity In Unity". jmorris882@aol.com

MORRIS, Janie Leigh Kirt (Tex) 12411 Honeywood Trl, Houston TX 77077 **Wrld Mssn Bd Dio Texas Houston TX 2009-; R Emm Ch Houston TX 2003-** B Oklahoma City OK 8/24/1945 d Glenn Leland Potts & Lila Elizabeth. BA U of Oklahoma 1967; MDiv Epis TS of The SW 1990. D 6/23/1990 P 2/1/1991 Bp Robert Manning Moody. m 5/28/1994 William Arthur Deceased c 2. Dn W Harris Dio Texas Houston TX 2007-2009; Com for Diac Dio Texas Houston TX 2004-2008; R Emm Epis Ch Shawnee OK 1992-2003; Dioc Coun Dio Oklahoma Oklahoma City OK 1992-1995; Asst R S Mary's Ch Edmond OK 1991-1992; Yth Min/Sch Chapl All SS Epis Ch Austin TX 1990-1991. jkirtmorris@earthlink.net

MORRIS, J. Anthony Grant (Alb) 163 N Pole Rd, Melrose NY 12121 B Mansfield Notts UK 12/28/1924 s Arthur Le Blanc Grant Morris & Alison Emily. BA Harv 1949; BD Harvard DS 1959. D 5/1/1959 Bp Frederic Cunningham Lawrence P 11/1/1959 Bp Conrad Gesner. m 7/9/1949 Sheila Emily Forster. S Paul's Ch Troy NY 1982; S Ptr's Ch Albany NY 1975-1977; R Ch Of The H Cross Troy NY 1960-1972.

MORRIS, John Burnett (SC) 4275 Owens Rd Apt 1140, Evans GA 30809 **Died 12/28/2010** B Brunswick GA 2/10/1930 s Hervey Clark Morris & Annie Burnett. BA Col 1951; BD VTS 1954; Fllshp U of Virginia 1977. D 6/13/1954 Bp Horace W B Donegan P 3/26/1955 Bp Thomas N Carruthers. Auth, "arts," *On The Battle Lines*; Ed, "So Carolinians Spea," *So Carolinians Speak*.

MORRIS, John Charles (Vt) 37 Thompson Rd, East Corinth VT 05040 **R S Mart's Epis Ch Fairlee VT 2002-** B Lincoln NE 5/21/1943 s Robert Earl Morris & Margaret Janice. BA Midland Luth 1965; Bos 1967; STB GTS 1968. D 6/14/1968 P 12/13/1968 Bp Russell T Rauscher. c 3. Int R S Lk's Ch Chester VT 2000-2002; R S Mary's In The Mountains Wilmington VT 1971-2000; Cur The Ch of S Edw The Mtyr New York NY 1968-1971. Auth, *First Comes Love?*, Pilgrim Press, 2007; Auth, "Living by the Word," *Chr Century*; Auth, "essays," *Educational Ldrshp*; Auth, "essays," *Teachers' Journ*. morrisvt@tops-tele.com

MORRIS III, John Glen (Va) 1021 Aquia Dr, Stafford VA 22554 **Asst R Aquia Ch Stafford VA 2004-** B Burlington NC 7/27/1970 BA Wake Forest U. D 6/26/2004 P 1/10/2005 Bp Peter James Lee. assistant@aquiachurch.com

MORRIS, John Karl (NCal) 46 Falcon Crest Circle, Napa CA 94558 **Assoc S Mary's Epis Ch Napa CA 2011-; Assoc S Mary's Epis Ch Napa CA 2011-** B Denver CO 2/27/1939 s Bryce Morris & Grace Rose. U CO; BS USNA 1961; MS MIT 1973; OE MIT 1973; BA California Sch for Deacons 1988; CAS CDSP 2011. D 2/19/1992 Bp Jerry Alban Lamb P 9/8/2011 Bp Barry Leigh Beisner. m 6/15/1961 Patricia Marie Bybee c 4. D S Mary's Epis Ch Napa CA 1994-2011; D H Sprt Epis Ch Houston TX 1993-1994. "Regulatory Consideration in the Design of Teusion Leg Platforms," SPE Journ Soc of Petroleum Egineer, 1988; "Measurement of Low-Wavenumber Components of Turbulout Boundary Layer Wall Pressure Fluctuations," ASA Journ Acoustic Soc of Amer, 1973. jkmorris61@comcast.net

MORRIS, John William (CPa) St. John's Episcopal Church, 321 W. Chestnut St., Lancaster PA 17603 **Archd S Jn's Epis Ch Lancaster PA 2005-** B York PA 2/1/1952 s Elmer Manuel Morris & Nancy Marie. BA Susquahanna U 1974; MDiv EDS 1979. D 6/15/1979 P 2/10/1980 Bp Dean T Stevenson. m 8/24/1974 Cynthia Kay Cromis c 2. R S Thos Epis Ch McLean VA 1988-2005; R S Marg's Epis Ch Baltimore MD 1983-1988; Asst St Martins-In-The-Field Ch Severna Pk MD 1979-1983. holysmoke52@aol.com

MORRIS, Jonathan Edward (USC) 717 Dupre Dr, Spartanburg SC 29307 **R Ch Of The Adv Spartanburg SC 2009-** B Williamsburg VA 9/18/1966 s Harry Arthur Morris & Lillian Susan. BA Roa 1988; MSW Virginia Commonwealth U 1993; MDiv GTS 2001. D 2/23/2001 P 9/14/2001 Bp Frank Neff Powell. m 5/15/1993 Ellen E Oostdyk c 4. R Calv Ch Louisville KY 2004-2009; Assoc R Trin Ch Staunton VA 2001-2004. nedmorris01@gmail.com

MORRIS, Judy Lane (Miss) 1954 Spillway Rd, Brandon MS 39047 **Assoc S Ptr's By The Lake Brandon MS 2011-** B Belden MS 12/23/1945 d Otho Morris & Jewel. BA Memphis St U 1975; MA Memphis St U 1979; MDiv The TS at The U So 2009. D 5/30/2009 Bp Joe Goodwin Burnett P 4/11/2010 Bp Duncan Montgomery Gray Jr. judymorris63@gmail.com

MORRIS, Julie H. (Los) P.O. Box 2305, Camarillo CA 93011 **P The Abundant Table Camarillo CA 2010-** B Fullerton CA 11/11/1970 d John E Morris & Gerlinde H. BA Loyola Marymount U 1992; MA Boston Coll 1994; MDiv Claremont TS 2001. D 6/16/2001 Bp Robert Marshall Anderson P 1/12/2002 Bp Frederick Houk Borsch. m 9/21/1996 Paul DeBusschere c 3. R Trin Par Fillmore CA 2006-2010; Asst S Columba's Par Camarillo CA 2001-2005. juliehmorris@yahoo.com

MORRIS, Kevin Larry (Nwk) 176 Palisade Ave, Jersey City NJ 07306 **Chr Hosp Jersey City NJ 2008-** B Melbourne FL 1/8/1979 s Larry Morris & Sandra. BA U of Miami 2000; MDiv Yale DS 2004. D 4/17/2004 P 11/30/2004 Bp Leopold Frade. Ch Of The Resurr New York NY 2004-2005. kmorris@christhospital.org

MORRIS, Richard Melvin (O) 7 Malcolm St, Norfolk MA 02056 B North Attleboro MA 6/15/1923 s George Henry Morris & Etta May. BA Br 1947; BD EDS 1950. D 5/31/1950 P 12/1/1950 Bp Norman B Nash. m 12/29/1951 Marjorie Miner c 6. Chair of The Stndg Com Dio Ohio Cleveland OH 1988-1989; Chairman of the Dept of CE Dio Ohio Cleveland OH 1985-1988; Chair of the Dept Chr Soc Relatns Dio Ohio Cleveland OH 1971-1985; Chair of the Dept of Chr Soc Relatns Dio Ohio Cleveland OH 1967-1970; Exec Coun Dio Ohio Cleveland OH 1967-1968; R S Ptr's Epis Ch Lakewood OH 1965-1985; Exec Coun Dio Cntrl New York Syracuse NY 1962-1965; R S Thos' Epis Ch Syracuse NY 1952-1965; Asst All SS' Epis Ch Belmont MA 1950-1952. pittphil@verizon.net

MORRIS, Robert Corin Veal (Nwk) 422 Clark, South Orange NJ 07079 **Bp's Chapl to Cler Dio Newark Newark NJ 2009-; Exec Dir Interweave Summit NJ 1981-** B Detroit MI 4/17/1941 s John Franklin Morris & Lorene Wilma. BA Ya 1963; STB GTS 1966. D 6/29/1966 Bp C Kilmer Myers P 1/26/1967 Bp Richard S M Emrich. m 7/26/1969 Suzanne G Bate. COM Dio Newark Newark NJ 2002-2004; Fac, Epis Coll Stdt Gatherings Epis Ch Cntr New York NY 1985-1994; Chr Ed. Asst. The Ch Of The Sav Denville NJ 1985-1988; Asstg P S Bern's Ch Bernardsville NJ 1983-1985; Assoc R Calv Epis Ch Summit NJ 1968-1981; Asstg P S Ptr's Ch Essex Fells NJ 1967-1968. Contrib, "Provocative Gr:," Upper Room Books, 2006; Auth, "Suffering and the Courage of God," Paraclete, 2005; Auth, "Prayers to Green the Earth," Interweave, 2004; Auth, "Wrestling w Gr: A Sprtlty for the Rough Edges," Upper Room Books, 2003; Auth, "Sprtl Formation Bible: Sprtl Exercises for Isaiah," Zondervan/Upper Room, 1999. DD The GTS 2009; Cert of Merit Epis Dio Newark 1993; Phi Beta Kappa Key Phi Beta Kappa 1963. angelhold@earthlink.net

MORRIS, Robert Lee (Fla) 400 San Juan Dr, Ponte Vedra Beach FL 32082 **Assoc Chr Epis Ch Ponte Vedra Bch FL 2004-** B South Charleston WV 3/30/1947 s Lewis Henry Morris & Thursta Mae. BA W Virginia U 1969; MDiv GTS 1973. D 6/7/1973 P 2/24/1974 Bp Wilburn Camrock Campbell. m 8/26/1973 Cathleen Linda Gillis c 2. Assoc S Dunst's Epis Ch Houston TX 1999-2004; Vic All SS Epis Ch Brighton Heights Pittsburgh PA 1994-1999; Asst Chr Epis Ch No Hills Pittsburgh PA 1992-1994; Asst All SS Ch Aliquippa PA 1985-1990; D S Pauls Epis Ch Williamson WV 1973-1974. bobmorris@christepiscopalchurch.org

MORRIS, Stephen B (SwFla) 140 4th St N, St Petersburg FL 33701 B Alexandria LA 5/4/1965 s James Stephen Morris & Dorothy Jean. BBA Loyola U 1988; MDiv Epis TS of The SW 1994. D 10/30/1993 Bp Robert Jefferson Hargrove Jr P 5/1/1994 Bp James Monte Stanton. m 10/6/1989 Jayne L Morris c 4. Cathd Ch Of S Ptr St Petersburg FL 2004-2008; S Jas Epis Ch Ormond Bch FL 2004-2008; S Lk's Ch Salisbury NC 2000-2003; Upper Yellowstone Epis Ch Livingston MT 1999-2000; The Epis Ch Of The Gd Shpd Vidalia LA 1996; Epis Sch Of Dallas Dallas TX 1993-1995. sbm@spcathedral.com

MORRIS, Thomas Rand (Tenn) PO Box 173, Sewanee TN 37375 **S Mary's Sewanee Sewanee TN 2009-** B Lake Charles LA 12/28/1962 s Walter Jackson Morris & Bonnie. BA LSU 1986; MDiv PrTS 1990. D 6/7/1999 Bp Robert Jefferson Hargrove Jr P 2/5/2000 Bp Frank Kellogg Allan. m 4/11/1999 Hadley Simmonds c 1. R S Paul's Ch Wilkesboro NC 2004-2009; R Trin Ch Spruce Pine NC 2001-2004; Assoc R All SS Epis Ch Atlanta GA 1999-2001. thomas.morris@stmaryssewanee.org

MORRIS JR, William Collins (La) 734 Newman Avenue, Jefferson LA 70121 B Cleveland OH 4/27/1936 s William Collins Morris & Janet. BA Duke 1958; BD Epis TS of The SW 1961. D 6/24/1961 P 12/30/1961 Bp Thomas Augustus Fraser Jr. m 6/18/1963 Sarah W Weaver c 2. R All SS Epis Ch River Ridge LA 1971-1998; Stff S Ptr's Ch Oxford MS 1966-1968; Vic S Alb's Ch Davidson NC 1962-1966. Auth, "Avoiding the Dangers of a Monumental Ch, A New Conversation," Ch Pub Inc, 1999. ECom; LA Epis Cleric Assn. Hal Brook Perry Awd Epis TS of the SW 2000. wcmj1234@gmail.com

MORRIS-KLIMENT, Nicholas McClure (Mass) 44 Seminole Rd, Acton MA 01720 **Asst Trin Ch Concord MA 2004-** B Philadelphia PA 6/7/1963 s Robert Michael Kliment & Janet Drury. BA Ya 1985; MA Br 1988; ABD Br 1990; MDiv Ya Berk 2001. D 6/15/2002 P 5/31/2003 Bp M(arvil) Thomas Shaw III. m 12/20/1997 Jameson Lynn Morris-Kliment c 2. Asst S Ptr's Ch Weston MA 2002-2004. nmorriskliment@yahoo.com

MORRISON, Enid Ann (Ind) 8320 E. 10th St., Indianapolis IN 46219 **D S Matt's Ch Indianapolis IN 2008-** B London England 7/16/1937 d Frederick Charles Morrison & Enid. AGS Indiana U-Pur-Indianapolis 1985; BGS Indiana U-Pur 1987; MTS Chr TS Indianapolis IN 1997. D 10/26/2008 Bp Catherine Elizabeth Maples Waynick. c 2. NAAD 2006. deacon@stmattsindy.org

MORRISON, Gordon Lee (Eas) 7035 Pine Ridge Road, Easton MD 21601 **R S Paul's Ch Trappe MD 2009-** B Princeton IN 3/16/1940 s Leland Maxam Morrison & Ruth Alene. BA Indiana U 1961; MS Indiana U 1971; MDiv TS 1984; Spec Stds McGill U 1997. D 6/16/1984 Bp Quintin Ebenezer Primo Jr P 12/18/1984 Bp Furman Stough. m 10/29/1966 Lynda Sanderford c 2. Int S Ptr's Ch Salisbury MD 2008-2009; Asst Chr Ch S Ptr's Par Easton MD 2005-2008; R S Paul's Ch Henderson KY 1995-2005; Int S Jn's Epis Ch Odessa TX 1993-1995; R S Paul's Ch Selma AL 1987-1993; Chair of the Dept of Wrld Missions Dio Alabama Birmingham AL 1987-1992; R S Steph's Ch Eutaw AL 1984-1987. "A View from the Other Side, Pstr Care in a Damascus Hosp," *The Journ of Pstr Care and Counslg*, 2005; "Fiji - Interfaith Challenge," *Zion's Herazld*, 2005. Cmnty of S Mary 1983; Int Mnstrs Ntwk 1994. Interfaith Prchr's Gown Kuftaro Inst, Damascus, SY 2009; DuBose Awd for Serv TS, Univ. of the So, Sewanee, TN 2005; Cler Renwl Grant, Where Islam and Chrsnty Interface Ar Lilly Endwmt, Inc. 2004. episcopalgordon@hotmail.com

MORRISON JR, Henry T (Nick) (Az) Po Box 610, Ketchum ID 83340 B Mount Pleasant NY 12/21/1939 s Henry Terry Morrison & Mary Peavey. BA U MN 1963; Pedi Imede Lausanne Ch 1971; MA Yale DS 1980. D 6/24/1982 Bp Robert Marshall Anderson P 3/1/1983 Bp David Bell Birney IV. m 3/10/1979 Karen Anne Nelson c 6. Asstg Chr Ch Of The Ascen Paradise Vlly AZ 1993-1998; Asst Ch Of The Epiph Epis Plymouth MN 1986-1991; R Emm Ch Hailey ID 1983-1984; R S Thos Epis Ch Sun Vlly ID 1983-1984. Auth, "Intercept". Knights Of Malta (Ord S Jn Jerusalem). htnickmorrison@aol.com

MORRISON, John Ainslie (SO) Calvary Episcopal Church, 3766 Clifton Ave, Cincinnati OH 45220 B Cincinnati OH 12/3/1939 s Marion Edwin Morrison & Mary Ainslie. BA U Cinc 1962; BD EDS 1965; MA U Cinc 1971; PhD U Cinc 1977. D 9/25/1965 P 3/27/1966 Bp Roger W Blanchard. m 8/17/1963 Patricia Morrison. Vol Assoc R Calv Ch Cincinnati OH 1998-2008; P-in-c S Steph's Epis Ch Cincinnati OH 1987-1991; H Sprt Epis Ch Cincinnati OH 1975-1976; Asst Min Chr Ch - Glendale Cincinnati OH 1965-1968. Auth, "Var arts & Chapters On Med & Epidemiology". john.morrison@cchmc.org

MORRISON III, John E (LI) 510 Manatuck Blvd, Brightwaters NY 11718 **Int S Jn's Ch Huntington NY 2007-; Asst S Ptr's by-the-Sea Epis Ch Bay Shore NY 1999-** B New York NY 9/21/1941 s John Emerson Morrison & Constance Ruth. BA Dart 1963; Med Hofstra U 1968; MLS SUNY 1973; CTh Mercer TS 1980. D 6/7/1980 Bp Robert Campbell Witcher Sr P 5/15/1982 Bp Henry Boyd Hucles III. m 6/5/1965 Susan Morrison. Geo Mercer TS Garden City NY 1994-2000; Asst Gr Epis Ch Massapequa NY 1980-1999. Auth, "Idea Of Cov In Narnia"; Auth, "God Means What He Says: Cs Lewis On Forgiveness"; Auth, "Bulletin Of Ny Cs Lewis Soc"; Auth, "A Pleasure Is Full Growth Only When It'S Remembered". frlion@aol.com

MORRISON, Karl Frederick (NJ) 75 Linwood Circle, Princeton NJ 08540 B Birmingham AL 11/3/1936 s Karl Morrison & Margaret Gladys. BA U of Mississippi 1956; MA Cor 1957; PhD Cor 1961. D 5/9/1998 P 4/10/1999 Bp Joe Morris Doss. m 8/29/1964 Anne Caroline Blunt c 2. P-in-c The Epis Campus Mnstry at Rutgers New Brunswick NJ 2003; D Chr Ch New Brunswick NJ 1998-2003. Co-Ed, "Empathy in the Middle Ages," Brepols, 2012; Co-Ed, "Seeing the Invisible," Brepols, 2005; Auth, "Understanding Conversion," U of Virginia Press, 1992; Auth, "Conversion and Text," U of Virginia Press, 1992; Auth, "Hist as a Visual Art," Pr Press, 1990; Auth, "I am You," Pr Press, 1988; Auth, "The Mimetic Tradition of Reform," Pr Press, 1982; Auth, "Europe's Middle Ages," Scott, Foresman, 1970; Auth, "Tradition and Authority," Pr Press, 1969; Auth, "Carolingian Coinage," Amer Numismatic Soc, 1967; Auth, "The Two Kingdoms," Pr Press, 1964; Auth, "Rome and the City of God," Amer Philos Soc, 1964; Co-Transltr, "Imperial Lives and Letters," Col Press, 1962. Amer Cath Hist Soc 1970; Amer Hist Assn 1965; Amer Soc of Ch Hist 1970; Medieval Acad of Amer 1960; Soc of Biblic Theologians 1999. Vstng Mem Inst for Advncd Study 2004; Carey Sr Fac Fell U of Notre Dame 2001; Haskins Medal Medieval Acad of Amer 1994; Fell Medieval Acad of Amer 1986. ankamor@verizon.net

MORRISON, Larry Clair (NJ) PO Box 100, Front Royal VA 22630 B West Buffalo Township PA 10/23/1940 s Robert Carl Morrison & Helen Annabelle. BA Pr 1970; MDiv Westminster TS 1975. D 6/5/1982 P 10/1/1982 Bp Albert Wiencke Van Duzer. m 12/22/1972 Priscilla Jane Knox c 1. P-in-c S Jn The Evang Ch Blackwood NJ 1997-1999; Supply P S Jn's Epis Ch Maple Shade NJ 1996-1997; Vic Ch Of S Jn-In-The-Wilderness Gibbsboro NJ 1984-1992; Cur Trin Cathd Trenton NJ 1982-1984. oatmeal@shentel.net

MORRISON, Leroy Oran (NwT) 6535 Amber Dr, Odessa TX 79762 B Sharon PA 4/23/1953 s Oran Jacob Morrison & Ruth Elizabeth. AA Penn 1992. D 5/24/1998 Bp Robert Deane Rowley Jr. m 4/25/1975 Kathy Sue DeHoff c 2.

MORRISON, Mary K (ECR) PO Box 1160, Los Gatos CA 95031 **R S Jas Ch Paso Robles CA 2002-** B Sacramento CA 12/26/1946 d Robert Morrison & Janet Duncan. BA U CA 1969; Cert U CA 1970; BA Sch for Deacons 1985; MDiv CDSP 2000. D 6/24/2000 P 4/26/2001 Bp Richard Lester Shimpfky. m 7/15/2008 Claudia Jo Weber c 2. Pstr Assoc S Lk's Ch Los Gatos CA 2002-2008; Prog Dir CDSP Berkeley CA 2000-2002; Asstg Cler S Lk's Ch Los Gatos CA 2000-2002. mkmorrison1@me.com

MORRISON, Mikel Anne (Oly) 760 Kristen Ct, Santa Barbara CA 93111 **D S Andr's Epis Ch Ojai CA 2000-; D S Mich's U Mssn Island Isla Vista CA 1992-** B Cleveland OH 5/28/1941 d Stephen Ralph Kranek & Ethel Mae. BA Coll of Wooster 1962; MS U IL 1964; Oxf 1989; MA Fuller TS 1990. D 6/27/1992 Bp Chester Lovelle Talton. m 6/10/1964 Rollin John Morrison c 2. NAAD. revmikel@silcom.com

MORRISON, Paul Charles (NC) 77 W Coolidge St #227, Phoenix AZ 85013 B Conneaut OH 4/6/1933 s Paul N Sabo & Mary Blanch. BA Case Wstrn Reserve U 1955; MDiv Bex 1964; ThM Duke 1971. D 6/13/1964 Bp Nelson Marigold Burroughs P 1/1/1965 Bp Robert Lionne DeWitt. m 6/15/1957 Marlene R McKensie c 4. R S Jos's Ch Durham NC 1968-1975; R Chr Ch Albemarle NC 1966-1968; Cur S Mk's Ch Philadelphia PA 1964-1966. azpmorri@gmail.com

MORRISON, Pauline Ruth (Ore) St John's Episcopal Church, PO Box 332, Toledo OR 97391 **S Jn's Epis Ch Toledo OR 2007-** B Santa Ana CA 12/15/1950 d Paul Wickham Randall & Anita May. AS Judson Bapt Coll Portland OR 1971; Portland St U 1976; Oregon Cntr for the Diac 2004. D 9/18/2004 Bp Johncy Itty. m 5/26/1979 Robert Paterson Morrison c 2. monnshadowducky@yahoo.com

MORRISON, Richard Neely (Az) 720 West Elliot Road, Gilbert AZ 85233 B Mesa AZ 6/4/1947 s Marvin Richard Morrison & Eunice June. BS Nthrn Arizona U 1970; JD U of Houston 1977; MA SFTS 1991. D 2/8/1997 P 6/28/2003 Bp Robert Reed Shahan. m 12/8/1973 Elaine Morrison c 2. Ch Of The Epiph Flagstaff AZ 2003-2005; D S Matt's Ch Chandler AZ 2000-2003; D Ch Of The Epiph Tempe AZ 1997-2000. Distinguished Achievement Arizona St U 1989. rnmorrison@msn.com

MORRISON JR, Robert Dabney (EC) 119 Briarwood St., Lynchburg VA 24503 B Lynchburg VA 10/1/1941 s Robert Dabney Morrison & Margaret West. BS Davidson Coll 1963; MDiv VTS 1971. D 6/4/1971 P 12/9/1971 Bp William Henry Marmion. m 8/9/1969 Julia R Read c 2. R S Jn's Epis Ch Wilmington NC 2000-2007; R S Mths Epis Ch Midlothian VA 1979-2000; R S Jas Ch Roanoke VA 1974-1979; S Mary's Ch Wayne PA 1971-1974; Asst S Dav's Ch Wayne PA 1971-1973. bobmorrison63@gmail.com

MORRISON, Robert Paterson (Ore) Po Box 789, Lincoln City OR 97367 B Kilmaurs Scotland GB 2/27/1944 s Robert Morrison & Edith Patricia. Duquesne U; DD U Of Edinburgh Edinburgh Gb 1969; STM Drew U 1970; BA Portland St U 1976. D 6/28/1983 P 6/1/1984 Bp Matthew Paul Bigliardi. m 5/26/1979 Pauline Ruth Morrison c 4. S Jas Ch Lincoln City OR 2000-2010; Vic S Jas Ch Lincoln City OR 1987-1991; Asst Trin Epis Cathd Portland OR 1984-1987; Legacy Gd Samar Hosp Portland OR 1983-1984. Fllshp S Alb & S Sergius. robertpmorrison@charterinternet.com

MORRISON, Samuel Warfield (FdL) 101 S Wythe St, Pentwater MI 49449 **R S Jas' Epis Ch Of Pentwater Pentwater MI 2007-** B Iowa City IA 2/4/1951 s William Frisbie Morrison & Elizabeth Jane. BS Wstrn Michigan U 1972; MA SWTS 1975. D 6/2/1975 P 6/2/1976 Bp Charles Bennison. m 7/8/1972 Jane M Gustafson c 3. Vic S Paul's Ch Plymouth WI 1996-2007; Vic St Bon Ch Hilbert WI 1996-2004; R S Aid's Ch Michigan Cntr MI 1986-1996; Vic S Paul's Ch Greenville MI 1978-1986; Cur S Lk's Par Kalamazoo MI 1978; R S

Ptr's By-The-Lake Ch Montague MI 1976-1977; D S Dav's Ch Lansing MI 1975-1976. Cler Assn; Curs; Ord of S Lk. sampentwater@frontier.com

MORRISON-CLEARY, Douglas Vaughn (Minn) No address on file. **S Paul's Ch Virginia MN 2007-** B Newcastle Australia 3/8/1965 s James E R Cleary & Lurline L. D 6/8/2006 P 12/21/2006 Bp James Louis Jelinek. m 10/5/1991 Jennifer Morrison-Cleary c 2. Cong of the Gd Shpd Keewatin MN 2007-2009. doug.mc@stjames.hibbing.mn.us

MORRIS-RADER, Patricia (Ore) 8045 Sw 56th Ave, Portland OR 97219 **D Gr Epis Ch Astoria OR 2007-; D S Jn The Evang Ch Milwaukie OR 2007-** B Brementon WA 12/6/1939 d George M Thomas & Liela M. BA Linfield Coll 1963; MS OR SU 1978. D 9/29/2001 Bp Robert Louis Ladehoff. m 6/8/2002 Donald D Rader c 2. D Epis Par Of S Jn The Bapt Portland OR 2001-2006.

MORRISS, Jerry Davis (Dal) 132 Baywood Blvd, Mabank TX 75156 **R S Jas' Epis Ch Kemp TX 2003-** B Matador TX 8/29/1941 s Malcolm D Morriss & Eunice C. Baylor U 1961; U of No Texas 1967; BA Sch for Deacons 1991. D 12/7/1991 Bp William Edwin Swing P 2/15/2003 Bp James Monte Stanton. m 12/29/1961 Carroll Reeves. Archd Dio Dallas Dallas TX 2001-2002; D S Clem's Ch Berkeley CA 2001-2002; D S Jas' Epis Ch Kemp TX 1994-2002; D H Cross Epis Ch Castro Vlly CA 1992-1994; S Clem's Ch Berkeley CA 1991-1992. Amer Assn Chr Counslrs. revjerrymorriss@aol.com

MORRISSETTE, Paul E (WMass) 14 Enaya Circle, Worcester MA 01606 B Berlin NH 12/9/1930 s Henry Morrissette & Lumina. BA S Mary's Sem Baltimore MD 1952; St.Mary's Sem, Baltimore, MD 1957; Masters of Educ Rivier Coll 1970; C. A.G.S. Univ. of NH 1973; D. Min. Boston Univ. 1976. Rec from Roman Catholic 12/16/1987 as Priest Bp Andrew Frederick Wissemann. m 11/20/1983 Judith Ann Morrissette. Supply Chr Ch So Barre MA 2005-2007; P-in-c Chr Memi Ch No Brookfield MA 1996-2000; Int S Matt's Ch Worcester MA 1991-1993; Int H Trin Epis Ch Southbridge MA 1989-1990; Dio Wstrn Massachusetts Springfield MA 1988-1989. Auth, "The Relatedness and their Contributions to Counslg," *AMHC Forum*, The Assn of Mntl Hlth Chapl, 1975; Auth, "The Role Functions of Chapl At New Hampshire Hosp," *AMHC Forum*, The Assn of Mntl Hlth Cler, Inc., 1975; Auth, "Taking a Second Look at Psych Treatment: Ther Is Not Enough," *Hosp and Cmnty Psychiaty*, 1975; Auth, "A study of Rel Values: Psych Patients Are Compared To Non- Patietnts," *AMHC Forum*, The Assn pf Mntl Hlth Chapl, 1974; Auth, "CPE For Sis," *The Camillian*, NACC, XII, 1974; Auth, "Three Chapl Models," *AMHC News Letters*, 1973. AAPC; Massachusets Lic Clincl Psychol; Massachusetts Psychol Assn 1995. pmjm2@hotmail.com

MORRISSEY, Mike (Oly) 1120 Heron Ridge Ave, Port Orchard WA 98366 **VP Mssn to Seafarers Seattle WA 2011-; Bd Mem Mssn to Seafarers Seattle WA 2009-; Vic St Bede Epis Ch Port Orchard WA 2003-** B Glasgow MT 4/13/1946 s John Elmer Morrissey & Patricia Jean. BS OR SU 1968; MDiv TESM 1992; DMin TESM 2009. D 6/13/1992 Bp James Barrow Brown P 12/19/1992 Bp Charles Jones III. m 12/9/1973 Penny M Irwin c 1. Evang Com Dio Olympia Seattle WA 2006-2009; P-in-c Calv Epis Ch Red Lodge MT 1997-2003; P-in-c Our Sav Epis Joliet MT 1997-2003; P-in-c S Alb's Epis Ch Laurel MT 1997-2003; P-in-c S Paul's of the Stillwater Ch Absarokee MT 1997-2003; Chair, Stwdshp Com Dio Montana Helena MT 1995-1996; Coun Dio Montana Helena MT 1994-1997; Fin Com Dio Montana Helena MT 1992-2003; R S Pat's Epis Ch Bigfork MT 1992-1996. Bp's Soc, Dio Olympia 2004; BroSA 2007. skypilot1992@gmail.com

MORROW, Daniel R (Los) 202 Avenida Aragon, San Clemente CA 92672 **S Paul's Par Oregon City OR 2011-; Yth Dir S Jn's Mssn La Verne CA 2004-** B Henryetta OK 9/24/1977 s David Michael Morrow & Deborah Kay. BA Oklahoma Bapt U 2001; MDiv Claremont TS 2006. D 6/9/2007 P 1/12/2008 Bp Joseph Jon Bruno. m 12/30/2000 Jenell Rae Bradley. S Clem's-By-The-Sea Par San Clemente CA 2007-2008. revdanmorrow@gmail.com

MORROW JR, Harold Frederick (CPa) 2453 Harrisburg Pike, Lancaster PA 17601 **Disaster Response Cmsn Dio Cntrl Pennsylvania Harrisburg PA 2010-; D S Edw's Epis Ch Lancaster PA 2010-; Cmsn on Liturg and Mus Dio Cntrl Pennsylvania Harrisburg PA 2008-** B Columbia PA 10/13/1952 s Harold Frederick Morrow & Lillian M. Sch of Chr Stds 2010. D 10/31/2010 Bp Nathan Dwight Baxter. m 9/23/1972 Deborah J Boyer c 3. Assn for Epis Deacons 2010. deaconhank@gmail.com

MORROW, Jerry Dean (Mass) 89 Msgr Patrick J Lydon Way, Dorchester MA 02124 **R S Jn's Ch Sharon MA 1983-** B Macomb IL 4/7/1944 s Harold Q Morrow & Vera R. BA MacMurray Coll 1966; SMM UTS 1968; MDiv UTS 1971; Bos 1976. D 6/5/1971 P 12/18/1971 Bp Horace W B Donegan. m 7/28/1984 Joyce Elaine Hempstead c 3. T/F on Catechumate Dio Massachusetts Boston MA 1993-1997; Chair, Mus Cmsn Dio Massachusetts Boston MA 1985-1989; Liturg Cmsn Dio Massachusetts Boston MA 1982-1989; Liturg Cmsn Dio Massachusetts Boston MA 1982-1989; Coordntr YA Netwk Dio Massachusetts Boston MA 1980-1982; P-in-c S Matt And The Redeem Epis Ch So Boston MA 1980-1982; Mssnr All SS Par Brookline MA 1979-1981; P-in-c S Lk's And S Marg's Ch Allston MA 1977-1979; Asst Zion Ch Douglaston NY 1971-1972. Associated Parishes 1984; ADLMC 1984-2002; Soc of Cath Priests 2009. jdm@bu.edu

MORROW, John Thomas (NJ) Po Box 424, Pine Beach NJ 08741 B Philadelphia PA 10/10/1934 s Lester Martin Robinson & Lillie Roberts. BA U So 1957; STB PDS 1960. D 4/30/1960 P 11/1/1960 Bp Alfred L Banyard. m 6/21/1958 Marilyn Divan c 3. R S Lk's Ch Gladstone NJ 1965-1996; R S Geo's Epis Ch Helmetta NJ 1962-1965; Cur Gr Ch Merchantville NJ 1960-1962. Cmnty Of S Jn The Bapt. Hon Cn Trin Cathd Trenton NJ. jtmorrow2@comcast.net

MORROW, Quintin Gregory (FtW) 917 Lamar St, Fort Worth TX 76102 B Yuma AZ 12/28/1963 s Richard Allen Marrow & Billie Joyce. BA Chr Heritage Coll 1991; MDiv TESM 1994. D 6/11/1994 P 2/24/1995 Bp Gethin Benwil Hughes. m 1/12/1991 Kathryn Nonnemacher c 2. S Andr's Ft Worth TX 2001-2005; R S Anne's Epis Ch Oceanside CA 1995-2001; Cur S Barth's Epis Ch Poway CA 1994-1995. stannes@pacbell.net

MORSCH, Joel (SwFla) 1903 - 85th Court NW, Bradenton FL 34209 **Dioc Endwmt Bd Dio SW Florida Sarasota FL 2011-; Dioc Fin Com Dio SW Florida Sarasota FL 2010-; Dioc Coun Dio SW Florida Sarasota FL 2007-; R Chr Ch Bradenton FL 2006-; Bd Mem S Steph's Epis Sch Bradenton FL 2006-** B Aurora IL 10/21/1950 s Byron James Morsch & Betty Joan. BA U of Wisconsin 1972; MDiv Nash 1998. D 12/8/1997 P 7/5/1998 Bp Keith Lynn Ackerman. m 1/11/1992 Barbara Bell c 3. Stndg Com Dio Tennessee Nashville TN 2005-2006; R The Epis Ch Of The Resurr Franklin TN 2002-2006; Assoc R S Jn's Epis Ch Naperville IL 1998-2002. joelmorsch@gmail.com

MORSE, Alice Janette (Mich) 11 W 3rd St, Monroe MI 48161 **R Trin Epis Ch Monroe MI 2003-** B Howell MI 6/18/1947 d Walter Suter & Ellamae. BA Estrn Michigan U 1971; MDiv Nash 1986. D 6/30/1987 Bp Henry Irving Mayson P 8/1/1993 Bp Roger John White. c 3. S Paul's Ch Milwaukee WI 1999-2003; P-in-c S Andr's Ch Kenosha WI 1994-1997. ALICEJMORSE@YAHOO.COM

MORSE, Davidson Rogan (FtW) 2916 Caprock Ct, Grapevine TX 76051 B Macon GA 7/10/1970 BA Mississippi St U. D 3/22/2003 P 9/30/2003 Bp Jack Leo Iker. m 7/30/1994 Amy Carolyn Morse c 4. Assoc R S Andr's Ft Worth TX 2006-2009; Cur S Laurence Epis Ch Grapevine TX 2003-2006. MORSEAMY@ATT.NET

MORSE, Elizabeth Bovelle (Los) 661 NW Kersey Dr, Dallas OR 97338 B Portland OR 3/9/1954 d William Bovelle Morse & Jean Patrica. Montana St U 1973; BS OR SU 1976; MDiv CDSP 1988. D 6/24/1988 Bp Charles Shannon Mallory P 1/1/1989 Bp Donald Purple Hart. R S Mich The Archangel Par El Segundo CA 2004-2011; Seamens Ch Inst Of Los Angeles San Pedro CA 2003-2004; S Thos Of Cbury Par Long Bch CA 2000-2002; Seamens Ch Inst Of Los Angeles San Pedro CA 1999-2002; S Cross By-The-Sea Ch Hermosa Bch CA 1997-1999; S Fran' Par Palos Verdes Estates CA 1992-1994; S Ptr's Par San Pedro CA 1991; Epis Ch On W Kaua'i Eleele HI 1989-1991; Vic S Jn's Ch Eleele HI 1989-1991; Asst Ch Of Our Sav Mill Vlly CA 1988-1989. revebm@gmail.com

MORTON, James Parks (NY) 285 Riverside Dr Apt 13-B, New York NY 10025 B Houston TX 1/7/1930 s Vance Mulock Morton & Virginia May. BA Harv 1951; BA U of Cambridge 1953; STB GTS 1954; MA U of Cambridge 1959; DD The New Sem 1985; DD Pratt Inst 1992; DD GTS 1996. D 6/12/1954 P 12/18/1954 Bp Horace W B Donegan. m 12/30/1954 Pamela Taylor c 4. Dn Cathd Of St Jn The Div New York NY 1972-1997; Assoc P in charge Gr Ch Van Vorst Jersey City NJ 1954-1962. Auth, "Lightworks: Explorations in Art," *Culture & Creativity*; Auth, "Intro," *Emergence: Rebirth of Sacr*; Auth, "Haut Liex: An Appreciation of Rene Dubus," *Orion*. Lindisfarne Assn; Ord of S Jn-Jerusalem. Distinguished Medal Barnard Coll 1987; Jn Phillips Awd Phillips-Exeter Acad 1985. deanjpmorton@interfaithcenter.org

MORTON, John Andrew (WNC) Po Box 185, Flat Rock NC 28731 **R Ch Of S Jn In The Wilderness Flat Rock NC 1999-** B Lancaster SC 7/20/1947 s Turner Harrison Morton & Mary Evelyn. BA Wofford Coll 1969; JD U of So Carolina 1974; LLM GW 1985; MDiv VTS 1994. D 6/5/1994 P 12/14/1994 Bp Robert Hodges Johnson. m 5/21/1992 Paula Karen Clegg c 2. Assoc S Jn's Epis Ch Chula Vista CA 1997-1999; S Phil's Ch Brevard NC 1994-1997. frjam@bellsouth.net

MORTON SR, Kell (Pa) 501 Upland St, Pottstown PA 19464 **P-in-c S Jn's Ch Norristown PA 2006-** B Toledo OH 11/8/1947 s Raymond Lipe Morton & Betty Lou. BS U of Toledo 1972; MDiv Nash 1978. D 6/24/1978 P 12/1/1978 Bp William Hampton Brady. m 6/6/1972 Constance Ann Crowley c 2. R Chr Epis Ch Pottstown PA 1991-2005; R Gr Ch Riverhead NY 1984-1991; Dioc Dir Liturg Com Dio Fond du Lac Appleton WI 1982-1984; Dio Fond du Lac Appleton WI 1980-1984; St Ambr Epis Ch Antigo WI 1980-1984; Vic S Barn Epis Ch Tomahawk WI 1980-1981; Cur Trin Epis Ch Oshkosh WI 1978-1980. CBS; SocMary; SocOLW; Soc Of The H Nativ. kellmorton@comcast.net

MORTON, Paula Karen Clegg (WNC) 901 Big Raven Ln, Saluda NC 28773 **R Ch Of The Trsfg Saluda NC 2002-** B Burlington NC 11/29/1960 d Robert Lawrence Clegg & Elois. BA Wstrn Carolina U 1986; MDiv VTS 1994. D 6/5/

1994 P 12/7/1994 Bp Robert Hodges Johnson. m 5/21/1992 John Andrew Morton. Spec Mobilization Spprt Plan Washington DC 2010-2011; Pension Fund Mltry New York NY 2005-2006; Gr Ch Morganton NC 2000-2001; Off Of Bsh For ArmdF New York NY 1996-1999; Cur Calv Epis Ch Fletcher NC 1994-1996. mothermorton2003@yahoo.com

MORTON, William Paul (EO) 1025 NE Paula Dr, Bend OR 97701 **Stndg Com & Dioc Coun Dio Estrn Oregon The Dalles OR 2009-2012** B Philadelphia PA 5/14/1945 s William Irwin Morton & Dorothy Grace. BA Dickinson Coll 1967; MDiv Ya Berk 1970; STM Ya Berk 1971. D 6/16/1970 P 4/1/1971 Bp Robert Lionne DeWitt. m 8/9/1969 Katharine Dresch Langham. Missional P Epis Ch Of The Trsfg Sis OR 2011; Missional P Dio Estrn Oregon The Dalles OR 2010-2011. Rotary 1998. wpm1025@bandbroadband.com

MORTON III, Woolridge Brown (Va) Po Box 158, Waterford VA 20197 **P Assoc Gr Ch The Plains VA 1996-** B Charlottesville VA 1/7/1938 s Woolridge Brown Morton & Louisa. BA U of Virginia 1961; Ministere Des Affaires Culturelles Paris Fr 1966. D 6/2/1974 Bp Edmond Lee Browning P 12/1/1974 Bp Albert Ervine Swift. m 6/26/1965 Margaret Anita Templeton. Asst R Trin Ch Fredericksburg VA 1977-1991; Assoc R S Ptr's Epis Ch Purcellville VA 1976-1986. Auth, "A Call For Bold Ldrshp," *Seaching For Sacr Space*, Ch Pub Co., 2002. Honary Mem Amer Inst Of Architects 1993; Fell Us/Icoms 1990. brownmorton@aol.com

MOSCOSO, Servio Rhadames (Tex) 38 W End Pl, Elizabeth NJ 07202 **Vic Gr Epis Ch Eliz NJ 1996-** B San Pedro Macoris DO 3/20/1950 s Servio Tulio Moscoso & Julia. BD U Of Santo Domingo Santo Domingo Do 1974; MDiv S Andrews TS Mex City Mx 1979. D 10/7/1979 P 12/14/1980 Bp Telesforo A Isaac. m 8/31/1975 Angela Gonzalez c 3. Dio Texas Houston TX 2009-2011; San Jose Epis Ch Eliz NJ 1986-2009; Gr Epis Ch Eliz NJ 1985; Vic Iglesia Epis Cristo el Rey San Felipe de Puerto Plat DO 1981-1985; Vic Dio The Dominican Republic (Iglesia Epis Dominicana) 100 Airport AvVenice FL 1979-1985; Iglesia Epis San Marcos Haitiana 1979-1981. Auth, "Religiosidad Paopular Dominicana," 1979. OHC 1979. smoscoso@msn.com

MOSER, Albert E (Alb) 133 Saratoga Rd Apt. 109-8, Glenville NY 12302 **D Chr Epis Ch Ballston Spa NY 1998-** B Reading PA 9/2/1928 s Paul Jones Moser & Helen Susan. BS Lebanon Vlly Coll 1953; MS SUNY 1959. D 10/16/1965 Bp Allen Webster Brown. m 11/23/1950 Mary Jane Wentzel c 3. S Andr's Ch Scotia NY 1965-1998. Scotia-Glenville Lions Serv Club 1954. Melvin Jones Fell Lions Intl 1985. aemjm50@juno.com

MOSER, Frederick Perkins (Mass) 138 W Plain St, Wayland MA 01778 **Coordntr of Dioc Ecum and Interreligious Off Epis Prov Of New Engl Dorset VT 2009-; Admin, Cler Cont Educ Fund Dio Massachusetts Boston MA 2006-; Dir, Bd Dir, Massachusetts Coun of Ch Dio Massachusetts Boston MA 2006-; Ecum Off Dio Massachusetts Boston MA 2006-; Natl Workshop on Chr Unity, Rep Dio Massachusetts Boston MA 2006-; R Ch Of The H Sprt Wayland MA 1994-** B Middletown CT 4/8/1953 s Theodore Pomeroy Moser & Beatrice Johanna. BA Connecticut Coll 1975; MDiv Yale DS 1979; DMin EDS 2004. D 6/13/1981 Bp Arthur Edward Walmsley P 2/13/1982 Bp William Bradford Hastings. m 5/28/1988 Kim Hardy c 2. Dio Jerusalem Relatns Grp Dio Massachusetts Boston MA 2009-2011; Cler Conf Design Grp Dio Massachusetts Boston MA 2000-2003; COM Dio Massachusetts Boston MA 1995-1997; COM Dio Rochester Rochester NY 1987-1994; Chapl Hobart And Wm Smith Colleges Geneva NY 1984-1994; Assoc R S Mary's Epis Ch Manchester CT 1981-1984. fpmoser@aol.com

MOSER, Gerard Stoughton (Eur) 15 Hoopoe Ave., Camps Bay, Cape Town 8005 South Africa B Knoxville TN 4/28/1938 s Arthur Hurst Moser & Sara. BA U So 1960; MDiv GTS 1964. D 6/30/1964 Bp William Evan Sanders P 5/1/1965 Bp John Vander Horst. m 7/10/1992 Carole Hambleton c 2. R Emm Epis Ch Geneva 1201 CH 1976-2000; Asst Min S Paul's Ch Rochester NY 1968-1973; Vic S Mary Magd Ch Fayetteville TN 1966-1967; Cur Gr - S Lk's Ch Memphis TN 1964-1966. jmoser@worldonline.co.za

MOSER, Paul Henry (Md) 16 E Broadway, Bel Air MD 21014 B Ossining NY 10/21/1938 s Henry Merritt Moser & Mary Naomi. BA W Virginia Wesleyan Coll 1960; BD Bex 1963; Ldrshp Acad for New Directions 1975. D 6/5/1963 P 12/1/1963 Bp Wilburn Camrock Campbell. m 5/1/1965 Christine W Woods c 1. Dio W Virginia Charleston WV 1983-2009; Prog Com Dio Maryland Baltimore MD 1979-1984; Com On Human Needs Dio Maryland Baltimore MD 1979-1980; Co-Chair Of The VIM Dio Maryland Baltimore MD 1978-2009; Dioc Coun Dio Maryland Baltimore MD 1978-1984; Plnng Cmsn Dio Maryland Baltimore MD 1978-1982; R Emm Ch Bel Air MD 1977-2008; Stndg Com Dio W Virginia Charleston WV 1973-1974; RurD Dio W Virginia Charleston WV 1972-1976; Exec Coun Dio W Virginia Charleston WV 1970-1972; Vic Trin Ch Shepherdstown WV 1969-1977; R Chr Memi Ch Williamstown WV 1965-1969; Vic Gr Ch S Marys WV 1965-1969; Asst S Matt's Ch Wheeling WV 1963-1965. fasamosa@comcast.net

MOSES, Donald Harwood (Kan) 2201 Sw 30th St, Topeka KS 66611 B Fort Wayne IN 11/26/1933 s Horace Smith Moses & Harriet Harwood. BS K SU 1956; BD Nash 1968; U of Wisconsin 1974; Int Mnstry Prog 1997. D 3/8/1968 Bp Edward Randolph Welles II P 9/28/1968 Bp Robert Rae Spears Jr. m 9/9/1956 Shirley R Garrison c 3. Int S Paul's Ch Manhattan KS 2001-2002; Int S Lk's Ch Wamego KS 1998-2000; Int S Ptr's Ch Pittsburg KS 1996-1997; Brewster Place (The Congrl Hm) Topeka KS 1992-1993; S Dav's Epis Ch Topeka KS 1989; Vic S Paul's Ch Claremore OK 1982-1986; Coun on Mssns Dio Oklahoma Oklahoma City OK 1982-1985; Yth Div Educ conf Dio W Missouri Kansas City MO 1979-1981; R S Ptr's Ch Harrisonville MO 1978-1982; R S Fran Ch Menomonee Falls WI 1971-1978; Coll Wk Chair Dio Milwaukee Milwaukee WI 1971-1975; Vic Trin Epis Ch Mineral Point WI 1969-1971; Vic Trin Epis Ch Platteville WI 1969-1971; Cur Ch Of The Gd Shpd Kansas City MO 1968-1969. RWF 1968; Soc of S Jn the Evang 1966. dsmoses33@yahoo.com

MOSES, George David (WVa) 20 Alexander Drive, Morgantown WV 26508 **Morgantown Pstr Counslg Cntr Inc Morgantown WV 1988-** B Charleston WV 10/8/1947 s Richard Moses & Lorise. BS W Virginia U 1970; MDiv GTS 1973; MA W Virginia U 1983; EdD W Virginia U 1990. D 6/7/1973 P 2/1/1974 Bp Wilburn Camrock Campbell. m 2/9/1975 Holly Christine Carhahan c 2. Dio W Virginia Charleston WV 1984-1988; Dioc Coun Dio W Virginia Charleston WV 1980-1982; Vic S Barn Bridgeport WV 1978-1982; Int Gr Ch Ravenswood WV 1977-1978; Ch Of The Redeem Houston TX 1974-1977. Auth, *Dyadic Adjustment: Its Impact on Ther Burnout*, 1990. Amer Assn Pstr Counslg Assn - Fell 1999; Amer Counslg Assn 1983. gdmoses@juno.com

MOSES, Michael David (Minn) 11078 Nichols Spring Dr, Chatfield MN 55923 B Mankato MN 2/5/1951 s Charles Henry moses & Edna. BS Minnesota St U Mankato 1985; MBA Minnesota St U Mankato 1986. D 7/29/2006 Bp Daniel Lee Swenson P 3/25/2007 Bp James Louis Jelinek. m 8/9/1975 Susan Durgin c 3. mike.moses@thomson.com

MOSES, Robert Emilio (CFla) 145 E Edgewood Dr, Lakeland FL 33803 **Asst to the R, DRE S Dav's Epis Ch Lakeland FL 2008-; Asst Trin Ch Edisto Island SC 2008-** B Lakewood OH 12/2/1971 s Robert Grant Moses & Mary Ann. BS Florida St U 1992; MA STB Pontifical Gregorian U Rome IT 1998; MA STL Pontifical Gregorian U Rome IT 2000. Rec from Roman Catholic 5/31/2008 Bp John Wadsworth Howe. m 9/27/2003 Nancy Brink Moses c 2. rmoses@stdavidslakeland.com

MOSHER, David Rike (SwFla) 6764 122nd St, Seminole FL 33772 **Winter Assoc S Anne Of Gr Epis Ch Seminole FL 1997-** B Los Angeles CA 2/9/1924 s Ezra Davis Mosher & Norine. BA U Denv 1949; MDiv Ya Berk 1952. D 3/25/1952 Bp Walter H Gray P 10/12/1952 Bp Harold L Bowen. m 11/26/2000 Maureen Sommerville Anderson. Sum Asst S Lk's Epis Ch Asheville NC 1989-1990; Int Ch Of The H Sprt Osprey FL 1987-1988; Cathd Ch Of S Ptr St Petersburg FL 1980-1989; Dio Colorado Denver CO 1959-1984; R Calv Ch Golden CO 1952-1959. Fell Amer Coll of Healthcare Admin 1985; Hon Past Pres Amer Hlth Care Assn 1985; Phi Beta Kappa U Denv 1949. drmasheville@yahoo.com

M

MOSHER, Steven Emerson (ETenn) 314 W. Broadway Ave, Maryville TN 38801 **R S Andr's Ch Maryville TN 2009-** B Atlanta GA 7/5/1962 s David Kenneth Mosher & Cynthia Compton. BBA U GA 1985; MDiv STUSo 2004. D 6/5/2004 P 12/2/2004 Bp J(ohn) Neil Alexander. m 11/29/1986 Kirsten K Kaufmann c 2. Assoc R Ch Of The Nativ Epis Huntsville AL 2004-2009. rev.steve.mosher@gmail.com

MOSIER, James David (EO) 1237 Sw 12th St, Ontario OR 97914 **D S Matt's Epis Ch Ontario OR 1985-** B The Dalles OR 1/16/1946 s Ernest Draper Mosier & Eleanor Virginia. BA U of Portland 1968. D 9/21/1985 Bp Rustin Ray Kimsey P 5/22/2010 Bp Bavi Rivera. m 7/12/1969 Vicki Dehaven c 2. jimosier@cableone.net

MOSIER, William Frank (Ore) 39361 Mozart Ter Unit 101, Fremont CA 94538 **D S Hilda's Ch Monmouth OR 1994-** B The Dalles OR 1/16/1946 s Ernest David Mosier & Elenor Virginia. BS Wstrn Oregon U 1984; MS Wstrn Oregon U 1986; Oregon Cntr for the Diac 1994. D 10/29/1994 Bp Robert Louis Ladehoff. The Epis Conf of the Deaf 1985. Elected Pres Epis Conf of the Deaf 2004; Meritorius Serv Awd Epis Conf of the Deaf 1999; Elected Bd Mem Epis Conf of the Deaf 1997. bmose@aol.com

MOSLEY, Carl Ernest (Eas) 111 76th St Unit 205, Ocean City MD 21842 **2007 Dio Easton Easton MD 2007-** B Washington DC 6/3/1942 s Carl N Mosley & Helen M. ABA Benjamin Franklin U Washington DC 1968; BS Benjamin Franklin U Washington DC 1972; Dipl. in Theol VTS 2007; MaMin Nash 2011. D 11/13/2007 Bp James Joseph Shand. m 10/23/1987 Virginia Monaco. carlmosleycpa@msn.com

MOSQUEA, Jesus (DR) Calle Santiago, #114 Dominican Republic **Dio The Dominican Republic (Iglesia Epis Dominicana) Santo Domingo DO 2007-** B Rio San Juan 12/25/1971 D 2/12/2006 Bp Julio Cesar Holguin-Khoury.

MOSS JR, Alfred Alfonso (Chi) 1500 N Lancaster St, Arlington VA 22205 **S Andr's Epis Ch Arlington VA 1993-** B Chicago IL 3/2/1943 s Alfred Alfonso Moss & Ruth. BA Lake Forest Coll 1965; STB EDS 1968; MA U Chi 1972; PhD U Chi 1977. D 6/15/1968 Bp James Winchester Montgomery P 12/21/1968 Bp Gerald Francis Burrill. c 1. Cur The Ch Of The H Sprt Lake Forest IL 1968-1970. Auth, *Dangerous Donations: Nthrn Philantrophy and Sthrn Black Educ 1902-1930*, Col of Missouri Press, 1999; Auth, "Alexander

Crummell," *Black Leaders of the 19th Century*; Auth, *From Slavery To Freedom: A Hist of Afr Americans*; Auth, *The Amer Negro Acad.* HSEC 1994; UBE. DD Virginia Theoloigal Sem 2006. lalmoss@umd.edu

MOSS III, David MacBeth (At) 3880 N Stratford Rd Ne, Atlanta GA 30342 B Saint Louis MO 1/12/1943 s Harry Nichols Moss & Helen Josephine. BA Washington U 1966; MDiv SWTS 1969; STM SWTS 1970; PhD NWU 1974; ThD Somerset U Gb 1990. D 6/22/1969 Bp James Loughlin Duncan P 4/13/1970 Bp James Winchester Montgomery. m 5/5/1984 Denise S Spickerman. Asst All SS Epis Ch Atlanta GA 1979-2004; Chair Dio Chicago Chicago IL 1972-1979; Asst R S Chrys's Ch Chicago IL 1969-1974. Ed, "Orgnztn & Admin Pstr Counslg Centers," Abingdon, 1981; Ed, "Journ Of Pstr Care"; Ed, "Alcoholic'S 12 Steps Into Life," Forw Mvmt; Ed, "Pstr Psychol"; Ed, "Amer Journ Of Pstr Counslg"; Ed, "Dialogues In Depth Psychol & Rel"; Ed, "Journ Rel & Hlth". Aamft; AAPC; Amer Coll Forensic Examiners; APA; ACPE; CDSP. DD SWTS Evaston IL 1997; Vstng Schlr Freud Museum 1991. dmoss154@earthlink.net

MOSS, Denise S (At) 3880 N Stratford Rd NE, Atlanta GA 30342 **R S Alb's Ch Elberton GA 2007-; R Ch Of The Medtr Washington GA 2002-** B Saint Louis MO 2/6/1942 d John Frederick Spickerman & Claire. BA Merc 1981; MDiv Merc 2000; DMin SWTS 2005. D 2/21/2004 P 1/16/2007 Bp J(ohn) Neil Alexander. m 5/5/1984 David MacBeth Moss c 2. Asst S Tim's Epis Ch Calhoun GA 2000-2002. Auth, "Feed Your Wk: Dispelling dangerous myth in a dangerouls Wrld," Libr of Congr, 2005. dmoss154@earthlink.net

MOSS III, Frank Hazlett (WMass) 17910 NW Chestnut Lane, Portland OR 97231 B Fredericksburg VA 6/3/1945 s Frank Hazlet Moss & Nancy Lancaster. BA Pr 1967; MDiv EDS 1970; MBA U of New Haven 1988. D 6/20/1970 Bp Philip Alan Smith P 5/15/1971 Bp Robert Bruce Hall. c 1. Int Ch Of The Redeem Pendleton OR 2006-2010; Dio Wstrn Massachusetts Springfield MA 1999-2006; R S Jas' Ch Greenfield MA 1999-2006; R Trin Ch Ft Wayne IN 1990-1999; S Andr's Ch Meriden CT 1979-1990; P-in-c Geth Ch Proctorsville VT 1974-1979; R S Lk's Ch Chester VT 1974-1979; Cur Gr Ch Utica NY 1972-1974; Cur S Paul's Memi Charlottesville VA 1970-1972. frankhmoss@msn.com

MOSS, J(ohn) Eliot Blakeslee (WMass) 7 Kestrel Ln, Amherst MA 01002 **GC Alt Dep Dio Wstrn Massachusetts Springfield MA 2010-; Dioc Coun Dio Wstrn Massachusetts Springfield MA 2008-; Vic S Jn's Ch Ashfield MA 2008-; Cathd Chapt Chr Ch Cathd Springfield MA 2007-** B Staunton VA 1/1/1954 s William Edwin Moss & Mary Frances. BS MIT 1975; MS MIT 1978; PhD MIT 1981. D 6/19/2004 P 4/23/2005 Bp Gordon Paul Scruton. m 5/29/1976 Hannah Allen Abbott c 2. Dioc Coun Dio Wstrn Massachusetts Springfield MA 2008-2010; GC Dep Dio Wstrn Massachusetts Springfield MA 2007-2010; Asst Ch Of The Atone Westfield MA 2005-2008; GC Alt Dep Dio Wstrn Massachusetts Springfield MA 2004-2007; D Ch Of The Atone Westfield MA 2004-2005. Fllshp of S Jn; Fllshp of the Way of the Cross 2004. moss@cs.umass.edu

M

MOSS SR, Ledly Ogden (SeFla) 4020 Nw 187th St, Carol City FL 33055 **D Epis Ch Of The H Fam Miami Gardens FL 1992-** B 8/19/1931 s Wellington Samuel Moss & Melwese Maud. D 4/4/1992 Bp Calvin Onderdonk Schofield Jr. m 10/24/1962 Muriel Martha Bonaby c 4.

MOSS, R Benjamin (WNY) 716 Gwinn St. Front, Medina NY 14103 B Horseheads NY 7/20/1926 s Robert Thomas Moss & Edna. BA Hob 1952; STB GTS 1956. D 6/23/1956 Bp Walter M Higley P 6/21/1957 Bp Malcolm E Peabody. m 7/12/1952 Judith Howard c 4. Int Dio Wstrn New York Tonawanda NY 1987-1993; Trin And S Mich's Ch Albany NY 1969-1980; R S Jn's Ch Medina NY 1966-1986; P-in-c Ch Of The Gd Shpd Irving NY 1963-1966; S Andr's Ch Buffalo NY 1963-1966; P-in-c S Ptr's Ch Forestville NY 1963-1966; Vic S Alb's Ch Silver Creek NY 1959-1966. fasted7403@yahoo.com

MOSS, Susan Maetzold (Minn) 175 Woodlawn Ave, Saint Paul MN 55105 **Comission on Mssn Dio Minnesota Minneapolis MN 2011-; Exam Chapl Dio Minnesota Minneapolis MN 2010-; Stndg Com Dio Minnesota Minneapolis MN 2010-; Reg Dn Dio Minnesota Minneapolis MN 2008-** B Red Wing MN 8/26/1950 d James Wallace Maetzold & Elizabeth Mary. BA Bowling Green St U 1972; MA Luther TS 1976; MDiv Untd TS of the Twin Cities 1984; GTS 1985; Seminario De San Andres 2001. D 6/11/1984 P 10/23/1985 Bp Robert Marshall Anderson. m 8/24/1974 Thomas V Moss c 3. Vic La Mision El Santo Nino Jesus S Paul MN 2008-2011; Vstng Fell Epis TS Of The SW Austin TX 2008; Stff Liason Mssn Strtgy Ntwk Dio Minnesota Minneapolis MN 2005-2007; Co Chair Comission on Mnstry Dio Minnesota Minneapolis MN 1996-2000; R S Jas On The Pkwy Minneapolis MN 1993-2000; Int R S Lk's Ch Minneapolis MN 1991-1993; Chair Wellness Com Dio Minnesota Minneapolis MN 1988-1990; Assoc S Jn The Bapt Epis Ch Minneapolis MN 1988-1990; Exam Chapl Dio Minnesota Minneapolis MN 1986-1990; Int R Ch Of The Epiph Epis Plymouth MN 1986-1987; Assoc Ch Of The Epiph Epis Plymouth MN 1984-1986; Dir of YA Mnstry S Steph The Mtyr Ch Minneapolis MN 1982-1984. susanmaetzoldmoss@gmail.com

MOSSBARGER, David Jefferson (NwT) 1402 Wilshire Dr, Odessa TX 79761 **R S Barn' Epis Ch Of Odessa Odessa TX 2003-** B La Jolla CA 4/16/1958 s John William Mossbarger & Jane Gordon. BA SMU 1980; MDiv Epis TS of The SW 1985. D 6/15/1985 P 12/21/1985 Bp Donis Dean Patterson. m 12/27/1986 Deborah Snyder c 2. Gr Ch Llano TX 1997-2002; Dept Of CE Dio W Texas San Antonio TX 1993-1997; Asst R S Peters Epis Sch Kerrville TX 1991-1997; S Ptr's Epis Ch Kerrville TX 1991-1997; S Geo's Epis Ch Dallas TX 1990-1991; Dept Of Missions Dallas TX 1987-1990; Cur S Lk's Epis Ch Dallas TX 1985-1986. rector41@sbcglobal.net

MOSSER, Kenneth Ison (USC) 12127 Oldfield Pointe Dr, Jacksonville FL 32223 B Ashland KY 2/19/1936 s Joseph Sheats Mosser & Draxie. BS Virginia Commonwealth U 1972; MDiv VTS 1984. D 6/8/1985 P 5/1/1986 Bp William Arthur Beckham. m 9/23/1961 Alice Evelyn England. R S Lk's Ch Newberry SC 1991-1998; R S Mk's Ch Palatka FL 1989-1991; Vic S Steph's Epis Ch Ridgeway SC 1986-1989; Cur Ch Of The Adv Spartanburg SC 1985-1986. kmosser137@comcast.net

MOSSO, Karen Ann (Ind) 721 Roma Ave., Jeffersonville IN 47130 B Saint Paul MN 12/29/1945 d Earl Henry Mosso & Carla. BS U MN 1967; MA Minnesota St U Mankato 1975; MDiv Bex 1978. D 6/24/1978 P 7/13/1980 Bp Robert Marshall Anderson. R S Paul's Jeffersonville IN 2002-2007; Int S Mk's Epis Ch Huntersville NC 2001-2002; Int All SS Epis Ch Charlotte NC 1999-2001; Dio Missouri S Louis MO 1995-1998; St Louis Urban Partnership S Louis MO 1995-1998; Int Trin Ch Litchfield MN 1993-1994; Int S Matt's Epis Ch Minneapolis MN 1992-1993; Supply Dio Minnesota Minneapolis MN 1989-1993; P-in-c S Edw's Ch Duluth MN 1988-1989; Asst S Paul's Epis Ch Duluth MN 1988-1989; R S Lk's Epis Ch Hastings MN 1983-1988. Oblate, Our Lady of Gr, Beech Grove, IN 2011; Wmn Touched by Gr, Our Lady of Gr Monstry, Beech Grove,IN 2003. kmosso@sbcglobal.net

MOTE, Doris Ellen (Ind) 2018 Locust St, New Albany IN 47150 B Anderson IN 12/12/1938 d Henry Evertt Bricker & Louise Ellen. BA Ball St U 1960; MDiv Untd TS Dayton OH 1973. D 6/22/1974 P 1/29/1977 Bp John Mc Gill Krumm. c 3. R S Paul's Epis Ch New Albany IN 1992-2004; Int Ch Of The Trsfg Braddock Heights MD 1990-1991; Int Chr Ch Forest Hill MD 1989-1990; H Cross Ch St MD 1989-1990; Ch of the H Evangelists Baltimore MD 1988-1989; Dio Maryland Baltimore MD 1986-1991; Assoc R S Barth's Ch Baltimore MD 1980-1986; Asst Chr Epis Ch Dayton OH 1975-1979; Dio Sthrn Ohio Cincinnati OH 1975-1979. dorisemote@msn.com

MOTE, Larry H. (RG) 1016 E 1st St, Portales NM 88130 **Vic Trin Ch Portales NM 2006-** B Claude TX 8/27/1943 s Paul Hobart Mote & Mildred O. BBA Estrn New Mex U 1978; Basic Chr Stds Trin/ Rio Grande Sch For Mnstry 2006. D 5/20/2006 P 11/30/2006 Bp Jeffrey Neil Steenson. m 2/14/1987 Nancy Strange c 7. BroSA 2007; The Intl Ord of St Lk the Physcn 2008. larry.mote@enmu.edu

MOTES, Brantley Eugene (Ala) Po Box 5556, Decatur AL 35601 B Sylacauga AL 2/13/1936 s Dewitt Brantley Motes & Dorma. BA Athens St U 1960; MDiv Van 1964; DMin Van 1976. D 6/4/1993 Bp Furman Stough P 12/1/1993 Bp Robert Oran Miller. m 5/21/1983 Glenda Carol Sanders. Gd Shpd Decatur AL 1995-1997; Dio Alabama Birmingham AL 1993-1995; H Cross-St Chris's Huntsville AL 1993-1994. Phi Tau Chi.

MOTHERSELL, Lawrence Lavere (Roch) Po Box 1, Geneseo NY 14454 B Potter NY 7/10/1939 s Sheldon Eugene Mothersell & Kathleen Marjorie. CRDS; BS SUNY 1961; MA SUNY 1967. D 9/20/1981 P 3/1/1983 Bp Robert Rae Spears Jr. m 6/20/1959 Patricia Ann Gage. Auth, "Mainstreaming". Ch Mssn Deaf People, Wrld Congr Jewish Deaf.

MOTLEY-FISCHER, Sarah Helen (NCal) Church of St Martin, 640 Hawthorne Ln, Davis CA 95616 B Sacramento CA 2/25/1952 d Edward Preble Motley & Cecily Clare. BA U CA 1974; MDiv Harvard DS 1988. D 6/9/1979 P 11/30/1980 Bp John Bowen Coburn. m 11/25/1989 J Christopher Fischer c 3. Dio Nthrn California Sacramento CA 2000-2007; Assoc Ch Of S Mart Davis CA 1997-1999; S Andr's Ch Trenton NJ 1995-1996; Pstr Asst Trin Ch Princeton NJ 1990-1991; Int Epis Ch at Pr Princeton NJ 1985-1986; The Wm Alexander Procter Fndt Trenton NJ 1985-1986; Cur Trin Ch Princeton NJ 1981-1984; D The Cathd Ch Of S Paul Boston MA 1979-1980. Writer, "Uc Davis Bioregional Proj," 1999; Ed, "Via Media," 1987. Epis Soc For Mnstry In Higer Educ 1986-1988; SCHC 1988. Writer-In-Res Uc Davis Bioregional Grp 1998. sarahmot@earthlink.net

MOTT, Pamela Jane (RI) 324 E Main Rd # 2871, Portsmouth RI 02871 **R S Mary's Ch Portsmouth RI 2004-** B White Plains NY 6/7/1957 d Willard S Mott & Charlotte. CAS Ya Berk; BA SUNY 1978; MDiv Yale DS 1985. D 6/8/1991 P 12/15/1991 Bp Richard Frank Grein. Cn Trin Epis Cathd Portland OR 1998-2004; R S Eustace Ch Lake Placid NY 1994-1998; Cur Gr Ch Millbrook NY 1991-1994. pamelamott@aol.com

MOTTL, Christine Elizabeth (Pa) 94 E Oakland Ave, Doylestown PA 18901 **Int R S Paul's Ch Doylestown PA 2009-** B New York NY 1/23/1951 d Alfred Hinek & Ann. CRDS; BA SUNY 1972; MA SUNY 1975; MDiv Trin TS Newburgh IN 1999. D 5/5/2000 P 11/5/2000 Bp James Edward Krotz. m 8/8/1978 Paul Edward Mottl c 2. Dio Nebraska Omaha NE 2004-2009; Int Ch Of

The H Apos Mitchell NE 2003-2004; All SS Med Cntr Racine WI 2003; Coordntr of Epis Serv S Lk's Hosp Racine WI 2002-2003; R Calv Ch Hyannis NE 2000-2002. Assoc of Profsnl Chapl 2004. DD, D.D. Prov. Theo. Sch. 2007; Bd Cert Chapl, BCC Assoc of Profsnl Chapl 2004. revchrism@aol.com

MOTTL, Paul Edward (Neb) 94 E Oakland Ave, Doylestown PA 18901 B Bay Shore NY 1/29/1944 s Edward Walter Mottl & Claire Johnson. BA Adel 1965; MRE Methodist TS In Ohio 1970; MDiv Colgate Rochester DS 1993; PhD Sheffield Univ 2003. D 4/24/1993 Bp Orris George Walker Jr P 11/1/1993 Bp George Clinton Harris. m 8/8/1978 Christine Elizabeth Hinek c 2. Cn to the Ordnry Dio Pennsylvania Philadelphia PA 2009-2010; Dio Nebraska Omaha NE 2005-2009; R S Jas' Epis Ch Fremont NE 2005-2009; Calv Ch Hyannis NE 2003; R S Matt's Ch Allnce NE 1997-2005; Asst S Ptr's by-the-Sea Epis Ch Bay Shore NY 1994-1997; COM Dio No Dakota Fargo ND 1993-1994; P-in-c S Ptr's Epis Ch Williston ND 1993-1994. Auth, "HEARTLAND HOPE," Morris Pub, 2000. FA 1992-1996; Naval Inst 1979. pemottl@aol.com

MOUER, Patricia Wade (WNC) 500 Christ School Road, Asheville NC 28704 **R S Lk's Epis Ch Asheville NC 2004-** B Richmond VA 11/6/1963 d James Adams Eichner & Dorothy. BA Br 1986; MS U of Tennessee 1993; MDiv Van 1994. D 6/10/2000 P 12/9/2000 Bp Robert Hodges Johnson. m 5/26/1990 Joseph Raber Mouer c 2. Gr Ch Asheville NC 2000-2004. stlukeschurch@charter.net

MOUILLE, David Ronald (Kan) 4786 Black Swan Dr, Shawnee KS 66216 B Church Pt LA 5/30/1942 s Joseph Cermit Mouille & Enola. BA Notre Dame Sem 1964; STB CUA 1968; STM GTS 1972; MSEd Kansas U 1982; PhD KANSAS U 1990. Rec from Roman Catholic 5/1/1971 as Priest Bp Iveson Batchelor Noland. m 7/2/1995 Cheryl Daugharty. S Mart-In-The-Fields Edwardsville KS 1981-1990; R Gr Epis Ch Ottawa KS 1976-1980; Asst S Mich And All Ang Ch Dallas TX 1973-1976; Asst Par Of Chr The Redeem Pelham NY 1971-1973; Asst Trin S Paul's Epis New Rochelle NY 1970-1971. AAPC.

MOULDEN, Michael Mackreth (NC) 401 Plainfield Road, Greenborough NC 27455 **R S Fran Ch Greensboro NC 2007-** B Washington DC 11/25/1951 s William Raymond Moulden & Mary Gwendolen. BA Guilford Coll 1974; MDiv STUSo 1979. Trans 10/8/2003 Bp Stephen Hays Jecko. m 1/2/2004 Celeste Krueger c 2. Ch Of Our Sav Jacksonville FL 2006; S Jn's Cathd Jacksonville FL 2006; Chr Ch Cleveland NC 2004-2005; Trin Epis Sch Charlotte NC 2003-2005; R All SS Epis Ch Jacksonville FL 1998-2003; R S Eliz's Epis Ch Knoxville TN 1992-1998; R Epis Ch of the Gd Shpd Charleston SC 1988-1992; R S Ann's Ch Nashville TN 1983-1988; D-in-Trng S Steph's Epis Ch Oak Ridge TN 1979-1980. mmoulden@hotmail.com

MOULTON, Elizabeth Jean (Be) 109 Cruser St, Montrose PA 18801 B Louisville KY 10/14/1941 d Newton Miller Cunningham & Elizabeth Louise. BS U IL 1963; MS Nthrn Illinois U 1972; MDiv Luth TS at Gettysburg 1987. D 6/12/1987 P 5/10/1988 Bp Charlie Fuller McNutt Jr. m 5/20/1962 John R Moulton c 2. Supply Chr Ch Susquehanna PA 2006-2010; Supply S Mk's New Milford PA 2006-2010; R S Paul's Ch Montrose PA 1999-2005; Supply Prince Of Peace Epis Ch Dallas PA 1998; R Chr Ch Stroudsburg PA 1992-1998; Vic S Alb's Ch Littleton NC 1992; R Gr Ch Weldon NC 1988-1992; Vic S Anna's Ch Littleton NC 1988-1992; Vic All SS Ch Roanoke Rapids NC 1988-1991; Asst Mt Calv Camp Hill PA 1987-1988. emoulton@stny.rr.com

MOULTON II, John Adkins (Fla) 1631 Blue Heron Ln, Jacksonville Beach FL 32250 B Richmond VA 11/4/1944 s John Adkins Moulton & Martha Demoval. BA U NC 1967; MDiv UTS 1970; Ripon Coll Cuddesdon 1971; DMin VTS 1986; S Geo's Coll Jerusalem IL 1989. D 6/24/1970 P 10/17/1971 Bp William Moultrie Moore Jr. m 1/28/1967 Harriet Jeffress c 2. Assoc S Geo's Epis Ch Jacksonville FL 2001-2008; S Paul's By-The-Sea Epis Ch Jacksonville Bch FL 1993-2000; Liturg Cmsn Dio Sthrn Virginia Norfolk VA 1981-1987; Ch Of The Redeem Midlothian VA 1979-1993; Exec Bd Dio E Carolina Kinston NC 1977-1979; R S Paul's Epis Ch Wilmington NC 1975-1979; Assoc H Trin Epis Ch Fayetteville NC 1973-1975; Cur Bruton Par Williamsburg VA 1971-1973. OHC 1973. jamtwo2@comcast.net

MOULTON, Roger Conant (Mass) 291 Washington St, Arlington MA 02474 **Asstg P Par Of The Epiph Winchester MA 2008-** B Boston MA 3/11/1929 s Stanley Windsor Moulton & Lina. BS Babson Coll 1950; MDiv EDS 1960. D 6/18/1960 Bp Anson Phelps Stokes Jr P 1/8/1961 Bp Dudley S Stark. m 7/11/1953 Barbara Holden c 3. P-in-c S Mk's Epis Ch Burlington MA 2005-2006; Asst Par Of The Epiph Winchester MA 2004-2005; Asstg P All SS Ch Chelmsford MA 2001-2003; Asst The Ch Of Our Redeem Lexington MA 1997-1999; R Ch Of The Gd Shpd Watertown MA 1979-1993; Int Ch Of Our Sav Arlington MA 1978-1979; Ecum All SS Epis Ch Portsmouth OH 1977-1978; R S Jn's Ch Huntington WV 1972-1975; Assoc S Mk's Epis Ch Columbus OH 1968-1972; R Trin Ch Newark OH 1964-1968; Cur S Paul's Ch Rochester NY 1960-1964. Auth, "E-Mail From Amer," *Sherborne Scene-Devon, U.K.*, Ecum Monthly, 2001. Phillips Brooks Club, Boston 1980-1992. Honoree of the Year Nature Conservancy, Boston 1996. rbcprjbjm@rcn.com

MOUNCEY, Perry Kathleen (CNY) 127 Brookview Ln, Liverpool NY 13088 **Reverend S Matt's Ch Moravia NY 2007-** B Toronto Canada 4/6/1948 d Theodore W Kober & Susan D. RN St Jos's Sch of Nrsng 1970; Loc Dioc Formation Prog 2006. D 10/7/2006 P 6/9/2007 Bp Gladstone Bailey Adams III. m 9/16/1972 Douglas W Mouncey c 2. Gr Ch Mex NY 2009. perryrev@hotmail.com

MOUNTFORD, Helen Harvene (Los) 1566 Edison St, Santa Ynez CA 93460 B Dallas TX 3/13/1942 d Roger Parkhurst Turner & Harvene. BS U of Iowa 1964; JD U of Kansas 1969. D 11/1/1985 Bp Richard Frank Grein. c 2. D Ch Of The Incarn San Francisco CA 1999-2000; D S Marg's Ch Lawr KS 1997-1999; Archd Dio Kansas Topeka KS 1994-1999; D S Mich And All Ang Ch Mssn KS 1985-1997. NAAD. helen_mountford@compuserv.com

MOUNTFORD SR, Robert (CFla) 160 Heron Bay Cir, Lake Mary FL 32746 B 11/7/1933 m 2/12/1952 Mildred Rideout. Assoc R S Ptr's Epis Ch Lake Mary FL 1999; Trin Ch Saco ME 1988-1999. bobamim@aol.com

MOURADIAN, Victoria Kirk (Los) 1411 Dalmatia Dr., San Pedro CA 90732 **Kensington Epis Hm Alhambra CA 2008-; Cur S Bede's Epis Ch Los Angeles CA 2008-; The Epis Hm Communities Pasadena CA 2008-** B Chicago IL 3/8/1950 d Kenneth Burson Kirk & Helen. Angl Stds ETS at Claremont; BA USC 1973; MAT Fuller TS 2007. D 6/7/2008 P 1/10/2009 Bp Joseph Jon Bruno. c 3. vickimour@aol.com

MOUSIN, Thomas Nordboe (Mass) 29 Lakeview Rd, Winchester MA 01890 **R S Jn's Ch Charlestown (Boston) Charlestown MA 2011-** B Hackensack NJ 1/3/1956 s Carl John Mousin & Dorothy Eleanor. BA Dart 1978; MDiv UTS 1983; Cert in Advncd Theol Stds EDS 2011. D 12/14/2010 P 6/25/2011 Bp Thomas C Ely. m 6/28/2003 Thomas James Brown. D Ch Of The Gd Shpd Reading MA 2011. tmousin@gmail.com

MOWERS, Culver Lunn (CNY) Po Box 130, Brooktondale NY 14817 **All SS Ch 1968-; Dio Cntrl New York Syracuse NY 1968-** B Syracuse NY 9/9/1942 s Jack Lunn Mowers & Erma. BA Syr 1964; MDiv EDS 1968. D 6/14/1968 Bp Walter M Higley P 5/28/1969 Bp Ned Cole. S Thos Epis Ch Brooktondale NY 1972-2006; R S Mk's Ch Candor NY 1972-1979; St Johns Epis Ch Berkshire NY 1972-1975; P-in-c S Paul's Ch Brownville NY 1968-1972; Cur S Paul's Ch Watertown NY 1968-1971. culliem@aol.com

MOWERY, Donald (WTenn) 231 Baronne Pl, Memphis TN 38117 B Chattanooga TN 8/2/1931 s Clarence Edgar Mowery & Myrtle. BS U of Tennessee 1953; MDiv Ya Berk 1956. D 7/1/1956 Bp Theodore N Barth P 1/18/1957 Bp John Vander Horst. m 4/10/1983 Julie L Bailey. Dio W Tennessee Memphis TN 1968-1995; Bridges Inc Memphis TN 1963-1995; Stff S Mary's Cathd Memphis TN 1963-1995; R S Andr's Ch Nashville TN 1956-1963. Bp's Mnstry Awd Dio W Tennessee 1985. don767@aol.com

MOYER, C(harles) (Miss) 4555 35th Ave Apt 206, Meridian MS 39305 B Joplin MO 1/8/1917 s Eldred Eugene Moyer & Emma Love. Houston Vocational Coll 1937; Road for Ord 1955. D 12/16/1953 Bp Clinton Simon Quin P 2/2/1955 Bp Duncan Montgomery Gray. c 2. S Columb's Ch Ridgeland MS 1968-1981; R The Epis Ch Of The Medtr Meridian MS 1963-1968; Vic Calv Ch Ripley MS 1957-1963; R Chr Ch Holly Sprg MS 1957-1963; Cur Palmer Memi Ch Houston TX 1955-1957; Cur S Jas Ch Greenville MS 1954-1955; Vic S Steph's Ch Liberty TX 1953-1954. CSB; CBS 1982; P Assoc, SocOLW 1972; SocMary 1984.

MOYER, Dale Luther (SeFla) 4851a Nursery Rd, Dover PA 17315 B New Ringgold PA 6/17/1937 s Irvin George Moyer & Catherine Irene. BA Albright Coll 1959; BD Evang TS 1962; STM Nash 1970. D 6/14/1964 Bp James Winchester Montgomery P 12/19/1964 Bp Gerald Francis Burrill. m 7/2/1966 Donna Stephanie Blake. P-in-c S Paul's Ch Columbia PA 1998-2003; S Jn's Epis Ch Midland MI 1996-1997; R S Mart's Epis Ch Pompano Bch FL 1987-1996; R S Paul's Ch Wallingford CT 1978-1987; R Par Of Chr The King Willingboro NJ 1970-1978; Dce S Jas Epis Ch Danbury CT 1969-1970; R S Mart-In-The-Fields Edwardsville KS 1966-1968; Cur S Dav's Ch Glenview IL 1964-1966. CHS.

MOYER, J Douglas (Be) 205 North Seventh Street, Stroudsburg PA 18360 **R Chr Ch Stroudsburg PA 2011-; R Chr Ch Stroudsburg PA 2011-; Cur Dio Bethlehem Bethlehem PA 2009-** B Chester PA 3/23/1949 s James Douglas Moyer & Helen Charlotte. BA Penn 1971; BS Widener U 1981; MDiv Nash 2009. D 2/2/2009 Bp John Palmer Croneberger P 9/29/2009 Bp Paul Victor Marshall. m 12/19/1983 Michelle Merlo c 3. Asst Chr Ch Reading PA 2011. jdm323@gmail.com

MOYER, Laureen H (Cal) 412 Centre Ct, Alameda CA 94502 **S Andr's Epis Ch San Bruno CA 2010-** B Albany NY 6/26/1946 d John William Hooker & Beatrice Helen. BA U of Tennessee 1968; MAPS Washington Theol Un 2001; VTS 2002. D 9/19/2002 P 6/7/2003 Bp William Michie Klusmeyer. c 2. Asst Chr Ch Alameda CA 2008-2010; Gr Epis Ch Middleway WV 2006-2007; Nelson Cluster Of Epis Ch Rippon WV 2004-2005; S Phil's Ch Chas Town WV 2002-2005; S Jn's Ch Harpers Ferry WV 2002. "Which is Better: Grid Listing or Grp Question Design for Data Collection in Establishment Surveys?," *Resrch Report Series*, U.S. Census Bureau, 1999; "Problem w Determining and Listing Grp. Qtrs. in Prep. for Enumeration," *Proceedings of the Survey Methods Sectn*, Amer Statistical Assn, 1998; "How Do People Answer Income Questions?," *Publ Opinion Quarterly*, AAPOR, 1998. lhm626@gmail.com

MOYER, Michael David (Eas) 203 S Main St, Berlin MD 21811 **R S Paul's Berlin MD 1999-** B Pottstown PA 5/6/1967 s David Andrew Moyer & Linda Kachel. AGS Montgomery Cnty Cmnty Coll 1987; MDiv Bangor TS 1992; BA U of Maine 1992; STM Nash 1996. D 6/21/1997 Bp Allen Lyman Bartlett Jr P 12/22/1997 Bp Jack Leo Iker. c 1. Assoc All SS' Epis Ch Ft Worth TX 1997-1999. CBS; GAS; P Assoc -- All SS Sis of the Poor; SocMary. frmoyer@aol.com

MOYERS, William Riley (SwFla) 2008 Isla De Palma Cir, Naples FL 34119 **Bp Gray Fndt Dio SW Florida Sarasota FL 2011-; D Coun Dio SW Florida Sarasota FL 2011-; Cler Ldr of Steph Mnstry S Monica's Epis Ch Naples FL 2011-; S Paul's Cathd Peoria IL 2003-** B Peoria IL 4/28/1944 s Arthur Moyers & Lenor Vivian. Illinois St U; Illinois Cntrl Coll 1974. D 11/2/2003 Bp Keith Lynn Ackerman. m 1/25/1969 Cheri Lynne Baker c 1. cherinbill@embarqmail.com

MOYLE, Sandra K (Fla) St. Mark's Episcopal Church, 4129 Oxford Ave, Jacksonville FL 32210 **Dioc Anniv Com Dio Florida Jacksonville FL 2011-; Pstr Care Cmsn, Chair- Cler Wellness Dio Florida Jacksonville FL 2009-; Assoc R S Mk's Epis Ch Jacksonville FL 2003-** B Huntingdon PA 6/20/1949 d Ralph Cypher Moyle & Mary Irene. BA Virginia Wstrn Cmnty Coll 1969; BA Old Dominion U 1972; MDiv VTS 1997. D 6/14/1997 Bp Rogers Sanders Harris P 1/15/1998 Bp John Bailey Lipscomb. Prcs, Stndg Com Dio Florida Jacksonville FL 2008-2009; Cmncatn Cmsn Dio Florida Jacksonville FL 2007-2008; Chair, Liturg and Wrshp Cmsn Dio Florida Jacksonville FL 2005-2008; Anchor-Reporter GC Epis News Serv New York NY 2003; Stndg Com Dio SW Florida Sarasota FL 2001-2003; Asstg R St Johns Epis Ch Tampa FL 1997-2002; Anchor-Reporter GC Epis News Serv New York NY 1997. smoyle@stmarksjacksonville.org

MOYSER, George H (Vt) 48 Munroe Dr, Shelburne VT 05482 **Eccl Crt Dio Vermont Burlington VT 2009-2012** B York UK 3/15/1945 s Herbert Ernest Moyser & Violet. BA(Econ) Hons. U of Manchester, UK 1966; MA U of Essex, UK 1968; MA U MI 1972; PhD U MI 1976; Montreal TS 1994. D 5/31/1994 P 12/18/1994 Bp Mary Adelia Rosamond McLeod. m 7/26/1969 Stella Mary Dann c 1. Int/Supply S Matt's Ch Enosburg Falls VT 2010; Int/Supply S Lk's Ch S Albans VT 2009-2010; R Calv Ch Underhill VT 1994-2006; COM Dio Vermont Burlington VT 1994-1997. Auth, "Rel and Politics," *The Roubledge Compinion to the Study of Rel*, Routledge, 2009; Auth, "The WCC," *Encyclopedia of Politics and Rel*, CQ Press, 2007; Auth, "European Rel in Comparison Perspective," *Political Theol*, 2005; Ed, "Politics & Rel In The Mod Wrld," Routledge, 1991; Co-Auth, "Ch & Politics In A Secular Age," Clarendon Press, 1988; Ed, "Ch & Politics Today," T & T Clarke, 1985. Amer Political Sci Assn 1970-2010; Fllshp Of Soc Of S Jn The Evang 1993; Friends Of York Min 1995; The Angl Soc 1997. Emer Prof U of Vermont 2010; The Robert V. Daniels Awd for Outstanding Contributions to Intl Educ U of Vermont 2010. george.moyser@uvm.edu

MOZELIAK JR, Leon Clement (WNY) Trinity Episcopal Church, 261 E. Main St., Hamburg NY 14075 **Int Trin Epis Ch Hamburg NY 2009-** B Carbondale PA 8/21/1951 s Leon Clement Mozeliak & Mary Irene. BA S Mary's Sem & U Baltimore MD 1977; MBA U of New Haven 1989; MDiv GTS 1996; D.Min. (candidate) SWTS 2008. D 6/14/1997 P 12/20/1997 Bp Clarence Nicholas Coleridge. m 11/25/1978 Lynn Ellen Terragna c 2. Int S Paul's Epis Ch Harris Hill Williamsville NY 2007-2009; S Thad Epis Ch Aiken SC 2000-2007; R Trin Epis Ch Collinsville CT 1998-2000; S Ptr's Epis Ch Cheshire CT 1997-1998; Pstr Assoc S Ptr's Epis Ch Cheshire CT 1996-1997. Chapl, Aiken Reg Med Cntr 2000-2004; DEC and Dioc. Stndg. Cmtee. EDUSC 2001-2004; Dn, Gravatt Convoc EDUSC 2000-2002; Pres. Exec. Coun EDUSC 2002-2004; Pres. Stndng. Cmtee. EDUSC 2002-2004; Pres, Mead Hall Epis Day Sch 2000-2006. leemozely@verizon.net

MRAZ, Barbara (Minn) 4201 Sheridan Ave S, Minneapolis MN 55410 **D S Jn The Evang S Paul MN 2002-; Dn The Epis Par Of S Dav Minnetonka MN 1988-** B 1/13/1944 d Harry Berg & Agnes. BS U MN 1966; MA U MN 1970. D 1/25/1982 Bp Robert Marshall Anderson. m 8/2/1969 Stephen L Bougie c 2. Dn S Jn The Bapt Epis Ch Minneapolis MN 1988-2000. Auth, "Sacr Strands". bmraz@blakeschool.org

MROCZKA, Mary Ann Catherine (Roch) PO Box 741506, San Diego CA 92174 B Washington DC 9/26/1949 d Joseph Andrew Mroczka & Virginia Lee. BS U Of Dayton 1973; MRE SW Bapt TS 1977; MDiv Bex 1979; BA Marist Coll 1993; M.S. No Carolina St U 2000; Duke DS 2005; Ph.D. No Carolina St U 2005; Grad Cert U of San Diego 2008; San Diego City Coll 2010. D 9/22/1984 Bp Robert Rae Spears Jr P 11/30/1985 Bp William George Burrill. Anti-Racism Com Dio No Carolina Raleigh NC 2004-2006; Bd Mem, NCSU Campus Mnstry Dio No Carolina Raleigh NC 2003-2004; Int S Barth's Ch Pittsboro NC 2001; Asst Ch Of The H Trin Pawling NY 1989-1990; Assoc Estrn Dutchess Min Coun Pawling NY 1986-1990; D Team Monticello NY 1985. OHC 1985. Alum Schlrshp Psychol Dept, NCSU 2004; Hon Soc Psi Chi 1993; Hon Soc Alpha Chi 1992; Rossiter Schlr Bex 1984. mmroczka@mindspring.com

MUDD, Gwynneth Jones (SVa) 214 Fairway Blvd, Columbus OH 43213 B CA 7/21/1937 d Edmund Hawley Jones & Eileen. U of Maryland 1957; BS U of Virginia 1972; MS Geo Mason U 1980; Postgrad Geo Mason U 1981; Postgrad VPI 1981; MDiv VTS 1992. D 6/13/1992 Bp Robert Poland Atkinson P 12/1/1992 Bp Peter James Lee. c 4. Ch Of S Edw Columbus OH 2005; Columbus Comm Mnstrs Columbus OH 2002-2004; P-in-c S Paul's Ch Columbus OH 2002-2004; R S Lk's Ch Granville OH 1998-2002; Cn Evang Chr Ch Cathd Lexington KY 1997-1998; Cn Pstr Chr Ch Cathd Lexington KY 1995-1996; Asst S Ptr's Epis Ch Washington NC 1993-1995; Asst S Aid's Ch Alexandria VA 1992-1993. Ord Of S Lk 1995-1998; Sigma Alpha Iota 1956; Steph Mnstry 1995. gwynnethm@prodigy.net

MUDGE, Barbara Duffield Covington (Ore) 88427 Trout Pond Ln, Bandon OR 97411 **S Paul Epis Ch Norwalk OH 1999-** B Laguna Bch CA 9/27/1930 d Luther Dow Covington & Harriet Ferris. BA Occ 1952; MA ETSBH 1981; Cert. CDSP 1982. D 11/4/1982 Bp Robert C Rusack P 5/8/1983 Bp George West Barrett. m 3/25/1951 John L Mudge c 3. Ecum Off Dio Oregon Portland OR 2002-2006; Vic S Jn-By-The-Sea Epis Ch Bandon OR 1999-2006; Vic S Fran Of Assisi Epis Ch Simi Vlly CA 1986-1995; S Mary's Par Laguna Bch CA 1984-1986. OHC 1992. Wmn of Achievement Bus & Profsnl Wmn Club 1980; Cn 93 Cathd Cntr; 85 in Rel YWCA So Orange Cnty. revmumm@aol.com

MUDGE OHC, Bede Thomas (Kan) PO Box 99, West Park NY 12493 B Cincinnati OH 3/15/1938 s Hiram Mudge & Maxine. BA Cor 1960; MDiv Nash 1964. D 2/22/1964 P 8/22/1964 Bp Donald H V Hallock. R S Lk's Ch Whitewater WI 1965-1967. Auth, *Tracts & arts on the Pryr Life*. Phi Kappa Phi; Phi Beta Kappa. bede@hcmnet.org

MUDGE, Julia Hamilton (Alb) 204 Worthington Ter, Wynantskill NY 12198 **SAMS Ambridge PA 2009-; Mem, Liturg & Ch Mus Com Dio Albany Albany NY 1998-** B Houston TX 10/20/1956 d Bill L Hamilton & Blanche Heywood. BA Ob 1979; MA St. Bern's TS & Mnstry 2004. D 6/12/2004 Bp Daniel William Herzog P 1/1/2005 Bp David John Bena. m 6/13/1981 Shaw Mudge c 3. Asst Chr's Ch Duanesburg NY 2004-2009. "Welcome Song (Mus composition)". mrsdalian@yahoo.com

MUDGE, Melanie Althea (Lex) 8 Redbud Ln, Winchester KY 40391 **R Emm Epis Ch Winchester KY 2006-** B Raleigh NC 8/19/1945 d Harley Lorenzo Mudge & Althea. BS Virginia Commonwealth U 1967; MDiv STUSo 1999. D 5/26/1999 Bp Robert Carroll Johnson Jr P 2/12/2000 Bp J(ames) Gary Gloster. R Epis Ch Of The H Sprt Cumming GA 2002-2006; Asst R All SS Ch Roanoke Rapids NC 1999-2002. Preaching Excellence Awd 1999. revmam@coastalnet.com

MUDGE JR, Shaw (Alb) c/o SAMS, P.O. Box 399, Ambridge PA 15003 B Greenwich Connecticut 7/28/1953 s Patricia. BA Dickinson Coll 1976; MDiv TESM 1988; DMin TESM 2004. D 6/14/1997 Bp Clarence Nicholas Coleridge P 8/29/1998 Bp Daniel William Herzog. m 6/13/1981 Julia Hamilton c 3. SAMS Ambridge PA 2009; R Chr's Ch Duanesburg NY 2002-2009; GC Dep Dio Albany Albany NY 2002-2009; R Chr Ch Walton NY 1998-2002; P-in-c S Paul's Ch Bloomville NY 1998-2002. shepherd110@yahoo.com

MUELLER, Denise Ray (SO) 412 Sycamore St., Cincinnati OH 45202 B Lincoln IL 3/5/1951 d Forrest R Mueller & Chiquita. Pre-Med The OH SU 1972; -Angl Acad 2008. D 6/14/2008 Bp Thomas Edward Breidenthal. m 5/28/1999 Karen Roberta Peeler. deniray@deniray.com

MUELLER, Heather May (Haw) 8992 Kula Hwy, Kula HI 96790 B Radford VA 4/28/1942 d Robert Rohn Selfridge & Esther Helen. BS MI SU 1966; MDiv CDSP 1978. D 6/21/1979 P 4/22/1981 Bp Edmond Lee Browning. c 2. R S Jn's Epis Ch Kula HI 1981-2010; H Innoc' Epis Ch Lahaina HI 1980-1981; Seabury Hall Makawao HI 1979-1981. Auth, "Hist Of S Jn'S," *Kula*, 2000. EWC 1982-1988; NNECA 1991. heathermaymueller@yahoo.com

MUELLER, Mary Margaret (WTex) 1045 Shook Ave Apt 105, San Antonio TX 78212 B San Antonio TX 1/12/1944 d James O Mueller & Margaret. BA Trin 1967; MDiv STUSo 1982. D 6/24/1982 Bp Stanley Fillmore Hauser P 1/6/1983 Bp Scott Field Bailey. Int Gr Ch Llano TX 2003-2010; Asst S Mk's Epis Ch San Antonio TX 1993-2001; Asst Chr Epis Ch San Antonio TX 1982-1990. marymargaretmueller@gmail.com

MUELLER, Susan Richards (Mil) 7018 Colony Dr, Madison WI 53717 **Exec Bd Dio Milwaukee Milwaukee WI 1981-** B Evanston IL 12/31/1946 d Stanleigh Baker Richards & Olive Pellage. Loyola U 1967; BS U of Wisconsin 1968; MA U of Wisconsin 1970; Nash 1983. D 4/7/1984 Bp Charles Thomas Gaskell. m 6/22/1968 William Mueller c 2. D S Andr's Ch Madison WI 2003-2010; Dir -Deacons' Formation Prog Dio Milwaukee Milwaukee WI 2001-2004; D Gr Ch Madison WI 1996-2000; Commision on Mnstry Dio Milwaukee Milwaukee WI 1991-1996; D S Dunst's Ch Madison WI 1987-1996; D S Fran Ch Madison WI 1984-1987. NAAD 1984. mueller@chorus.net

MUELLER, Warren Burke (CFla) 2334 S Conway Rd Apt H, Orlando FL 32812 **Min For Pstr Care S Mich's Ch Orlando FL 2002-** B Louisville KY 1/10/1952 s Jay Francis Mueller & Barbara Lee. AA S Petersburg Jr Coll 1972; BS Florida St U 1974; PhD MI SU 1978. D 2/28/1999 Bp Charles

Edward Jenkins III. D S Lk's Ch Baton Rouge LA 1999-2002. NAAD 1999. Phi Beta Kappa 1974. deaconsailor@hotmail.com

MUES, Steven Wayne (Kan) 144 Lake Mountain Dr, Boulder City NV 89005 **R S Steph's Ch Wichita KS 2005-** B Arapahoe NE 7/27/1948 s Wayne Frank Mues & Dorothy Cora. BA U of Nebraska 1970; MDiv PDS 1973; DMin Untd TS Of The Twin Cities 1994. Trans 11/3/2003 Bp James Louis Jelinek. m 9/2/1969 Marilyn Mues. S Judes Ranch Boulder City NV 2003-2005; R S Lk's Epis Ch Rochester MN 1989-2003; R Ch Of The H Trin Lincoln NE 1984-1989; P-in-c S Pauls Epis Ch Arapahoe NE 1978-1984; Cur Ch Of The H Trin Lincoln NE 1974-1978. Auth, "A Thinking Person'S Ch," *LivCh*, 2000; Auth, "Hist Theol Characteristics Making Evang Difficult," *ATR*, 1995; Auth, "Time," *Sermons That Wk*, Forw Mvmt Press, 1994. Louisville Inst Grant Rec 2000. smues@sbcglobal.net

MUGAN JR, Robert Charles (WNC) 894 Indian Hill Rd, Hendersonville NC 28791 **R Ch Of The Trsfg Bat Cave NC 1997-** B Sioux City IA 8/7/1940 s Robert Charles Mugan & Hazel Christian. Marq 1964; BA S Louis U 1966; MA S Louis U 1969; MA S Louis U 1973; MA St. Louis U 1973. Rec from Roman Catholic 4/16/1994 as Priest Bp Alfred Clark Marble Jr. m 6/27/1982 Susan H Harrison c 1. Chap Of The Cross Chap Hill NC 1996-1997; Asst R S Ptr's By The Lake Brandon MS 1994-1996. mmugan@bellsouth.net

MUHLHEIM, Nancy Colleen (Ore) 98 Fairway Loop, Eugene OR 97401 **D S Mary's Epis Ch Eugene OR 2001-** B Portland OR 1/28/1944 d Francis Lowell Collins & Isis Roselyn. BA U of Oregon 1965; Dio Oregon Cntr for the Diac 2001; 3 year course of study Dio Oregon Cntr for the Diac 2001. D 9/29/2001 Bp Robert Louis Ladehoff. m 9/11/1965 Wilson Caughey Muhlheim c 2. CHS 1998. nancy.muhlheim@gmail.com

MUINDE, Sandra LaVerne (FdL) 311 Division St, Oshkosh WI 54901 B Milwaukee WI 4/21/1950 d Alfonso E Miller & Shirley M. D 5/7/2011 Bp Russell Edward Jacobus. m 6/21/1969 Samuel Muinde c 3. muinde3@yahoo.com

MUIR, George Daniels (Chi) 60 Church Street, Asheville NC 28801 **Int Trin Epis Ch Asheville NC 2010-** B Goldsboro NC 5/25/1954 s J Harry Muir & Martha Elizabeth. BA U NC 1976; MDiv VTS 1982. D 6/7/1982 Bp Brice Sidney Sanders P 1/21/1983 Bp Hunley Agee Elebash. m 8/20/1977 Susan Byers c 3. R Gr Epis Ch Hinsdale IL 2001-2010; Assoc Gr & H Trin Epis Ch Richmond VA 1989-2000; R S Paul's Ch Beaufort NC 1984-1989; Asst S Jn's Epis Ch Fayetteville NC 1982-1984. Bd, Ymca 1989-2000; COM 1994-1997; Dir Middle Atlantic Paridh Trng Prog 1989-2000; Goe Rdr 1987-1994; Stndg Com 1986-1989. trgdm@aol.com

MUIR, Richard Dale (Chi) 181 Wildwood Rd, Lake Forest IL 60045 B Cincinnati OH 6/4/1932 s Virgil Raymond Muir & Virginia Annette. BS Mia 1954; MDiv Bex 1967; DMin Hartford Sem 1981. D 6/17/1967 Bp Nelson Marigold Burroughs P 2/6/1968 Bp John Harris Burt. m 8/8/1959 Ruth A Craighead c 3. Assoc The Ch Of The H Sprt Lake Forest IL 1992-1996; R S Mk's Barrington Hills IL 1986-1991; Int Gr Ch Vineyard Haven MA 1985-1986; R S Steph's Ch Cohasset MA 1970-1984; Pres Bex Alum Bex Columbus OH 1969-1976; Cur S Paul's Ch Akron OH 1967-1970. rdmuir59@comcast.net

MUIRURI, Jacob Ngobia (Dal) 12727 Hillcrest Rd, Dallas TX 75230 **Trin Angl Ch Dallas TX 2011-** B Muranga 5/20/1954 s Christopher Muiruri & Janet. B.Div St. Paul's U Kenya 1991; Mstr of Arts (Theol) Moore Theol Coll 1996. Trans from Anglican Church Of Kenya 5/13/2008 Bp James Monte Stanton. m 1/1/1983 Rodah M Ngobia c 3. Trin Epis Ch Dallas TX 2008-2010. jnmuiruri@trinityanglicanchurch.net

MUKHWANA-NAFUMA, Joel Eric (NY) 116 Hoover Rd, Yonkers NY 10710 B Uganda 12/5/1941 s Daniel Tsama Mukhwana & Susana Mutenyo. CTh Bp Tucker Theol Coll Mukono Ug 1969; LTh VTS 1975; BA U Of Charleston 1981; MA Marshall St U 1983; MDiv VTS 1983. Trans from Church of the Province of Uganda 12/3/2004 Bp Mark Sean Sisk. m 10/30/1970 Juliana Auma Nafuma c 3. P-in-c Trin Ch Mt Vernon NY 2003-2010. Auth, "Imbalu, Gisu Initiation Rite," UMI Dissertation Serv, 1991; Auth, "The Faith of Magd," 1980. Naming of Joel Nafuma Refugee Cntr Epis Ch, Rome 1985. trinityhistoric1856@yahoo.com

MULAC, Pamela Ann (Los) 7585 N Park Crest Ln, Prescott Valley AZ 86314 B Salem OH 12/6/1944 d Elmer John Mulac & Dorothy Adeline. Bryn 1964; BA U Chi 1966; MDiv SWTS 1974; PhD NWU 1988. D 9/21/1974 Bp James Winchester Montgomery P 12/13/1978 Bp Charles Bennison. m 8/8/1987 George Larse. Dio Los Angeles Los Angeles CA 2001-2005; R S Steph's Par Whittier CA 1998-2005; Int S Mich's Epis Ch Riverside CA 1996-1998; Int S Tim's Epis Ch Apple Vlly CA 1995-1996; The ETS At Claremont Claremont CA 1994-1998; Foothill Presb Hosp Glendora CA 1994-1995; Asst S Geo's Par La Can CA 1994-1995; Asst All SS Ch Pasadena CA 1992-1993; Asst S Ambr Par Claremont CA 1988-1991; Asst S Mk's Epis Ch Upland CA 1984-1987; Adj Instr SWTS Evanston IL 1979-1981. AAPC 1973; ACPE 2000; OHC 1973. Resrch Awd Aapc Pacific Reg 1989. revpammulac@msn.com

MULDER, Timothy John (Nwk) 2 Hunt Lane, Gladstone NJ 07934 **Chr Ch Short Hills NJ 2010-** B Englwood NJ 6/26/1954 s Edwin George Mulder & Luella Beth. BA Hope Coll 1976; MDiv PrTS 1982; DMin Drew U 1991. D 2/11/1998 P 8/1/1998 Bp Joe Morris Doss. m 1/1/2001 Linda Walker c 2. New Brunswick Theoloical Sem New Brunswick NJ 2008-2010; S Lk's Ch Gladstone NJ 1998-2006; S Bern's Ch Bernardsville NJ 1998; Assoc S Bern's Ch Bernardsville NJ 1996-1998. Auth, "Adv/Christmas Year C 2009-12010," *New Proclamation*, Fortress Press, 2009; "My, How You've Changed," *Sermons and Comments*, Epis Preaching Fndt, 2006; Auth, "Never the Point of the Story," *Preaching through the Year of Lk*, Morehouse Pub, 2000; Auth, *Liturg & Life*, Reformed Ch Press, 1996; Ed, *Sprtl Discipline of Tithing*, Reformed Ch Press, 1993. Cmnty of St. Jn Bapt 2006. tmulder@me.com

MULDOON, Maggie Rose Daniels (Minn) 18350 67 Avenue, Cloverdale BC V3S 1E5 Canada B Minneapolis MN 2/26/1939 d Cosmas Damian Daniels & Mary Ethel. BA U of St. Thos 1980; MDiv U Tor 1990. Trans from Anglican Church of Canada 11/5/2002 Bp James Louis Jelinek. c 5. S Lk's Epis Ch Rochester MN 2003-2004; P-in-c S Paul's Ch Winona MN 2002-2003. maggie_muldoon@mac.com

MULFORD, Marie Lynne (WVa) 2585 State Route 7 N, Gallipolis OH 45631 B Chicago IL 10/11/1948 d Willard R Gour & Shirley Dorothy. BA OH SU 1971; MA OH SU 1978; 2001. D 9/19/2002 P 6/7/2003 Bp William Michie Klusmeyer. m 8/21/1983 James Michael Mulford. River Bend Cluster Point Pleasant WV 2003-2008; P S Jn's Ripley WV 2002. mulford@eurekanet.com

MULKIN, Suzanne Devine (CFla) 875 Brock Rd, Bartow FL 33830 **D The Epis Ch Of The Gd Shpd Lake Wales FL 2008-** B Queens NY 5/19/1948 d Raymond Herbert Devine & Marion Louise. Reformed TS; AA Vernon Crt Jr Coll 1968; BA Barrington Coll 1971; Cert Natl Inst For Lay Trng New York NY 1978; Cert Inst for Chr Stds Florida 1998. D 12/11/1999 Bp John Wadsworth Howe. m 6/19/1976 Michael Mulkin. D All SS Epis Ch Lakeland FL 2004-2006; D S Steph's Ch Lakeland FL 2002-2003; D H Trin Epis Ch Bartow FL 1999-2002. NAAD 1999; OSL 2005. deacon.suzanne@gmail.com

MULL, Judson Gary (At) 499 Trabert Ave Nw, Atlanta GA 30309 **Cler Assoc All SS Epis Ch Atlanta GA 1994-** B Chattanooga TN 10/20/1946 s Julian Lake Mull & Grace Louise. BA U GA 1972; MDiv STUSo 1977. D 6/11/1977 Bp Bennett Jones Sims P 3/1/1978 Bp Charles Judson Child Jr. Cler Assoc Cathd Of S Phil Atlanta GA 1984-1993; Asst R S Anne's Epis Ch Atlanta GA 1978-1984; D/P Emm Epis Ch Athens GA 1977-1978. jgary@mindspring.com

MULLALY JR, Charles Francis (Va) 888 Summit View Ln, Charlottesville VA 22903 **Emm Epis Ch Greenwood VA 1997-** B Washington DC 9/25/1942 s Charles Francis Mullaly & Virginia Adelaide. BA E Carolina U 1967; MS Sthrn Illinois U 1979; MA Baylor U 1981; MDiv VTS 1994. D 6/11/1994 P 12/1/1994 Bp Peter James Lee. m 6/16/1966 Leith Merrow c 2. Asst S Ptr's Epis Ch Arlington VA 1994-1997.

MULLEN, Sean E (Pa) St Mark's Church, 1625 Locust St, Philadelphia PA 19103 **S Mk's Ch Philadelphia PA 2002-** B Jersey City NJ 6/19/1967 s Richard Francis Mullen & Anne Mary. BA W&M 1989; MDiv GTS 1996. D 6/1/1996 P 12/1/1996 Bp Richard Frank Grein. Asst R All SS Ch Richmond VA 1996-1998. curate@saintmarksphiladelphia.org

MULLER, Barbara L (SwFla) 504 Constitution Dr, Tampa FL 33613 B Chattanooga TN 4/5/1943 d Malbern Edington & Barbara Lefort. BA Ob 1966; MA Stetson U 1975; Cert Inst for Chr Stds 1977; MDiv STUSo 1987. D 11/18/1977 P 12/1/1987 Bp William Hopkins Folwell. Org/Mus Dir S Clem Epis Ch Tampa FL 1998-2001; Epis Campus Mnstry Orlando FL 1987-1990; Assoc R The Epis Ch Of S Jn The Bapt Orlando FL 1987-1990; Asst H Cross Epis Ch Sanford FL 1981-1984; Asst Trin Ch S Louis MO 1980-1981; Asst H Cross Epis Ch Sanford FL 1977-1980. Auth, "Memi Serv For Nrsng Hm". eclector@aol.com

MULLER, Donald Joseph (NJ) 4 Christopher Mill Rd, Medford NJ 08055 **Dn-Burlington Convoc Dio New Jersey Trenton NJ 2004-; R S Ptr's Ch Medford NJ 2004-; Dept Of Cmncatn Dio New Jersey Trenton NJ 1986-** B New York NY 4/28/1953 s Edward R Muller & Edith E. BA Manhattan Coll 1975; MDiv Nash 1980; DMin GTF 1997. D 6/7/1980 P 12/1/1980 Bp Paul Moore Jr. m 9/5/1982 Margaret Lynn VanDuzer. R S Steph's Epis Ch Wilkes Barre PA 1996-2004; Dioc Coun Dio New Jersey Trenton NJ 1990-1994; Chair - Evang Comm Dio New Jersey Trenton NJ 1988-1995; Evang Cmsn Dio New Jersey Trenton NJ 1987-1995; R The Ch Of The H Innoc Bch Haven NJ 1986-1996; R Ch Of The Div Love Montrose NY 1982-1986; Dir Dio New York New York City NY 1981-1985; Cur Par Of Chr The Redeem Pelham NY 1980-1982. Cn Dio Bethlehem 1999. frdon@stpetersmedford.org

MULLER JR, John (Colo) 513 E 19th St, Delta CO 81416 B Philadelphia PA 7/5/1942 s John Muller & Elizabeth Pauline. BA U of Pennsylvania 1964; MDiv VTS 1969. D 6/7/1969 Bp Chandler W Sterling P 12/7/1969 Bp David Ritchie Thornberry. m 10/14/1967 Linda Young c 2. Exec Coun Dio Colorado Denver CO 1979-1985; S Lk's Epis Ch Delta CO 1977-2008; Stff Ch Of The Redeem Houston TX 1976-1977; Dioc Coun Dio Colorado Denver CO 1972-1974; R S Barn Of The Vlly Cortez CO 1971-1975; Vic S Paul's Ch Mancos CO 1971-1975; Asst S Mk's Epis Ch Casper WY 1969-1971. jmuller621@msn.com

MULLER JR, Liam Charles (SD) 522 W 4th Ave, Mitchell SD 57301 **R S Mary's Epis Ch Mitchell SD 2006-** B Poughkeepsie NY 10/25/1961 s

William Muller & Katherine Loise. BA Marist Coll 1988; MDiv CDSP 2006. D 3/11/2006 Bp Mark Sean Sisk P 9/16/2006 Bp Creighton Leland Robertson. m 7/16/1988 Margaret Jean Muller c 3. rectorstmarys@mitchelltelecom.net

MULLIGAN IV, Edward Bowman (RI) 251 Canaan Rd, Salisbury CT 06068 **Emm Chap Manchester MA 2009-** B Kingston PA 4/1/1952 s Edward Mulligan & Ellen. BA Amh Amherst MA 1975; JD S Louis U Law Sch S Louis MO 1981; MDiv Ya Berk 2006. D 6/3/2006 Bp V Gene Robinson. m 8/29/1992 Pamela Bowman Mulligan c 3. nmulligan@salisburyschool.org

MULLIN, Mark Hill (Okla) 2091 Brownstone Ln, Charlottesville VA 22901 B Chicago IL 7/6/1940 s Francis Joseph Mullin & Alma Hill. BA Harv 1962; BA Oxf 1964; MDiv GTS 1968; MA Oxf 1968. D 6/15/1968 P 3/1/1969 Bp James Winchester Montgomery. m 7/23/1966 Martha Jane Leamy c 3. Cathd of St Ptr & St Paul Washington DC 1978-1999; Blue Ridge Sch Dyke VA 1976-1977; The Choate Sch Wallingford CT 1968-1976. Auth, "The Headmaster's Run," Rowman and Littlefield Educ, 2008; Auth, "Educ for the 21st Century," Madison Books, 1991; Auth, "Wstrn Europe 84," Stryke-Post, 1984; Auth, "Should Buffalo Bob Come to Chap?," *NAIS Journ*, 1975.

MULLINS, Andrew Jackson W (NY) 1393 York Ave, New York NY 10021 B Charleston WV 7/26/1939 s Andrew Jackson Mullins & Sallye Elizabeth. BA Bethany Coll 1962; STM GTS 1967; Col 1978; Cert Inst For Not-For-Profit Mgmt 1978. D 6/12/1967 P 12/16/1967 Bp Wilburn Camrock Campbell. m 6/15/1996 Cathy West c 1. R The Ch Of The Epiph New York NY 1998-2011; V-Dn S Mk's Cathd Seattle WA 1990-1998; The Assoc R S Barth's Ch New York NY 1968-1990; Vic Gr Ch Ravenswood WV 1967-1968; Vic S Jn's Ripley WV 1967-1968. Auth, "A Hist Of Missions In The Dio W Virginia". Hon Cn Dio Olympia 1998; Who'S Who In Rel. ajwmullins@aol.com

MULLINS, Edward Lee (Mich) 415 Church Rd, Bloomfield Hills MI 48304 **Int Epis Ch Of S Fran-In-The-Vlly Green Vlly AZ 2009-** B Wheeling WV 8/11/1944 s Ezekiel Weddie Mullins & Mayme Mae. BBA Marshall U 1966; MDiv VTS 1971; None PrTS 1982; None Harv 1987. D 6/11/1971 P 2/26/1972 Bp Wilburn Camrock Campbell. m 6/30/1973 Diana M Young c 2. R Chr Ch Cranbrook Bloomfield Hills MI 1996-2009; R S Barth's Epis Ch Poway CA 1985-1996; R Emm Ch Cumberland MD 1978-1984; Assoc Gr Epis Ch Silver Sprg MD 1974-1978; Vic S Mk's Epis Ch Berkeley Sprg WV 1971-1974. Auth, "Guidelines For Congrl Growth," *Dio San Diego*, Dioc, 1989; Auth, "Outline Notes on The NT," *Self Pub*, S Barth's, 1988; Auth, "Outline Notes On The OT," *Self Pub*, S Bartholomews, 1988; Auth, "Article on Ch Growth," *Alive Now*, Grp, 1973. Epis Ch Visual Arts 2007. Wrld Sabbath Peace Awd Outstanding Wk bewteen Rel 2009; ECVA's Best Relgious Prog TV 2005; Herald Awd Best Ecum Event TV 2004; Herald Awd Best Rel Prog TV 2003; Hometown Awd Best Rel TV Interview Show 2002. emullins@emzoom.com

M

MULLINS, Judith Pierpont (Oly) 80 E Roanoke St Apt 16, Seattle WA 98102 B Waterbury CT 2/15/1938 d Elvin W Pierpont & Bernice L. AS Dn Coll 1958; Ascp U of Tennessee 1966. D 6/22/1996 Bp Vincent Waydell Warner. m 6/25/1960 Donald Hugh Mullins.

MULLINS, Walter Earl (Md) 6922 Hollenberry Rd, Sykesville MD 21784 **R S Barn Epis Ch Sykesville MD 2000-** B Nash County NC 6/8/1945 s Walter Edison Mullins & Nancy Jane. BA E Carolina U 1967; MDiv SE Sem Wake Forest NC 1972; Inst Pstr Psychol 1975; Advncd CPE 1978. D 6/12/1982 P 4/1/1983 Bp John Thomas Walker. c 3. R S Paul's Ch Dedham MA 1988-1992; S Jn's Ch Georgetown Par Washington DC 1983-1985; VTS Alexandria VA 1983-1984. earlmullins@hotmail.com

MULLIS, Robert Bradley (NC) 405 Baymount Dr., Statesville NC 28625 **R Trin Epis Ch Statesville NC 2003-** B Winston-Salem NC 6/27/1961 s Starret Worth Mullis & Pauline Gertrude. BA Davidson Coll 1983; MA U NC 1991; MDiv Duke 1996; Cert. of Angl. Studi VTS 1996. D 6/29/1996 P 6/21/1997 Bp Robert Carroll Johnson Jr. m 8/13/1994 Ellyn Bain Pearson c 2. Dioc Coun Mem Dio No Carolina Raleigh NC 2006-2008; Asst Ch Of The Nativ Raleigh NC 1996-2003. rbmullis@roadrunner.com

MULRYAN, John Anthony (LI) 68 Grace Ave, Great Neck NY 11021 B New York NY 7/17/1936 s John Mulryan & Bridget. STL Gregorian U 1962; MA Col 1965. D 8/1/1981 Bp Walter Decoster Dennis Jr P 12/20/1981 Bp Paul Moore Jr. c 1. S Paul's Ch Great Neck NY 1982-2008. Woodrow Wilson Sum Schlr Prize 1994; Natl Endwmt For Hmnts Schlr S Jn'S U Collegeville MN.

MULVEY, Dorian Larsen (Az) 8951 E. Sutton Drive, Scottsdale AZ 85260 **R S Anth On The Desert Scottsdale AZ 2008-** B New York NY 7/25/1954 d Harold Clifford Larsen & Dorothy Sophie. BA CUNY 1975; MBA NYU 1981; MDiv SWTS 1998. D 6/20/1998 Bp Chilton Abbie Richardson Knudsen P 12/21/1998 Bp Herbert Alcorn Donovan Jr. m 5/30/1976 George Matthew Mulvey c 2. R Ch Of The Ascen Seattle WA 2003-2008; The Epis Ch Of S Jas The Less Northfield IL 1998-2003. Bd Dir, Olympia 2005-2008; Bdgt Com, Chicago 2001-2003; Chr Formation Comission, Chicago 2000-2003. dorianmulvey@st-anthony.net

MULVEY JR, Thomas Patrick (Mass) 3 Sayles Rd, Hingham MA 02043 **Emm Ch Braintree MA 2009-** B Boston MA 8/24/1955 BS Stonehill Coll 1977; JD Suffolk U 1985; MDiv EDS 2001. Trans from Anglican Church of Canada 9/6/2005 Bp M(arvil) Thomas Shaw III. m 12/11/1982 Elizabeth Friese c 2. Asst Ch Of S Jn The Evang Hingham MA 2004-2007. tommulvey@comcast.net

MULVEY SHERER, Valori (WNC) 506 W Sumter St, Shelby NC 28150 **R Ch Of The Redeem Shelby NC 2009-** B Perth Amboy NJ 12/11/1958 d Edward Joseph Mulvey & Manuela Rivera. AA Cnty Coll Of Morris 1978; BA Rutgers-The St U 1984; MDiv STUSo 2005. D 2/5/2005 P 9/7/2005 Bp Henry Irving Louttit. m 4/16/1988 Steven Sherer c 3. R S Mary's Epis Ch Cadillac MI 2007-2009; Cur S Paul's Epis Ch S Jos MI 2005-2007. vmsherer@gmail.com

MUMFORD, Nigel William David (Alb) 23 Sloan Dr, Greenwich NY 12834 **The Rev. Dio Albany Albany NY 2005-** B England 3/13/1954 D 6/11/2005 P 12/17/2005 Bp Daniel William Herzog. m 9/15/2001 Lynn French Mumford c 2. healing@albanydioceselc.org

MUN SSP, Paul Shinkyu (SVa) Grace Episcopal Church, 5181 Princess Anne Road, Virginia Beach VA 23462 **P-in-c Gr Epis Ch Virginia Bch VA 2008-** B Tokyo, Japan 3/8/1944 s Yong Oh Mun & Yang Ja. MDiv Sthrn Louisville KY 1989; PhD Sthrn Louisville KY 1995; Dipl. in Angl Stds SungKongHoe Angl U, Seou, Korea 2004. D 9/28/2007 P 3/31/2008 Bp John Clark Buchanan. m 10/24/1973 Grace Hahn c 2. paulmun308@gmail.com

MUNCIE, Margaret Ann (NY) 1 Columbus Pl, New York NY 10019 **Healthcare Chapl New York NY 2002-** B New York NY 2/4/1948 d James Ernest Muncie & Doris. BA Hood Coll 1970; MDiv GTS 1974; Bd Cert Chapl 1984; Cert U MI 1984. D 6/15/1974 P 4/25/1977 Bp Jonathan Goodhue Sherman. m 7/27/1974 Stephen M Bolle c 1. Fac Dio Sthrn Ohio Cincinnati OH 1994-2000; VP The GTS New York NY 1992-1993; St Lukes Cntr Cincinnati OH 1990-2000; Field Educ Supvsr Ya Berk New Haven CT 1984-1990; Cmsn On Aging Dio New York New York City NY 1983-1989; Greenwich Chapl Serv Inc Greenwish CT 1982-1990; Asst S Matt's Ch Bedford NY 1978-1980; Seminar Moderator The GTS New York NY 1978-1980; Bishops Advsry Com New York NY 1974-1976. Auth, "Sensory Stimulated Wrshp," 2003; Ed, "Aging Nwsltr," 1994; Co-Auth, "Dvlpmt Of Sprtl Awareness Prog In Ltc Settings," 1993. ACPE; Assn Prof Chapl; ESMA; Forsa. revpegg@aol.com

MUNCIE, Stephen Dee (LI) 1989 Madison Rd Apt 301, Cincinnati OH 45208 **Gr Ch Brooklyn NY 2004-** B Fort Knox KY 2/20/1955 s Russell Dee Muncie & Wilma Jean. BA Mia 1976; MDiv Van 1979. D 6/29/1982 P 1/18/1983 Bp William Grant Black. m 6/12/2003 Linette Powers c 2. Cn Dio Sthrn Ohio Cincinnati OH 2000-2004; S Fran Epis Ch Springboro OH 1982-2000. Comt. stephenmuncie@mac.com

MUNDAY, Robert Stevenson (SC) 2777 Mission Rd., Nashotah WI 53058 **Nash Nashotah WI 2001-** B Benton IL 10/19/1954 s Robert M Munday & Kathryn M. STUSo; AA Rend Lake Coll Ina IL 1974; BA Sthrn Illinois U 1976; MDiv Mid-Amer Bapt TS 1979; PhD Mid-Amer Bapt TS 1984; MLS Van 1986. D 11/25/1989 P 6/9/1990 Bp Edward Harding MacBurney. m 7/31/1976 Christina Ellen Karroll. TESM Ambridge PA 1986-2001. Auth, "Ontology In Process Theol". AAR; Bd NOEL. Who'S Who In Rel; Who'S Who In Amer. rmunday@nashotah.edu

MUNDAY, Sharon Boublitz (SVa) PO Box 3886, Chester VA 23831 B Baltimore MD 11/28/1942 d John Louis Boublitz & Ethel L. MS Madison U 1965; BA Mary Washington U 1965; Masters' Degree Loyola of New Orleans 1990. D 6/18/2011 Bp Herman Hollerith IV. c 1. sbmunday@verizon.net

MUNDY, Robert Lowry (RG) PO Box 663, Tome NM 87060 **Vic S Matt's Mssn Los Lunas NM 2006-** B Las Cruces NM 12/30/1963 Bachelor of Sci New Mex St U. 1988; Basic Chr Stds TESM 2005. D 7/30/2005 P 8/19/2006 Bp Jeffrey Neil Steenson. m 6/17/1953 Karen Lee Mundy. COM Dio The Rio Grande Albuquerque NM 2009-2011; Cathd Chapt Dio The Rio Grande Albuquerque NM 2008-2011. Valencia Civitan Club 2008; Valencia Cnty Jvnl Justice Bd 2011; Valencia Cnty Resiliency Corp. 2011. Paul Harris Fell Chama Rotary Club 2006. frrobert@mundy.com

MUNGOMA, Stephen Masette (Los) 1401 W 123rd St, Los Angeles CA 90047 B Mbale UG 4/4/1949 s Nicholas Masette & Kezia. BA Makerere U 1972; MA Makerere U 1977; MA Fuller TS 1987; PhD Fuller TS 2003. Trans from Church of the Province of Uganda 6/1/2000 Bp Frederick Houk Borsch. m 1/6/1973 Rachel Masete Kakai c 4. S Patricks Ch And Day Sch Thousand Oaks CA 2005-2006; P-in-c S Tim's Par Compton CA 2000-2006. smmungoma@yahoo.com

MUNOZ, Antonio (Dal) 5100 Ross Ave, Dallas TX 75206 **Cn For Hisp Mnstry S Matt's Cathd Dallas TX 2003-** B Mexicali Baja Mexico 2/2/1963 s Manuel Munoz & Maria Cecilia. MA Universidad Autonoma de Baja CA 1985; Cert S Andrews TS Guadalajara Mx 1990; Seminario San Andres 1990. D 11/30/1990 P 10/1/1991 Bp Samuel Espinoza-Venegas. c 4. Vic La Iglesia De San Pablo Seaside CA 1994-2003; Mssn San Pablo Monterey CA 1994-2002; Dio Wstrn Mex Zapopan Jalisco CP 45150 1990-1993. amunoz@episcopalcathedral.org

MUNOZ, Frank Peter (Spr) Naval Medical Center San Diego, 34800 Bob Wilson Dr., San Diego CA 92134 **Chapl Off Of Bsh For ArmdF New York NY 2004-** B CUBA 6/29/1958 s Frank Munoz & Lopez. BA Loyola U 1983; Jesuit TS 1984; MA Mt St Mary's Coll Los Angeles CA 1989; CTh ETSBH

1996; MA Natl U 2006; Naval War Coll 2008. D 6/1/1996 P 1/18/1997 Bp Frederick Houk Borsch. m 7/3/1982 Estella Gonzalez c 2. Sr. Assoc for Chr Ed. S Geo's Epis Ch Laguna Hills CA 2002-2003; R All Ang Ch Miami Sprg FL 1999-2002; Asst to the Dn Trin Cathd Miami FL 1997-1998; D S Barn' Epis Ch Los Angeles CA 1996-1997. semperfipadre@yahoo.com

MUNOZ, Maria E (Los) 1917 New Jersey St, Los Angeles CA 90033 **P-in-c Trin Epis Par Los Angeles CA 2006-** B Los Angeles CA 4/2/1957 d Fernando Munoz & Maria Consuelo. BA Pr Princeton NJ 1980; California St Los Angeles 1990; MDiv Epis TS of The SW 2005. D 6/11/2005 Bp Chester Lovelle Talton. lmunoz9568@aol.com

MUNOZ-LABRA, Manuel J (PR) PO Box 6795, Marina Station, Mayaguez PR 00681 B Cienfuegos Cuba 6/1/1929 s Victor Manuel Munoz & Josefa. ThB Seminario Evangelico De Matanza 1958; PhD Universidad De Oriente Cu 1963. D 4/13/1958 P 2/24/1959 Bp A H Blankingship. m 6/5/1961 Oneida F Munoz c 2. Dio Puerto Rico S Just PR 1980-2000; Dio Puerto Rico S Just PR 1972-1979. "Lit," Juan De Valdes:His Living & Writings, 1958. Ymca Of The Usa, E Field Cluster Awd 1992; Bp Medal Bp Reus Awd 1978. majumu@yahoo.com

MUNRO BSG, Edward Henry (Md) 12310 Firtree Ln, Bowie MD 20715 B New York NY 10/13/1943 s Edward Henry Munro & Cecilia. Nthrn Virginia Cmnty Coll 1972; U of Maryland 1977; Cert STUSo 1985; Maryland TS 1991. D 6/15/1991 Bp A(lbert) Theodore Eastman. m 12/8/1962 Barbara Gail Lof c 4. Asst S Geo's And S Matthews Ch Baltimore MD 1996-2004; D/ Asst The Ch Of The H Apos Halethorpe MD 1991-1992. No Amer Maritime Mnstry Assn. Hon Chapl Missions to Seamen Baltimore MD. broedbsg@comcast.net

MUNRO, JoAnn Reynolds (Ct) 27 Chateau Margaux, Bloomfield CT 06002 B Walla Walla WA 10/20/1934 d Harry Jay Reynolds & Sarah Margaret. BS U of Idaho Moscow ID 1956; MA NYU 1975; MDiv Ya Berk 1985. D 6/13/1987 P 2/1/1988 Bp Arthur Edward Walmsley. m 6/22/1996 David Livingston Simpson c 2. Cn for Transitional Mnstry Dio Connecticut Hartford CT 1999-2006; R S Mich's Ch Naugatuck CT 1993-1999; S Paul's Ch Fairfield CT 1987-1993. "It's a Journey: Calling a P to Your Par," The Epis Dio Connecticut. Cn Chr Ch Cathd 2005; Cn Chr Ch Cathd 2000; Cler Ldrshp Proj, Class IX Trin Ch, Wall St, NYC. munro.j.34@gmail.com

MUNRO, Michael Gregory (Kan) 804 Cottonwood Dr, Lansing KS 66043 **Dn, NE Convoc Dio Kansas Topeka KS 2004-; R S Paul's Ch Leavenworth KS 2000-** B San Mateo CA 3/14/1952 s Francis Raymond Munro & Theresa Marie. AA Coll of San Mateo 1972; BA WA SU 1974; MDiv CDSP 1983; Cert Cler Ldrshp Proj - Class XXI 2008. D 6/25/1983 P 6/9/1984 Bp William Edwin Swing. m 8/20/1983 Machrina Loris Blasdell c 2. Coun of Trst Dio Kansas Topeka KS 2004-2010; Bp Search Com Dio Kansas Topeka KS 2003-2004; Vic S Mths Epis Ch San Ramon CA 1995-2000; St Johns Epis Ch Ross CA 1992-1995; Int S Anselm's Epis Ch Lafayette CA 1991-1992; P-in-c Emm Epis Ch (Piedmont Par) Delaplane VA 1987; Asst Min Ch Of The Gd Shpd Burke VA 1985-1987; Asst Min Chr Epis Ch Los Altos CA 1983-1985. Tertiary of the Soc of S Fran 1982. michaelmunro@sbcglobal.net

MUNROE, James Granger (WMass) 235 State St Apt 413, Springfield MA 01103 **Chr Ch Cathd Springfield MA 1982-** B Boston MA 12/29/1946 s William Abbot Munroe & Jeannette Granger. BA Wms 1972; MDiv VTS 1975. D 6/15/1975 P 1/6/1976 Bp Alexander Doig Stewart. S Jn's Ch Northampton MA 1983-1986; Stff Off Dio Wstrn Massachusetts Springfield MA 1982-1983; Int S Thos Epis Ch Auburn MA 1982; Asst Gr Epis Ch New York NY 1977-1981; S Andr's Ch Turners Falls MA 1975-1977; Cur S Jas' Ch Greenfield MA 1975-1977. dean.javanet@rcn.com

MUNROE, Sally G (Colo) 1127 Westmoreland Rd, Colorado Springs CO 80907 **S Andr's Ch Manitou Sprg CO 2010-** B Charleston WV 1/1/1942 BS SMU. D 6/8/2002 P 12/14/2002 Bp William Jerry Winterrowd. Ch Of S Mich The Archangel Colorado Sprg CO 2002-2009. sallygo2@me.com

MUNSON, Peter Alan (Colo) 9972 W 86th Ave, Arvada CO 80005 **R S Ambr Epis Ch Boulder CO 2001-** B London UK 8/22/1957 s Holger William Munson & Coranelle Campbell. BA U CO 1979; JD U CO 1982; MDiv VTS 1991. D 6/15/1991 P 12/1/1991 Bp William Jerry Winterrowd. m 8/1/1987 Julia Gordon Smith c 1. Vic S Martha's Epis Ch Westminster CO 1992-2001; Cur Ch Of S Jn Chrys Golden CO 1991-1992. PETERMUNSON3@COMCAST.NET

MUNTEAN, Aurel Henry (Ga) 2820 Peachtree Rd NW Apt 302, Atlanta GA 30305 B Detroit MI 10/29/1923 s Nick Muntean & Dolly. Emory U; BS Wayne 1950; BD SWTS 1960; Emory U 1968. D 6/8/1960 P 4/1/1961 Bp Albert R Stuart. m 7/5/1958 Barbara Tillman c 3. Asst S Barth's Epis Ch Atlanta GA 1968-1969; Cur The Ch Of The Gd Shpd Augusta GA 1963-1967; Vic Ch Of The Gd Shpd Swainsboro GA 1961-1963; Vic The Epis Ch Of The Annunc Vidalia GA 1961-1963; Vic Ch Of The H Sprt Dawson GA 1960-1961; Vic H Trin Epis Ch Blakely GA 1960-1961. aurelmunt@aol.com

MUNZ, Catherine A (Pgh) 5 Willow Circle, Easthampton MA 01027 **R S Jn's Ch Northampton MA 2008-** B Detroit MI 10/17/1953 d Charles Munz & Jo Ann Marguaritte. Schoolcraft Cmnty Coll; ABS Nthrn Michigan U 1976; MDiv GTS 1993. D 6/19/1993 P 7/2/1994 Bp R(aymond) Stewart Wood Jr. m 5/26/1978 William D Phelps c 2. Chair, Com on the Status of Wmn Exec Coun Appointees New York NY 2007-2010; Com on the Status of Wmn Exec Coun Appointees New York NY 2004-2007; R S Brendan's Epis Ch Sewickley PA 1998-2008; S Jn's Ch Royal Oak MI 1993-1997. Contrib, "Wmn Uncommon Prayers," Morehouse Pub, 2000. link2cat@mac.com

MURASAKI-WEKALL, Ellen (Los) 330 East Cordova St Unit 366, Pasadena CA 91101 **P for Engl-Spkng Cong Cathd Cntr Of S Paul Cong Los Angeles CA 2010-; Supply P Dio Los Angeles Los Angeles CA 2010-** B Cologne DE 1/30/1930 d Ludwig Speyer & Lucy. BS NYU 1956; MS USC 1961; PhD Colorado Chr U 1973; ETSBH 1986. D 11/9/1996 Bp Chester Lovelle Talton P 1/22/2005 Bp Joseph Jon Bruno. m 10/13/1984 Gene Wekall. Assoc Ch Of The Ascen Tujunga CA 2008-2010; Assoc R S Geo's Par La Can CA 2005-2006; D S Geo's Par La Can CA 1996-2005. "Grp Wk w Adolescents," Journ of Psychol, 1963. ellenwek@aol.com

MURAY, Leslie Anthony (Mich) 241 Douglas Ave, Lansing MI 48906 B Budapest HU 12/30/1948 s Remus F Muray & Marianna Tohati. BA Whittier Coll 1971; BA Claremont TS 1973. P 10/1/1975 Bp J(ohn) Joseph Meakins Harte. All SS Ch Brooklyn MI 1997-2001; P S Jn's Epis Ch S Johns MI 1990-1996; Cbury MI SU E Lansing MI 1986-1989; R S Jn The Bapt Globe AZ 1986-1988; S Geo's Epis Ch Holbrook AZ 1984-1985; S Paul's Epis Ch Winslow AZ 1984-1985; R Epiph On The Desert Gila Bend AZ 1980-1981; Epis Cmnty Serv Phoenix AZ 1978-1979; S Lk's At The Mtn Phoenix AZ 1976-1978.

MURCHISON, Joel Williams (EC) 259 W 19th St, Chattanooga TN 37408 B Wilmington NC 7/27/1924 s David Reid Murchison & May. BS U NC 1948; MDiv VTS 1952. D 6/23/1952 Bp Thomas H Wright P 6/18/1953 Bp Richard S M Emrich. R S Columba Ch Detroit MI 1957-1962; Cur Chr Ch Cranbrook Bloomfield Hills MI 1952-1953. Integrity-E.T. 2001. murtal@comcast.net

MURCHISON, Malcolm Fraser (CFla) 1603 E Winter Park Rd, Orlando FL 32803 **R Emm Ch Orlando FL 2003-** B Rockville Centre NY 9/29/1948 s Kenneth Fraser Murchison & Victoria Jane. BA Colg 1970; ThM Gordon-Conwell TS 1985; MDiv VTS 1985; DMin STUSo 1999. D 5/20/1985 Bp Robert Campbell Witcher Sr P 11/1/1985 Bp George Nelson Hunt III. m 6/11/1972 Linda Louise White c 2. Ch Of Our Sav Palm Bay FL 1997-1998; Trst The TS at The U So Sewanee TN 1996-2002; S Edw's Sch Vero Bch FL 1992-2002; Assoc R Trin Ch Vero Bch FL 1987-1992; Cur S Jn's Ch Barrington RI 1985-1987. Auth, "arts & Revs," *Sewanee Theol Revs*, Vts Journ. mfmurchison@bellsouth.net

MURDOCH, Brian J(oseph) P(aul) (Mass) 38 Highland Park Ave, Roxbury MA 02119 **P In Res Emm Ch W Roxbury MA 2004-** B Peabody MA 4/3/1954 s Urban John Murdoch & Helen Marie. Gordon-Conwell TS; UTS; BA Boston Coll 1977; MDiv GTS 1985. D 6/4/1986 Bp John Bowen Coburn P 4/1/1987 Bp David Elliot Johnson. Int S Paul's Epis Ch Hopkinton MA 2002-2004; Assoc S Mary's Epis Ch Dorchester MA 1997-2004; R Ch Of S Jn The Evang Boston MA 1986-1990; S Jn's Ch Charlestown (Boston) Charlestown MA 1986-1990. Soc Of S Jn The Evang - Assoc. brianmurd@aol.com

MURDOCH, Judith Carolyn (Ga) 4227 Columbia Rd, Martinez GA 30907 B Plainfield NJ 8/28/1943 d John Davis Bartlett & Eleanor McKay. BS Ed Monmouth U 1975; MS Nova SE U 2000. D 1/29/2011 Bp Scott Anson Benhase. m 7/25/1981 Francis J Murdoch c 3. cmurdoch@bygracedesign.net

MURDOCH, Julie Brady (WVa) 75 Old Cheat Rd., Morgantown WV 26508 **R S Thos a Becket Epis Ch Morgantown WV 2008-** B Bethesda MD 12/4/1958 MDiv VTS 2004. D 7/26/2003 P 6/13/2004 Bp John Chane. m 9/6/1986 Scott Orlo Murdoch c 3. S Barn' Ch Leeland Upper Marlboro MD 2004-2008; D H Trin Epis Ch Bowie MD 2003-2004. murdochj@aol.com

MURDOCH, Richard Dorsey (SVa) 214 Archers Mead, Williamsburg VA 23185 B Frederick MD 12/19/1939 s Richard Burgess Murdoch & Martha Blanche. BA U of Maryland 1961; MDiv VTS 1970; MBA Syr 1989; DMin Asbury TS 1991. D 6/27/1970 P 2/1/1971 Bp William Foreman Creighton. m 2/1/1964 Jane Lynn Helm c 2. Off Of Bsh For ArmdF New York NY 1978-1995; S Jn Wheeling WV 1976-1977; R Gr Ch Elkridge MD 1973-1976; Assoc R S Phil's Epis Ch Laurel MD 1970-1973. murdoch214@cox.net

MURDOCH JR, William Henry (Me) Po Box 639, Damariscotta ME 04543 B Philadelphia PA 11/6/1931 s William Henry Murdoch & Hannah Maud. Penn 1956; BA Villanova U 1968; MDiv EDS 1971. D 6/19/1971 P 2/1/1972 Bp Robert Lionne DeWitt. m 9/12/1953 Jane Hallam c 2. Estrn Upper Peninsula Epis Convoc Moran MI 1999-2001; R S Giles Ch Jefferson ME 1993-1994; Archd Dio Iowa Des Moines IA 1989-1993; Vic Ch Of The Epiph Centerville IA 1986-1989; Vic Gr Ch Albia IA 1986-1989; Vic S Andr's Ch Chariton IA 1986-1988; Vic/R S Giles Ch Jefferson ME 1979-1986; R S Fran-In-The-Fields Malvern PA 1973-1978; Cur Trin Memi Ch Binghamton NY 1971-1973. bmurdoch@tidewater.net

MURDOCK, Audrey (Ct) 300 Grove St Unit 26, Rutland VT 05701 B Burnley Lancashire UK 4/7/1938 d Dennis Copping & Evelyn Jean. BA Southport Coll Southport GB 1952; GTS 2000. D 6/15/2000 P 10/19/2000 Bp Mary Adelia Rosamond McLeod. c 2. Vic S Jn's Epis Ch Bristol CT 2006-2009; Rectr Trin Ch Jersey Shore PA 2002-2005; Assoc R Trin Ch Rutland VT 2000-2001.

Auth, "Hist of Trin Epis Ch," *Rutland VT 1794-1994*, 1994. SSJE 1994. amurdock38@aol.com

MURDOCK, Thomas Lee (Cal) 14821 N E Eugene St, Portland OR 97230 **Asst Gr S Paul's Epis Ch Tucson AZ 1995-; Assoc Iglesia Epis Del Buen Samaritano San Francisco CA 1992-; Assoc S Jn-By-The-Sea Epis Ch Bandon OR 1988-; Assoc S Mk's Par Berkeley CA 1988-** B San Mateo CA 5/2/1934 s James Maynard Murdock & Lillian Ada. BA Willamette U 1957; NWU 1958; MDiv CDSP 1962; VTS 1982. D 6/11/1962 P 12/1/1962 Bp James Walmsley Frederic Carman. m 8/30/1959 Esther Gwilliam c 2. R Trsfg Epis Ch San Mateo CA 1984-1987; Stndg Com Dio Oregon Portland OR 1977-1980; Bd Trst CDSP Berkeley CA 1975-1990; R Emm Ch Coos Bay OR 1970-1984; Stndg Com Dio Oregon Portland OR 1969-1972; R S Aid's Epis Ch Gresham OR 1966-1970. U Fell NWU; Legislativee Res Untd States Senate 85th Congr. thomas.murdock@comcast.net

MURGUIA, James Raphael (WTex) 618 Williamson Pl, Corpus Christi TX 78411 B San Antonio TX 6/1/1968 s Clemente Joseph Murguia & Priscilla. U So 1988; BA Texas A&M U 1992; MDiv Epis TS of The SW 1998. D 6/3/1998 P 2/5/1999 Bp James Edward Folts. m 6/20/1998 Elisabeth B Lester c 2. S Dav's Epis Ch San Antonio TX 2004-2011; R S Phil's Ch Uvalde TX 2000-2004; Cur Ch Of The Gd Shpd Corpus Christi TX 1998-2000. murguiajr@aol.com

MURPH, Jeffrey David (Pgh) 530 10th St, Oakmont PA 15139 **Stndg Com Dio Pittsburgh Monroeville PA 2008-2012; R S Thos Memi Epis Ch Oakmont PA 1994-** B Concord NC 10/9/1959 s Charles Robert Murph & Doris Annette. BA U NC 1980; MDiv VTS 1986. D 12/14/1986 Bp Robert Whitridge Estill P 12/1/1987 Bp Frank Harris Vest Jr. m 10/11/1986 Meloni J Craig c 3. Stndg Com Dio Pittsburgh Monroeville PA 1997-2001; Assoc S Paul's Epis Ch Winston Salem NC 1986-1994. PGHMURPH@CS.COM

MURPHEY, William Frederick (CPa) 2306 Edgewood Rd, Harrisburg PA 17104 **R Bangor Ch Of Churchtown Narvon PA 2008-** B Scranton PA 9/28/1932 s Howard Frederick Murphey & Frances Ann. BA Leh 1954; STB Ya Berk 1957. D 6/15/1957 P 12/21/1957 Bp Frederick J Warnecke. m 5/24/1958 Marian Lois Murphey c 2. Int S Jn's Ch Marietta PA 2000-2002; Epis Hm Shippensburg PA 1984-1998; S Andr's Epis Ch Shippensburg PA 1984-1998; Cn Pstr Cathd Ch Of S Steph Harrisburg PA 1979-1984; R S Paul's Ch Wellsboro PA 1974-1979; R All SS Ch Hanover PA 1965-1974; R S Steph's Ch Whitehall PA 1960-1965; Cur Trin Ch Bethlehem PA 1957-1960. Hon Cn S Steph's Cathd/Harrisburg PA Harrisburg PA 1991. canonwfm@comcast.net

M

MURPHREE, James Willis (Dal) 5426 Meadowcreek Dr Apt 2037, Dallas TX 75248 B Fort Worth TX 12/6/1934 s J W Murphree & C D. BA Ya 1957; MDiv UTS 1970; Cert PDS 1971. D 2/26/1972 P 12/1/1972 Bp William Henry Mead. S Lk's Epis Ch Dallas TX 1996-2003; Asst Ch Of The Epiph Richardson TX 1984-1989; Asst All SS Epis Ch Dallas TX 1982-1984; P-in-c Ch Of The Epiph Dallas TX 1979-1982; Asst Chr Epis Ch Dallas TX 1977-1979; Cur S Alb's Wilmington DE 1972-1973. AEHC.

MURPHY, Diane Gensheimer (Va) 9374 Mount Vernon Cir, Alexandria VA 22309 **Dioc Hm Bd Trst Dio Virginia Richmond VA 2011-2014; Assoc Chr Ch Alexandria VA 2006-** B Erie PA 11/12/1948 d Herbert F Gensheimer & Jeanne Lenore. BA Gannon U 1970; MA U of Maryland 1971; PhD U of Maryland 1978; MDiv VTS 2003. D 6/14/2003 P 12/20/2003 Bp Peter James Lee. m 6/6/1980 James Jerome Murphy c 1. Assoc S Paul's Epis Ch Alexandria VA 2005; Asst S Paul's Epis Ch Alexandria VA 2003-2005. dgmprop@aol.com

MURPHY, Edward John (NJ) 10 Rupells Rd, Clinton NJ 08809 **Pstr Assoc S Mart's Ch Bridgewater NJ 2008-** B Brooklyn NY 2/1/1946 s Edward Benjamin & Helen. BA CUNY; Drew U; MA FD; Eid Rutgers-The St U. D 5/22/1999 Bp Joe Morris Doss P 1/15/2000 Bp Herbert Alcorn Donovan Jr. m Marguerite Hanlon. R S Paul's Epis Ch Bound Brook NJ 2002-2008; Calv Epis Ch Flemington NJ 2000-2001; Ch Of The H Sprt Lebanon NJ 1999-2002. APA.

MURPHY JR, Edward John (CNY) 27 Bridge St Apt 2, Carthage NY 13619 **Shared Epis Mnstry E Carthage NY 2006-** B Brooklyn NY 9/14/1952 s Edward Murphy & Marie. Bex; BS Tenn Tech Univ 1979; MS SUNY 1988. D 10/7/2006 P 6/16/2007 Bp Gladstone Bailey Adams III. m 7/20/1996 Susan Everard. emurphy@carthagecsd.org

MURPHY, Genevieve Margaret (Va) 501 Simmons Gap Road, Box 172, Earlysville VA 22936 B York Yorkshire UK 1/8/1934 d Louis Johnson & Elsie May. BA Mary Baldwin Coll 1982; Med U of Virginia 1985; EdD U of Virginia 1990; MA VTS 1998. D 12/10/1998 P 6/10/1999 Bp Peter James Lee. m 12/16/1961 Richard Alan Murphy c 2. R Buck Mtn Epis Ch Earlysville VA 1998-2006.

MURPHY, Gwyneth MacKenzie (NY) 161 Main St, New Paltz NY 12561 **Muslim-Chr Relatns Com Dio New York New York City NY 2011-; Chapl Dio New York New York City NY 2007-; Prog Plnng Com Dio New York New York City NY 2007-; Vic S Andr's Epis Ch New Paltz NY 2007-** B Mount Vernon NY 5/30/1955 d Frank Mackenzie Murphy & Bronwen Griffiths. BA Barnard Coll of Col 1976; JD Ford 1981; MDiv Harvard DS 1991; Cert Sursum Corda Sprtl Dir Trng 2006. D 12/18/1994 P 6/1/1995 Bp George Edmonds Bates. COM Dio Utah Salt Lake City UT 2003-2006; Retreat Ldr, Int Dio Utah Salt Lake City UT 2003-2006; Assoc Cathd Ch Of S Mk Salt Lake City UT 2001-2003; Assoc R S Jn's Epis Ch Oakland CA 2000-2001; 150th Anniv Plnng Com Dio California San Francisco CA 1999-2000; Pstr Assoc Gr Cathd San Francisco CA 1998-2000; Stndg Com Dio Utah Salt Lake City UT 1996-1998; P-in-c S Mich's Ch Brigham City UT 1996-1998; Hosp Chapl Epis Cmnty Serv Inc Salt Lake City UT 1994-1996; Assoc All SS Ch Salt Lake City UT 1993-1996. Auth, "Var," *GraceCom Website*, Gr Cathd, San Francisco; Auth, "Var," *Utah Dioc Dialogue*, Dio Utah. Sacr Dance Gld 1995; Utah Pstr Care Assoc 1994-1998. Wmn of the Year YWCA Salt Lake City 2003. revgwyneth@gmail.com

MURPHY JR, Hartshorn (Los) 1630 Greenfield Ave. Apt 105, Los Angeles, Los Angeles CA 90025 B Baltimore MD 8/29/1948 s Hartshorn Murphy & Mildred. BA U of Maryland 1970; MDiv VTS 1973. D 5/24/1973 P 2/1/1974 Bp David Keller Leighton Sr. m 5/27/1973 Marla Harris c 1. R S Aug By-The-Sea Par Santa Monica CA 1997-2009; Archd For Congrl Dvlpmt Dio Los Angeles Los Angeles CA 1988-1997; S Aug By-The-Sea Par Santa Monica CA 1988-1996; R S Phil's Par Los Angeles CA 1980-1988; St Georges Ch Milwaukee WI 1975-1980; Cur Ch Of The H Nativ Baltimore MD 1973-1975. hartshorn@saint-augustine.org

MURPHY, James Tracy John (SwFla) 1605 Banchory Cir, Walhalla SC 29691 B Cleveland OH 9/12/1952 s James Thomas Murphy & Pauline. Cert OH SU 1973; BS U of So Florida 1989; MDiv STUSo 1993. D 6/26/1993 P 1/6/1994 Bp Rogers Sanders Harris. m 8/20/1988 Sharon L White c 1. R Ch of the Nativ Sarasota FL 1995-2004; Asst R S Dav's Epis Ch Englewood FL 1993-1995; Yth Dir Ch Of The H Sprt Osprey FL 1986-1990. AFP 1990; Bro Of S Andr 1993; ERM 1987; Fllshp Wit 1992-1997; Intl Ord Of S Lk 1988. frmurf@msn.com

MURPHY, Jo-Ann Rapp (Va) 3605 S Douglas Rd, Miami FL 33133 **Asst S Steph's Ch Coconut Grove Coconut Grove FL 2009-** B Queens NY 8/28/1941 d John Leroy Rapp & Hulda Ann. BA Mar 1963; Cert 1985; MDiv VTS 1987; Cert Shalem Inst 1993; DMin Drew U 1998. D 6/13/1987 Bp Peter James Lee P 5/14/1988 Bp David Henry Lewis Jr. m 7/4/1965 Russell Francis Murphy c 2. Dir. Chr. Formation Ware Epis Ch Gloucester VA 2005-2008; Ch Of The H Comf Richmond VA 2002-2006; Ch Of The Gd Shpd Burke VA 1998-2002; R S Paul's Epis Ch Morris Plains NJ 1997-1998; Ch Of The Trsfg Towaco NJ 1989-1997; Asst to R Ch Of The Resurr Alexandria VA 1987-1989. Writer, "Conv Daily," 1979; Writer/Ed, "Voice Dio Newark"; Ed, "Rauch". Ord of S Helena 1989. joannrmurphy@aol.com

MURPHY, Linda Estelle (Va) 3606 Seminary Rd, Alexandria VA 22304 **Com on the Diac Dio Virginia Richmond VA 2011-; Pstr Assoc Imm Ch-On-The-Hill Alexandria VA 2010-** B Woburn MA 7/18/1947 d Howard William Redmond & Martha Elaine. Dplma in Theol Stds VTS 2005. D 2/5/2011 Bp Shannon Sherwood Johnston. m 6/14/1997 Cyrus Murphy c 6. lem1624@aol.com

MURPHY, Michael John (Tenn) 203 Austell Dr, Columbia TN 38401 **R S Barn Ch Tullahoma TN 2007-** B Waukesha WI 10/17/1975 s William Lester Murphy & Dorothy Costner. BA MI SU 1999. D 12/6/2001 P 9/1/2002 Bp Keith Lynn Ackerman. m 8/2/1997 Erica E Geramel c 1. Asst S Ptr's Ch Columbia TN 2002-2007. FRMMURPHY@YAHOO.COM

MURPHY, Michael Robert (SVa) 2315 Mary Goodwyn Rd., Powhatan VA 23139 B Portsmouth OH 11/25/1944 s Robert Truman Murphy & Margaret Anne. OH SU 1964; MDiv Epis TS In Kentucky 1978; BS U Of Kentucky 1978. D 5/14/1978 P 12/1/1978 Bp Addison Hosea. m 11/28/1964 Sally Curchin. Police Off Chr Ch Amelia Crt Hse VA 1996-2004; S Matt's Epis Ch Chesterfield VA 1996-1997; Archd Dio Sthrn Virginia Norfolk VA 1990-1996; Dio Sthrn Virginia Norfolk VA 1987-1989; Dio Sthrn Virginia Norfolk VA 1981-1986; R S Dav's Epis Ch Richmond VA 1980-1989; R S Paul's Ch Newport KY 1978-1980; Dio Lexington Lexington KY 1976-1980. padre44@comcast.net

MURPHY, Patricia A (Kan) 7515 W 102nd St, Overland Park KS 66212 B Tampa FL 9/13/1943 AA Richland Coll. D 3/1/2003 Bp William Edward Smalley. D S Paul's Ch Kansas City KS 2003-2010. deacon.pat@sbcglobal.net

MURPHY JR, P L (Dal) 7900 West Lovers Lane, Dallas TX 75225 **Int S Chris's Ch Dallas TX 2007-** B Lufkin TX 11/21/1943 s Pleasant Lawrence Murphy & Margaret Hortense. D 6/15/1978 P 12/18/1978 Bp Scott Field Bailey. m 7/28/1967 Susan Diane Frehner c 2. larrymurphyjr@yahoo.com

MURPHY, Richard William (RG) 4717 Sundial Way, Santa Fe NM 87507 **R S Bede's Epis Ch Santa Fe NM 1997-** B New Haven CT 10/25/1945 s Richard William Murphy & Margaret Mary. AA S Thos Sem 1968; BA S Jn's Sem 1970; MDiv GTS 1988; DMin GTF 2003. D 6/3/1989 P 6/23/1990 Bp David Elliot Johnson. m 4/6/1974 Carol Fransen c 1. Cn Dio The Rio Grande Albuquerque NM 1997; Field Educ Supvsr EDS Cambridge MA 1993-1997; R The Par Of S Chrys's Quincy MA 1991-1997; Cur S Ptr's Ch Osterville MA 1989-1991. Asst. Producer, *Odyssey Toward Unity*, Boston Theol Inst, 1997; Asst. Producer, *Out of Ashes: Nthrn Ireland's Fragile Peace*, Boston Theol Inst, 1996. Fllshp of SSJE 1985; SBL 1988. frrichardsf@gmail.com

MURPHY, Robert A (WMo) 4225 Sw Clipper Ln, Lees Summit MO 64082 B Kansas City MO 5/4/1937 s AL Murphy & Dorothy. BA Cntrl Methodist U 1960. D 3/27/1993 Bp John Clark Buchanan. m 8/11/1962 B Kathleen Moore c 3. D S Ptr's Epis Ch Kansas City MO 1993-2006.

MURPHY JR, Russell Edward (Wyo) PO Box 909, Buffalo WY 82834 B Saint Louis MO 3/1/1945 s Russell Edward Murphy & Marion Ruth. BA Washington U 1967; MA U of Missouri 1972; MDiv S Paul TS 1980; Nash 1982. D 8/6/1982 P 2/9/1983 Bp Arthur Anton Vogel. c 1. R S Lk's Epis Ch Buffalo WY 2007-2010; Mssnr S Steph's Epis Ch DeTour Vill MI 2002; R / Mssnr S Jas Ch Of Sault S Marie Sault Ste Marie MI 2001-2007; Vic Dio Utah Salt Lake City UT 1999-2001; Vic S Mich's Ch Brigham City UT 1998-2000; Chapl Mssnr Calv Epis Ch Osceola AR 1998-1999; Vic Dio Arkansas Little Rock AR 1998-1999; Chapl Mssnr S Steph's Ch Blytheville AR 1998-1999; R S Paul's Ch Fayetteville AR 1993-1997; R S Jn's Epis Ch Mankato MN 1984-1993; Cur Chr Epis Ch S Jos MO 1982-1984. Mn Coun Ch, Alb Inst 1986-1993; WY Cltn of Chruches 2007. remurphy99@hotmail.com

MURPHY, Susan Marie (Me) 100 Clearwater Dr Unit 160, Falmouth ME 04105 **R S Geo's Epis Ch Sanford ME 2008-** B Pittsfield MA 6/13/1946 d Francis John Murphy & Sophie Mary. BA Elms Coll 1971; Westfield St Coll 1976; Westfield St Coll 1981; MDiv EDS 1999. D 5/22/1999 P 12/4/1999 Bp Chilton Abbie Richardson Knudsen. S Alb's Epis Ch St Pete Bch FL 2002; Aroostook Epis Cluster Caribou ME 2001-2006; P Ch Of The Adv Caribou ME 1999-2006; P S Anne's Ch Mars Hill ME 1999-2006; P S Jn's Ch Presque Isle ME 1999-2006; P S Lk's Ch Caribou ME 1999-2006; P S Paul's Ch Ft Fairfield ME 1999-2006; Dio Maine Portland ME 1999-2000. revsmurph@metrocast.net

MURPHY, T(eresa) Abigail (LI) 15 Stewart Ave, Stewart Manor NY 11530 **P-in-c S Elis's Epis Ch Floral Pk NY 2000-; P-in-c S Thos' Epis Ch Bellerose Vill NY 2000-** B Indianapolis IN 2/28/1959 d Leroy Rogers & Ruth Eileen. Taylor U Upland IN 1979; MA Bos 1981; MDiv SWTS 1995. D 6/23/1995 P 3/25/1996 Bp Orris George Walker Jr. m 6/3/1995 Roy Murphy. Cur Cathd Of The Incarn Garden City NY 1995-1999. Associated Parishes 1995-1998; EWC 1995. abby@panix.com

MURPHY, Thomas Christopher (WA) 4667 36th St S # B, Arlington VA 22206 **Assitant To The R Chr Ch Georgetown Washington DC 2007-** B St Amford CT 8/26/1948 s Thomas Christopher Murphy & Patricia Link. BA Sacr Heart U Fairfield CT 1972; MTS VTS 2007. D 6/9/2007 P 1/19/2008 Bp John Chane. m 12/10/1977 Mary Rieser c 1. father.tom.murphy@gmail.com

MURPHY, Thomas Edward (Spok) 215 Tolman Creek Rd Unit 34, Ashland OR 97520 **Asst S Mk's Epis Par Medford OR 2006-; Asst Trin Epis Ch Ashland Ashland OR 2005-** B Natick MA 9/30/1935 s Edward Francis Murphy & Gladys May. BA U of Redlands 1957; MDiv Berkeley Bapt DS 1961; CAS EDS 1966. D 6/29/1966 P 2/24/1967 Bp Ivol I Curtis. m 11/24/1979 Huberta Imilda Murphy c 3. S Jn's Epis Ch Colville WA 2001; S Paul's Ch Cheney WA 1994-2001; R S Andr's Ch Spokane WA 1989-2001; R S Lk's Ch Ft Madison IA 1986-1988; Dio Olympia Seattle WA 1986; H Trin Ch Seattle WA 1979-1986; Vic S Christophers Epis Ch Westport WA 1979-1983; Assoc S Eliz's Ch Burien WA 1973-1978; S Dav Emm Epis Ch Shoreline WA 1967-1973; Assoc Min Ch Of The Epiph Seattle WA 1966-1967. CHS 1992. tommurphy930@q.com

MURPHY, Thomas Lynch (WNC) 9 Swan St, Asheville NC 28803 **R The Cathd Of All Souls Asheville NC 2010-** B Oklahoma City OK 12/22/1977 s Thomas Lynch Murphy & Nancy Clark. BA U of NC, Chap Hill 2000; MTS Harvard DS 2005; Angl Stds VTS 2008. D 5/23/2010 P 12/11/2010 Bp Granville Porter Taylor. m 5/29/2004 Amanda Murphy c 2. thomas@allsoulscathedral.org

MURPHY, Thomas M (Nwk) Grace Episcopal Church, 4 Madison Ave, Madison NJ 07940 **Cathd Chapt Trin And S Phil's Cathd Newark NJ 2009-; COM Dio Newark Newark NJ 2008-** B Jersey City NJ 5/13/1967 s Thomas Michael Murphy & Catherine Mary. BA New Jersey City U Jersey City NJ 1989; MA St Peters Coll Jersey City NJ 1991; MDiv GTS 2007. D 6/2/2007 P 12/22/2007 Bp Mark M Beckwith. m 7/12/1997 Susan R Suarez. Ch Of The Incarn Gainesville FL 2010-2011; S Mich's Ch Gainesville FL 2010-2011; Cur Gr Ch Madison NJ 2007-2010. tommurphe@gmail.com

MURPHY, Timothy Hunter (Ala) 801 The Trce W, Jasper AL 35504 **R S Mary's Epis Ch Jasper AL 2008-** B Decatur AL 11/8/1949 s Charles Hurt Murphy & Anne. BS U of Alabama 1972; MDiv VTS 1978. D 6/14/1978 P 12/15/1978 Bp Furman Stough. m 11/24/2009 Kate J Davis c 4. Vic Ch Of The H Nativ St Simons Island GA 2006-2008; R Trin Epis Ch Florence AL 1995-2006; R Trin Epis Ch The Woodlands TX 1993-1995; R S Lk's Ch Scottsboro AL 1984-1993; R Ch Of The H Comf Sumter SC 1983-1984; R S Ptr's Epis Ch Talladega AL 1980-1983; R Trin Epis Ch Alpine AL 1980-1983; Cur S Jn's Ch Decatur AL 1978-1980. thm1995@yahoo.com

MURPHY, Warren Charles (Wyo) 50 Diamond View Rd, Cody WY 82414 B Philadelphia PA 5/6/1944 s Warren Nixon Murphy & Frances Emma. BA Bridgewater Coll 1967; MDiv EDS 1972. D 6/24/1972 P 1/15/1973 Bp Harold B Robinson. m 6/25/1977 Katharine Linde c 2. Chair , COM Dio Wyoming Casper WY 2003-2010; Stndg Com Dio Wyoming Casper WY 1992-1995; R Chr Ch Cody WY 1989-2004; Dioc Coun Dio Wyoming Casper WY 1989-1992; GC Dep Dio Wyoming Casper WY 1988-2011; Vstng P Shoshone Epis Mssn Ft Washakie WY 1986-1989; Chair Ch Cltn Dio Wyoming Casper WY 1984-1991; P in Charge S Andr's Mssn Lander WY 1982-1989; R Trin Ch Lander WY 1982-1989; R S Paul's Epis Ch Dixon WY 1977-1982; Asst Trin Trin Epis Ch Buffalo NY 1973-1977. Auth, "On Sacr Ground: A Rel and Sprtl Hist of Wyoming," *Bk*, Wordsworth Pub, 2011. warrencmurphy@gmail.com

MURPHY, William McKee (WMich) N 2794 Summerville Park Road, Lodi WI 53555 B Champaign IL 6/9/1946 s William Grove Murphy & Eunice Mary. BA U of Wisconsin 1969; MDiv Nash 1973. D 4/28/1973 Bp Donald H V Hallock P 10/27/1973 Bp Charles Thomas Gaskell. m 8/26/1989 Mary Elizabeth Berkes c 2. R St Jn's Epis Ch of Sturgis Sturgis MI 1989-2003; R Geth Epis Ch Marion IN 1976-1989; P-in-c S Alb's Ch Sussex WI 1973-1976; P-in-c S Barth's Ch Pewaukee WI 1973-1976. wmurphy@charter.net

MURRAY III, Alfonso Jerome (SanD) 8001 Hough Ave, Cleveland OH 44103 **S Jn's Ch Indio CA 2008-** B Miami FL 11/15/1954 s Alfonso Jerome Murray & Valez. BS Cameron U 1987; MDiv Candler TS Emory U 1990. D 12/13/1999 P 6/24/2000 Bp Gethin Benwil Hughes. m 4/4/1994 Carmelita Ruiz. S Marg's Epis Ch Palm Desert CA 2009; S Marg's Epis Sch Palm Desert CA 2008-2010; S Andr's Ch Cleveland OH 2002-2006; Assoc R S Marg's Epis Ch Palm Desert CA 2000-2001. amblackfriar@gmail.com

MURRAY, Austin B (Haw) PO Box 813, Kihei HI 08752 **P-in-c Trin Ch By The Sea Kihei HI 2008-** B Monaghan IE 3/21/1950 s Eamonn Patrick Murray & Rose Ann. U Coll Dublin 1973; ThM S Patricks Coll/Sem 1974; GTS 1989; ThM NBTS 1995. Rec from Roman Catholic 9/12/1987 as Priest Bp Vincent King Pettit. m 8/6/1980 Maureen F Murray c 5. S Steph's Ch Waretown NJ 1989-2008; Par Of S Jas Of Jerusalem By The Sea Long Bch NY 1987-1989; S Jas Ch Long Branch NJ 1987-1988. oistinb682@yahoo.com

MURRAY IV, Bill S (WTenn) 2911 Elmore Park Road, Bartlett TN 38134 **R S Elis's Epis Ch Memphis TN 2007-** B Memphis TN 11/30/1973 s William Seldon Murray & Lela Carolyn. BA U of Memphis 1997; MDiv VTS 2006. D 6/10/2006 P 2/15/2007 Bp Don Edward Johnson. m 3/1/2003 Jessica McCutchen c 2. Cur S Geo's Ch Germantown TN 2006-2007; Yth Dir Gr - S Lk's Ch Memphis TN 1998-2003. billmurray4@hotmail.com

MURRAY, Cicely Anne (Pa) 600 E Cathedral Rd Apt D104, Philadelphia PA 19128 B Harpenden Herts UK 9/10/1927 d Percy John Bolesworth & Constance Frances. MS Middlesex Hosp London GB 1949; Pennsylvania Diac Sch 1996. D 11/2/1996 Bp Allen Lyman Bartlett Jr. D S Mary's Ch Wayne PA 1998-2005; D S Matt's Ch Maple Glen PA 1996-1998. NAAD 1995; Soc of Comp of H Cross 1982. murrayrevs@earthlink.net

MURRAY, Diane Marie (FdL) W5766 Winooski Rd, Plymouth WI 53073 **S Jas Ch Manitowoc WI 2009-; Dio Fond du Lac Appleton WI 2006-** B Pocatello ID 6/4/1957 d Leo Clarence Dobrzynski & Betty Jeanine. U of Wisconsin 1982; Milwaukee Area Tech Coll 1996; BA Marian Coll of Fond Du Lac 2001; Lakeland Coll 2002. D 8/23/1998 P 5/23/2009 Bp Russell Edward Jacobus. c 3. Dio Fond du Lac Appleton WI 2009; D S Paul's Ch Plymouth WI 2000-2007; S Ptr's Epis Ch Sheboygan Falls WI 1998-2000. Bp's Cross Dio Fond du Lac 2003. dianemarie.murray@gmail.com

MURRAY, Elizabeth Ann (CFla) 144 Sea Park Blvd, Satellite Beach FL 32937 **Yth Dir S Jn's Ch Melbourne FL 2008-** B East Chicago IN 11/2/1951 d John W Murray & Shirley A. U of Wisconsin 1972; BA U of Nthrn Colorado 1974. D 12/8/2001 Bp John Wadsworth Howe. m 6/21/1980 Douglas Alan Ludwig. yarrumea@gmail.com

MURRAY JR, George Ralph (Eas) 4453 Eastwicke Dr, Salisbury MD 21804 **Pstr Assoc All Hallow's Ch Snow Hill MD 2009-** B Washington DC 2/28/1936 s George Ralph Murray & Dorothy Myrtene. AA w hon Montgomery Coll 1959; BSBA mcl Amer U 1963; Mstr of Liberal Stds Geo 1981. D 4/6/2002 Bp Charles Lindsay Longest. m 8/19/1955 Mary Barbara Woolard c 2. D Pstr S Mary's Epis Ch Tyaskin MD 2006-2009; Supply Dio Easton Easton MD 2005-2006; D Pstr S Paul's Epis Ch Hebron MD 2004-2005; Asstg D S Mary's Epis Ch Tyaskin MD 2002-2004. grmurray@hotmail.com

MURRAY, John Patrick (RG) 110 W. Texas, Marfa TX 79843 **Big Bend Epis Mssn Alpine TX 2001-** B 3/17/1925 D 9/1/2001 P 9/21/2002 Bp Terence Kelshaw. m 5/5/2004 Greta Grace Rogers c 2. jpmurray@christophers.net

MURRAY III, John William (CGC) 11 George St, Charleston SC 29401 B Charleston SC 6/30/1940 s John William Murray & Mary Elizabeth. BS Emory U 1961; BS Coll of Charleston 1964; MDiv VTS 1967. D 6/22/1967 P 6/1/1968 Bp Gray Temple. m 8/27/1966 Sara Ann Lofton c 2. H Trin Epis Ch Pensacola FL 1983-2002; S Barth's Epis Ch Atlanta GA 1975-1983; Cur S Jn's Coll Pk GA 1971-1975; Vic Chr Ch Denmark SC 1967-1971; Vic S Alb's Ch Blackville SC 1967-1971. OHC. mail@fantasiabb.com

MURRAY, Kathleen Fontaine (Okla) 1255 Canterbury Blvd, Altus OK 73521 **P-in-c S Paul's Ch Altus OK 2009-** B Huntington WV 9/30/1963 d Hershell Belmont Murray & Imogene Fontaine. BA Marshall U 1985; MDiv VTS 1991; MBA U of Phoenix 2000; DO OSU-COM 2008; SW OK Fam Med Residency

M

2011. D 6/11/1991 P 6/13/1992 Bp John H(enry) Smith. R S Basil's Epis Ch Tahlequah OK 2000-2005; Asst Trin Ch Tulsa OK 1998-2000; Int Cathd Of S Lk And S Paul Charleston SC 1997-1998; Int S Jn's Epis Par Johns Island SC 1996-1997; Chapl Off Of Bsh For ArmdF New York NY 1994-1996; Vic Nelson Cluster Of Epis Ch Rippon WV 1991-1994. katmurok@yahoo.com

MURRAY, Lewellyn St Elmo (LI) 590 Flatbush Ave, Brooklyn NY 11225 **P-in-c S Lydia's Epis Ch Brooklyn NY 1981-** B Colon PA 3/25/1926 s F Robert Murray & Ida. Merc TS. D 6/17/1978 P 1/1/1981 Bp Robert Campbell Witcher Sr. m 11/24/1955 Dorothy Hinds. E Bklyn Ch, OHC.

MURRAY, Lois Thompson (SeFla) 1521 Alton Rd # 219, Miami Beach FL 33139 B PA 9/23/1942 d Jack Burn Thompson & Lois. MDiv PrTS; BA Swarthmore Coll 1965. D 7/23/2004 Bp Leopold Frade P 2/18/2005 Bp James Hamilton Ottley. c 2.

MURRAY, Mac (WMass) 23 Dana Park, Hopedale MA 01747 **R Trin Epis Ch Milford MA 2006-** B Buffalo NY 5/16/1952 s Gerard Eareckson Murray & Eleanor Jean. BS New Mex St U. 1976; PMD Harv 1986; MDiv VTS 2002. D 6/15/2002 P 12/18/2002 Bp Peter James Lee. m 6/12/1976 Merline Roush c 2. Asst R Gr Ch The Plains VA 2002-2006. mac.murray@gmail.com

MURRAY, Michael Hunt (Va) 700 Port St Apt 226, Easton MD 21601 B Cambridge UK 4/21/1922 s Cecil Dunmore Murray & Veronica. BA Harv 1948; MA Jn Hopkins U 1950; ThB ETSBH 1965; CAS W&M 1982. D 6/24/1965 P 12/1/1965 Bp Robert McConnell Hatch. m 11/16/1955 Eliane C Cadilhac c 2. R Ware Epis Ch Gloucester VA 1975-1983; Cur All SS Ch Worcester MA 1965-1966. Auth, "Chance or Providence," Easterly Press, MD, 2001; Auth, "The Thought of Teilhard de Chardin," Seabury Press, NY, 1966; Auth, "In Sight of Eden," Jonathan Cape, London, 1961. Amer Assn Counslg & Devolpment, VA Mntl Hlth 1979; Amer Teilhard de Chardin Assoc. 1964. mhmurray@goeaston.net

MURRAY, Milton Hood (Fla) 3750 Peachtree Rd NE # 422, Atlanta GA 30319 B Athens GA 1/22/1929 s William Mercer Murray & Tulley Lourine. BS U GA 1950; Cert CPE 1956; MDiv VTS 1958. D 6/21/1958 Bp Robert E Gribbin P 12/22/1958 Bp Randolph R Claiborne. m 6/8/1960 Jane R Ringo c 1. Assoc Chr Epis Ch Ponte Vedra Bch FL 1999-2004; Assoc R Chr Epis Ch Ponte Vedra Bch FL 1984-1991; Stndg Com Dio Atlanta Atlanta GA 1976-1979; Chair Dept Stwdshp Dio Atlanta Atlanta GA 1976-1978; Chair Dept Par Serv Dio Atlanta Atlanta GA 1971-1973; R S Bede's Ch Atlanta GA 1970-1984; Dep GC Dio Atlanta Atlanta GA 1970-1973; Chair Bd Gvnrs Dio Atlanta Atlanta GA 1964-1970; R S Steph's Ch Milledgeville GA 1964-1970; Vic Gr-Calv Epis Ch Clarkesville GA 1958-1964.

MURRAY, Noland Patrick (Ark) 14300 Chenal Pkwy Apt 1316, Little Rock AR 72211 B Springfield MO 3/26/1934 s Woody Murray & Clara. BA Baylor U 1955; BD Sthrn Bapt TS Louisville KY 1958; PhD Duke 1963. D 5/7/1977 P 3/15/1978 Bp Christoph Keller Jr. c 3. S Mk's Epis Ch Jonesboro AR 1983-1999; R All SS Epis Ch Russellville AR 1978-1982; Cur S Paul's Ch Fayetteville AR 1976-1978. Auth, "Living Beyond Your Losses," Morehouse Pub, 1997; Auth, "Creationism and Evolution: The Real Issues," 1981. nolmur2003@yahoo.com

MURRAY, Robert Scott (EpisSanJ) 1104 Kitanosho-Cho, Ohmihachiman, Shiga 523-0806 Japan B Visalia CA 12/26/1957 s Robert Cicero Murray & Norma Jean. Nash; S Jn Coll Sante Fe NM; BS California St U 1980; MDiv CDSP 1986. D 7/25/1987 P 5/1/1988 Bp Victor Manuel Rivera. m 7/10/1988 Hiroko Hasegawa. St Stephans Ch 0 1993-1994; S Thos Of Cbury Mammoth Lakes CA 1990-1992; Asst P Ch Of The H Fam Chap Hill NC 1988-1989; Mssnr-In-Charge Ch Of The Epiph Corcoran CA 1987-1988. tektonhouse@yahoo.com

MURRAY, Robin George Ellis (SwFla) 27439 Edenfield Dr, Wesley Chapel FL 33543 B Glenelg AU 12/27/1935 s George Alfred Murray & Lillian Venitia. BA MI SU 1959; MBA MI SU 1963; MDiv VTS 1968; Amer Inst Of Fam Relatns 1975; Bethel Bible Inst Madison WI 1976; DMin Andover Newton TS 1982. D 6/29/1968 Bp Archie H Crowley P 1/11/1969 Bp Richard S M Emrich. m 9/8/1962 Dorothy Ann Remsburg. Assoc S Mary's Par Tampa FL 2008-2011; R S Andr's Epis Ch Sprg Hill FL 1986-2004; R S Paul's Ch Lynnfield MA 1978-1986; Off Of Bsh For ArmdF New York NY 1973-1978; Assoc The Falls Ch Epis Falls Ch VA 1970-1972; Asst Chr Ch Dearborn MI 1968-1969. Auth, "Symptomatology & Mgmt Of Acute Grief As Experienced By Death & Dying," *Doctoral Thesis*, 1982. Acad Of Par Cler; ACPE. Outstanding Young Men Of Amer 1971. robhome@iname.com

MURRAY III, Roderic Lafayette (Ala) 634 Timber Ln, Nashville TN 37215 **Assoc Chr Ch Cathd Nashville TN 2007-; Ch Pension Fund Benefici New York NY 2005-** B Beattyville KY 8/6/1940 s Roderic Lafayette Murray & Mattie Ellen. U Of Kentucky 1960; BA Wstrn Kentucky U 1962; MDiv Van 1969; TS 1971; DDiv Van 1971; DMin Van 1973. D 5/24/1969 Bp William R Moody P 11/30/1969 Bp John Vander Horst. m 6/4/1966 Jennie Diana Bush c 2. R Ch Of The Nativ Epis Huntsville AL 1988-2002; Dn S Andr's Cathd Jackson MS 1980-1988; R S Paul's Ch Augusta GA 1975-1980; R S Andr's Ch Maryville TN 1971-1975; Cur Chr Ch Cathd Nashville TN 1969-1971. Auth, "arts Var mag". Fllshp Un Theiological Sem 1986; Fllshp Emory 1984; S.T.D. (Doctor of Sacr Theol) Epis TS 1983; Fllshp VTS 1983; Outstanding Citizen Awd Human Relatns Cmsn 1980. tanglewood1966@gmail.com

MURRAY III, Thomas Holt (WTex) 1120 Lake Dr, Kerrville TX 78028 **S Peters Epis Sch Kerrville TX 2005-; Assoc S Ptr's Epis Ch Kerrville TX 2005-** B Oklahoma OK 7/27/1965 s Thomas Holt Murray & Julia Catherine. BS Texas A&M U 1987; MA U of Mary Hardin-Baylor 1989; MA VTS 1996. D 12/5/1998 Bp Leopoldo Jesus Alard P 12/13/1999 Bp Claude Edward Payne. m 7/6/2004 Julie Ann Utzman c 1. Dio Texas Houston TX 2005; R S Mich And All Ang' Epis Ch Longview TX 2004-2005; Asst Trin Ch Marshall TX 2003-2004; All SS Epis Sch Tyler TX 2000-2002; Assoc P Chr Epis Ch Tyler TX 2000-2002; P S Cuth's Epis Ch Houston TX 1998-2000. frtommurray@Yahoo.com

MURRAY, Thomas Padraic (NC) 520 Summit St., Winston Salem NC 27101 **Assoc R S Paul's Epis Ch Winston Salem NC 2006-** B Madison WI 3/18/1968 s Richard Murray & Martha. BA No Carolina St U 1992; MDiv STUSo 1999. D 5/29/1999 P 12/4/1999 Bp Edward Lloyd Salmon Jr. m 11/12/2009 Perrin S Steele c 4. R S Dav's Ch Cheraw SC 2003-2006; Assoc For Fam Mnstry Par Ch of St. Helena Beaufort SC 1999-2003. perrinmurray@bellsouth.net

MURRAY, Vincent Devitt (Oly) 306 Lopez Ave, Port Angeles WA 98362 B Jersey City NJ 1/31/1935 s William Russell Murray & Jeannette Marie. BA Loyola U 1959; PHL Loyola U 1960; MA Ford 1961; STB Wood 1967; MA GW 1972. Rec from Roman Catholic 11/12/1993 as Priest Bp Vincent Waydell Warner. m 10/5/1974 Anne Carlyle Hastings c 1. murray@olympus.net

MURRELL, William Lewis (NY) 2400 Johnson Ave Apt 10c, Bronx NY 10463 **Int P All Souls Ch New York NY 1998-; Hon Asst Ch Of The Intsn New York NY 1982-** B BB 9/17/1922 s Arthur Hampden Murrell & Inez Henrietta. BA SUNY 1978; SUNY 1981; NYTS 1983; GTS 1986; Med U of No Texas 1994. D 6/6/1983 Bp Paul Moore Jr P 9/1/1989 Bp James Stuart Wetmore. m 12/29/1971 Luisa Pommou. P-in-c Ch Of The Ascen Mt Vernon NY 1992-1996; Int Trin Ch Of Morrisania Bronx NY 1991-1992.

MURSULI, Modesto E (LI) 399A Himrod St, Brooklyn NY 11237 B Camaguey CU 12/1/1952 s Orlando Modesto Mursuli & Maria de Jesus. Graduated TS of Havana Havana CU 1980; CIAM Rome IT 1989; Angl Educ Havana CU 1993. Trans from Iglesia Episcopal de Cuba 4/20/1999 as Priest Bp Robert Reed Shahan. m 4/26/1990 Annie Gomez Montalvan c 1. Dio Arizona Phoenix AZ 1999-2008; Vic Iglesia Epis De San Pablo Phoenix AZ 1999-2008. fathermursuli@optimum.net

MUSGRAVE, David Charles (Chi) 11112 Bayberry Hills Dr, Raleigh NC 27617 B New York NY 8/15/1948 s Howard Albert Musgrave & Dorothy Elizabeth. BA Hob 1970; MDiv GTS 1973; DMin Eden TS 1978. D 6/16/1973 Bp Jonathan Goodhue Sherman P 12/15/1973 Bp George Leslie Cadigan. m 8/22/1970 Donna Borkhuis c 1. R S Aug's Epis Ch Wilmette IL 1993-2010; R S Alb's Ch Indianapolis IN 1984-1993; R S Mk's Ch S Louis MO 1978-1984; Asst Ch Of The H Comm U City MO 1973-1978. d2musgrave@gmail.com

MUSGRAVE, John Barrett (Mo) 14216 Woods Mill Cove Dr, Chesterfield MO 63017 B Goiania BR 1/29/1952 s James Everett Musgrave & Jane A. BA Baylor U 1974; U of New Orleans 1977; MDiv Epis TS of The SW 1992. D 6/27/1992 Bp Maurice Manuel Benitez P 1/26/1993 Bp William Jackson Cox. m 1/14/1984 Nannette Bert c 3. R Ch Of The Gd Shpd S Louis MO 2006-2010; Sr Assoc S Ptr's Epis Ch St Louis MO 2004-2006; S Thos The Apos Epis Ch Houston TX 1999-2004; Vic S Alb's Epis Ch Austin Manchaca TX 1994-1999; Asst to R S Lk's On The Lake Epis Ch Austin TX 1992-1994. jnmusgrave@sbcglobal.net

MUSHORN, Richard C (LI) 2206 Cloverleaf Cir SE, Cleveland TN 37311 B Kew Gardens NY 3/21/1946 s Harold Frederick Mushorn & Frances Helen. BA Cathd Coll of the Immac Concep 1966; MDiv Our Lady Of Ang Sem (Niagara U) 1971. Rec from Roman Catholic 12/1/1987 as Priest Bp Robert Campbell Witcher Sr. R Epis Ch Of S Mk The Evang No Bellmore NY 1990-1994; Chr Ch Brentwood NY 1988. rcm46@aol.com

MUSOKE-LUBEGA, Benjamin Kiwomutemero (NY) 27 Compton Dr, East Windsor NJ 08520 **Trin Par New York NY 2005-** B MengoUG 9/24/1956 s Benjamin K Musoke-Lubega & Theorphlis. BA Shimer Coll 1975; BD Bp Tucker Theol Coll Mukono Ug 1980; MA McCormick TS 1985; STM Nash 1987. Trans from Church of the Province of Uganda 9/25/1990 Bp William Grant Black. m 7/16/1994 Edith L Senyumba c 2. Epis Ch Cntr New York NY 2002-2005; R S Matt's And S Jos's Detroit MI 1997-2002; H Sprt Epis Ch Cincinnati OH 1991-1997. Cmnty Of Trsfg. musokelubega@wwnet.net

MUSSATTI, David James (Nev) Po Box 5572, Incline Village NV 89450 **Assoc S Pat's Ch Incline Vill NV 1982-** B Los Angeles CA 3/22/1934 s James Mussatti & Louise Evans. BA San Jose St U 1957; MA U of Nevada at Reno 1968; EdD U Pac 1981. D 3/17/1982 P 11/1/1982 Bp Wesley Frensdorff. m 7/25/1981 Stephanie Irene Finlay c 4. Bro of S Andr 1958; Ord of S Lk 1999. Phi Delta Kappa 1968; Phi Beta Kappa 1957; Phi Kappa Phi 1957. dmussatti@tahoeepiscopal.org

MUSSELMAN JR, William Stanley (Pa) 93 Willow Way, Lansdale PA 19446 B Norristown PA 8/10/1929 s William S Musselman & Kathryn. BA Ge 1951; BD PDS 1954. D 6/5/1954 Bp Joseph Gillespie Armstrong P 12/11/1954 Bp

M

Oliver J Hart. m 6/23/1951 Janet Schultz c 3. Ch Of The H Sprt Harleysville PA 1995-2000; Asst S Jn's Epis Ch Carlisle PA 1990-1993; R Chr Ch Epis Ridley Pk PA 1956-1989; Cur Ch Of Our Sav Jenkintown PA 1954-1956. jzmusselman@hotmail.com

MUSTARD, G Thomas (SwVa) 6437 Monarch Ct, Hoschton GA 30548 B Tazewell VA 3/29/1944 s George Newton Mustard & Lina Elizabeth. BA Berea Coll 1974; MDiv VTS 1977; VTS 1984. D 6/12/1977 P 12/18/1977 Bp William Henry Marmion. m 11/27/1965 Shirley Snider c 2. Asst S Jn's Ch Roanoke VA 2009-2011; R S Jn's Ch Bedford VA 1999-2008; R Chr Ch Pocahontas VA 1991-1999; R S Mary's Ch Bluefield VA 1991-1999; R Trin Ch Richlands VA 1991-1999; R The Tazewell Cnty Cluster Of Epis Parishes Tazewell VA 1991-1998; R S Geo's Epis Ch Griffin GA 1986-1991; R S Jas Ch Roanoke VA 1980-1986; Asst Chr Epis Ch Roanoke VA 1977-1979. "Preaching as Prophetic Calling," *Harvest Evang*, Morehouse Pub. Alling and Schlafer, Editors. Phi Kappa Phi. tmustard74@gmail.com

MUTH, David Philip (NCal) 1429 Spring Valley Dr, Roseville CA 95661 B New Orleans LA 9/23/1933 s Philip George Muth & Dorothy Lorraine. BS Tul 1955; MDiv STUSo 1967; JD U NC 1985. D 6/29/1967 P 1/1/1968 Bp William G Wright. m 6/4/1960 Deborah Jean Young. S Andr's In The Highlands Mssn Antelope CA 1973-1986; Cur Gr Ch New Orleans LA 1969-1973; LocTen S Paul's Epis Ch Wilmington NC 1967-1968.

MUTH, Donald Charles (La) 4920 Cleveland Pl, Metairie LA 70003 **Int R S Lk's Ch New Orleans LA 2000-** B New Orleans LA 9/23/1933 s Philip George Muth & Dorothy Lorraine. BA Tul 1955; SWTS 1958. D 6/18/1958 Bp Girault M Jones P 5/23/1959 Bp Iveson Batchelor Noland. m 5/24/1958 Nancy E Evans c 4. S Paul's Ch New Orleans LA 2002-2003; S Paul's Ch New Orleans LA 1998-1999; Asst S Mart's Epis Ch Metairie LA 1985-1997; Chair Dio Chicago Chicago IL 1972-1976; Advsry Liturg Cmsn Dio Chicago Chicago IL 1968-1976; Ch Of The H Nativ Clarendon Hills IL 1966-1985; Cur Gr Ch New Orleans LA 1961-1966; P-in-c S Paul's Ch Abbeville LA 1958-1961; Cur Ch Of The Ascen Lafayette LA 1958-1960. dnmuth@att.net

MUTOLO, Frances (Colo) 85 Long Bow Cir, Monument CO 80132 **D S Andr's Ch Manitou Sprg CO 2009-** B McKeesport PA 2/22/1953 d Frank Joseph Mutolo & Angela Ann. RN Mercy Hosp Sch of Nrsng 1973. Rec from Roman Catholic 11/8/1992 Bp Alden Moinet Hathaway. m 4/20/1977 Michael M Malivuk c 2. D Ch of the Gd Shpd Colorado Sprg CO 2003-2008; D Chr's Epis Ch Castle Rock CO 2000-2003. deaconfam@hotmail.com

MUTZELBURG, Michael Kenneth (Mich) 110 W South Holly Rd, Fenton MI 48430 B Detroit MI 11/17/1940 s Herman Kenneth Mutzelburg & Ruth Mildred. BA Wayne 1967; MDiv Ya Berk 1970; MS U MI 1985. D 6/29/1970 Bp Archie H Crowley P 3/12/1971 Bp Richard S M Emrich. m 7/24/1965 Linda Lou Morgan c 1. R S Pat's Epis Ch Madison Heights MI 1992-1995; S Andr's Epis Ch Flint MI 1989-1992; P-in-c S Paul's Epis Ch Corunna MI 1982-1987; Trin Epis Ch Flushing MI 1974-1977; Asst Min S Andr's Ch Ann Arbor MI 1970-1974. Acad of Cert Soc Workers; NASW.

MYCOFF JR, Walter Joseph (SO) 892 W Webster Rd, Summersville WV 26651 B Pittsburgh PA 10/5/1942 s Walter Joseph Mycoff & Marguerite Jane. BA Ohio U 1964; MDiv VTS 1971. D 6/11/1971 P 2/1/1972 Bp Wilburn Camrock Campbell. m 6/19/1965 Martha H Henry c 1. P-in-c S Matt's Ch Westerville OH 2007-2008; Cn Dio Sthrn Ohio Cincinnati OH 2005-2008; R The Epis Ch Of The Ascen Middletown OH 1997-2005; Vic All Souls Epis Ch No Ft Myers FL 1990-1997; R Trin Ch Morgantown WV 1983-1990; R S Andr's Ch Oak Hill WV 1972-1983; R Ch Of The Incarn Ronceverte WV 1971-1972. Personalities Of The So Awd. wmycoff@siscom.net

MYERS, Annwn Hawkins (Miss) 735 University Ave, Sewanee TN 37383 **The TS at The U So Sewanee TN 1989-** B Aurora IL 12/31/1953 d Paul Minor Hawkins & Beatrice Maureen. BA Millsaps Coll 1981; MDiv VTS 1984. D 6/23/1984 P 5/24/1985 Bp Duncan Montgomery Gray Jr. m 1/23/1988 Samuel Dixon Myers c 2. S Andr's Cathd Jackson MS 1989; The Chap Of The Cross Madison MS 1989; Int R The Chap Of The Cross Madison MS 1988-1989; Asst R S Jn's Epis Ch Pascagoula MS 1987-1988; Cur S Jn's Epis Ch Pascagoula MS 1984-1986. amyers@sewanee.edu

MYERS, Bethany Leigh (Colo) 800 N Saint Asaph St # 202, Alexandria VA 22314 B Sterling CO 1/24/1983 d Robert Paul Davidson & Linda Leigh. BA Willamette U 2005; MSW U of Connecticut 2009; MDiv Ya Berk 2010. D 11/20/2010 Bp Robert John O'Neill. m 6/12/2010 Nicholas Allen Myers. bethanyleighmyers@gmail.com

MYERS, Brooke (Mo) 7401 Delmar Blvd, University City MO 63130 **R Ch Of The H Comm U City MO 2002-** B Charleston SC 7/7/1951 s deRosset Myers & Barbara Mordecai. BA Coll of Charleston 1974; MDiv CDSP 1979. D 6/7/1980 P 12/22/1980 Bp John Lester Thompson III. m 9/30/1995 Anne Kelsey c 2. R H Cross Epis Ch Castro Vlly CA 1989-2001; Asst All Souls Par In Berkeley Berkeley CA 1986-1989; Vic S Tim's Ch Gridley CA 1980-1986; Co-Pstr Chr The King Quincy CA 1979-1980. bmyers@holycommunion.net

MYERS III, Bruns Mckie (Miss) 107 Sundown Rd, Madison MS 39110 B Jackson MS 7/27/1950 s Bruns Mckie Myers & Evelyn. BA Belhaven Coll 1986; MDiv Reformed TS 1988. D 6/21/2001 Bp Duncan Montgomery Gray III P 1/24/2002 Bp Alfred Clark Marble Jr. S Phil's Ch Jackson MS 2002-2003. Kappa Alpha Ord, Alpha Upsilon Chapt 1972. Gd Will Cmnty Serv Awd Gd Will Industries Of Mississippi 2000; Golden Deeds Awd Exch Club Of No Jackson 1996; ABS Awd In Biblic Stds Belhaven Coll 1986; Mich Landon Grad Schlrshp Awd Mississippi Dept Of Rehab Serv 1986. bmm03@bellsouth.net

MYERS, David John (WMo) 12599 Timberline Dr, Garfield AR 72732 B Pueblo CO 7/23/1940 s Lawrence David Myers & Dorothy Arlene. Cntrl Bapt TS; U of Kansas. D 2/1/2003 Bp Barry Robert Howe. m 12/30/1989 Susan Ann Francis c 2. dmyers005@centurytel.net

MYERS, Dorothy Helen (WNY) 5234 E River Rd, Grand Island NY 14072 **Died 7/6/2010** B Fonthill ON CA 12/22/1924 d Henry George Leonard Clarke & Florence. BS SUNY 1966; Med SUNY 1974. D 2/28/1987 Bp David Charles Bowman. c 4.

MYERS, Elizabeth Williams (Be) Hc 67 Box 47, Dingmans Ferry NJ 18328 **S Ptr's Ch Mt Arlington NJ 2010-** B New York NY 9/4/1935 d Darwood Gillespie Myers & Elizabeth. BA Smith 1957; MDiv EDS 1962. D 5/24/1974 Bp John Alfred Baden P 1/14/1977 Bp Dean T Stevenson. Int S Lk's Ch Hope NJ 2008-2009; R Ch Of The Gd Shpd And S Jn Milford PA 1980-2000; Assoc Chr Ch Cranbrook Bloomfield Hills MI 1978-1980; Int S Jas Ch Lancaster PA 1974-1978; Asst to R Emm Ch Middleburg VA 1973-1974. myers22@comcast.net

MYERS, Frederick Martin (RG) 1500 Chelwood Park Blvd Ne, Albuquerque NM 87112 **D S Mary's Epis Ch Albuquerque NM 1989-** B Upper Sandusky OH 4/3/1916 s Bertram Derrington Myers & Donna Adeline. BA Indiana U 1951; MA U of New Mex 1953. D 10/27/1982 Bp Richard Mitchell Trelease Jr. m 5/12/1940 Margaret Louise Roundy c 3. D S Jn's Cathd Albuquerque NM 1990-1996.

MYERS, Fredrick Eugene (SanD) 403 Traverse St, Elk Rapids MI 49629 B Elyria OH 7/4/1935 s Ford Eugene Myers & Alberta Lillian. BA Ob 1977; MDiv SWTS 1980. D 6/28/1980 Bp John Harris Burt P 1/1/1981 Bp Charles Bennison. m 11/7/1954 Janet Yvonne Rickel. Stndg Com Dio Wstrn Michigan Kalamazoo MI 1995-1997; Dn Of The Traverse Dnry Dio Wstrn Michigan Kalamazoo MI 1989-1993; Exec Coun Dio Wstrn Michigan Kalamazoo MI 1987-1993; Stndg Com Dio Wstrn Michigan Kalamazoo MI 1985-1989; R S Paul's Epis Ch Elk Rapids MI 1982-2000; Asst Gr Epis Ch Traverse City MI 1980-1982; Grand Traverse City Area Mssn Traverse City MI 1980-1982. OHC. femyers@aol.com

MYERS, Henry Lee Hobart (Tenn) 237 Villa Creek Pkwy, Canton GA 30114 B Sewanee TN 11/14/1927 s George Boggan Myers & Margaret Jefferys. BA U So 1951; MDiv GTS 1954; DMin Van 1973. D 7/1/1954 Bp Edmund P Dandridge P 6/1/1955 Bp Theodore N Barth. m 11/19/1978 Carole A Williams c 4. P-in-c Trin Ch Russellville KY 1996-2001; Chapl S Aug's Chap Nashville TN 1988-1993; R S Barth's Epis Ch Florence AL 1983-1988; R Chr Ch Capitol Hill Washington DC 1978-1983; The TS at The U So Sewanee TN 1964-1978; Asst S Paul's Epis Ch Chattanooga TN 1957-1959; Vic S Fran' Ch Norris TN 1954-1957. hlhm@comcast.net

MYERS, Herbert Gardner (SeFla) 800 S 15th St Apt 5103, Sebring OH 44672 **Died 8/6/2009** B Toronto OH 3/11/1918 s Walter Myers & Stephanie Myers. BS Kent St U 1943; U of Wisconsin 1950; MDiv Bex 1953; MA U MI 1970. D 6/9/1953 P 12/29/1953 Bp Nelson Marigold Burroughs. c 2. Auth, "Don't Just Sit There," *LivCh*, LivCh Fndt. BSP. Hon Asst Trin Ch Allnce OH 1995; Hon Asst Chr Ch Blacksburg VA 1983. hmyersco@cannet.com

MYERS, Jeannette Anne Harrell (Haw) 1858 Kaumana Dr, Hilo HI 96720 B Petaluma CA 6/12/1950 d William Dewey Harrell & Irene Natalie. BA Sonoma St Coll Rohnert Pk 1975; MDiv CDSP 1979; CTh Jesuit TS 1987. D 11/1/1979 P 10/1/1983 Bp John Lester Thompson III. Ch Of The H Apos Hilo HI 2001-2004; S Jude's Hawaiian Ocean View Ocean View HI 1999-2001; R Ch Of S Jn The Evang Boston MA 1996-1999; Dio California San Francisco CA 1991-1996; Asst Chr Ch Alameda CA 1988-1991; DCE S Clem's Ch Berkeley CA 1987-1988; Vic S Clare Assisi Challenge Forbestown CA 1983-1986; Co-Pstr Chr The King Quincy CA 1979-1980. nobrainerjenny@yahoo.com

MYERS, John Geenwood (WLa) 117 Pithon Street, Lake Charles LA 70601 **Epis Ch Of The Gd Shpd Lake Chas LA 2004-** B Ridgway PA 6/25/1956 s Paul Robert Myers & Mabel. BA Alleg 1979; MDiv SWTS 1990. Trans 2/25/2004 Bp Robert R Gepert. m 6/9/1990 Joan Kickel c 2. Emm Ch Petoskey MI 1995-2004; Asst R S Andr's Ch Downers Grove IL 1992-1995; Gr Ch Lake City PA 1990-1992. 4myers@suddenlink.net

MYERS, Max Arthur (Ct) 247 New Milford Tpke, Marble Dale CT 06777 **S Andr's Epis Ch New Preston Marble Dale CT 2007-** B Coffeyville KS 10/19/1943 s Arthur Elmer Myers & Gwendolyn Ione. BA Cornell Coll 1965; BD Harvard DS 1968; PhD Harv 1976. D 12/13/1999 P 6/18/2000 Bp J Michael Garrison. m 7/14/1984 Maureen Elizabeth Fox c 3. S Mary's Epis Ch Gowanda NY 2002-2007; P-in-c S Mary's Ch Salamanca NY 2001-2002; S Steph's Ch Olean NY 2000-2002; Cn Theol S Paul's Cathd Buffalo NY 2000. Auth, "Christmas On Celluloid," *Christmas Unwrapped*, Trin Press Intern, 2001;

Auth, "Stds In The Theol Ethics Of Ernest Troeltsch," Edwin Mellen Press, 1991; Auth, "The Contemporary Crisis Of Marxism And Our Responsibility," *Thought: A Revs Of Culture And Ideas*, 1987; Auth, "Toward What Is Rel Thinking Underway," *De-Construction And Theol*, Crossroads, 1982; Auth, "Ideology And Legitimation As Necessary Concepts For Chr Ethics," *Journ Of The AAR*, 1981; Auth, "Santa Claus As An Icon Of Gr," *Ibid.* AAR; Conf Of Angl & Luth Theol; Soc Of Chr Ethics. mmyers7165@aol.com

MYERS, Nicholas Allen (NI) 118 N Washington St, Alexandria VA 22314 B South Bend IN 2/22/1983 s James Lynn Myers & Trudy Jeanine. BA Wabash Coll 2005; MDiv Ya Berk 2009. D 5/31/2009 Bp Edward Stuart Little II P 12/7/2009 Bp Shannon Sherwood Johnston. m 6/12/2010 Bethany Leigh Davidson. Cler Res Chr Ch Alexandria VA 2009-2011. nam8502@gmail.com

MYERS JR, Robert Keith (Chi) 333 Warwick Rd, 7050 N Oakley Ave, Chicago IL 60645 B Clinton IA 7/2/1945 s Robert Keith Myers & Corine Garnet. BA Illinois Coll 1968; MDiv SWTS 1975; PhD NWU 1984. D 6/14/1975 P 12/13/1975 Bp James Winchester Montgomery. c 2. R Ch Of The H Comf Kenilworth IL 1986-2011; Assoc R Ch Of The H Comf Kenilworth IL 1979-1985; Cur Ch Of The H Comf Kenilworth IL 1975-1978. Auth, "The Relatns Between Dreams & Dreamers In Mod Psychol Lit," 1984. Friend; Soc Of S Jn The Evang 1988. Bp Whipple Schlr SWTS Evanston IL 1975. robertkmyers@gmail.com

MYERS II, Robert W. (Ind) 8014 River Bay Drive West, Indianapolis IN 46240 **Chapl to the Ret Cler & Surviving Spouses Dio Indianapolis Indianapolis IN 2011-** B Gainesville FL 7/11/1944 s Robert Ware Myers & Alice Muriel. BA Jacksonville U 1967; MDiv STUSo 1973. D 6/13/1973 P 5/7/1974 Bp Edward Hamilton West. m 6/23/1979 Evelyn Wiley c 1. Assoc S Paul's Epis Ch Indianapolis IN 2008-2010; Sacramentalist S Tim's Ch Indianapolis IN 2006-2008; S Paul's Epis Ch Indianapolis IN 2000-2006; S Chris's Epis Ch Carmel IN 1991-2000; Chr Ch Cathd Indianapolis IN 1984-1991; Assoc S Chris's Ch Pensacola FL 1979-1984; H Innoc Ch Atlanta GA 1978-1979; Asst Ch Of The Epiph Jacksonville FL 1975-1977; Vic S Mary's Ch Jacksonville FL 1975-1977; S Fran Of Assisi Epis Ch Tallahassee FL 1974-1976. Auth, "Play," *The White Horse*, 1992; Auth, "Play," *What's Best For Billy?*, 1992; Auth, "Play," *Airwaves*, 1991. robin710710@yahoo.com

MYERS, Roy Clarence (WLa) 1906 Evangeline Dr, Bastrop LA 71220 B Glenshaw PA 3/29/1949 s Julius Myers & Viola. BA Geneva Coll 1971; MDiv Epis TS In Kentucky 1977; DMin Covington TS 1986. D 6/26/1977 P 12/11/1977 Bp Robert Bracewell Appleyard. m 8/28/1971 Benetta L Bates c 1. Chr Ch Bastrop LA 2004-2007; R H Trin Epis Ch Wyoming MI 2000-2004; R S Jas Ch Manitowoc WI 1998-2000; R S Tim's Ch Bp CA 1992-1998; P-in-c Gr Ch Pomeroy OH 1990-1992; Vic Gr Ch Ravenswood WV 1986-1992; Vic S Andr's Epis Ch Rose City MI 1981-1986; R Trin Epis Ch W Branch MI 1981-1986; R Chr Ch Brownsville PA 1977-1981. EFAC.

MYERS, Thomas (NJ) 2502 Central Ave, North Wildwood NJ 08260 **P-in-c S Simeon's By The Sea No Wildwood NJ 2008-** B Plainfield NJ 12/22/1942 s Richard Carl Myers & Jane. DEUG Inst Prot Theologie 1999; BTh Cambridge Theol Fed 2004; Angl Stds Nash 2007. D 5/31/2007 Bp Keith Lynn Ackerman P 12/21/2007 Bp George Edward Councell. m 12/16/1988 Sophie Roy c 3. Assoc The Ch Of S Uriel The Archangel Sea Girt NJ 2007-2008. FRTHOMASMYERS@AOL.COM

MYERS, Vernon (Colo) 21647 Hill Gail Way, Parker CO 80138 B Mountain Home AR 7/3/1923 s Austin L Myers & Amy Bertha. BA U Denv 1949; MDiv Ya Berk 1952. D 3/25/1952 Bp Duncan Montgomery Gray P 10/12/1952 Bp Harold L Bowen. c 3. Int Ch Of The H Redeem Denver CO 1992-1993; Coord. - Prov. VI Comm. on Alco & Drug Abuse Dio Colorado Denver CO 1991-1996; Int Ch Of S Jn Chrys Golden CO 1991-1992; Int S Matt's Parker CO 1990-1991; Chair - Comm. on Alco and Drug Abuse Dio Colorado Denver CO 1979-1988; Stndg Com Dio Colorado Denver CO 1975-1983; Ch Of S Phil And S Jas Denver CO 1956-1986; DCE S Jn's Cathd Denver CO 1952-1958. vernmyers@comcast.net

MYERS, William Francis (Va) 11142 Beaver Trail Ct, Reston VA 20191 B Washington DC 7/12/1933 s Raymond Cassius Myers & Matilda Martin. BA U of Maryland 1955; MDiv VTS 1960; MA Colg 1970; DMin Wesley TS 1979. D 6/18/1960 P 12/1/1960 Bp Angus Dun. S Jn's Epis Ch McLean VA 1972-1993; R S Thos Ch Hamilton NY 1967-1970; R Trin Ch St Chas MO 1963-1967; Vic S Geo's Ch Glenn Dale MD 1960-1963; Vic S Jas Epis Ch Bowie MD 1960-1963. Auth, "Brightness Of His Presence". wfmyers712@aol.com

MYHR, Laura Parmer (WNC) 95 Summit Street, Marion NC 28752 B Nashville TN 12/18/1946 d Henry Elmer Parmer & Mitylene. E Tennessee St U 1967; BS U of Tennessee 1974; MDiv Van 1990; STUSo 1992. D 6/14/1992 P 2/21/1993 Bp William Evan Sanders. m 7/6/2008 Harold Henline c 3. R S Jn's Epis Ch Marion NC 2000-2008; Cn Pstr S Jn's Epis Cathd Knoxville TN 1995-2000; Asst S Phil's Ch Nashville TN 1992-1995. laura.myhr@verizon.net

MYNATT, B(elva) Chari (Charlene) (WMo) 3523 S Kings Hwy, Independence MO 64055 B Independence MO 2/9/1942 d Charles Edwin Winn & Belva Ineatus. BA U of Missouri 1964; MS Cntrl Missouri St U 1972; Pk Coll Parkville MO 1987; Rockhurst Coll 1988; S Paul TS Kansas City MO 1988. D 1/18/1989 Bp Arthur Anton Vogel. m 8/1/1964 Kenneth Edward Mynatt c 2. Co-Dn WMO Sch for Mnstry Dio W Missouri Kansas City MO 2000-2010; Strng Com Parenting Life Skills Dio W Missouri Kansas City MO 1996-1999; Epis Soc Serv Dio W Missouri Kansas City MO 1996-1998; D S Anne's Ch Lees Summit MO 1991-2008; D Trin Ch Independence MO 1989-1991; Chair Hisp Mnstry Dio W Missouri Kansas City MO 1987-1992. Auth, "First Article, Scrub Oaks and Pines," *LivCh*, 1990; Auth, *Seventh Grade Spanish Curric*, 1965. NAAD 1989. Bp's Shield Dio W Missouri 2008; Loc org Mortar Bd UMKC 1964; Torch and Scroll, Loc Phi Beta Kappa UMKC 1964. mynatts@comcast.net

MYRICK, H (Harry) Eugene (RG) 708 E Lockhart Ave, Alpine TX 79830 B Gallup NM 9/9/1927 s John Thomas Myrick & Mary Frances. BA U of New Mex 1957; MDiv CDSP 1960. D 6/10/1960 P 4/11/1961 Bp C J Kinsolving III. Providence Meml Hosp El Paso TX 1984-1992; R S Fran On The Hill El Paso TX 1976-1984; Assoc Pro Cathd Epis Ch Of S Clem El Paso TX 1960-1976. amen.1@sbcglobal.net

MYRICK, William Harris (Mil) 503 E Walworth Ave P.O. Box 528, Delavan WI 53115 **Chr Epis Ch Of Delavan Delavan WI 1998-** B Sault Saint Marie MI 12/31/1946 s William John Myrick & Betty Lorraine. BS Nthrn Michigan U 1981; MDiv Nash 1984. D 2/23/1984 P 9/22/1984 Bp Thomas Kreider Ray. Chr Ch Epis Madison WI 1992-1998; R Gr Ch Madison WI 1987-1992; Epis Ch-Wstrn Reg Crystal Falls MI 1987. Auth, "Index Guide," *BCP*. 4wmharris@gmail.com

MYSEN, Andrea Leigh (Chi) 411 Laurel Ave, Highland Park IL 60035 **Trin Ch Highland Pk IL 2005-** B Pensacola FL 9/23/1964 BBA TCU 1986; MA Denver Sem 1995; MDiv SWTS 2004. D 3/30/2004 P 9/30/2004 Bp Victor Alfonso Scantlebury. m 1/9/2004 Rene Mysen c 2. All SS Epis Ch Chicago IL 2004-2005. mysen64@aol.com

MZIMELA, Sipo E (At) 245 Jefferson Pl, Decatur GA 30030 B Durban Natal ZA 6/19/1935 s Allison Mzimela & Maria. MBA Ruhr-Bochum Universitat 1970; STM GTS 1977. D 6/12/1976 Bp Paul Moore Jr P 12/1/1976 Bp Richard Beamon Martin. m 6/17/1989 Esther Munyaradzi c 2. Asst S Barth's Epis Ch Atlanta GA 2003-2006; Exec Coun Appointees New York NY 1983-1988; Epis Ch Of The Epiph Ventnor City NJ 1980-1983; S Lk's Epis Ch Bronx NY 1977.

N

NABE, Clyde Milton (Mo) 4742 Burlington Ave N, Saint Petersburg FL 33713 B Saint Louis MO 7/19/1940 s Loretta Emelia. BS Pur 1962; MA U of Missouri 1965; MA Pur 1972; PhD Pur 1975. D 12/22/1979 P 11/30/1980 Bp Albert William Hillestad. c 4. Affiliated Cler Cathd Ch Of S Ptr St Petersburg FL 2005-2006; Affiliated Cler S Bede's Ch St Petersburg FL 2001-2005; Affiliated Cler Trin Ch S Louis MO 1990-2001; P S Thos Epis Ch Glen Carbon IL 1985-1990; Asst Min S Paul's/Trin Chap Alton IL 1982-1983; Asst Min S Andr's Epis Ch Edwardsville IL 1979-1981. Auth, "Death & Dying/ Life & Living," *6th Ed.*, Wadsworth, 2009; Auth, "Mystery & Rel: Newman'S Epistemology Of Rel," 1988; Auth, "Morality Of Rel Beliefs," *Rel Stds*, 1986; Auth, "Confessionalism & Philos Of Rel," *Amer Journ Theol & Philos*, 1983. c8813nabe@verizon.net

NACHTRIEB, John David (Chi) 131 N Brainard Ave, La Grange IL 60525 **D Ch Of The Trsfg Palos Pk IL 1998-** B Chicago IL 8/7/1948 s Robert Walter Nachtrieb & Elizabeth. BA DePauw U 1970; Cert Chicago D Sch Chicago IL 1997. D 2/7/1998 Bp Herbert Alcorn Donovan Jr. m 1/23/1971 Beverly Lynn Herrin c 2. jnachtrieb@worldnet.att.net

NAECKEL, Lynn Miles (Minn) Po Box 43, Ranier MN 56668 **H Trin Intl Falls MN 2006-** B Kansas City MO 9/22/1938 d Arno Carl Naeckel & Mildred. BA NWU 1960; MA NWU 1970; PhD (Qualified) NWU 1972. D 10/23/2005 Bp Daniel Lee Swenson P 7/8/2006 Bp James Louis Jelinek. c 1. Lay Prchr H Trin Intl Falls MN 1995-2005. naeckel@charter.net

NAEF, Linda (Miss) 655 Eagle Ave, Jackson MS 39206 B Philadelphia PA 9/1/1953 d Richard Wick Naef & Jane Ellen. Harv; BS U of Sthrn Mississippi 1974; MS U of Sthrn Mississippi 1976; MS U of Sthrn Mississippi 1978; MDiv EDS 1986. D 5/31/1986 Bp Duncan Montgomery Gray Jr P 5/1/1987 Bp Otis Charles. m 11/24/1982 Richard Lewis Hudson. Asst R S Mich's Ch Milton MA 1991-1992; S Paul's Ch Brookline MA 1987-1990.

NAEGELE III, John Aloysius (CPa) 982 Spa Rd. Apt. 201, Annapolis MD 21403 **Assoc S Phil's Ch Annapolis MD 2007-** B Philadelphia PA 1/11/1933 s John Aloysius Naegele & Natalie. BA W Liberty St Coll 1955; LTh Epis TS In Kentucky 1963; MDiv Epis TS In Kentucky 1986. D 12/1/1963 P 7/1/1964 Bp William R Moody. m 8/21/1988 Ellen W Sleat c 3. Int S Lk's Epis Ch Mechanicsburg PA 2002-2004; Int Hope Epis Ch Manheim PA 2001-2002; R Hope Epis Ch Manheim PA 1992-2001; R Trin And S Phil's Epis Ch Lansford

PA 1977-1984; P-in-c S Mk's Ch Hazard KY 1962-1966. jasonn123@verizon.net

NAGATA, Ada Yuk-Ying (Los) The Mission of Saint Thomas, 2323 Las Lomitas Dr, Hacienda Heights CA 91745 **Ch Of Our Sav Par San Gabr CA 2009-** B Hongkong China 4/20/1953 d Nam Wong & Lin-Chan. BSN California St U 1999; MDiv The ETS At Claremont 2007. D 6/9/2007 P 1/12/2008 Bp Joseph Jon Bruno. m 9/21/1985 Ronnie Nagata c 1. revadarn@pacbell.net

NAGEL, Virginia Otis Wight (CNY) 100 Wilson Pl, Syracuse NY 13214 **Vic Ephphatha Epis Par Of The Deaf Syracuse NY 1988-** B Schenectady NY 9/29/1939 d Otis Martin Wight & Marjorie Marie (Hillman). BA Gallaudet U 1959; MDiv Estrn Bapt TS 1988. D 11/22/1986 Bp Lyman Cunningham Ogilby P 6/1/1988 Bp Allen Lyman Bartlett Jr. m 10/3/1959 Robert V Nagel c 3. Mssnr Ephphatha Mssn For The Deaf Henrietta NY 1998; Ephphatha Epis Par Of The Deaf Syracuse NY 1997-2009; Dio Cntrl New York Syracuse NY 1988-2008; Dio Pennsylvania Philadelphia PA 1987-1988; Jubilee Intern All Souls Ch For The Deaf Philadelphia PA 1986-1988. Auth, "Sunday Sermons For Everyday People," *Year A*, Privately Printed, 2002; Auth, "Bcp Lections Translated Into Amer Sign Lang," *Year B*, Privately Printed, 2002; Auth, ",BCP Lections Translated Into Amer Sign Lang," *Years A, B & C*, Privately Printed, 2002; Auth, ",Sunday Sermons For Everyday People," *Years B & C*, Privately Printed, 2002; Auth, "Jubilee Journ," 1988; Auth, "To Remember Means To Live," *Bapt Ldr*, 1988. ECom 1989-1996; Epis Conf Of The Deaf 1961; Ord Of S Lk 1977; OHC, Assoc 1970. D.D. (honoris causa) Palmer TS 2007; Thos Gallaudet Awd Epis Conf Of The Deaf 2004. revginger@aol.com

NAGLE, George Overholser (CNY) 65 Glenwood Dr, Saranac Lake NY 12983 B West Reading PA 3/1/1936 s Warren Thomas Nagle & Elizabeth. BA Cor 1957; STB Ya Berk 1960; STM STUSo 1972. D 6/18/1960 P 6/29/1961 Bp Walter M Higley. m 6/13/1959 Margaret Mae Benoit. P-in-c S Jn In The Wilderness (Sum Chap) Onchiota NY 1977-1996; P-in-c S Mk's Ch Malone NY 1976-1977; R S Steph's Ch New Hartford NY 1967-1974; R Chr Epis Ch Jordan NY 1961-1967; D Chr Epis Ch Jordan NY 1960-1961. Auth, "Rel Attitudes And Symbols In The Writing Of Jn Updike". gnagle@roadrunner.com

NAGLEY, Stephanie Jane (WA) 6030 Grosvenor Lane, Bethesda MD 20814 **S Lk's Ch Trin Par Beth MD 2003-** B Colfax WA 1/29/1953 d Harold Dean Nagley & Violet Leota. BD Estrn Washington U 1975; MS U of Texas 1977; PhD Case Wstrn Reserve U 1984; MDiv VTS 1993. D 6/5/1993 Bp James Russell Moodey P 2/1/1994 Bp Gethin Benwil Hughes. m 8/22/2008 Joann Hallet. Bd Trst VTS Alexandria VA 2000; Assoc R S Mk's Ch Washington DC 1999-2003; Assoc R S Jas By The Sea La Jolla CA 1993-1999; Bd Trst VTS Alexandria VA 1993-1994. Harris Awd VTS 1993. rector@stlukesbethesda.org

NAGY, Robert Arthur (SanD) 33396 Alagon St, Temecula CA 92592 **Vic S Thos Epis Ch Temecula CA 2006-** B Bridgeport CT 4/10/1952 s Frank Alexander Nagy & Joan Mable. BS Arizona St U 1981; MBA Arizona St U 1984; MDiv STUSo 1994. D 6/11/1994 P 12/17/1994 Bp Robert Reed Shahan. m 8/10/1974 Beatrice Joan Dobi c 2. R Trin Ch Portsmouth VA 2002-2006; R Prince Of Peace Epis Ch Dallas PA 1998-2002; S Mary's Epis Ch Phoenix AZ 1995-1998; Dio Arizona Phoenix AZ 1994-1995. beanagy@yahoo.com

NAHIKIAN, Patricia Ann Loveridge (Fla) Po Box 1057, Melrose FL 32666 **D Trin Epis Ch Melrose FL 1997-** B Washington DC 7/11/1939 d Lloyd Edison Loveridge & Edna Monford. AA Mars Hill Coll 1959; BA U NC 1965; MA U Of Cntrl Florida 1980; Inst for Chr Stds 1996. D 11/23/1996 Bp John Wadsworth Howe. m 3/30/1959 Robert Lavon Nahikian.

NAIRN, Frederick William (Minn) 5895 Stoneybrook Dr, Minnetonka MN 55345 B IE 8/20/1943 s Frederick Nairn & Maureen Beatrice. GOE Trin-Dublin Ie 1967; Luther TS 1987; DMin 1988. Trans from Church Of England 8/5/1987 Bp Robert Marshall Anderson. m 8/1/2002 Mary Jo Montenegro c 1. S Anne's Ch De Pere WI 1999-2000; S Paul's Ch Brainerd MN 1998; R Ch Of The Epiph Epis Plymouth MN 1987-1996; Int S Geo's Ch St Louis Pk MN 1986-1987; Exch R The Epis Par Of S Dav Minnetonka MN 1985-1986. fwnairn@stthomas.edu

NAKAMURA, Katherine Toshiko (Ala) 521 20th St N, Birmingham AL 35203 **Dio Alabama Birmingham AL 2011-** B Birmingham AL 7/21/1985 BMusic NWU 2007; MDiv VTS 2011. D 5/20/2011 Bp John McKee Sloan. m 5/22/2010 Josiah Daniel Rengers. KTNAKAMURA@GMAIL.COM

NAKATSUJI, Dorothy Masako Kamigaki (Haw) 1725 Fern St, Honolulu HI 96826 **D The Par Of S Clem Honolulu HI 2002-** B Peru WY 11/7/1932 d Nobuo Kamigaki & Ida. MS U of Utah 1962; Dio Trng Prog HI 1983. D 11/11/1983 Bp Edmond Lee Browning. m 6/23/1962 Ronald M Nakatsuji c 1. The Par Of S Clem Honolulu HI 1990-1991. Naeyc; NAAD; Third Ord At Soc Of S Fran.

NAKAYAMA, Timothy Makoto (Oly) 700 6TH AVE S APT 321, Seattle WA 98104 B Vancouver BC CA 10/5/1931 s Gordon Goichi Nakayama & Lois Masui. BA U of British Columbia Vancouver BC CA 1953; ATC 1956; LTh ATC 1964. Trans from Anglican Church of Canada 3/28/1966 as Priest Bp Ivol I Curtis. m 9/18/1961 Lois Keiko Furumoto c 4. P in Charge All Soul's Epis Ch 1991-1997; R Dio Olympia Seattle WA 1977-1991; R St Ptr's Epis Par Seattle WA 1977-1991; Par P, Appointed Natl Convenor, Epis Asiamerica Mnstry, Japanese Convoc St Ptr's Epis Par Seattle WA 1973-1979. Auth, "Wrld War II internment as a Japanese-Can Chld," *Too Young To Fight*, Stoddard, 1999; Auth, "Hist of Angl Japanese Missions in Can," *Can Ch Hist Journ*, 1967. Cmnty of Nazareth 1993. Epis Asiamerica Mnstry Cross Natl EAM 1985; Bp's Cross Bp Curtis of Olympia 1972. frtim@yahoo.com

NAKO, James Walter (Chi) 9300 S Pleasant Ave, Chicago IL 60620 **R Ch Of The H Nativ Chicago IL 1992-** B Chicago IL 11/1/1937 s Walter Nako & Eleanora. MA U Chi 1953; Ph.D. U Chi 1959; MDiv SWTS 1962; Ph.D. Loyola U 1972. D 6/23/1962 Bp Charles L Street P 12/1/1962 Bp Gerald Francis Burrill. Min of Pstr Care Chr Ch River Forest IL 1981-1991; R Gr Ch Chicago IL 1966-1972; Asst to Dn Cathd Of S Jas Chicago IL 1962-1965. jwnako@sbcglobal.net

NALVEN, Claudia (Chi) 327 S 4th St, Geneva IL 60134 **Asst. R S Mk's Ch Geneva IL 2007-** B Mt Kisco, NY 12/4/1958 d Joseph Weckessar & Josephine. BS Nyack Coll 1999; MDiv TESM 2006. D 3/30/2007 P 10/12/2007 Bp Henry William Scriven. c 2. cnalven@comcast.net

NANCARROW, Arthur Paul (Mich) 148 W Eagle Lake Dr, Maple Grove MN 55369 B Houghton MI 11/20/1930 s Arthur James Nancarrow & Elsie Bertha. BA Ripon Coll Ripon WI 1952; MDiv SWTS 1955; MA U of Detroit 1973. D 6/15/1955 P 12/18/1955 Bp Herman R Page. m 10/12/1955 Deborah A Clapp c 3. Archd Dio Michigan Detroit MI 1986-1992; Stndg Comm Dio Michigan Detroit MI 1982-1985; R S Jude's Epis Ch Fenton MI 1978-1992; Asst to Bp for Faith & Wrshp Dio Michigan Detroit MI 1973-1978; Assoc Dir Whitaker TS Dio Michigan Detroit MI 1964-1978; Stndg Comm Dio Nthrn Michigan Marquette MI 1959-1964; Cn Res Gr Epis Ch Menominee MI 1958-1959; Vic Ch Of The Ascen Ontonagon MI 1956-1958; S Mk's Ch Ewen MI 1956-1958; Asst S Jas Ch Of Sault S Marie Sault Ste Marie MI 1955-1956. Hon Cn S Paul's Cathd Detroit MI 1993; Phi Beta Kappa Ripon Coll 1983. debnancarrow@comcast.net

NANCARROW, Paul Steven (SwVa) 25 Church St, Staunton VA 24401 **R Trin Ch Staunton VA 2008-** B Ontonagon MI 9/9/1956 s Arthur Paul Nancarrow & Deborah Ann. BA Ripon Coll Ripon WI 1978; MA U MN 1984; MDiv SWTS 1986; PhD Van 2000. D 6/28/1986 P 2/24/1987 Bp Henry Irving Mayson. m 4/29/2006 Lee M Morris c 2. R S Geo's Ch St Louis Pk MN 1999-2008; Int S Barth's Ch Bristol TN 1997-1999; Int Otey Memi Par Ch Sewanee TN 1996-1997; P-in-c The Epis Ch Of The Resurr Franklin TN 1995-1996; P Ch Of Our Sav Gallatin TN 1993-1995; Assoc Chr Ch Dearborn MI 1988-1993; Asst Gr Epis Ch Port Huron MI 1986-1988. "The Call of the Sprt: Process Sprtlty in a Relational Wrld," P&F Press, 2005; Auth, "Wisdom's Info," *Zygon: Journ Rel & Sci*, 1997; Auth, "Realism and Anti-Realism," *Process Stds*, 1995. psnancarrow@gmail.com

N

NANCARROW, Philip John (NMich) 115 W Douglass Ave, Houghton MI 49931 **Died 9/22/2011** B Hancock MI 8/23/1943 s Willard George Nancarrow & Dorothy Edna. MCMT Houghton MI 1962; BA Ripon Coll Ripon WI 1965; BD SWTS 1968. D 6/22/1968 P 3/30/1969 Bp George R Selway. m 9/26/2011 Gary Evans. philnan@chartermi.net

NANCEKIVELL, Diane (NJ) 1008 Hemenway Rd, Bridport VT 05734 B Montreal QC CA 7/6/1946 d Arthur Frank Nancekivell & Beatrice L. BEd U of Alberta Edmonton AB CA 1976; Med S Mich's Coll Colchester VT 1984; MDiv Bangor TS 1992. D 11/7/1998 P 5/1/1999 Bp Joe Morris Doss. m 5/21/1994 Thomas Roland Baskett c 1. Dn Trin Cathd Trenton NJ 2000-2006; S Paul's Epis Ch Westfield NJ 1998-2000. dianenan@gmaut.net

NANNY, Susan Kathryn (Mo) 2831 Eads Ave, Saint Louis MO 63104 B Tulsa OK 4/22/1955 d Joe David Nanny & Patricia Lou. BS U of Texas 1977; MDiv SWTS 1989. D 6/17/1989 Bp Robert Manning Moody P 1/1/1990 Bp Bob Gordon Jones. Cn Chr Ch Cathd S Louis MO 2000-2008; Int S Fran Epis Ch Eureka MO 1997-2000; Trin Ch S Louis MO 1989-1994. sknanny@aol.com

NANTON-MARIE, Allan (Fla) PO Box 1-5442, Fort Lauderdale FL 33318 **LocTen Dio SE Florida Miami FL 2000-; LocTen Dio Florida Jacksonville FL 1996-** B Port of Spain Saint George TT s Anselm Marie & Ira. Dplma (Honours) Jamaica Bible Coll; B. A. SUNY, Empire St Coll 1975; UTS 1975; M. Div. Yale DS 1978; Paralegal Cert NYU 1986. D 12/8/1996 P 6/15/1997 Bp Stephen Hays Jecko. Int Vic S Kevin's Epis Ch Opa Locka FL 2002-2004; Assoc Pstr S Agnes Ch Miami FL 2000-2002; Par Mssnr S Paul's By-The-Sea Epis Ch Jacksonville Bch FL 1995-1996. Auth, "Caribbean Roots People: The Struggle for Amerindian Survival in the Caribbean," (In press) Cedar Press, Barbados, W.I.; Auth, "Mandate for Caribbean Rituals in Rel Drama," (In press)Jnl of Intl Theol Cntr Atlanta GA. Phi Alpha Delta Law Fraternity, Intl 1987. fathernantonmarie@hotmail.com

NAPOLI, Michael Anthony (CGC) 551 W Barksdale Dr, Mobile AL 36606 **Died 9/8/2009** B Lafayette LA 7/15/1946 s Leon Joseph Napoli & Lizzie Ann. BS U of SW Louisiana 1968; MBA U of W Florida 1972; MDiv Nash 1985. D 5/30/1985 P 4/1/1986 Bp Charles Farmer Duvall. mikelal@earthlink.net

NARAIN, Errol Lloyd (Chi) 125 E 26th St, Chicago IL 60616 **R Trin Ch Chicago IL 1989-** B Durban ZA 3/3/1949 s Haricharan Rhambowan & Mona. LSED Springfield Durban ZA 1971; AFTS Fed TS 1980; BA U of Natal 1981;

MA U Chi 1985. Trans from Church of the Province of Southern Africa 4/1/1988 Bp A(lbert) Theodore Eastman. m 12/29/1973 Louisa S Narain c 3. Int S Marg's Epis Ch Baltimore MD 1988-1989. Auth, *Word & Witness*. Fulbright Schlr Fulbright 1984. elnarain@yahoo.com

NARD, David (WNC) 14 Red Oak Rd, Asheville NC 28804 **D The Cathd Of All Souls Asheville NC 2002-** B Paintsville KY 2/19/1947 s Frank Edward Nard & Billy Palmer. BFA E Carolina U 1970; MA U NC 1972. D 12/11/1985 Bp William Gillette Weinhauer. m 6/12/1976 Mary Alice Nard c 3. D Gr Ch Asheville NC 2000-2002; D S Jn's Ch Asheville NC 1999-2000; Archd Dio Wstrn No Carolina Asheville NC 1996-2005; D Gr Ch Asheville NC 1985-1998. AEHC 1988; NC Chapl Assn 1993; Tertiary of the Soc of S Fran 1978. Pres NAAD 2002. david.nard@msj.org

NARVAEZ, Alfonso Anthony (WTex) Po Box 3003, Laredo TX 78044 B New York NY 8/1/1930 s Alfonso Narvaez & Isabel. BA CUNY 1962; MS Col 1964; NYTS 1984; Inst Pstr Hisp 1985. D 6/8/1985 P 6/1/1986 Bp John Shelby Spong. m 4/18/1971 Dabney Harfst c 4. Supply Cler Chr Ch Creswell NC 2006-2010; Asst S Paul's Epis Ch Edenton NC 2000-2003; Chr Ch Epis Laredo TX 1993-1998; Vic Trin Ch Paterson NJ 1986-1993. alnarv@net-change.com

NASH, Penny Annette (At) 183 Cutspring Arch, Williamsburg VA 23185 **Assoc R for Yth, Chld & Families Bruton Par Williamsburg VA 2011-** B Louisburg NC 5/9/1955 d Willis Winfield Nash & Catherine Oldham. BA Florida St U 1978; MDiv Candler TS Emory U 2008. D 12/21/2007 Bp J(ohn) Neil Alexander P 8/9/2008 Bp Keith Bernard Whitmore. m 6/16/1989 Thomas Alan Cox c 2. Sabbatical P-in-c S Simon's Epis Ch Conyers GA 2010; Assoc R S Pat's Epis Ch Atlanta GA 2008-2010. nash.penny@gmail.com

NATERA, Marivel Natura (SeFla) 6744 N Miami Ave, Miami FL 33150 B Dominican Republic 7/24/1966 d Juan Natera & Paula. D 10/28/2007 Bp Leopold Frade. m 12/22/1991 Jean Baptiste Smith Milien c 3. fmiliena@yahoo.com

NATERS-GAMARRA, Floyd (Butch) (Los) 623 Prospect Ave Unit 6, South Pasadena CA 91030 **Asst S Mary's Epis Ch Los Angeles CA 2007-** B Colon Colon PA 10/3/1941 s Septimo Leonardo Naters & Policarpa. MDiv ETSC 1966; U Of Panama Panama City PA 1967. D 6/11/1966 P 12/17/1966 Bp Reginald Heber Gooden. c 2. S Phil's Par Los Angeles CA 2003-2006; Dio Los Angeles Los Angeles CA 2000-2003; Mssnr Multicultrl Mnstries & Congreg Dvlpmnt Dio Los Angeles Los Angeles CA 1999-2003; Dio Los Angeles Los Angeles CA 1997; Dio Massachusetts Boston MA 1995-1999; Com Dio Los Angeles Los Angeles CA 1995; S Steph's Epis Ch Boston MA 1989-1994; Dio Pennsylvania Philadelphia PA 1988-1989; S Barn Kensington Philadelphia PA 1983-1988; S Mary's Manhattanville Epis Ch New York NY 1982-1983; Hisp Epis Cntr San Andres Ch Yonkers NY 1979-1982; Chr Ch By The Sea 1976-1979; Dio Panama 1974-1979. multicultural@ladiocese.org

N

NATHANIEL, Mary (Ak) PO Box 56, Chalkyitsik AK 99788 B Fort Yukon AK 8/28/1956 d Fred Paul & Sophie. Cook Coll & TS Tempe AZ. D 6/30/1990 Bp George Clinton Harris P 12/26/2003 Bp Mark Lawrence Mac Donald. m 3/26/1983 David Nathaniel c 4. marynathaniel@hotmail.com

NATION, Michael Christopher (Miss) 580 Hutchinson St, Mandeville LA 70448 **Seamens Ch Inst Income New York NY 2011-; Ecum Off Dio Mississippi Jackson MS 2007-** B Mobile AL 3/16/1970 s Lewis Douglas Nation & Annie Ruth. BA U of Mobile 1992; Cert Hebr U of Jerusalem 1993; MDiv Duke 1997; CAS VTS 1997; Cert Duke 2006. D 9/20/1997 P 6/13/1998 Bp Clifton Daniel III. m 8/6/1994 Cheryl Ann Presnall c 3. R Ch of the H Trin Vicksburg MS 2001-2011; Trin Epis Ch Chocowinity NC 1997-2001. michaelnation@bellsouth.net

NATOLI, Anne M (EC) 104 S Madison St, Whiteville NC 28472 **R Gr Ch Whiteville NC 2003-** B Watertown NY 11/6/1950 d Anthony Carmen Sylvester & Ethel Elizabeth. BS Russell Sage Coll 1972; MS Med Coll of Virginia 1979; MDiv VTS 1998. D 5/26/1998 P 12/8/1998 Bp Henry Irving Louttit. c 1. S Paul's Ch Albany GA 1999-2003; Dio Georgia Savannah GA 1998. Oblate, Ord of Julian of Norwich 2006; Ord of S Lk. amnatoli@aol.com

NATTERMANN, Margaret (Peggy) Ann (WMich) 06685 M-66n, Charlevoix Estates Lot 124, Charlevoix MI 49720 **Ch Of The Nativ Boyne City MI 2006-** B Philadelphia PA 10/16/1948 d Elmer Frederick Nattermann & Edith Margaret. BS Alma Coll 1970; MDiv SWTS 1991. D 7/6/1991 P 6/26/1993 Bp Edward Lewis Lee Jr. Int Chr Epis Ch Charlevoix MI 1998-1999; Emm Ch Petoskey MI 1994-1995; Emm Ch Petoskey MI 1992-1993.

NATZKE, Vicki Jo (FdL) 7221 Country Village Dr, Wisconsin Rapids WI 54494 **P St Johns Epis Ch Wisconsin Rapids WI 2004-** B Wis Rapids WI 11/15/1955 d Charles Alan Patterson & Joan Ruth. BS U of Wisconsin 1978; MEPD U of Wisconsin 1983; MDiv Nash 2002. D 12/8/2001 P 6/8/2002 Bp Russell Edward Jacobus. m 8/7/1981 David Ken Natzke c 2. Assoc S Thos Ch Menasha WI 2002-2004. vnatzke@charter.net

NAUGHTON, Ezra A (VI) 398 N St Sw, Washington DC 20024 B 11/16/1926 s James E Naughton & Mary Evelyn. BS Dist Of Columbia Teachers Coll Washington DC 1962; MA How 1965; PhD CUA 1973; MA Washington Theol Consortium 1993. D 12/7/1993 Bp E(gbert) Don Taylor P 3/1/1995 Bp James Winchester Montgomery. m 5/8/1989 LaVerne Glasgow. Dio Washington Washington DC 1993-1998. Cath Fllshp Of Epis Ch; Washington Dc Cleric Assn.

NAUGHTON, Sharon Yvonne (EMich) St Paul's Episcopal Church, 711 S Saginaw St, Flint MI 48502 **D S Paul's Epis Ch Flint MI 2003-** B Grand Rapids MI 9/29/1937 d Anthony Schumaker & Isla. BA U of Detroit Mercy 1959. D 10/11/2003 Bp Edwin Max Leidel Jr. Dio Estrn Michigan Saginaw MI 2008-2009. naughtonatstpauls@ameritech.net

NAUGLE, Gretchen Rohn (Neb) PO Box 306, Columbus NE 68602 **Chr Ch Epis Beatrice NE 2010-; S Chas The Mtyr Beatrice NE 2010-; S Lk's Ch Wymore NE 2010-** B Allentown PA 1/5/1943 d Benjamin Rohn & Elizabeth. BA Pur 1964; MA U of Iowa 1980; MDiv Luth TS 1994. Rec from Evangelical Lutheran Church in America 9/3/2009 as Priest Bp Joe Goodwin Burnett. m 6/2/1963 Ronald C Naugle c 1. Int Gr Ch Par -Epis Columbus NE 2009-2010. prgrn@earthlink.net

NAUMANN, John Frederick (Mont) 1241 Crawford Dr., Billings MT 59102 B Toowoomba Queensland AU 1/21/1940 s John Frederick Naumann & Elsie. Lic S Fran Sem 1966. Trans from Anglican Church Of Australia 3/21/1989 as Priest Bp Charles Jones III. R S Steph's Ch Billings MT 1989-2005. jfnaumann@yahoo.com

NAUMANN, Richard Donald (Wyo) 1251 Inca Dr, Laramie WY 82072 **Archd Dio Wyoming Casper WY 2011-; D S Matt's Epis Cathd Laramie WY 2005-** B Columbia MO 6/29/1946 s Hugh Donald Naumann & Geraldine Coleman. BA U of Missouri 1971; Med U of Missouri 1972; EDS U of Wyoming 1998. D 2/17/2005 Bp Bruce Edward Caldwell. m 11/16/1968 Mary Barninger Naumann c 2. AED 2005. naumann@wyo2u.com

NAUSKA, Gayle Lynn (Ak) 1703 Richardson Dr, Anchorage AK 99504 **P S Mary's Ch Anchorage AK 2007-** B Normal IL 11/16/1955 d Omer L Carey & Carol Lucille. AAS U of Alaska 1988; BA Alaska Pacific U 1990; MS U of LaVerne 1993; M.Div. Vancouver TS 2009; Grad Cert U of Alaska, Anchorage 2010. D 5/11/1997 Bp A(lbert) Theodore Eastman P 3/25/2004 Bp Mark Lawrence Mac Donald. Chr Ch Anchorage AK 2003-2007; D All SS' Epis Ch Anchorage AK 1997-2001. AAPC 1994; Amer Counslg Assn 2010. gnauska@gmail.com

NAWROCKI, Cynthia Lynn (WMich) 3006 Bird Ave Ne, Grand Rapids MI 49525 **D S Mk's Ch Grand Rapids MI 2006-** B Lansing MI 4/8/1947 D 9/20/2003 Bp Robert R Gepert. m 12/29/1984 Frederick Edwin Nawrocki c 3. S Andr's Ch Grand Rapids MI 2003-2008. rocki@att.net

NAYLOR, Susan Bernadine Rice (Mo) 2905 Wingate Ct, Saint Louis MO 63119 **Chapl to the Cmnty of Deacons Dio Missouri S Louis MO 2010-; D S Mart's Ch Ellisville MO 2010-** B Ypsilanti MI 5/1/1957 d Warren Albert Rice & Ramona Ann. Dplma Barnes Hosp Sch Of Nrsng 1991; Dplma The Epis Sch for Mnstry 2002. D 6/3/2004 Bp George Wayne Smith. m 8/17/1996 Earl Carleton Naylor. D / Pstr Assoc Emm Epis Ch Webster Groves MO 2004-2010. "Mnstry Of Hlth And Wholeness: A Par Nrsng Prog," Circut Rider mag /, 2001. sricenaylor@yahoo.com

NAZRO JR, A(rthur) Phillips (Tex) 1109 W 31st St, Austin TX 78705 B New York NY 8/20/1937 s Arthur Phillips Nazro & Frances Anna. BA Rice U 1958; BS Rice U 1959; BD Epis TS of The SW 1966. D 6/8/1966 Bp J Milton Richardson P 5/29/1967 Bp Frederick P Goddard. m 5/29/1964 Lucy Collins c 3. All SS Epis Ch Austin TX 2001-2009; S Steph's Epis Sch Austin TX 1983-1994; Assoc Trin Ch Galveston TX 1978-1980; R S Paul's Epis Ch Orange TX 1975-1978; Asst R Ch Of The Ascen Clearwater FL 1970-1975; R S Jn's Epis Ch Sealy TX 1968-1970; R S Mary's Ch Bellville TX 1968-1970; Min in charge S Mk's Ch Gladewater TX 1966-1967; Min in charge S Mich And All Ang' Epis Ch Longview TX 1966-1967. Texas Coun for the Hmnts 1997-2002. pnazro@aol.com

NDAI, Domenic Muthoga (Pa) 801 Macdade Blvd, Collingdale PA 19023 **Trin Ch Boothwyn PA 1997-** B 12/15/1947 s Ndai Gitonga & Beth Njeri. Kamwenja Coll 1968; BD S Paul Untd TS 1985; STM GTS 1989; MA Evang TS 1996. Trans from Anglican Church Of Kenya 2/1/1998 Bp Allen Lyman Bartlett Jr. m 11/8/2011 Anne W Kanyari c 5. domenicndai@yahoo.com

NDISHABANDI, William K (Miss) 147 Daniel Lake Blvd, Jackson MS 39212 **R All SS Ch Jackson MS 2006-** B Kilembe Uganda 4/14/1959 BA Haggai Inst for Ldrshp; Bachelor of Arts Afr Bible Coll 1995; Mstr of Arts Reformed TS 1999; Doctor of CE Carolina U of Theol 2002. Trans from Church of the Province of Uganda 11/1/2002 Bp Duncan Montgomery Gray III. m 5/24/1986 Naomi Muhindo Ndishabandi c 5. Int All SS Ch Jackson MS 2008-2009; Vic S Jn's Ch Leland MS 2001-2006; Vic Ch Of The Redeem Greenville MS 1999-2006. wndishab@gmail.com

NEAD III, Prescott Eckerman (USC) 714 Michaels Creek, Evans GA 30809 B Albany,NY 7/29/1947 s Prescott Edkerman Nead & Clara. BA Alfred U 1972; MDiv STUSo 1975. D 5/31/1975 P 12/20/1975 Bp Wilbur Emory Hogg Jr. m 6/9/2001 Susan Payne c 3. Vic S Aug Of Cbury Aiken SC 1990-2005; R All SS Epis Ch Clinton SC 1984-1990; Coordntr Dio Upper So Carolina Columbia SC 1981-1990; Asst R Ch Of Our Sav Rock Hill SC 1980-1984; R S Andr's

Epis Ch Douglas GA 1979-1980; R S Paul's Ch Albany GA 1976-1979; R Chr's Ch Duanesburg NY 1975-1976. scottynead@comcast.net

NEAL, Ashley Cosslett (WNC) 449 Crowfields Drive, Asheville NC 28803 B Hitchin UK 10/21/1952 d Kenneth Edward Cosslett & Margot. Bard Coll 1972; U of Paris-Sorbonne FR 1973; BA U of San Francisco 1982; MDiv Ya Berk 1991. D 6/8/1991 Bp John Shelby Spong P 12/14/1991 Bp Jack Marston McKelvey. Assoc S Paul's By-The-Sea Epis Ch Jacksonville Bch FL 2000-2001; R All SS' Epis Ch Glen Rock NJ 1993-1999; P-in-c S Eliz's Ch Ridgewood NJ 1991-1993. acosslett@gmail.com

NEAL, Deonna Denice (WA) Department of Theology, 130 Malloy Hall, Notre Dame IN 46556 B Glendale CA 5/13/1972 d William Whitney Neal & Jodelle Denice. B.S. The USAF Acad 1994; M.Div GTS 2002; M.Phil Oxf 2005. D 6/15/2002 P 5/5/2004 Bp John Chane. Promising Schlr Awd ECF 2003. dneal@nd.edu

NEAL, James Frederick (Oly) 1831 E South Island Dr, Shelton WA 98584 **P S Hugh Of Lincoln Allyn WA 2003-** B Hailey ID 8/12/1941 s Harry Herford Neal & Maxine. BS Idaho St U 1963. D 11/30/2002 Bp Sanford Zangwill Kaye Hampton P 6/23/2003 Bp Vincent Waydell Warner. m 6/1/1962 Wilma Larae Bingham. jfneal@hctc.com

NEAL, Kristi Hasskamp (WNC) 100 Spring Ln, Black Mountain NC 28711 **Archd Dio Wstrn No Carolina Asheville NC 2011-** B Marion NC 6/19/1947 d Harry William Hasskamp & Patricia Adair. BA Duke 1969; MAEd Wstrn Carolina U 1979. D 1/28/2006 Bp Granville Porter Taylor. m 11/28/1998 John Culbreth c 2. dn_kneal@att.net

NEAL, Linda (ECR) 41-884 Laumilo St, Waimanalo HI 96795 B Dayton KY 11/18/1949 d Lloyd D Kendall & Mary Ellen. D 12/18/1985 Bp Edmond Lee Browning. coaster1149@aol.com

NEAL JR, Millard Fillmore (SwFla) 14820 Rue De Bayonne, Clearwater FL 33762 B Clearwater FL 7/26/1929 s Millard Fillmore Neal & Nettie Viola. BS Bethune-Cookman Coll 1950; S Mary U 1971; MDiv Iliff TS 1973. D 6/11/1988 Bp Gerald Francis Burrill P 2/1/1989 Bp James Winchester Montgomery. c 3. Cn Dio SW Florida Sarasota FL 2002-2004; Cn Cathd Ch Of S Ptr St Petersburg FL 1998-2008; Int S Jn's Epis Ch Clearwater FL 1996-1997; Assoc Pstr S Mk's Epis Ch Of Tampa Tampa FL 1990-1995; Assoc R S Giles Ch Pinellas Pk FL 1989-1990. fatherfill@aol.com

NEAL, Scott Bradley (Vt) PO Box 410, Arlington VT 05250 **R S Jas Epis Ch Arlington VT 2007-** B Lincoln NE 8/2/1957 s William Summer Neal & Maxine. BS U of Maine 1979; MDiv GTS 2007. D 11/29/2006 P 12/1/2007 Bp Thomas C Ely. m 2/16/1980 Elizabeth Capelle c 2. rectorstjames@gmail.com

NEAL, William Everett (FdL) No address on file. B Santa Rosa CA 10/27/1940 D 1/10/1965 P 8/9/1965 Bp William Hampton Brady.

NEALE, Alan James Robert (Pa) 316 S 16th St, Philadelphia PA 19102 **R The Ch Of The H Trin Rittenhouse Philadelphia PA 2004-** B London UK 4/16/1952 s James Samuel Neale & Lilian Frances. BSc(Econ) Lon 1973; BA Oxf 1976; CTh Oxf 1977; MA Oxf 1979. Trans from Church Of England 12/2/1988 Bp Craig Barry Anderson. m 3/9/1987 Wendy Elizabeth Marsh c 4. R S Columba's Chap Middletown RI 1991-2004; Assoc Trin Ch Newport RI 1991; R S Paul's Ch Brookings SD 1988-1990. ajrn316@gmail.com

NEALE, Hedwig Brown (RI) 143 Spring St, East Greenwich RI 02818 B Providence RI 4/2/1927 d Frederick Gregory Brown & Grace Eugenie. BA McGill U 1947; MA Harv 1948; Rhode Island Sch for Deacons 1989. D 6/23/1990 Bp George Nelson Hunt III. c 5. D S Lk's Epis Ch E Greenwich RI 1993-1998; D All SS' Memi Ch Providence RI 1990-1993. hbneale@aol.com

NEAR, Kenneth Mark (Nwk) 6-376 av Redfern, Westmount QC H3Z 2G5 Canada B Grosse Pte Farms MI 1/30/1952 s Donald Jacob Near & Barbara Marie. BA Wayne 1976; MDiv U of Trin, U Tor 1978. D 6/17/1978 P 12/1/1978 Bp William J Gordon Jr. m 6/22/1974 Karen Williamson c 2. R S Paul's Ch Englewood NJ 1991-2009; Vic S Andr's Ch Denver CO 1987-1991; Cn S Jn's Cathd Denver CO 1985-1991; R Chr Epis Ch E Tawas MI 1978-1984. circak@aol.com

NEARY, Marlyn Mason (NH) 1935 Us Route 3, Colebrook NH 03576 **Vic S Steph's Epis Mssn Colebrook NH 1998-** B Barton VT 9/5/1946 d Percy Maurice Mason & Eva Louise. D 3/14/1998 P 9/20/1998 Bp Douglas Edwin Theuner. m 2/25/1967 William Henry Neary

NEAT, William Jessee (Lex) 311 Washington St, Frankfort KY 40601 **Ch Of The Ascen Frankfort KY 2011-** B Glasgow KY 12/9/1953 s James Arlo Neat & June. BS Estrn Kentucky U 1975; MA Wichita St U 1981; MDiv Nash 1999. D 6/11/1999 P 5/13/2000 Bp Michael Whittington Creighton. m 12/16/1973 Virginia S Sherrod c 1. R Chr Ch Chaptico MD 2003-2011; Assoc R S Jas Ch Lancaster PA 1999-2003. OHC - Assoc 1991. fatherjessee@aol.com

NEBEL, Sue (Chi) 2023 Lake Ave, Wilmette IL 60091 **D Gr Ch Chicago IL 2011-** B Grand Rapids MI 3/20/1940 d Edson Hemingway Fuller & Elisabeth. BA Albion Coll 1961; MA U CO 1963; PhD NWU 1969; MDiv SWTS 2007. D 2/7/1998 Bp Herbert Alcorn Donovan Jr. m 7/13/1967 Henry Martin Nebel c 2. D S Simons Ch Arlington Heights IL 2008-2011; D The Annunc Of Our Lady Gurnee IL 2004-2008; D Gr Ch Oak Pk IL 2001-2005; D Ch Of The H Fam Lake Villa IL 1999-2000; D S Matt's Ch Evanston IL 1998-1999. Assn for Epis Deacons 1998. Recognition Of Diac Mnstry In The Traditional Of St. Step N Amer Associateion For The Dracuete 2005. s-hnebel@comcast.net

NECKERMANN, Ernest Charles (Los) 1107 Foothills Dr, Newberg OR 97132 B Oak Park IL 9/8/1937 s Edwin Neckermann & Martha. BA Elmhurst Coll 1962; STB PDS 1965; MA Untd States Intl U San Diego CA 1977. D 6/24/1965 P 1/2/1966 Bp Chandler W Sterling. m 12/6/1995 Barbara Ann Sager c 1. S Columba's Epis Mssn Big Bear Lake CA 2000-2003; P-in-c S Paul's Mssn Barstow CA 1995-2000; Asst R The Epis Ch Of S Andr Encinitas CA 1988-1990; S Ptr's Epis Ch Del Mar CA 1977-1981; Vic All SS Epis Ch Whitefish MT 1968-1976; Vic S Matt's Ch Columbia Falls MT 1968-1976; Dioc Yth Dir Dio Montana Helena MT 1966-1976; Vic Chr Ch Sheridan MT 1965-1967; Vic S Paul's Ch Virginia City MT 1965-1967; Vic Trin Ch Ennis MT 1965-1967.

NEDELKA, Jerome Joseph (LI) 55 Harbor Beach Rd, PO Box 2016, Miller Place NY 11764 **Chapl to Ret Cler Dio Long Island Garden City NY 2009-** B Flushing NY 2/27/1938 s Frank Josef Nedelka & Marie. BA Wag 1959; MDiv/STB PDS 1965; MDiv EDS 1987. D 6/19/1965 P 12/21/1965 Bp Jonathan Goodhue Sherman. m 10/9/1960 Ruth Ann Falbee c 2. Archdnry of Suffolk Dio Long Island Garden City NY 1998-2005; Great So Bay Dnry Dio Long Island Garden City NY 1979-1998; R S Mk's Ch Islip NY 1978-2000; Vic Ch Of Chr The King E Meadow NY 1968-1978; Cur All SS Ch Bayside NY 1965-1967. New York St Associatoon of Fire Chapl 1979; Ord of S Lk 1980-2000; P Assoc, OHC 1965. Cn of the Cathd of the Incarn Dio Long Island 2002; Bp's Cross for Distinguished Dioc Serv Dio Long Island 2000; R Emer S Mk's Ch,Islip,NY Islip NY 2000; Distinguished Trst Untd Hosp Fund/Epis Hlth Serv 2000; Paul Harris Fell Rotary Intl 1995. jeromej.nedelka@gmail.com

NEDS, Walter Eugene (SeFla) 1120 SE 46th St Apt 1E, Cape Coral FL 33904 B Lima OH 12/1/1926 s John Calvin Neds & Florence Mae. Creighton U 1945; Cert of Completion VTS 1962; LTh VTS 1976. D 6/9/1962 Bp Nelson Marigold Burroughs P 12/22/1962 Bp William Foreman Creighton. c 3. Cn Dio SE Florida Miami FL 1979-1990; LocTen H Sprt Epis Ch W Palm Bch FL 1977-1979; Asst S Margarets Epis Ch Miami Lakes FL 1975-1977; Asst Ch Of The Ascen Miami FL 1974-1975; Vic S Jas The Fisherman Islamorada FL 1972-1974; Assoc Chr Ch Cranbrook Bloomfield Hills MI 1965-1972; Asst S Thos' Par Washington DC 1962-1965. Auth, *The Orgnztn Bridge*, Self-Pub, 1974. weneds@comcast.net

NEED, Merrie Anne Dunham (Colo) 7726 S Trenton Ct, Englewood CO 80112 **S Anne's Epis Sch Denver CO 2005-** B Denver CO 9/28/1947 d Herbert Ralston Dunham & June. U Of Puget Sound 1966; BA U CO 1969; Med U Of Delaware Newark 1976; U of Sthrn Mississippi 1979; MDiv Bex 1991. D 6/13/1992 P 11/16/1993 Bp William George Burrill. m 7/20/1974 Harry Need c 1. Gd Shpd Epis Ch Centennial CO 2004-2005; The Ch Of The Ascen Denver CO 2002; Peace in Chr Ch Eliz CO 2000-2002; Asst Chr's Epis Ch Castle Rock CO 1999-2000; Non-par Dio Colorado Denver CO 1998-1999; Zion Ch Avon NY 1995; Calv/St Andr's Par Rochester NY 1993-1994. mneed@hotmail.com

NEEL, Douglas E (Colo) 225 S Pagosa Blvd, Pagosa Springs CO 81147 **R S Pat's Epis Ch Pagosa Sprg CO 2008-** B Fort Benning GA 5/2/1954 s Earl Myers Neel & Alice. BD U of Arkansas 1976; MDiv Nash 1983. D 6/11/1983 Bp Robert Elwin Terwilliger P 5/5/1984 Bp Donis Dean Patterson. m 6/25/1989 Sarah Louise Logee c 3. R H Trin Ch Rockwall TX 2000-2004; Assoc The Epis Ch Of The Trsfg Dallas TX 1999-2000; Cur S Lk's Epis Ch Dallas TX 1983-1986. dougneel@sbcglobal.net

NEELEY II, Harry Edwin (Mont) 100 W Glendale St #8, Dillon MT 59725 B Sioux Falls SD 8/8/1934 s Thomas John Neeley & Alice Katherine. Ldrshp Acad for New Directions; BS Augustana Coll 1957; BD Epis TS of The SW 1964. D 5/30/1964 P 12/1/1964 Bp James W Hunter. m 8/22/1954 Valrae Hill c 3. S Andr's Ch Anaconda MT 1992-1994; S Marks Pintler Cluster Anaconda MT 1987-1994; Vic S Mich Ch Alturas CA 1982-1984; Calv Epis Ch Red Lodge MT 1981-1984; Our Sav Epis Joliet MT 1981-1984; S Paul's of the Stillwater Ch Absarokee MT 1981-1984; Stndg Com Dio Montana Helena MT 1980-1983; R St Jas Epis Ch Dillon MT 1977-1981; Vic S Lk's Ch Lakeview OR 1976-1977; Dn Dio Nthrn California Sacramento CA 1974-1976; Vic S Mich Ch Alturas CA 1971-1977; R S Lk's Par Monrovia CA 1970-1971; Exec Coun Dio Wyoming Casper WY 1965-1994; R H Trin Epis Ch Thermopolis WY 1965-1969; Chair C&C Dio Wyoming Casper WY 1965-1967. relicx2@msn.com

NEEL-RICHARD, Joanne Louise (Ct) 39 Mckinley Ave, New Haven CT 06515 B San Francisco CA 1/28/1945 d H(arry) Clayton Neel & Phyllis Louise. BS U Pgh 1966; MDiv Ya Berk 1988; MS Col 1993. D 6/12/1988 Bp Frank Stanley Cerveny P 1/28/1989 Bp Clarence Nicholas Coleridge. m 12/31/2008 Mary Anne Osborn c 3. Int Pstr Chr Ch New Haven CT 2008-2009; Int Ch of the H Sprt W Haven CT 2008-2009; P-in-c Trin Ch Wethersfield CT 2001-2006; Dio Connecticut Hartford CT 1999-2007; Stndg Com Dio Connecticut Hartford CT 1999-2004; Grtr Waterbury Mnstry Middlebury CT 1998-2001; P-in-c All SS Ch Wolcott CT 1997-2001; P-in-c S Geo's Ch Middlebury CT 1997-2001; P-in-c Trin Ch Litchfield CT 1997-2001; Int Old S Andr's Ch Bloomfield CT 1996-1997; Chr Ch Stratford CT 1990-1996; Asst Trin Ch Torrington CT 1988-1990. Connecticut Soc Clincl Soc Workers Ethics Chair 1996-2000. jneelrichard@aol.com

NEELY, Christopher Fones (SO) 2508 Meadowmar Ln, Cincinnati OH 45230 B Cincinnati OH 4/28/1927 s Uberto Neely & Barbara Cline. BS MIT 1948; MS U of Tulsa 1949; MDiv CDSP 1961; Shalem Inst. for Sprtl Gdnc Washington DC 1987. D 6/25/1961 Bp James Albert Pike P 1/19/1962 Bp Roger W Blanchard. c 3. Vic S Phil's Ch Cincinnati OH 1995-2001; R S Jas Epis Ch Cincinnati OH 1967-1988; R The Epis Ch Of The Ascen Middletown OH 1961-1967. *October*, October Fwd Day by Day, 1991. chrisn1@fuse.net

NEFSTEAD, Eric (Cal) 275 Burnett Ave Apt 8, San Francisco CA 94131 **Sojourn Multifaith Chapl San Francisco CA 2010-** B Staples MN 4/21/1966 s Melvin John Nefstead & Sonja Kaye. BA S Olaf Coll 1988; MDiv UTS 1995; CAS CDSP 2005. D 6/1/2002 P 6/7/2003 Bp William Edwin Swing. ERIC_NEFSTEAD2002@YAHOO.COM

NEGLIA, Dwight Louis (Nwk) 116 Oakmont Dr, Mays Landing NJ 08330 B Long Island NY 4/14/1943 s Louis Anthony Neglia & Gladys Kathryn. BA LIU CW Post Coll 1966; MDiv PDS 1969. D 6/14/1969 P 12/1/1969 Bp Jonathan Goodhue Sherman. m 1/22/1966 Nancy Ruth Earl c 2. R S Agnes Ch Little Falls NJ 1997-2006; R S Jn's Ch Dover NJ 1981-1997; R Trin Epis Ch Beaver PA 1972-1981; Cur S Geo's Ch Hempstead NY 1969-1972. Ord of S Lk. neglia@aol.com

NEGROTTO, John Joseph (Nwk) 714 Laurel Blvd, Lanoka Harbor NJ 08734 **Int S Thos Epis Ch Red Bank NJ 2011-; Dio Newark Newark NJ 2009-; Assoc S Steph's Ch Waretown NJ 2000-** B Paterson NJ 9/24/1943 s John Angelo Negrotto & Josephine. BA Seton Hall U 1965; STB Immac Concep Sem 1969; MDiv GTS 1972; Sr Cert. Intl Conf of Police Chapl Destin FL 1991; Cert Bergen Cnty Law and Publ Sfty Inst 1998. Rec from Roman Catholic 6/17/1972 as Priest Bp George E Rath. m 5/27/1972 Susan V Giagiari c 2. Int S Paul's Ch In Bergen Jersey City NJ 2007-2010; Dioc Dept Mssn Dio Newark Newark NJ 1994-1998; R H Trin Epis Ch Hillsdale NJ 1976-2004; Asst S Mich's Epis Ch Wayne NJ 1972-1976; Intern Trin Ch Cliffside Pk NJ 1971-1972. ESMHE 1987-2000. Jn A Price Awd Intl Conf. Police Chapl 1991. fr_negrotto@yahoo.com

NEIDLINGER, Theodore Paul (NI) 125 S Mccann St, Kokomo IN 46901 **S Andr Epis Ch Kokomo IN 2010-** B Peoria IL 2/13/1950 s Paul Howard Neidlinger & Mildred Janet. BS Indiana St U 1972; MHA Indiana U 1976. D 10/9/1991 Bp Francis Campbell Gray P 2/8/2002 Bp Edward Stuart Little II. m 12/17/1971 Dianne Sheetz c 2. P-in-c Trin Epis Ch Logansport IN 2005-2010; Asstg P S Andr Epis Ch Kokomo IN 2002-2005; Cn for Diac Dio Nthrn Indiana So Bend IN 1991-2002. tneidlinger@yahoo.com

NEIGHBORS, D(olores) Maria (Chi) 5555 S Everett Ave Apt C-4, Chicago IL 60637 **Hon Cn Cathd Of S Jas Chicago IL 2003-** B Chicago IL 8/21/1929 d Roscoe Cokiegee & Ruth Mae. Cert Kennedy-King Coll 1948; Chicago St U 1973; MDiv SWTS 1988. D 6/18/1988 P 12/1/1988 Bp Frank Tracy Griswold III. c 3. Assoc Ch Of S Paul And The Redeem Chicago IL 2001-2006; Asstg Cler Cathd Of S Jas Chicago IL 2001-2002; S Chrys's Ch Chicago IL 2000-2001; Cn Pstr Cathd Of S Jas Chicago IL 1997-2000; Dio Chicago Chicago IL 1997-2000; S Edm's Epis Ch Chicago IL 1990-1997; Assoc Ch Of The Epiph Chicago IL 1988-1990. Ntwk of Biblic Story Tellers 1990-2000; UBE 1980-1998. dm9899@aol.com

NEIL, Earl Albert (WA) 4545 Connecticut Ave Nw Apt 929, Washington DC 20008 B Saint Paul MN 12/17/1935 s Earl Willus Neil & Katherine Louise. BA Carleton Coll 1957; BD SWTS 1960; MS U CA 1973. D 6/18/1960 Bp Hamilton Hyde Kellogg P 12/17/1960 Bp Edward Clark Turner. m 4/2/1992 Angela Kazzie c 1. Int Calv Ch Washington DC 1997-2000; Cn Cathd of St Ptr & St Paul Washington DC 1994-1997; Epis Ch Cntr New York NY 1974-1994; R S Aug's Ch Oakland CA 1967-1974. Hon DD SWTS 1989; Carl Alum Awd Carleton Coll 1971; Outstanding Young Man In Amer 1970. ealneil@aol.com

NEILL III, James Raleigh (USC) 311 Hickory Ln, Seneca SC 29678 B Hendersonville NC 7/10/1939 s James Raleigh Neill & Sarah Estelle. BS E Tennessee St U 1963; MDiv STUSo 1969. D 6/15/1969 P 2/1/1970 Bp Matthew G Henry. m 4/16/1983 Fiona Mary Baker c 3. R Ch Of The Ascen Seneca SC 1995-2005; R S Ptr's Epis Ch Norfolk VA 1992-1995; Off Of Bsh For ArmdF New York NY 1973-1992; R Calv Epis Ch Fletcher NC 1971-1973; P-in-c S Andr's Ch Bessemer City NC 1969-1971; P-in-c Trin Ch Kings Mtn NC 1969-1971. jrn3@nctv.com

NEILL, Margaret Kathryn James (EC) 42 Warwick Dr, Hampstead NC 28443 **EFM Mentor Dio Wstrn Michigan Kalamazoo MI 1992-** B Lee County SC 3/8/1939 d Moses Edwards James & Geneva Catherine. BS Tennessee St U 1961; MA Peabody Coll 1971; EdD Wstrn Michigan U 1975; MDiv Nash 1990. D 6/3/1990 P 12/1/1990 Bp Peter James Lee. m 6/28/1973 James Donald Neill c 3. Gr S Paul's Epis Ch Tucson AZ 2004-2005; S Fran by the Sea Bogue Banks Salter Path NC 2004; DCE S Paul's Epis Ch Wilmington NC 2000-2002; S Paul's Ch Muskegon MI 1997-1998; Chapl - Ecw Dio Wstrn Michigan Kalamazoo MI 1996-2002; Trnr Dio Wstrn Michigan Kalamazoo MI 1994-2002; Chapl Of DOK; Stndg Com Dio Wstrn Michigan Kalamazoo MI 1994; S Phil's Epis Ch Grand Rapids MI 1990-1996. Ord Of S Lk-Physcn. Cleric Ldrshp Proj 1994. mjneill@charter.net

NEILS, Leonard Faulkner (NY) 7 Harter Ln, Rhinebeck NY 12572 **Died 7/30/2011** B Troy NY 5/23/1927 s Frederick Benjamin Neils & Helen May. BA Hob 1953; MDiv/STB Ya Berk 1956; MS/CSW Adams St Coll 1985. D 5/27/1956 Bp Frederick Lehrle Barry P 12/15/1956 Bp David Emrys Richards. c 2. Auth, *Welcome Happy Morning*, Davey Tree Co, 1962. Monday Club - Dio New York 1962.

NEILSEN, Eloise (RI) 20 Exeter Blvd, Narragansett RI 02882 **D S Ptr's By The Sea Narragansett RI 1994-** B Pawtucket RI 6/3/1930 d Harold Springthorpe & Matilda. RN Newton-Wellesley Hosp Sch of Nrsng Lower Falls MA 1951; Sch for Deacons 1988. D 2/4/1989 Bp George Nelson Hunt III. m 8/22/1953 Erling Hugh Neilsen c 4. NAAD; Ord of Julian of Norwich 1987. S S Steph's Awd for Diac Mnstry NAAD 1997. RevLoisN@aol.com

NEILSON, Albert Pancoast (Del) 10 Chickadee Dr, Topsham ME 04086 B Philadelphia PA 6/27/1930 s Harry Rosengarten Neilson & Alberta. BA Ya 1952; STB GTS 1957; STM NYTS 1972. D 6/1/1957 Bp Charles F Hall P 12/12/1957 Bp Richard S M Emrich. m 5/2/1953 Julie Neilson c 3. Assoc Trin Par Wilmington DE 1964-1990; Vic S Clare Of Assisi Epis Ch Ann Arbor MI 1957-1963. AAPC, Fell 1976. sumtrash@aol.com

NEILSON, Jack Drew (WVa) 15 Fairview Hts, Parkersburg WV 26101 **Pstr Assoc Trin Ch Parkersburg WV 2008-** B Brooklyn NY 5/18/1926 s Rudolph Carl Neilson & Dorothy. BS W Virginia U 1945; BS Penn 1948. D 6/3/1981 P 6/10/1982 Bp Robert Poland Atkinson. m 2/21/1948 Lynette Lundquist. Asst Trin Ch Parkersburg WV 1981-2000. jneilson@suddenlink.net

NEILSON, John Robert (NJ) 39 Yarmouth Ct, Scotch Plains NJ 07076 B New York NY 11/23/1932 s John Neilson & Elizabeth. BA Lycoming Coll 1958; MDiv PDS 1961. D 4/21/1961 P 10/28/1961 Bp Alfred L Banyard. m 5/11/1963 Sandra Irwin. R All SS' Epis Ch Scotch Plains NJ 1969-1997; Vic S Barth's Ch Cherry Hill NJ 1963-1969; Cur Gr Ch Merchantville NJ 1961-1962. Chapl Ord of the Noble Comp of the Swan 1992; Oblate - OSB, Portsmouth Abbey, RI. Phi Alpha Theta.

NEILSON, Kurt Brian (Ore) 2736 SE 63rd Ave, Portland OR 97206 **S Ptr And Paul Epis Ch Portland OR 2000-** B Huntington NY 8/18/1958 s Henry Frederick Neilson & Margaret Bernadette. S Fidelis Coll 1978; BA SUNY 1980; MA Cath Theol Un 1988; MDiv SWTS 1991. Rec from Roman Catholic 11/30/1986 Bp Frank Tracy Griswold III. m 9/27/1986 Diane Urbano c 3. R S Ptr And Paul Epis Ch Portland OR 1995-2000; Cur Emm Epis Ch Webster Groves MO 1991-1995. "Urban Iona," Morehouse 2007. ORCA 1995. urbanoneilson5@yahoo.com

NEILY, Robert Edward (Mich) 37443 Stonegate Cir, Clinton Township MI 48036 B Swampscott MA 2/1/1938 s Fred Ernest Neily & Gertrude Louise. BA San Jose St U 1959; MDiv CDSP 1962; MA San Jose St U 1970. D 6/24/1962 Bp James Albert Pike P 6/18/1963 Bp George Richard Millard. m 4/13/1996 Martie J Wernz c 2. R S Mich's Ch Grosse Pointe Woods MI 1980-2006; R S Jn's Par San Bernardino CA 1971-1980; Assoc R Ch Of Our Sav Par San Gabr CA 1969-1971; Asst S Clem's Ch Berkeley CA 1966-1969; Vic S Jn The Div Epis Ch Morgan Hill CA 1964-1966; Vic Ch Of S Jos Milpitas CA 1964-1965; Asst S Mk's Epis Ch Santa Clara CA 1962-1964. RNEILY@WOWWAY.COM

NEILY BARBERIA, Kristin Noel (Los) c/o St. Matthew's Parish School, 1031 Bienveneda Avenue, Pacific Palisades CA 90272 **Sch Chapl The Par Of S Matt Pacific Palisades CA 2007-** B San Jose CA 12/23/1964 d Robert Edward Neily & Nancy Sue. BA Kalamazoo Coll 1987; Ya Berk 1990; Cert Other 1990; MDiv Ya 1990. D 6/23/1990 P 1/23/1991 Bp R(aymond) Stewart Wood Jr. m 7/3/1993 Frank C Barberia c 2. Assoc for Formation and Inclusion S Jas Par Los Angeles CA 2006-2007; Chld & Yth All SS Ch Pasadena CA 2002-2003; Assoc R The Par Of S Matt Pacific Palisades CA 1995-2000; Yth Mnstry All SS Ch Pasadena CA 1990-1995. Berkeley Grad Soc. Rel and Arts Prize Berk New Haven CT 1990. fbarberia@earthlink.net

NEIMAN, Joseph Clayton (WMich) 34462 1st St, Paw Paw MI 49079 B Traverse City MI 1/21/1939 s Francis Joseph Neiman & Virginia Ryckman. BA U MI 1960; MA MI SU 1967; Dplma Div Word Intnl Cntr London CA 1968; Phd Stds Pontifical Gregorian U Rome It 1974; DIT SWTS 1980; CPE Pinerest Psch Hosp 1981. D 11/16/1980 P 6/13/1981 Bp Charles Bennison. m 10/13/1974 Judi Ann Guza. S Mk's Epis Ch Paw Paw MI 1984-2006; Cmcatn/Ed WME Dio Wstrn Michigan Kalamazoo MI 1981-2003. Auth, "Coordinators: A New Focus In Par Rel Educ," St. Mary Press, 1971; Auth, "arts," *Amer*; Auth, "arts," *Angl Dig*; Auth, "arts," *Rel Teachers Journ*; Auth, "arts," *Rel Educ*; Auth, "arts," *The Catechist*; Auth, "arts," *The Epis*; Auth, "arts," *LivCh*; Auth, "arts," *Today'S Par*; Auth, "arts," *Traverse City Record Eagle*; Auth, "arts," *Wstrn Michigan Epis*, Dio Wstrn MI. ECom 1984-2002; Rotary Intl 1991. Citizens of the Year Paw Paw ChmbrCom 2007; Outstanding Serv Awd Traverse City Human Rts Cmsn 1976. jneiman@btc-bci.com

NEIMAN, Judi Ann (WMich) 34462 1st St, Paw Paw MI 49079 B Flint MI 11/16/1938 d Francis Phillip Guza & Geraldine Leona. AA Aquinas Coll 1958; RN Mercy Cntrl Nrsng Sch 1961; Dplma Div Word Intl Cntr 1971; Dioc study Prog 1987; Cert CPE 1990. D 10/13/1990 Bp Edward Lewis Lee Jr. m 10/13/1974 Joseph Clayton Neiman. D Coordntr Dio Wstrn Michigan Kalamazoo MI 1991-2002; D S Mk's Epis Ch Paw Paw MI 1990-2006. NAAD 1992-2006. Diac Awd Naad 2000. jneiman@btc-bci.com

NEITZEL, Anna C (Dal) 6525 Inwood Road, Dallas TX 75209 **D The Epis Ch Of S Thos The Apos Dallas TX 2009-** B Dallas TX 1/30/1946 d Howard Earl Cannon & Mary Louise. BS U of Texas 1992; MTS SMU 2004. D 6/4/2005 Bp James Monte Stanton. m 12/27/1967 James Neitzel c 2. Dir. Missions Trips & Pilgrimages S Mich And All Ang Ch Dallas TX 2005-2007. doubteranna@aol.com

NELIUS, Albert Arnold (NC) 26 Old Oak Ct, Durham NC 27705 B Memphis TN 12/9/1925 s Engel Woerne Nelius & Eva Emilia. BA Rhodes Coll 1951; STUSo 1951; MDiv VTS 1954; MLS U NC 1969. D 7/9/1954 Bp Theodore N Barth P 5/5/1955 Bp John Vander Horst. m 6/19/1955 Sigrid von Von Renner c 1. S Andrews Ch Durham NC 1970-1993; Cur S Phil's Ch Durham NC 1960-1967; Vic S Barn Ch Florissant MO 1957-1960; Asst S Geo's Ch Nashville TN 1954-1957.

NELSON, Ann J (Colo) 2002 Warwick Ln, Colorado Springs CO 80909 B Providence RI 2/19/1935 d Edgar Thomson Nelson & Zabelle. BA Br 1956; MA Br 1959; Cert Epis TS of The SW 1984. D 12/27/1984 Bp William Carl Frey P 6/27/1985 Bp William Harvey Wolfrum. Com Diac Dio Colorado Denver CO 1995-2002; R S Andr's Ch Cripple Creek CO 1991-1996; COM Dio Colorado Denver CO 1987-1991; Asst S Fran Of Assisi Colorado Sprg CO 1986-1990. Auth, "A P Looks at D Formation," *DiaKoneo*, 1999. NAAD 1995. ajnelson@q.com

NELSON III, Ben (Haw) PO Box 1415, Kapaa HI 96746 **P All SS Ch Kapaa HI 2008-** B Sewanee TN 9/17/1974 s Benjamin Howard Nelson & Cammie. BA Millsaps Coll 1996; MDiv STUSo 2002. D 6/24/2002 Bp Robert Boyd Hibbs P 2/28/2003 Bp James Edward Folts. m 12/14/2002 Linda Carole Latchford c 1. Asst to the R S Paul's Epis Ch Chattanooga TN 2004-2008; Cur Ch Of The Gd Shpd Corpus Christi TX 2002-2004. bennelson3@gmail.com

NELSON SR, Bob (SanD) 330 11th St, Del Mar CA 92014 **Cler-in-charge, St. Anne's Mssn, Oceanside Dio San Diego CA 2010-; D S Anne's Epis Ch Oceanside CA 2010-** B Saint Louis MO 9/30/1939 s Arthur Alexius Nelson & Lillian Margaret. AA MiraCosta Coll 1960; BS U CA 1962; ETSBH 1998. D 6/9/2001 Bp Gethin Benwil Hughes. m 1/26/1974 Suzanne Elizabeth Foucault c 4. S Ptr's Epis Ch Del Mar CA 2005-2009; D Ch Of The Gd Samar San Diego CA 2001-2003. Rotary Grp Study Fell Rotary Intl Fndt 1974. bobnelson1@hotmail.com

NELSON, Charles Herbert (LI) 194-51 Murdock Ave, Saint Albans NY 11412 **D S Dav's Epis Ch Cambria Heights NY 2008-; S Paul's And Resurr Ch Wood Ridge NJ 2004-** B Newark NJ 3/31/1938 s Thomas & Mabel. D 6/5/2004 Bp John Palmer Croneberger. m 4/1/2000 Veronica Nelson c 1. D S Jos's Ch Queens Vill NY 2006-2008; D S Agnes And S Paul's Ch E Orange NJ 2006-2007. Bro of St Andr 1996; UBE. Cert of Recognition Trin Cathd 1990. cpreciouscharles@aol.com

NELSON, Charles Nickolaus (Minn) Rt 2 Box 283, Park Rapids MN 56470 B Minneapolis MN 4/13/1930 s Oscar Nickolaus Nelson & Anna. D 5/30/1986 Bp Harold Anthony Hopkins Jr. m 5/30/1955 Adele Elizabeth Scott c 3. D Geth Cathd Fargo ND 1986-1995. NAAD, ABS.

NELSON, David Scott (O) 1505 E Wooster St, Bowling Green OH 43402 **Chr The King Epis Ch Humble TX 2011-** B Houston TX 4/10/1979 s Steven A Nelson & Susan K. BBA S Mary U at San Anonio Texas 2002; MDiv VTS 2005. D 6/13/2009 Bp Mark Hollingsworth Jr P 1/30/2010 Bp David Charles Bowman. m 7/25/2009 Beth A Nelson. Campus Mssnr/D in Charge S Jn's Epis Ch Bowling Green OH 2009-2011. bgchaplain@gmail.com

NELSON, Elizabeth Lane (CFla) 321 Belle Tower Ave, Lake Placid FL 33852 **D S Fran Of Assisi Epis Ch Lake Placid FL 1998-** B Fall River MA 1/1/1948 d Everett Lane & Lottie May. BD U of Rhode Island 1991; MDiv VTS 1996. D 12/1/1998 P 6/13/1999 Bp John Wadsworth Howe. m 5/14/2011 Joel Nelson c 5. BStA Chapl 2006; DOK Dioc Chapl 2006; Ord of S Lk 1994. elm48@mac.com

NELSON, Geri Lee (Ga) 129 Viewcrest Dr, Hendersonville NC 28739 **S Thos Ch Savannah GA 2005-; D Ch Of The H Fam Mills River NC 1999-** B Pikeville KY 10/23/1948 d Frelin J Thacker & Edith. D 12/18/1999 Bp Robert Carroll Johnson Jr. m 6/9/1990 Richard A Nelson. GERILEENELSON@AOL.COM

NELSON, James Craig (WTex) 2500 N 10th St, McAllen TX 78501 **R S Jn's Ch McAllen TX 2011-** B Woodward OK 10/6/1949 s Gene Andrew Nelson & Eula Florence. SW Oklahoma St U 1969; BS Oklahoma St U 1971; MDiv VTS 1989. D 6/17/1989 P 1/1/1990 Bp Robert Manning Moody. m 9/7/1968 Linda R Caruthers c 1. R Ch Of The Gd Shpd Friendswood TX 2000-2011; R Epis Ch Of The Resurr Oklahoma City OK 1989-2000. rector@stjohns-mcallen.org

NELSON, James Lowell (Mass) 1218 Heatherwood, Yarmouth Port MA 02675 B Owatonna MN 11/16/1926 s Robert Dibble Nelson & Carol Laura. BS U of Arizona 1950; MDiv Bex 1964. D 6/1/1964 Bp Anson Phelps Stokes Jr P 5/30/1965 Bp Frederic Cunningham Lawrence. m 3/28/1976 Anne V R Van Rensselaer. R Ch Of The H Nativ So Weymouth MA 1972-1989; Founding S Dav's Epis Ch So Yarmouth MA 1966-1973; Cur S Andr's Ch Framingham MA 1964-1965. Boston Cleric Club 1964-1990. dutnel@verizon.net

NELSON, Jeffrey Scott (Neb) 607 Spruce Street, North Platte NE 69101 B Milwaukee WI 9/17/1959 s Kenneth Walter Nelson & Sharon Rae. BA Valparaiso U 1982; MDiv Luth TS 1986; ThD Luther Sem 1997. Rec from Evangelical Lutheran Church in America 1/7/2010 Bp James Louis Jelinek. c 3. jsfnelson@gmail.com

NELSON, John Douglas (SD) 12 Bis Rue Monmory, Vincennes France B Whitefish MT 1/10/1952 s Thurlow Christian Nelson & Joann Louise. BA MI SU 1974; MDiv CRDS 1978. D 11/10/1978 Bp George Theodore Masuda P 7/1/1979 Bp Walter H Jones. m 7/11/1981 Christel Thobois. M-in-c Chr Epis Ch Milbank SD 1978-1981; Dio So Dakota Sioux Falls SD 1978-1981; S Mary's Epis Ch Roslyn SD 1978-1981.

NELSON, Joseph Reed Peter (NJ) 715 Magie Ave, Elizabeth NJ 07208 B Tuscaloosa AL 5/18/1941 s Hugh Reavis Nelson & Sarah Beth. BA U NC 1964; BD EDS 1967; MS Col 1971; PhD NYU 1976. D 12/18/1970 P 6/1/1971 Bp Horace W B Donegan. m 3/16/1968 Lynne Newbold c 1. Int St Jn the Bapt Epis Ch Linden NJ 1991-1992; Vic Ascen Ch New Haven CT 1971-1983; Serv All Ang' Ch New York NY 1970-1971. Karatana 1971. Morehead Schlr U Nc 1959; Spec Citation For Serv 83 Mayor New Haven CT; Ml King Awd 82 New Haven Publ Schs. jrpnelson@addabbo.org

NELSON, Julia Marie (ECR) 375 Benfield Rd, Severna Park MD 21146 **Assoc S Edw The Confessor Epis Ch San Jose CA 2011-** B Fort Rucker AL 11/3/1969 d James Lee Brenneman & Judy Marie. BS California St U Fresno 1993; MDiv 2008 The GTS 2008. D 6/21/2008 Bp Mary Gray-Reeves P 1/24/2009 Bp Eugene Sutton. m 5/25/1996 Dale R Nelson c 2. Assoc R St Martins-In-The-Field Ch Severna Pk MD 2008-2010. Julien650@gmail.com

NELSON, Julie F (NwPa) 140 Oyster Pond Rd, Falmouth MA 02540 B Philadelphia PA 10/13/1931 d William Thomas Fleming & Isabel A. BA Col 1972; CTh EDS 1992; MDiv VTS 1994. D 7/8/1995 P 1/13/1996 Bp Robert Deane Rowley Jr. Ch of the Ascen Munich 81545 DE 2001-2002; COM Dio NW Pennsylvania Erie PA 1996-2002; Vic Ch Of The H Cross No E PA 1995-2002.

NELSON, Leilani Lucas (Cal) 3973 17th St, San Francisco CA 94114 B Honolulu HI 1/19/1948 d Joseph Timothy Lucas & Lois Eileen. Lewis & Clark Coll; U of Hawaii; BTh California Sch for Deacons 1988. D 12/2/1989 Bp William Edwin Swing. m 12/27/1973 Lowell Thomas Nelson c 2. S Andr's Epis Ch San Bruno CA 2002-2010; D Fam Assoc S Paul's Epis Ch Burlingame CA 1999-2002; Yth Min S Matt's Epis Ch San Mateo CA 1990-1999; Ch Adminstrator S Fran' Epis Ch San Francisco CA 1988-1990.

N

NELSON JR, L(evine) Stephen (Pa) Po Box 1105, Norristown PA 19404 **Asst All SS Ch Norristown PA 1986-** B Buffalo NY 2/28/1945 s Levine Nelson & Marian Jean. BA Hob 1967; MDiv PDS 1970. D 6/29/1970 Bp Harold B Robinson P 4/27/1973 Bp Robert Lionne DeWitt. m 7/3/1967 Louise Passarelli. Asst S Christophers Epis Ch Oxford PA 1972-1976.

NELSON, Raymond Allen (SVa) 3850 Pittaway Dr, Richmond VA 23235 **Asst The Epis Ch Of The Adv Kennett Sq PA 2009-** B Brooklyn NY 2/10/1932 s Raymond Eric Nelson & Georgena Beatrice. Wms 1954; Harv 1957; EDS 1960. D 10/9/1966 Bp George E Rath P 12/1/1967 Bp Leland Stark. m 8/13/1955 Rosemary Davenport King. Cur S Lk's Ch Gladstone NJ 1966-1967.

NELSON, Richard A (Ga) 7607 Lynes Ct, Savannah GA 31406 **R S Thos Ch Savannah GA 2004-** B Cadillac MI 7/16/1953 s Leonard Emmanuel Nelson & Ruth Marie. BA Cntrl Michigan U 1976; MDiv SWTS 1983. D 3/25/1983 Bp Quintin Ebenezer Primo Jr P 9/29/1983 Bp James Winchester Montgomery. m 6/9/1990 Geri Lee Thacker c 2. R Ch Of The H Fam Mills River NC 1997-2004; Assoc S Jas Epis Ch Hendersonville NC 1993-1997; Asstg S Wlfd's Epis Ch Sarasota FL 1989-1992; S Bon Ch Sarasota FL 1988-1989; R S Alb's Ch Chicago IL 1985-1987; Cur Ch Of The Ascen Chicago IL 1983-1985. Assoc, CT 1994. frrichard388@aol.com

NELSON JR, Richard Louis (NwT) Po Box 82, Burton TX 77835 **Pstr Emm Luth Ch of Greenvine Burton TX 2007-** B Sedalia MO 9/18/1976 s Carol. BA U of Missouri 1998; MDiv Epis TS of The SW 2004. D 6/5/2004 P 12/11/2004 Bp C(harles) Wallis Ohl. m 8/22/1997 Karen Rochelle Buck c 2. Assoc R S Steph's Ch Lubbock TX 2004-2007. revrichnelson@gmail.com

NELSON, Rita Beauchamp (Del) 30895 Crepe Myrtle Dr Unit 66, Millsboro DE 19966 **COM Dio Delaware Wilmington DE 2003-** B Detroit MI 5/23/1939 d Edgar Albert Beauchamp & Antoinette Mardel. BS Sacr Heart U Fairfield CT 1975; MBA U of Connecticut, Storrs 1981; MDiv VTS 1999. D 6/12/1999 P 12/12/1999 Bp John Bailey Lipscomb. m 3/21/1980 Ralph William Peters c 2. Dep - GC Dio Delaware Wilmington DE 2006-2009; Diac Formation Dir Dioc Coun Inc Wilmington DE 2005-2011; R S Phil's Ch Laurel DE 2005-2009; Personl Com Dio Delaware Wilmington DE 2002-2005; R The Ch

Of The Ascen Claymont DE 2001-2005; Cur S Jn's Epis Ch Clearwater FL 1999-2000. Auth, "It's 'T' Time," *LivCh*, LivCh, 2003. Integrity 2009. revrita@verizon.net

NELSON JR, Robert Mitchell (Nev) 3609 Casa Grande Ave, Las Vegas NV 89102 **Cn To The Ordnry Dio Nevada Las Vegas NV 2002-; Assoc All SS Epis Ch Las Vegas NV 1998-** B Evanston IL 7/8/1941 s Robert Mitchell Nelson & Ruth. BS U of New Mex 1966. D 5/19/1987 P 11/1/1987 Bp Stewart Clark Zabriskie. m 8/15/1964 Kathy Amanda Atchison. nelsonrk@ix.netcom.com

NELSON, Robert William (Ak) 2777 S Kihei Rd Apt G209, Kihei HI 96753 B Torrance CA 4/18/1939 s Lee George Nelson & Marie Blanche. AA El Camino Coll 1958; BA U CA 1961; BA ETSBH 1965. D 1/7/1979 P 12/1/1979 Bp David Rea Cochran. m 6/6/2005 Norma Lee Trennert c 2. Assoc R S Mary's Ch Anchorage AK 1979-2001. Auth, *Counslg & Values*. AAPC, AAMFT; Mar Fam Ther. bobnorma@verizon.net

NELSON, Roger Edwin (Mass) 557 Salem St, Malden MA 02148 **Assoc Par Of The Epiph Winchester MA 2003-** B Weymouth MA 3/29/1940 s Carl Edwin Nelson & Marjorie May. BA Trin Hartford CT 1962; MDiv EDS 1966. D 6/25/1966 P 6/3/1967 Bp Anson Phelps Stokes Jr. m 9/10/1966 Dorothy Whitney c 1. R S Jn's Epis Ch Saugus MA 1973-2003; Cur Epis Ch Of S Thos Taunton MA 1966-1973. Bd Ch & Hm Soc 1973; Marg Coffin PB Soc 1998. Phi Beta Kappa Trin, Hartford, CT 1961; Pi Gamma MU Trin, Hartford, CT 1961. revrogernelson@gmail.com

NELSON, Sarah Lee (Nwk) 576 Concord Rd, Glen Mills PA 19342 **S Jas Epis Ch Newport Newport DE 2002-; S Jas' Epis Ch Los Angeles CA 2002-** B Washington DC 2/24/1957 d Thomas Frank Johnson & Margaret Ann. BA Duke 1979; MS CUA 1982; MDiv Duke 1986. D 6/13/1987 Bp Edward Lewis Lee Jr P 6/1/1989 Bp John Shelby Spong. m 1/3/1987 Luke Richard Nelson c 6. The Epis Ch Of The Adv Kennett Sq PA 1995-1997; Vic S Gabr's Ch Oak Ridge NJ 1990-1993; Asst to R S Ptr's Ch Mtn Lakes NJ 1988-1990; D S Ptr's Epis Ch Arlington VA 1987-1988. sljn@comcast.net

NELSON, Wesley Theodore (Dal) 2525 Ohio Dr Apt 1303, Plano TX 75093 B Enid OK 7/12/1926 s Boyce Nelson & Carolyn Elizabeth. BFA U of Texas 1958; MDiv VTS 1965; STM SMU 1969. D 6/1/1965 P 12/1/1965 Bp Charles A Mason. m 1/21/1955 Lee Ann Lane c 2. Dep Gc Dio Dallas Dallas TX 1985-1988; Exec Com Of FA Dio Dallas Dallas TX 1970-2002; Chair Of The Dept Of Cmncatn Dio Dallas Dallas TX 1965-2002; R The Epis Ch Of The Resurr Dallas TX 1965-1988. Auth, "Cs Lewis: Prophet For Today". OHC, Ord Of S Lk, Comt, CCU, NOEL, Ebs, ERM, Epis Untd. Who'S Who Rel 1975. nelson.523@yahoo.com

NELSON-AMAKER, Melana (Va) 1042 Preston Ave., Charlottesville VA 22903 B Pittsburgh PA 5/16/1955 d Frank Arnold Nelson & Alberta Elizabeth. BA Carnegie Mellon U 1981; MDiv Pittsburgh TS 1988. D 6/4/1988 P 5/1/1989 Bp Alden Moinet Hathaway. m 9/26/1981 Derek Leon Amaker. S Phil's Ch Annapolis MD 2010-2011; Trin Ch Washington DC 2009-2010; Trin Epis Ch Charlottesville VA 1996-2007; Sacrementalist All SS Ch Aliquippa PA 1993-1994; Int Ch Of The Epiph Pittsburgh PA 1990-1992; Cur Emm Ch Pittsburgh PA 1989-1990. nelsamak@cstone.net

NELSON-LOW, Jane (Spok) 719 W. Montgomery Ave, 719 W Montgomery Ave, Spokane WA 99205 B San Jose CA 11/9/1943 d Clifton Stewart Nelson & Margaret Jane. Arizona St U 1961; BA Linfield Coll 1970; MDiv CDSP 1991. D 6/18/1991 Bp Robert Louis Ladehoff P 2/27/1992 Bp William Benjamin Spofford. c 3. Vic H Trin Epis Ch Wallace ID 2004-2010; Vic Emm Ch Kellogg ID 2004-2007; Assoc Cathd Of S Jn The Evang Spokane WA 2000-2004; Sr Assoc S Barn On The Desert Scottsdale AZ 1998-2000; Asst Chr Ch Par Lake Oswego OR 1991-1998. janenelsonlow@yahoo.com

NEMBHARD, Ralston Bruce (CFla) 8413 Clematis Ln, Orlando FL 32819 B Manchester Jama CA 6/6/1955 s David Solomon Nembhard & Iris Elizabeth. BA U of The W Indies 1981; STM Ya Berk 1988. Trans from Church Of England 1/19/1998 Bp John Wadsworth Howe. m 9/4/1982 Heather Yvonne Grant c 2. R The Epis Ch Of S Jn The Bapt Orlando FL 1997-2009. Auth, "Prayers From The Cross," 1983; Auth, "You & Your Neighbour In A Broken Wrld," 1982. BSA; Steadfast Ministers. stead6655@aol.com

NEMES, John Dale (Oly) No address on file. **D S Lk's Epis Ch Elma WA 1981-** B Glenwood MN 7/23/1944 s John Nemes & Beth Irene. BS U MN 1969; LLD Wm Mitchell Coll 1974. D 12/14/1981 Bp Robert Marshall Anderson. m 8/20/1966 Mary Elizabeth Brooks c 2. Asst S Paul's Ch Winona MN 1982-1986.

NENSTIEL, George Charles (LI) Montauk Highway, Oakdale NY 11769 B New York NY 9/4/1921 s George Nenstiel & Katherine Rose. Merc TS 1966. D 6/16/1966 P 12/1/1966 Bp Jonathan Goodhue Sherman. m 9/4/1948 Mae Duffy. Asst Trin Ch Vero Bch FL 1990-2001; Cur S Jas Epis Ch S Jas NY 1966-1967.

NERN JR, William Baker (Cal) 971 Sanchez St, San Francisco CA 94114 B Wheeling WA 5/7/1940 s William Baker Nern & Ruth Elizabeth. BA Bethany Coll 1962; MDiv CDSP 1971. D 6/26/1971 Bp George Richard Millard P 1/2/1972 Bp C Kilmer Myers. c 2. Epis Sanctuary San Francisco CA 1986-1993; Ch Of The Redeem San Rafael CA 1974-1986; Asst S Andr's Ch Saratoga CA 1971-1974. susbuzz2003@yahoo.com

NERUD, Barbara Jeanne (Neb) PO Box 436, Oshkosh NE 69154 B Norrill NE 3/6/1931 d Glen Logan Morris & Ethel Elizabeth. D 9/6/2005 Bp Joe Goodwin Burnett. m 8/27/1950 Jack Nerud c 4. D Dio Nebraska Omaha NE 2005-2011. nerudagency@lakemac.net

NESBIT, Pamela Mcabee (Pa) Po Box 128, Wycombe PA 18980 **D Gd Shpd Ch Hilltown PA 1996-** B Montebello CA 8/5/1947 d Bud McAbee & Silva Terese. BA U CA 1968; MA Tem 1970; PhD Tem 1976; Pennsylvania Diac Sch 1996. D 9/22/1996 Bp Franklin Delton Turner. m 11/26/1988 C Clifton Nesbit c 1. NAAD. pamelamnesbit@gmail.com

NESBIT JR, William Reed (Chi) 917 Wildwood Ct, St. Charles IL 60174 **Stndg Com Dio Chicago Chicago IL 2005-; R S Chas Ch S Chas IL 2000-** B Chicago Heights IL 2/26/1958 s William Reed Nesbit & Nancy Carolyn. AA Valparaiso U 1979; BPharm U IL 1982; MDiv SWTS 1996. D 6/15/1996 P 12/1/1996 Bp Frank Tracy Griswold III. m 9/22/1984 Beverly Kaye Sneed c 2. Asst R S Andr's Ch Downers Grove IL 1996-2000; Yth Coun Dio Chicago Chicago IL 1996-1998. scecrector@sbcglobal.net

NESBITT, John Russell (Ore) 3846 NE Glisan St, Portland OR 97232 **R S Dav's Epis Ch Portland OR 1990-** B Poughkeepsie NY 11/1/1936 s Garven Stokes Nesbitt & Mary. BS SUNY 1958; MS WA SU 1980; SWTS 1998. D 12/16/1973 Bp James Walmsley Frederic Carman P 1/2/1987 Bp Rustin Ray Kimsey. m 8/20/1960 Ellen Ascherfeld c 2. Vic S Lk's Ch Lakeview OR 1986-1990; S Andr's Epis Ch Florence OR 1974-1979. NNECA 1988; ORCA 1988. nesbitt11@msn.com

NESBITT, Margot Lord (Okla) 1703 N Hudson Ave, Oklahoma City OK 73103 **P S Paul's Cathd Oklahoma City OK 1994-** B Tonbrigde Kent UK 2/13/1927 d Douglas Gerald R Lord & Octave Wilhelmenia. BA U of Oklahoma 1950; BFA U of Oklahoma 1971; MA U of Oklahoma 1975; Cert Oklahoma Diac Trng Sch 1988; PhD U of Oklahoma 1988; Epis TS of The SW 1994. D 6/26/1988 Bp Gerald Nicholas McAllister P 6/18/1994 Bp Robert Manning Moody. m 6/6/1948 Charles Rudolph Nesbitt c 3. Benedictine Oblate 1995. Hon Cn Dio Oklahoma 1997. margotnesbitt@sbcglobal.net

NESBITT, Paula Diane (Cal) 577 Forest St., Oakland CA 94618 **ECCSW, Mem Exec Coun Appointees New York NY 2009-2012; non-stipendiary P Assoc All Souls Par In Berkeley Berkeley CA 2002-** B Seattle WA 6/7/1948 d John Paul Nesbitt & Ellen Marie. BS U of Oregon; MDiv Harvard DS 1987; MA Harv 1987; PhD Harv 1990. D 7/5/1991 Bp Robert Louis Ladehoff P 2/26/1992 Bp William Jerry Winterrowd. m 3/26/2000 Lloyd Kirk Miller. CALL online Instr CDSP Berkeley CA 2009; Grad Fllshp Selection Com The ECF New York NY 1995-2000; BEC, Mem Dio Colorado Denver CO 1992-1996; Cmsn on Human Sxlty, Mem Dio Colorado Denver CO 1992-1996; non-stipendiary Asstg P/D S Barn Epis Ch Denver CO 1991-2001. Auth, "Keepers of the Tradition: Rel Professionals and their Careers," *Handbook of the Sociol of Rel*, Sage, 2007; Ed, "Rel and Soc Plcy," *Rel and Soc Plcy*, AltaMira, 2001; Auth, "Epis Ch and Bk of Common Pryr," *Contemporary Amer Rel*, Macmillan Libr Reference, 2000; Co-Auth, "Wmn Status in the Ch," *Gender Mosaics*, Roxbury Press, 2000; Co-Auth, "Wmn Cler Resrch and the Sociol of Rel," *Sociol of Rel*, 2000; Auth, "Feminization of the Cler in Amer," *Feminization of the Cler in Amer*, Oxford Press, 1997; Auth, "Sexual Orientation as a Justice Issue Dilemmas of Postmodern Soc Philos and Rel for Civil Rts," *Soc Justice Resrch*, 1997; Auth, "First and Second Career Cler," *Journ for the Sci Study of Rel*, 1995; Auth, "Mar, Parenthood and the Mnstry," *Sociol of Rel*, 1995. AABS 2005-2006; SSA 2005. nesbitt.p@sbcglobal.net

NESHEIM, Donald Oakley (Minn) 4400 36th Ave N Apt 116, Robbinsdale MN 55422 **Long Term Supply Epiph Epis Ch S Paul MN 2007-** B Dupree SD 12/18/1937 s Melvin Alfred Nesheim & Marjorie Ruth. BD U of Nebraska 1971; GW 1973; MDiv STUSo 1984. D 6/17/1984 Bp Walter H Jones P 12/21/1984 Bp Craig Barry Anderson. c 3. S Matt's Epis Ch Minneapolis MN 1997-1999; R S Andr's Epis Ch Minneapolis MN 1992-2002; Cn Adminstrator Dio Minnesota Minneapolis MN 1992-1997; P-in-res S Chris's Epis Ch Roseville MN 1991-1992; Dn of the Pine Ridge Dnry Dio So Dakota Sioux Falls SD 1987-1991; Adminstrator of the Pine Ridge Dnry Dio So Dakota Sioux Falls SD 1985-1986; R S Katharine's Ch Mart SD 1984-1991. Ord of S Lk 1981. Legion of Merit US-A 1977. dnesheim@earthlink.net

NESIN, Leslie Frances (Me) Po Box 358, Howland ME 04448 **Transitional D S Mart's Epis Ch Pittsfield ME 2003-** B Dayton OH 5/14/1944 RN Jn Hopkins U. D 4/26/2003 P 11/9/2003 Bp Chilton Abbie Richardson Knudsen. Ch Of The Gd Shpd Houlton ME 2004-2011; Dio Maine Portland ME 2003-2004. lnesin@telplus.net

NESKE JR, Robert Norman (Neb) 1722 E Kachina Trail, Sierra Vista AZ 85650 B Paterson NJ 6/14/1947 s Robert Norman Neske & Marion Clarina. BA Transylvania U 1969; MDiv GTS 1973; MA Command and Gnrl Stff Coll 1999. D 10/28/1972 Bp George E Rath P 4/28/1973 Bp Leland Stark. m 5/1/2010 Katiri A Neske. S Mk's Epis Pro-Cathd Hastings NE 2006-2010; Off Of Bsh For ArmdF New York NY 1986-2006; R Trin Ch Irvington NJ 1977-1986; Chr Ch Teaneck NJ 1976; Dio Newark Newark NJ 1976; Gr Ch

N

Madison NJ 1975-1976; Cur Chr Ch Teaneck NJ 1972-1973. Assoc / OHC 2004; Conf of St Ben 1981; CBS 1978. Dn Emer St Mk's Pro-Cathd 2010. robertneske@aol.com

NESMITH, Elizabeth Clare (LI) 305 Carlls Path, Deer Park NY 11729 **P-in-c Chr Ch Babylon NY 2011-; P-in-c Chr Ch Babylon NY 2011-; P-in-c Chr Ch Babylon NY 2011-; P-in-c Chr Ch Babylon NY 2011-; Bp's Dep for Stwdshp Dio Long Island Garden City NY 2007-; Bp's Dep for Stwdshp Dio Long Island Garden City NY 2007-; Exec Dir, Epis Chars Dio Long Island Garden City NY 2007-** B Marietta GA 8/25/1953 BS Wstrn Carolina U 1976; MA U IL 1981; MDiv GTS 2005. D 6/11/2005 P 2/11/2006 Bp John Palmer Croneberger. Epis Chars of Long Island Inc. Garden City NY 2007-2011; S Jn's Of Lattingtown Locust Vlly NY 2005-2007. ecnesmith@aol.com

NESS, Jerry (Neb) 803 Avenue E Pl, Kearney NE 68847 **R S Lk's Ch Kearney NE 2007-** B Chicago IL 4/10/1952 BA Wabash Coll Crawfordsville IN 1976; MA Loyola U 1996; MDiv SWTS 1999. Rec from Roman Catholic 4/18/1992 Bp Frank Tracy Griswold III. R Ch Of The Medtr Chicago IL 2002-2007; Cathd Of S Jas Chicago IL 2002; Dio Minnesota Minneapolis MN 1999-2002; S Mart's Epis Ch Fairmont MN 1999. frjerry@rcom-ne.com

NESS, Louisett Marie (Chi) 466 W Jackson St, Woodstock IL 60098 **D Ch Of The Incarn Bloomingdale IL 2008-** B 9/15/1948 D 2/5/2005 Bp William Dailey Persell. c 4. whistlestop466@comcast.net

NESS, Zanne Bartlett (ND) 1971 Mesquite Loop, Bismarck ND 58503 **Cn Dio No Dakota Fargo ND 2011-** B Canadian TX 9/4/1941 d William Bartlett & Fermanetta. BS W Texas A & M U 1987; MA W Texas A & M U 1990; PhD U of So Dakota 1994. D 6/8/2007 Bp Michael Gene Smith. m 7/19/2003 Terrance Ness c 3. zannec@bis.midco.net

NESTLEHUTT, Abigail Nestlehutt (Eas) Po Box 517, Saint Michaels MD 21663 B Boston MA 2/22/1969 d William Marshall Crozier & Prudence. BA Ya 1991; MDiv Harvard DS 1995; STM GTS 1998. D 12/19/1998 P 12/4/1999 Bp M(arvil) Thomas Shaw III. m 1/13/2001 Mark Stevens Nestlehutt c 2. Chr Ch St Michaels MD 2003-2010; Assoc R S Chrys's Ch Chicago IL 2001-2003; Asst to R S Barn Ch Falmouth MA 1999-2001. revabigail@christstmichaels.org

NESTLEHUTT, Mark Stevens (Eas) 115 West Chestnut, PO Box 517, Saint Michaels MD 21663 **R Chr Ch St Michaels MD 2003-** B Atlanta GA 2/3/1962 s Milton Bruce Nestlehutt & Betty Ruth. AB U GA 1984; BA Georgia St U 1985; MA Georgia St U 1986; MDiv EDS 1997. D 6/5/1999 P 6/3/2000 Bp M(arvil) Thomas Shaw III. m 1/13/2001 Abigail Nestlehutt Crozier c 2. Assoc R S Chrys's Ch Chicago IL 2001-2003; Bp's Stff Dio Massachusetts Boston MA 2000-2001; Ch Of S Jn The Evang Hingham MA 1999-2000. Auth, *Sprtlty for You*, Forw Mvmt Press, 1999; Auth, "Chalcedonian Christology," *Journ of Ecum Stds*, Temple Press, 1998; Auth, "Anglicans in Greece," *Angl and Epis Hist*, 1996. revmark@christstmichaels.org

NESTLER, Mary June (U) 8700 S. Kings Hill Dr, Cottonwood Heights UT 84121 **Exec Off Dio Utah Salt Lake City UT 2010-** B Colorado Springs CO 5/27/1951 d Karl Otto Nestler & Margaret Louise. B.Mus. The Curtis Inst of Mus 1975; MDiv GTS 1979; M.A. S Mary Sem Baltimore MD 1985; C.Phil. U CA 1992. D 6/12/1979 Bp David Keller Leighton Sr P 12/16/1979 Bp Robert Bruce Hall. c 2. Cn for Mnstry Formation Dio Utah Salt Lake City UT 2006-2010; Schlr In Res S Jas Par Los Angeles CA 1998-2006; Asst All SS Ch Pasadena CA 1993-1997; Dn and Pres The ETS At Claremont Claremont CA 1992-2006; P-in-c Epis Ch Of S Andr And S Chas Granada Hills CA 1991-1992; P-in-c S Geo's Mssn Hawthorne CA 1989-1991; Asst to R S Greg's Par Long Bch CA 1983-1986; P-in-c S Jn's And H Chld Wilmington CA 1981; Asst All SS Par Beverly Hills CA 1980-1981; Chapl S Marg's Sch Tappahannock VA 1979-1980. Cn Of Cathd Cntr Of S Paul Bp Borsch Of Dio Los Angeles 2001; Fell The ECF 1985. mjnestler@comcast.net

NESTOR, Elizabeth M (RI) 57 South Rd, Wakefield RI 02879 B Wakefield RI 6/5/1952 d Thomas Agnew Nestor & Mary Virginia. BA U of Rhode Island 1973; MDiv Yale DS 1979; MD NWU 1991. D 6/29/1979 Bp Frederick Hesley Belden P 12/23/1980 Bp George Nelson Hunt III. Asst S Aug's Ch Kingston RI 1994-2000; Asst Gr Ch Chicago IL 1987-1991; Asst Vic S Aug's Ch Kingston RI 1983-1987; Asst Ch Of The Redeem Bryn Mawr PA 1982; Int S Andr's Ch New Haven CT 1979-1982. Auth, "The Only Law I've Got," *Acad Emergency Med*, AEM, 2012; Auth, "I speak Doctor," *Acad Emergency Med*, AEM, 2012; Auth, "The Challenges of Treating Pain in the Emergency Dept," *Med and Hlth Rhode Island*, Med Soc of RI, 2011; Auth, "The Intimate Sci," *Acad Emergency Med*, AEM, 2009; Auth, "The Obligation of Narrative," *Canadien Journ of Emergency Med*, CJEM, 2006. Fell Of The Amer Coll Of Emergency Physicians 1996; Soc for Acad Emergency Med 2006. Jacob Franaszek Fac Tchg Awd Brown Emergency Med Residency 2010; Excellence in Tchg Awd Brown Med Sch 2008; Wmn Physcn of the Year RIMWA 2008; Outstanding Physcn UEMF 2008; Tchg Recognition Awd Brown Med Sch 2006; Fllshp and Resrch Grant Smithkline Beecham 1988. libbynestor@gmail.com

NESTROCK, Frederick Richard (Chi) 4633 Fairway Ct, Waterford MI 48328 **P Cathd Ch Of S Paul Detroit MI 2010-** B Bronx NY 10/4/1944 s Frederick Leonard Nestrock & Martha. BA Hob 1967; DPS Queens Coll (U of Birmingham) 1970; MDiv SWTS 1970; DDS Loyola U 1987. D 11/29/1972 Bp Quintin Ebenezer Primo Jr P 6/1/1973 Bp James Winchester Montgomery. m 9/18/1971 Katherine L Nestrock c 1. Stff Assoc S Paul's Ch No Kingstown RI 2008-2009; Int Chr Ch Ridgewood NJ 2005-2006; Chr Ch Westerly RI 2005-2006; Int S Dav's Ch Cranbury NJ 2003-2004; Int H Comf Ch Rahway NJ 2001-2003; Int S Mk's Ch Islip NY 2000-2001; Chr Ch Joliet IL 1996-2000; S Ambr Ch Chicago Heights IL 1995; Ch Of The H Fam Pk Forest IL 1993-1994; Int S Paul's Ch Kankakee IL 1991-1992; Assoc S Ptr's Epis Ch Chicago IL 1988-2002; Int Ch Of The H Nativ Clarendon Hills IL 1985-1988; Int S Dav's Epis Ch Aurora IL 1985-1988; Asst Gr Epis Ch Hinsdale IL 1978-1984; R S Jn's Epis Ch Chicago IL 1975-1978; Assoc S Thos Epis Ch Battle Creek MI 1973-1975. Int Mnstry Ntwk 1990-1999; Safe Ch Trnr (Dio Michigan) 2010; Safe Ch Trnr (Dio Rhode Island) 2006-2009. fnest44@aol.com

NETTLETON, Edwin Bewick (Colo) Po Box 22, Lake City CO 81235 B Oakmont PA 2/4/1940 s Lewis Lomax Nettleton & Marion. BS Texas Tech U 1962; BD Epis TS of The SW 1966; DD Epis TS of The SW 1989. D 6/3/1966 P 12/1/1966 Bp George Henry Quarterman. m 9/3/1960 Mary Lou Ford. S Jas Ch Lake City CO 2005-2010; R S Jas Epis Ch Taos NM 1976-1991; S Vincents Hse Galveston TX 1969-1976; Vic Chr Ch San Aug TX 1967-1969; Vic S Jn's Epis Ch Carthage TX 1967-1969; Vic S Jn's Epis Ch Cntr TX 1967-1969; Cur S Chris's Epis Ch Lubbock TX 1966-1967; Cur The Epis Ch Of The Gd Shpd Brownfield TX 1966-1967. Auth, "Why Were You Searching for Me," *Bk*, Peak Pub, 2006. PILGRIMSREST@CENTURYTEL.NET

NETTLETON, Jerome Paul (Eas) 525 E 6th St, Cookeville TN 38501 B Omaha NE 9/28/1937 s Paul Howard Nettleton & Beryl Elizabeth. BS U of Maryland. D 9/15/2001 Bp Martin Gough Townsend. m 11/27/1958 Myrna Sue Gentry.

NETZLER, Sherryl Kaye (Nev) 1631 Esmeralda Pl, Minden NV 89423 B New Zealand 12/13/1948 d Trevor Thomas Eyre & Lola Inez. D 10/6/2006 Bp Katharine Jefferts Schori P 9/14/2008 Bp Dan Thomas Edwards. m 8/2/1974 Serwind Netzler c 2. sherryl@netzlers.com

NEUBERGER, Jeffrey Lynn (Spok) 9106 N Bradbury St, Spokane WA 99208 B Sioux Falls SD 12/20/1949 s Harold Chester Neuberger & Mavis Jeanette. BS So Dakota St U 1977; MDiv SE Bapt TS Wake Forest NC 1981. D 9/8/2004 P 5/7/2005 Bp Daniel William Herzog. m 6/11/1981 Kathryn Arthur c 3. Conv Coordntr Dio Spokane Spokane WA 2011; Cn for Admin Dio Spokane Spokane WA 2009-2010. jeffrey.neuberger@comcast.net

N

NEUBURGER, James Edward (USC) 301 W Liberty St, Winnsboro SC 29180 **R S Jn's Ch Winnsboro SC 2008-** B St Louis MO 5/7/1947 s Maurice Edwin Neuburger & Elizabeth Ann. BA U of Notre Dame 1969; Angl Stds The U So (Sewanee) 2006. D 6/24/2006 Bp Dorsey Felix Henderson. m 10/23/2008 Carol Jenkins c 3. jeneuburger@att.net

NEUER, Paul Edward (NJ) 30 Shaw Springs Rd, Littleton NC 27850 **Died 12/5/2010** B Oak Tree NJ 7/28/1939 s Ellwood Irving Neuer & Pauline. BA Trenton St Coll 1965; MA Trenton St Coll 1970; MDiv Nash 1977. D 6/4/1977 P 12/14/1977 Bp Albert Wiencke Van Duzer. Credo; Curs; Epis Untd. Vol Of The Year - Cape May Cnty, Alco & Drug Abuse Gvnr Coun 2002; Mntl Hlth, Alco, And Drug Abuse Vol Of The Year 1996; Nomination For Bp Suffr Of New Jersey 1983. hopeneuer@earthlink.net

NEUFELD, Ellen Christine Hirsch (Alb) 6349 Milgen Rd Apt 12, Columbus GA 31907 **S Lk's Ch Chatham NY 2007-** B Jamaica NY 6/22/1950 d William P Hirsch & Catherine E. BS SUNY 1974; MS SUNY 1979; MA Ford 1982; CAS GTS 1993. D 1/6/1994 Bp John Shelby Spong P 7/1/1994 Bp Jack Marston McKelvey. m 1/11/1986 Michael John Neufeld. Trin Ch Gloversville NY 2004-2005; Ch Of The Ascen Troy NY 2001-2004; S Thos Of Cbury Thomaston GA 1998-1999; Trin Epis Ch Columbus GA 1998; P-in-c Ch Of The Gd Shpd Sumter SC 1996-1997; S Aug's Epis Ch Wedgefield SC 1996-1997; S Dav's Ch Cheraw SC 1996; Asst to R S Lk's Epis Ch Montclair NJ 1994-1995; D / Asst To R S Mk's Ch Teaneck NJ 1994. therevsec-mj@worldnet.att.net

NEUFELD, Michael John (Alb) 52 Sacandaga Rd, Scotia NY 12302 **R S Andr's Ch Scotia NY 2000-; Off Of Bsh For ArmdF New York NY 1997-** B Jamaica NY 8/31/1953 s Michael John Neufeld & Ethel Josephine. BA Seton Hall U 1974; MA Ford 1983; CAS GTS 1993. D 1/6/1994 Bp John Shelby Spong P 7/10/1994 Bp Jack Marston McKelvey. m 1/11/1986 Ellen Christine Hirsch. Gr Epis Ch And Kindergarten Camden SC 1995-1997; S Lk's Epis Ch Montclair NJ 1994-1995; S Mk's Ch Teaneck NJ 1994. ecmjneuf@prodigy.net

NEUHARDT, Kerry Coford (Az) 975 E Warner Rd, Tempe AZ 85284 **S Jn's Ch Christiansted VI 2011-** B Butte MT 12/26/1954 s Roy Walter Neuhardt & Shirley Jean. BA Carroll Coll at Helena 1978; MDiv Epis TS of The SW 1981. D 9/21/1982 Bp Leigh Wallace Jr P 3/1/1983 Bp Jackson Earle Gilliam. m 10/19/1984 Diana Lynn Fields c 2. P-in-c S Jas The Apos Epis Ch Tempe AZ 2002-2011; Pstr Asst S Barn On The Desert Scottsdale AZ 1998-2002; S Steph's Ch Phoenix AZ 1998-1999; R S Andr's Epis Ch Sedona AZ

1990-1997; All SS Ch Phoenix AZ 1985-1990; Assoc R Trin Epis Ch Everett WA 1983-1985; Asst S Jas Ch Bozeman MT 1982-1983. Ord Of S Lk. kneuhardt1@gmail.com

NEUHAUS, Beverly Ruth (NY) 277 Garrison Ave, Staten Island NY 10314 **D S Jn's Ch Staten Island NY 2010-; D S Simon's Ch Staten Island NY 1998-** B Staten Island NY 9/28/1944 d Edward Wurth & Ruth. BA St. Johns U 1987. D 6/4/1994 Bp Richard Frank Grein. m 10/3/1964 Robert Neuhaus c 2. D Chr Ch New Brighton Staten Island NY 1994-1997. bevneu@yahoo.com

NEUHAUS, Theodore James (Minn) 290 Dayton Ave Apt 1w, Saint Paul MN 55102 B Milwaukee WI 10/11/1940 s Lawrence Frederick Neuhaus & Marjorie Elizabeth. BSc U of Wisconsin-Milwaukee 1963; Coll of the Resurr 1966; D.Arts Ashworth U 2005. D 8/15/1975 Bp Philip Frederick McNairy P 11/23/1982 Bp Robert Marshall Anderson. S Paul's Ch Minneapolis MN 2004-2006; Int S Paul's On-The-Hill Epis Ch St Paul MN 1999-2004; Int Ch Of The Epiph Epis Plymouth MN 1997-1998; Dio Wstrn Massachusetts Springfield MA 1995-1996; Int Gr Ch Amherst MA 1995-1996; Int S Jn's Ch Massena NY 1993-1995; Int S Jn The Bapt Epis Ch Minneapolis MN 1992-1993; Int S Jas On The Pkwy Minneapolis MN 1987-1990; Int H Trin Epis Ch Elk River MN 1985-1986; Serv S Clem's Ch S Paul MN 1981-1983; Asst The Angl/Epis Ch Of Chr The King Frankfurt am Main 60323 DE 1978-1981; Serv S Chris's Epis Ch Roseville MN 1975-1978. CBS 1962; Friends of St Geo and Descendants of the Knights of the Garter 1982; GAS 1962; Sovereign Mltry Ord of the Temple of Jerusalem 2001. chevted@gmail.com

NEVAREZ, Christine M. (Los) Po Box 6036, Rosemead CA 91770 **Died 9/25/2009** B Santa Barbara CA 6/24/1945 d George Nevarez & Lillian. AA Pasadena City Coll 1965; Cert ETSBH 2006. D 12/2/2006 Bp Chester Lovelle Talton. christinenevarez@aol.com

NEVELS JR, Harry V (O) 2532 Potomac Hunt Ln Apt 1B, Richmond VA 23233 B Savannah GA 2/7/1938 s Harry Nevels & Mary. Fllshp Coll of Preachers; Savannah St Coll 1958; GW 1959; VTS 1962; U GA 1964; Case Wstrn Reserve U 1990. D 6/16/1962 P 5/1/1963 Bp Albert R Stuart. m 12/29/1962 Susie Morris. Ch Of The Trsfg Cleveland OH 1982-1998; S Aug's Ch New York NY 1976-1982; Vic S Aug's Ch New York NY 1974-1976; Vic The Epis Ch Of S Jn And S Mk Albany GA 1962-1968; R S Matt's Ch Savannah GA 1958-1974. harryvn2@msn.com

NEVILLE, Robyn-Michelle (Va) 1299 Quaker Hill Dr, Alexandria VA 22314 **Asst H Trin Par Decatur GA 2010-** B Wilmington NC 4/28/1976 BA W&M. D 6/14/2003 P 12/20/2003 Bp Peter James Lee. m 11/23/2002 Robert Damian Reeder. Chr Ch Cambridge Cambridge MA 2006; Asst S Andr's Ch Burke VA 2003-2005.

N

NEVILS, William Howard Paul (ETenn) PO Box 965, Tazewell TN 37879 **Supply S Clare's Ch La Follette TN 2005-** B New Tazewell TN 4/25/1940 s George Howard Nevils & Thelma Ruth. BA Carson-Newman Coll 1961; L. Th Nash 1964. D 10/28/1964 Bp William Evan Sanders P 12/1/1966 Bp John Vander Horst. c 3. Supply S Mths Rogersville TN 2005; Vic S Mths Rogersville TN 1993-2005; Vic S Clare's Ch La Follette TN 1992-2002; Supply Dio Olympia Seattle WA 1987-1991; LocTen S Dunst-The Highlands Shoreline WA 1986-1987; Supply Dio Olympia Seattle WA 1983-1985; LocTen Chr Epis Ch Blaine WA 1981-1982; LocTen S Paul's Epis Ch Poulsbo WA 1981-1982; LocTen S Paul Epis Ch Bellingham WA 1980-1981; LocTen S Geo's Ch Seattle WA 1978-1979; Cn S Mk's Cathd Seattle WA 1970-1978; R S Clem's Epis Ch Seattle WA 1969-1978; Asst Ch Of The H Comm Memphis TN 1965-1966; Vic Trin Ch Mason TN 1965-1966; D S Jn's Epis Cathd Knoxville TN 1964-1965. Auth, "All Around Us: Poems From The Vlly," *All Around Us: Poems From The Vlly*; Auth, "Hist of Claiborne Cnty TN 1801-2005," *Hist of Claiborne Cnty TN 1801-2005, Vol. 2*; Auth, *The Bicentennial Hist of Lee Cnty VA 1792-1992*.

NEVIN-FIELD, Claire Margaret (Pa) 816 Derby Dr, West Chester PA 19380 **S Ptr's Ch Philadelphia PA 2006-** B Cannock England 4/2/1963 d Ronald Nevin & Sadie. BSN U of Delaware Newark 1984; MS U of Pennsylvania 1994; MDiv GTS 2006. D 6/10/2006 P 12/16/2006 Bp Charles Ellsworth Bennison Jr. m 4/5/1980 Andrew Field c 2. claire@fieldsystem.com

NEVINS, Nancy Ruth (WMo) 416 SE Grand, Lee's Summit MO 64063 **D S Paul's Epis Ch Lees Summit MO 2011-** B Kansas City MO 5/2/1945 d Percy Earl Welsh & Mary Isabel. Lamar U 1981; no degree Lousiana St U 1982. D 6/5/2010 Bp Barry Robert Howe. m 12/28/1991 Stanley Nevins c 5. nnevins@aol.com

NEVITT, Benjamin Wilson (Alb) 1055 Belmont Rd, Gettysburg PA 17325 **Died 11/1/2009** B Washington DC 9/2/1918 s Benjamin Argyle Nevitt & Estelle Amanda. BA Bow 1947; MDiv Ya Berk 1950; Connecticut Vlly Hosp CT 1968. D 6/14/1950 P 12/22/1950 Bp Angus Dun. Hon Cn All SS Cathd Albany NY 1976.

NEW, Robert Henry (SVa) 2804 Cove Ridge Road, Midlothian VA 23112 B Rochester MN 9/23/1927 s Gordon Balgarnie New & Ethel Margaret. MDiv Bex; BA U MN 1961; BD Bex 1964; Cert Gestalt Inst 1978. D 6/13/1964 P 2/2/1965 Bp Nelson Marigold Burroughs. m 7/7/1951 Marian Merchant. LocTen S Dav's Epis Ch Richmond VA 2003-2004; Asst R S Mich's Ch Bon Air VA 1998-2000; Int Emm Ch Virginia Bch VA 1996-1997; Int S Steph's Ch Newport News VA 1995-1996; Int Trin Ch Portsmouth VA 1993-1994; Int Chr Epis Ch Raleigh NC 1992-1993; Vic Trin Ch Highland Sprg VA 1990-1992; Int S Mich's Ch Bon Air VA 1988-1989; Int Estrn Shore Chap Virginia Bch VA 1986-1988; Int S Tim's Epis Ch Creve Coeur MO 1985-1986; Int S Andr's Ch Ann Arbor MI 1984-1985; Gr Epis Ch Sandusky OH 1983-1984; Int R S Andr's Ch Ann Arbor MI 1983-1984; Int Ch Of The Epiph Euclid OH 1982-1983; R S Tim's Epis Ch Perrysburg OH 1977-1982; Assoc S Paul's Ch Akron OH 1973-1977; R S Paul's Ch Mt Vernon OH 1973-1974; Asst S Paul Epis Ch Norwalk OH 1964-1967. Acad Of Par Cler 1971-1995; Acad Of Par Cler Bd 1986-1988; Acad Of Par Cler Bd 1982-1984. bobnew@imanew.com

NEWBERRY, Hancella Warren (SO) 840 Middlebury Dr N, Worthington OH 43085 B Fort Sill OK 3/29/1957 d Hancel Warren & Annabelle Beatrice. BA W&M 1978; MDiv Harvard DS 1981. D 6/7/1982 Bp David Henry Lewis Jr P 1/31/1983 Bp William Grant Black. m 4/4/1987 Mervin Orin Newberry c 3. Int Ch Of S Edw Columbus OH 1988-1989; Int S Jas Epis Ch Columbus OH 1987-1988; Chapl Chap of the H Chld at Chld's Hosp Cincinnati OH 1982-1984. hanci.newberry@osumc.edu

NEWBERRY III, Jay Lamar (Mass) 205 Oxbow Rd, Wayland MA 01778 B Detroit MI 4/27/1936 s Jay Lamar Newberry & Anna. BA U MI 1958; BD EDS 1966. D 6/25/1966 P 5/1/1967 Bp Anson Phelps Stokes Jr. m 3/14/1964 Jane Wendell Hastings. Gr Ch Norwood MA 2000-2001; S Ptr's Ch Osterville MA 1999-2000; S Ptr's Ch Beverly MA 1998-1999; S Anne's Ch Lowell MA 1996; S Eliz's Ch Sudbury MA 1990; Gr Ch Newton MA 1983-1984; S Paul's Ch Peabody MA 1983; S Paul's Ch In Nantucket Nantucket MA 1982; R S Jn's Ch Frostburg MD 1968-1969; Cur The Ch Of Our Redeem Lexington MA 1966-1967.

NEWBERT, Russell Anderson (WNY) 185 Norwood Ave, Buffalo NY 14222 B Gardiner ME 7/19/1937 s Russell Copeland Newbert & Gwendolyn May. BS U of Maine 1959; STB GTS 1964; MA U of Notre Dame 1989. D 6/13/1964 Bp Oliver L Loring P 12/12/1964 Bp Roger W Blanchard. R S Simon's Ch Buffalo NY 1975-1998; R S Paul's Ch Martins Ferry OH 1972-1975; Cur Ch Of S Mich And All Ang Cincinnati OH 1964-1972. newbert185@hotmail.com

NEWBERY, Charles Gomph (LI) 1322 Shattuck Ave., #306, Berkeley CA 94709 B Chicago IL 4/17/1928 s Alfred Newbery & Helen Louise. BA Ya 1951; STB GTS 1954. D 6/12/1954 P 12/18/1954 Bp Benjamin M Washburn. m 6/23/1954 Jane Bollwinkel c 5. R S Jn's Of Lattingtown Locust Vlly NY 1974-1994; R S Jn's Ch Roanoke VA 1969-1974; R Chr Ch New Brunswick NJ 1966-1969; Vic All SS Ch Princeton NJ 1960-1966; Asst Trin Ch Princeton NJ 1956-1960; Cur Chr Ch Poughkeepsie NY 1954-1956. DD GTS New York NY 1986. charlesnewbery@att.net

NEWBOLD SR, Simeon Eugene (Va) 1719 N 22nd St, Richmond VA 23223 B Miami FL 9/4/1954 s David Jerone Newbold & Catherine Melvina. BSW Tuskegee Inst 1977; M.Ed Tuskegee Inst 1979; MDiv SWTS 1989; DMin Samuel Dewitt Proctor TS 2005. D 12/23/1989 P 1/1/1992 Bp Calvin Onderdonk Schofield Jr. m 8/21/1982 Audrea Stitt c 2. S Paul's Coll Lawrenceville VA 2005-2006; Dio Virginia Richmond VA 2003-2005; R S Ptr's Epis Ch Richmond VA 2000-2005; Comm on Mnstry Mem Dio Cntrl Florida Orlando FL 1993-1996; R Ch Of S Simon The Cyrenian Ft Pierce FL 1992-1994; Asst Mssh-S Barth Epis Ch Chicago IL 1989-1991. Reseacher/Writer, "Choosing Life Over Death: The Dvlpmt of a Strategic Growth Plan for S Ptr's Epis Ch," Samuel DeWitt Proctor TS, 2005. simeon.newbold@hamptonu.edu

NEWBURY, Edwards B (Neb) 210 S Howard St, Kimball NE 69145 B Lakewood NJ 6/8/1938 s Amos Birdsall Newbury & Elizabeth. NYTS; BA Kings Coll 1952; MDiv Conwell TS 1966. D 10/5/1986 P 2/1/1987 Bp Don Adger Wimberly. c 2. S Hildas Ch Kimball NE 1995-2010; Ch Of The Gd Shpd Bridgeport NE 1993-1995; Panhandle Mnstrs Inc. Sidney NE 1993-1995; Chr Ch Sidney NE 1993; S Mary's Ch: Holly Rushville NE 1991-1993; Calv Ch Hyannis NE 1990-1991; Vic S Jos's Ch Mullen NE 1990-1991. ednewbury@earthlink.net

NEWBY, Robert LaVelle (Colo) 265 Meadows Cir, # Th120, Bayfield CO 81122 B Topeka KS 11/14/1934 s Robert Henry Newby & Loretta. BS Sterling Coll 1962; BD Denver Sem 1967. D 6/10/1995 P 1/27/1996 Bp William Jerry Winterrowd. m 8/4/1957 Shirley Miller c 4. Ch Of The Gd Samar Gunnison CO 1999-2002; Asst S Mk's Epis Ch Durango CO 1998-1999; Supply S Jn's Ch Farmington NM 1997-1998; S Geo Epis Mssn Leadville CO 1996-1998; D S Mk's Epis Ch Durango CO 1995.

NEWBY, William Russell Michael (WLa) 705 N. Moffet Ave, Joplin MO 64801 B Moberly MO 9/29/1950 s William Russell Newby & Janice Malen. BA Cntrl Methodist U 1972; MEd U of Missouri 1975; MDiv Nash 1983. D 6/29/1981 P 7/1/1983 Bp Charles Thomas Gaskell. m 8/9/1975 Deborah Million. R S Jas Epis Ch Shreveport LA 2003-2005; Vic S Jn's Ch Neosho MO 1993-2003; Vic S Nich Ch Noel MO 1993-1995; Assoc S Phil's Ch Joplin MO 1988-1993; Int Trin Ch Michigan City IN 1988; R S Mich And All Ang Ch So Bend IN 1986-1988; Cn Mssnr To The Deaf Dio Ft Worth Ft Worth TX

1983-1986; Assoc R S Steph's Epis Ch Hurst TX 1983-1986; Secy-Gnrl Ord Of St Vinc Little Neck NY 1981-1996; Cn Mssnr To The Deaf Dio Milwaukee Milwaukee WI 1981-1983; P-n-c, All Souls deaf Cong S Jas Epis Ch Milwaukee WI 1981-1983. Ed, "The Angl Way"; Auth, "Osv Tracts". Assn Chr Therapists; Ord Of S Ben, Cbsaint, Som, Epis Conf Of The Deaf Of The Epis Ch In The USA, SSC, Secy Gnrl Ord S Vincents. Counslr Of The Year Natl Counslr Assn 1981. wdnewby@hotmail.com

NEWCOMB, Blair Deborah (Md) 2214 Grove Ave, Richmond VA 23220 B Ithaca NY 5/11/1947 d Edward Lindsay Newcomb & Carol. BA Mt Holyoke Coll 1969; Med Duke 1972; MDiv Ya Berk 1980; PhD U MI 1999. D 6/14/1980 P 2/15/1981 Bp Alexander Doig Stewart. m 1/11/2011 Paul Henle. Assoc The Ch Of The Redeem Baltimore MD 1986-1989; Asst Trin Ch On The Green New Haven CT 1981-1983; S Steph's Ch Westborough MA 1981. Amer Soc For Legal Hist; Amer Soc Of Ch Hist; Medieval Acad. Vstng Fellowow Univ Of Richmond Richmond VA 1999; Inst For The Hmnts Fellowowship U MI Ann Arbor MI 1995; Lurcy Fllshp 1993. BDNEWCOMB@EARTHLINK.NET

NEWCOMB, Deborah Johnson (Va) 25260 County Route 54, Dexter NY 13634 B Watertown NY 7/25/1949 d John Brayton Johnson & Catherine. BA Dickinson Coll 1972; MDiv STUSo 1987; DMin STUSo 1995. D 6/27/1987 P 1/16/1988 Bp George Lazenby Reynolds Jr. m 5/26/2002 Robert Newcomb c 3. R Emm Ch King Geo VA 2000-2004; R Hanover w Brunswick Par - S Jn King Geo VA 2000-2004; Int Trin Ch Upper Marlboro MD 1999-2000; Assoc The Ch Of The Redeem Baltimore MD 1996-1999; Assoc Chr Ch Alexandria VA 1988-1995; P-in-c S Barn Ch Tullahoma TN 1988; D S Barn Ch Tullahoma TN 1987-1988. dnewcomb@twcny.rr.com

NEWCOMB, Thomason League (NY) 10 Church Ln, Scarsdale NY 10583 **R Ch Of S Jas The Less Scarsdale NY 2000-** B New York NY 4/1/1947 s Wyllys Stetson Newcomb & Frances Annette. BA Baldwin-Wallace Coll 1969; MDiv GTS 1975. D 6/21/1975 Bp John Harris Burt P 2/14/1976 Bp Gray Temple. m 6/29/1974 Lee Ann Stutzman c 2. Dn Bridgeport Deanry Dio Connecticut Hartford CT 1996-1998; Chair Angl-Rc Dialogue Fairfield Cnty Dio Connecticut Hartford CT 1990-1998; Excoun Dio Connecticut Hartford CT 1985-1988; R S Tim's Ch Fairfield CT 1983-2000; Dir Happ Dio Georgia Savannah GA 1980-1983; Asst Chr Ch Epis Savannah GA 1978-1983; Asst S Mich's Epis Ch Charleston SC 1975-1978. frtomnewcomb@gmail.com

NEWCOMBE, D G (NY) 113 Gilbert Road, Cambridge CB4 3NZ Great Britain (UK) B Bronxville NY 11/7/1952 s Gordon Irving Newcombe & Virginia Olive. BA U of Vermont 1975; MDiv GTS 1978; STM GTS 1982; PhD U of Cambridge 1990. D 5/18/1978 Bp Harold Louis Wright P 11/1/1979 Bp Harvey D Butterfield. m 6/26/1976 Barbara Lynn Johnson c 4. Ch Of S Jas The Less Scarsdale NY 1979-1985. Auth, "Jn Hooper," Davenant Press, 2009; Auth, "Jn Hooper," *Cambridge Dictionary of Chrsnty*, Camb Press, 2009; Auth, "Nich Hawkins," *New Oxford Dictionary of Natl Biography*, Oxf Press, 2004; Auth, "Jn Hooper," *New Oxford Dictionary of Natl Biography*, Oxf Press, 2004; Auth, "Jn Ponet," *New Oxford Dictionary of Natl Biography*, Oxf Press, 2004; Auth, "Wm Rokeby," *New Oxford Dictionary of Natl Biography*, Oxf Press, 2004; Auth, "Jas Stanley," *New Oxford Dictionary of Natl Biography*, Oxf Press, 2004; Auth, "Richard Mayew," *New Oxford Dictionary of Natl Biography*, Oxf Press, 2004; Auth, "Geoffrey Blythe," *New Oxford Dictionary of Natl Biography*, Oxf Press, 2004; Auth, "Henry Man," *New Oxford Dictionary of Natl Biography*, Oxf Press, 2004; Auth, "Hugh Inge," *New Oxford Dictionary of Natl Biography*, Oxf Press, 2004; Auth, "Jn Kite," *New Oxford Dictionary of Natl Biography*, Oxf Press, 2004; Auth, "Jn Skip," *New Oxford Dictionary of Natl Biography*, Oxf Press, 2004; Auth, "Chas Booth," *New Oxford Dictionary of Natl Biography*, Oxf Press, 2004; Auth, "Jn Howden," *New Oxford Dictionary of Natl Biography*, Oxf Press, 2004; Auth, "Cuth Tunstall," *New Oxford Dictionary of Natl Biography*, Oxf Press, 2004; Ed, "Facsimilie of Foxe's Bk of Martyrs, 1583...on CD-ROM," Oxf Press, 2001; Auth, "Electric Foxe, A Digital Case Hist.," *Jn Foxe: An Hist Perspective*, Ashgate Press, 1999; Auth, "A Finding List of editions of Jn Foxe's Acts and Monuments.," *Jn Foxe and the Engl Reformation*, Scolar Press, 1997; Auth, "The Visitation of the Dio Gloucester and the St of the Cler, 1551.," *Transactions of the Bristol and Gloucestershire Archeol Soc*, 1996; Auth, "Henry VIII and the Engl Reformation," Routledge, 1995; Auth, "Jn Hooper's visitation and examination of the Cler in the Dio Gloucester, 1551," *Reformations Old and New: essays on the socio Econ impact of Rel change, c. 1470 - 1630.*, Scolar Press, 1995. dgn71152@ntlworld.com

NEWELL, John E (SVa) 501 Old Town Dr, Colonial Heights VA 23834 **S Mich's Ch Colonial Heights VA 1993-** B Cleveland OH 9/29/1951 s John Newell & Mildred. BA U Denv 1974; MDiv Nash 1989. D 6/12/1989 Bp John Wadsworth Howe P 12/13/1989 Bp William Hopkins Folwell. m 3/15/1975 Courtney Hawley c 3. Gr Epis Ch Inc Port Orange FL 1989-1993. tcnewell@comcast.net

NEWELL, Tamara Locke (Dal) 464 Ne 16th St, Miami FL 33132 B Mexico DF MX 3/19/1947 d Thomas Henry Locke & DeNeen. BA U Of Amer 1973; Cert U of Texas 1975; SMU 1986; MA Usiu 1988. D 7/2/1982 P 5/1/1983 Bp Jose Guadalupe Saucedo. m 12/7/1967 Roberto E Newell. Trin Cathd Miami FL 1997-2004; S Mich And All Ang Ch Dallas TX 1989-1993. tamarane@mac.com

NEWHART, David George (CFla) 120 Larchmont Ter, Sebastian FL 32958 **Congrl Dvlpmt Dio Cntrl Florida Orlando FL 2011-; Dioc Bd Dio Cntrl Florida Orlando FL 2011-; Chair, ICS Cmsn Dio Cntrl Florida Orlando FL 2010-; COM Dio Cntrl Florida Orlando FL 2010-; R S Eliz's Epis Ch Sebastian FL 2007-** B Scranton PA 3/14/1955 s William Henry Newhart & Barbara Ann. BS Arizona St U 1982; MDiv TESM 2005. D 5/28/2005 Bp John Wadsworth Howe P 12/11/2005 Bp Gary Richard Lillibridge. m 7/22/1998 Matilda Mae Pirlo c 3. Chair, ICS Cmsn Dio Cntrl Florida Orlando FL 2010-2011; Curs Cmsn Dio Cntrl Florida Orlando FL 2009-2011; Cur S Helena's Epis Ch Boerne TX 2005-2007. dgnewhart@yahoo.com

NEWLAND, Benjamin John (Oly) 210 W Pioneer Unit 215, Puyallup WA 98371 **R Chr Epis Ch Puyallup WA 2007-** B Richland WA 1/17/1975 s Dennis John Newland & Judy Marie. BA Gonzaga U 1997; MDiv CDSP 2000. D 6/24/2000 Bp John Stuart Thornton P 1/7/2001 Bp Barry Robert Howe. m 6/12/2004 Jieun Kim. S Andr's Ch Madison CT 2006-2007; Yth Min Coordntr Gr And H Trin Cathd Kansas City MO 2000-2005. ben.newland@gmail.com

NEWLAND, Robert Bruce (Me) 2321 Enchanted Forest Ln, Virginia Beach VA 23453 **Died 11/14/2010** B Long Beach CA 10/29/1933 s Paul Tyler Newland & Margaret Elora. BS California St Polytechnic U 1955; MDiv EDS 1966; Fllshp EDS 1986. D 6/24/1966 P 1/1/1969 Bp George P Gunn. Auth, "Relatives Of Aid To The 20th Century"; Auth, "Peregrini Pro Amore Christi"; Auth, "Wherever Two Or Three Are Gathered".

NEWLAND, William Trent (Va) 43506 Shalimar Pointe Ter, Leesburg VA 20176 B Roanoke VA 4/18/1934 s William Trent Newland & Josephine. BS VMI 1958; MDiv VTS 1966. D 9/17/1966 Bp John Brooke Mosley P 5/1/1967 Bp William Foreman Creighton. m 6/12/1958 Ann C Newland c 3. S Jas' Epis Ch Leesburg VA 1993-2006; Pstr Counslr Ch Of The H Comf Vienna VA 1986-2003; P-in-c S Jn's Epis Ch Arlington VA 1967-1971; Cur S Jn's Epis/Angl Ch Mt Rainier MD 1966-1967. Amer Assn of Mar and Fam Therapists 1975; AAPC 1973. bnewland55@verizon.net

NEWLIN, Melissa Dollie (ECR) 1514 Hilby Ave, Seaside CA 93955 B Fort Knox KY 5/22/1946 d Charles Albert Newlin & Mary Pearl. BA San Francisco St U 1972; MDiv CDSP 1973. D 6/23/1973 Bp C Kilmer Myers. m 10/5/1985 Jeff Lucas. D Santa Lucia Chap Big Sur Carmel CA 1991-2007; D All SS Ch Carmel CA 1991-2004; Natl Coun Of Ch New York NY 1978-1979; S Andr's Ch Hanover MA 1976-1977.

NEWMAN, Allen Ray (NY) 27 Mariners Cove, Edgewater NY 07020 **Supply P Trin Ch Of Morrisania Bronx NY 2007-** B Ashland KY 5/5/1943 s William Raymond Newman & Virginia Allen. BA Stetson U 1964; MA U NC 1966; PhD U NC 1975; MDiv UTS 1986. D 8/10/1986 Bp Walter Decoster Dennis Jr P 5/1/1987 Bp Paul Moore Jr. S Anne's Ch Washingtonville NY 1998-2009; Calv Epis Ch Flemington NJ 1996-1998; Int S Andr's Epis Ch Hartsdale NY 1994-1996; Vic S Jos's Ch Bronx NY 1988-1994; Assoc Chr And S Steph's Ch New York NY 1987-1988. newman@brasington.com

NEWMAN, Georgia A(nn) (At) **D S Steph's Ch Milledgeville GA 2008-** D 5/17/2008 Bp J(ohn) Neil Alexander.

NEWMAN JR, Harry George (Spr) 5 Hackberry Ln, Springfield IL 62704 **Asst Chr Ch Springfield IL 1986-** B Hammond IN 5/28/1928 s Harry G Newman & Dorothy. BA; MA. m 9/20/1952 Elizabeth Johnson. hnewman@springnet1.com

NEWMAN II, James Arthur (Los) 1445 Westerly Ter, Los Angeles CA 90026 **Area Dn Dio Los Angeles Los Angeles CA 2005-; R S Bede's Epis Ch Los Angeles CA 1990-** B Long Beach CA 11/15/1949 s James Arthur Newman & Lillian Anna. BS U MN 1973; MDiv VTS 1978. D 6/24/1978 P 2/2/1979 Bp Robert Marshall Anderson. m 8/17/1978 Michael M Mullins. Int Chr Ch Par Redondo Bch CA 1988-1990; R and Chapl All SS Ch Northfield MN 1980-1988; R Ch Of The H Cross Dundas MN 1980-1988; Asst S Chris's Epis Ch Roseville MN 1978-1980. AAM 2009; Assn of Dioc Liturg & Mus Commissions 1982-2002; EPF 1978; ESMHE 1980-1992; Integrity 1976; OHC 1974. westerr45@yahoo.com

NEWMAN, Michael Werth (Pa) 1705 Varsity Ln, Bear DE 19701 B Boston MA 9/10/1944 s Byron Werth Newman & Mary Margaret. MDiv S Mary Sem 1974; MEd U of Maine 1980; STM GTS 1984. Rec from Roman Catholic 3/1/1984 as Priest Bp Frederick Barton Wolf. m 1/18/1982 Melda Mary Brandt. Supply S Mart's Epis Ch Upper Chichester PA 2000-2004; Supply Dio Pennsylvania Philadelphia PA 1999; R Chr Ch Epis Ridley Pk PA 1991-1999; R Chr Ch Stroudsburg PA 1986-1991; R Trin Ch Buchanan VA 1984-1986. AAPC 1978. Citizen Year Botetourt Cnty 1986. bigandlittle009@comcast.net

NEWMAN JR, Murray Lee (Va) 10450 Lottsford Rd Apt 1206, Mitchellville MD 20721 B Checotah OK 8/22/1924 s Murray Lee Newman & Sally. BA Phillips U 1945; MA Phillips U 1947; BD/THD UTS 1951; S Geo's Coll Jerusalem 1984; Ecumencial Inst Jerusalem 1986; Institut Catholique De Paris 1992. D 1/29/1956 P 9/26/1956 Bp William A Lawrence. m 6/6/1946 Janice Hood c 4. Prof VTS Alexandria VA 1956-1996. Auth, "Erodus," *Forw Mvmt*,

N

2000; Auth, "The Old Convenantand The New," *Sead*, 2000; Auth, "Genesis," *Forw Mvmt*, 1999; Auth, "Interp Of Scripture," *The Afr Amer Jubilee*, 1999; Auth, "People Of The Cov," 1962; Auth, "Israels Prophetic Heritage"; Auth, "Stds In Deuteronomy"; Auth, "Idb Supplement"; Auth, "Rahab & Conquest"; Auth, "The Cont Quest For The Hist Cov". Cath Of Biblic Assn; SBL. mlnewman@aol.com

NEWMAN, Peggy Williams (SVa) 1969 Woodside Ln, Virginia Beach VA 23454 **D All SS' Epis Ch Virginia Bch VA 2008-** B Memphis TN 12/8/1948 d Henry M Williams & Mildred Elizabeth. BS U GA GA 1971; MA Bowie St Coll 1981; MSW Norfolk St U 1988. D 6/14/2008 Bp John James Buchanan. pnewman@okgov.com

NEWMAN, Richard Barend (Pa) 14 Princess Ln, Newtown PA 18940 B Trenton NJ 3/24/1936 s John Arnold Newman & Jennie Martha. Moody Bible Inst 1957; BA Westmont Coll 1960; MA Tem 1971. D 11/2/1991 Bp Franklin Delton Turner. m 6/19/1965 Dorothy Jean Banks c 2. Trin Ch Buckingham PA 1999-2000; Dio Pennsylvania Philadelphia PA 1995-1997; Cur S Lk's Ch In The Cnty Of Buck Newtown PA 1994-1995; Asst Washington Memi Chap Vlly Forge PA 1992-1994. Auth, "A Photographic View Of Bucks Cnty, Pa," *Bucks Cnty Town And Country Living*, 1999; Auth, "Farms & Barns Of Bucks Cnty". rndn@bellatlantic.net

NEWMAN, Ryan Douglas (Los) 4533 Laurel Canyon Blvd, N Hollywood CA 91607 **Campbell Hall Vlly Vill CA 2002-** B Tarzana CA 4/24/1976 s Stephen Lee Newman & Charlotte Irene. BA USC 1998; MDiv VTS 2002. D 6/29/2002 P 1/11/2003 Bp Joseph Jon Bruno. newmanr@campbellhall.org

NEWMAN, Thomas Frank (SD) 10 Red Oak Rd, Shawnee OK 74804 B Waukesha WI 1/19/1945 s Howard Newman & Gertrude. BA U of Texas 1974; MDiv STUSo 1977. D 6/26/1977 P 6/16/1978 Bp Walter H Jones. m 2/5/1966 Shirlene Barton c 2. Chr Epis Ch Forrest City AR 2004; Ch Of The Gd Shpd Forrest City AR 2004; Delta Epis Cluster Mnstry Forrest City AR 2000-2003; Ch Of The Gd Shpd Forrest City AR 1996-2000; R S Andr's Ch Marianna AR 1995-2000; P Ch Of The Epiph Dallas TX 1986-1995; P S Mk's Ch Seminole OK 1983-1985; R S Thos Epis Ch Sturgis SD 1980-1982; Dio So Dakota Sioux Falls SD 1977-1980; P Trin Epis Ch Mssn SD 1977-1980. wiztex@sbcglobal.net

NEWNAM, Elizabeth Ann (Cal) 555 4th St Unit 530, San Francisco CA 94107 B Galveston TX 8/16/1943 d Frank Hastings Newnam & Martha Elizabeth. BA Randolph-Macon Wmn's Coll 1965; MA Eastman Sch of Mus 1967; Dm Florida St U 1972; MDiv CDSP 1989. D 5/31/1989 P 12/1/1989 Bp Sam Byron Hulsey. Assoc Trin Ch San Francisco CA 1999-2005; P-in-c S Barn Ch San Francisco CA 1996-2005; Epis Ch Of S Geo Canyon TX 1989-1995. enewnam@comcast.net

NEWSOM, James Cook (WTenn) St Matthew's Episcopal Church, 303 S Munford St, Covington TN 38019 **St Geo's Indep Sch Collierville TN 2009-** B Memphis TN 10/20/1954 s William Andrew Newsom & Sarah Cook. Cert. of Theol Stds U So Sewanee TN; BA Memphis St U 1977; MDiv Memphis TS 2007. D 1/19/2008 P 8/9/2008 Bp Don Edward Johnson. m 4/27/1997 Patti Newsom c 6. Bishops Vic S Matt's Ch Covington TN 2007-2009. jcnewsom@comcast.net

NEWTON, John David (Minn) 1631 Ford Pkwy, Saint Paul MN 55116 **R Mssh Epis Ch S Paul MN 2004-** B Halifax Nova Scotia 10/6/1948 s John Matthew Newton & Flora. MA McGill U 1973; Dplma in Mnstry Montreal Dioc Theol Coll 1974. Trans from Anglican Church of Canada 11/1/2004 Bp James Louis Jelinek. m 9/7/1973 Karen A Johnson c 3. j.newton@messiahepiscopal.org

NEWTON IV, John Wharton (Tex) 209 W 27th St, Austin TX 78705 **Dio Texas Houston TX 2011-; Campus Mssnr Dio Texas Houston TX 2008-** B Beaumont TX 9/11/1981 s John Wharton Newton & Martha S. BBA U of Texas 2004; MDiv VTS 2008. D 6/28/2008 Bp Don Adger Wimberly P 1/31/2009 Bp Dena Arnall Harrison. jwnewt@gmail.com

NEWTON, Willoughby (Ct) 1623 - 3rd Avenue #18-KW, New York NY 10128 B Orange VA 4/8/1925 s Frederick Griffith Newton & Kathleen Sutherland. BA U of Virginia 1949; BA/MA U of Cambridge 1951; DD S Paul's Coll Lawrenceville VA 1981. D 6/14/1956 Bp Walter H Gray P 5/10/1957 Bp Robert McConnell Hatch. VP Extrnl Affrs The GTS New York NY 1987-1990; Venture In Missions- Epis Ch Cntr New York NY 1977; Wykeham Rise Sch 1963-1976; Asst S Jn's Ch Salisbury CT 1956-1957. D.D. (Hon) S Paul's Coll, Lawrenceville, Va. 1986.

NEYLAND, Thomas Allen (Colo) PO Box 228, Hygiene CO 80533 B Beaumont TX 9/11/1936 s Allen Carroll Neyland & Winnie Helen. BA U of Texas 1959; MDiv SWTS 1963; Ldrshp Acad for New Directions 1989; Grad Int Mnstry Ntwk 1996. D 6/15/1963 Bp James Winchester Montgomery P 3/21/1964 Bp Theodore H McCrea. m 4/23/1972 Charlotte A Smith c 4. Supply H Cross Epis Mssn Sterling CO 2010-2011; Int The Ch Of Chr The King (Epis) Arvada CO 2006-2007; Int S Mk's Ch Cheyenne WY 2004-2005; Int S Andr's Ch Omaha NE 2002-2003; Int Trin Ch Ennis MT 2001-2002; Int S Jas Epis Ch Wheat Ridge CO 2000-2001; Int S Jos's Ch Lakewood CO 1999-2000; Int S Alb's Epis Ch McCook NE 1998-1999; Int Ch Of Our Sav No Platte NE 1997-1998; R Par Ch Of S Chas The Mtyr Ft Morgan CO 1992-1996; R - Reg Coordntr S Mk's Epis Ch Pecos TX 1990-1991; Dio WK SE Rgnl Coordntr Dio Wstrn Kansas Hutchinson KS 1988-1990; R S Jn's Ch Great Bend KS 1985-1990; R S Paul's Epis Ch Coffeyville KS 1981-1985; R S Thos Ch Ennis TX 1977-1980; Int Ch Of The H Apos Aledo TX 1976-1977; Chapl S Aid's Epis Ch Boulder CO 1967-1968; Cur All SS' Epis Ch Ft Worth TX 1965-1967; Vic S Mart's Ch Lancaster TX 1963-1964. Phi Mu Alpha 1957-1960. tomneyland@msn.com

NEYLON, Jean Carla (Md) 110 W Ruffin St, Mebane NC 27302 B 11/22/1936

NG, Joshua (Los) 15930 Annellen St, Hacienda Heights CA 91745 **S Thos' Mssn Hacienda Heights CA 2005-** B Kota Kinabalu Sabah 2/7/1963 s Huat-Lang Ng & Jingguni. Trans from Church of the Province of South East Asia 8/30/2005 Bp Joseph Jon Bruno. m 11/23/1991 Pit-Lin Chin c 2. yosshua@yahoo.com

NGUYEN, Duc Xuan (Los) 9097 Crocus Ave, Fountain Valley CA 92708 B 10/28/1941 s Ba Xuan Nguyen & Lai. BA U Saigon 1965; MDiv Golden Gate Bapt TS 1971; MLS CUNY 1975; PhD Drew U 1978. D 2/27/1984 P 7/7/1984 Bp Robert C Rusack. m 5/29/1977 Thuan Nguyen c 1. Ch Of Redeem Mssn Garden Grove CA 1985-1992. dxnguyen@worldnet.att.net

NGUYEN, Hong Xuan (Los) 9051 Biola Ln, Garden Grove CA 92844 B Caobang VN 9/21/1936 s Ba Xuan Nguyen & Lai. BA Saigon U 1967; MS Natl Inst Admsntr 1974; MDiv CDSP 1990. D 6/16/1990 P 1/1/1991 Bp Frederick Houk Borsch. m 11/18/1962 Baoan Thi Le. Vic Ch Of Redeem Mssn Garden Grove CA 1991-2005. Auth, "A Moment Of Meditation". nguyenredeemer@yahoo.com

NI, Hui Liang (Los) St Edmunds Episcopal Church, 1175 S San Gabriel Blvd, San Marino CA 91108 **Assoc, PhD S Edm's Par San Marino CA 2007-** B Shanghai China 1/30/1962 s Ni Chen Biao & Cha Hua. BA E China Normal U 1984; BA Oak Hill Theol Coll 1994; MA E China Normal U Shanghai China 1997. D 6/9/2007 P 1/12/2008 Bp Joseph Jon Bruno. m 2/14/1989 Yuan Zhi Wu c 1. thomasni@yahoo.com

NICHOLAS, John Robert (Nev) 116 Ocotillo St, Henderson NV 89015 B San Francisco CA 11/20/1922 s Frederick John Nicholas & Charlotte Margaret. BS California Inst of Tech 1944; MDiv CDSP 1948. D 5/15/1948 P 12/1/1948 Bp William Hawley Clark. c 3. Vic S Tim's Epis Ch Henderson NV 1960-1968; Vic S Lk's Ch Weiser ID 1956-1960; R S Mary's Ch Emmett ID 1953-1956; Vic All SS Ch Salt Lake City UT 1952-1953.

NICHOLS, Alice S (Ky) 216 E 6th St, Hopkinsville KY 42240 **R Gr Ch Hopkinsville KY 2011-** B Wadesboro NC 6/7/1947 d Vernon Bradford Smith & Margaret Tice. BA Meredith Coll 1969; MSSW U of Tennessee 1972; MDiv Van 2004. D 4/14/2007 P 10/27/2007 Bp Edwin Funsten Gulick Jr. c 1. R Chr Ch Elizabethtown KY 2007-2011. alicenichols@gmail.com

NICHOLS, Catherine Palmer (Vt) Trinity Episcopal Cathedral, 147 NW 19th Ave, Portland OR 97209 **Cn Pstr Trin Epis Cathd Portland OR 2005-** B North Conway NH 7/7/1944 d Fessenden Arenberg Nichols & Ethel Jourdan. a.b. Harv 1966; M.M. U MI 1970; M.M. U MI 1971; MDiv EDS 1983. D 5/28/1983 Bp John Bowen Coburn P 3/14/1984 Bp Maurice Manuel Benitez. c 2. Int S Jn's Ch Portsmouth NH 2004-2005; Mus & Liturg Cmsn, Chair Dio Vermont Burlington VT 1993-2003; R S Steph's Ch Middlebury VT 1991-2003; Dioc Coun Dio Vermont Burlington VT 1991-1997; Cler Pstr Care Com Dio Texas Houston TX 1987-1991; Cn Pstr Chr Ch Cathd Houston TX 1985-1991; COM Dio Texas Houston TX 1984-1985; Exam Chapl Dio Texas Houston TX 1983-1986; Asst to R H Sprt Epis Ch Houston TX 1983-1985; Mus Com Dio Massachusetts Boston MA 1980-1983. EWC 1998; Middlebury Area Cler 1991-2004; St. Jn's Soc, EDS 1991-2004. Preaching Prize EDS 1983; Avon Schlr Suffern HS 1962. revcpn@gmail.com

NICHOLS, Dennis Witt (NJ) 200 Kings Hwy, Mount Royal NJ 08061 **R S Ptr's Ch Clarksboro NJ 1995-** B Bedford VA 10/20/1955 s Heenan Witt Nichols & Betty Ann. Oriental Stds Oxf; BME/BCM Shenandoah U 1978; MDiv GTS 1992. D 6/6/1992 Bp A(rthur) Heath Light P 12/1/1992 Bp George Phelps Mellick Belshaw. m 5/29/1982 Linda Wintersteen c 2. R Ch Of S Jn-In-The-Wilderness Gibbsboro NJ 1992-1995. Affirming Catholicism 2000. Oxford Round Table Harris Manchester Coll 2007; Alum Exec Com GTS 2003. dn4116@comcast.net

NICHOLS, Kevin Donnelly (NH) 21 Hampshire Hills Dr, Bow NH 03304 **Chair, Bp Search Com Dio New Hampshire Concord NH 2011-; Stndg Com Dio New Hampshire Concord NH 2007-; R S Andr's Epis Ch Hopkinton NH 2006-** B Inglewood CA 2/7/1962 s Thomas Nichols & Virginia. BA S Bonaventure U 1984; MDiv S Mary Sem 1992. Rec from Roman Catholic 12/1/1999 as Priest Bp Douglas Edwin Theuner. m 4/20/1996 Patti Ann Mather Oakland c 3. R S Steph's Ch Pittsfield NH 2000-2006; Asst Chr Ch Exeter NH 2000. rectorst.andrews@comcast.net

NICHOLS, Liane Christoffersen (Ia) 2013 Minnetonka Dr, Cedar Falls IA 50613 **D S Lk's Epis Ch Cedar Falls IA 1992-** B Dubuque IA 5/16/1934 d Iver Hvidtfeldt Christoffersen & Veronica Marie. BA Iowa St Teachers Coll 1956; MA St Coll of Iowa 1966. D 10/18/1992 Bp Carl Christopher Epting. m 1/14/1956 Raymond Charles Nichols c 3. NAAD 1993. lianebud@cfu.net

NICHOLS, Nancy Brewster Clifton (SwFla) 7151 22nd St N, Saint Petersburg FL 33702 **D S Bede's Ch St Petersburg FL 1990-** B Cincinnati OH 4/6/1938 d Edward Nelson Clifton & Eleanor Benedict. D Formation Prog 1959; S Leo Coll For Psychol 1977; Dio Sthrn Florida D Trng FL 1990. D 6/30/1990 Bp Rogers Sanders Harris. m 7/1/1965 Earl Scott Nichols c 2. NAAD.

NICHOLS III, Robert George (Tex) 15 Hannon Ave, Mobile AL 36604 **Chap Of S Jn The Div Champaign IL 2011-; S Ptr's Ch Jackson AL 2008-** B Jackson MS 2/16/1955 s Robert George Nichols & Mary Maude. BA Millsaps Coll 1977; MDiv VTS 1988; DMin STUSo 1995; Basic Int Mnstry Ntwk 2005. D 5/26/1988 P 10/26/1989 Bp Duncan Montgomery Gray Jr. m 5/29/1993 Diana K Kahalley c 2. R S Chris's Ch Houston TX 2007-2008; S Ptr's Ch Jackson AL 2005-2007; S Jn's Ch Monroeville AL 2003-2006; S Lk's Epis Ch Mobile AL 2000-2003; Asst R S Mk's Epis Ch Little Rock AR 1997-2000; Chr Epis Ch Little Rock AR 1997; Ch Of The Ascen Hattiesburg MS 1996-1997; All SS Epis Ch Mobile AL 1990-1996; Cur S Jn's Epis Ch Pascagoula MS 1988-1990. robbie0216@comcast.net

NICHOLS, Robert Lee (Chi) 24826 Gates Ct. # 85, Plainfield IL 60585 **Died 10/21/2009** B Savannah GA 1/20/1930 s Ira Lee Nichols & Gertrude. BA Dbc 1952; BD SWTS 1955. D 7/4/1955 P 5/1/1956 Bp Albert R Stuart. big.cats2@sbcglobal.net

NICHOLS, Sarah Winn (Los) 1125 S Orange Grove Blvd, Pasadena CA 91105 **Dir of Pstr Care The Epis Hm Communities Pasadena CA 2008-; Dioc Stwdshp Prog Grp Dio Los Angeles Los Angeles CA 2006-** B Madison WI 9/11/1965 d Stephen George Nichols & Mary Jordan. BS Van 1986; MDiv Fuller TS 2004; Cert CDSP 2005. D 6/11/2005 Bp Joseph Jon Bruno P 1/14/2006 Bp Frank Tracy Griswold III. Dioc Stwdshp Prog Grp Dio Los Angeles Los Angeles CA 2006-2007; Assoc R S Mich and All Ang Epis Ch Studio City CA 2005-2007. Contributing Auth, "Caring for Protestants: Asking the Rt Questions," *Living w Grief: Sprtlty and End-of-Life Care*, Hospice Fndt of Amer, 2011; Auth, "Exam the Impact of Sprtl Care in Long Term Care," *Omega: The Journ of Death and Dying*, Baywood Pub Co., Inc., 2011. sarah@winnwares.com

NICHOLSON, A(leathia) Dolores (Tenn) 3729 Creekland Ct, Nashville TN 37218 **D Chr Ch Cathd Nashville TN 2007-** B Salisbury NC 4/10/1937 d John Wadsworth Nicholson & Leathia Geraldine. BS Hampton U 1959; MA U of Connecticut 1965; EDS Peabody Coll 1969; Lic Epis TS In Kentucky 1989. D 10/28/1989 Bp George Lazenby Reynolds Jr. D S Anselm's Epis Ch Nashville TN 2002-2007; D/Asst S Mths Ch Nashville TN 1989-2000. Auth, "Encyclopedia Of Afr-Amer Culture And Hist Supplement," 2001; Auth, "Notable Black Amer Men," Gale Resrch, 1998; Auth, "Notable Black Amer Wmn Bk Ii," Gale Resrch, 1996; Auth, "Notable Black Amer Wmn Bk I," Gale Resrch, 1992. Intl Ord Of S Lk Physcn 2001-2002; NAAD 2001. Fell Tennessee Collaborative Ldrshp Acad TN 1996; Experienced Tchr Fllshp in the Hmnts Peabody Coll 1968. a_d_nicholson@yahoo.com

NICHOLSON, David Owen (WMass) 850 Parker St, Springfield MA 01129 B Salem MA 12/6/1931 s Harold Forbes Nicholson & Anne Mccoll. BA MI SU 1958; MDiv EDS 1968; Med Springfield Coll 1982. D 6/11/1968 Bp Walter H Gray P 12/21/1968 Bp Joseph Warren Hutchens. m 8/24/1979 Judith Allan Allen c 1. P-in-c S Lk's Ch Springfield MA 1999-2002; Int S Jn's Ch Northampton MA 1998-1999; Int S Steph's Epis Ch Bloomfield CT 1995-1998; Int S Jn's Ch Athol MA 1994-1995; Int S Alb's Ch Simsbury CT 1993-1994; No Cntrl Reg Mnstry Enfield CT 1993; Calv Ch Enfield CT 1991-1992; H Trin Epis Ch Enfield CT 1991-1992; S Phil's Epis Ch Putnam CT 1991; Int S Jn's Epis Ch Vernon Rock Vernon CT 1990-1992; Dio Wstrn Massachusetts Springfield MA 1989-2002; Int Ch Of The Gd Shpd W Springfield MA 1989-1990; Int Gr Ch Chicopee MA 1988-1989; S Jn's Epis Ch Vernon Rock Vernon CT 1988-1989; Int Ch Of The Recon Webster MA 1987-1988; Int S Andr's Epis Ch Enfield CT 1984-1985; Supply P Dio Connecticut Hartford CT 1980-1984; Asst to R S Jn's Ch W Hartford CT 1971-1975; Vic S Jas' Ch New Haven CT 1968-1971. Int Mnstry Ntwk 1987-2002. nichnak@aol.com

NICHOLSON, Donald Robert (HB) 104 42nd St. NW, Bradenton FL 34209 B Hartford CT 5/19/1935 s Robert Nicholson & Mary. BA GW 1960; STB Ya Berk 1964; DMin Acad of Chinese Healing Arts Sarasota FL 1999. D 6/22/1964 P 6/3/1965 Bp Harry Lee Doll. m 11/27/2004 Beverly Hunt c 2. Int Gd Samar Epis Ch Clearwater FL 2008-2009; Asst Chr Ch Bradenton FL 1997-2006; Dio Wstrn Massachusetts Springfield MA 1968-1970; Asst S Ptr's Ch Springfield MA 1968-1970; Ch Of The H Sprt 1966-1968; Dio Maryland Baltimore MD 1964-1966. nicholosondr@mac.com

NICHOLSON, Kedron Jarvis (Ala) 113 Madison Ave, Montgomery AL 36104 B Columbus GA 5/4/1977 d Michael Andrew Jarvis & Eleanor Drake. BA U GA 1998; MDiv VTS 2002. Trans 9/29/2003 Bp J(ohn) Neil Alexander. Assoc R S Jn's Ch Montgomery AL 2008-2011; Gr Ch The Plains VA 2006-2008; Epis Ch Cntr New York NY 2005-2006; S Tim's Ch Herndon VA 2003-2005; Asst H Innoc Ch Atlanta GA 2002-2003. VTS Alum Exec Coun 2008-2010. kedronnicholson@gmail.com

NICHOLSON, Wayne Philip (WMich) 405 E High St, Mount Pleasant MI 48858 **R S Jn's Ch Mt Pleasant MI 2006-** B Los Angeles CA 7/31/1948 s Eugene Nicholson & Shirley. BA U of Washington 1971; MDiv GTS 2002. D 6/1/2002 Bp William Edwin Swing P 12/7/2002 Bp Catherine Scimeca Roskam. m William Denison Kelley. P-in-c S Paul's Ch Chester NY 2002-2006. revwayne@mac.com

NICKEL, Rebecca (Ind) St. Timothy's Episcopal Church 2601 E. Thompson Road, Indianapolis IN 46227 **P-in-c S Tim's Ch Indianapolis IN 2011-** B McPherson KS 12/7/1957 d John William Ferrell & Claudine May. AA Cntrl Coll 1978; BA Azusa Pacific U 1980; MDiv Fuller TS 1986; Iliff TS 1997. D 6/6/1998 P 12/16/1998 Bp William Jerry Winterrowd. m 7/24/1981 David Nickel c 2. Vic S Steph's Elwood IN 2008-2011; P-in-c H Fam Ch Angola IN 2007; Dio Nthrn Indiana So Bend IN 2004-2006; R Trin Ch Ft Wayne IN 2001-2004; Assoc S Jn's Epis Ch Boulder CO 1999-2000; Cur S Andr's Ch Denver CO 1998-1999. rjfnickel@gmail.com

NICKELSON, Jay Victor (At) 870 Winnbrook Dr, Dacula GA 30019 B Atlanta GA 8/15/1923 s Ansel Lorenzo Nickelson & Ella Rutherford. BA Emory U 1947; BD UTS 1950. D 4/7/1951 Bp John M Walker Jr P 10/8/1951 Bp Edwin A Penick. m 6/16/1945 Mary Bell c 4. S Edw's Epis Ch Lawrenceville GA 1998-2001; Bp's Chapl S Edw's Epis Ch Lawrenceville GA 1989-1997; S Anth's Epis Ch Winder GA 1974-1988; S Edw's Epis Ch Lawrenceville GA 1972-1976; Vic Ch Of The Medtr Washington GA 1950-1952; Vic S Alb's Ch Elberton GA 1950-1952. Bro of S Andr. Omicron Delta Kappa (Mu Chapt). mjandv@msn.com

NICKELSON, Marian Lorraine (Ak) PO Box 8525, Nikiski AK 99635 **Co - Vic S Augustines' Epis Ch Homer AK 2002-; D S Fran By The Sea Ch Kenai AK 1997-** B Livingston MT 11/21/1937 d H Lawrence Carpenter & Ruby Ellen. Montana St U 1957; BS Montana St U 1960; MS Montana St U 1969. D 5/15/1997 Bp A(lbert) Theodore Eastman. m 11/25/1960 Ray Clifford Nickelson. No Amer Assn of Deaconate. dmpbd@acsalaska.net

NICKERSON, Audra M (WMich) 141 Broad St N, Battle Creek MI 49017 **D Dio Wstrn Michigan Kalamazoo MI 1986-** B Marshall MI 10/28/1926 d Blaine Willard Hatch & Mabel Adah. BA MI SU 1948. D 5/3/1986 Bp Howard Samuel Meeks. m 1/6/1951 Ralph Dale Nickerson c 1. Ord Of S Ben.

NICKERSON, Bruce Edward (Mass) 77 South Rd, Bedford MA 01730 B Boston MA 6/8/1938 s Bernard Everett Nickerson & Edith Estelle. AS Tufts U 1960; BA Tufts U 1965; MA NEU 1967; PhD Indiana U 1976. D 6/23/1990 Bp George Nelson Hunt III. m 9/1/1973 Joanna Gay Doob. D S Barth's Ch Cambridge MA 2000-2009; D Chr Ch Somerville MA 1991-2002; D S Jas Epis Ch At Woonsocket Woonsocket RI 1990-1991. NAAD; Soc Of S Jn The Evang. JBIV4338@verizon.net

NICKERSON JR, Donald Albert (Me) Po Box 855, Intervale NH 03845 B Boston MA 5/19/1939 s Donald Albert Nickerson & Mildred. BS Springfield Coll Springfield MA 1961; STB Ya Berk 1964. D 6/20/1964 Bp Anson Phelps Stokes Jr P 6/4/1965 Bp John Melville Burgess. m 8/25/1962 Susan M Martin c 3. Epis Ch Cntr New York NY 1989-1998; Exec & Secy Off New York NY 1986-1988; Ex Coun Dio Maine Portland ME 1982-1986; Liaison To Trien Com Wrld Mssn Com Epis Ch Cntr New York NY 1982-1985; R S Paul's Ch Brunswick ME 1974-1986; Stndg Com Dio New Hampshire Concord NH 1973-1974; R Chr Ch No Conway NH 1966-1974; Cur Trin Ch Newton Cntr MA 1964-1966. padresway@aol.com

NICKLES, Amanda Lynn (Fla) PO Box 10472, Tallahassee FL 32302 **Gr Mssn Ch Tallahassee FL 2010-** B Columbia SC 9/17/1956 d Robert J Nickles & Carole Barbara. MDiv TESM 2003. Trans 3/13/2004 Bp Robert William Duncan. c 2. R The Ch Of The Gd Shpd Canajoharie NY 2004-2009. panickles@gmail.com

NICKLES, Brenda Joyce (Alb) 12 Woodbridge Ave., Chatham NY 12037 B Catskill, NY 2/5/1953 d Herbert C Scott & Helen B. D 5/10/2008 Bp William Howard Love. c 3. brendanickles2000@yahoo.com

NICKLES, Megan Woods (Wyo) 349 N Douglas St, Powell WY 82435 **S Jn's Ch Powell WY 2005-** B Powell WY 4/15/1964 d William Woods & Dolores. BA U of Wyoming 1986. D 6/30/2005 P 2/10/2006 Bp Bruce Edward Caldwell. m 8/19/1989 Lloyd Steven Nickles c 3. mnickles@bresnan.net

NICKSON, Donald Monroe (SO) 3812 Floral Ave, Norwood OH 45212 B Buffalo NY 6/29/1924 s Thomas Barrow Nickson & Agnes. BA SUNY 1949; GTS 1952. D 6/9/1952 P 12/1/1952 Bp Lauriston L Scaife. m 9/22/1947 Billie Rathgber. Epis Ret HmInc. Cincinnati OH 1985-1990; Dio Sthrn Ohio Cincinnati OH 1975-1990; St Marks Ch Cincinnati OH 1955-1986; Asst S Chrys's Ch Chicago IL 1952-1955. melvin381@webtv.com

NICOLL, Thomas Eugene (NY) 4 Fountain Sq, Larchmont NY 10538 **R S Jn's Ch Larchmont NY 1993-** B Greenville SC 5/16/1953 s Ernest Eugene Nicoll & Mary Jo. BA Davidson Coll 1975; MA U of Virginia 1981; MDiv GTS 1982. D 6/12/1982 P 5/21/1983 Bp William Arthur Beckham. m 8/7/1982 Mary F Forbes c 2. Assoc Chr Ch Charlotte NC 1990-1993; Vic H Trin Epis Ch Baltimore MD 1984-1989; Asst Chr Epis Ch Charlottesville VA 1982-1984. Omicrom Delta Kappa; Phi Beta Kappa. tenicoll@optonline.net

NICOLOSI, Gary Garbriel (Nwk) St. James Westminster Church, 115 Askin Street, London ON V6C 1E7 Canada B Brooklyn NY 7/2/1950 s Joseph Nicolosi & Carol Toia. BA Ford 1972; MA Geo 1973; JD Tem 1976; MDiv U Tor

1983; DMin Pittsburgh TS 1997. Trans from Anglican Church of Canada 4/16/1985 Bp William George Burrill. c 1. R S Ptr's Ch Morristown NJ 2005-2007; R S Barth's Epis Ch Poway CA 1997-2005; R S Thos Ch Lancaster PA 1990-1997; Cn For Mnrtrs Cathd Ch Of The Nativ Bethlehem PA 1987-1990; R Gr Ch Scottsville NY 1985-1987; R S Andr's Epis Ch Caledonia NY 1985-1987. Auth, "Come Hm Again," *The Angl Journ*, 2011; Auth, "The Sprtl Compass of the Ch," *The Angl Journ*, 2011; Auth, "One Chr's Perspective on Norway," *The Angl Journ*, 2011; Auth, "The Case For Open Comm," *The Angl Journ*, 2011; Auth, "What Steve Jobs Can Teach the Ch," *The Angl Journ / ENS*, 2011; Auth, "Anxious Times Demand a Courageous Response," *Networking*, 2009. gary.nicolosi@gmail.com

NIEHAUS, Thomas Kenneth (WNC) 12503 N Woodberry Dr, Mequon WI 53092 **R Emer S Thos Epis Ch Burnsville NC 2004-** B Cincinnati OH 8/3/1939 s Sylvester Joseph Niehaus & Lucille. BA Xavier U 1963; MA U Cinc 1964; PhD U of Texas 1976; MLS U of Texas 1976; MDiv STUSo 1993. D 7/10/1993 Bp James Barrow Brown P 1/1/1994 Bp Robert Hodges Johnson. m 6/13/1964 Julia Loftus c 2. Dioc Ecum Off Dio Wstrn No Carolina Asheville NC 1998-2004; R S Thos Epis Ch Burnsville NC 1997-2003; S Jn's Ch Sylva NC 1993-1997. Auth, "Liberation Theol," *Encyclopedia of Latin Amer Hist*, Chas Scribner's Sons, 1993; "Cath Rt in Contemp. Brazil," *Rel in Latin Amer. Life & Liter.*, Baylor U Press, 1980; "Lorenzo Hervas y Panduro, S.J.," *Archivum historicum Societatis Iesu*, Rome: Jesuit Hist Soc, 1975. Fulbright Prof Cntrl U of Venezuela Caracas Venezuela 1983; Fulbright Schlr (grad Stdt) U of Madrid, Spain Madrid Spain 1967. tomniehaus@gmail.com

NIELSEN III, Peter W (O) 5811 Vrooman Rd, Painesville OH 44077 **Cedar Hills C&C Painesville OH 2004-; Dio Ohio Cleveland OH 2004-** B Darby PA 3/5/1955 s Peter W Nielsen & Lois Anne. RBA Shpd Coll Shepherdstown WV 1989. D 11/13/2004 Bp Mark Hollingsworth Jr. m 6/28/1975 Laura J Grant c 4. ECCC, Inc. 1987. cedarhills@dohio.org

NIEMAN, John S (USC) 193 Old Greenville Highway, Clemson SC 29631 **R H Trin Par Epis Clemson SC 2006-; S Paul's Pendleton Clemson SC 2006-** B Passaic NJ 8/5/1959 s Thomas Nieman & Audrey. BA Drew U 1984; MDiv Harvard DS 1987. D 5/30/1987 P 12/12/1987 Bp John Shelby Spong. m 7/28/1984 Margaret Lynn Snider c 1. R S Andr's Ch Ann Arbor MI 1997-2006; R S Mary's Ch Sparta NJ 1993-1997; R S Dunst's Ch Ellsworth ME 1990-1993; Cur S Eliz's Ch Ridgewood NJ 1987-1989. Auth, *Epis Life*. Phi Beta Kappa 1983. jnieman2@bellsouth.net

NIEMEYER, John D (Va) 501 W Nine Mile Rd, Highland Springs VA 23075 **Co-Chair, Com on Race Relatns Dio Virginia Richmond VA 2009-; Vic Trin Ch Highland Sprg VA 2008-** B Hattiesburg MS 12/23/1953 s Carl Fred Niemeyer & Betty Sue Avery. B.S. Acctg U of Sthrn Mississippi 1977; M. Div. St. Meinrad Sem 1982; M.A. Liturg U of Notre Dame 1986; M.S. M.F.T. U of St. Thos 1994. Rec from Roman Catholic 6/7/2008 Bp Peter James Lee. m 5/20/1989 Arielle F Niemeyer c 2. Amer Assn of Mar and Fam Ther 1993; Virginia Assn of Mar and Fam Ther 2002. therev.jdavidniemeyer@gmail.com

NIESE JR, Alfred Moring (NJ) 269 Montsweag Rd, Woolwich ME 04579 B New York NY 9/12/1937 s Alfred M Niese & Anne Louise. BA Rutgers-The St U 1959; STB GTS 1963; STM NYTS 1971. D 6/8/1963 P 12/21/1963 Bp Leland Stark. m 2/5/1966 Brenda Anne Munch c 2. Int S Aug's Epis Ch Dover Foxcroft ME 1999-2001; Pres Stndg Com Dio New Jersey Trenton NJ 1996-1997; Chair Dioc Com for Unified Bdgt Dio New Jersey Trenton NJ 1991-1992; Chair Dio Bdgt Com Dio New Jersey Trenton NJ 1989-1990; Dioc Fndt Dio New Jersey Trenton NJ 1985-1990; Chair D Polity Com Dio New Jersey Trenton NJ 1984-1985; R Ch of S Jn on the Mtn Bernardsville NJ 1980-1997; Chr Ch Short Hills NJ 1976-1980; Ch Of The Atone Fair Lawn NJ 1967-1976; Asst Trin And S Phil's Cathd Newark NJ 1963-1967. AAPC 1975-1985. R Emer Ch of St. Jn on the Mtn 2002. aniese@suscom-maine.net

NIETERT, Jack Frederick (SC) 2830 W Royal Oaks Dr, Beaufort SC 29902 **P All SS Ch Hilton Hd Island SC 2009-** B New York NY 7/27/1941 s Rudolph Albert Nietert & Elsa. BA Hob 1963; MDiv GTS 1966. D 6/16/1966 P 12/21/1966 Bp Jonathan Goodhue Sherman. m 6/23/1990 Christina Nelson c 4. All SS Epis Ch Hampton SC 1998; Int S Jas Ch Charleston SC 1998; R Ch Of The Gd Shpd Kansas City MO 1989-1998; Assoc S Andr's Ch Mt Pleasant SC 1975-1989; R Gr Ch Hastings On Hudson NY 1974-1975; R Zion Ch Dobbs Ferry NY 1969-1975; Asst S Jas Ch Hyde Pk NY 1966-1969. Hon Cn, Gr and H Trin Cathd Kansas City MO 1997. jcnietert@hargray.com

NILSEN, Stan (LI) 31 Patchogue Ave, Mastic NY 11950 **Died 10/23/2009** B Brooklyn NY 3/15/1933 s Nilmar Nilsen & Gudren. BBA Pace Coll 1963; Cert Mercer Hosp Sch of Nrsng 1968. D 6/15/1968 P 12/1/1968 Bp Jonathan Goodhue Sherman. c 2.

NIPPS, Leslie (Cal) 592 Jean St #202, Oakland CA 94610 B Mount Kisco NY 12/12/1963 d John William Nipps & Helen Firman. BA Cor 1987; MDiv GTS 1994. D 6/4/1995 P 12/16/1995 Bp Joe Morris Doss. S Mich And All Ang Concord CA 2003-2006; Dir Of Fam And Chld'S Mnstrs S Greg Of Nyssa Ch San Francisco CA 2001-2003; Asst S Mk's Epis Ch Toledo OH 1998-2001; Vic Ch Of The H Sprt Tuckerton NJ 1995-1998. Auth, "Practical Postmodernism For Parishes," 'Open'. AP, 2001. Coun Mem AP (Aplm) 2001. lnipps@gmail.com

NISBETT, Joshua Mastine (LI) 11738 Cross Island Pkwy, Cambria Heights NY 11411 **R S Dav's Epis Ch Cambria Heights NY 1985-** B Nevis West Indies 9/10/1946 s Clarence Mastine Nisbett & Alice Maude. BA Untd Theol 1975. D 6/29/1974 P 7/1/1975 Bp The Bishop Of Antigua. m 12/4/1976 Enid Fay Gabbidon c 3. fatherjmn@hotmail.com

NISSEN, Peter Boy (WK) 312 S Kansas Ave, Norton KS 67654 **S Andr's Ch Hays Hays KS 1999-** B Seattle WA 11/29/1946 s Boy Andreas Nissen & Roma Caldwell. BA U of British Columbia 1969; MDiv Vancouver TS 1973. P 5/1/1975 Bp Furman Stough. Serv Ch Of The Epiph Concordia KS 1996-1998; Vic Trin Epis Ch Norton KS 1993-1996; Off Of Bsh For ArmdF New York NY 1980-1993; Assoc S Mk's Epis Ch Casper WY 1979-1980. boyandreas@hotmail.com

NISSING, Douglas (Ct) PO Box 300189, University City MO 63130 B Saint Louis MO 11/20/1960 s Burton John Nissing & Mary Ann. BA Rice U 1983; MDiv GTS 1988; Cert Blanton-Peale Grad Inst 1994; MBA S Louis U 2012. D 6/11/1988 Bp William Augustus Jones Jr P 2/1/1989 Bp Jeffery William Rowthorn. m 8/4/1991 Daniel John Kelly. Vic Calv St Geo's Epis Ch Bridgeport CT 2001-2008; Int Zion Epis Ch No Branford CT 1993-1994; Asst S Mk's Ch New Britain CT 1988-1991. AAPC. douglas@nissing.com

NITZ, Theodore Allen (Spok) 2300 NW Ridgeline Drive, Pullman WA 99163 **Archd Dio Spokane Spokane WA 2003-; Archd S Jas Pullman WA 1991-** B Oakland CA 5/6/1946 s Jack Henry Nitz & Beverly Jane. BA U of Washington 1968; MA WA SU 1975; PhD WA SU 1999. D 9/26/1982 Bp Harold Anthony Hopkins Jr. m 8/16/1970 Sharon Ann Krause c 2. Asst Dio No Dakota Fargo ND 1988-1991; D/Asst S Geo's Epis Ch Summerville SC 1988-1991; D/Asst Zion Ch Rome NY 1984-1988; Asst Geth Cathd Fargo ND 1982-1984. "Messengers, Agents, and Attendants: Deacons in the Body of Chr," *Diakoneo*, 2006; "Commentary on New D Cn w Ormonde Plater," *Diakoneo*, 2003. HSEC 1994; NAAD 1982. ted_nitz@hotmail.com

NIX JR, William Dale (NwT) 11355 Nix Ranch Road, Canadian TX 79014 B Amarillo TX 6/9/1941 s William Dale Nix & Mary Alice. CDSP 1963; BA Texas A&M U 1963; MDiv Epis TS of The SW 1975. D 6/7/1975 P 6/18/1976 Bp Willis Ryan Henton. m 8/3/1963 Nelwyn H Hermann c 3. Panhandle Reg Mssnr Dio NW Texas Lubbock TX 2000-2004; Joint Stndg Cmsn on Prog Bdgt & Fin Epis Ch Cntr New York NY 1994-2003; Dio NW Texas Lubbock TX 1993-1996; R S Andr's Epis Ch Amarillo TX 1992-2000; Dn All SS' Epis Ch Ft Worth TX 1986-1992; Cn to the Ordnry Dio NW Texas Lubbock TX 1981-1986; COM Dio NW Texas Lubbock TX 1978-1981; R S Steph's Ch Lubbock TX 1977-1981; Cur S Jn's Epis Ch Odessa TX 1975-1977; Epis TS Of The SW Austin TX 1970-1971. OSB 1993; Ord of St. Jn of Jerusalem 1987. Hon Cn Dio NW Texas 1986; Who's Who in Rel 1985. wdnix@nixranch.com

NIXON, Barbara Elizabeth (Ct) 445 Spinnaker Way, Sacramento CA 95831 **S Lk's Ch Galt CA 2005-** B Detroit MI 8/3/1954 d Glenn Curry Nixon & Irma Mary. BA Kirkland (Hamilton) Coll 1976; MA Col 1981; Dip. Chr Stud 1983; Dip. Chr Stud. Regent Coll Vancouver BC CA 1983; Dip.Ang.Stds Ya Berk 1987; MDiv Yale DS 1987. D 6/13/1987 Bp Arthur Edward Walmsley P 6/17/1989 Bp William Bradford Hastings. m 1/10/1998 James R Wirrell. Assoc All SS Meml Sacramento CA 2003-2005; Int Varina Epis Ch Richmond VA 2000-2001; S Chris's Sch Richmond VA 1998-2000; Assoc R S Paul's Ch Fairfield CT 1994; Dio Ottawa 1992; Asst S Jn's Epis Ch Vernon Rock Vernon CT 1990-1992; Asst Calv Ch Danvers MA 1989; S Paul's Sch Concord NH 1987-1988. Curs 1989. "Who's Who In Amer Wmn". barb_nixon@hotmail.com

NIXON, James Thomas (At) 2700 Bennington Dr Ne, Marietta GA 30062 **R S Cathr's Epis Ch Marietta GA 1998-** B Kingston PA 4/25/1948 s James Nixon & Constance Caroline. Ame Penn 1968; BD U Cinc 1980; MDiv STUSo 1990. D 5/26/1990 Bp John M Allin P 3/16/1991 Bp Alex Dockery Dickson. m 5/22/1971 Joan Anita Lange c 2. Vic Gr Epis Ch New Lenox IL 1992-1998; S Thos The Apos Humboldt TN 1990-1992. Woods Ldrshp Awd U So Sewanee TN 1988. fatherjim@bellsouth.net

NIXON, Thomas E (CGC) 1580Deese Road, Ozark AL 36360 **Vic S Mich's Ch Ozark AL 2007-** B Batavia NY 11/2/1948 s Donald O Nixon & Janet G. BA SUNY 1973; Med Bos 1976; MDiv EDS 1976; DMin STUSo 1996. D 9/25/1982 P 8/1/1983 Bp Charles Farmer Duvall. c 2. Ch Of The Epiph Enterprise AL 1992-1995; S Mich's Ch Ozark AL 1982-1991. revdr112@juno.com

NOALL, Nancy J(o) (WA) 312 Hillmoor Dr, Silver Spring MD 20901 B Clarksburg WV 7/8/1936 d Joseph Lawrence Flowers & Mabel. Kent St U 1957; LTh VTS 1981. D 6/20/1981 Bp John Thomas Walker P 1/6/1982 Bp William Benjamin Spofford. m 7/20/1957 William Frederick Noall c 3. R S Paul's Epis Ch Piney Waldorf MD 2000-2006; P-in-c S Mk's Ch Fairland Silver Sprg MD 1998-2000; Int S Jn's Epis Ch Zion Par Beltsville MD 1995-1997; Int S Tim's Ch Herndon VA 1990-1994; Int S Mk's Ch Alexandria VA 1987-1989; Asst S Paul's Epis Ch Alexandria VA 1981-1987. nancynoall@aol.com

NOBLE, Mitzi McAlexander (WA) 508 Tranquility Rd., Moneta VA 24121 B Kingsport TN 2/6/1941 d Buren McAlexander & Ruby. RBA Shpd Coll Shepherdstown WV 1985; How 1988; Wesley TS 1988; MDiv GTS 1990. D 6/15/1991 Bp Ronald Hayward Haines P 12/21/1991 Bp Orris George Walker Jr. m 6/29/1957 Paul Benjamin Noble c 2. P-in-c S Barn' Epis Ch of The Deaf Chevy Chase MD 1998-2001; Liturg Advsr, Chap of the H Sprt Dio Washington Washington DC 1998-1999; P-in-c H Sprt Epis Ch Gaithersburg MD 1998-1999; R Trin Ch Lakeville CT 1993-1998; Asst S Jn's Of Lattingtown Locust Vlly NY 1990-1993. Auth, *Planned Giving Bklet*. Angl-Luth Soc; The Angl Soc. pmnoble@earthlink.net

NOBLE, Tony (SanD) 625 Pennsylvania Ave, San Diego CA 92103 B Australia 5/18/1947 s Norman Moreton Noble & Alice June. BTh St. Barn Coll Australia 1978. R All SS Ch San Diego CA 2003-2011. Ord of St Corentin 1995; SSC 1980; SSM 1998; Shrine of Our Lady of Walsingham 1980. frtonynoble@ymail.com

NOBLE, William C. (NJ) 1941 Wayside Rd, Tinton Falls NJ 07724 B Vidalia GA 7/29/1940 s Bennett Arthur Noble & Lucy Swearingen. BA U So 1962; MDiv GTS 1969; MS USC 1980; DMin GTF 1995; Cert Postgraduate Cntr For Mntl Hlth New York NY 2002; Cert Blanton-Peale Grad Inst 2006; Cert Blanton-Peale Grad Inst 2006; Psy.D. GTF 2010. D 6/14/1969 P 3/8/1970 Bp Albert R Stuart. m 6/19/1976 Liliane G Guyon c 4. P-in-c S Jas Memi Ch Eatontown NJ 1997-2002; Exec Asst To Bp Armdf Epis Ch Cntr New York NY 1995-2002; Off Of Bsh For ArmdF New York NY 1975-1995; Chapl S Barn' Ch Leeland Upper Marlboro MD 1972-1975; Vic Trin Ch Statesboro GA 1970-1972; Cur S Paul's Ch Albany GA 1969-1970. Auth, "'Reflections On A Vision," *Journ Of Rel And Hlth*, Blanton-Peale Inst, 2003; Auth, "In The Shadow Of Death," *A New Conversation*, Ch Publilshing Co, 2001; Auth, "arts And Bk Revs," *LivCh*, LivCh, 1985; Auth, "A Theol Of Mnstry," *Mltry Chapl Revs*, 1982. Amer Assn Of Mar And Fam Therapists 2002; AAPC 2002; APA 2009; Natl Assn for the Advancement of Psychoanalysis 2006. wcnoble@aol.com

NOBOA VITERI, Eugenio (EcuC) Casilla 0901-5250, Guayaquil Ecuador **Vic Iglesia San Marcus 24ava y la O Guayas EC 1984-; Vic Iglesia San Pedro Guayaquil EC 1984-; Vic Iglesia Todos los Santos 25ava y la S Guayaquil EC 1984-** B Parroquia Simon Bolivar EC 11/15/1955 s Terencio Noboa & Ninfa. D 12/16/1984 Bp Adrian Delio Caceres-Villavicencio P 6/1/1992 Bp Martiniano Garcia-Montiel. Litoral Dio Ecuador Guayaquil EQ EC 1991-2008.

NOCHER, Janet Gregoire (FtW) 4408 Foxfire Way, Fort Worth TX 76133 **COM Dio Ft Worth Ft Worth TX 2008-; ER-D Dioc Chair Dio Ft Worth Ft Worth TX 2008-; Epis Relief & Dvlpmt Chair Dio Ft Worth Ft Worth TX 2008-; D Trin Epis Ch Ft Worth TX 2000-** B Miami FL 3/1/1940 d Louis Bernard Gregoire & Sarah Irene. U Of Florida 1960; Angl TS, Dallas, TX 1995. D 6/5/1996 Bp Jack Leo Iker. m 10/27/1962 John Nocher c 2. COM for the Diac Dio Ft Worth Ft Worth TX 1996-2008; D S Chris's Ch And Sch Ft Worth TX 1996-2000. janet.nocher@sbcglobal.net

NOE, Thomas Darst (EC) Sitter and Barfoot Veteran Care Ctr, 1601 Broadrock Boulevard, Richmond VA 23224 B Wilmington NC 1/26/1923 s Walter Raleigh Noe & Sallie London. E Carolina U; Epis TS In Kentucky; U NC 1964; Campbell U 1973; U Rich 1976; Berea Coll 1985. D 12/8/1984 Bp Addison Hosea P 6/1/1985 Bp Brice Sidney Sanders. c 4. P-in-c S Jn's And S Mk's Grifton NC 1989-2004; P-in-c S Paul's Ch Vanceboro NC 1989-2004; P-in-c S Aug's Epis Ch Kinston NC 1988-1989; P-in-c S Cyp's Ch New Bern NC 1988-1989; P-in-c S Marys Epis Ch Burgaw NC 1985-1988; Asst R Chr Ch Cathd Louisville KY 1984-1986. ncborn52@gmail.com

NOE, William Stanton (Va) Po Box 2078, Ashland VA 23005 B Greenville NC 12/7/1929 s Alexander Constantine Davis Noe & Sarah Elizabeth. U Vienna 1953; BA U So 1954; U Heidelberg DE 1955; MDiv STUSo 1961; PhD U of Virginia 1973. D 6/21/1961 P 3/1/1962 Bp Thomas H Wright. m 11/27/1964 Anita Christie Rabe. P-in-c Ch Of Our Sav Montpelier VA 1964-1984; P-in-c Ch of the Incarn Mineral VA 1963-1964; Vic S Ptr's By-The-Sea Swansboro NC 1961-1963. wmstantonnoe@juno.com

NOEL, Virginia Lee (Mo) 15826 Clayton Rd Apt 131, Ellisville MO 63011 B Little Rock AR 2/14/1934 d William Roscoe Lee & Mabel Virginia. BS U of Wisconsin 1957; MDiv Nash 1977; ABD S Louis U 1989. D 4/16/1977 Bp Charles Thomas Gaskell P 2/16/1980 Bp Robert Marshall Anderson. c 4. Cn Chr Ch Cathd S Louis MO 1984-1986; Screening Com Dio Minnesota Minneapolis MN 1980-1984; S Andr's Ch Milwaukee WI 1977-1979. Auth, "Darkness," *Plumbline*, 1977; Auth, "Mysticism: Its Relatns to Other Spiritualities," *Nashotah Revs*, 1976. Ord of S Helena, Assoc 1984. veelee03@yahoo.com

NOETZEL, Joan Lois (SeFla) 7300 W Lake Dr, West Palm Beach FL 33406 B Rye NY 12/3/1932 d Corneilius Graham VanderFeen & Joan H. BA Palm Bch Atlantic Coll; AA Lasell Coll 1952. D 11/27/1987 Bp Calvin Onderdonk Schofield Jr. m 10/1/1955 Everett Llewellyn Noetzel. D H Trin Epis Ch W Palm Bch FL 1987-2002.

NOISY HAWK SR, Lyle Maynard (SD) Po Box 257, Kyle, SD 57752 B Fort Yates ND 5/2/1942 CTh Nash 1973; BA So Dakota St U 2000; MS So Dakota St U 2004. D 6/15/1973 P 12/21/1974 Bp Walter H Jones. m 1/1/1966 Mary Emily Last Horse c 4. S Lk's Veblen Brookings SD 2000-2002; Geth Epis Ch Sisseton SD 1995-2000; S Lk's Sta Sisseton SD 1995-2000; Vic Bp Whipple Mssn Morton MN 1990-1995; Dio Minnesota Minneapolis MN 1990-1995; S Thos Ch Mssn SD 1990-1995; Dio Colorado Denver CO 1989-1990; Vic Living Waters Ch Denver CO 1989-1990; Geth Epis Ch Mart SD 1988-1989; Vic S Matt's Epis Ch Rapid City SD 1976-1989; Dio So Dakota Sioux Falls SD 1973-1999; Pine Ridge Mssn Mart SD 1973-1976. Fam of the Year SDSU/Alumini 2001. lmnoisyhawk@yahoo.com

NOLAN, Richard Thomas (Ct) 451 Heritage Drive, Apt 1014, Pompano Beach FL 33060 B Waltham MA 5/30/1937 s Thomas Michael Nolan & Elizabeth Louise. BA Trin Hartford CT 1959; MDiv Hartford Sem 1963; MA Ya 1967; PhD NYU 1973; Harv 1991. D 6/29/1963 Bp John Melville Burgess P 6/1/1965 Bp Frederic Cunningham Lawrence. m 6/4/2009 Robert C Pingpank. Ret P-in-res S Andr's Ch Lake Worth FL 2002-2004; Ret Hon Life Cn Chr Ch Cathd Hartford CT 1994-2004; Vic S Paul's Epis Ch Bantam CT 1974-1988; D Cathd Of St Jn The Div New York NY 1963-1964. Ed, "Soul Mates: More Than Partnr," *online Ed*, www.nolan-pingpank.com, 2004; "The Diac Now," *online Ed*, Corpus/Wrld, 2002; Auth, "Living Issues In Ethics," *online Ed*, iUniverse, 2002; Ed, "Living Issues in Ethics," *revised Ed*, iUniverse, 2000; Ed, "www.Philos-Rel.org," *www.Philos-Rel.org*, online educational website, 2000; Ed, "Living Issues In Philos," *9th Ed*, Oxford, 1995; Auth, "Living Issues in Ethics," *Chinese Ed*, Huaxia, 1988; Ed, "Living Issues In Philos," *8th Ed*, Wadsworth, 1986; Ed, "Living Issues In Philos," *Indonesian Ed*, PT Bulan Bintang, 1984; "Living Issues in Ethics," *1st Ed*, Wadsworth, 1982; Auth, "Living Issues In Philos," *7th Ed*, Wadsworth, 1979; "The Diac Now," *1st Ed*, Corpus/Wrld, 1968. AAR 1965; Amer Philos Assn 1965; Angl Assn of Biblic Scholars 1998; Hemlock Soc of Florida 1994; Integrity, Inc 1980; Interfaith Allnce 2000; Lambda Legal 2001. Soc of Rgnts Cathd of S Jn the Div 2004. canon@rtnolan.com

NOLAND, Elisabeth Hooper (RG) No address on file. **D Epis Ch Of The H Fam Santa Fe NM 2004-** B Waltham MA 6/27/1939 d Richard Hooper & Katharine. Goucher Coll; BA Trin TS Albuquerque NM. D 7/28/2001 Bp Terence Kelshaw. m 6/27/1987 Charles Donald Noland c 1. ehnoland@aol.com

NOLTA, Hugh Gregg (NCal) 556 E Sycamore St, Willows CA 95988 B Willows CA 2/10/1942 s Dale E Nolta & Gretchen Eileen. D 10/30/2010 P 7/9/2011 Bp Barry Leigh Beisner. m 6/28/1971 Vicki Ann Nolta c 3. gnolta@digitalpath.net

NOON, Anna Catherine Christian (SVa) 100 W Queens Way, Hampton VA 23669 **Assisant R S Jn's Ch Hampton VA 2010-** B Springfield TN 7/25/1970 d Dennis Allen Noon & Carol Schutz. BA The U So (Sewanee) 1992; MDiv The GTS 2010. D 6/12/2010 P 12/18/2010 Bp Herman Hollerith IV. anna-noon@verizon.net

N

NOONAN, Deborah Anne (Az) 2331 E. Adams St., Tucson AZ 85719 **Asst Dio Arizona Phoenix AZ 2010-; Cn Trin Cathd Phoenix AZ 2010-** B Panorama City CA 7/19/1979 d John Thomas Noonan & Catherine Louise. BA U of Virginia 2001; MDIV Ya Berk 2010. D 6/6/2009 P 7/10/2010 Bp Kirk Stevan Smith. debbienoonan@yahoo.com

NORBY, Laura L (Mil) 508 Rupert Rd, Waunakee WI 53597 B Kankakee IL 2/9/1949 d Lloyd W Verhoeks & Jeanine G. BA Wartburg Coll 1971; MA Peabody Coll 1972; EDS Peabody Coll 1973; A.D.N Maysville Cmnty and Tech Coll 1978. D 6/5/1993 Bp Roger John White. m 11/1/1983 Terry Raymond Norby. D Dio Milwaukee Milwaukee WI 1993-2003. ll.norby@hosp.wisc.edu

NORCROSS, Stephen Carl (Ore) 8949 SW Fairview Pl, Portland OR 97223 B Charleston WV 12/29/1941 s Robert Norcross & Helen F. BA W Virginia U 1963; MDiv SMU 1966; Cert CDSP 1968; Fllshp STUSo 1975; Fllshp VTS 1998. D 8/5/1968 P 5/15/1969 Bp Ivol I Curtis. m 10/19/1985 Sandra Norcross c 2. P-in-c Ascen Par Portland OR 2004-2011; Int S Jn's Epis Ch Olympia WA 2002-2003; Chapl Wm Temple Hse Portland OR 2002; Int All SS Ch Hillsboro OR 1999-2002; R S Mart's Ch Lebanon OR 1991-1999; Int Epis Par Of S Mich And All Ang Tucson AZ 1987-1988; R S Mk's Ch Havre MT 1983-1987; R Meade Memi Epis Ch Alexandria VA 1980-1983; Int S Jas Epis Ch Westernport MD 1975-1976; R Ch Of The Gd Shpd Charleston WV 1972-1974; Assoc Chr Ch Tacoma WA 1970-1972; Cur S Jn's Epis Ch Olympia WA 1968-1970. Auth, *The Bivocational Option*, The Sm Ch / Alb Institue, 2000; Auth, *Var arts Hymnody & Ch Mus*. ADLMC; CBS 1975; EPF 1968; Integrity 1980; OHC 1972. snorx@hevanet.com

NORDQUIST, Conrad (Los) 4063 Ruis Ct, Riverside CA 92509 B Minneapolis MN 7/16/1933 s Conrad Adolph Nordquist & Lucy-Lee Fessenden. BS U MN 1955; LTh SWTS 1959; MA USC 1977. D 6/20/1959 P 12/21/1959 Bp Philip Frederick McNairy. c 3. Asst All SS Epis Ch Riverside CA 2001-2003; R S Jn The Div Epis Ch Costa Mesa CA 1977-2000; Prof The ETS At Claremont Claremont CA 1974-1984; Assoc S Nich Par Encino CA 1965-1978; Asst Chr Ch Las Vegas NV 1963-1964; Cur Ch Of The Mssh Santa Ana CA 1960-1963; Vic S Ptr's Ch Warroad MN 1959-1960. conrad@cnordquist.net

NORDSTROM JR, Eugene Alexander (HB) No address on file. B Portland OR 12/30/1939 s Eugene Alexander Nordstrom & Kathleen Alberta. BA Whitman

Coll 1962; STB ATC 1965; MS U of Washington 1967; DSW USC 1973. D 12/21/1965 Bp Ivol I Curtis. Stff S Lk's Epis Ch Vancouver WA 1967-1969. Auth, "A Study Of Love In Parent-Chld Relationships"; Auth, "Experiment In Upgrading The Nonprofessional Worker".

NORDWICK, Brian Paul (ECR) 670 Clearview Dr, Hollister CA 95023 **Cn for Admin & Fin Dio El Camino Real Monterey CA 2004-** B Medford OR 5/12/1953 s Harry Allen Nordwick & Jeanette Francis. BS California Luth U 1976; BA California Sch for Deacons 1993. D 5/28/1994 Bp Richard Lester Shimpfky. m 3/20/1982 Sheila Marie Donovan c 1. brian@edecr.org

NORGARD, David Lee (Los) PO Box 691458, West Hollywood CA 90069 B Hibbing MN 6/11/1958 s Theodore Ethan Norgard & Gladys Ida. BA Augsburg Coll 1980; MDiv Ya Berk 1983; MAOM Antioch U 2008. D 6/11/1984 P 12/20/1984 Bp Robert Marshall Anderson. m 10/11/2011 Joseph Oppold. Assoc for Congrl Dvlpmt Cathd Ch Of S Paul San Diego CA 2004-2005; VP for Prog Epis Cmnty Serv San Diego CA 2003-2004; Exec Dir Epis Cmnty Serv Inc Minneapolis MN 2000-2003; R The Epis Ch Of S Jn The Evang San Francisco CA 1994-2000; Exec Dir & Mssnr The Oasis Newark NJ 1990-1994; Assoc All SS Epis Par Hoboken NJ 1990-1992; Asst R Ch Of The H Apos New York NY 1985-1990. Awd Of dist Among Recent Graduates Yale DS 1995; Dn'S Citation For Cmnty Serv Berk New Haven CT 1983. davidnorgard@od180.com

NORGREN, William Andrew (NY) 10 Bucks Path, East Hampton NY 11937 B Frostburg MD 5/5/1927 s William Andrew Norgren & Martha Elizabeth. BA W&M 1948; STM GTS 1953; BLitt Oxf 1959. D 5/31/1953 P 12/20/1953 Bp Horace W B Donegan. Theol Consult Epis Ch Cntr New York NY 1995-2000; Ecum Off Epis Ch Cntr New York NY 1979-1994; Assoc Ecum Off Epis Ch Cntr New York NY 1975-1979; Par of Trin Ch New York NY 1972-1974; Asst Ch Of The Resurr Kew Gardens NY 1953-1955; Fell/Tutor The GTS New York NY 1953-1955. Ed, *Ecum of the Possible*, Forw Mvmt Press, 1994; Ed, *Toward Full Commitment & Concordat of Agreement*, Forw Mvmt Press, Augsburg, 1991; Ed, *Implications of the Gospel*, Forw Mvmt Press, Augsburg, 1988; Ed, *Living Room Dialogues*, Paulist Press, Friendship Press, 1965. DD Ya Berk 1995; DD GTS 1984.

NORMAN, Curtis Kemper (FtW) 595 N McIlhaney St, Stephenville TX 76401 **R S Lk's Epis Ch Stephenville TX 2011-** B Norfolk VA 2/25/1969 s Worth Earlwood Norman & Patricia Ann. BA U of No Texas 1996; MDiv STUSo 2001. D 6/9/2001 Bp D(avid) Bruce Mac Pherson P 5/18/2002 Bp James Monte Stanton. m 1/11/2003 Margaret L Link c 2. Ch of the H Faith Santa Fe NM 2009-2011; R S Lk's Ch Denison TX 2004-2009; S Ptr's Epis Ch Del Mar CA 2003-2004; Chr Epis Ch Plano TX 2001-2003. curt.norman@gmail.com

NORMAN, Harold Gene (Dal) 406 Dula Cir., Duncanville TX 75116 B Waco TX 12/24/1927 s Ulma John Norman & Lena. BA U of Texas 1950; MDiv Bex 1954. D 7/2/1954 P 7/1/1955 Bp Clinton Simon Quin. m 2/16/1974 Patsy Vinson c 1. Dept Of Missions Dallas TX 1984-1985; St Gabriels Ch De Soto TX 1975-1986; R S Geo's Epis Ch Dallas TX 1970-1975; R S Barth's Ch Hempstead TX 1956-1960; Cur St Andrews Epis Ch Houston TX 1954-1956. Auth, "Manual Para Lectores Laicos," 1963. normandie406@sbcglobal.net

NORMAN, J(oseph) Gary (Alb) Po Box 800, Morris NY 13808 **D Zion Ch Morris NY 2006-** B Richmond VA 5/28/1959 s Jospeh Henry Norman & Nancy LaVerne. BA U of Virginia 1981; MA W&M 1987. D 6/10/2006 Bp Daniel William Herzog. m 8/15/1987 Stacia Gregory Stacia Guild Gregory c 2. gary@gatehousebooks.net

NORMAN, Lynn (Miss) 302 Vermont Ave, Oak Ridge TN 37830 **Calv Epis Ch Cleveland MS 2009-** B Chattanooga TN 4/21/1979 s Lynn Albert Norman & Suzanne. BA U So 2001; MDiv VTS 2006. D 5/27/2006 P 1/21/2007 Bp Charles Glenn VonRosenberg. m Sara N Norman. Asst S Steph's Epis Ch Oak Ridge TN 2006-2009. bailey@calvaryclevelandms.org

NORMAN JR, Richard Hudson (Minn) 3734 Pleasant Ave, Minneapolis MN 55409 **Cn Liturg Cathd Ch Of S Mk Minneapolis MN 2005-** B Alexandria LA 3/1/1958 s Richard Hudson Norman & Frances Elizabeth Bradford. Wake Forest U 1977; NW St U, Natchitoches 1980; BS LSU 1984; MA LSU 1988; STM GTS 1993; MDiv GTS 1993. D 6/6/1992 P 5/15/1993 Bp Robert Jefferson Hargrove Jr. m 5/29/1993 Adrienne Judith McKee c 2. R Epis Ch Of The Redeem Greenville SC 2002-2005; Assoc R All SS' Epis Ch Chevy Chase MD 1995-1997; S Paul's Ch Abbeville LA 1993-1995; D The Ch of S Matt And S Tim New York NY 1992-1993; Pstr Asst The Amer Cathd of the H Trin Paris 75008 FR 1991-1992. richardn@ourcathedral.org

NORMAND, Ann Dennison (Tex) 1 Hermann Museum Cir Apt 3021, Houston TX 77004 **Cn to the Ordnry Dio Texas Houston TX 2008-** B Beaumont TX 3/4/1942 d George Dennison & Elouise Foley. BS Texas Tech U 1964; Baylor U 1984; MDiv Austin Presb TS 1995; Cert VTS 1995; DMin Austin Presb TS 2001. D 6/17/1995 Bp Claude Edward Payne P 2/18/1996 Bp Leopoldo Jesus Alard. c 3. R Trin Epis Ch Marble Falls TX 1998-2008; Asst to the R S Paul's Ch Waco TX 1995-1998. Auth, "The Vow of Stability: Rooting the Contermporary Epis Par in Benedictine Sprtlty," Austin Presb TS, 2001. Cler Renwl Grant Lilly Endwmt, Inc. 2005; WP Newell Memi Fllshp Austin Presb TS 1995. anormand@epicenter.org

NORMANN, Margaret E(lla) (Monroe) (Ct) 888 B Heritage Vlg, Southbury CT 06488 B Providence RI 1/13/1931 d Parker Edward Monroe & Margaret Millard. BA Vas 1952; MA NYU 1966; MS Sthrn Connecticut St U 1978. D 6/15/1993 Bp Walter Decoster Dennis Jr. m 7/17/1953 Conrad Neil Normann c 4. D S Paul's Ch Woodbury CT 2002-2005; D Ch Of The H Comm Mahopac NY 1996-2002. Auth, "Stand Up & Be Counted," 1990; Auth, "In My Hm Town," 1989; Auth, "There Goes The Nbrhd," Nys Dept Of Mntl Hlth; Auth, "Swear To Uphold". Spec Citation Westchester Cnty Bd Legislators 1994; Cert Of Nerit For Wk w Homeless Gvnr Cuomo 1991; Mickey Loland 2nd Annual Hope For The Homeless Awd St Of Ny 1991; DSA Lincoln Sch 1988.

NORQUIST-HINSE, Mary Christine (Cal) 2230 Huron Dr., Concord CA 94519 **D S Geo's Epis Ch Antioch CA 2011-** B Portland OR 8/8/1952 d Nels Leroy Norquist & Janet Lake. BA Augustana Coll 1973; Anthropology U IL 1984; CDM,CFPP Merritt Coll Oakland CA 1996; BTS Epis Sch For Deacons 2008. D 12/6/2008 Bp Marc Handley Andrus. c 3. mcnh@comcast.net

NORRIS, David (Ct) 5 Briar Brae Rd, Stamford CT 06903 **P-in-c Trin-S Mich's Ch Fairfield CT 2008-** B 11/14/1935 BA Harv; MS Iona Coll; MDiv UTS; MA UTS; PhD UTS. D 10/20/1982 P 11/1/1983 Bp William Bradford Hastings. m Enid Norris. TRINITY.ST.MICHAELS@SNET.NET

NORRIS JR, Edwin Arter (Chi) 2866 Vacherie Ln, Dallas TX 75227 **Nash Nashotah WI 1990-** B Akron OH 9/4/1929 s Edwin Arter Norris & Elizabeth Palmer. BA U Denv 1955; Nash 1956; DD Nash 1986. D 6/15/1962 P 10/28/1963 Bp James R Mallett. Nash Nashotah WI 1978-1980; R Ch Of The Ascen Chicago IL 1971-1993. CCU, ECM, ESA. gregorynaz@sbcglobal.net

NORRIS, John Roy (Okla) 6310 E 111th Place, Tulsa OK 74137 B Oklahoma City OK 10/2/1940 s John Lee Norris & Eleanor Adaline. Cntrl St Coll Chadron NE 1960; BS Oklahoma City U 1964; MDiv Epis TS In Kentucky 1977; DMin Phillips Grad Sem 1988. D 6/18/1977 Bp Gerald Nicholas McAllister P 12/18/1977 Bp Frederick Warren Putnam. m 11/21/1962 Linda Carol Intemann c 2. Chapl S Simeons Epis Hm Tulsa OK 1986-2005; R S Ptr's Ch Tulsa OK 1982-1986; S Jn's Ch Oklahoma City OK 1977-1982; Cur Dio Oklahoma Oklahoma City OK 1977-1980. j6630@cox.net

NORRIS, Mark Joseph Patrick (Neb) 155 Strozier Rd # B, West Monroe LA 71291 **Ch Of The Trsfg Evergreen CO 2010-** B Omaha NE 5/23/1961 s Richard Frederick Norris & Roberta Clare. BA Creighton U 1990; ThM S Jn's U Collegeville MN 1995; CTh Epis TS of The SW 1999; CPE Nebraska Med Cntr 2003. Rec from Roman Catholic 1/17/1999 as Priest Bp Robert Jefferson Hargrove Jr. S Mary's Epis Ch Blair NE 2006-2009; H Fam Epis Ch Omaha NE 2003-2005; R S Pat's Epis Ch W Monroe LA 1999-2002. marknorris@juno.com

NORRIS, M Brent (Ala) 339 Charlotte St, Asheville NC 28801 **R S Mary's Ch Asheville NC 2005-** B Easley SC 5/17/1962 s Robert Joel Norris & Margie Miller. BA Furman U 1984; MDiv STUSo 1996. D 5/31/1996 P 12/7/1996 Bp Henry Irving Louttit. m 2/24/1989 Cynthia Ann Baker c 1. R Gr Ch Cullman AL 1999-2005; Cur Chr Ch Frederica St Simons Island GA 1996-1999. CSM Assoc 1996. rector@stmarysasheville.org

NORRIS III, Paul Haile (At) 951 Williams St, Madison GA 30650 **S Columba Epis Ch Suwanee GA 2004-** B Atlanta GA 8/13/1965 s Paul Haile Norris & Carolyn Ann. BA Davidson Coll 1987; MDiv GTS 1994. D 6/4/1994 P 12/10/1994 Bp Frank Kellogg Allan. m 7/27/1991 Theresa B Barrett c 2. Dio Atlanta Atlanta GA 2002-2003; The Epis Ch Of The Adv Madison GA 1996-2002; S Mk's Ch Dalton GA 1994-1996. pauln@mindspring.com

NORRIS, Rollin Bradford (Mich) 1626 Strathcona Dr, Detroit MI 48203 B Nevilly FR 3/4/1934 s Whitton Evens Norris & Carolyn. BA Harv 1956; BD EDS 1959. D 6/20/1959 Bp Hamilton Hyde Kellogg P 12/20/1959 Bp Philip Frederick McNairy. m 7/18/1959 Margo Pinney. Chr Ch Dearborn MI 1993; S Jn's Ch Royal Oak MI 1991-1992; Int Dio Michigan Detroit MI 1990-1994; S Lk's Ch Shelby Twp MI 1990-1991; All SS Ch Detroit MI 1985-1990; R S Paul's Epis Ch Port Huron MI 1971-1985; Assoc Chr Ch Cranbrook Bloomfield Hills MI 1968-1971; Vic Ch Of The Resurr Minneapolis MN 1962-1968; Cur S Lk's Ch Minneapolis MN 1959-1962.

NORRIS, Stephen Allen (Ga) 2493 Chandler Dr, Valdosta GA 31602 B Valdosta GA 5/7/1975 s Kenneth Allen Norris & Terrie Ann. BA SE U Lakeland FL 1997; MDiv VTS 2003. D 2/8/2003 P 8/20/2003 Bp Henry Irving Louttit. m 8/9/1997 Stephany A Christian c 2. yes S Jn's Ch Moultrie GA 2003-2004. Assn of Profsnl Chapl 2007. stephen.norris@sgmc.org

NORRIS, Susan Beatrice Priess (NJ) 6355 Pine Dr., Chincoteague VA 23336 B Jefferson City MO 3/23/1943 d Harold Edwin Oswald Priess & Alice Elizabeth. BD DePauw U 1965; SMM UTS 1968; MDiv Drew U 1981; GTS 1986. D 6/14/1986 P 1/10/1987 Bp George Phelps Mellick Belshaw. m 8/20/1966 Kenneth Scott Norris c 2. P Assoc Gr Ch Newark NJ 2008-2009; P Gr-S Paul's Ch Mercerville NJ 2000-2008; Dir D Formtn Dio New Jersey Trenton NJ 1995-2002; R H Trin Ch So River NJ 1993-1994; Field Spvsr The GTS New York NY 1991-1994; Assoc Gr Epis Ch Plainfield NJ 1991-1993; Asst Min S Jn's Ch Eliz NJ 1986-1987. Claiming the Blessing 2006-2009; Cmnty

N

Of S Jn The Bapt 1984; EWC 1976-1982; Integrity 1982; Interfaith Hosp Ntwk 1994-2006; NAAD 1992; Oasis New Jersey 2004-2009. susyplus@juno.com

NORRO, Hugo Pablo (Los) 4200 Summers Ln Unit 15, Klamath Falls OR 97603 B Buenos Aires Argentina 4/9/1942 s Hector Norro & Giovanna Maria. BA California St U 1973; BS California St U at Los Angeles 1975; MDiv CDSP 1985; PsyD USC 2001. D 6/15/1985 P 12/21/1985 Bp Oliver Bailey Garver Jr. m 8/19/2006 Bernice Watterson c 3. R S Jos's Par Buena Pk CA 2001-2008; Int S Jas' Par So Pasadena CA 2000-2001; R S Mary's Epis Ch Mitchell SD 1988-2000; Asst S Wilfrid Of York Epis Ch Huntington Bch CA 1985-1988. saintjosephs@sbcglobal.com

NORTH, Joseph James (Alb) No address on file. **Trin Ch Gloversville NY 2002-** B Binghamton NY 10/15/1946 D 9/8/2002 Bp David John Bena P 3/7/2009 Bp William Howard Love. m 6/13/1970 Monica Young.

NORTH, Robert David (Chi) 7 Huron Trce, Galena IL 61036 **PT SUNDAY'S S Paul's Ch Savanna IL 2001-** B Rochester MN 4/12/1942 s Clarence W North & Phyllis R. BA Macalester Coll 1964; BD-hon Bex 1967; DMin Luther Sem 1982. D 7/25/1967 P 4/6/1968 Bp Hamilton Hyde Kellogg. m 5/27/1967 Karen Kunzman c 4. Gr Epis Ch Galena IL 2001-2011; R Gr Epis Ch Freeport IL 1995-2001; Mssy S Lk's Ch Pk City UT 1993-1995; Dio Utah Salt Lake City UT 1992-1995; Calv Cathd Sioux Falls SD 1990-1992; R Gr Ch Holland MI 1983-1989; R Chr Epis Ch Grand Rapids MN 1976-1982; Asst S Mary's Ch St Paul MN 1974-1976; Assoc The Epis Par Of S Dav Minnetonka MN 1970-1973; R Epiph Epis Ch S Paul MN 1967-1970. Galena Cultural Arts Allnce Pres 2006; Habitat of Jo Daviess Cnty Founding Pres 2005; YMCA Founders 1980; Bush Ldrshp Fellowowship 1973. robertdavidnorth@gmail.com

NORTH, Susan Jane (RI) 350 Grange Rd, North Smithfield RI 02896 **D S Thos Ch Greenville RI 2001-** B Woonsocket RI 10/15/1953 d Alfred Byron Gardner & Alice Phyllis. Bryant U; Massachusetts Gnrl Hosp Inst for Hlth Plcy; BA Barrington Coll 1975; Cert Sch for Deacons 1989. D 3/16/1991 Bp George Nelson Hunt III. m 10/24/1987 Christopher Roberts North c 1. NAAD. suenor1@aol.com

NORTH JR, William Miller (Tex) 11209 SW Southridge Dr, Portland OR 97219 B Buffalo NY 10/19/1942 s William Miller North & Carolyn. BA Coll of Wooster 1964; Col 1967; MDiv UTS 1967; Cert Blanton-Peale Grad Inst 1971. D 8/1/1995 P 3/5/1996 Bp Hays H. Rockwell. m 6/26/1965 Mary D North c 2. Chapl to the Cler Dio Arizona Phoenix AZ 2005; Int Assoc Dn Trin Cathd Phoenix AZ 2005; Assoc Chr Ch Of The Ascen Paradise Vlly AZ 1999-2004; Assoc S Mich & S Geo Clayton MO 1993-1999. Amer Assn of Mar and Fam Therapists; AAPC; Soc of S Jn the Evang. revbillnorth@comcast.net

NORTHCRAFT, Linda Louise (Mich) 26998 Woodward Ave, Royal Oak MI 48067 **R S Jn's Ch Royal Oak MI 1997-** B Cumberland MD 7/30/1945 d Howard Leroy Northcraft & Sidna Rebecca. BS Frostburg St U 1967; Mstr's Wstrn Maryland Coll 1973; MDiv Ya Berk 1987. D 6/20/1987 P 5/19/1988 Bp A(lbert) Theodore Eastman. m 6/22/2011 Ellen C Ehrlich. COM Dio Michigan Detroit MI 1999-2003; Com of the Episcopate Dio Maryland Baltimore MD 1994-1997; R S Mths' Epis Ch Baltimore MD 1990-1997; COM Dio Maryland Baltimore MD 1990-1996; Liturg Com Dio Maryland Baltimore MD 1990-1994; Int S Mary Anne's Epis Ch No E MD 1989; Ch Of The H Comf Luthvle Timon MD 1987-1989; Peace & Justice Cmsn Dio Maryland Baltimore MD 1987-1989. Chas E Mersick Prize for Preaching Yale DS 1987. lindanorthcraft@stjohnro.org

NORTHUP, Frederick Bowen (At) 1118 Chicory Lane, Asheville NC 28803 **Fndr/Pres Athletes For A Better Wrld Atlanta GA 1998-** B Asheville,NC 11/6/1945 s Isaac Noyes Northup & Josephine Manigault. Institut des Etudes Politiques 1966; BA U So 1968; MDiv GTS 1973. D 6/16/1973 Bp Robert E Gribbin P 6/23/1974 Bp William F Gates Jr. m 6/29/1968 Jule S Seibels c 2. Assoc S Geo's Epis Ch Griffin GA 2002-2003; Dn S Mk's Cathd Seattle WA 1988-1998; R Epis Ch Of The Gd Shpd Lake Chas LA 1982-1988; Asst S Barth's Ch New York NY 1978-1982; Cn Convoc of Amer Ch in Europe Paris FR 1975-1978; Cn The Amer Cathd of the H Trin Paris 75008 FR 1975-1978; Asst S Jn's Epis Ch Memphis TN 1973-1975. Auth, "Mass For The Universe"; Auth, "Dav". fnorthup@aol.com

NORTHUP, Lesley Armstrong (NY) 1298 NE 95th St, Miami FL 33138 **Cn Theol Dio Bethlehem Bethlehem PA 1996-** B Bronx NY 12/2/1947 d Edmund Dwight Northup & Ruth. BA U of Wisconsin 1970; MDiv EDS 1980; MA CUA 1983; PhD CUA 1991. D 6/7/1980 P 1/19/1981 Bp Paul Moore Jr. c 1. Instr of Liturg VTS Alexandria VA 1987; Liturg Comm. Consult Dio Washington Washington DC 1985-1988; Educ Coordntr S Aug's Epis Ch Washington DC 1983-1985. Ed, "Years 1999-2004," *Rel Documents, No Amer Annual*, Amer Intl Press, 2004; Co-Ed, "Leaps & Boundaries: Lit Rev in the 21st Cent," Continuum/Morehouse, 1997; Auth, "Ritualizing Wmn," Pilgrim Press, 1997; Auth, "The 1892 Revs of BCP," Edwin Mellen Press, 1993; Ed, "Wmn and Rel Ritual," Pstr Press, 1993. Florida Hmnts Coun 2001-2007; HSEC 2005; Nat Coun of hon Colleges 2004; No Amer Acad of Liturg 1997; Societas Liturgica 1997. Cn Theol Dio Bethlehem 1996. northupl@fiu.edu

NORTHWAY, Dan P (Kan) 3531 SW Ashworth Ct, Topeka KS 66614 **Assoc Trin Ch Lawr KS 2008-** B Oneida NY 6/17/1942 s David William Northway & Virginia Augusta. Topeka Inst for Psychoanalysis; Ya 1965; BA/BS U of Miami 1970; MD U of Miami 1974; Menninger Clnc 1979. D 9/29/1988 Bp Richard Frank Grein P 8/1/1989 Bp John Forsythe Ashby. m 3/6/1970 Kathryn Ann Sweeney. Vic S Mk's Ch Blue Rapids KS 1988-2008; Vic S Paul's Ch Marysville KS 1988-2008. OHC, RWF, Associated P.

NORTON, Ann Elizabeth (EMich) PO Box 217, Otter Lake MI 48464 B Detroit MI 4/13/1946 d David Edgar Garbutt & Doris Mac Green. BA Cntrl Michigan U 1968. D 9/23/2008 P 3/21/2009 Bp S(teven) Todd Ousley. m 8/15/1970 Joseph Norton c 2. annorton46@gmail.com

NORTON JR, James Frederick (Ia) 1624 E River Ter, Minneapolis MN 55414 B Cleveland OH 12/10/1946 s James Frederick Norton & Barbara Ann. BA Baldwin-Wallace Coll 1969; MDiv Bex 1981. D 9/24/1981 Bp Harold Anthony Hopkins Jr P 3/1/1982 Bp William Grant Black. m 12/27/1970 Susan Lee Croy. R S Jn's Ch Mason City IA 1984-1986; Asst R Chr Epis Ch Of Springfield Springfield OH 1981-1984. Ord Of S Lk.

NORTON, Jerry R (Ak) Kivalina AK 99750 **Epiph Ch Kivalina AK 1974-** B Kivalina AK 7/20/1942 s Daniel S Norton & Betty. D 7/28/1974 Bp William J Gordon Jr. m 1/15/1967 Rebecca Swan c 1.

NORTON, Julie L (Va) PO Box 169, Keswick VA 22947 **R Gr Ch Keswick VA 1995-** B Shreveport LA 3/7/1947 d Floyd Ligon Norton & Grace Louise. BA Randolph-Macon Wmn's Coll 1969; MA Virginia Commonwealth U 1975; MDiv EDS 1982; S Geo's Coll Jerusalem Israel 1986. D 6/9/1982 Bp David Henry Lewis Jr P 5/18/1983 Bp Robert Bruce Hall. c 2. R Par Of S Paul Newton Highlands MA 1988-1995; Assoc S Paul's Ch Newburyport MA 1985-1988; Ch Of The H Sprt Wayland MA 1983-1985. Winner Best Sermon Competition Epis Evang Fndt 1993. parsonjulie@earthlink.net

NORTON, Marlee R (Va) 2416 N Florida St, Arlington VA 22207 **S Jas Epis Ch Bristol PA 2009-** B Chicago, IL 1/6/1959 d Donald Edward Norton & Jane Bertholi. BA U of Iowa Iowa City IA 1977; MDiv VTS 2006. D 6/16/2007 Bp Peter James Lee P 12/17/2007 Bp David Colin Jones. marleenorton@gmail.com

NORTON, Mary K (NwPa) 218 Center St, Ridgway PA 15853 **Dnry Dn Dio NW Pennsylvania Erie PA 2009-; P-in-c Gr Epis Ch Ridgway PA 2009-; P-in-c S Agnes' Epis Ch S Marys PA 2009-; Prov 3 Syn Rep Dio NW Pennsylvania Erie PA 2007-; Stndg Com Dio NW Pennsylvania Erie PA 2007-** B Pittsburgh PA 10/16/1957 d Thomas W Norton & Mary J. BA Alleg 1979; MBA Duquesne U 1988; MDiv VTS 2006. D 10/29/2005 P 6/10/2006 Bp Robert Deane Rowley Jr. Dnry Dn Dio NW Pennsylvania Erie PA 2009-2010; Dioc Hlth Team Dio NW Pennsylvania Erie PA 2008-2010; Cur Ch Of Our Sav DuBois PA 2006-2009. The Ford Chair VTS 2006. mnorton7@windstream.net

NORVELL, John David (Okla) 530 Northcrest Dr, Ada OK 74820 **R S Lk's Epis Ch Ada OK 1995-** B 4/17/1952 s James Edgar Norvell & Billie Jean. BS SW Oklahoma St U 1976; MDiv Epis TS of The SW 1988. D 6/18/1988 Bp Gerald Nicholas McAllister P 3/17/1989 Bp Robert Manning Moody. m 7/17/2003 Susan Norvell c 1. Ch Of The Redeem Okmulgee OK 1990-1995; S Paul's Cathd Oklahoma City OK 1988-1990. stlukesada@gmail.com

NORVILLE, Colbert Mitchell (CFla) 688 Canopy Ct, Winter Springs FL 32708 B Bridgetown Saint Michael BB 11/3/1930 s Proctor Norville & Sylvia. BA Coll of New Rochelle 1976; MA LIU 1978; Cert Mercer TS 1990. D 6/15/1991 P 6/1/1992 Bp Orris George Walker Jr. m 4/14/1956 Vilma Meredith Thorington. Vic S Tim's Epis Ch Daytona Bch FL 2000-2002; Ret Assoc Cathd Ch Of S Lk Orlando FL 1999-2002; S Mary Of The Ang Epis Ch Orlando FL 1998-2002; Asst Ch Of The New Cov Winter Sprg FL 1997-1998; P-in-c Trin Ch Mt Vernon NY 1996-1997; Sup P Trin Ch Mt Vernon NY 1994-1995; P Asst S Jos's Ch Queens Vill NY 1992-1994; D S Jos's Ch Queens Vill NY 1991. Bro Of S Andr 1968; Epis Caring Fund, Dio Cntrl Florida 2002; Int Mnstry Ntwk 1996; UBE 1997. The Bp'S Cross Dio Long Island 1983; Congressional Cert Of Merit For Serv To Economically. bertandvil@bellsouth.net

NORWOOD, Douglas Milton (CNY) 25 Village Inn Rd, Apt 107, Bar Harbor ME 04609 B Bar Harbor ME 7/24/1926 s Milton Webster Norwood & Meda Alice. BA Aurora U 1951; EDS 1957. D 6/28/1957 Bp Malcolm E Peabody P 6/14/1958 Bp Walter M Higley. Assoc All SS Ch Brooklyn NY 1990-1994; Int Ch Of The H Sprt Brooklyn NY 1987-1990; Dio Long Island Garden City NY 1987-1990; Asst All SS Ch Brooklyn NY 1986-1987; Asst Calv Ch Syracuse NY 1965-1967; Mssnr-In-C Gr Ch Copenhagen NY 1957-1965; Mssnr-In-C S Jn's Ch Black River NY 1957-1965.

NORWOOD, James Ulyses (FtW) No address on file. B Houston TX 5/17/1924 s Wyatt Norwood & Alma G. BA Baylor U 1951; MDiv Epis TS of The SW 1959; Natl Chr U 1982. D 7/10/1959 Bp Everett H Jones P 2/1/1960 Bp Richard Earl Dicus. m 5/11/1997 Marietta Norwood c 4. Assoc S Chris's Ch And Sch Ft Worth TX 2000-2002; R S Jas Epis Ch Oklahoma City OK

1964-1969; Chair Of The Yth Div Dio Oklahoma Oklahoma City OK 1963-1966; P-in-c S Mich And All Ang Ch Lindsay OK 1962-1964; D S Jas Epis Ch Hebbronville TX 1959-1960. Auth, "Notes On Gestalt Ther"; Auth, "Integrating Ta & Gestalt Theory & Process". Ok Pstr Counselors Assn. fatherjimshouse@juno.com

NOVAK, Barbara Ellen Hosea (Spok) 1107 E 41st Ave, Spokane WA 99203 **D Asst Cathd Of S Jn The Evang Spokane WA 1978-** B Spokane WA 7/4/1949 d Noel Earl Hosea & Margaret Louis. BA WA SU 1972; MA Sthrn Illinois U 1974. D 11/19/1978 Bp John Raymond Wyatt. m 8/29/1981 Terry Novak. banovak@iea.com

NOVAK, M(argaret) Anne (Oly) 15502 30th Ave Ne, Shoreline WA 98155 B Bellingham WA 1/29/1940 d John Clifton Cheney & Margaret Elma. BS WA SU 1962; MA Seattle U 1991. D 6/24/2000 Bp Sanford Zangwill Kaye Hampton. m 8/11/1962 Stuart Raymond Novak c 3. S Andr's Ch Seattle WA 2002-2005. srnovak@attglobal.net

NOVAK, Nicky Don (Tex) 5215 Honey Creek, Baytown TX 77523 **Trin Epis Ch Baytown TX 2001-** B San Antonio TX 11/18/1950 s Donald Edward Novak & Oleta Margarite. AA San Jacinto Coll 1975; BBA U of Houston Clear Lake 1984; MDiv TESM 1991. D 6/23/1991 P 2/17/1992 Bp Maurice Manuel Benitez. m 5/9/1971 Pamela Gay Rogers c 2. S Mk's Ch Bay City TX 1994-2001; Vic S Paul's Epis Ch Woodville TX 1991-1994. nnovak1@verizon.net

NOVES, W David Peter (WNY) 840 Bataan Ave, Dunkirk NY 14048 **P-in-c S Mary's Epis Ch Gowanda NY 2008-** B Buffalo NY 10/18/1943 s William David Noves & Doris Mary. BA SUNY 1966; STB Ya Berk 1969; DMin GTF 1991. D 6/21/1969 Bp Lauriston L Scaife P 12/9/1976 Bp John Harris Burt. m 6/22/1968 Diane R Richardson c 4. R Gr Ch Randolph NY 1997-2007; P-in-c Chr Ch Punxsutawney PA 1987-1997; R Emm Ch Corry PA 1978-1987; Assoc Ch Of Our Sav Akron OH 1975-1978; Cur S Paul's Ch Akron OH 1969-1971.

NOWLIN, Ben Gary (Mo) 61 Dames Ct, Ferguson MO 63135 B Fort Smith AR 2/4/1953 s Ben Wade Nowlin & Reba Sue. BA U Of Cntrl Arkansas Edmond 1975; PhD U of Oklahoma 1981; MDiv Epis TS of The SW 1984. D 6/16/1984 Bp William Jackson Cox P 5/1/1985 Bp Herbert Alcorn Donovan Jr. m 12/20/1975 Susan Mary c 1. S Steph's Ch Ferguson MO 1993-2001; S Jas Ch Magnolia AR 1992-1993; S Mary's Epis Ch El Dorado AR 1990-1991; Dio Arkansas Little Rock AR 1989-1990; R S Mk's Ch Crossett AR 1987-1989; Asst R S Paul's Ch Fayetteville AR 1984-1987. revbgary@myway.com

NOYES, Daphne Bess (Mass) Church of the Advent, 30 Brimmer St, Boston MA 02108 B Boston MA 1/23/1947 d Thomas Henry Lehman & Tenney Barbara. MA EDS 1995; Dioc D Prog 2001. D 10/6/2001 Bp M(arvil) Thomas Shaw III. c 2. Ch Of S Jn The Evang Boston MA 2001-2007; Emm Ch Boston MA 2001-2007; The Cathd Ch Of S Paul Boston MA 2001-2007. Assembly of Epis Healthcare Chapl 1996-2006; Assn of Epis Deacons (life Mem) 2011; Assn of Profsnl Chapl 1996-2006; NAAD 2001-2005. dbnoyes@gmail.com

N

NOYES, Roger Bow (Az) 1830 W Dart Cir, Cottonwood AZ 86326 B Tulsa OK 8/2/1923 s Roger B Noyes & Gladys V. LSU. D 4/10/1971 P 1/1/1972 Bp Jose Guadalupe Saucedo. m 10/3/1945 Henrietta P Noyes. S Andr's Epis Ch Sedona AZ 1989; Int P S Andr's Epis Ch Sedona AZ 1988; The Verde Vlly Par Sedona AZ 1987-1989; Vic S Mary's/Santa Maria Virgen Imperial Bch CA 1978-1985. roger300@cableone.net

NSENGIYUMVA, Samuel (FdL) 1223 Huron Trail, Sheboygan Falls WI 53085 **R S Ptr's Epis Ch Sheboygan Falls WI 2003-** B Cyeru Rwanda 1/26/1961 s Petero Nsekuye & Agnesta. BA SeminaryDaystar U Nairobi Kenya 1996; MA Associated Mennonite Biblic Sem 1999. Trans from Anglican Church Of Kenya 8/11/2004 Bp Russell Edward Jacobus. m 12/26/1987 Marie Rose Nirere c 4. Exec Coun Dio Fond du Lac Appleton WI 2005-2011; RurD, Lake Winnebago Dnry Dio Fond du Lac Appleton WI 2005-2011; Stndg Com Dio Fond du Lac Appleton WI 2004-2008. nsengasa@yahoo.com

NSUBUGA, Thomas Timothy (WLa) 538 Main St, Grambling LA 71245 **Vic S Lk's Chap Grambling LA 2008-** B Uganda 2/22/1969 s Lameka Nsubuga & Agiri-Norah. Bachelor of Commerce Makerere U 1992; Bachelor of Div Bp Tucker Theol Coll 1995; Mstr of Div Cranmer Theol Hse 2001. Trans from Church of the Province of Uganda 12/23/2008 Bp D(avid) Bruce Mac Pherson. m 1/4/1997 Erinah E Nambirige c 2. ttnsubuga@yahoo.com

NTAGENGWA, Jean Baptiste (Mass) 149 Roxbury Street, Roxbury MA 02119 **P-in-c S Jn's S Jas Epis Ch Roxbury MA 2011-** B Rwanda 2/5/1966 s Francois Ugirashebuja & Marisiyana. BD St. Paul's U, Limuru-Kenya 1998; MTS Harvard DS 2001; ThD Bos TS 2008. Trans from L'Eglise Episcopal au Rwanda 5/29/2008 Bp M(arvil) Thomas Shaw III. m 8/21/1993 Christine Karangwa c 3. Asst Ch Of The H Sprt Mattapan MA 2009-2011. Auth, "Bk," *Overcoming Cycles of Violence in Rwanda: Ethical Ldrshp and Ethnic Justice*, Edwin MellenPress, 2010. jbntagengwa@hotmail.com

NUAMAH, Reginald (LI) 3607 Glenwood Rd, Brooklyn NY 11210 B 7/29/1948 Trans from Church of the Province of West Africa 5/13/2002 Bp Orris George Walker Jr. m 8/7/1979 Rebecca Nixon c 1. Int S Paul's Epis Ch Bound Brook NJ 2008-2010; S Mary's Ch Brooklyn NY 2001-2008.

NULL, John Ashley (WK) PO Box 2507, Salina KS 67402 **Cn Theol Dio Wstrn Kansas Hutchinson KS 2005-** B Birmingham AL 7/11/1960 s William George Null & Peggy Jean. BA, mcl SMU 1982; MDiv Yale DS 1985; STM, Yale DS 1989; PhD U of Cambridge 1995. D 8/31/1985 Bp John Forsythe Ashby P 6/8/1986 Bp C(hristopher) FitzSimons Allison. Caritas Fndt Of Wstrn Kansas Assaria KS 2008; Epis TS Of The SW Austin TX 2008; Prof VTS Alexandria VA 2007; R S Andr's Epis Ch Liberal KS 1988-1990; Asst S Jas' Ch New Haven CT 1987-1988; Asst & Chapl Gr Epis Ch New York NY 1985-1987. "Thos Cranmers Theol of the Heart," *Trin Journ for Theol and Mnstry*, 2007; "The Marian Exiles in Switzerland," *Jahrbuch für Europäische Geschichte*, 2006; "Real Joy: Freedom to be Your Best," Hänssler, 2004; "Jn Redman, the Gentle Ambler," *Westminster Abbey Reformed, ed. Knighton and Mortimer*, Ashgate, 2003; "Thos Cranmer's Doctrine of Repentance: Renewing the Power to Love," Oxford, 2000. Fell Royal Hist Soc 2008; Spec Discretionary Grant Rec ECF 2006; Guggenheim Fell Jn Simon Guggenheim Memi Fndt 2006; NEH Fell Natl Endwmt for the Hmnts 2005; Grant Rec HSEC 2002; Fulbright Schlr Fulbright Fndt 1990. JANULL@ATT.NET

NUNEZ, Carlos Enrique (Ore) 3052 Se 158th Ave, Portland OR 97236 B Santiago CL 12/31/1936 s Carlos Nunez & Marina. BTh UTS Buenos Aires AR 1961; MDiv UTS Buenos Aires AR 1964; DMin SFTS 2000. D 6/22/2002 Bp Robert Louis Ladehoff. m 12/10/1964 Susy O'Campo c 2. H Cross Epis Ch Portland OR 2002.

NUNEZ, Timothy Charles (CFla) 10481 Se 68th Ct, Belleview FL 34420 **R Epis Ch Of S Mary Belleview FL 2003-** B Bartow FL 9/21/1961 BA U Of Florida. D 5/24/2003 P 12/7/2003 Bp John Wadsworth Howe. m 10/21/1988 Mary Norris c 2. tcnunez@yahoo.com

NUNLEY, Janet Worth (RI) 1414 Elm St, Peekskill NY 10566 **Int Dir of Cmncatn & Marketing EDS Cambridge MA 2011-; P S Thos Epis Ch New Windsor NY 2010-; P St Fran of Assisi Montgomery NY 2010-; Assoc P S Ptr's Epis Ch Peekskill NY 2001-** B Gulfport MS 11/16/1954 d Lolan Earl Nunley & Worth. BA Trin U San Antonio TX 1975; MDiv EDS 1992. D 12/10/1994 Bp George Nelson Hunt III P 7/15/1995 Bp Barbara Clementine Harris. m 11/10/2004 Susan T Erdey. Int Dir of Cmncatn & Marketing EDS Cambridge MA 2010; Dep for Cmncatn Epis Ch Cntr New York NY 2005-2009; Dep Dir, Epis News Serv Epis Ch Cntr New York NY 2000-2005; Cmncatn Dir Dio Rhode Island Providence RI 1997-2000; R S Ptr's And S Andr's Epis Providence RI 1996-2000; Assoc P Ch Of The H Trin Tiverton RI 1995-1996; D Ch Of The H Trin Tiverton RI 1994-1995. Co-Auth, "Many Parts, One Body: How the Epis Ch Works," Ch Pub, 2009; Auth, "How Many Lightbulbs Does It Take To Change A Chr?," Ch Pub, 2008; Auth, "Understanding the Windsor Report," Ch Pub, 2005; Auth, "Var arts," *Epis News Serv*, 2000. ECom 1990-2009. erdeynunley@earthlink.net

NUNN, Frances Louise (Va) No address on file. B Washington DC 3/29/1925 d Ira Hudson Nunn & Esther Louise. BA Vas 1948; JD GW 1952. D 10/14/1978 Bp Robert Bruce Hall P 11/1/1982 Bp David Henry Lewis Jr. Epis Ch Cntr New York NY 1989.

NUNNALLY, J Ellen (WA) 937 Moss Hill Dr, Ashland OH 44805 **Died 8/31/2010** B Akron OH 6/5/1945 d Alvon Cox & Harriet. BD Ashland U 1967; MDiv VTS 1978; MFA Geo Mason U 1988. D 6/24/1978 P 2/18/1979 Bp John Thomas Walker. c 2. Auth, *Deep Peace: Healing Our Lives*, Cowley, 2003; Auth, *Foremothers: Wmn of the Bible*, 1981. ohiofive@zoominternet.net

NURDING, Brian Frank (Haw) 1144 Kumukumu St. Apt. E, Honolulu HI 96825 B Tacoma WA 3/10/1935 s Frank John Nurding & Jessie Elizabeth. BA Stan 1957; MDiv CDSP 1960. D 6/24/1960 P 3/13/1961 Bp William F Lewis. m 6/2/1990 Joe Ellen Katamoto c 2. Int Waikiki Chap Honolulu HI 2000-2001; Int Gd Samar Epis Ch Honolulu HI 1997-1999; Int S Ptr's Ch Honolulu HI 1995-1997; R The Par Of S Clem Honolulu HI 1979-1990; R S Jn The Bapt Epis Ch Seattle WA 1970-1979; R Gr Ch Ellensburg WA 1964-1970; Asst Trin Epis Ch Everett WA 1960-1964. Alum Preaching Prize CDSP BerkeleyCA 1960. bnurd@aol.com

NUSSER-TELFER, Hiltrude Maria (O) 9868 Ford Rd, Perrysburg OH 43551 B 2/17/1937 d Karl Nusser & Margareta. Kaufmansgehilfe Bus Sch Industries and Handels Kammer 1956; BA Cath U Louvain 1992; MA Katholike Universitaet 1994; Dplma GTS 2002; D Min GTF 2010. D 6/8/2002 Bp Arthur Benjamin Williams Jr P 12/18/2002 Bp J Clark Grew II. D Epis Shared Minist Of Nwohio Sherwood OH 2002. Auth, "Pstr Care," *Outcomes of Faith During Hospitalization A Case Study Method*, Auth Hse, 2010. Assn of Profsnl Chapl 2004; Epis Hlth Care Chapl Assn 2002; Flower Hosp Aux 1999; Flower Hosp Gld 1999; Ohio Chapl Orgnztn 2008. HNussertelfer@aol.com

NUTTER, James Wallace (Tex) 6221 Main St, Houston TX 77030 **R Palmer Memi Ch Houston TX 1994-** B Minden LA 5/22/1956 s James Bertrand Nutter & Alice Anne (Wallace). BA Bates Coll 1979; MDiv Nash 1983. D 5/28/1983 P 12/1/1983 Bp Frederick Barton Wolf. m Lucy Nutter c 2. R S Ptr's Ch Rockland ME 1987-1994; Cur Cathd Ch Of S Lk Portland ME 1983-1987. Soc Of S Jn The Evang. jnutter@palmerchurch.org

NYATSAMBO, Tobias Dzawanda (NH) PO Box 737, Ashland NH 03217 **R S Jas Epis Ch Laconia NH 2011-** B Kadoma Zimbabwe 1/3/1947 s Masiwa

Nyatsambo & Norah Jessica. DRS All Nations Chr Coll, UK 1980; MRE Gordon-Conwell TS 1991. Trans from Church of the Province of Central Africa 9/11/2008 Bp V Gene Robinson. m 12/23/1973 Rozina Matonhodze c 3. P-in-c S Mk's Ch Ashland NH 2007-2009. tnyatsambo@gmail.com

NYBACK, Rachel Anne (Los) 1818 Monterey Blvd, Hermosa Beach CA 90254 **R S Cross By-The-Sea Ch Hermosa Bch CA 2010-** B California 2/24/1970 d Warren Stanley Nyback. BA Smith 1992; MA Claremont Grad U 1995; MDiv VTS 2004. D 6/19/2004 P 1/22/2005 Bp Joseph Jon Bruno. rnyback@stcross.org

NYBACK, Warren Stanley (Los) 242 E Alvarado St, Pomona CA 91767 B Los Angeles CA 8/2/1939 s Martin Nyback & Beula Iona. BA USC 1961; BD CDSP 1964. D 9/10/1964 P 3/1/1965 Bp Francis E I Bloy. c 1. S Paul's Pomona Pomona CA 1972-2001; R S Tim's Par Compton CA 1967-1972; Cur The Par Ch Of S Lk Long Bch CA 1964-1967. warrennyback@aol.com

NYE, Linda Wade (NC) Grace Memorial Episcopal Church, 871 Merrimon Ave, Asheville NC 28804 **Ch Of The Epiph Eden NC 2010-** B Concord NC 9/9/1959 d Jack Wade & Doris Cline. BA Wstrn Carolina U 1981; MDiv STUSo 2007. D 6/9/2007 P 12/15/2007 Bp Granville Porter Taylor. m 3/3/1984 Steven Nye. Assoc Gr Ch Asheville NC 2007-2009. gracerevnye@bellsouth.net

NYE, Max Ormsbee (Nev) 150 Cortona Way Apt 331, Brentwood CA 94513 **P S Alb's Epis Ch Brentwood CA 2010-** B Oakland CA 9/19/1928 s Berthold Max Nye & Virginia Parcells. U CA 1953; VTS 1971. D 6/26/1971 P 12/1/1971 Bp C Kilmer Myers. m 6/30/1951 Nadeane Berry c 4. Assoc S Thos Epis Ch Temecula CA 2003-2010; Int R S Fran Ch Pauma Vlly CA 2002; Assoc S Mich And All Ang Ch Ft Bragg CA 1997-2001; Assoc Epis Ch Of S Fran-In-The-Vlly Green Vlly AZ 1995-1997; Int Chr Memi Ch Kilauea HI 1992; Assoc R Trin Epis Ch Reno NV 1990-1995; P Gr Ch Martinez CA 1987-1988; R All SS Epis Ch Redding CA 1982-1986; Vic Gd Shpd Epis Ch Susanville CA 1978-1982; R St Johns Epis Ch Ross CA 1973-1977. denamax2008@yahoo.com

NYGAARD, Steven Bickham (NMich) 6144 Westridge 21.25 Dr, Gladstone MI 49837 B Evanston IL 7/1/1948 s Dorrance Nygaard & Margaret. D 5/4/2002 Bp James Arthur Kelsey. m 4/18/1987 Pamela Martin-Nygaard c 1. spmnygaard@chartermi.net

NYRE-THOMAS, Beryl Jean (Los) 1117 Bennett Ave, Long Beach CA 90804 **Asst The Par Ch Of S Lk Long Bch CA 2005-** B London UK 7/22/1936 d Maurice James Allmen & Evelyn May. BA Gld Hall Sch Mus 1956; BA California St U 1975; MA California St U 1978; MA ETSBH 1986. D 6/22/1986 Bp Robert C Rusack P 1/10/1987 Bp Oliver Bailey Garver Jr. m 1/4/2005 Gordon Thomas c 1. Ch Of The H Comm Gardena CA 2001-2004; The Par Ch Of S Lk Long Bch CA 2000-2001; Assoc S Greg's Par Long Bch CA 1989-2000; Asst S Anselm Of Cbury Par Garden Grove CA 1986-1989; Refugee Coordntr Dio Los Angeles Los Angeles CA 1982-1985. reverendberyl@gmail.com

O

OAK, Carol Pinkham (Md) St. John's Episcopal Church, 9120 Frederick Road, Ellicott City MD 21042 **R S Jn's Ch Ellicott City MD 2006-** B Jamaica NY 11/5/1954 d Gilbert Edward Pinkham & Doris Elizabeth. BA U CO 1976; MDiv Ya Berk 1985; DMin Seabury-Wstrn TS 2003. D 8/24/1985 Bp Andrew Frederick Wissemann P 4/27/1986 Bp Robert Rae Spears Jr. m 10/11/1986 Jeffrey C Oak c 2. Assoc Chr Ch Alexandria VA 2000-2006; R S Jas' Ch Goshen NY 1990-1999; Asst All SS Ch Staten Island NY 1988-1990; Cur S Jas Ch New York NY 1985-1987. Auth, "Creating the Conditions for New Pastors' Success," *Congregations*, The Alb Inst, 2006; Auth, "Help, The R Is Pregnant," *Alb Inst*, The Alb Inst, 1994. cpoak@stjohnsec.org

OAKES, Leonard (Cal) 777 Southgate Ave, Daly City CA 94015 **Vic H Chld At S Mart Epis Ch Daly City CA 2009-** B Philippines 7/3/1971 s Benedicto F Oakes & Teresa B. Trans from Episcopal Church in the Philippines 6/6/2009 Bp Marc Handley Andrus. m 4/27/1993 Haidee Salbino c 3. revleonardoakes@gmail.com

OAKES, Louise K (NC) 201 N Walbridge Ave Apt 335, Madison WI 53714 B Watertown WI 1/24/1936 d Raymond Henry Kaercher & Cora Emilie. AA U of Wisconsin 1957; ACS Herzing Inst Madison WI 1973; Cert Nash 1984; Cert SWTS 1992. P 1/1/1994 Bp Roger John White. c 4. Vic Ch Of The H Sprt Greensboro NC 1997-2001; Vic S Helena's Ch Willowbrook IL 1994-1996; D S Matt's Ch Evanston IL 1991-1994; D Gr Ch Madison WI 1987-1991.

OAKES OJN, Sara Elizabeth Herr (Cal) 622 Terra California Dr Apt 7, Walnut Creek CA 94595 **Asst S Giles Ch Moraga CA 1997-** B New York NY 11/20/1933 d Edwin Dean Herr & Aline. BA U Of Detroit 1981; Michigan TS 1982. D 6/22/1983 Bp H Coleman McGehee Jr P 8/17/1994 Bp Jerry Alban Lamb. m 1/1/1975 Robert C Oakes. D S Anselm's Epis Ch Lafayette CA 1988-1994; Pstr Assoc S Paul's Epis Ch Walnut Creek CA 1987-1988; D All SS Epis Ch Pontiac MI 1983-1984. OHC 1977; Wrdn Of Oblates For Ord Of Julian Of Norwich 1985. objn1@attbi.com

OAKLAND, Mary Jane (Ia) 1612 Truman Dr, Ames IA 50010 **Chair of COM Dio Iowa Des Moines IA 2009-; R S Paul's Ch Marshalltown IA 2006-** B Madison SD 2/27/1944 d Charles Thomas Kaisersatt & Lilah Lorraine. BS So Dakota St U 1967; MS Iowa St U 1970; PhD Iowa St U 1985. D 6/7/1995 Bp Carl Christopher Epting P 6/18/2005 Bp Alan Scarfe. m 8/13/1966 David Oliver Oakland c 3. Asst S Paul's Ch Marshalltown IA 2005-2006; D S Paul's Ch Marshalltown IA 2001-2005; D S Jn's By The Campus Ames IA 1995-2001. Cler Assn 1999; The Ord of Julian of Norwich-Oblate 1984. mary.j.oakland@gmail.com

OASIN, (Elizabeth) (NJ) 344 B Delancey Pl, Mount Laurel NJ 08054 **Stff Off for Anti-Racism and Gender Equality Epis Ch Cntr New York NY 2000-** B PhiladelphiaPA 7/31/1944 d J Arthur Jones & Marion. BA How 1968; MA Tem 1970; MDiv EDS 2000. D 5/20/2000 Bp David B(ruce) Joslin P 4/28/2001 Bp Herbert Alcorn Donovan Jr. c 2. Epis Ch Cntr New York NY 2000-2010. "Kaleidscopic God," *Race and Power*, Morehouse, 2003; "Pryr to a Sheltering God," *Wmn Uncommon Prayers*, Morehouse, 2000. scl How 1968. revjayne@comcast.net

OATS, Louis (NC) 712 East 9th Street, Charlotte NC 28202 **S Jas Epis Sch Of Corpus Christi Inc. Corpus Christi TX 2011-; Trin Epis Sch Charlotte NC 2000-** B Nashville TN 5/16/1951 s Paul Eugene Oats & Bettye Jane. BA U So 1973; MDiv SWTS 1980; DMin Columbia TS 1998. D 6/29/1980 P 5/1/1981 Bp William Evan Sanders. m 4/10/1976 Sharon Langley c 2. R All SS' Epis Ch Morristown TN 1987-1999; Asst to R Ch Of The Ascen Knoxville TN 1984-1987; Vic S Thos Ch Elizabethton TN 1981-1984; D-in-trng Ch Of The H Comm Memphis TN 1980-1981. Auth, *Preparing for Priesting: A Trng Prog*, CTS Press, 1998. Untd Way Vol Awd 1989. soats@tescharlotte.org

OBARSKI, Sandra Ruth (Minn) 1111 Lowell Cir, Apple Valley MN 55124 **Part TIme Geth Ch Minneapolis MN 2006-** B Milwaukee WI 9/2/1938 d Arnold Otto Sedenquist & Ruth Mrytle. RN Milwaukee Cnty Gnrl Hosp, Sch of Nrsng 1959; AS Inver Hills Cmnty Coll 2004; D D Formation Prog 2006. D 6/29/2006 Bp James Louis Jelinek. m 9/17/1960 Marvin Leonard Obarski c 2. Assn for Epis Deacons 2007. sobarski@gmail.com

OBENCHAIN, John Colin (Pa) 3401 Compass Rd, Gap PA 17527 **P-in-c S Jn's Ch Gap PA 2007-** B Chester PA 4/23/1943 s Colin Sears Obenchain & Lillian Bamforth. BA Heidelberg Coll 1966; MDiv PDS 1969. D 8/29/1969 P 2/1/1970 Bp Chandler W Sterling. m 3/17/2000 Margaret Doffy c 2. The Epis Ch Of The Adv Kennett Sq PA 2000-2001; R S Christophers Epis Ch Oxford PA 1972-1999; R Incarn H Sacr Epis Ch Drexel Hill PA 1970-1972; Asst S Paul's Ch Philadelphia PA 1969-1970. padreatstjohuse@yahoo.com

OBERHEIDE, Richard Dean (Ala) 155 N Twining St, Montgomery AL 36112 **Gr Ch Sheffield AL 2004-; Off Of Bsh For ArmdF New York NY 1984-** B Kansas City MO 10/25/1949 s Harold Junin Oberheide & Virginia Lee. BA Winona St U 1975; MDiv SWTS 1978. D 6/24/1978 Bp Robert Marshall Anderson P 1/6/1979 Bp Charles Bennison. m 9/21/1971 Nancy Palmer Schmauss c 2. Vic S Jn's Ch Fremont MI 1978-1984. Auth, "Easter In The Er," *Sermons That Wk*, Random Hse, 1996; Auth, "Best AF Sermons 1985". rickober@comcast.net

OBIER, Cynthia Andrews (La) 4255 Hyacinth Ave, Baton Rouge LA 70808 **D Trin Epis Ch Baton Rouge LA 2003-** B Opelika AL 9/22/1957 d Newton Steele Andrews & Ann Allen. BA LSU 1980. D 9/13/2003 Bp Charles Edward Jenkins III. m 12/18/1982 Robert Row Obier. cindyobier@cox.net

OBREGON, Ernesto M (Ala) 8123 Highway 75, Pinson AL 35126 B Havana CU 11/7/1951 s Patricio Obregon-Zamora & Gloria E. Ken; TESM; AA Dekalb Cmnty Coll Clarkston GA 1973; MA Ashland TS 1977; BS Kent St U 1977; MA Cleveland St U 1981. D 11/1/1990 P 4/1/1991 Bp The Bishop Of Peru and Bolivia. m 7/8/1978 Denise Ruth Lockney c 3. Hisp Mssnr Dio Alabama Birmingham AL 2000-2004; Mssy SAMS Ambridge PA 1989-1993. Bro Of S Andr 1990-2000. eobregon@bellsouth.net

O'BRIEN, Charles Harold (Q) 738 Simonds Rd, Williamstown MA 01267 B Oshkosh WI 10/17/1927 s Erwin Joseph O'Brien & Margaret Alice. BA U of Notre Dame 1951; MA U of Notre Dame 1952; STB Gregorian U 1957; STL Gregorian U 1959; PhD Col 1967. Rec from Roman Catholic 10/9/1979 as Priest Bp Donald James Parsons. m 12/21/1964 Elvy Setterqvist. Vic S Paul's Ch Warsaw IL 1984-1989; Assoc S Geo's Ch Macomb IL 1979-1984. Auth, "Assassins' Rage," Severn Hse, 2008; Auth, "Cruel Choices," Severn Hse, 2007; Auth, "Black Gold," Poisoned Pen Press, 2002; Auth, "Mute Witness," Poisoned Pen Press, 2001; Auth, "Ideas of Rel Toleration in Austria," Amer Philos Assn, 1969; Auth, "Jansenist Cmpgn for Toleration of Protestants," *Journ of Hist of Ideas*. obrien@bcn.net

O'BRIEN, Craig Edward (Ga) 201 E 49th St, Savannah GA 31405 **P Assoc S Jn's Ch Savannah GA 2007-** B Halifax Nova Scotia Canada 5/24/1972 s Daniel William O'Brien & Valerie Ruth. BA The U Of Kings Coll Halifax Nova Scotia 1995; MDiv Regent Coll/Wycliffe Hall Oxford 1997. Trans from Anglican Church of Canada 10/22/2004 Bp Leopold Frade. The Ch Of The Guardian Ang Lantana FL 2005-2007. cobrien@stjohnssav.org

O'BRIEN, Donald Richard (SwFla) No address on file. B Opelika AL 9/9/1952 AA Manatee Cmnty Coll 1972. D 6/11/1980 Bp Emerson Paul Haynes. m 8/4/1972 Deborah Fox.

O'BRIEN, Julie Lynn (Az) 1735 S College Ave, Tempe AZ 85281 **Epis Ch of the H Sprt Phoenix AZ 2009-; P Dio Arizona Phoenix AZ 2008-** B Bloomington IN 4/1/1956 d Robert Denis O'Brien & Edna Anne. MDiv Epis TS of the SW 2009. D 6/7/2008 P 6/13/2009 Bp Kirk Stevan Smith. c 1. D S Aug's Epis Ch Tempe AZ 2008. julielynnobrien@gmail.com

O'CALLAGHAN, Elizabeth Putnam (WA) 205 S Summit Ave, Gaithersburg MD 20877 **Asst R Ch Of The Ascen Gaithersburg MD 2009-** B Pittsburgh PA 4/25/1958 d Horace Lynn Mann & Prudence Putnam. BS U of Maryland 1980; MHS JHU 1987; MDiv VTS 2009. D 6/13/2009 P 1/16/2010 Bp John Chane. m 9/3/1998 Marla Aizenshtat. revbethoc@gmail.com

O'CARROLL, Bryan Douglas (SwFla) 912 63rd Ave W, Bradenton FL 34207 **S Geo's Epis Ch Bradenton FL 2011-** B Michigan 3/22/1967 s Kevin O'Carroll & A Lorraine. BA Eckerd 2008; MDiv Nash 2011. D 2/27/2011 P 8/28/2011 Bp Dabney Tyler Smith. m 8/31/1991 Susan Leslie Heiland c 3. revboc@gmail.com

O'CONNELL, Kelly Ann (O) 2602 Parkwood Ave., Toledo OH 43610 **R S Mk's Epis Ch Toledo OH 2005-** B Euclid OH 10/22/1967 d Jerome Michael O'Connell & Bernadette Jean. BA Ken 1989; MDiv EDS 1995. D 6/5/1999 P 6/4/2000 Bp M(arvil) Thomas Shaw III. m 8/25/1988 Frances Virginia Carr. Int S Lk's Epis Ch Scituate MA 2004-2005; Asst to R S Anne's In The Fields Epis Ch Lincoln MA 2000-2004; Bp's Aide Dio Massachusetts Boston MA 1999-2000. revkao@gmail.com

O'CONNOR, Andrew T (Kan) 3586 N. Forest Ridge St., Wichita KS 67205 **R Gd Shpd Epis Ch Wichita KS 2009-** B Glendale CA 7/19/1978 s Lawrence O'Connor & Mary. AB Boston Coll 2000; MDiv VTS 2005. D 6/11/2005 Bp Chester Lovelle Talton P 1/14/2006 Bp Frank Tracy Griswold III. m 8/10/2002 Heather S Killpatrick c 6. P-in-c S Mk's Par Altadena CA 2007-2009; Assoc R All SS-By-The-Sea Par Santa Barbara CA 2005-2007. frandrewoconnor@gmail.com

O'CONNOR JR, Edward Francis (Miss) 305 East Capitol, Jackson MS 39215 **Cler Dep GC Dio Mississippi Jackson MS 2009-; Presb's Discernment Com Dio Mississippi Jackson MS 2007-; Dn S Andr's Cathd Jackson MS 2007-; COM Dio Mississippi Jackson MS 2006-** B Memphis TN 11/5/1967 s Edward F O'Connor & Sandra Louise. BS U of Mississippi 1990; MS U of Sthrn Mississippi 1993; MDiv STUSo 2001. D 5/27/2001 Bp Duncan Montgomery Gray III P 1/16/2002 Bp Alfred Clark Marble Jr. m 12/28/1991 Deidra K Kirchmayr c 3. Stndg Com Dio Mississippi Jackson MS 2008-2010; Presb's Discernment Com Dio Mississippi Jackson MS 2007-2010; R S Ptr's By The Sea Gulfport MS 2004-2007; Cur S Paul's Epis Ch Meridian MS 2001-2004. eoconnor@standrewscathedral.org

O'CONNOR, Mary Colleen Mchale (WNY) 82 Clay St, Le Roy NY 14482 **R S Mk's Epis Ch Le Roy NY 2005-** B Binghamton NY 9/28/1957 d Edward G McHale & Nancy J. BA Mid 1979; MDiv EDS 1988. D 4/6/2002 P 10/6/2002 Bp Roger John White. m 8/17/1985 Christopher O'Connor. P-in-c S Paul's Ch Watertown WI 2002-2005.

ODA-BURNS, John MacDonald (Cal) 611 La Mesa Dr, Portola Valley CA 94028 **Asst S Bede's Epis Ch Menlo Pk CA 2011-** B Exeter UK 6/18/1931 s Hector MacDonald Burns & Marjorie Edith. AKCL Lon, King's Coll 1956; S Bon Coll Warminster GB 1957. Trans from Church Of England 4/1/1967 Bp C Kilmer Myers. m 5/18/1985 Marjorie Oda c 3. Assoc P Chr Ch Portola Vlly CA 2002-2009; Assoc Trsfg Epis Ch San Mateo CA 1999-2002; R Chr Ch Portola Vlly CA 1971-1996; Pstr S Bede's Epis Ch Menlo Pk CA 1967-1971; Assoc Trin Par Menlo Pk CA 1967-1971. bussels@batnet.com

ODDERSTOL, Sarah D (Chi) St. Mary's Episcopal Church, 306 S Prospect Avenue, Park Ridge IL 60068 **R S Mary's Ch Pk Ridge IL 2008-** B Philadelphia PA 6/20/1964 BSBA The Amer U; MDiv VTS 2003. D 6/14/2003 P 2/21/2004 Bp Carol Joy Gallagher. m 12/29/1990 Eric Odderstol c 2. Int R S Cyp's Epis Ch Hampton VA 2007-2008; Assoc R S Ptr's By The Sea Gulfport MS 2005-2007; Cur All Souls' Epis Ch San Diego CA 2004-2005; Asstg P Chr Ch Coronado CA 2004. sdodderstol@yahoo.com

ODEKIRK, Dennis Russell (Los) 830 Columbine Ct, San Luis Obispo CA 93401 B Mauston WI 1/13/1938 s Charles Russell Odekirk & Evelyn Alma. BA Lawr 1959; Rotary Fndt Fe U of Brussels Brussels BE 1960; BD SWTS 1963; MA U of Notre Dame 1977; PhD U CA 1990. D 6/3/1963 Bp William Hampton Brady P 12/21/1963 Bp Charles Bennison. m 6/20/1959 Charlene Elizabeth Sanford c 4. R All SS-By-The-Sea Par Santa Barbara CA 1993-2001; R S Mich's Epis Ch Carmichael CA 1986-1993; Sr Asst S Jas By The Sea La Jolla CA 1981-1986; Ecum Off Dio Wstrn Michigan Kalamazoo MI 1977-1981; R St Jn's Epis Ch of Sturgis Sturgis MI 1968-1981; Asst S Thos Epis Ch Battle Creek MI 1966-1968; Vic S Fran Ch Orangeville Shelbyville MI 1963-1966. Auth, *Bk Revs*. drdro@charter.net

O'DELL, Andrew Rivers (SC) Saint Matthew's Church, 210 S Main St, Darlington SC 29532 **R S Matt's Epis Ch Darlington SC 2007-** B Charleston SC 11/12/1974 s Robert & Carolyn. BS Davidson Coll 1997; MDiv STUSo 2003. D 5/21/2003 P 12/4/2003 Bp Edward Lloyd Salmon Jr. m 2/19/2000 Ellen Megan Timoney c 2. Cathd Of S Lk And S Paul Charleston SC 2003-2007. andrew@saintmatthews.us

O'DELL, Thomas Peyton (Neb) 123 W Washington St, Lexington VA 24450 **All SS Epis Ch Omaha NE 2006-** B Hodgenville KY 10/7/1950 s John Thomas O'Dell & Helen Catherine. BS Murray St U 1973; JD W&L 1976; MDiv GTS 1987. D 7/22/1987 P 3/1/1988 Bp David Reed. m 5/20/2000 Margaret L O'Dell c 3. P-in-c R E Lee Memi Ch (Epis) Lexington VA 2000-2005; R S Jn's Ch Roanoke VA 1992-2000; Asst R S Fran In The Fields Harrods Creek KY 1987-1992. todell@allsaintsomaha.org

ODGERS, Marie Christine Hanson (Neb) 8800 Holdrege St, Lincoln NE 68505 B Fremont NE 12/2/1932 d Willard Barton Hanson & Mathilda Truelsen. BA Nebraska Wesl 1955; AS Nebraska Wesl 1993. D 4/29/2010 Bp Joe Goodwin Burnett. m 5/31/1955 Richard Varney Odgers c 2. modgers@un1serve.un1.edu

ODIERNA, Robert William (NH) Po Box 412, Nashua NH 03061 **R Ch Of The Gd Shpd Nashua NH 1986-** B New York NY 8/7/1949 s Frank Charles Odierna & Carolyn Ruth. BA Hob 1971; MDiv GTS 1975; Cert Blanton-Peale Grad Inst 1981; DMin Andover Newton TS 1996. D 6/7/1975 Bp Jonathan Goodhue Sherman P 12/1/1975 Bp George E Rath. m 12/22/2001 Kim L Auger c 3. R All SS Epis Ch Oakville CT 1977-1986; P-in-c Chr Ch Ridgewood NJ 1975-1977. AAPC.

ODOM, Robert Martial (Dal) 5923 Royal Ln, Dallas TX 75230 **R S Lk's Epis Ch Dallas TX 2008-** B Baton Rouge LA 7/15/1968 s Harold Louis Sorrel Odom & Bonnie Earp. BA LSU 1990; MDiv Nash 2001. D 12/27/2000 P 9/8/2001 Bp Charles Edward Jenkins III. m 6/17/1995 Mary Inez Tannehill c 2. Assoc S Jas Epis Ch Baton Rouge LA 2004-2008; Cur Chr Ch Covington LA 2001-2004. rodom@stlukesdallas.org

O'DONNELL, Elizabeth Anne (Me) 16726 Lauder Ln, Dallas TX 75248 **D The Epis Ch Of The Trsfg Dallas TX 2009-** B Jamestown NY 12/3/1942 d Stanton Wood Gibbs & Grace Adele. BS Cor 1964; MA U Denv 1966. D 6/19/2004 Bp Chilton Abbie Richardson Knudsen. m 7/17/2003 S Bruce O'Donnell c 2. D S Jn's Ch Bangor ME 2004-2008. liz-bruceod2@netzero.net

O'DONNELL, John J (NH) 315 Mason Rd, Milford NH 03055 B Holyoke MA 10/31/1932 s John Joseph O'Donnell & Evelyn. BS U of Massachusetts 1954; Sem of Niagara Niagara NY 1960; DMin Andover Newton TS 1975. Rec from Roman Catholic 11/1/1974 as Priest Bp Robert Shaw Kerr. m 10/13/1973 Mary Wynne. Amer Assn for Mar & Fam Ther; AAPC; ACPE; NHAPP.

O'DONNELL, Michael Alan (Colo) 4940 Shirley Pl, Colorado Springs CO 80920 **VP & CDO Cath Chars of Colorado Sprg Colorado Sprg CO 2009-** B Bryn Mawr PA 6/17/1956 s William Francis O'Donnell & Valia Rich. BS Manhattan Coll 1979; MA Palmer TS 1981; post-Grad PrTS 1982; MA Cincinnati Chr U & Sem 1983; PhD K SU 1986. Trans from L'Eglise Episcopal au Rwanda 6/24/2004 Bp Keith Lynn Ackerman. m 6/9/1987 Rachel O'Donnell c 3. P-in-c Gr And S Steph's Epis Ch Colorado Sprg CO 2007-2009; 1. Clincl Pstr Counslr & Asstg P; 2. Assoc R Gr And S Steph's Epis Ch Colorado Sprg CO 2004-2007. Auth, "How A Man Prepares His Sons for Life," *Bk*, Bethany Hse, 1996; co-Auth, "Question of hon," *Bk*, Harper Collins/Zondervan, 1996; co-Auth, "Gd Kids," *Bk*, Doubleday, 1996; Auth, "Hm from Oz," *Bk*, Word Pub, 1994; co-Auth, "Heart of the Warrior (for fathers)," *Bk*, ACU Press, 1993. fathermichael3@comcast.net

OECHSEL JR, Russell Harold (Tex) 15811 Mesa Gardens Dr, Houston TX 77095 **Archd Dio Texas Houston TX 2008-; D S Mary's Epis Ch Cypress TX 2007-** B Bryn Mawr PA 12/25/1948 s Russell Harold Oechsel & Rita. BS Nthrn Illinois U Dekalb IL 1974; The Iona Sch for Mnstry 2007. D 2/9/2007 Bp Don Adger Wimberly. m 11/21/1998 Linda Sue Quesinberry c 3. roechsel@sbcglobal.net

OEHMIG, Henry King (ETenn) 14 Lindsay Ct, Chattanooga TN 37403 B Chattanooga TN 6/19/1951 s Lewis West Oehmig & Mary Augusta. BA U of Virginia 1973; MDiv STUSo 1977; DMin STUSo 1987. D 6/19/1977 P 4/17/1978 Bp William Evan Sanders. m 8/14/1976 Margaret Marie Davenport c 2. S Barn Ch Trion GA 1990-2007; S Andr's Cathd Jackson MS 1980-1983; R S Anne's Ch Millington TN 1979-1980; Vic Ravenscroft Chap Brighton TN 1978-1980; D-In-Trng S Jn's Epis Cathd Knoxville TN 1977-1978. Ed, "Between The Lines: Reflection On The Gospels Through The Ch," 1999; Auth, "Soul Openings I & Ii Through The Ch Year," 1999; Auth, "Synthesis: A Weekly Resource For Preaching & Wrshp In The Epis Tradition"; Auth, "Synthesis CE: A Lectionary Study Guide In The Epis Tradition"; Auth, "Syntheisis CE: A Weekly Comentary On The Epis Lectionary"; Ed, "Understanding The Sunday Scriptures: The Syntheisis Commentary". Ord Of S Lk; Ord S Mary; Royal & Ancient Golf Club; Seth Raynor Soc; Co-Pres. Outstanding Awd For Achievement Tennesssee Sports Hall Of Fame. kingowf@aol.com

OESTERLIN, Kathy E (RG) 1304 #East, Nakomis NE 87112 B Chicago IL 8/24/1944 d Everett Roland Champney & Helen. D 2/21/1998 Bp Terence Kelshaw. D S Mary's Epis Ch Albuquerque NM 1998-2002.

OESTERLIN, Peter William (RG) 3232 Renaissance Dr SE, Rio Rancho NM 87124 B Milwaukee WI 1/15/1933 s Ernst Oesterlin & Gertrude. BA U of

Vermont 1959; STB GTS 1962. D 6/6/1962 P 12/15/1962 Bp Harvey D Butterfield. m 8/1/1992 Jeanette Henderson c 2. R S Matt's Epis Ch Newton KS 2002-2004; Int Trin Ch Lawr KS 2000-2002; Int Gr Epis Ch Winfield KS 1999-2000; Int Trin Ch Arkansas City KS 1999-2000; Trin Epis Ch El Dorado KS 1998-1999; Int Gd Shpd Epis Ch Wichita KS 1996-1998; S Jn's Ch Wichita KS 1994-1998; Int Gr Epis Ch Ottawa KS 1993-1994; P-in-c S Andr's Epis Ch McCall ID 1977-1979; Bp Of ArmdF- Epis Ch Cntr New York NY 1969-1993; BEC Dio Vermont Burlington VT 1963-1967; S Paul's Epis Ch White River Jct VT 1962-1968; Cur S Jas Ch Woodstock VT 1962-1963. Coll of Chapl 1967. peteroesterlin@yahoo.com

OETJEN, Sandra Lee (Nev) 4613 Steeplechase Ave, North Las Vegas NV 89031 **D All SS Epis Ch Las Vegas NV 2006-** B Reno NV 12/6/1948 d William Lee Hiett & Adelma Emma. CDSP; UNR. D 10/14/2006 Bp Katharine Jefferts Schori. m 3/13/1993 Jack Oetjen c 1. NAAD (No Amer Assoc. for the Diac) 2006. theoetjens@earthlink.net

O'FLYNN, Donnel (CNY) 14 Madison Street, Hamilton NY 13346 **R S Thos Ch Hamilton NY 2004-** B Helena MT 3/1/1952 s John F O'Flynn & Dorothy. BA St. Jn's Coll Annapolis MD 1974; MDiv VTS 1985. D 6/8/1985 P 1/4/1986 Bp John Thomas Walker. m 6/28/1985 Janet Lee Christhilf c 2. R Gr Ch Vineyard Haven MA 1998-2004; Vic S Jn The Evang Yalesville CT 1989-1998; Cur Chr Ch New Haven CT 1985-1989. donnel_oflynn@hotmail.com

OFOEGBU, Daniel Okwuchukwu (Dal) Church Of The Ascension, 8787 Greenville Ave., Dallas TX 75243 **Asst Epis Ch Of The Ascen Dallas TX 2011-** B Nkpologwu Nigeria 11/28/1957 s Chikezie Ofoegbu & Agnes. BA Tougaloo Coll 1987; LM Angl TS 2005. D 8/19/2006 Bp James Monte Stanton P 9/6/2008 Bp Paul Emil Lambert. m 8/27/1992 Roseline Roseline Chijioke c 5. ascensiondaniel@yahoo.com

OGBURN JR, John Nelson (NC) 330 W Presnell St Apt 44, Asheboro NC 27203 B Greensboro NC 11/26/1932 s John Nelson Ogburn & Jean Sheldon Funk. BS U NC 1955; JD U NC 1957. D 5/31/1992 Bp Robert Whitridge Estill. m 2/18/1961 Edith Junkins. D S Andr's Ch Haw River NC 1993-1999; D The Epis Ch Of Gd Shpd Asheboro NC 1992-1999. jogburn1@triad.rr.com

OGDEN, Virginia Louise (Alb) 51 Brockley Dr, Delmar NY 12054 B New York City 2/7/1949 d Julius Baldy & Mildred. MA St. Bernards TS And Mnstry Rochester NY 2006. D 6/10/2006 Bp Daniel William Herzog P 1/6/2007 Bp William Howard Love. m 5/24/1980 Kenneth Ogden c 2. Int S Steph's Ch Delmar NY 2008-2010. gogden1@verizon.net

OGEA, Herman Joseph (WLa) 110 W 13th St, PO Box 912, Jennings LA 70546 **R Trin Ch Crowley LA 2009-** B Lake Charles LA 12/7/1947 s Jasper Ogea & Gladys Marie. MDiv Notre Dame Sem; CAS STUSo. Rec from Roman Catholic 6/23/2000 as Priest Bp Robert Jefferson Hargrove Jr. m 4/2/1994 Kathleen Lambert Doherty. S Barn Epis Ch Lafayette LA 2004-2005; R Chr Ch Bastrop LA 2000-2004. hermanog@bellsouth.net

OGIER JR, Dwight Eugene (At) 125 Betty Street, Clarkesville GA 30523 B Fort Benning GA 3/7/1942 s Dwight E Ogier & Constance. BA U So 1964; MDiv Ya Berk 1971; VTS 1977; DMin Pittsburgh TS 1989. D 6/20/1971 Bp James Loughlin Duncan P 4/29/1972 Bp Albert Ervine Swift. m 7/20/1962 Barbara Watts c 2. Int S Ptr the Apos Ch Christiansted VI 2009-2010; Asst S Dav's Ch Roswell GA 2001-2002; Assoc H Trin Par Decatur GA 1999-2001; R Epis Ch Of The H Sprt Cumming GA 1994-1999; Dio No Carolina Raleigh NC 1991-1992; Trst The TS at The U So Sewanee TN 1990-1994; Assoc R S Mich's Ch Raleigh NC 1987-1994; Assoc S Lk's Epis Ch Mobile AL 1984-1987; Trst The TS at The U So Sewanee TN 1984-1986; Vic H Fam Ch Orlando FL 1981-1984; R H Trin Epis Ch Bartow FL 1977-1981; Asst S Mk's Epis Ch Jacksonville FL 1972-1977; Cur H Trin Epis Ch W Palm Bch FL 1971-1972. Auth, *Forsyth Cnty News*. OHC 1978. dwightogier@windstream.net

OGILBY, Alexander (Del) 42 Meadow Ave, Westerly RI 02891 B Hartford CT 1/13/1928 s Remsen B Ogilby & Lois M. BA Harv 1948; STB EDS 1954. D 6/9/1954 Bp Walter H Gray P 3/18/1955 Bp Robert McConnell Hatch. S Andrews Sch Of Delaware Inc Middletown DE 1961-1991; Dio Delaware Wilmington DE 1959-1991; Asst Trin Ch On The Green New Haven CT 1954-1955. Pres Weekapaug RI Chap Soc 1956-1996.

OGLE, Albert Joy (Los) 3634 Seventh Ave Unit 6B, San Diego CA 92103 **St. Paul's Fndt for Int Reconcil. Cathd Ch Of S Paul San Diego CA 2010-; P Res Cathd Ch Of S Paul San Diego CA 2007-** B Belfast IE 3/9/1954 s Albert Joy Ogle & Thelma. BD U of Wales 1975; Trin-Dublin IRE 1976; PGCE Lon 1977; MA Trin-Dublin IRE 2007. Trans from Church of Ireland 2/1/1982 as Priest Bp Robert C Rusack. R S Geo's Epis Ch Laguna Hills CA 1999-2006; Int Pstr S Geo's Epis Ch Laguna Hills CA 1997-1998; Dio Los Angeles Los Angeles CA 1991-1996; Assoc All SS Ch Pasadena CA 1987-1991. Chapt, "Returning to Places of Wounded Memory," *The Sprt of Place*, U of Laval, 2010; Chapt, "Pstr Handbook for HIV," *The Gospel Imperative in the Midst of AIDS*, 1989; Auth, "Cnfrmtn Prog," *Stand Out in a Crowd*, 1978. Cn Dio Los Angeles 2003; Epis Relief and Deveopment Off Dio Los Angeles 2003. aogle@cox.net

OGLE SR, Louis Knox (La) 43 Hyacinth Dr, Covington LA 70433 B Galveston TX 5/6/1942 BA SE Louisiana U 1985. D 2/23/2002 Bp Charles Edward Jenkins III. m 2/3/1962 Margaret Berger c 3. D S Mich's Epis Ch Mandeville LA 2006-2011. ogle_l@bellsouth.net

OGLESBY, Charles Lucky (NC) 325 Glen Echo Ln Apt J, Cary NC 27518 **D Dio No Carolina Raleigh NC 1997-** B Breckenridge TX 8/22/1935 s Thomas Bryan Oglesby & Ava. BA U of Texas 1957; MA U Of Kentucky 1971; EdD No Carolina St U 1979. D 10/4/1987 Bp Robert Whitridge Estill. m 7/11/1992 Hilda Phillips c 2. D St Elizabeths Epis Ch Apex NC 2000-2002; D Dio Wstrn No Carolina Asheville NC 1993-1997; D Dio No Carolina Raleigh NC 1987-1993. NAAD. oglesbycl@aol.com

OGLESBY, Keith W (At) 3087 Monarch Pine Dr, Norcross GA 30071 B Atlanta GA 10/21/1958 s Joseph Preston Oglesby & Margaret Cole. BA Georgia St U 1980; MDiv Candler TS Emory U 2007. D 12/21/2006 P 6/27/2007 Bp J(ohn) Neil Alexander. m 9/1/1979 Lynn Howard c 3. R Epis Ch Of The H Sprt Cumming GA 2009; Asst S Aid's Epis Ch Milton GA 2007-2009. keith.oglesby@gmail.com

OGLESBY, Patricia (Ct) 1734 Huntington Tpke, Trumbull CT 06611 **P-in-c S Faith Ch Havertown PA 2003-** B Washington DC 2/19/1950 d Nicholas E Oglesby & Alma Lois. BA Connecticut Coll 1971; MDiv Yale DS 1976. D 6/18/1977 P 5/1/1978 Bp William Hawley Clark. Trin Epis Ch Trumbull CT 1997-2002; S Paul's Ch Elkins Pk PA 1993-1994; Epis Cmnty Serv Philadelphia PA 1987-1993; Trin Ch Swarthmore PA 1985-1986; P-in-c S Aidans Ch Cheltenham PA 1981-1982; Serv Ch of St Andrews & St Matthews Wilmington DE 1979-1980; Dio Delaware Wilmington DE 1979-1980.

OGUIKE, Martin Ugochukwu (NJ) 17 Woodbridge Ave, Sewaren NJ 07077 **Raritan Bay Epis Team Mnstry Sewaren NJ 2003-** B NG 9/12/1956 s Harold Oguike & Cordelia. DIT Trin Umuahia Ng 1983; MPhil U of Birmingham Gb 1988; PhD U of Port-Harcourt Ng 2005. Trans from Church Of Nigeria 1/1/2003 Bp David B(ruce) Joslin. m 11/17/1990 Ngozi Martin-Oguike c 4. Vic S Cyp's Epis Ch Hackensack NJ 1999-2002. moguike@aol.com

OGUS, Mary Hutchison (EC) 175 9th Ave, New York NY 10011 **R S Paul's Epis Ch Clinton NC 2011-** B Lake Charles LA 3/12/1954 BA U Denv. D 6/14/2003 P 6/26/2004 Bp Clifton Daniel III. m 12/2/1989 Richard Ogus. D The Ch Of The Epiph New York NY 2003-2004. mogus@ec.rr.com

OGWAL-ABWANG, Benoni Y (NY) 135 Remington Pl, New Rochelle NY 10801 B Adilang UG 10/9/1942 s Yovani Otto & Gladys. CTh Buwalasi Theol Coll 1962; DIT Bp Tucker Theol Coll Mukono Ug 1968; BD Hur 1974. Trans from Church of the Province of Uganda 6/1/1990 Bp Edmond Lee Browning. m 9/25/1971 Alice A Okoth c 1. Ch Of S Simon The Cyrenian New Rochelle NY 2001-2009; S Paul's Epis Ch Harrisburg PA 1989-2001. Hononary DD Hur U, London, Ontarion 1975. bishopogwal@aol.com

OH, David Yongsam (Nwk) 1224 McClaren Drive, Carmichael CA 95608 **S Mich's Epis Ch Carmichael CA 1991-** B Sinchun Korea 12/5/1933 s Chang Hai Oh & Sun Ai. BD Presb Theol Coll 1960; BA Sung Jeon U 1962; BD S Mich's TS 1967; VTS 1978; MDiv SFTS 1996. Trans from Anglican Church Of Korea 2/21/1990 as Priest Bp John Shelby Spong. m 8/15/1972 Anna Shin. davidoh@surewest.net

OH, KyungJa (Chi) 519 Theodore St., Loves Park IL 61111 **Vic S Chad Epis Ch Loves Pk IL 2003-** B Chicago IL 11/11/1951 d Fred F Ohr & Esther. BA IL Wesl 1973; MDiv SWTS 2000. D 6/15/2002 P 12/21/2002 Bp William Dailey Persell. c 2. Asst The Annunc Of Our Lady Gurnee IL 2002. revkjoh@gmail.com

O'HAGIN, Zarina Eileen Suarez (Vt) 215 Corner Rd, Hardwick VT 05843 **D S Jn The Bapt Epis Hardwick VT 2000-** B Ruislip UK 4/6/1954 d Harry O'Hagin & Czarina Ruth. BA U Chi 1976; JD U Chi 1984. D 2/7/1998 Bp Herbert Alcorn Donovan Jr. D Ch Of S Paul And The Redeem Chicago IL 1998-2000. zetso@aol.com

O HALLORAN, John Dennis (LI) 9526 92nd St Fl 2, Ozone Park NY 11416 **Died 7/1/2011** B Brooklyn NY 9/8/1928 s William Harold O'Halloran & Katherine Frances. Mercer TS. D 6/16/1962 P 12/21/1962 Bp James P De Wolfe. Auth, "Hist Of Massapequa Ny"; Auth, "Hist Of Sabine Par". Angl Orth Fllshp - Fndr, First Pres, Long Island Chapt, 1962.

O'HALLORAN, Shirley Joan (Colo) **H Apos Epis Ch Englewood CO 2003-** D 11/8/2003 Bp Robert John O'Neill.

O'HARA, Christina Swenson (SD) 2707 W 33rd St, Sioux Falls SD 57105 **DCE Ch Of The Gd Shpd Sioux Falls SD 2010-** B Toronto Canada 4/29/1968 d John Milton Swenson & Catherine Hafey. BA Mid 1991; MDiv Sioux Falls Sem 2010. D 4/30/2011 Bp John Thomas Tarrant. m 6/8/1991 David O'Hara c 3. cohara@sio.midco.net

O'HARA, Ellen (NY) 794 Traver Rd, Pleasant Valley NY 12569 **Mem Cler Critical Concerns Dio New York New York City NY 2007-; R S Paul's Ch Pleasant Vlly NY 1997-** B New York NY 5/18/1942 d Thomas Patrick O'Hara & Rebecca Vansant. BA CUNY 1964; MA Ford 1969; MDiv GTS 1997. D 6/14/1997 P 12/13/1997 Bp Richard Frank Grein. Soc Of S Jn The Evang. ellieo1@verizon.net

O'HARA-TUMILTY, Anne (Los) 26029 Laguna Court, Valencia CA 91355 **R S Jas' Par So Pasadena CA 2002-** B Utica NY 5/24/1950 d James Joseph O'Hara & Mary Agnes. BA California St U 1988; ETSBH 1991; MDiv Claremont TS 1993. D 6/13/1993 Bp Chester Lovelle Talton P 1/1/1994 Bp Frederick Houk Borsch. m 8/29/1981 David Tumilty c 2. Assoc All SS Par Beverly Hills CA 1993-2002. amtoht@aol.com

O'HEARNE, John Joseph (WMo) 4550 Warwick Blvd Apt 1212, Kansas City MO 64111 **Asstg P Gr And H Trin Cathd Kansas City MO 1992-** B Memphis TN 2/5/1922 s John Joseph O'Hearne & Norma Rose. Hendrix Coll 1940; BS Rhodes Coll 1944; MD U of Tennessee 1945; MS U CO 1951. D 5/30/1992 P 12/1/1992 Bp John Clark Buchanan. m 12/30/1982 Barbara Vanneman c 4. Auth, "Nonverbal Behavior In Groups &"; Auth, "Comprhensive Grp Psychol".

✠ **OHL, Rt Rev C(harles) Wallis** (NwT) 1802 Broadway St, Lubbock TX 79401 **Provsnl Bp Dio Ft Worth Ft Worth TX 2009-** B Bay City TX 10/21/1943 s Charles Wallis Ohl & Marguerite Olivia. BA U So 1965; MDiv Nash 1974; DD Nash 1998; DD STUSo 1998. D 12/20/1973 P 6/20/1974 Bp Chilton Powell. m 9/4/1964 Sheila K Byrd c 3. Bp Dio NW Texas Lubbock TX 1997-2008; Eccl Crt Dio Colorado Denver CO 1992-1994; R Ch Of S Mich The Archangel Colorado Sprg CO 1991-1997; Stndg Com Dio Oklahoma Oklahoma City OK 1987-1990; Chair COM Dio Oklahoma Oklahoma City OK 1985-1991; Chair - BEC Dio Oklahoma Oklahoma City OK 1983-1986; R S Mich's Epis Ch Norman OK 1977-1991; Stndg Com Dio Oklahoma Oklahoma City OK 1977-1982; Trst Nash Nashotah WI 1977-1981; Assoc S Paul's Cathd Oklahoma City OK 1974-1977. Auth, *Into the Household of God*, 1989. Hon DD Nash Nashotah WI 1998; Hon DD STUSo Sewanee TN 1998. cwo1021@aol.com

OHLSON, Elizabeth Anderson (NJ) 5752 West Ave, Ocean City NJ 08226 **D H Trin Epis Ch Ocean City NJ 2003-** B Winchester MA 6/6/1939 d Elmer Charles Anderson & Mary Caroline. Pennsylvania Johnson Cnty Cmnty Coll; Penn St U 1959; Penna Acad of the Fine Arts 1962; BFA U of Kansas 1980. D 2/3/1996 Bp Frank Tracy Griswold III. m 7/29/1961 Richard Frank Ohlson. D Ch Of The H Nativ Clarendon Hills IL 1996-2001. SCHC 1990. elizabeththohlson@aol.com

OHLSTEIN, Allen Michael (Ark) 310 W 17th St, Little Rock AR 72206 B Paterson NJ 11/6/1949 s Herbert Ohlstein & Anna Marie. BA Seton Hall U 1971; MPA Jacksonville St U 1978. D 6/11/2005 Bp Dean Elliott Wolfe. m 10/14/2000 Kimberly S Venzke c 4. Trin Cathd Little Rock AR 2010-2011; Epis Cmnty Serv Kansas City MO 2005-2009. NAAD 2004. aohlstein@trinitylittlerock.org

OHMER, John Richard (Va) 102 Cornwall St NW, Leesburg VA 20176 **R S Jas' Epis Ch Leesburg VA 1999-** B Grand Rapids MI 9/10/1961 s Donald Ohmer & Sofka. BA Wabash Coll 1984; Van 1985; MDiv VTS 1994. D 6/24/1994 Bp Edward Witker Jones P 1/22/1995 Bp Peter James Lee. m 12/17/1988 Mary Elizabeth Butler c 2. Assoc R S Mary's Epis Ch Arlington VA 1994-1999. Auth, "Epis Ch Curric For The Yth," 1999. Soc Of S Jn The Evang. maryohmer@msn.com

O'KEEFE, Gay Boggs (SO) 215 Henry St, Urbana OH 43078 B Chicago IL 5/31/1927 d George Warren Boggs & Dorothy Elizabeth. AA Clark St Cmnty Coll 1984; BA Antioch Coll 1986. D 12/3/1993 Bp Herbert Thompson Jr. c 2. D Ch Of The H Trin Epis Bellefontaine OH 1997-2002. NAAD.

O'KEEFE, Lloyd Frost (O) 970 Cottage Gate Dr, Kent OH 44240 B Columbus OH 7/12/1939 s Thomas George O'Keefe & Agnes. BA Heidelberg Coll 1962; BD VTS 1967. D 6/17/1967 P 12/16/1967 Bp Nelson Marigold Burroughs. m 12/27/1966 Roberta Ann Bode. Dio Ohio Cleveland OH 1988-2002; Asst To Bp Peace/Justice Dio Ohio Cleveland OH 1988-2001; Gr Ch Ravenna OH 1987-1988; R Chr Epis Ch Kent OH 1971-1980; Assoc Chr Epis Ch Warren OH 1969-1971; Cur Trin Ch Toledo OH 1967-1969. EPF 1988. rlokeefe@sbc.global.net

OKEREKE, Ndukaku Shadrack (Dal) 9624 Valley Mills Ln, Dallas TX 75227 B Nigeria 2/2/1950 s Isaiah Uba Okereke & Phube Manu. BS Bp Coll 1995; MDiv TESM 2005. Trans from Church Of Nigeria 8/15/2003 Bp James Monte Stanton. m 6/2/1984 Christiana Okeke c 4. St Peters Angl Ch Dallas TX 2006-2010. ndukakuokereke@sbcglobal.net

OKIE, Packard Laird (Fla) 35415 Beach Rd, Capistrano Beach CA 92624 **Died 10/4/2010** B Marshalton DE 6/28/1917 s William Richardson Okie & Charlotte Goldsborough. BA Pr 1939; MDiv VTS 1942; STM GTS 1962. D 5/30/1942 P 11/1/1942 Bp Henry St George Tucker. c 3. Auth, *Folk Mus of Liberia*, Ashe Records, 1954.

OKKERSE, Kenneth Howland (FdL) 4078 Valley View Trl, Sturgeon Bay WI 54235 **Chr Ch Green Bay WI 2000-** B Rye NY 11/10/1928 s Bertram Macpherson Okkerse & Jennie Aoita. BA U of Virginia 1951; GTS 1955. D 6/11/1955 Bp Benjamin M Washburn P 12/21/1955 Bp Henry Hean Daniels. m 6/18/1955 Grace van de Wint c 3. Int S Paul's Ch Suamico WI 2000-2001; Int S Jas Ch Manitowoc WI 1997-1998; Asst R S Anne's Ch De Pere WI 1994-1997; R Ch Of The Intsn Stevens Point WI 1990-1991; Dio Coun Dio Maine Portland ME 1985-1990; R S Andr's Ch Millinocket ME 1985-1990; Chr the King/H Nativ (Sturgeon Bay) Sturgeon Bay WI 1981-1985; Vic Ch Of The H Nativ Jacksonport Sturgeon Bay WI 1981-1985; Yth Camps Dio Fond du Lac Appleton WI 1980-1982; Asst R S Thos Ch Menasha WI 1978-1981; Ch Of The Epiph Norfolk VA 1973-1978. Sis Of H Nativ. kgokk@att.net

OKRASINSKI, Ronald Stanley (Va) Po Box 420, Colonial Beach VA 22443 **R S Mary's Ch Colonial Bch VA 1980-** B Irvington NJ 7/12/1941 s Stanley A Okrasinski & Helen C. GTF; BA Seton Hall U 1963; MDiv Immac Concep Sem 1968; VTS 1979; DMin U of Notre Dame 1986. Rec from Roman Catholic 6/1/1980 as Priest Bp Robert Bruce Hall. m 5/27/1972 Claudette J Okrasinski c 2. Chapl Cathd of St Ptr & St Paul Washington DC 1996; S Geo's Ch Fredericksburg VA 1980; Asst S Geo's Ch Fredericksburg VA 1978-1980. Auth, *Liturg*. smchurchmouse@verizon.net

OKTOLLIK, Carrie Ann (Ak) PO Box 29, Point Hope AK 99766 **Dio Alaska Fairbanks AK 2010-; S Thos Ch Point Hope AK 2010-** B Kotzebue AK 3/9/1952 d Howard Monroe & Emily. D 2/13/2010 Bp Mark Lawrence Mac Donald. m 8/31/1973 Martin Oktollik c 3. oktollikcarrie@yahoo.com

OKUNSANYA, Adegboyega Gordon (At) 4895 Gladstone Pkwy, Suwanee GA 30024 **R Ch Of The Incarn Atlanta GA 2005-** B Igbara-Oke ON NG 10/1/1942 s Isaac Oyelaja Sondla Okunsanya & Julie Adeyinka. Ripon Coll Cuddesdon Oxford Gb 1966; Westminster Coll 1969; Emml 1981; PrTS 1981; MDiv Van 1985; DMin Van 1988. Trans from Church Of Nigeria 2/17/1992 Bp R(aymond) Stewart Wood Jr. m 12/11/1965 Jean P Thomas-Cavalier. Dio Atlanta Atlanta GA 2003-2004; S Paul's Epis Ch Flint MI 2000-2003; S Jn The Div Epis Ch Burlington WI 2000; Dio Milwaukee Milwaukee WI 1998-2000; Dep Cong Dvlpmt Dio Milwaukee Milwaukee WI 1992-1998; Cathd Ch Of S Paul Detroit MI 1991-1998; Int The TS at The U So Sewanee TN 1988-1989; Assoc S Ann's Ch Nashville TN 1987-1988. Auth, "Issues Of Death Comparative Analysis On Jewish, Wstrn," *Afr Funeral Rites*; Auth, "Wstrn," *Afr Funeral Rites*. Iha; Ord For SS Of S Mary. agokun@hotmail.com

OKUSI, George Otiende (Los) 312 S Oleander Ave, Compton CA 90220 **P-in-c S Tim's Par Compton CA 2009-** B Kisumu 3/15/1964 s Petro Okusi Odida & Lona. Dip in Theol St. Jn's Sch of Mssn; MDiv Intl TS 2004; DMin Intl TS 2006. Trans from Anglican Church Of Kenya 4/29/2010 Bp Joseph Jon Bruno. m 12/11/1993 Christine Otiende. calleb48@yahoo.com

OLANDESE, Jan Susan (Nev) 2830 Phoenix St, Las Vegas NV 89121 B Seattle WA 11/22/1948 d Jerry J Klein & Freda. BA California St U 1970; MA U of Nevada at Las Vegas 1972; MDiv Oxf 2000; MDiv CDSP 2001; Clincl Residency CPE U of Iowa 2002. D 5/29/2001 Bp Katharine Jefferts Schori P 12/1/2001 Bp William Edwin Swing. m 2/26/2010 Carlo Olandese. Assoc R S Fran' Epis Ch San Francisco CA 2001-2002. Co-Auth, "Sex and Satanism in Susan Howatch's The High Flyer and The Heartbreaker," *Sprtl Identities: Lit and the Post Secular Imagination*, Ptr Lang Intl Acad Pub, 2010; Co-Auth, "Scandalous Risks: Sex, Scandal and Sprtlty in the Sixties," *Scandalous Truths: Essays by and about Susan Howatch*, Susquehanna U Press, 2005; Co-Auth, "Revs of The Novel, Sprtlty and Mod Culture," *The Angl Cath*, 2003; Co-Auth, "Psychic Sprtlty and Theol Romance in Susan Howatch's," *Chrsnty and Lit*, 2001. Who's Who in Amer Marquis Who's Who 2011; Who's Who in Amer Marquis Who's Who 2010. janwaples@aol.com

OLBRYCH, Jennie Clarkson (SC) 26 Saint Augustine Dr, Charleston SC 29407 **Porter-Gaud Sch Charleston SC 2006-; S Jas Santee Ch McClellanville SC 2006-** B Columbia SC 9/18/1950 d Andrew Crawford Clarkson & Sarah Fairbanks. S Mary's Jr Coll Raleigh NC 1969; BA U of So Carolina 1977; MDiv VTS 1988. D 6/23/1988 P 5/13/1989 Bp C(hristopher) FitzSimons Allison. m 6/2/1979 John Olbrych c 5. Dn of Charleston Convoc Dio So Carolina Charleston SC 1999-2002; Dn of W Charleston Convoc Dio So Carolina Charleston SC 1999-2002; R Epis Ch of the Gd Shpd Charleston SC 1998-2005; S Steph's Epis Ch Charleston SC 1996-1997; Cong Dvlpmnt Com Dio So Carolina Charleston SC 1996; S Mich's Epis Ch Charleston SC 1994; Cn Dio So Carolina Charleston SC 1993-1998; Cn for Int Mnstry Dio So Carolina Charleston SC 1993-1998; S Jude's Epis Ch Walterboro SC 1993-1994; Asst to R S Paul's Epis Ch Summerville SC 1989-1993; Asst Cathd Of S Lk And S Paul Charleston SC 1988. jolbrych@portergaud.edu

OLDFATHER, Susan Kay (Kan) PO Box 187, Kingsville MD 21087 **Int R S Jn's Ch Kingsville MD 2010-** B Bloomington IN 3/9/1947 d Frank L Oldfather & Mary Ellen West. Dplma in Angl Stds The TS at The U So; MLS U of Maryland Coll Pk 1994; MDiv Jesuit TS at Berkeley 2003. D 6/6/2009 P 6/5/2010 Bp Dean Elliott Wolfe. c 2. chaplainsue@gmail.com

OLDHAM ROBINETT, Lynn Margaret (Cal) 42 Glen Dr, Fairfax CA 94930 **Ch Of The H Innoc Corte Madera CA 2006-** B Oakland CA 5/29/1966 d Donald Keith Oldham & Susan. BA U CA 1988; MDiv CDSP 1998. D 12/5/1998 P 6/5/1999 Bp William Edwin Swing. m 8/31/1997 Ryan Robinett c 3. Asst R S Paul's Epis Ch San Rafael CA 1998-1999. lynnmor@gmail.com

OLDLAND, William Daniel (SC) 212 Virginia Ave., Cheraw SC 29520 **S Dav's Ch Cheraw SC 2007-** B Charleston SC 10/13/1959 s William Albut Oldland & Joan Jeannette. BS Coll of Charleston 1981; MDiv VTS 2000. D 5/27/2000 Bp Robert Carroll Johnson Jr P 6/9/2001 Bp J(ames) Gary Gloster. m 4/16/1983 Ellen Walker Taylor c 2. S Thos Epis Ch Reidsville NC

2000-2007; S Fran Ch Greensboro NC 1991-1997. Oral Interp Of Scripture VTS 2000. swcreekbillo@bellsouth.net

OLDS, Kevin (Mass) 8 Prospect Street, Saugus MA 01906 **R S Jn's Epis Ch Saugus MA 2010-** B Oswego NY 9/8/1975 s Don Ivan Olds & Sherry Ann. BA Un Coll 1997; MDiv Drew TS 2008; STM The GTS 2010. D 11/14/2009 P 6/19/2010 Bp George Edward Councell. m 7/4/2009 Jill Rumpf. kevinolds@comcast.net

O'LEARY, Jane (Md) 6011 Chesworth Rd., Baltimore MD 21228 **Eccl Crt Dio Maryland Baltimore MD 2008-; Eccl Crt Dio Maryland Baltimore MD 2008-; D Ch Of The Guardian Ang Baltimore MD 2003-** B Rochester NY 2/21/1949 d John Francis O'Leary & Joyce C. BA GW 1971; MS Sthrn Connecticut St U 1976; MSW U of Maryland 2004. D 12/2/1989 Bp Arthur Edward Walmsley. m 11/20/2005 William Thomas Mundy c 3. D Chr Epis Ch Norwich CT 2000-2002; D Chr Epis Ch Middle Haddam CT 1997-1998; Eccl Crt Dio Connecticut Hartford CT 1995-2002; Ecclesiatical Crt Dio Connecticut Hartford CT 1995-2002; D S Jas Ch Preston CT 1990-1996; S Paul's Epis Ch Willimantic CT 1990-1991. NAAD 1989. janeoleary@yahoo.com

OLER, Clarke Kimberly (Los) 407 W Walnut St, Pasadena CA 91103 B Brightwaters NY 11/14/1925 s Wesley Marion Oler & Imogene Mary. BA Ya 1949; MDiv VTS 1956; Med S Jn 1974; MA California 1985. D 6/3/1956 Bp Horace W B Donegan P 12/1/1956 Bp Beverley D Tucker. c 3. All SS Ch Pasadena CA 1982-1989; All SS Par Beverly Hills CA 1975-1982; Chair Of The Stndg Com Dio New York New York City NY 1971-1972; Com Dio New York New York City NY 1970-1974; Dioc Coun Dio New York New York City NY 1970-1972; Stndg Com Dio New York New York City NY 1968-1971; Chair Of The Dept Of CE Dio New York New York City NY 1964-1966; Dioc Coun Dio New York New York City NY 1964-1966; R Ch Of The H Trin New York NY 1962-1975; Dept Of CE Dio New York New York City NY 1962-1964; Dept Of CE Dio Ohio Cleveland OH 1960-1962; Coll Wk Dept Dio Ohio Cleveland OH 1958-1962; Asst S Jn's Ch Youngstown OH 1956-1959. ckoler@earthlink.net

OLIFIERS JR, Edmund Wilbur (LI) 2129 Bucknell Ter, Silver Spring MD 20902 **Died 8/24/2011** B Brooklyn NY 1/10/1929 s Edmund Wilbur Olifiers & Emma. BA St. Johns U 1950; STB GTS 1959; MDiv GTS 1971. D 4/11/1953 P 10/31/1953 Bp James P De Wolfe. c 6. Contrib, *The Pat Bk*, Macmillan, 1983; Auth, *Contrib The Pat Bk*. Hon Cn Sao Paulo Cathd, Lisbon, Portugal 1971.

OLIVER, Eugene Emery (O) 250 East Alameda St #418, Santa Fe NM 87501 B Independence KS 4/2/1926 s Leonard Leo Oliver & Juanita Elizabeth. BA OH SU 1959; MDiv Bex 1962. D 6/9/1962 P 12/15/1962 Bp Nelson Marigold Burroughs. m 4/19/1947 Blanche Marie Conaway c 2. R S Paul's Ch Steubenville OH 1965-1986; Cur S Paul's Ch Akron OH 1962-1965. eeobmo@msn.com

OLIVER, Robert Gordon (Los) 3750 Peachtree Rd Ne, Atlanta GA 30319 B Hazlehurst GA 4/4/1930 s William Frazier Oliver & Lorrayne. BS U Of Florida 1951; MDiv STUSo 1959. D 6/24/1959 P 4/1/1960 Bp Edward Hamilton West. Corp Dio Los Angeles Los Angeles CA 1987-1990; R S Jas Par Los Angeles CA 1979-1990; The Amer Cathd of the H Trin Paris 75008 FR 1974-1979; Stndg Com Dio Mississippi Jackson MS 1972-1974; Dn S Andr's Cathd Jackson MS 1971-1974; R H Innoc Ch Atlanta GA 1968-1971; Sr Cn In Res S Jn's Cathd Jacksonville FL 1961-1968; M-in-c Ch Of The H Comm Hawthorne FL 1959-1961; M-in-c S Andr's Ch Interlachen FL 1959-1961. Auth, "Cathd Age". Ord S Jn Jerusalem.

OLIVERO, Cesar Olivero (SwFla) 17241 Edgewater Dr, Port Charlotte FL 33948 **M-in-c S Jas Epis Ch Port Charlotte FL 2003-** B Elmhurst NY 6/12/1959 Lic VTS. D 6/14/2003 P 12/19/2003 Bp John Bailey Lipscomb. m 5/26/1994 Mireya Olivero c 5. Dio SW Florida Sarasota FL 2003. mirces2@comcast.net

OLIVO, David Andrew (ETenn) 305 W 7th St, Chattanooga TN 37402 **Cur S Paul's Epis Ch Chattanooga TN 2011-** B Portsmouth VA 6/4/1986 s David Olivo & Maxine. BA Milligan Coll 2008; MDiv The TS at The U So 2011. D 6/4/2011 Bp Charles Glenn VonRosenberg. d.andy.olivo@gmail.com

OLLER, Janet Petrey (Ind) St. Andrew's Episcopal Church, 520 E. Seminary St, Greencastle IN 46135 **Anti-Racism Com Dio Indianapolis Indianapolis IN 2011-; Safeguarding God's People Trnr Dio Indianapolis Indianapolis IN 2011-; Stndg Com Dio Indianapolis Indianapolis IN 2011-; Int S Andr's Epis Ch Greencastle IN 2011-** B Washington DC 3/24/1952 d Harry Grady Petrey & Genevieve Frederick. BA U CO 1973; JD U of Houston 1983; MDiv SWTS 2009. D 6/20/2009 Bp Catherine Elizabeth Maples Waynick P 1/24/2010 Bp Duncan Montgomery Gray III. m 6/12/1999 Jeffery Scott Oller. Judicial Crt Dio Mississippi Jackson MS 2010-2011; Asst R and Chapl S Ptr's Ch Oxford MS 2009-2011. janet.oller@gmail.com

OLMEDO-JAQUENOD, Nina (Cal) 1321 Webster St, Alameda CA 94501 B Rosario Santa Fe AR 2/15/1928 d Carlos Maria Olmedo & Irma Roberta. MA U Of Bueno Aires AR 1942; MRE New Orleans Bapt TS 1957; MDiv CDSP 1980; MA California St U 1981. D 6/24/1978 Bp William Foreman Creighton P 6/1/1980 Bp John Raymond Wyatt. P-in-c S Mths Epis Ch San Ramon CA 1984-1985; Centro Hispano (Siruiendo El Delta) Walnut Creek CA 1979-1985; Vic S Alb's Epis Ch Brentwood CA 1978-1980; Dio California San Francisco CA 1978-1979. Auth, "Var arts," *Journ Of Wmn Ministers*; Auth, "Chld'S Stories & Poetry," *Versos Para Ninos*; Auth, "Var arts," *Wit*. bobo52000@comcast.net

OLMO, Manuel (PR) PO Box 2930, Bayamon PR 00960 **Died 11/17/2009** B 5/11/1938 D.

OLMSTED, Nancy Kay Young (RI) Po Box 245, Lincoln RI 02865 B Duluth MN 2/23/1947 d Telford Evan Young & Evelyn Winnifred. BA Gri 1969; JD U Chi 1972; MDiv EDS 1990. D 8/4/1990 P 2/23/1991 Bp Douglas Edwin Theuner. m 8/23/1969 David Lester Olmsted. Chr Ch In Lonsdale Lincoln RI 1994-2005; S Paul's Ch Pawtucket RI 1990-1993. Phi Beta Kappa; Phi Beta Kappa. nkdlolmsted@comcast.net

OLOIMOOJA, Joseph Mtende (Los) 1501 N Palos Vevoler Dr. #128, Harbor City CA 90710 **Chr The Gd Shpd Par Los Angeles CA 2010-** B Kenya 5/19/1972 s Kanchori Oloimooja Olimbolo & Lente. Bible Coll Of E Afr Kenya 1994; MDiv Intl Theol Los Angeles CA 2003. Trans from Anglican Church Of Kenya 11/1/2005 Bp Joseph Jon Bruno. c 4. Epis Ch Of The Adv Los Angeles CA 2007-2010; Asstg P Par Of S Mary In Palms Los Angeles CA 2006-2007. oloimooja@yahoo.com

OLSEN, Christiana (CGC) 1 Saint Francis Dr, Gulf Breeze FL 32561 **R S Fran Of Assisi Gulf Breeze FL 2010-** B New York NY 9/29/1964 d James Carl Olsen & Judith Riggs. BA Sweet Briar Coll 1986; Angl Stds Ya Berk 2002; MDiv Yale DS 2002. D 6/15/2002 Bp M(arvil) Thomas Shaw III P 6/27/2003 Bp James Monte Stanton. S Mich And All Ang Ch Dallas TX 2008-2010; Cathd of St Ptr & St Paul Washington DC 2007-2008; S Peters-In-The-Woods Epis Ch Fairfax Sta VA 2007; Assoc for Pstr Care S Mich And All Ang Ch Dallas TX 2002-2007. Daugthers of the King 2005. christianaolsen@hotmail.com

OLSEN, Daniel Kevin (Pa) Box 681, Oaks PA 19456 **R St Pauls Epis Ch Oaks PA 1995-** B Indianapolis IN 9/2/1954 s Bernhard Olsen & Elizabeth Ann. Ball St U 1973; BA Taylor U Upland IN 1976; MA No Pk TS 1978; MDiv TESM 1992. D 6/3/1992 Bp Edward Harding MacBurney P 12/1/1992 Bp Alexander Doig Stewart. m 4/25/1981 Katharine Ellen Chambers c 3. Cur All SS Ch Wynnewood PA 1992-1995. Amer Angl Coun; Angl Comm Ntwk.

OLSEN, David Logie (Ore) 10445 Sw Greenleaf Ter, Tigard OR 97224 B Portland OR 9/6/1936 s Oscar Nels Olsen & Melva Burton. Lewis & Clark Coll 1954; BA U Denv 1959; MDiv Nash 1972. D 8/10/1972 P 2/15/1973 Bp James Walmsley Frederic Carman. Chr Ch S Helens OR 1990-2000; Treas Cler Assn Dio Oregon Portland OR 1986-1998; Chair, Oregon Liturg Comm. Dio Oregon Portland OR 1985-1998; R S Dav's Epis Ch Portland OR 1980-1990; COM Dio Oregon Portland OR 1980-1983; Bd of Trst Dio Oregon Portland OR 1979-1987; Liturg Cmsn Dio Oregon Portland OR 1974-2000; Vic S Jn's Epis Ch Toledo OR 1973-1980; Vic S Lk's Ch Waldport OR 1973-1980; Vic S Steph's Ch Newport OR 1973-1980; Asst All SS Ch Portland OR 1972-1973. dav36@earthlink.net

OLSEN, Donna Jeanne Hoover (Ind) 2601 East Thompson Road, Indianapolis IN 46227 B Chicago IL 11/24/1943 d Donald Jean Hoover & Cosette. BA U of Indianapolis 1974; MA Chr TS 1993; U of Iowa 1999; Ivy Tech St Coll 2010. D 6/23/1995 Bp Edward Witker Jones. m 6/7/1963 Harold Nelvin Olsen c 3. Chapl Trin Ch Indianapolis IN 2001-2003; D S Tim's Ch Indianapolis IN 1995-2001; DRE S Paul's Epis Ch Indianapolis IN 1995; DRE S Paul's Epis Ch Indianapolis IN 1989-1995; DRE Chr Ch Cathd Indianapolis IN 1982-1989. Auth, "Journey to Easter," *Journey to Easter*; Auth, "Ldr Resources," *Ldr Resources*; Auth, "Ldr Resources," *Ldr Resources*; Auth, "Words of Truth," *Words of Truth*. elsnert@aol.com

OLSEN, Jean (RI) 35-C W Castle Way, Charlestown RI 02813 B Providence RI 7/31/1943 d Bernard Joseph Barry & Florence Mable. D 7/13/1985 Bp George Nelson Hunt III. warm@ids.com

OLSEN JR, Lloyd Lein (CFla) 992-B E Michigan St, Orlando FL 32806 **R Epis Ch Of The H Sprt Apopka FL 2007-** B Richmond VA 6/21/1951 s Lloyd Lein Olsen & Martha Jean. BGS U MI 1984; MDiv VTS 1984; DMin Reformed TS 2004; U of Bristol 2005; London TS 2009. D 10/11/1984 Bp H Coleman McGehee Jr P 9/30/1985 Bp William Hopkins Folwell. m 2/21/1982 Ginette Eustache c 2. P-in-c S Chris's Ch Orlando FL 2002-2005; Cathd Ch Of S Lk Orlando FL 2002; R S Paul's Epis Ch Jackson MI 1991-1998; R S Ptr's Ch Fernandina Bch FL 1989-1991; Assoc R S Mich's Ch Orlando FL 1987-1989; Dio Cntrl Florida Orlando FL 1986-1987; Asst R Trin Ch Vero Bch FL 1985-1987. "Theodicy And Chr Mnstry: The Practical Theol Of Suffering," 2004. olseninc@hotmail.com

OLSEN, Loren Michael (Los) St. Cross by-the Sea, 1818 Monterey Blvc., Hermosa Beach CA 90254 **Assoc S Cross By-The-Sea Ch Hermosa Bch CA 2008-; D S Cross By-The-Sea Ch Hermosa Bch CA 2008-** B Denver CO 3/7/1948 s Lawrence Frederich Olsen & Lela Maxine. BA Pk U 1976; MA Webster U 1980; ETSBH 2007; MDiv CDSP 2008. D 6/7/2008 P 1/10/2009 Bp Joseph Jon Bruno. m 5/21/1966 Cassandra Althea Cassandra Athea Potter c 2. molsen@stcross.org

O

OLSEN, Meredith DK (Md) 4127 Chadds Crossing, Marietta GA 30062 B Drexel Hill PA 2/7/1975 d Joseph Dawson Kefauver & Jayne Elenor. BA Birmingham-Sthrn Coll 1998; MDiv Candler TS Emory U 2002; STM GTS 2005. D 6/12/2005 P 7/26/2006 Bp J(ohn) Neil Alexander. m 8/21/1999 Derek A Olsen c 2. S Mk's Ch Highland MD 2010-2011; S Jn's Ch Reisterstown MD 2008-2009; S Marg's Ch Carrollton GA 2007-2008; The Epis Ch Of S Ptr And S Paul Marietta GA 2006. mkefauverolsen@hotmail.com

OLSEN, Robert M (NCal) 8070 Glen Creek Way, Citrus Heights CA 95610 **D S Geo's Ch Carmichael CA 2011-; Epis Cmnty Serv Dio Nthrn California Sacramento CA 2001-** B Maderra CA 7/12/1947 s Hans C Olsen & Ida Francis. BA California St U 1969; MS USC 1988; BA Sch for Deacons 2001. D 7/28/2001 Bp Jerry Alban Lamb. m 9/14/1968 Sandra J Schlotthauer c 2. rolsen@surewest.net

OLSEN, William Henry (O) 800 Southerly Rd. Apt. 1808, Baltimore MD 21286 **Died 10/5/2009** B Elyria OH 11/21/1922 s Clarence Albert Olsen & Natalie Hill. BS USNA 1943; MDiv VTS 1981. D 6/27/1981 P 1/7/1982 Bp John Harris Burt. c 4. billolsen2@verizon.net

OLSON, Alice Ingrid (Minn) 7218 Hill Rd, Two Harbors MN 55616 **D S Andr's By The Lake Duluth MN 2002-** B Duluth MN 7/30/1947 d Walter Pylkkanen & Ina Ingrid. D 6/17/2001 Bp James Louis Jelinek. m 7/2/1966 Quentin William Olson.

OLSON, Anna Burns (Los) 4274 Melrose Ave, Los Angeles CA 90029 **S Mary's Epis Ch Los Angeles CA 2011-** B Hanover NH 9/3/1971 BA Stan 1993; MDiv UTS 1998. D 6/24/2000 Bp Joseph Jon Bruno P 1/6/2001 Bp Frederick Houk Borsch. m Steven K Ury c 2. The Par Ch Of S Lk Long Bch CA 2008-2011; P-in-c Trin Epis Par Los Angeles CA 2002-2006; H Faith Par Inglewood CA 2000-2002; Assoc R H Faith Par Inglewood CA 1998-2000. ao90004@gmail.com

OLSON, Britt Elaine (NCal) 262 Swenson Ct., Auburn CA 95603 **Cn to the Ordnry Dio Nthrn California Sacramento CA 2006-** B Fairbanks AK 11/19/1959 d Charles Edward Olson & Zoe Elaine. BA U of Oregon 1981; MDiv CDSP 1996. D 6/15/1996 P 12/13/1996 Bp Robert Louis Ladehoff. m 8/11/2007 Bryon H Hansen. Cn for Evang & Cong. Dev. Dio El Camino Real Monterey CA 2005-2006; R S Paul's Epis Ch Sparks NV 1998-2005; Asst Chr Ch Par Lake Oswego OR 1996-1998; Prog Assoc S Mich And All Ang Ch Portland OR 1992-1993. britt-olson@sbcglobal.net

OLSON, Corinna (SeFla) 8888 SW 131st Ct Apt 205, Miami FL 33186 **P-in-c S Lk The Physcn Miami FL 2006-** B Baton Rouge LA 4/1/1958 d John Ernest Olson & Karen Ann. BA Florida Atlantic U 1982; MDiv GTS 2004. D 4/17/2004 P 12/10/2004 Bp Leopold Frade. cori.olson@gmail.com

OLSON, Ellen Elizabeth (Neb) 609 Avenue C, Plattsmouth NE 68048 B Sioux City IA 9/12/1946 D 1/6/2003 Bp James Edward Krotz. m 4/24/1965 Merlin Leroy Olson.

OLSON, Kurt Allan (Chi) 5057 W Devon Ave, Chicago IL 60646 **Asst Ch Of The Ascen Chicago IL 2008-** B Chicago IL 5/12/1944 s Sigfrid John Olson & Karen E. DMin U Chi; BD Roosevelt U 1977; MDiv SWTS 1977. D 6/8/1974 Bp Quintin Ebenezer Primo Jr P 12/1/1974 Bp James Winchester Montgomery. m 10/19/1966 Nancy Lamkin. Advoc Hlth Care Oak Brook IL 1992-1993; R S Richard's Ch Chicago IL 1976-2002; Cur Trin Epis Ch Wheaton IL 1974-1976. Soc Of S Jn The Evang.

OLSSON, Paul V (Nwk) 32 Hillview Ave, Morris Plains NJ 07950 **Bp's Human Resource Advsry Com Dio Newark Newark NJ 2010-; Comm. on Constitutions & Cn Dio Newark Newark NJ 2010-; Diac Ord Com, COM Dio Newark Newark NJ 2004-2012; R S Paul's Epis Ch Morris Plains NJ 2003-** B Woodbury NJ 5/14/1963 s Victor Edward Olsson & Virginia Lee. BA JHU 1985; MIA Col 1987; MDiv GTS 1999. D 2/6/1999 P 9/11/1999 Bp Richard Frank Grein. Dioc Coun Dio Newark Newark NJ 2004-2008; Asst Chr And S Steph's Ch New York NY 1999-2003. rectorstpaulsmp@optonline.net

OLVER, Matthew Scott Casey (Dal) 6569 Kingsbury Dr, Dallas TX 75231 **Cur for Liturg and Chr Formation Ch Of The Incarn Dallas TX 2010-; Angl-RC Theol Consult in the USA (ARC-USA) Epis Ch Cntr New York NY 2008-** B Waynesboro PA 2/20/1980 BA Wheaton Coll 2001; MDiv Duke DS 2005. D 11/1/2005 P 5/27/2006 Bp James Monte Stanton. m 7/27/2001 Kristen Casey Cacsey c 2. Exec Coun Dio Dallas Dallas TX 2008-2011; Cur for Chr Formation Ch Of The Incarn Dallas TX 2008-2009; Cur for Yth and Young Families Ch Of The Incarn Dallas TX 2006-2008; Ecum Off Dio Dallas Dallas TX 2005-2009; Epis Rep on Plnng Team, Ecum Conf for Young Cler Epis Ch Cntr New York NY 2005-2007; Cur and Sch Chapl S Jn's Epis Ch Dallas TX 2005-2006. Auth, "Impassioned Unity: The Sprtl Grammar of Cbury's Visit to Rome," *Esprit*, Jan/Feb, 2007; co-Auth, "True Ecum," *LivCh*, 1921-01-01, 2007; Auth, "A New Annunc," *Esprit*, April, 2006; Auth, "Re-Reception: A Fundamental Tool for Chr Unity," *LivCh*, 1915-01-01, 2006. No Amer Patristic Soc 2007; The AAR (AAR) 2005; The No Amer Acad of Ecumenists (NAE) 2005. mcl, Mstr of Div Duke DS 2005. matthewscolver@gmail.com

O'MALLEY, Donald Richard (WNC) 101 Piney Rd, Hayesville NC 28904 B Camden NJ 8/7/1952 D 6/7/1997 P 12/21/1997 Bp Robert Hodges Johnson. m 6/8/1974 Deborah O'Mallley. Ch Of The Gd Shpd Hayesville NC 1997-2003. domalley@dnet.net

OMERNICK, Marilyn (Los) St. Michael the Archangel Church, 361 Richmond St., El Segundo CA 90245 **S Mich The Archangel Par El Segundo CA 2011-** B Stevens Point WI 6/9/1955 d Raymond Omernick & Victoria. BS Viterbo Coll 1977; MA MI SU 1980; MS MI SU 1983; MDiv ETSBH 1999. D 6/26/1999 P 1/8/2000 Bp Frederick Houk Borsch. m 6/17/2008 Carol Grosvenor. P-in-c S Mary's Epis Ch Los Angeles CA 2008-2011; P-in-c S Mich and All Ang Epis Ch Studio City CA 2007; P-in-c S Jn's Mssn La Verne CA 2006-2007; Int St Johns Pro-Cathd Los Angeles CA 2004-2005; Int S Alb's Epis Ch Los Angeles CA 2004; Int S Mich and All Ang Epis Ch Studio City CA 2003-2004; Sr Assoc S Cross By-The-Sea Ch Hermosa Bch CA 1999-2003. laomernick@yahoo.com

ONATE-ALVARADO, Gonzalo Antonio (EcuC) Apartado Postal #5250, Guayaquil Ecuador B Celica Loja EC 10/4/1957 s Gerardo Onate-Urrutia & Ana Maria. U Cuenca 1981; MA U Havana 1983; Cert Cntr Theol Stds 1985. D 2/2/1986 Bp Adrian Delio Caceres-Villavicencio. m 8/31/1981 Deyce Aquilar-Ordonez. Litoral Dio Ecuador Guayaquil EQ EC 1987-1991; Iglesia Epis Del Ecuador Ecuador 1986. Auth, "Var Lectures On Publ Hlth U Of Cuenca".

O'NEIL, Janet Anne (Mo) 808 N Mason Rd, Saint Louis MO 63141 **D S Tim's Epis Ch Creve Coeur MO 2007-** B St Paul MN 5/4/1944 d Percy T Watson & Jeanne. BA Lawr 1966; Med U of Missouri 1989. D 5/17/2007 Bp George Wayne Smith. m 8/20/1966 Michael O'Neil c 2. jawoneil@gmail.com

O'NEILL, Bruce (Cal) 2833 Claremont Blvd, Berkeley CA 94705 **Chair of Personl Practices Com Dio California San Francisco CA 2003-; R S Clem's Ch Berkeley CA 1997-** B Walnut Creek CA 8/4/1966 s Robert Gardiner O'Neill & Inge. BA U CA 1988; MDiv VTS 1994. D 6/4/1994 P 6/3/1995 Bp William Edwin Swing. m 7/2/1994 Elizabeth Lemm c 1. Asst R S Bede's Epis Ch Menlo Pk CA 1994-1997. bruceoneill@earthlink.net

O'NEILL, Dennis Topliss (Fla) 645 S Lawrence Blvd, Keystone Heights FL 32656 **R S Mk's Ch Starke FL 2003-** B Jacksonville FL 9/1/1946 BS SUNY 1983; MDiv STUSo 2003. D 6/8/2003 P 12/7/2003 Bp Stephen Hays Jecko. m 8/10/1984 Marianne Katherine Harrison c 2. doneill@sc.rr.com

O'NEILL, Grayce Margo (Va) 6800 Columbia Pike, Annandale VA 22003 **R S Alb's Epis Ch Annandale VA 2005-** B Huntington NY 9/28/1947 d George William Westerfield & Marion Christine. AAS Suffolk Cnty Cmnty Coll 1967; BS SUNY 1974; no degree Duke DS 1993; MDiv GTS 1994. D 6/23/1994 Bp Robert Carroll Johnson Jr P 12/23/1994 Bp Huntington Williams Jr. m 3/5/2011 James Rowe c 3. Fin Fac - CREDO II Credo Inst Inc. Memphis TN 2008-2011; Assoc R S Paul's Epis Ch Winston Salem NC 1999-2004; Vic S Mk's Epis Ch Roxboro NC 1994-1998. goneill928@gmail.com

O'NEILL, Joanne Carbone (Nwk) 97 Highwood Ave., Tenafly NJ 07670 **S Barn Epis Ch Williston FL 2007-; D Ch Of The Atone Tenafly NJ 2006-** B Bronx NY 1/5/1948 d Rocco Carbone & Rita. BA Rutgers St U 1983; MS Ford 1993. D 12/9/2006 Bp Carol Joy Gallagher. m 4/16/1983 James O'Neill. jrconeill@yahoo.com

✠ **O'NEILL, Rt Rev Robert John** (Colo) 7937 E 24th Ave, Denver CO 80238 **Bp of Colorado Dio Colorado Denver CO 2003-** B Pasadena CA 2/6/1955 s Richard Hugh O'Neill & Joanne Ross. BA TCU 1977; MDiv Yale DS 1981. D 6/28/1981 Bp William Grant Black P 1/1/1982 Bp William Carl Frey Con 10/4/2003 for Colo. m 8/6/1977 Virginia L Lughes c 3. R Par Of The Epiph Winchester MA 1991-2003; Cn S Jn's Cathd Denver CO 1981-1991. Auth, "Exploring The Liturg," S Jn'S Cathd, 1991; Auth, "Focus On Lk," *Living The Gd News*, 1991. gingeroneill1@gmail.com

O'NEILL, Vincent DePaul (Haw) 98-939 Moanalua Rd, Aiea HI 96701 B Hartford CT 9/5/1938 s John Francis O'Neill & Gertrude Mary. BA S Columban Milton MA 1961; MDiv S Columban Milton MA 1965; Med NEU 1970; MA Cntrl Michigan U 1974; DMin SFTS 1980. Rec from Roman Catholic 11/1/1975 as Priest Bp Edwin Lani Hanchett. m 3/10/1969 Maria Choi O'Neill. Ecum Off Dio Hawaii Honolulu HI 1988-2008; R S Tim's Ch Aiea HI 1984-2007; Cn Pstr S Andr's Cathd Honolulu HI 1977-1984; Dio Hawaii Honolulu HI 1977-1978. Auth, "Toward A Theol Of AA". vince9028@yahoo.com

O'NEILL, William Haylett (Chi) 4899 Montrose Blvd. Apt. 703, Houston TX 77006 B Houston TX 2/10/1939 s Haylett O'Neill & Kate. BA U of No Texas 1967; MDiv SWTS 1970; MS Loyola U 1980. D 6/18/1970 Bp Theodore H McCrea P 5/4/1971 Bp James Winchester Montgomery. m 1/1/1996 Elizabeth Boushall. Adj Prof Field Educ SWTS Evanston IL 1984-1991; S Jn's Epis Ch Chicago IL 1982-1993; P Epis Ch Of The Atone Chicago IL 1972-1978; Gr Ch Chicago IL 1972-1978; Asst Chr Ch Winnetka IL 1970-1972. willamhoneill@prodigy.net

ONG, Dian Marie (Ia) 803 W Tyler Ave, Fairfield IA 52556 **D S Mich's Ch Mt Pleasant IA 1997-** B Anamosa IA 6/3/1940 d Arthur Dane Whitney & Helen Marie. BA Parsons Coll Fairfield IA 1962. D 9/17/1997 Bp Carl Christopher Epting. m 7/27/1996 John Nathan Ong c 2. DOK 1996; Sis of S Helena 1996. djong@iowatelecom.net

ONG, Merry Chan (Cal) 1011 Harrison St, Oakland CA 94607 **R Epis Ch Of Our Sav Oakland CA 2010-; R Epis Ch Of Our Sav Oakland CA 2010-** B Philippines 7/7/1957 d Manuel Chan Hong & Leticia. BBA U of Santo Tomas 1980; MAEd Notre Dame Coll 1997; Mstr of Div Biblic Sem of the Philippinese 2000; Angl Stds Ch of the DS in Pacific 2007. D 6/13/2008 P 6/6/2009 Bp Marc Handley Andrus. m 11/2/2008 James Panzarella c 1. Int Vic Chr Epis Ch Sei Ko Kai San Francisco CA 2009-2010; Area Mssnr Dio California San Francisco CA 2009-2010; D S Jas Epis Ch San Francisco CA 2008-2009; Ch Admin, Prog. Dir True Sunshine Par San Francisco CA 2002-2006. revmerry@oursaviouroakland.org

ONKKA, Marcia Rauls (Minn) 1200 Autumn Dr Apt 211, Faribault MN 55021 B Paynesville MN 3/27/1926 d J H Rauls & Hazel Isabelle. U MN 1946. D 2/14/1990 Bp Sanford Zangwill Kaye Hampton. m 5/25/1946 Paul William Onkka. D All SS Ch Northfield MN 1992-1994; D Ch Of The H Cross Dundas MN 1992-1994; D The Epis Cathd Of Our Merc Sav Faribault MN 1990-1992. NAAD. ponkka@cs.com

ONKKA SR, Paul William (Minn) 1200 Autumn Dr Apt 211, Faribault MN 55021 B Virginia MN 12/25/1919 s Elno Ferdinand Onkka & Inga Mathilda. BS U MN 1943. D 2/14/1990 Bp Sanford Zangwill Kaye Hampton. m 5/25/1946 Marcia Rauls. D S Paul's Ch Yuma AZ 2001-2007; D The Epis Cathd Of Our Merc Sav Faribault MN 1990-1993. NAAD. ponkka@cs.com

ONYENDI, Matthias E (Tex) PO Box 42220, Houston TX 77242 B MBA Nigeria 9/2/1968 s Godwin Onyendi & Catherine Onwutuebe. Dipl. in Theol Imm Coll 1993; MArts U of Ibadan 1997; Post Grad Dplma Virginia Theol Sem 2001. Trans from Church Of Nigeria 10/31/2006 Bp Don Adger Wimberly. m 2/13/1999 Goodness Ueoma Nzeadibe c 3. S Fran Of Assisi Epis Prairie View TX 2006-2007. nwaonyendi@hotmail.com

OPAT, Kris (Pgh) 1066 Washington Rd, Pittsburgh PA 15228 **Assoc R S Paul's Epis Ch Pittsburgh PA 2008-** B Pittsburgh PA 4/20/1980 s Robert Opat & Lou Ann. BSME Grove City Coll 2002; MDiv TESM 2008. D 6/7/2008 Bp Robert William Duncan P 12/13/2008 Bp David Colin Jones. m 9/13/2011 Shauna E McInnes. D in Charge Three Nails Mssy Fllshp Pittsburgh PA 2008-2009. kris@stpaulspgh.org

OPEL, William A(ndrew) (NH) 395 Locust Road, Eastham MA 02642 B Kansas City MO 10/17/1926 s Frederick Nicholas Opel & Bertha Nieman. BA Harv 1949; BD EDS 1952; MA UTS 1954; EdD UTS 1960. D 6/14/1952 Bp Goodrich R Fenner P 12/13/1952 Bp Granville G Bennett. m 6/9/1951 Nina Ule Emerson c 3. Int Faith Epis Ch Merrimack NH 1984-1987; Int S Barn Ch Berlin NH 1984; Int Ch Of The Gd Shpd Reading MA 1982-1983; R S Dunstans Epis Ch Dover MA 1980-1982; R S Jn's Ch Ft Washington MD 1971-1980; R S Thos Epis Ch McLean VA 1961-1967; Assoc R All SS' Epis Ch Chevy Chase MD 1959-1961; Asst Gr Ch Jamaica NY 1952-1954. w. opel@comcast.net

O'PRAY, Denis Michael (Minn) 2412 Seabury Ave, Minneapolis MN 55406 **Vic Ch Of The Nativ Burnsville MN 2008-** B Buffalo NY 7/17/1941 s George Francis O'Pray & Elsie Mary. BA Hob 1963; MA U MN 1970. D 6/11/1975 P 3/25/1976 Bp Philip Frederick McNairy. m 8/30/1964 Lynette Christine Carlson c 3. R Ch Of Our Sav Par San Gabr CA 1990-2007; Assoc R All SS Ch Pasadena CA 1983-1990; R S Jas On The Pkwy Minneapolis MN 1976-1983; Dio Minnesota Minneapolis MN 1976; Cur S Lk's Epis Ch Jamestown NY 1975-1976. denisopray@gmail.com

ORBAUGH, Phyllis J (RG) 6626 Shpaati Ln, Cochiti Lake NM 87083 B Clay City IL 3/5/1938 d Raymond Mize Jones & Viola Alexine. Cert Oklahoma City SW Oklahoma City OK; U of Tulsa; Cbs TESM 2001. D 7/28/2001 Bp Terence Kelshaw. m 8/23/1960 Harry Whitman Orbaugh c 3. Ch of the H Faith Santa Fe NM 2001-2004; S Mths Epis Ch Shreveport LA 1980-1992. porbaugh2000@42.80

ORCHARD, Carolyn Gertrude (NMich) 311 S 4th St, Crystal Falls MI 49920 **P S Mk's Ch Crystal Falls MI 1991-** B Stambaugh MI 4/16/1936 d Frank Lloyd Symmonds & Gertrude Winnifred. BSN U MI 1959. D 5/20/1990 P 1/27/1991 Bp Thomas Kreider Ray. m 6/16/1956 David George Orchard c 3. D Dio Nthrn Michigan Marquette MI 1990-1991. dcorchard@sbcglobal.net

O'REILLY, Eileen C (SO) 6873 Fieldstone Pl, Mason OH 45040 **Cmsn on Congrl Life Dio Sthrn Ohio Cincinnati OH 2011-; R All SS Ch Cincinnati OH 2009-** B San Francisco CA 8/17/1947 d Austin Thomas O'Reilly & Sarah M. BA San Francisco St U 1970; JD Natl U 1975; EdD - ABD USC 1986; MDiv Trin Dublin 1995; MDiv Trin Dublin, Ch of Ireland Theol Colleg 1995. Trans from Church of Ireland 11/1/2001 as Priest Bp Kenneth Lester Price. m 9/17/2008 Dana Speer. Dio Sthrn Ohio Cincinnati OH 2010; The Epis Ch Of The Ascen Middletown OH 2008-2009; S Andr's Epis Ch Washington Crt Hse OH 2007-2008; Int H Trin Epis Ch Oxford OH 2005-2006; Dioc Coun Dio Sthrn Ohio Cincinnati OH 2001-2003; Int S Jas Ch Piqua OH 2001. eoreilly@cinci.rr.com

O'REILLY, John Thomas (SwFla) 5321 Laurelwood Pl, Sarasota FL 34232 B Hartford CT 3/17/1937 s Myles Joseph O'Reilly & Violet Irene. D 6/13/1998 Bp John Bailey Lipscomb. m 1/17/1959 Ina Marie Johnson.

O'REILLY, Patricia (Los) 402 S. Oakland Ave Apt 6, Pasadena CA 91101 **Asst S Steph's Par Los Angeles CA 2000-** B Boston MA 9/6/1950 d Patrick Joseph O'Reilly & Sara Ellen. BA Newton Sacr Heart 1971; MA Boston Coll 1972; MDiv EDS 1982. D 6/5/1982 Bp John Bowen Coburn P 1/22/1983 Bp Robert C Rusack. P-in-c Mssh Luth Ch Pasadena CA 2005-2006; Vic S Fran Mssn Norwalk CA 2002-2004; Chapl The Par Of S Matt Pacific Palisades CA 1995-2002; Asst S Aid's Epis Ch Malibu CA 1992-1994; Chapl Cong Of S Athan Los Angeles CA 1987-1995; Dir Epis Chaplncy La Cnty Facilities Dio Los Angeles Los Angeles CA 1987-1995; Asst S Phil's Par Los Angeles CA 1987-1989; Co-R Ch Of The Epiph Los Angeles CA 1982-1987. trishor@aol.com

ORENS, Elizabeth Mills (Md) St James Church, 19200 York Rd, Parkton MD 21120 **S Jas' Epis Ch Parkton MD 2007-** B Washington DC 10/24/1939 d George Wallace Allan & Charlotte. Dplma Juilliard Sch 1961; BA Amer U 1963; MRE UTS 1967; MA Col 1969; ABD Drew U 1976; MDiv EDS 1978. D 10/19/1978 Bp John Shelby Spong P 10/14/1979 Bp George E Rath. m 6/6/1971 John Richard Orens c 1. Ecum Cmsn Dio Washington Washington DC 1991; Cathd of St Ptr & St Paul Washington DC 1987-2007; Dio Wstrn Massachusetts Springfield MA 1982-1987; Assoc R Gr Ch Amherst MA 1982-1987; Cur S Andr's Ch Belmont MA 1978-1979. Auth, "Bk Revs," *Julia Gatta's*, The Sewanee Revs, 2010; Auth, "Bk Revs," *Julia Gatta's*, The Sewanee Revs, 2010; Auth, "Article," *The Heir of Redclyffe*, Fllshp Papers, 1990. SSJE 1987. eorensnoel@earthlink.net

ORESKOVICH JR, Steve John (Mont) 1405 Sunflower Dr, Missoula MT 59802 B Butte MT 1/6/1945 s Steve Oreskovich & Zorka. BA Carroll Coll 1973; ThM Aquinas Inst of Theol 1975; VTS 1981. D 8/16/1981 P 3/1/1982 Bp Jackson Earle Gilliam. m 6/22/1973 Brenda Dirkes. Ch Of The H Sprt Missoula MT 1981-2010. holyspiritparish@qwestoffice.net

ORLANDO, Helen Marie (NJ) 10 Iris Ct, Marlton NJ 08053 **Mem, Dioc MDG T/F Dio New Jersey Trenton NJ 2010-; D S Ptr's Ch Medford NJ 2000-** B Toledo OH 1/4/1951 d George Henry Gruenwald & Corrine Rae. Rutgers U; Universtiy of Minnesota 1972; BA Smith 1973; EFM 1997; Ord as D D Formation Prog 2000. D 10/21/2000 Bp David B(ruce) Joslin. m 6/23/1973 Michael Thomas Orlando c 2. Mem, Comp Dio Com Dio New Jersey Trenton NJ 2007-2011; Par Secy Dio New Jersey Trenton NJ 2006-2007; Par Admin Dio New Jersey Trenton NJ 2002-2006. NAAD 1997. dcnhelen@stpetersmedford.org

ORME-ROGERS, Charles Arthur (Mo) 7634 Mid Town Rd - #212, Madison WI 53719 B Robinson Illinois 5/4/1949 s Roy Roscoe Rogers & Ardis Melva. BA Wabash Coll 1973; MA U of Notre Dame 1979; MDiv Eden TS 2006; Cert Epis Sch for Mnstry 2008; CPE Supvsr St. Lk's Epis/Presb Hosp 2008. D 5/31/2006 P 1/6/2007 Bp George Wayne Smith. m 12/11/1976 Catherine Marie Orme c 2. "A field dependency explanation of age differences in the persuasibility of irrelevant stimuli," *Intl Journ of Aging and Human Dvlpmt*, 1979; "Examination of stimulus persistence as the basis for superior visual identification performance among adults," *Journ of Gerontology*, 1978. chuck_rogers@swbell.net

ORMOND, John James (EC) 2324 S 41st St Apt 252, Wilmington NC 28403 B Houston TX 11/3/1926 s Lewis Fisher Ormond & Mary. BA U NC 1950; MDiv VTS 1953; VTS 1972. D 9/29/1953 P 6/3/1954 Bp Thomas H Wright. Transition Com Dio E Carolina Kinston NC 1984-1986; Secy Dio E Carolina Kinston NC 1980-1983; R S Paul's Epis Ch Wilmington NC 1979-1988; Pres, Stndg Com Dio E Carolina Kinston NC 1978-1979; Dep, GC Dio E Carolina Kinston NC 1976-1979; R S Fran Ch Goldsboro NC 1967-1979; R S Paul's Ch Petersburg VA 1962-1967; R Ch Of The Adv Williamston NC 1958-1962; Cur S Jas Epis Ch Baton Rouge LA 1955-1958; D Chr Epis Ch Hope Mills NC 1953-1954; D Gd Shpd Epis Ch Fayetteville NC 1953-1954. Sem Hill Soc 1953.

ORMOS, C(laude) Patrick (WTex) c/o Saint Francis Chruch, 4242 Bluemel Rd, San Antonio TX 78240 B Paris FR 2/22/1951 s Paul S Ormos & Jacqueline R N. BA Indiana U 1975; MA Chicago TS 1977; Dplma in Mnstry Montreal TS 1978; STM McGill U 1990; DMin SWTS 1997. Trans from Anglican Church of Canada 1/1/1992 Bp Francis Campbell Gray. m 6/30/1982 Kristine Helen Graunke c 1. St Fran Epis Ch San Antonio TX 2007-2011; R S Andr's Epis Ch Valparaiso IN 1991-2007; Int Gr Epis Ch Freeport IL 1990-1991. Auth, "The Place of Self-Revelation in Preaching," *Pract of Mnstry in Can.* patrick.ormos@gmail.com

O'ROURKE, Brian Alexander (Los) 47535 State Highway 74, Palm Desert CA 92260 **P Assoc S Marg's Epis Ch Palm Desert CA 2011-** B Wiesbaden Germany 8/9/1976 s Kelly Krapivin O'Rourke & Cynthia Ann. BS Menlo Coll 1998; MDiv VTS 2011. D 6/11/2011 Bp Diane M Jardine Bruce. m 9/28/2002 Jennifer Wachtel. borourke@stmargarets.org

OROZCO, Benjamin Manuel (SanD) 3568 Elmwood Ct, Riverside CA 92506 B Glendale AZ 2/18/1933 s Antonio Orozco & Esther. BA U CA 1959; BD CDSP 1962; U of Texas 1971. D 6/28/1962 Bp Everett H Jones P 1/4/1963 Bp Richard Earl Dicus. m 6/25/1967 Irene Emma Rios c 2. Vic S Andr's By The Lake Temecula CA 1995-1998; P S Andr's By The Lake Temecula CA

O

1977-1978; Vic S Gabr's Ch Dallas TX 1966-1970; Cur S Paul's Epis Ch San Antonio TX 1964-1966; P Santa Fe Epis Mssn San Antonio TX 1963-1964. SSC.

ORPEN JR, J(ohn) Robert (Chi) 5550 S Shore Dr Apt 512, Chicago IL 60637 **Cathd Of S Jas Chicago IL 2002-** B Providence RI 3/30/1921 s John Robert Milner Orpen & Mary Lydia Brook. BA Br 1942; STB GTS 1948; STM Nash 1949. D 3/31/1948 P 4/23/1949 Bp Granville G Bennett. m 5/30/1957 Lavinia Lutz c 3. Asst S Mich's Ch Barrington IL 1990-2008; Dioc Coun Dio Chicago Chicago IL 1974-1986; Dio Chicago Chicago IL 1970-1973; St Stephens Ch Chicago IL 1969-1985; Dioc Coun Dio Chicago Chicago IL 1961-1964; R Ch Of The Adv Chicago IL 1958-1986; Chair Dept & Prom Dio Nevada Las Vegas NV 1950-1951; Vic H Trin Epis Ch Fallon NV 1949-1953; Asst S Matt's Ch Kenosha WI 1948-1949. jrorpenjr@yahoo.com

ORR, Daniel Longsworth (O) 433 E Maple St, Bryan OH 43506 **S Paul's Ch Fremont OH 2006-** B Decatur GA 12/30/1971 BA Ob. D 1/30/2004 Bp J Clark Grew II P 10/6/2004 Bp Mark Hollingsworth Jr. m 5/31/1997 Ann Longsworth Orr c 2. Dio Ohio Cleveland OH 2004-2006. zlorr@yahoo.com

ORR, Kristin Elizabeth (Chi) P. O. Box 25, Flossmoor IL 60422 **R The Ch Of S Jn The Evang Flossmoor IL 2004-** B Berkeley CA 4/25/1958 d Charles Ross Orr & Carol. BS Ya 1980; MS U of Washington 1982; PhD U of Washington 1985; MDiv VTS 1991. Trans 3/11/2004 Bp Chilton Abbie Richardson Knudsen. R S Pat's Ch Brewer ME 1999-2003; Dioc Liturg Cmsn Dio Texas Houston TX 1995-1999; S Mk's Ch Houston TX 1991-1999. krisorr@att.net

ORRIN, Dyana Vail (Ak) 1501 N Adams St, Fredericksburg TX 78624 B Glendale CA 6/14/1937 d Ande Ross Vail & Lillian Maude. AA Anchorage Cmnty Coll 1983; BA Alaska Pacific U 1988; MDiv CDSP 1991; DMin Vancouver TS 2004. D 12/19/1987 Bp George Clinton Harris P 9/1/1991 Bp Steven Charleston. m 7/22/1994 Robert Dennis Orrin c 1. R S Jas The Fisherman Kodiak AK 2005-2006; R S Dav's Ch Wasilla AK 1992-2005; Asst Dio Alaska Fairbanks AK 1991-1992. DOK 2008; OHC 1989. revdyana@gmail.com

ORSO, Thomas Ray (NY) Episcopal Diocese Of New York, 1047 Amsterdam Ave., New York NY 10025 **Cn For Deploy Dio New York New York City NY 2001-** B Williamsport PA 8/30/1947 s Max Lester Orso & June Lucille. BFA Witt 1969; MDiv EDS 1977; MS Wstrn Connecticut St U 1991. D 6/18/1977 P 9/9/1978 Bp William Hawley Clark. P-in-c S Andr's Epis Ch Staten Island NY 2000-2001; P-in-c S Mk's Epis Ch Yonkers NY 1997-2000; P-in-c Ch Of The H Comm Mahopac NY 1991-1994; R Ch Of The Ascen And H Trin Highland NY 1981-1983. tomorso@dioceseny.org

ORTEGA, Guido Andres (EcuC) Avenue Amazonas 4430 Y Villalengua, Casilla 17116 Ecuador B Bolivar Carchi EC 2/13/1965 s Maria Orfelina Ortega. U Cath Ecu 5 Yrs. m 4/21/1995 Jenny J P Quiroz. Ecuador New York NY 1999-2010; Vic Iglesia Nueva Jerusalem Pelileo EC 1999-2010.

ORTEZ, Jose Leonel (SeFla) 3635 NE 1st Ave, PO Box 370748, Miami FL 33137 **H Cross Epis Ch Miami FL 2003-** B 12/15/1965 s Enrique Ortez & Eva. Mstr's Honduras 1990; Bachelor's Honduras 1994. Rec 4/15/1998 Bp Calvin Onderdonk Schofield Jr. m 12/17/1994 Wendy Molina De Pena c 5. Dio Honduras Miami FL 1998-2002. reverendortez@bellsouth.net

ORTT, William Jeffrey (Eas) 111 S Harrison St, Easton MD 21601 **R Chr Ch S Ptr's Par Easton MD 1999-** B Niagara Falls NY 5/7/1958 s John Franklin Ortt & Molly Pryce. Niagara U 1978; BA and BA SUNY 1980; MDiv GTS 1986; DMin Drew U 1993. D 5/31/1986 P 5/29/1987 Bp Harold B Robinson. m 5/10/1990 Susan E H Harris. R S Steph's Ch Newton IA 1990-1999; Asst S Fran Ch Greensboro NC 1986-1990. OHC 1985. wjortt@goeaston.net

ORTUNG, Thomas Edward (Alb) 105 State St, Kirkland WA 98033 **Dio Olympia Seattle WA 2011-** B Poughkeepsie NY 11/1/1962 s Edward M Ortung & Teresa M. BA The U of Albany 1999; MDiv Nash 2007. D 6/9/2007 Bp William Howard Love P 1/25/2009 Bp Gregory Harold Rickel. m 7/1/1989 Jami L Fowler c 3. S Lk's Ch Cambridge NY 2007-2008. tomortung@yahoo.com

ORVILLE, Lynn Denise (NwPa) 103 Clinton St., Greenville PA 16125 B Jackson MI 10/3/1958 d James Leroy Burden & Eloise Charmaine. Cntrl Wyoming Coll Riverton WY; BS Bellevue U 1991; MDiv VTS 1998. D 4/21/1998 P 10/23/1998 Bp James Edward Krotz. m 9/30/1978 Douglas Duvall Orville c 1. P-in-c S Clem's Epis Ch Hermitage PA 2009-2010; S Barth's Epis Ch Bemidji MN 2005-2007; Epis Cmnty Serv Benidji MN 2004-2005; R Gr Epis Ch Chadron NE 2000-2004; Cn Pstr Cathd Of S Paul Erie PA 1998-1999. lynnorville98@gmail.com

ORWIG, Dana Lynn Maynard (Okla) 2710 Nw 17th St, Oklahoma City OK 73107 **S Jn's Ch Oklahoma City OK 2005-** B Julesburg CO 6/13/1954 d Judson Dana Maynard & Gladys Rose. Texas Tech U 1974; BA U of Texas 1978. D 6/27/1992 Bp Robert Manning Moody. m 9/21/1974 Steven Rhea Orwig c 2. NAAD.

OSBERGER, Charles Edward (Eas) 14084 Old Wye Mills Rd, Wye Mills MD 21679 **R Old Wye Ch Wye Mills MD 1986-** B Houston TX 1/6/1954 s Charles Robert Osberger & Margeurite Mary. BA USC 1976; MA Fuller TS 1978; MDiv TESM 1980. D 6/5/1982 P 12/1/1982 Bp Robert Bracewell Appleyard. c 2. R S Lk's Chap Wye Mills MD 1986; Assoc S Mart's Ch Chagrin Falls OH 1982-1985. Bd India Mssn; Bro Of S Andr; Ecmc Casa; Theol Stdt Fllshp. wrectory@intercom.net

OSBORN, Mary Anne (Ct) 560 Lake Dr., Guilford CT 06437 B Mobile AL 6/3/1951 d Prime Francis Osborn & Grace. BA Florida St U 1974; MA U of No Florida 1976; U of Florida 1983; MDiv EDS 1986. D 6/8/1986 P 12/14/1986 Bp Frank Stanley Cerveny. m 12/31/2008 Joanne Louise Neel. Zion Epis Ch No Branford CT 2009-2011; S Paul's Ch Fairfield CT 1999-2007; Trin Ch Torrington CT 1999; S Paul And S Jas New Haven CT 1996-1998. revmao28@gmail.com

OSBORN, Sherry E (Vt) 31 Fairground Rd, Springfield VT 05156 **Stndg Com Dio Vermont Burlington VT 2010-; COM Dio Vermont Burlington VT 2007-; R S Mk's Ch Springfield VT 2006-** B Springfield MA 4/26/1961 d Jonathan Webster Osborn & Sue Harman. BS Green Mtn Coll 1983; Med Bos 1987; Angl Dplma Ya Berk 2002; MDiv Ya 2002. D 6/21/2003 P 12/20/2003 Bp Andrew Donnan Smith. m 2/18/2005 Margaret King. Assoc R S Mich's Ch Milton MA 2003-2006. Seminarians Interacting Yale DS 2001; Jess H. and Hugo A. Norenbuerg Preaching Prize Yale DS 2000; Pres's Publ Serv Fllshp Ya 2000. sherryosborn@vermontel.net

OSBORN DE ANAYA, Archie (NAM) 1115 Main St, Vicksburg MS 39183 **Navajoland Area Mssn Farmington NM 2011-** B Florence AL 4/27/1951 RN Coll of Santa Fe. D 6/21/2003 Bp Terence Kelshaw P 1/3/2004 Bp Duncan Montgomery Gray III. m 11/30/1996 Vernon L Anaya c 2. R Chr Epis Ch Vicksburg MS 2003-2010. chanoanaya@gmail.com

OSBORNE, C(harles) Edward (ETenn) 1540 Belmeade Dr, Kingsport TN 37664 B Mount Croghan SC 8/5/1929 s Edward Ruffin Osborne & Emeline Gladys. BS U NC 1951; MS U of Maine 1953; PhD NWU 1956. D 6/21/1981 Bp William Evan Sanders. m 8/6/1955 Columbine Vera Amici c 2. D S Chris's Ch Kingsport TN 1997-2002; D S Paul's Epis Ch Kingsport TN 1981-1996. edosborne@alumni.northwestern.edu

OSBORNE, Janne Alro (Tex) 6001 Shepherd Mountain Cv, Apt 227, Austin TX 78750 **S Mich's Ch Austin TX 2005-; Assoc R S Mich's Epis Ch San Antonio TX 2005-** B Skalskor DK 12/3/1952 d Merritt H Nielsen & Inga Alro. Austin Coll 1973; BD U of Texas 1989; MDiv VTS 1994. D 7/6/1994 Bp John Herbert MacNaughton P 1/18/1995 Bp James Edward Folts. c 2. R S Alb's Epis Ch Waco TX 2002-2005; Assoc R S Dav's Ch Austin TX 1997-2002; Vic Ch Of Our Sav Aransas Pass TX 1994-1997; Vic Trin-By-The-Sea Port Aransas TX 1994-1997; Secy S Mich's Epis Ch San Antonio TX 1989-1991; CE Coordntr S Alb's Epis Ch Arlington TX 1984-1989. Sis of the H Sprt 2006. jannealro@mac.com

OSBORNE III, Joseph E (Okla) 418 N Park St, Guthrie OK 73044 B Wichita KS 6/3/1924 s Joseph Erle Osborne & Eleanor. GTS 1968. D 6/23/1962 P 6/22/1968 Bp Chilton Powell. m 11/2/1975 Luann Williamson c 4. Asst P S Aug Of Cbury Oklahoma City OK 1995-1999; R Trin Ch Guthrie OK 1968-1974; D S Jn's Epis Ch Woodward OK 1962-1966. lujo2437@cox.net

OSBORNE, Ralph Everett (FdL) 2420 Marathon Ave, Neenah WI 54956 **S Thos Ch Menasha WI 2010-** B Chicago IL 10/29/1956 s Ralph Everett Osborne & Martha. DePaul U 1974; BA Olivet Nazarene Coll 1978; MA U of Missouri Kansas City 1983; MDiv Nazarene TS 1985. D 6/17/1995 P 1/6/1996 Bp David B(ruce) Joslin. m 8/12/1978 Cindy Jo Prior c 7. Dio Cntrl New York Syracuse NY 2005; R Zion Epis Ch Greene NY 1996-2010. rosbornejr@yahoo.com

OSBORNE, Richard L (RG) 164 Chrissa Dr., Pottsboro TX 75076 B Syracuse NY 3/9/1942 s Leo Osborne & Dorothy. Le Moyne Coll 1963; BA St. Bern's Sem Rochester NY 1964; MDiv St. Bern's Sem Rochester NY 1968. Rec from Roman Catholic 6/26/1995 Bp William Edward Smalley. m 5/30/1992 Connie Shelstad c 1. S Chris's Epis Ch Hobbs NM 2002-2007; S Chris's Epis Ch Wichita KS 2002-2007; Vic S Mary's Ch Lovington NM 2002-2007. rosborne09@windstream.net

OSBORNE, Ronald Douglas (Ia) 2325 E Highview Dr., Des Moines IA 50320 **Assoc S Andr's Ch Des Moines IA 2007-** B Kearney NE 6/28/1940 s Rolland H Osborne & Esther Joanna. BA Westmar Coll 1962; BD SWTS 1965; U of Iowa 1989; Creighton U 1993; Cert St. Jos Cntr 1995; DMin SWTS 2005. D 6/24/1965 P 1/1/1966 Bp Gordon V Smith. m 4/6/1991 Sara Jane Hauff c 2. R Trin Epis Par Waterloo IA 1998-2006; Vic S Mart's Ch Perry IA 1990-1998; Coll Field Des Moines IA 1972-1990. Auth, "Mar Of Christians And Jews," Plumbline, 1984; Auth, "Rendering Resrch From Caesar," Plumbline, 1982. Affirming Angl Catholicism 1966. Chapl Sons Of Knutt--Lake Wobegon 1998. parson3333@aol.com

OSBORNE, William Paul (NCal) 101 Dennison Lane, Fort Bragg CA 95437 **S Steph's Epis Ch Spokane WA 2011-** B Tacoma WA 7/16/1955 s Robert Wesley Osborne & Evelyn Anne. BA Gri 1977; MS Humboldt St U 1991; MDiv CDSP 2001. D 1/14/2001 Bp Mark Lawrence Mac Donald P 8/5/2001 Bp Jerry Alban Lamb. m 1/7/1995 Margaret Ann Drumm c 5. R S Mich And All Ang Ch Ft Bragg CA 2006-2009; Asst P S Mary's Epis Ch Napa CA 2001-2006. billandmargaret@mcn.org

OSBORNE-MOTT, Susan (Chi) 503 Asbury Ave, Asbury Park NJ 07712 **Asst R Trin Ch Asbury Pk NJ 2008-** B Minneapolis MN 8/4/1950 d Lawrence Eric Osborne & Mary. BA U Of Minneapolis MN 1974; MDiv SWTS 2007. D 6/2/2007 Bp William Dailey Persell P 12/15/2007 Bp Victor Alfonso Scantlebury. m 8/24/1985 Bradley A Mott c 2. momott@trinitynj.com

OSGOOD, John Albert (NY) 1047 Amsterdam Ave, New York NY 10025 **Cn Ordnry Dio New York New York City NY 1996-** B New Berlin NY 9/5/1948 BA Un Coll Schenectady NY 1970; Dipl. Th U of Birmingham GB 1972; MDiv GTS 1973; STM GTS 1975. D 6/9/1973 Bp Paul Moore Jr P 12/20/1973 Bp Horace W B Donegan. m 6/20/1985 Maribeth Goewey c 2. Stndg Com Dio New York New York City NY 1988-1992; R Gr Ch Middletown NY 1979-1996; Tutor The GTS New York NY 1977-1983; Chair Angl-Roman Cath Com Dio New York New York City NY 1976-1983; The Epis Ch Of Chr The King Stone Ridge NY 1975-1979; Cur Chr Ch Of Ramapo Suffern NY 1973-1975. Auth, *Angl-RC Consult Inter-Par Dialogue*; Auth, *Ecum Study Guide on Authority*; Auth, *Ecum Study Guide on Mnstry & Ord.* josgood@dioceseny.org

OSGOOD, Thomas Marston (Cal) 6471 Coopers Hawk Rd, Klamath Falls OR 97601 **Asst S Paul's Ch Klamath Falls OR 2006-** B Pittsburgh PA 2/2/1932 s Thomas Harris Osgood & Dorothy Marston. BA Ya 1954; BD CDSP 1957. D 6/23/1957 Bp Russell S Hubbard P 3/1/1958 Bp William J Gordon Jr. m 5/21/1991 Margaret Pring c 3. Epis Sr Communities Walnut Creek CA 1978-2001; Assoc Ch Of The Epiph Seattle WA 1969-1975; Vic S Lk's Ch Sequim WA 1964-1969; Cur S Steph's Epis Ch Longview WA 1962-1964; Vic S Geo In The Arctic Kotzebue AK 1957-1962. tommarley@charter.net

O'SHEA, Nancy Corinne Tucker (WTenn) 6294 Venus Ave, Bartlett TN 38134 **D Imm Ch Ripley TN 2009-** B Kansas City MO 4/27/1942 d Dean Whitcomb Tucker & Martha Marie. BS U of Missouri 1964. D 10/28/1985 Bp Arthur Anton Vogel. m 8/10/1985 Donald Patrick O'Shea. D S Mary's Cathd Memphis TN 1986-1999. DOK 1987; Oblates of St. Ben 1980. swopepark1@bellsouth.net

O'SHEA, Susan J (Oly) 1736 Belmont Ave Apt 210, Seattle WA 98122 B San Diego CA 9/12/1944 d Fredrick Adolf Jeswine & Edna M. BS U of Kansas 1979; MDiv Epis TS of The SW 1988. D 6/19/1988 Bp Richard Frank Grein P 9/1/1991 Bp Vincent Waydell Warner. m 5/10/1980 Jerry N O'Shea. Chapl/Dir Chap of S Martha and S Mary of Bethany Seattle WA 1991-2011; Chapl/Dir Chap of S Martha and S Mary of Bethany Seattle WA 1991-2006; Port Chapl Mssn to Seafarers Seattle WA 1990-1991; Urban Chapl S Mk's Cathd Seattle WA 1989-1991. chaplain.oshea@gmail.com

OSHRY, Michael (Ind) 534 Nuthatch Dr, Zionsville IN 46077 **Guest Celebrant S Mary's Epis Ch Martinsville IN 2009-; Guest Celebrant S Geo Epis Ch W Terre Haute IN 2006-** B Crawfordsville IN 3/25/1955 s Harold Morton Oshry & Barbara Jo. Ball St U; MDiv Chr TS; BS Indiana Wesl; CAS SWTS. D 6/18/2005 P 5/28/2006 Bp Catherine Elizabeth Maples Waynick. m 5/14/1976 Sharon Turner c 1. Assoc P S Chris's Epis Ch Carmel IN 2005-2009. Assn of Profsnl Chapl 2008. mike.oshry@gmail.com

OSMUN, Andrew Gilbert (Ct) 4 Glen St, Milford CT 06460 **R S Ptr's Epis Ch Milford CT 1999-** B Wilmington DE 11/13/1948 s William Gilbert Osmun & Priscilla. BA Wms 1971; CTh Oxf 1975. D 10/5/1975 P 4/4/1976 Bp Robert Bracewell Appleyard. m 8/31/1974 Terry Ann Oppee c 2. R S Lk's Ch Chester VT 1980-1999; Vic Geth Ch Proctorsville VT 1980-1985; Vic Ch Of The Trsfg Clairton PA 1975-1980; Cur S Steph's Epis Ch Mckeesport PA 1975-1980. SAMS 1976. andrewgosmun@sbcglobal.net

OSNAYA-JIMENEZ, Uriel (Tex) 9600 Huntington Place Dr, Houston TX 77099 B Mexico City MX 7/7/1956 s Aaron Osnaya-Hernandez & Evangelina. BA Jose Vasconcelos 1976; Cert S Andr's TS Ph 1979; Cert Epis TS of The SW 1980. D 12/1/1979 Bp Donald James Davis P 1/23/1982 Bp Robert Elwin Terwilliger. m 11/8/1997 Maria Elena Osnaya-Jimenez c 1. Dio Dallas Dallas TX 1990-1997; Vic Iglesia Epis Santa Maria Virgen Houston TX 1990-1997; S Matt's Cathd Dallas TX 1982-1990; Dio Dallas Dallas TX 1981; Asst Hisp Mnstry Dio Dallas Dallas TX 1980-1982. CHS. frosnaya@msn.com

OST, Gary Wilbert (Cal) 712 Bancroft Rd # 194, Walnut Creek CA 94598 **Dio California San Francisco CA 2000-** B Renton WA 6/1/1947 s Wilbert Ost & Irene. BA U of Washington 1969; MDiv CDSP 1972. D 8/26/1972 P 12/1/1973 Bp Ivol I Curtis. c 2. R S Lk's Ch Walnut Creek CA 1982-2007; S Eliz's Ch Burien WA 1977-1979; Vic S Lk's Ch Sequim WA 1974-1977; Cur S Lk's Ch Tacoma WA 1972-1974. Integrity; Tertiary Of The Soc Of S Fran. shambhalagary@gmail.com

O'STEEN, Joe Arnold (LI) 2312 Halbert Dr, Pearland TX 77581 **Assoc S Andr's Epis Ch Pearland TX 1999-; Supply S Jn's Ch Brooklyn NY 1993-** B Hope AR 11/28/1935 s A(lpha) Noel O'Steen & Ola. BA Henderson St U 1957; MDiv UTS 1960; GTS 1961; Blanton-Peale Grad Inst 1971; New York Cntr for Psychodrama Trng Brooklyn NY 1978. D 6/10/1961 P 12/16/1961 Bp Horace W B Donegan. Assoc Ch Of The Redeem Brooklyn NY 1976-1993; Asst S Ann And The H Trin Brooklyn NY 1971-1976; Vic S Anselm's Ch Shoreham NY 1967-1971; Asst Ch Of S Jas The Less Scarsdale NY 1964-1966; Asst Chr Ch Greenwich CT 1961-1964. Amer Soc for Grp Psych & Psychodrama 1973-1990. MCL Henderson St U 1957. fatherjoeosteen@gmail.com

OSTENSON, Roy Oliver (SwFla) 4009 Wonderland Hill Ave, Boulder CO 80304 B Hallock MN 4/20/1921 s Edwin Oliver Ostenson & Lillian Caroline. BA Montana St U 1948; BD EDS 1951; Fllshp Coll of Preachers 1963; MA Wstrn Michigan U 1982. D 8/6/1951 P 2/6/1952 Bp Henry Hean Daniels. m 1/30/1982 Sondra Jean. Dio SW Florida Sarasota FL 1982-1989; Gr Ch Grand Rapids MI 1968-1983; Chapl U Roch Dio Rochester Rochester NY 1954-1960; Vic S Matt's Ch Glasgow MT 1951-1954.

OSTERTAG, Edward Frederick (Colo) 4611 35th Ave SW, #302, Seattle WA 98126 B Albuquerque NM 6/5/1925 s Carl John Ostertag & Kathryn Winifred. BA U So 1950; MDiv GTS 1952; Colorado St U 1966. D 6/22/1952 Bp James M Stoney P 3/27/1953 Bp C J Kinsolving III. c 4. P-in-c Chr Ch Hillsboro NM 1991-2001; P-in-c S Paul's Epis Ch Truth or Consequences NM 1991-1998; R S Barn Epis Ch Denver CO 1984-1990; Stndg Com Dio Colorado Denver CO 1965-1967; Dn Dio Colorado Denver CO 1962-1964; Trst Dio Colorado Denver CO 1961-1965; R S Lk's Epis Ch Ft Collins CO 1960-1981. Human Relatns Awd Ft Collins CO 1982.

OSTLUND, Holly Lisa (SeFla) 15730 88th Pl N, Loxahatchee FL 33470 **S Mk's Ch Palm Bch Gardens FL 2009-** B Miami FL 12/24/1954 d Grant Jung Ostlund & Mary B. BS U of Tennessee 1976; MA Barry U 2002; Cert. Epis TS of the SW 2002. D 2/8/2003 P 9/6/2003 Bp Leopold Frade. c 1. Trin Ch Towson MD 2009; Dio SE Florida Miami FL 2007-2009; Asst R S Mary's Epis Ch Stuart FL 2003-2006. hollyostlund@aol.com

OSTRANDER, Paul Copeland (Okla) 2321 Northwest 48th Street, Oklahoma City OK 73112 **S Alb's Ch Cushing OK 2003-** B Ponca City OK 10/27/1926 s Quintus Paul Ostrander & Martha Fay. BA U of Oklahoma 1950; SWTS 1964; Epis TS In Kentucky 1966; Cert Presb Hosp Oklahoma City OK 1982. D 6/17/1966 P 10/17/1968 Bp Chilton Powell. m 4/23/1977 Patsy Ruth Walsh c 4. Vic Chr Memi Epis Ch El Reno OK 1977-1986; Cmncatn Off Dio Oklahoma Oklahoma City OK 1977-1981; P S Mich And All Ang Ch Lindsay OK 1974-1977; P S Tim's Epis Ch Pauls Vlly OK 1974-1977; Vic S Paul's Epis Ch Holdenville OK 1972-1974; Cur S Jn's Ch Norman OK 1971-1972; Asst S Jas Epis Ch Oklahoma City OK 1970-1971; S Marg's Ch Lawton OK 1970-1971; Asst S Paul's Cathd Oklahoma City OK 1967-1969; Cur All SS Epis Ch Miami OK 1966-1967. poeastbank@cex.net

OSTUNI, Elizabeth Ellen (Nwk) 10 Hampton Downes, Newton NJ 07860 **Archd Ch Of The Gd Shpd Sussex NJ 2009-** B Parsons KS 5/8/1937 d Walter Jarboe & Ferne. BA U of Kansas 1959; MA U of Kansas 1972; Cert GTS 2001. D 6/5/2004 Bp John Palmer Croneberger. m 9/9/1984 Lawrence Ostuni c 3. D S Jn's Ch Dover NJ 2004-2008. "Successful Cmncatn w Alzheimer's Disease Patients," *Elsivir*; "Getting Through: When someone you care for has Alzheimer's Disease," *Speech Bin*.

OSWALD, Todd Dennis (SC) 2362 Parsonage Rd Apt 9C, Charleston SC 29414 B 12/8/1964 s Ronald Oswald & Ann. BS U of So Carolina 1988; MA U of So Carolina 1989; MDiv Duke 2001; Cert Nash 2002. D 7/1/2006 P 1/20/2007 Bp Edward Lloyd Salmon Jr. toddoswald@hotmail.com

OTA, David Yasuhide (Cal) 900 Edgewater Blvd, Foster City CA 94404 **Mem, Stndg Com Dio California San Francisco CA 2009-2013; Dep, GC Dio California San Francisco CA 2004-2013; R S Ambr Epis Ch Foster City CA 1997-** B San Francisco CA 5/8/1954 s Ichiro Ota & Mary. BS U CA 1976; MDiv CDSP 1983. D 6/25/1983 Bp William Edwin Swing P 6/10/1984 Bp Edmond Lee Browning. m 2/4/1984 Karen Swanson c 1. Pres, Stndg Com Dio California San Francisco CA 2010-2011; Dep, GC Dio Hawaii Honolulu HI 1986-1995; Vic/R Gd Samar Epis Ch Honolulu HI 1983-1997. dyota@mindspring.com

OTIS, Violetta Lansdale (Me) 17 Foreside Rd, Falmouth ME 04105 B Evanston IL 11/5/1947 d James Sanford Otis & Violetta Lansdale. AA Bradford Jr Coll 1967; BA U of Wisconsin 1969; MDiv EDS 1998. D 7/2/1998 P 1/30/1999 Bp Chilton Abbie Richardson Knudsen. c 2. P-in-c Trin Epis Ch Lewiston ME 1999-2006.

OTT, Janet Sanderson (Miss) 1200 Meadowbrook Rd Apt 44, Jackson MS 39206 B Laurel MS 11/6/1951 d Joe Franklin Sanderson & Ann. BS Mississippi Coll 1989; MDiv EDS 1996. D 6/22/1996 P 3/1/1997 Bp Alfred Clark Marble Jr. m 3/31/1970 Luther Smith Ott c 2. Assoc Ch Of The Creator Clinton MS 2003-2007; S Columb's Ch Ridgeland MS 1996-2003. nanatt@comcast.net

OTT, Luther Smith (Miss) 1200 Meadowbrook Road, #44, Jackson MS 39206 **S Paul's Epis Ch Meridian MS 2010-** B Oxford MS 2/26/1949 s Thomas De Vecmon Ott & Lorraine. BA Millsaps Coll 1971; JD U of Mississippi 1973; MA EDS 1996. D 4/15/1998 P 10/28/1998 Bp Alfred Clark Marble Jr. m 3/31/1970 Janet Sanderson Ott c 2. Ch Of The Creator Clinton MS 2002-2006; Cur S Phil's Ch Jackson MS 1998-2000. lutherott@bellsouth.net

OTT, Paula Lee (Lex) 2410 Lexington Rd, Winchester KY 40391 B Cincinnati OH 12/5/1951 d Eli J Rishty & Arvilla Marie. BSEd U Cinc 1973; MAEd U of Kentucky 1979. D 6/5/2011 Bp Stacy F Sauls. m 6/18/1978 John Stephen Ott c 1. autumn51@bellsouth.net

O

OTT, Robert Michael (ECR) 1490 Mark Thomas Dr., Monterey CA 93940 B Seoul Korea 9/19/1947 D 5/30/2004 Bp Samuel Johnson Howard P 12/5/2004 Bp Edward Lloyd Salmon Jr. m 12/14/1974 Bonnie Ellen Morgan c 2. Ch Of The H Cross Sullivans Island SC 2004-2009. bobstjohnschappel@redshift.com

OTTAWAY, Richard Napoleon (NJ) 16 Bell Ter, Bernardsville NJ 07924 **Part Time Epis Ch Of S Thos Taunton MA 2008-** B Ypsilanti MI 12/26/1931 s Henry Jackson Ottaway & Ruth Marie. BA Ecu 1954; MDiv VTS 1957; PhD U of Manchester 1979. D 6/27/1957 P 5/1/1958 Bp Thomas H Wright. m 6/28/1981 Elaine Davis c 2. Ch of S Jn on the Mtn Bernardsville NJ 1992-1995; Dioc Coun Dio No Carolina Raleigh NC 1970-1973; The Ch & Industry Inst Winston Salem NC 1969-1972; Chair Of The Pitt Cnty Inter-Racial Com Dio E Carolina Kinston NC 1962-1964; Cur S Paul's Epis Ch Greenville NC 1959-1964; D S Paul's Ch Vanceboro NC 1957-1958; D Trin Epis Ch Chocowinity NC 1957-1958. Auth, "Humanising The Workplace"; Auth, "Intro-Ing Orgnztns Behavior". ottaway@fdu.edu

OTTERBURN, Margaret K (Nwk) 50 Route 24, Chester NJ 07930 **R Ch Of The Mssh Chester NJ 2007-** B Stoke-on-Trent GB 9/5/1946 d Benjamin Guy Vernon & Winifred Kathleen. BS Lon 1968; MA Belfast U Belfast 1975; MDiv Drew U 1999. D 6/1/2002 P 12/7/2002 Bp John Palmer Croneberger. m 7/26/1969 Michael S Otterburn c 3. Cathd Ch Of S Mk Minneapolis MN 2004-2007; Cur Gr Ch Newark NJ 2003-2004. margaretotterburn@msn.com

OTTERY JR, Willis Dee (NH) 83 Irving Dr, Weare NH 03281 **D S Paul's Ch Concord NH 2007-** B Fond du Lac WI 7/7/1927 s Willis Dee Ottery & Irene Elizabeth. BS U of Wisconsin 1950. D 11/1/1997 Bp Douglas Edwin Theuner. m 3/26/1994 Linda Messenger c 4. D Ch Of S Jn The Evang Dunbarton NH 1997-2000. Auth, *A Man Called Sampson*, Penobscot, 1989. NAAD 1995. Recognition of Diac Mnstry in the Tradition of S Step Natl Amer Assn for the Diac 2001. deaconwill@comcast.net

✠ OTTLEY, Rt Rev James Hamilton (LI) 3 E Fairway Ct, Bay Shore NY 11706 B Colon PA 6/27/1936 s Lipton Cornelius Ottley & Mirell. STB ETSC 1964; MS ETSC 1973; Fllshp Epis TS of The SW 1980; VTS 1982; DD Epis TS of The SW 1986; DD STUSo 1986; DD Ya Berk 1991. Trans from Iglesia Anglicana de la Region Central de America 4/30/2000 Bp Orris George Walker Jr Con 1/21/1984 for RP. m 1/15/1965 Lillian Garcia. Asst Dio SE Florida Miami FL 2001-2004; Ch Of The Mssh Cntrl Islip NY 1999-2001; Dio Long Island Garden City NY 1999-2000; Epis Ch Cntr New York NY 1994-1999; St Pauls Ch 1977-1984; Mntl Hlth Prog 1974-1994; Dio Panama 1964-1994. Auth, "Making Sense Of Things"; Auth, "We Are Angls"; Auth, "The Challenge Of The Past," *The Challenge Of The Future*. jottley@aol.com

OTTSEN, David K (Tex) 3007 Live Oak Dr., Brenham TX 77833 **R S Ptr's Epis Ch Brenham TX 2008-** B Charles City IA 5/20/1952 s George Maurice Ottsen & Katherine Viola. BA Coe Coll 1974; MDiv Epis TS of The SW 1982. D 4/2/1982 Bp Charles Thomas Gaskell P 3/1/1983 Bp William Jackson Cox. m 5/25/1974 Deborah Usher c 1. S Paul's Ch Mishawaka IN 1997-2008; Mssnr Dio Nthrn Indiana So Bend IN 1994-1996; Stndg Com Dio Oklahoma Oklahoma City OK 1992-1994; St Andrews Ch Broken Arrow OK 1988-1994; Cn S Paul's Cathd Oklahoma City OK 1985-1988; Cur S Andr's Ch Stillwater OK 1982-1985. Drum Major Awd Mayors' Off, MIshawaka and So Bend, IN 2003; Drum Major Awd Mayors' Off, Mishawaka and So Bend, IN 2001. frdavid@stpetersbrenham.org

OU, Chun Shih (Tai) 200 Chu Chang 1st Road, Kaohsiung Taiwan B Kao Sung TW 1/27/1934 s Ching I Ou & Hsi. BTh Tainan Theol Coll Tw 1962; Tokyo Cntrl TS 1967. D 4/25/1965 P 2/1/1966 Bp James Chang L Wong. m 2/24/1959 Tung-Yin Chang c 4.

OUGHTON, Marjorie Knapp (Ore) PO Box 1556, Albany OR 97321 B Philadelphia PA 3/13/1944 d Joseph Edward Knapp & Ruth Fabeck. BS Wag 1965; MBA Marymount U Arlington VA 1987; Cert. of Theol Stds NW Hse of Theol Stds 2008. D 2/28/2009 Bp Sanford Zangwill Kaye Hampton. c 2. oughtonm@aol.com

OUSLEY CSF, David K (Alb) 1040 State Route 9N, Keeseville NY 12944 **Stndg Com Dio Albany Albany NY 2009-; D Vic S Jas Ch Au Sable Forks NY 2005-; D Assoc, Vol Trin Ch Plattsburgh NY 2001-** B Bellingham WA 6/16/1943 Wstrn Washington U; Mstr Art in Mnstry Nash 2008. D 6/29/2002 Bp Daniel William Herzog P 2/27/2008 Bp William Howard Love. c 3.

OUSLEY, John Douglas (NY) 209 Madison Ave, New York NY 10016 **R Ch Of The Incarn New York NY 1985-** B Kansas City MO 12/7/1947 s Jack Marston Ousley & Nancy Ann. BA Ya 1969; MRE NYTS 1971; ThM Lon 1972; MA New Sch for Soc Resrch 1975. D 11/12/1972 P 9/30/1973 Bp Horace W B Donegan. m 5/1/1971 Mary Young c 2. S Paul's Within the Walls Rome 00184 IT 1981-1985; The Amer Cathd of the H Trin Paris 75008 FR 1978-1981; Asst S Thos Ch New York NY 1973-1978. Auth, "arts," *ATR*; Auth, "arts," *Rel Stds*; Auth, "arts," *Wall St Journ*. Cler Liaison - NYPD 2004; Cmnty of S Mary; Soc of Chr Philosophers; Sons of the Amer Revolution. Phi Beta Kappa. ousleyjd@churchoftheincarnation.org

OUSLEY, Patrick Lance (Tex) 301 Avenue A, Wharton TX 77488 B Dallas TX 10/20/1964 s John R Ousley & Faye Holcomb. BBA Baylor U 1987; MDiv STUSo 2001. D 6/16/2001 Bp Claude Edward Payne P 6/19/2002 Bp Don Adger Wimberly. m 4/13/1991 Elizabeth Jenness Bundy c 2. R S Thos Ch Wharton TX 2004-2011; Dio Texas Houston TX 2003; S Dunst's Epis Ch Houston TX 2001-2004. lance@ecww.org

✠ **OUSLEY, Rt Rev S(teven) Todd** (EMich) 1821 Avalon Ave, Saginaw MI 48638 **Bp Dio Estrn Michigan Saginaw MI 2006-** B Palestine TX 7/10/1961 s John Roy Ousley & Faye Holcomb. BA Baylor U 1983; MS Texas A&M U 1984; MDiv Epis TS of The SW 1991; DMin SWTS 2004. D 6/22/1991 P 2/1/1992 Bp Maurice Manuel Benitez Con 9/9/2006 for EMich. m 10/27/1984 Ann M Schumann c 3. Mssnr for Congrl Dvlpmt Dio Estrn Michigan Saginaw MI 2001-2006; R S Fran Par Temple TX 1997-2001; R Ch Of The H Comf Angleton TX 1993-1997; Cur The Ch of the Gd Shpd Austin TX 1991-1993. DD Seabury-Wstrn 2008; DD Sem of the SW 2007. tousley@eastmich.org

OUTMAN-CONANT, Robert Earl (Mass) 482 Beech St, Rockland MA 02370 B Middlebury VT 11/28/1947 s Robert Earl Outman & Dorothy Elizabeth. BA W Maryland Coll 1969; MDiv VTS 1973; DMin Andover Newton TS 1981. D 6/7/1973 P 3/13/1974 Bp David Keller Leighton Sr. m 10/3/1981 Judith Conant c 2. R S Jn's Epis Ch Holbrook MA 1995-2011; Assoc R Ch Of The H Nativ So Weymouth MA 1992-1995; P Assoc Ch Of The H Nativ So Weymouth MA 1987-1992; Trin Epis Ch Rockland MA 1977-1986; S Mk's Ch Brooklyn NY 1976-1977; Cur Par Of Chr Ch Andover MA 1973-1975. AAPC 1981.

OUTWIN, Edson Maxwell (WNY) 316 Park Ave, Medina NY 14103 B New York NY 2/26/1943 s Edson Schreinert Outwin & Mary Elizabeth. ABS Washington U 1965; MDiv GTS 1969. D 6/14/1969 Bp Leland Stark P 5/26/1973 Bp George E Rath. m 6/8/1968 Kay Anna Bulbrook c 2. Vic S Jn's Ch Medina NY 2002-2009; Vic S Mich's Epis Ch Oakfield NY 2002-2009; Vic S Mary's Epis Ch Gowanda NY 1990-2002; Dio Rochester Rochester NY 1989-1990; Vic Allegany Cnty Epis Mnstry Belfast NY 1985-1989; P-in-c Gr Ch No Attleborough MA 1985; P-in-c S Ptr's Ch On The Canal Buzzards Bay MA 1982-1984; Asst Gr Ch Middletown NY 1978-1979; Asst All Ang' Ch New York NY 1973-1977; Cur Chr Ch Hackensack NJ 1969-1970. LAND 1966; Phi Delta Theta 1962. kaynedo360@comcast.net

OUZTS, Peter Daniel (WNC) 805 13th Ave Nw, Hickory NC 28601 B Ware Shoals SC 5/7/1930 s William Daniel Nelson Ouzts & Emmie Lloyd. BA Ya 1951; MA U of So Carolina 1955; STB GTS 1960; STM GTS 1963. D 6/24/1960 Bp Clarence Alfred Cole P 1/18/1964 Bp John Adams Pinckney. m 8/14/1971 Henrietta Eve Hughes c 2. R S Jas Epis Ch Lenoir NC 1987-1994; All SS Epis Ch Hampton SC 1986-1987; P-in-c Epis Ch Of The H Trin Ridgeland SC 1978-1987; P-in-c The Ch Of The Cross Bluffton SC 1978-1986; Asst to R Chr Ch Greenville SC 1971-1978; Vic All SS Epis Ch Clinton SC 1966-1971; Asst Ch Of Our Sav Rock Hill SC 1963-1966; Asst Gr Epis Ch New York NY 1960-1961. peterouzts@hotmail.com

OVENSTONE, Jennifer (SanD) 810 Mockingbird Ln Apt 301, Towson MD 21286 **Assoc R S Jn's Ch Ellicott City MD 2008-** B Dundee Scotland 3/10/1978 BA Azusa Pacific U 2000; MDiv VTS 2003. D 6/7/2003 Bp Gethin Benwil Hughes P 1/17/2005 Bp DM Tutu. m Sidney Smith. Cler Res S Geo's Epis Ch Griffin GA 2005-2008; S Paul's Par Baltimore MD 2005-2008; Cler Res Chr Ch Alexandria VA 2003-2005. josmith@stjohnsec.org

OVERALL, Martha Rollins (NY) 345 E 86th St Apt 16-D, New York NY 10028 **S Ann's Ch Of Morrisania Bronx NY 1996-** B New York NY 11/29/1947 d John Henry Overall & Vera. BA Rad 1969; JD NYU 1976; MDiv UTS 1991; DD Ursinus Coll 2000. D 6/8/1991 P 12/14/1991 Bp Richard Frank Grein. c 1. Pres - Stndg Com Dio New York New York City NY 2001-2002; Stndg Com Dio New York New York City NY 1998-2001; Dio New York New York City NY 1996-2001; Dio Coun Dio New York New York City NY 1995-2002; Diocn Msnry & Ch Extntn Socty New York NY 1993-1995; Vic S Ann's Ch Of Morrisania Bronx NY 1993; Ecum Cmsn Dio New York New York City NY 1991-1999; Asst S Ann's Ch Of Morrisania Bronx NY 1991-1992. Auth, *Var arts*. Trin Transformational Fllshp Trin Ch Wall St 2006; DD Ya Berk 2001. overallmartha@mac.com

OVERFIELD, Brenda S (LI) 87 7th St, Valley Stream NY 11581 **Archd Dio Long Island Garden City NY 2011-; Archd, Nassau Cnty Dio Long Island Garden City NY 2011-; R H Trin Epis Ch Vlly Stream NY 1998-** B 1/18/1959 d Rolland Crane Smiley & Katherine R. BA U of Missouri 1981; MDiv GTS 1993. D 4/24/1993 P 11/7/1993 Bp Orris George Walker Jr. All SS Ch Great Neck NY 1998; Asst S Thos Of Cbury Ch Smithtown NY 1995-1998; Epis Hlth Serv Bethpage NY 1993-1998; Asst Ch of S Jude Wantagh NY 1993-1995. Chair, COM 1998-2001; Chair, Dept of Mssn 2006-2011; Congrl Dvlpmt, Prov II 2006-2011; Dioc Coun 2006-2011; Trst of the Estate, Dioc. of LI 2006-2010. Bd Cert Chapl Assn of Profsnl Chapl 1995. boverf1025@aol.com

OVERTON, Donald Ernest (EC) 2912 Hewitt Place Ct, Louisville KY 40299 B Alliance NE 3/9/1936 s Kenneth Hubert Overton & Dorothy Maxine. BS U of Nebraska 1957; MDiv SWTS 1960; MA U of New Mex 1970. D 6/15/1960 P 12/21/1960 Bp Howard R Brinker. m 6/4/1957 Idona A Vodehnal c 2. R Chr Epis Ch Hope Mills NC 1995-2000; Ch Of The H Sprt Bellevue NE 1988-1993; Off Of Bsh For ArmdF New York NY 1970-1988; Vic Epis Ch Of

O

The Incarn Salina KS 1964-1966; Vic S Chas The Mtyr Beatrice NE 1960-1964. DEOVERTON2@AOL.COM

OWEN, Charles Bryan (Miss) 5246 Saratoga Dr, Jackson MS 39211 **R S Andr's Cathd Jackson MS 2006-** B Memphis TN 1/6/1969 s Sterling Williamson Owen & Ruby Bankeston. BA Ken 1991; MA Van 1994; PhD Van 2000; CAS STUSo 2001. D 9/18/2001 Bp Alfred Clark Marble Jr P 3/20/2002 Bp Duncan Montgomery Gray III. m 5/31/1997 Julie Ann Nolte c 2. R Epis Ch Of The Incarn W Point MS 2001-2006. frbryanowen@yahoo.com

OWEN, David Allen (Ct) 92 E Hill Rd, Canton CT 06019 B Toledo OH 2/26/1936 s Allen Owen & Marion. BA W&L 1958; STM EDS 1962. D 6/9/1962 P 12/1/1962 Bp Nelson Marigold Burroughs. m 11/27/1986 Anne B Batterson c 2. Trin Epis Ch Collinsville CT 1997-1998; Int Dio Connecticut Hartford CT 1996-1998; R Old S Andr's Ch Bloomfield CT 1983-1996; Kent Sch Kent CT 1977-1983; Assoc The Ch Of The H Sprt Lake Forest IL 1970-1976; Stff Gr Ch Chicago IL 1966-1970; Cur S Chrys's Ch Chicago IL 1962-1966. davidowen@snet.net

OWEN, Donald Edward (Ala) 1921 Chandaway Ct, Pelham AL 35124 **D (non-stipendiary) The Epis Ch Of S Fran Of Assisi Indn Sprg Vill AL 2004-** B Florence AL 10/29/1949 s Wallace Owen & Mittie. BA U of Alabama 1974; MA U of Alabama 1977; BS U of Alabama 1995; MBA Samford U 1999. D 10/30/2004 Bp Henry Nutt Parsley Jr. m 7/7/1972 Teresa Owen c 1.

OWEN II, G Keith (O) 18001 Detroit Ave, Lakewood OH 44107 **R S Ptr's Epis Ch Lakewood OH 2004-; Vstng P Trsfg Sum Chap Whitefield NH 1994-** B Petersburg VA 12/25/1959 s Gordon Keith Owen & Mable Jean. Cleveland St U; PrTS; BA U of Virginia 1982; MDiv GTS 1988. D 6/9/1988 P 3/16/1989 Bp C(laude) Charles Vache. m 9/4/1994 Monica Marie Miller c 3. R S Paul's Epis Ch Albany NY 1994-2004; Assoc R S Steph's Ch Newport News VA 1988-1994. Study Grants For Leaders Louisville Inst Louisville VA 2000. keithowen@stpeterslakewood.org

OWEN, Harrison Hollingsworth (WA) 7808 River Falls Dr, Potomac MD 20854 B Evanston IL 12/2/1936 s Raymond Smith Owen & Mary Crawford. BA Wms 1957; BD VTS 1960; MA Van 1965. D 5/14/1960 Bp Oliver J Hart P 7/1/1961 Bp Chilton Powell. m 8/12/1967 Ethelyn Rose Abbott c 2. Assoc Team Mnstry S Marg's Ch Washington DC 1965-1967; Coll Chapl Cathd Of The Incarn Baltimore MD 1960-1962. Auth, "Wave Rider: Ldrshp for High Performance in a Self Organizing Wrld," Berrett-Koehler, 2008; Auth, "Open Space Tech: A User's Guide (3rd Ed)," Berrett- Koehler, 2008; Auth, "The Pract of Peace," Human Systems Dynamics Inst., 2004; Auth, "The Power of Sprt," Berrett-Koehler, 2003; Auth, "The Sprt of Ldrshp," Berrett-Koehler, 2000; Auth, "Expanding our Now," Berrett Koehler, 1997; Auth, "The Millennium Organiztion," Abbott Pub, 1993; Auth, "Riding the Tiger," Abbott Pub, 1992; Auth, "Sprt: Transformation and Dvlpmt in Orgnztn," Abbott Pub, 1987. Share the Wealth Awd Orgnztn Dvlpmt Ntwk 2007. HHOWEN@VERIZON.NET

OWEN, Ronald M (Fla) 100 NE First St, Gainesville FL 32601 **H Trin Ch Gainesville FL 2011-** B Sikeston MO 2/13/1949 s Bryan Yancey Owen & Jean Martin. BA U of Kentucky 1971; JD U of Florida Coll of Law 1973; MDiv VTS 2008. D 6/1/2008 P 12/7/2008 Bp Samuel Johnson Howard. m 6/5/1993 Janet Davis Taylor c 2. Asst R S Ptr's Ch Fernandina Bch FL 2010-2011; S Eliz's Epis Ch Jacksonville FL 2008-2009. ron.m.owen@gmail.com

OWEN, Shelby Ochs (SwVa) PO Box 208, Staunton VA 24402 **Assoc Trin Ch Staunton VA 2009-** B Chattanooga TN 5/2/1958 d Martin Shelby Ochs & Celia Latimer. BA W&M 1980; MDiv VTS 2005. D 6/4/2005 P 12/15/2005 Bp David Conner Bane Jr. m 8/15/1981 Stephen Owen c 3. Assoc S Paul's Ch Ivy VA 2007-2009; Asst R for Yth and Fam Mnstrs S Anne's Epis Ch Reston VA 2005-2007. sowen61331@aol.com

OWENS, Bennett Lee (SO) 1062 Fearrington Post, Pittsboro NC 27312 **Died 4/15/2010** B Cincinnati OH 7/25/1926 s Burleigh Lloyd Owens & Esther Louise. BA Denison U 1949; BD Yale DS 1952. D 10/22/1961 P 4/19/1962 Bp Roger W Blanchard. c 4. Auth/Ed, *ABC People*; Auth/Ed, *Tomorrow*. bowens4161@aol.com

OWENS IV, Bernard J (NC) 4407 Westbourne Rd, Greensboro NC 27410 **R S Andr's Ch Greensboro NC 2010-** B Charlotte NC 8/20/1975 s Bernard Owens & Janet. BA U NC 1997; DAS Ya Berk 2004; MDiv Yale DS 2004. D 12/17/2005 P 6/25/2006 Bp Michael Bruce Curry. m 10/4/2010 Johanna Owens c 1. Assoc R S Paul's Epis Ch Cary NC 2006-2010. bernard.owens@gmail.com

OWENS, Brent A (At) PO Box 655, Monroe GA 30655 **R S Alb's Ch Monroe GA 2008-** B Phildelphia PA 3/22/1962 BS Indiana U 1984; JD Stetson U 1987; MDiv Epis TS of The SW 2005. D 4/17/2005 Bp Leopold Frade P 10/29/2005 Bp Kirk Stevan Smith. m 7/20/1985 Malinda Sue Higginbotham c 3. Cur S Barn On The Desert Scottsdale AZ 2005-2008. fatherbrent@live.com

OWENS III, Charles Edward (SC) Po Box 1038, Bluffton SC 29910 **R The Ch Of The Cross Bluffton SC 1996-** B Sumter SC 11/19/1943 s Charles Edward Owens & Margaret Adaline. BS Auburn U 1965; Med Auburn U 1966; DMin GTF 1994. D 1/23/1994 P 8/1/1994 Bp Edward Lloyd Salmon Jr. m 3/6/1971 Rebecca Duren Edens c 2. Asst Ch Of The Redeem Orangeburg SC 1994-1996. thepadre@thechurchofthecross.net

OWENS JR, Donald P (La) 5 Mary Ridge Ct, River Ridge LA 70123 **Dio Louisiana Baton Rouge LA 2000-; Chapl/ Prof Epis Mnstry To Med Educ New Orleans LA 2000-; P-in-c S Tim's Ch La Place LA 2000-** B Fort Worth TX 2/14/1942 s Donald Phil Owens & Marguerite Ione. Arlington St Arlington TX 1962; BA Trin U San Antonio TX 1966; MDiv Pittsburgh TS 1969; PhD U of Oklahoma 1986. D 6/11/1975 P 10/17/1975 Bp Chilton Powell. m 4/9/1966 Barbara John c 4. Int S Dav's Ch Oklahoma City OK 1999-2000; Int S Jas Epis Ch Oklahoma City OK 1997-1998; Int S Dav's Ch Oklahoma City OK 1995-1997; Int S Fran Ch Edmond OK 1989-1990; Int Emm Epis Ch Shawnee OK 1987-1989; Chapl S Anselm Cbury Norman OK 1975-2000; Cur S Jn's Ch Norman OK 1975-1981. Auth, "Healing and Hope in the midst of Devastation: Reflections on Katrina in the light of 9/11," *Journ of Rel and Hlth*, Journ of Rel and Hlth, Volume 50, Issue 1, 2011; Auth, "The Med Sch Cur: An Examination of Stdt Need," *Journ of Rel and Hlth*, Journ of Rel and Hlth Volume 50, Issue 3, 2011; Auth, "Organ Donation by a Prisoner: Legal and Ethical Considerations," *Journ Louisiana St Med Soc*, Journ Louisiana St Med Soc, Vol. 162, 2010; Auth, "Hist of the Epis Mnstry to Med Educ," *Churchwork*, Epis Dio Louisiana, 2008; Auth, "Psych Issues and Answers Following Hurricane Katrina," *Acad Psych*, Acad Psych, 31:200-204, 2007; Auth, "Beyond Sprtlty: The role of Med Sch Chapl," *Healing Mnstry*, Healing Mnstry, Volume 14, Number 4, Fall, 2007; Auth, "Perspectives on the Cancer Death of a Med Stdt," *Amer Journ of Hospice and Palliative Care*, Journ of Hospice and Palliative Care, Vol 22, No 5, 2005; Auth, "Allowing Patients To Die: Practical Ethical And Rel Concerns," *Journ of Clincl Oncology*, Journ Of Clincl Oncology Vol 21 No 15, 2003. Amer Assn for Mar and Fam Ther 2003; Amer Counslg Assn 2001; Amer Psych Assn 1998; Amer Soc for Bioethics and Hmnts 2000; Arnold P. Gold Humanism in Med hon Soc 2006; ESMHE 1985-2003; Louisiana Counslg Assn 2000. Distinguished Alum Awd Pittsburgh TS 2002. dowens@tulane.edu

OWENS, Gene Waller (At) 3260 Indian Valley Trl, Atlanta GA 30341 B Atlanta GA 10/27/1933 d Hugh Sturgis Waller & Lauree Maude. BA Merc 1983; Cert EFM 1995. D 10/28/1995 Bp Frank Kellogg Allan. m 7/26/1980 J Robert Owens c 3. D Ch Of The H Comf Atlanta GA 1999-2003; D S Bede's Ch Atlanta GA 1995-1998. NAAD 1994. deacongeneo@bellsouth.net

OWENS JR, Jack R (SC) 673 Palisades Dr, Mount Pleasant SC 29464 **Asst R S Phil's Ch Charleston SC 2006-** B Steubenville OH 5/4/1954 s Jack Raymond Owens & Nancy. MA Med U Of So Carolina Charleston SC; BD Med U Of So Carolina Charleston SC 1987; MDiv Trin Sch For Mnstry Ambridge PA 2006. D 7/1/2006 P 1/13/2007 Bp Edward Lloyd Salmon Jr. c 2. owensjack@comcast.net

OWENS, John (Fla) 8373 Normandy Blvd, Jacksonville FL 32221 B Annapolis MD 2/15/1947 s William Thomas Owens & Audry Rita. Angl Inst of Theol 2007. D 6/1/2008 P 12/7/2008 Bp Samuel Johnson Howard. m 10/19/1968 Ellen B Congor c 2. padrejohn@bellsouth.net

OWENS JR, John Evan (Md) 260 S Reynolds St, Alexandria VA 22304 B Portsmouth OH 7/20/1918 s John Evan Owens & Hilda Griffith. BS Towson U 1939; STB GTS 1948; STD GTS 1970. D 6/15/1948 P 5/1/1949 Bp Noble C Powell. S Jas Sch St Jas MD 1955-1984. Chapl Gnrl All SS Sis of the Poor; Contemplative Pryr.

OWENS, Miriam Elizabeth (Roch) 515 Oakridge Dr, Rochester NY 14617 **P-in-c Ch Of The Incarn Penfield NY 2008-** B Amityville NY 5/20/1937 d Joseph Louis Meyer & Edith Crosley. BA Queens Coll 1959; MDiv Bex 1980. D 10/18/1980 P 10/17/1981 Bp Robert Rae Spears Jr. m 7/12/1960 Raymond L Owens c 3. R S Jn's Epis Ch Honeoye Falls NY 1983-1988; Ch Of The Ascen Rochester NY 1982-1999; Int R S Jn's Epis Ch Honeoye Falls NY 1981-1983. mimio76@aol.com

OWENS, Robert Michael (At) P.O. Box 86, Sewanee TN 37375 B Birmingham AL 4/26/1947 s Robert Howard Owens & Edythe Virginia. BS U of Alabama 1969; MS U of Alabama 1970; MS U GA 1973; MDiv STUSo 1983. D 6/11/1983 P 4/1/1984 Bp Charles Judson Child Jr. m 10/13/2006 Jeannine Clements c 4. Ch Of The Trsfg Rome GA 2002-2011; R Trin Epis Ch Asheville NC 1994-2000; Exec Coun Appointees New York NY 1994; Dio Atlanta Atlanta GA 1991-1994; Assoc R The Epis Ch Of S Ptr And S Paul Marietta GA 1985-1990; Cur S Paul's Ch Macon GA 1983-1985. Cmnty of S Mary 1983; Tertiary Ord S Mary the Vrgn 1983; Tertiary Ord of the Precious Blood of Jesus 1987. Cn Angl Dio Capetown, Ch. of the Prov. of Sthrn Afri 1991. robertmichaelowens@me.com

OWENS, U'Neice Yvette (Ga) 4033 Foxborough Blvd, Valdosta GA 31602 B Austin TX 2/7/1963 d Pauris W Kelly & Laura. Physiology Pk U. D 6/28/2006 Bp Henry Irving Louttit. m 8/19/1990 Augustine Owens c 4. yvette.owens@moody.af.mil

OWENSBY, Jacob W (WLa) 908 Rutherford St, Shreveport LA 71104 **Dn S Mk's Cathd Shreveport LA 2009-** B Spartanburg SC 10/30/1957 s James W Owensby & Trudy. BA Emory U 1980; MA Emory U 1983; PhD Emory U 1985; MDiv STUSo 1997. D 6/8/1997 P 12/7/1997 Bp Stephen Hays Jecko. m

4/30/1983 Joy B Bruce c 3. R Emm Epis Ch Webster Groves MO 2003-2008; R S Steph's Epis Ch Huntsville AL 1999-2003; Asst S Mk's Epis Ch Jacksonville FL 1997-1999. Auth, "Dilthey & The Narrative Of Hist". revdrjake@me.com

OWREN, David (NCal) 99 Pampas Ln, Fortuna CA 95540 B Schenectady NY 3/16/1947 s Harvey Owren & Doris. BA San Jose St U 1969; MDiv Pacific Luth Sem 1974; ThM Pacific Luth Sem 1977. Rec from Evangelical Lutheran Church in America 12/30/2005 Bp Jerry Alban Lamb. m 7/25/1992 Carol Arnold Deffner c 2. Vic S Fran Ch Fortuna CA 2006-2010. dowren@suddenlink.net

OWUSU-AFRIYIE, Kwabena (Pa) 811 Longacre Blvd, Yeadon PA 19050 **S Mich's Ch Yeadon PA 2004-** B Kumasi Ghana 11/23/1954 s Sampson Asokwa-Mann & Adwoa. Teachers Coll, Ghana 1971; B Th Trin, Ghana 1979; MTS VTS 1988; Geo Mason U 1990. Trans 1/1/2005 Bp Charles Ellsworth Bennison Jr. c 4. Asst S Paul's Ch Bailey's Crossroads Falls Ch VA 1990-1993; Int Asst S Andr's Epis Ch Arlington VA 1987-1988. revkoafriyie@aol.com

OXFORD, Scott Alexander (WNC) 520 New Haw Creek Rd, Asheville NC 28805 **Stndg Com Dio Wstrn No Carolina Asheville NC 2005-; R S Jas Ch Black Mtn NC 2003-** B Morganton NC 1/22/1957 s John Tipton Oxford & Nancy Caroline. BS Appalachian St U 1980; MDiv STUSo 1987; DMin Drew U 1994. D 5/15/1987 P 11/22/1987 Bp William Gillette Weinhauer. m 10/9/1993 Partrica Diane Stoupe c 2. Cn To Bp Dio Wstrn No Carolina Asheville NC 2000-2003; R Ch Of The H Cross Valle Crucis NC 1993-1999; Chair Stwdshp Cmsn Dio Wstrn No Carolina Asheville NC 1990-1997; Congreg Mnstrs Dio Wstrn No Carolina Asheville NC 1988-1994; Congreg Mnstrs Dio Wstrn No Carolina Asheville NC 1988-1994; Stndg Com Dio Wstrn No Carolina Asheville NC 1988-1994; R S Mary's Ch Morganton NC 1988-1993; Assoc R Ch Of The Ascen Hickory NC 1987-1988. Auth, "St"; Auth, "Re-Memberance At Christmas". OHC 1998. canon@diocesewnc.org

P

PACE, Bradley Warren (O) 323 Wick Ave, Youngstown OH 44503 **R S Jn's Ch Youngstown OH 2010-** B Louisville KY 10/13/1975 s Robert Thomas Pace & Teressa Jo. BA Berea Coll 1997; MA U of Arkansas 1999; PhD U IL at Urbana-Champaign 2006; MDiv SWTS 2008. D 6/7/2008 P 12/6/2008 Bp Jeffrey Dean Lee. m 1/6/1998 Mary Katharine Elder c 3. Assoc Trin Epis Ch Wheaton IL 2008-2010. Auth, "Publ Reason and Publ Theol," ATR, 2009. bradleypace@gmail.com

PACE, David Frederick (ECR) 514 Central Ave, Menlo Park CA 94025 B Haverhill MA 12/28/1940 s Frederick Benjamin Pace & Dorothy May. STM Jesuit TS; BS Menlo Coll; MA/STB U of San Francisco. D 3/4/1977 Bp C Kilmer Myers P 4/1/1978 Bp Wesley Frensdorff. Ch Of S Jos Milpitas CA 2002-2005; R S Jas' Ch Monterey CA 1998-2000; S Ptr's Ch Honolulu HI 1997-1998; Chr Ch Alameda CA 1981-1985; Trin Par Menlo Pk CA 1980-1981. padav381@aol.com

PACE, David Taylor (Ore) 1729 Northeast Tillamook St, Portland OR 97212 B Honolulu HI 12/10/1941 s John Edward Pace & Kathryn. BS OR SU 1965; Oregon Hlth Sci U. Dental Sch 1968; MDiv CDSP 1972. D 8/10/1972 P 6/1/1973 Bp James Walmsley Frederic Carman. m 1/22/1966 Jeanne Frances Lance c 1. Oregon Epis Sch Portland OR 2001-2002; Ch Of The Trsfg Brightwood OR 1978-1980; S Mich And All Ang Ch Portland OR 1975-1976; Asst S Barn Par Portland OR 1972-1974. jeanneanddavidpace@gmail.com

PACE, James Conlin (At) 510 Gay St Apt 1002, Nashville TN 37219 **Asst Ch Of S Mary The Vrgn New York NY 2011-; Supply P Dio Tennessee Nashville TN 2002-** B Bradenton FL 5/30/1954 s Jack Wilbur Pace & Jayne Lee. BA U So 1976; BSN Florida St U 1978; MSN Van 1981; DSN U of Alabama 1986; MDiv Van 1988. D 6/25/1988 P 4/1/1989 Bp George Lazenby Reynolds Jr. m 5/10/1980 Margaret Ellen Olsen. S Anselm's Epis Ch Nashville TN 2006-2007; S Clem's Epis Ch Canton GA 1996-2002; S Jn's Epis Ch Mt Juliet TN 1995. jcp12@nyu.edu

PACE JR, Johnson Hagood (Ga) PO Box 13151, Jacksonville FL 32206 B Brunswick GA 8/15/1918 s Johnson Hagood Pace & Margaret Ruth. BA U of Florida 1941; U So 1948. D 9/26/1948 P 10/20/1949 Bp Middleton S Barnwell. m 8/11/1948 Phyllis Zeuch c 4. Vic Chr Ch S Marys GA 1980-1984; S Mk's Ch Brunswick GA 1980-1984; S Mk's Epis Ch Woodbine GA 1980-1984; R S Lk's Epis Ch Jacksonville FL 1972-1980; LocTen H Trin Ch Gainesville FL 1959-1960; Asst S Jn's Epis Ch Tallahassee FL 1957-1959; Vic Trin Ch Cochran GA 1952-1959; Vic S Andr's By The Sea Epis Ch Destin FL 1952-1957; R S Simon's On The Sound Ft Walton Bch FL 1952-1957; Vic Chr Epis Ch Dublin GA 1950-1952; Archd & Secy Dio Georgia Savannah GA 1950-1952; Vic S Lk's Epis Hawkinsville GA 1950-1952; Vic S Mich's Ch Waynesboro GA 1948-1950; Cur S Paul's Ch Augusta GA 1948-1950.

PACE, Joseph Leslie (Ct) 679 Farmington Ave, West Hartford CT 06119 **R S Jn's Ch W Hartford CT 1991-** B Knoxville TN 7/2/1951 s Norman Alfred Pace & Doris. BA U So 1973; MDiv GTS 1979; MA Hartford Sem 2000. D 6/17/1979 Bp William F Gates Jr P 6/1/1980 Bp William Evan Sanders. Com Dio Connecticut Hartford CT 1992-1998; Rdr Goe Dio Connecticut Hartford CT 1984-1991; Asst S Geo's Ch Nashville TN 1984-1991; Vic S Raphael's Epis Ch Crossville TN 1980-1984; Asst S Lk's Epis Ch Jackson TN 1979-1980. Auth, "Var Bk Revs". Muslim-Chr Relatns, Hartford Sem: Advsry Committ 1999; Soc For Increase Of Mnstry: Exec Com 1995; Soc Of S Marg: Assoc; SCHC: Chapl. Ord of Hosp of St. Jn Jerusalem 2006. pacjos@aol.com

PACE, Stephanie Anne Heflin (O) 3677 Hughstowne Dr, Akron OH 44333 **P-in-c S Matt's Epis Ch Brecksville OH 2010-** B 4/14/1956 Trans from La Iglesia Anglicana de Mex 7/26/2001 Bp J Clark Grew II. m 4/15/1978 Hugh D Pace c 3. P-in-c S Barn Ch Trion GA 2008-2010; R New Life Epis Ch Uniontown OH 2001-2007.

PACHECO, Jose (SanD) 209 Clay St, Weed CA 96094 B 11/3/1941 s Jose Pacheco & Adelina. Immac Concep Sem 1967. Rec from Roman Catholic 8/1/1994 as Priest Bp Jerry Alban Lamb. m 7/15/1972 Linda Alvarado c 4. S Andr's By The Lake Temecula CA 2006-2009; Dio San Diego San Diego CA 1998-2005; S Barn Ch Mt Shasta CA 1994-1998. standrews.episcopal@verizon.net

✠ **PACKARD, Rt Rev George Elden** (NY) 815 2nd Ave, New York NY 10017 B New Rochelle NY 2/23/1944 s George Crissy Packard & Catherine Anna. BA Hob 1966; US-A Chapl Sch 1973; MDiv VTS 1974; US-A Advncd Course Command and Gnrl Stff 1987; DD VTS 2000. D 6/5/1974 P 12/15/1974 Bp William Henry Marmion Con 2/12/2000 for Armed Forces and Micr. m 6/19/1999 Brook Hedick c 4. Chair, Dioc Bdgt Com Dio New York New York City NY 2000-2002; Suffr Bp Armed Serv Fed Mnstrs Epis Ch Cntr New York NY 1999-2010; P-in-c Chr's Ch Rye NY 1997-1999; P-in-c The Ch Of The Epiph New York NY 1995-1997; Cn to the Ordnry Dio New York New York City NY 1994-1995; Supply P S Jn's Ch New Rochelle NY 1992-1993; Mssn Wk Diocn Msnry & Ch Extntn Socty New York NY 1989-1994; Mssn Wk Dpt Of Missions Ny Income New York NY 1989-1994; R Gr Ch Hastings On Hudson NY 1980-1989; R Chr Ch Martinsville VA 1976-1980; Asst S Paul's Epis Ch Lynchburg VA 1974-1976. Co Auth, "Pstr Tchg," *Pstr Tchg on Just War*, HOB, 2003. First Infantry Div 1995; The Druid Soc 1965. September 11th 2001. geopackard@gmail.com

PACKARD, Jeffrey Alan (Va) 220 Morgan Ln, Spotsylvania VA 22551 **R Chr Epis Ch Spotsylvania VA 2000-** B Bellefonte PA 2/10/1966 s Richard L Packard & Janet L. BA Penn 1989; MDiv VTS 1995; STUSo 1999. D 6/9/1995 Bp Charlie Fuller McNutt Jr P 2/10/1996 Bp Michael Whittington Creighton. m 7/1/1989 Sian A MacKey c 4. Vic All SS Ch Coudersport PA 1996-2000; R Chr Ch Coudersport PA 1996-2000; Cur S Andr's Ch St Coll PA 1995-1996. Auth, "Experiencing H Week," *LivCh*, 2008; Auth, "The Scam Artist," *LivCh*, 2002; Auth, "Faith Like a River," *Preaching Through the Year of Lk: Sermons that Wk IX*, Morehouse Pub, 2000; Auth, "Ang in the Flames," *LivCh*, 2000. rector@christchurchspotsy.com

PACKARD, Laurence Kent (Va) 9350 Braddock Rd, Burke VA 22015 **Ch Of The Gd Shpd Burke VA 1997-** B Rockville Centre NY 8/6/1952 s Henry Darrach & Jane. DMin PrTS; BA Wake Forest U 1975; U of Tennessee 1976; MDiv VTS 1979. D 6/28/1979 Bp William F Gates Jr P 5/3/1980 Bp William Evan Sanders. m 11/1/1980 Melissa Armour. S Cathr's Epis Ch Marietta GA 1989-1996; Dept Of Chr Nurture Dio Wstrn Louisiana Alexandria LA 1985-1989; Dept Of CE Dio Wstrn Louisiana Alexandria LA 1984-1989; Asst to R S Mk's Cathd Shreveport LA 1983-1989; Dio W Tennessee Memphis TN 1983; Bd Dir S Columba's Epis Ch Bristol TN 1981-1983; Vic S Jn's Ch Mart TN 1980-1983; Dio Tennessee Nashville TN 1980-1982; Yth Advsr Dio Tennessee Nashville TN 1979-1983; D-In-Trng S Elis's Epis Ch Memphis TN 1979-1980. Auth, "Being There: A New Vision Of Yth Mnstry"; Auth, "Celebrating Yth Mnstry". Ord Of S Mary.

PACKARD, Linda Axelson (Chi) 2 Currant Ct, Galena IL 61036 B Chicago IL 3/7/1942 d William Mandus Axelson & Elin Christina. BA Lawr 1964; MDiv McCormick TS 1989; Cert SWTS 1989; Cert Int Mnstry Prog 1992. D 12/2/1989 P 7/2/1990 Bp Frank Tracy Griswold III. m 10/18/1980 C Anthony Packard c 3. Int Gr Epis Ch Galena IL 2010-2011; R Ch Of Our Sav Chicago IL 1997-2008; Int Gr Ch Oak Pk IL 1994-1997; Pres, Stndg Commitee Dio Chicago Chicago IL 1993-1996; Asst S Greg's Epis Ch Deerfield IL 1993-1994; Int S Andr's and Pentecostal Epis Ch Evanston IL 1992; Admssns Coordntr SWTS Evanston IL 1990-1992. Coll Chapl. lindapack@jcwifi.com

PACKARD, Nancy Meader (Be) 359 Whitehall Rd, Hooksett NH 03106 **R S Mary's Epis Ch Reading PA 2004-** B Waterville ME 7/30/1946 d Harold Arthur Meader & Arlene White. Med Notre Dame Coll 1983; Cert. EDS 1997; MA Notre Dame Coll 1997. D 6/17/2001 P 12/22/2001 Bp Douglas Edwin Theuner. c 2. Gr Ch Manchester NH 2001-2004. npackard@juno.com

PACKER, Barbara Jean (Nwk) Po Box 240, Mendham NJ 07945 B Abington PA 3/18/1942 d Walter Hamilton Packer & Margaret Mary. BS Millersville U 1963; MDiv Drew U 1989. D 6/10/1989 P 2/19/1994 Bp George Phelps

Mellick Belshaw. S Jn's Ch Eliz NJ 1989. Auth, "The Calling of S Pat," *Living Ch*, 1997; Auth, "S Teresa & The Priority of Pryr," *Living Ch*, 1996; Auth, "Catherineof Siena," *Living Ch*, 1996; Auth, "In A Quiet Time & Place," *Living Ch*, 1992. Cmnty of St. Jn Bapt 1964. csjb@csjb.org

PADASDAO, Imelda Sumaoang (Haw) 1326 Konia St, Honolulu HI 96817 **Assoc S Eliz's Ch Honolulu HI 2008-; Dioc Coun Dio Hawaii Honolulu HI 1990-** B Masikil Bangui Ilocos PH 4/1/1953 d Florentino N Padasdao & Iluminada Sumaoang. Cannon's Coll Of Commerce 1973; Hawaii Sch Of Bus 1976; Dio Hawaii Diac Trng Prog HI 1986. D 12/14/1986 P 10/7/1990 Bp Donald Purple Hart. P S Paul's Epis Ch Honolulu HI 1990-1999; Treas Dio Hawaii Honolulu HI 1977-1990. revemeeh@aol.com

PADDOCK, Andrea Lee (Los) 31551 Catalina St,, Laguna Beach CA 92651 **Mem Prog Grp on Sr Adult Mnstry Dio Los Angeles Los Angeles CA 2007-; Mem and Chairman Prog Grp on Single Adult Mnstry Dio Los Angeles Los Angeles CA 2007-** B Oakland CA 10/10/1944 d Dexter Sherman Paddock & Dorothy Bonner. BA U CA 1966; California St U 1969; ETSBH 2006. D 12/2/2006 Bp Chester Lovelle Talton. c 3. Sr Adult Mnstry S Marg Of Scotland Par San Juan Capistrano CA 2006-2009. Assn for Epis Deacons 2007. apaddock01@aol.com

PADDOCK, John Sheldon (SO) 1837 Ruskin Rd, Dayton OH 45406 **R Chr Epis Ch Dayton OH 1999-** B Rochester NY 8/25/1946 s William Sheldon Paddock & Jane Isabel. BA U Roch 1968; MDiv VTS 1972; D.Min Untd TS 2004. D 6/15/1972 P 12/24/1972 Bp John Mc Gill Krumm. m 1/19/1974 Ann V Wilhelm c 8. R Gr Epis Ch Bath ME 1988-1999; R S Jas Ch Great Barrington MA 1980-1988; R S Paul's Epis Ch Greenville OH 1974-1980; Asst Ch Of S Edw Columbus OH 1972-1974. johnpaddock@mac.com

PADEN III, Carter Northen (ETenn) 848 Ashland Ter, Chattanooga TN 37415 **R S Ptr's Ch Chattanooga TN 1994-** B Chattanooga TN 2/9/1953 s Carter Northen Paden & Janet Cheves. BA Van 1975; MA U of Wales, U.K 1980; MDiv STUSo 1987. D 6/21/1987 P 4/24/1988 Bp William Evan Sanders. m 8/30/1980 J Paden c 4. Dio E Tennessee Knoxville TN 2002-2005; Dio E Tennessee Knoxville TN 1996-1999; Bp Coun Dio E Tennessee Knoxville TN 1993-1994; Dio Ecum Off Dio E Tennessee Knoxville TN 1990-1994; R S Fran' Ch Norris TN 1988-1994; D & Cur S Lk's Ch Cleveland TN 1987-1988. Assoc Of The Soc Of St Marg 2001; Childrens Med Missions of Haiti 1993. Fell Coll Of Preachers 1992. carterpaden@stpeters.org

PADGETT, John Elliott (WTex) 12431 Modena Bay, San Antonio TX 78253 B McKenzie TN 10/29/1943 s John Ethelbert Padgett & Martha Ruth. BS USNA 1965; MS Untd States Naval Postgraduate Sch 1972; MDiv Epis TS of the SW 1988. D 5/23/1988 Bp Earl Nicholas McArthur Jr P 12/1/1988 Bp John Herbert MacNaughton. m 6/17/2006 Leslie Watson c 2. Cn Mssnr Partnr In Mnstry Estrn Convoc Kennedy TX 2005-2011; R S Andr's Epis Ch San Antonio TX 1995-2005; Vic/R S Chris's By The Sea Portland TX 1990-1995; Asst/Int R S Thos Epis Ch And Sch San Antonio TX 1988-1990. Ord Of S Lk - Chapl 1992. jpadg43@gmail.com

PADGETT, Judy Malinda Pitts (At) 980 W Mill Bnd Nw, Kennesaw GA 30152 **D S Cathr's Epis Ch Marietta GA 1998-** B Knoxville TN 7/9/1945 d John Franklin Pitts & Nan. D 10/18/1998 Bp Onell Asiselo Soto. m 10/19/1963 Robert Micheal Padgett. judypadgett@cobbfamilyresources.org

PADILLA, Manuel Jack (NMich) 711 Michigan Ave, Crystal Falls MI 49920 **Reg Cleric For The Wstrn Reg Dio Nthrn Michigan Marquette MI 1988-; Reg Cleric For The Wstrn Reg Dio Nthrn Michigan Marquette MI 1988-; Epis Ch-Wstrn Reg Crystal Falls MI 1988-; Mssnr/P S Mk's Ch Crystal Falls MI 1988-** B Paterson NJ 3/12/1955 s Diego Padilla & Laurinda Manuela. BA U of Maryland 1982; MDiv SWTS 1988; DMin SWTS 2004. D 12/22/1987 P 6/1/1988 Bp Thomas Kreider Ray. m 6/22/1974 Margaret Evangeline Dishaw c 2. mpadilla@up.net

PADILLA, Margaret Evangeline (NMich) 711 Michigan Ave, Crystal Falls MI 49920 **P S Mk's Ch Crystal Falls MI 1997-** B Crystal Falls MI 7/12/1953 d Norbert Raymond Dishaw & Mary Lillian. D 12/4/1996 P 6/22/1997 Bp Thomas Kreider Ray. m 6/22/1974 Manuel Jack Padilla c 2. ppadilla@up.net

PADZIESKI, Virginia Sue (Minn) 4409 Ettenmoor Ln SW, Rochester MN 55902 **D Calv Ch Rochester MN 1992-** B Independence KS 7/14/1952 d Douglass Lee Clark & Doris Irene. U of Oklahoma 1970; Simpson Coll Indianola IA 1971; Winchester Art Coll 1985. D 10/17/1992 Bp Sanford Zangwill Kaye Hampton. m 10/8/1983 Robert Joseph Padzieski. Stndg Com Dio Minnesota Minneapolis MN 1996-1998; Dioc Coun Dio Minnesota Minneapolis MN 1994-1996. gonpeas@attglobal.net

PAE, Joseph S (LI) 191 Kensington Rd, Garden City NY 11530 **S Paul's Ch Great Neck NY 2010-** B Chunan South Korea 4/30/1971 BA U of Pennsylvania 1994; MDiv Ya Berk 2001. D 6/24/2003 P 1/17/2004 Bp Orris George Walker Jr. m 5/12/2007 Ju Young Lee-Pae c 2. Cn Cathd Of The Incarn Garden City NY 2004-2010; P Chr Ch Alexandria VA 2003-2004. superjoe1@aol.com

PAGANO, Joseph Samuel (Md) 3 Ashford Ct, Annapolis MD 21403 **S Anne's Par Annapolis MD 2010-** B Fontana CA 12/30/1964 s Stephen Pagano & Mary. BA U of Pennsylvania 1987; MDiv PrTS 1993; PhD Marq 2001. D 6/5/2004 P 12/8/2004 Bp Steven Andrew Miller. m 8/26/1990 Amy Elizabeth Richter. R Emm Ch Baltimore MD 2006-2010; Asst S Paul's Ch Milwaukee WI 2005-2006; S Jas Epis Ch Milwaukee WI 2001-2002. jspagano@loyola.edu

PAGE, Donald Eugene (LI) PO Box 417, 29 East Street, Nunda NY 14517 **Died 3/12/2010** B Buffalo NY 9/26/1943 s Gerald David Chandler Page & Arlowene Anna. BA NYU 1966; MDiv GTS 1969. D 6/21/1969 Bp Lauriston L Scaife P 12/22/1969 Bp Richard Beamon Martin. m 3/18/2010 Trevor A Earley. CCU. donbklyn@aol.com

PAGE, Donald Richard (Ct) 44 Tolland Ave - Unit 47, Stafford Springs CT 06076 B Audubon NJ 7/7/1943 s Victor Page & Allene. Assoc. In Sci Pierce Jr Coll 1965; BA Trenton St Coll 1968; MDiv PDS 1971. D 4/24/1971 P 10/23/1971 Bp Alfred L Banyard. m 6/13/1970 Elizabeth R Dornfeld c 2. No Cntrl Reg Mnstry Enfield CT 1996-2008; Sunday Celebrant Calv Ch Enfield CT 1993-2007; Sunday Celebrant Gr Ch Broad Brook CT 1993-2007; Sunday Celebrant H Trin Epis Ch Enfield CT 1993-2007; Sunday Celebrant S Andr's Epis Ch Enfield CT 1993-2007; Aids T/F Dio Connecticut Hartford CT 1987-1990; Gr Ch Broad Brook CT 1979-1992; R Gr Ch Stafford Sprg CT 1979-1992; Rep Afp Dio New Jersey Trenton NJ 1978-1979; R S Mk's Ch Hammonton NJ 1973-1979; R S Mich's Ch Trenton NJ 1971-1973. Assn Of Epis Chapl 1992-2008; Coll Of Chapl 1992-2008. Citation For Cleric Activities Kessler Hosp Hammonton NJ 1979. dpagesun@yahoo.com

PAGE, Herman (Kan) Po Box 5167, Topeka KS 66605 B Boston MA 3/30/1927 s Herman Riddle Page & Lois Dickinson. BA Harv 1950; MDiv EDS 1952. D 6/1/1952 P 12/13/1952 Bp Herman R Page. m 6/6/1952 Mary Waldo c 3. Assoc S Dav's Epis Ch Topeka KS 1990; Int Dio Kansas Topeka KS 1987-1990; Vic S Phil's Epis Ch Topeka KS 1980-1987; R S Andr's Epis Ch Liberal KS 1967-1980; R Trin Epis Ch Houghton MI 1957-1963; Vic S Jn's Ch Iron River MI 1952-1957; Vic S Mk's Ch Crystal Falls MI 1952-1957.

PAGE JR, Hugh Rowland (EC) 2043 S Bend Ave Pmb 112, South Bend IN 46637 B Baltimore MD 8/18/1956 s Hugh Rowland Page & Elaine. BA Hampton U 1977; Pittsburgh TS 1978; MDiv GTS 1980; STM GTS 1983; MA Harv 1988; PhD Harv 1990. D 6/28/1980 P 12/30/1980 Bp David Keller Leighton Sr. Tutor The GTS New York NY 1982-1983; R S Jos's Epis Ch Fayetteville NC 1981-1982; S Jas' Epis Ch Baltimore MD 1981. poet@hrpj.com

PAGE, Marilyle Sweet (Roch) 401 Beresford Rd, Rochester NY 14610 B Saint Louis MO 7/10/1942 d Martin Pierce Sweet & Vera Bigings. BS Ohio U 1964; MDiv Bex 1975; DMin Bex 1986. D 6/7/1975 Bp John Mc Gill Krumm P 1/4/1977 Bp Robert Rae Spears Jr. R S Mk's And S Jn's Epis Ch Rochester NY 2001-2008; Int S Mk's And S Jn's Epis Ch Rochester NY 2001; P-in-c Chr Ch Rochester NY 2000; Int The Ch Of The Epiph Rochester NY 1999; Int S Thos Epis Ch Rochester NY 1995-1996; R Ch Of The Atone Westfield MA 1989-1995; R S Ptr's Epis Ch Henrietta NY 1979-1989; Assoc S Steph's Ch Rochester NY 1977-1979; Dio Rochester Rochester NY 1975-1984. Auth, "The Ch & The Alco Addicted Fam: A Co-Dependent Perspective," *D. Min. Thesis*, 1986. AAMFT 1990-2010; AAPC 1995-2008; MFT Lic 1993. Outstanding Serv Awd as Pres Genesee Vlly Chapt - NY Assn for MFT 2000. marilyle@aol.com

PAGE, Michelle (EC) 18115 State Road 23 Ste 112, South Bend IN 46637 B San Antonio TX 12/27/1954 d Orah Garfield Thornton & Barbara Jan. Ya; BA Gri 1977; MDiv GTS 1980. D 11/22/1980 Bp James Winchester Montgomery P 12/1/1981 Bp Hunley Agee Elebash. Vic S Andr's Ch Goldsboro NC 1981-1982; Vic S Aug's Epis Ch Kinston NC 1981-1982.

PAGE, Rufus Lee (NCal) 2636 5th Ave, Sacramento CA 95818 B Ionia MI 7/16/1934 s Rufus Lee Page & Mary. BA Shimer Coll 1954; STB PDS 1958. D 4/26/1958 P 11/1/1958 Bp Alfred L Banyard. m 10/22/1982 Gayle I Sutton c 2. Assoc All SS Memi Sacramento CA 1990-1992; R S Matt's Epis Ch Sacramento CA 1969-1970; R S Paul's Epis Ch Sacramento CA 1966-1968; Cur S Steph's Par Whittier CA 1962-1966; Cur S Jas Par Los Angeles CA 1960-1962; In-Charge S Barn By The Bay Villas NJ 1958-1960. Auth, "Funk & Wagnalls New Encyclopedia"; Auth, "Students Needs As A Clergyman Sees Them Ca Educ Agcy 73". Annual Awd For Outstanding Soc Wk For A Non-Profsnl Natl Assn Soc Wkrs 1968. lpage@hhsdc.ca.gov

PAGE, Sherrill Lee (WA) 21641 Great Mills Rd, Lexington Park MD 20653 **R The Ch Of The Ascen Lexington Pk MD 2011-** B Baton Rouge LA 5/26/1953 d Marvin Edward Lee & Alice Leone. BA LSU 1975; MDiv STUSo 1990. D 7/14/1990 P 4/13/1991 Bp George Lazenby Reynolds Jr. m 1/15/1977 William Preston Page Jr c 3. Int S Mary Magd Ch Silver Sprg MD 2009-2010; R S Barn Epis Ch Temple Hills MD 1998-2009; Asst Ch Of The Gd Shpd Rocky Mt NC 1993-1997; Asst To R S Dav's Epis Ch Nashville TN 1991-1993; D-In-Trng S Phil's Ch Nashville TN 1990-1991. Integrity 1999. storyrev@aol.com

PAGE JR, William Russell (Mass) 217 Holland St Pt 2A, Somerville MA 02144 B Evanston IL 5/3/1949 s William Russell Page & Ann Whiting. BA Trin 1971; MDiv GTS 1975. D 6/14/1975 Bp Quintin Ebenezer Primo Jr P 12/1/1975 Bp James Winchester Montgomery. P S Jn's Chap Cambridge MA

1979-2005; Asst Ascen Memi Ch Ipswich MA 1975-1978. page_217@comcast.net

PAGLIARO, Lois Anne (NY) 18818 89th Ave, Hollis NY 11423 B New York NY 12/6/1948 d Salvatore Robert Pagliaro & Muriel Beatrice. BA CUNY 1977; MDiv EDS 1980. D 6/7/1980 Bp Paul Moore Jr. The Ch Of S Lk In The Fields New York NY 1986-2003. loisp@stlukeschool.org

PAGLINAUAN, Cristina (Md) 5603 N Charles St, Baltimore MD 21210 **Assoc R The Ch Of The Redeem Baltimore MD 2010-** B Newark NJ 4/26/1970 d Teodulo J Paglinauan & Wilhelmina Cafugauan. AB Harv 1992; MDiv The GTS 2010. D 6/19/2010 Bp John Leslie Rabb P 1/6/2011 Bp Eugene Sutton. m 11/24/2007 David Warner c 2. cpaglinauan@gmail.com

PAGUIO, Ruth Alegre (ECR) 212 Swain Way, Palo Alto CA 94304 **Vic H Chld Epis Ch San Jose CA 2006-** B Philippines 5/29/1969 d Wilfrido Casipit & Leonor. MDiv CDSP; BA Harris Memi Coll; Med Tariac St U Tariac Philippines. D 12/21/2005 P 8/24/2006 Bp Sylvestre Donato Romero. m 6/5/2004 Adorlito Paguio. Lay H Chld Epis Ch San Jose CA 2005-2006. ruth_casipit@hotmail.com

PAHL JR, James Larkin (NC) 302 College St, Oxrford NC 27565 **R S Steph's Ch Oxford NC 2008-** B Winston Salem NC 12/19/1971 s James Larkin Pahl & Alice Greene. BA No Carolina St U 1995; MDiv VTS 2005. D 6/26/2005 P 1/6/2006 Bp Michael Bruce Curry. m 3/2/1996 Susan Norris Pahl c 4. Asst S Jas Par Wilmington NC 2005-2008. jpahljr@gmail.com

PAHLS JR, John Bernard (Colo) 1713 N Royer St, Colorado Springs CO 80907 B Colorado Springs CO 9/15/1945 s John Bernard Pahls & Mary Louise. BMus U CO 1968; MDiv Nash 1973; S Tikhon Orth TS So Canaan PA 1991; STM Nash 2005. D 9/22/1973 Bp Stanley Hamilton Atkins P 5/11/1974 Bp Edward Clark Turner. Asst Gr And S Steph's Epis Ch Colorado Sprg CO 2007-2009; P-in-c Gr Ch Buena Vista CO 2001-2002; Vstng P Par Ch Of S Chas The Mtyr Ft Morgan CO 1997-1998; Cler Assoc Ch Of S Mich The Archangel Colorado Sprg CO 1995-2001; S Lk's Epis Ch Anth NM 1993-1994; Hon Assoc S Raphael Epis Ch Colorado Sprg CO 1992-1993; H Cross Epis Mssn Sterling CO 1987-1988; Dio Fond du Lac Appleton WI 1983-1987; S Mk's Ch Oconto WI 1983-1987; S Mk's Ch Waupaca WI 1983-1987; Vic S Paul's Ch Suamico WI 1983-1987; Chap Of The Resurr Limon CO 1981-1983; Secy Sthrn Dnry Dio Colorado Denver CO 1981-1983; St Pauls Epis Ch Deer Trail CO 1981-1983; Secy-Treas Saw Mill River IPC Dio New York New York City NY 1978-1980; S Andr's Ch Brewster NY 1975-1980; S Jn's Ch Ulysses KS 1973-1975. CBS - Life Mem 1973; GAS - Life Mem 1973; SHN - Assoc 1983; Soc of King Chas the Mtyr 1975; Soc of Mary - Life Mem 2001; Soc of Our Lady of Walsingham - P Assoc of the H Ho 1975. rev.john.pahls@gmail.com

PAIN, Mary Reed (Mil) 10400 W Dean Rd Apt 102, Milwaukee WI 53224 **D S Simon The Fisherman Epis Ch Port Washington WI 2005-** B Cambria WI 4/29/1938 d James Ellsworth Reed & Ethel Mae. BA U of Wisconsin 1960; MA SWTS 1962. D 12/7/2002 Bp Roger John White. m 11/17/1967 Jack Pain c 2. D S Fran Ch Menomonee Falls WI 2002-2005. painmary@hotmail.com

PAINE, Michael Jackson (WVa) 13 Byron St, Boston MA 02108 B Boston MA 4/18/1940 s Francis Ward Paine & Frances Moyer. BA Pr 1962; BD UTS 1965. D 6/9/1965 P 12/15/1965 Bp Wilburn Camrock Campbell. m 8/22/1964 Victoria Landel Moore. R Trin Ch Morgantown WV 1966-1968; Cur S Matt's Ch Charleston WV 1965-1966.

PAINTER JR, Borden Winslow (Ct) 110 Ledgewood Rd, West Hartford CT 06107 B Brooklyn NY 2/20/1937 s Borden W Painter & Gladys S. BA Trin Hartford CT 1958; MA Ya 1959; STB GTS 1963; PhD Ya 1965. D 6/11/1963 P 12/21/1963 Bp Horace W B Donegan. m 8/29/1959 Ann Deborah Dunning. Dio Connecticut Hartford CT 1974-1987; Asst S Jn's Ch New Haven CT 1963-1966. "Mussolini's Rome," Palgrave-Macmillan, 2005; Auth, "Renzo DeFelice and Historiography of Italian Fascism," *Amer Hist Revs*; Auth, "Angl Terminology in Recent Tudor and Stuart Historiography," *Angl and Epis Hist*; Auth, "The Vstry in Colonial New Engl," *Hist mag of the Prot Epis Ch*; Auth, "The Vstry in the Middle Colonies," *Hist mag of the Prot Epis Ch*; Auth, "Bp Walter H Gray & the Angl Cong of 1954," *Hist mag of the Prot Epis Ch.* DD GTS 2005. borden.painter@mail.trincoll.edu

PAISLEY, David Metsch (Haw) 1307 E Ave De Los Arbolas, Thousand Oaks CA 91360 **Died 3/1/2010** B East Liverpool OH 2/28/1917 s Jesse M Paisley & Martha. BIE OH SU 1948; EDS 1952. D 7/13/1952 Bp Richard S M Emrich P 2/1/1953 Bp Russell S Hubbard. c 2.

PALACIO BEDOYA, Luis Hernan (Colom) Carrera 6 No 49-85, Piso 2, Bogota Colombia B Yarumal Antioguia 12/5/1959 s Javier Antonio Palacio & Matha Ines. D 10/18/2008 Bp Francisco Jose Duque-Gomez. luishpalacio@hotmail.com

PALAGYI, Addyse Lane (Ore) 3697 Croisan Creek Rd S, Salem OR 97302 **Mssy to Ukraine Dio Oregon Portland OR 2008-; Mssy to China Dio Oregon Portland OR 2006-; Mssy to China Dio Oregon Portland OR 2006-; Mssy to Hungary Dio Oregon Portland OR 2005-; D S Thos Epis Ch Dallas OR 2000-** B Salem OR 7/3/1927 d Addison W Lane & Gladys A. BA Willamette U 1949; MA Stan 1952; Doctorate SUNY 1975; Cntr for the Diac 2000. D 9/30/2000 Bp Robert Louis Ladehoff. c 3. "Families: The Artistic Chld," *Fam Focus mag*, 1997; "Tapestries," The E River Anthology Addison Pacific, 1992; "Behavior Modification Through Theatre," Parker, 1980; "The Assembly Prog," Parker, 1975; "The Writer's Corner (monthly column 1992--1998)," *Mid-Vlly Arts mag*.

PALARINE, John Renald (Fla) 12236 Mandarin Rd, Jacksonville FL 32223 **R Ch Of Our Sav Jacksonville FL 1996-** B Saint Paul MN 4/27/1948 s Fiori Leandro Palarine & Lorayne. BA S Thos 1970; MDiv SWTS 1973. D 6/29/1973 P 3/22/1974 Bp Philip Frederick McNairy. m 10/26/1991 Joanne Evanisko c 2. Stndg Com Dio Florida Jacksonville FL 2007-2009; Dio Florida Jacksonville FL 2000-2004; Att Dep Dio Florida Jacksonville FL 2000-2003; Dioc Coun Dio Florida Jacksonville FL 1997-1998; Ch Of The Ascen Clearwater FL 1992-1996; Pstr Response Team Dio SW Florida Sarasota FL 1992-1995; Cn For Yth & Educ Dio Cntrl Florida Orlando FL 1981-1991; Natl Ch Yth Coordntr Dio Minnesota Minneapolis MN 1978-1981; Asst S Jn The Evang S Paul MN 1976-1978; Cur S Ptr's Epis Ch Chicago IL 1974-1976; Yth Coordntr Dio Minnesota Minneapolis MN 1973-1981. jejpal@aol.com

PALASI, Dario Palasi (LI) 13424 96th St, Ozone Park NY 11417 **S Jn's Ch Flushing NY 2004-** B 3/10/1960 Assoc in Arts U of Asia 1981; Masters in Div St. Andr's TS 1985. Trans from Episcopal Church in the Philippines 3/5/2003 Bp Orris George Walker Jr. m 12/28/1989 Catherine Taclobao c 3. Dio No Cntrl Philippines 1990-1993; Dio Cntrl Philippines 1986-1989.

PALLARD, John J (RI) PO Box 142, Peckham Lane RR#2, Coventry RI 03/01/2816 **R S Barn Ch Warwick RI 2009-; P-in-c St Fran Epis Ch Coventry RI 2008-** B Scramton PA 4/19/1945 s John Paul Pallard & Mary Ann. BA Oblate Coll 1969; MRE Fairfield U 1975; MA Oblate Coll 1975; EdD Boston Coll 1982; MSEd Niagara U Niagara Falls NY 1982. Rec from Roman Catholic 10/9/2008 Bp John Wadsworth Howe. m 11/24/2009 Erin Lee Mahoney c 1. Dio Rhode Island Providence RI 2009. P-Tchr, "The Ch's Soc Mssn," Cntr for Lrng, 1979. palgel@aol.com

PALLARES-ARELLANO, Jorge Enrique (Los) 10154 Mountair Ave, Tujunga CA 91042 **Vic Ch Of The Ascen Tujunga CA 2008-** B Puebla Mexico 6/19/1957 s Enrique Pallares-Mendoza & Lidia. Bachelor Universidad Autonoma de Puebla 1980; Dplma w hon Comunidad Teologica de Mex 2005; Bachelor Seminario de San Andres 2005. Trans from La Iglesia Anglicana de Mex 11/5/2008 Bp Joseph Jon Bruno. m 8/1/1987 Rosa Patricia Pezzat-Said c 2. jorgeepallaresa2007@hotmail.com

PALMA, Jose Leandro (WMo) 420 West 14th St, Kansas City MO 64105 **Dio W Missouri Kansas City MO 2009-** B SV 4/2/1963 s Jose Erasmo Palma & Maria Luz. BA Santiago de Maria Usulutan 1993. Rec from Roman Catholic 8/25/2001 as Priest Bp Claude Edward Payne. m 11/18/1994 Mercedes Arias c 4. Pstr San Francisco De Asisi Austin TX 2001-2008. jose_palma2002@yahoo.com

PALMER, Albert Henry (NC) 638 N Stratford Rd, Winston Salem NC 27104 B London UK 10/19/1927 s Frederick Walter Palmer & Eliza. BA Kent St U 1952; MDiv Nash 1961. D 4/16/1955 P 11/5/1955 Bp James P De Wolfe. m 6/27/1959 Arden Farris c 3. Asst Secy Dioc Conv Dio Long Island Garden City NY 1974-1976; Dioc Coun Dio Long Island Garden City NY 1969-1972; R S Thos Ch Farmingdale NY 1965-1992; Vic S Lydia's Epis Ch Brooklyn NY 1955-1958. Bishops DSC; Hon Cn Cathd Of The Incarn Garden City NY. k4ahp@triad.rr.com

PALMER, Alison (WA) 70 Lookout Rd, Wellfleet MA 02667 B Medford MA 11/22/1931 d Charles Burbank Palmer & Lois Mead. BA Br 1953; MA Bos 1970; Dio Washington Spec Preparatory Prog 1974. D 6/9/1974 Bp William Foreman Creighton P 9/7/1975 Bp George West Barrett. Assoc The Ch Of The H Sprt Orleans MA 1995-1998; Assoc Min Chap Of S Jas The Fisherman Wellfleet MA 1982-1983; Assoc Min S Columba's Ch Washington DC 1974-1975. Wm Scarlett Awd Epis Ch Pub Soc 1994.

PALMER, Andrew Wallace (Okla) 2149 S Erie Pl, Tulsa OK 74114 **D S Ptr's Ch Tulsa OK 1983-** B New York NY 6/12/1921 s Willis Edwin Palmer & Kathryn Florence. Dutchess Cmnty Coll Poughkeepsie NY; NYU. D 6/7/1969 Bp Horace W B Donegan. m 3/29/1947 Virginia Maitland Smucker c 4. Asst S Jas Epis Ch Wagoner OK 1974-1975; D Zion Epis Ch Wappingers Falls NY 1969-1973. NCD.

PALMER JR, Archie Macinnes (Nwk) 18 Ridgewood Ave, Glen Ridge NJ 07028 B Chattanooga TN 12/17/1939 s Archie Macinnes Palmer & Elizabeth Cheatham. BA Wms 1962; MDiv PDS 1969. D 6/14/1969 P 12/17/1969 Bp Leland Stark. m 6/24/1967 Lynne Witte. S Andr's Epis Ch Lincoln Pk NJ 2001; R Trin Epis Ch Cranford NJ 1982-1984; Trin Epis Ch Kearny NJ 1971-1982; Asst to R S Jas Ch Upper Montclair NJ 1969-1971. Trst For Bloomfield Coll 2000. lynnearch@verizon.net

PALMER, Beth Ann (Va) Po Box 829, West Point VA 23181 **D-in-c S Jn's Ch W Point VA 2003-; The Falls Ch Epis Falls Ch VA 2003-** B Danville PA 7/30/1953 BS Bloomsburg U of Pennsylvania 1975; MBA Penn 1981; MDiv VTS 2003. D 6/14/2003 P 12/20/2003 Bp Peter James Lee. m 11/27/1981 David Ralph Rorick c 1. beth.palmer@verizon.net

PALMER, Brian Gerald (Los) PO Box 37, Pacific Palisades CA 90272 **The Par Of S Matt Pacific Palisades CA 2009-** B 8/3/1949 s Charles Edward Palmer & Jean Ruby. MDiv VTS 2009. D 1/24/2009 Bp Chester Lovelle Talton. bpalmer@stmatthews.org

PALMER, Earle Jason (Ak) Po Box 1002, Ward Cove AK 99928 **Asst P S Jn's Ch Ketchikan AK 1978-** B Elma WA 12/4/1930 s Ben I Palmer & Ina Dunfee. D 10/9/1972 P 4/1/1973 Bp William J Gordon Jr. m 5/24/1963 Lana Jaquith.

PALMER, Hubert Charles (Tex) Po Box 353, Ingram TX 78025 B Gwent Wales GB 2/21/1921 s Albert Palmer & Daisy Everson. BA U Pgh 1942; MDiv VTS 1944; MA SW Texas St U San Marcos 1946. D 6/16/1944 Bp Frederick D Goodwin P 2/21/1945 Bp Everett H Jones. m 6/3/1947 Donna Wilson Duff c 2. Int Epis Ch Of The Gd Shpd San Angelo TX 1992-1993; Int S Mk's Epis Ch San Antonio TX 1991-1992; Int Emm Epis Ch San Angelo TX 1989-1990; R H Sprt Epis Ch Houston TX 1960-1987; R All SS Epis Ch Corpus Christi TX 1950-1959; Assoc Ch Of The Gd Shpd Corpus Christi TX 1948-1950; R S Andr's Epis Ch Seguin TX 1944-1948.

PALMER, John Avery (ECR) 981 South Clover Ave, San Jose CA 95128 **D/H Sprt Mssn; Lake Almanor, CA Dio Nthrn California Sacramento CA 2009-; Dio's Liaison, Natl Epis Hlth Mnstrs S Paul's Epis Ch Indianapolis IN 2009-; Chapl / Pstr Care S Fran Epis Ch San Jose CA 2003-** B Cooperstown, New York 5/30/1944 s Kenneth Alfred Palmer & Helen Avery. BS OH SU 1969; MA U CA/Berkeley: Sch of Publ Hlth 1971; BS CDSP 1988; PhD Canbourne U 2005. D 9/20/1991 Bp Richard Lester Shimpfky. m 9/2/1989 Sherrill Carlton Butler c 2. Presiding Judge, Eccl Trial Crt Dio El Camino Real Monterey CA 2010-2011; Ch Of The H Sprt Campbell CA 2000-2002; S Mk's Epis Ch Santa Clara CA 1991-1999. Auth, "Hlth Instrn in California's Publ Schools," *Hlth Framework in California*, CA St Dept of Ed., 1977; Auth, "Childrens' Mntl Hlth," *NMHA*, NMHA, 1972. (Am Red Cross) Vol. Org. Active in Disasters (VOAD) 1976; Amer Publ Hlth Assn 1971; Intl Conf of Police Chapl 1996; No Amer Assn Diac 1988. Hall Of Fame Mt. Markham HS 2007; Knight of Gr Ord of S Jn of Jerusalem, Knights Hospitallier 2003; Employee of the Year Santa Clara Cnty Hlth & Hosp System 1998; Knight of hon Ord of S Jn of Jerusalem, Knights Hospitallier 1989; Employee of the Year Santa Clara Cnty Publ Hlth Dept 1982; Pres'sScholarship Awd The OH SU 1968; Natl hon Soc W Winfield Cntrl Sch 1960. Avery-s_Aloha@Juno.Com

PALMER III, John Milo (NY) 33 E 10th St Apt 2-G, New York NY 10003 B Kansas City MO 12/19/1945 s Milo Palmer & Carrie Winifred. BA Wm Jewell Coll 1967; STB GTS 1970. D 6/20/1970 Bp Robert Rae Spears Jr P 1/1/1971 Bp Edward Randolph Welles II. Assoc S Jn's Ch New York NY 1998-2000; Dir Of Spec Par Ministers Par of Trin Ch New York NY 1984-1988; Trin Educ Fund New York NY 1979-1986; R Ch Of The Trsfg Bat Cave NC 1977-1979; Asst To Bp Of SE Florida Dio SE Florida Miami FL 1975-1977; Dio SE Florida Miami FL 1974-1977; Yth Coordntr Dio SE Florida Miami FL 1973-1975; Asst S Steph's Ch Coconut Grove Coconut Grove FL 1970-1973. Auth, "Unicorn". Comt.

PALMER, Richard Rainer (Colo) 755 S Dexter St Apt 614, Denver CO 80246 B Bogota CO 5/18/1928 s Thomas Waverly Palmer & Marguerite. BS U Denv 1954; MDiv Nash 1959. D 6/29/1959 P 2/1/1960 Bp Joseph Summerville Minnis. R S Lk's Ch Denver CO 1983-1992; Chair - COM Dio Colorado Denver CO 1971; Chair - COM Dio Colorado Denver CO 1971; R Ch Of S Mich The Archangel Colorado Sprg CO 1967-1983; R Chr The King Epis Ch Ft Worth TX 1963-1967; Vic Chr Epis Ch Aspen CO 1959-1963. Auth, "7 Ways God Helps You," 1969. rainer7mx@yahoo.com

PALMER, Richard William (Wyo) 4753 Estero Blvd Apt 1601, Fort Myers Beach FL 33931 B Cleveland OH 5/26/1923 s Leon Thomas Palmer & Myrtle Rose. BA Pr 1944. D 6/30/1984 P 3/1/1985 Bp John Harris Burt. m 11/27/1969 E Allyene Chrisman. P Lamb Of God Epis Ch Ft Myers FL 2000-2002; S Raphael's Ch Ft Myers Bch FL 1998-2003; Archd Dio Colorado Denver CO 1992-1994; Dio Wyoming Casper WY 1992-1994; Archd Dio Wyoming Casper WY 1985-1990; Pres Equipment Co Dio Colorado Denver CO 1975-1985. allyene_palmer@yahoo.com

PALMER, Sara Elizabeth (NC) 108 W Farriss Ave, High Point NC 27262 **Asst to the R S Mary's Epis Ch High Point NC 2010-** B Redhill, Surrey England 4/27/1957 d David S Harding & Elizabeth Margaret. BA Bristol U 1979; Post Grad Cert. of Educ King Alfred's Teachers' Trng Coll 1980; MDiv VTS 2010. D 6/19/2010 P 1/15/2011 Bp Michael Bruce Curry. m 2/22/1986 David Palmer c 1. sarahp@stmarysepisc.org

PALMGREN, Charles Leroy (At) 4482 Hunters Ter, Stone Mountain GA 30083 **Asst S Marg's Epis Ch Waxhaw NC 1988-** B Peoria IL 9/28/1933 s Elmer Sidney Palmgren & Iantha. BA Drake U 1955; MA U Chi 1963; PhD Un Grad Sch 1972. D 10/2/1985 Bp William Carl Frey P 10/1/1986 Bp Peter James Lee. m 8/17/1957 Marian Robertson. Asst S Ptr's Epis Ch Arlington VA 1985-1988. Soc Of S Fran.

PAMATMAT, Roberto Delos Reyes (Chi) 509 N. 6th Avenue, Des Plaines IL 60016 B Manila Philippines 7/29/1966 s Roberto Cosio Pamatmat & Teodora Delos Reyes. BS U of So Tomas Manila PH 1989; BD U of So Tomas Manila PH 1992; MDiv SWTS 2000. D 6/16/2001 P 12/15/2001 Bp William Dailey Persell. S Raphael The Archangel Oak Lawn IL 2001-2005. Epis Asiamerica Mnstry 1995. jopam729@gmail.com

PANASEVICH, Eleanor J. (Mass) 104 Oak St, Weston MA 02493 B New York NY 5/29/1941 d Albert Ross Jones & Eleanor. BA Smith 1963; MDiv EDS 1995. D 6/6/1998 Bp Barbara Clementine Harris P 5/29/1999 Bp M(arvil) Thomas Shaw III. m 4/22/1978 Leo N Panasevich c 1. S Mich's Ch Milton MA 2001-2003; Asst R S Ptr's Epis Ch Cambridge MA 1999-2001; D S Ptr's Epis Ch Cambridge MA 1998-1999. epanasevich@comcast.net

PANG, Pui-Kong Thomas (Mass) 138 Tremont St, Boston MA 02111 **Asiamerica Mnstry The Cathd Ch Of S Paul Boston MA 2000-; Mssnr, Chinese Mnstrs Dio Massachusetts Boston MA 1996-** B Hong Kong,,HK 12/21/1954 s Chun Kung Pang & Gick Luen. B.A. Chinese U HK 1982; M. Ed. Boston Coll 1988; D Min Bos 1996. D 10/18/1982 P 11/30/1993 Bp The Bishop of Hong Kong. m 1/1/1983 Wendy Luk c 3. tompang12@gmail.com

PANKEY, Steven John (CGC) 1780 Abbey Loop, Foley AL 36535 **Cur S Paul's Ch Foley AL 2007-** B Harvey IL 1/12/1980 s John Steven Pankey & Patricia Joan. BS Millersville U PA 2002; MDiv VTS 2007. D 6/9/2007 P 1/24/2008 Bp Nathan Dwight Baxter. m 3/1/2003 Catherine Rae Thomas c 1. steve@saintpaulsfoley.com

PANNELL, Terry Randolph (Mass) 519 Commercial St, Provincetown MA 02657 **The Ch Of S Mary Of The Harbor Provincetown MA 2006-; Dio Wstrn Louisiana Alexandria LA 2003-** B Ripley MS 12/2/1956 s Clayton Randolph Pannell & Dollie. BS U of No Alabama 1985; MTS Van 2001; MDiv STUSo 2003. D 6/7/2003 P 3/6/2004 Bp D(avid) Bruce Mac Pherson. S Clem's Ch New York NY 2006. Writer, "Rite of Passage," *The Spire*, Van Off of Cmncatn & Pub, 2004. ptownvicar50@gmail.com

PANTLE, Thomas Alvin (Dal) 617 Star St # 81, Bonham TX 75418 **The Epis Ch Of The Resurr Franklin TN 1966-** B Portland OR 7/21/1939 s Alvin Thomas Pantle & Marian Lyall. BS Portland St U 1963; LTh SWTS 1966. D 6/22/1966 Bp James Walmsley Frederic Carman P 1/1/1967 Bp William Evan Sanders. S Dunst's Ch Mineola TX 2002-2011; Vic All SS Ch Atlanta TX 1998-2002; Vic S Mart Epis Ch New Boston TX 1998-2002; Ch Of The H Trin Bonham TX 1995-1997; The Epis Ch Of The H Nativ Plano TX 1993-1994; P-in-c S Edw's Ch Silverton OR 1989-1998; Dio Oregon Portland OR 1988-1991; S Mary's Ch Woodburn OR 1984-1988; Int Ch Of The Resurr Eugene OR 1982-1983; The Epis Ch Of The Gd Samar Corvallis OR 1981-1982; Int S Mary's Epis Ch Eugene OR 1980-1981; R Ch Of The H Cross Paris TX 1974-1978; R The Epis Ch Of The H Nativ Plano TX 1969-1974. dunstan@lcii.net

PANTON, Rosalyn Way (Ga) 2200 Birnam Pl, Augusta GA 30904 **D S Alb's Epis Ch Augusta GA 1994-** B Augusta GA 7/2/1942 d Raymond Way & Mary Elizabeth. BA Fisk U 1964. D 10/28/1994 Bp Henry Irving Louttit. c 2. Ord Of S Helena. rpa1760100@aol.com

PANTON, Thelma Monique (At) 306 Peyton Rd SW, Atlanta GA 30311 **Assoc R S Paul's Epis Ch Atlanta GA 2008-** B Fort Monmouth NJ 10/1/1965 d Gordon Joseph Panton & Rosalyn Way. BA Emory U 1987; MSW U GA 1992; MDiv U So TS 2008. D 12/21/2007 P 8/9/2008 Bp J(ohn) Neil Alexander. stpauls731@aol.com

PAOLOZZI, Joann Lee (Oly) No address on file. B Pendleton OR 7/10/1941 d Don Daniel Allstott & Alma Eunice. BEd Estrn Oregon U 1963; Cert Westcott Hse Cambridge 1987; MDiv CDSP 1989. D 6/27/1989 P 5/1/1990 Bp Robert Louis Ladehoff. c 1. Dio Olympia Seattle WA 2002-2003; S Matt Ch Tacoma WA 2001-2002; R S Tim's Epis Ch Chehalis WA 1992-2001; Asst S Mich And All Ang Ch Portland OR 1989-1991. Dok.

PAPANEK, Nicolette (Kan) 545 Greenup St #3, Covington KY 41011 **Int R Trin Ch Covington KY 2010-** B San Francisco CA 11/23/1951 d Victor Joseph Papanek & Winifred. BA Webster U 1985; MDiv SWTS 2002. D 4/6/2002 P 10/12/2002 Bp William Edward Smalley. Int Trin Ch Russellville KY 2009-2010; Int Chr Epis Ch Bowling Green KY 2007-2008; Int S Jn's Ch Wichita KS 2006-2007; Int S Thos The Apos Ch Overland Pk KS 2004-2006; Cur/Assoc R Gd Shpd Epis Ch Wichita KS 2002-2004. npapanek@gmail.com

PAPAZOGLAKIS, Elizabeth Brumfield (Mil) 1717 Church Street, Wauwatosa WI 53213 **Trin Ch Wauwatosa WI 2010-** B 7/24/1950 d John Burke Brumfield & JoAnn R. BS LSU 1977; MA Nicholls St U 1990; MA Sacr Heart TS Hales Corners WI 2009. D 6/6/2009 P 5/1/2010 Bp Steven Andrew Miller. m 9/17/1977 Thomas Weston Pakis c 3. Dio Milwaukee Milwaukee WI 2009-2010; Mus Dir S Barth's Ch Pewaukee WI 2009; Zion Epis Ch Oconomowoc WI 2002-2007. mother.elizabethp@gmail.com

PAPAZOGLAKIS, Thomas Weston (Mil) N27w 2400 Paul Court, Pewakee WI 53072 **P-in-c/Vic S Barth's Ch Pewaukee WI 2002-** B Brooklyn NY 3/10/1955 s James Pakis & Janis J. BA LSU 1978; MBA Tul 1989; MDiv Nash 2002. D 12/27/2001 Bp Charles Edward Jenkins III P 6/30/2002 Bp Roger John White. m 9/17/1977 Elizabeth Brumfield c 1. fr.tomp@gmail.com

PAPE, Cynthia Dale (Mass) 1 Linden St, Quincy MA 02170 B Flemington NJ 10/15/1956 d Richard Douglas Pape & Beverly Dale. NEU; AA Roger

Willliams Coll. D 6/6/2009 Bp M(arvil) Thomas Shaw III. m 8/13/2004 Anne Campbell Moore. cynthpp@yahoo.com

PAPILE, James Allen (Va) 3241 Brush Dr, Falls Church VA 22042 **R S Anne's Epis Ch Reston VA 1999-** B Chelsea MA 2/21/1951 s James Dominic Papile & Phyllis Roberta. U of New Hampshire 1971; BS Geo Mason U 1989; MDiv VTS 1992. D 6/13/1992 Bp Robert Poland Atkinson P 12/1/1992 Bp Peter James Lee. m 10/7/1978 Barbara Kay Evans. Epis EvangES Arlington VA 1998-1999; S Patricks Ch Falls Ch VA 1994-1999; Asst to R Imm Ch-On-The-Hill Alexandria VA 1992-1994. Treas Eees. rector@stannes-reston.org

PAPINI, Heber Mauricio (Tex) 3002 Six Gun Trl, Austin TX 78748 B Cumari Goias BR 11/19/1950 s Uberdon Papini & Maria Antonia. BA Fach Brazil Br 1981; MDiv Epis TS of The SW 1993. D 10/28/1995 Bp Leopoldo Jesus Alard P 5/1/1996 Bp Claude Edward Payne. m 7/4/2008 Marlaine Carneiro c 4. Trin Ch Houston TX 2004; R S Ptr's Ch Pasadena TX 2000-2009; Vic S Alb's Ch Houston TX 1995-2000. hebermpapini@hotmail.com

PAPPAS, Christopher A (RI) 4 Sesame St, Westerly RI 02891 Canada B Plainfield NJ 9/4/1962 BS Trin Hartford CT 1980; PhD U of Connecticut 1992; MDiv Ya Berk 2004; DAS Ya Berk 2004. D 12/13/2003 Bp Keith Bernard Whitmore. m 5/16/1970 Elisabeth J Thompson c 4. R Chr Ch Westerly RI 2008-2010. christ-church@verizon.net

PAPPAS III, James Christopher (At) 735 University Ave, Sewanee TN 37383 B Belleville IL 10/9/1973 s James Christopher Pappas & Rose Marie. Quincy U; Althoff Cath HS 1991; BA McKendree U 1997; MDiv The U So (Sewanee) 2005. D 12/20/2008 P 2/10/2010 Bp J(ohn) Neil Alexander. m 5/25/2008 Jennifer Davis. P-in-c Trin Ch Winchester TN 2010. pappajc9@sewanee.edu

PARAB, Elizabeth Anne (Cal) Saint Timothy's Episcopal Church, 2094 Grant Road, Mountain View CA 94040 **Dir, Chld, Yth and Fam Mnstrs S Tim's Epis Ch Mtn View CA 2011-** B Modesto CA 1/14/1974 d Steven MacDonald Ellis. BA Santa Clara U 1996; MDiv VTS 2001. D 6/23/2001 P 2/1/2002 Bp Richard Lester Shimpfky. m 4/3/2005 Sameer Dattatray Parab. Asst S Edm's Epis Ch Pacifica CA 2009-2011; Asst S Matt's Epis Ch San Mateo CA 2003-2009; Cur S Dunst's Epis Ch Carmel Vlly CA 2001-2003. The DOK 1993. bethparab@gmail.com

PARACHINI, David Charles (Ct) 42 Blue Jay Dr, Northford CT 06472 **Int S Steph's Ch E Haddam CT 2011-** B Philadelphia PA 9/20/1942 s Harold Charles Parachini & Ruth Irene. BA U of Pennsylvania 1965; BTh Hur 1968; STM Andover Newton TS 1969. Trans from Anglican Church of Canada 12/1/1970 Bp John Melville Burgess. m 5/24/1965 Mary Vickery c 1. R Gr Epis Ch Windsor CT 2001-2011; Int S Andr's Ch Madison CT 1998-2001; Dio Connecticut Hartford CT 1997-2005; Int Imm S Jas Par Derby CT 1997-1998; Int Chr Ch Guilford CT 1995-1997; Litchfield Hills Reg Mnstry Bridgewater CT 1991-1995; Int S Jn's Ch W Hartford CT 1990-1991; Ya Berk New Haven CT 1986-1990; Int S Jas On The Pkwy Minneapolis MN 1984-1985; Minnesota Epis Fndt Inc Minneapolis MN 1981-1986; Int S Clem's Ch S Paul MN 1981-1983; Int S Matt's Ch St Paul MN 1979-1980; Gr Ch Newton MA 1970-1972. Auth, "Prog In a Cnty Jail"; Auth, "A Guide to Human Serv for Sch Managers". Fllshp Natl Educ Plcy Massachusetts 1976. eakp@aol.com

PARADINE, Philip James (Va) 118 Monte Vista Ave., Charlottesville VA 22903 **Vic S Lk's Simeon Charlottesville VA 2008-** B London UK 2/24/1946 s Albert James Paradine. BS Lon 1967; MA U of Ottawa 1976; MDiv VTS 1997; DMin SWTS 2003. Trans from Anglican Church of Canada 4/4/1998 Bp Peter James Lee. m 2/5/1994 Carter Kimsey c 4. S Paul's Epis Ch Port Townsend WA 2005-2006; Trin Epis Ch Martinsburg WV 2003-2005; R S Thos Epis Christiansburg VA 1999-2003; Asst R Emm Epis Ch Alexandria VA 1997-1999. pjparadine@juno.com

PARADISE, Gene Hooper (Ga) 3645 Peachtree Rd NE, Apt 313, Atlanta GA 30319 **Assoc for Sr. Pstr Care S Lk's Epis Ch Atlanta GA 2002-** B Nashville TN 11/21/1936 s Ira Gilbert Paradise & Lois Schardt. BA Van 1958; MDiv Epis TS In Kentucky 1983. D 1/22/1983 P 10/28/1983 Bp (George) Paul Reeves. Cur The Ch Of Our Sav Atlanta GA 2000-2001; Dio Georgia Savannah GA 1987-1995; R S Mich's Ch Waynesboro GA 1984-1999; Asst R S Thos Ch Savannah GA 1983-1984. paradise@stlukesatlanta.org

PARADISE, Scott Ilsley (Mass) 305 Badger Terrace, Bedford MA 01730 B Winchester MA 4/6/1929 s Scott Hurtt Paradise & Alma Sherman. BA Ya 1950; BD EDS 1953. D 6/6/1953 Bp Norman B Nash P 6/13/1954 Bp The Bishop Of Sheffield. m 12/20/1958 Mary Jeanne McKay c 2. Boston Indstrl Mssn Cambridge MA 1965-1978. Auth, "Unequal Battle," *MA Audubon*, 1969; Auth, "Vandal Ideology," *The Nation*, 1969; Auth, "Detroit Indstrl Mssn: A Personal Narrative," Harper & Row, 1968. EPF; ESMHE 1978-1994. sparadise35@comcast.net

PARAISON, Edwin Mardochee (DR) Calle Tony Mota Ricart #16, Box 132, Barahona Dominican Republic B Cap Haitien HT 10/12/1962 s Jean M Paraison & Yolanda. D 10/26/1986 P 12/1/1987 Bp Telesforo A Isaac. m 8/26/1990 Angie Dinorah Polanco Monegro. Dio The Dominican Republic (Iglesia Epis Dominicana) Santo Domingo DO 1986-1994. Anti-Slavery Awd London 1994; Haitian Consul In Dominican Republic.

PARAISON, Maud (Hai) PO Box 5826, Fort Lauderdale FL 33310 **P S Benedicts Ch Plantation FL 2011-** B 11/26/1945 d Enoch Paraison & Madeleine. Dioc Sch for Mnstry; BA Florida Intl U; AA Miami-Dade Cmnty Coll; So Florida Theol Cntr for Theol Stds. D 5/26/1994 P 12/19/1998 Bp Calvin Onderdonk Schofield Jr. c 4. Ch Of The Intsn Ft Lauderdale FL 2000-2008; H Sacr Pembroke Pines FL 1999-2000. peremaud@live.com

PARAN, William John (Mich) 435 S Gulfstream Ave Unit 1005, Sarasota FL 34236 B Springfield MA 4/21/1928 s John Paran & Marion Evelyn. BS U of Detroit 1952; MDiv Bex 1968. D 6/29/1968 P 12/30/1968 Bp Archie H Crowley. m 7/26/2003 Patricia Ann Davenport. Int S Thos Epis Ch Battle Creek MI 1994; S Andr's Ch Grand Rapids MI 1991-1992; Int S Paul's Epis Ch Port Huron MI 1990-1991; S Paul's Epis Ch Lansing MI 1985-1991; R S Jas Ch Piqua OH 1974-1985; Assoc R S Jn's Epis Ch Midland MI 1968-1974. Life Mem MI Assn CPA's. bnp2@verizon.net

PARDINGTON III, G(eorge) Palmer (Ore) 3033 Ne 32nd Ave, Portland OR 97212 B Mobile AL 7/12/1939 s George Palmer Pardington & Mary Gladden. BA W&L 1961; MDiv GTS 1966; PhD Grad Theol Un 1972; STM GTS 1988. D 6/29/1966 Bp Iveson Batchelor Noland P 5/11/1967 Bp Girault M Jones. m 6/7/1965 Anne S Simpson c 2. Chapl Assoc S Steph's Epis Par Portland OR 1995-1997; Portland Metro Epis Campus Mnstry Portland OR 1992-1997; Epis Par Of S Jn The Bapt Portland OR 1985-1991; Dio Oregon Portland OR 1978-1984; Vic Chr Epis Ch Danville VA 1974-1978; Asst Ch Of The Epiph Danville VA 1974-1978; Cur and Chapl Gr Memi Hammond LA 1966-1968. Auth, *Rel Experience and Process Theol*, Paulist, 1976; Auth, "Transcendance & Models of God," *ATR*; Auth, "H Ghost is Dead, H Sprt Lives," *ATR*; Auth, "Theol & Sprtl Renwl," *ATR*. ARIL 1985-1998; ESMHE 1978-1998; SVHE 1995-1998; Soc of S Jn the Evang 1985. Fllshp ECF 1968; Phi Beta Kappa 1960. gpardington@mindspring.com

PARDOE, Edward (NY) 111 E 60th St, New York NY 10022 **Gr Epis Ch New York NY 2010-** B Abington PA 10/3/1956 s Edward D Pardoe & Edith Wells. BS Trin 1978; MDiv UTS 2005. D 3/7/2009 P 9/12/2009 Bp Mark Sean Sisk. m 4/26/1986 Helen Pardoe c 4. rgranch@aol.com

PARHAM, A(lfred) Philip (RG) 6148 Los Robles Dr, El Paso TX 79912 B Fort Benning GA 12/20/1930 s Alfred Henry Parham & Elisa Dechoisel. BA Ya 1952; MDiv Epis TS of The SW 1963; Fllshp Coll of Preachers 1972; DMin SFTS 1983. D 6/30/1963 Bp Richard Earl Dicus P 1/8/1964 Bp Everett H Jones. m 3/7/1953 Ruth A Clauser. Vic S Brendan's Ch Horizon City TX 1997-2000; Asst S Fran On The Hill El Paso TX 1991-1994; Pstr Counslg Serv of El Paso El Paso TX 1990-1995; R S Steph's Epis Ch Wimberley TX 1988-1989; S Paul's Epis Ch San Antonio TX 1982-1988; S Thos Epis Ch And Sch San Antonio TX 1966-1981; P-in-c S Tim's Ch Cotulla TX 1965-1966; P-in-c All SS Epis Ch Pleasanton TX 1963-1966. Auth, "Letting God: Chr Meditations For Recovering Persons," Harper'S, 1987. Yale Club Pres San Antonio Tx 1975. alfredparham@att.net

PARINI, Barbara Dennison Biggs (Mass) 2957 Barbara St., Ashland OR 97520 B Brooklyn NY 6/23/1931 d Thomas West Biggs & Florence Elizabeth. AA Centenary Coll 1951; BA S Thos Aquinas Grand Rapids MI 1984; MDiv VTS 1988. D 6/11/1988 P 2/26/1989 Bp Lyman Cunningham Ogilby. m 1/24/1953 Joseph Gregg Parini c 3. Assoc S Mary's Epis Ch Bonita Sprg FL 2002-2004; Asst S Mary's Epis Ch Bonita Sprg FL 2000-2001; Vic Chr Ch Sag Harbor NY 1996-1999; Vic S Dav's Epis Mssn Pepperell MA 1993-1994; All SS Ch Chelmsford MA 1991-1992; Cur S Andr's Ch Grand Rapids MI 1988-1991. Oblate Ord Julian of Norwich 1988-2006. bobbieparini@aol.com

PARISH, Nurya Love (WMich) 1025 3 Mile Rd NE, Grand Rapids MI 49505 **Assoc Cler S Andr's Ch Grand Rapids MI 2011-** B Las Vegas NV 1/15/1971 d John Dian Lindberg & Sherrill Love. BA U of Redlands 1992; M.Div. Harvard DS 1996; Cert SWTS 2011. D 5/23/2011 Bp Robert R Gepert. m 3/4/2000 David Parish c 2. nuryaloveparish@gmail.com

PARK, Ciritta Ann Boyer (SO) 5000 Shannonbrook Dr, Columbus OH 43221 **Conv Mgr Dio Sthrn Ohio Cincinnati OH 2006-; Asst R S Pat's Epis Ch Dublin OH 2006-** B South Bend IN 4/28/1959 d Byron Oliver Boyer & Betty Jo. BA Pur 1980; D Formation Prog 1989; EFM 1990; MDiv Bex 2006. D 11/9/1990 Bp William Grant Black P 6/24/2006 Bp Kenneth Lester Price. m 8/16/1980 Stephen William Park c 1. D S Pat's Epis Ch Dublin OH 2003-2006; Conv Mgr NEAC Washington DC 1995-2000; D S Paul's Ch Columbus OH 1993-2002; AIDS T/F Chair Dio Sthrn Ohio Cincinnati OH 1991-2000; D S Steph's Epis Ch And U Columbus OH 1990-1992. Auth, "Easter Vigil Sermon," *Sermons that Wk: Prophetic Preaching*, Epis Preaching Fndt, 2004; co-Auth, "Accessible Meetings & Conventions," *same*, Assn. on Higher Educ. & Disabil, 2002. Amer Soc of Assn Executives 1988-2003; Integrity/Intl 1991; NEAC 1991-2000; NAAD 1989-2005. Auth of the Year Profsnl Conv Mgmt Assn. 1998; Best Educ Pub Amer Soc of Assn. Executives 1992; Best FIrst Auction Publ Broadcasting Serv 1984. cbpark@aol.com

PARK, Cynthia Bryant (Ala) 3420 Stafford St. So., Arlington VA 22206 **The Ch of S Clem Alexandria VA 2008-** B Dallas TX 10/14/1952 d Forest Leon Bryant & Richard Marie. BA St. Leo U Norfolk VA 1989; Phd Cath U 2000; MS Troy St U-Montgomery AL 2000; MTS VTS 2008. D 10/30/2004 Bp

Henry Nutt Parsley Jr. m 4/21/2001 John J Park c 4. Gr Epis Ch Mt Meigs AL 2004-2006. 88park@cua.edu

PARK III, Howard Franklin (Mo) 14133 Baywood Village Dr, Chesterfield MO 63017 **Asstg Cler Ch Of The Trsfg Lake S Louis MO 2002-** B Philadelphia PA 7/6/1933 s Howard Franklin Park & Mary Gessner. BA Ya 1955; MDiv VTS 1962. D 6/16/1962 P 1/23/1963 Bp George Leslie Cadigan. m 3/31/1975 Helen Wickline c 3. Stndg Com Dio Missouri S Louis MO 1977-1988; S Mart's Ch Ellisville MO 1965-1998; Cur Chr Ch Cathd S Louis MO 1962-1965. parkhf@aol.com

PARK, John Hayes (Pgh) Av Santa Cruz 491, Miraflores, Lima 18 Honduras B New Brighton PA 12/24/1945 s Robert Park & Jennie Hayes. TESM; BA Geneva Coll 1967; MA Duke 1970; MDiv Epis TS of The SW 1984. D 6/2/1984 Bp Alden Moinet Hathaway P 7/1/1985 Bp Sam Byron Hulsey. m 5/29/1976 Susan Delgado c 1. Mssy SAMS Ambridge PA 1995-2010; Archd Dio Honduras Miami FL 1991-2003; Mssy Exec Coun Appointees New York NY 1985-1994; Int Asst Ch Of The Heav Rest Abilene TX 1985. Cn Buen Pstr Cathd, San Pedro Sula 2000. johnpark@sams-usa.org

PARK, Stephen Radcliffe (NH) 14715 Edgewood Dr Ste 7, Baxter MN 56425 B Washington DC 7/22/1947 s Edward Radcliffe Park & Betty. BS Shimer Coll; MDiv VTS 1980. D 10/21/1973 P 11/1/1974 Bp John Alfred Baden. m 9/5/1970 Denise Zapffe c 1. Vic Faith Epis Ch Merrimack NH 1981-1984; Cur Ch Of The H Comf Vienna VA 1974-1976; Cur Chr Ch Alexandria VA 1973-1974.

PARK, Theodore A(llen) (Minn) 19 S 1st St Apt B2208, Minneapolis MN 55401 **Chr Ch Red Wing MN 2010-** B Saint Louis MO 5/18/1951 s Alvin Loren Park & Jean Ann. BA U MN 1975; MA The Coll of St. Cathr 1991; DAS GTS 1993; DMin Untd TS 2010. D 6/24/1993 Bp Robert Marshall Anderson P 2/21/1994 Bp Sanford Zangwill Kaye Hampton. m 12/26/1975 Dennis Vernon Christian. R S Jas On The Pkwy Minneapolis MN 2002-2009; P S Jas On The Pkwy Minneapolis MN 2000-2002; Int S Alb's Epis Ch Edina MN 1998-2000; Chair, Liturg Com Dio Minnesota Minneapolis MN 1996-2002; Int S Anne's Epis Ch Sunfish Lake MN 1996-1998; Assoc The Epis Par Of S Dav Minnetonka MN 1995-1996. Cntr for Progressive Chrsnty. Phi Beta Kappa 1975. rectorstjames@comcast.net

PARKE, John Holbrook (WMass) 213 Reeds Landing, Springfield MA 01109 B Amherst MA 10/2/1916 s Hervey Coke Parke & Ethel Margaret. BA Pr 1938; MDiv GTS 1942. D 6/7/1942 P 2/3/1943 Bp William A Lawrence. m 7/10/1982 Eleanor Anderson c 4. Asst S Dav's Ch Feeding Hills MA 1989-2001; Int All SS Ch So Hadley MA 1986-1987; Asst The Falls Ch Epis Falls Ch VA 1980-1982; R S Steph's Ch Heathsville VA 1978-1980; Vic Chr Ch Rochdale MA 1971-1978; R S Barn On The Desert Scottsdale AZ 1965-1970; R S Jas' Epis Ch Los Angeles CA 1955-1965; R Gr Ch Norwood MA 1952-1955; R S Jn's Ch Worcester MA 1946-1952; Vic S Andr's Ch Turners Falls MA 1942-1944; Asst S Jas' Ch Greenfield MA 1942-1944. Auth, "Manual of Chr Healing"; Auth, "Cler Manual for Chr Healing". Natl Wrdn, Ord of S Lk 1971-1978; Ord of S Lk 1952. parkeplace@aol.com

PARKE, Thomas Taylor (Alb) 41 Washington St, Saratoga Springs NY 12866 B Cooperstown NY 7/27/1939 s Nelson Fremont Parke & Emily Florence. BS Syr 1961; STB GTS 1964. D 5/23/1964 P 12/21/1964 Bp Allen Webster Brown. m 5/26/2002 Allison Vassallo c 2. Const & Cns Com Dio Albany Albany NY 1984-1989; Fin Com Dio Albany Albany NY 1984-1989; Dn - Troy Deanry Dio Albany Albany NY 1971-1981; Liturg Cmsn Dio Albany Albany NY 1971-1980; R Ch Of Beth Saratoga Sprg NY 1968-2011; Cur S Geo's Epis Ch Schenectady NY 1964-1968. frparke@bethesdachurch.org

PARKER JR, Allan Curtis (Oly) 720 Seneca St Apt 211, Seattle WA 98101 **R Emer Trin Par Seattle WA 2002-** B Los Angeles CA 9/11/1930 s Allan Curtis Parker & Edith Elizabeth. BA U of Washington 1953; MDiv SFTS 1956; Fllshp Coll of Preachers 1971; Cert Case Wstrn Reserve U 1972. D 3/14/1963 P 7/16/1963 Bp William F Lewis. c 6. Hstgr Dio Olympia Seattle WA 1996-1999; Stndg Com Dio Olympia Seattle WA 1994-1995; Pres of the Seattle So Convoc Dio Olympia Seattle WA 1992-1993; VP of the Seattle So Convoc Dio Olympia Seattle WA 1991-1992; Vice-Pres of the Seattle So Convoc Dio Olympia Seattle WA 1991-1992; Pres Stndg Com Dio Olympia Seattle WA 1988-1989; Stndg Com Dio Olympia Seattle WA 1985-1989; R Trin Par Seattle WA 1984-1996; Instr DSOT Dio Olympia Seattle WA 1979-1993; Hosp Chapl Dio Olympia Seattle WA 1976-1979; R Ch Of S Phil The Apos Cleveland OH 1970-1974; P-in-c S Agnes Ch Cleveland OH 1970-1974; Asst S Paul's Epis Ch Cleveland Heights OH 1968-1970; Assoc S Mich & S Geo Clayton MO 1967-1968; Vic Ch Of The Resurr Bellevue WA 1964-1966; Cur Emm Epis Ch Mercer Island WA 1963-1964. Auth, *arts Var mag*. Affirming Catholicism USA; Affirming Catholicism of Ch of Engl; Cmnty of the Cross of Nails; Conf of S Ben. Cont Educ Fell VTS Alexandria VA 1992. allan@parkerseattle.com

PARKER, Andrew David (Tex) 200 Oyster Creek Dr, Lake Jackson TX 77566 **R S Tim's Epis Ch Lake Jackson TX 2001-** B Bartlesville OK 6/28/1957 s Harry William Parker & Phyllis. BS Texas Tech U 1978; MA Texas A&M U 1984; MDiv Ya Berk 1989. D 6/9/1989 P 12/11/1989 Bp Sam Byron Hulsey. m 10/17/1987 Elizabeth Denny Welch c 3. S Andr's Epis Ch Amarillo TX 1993-2001; Asst Ch Of The Heav Rest Abilene TX 1989-1993. Auth, "Keeping The Promise," Morehouse, 1994. Bd No Amer Assn For The Catechumenate 1996. aparker@stimothy.org

PARKER, Betsee (Va) 110 W Franklin St, Richmond VA 23220 B Minneapolis MN 8/18/1951 d Owen William Parker & Betsy. BA Wellesley Coll 1982; MDiv Harvard DS 1985. D 6/11/1988 Bp David Elliot Johnson P 4/1/1993 Bp Barbara Clementine Harris. m 3/17/1984 Michael Rod Zalutsky c 1. S Jas' Epis Ch Leesburg VA 1994-1998; Emm Ch Middleburg VA 1994; Trin Ch Fuquay Varina NC 1988-1996.

PARKER, Carol Ann (EO) 9333 Nw Winters Ln, Prineville OR 97754 B Glascow MT 7/1/1944 d Lowell Eugene Carpenter & Dorothy Lorraine. Cntrl Oregon Cmnty Coll Bend OR. D 3/15/1992 P 9/5/1992 Bp Rustin Ray Kimsey. m 8/12/1961 Jerold Corwin Parker. jcparker@coinet.com

PARKER, David Clinton (Ind) 224 Davis Ave, Elkins WV 26241 B Springfield MA 7/28/1949 s Ward Morris Parker & Helen Robertson. BA Wilmington Coll 1980; MDiv GTS 1983. D 6/4/1983 P 12/14/1983 Bp William Grant Black. m 7/8/2001 Connie Sue Townsend c 3. R S Matt's Ch Indianapolis IN 1991-1997; S Barn Bridgeport WV 1990-1991; R Ch Of The Heav Rest Princeton WV 1985-1990; Asst S Mk's Epis Ch Columbus OH 1983-1985. rooster@ginsangmusic.com

PARKER, Dennis J (Ore) 4320 SW Corbett Ave, Unit # 317, Portland OR 97239 **GC Del Dio Oregon Portland OR 2010-2012; COM Chair Dio Oregon Portland OR 2010-; Jubilee Mnstry Off Dio Oregon Portland OR 2008-; R S Steph's Epis Par Portland OR 2008-** B Morristown NJ 11/28/1952 s Thomas G Parker & Loretta V. BFA Emerson Coll 1982; MDiv CDSP 2003. D 6/22/2002 P 1/11/2003 Bp Robert Louis Ladehoff. m 11/26/2010 Michael S Sagun. Int Ch Of The Resurr Eugene OR 2004-2008; Cur Chr Ch Par Lake Oswego OR 2002-2004; Assoc Legacy Gd Samar Hosp Portland OR 2001-2004. revdennisj@comcast.net

PARKER, Donald Harry (Mass) 28 Cambridge Cir., Smithfield RI 02917 **Int Emm Epis Ch Cumberland RI 2010-** B Bridgeport CT 2/27/1943 s Albert S Parker & Mildred. BA Cntrl Connecticut St U 1965; MDiv Ya Berk 1968; MS Sthrn Connecticut St U 1978. D 6/11/1968 Bp Walter H Gray P 3/1/1969 Bp John Henry Esquirol. m 8/21/1965 Carol Miller c 2. Int S Jn's Ch Cumberland RI 2009-2010; Int S Mary's Ch Warwick RI 2006-2008; Int S Ptr's Ch Dartmouth MA 2004-2006; Int S Jas Epis Ch At Woonsocket Woonsocket RI 2001-2004; Int S Paul's Ch Boston MA 1999-2001; R Ch Of The H Nativ Seekonk MA 1986-1998; S Lk's Epis Ch E Greenwich RI 1981-1985; S Jn's Ch Sodus NY 1979-1981; Chr Ch Trumbull CT 1974-1979; Cur Trin Ch Wethersfield CT 1968-1970. seekonkdon@cox.net

PARKER, Elizabeth Denny Welch (Tex) 200 Oyster Creek Dr, Lake Jackson TX 77566 **Assoc R S Tim's Epis Ch Lake Jackson TX 2001-** B Bellefonte PA 6/21/1954 d William Lee Welch & Betty Tamazine. BA Penn 1976; MDiv Ya Berk 1988. D 6/11/1988 Bp Paul Moore Jr P 2/18/1989 Bp William Bradford Hastings. m 10/17/1987 Andrew David Parker c 3. S Andr's Epis Ch Amarillo TX 1993-2001; Dn Dio NW Texas Lubbock TX 1990-1991; Ch Of The Heav Rest Abilene TX 1989-1993; D Chr Ch Greenwich CT 1988-1989. Catechesis of the Gd Shpd 1993. lparker@stimothy.org

PARKER, Gary Joseph (LI) 257 Middle Rd., Sayville NY 11782 B Potsdam NY 8/25/1948 s Joseph Parker & Florence. BA SUNY 1971; MDiv GTS 1975. D 6/15/1974 P 12/16/1974 Bp Wilbur Emory Hogg Jr. S Paul's Ch Glen Cove NY 2006-2009; Epis Ch Cntr New York NY 2004-2006; Off Of Bsh For ArmdF New York NY 1983-2004; Trin Ch Whitehall NY 1982-1983; The Epis Ch Of The Cross Ticonderoga NY 1977-1982; Cur S Andr And H Comm Ch So Orange NJ 1974-1977. gjparker1@optonline.net

PARKER, James Frank (HB) 2409 Cheshire Woods Rd, Toledo OH 43617 B Omaha NE 12/3/1946 s Frank Parker & Viola. BS U of Nebraska 1983; MDiv STUSo 1987. D 8/24/1987 Bp James Daniel Warner P 5/1/1988 Bp Arthur Benjamin Williams Jr. m 6/10/1967 Wanda Marie Eddy. All SS Epis Ch Toledo OH 1991; All SS Ch McAlester OK 1990-1991; Asst S Andr's Epis Ch Toledo OH 1987-1989.

PARKER JR, James Nahum (Ga) 402 E 46th St, Savannah GA 31405 **R S Geo's Epis Ch Savannah GA 2004-** B Camp Kilmer NJ 7/10/1948 s James Nahum Parker & Inez Gloria. STUSo; BA Augusta St U 1970; MS Bos 1975. D 8/24/1982 Bp (George) Paul Reeves P 11/16/1998 Bp Henry Irving Louttit. m 10/23/1999 Leslie D Grayson c 3. Vic St Patricks Ch Pooler GA 1998-2000; D S Geo's Epis Ch Savannah GA 1997-1998; D in Charge S Eliz's Epis Ch Richmond Hill GA 1994-1997; D S Paul's Ch Savannah GA 1992-1994; D S Ptr's Epis Ch Savannah GA 1990-1992; D S Thos Ch Savannah GA 1986-1989; D S Paul's Ch Savannah GA 1982-1986. CBS 1982. parker.j@comcast.net

PARKER, Jesse Leon Anthony (Md) 3001 Old York Rd, Baltimore MD 21218 **Dioc Ecum Off Dio Maryland Baltimore MD 2010-; Mem, COM Dio Maryland Baltimore MD 2010-; Mem, Com on Liturg and Mus Dio Maryland Baltimore MD 2010-; Ch Of S Paul The Apos Baltimore MD 1991-; R S Jn's Ch Huntingdon Baltimore MD 1991-; Hon Vic S Paul's**

P

Par Baltimore MD 1991- B Saint Augustine FL 2/19/1951 s Jesse Leon Parker & Verna Marie. BA S Mary TS & U 1974; MDiv GTS 1981. D 10/17/1981 P 6/28/1982 Bp David Keller Leighton Sr. m Gene Sartori c 1. Mem, Com on Aging Dio Maryland Baltimore MD 1991-1994; Hon Vic S Paul's Par Baltimore MD 1991; Chair, Cmsn on Soc Mnstry Dio Maryland Baltimore MD 1990-1992; Ch Of S Paul The Apos Baltimore MD 1990-1991. GAS 1979; Ord of S Ben (Confrater) 1986; SocMary 1989; SocOLW 2009. rectorstjn@mac.com

PARKER, John Winston (Ct) 273 Hickory Hill Dr, Waterbury CT 06708 **Died 9/12/2009** B Fitchburg MA 6/3/1923 s Carol A Parker & Cynthia J. BA Trin Hartford CT 1949; MLS Col 1951; MDiv EDS 1961. D 6/13/1961 Bp Walter H Gray P 12/16/1961 Bp John Henry Esquirol. c 5.

PARKER, L(ilbern) Lynn (Los) 516 Via La Paloma, Riverside CA 92507 **Died 4/15/2010** B Edmond OK 3/6/1925 s Lilbern L Parker & Georgia. AA Citrus Jr Coll Covine CA 1947; BA Whittier Coll 1949; MDiv CDSP 1953. D 6/22/1953 Bp Francis E I Bloy P 2/23/1954 Bp Donald J Campbell. c 3.

PARKER, Matthew Ross (Dal) 1908 E Spring Valley Rd, Richardson TX 75081 **S Jos's Par Buena Pk CA 2005-** B Plano TX 1/15/1979 MDiv Nash 2005. D 6/4/2005 Bp James Monte Stanton. Cur Ch Of The Annunc Lewisville TX 2005-2006. mrp011579@netscape.net

PARKER, Robert Coleman (Tex) 832 W Jones St, Livingston TX 77351 B Philadelphia PA 5/29/1936 s William Parker & Mary. Epis TS of The SW. D 6/12/1972 Bp Richard Earl Dicus P 12/1/1972 Bp Harold Cornelius Gosnell. R S Paul's Epis Ch Orange TX 1998-2003; Vic S Lk's Ch Livingston TX 1993-1998; Asst All SS Epis Ch Austin TX 1977-1984; Asst S Barth's Ch Corpus Christi TX 1974-1977; Vic Ch Of Our Sav Aransas Pass TX 1972-1974.

PARKER, Ronald Mark (FtW) 200 N Bailey Ave, Fort Worth TX 76107 B Kansas City MO 11/5/1952 s Robert Washington Parker & Mary Catherine. D 10/22/1999 Bp Roger John White. m 10/24/1987 Denise Dawn Rodenhause. All SS' Epis Sch Of Ft Worth Ft Worth TX 2000-2004; All SS' Epis Ch Ft Worth TX 2000.

PARKER, Ronald Wilmar (Pa) 254 Williams Rd, Bryn Mawr PA 19010 B Philadelphia PA 11/26/1938 s Charles Wilmar Parker & Nydia Lavinia. BA Combs Mus 1962; B.Mus.ED Combs Mus 1975; MA GTS 1978; MPS NYTS 1980; D Min GTF 1986; DMin U of Notre Dame 1986; Cert Oxf 2002. D 6/2/1979 P 12/1/1979 Bp Albert Wiencke Van Duzer. m 4/20/1963 Josephine Parker. Dioc Nomin Com Dio Pennsylvania Philadelphia PA 1998; Emer Chr Epis Ch Villanova PA 1992-2009; R S Paul's Epis Ch Bound Brook NJ 1980-1992; Cur S Lk's Epis Ch Metuchen NJ 1979-1980. Auth, "GTF Yearbook," *(sermons)*, GTF, 1986; Auth, "Living Ch," *(Var mag arts)*, 1986; Auth, "St. Jn's Mass," *S Jn's Mass*, 1976. CBS; Ord of S Lk 1979; Ord of S Lk - Chapl. Outstanding Life Achievement in Mus & Mnstry Abraham Lincoln HS 2005. frjo@aol.com

PARKER JR OHC, Roy Earl (Mass) PO Box 1296, Santa Barbara CA 93102 B Los Angeles CA 9/14/1933 s Roy Earl Parker & Amy Elizabeth. BS MIT 1955; MDiv EDS 1964; STM Jesuit TS 1981. D 6/20/1964 P 1/25/1967 Bp Anson Phelps Stokes Jr. Liturg Com Dio New York New York City NY 1985-1992; Stff Dio Massachusetts Boston MA 1970-1971. OHC 1972; Soc of S Jn the Evang 1958-1970. parkerearl@aim.com

PARKER, Stephanie Eve (Oly) 4805 NE 45th St, Seattle WA 98105 **R S Steph's Epis Ch Seattle WA 2010-** B Anchorage AK 3/7/1962 d Paul James Parker & Cora Belle. MDiv VTS 2003. D 2/8/2003 P 8/14/2003 Bp Henry Irving Louttit. S Paul In The Desert Palm Sprg CA 2005-2009; Vic Ch Of The Gd Shpd Swainsboro GA 2003-2005. stephnsea@gmail.com

PARKER JR, Stephen D (Ct) 4607 Chandlers Forde, Sarasota FL 34235 B New York NY 5/23/1940 s Stephen Dwight Parker & Elizabeth. BA W&M 1964; MDiv Ya Berk 1967. D 6/14/1967 P 2/5/1968 Bp Albert Ervine Swift. m 8/2/1985 Barbara F Parker c 2. S Jn's Epis Ch Fishers Island NY 1997-2008; Asst R S Jas The Fisherman Islamorada FL 1993-1994; Exec Coun Dio Connecticut Hartford CT 1988-1990; COM Dio Connecticut Hartford CT 1982-1984; R S Matt's Epis Ch Wilton CT 1978-1993; R Trin Epis Ch Collinsville CT 1969-1978; Cur S Lk's Par Darien CT 1967-1969. Auth, "Bridges, Reconnecting Sci and Faith," Tate Pub, 2012. Endowed Chapl Chair Salisbury Sch class of 59 2004; Sr Class Awd Salisbury Sch 1995; Epis Evang Fndt Sermon Prchng Prize 1992. parsonparker@gmail.com

PARKER, Walter Scott Hammett (Ore) Po Box 150, Gold Beach OR 97444 **Died 11/11/2009** B Philadelphia PA 6/13/1922 s Ellis Branson Parker & Josephine Augusta. BS OR SU 1950; BD CDSP 1953. D 6/23/1953 P 12/21/1953 Bp Benjamin D Dagwell.

PARKER, William C(urtis) (NJ) 200 Armitage Court, Lincoln University PA 19352 **Int R Ch Of The Ascen Parkesburg PA 2011-; Com on the Diac Dio New Jersey Trenton NJ 2008-** B Seaford DE 4/15/1958 s Joseph Farris Parker & Pearl Guerant. U of Delaware Newark 1978; City Coll of San Francisco 1982; BA - cum laud U of San Francisco 1984; MDiv GTS 1996. D 6/22/1996 Bp Vincent Waydell Warner P 12/7/1996 Bp Richard Frank Grein. m Robert S Monitto. R Epis Ch Of The Epiph Ventnor City NJ 2007-2010; Bdgt Com Dio Long Island Garden City NY 2000-2007; Commision on Mnstry Dio Long Island Garden City NY 2000-2007; R S Bede's Epis Ch Syosset NY 1999-2007; Cur/Int Vic Ch Of S Mary The Vrgn New York NY 1996-1999. Affirming Angl Catholicism 1996. thebcp@juno.com

PARKIN, Jason Lloyd (Chi) 222 Kenilworth Ave, Kenilworth IL 60043 **R Ch Of The H Comf Kenilworth IL 2011-** B Chicago IL 10/9/1958 s Joseph Louis Parkin & Louise. B.Mus. Chicago Coll of Performing Arts Chicago IL 1979; M.Mus. NWU 1980; MDiv Nash 1985; DMin SWTS 1998. D 6/15/1985 Bp Frank Tracy Griswold III P 12/21/1985 Bp James Winchester Montgomery. m 6/19/1984 Janice Dymitro c 3. R The Epis Ch Of S Mary The Vrgn San Francisco CA 2000-2011; Ways and Means Com Dio Iowa Des Moines IA 1995-2000; Cler Wellness Cmsn Dio Iowa Des Moines IA 1993-1996; New Ch Starts Com Dio Iowa Des Moines IA 1993-1996; R Trin Ch Iowa City IA 1991-2000; Assoc Ch Of The H Comf Kenilworth IL 1987-1991; Asst Gr Epis Ch Hinsdale IL 1985-1987. Phi Beta Kappa 1979. parkin.jason@gmail.com

PARKINSON, Caroline Smith (Va) 4614 Riverside Drive, Richmond VA 23225 B Washington DC 10/29/1943 d Sydney Strother Smith & Elizabeth. BA U of Virginia 1965; Amer U 1969; MDiv VTS 1984. D 6/14/1986 P 1/11/1987 Bp John Thomas Walker. m 10/10/1998 James T Parkinson c 2. R Gr Ch The Plains VA 1997-2010; Assoc R S Alb's Par Washington DC 1986-1997. Auth, "From Ashes To Fire," *Trin News Occasional Paper*, 1994. csp@activated.com

PARKS, James Joseph (Fla) 7151 Nw 105th St, Chiefland FL 32626 **D (Vol) S Alb's Epis Ch Chiefland FL 2007-** B Jacksonville FL 12/22/1936 D 12/8/2002 Bp Samuel Johnson Howard. m 9/6/1958 Barbara Parks. jparks@swic.net

PARKS, Kenneth Thomas (Ark) 1001 Kingsland Rd, Bella Vista AR 72714 **R S Theo's Epis Ch Bella Vista AR 2005-** B Atlanta GA 5/16/1945 s Roy Gilbert Parks & Lillian Fern. BA Henderson St U 1970; MA U of Arkansas 1971; PhD U of Mississippi 1979; MDiv STUSo 1987. D 3/6/1988 P 9/9/1988 Bp Herbert Alcorn Donovan Jr. m 7/7/1968 Brenda Kay Green c 1. R S Barth's Ch Corpus Christi TX 1997-2005; R S Barth's Epis Ch Ft Smith AR 1989-1997; Cur S Lk's Ch Hot Sprg AR 1988-1989; Dio Arkansas Little Rock AR 1988. Auth, "The Way of the Cradle"; Auth, "Adv Meditations". Oblate, Ord of Julian of Norwich 1985. DuBose Awd for Serv The TS U So 2011. frkenparks@sbcglobal.net

PARKS JR, Limuel Guy (Miss) 229 Westwood Dr, Batesville AR 72501 **Died 9/2/2011** B Batesville AR 7/11/1929 s Limuel Guy Parks & Emily Ellen. BS U of Arkansas 1951; MA U of Arkansas 1956; MDiv STUSo 1958. D 6/11/1958 P 4/14/1959 Bp Robert Raymond Brown. c 2. AFP 1975; Evang Cath Mssn; Rural Mnstrs Ntwk 1958. llparks@aristotle.net

PARKS, Robert Ray (NY) 333 E 57th St Apt 9-A, New York NY 10022 **Died 10/18/2009** B Ty Ty GA 1/2/1918 s Aaron Parks & Addie Miller. BA U of Florida 1940; BD STUSo 1949; DD STUSo 1970; STD GTS 1972; STD Hobart and Wm Smith Colleges 1973; DD Trin 1974; DD U of King's Coll Halifax NS CA 1987. D 6/19/1949 P 2/3/1950 Bp Frank A Juhan. c 2. Epis Mssn Soc, Bible & Bible and Common Pryr Soci. Robert Ray Parks Awd for Outstdng Contrib in the Field of Agi; Bp's Cross Awd for Distinguished Serv Dio New York; Lawr T Cole Alum Awd for Distinguished Serv Trin Sch, NY New York NY.

PARKS, T(heodore) E(dward) Michael (Mil) Po Box 590, Milwaukee WI 53201 B Chathan NY 7/3/1944 s Elba Keefer Parks & Caroline Louise. BS SUNY 1967; MDiv Nash 1971; BBA U of Wisconsin 1984. D 1/25/2003 Bp Roger John White P 7/26/2003 Bp Keith Bernard Whitmore. P-in-c Epis Ch Of The Resurr Mukwonago WI 2003-2006; D S Ptr's Ch W Allis WI 2003. 70741.2122@compuserve.com

PARLIER, Susan Taylor (USC) 1238 Evergreen Ave, West Columbia SC 29169 B Wilmington DE 1/5/1952 d Dixon Kirby Parlier & Louise Terry. BA Columbia Coll 1973; MS Virginia Commonwealth U 1975; MA Luth Theol Sthrn Sem 2003. D 12/14/2002 Bp Dorsey Felix Henderson. m 4/12/1980 John Russell Metz c 1.

PARMETER JR, George Edward (SD) Po Box 1361, Huron SD 57350 B Deer River MN 4/15/1946 s George Edward Parmeter & Margeret Elizabeth. BA Bemidji St U 1969; SWTS 1972; Johnston Inst 1973; Ldrshp Acad for New Directions 1976; Alte 86 88 1988; SWTS 1997; Knights Templars H Land Pilgrimage 1998. D 6/28/1973 P 4/1/1974 Bp Philip Frederick McNairy. m 10/26/1974 Gayle Harriet Parmeter c 3. R Gr Epis Ch Huron SD 1993-2010; R Ch Of The H Comm Lake Geneva WI 1989-1993; Del Of Prov Vi Syn Dio Wyoming Casper WY 1986-1987; Fin Com Dio Wyoming Casper WY 1985-1989; Yth Ministers Coordntr Dio Wyoming Casper WY 1985-1988; Yth Ministers Coordntr Dio Wyoming Casper WY 1985-1988; EYC Cler Advsr Dio Wyoming Casper WY 1982-1985; Stndg Com Dio Wyoming Casper WY 1980-1983; R H Trin Epis Ch Thermopolis WY 1979-1989; EYC Cler Advsr Dio Wyoming Casper WY 1979-1980; Dioc Coun Dio Minnesota Minneapolis MN 1975-1979; Stff Dir Dio Minnesota Minneapolis MN 1974-1986; P-in-c Breck Memi Mssn Naytahwaush MN 1974-1979; Bd Cass Lake Epis Camp Dio Minnesota Minneapolis MN 1974-1979; Com Of Indn Wk Dio Minnesota

Minneapolis MN 1974-1979; P-in-c S Columba White Earth MN 1974-1979; P-in-c Trin Epis Ch Pk Rapids MN 1974-1979; Dio Minnesota Minneapolis MN 1973-1979. Auth, "Dioc Yth Mnstrs Structure Plan". georgep@hur.midco.net

PARMLEY, Ingram Cannon (WNC) 924 Plantation Dr, Lenoir NC 28645 B Sewanee TN 4/20/1938 s Ingram Bedford Parmley & Rebecca. BA Scarritt Coll 1961; MA Scarritt Coll 1962; MDiv Duke 1964; MA Peabody Coll 1965; PhD No Carolina St U 1973. D 4/20/1974 P 12/14/1974 Bp Gray Temple. m 5/24/1959 Jane Dowlen c 3. S Jas Epis Ch Lenoir NC 1994-2004. Auth, "Mntl Hlth Tech". saintjames@w3link.com

PARNELL, William Clay (NY) 1047 Amsterdam Ave, New York NY 10025 **Archd for Mssn Dio New York New York City NY 2010-; Alum/ae Exec Com VTS Alexandria VA 2009-** B Atlanta GA 11/9/1956 s James R Parnell & Salena Victoria. BA U GA 1977; MA U GA 1979; MDiv VTS 1989. D 6/12/1989 Bp Calvin Onderdonk Schofield Jr P 2/2/1990 Bp James Winchester Montgomery. m 11/15/2009 Thomas Arndt. Dio Newark Newark NJ 2007-2010; ACTS/VIM Bd Mem Dio Newark Newark NJ 2007-2010; GC Alt Dep Dio Newark Newark NJ 2006-2009; GC Alt Dep Dio Newark Newark NJ 2006-2009; Dio Newark Newark NJ 1997-2001; R Chr Ch Hackensack NJ 1994-2010; Asst to R S Mary's Epis Ch Arlington VA 1989-1994. Phi Kappa Phi U GA 1977. wmcparnell@aol.com

PARODI, Louis M (NJ) Po Box 192682, San Juan PR 00919 B Genoa 7/5/1926 s James Parodi & Madeline. BA Lyceum Savona 1948; ThM Gregorian U 1954; PhD Gregorian U 1957; Med U of Puerto Rico 1970; Med Kean U 1981. Rec from Roman Catholic 3/1/1971 as Priest Bp Francisco Reus-Froylan. m 4/2/1971 Ludy M Collins. San Jose Epis Ch Eliz NJ 1977-1984. Auth, "Educacion Epspecial Y Sus Servicios, Spec Educ," *2nd Ed*, 2002; Auth, "Ecumenismo: Confluencia De Valores," *Ecum Theol Textbook*, 1997; Auth, "La Sexualidad Humana," *Sex Educ*, 1993; Auth, "La Cathechesi," *Educ Of Catechumens*, 1957. Lmp Fndt For Spec Educ 1997. Acad Recognition Inter Amer U Of Puerto Rico 2000.

PARR, Heather Katheryn (Ore) 835 E 43rd Ave, Eugene OR 97405 B Portland OR 11/11/1948 d Gregory Tuclay Parr & Vera Ebba. U of Oregon; BA Dalhousie U 1984. D 10/18/1997 Bp Robert Louis Ladehoff P 6/12/2004 Bp Johncy Itty. c 2. Exec Coun Appointees New York NY 2004-2005; Dio Oregon Portland OR 2001; S Mary's Epis Ch Eugene OR 1997-2000. Ord Of S Lk. heatherparr@hotmail.com

PARRIS, Cheryl A E (Ga) 1401 Martin Luther King Jr Blvd, Savannah GA 31415 **R S Matt's Ch Savannah GA 2007-** B Bronx NY 1/8/1968 d Kenneth Gilkes & Cynthia. BS Iona Coll 1988; MA NYU 1991; MA Bex 2000; MDiv Bex 2002. D 12/21/2002 P 9/13/2003 Bp J Michael Garrison. S Jas' Ch Batavia NY 2006; St Bonaventure U S Bonaventure NY 2002-2007; D S Steph's Ch Olean NY 2002-2006. "Words From The Hill: Black Stdt Caucus 1997-2000," Colgate Rochester DS, 2000; "Bp. Geo Barrett'S Role In The Fight-Kodak Conflict: An Examination Of Epis Authority And Soc Justice," Colgate Rochester DS, 2000. caeparris@gmail.com

PARRIS, Kenneth W (Cal) **Police Chapl Dio California San Francisco CA 2009-** D 12/2/1995 Bp William Edwin Swing.

PARRISH, David LeRoy (Neb) 647 Sussex Dr, Janesville WI 53546 B Marshfield WI 9/17/1937 s Clarence Lester Parrish & Georgia Jane. BA U MN 1960; MDiv SWTS 1963. D 6/29/1963 P 5/19/1964 Bp Hamilton Hyde Kellogg. m 9/2/1961 Karen Lorraine Brunet c 3. Dio Nebraska Omaha NE 1990-1993; R Ch Of The H Trin Lincoln NE 1989-1993; Int S Andr's Ch Kansas City MO 1985-1986; St Lk's So Chap Overland Pk KS 1982-1989; S Ptr's Epis Ch Kansas City MO 1982-1983; Other Lay Position Dio Minnesota Minneapolis MN 1978-1980; R Trin Ch Litchfield MN 1977-1982; S Mk's Ch Erie PA 1975-1977; S Mths Ch St Paul Pk MN 1971-1974; Asst S Paul's Ch Minneapolis MN 1969-1970; Dioc Coun Dio Minnesota Minneapolis MN 1968-1970; P-in-c S Helen's Ch Wadena MN 1968-1969; R Ch Of Our Sav Little Falls MN 1965-1969; P-in-c Gr Ch S Cloud MN 1965-1969; Cur S Jn's Epis Ch Mankato MN 1963-1965. Coll of Chapl; Assembly of Epis Hospitals and Chapl 1970. Who's Who Rel 1975. brunet3@att.net

PARRISH JR, Joseph R (NJ) 300 E 56th St Apt 2B, New York NY 10022 **R S Jn's Ch Eliz NJ 1989-** B Knoxville TN 6/5/1941 s Joseph Raymond Parrish & Virginia. BS U of Tennessee 1963; PhD Harv 1969; MBA Harv 1974; GTS 1986; MDiv UTS 1986. D 6/7/1986 P 12/11/1986 Bp Paul Moore Jr. m 6/7/1975 Janice Lynn Zepik. Unified Bdgt Com Dio New Jersey Trenton NJ 1991-1993; S Jn's Ch New York NY 1989-2000; Assoc R Trin Epis Ch Southport CT 1988-1989; Asst S Barth's Ch New York NY 1986-1993; Asst R All Ang' Ch New York NY 1986-1988; Cur Dio New York New York City NY 1986-1988; Asst S Jas Ch New York NY 1986-1987; S Simeon's Ch Bronx NY 1986-1987. Auth, "Water, Environ and Sprtlty," 1992. ACPE 1985; Cmnty of S Jn the Bapt 1989; NNECA 1989. joeparrish@compuserve.com

PARRISH, Judy Kay (SwVa) 989 Pigeon Hill Rd, Roseland VA 22967 **Gr Ch Tyro VA 2011-; Nelson Par Cluster Howardsville VA 2002-** B Norfolk VA 4/18/1945 d Bernard Lee Parrish & Eva Curtis. BS Oklahoma St U 1972; MA W&M 1998; MDiv STUSo 2001. D 6/9/2001 Bp David Conner Bane Jr P 12/21/2001 Bp John Lewis Said. P-in-c Trin Ch Arrington VA 2002-2011; Cur S Paul's Ch Delray Bch FL 2001-2002. revgrhugger@msn.com

PARRISH, Larry A (Neb) PO Box 117, Falls City NE 68355 **R S Thos' Epis Ch Falls City NE 2010-** B Richmond Heights MO 6/19/1946 s Dale Henderson Parrish & Margaret. AB Butler Cnty Cmnty Coll 1966; BA SW Coll 1968; MDiv St Paul TS 1973. D 10/28/2009 P 5/4/2010 Bp Joe Goodwin Burnett. m 9/22/1984 Mary Mary Schlicher Hirst c 3. larry.parrish1@us.army.mil

PARRISH, William Potter (SwVa) 3708 Manton Dr, Lynchburg VA 24503 B Carrolltown PA 10/5/1925 s Harry Lawrence Parrish & Ruth. BS S Fran Coll Loretto PA 1949; MS Geo 1952; PhD Geo 1955; Cert VTS 1959. D 6/12/1959 Bp Frederick D Goodwin P 7/1/1960 Bp Robert Fisher Gibson Jr. Asst S Jn's Ch Lynchburg VA 1992; R Emm Epis Ch Chatham VA 1988-1992; Vic Trin Ch Gretna VA 1988-1992; Vic S Ptr's Ch Altavista VA 1973-1982; Asst S Paul's Epis Ch Lynchburg VA 1966-1971; Asst Truro Epis Ch Fairfax VA 1960-1961; D Trin Epis Ch Washington VA 1959-1960. Auth, "Var arts," *Living Ch*. bp3708@aol.com

PARROTT, Edgar George (NI) 17 Bowdoin Ave, Waltham MA 02451 B Nipawin SK CA 7/25/1935 s Harold Ernest Parrott & Selina Ann. BA Whitman Coll 1957; BD CDSP 1960; STM SFTS 1965; MA California St U 1986. D 6/4/1960 Bp Clarence Rupert Haden Jr P 1/5/1961 Bp Ivol I Curtis. m 4/4/1964 Beatrice Schellenberg c 2. Int S Alb's Epis Ch Ft Wayne IN 2000-2001; R S Fran' Epis Ch Turlock CA 1990-1999; P-in-c Trin Epis Ch Redlands CA 1979-1981; Consult for CE Epis Dio San Joaquin Modesto CA 1975-1979; Vic Chr The Lord Epis Ch Pinole CA 1969-1975; Instr of Ch Mus CDSP Berkeley CA 1963-1965; Asst Ch Of The H Trin Richmond CA 1963-1965; Cur All Souls Par In Berkeley Berkeley CA 1961-1963; Cur S Mk's Par Altadena CA 1960-1961. Cal. Assoc. Marr. and Fam. Therapists 1989-2001. eparrott@rcn.com

PARROTT, Sally F (USC) 100 Deerfield Dr, Greer SC 29650 B Albany GA 2/17/1951 d William Howard Fowler & Sally Charlyne. BA Van 1976; MDiv STUSo 1993. D 6/12/1993 P 5/1/1994 Bp William Arthur Beckham. m 6/16/1973 John Flick Parrott c 2. Chr Ch Greenville SC 2007-2009; S Jas Epis Ch Greenville SC 2001-2004; Chr Ch Greenville SC 1993-1996. sparrott@ccgsc.org

PARRY, Bede James McKinley (Nev) 5733 Capitola Ave, Las Vegas NV 89108 B Seattle WA 2/28/1942 s Charles Earl McKinley & Cynthia Elizabeth. BA Concep Sem Coll 1977; BA St. Johns U 1981; MA St. Johns U 1982. Rec from Roman Catholic 10/15/2004 Bp Katharine Jefferts Schori. Mus Dir & Asstg P All SS Epis Ch Las Vegas NV 2004-2011. bedeparry@aol.com

PARRY, James William (ETenn) 2740 Joneva Rd, Knoxville TN 37932 B Knoxville TN 10/24/1928 s Lawrence Meade Parry & Gladys. BD U of Tennessee 1954. D 1/26/1986 Bp William Evan Sanders. m 9/13/1948 Georgia Ruth Ayre c 3.

PARRY-MOORE, Joyce Marie (Ak) 4001 7th St, Oakland CA 94607 **Seamens Ch Inst Income New York NY 2011-** B Seattle WA 4/29/1961 d Mark Parry & Sally. BA Wstrn WA U 1982; Opera Cert Boston Conservatory 1986; MDiv PSR 2010. D 6/4/2010 Bp Marc Handley Andrus P 3/31/2011 Bp Mark A Lattime. m 6/8/1996 Patrick Moore c 5. jparrymoore@gmail.com

PARSELL, Harry Irvan (SwFla) 4408 Gulf Dr, Holmes Beach FL 34217 **Vic S Matt's Ch St Petersburg FL 2010-** B Saint Albans NY 3/22/1953 s Harry Irvin Parsell & Erie Elizabeth. BA Stetson U 1975; MDiv Nash 1980. D 6/22/1980 Bp William Hopkins Folwell P 1/21/1981 Bp Emerson Paul Haynes. Cncl Dn Dio SW Florida Sarasota FL 2008-2010; R Ch Of The Annunc Holmes Bch FL 2003-2010; Dio SW Florida Sarasota FL 2000; COM Dio SW Florida Sarasota FL 1999-2001; Comp Dioc Com Dio SW Florida Sarasota FL 1998-2000; Dioc Coun Dio SW Florida Sarasota FL 1997-2000; Ch Ext Com Dio SW Florida Sarasota FL 1993-1995; R S Barth's Ch St Petersburg FL 1989-2003; Com Cont Educ For Cler Dio SW Florida Sarasota FL 1986-1996; Yth Cmsn Dio SW Florida Sarasota FL 1984-1988; Asst Gd Samar Epis Ch Clearwater FL 1983-1989; Ecum Cmsn Dio SW Florida Sarasota FL 1981-1985; Asst S Thos' Epis Ch St Petersburg FL 1980-1983. myfriends@tampabay.rr.com

✠ **PARSLEY JR, Rt Rev Henry Nutt** (Ala) 4133 Crescent Rd, Birmingham AL 35222 **Bp of Alabama Dio Alabama Birmingham AL 2005-; Bp of Alabama Dio Alabama Birmingham AL 1999-** B Memphis TN 10/29/1948 s Henry Nutt Parsley & Barbara Brown. BA U So 1970; MDiv GTS 1973; DD GTS 1998; DD STUSo 1998. D 6/16/1973 P 4/1/1974 Bp Gray Temple Con 9/28/1996 for Ala. m 8/8/1970 Rebecca Allison Parsley c 1. Bp Coadj of Alabama Dio Alabama Birmingham AL 1996-1998; Bd, PBp's Fund Dio No Carolina Raleigh NC 1990-1993; Chair, AIDS Com Dio No Carolina Raleigh NC 1988-1990; Kanuga Prog Com Dio No Carolina Raleigh NC 1987-1992; R Chr Ch Charlotte NC 1986-1996; Stndg Com Dio So Carolina Charleston SC 1983-1986; Dep, GC Dio So Carolina Charleston SC 1982-1994; R S Paul's Epis Ch Summerville SC 1982-1986; Exexutive Coun Dio So Carolina Charleston SC 1981-1986; BEC Dio So Carolina Charleston SC 1978-1986; R All SS Ch Florence SC 1977-1982; Chair, Div of Yth Mnstry Dio So Carolina Charleston SC 1976-1979; Asst S Phil's Ch Charleston SC 1975-1977; Asst Trin Ch

Myrtle Bch SC 1973-1974. Auth, "Conflict and Controversy: Bringing Wounds and Blessings," *Vstry Papers*, 2004. DD GTS 1997; DD U So, Sewanee 1997. hparsley@dioala.org

PARSLEY, Jamie A (ND) 117 20 Ave. N., Fargo ND 58102 **Dep to GC Dio No Dakota Fargo ND 2010-; Rep, Epis News Serv Advsry Commitee Prov VI 2010-; Asst Dio No Dakota Fargo ND 2009-; P-in-c S Steph's Ch Fargo ND 2008-; COM Dio No Dakota Fargo ND 2007-; Dio No Dakota Fargo ND 2006-; Edtior, The Sheaf Dio No Dakota Fargo ND 2002-** B Fargo ND 12/8/1969 s Albert Harold Parsley & Joyce Marie. MFA Vermont Coll 1999; MA Nash 2008. D 7/25/2003 Bp Andrew Hedtler Fairfield P 6/11/2004 Bp Michael Gene Smith. Rep, Epis News Serv Advsry Commitee Prov VI 2010; Chapl All SS Ch Vlly City ND 2006-2008; Rep, Epis Life Bd Gvnr Prov VI 2005-2010; P Geth Cathd Fargo ND 2004-2008. Auth, "Bk," *Fargo, 1957; an elegy*, The Insitute for Reg Stds, NDSU, 2010; Auth, "Bk," *This Grass: poems*, Enso, 2009; Contrib, "prayers," *Evang Luth Wrshp Pstr Care*, Augsburg, 2008; Auth, "nook," *Just Once: poems*, Loonfeather, 2007; Auth, "Bk," *Ikon: poems*, Enso, 2005; Auth, "Bk," *no stars, no moonL new and selected haiku*, Mellen, 2004; Contrib, "A Pryr on the Feast Day of Jonathan Myrick Daniels," *Race and Pryr: Collected Voices Many Dreams*, Morehouse, 2003; Contrib, "Jesus in Showbiz," *Up Off Your Knees: Preaching the U2 Songbook*, Cowley, 2003; Auth, "Bk," *earth into earth: poems*, Enso, 2000; Auth, "Bk," *The Wounded Table.: prose poems*, Pudding Hse, 1999; Auth, "Bk," *Cloud: a poem in 2 acts*, Mellen, 1997; Auth, "Bk," *The Loneliness of Blizzards: poems*, Mellen, 1995; Auth, "Bk," *Paper Doves, Falling and other poems*, Sunstone, 1992. Fllshp of SSJE 2002; Oblate of St. Ben 1992; Soc of Cath Priests 2009. Assoc Poet Laureate of No Dakota 2004. apium@aol.com

PARSONS, Ann Roberts (Ak) Po Box 1445, Sitka AK 99835 B Evanston IL 8/29/1925 d Keith Roberts & Helen. Chicago Art Inst Chicago IL. D 5/1/1984 Bp George Clinton Harris. m 6/21/1947 Francis John Parsons. Sec - Com Dio Alaska Fairbanks AK 1977-1985.

PARSONS, Berry Ed (LI) 20 Apache Ln, Sedona AZ 86351 B Brownsville TX 8/26/1946 s Givon Monroe Parsons & Nida Belle. BA U Cinc 1969; MDiv GTS 1975. D 6/7/1975 Bp William Foreman Creighton P 6/7/1976 Bp Robert Bruce Hall. S Jn's Epis Ch Ft Hamilton Brooklyn NY 2004-2008; Vic Ch Of S Fran Of Assisi Levittown NY 1994-2004; Vic Epis Ch of The Resurr Williston Pk NY 1994-2004; Vic S Phil And S Jas Ch New Hyde Pk NY 1992-1994; The Ch of S Ign of Antioch New York NY 1988-1990; P-in-c Ch Of The Ascen And S Agnes Washington DC 1985; S Andr's Epis Ch Arlington VA 1983-1984; Cur S Dunst's McLean VA 1975-1983. berry14@me.com

✠ **PARSONS, Rt Rev Donald James** (Spr) 6901 N Galena Rd Apt 111, Peoria IL 61614 **Ramsey Prof of Ascetical Theol Nash Nashotah WI 2001-; Ret Bp of Quincy Dio Quincy Peoria IL 1988-** B Philadelphia PA 3/28/1922 s Earl Parsons & Helen. DCL Nash; BA Tem 1943; ThB PDS 1946; ThM PDS 1948; ThD PDS 1952; DD PDS 1974. D 2/1/1946 Bp William P Remington P 10/6/1946 Bp Arthur R Mc Kinstry Con 9/8/1973 for Q. c 3. Bp Dio Quincy Peoria IL 1973-1987; Dn & Pres Nash Nashotah WI 1963-1973; Prof Nash Nashotah WI 1956-1973; Instr NT Nash Nashotah WI 1950-1954; R S Ptr's Ch Smyrna DE 1949-1950; Asst Imm Ch Highlands Wilmington DE 1946-1949; Cur The Ch Of The H Trin Rittenhouse Philadelphia PA 1946-1947. Auth, *Euch: Rite 2*, Seabury Press; Auth, *In Time w Jesus*, Par Press; Auth, *Lifetime Road to God*, Par Press. Epis Visitor, All SS Sis of Poor 2005; Epis Visitor, S Greg Abbey 1996-2000.

PARSONS, Susan Diane (Cal) 9 Ruben Ct., Novato CA 94947 **Assoc The Epis Ch Of S Mary The Vrgn San Francisco CA 2011-** B Beaumont TX 1/29/1952 d John Kenneth Parsons & Grova Maye. BA Sonoma St U Rohnert Pk 1994; MA CDSP 1997; MA CDSP 1997. D 6/5/2004 P 12/4/2004 Bp William Edwin Swing. m 1/11/1997 Bruce Alan Murphy c 2. Assoc S Fran Of Assisi Ch Novato CA 2004-2011. susandparsons@aol.com

PARSONS, Timothy Hamilton (CNY) 12 Oak Ave, Norway ME 04268 **Grants Revs Com Dio Maine Portland ME 2007-; P S Barn Ch Rumford ME 2006-** B Boston MA 10/6/1941 s Kenneth Hamilton Parsons & June Frances. BA Ge 1964; MDiv VTS 1968; DMin Drew U 1977. D 6/8/1968 Bp Leland Stark P 6/4/1969 Bp Paul Moore Jr. m 12/23/1983 Susan Sommers c 3. R S Matt's Epis Ch Liverpool NY 1993-2006; R Emm Ch Adams NY 1990-1993; R Zion Ch Adams NY 1990-1993; S Ptr's Ch Newark NJ 1989-1990; R S Andr's Ch Harrington Pk NJ 1986-1989; R Ch Of The H Comm Norwood NJ 1986-1987; R S Jn's Ch Clinton IA 1981-1986; Ce Com Dio Sthrn Ohio Cincinnati OH 1978-1981; Gr Ch Hastings On Hudson NY 1972-1978; Assoc Zion Ch Dobbs Ferry NY 1972-1975; Asst P In Charge S Pat's Ch Washington DC 1970-1972; Asst S Phil The Evang Washington DC 1968-1970. timothyprsns@yahoo.com

PARSONS-CANCELLIERE, Rebecca Anne (Be) 350 Spruce Rd, Palmerton PA 18071 B Kingston PA 11/2/1961 d Winfield L Parsons & Jeanne Carol Evans. BS Millersville U 1983; MDiv Moravian TS 1997. D 2/2/2009 Bp John Palmer Croneberger. m 9/18/1999 Thomas Cancelliere c 2. rapcancelliere@aol.com

PARTANEN, Robert C (Cal) 62 Valais Ct, Fremont CA 94539 **D S Anne's Ch Fremont CA 2006-** B Syracuse NY 9/27/1947 s John Emil Partanen & Alice Aliene. BS San Jose St U 1972; BA Sch for Deacons 2003. D 6/3/2006 Bp William Edwin Swing. m 3/31/2000 Diana Lynn Miller c 1. No Amer Assoc. of Deacons 2001. singer-rep@yahoo.com

PARTEE, Mariclair Elizabeth (Be) 321 Wyandotte St, Bethlehem PA 18015 **Cn Cathd Ch Of The Nativ Bethlehem PA 2009-** B Atlanta GA 10/11/1977 d Norman Partee & Amanda. BA The U GA Athens GA 1999; JD U GA 2002; MDiv The GTS 2007. D 12/21/2006 P 7/8/2007 Bp J(ohn) Neil Alexander. Assoc R Trin Ch Solebury PA 2007-2009. mpartee@mindspring.com

PARTENHEIMER, Gary Hoffman (Pa) East Hall - Northfield Mt Hermon, Northfield MA 01360 B Philadelphia PA 11/7/1949 s Raymond Partenheimer & Ella Evelyn. BA Dart 1971; MDiv EDS 1977. D 6/11/1977 Bp Lyman Cunningham Ogilby P 6/1/1978 Bp John Brooke Mosley. m 6/23/1979 Sarah Ogden Hoffman. cl Soc; Phi Beta Kappa.

PARTHUM II, Charles Frederick (Mass) 1415 N Victoria Cir, Elm Grove WI 53122 B Kansas City MO 3/2/1947 s Charles Frederick Parthum & Mary Louise. BS U of Wisconsin 1969; JD U of Wisconsin 1975; MDiv VTS 1987. D 6/13/1987 Bp Ronald Hayward Haines P 6/19/1988 Bp Robert Whitridge Estill. c 2. Dn Calv Cathd Sioux Falls SD 2006-2008; Calv Cathd Sioux Falls SD 2004-2006; S Steph's Epis Ch Wilkes Barre PA 2004-2006; Int S Jn's Ch Cornwall NY 2002-2004; Dio Wstrn Massachusetts Springfield MA 2001-2002; Int S Steph's Ch Westborough MA 2001-2002; Int S Paul's Epis Ch Willimantic CT 1999-2001; Int Emm Epis Ch Wakefield MA 1997-1999; Mssn Plcy & Plnng Cmte Dio Massachusetts Boston MA 1994-1995; Const & Cns Cmte Dio Massachusetts Boston MA 1993-1998; R S Ptr's Ch Weston MA 1992-1997; COM Dio No Carolina Raleigh NC 1990-1992; Bd Dir Urban Mnstry Cntr Dio No Carolina Raleigh NC 1988-1992; Asst to R Chr Epis Ch Raleigh NC 1987-1992. Connecticut Int Mnstry Assn 1999-2001; Exec Bd, Wis Law Rev 1974-1975; Int Mnstry Ntwk 1999; Natl Assn of Epis Int Mnstry Specialists 2000-2006; Transition Mnstry Ntwk 2007. AG hon US Dept Justice 1983; Ord Coif Univ Wisconsin 1975. cfp3@mac.com

PARTINGTON, Richard Ogden (Pa) 4116 Twin Silo Dr, Blue Bell PA 19422 B Philadelphia PA 4/30/1922 s Harold Charles Partington & Ida May. BS Tem 1944; STB Tem 1947; STM Tem 1949. D 12/28/1951 Bp Oliver J Hart P 6/1/1952 Bp William P Roberts. m 11/11/1944 Shirley T Thomas c 2. Vic Ch Of S Jude And The Nativ Lafayette Hill PA 1952-1954; Asst Chr Ch And S Mich's Philadelphia PA 1951-1952.

PARTLOW, John Michael Owen (WVa) No address on file. B Parkersburg WV 4/16/1951 s Walter Woodworth Partlow & Mary Margaret. BA W Virginia U 1974; MDiv VTS 1988. D 6/1/1988 Bp Robert Poland Atkinson P 6/1/1989 Bp William Franklin Carr. Chr Ch Winnetka IL 1990; D-In-Trng Trin Epis Ch Martinsburg WV 1988-1990.

PARTLOW, Robert Greider (SVa) 2245 Huguenot Trl, Powhatan VA 23139 B Rochester NY 9/12/1938 s James Ross Partlow & Margaret Ellen. BS USNA 1961; MDiv SWTS 1971; MBA Stan 1971; DMin SWTS 2000. D 6/24/1989 Bp C(laude) Charles Vache P 3/4/1990 Bp Robert Hodges Johnson. m 6/23/1962 Ruth Goodrich. Int S Matt's Epis Ch Chesterfield VA 2010; Int Johns Memi Epis Ch Farmville VA 2006-2008; co-R S Lk's Ch Powhatan VA 1999-2000; Co-R Chr Epis Ch Of Springfield Springfield OH 1992-1999; Ch Of The Mssh Murphy NC 1989-1992. rgpx2@aol.com

PARTLOW, Ruth Goodrich (SVa) 3358 Medway Lane, Powhatan VA 23139 B Hannibal MO 10/9/1940 d Howard Brant Goodrich & Ruth. BA Duke 1962; MA Regent U Virginia Bch VA 1983; MDiv SWTS 1989. D 6/24/1989 Bp C(laude) Charles Vache P 3/4/1990 Bp Robert Hodges Johnson. m 6/23/1962 Robert Greider Partlow c 2. Int Co-R S Matt's Epis Ch Chesterfield VA 2010; Int Co-R Johns Memi Epis Ch Farmville VA 2007-2008; Co-R S Lk's Ch Powhatan VA 1999-2006; Co-R Chr Epis Ch Of Springfield Springfield OH 1992-1999; Int S Cyp's Ch Franklin NC 1992; R S Jn's Epis Ch Franklin NC 1990-1992. rugpart@aol.com

PARTRIDGE, Cameron Elliot (Mass) 34 Hatch Rd, Medford MA 02155 **Epis Chapl at Bos Dio Massachusetts Boston MA 2011-** B Berkeley CA 11/20/1973 s David Partridge & Rebecca. BA Bryn 1995; MDiv Harvard DS 1998; STM Ya Berk 2001; ThD Harvard DS 2008. D 6/12/2004 P 1/8/2005 Bp M(arvil) Thomas Shaw III. m 10/29/2005 Kateri Paul c 1. Int Epis Chapl at Harv Epis Chapl At Harvard & Radcliffe Cambridge MA 2010-2011; Vic S Lk's And S Marg's Ch Allston MA 2006-2010; D Chr Ch Somerville MA 2004-2005. Auth, "Transfigured Name," *Crossing Paths: Where Transgender & Rel Meet*, Unitarian Universalist Assn of Congregations, 2003; Auth, "H Week," *Crossing Paths: Where Transgender & Rel Meet*, Unitarian Universalist Assn of Congregations, 2003. AAR 2005; No Amer Patristics Soc 2006; SBL 2007. cepart@yahoo.com

PARTRIDGE, Edmund Bruce (Nwk) 106 Cambridge Ln, Williamsburg VA 23185 B Orange NJ 7/6/1932 s Harold Raymond Partridge & Dorothy Shute. BA U Pgh 1959; MDiv GTS 1962; LHD London Inst GB 1972. D 6/9/1962 P 12/1/1962 Bp Leland Stark. Int S Geo's Epis Ch Newport News VA 2000; Dn Trin And S Phil's Cathd Newark NJ 1990-1993; R/P Dstrssd Congs Dio Newark Newark NJ 1978-1990; 11 Int Retorates Dio Newark Newark NJ 1971-2000; R S Jas Ch Wichita KS 1968-1971; Cur S Ptr's Ch Essex Fells NJ

P

1962-1964. Auth, "The New Sprtlty for Lymn," Forw Mvmt; Auth, "Anger, Rage & Resentment," St. Ive's Press; Auth, "The Guide for Lay Readers," Morehouse / Barlow; Auth, "The Ch in Perspective". GTS Alum Assn 1962; Newark Epis Cler Assn 1982; Virginia Epis Cler Assn 2002. Hon Cn Trin & S Phil's Cathd Newark NJ 1993. ebparty@cox.net

PARTRIDGE JR, Henry Roy (Me) 3 Old Colony Ln, Scarborough ME 04074 B Tuskegee AL 4/23/1947 s Henry Roy Partridge & Olive Deborah. MS U MI 1971; MA U MI 1983; PhD U MI 1985; MDiv Harvard DS 1988. D 6/4/1988 P 12/1/1988 Bp Edward Cole Chalfant. m 9/22/1978 Susan Elizabeth Murray c 3. R S Ann's Epis Ch Windham Windham ME 1997-2005; Int S Dav's Epis Ch Kennebunk ME 1996-1997; Cur Cathd Ch Of S Lk Portland ME 1988-1989. spartri1@maine.rr.com

PARTRIDGE, Ivan Harold (Nwk) Po Box 235, Cotuit MA 02635 B Stockport, England 10/30/1925 s Harold Raymond Partridge & Dorothy Victoria. BA Hob 1950; MDiv GTS 1953. D 6/1/1953 P 1/1/1954 Bp Benjamin M Washburn. m 6/17/1950 Jean MacGregor c 4. Acts/VIM Bd Dio Newark Newark NJ 1981-1985; Pres Of The Newark Cler Assn Dio Newark Newark NJ 1971-1972; R All SS' Epis Ch Glen Rock NJ 1956-1988; Asst R S Lk's Epis Ch Montclair NJ 1953-1956.

PASCHALL JR, Fred William (NC) 4341 Bridgewood Ln, Charlotte NC 28226 B Burlington NC 11/26/1935 s Fred William Paschall & Emily Spencer. BS No Carolina St U 1958; MA STUSo 1992; DMin STUSo 1996. D 6/25/1978 Bp William F Gates Jr P 6/1/1979 Bp William Evan Sanders. m 2/14/1964 Winston Conner. Chr Ch Charlotte NC 1998-2004; Asst to R Chr Ch Charlotte NC 1994-1996; Asst to R S Jn's Epis Ch Charlotte NC 1990-1994; P-in-c S Tim's Ch Signal Mtn TN 1988-1989; Int Chr Ch Epis So Pittsburg TN 1987-1988; P-in-c S Tim's Ch Signal Mtn TN 1984-1985; P-in-c S Alb's Epis Ch Hixson TN 1983-1984; Assoc Ch Of The Gd Shpd Lookout Mtn TN 1982-1990; Assoc S Mart Of Tours Epis Ch Chattanooga TN 1981-1982; D S Lk's Ch Cleveland TN 1978-1979.

PATIENCE, Alexander Theodore (ECR) 3255 De Forest Rd, Marina CA 93933 **S Matt's Ch San Ardo CA 2005-** B Hoboken NJ 3/8/1931 s Alexander Patience & Magdelene Erna. Cert ECA Trng Cntr 1952; BA Pk Coll Parkville MO 1959; BD CDSP 1962. D 6/24/1961 P 6/12/1962 Bp William G Wright. m 6/8/1958 Roberta Fehlman c 3. Asst S Jas' Ch Monterey CA 1997-1998; R S Jn's Chap Monterey CA 1990-1997; P-in-c H Comm Ch Dallas TX 1988-1990; Chair Dioc Com New Pars & Mssns Epis Dio San Joaquin Modesto CA 1984-1988; R Epis Ch Of The Sav Hanford CA 1979-1987; Stndg Com Epis Dio San Joaquin Modesto CA 1976-1980; Cn Pstr S Jas Epis Cathd Fresno CA 1975-1979; R S Mich And All Ang' Ch Denver CO 1971-1975; R All SS Epis Ch Denver CO 1969-1970; R S Mk's Epis Ch Durango CO 1965-1969; Cur S Thos Epis Ch Denver CO 1964-1965; Vic S Jn's In The Wilderness Ch Glenbrook NV 1961-1964. ALEX.REV@SBCGLOBAL.NET

PATIENCE, Rodger Lindsay (FdL) 130 Cherry Ct, Appleton WI 54915 **D S Thos Ch Menasha WI 2010-** B Winter Haven FL 3/4/1968 s Lindsay Garrett Patience & Christine Ellen. BA Estrn Illinois U 1989; Sch for Deacons - Dio Chicago 1995. D 2/3/1996 Bp Frank Tracy Griswold III. m 5/13/1989 Katharina Elisabeth Prohaska. D S Lk's Ch Racine WI 2007-2010; D S Lk's Ch Whitewater WI 2002-2007; Instr, Sch for Deacons Dio Milwaukee Milwaukee WI 1998-2010; D Ch Of The H Comm Lake Geneva WI 1996-2001; D S Paul's Ch Milwaukee WI 1996. Contrib, "An Epis Dictionary of the Ch," Ch Pub Inc, 2000. Assn for Epis Deacons (NAAD) 1993; Fllshp of St. Jn, SSJE 1996. dcnpatience@gmail.com

PATNAUDE, Robert J (O) 1160 Fulton St, Palo Alto CA 94301 B Saratoga Sprgs NY 12/19/1949 s Robert West & Elsa Margaret. MDiv Bex; Hob 1969; BS SUNY 1971. D 6/15/1974 Bp Wilbur Emory Hogg Jr P 12/1/1974 Bp H Coleman McGehee Jr. R Chr Ch Shaker Heights OH 1987-1988; R Trin Par Menlo Pk CA 1976-1987; Asst S Jas Epis Ch Birmingham MI 1974-1976. Auth, "Penny," White Rhino Press, 2002; Auth, "Leading From The Maze," Ten Speed Press, 1997. Cleric Of Year Awd Kiwanis Intl 1985. jeff@patnaude.com

PATRONIK JR, Joseph Andrew (SanD) P.O. Box 1220, Pauma Valley CA 92061 **R S Fran Ch Pauma Vlly CA 2003-** B Chicago IL 11/11/1951 s Joseph Andrew Patronik & Mary Louise. BS The OH SU 1973; MBA Santa Clara U 1980; U Of Geneva Ch 1987; MDiv CDSP 1988. D 6/4/1988 P 6/3/1989 Bp William Edwin Swing. m 10/6/1990 Leslie Lynn Patronik c 4. R H Trin Ch So River NJ 1999-2003; Chapl Washington Epis Sch Beth MD 1998-1999; R S Ptr's By-The-Sea Epis Ch Morro Bay CA 1992-1994; Asst Chr Ch Portola Vlly CA 1990-1991; Int S Bede's Epis Ch Menlo Pk CA 1989. Allin Fllshp 1987. PAUMAFAM@AOL.COM

PATSTON, John Ralph Ansell (NI) 502 N James St, Ludington MI 49431 B Vancouver BC CA 9/13/1927 s Percival John Patston & Lydia Fredericka. BA U So 1954; BD Nash 1957; Rutgers-The St U 1966; STM Nash 1979. D 6/15/1957 Bp Charles L Street P 12/21/1957 Bp Gerald Francis Burrill. m 8/30/1952 Nancy Higgins c 5. R S Paul's Ch Henderson KY 1986-1994; R Gr Epis Ch Of Ludington Michigan Ludington MI 1970-1986; Vic S Jas' Epis Ch Of Pentwater Pentwater MI 1970-1986; Vic Ch Of The Medtr Harbert MI 1968-1970; Asst Dir, Cathd Shltr Cathd Of S Jas Chicago IL 1966-1968; P Chr The King Epis Ch Huntington IN 1960-1966; Cur Chr Ch Waukegan IL 1957-1960. Auth, "The Symbolism Of The Cntr & The Euch". SSC 1976.

PATTEN, John Frederick (WLa) 44 Tealwood, Shreveport LA 71104 B Alexandria LA 12/14/1926 s Albert Burkett Patten & Ada. BA Col 1948; MBA U of Pennsylvania 1958; BD VTS 1967. D 6/28/1967 P 5/28/1968 Bp J Milton Richardson. m 7/2/1980 Sybil Tyrrell c 2. Chair. Comm. on Structure, New Dio Dio Wstrn Louisiana Alexandria LA 1977-1979; Dep. Gen'l. Conv, Dio Louisiana Baton Rouge LA 1976-1982; Pres, Stndg Com Dio Louisiana Baton Rouge LA 1974-1977; S Mk's Cathd Shreveport LA 1973-1989; R S Matt's Ch Austin TX 1969-1972; Vic S Fran Par Temple TX 1967-1969. Hon Cn St. Mk'S Cathd Shreveport La. Dio WLa 1989. pattenfred@aol.com

PATTEN, Kenneth Lloyd (Hond) No address on file. B Glace Bay NS CA 4/1/1941 s Frederick Thomas Patten & Florence Christine. BA Kings Coll Edmonton Ab CA 1961; STB U Tor 1965.

PATTERSON, Barbara Anne Bowling (At) 437 S Candler St, Decatur GA 30030 B Tucson AZ 3/16/1952 d Lawson Hamilton Bowling & Anne Glenn. Candler TS Emory U; BA Smith 1973; MDiv Harvard DS 1977; PhD Emory U 1994. D 6/9/1984 P 5/1/1985 Bp Charles Judson Child Jr. m 7/30/1977 Joe Steadman Patterson. Dn S Jn's Coll Pk GA 1984-1985. Auth, "Campus Calling"; Auth, "Redeemed Bodies Simone Weil: Distance & Fasting". Soc Of S Jn The Evang.

PATTERSON, Beverly A (WTex) 614 Swift St, Refugio TX 78377 **R S Andr's Ch Port Isabel TX 2011-** B Hondo TX 1/17/1958 d Otway Frederick James & Geraldine Daniel. BS Amberton U 2002; MDiv The TS at The U So 2009. D 6/20/2009 Bp James Monte Stanton P 4/2/2011 Bp Gary Richard Lillibridge. c 5. bevpat46@gmail.com

PATTERSON JR, Dennis Delamater (SVa) 1242 W Queens St, Hampton VA 23669 **R S Cyp's Epis Ch Hampton VA 2008-** B Norfolk VA 8/13/1977 s Dennis Patterson & Annie. BA Psycology Norfolk St U; Masters of Div/M.Div UTS; Post Grad Angl Stds VTS. D 4/19/2008 P 10/25/2008 Bp John Clark Buchanan. m 5/21/2005 Monica E Edwards. revddpj@gmail.com

PATTERSON, Edith Croessmann (Minn) 8010 Corey Path, Invergrove Heights MN 55076 B Buffalo NY 3/19/1923 d Richard Jacob Croessmann & Anna H. BS SUNY 1974. D 2/28/1987 Bp J Michael Garrison. m 6/12/1948 John Reeves Patterson c 3. D The Epis Ch Of The Gd Shpd Buffalo NY 1987-2008.

PATTERSON, Jane Lancaster (WTex) St. Mark's Episcopal Church, 315 Pecan St., San Antonio TX 78205 **Asst R S Mk's Epis Ch San Antonio TX 2005-** B Miami FL 7/1/1954 d James William Lancaster & Claudia Mary. SMU; BA Smith 1977; MTS SMU 1992; CTh Epis TS of The SW 1993. D 1/18/1994 P 6/15/1995 Bp John Herbert MacNaughton. m 11/22/1997 Lorenzo D Patterson IV c 2. Int Epis TS Of The SW Austin TX 2003-2005; S Lk's Epis Ch San Antonio TX 2003; Assoc All SS Epis Ch Corpus Christi TX 2001-2002; Ch Of Recon San Antonio TX 1995-2000. AAR 1993; Angl Assn Of Biblic Scholars 1996; Cltn for Mnstry in Daily Life 1995; SBL 1993. Fllshp ECF 1994. jpatterson@theworkshop-sa.org

P

PATTERSON, John (EpisSanJ) 9 Simpson Close, Barrow on Humber, North Lincolnshire DN19 7BL Great Britain (UK) B Croydon Surrey UK 12/5/1927 s Eric Munn Patterson & Gladys Edith. GOE Bp's Coll Cheshunt GB 1961; MA Regent St Polytechnic/Univ of Westminster London GB 1976; MA Regent St Polytechnic/Univ of Westminster London GB 2003. D 12/1/1961 P 12/1/1962 Bp The Bishop Of Oxford. m 6/8/1949 Olive Jean Orchard c 2. Dioc Coun Epis Dio San Joaquin Modesto CA 1987-1990; Dn, Sierra Dnry Epis Dio San Joaquin Modesto CA 1979-1990; Dioc Coun Epis Dio San Joaquin Modesto CA 1979-1982; R S Mich's Epis Par Ridgecrest CA 1978-1989. Chapl of the Year NV Wing CAP 1985.

PATTERSON, John Willard (NJ) 2885 Citrus Lake Dr, Naples FL 34109 **S Monica's Epis Ch Naples FL 1995-** B Hackensack NJ 3/9/1926 s John Joseph Patterson & Edna. Seton Hall U; BA U NC 1948; MDiv GTS 1951; Montclair St U 1956. D 5/26/1951 P 12/8/1951 Bp Benjamin M Washburn. m 3/31/1964 Elena Gonzalez c 1. R Epis Ch Of The Epiph Ventnor City NJ 1984-1991; Vic S Jas Memi Ch Eatontown NJ 1976-1984; S Andr The Apos Highland Highlands NJ 1976; Asst S Ptr's Ch Freehold NJ 1973-1974; Asst Ch Of The H Comm Paterson NJ 1954-1955; Vic Ch Of S Mary The Vrgn Ridgefield Pk NJ 1951-1954. lumbiedog@aol.com

PATTERSON, Margaret Pittman (Del) 10 Concord Ave, Wilmington DE 19802 B Macon GA 12/27/1944 d Charles Wood Pittman & Margaret Lucile. BA Sweet Briar Coll 1967; MRE SMU 1969; MDiv SMU 1985; DMin SMU 1995. D 6/17/1989 P 5/26/1990 Bp Donis Dean Patterson. c 3. Dioc Coun Dio Delaware Wilmington DE 1997-2002; Dep Gc Dio Delaware Wilmington DE 1997-2000; Cathd Ch Of S Jn Wilmington DE 1995-2005; Excoun Fin Com Dio Dallas Dallas TX 1992; S Matt's Cathd Dallas TX 1989-1995. Auth, "Cathederals In The Twenty First Century," Wash Natl Cathederals, 2000. AAM (AAM) 1999; EWC; Integrity Inc. revpeggy@gmail.com

PATTERSON, Michael Steven (Nev) PO Box 1041, Fernley NV 89408 B Alameda CA 8/27/1948 s Robert Owen Patterson & Dolores Francis. D 7/25/

2009 P 3/27/2010 Bp Dan Thomas Edwards. m 4/29/1995 Connie Dixon c 4. mcp4675@charter.net

PATTERSON, Robert Place (Md) 3 Cobb Ln, Topsham ME 04086 B Taunton MA 11/15/1930 s Alvah Greenleaf Patterson & Alice Williams. BA Bos 1952; MDiv Ya Berk 1955; Harvard DS 1957. D 6/25/1955 Bp Norman B Nash P 1/21/1956 Bp Anson Phelps Stokes Jr. m 8/25/1956 Edith M Melcher c 4. Chr Crossroads Oprtns Commitee Dio Maryland Baltimore MD 1988-1992; Stndg Com Dio Maryland Baltimore MD 1985-1989; Co-Fndr of the Chr/Jewish Dialogue Grp Dio Maryland Baltimore MD 1982-1987; Dep GC Dio Maryland Baltimore MD 1979-1988; Dioc Coun Dio Maryland Baltimore MD 1977-1979; Dioc Coun Dio Maryland Baltimore MD 1968-1971; R The Ch Of The Redeem Baltimore MD 1965-1993; Assoc Chr Ch Cranbrook Bloomfield Hills MI 1961-1965; R S Mary's Epis Ch Rockport MA 1958-1961; Assoc Ch Of The Redeem Chestnut Hill MA 1957-1958; Cur S Jn's Ch W Hartford CT 1955-1956. Auth, *Reflections*, Ch of the Redeem, 1990; Auth, *Selected Sermons*. Bp's Awd for Distinguished Serv Dio Maryland 1989. bob1130@gmail.com

PATTERSON, Siobhán (WVa) 913 Sylvan Avenue, Fairmont WV 26554 **R Chr Ch Fairmont WV 2008-** B Cheverly Maryland 10/2/1981 d Robert William Patterson & Joan Marie. BA Wheeling Jesuit U 2003; MDiv SWTS 2006. D 12/10/2005 P 6/10/2006 Bp William Michie Klusmeyer. Cur/Campus Min Trin Ch Huntington WV 2007-2008; Cur Trin Ch Shepherdstown WV 2006-2007. christchfmt.rector@gmail.com

PATTERSON, Timothy Jay (NC) 607 N Greene St, Greensboro NC 27401 **R H Trin Epis Ch Greensboro NC 1996-** B Upper Darby PA 9/25/1952 s Robert Eugene Patterson & Helen Jacqueline. BA Duke 1975; MDiv Duke 1980; CAS GTS 1989. D 6/3/1989 P 8/15/1990 Bp Robert Whitridge Estill. m 10/30/1982 Kathleen Elizabeth Forbes. Asst H Trin Epis Ch Greensboro NC 1989-1996. tim@holy-trinity.com

PATTERSON JR, W(illiam) Brown (NC) 195 N Carolina Ave, Sewanee TN 37375 B Charlotte NC 4/8/1930 s William Brown Patterson & Eleanor Selden. BA U So 1952; MA Harv 1954; BA Oxf 1955; MDiv EDS 1958; MA Oxf 1959; PhD Harv 1966. D 6/29/1958 Bp Edwin A Penick P 2/8/1959 Bp Richard Henry Baker. m 11/27/1959 Evelyn Byrd Hawkins c 4. ExCom EDS Alum/ae Assn EDS Cambridge MA 1984-1987; S Alb's Ch Davidson NC 1971-1978; Fell The GTS New York NY 1961-1962. Auth, *King Jas VI & I & Reunion of Christendom*, Cambridge U Press, 1997; Contrib, *Richard Hooker and the Construction of Chr Cmnty*, Med & Ren Texts & Stds, 1997; Contrib, *This Sacr Mnstry: Angl Reflections for Jn Booty*, Cowley Press, 1990; Auth, *Var arts on Hist*. Amer Soc of Ch Hist 1963; Eccl Hist Soc (UK) 1967; Royal Hist Soc 2000. Distinguished Fac Awd U So 2002; Albert C. Outler Prize in Ecum Ch Hist Amer Soc of Ch Hist 1999; Rhodes Schlr Rhodes Trust 1953; Phi Beta Kappa U So 1951. bpatters@sewanee.edu

PATTERSON-URBANIAK, Penelope Ellen (CFla) 676 Nettles Ridge Rd, Banner Elk NC 28604 B New Rochelle NY 2/22/1948 d John Dexter Patterson & Mary Katherine. BFA U GA 1970; MDiv STUSo 1992. D 6/20/1992 P 1/1/1993 Bp John Wadsworth Howe. m 7/8/1985 Ronald Lee Urbaniak. Emm Ch Orlando FL 1993-1999; S Mich's Ch Orlando FL 1992. PPATTURB@GMAIL.COM

PATTISON, Benno David (At) 634 W Peachtree St Nw, Atlanta GA 30308 **Ch Of The Epiph Atlanta GA 2006-** B Cincinnati OH 4/14/1963 s Edward Mansell Pattison & Myrna Loy. BA U GA 1985; MDiv GTS 1988. D 6/4/1988 P 6/1/1989 Bp Harry Woolston Shipps. c 3. S Lk's Epis Ch Atlanta GA 2001-2006; All SS Epis Ch Atlanta GA 1991-1997; Assoc R S Aug Of Cbury Ch Augusta GA 1988-1991. RECTOR@EPIPHANY.ORG

PATTON, David C (Mich) 2027 E 93rd St N, Valley Center KS 67147 B San Diego CA 12/23/1929 BA MI SU 1951; MDiv ETS 1954; MA San Francisco St U 1969. D 6/26/1954 Bp Richard S M Emrich P 4/9/1955 Bp Archie H Crowley. m 7/24/1982 Margaret Wagner. S Mary's/Santa Maria Virgen Imperial Bch CA 1986-1991; S Fran In The Redwoods Mssn Willits CA 1983-1986; H Trin Epis Ch Ukiah CA 1978-1986. "Dynamis," St Geo Orth Cathd Wichita Ks, 1996. dynamis@dynamispublications.org

PATTON, Kathleen (Oly) 1645 24th Ave, Longview WA 98632 **R S Steph's Epis Ch Longview WA 2011-; Conv Deputation Dio Olympia Seattle WA 2010-2012** B Cherry Point NC 9/18/1958 d Harvey M Patton & Jane D. U CA 1978; BA U CA 1980; MDiv CDSP 1990. D 6/9/1990 P 6/8/1991 Bp William Edwin Swing. m 4/6/1991 Richard Lee Green c 1. P in Charge S Steph's Epis Ch Longview WA 2010-2011; Conv Deputation Dio Olympia Seattle WA 2006-2009; COM Dio Olympia Seattle WA 2005-2011; Assoc R S Steph's Epis Ch Longview WA 2000-2010; Co-R S Mk's Ch Yreka CA 1995-2000; Consult -- Chld's Mnstry Ch Of The Epiph San Carlos CA 1994-1995; Assoc R S Steph's Par Belvedere CA 1990-1994. kpatton@sslv.org

PATTON, Thomas Dunstan (Spr) 1904 S Glenwood Ave, Springfield IL 62704 B Springfield IL 7/13/1947 s Robert J Patton & Helen Dunstan. BA U IL 1969; MDiv McCormick TS 1996; DAS VTS 1997. D 6/8/2003 P 6/29/2004 Bp Peter Hess Beckwith. c 2. tpatton@springnet1.com

PATTON-GRAHAM, Heather Lynn (Pa) 338 Riverview Ave, Drexel Hill PA 19026 B Dover DE 6/13/1973 d Robert Wayne Patton & Judith Aileen. BA U Of Delaware Newark 1995; MDiv GTS 2003. D 1/18/2003 P 9/26/2003 Bp Wayne Parker Wright. m 12/22/1995 Alexander C Graham c 1. S Thos' Ch Whitemarsh Ft Washington PA 2009-2011; All SS Ch Norristown PA 2006; The Epis Acad Newtown Sq PA 2005-2009; Asst R Chr Ch Greenville Wilmington DE 2003-2005. hpatton-graham@cathedral.org

PAUL, Jeffrey (Nev) 305 N Minnesota St, Carson City NV 89703 **Dn Dio Nevada Las Vegas NV 2009-; R S Ptr's Epis Ch Carson City NV 1995-** B Cleveland OH 10/31/1954 s Donald Jack Paul & Florence Teresa. AA Orange Coast Coll 1975; BS California St U 1977; MDiv CDSP 1983. D 6/18/1983 Bp Albert Wiencke Van Duzer P 12/21/1983 Bp Robert C Rusack. c 4. Assoc S Paul's Epis Ch Ventura CA 1990-1995; R S Andr's Par Torrance CA 1986-1989; Asst to R S Jas Par Los Angeles CA 1983-1986; S Jas' Sch Los Angeles CA 1983-1986. godguy@stpeterscarsoncity.org

PAUL, Kenneth Wayne (WLa) 720 Wilder Pl, Shreveport LA 71104 **Stndg Com Dio Louisiana Baton Rouge LA 1988-** B Alexandria LA 3/10/1935 s Newton Jefferson Paul & Mellie. BA Asbury Coll 1957; BD SMU 1960; DIT Oxf 1962; GTS 1965; STUSo 1965; ThM SMU 1972. D 6/30/1965 Bp Girault M Jones P 5/18/1966 Bp Iveson Batchelor Noland. m 9/26/1976 Virginia M Millener c 2. Pres Dio Louisiana Baton Rouge LA 1996-1997; R Ch Of The H Cross Shreveport LA 1968-2007; Chapl Centenary Coll Dio Louisiana Baton Rouge LA 1965-1993; P-in-res S Mk's Cathd Shreveport LA 1965-1968. Auth, "Rel & Psychol," *Louisiana Med Journ*.

PAUL, Linda Joy (Okla) 10901 S Yale Ave, Tulsa OK 74137 B Tulsa OK 6/21/1951 d C E Gene Barton & Mona Lee Carroll. BFA-MEd Oklahoma U 1972; Liberal Arts Oklahoma St 1996. D 6/16/2007 Bp Robert Manning Moody. m 12/21/1986 Arthur Paul. harplinda1@gmail.com

PAUL, Michael Kiju (Md) 1321 Charlestown Dr, Edgewood MD 21040 B Sudan 5/12/1960 s Paul K Mulamu & Roa P. Trans 3/22/2005 Bp Robert Wilkes Ihloff. m 7/6/1985 Veronica M Kiju c 4. S Lk's Ch San Diego CA 2006-2010; Dio Maryland Baltimore MD 2006. kijupaul@yahoo.com

PAUL, Rocks-Anne (SwFla) 1200 4th St W, Palmetto FL 34221 **Ch Of The H Sprt Osprey FL 2006-** B Bradenton FL 4/8/1951 d Richard Hamilton Edwards & Lois Hale. BA Sonoma St U Sonoma 1995. D 6/12/2004 Bp John Bailey Lipscomb. c 3. d the King 1986. rocks-anne@nerdyben.com

PAUL, Wectnick (Ct) Box 1309, Port-Au-Prince Haiti B Hinche HT 11/23/1946 s Claudius Paul & Anne Marie. BA Lycee Dumarsais Estime 1965; BA Lycee Alexandre Petion 1966; Cert Ufcwi 1976; Ceteh 1977. D 9/18/1977 P 5/1/1978 Bp Luc Anatole Jacques Garnier. m 12/4/1980 Marie Derissaint c 3. Dio Connecticut Hartford CT 2005-2009; L'Eglise de L'Ephiphanie Stamford CT 1997-2009; S Jn's Ch Stamford CT 1997-2004; Dio Haiti Ft Lauderdale FL 1977-1995.

PAUL, William H (NJ) 2 Illinois Dr, Whiting NJ 08759 **Died 3/5/2011** B Mechanicsburg PA 6/11/1922 s John Heiks Paul & Matilda Claire. BS Penn St U 1943; STB PDS 1958; ThM PrTS 1987. D 4/26/1958 P 11/1/1958 Bp Alfred L Banyard. c 3. ASSP 1982; Rotarian 1963-1986. Hon Resolution The New Jersey Legislature New Jersey 1993; Paul Harris Fell Rotary Intl 1983; Hon Cn Trin Cathd Trenton NJ 1969; R Emer S Stephens Ch Waretown NJ.

PAULIKAS, Steven D (LI) 286-88 7th Ave, Brooklyn NY 11215 **All SS Ch Brooklyn NY 2011-** B Royal Oak MI 12/9/1978 s Alfonsas Jospeh Paulikas & Janet Florence. BA Ya New Haven CT 2001; MA Camb Cambridge Engl 2002; MDiv GTS 2008. D 6/23/2007 Bp Kenneth Lester Price P 6/28/2008 Bp Thomas Edward Breidenthal. Gr Ch Brooklyn NY 2008-2011. stevenpaulikas@yahoo.com

PAULL JR, Lorin (Colo) 967 Nevada Ave, San Jose CA 95125 **Died 12/5/2009** B San Jose CA 10/29/1927 s Lorin Albert Paull & May Eunice. BA Stan 1950; MDiv VTS 1953. D 7/15/1953 Bp Henry H Shires P 2/1/1954 Bp Karl M Block. AEHC.

PAULSON, Diane Theresa (Ida) 1785 Arlington Dr, Pocatello ID 83204 **Trin Epis Ch Pocatello ID 1998-** B Chicago IL 4/19/1943 d Jacob Andrew Pavlik & Theresa. BS Nthrn Illinois U 1966; Med Indiana U 1969. D 4/25/1998 Bp John Stuart Thornton P 5/12/2001 Bp Harry Brown Bainbridge III. m 2/1/1969 Donald Leonard Paulson c 3.

PAULSON, Donald Leonard (Ida) 1785 Arlington Dr, Pocatello ID 83204 B Minneapolis MN 11/20/1944 s Donald Leonard Paulson & Eleanor Louisa. BA Hamline U 1966; Med Indiana U 1968; PhD U of Iowa 1972. D 4/25/1998 P 10/1/1998 Bp John Stuart Thornton. m 2/1/1969 Diane Theresa Paulik. Asst Trin Epis Ch Pocatello ID 1998-2002.

PAULUS II, Garrett Keith (RG) 12211 Mountain Haze Rd NE, Albuquerque NM 87122 B Albuquerque NM 6/28/1976 D 7/30/2005 P 3/25/2006 Bp Jeffrey Neil Steenson. m 2/28/2006 Cindy Thu-Van Bartolotta. D And Dir Of Stdt Mnstrs S Mk's On The Mesa Epis Ch Albuquerque NM 2005. gadosii@aol.com

PAULUS, Ruth B (SO) 1472 Blake Ct, Fairborn OH 45324 **R S Chris's Ch Fairborn OH 2005-** B Piqua OH 10/1/1953 d William Francis Bodine & Ruth Lucille. BSN Franklin U 1994; MSN Wright St U 1997; MDiv Bex 2005. D

P

11/17/2004 P 6/25/2005 Bp Herbert Thompson Jr. m 9/18/1981 Richard J Paulus c 4. ruthpaulusmdiv@yahoo.com

PAVLAC, Brian Alexander (Be) 365 Rutter Ave, Kingston PA 18704 **Assoc S Steph's Epis Ch Wilkes Barre PA 2010-** B Berea OH 7/11/1956 s Charles Pavlac. BA Bowling Green St U 1978; MA Bowling Green St U 1980; MA U of Notre Dame 1982; PhD U of Notre Dame 1986. D 12/21/2009 P 6/29/2010 Bp Paul Victor Marshall. m 10/28/1981 Elizabeth Lott c 2. Auth, "A Concise Survey of Wstrn Civilization: Supremacies and Diversities throughout Hist," Rowman & Littlefield, 2011; Auth, "Witch Hunts in the Wstrn Wrld: Persecution and Punishment from the Inquisition through the Salem Trials," Greenwood, 2009; Transltr, "A Warrior Bp of the 12th Century: The Deeds of Albero of Trier, by Balderich," Pontifical Inst of Medieval Stds, 2008. therev@brianpavlac.org

PAXTON, Richard Edwin (Ky) 820 Broadway St, Paducah KY 42001 B Paducah KY 9/11/1962 s James Paxton & Peggy. BBA Notre Dame 1984; MBA Stanford 1989; Grad Sch of Mnstry 2009. D 5/2/2010 Bp Edwin Funsten Gulick Jr. m 9/28/1985 Cheryl O'Meara c 4. rpaxton@paxtonmedia.com

PAYDEN-TRAVERS, Christine Ann (SwVa) 1711 Link Rd, Lynchburg VA 24503 B Washington DC 6/18/1945 d Carl Irvin Payden & Helen Irma. BA U MI 1967; MS Col 1968; MDiv GTS 1984. D 6/11/1984 Bp Charles Bennison P 5/1/1985 Bp Peter James Lee. m 9/16/1972 John Travers c 2. R Gr Memi Ch Lynchburg VA 1996-2006; Dio SW Virginia Roanoke VA 1988-1996; R S Ptr's Epis Ch Callaway VA 1988-1996; Cur S Jas' Ch Richmond VA 1984-1988. paydentravers@verizon.net

PAYER, Donald R (Ia) 1809 Waterbury Circle, Ames IA 50010 **D S Jn's By The Campus Ames IA 1995-** B Fargo ND 12/12/1928 s Roy L Payer & Catherine M. LLB U of Iowa 1954. D 12/19/1995 Bp Carl Christopher Epting. m 9/6/1952 Janet Mae Supernois c 2. salset@aol.com

✠ **PAYNE, Rt Rev Claude Edward** (Tex) 617 Indian Trl, Salado TX 76571 B Abilene TX 6/19/1932 s Victor Duaine Payne & Katherine. BA Rice U 1954; BS Rice U 1955; MDiv CDSP 1964. D 7/10/1964 Bp Everett H Jones P 1/14/1965 Bp Richard Earl Dicus Con 10/9/1993 for Tex. m 7/9/1955 Barbara King. Bp Dio Texas Houston TX 1993-2003; Trst CDSP Berkeley CA 1989-1993; Trst Epis TS Of The SW Austin TX 1988-2001; R S Mart's Epis Ch Houston TX 1983-1993; R S Mk's Ch Beaumont TX 1968-1983; Asst S Mk's Ch Houston TX 1966-1968; Asst Ch Of The Epiph Kingsville TX 1964-1966. Auth, "Reclaiming the Great Cmsn," Jossey-Bass, 2000. Distinguished Alum Rice U 1996; DD U So 1994; DD CDSP 1988. bpclaudepayne@gmail.com

PAYNE, Edward Thomas (SO) 8363 Cannon Knoll Ct, West Chester OH 45069 **S Fran Epis Ch Springboro OH 2010-** B Cleveland OH 5/16/1948 s Brady C Payne & Betty. BA Cleveland Inst of Mus 1971; MA Cleveland Inst of Mus 1972; MDiv GTS 1996. D 5/24/1997 P 5/1/1998 Bp Herbert Thompson Jr. m 8/12/1978 Gail Annette Donnelly c 4. S Paul's Ch Chillicothe OH 2007-2009; Gr Ch Pomeroy OH 2006-2007; S Mary's Ch Waynesville OH 2002-2003; S Simon Of Cyrene Epis Ch Cincinnati OH 1997-2001. UBE 1997. Cert for Serv as Chf Precentor The Gnrl Sem New York 1996; The Seymour Prize for Extemporaneous Preaching The Gnrl Sem New York 1995. edrevsing@aol.com

PAYNE, Harold Womack (Ark) 3412 W 7th St, Little Rock AR 72205 B Moore County NC 5/4/1941 s Augustus Wilbur Payne & Edna Louise. BA Pfeiffer Coll Misenheimer NC 1963; BD VTS 1966. D 6/29/1966 P 6/24/1967 Bp Thomas Augustus Fraser Jr. Mssnr S Jn's Ch Camden AR 2000-2003; Mssnr S Jas Ch Magnolia AR 2000-2002; Dio E Tennessee Knoxville TN 1996-1999; Vic S Thos Ch Elizabethton TN 1995-1996; Vic S Mary Magd Ch W End NC 1992-1995; P Gr Ch Chanute KS 1988-1991; Neosho Vlly Epis Cluster Chanute KS 1988-1991; Stff Mnstry Devmt Dio Nevada Las Vegas NV 1979-1988; S Paul's Ch Salisbury NC 1975-1976; Novc Ch Of The Ascen And H Trin Highland NY 1971-1975; Asst S Mart's Epis Ch Charlotte NC 1969-1971; Vic S Andr's Ch Haw River NC 1967-1969; D Chr Ch Walnut Cove NC 1966-1967.

PAYNE, John Douglas (FtW) 4902 George St, Wichita Falls TX 76302 **P-in-c S Steph's Epis Ch Wichita Falls TX 2008-** B Monohans TX 1/21/1937 s John Clark Payne & Annie. BA NWU 1959; USA Security Agcy Sch 1960; MDiv GTS 1965. D 6/22/1965 Bp Girault M Jones P 5/5/1966 Bp Iveson Batchelor Noland. m 8/14/1965 Mildred Kay McIntosh c 2. Chair - COM Dio Ft Worth Ft Worth TX 1983-1985; Exec Coun Dio Dallas Dallas TX 1976-1978; R All SS Ch Wichita Falls TX 1973-2006; R Ch Of The Epiph Opelousas LA 1968-1973; Cur S Jas Epis Ch Alexandria LA 1965-1968.

PAYNE, Nona Marie Jones (Dal) 736 Valiant Cir, Garland TX 75043 B Winthrop AR 8/12/1931 d Thomas Elias Jones & Pearl Quindora. STL Dio Dal Angl TS 1986; BA U of Texas 1987. D 6/20/1992 Bp Donis Dean Patterson. c 1. Asst Ch Of Our Sav Dallas TX 1997-1999; D The Epis Ch Of The Trsfg Dallas TX 1986-1997.

PAYNE, Richard Leeds (Mass) Po Box 289, Brewster MA 02631 B Boston MA 2/21/1933 s William James Payne & Alice Beatrice. BA Wms 1954; BD EDS 1957; Med Boston Coll 1972. D 6/8/1957 Bp William A Lawrence P 12/16/1957 Bp Lane W Barton. m 6/6/1953 Joan Alida Wilson c 4. Vic S Steph's Ch E Haddam CT 1982-1985; Asst The Ch Of S Mary Of The Harbor Provincetown MA 1969-1970; R Ch Of The Redeem Pendleton OR 1964-1969; P-in-c S Thos Ch Canyon City OR 1957-1960. baybreez02631@yahoo.com

PAYNE, Susan Strauss (Ark) 1723 Center St, Little Rock AR 72206 B Malvern AR 6/13/1940 d Wilfred L Payne & Janet Strauss. BA U of Arkansas 1989; MDiv SWTS 1995. D 6/15/1995 P 12/16/1995 Bp Larry Earl Maze. m 2/2/1991 Barry Coplin c 2. Asst to the R, Chld & Fam Mnstry Chr Epis Ch Little Rock AR 2004-2010; Vic S Mich's Epis Ch Little Rock AR 1999-2004; Dio Arkansas Little Rock AR 1998-1999; Mssnr S Jas Ch Magnolia AR 1998-1999; H Trin Epis Ch Hot Sprg Vill AR 1997-1998; Cur S Mk's Epis Ch Little Rock AR 1995-1997; Dio Arkansas Little Rock AR 1991-1993; Yth Coordntr Dio Arkansas Little Rock AR 1991-1993. susanspayne@gmail.com

PAYNE-CARTER, Gloria Edith Eureka (WNY) 15 Fernhill Ave, Buffalo NY 14215 **S Phil's Ch Buffalo NY 2005-** B Laventille TT 11/20/1945 d Clyde Fitzgerald Payne & Phyllis Joan. AAS CUNY 1969; BS CUNY 1974; MA NYU 1976; MDiv GTS 1996; Epis Hlth Serv 2001. D 4/21/1997 Bp Orris George Walker Jr P 6/5/1999 Bp Rodney Rae Michel. c 1. All SS Ch Bayside NY 2003-2005; Vic S Gabr's Ch Brooklyn NY 2001-2002; Epis Hlth Serv Bethpage NY 1998-2000; Cur Ch Of SS Steph And Mart Brooklyn NY 1998-1999; Dio Long Island Garden City NY 1997-1998; Cur S Barn Epis Ch Brooklyn NY 1997-1998. Black Cleric Caucus Dio Li 1997-2003; CHS (Assoc) 1997-2003; ECW 1988-2003; UBE 1988-2003. geepcar@hotmail.com

PAYNE-WIENS, Reginald Anton (Tex) 1941 Webberville Rd, Austin TX 78721 **S Jas Ch Austin TX 2010-** B Miami FL 11/24/1968 s Charles Reginald Payne & Gladys. BA Valdosta St U 1993; MDiv VTS 1997. D 5/24/1997 P 6/1/1998 Bp Henry Irving Louttit. m 10/11/1997 Elena Wiens c 2. S Marg Of Scotland Par San Juan Capistrano CA 2003-2009; Yth Min Dio SE Florida Miami FL 2000-2003; S Paul's Epis Ch Paterson NJ 1999-2000; S Paul's Rock Creek Washington DC 1997-1999. REGGIEPW40@ME.COM

PAYSON, Charles Beck (Chi) N1133 Vinne Haha Rd, Fort Atkinson WI 53538 B Portsmouth VA 10/17/1942 s Harold Payson & Anne Marie. AB Harv 1964; MDiv EDS 1972. D 10/3/1972 P 6/1/1973 Bp Frederick Hesley Belden. m 6/12/1964 Evelyn Howe c 3. R S Anskar's Ch Rockford IL 1993-2002; R S Peters Epis Ch Ft Atkinson WI 1977-1993; Cur Chr Ch Cooperstown NY 1973-1977; Cur Gr Ch Lawr MA 1972-1973. cepayson@charter.net

PAYSON, Deborah (Pa) 531 Maison Place, Bryn Mawr PA 19010 B Albany NY 5/11/1943 d George Payson & Mary. BA W Chester St Coll 1975; MA Luth TS at Gettysburg 2006. D 6/18/2004 Bp Charles Ellsworth Bennison Jr. c 1. debpayson@comcast.net

PAYSON, Evelyn (Mil) 4903 Danforth Dr, Rockford IL 61114 **D S Anskar's Ch Rockford IL 1993-** B Providence RI 4/18/1943 d Herbert Marshall Howe & Evelyn Grace. BA Rad 1963; MLS Simmons Coll 1964. D 6/13/1992 Bp Roger John White. m 6/12/1964 Charles Beck Payson c 3. D S Andr's Ch Madison WI 1992-1993; D S Peters Epis Ch Ft Atkinson WI 1992-1993. epayson@uwc.edu

PEABODY, Morrill Woodrow (RG) Po Box 247, Lemitar NM 87823 **P Epis Ch Of The Epiph Socorro NM 2003-** B Biddeford ME 6/12/1942 s Morrill Woodrow Peabody & Eleanor Eunice. BA U Pac 1965; MDiv CDSP 1969. D 9/13/1969 P 8/8/1970 Bp Victor Manuel Rivera. m 7/30/1980 Ginny Patricia Romero c 3. Gd Samar Epis Ch Sammamish WA 2000-2002; Dio Olympia Seattle WA 1998-1999; Vic S Dav Emm Epis Ch Shoreline WA 1995-1998; Int S Paul's Epis Ch Bremerton WA 1994-1995; Assoc S Thos Ch Medina WA 1992-1994; Asst S Marg's Epis Ch Palm Desert CA 1991-1992; Vic S Matt's Ch San Andreas CA 1989-1991; S Paul In The Desert Palm Sprg CA 1976; S Ptr's Epis Ch Kernville CA 1975-1976; Yth Dir Epis Dio San Joaquin Modesto CA 1973-1974; Epis Dio San Joaquin Modesto CA 1971-1976; R S Phil's Ch Coalinga CA 1971-1973; Cur S Paul's Epis Ch Visalia CA 1970-1971. TWPeabody@yahoo.com

PEABODY, S Walton (Pa) 234 Yahoola Shoals Dr, Dahlonega GA 30533 B Atlanta,GA 1/24/1938 s S Walton Peabody & Louise Dean. BA Emory U 1960; Edinburgh U 1961; MDiv Candler TS Emory U 1963; MA U Denv 1974; U of Maryland 1977; U So 1992. D 6/13/1992 P 12/12/1992 Bp William Arthur Beckham. m 3/19/1963 Jacqueline Anne Lamb. peabs56@windstream.net

PEABODY, William Nelson (Mo) 852 Water Andric Rd, Saint Johnsbury VT 05819 B Boston MA 5/21/1936 s Frank Peabody & Virginia. BA Cor 1959; MDiv VTS 1963; DMin Eden TS 1972. D 6/15/1963 P 12/1/1963 Bp Roger W Blanchard. m 7/2/1960 Elizabeth C Benedict c 3. Assoc R S Paul's Ch Englewood NJ 1965-1968; Asst Ch Of The H Trin Oxford MD 1963-1965. bill.betsy.peabody@gmail.com

PEACOCK, George Hunt (RG) 604 Aredo De Carlos, Farmington NM 87401 **Assoc Rectort Navajoland Area Mssn Farmington NM 1998-; Assoc R S Jn's Ch Farmington NM 1998-** B Farmington NM 1/17/1940 s Wendell Hunt Peacock & Mary. Trin Sem; BA Stan 1963; MD U of New Mex 1968; MA Jn Hopkins U 1974. D 2/21/1998 P 3/17/1999 Bp Terence Kelshaw. m 3/11/1978 Charlotte Gibbs Carmines c 2. hpeacock@advantas.net

PEACOCK, Heber Fletcher (WNC) PO Box 647, Whittier NC 28789 **Died 3/9/2010** B Tucson AZ 2/4/1918 s Heber Fletcher Peacock & Mazie. U of Zurich; BA Hardin-Simmons U 1938; U CA 1939; ThM Sthrn Bapt TS Louisville KY 1944; ThD Sthrn Bapt TS Louisville KY 1949. D 6/26/1976 P 12/10/1976 Bp William Gillette Weinhauer. c 4. Auth, *Bible Translater*, ABS; One of Translators, "The Gd New Bible," *Today's Engl Version*, ABS. SBL, Novi Testamenti Soc. heberpeacock@juno.com

PEACOCK, Joan Louise (Va) 7515 Snowpea Ct Unit M, Alexandria VA 22306 **Assoc All SS Ch Alexandria VA 2008-** B Washington DC 2/28/1955 d Bernard Francis Peacock & Mary Louise. BA Geo Mason U 1994; MDiv VTS 1994. D 6/11/1994 P 12/14/1994 Bp Peter James Lee. m 5/19/1972 William Christopher Clark c 3. Int S Geo's Ch Fredericksburg VA 2003-2005; R Ch Of The H Cross Dunn Loring VA 2001-2003; Assoc S Lk's Ch Alexandria VA 1994-2001. CELTICJLP@YAHOO.COM

PEACOCK, Margaret Ann (NMich) Po Box 66, Saint Ignace MI 49781 B Durham NC 10/20/1953 d William Henry Peacock & Helen Virginia. Roa 1972; Amer Inst for Frgn Study Richmond Surrey GB 1973; BA Untd States Intl U San Diego CA 1975. D 9/12/1992 Bp Thomas Kreider Ray. Auth, "A Poem Called Lost," Forw Mvmt Press, 1999. p_meg@hotmail.com

PEACOCK, Virginia A (NMich) PO Box 165, Stonington ME 04681 **R S Brendan's Epis Ch Stonington ME 2008-; Dio Maine Portland ME 1982-** B Oak Park IL 5/2/1941 d Daura Vance Peacock & Maryella. BSEd U MI 1965; MDiv EDS 1977; MA U of St Mich's Coll, Toronto 1979; PhD U of St Mich's Coll, Toronto 1987. D 6/20/1982 P 11/1/1983 Bp H Coleman McGehee Jr. c 2. R Trin Epis Ch Houghton MI 2005-2008; R S Jn's Ch Negaunee MI 1995-2005; Dio Nthrn Michigan Marquette MI 1995-2000; Gr Ch Ishpeming MI 1995-2000; Dio Michigan Detroit MI 1990-1992; Dio Michigan Detroit MI 1987-1989; Vic Ch Of The Incarn Pittsfield Twp Ann Arbor MI 1986-1987. ginnypeacock@gmail.com

PEAK, Ronald Robert (Kan) 1150 Beach Road, Riviera Beach FL 33404 B Oakland CA 6/9/1944 s John Peak & Marian Virginia. ArmdF; Ft Hays St U; San Diego City Coll; Trident Tech Coll; Dplma Epis TS of The SW 1979. D 9/25/1979 P 4/30/1980 Bp Gerald Nicholas McAllister. m 12/9/2000 Sheila Tice Rader c 3. R Trin Epis Ch El Dorado KS 2004-2009; R All SS Epis Ch Miami OK 2002-2004; P-in-c S Ptr's Epis Ch Key W FL 1999-2002; R Ch Of The Atone Lauderdale Lakes FL 1991-1993; Port Chapl - Port Of Palm Bch Dio SE Florida Miami FL 1988-1991; R S Geo's Epis Ch Riviera Bch FL 1986-1991; R S Mich's Ch Hays KS 1983-1986; Assoc R S Lk's Epis Ch Bartlesville OK 1981-1983; Founding Vic Ch Of The H Cross Owasso OK 1980-1981; Cur S Lk's Ch Tulsa OK 1979-1981; M-in-c S Barn Ch Dillon SC 1978-1979. ron.w5rrp@gmail.com

PEALER, Judson Paul (Me) 2614 Main St, Rangeley ME 04970 **Ch Of The Gd Shpd Rangeley ME 2009-; Dio Maine Portland ME 2009-** B Mount Vernon OH 9/19/1950 s Arlo Paul Pealer & Martha Jean. BFA OH SU 1973; MDiv SWTS 1987. D 6/11/1987 P 12/11/1987 Bp Daniel Lee Swenson. m 6/19/1971 Sandra L Thompson c 3. P-in-c S Paul's Ch Windsor VT 2004-2009; R S Eustace Ch Lake Placid NY 1999-2004; R Emm Ch Keyser WV 1993-1999; R Gr Ch Sheldon VT 1989-1993; R H Trin Epis Ch Swanton VT 1989-1993; R S Jn's Ch Swanton VT 1989-1993; R S Lk's Ch Alburgh VT 1989-1993; Trin Ch Rutland VT 1987-1989. studio32@myfairpoint.net

PEARCE, Clyde Willard (Ala) 1301 Paradise Cove Ln, Wilsonville AL 35186 B Tuscaloosa AL 1/7/1940 s Rachel Dean. D 10/30/2004 Bp Marc Handley Andrus. m 6/17/1960 Eunice Carole Smith c 1.

PEARCE JR, R(obert) Charles (Kan) 1720 Westbank Way, Manhattan KS 66503 **Archd S Paul's Ch Manhattan KS 2000-** B Denver CO 6/11/1946 s Robert Charles Pearce & Mildred Elizabeth. BFA U of Alabama 1971; MA U of Alabama 1975; PhD U of Tennessee 1984. D 2/19/2000 Bp William Edward Smalley. m 12/11/1980 Demerilus Ann DeJarnatt c 2. pearce@flinthills.com

PEARCE, (William) Philip (Daniel) (ECR) 1037 Olympic Ln, Seaside CA 93955 B New Orleans LA 5/28/1926 s William Stanley Howe Pearce & Henrietta Tupper. BA Stan 1948; Ripon Coll Cuddesdon 1957; Cert U Of Leeds Gb 1964; MA U Of Leeds Gb 1975. Trans from Church Of England 7/1/1989 Bp Charles Shannon Mallory. S Mths Ch Seaside CA 1994-1995; Dio El Camino Real Monterey CA 1990-1993; York Sch Monterey CA 1989-1992; Asst S Matt's Epis Ch San Mateo CA 1957-1958. Auth, "Generation Gap," *Mambo Press*, 1983. danielp@mbay.net

PEARSALL, Arlene Epp (SD) 909 E 14th St Apt 305, Sioux Falls SD 57104 **D Calv Cathd Sioux Falls SD 2000-** B York NE 7/26/1943 d Jacob Epp & Emma. BA Bethel Coll 1965; MA Stan 1969; PhD U IL 1991; MS U IL 1995. D 6/12/2000 Bp Creighton Leland Robertson. m 12/10/1980 Robert Pearsall. Auth, *Johannes Pauli (1450-1520) on the Ch & Cler*, Edwin Mellen Press, 1994; Auth, "Johannes Pauli and the Papal Indulgences," *Reform and Counter-reform: Dialectics of the Word in the Wstrn Chrsnty since Luther*, 1994; Auth, "Murders in Saxony: Dateline1500," *Clues: A Journ of Detection 14*, 1993. Ch & Synagogue Libr Assn 1996; Natl Ch Libr Assn 1996; NAAD 1999.

PEARSALL, Martin A (Colo) 4939 Harvest Rd, Colorado Springs CO 80917 **Assoc Gr And S Steph's Epis Ch Colorado Sprg CO 2009-** B Norwalk CT 3/4/1946 s Raymond Smith Pearsall & Elizabeth Thornton. Epis TS of The SW; BA Alleg 1967; MA U Denv 1970. D 11/10/1983 P 5/16/1984 Bp William Harvey Wolfrum. m 6/19/1976 Mary Sukys c 2. S Fran Of Assisi Colorado Sprg CO 1986-2007; Vic H Cross Epis Mssn Sterling CO 1984-1986. MANDMPAR@AOL.COM

PEARSON, Albert Claybourn (Cal) 261 Fell St, San Francisco CA 94102 **Ch Of The H Innoc San Francisco CA 2011-; P-in-c The Epis Ch Of S Jn The Evang San Francisco CA 2011-** B Lubbock TX 3/1/1978 s Anthony Claybourn Pearson & Tomijann Christina. BA New Coll 2004; MDiv CDSP 2007. D 6/13/2008 P 12/6/2008 Bp Marc Handley Andrus. m 4/8/2009 Rahel R Pearson. Dio California San Francisco CA 2008-2010. bertie@holyinsf.org

PEARSON II, Alonzo Lawrence (FdL) 205 Columbus Dr, Marshfield WI 54449 B Columbus OH 12/23/1949 s Alonzo Lawrence Pearson & Barbara. BA OH SU 1973; MDiv TESM 1979. D 6/20/1981 P 5/19/1982 Bp A Donald Davies. m 6/10/1972 Kathy Shay. S Alb's Epis Ch Marshfield WI 1997-2003; Assoc S Thos Ch Menasha WI 1988-1997; Asst Ch Of The Annunc Lewisville TX 1983-1988; Cur S Andr's Ft Worth TX 1981-1983. pearson@tznet.com

PEARSON JR, Andrew Christian (SC) Cathedral Church of the Advent, 2017 Sixth Avenue North, Birmingham AL 35203 **Cn for Theol and Evang The Cathd Ch Of The Adv Birmingham AL 2011-** B Washington DC 1/10/1980 s Andrew Christian Pearson & Denise Anne. BA U of Virginia 2002; BTh Oxf 2007. D 4/14/2007 P 10/13/2007 Bp Edward Lloyd Salmon Jr. m 6/24/2006 Lauren Woods Lauren Woods Saddler. Dioc Coun Dio So Carolina Charleston SC 2008-2011; Assoc R Par Ch of St. Helena Beaufort SC 2007-2011. andrew@cathedraladvent.com

PEARSON, Anna S (NY) 78 Main St, Hastings On Hudson NY 10706 **Gr Ch Hastings On Hudson NY 2000-** B Bethesda MD 9/14/1963 d John Godfrey Keller & Hester. BA Barnard Coll of Col 1985; MDiv Ya Berk 1992; D Min Hartford Sem 2007. D 5/30/1992 P 2/15/1993 Bp David Elliot Johnson. m 5/9/1992 Charles Woods Pearson c 3. Asst S Jn's Ch W Hartford CT 2000-2008; Chapl Kent Sch Kent CT 1992-2000. annaspearson@yahoo.com

PEARSON, Bill (Alb) 27 Trottingham Road, Saratoga Springs NY 12866 **D Chr Epis Ch Ballston Spa NY 2003-** B Columbus NE 10/17/1950 s William Robert Pearson & Geraldine. D 1/11/2003 Bp Daniel William Herzog. m 5/26/1974 Elaine Lorraine Salegna c 2. wpearson@nycap.rr.com

PEARSON, Cedric Eugene (O) 14778 Dexter Falls Rd, Perrysburg OH 43551 **P-in-c Gr Ch Defiance OH 2009-** B Fairfield AL 12/6/1945 s Junior Arthur Pearson & Flora Barbara. BA w hon U of Virginia 1967; U MI 1968; MA Chicago TS 1973; Cert of Spec Stds SWTS 1973; Cert of Advncd Pstr Ldrshp Trin Sch For Mnstry 2011. D 5/12/1973 Bp Quintin Ebenezer Primo Jr P 12/8/1973 Bp James Winchester Montgomery. m 4/22/1967 Judy Osborn c 2. Int S Andr's Epis Ch Toledo OH 2007-2009; R S Tim's Epis Ch Perrysburg OH 1982-2004; R Gr Ch Defiance OH 1975-1982; Cur S Mk's Ch Evanston IL 1973-1975. Phi Beta Kappa U of Virginia Chapt of PBK 1967; Woodrow Wilson Natl Fllshp WW Natl Fllshp Fndt 1967. cepjop422@earthlink.net

PEARSON, Daniel V (Minn) 1970 Nature View Lane, W. St. Paul MN 55118 **Int S Ptr's Epis Ch St Louis MO 2011-** B Minneapolis MN 9/12/1941 s Claude Sigried Pearson & Florence Mertens. BA U MN 1964; STB GTS 1968. D 6/24/1968 Bp Hamilton Hyde Kellogg P 3/17/1969 Bp Philip Frederick McNairy. c 2. Int S Mart's By The Lake Epis Minnetonka Bch MN 2009-2011; Int The Epis Par Of S Dav Minnetonka MN 2007-2009; Int S Steph The Mtyr Ch Minneapolis MN 2005-2007; R S Clem's Ch S Paul MN 1983-2005; R Par Of The H Trin And S Anskar Minneapolis MN 1982-1983; Chapl U Epis Cntr Minneapolis MN 1981-1983; R Trin Ch Excelsior MN 1976-1981; Cn Theol Cathd Ch Of S Mk Minneapolis MN 1972-1976; R S Paul's Epis Ch Owatonna MN 1968-1969. dpearson@stpetersepiscopal.org

PEARSON, Francis John Peter (Pa) 10 Chapel Rd, New Hope PA 18938 **P-in-c S Phil's Ch New Hope PA 2005-** B Williamsport PA 6/28/1957 s William Pearson & Sarah. Liturg Stds Geo; MDiv St. Jn's TS; MDiv St. Vinc Sem; BS U Of Scranton. Rec from Roman Catholic 7/10/2004 Bp Paul Victor Marshall. pearson@nb.net

PEARSON, James Thomas (SD) 513 Douglas Ave, Yankton SD 57078 **R Chr Epis Ch Yankton SD 2000-** B Sisseton SD 10/12/1954 s Julian Horatio Pearson & Charlotte Maxine. U So; BS So Dakota St U 1980; MDiv VTS 1988. D 6/28/1988 P 3/1/1989 Bp Craig Barry Anderson. m 8/25/1973 Gloria Jane Bladow c 3. Dio So Dakota Sioux Falls SD 1988-2000; D Chr Ch Chamberlain SD 1988-1989; D H Comf Ch Lower Brule SD 1988-1989. Bro Chr Unity. fatherjim@iw.net

PEARSON, Janice Von (Colo) 9706 Quay Loop, Broomfield CO 80021 **Our Merc Sav Epis Ch Denver CO 2006-** B 8/11/1947 D 11/13/2004 Bp Robert John O'Neill. m 8/21/1976 Alexander Pearson c 2. janvcp@aol.com

PEARSON, John Norris (Oly) 2831 Marietta St, Steilacoom WA 98388 B Everett WA 3/28/1924 s John Norris Pearson & Margaret May. BD WA SU 1949; Olympia TS 1968. D 10/5/1968 Bp Ivol I Curtis P 2/1/1979 Bp Robert Hume

Cochrane. m 8/26/1949 Carol Deane Abernethy. Int S Jn's Ch Chehalis WA 1986-1988; Inst Chapl Dio Olympia Seattle WA 1978-1980. Curs; Kairos.

PEARSON, Joseph Herbert (At) 1280 Berkeley Rd, Avondale Estates GA 30002 **D H Trin Par Decatur GA 2009-** B N. Charlerol PA 9/18/1937 s Joseph Pearson & Mary. BS Kansas .Univesity Lawr KS 1961. D 8/6/2006 Bp J(ohn) Neil Alexander. c 2. jhpatl@earthlilnk.net

PEARSON, Kevin David (Oly) 16617 Marine View Dr SW, Burien WA 98166 **R S Lk's Epis Ch Renton WA 2004-** B Bellingham WA 11/21/1961 s Richard Duane Pearson & Carol Ann. BA Seattle Pacific U 1984; MDiv GTS 1991. D 6/15/1991 Bp Frank Tracy Griswold III P 2/13/1992 Bp Vincent Waydell Warner. m 2/10/2010 Thomas Kenison. R The Epis Ch Of S Jn The Evang San Francisco CA 2001-2003; Cathd Of S Jas Chicago IL 2000-2001; Assoc S Lk's Ch Evanston IL 1996-1999; Int S Columba's Epis Ch And Chilren's Sch Kent WA 1994-1995; Int S Paul's Ch Seattle WA 1993-1994; Cur Ch Of The Ascen Seattle WA 1991-1993. kevindavidpearson@yahoo.com

PEARSON, Lennart (USC) 402 Chestnut St, Clinton SC 29325 B New York NY 1/29/1935 s Gunnar Pearson & Linea. BA Wheaton Coll 1955; U of Edinburgh GB 1957; BD UTS Richmond VA 1959; ThM UTS Richmond VA 1965; MLS U NC 1967; DMin UTS Richmond VA 1974. D 12/5/1989 P 5/1/1990 Bp William Arthur Beckham. m 8/4/1956 Carol Elizabeth Landon c 4. P-in-c Ch Of The Nativ Un SC 1991-2001; Prof Presb Coll Clinton SC 1990-1997; Int All SS Epis Ch Clinton SC 1990-1991. Bk, "Calligraphy and Poetry," Amazon, 2011; Bk, "The Prism of Metaphor," Amazon, 2011; Bk, "Food for the Journey," Amazon, 2011; Bk, "No Abiding City (2v.)," Amazon, 2011; Bk, "Bits and Pieces," Amazon, 2011; Bk, "Ch of the Nativ," Amazon, 2011; Bk, "Hemresan (Swedish)," Amazon, 2011; Bk, "Three Transatlantic Adventures," Amazon, 2011; Article, "The True Voice of Orthodoxy," *Crosswalk*; Article, "Lutherans in New Iceland," *Luth Quarterly*; Article, "The Ch of the Nativ and the Frank Wills Connection," *So Carolina Hist mag*; Article, "When Fredrika Bremer Came to Charleston," *Swedish-Amer Hist Quarterly*; Article, "Salve Regina and Salve Redemptor," *The Hymn*. Ecum Soc Blessed Vrgn Mary 1981; OHC 1985. Outstanding Libr Awd So Carolina Libr Assn 1997; Chr Action in Serv Awd So Carolina Chr Action Coun 1996; Lennart Pearson Sacr Choral Mus Endwmt Presb Coll (Clinton, SC) 1991. lpearson@presby.edu

PEARSON, Michael A (Pa) 104 Louella Ave, Wayne PA 19087 **R S Mary's Ch Wayne PA 2001-** B Detroit MI 7/27/1950 s Archibald Pearson & Mable Marie. BA Duke 1972; MDiv PrTS 1975; GTS 1977. D 9/14/1977 P 4/7/1978 Bp William Gillette Weinhauer. m 9/13/1986 Julia Matteus Blackwood c 1. R S Lk's Ch Anchorage KY 1992-2001; S Mk's Ch New Canaan CT 1989-1992; R Ch Of The Epiph Providence RI 1981-1989; Dio Rhode Island Providence RI 1978-1989; S Steph's Ch Providence RI 1977-1981. surfnclyde@aol.com

PEARSON, Patricia Ann Waychus (Cal) PO Box 2088, Walnut Creek CA 94595 **Gift Plnng Com Mem Dio California San Francisco CA 2011-; D S Lk's Ch Walnut Creek CA 2011-** B Kansas City MO 11/12/1956 d Felix John Waychus & Harriet Elizabeth. BA U of San Francisco 1978; Paralegal Cert S Mary's Coll 2002; BDS Epis Sch for Deacons 2010. D 6/4/2011 Bp Marc Handley Andrus. m 6/20/2008 Sharyn Leslie Mitzo. Assn for Epis Deacons 2007. rev.dcn.patricia@gmail.com

PEASE JR, Edwin C (Mass) 2 Kennedy Ln, Walpole MA 02081 B Philadelphia PA 8/18/1938 s Edwin C Pease & Rebecca Elizabeth. BA U of Manitoba 1963; MDiv EDS 1979; Ldrshp Acad for New Directions 1984; DMin EDS 1992. D 6/2/1979 Bp Paul Moore Jr P 2/1/1980 Bp Roger W Blanchard. m 10/6/1984 Linda J Clark. Dio Wstrn Massachusetts Springfield MA 1997-2004; Vic S Andr's Ch No Grafton MA 1997-2004; R Epis Ch Of S Thos Taunton MA 1996-1997; Int Chr Ch New Haven CT 1995-1996; Dep For Cong & Cler Dvlpmt Dio SW Virginia Roanoke VA 1992-1995; R Chr Ch Medway MA 1981-1992; Cur S Anne's Ch Lowell MA 1979-1981. Acad Of Homil; Cert Int Pstr, Int Mnstry Ntwk. clarkpease2@cs.com

PEAY, Steven Allen (Alb) 2777 Mission Rd, Nashotah WI 53058 **Assoc Prof of Ch Hist Nash Nashotah WI 2010-** B Indianapolis IN 6/8/1954 s Willard Raymond Peay & Doris Juanita Furnish. BA Greenville Coll 1977; MA St Vinc Sem 1981; MA U Pgh 1983; MDiv St Vinc Sem 1984; PhD St Louis U 1990. Rec from Roman Catholic 8/12/2010 Bp William Howard Love. m 7/5/1996 Julie Ann Strandt c 2. speay@nashotah.edu

PECARO, Bernard Joel (SeFla) 140 Se 28th Ave, Pompano Beach FL 33062 **S Mart's Epis Ch Pompano Bch FL 1998-** B Fort Lauderdale FL 7/27/1955 s John Frank Pecaro & Josephine Margaret. BS Nova U 1980; MDiv Nash 1984. D 6/11/1984 P 6/11/1985 Bp Calvin Onderdonk Schofield Jr. m 9/18/1993 Sylvia Pecaro c 2. Cur S Paul's Ch Delray Bch FL 1990-1998; Cur S Mary's Epis Ch Stuart FL 1984-1990. SHN 1984. fpecaro@stmartinchurch.com

PECH, Meredith Ayer (Ore) 371 Idaho St, Ashland OR 97520 **D Trin Epis Ch Ashland Ashland OR 1996-** B San Jose CA 5/25/1947 d Cecil Ayer & Jean Meredith. BA U CA 1969; Cert U of Oregon 1972; Cntr for the Diac, Dio Oregon 1996. D 11/30/1996 Bp Robert Louis Ladehoff. m 8/20/1973 Robert Steven Pech c 3. Ashland Educ Assn 1981-2006; NEA 1972-2006; Oregon Educ Assn 1972-2006. Favorite Elem Tchr, Ashland, Oregon Sneak Preview 1996. meredith@mind.net

PECK, David W (CPa) 119 N Duke St, Lancaster PA 17602 **S Jas Ch Lancaster PA 2008-** B Evansville IN 3/12/1966 s David Peck & MacGregor. BA Amer U 1988; MA Camb 1994; CTM Westcott Hse 1995. Trans from Church Of England 8/19/2008 Bp Nathan Dwight Baxter. m 5/30/1992 Cordelia A Moyse c 1. rector@stjameslanpa.org

PECK SR, Donald Morrow (Ore) 304 Spyglass Dr, Eugene OR 97401 **D S Matt's Epis Ch Eugene OR 1996-** B Portland OR 10/17/1936 s Edward Wade Peck & Hazel. U of Oregon. D 3/16/1996 Bp Robert Louis Ladehoff. m 11/23/1957 Beverly Jane Hall c 3. NAAD.

PECK JR, Edward Jefferson (CPa) 7041 Fairway Oaks, Fayetteville PA 17222 B Cincinnati OH 2/22/1943 s Edward Jefferson Peck & Emmadora. BA Juniata Coll 1970; MDiv PDS 1973. D 6/8/1973 P 3/25/1974 Bp Dean T Stevenson. m 4/11/2010 Sandra Steinmetz c 2. R S Andr's Epis Ch Shippensburg PA 1999-2004; R S Paul's Epis Ch Bound Brook NJ 1994-1999; R Gr Ch Merchantville NJ 1984-1994; COM Dio Cntrl Pennsylvania Harrisburg PA 1983-1984; R S Andr's Epis Ch York PA 1978-1984; Chair Dio CPa Dept Yth Mnstrs Dio Cntrl Pennsylvania Harrisburg PA 1977-1979; R S Mary's Epis Ch Waynesboro PA 1975-1978; Cur S Jn's Epis Ch Lancaster PA 1973-1975. ejpj43@comcast.net

PECK, Felicity Lenton Clark (ETenn) 3333 Love Cir, Nashville TN 37212 **D Chr Ch - Epis Chattanooga TN 2002-; D S Raphael's Epis Ch Crossville TN 2001-** B Falmouth UK 6/4/1942 d Edward William Lenton Clark & Bettina Forbeck. Cert Croydon Tech Coll Surrey Gb. D 6/16/2001 Bp Charles Glenn VonRosenberg. m 2/21/1965 Herbert Jefferson Peck c 1. fcpeck@comcast.net

PECK, Frederick (Ore) 18205 SE 42nd St, Vancouver WA 98683 B Waverly NY 4/11/1941 s Walter Sylvester Peck & Marjorie. BA Duke 1963; MDiv VTS 1966; PhD Cor 1974. D 6/25/1966 P 12/27/1966 Bp Edward Hamilton West. m 6/23/1985 Kim Huynh. pecksmessage@gmail.com

PECK JR, Jordan Brown (Haw) 1254 Cordova Blvd Ne, Saint Petersburg FL 33704 B Miami FL 11/8/1929 s Jordan Brown Peck & Virginia Freeman. BA Van 1951; JD U Of Florida 1956; MDiv VTS 1963. D 7/10/1963 P 2/1/1964 Bp Thomas H Wright. m 6/15/1951 Maryly VanLeer c 4. Dio Micronesia Tumon Bay GU GU 1978-1987; Exec Coun Appointees New York NY 1966-1987; Vic S Paul's In The Pines Epis Ch Fayetteville NC 1964-1966; Asst S Jn's Epis Ch Fayetteville NC 1963-1964.

PECKHAM, Ashley Hall (RI) 31 W Main Rd, Portsmouth RI 02871 B Fall River MA 9/10/1940 s Richard Adelburt Peckham & Marjorie Amy. BA Barrington Coll 1966; Merc TS 1971. D 6/27/1970 Bp John S Higgins P 10/1/1971 Bp Frederick Hesley Belden. m 7/18/1964 Gudrun Elinor Peckham c 2. New Engl Seafarers Mssn Boston MA 1998-2006; The Ch Of The H Cross Middletown RI 1993-1998; R S Barn Ch Warwick RI 1988-1991; Dio Rhode Island Providence RI 1975-1978; Cur Emm Ch Newport RI 1971-1974; Cur S Bon Epis Ch Lindenhurst NY 1970-1971. gestemor31@aol.com

PECKHAM, Laura Lee (Me) 597 Indiana Rd, West Gardiner ME 04345 **S Andr's Ch Newcastle ME 2011-** B Chelsea ME 12/19/1967 d Robert Scottie Burns & Leonetta Faye. BA U of Maine 1990; MDiv Bangor TS 2008. D 6/25/2011 Bp Stephen Taylor Lane. m 12/5/1992 Keith Peckham c 2. lkhkv@yahoo.com

PEDERSEN, John Charles (Kan) 9408 San Rafael Ave Ne, Albuquerque NM 87109 B Omaha NE 7/28/1927 s Henry Fredrick Pedersen & Jessie. BA U of Nebraska 1949; MDiv SWTS 1952. D 3/17/1952 P 11/3/1952 Bp Howard R Brinker. m 2/8/1954 Sharon Fritzler c 2. R Chr Ch Overland Pk KS 1982-1990; R S Matt's Epis Ch Newton KS 1978-1982; Chapl Epis Ch Of S Geo Canyon TX 1965-1970; Cur S Andr's Epis Ch Amarillo TX 1962-1965; Vic Gr Ch Vernon TX 1957-1962; Vic Trin Ch Quanah TX 1957-1962; Vic S Paul's Ch Ogallala NE 1952-1955. FRITZPED@MSN.COM

PEDERSEN, Kenneth Mark (Ia) 928 Seeland Dr, Grinnell IA 50112 **D S Paul's Epis Ch Grinnell IA 2005-** B Grinnell IA 2/6/1928 s Edwin Bernard Pedersen & Hattie Mae. BA Gri 1952. D 12/26/1987 Bp Frank Tracy Griswold III. m 5/30/1955 Mary Virginia Graham c 2. D Trin Epis Ch Wheaton IL 1987-2004. mmpedersen@minspring.com

PEDRICK, Jennifer L (RI) 1336 Pawtucket Ave, Rumford RI 02916 **Mem of Stndg Com Dio Rhode Island Providence RI 2009-; Dep to GC Dio Rhode Island Providence RI 2008-; R Ch of the Epiph Rumford RI 2002-; R St Mich & Gr Ch Rumford RI 2002-** B Philadelphia PA 7/14/1966 d Daniel Webster Pedrick & Judith Lee. BA Sweet Briar Coll 1988; MDiv Harvard DS 1998. D 6/13/1998 P 1/24/1999 Bp Geralyn Wolf. m 8/20/1994 Michael John DeAngelo c 2. Dn, E Bay Dnry Dio Rhode Island Providence RI 2005-2010; Mem of COM Dio Rhode Island Providence RI 2003-2009; Mem of Dioc Coun Dio Rhode Island Providence RI 1999-2000; Asst to R S Mary's Ch Portsmouth RI 1998-2002. Phi Beta Kappa Sweet Briar Coll 1988. jennifer@epiphanyep.org

PEEK, Charles Arthur (Neb) St. Stephen's Episcopal Church, 410 W. 2nd St. Suite 10, Grand Island NE 68801 **R S Steph's Ch Grand Island NE 2008-** B

Greeley CO 10/8/1942 s George Hooper Peek & Dorothy Lucille. BA UNL 1964; MA UNL 1966; PhD UNL 1971. D 12/20/1970 P 6/29/1971 Bp Russell T Rauscher. m 6/19/1965 Nancy Resler c 2. S Steph's Ch Grand Island NE 1995-2007; Dio Nebraska Omaha NE 1990-1991; Supply P Chr Ch Cntrl City NE 1989-1994; P-in-c Calv Ch Hyannis NE 1987-1989; P-in-c S Jos's Ch Mullen NE 1987-1989; Reg Coordntr - Evang Prv. VIII S Lk's Ch Kearney NE 1983-1986; Cur Ch Of The Epiph Flagstaff AZ 1972-1977; Vic S Jn's Ch Williams AZ 1972-1977. Auth, "Critical Comp to Wm Faulkner," Greenwood, 2002; Auth, "A Wm Faulkner Encyclopedia," Greenwood, 1999. Fulbright Sr Lectr Fulbright Assn 2005; Distinguished Fac Awd Leland Holdt/Security Mutual 2005; Excellence in Tchg Awd Pratt-Heins Fndtn./U. of Nebraska 2002. twinpeeks@charter.net

PEEK, Guy Richardson (WNY) 217 E Delavan Ave Apt 315, Buffalo NY 14208 B Helena MT 1/2/1941 s Tate Wilbur Peek & Imogene Boyce. BA U of Montana 1964; MDiv Ya Berk 1967. D 6/18/1967 P 12/1/1967 Bp Chandler W Sterling. c 2. R S Ptr's Ch Niagara Falls NY 1992-2001; R St Johns Epis Youngstown NY 1978-1992; R Chr Ch Deposit NY 1969-1978; Cur Ch Of The Incarn Great Falls MT 1967-1969; Cur S Mk's Ch Havre MT 1967-1969. frpeek@adelpkia.net

PEEL, Richard Charles (Mont) No address on file. B Harrisburg PA 9/7/1940 s Charles Ralph Peel & Helen Marie. BA Buc 1962; MDiv PDS 1965; MLS U Of British Columbia Vancouver Bc CA 1971. D 6/26/1965 P 1/1/1966 Bp Joseph Thomas Heistand. Assoc S Ptr's Par Helena MT 1995-2004; Assoc Ch Of The Epiph Tempe AZ 1977-1995; Cur S Ptr's Par Helena MT 1967-1969; Cur The Epis Ch Of S Jn The Bapt York PA 1965-1967. Fran Jos Campbell Citation Amer Libr Assn 1994; Libr Of The Year Outreach Serv 1989; Outstanding Serv To The Blind Laura Bridgeman Awd 1975.

PEELER, Lance Vernon (Ore) 333 NW 35th St, Corvallis OR 97330 **Gd Samar Med Cntr Corvallis OR 2010-; Samar Hlth Serv Corvallis OR 2010-; Asst The Epis Ch Of The Gd Samar Corvallis OR 2008-** B Roseburg OR 8/8/1969 s Vernon Delbert Peeler & Patsy Ann. BS Willamette U 1991; MDiv Epis TS of the SW 2008. D 6/25/2008 P 4/4/2009 Bp Sanford Zangwill Kaye Hampton. m 8/5/2000 Stacie Dyan-Jackson Peeler c 2. revlance@peak.org

PEEPLES, David H (Ala) 1268 Gregory Ave, Montgomery AL 36111 **R Gr Epis Ch Mt Meigs AL 2005-** B Indianapolis IN 2/28/1961 s John Dorsey Peeples & Sarah June. BS Trin U San Antonio TX 1983; MDiv STUSo 2000. D 6/4/2000 P 12/12/2000 Bp Henry Nutt Parsley Jr. m 8/10/1996 Margaret F Freeman c 3. Cur S Jn's Ch Montgomery AL 2000-2005. dhpeeples@gmail.com

PEERMAN III, C(harles) Gordon (Tenn) 4416 Harding Pl, Nashville TN 37205 **Assoc S Aug's Chap Nashville TN 2005-** B Nashville TN 4/24/1951 s Charles Gordon Peerman & Mary Alice. BA U of Virginia 1973; MDiv Yale DS 1976; DMin Van 1990. D 11/7/1976 P 6/1/1977 Bp Robert Bruce Hall. m 6/19/1998 Kathleen Elizabeth Woods c 1. Asst R for Pstr Counslg Chr Ch Cathd Nashville TN 1985-1995; Asst S Steph's Ch Richmond VA 1976-1982. "Blessed Relief: What Christians Can Learn from Buddhists About Suffering," *Skylight Paths*, 2008; Auth, "Gordon Peerman," *Weavings*. gpeerman@nsh1sth1.stthomas.org

PEET, Donald Howard (Ct) PO Box 681, Sandisfield MA 01255 B Waterbury CT 1/12/1932 s Howard Andrew Peet & Hazel Martha. BA U of Connecticut 1953; BD VTS 1958. D 6/11/1958 P 3/1/1959 Bp Walter H Gray. m 6/6/1953 Charlene N Foster c 3. R S Jn's Ch E Windsor CT 1979-1996; S Andr's Ch Milford CT 1964-1979; Vic S Paul's Ch Plainfield CT 1958-1964. dandcpeet@gmail.com

PEETE, Brandon Ben (At) 3404 Keaton AVe, Tyler TX 75701 **All SS Epis Sch Tyler TX 2011-; Cathd Of S Phil Atlanta GA 2002-** B Huntsville AL 9/8/1978 s Ben B Peete & Gail Young. BS U of Alabama 2002; MDiv Candler TS 2010. D 4/30/2011 Bp Keith Bernard Whitmore. m 10/31/2009 Hillary S Hillary Olga Stewart. Ch Of The Gd Shpd Dallas TX 2002-2004. bbpeete1@gmail.com

PEETE, Nan Olive Arrington (WA) 3001 Veazey Ter Nw Apt 1208, Washington DC 20008 **Mem of the Bd The GTS New York NY 2008-** B Chicago IL 8/19/1938 d Maurice Daniel Arrington & Phoebe Nan. BA Occ 1975; MA U of Redlands 1978; MDiv GTS 1984; DD SWTS 1990. D 6/16/1984 P 2/2/1985 Bp Robert C Rusack. c 2. Cn For Deploy And Ord Dio Washington Washington DC 2003-2005; Cn Min Dio Sthrn Ohio Cincinnati OH 1999-2003; Assoc P Par of Trin Ch New York NY 1994-1999; Mem of the Bd The GTS New York NY 1989-1999; Cn to the Ordnry Dio Atlanta Atlanta GA 1989-1994; Urban & Soc Mnstrs Cmsn Dio Indianapolis Indianapolis IN 1986-1988; R All SS Ch Indianapolis IN 1985-1988; Cur S Mk's Epis Ch Upland CA 1984-1985. Auth, "Wit"; Auth, "Shaping Our Future"; Auth, "Angl Theol Revs". Bd Dir EWC 1998-2002; UBE 1982. npeete@comcast.net

PEETS, Patricia Ann Dunne (Mo) 429 Martindale Dr, Albany GA 31721 **D S Patricks Ch Albany GA 1996-** B Norman OK 9/20/1952 d Richard Michael Dunne & Shirley Faye. BA U of Missouri 1974. D 2/18/1996 Bp Alfred Clark Marble Jr. m 8/25/1973 Roy Ashby Peets. ppeets@surfsouth.com

PELKEY, Richard Elwood (Fla) 7860 SW 86th Way, Gainesville FL 32608 **R S Jos's Ch Newberry FL 2011-** B Garden Grove CA 5/23/1974 s Glenn Earl Pelkey & Christine L. BM U of Nevada Las Vegas 1996; MDiv Epis TS of the SW 2008. D 6/14/2008 Bp Barry Leigh Beisner P 12/14/2008 Bp C(harles) Andrew Doyle. m 10/23/1999 Helen K F Fowler c 3. Assoc Trin Epis Ch Marble Falls TX 2008-2010. rev.richard.pelkey@gmail.com

PELKEY, Wayne Lloyd (Ia) 13218 State Road #17, West Plains MO 65775 **Supply P Dio W Missouri Kansas City MO 2008-** B Canton NY 2/18/1946 s Lloyd Lyndon Pelkey & Thelma Mary. BA Cntrl Missouri St U 1968; MDiv SWTS 1971; EMT SUNY 1973. D 6/6/1971 P 12/1/1971 Bp Allen Webster Brown. Supply P Dio Arkansas Little Rock AR 2006-2007; Supply P Dio Iowa Des Moines IA 1977-2006; Clncl Psych Dio Iowa Des Moines IA 1976-1983; Dio W Missouri Kansas City MO 1974-1976; P S Oswald In The Field Skidmore MO 1974-1976; P S Paul's Ch Maryville MO 1974-1976; P Ch Of The Nativ Star Lake NY 1971-1974. Auth, "Dare We Say God"; Auth, "Curric Dvlpmt Of Sxlty Of The Mentally Retardeddare We Say God"; Auth, "Residential Needs Survey". Masters Thesis Seabury Wstrn TS 1971. wpelkey@yahoo.com

PELLA, Diane Maria (Az) Po Box 753, Hartsdale NY 10530 B New York NY 10/16/1952 d Anthony A Pella & Dora C. BA NYU 1974; MBA Iona Coll 1977; MDiv Ya Berk 1989. D 10/6/1991 Bp Joseph Thomas Heistand P 4/1/1992 Bp Walter Decoster Dennis Jr. Supply P Dio Arizona Phoenix AZ 1993-1996; Assoc S Andr's Epis Ch Tucson AZ 1992-1993; Assoc S Andr's Epis Ch Hartsdale NY 1991-1992.

PELLATON, Thomas Jean-Pierre (LI) 98 Plymouth Rd, Rockville Centre NY 11570 B New York NY 6/8/1944 s Pierre Jean-Jacques Pellaton & Anne Marie. BA/BMUS Ob 1967; MFA Carnegie Mellon U 1969; MDiv Ya Berk 1991. D 6/8/1991 P 12/1/1991 Bp Richard Frank Grein. R The Ch Of The Ascen Rockville Cntr NY 2008-2010; Ch of the Ascen Munich 81545 DE 1997-2008; S Mich's Ch New York NY 1991-1997. Auth, "Dear Amer: Letters From Viet-Nam"; Auth, "Sciences Emmy For Writing Documentary Dear Amer 91". revtjpp@yahoo.com

PELLEGRINI, Lucy Carr (Vt) 48 East St, Bristol VT 05443 **Deacons' Coun Dio Vermont Burlington VT 2009-; D S Steph's Ch Middlebury VT 2009-** B Dayton OH 9/6/1950 d Charles S Bergen & Sylvia Anne. BS Skidmore Coll 1972. D 6/5/2004 Bp Thomas C Ely. c 3. D S Paul's Epis Ch On The Green Vergennes VT 2004-2009. lcbpellegrini48@gmail.com

PELLETIER, Ann Dietrich (RI) 669 W Main Rd, Portsmouth RI 02871 **D Ch Of The Ascen Cranston RI 2010-** B Chicago IL 12/11/1931 d Harold Eugene Dietrich & Jane. BA W&M 1954; MA Mid 1960; Rhode Island Sch For Deacons 1988. D 6/23/1990 Bp George Nelson Hunt III. D S Ptr's And S Andr's Epis Providence RI 1997-2006; D S Matt's Ch Barrington RI 1992-1997; D S Geo And San Jorge Cntrl Falls RI 1989-1992. NAAD; Ord Of S Helena. Lind Botetort Medal Coll Of Wm & Mary Williamsburg Virginia 1954; Phi Beta Kappa Coll Of Wm & Mary Williamsburg Virginia 1953.

PELNAR, William Donald (Mil) 2544 Tilden Ave, Delavan WI 53115 B Berwyn IL 11/25/1950 D 1/13/2001 Bp Roger John White. m 5/15/1976 Michelle Ann Gifford c 3. pelnar@pensys.com

PEMBERTON, Barbara Louise (CFla) 668 Whispering Pines Ct, Inverness FL 34453 **D S Marg's Ch Inverness FL 2002-** B Miami FL 7/9/1952 d William Walker Radebaugh & Helen Louise. AS Hillsborough Cmnty Coll Tampa FL 1989. D 12/14/2002 Bp John Wadsworth Howe. m 6/6/1979 Kirby Pemberton. stmaggies@embarqmail.com

PENA-REGALADO JR, Jose Francisco (Hond) Col Victoria, Bloque J-3, Choloma Cortes Honduras **Dio Honduras Miami FL 1995-; Vic Iglesia Epis San Jose De La Montana San Pedro Sula HN 1993-; Vic Iglesia Epis Santa Rosa Cisneros Villanueva Cortes 1993-; Vic Iglesia Epis de la Epifania San Pedro Sula HN 1993-** B La Labor Ocotepeque HN 1/25/1957 s Ignacio Pena Pinto & Maria Refugio. Centro U Reg Del No; Sem Mayor Nuestro Senora De Suyapa. Rec from Roman Catholic 2/1/1995 as Priest Bp Leopold Frade. m 7/23/1993 Carmen Patricia Melgar Martinez c 2.

PENA TAVAREZ, Vicente A (DR) Iglesia Episcopal Todos Los Santos, Calle Dr. Ferry Esq Eugenio Miranda, La Romna Dominical Republic Dominican Republic **Dio The Dominican Republic (Iglesia Epis Dominicana) Santo Domingo DO 2008-** B Dominican Republic 7/19/1964 s Valentin Pena & Rosa Julia. Licenciado en Teologia Centro De Estudio Teologico Int. Latino Amer y El Caribe; Dplma En Relaciones Humana Ins. Polotechnico J.P.D.; BA Miami Tech Coll; 2 yrs Law Sch Univesida (UAPA). D 2/4/2007 P 2/10/2008 Bp Julio Holguin. m 7/10/1993 Nancy Miossotte Fondeur Cabrera. vvpenna@hotmail.com

PENCE, George E. (Spr) 8103 Donna Lane, Edwardsville IL 62025 **Int R S Jn's Epis Ch Kewanee IL 2009-; Asst S Andr's Epis Ch Edwardsville IL 2001-** B Milwaukee WI 9/24/1939 s Ivan E Pence & Virginia H. BA McKendree U 1961; MA U IL 1962; SMU 1963; PhD S Louis U 1971; MTS SWTS 1979. D 6/15/1975 P 6/29/1979 Bp William Hopkins Folwell. m 12/29/1962 Ione Kolm. Dioc Admin Dio Quincy Peoria IL 1996-2003; R S Jn's Epis Ch Kewanee IL 1993-2001; Vic Ch of the Trsfg Peoria IL 1991-1996; Chapl S

P

Jn's Mltry Acad Delafield WI 1986-1991; Assoc R S Andr's Epis Ch Ft Pierce FL 1984-1985; Headmaster/Assoc R S Cyp's Ch Lufkin TX 1979-1984; Asst The Epis Ch Of S Jas The Less Northfield IL 1978-1979. Auth, "Bibliography of Med Ethics," *Bibliography of Med Ethics*, Self-Pub, Sem Proj, 1978. Sigma Chi 1973. Who's Who in Amer Educ Who's Who in Amer 1990; Most Prominent Eductr of Texas Texas 1983; Outstanding Young Men in Amer Who's Who in Amer 1972; Phi Delta Kappa S Louis U 1970. gepence39@empowering.com

PENDERGRAFT, Randall Scott (Mont) Po Box 367, Red Lodge MT 59068 **Our Sav Epis Joliet MT 2006-; S Alb's Epis Ch Laurel MT 2006-; S Paul's of the Stillwater Ch Absarokee MT 2006-** B Billings MT 3/29/1949 s Lawrence William Pendergraft & Dorothy Mavis. BS Montana St U 1972; Mnstry Formation Prog 1999. D 10/2/1999 P 4/15/2000 Bp Charles Jones III. m 6/1/1985 Susan Jean Blackburn. Asst Vic Calv Epis Ch Red Lodge MT 2006-2010. lili@cablemt.net

PENDLETON, Dudley Digges (NJ) 3604 Crestside Rd, Birmingham AL 35223 **P Assoc S Barth's Ch Cherry Hill NJ 1984-** B Elizabeth NJ 8/25/1914 s Dudley Digges Pendleton & Marguerite Brunell. BS Carnegie Mellon U 1935. D 12/21/1963 P 6/1/1964 Bp Alfred L Banyard. m 5/26/1990 Joan Marie Herrera. St Marks At The Crossing Sicklerville NJ 1975-1979; Vic S Mk's Ch Hammonton NJ 1963-1971. dudleypendleton@hotmail.com

PENDLETON JR SSJE, Eldridge H (Mass) 21 Emery Ln, West Newbury MA 01985 B McKinney TX 2/23/1940 s Eldridge Honaker Pendleton & Kathryn. BA U of No Texas 1962; MA U of No Texas 1968; PhD U of Virginia 1974; MDiv Duke 1992. D 4/16/1993 P 11/29/1993 Bp Robert Whitridge Estill. S Jn's Chap Cambridge MA 1993-2005. eldridge@ssje.org

PENDLETON, Mark Bruce (Ct) 118 Westerly Ter, Hartford CT 06105 **Dn Chr Ch Cathd Hartford CT 2004-** B Cincinnati OH 5/10/1963 s Bruce Norman Pendleton & Judith Ann. Mia 1983; BA Florida St U 1986; MDiv GTS 1991. D 6/9/1991 Bp Frank Stanley Cerveny P 2/1/1992 Bp John Shelby Spong. m 6/2/1990 Leslie Glover c 2. R Ch Of Our Sav Silver Sprg MD 1998-2004; R S Lk's Ch So Glastonbury CT 1993-1998; Asst Chr Ch Short Hills NJ 1991-1993. Cmnty Of The Cross Of Nails No Amer, Pres 2000. Cn St. Andr'S Cathd, Aberdeen Scotland 2004. mpendleton@cccathedral.org

PENDLETON, William Beasley (NC) 1205-B Brookstown Ave. NW, Winston Salem NC 27101 B Mt. Airy NC 3/30/1954 s William Rosser Pendleton & Rebecca Anne. BS No Carolina St U; No Carolina St U 1987. D 6/13/2004 Bp Michael Bruce Curry. Bp's Com for the Diac 2007; OSL 2006; St. Frances Fllshp 2003. bpend@triad.rr.com

PENFIELD, Joyce Ann (RI) 25 Pomona Ave, Providence RI 02908 **Mem, Hisp Mnstry Com Dio Rhode Island Providence RI 2011-; P-in-c S Ptr's And S Andr's Epis Providence RI 2004-** B Urbana-Champaign IL. 10/1/1946 d John Glenn Sappenfield & Helen Irene. BA Illinois St U 1968; MA Amer U 1973; PhD SUNY 1977; MA Maryknoll TS 1995; MDiv EDS 2001. D 6/2/2001 Bp David B(ruce) Joslin P 2/3/2002 Bp Geralyn Wolf. m 8/26/2000 Ulick Mahoney c 3. Mem Soc Concerns Com Dio Rhode Island Providence RI 2001-2005; Assoc Cler S Lk's Epis Ch E Greenwich RI 2001-2004. Handbook, "Respecting Dignity: Working for Equity," *Handbook for trainers*, Penfield Assoc, 1997; Video & Bklet, "When Cultures Meet Face to Face," *Video and Bklet for cross-cultural Trng*, Penfield Assoc, 1992; Edited Bk, "Wmn and Lang in Transition," *Edited collection*, St Univ. of NY Press, 1987; reviewed Article, "The Afr Proverb: Sacr Text in praxis," *Symposium on Afr Proverbs*, U of So Afr, 1986; Reviewed Bk, "Communicating w Quotes: The Igbo Case," *Academically reviewed Bk*, Greenwood Press, Ct., 1983; Reviewed Bk, "Chicano Engl: A Dialectical Study," *by Penfield and Ornstein-Galicia*, Belgium Press, 1982. Outstanding Prof Rutgers U, Grad. Sch Ed. 1996; Hon Awd AARP, Rutgers U 1994. blessingwayinfo@yahoo.com

PENICK, Charles Inglesby (NC) 1417 Lafayette Ave, Rocky Mount NC 27803 B Charlotte NC 7/3/1925 s Edwin A Penick & Caroline. BA U NC 1948; BD STUSo 1951. D 8/21/1951 P 3/4/1952 Bp Edwin A Penick. m 9/3/1949 Nancy C Steele c 3. R Ch Of The Gd Shpd Rocky Mt NC 1964-1990; R S Ptr's Epis Ch Washington NC 1962-1964; R S Steph's Ch Goldsboro NC 1954-1962; R Gr Ch Whiteville NC 1951-1954.

PENICK, Fern Marjorie (Eau) 538 N 4th St, River Falls WI 54022 B Mason City IA 1/14/1942 d Donavon Veech & Marjorie Evelyn. D 7/24/1994 Bp William Charles Wantland. D Ch Of The Ascen Hayward WI 1998-2007.

PENN, John William (RG) 116 Kansas City Rd, Ruidoso NM 88345 B Tulsa OK 9/1/1936 s John D Penn & Odessa Angeline. U of Tulsa 1955; U Denv 1956; BFA U of New Mex 1963; MDiv SWTS 1966. D 6/18/1966 Bp C J Kinsolving III P 12/21/1966 Bp George Theodore Masuda. c 4. S Anne Chap Ruidoso NM 2000-2003; Cn Ltrgcs Dio The Rio Grande Albuquerque NM 1994-2002; Dio The Rio Grande Albuquerque NM 1993-2003; Dn - SE Deanry Dio The Rio Grande Albuquerque NM 1993-2002; R S Lk's Epis Ch Anth NM 1981-1988; R Ch Of The Gd Shpd Silver City NM 1978-1981; Cn Pstr Cathd Of S Jas Chicago IL 1968-1972; R S Jn's Epis Ch Dickinson ND 1966-1968. Auth, "arts RG Epis," *Living Ch*, 2003. Cn Liturg/ Dioc Cn Dio the Rio Grande 1994; Cn Pstr Dio Chicago 1968. susnjohn@beyondbb.com

PENNEKAMP, Nancy (Cal) 556 40th Ave, San Francisco CA 94121 **The Edge Chr Campus Cntr San Francisco CA 2006-** B Oakland CA 2/26/1950 d Arthur Eugen Pennekamp & Eleanor Marie. BA U CA 1972; MA Humboldt St U 1992; BA Sch for Deacons 2005. D 12/2/2006 Bp Marc Handley Andrus. m 7/26/1987 John Cumming. njpennekamp@yahoo.com

PENNER, Loree Anne (Md) 623 Monkton Rd, Monkton MD 21111 **R S Thos Epis Ch Towson MD 2011-** B Los Angeles CA 1/22/1956 d Paul Kinney Kinney & Mary Jo Kinney. BA Bethany Coll 1982; MA California St U 1990; MDiv STUSo 2004. D 6/4/2004 Bp Jerry Alban Lamb P 12/2/2004 Bp Henry Nutt Parsley Jr. m 6/9/1984 Steven Bruce Penner c 2. Assoc R S Jas Ch Monkton MD 2005-2011; Assoc S Jas Sewanee TN 2004-2005. Ord of the DOK 2004. lapenner@gmail.com

PENNIMAN JR, Charles Frederic (Pa) 2315 South Street, Philadelphia PA 19146 **Ch Without Walls Gwynedd PA 2003-** B Meridian MS 6/9/1928 s Charles Frederic Penniman & Lucile S. BA Amh 1950; MDiv VTS 1957. D 6/15/1957 P 6/20/1958 Bp John Brooke Mosley. m 8/5/1960 Annette Eckert c 1. R Trin Memi Ch Philadelphia PA 1962-1972; Cur Gr Ch Jamaica NY 1957-1959. cpenni2@verizon.net

PENNINGTON, Jasper Green (Mich) 204 Elm St, Ypsilanti MI 48197 B Clio MI 3/20/1939 s Walter Columbus Pennington & Hazel Sutton. BA Wstrn Michigan U 1967; MLS Wstrn Michigan U 1968; MDiv STUSo 1973; DMin GTF 1988. D 6/30/1973 Bp H Coleman McGehee Jr P 5/1/1974 Bp Robert Rae Spears Jr. m 10/13/1962 Carole Cecile Lynch c 3. Ecum Off Dio Michigan Detroit MI 1986-1992; R S Lk's Epis Ch Ypsilanti MI 1983-2001; Dio Maine Portland ME 1983; S Alb's Ch Cape Eliz ME 1981-1983; R S Jn's Ch Clifton Sprg NY 1978-1981; Ch Of The Ascen Rochester NY 1974-1977. Auth, "The Penningtons & their Rel vocations through the centuries.," *As We Knew Him: reflections on M. Basil Pennington*, Paraclete Press, Brewster, Mass., 2008; Auth, "Par Hist," *Fulton J Sheen; Chronology & Bibliography*, St. Bern's Sem, Rochester NY, 1976. Dir Archbp Fulton Jn Sheen Archv 1973-1981; Exec Secy No Amer Fllshp SS Alb & Se 1989-1990. muncaster@sbcglobal.net

PENNINGTON, (John) Joseph (Lex) 24 Thompson Ave, Ft Mitchell KY 41017 **P-in-c S Andr's Ch Ft Thos KY 2011-** B New Bedford MA 12/10/1943 s John Pennington & Sarah. BS U of Massachusetts 1965; MDiv VTS 1971. D 6/26/1971 P 12/29/1971 Bp John Melville Burgess. m 5/20/1973 Gail Savage. Stndg Com Dio Lexington Lexington KY 2004-2007; Stndg Com Dio Lexington Lexington KY 1996-1999; Dioc Coun Dio Lexington Lexington KY 1991-1995; R Trin Ch Covington KY 1989-2010; R Chr Ch Par Plymouth MA 1974-1989. johnjosephpennington@yahoo.com

PENNYBACKER, Kathleen Joanne (CFla) 320 S Canaday Dr, Inverness FL 34450 **D S Marg's Ch Inverness FL 1998-** B DesPlaines 2/15/1942 d John Schneider & Jennie Braida. Texas Wmn's U-Denton 1963; Orange Memi Hosp Sch 1965; Inst for Chr Stds 1998. D 6/6/1998 Bp John Wadsworth Howe. ksp0199@yahoo.com

PENROD, Roger Scott (WTex) 114 S. Cypress Cir, Pharr TX 78577 **R Trin Epis Ch Pharr TX 2004-** B San Antonio TX 3/12/1953 s Roger Harry Penrod & Texas Scott. AA San Antonio Coll 1977; BA U of Texas 1987; MDiv Epis TS of The SW 1993. D 6/29/1993 P 1/2/1994 Bp John Herbert MacNaughton. m 11/10/1996 Alice Lee Williams c 1. Vic S Mich's Epis Ch San Antonio TX 2003-2004; R Trin Ch San Antonio TX 1998-2003; Asst R S Thos Epis Ch And Sch San Antonio TX 1995-1998; R Trin Epis Ch Edna TX 1993-1995. salpenrod@yahoo.com

PEOPLES, David Brandon (CFla) 2627 Brookside Bluff Loop, Lakeland FL 33813 **R S Steph's Ch Lakeland FL 2010-** B Orlando FL 7/25/1974 s William Randolph Peoples & Mary Jo. BS U of Florida 1995; MDiv STUSo 2001. D 5/26/2001 Bp John Wadsworth Howe P 11/25/2001 Bp John Bailey Lipscomb. m 8/3/1996 Loudes Maria Ungaro c 5. R S Ambr Epis Ch Ft Lauderdale FL 2002-2009; Cur All SS Ch Tarpon Sprg FL 2001-2002. dbpeoples@aol.com

PEOPLES JR, E(dward) Moray (Ky) 3604 Fallen Timber Dr, Louisville KY 40241 **Vic H Trin Ch Brandenburg KY 2011-; P Assoc S Matt's Epis Ch Louisville KY 2004-** B Huntington WV 1/12/1939 s Edward M Peoples & Betty Jo. BA Marshall U 1968; MDiv STUSo 1972; Postgrad Louisville Presb TS 1991. D 6/19/1972 Bp David Shepherd Rose P 12/1/1972 Bp John B Bentley. m 12/17/1977 Judith Burnside. Assoc S Fran In The Fields Harrods Creek KY 1996-2003; Ch of the Gd Samar Louisville KY 1996; S Matt's Epis Ch Louisville KY 1993-1995; Stff Dio Kentucky Louisville KY 1988-1992; S Fran Sch (K-8) Goshen KY 1984-1988; Dio W Virginia Charleston WV 1979-1984; R S Andr's in the Vill Ch Barboursville WV 1979-1984; R Abingdon Epis Ch White Marsh VA 1975-1979; Vic Emm Ch Glenmore Buckingham VA 1972-1975; Emm Ch Scottsville VA 1972-1975; Vic S Anne's Ch Appomattox VA 1972-1975. mpeoples@bellsouth.net

PEPIN, Kenneth Raymond (O) 53 Lee Road 974, Phenix City AL 36870 **S Tim's Epis Ch Perrysburg OH 2006-** B New Bedford MA 10/16/1957 s Jean M Pepin & Alma L. BA Worcester St Coll 1980; MDiv S Jn Sem Boston MA 1985; VTS 2000. Rec from Roman Catholic 6/24/2000 as Priest Bp Peter

James Lee. m 4/18/1998 Mery Panozo Butron c 2. R S Steph's Epis Ch Smiths Sta AL 2002-2006; Vic S Jas Epis Ch Belhaven NC 2000-2002; Vic San Mateo (S Matt's) Washington NC 2000-2002; Vic San Mateo Mssn Yeatesville Washington NC 2000-2002. revkenmery@aol.com

PEPPLER, Connie Jo (Ind) 4131 W Woodyard Rd, Bloomington IN 47404 **Co-Dir of D Formation Prog Dio Indianapolis Indianapolis IN 2007-; D Trin Epis Ch Bloomington IN 2002-** B Anderson IN 11/29/1947 d Russell Nile Killian & Wanda Marie. BA Indiana U 1970; AA Indiana Bus Coll Vincennes IN 1978; BSN Indiana U 1994. D 6/29/2002 Bp Catherine Elizabeth Maples Waynick. m 3/20/1976 Michael Lynn Peppler. D S Mary's Epis Ch Martinsville IN 2002. dcncpep@att.net

PERALTA, Ercilia (DR) Santiago 114 Apt 764, Santo Domingo Dominican Republic **Dio The Dominican Republic (Iglesia Epis Dominicana) Santo Domingo DO 2003-** B Jarbacoa DR 6/14/1959 D 9/7/2002 Bp Julio Cesar Holguin-Khoury P 9/13/2003 Bp William Jones Skilton.

PERCIVAL, Herbert Duvall (Chi) 5550 S Shore Dr Apt 507, Chicago IL 60637 B Chicago IL 5/5/1926 s Francis Sanderson Percival & Elizabeth Hamilton. BS U IL 1949; MDiv Bex 1967. D 6/17/1967 Bp James Winchester Montgomery P 12/16/1967 Bp Gerald Francis Burrill. c 2. Dn of the Chicago W Dnry Dio Chicago Chicago IL 1986-1988; Dioc Counc Dio Chicago Chicago IL 1978-1985; Bishops Advsry Cmsn for Audio Visuals Dio Chicago Chicago IL 1977-1982; Vic/R S Mart's Ch Chicago IL 1971-1991; Cur S Dav's Ch Glenview IL 1969-1971; Vic Ch Of The Gd Shpd Momence IL 1967-1969; Asst S Paul's Ch Kankakee IL 1967-1969. Herbert D. Percival Schlrshp Cmnty Chr Alternative Acad 1992; Hon Pres Cmnty Chr Alternative Acad 1985.

PERCIVAL, Joanna Vera (ECR) 35 Shirley Park Road, Shirley, Southampton S0164FQ Great Britain (UK) B New York NY 4/11/1952 d David Arthur Percival & Elizabeth Jane. Cert Kingston Polytech 1975; BA U of San Francisco 1987; MDiv CDSP 1994. D 4/23/1994 P 11/1/1994 Bp Richard Lester Shimpfky. The Epis Ch In Almaden San Jose CA 1994-1995. Associated Parishes. Joanna.Percival@btinternet.com

PERCIVAL, Jonathan Beach (NJ) 18 Oak Ave, Metuchen NJ 08840 **R S Lk's Epis Ch Metuchen NJ 2000-** B Kabul AF 11/9/1949 s LeRoy Frederick Percival & Barbara Marion. BA Bard Coll 1971; MDiv GTS 1975; MBA Ya 1987. D 6/14/1975 Bp Paul Moore Jr P 12/21/1975 Bp Frederick Hesley Belden. m 6/21/1986 Evaleon Hill c 1. R S Andr And H Comm Ch So Orange NJ 1987-2000; R S Marg's Ch Staatsburg NY 1978-1981; Cur S Mich's Ch Bristol RI 1975-1977. arbocy@optonline.net

PERCIVAL, Michael John (Colo) 1301 Ferguson Ln, Santa Fe NM 87505 B Des Moines IA 10/1/1941 s Wright Courtney Percival & Mary Margaret. BA Stan 1964; MA U of Wisconsin 1968; MDiv CDSP 2000. Rec from Roman Catholic 4/30/1997 Bp Carl Christopher Epting. m 6/30/1991 Constance McBurney. Vic S Lk's Ch Westcliffe CO 2002-2006. frmichael01@gmail.com

PERDUE, David (NwT) 1101 Slide Rd, Lubbock TX 79416 **S Steph's Ch Lubbock TX 2010-** B Duncan OK 4/13/1949 s Jack R Perdue & Georgia Louise. Pharm Degree U of Oklahoma 1972; MDiv Epis TS of the SW 2008. D 6/28/2008 P 1/3/2009 Bp Edward Joseph Konieczny. m 6/7/1968 Donna Kay Pearson c 2. Vic Ch Of The H Cross Owasso OK 2008-2010; Dio Oklahoma Oklahoma City OK 2008-2010. ddperdue@sbcglobal.net

PERDUE, Thomas Hayes (EC) 3981 Fairfax Sq, Fairfax VA 22031 B Huntington WV 6/5/1969 s Thomas Henry Perdue & Mary Ann. BA Samford U 1993; MA Geneva Coll 1997; MDiv TESM 2002. D 11/9/2002 P 5/17/2003 Bp Robert William Duncan. m 8/12/2000 Melody Mae Miloszewski c 3. Assoc Ch Of The Apos Fairfax VA 2002-2005. thomas.perdue@navy.mil

PEREZ, Altagracia (Los) 1235 Westchester Pl, Los Angeles CA 90019 **R H Faith Par Inglewood CA 2003-** B New York NY 9/19/1961 d Ramon Eduardo Perez & Esther Zoraida. BS NYU 1982; MDiv UTS 1985; STM UTS 1986. D 6/15/1991 P 5/29/1993 Bp Frank Tracy Griswold III. m 4/24/1993 Carlos Rafael Alvarado. S Phil's Par Los Angeles CA 1994-2003; Dio Chicago Chicago IL 1991-1993. Auth, "Abundant Life," *The Bk Of Wmn Sermons*, Riverhead Books, 1999; Auth, "Este Es Mi Cuerpo," *A Faith Of One'S Own Explorations By Cath Lesbians*, The Crossing Press, 1986. Who'S Who In Black Amer 2002; Econ Justice And Worker'S Rts Los Angeles Allnce For A New Econ 2002; Golden Ang Rel Advoc Awd Natl Institutes Of Mntl Hlth 2001; Outstanding Serv Awd Second Bapt Ch Los Angeles CA 2000. revaltagracia@pacbell.net

PEREZ, Gregory Gerard (Nwk) 141 Broadway, Bayonne NJ 07002 **P-in-c Calv Ch Bayonne NJ 2011-; Trin Ch Bayonne NJ 2007-; Windmill Allnce Inc. Bayonne NJ 2007-** B Giddings TX 1/5/1960 s Butchild Perez & Herminia. BA Coll of Santa Fe 1982. Rec from Roman Catholic 12/15/2005 Bp John Palmer Croneberger. m 7/9/2009 Douglas Flores. Cur Gr Ch Van Vorst Jersey City NJ 2006-2007; S Barn Ch Newark NJ 2003-2006. greg.perez@comcast.net

PEREZ, Jesus Eduardo (Colom) Ap Aer 2704, Barranquilla, Atlantico Colombia B Sta Rosa de Osos Antioquia CO 4/30/1948 s Jose De Los Santos Perez Rua & Maria Mercedes. Arquidiocesano TS; Valmaria TS. Rec from Roman Catholic 3/1/1982 as Priest Bp Bernardo Merino-Botero. m 8/12/1978 Janette Cecilia Fernandez. Iglesia Epis En Colombia 1982-1998.

PEREZ, Jon Arnold (ECR) 949 Nantucket Blvd Unit 6, Salinas CA 93906 **Vic Epiph Luth & Epis Ch Marina CA 2005-** B Carmel CA 8/3/1959 Sch for Deacons 2003. D 4/16/2005 P 12/3/2005 Bp Sylvestre Donato Romero. vicarjon@sbcglobal.net

PEREZ MOREIRA, Hector (EcuC) Cd Sauces 5 Mz 225 V2, Guayaquil Ecuador **Vic Iglesia Santiago Apostolo Enrique Drouet Peninsula EC 1988-; Vic Iglesia Virgen Maria Salanguillo Peninsula St Elena 1988-; Vic Iglesia de la Santisima Trinidad (La Libertad) La Libertad EC 1988-; Litoral Dio Ecuador Guayaquil EQ EC 1988-** B Guayaquil EC 5/26/1940 s Hector Alciviades Perez & Juana. D 3/12/1988 Bp Adrian Delio Caceres-Villavicencio P 6/1/1992 Bp Martiniano Garcia-Montiel. m Eugenia Ruiz.

PERINE, Everett Craig (Ct) 60 Church St # 6248, Hebron CT 06248 **R S Ptr's Epis Ch Hebron CT 2004-** B New York NY 9/22/1949 s Gordon Condit Perine & Alice Neef. BA Mid 1971; None Gordon-Conwell TS 1981; MDiv Ya Berk 1986. D 6/11/1986 P 12/21/1986 Bp Robert Shaw Kerr. c 2. Assoc S Barn Epis Ch Greenwich CT 2000-2004; R S Jn's Ch New Milford CT 1997-1999; R Ch Of The Gd Shpd Pitman NJ 1991-1997; Cn Res Cathd Ch Of S Paul Burlington VT 1988-1991; Cur Cathd Ch Of S Paul Burlington VT 1986-1987. Cmnty Cross Of Nails 1981-1991. fatherperry1986@hotmail.com

PERKEY, Hayward Roger (WVa) 2503 S Pleasants Hwy, Saint Marys WV 26170 **S Paul's Ch Sistersville WV 2003-** B Weston WV 4/28/1922 s John B Perkey & Evelyn. Epis TS In Kentucky. D 7/22/1973 P 2/1/1974 Bp Wilburn Camrock Campbell. m 3/3/1950 Virginia Rexroad c 2. Vic S Mk's Ch Glenville WV 1977-1985; Gr Ch S Marys WV 1973-1993. hperkey@citlink.net

PERKINS, Aaron C. (Me) 26 Moulton Ln, York ME 03909 **D S Geo's Epis Ch York Harbor ME 2008-** B Boston MA 6/23/1968 s Richard Perkins & Cynthia. BArch Roger Wms 1991. D 6/24/2006 Bp Chilton Abbie Richardson Knudsen. m 5/21/1995 Cynthia Weiss c 1. St. Steph Awd NAAD 2010. aperkins@stgeorgesyorkharbor.org

PERKINS III, Albert Dashiell (Ala) 425 N Moye Dr, Montgomery AL 36109 B Chattanooga TN 3/2/1929 s Albert Dashiell Perkins & Kathryn Lucille. BA U of Mississippi 1954; MDiv STUSo 1961; DMin TCU 1980. D 6/18/1961 Bp George Mosley Murray P 5/1/1962 Bp Charles C J Carpenter. m 4/6/1956 Virgie R Richerson c 3. R S Barn Epis Ch Roanoke AL 1994-1995; Secy Dio Dio Alabama Birmingham AL 1991-1994; Cn Revs Com Dio Alabama Birmingham AL 1989-1991; Evang & Renwl Dept Dio Alabama Birmingham AL 1979-1982; S Jn's Ch Montgomery AL 1974-1995; Chair Dept Mssn Dio Alabama Birmingham AL 1967-1971; Chair Yth Div Dio Alabama Birmingham AL 1965-1967; Vic S Barn Epis Ch Roanoke AL 1961-1974; Vic S Jas' Epis Ch Alexander City AL 1961-1974. Auth, "Along The Way," *Montgomery Advert*, 1994. St Geo Medal For Scouting 1992.

PERKINS, Calhoun W (SC) 464 Golf Dr, Georgetown SC 29440 **Gr Ch Charleston SC 2009-** B Charleston SC 8/14/1968 BA Clemson U 1990; MDiv STUSo 2005. D 6/25/2005 P 12/17/2005 Bp Edward Lloyd Salmon Jr. m 5/22/1993 F Wilson Perkins. Asst H Cross Faith Memi Epis Ch Pawleys Island SC 2005-2008; Dio So Carolina Charleston SC 1999-2003. calhounperkins@aol.com

PERKINS, David William (Lex) 3509 Falcon Ridge Ct, Montgomery AL 36111 **Int Ch Of The H Comf Montgomery AL 2011-; Int Ch Of The H Comf Montgomery AL 2011-** B Oakdale LA 9/16/1944 s William Perkins & Ruth Katherine. STM (in progress) STUSo; BS U of Louisiana, Monroe 1967; ThM New Orleans Bapt TS 1972; ThD New Orleans Bapt TS 1977; Emory U 1987; LSU 1992. Trans 1/21/2004 Bp J(ohn) Neil Alexander. c 2. Int S Jn's Ch Versailles KY 2010-2011; Chair, Com on the Diac Dio Virginia Richmond VA 2006-2009; Ch planter/Vic All Soul's Epis Ch Mechanicsville VA 2002-2010; Int S Marg's Ch Carrollton GA 2001-2002; Assoc S Jas Epis Ch Marietta GA 1998-2001; P-in-c S Pat's Epis Ch W Monroe LA 1998; Vic The Epis Ch Of The Gd Shpd Vidalia LA 1996-1998. Auth, *Var arts*. Amer Academy of Religioni 1995; SBL, AAR 1974. davidwperk@gmail.com

PERKINS, Gloria Eade Gallic (SanD) 2556 Via Torina, Del Mar CA 92014 **Died 3/9/2010** B Plainfield NJ 9/21/1924 d Harold Eugene Gallic & Elizabeth Holmes. BA Wellesley Coll 1945; MA Harv 1946. D 11/19/1992 Bp Gethin Benwil Hughes.

PERKINS, Jesse S (Ark) 531 W College Ave, Jonesboro AR 72401 **S Mk's Epis Ch Jonesboro AR 2009-** B Hot Springs AR 7/12/1980 s Alvis Joe Perkins & Kathy Jean. BS U of Cntrl Arkansas 2002; MDiv SWTS 2009. D 3/21/2009 Bp Larry Earl Maze P 9/29/2009 Bp Larry R Benfield. m 6/8/2002 Kathryn A Hohrine c 1. jesse.perkins@gmail.com

PERKINS, Lynn Jones (RG) 1409 Linda Drive, Gallup NM 87301 **Co-Vic Ch Of The H Sprt Gallup NM 2007-** B Atlanta GA 7/26/1947 d Oliver Steadum Jones & Roselyn Weisman. BS U of Tennessee 1969; MS U of Tennessee 1975; MDiv TESM 2007. D 6/26/2007 Bp Jeffrey Neil Steenson P 11/10/2007 Bp William Carl Frey. m 12/27/1983 Roger S Perkins. jonesmlynn@aol.com

PERKINS, Patrick Ryder (Ct) 679 Farmington Ave, West Hartford CT 06119 **Asst to the R S Jn's Ch W Hartford CT 2009-** B New Britain CT 8/9/1964 s John H Perkins & Betsy C. BS US Naval Acad 1987; MS RPI 1993; MDiv

VTS 2009. D 6/6/2009 Bp Jeffrey Dean Lee P 12/19/2009 Bp James Elliot Curry. m 8/20/1988 Carol C Cone c 2. prknz87@yahoo.com

PERKINS, Roger S (RG) 1409 Linda Drive, Gallup NM 87301 **Co-Vic Ch Of The H Sprt Gallup NM 2007-** B Louisville KY 7/26/1947 s Lloyd S Perkins & Harriet S. BEd Keene St Coll Keene NH 1966; MS U of Tennessee 1969; MDiv TESM 2007. D 6/27/2007 Bp Jeffrey Neil Steenson P 11/10/2007 Bp William Carl Frey. m 12/27/1983 Lynn Jones c 1. perkinsrs@aol.com

PERKINSON, Edward Myron (O) 1683 N Hametown Rd, Akron OH 44333 **Asst S Paul's Ch Akron OH 2010-** B Forest Park IL 3/27/1935 s Myron Boyer Perkinson & Rhoda. BA Mt Un Coll 1956; MDiv Garrett Evang TS 1959; MA NWU 1961. D 12/21/1965 P 5/9/1966 Bp Nelson Marigold Burroughs. m 2/24/1978 Susannah Watson c 3. Int Ch Of Our Sav Akron OH 2002-2003; Int Trin Ch Allnce OH 1984-1985; Assoc S Mk's Ch Canton OH 1978-1984; Vic Adv Epis Ch Westlake OH 1968-1972; Asst Chr Ch Epis Hudson OH 1965-1968. Auth, "Step Families: Another Chance," *The Script*. Amer Assn of Mar and Fam Therapists; ITAA. perkatak@gmail.com

PERKO, F Michael (RG) 2 Paa Ko Ct, Sandia Park NM 87047 **Cn for Cncl Affrs Dio The Rio Grande Albuquerque NM 2011-; P-in-c S Alb's Ch El Paso TX 2011-; Dioc Coun Vice Pres./Secy Dio The Rio Grande Albuquerque NM 2006-; Asst S Jn's Cathd Albuquerque NM 2005-** B Chicago IL 11/6/1946 s Frank Perko & Mary Josephine. AB/MA Boston Coll 1970; MDiv Loyola U Chi 1975; MA Stan 1976; PhD Stan 1981. Rec from Roman Catholic 9/18/2005 Bp Jeffrey Neil Steenson. m 2/5/2005 Lisa Gruber. P-in-c Ch of the H Faith Santa Fe NM 2007; Cn Dio The Rio Grande Albuquerque NM 2006-2011; Cn to the Ordnry/Eccl Authority Dio The Rio Grande Albuquerque NM 2006-2011; Dioc Coun Vice-Pres/Secy Dio The Rio Grande Albuquerque NM 2006-2011; Secy of Dioc Conv Dio The Rio Grande Albuquerque NM 2006-2011; Int Ch Of The H Cross Edgewood NM 2006-2007. Auth, "Cath and Amer," OSV Press, 1989; Auth, "A Time to Favor Zion," Educational Stds Press, 1988; Auth, "Enlighting the Next Generation," Garland Press, 1988; Auth, "numerous Bk Revs, Journ arts and Bk chapters". Dn Dio the Rio Grande 2007; Dioc Cn Dio the Rio Grande 2006. mperko@luc.edu

PERRIN, Charles Leonard (LI) 13530 Grand Central Pkwy Apt 317, Jamaica NY 11435 **Cluster D S Jn's Of Lattingtown Locust Vlly NY 2011-; Cluster D S Lk's Ch Sea Cliff NY 2011-; Cluster D S Paul's Ch Glen Cove NY 2011-; Cluster D Trin Epis Ch Roslyn NY 2011-; Admin Trin Epis Ch Roslyn NY 2010-; D Asst S Elis's Epis Ch Floral Pk NY 2002-; D Asst S Thos' Epis Ch Bellerose Vill NY 2002-** B Brooklyn NY 9/25/1946 s Dwight Richard Perrin & Evelyn. Adel 1965; Pratt Inst 1974; Cert Geo Mercer Memi TS 1987. D 12/15/1986 Bp Robert Campbell Witcher Sr. m 11/5/2005 Marana Hall. D Gr Ch Jamaica NY 2008-2011; Asst S Mk's Ch Jackson Heights NY 2001-2002; Asst Ch Of S Alb The Mtyr S Albans NY 1996-2000; D All SS' Epis Ch Long Island City NY 1994-1996; Asst Ch Of The Redeem Astoria NY 1990-1994; Asst S Mk's Ch Jackson Heights NY 1986-1990. Assn of Epis Deacons 1986. charlie-perrin@nyc.rr.com

PERRIN, Henry Keats (SO) 10129 Springbeauty Ln, Cincinnati OH 45231 B El Dorado AR 12/11/1945 s Howard Keats Perrin & Vera A. BA U So 1967; MDiv STUSo 1974. D 6/29/1974 P 11/1/1975 Bp Christoph Keller Jr. m 5/26/1974 Margaret Ann Barnum. S Phil's Ch Cincinnati OH 1992; Vic S Steph's Epis Ch Cincinnati OH 1991-2001; Assoc R The Ch of the Redeem Cincinnati OH 1990; Chair Of The Cong Dvlpmt Com Dio Sthrn Ohio Cincinnati OH 1989-1990; Int S Jas Epis Ch Cincinnati OH 1989-1990; Dio Sthrn Ohio Cincinnati OH 1988-1989; S Jn's Ch Clinton IA 1987; Assoc R S Tim's Epis Ch Cincinnati OH 1983-1987; Vic S Andr's Ch Grove OK 1982-1983; Coun On Mssn Dio Oklahoma Oklahoma City OK 1979-1983; Vic S Jn's Epis Ch Vinita OK 1979-1983; Vic All SS Epis Ch Paragould AR 1975-1979; Asst S Mk's Epis Ch Jonesboro AR 1975-1979; Cur S Andr's Ch Rogers AR 1974-1975. Ord Of Ascen; RACA, NECAD, Cath Fllshp Of The Epis Ch. HOGWILD@FUSE.NET

PERRIN, Mary Elizabeth (WMich) 2512 Highpointe Dr, Kalamazoo MI 49008 **R S Mart Of Tours Epis Ch Kalamazoo MI 2004-** B Grand Rapids MI 7/6/1952 d Benjamin Ivan Judy & Nettie Esther. BA MI SU 1979; MDiv SWTS 2000. D 4/22/2001 P 10/27/2001 Bp Edward Lewis Lee Jr. m 6/15/1974 Tomas Wesley Perrin. S Andr's Ch Grand Rapids MI 2001-2004. perrinm@sbcglobal.net

PERRIN, Ronald Van Orden (NY) No address on file. B Greenfield MA 4/20/1933 s Robert Anthony Perrin & Clara Mildred. BA Wesl 1955; BD UTS 1958. D 6/30/1960 P 1/1/1961 Bp Conrad Gesner. m 6/11/1955 Aletheia Nevius Reeves c 4. Asst Min Calv and St Geo New York NY 1963-1965; Vic Chr Epis Ch Gettysburg SD 1961-1963.

PERRINE JR, Paul Austin (CFla) 7815 Winona Rd, Melbourne Beach FL 32951 **Assoc H Trin Epis Ch Melbourne FL 2007-** B Detroit MI 1/26/1935 s Paul Austin Perrine & Dorothy Maude. BS U of Tampa 1959; MDiv CDSP 1962. D 6/29/1962 Bp William Loftin Hargrave P 12/31/1962 Bp Henry I Louttit. m 6/11/1966 Rose A Scarbrough c 1. S Lk's Epis Ch Merritt Island FL 1962-2000. perrineap@cfl.rr.com

PERRINO, Robert Anthony (SeFla) 1103 Duncan Cir Apt 103, Palm Beach Gardens FL 33418 **S Mk's Ch Palm Bch Gardens FL 2004-** B Providence RI 1/29/1933 BS Providence Coll 1954. D 11/12/2003 Bp Leopold Frade. m 2/7/1976 Bernice Leger. perrimoleger@gmail.com

PERRIS, John David (Nwk) 581 Valley Rd, Upper Montclair NJ 07043 **R S Jas Ch Upper Montclair NJ 2006-** B Oak Park IL 8/30/1960 s John Perris & Elenor. BA w dist Cor 1982; JD Ya 1986; M.Div. cl GTS 1998. D 6/10/1998 P 12/10/1998 Bp Orris George Walker Jr. m 4/21/1990 Catharine Hereford Doherty c 3. R Chr Ch Epis Harwich Port MA 2002-2006; Asst S Jn's Ch Roanoke VA 1998-2002. Assoc of the OHC 2003; The Angl Soc 1998. Phi Beta Kappa Cor 1981. johnperris@yahoo.com

PERRIZO, Faith Crook (WVa) 405 E Montgomery St, Marietta OH 45750 **Archd/Mnstry Dvlpmt and Transitions Off Dio W Virginia Charleston WV 2004-** B Marietta OH 4/25/1953 d Clifford Crook & Lillian Alison. Cert The Wstrn Coll 1974; BA Macalester Coll 1975; MDiv SWTS 1980. D 6/24/1980 P 9/23/1981 Bp Robert Marshall Anderson. c 3. Dio Sthrn Ohio Cincinnati OH 2002; Epis Ch Serv Fndt Dio Sthrn Ohio Cincinnati OH 2000-2002; COM Dio Sthrn Ohio Cincinnati OH 1997-1999; R S Lk's Ch Marietta OH 1995-2004; Asst for Mnstry/Dioc Dio Chicago Chicago IL 1990-1994; Chris Ed Dir, Gr Ch-in-the-Loop Dio Chicago Chicago IL 1987-1989; Vic S Fran Epis Ch Chicago IL 1982-1987; Search Consult Dio Chicago Chicago IL 1981-1982; DCE & Yth S Mary's Ch Pk Ridge IL 1980-1981. fperrizo@wvdiocese.org

PERRY, Ally (Dal) 3212 Crawford Ln, Denison TX 75020 **The Rev. Ally Perry S Jn's Epis Ch Pottsboro TX 2001-** B Cincinnati OH 11/9/1949 d Edward Milton Wilcox & Queenie. BA Franconia Coll 1975; MDiv Yale DS 1978; MBA GTF 1990; St. Geo's Coll 1995; Hebr U of Jerusalem 1996. D 6/1/1984 P 12/21/1984 Bp Walter Cameron Righter. m 5/23/2004 Lowry Gene Perry. Vic S Anne's By The Fields Ankeny IA 1985-1997; Int S Andr's Ch Des Moines IA 1984-1985. therev.allyperry@gmail.com

PERRY, Bonnie Anne (Chi) 4550 N Hermitage Ave # 103, Chicago IL 60640 **Vic All SS Epis Ch Chicago IL 1992-** B San Diego CA 4/15/1962 d Raymond F Perry & Mary Jane. SWTS; BA H Cross Coll 1984; MDiv UTS 1988; DMin 1998. D 6/2/1990 P 12/1/1990 Bp John Shelby Spong. Int S Ptr's Ch Clifton NJ 1991-1992; Chr Ch Ridgewood NJ 1990-1991; Mssnr Chr Ch Hackensack NJ 1988-1989. Ord Of S Helena 1998. bonnie@allsaintschicago.org

PERRY, Cecilia C (RI) PO Box 872, Bristol RI 02809 B Bristol RI 8/9/1936 d Calbraith Bourne Perry & Marie Lea. BA U of Rhode Island 1970; MEd Rhode Island Coll 1977; MDiv EDS 1994. D 1/27/1996 Bp Morgan Porteus P 2/8/1997 Bp Geralyn Wolf. c 3. Supply P Ch Of The Adv Pawtucket RI 2003-2005; Int Ch Of The Mssh Providence RI 2002; R S Paul's Ch Portsmouth RI 2000-2001; Vic Calv Ch Providence RI 1997-2000; D S Paul's Ch No Kingstown RI 1996-1997. Sis of St. Marg, Boston, MA 2003. ccperryrev1@aol.com

PERRY, Charles Austin (Cal) 250 Pantops Mountain Rd Apt 5411, Charlottesville VA 22911 **Died 10/24/2010** B White Plains NY 11/5/1928 s Russell Elven Perry & Jennie-Belle. DD CDSP; DD VTS; BA Cor 1950; MDiv VTS 1961; Fllshp Coll of Preachers 1966; MA U MN 1969. D 6/23/1961 P 6/1/1962 Bp Robert Fisher Gibson Jr. c 2. Auth, "The Ressurection Promise," Eerdmans, 1986. charlesperry@wcbr.us

PERRY, David Warner (Ore) 715 Se 34th Ave, Portland OR 97214 B Salem OR 6/2/1941 s Leon Clarence Perry & Josephine Bertha. W&M 1961; BA U of Oregon 1963; STB GTS 1966; DD VTS 2001; DD CDSP 2002. D 6/22/1966 P 12/27/1966 Bp James Walmsley Frederic Carman. m 6/19/1965 Fredrika Ann Wood c 2. Asst S Mich And All Ang Ch Portland OR 2001; Epis Ch Cntr New York NY 1987-1995; Assoc All SS Ch Pasadena CA 1982-1986; Rel Educ Coordntr Epis Ch Cntr New York NY 1973-1982; Dir. CE Dio Oregon Portland OR 1971-1973; Assoc Chr Ch Par Lake Oswego OR 1966-1971. Ed, *Making Sense of Things*, Seabury Press, 1981; Ed, *Homegrown CE*, Seabury Press, 1979; Ed, "AWARE (Rel Educ Notebooks)," *10 v)*, Epis Ch Cntr, 1974. Hon Cn S Lk's Cathd Dio Panama 1995. perrypdx@comcast.net

PERRY, John Wallis (Alb) 431 Union St, Hudson NY 12534 **R Chr Ch Epis Hudson NY 2004-** B Bronx NY 12/22/1948 s John Wallis Perry & Helen. BA Ford 1970; MDiv EDS 1999. D 6/5/1999 Bp Arthur Edward Walmsley P 12/18/1999 Bp Robert Deane Rowley Jr. m 4/22/1972 Eleanor Cawley c 3. R S Jas Memi Epis Ch Titusville PA 1999-2004. Cmnty Cross Nails. jpchristch@mhcable.com

PERRY, Kenneth M (Roch) PO Box 147, Geneva NY 14456 B Queens NY 1/28/1940 s Lester Perry & Gertrude. BS SUNY 1962; MScEd SUNY 1997. D 3/29/2008 Bp Jack Marston McKelvey. m 8/25/1962 Josephine V Valenti c 2. jperry97@rochester.rr.com

PERRY, Margaret Rose (Az) St Francis in-the-Valley, 600 S La Canada Dr, Green Valley AZ 85614 **D Epis Ch Of S Fran-In-The-Vlly Green Vlly AZ 2008-** B Jackson MI 3/16/1941 d William Parker Rose & Betty Margaret. AA Elgin Cnty Coll 1975; AS DuPage Glen Ellyn IL 1981. D 1/26/2008 Bp Kirk Stevan Smith. m 8/28/1959 Carl Perry c 2. cmperry@cox.net

PERRY, Marvin Collier (SC) 135 Lake Hills Rd, Pinehurst NC 28374 B Savannah GA 3/5/1920 s Marvin Perry & I'Dell. BS No Carolina St U 1943. Trans from Igreja Episcopal Anglicana do Brasil 11/20/1978 Bp Robert Bracewell Appleyard. m 11/7/1942 Catherine Smith. P-in-c S Marys Epis Ch Mt Pleasant SC 1984-1987; P-in-c Ch Of The H Fam Moncks Corner SC 1983-1984.

PERRY, Pauline Tait (WMass) 49 Briarwood Cir, Worcester MA 01606 **D Dio Wstrn Massachusetts Springfield MA 2002-** B Springfield MA 9/1/1925 d Richard Hare Tait & Ethel Lucy. BA Clark U 1947; MA Assumption Coll 1975; Cert SWTS 1992. D 6/13/1992 Bp Andrew Frederick Wissemann. m 9/13/1947 Roger Newton Perry c 4. D S Lk's Ch Worcester MA 1998-1999; D S Jn's Ch Worcester MA 1997-2001; D S Fran Ch Holden MA 1992-1997. FVC 1993; Soc of S Marg 1986-1998. spd25@charter.net

PERRY, Raymond Glenn (NMich) 251 Monongahela Rd, Crystal Falls MI 49920 B Crystal Falls MI 3/9/1928 s Thomas Perry & Elsie. BD Michigan Tech U 1959. D 5/20/1990 P 12/1/1990 Bp Thomas Kreider Ray. m 1/7/1954 Helen Eckola. P (Ret) S Mk's Ch Crystal Falls MI 1990-2005.

PERRY, Robert Kendon (Ida) 411 Capitol Ave, Salmon ID 83467 **Asst Ch Of The Redeem Salmon ID 1994-** B Salmon ID 5/3/1949 s William N Perry & Aloha J. D 1/29/1994 P 9/1/1994 Bp John Stuart Thornton. m 5/23/1969 Barbara Ann Cool.

PERSCHALL JR CSF, Donald Richard (Dal) 909 W Gandy St, Denison TX 75020 **R S Lk's Ch Denison TX 2011-** B Bloomington IL 10/14/1949 s Donald Richard Perschall & Virginia Pearl. BS U Of Dubuque 1976; MDiv U Of Dubuque TS 1978. Rec from The American Anglican Church 3/1/2003 Bp Peter Hess Beckwith. m 3/25/1979 Andrea Morine c 3. R S Mths' Epis Ch Athens TX 2006-2010; R Trin Ch Mt Vernon IL 2003-2006. graycoparson@gmail.com

✠ **PERSELL, Rt Rev William Dailey** (Chi) 28 Haskell Dr., Bratenahl OH 44108 B Rochester NY 5/6/1943 s Charles Bowen Persell & Emily Elizabeth. BA Hob 1965; MDiv EDS 1969; Fllshp Intl Coll LB 1969; Fllshp EDS 1981. D 6/21/1969 Bp Charles Bowen Persell Jr P 12/21/1969 Bp Robert C Rusack Con 3/13/1999 for Chi. m 5/5/1973 Nancy Pollard c 6. Bp Dio Chicago Chicago IL 1999-2008; Mem, Bd Trst SWTS Evanston IL 1999-2008; Dn Trin Cathd Cleveland OH 1991-1999; Soc Concerns & Peace Cmsn Dio Long Island Garden City NY 1983-1991; R S Ann And The H Trin Brooklyn NY 1982-1991; Trst Dio Los Angeles Los Angeles CA 1977-1981; R St Johns Pro-Cathd Los Angeles CA 1972-1982; Dept Soc Rela Dio Los Angeles Los Angeles CA 1972-1974; P S Paul's Epis Ch Tustin CA 1969-1972. Phi Beta Kappa Hob 1965. wpersell@dohio.org

PERSON, Dorothy Jean (NMich) 208 Lane Ave, Kingsford MI 49802 B 9/25/1926 D 2/29/2004 Bp James Arthur Kelsey. m 6/7/1947 William Jay Person c 5.

PERSON, Kathryn Jeanne (Mass) 1803 Glenwood Rd, Brooklyn NY 11230 **Com on Status of Wmn Exec Coun Appointees New York NY 2009-; Dir, Cntr for Chr Sprtlty The GTS New York NY 2009-** B New Orleans LA 7/26/1962 d Daniel Joseph Person & Sandra Kathryn. BA Pr 1984; MS Col 1985; MDiv Harvard DS 1996; STM GTS 2000. D 12/19/1998 P 12/4/1999 Bp M(arvil) Thomas Shaw III. m 2/18/1996 Kamal Abdullah. Assoc R Ch Of The H Trin New York NY 2004-2010; Assoc R Gr Ch Brooklyn NY 1999-2004. "Lifting Wmn Voices," Morehouse, 2009; "Where You Go I Shall: Gleanings From The Stories Of Biblic Widows," Cowley Pub, 2005. Fllshp of St. Jn 2002. kjeanne@glenwoodgrace.net

PERSONS, Alfred Ernest (Colo) Po Box 1741, Estes Park CO 80517 B Tulsa OK 10/7/1922 s Charles Alfred Persons & Edna Maude. BA U of Tulsa 1943; MDiv GTS 1946. D 6/2/1946 P 12/1/1946 Bp Thomas Casady. m 3/16/2003 Jo Ann Jones. Asst S Barth's Ch Estes Pk CO 2001-2002; DCE Dio Texas Houston TX 1961-1970; Asst S Lk's Par Darien CT 1959-1961; Vic S Paul's Ch Darien CT 1959-1961; R S Matt's Ch Enid OK 1953-1955; Vic S Steph's Alva Alva OK 1953-1954; Vic All SS Epis Ch Miami OK 1946-1953; Vic S Jn's Epis Ch Vinita OK 1946-1953. Auth, "One God, One Fam," *One Earth*, Exec Coun, Nyc, 1996; Auth, "Human Sxlty: A Chr Perspective," Exec Coun, Nyc, 1993; Auth, "The Use Of Applied Behavorial Sci In Rel Systems," Nat'L Dept. Of Educ, 1956. Aci 1978; Cts 1977-1992. Consult/ Trnr Emer Aci 1999. alpersons@aol.com

PETERMAN, Lynn Ceremuga (EC) 115 John L Hurst Dr, Swansboro NC 28584 B Greenville PA 10/25/1960 d Paul Ceremuga & Nancy Carol Ann. BA/BS U of So Carolina 1987; MS Clemson U 1991; MDiv VTS 2002. D 4/10/2002 P 10/19/2002 Bp Clifton Daniel III. m 12/8/1993 Thomas R Peterman c 1. Assoc S Cyp's Ch New Bern NC 2006-2009; Asst S Jas Par Wilmington NC 2002-2004. lynnpeterman@yahoo.com

PETERS, Albert Fitz-Randolph (Del) 1001 Middleford Rd # 184, Seaford DE 19973 B Washington DC 9/13/1927 s Albert Fitz-Randolph Peters & Marquerite. BA Amer U 1952; GTS 1955. D 6/18/1955 P 12/21/1955 Bp Angus Dun. m 5/27/1978 Margaret Robinson. Primary Pstr S Mary's Ch Bridgeville DE 2000-2005; Mssn Supply P Dio Delaware Wilmington DE 1989-2001; Sup P Dio Delaware Wilmington DE 1989-1997; Vic All SS Epis Ch Delmar DE 1983-1989; Dio Delaware Wilmington DE 1983-1989; R S Mary's Ch Bridgeville DE 1983-1989; The Sussex Cnty Mssn Of The Epis Ch Wilmington DE 1975-1983; R S Marg's Ch Chicago IL 1962-1975; Cur Gr Ch White Plains NY 1957-1959; Cur All SS' Epis Ch Chevy Chase MD 1955-1957.

PETERS, Arthur Edward (Alb) 35 North St, Granville NY 12832 **D/Vic Trin Ch Granville NY 2005-** B Paterson NJ 2/5/1952 D 6/22/2003 Bp Daniel William Herzog. m 10/20/1979 Sue Anne Boerner.

PETERS JR, August William (WA) 1000 Hilton Ave, Catonsville MD 21228 **Pstr Assoc S Tim's Ch Catonsville MD 2002-** B Baltimore MD 10/23/1933 s August William Peters & Sarah Elizabeth. Cert Towson U 1953; BS U of Maryland 1957; STB Ya Berk 1961. D 7/6/1961 P 6/18/1962 Bp Noble C Powell. m 4/13/1958 Donaleen Schlegel c 3. S Paul's Par Washington DC 1985-1996; Asst to R S Paul's Rock Creek Washington DC 1985-1996; R S Lk's Par Bladensburg MD 1972-1985; Cur Chr Ch Prince Geo's Par Rockville MD 1965-1970; Asst Emm Ch Cumberland MD 1961-1962. CAP; CBS; ESA; Foward In Faith; Soc Of All SS; Soc Of S Mary, Ward Superior. lotsotrains@aol.com

PETERS, Diana Wray (Colo) 13495 Monroe St, Thornton CO 80241 **R Intsn Epis Ch Thornton CO 2001-** B South Joseph MO 12/18/1949 d John Wrayman Strickland & Doris Eileen. S Thos Theol Sem; BS Missouri Wstrn St U 1974; MA U of Kansas 1981; MDiv CDSP 1996. D 6/8/1996 P 12/21/1996 Bp William Jerry Winterrowd. m 5/22/1981 Gary L Peters c 2. All Souls Mssn Of The Deaf Thornton CO 2001; S Lk's Ch Denver CO 1999-2001; Dio Colorado Denver CO 1999-2000; Cur Chr's Epis Ch Castle Rock CO 1996-1998. Celtic Cross Soc. dianapetrs@msn.com

PETERS, Gregory William (Oly) 4424 SW 102nd Street, Seattle WA 98146 B Elkhorn WI 8/13/1961 s Joseph Thomas Peters & Alma Jane. BA Evergreen St Coll 1988; MDiv GTS 1995. D 6/28/1997 P 6/1/1998 Bp Vincent Waydell Warner. m 5/8/1999 Erika Diane Schreder c 2. Vic All SS Ch Seattle WA 2003-2009; Int St Bede Epis Ch Port Orchard WA 2001-2003; S Mk's Cathd Seattle WA 1998-2001; S Andr's Ch Seattle WA 1997-1998. msandrev@mindspring.com

PETERS, Helen Sarah (Ak) 1340 23rd Ave, Fairbanks AK 99701 B Tanana AK 6/11/1929 d Elijah Joseph & Helen. Cert Cook Chr Trng Sch 1984. D 8/11/1974 Bp William J Gordon Jr. m 9/2/1956 Hardy A Peters.

PETERS, John T (Minn) 14434 Fairway Dr # 55734-4, Eden Prairie MN 55344 **R S Alb's Epis Ch Edina MN 2000-** B Greenwich CT 8/13/1958 s John Peters & Shirley. DPS St. Jn's Coll Nottingham Gb; BA U of Connecticut 1980; LTh St. Jn's Coll Nottingham Gb 1987. Trans from Church Of England 10/4/1994 Bp James Louis Jelinek. R Chr Epis Ch Grand Rapids MN 1994-2000. johnpeters@isd.net

PETERS, J Patrick Patrick (CPa) 465 Zachary Dr, Manheim PA 17545 **R S Paul's Ch Columbia PA 2003-** B Trenton NJ 7/31/1946 s Martin Henry Peters & Edyth. BA S Mary Sem & U 1971; CUA 1974; MA JHU 1984. Rec from Roman Catholic 1/12/2002 as Priest Bp Michael Whittington Creighton. m 11/15/1980 Danielle Joyce Guraleczka c 4. P The Epis Ch Of S Jn The Bapt York PA 2002-2003. jpp001@earthlink.net

PETERS, Peter William (Roch) 239 Yarmouth Rd, Rochester NY 14610 **Vocation & Ldrshp Dvlpmt Dio Rochester Rochester NY 2010-; Int S Jn's Ch Canandaigua NY 2009-** B Tidworth UK 7/8/1939 s George Peters & Harriet. ThL Moore Theol Coll, Sydney 1962; BA U Of New Engl Armidale Nsw Au 1966; MA Yale DS 1969; PhD Van 1979. Trans from Anglican Church Of Australia 6/1/1969 Bp John Vander Horst. c 3. P-in-c S Andr's Ch No Grafton MA 2004-2005; P-in-c S Paul's Ch Boston MA 2003-2004; Dioc Coun Dio Rochester Rochester NY 1999-2002; R S Lk's Ch Fairport NY 1992-2003; Dio Washington Washington DC 1986-1992; Cathd of St Ptr & St Paul Washington DC 1984-1986; R Trin Ch Clarksville TN 1974-1982; Asst S Geo's Ch Nashville TN 1970-1974. Auth, "Ch And Publ Plcy," Dio Rochester, 1999; Auth, "Some Considerations Concerning Ch & Educ For Morality"; Auth, "Evang: Angl Witness In A Pluralistic Soc"; Auth, "Ch & Publ Plcy". EPF 1987; ESMHE 1986-1992; Eposcopal Urban Caucus 1987-2005; Interfaith Allnce 1993. peterwpeters@frontiernet.net

PETERS, Yejide S (NY) 1414 Greycourt Ave, Richmond VA 23227 **All SS' Epis Ch Briarcliff Manor NY 2010-** B New York, NY 8/16/1976 d William Arthur Peters & Jacquelyn. BA The U MI 2002; MDiv Ya Berk 2008. D 3/15/2008 Bp Mark Sean Sisk P 12/6/2008 Bp Peter James Lee. S Steph's Ch Richmond VA 2008-2010. yejidep@yahoo.com

PETERSEN, Barbara Jean (WNC) 2047 Paint Fork Rd, Mars Hill NC 28754 **Assoc St Georges Epis Ch Asheville NC 2010-** B Evanston IL 7/29/1948 d Frank Joseph Dudek & Mary Louise. BS U of Nebraska 1970; MDiv TS 2000. D 5/30/2000 P 11/30/2000 Bp James Edward Krotz. m 9/4/1969 Lyle Petersen. St Georges Epis Ch Asheville NC 2009-2010; Epis Ch Of The H Sprt Mars Hill NC 2002-2008; Mssnr S Christophers Ch Cozad NE 2000-2002; Mssnr S Eliz's Ch Holdrege NE 2000-2002; Mssnr S Jn's Ch Broken Bow NE 2000-2002; Cur S Mk's Epis Pro-Cathd Hastings NE 2000-2002; Mssnr S Pauls Epis Ch Arapahoe NE 2000-2002; Mssnr S Ptr's In The Vlly Lexington NE 2000-2002. Writer/article, "Renwl of Vows," *Highland Epis*, Dio Wstrn No Carolina, 2007. Ord of S Helena, Assoc 2004. CE Prize ABS 2000; Urban

T Holmes III Prize U So TS 2000; Wm A Griffin Schlrshp U So TS 2000. barbarajpetersen@yahoo.com

PETERSEN, Carolyn Petersen (CFla) 4708 Waterwitch Point Dr, Orlando FL 32806 **D Cathd Ch Of S Lk Orlando FL 1999-** B Cheyenne WY 7/2/1937 D 1/16/1999 Bp John Wadsworth Howe. m 8/1/1959 Leon Louis Petersen c 3. leonpete@gate.net

PETERSEN, Duane Eric (WLa) 1030 Johnston Street, Lafayette LA 70501 **P Asstg Ch Of The Ascen Lafayette LA 2009-; Assoc R Ch Of The Ascen Lafayette LA 1998-** B Rio Hondo CA 10/17/1956 s Donald Maxwell Petersen & Mavis Eleanor. BS Sthrn California Coll Costa Mesa 1978; Cert Sthrn California Coll Costa Mesa 1980; MDiv TESM 1992; DMin TESM 2006. D 6/27/1992 Bp Gethin Benwil Hughes P 1/9/1993 Bp James Michael Mark Dyer. m 6/13/1981 Mirinda Kay Miles c 2. Vic S Dunstans Epis Ch Modesto CA 1995-1998; Supply Cler Dio Oregon Portland OR 1994-1995; Asst R S Steph's Epis Ch Wilkes Barre PA 1992-1994. felizfour@yahoo.com

PETERSEN, Judith R. (SD) 1002 2nd St, Brookings SD 57006 B Dallas TX 6/26/1935 D 4/25/2003 Bp Creighton Leland Robertson. m 10/15/1976 Daryl Dee Petersen. ctrstage@brookings.net

PETERSEN, Scott B (WNC) 200 E Cowles St, Wilkesboro NC 28697 **R S Paul's Ch Wilkesboro NC 2010-** B 5/7/1971 s Eric Peter Petersen & Joan. St. Thos U; BA U of Massachusetts 1993; MDiv VTS 2007. D 1/6/2007 Bp Leopold Frade. m 3/17/1998 Rasmira Petersen c 3. The Epis Ch Of The Gd Shpd Tequesta FL 2007-2010. revpetersen@gmail.com

PETERSEN, William Herbert (Roch) 49 Winding Brook Dr., Fairport NY 14450 B Davenport IA 2/13/1941 s William August Petersen & Dorothea Cathleen. WCC Ecumencial Inst; BA Gri 1963; MDiv CDSP 1966; Oxf 1971; U CA 1971; PhD Grad Theol Un 1976; Deem Inst Of Sem Mgmt 1985. D 6/24/1966 P 12/27/1966 Bp Gordon V Smith. m 7/20/1963 Priscilla Ruth Eide c 2. Ecum Off Dom And Frgn Mssy Soc- Epis Ch Cntr New York NY 2011; Provost Bex Columbus OH 1995-2009; Dn Bex Columbus OH 1983-1995; Prof Nash Nashotah WI 1973-1983; Tchg Fell CDSP Berkeley CA 1970-1972; Asst Trsfg Epis Ch San Mateo CA 1968-1970; P-in-c All SS Epis Ch Storm Lake IA 1966-1968. Auth, "Ecum Ord," *Equipping the SS: Ord in Anglicanism Today*, Columba Press, 2006; Co-Auth, "Diac as Ecum Opportunity," *Hanover Report of ALIC*, ACC & Luth Wrld Fed, 1996; Co-Auth, "Implications Of The Gospel," Augsburg & Forwared Mvmt, 1988; Co-Auth, "A Hist of Mus in the Epis Ch," AAM, 1987; Auth, "On the Pattern & in the Power," *Angl Theol & Pstr Care*, Morehouse-Barlow, 1985; Auth, "Traditions Transplanted: Story Of Angl & Luth Ch In Amer," Forw Mvmt, 1981; Auth, "Clio in Ch," *Wrshp Points the Way*, Seabury, 1981. Amer Soc Ch Hist, Hist Soc Of The Episcop 1970; Angl Luth Intl Cmsn 1993; Associated Parishes for Liturg & Mssn 1973; HSEC 1973; Intl Angl Liturg Conf 1995; No Amer Acad of Ecumenists 1990; No Amer Acad of Liturg 1998; Societas Liturgica 1997. Cnvnr, Adv Proj Seminar No Amer Acad of Liturg 2007; Co-Cnvnr, Angl Colloquium No Amer Acad of Liturg 2004; Pres No Amer Acad of Ecumenists 2003; DD, honoris causa CDSP 1997; Pres Coun of Epis Sem Deans 1993. whpetersen@aol.com

PETERSEN-SNYDER, Christine Lynn (LI) 290 Conklin St, Farmingdale NY 11735 **S Thos Ch Farmingdale NY 2006-** B Brooklyn NY 12/2/1958 d Alfred B Petersen & Marjorie M. BA CUNY 2000; MDiv GTS 2004. D 5/26/2004 Bp Orris George Walker Jr P 12/18/2004 Bp Rodney Rae Michel. m 6/12/1977 Daniel Snyder c 2. Cur S Ptr's by-the-Sea Epis Ch Bay Shore NY 2004-2006. DOK 1996. therevcps@optonline.net

PETERSON, Barbara Ann (Mass) 249 Highland St, Marshfield MA 02050 **R Trin Ch Marshfield Hills MA 1999-** B Philadelphia PA 9/18/1951 d William Ellis & Joanne Dufur. BA U of New Mex 1979; MA U of New Mex 1983; MDiv Harvard DS 1986. D 6/10/1988 P 6/17/1989 Bp Don Edward Johnson. m 7/4/1991 William Charles Wrenn c 1. S Matt And The Redeem Epis Ch So Boston MA 1989-1999; D Chr Ch Cambridge Cambridge MA 1988-1989. revbap@aol.com

PETERSON, Diane Mildred (Ct) 4670 Congress St, Fairfield CT 06824 **D S Tim's Ch Fairfield CT 2009-** B Bridgeport CT 5/30/1947 d Ralph Kenneth Peterson & Phyllis Marie. D 9/12/2009 Bp Andrew Donnan Smith. c 2. peterson6@optonline.com

PETERSON JR, Frank Lon (NY) 969 Park Ave Apt 8C, New York NY 10028 **D Dio Connecticut Hartford CT 2009-; Mem - COM Dio New York New York City NY 2003-** B Miami FL 6/16/1936 s Frank Lon Peterson & Helen Evelyn. Florida St U; BS NYU 1964; MA GTS 1999. D 5/18/2002 Bp Mark Sean Sisk. D S Mich's Ch New York NY 2002-2009. Auth, "The Theol and Christology of the Prologue of theGospel of Jn," GTS, 1999. Soc of S Jn The Evangeliist 1997. fprm@comcast.net

PETERSON, Iris (Be) 56 Franklin St Unit 16, Danbury CT 06810 **S Jas Epis Ch Danbury CT 2002-** B Chester PA 1/5/1958 BA Cedar Crest Coll. D 4/6/2002 P 10/6/2002 Bp Paul Victor Marshall. IPETERSON@EARTHLINK.NET

PETERSON, John Edward (ND) PO Box 144, West Fargo ND 58078 **Geth Cathd Fargo ND 2006-** B Minneapolis MN 1/12/1929 s John Edward Peterson & Florence. MDiv NW Luth Sem; BA U MN 1954. Rec from Evangelical Lutheran Church in America 10/10/2006 Bp Michael Gene Smith. c 8. jehp@multipband.tv

PETERSON JR, John Henry (FdL) 129 5th St, Neenah WI 54956 B Providence RI 4/14/1941 s John Henry Peterson & Connie. BA U of Rhode Island 1963; MDiv Ya Berk 1966; MS U of Rhode Island 1987. D 6/18/1966 P 3/18/1967 Bp John S Higgins. m 12/30/1967 Kathleen Ann Aubert c 3. S Mk's Ch Westhampton Bch NY 1994-1997; Dio Milwaukee Milwaukee WI 1988-1993; R Ch Of The H Trin Tiverton RI 1973-1988; Cur S Mich's Ch Bristol RI 1967-1973; Cur Chr Ch Hackensack NJ 1966-1967. Auth, *Healing Touch*; Auth, *Origami for Christians*. kapeters3@earthlink.net

PETERSON, John Louis (WA) 1001 Red Oak Dr, Hendersonville NC 28791 B Wadena MN 12/17/1942 s John Harold Peterson & Edythe Victoria. BA Concordia Coll 1965; STB Harvard DS 1968; ThD Chicago Inst Of Advncd Theol Chicago MA 1977; DD VTS 1992; DCL STUSo 1996; DD SWTS 1997. D 6/6/1976 Bp Charles Ellsworth Bennison Jr P 6/1/1977 Bp Charles Bennison. m 8/20/1966 Kirsten R Bratlie c 2. Cathd of St Ptr & St Paul Washington DC 2005-2009; Dio Washington Washington DC 2005-2009; Epis Ch Cntr New York NY 1995-2004; Exec Coun Appointees New York NY 1982-1994; Dio Wstrn Michigan Kalamazoo MI 1978-1982; Asst To The Bp Of Wstrn Michigan Dio Wstrn Michigan Kalamazoo MI 1976-1982; Cn Theol Dio Wstrn Michigan Kalamazoo MI 1976-1982; Vic S Steph's Epis Ch Plainwell MI 1976-1982; Instr SWTS Evanston IL 1972-1973. Auth, "A Walk In Jerusalem," Morehouse, 1998; Auth, "36 arts," *Anchor Bible Dictionary*, 1992. Hon Cn All SS' Cathd Mpwapwa Tanzania 2002; Hon Cn S Paul'S Cathd London Engl 2001; Hon Cn S Mich'S Cathd Kaduna Nigeria 1999; Hon Cn Cbury Cathd Cbury Engl 1995; Hon Cn S Geo Cathd Jerusalem 1984; Hon Cn Chr King Cathd Kalamazoo MI 1982. jpeterson@cathedral.org

PETERSON JR, John Raymond (SwFla) 5020 Bayshore Blvd Apt 301, Tampa FL 33611 B Detroit MI 9/2/1936 s John Raymond Peterson & Shirley. BA MI SU 1959; MDiv VTS 1962. D 6/29/1962 Bp Archie H Crowley P 2/1/1963 Bp Richard S M Emrich. m 8/22/1959 Kay Slappey. Dio SW Florida Sarasota FL 1998-2001; Common Mnstry Dio SW Florida Sarasota FL 1998-2000; Chair Of Prog Dio SW Florida Sarasota FL 1987-1993; Ext Cmsn Dio SW Florida Sarasota FL 1987-1992; In Vitro Instnl Reviwe Bd Dio SW Florida Sarasota FL 1986-1995; Chair Of The Dnry Ext Com Dio SW Florida Sarasota FL 1984-1986; R St Johns Epis Ch Tampa FL 1979-2000; R S Mk's Barrington Hills IL 1965-1979; Asst S Paul's Epis Ch Lansing MI 1962-1965. jkpetersons@yahoo.com

PETERSON, Mainert Jordan (Ky) 7504 Westport Rd #A-17, Louisville KY 40222 **Died 5/20/2010** B Jersey City NJ 10/9/1917 s Charles Henry Peterson & Carrie. BS St Coll of New Jersey 1939; STB GTS 1943; MDiv GTS 1973. D 2/14/1943 P 9/11/1943 Bp Wallace J Gardner. c 4. Ord of S Lk 1979; Ord of S Lk, Wrdn Reg IV 1979-1985. Sovereign Red Cross of Constantine Kentucky Knights Templars KY 1991; Gd Turn Awd Intl BSA 1965; Grand Prelate Kentucky Knights Templars KY; Medal Meritorious Serv Kentucky Knights Templars KY; Celebrant Rose and Cross Kentucky Knights Templars KY.

PETERSON, Paul Douglas (SC) 142 Church St, Charleston SC 29401 **Chr Memi Chap Hobe Sound FL 2008-; Asst R S Phil's Ch Charleston SC 1998-** B Chicago IL 11/26/1936 s Paul Gilbert Peterson & Hazel Victoria. BD Cor; BA/MA U of Cambridge; MA Ya. D 6/24/1972 P 1/28/1973 Bp John Melville Burgess. m 6/17/1967 Joanne Vickers. Asst R Chr Ch Epis Ridley Pk PA 1991-1998; Assoc Ch Of The Ascen Knoxville TN 1989-1990; Assoc Ch Of The Gd Samar Knoxville TN 1984-1989; Assoc S Nich' Epis Ch Midland TX 1976-1984; Locten S Paul's Epis Ch No Andover MA 1975-1976; Assoc Trin Ch Topsfield MA 1972-1975; Mstr Brooks Sch Chap No Andover MA 1969-1976. douglas.peterson@citadel.edu

PETERSON, Peter Megill (HB) 1055 Wofford Dr, Las Cruces NM 88001 B Camden Pt MO 9/8/1929 s FF Peterson & LC. BA U NB 1951; ThD U of Basel 1958. D 5/12/1962 P 4/1/1963 Bp Joseph Gillespie Armstrong. m 7/3/1999 Lois Marion Welch. P Dio Mississippi Jackson MS 1978-1991; Vic S Patricks Epis Ch Long Bch MS 1974-1977; Vic S Paul's Ch Batesburg SC 1970-1974; Vic S Martins-In-Fields Summersville WV 1967-1970; Cur The Afr Epis Ch Of S Thos Philadelphia PA 1963-1967; M-in-c & Vic Hse Of Pryr Philadelphia PA 1962-1963; DCE Chr Ch Philadelphia Philadelphia PA 1961-1962. "Andr, Bro of Simon Ptr: Hist and Legend," *Supp. to Novum Testamentum*.

PETERSON, Philip Leonard (Oly) 14040 15th Ave Ne, Seattle WA 98125 B Spokane WA 2/25/1927 s Philip L Peterson & Thelma. BA U of Washington 1953. D 3/20/1972 Bp Ivol I Curtis. m 1/5/1951 Mary Little. D S Dunst-The Highlands Shoreline WA 1972-1974.

PETERSON, Ralph Edward (NY) 202 Shaker Ridge Drive, Canaan NY 12029 B Duluth MN 4/12/1932 s Harold Edward Peterson & Verna Muriel. BA U MN 1954; AMT Harv 1955; EDS 1956; MDiv Luth TS at Chicago 1960; Cert, AMP Harv Bus Sch 1977. Rec from Church of Sweden 1/24/1989 as Priest Bp Richard Frank Grein. m 5/31/1969 Birgitta E Esselius c 1. Int Chr Ch Oyster Bay NY 2002-2004; Int Chr Ch Warwick NY 2000-2002; Int Par Of

P

Chr The Redeem Pelham NY 2000; Int Ch Of S Jas The Less Scarsdale NY 1999-2000; Int All SS' Epis Ch Briarcliff Manor NY 1997-1998; Int S Paul's Ch Kinderhook NY 1996-1997; Int S Mk's Ch Mt Kisco NY 1994-1996; P-in-c Hse Of The Redeem New York NY 1992-1994. Auth, "The Healing Ch: Hlth Care Apostolate," 1981. Ch Club 1992; Fllshp of St. Alb and St. Sergius 1979; Societas Sanctae Birgittae 1982. Fell The Sophia Inst 2009; Fell Soc of Art Rel and Culture 1972; D.D. Ge 1971; Phi Delta Kappa Harvard 1955. ralphepete@mac.com

PETERSON, Richard Trenholm (Cal) 883 Roble Dr, Sunnyvale CA 94086 B San Francisco CA 3/30/1934 s Franklin Trenholm Peterson & Etta Mernelva. Trin San Antonio TX 1954; Tchr Cred. San Francisco St U 1968; California Sch for Deacons 1979; BA California Sch for Deacons 1984; Cert U CA 1987. D 6/28/1980 Bp William Edwin Swing. m 6/24/1962 Marilyn Ann Koyen c 2. S Mk's Epis Ch Palo Alto CA 2000-2003; Assoc S Lk's Ch Los Gatos CA 1984-1992; Pstr Asst S Tim's Epis Ch Mtn View CA 1980-1984. *Var Mus Pub.* OHC 1976. Letter of Commendation for Wk as Ther / Counslr Phoenix Prog, El Camino Hosp Mtn View CA 1987; Cert of Appreciation for Years of Serv Foothill-DeAnza Cmnty Coll Distr 1985; Janacek Medal Mus/Conducting Awd Republic of Czechoslovakia 1971; Cert of Merit and Appreciation USAF Chapl Off Headqu 12th AF Germany Germany 1956.

PETERSON, S(ally) Suzanne (Ia) Diocese of Cape Town, PO Box 1932, Cape Town 8000 South Africa **Exec Coun Appointees New York NY 1999-; Hon Cn The Cathd Ch Of S Paul Des Moines IA 1998-** B Bradenton FL 4/26/1948 d Harry Wheeler Peterson & Mildred Polly. BA Florida St U 1970; MA VTS 1972. D 12/18/1976 P 9/25/1977 Bp Walter Cameron Righter. Iowa Inter-Ch Agcy For Peace & Justice Des Moines IA 1983-1991; The Cathd Ch Of S Paul Des Moines IA 1976-1982. Comm Res Lord Grahamstown So Afr 1994. Proctor Fell EDS 1994; Hon Cn 98 S Paul Cath Des Moines IA. ppo@anglicanchurchssa.org.sa

PETERSON-WLOSINSKI, Cynthia M E (Minn) 1121 W Morgan St, Duluth MN 55811 B Saint Paul MN 7/9/1950 d Glenn Richard Peterson & Margaret Mae. BS San Jose St U 1974; MDiv VTS 1982. D 6/24/1982 P 12/29/1982 Bp Robert Marshall Anderson. m 12/28/1983 Stephen Stanley Peterson Wlosinski c 1. S Andr's By The Lake Duluth MN 1994-1998; Cur S Lk's Ch Minneapolis MN 1982-1986. cmpetefarm@aol.com

PETIPRIN, Andrew Kirk (CFla) 7142 Lake Drive, Orlando FL 32809 **R S Mary Of The Ang Epis Ch Orlando FL 2011-** B Plattsburgh NY 12/26/1979 s Eric Kemp Petiprin & Mary. BA U Pgh 2001; MPhil Oxf 2003; MDiv Ya Berk 2010. D 6/5/2010 Bp John Wadsworth Howe P 12/21/2010 Bp Kirk Stevan Smith. m 12/31/2005 Amber R Morris c 1. Asst to the R Chr Ch Of The Ascen Paradise Vlly AZ 2010-2011. andrew.petiprin@gmail.com

PETIT, Charles David (USC) 5220 Clemson Ave, Columbia SC 29206 B Huntington WV 1/14/1951 BA Marshall U. D 6/14/2003 P 5/27/2004 Bp Dorsey Felix Henderson. m 6/7/1997 Michelle Maria Petit c 3. D H Cross Epis Ch Simpsonville SC 2003-2005. External Serv Awd Unoiversity Of The So TS 2003. cpetit@sc.rr.com

PETITE, Robert (Chi) 2038 N Sayre Ave, Chicago IL 60707 **The Ch Hm At Montgomery Place Chicago IL 1993-** B Belloram CA 11/2/1946 s Robert Henry Petite & Olive. BA U Of King's Coll Halifax Ns CA 1969; MDiv U Tor 1972; DMin Chicago TS 1998. Trans from Anglican Church of Canada 7/23/1993 Bp Frank Tracy Griswold III. c 3. Chapl And Exec Dir S Anna's Chap Chicago IL 1993-2003. Bd Cert Chapl Assn Prof Chapl; Clincl Mem Assn Mar & Fam Ther; Supvsr ACPE. rpetite@montplace.com

PETLEY, Dale Alfred (Okla) 1813 Westminster Pl, Oklahoma City OK 73120 **Assoc R All Souls Epis Ch Oklahoma City OK 1997-** B Summerside CA 1/31/1958 s Melvin Harold Petley & Rita Mary. BA U Of King's Coll Halifax Ns CA 1979; MDiv Atlantic TS 1982. Trans 9/1/1997 Bp Robert Manning Moody. Auth, "The H Sprt". Royal Can Legion. dpetley@allsoulsokc.com

PETRASH, David Lloyd (Dal) PO Box 745, Kaufman TX 75412 B Waxahachie TX 3/18/1948 s John Joseph Petrash & Mary Frances. BA U of No Texas 1969; MA U of No Texas 1971; DMA U of No Texas 1975; Angl TS 2005. D 6/5/2004 P 5/29/2008 Bp James Monte Stanton. m 1/21/1984 Laura Petrash c 4. Ch Of Our Merc Sav Kaufman TX 2009; S Lk's Ch Denison TX 2008-2009; Int Hd of Sch S Lk's Ch Denison TX 2007-2008; D S Steph's Epis Ch Sherman TX 2004-2005. david.petrash@gmail.com

PETROCCIONE, James Victor (Nwk) 28 Ross Rd, Stanhope NJ 07874 B Elizabeth NJ 9/4/1963 s Vincent P Petroccione & Alice E. BA U of Memphis 1995; MDiv Memphis TS 1998. D 4/13/2002 P 10/20/2002 Bp John Palmer Croneberger. R Ch Of The H Comm Norwood NJ 2008; S Mary's Ch Sparta NJ 2007-2008; All SS Ch Orange NJ 2003-2006; Asst S Jn's Meml Ch Ramsey NJ 2002-2003; Assoc S Mary's Ch Sparta NJ 2002. frjimpetroccione@aol.com

PETROTTA, Anthony Joseph (Ore) PO Box 445, Wilsonville OR 97070 **P S Fran Of Assisi Epis Wilsonville OR 2005-** B San Francisco CA 10/12/1950 BA Westmont Coll 1975; MA Fuller TS 1977; MPhil U of St. Andrews 1984; PhD Sheffield U Engl 1990. D 7/18/2004 P 4/24/2005 Bp Jerry Alban Lamb. m 7/10/2000 Pamela Berta-Petrotta c 2. Ch Of The Incarn Santa Rosa CA 2005; S Paul's Epis Ch Benicia CA 2004-2005. co-Auth, "Pocket Dictionary of Biblic Stds," InterVarsityPress, 2002. SBL 1980. apetrott@ix.netcom.com

PETTENGILL, David Eugene (Az) 1558 E Gary St, Mesa AZ 85203 **Asst Chr Ch Of The Ascen Paradise Vlly AZ 2010-; Chapl to Ret Cler and spouses Dio Arizona Phoenix AZ 2010-** B Polk City IA 5/29/1932 s Claude Edward Pettengill & Liane Anna. BA Arizona St U 1958; MDiv CDSP 1960. D 6/12/1960 P 12/11/1960 Bp Arthur Kinsolving. m 9/5/1953 Lois Midkiff c 1. Asst S Matt's Ch Chandler AZ 1999-2009; Int Chr Ch Of The Ascen Paradise Vlly AZ 1998-1999; R S Mk's Epis Ch Mesa AZ 1978-1994; R S Lk's Ch Prescott AZ 1967-1978; Mem of Dioc Coun Dio Arizona Phoenix AZ 1965-1990; Cur Gr S Paul's Epis Ch Tucson AZ 1964-1967; R SS Phil And Jas Morenci AZ 1960-1964. Hon DD The CDSP 2011; Hon Cn To Ordnry Dio Az 1992. dalopet@juno.com

PETTERSON, Ted Ross (La) 25 Signature Dr, Brunswick ME 04011 B Amsterdam NY 4/20/1935 s John Christian Petterson & Mary Kathrine. BA Tem 1964; MDiv PDS 1970. D 6/6/1970 P 12/12/1970 Bp Robert Lionne DeWitt. m 4/15/1961 Joan Bellows c 2. S Paul's Ch New Orleans LA 1985-1998; The Cathd Ch Of S Paul Des Moines IA 1984-1985; The Ch Of Our Redeem Lexington MA 1974-1984. tpetterson@comcast.com

PETTITT, Robert Riley (ND) 1201 49th Avenue, Rt 6, Fargo ND 58103 B Saint Cloud MN 3/19/1923 s William Riley Pettitt & Erma Mae. D 12/21/1985 P 10/1/1987 Bp Harold Anthony Hopkins Jr. m 7/20/1946 Elizabeth Mae Bensen.

PETTY, Carol Ross (Tex) Holy Comforter Episcopal Church, PO Box 786, Angleton TX 77516 B Hamilton Ohio 12/27/1953 d Max Ross Petty & Priscilla Jean. BS Texas Wmn's U-Denton 1974; MDiv SW Bapt TS 2001; MA SW Bapt TS 2001; CTh Epis TS of The SW 2005; D. Min. Austin Presb TS 2012. D 6/11/2005 Bp Don Adger Wimberly P 12/19/2005 Bp Rayford Baines High Jr. m 5/14/2011 George Haggas Zwicker c 2. Ch Of The H Comf Angleton TX 2005-2007; Assoc. R Trin Ch Longview TX 2005-2007. carolpetty@gmail.com

PETTY JR, Jess Joseph (O) 568 101st Ave N, Naples FL 34108 B Berea OH 8/17/1936 s Jess Joseph Petty & Arline. BA Baldwin-Wallace Coll 1958; MDiv Bex 1961. D 6/10/1961 P 1/24/1962 Bp Nelson Marigold Burroughs. m 8/8/1969 Gillian Wilkins c 4. St Johns Epis Ch Tampa FL 2001-2002; Int S Jn's Epis Ch Clearwater FL 2000; Int Ch Of The Ascen Clearwater FL 1999-2000; Int Trin By The Cove Naples FL 1998-1999; Int S Hilary's Ch Ft Myers FL 1996-1997; Int Gr And H Trin Cathd Kansas City MO 1995-1996; Int S Mart's Ch Chagrin Falls OH 1994-1995; R S Paul's Epis Ch Medina OH 1981-1994; Int S Ptr's Ch Clifton NJ 1980-1981; Cathd Of St Lk Balboa PANAMA CITY 1977-1980; Vic S Lk's Epis Ch Chardon OH 1973-1977; Cur Chr Ch Shaker Heights OH 1961-1963; S Alb Epis Ch Cleveland Heights OH 1961-1963. Hon Cn Gr and H Trin Cathd 1996. gilljess@aol.com

PETTY JR, Tyrus Cecil (Kan) 5841 Sw 26th St, Topeka KS 66614 B Teague TX 1/16/1944 s Tyrus C Petty & Maybelle. BA TCU 1967; MDiv SWTS 1972; MS U of Kansas 1991. D 4/10/1972 Bp William Paul Barnds P 10/1/1972 Bp Edward Clark Turner. m 7/27/1968 Marjorie D McColl. S Dav's Epis Ch Topeka KS 1976-1978; Cn Gr Cathd Topeka KS 1972-1975. Aamft; Supvrs ACPE.

PETZAK, Rodney Ross (Nev) 1965 Golden Gate Dr, Reno NV 89511 B Manistee MI 2/10/1933 s Joseph Petzak & Elsie. AA Orange Coast Coll Costa Mesa CA 1957. D 9/6/1996 P 3/1/1997 Bp Stewart Clark Zabriskie. m 9/20/1980 Sharyn L Petzak. P S Jn's In The Wilderness Ch Glenbrook NV 1997-2011.

PETZAK, Sharyn L (Nev) 1965 Golden Gate Dr, Reno NV 89511 B Wausau WI 8/5/1953 d Albert Joseph & Leone. BA Gonzaga U 1984; MA Gonzaga U 1986; EdD U of Nevada at Reno 1993. D 3/15/1997 Bp Stewart Clark Zabriskie. m 9/20/1980 Rodney Ross Petzak. D S Jn's In The Wilderness Ch Glenbrook NV 1997-2003.

PEVERLEY, Stephen Richard (LI) 1 Araca Ct, Babylon NY 11702 **Gr Epis Ch Massapequa NY 2004-** B Mineola NY 2/6/1937 s Norman Peverley & Eleanor. BA Adel 1961; MA Adel 1966; Mercer TS 1978. D 6/23/1979 P 2/1/1981 Bp Robert Campbell Witcher Sr. m 7/3/1965 Susan Combs c 4. Epis Ch Of S Mk The Evang No Bellmore NY 2004-2006; Chr Ch Manhasset NY 2003-2004; Int Chr Ch Garden City NY 2002-2003; Ch of S Jude Wantagh NY 2001-2009; Int S Mk's Ch Westhampton Bch NY 2000-2001; Int Ch of S Jude Wantagh NY 1998-1999; Int S Ptr's by-the-Sea Epis Ch Bay Shore NY 1997-1998; Int Trin Epis Ch Roslyn NY 1996; Int Ch of S Jude Wantagh NY 1995-1999; Int S Bon Epis Ch Lindenhurst NY 1994-1995; Int Trin Ch Northport NY 1992-1994; Int S Ann's Epis Ch Bridgehampton NY 1991-1992; Int S Phil And S Jas Ch New Hyde Pk NY 1990-1991; Int S Jas Epis Ch S Jas NY 1989-1990; Int S Paul's Ch Patchogue NY 1986-1989; Int Epis Ch Of S Mk The Evang No Bellmore NY 1985-1986; Int Epis Ch Of S Mk The Evang No Bellmore NY 1983-1984; Assoc Emm Epis Ch Great River NY 1980-1983; Asst Chr Ch Babylon NY 1979-1980. Ord of S Lk Chapl. revpev@verizon.net

PEYTON III, Allen Taylor (Alb) 2401 Ben Hill Rd, Atlanta GA 30344 B Copenhagen DK 11/15/1957 s Allen Taylor Peyton & Margaret. BA U So 1980; MDiv GTS 1988. D 6/11/1988 P 6/28/1989 Bp Frank Kellogg Allan. m 5/22/1988 Suzanne Darlington Cohen. R S Paul's Epis Ch Greenwich NY

2002-2010; R S Paul's Ch Palmyra MO 1992-1995; Vic S Jas Epis Ch Clayton GA 1989-1992; D The Epis Ch Of S Ptr And S Paul Marietta GA 1988-1989. alleniii@iwon.com

PEYTON IV, F(rancis) (WA) 5 Barthel Ct, Lutherville Timonium MD 21093 B Charlottesville VA 12/26/1950 s F Bradley Peyton & Gertrude. Deerfield Acad Deerfield MA 1968; BA U of Virginia 1972; JD U of Virginia 1975; MDiv VTS 1984. D 5/23/1984 Bp Peter James Lee P 6/11/1985 Bp David Keller Leighton Sr. m 8/1/1987 Joan A D'Adamo c 2. Int S Jn's Ch Kingsville MD 2004-2005; St Philips Luth Ch Baltimore MD 2001-2004; Eccl Trial Crt Dio Washington Washington DC 1998-2003; Epis Cler Assn Dio Washington Washington DC 1996-1999; R S Paul's Epis Ch Piney Waldorf MD 1992-2000; Int S Anne's Par Scottsville VA 1991-1992; R Emm Ch At Brook Hill Richmond VA 1988-1990; Cur Chr Ch St Michaels MD 1985-1988; Asst S Jn's Ch Reisterstown MD 1984. fb.peyton@yahoo.com

PEYTON, Linda (Me) 42 Flying Point Rd, Freeport ME 04032 B New York NY 2/8/1952 d Bernard Peyton & Joan. BA Sarah Lawr Coll 1976; MDiv EDS 1980. D 6/7/1980 Bp Paul Moore Jr P 12/20/1980 Bp Lyman Cunningham Ogilby. m 10/29/1983 Morris C Hancock c 2. Asst Ch Of The Redeem Bryn Mawr PA 1980-1983. peytol@comcast.net

PEYTON JR, Robert Lee (At) 579 Fairview Ave, Hartwell GA 30643 **R S Andr's Ch Hartwell GA 2008-** B Austin TX 9/22/1950 BS Louisiana Tech U 1972; MS U of Texas at Austin 1975; PhD Colorado St U 1985; MA UTS 2004; Angl Dplma GTS 2008. D 12/21/2007 P 6/21/2008 Bp George Wayne Smith. leepeyton.standrews@gmail.com

PEYTON, William Parish (Va) 865 Madison Ave., New York NY 10021 **Assoc R S Jas Ch New York NY 2010-** B Alexandria VA 10/5/1970 s Gordon Pickett Peyton & Marjorie Parish. BA U of Virginia 1993; MDiv GTS 2006. D 6/24/2006 P 2/3/2007 Bp Peter James Lee. m 6/19/1991 Elizabeth Moomaw c 3. Asst R S Paul's Ch Ivy VA 2006-2010. willpeyton@gmail.com

PFAB, Martin William (Fla) 724 Lake Stone Cir, Ponte Vedra Beach FL 32082 B Bernard IA 9/27/1935 s Henry Pfab & Regina. BA Loras Coll 1958; MDiv Mt S Bern Sem Dubuque IA 1962; CTh SWTS 1987. Rec from Roman Catholic 6/7/1987 as Priest Bp Walter Cameron Righter. m 11/21/1984 Penny L Pfab. S Mary's Epis Ch Green Cove Sprg FL 2007-2009; Adv Ch Farmington MN 2001-2003; S Ptr's Epis Ch Kasson MN 1997-2000; Dio Minnesota Minneapolis MN 1988-1997; Int Trin Epis Par Waterloo IA 1987-1988. Assembly of the Epis Hospitals and Chapl 1988; Coll Of Chapl 1988. mpfab@stpatricksepiscopal.org

PFAB, Penny L (Fla) 724 Lake Stone Cir, Ponte Vedra Beach FL 32082 **R S Paul's By-The-Sea Epis Ch Jacksonville Bch FL 2006-** B Cedar Rapids IA 7/8/1947 d John G Willman & Mildred D. BD Mt Mercy Coll 1983; CTh SWTS 1994; MDiv Untd TS of the Twin Cities 1994. D 6/29/1994 Bp James Louis Jelinek P 1/7/1995 Bp Sanford Zangwill Kaye Hampton. m 11/21/1984 Martin William Pfab c 4. R S Lk's Ch Minneapolis MN 2001-2006; R S Paul's Epis Ch Owatonna MN 1995-2001; Mayo Clnc Rochester Rochester MN 1994-1995. ppfab@spbts.net

PFAFF, Brad Hampton (NY) 126 W 83rd St Apt 3-P, New York NY 10024 B Carlinville IL 8/1/1948 s Harold Bernard Pfaff & Lucille. BA, cl IL Wesl 1970; MDiv GTS 1975. D 3/24/1977 P 1/25/1978 Bp Harold Louis Wright. Vic Ch Of The H Nativ Bronx NY 1997-2008; P Dio New York New York City NY 1981-1997; Cur The Ch of S Ign of Antioch New York NY 1978-1981; Assoc Chr Ch Bronxville NY 1977-1978. CBS. bradderpfaff@gmail.com

PFAFF, David Anthony (Mil) Diocese of Milwaukee, 804 East Juneau Avenue, Milwaukee WI 53202 **GC Dep Dio Milwaukee Milwaukee WI 2012** B Oxford England UK 7/7/1964 s Richard William Pfaff & Margaret. BA U NC 1986; MDiv GTS 1992. D 5/28/1992 Bp Robert Whitridge Estill P 5/29/1993 Bp Huntington Williams Jr. m 8/26/1989 Emily Susan Vaill c 3. GC Dep Dio Milwaukee Milwaukee WI 2009; GC Dep Dio Milwaukee Milwaukee WI 2006; COM Chair Dio Milwaukee Milwaukee WI 2003-2007; R S Mk's Ch Milwaukee WI 1999-2007; P-in-c Ascen Memi Ch Ipswich MA 1997-1999; Assoc Chr Epis Ch Raleigh NC 1992-1997. pfaff@diomil.org

PFAFF, Richard William (NC) 750 Weaver Dairy Road, #190, Chapel Hill NC 27514 B Oklahoma City OK 8/6/1936 s Frederick Erwin Pfaff & Flora. AB Harv 1957; BA Oxf 1959; MA Oxf 1963; DPhil Oxf 1965; Cert GTS 1966. D 6/11/1966 Bp Robert Lionne DeWitt P 12/17/1966 Bp Horace W B Donegan. m 12/27/1962 Margaret Campbell c 1. Auth, "The Liturg in Medieval Engl. A Hist," 2009; Auth, "Liturg Calendars, Books & SS in Medieval Engl," 1998; Co-Auth & co-Ed, "The Eadwine Psalter. Text, Image, & Monastic Culture in Twelfth-Century Cbury," 1992; Auth, "Medieval Latin Liturg: Select Bibliography," 1982; Auth, "Montague Rhodes Jas," 1980; Auth, "New Liturg Feasts In Later Medieval Engl," 1970. Assn Amer Rhodes Scholars 1959; Henry Bradshaw Soc (Hon VP) 1987; Phi Beta Kappa 1957. Fell of Medieval Acad of Amer 2000; DD U of Oxford 1995; Fell of Soc of Antiquaries of London London 1993; Fell of Royal Hist Soc 1983. pfaffrw@live.unc.edu

PFEIFFER, Dorothea Koop (WNC) 2 Sweet Gum Ct, Hilton Head SC 29928 **D S Lk's Epis Ch Hilton Hd SC 1996-** B Omaha NE 3/12/1927 d Harvey Brian Koop & Gertrude. BA U of Nebraska 1948; MA U Denv 1965; Illinois St U 1982; Inst of Pstr Stds, Chicago 1992. D 12/18/1993 Bp Edward Harding MacBurney. m 5/27/1977 Frederick W Pfeiffer c 2. D Dio Quincy Peoria IL 1993-1996. Auth, "The View From My Car," Vantage, 2001. Chapl/St Lukes Chapt Of Dok 1997; Cnvnt Trsfg 1988; Mem/Chapl Dok 1997. dkpfeiffer@verizon.net

PFEIL, Benjamin Oliver (Fla) Po Box 611, Madison FL 32341 **Vic S Mary's Epis Ch Madison FL 1992-** B Cementon NY 4/22/1924 s Benjamin James Pfeil & Anna Elizabeth. D 5/24/1992 P 11/1/1992 Bp Frank Stanley Cerveny. m 11/19/1944 Mary Jane Smith c 1. S Mary's Epis Ch Madison FL 1994-1996.

PFISTER, Kathleen Rock (NC) PO Box 5176, Austin TX 78763 **Cur The Ch of the Gd Shpd Austin TX 2010-** B New Orleans LA 10/5/1969 d William A Rock & Eileen B. BA The Amer U Washington DC 1990; MDiv Epis TS Of The SW 2010. D 6/19/2010 P 1/28/2011 Bp Michael Bruce Curry. m 8/8/1997 Phillip Julian Pfister c 2. Dio No Carolina Raleigh NC 2000-2007. salshouse@gmail.com

PFOTENHAUER, Leon Henry (Ia) 1613 S Nicollet St, Sioux City IA 51106 **D S Paul's Indn Mssn Sioux City IA 2001-** B Pierre SD 12/15/1929 s William C Pfotenhauer & Frances Ann. BS So Dakota St U 1956. D 4/25/1995 Bp Carl Christopher Epting. m 5/29/1955 Lorraine Joyce Snyder c 2. D Calv Epis Ch Sioux City IA 1995-2001. asvcitw13@msn.com

PHALEN, John Richard (Los) 5772 Garden Grove Blvd Spc 487, Westminster CA 92683 B Eden NY 6/14/1936 s James Robert Phalen & Marguerite Mary. BA Un 1958; MDiv Ya Berk 1962; GTS 1967; Cert U CA 1977; STD SFTS 1987. D 6/22/1962 P 3/31/1963 Bp Lauriston L Scaife. m 9/23/2000 Sherry Tao Sha c 2. Int R St Johns Pro-Cathd Los Angeles CA 2001-2009; Int Ch Of The H Comm Gardena CA 2000-2002; Cur Trin Epis Ch Buffalo NY 1962-1964. Auth, "Screenplay, Petals of the Midnight Rose," 2011; Auth, "Screenplay Snow Without Name," 2009; Auth, "Pathways Through theNight," *Pathways Through the Night*, Publish Amer, 2009; Auth, "Beneath the Eyes of God, The Ord," Gateways Pub, 2004; Auth, "Plays, Wastelands, Second Sunday, Midnight Video, Choir Without Song, Orphans," *Beneath the Eyes of God*, Gateways Pub, 2001; Auth, "Poems, Diary of Fallen Warriors, Snake Eyes In The Garden, Ang City Light," *Beyond the Poetry of God*, Gateways Pub, 1995. pacificdirections@yahoo.com

PHAM, J Peter (Q) 119 E 74th St, New York NY 10021 **Hon Asst S Paul's Par Washington DC 2011-** B Paris France 12/27/1970 s Joseph Yen Van Pham & Catherine Mai. AB U Chi 1990; STB Pontifical Gregorian U 1994; STL Pontifical Gregorian U 1996; STD Pontifical Gregorian U 1999; JCL Pontifical Gregorian U 2001. Rec from Roman Catholic 5/9/2008 as Priest Bp Keith Lynn Ackerman. m 6/30/2007 Soo Chu Yee. Hon Asst Ch Of The Resurr New York NY 2008-2011. drjppham@aol.com

PHANORD, Jn. Berthold (Hai) PO Box 407139, C/O Lynx Air, Fort Lauderdale FL 33340 **Dio Haiti Ft Lauderdale FL 2003-** B 8/5/1966 D.

PHELAN, Shane (Nwk) 43 Massachusetts Ave., Haworth NJ 07641 **P-in-c/ Pstr S Lk's Epis Ch Haworth NJ 2010-** B Lakewood OH 11/15/1956 s William Dallas Baker & Dorothy Wyckoff. BA California St U 1980; PhD U of Massachusetts 1987; MDiv Drew TS 2009. D 6/6/2009 P 12/12/2009 Bp Mark M Beckwith. Ed, "We Are Everywhere," Routledge, 2007; Ed, "Playing w Fire," Routledge, 2007; Auth, "Sexual Strangers: Gays, Lesbians, and the Dilemmas of Citizenship," Tem Press, 2000; Auth, "Getting Specific: Postmodern Lesbian Politics," U Minnesota Press, 1994; Auth, "Identity Politics: Lesbian Feminism and the Limits of Cmnty," Tem Press, 1989. revdrshane@gmail.com

PHELPS, Cecil Richard (NI) 4525 Baring Ave, Box 2293, East Chicago IN 46312 B Gary IN 12/8/1938 s Cecil Arthur Phelps & Elizabeth. BA W&M 1960; STB GTS 1963. D 4/20/1963 P 10/28/1963 Bp James R Mallett. Ch Of The Gd Shpd E Chicago IN 1980-2003; P S Augustines Ch Gary IN 1975-1978; Vic H Fam Ch Angola IN 1970-1974; Asst The Ch of S Matt And S Tim New York NY 1964-1967; Cur S Paul's Epis Ch Munster IN 1963-1964. SSC 1973.

PHELPS, H(oward) Neal (Ga) 611 E Bay St, Savannah GA 31401 B Franklin County NC 9/4/1937 s Jim Collie Phelps & Emma Line. Louisburg Coll 1956; LTh Nash 1975. D 2/4/1975 P 8/5/1975 Bp (George) Paul Reeves. m 4/5/1958 Chris Shearin c 1. Cn Dio Georgia Savannah GA 2003-2009; R S Aug Of Cbury Ch Augusta GA 1977-2003; Vic S Matt's Epis Ch Fitzgerald GA 1975-1977. Soc of S Jn the Evang 1975. chrisnealp@knology.net

PHELPS, Joan Priscilla (Ct) 15 Freedom Way Unit 101, Niantic CT 06367 B Farmington CT 2/13/1941 d Herbert Arthur Phelps & Marie Lucy. BS U of Connecticut 1963; MA U of Connecticut 1966; MDiv GTS 1990. D 6/9/1990 P 4/19/1991 Bp Arthur Edward Walmsley. Assoc Trin Epis Ch Hartford CT 2006-2007; Assoc S Jas's Ch W Hartford CT 2000-2006; R S Barn And All SS Ch Springfield MA 1994-1999; Asst S Paul's Epis Ch Willimantic CT 1990-1994; Asst S Jn's Epis Ch Niantic CT 1990. Ord Of S Helena. rev@ct.metrocast.net

P

PHELPS, John Edward (Me) 4 Glendale Rd, Kennebunk ME 04043 B Boston MA 12/7/1937 s Houston Street Phelps & Barbara Darling. BA Bos 1961; MDiv VTS 1965. D 6/1/1965 Bp John Melville Burgess P 5/1/1966 Bp Anson Phelps Stokes Jr. m 6/10/1961 Janet Dane Smerage c 4. Dioc Search Com Dio Maine Portland ME 1997-1998; Vic/R Chr Epis Ch Eastport ME 1990-2002; R S Andr's Ch Methuen MA 1977-1989; Supplement Accounts Boston MA 1971-1976; R St Johns Ch Taunton MA 1967-1977; Cur Ch Of The H Nativ So Weymouth MA 1965-1967. Nash Fllshp Dio Massachusetts 1986.

PHELPS JR, Kenneth O (Md) 6401 Solomons Island Rd N, Sunderland MD 20689 **R All SS Epis Par Sunderland MD 2004-** B Baltimore MD 7/11/1951 s Kenneth Oliver Phelps & Anne Henrietta. BA Buc 1973; MDiv Luth TS at Gettysburg 1978; U of Baltimore 1985; VTS 1997. D 11/30/1999 Bp John Leslie Rabb P 6/2/2000 Bp Robert Wilkes Ihloff. m 2/13/1988 Dianne Lynne Martin c 3. Assoc S Thos Epis Ch Towson MD 1999-2004. phelpsjrko@yahoo.com

PHELPS, Mary M (Minn) 7350 Bristol Village Dr., Apt. 327, Bloomington MN 55438 **Int P S Mary's Basswood Grove Hastings MN 2010-** B Minneapolis MN 5/21/1951 d Douglas Keith Millett & Dorothy Deen. BA The Coll of St. Cathr St. Paul MN 1990; Cert SWTS 2004; MDiv Untd TS of the Twin Cities 2005. D 6/15/2005 P 12/15/2005 Bp James Louis Jelinek. c 2. Asstg P Ch Of The Nativ Burnsville MN 2009-2010; Asst to the R S Geo's Ch St Louis Pk MN 2005-2007. marypl@aol.com

PHELPS, Nicholas Barclay (Pa) 1906 Trenton Ave, Bristol PA 19007 **Asst P S Mk's Ch Philadelphia PA 1999-** B Grosse Pte MI 10/17/1933 s Charles Blanchard Phelps & Constance. BA Wms 1956; MDiv EDS 1959. D 6/14/1959 Bp Oliver J Hart P 12/21/1959 Bp Robert McConnell Hatch. R S Jas Epis Ch Bristol PA 1981-1997; R Trin Ch Buckingham PA 1970-1980; Asst S Jn's Ch Williamstown MA 1959-1962. ESMHE.

PHELPS, Shannon David (SanD) Po Box 234, Del Mar CA 92014 B Pana IL 10/12/1948 s Marion Phelps & Esther Garnet. BA Stan 1980; MA Harvard DS 1990; MDiv Ya Berk 1993. D 6/5/1993 P 3/1/1994 Bp Gethin Benwil Hughes. m 9/24/1977 Kit Claire Warfield. H Cross Mssn Carlsbad CA 1999-2001; S Ptr's Epis Ch Del Mar CA 1993-1997. phelps@inetworld.net

PHELPS, Walter E (Cal) 120 Lorraine Ct, Vacaville CA 95688 B Brooklyn NY 3/17/1922 s Walter Sinclair Phelps & Anna. BA CUNY 1949; MA U CA 1955; BD CDSP 1959; MS U CA 1966. D 6/21/1959 P 1/9/1960 Bp James Albert Pike. m 11/20/1996 Lucretia Ann Jevne. Asst P S Aid's Mssn Bolinas CA 1987-1991; S Paul's Epis Ch San Rafael CA 1982-1983; Asst S Paul's Epis Ch San Rafael CA 1965-1968; Asst St Johns Epis Ch Ross CA 1965-1968; Assoc S Mk's Epis Ch Santa Clara CA 1960-1961. Auth, *An Intro to Eliots Murder in the Cathd*; Auth, *Hello Thorton!; Thoughts on The Matchmaker*. walterephelps@comcast.net

PHILIP, Kristi (Spok) 245 E 13th Ave, Spokane WA 99202 **Dioc Coun Chair Dio Spokane Spokane WA 1988-** B Bremerton WA 2/2/1946 d Howard Bruce Henderson & Virginia Ethelyn. BA U of Washington 1967; Cert CDSP 1985; MA Gonzaga U 1989. D 2/27/1977 Bp John Raymond Wyatt P 7/13/1985 Bp Leigh Wallace Jr. c 2. Dio Spokane Spokane WA 2006-2007; Cn Cong Resources Dio Spokane Spokane WA 1997-2000; Cn Pstr Care & Educ Cathd Of S Jn The Evang Spokane WA 1985-1997; Dioc Coun Dio Spokane Spokane WA 1985-1989; COM Dio Spokane Spokane WA 1980-1984; Asst S Paul's Epis Ch Kennewick WA 1977-1985. Auth, "A Pryr for Transition," *Wmn Uncommon Prayers*, Morehouse, 2000; Auth, "w God as our Comp," *Congregations*, Alb Inst, 1997. DD CDSP 2004; Fell Coolidge Colloquim 1993. kristip@spokanediocese.org

PHILIPS, John Kevin (ECR) 1190 Alta Mesa Road, Monterey CA 93940 **Chapl Epis Sr Communities Walnut Creek CA 1991-** B Kingsville TX 5/28/1955 s Ronald William Philips & Marian Rhoades. BA U So 1977; MDiv Nash 1982; MA Santa Clara U 1999. D 6/5/1982 Bp Paul Moore Jr P 12/1/1982 Bp Charles Alfred Voegeli. Chair Of HIV/AIDS Taskforce Dio El Camino Real Monterey CA 1991-1996; R Trin Epis Ch Ossining NY 1985-1989; Cur S Geo's Epis Ch Schenectady NY 1982-1985; Mem of Ecum Com Dio Albany Albany NY 1982-1984. Ord S Mary 1985; Sons of the Amer Revolution 2004. kevin2216@comcast.net

PHILLIPS, Alvin Kenneth James (Pa) Po Box 200, Morton PA 19070 **Died 4/22/2011** B 9/30/1946 s Alvin Samuel James Phillips & Edna Grace. Codrington Coll; LTh U of The W Indies 1971; ThM VTS 1994. D 9/1/1977 P 1/1/1978 Bp The Bishop Of Jamaica. Pres Earl B. Scott Chapt UBE. kena_jp@verizon.net

PHILLIPS III, Arthur William (Tex) 407 Cordell Dr, Crockett TX 75835 B KS 6/18/1953 D 6/22/2002 Bp Claude Edward Payne P 1/29/2003 Bp Don Adger Wimberly. m 4/14/1973 Lynn A Passmore c 2. S Paul's Epis Ch Orange TX 2005-2010; All SS Epis Ch Crockett TX 2002-2004. fr.bill@stpaulschurch.us

PHILLIPS, Benjamin Thomas (SO) 41 Manor Ln, Dayton OH 45429 **R S Geo's Epis Ch Dayton OH 2010-** B 8/29/1977 BS U of Arizona 2000; MDiv TESM 2006. D 6/3/2006 Bp James Robert Mathes P 12/6/2006 Bp Don Adger Wimberly. m 1/14/2006 Amy A Kreis c 1. Asst S Jn The Div Houston TX 2006-2010. benamyphillips2@gmail.com

PHILLIPS, Catharine Seybold (Chi) 458 Dee Ln, Roselle IL 60172 B Minneapolis MN 3/29/1955 d William Laney Phillips & Marjorie. BA Earlham Coll 1977; MDiv SWTS 1983. D 6/23/1983 P 5/1/1984 Bp Edward Witker Jones. m 6/24/1995 Jeffrey S Hill. Ch Of S Ben Bolingbrook IL 2003-2007; P-in-c Ch Of Our Sav Elmhurst IL 2000-2002; S Chas Ch S Chas IL 1998-2000; S Dav's Epis Ch Aurora IL 1997-1998; S Mk's Epis Ch Glen Ellyn IL 1997; Ch Of The Incarn Bloomingdale IL 1995-1997; Int R S Dav's Epis Ch Aurora IL 1995-1997; R S Lk's And S Marg's Ch Allston MA 1993-1995; Int Trin Epis Ch Marshall MI 1992-1993; Assoc R All SS Ch E Lansing MI 1987-1991; Epis Ch Coun U Chi Chicago IL 1984-1987. ESMHE. catharinephillips@ameritech.net

PHILLIPS, Craig Arnold (Va) 4818 Old Dominion Dr, Arlington VA 22207 **Chair, Dioc BEC Dio Virginia Richmond VA 2006-; COM Dio Virginia Richmond VA 2006-; R S Ptr's Epis Ch Arlington VA 2002-** B Tulsa OK 7/1/1954 s Milton Arnold Phillips & Shirley Jane. BA Br 1976; MDiv Harvard DS 1979; PhD Duke 1993. D 11/1/1980 Bp William Jackson Cox P 5/1/1981 Bp Gerald Nicholas McAllister. m 6/11/1977 Marguerite Eustis Spruance Pool c 2. Adj Instr VTS Alexandria VA 2010; Race Relatns Com Dio Virginia Richmond VA 2007-2010; Chair, Dioc BEC Dio Virginia Richmond VA 2006-2010; Dn, Conestoga Dnry Dio Pennsylvania Philadelphia PA 1999-2002; Ecum Cmsn Dio Pennsylvania Philadelphia PA 1998-2002; R Incarn H Sacr Epis Ch Drexel Hill PA 1997-2002; P in Charge S Geo S Barn Ch Philadelphia PA 1996; Int R S Barth's Ch Pittsboro NC 1994; Int R Ch Of The Gd Shpd Raleigh NC 1992-1993; Int R Ch Of The Nativ Raleigh NC 1992; Int R S Tit Epis Ch Durham NC 1990-1991; Ecum Cmsn Dio No Carolina Raleigh NC 1988-1994; Assoc R S Ptr's Epis Ch St Louis MO 1984-1986; COM Dio Oklahoma Oklahoma City OK 1982-1984; Vic Trin Ch Eufaula OK 1980-1984. Auth, "Hegel, Kierkegaard," *The Blackwell Comp to the Theologians*, Wiley Blackwell, 2009; Auth, "Postmodernism, Literary Criticism, Lang, Interp, Hermeneutics, and Fundamental Theol," *Encyclopedia of Chrsnty*, Eerdmans/ Brill, 2005; Auth, "From Aesthetics to Redemptive Politics: A Political Reading of the Theol Aesthetics of Hans Urs von Balthasar and the M," UMI, 1993. AAR, 1986; Amer Soc Of Ch Hist 1976-1990; SBL 1986. craigphillips@me.com

PHILLIPS, Deborah Anne (Mass) 35 Settlers Way, Salem MA 01970 **Dio Massachusetts Boston MA 2005-; Hisp Mnstry Cmsn Dio Massachusetts Boston MA 2005-; R Gr Ch Salem MA 1997-** B Albany NY 11/24/1954 d William Frederick Phillips & Helen. BA Bos 1976; MDiv EDS 1990. D 6/1/1991 Bp David Elliot Johnson P 5/23/1992 Bp David Bell Birney IV. m 7/16/1983 Alan Paulsen. Dioc Coun Dio Massachusetts Boston MA 1998-2002; S Eliz's Ch Wilmington MA 1995-1997; Chapl Dioc Young Singers Camp Dio Massachusetts Boston MA 1993-2002; Liturg & Mus Cmsn Dio Massachusetts Boston MA 1992-1995; Dio Massachusetts Boston MA 1992-1994; Asst S Mary's Ch Newton Lower Falls MA 1991-1993. Excellence in Preaching Awd Epis Evang Fndt 1989. dphillips54@verizon.net

PHILLIPS, Douglas Cecil (Ind) No address on file. B Columbus IN 10/15/1947 BA Indiana U 1969; MA Indiana U 1971; MDiv Indiana U 1978. D 12/21/1974 P 8/2/1975 Bp John P Craine. m 8/30/1979 Jean Marie Stoner.

PHILLIPS, Jennifer Mary (RG) 2903 Cabezon Blvd SE, Rio Rancho NM 87124 **R S Fran Ch Rio Rancho NM 2001-** B Dartford Kent UK 2/7/1952 d Victor Arthur Phillips & Mavis Adelaide. BA Wellesley Coll 1973; MDiv Andover Newton TS 1981; DMin Andover Newton TS 1984. D 6/2/1984 Bp John Bowen Coburn P 7/22/1985 Bp Edward Randolph Welles II. R S Aug's Ch Kingston RI 2000-2011; R Trin Ch S Louis MO 1995-2000; R Ch Of S Jn The Evang Boston MA 1987-1995. Auth, *Simple Prayers for Complicated Lives*, Ch Pub, Inc., 2007; Auth, *Preaching Creation*, Cowley Pub., 2000; Auth, *Prayers for Penitents*, Ch Pub, Inc.; Auth, "Pryr of the Eucharistic Cmnty & Abuse Survivor," *Sewanee Theol Revs*. ASSOC Soc of S Jn the Evang; Assn of Parishes for Liturg & Mus; Coll of Chapl; Naitonal Assn of Campus Ministers. revjphillips@earthlink.net

PHILLIPS, Jerry Ray (La) 2386 Louisiana Ave, Lutcher LA 70071 **P-in-c Ch Of The Nativ Rosedale LA 2009-** B Saint Louis MO 1/2/1941 s Edgar James Phillips & Zelda Mae. AA Florida Chr Coll Tampa FL 1962; BA LSU 1968; Concordia TS 1972; MA Washington U 1978; EDS LSU 1997; TESM 1999; Cert Dioc Sch for Mnstry 2002; Cert McFarland Inst 2003. D 12/21/2005 P 11/19/2006 Bp Charles Edward Jenkins III. c 3. jerphi@hotmail.com

PHILLIPS, John Bradford (Cal) 891 Skeel Drive, Camarillo CA 93010 B Brooklyn NY 8/3/1940 s Charles Edwin Phillips & Sara Elizabeth. BS USNA 1962; BD EDS 1971. D 6/26/1971 Bp George Richard Millard P 4/7/1972 Bp C Kilmer Myers. m 3/26/1967 Muriel HC Phillips c 3. Int All SS Epis Ch Oxnard CA 2008-2009; R Ch Of The H Trin Richmond CA 1974-1979. jackn.phyls@verizon.net

PHILLIPS II, John Walter (CGC) 590 Parker Cr., Pensacola FL 32504 **Asst Chr Ch Par Pensacola FL 2003-** B Mobile AL 5/28/1931 s Sidney Clarke Phillips & Kate. BS OH SU 1952; MDiv Epis TS of The SW 1960. D 6/26/1960 Bp George Mosley Murray P 6/17/1961 Bp Charles C J Carpenter. m 5/21/1955 Ann V Vasser c 3. P-in-c S Paul's Chap Magnolia Sprg AL

1999-2002; Vic S Anna's Ch Atmore AL 1995-1998; R Trin Epsicopal Ch Atmore AL 1995-1998; Asst Chr Ch Par Pensacola FL 1976-1995; P-in-c Gd Shpd Ch Montgomery AL 1970-1976; Asst Ch Of The Ascen Clearwater FL 1967-1969; Vic Trin Ch Wetumpka AL 1961-1967; Vic All SS Ch Montgomery AL 1960-1967. jwp2@cox.net

PHILLIPS, Julia Coleman (CGC) 127 Hamilton Ave, Panama City FL 32401 **P-in-c S Pat's Epis Ch Panama City FL 2001-** B Liberty MO 11/2/1928 d Mathias Stephen Coleman & Florence Elizabeth. JD U of Missouri 1952; BA Wm Jewell Coll 1952; DIT ETSBH 1980. D 7/25/1989 P 2/24/1990 Bp Charles Farmer Duvall. m 7/14/1965 Richard Alexander Phillips c 1. Vic S Pat's Epis Ch Panama City FL 1990-2001; D-in-trng H Nativ Epis Ch Panama City FL 1989-1990. CPC 2002; HSEC 1980. revmrs@comcast.net

PHILLIPS, Kathleen French (SC) 38 W Morgan Ct, Hilton Head Island SC 29926 B Worcester MA 4/12/1941 D 9/10/2005 Bp Edward Lloyd Salmon Jr. m 8/1/1964 William Phillips c 3. S Lk's Epis Ch Hilton Hd SC 1998-2004. kfphillips@yahoo.com

PHILLIPS, Marcella W (Ind) 3017 Peaceful Pl, Evansville IN 47720 **Died 1/9/2010** B Baltimore MD 7/9/1927 d Harold Auringer & Marcella. GW 1975. D 6/24/1994 Bp Edward Witker Jones. c 3. NAAD 1994.

PHILLIPS, Marie (O) Trinity Commons, 2230 Euclid Avenue, Cleveland OH 44115 **Cn for Mssn Dio Ohio Cleveland OH 2011-** B Dearborn MI 1/30/1960 d George Archibald Phillips & Dorothy Marie. BA MI SU 1982; MA Marygrove Coll 1987; MDiv EDS 1990. D 6/21/1991 Bp Henry Irving Mayson P 11/1/1994 Bp Ronald Hayward Haines. m 10/29/2010 Kristi A Ballinger. R Ch Of The Epiph Euclid OH 2002-2011; Assoc Epis. Shared Mnstrs Nw Lakewood OH 1998-2000; Cur All Faith Epis Ch Charlotte Hall MD 1994-1996. mphillips@dohio.org

PHILLIPS, Michael Albin (NY) 316 E 88th St, New York NY 10128 **R Ch Of The H Trin New York NY 2005-** B Lexington KY 3/22/1951 s Donald McCracken Phillips & Bernice Marie. BA U Of Dallas Irving 1973; MDiv CDSP 1978. D 10/6/1979 Bp C Kilmer Myers P 9/26/1980 Bp Robert Hume Cochrane. m 7/29/1978 Sarah Easton c 2. R Chr Ch Poughkeepsie NY 1995-2005; R S Phil's Epis Palatine IL 1986-1995; Assoc For Cmnty Mnstry Chr Ch Poughkeepsie NY 1982-1986; Cur Trin Epis Ch Everett WA 1979-1982. michael.phillips@holytrinity-nyc.org

PHILLIPS, Paul Henry (SVa) Po Box 374, Kenbridge VA 23944 **R Gibson Memi Crewe VA 1977-** B Spokane WA 7/7/1941 s Paul Henry Phillips & Elizabeth A. BA U CA 1964; MA U CA 1966; PhD U CA 1975; MDiv STUSo 1997. D 6/14/1997 P 12/13/1997 Bp David Conner Bane Jr. R Epis Ch Of S Paul And S Andr Kenbridge VA 1997-2008; The Epis Cluster Of Southside Kenbridge VA 1997-2008.

PHILLIPS JR, Raymond Leland (USC) 701 Unity St, Fort Mill SC 29715 B Towson MD 8/14/1935 s Raymond Leland Phillips & Minnie Leita. BS Wofford Coll 1956; MDiv STUSo 1962; Cert Appalachian Reg Hosps Inc Ape 1972. D 11/1/1962 Bp Clarence Alfred Cole P 11/1/1963 Bp John Adams Pinckney. m 6/5/1964 Nikki Ann McGinley. S Paul's Epis Ch Ft Mill SC 1974-1996; R S Andr's Epis Ch Canton NC 1972-1974; R S Mich's Epis Ch Easley SC 1965-1971; Asst R S Thad Epis Ch Aiken SC 1962-1965. phillipsn@comporium.net

PHILLIPS, Richard Oliver (NY) 10 Badger St, Littleton NH 03561 B Yonkers NY 9/25/1935 s John Preston Phillips & Louise. BA Ken 1957; STB Ya Berk 1960. D 6/11/1960 P 12/17/1960 Bp Horace W B Donegan. m 6/22/1957 Judith C Cargill c 2. R S Andr's Ch Brewster NY 1969-1973; R Par Of Chr The Redeem Pelham NY 1962-1969; Cur All SS Ch Bayside NY 1960-1962. judiphil@together.net

PHILLIPS, Robert W (CFla) 1620 Mayflower Ct Apt A-610, Winter Park FL 32792 B Duluth MN 8/12/1920 s Chester Worden Phillips & Doris Robena. BA Rol 1966; MS Rol 1971; CTh Oxf 1978. D 6/15/1975 P 2/24/1979 Bp William Hopkins Folwell. m 8/28/2007 Sallie M Guyon c 2. Asst Ch Of The Gd Shpd Maitland FL 1991-2009; R All SS Epis Ch Enterprise FL 1979-1984; D Dio Cntrl Florida Orlando FL 1975-1979. SSC 1983. frphillips@sprintmail.com

PHILLIPS, Roger V (Minn) 1801 Santa Maria Pl, Orlando FL 32806 **P, Total Mnstry S Steph's Epis Ch Paynesville MN 2004-; D Ch Of The Gd Samar Sauk Cntr MN 2003-** B Philipsburg PA 10/8/1937 s Roger Earle Phillips & Maud Amy. U of Florida 1959; BA U of Florida 1959; Cert U So 2005. D 11/11/2003 Bp James Louis Jelinek P 10/24/2004 Bp Daniel Lee Swenson. m 11/13/1970 Rosemary Burger c 4. P,Total Mnstry Ch Of Our Sav Little Falls MN 2004-2009; Asst P S Chris's Ch Orlando FL 2004-2005; D S Chris's Ch Orlando FL 2003-2004. frrophill@gmail.com

PHILLIPS, Stuart John Tristram (Tenn) 654 Long Hollow Pike, Goodlettsville TN 37072 B Montreal QC CA 1/19/1933 s Arthur John R Phillips & Beryl Emily. MDiv STUSo 1987. D 7/25/1979 Bp William Evan Sanders P 6/1/1980 Bp William F Gates Jr. m 6/3/1955 Aldona Lazarenko. S Jas The Less Madison TN 1993-2005; Gr Ch Sprg Hill TN 1987-1991; Assoc Ch Of The Adv Nashville TN 1981-1984; Asst S Barth's Ch Bristol TN 1979-1981.

PHILLIPS, Susan Elizabeth (Del) 18 Olive Ave, Rehoboth Beach DE 19971 B Philadephia PA 2/5/1944 d Henry W Shuttleworth & Elizabeth. BSN U of Pennsylvania 1968; MSN U of Virginia 1975. D 12/5/2009 Bp Wayne Parker Wright. c 2. ss.phillips@verizon.net

PHILLIPS, Thomas Goldsmith (Minn) 2397 Driftwood Ln, Stillwater MN 55082 B Saint Paul MN 10/15/1930 s Lewis Goldsmith Phillips & Edith Lydia. BA Macalester Coll 1952; BD SWTS 1955. D 6/29/1955 Bp Hamilton Hyde Kellogg P 12/21/1955 Bp Stephen E Keeler. m 7/6/1955 Priscilla G Gooch c 4. R Ch Of The Ascen Stillwater MN 1970-1990; Vic S Edw's Ch Duluth MN 1964-1970; R S Mk's Barrington Hills IL 1959-1964; Asst S Jas Epis Ch Birmingham MI 1957-1959; P-in-c S Antipas Ch Redby MN 1955-1957; P-in-c S Jn-In-The-Wilderness Redlake MN 1955-1957. Henry Benjamin Wipple Schlr Seabury Wstrn 1955; Chas Palmerston Anderson Schlr Seabury Wstrn 1954. tomandpercy@usfamily.net

PHILLIPS, Thomas Larison (Spr) 1015 Frank Dr, Champaign IL 61821 B Lincoln IL 2/25/1939 s Thomas Lenon Phillips & Elizabeth Josephine. BS Illinois St U 1963; M Div Nash 1966; MS Sthrn Illinois U 1968. D 6/11/1966 P 12/19/1966 Bp Albert A Chambers. m 8/11/1962 Patricia Ann Billings c 3. S Paulinus Ch Watseka IL 1994-2001; Vic Ch Of S Chris Rantoul IL 1986-2001; Assoc R Emm Memi Epis Ch Champaign IL 1978-1986; Chapl SIU Dio Springfield Springfield IL 1973-1977; Assoc S Andr's Ch Carbondale IL 1968-1973; Vic S Annes Epis Ch Caseyville IL 1966-1968. Auth, "Outdoor Living & Lrng Complement Each Other"; Auth, "Emotionally Distrurbed Chld Try Camping". ESMHE. Outstanding Ldrshp In Cmnty Mntl Hlth Awd Carbondale 1977. paphilli@yahoo.com

PHILLIPS, Wendell Roncevalle (NC) 4211 Sharon View Rd, Charlotte NC 28226 **P-in-c S Mich And All Ang Epis Ch Charlotte NC 2002-** B New Rochelle NY 1/27/1939 s Wendell Wert Phillips & Marguerite Virgine. BA Denison U 1963; MDiv GTS 1966. D 6/4/1966 P 12/17/1966 Bp Horace W B Donegan. m 8/12/1972 Linda I Vigen c 2. S Matt Ch Salisbury NC 2000-2001; Vic S Paul's Ch Salisbury NC 1993-2001; P/Org All SS Epis Ch Charlotte NC 1990-1993; Vic All SS Epis Ch Whitefish MT 1985-1989; P / Org S Fran Of Assisi Epis Wilsonville OR 1983-1985; Asst All SS Ch Hillsboro OR 1976-1982; R S Andr's Ch Brewster NY 1974-1975; Mus Cmsn Dio Long Island Garden City NY 1969-1974; R S Geo's Ch Astoria NY 1969-1974; Cur S Jn's Epis Ch Lancaster PA 1967-1968. AGO 1975-, Bd Shltr Inc Hillsboro OR; Bd Arc of Mecklenburg Co 2003; Mus Cmsn Dio Ore 1983-1985. revwendellphillips@gmail.com

PHILLIPS-GAINES, Lynn (Miss) 105 N Montgomery St, Starkville MS 39759 B Jacksonville FL 1/18/1956 d CE Phillips & Teresa Ann. BA Mississippi St U 1978; MS Sthrn Illinois U 1980. D 1/15/2011 Bp Duncan Montgomery Gray III. m 4/15/2005 James Russell Gaines c 1. therevlynngaines@gmail.com

PHILLIPS-MATSON, Wesley A (EpisSanJ) 333 Kentfield Dr, San Marcos CA 92069 B Los Angeles CA 7/6/1926 s Archie Matson & Martha. MDiv CDSP 1965. D 6/24/1968 Bp Sumner Walters P 7/11/1973 Bp CE Crowther. c 1. P S Clare of Assisi Epis Ch Avery CA 1999-2001; Assoc S Jas Epis Ch Sonora CA 1991-1998; S Mk's Ch KING CITY CA 1980-1983; P S Mk's Ch KING CITY CA 1969-1972. wpm@volcano.net

PHILPUTT JR, Frederick Chapman (Dal) 5811 Penrose Ave, Dallas TX 75206 **Vic Ch Of The Incarn Dallas TX 1995-** B White Plains NY 3/30/1945 s Frederick Chapman Philputt & Ragnhild. BA TCU 1971; MDiv Nash 1987. D 7/25/1987 P 1/25/1988 Bp Clarence Cullam Pope Jr. m 12/29/1973 Nancy McCoy c 2. Ch Of The Incarn Dallas TX 1992-2010; R Calv Ch Americus GA 1989-1992; Cur All SS' Epis Ch Ft Worth TX 1987-1989. CHS 2008; SHN 2006. ricknancy.philputt@att.net

PHINNEY, Frederick Warren (Mass) 67 Pasture Path, Randolph NH 03593 B Lawrence MA 5/15/1922 s Arthur Osgood Phinney & Lucile Snow. BA Harv 1943; MDiv EDS 1948. D 6/1/1948 P 12/17/1948 Bp Norman B Nash. c 6. Int S Andr's Ch Wellesley MA 1989-1990; Chr Ch Cambridge Cambridge MA 1986; S Paul's Within the Walls Rome 00184 IT 1985; Exec Coun Appointees New York NY 1981-1983; Chair Comp Dio Cmsn Dio Chicago Chicago IL 1980-1981; Chair - Iran Dioc Assn. Dio Chicago Chicago IL 1973-1978; Dn - Waukegan Dnry Dio Chicago Chicago IL 1971-1981; Pres - Stndg Com Dio Chicago Chicago IL 1970-1972; Stndg Comm. Dio Chicago Chicago IL 1969-1970; ExCoun & BEC Dio Chicago Chicago IL 1965-1971; Chair Dept Mssn Dio Chicago Chicago IL 1964-1968; R The Ch Of The H Sprt Lake Forest IL 1963-1981; R S Jn's Ch Beverly Farms MA 1956-1963; R Ch Of Our Sav Brookline MA 1950-1956; Cur S Jn's Epis Par Waterbury CT 1948-1950. Hon Cn St. Lk's Cathd, Dio Maseno No, Kenya 1987.

PHINNEY, James Mark (Oly) 4246 South Discovery Road, Port Townsend WA 98368 B Glasgow MT 5/30/1937 s Harold Mathers Phinney & Anna Gertrude. BA WA SU 1959; MDiv CDSP 1967. D 8/10/1967 P 3/30/1968 Bp Ivol I Curtis. c 2. Assoc Gr Ch Bainbridge Island WA 1999-2008; R S Paul's Epis Ch Port Townsend WA 1990-1997; Vic Chr Ch S Helens OR 1977-1990; Dio Oregon Portland OR 1977-1990; R S Paul's Epis Ch Elko NV 1970-1977. jimph@cablespeed.com

PHIPPS, Joy Ogburn (Ala) 3919 Westminster Ln, Birmingham AL 35243 B Birmingham AL 3/20/1932 d Frank McCord Ogburn & Lottie Mays. BA Monmouth U 1974; MS Rutgers-The St U 1980; MDiv VTS 1988. D 6/4/1988 Bp Furman Stough P 12/14/1988 Bp Robert Oran Miller. m 7/18/1952 Donald Miller Phipps c 2. Stndg Com Dio Alabama Birmingham AL 1994-1997; Assoc S Lk's Epis Ch Birmingham AL 1990-2001; COM Dio Alabama Birmingham AL 1988-1993; Asst Ch Of The Nativ Epis Huntsville AL 1988-1990. joyphipps@bellsouth.net

PHIPPS, Marion E (Chi) 5403 W Greenbrier Dr, McHenry IL 60050 **S Hugh Of Lincoln Epis Ch Elgin IL 2010-** B Oak Park IL 8/6/1958 d Paul Scholl Kyger & Marion Elizabeth. BA Illinois St U 1980; Cert Elgin Cmnty Coll 1992; MDiv SWTS 2009. D 6/6/2009 P 12/5/2009 Bp Jeffrey Dean Lee. m 1/23/1988 Michael J Phipps c 1. phipps54@sbcglobal.net

PHIPPS JR, Robert Stirling (Va) Po Box 33430, San Antonio TX 78265 B Baltimore MD 5/25/1935 s Robert Stirling Phipps & Rose Marvlyn. BA U Rich 1957; MDiv VTS 1960. D 6/1/1960 Bp Leland Stark P 1/1/1961 Bp John E Hines. m 6/2/1956 Mary Barbee Gilliam. S Steph's Epis Sch Austin TX 1960-1984.

PIATKO, Joanne M (NwPa) 26 Chautauqua Pl, Bradford PA 16701 **S Jos's Ch Port Allegany PA 2010-** B Buffalo NY 6/25/1955 d Thomas Murschel & Margaret Murschel. AAS Trocaire Coll 1975; BA Pk Coll Parkville MO 1981; MDiv Bex Sem 2008. D 5/9/2009 P 6/6/2010 Bp Sean Walter Rowe. c 2. jpiatko123@yahoo.com

PICCARD, Kathryn Ann (Mass) 68 Baldwin St Apt 2, Charlestown MA 02129 B Buffalo NY 9/19/1949 d J A Piccard & E M. BA Simpson Coll Indianola IA 1971; MDiv EDS 1975; ThM Harvard DS 1990. D 6/28/1975 P 3/16/1977 Bp Walter Cameron Righter. m 10/26/1997 Mary Jo Campbell. Supply P Dio Massachusetts Boston MA 1995-1998; Ch Of S Jn The Evang Boston MA 1987-1988; S Matt And The Redeem Epis Ch So Boston MA 1986-1987; Dio Iowa Des Moines IA 1980; Asst Emm Ch Boston MA 1979-1982; D's Sch For Mnstry And Formation Wilmette IL 1977-1980; EDS Cambridge MA 1977. Auth, "arts On Liturg". Mass Dioc Disabil Concerns Com. KAPICCARD@COMCAST.NET

PICCATE, Thomas (Nwk) 199 Woodward Ave, Rutherford NJ 07070 **COM Dio Newark Newark NJ 2011-; D S Jas' Ch Ridgefield NJ 2006-; Port Chapl Seamens Ch Inst Income New York NY 2001-** B Newark NJ 12/22/1944 s Alexander Piccate & Ruth H. Dio Newark Sch for Diac Formation; BS FD 1966; MA FD 1967. D 11/18/2006 Bp John Palmer Croneberger. m 9/24/1972 Mary Jane Cunningham c 1.

PICKARD, Joseph Shearer (Nwk) 115 Oak Grove Ave, Hasbrouck Heights NJ 07605 **Int S Mart's Ch Maywood NJ 2009-; Vic Ch Of S Jn The Div Hasbrouck Heights NJ 1996-** B Hollywood CA 11/18/1945 s Judson Eugene Pickard & Jayne Elizabeth. BArchitecture U of Arizona 1973; MDiv VTS 1984. D 6/20/1984 P 5/1/1985 Bp Joseph Thomas Heistand. m 7/28/2007 Louis Ewald Fifer c 3. Vic Ch Of S Mary The Vrgn Ridgefield Pk NJ 1996-1999; Int S Paul's Ch Montvale NJ 1994-1996; Int S Greg's Epis Ch Parsippany NJ 1993-1994; Vic Ch Of The Mssh Chester NJ 1986-1993; Asst S Dunst's McLean VA 1984-1986. vicar@saintjohnthedivine.com

PICKEN, Robert Andrew (LI) 191 Kensington Road, Garden City NY 11530 **Cn Cathd Of The Incarn Garden City NY 2010-; Chair, Cmsn on Liturg & Ch Mus Dio Long Island Garden City NY 2009-** B Bethpage NY 4/8/1980 s James Edward Picken & Barbara Mary. BA CUA 2002; M.Div. GTS 2006. D 4/25/2006 P 10/28/2006 Bp Orris George Walker Jr. Bd Managers of Camp DeWolfe Dio Long Island Garden City NY 2007-2009; P-in-c Ch Of The Ascen Greenpoint Brooklyn NY 2006-2010. rpicken@gmail.com

PICKENS, Gregory Doran (Dal) 8011 Douglas, Dallas TX 75225 **Assoc S Mich And All Ang Ch Dallas TX 2011-; P-in-c S Mk's Ch Irving TX 2006-** B Oklahoma City OK 8/22/1961 B.A. Univ. of Texas at Austin 1986; M.Div. Nash 2005. D 5/14/2005 P 4/25/2006 Bp James Monte Stanton. m 1/6/2007 Noralyn Pickens. Cur H Trin Epis Ch Garland TX 2005-2006. gpickens@saintmichael.org

PICKERAL, Gretchen Marta Benson (Minn) 404 Trout Lake Rd, Grand Rapids MN 55744 **S Paul's Ch Brainerd MN 2011-; Total Mnstry Mentor S Barth's Epis Ch Bemidji MN 2008-; Dio Minnesota Minneapolis MN 2006-** B Minneapolis MN 1/8/1952 d David Howard Benson & Betty Ann. BA St. Cloud St U 1977; MDiv SWTS 1992. D 6/6/1992 Bp William Augustus Jones Jr P 4/27/1994 Bp Hays H. Rockwell. m 5/12/1973 Larry Allen Pickeral c 2. R Chr Epis Ch Grand Rapids MN 2001-2006; Int S Mich & S Geo Clayton MO 1999-2001; P S Tim's Epis Ch Creve Coeur MO 1998-1999; P S Barn Ch Florissant MO 1997-1998; Mnstry Coordntr Dio Missouri S Louis MO 1993-1995; Assoc S Barn Ch Florissant MO 1993-1995. Auth, "Confession Of Possession," *Wmn Uncommon Pryr*, 2000; Auth, "Gender-Defined Sin," *Wit*, 1995. Minneca 2001; Moca 1992-2001; Natl Ntwk Of Epis Cler Assns 1994. pickeral@uslink.net

PICKERING, LouAnn Kisor (Ore) 7610 Sw 49th Ave, Portland OR 97219 **Vic S Gabr Ch Portland OR 2005-; Asst Epis Par Of S Jn The Bapt Portland OR 2001-** B Oskaloosa IA 8/14/1954 d Morgan Thomas Kisor & Ruth Kisor. BA Pacific U 1976. D 10/18/1996 P 5/31/1997 Bp Robert Louis Ladehoff. m 9/9/1978 James M Pickering c 2. Epis Par Of S Jn The Bapt Portland OR 2001; Asstg P Gr Memi Portland OR 1998-2001. pickering18@comcast.net

PICKERING, Roger Alan (Pa) 655 Willow Valley Sq. Apt. L302, Lancaster PA 17602 B Pontiac MI 2/18/1931 s John Wayne Pickering & Astrid. BA Kalamazoo Coll 1953; MS U Chi 1957; MDiv CDSP 1962; DD CDSP 1990. D 6/1/1962 Bp Matthew G Henry P 1/6/1963 Bp George Richard Millard. m 7/12/1962 Sandra Verda Richie c 2. P-in-c All Souls Ch For The Deaf Philadelphia PA 2006-2007; Alt Dep Gc Dio Pennsylvania Philadelphia PA 1993-1996; Alt Dep Gc Dio Pennsylvania Philadelphia PA 1982-1988; Vic All Souls Ch For The Deaf Philadelphia PA 1969-2001; Vic H Sprt Ch Of The Deaf San Lorenzo CA 1962-1968. Epis Conf Of The Deaf Of The Epis Ch In The 1959. Geo W. Nevil Awd Of Merit The Pennsylvania Sch For The Deaf 1996; Raoul Wallenberg Awd Hebr Assn For The Deaf, Philadelphia, Pa 1995; Ralph Harwood Memi Awd Delaware Vlly Telecommunications For The Deaf 1985; DSA Epis Conf Of The Deaf 1980; Deaf Cmnty Serv Awd. revpickering@comcast.net

PICKERING, William Todd (Va) 208 N 28th St, Richmond VA 23223 **P-in-c S Jn's Epis Ch Tappahannock VA 2006-** B Pittsburgh PA 5/24/1946 s Thomas Edwin Pickering & Lucile. BA Randolph-Macon Coll 1968; MDiv GTS 1971. D 6/19/1971 P 12/1/1971 Bp Robert Bracewell Appleyard. m 9/5/1970 Lee Ann Bunnell c 3. R S Mk's Ch New Canaan CT 1997-2005; R S Paul's Epis Ch Pittsburgh PA 1983-1997; R Chr Ch Greensburg PA 1976-1983; Exec Com of Alum The GTS New York NY 1976-1982; Vic S Alb's Epis Ch Murrysville PA 1971-1976. Dio Pgh Cleric Assn 1971-1996. Who's Who in Rel 92. billytodd@comcast.net

PICKERRELL, Nina (Cal) 1100 California St, San Francisco CA 94108 **D Gr Cathd San Francisco CA 1999-** B Oakland CA 7/17/1951 d George Robert Pickerrell & Evelyn Alice. BA Sch for Deacons 1996. D 6/1/1996 Bp William Edwin Swing. m 10/28/1973 William Gene Hendirckson c 2. ESMA. ninap@gracecathedral.org

PICKUP JR, Edmund (SVa) Po Box 146, Franklin VA 23851 **Mem Stndg Com Dio Sthrn Virginia Norfolk VA 2011-2014; R Emm Ch Franklin VA 1991-** B Eden NC 6/12/1952 s Edmund Pickup & Edna Earl. BA U NC 1974; JD U NC 1976; MDiv Nash 1988. D 5/27/1988 Bp Frank Harris Vest Jr P 5/31/1989 Bp Robert Whitridge Estill. Mem Exec Bd Dio Sthrn Virginia Norfolk VA 2008-2011; Asst S Mary's Epis Ch High Point NC 1988-1991. Alb Inst 1987; RSCM in Amer 1995; Soc of S Marg 1992. Assoc RSCM 2011. edmundpickup@gmail.con

PICKUP JR, Ezra Alden (Vt) 37 S Main St, Alburgh VT 05440 B Hartford CT 6/8/1935 s Ezra Alden Pickup & Lois Westwood. BA McGill U 1957; STB Ya Berk 1960. D 4/17/1960 Bp Vedder Van Dyck P 2/18/1961 Bp Harvey D Butterfield. P-in-c S Dav's Epis Ch E Greenbush NY 1984-1997; Consult Ch Of The H Cross Troy NY 1983-1990; Int Trin Ch Gloversville NY 1983-1984; Brookhaven Hm For Boys Chelsea VT 1966-1983; Chr Ch Bethel VT 1966-1982; R Chr Ch Island Pond VT 1961-1966; Vic S Ptr's Mssn Lyndonville VT 1961-1966; Cur Chr Ch Montpelier VT 1961; Cur S Lk's Ch S Albans VT 1960-1961. Auth, *Massbook/Missel (bilingual) (together w: Ainsi que / Other Devotions / Autres devotions*, Montreal, 2002; Co-Ed, *Le Missel Anglo-Catholique en Français*, 2000; Auth/Ed, *Cath, Evang &Chrsmtc Renwl*. SBL 1957-2005. ezrap@fairpoint.net

PICOT, Katherine Frances (Tex) 717 Sage Rd, Houston TX 77056 **Cur S Mart's Epis Ch Houston TX 2010-** B Gloucester England 6/16/1973 d Lewis Picot & Judith. BA Oxford Brookes; BA Ridley Hall 2009. Trans from Church Of England 10/24/2010 as Deacon Bp C(harles) Andrew Doyle. PICOTK@GOOGLEMAIL.COM

PIELEMEIER, Gary L. (Minn) 1268 Masters Drive, Arnold MD 21012 **Died 5/4/2011** B Cincinnati OH 9/10/1931 s Harold Ernest Pielemeier & Virginia. BA U Of Florida 1952; MDiv SWTS 1955; MA U MN 1971; PhD U MN 1976. D 6/18/1955 Bp Charles L Street P 12/21/1955 Bp Gerald Francis Burrill. m 6/28/1984 Averil Stephenson. Usaf Medal Merit USAF 1988; Oak Leaf Cluster 1981; Usaf Commendation Medal USAF 1980; Phi Kappa Phi. glpielemeier@comcast.net

PIERCE, Charles Christian (Va) 73 Culpeper St, Warrenton VA 20186 **R S Jas' Epis Ch Warrenton VA 2007-** B Memphis TN 11/23/1964 s Charles Alfred Pierce & Patti-Ann. BA Estrn Nazarene Coll 1987; MDiv Andover Newton TS 1992. D 11/18/1992 P 5/20/1993 Bp Edward Harding MacBurney. m 6/27/1987 Julie Ann Pierce c 4. Off Of Bsh For ArmdF New York NY 1999-2007; S Matt's Ch Lincoln NE 1996-1999; S Paul's Cathd Peoria IL 1993-1996; Ch Of S Jn The Evang Duxbury MA 1992-1993.

PIERCE, Donald Buckley (Ct) 515 E 5th St, Kinsley KS 67547 **Died 7/19/2010** B Syracuse NY 12/11/1927 s James Edward Pierce & Florence Elizabeth. BA Trin Hartford CT 1951; MDiv Ya Berk 1954; MS Sthrn Connecticut St U 1968. D 6/2/1954 P 12/21/1954 Bp Shirley Hall Nichols. c 1. Cwc; RWF. piercedm@cox.net

PIERCE, Dorothy Kohinke (CNY) PO Box 458, Chenango Bridge NY 13745 B Cooperstown NY 3/18/1947 d Theodore Kohinke & Marion Howard. BA St U

Coll 1969; MS St U Coll 1981. D 11/14/2009 Bp Gladstone Bailey Adams III. m 9/28/1991 James Pierce c 3. dorothy.k.pierce@gmail.com

PIERCE, Graham Towle (Me) 35 Pine Ledge Dr, Scarborough ME 04074 B Providence RI 7/22/1930 s Frederick Goddard Pierce & Elizabeth. BA Colby Coll 1952; BD Bex 1968. D 6/25/1968 P 12/21/1968 Bp Robert McConnell Hatch. m 10/9/1976 Judith Hunter c 4. Dio Maine Portland ME 2005-2006; R Chr Ch Biddeford ME 1997-2002; P-in-c Ch Of The Gd Shpd So Lee MA 1995-1997; All SS Epis Ch Kansas City MO 1994-1995; R S Andr's Epis Ch St Johnsbury VT 1991-1993; S Jas Epis Ch Essex Jct VT 1990-1994; Int S Lk's Ch S Albans VT 1989-1990; R S Jas Epis Ch Arlington VT 1984-1989; Vic S Ann's Epis Ch Windham Windham ME 1970-1974; Admin Asst to Bp Dio Maine Portland ME 1969-1974; Admin Intern Dio Wstrn Massachusetts Springfield MA 1968-1969. 2graj@verizon.net

PIERCE, Jay Ross (Lex) 205 Cardinal Ave, Versailles KY 40383 B Rockmart GA 8/15/1935 s J W Pierce & Billie. BA Coll of Mt St. Jos 1978; MDiv Epis TS In Kentucky 1982. D 5/13/1978 P 5/1/1979 Bp Addison Hosea. m 5/12/1971 Patti Agnes Peters c 2. Int S Phil's Ch Harrodsburg KY 1992-1995; Epis TS Lexington KY 1979-1980; D-In-Trng Ch Of The Gd Shpd Lexington KY 1978-1980. frpierce@earthlink.net

PIERCE, Karen Lee (Oly) PO Box 753, Port Townsend WA 98368 B Port Townsend WA 6/13/1964 d William M Bennett & Patricia M. Certification U of Washington; BA WA SU 1985. D 10/17/2009 Bp Gregory Harold Rickel. m 10/3/1987 Douglas Dale Pierce c 1. D S Paul's Epis Ch Port Townsend WA 2009; Resource Mgr S Paul's Epis Ch Port Townsend WA 2009. kpierce@cablespeed.com

PIERCE, Nathaniel W (Eas) 3864 Rumsey Dr, Trappe MD 21673 **Wrshp Ldr S Phil's Ch Quantico MD 2002-** B Boston MA 8/18/1942 s Alvah Nathaniel Pierce & Anne. BS Cor 1966; MDiv CDSP 1972; MA Grad Theol Un 1972. D 5/15/1972 P 6/3/1973 Bp Ned Cole. c 3. R Chr Epis Ch Great Choptank Par Cambridge MD 1991-2003; Dio Easton Easton MD 1990-1999; Chapl Dio Massachusetts Boston MA 1990-1991; Stndg Cmsn on Peace (GC) Dio Massachusetts Boston MA 1986-1988; All SS Par Brookline MA 1984-1990; Dioc Coun Dio Massachusetts Boston MA 1984-1988; JCP Dio Idaho Boise ID 1980-1985; R Gr Epis Ch Nampa ID 1975-1984; Asst Chr Ch Portola Vlly CA 1973-1975. Auth, "Chiara Lubich," *LivCh*, 2011; Auth, "Proposed Angl Cov," *LivCh*, 2011; Auth, "The Arrival of Feminine Theol," *LivCh*, 1997; Co-Auth, "The Voice of Conscience," EPF, 1989; Auth, "Stained Glass Windows," *LivCh*, 1987; Auth, "selected Chapt," *Rumors of War: a Moral and Theol Perspective on the Arms Race*, Seabury Press, 1982. Assoc. Ord of S Helena 1965. Bray Tubman Awd Dio Easton 2002; Who's Who in Rel 1992. nwpierce@verizon.net

PIERCE, Nicholas Dana (Q) 1517 N Bigelow St, Peoria IL 61604 **Died 7/8/2010** B Boston MA 3/11/1919 s Henderson Guilford Pierce & Elizabeth De Long. Nash 1945; BS Bradley U 1970; BD Nash 1970; MDiv Nash 1970. D 12/31/1944 Bp Charles Clingman P 8/1/1945 Bp Edward P Wroth. c 8. Forw in Faith 2004. lucynnick@aol.com

PIERCE, Patricia Daniels (NJ) 203 Wildwood Ave, Pitman NJ 08071 **R Ch Of The Gd Shpd Pitman NJ 1999-** B Brooklyn NY 6/21/1942 d Ralph Randolf Daniels & Bertha. AA Fashion Inst of Tech 1962; BA SUNY 1992; MDiv GTS 1995. D 6/23/1995 Bp Orris George Walker Jr P 5/7/1997 Bp Brice Sidney Sanders. m 9/7/1963 John O Pierce c 2. Assoc R S Ptr's Epis Ch Washington NC 1997-1999; Int S Phil And S Jas Ch New Hyde Pk NY 1996-1997; Asst S Andr's Astoria NY 1995-1996. Auth, "God's Time," *Wmn Uncommon Prayers*, Morehouse Pub, 2000. Wmn of the Year in Rel and Philosphy Gloucester Cnty, NJ 2006. patjac@verizon.net

PIERCE, Patrick Arthur (CPa) 306 N Main Street, Mercersburg PA 17236 **R Trin Epis Ch Chambersburg PA 2009-** B Evanston IL 2/10/1949 s Charles Frank Pierce & Carol Grey. BA Mia 1971; MA Roosevelt U Chicago IL 1975; MDiv GTS 1979. D 6/9/1979 Bp Quintin Ebenezer Primo Jr P 12/12/1979 Bp James Winchester Montgomery. c 3. P-in-c Mt Zion Epis Ch Hedgesville WV 2006-2009; P-in-c S Mk's Epis Ch Berkeley Sprg WV 2006-2009; Int S Andr's Epis Ch Shippensburg PA 2004-2005; P-in-c Ch Of The Trsfg Blue Ridge Summit PA 2002-2004; P-in-c Calv Chap Beartown Blue Ridge Summit PA 2002; Int S Jn's Par Hagerstown MD 1999-2001; Int S Jas Epis Ch Westernport MD 1997-1999; Advsry Bd Chr Mnstry Cntr Dio Sthrn Ohio Cincinnati OH 1993-1997; R Calv Ch Cincinnati OH 1990-1997; Yth & YA Com Dio Maryland Baltimore MD 1985-1987; R Ch Of The Trsfg Braddock Heights MD 1984-1990; Asst S Lk's Epis Ch Montclair NJ 1982-1984; Assoc Chr Ch Poughkeepsie NY 1979-1982. frbaldy@yahoo.com

PIERCE, Robert Hamilton (LI) 1827 Eisenhower Dr, Louisville CO 80027 B Philadelphia PA 5/3/1928 s William Hamilton Pierce & Sophia Irene. BA CUNY 1948; MDiv Ya Berk 1951; STM GTS 1957; MBA CUNY 1972; JD S Louis U 1989. D 3/31/1951 P 5/3/1952 Bp James P De Wolfe. m 6/23/1956 Patricia Kotraschek c 3. Int S Paul's Ch S Louis MO 1991-1994; Asst S Tim's Epis Ch Creve Coeur MO 1990-1991; Sup P S Jn's Ch Centralia IL 1988-1989; Sup P S Thos Ch Salem IL 1988-1989; S Andr's Ch Paris IL 1983-1985; Vic S Ambr Epis Ch Boulder CO 1980-1985; Dio Long Island Garden City NY 1973-1976; Vic S Andr's Ch Mastic Bch NY 1973-1976; Evang Cmsn Dio Long Island Garden City NY 1960-1965; Asst Secy Dio Long Island Garden City NY 1958-1965; Asst Ch Of The Trsfg Freeport NY 1953-1957; Asst S Jos's Ch Queens Vill NY 1951-1953. Auth, "The Sch Pryr Decision," *H Cross mag*, 1963; Auth, "Rel and the Presidency," *The Churchman*, 1960. Beta Gamma Sigma 1972. crisocor@aya.yale.edu

PIERCE, Roderick John (Tex) 2311 Ann St, Houston TX 77003 B Buffalo NY 8/28/1947 s John Button Pierce & Lois Elizabeth. AA Brevard Cmnty Coll 1972; BS HCA GW 1979; MDiv Candler TS Emory U 1987. D 1/11/1988 Bp Anselmo Carral-Solar P 12/14/1988 Bp Maurice Manuel Benitez. m 6/20/1970 Susan Hibbs c 2. Assoc Trin Epis Ch Baytown TX 1993; R S Tim's Epis Ch Houston TX 1989-1991; Cur S Chris's Ch League City TX 1988-1989. Bd Cert Chapl, APC 1993; Chair, Cmsn on Quality in Pstr Serv, APC 1998-2002; Clincl Mem, ACPE 1987; Endorsed Mem, AEHC 1992; Mem, Assn of Profsnl Chapl (APC) 1991; Pres, Assembly Of Epis Healthcare Chapl (Aehc) 1997-1999. rodpierce1@gmail.com

PIERSON, Paul Hamilton (Alb) PO Box 183, 156 Josh Hall Pond Road, Grafton NY 12082 **P Cathd Of All SS Albany NY 2011-** B Milwaukee WI 8/25/1950 s Paul Starrett Pierson & Patricia Hewes. BA Wms 1973; Dip. Th. St. Jn's Coll Nottingham GB 1974; DPS St. Jn's Coll Nottingham GB 1975; Cert VTS 1976. D 6/13/1976 Bp Alexander Doig Stewart P 6/1/1977 Bp Albert Wiencke Van Duzer. m 8/26/1972 Mary Dickerson c 2. R S Jn's Epis Ch Troy NY 2010-2011; Asst S Mk's Epis Ch Jacksonville FL 1999-2000; Chapl Jacksonville Epis HS Jacksonville FL 1994-2002; Yth Mnstry All Souls Epis Ch Jacksonville FL 1987-1993; R Chr Epis Ch Sheffield MA 1982-1987; Assoc Trin Epis Ch Portland ME 1980-1982; Asst S Lk's Ch Gladstone NJ 1976-1980. FOCUS; SHORESH; SAMS. phpierson@mac.com

PIERSON, Stewart (Vt) 232 High Rock Rd, Hinesburg VT 05461 B New York NY 6/25/1937 s Richard Pierson & Dorothy. BA Colg 1959; BD UTS 1963. D 6/1/1963 P 12/20/1963 Bp Horace W B Donegan. m 8/25/1962 Julie Gray Pierson c 2. R All SS' Epis Ch S Burlington VT 2000-2008; R S Ptr's Epis Ch Lakewood OH 1986-1998; R S Steph's Epis Ch Wilkes Barre PA 1972-1986; Cur Calv Ch Pittsburgh PA 1963-1972. Ldrshp Journalism S Peters 1984. stewjulie@juno.com

PIETSCH, Louise Parsons (NY) 80 Lyme Rd Apt 347, Hanover NH 03755 B New York NY 4/7/1940 d William Parsons & Louise Bigelow. BS Col 1963; MDiv UTS 1982; DMin Drew U 1988. D 6/5/1982 Bp Paul Moore Jr P 12/21/1982 Bp James Stuart Wetmore. m 9/25/1988 William Vincent Pietsch c 3. S Steph's Ch Ridgefield CT 1998-1999; Dio New York New York City NY 1997-1998; Ch Of The H Trin Pawling NY 1996; R S Lk's Ch Katonah NY 1992-1996; Chair Diac Form Dio New York New York City NY 1991-1993; Assoc S Lk's Ch Katonah NY 1984-1988; Cur S Matt's Ch Bedford NY 1983-1984. Auth, "Wmn in Prison: A Par in Search of a Mnstry (Doctoral Paper)," Drew U, 1988. Phi Beta Kappa Col 1963. lppietscg@gmail.com

PIETTE, Joseph Leroy (Minn) 204 8th St, Cloquet MN 55720 B Moose Lake MN 5/9/1950 s James Don Piette & Mary Ellen. D 7/20/2008 Bp Daniel Lee Swenson P 2/19/2009 Bp James Louis Jelinek. m 8/3/1974 Diane Elizabeth Hendrickson c 2. jlpiette@cpinternet.com

PIFKE, Lauran Kretchmar (Cal) 3400 Stevenson Blvd. #Q37, Fremont CA 94538 **R S Anne's Ch Fremont CA 2007-** B Flint MI 10/31/1953 d James Kretchmar & Beverley. BS U IL 1975; MDiv CDSP 2006. D 6/3/2006 Bp William Edwin Swing P 12/2/2006 Bp Marc Handley Andrus. m 12/26/2006 Frederick M Hansen c 3. Int Calv Epis Ch Santa Cruz CA 2006. rector@stanneschurch.org

PIGGINS, Deborah Ann (NJ) 179 Rector St, Perth Amboy NJ 08861 **S Ptr's Ch Perth Amboy NJ 2009-; S Lk's Hosp Bethlehem PA 2005-** B Glen Ridge NJ 11/5/1945 D 6/11/2005 P 5/27/2006 Bp George Edward Councell. Ch Of The Ascen Gloucester City NJ 2008-2009; Calv Epis Ch Flemington NJ 2005-2007. revdebstpetes@gmail.com

PIKE, Clifford Arthur Hunt (Pa) 105 Elm St, Lawrenceburg KY 40342 B Worcester MA 9/9/1946 s Joseph Edison Colbourne Pike & Louise. BA Transylvania U 1968; MDiv VTS 1971. D 12/8/1971 Bp William Foreman Creighton P 6/1/1972 Bp (George) Paul Reeves. m 10/20/2011 Nancy G Geoghegan c 1. R The Ch Of The H Trin W Chester PA 1999-2004; S Lk's Ch Salisbury NC 1994-1999; R S Ptr's Ch Paris KY 1977-1994; Assoc S Columba's Epis Ch Bristol TN 1974-1977; Calv Ch Memphis TN 1973-1977; Asst Dio Georgia Savannah GA 1971-1973. cliffpike@hotmail.com

PIKE, David Robert (WMich) 1519 Elmwood Rd, Lansing MI 48917 **R S Dav's Ch Lansing MI 1993-** B Port Sulpher LA 4/1/1955 s Charles Edward Pike & Bunny Marie. BA Grand Vlly St U 1977; MDiv EDS 1982. D 6/5/1982 Bp Charles Ellsworth Bennison Jr P 12/1/1982 Bp Charles Bennison. m 5/27/1978 Nancy L Strong c 2. Co-Chair Of Dioc Realignment Dio Michigan Detroit MI 1988-1990; R S Jas' Epis Ch Of Albion Albion MI 1984-1993; Cur S Paul's Ch Muskegon MI 1982-1984. frdavid.stdavids@sbcglobal.net

PIKE, Diane Marie (WMo) 324 E Main Rd, Portsmouth RI 02871 **S Mary's Ch Portsmouth RI 2011-** B Kalamazoo MI 7/22/1955 d Robert Gene Pike &

Loraine Mary. BA Nazareth Coll 1977; MA Oakland U 1983; MDiv Epis TS Of The SW 2011. D 7/15/2011 Bp Martin Scott Field. dmpike22@yahoo.com

PIKE, Stephen Phillip (Ky) RCT 1 HQ Co, UIC 40145, FPO AP 96426 **Off Of Bsh For ArmdF New York NY 1991-** B Montebello CA 8/27/1956 s Joseph Oscar Pike & Margaret Lydia. BA Baylor U 1983; MDiv Sthrn Bapt TS Louisville KY 1986; VTS 1988. D 5/31/1988 P 5/1/1989 Bp David Reed. m 8/7/1982 Dawna Linette Jeane. Asst S Matt's Epis Ch Louisville KY 1988-1991.

PIKE, Thomas Frederick (NY) 26 Gramercy Park S Apt 9h, New York NY 10003 **Collegial Cn Trin And S Phil's Cathd Newark NJ 2008-** B Dobbs Ferry NY 1/10/1938 s Frederick Roy Pike & Elizabeth Marion. BS SUNY 1960; MDiv Ya Berk 1968; DD Ya Berk 1977; DMin NYTS 1977. D 6/1/1963 P 12/1/1963 Bp Horace W B Donegan. m 10/1/1981 Lys McLaughlin c 3. Calv and St Geo New York NY 1976-2008; Trst Cathd Of St Jn The Div New York NY 1976; Calv and St Geo New York NY 1971-1975; Trst Ya Berk New Haven CT 1969; R San Andres Ch Yonkers NY 1965-1971; Cur S Mk's Ch In The Bowery New York NY 1963-1965. "Filosfia del Exito," Grijalbo, Mexica, 1991; "Is It Success? Or Is It Addiction?," Nelson Pub., 1988. revtpike@aol.com

PILARSKI, Terri C (Az) 600 S La Canada Dr, Green Valley AZ 85614 **R Chr Ch Dearborn MI 2011-** B Salt Lake City UT 2/15/1957 d Paul Cole & Shannon. D 12/28/1999 P 6/28/2000 Bp William Dailey Persell. m 8/17/1985 Daniel Pilarski c 3. Epis Ch Of S Fran-In-The-Vlly Green Vlly AZ 2008-2010; Dn Elgin Deann Dio Chicago Chicago IL 2003; S Hilary's Ch Prospect Hts IL 2001-2008; Ch Of The H Comf Kenilworth IL 2000-2001. family@pilarski.com

PILCHER III, William Edward (NC) 305 Jackson Rd, Mount Airy NC 27030 B Brooklyn NY 11/24/1930 s William Pilcher & Caroline Camille. BA U So 1952; MDiv GTS 1960; Cert Command and Gnrl Stff Coll 1969. D 6/21/1960 Bp Richard Henry Baker P 12/21/1960 Bp Thomas Augustus Fraser Jr. m 10/6/1979 Carolyn Dolores Whisonant c 4. Int Vic Galloway Memi Chap Elkin NC 2000-2005; Int S Steph's Epis Ch Winston Salem NC 2000-2002; Int Galloway Memi Chap Elkin NC 1997-1999; Int S Mary's Epis Ch Shltr Island NY 1993-1995; Int S Jas Ch Oneonta NY 1992-1993; Int All SS' Epis Ch Gastonia NC 1990-1991; Int Par Of The H Comm Glendale Sprg NC 1987-1989; Int Chr Epis Ch Danville VA 1986-1987; P-in-c Galloway Memi Chap Elkin NC 1981-1986; R Trin Ch Mt Airy NC 1963-1981; R Ch Of The Adv Enfield NC 1960-1963; S Mk Ch Roanoke Rapids NC 1960-1963. Mltry Off Assn of Amer 1991; NC Consultants Ntwk 2001-2004; NG Assn 1983. Legion of Merit US-A 1991. wepilcher3@gmail.com

PILLOT, Anne Marie (O) 4292 Elmwood Rd, South Euclid OH 44121 **D Ch Of The Gd Shpd Beachwood OH 2011-; D S Chris's By-The River Gates Mills OH 2011-; D S Tim's Ch Macedonia OH 2011-** B Cleveland Heights OH 6/29/1960 d Lawrence William Pillot & Jane Louise. BFA Kent St U 1985; locally trained Dio Ohio D Formation 2011. D 6/4/2011 Bp Mark Hollingsworth Jr. a_pillot@yahoo.com

PILLSBURY, Samuel (Los) 919 Albany St, Los Angeles CA 90015 B Princeton NJ 10/24/1954 s Samuel Pillsbury & Katherine H. ABS Harv 1976; JD Usc Law Cntr 1983; Cert In Diac Stds ETSBH 2006. D 12/2/2006 Bp Chester Lovelle Talton. c 1.

P

PILTZ, Guy Hiwa (Haw) 62-2145 Ouli St, Kamuela HI 96743 B Honolulu HI 9/7/1938 s Guy Cecil Piltz & Marguerite Kristine. AB Dart 1960; BD CDSP 1963. D 5/17/1963 P 12/1/1963 Bp Harry S Kennedy. m 6/16/1960 Josephine Irene Amanti c 3. S Jas Epis Ch Kamuela HI 1976-1980; Leeward Missions Ewa Bch HI 1970-1973; Stndg Com Dio Hawaii Honolulu HI 1969-1971; Assoc S Mary's Epis Ch Honolulu HI 1968-1969; Vic S Matt's Epis Ch Waimanalo HI 1963-1966; Vic Emm Epis Ch Kailua HI 1963-1964. ghp2038@gmail.com

PIMM, Douglas Fraser (LI) No address on file. B 4/3/1929 Trans from Nova Scotia 3/1/1954.

PINA, David Ray (ETenn) 5300 Ironhorse Pkwy Unit 356, Dublin CA 94568 **S Lk's Ch Knoxville TN 2010-; Vic S Mk's Epis Ch French Camp CA 2008-** B Oakland CA 3/5/1947 s Manuel Baptiste Pena & Doris Rich. MTh SMU 1972; MA U of Houston 1994; DAS CDSP 2008. D 8/24/2008 P 2/28/2009 Bp Jerry Alban Lamb. m 1/29/2008 Cassandra Woodroof Woodroof Neaves c 2. Epis Dio San Joaquin Modesto CA 2008-2009. dpina@live.com

✠ **PINA-LOPEZ, Rt Rev Hugo Luis** (CFla) 2911 S Whisperbay Ct, Oviedo FL 32765 **Asstg Bp Dio Cntrl Florida Orlando FL 2000-** B La Gloria Camaguey CU 11/3/1938 s Humberto Eugenio Pina & Hortensia. BA La Progresiva Sch of Cuba 1960; BD UTS Cuba 1964. Trans from Iglesia Episcopal de Cuba 2/1/1967 Bp Agueros R Gonzalez Con 8/23/1978 for Hond. m 8/4/1965 Minerva Azucena Arias c 3. Asst Dio Cntrl Florida Orlando FL 1995-2000; R The Epis Ch Of The Redeem Avon Pk FL 1991-1995; Hisp Mssnr Dio Oklahoma Oklahoma City OK 1987-1991; Vic Santa Maria Virgen Epis Oklahoma City OK 1987-1991; S Matt's Ch Bellaire TX 1984-1987; Assoc San Mateo Epis Ch Bellaire TX 1984-1987; Exec Coun Appointees New York NY 1982-1984; Bp Dio Honduras Miami FL 1978-2011; R S Simons Ch Miami FL 1973-1975. R Emer Ch of the Redeem 1995. duncan3@rocketmail.com

PINDER, Churchill G (CPa) St. Stephens Episcopal Cathedral, 221 N. Front St., Harrisburg PA 17101 **Dn Cathd Ch Of S Steph Harrisburg PA 2005-** B Wicomico Church VA 9/8/1953 s Joseph William Pinder & Gay. BA U of Virginia 1976; MDiv VTS 1983. D 8/14/1983 P 2/16/1984 Bp Rustin Ray Kimsey. m 5/28/1988 Sally Reeves Gambill c 2. S Jn's Ch Cold Sprg Harbor NY 1995-2005; R All SS Ch Portland OR 1990-1995; Cn Cathd Ch Of S Steph Harrisburg PA 1986-1990; S Steph's Baker City OR 1983-1986. churchillp3@gmail.com

PINDER, Nelson Wardell (CFla) 2632 Marquise Ct, Orlando FL 32805 B Miami FL 7/27/1932 s George Pinder & Colleen. BA Bethune-Cookman Coll 1956; Nash 1959; Urban Trng Cntr 1965; Med Florida A&M U 1974. D 7/5/1959 Bp Henry I Louttit P 1/9/1960 Bp William Francis Moses. m 8/15/1959 Marian G Grant c 2. R The Epis Ch Of S Jn The Bapt Orlando FL 1977-1995; Vic The Epis Ch Of S Jn The Bapt Orlando FL 1959-1969. Auth, "The Legacy," Ch Pension Fund, 2003; Auth, "The Vintage Voice," Ch Pension Fund, 2003. Alpha Phi Alpha Fraternity 1999; Kappa Delta Pi (Fraternity for Educators) 1968; Phi Beta Kappa 1968. NAACP Freedom Awd 2011; Hall of Frame for Preachers More Hse 2011; Hall of Frame for Priestors More Hse 2011; Hall of Frame for Pastors More Hse 2011; Doctor of Human Letters Voohees Coll 2011; DD VTS DD 2010; DD VTS 2010; DD Nash 2004; Orlando Black Human Relatns Awd Orlando Black Hall of Fame and Florida Rel Hall of Fame 2002; Orlando Black Human Relatns Awd Orlando Black Hall of Fame 1987; Orlando Black Human Relatns Awd Orlando Black Hall of Fame 1978; DD Bethune-Cookman Coll 1976; Hon Cn Cathd of S Lk Orlando Florida 1971; Alum Awd Bethune Cookman Coll 1965. thecanonp@hotmail.com

PINEO, Linda Baker (At) 3404 Doral Ln, Woodstock GA 30189 **Int All SS' Epis Ch Gastonia NC 2010-** B Minneapolis MN 5/24/1947 d Roger Lyman Baker & Joan. BA Mt Holyoke Coll 1969; MA Stan 1975. D 6/24/1988 P 1/5/1989 Bp Bob Gordon Jones. m 9/11/1971 Charles C Pineo c 2. Int Ch Of The Ascen Cartersville GA 2008-2010; S Gabr's Epis Ch Oakwood GA 2006-2007; S Jas Epis Ch Marietta GA 2004-2005; S Clem's Epis Ch Canton GA 2002-2004; Assoc R Chr Epis Ch Kennesaw GA 1998-2002; Chapl Dok Bd Dio Atlanta Atlanta GA 1997-2000; Asst Cleric Chr Epis Ch Kennesaw GA 1994-1997; Serv Convoc of Amer Ch in Europe Paris FR 1992-1994; Chapl Ecw Bd Dio Colorado Denver CO 1990-1992; Assoc Gd Shpd Epis Ch Centennial CO 1990-1992; Vic S Barth's Ch Cokeville WY 1988-1989; Vic S Jas Ch Kemmerer WY 1988-1989. lbpineo@aol.com

PINHO, Joseph T (Mass) 1 Summit Dr Apt 48, Reading MA 01867 **R S Eliz's Ch Wilmington MA 1998-** B Waterbury CT 6/19/1947 s Jose Pinho & Ivone Naif. Rec from Roman Catholic 5/1/1997 as Priest Bp M(arvil) Thomas Shaw III. D Ch Of S Jn The Evang Boston MA 1996-1998.

PINKERTON, Patricia Edith Long (ECR) Highfield House, New Road, Coalway, Coleford, Gloucestershire GL1 67JA Great Britain (UK) B London UK 8/1/1938 d George Matthew Long & Florence Jessica. BA San Jose St U 1969; MA San Jose St U 1975; CDSP 1985. D 5/4/1981 P 12/1/1982 Bp Charles Shannon Mallory. m 6/8/1974 Robert William Pinkerton. Santa Maria Urban Mssn San Jose CA 1985-1987; S Phil's Ch San Jose CA 1984-1985; Asst S Fran Epis Ch San Jose CA 1981-1982. Mow. Phi Kappa Phi. lammascottage@yahoo.com

PINKERTON, Susan Beth (WA) 118 3rd St SE, Washington DC 20003 **The Ch Of The H Sprt Lake Forest IL 2011-** B Ft Riley KS 8/20/1952 d Bobby Joe Pinkerton & Barbara Grandy. BA U of Texas 1993; JD U of Oklahoma 1997; MDiv Ya Berk 2008. D 6/28/2008 P 1/24/2009 Bp Edward Joseph Konieczny. c 3. Asst S Mk's Ch Washington DC 2008-2011; D Trin Par New York NY 2008. sbp2115@hotmail.com

PINKSTON JR, Frederick William (NC) 7225 Saint Clair Dr, Charlotte NC 28270 B Salisbury NC 1/28/1942 s Frederick William Pinkston & Alice Elizabeth. BS No Carolina St U 1965; MDiv TESM 1981. D 1/6/1982 Bp William Gillette Weinhauer P 7/1/1982 Bp Furman Stough. m 6/1/1968 Carolyn Jeanette Plecker. Assoc S Marg's Epis Ch Waxhaw NC 1989-2000; Chap Of Hope Charlotte NC 1986-1989; Chr The Redeem Ch Montgomery AL 1982-1985.

PINNEO, Kent Hubbard (SanD) Po Box 3302, Idyllwild CA 92549 B Alta IA 11/6/1927 s Carroll Mccaulay Pinneo & Evelyn Leone. BA Drake U 1951; GTS 1954. D 6/29/1954 P 2/1/1955 Bp Gordon V Smith. m 4/1/1991 Karen Doreen Walker. Asst Chr The Lord Epis Ch Pinole CA 1985-1987; Ch Of The H Trin Richmond CA 1979-1985; Epis Sr Communities Walnut Creek CA 1979-1982; Actg R S Barth's Epis Ch Livermore CA 1978; Asst S Steph's Epis Ch Orinda CA 1976-1977; Assoc S Clem's Ch Berkeley CA 1974-1975; R All SS' Ch San Francisco CA 1971-1973; Cn S Mk's Cathd Seattle WA 1967-1971; Vic S Geo's Ch Riverside CA 1962-1964; Assoc All SS Epis Ch Riverside CA 1962-1963; R Chr Ch - Epis Chattanooga TN 1958-1962; Assoc Gr - S Lk's Ch Memphis TN 1956-1958; Vic Trin Ch Emmetsburg IA 1954-1956. karenpinneo@yahoo.com

PINNER JR, Joseph W (ETenn) 818 Hill St, Kingston TN 37763 **R S Andr's Ch Harriman TN 1999-** B Memphis TN 6/5/1950 s Joseph Walter Pinner & Dorothy Ethel. BA SW at Memphis 1972; MDiv VTS 1975. D 5/24/1975 P 4/1/1976 Bp William F Gates Jr. m 1/26/1981 Sharon Philpott c 3. Hstgr Dio Wstrn Louisiana Alexandria LA 1992-1999; Dio Wstrn Louisiana Alexandria LA 1992; PBp's Dioc Fund Coordntr Dio Wstrn Louisiana Alexandria LA 1991-1999; Chair of the Pvrty Cmsn Dio Wstrn Louisiana Alexandria LA 1991-1995; Dio Wstrn Louisiana Alexandria LA 1991; Dio Wstrn Louisiana Alexandria LA 1991; Vic S Lk's Ch Jennings LA 1990-1999; R S Lk's Ch Brandon MS 1989-1990; Dept of Chr Nurture Dio Wstrn Louisiana Alexandria LA 1988-1989; Pvrty Cmsn Dio Wstrn Louisiana Alexandria LA 1987-1989; R Ch Of The Epiph Opelousas LA 1986-1989; CE Com Dio Wstrn Louisiana Alexandria LA 1986-1987; Evang & Renwl Cmsn Dio Mississippi Jackson MS 1983-1986; R S Paul's Epis Ch Picayune MS 1982-1986; Vic S Thos The Apos Humboldt TN 1976-1981; D-in-Trng S Ptr's Ch Columbia TN 1975-1976.

PINNOCK, Betty Lou (Ore) 459 Herbert St, Ashland OR 97520 **D S Mk's Epis Par Medford OR 2000-** B Denver CO 7/29/1932 d William Fisher Emery & Josephine Elizabeth. BA U CO 1953; Med Sthrn Oregon U 1963. D 11/4/2000 Bp Robert Louis Ladehoff. deaconbp@hotmail.com

PINTI, Daniel John (WNY) 13021 W. Main St., Alden NY 14004 **Vic S Aid's Ch Alden NY 2011-** B Warren OH 10/6/1963 s Daniel Frank Pinti & Jean Anne. BA Kent St U 1986; MA OH SU 1988; PhD OH SU 1992; M.Div. Chr the King Sem 2011. D 11/22/2008 Bp J Michael Garrison. m 8/27/1988 Maria Pinti c 3. Auth, "Tyndale's Gospel of St.Jn: Translation and the Theol of Style," *Journ of Angl Stds*, 2008; Auth, "Julian's Audacious Reticence: Perichoresis and the Showings," *ATR*, 2006. dpinti@roadrunner.com

PINZON, Samuel E(duardo) (WA) 15570 Sw 143rd Ter, Miami FL 33196 B Bogota CO 5/13/1932 s Eduardo Pinzon & Ana Rosa. AA Warren Wilson Coll 1957; BA Tusculum Coll 1959; MDiv UTS Cuba 1962; ThM PrTS 1971; ThD Covington TS 1982. Rec 12/12/1954 Bp Matthew G Henry. m 5/10/1961 Rosa Maria Treto Moina c 3. All Souls Memi Epis Ch Washington DC 1979-1980; Com Affrs Dio Washington Washington DC 1976-1978; Mssn San Juan Washington DC 1974-1980. Auth, *The Epis Ch in Columbia*, 1980; Auth, "La Gran Colombia," *The Chr Challenge*, 1974; Auth, "Homilia para el Dia Ecum," *Comunidad Teologica*; Auth, "El Significado de la Navidad para el Epis Anglicano," *Temas*; Auth, "Biblia v Ecum," *Vida Espiritual*; Auth, "La Praxis de la Liberacion en Miami," *Voces Luteranas*. Assn of Ministers of Grtr Miami 1982-1996; Consejo Hispano de Ministros Evangelicos / Metro Area Washingto 1978-1980; Hsng Counslg Serv - Washington, DC 1977-1980; Wilson Cntr, Washington, DC 1975-1978. Ecum Speaker representing the Prot Ch of Colo Intl Eucharistic Congr of the RC Ch Bogota Colombia 1968. pinzon96@hotmail.com

PINZON CASTRO, Luis Alberto (Colom) Carrera 6 No 49-85, Piso 2, Bogota Colombia B Buenos Dios Colombia 4/22/1948 s Teofilo Pinzon & Maria Teresa. Licenciatur-Eclesiast Seminario Mayor-Escuela 2000; Filosofo-Teologo Seminario Diocesano 2003; Teologia-Sistematica Facultad Estudios Teologilos 2004. D 6/16/2007 P 9/14/2008 Bp Francisco Jose Duque-Gomez. m 8/24/1969 Maria Eugenia Salcedo c 4. ebeto48@hotmail.com

PIOTROWSKI, Mary Triplett (Az) 2035 N Southern Hills Dr, Flagstaff AZ 86004 **D S Andr's Epis Ch Sedona AZ 2003-; R S Andr's Epis Ch Sedona AZ 2003-** B Oak Hill WV 11/12/1948 d John B Long & Katharine Lumkin. BA Hollins U 1970; MBA Ball St U 1975; MA Nthrn Arizona U 2000; Mdiv Epis TS of the SW 2003. D 5/14/2003 P 12/13/2003 Bp Robert Reed Shahan. m 1/22/1972 Ronald James Piotrowski c 3. marypiotrowski@hotmail.com

PIOVANE, Michael F (Be) Po Box 368, Trexlertown PA 18087 **R S Anne's Epis Ch Trexlertown PA 1998-** B Coaldale PA 9/8/1943 s Rocco Piovane & Veronica. BA S Chas Sem Philadelphia PA 1965; MDiv S Chas Sem Philadelphia PA 1969; EdD Nova SE U 1996. Rec from Roman Catholic 10/31/1993 Bp James Michael Mark Dyer. m 11/15/1986 Rita M Valenti. Int S Mich's Epis Ch Bethlehem PA 1997-1998; Asstg P S Anne's Epis Ch Trexlertown PA 1993-1998. michael.piovane@stannesepiscopal.net

PIPER, Charles Edmund (NMich) 632 Woodward Ave, Iron Mountain MI 49801 B Rockville Center NY 6/30/1947 s Charles Piper & Alys Maude. BA Trin Hartford CT 1969; STB GTS 1972. D 6/17/1972 Bp Jonathan Goodhue Sherman P 12/21/1972 Bp Samuel Joseph Wylie. m 8/22/1970 Linda Lee Jauck c 2. So Cntrl Reg Manistique MI 2000-2010; Pres Stndg Com Dio Nthrn Michigan Marquette MI 1990-1994; Mssnr Gr Epis Ch Menominee MI 1989-1990; R H Trin Ch Iron Mtn MI 1979-2009; Dep GC Dio Nthrn Michigan Marquette MI 1979-1988; Vic Ch Of The Gd Shpd S Ignace MI 1974-1979; Dio Nthrn Michigan Marquette MI 1972-1979. chaspiper@gmail.com

PIPER, Geoffrey Tindall (Mass) 124 Front St, Marion MA 02738 **R S Gabr's Epis Ch Marion MA 2008-** B Burlington VT 9/20/1955 s Winthrop Walker Piper & Emilie. BA Amh 1977; MA Regent U Virginia Bch VA 1981; B.A., 1st honours Bp's U, Lennoxville, Quebec 1988. Trans from Anglican Church of Canada 9/1/1990 Bp Andrew Frederick Wissemann. m 12/28/1983 Leslie T Thayer c 3. Asst for CE Chr Ch Detroit MI 2006-2008; Asst R The Epis Ch Of The Adv W Bloomfield MI 1998-2006; Dio Wstrn Massachusetts Springfield MA 1990-1998; P-in-c S Phil's Ch Easthampton MA 1990-1992. gtpiper55@hotmail.com

PIPER, Linda Lee (NMich) 632 Woodward Ave, Iron Mountain MI 49801 **D H Trin Ch Iron Mtn MI 2003-** B Brooklyn NY 5/14/1947 d Robert Hugh Jauck & Barbara Ann. BSN U of Vermont 1969; MPH U MI 1994. D 8/13/2003 P 2/29/2004 Bp James Arthur Kelsey. m 8/22/1970 Charles Edmund Piper c 2. Pres of the Stndg Com Dio Nthrn Michigan Marquette MI 2006-2011. lindapiper@charter.net

PIPER, Mary Meacham (Ore) 1399 Old Hwy 234, Eagle Point OR 97524 B Minneapolis MN 11/29/1956 d Harris R Meacham & Betty Lou. BS U MN 1979; EFM 1992; Cert Cpt 1993; ORD D Formation Prog 1994; 5 Units Cpe Units 2000. D 6/11/1994 P 10/7/2000 Bp Charles Jones III. m 11/5/1989 Harry C Piper c 3. COM/Baptized Dio Oregon Portland OR 2010-2011; Transition Com Co-Chair Dio Oregon Portland OR 2008-2010; Dn Dio Oregon Portland OR 2006-2007; Asst S Mart's Ch Shady Cove OR 2004-2011; Asstg P S Jas Ch Bozeman MT 2000-2004; Dio Montana Helena MT 1994-2004; D Geth Ch Manhattan MT 1994-2000. shaggypiper1@gmail.com

PIPKIN, Michael (Va) St. John's Episcopal Church, 1623 Carmel Rd., Charlotte NC 28226 **The R's Assoc (Sr Assoc) S Jn's Epis Ch Charlotte NC 2011-** B Houston TX 5/3/1976 s Robert Joseph Pipkin & Jane Elizabeth. BA Texas Tech U 1998; MDiv VTS 2002. D 12/15/2001 P 6/22/2002 Bp C(harles) Wallis Ohl. m 11/1/2008 Molly Hamon. P-in-c The Falls Ch Epis Falls Ch VA 2008-2011; U.S. Navy Chapl Off Of Bsh For ArmdF New York NY 2004-2008; Assoc R Ch Of The Gd Shpd Burke VA 2002-2004; Cur S Dav's Ch Ashburn VA 2002; S Dav's Ch Ashburn VA 2000-2002. Auth, "Reflections on God and 9/11," *Epis News Serv*, Epis Ch, 2011; Auth, "The Romance of War (three-part series)," *Epis Cafe*, Epis Cafe, 2010; Auth, "Repealing Dont Ask Dont Tell could strengthen Rel freedom in the Mltry," *Epis Life Online*, Epis News Serv, 2010; Auth, "Top 10 iPhone Apps for Organizing a Ps Life," *Epis Life Online*, Epis News Serv, 2010. S Andr's Soc 2009. michael@pipkin.com

PIPPIN, J(ames) Edwin (Va) 2 Florida Ave, Earleville MD 21919 **Died 1/6/2010** B Dover DE 10/29/1938 s William E Pippin & Mary Pryor. AA Wesley Coll 1969; LTh VTS 1972; DMin S Mary Sem 1987. D 5/13/1972 P 11/18/1972 Bp George Alfred Taylor. c 2. SOM, CBS, GAS 1977. james.e.pippin@att.net

PIPPIN, Tina (At) 25 Second Avenue, Atlanta GA 30317 B Kinston NC 9/10/1956 d Leon Louis Pippin & Jean. BA Mars Hill Coll 1977; MDiv Candler TS Emory U 1980; ThM Sthrn Bapt TS Louisville KY 1984; PhD Sthrn Bapt TS Louisville KY 1987. D 5/31/1988 Bp David Reed. m 7/28/1984 Jerry Gentry. D S Matt's Epis Ch Louisville KY 1988-1989. Auth, "Death & Desire: The Rhetoric Of Gender In The Apocalypse Of Jn"; Auth, "The Postmodern Bible".

PISANI JR, Gerard Alexander (Nwk) 141 Broadway, Bayonne NJ 07002 B Pompton Lakes NJ 5/17/1938 s Gerard Alexander Pisani & Dorothy Louise. BS Nyack Coll 1963; GTS 1966. D 6/11/1966 Bp Leland Stark P 10/15/1966 Bp George E Rath. m 7/17/2003 Dwight A Tintle. Windmill Allnce Inc. Bayonne NJ 1999-2009; R Trin Ch Bayonne NJ 1974-2009; R Chr Ch Pompton Lakes NJ 1969-1974; Vic S Gabr's Ch Oak Ridge NJ 1966-1969. "The Apparent Heresy Of Jesus," Bk - Dorrance Pub, 2002. jpisani@janddhealth.com

PITA-PARRALES, Ubaldo (EcuC) Manabi Y Tayapi, Puyo Ecuador B Cataraama EC 5/16/1948 s Segundo Pita & Iberible. Sem 1989. D 3/14/1987 P 12/1/1988 Bp Adrian Delio Caceres-Villavicencio. Ecuador New York NY 1993-2003. UBI.PIT@HOTMAIL.COM

PITCHER, Trenton Langland (Chi) 145 E Columbia Ave, Elmhurst IL 60126 **Chapl Bp Anderson Hse Chicago IL 2002-** B Marshalltown IA 5/4/1938 s Elbert Austin Pitcher & Ida. BS U of Wisconsin 1962; Tufts U 1965; MDiv SWTS 1970. D 10/17/1971 P 6/18/1972 Bp James Winchester Montgomery. Cn Res Cathd Of S Jas Chicago IL 1978-1988; Dio Chicago Chicago IL 1973-1977; Asst Trin Ch Highland Pk IL 1971-1978.

PITMAN JR, Omar W (WTex) 11919 El Sendero St, San Antonio TX 78233 **Cntrl Convoc Partnership In Mssn San Antonio TX 2000-** B Big Spring TX 8/26/1933 s Omar William Pitman & Daphne. BA Nm Mltry Inst NM 1954; MDiv GTS 1957. D 7/7/1957 P 2/4/1958 Bp C J Kinsolving III. m 11/27/1965 Mary Engels. S Lk's Epis Ch San Antonio TX 1993-2005; Vic S Jn's Ch Ft Sumner NM 1957-1959; Vic S Mich's Ch Tucumcari NM 1957-1959. fr.omarpitman@sbcglobal.net

PITMAN JR, Ralph William (O) 3044 Edgehill Rd, Cleveland Heights OH 44118 **Luth Metro Mnstry Cleveland OH 1999-** B Bryn Mawr PA 10/24/1947 s Ralph William Pitman & Martha Louise. BA U of Virginia 1969; MDiv EDS 1972; Virginia Commonwealth U 1987; Cert Case Wstrn Reserve U 1998; Cert Case Wstrn Reserve U 2001. D 6/28/1972 Bp Robert Lionne DeWitt P 2/9/1973 Bp Lyman Cunningham Ogilby. m 11/30/1974 Jane Buch c 2. Gr Epis Ch Willoughby OH 2001-2007; R S Mart's Ch Chagrin Falls OH 1995-1999; S Paul's Epis Ch Cleveland Heights OH 1991-1995; Yth Cmsn

Dio Ohio Cleveland OH 1988-1995; Asst S Paul's Epis Ch Cleveland Heights OH 1988-1991; Chair: Cmsn on Alco and Drugs Dio Virginia Richmond VA 1985-1988; S Ptr's Ch Philadelphia PA 1985-1988; Asst S Steph's Ch Richmond VA 1982-1985; Virginia Epis Sch Lynchburg VA 1980-1982; R S Paul's Ch Columbia PA 1976-1980; Asst Nevil Memi Ch Of S Geo Ardmore PA 1975-1976; Cmncatn Consult Dio Pennsylvania Philadelphia PA 1972-1974. Auth, *Chld of Alcoholics in Schools*, CRIS, 1982; Auth, *Baby Jesus Childrens Wrshp Bk*, PS Mus, Inc, 1978; Auth, *The Fast I Choose-Mus & Pryr on Wrld Hunger*, PS Mus, Inc, 1974; Auth, *Cmncatn Media & Orgnztn Values: A Study of Uses of Video Tape in a Par Ch*, Consult Search, Inc, 1972. EPF. rjpit74@gmail.com

PITNER JR, William Cleghorn (Ga) 230 Alabama St, Saint Simons Island GA 31522 **Died 11/30/2009** B Chattanooga,TN 10/12/1938 s William C Pitner & Edna Susan. BA U So 1960; MS U GA 1983; MDiv VTS 1990. D 2/8/1990 P 8/1/1990 Bp Harry Woolston Shipps. pitnerp@bellsouth.net

PITT JR, Louis Wetherbee (Mass) 59 Dartmouth Ct, Bedford MA 01730 B Newark NJ 3/31/1923 s Louis Wetherbee Pitt & Blanche. BA Col 1944; MDiv EDS 1947. D 1/6/1947 P 10/18/1947 Bp William A Lawrence. Exec Coun Appointees New York NY 1983-1986; Cn Pstr The Cathd Ch Of S Paul Boston MA 1980-1983; Dio Massachusetts Boston MA 1979-1986; Zambia New York NY 1972-1979; R All SS Par Brookline MA 1954-1972; R S Mk's Ch Foxborough MA 1949-1954; Assoc Gr Ch Manchester NH 1947-1949. lwpitt@yahoo.com

PITT JR, R Douglas (Md) 615 Chestnut Ave., Towson MD 21204 **Died 1/27/2011** B Richmond VA 4/11/1925 s Robert Douglas Pitt & Grace Estelle. BA U Rich 1951; BD Bex 1954. D 6/4/1954 Bp Robert Fisher Gibson Jr P 6/24/1955 Bp Wiley R Mason.

PITTENGER II, Thomas Tracy (SeFla) 623 Se Ocean Blvd, Stuart FL 34994 B Akron OH 3/24/1937 s Thomas Tracy Pittenger & Bertha. BS Florida St U 1963; MDiv SWTS 1979. D 6/25/1979 P 1/6/1980 Bp William Hopkins Folwell. m 1/30/1988 Diane Crocker c 3. Pres Dio SE Florida Miami FL 1999-2000; Chair Dio SE Florida Miami FL 1998-2000; Brf Bd Dio SE Florida Miami FL 1994-1996; Curs Sec Dio SE Florida Miami FL 1994-1996; Exec Bd Dio SE Florida Miami FL 1993-1996; R S Mary's Epis Ch Stuart FL 1991-2009; Secy Excoun Dio Colorado Denver CO 1989-1990; R Ch Of S Phil And S Jas Denver CO 1987-1991; Sr Cn S Jn's Cathd Jacksonville FL 1985-1987; Cn S Jn's Cathd Jacksonville FL 1982-1984; Assoc All SS Epis Ch Jacksonville FL 1981-1982; D-in-c The Epis Ch Of The Redeem Avon Pk FL 1979-1980. Oblate, Ord Of S Ben 1979. Trst Bp Gray Inns 1995; Vice Chair Cathd Fndt 1986. pittenger@stmarys-stuart.org

PITT-HART, Barry Thomas (SD) 1409 S 5th Ave, Sioux Falls SD 57105 B Liverpool England UK 9/16/1935 s Eric Pitt-Hart & Ida Olive. MD U of Liverpool 1959. D 2/2/1987 Bp Craig Barry Anderson. m 5/8/1958 Mary Jones. D Calv Cathd Sioux Falls SD 1987-1996.

PITTMAN, Albert Calhoun (WA) 403 Russell Ave # 812, Gaithersburg MD 20877 B Greenville MS 1/1/1930 s Albert Sydney Pittman & Mollie Byrd. BA U Rich 1951; BD CRDS 1954; DD Kalamazoo Coll 1974; Cert VTS 1981. D 5/31/1981 Bp Charles Bennison P 11/1/1981 Bp John Thomas Walker. m 8/21/1953 Julia W Wann c 3. R Chr Ch Port Tobacco Paris La Plata MD 1981-1991.

PITTMAN, David West (NC) 218 Pine Cove Drive, Inman SC 29349 B Greenville SC 6/12/1948 s Wayne Creekmore Pittman & Dorothy Ethel. BA VMI 1970; MDiv VTS 1973. D 6/5/1973 P 12/12/1973 Bp William Henry Marmion. m 5/17/1970 Alene Belle Wright c 2. R S Ptr's Epis Ch Charlotte NC 2001-2011; R H Trin Ch Gainesville FL 1986-2001; R Trin Ch Staunton VA 1973-1986. dpittman517@gmail.com

PITTMAN, Warren Lewis (NC) 4211 Wayne Rd, Greensboro NC 27407 **R All SS Ch Greensboro NC 1996-** B Los Angeles CA 12/16/1949 s Frank Alexander Pittman & Helen Germaine. BA Duke 1971; MDiv VTS 1974. D 6/15/1974 P 1/4/1975 Bp Robert C Rusack. m 5/17/2007 Ayliffe Blake Mumford c 2. S Anselm Of Cbury Par Garden Grove CA 1980-1993; S Mich's Mssn Anaheim CA 1976-1980; Yth Dir All SS-By-The-Sea Par Santa Barbara CA 1974-1975; Yth Dir Chr The King Epis Ch Santa Barbara CA 1974-1975; Yth Dir Trin Epis Ch Santa Barbara CA 1974-1975. wlpplus@aol.com

PITTS, John Robert (Tex) 6324 Bon Terra Dr, Austin TX 78731 **Exec Coun Dio Texas Houston TX 1992-** B Dallas TX 1/1/1947 s Roy Eugene Pitts & Agnes. BBA SMU 1968; MBA SMU 1969; JD SMU 1972; MDiv VTS 1987. D 6/29/1987 Bp Gordon Taliaferro Charlton P 2/1/1988 Bp Maurice Manuel Benitez. S Paul's Epis Ch Pflugerville TX 1998; S Matt's Ch Austin TX 1991-1996; Cn To Ordnry For Mssn & Prog Dio Texas Houston TX 1990-1991; Asst to R S Jn The Div Houston TX 1987-1989.

PIVER, Jane Duncan (Va) 53 Ridgemont Road, Ruckersville VA 22968 **Vic Gr Ch Stanardsville VA 2007-** B Rochester NY 2/16/1950 d Edward Lee Piver & Frances Louise. BSN U Roch 1972; MSN U of Pennsylvania 1980; MDiv VTS 2000. D 6/24/2000 Bp Clifton Daniel III P 2/6/2001 Bp Peter James Lee. c 2. Asst Pohick Epis Ch Lorton VA 2002-2007; Vic S Andr's Ch Burke VA 2000-2002; Trin Epis Ch Lorton VA 2000-2002. janedpiver@prodigy.net

PIXCAR-POL, Tomas Pixar (PR) Apartado R, Balboa Panama **Mision La Santa Cruz Castaner PR 2009-** B El Quiche GT 2/8/1963 s Manuel Pixcar Sente & Petronila. Rafael Landivar U 1987; RC Sem 1989; Panama Natl U PA 1991; CTh Epis TS of The SW 1993. D 9/21/1993 Bp James Hamilton Ottley. Dio Guatemala Guatemala City 2005-2009; Dio The Dominican Republic (Iglesia Epis Dominicana) Santo Domingo DO 1999-2003; Dio Panama 1994-1997.

PIZZONIA, Wanda Strong (Mass) Post Road & Ring'S End Road, Darien CT 06820 B Roanoke VA 6/2/1953 d Joseph Wheeler Strong & Nellie Catherine. BD Roa 1975; MDiv Ya Berk 1998. D 6/12/1999 Bp Clarence Nicholas Coleridge P 2/1/2000 Bp Andrew Donnan Smith. m 5/24/1980 Daniel George Pizzonia c 4. Ch Of The Adv Medfield MA 2004-2008; Assoc R S Lk's Par Darien CT 1999-2003. revmom@optonline.net

PLACE, Donald Gordon (WMass) 52 County Road, Pownal VT 05261 B Worcester MA 5/3/1951 s Robert Edward Place & Martha. BA Wms 1974; MDiv Yale DS 1977. D 6/15/1977 P 1/14/1978 Bp Morris Fairchild Arnold. m 7/18/1981 Catherine M Ross. Dio Wstrn Massachusetts Springfield MA 1996-2003; R S Jn's Ch No Adams MA 1996-2002; R Emm Ch Braintree MA 1989-1995; S Asaph's Par Ch Bowling Green VA 1984-1989; St Peters Ch Fredericksburg VA 1984-1989; R S Ptr's Port Royal Port Royal VA 1983-1989; S Paul's Sch Clearwater FL 1981-1983; Cur Epis Ch Of S Thos Taunton MA 1977-1979. Fllshp of the Way of the Cross 2002. dplace@bcn.net

PLACE, Donald Lee Andrew (NY) 111 5th Ave Apt 1206, Pittsburgh PA 15222 B Olean NY 10/7/1937 s Harold Burton Place & Margaret Ethel. Cert Diac Sch 1974; Cert GTS 1976. D 2/23/1974 Bp Kenneth Daniel Wilson Anand P 4/1/1979 Bp James Stuart Wetmore. m 6/6/1970 Mary Jane Hastings. D Ch Of The H Apos New York NY 1977-1978; Cur S Ptr's Ch Bronx NY 1977-1978. Auth, "Living Ch". frplace@yahoo.com

PLANK, David Bellinger (LI) PO Box 693, Palatine Bridge NY 13428 B Little Falls NY 7/8/1938 s Harold William Plank & Doris Bertha. BS U Roch 1960; MDiv PDS 1967; Med St. Lawr Canton NY 1975. D 6/3/1967 Bp Allen Webster Brown P 12/24/1967 Bp Charles Bowen Persell Jr. m 6/25/1960 Francelia R Roider c 4. P-in-c S Jas Ch Brookhaven NY 1996-2002; P-in-c S Andr's Ch Mastic Bch NY 1990-2002; Asst to R S Mk's Ch Westhampton Bch NY 1984-1990; Vic Trin Ch Castine ME 1977-1984; R S Phil's Ch Norwood NY 1969-1977; R Zion Ch Colton NY 1969-1977; Cur S Steph's Ch Delmar NY 1967-1969. davefran@adelphia.net

PLANTZ, Christine Marie (Neb) 2526 Queen Dr, Sidney NE 69162 **Dio Nebraska Omaha NE 2010-** B Moscow ID 7/28/1946 d John Albert Holmes & Marian Malm. AB Shimer Coll 1968; BS Chadron St Coll 1977; MDiv SWTS 2009. D 12/11/2009 P 6/19/2010 Bp Joe Goodwin Burnett. m 5/19/1973 Charles Plantz. chrisplantz@hotmail.com

PLASKE, Susan Ann (Alb) 68 S Swan St, Albany NY 12210 B Albany NY 1/12/1959 d Gordon Peter Ahl & Eileen Frances. AAS Maria Coll 1979. D 6/4/2011 Bp William Howard Love. m 10/3/1981 Kenneth Plaske c 5. deaconsusanplaske@gmail.com

PLATER, Ormonde (La) 1453 Arabella St, New Orleans LA 70115 **D Trin Ch New Orleans LA 2007-** B New York NY 9/6/1933 s Richard Cheatham Plater & Eleanore Mundé. BA Van 1955; MA Tul 1965; PhD Tul 1969. D 7/11/1971 Bp Iveson Batchelor Noland. m 7/19/1957 Kathleen Treadway c 3. Archd Dio Louisiana Baton Rouge LA 1998-2005; D Gr Ch New Orleans LA 1996-2006; D S Anna's Ch New Orleans LA 1971-1995. Auth, "Deacons in the Liturg," Ch Pub, 2009; Auth, "Passion Gospels," Ch Pub, 2007; Auth, "Many Servnt," Cowley, 2004; Auth, "Intsn," Cowley, 1995; Co-Auth, "Cajun Dancing," Pelican Pub Co, 1993. Associated Parishes 1977; NAAD 1987. oplater@cox.net

PLATSON, Julie Lynn (Nev) 171 Cindy Drive, Pahrump NV 89048 **P S Mart's In The Desert Pahrump NV 2001-** B St Petersburg FL 2/27/1961 d Daniel Wilber Marcotte & Margaret Ann. Berklee Sch Of Mus. D 10/1/2000 Bp George Nelson Hunt III P 5/6/2001 Bp Katharine Jefferts Schori. m 10/1/2005 Loyd Platson. Transitional D S Mart's In The Desert Pahrump NV 2000-2001. julie@stmartinspv.org

PLATT, Gretchen Mary (SwFla) 1562 Dormie Dr, Gladwin MI 48624 **D Chr Ch Bradenton FL 2002-; D H Fam Epis Ch Midland MI 2002-** B Biwabik MN 1/9/1936 d Ernest W Ostby & Gladys M. BS Estrn Michigan U 1958; Med Wayne 1973; Med Saginaw Vlly St U 1988. D 10/20/2002 Bp Edwin Max Leidel Jr. m 5/11/1985 Kenneth E Platt. gmkeplatt@sbcglobal.net

PLATT, Nancy Grace Van Dyke (Me) 192 Cross Hill Rd, Augusta ME 04330 B Kane PA 9/18/1937 d William Robert Van Dyke & Alice Ida. BA Hobart and Wm Smith Colleges 1959; MTASCP Montfiore Hosp 1960; SCAC SCAC Chicago IL 1975; MDiv SWTS 1975; CPE Chicago IL 1976. D 6/16/1975 Bp Quintin Ebenezer Primo Jr P 4/30/1980 Bp Morris Fairchild Arnold. c 3. R S Matt's Epis Ch Hallowell ME 1984-2003; Chr Ch Joliet IL 1983-1984; Asst Ch Of The Epiph Chicago IL 1977-1983. "Closed Doors, Open Hearts," *Forw Mvmt*, 2008; Auth, "Healing P & Par," *Addiction*, 1996; Auth, "Pstr Care To

Cancer Patients," 1977; Auth, "Alcoholic's 12 Steps Into Life," 1976. APHA. CPE Resrch Awd 1976. nplatto@aol.com

PLATT, Thomas Walter (Pa) 824 S New St, West Chester PA 19382 B Harmony PA 7/21/1933 s Ira Walter Platt & Frances Gertrude. BA Washington and Jefferson U 1955; MA U Pgh 1960; PhD U of Pennsylvania 1966; STB PDS 1967. D 6/10/1967 P 12/1/1967 Bp Robert Lionne DeWitt. m 6/1/1957 Patricia Ann Schweingruber. Assoc R Emer The Ch Of The H Trin W Chester PA 1971-2002. Auth, "The Conflict Of Sci & Rel A Confusion Re-Visited"; Auth, "Fact & Value: Reflections In Contextual Relativity"; Auth, "The Pitfall Of Postmodernism Chance & Equity"; Auth, "Sci As Human Value"; Auth, "The Concept Of Violence As Discriptive," *The Concept Of Violence As Discriptive & Polemic*. Assoc R Emer Ch Of The H Trin 2002. t.platt@verizon.net

PLATT, Warren Christopher (NY) 255 W 23rd St Apt 3-DE, New York NY 10011 B Far Rockaway NY 6/12/1945 s William J Platt & Ida Dolores. BA Cor 1966; BD UTS 1969; PhD Col 1982. D 6/1/1969 P 12/1/1969 Bp Horace W B Donegan. Hon Asst Ch Of The Trsfg New York NY 1972-2004; Cur All SS Ch Orange NJ 1969-1970. "Translations of BCP in the Resrch Libraries," *Biblion 1, No. 1*, 1992; Auth, "The Polish Natl Cath Ch," *Ch Hist*, 1992; Auth, "Var arts"; Auth, "The Afr Orth Ch," *Ch Hist*. HSEC; SocMary. wplatt@nypl.org

PLATTENBURG, George Smith (Mo) 9 Brentmoor Ct, Saint Charles MO 63303 B Oxford OH 12/1/1933 s Stanley Wilbur Plattenburg & Mary Ann. BA U So 1955; MDiv Bex 1962. D 6/17/1962 P 12/15/1962 Bp Roger W Blanchard. m 5/31/1986 Barbara W Winter c 3. S Steph's Ch S Louis MO 1998-2000; St Louis Urban Partnership S Louis MO 1995-1998; S Jn's Ch St Louis MO 1990-1995; S Ptr's Epis Ch St Louis MO 1976-1981; Vic S Barth's Ch Cokeville WY 1965-1972; Vic S Jas Ch Kemmerer WY 1965-1972; S Mk's Ch Augusta ME 1962-1965.

PLATT-HENDREN, Barbara (NC) 222 Normandy Dr, Clayton NC 27527 **Vic Gr Epis Mssn Clayton NC 1998-** B UK 1/21/1946 d Frederick J Platt & Marguerite May. BA Elmhurst Coll 1968; MRE Andover Newton TS 1970; Cert EDS 1985. D 6/1/1985 Bp John Bowen Coburn P 5/1/1986 Bp Roger W Blanchard. m 6/26/1982 Shelby Ion Hendren c 2. Wendell Epis Explorers Wendell NC 1998-2001; Asst R S Jn's Ch Beverly Farms MA 1986-1996; Asst Min S Ptr's Ch Beverly MA 1985-1986. SCHC 2008. joyfulgrammie@aol.com

PLAZAS, Carlos Alberto (Chi) 1333 W Argyle St, Chicago IL 60640 B Iza Columbia 5/12/1931 s Jose De Los Reyes Plazas & Rosa Ines. LTh Colombia Sa CO; PhD Loyola U; PhD U Chi; PhD Xavier U. Rec from Roman Catholic 8/7/1972 Bp James Winchester Montgomery. m 8/26/1972 Blanca Rosa de la Torre. S Aug Coll Chicago IL 1989-2000; Vic Cristo Rey Chicago IL 1979-1984; Soc And Educational Serv Chicago IL 1978-1988. Auth, "A Proposal On Mntl Hlth Educ & Consult In The Uptown Edgewater Area"; Auth, "Parent Chld Latino Cntr"; Auth, "S Aug Bilingual Cmnty Coll"; Auth, "Relationships Between The Stable m"; Auth, "A Proposal On Mntl Hlth Educ". Amer Coll Of Forensic Examinery; APA; Illinois Psychol Assn; Illionois Alco And Other Drug Abuse Profsnl Certification Assn. El Puente Awd S Aug Coll 2000; The Humanitarian Awd For The Year Pr ChmbrCom 1985; Thos & Elinor Wright Awd; DD GTS New York NY. capalzas@aol.com

PLESTED, Robert William Harvey (LI) 5402 Timber Trace St, San Antonio TX 78250 B Queens NY 12/14/1939 s Leslie William Ferguson Plested & Janet Smith. BA C.W. Post Coll of LIU 1966; MDiv PDS (EDS) 1969; Dplma Command and Gnrl Stff Coll 1984; Dplma Air War Coll 1987; MA St. Mary's U San Antonio TX 1990. D 6/14/1969 P 12/20/1969 Bp Jonathan Goodhue Sherman. m 12/21/1963 Denise Elizabeth Gomichon des Granges. Assoc Ch Of The Resurr San Antonio TX 1996-2002; Int S Fran Epis Ch Victoria TX 1994-1995; Int S Alb's Ch Harlingen TX 1994; Dept. U.S. AF Off Of Bsh For ArmdF New York NY 1972-1988; Vic S Anselm's Ch Shoreham NY 1970-1972; Cur S Jn's Ch Huntington NY 1969-1970. Auth, "arts & Study Papers On Chaplncy, Mnstry & Pstr Care Mgmt," 2003; Auth, "Var Loc And Natl Pubs," 1979. Fed Of Fire Chapl 1988; Intl Conf Of Police Chapl 1979; New York St Assn Of Fire Chapl 1971; Texas Police Assn 1997. Profsnl Mltry Homors U.S. AF 1972-88 1988.

PLIMPTON, Barbara Wilson (WNC) PO Box 968, Marion 28752 B Worcester MA 11/6/1941 d Chester Joseph Wilson & Stella Paula. MA EDS; BA Emml 1963; MSEd Tray St U 1969; Dipl. in Angl Stds TS 2007. D 9/15/2007 P 2/15/2009 Bp Granville Porter Taylor. m 3/23/1968 Fred Plimpton. bwplimpton@aol.com

PLOVANICH, Ede Marie (CGC) 200 Virginia Dr, Dothan AL 36301 B Hattiesburg MS 9/28/1959 BS U Of Mississippi Oxford MS 1983; MDiv Epis TS of The SW 2003. D 6/4/2006 P 4/21/2007 Bp Philip Menzie Duncan II. m 7/31/2003 Robert Plovanich c 1. The Epis Ch Of The Nativ Dothan AL 2007-2008. rplovanich@aol.com

PLUCKER, Susan Elizabeth (NCal) Our Saviour Episcopal Church, P.O. Box 447, Placerville CA 95667 **Assoc Epis Ch Of Our Sav Placerville CA 2011-** B Philadelphia PA 3/4/1947 d Charles Jackson Raiffeisen & Mary Margaret. AS Northland Pioneer Coll Winslow AZ 1980; BA U of Arizona 1988; MDiv CDSP 1991. D 6/8/1991 Bp Joseph Thomas Heistand P 12/6/1991 Bp Jerry Alban Lamb. c 2. R S Lk's Ch Auburn CA 2004-2010; R S Ptr's Epis Ch Red Bluff CA 1993-2004; Asst Trin Ch Folsom CA 1991-1993. grandfathersage@nccn.net

PLUMMER, Ann Hills (LI) 10 Mill Pond Rd, Stony Brook NY 11790 **Died 7/17/2009** B New Rochelle NY 11/28/1935 d George Strough Hills & Alice Gertrude. BA Vas 1957; Cert Mercer TS 1990; STM GTS 1996. D 6/22/1990 P 5/19/1991 Bp Orris George Walker Jr. m 10/20/1962 William Hurbert Plummer c 3. Int Mnstry Ntwk. ahplummer@yahoo.com

PLUMMER, Dale Wilkinson (Kan) 505 N. Pennsylvania, Roswell NM 88201 **R S Andr's Ch Roswell NM 2011-** B Newton KS 9/5/1958 s John Watrous Plummer & Evelyn May. BS Wichita St U 1992; MDiv STUSo 2001. D 3/17/2001 P 10/14/2001 Bp William Edward Smalley. m 11/3/1984 Sharon K Janzen c 2. P-in-c Ch Of The Cov Jct City KS 2003-2011; D S Dav's Epis Ch Topeka KS 2001-2003. rectorstandrews@yahoo.com

PLUMMER, Mark Alton (O) Trinity Episcopal Church on Capitol Square, 125 East Broad Street, Columbus OH 43215 **Gr Epis Ch Willoughby OH 2010-; Asst Trin Ch Columbus OH 2008-** B N Tonowanda NY 2/24/1955 s Berton Porter Plummer & Coletta Smith. BA St Jn Fish Hsc Coll 1998; MDiv Methodist TS in Ohio 2002; Cert. in Angl St Bex Sem 2006. D 6/23/2007 Bp Kenneth Lester Price P 6/28/2008 Bp Thomas Edward Breidenthal. m 6/21/2003 Cathleen Marie Carey c 2. D Chr Epis Ch Of Springfield Springfield OH 2007-2008. alton.plummer@gmail.com

PLUMMER JR, William Morsell (Md) 411 High St, Chestertown MD 21620 **Died 1/5/2011** B Baltimore MD 10/8/1920 s William Morsell Plummer & Mary Isabel. BA Loyola Coll 1942; MDiv GTS 1945. D 6/4/1945 P 6/26/1946 Bp Noble C Powell. c 3.

PLUNKETT, Phillip Riley (Ark) 7 Sonata Trail, Little Rock AR 72205 **Asst P S Mk's Epis Ch Little Rock AR 2003-** B Little Rock AR 10/7/1932 s Benjamin Riley Plunkett & Florence. BS U of Cntrl Arkansas 1954; Med U of Arkansas 1966; MDiv Epis TS of The SW 1970. D 6/17/1970 Bp Robert Raymond Brown P 12/1/1970 Bp Christoph Keller Jr. m 5/6/2006 Jo Ann Gates c 2. Chr Epis Ch Forrest City AR 1985-1986; P-in-c S Lk's Brinkley AR 1981-1992; Gr Ch Wynne AR 1981-1982; S Alb's Ch Stuttgart AR 1970-1976. phil72a@gmail.com

PLUVIOSE, Germaine Auguste (NY) 8915 205th St, Hollis NY 11423 **Died 1/21/2011** B Hinche HT 7/31/1926 s Rosamulaire C Pluviose & Resia. BA Philippe Guerier Coll Ht 1947; BTh Epis TS 1951. D 12/24/1951 P 6/1/1952 Bp Charles Alfred Voegeli. c 2. akavev@yahoo.com

POBJECKY, J Richard (CFla) 414 Pine St, Titusville FL 32796 **R S Gabriels Ch Titusville FL 1978-** B 1/6/1940 Rec 1/31/1975 Bp William Hopkins Folwell. m 9/15/1973 Judith A Pobjecky c 4. S Gabriels Ch Titusville FL 1977-2009; S Andr's Epis Ch Ft Pierce FL 1975-1977. rpobjecky@cfl.rr.com

POCALYKO, Richard Peter (Pgh) 415 Stone Mill Trl Ne, Atlanta GA 30328 B Palmerton PA 11/15/1946 s Peter N Pocalyko & Ruth Helen. Fuller TS; BA Leh 1968; MDiv VTS 1971; Fllshp PrTS 1997. D 6/26/1971 P 2/26/1972 Bp William Foreman Creighton. m 8/16/1969 Cynthia Gail Austin. Dn Trin Cathd Pittsburgh PA 2000-2004; Cathd Of S Phil Atlanta GA 1993-2000; Dept Of Stwdshp Dio Atlanta Atlanta GA 1990-1994; Assoc Cathd Of S Phil Atlanta GA 1990-1993; Com Dio Atlanta Atlanta GA 1987-1989; Chair - Cmsn On Consulting Dio Atlanta Atlanta GA 1982-1983; Strng Com Cler Assn Dio Atlanta Atlanta GA 1982-1983; Strng Com Cler Assn Dio Atlanta Atlanta GA 1982-1983; S Dunst's Epis Ch Atlanta GA 1980-1992; Chair - Dept Of Stwdshp Dio Atlanta Atlanta GA 1978-1979; Dept Of Stwdshp Dio Atlanta Atlanta GA 1976-1981; Chair - Cmsn On Consulting Dio Atlanta Atlanta GA 1975-1977; Cmsn On Consulting Dio Atlanta Atlanta GA 1974-1984; Assoc S Lk's Epis Ch Atlanta GA 1973-1980; Assoc S Andr's Epis Ch Coll Pk MD 1971-1973. rppocalyko@bellsouth.net

POFFENBARGER II, George (NMich) 5002 Green Oak Dr, Durham NC 27712 B Charleston WV 3/26/1930 s Nathan Simpson Poffenbarger & Harriet. BS Ohio U 1956; MDiv Epis TS In Kentucky 1966. D 6/3/1966 P 12/14/1966 Bp Wilburn Camrock Campbell. m 11/29/1958 Sandra Courtney c 2. P S Mk's Epis Ch Roxboro NC 1999-2001; Int S Steph's Epis Ch Erwin NC 1997-1998; Int Trin Ch Mt Airy NC 1996-1997; Cn To E Upper Peninsula Convoc Dio Nthrn Michigan Marquette MI 1985-1995; R S Jas Ch Of Sault S Marie Sault Ste Marie MI 1985-1995; Dept Mssn Dio Newark Newark NJ 1979-1985; Ch Of The Gd Shpd Sussex NJ 1978-1985; S Jn's Memi Ch Ramsey NJ 1978; Epis Cntr Newark NJ 1976-1978; Assoc Chr Ch Short Hills NJ 1973-1976; R Ch Of The Heav Rest Princeton WV 1970-1973; Vic All SS Ch Un WV 1967-1970; Vic Ch Of The Incarn Ronceverte WV 1967-1970; Vic S Andr's Ch Mullens WV 1966-1967; Cur S Steph's Epis Ch Beckley WV 1966-1967. Int Mnstry; Ldrshp Acad For New Directions; Ord Of S Lk. geopoff@mindspring.com

POGGEMEYER JR, Lewis Eugene (U) 2849 Polk Ave, Ogden UT 84403 **D Ch Of The Gd Shpd Ogden UT 1980-** B McKeesport PA 10/28/1946 s Lewis

P

Eugene Poggemeyer & Aureline Margaret. BA K SU 1971. D 9/13/1980 Bp Otis Charles. m 6/7/1969 Karen Joyce West c 3.

POGOLOFF, Stephen Mark (NC) 218 Forestwood Dr, Durham NC 27707 B Washington DC 11/27/1949 s David Pogoloff & Florence. BA Jn Hopkins U 1971; BA Oxf 1978; MDiv GTS 1979; MA Oxf 1984; PhD Duke 1990. D 8/11/1979 Bp David Keller Leighton Sr P 3/1/1980 Bp Walter Decoster Dennis Jr. m 9/23/1973 Christina Askounis. P-in-c St Elizabeths Epis Ch Apex NC 1993-1999; Assoc S Jos's Ch Durham NC 1984-1993; Assoc R All Ang' Ch New York NY 1980-1984; Cur S Jn's Ch Larchmont NY 1979-1980. Auth, "Isocrates & Contemporary Hermeneutics"; Auth, "Logos & Sophia: The Rhetorical Situation Of 1 Corinthians". SBL.

POGUE, Blair A (Minn) 2136 Carter Avenue, Saint Paul MN 55108 **R S Matt's Ch St Paul MN 2005-** B Los Angeles CA 12/26/1964 d William Lloyd Pogue & Gwen Jeannine. BA Whitman Coll 1986; MDiv Ya Berk 2000. D 6/24/2000 P 2/6/2001 Bp Peter James Lee. m 5/27/2000 Dwight J Zscheile c 1. Assoc R Ch Of The H Comf Vienna VA 2002-2005; Asst R Trin Ch Upperville VA 2000-2002. Auth, "Three Essays on Romans 8," *Feasting on the Word: Preaching the Revised Common Lectionary*, Westminster Jn Knox Press, 2011; Auth, "Cultivating a Culture of Discernment," *Vstry Papers July/August 2010*, ECF, 2010; Auth, "I Cannot Believe The Gospel That Is So Much Preached: Gender, Belief, And Discipline In Kentuckey Bapt Rel Culture, 1780-1860," *Kentucky: Settl*, U Of Kentucky Press, 1999. R. Lansing Hicks Prize Ya Berk New Haven CT 2000. rector@stmatthewsmn.org

POGUE, Ronald Dennis (Tex) 3017 Avenue O, Galveston TX 77550 **Int Ch Of The Gd Shpd Lexington KY 2010-** B Houston TX 2/4/1948 s Alfred Coy Pogue & Velma Ethel. BS U of Houston 1970; MDiv Candler TS Emory U 1973; DMin Houston Grad TS 1997. D 12/3/1997 Bp Claude Edward Payne P 6/1/1998 Bp Leopoldo Jesus Alard. m 2/9/1969 Gay Elva Wunderlich c 2. Int Trin Ch Lawr KS 2009-2010; R Trin Ch Galveston TX 1999-2009; Cn Chr Ch Cathd Houston TX 1997-1999. Auth, *Equipping Empowering Chr Leaders in Congregations*. Theta Phi. ron@e-piphanies.com

POINDEXTER, Charles (Pa) 5421 Germantown Ave, Philadelphia PA 19144 B Richmond VA 4/11/1932 s Walter Edward Poindexter & Pearl Marie. GTS; MDiv PDS; BA W Virginia St U; LHD S Aug 1988. D 6/11/1958 P 12/1/1958 Bp Horace W B Donegan. m 2/24/1962 Judith Owens. P-in-c S Phil's Ch Richmond VA 1997-1999; S Lk's Ch Philadelphia PA 1968-1994; R S Geo S Barn Ch Philadelphia PA 1965-1968; R S Monica's Ch Hartford CT 1963-1965; Vic S Fran Assisi And S Martha White Plains NY 1958-1963. Auth, "Boule Journ". OHC, CCU; Soc Of S Marg. Who'S Who Amer & Colls 53-54; Who'S Who Rel 75,.

POINTER, Ivan Edward (EO) 1723 Nw Carden Ave, Pendleton OR 97801 **D Ch Of The Redeem Pendleton OR 1999-** B Baker City OR 1/6/1936 s Edward Eugene Pointer & Margaret Eva. EFM. D 6/16/1999 Bp Rustin Ray Kimsey. m 7/7/1957 Nora Doreen Roberts c 4.

POIRIER, Esther H (Oly) PO Box 3108, Federal Way WA 98063 **P Ch Of The Gd Shpd Fed Way WA 2006-** B 1/6/1948 d Frank Edward Holley. BA Coll of Wooster 1970; MA Natl Coll of Educ 1971; MDiv CDSP 2002. D 6/29/2002 Bp Sanford Zangwill Kaye Hampton P 1/25/2003 Bp Vincent Waydell Warner. Dio Olympia Seattle WA 2006; Vic Ch Of Our Sav Monroe WA 2002-2006. estherpoirier@hotmail.com

POISSON OSH, Ellen Francis (USC) Convent of St. Helena, 3042 Eagle Drive, Augusta GA 30906 **P-in-c All SS Ch Beech Island SC 2011-; Int S Aug Of Cbury Ch Augusta GA 2008-** B New London CT 10/13/1946 d Robert A Poisson & Eleanor. BA Smith 1968; MLS Teheran U Teheran IR 1972; DLS Col 1983; MDiv GTS 2000. D 3/18/2000 P 9/16/2000 Bp Richard Frank Grein. Serv The Ch Of The Epiph New York NY 2000-2001. Auth, "Citizen Diplomacy in Iran," *Natl Cath Reporter, Sept 22, 2006*, 2006. Alum/ae Prize in Eccl. Hist The GTS 2000; Wmn Hist Proj Prize The GTS 2000; H Land Travel Prize The GTS 1999; H.P. Montgomery Prize The GTS 1998. ellenfrancisosh@yahoo.com

POIST, David Hahn (Va) 341 Woodlands Rd, Charlottesville VA 22901 **R Emer S Paul's Memi Charlottesville VA 2008-** B Baltimore MD 10/24/1940 s Emmett Curtis Chase Poist & Yolanda Carolyn. BA W&M 1962; MDiv Ya Berk 1965; MA Jn Hopkins U 1969. D 6/22/1965 P 5/19/1966 Bp Harry Lee Doll. m 6/27/1970 Elizabeth Patterson Williams c 2. Peace Cmsn Dio Virginia Richmond VA 1986-1992; S Paul's Memi Charlottesville VA 1977-2006; Koinonia Fndt Baltimore MD 1970-1977; DP Ecum Campus Mnstry Dio Maryland Baltimore MD 1966-1970; Asst S Paul's Par Baltimore MD 1966-1968; Asst Ch Of The Ascen Westminster MD 1965-1966. dhpoist@cstone.net

POITIER, Marlon Stanley (EC) Po Box 2338, Kinston NC 28502 **Died 8/11/2009** B Deerfield Bch FL 10/9/1934 s Stanley Poitier & Drucilla. BA S Aug 1959; VTS 1962. D 11/10/1963 P 6/1/1964 Bp Thomas H Wright. c 2. lpoiter@eastlink.net

POKORNY, Wayne Douglas (Ct) 30 Woodland St Apt 11NP, Hartford CT 06105 **Assoc Gr Epis Ch Hartford CT 2000-** B Oak Park IL 7/30/1938 s Frank Albert Pokorny & Anna. BA Beloit Coll 1960; MDiv GTS 1967; DMin GTF 1986. D 6/10/1967 Bp Robert Lionne DeWitt P 2/1/1968 Bp Ned Cole. c 3. Bp Of ArmdF- Epis Ch Cntr New York NY 1987-2000; Vic Ch Of S Jn By The Sea W Haven W Haven CT 1978-1986; Yth Mnstry Off Dio Connecticut Hartford CT 1978-1982; Dn of the Bridgeport Dnry Dio Connecticut Hartford CT 1977-1978; Exec Coun Dio Connecticut Hartford CT 1976-1978; Sub-Dn, Bridgeport Dnry Dio Connecticut Hartford CT 1976-1977; R Trin-S Mich's Ch Fairfield CT 1974-1978; Dn, Ithaca-Cortland Dist Dio Cntrl New York Syracuse NY 1972-1974; R Calv Ch Homer NY 1969-1974; Cur Emm Ch Norwich NY 1967-1969. Auth, "arts & Bk Revs". AASECT 1981; Societas Liturgica 1977.

POLGLASE, Kenneth Alexis (Nwk) 2796 Rudder Dr, Annapolis MD 21401 B Brooklyn NY 9/10/1931 s Alexis Talmadge Polglase & Hazel Ruth. BA Wag 1953; CTh GTS 1956; MA FD 1972. D 9/1/1956 P 4/27/1957 Bp James P De Wolfe. m 5/3/1953 Carolyn H Honeycutt c 4. Ch Of The Epiph Allendale NJ 1964-1984; R S Mart's Ch Maywood NJ 1960-1964; Cur Gr Epis Ch Massapequa NY 1957-1960; Cur Trin Epis Ch Roslyn NY 1956-1957. polglaka@yahoo.com

POLGLASE, Robert Ferris (Ga) 1904 Greene Street, Augusta GA 30904 **Vic Chr Ch Augusta GA 2011-** B Bloomfield NJ 11/18/1956 s Robert J Polglase & Lydia M. BA Davidson Coll 1979; JD Merc Sch of Law 1982; MD Merc Sch of Med 1991; MDiv Erskine TS 2012. D 8/20/2010 P 3/6/2011 Bp Scott Anson Benhase. m 10/9/1999 Amanda Robinson c 1. P Chr Ch Augusta GA 2011; Transitional D S Paul's Ch Augusta GA 2010-2011. rpolglase@gmail.com

POLITZER, Jerome Foute (ECR) Po Box 221115, Carmel CA 93922 B San Francisco CA 12/13/1926 s Jerome Politzer & Augusta. BA Stan 1948; BD VTS 1951; STM PSR 1965. D 8/4/1951 P 4/5/1952 Bp Karl M Block. m 5/5/1953 Beverly Reeves c 3. Dept Mssns Dio California San Francisco CA 1974-1977; ExCoun Dio California San Francisco CA 1969-1973; R S Jn's Chap Monterey CA 1968-1995; Dn Monterey Convoc Dio California San Francisco CA 1956-1960; Vic Epis Ch Of The Gd Shpd Salinas CA 1955-1968; Vic S Geo's Ch Salinas CA 1951-1968. "A Light Unto My Paths," Silver Bch Books, 2005; Auth, "A Lantern Unto My Feet," PB Soc, 2001; Ed, "Lex Orandi," PB Soc, 1983. ESA; SPBCP 1976. jeromep@mncmail.com

POLK, Perry Willis (NCal) Grace Episcopal Church, 1405 Kentucky St, Fairfield CA 94533 **Assoc Gr Epis Ch Fairfield CA 2008-** B Waco TX 11/26/1940 s Willis Houston Polk & Florence Nyander. BBA Baylor U 1962; MBA U of Oklahoma 1967; MA NW Nazarene U 2006; MDiv CDSP 2008. D 11/22/2008 P 6/13/2009 Bp Barry Leigh Beisner. m 4/11/1970 Sylvia Marie McClard c 3. revperrypolk@aol.com

POLK JR, Rollin Saxe (WTex) 207 Veda Mae Drive, San Antonio TX 78216 B Troy NY 5/5/1921 s Rollin Saxe Polk & Anna Elizabeth. BA Wesl 1943; MDiv VTS 1955; MS OLLU Soc Wk 1974. D 2/8/1945 Bp Frederick D Goodwin P 10/18/1945 Bp George Ashton Oldham. c 2. Asst S Andr's Epis Ch San Antonio TX 1981-1988; Vic S Matt's Epis Ch Kenedy TX 1980-1983; Vic S Tim's Ch Cotulla TX 1975-1980; R Epis Ch Of The Gd Shepard Geo W TX 1967-1972; R S Phil's Ch Beeville TX 1967-1972; R S Jn's Epis Ch Sonora TX 1965-1967; Asst Ch Of The Incarn Dallas TX 1957-1965; R S Ptr's Epis Ch Hillsdale MI 1951-1957; P-in-c Ch Of The Epiph Nelsonville OH 1947-1951; P-in-c S Paul's Epis Ch Logan OH 1947-1951; Asst S Paul's Epis Ch Albany NY 1945-1947. Auth, "Cmnty Hospice Care," *Hospice Soc Serv*, 1979. AEHC 1972-2000. rollinpolk@gmail.com

POLK, Thomas Robb (RG) 90 S Longspur Dr, The Woodlands TX 77380 B Memphis TN 5/2/1926 s Oscar Boyle Polk & Mary Elizabeth. BD U of Oklahoma 1946; MS U of Oklahoma 1948; MDiv STUSo 1973. D 6/10/1973 Bp Girault M Jones P 3/12/1976 Bp Reginald Heber Gooden. c 1. R S Mary's Ch Lovington NM 1981-1986; Vic All SS Epis Ch Ponchatoula LA 1977-1980; Vic Ch Of The Incarn Amite LA 1977-1980; Epis Coll Cntr Hammond LA 1977; Cur S Paul's Ch New Orleans LA 1976-1977; Asst S Paul's Ch New Orleans LA 1975-1976; Vic All SS Ch Wheatland WY 1973-1975; Asst All SS Epis Ch Torrington WY 1973-1975; Vic Ch Of Our Sav Hartville WY 1973-1975; Vic S Geo's Ch Lusk WY 1973-1975; Asst Chr Ch Epis So Pittsburg TN 1970-1973. Tau Beta Pi U of Oklahoma, Norman 1948; Sigma Xi U of Oklahoma, Norman 1946; Sigma Tau. tpolk80@gmail.com

POLLACH, Gideon Liam Kavanaugh (Va) 125 Court Street, 11SH, Brooklyn NY 11201 **Epis HS Alexandria VA 2008-** B Long Beach CA 1/31/1975 s Samuel Pollach & Mary Suzanne. St. Albans Sch for Boys 1992; BA Trin 1996; MDiv GTS 2006. D 6/24/2006 P 2/12/2007 Bp Peter James Lee. m 6/1/2002 Sarah Broaddus. Assoc S Barth's Ch New York NY 2006-2007; S Steph's Ch Richmond VA 1999-2003. gpollach@gmail.com

POLLAK, Charles Duane (SC) PO Box 1043, Beaufort SC 29901 **P Assoc Par Ch of St. Helena Beaufort SC 2009-** B Detroit MI 10/11/1930 s Edward Charles Pollak & Gladys Horne. BS US Naval Acad 1952; MSEE US Naval Postgraduate 1961. D 10/31/2009 P 5/16/2010 Bp Mark Joseph Lawrence. m 8/5/1972 Anne Jones c 3. chuckpollak@lowcountry.com

POLLARD, Richard Allen (Pgh) 1750 Hastings Mill Rd, Pittsburgh PA 15241 **R All SS Epis Ch Bridgeville PA 2009-; Asst Chr Epis Ch No Hills**

P

Pittsburgh PA 2007- B Ridgway PA 10/17/1946 s Ernest Isaac Pollard & Mary Campbell. TESM; BS Penn 1968; JD Duquesne U 1976. D 6/12/2004 P 12/17/2004 Bp Robert William Duncan. m 11/5/1988 Susan Hurlbut Compton c 4. Asst S Paul's Epis Ch Pittsburgh PA 2007-2009; Vic Ch Of The Adv Pittsburgh PA 2004-2007. richardpollard@verizon.net

POLLARD III, Robert (NY) 400 S Ocean Blvd, Palm Beach FL 33480 B Asheville NC 11/10/1927 s Robert Pollard & Mary Gladys. MIT; BA Hav 1950; MDiv VTS 1954; Fllshp Coll of Preachers 1966. D 6/9/1954 P 7/23/1955 Bp Matthew G Henry. m 8/18/1985 Cornelia Bertles c 2. Asst The Epis Ch Of Beth-By-The-Sea Palm Bch FL 1992-2010; Vic S Matt's Sum Chap Sugar Hill NH 1986-2000; Alt Del Dio Coun Dio New York New York City NY 1980-1984; Evan Com Dio New York New York City NY 1978-1984; R S Paul's Ch Yonkers NY 1978-1984; Adj Prof Cathd Of St Jn The Div New York NY 1978-1979; Wkr P Coordntr Dio New York New York City NY 1977-1984; Chair Dio New York New York City NY 1965-1969; Vic All SS Epis Ch Vlly Cottage NY 1961-1970; Cur H Trin Epis Ch W Palm Bch FL 1958-1961; P S Fran Of Assisi Cherokee NC 1954-1956; P S Jn's Ch Sylva NC 1954-1956. "Power, Save, and Chr Discipliaship," *These*, Self-Pub, 2007. Soc Of The Cincinnati In The St Of Virginia 1951; Soc Of The Cincinnati In The St Of Virginia, Chapl 1986. pollardr@earthlink.net

POLLEY, Bonnie (Nev) 1631 Ottawa Drive, Las Vegas NV 89169 **D Chr Ch Las Vegas NV 1983-** B Lake Charles LA 2/8/1939 d Robert Bonnabel Lawes & Rose. Colorado Inst of Bus; U CO; U of New Mex. D 12/9/1982 Bp Wesley Frensdorff. m 8/30/1958 David Cleland Polley c 3. NAAD 1984; Ord of S Lk 1987. bbelpolley@cox.net

POLLEY, Seth Alexander (Az) 5 Gardner St, Bisbee AZ 85603 **Vic/Border Mssnr Dio Arizona Phoenix AZ 2006-** B Albuquerque NM 6/8/1962 s David Cleland Polley & Bonnie. BA U of Nevada at Reno 1986; MDiv CDSP 1992; MA U of Nevada at Reno 1998. D 4/2/1995 P 1/27/1996 Bp Stewart Clark Zabriskie. m 2/15/1997 Lori Valerie Keyne c 1. Int Chapl Emmaus Collgt Chap at UofA Tucson AZ 2005-2006; Asst R S Jn's Ch Roanoke VA 2002-2005; Mssy Dio Panama Exec Coun Appointees New York NY 2001-2002; P in Charge, Catedral de San Lucas Dio Panama 1999-2002; San Jose St. Cantebury Dio El Camino Real Monterey CA 1998; Yth Asst Chr Epis Ch Los Altos CA 1997-1999; LP/P-in-c ELM Cmnty Ch Reno NV 1992-1997. Auth, "Borders and Blessings: Reflections on Our Natl Immigration Crisis from the Arizona Desert," *ATR*, 2010. seteo@q.com

POLLINA, Roy Glen (SwVa) PO Box 4162, Martinsville VA 24115 **R Chr Ch Martinsville VA 2011-** B Oak Park IL 4/20/1951 s Roy Dominic Pollina & Dolores. BA Nthrn Illinois U 1973; MDiv Epis TS of The SW 1985. D 6/23/1985 P 5/4/1986 Bp James Barrow Brown. m 8/18/1973 Susan Crowley c 2. P-in-c All SS Epis Ch Ponchatoula LA 2011; R S Mich's Epis Ch Mandeville LA 1986-2009; D Trin Ch New Orleans LA 1985-1986. Auth, "To Bless A Chld," *To Bless A Chld*, Ch Pub, 2009. roy@christchurchmvl.org

POLLITT, Michael James (Q) 1376 Telegraph Rd., West Caln MI 19320 B Glens Falls NY 9/30/1949 s James Joseph Pollitt & Dorothy Marian. BA Providence Coll 1975; MDiv Mt St. Mary's Sem 1983; MA Mt St. Mary's Sem 1985; Cert Wstrn Michigan U 1996; DMin Cornerstone U 2001. Rec from Antiochian Orthodox Church 6/25/2001 as Priest Bp Keith Lynn Ackerman. m 8/2/1993 Patricia Pollitt. Auth, "Addiction, Relapse, And Existentialism," *Chapl Today*, Assn Of Profsnl Chapl, 2003. Assembly Of Epis Healthcare Chapl 2001-2003; Natl Assn Of Veterans Affrs Chapl 1998-2003. "Best Pract In Chapl" Dept Of Veterans Affrs 2001. michael.pollitt2@med.va.gov

POLLOCK, Alma Harward (Ct) 128 Litton Ave, Groton CT 06340 **Middlesex Area Cluster Mnstry Higganum CT 2006-** B White Plains NY 5/6/1954 d Vernon Judson Harward & Marian Eleanor. BA Harv 1975; BA Oxf 1977; MDiv Yale DS 1982. D 6/13/1982 P 3/1/1983 Bp Alexander Doig Stewart. m 2/7/1981 Stewart Andrew Pollock. Oneida Area Epis Consortium Oneida NY 1984-1987; Par Assoc S Jn's Ch Bridgeport CT 1982-1984.

POLLOCK, Christina (Spok) St. John the Evangelist Cathedral, 127 E. 12th Ave., Spokane WA 99202 **D Cathd Of S Jn The Evang Spokane WA 2002-** B Spokane WA 5/8/1951 d Marvin Cordie Taylor & Alyce Mary. BA Estrn Washington U 1973; CPE D Formation Prog 1996. D 5/16/1998 Bp Frank Jeffrey Terry. m 12/18/1974 Wayne Thomas Pollock c 2. D Emm Ch Kellogg ID 2000-2002; COM Dio Spokane Spokane WA 1998-2004; D Ch Of The Resurr Spokane Vlly WA 1998-2000. deaconchristina@yahoo.com

POLLOCK, David Stanton (WA) 21517 Laytonsville Rd, Laytonsville MD 20882 **Int S Anne's Ch Damascus MD 2011-** B West Chester,PA 3/21/1944 s Thomas Martin Pollock & Lois Hutten. BA Ohio Wesl 1966; MDiv PDS 1971; DMin Wesley TS 1978. D 9/2/1971 P 1/1/1972 Bp Robert Lionne DeWitt. m 11/17/1989 Margaret Fowler c 2. R S Barth's Ch Laytonsville MD 2001-2004; Stndg Com Dio Washington Washington DC 1988-1990; R S Lk's Ch Trin Par Beth MD 1980-2001; Assoc Chr Ch Georgetown Washington DC 1974-1980. Washington Dc Cleric Assn, NNECA. dspollock44@hotmail.com

POLLOCK, Douglas Stephen (Oly) 7701 Skansie Ave, Gig Harbor WA 98335 B Chicago IL 10/10/1942 s Neil John Pollock & Frances. BS U IL 1965; MDiv Epis TS of The SW 1979. D 12/9/1978 P 6/17/1979 Bp Otis Charles. m 5/27/1967 Carol Ann McKinley c 2. R S Jn's Epis Ch Gig Harbor WA 1991-2010; R S Paul's Ch Klamath Falls OR 1983-1991; Ch Of The Gd Shpd Ogden UT 1980-1983; Dio Utah Salt Lake City UT 1979-1980. dougpollock@clearwire.net

POLLOCK, Elizabeth Good (Me) Po Box 896, York Harbor ME 03911 B Van Wert OH 8/26/1926 d Roland Haven Good & Myrtle Marguerite. BS NWU 1948; MA Methodist TS In Ohio 1977; MDiv Methodist TS In Ohio 1979. D 4/14/1982 Bp William Grant Black P 6/2/1984 Bp Frederick Barton Wolf. m 3/26/1949 Clark Pollock. P-in-c S Steph The Mtyr Epis Ch E Waterboro ME 1989-1994; Assoc S Geo's Epis Ch York Harbor ME 1984-1989; Asst S Jn's Ch Worthington OH 1982-1984; Dce Dio Sthrn Ohio Cincinnati OH 1979-1984.

POLLOCK, John Blackwell (EC) 1912 Shepard St, Morehead City NC 28557 **Trst Dio E Carolina Kinston NC 2011-; Dep to GC Dio E Carolina Kinston NC 2006-2013; R S Andr's Ch Morehead City NC 2004-** B Georgetown SC 11/13/1959 s James Furman Pollock & Elsie Alice. Spartanburg Methodist Coll 1980; BA U of So Carolina 1983; Med U of So Carolina 1985; Luth Theol Sthrn Sem 1994; M.Div. STUSo 1996; D.Min VTS 2011. D 6/8/1996 P 5/15/1997 Bp Dorsey Felix Henderson. m 12/6/1997 Mary Deborah Withington. Stndg Com Dio E Carolina Kinston NC 2006-2009; R S Paul's Epis Ch Clinton NC 1999-2004; Asst Chr Ch Greenville SC 1998-1999; Chapl Chr Ch Epis Sch Greenville SC 1997-1999; D S Matt's Epis Ch Spartanburg SC 1996-1997. jbpollock@aol.com

POLLOCK, Margaret (Va) 21517 Laytonsville Rd, Laytonsville MD 20882 **Asst S Barth's Ch Laytonsville MD 2001-** B Washington DC 4/10/1951 d George Randolph Cooper & Nancy Louise. Smith 1970; BA GW 1973; MBA GW 1977; MDiv VTS 1994. D 4/14/1998 P 5/8/1999 Bp Leopold Frade. m 11/17/1989 David Stanton Pollock. Epis Ch Cntr New York NY 2000-2001; Assoc S Geo's Epis Ch Arlington VA 1998-2000. Bd, Inter Ch Med Assistance; NNECA. margaretpollock@hotmail.com

POLLOCK, Ronald Neal (NJ) 154 W High St, Somerville NJ 08876 **R S Jn's Ch Somerville NJ 1998-** B Riverside NJ 2/6/1965 s Ronald Jay Pollock & Phaedra. BA Elon U 1987; Cert S Geo's Coll Jerusalem IL 1993; MDiv GTS 1994. D 6/11/1994 P 12/17/1994 Bp George Phelps Mellick Belshaw. Cur Ch of S Jn on the Mtn Bernardsville NJ 1994-1998. CHS, Nyc 1994. frronpollock1@verizon.net

POLVINO, Andrea Regina (WNY) 515 Columbus Ave., Waco TX 76701 B New Brunswick NJ 3/1/1958 d Joseph Andrew Polvino & Esther Mary Beia. BA Wm Smith 1980; JD SUNY at Buffalo Sch of Law 1983; MDiv The TS at The U So 2008. D 4/29/2007 Bp J Michael Garrison P 11/15/2008 Bp Dena Arnall Harrison. c 1. Dio Texas Houston TX 2011; Cur S Paul's Ch Waco TX 2008-2010. andrea@stpaulswaco.org

POMPA, Anthony R (Be) 19 E Cochran St, Middletown DE 19709 **Dn and R Cathd Ch Of The Nativ Bethlehem PA 2007-** B Jim Thorpe PA 1/2/1965 s Robert Anthony Pompa & Rose Marie. BS Penn 1987; MDiv Epis TS of The SW 1991. D 6/8/1991 P 2/1/1992 Bp James Michael Mark Dyer. m 10/2/1993 Felicia Salventi c 2. St Annes Epis Ch Middletown DE 2003-2007; Dio Virginia Richmond VA 1998-2003; Imm Ch Mechanicsville VA 1995-2000; Cathd Ch Of The Nativ Bethlehem PA 1991-1995. Mk Armin Jojorian Awd Epis TS Of The SW 1991. rocco1234@verizon.net

PONADER, Martha Downs (Ind) 1337 Eagle Run Dr, Sanibel FL 33957 B Sturgis MI 6/20/1933 d Howard Wilson Downs & Elizabeth Williams. BA Indiana U 1955; MA Butler U 1984; Chr TS 1984. D 6/24/1988 Bp Edward Witker Jones. m 6/23/1956 Wayne Carl Ponader c 4. D Dio Indianapolis Indianapolis IN 1988-1996. NAAD.

PONCE, Jacqueline (PR) 1 Calle Brandon, Ensenada PR 00647 Puerto Rico **Mision Santa Cecilia Ensenada PR 2004-** B New York NY 11/19/1955 d Anastacio Ponce & Ana. CTh San Pedro Y San Pablo Sem S Just Puerto Rico; Universidad Interamericana San German PR; Luth TS at Gettysburg 2000. D 6/24/2000 Bp Charles Ellsworth Bennison Jr P 8/29/2004 Bp David Andres Alvarez-Velazquez. m 10/6/2007 José A Estrada c 2. revponce@aol.com

POND, Finn Richard (Spok) 7315 N Wall St, Spokane WA 99208 B Santa Monica CA 11/28/1951 s Gene N Pond & Louise A. BS Biola U 1974; MS OR SU 1977; PhD OR SU 1981. D 12/21/2002 Bp James Edward Waggoner. m 8/1/1981 Jean Bertelsen c 2. fpond@whitworth.edu

POND JR, Walter Edward (WNY) 4345 Clear View Dr Apt 7, Geneseo NY 14454 **Reg Mnstry Dvlp Dio Wstrn New York Tonawanda NY 2000-** B Jacksonville FL 3/5/1933 s Walter Edward Pond & Marie Louise. BA Newberry Coll 1955; MDiv Luth TS 1958; ThM Columbia TS 1964; Cert Bex 1999. D 5/30/1999 P 12/5/1999 Bp J Michael Garrison. m 5/19/1956 Jane McCants Weeks c 2. P-in-c The Ch Of The H Apos - Epis Perry NY 2000-2004; D S Lk's Epis Ch Attica NY 1999-2000. frwalter@earthlink.net

PONDER, J(ames) Brian (WTenn) 1116 23rd Ave., Meridian MS 39301 **S Paul's Epis Ch Meridian MS 2011-; S Paul's Epis Ch Meridian MS 2011-; R S Paul's Epis Ch Meridian MS 2011-** B Jackson MS 12/17/1974 s James Harold Ponder & Mary Frances. BA Millsaps Coll 1997; MDiv GTS 2004. D 6/18/2004 P 1/22/2005 Bp Duncan Montgomery Gray III. Discerning Young

Vocations Experience, Fac Dio W Tennessee Memphis TN 2010-2011; Stndg Cmsn on Liturg & Mus, Chair Dio W Tennessee Memphis TN 2010-2011; Assoc Gr - S Lk's Ch Memphis TN 2008-2011; Exec Com Dio Mississippi Jackson MS 2008; Vocare in MS, Sprtl Dir Dio Mississippi Jackson MS 2007-2008; Asst & Chapl Ch Of The Resurr Starkville MS 2004-2008. jbponder@hotmail.com

PONG, Tak Yue (Tai) 11 Pak Po Street, Homantin Hong Kong B HK 7/28/1946 s Paul Yui Tim Pong & Wei Ching. BEd Natl Taiwan Normal U 1971; MS U of Wisconsin 1972; MDiv VTS 1978; PhD Penn 1982. D 6/24/1978 Bp John Thomas Walker P 9/1/1979 Bp James T M Pong. m 8/2/1975 Li-jiuan Yu. All SS Middle Sch 1990-2010; Gr And S Ptr's Ch Baltimore MD 1979-1980; Cur Calv Ch Washington DC 1978.

PONS, Albert Erskine (Okla) 2700 Vista Grande Dr. N.W. Unit 29, Albuquerque NM 87120 B New Orleans LA 8/21/1926 s Albert Pons & Clara Louise. BA U So 1946; BD STUSo 1949; Fllshp Coll of Preachers 1954; S Aug's Coll Cbury Gb 1963. D 7/10/1949 P 9/5/1950 Bp Girault M Jones. m 3/8/1975 Madelyn Marie Edwards c 4. Asst R S Jn's Ch Oklahoma City OK 1965-1970; Chair Of The Dept Of CE Dio Dallas Dallas TX 1956-1959; R S Mich's Ch Richland Hills Richland Hills TX 1953-1965; Vic S Paul's Ch Abbeville LA 1951-1953. ponsmgmt@comcast.net

POOL, Jayne Collins (Ala) 106 Stratford Road, Birmingham AL 35209 **P-t P affiliate S Mary's-On-The-Highlands Epis Ch Birmingham AL 2009-; Rel Tchr Adv Epis Day Sch Birmingham AL 2007-; T/F on the Stwdshp of Creation Dio Alabama Birmingham AL 2004-** B Birmingham AL 8/10/1959 d James Austin Collins & Katherine Louise. MA Birmingham-Sthrn Coll 1981; Candler TS Emory U 1982; MDiv Yale DS 1984; DMin STUSo 2011. D 5/21/1998 Bp Robert Oran Miller P 12/1/1998 Bp Henry Nutt Parsley Jr. m 5/30/1981 James Marion Pool c 1. Asst for Pstr Care and Outreach S Mary's-On-The-Highlands Epis Ch Birmingham AL 2004-2006; Stndg Com Dio Alabama Birmingham AL 2002-2005; Dioc Revs Bd Dio Alabama Birmingham AL 2001-2003; Cur S Mary's-On-The-Highlands Epis Ch Birmingham AL 1998-2002; COM Dio Alabama Birmingham AL 1993-1996; Dioc Coun Dio Alabama Birmingham AL 1992-1996; Cmsn on Chr Formation Dio Alabama Birmingham AL 1991-1994. writer, "A Revs of "What Are You Going To Do w Your Life?"," *Sewanee Theol Journ*, The U So, 2010. Phi Beta Kappa Birmingham Sthrn Coll 1981; ABS Awd Emory U Decatur GA 1981. poolja123@bellsouth.net

POOL, Mart Gayland (FtW) 1870 Ederville Rd S, Fort Worth TX 76103 B Plainview TX 4/23/1937 s Mart Greenwood Pool & Mattie Lou. TCU; BA Texas Tech U 1959; UTS 1960; STB GTS 1962. D 4/27/1962 P 11/1/1962 Bp George Henry Quarterman. m 11/2/1991 Katie Sherrod. Int R S Paul's Epis Ch Dallas TX 1999; S Paul's Epis Ch Dallas TX 1997; Asst S Greg's Epis Ch Mansfield TX 1995-1997; Associated Parishes Inc. Ft Worth TX 1995-1996; All SS' Epis Ch Ft Worth TX 1993-1997; R S Lk's In The Meadow Epis Ch Ft Worth TX 1985-1990; St Mich All Ang Ch 1980-1982; Chr The King Epis Ch Ft Worth TX 1974-1996; Cur S Lk's Epis Ch Dallas TX 1963-1966; Vic S Jn's Ch Lamesa TX 1962-1963; Cur The Epis Ch Of S Mary The Vrgn Big Sprg TX 1962-1963. Coun Associated Parishes 1970-2001. mgpool@charter.net

POOLE, Charles Lane (NCal) 6342 Paso Dr, Redding CA 96001 **Stndg Com Dio Nthrn California Sacramento CA 1978-** B Chicago IL 2/20/1933 s Charles Lane Poole & Helen Amelia. BS IL Wesl 1956; BD CDSP 1959. D 7/1/1959 Bp William F Lewis P 2/27/1960 Bp William G Wright. m 7/11/1959 Evelyn Rose Taylor c 2. S Mich's Ch Anderson CA 1973-1995; R S Paul's Epis Ch Oroville CA 1966-1971; Assoc Trin Epis Ch Reno NV 1965-1966; Yth Advsr Dio Nevada Las Vegas NV 1961-1966; Vic Chr Ch Pioche NV 1961-1965; Vic S Barth's Ch Ely NV 1961-1965; Vic S Philips-in-the-Desert Hawthorne NV 1959-1961. Hon Cn to the Ordnry Dio Nthrn California 1984. clp39erp@att.net

POOLE, John Huston (CFla) 603 Spring Island Way, Orlando FL 32828 **D S Chris's Ch Orlando FL 2002-** B Franklin NJ 11/5/1947 s Huston A Poole & Marjorie. D 2/13/1982 Bp Wilbur Emory Hogg Jr. m 11/19/1965 Denice R Seale. Assoc Chr Ch Gilbertsville NY 1987-1988; Assoc S Matt's Ch Unadilla NY 1982-1987.

POOLEY, Nina Ranadive (Me) 152 Princes Point Rd, Yarmouth ME 04096 **Mem Cler Day Plnng Com Dio Maine Portland ME 2009-; Fin Com Mem Dio Maine Portland ME 2007-; R S Barth's Epis Ch Yarmouth ME 2007-** B Providence RI 3/6/1965 d Manmohan Vishwanath Ranadive & Gail Eileen. BA W&M 1987; Med U of Virginia 1991; MDiv STUSo 2004. D 12/11/2004 P 9/10/2005 Bp Charles Glenn VonRosenberg. m 8/1/1993 Kenneth T Pooley c 2. Mem Mssn Priorities Study Grp Dio Maine Portland ME 2009-2011; Assoc Chapl S Paul's Sch Brooklandville MD 2006-2007; Yth Min Ch Of The Gd Shpd Lookout Mtn TN 2004-2006. nina@wickednifty.com

POOSER, W(illiam) Craig (Chi) 2423 Blue Quail, San Antonio TX 78232 B Jacksonville FL 7/23/1944 s William W Pooser & Louise O'Quinn. BA Stetson U 1967; Massachusetts Gnrl Hosp 1969; MDiv SWTS 1973; MS Texas A&M U 1985. D 6/13/1973 P 12/15/1973 Bp William Hopkins Folwell. m 2/16/1984 Patricia Bode c 2. Ch Of The Resurr San Antonio TX 2003-2010; Int S Andr's Epis Ch Corpus Christi TX 2002-2003; Supply P (Weekends) Calv Ch Menard TX 2001-2002; Supply P (Weekends) Trin Ch Jct TX 2001-2002; Int S Andr's Epis Ch Corpus Christi TX 2000-2001; Supply P Dio W Texas San Antonio TX 1998-2000; S Jude's Epis Ch Rochelle IL 1991-1993; Cbury Epis Cntr Dekalb IL 1989-1991; Gr Ch Of W Feliciana S Francisville LA 1985-1986; Asst S Andr's Ch Bryan TX 1980-1983; Off Of Bsh For ArmdF New York NY 1976-1981; Vic H Faith Epis Ch Port S Lucie FL 1973-1976. padre@pooserville.com

POPE, Alicia Hale (RG) 432 Aragon Ave, Los Alamos NM 87544 B 5/16/1973 BAAS U of No Texas 1996; MPA U of New Mex 2001; Dplma in Basic Christians Stds TESM 2006. D 10/21/2006 Bp Jeffrey Neil Steenson P 11/10/2007 Bp William Carl Frey. c 1. ahale@lanl.gov

POPE, Charles Maurice (Ia) 671-18th Street, Des Moines IA 50314 **R S Paul's Epis Ch Grinnell IA 2003-** B Bremen GA 5/5/1947 s Hughlan William Pope & Ruby Pope. BA W Georgia Coll 1969; MDiv Sthrn Bapt TS Louisville KY 1972; U So 1984. D 11/30/1993 P 5/31/1994 Bp Carl Christopher Epting. m 12/22/1970 Mary Leah Bhame c 3. Mem of Com to Selcect Candidates for Bp Dio Iowa Des Moines IA 2002; Cn The Cathd Ch Of S Paul Des Moines IA 1999-2003; P-in-c S Anne's By The Fields Ankeny IA 1998-1999; Int S Paul's Epis Ch Grinnell IA 1997-1998; Supply P Dio Iowa Des Moines IA 1995-1997; COM Dio Iowa Des Moines IA 1994-1997; P S Andr's Ch Des Moines IA 1994-1995. "Deciding Before the Draft," Epis Life, 2005; "Journey Outward," Living Ch, 2000. Natl Bd for Cert Counselors 1993. chasmpope@hotmail.com

POPE III, Daniel Stuart (Roch) 406 Canandaigua St, Palmyra NY 14522 B Natick MA 8/8/1930 s Daniel Stuart Pope & Marguerite. BA Ya 1952; STB Ya Berk 1963. D 5/10/1989 P 11/18/1989 Bp William George Burrill. m 5/21/1966 Patricia Ann Smith c 3. R S Jn's Ch Sodus NY 1997-2002; P-in-c S Steph's Ch Wolcott NY 1989-2004; D-In-C S Steph's Ch Wolcott NY 1989. dpope@rochester.rr.com

POPE, Kristin (Stina) (Cal) 790 Linda Mar Blvd, Pacifica CA 94044 **Vic Chr Epis Ch Sei Ko Kai San Francisco CA 2010-** B Moscow ID 11/9/1950 d Kenneth Pope & Kathleen. Emory U; BA Pitzer Coll 1973; MDiv Untd Theo Sem MN 1977; MA Jn F Kennedy U 2011. D 8/6/1977 Bp Philip Frederick McNairy P 4/24/1978 Bp Robert Marshall Anderson. m 7/8/2001 Sue Thompson c 2. Actg Vic Chr Epis Ch Sei Ko Kai San Francisco CA 2008-2009; Int H Chld At S Mart Epis Ch Daly City CA 2007-2008; Assoc Ch Of The H Innoc San Francisco CA 2003-2005; S Mk's Par Berkeley CA 2003; Int Trin Ch San Francisco CA 2002-2003; Dir Admssns CDSP Berkeley CA 1999-2002; Int S Phil's Ch San Jose CA 1999; Int Chr Ch Alameda CA 1997-1999; Asst S Barth's Epis Ch Atlanta GA 1993-1997; Asst S Lk's Ch Minneapolis MN 1978-1979. Auth, *Cler Journ*; Auth, *Open Hands*. stinapope@gmail.com

POPE, Robert Gardner (Colo) 108 Sawmill Cir, Bayfield CO 81122 **Vic S Aug's Ch Creede CO 2009-** B Newton MA 8/13/1936 s Daniel Stuart Pope & Marguerite. BA Mar; St Jn Vianney TS (R.C.) Denver CO; MA Ya 1961; PhD Ya 1967. D 11/6/1976 P 6/9/1977 Bp Harold B Robinson. m 11/22/1986 Alice Robinson c 3. P-in-c Trin Epis Ch Hamburg NY 1988-1989; Vic Ch Of All SS Buffalo NY 1982-1986; P-in-c S Phil's Ch Buffalo NY 1981-1982; Asst S Jn's Gr Ch Buffalo NY 1978-1981; P-in-c S Phil's Ch Buffalo NY 1977-1978; Cur S Pat's Ch Cheektowaga NY 1976-1977. Auth, "The Halfway Cov," Pr, 1969. Guggenheim Fellowowship 1976.

POPE, Steven Myron (Tex) 905 Whispering Wind, Georgetown TX 78633 B Saint Paul MN 5/21/1941 s Myron Robert Pope & June Nan. BA California St U 1965; MDiv VTS 1984; DMin SWTS 2001. D 6/22/1984 Bp Joseph Thomas Heistand P 2/14/1985 Bp Maurice Manuel Benitez. m 9/1/1962 April Lion c 2. R S Andr's Ch Breckenridge TX 2005-2008; R Trin Ch Victoria TX 2001-2005; Chair Div Renwl Dio Texas Houston TX 1995-1996; R Calv Epis Ch Richmond TX 1990-2001; Bd Dir EP Amnesty Prog Dio Texas Houston TX 1989-1991; S Matt's Ch Bellaire TX 1988-1990; R San Mateo Epis Ch Bellaire TX 1988-1990; Asst R S Lk's On The Lake Epis Ch Austin TX 1984-1988. frsteven2@yahoo.com

POPLE, David A (Ct) 95 Greenwood Ave, 22 Golden Hill St, Bethel CT 06801 B Hollis NY 11/13/1945 s John Franklin Pople & Virginia May. BA Syr 1967; MDiv Hartford Sem 1970. D 6/12/1971 Bp Joseph Warren Hutchens P 1/15/1972 Bp Morgan Porteus. R Ch Of S Thos Bethel CT 1980-2011; Vic All SS Ch Wolcott CT 1974-1980; Cur S Andr's Ch Meriden CT 1971-1974. dapople@yahoo.com

POPPE, Bernard William (Nwk) 18 De Hart Rd, Maplewood NJ 07040 **R S Geo's Epis Ch Maplewood NJ 2002-** B Newport RI 6/6/1957 s Norman Howard Poppe & Hilda. BA H Cross Coll 1979; MDiv GTS 1984. D 6/23/1984 P 1/12/1985 Bp George Nelson Hunt III. Geo Mercer TS Garden City NY 1999-2000; Geo Mercer TS Garden City NY 1994-1995; R S Mk's Ch Jackson Heights NY 1992-2002; Assoc R S Ann And The H Trin Brooklyn NY 1987-1992; Cur Gr Ch Newark NJ 1984-1987. bwpoppe@verizon.net

P

POPPE, Kenneth Welch (Vt) 2 Cherry St, Burlington VT 05401 **Dn And R Cathd Ch Of S Paul Burlington VT 1998-** B Philadelphia PA 3/2/1949 s Herman Ernest Poppe & Mary Laura. BA Hob 1971; MDiv ETS 1975; Col 1978; UTS 1978. D 6/14/1975 Bp Lyman Cunningham Ogilby P 3/1/1976 Bp William Hawley Clark. m 9/12/1970 Margaret Shawn Sussman c 1. R Chr Ch Shaker Heights OH 1989-1998; R S Dav's Ch Kinnelon NJ 1983-1989; Asst S Eliz's Ch Ridgewood NJ 1981-1983; P-in-c S Andr's Epis Ch Lincoln Pk NJ 1980-1981; Serv Chr Ch Short Hills NJ 1978-1980; Asst Chr Ch Greenville Wilmington DE 1975-1978. Auth, "Liturg On The Holocaust". AAR, SBL. kpoppe@stpaulscathedralvt.org

POPPLEWELL, Elizabeth Carol Duff (Ia) 1808 Nw 121st Cir, Clive IA 50325 **R S Lk's Epis Ch Cedar Falls IA 2010-** B Roswell NM 7/26/1963 d Donald Hemings Duff & Phyllis Carol Bradt. BA Drake U 1985; MDiv SWTS 2007. D 12/16/2006 P 6/16/2007 Bp Alan Scarfe. m 10/24/1987 Dennis Ray Popplewell c 2. Asst S Tim's Epis Ch W Des Moines IA 2007-2010. edpopplewell@msn.com

PORCHER, Philip Gendron (SVa) 1494 Stratton Pl, Mount Pleasant SC 29466 B Mount Pleasant SC 3/12/1932 s Philip Porcher & Wilhelmina. BS Clemson U 1954; MDiv VTS 1957. D 6/27/1957 P 5/19/1958 Bp Thomas N Carruthers. m 8/24/1963 Georgia A Jenkins c 3. Int S Thos Epis Ch No Charleston SC 2002-2003; Asst to Bp of SC Dio Sthrn Virginia Norfolk VA 1975-1995; Dio Sthrn Virginia Norfolk VA 1967-1995; Vic S Thos Epis Ch Chesapeake VA 1967-1972; Assoc Ch Of The Gd Shpd Sumter SC 1965-1967; Assoc Ch Of The H Comf Sumter SC 1965-1967; P-in-c The Ch Of The Epiph Eutawville SC 1957-1960. Auth, *Why Use Int Pstr or Int Consult*. Alb Inst 1975; CODE 1982-1995; Int Mnstry Ntwk 1980. vipgp@aol.com

PORTARO JR, Sam Anthony (Chi) 1250 N Dearborn St Apt 19C, Chicago IL 60610 **Fac Credo Inst Inc. Memphis TN 2006-** B Bethesda MD 1/9/1948 s Sam Anthony Portaro & Frances Louise. BA U NC 1970; MDiv VTS 1973; DMin PrTS 1982. D 1/25/1975 Bp Matthew G Henry P 12/20/1975 Bp William Gillette Weinhauer. m 3/15/1995 Christopher Mark Dionesotes. Trst VTS Alexandria VA 2003-2008; Pres, Alum/ae Assn Exec Com VTS Alexandria VA 2002-2003; Alum/ae Assn Exec Com VTS Alexandria VA 2000-2003; Pres, Stndg Com Dio Chicago Chicago IL 1995; Stndg Com Dio Chicago Chicago IL 1993-1995; Coordntr for MHE Fifth Prov of the Epis Ch Epis Ch Cntr New York NY 1987-1990; Int Dir of Field Educ SWTS Evanston IL 1987-1988; Int R Trin Ch Chicago IL 1986; Exam Chapl/COM Dio Chicago Chicago IL 1983-2005; Cmsn on Higher Educ Dio Chicago Chicago IL 1982-2005; Epis Chapl to The U Chi Epis Ch Coun U Chi Chicago IL 1982-2005; Assoc To The R Bruton Par Williamsburg VA 1976-1982; Cmsn on Coll Wk Dio Sthrn Virginia Norfolk VA 1976-1982; Cmsn on Human Sxlty Dio Sthrn Virginia Norfolk VA 1976-1982; Vic Ch Of The Epiph Newton NC 1975-1976; Angl/RC T/F Dio Wstrn No Carolina Asheville NC 1975-1976; Cmsn on Arts, Liturg, Mus and Sacristans Dio Wstrn No Carolina Asheville NC 1975-1976; Cmsn on St of the Ch Dio Wstrn No Carolina Asheville NC 1975-1976. Auth, "Transforming Vocation," Ch Pub, 2008; Auth, "Mind the Gap: Forming a New Generation for Ldrshp in an Aging Ch," Forw Mvmt Press, 2004; Auth, "Sheer Chrsnty: Conjectures on a Catechism," Cowley Pub, 2004; Auth, "Daysprings: Meditations For The Weekdays Of Adv," *Lent And Easter*, Cowley Pub, 2000; Auth, "Crossing The Jordan: Meditations On Vocation," Cowley Pub, 1999; Auth, "Brightest & Best: A Comp To The Lessons Feasts And Fasts," Cowley Pub, 1998; Auth, "Conflict And A Chr Life," Morehouse Pub, 1996; Auth, "Inquiring & Discerning Hearts: Mnstry And Vocation w YA On Campus," Scholars Press, 1993. ESMHE 1982-2003. samportaro@ameritech.net

PORTER, Elizabeth Streeter (Ark) 10 Thunderbird Dr, Holiday Island AR 72631 **P S Jas Ch Eureka Sprg AR 2004-** B Elkhart IN 7/8/1940 D 5/4/2002 P 11/23/2002 Bp Andrew Hedtler Fairfield. c 2. S Geo's Epis Ch Bismarck ND 2002-2004. betsyporter@cox.net

PORTER, Ellis Nathaniel (WA) 118 Seaton Pl Nw, Washington DC 20001 B Sumter SC 4/26/1931 s Nathaniel Jerome Porter & Francis Juanita. BS So Carolina St U 1959; MDiv PDS 1963; DMin How 1985. D 6/21/1963 P 6/1/1964 Bp Gray Temple. Int S Mk's Ch Brooklyn NY 1994-1995; Epis Ch Cntr New York NY 1988-1994; Vic S Tit Epis Ch Durham NC 1966-1972; Vic Ch Of The Redeem Pineville SC 1963-1965. Auth, "Charity & The Black Man," 1965. Bd UBE 1975-1989; Cmsn On Peace 1974-1987; Mnstuntdrs In Educ 1973-1985; OHC 1965-1971. Ldrshp Awd Natl Ube UBE 1996; Chpl To Bp Tutu 1984.

PORTER III, Fulton Louis (Chi) 2720 2nd Private Rd, Flossmoor IL 60422 **Dn, Chicago So Dnry Dio Chicago Chicago IL 2009-; R Ch Of S Thos Chicago IL 2005-** B Jackson MS 10/11/1967 s Fulton Louis Porter & Clara Womack. BS Morehouse Coll 1989; MD NWU 1993; MDiv SWTS 2004. D 6/12/2004 Bp Dorsey Felix Henderson P 4/9/2005 Bp Victor Alfonso Scantlebury. m 11/26/1994 Lisa C Cochran c 2. Cur S Edm's Epis Ch Chicago IL 2004-2005. Benjamin Whipple Schlr Seabury-Wstrn 2004. fultonp@aol.com

PORTER, George Vernon (Ga) 1201 Fairfield St, Cochran GA 31014 **P Trin Ch Cochran GA 2005-** B Bainbridge GA 8/21/1936 s Vernon Smith Porter & Alice. Gordon Mltry Barnesville GA; Merc; Middle Georgia Coll. D 2/5/2005 P 8/7/2005 Bp Henry Irving Louttit. m 3/2/1974 Mary Sue Chance Chacne c 5. portergvp@aol.com

PORTER, Gerald William (Oly) PO Box 488, Kingston WA 98346 **Assoc Gr Ch Bainbridge Island WA 2005-** B McCook NE 8/30/1942 s Robert Hervey Porter & Doris Fay. BA U Denv 1964; Harvard DS 1965; MDiv EDS 1968. D 6/22/1968 P 5/31/1969 Bp Anson Phelps Stokes Jr. m 6/23/1968 Barbara Worrell. Provost S Mk's Cathd Seattle WA 1998-2000; Provost Dio Olympia Seattle WA 1991-2002; Provost The Cathd Ch Of S Paul Boston MA 1989-1990; Asst Dio Massachusetts Boston MA 1978-1991; P-in-c S Paul's Ch Brookline MA 1976-1977; Dio Massachusetts Boston MA 1970-1977; Cur/R Gr Ch Salem MA 1968-1978. alphahusky@comcast.net

PORTER, James Robert (Az) 7014 E Golf Links Rd #194, Tucson AZ 85730 B Springfield MO 12/10/1941 s James Newton Porter & Margaret. BA U of Texas at Arlington 1970; MDiv CDSP 1973. D 7/11/1973 P 1/18/1974 Bp Clarence Rupert Haden Jr. m 2/17/1979 Candy Carey c 2. Int S Ptr's Ch Casa Grande AZ 2008-2011; R Ch Of Our Sav Lakeside AZ 1997-2007; Vic S Jn's Epis Ch Colville WA 1990-1997; Epis Ch Of The Redeem Republic WA 1990-1996; R Trin Ch Folsom CA 1987-1990; Int Ch Of The Incarn Santa Rosa CA 1985-1987; R S Ptr's Epis Ch Red Bluff CA 1979-1985; Cur S Barn' Epis Ch Of Odessa Odessa TX 1977-1979; Vic S Mk's Epis Ch Coleman TX 1976-1977; Vic Trin Ch Albany TX 1976-1977; Vic S Tim's Ch Gridley CA 1973-1976. Barbershop Harmony Soc 2000; RACA 1984; SocMary 1997. jrporter1941@gmail.com

PORTER, Joe T(homas) (WTenn) 43 Carriage Ln, Sewanee TN 37375 B Rena Lara MS 1/9/1945 s Ulysses Selby Porter & Shirley Hayes. BA U of Memphis 1971; MDiv STUSo 1985. D 6/11/1985 P 6/11/1986 Bp Alex Dockery Dickson. m 11/24/1967 Claudia W Williams. Cur Gr - S Lk's Ch Memphis TN 2001-2007; S Lk and S Jn's Caruthersville MO 1999-2003; R S Mary's Epis Ch Dyersburg TN 1989-2001; P-in-c S Thos The Apos Humboldt TN 1986-1989; D S Mary's Cathd Memphis TN 1985-1986. PORTER45@BELLSOUTH.NET

PORTER, John Harvey (Cal) 551 Ivy St, San Francisco CA 94102 B CA 6/2/1944 Rec from Roman Catholic 12/3/2005 Bp William Edwin Swing. johncantuar@yahoo.com

PORTER, John Joseph (At) 215 Abington Dr NE, Atlanta GA 30328 B Newark NJ 4/24/1939 s John Joseph Porter & Catherine Elizabeth. MA CUA; BA/MA S Bonaventure U; VTS 1970. Rec from Roman Catholic 3/21/1974 as Priest Bp Matthew G Henry. m 7/14/1973 Mary Kirchhoffer c 2. P-in-c H Innoc Ch Atlanta GA 2002-2009; R S Bede's Ch Atlanta GA 1985-2002; Asst H Innoc Ch Atlanta GA 1978-1985; Cn to Bp for Cler Dvlpmt Dio Atlanta Atlanta GA 1975-1978; Cur Chr Ch Greenwich CT 1973-1975; Dir of the Cntr for Cont Educ VTS Alexandria VA 1971-1973. Ldrshp Awd Ldrshp Atlanta Atlanta 1977. mary@sterlingtvl.com

PORTER, Lloyd Brian (Tex) 1701 W TC Jester Blvd, Houston TX 77008 B Houston TX 12/16/1945 s Lloyd Alexander Porter & Margaret Emma. BA U of Texas 1968; MDiv Epis TS of The SW 1983. D 6/8/1984 P 12/13/1984 Bp Scott Field Bailey. c 2. St Andrews Epis Ch Houston TX 2004-2005; Emm Ch Houston TX 2001-2002; S Jas Epis Ch Houston TX 2000-2001; S Ptr's Ch Pasadena TX 1999-2000; R S Paul's Epis Ch Orange TX 1995-1997; S Steph's Epis Ch Houston TX 1993-1995; Assoc R S Mk's Ch Houston TX 1990-1992; St Lk's Epis Hosp Houston TX 1989-1990; R S Jas' Epis Ch La Grange TX 1986-1989; Asst R S Jn's Ch McAllen TX 1984-1986. EFM Mentor, AFP. porter6375@sbcglobal.net

PORTER, Nicholas Tewkesbury (Ct) Trinity Church, 651 Pequot Ave, P.O. Box 400, Southport CT 06890 **Trst Ya Berk New Haven CT 2008-; R Trin Epis Ch Southport CT 2005-** B New York NY 6/3/1964 s Harry Boone Porter & Violet. BA Yale Coll 1986; MA Amer U in Cairo 1990; MA King's Coll, Lon 1991; MDiv Ya Berk 1994. D 6/11/1994 Bp Clarence Nicholas Coleridge P 6/11/1995 Bp Samir H Kafity. m 8/10/1991 Dorothy Meek c 3. Mem of Bp's Coun of Advice Amer Ch In Europe 2001-2004; R Emm Epis Ch Geneva 1201 CH 2000-2005; Chairman of Mnstry in Daily Life Com Amer Ch In Europe 1998-2001; Sub-Dn &Cn Pstr The Amer Cathd of the H Trin Paris 75008 FR 1997-2000; Intl Chapl to Angl Bp in Jerusalem Exec Coun Appointees New York NY 1995-1997; Cur of St. Geo's Cathd Dio Jerusalem 1994-1996. Fllshp of St Alb & St Sergius 1995; Ord S Jn of Jerusalem 1995. Knight Ord of St. Jn of Jerusalem 2008. nporter@trinitysouthport.org

PORTER, Pamela (WMass) Po Box 19, Heath MA 01346 B Mount Clemens MI 1/31/1948 d John Francis Porter & Nelle Bea. BA U of Detroit 1973; Wayne Elem Tchg Detroit MI 1974; MDiv EDS 1986. D 6/28/1986 Bp Henry Irving Mayson P 1/17/1988 Bp Daniel Lee Swenson. m 8/3/1974 Brian Michael DeVriese c 2. S Jas Epis Ch Arlington VT 2006-2007; S Mary's In The Mountains Wilmington VT 2000-2001; Asst Gr Ch Amherst MA 1993-1996; Dio Wstrn Massachusetts Springfield MA 1993-1995; Asst Vic S Mary's In The Mountains Wilmington VT 1987-1990. pam_porter@verizon.net

PORTER, Roger Cliff (CGC) 6500 Middleburg Ct, Mobile AL 36608 **S Paul's Ch Mobile AL 1975-** B Jacksonville Bch FL 11/15/1933 s Cliff Porter &

Annie Ruth. BA Stetson U 1956; MDiv VTS 1960. D 6/22/1960 P 3/1/1961 Bp Edward Hamilton West. m 8/16/1957 June Mims c 1. All SS Epis Ch Mobile AL 2003-2004; S Paul's Ch Mobile AL 1970-2001; Asst R S Jn's Epis Ch Tallahassee FL 1962-1970; In-Charge Chr Ch Monticello FL 1960-1962; In-Charge S Mary's Epis Ch Madison FL 1960-1962. Auth, "Selected Sermons".

PORTER-ACEE III, John M (NC) 8828 Rittenhouse Cir, Charlotte NC 28270 **Asst To The R Chr Ch Charlotte NC 2005-** B Asheville NC 4/3/1978 MDiv VTS 2005. D 6/25/2005 P 1/14/2006 Bp Clifton Daniel III. m 11/16/2009 Whitney A Porter c 2. porter-aceej@christchurchcharlotte.org

PORTER CADE, Wendy M (At) 1323 N Dupont St, Wilmington DE 19806 **Gr Ch Asheville NC 2005-** B Atlanta GA 1/29/1979 d Everett E Porter & Arlene Goodroe. BS Shorter Coll 2001; MDiv GTS 2005. D 12/21/2004 P 12/21/2004 Bp J(ohn) Neil Alexander. m 4/19/2010 Shaun Cade. S Edw's Epis Ch Lawrenceville GA 2009-2011; S Anne's Epis Ch Atlanta GA 2007-2009; Chr Ch Greenville Wilmington DE 2005-2007. portercade@gmail.com

PORTEUS, Beverly S (Eas) 39 Norman Allen St, Elkton MD 21921 B Freeport NY 4/28/1947 d Arthur Lugrin & Beatrice Faye. BA Buc 1969; MDiv GTS 1988. D 6/11/1988 P 12/11/1988 Bp Paul Moore Jr. m 4/9/1988 Christopher Porteus. R Trin Ch Elkton MD 1995-2010; Vic All SS Epis Ch Delmar DE 1990-1995; Asst S Ptr's Ch Salisbury MD 1990-1995; Asst Min The Epis Ch Of The Adv Kennett Sq PA 1988-1990. reverendbev@verizon.net

PORTEUS, Christopher (Eas) 27 Woods Way, Elkton MD 21921 B Waterbury CT 5/25/1947 s Morgan Porteus & Martha Adelaide. BA Bos 1973; MDiv GTS 1982. D 5/29/1982 P 4/25/1983 Bp Robert Shaw Kerr. m 4/9/1988 Beverly S Porteus c 1. R S Steph's Ch Earleville MD 2005-2008; S Steph's Ch Earleville MD 1995-2004; H Cross Millington Massey MD 1995; No Kent Par S Clem's Massey MD 1995; Mssnr Dioc S Mary's Epis Ch Tyaskin MD 1990-1995; Mssnr S Paul's Ch Vienna MD 1990-1995; Mssnr Dioc S Paul's Epis Ch Hebron MD 1990-1995; Mssnr Dioc S Phil's Ch Quantico MD 1990-1995; Int S Steph's Ch Earleville MD 1989-1990; S Tim's Ch Roxborough Philadelphia PA 1988-1989; Asst S Jas Epis Ch S Jas NY 1985-1988; Vic S Ann's Ch Sheldon VT 1982-1985; R S Matt's Ch Enosburg Falls VT 1982-1985. mozoman@comcast.com

PORTEUS, James Michael (Az) Triskele, Rinsey, Ashton, Helston TR13 9TS Great Britain (UK) B Chester-le-Street UK 2/21/1931 s Charles Frederick Porteus & Agnes Emilie. BA Oxf 1955; GLE Ripon Coll Cuddesdon 1957; MA Oxf 1958. Trans from Church Of England 8/1/1986 as Priest Bp Joseph Thomas Heistand. m 7/4/1998 Kate Money c 3. Epis Campus Mnstry - U of Arizona Tucson AZ 1986-1991. Hon Cn Cathd of the Isle, Isle of Cumbrae, Scotland 2006; Hon Alum CDSP 1991.

✠ **PORTEUS, Rt Rev Morgan** (Ct) Po Box 782, Wellfleet MA 02667 **Ret Bp of Ct Dio Connecticut Hartford CT 1981-** B Hartford CT 8/10/1917 s Robert William Porteus & Ruth. BA Bates Coll 1941; BD EDS 1943. D 9/29/1943 P 6/1/1944 Bp Frederick G Budlong Con 10/13/1971 for Ct. c 3. Asstg Bp of Mass Dio Massachusetts Boston MA 1986-2009; Dio Massachusetts Boston MA 1986-2003; Asst Dio Massachusetts Boston MA 1982-1984; Bp of Ct Dio Connecticut Hartford CT 1977-1981; Bp Coadj of Ct Dio Connecticut Hartford CT 1976-1977; Bishops Fund Hartford CT 1971-1981; Bp Dio Connecticut Hartford CT 1971-1976; R S Ptr's Epis Ch Cheshire CT 1944-1971; Cur Trin Ch Torrington CT 1943-1944. DD Trin, Hartford, CT 1981; DD Ya Berk 1972.

POST, Suzanne Marie (SwFla) 14511 Daffodil Dr Apt 1402, Fort Myers FL 33919 B New York NY 11/29/1963 d John Post & Doris Marie. BS Pace U 1988; MDiv Yale DS 1991. D 6/8/1991 P 12/14/1991 Bp Richard Frank Grein. Eccl Crt Dio SW Florida Sarasota FL 2004-2007; Bp Search Com Dio SW Florida Sarasota FL 2004-2006; COM Dio SW Florida Sarasota FL 2003-2007; Assoc R Ch Of S Mich And All Ang Sanibel FL 2002-2007; COM Dio New York New York City NY 1995-1997; R S Jas' Ch No Salem NY 1994-1997; Asst Chr Chr Ch Greenwich CT 1992-1994; Cur S Thos Ch Mamaroneck NY 1991-1992. Auth, "Preaching as Pstr Care". postsuzy@aol.com

POSTON, Ronald Glen (Az) 2174 E Loma Vista Dr, Tempe AZ 85282 **R Ch Of The Epiph Tempe AZ 1994-** B Franklin KY 1/13/1951 s William Thomas Poston & Violetta. BS Pur 1976; MA Pur 1983; MDiv Nash 1986. D 5/16/1986 P 12/12/1986 Bp William Cockburn Russell Sheridan. c 2. Ecum Off Dio Arizona Phoenix AZ 1998; Assoc All SS Ch Phoenix AZ 1991-1994; The Bp's Sch La Jolla CA 1989-1991; Trin Ch Ft Wayne IN 1986-1989. rposton@gateway.net

POTEAT, Sally Tarler (WNC) No address on file. **D Gr Ch Morganton NC 1996-** B Baltimore MD 3/3/1955 d Craig Cornell Tarler & Joanne Diehl. BA Duke 1977. D 12/9/1995 Bp Robert Hodges Johnson. m 10/6/1979 William Larry Poteat c 2. sallypoteat@yahoo.com

POTEET, David Bertrand (Tex) Po Box 6828, Katy TX 77491 B Tulsa OK 10/10/1942 s Albert Leroy Poteet & Muriel. BS U of Texas 1965; MDiv VTS 1969. D 7/1/1969 Bp Scott Field Bailey P 5/1/1970 Bp J Milton Richardson. m 5/9/1979 Iris Poteet. S Paul's Ch Katy TX 1978-1983; Asst S Mart's Epis Ch Houston TX 1969-1973. davidpoteet142@msn.com

POTEET, Fred (SVa) 1555 Genesee Ridge Road, Golden CO 80401 **Dio Colorado Denver CO 2011-** B Huntington WV 1/2/1948 s Henry Swann Poteet & Hilda Lee. BS Virginia Commonwealth U 1973; VTS 2004. D 6/4/2005 Bp David Conner Bane Jr P 5/13/2006 Bp Robert Hodges Johnson. m 6/15/1969 Mary Poteet c 2. Int R S Jn's Ch Portsmouth VA 2009-2010; Archd Dio Sthrn Virginia Norfolk VA 2007-2009; P-in-c S Steph's Ch Norfolk VA 2006-2007; D Old Donation Ch Virginia Bch VA 2005-2006; Yth Dir Dio Sthrn Virginia Norfolk VA 2002-2003. fred@poteet.com

POTTER, Frances Dickinson (NH) 38 Little Pond Rd, Concord NH 03301 B Chicago IL 4/2/1929 d Truman Squire Potter & Jean. BA Smith 1950; MA U CA 1961; MDiv EDS 1978. D 10/20/1979 P 5/1/1980 Bp Philip Alan Smith. m 10/16/1955 Richard B Gamble c 4. Assoc R S Paul's Ch Concord NH 1984-1987; Vic Ch Of The Mssh No Woodstock NH 1981-1987; Nthrn Grafton Shared Mnstry Lyman NH 1981-1984; Vic S Lk's Ch Woodsville NH 1981-1984; Asst Ch Of Our Sav Milford NH 1980-1981; Chr Ch Exeter NH 1980. Phi Beta Kappa.

POTTER, Jack C (U) 231 E 100 S, Salt Lake City UT 84111 B Union City IN 3/15/1936 s James Clarence Potter & Mary Henrietta. BA Hanover Coll 1958; MA U Of Delaware Newark 1960; MDiv Bex 1965. D 6/12/1965 P 12/19/1965 Bp Robert Lionne DeWitt. m 10/2/1987 Patricia A Plunk c 4. Cathd Ch Of S Mk Salt Lake City UT 1990-2002; Gr Ch Tucson AZ 1982-1990; St Johns Epis Ch Lafayette IN 1977-1982; Dio Indianapolis Indianapolis IN 1972-1977. jpotter@episcopal-ut.org

POTTER, Linda Gail (Chi) 130 N West St, Wheaton IL 60187 **R Trin Epis Ch Wheaton IL 2003-** B Duncan OK 10/29/1949 d Ben Thomas Inscore & Myrtle Lucille. BA Portland St U 1971; S Thos Sem Denver CO 1990; MDiv CDSP 1994. D 6/15/1994 P 1/20/1995 Bp Robert Louis Ladehoff. m 5/28/1971 Thomas I Potter c 2. Cn to the Ordnry Dio Oregon Portland OR 1999-2003; R All SS Ch Hillsboro OR 1996-1999; Asst Chr Ch Par Lake Oswego OR 1994-1996; Dioc Chair of the Evang Com Dio Oregon Portland OR 1991-1992. lpotter@trinitywheaton.org

POTTER, Lorene Heath (WNY) 537 S Park Ave, Buffalo NY 14204 B Norfolk VA 3/22/1932 d William Rufus Heath & Lorene Elisabeth. BA Barnard Coll of Col 1953; MA SUNY 1976; MDiv Bex 1987. D 6/13/1987 P 4/1/1988 Bp David Charles Bowman. m 6/10/1953 Milton Grosvenor Potter. S Thos Ch Buffalo NY 1989-1991; Asst St Mk Epis Ch No Tonawanda NY 1987-1988. Auth, "The Afr Collection Of The Buffalo Soc Of Natural Sciences"; Auth, "Afr Arts"; Auth, "Collections".

POTTER, Meredith Woods (Chi) 2702 Princeton Ave, Evanston IL 60201 **Vic S Greg's Epis Ch Deerfield IL 2004-** B Chicago IL 8/10/1934 d Charles Scott Woods & Mary Ruth. Tufts U; BA San Jose St U 1955; MA Wstrn Michigan U 1967; Spec in Arts Wstrn Michigan U 1968; MDiv SWTS 1985; DMin SWTS 2000. D 3/23/1985 Bp James Winchester Montgomery P 9/29/1985 Bp Frank Tracy Griswold III. c 3. Int Dir of D. Min. in Congrl Dvlpmt SWTS Evanston IL 2007-2009; Sch for Deacons Fac Dio Chicago Chicago IL 2004-2009; Lectr in Congrl Stds and Dir. Ext, Seabury Inst SWTS Evanston IL 2001-2005; Asst and Supply Int P Emm Epis Ch Rockford IL 2000-2002; Assoc S Greg's Epis Ch Deerfield IL 1997-2004; Vic One In Chr Ch Prospect Heights IL 1995-1996; Vic S Mary's Ch Pk Ridge IL 1985-1995. Auth, "Thy Will Be Done: Discerning Pryr," *Luth Wmn Today*, ELCA, 1997; Auth, "Power of Pryr," *Luth Wmn Today*, ELCA, 1996; Auth, "This Is Not The Most Important Day Of Your Life," *Preaching As The Art Of Sacr Conversation*, Morehouse Pub, 1977. EPF; Fllshp Of S Jn The Evang 1987. DSA SWTS Evanston IL 1994. meredithpotter@comcast.net

POTTER, Paul Christopher (Los) 10925 Valley Home Ave, Whittier CA 90603 **S Steph's Par Whittier CA 2011-** B Fontana CA 10/24/1956 s William Daniel Potter & Georgia Rose. BA U of San Diego 1978; MDiv St Jn's 1982. Rec from Roman Catholic 5/16/2011 Bp Joseph Jon Bruno. c 1. rev.christopherpotter@gmail.com

POTTER, Raymond J (NCal) 6508 Blue Spruce Ct, Elk Grove CA 95758 **Associte P - Vol St Marys Ch Elk Grove Sacramento CA 2008-** B Providence RI 8/3/1950 s Raymond Joseph Potter & Claire Sylvia. BA Wadhams Hall Sem Coll 1974; MDiv St. Bern's Sem Rochester NY 1978; DMin SWTS 1995. Rec from Roman Catholic 6/1/1988 as Priest Bp William Augustus Jones Jr. m 11/30/1985 Roberta Shapard. All SS Meml Sacramento CA 2000-2005; S Dunst's Ch Tulsa OK 1995-2000; Dioc Coun Dio Rhode Island Providence RI 1991; Yth Dir Dio Missouri S Louis MO 1988-1990; Asst Trin Ch St Chas MO 1988-1990. Auth, "A Fifty-Two Week Model Of Cathechesis". St Geo Awd 1995.

POTTER, Roderick Kenneth (Me) 16 Alton Rd Apt 215, Augusta ME 04330 B Gardiner ME 3/18/1933 s Clyde James Potter & Zilphaetta. BA Bates Coll 1960; MDiv GTS 1963. D 6/8/1963 P 12/14/1963 Bp Oliver L Loring. m 6/25/1955 Barbara Jones c 2. S Lk's Ch Farmington ME 1963-1981. rkpotter@aol.com

POTTER, Sara (NCal) 1776 Old Arcata Road, Bayside CA 95524 **R S Alb's Ch Arcata CA 2008-** B Sonora CA 3/29/1970 d Donald Allen Potter & Janice Ann. BA U CA 1993; MDiv Ya Berk 2004. D 7/3/2004 P 1/29/2005 Bp Jerry Alban Lamb. m 6/29/2002 Aaron M Hohl c 2. Cur/Dir of Chr Formation Calv Ch Stonington CT 2004-2008. revsara@stalbansarcata.org

POTTER JR, Spencer B (SeFla) 19000 SW 89th Ave, Cutler Bay FL 33157 **S Andr's Epis Ch Palmetto Bay FL 2007-** B 1/30/1975 BA Bates Coll 1997; MDiv VTS 2005. D 3/19/2005 P 9/17/2005 Bp Mark Sean Sisk. m 7/6/2005 Erin Stokes c 1. Assoc S Mk's Ch Palm Bch Gardens FL 2007-2009; Lilly Fell S Jas Ch New York NY 2005-2007; Yth Dir Calv and St Geo New York NY 1999-2002. revspencerpotter@gmail.com

POTTER, William A (VI) Po Box 415, Hope NJ 07844 **Died 5/29/2011** B Glen Cove NY 6/13/1948 s Earl S Potter & Mary C. GTS; BA GW 1970; MDiv ETSC 1974; ThM PrTS 1978; MPA Pr 1983. D 5/25/1974 P 5/15/1975 Bp Francisco Reus-Froylan. c 3. Auth, *Hsng Crisis: Responses to New Federalism*. potter1832@gmail.com

POTTER-NORMAN, Ricardo T (DR) Camila Alvarez #7 Urb. Mallen, San Pedro De Macoris Dominican Republic **Ret Dio The Dominican Republic (Iglesia Epis Dominicana) 100 Airport AvVenice FL 1964-** B San Pedro de Macoris DO 10/31/1936 s Alfred Grandison Potter & Louise Mabel. Instituto Comercial Vazques San Pedro De Macoris 1958; STB ETSC 1964. D 5/31/1964 P 12/6/1964 Bp Paul Axtell Kellogg. m 1/8/1965 Mercedes Benitez Garcia c 2. Hon Assoc Ch Of The Medtr Bronx NY 2000-2001; Assoc Dir Epis Ch Cntr New York NY 1994-2000; R Iglesia Epis de Todos los Santos La Romana La DO 1980-1986; Vic Ch Of The Intsn New York NY 1976-1980; Natl Coun Of Ch New York NY 1976-1978; Vic Iglesia Epis Cristo el Rey San Felipe de Puerto Plat DO 1966-1972; Ret Dio The Dominican Republic (Iglesia Epis Dominicana) 100 Airport AvVenice FL 1964-1980; Asst Iglesia Epis San Andres Santo Domingo DO 1964-1965. Hon Cn Dio Dr 1991; Hon Cn 97 Dio Cecu (Cntrl Ecuador). rpotter@codetel.net.do

POTTERTON, Carol Thayer (SO) 5825 Woodmont Ave, Cincinnati OH 45213 **D All SS Ch Cincinnati OH 2011-; D The Ch of the Redeem Cincinnati OH 2011-** B Jersey City NJ 2/14/1945 d Sanford Thayer Potterton & Susan Shaw. Duke; BA Emory U 1969; MSW OH SU 1980; MATS Untd TS Dayton OH 1992. D 5/4/1991 Bp Herbert Thompson Jr. m 2/14/1981 Jerry Eckart c 2. D S Mary Magd Ch Maineville OH 2006-2011; D H Trin Epis Ch Oxford OH 1998-2006; D S Barn Epis Ch Montgomery OH 1991-1998. carol_potterton@yahoo.com

POTTS, David Gary (SD) 1728 Mountain View Rd, Rapid City SD 57702 B Rapid City SD 4/2/1946 s Bernard Potts & Harriet Bernice. So Dakota Sch Mines & Tech. D 11/19/1988 Bp Craig Barry Anderson. m 12/31/1989 Cheryl L Heil c 2. D S Andr's Epis Ch Rapid City SD 1988-2000. dgpotts@rushmore.com

POTTS, Kathleen Kirkland (Miss) 1421 Goodyear Blvd., Picayune MS 39466 **S Paul's Epis Ch Picayune MS 2005-** B Vicksburg MS 1/3/1951 d Frederick Clifford Kirkland & Jean Zoe. BA U of Sthrn Mississippi 1975; MDiv STUSo 2002. D 6/22/2002 Bp Alfred Clark Marble Jr P 1/11/2003 Bp Duncan Montgomery Gray III. Cur Chap Of The Cross ROLLING FORK MS 2002-2005. revkkpotts@yahoo.com

POTTS, Matthew L (WMich) P.O. Box 298, Falmouth MA 02541 **S Barn Ch Falmouth MA 2009-** B E Grand Rapids MI 1/3/1977 s Daniel Lawrence Potts & Miyoko. BA U of Notre Dame 1999; MDiv Harvard DS 2008. D 6/9/2008 Bp Robert Alexander Gepert Jr P 12/21/2008 Bp Robert R Gepert. m 8/9/2008 Colette P Sgambati c 2. cpotts@post.harvard.edu

POULIN, Suzanne Gordon (NH) Saint John the Baptist, 118 High St, Sanbornville NH 03872 **The Epis Ch Of S Jn The Bapt Sanbornville NH 2007-** B Portland ME 9/17/1960 d John Gordon & Grace. BS Plymouth St Coll 1983; MDiv Andover Newton TS 2003. D 6/14/2003 P 8/7/2005 Bp Chilton Abbie Richardson Knudsen. m 6/23/1990 Daniel S Poulin c 2. Asst. P S Dav's Epis Ch Kennebunk ME 2005-2007. suepoulin1098@aol.com

POULOS, G(eorge) (NC) 3308 Northampton Dr, Greensboro NC 27408 B Rome GA 5/29/1934 s James Poulos & Farris. BS U GA 1956; MDiv STUSo 1966. D 6/25/1966 P 3/11/1967 Bp Randolph R Claiborne. m 6/7/1955 Nancy Leckie c 4. Mem, COM Dio No Carolina Raleigh NC 1996-2000; Chair Dept Coll Wk Dio No Carolina Raleigh NC 1988-1990; Mem, Dioc Coun Dio No Carolina Raleigh NC 1987-1990; R S Andr's Ch Greensboro NC 1977-1999; Assoc S Paul's Epis Ch Winston Salem NC 1975-1977; R S Tim's Decatur GA 1969-1975; Cur S Mart In The Fields Ch Atlanta GA 1966-1969; Chr Ch Walnut Cove NC 2005.

POULOS, John William (Mass) 16 S Main St Apt 508, Barre VT 05601 B Montpelier VT 12/11/1930 s Spero Eanou Poulos & Winifred Elizabeth. BA Ya 1952; MDiv GTS 1960; STM GTS 1967. D 4/17/1960 Bp Vedder Van Dyck P 10/22/1960 Bp Roger W Blanchard. c 1. Archv Asst Casserley Resrch Cntr The GTS New York NY 1987-1993; R S Mk's Epis Ch Fall River MA 1979-1981; Asst / Chapl / Tchr S Jos's Ch Queens Vill NY 1977-1986; Ch of the Ascen Jersey City NJ 1974-1977; R S Steph's Ch Jersey City NJ 1970-1972. Collaborator, "Foundations for an Ethic of Dignity," 1993; Collaborator, "Gazello Boy," 1976; Collaborator,, "Bk, Play, arts". Medill-McCormick Full Schlrshp Yale Coll 2048; Bd Deacons, Battell Chap Ya 1952; Elihu Sr Soc Ya 1952. goodshep@saver.net

POUNDERS, Marci (Dal) St James Episcopal Church, 9845 McCree Rd, Dallas TX 75238 **Asst. S Jas Ch Dallas TX 2008-** B Louisville KY 9/7/1961 d Lawrence Orr & Ann. BAS U of Louisville 1983; MDiv SMU 2005. D 1/26/2008 P 11/1/2008 Bp James Monte Stanton. m 8/10/1985 Tracy Pounders c 2. Bd Certification Assn of Profsnl Chapl 2009. chaplainmarci@yahoo.com

POUNDS, Elton William (Colo) 1576 E Mineral Ave, Centennial CO 80122 B Smith County KS 6/27/1935 s Elton Lee Pounds & Thelma I. BA Hastings Coll of Law 1957; BD SWTS 1960. D 6/15/1960 P 12/21/1960 Bp Howard R Brinker. m 8/20/1989 Ann Muehleisen. Com Dio Colorado Denver CO 1978-1992; P Gr And S Steph's Epis Ch Colorado Sprg CO 1976-1985; Dio Colorado Denver CO 1975-1976; R H Trin Epis Ch Gillette WY 1970-1973; Stndg Com Dio Nebraska Omaha NE 1968-1970; R Gr Ch Par -Epis Columbus NE 1965-1970; Cur S Andr's Ch Omaha NE 1960-1965. Auth, "Ret: Boom Or Bust"; Ed, "Bk Of Common Pryr Lg Print". ACPE Supvsr 1989-2011. bill@billpounds.org

POVEY, J Michael (Mass) 3901 Glen Oaks Drive E, Sarasota FL 34232 **Assoc S Bon Ch Sarasota FL 2007-** B Bristol England UK 5/26/1944 s Henry John Povey & Evelyn Maud. BTh S Jn's Coll U of Nottingham GB 1976. Trans from Church Of England 12/1/1978 as Priest Bp Alexander Doig Stewart. R S Jas' Epis Ch Cambridge MA 2000-2006; R S Steph's Ch Pittsfield MA 1984-1986; Dio Wstrn Massachusetts Springfield MA 1980-2000; Vic S Chris's Ch Fairview Chicopee MA 1980-1984; R Ch Of The Gd Shpd Fitchburg MA 1978-1980. retiredpove@comcast.net

POWELL, Anna Marie Stewart (NJ) 485 Main St, Lumberton NJ 08048 **COM Dio New Jersey Trenton NJ 2003-; COM Dio New Jersey Trenton NJ 2003-; R S Mart-In-The-Fields Lumberton NJ 2001-** B Neosho MO 6/19/1945 d James Duard Marshall & Helen Eileen. AA Arapahoe Cmnty Coll 1970; BA Metropltn St Coll of Denver 1977; MDiv GTS 1984. D 8/7/1984 Bp Richard Mitchell Trelease Jr P 5/31/1985 Bp Walter Decoster Dennis Jr. m 8/25/1974 John Charles Powell c 1. Dn of the Burlington Convoc Dio New Jersey Trenton NJ 1996-1998; Trial Crt Dio New Jersey Trenton NJ 1992-1999; Vic S Mart-In-The-Fields Lumberton NJ 1986-2011; Ecum Cmsn Dio New Jersey Trenton NJ 1986-1998; Dio New Jersey Trenton NJ 1986-1990; Liturg Cmsn Dio New Jersey Trenton NJ 1986-1990; Asst S Ptr's Ch Bronx NY 1985; Cur S Ptr's Ch Bronx NY 1985; Asst Epis Ch Of SS Jn Paul And S Clem Mt Vernon NY 1984-1985. CBS 1984; OHF Dir of Oblates and Assoc 1984-1985. Ch and Soc Prize Gnrl Sem 1983. motherpowell@gmail.com

POWELL, Anne Margrete (NCal) 20248 Chaparral Cir, Penn Valley CA 95946 **D Emm Epis Ch Grass Vlly CA 2004-; D S Edm's Epis Ch Pacifica CA 2001-** B DK 9/15/1943 d Erik Viggo Larsen & Agnete. BA Sch for Deacons 1999. D 11/20/1999 Bp William Edwin Swing. m 3/25/1964 Eric Nielsen c 3. anne.nielsen@earthlink.net

POWELL, Armistead Christian (Tex) 802 Old Sayers Rd, Elgin TX 78621 B Mobile AL 3/15/1939 s Edward Lewis Powell & Edith Redwood. BA Trin U 1962; BD VTS 1965. D 8/11/1965 P 7/1/1966 Bp J Milton Richardson. m 8/31/1962 Virginia Dowdell Thomas c 2. Vic St Jas Ch Mcgregor TX 2011; S Chris's Epis Ch Austin TX 2001-2002; Calv Epis Ch Bastrop TX 2000-2001; S Paul's Epis Ch Pflugerville TX 1997; All SS Epis Ch Austin TX 1967-1994; Vic S Fran Par Temple TX 1966-1967; Vic S Lk's Epis Ch Belton TX 1965-1967.

POWELL, Arthur Pierce (NJ) 16 Copperfield Dr, Hamilton NJ 08610 **R S Jas Ch Trenton Yardville NJ 1990-** B Camden NJ 7/7/1957 s Lawrence Kenneth Powell & M Carol. BA Rutgers-The St U 1980; MDiv GTS 1983. D 6/4/1983 Bp George Phelps Mellick Belshaw P 12/10/1983 Bp Albert Wiencke Van Duzer. m 10/26/1985 Linda Powell c 1. R The Epis Ch Of The H Comm Fair Haven NJ 1986-1990; Cur S Andr's Ch Mt Holly NJ 1983-1986; Vic S Mart-In-The-Fields Lumberton NJ 1983-1986. alapowell@ah.net

POWELL, Blanche Lee (Del) 304 Taylor Ave, Hurlock MD 21643 **Pstr S Steph's Ch Harrington DE 2002-** B Cambridge MD 1/1/1940 d Adam Alexander Powell & Lula Blanche. BS Winthrop U 1961; MDiv VTS 1975. D 5/24/1975 P 1/8/1977 Bp Robert Bruce Hall. Team Ldr Chr Ch Delaware City DE 1994-2001; Dio Delaware Wilmington DE 1994-2001; Primary Pstr S Jas Epis Ch Newport Newport DE 1994-2001; Team Ldr S Nich' Epis Ch Newark DE 1994-2001; R Chr Ch Pearisburg VA 1984-1994; St Davids Ch Alexandria VA 1975-1982.

POWELL, Brent Cameron (WTenn) 346 Hawthorne St, Memphis TN 38112 B Tupelo MS 11/26/1953 s Fred C Powell & Laura. BA Blue Mtn Coll 1984; MDiv Mid-Amer Bapt TS 1987. D 12/4/2002 Bp Don Edward Johnson. m 3/6/1993 Jo Ann Howton c 3.

POWELL, Catherine Ravenel (EC) 314 S. 4th St., Wilmington NC 28401 **Dn, Lower Cape Fear Dio E Carolina Kinston NC 2011-; R Ch Of The Servnt Wilmington NC 2008-** B Fayetteville NC 9/5/1952 d Robert Jackson Powell & Catherine. BA Hollins U 1974; Inter/Met 1977; MDiv UTS 1979; Cert

P

Catechesis of the Gd Shpd 1994. D 6/23/1979 P 1/10/1980 Bp John Thomas Walker. c 2. Chapl Washington Epis Sch Beth MD 2001-2002; R S Ptr's Ch Salem MA 1997-2001; Assoc The Ch Of Our Redeem Lexington MA 1996-1997; Assoc S Ptr's Ch Weston MA 1993-1996; Chr Formation Com Dio Massachusetts Boston MA 1993-1995; P-in-c S Andr's Ch Belmont MA 1993; COM Dio No Carolina Raleigh NC 1990-1992; Vic Trin Ch Fuquay Varina NC 1990-1992; Dio No Carolina Raleigh NC 1988-1992; Assoc R Gr Ch Washington DC 1985-1987; Asst Cathd of St Ptr & St Paul Washington DC 1979-1981; Asst S Dunst's Epis Ch Beth MD 1979-1980. Chapt Auth, "Preschool Sprtlty," *Gateways to Sprtlty*, Ptr Lang Pub, 2005; Auth, "Let The Chld Come," Living the Gd News, 1990. Phi Beta Kappa Hollins Coll 1974. revcrp@gmail.com

POWELL, Christopher (Miss) 3921 Oakridge Drive, Jackson MS 39216 **R S Jas Ch Jackson MS 2002-** B Louisville KY 4/30/1959 s Robert Charles Powell & Alice Karen. BA Tul 1981; MDiv Nash 1985. D 12/21/1985 P 6/24/1986 Bp David Standish Ball. m 8/9/1986 Lauren Smith c 2. R Trin Ch Rutland VT 1990-2002; Ch Of S Jn The Evang Red Hook NY 1986-1990; S Jn The Evang Columbiaville NY 1986-1990. Chapl Gnrl 3rd Ord of Cubs Fans in Exile. capowell12@aol.com

POWELL, David Brickman (Ala) PO Box 1306, Selma AL 36702 **R S Paul's Ch Selma AL 2010-** B Orlando FL 11/26/1952 s Bruce Taylor Powell & Mary-Frances. BA Florida Atlantic U 1976; MDiv GTS 1982. D 5/26/1982 P 12/21/1982 Bp Calvin Onderdonk Schofield Jr. m 7/11/1987 Elizabeth Jennings c 1. Int S Jn's Ch Pensacola FL 2009; R S Andr's By The Sea Epis Ch Destin FL 2004-2009; Int Ch Of The Nativ Mineola NY 2003-2004; R The Epis Ch Of The Nativ Dothan AL 1994-2002; R S Steph's Ch Brewton AL 1990-1994; Assoc S Mk's Epis Ch Venice FL 1987-1990; Asst Ch Of The Atone Lauderdale Lakes FL 1986; Cur S Mk's Ch Palm Bch Gardens FL 1982-1985. rector@stpaulselma.org

POWELL, David Richardson (NCal) 122 Main, Cloverdale CA 95425 B Cambridge MA 3/18/1935 s Wilson Marcy Powell & Fredrika Taber. BA CUNY 1977; MS Amer U 1981; MDiv CDSP 1986. D 6/14/1986 P 2/1/1987 Bp John Lester Thompson III. m 1/5/1995 Margaret Kelly c 2. Vic Ch Of The Gd Shpd Cloverdale CA 1998-2000; Chr Ch Santa Rosa CA 1994-1998; Vic Chr Epis Ch Windsor CA 1993-1998; Dio Nthrn California Sacramento CA 1986-2000; S Andr's In The Highlands Mssn Antelope CA 1986-1994. Associated Parishes, EPF. lazarus495@aol.com

POWELL, Elizabeth Jennings (Ala) PO Box 1306, Selma AL 36702 **Assoc R S Paul's Ch Selma AL 2010-** B Atlanta GA 10/15/1949 d Henry Smith Jennings & Elizabeth Martin. BA Agnes Scott Coll 1971; MD Van Sch of Med 1976; MDiv w hon GTS 2005. D 6/4/2005 P 5/27/2006 Bp Philip Menzie Duncan II. m 7/11/1987 David Brickman Powell c 1. R St Aug of Cbury Navarre FL 2008-2009; Assoc R S Simon's On The Sound Ft Walton Bch FL 2005-2008. Assoc - OSH 2007; DOK 1984. associaterector@stpaulselma.org

POWELL, Everett (Cal) 417 44th Ave, San Francisco CA 94121 **D Ch Of The Incarn San Francisco CA 2009-; D The Epis Ch Of S Mary The Vrgn San Francisco CA 2001-** B Corpus Christi TX 4/25/1934 s Everett L Powell & Imogene B. BA U of Corpus Christi Corpus Christi TX 1955; MA Texas A&M U 1961; PhD U of Texas 1970; BTS Sch for Deacons 1999. D 12/1/2001 Bp William Edwin Swing. m 6/5/1953 Gloria Katherine Hood c 1. Dn Emer, Del Mar Coll 1996; Who's Who in Amer Educ 1995; Who's Who in the SW 1995. gloev@sbcglobal.net

POWELL JR, Festus Hilliard (Ark) Po Box 21162, Hot Springs AR 71903 B Russellville AR 5/7/1943 s Festus Powell & Dortha. BA Alaska Tech 1968; MDiv STUSo 1972. D 5/27/1972 P 3/1/1973 Bp Christoph Keller Jr. m 6/16/1966 Brenda Norton. Vic S Ptr's Ch Conway AR 1977-1984; S Mary's Epis Ch Monticello AR 1973-1977; S Paul's Ch McGehee AR 1973-1977; Cur S Paul's Ch Fayetteville AR 1972-1973. Auth, "Var arts & Poems".

✠ **POWELL, Rt Rev Frank Neff** (SwVa) Po Box 2279, Roanoke VA 24009 **Bp Dio SW Virginia Roanoke VA 1996-** B Salem OR 12/28/1947 s G Bingham Powell & Gretchen Spencer. Fllshp Coll of Preachers; BA Claremont Mckenna Coll 1970; MDiv EDS 1973. D 7/15/1973 P 1/20/1974 Bp James Walmsley Frederic Carman Con 10/26/1996 for SwVa. m 6/13/1970 Dorothy R Houck c 3. Archd Dio No Carolina Raleigh NC 1983-1991; Asst Dio Oregon Portland OR 1975-1996; Vic S Bede's Ch Forest Grove OR 1975-1983; Asst Trin Epis Cathd Portland OR 1973-1975. Associated Parishes. DD VTS 1997. npowell@dioswva.org

POWELL, Gregory Lane (Eas) 29497 Hemlock Ln, Easton MD 21601 **Dn Trin Cathd Easton MD 2009-** B Daytona Bch FL 7/26/1959 s John Barrow Powell & Diane Lee. BA Gordon Coll 1984; MDiv U Tor 1993. D 6/12/1993 Bp William Jerry Winterrowd P 12/1/1993 Bp Robert Gould Tharp. m 6/8/1985 Laura Blohm c 4. R S Mary's Epis Ch Pocomoke City MD 1999-2009; Chr Epis Ch San Antonio TX 1996-1999; Ch Of The Ascen Knoxville TN 1993-1995. Auth, "God'S Chosen People Exploring The Jewish Roots In Chr Faith". greg@trinitycathedraleaston.com

POWELL, John Charles (NJ) 485 Main St, Lumberton NJ 08048 **P-in-c S Jn's Epis Ch Maple Shade NJ 2009-** B Los Angeles CA 8/19/1944 s Charles Carroll Powell & Carolyn Ann. Metropltn St Coll of Denver; U CO; U Denv 1963; GTS 1984. D 8/7/1984 Bp Richard Mitchell Trelease Jr P 5/31/1985 Bp Henry Boyd Hucles III. m 8/25/1974 Anna Marie Stewart Marshall. P-in-c S Fran Ch Dunellen NJ 2006-2008; Int Gr Epis Ch Whitestone NY 2001-2004; Int S Ptr's Ch Spotswood NJ 1999-2001; Int Ch Of S Mk And All SS Absecon Galloway NJ 1998-1999; Int H Trin Ch Collingswood NJ 1997-1998; Int Gr Ch In Haddonfield Haddonfield NJ 1996-1997; Int Gr Ch Merchantville NJ 1994-1996; Int Trin Epis Ch Cranford NJ 1993-1994; Int S Geo's Epis Ch Helmetta NJ 1992; R Par Of Chr The King Willingboro NJ 1985-1991; Cur Chr Ch Manhasset NY 1984-1985. Accredited Int Specialists 1994-2000; CBS; Int Mnstry Ntwk 1994-2000. Ch And Soc Prize GTS New York NY 1983. john.charles.powell@comcast.net

POWELL, John Lynn (Cal) 180 Westbury Cir Apt 327, Folsom CA 95630 B Wichita KS 5/9/1923 s Roxie Thomas Powell & Minya Temple. BA Duke 1944; BD Yale DS 1947. D 6/18/1951 P 2/1/1952 Bp Francis E I Bloy. m 6/17/1948 Shirley Ann Stewart c 4. Asst Trin Par Menlo Pk CA 1985-1988; R S Andr's Epis Ch San Bruno CA 1958-1985; R Ch of S Mary's by the Sea Pacific Grove CA 1953-1958; Cur S Edm's Par San Marino CA 1951-1953. jlynnpow@juno.com

POWELL, Kenneth James (Cal) All Saints Parish, 1355 Waller St, San Francisco CA 94117 B Mt Holly NJ 7/20/1950 s Walter Franklin Powell & June Ann. BA San Francisco St U 1984; BTS Epis Sch for Deacons Berkeley CA 2007. D 12/1/2007 Bp Marc Handley Andrus. m 9/17/2005 Karen Freeman c 2. kennethjpowell@yahoo.com

POWELL, Lewis (NCal) 20248 Chaparral Cir, Penn Valley CA 95946 **Native Amer Mnstrs Mssnr Dio Nthrn California Sacramento CA 2010-; D Emm Epis Ch Grass Vlly CA 2010-; Exec Coun Com for Indigenous Mnstrs Exec Coun Appointees New York NY 2006-; D S Thos Of Cbury Epis Ch Albuquerque NM 2000-** B Churchland VA 8/28/1942 s James Powell & Myrtle Annabelle. BS U of Maryland 1964; BA Sch for Deacons 1999. D 11/20/1999 Bp William Edwin Swing. c 2. lp4golf@comcast.net

POWELL, Marilyn (SC) 577 Water Turkey Retreat, Charleston SC 29412 **D S Steph's Epis Ch Charleston SC 2002-** B Oakland CA 11/10/1924 d Niels David Lindeberg & Azalia Ouita. U So. D 7/13/1985 Bp George Lazenby Reynolds Jr. m 9/14/1943 Joseph Harllee Powell c 3. D Ch Of Our Sav Johns Island SC 1992-2000; Team-In-Charge Ch Of The H Comf Monteagle TN 1988-1992; D S Jas Sewanee TN 1985-1988. marpow@concentric.net

POWELL, Mark M (EC) St Andew's On-The-Sound Episcopal Church, 101 Airlie Rd, Wilmington NC 28403 **Cur S Andr's On The Sound Ch Wilmington NC 2007-** B Washington NC 10/13/1978 s Charles Edward Powell & Virginia Garettson. BSN E Carolina U 2001; MDiv VTS 2007. D 6/9/2007 P 6/28/2008 Bp Clifton Daniel III. markpowell@ec.rr.com

POWELL, Murray Richard (Tex) 951 Curtin St # 920564, Houston TX 77018 **Asst S Mk's Ch Houston TX 2011-** B Lookout Mountain TN 4/17/1950 s Edward Lewis Powell & Edith Redwood. BA U of Texas 1976; MDiv VTS 1977. D 6/22/1977 Bp Roger Howard Cilley P 6/1/1978 Bp J Milton Richardson. m 4/16/1983 Sarah T Jones c 2. Asst Trin Ch Houston TX 2005-2010; R Hope Epis Ch Houston TX 1992-2005; S Jn's Epis Ch Austin TX 1984-1992; Chr Ch Cathd Houston TX 1981-1984; Chr Epis Ch Tyler TX 1978-1981; St Jas Ch Houston TX 1977-1978; St Matthews Ch Beaumont TX 1977-1978. powellmrp@earthlink.net

POWELL JR, Peter Ross (Ct) 6 Gorham Ave, Westport CT 06880 B Philadelphia PA 1/8/1948 s Peter Ross Powell & Rosalie Watson. BS No Carolina St U 1970; M. Div VTS 1976; ThM PrTS 1979; Coll of Preachers 1982; D.Min TS 1997; Kennedy Sch of Govt 2000; S Geo's Coll Jerusalem IL 2000; Harvard Bus Sch 2006. D 6/12/1976 P 12/18/1976 Bp John Mc Gill Krumm. m 8/12/1992 Barbara Smith c 3. Int Gr Epis Ch Norwalk CT 1993; Int S Ptr's Epis Ch Oxford CT 1992-1993; Pres/CEO Interfaith Hsng Assoc. Westport CT 1988-2010; R The Par Of Emm Ch Weston CT 1985-1987; Adj Prof VTS Alexandria VA 1981-1984; R Chr Ch S Jn's Par Accokeek MD 1979-1985; Assoc All SS Ch Princeton NJ 1977-1979; Cur S Andr's Epis Ch New Providence NJ 1976-1977. Auth, "Homeless In The Suburbs," *Festschrift for Donald Armentrout*, Sewanee, 2000. Cath Biblic Associaton 1976-2003; SBL 1975-2003. Danver's Fell Harvard Bus Sch 2006; Fllshp Jn F. Kennedy Sch of Govt 2003; Faces Of Achievement Westport/Weston Ymca 2001; Distinguished Cmnty Serv Awd ADL 2000; Fllshp Jn F Kennedy Sch Of Govt Harvard 2000. petepowell@yahoo.com

POWELL, Rita Teschner (SD) 500 S Main Ave, Sioux Falls SD 57104 **Vic S Paul's Epis Ch Vermillion SD 2010-; Coordntr for Yth Mnstry Dio So Dakota Sioux Falls SD 2008-** B Worcester MA 1/13/1978 d Russell Steven Powell & Anne F. BA Barnard Coll 1999; MDiv Ya Berk 2005. D 6/14/2008 Bp Andrew Donnan Smith P 1/17/2009 Bp Creighton Leland Robertson. m 5/4/2008 Justin Andrew Beebe. Yth Min S Mk's Ch New Canaan CT 2005-2007. ritateschnerpowell@gmail.com

POWELL, Robert Bingham (Ore) St Mary's Episcopal Church, PO Box 50428, Eugene OR 97405 **P-in-c S Mary's Epis Ch Eugene OR 2007-** B Hillsboro OR 6/1/1981 s Frank Neff Powell & Dorothy Ruth. BA Wake Forest U 2003;

MDiv VTS 2007. D 6/2/2007 P 12/22/2007 Bp Frank Neff Powell. m 1/2/2010 Christine Elizabeth Tyson Zeller-Powell c 1. bingham.powell@gmail.com

POWELL JR, Stanley Anthony (Pa) 11 Peachtree Ln, Levittown PA 19054 **Died 10/20/2011** B West Chester PA 1/6/1922 s Stanley Anthony Powell & Anne Matlack. BA U of Virginia 1943; BD VTS 1949. D 5/1/1949 P 11/1/1949 Bp Oliver J Hart.

POWELL, Sydney Roswell (NY) 3405 Grace Ave, Bronx NY 10469 B Alligator Pond Jama CA 8/29/1923 s Hubert Powell & Margaret Elizabeth. S Ptr's Coll Jersey City NJ 1959; GTS 1968. Trans from Church in the Province Of The West Indies 3/25/1969. m 7/26/1978 Daisy Belle c 3. Asst The Ch of S Matt And S Tim New York NY 1967-1972. Ecum Chr Coun.

POWELL, Thomas Alvin (FtW) 7536 Meadow Creek Drive, Fort Worth TX 76123 B Selma AL 1/28/1932 s Norborne Alvin Powell & Bessie. BA U of Alabama 1954; MDiv STUSo 1959. D 5/1/1959 P 6/27/1960 Bp George Mosley Murray. m 8/14/1953 Ann Ross c 2. Assoc S Tim's Ch Ft Worth TX 1996-1997; Dio Ft Worth Ft Worth TX 1991-1996; Stndg Com Dio Ft Worth Ft Worth TX 1980-1984; S Andr's Ft Worth TX 1978-1991; Chair of the Hunger Taskforce Dio Alabama Birmingham AL 1977-1979; S Jn's Ch Monroeville AL 1970-1978; Trin Epsicopal Ch Atmore AL 1970-1978; Assoc S Mary's-On-The-Highlands Epis Ch Birmingham AL 1966-1970; R S Thos Ch Greenville AL 1961-1966; Vic S Paul's (Carlowville) Minter AL 1959-1961; DCE S Paul's Ch Selma AL 1959-1961. CCU. taross@wans.net

POWELL, Tony (Ga) 615 Mallory St, St Simons Is GA 31522 **Vic Ch Of The H Nativ St Simons Island GA 2008-; Vic S Richard's Of Chichester Ch Jekyll Island GA 2008-** B Valdosta GA 4/15/1954 s Frank D Powell & Ruth Hill. BA Valdosta St U 1978; MDiv The U So (Sewanee) 2008. D 5/31/2008 Bp John Wadsworth Howe P 12/20/2008 Bp Henry I Louttit. m 6/17/1978 Anita Ann Royal c 2. arapowell@gmail.com

POWELL, William Vincent (Okla) 124 Randolph Ct, Stillwater OK 74075 **Vic S Mk's Ch Perry OK 1989-** B Pampa TX 4/18/1927 s Earl L Powell & Olive Alice. Oklahoma A&M Coll 1947; Oklahoma City U 1951; Nash 1958. D 12/1/1957 P 9/27/1958 Bp Chilton Powell. m 8/7/1947 Jacqueline Hoshall c 3. Vic Ch Of The Ascen Pawnee OK 1988-1989; Vic S Alb's Ch Cushing OK 1988-1989; R S Andr's Ch Stillwater OK 1970-1987; DCE Chr Cathd Salina KS 1967-1970; Prog Dir Dio Wstrn Kansas Hutchinson KS 1967-1970; Vic S Ptr's Ch Tulsa OK 1963-1967; P-in-c Trin Ch Guthrie OK 1960-1963; Vic S Mk's Ch Perry OK 1958-1963. Provence VII Syn-2 Terms 1979; Chair of Educ Com Provence VII 1976; Rep to Exec Coun Provence VII 1972. jpowellst@aol.com

POWELL IV, Woodson Lea (NC) 560 Water Tower Road, Moncure NC 27559 B Wadesboro NC 11/6/1935 s Woodson Lea Powell & Evelyn. BA U NC 1957; MDiv VTS 1960. D Bp Thomas Augustus Fraser Jr P 4/29/1961 Bp Richard Henry Baker. m 8/12/1978 Susan Henderson c 3. Vic Ch Of The Adv Enfield NC 1999-2001; Vic Ch Of The Epiph Rocky Mt NC 1999-2001; Vic S Jn's Ch Battleboro NC 1999-2001; Vic S Mich's Ch Tarboro NC 1999-2001; Vic St Marys Epis Ch Speed NC 1999-2001; Asst S Tim's Ch Raleigh NC 1999-2000; Gr Ch Weldon NC 1995-1999; Ch Of The Adv Enfield NC 1987-1995; Vic S Jn's Ch Battleboro NC 1987-1992; R Gr Epis Ch Lexington NC 1963-1969; P-in-c S Paul's Epis Ch Thomasville NC 1960-1963. Mayor'S Civic Awd Williston Nd 1987. susanpowell@embarqmail.com

POWER, William Joseph Ambrose (Dal) 8011 Douglas Ave, Dallas TX 75225 B 5/16/1931 s William James Power & Florence Miriam. BA U Tor 1953; MA U Tor 1954; ASOR 1955; U Tor 1959; PhD U Tor 1961. D 10/8/1972 P 4/29/1973 Bp A Donald Davies. m 8/5/1966 Waldine Ann Peterson Little. Assoc S Mich And All Ang Ch Dallas TX 1974-2004. SBL. DD Epis TS Austin TX 1999. wjup@charter.net

POWERS JR, Clarence Hall (LI) 139 Saint Johns Pl, Brooklyn NY 11217 **R S Jn's Ch Brooklyn NY 1987-** B Memphis TN 5/15/1947 s Clarence Hall Powers & Agnes. BA U of Memphis 1970; MDiv GTS 1976. D 6/26/1976 Bp John Vander Horst P 4/14/1977 Bp William F Gates Jr. R Ch Of SS Steph And Mart Brooklyn NY 1981-1987; D Chr Ch Cathd Nashville TN 1976-1977. Auth, "Faith, Fear, And Future," *Ecum Bulletin*, 1975. fatherpowers@gmail.com

POWERS, David Allan (CGC) 959 Charleston St, Mobile AL 36604 **S Simon's On The Sound Ft Walton Bch FL 2000-** B Reading PA 4/29/1938 s Edward O Powers & Frances. BS So Georgia Coll 1960; MA U GA 1961; MDiv STUSo 1973; DMin STUSo 1993. D 6/14/1961 P 3/1/1974 Bp (George) Paul Reeves. m 5/26/1979 Celeste Stanfield c 3. Trin Epis Ch Mobile AL 2008; S Lk's Epis Ch Birmingham AL 2003-2004; R All SS Epis Ch Mobile AL 1995-2002; R S Matt's Epis Ch Houma LA 1986-1995; Vic/R S Marg's Epis Ch Baton Rouge LA 1978-1986; Cur Epis Ch Of The Gd Shpd Lake Chas LA 1975-1978; Cur S Aug Of Cbury Ch Augusta GA 1973-1975. Woods Ldrshp Awd U So.

POWERS, Elizabeth Ann (SD) 209 S Main S, Chamberlain SD 57325 **P-in-c Chr Ch Chamberlain SD 2008-; P-in-c Chr Epis Ch Ft Thompson SD 2008-; P-in-c H Comf Ch Lower Brule SD 2008-; P-in-c S Jn's Ch Chamberlain SD 2008-** B Minneapolis MN 5/22/1950 d John Hamlin Powers & Mercedes Catherine. BA Metropltn St U; M. Div. TS 2004. D 6/19/2004 P 12/18/2004 Bp Michael Gene Smith. m 9/2/1995 Samuel N Robertson c 2. Dio So Dakota Sioux Falls SD 2008; S Steph's Ch Fargo ND 2004-2008. revlpowers@yahoo.com

POWERS, Fairbairn (Nwk) 8E Nobhill, Roseland NJ 07068 B Detroit MI 3/27/1939 d Frank Alfred Reid & Marian Jane. BA Smith 1960; MBA Cntrl Michigan U 1986; MDiv EDS 1992; CAGS Andover Newton TS 2009. D 11/1/1997 P 5/14/1998 Bp Douglas Edwin Theuner. m 7/17/2003 Joanna B Dewey c 3. Ch Of The H Innoc W Orange NJ 2006-2010; Chr Hosp Jersey City NJ 2004-2006; Int Ch Of The Adv Medfield MA 2003-2004; Assoc S Ptr's Ch Beverly MA 2000-2003; S Agnes Ch Little Falls NJ 1997-2006; Dio Wstrn Massachusetts Springfield MA 1997-2000. fairbairn.powers@verizon.net

POWERS JR, Frederick Forrest (Mil) 29 Beal Pl, Scituate MA 02066 **Died 7/16/2011** B Arlington MA 3/10/1927 s Frederick Forrest Powers & Mildred. BA Harv 1950; MDiv Nash 1955; Med Tem 1963; STM PDS 1971; MBA Tem 1976; DMin PrTS 1982. D 6/24/1955 P 3/24/1956 Bp John S Higgins. c 5. "One's Sense of Idenity:Losing It, Regaining It, StrengtheningIt," *The Journ of Pstr Care, Vol. 47 No.3*, The Journ of Pstr Care Pub . inc., 1993. Coll of Chapl; SSC. jpowers849@aol.com

POWERS, John Carter (Okla) 2431 Terwilleger Blvd, Tulsa OK 74114 **Supply P S Bede's Ch Cleveland OK 2000-** B Tulsa OK 12/21/1936 s Harold Robert Powers & Edith Carter. BA U of Oklahoma 1958; MDiv GTS 1962; U of Cambridge 1975. D 6/21/1962 P 12/20/1962 Bp Chilton Powell. c 3. The AEC New York NY 1994-2000; Sunday Assoc Calv and St Geo New York NY 1993-2000; Dio Oklahoma Oklahoma City OK 1992-1993; R Trin Ch Tulsa OK 1975-1991; R S Mary's Ch Edmond OK 1964-1974; Vic H Fam Ch Langston OK 1964-1968; Vic S Lk The Beloved Physcn Idabel OK 1962-1964. Soc of S Jn the Evang. Doctor of Humane Letters, Honoris Causa Cuttington U Coll (Liberia) 2001; Jas Mills Fllshp 1974; Hon Cn Dio Oklahoma; Chapl 95 S Geo's Cociety New York NY. jackpowers@cox.net

POWERS, Lee (NJ) 119 St. Georges Drive, Galloway NJ 08205 **Cn to the Ordnry Dio New Jersey Trenton NJ 2004-; Fac Credo Inst Inc. Memphis TN 2000-** B Brooklyn NY 10/15/1949 s Fredrick John Powers & Dorothy. BBA U of Pennsylvania 1973; MDiv GTS 1981. D 6/6/1981 P 12/11/1981 Bp Albert Wiencke Van Duzer. m 5/28/1988 Nancy Kleinfelder c 2. Vic Ch Of S Mk And All SS Absecon Galloway NJ 2001-2004; R S Mary's Epis Ch Daytona Bch FL 1999-2001; R S Ptr's Ch Spotswood NJ 1988-1999; Int H Trin Ch So River NJ 1987; Vic Trin Epis Old Swedes Ch Swedesboro NJ 1981-1984. revlpowers@comcast.net

POWERS, Nancy Chambers (Dal) 7934 Glade Creek Court, Dallas TX 75218 **Cn Pstr S Matt's Cathd Dallas TX 2005-** B Houston TX 6/1/1953 BS U of Texas 1975; M. Ed. U of No Florida 1979; Angl TS 2005. D 5/14/2005 Bp James Monte Stanton. m 4/29/1977 Frank Norman Powers c 1. No Amer Assn of the Diac 2005. npowers@episcopalcathedral.org

POWERS, Patricia Ann (SwFla) Caixa Postal 11510, Porto Alegre 91720 Brazil **R S Nath Ch No Port FL 2001-** B Cleveland OH 5/25/1946 d Frank Joseph Powers & Eleanor Jeannette. CRDS; AA Lakeland Cmnty Coll 1977; BA Cleveland St U 1979; ThM Crozer TS 1987. Rec 12/1/1990 as Priest Bp David Charles Bowman. c 2. Exec Coun Appointees New York NY 1998-2001; S Mk's Ch Buffalo NY 1992-1996; Exec Coun Appointees New York NY 1990-1992. Dok, SCHC. revpatriciapowers@yahoo.com

POWERS, Robert Leonard (Chi) 675 Root St, Port Townsend WA 98368 **Asstg Cler S Paul's Epis Ch Port Townsend WA 1998-** B Buffalo NY 12/29/1929 s Leonard Philip Powers & Amelia Isabelle. BA Capital U 1951; MDiv Yale DS 1955; Sometime Stdt GTS 1956; Fllshp SWTS 1963; Cert Alfred Adler Inst 1965; MA U Chi DS 1969. D 6/29/1956 P 6/28/1957 Bp Lauriston L Scaife. m 8/1/1979 Jane Serrill Griffith c 3. Asstg Cler S Chrys's Ch Chicago IL 1994-1998; Asstg Cler Ch Of S Paul And The Redeem Chicago IL 1963-1967; Grad Fell & Lectr SWTS Evanston IL 1962-1963; Cur S Jn The Evang Ch Elkhart IN 1957-1960. Co-Auth, "The Lexicon of Adlerian Psychol," Adlerian Psychol Assoc, 2007; Auth, "Understndg Life-Style: The Psycho-Clarity Process," Adlerian Psychol Assoc, 1987; Co-Auth, "Winning Chld Over: A Manual For Teachers," *Counselors Principals & Parents*, Adlerian Chld Care, 1974; Auth, "Myth & Memory," *Alfred Adler: His Influence on Psychol Today*, Noyes, 1973. EPF 2002; Epis Soc For Cultural & Racial Unity 1964-1968; Illinois Pyschology Assn 1972; No Amer Soc Of Adlerian Psychol 1965. Disting Serv Prof Of Adlerian Stds In Culture & Personali Adler Sch Of Profsnl Psychol 1995. adlerpsy@olypen.com

POWERS, R(oy) Stephen (SVa) 1829 Pittsburg Landing, Virginia Beach VA 23464 **R S Bride's Epis Ch Chesapeake VA 2004-; Off Of Bsh For ArmdF New York NY 1987-** B Koahsiung CN 8/14/1953 s James Garfield Powers & Vivian. BA Anaheim Chr Coll 1979; MDiv GTS 1982; Harvard DS 1996. D 6/10/1982 Bp Robert Munro Wolterstorff P 12/21/1982 Bp Charles Brinkley Morton. Cur H Trin Epis Ch Spokane WA 1985-1987; Cur All SS Ch Vista CA 1982-1985. SSC 1986. 4 Navy Commendation Medals US Navy; Nato Medal US Navy; Kosovo Liberation Medal US Navy; SW Asia Medal US

P

Navy; Kuwaiti Liberation Medal US Navy; 2 Navy Achievement Medals US Navy. frstephenp@mac.com

POWERS, Sharon Kay (Mass) 49 Puritan Rd, Buzzards Bay MA 02532 B Warebam MA 9/22/1946 d Edgar Burgess Johnson & Charlotte Smith. D 6/4/2005 Bp M(arvil) Thomas Shaw III. m 9/24/1966 John R Powers c 2. skp91946@msn.com

POWLESS, Edmund Cornelius (FdL) 2584 Indian Hill Dr, Green Bay WI 54313 **Died 12/30/2010** B Oneida WI 6/14/1923 s Benjamin & Philomene. D 8/25/1990 Bp William L Stevens. c 5.

POZO, Francisco (NJ) 61 Kristopher Dr, Yardville NJ 08620 **Chr Ch Trenton NJ 1995-** B DO 12/17/1956 s Marcelino Pozo & Rosa. BA CUA 1982; BTh S Thos Sem 1986; ThM Cath U of Paris 1989; STM GTS 1995. Rec from Roman Catholic 6/16/1994 Bp Joe Morris Doss. m 4/4/1991 Carmen Angelin Pozo c 3. Trin Epis Ch Cranford NJ 1994-1995. fpchildrenfirst1@verizon.net

PRADAT, Paul Gillespie (Miss) 323 N Main St, Yazoo City MS 39194 B Meridan MS 9/13/1960 s Ray William Pradat. BA U of Alabama 1983; MDiv Epis TS of The SW 1989. D 5/27/1989 P 12/8/1989 Bp Robert Oran Miller. c 1. The Chap Of The Cross Madison MS 2003-2004; Ch Of The Ascen Hattiesburg MS 1997-2003; Trin Ch Yazoo City MS 1992-1997; Cur S Lk's Epis Ch Birmingham AL 1989-1992.

PRADAT, Ray William (Ala) 1747 Jack Warner Pkwy Apt 208, Tuscaloosa AL 35401 B Birmingham AL 3/29/1930 s Joseph Edward Pradat & Susie Pearce. BA/BS U of Alabama 1951; MDiv STUSo 1966. D 5/30/1966 P 5/20/1967 Bp John M Allin. c 3. R Chr Ch Tuscaloosa AL 1973-1997; Vic Calv Epis Ch Cleveland MS 1970-1973; Vic Gr Ch Rosedale MS 1970-1973; Vic All SS Ch Inverness MS 1968-1970; Vic S Thos Ch Belzoni MS 1968-1970; Cur S Geo's Epis Ch Clarksdale MS 1966-1968.

PRAKTISH, Carl Robert (Va) No address on file. B Clayton MO 9/16/1932 s Carl Praktish & Clara Amelia. BS U of Wisconsin 1953; MA VTS 1971. D 4/15/1972 Bp Philip Alan Smith P 5/1/1973 Bp Robert Bruce Hall. m 9/21/1951 Betty Rhomberg. Supply P Dio Virginia Richmond VA 1986-2004; Asst Ch Of The Apos Fairfax VA 1983-1986; Pryr & Praise Tchr S Paul's Ch Bailey's Crossroads Falls Ch VA 1981-1983; Int Ch Of The H Comf Washington DC 1979-1981; S Pat's Ch Washington DC 1973-1979. Auth, "Case Hist Of Tentmakers".

PRATER, John Stockham (Be) 1040 Jesse Rd, Plymouth PA 18651 B Kingston PA 1/14/1934 s Willard George Prater & Elizabeth Muriel. BA Wilkes Coll U 1955; MDiv VTS 1958. D 6/17/1958 P 12/20/1958 Bp Frederick J Warnecke. m 11/23/1957 Ingrid E Forck c 3. R Prince Of Peace Epis Ch Dallas PA 1962-1997. jprater@epix.net

PRATER, Willard Gibbs (O) 50 Green St, Thomaston ME 04861 **Lic Supply P Dio Maine Portland ME 1998-** B Forty Fort PA 4/4/1928 s Willard George Prater & Elizabeth Muriel. BA Wilkes Coll 1951; MDiv Bex 1954. D 6/9/1954 P 12/17/1954 Bp Frederick J Warnecke. m 6/19/1954 Phyllis Deisher c 3. Lic Supply P Dio Sthrn Ohio Cincinnati OH 1995-1997; Supply P Dio Ohio Cleveland OH 1993-1997; R Ch Of The H Trin Epis Bellefontaine OH 1966-1993; Vic S Geo's Epis Ch Hellertown PA 1957-1966; M-in-c Chr Ch Susquehanna PA 1954-1957; M-in-c S Mk's New Milford PA 1954-1957. willphyl@midcoast.com

PRATHER, Joel A (Dal) 6400 Stonebrook Pkwy, Frisco TX 75034 B Elmhurst IL 7/3/1973 s Gerald A Prather & Catherine A. AA Coll of Dupage 1994; BS Illinois St U 1996; MDiv Nash 2009. D 10/23/2008 P 5/16/2009 Bp Keith Lynn Ackerman. m 9/5/1998 Tammy M Suppes c 1. S Phil's Epis Ch Frisco TX 2009-2010. japrather@gmail.com

PRATHER, Lynn (Ga) 3504 Professional Cir Ste A, Martinez GA 30907 **H Comf Ch Martinez GA 2010-** B Augusta GA 2/3/1958 d David N Barnes & Elizabeth A. BS Augusta St 1996; MDiv TS U So 2010. D 2/6/2010 P 8/21/2010 Bp Scott Anson Benhase. m 6/12/1982 Stuart Prather c 2. pratheraugusta@aol.com

PRATLEY JR, Frederick Harold (SeFla) 707 Elm St Apt 304, San Carlos CA 94070 B Camden NJ 10/27/1928 s Frederick Harold Pratley & Elsie Augusta. BS Tem 1954; PDS 1963; Ya Berk 1967; Sthrn Connecticut St U 1974; Indn River Cmnty Coll & Florida Atlantic U 1988; Oxf 1993. D 4/27/1963 P 11/2/1963 Bp Alfred L Banyard. c 4. S Monica's Ch Stuart FL 1986-1993; S Mk's Epis Sch Ft Lauderdale FL 1978-1979; Com Of Constitutions & Cn Dio Pennsylvania Philadelphia PA 1976-1978; R S Paul's Ch Philadelphia PA 1976-1978; Ch Of The Epiph Southbury CT 1970-1976; Vic S Ptr's Epis Ch Oxford CT 1970-1976; Cur S Mich's Ch Naugatuck CT 1968-1969; Vic Ch Of S Jn By The Sea W Haven W Haven CT 1964-1967; Vic S Jas Epis Ch Cape May NJ 1963-1964. Intl Assn For Hosp Security 1982-1986. Fl St Nrsng Assn Cert 85-94; Fire Sfty In Hlth Care Facilities Natl Fire Protection Assn.

PRATOR, Lloyd (Eugene) (NY) 224 Waverly Pl, New York NY 10014 **R S Jn's Ch New York NY 1988-** B Martinez CA 11/11/1944 s James Olen Prator & Hortense. BA Stan 1966; MDiv ETS 1974; Cert GTS 1992. D 6/29/1974 P 5/24/1975 Bp C Kilmer Myers. Adj Instr Liturg The GTS New York NY 2000-2002; Trst Cathd Of St Jn The Div New York NY 1998; Stwdshp Dept Dio New York New York City NY 1988-1992; Chair COM Dio California San Francisco CA 1984-1987; All SS' Ch San Francisco CA 1979-1988; Chapl Dio California San Francisco CA 1978-1979; Cur Trsfg Epis Ch San Mateo CA 1974-1978. Auth, "A P on the Line," *From The Ashes*, 2001; Auth, *Selected Sermons*, 1987. Associated Parishes 1977-1990; Assn of Angl Mus 1990-2000. Polly Bond Awd for Rel Writing 2002. lprator@stjvny.org

PRATT CHS, Carl Walter (Alb) No address on file. **D Ch Of The H Cross Warrensburg NY 2000-; D Chr Ch Pottersville NY 1981-; D Ch Of The Gd Shpd Brant Lake NY 1981-; D S Andr's Ch Brant Lake NY 1981-; D S Barbara's Ch Brant Lake NY 1981-; D S Chris's Ch Brant Lake NY 1981-; D S Paul's Ch Brant Lake NY 1981-** B Glens Falls NY 6/12/1945 s Murton C Pratt & Florence Gertrude. BA SUNY 1968. D 12/19/1981 Bp Wilbur Emory Hogg Jr. Conf Of CHS.

PRATT, Dorothy Louise (WNC) 84 Church Street, Franklin NC 28734 **R S Agnes Epis Ch Franklin NC 2005-; R S Cyp's Ch Franklin NC 2005-** B Abington PA 11/3/1957 d Charles Douglas Pratt & Louise. MA U NC 1987; MDiv GTS 2005. D 5/28/2005 P 12/10/2005 Bp Granville Porter Taylor. m 2/14/1986 John Allyn Miller. revdorothypratt@gmail.com

PRATT JR, Earle Wilson (LI) 3240 N Caves Valley Path, Lecanto FL 34461 B New Castle PA 11/12/1941 s Earle Wilson Pratt & Mary Jane. BA Youngstown St U 1963; MA Colg 1964; MDiv EDS 1969; PhD Untd States Intl U San Diego CA 1973. D 6/11/1969 P 6/1/1970 Bp Ned Cole. m 12/31/1966 Susan H Walling. R Trin-St Jn's Ch Hewlett NY 1974-2002. Auth, "Case Stds". prattew@aol.com

PRATT, Jennifer Julian (Oly) 2109 N Lafayette Ave, Bremerton WA 98312 **P - Vol S Hugh Of Lincoln Allyn WA 1997-** B San Francisco CA 10/11/1948 d Phillip Harmon Pratt & Frances Helen. BA U CA 1966; MDiv Seattle U 1996. D 11/5/1997 Bp Vincent Waydell Warner P 6/20/1998 Bp Sanford Zangwill Kaye Hampton. m 6/13/1992 William Frederick Smith.

PRATT, Mary Florentine Corley (Vt) 865 Otter Creek Hwy, New Haven VT 05472 B Saint Johnsbury VT 2/17/1949 d William H Corley & Ruth M. BS U of Vermont 1972. D 1/30/1981 Bp Robert Shaw Kerr. m 8/2/1969 John Arthur Pratt. D Trin Ch Rutland VT 1993-1997; Asst S Steph's Ch Middlebury VT 1990-1993; Asst S Paul's Epis Ch On The Green Vergennes VT 1983-1990; Asst S Lk's Epis Ch New Haven CT 1981-1983; Asst S Mk's-S Lk's Epis Mssn Castleton VT 1981-1983.

PRATT-HORSLEY, Mary Elizabeth (ECR) 308 Lilac Dr, Los Osos CA 93402 B Kenosha WI 10/2/1946 d Ernest Elwood Pratt & Ruth Margaret. AA Un Coll Cranford NJ 1982; BA Rutgers-The St U 1986; MA California St U 1990; MDiv CDSP 1995. D 5/16/1995 P 12/2/1995 Bp Richard Lester Shimpfky. m 7/12/1969 John Anthony Horsley c 2. R S Ben's Par Los Osos CA 2000-2006; D, Asstg P S Thos Epis Ch Sunnyvale CA 1995-2000; Santa Maria Urban Mssn San Jose CA 1995-2000. scl Rutgers U, NJ 1986; Phi Beta Kappa. mepratthorsley@aol.com

PRAY, Frederick Russell (NJ) 221 Ivy Rd, Edgewater Park NJ 08010 **D S Steph's Epis Ch Beverly NJ 2005-** B Philadelphia PA 5/20/1944 s Frederick Wesley Pray & Marie Claire. D 4/13/1985 Bp George Phelps Mellick Belshaw. m 9/9/1967 Roberta Louise Thompson c 2. D/Asst Par Of Chr The King Willingboro NJ 1985-1993. Keiros Prison Mnstry 1981-2008; Ord S Lk 2006. frpray@comcast.net

PREAS, Barbara Jean (Nev) 6475 Mondell Pines Cir, Las Vegas NV 89146 **D Gr In The Desert Epis Ch Las Vegas NV 1994-** B Milwaukee WI 7/17/1939 d Howard Dickinson & Mildred. BS U of Wisconsin 1961. D 10/1/1994 Bp Stewart Clark Zabriskie. m 7/24/1982 Rhine F Preas c 4. Claims Person Of The Year Sthrn Nevada Claims Assn 1995. rpreas@aol.com

PREBLE, Charles William (Minn) Rr 2 Box 844, Saint Joseph MN 56374 B Santa Ana CA 10/19/1936 s Donovan Herrick Preble & Charlotte Amanda. BA U CA 1957; PSR 1962; Natl Trng Lab 1976; Guelph Inst Chr Sprtlty 1978; Creighton U 1980; Arizona St U 1981; BD CDSP 1984; U of Nebraska 1984. D 6/14/1962 Bp Ivol I Curtis P 12/14/1962 Bp Gordon V Smith. m 7/3/1963 Jana M B Bollman. Dn Of Reg 3 Dio Minnesota Minneapolis MN 1988-1998; Ch Of Our Sav Little Falls MN 1987-1997; S Jn's Ch S Cloud MN 1986-1987; Stndg Com Dio Nevada Las Vegas NV 1979-1982; Com Dio Nevada Las Vegas NV 1974-1979; Dir Of The Discovery Proj Dio Nevada Las Vegas NV 1974-1978; R S Steph's Epis Ch Reno NV 1973-1986; Secy Of The Dioc Conv Dio Utah Salt Lake City UT 1971-1973; Secy Of The Exec Coun Dio Utah Salt Lake City UT 1970-1973; Vic S Barn EpiscopalChurch Tooele UT 1967-1973; Cur S Mich's Ch New York NY 1965-1967; Vic S Paul's Epis Ch Grinnell IA 1962-1965. Auth, "U Churchmen". Ord Of Agape And Reconciliation; Soc Of S Marg.

PREBLE, Joan (Me) 55 Union St # 4606, Ellsworth ME 04605 B Portland ME 3/23/1940 BS Gorham St Teachers Coll Gorham ME. D 5/3/2003 Bp Chilton Abbie Richardson Knudsen. m 8/10/1963 Ralph Allen Preble c 2.

PRECHTEL, Daniel L (Chi) 2337 Greenwich Rd, San Pablo CA 94806 **Assoc P All Souls Par In Berkeley Berkeley CA 2010-; Adj Instr CALL and Theol Field Educ CDSP Berkeley CA 2010-** B Battle Creek MI 9/9/1948 s Earl Otto Prechtel & Joyce Doreen. BA Wstrn Michigan U 1972; MDiv SWTS 1984; Cert Upper Room Acad Of Sprtl Formation Nashville TN 1990; DMin

SWTS 2002. D 6/11/1984 Bp Charles Bennison P 12/22/1984 Bp Howard Samuel Meeks. m 6/10/1989 Ruth Meyers c 2. Inst of Sprtl Comp Evanston IL 2008-2009; S Aug's Epis Ch Wilmette IL 2006; S Aug's Epis Ch Wilmette IL 2004; S Clem's Ch Harvey IL 2001-2002; SWTS Evanston IL 1999-2008; S Matt's Ch Evanston IL 1997; The Annunc Of Our Lady Gurnee IL 1996-1997; R S Jn's Epis Ch Charlotte MI 1984-1995. Auth, "Where Two or Three are Gathered: Sprtl Direction for Sm Groups," Morehouse-Ch Pub, 2012; Interviewed by Auth Laura Br, "Interview w a Sprtl Dir," *If I Only Had a Brain Injury*, XLibris, 2008; Auth, "From Discord To Discernment," *Open: Journ Of AP*, 2001; Auth, "A Chr Reawakening To The Dream," *Dream Ntwk: A Journ Exploring Dreams & Mythology*, 2000; Auth, "Angl Sprtl Direction By Ptr Ball (Bk Revs)," *Open: Journ Of AP*, 1999; Auth, "Well Sprg," 1993; Auth, "Guidelines For Chr Living Baptismal Preparation," 1992; Auth, "Guidelines For Chr Living: Conscious Beginnings," 1992. Soc For The Study Of Chr Sprtlty 2001; Sprtl Dir Intl 1991; St. Greg'S Abbey - Three Rivers, Mi - Oblate 2000. dprechtel@sbcglobal.net

PREECE, Mark W (Pa) 220 E 6th Ave, Conshohocken PA 19428 **S Jn's Epis Ch Randolph VT 2011-** B Norwalk CT 12/29/1953 s Warren E Preece & Deborah. BA Dart 1975; MA EDS 1978. D 6/23/2001 P 12/23/2001 Bp Charles Ellsworth Bennison Jr. m 6/25/1995 Patricia Anne Horne c 1. Int Pstr Imm Ch Bellows Falls VT 2008-2011; Trin Ch Gulph Mills King Of Prussia PA 2003-2008; Dio Pennsylvania Philadelphia PA 2001-2003; P-in-c S Steph's Epis Ch Norwood PA 2001-2003. mwp@ix.netcom.com

PREGNALL, William Stuart (WA) 132 Lancaster Dr #410, Irvington VA 22480 B Charleston SC 3/26/1931 s Alexander Howard Pregnall & Marion Lockwood. BA U NC 1952; MDiv VTS 1958; DMin STUSo 1977. D 6/12/1958 P 5/26/1959 Bp Thomas N Carruthers. m 12/20/1952 Gabrlelle Joye Uzzell c 3. S Geo's Ch Fredericksburg VA 1993-2001; R St Marys Par St Marys City MD 1989-1993; Dn & Pres CDSP Berkeley CA 1981-1989; Prof VTS Alexandria VA 1973-1981; Vic/R S Aug's Epis Ch Washington DC 1970-1973; R S Jn's Epis Ch Charleston WV 1962-1966; Asst S Jn's Epis Ch Charleston WV 1961-1962; DCE Dio So Carolina Charleston SC 1960-1961; In-c Epis Ch Of The H Trin Ridgeland SC 1958-1960; S Jn's Epis Ch Charleston WV 1958-1960; In-c The Ch Of The Cross Bluffton SC 1958-1960. Auth, *Epis Sem System during the Decline of the Amer Empire*, 1988; Auth, *Laity & Liturg*, 1975; Auth, "Intro," *PB Renwl*. DD CDSP 1990; Doctor in Div VTS 1987. wpregnall@va.metrocast.net

PREHM, Katherine T. (Spok) 3401 W Lincoln Ave, Yakima WA 98902 B Bellingham WA 4/4/1939 d Norman Ralph Townsend & Margaret Hall. BA Wstrn Washington U 1964; EdM Wstrn Washington U 1966; Dioc Sch Of Mnstry Spokane WA 1995; EFM STUSo 1997. D 6/8/1997 Bp Frank Jeffrey Terry P 6/2/2002 Bp James Edward Waggoner. m 11/20/1970 James Lee Prehm c 4. D S Tim's Epis Ch Yakima WA 1997-2002. kjprehm@charter.net

PREHN III, Walter Lawrence (NwT) 3500 W Wadley Ave, Midland TX 79707 **Headmaster Trin Sch Of Midland Midland TX 2010-** B Palo Alto CA 4/3/1957 s Walter Lawrence Prehn & Rebecca Annette. BA Texas A&M U 1979; MDiv Nash 1985; Ph.D U of Virginia 2005. D 6/13/1985 P 12/21/1985 Bp Donis Dean Patterson. m 4/30/1988 Cecilia Anne Jones c 3. S Lk's Epis Ch San Antonio TX 2005-2010; R S Marg's Epis Ch San Antonio TX 1990-1996; Chair Of Liturg And Mus Cmsn Dio W Texas San Antonio TX 1990-1993; Cur The Ch Of The Gd Shpd Bryn Mawr PA 1987-1990; Cur Ch Of The H Cross Dallas TX 1985-1987. Auth, "Epis Schools: Hist & Mssn," *Handbook of Faith-based Educ in Amer*, Clio/Praeger Acad, 2011; Auth, "Bk Revs," *LivCh mag*, TLC Fndt; Auth, "poems," *LivCh, San Antonio Express-News*. Amer Hist Assn 2003; HSEC 2005; Orgnztn of Amer Historians 2003; St. Mich's Soc for the Prom of the Ch Sch 2003. Distinguished Alum Chamberlain-Hunt Acad 1990; Distinguished Alum Chamberlain-Hunt Acad MS 1990; cl Nash 1985. c_prehn@trinitymidland.org

PRESCOTT, Benjamin Tyler (SC) 111 Waring St, Summerville SC 29483 **S Paul's Epis Ch Summerville SC 2011-** B Columbia SC 8/5/1980 s Roy Wayne Prescott & Susan Cox. BS U of So Carolina 2002; MDiv Trin Sch for Mnstry 2010. D 1/3/2011 P 7/7/2011 Bp Mark Joseph Lawrence. m 12/27/2003 Lanier Simmons c 4. tylerp@stpaulssummerville.org

PRESCOTT, Vicki Lee (Roch) 2500 East Avenue, Apartment 5H, Rochester NY 14610 **R Ch Of The Incarn Penfield NY 2001-** B Sterling IL 4/20/1950 d Richard Prescott & Juanita Jean. Syr; BS U IL 1973; MDiv UTS 1980. D 6/20/1981 P 6/20/1982 Bp Ned Cole. m 9/1/1973 Paul L Couch c 1. R All SS Ch Cincinnati OH 1999-2001; S Barn Epis Ch Greenwich CT 1994-1998; S Fran Ch Stamford CT 1994-1995; S Steph's Ch Ridgefield CT 1993-1994; Ch Of The Resurr Oswego NY 1992; Yth Coordntr Dio Cntrl New York Syracuse NY 1990-1992; Int Chr Epis Ch Jordan NY 1988-1989; Asst S Paul's Cathd Syracuse NY 1981-1983. vprescot@rochester.rr.com

PRESCOTT, W Clarke (Los) 8830 Mesa Oak Dr, Riverside CA 92508 **Vic S Steph's Mssn Menifee CA 2011-** B Atlanta GA 1/13/1943 s Ralph Bimonte & Ethel. BA Manhattan Coll 1969; MDiv Bex 1972; MA US Intl U San Diego CA 1987; Naval Chapl Sch 1991. D 6/3/1972 Bp Paul Moore Jr P 12/16/1972 Bp Robert Rae Spears Jr. m 3/17/2007 Jeanette Wiley c 2. Asst S Geo's Ch Riverside CA 2008-2009; R All SS Epis Ch Riverside CA 1996-2005; Chapl S Marg's Epis Sch San Juan Capo CA 1994-1996; Asst Par of Trin Ch New York NY 1992-1993; Chapl Off Of Bsh For ArmdF New York NY 1982-1992; Assoc Par Ch of St. Helena Beaufort SC 1980-1982; R S Paul's Ch Washington NC 1979-1980; R Zion Epis Ch Washington NC 1978-1980; Asst S Paul's Ch Rochester NY 1973-1976; Asst Chr Ch Pittsford NY 1972-1973. apadre@apadre.com

PRESLER, Henry Airheart (NC) Po Box 293, Monroe NC 28111 **Assoc S Tim's Ch Raleigh NC 2010-** B Naini Tal Uttar Pradesh IN 4/8/1940 s Henry Hughes Presler & Marion Constance. BA U NC 1973; MA U NC 1976; MDiv GTS 1985. D 6/2/1985 P 6/7/1986 Bp Frank Harris Vest Jr. m 10/5/1963 Judith L Heiss c 4. R S Paul's Ch Monroe NC 1988-2008; Vic Chap Of The Gd Shpd Ridgeway NC 1987-1988; Vic All SS Ch Warrenton NC 1986-1988; R Emm Ch Warrenton NC 1986-1988. hpresler@gmail.com

PRESLER, Titus Leonard (Tex) 175 9th Ave, New York NY 10011 B Mussoorie Uttar Pradesh IN 8/7/1950 s Henry Hughes Presler & Marion Constance. MDiv GTS 1972; BA Harv 1972; ThD Bos 1995. D 6/9/1979 Bp John Bowen Coburn P 2/9/1980 Bp Morris Fairchild Arnold. m 4/6/1974 Jane Butterfield-Presler c 4. The GTS New York NY 2005-2009; Dn And Pres Epis TS Of The SW Austin TX 2002-2005; Nomin Com Pbp Dio Massachusetts Boston MA 1997-2000; EDS Cambridge MA 1993-1997; R S Ptr's Epis Ch Cambridge MA 1991-2002; Co Chair Dioc Wider Mssn Cmsn Dio Massachusetts Boston MA 1990-1993; Int The Par Of S Chrys's Quincy MA 1990-1991; Dep Gc Dio Massachusetts Boston MA 1988-2000; Assoc All SS' Epis Ch Belmont MA 1988-1990; Stwdshp Cmsn Dio Massachusetts Boston MA 1987-2000; Chr Ch Cambridge Cambridge MA 1987-1988; Exec Coun Appointees New York NY 1983-1987; Chr Ch So Hamilton MA 1979-1983. Auth, "Old And New In Wrshp And Cmnty," 2000; Auth, "Chrsnty Rediscovered:," 1992; Auth, "Mssy Englicanism Meets An Afr Traditional Relatns: A Restropective On The Centenary Of Bp Knight-Bruce'S Entry Into Zimbabwe," 1989; Auth, "Transfigured Night," U Of So Afr Press; Auth, "Transfigured Night: Mssn & Culture In Zimbabwe'S Vigil Mvmt"; Auth, "Horizon Of Mssn (To Be Pub In 2001)," Cowley Press. Amer Soc Of Missiology 1988; EPF 1997; Intl Assn Of Mssn Stds 1985. tituspresler@earthlink.net

PRESSENTIN, Elsa Ann (EMich) 7562 Alex Ct, Freeland MI 48623 **Mnstry Develoopment and Transition Mnstry Dio Estrn Michigan Saginaw MI 2008-** B Holland MI 4/10/1944 d Paul Henry Pressentin & Vera Annetta. AB Cntrl Michigan U 1966; BTS Sch for Deacons 1984. D 6/7/1986 Bp William Edwin Swing P 5/23/1998 Bp Jerry Alban Lamb. R S Paul's Epis Ch Bad Axe MI 2000-2009; Asst S Jn's Epis Ch Saginaw MI 2000-2003; Vic H Sprt Ch Of The Deaf San Lorenzo CA 1989-2000. revelsap@gmail.com

PRESSEY, Stephen Palmer (Mich) 1792 Celeste Circle, Youngstown OH 44511 B Baker OR 3/5/1929 s Herbert Ernest Palmer Pressey & Alma Wheaton. BA Trin 1951; BD Bex 1958. D 5/30/1958 P 12/19/1958 Bp Nelson Marigold Burroughs. m 12/27/1970 Constance Jeswald c 4. S Andr's Ch Jackson MI 1985-1994; R S Kath's Ch Williamston MI 1977-1985; Vic S Rocco's Ch Youngstown OH 1969-1977; R S Mk's Epis Ch Shelby OH 1958-1965. Auth, *Habakkuk*; Auth, *Jeremiah's Confession*. presseycm@zoominternet.net

PRESSLEY JR, Dennis Charles (Alb) Po Box 206, Greenwich NY 12834 **Dio Albany Albany NY 2003-; Asst Chr Ch Pottersville NY 2000-; Asst Ch Of The Gd Shpd Brant Lake NY 2000-; Asst S Andr's Ch Brant Lake NY 2000-; Asst S Barbara's Ch Brant Lake NY 2000-; Asst S Chris's Ch Brant Lake NY 2000-; Asst S Paul's Ch Brant Lake NY 2000-** B Riverside NJ 4/27/1952 s Dennis C Pressley & Margaret F. Cert Berean U 1973. D 5/10/1999 P 11/13/1999 Bp Daniel William Herzog. m 12/8/1973 Veronica Lynn Mackey c 3. Barry Hse Retreat Cntr Albany NY 1999-2002; Dio Albany Albany NY 1997-1999. frdenny@nycap.rr.com

PREST JR, Alan Patrick Llewellyn (Va) 3920 Custis Rd, Richmond VA 23225 B Detroit MI 2/28/1928 s Alan Patrick Prest & Mary Naomi. BS Leh 1951; MDiv EDS 1954. D 6/9/1954 P 3/26/1955 Bp Walter H Gray. m 6/16/1956 Joan Moyniham c 5. Asst S Andr's Ch Meriden CT 1954-1956. Auth, "Uncommon Pryr," Lulu Publ., 2005; Auth, "Prayers," *Hymnal for Wrshp*, NCCC, 1982; Auth, "By What Authority," *Journ Pstr Care*, Vandenhoeck, 1976; Auth, *Care for Dying*, Jn Knox, 1975; Auth, *Psychoanalytic Contributions to Cmnty Psychol*, Chas Thos, 1971; Auth, "By What Authority," Journ Pstr Care, 1970; Auth, "Suicide," *A Psych's Friend*, Journ Pstr Care. Amer Assn for Pstr Counselors 1972; ACPE 1959; Coll of Chapl 1975. Helen Flanders Dunbar Awd Coll of Pstr 2006; DD STUSo Sewanee TN 1977. JOPA3920@COMCAST.NET

PRESTEGARD, Joann (Oly) 55 Irving St, Cathlamet WA 98612 **Serv S Jas Epis Ch Cathlamet WA 1999-** B Woodland WA 3/26/1938 d Walter Alan Irving & Inez Marie. D 10/3/1998 Bp Vincent Waydell Warner P 5/4/1999 Bp Sanford Zangwill Kaye Hampton. m 9/16/1967 Ray Elton Prestegard. jo38@centurytel.net

PRESTON II, James Montgomery (Tex) 1310 Malmaison Ridge Dr, Spring TX 77379 B San Antonio TX 8/3/1936 s Allan Hill Preston & Jenna Mae. BA U Of Houston 1963; MDiv STUSo 1967; Cert Oll Prof Tchr 1973. D 7/13/1967

P

Bp Everett H Jones P 1/27/1968 Bp Richard Earl Dicus. m 8/22/1964 Barbara Ann Killebrew c 1. Int P S Jas' Par So Pasadena CA 1999-2000; St Johns Pro-Cathd Los Angeles CA 1995-1997; R Gr Epis Ch Houston TX 1979-1983; Dio The Dominican Republic (Iglesia Epis Dominicana) 100 Airport AvVenice FL 1974-1979; P-in-c S Jas Epis Ch Hebbronville TX 1968-1971. Auth, "Mortal," *The Atlantic Contest*, 1963. prest829@yahoo.com

PRESTON, Leigh C (Ct) St. James' Episcopal Church, 45 Church St., Hartford CT 06103 **Dio Connecticut Hartford CT 2010-; Dom And Frgn Mssy Soc-Epis Ch Cntr New York NY 2007-** B Oakland, CA 5/6/1981 d Kenneth Amos Preston & Nancey Green. AB, BS U GA, Athens GA 2003; MDiv Ya Berk 2007. D 12/21/2006 P 7/1/2007 Bp J(ohn) Neil Alexander. m 7/31/2004 Andrew Thompson c 1. Grtr Hartford Reg Mnstry E Hartford CT 2008-2009; Exec Coun Appointees New York NY 2007-2008. leighpreston@gmail.com

PRESTON, Robert George (SeFla) 401 Sw 6th Ave, Hallandale FL 33009 B Tecumseh MI 11/18/1924 s John James Preston & Margaret. BA Carroll Coll 1950; Nash 1953. Trans from Anglican Church of Canada 8/3/1955 as Priest Bp Martin J Bram. R S Andr's Epis Ch Of Hollywood Dania Bch FL 1977-1991; R S Anne's Epis Ch Hallandale Bch FL 1977-1991; Asst S Benedicts Ch Plantation FL 1974-1976; Asst San Jose Epis Ch Jacksonville FL 1969-1974; Secy Dio Quincy Peoria IL 1964-1969; Asst S Paul's Cathd Peoria IL 1959-1962. frbob1@bellsouth.net

PRETTI, Victoria Ann (Mass) 893 Main St, West Newbury MA 01985 **All SS Ch W Newbury MA 2009-** B Winthrop MA 1/14/1958 d Joseph Borkowski & Diana. ADN No Shore Coll 1984; MDiv Weston Jesuit TS 2004; Cert Epis Div 2008. D 6/6/2009 Bp M(arvil) Thomas Shaw III. m 9/27/2007 Anthony Pretii c 1. vikiannb@hotmail.com

PREVATT JR, Jim (NC) 5104 Ainsworth Dr, Greensboro NC 27410 B Monticello GA 4/25/1938 s James Thomas Prevatt & Vida Edna. BA Emory U 1960; BD Duke 1963; ThM Duke 1964; GTS 1965; VTS 1981. D 6/29/1965 P 6/29/1966 Bp Thomas Augustus Fraser Jr. m 4/16/1966 Muriel E Wegel c 2. S Barn' Ch Greensboro NC 1971-2001; Cur Ch Of The Atone Tenafly NJ 1965-1967. The Fllshp of St. Jn the Evang. mjprevatt@bellsouth.net

PREVOST, Edward Simpson (Chi) 470 Maple St, Winnetka IL 60093 **S Matt's Epis Ch Bloomington IL 2007-; Bd Trst The GTS New York NY 2007-; R Chr Ch Winnetka IL 1992-** B Elizabeth NJ 11/8/1944 s Sterett Ridgely Prevost & Elizabeth Durrie. BA Trin Sch 1967; MDiv GTS 1970. D 6/10/1970 Bp John Henry Esquirol P 12/20/1970 Bp Joseph Warren Hutchens. m 6/6/1970 Beverly Holmes c 2. COM Chair Dio Chicago Chicago IL 1995-1999; COM Dio Chicago Chicago IL 1993-1999; Alum Assn Pres The GTS New York NY 1988-1992; R S Paul's Ch Fairfield CT 1981-1992; COM Dio Connecticut Hartford CT 1977-1992; R S Paul's Ch Southington CT 1973-1981; Cur S Jn The Evang Yalesville CT 1970-1973; Cur S Paul's Ch Wallingford CT 1970-1973. Auth, "R's Sermon," *On the Sabbath After 9/11*, Brandylane, 2002. Bp of Newark Preaching Prize GTS 1970. rectorned@gmail.com

PRICE, Ashburn Birdsall (CFla) 1781 Pocahontas Path, Maitland FL 32751 B New York NY 7/15/1915 s Charles Price & Margaret. BA NYU 1936. D 1/18/1980 Bp William Hopkins Folwell. m 4/29/1943 Dorothy Brown.

P

PRICE, Barbara Deane (Ak) 1560 Westwood Way, Fairbanks AK 99709 B Lakewood OH 11/4/1944 d Richard Erwin Austin & Florence Marie. BA Coll of Wooster 1966; MA U of Texas 1969; Med Duquesne U 1984; Paths To Serv Trng AK 1996; Psyd Sthrn California U For Profsnl Stds 2002. D 12/9/1996 Bp Howard Samuel Meeks. m 6/16/1990 Murray D Price. Auth, "Meditation On Adv," *Coun Of Wmn Mnstrs Dom & Frgn Mssy Soc Pecusa*, 2000; Auth, "Meditation On Untimely Death," *Coun Of Wmn Mnstrs Dom &Frgn Mssy Soc Pecusa*, 2000. AAPC; Amer Counslg Assn 1984. Appreciation Tanana Chiefs Conf 2000.

PRICE, Barbara Jean (WNY) 77 Huntington Ave, Buffalo NY 14214 **S Ptr's Epis Ch Eggertsville NY 2000-** B Buffalo NY 8/18/1949 d LeRoy Jesse Farley & Doris Winifred. RN EJ Meyer Memi Hosp Nrsng Sch 1970; BS S Jos's Coll 1988; MDiv Bex 1997. D 6/7/1997 P 12/20/1997 Bp David Charles Bowman. m 9/26/1992 Alfred Price c 3. Int Vic Ephphatha Epis Ch Of The Deaf Eggertsville NY 2001-2003; Bex Columbus OH 2000-2008; Dio Wstrn New York Tonawanda NY 1997-2004; Cn to the Ordnry Dio Wstrn New York Tonawanda NY 1989-2001; Int Trin Ch Lancaster NY 1988-1999. Auth, "Psalm For A Widow," *Wmn Uncommon Prayers*. SCHC 1997; Sprtl Dir Intl 1995. morningstar228@verizon.net

PRICE, Darwin Ladavis (LI) PO Box 280, Brewster MA 02631 B Hopewell VA 4/22/1943 s Baldy Davis Price & Reathella. BA U Of Hartford 1967; MDiv Harvard DS 1970; EDS 1971. D 6/10/1970 Bp John Henry Esquirol P 2/21/1971 Bp Anson Phelps Stokes Jr. m 12/23/1967 Grace Dunn c 3. R S Lk's Ch E Hampton NY 1997-2009; Bd Trsts Pediatric Care Hiv/Aids Dio Washington Washington DC 1992-1997; Chapl Cathd of St Ptr & St Paul Washington DC 1991-1997; Stndg Com Dio Washington Washington DC 1991-1997; R S Mary's Epis Ch Foggy Bottom Washington DC 1990-1997; R Calv Ch Enfield CT 1981-1990; S Geo's Sch Newport RI 1975-1978; Chapl S Geo's Ch Portsmouth RI 1973-1978; Assoc S Mary's Ch Portsmouth RI 1973-1978; Assoc The Ch Of The H Sprt Orleans MA 1972-1975; Asst All SS Par Brookline MA 1970-1972. Auth, "Rel Indep Sch," 1978; Auth, "Rel Indep Sch," *Coffee Hse Mnstry & Counter Culture*, Parnass, 1971. EME. darwinlprice@gmail.com

PRICE, David Lee (Oly) 15967 169th Ave Se, Monroe WA 98272 **P-in-c Ch Of The Trsfg Darrington WA 2008-; Supply P S Fran Epis Ch Mill Creek WA 2008-** B Indianapolis IN 11/8/1947 s Anthony Hubert Price & Mary. BA U of Alaska 1995; MDiv SWTS 1999. D 5/1/1999 Bp Mark Lawrence Mac Donald P 12/6/1999 Bp Sanford Zangwill Kaye Hampton. m 10/4/2003 Donna Price c 1. S Fran Epis Ch Mill Creek WA 1999-2006. fatherprice@yahoo.com

PRICE, David William (Tex) 302 S Hardie St, Alvin TX 77511 **R Gr Epis Ch Alvin TX 2006-** B Tucson AZ 9/19/1956 s Hermon T Price & Margaret Lois. BA U of Arizona 1979; MDiv Epis TS of The SW 1984. D 6/16/1984 Bp Joseph Thomas Heistand P 6/1/1985 Bp Sam Byron Hulsey. m 6/27/1981 Jennifer Randal c 3. R S Mk's Ch Houston TX 1994-2006; R S Phil's Epis Ch Palestine TX 1990-1994; S Paul's On The Plains Epis Ch Lubbock TX 1986-1990; Cur Ch Of The H Trin Midland TX 1984-1986. davidprice56@yahoo.com

PRICE, Gary Kilmer (Va) 18 Witherell Rd, Wales ME 04280 B Swarthmore PA 3/28/1923 s William Stanley Price & Ethel Marie. BA Un Coll Schenectady NY 1944; BD VTS 1947; DD VTS 1973. D 12/28/1946 Bp Oliver J Hart P 6/30/1947 Bp William P Remington. Epis EvangES Arlington VA 1976-1986; Treas VTS Alexandria VA 1954-1958; R Trin Ch Arlington VA 1949-1975; Asst S Mary's Epis Ch Ardmore PA 1947-1949. Phi Beta Kappa Un Coll 1944.

PRICE, Geoffrey Masefield (WA) 199 Rolfe Rd., Williamsburg VA 23185 **Int Epis Ch Of Leeds Par Markham VA 2011-** B Youngstown OH 12/11/1946 s Howard Randall Price & Gertrude Jane. Lon (Queen Mary Coll) 1969; BS Youngstown St U 1970; LTh Salisbury Theol Coll, Sarum GB 1973; MDiv VTS 1974; DMin VTS 1992. D 6/15/1974 P 4/26/1975 Bp John Harris Burt. m 4/22/1995 Kathleen Vermillion Farmer c 4. Int Abingdon Epis Ch White Marsh VA 2005-2010; Int S Ptr's Par Ch New Kent VA 2003-2005; R S Paul's Rock Creek Washington DC 1988-2004; Assoc The Ch Of The Epiph Washington DC 1983-1988; Vic S Jas Epis Ch Bowie MD 1978-1983; Prof VTS Alexandria VA 1977-2007; Asst S Andr's Epis Ch Arlington VA 1976-1978; Cur S Paul's Ch Maumee OH 1974-1976. Auth, "A Gd Conscience (Doctoral Thesis)," VTS, Libr, 1992; Auth, "Serv For The Ending Of Pstr Relatns, Etc.," *Bk Of Occasional Serv*, Ch Hymnal, 1982. Natl Eagle Scout Assn, Life Mem 1963; Natl Rifle Assn. gmprice46@aol.com

PRICE, George Harry (SeFla) 2300 Spanish River Rd, Boca Raton FL 33432 B Mount Holly NJ 11/12/1938 s George Hartman Price & Naomi Margaret. BA Hob 1961; MDiv PDS 1964; STM STUSo 1974. D 4/25/1964 P 10/31/1964 Bp Alfred L Banyard. m 6/27/1964 Barbara Wade c 2. R S Greg's Ch Boca Raton FL 1981-2003; R S Lk's Ch Fairport NY 1975-1981; R St Andrews Epis Ch Rome NY 1971-1975; P-in-c St Andrews Epis Ch Rome NY 1969-1971; R Trin Epis Par Hughesville MD 1966-1969; Cur H Trin Ch Collingswood NJ 1964-1965. ghprice6583@att.net

PRICE, George N (Me) 290 Baxter Blvd Apt B3, Portland ME 04101 B Elgin IL 4/27/1935 s Lyle G Price & Marian J. BA NWU 1957; MDiv VTS 1960. D 6/18/1960 Bp Gerald Francis Burrill P 12/17/1960 Bp Charles L Street. m 11/3/1962 Harriet Farr Hemenway c 2. Cn Mssnr Dio Maine Portland ME 1990-1992; Chair - Commision for Outreach & Serv Dio Maine Portland ME 1990-1992; Chair of the Liturg Com Dio Maine Portland ME 1990-1992; Chair of Comp Relatns Dio Maine Portland ME 1986-1989; Exec Com of the Alum Assn VTS Alexandria VA 1983-1990; R S Andr And S Jn Epis Ch SW Harbor ME 1969-1996; Assoc S Chrys's Ch Chicago IL 1966-1969. Doctor in Div, Honoris Causa VTS 1991; Fell Cntr for Cont Educ, VTS 1986. ghhprice@mac.com

PRICE, Gloria M (EC) 130 Quail Dr, Dudley NC 28333 B Winthrop MA 6/23/1931 d John Stewart MacCormack & Veronica. Dio Diac Trng; NYU; San Mateo Jr Coll. D 11/2/1988 Bp Brice Sidney Sanders. m 12/24/1950 Hillery Price c 5. D S Fran Ch Goldsboro NC 1997-2000; D S Steph's Ch Goldsboro NC 1988-1997. NAAD; Ord Of S Lk. g2price@earthlink.net

PRICE, Gordon Stephen (SO) 2849 Dwight Ave, Dayton OH 45420 **R Emer Chr Epis Ch Dayton OH 1993-** B Fitchburg MA 10/25/1916 s Hugh Terry Price & Nellie E. MATC; BA Clark U 1944; MDiv EDS 1947; DHum U of Dayton 1974. D 1/25/1947 Bp William A Lawrence P 7/25/1947 Bp Richard Ainslie Kirchhoffer. m 9/13/1947 Ruth D Dufresne c 3. Cn Dio Sthrn Ohio Cincinnati OH 1997-2008; Int S Anne Epis Ch W Chester OH 1995-1996; Ch Of S Mich And All Ang Sanibel FL 1991-1994; Int S Jas Epis Ch Columbus OH 1989-1991; Int Ch Of The Epiph Urbana OH 1988-1989; P-in-c S Paul's Ch Palmyra MO 1982-1987; R Chr Epis Ch Dayton OH 1958-1982; R S Steph's Ch Ferguson MO 1950-1958; Asst Trin Ch Columbus OH 1947-1950. Auth, *Early Age Comm*; Auth, *Us on a Bus*. Comp Cmnty Cross Nails, Coventry, Engl 1983. gsrd_price@pocketmail.com

PRICE, Harold Thomas (Ky) 409 Wendover Ave, Louisville KY 40207 **The Reverend Ch Of Our Merc Sav Louisville KY 2005-; S Phil Naytahwaush MN 2005-** B Cincinnati OH 3/20/1957 s Robert Edwin Price & Joyce Ann. BA U Cinc 1979; MDiv Sthrn Bapt TS Louisville KY 1983. D 6/4/2005 P 12/10/

2005 Bp Edwin Funsten Gulick Jr. m 8/6/1983 Mary Virginia Burks c 2. HEIDRON@INSIGHTBB.COM

PRICE, John Randolph (Md) 772 Ticonderoga Ave, Severna Park MD 21146 **S Mk's Ch Highland MD 2010-** B Coolemee NC 8/9/1947 s William Penn Price & Betsy. BA Laf 1969; STM GTS 1973; DMin VTS 1986. D 6/9/1973 P 12/22/1973 Bp Horace W B Donegan. m 8/11/2007 Laura Lee Hall c 2. Chr Ch Greenville Wilmington DE 2006-2007; Liturg Com Dio Maryland Baltimore MD 1998-2000; Comm on the Mnstry Dio Maryland Baltimore MD 1990-1996; Episcopate Cmsn Dio Maryland Baltimore MD 1990-1991; R S Anne's Par Annapolis MD 1989-2006; Asst To Bp For Diac Dio E Carolina Kinston NC 1988-1989; Asst To Bp For Diac Dio E Carolina Kinston NC 1988-1989; Asst To Bp For Diac Dio E Carolina Kinston NC 1988-1989; Evang Consult Dio E Carolina Kinston NC 1988-1989; Stndg Com Dio E Carolina Kinston NC 1988-1989; Excoun Dio E Carolina Kinston NC 1986-1987; Excoun Dio E Carolina Kinston NC 1980-1983; Liturg Cmsn Dio E Carolina Kinston NC 1977-1989; S Tim's Epis Ch Greenville NC 1976-1988; Deptce Dio E Carolina Kinston NC 1976-1980; Assoc S Paul's Epis Ch Greenville NC 1976-1978; Assoc Ch Of The Intsn New York NY 1973-1976. johnranprice@gmail.com

PRICE, Joyce Elizabeth (WNC) 75 Echo Lake Dr, Fairview NC 28730 B Asheville NC 9/26/1955 d Fred Hamilton Price & Betty Caroline. BA Warren Wilson Coll 1977; MDiv Yale DS 1981. D 6/20/1981 P 6/1/1983 Bp William Gillette Weinhauer. m 3/3/1984 Jay Carter Paul. Asst Ch Of The Epiph Commerce TX 1981-1983. City Allnce For Mnstry. Danforth Fell 1978.

PRICE, Kathleen Vermillion (WA) 199 Rolfe Rd, Williamsburg VA 23185 **R All SS Ch Oakley Av MD 1999-** B Newport News VA 4/11/1946 d Ervin Davis Farmer & Charlotte Mae. BS U NC 1968; Certification U So,EFM 1990; M Ed W&M 1991; Certification Maryknoll Inst of Afr Stds 1994; MDiv VTS 1994; Certification Myers-Briggs Type Indicator 1997; DMin How 1998; Certification CREDO I 2003; Certification Cler Ldrshp Proj XIV 2003; Certificsation CREDO II 2008. D 5/28/1994 P 2/11/1995 Bp Frank Harris Vest Jr. m 4/22/1995 Geoffrey Masefield Price c 3. Chapl, DOK Prov III Chester Sprg PA 2000-2006; Chapl, DOK Dio Washington Washington DC 1997-2000; Asst R S Jn's Ch Chevy Chase MD 1995-1998. *Biblic Narrative Experienced Through Visual Arts*, 1998. DOK 1990. Grant: Cler Renwl ("Following the Footsteps of Van Gogh") Lilly Fndt 2005. kvprice11@aol.com

✠ **PRICE, Rt Rev Kenneth Lester** (SO) 125 E Broad St, Columbus OH 43215 **Provsnl Bp Dio Pittsburgh Monroeville PA 2010-; Vice Chair, Bd Trst Bex Columbus OH 1999-; Bp Suffr Dio Sthrn Ohio Cincinnati OH 1994-** B Charleston WV 6/12/1943 s Kenneth Lester Price & Margaret. BA W Virginia U 1965; STB GTS 1968; MA Marshall U 1974. D 6/11/1968 P 12/18/1968 Bp Wilburn Camrock Campbell Con 10/29/1994 for SO. m 6/21/1968 Mary Ann Prosser c 2. Archd, Nthrn Dearery Dio W Virginia Charleston WV 1990-1994; Dio W Virginia Charleston WV 1987-1990; The GTS New York NY 1986-1994; R S Matt's Ch Wheeling WV 1984-1994; Dep to GC Dio W Virginia Charleston WV 1982-1994; Chair - COM Dio W Virginia Charleston WV 1981-1994; R Trin Ch Parkersburg WV 1974-1984; Dn Lay Mnstry Dio W Virginia Charleston WV 1974-1982; Vic S Andr's in the Vill Ch Barboursville WV 1970-1974; Cur Trin Ch Parkersburg WV 1968-1970. DD GTS 1995. bishopken@aol.com

PRICE, Marston (Ct) 33 Old Field hill Rd. Unit48, Southbury CT 06488 B Washington DC 11/29/1944 s Hickman Price & Margaret. BA U of Miami 1969; MA U of Washington 1975; MDiv EDS 1982; Certificat Mssy Traning Prog 1987; Certificat Int Mnstry Trng 2000; Certificat Pstr Gestault Ther Traning 2007. D 8/3/1982 Bp Robert Hume Cochrane P 5/1/1983 Bp George Nelson Hunt III. m 8/26/2006 Pamela Rorholm c 4. Mem Bishops Fund Hartford CT 2003-2011; R S Mich's Ch Naugatuck CT 2001-2010; Int S Paul's Epis Ch Shelton CT 2000-2001; R The Ch Of The H Sprt Orleans MA 1994-1998; R S Jn's Ch Georgetown Par Washington DC 1990-1994; R S Jn's Ch Lafayette Sq Washington DC 1990-1994; ECUSA Mssy Exec Coun Appointees New York NY 1987-1990; Assoc R Trin Ch Newport RI 1982-1987. marston_price@yahoo.com

PRICE, Paul Alexander (Los) 113 Tierra Plano, Rancho Santa Margarita CA 92688 **S Tim's Epis Ch Apple Vlly CA 2011-** B Berlin DE 3/8/1962 BS Azusa Pacific U. D 6/19/2004 Bp Joseph Jon Bruno P 12/19/2004 Bp Robert Marshall Anderson. m 11/1/1985 Cheryl A Simon c 1. S Geo's Ch Riverside CA 2006-2011; Cur S Jn Chrys Ch And Sch Rancho Santa Margarita CA 2004-2006. fr.paul@mac.com

PRICE, Phyllis Anne (Mass) 12191 Clipper Dr, Lake Ridge VA 22192 B New York NY 7/14/1940 d Ralph G Price & Beatrice H. BA Randolph-Macon Wmn's Coll 1962; MA U Chi 1964; MA CUA 1978; CAS GTS 1998. D 2/6/1999 P 9/11/1999 Bp Richard Frank Grein. Trin Chap Shirley MA 2003-2004; Asst S Jas' Epis Ch Warrenton VA 2000-2002; Ce Dir Ch Of The H Trin New York NY 1999-2000.

PRICE, Raymond Estal (Wyo) 417 S 2nd St, Lander WY 82520 **Trin Ch Lander WY 2004-** B Niles MI 5/12/1948 D 2/8/2004 P 10/31/2004 Bp Bruce Edward Caldwell. c 2. rprice@wyoming.com

PRICE JR, Richard Elwyn (WNC) 185 Macon Ave Apt A-3, Asheville NC 28804 B Florence AL 1/1/1926 s Richard Elwyn Price & Beulah May. BA Mississippi Coll 1949; BD Sthrn Bapt TS Louisville KY 1952; MDiv(supercedes BD) Sthrn Bapt TS Louisville KY 1973. D 5/20/1988 P 10/22/1988 Bp William Gillette Weinhauer. m 2/28/1953 Ellen Gray Honts c 2. Assoc S Mary's Ch Asheville NC 1996-2001; Int S Jn's Ch Asheville NC 1989-1990; Asst Gr Ch Asheville NC 1988-1989. Assoc, CSM; Assoc, Fllshp of St. Jn. padreprice@bellsouth.net

PRICE, Robert David (WMass) 12 Oxford Dr, Suffield CT 06078 **Assoc S Andr's Ch Longmeadow MA 1999-** B Worcester MA 5/8/1932 s Hugh Terry Price & Josephine Lura. BA Tufts U 1957; BD VTS 1960. D 6/4/1960 P 12/7/1960 Bp Robert McConnell Hatch. c 3. Dio Wstrn Massachusetts Springfield MA 1980-1992; S Chris's Ch Fairview Chicopee MA 1971-1980. sbogstream@cox.net

PRICE, Robert H(ampton) (NC) 175 Springmoor Dr, Raleigh NC 27615 **R Emer S Jas Ch Black Mtn NC 1979-** B Mayodan NC 12/3/1913 s John Randolph Price & Elcana Virginia. BA Guilford Coll 1940; MDiv STUSo 1943. D 1/24/1943 P 12/21/1943 Bp Edwin A Penick. m 6/25/1947 Frances Humphries c 2. R S Jas Ch Black Mtn NC 1969-1978; P Our Sav Epis Ch Lincolnton NC 1966-1969; P S Thos Epis Ch Sanford NC 1958-1966; P S Barth's Ch No Augusta SC 1955-1958; R S Mk's Ch Chester SC 1952-1955; Asst S Mart's Epis Ch Charlotte NC 1951-1952; R Ch Of The Epiph Eden NC 1946-1951; R S Paul's Epis Ch Smithfield NC 1945-1946; P S Steph's Epis Ch Erwin NC 1945-1946; Min in charge Chr Ch Albemarle NC 1943-1945.

PRICE, Robert Paul (Tex) 1023 Compass Cove Cir, Spring TX 77379 **Leading Pstr S Dunst's Epis Ch Houston TX 2005-** B La Jolla CA 9/27/1970 s Robert Preston Price & Jean. BA Stan 1996; MA Stan 1996; MDiv Yale DS 2002; MA Ya 2002. D 11/27/2001 Bp Hays H. Rockwell P 5/2/2002 Bp George Wayne Smith. m 6/29/1996 Kate Ellen Price c 3. First Alt Dep to GC Dio Texas Houston TX 2009; Ch Of The Incarn Dallas TX 2004-2005; Cur S Mich & S Geo Clayton MO 2002-2004. Ord of St. Jn of Jerusalem 2005. rprice@saintdunstans.org

PRICE III, Robert Preston (Tex) 2312 Steel Street, Houston TX 77098 **Assoc Palmer Memi Ch Houston TX 2004-** B Corpus Christi TX 11/24/1938 s William Armstrong Price & Evelyn Tyson. BA U of Texas 1961; MDiv VTS 1964; Pecos Monstry Sch Sprtl Dirs Pecos NM 1986. D 6/29/1964 Bp Richard Earl Dicus P 1/13/1965 Bp Everett H Jones. m 6/25/1966 Arlene Bruchmiller c 2. Chapl Cullen Memi Chap Houston TX 1996-2004; Chapl St Lk's Epis Hosp Houston TX 1996-2004; Sprtl Dvlpmnt Div Dio Texas Houston TX 1995-2004; R H Comf Epis Ch Sprg TX 1988-1996; Curs Strng Com Dio Texas Houston TX 1978-1982; Dir Sum Camping Prog Dio Texas Houston TX 1972-1975; Retor S Geo's Ch Austin TX 1968-1988; Asst R S Mk's Epis Ch San Antonio TX 1965-1968; Asst R Trin Ch San Antonio TX 1964-1965. Internat'l Assoc Near Death Stds 2010; Near Death Experience Resrch Fndn 2001; Sprtl Dir Internat'l 2010. johnwprice38@gmail.com

PRICE, Stephen Marsh (NY) 117 Washington Street, Keene NH 03431 B Zanesville OH 4/26/1941 s James Robert Price & Jane Ann Marsh. BA Muskingum Coll 1964; STB GTS 1967; STM UTS 1970; Cert Amer Fndt of Rel & Psych 1973; DMin Andover Newton TS 1974. D 6/17/1967 Bp Roger W Blanchard P 12/19/1967 Bp Joseph Warren Hutchens. Par Of S Jas Ch Keene NH 1993-1998; S Barth's Ch New York NY 1978-1984; Counslg And Human Dvlpmt Cntr New York NY 1976-1991; Interchurch Counslg Serv New York NY 1974-1976; Cur S Mary's Epis Ch Manchester CT 1967-1969. Auth, "No More Lonely Nights: Overcoming The Hidden Fears That Keep You From Getting m," Putnam, 1987. Amer Associaion Of Mar And Fam Therapists 1973; AAPC 1973. stephenprice4@gmail.com

PRICE, Stephen Wright (Pa) 3724 E Fisherville Rd, Downingtown PA 19335 B Danbury CT 11/6/1942 s Louis Henry Price & Elizabeth Salisbury. BA Wesl 1965; MDiv Ya Berk 1968. D 6/20/1981 P 7/1/1981 Bp Lyman Cunningham Ogilby. m 6/12/1965 Dawn Marie Hauptman.

PRICE, Susan Medlicott (Spok) 6965 Bent Grass Dr, Naples FL 34113 **Asstg P S Mk's Ch Marco Island FL 2010-** B Evansville IN 7/12/1947 B.S. Indiana St U 1969; Ph.D. U of Idaho 1977. D 4/14/1999 Bp Cabell Tennis P 10/16/1999 Bp John Stuart Thornton. m 5/24/1969 William Hugh Price. Asstg P S Jn's Epis Ch Of Kissimmee Kissimmee FL 2005-2009; P S Matt's Ch Prosser WA 1999-2004. sueprice@hughes.net

PRICE, Terrell Wells (Roch) 23 Main St, Geneseo NY 14454 **D S Mich's Ch Geneseo NY 2008-** B Huntington NY 8/17/1936 s John B Price & Isobel R. BS SUNY; Cert EFM Univ. of the So 1980; 5 courses CRDS 1986; Dioc Diac Trng Prog Bex 2007. D 3/29/2008 Bp Jack Marston McKelvey. m 8/22/1959 Dianne Tanner c 2. Dioc Coun Dio Rochester Rochester NY 2008-2010. NAAD 2008; Third OSF 1986; Vergers Gld of Epis Ch 2001-2007. tprice7552@rochester.rr.com

PRICE, William Penn (NC) Po Box 2004, Southern Pines NC 28388 **Died 8/4/2010** B Mayodan NC 3/11/1915 s John Randolph Price & Elcana. BA Guilford Coll 1936; MDiv VTS 1939. D 6/18/1939 P 6/19/1940 Bp Edwin A Penick. m 8/17/2010 Mary Davis c 4.

PRICHARD, Robert Walton (Va) Virginia Theological Seminary, 3737 Seminary Rd., Alexandria VA 22304 **GC Dep Dio Virginia Richmond VA 2006-; Prof of Ch Hist and Instr in Liturg VTS Alexandria VA 2000-** B Washington DC 5/14/1949 s Edgar Allen Prichard & Nancy Montague. BA Pr 1971; MDiv Yale DS 1974; PhD Candler TS Emory U 1983. D 5/24/1974 P 10/1/1976 Bp John Alfred Baden. m 5/27/1973 Marcia Cassidy c 2. Prof Of Ch Hist VTS Alexandria VA 1994-2000; Assoc Prof VTS Alexandria VA 1989-1994; Asst Prof Of Ch Hist VTS Alexandria VA 1983-1989; R Gr Ch Berryville VA 1980-1983; Vic S Mary's Memi Berryville VA 1980-1983; Int All SS Epis Ch Woodbridge VA 1979-1980; Cur S Geo's Epis Ch Arlington VA 1974-1977. Auth, "Cohabiting Couples & Cold Feet," Ch Pub, 2008; Auth, "A Hist Of The Epis Ch, rev. ed.," Morehouse, 1999; Ed, "A Hist Of Ch Schools In The Dio Virginia," Morehouse for Ch Schools in the Dio Virginia, 1999; Auth, "The Nature Of Salvation," U IL Press, 1997; Ed, "A Wholesome Example," Bristol Books, 1993; Auth, "The Bat And The Bp," Morehouse, 1989; Auth, "Readings From The Hist Of The Epis Ch," Morehouse-Barlow, 1986. Amer Hist Assn 2006; Amer Soc of Ch Hist 1989; Conf of Angl Ch Historians 1985; HSEC 1979. Fllshp ECF 1978. rprichard@vts.edu

PRICHARD, Thomas Morgan (Pgh) 809 18th St, Ambridge PA 15003 B Alexandria VA 4/23/1952 s Edgar Allen Prichard & Nancy Montague. BA Ken 1974; MDiv VTS 1978. D 6/3/1978 Bp John Alfred Baden P 3/24/1979 Bp Christoph Keller Jr. m 9/17/2006 Nancy Richey Prichard. Chr Ch Overland Pk KS 2003-2005; Pres - Com Dio Colombia Bogota CO 1986-1987; Stndg Com Dio Colombia Bogota CO 1985-1986; SAMS Ambridge PA 1983-2003; Asst Trin Cathd Little Rock AR 1978-1983. Amer Angl Coun. TOMPRICHARD@SUDANSUNRISE.ORG

PRICKETT, Gerald Stanley (WNC) 360 Asheville School Rd., Asheville NC 28806 B Toccoa, GA 10/29/1947 AB U GA 1969; MDiv Sthrn Bapt TS 1973; MEd Van 1983. D 1/13/2008 P 8/10/2008 Bp Granville Porter Taylor. m 6/12/2000 Patricia Prickett c 4. prickettj@ashevilleschool.org

PRIDEMORE JR, Charles Preston (NY) PO Box 149, Ossining NY 10562 **R Trin Epis Ch Ossining NY 1993-** B Fort Worth TX 10/9/1949 s Charles Preston Pridemore & Patricia Ann. GTS; BA U of No Texas 1971. D 6/9/1984 Bp James Stuart Wetmore P 12/4/1984 Bp Paul Moore Jr. c 1. Cathd Of St Jn The Div New York NY 1984-1993. Ed, *Plnng and Control of Municipal Revenues and Expenditures*, Natl Assn of Accountants, 1984; Ed, *The Capital Expenditure Decision*, Natl Assn of Accountants, 1983. Advsry Bd Epis Chars 1993; Dio New York Prison Mnstry Ntwk 2000; Dio New York Soc Concerns Cmsn 2000; Hudson No Cler 1993; Ossining Agencies Coun 1993; Ossining Mnstrl Assn 1993. cprectortrinity@aol.com

PRIDGEN III, J(ohn) Blaney (USC) 170 Saint Andrews Rd, Columbia SC 29210 B Valdosta GA 2/22/1947 s John Blaney Pridgen & Dorothy. MA U of So Carolina 1975; MDiv STUSo 1979. D 6/9/1979 Bp George Moyer Alexander P 12/19/1981 Bp William Arthur Beckham. m 12/26/1992 Helen Rogers c 2. R S Mary's Ch Columbia SC 1996-2011; R Ch Of Our Sav Rock Hill SC 1988-1996; S Andr's On The Sound Ch Wilmington NC 1984-1988; Chr Ch Greenville SC 1982-1984; S Fran of Assisi Chapin SC 1979-1980. bpridgin@stmaryscolumbiasc.org

PRIEBE JR, Charles M (Del) 124 Highview Ave, Dover DE 19901 B Fulton NY 6/3/1918 s Charles Martin Priebe & Florence Marie. BA Houghton Coll 1947; BD Bex 1950; U of Delaware Newark 1966; MDiv Bex 1973; Oxf - Oxford, Engl 1976. D 6/1/1950 P 12/20/1950 Bp Dudley S Stark. c 2. Chr Ch 1977-1985; Serv Cathd Ch Of S Jn Wilmington DE 1958-1962; R S Jas Epis Ch Newport Newport DE 1954-1976; Asst R Trin Par Wilmington DE 1952-1954; S Jn's Ch Mt Morris NY 1950-1952. "Var columns and arts," *Var newpapers, other Pub*. Hon Cn Cathd of SS Mary, Mich, Geo (Caracas, VZ) Caracas Venezuela 1985.

PRIEST JR, W(illiam) Hunt (Oly) 4400 86th Ave SE, Mercer Island WA 98040 **R Emm Epis Ch Mercer Island WA 2008-** B Mount Sterling KY 6/22/1964 s William Priest & Rebecca. BA Hanover Coll 1986; M.Div. Epis TS of the SW 2005. D 12/21/2004 P 8/21/2005 Bp J(ohn) Neil Alexander. m 9/17/1994 Lisa Lee Priest c 1. Assoc R S Paul's Epis Ch Newnan GA 2005-2008. huntpriest@gmail.com

PRINCE, Christopher Carl (Tex) 8306 Spring Wind Dr, Houston TX 77040 **Died 10/7/2009** B Flint MI 4/14/1945 s Kenneth Carl Prince & Doris Lenore. BA Centenary Coll 1969; MS Texas A&M U 1970; MDiv EDS 1978. D 6/21/1978 P 6/29/1979 Bp J Milton Richardson. ADLMC, Cath. cyfairkid@gmail.com

PRINCE, Elaine (Md) 10913 Knotty Pine Dr, Hagerstown MD 21740 **Epis Mnstrs To The Aging Sykesville MD 2004-** B Indianapolis MD 10/25/1944 d John William Hardwick & Dorothy. Antioch Coll; BA Ohio Wesl 1966; MA Hrod 1979; MDiv EDS 1986. D 6/7/1986 P 3/1/1987 Bp A(lbert) Theodore Eastman. S Anne's Epis Ch Smithsburg MD 2001-2004; S Andr's Ch Clear Sprg MD 2001; Dio Maryland Baltimore MD 1995-2000; Dioc Coun Dio Maryland Baltimore MD 1995-1998; Bp Clagget Cntr Buckeystown MD 1992-1995; Dioc Coun Dio Maryland Baltimore MD 1988-1991; Assoc Chr Ch Columbia MD 1986-1992; Chair Of The CE Com Dio Maryland Baltimore MD 1982-1983; DCE Ch Of The Ascen Westminster MD 1980-1983; Dioc Coun Dio Maryland Baltimore MD 1980-1983; Chair Of Yth And YA Cmsn Dio Maryland Baltimore MD 1980-1982; DCE Emm Ch Baltimore MD 1972-1980; DCE S Barth's Ch Baltimore MD 1970-1972. princee@emaseniorcare.org

PRINGLE, Amy Fay (Los) 5332 Mount Helena Ave, Los Angeles CA 90041 **R S Geo's Par La Can CA 2005-** B Ann Arbor MI 7/6/1962 d David Lee Pringle & Mary Elizabeth. BA U MI 1988; MDiv SWTS 1992. D 6/8/2002 Bp Robert Marshall Anderson P 1/11/2003 Bp Joseph Jon Bruno. m 11/11/2005 Bryan William Jones. Asst S Wilfrid Of York Epis Ch Huntington Bch CA 2002-2005. guruamy@yahoo.com

PRINGLE, Charles Derek (SVa) 419 Elizabeth Lake Dr, Hampton VA 23669 B Clones MO IE 6/2/1946 s Joseph Charles Pringle & Isabel. BA Trin-Dublin IE 1970; MA Trin-Dublin IE 1972; DMin VTS 1996. Trans from Church of Ireland 9/1/1999 Bp David Conner Bane Jr. m 6/18/1976 Pamela Olliffe c 3. Mem of SoVeca Bd Natl Ntwk Of Epis Cler Assn Lynnwood WA 2011; R Emm Epis Ch Hampton VA 1999-2011. Ed, "New Life," *Toronto*, Angl Bk Cntr, 1989; Auth, "Pstr's Page," *Welland Tribune, Ont*, 1985. Alb Inst 1994; Coll of Preachers Participant 2000; SoVECA 2001. Reg Dn Dio Niagara 1995; Hon Cn Dio Niagara 1987. cdpringle@verizon.net

PRINZ, Susan Moore (USC) 6408 Bridgewood Rd, Columbia SC 29206 **S Mich And All Ang' Columbia SC 2010-** B Sanford FL 1/4/1958 d James Gates Moore & Barbara Chapman. BA U of So Carolina-Columbia 1980; MEd U of So Carolina-Columbia 1983; PhD U of So Carolina-Columbia 1998; MDiv VTS 2010. D 6/3/2010 P 6/14/2011 Bp W(illiam) Andrew Waldo. m 5/16/1981 Ronald J Prinz c 1. sprinz42@gmail.com

✠ **PRIOR, Rt Rev Brian N** (Minn) 1730 Clifton Place Suite 201, Minneapolis MN 55403 **Bp Dio Minnesota Minneapolis MN 2010-** B Prosser WA 10/16/1959 s Robert Lincoln Prior & Norma Ann. BA Whitworth U 1984; MDiv CDSP 1987. D 6/20/1987 P 4/22/1989 Bp Leigh Wallace Jr Con 2/13/2010 for Minn. m 7/25/1987 Staci H Hubbard c 2. R Ch Of The Resurr Spokane Vlly WA 1996-2009; Dir of Educ and Dvlpmt Dio Spokane Spokane WA 1990-1996; Assoc R S Steph's Epis Ch Spokane WA 1987-1990. Auth, *Epis Curric for Yth*; Auth, *Yth & YA Resource Bk*. brian.p@episcopalmn.org

PRIOR, John Gregory (RI) 100 Sakonnet Point Road, Little Compton RI 02837 **Int S Lk's Epis Ch E Greenwich RI 2010-** B Providence RI 1/20/1944 s Gerald Joseph Prior & Emma. BA Providence Coll 1965; MDiv STUSo 1983; DMin STUSo 2005. D 6/29/1983 P 6/24/1984 Bp C(hristopher) FitzSimons Allison. m 11/12/1966 Anna de Brux c 4. R S Andr's By The Sea Little Compton RI 2002-2009; Dn Beaufort Convoc Dio So Carolina Charleston SC 1994-2002; Stndg Com Dio So Carolina Charleston SC 1994-1999; R All SS Ch Hilton Hd Island SC 1993-2002; R S Paul's Epis Ch Conway SC 1985-1993; Stndg Com Dio So Carolina Charleston SC 1985-1989; Asst S Jas Ch Charleston SC 1983-1985. frpriorinri@aol.com

PRIOR, Randall Leavitt (Va) 9515 Holly Prospect Ct, Burke VA 22015 B Jacksonville FL 9/22/1945 s Lyman Wolcott Prior & Gladys Victoria. BA W&L 1967; BD VTS 1970; DMin Estrn Bapt TS 1990. D 6/24/1970 Bp Edward Hamilton West P 4/16/1971 Bp George Mosley Murray. m 12/29/1966 Clotilde V Van Aken c 3. Adj Fac VTS Alexandria VA 1992-1994; R S Andr's Ch Burke VA 1974-2010; Asst S Steph's Ch Richmond VA 1971-1974; P-in-c S Matt's Chipley FL 1970-1971; P-in-c S Mich's Ch Gainesville FL 1970-1971. "Faith Based Serv Prog in the Publ Sector: Illustrations from Virginia," Participatory Governance Plnng Conflict Mediation, 2004. AAPC 1983; CFLE, Natl Coun on Fam Relatns 1990. rprior1@verizon.net

PRITCHARD, David Gatlin (Ct) 16 Ashlar Vlg, Wallingford CT 06492 B Washington DC 12/12/1927 s David Dennison Pritchard & Elizabeth Porter. BA CUA 1951; GTS 1954. D 6/12/1954 Bp Angus Dun P 12/18/1954 Bp Norman B Nash. m 6/26/1954 Helen L Hollis c 4. P-in-c Chr Ch Bethlehem CT 1997-2008; Int Calv St Geo's Epis Ch Bridgeport CT 1995-1996; R Chr Ch Waterbury CT 1983-1994; Asst S Mk's Ch New Britain CT 1982-1983; Vic St Gabr's Ch E Berlin CT 1978-1983; Cmncatns Off Dio Connecticut Hartford CT 1978-1982; R H Apos Savannah GA 1970-1978; R Calv Ch Americus GA 1962-1970; R Chr Ch Augusta GA 1958-1962; Vic S Mary's Epis Ch Madison FL 1956-1958; Cur S Anne's Ch Lowell MA 1954-1956. ECom 1973-1983; Epis Curs 1976. dpritchard@ashlarvlg.org

PRITCHARTT, Paul Waddell (Dal) 106 Commons Dr, Spartanburg SC 29302 B Memphis TN 10/11/1929 s A Van Court Pritchartt & Winifred. BA SW At Memphis 1958; MDiv STUSo 1961; DD Nash 1992. D 6/18/1961 P 5/1/1962 Bp John Vander Horst. m 10/1/1955 Dale Smith c 2. R Ch Of The Incarn Dallas TX 1974-1992; R S Jn's Ch Savannah GA 1970-1973; R Chr Ch Martinsville VA 1967-1970; Asst Ch Of The Adv Spartanburg SC 1964-1967; Sum Prchr All SS Epis Chap Linville NC 1960-1992.

PRITCHER, Joan Jean (At) 1098 Saint Augustine Pl Ne, Atlanta GA 30306 **Int H Trin Par Decatur GA 2010-** B Atlanta,GA 1/21/1954 d Gerald Marquis Pritcher & Jeannine Ellis. BA Tift Coll 1975; MRE SW Sem 1976; PhD Emory U 1985. D 6/4/1994 P 12/10/1994 Bp Frank Kellogg Allan. Ch S Mich

P

The Archangel Lexington KY 2008-2010; Chr Ch Macon GA 2005-2006; S Aid's Epis Ch Milton GA 2003-2004; The Epis Ch Of The Adv Madison GA 2002-2003; Ch Of The Atone Sandy Sprg GA 1994-2002. joanpritcher@aol.com

PRITCHETT JR, Harry Houghton (NY) 1290 Peachtree Battle Ave Nw, Atlanta GA 30327 B Tuscaloosa AL 10/11/1935 s Harry Pritchett & Margaret. BA U of Alabama 1957; MDiv VTS 1964; DD Cntr Coll 1981; DD STUSo 2007. D 6/24/1964 P 5/16/1965 Bp George Mosley Murray. m 9/1/1956 Allison McQueen c 3. Dn Cathd Of St Jn The Div New York NY 1997-2001; R All SS Epis Ch Atlanta GA 1981-1997; Dio Alabama Birmingham AL 1975-1981; St Thos Epis Ch Huntsville AL 1975-1979; Dir Field Educ The TS at The U So Sewanee TN 1975-1979; Asst R S Lk's Epis Ch Birmingham AL 1964-1967. Auth, *God is a Surprise Songbook*; Auth, *Morning Run: Sabbatical Reflections on the Ch & the City*; Auth, *Patterns for Par Dvlpmt*; Auth, *Sermons That Wk*. Phi Beta Kappa. harryandallison@aol.com

PRITCHETT JR, James Hill (WNC) 209 Nut Hatch Loop, Arden NC 28704 B Atlanta GA 7/12/1956 s James Hill Pritchett & Anne C. W&L 1976; BA U GA 1978; JD U GA 1981; MDiv STUSo 1991. D 6/8/1991 P 1/25/1992 Bp Frank Kellogg Allan. m 11/17/1984 Charlotte J Perry c 2. GC Dep Dio Wstrn No Carolina Asheville NC 2009; GC Dep Dio Atlanta Atlanta GA 2006; Chair, New Ch Starts Cmsn Dio Atlanta Atlanta GA 2005-2007; Co-Chair, Cong Growth & Dev. Dio Atlanta Atlanta GA 2002-2006; Co-Chair, Bp Search Com Dio Atlanta Atlanta GA 2000-2001; R S Jn's Coll Pk GA 1998-2007; Assoc R All SS Epis Ch Atlanta GA 1992-1998; Assoc R The Epis Ch Of S Ptr And S Paul Marietta GA 1991-1992. Preaching Awd U So, TS 1991; Ord of the Coif hon Soc UGA Sch of Law 1981; Golden Key hon Soc UGA Chapt 1978; Phi Kappa Phi hon Soc UGA Chapt 1978; Phi Beta Kappa U of GA Chapt 1978. jimpritchett1@mac.com

PRITTS, Clarence Edward (NJ) 7 E Maple Ave, Merchantville NJ 08109 B Baltimore MD 6/16/1946 s Clarence Otis Pritts & Eleanor Mary. BA Frostburg St U 1968; MLa Jn Hopkins U 1971; MDiv GTS 1984. D 6/16/1984 Bp A(lbert) Theodore Eastman P 2/8/1985 Bp David Keller Leighton Sr. R Gr Ch Merchantville NJ 1995-2007; R Chr Ch W River MD 1988-1995; Cur S Jn's Ch W Hartford CT 1984-1988. wce1893@aol.com

PRIVETTE, William Herbert (EC) 1119 Hendricks Ave., Jacksonville NC 28540 B Salisbury NC 12/30/1949 s William Cecil Privette & Lena Wellman. BA Duke 1972; MDiv STUSo 1975. D 6/24/1975 P 3/25/1976 Bp Hunley Agee Elebash. m 5/20/1972 Karen P Perten c 3. R S Anne's Epis Ch Jacksonville NC 2002-2006; Dioc Coun Dio Springfield Springfield IL 1993-2002; R Chr Ch Springfield IL 1992-2002; Com Dio Springfield Springfield IL 1992-1995; Congreg Dvpmt Dio Sthrn Ohio Cincinnati OH 1986-1991; Assoc R S Paul's Epis Ch Dayton OH 1985-1992; S Thos' Epis Ch Ahoskie NC 1981-1985; Chr Epis Ch Hope Mills NC 1979-1981; Gd Shpd Epis Ch Fayetteville NC 1978; Com Dio E Carolina Kinston NC 1976-1982; Asst S Jn's Epis Ch Fayetteville NC 1975-1978. bill@turkeyhuntbooks.com

PRIVITERA, Linda Fisher (Mass) 21 Marathon St, Arlington MA 02474 B Pittsburgh PA 10/30/1946 d Cecil Blaine Fisher & Jean Elisabeth. BS/RN Med Coll of Virginia 1968; MDiv Ya Berk 1986. D 6/13/1987 P 1/21/1988 Bp Arthur Edward Walmsley. c 3. R Ch Of Our Sav Arlington MA 1997-2005; Assoc R S Mk's Ch Southborough MA 1995-1996; Cler Sexual Misconduct Taskforce Dio Wstrn Massachusetts Springfield MA 1993-1994; Dio Wstrn Massachusetts Springfield MA 1990-1995; Assoc All SS Ch Worcester MA 1990-1994; Prov I Aids Taskforce Dio Wstrn Massachusetts Springfield MA 1990-1993; Asst to R All SS Epis Ch Meriden CT 1987-1990. Auth, "Reviving Ophelia - Girls Ldrshp Experience," *Journ Of Wmn Mnstrs*, 1998; Auth, "The Trees," *Angl Dig*, 1994. NCA, Alb Inst; Trst Ma Bible Soc 1990-1995. Altrusa Club Serv Awd; Wmn Awd In Ldrshp Meriden 89 Ywca. lprivitera@eds.edu

PROBERT, Walter Leslie (Mil) 125 Cedar Ridge Dr, West Bend WI 53095 B Milwaukee WI 1/22/1925 s Walter Jordan Probert & Mildred Adele. BS Marq 1950. D 11/6/1960 Bp Donald H V Hallock. m 8/20/1949 Jane Beverly Lundquist c 5. Asst S Mk's Ch Milwaukee WI 1978-1990; Asst S Jas Epis Ch Milwaukee WI 1970-1977; Asst S Mart's Ch Brown Deer WI 1968-1970; Asst S Jn Ch/Mision San Juan Milwaukee WI 1960-1961. wlprobert@charter.net

PROBST, David Charles (At) 139 Country Club Rd, Macon GA 31210 **Assoc R Chr Ch Macon GA 2007-** B Columbia GA 9/26/1966 s William Probst & Gayle Balte. BA Berry Coll, Rome GA 1989; MDiv Candler TS, Emory U 2007. D 12/21/2006 P 9/14/2007 Bp J(ohn) Neil Alexander. m 1/20/1990 Marie Patellis Probst c 2. david@christchurchmacon.com

PROCTOR, F(rederick) Gregory (Miss) 4220 Oakridge Dr, Jackson MS 39216 B Lakeland FL 2/26/1952 s William Con Proctor & Ruth Shaw. BA No Carolina St U 1975; MDiv VTS 1993. D 6/19/1993 Bp Huntington Williams Jr P 6/22/1994 Bp Robert Carroll Johnson Jr. m 11/18/1972 Deborah McQuaid c 2. R S Paul's Epis Ch Meridian MS 2003-2009; Dioc Exec Com Dio Mississippi Jackson MS 2002-2005; Dio Mississippi Jackson MS 1998; R All SS Epis Ch Grenada MS 1997-2003; Asst to R S Cyp's Ch Oxford NC 1993-1997; Asst to R S Steph's Ch Oxford NC 1993-1997. Associated Parishes for Mssn & Liturg 1993. fgproc@gmail.com

PROCTOR, Judith Harris (Va) St Paul's Episcopal Church, 228 S Pitt St, Alexandria VA 22314 **S Paul's Epis Ch Alexandria VA 2001-** B Baltimore MD 11/12/1944 d Charles David Harris & Janet Bartam. BA Goucher Coll 1968; MS U of Maryland 1992; LCSWC U of Maryland 1994; MDiv VTS 1996. D 6/23/2000 P 4/17/2002 Bp Hays H. Rockwell. m 8/2/1969 Kenneth Donald Proctor c 3. Auth, "Liturg Skirmishes in the Dio Maryland, Angl and Epis Hist v. LSVIII," *no. 4*, 1999; Auth, "Therapists and the Clincl Use of Forgiveness, The Amer Journ of Fam Ther, v.21," *number 2*, 1993. judith@stpaulsalexandria.com

PROCTOR, Richard G (At) 3738 Butler Rd, Glyndon MD 21136 **S Jn's Ch Reisterstown MD 2011-** B Tallahassee FL 12/19/1972 s Maurice Julian Proctor & Elizabeth Gillespie. BA Florida St U 1996; MDiv Columbia TS 2009; STM The GTS 2011. D 12/18/2010 P 6/26/2011 Bp J(ohn) Neil Alexander. m 7/25/2010 Emily Rose Martin. proc72@gmail.com

PROFFITT, Darrel D (Tex) 1225 W Grand Pkwy S, Katy TX 77494 **R Ch Of The H Apos Katy TX 2007-** B Oklahoma City OK 1/21/1956 s Jimmy Darrel Proffitt & Patsy Darline. BS U of Kansas 1979; MDiv SWTS 1991; DMin SWTS 1999. D 6/15/1991 P 12/14/1991 Bp William Edward Smalley. m 8/6/1979 Julie M Mills c 3. R S Marg's Ch Lawr KS 1999-2007; R Gr Ch Sterling IL 1993-1999; Assoc Ch Of The H Comf Kenilworth IL 1991-1993. Doctoral Stds, "Dissertation," *It is No Sm Pity When We Fail to Understand Ourselves: Seeking Excellence in Congregations*, Seabury-Wstrn, 1999. Merit Awd SWTS 2004. darrel@holyapostles.cc

PROFFITT III, John (Ark) Saudi Aramco, P.O. Box 1888, Ras Tanura AR 31311 Saudi Arabia **The Centeburry Grp Dhahran 31311 2008-** B Waynesboro VA 8/24/1951 s John Roscoe Proffitt & Sybil Joyce. BS Emory U 1973; MS U of Memphis 1975; MDiv STUSo 1990. D 6/16/1990 P 12/1/1990 Bp Robert Jefferson Hargrove Jr. m 6/30/1973 Margaret P Pittenger c 2. R S Mk's Epis Ch Little Rock AR 2003-2008; S Jas Epis Ch Baton Rouge LA 2001-2003; S Paul's Ch New Orleans LA 1999-2001; R S Jas Epis Ch Shreveport LA 1992-1998; Trin Ch Tallulah LA 1990-1992. frocki@aol.com

PROUD, James (Pa) 111 W Walnut Ln, Philadelphia PA 19144 **Vic S Dav's Ch Philadelphia PA 1997-** B Little Falls NY 5/16/1931 s Cecil James Proud & Elsa Blair. BA Ob 1953; LLB Ya 1956. D 6/12/1965 P 12/18/1965 Bp Horace W B Donegan. m 9/11/1987 Kathleen Pasco. Assoc S Jn's Ch New York NY 1976-1988; Assoc Ch Of The H Comm Paterson NJ 1972-1976; P-in-c Gr Ch (W Farms) Bronx NY 1970-1972; Assoc S Edm's Ch Bronx NY 1967-1970; Assoc S Simeon's Ch Bronx NY 1967-1970; Asst S Ptr's Ch New York NY 1965-1967. Ed, "Jn Woolman and the Affrs of Truth: The Jrnlst's Essays, Epistles, and Ephemera," *same*, Inner Light Books, 2010; Auth, "Jn Woolman and the Affrs of Truth". james.proud@verizon.net

✠ **PROVENZANO, Rt Rev Lawrence C** (LI) Episcopal Diocese of Long Island, 36 Cathedral Avenue, Garden City NY 11530 **Bp Dio Long Island Garden City NY 2009-; Pres/CEO Epis Hlth Serv Bethpage NY 2009-** B Brooklyn NY 1/25/1955 s Larry Provenzano & Marie. BS SUNY 1980; MDiv Chr The King Sem 1982. Rec from Roman Catholic 12/22/1984 as Priest Bp George Nelson Hunt III Con 9/23/2009 for LI. m 1/8/1983 Jeanne M Ross c 3. Dep-Gc Dio Wstrn Massachusetts Springfield MA 2000-2003; Chair - Fin Com Dio Wstrn Massachusetts Springfield MA 1995-1998; Del Prov I Syn Dio Wstrn Massachusetts Springfield MA 1989-1995; Dio Wstrn Massachusetts Springfield MA 1987-2009; Bp S Andr's Ch Longmeadow MA 1987-2009; R S Jn's Ch No Adams MA 1987-1994; Asst R Chr Ch Westerly RI 1984-1987; Litgurg Com Dio Rhode Island Providence RI 1984-1987; Liturg Com Dio Rhode Island Providence RI 1984-1987. Auth, "A Model Of Priestly Mnstry - The Pachomius Proj," *Sabbatical Wk*, 1999; Auth, "Reflections On The Litugies Of H Week," *The St. Jn'S Record (Par Pub.)*, 1988. Angl Soc 1986; Massachusetts Corps Of Fire Chapl 1999. Citizen Of The Year - For Outstanding Cmnty Serv Town Of Longmeadow 2002; Recognition Awd - For Serv w The Fire Dept At "Ground Zero" Fed Emergency Managment Admin 2001. lprovenzano@dioceseli.org

PROVINE, (Marion) Kay (Minn) 3424 Willow Ave, White Bear Lake MN 55110 B Tallulah LA 2/16/1949 d Henry Sproles Provine & Dorothy Kayser. BA LSU 1972; MDiv GTS 2005. D 6/8/2006 P 12/21/2006 Bp James Louis Jelinek. c 3. kprovine@ehomesmn.org

PRUEHER JR, Roi Francis (Az) 19303 N New Tradition Rd Apt 204, Sun City West AZ 85375 B La Crosse WI 6/25/1929 s Roi Prueher & Gertrude G. BS USNA 1952; MS U IL 1956; PhD U IL 1967. D 10/19/1996 Bp William Charles Wantland. m 6/21/1952 Margaret M Prueher c 2. D Ch Of The Adv Sun City W AZ 2008-2010; D All SS Of The Desert Epis Ch Sun City AZ 1999-2008; D Ch Of The Adv Sun City W AZ 1996-1997. Eta Kappa Nu.

PRUITT, Albert Wesley (CGC) 729 Brown Pl, Decatur GA 30030 B Anderson SC 1/1/1940 s James Ernest Pruitt & Jennie. BA Emory U 1961; MD Emory U 1965; MDiv GTS 2000; STM GTS 2000. D 6/3/2000 P 2/2/2001 Bp Charles Farmer Duvall. m 6/3/1961 Ellanor Frances Hanson c 1. S Jn's Ch Pensacola FL 2010; R S Fran Of Assisi Gulf Breeze FL 2002-2009; Cur S Chris's Ch

Pensacola FL 2000-2002. Alpha Omega Alpha Med Soc; Amer Acad Of Pediatrics; AMA. prugts422@aol.com

PRUITT, Allen (At) 5825 Greenlawn Dr, Bethesda MD 20814 **R S Mk's Epis Ch Lagrange GA 2010-** B Rome GA 5/21/1980 s Welton Lee Pruitt & Jean R. BS Shorter Coll Rome GA 2002; MDiv VTS 2007. D 12/21/2006 P 7/1/2007 Bp J(ohn) Neil Alexander. Asst S Fran Epis Ch Great Falls VA 2007-2010. allenpruitt@gmail.com

PRUITT, Alonzo Clemons (Va) Saint Philip's Church, 2900 Hanes Ave, Richmond VA 23222 **Vic Calv Ch Hanover VA 2011-** B Chicago IL 2/20/1951 s Alonzo Pruitt & Louise. BA Roosevelt U 1975; MS U IL 1978; MDiv SWTS 1984; DMin GTF 1998. D 6/16/1984 Bp Quintin Ebenezer Primo Jr P 4/1/1985 Bp James Winchester Montgomery. m 2/21/2003 Linda Powell c 2. R S Phil's Ch Richmond VA 2004-2009; Alt Dep G C Dio Long Island Garden City NY 2003; Stndg Com Dio Long Island Garden City NY 2001-2004; Dn Dio Long Island Garden City NY 1998-2001; Bdgt Com Dio Long Island Garden City NY 1997-2000; S Phil's Ch Brooklyn NY 1993-2009; Adj Prof of Mnstry SWTS Evanston IL 1989-1991; S Geo/S Mths Ch Chicago IL 1984-1993; Dio Chicago Chicago IL 1984. Auth, "Recruitment Of Minority Cler," *Hisp Ministers Journ*, 1989. Tertiary Of The Soc Of S Fran 1982; UBE 1994. DD St Paul Coll 1996; Hon Cn St Peters Cathd Dio Kigezi 1994; Cotton Memi Awd SWTS 1984; Field Prize SWTS 1984. dracpruitt@comcast.net

PRUITT JR, George Russell (Md) 1246 Summit Ave SW, Roanoke VA 24015 B Atlanta GA 2/7/1936 s George Russell Pruitt & Nell Jane. Truett McConnell Jr Coll 1956; Georgia St U 1959; LTh VTS 1974. D 6/10/1974 Bp Robert Poland Atkinson P 2/22/1975 Bp Wilburn Camrock Campbell. m 9/8/1956 Peggy R Reese c 3. R Ch Of The H Cross Cumberland MD 1991-1997; Vic S Mich's Epis Ch Easley SC 1986-1991; R Chr Ch Norway ME 1982-1986; S Andr's Ch Clifton Forge VA 1978-1980; R Emm Ch Covington VA 1976-1982; Vic S Ann's Ch New Martinsville WV 1974-1976. padrep@cox.net

PRUITT, Mark James (O) Po Box 1910, Newport RI 02840 **R S Paul's Ch Akron OH 2007-** B Pittsburgh PA 6/9/1958 s James Jesse Pruitt & Ellen Marie. U of Cambridge; BA Wheaton Coll 1980; MA VTS 1991. D 9/29/1992 Bp Stephen Whitfield Sykes P 9/1/1993 Bp Alden Moinet Hathaway. m 6/24/1989 Rebecca Jo Shaffer. S Geo's Sch Newport RI 1999-2007; R S Ptr's Epis Ch Butler PA 1995-1999; Dir Of Yth Mnstry S Jas Ch Potomac MD 1987-1992. ECF 1992-1995. mpruitt@stpaulsakron.org

PRYNE, Carla Valentine (Oly) 1745 Ne 103rd St, Seattle WA 98125 **R Ch Of The H Sprt Vashon WA 2010-; Dio Olympia Seattle WA 2006-; BEC Dio Olympia Seattle WA 2006-** B Chicago IL 3/12/1954 d Michael James Valentine & Mary Catherine. BA Bow 1976; MDiv Ya Berk 1979. D 7/21/1983 P 7/24/1984 Bp Robert Hume Cochrane. m 8/13/2000 Eric Bruce Pryne c 2. P-in-c Ch Of The Ascen Seattle WA 2008-2010; S Alb's Ch Edmonds WA 2007; Assoc Emm Epis Ch Mercer Island WA 1994-2004; Exec Dir - Earth Mnstry Dio Olympia Seattle WA 1992-1996; Earth Mnstry Seattle WA 1992-1995; Asst S Steph's Epis Ch Seattle WA 1992-1994; Chr Initiation Dio Olympia Seattle WA 1988-1991; Cn Pstr & Eductr S Mk's Cathd Seattle WA 1988-1991; Pres Stndg Com Dio Olympia Seattle WA 1987-1988; Bd Dir Dioc Ts Dio Olympia Seattle WA 1985-1988; D S Mk's Cathd Seattle WA 1983-1984. Auth, "2 Poems By Sappho," *Gk Attitudes*, 1976. "Renewing Hope" Awd Yale DS 2008; Conservation Awd Washington Wildlife Fed 1997; Bloedel Fell 1995; Bloedel Reserve 1995; Environ Of Year Seattle Audubon 1995. cpryne@zipcon.com

PUCKETT, David Forrest King (Tex) 12535 Perthshire Rd, Houston TX 77024 **R H Sprt Epis Ch Houston TX 2002-** B San Angelo TX 3/12/1950 s Henry Clay Tompkins Puckett & Mary-Jack. BA Texas Wesl 1974; MDiv VTS 1977. D 6/22/1977 Bp Roger Howard Cilley P 6/22/1978 Bp J Milton Richardson. m 11/29/1997 Elizabeth Dabney c 2. Dn S Jn's Cathd Albuquerque NM 1992-2001; Stndg Com Dio The Rio Grande Albuquerque NM 1991-2000; Stndg Com Dio NW Texas Lubbock TX 1986-1992; R Ch Of The Heav Rest Abilene TX 1985-1992; R S Jas' Epis Ch La Grange TX 1980-1985; Asst S Dunst's Epis Ch Houston TX 1977-1980. rector@hsechurch.org

PUCKETT, Douglas Arnold (USC) 111 Aiken Rd # 323, Graniteville SC 29829 **R S Paul's Ch Graniteville SC 1991-** B Reidsville NC 12/19/1952 s Joel H Puckett & Doris S. AA Rockingham Cmnty Coll 1973; BA Gardner-Webb Coll 1975; Luth Theol Sthrn Sem 1978; MDiv GTS 1979; BA Augusta St U 1995. Trans from Anglican Church of Canada 9/1/1981 Bp William Arthur Beckham. m 6/9/1979 Linda B Bedenbaugh c 2. Vic S Geo's Ch Stanley VA 1982-1991; Vic S Paul's Ch Shenandoah VA 1982-1991; Asst S Alb's Ch Lexington SC 1981-1982; Assoc S Jn's Epis Ch Columbia SC 1980-1981. Auth, "The Ord of the Thousandfold," Forw Mvmt Press, 1988. Alpha Chi Soc 1974. dap@gforcecable.com

PUCKLE, Donne Erving (Az) 125 E Kayetan Dr, Sierra Vista AZ 85635 B London England UK 6/17/1940 s Raymond Donne Aufrere Puckle & Elizabeth. AA Phoenix Jr Coll Phoenix AZ 1960; BA Arizona St U 1963; MDiv Bex 1966; Cert Pima Cmnty Coll 1993; MC U of Phoenix 1994. D 6/22/1966 P 12/26/1966 Bp J(ohn) Joseph Meakins Harte. c 2. S Steph's Ch Sierra Vista AZ 2000-2005; P-in-c S Steph's Epis Ch Douglas AZ 1996-2005; Vic S Jn's Epis Ch Bisbee AZ 1993-2002; RurD Dio Eau Claire Eau Claire WI 1985-1990; R Chr Ch Chippewa Falls WI 1981-1990; Vic S Simeon's Ch Stanley WI 1981-1990; Dio Springfield Springfield IL 1979-1981; R Trin Epis Ch Mattoon IL 1979-1981; Asst Chr Ch Par La Crosse WI 1976-1978; Gr Epis Ch Lake Havasu City AZ 1976; Vic Gr Epis Ch Lake Havasu City AZ 1973-1976; Vic S Phil's Preaching Sta Parker AZ 1973-1976; Liturg Off Dio Arizona Phoenix AZ 1969-1976; Vic S Jn's Epis Ch Bisbee AZ 1967-1973; Vic S Paul's Ch Tombstone AZ 1967-1973. Auth, "Article," *Arizona Ch Record*; Auth, "Prayers for Adv," *Christmas and Epiph*, Forw Mvmt Press; Auth, "Handbook," *Handbook for Altar lGuild Proposed Bk of Common Pryr*. SSC 1980. padre1226@cox.net

PUGH, Charles Dean (Md) 128 S Hilltop Rd, Catonsville MD 21228 **D Trin Ch Glen Arm MD 1998-** B VA 6/19/1937 s Charles M Pugh & Martha. Catonsville Cmnty Coll; U Of Baltimore; EFM STUSo 1997. D 6/14/1997 Bp Charles Lindsay Longest. m 12/15/1958 Mary Ives Maxwell.

PUGH II, Joel Wilson (Ark) 9, The Close, Salisbury SP12E B Great Britain (UK) B Little Rock AR 7/28/1932 s Robert Dean Pugh & Mary Louise. BA U So 1954; BD STUSo 1957; Oxf 1960; DD STUSo 1988. D 6/29/1957 P 3/17/1958 Bp Robert Raymond Brown. m 7/15/1967 Caroline Mary Stewart Maud c 2. Chapl Chr Memi Chap Hobe Sound FL 1995-2002; The TS at The U So Sewanee TN 1987-1990; TESM Ambridge PA 1980-1994; Dep GC Dio Arkansas Little Rock AR 1979-1991; Dn Trin Cathd Little Rock AR 1977-1994; Pres Alum The TS at The U So Sewanee TN 1975-1977; R The Falls Ch Epis Falls Ch VA 1972-1977; D-in-c Ch Of The Gd Shpd Little Rock AR 1957-1958. Fllshp of Witness.

PUGH III, Willard Jerome (HB) 1700 E 56th St Apt 3806, Chicago IL 60637 B Louisville KY 12/31/1945 s Willard J Pugh & Jane C. BA Ken 1967; MDiv EDS 1970; PhD U Chi 1990. D 6/27/1970 P 5/1/1971 Bp John Harris Burt. c 1. Assoc S Mart's Ch Chagrin Falls OH 1973-1976; Cur S Andr's Epis Ch Elyria OH 1971-1973.

PUGLIESE, Richard A (Spr) 744 Parker Road, West Glover VT 05875 B Los Angeles CA 5/6/1943 s Dominick Michael Pugliese & Equina. BA U of Washington 1966; California St U 1967; MDiv GTS 1970. D 6/24/1970 P 1/31/1971 Bp Charles F Hall. c 3. The Cathd Ch Of S Paul Springfield IL 1984-1991; Stndg Com Dio Springfield Springfield IL 1983-1987; Dep GC Dio Springfield Springfield IL 1982-1991; Secy Dio Dio Springfield Springfield IL 1981-1984; COM Dio Springfield Springfield IL 1980-1986; Vic S Alb's Epis Ch Olney IL 1977-1983; Vic S Mary's Ch Robinson IL 1977-1983; R S Mary's Epis Par Northfield VT 1973-1977; Cur S Paul's Ch Concord NH 1970-1973. Auth, *Hist of S Matt's Ch*, S Matt's Ch Press, 2002. loonsongoldenpond@hotmail.com

PUGLIESE, William Joseph (Ia) 108 Eden Way Ct, Cranberry Twp PA 16066 **Int S Brendan's Epis Ch Sewickley PA 2008-** B New Kensington PA 5/10/1942 s William Joseph Pugliese & Anne Marie. BA Pontifical Coll Josephinum 1965; BD Pontifical Coll Josephinum 1969; DMin Drew U 1980. Rec from Roman Catholic 2/1/1975 as Deacon Bp Wilburn Camrock Campbell. m 2/14/1987 Arlena Ingraham c 5. Chr Ch Cedar Rapids IA 2003-2008; Stndg Com Dio Spokane Spokane WA 2001-2003; R S Dav's Ch Spokane WA 1996-2003; Dio Spokane Spokane WA 1996; R Trin Memi Ch Warren PA 1991-1995; R Trin Ch Parkersburg WV 1985-1991; Dio W Virginia Charleston WV 1985-1988; S Jn Wheeling WV 1980-1985; Dioc Coun Dio W Virginia Charleston WV 1980-1983; Vic Olde S Jn's Ch Colliers WV 1975-1980; Ch Of The Gd Shpd Follansbee WV 1975-1979. Auth, *EDEO News*, 1991; Auth, *Epis-RC Par for WV: Proposed Model*, 1980. wjpugliese@aol.com

PULIMOOTIL, Cherian Pilo (Va) 6744 S Kings Hwy, Alexandria VA 22306 B 11/28/1940 s Pilo C Pulimootil & Annamma. BA Bridgewater Coll 1975; MA Middle Tennessee St U 1978; DMin The TS at The U So 1986. D 6/6/2009 Bp Peter James Lee P 12/6/2009 Bp Shannon Sherwood Johnston. m 10/23/1977 Ann Pulimootil c 2. D S Mk's Ch Alexandria VA 2009-2010. cheriapp@hotmail.com

PULLIAM, James Millard (WMo) 80 Council Trl, Warrensburg MO 64093 B Hannibal MO 2/26/1928 s Albert Franklin Pulliam & Wilma Eubank. BA U of Missouri 1954; MA U of Missouri 1955; MDiv STUSo 1970. D 5/19/1970 P 5/9/1971 Bp John M Allin. m 6/19/1954 Sandra Chullino c 5. R Chr Ch Warrensburg MO 1978-1993; Vic Calv Epis Ch Cleveland MS 1973-1978; Vic Gr Ch Rosedale MS 1973-1978; Cur S Bernards Ch Okolona MS 1970-1973; Cur S Jn's Ch Aberdeen MS 1970-1973. jspulliam@yahoo.com

PULLIAM JR, James Phillip (Va) Po Box 12042, Richmond VA 23241 **Died 11/2/2009** B Roanoke VA 3/12/1923 s James Phillip Pulliam & Margaret Inez. BA Wheaton Coll 1944; BD EDS 1962; MDiv EDS 1972. D 6/9/1962 Bp Robert Fisher Gibson Jr P 8/1/1963 Bp John P Craine. Auth, "Living Ch". Chapl Ord Of S Lk The Physcn.

PUMMILL, Joe H (Cal) 2550 Dana St Apt 2D, Berkeley CA 94704 B Covina CA 2/15/1926 s Joseph Howard Pummill & Volora Jean. AA Mt San Antonio Coll 1953; BA U CA at Santa Barbara 1955; MDiv Ya Berk 1958; EDS 1970. D 6/16/1958 P 2/1/1959 Bp Donald J Campbell. m 11/14/1990 Doris YS Kim c 2. P Ch Of Our Sav Mill Vlly CA 2000-2001; Asst The Epis Ch Of S Mary

The Vrgn San Francisco CA 1991-1998; Mgr The Bp's Ranch Healdsburg CA 1983-1988; Asst The Epis Ch Of S Mary The Vrgn San Francisco CA 1982-1983; Vic Epis Ch On W Kaua'i Eleele HI 1977-1979; Chair Of The Com On Campus Mnstry Dio Hawaii Honolulu HI 1976-1977; Asst The Par Of S Clem Honolulu HI 1975-1977; Chair Of The Dept Of CSR Dio Hawaii Honolulu HI 1970-1975; R S Mk's Ch Honolulu HI 1960-1969; Cur Trin Epis Ch Santa Barbara CA 1958-1960. joepummill@mac.com

PUMPHREY, Charles Michael (Ia) Naval Medical Center, Portsmouth, 620 John Paul Jones Cir, Portsmouth VA 23701 **Off Of Bsh For ArmdF New York NY 1993-** B Baltimore MD 7/22/1956 s Charles Merritt Pumphrey & Dorothy May. BA Randolph-Macon Coll 1978; MDiv VTS 1981. D 6/27/1981 Bp David Keller Leighton Sr P 1/1/1982 Bp Paul Moore Jr. m 8/12/1978 Donna Jean Gambill c 3. Curs Secy Dio Iowa Des Moines IA 1992-1993; Cmncatn Cmsn Dio Iowa Des Moines IA 1991-1993; Vic S Paul's Ch Durant IA 1991-1993; R S Matt's Par Oakland MD 1986-1991; P-in-c S Mary's Epis Ch Tyaskin MD 1982-1986; Cur S Ptr's Ch Salisbury MD 1981-1986. Achievement Medal Usn. cmpumphrey@mar.med.navy.mil

PUMPHREY, David William (O) 2385 Covington Rd, Apt 201, Akron OH 44313 B Warren OH 4/23/1927 s Claude Emory Pumphrey & Sarah. BBA U Cinc 1949; MDiv Bex 1955. D 6/18/1955 Bp Nelson Marigold Burroughs P 1/15/1956 Bp Beverley D Tucker. m 1/5/1951 Sarah Jeannine Appleton c 3. Dio Ohio Cleveland OH 1995-1998; Int S Jn's Epis Ch Cuyahoga Falls OH 1992-1993; ExCoun Dio Ohio Cleveland OH 1989-1992; Sprtl Dir Curs Dio Ohio Cleveland OH 1977-1988; Assoc S Paul's Ch Akron OH 1974-1992; Assoc Ch Of The Redeem Houston TX 1973-1974; R Ch Of S Thos Berea OH 1965-1973; R S Paul's Ch Steubenville OH 1960-1964; Cur Chr Ch Shaker Heights OH 1955-1960. Int Mnstry Ntwk. davidwpumphrey@sbcglobal.net

PUMPHREY, John B (WMo) 5519 Chadwick Road, Fairway KS 66205 **S Barn Ch Wilmington DE 2011-** B Warren OH 4/30/1947 s James Rezin Pumphrey & Jean. BA Ge 1969; MDiv GTS 1972. D 6/10/1972 P 12/1/1972 Bp Leland Stark. m 5/5/2007 Margaret K Kay c 2. St Lk's So Chap Overland Pk KS 2005-2011; Nevil Meml Ch Of S Geo Ardmore PA 2001-2005; Ch Of The H Apos Wynnewood PA 1987; Epis Cmnty Serv Philadelphia PA 1975-1988. jblair430@gmail.com

PUMPHREY, Margaret K (Del) 146 Fairhill Dr, Wilmington DE 19808 **R S Alb's Wilmington DE 2010-** B Richland WA 2/20/1945 d William Cameron Kay & Margaret Jane. BA Neumann Coll Aston PA 1997; MDiv GTS 2003; MS Neumann Coll Aston PA 2006. D 1/18/2003 P 12/4/2003 Bp Wayne Parker Wright. m 5/5/2007 John B Pumphrey c 4. Dn of Metro Dnry Dio W Missouri Kansas City MO 2009-2010; Metro Dnry Dio W Missouri Kansas City MO 2008-2010; Asst S Paul's Ch Kansas City MO 2008-2010; R S Aug's Ch Kansas City MO 2007-2008; P-in-c Ch Of The Nativ New Castle DE 2004-2007; Dio Delaware Wilmington DE 2003-2004; D Imm Ch Highlands Wilmington DE 2003-2004. mkpumphrey@gmail.com

PUMPHREY, Thomas Claude (Pa) 64 Powderhorn Dr, Phoenixville PA 19460 **Assoc S Dav's Ch Wayne PA 2009-** B Berea OH 8/14/1967 s David William Pumphrey. Cleveland St U; BS Cor 1989; MDiv, cl VTS 2004. D 6/12/2004 Bp Mark Hollingsworth Jr P 12/18/2004 Bp Charles Ellsworth Bennison Jr. m 10/18/1997 Silke Pumphrey c 2. Chair, Stwdshp Com Dio Pennsylvania Philadelphia PA 2008-2010; Nomin Com Dio Pennsylvania Philadelphia PA 2008-2010; R S Mk's Ch Honey Brook PA 2004-2009. Auth, "Hearts and Minds," *Angl Dig*, SPEAK, 2006. tpumphrey@stdavidschurch.org

PUNNETT, Ian Case (Minn) 901 Portland Ave, Saint Paul MN 55104 **D S Clem's Ch S Paul MN 2009-** B Wilmette, IL 3/3/1960 s Edwin Cockard Punnett & Ann Hill. BA U IL 1998; MDiv Columbia Theol Seminiary 2003. D 7/8/2008 Bp James Louis Jelinek. m 5/30/1985 Margery Campbell Punnett c 2. punnett@visi.com

PUNZO, Thomas Edward (WMo) 7055 N Highland Ct, Gladstone MO 64118 **R Ch Of The Gd Shpd Kansas City MO 1999-** B Saint Joseph MO 6/30/1943 s Ferdinand Punzo & Cecelia C. BA Concep Sem Coll; MDiv Concep Sem Coll 1969; STL (Hon.) No Amer Coll Rome IT 1974. Rec from Roman Catholic 9/1/1981 as Priest Bp Edward Clark Turner. m 2/1/1980 Sharon Louise Seip c 1. Int S Alb's Epis Ch Wichita KS 1997-1999; Asstng P S Dav's Epis Ch Topeka KS 1996-1997; Convoc Dn Dio Kansas Topeka KS 1994; R Ch Of The Cov Jct City KS 1984-1996; Vic Ch of SS Jn & Geo Jct City KS 1984-1994; Assoc S Mich And All Ang Ch Mssn KS 1982-1984; P-in-c Gr Epis Ch Ottawa KS 1981-1982. Auth, "Study of Ecum," *Ecum*, Archdio of Kansas City KS, 1972. tom.punzo@goodshepherdkc.org

PUOPOLO JR, Angelo Joseph (SO) 2366 Kemper Ln, 1801 Rutland Ave., Cincinnati OH 45207 **Int S Andr's Epis Ch Cincinnati OH 2011-** B Baltimore MD 9/9/1947 s Angelo Puopolo & Rose Marie. AA Catonsville Cmnty Coll 1974; BS Towson U 1975; M.Div VTS 1979. D 6/17/1979 P 6/17/1980 Bp David Keller Leighton Sr. m 2/14/1970 Mary L Lauer c 3. Int S Jas Epis Ch Cincinnati OH 2010-2011; R Ch Of The Adv Cincinnati OH 1987-2009; Assoc R S Thos Ch Lancaster PA 1984-1987; Asst S Tim's Ch Catonsville MD 1983-1984; Vic H Cross Ch Baltimore MD 1979-1983. angpuopolo@yahoo.com

PURCELL, Christine Funk (CPa) 445 Alta Vista Dr, Williamsport PA 17701 **Int S Andr's Epis Ch Shippensburg PA 2010-** B Los Angeles CA 3/6/1957 BA Dart 1978; MBA U of Connecticut 1988; MDiv GTS 2004. D 6/19/2004 P 2/3/2005 Bp Michael Whittington Creighton. m 6/23/1979 Robert E Purcell c 2. S Lk's Epis Ch Altoona PA 2009-2010; Chr Soc Mnstry Harrisburg PA 2006-2008; Cur S Andr's Epis Ch Lewisburg PA 2004-2005. cpurcell2@comcast.net

PURCELL-CHAPMAN, Diana Barnes (Roch) Po Box 492, Wellsville NY 14895 **Assoc Dio Rochester Rochester NY 1994-** B Brooklyn NY 11/14/1933 d Erwin Edward Barnes & Gertrude Henrietta. AA SUNY; BA S Jos Coll W Hartford CT 1980; MDiv Bex 1986. D 6/26/1993 P 1/22/1994 Bp William George Burrill. m 11/24/1990 G Fred Chapman. Pstr Care Coordntr Dio Rochester Rochester NY 1993-1999. dinfre@netsync.net

PURCHAL, John Jeffrey (WMass) 45 Willow St. Apt. 420, Springfield MA 01103 B Auroroa NE 10/23/1963 s John Frederick Purchal & Joyce Marilyn. BA U of Nebraska at Kearney 1995; MDiv GTS 2004. D 6/19/2004 P 10/17/2004 Bp Gordon Paul Scruton. S Andr's Ch Longmeadow MA 2004-2010; Vic S Jn's Ch Millville MA 2004-2007. revpurchal@yahoo.com

PURDOM III, Allen Bradford (O) 6809 Mayfield Rd Apt 1071, Cleveland OH 44124 **Dio Ohio Cleveland OH 2009-** B New Haven CT 8/1/1956 s Allen Bradford Purdom & Joan F. U Of Akron; BA U Of Cntrl Florida 1979; MDiv STUSo 1996. D 6/22/1996 P 12/14/1996 Bp J Clark Grew II. m 3/17/1979 Mary J Wade c 3. R Ch Of The Gd Shpd Beachwood OH 2001-2009; R Trin Ch Allnce OH 1996-2001. bpurdom@dohio.org

PURDUM, Ellen Echols (At) 3098 Saint Annes Ln Nw, Atlanta GA 30327 B Asheville NC 11/28/1959 BA Emory U 1981; MDiv Candler TS Emory U 2001; CAS GTS 2004. D 6/5/2004 P 12/5/2004 Bp J(ohn) Neil Alexander. m 6/8/1991 David Herbert Purdum. S Anne's Epis Ch Atlanta GA 2004-2006. "Mary And Martha And The Myers-Briggs," Abingdon Press, 2005. epurdum@thefund.org

PURDY, James Elliott (NJ) 309 Bridgeboro Rd Apt 4466, Moorestown NJ 08057 B Bath NY 9/24/1913 s Charles Edwin Purdy & Mary Frances. BA Bps 1936; MA Bps 1937; GTS 1938. D 6/8/1938 P 12/18/1938 Bp Frank W Sterrett. m 9/13/1941 Eloise Hughes c 1. Stndg Com Dio New Jersey Trenton NJ 1973-1975; COM Dio New Jersey Trenton NJ 1971-1984; Pres Ecum Rel Ldrs Conf Sthrn NJ Dio New Jersey Trenton NJ 1968-1980; R Gr Ch Merchantville NJ 1966-1983; Depts CSR & DRE Dio New Jersey Trenton NJ 1963-1978; Stndg Com Dio New Jersey Trenton NJ 1960-1962; BEC Dio New Jersey Trenton NJ 1959-1971; Dn Boys Conf (Sum) Dio New Jersey Trenton NJ 1945-1951; R Chr Ch Bordentown NJ 1943-1966; Gr-S Paul's Ch Mercerville NJ 1939-1941. Bp Dioc Ring 1965; Bp Dioc Medal Hon 1962; Hon Cn Trin Cathd Trenton NJ 1958.

PURDY, James Hughes (Mo) 53 Chaminade Dr, Saint Louis MO 63141 B Trenton NJ 7/7/1945 s James Elliott Purdy & Eloise Hughes. BA Trin Hartford CT 1967; MDiv PDS 1970. D 4/11/1970 P 10/24/1970 Bp Alfred L Banyard. m 1/22/1972 Emma Sarosdy c 2. R S Ptr's Epis Ch St Louis MO 1998-2011; R S Jn's Ch Beverly Farms MA 1984-1998; R S Bern's Ch Bernardsville NJ 1973-1983; Asst S Thos' Ch Garrison Forest Owings Mills MD 1970-1973. Alb Inst 1973; AGO 1978; CEEP 1999; Epis EvangES 1993; Missouri Cler Assn 1998. jhpurdy11@aol.com

PURDY, Steward Edward (CNY) 2 Highland Ave, Binghamton NY 13905 **Vic Gr Epis Ch Whitney Point NY 1997-; Vic S Jn's Ch Marathon NY 1997-** B Easton PA 4/12/1929 s Ira James Purdy & Mary Alice. Laf. D 6/8/1985 P 5/4/1986 Bp O'Kelley Whitaker. m 1/11/1999 Ellen Bennett. Asst R Trin Meml Ch Binghamton NY 1986-1997.

PURDY, Thomas Clayton (CPa) 111 Dickinson Ave, Lancaster PA 17603 **R S Ptr's Ch Poolesville MD 2008-** B Newport News VA 5/13/1978 s Philip Clayton Purdy & Susan Stall. BA Millersville U 2000; MDiv STUSo 2005. D 6/11/2005 P 2/4/2006 Bp Michael Whittington Creighton. m 8/19/2000 Donna JM Purdy c 2. Asst To The R S Jas Ch Lancaster PA 2005-2008. tom@stjameslanpa.org

PURKS III, Jim (Ga) c/o St Paul's Episcopal Church, 212 N Jefferson St, Albany GA 31701 **D S Paul's Ch Albany GA 2008-** B Atlanta GA 8/21/1936 s James Harris Purks & Mary Brown. BA U No Carolina 1959; MA Stan 1963. D 12/7/1999 Bp Henry Irving Louttit. D Calv Ch Americus GA 1999-2007. Ord of S Lk. jimpurks@vol.com

PURNELL, Erl Gould (Ct) 46 Overlook Ter, Simsbury CT 06070 **R Old S Andr's Ch Bloomfield CT 1997-** B Philadelphia PA 7/2/1946 s James Stanley Purnell & Margaret Gould. BA U Pgh 1969; MA Goddard Coll 1989; MA Ya Berk 1993. D 8/7/1993 Bp Arthur Edward Walmsley P 2/12/1994 Bp Clarence Nicholas Coleridge. m 7/26/2002 Joanne Kimball c 4. Cur S Paul's Ch Riverside CT 1993-1997; Dir Dvlpmt Ya Berk New Haven CT 1991-1992. Auth, "Through Mk's Eyes," *Through Mk's Eyes*, Abingdon Press, 2006; Auth, "A Sampler Of Poems," Featherstone Press, 1998; Auth, "A Sea Kayaker'S Trip Planner & Log Bk," GoThereDoThat, 1996. Distinguished Naval Grad U.S. Navy 1970. puckpurnell@mac.com

P

PURNELL, Susan Ann (Los) 19682 Verona Ln, Yorba Linda CA 92886 B Los Angeles CA 10/22/1943 d Joseph Bennett Moody & Ethel. BS California St U 1980; MS California St U 1982; MDiv CDSP 1989. D 6/10/1989 P 1/1/1990 Bp Frederick Houk Borsch. m 1/20/1962 Arnold Lee Purnell. Asst S Geo's Mssn Hawthorne CA 1994; Asst S Lk's Par Monrovia CA 1991-1993; Asst S Andr's Par Fullerton CA 1990-1991; Asst R S Geo's Epis Ch Laguna Hills CA 1989-1990.

PURSEL, Robert Howard (CPa) 150 E 9th St Ste 1-229, Bloomsburg PA 17815 **Died 11/23/2009** B Bloomsburg PA 12/8/1941 s Russell Herbert Pursel & Mary Martha. BS Bloomsburg U of Pennsylvania 1963; STB Wesley TS 1966; STM GTS 1970; Fllshp U Tor 1974; ThD U Tor 1975. D 6/28/1970 P 1/17/1971 Bp Dean T Stevenson. GAS 1982; Soc of King Chas the Mtyr 1985. barsetbiblion1@yahoo.com

PURSER, J Philip (USC) P.O. Box 265, Chapin SC 29036 **R S Fran of Assisi Chapin SC 2006-** B Fayetteville NC 5/24/1947 s John Graham Purser & Mary Ann. BA Methodist U 1969; MDiv STUSo 1973. D 6/23/1973 P 4/4/1974 Bp Hunley Agee Elebash. m 12/27/1970 Nancy Autry c 2. Cn Dio Upper So Carolina Columbia SC 2003-2005; R All SS' Epis Ch Morristown TN 2000-2003; R Epis Ch Of The Redeem Greenville SC 1981-2000; Asst S Jn's Epis Ch Columbia SC 1975-1981; R H Trin Epis Ch Hertford NC 1973-1975. rector@stfrancischapin.org

PURSLEY, George William (SO) 332 Mount Zion Rd NW, Lancaster OH 43130 **R S Jn's Epis Ch Lancaster OH 1998-** B Muncie IN 1/9/1954 s George Oscar Pursley & Billie Faye. BA Asbury Coll 1976; MDiv Asbury TS 1979; MS Ohio U 1989; DMin STUSo 1998. D 12/18/1993 P 8/1/1994 Bp Herbert Thompson Jr. m 6/10/1978 Rebecca Lynn Mathias c 2. Dn, NE Dnry Dio Sthrn Ohio Cincinnati OH 1998-2003; P-in-c Ch Of The Epiph Nelsonville OH 1995-1998; Vic S Paul's Epis Ch Logan OH 1994-1998. rector@stjohnlancaster.org

PURVIS, Howard Byrd (SVa) 245 Dexter St E, Chesapeake VA 23324 B Williamston NC 11/16/1932 s James Henry Robinson & Cora B. Cert VTS. D 10/2/1999 P 5/30/2000 Bp David Conner Bane Jr. m 2/18/1989 Delores Banks Jordan. Asst Emm Ch Virginia Bch VA 2000-2002.

PURVIS OSB, R(obert) David (Ind) 31 Hampshire Ct, Noblesville IN 46062 B Indianapolis IN 10/13/1938 s Cecil Purvis & Dorothy B. Int Mnstry Prog; Butler U 1957; U of Maryland 1961; Indiana U 1964; Ind Non-Res Sem Prog IN 1975. D 9/28/1974 P 4/15/1975 Bp John P Craine. m 10/11/1958 Donna Louetta Cunningham c 4. Int H Fam Epis Ch Fishers IN 2002-2003; Int All SS Ch Indianapolis IN 2001-2002; Ch Of S Mich And All Ang Sanibel FL 1997-2000; Dioc Bdgt Com Dio Indianapolis Indianapolis IN 1989; Bp Advsry Coun Applicants Mnstry Dio Indianapolis Indianapolis IN 1982-1988; Com Dio Indianapolis Indianapolis IN 1978-1981; S Mich's Ch Noblesville IN 1977-1997; Chair Dioc Personl Com Dio Indianapolis Indianapolis IN 1976-1982; S Chris's Epis Ch Carmel IN 1975-1976. davdon58@comcast.net

PURYEAR, Jim (SwFla) 339 Meadow Beauty Ct, Venice FL 34293 **R S Mk's Epis Ch Venice FL 2001-** B South Hill VA 3/15/1947 s James A Puryear & Ruby. BS Old Dominion U 1972; MDiv VTS 2001. D 6/9/2001 Bp David Conner Bane Jr P 12/16/2001 Bp John Bailey Lipscomb. m 5/19/2001 Carol Brenoltz c 1. jimpuryear@stmarksvenice.com

PUTMAN, Richard Byron (Ala) 408 Thornberry Cir, Birmingham AL 35242 **Asstg P S Thos Epis Ch Birmingham AL 2003-** B Birmingham AL 12/24/1943 s Herman Braxton Putman & Gertrude Smithers. BA U of Alabama 1966; MDiv Candler TS Emory U 1974. D 10/28/1976 P 5/26/1977 Bp Furman Stough. m 10/25/1985 Sharon H Harris c 3. Chapl Birmingham Epis Campus Mnstrs Birmingham AL 1981-1983; R S Jn's Ch Birmingham AL 1979-1983; R S Lk's Ch Scottsboro AL 1978-1979; Cn Dio Alabama Birmingham AL 1976-1978; Cur S Andrews's Epis Ch Birmingham AL 1976-1977. Theta Phi Intl Theol Soc 1974. Cert Fin Planner CFP Bd 1992; Var Combat Medals USAF 1969; Air Medal USAF 1969. rick@rputman.com

PUTNAM, Kevin Todd (Cal) 849 Spruance Ln, Foster City CA 94404 **S Andr's Ch Saratoga CA 2003-** B Portsmouth VA 10/5/1973 s Frank William Putnam & Fay Louise. BA/BS VPI 1995; MA VPI 2000; MDiv CDSP 2003. D 8/17/2003 Bp Otis Charles P 12/4/2004 Bp William Edwin Swing. m 5/21/2000 Nelzine Delia Grenville c 1. Dio Oregon Portland OR 2006; S Andr's Sch Saratoga CA 2004-2006. kt_putnam@yahoo.com

PUTNAM, Sarah (Sally) Thompson (SC) Po Box 888, Marion SC 29571 B Nashville TN 6/29/1940 d William Preston Thompson & Sarah. BA U of So Carolina 1961; MS U GA 1974; MDiv VTS 1997. D 3/31/1997 P 10/4/1997 Bp Edward Lloyd Salmon Jr. m 9/2/1961 Samuel Franklin Putnam. Vic Ch Of The Adv Marion SC 1998-2006; Int S Paul's Epis Ch Conway SC 1997-1998. sputnam629@aol.com

PUTNAM, Thomas Clyde (Ia) 397 Huron Ave, Cambridge MA 02138 B Des Moines IA 8/30/1948 s Clyde Charles Putnam & Dorothy Elizabeth. BA Westminster Coll 1971; MDiv EDS 1977; NCPsyA CG Jung Inst 1985; PhD Un U 1988. D 6/23/1977 P 4/27/1978 Bp Walter Cameron Righter. m 8/7/1988 Susan Lawrence. Mssnr All SS Par Brookline MA 1977-1979. Auth, "A Jungian Perspective On A Repetitive Nightmare". AAPC 1978; Amer Coll Chapl 1978; Intl Assn Of Analytical Psychol 1987; New Engl Soc Of Jungian Psychoanalysts 1990; New York Assn of Analytical Psychologists 1990. putnamtc@comcast.net

PUTZ, Shirley (Joyce) B(aynham) (Nev) 1453 Rawhide Rd, Boulder City NV 89005 **D S Chris's Epis Ch Boulder City NV 1992-** B Glasgow MT 11/18/1926 d Walter Alexander Baynham & Myrtle Alice. RN Montana Consolidated Sch Of Nrsng 1947. D 7/3/1992 Bp Stewart Clark Zabriskie. m 1/19/1946 Wayne Joseph Putz.

PYATT, Petrina Margarette (NJ) 100 East Maple Ave, Penns Grove NJ 08069 **R Ch Of Our Merc Sav Penns Grove NJ 2005-** B New York NY 6/26/1949 d Samuel E Francis & Juanita G. BA CUNY 1988; MDiv GTS 2003. D 6/12/2004 P 1/15/2005 Bp George Edward Councell. c 2. Chair, Nomin Com Dio New Jersey Trenton NJ 2006-2009; Visioning Com Mem Dio New Jersey Trenton NJ 2006-2008; Liturg & Mus Com Mem Dio New Jersey Trenton NJ 2005-2007; Asst S Andr's Ch Bronx NY 2004-2005. pniknu@aol.com

PYLES, Christopher V (CPa) 120 W Lamb St, Bellefonte PA 16823 **R S Jn's Epis Ch Bellefonte PA 2010-** B Washington DC 11/24/1976 BA Ford 1998; MDiv GTS 2005. D 3/19/2005 P 9/17/2005 Bp Mark Sean Sisk. Assoc R S Lk's Ch Philadelphia PA 2007-2010; Asst to the R Washington Memi Chap Vlly Forge PA 2005-2007. cvpyles@aol.com

PYRON JR, Nathaniel (Mo) 1422 Shady Creek Ct, Saint Louis MO 63146 B El Dorado AR 5/1/1943 s Wilson Nathaniel Pyron & Kathryn. BS U of Arkansas 1965; MDiv VTS 1973. D 6/25/1973 P 3/23/1974 Bp Christoph Keller Jr. c 2. Asst Ch Of The Adv S Louis MO 2006-2009; Assoc Emm Epis Ch Webster Groves MO 2005-2006; R S Matt's Epis Ch Warson Warson Woods MO 1999-2005; S Lk and S Jn's Caruthersville MO 1998-1999; R S Paul's Epis Ch Sikeston MO 1996-1999; S Lk's Ch Hot Sprg AR 1986-1996; R S Paul's Epis Ch Sikeston MO 1981-1986; R S Paul's Newport AR 1976-1981; Cur & Vic S Jas Ch Magnolia AR 1973-1976; Cur & Vic S Mary's Epis Ch El Dorado AR 1973-1976. wilsonpyron@sbcglobal.net

Q

QUACKENBUSH, Margaret Haight (Alb) Rr 1 Dunbar Road, Cambridge NY 12816 **D S Paul's Epis Ch Greenwich NY 1996-** B Syarcuse NY 7/8/1947 d Alfred Ward Haight & Ruth. Core Epis Dio Albany Albany NY; D Formation Prog 1995; EFM STUSo 1995. D 11/18/1995 Bp David Standish Ball. m 4/29/1972 Peter David Quackenbush.

QUAINTON, Rodney F (Chi) 154 South Cranbrook Cross, Bloomfield Hills MI 48301 B Seattle WA 7/9/1941 s Cecil Eden Quainton & Marjorie Oates. BA Ya 1962; MBA Harv 1970; MDiv Epis TS of The SW 1988. D 6/15/1988 Bp Gordon Taliaferro Charlton P 1/6/1989 Bp Maurice Manuel Benitez. m 6/18/1999 Nanci J Priest c 3. R Ch Of The Heav Rest Abilene TX 1993-1995; Assoc R All SS Prot Epis Ch Ft Lauderdale FL 1990-1993; Asst to R S Dunst's Epis Ch Houston TX 1988-1990. fatherq@fumcbirmingham.org

QUATORZE, Jean Lenord (Hai) PO Box 407139, C/O Lynx Air, Fort Lauderdale FL 33340 **Dio Haiti Ft Lauderdale FL 2002-** B 11/23/1969 D. m 4/7/2005 Michaud Ilomene. quaj23@hotmail.com

QUEEN, Jeffrey (SO) 1156 Dogwood Ridge Rd., Wheelersburg OH 45694 **R All SS Epis Ch Portsmouth OH 2006-** B Little Rock AR 7/3/1972 s James Queen & Beverly. BA Wilmington Coll 1994; MDiv Untd TS 2000; Angl Stds Bex 2002. D 5/22/2004 P 2/5/2005 Bp Herbert Thompson Jr. m 11/8/1997 Richelle T Thompson c 2. S Mary Magd Ch Maineville OH 2004-2005. GAS 2004; Soc of King Chas the Mtyr 2009; SocOLW 2006. jeffreyqueen@yahoo.com

QUEEN, Laura Virginia (Los) 445 Fifth Avenue, New York NY 10016 **VP for Pstr Care and Educ Ch Pension Fund New York NY 2011-** B Tampa FL 6/9/1960 d William Wesley Queen & Laura DeWalt. BS U of W Florida 1982; MDiv GTS 2003. D 6/21/2003 P 1/24/2004 Bp Joseph Jon Bruno. m 8/8/2008 Karen K Clark. R S Alb's Ch Simsbury CT 2008-2011; Asst S Aug By-The-Sea Par Santa Monica CA 2005-2008; Assoc S Cross By-The-Sea Ch Hermosa Bch CA 2003-2008; Chapl The Epis Hm Communities Pasadena CA 2003-2005; Mssnr for Yth Dio Los Angeles Los Angeles CA 1994-2001; Mssnr for Yth Dio Massachusetts Boston MA 1989-1993. cl The GTS 2003. lqueen@cpg.org

QUEEN JR, William L (Va) 8639 Brown Summit Rd, Richmond VA 23235 **Assoc R All SS Ch Richmond VA 2002-** B Jacksonville FL 4/1/1957 s William Lee Queen & Jo Ann. BA Eckerd Coll 1979; MA Amer Grad Sch of Intl Mgmt Glendal 1984; MDiv VTS 1994. Trans 11/6/2003 Bp David Conner Bane Jr. m 5/3/1986 Lynn E Haskett c 3. R S Barn Epis Ch Richmond VA 1997-2002; Assoc R S Paul's By-The-Sea Epis Ch Jacksonville Bch FL 1994-1997. bill.queen@verizon.net

QUEHL-ENGEL, Catherine Mary (Ia) 103 Oak Ridge Dr Se, Mount Vernon IA 52314 **Dioc Strategic Plnng Com Dio Iowa Des Moines IA 2011-; P Trin**

Ch Iowa City IA 2005- B 6/9/1967 d Gary Howard Quehl & Janeen Joy. BA Cornell Coll 1989; MDiv PSR 1994; MA PSR 1994. D 9/2/2005 Bp Alan Scarfe. m 5/28/1989 Craig Engel c 1. Bd Dir Dio Iowa Des Moines IA 2007-2010; Angl Comm Dialogue & Recon Grp Dio Iowa Des Moines IA 2006-2009; Dir of Sum Mnstry Sch & Retreat Dio Iowa Des Moines IA 2006-2009. cquehl-engel@cornellcollege.edu

QUERIDO, Manuel Tablante (Los) 357 Gardenia Ave, Mangilao GU 96913 Guam **St Andrews Ch Agat 1996-** B Manila Philippines 6/8/1968 s Manuel V Querido & Lucila T. BTh St. Andr's TS Quezon City Ph 1991; MDiv St. Andr's TS Quezon City Ph 2000. Rec from Philippine Independent Church 6/6/2006 Bp Joseph Jon Bruno. m 12/28/1987 Jeannie Linsao Querido c 2. Dio Micronesia Tumon Bay GU GU 2006-2007. manuel.querido@navy.mail

QUEVEDO-BOSCH, Juan A (LI) 3014 Crescent St S, Astoria NY 11102 **Archd of Queens Dio Long Island Garden City NY 2011-** B Puerto Padre Tunas CU 9/26/1955 s Juan Quevedo-Gonzalez & Alaria. M.Th. Seminario Evangelico de Teologia; MDiv U Tor; ThM U Tor; in process Vrieje Univrsiteit Amsterdam 2007. Trans from Iglesia Episcopal de Cuba 10/9/2000 Bp Orris George Walker Jr. m 2/15/1987 Adria Castillo-Raymond. R Ch Of The Redeem Astoria NY 2000-2006. Auth, "Ancestors in the cloud of witnesses : El Dia de Muertos in the Mex migrant experience in New York City," *Studia Liturgica*, 2004, vol. 34, no1, 2004; Auth, "Compasrose Liturg Tourists?," *The Chant of Life: Inculturation and the People of the Land*, Ch Pub, 2003; Auth, "The Influence of Afr Rel in Cuban Chrsnty.," *Theol in Afr*, http://theologyinafrica.com/blog/?page_id=133, 1998; Auth, "The Liturg Species," *Revising the Euch : groundwork for the Angl Comm : Stds in preparation for the 1995 Dublin Consult*, lcuin/GROW Liturg study,, 1994; Auth, "The Visigothic-Mozarabic Liturg : Reg expression of the integrity of the Chr initiation rite 300-1085," *Thesis*, 1991. SOCIETAS LITURGICA 1991. Hon Cn of the Cathd of the Incarn The Epis Dio Long island 2005. fatherjuan@rcn.com

QUEZADA MOTA, Moises (DR) Calle Costa Rica No 21, Ens. Ozama, Santo Domingo Dominican Republic **Iglesia Epis La Encarnacion La Romana DO 1998-; Iglesia Epis de Todos los Santos La Romana La DO 1998-; Dio The Dominican Republic (Iglesia Epis Dominicana) Santo Domingo DO 1982-** B La Romana DO 12/3/1956 s Virgilio Quezada & Mercedes. Centro De Estudios Teologicas 1982. D 8/15/1982 P 5/1/1983 Bp Telesforo A Isaac. m 7/31/1983 Mary Jeannette P Pringle de Quezada c 4. Vic Iglesia Epis San Andres Santo Domingo DO 1998-2007; Vic Iglesia Epis San Esteban San Pedro de Macoris DO 1983-1988. revquezadam@yahoo.com

QUIGGLE, George Willard (Ala) 384 Windflower Dr, Dadeville AL 36853 B Birmingham AL 9/30/1941 s George Willard Quiggle & Mary Cumi. U So; BA Birmingham-Sthrn Coll 1964; BD Candler TS Emory U 1969. D 6/21/1986 P 12/1/1986 Bp Furman Stough. m 12/16/1961 Dale C Callahan. Dio Alabama Birmingham AL 1998-2003; S Mich And All Ang Millbrook AL 1998-2003; P S Lk's Epis Ch Jacksonville AL 1986-1998. georgequiggle@aol.com

QUIGLEY JR, Frank Vernon (CFla) 2043 Country Side Cir S, Orlando FL 32804 B Baltimore MD 11/4/1921 s Frank Vernon Quigley & Ellen. BA U Of Florida 1943; MDiv VTS 1949; DMin VTS 1979. D 6/29/1949 P 4/27/1950 Bp Frank A Juhan. m 11/13/2005 Mary Watts c 3. Pres Stndg Com Dio Cntrl Florida Orlando FL 1970-1975; R S Mich's Ch Orlando FL 1958-1986. Golden Bell Awd MHA . eellis@cfl.rr.com

QUIGLEY, James E (Ky) 402 Sumpter Ave, Bowling Green KY 42101 **S Geo's Epis Ch New Orleans LA 2007-** B Lombard IL 10/26/1964 s John C Quigley & Frances. BFA The Art Acad Of Cincinnati 1987; VTS 2001; MDiv VTS 2001. Trans from Anglican Church of Canada 2/1/1972 Bp Leland Stark. m 8/19/1989 Ellen Land c 1. Assoc Chr Epis Ch Bowling Green KY 2001-2007. Alum/Alum Exec Com, VTS 2001-2003. jim@stgeorge-nola.org

QUILA GARCIA, Pedro Perfecto (EcuC) Box 235, Tena Ecuador B Los Rios 8/4/1944 s Pedro Quila Mejia & Ignacia. D 12/16/1984 P 6/1/1985 Bp Adrian Delio Caceres-Villavicencio. Iglesia Epis Del Ecuador Ecuador 1985-1989.

QUILL, Margaret M (Chi) Guardian Angels of Elk River, Inc., 400 Evans Avenue, Elk River MN 55330 B Milwaukee WI 5/7/1948 d Harold William Schwertfeger & Marvel Sedate. BA U of Wisconsin 1971; MA U Hawaii-Manoa Manoa HI 1974; MDiv EDS 1987. D 6/28/1987 Bp Donald Purple Hart P 1/1/1988 Bp Andrew Frederick Wissemann. P-in-c H Trin Epis Ch Elk River MN 2010-2011; R Emm Epis Ch Rockford IL 2004-2006; R Chr Ch Medway MA 1992-2004; Vic S Steph's Ch Pittsfield MA 1990-1992; Cur All SS Ch Worcester MA 1987-1990. mquill@earthlink.net

QUILLMAN, Bard (Tenn) 4215 Harding Pike Apt 509, Nashville TN 37205 **Asst To R S Geo's Ch Nashville TN 1986-** B Norristown PA 5/24/1921 s Charles Jacob Quillman & Sara Harley. BD Cor 1943. D 6/22/1986 Bp George Lazenby Reynolds Jr. m 8/11/1945 Barbara Jane Paul c 3. Auth, "Aiche," *Combustion Engr*.

QUIN, Alison Joan (NY) 3021 State Route 213 E, Stone Ridge NY 12484 **R The Epis Ch Of Chr The King Stone Ridge NY 2007-** B Washington D.C. 6/14/1959 d Frederick Sherman Quin & Diana. BA Swarthmore Coll 1982; JD Cor 1987; MDiv VTS 2001. D 6/9/2001 Bp Jane Hart Holmes Dixon P 12/18/2001 Bp Allen Lyman Bartlett Jr. m 5/28/1983 Timothy David Shapiro c 2. S Nich Epis Ch Germantown MD 2005-2007; S Dav's Par Washington DC 2002-2005; S Geo's Ch Glenn Dale MD 2002. tsharpe859@gmail.com

QUINBY, Congreve H. (Alb) 51 High Grove Ct, Burlington VT 05401 B Rochester NY 11/27/1928 s Henry Dean Quinby & Alice Hamilton. BA cl Wms 1950; MDiv SWTS 1958. D 6/16/1958 P 2/18/1959 Bp Donald J Campbell. m 5/31/1958 Constance Philp c 2. Stndg Com Dio Albany Albany NY 1987-1991; R Trin Ch Potsdam NY 1985-1993; P-in-c S Aug's Ch Kansas City MO 1982-1985; Dept Evang & Renwl Dio W Missouri Kansas City MO 1978-1982; Cn Pstr Gr And H Trin Cathd Kansas City MO 1978-1982; Corp Dio Los Angeles Los Angeles CA 1976-1978; R Chr The Gd Shpd Par Los Angeles CA 1962-1977; Vic S Jos's Par Buena Pk CA 1958-1962. quinby1@myfairpoint.net

QUINN, Carolee Elizabeth Sproull (USC) 1402 Wenwood Ct, Greenville SC 29607 **D S Andr's Epis Ch Greenville SC 2011-** B Detroit MI 2/27/1927 d William Cargill Sproull & Carolee Bedford. U of Kansas 1947; Dio SE Florida Sch for Mnstry FL 1993. D 5/20/1993 Bp Calvin Onderdonk Schofield Jr. m 9/25/1948 Hubert James Quinn c 3. D S Jas Epis Ch Greenville SC 2006-2010; D S Fran Ch Greenville SC 2004-2006; D Epis Ch Of The Redeem Greenville SC 1994-2004; D S Mart's Epis Ch Pompano Bch FL 1993-1994. NAAD. csquinn@charter.net

QUINN, Catherine Alyce Rafferty (Nwk) 66 Pomander Walk, Ridgewood NJ 07450 **S Eliz's Ch Ridgewood NJ 2011-** B Boston MA 9/18/1974 d James A Rafferty & Alyce Lee. BS U So 1996; MDiv Ya Berk 2003. D 11/22/2004 P 5/22/2005 Bp Peter James Lee. m 1/15/2005 Peter Devlin Quinn c 2. S Jn's Ch Lafayette Sq Washington DC 2005-2008; Chr Ch Alexandria VA 2004-2005. cathyraffertyquinn@gmail.com

QUINN, Eugene Frederick (WA) 5702 Kirkside Dr, Chevy Chase MD 20815 B Oil City PA 9/16/1935 s Frederick Anthony Quinn & William Lee. BA Alleg 1957; MA U CA 1966; MA U CA 1969; PhD U CA 1970. D 6/22/1974 Bp William Foreman Creighton P 2/22/1975 Bp John Thomas Walker. m 6/16/2001 Carolyn Tanner Irish. Chapl Cathd of St Ptr & St Paul Washington DC 1987; Chr Ch S Jn's Par Accokeek MD 1985; S Columba's Ch Washington DC 1973-1978. Auth, "The French Ovrs Empire," 2000; Auth, "You & Human Rts," 1999; Auth, "Democracy At Dawn," 1998; Auth, "To Heal The Earth," 1994; Auth, "Human Rts & The Judiciary," 1994; Auth, "The Federalist Papers Rdr," 1992; Auth, "Bk Revs Of Afr Stds & Frgn Affrs"; Auth, "The Angl Ethos In Hist". frederickquinn@hotmail.com

QUINN, Marjory Keith (Cal) 110 Wood Rd Apt C-104, Los Gatos CA 95030 **Died 10/16/2010** B Berkeley CA 10/18/1926 d Harold Allen Keith & Kathleen. BA U CA 1967; MS California St U 1974. D 6/24/1972 P 1/8/1977 Bp C Kilmer Myers.

QUINN, Peter Darrell (Ct) 120 Ford Ln, Torrington CT 06790 **P-in-c S Jn The Evang Yalesville CT 2006-** B Providence RI 11/26/1941 s Ernest Raymond Quinn & Marjorie Morse. BA Barrington Coll 1973; MA Providence Coll 1976; DMin Hartford Sem 2004. D 12/22/1973 P 6/1/1974 Bp Frederick Hesley Belden. m 9/11/1965 Janet E Drinwater c 2. R St Gabr's Ch E Berlin CT 1992; R Ch of our Sav Plainville CT 1985-2004; R Calv Ch Stonington CT 1977-1985; Chr Ch Westerly RI 1974-1977; Cur St Mich & Gr Ch Rumford RI 1974-1976. pdqfriartuck@yahoo.com

QUINN, Scott Thomas (Pgh) 537 Hamilton Rd, Pittsburgh PA 15205 **Cn Dio Pittsburgh Monroeville PA 2009-; R Ch Of The Nativ Crafton PA 1983-** B Pittsburgh PA 9/10/1954 s Thomas Henry Quinn & Lucille Caroline. BA U Pgh 1977; MDiv TESM 1982. D 6/5/1982 Bp Robert Bracewell Appleyard P 2/1/1983 Bp Alden Moinet Hathaway. m 6/1/1980 Vera Lee c 3. S Mk Pittsburgh PA 1982-1986. quinnsrus@comcast.net

QUINN-MISCALL, Michele (Colo) 3153 S Forest St, Denver CO 80222 **R S Jos's Ch Lakewood CO 2008-** B Portsmouth NH 11/23/1954 d John William Affourtit & Joan Marie. S Thos Sem; BA Trin 1976; MAR/MDIV Iliff TS 1997. D 6/6/1998 P 12/1/1998 Bp William Jerry Winterrowd. m 6/23/1996 Peter Miscall c 2. Dio Colorado Denver CO 2002-2005; R Epis Ch Of S Ptr And S Mary Denver CO 2001-2008; Asst S Steph's Epis Ch Aurora CO 1999-2000. revquinn@aol.com

QUINONEZ-MERA, Juan Carlos (EcuC) Francisco Sormiento N Y Portete, Quito Ecuador B Esmeraldas 3/10/1985 s Juan Quinonez Suillano & Sara. Programa De Educacion Teologia; Universidad Cntrl Del Ecuador. D 2/11/2006 Bp Orlando Jesus Guerrero P 1/6/2007 Bp Wilfrido Ramos-Orench. Ecuador New York NY 2006-2009. jcgmera@latinmail.com

QUINTERO, Timoteo Petines (Haw) 99-443 Waoala Pl, Aiea HI 96701 B Sta. Maria Pangasinan PH 1/24/1929 s Felomino Quintero & Consolacion. BTh S Andr's TS Manila PH 1954; MDiv S Andr's TS Manila PH 1994. Rec from Roman Catholic 5/1/1969 Bp Edmond Lee Browning. m 6/7/1958 Louisa Yamashita Bacayan c 2. S Pauls Ch Honolulu HI 1976-1997; Coun Advice Dio Hawaii Honolulu HI 1968-1969. luczaktool@hawii.ii.com

QUINTON, Dean Lepidio (Nev) FCI La Tuna - Religious Services Dept, 8500 Doniphan Dr House 17, Anthony TX 79821 **Off Of Bsh For ArmdF New**

Q

York NY 1995- B Daqupan City PH 3/9/1949 s Crispin Quinton & Angelita Tanguilig. BA Div Word Sem 1971; MA Div Word Sem 1977. Rec from Roman Catholic 4/1/1995 as Priest Bp Stewart Clark Zabriskie. m 3/18/1994 Paulyn de las Alas. dquinton@bop.gov

QUIROGA, Luis Alberto (LI) 14755 Sw 154th Ct, Miami FL 33196 B Bogota CO 12/7/1919 s Luis Filipe Quiroga de la Torre & Julia. BA Amer Coll De Bogota Bogota CO 1939; BD PrTS 1945; ThM PrTS 1946; PhD U De Antioquia CO 1950. D 4/24/1955 P 12/1/1955 Bp Albert Ervine Swift. Exec Coun Appointees New York NY 1983-1988; Chr Ch Cobble Hill Brooklyn NY 1977-1982; Dio Long Island Garden City NY 1961-1976. Auth, "Word and Sacraments," 1975.

QUITO-PAGUAY, Luis Eulogio (EcuC) Calle Hernando Sarmiento, N 39-54 Y Portete Ecuador **Ecuador New York NY 2009-; Iglesia Epis Del Ecuador Ecuador 2009-** B 1/7/1968 s Pedro Nicolas Quito & Ascencia. Rec from Roman Catholic 5/17/2009 as Priest Bp Wilfrido Ramos-Orench. m 11/20/2009 Rosa Lemay-Inga c 2.

R

RAASCH, Timothy D (Minn) 408 N 7th St, Brainerd MN 56401 **S Ptr's Epis Ch Charlotte NC 2011-** B Macon GA 2/1/1954 s Harold Arthur Raasch & Janice Marie. BA U CA 1976; MDiv CDSP 1982. D 6/25/1983 P 6/1/1984 Bp William Edwin Swing. P-in-c S Paul's Ch Brainerd MN 2008-2011; Ch Of The Adv Louisville KY 2004-2006; S Barn Ch Norwich VT 2003-2004; Chr Ch St Michaels MD 2002-2003; S Fran Epis Ch San Jose CA 1994-1999; Int S Mary's Ch Portsmouth RI 1993-1994; Int Calv Ch Stonington CT 1992-1993; Int S Steph's Epis Ch Bloomfield CT 1990-1991; R Ch Of The Nativ San Rafael CA 1986-1989; Com Dio California San Francisco CA 1984-1989; Cur S Bede's Epis Ch Menlo Pk CA 1983-1986. OHC. traasch@st-peters.org

RAASCH, Werner Henry (Mil) 1121 N Waverly Pl Apt 1304, Milwaukee WI 53202 **Died 11/12/2009** B Milwaukee,WI 1/23/1942 s Werner Herman Raasch & Virginia Teresa. BS U of Wisconsin 1964; MS U of Wisconsin 1966; PhD Marq 1978; MDiv GTS 1981. D 4/11/1981 Bp Charles Thomas Gaskell P 10/11/1981 Bp Robert C Rusack. Auth, "Helping the Retarded to Know God," Concordia Pub, 1969. revisionist2@sbcglobal.net

RABAGO-NUNEZ, Luis Antonio (U) 1211 N Redwood Rd Apt 165, Salt Lake City UT 84116 **Dio Mex 2004-** B Mexico City Mexico 6/11/1973 Lt Seminario De San Andres Mex City Df Mx. Trans from La Iglesia Anglicana de Mex 5/21/2003 Bp Carolyn Tanner Irish. c 2. Dio Utah Salt Lake City UT 2004; D S Steph's Ch W Vlly City UT 2003. PLUISRABAGO@YAHOO.COM.MX

✠ **RABB, Rt Rev John Leslie** (Md) 4 E University Pkwy, Baltimore MD 21218 B Des Moines IA 10/11/1944 s Carleton A Rabb & JoAnn R. BA DePauw U 1966; MA U of Iowa 1969; MDiv EDS 1976; Cert Franciscan Intl Study Cntr Cbury GB 2004. D 6/26/1976 P 1/8/1977 Bp William Foreman Creighton Con 10/10/1998 for Md. m 4/17/1976 Sharon Freeman c 2. Bp Suffr of Maryland Dio Maryland Baltimore MD 1998-2010; COM Dio Atlanta Atlanta GA 1989-1998; Pres, Cler Orgnztn Dio Atlanta Atlanta GA 1989-1993; R S Anne's Epis Ch Atlanta GA 1988-1998; R The Ch Of The H Apos Halethorpe MD 1979-1988; Cur Ch Of The Ascen Gaithersburg MD 1976-1978. ACPE; EUC 2005. Bryce Shoemaker for Chr Unity Cntrl Maryland Ecum Coun 2005; Outstanding Alum - Profsnl Wk DePauw U 2005; Atlanta Mayor's Awd for Serv City of Atlanta 1993. rabbfamily@msn.com

RABUSA, Romeo Redoble (Az) 7309 W Crown King Rd, Phoenix AZ 85043 B Philippines 8/10/1966 MA Pontifical U Of S Thos Manila Ph 1989; MA Pontifical U Of S Thos 1992; MS De La Salle U 1993; MA La Salle U 1999. Rec from Roman Catholic 6/13/2004 Bp Kirk Stevan Smith. m 6/14/2000 Elizabeth Albores c 2. "Facing The Crises Of Sch Crimes And Violence: A Thesis On Moral Mgmt And Admin Of Sch Discipline," Mstr Of Arts In Educ Thesis, 1999; "The Pstr Ecclesial And Theol Dimension Of Dioc Syn," Hawaiian Cath Herald Article, 1998; "Computer-Based Mgmt Info Systems Of S Aug Coll," Mstr Of Sci In Educational Mgmt Thesis, 1993; "S Aug'S Ethical Principles On Violence," Mstr Of Philos Thesis, 1989. Employee Excellence Awd City Of Phoenix, Arizona 2005; Youngest Dioc Cler Cath Dio Honolulu, Hawaii 1996; Youngest Sch Prncpl Cath Educ Assn Of The Philippines 1994. adeoffer@cox.net

RACHAL, Paula Choquette (NC) 2803 Watauga Dr, Greensboro NC 27408 B Madison IN 8/17/1957 d Henry Holmes Choquette & Martha Elizabeth. BS MI SU 1980; MDiv SWTS 2000. D 6/10/2000 Bp C(laude) Charles Vache P 5/26/2001 Bp J(ames) Gary Gloster. m 9/15/1990 Robert T Rachal c 1. Asst All SS Ch Greensboro NC 2000-2002. paularachal@yahoo.com

RACHAL, Robert T (NC) 2803 Watauga Dr, Greensboro NC 27408 **Supply Ch Of The Mssh Mayodan NC 2003-** B New Iberia LA 12/28/1962 s Richard Stephen Rachal & Margaret Lynn. BS LSU 1985; MDiv SWTS 1991; CSD Haden Inst 2004. D 6/8/1991 P 12/22/1991 Bp Robert Jefferson Hargrove Jr. m 9/15/1990 Paula Choquette c 1. Asst Trin Ch Huntington WV 1997-1999; Campus Mnstr Cbury Fllshp Huntington WV 1997-1998; Campus Mnstr Calv Ch Columbia MO 1993-1997; Asst Epis Ch Of The Gd Shpd Lake Chas LA 1992; Chapl Epis Sch Of Acadiana Inc. Cade LA 1991; Asst S Barn Epis Ch Lafayette LA 1991. Auth, "Voices of Life & Hope in Cntrl Amer," *Plumbline*, 1997. rocky.rachal@gmail.com

RACINE, Jean-Joel (Hai) Box 1309, Port-Au-Prince Haiti **Dio Haiti Ft Lauderdale FL 2006-** B Bon Repos HT 6/19/1950 s Joseph Kleber Racine & Marie Cleomise. BA Normal Sch U Ht 1976. D 8/4/1985 P 6/1/1986 Bp Luc Anatole Jacques Garnier. m 12/16/1976 Marie Monique Senat Racine. Dio Haiti Ft Lauderdale FL 1985-2003. Auth, "Cours De Mathematiques 6 & 5". MARMOSTEE@YAHOO.FR

RACKLEY, M Kathryn (O) 41 Owen Brown St, Hudson OH 44236 B Jacksonville FL 3/21/1962 d Otis Dowe Rackley & Betty Coleman. BA Lee Coll 1984; BA Stetson U 1986; MDiv STUSo 1999; MA Wisdom U 2011. D 5/29/1999 Bp Henry Irving Louttit P 11/28/1999 Bp Robert Hodges Johnson. Assoc R Chr Ch Epis Hudson OH 2006-2011; Vic Ch Of The Ascen At Fork Advance NC 2001-2006; Asst R S Paul's Ch Wilkesboro NC 1999-2001. krackley@roadrunner.com

RACUSIN, Michele (EpisSanJ) 5267 San Jacinto Ave, Clovis CA 93619 **1st Dep Alt GC Epis Dio San Joaquin Modesto CA 2010-; Stndg Com Epis Dio San Joaquin Modesto CA 2010-; R Ch Of H Fam Fresno CA 2009-; Dep to GC Epis Dio San Joaquin Modesto CA 2009-; EfM Coordntr Epis Dio San Joaquin Modesto CA 2008-** B Honolulu HI 1/9/1958 d Bill Lowell Corwin & Barbara Lee. BA U CA Los Angeles 1981; MBA Pepperdine U 1984; MDiv Mennonite Brethren Biblic Sem 2003. D 6/12/2004 Bp John-David Mercer Schofield P 6/4/2005 Bp William Edwin Swing. m 11/10/1984 Samuel Racusin c 4. Vice Chair Dioc Coun Epis Dio San Joaquin Modesto CA 2008-2010; Assoc Gr Cathd San Francisco CA 2005-2009; D S Mary's Epis Ch Fresno CA 2004-2005. Amer Assn of Cert Publ Accountants 1987; California Soc of Cert Publ Accountants 1987. micheleracusin@comcast.net

RADANT, William F (Mil) PO Box 442, Manitowish Waters WI 54545 **P-in-c Our Sav's Phillips WI 1999-** B Oklahoma City OK 7/27/1930 s Milo H Radant & Estella. BA Oklahoma City U 1952; MA U MI 1954; MDiv Nash 1980. D 5/24/1980 P 11/29/1980 Bp Walter Cameron Righter. c 3. R S Mk's Ch Beaver Dam WI 1982-1995; P-in-c Ch Of The Epiph Centerville IA 1980-1982; P-in-c Gr Ch Albia IA 1980-1982. AFP; RWF; SHN. wfr@centurytel.net

RADCLIFF III, Cecil Darrell (CFla) 3010 Big Sky Blvd, Kissimmee FL 34744 **R S Jn's Epis Ch Of Kissimme Kissimmee FL 2001-** B Morgantown WV 11/10/1948 s Cecil Darrell Radcliff & Betty Jean. BA U of Cntrl Florida 1979; MDiv STUSo 1982. D 6/16/1982 P 3/1/1983 Bp William Hopkins Folwell. m 8/24/1968 Rhoda Jane Werner c 4. R H Trin Epis Ch Bartow FL 1995-2001; The Ch Of The H Presence Deland FL 1994-1995; All SS Epis Ch Enterprise FL 1985-1993; Cur S Mk's Ch Cocoa FL 1982-1985. Chapl Ord of S Lk 1982. fathercr@earthlink.net

RADCLIFF, Irene Evelyn (SO) 1094 Oakland Park Ave, Columbus OH 43224 B Charleston WV 6/14/1935 d John Miller & Mary. BS W Virginia St 1956; BSW The OH SU 1980; MSW The OH SU 1982. D 5/13/2006 Bp Kenneth Lester Price. imradcliff@yahoo.com

RADCLIFFE, Ernest Stanley (Oly) 3732 Colonial Ln Se, Port Orchard WA 98366 B Calgary AB CA 5/27/1926 s Joseph Ernest Radcliffe & Claire Musgrove. ATC 1952. Trans from Anglican Church of Canada 6/1/1967. c 2. Int S Catherines Ch Enumclaw WA 1989-1992; P-in-c St Bede Epis Ch Port Orchard WA 1974-1988; Vic S Lk's Epis Ch Elma WA 1966-1969; Vic S Mk's Epis Ch Montesano WA 1966-1969; Asst S Paul's Ch Seattle WA 1963-1966.

RADCLIFFE JR, William Eugene (Md) 2846 Angus Circle, Molino FL 32577 B Mount Airy NC 6/25/1944 s William Eugene Radcliffe & Mary. BS New Mex St U. 1973; MS OH SU 1981. D 6/10/1995 Bp Charles Lindsay Longest. m 1/7/1966 Patricia Ann Maccarone c 4. D Chr Ch Port Republic MD 1998-2007; D Middleham & S Ptr's Par Lusby MD 1995-1996; Serv S Andr The Fisherman Epis Mayo MD 1983-1995. billradcliffe@mail.com

RADELMILLER OHC, William Lawrence Nicholas (FdL) Po Box 1296, Santa Barbara CA 93102 B Pasco WA 11/18/1939 s Merle Gifford Radelmiller & Lucy Mary. BA U of Washington 1962; BD Nash 1965. D 6/29/1965 P 3/21/1966 Bp Ivol I Curtis. Iglesia Epis Del Ecuador Ecuador 1983-1984; Vic Dio Fond du Lac Appleton WI 1967-1970; S Mk's Ch Oconto WI 1967-1970; Dio Olympia Seattle WA 1965-1967; Cur S Dunst-The Highlands Shoreline WA 1965-1967. radelohc@aol.com

RADLEY, C(harles) Perrin (Me) 3701 R St NW, Washington DC 20007 B Washington DC 2/9/1942 s H Monroe Radley & Ellen Gray. BA Ken 1963; Queens TS GB 1967; Cert ETS 1968; MA U of Cambridge 1969; MA U of Birmingham GB 1974. D 6/29/1968 Bp William Foreman Creighton P 3/1/1969 Bp Alfred L Banyard. m 10/7/1969 Laurel Cargill c 2. R S Mk's Ch Waterville ME 1989-1999; R S Paul's Ch Pawtucket RI 1984-1989; EDS Cambridge MA 1983-1984. pandlradley@alumni.unh.edu

RADNER, Ephraim Louis (Colo) 410 W 18th St, Pueblo CO 81003 **Wycliffe Coll 2007-** B New Haven CT 12/27/1956 s Roy Radner & Virginia Honoski.

BA Dart 1978; MDiv Ya Berk 1981; PhD Yale DS 1994. D 6/27/1981 P 6/1/1982 Bp William Edwin Swing. m 1/24/1987 Annette Geoffrian Brownlee c 2. Cn Dio Colorado Denver CO 1998; R Ch Of The Ascen Pueblo CO 1997-2007; S Jn's Ch Stamford CT 1996-1997; Emm Epis Ch Stamford CT 1994-1997; Chr Ch Shaker Heights OH 1988-1989; Calv Ch Cleveland OH 1987-1989; Gr Ch Brooklyn NY 1985-1987; Exec Coun Appointees New York NY 1981-1985. Auth, "The End Of The Ch," Eerdmans, 1999; Auth, "Cn And Creed," Morehouse Pub, 1998; Auth, "Inhabiting Unity," Eerdmans, 1997; Auth, "Reclaiming Faith," Eerdmans, 1993. Scholarly Engagement w Angl Doctrine 1997. e.radner@wycliffe.utoronto.ca

RADTKE, Warren Robert (Mass) 32 Breakwater Cv, Chelsea MA 02150 **Assoc R Trin Ch In The City Of Boston Boston MA 2011-** B Chicago IL 5/25/1935 s Lawrence Carl Radtke & Meta. BS NWU 1957; BD EDS 1964. D 6/1/1964 Bp Archie H Crowley P 2/10/1965 Bp C Kilmer Myers. m 5/14/1960 Judith Ann Lockhart c 3. Assoc R Trin Ch In The City Of Boston Boston MA 2011; Assoc R Trin Ch In The City Of Boston Boston MA 2008-2011; R Trin Par Melrose MA 1965-1981; Marguis Fell Chr Ch Cranbrook Bloomfield Hills MI 1964-1965. Auth, *Kellogg Lectures EDS 92*. Mass. Cler Assn; Phillips Brooks Club. Kellog Lecturers EDS Cambridge MA 1992. radtkew@aol.com

RAEHN, J Sid (CFla) 106 Jim Dedmon Rd, Dyer TN 38330 B Orlando FL 1/24/1944 s Henry Joseph Raehn & Martha Mattox. BS Florida St U 1969; PhD Columbia St U 1995; DMin Oxf 2005; St. Stephens Hse 2005. Trans from Church Of England 2/10/2006 Bp John Wadsworth Howe. m 7/9/1988 Deborah Happy Tinsley c 2. Int S Phil Ch Bartlett TN 2007; Pstr Care S Mich's Ch Orlando FL 2005-2006. "The 1st Blessing," *The Innkeeper*, My Story Pub, 2001. OSL 2005. jsidraehn@aol.com

RAEZER, C Thomas (CFla) 11580 Camp Dr, Dunnellon FL 34432 **Died 1/16/2011** B Lancaster PA 2/16/1944 s Clyde B Raezer & Erna M. Lic VTS 1991. D 6/14/1991 Bp Charlie Fuller McNutt Jr P 9/1/1993 Bp John Wadsworth Howe. c 4. frtuc@aol.com

RAFFALOVICH, Francis Dawson (Dal) 306 Cobalt Cv, Georgetown TX 78633 B Florence IT 11/20/1922 s George Raffalovich & Dorothy Harmon. BS U of Oklahoma 1950; Angl TS 1978. D 6/24/1977 P 7/1/1978 Bp Robert Elwin Terwilliger. m 1/6/2006 Georgia Dawson Strickland c 3. Pstr Assoc Gr Epis Ch Georgetown TX 2005-2010; R S Lk's Ch Denison TX 1983-1988; Cur And Assoc Chr Epis Ch Dallas TX 1977-1981. Auth, "Use Of Seismic Stratigraphy For Minnelusia Exploration Ne Wy"; Auth, "Geophysics". frraff@suddenlink.net

RAFFERTY, Joseph Patrick (Be) 220 Montgomery Ave, West Pittston PA 18643 **Supply P S Ptr's Epis Ch Tunkhannock PA 2011-** B Scranton PA 8/9/1956 s Joseph Rafferty & Dolores. BS U of Scranton 1979; MDiv St Jn Sem 1983. Rec from Roman Catholic 12/7/2010 Bp Paul Victor Marshall. m 6/14/2005 Deborah Montel. jpr20051@hotmail.com

RAFFERTY, Robert Douglas (NMich) 421 Cherry St, Iron River MI 49935 B L'Anse MI 11/22/1954 s Robert Rafferty & Joan. BS MI SU 1978. D 8/4/2005 P 3/12/2006 Bp James Arthur Kelsey. m 12/20/1997 Elke Heyer. rafferty@fast-air.net

RAFTER, John Wesley (Me) PO Box 527, Camden ME 04843 **Ch Of S Thos Camden ME 2007-; Dio Maine Portland ME 2007-** B Manchester NH 6/11/1946 s J Wesley Rafter & Ernagene. BA Estrn U 1968; MDiv STUSo 1984. D 6/9/1984 Bp William Grant Black P 12/18/1984 Bp Furman Stough. m 11/29/1969 Michele Linde c 2. S Matt's Epis Ch Horseheads NY 2003-2007; R Ch Of The Gd Samar Knoxville TN 1996-2003; Stndg Com Dio E Tennessee Knoxville TN 1994-2003; Evang Resource Team Dio E Tennessee Knoxville TN 1993-2003; Dio E Tennessee Knoxville TN 1993; S Tim's Epis Ch Kingsport TN 1992-1996; Stndg Com Dio W Tennessee Memphis TN 1988-1992; Assoc S Geo's Ch Germantown TN 1987-1992; Int S Mary's Epis Ch Jasper AL 1986-1987; COM Dio Alabama Birmingham AL 1985-1987; R S Mich's Epis Ch Fayette AL 1984-1987. Mem of Year Fayette-Lamar ARC Bd 1985. jrafter@webmail.us

RAGAN, Raggs (Ore) 640 Southshore Blvd., Lake Oswego OR 97034 **R S Jas Epis Ch Tigard OR 2006-; Rowland Hall/S Mk's Sch Salt Lake Cty UT 2004-** B Lake Forest IL 8/19/1945 d Randall Creech Ragan & Nathalie Merriam. BA Stan 1967, MA Stan 1971; MDiv CDSP 1979. D 6/24/1979 Bp C Kilmer Myers P 6/1/1980 Bp William Edwin Swing. m 9/11/1977 Robert Alan Kelly c 2. Int S Paul's Ch Salt Lake City UT 2004-2006; Dio Utah Salt Lake City UT 1994-2004; S Paul's Ch Salt Lake City UT 1990; S Mk's Chap Salt Lake City UT 1988-1994; St Marks Sch Salt Lake City UT 1988-1994; S Marg's Chap Salt Lake City UT 1988; S Steph's In-The-Field Epis Ch San Jose CA 1987; CE Min S Mk's Epis Ch Palo Alto CA 1986-1988; CE Min Trsfg Epis Ch San Mateo CA 1983-1984; Asst R S Mk's Epis Ch Palo Alto CA 1980-1982. raggs.ragan@gmail.com

RAGLAND, Rebecca Louise (Mo) 7401 DELMAR BLVD, UNIVERSITY CITY MO 63130 **Chf Ecum Off Dio Missouri S Louis MO 2010-; Ch Of The H Comm U City MO 2009-** B 6/24/1968 d Larry Bogart & Deanne. BA Asbury Coll 1990; MA U of Wisconsin 1994; MDiv Eden TS 2008. D 12/21/2007 P 6/21/2008 Bp George Wayne Smith. m 8/3/1991 Clyde Ragland c 2. Dioc Yth Coordntr Dio Missouri S Louis MO 2007-2009. Auth, "Prayers of the People," *ATR*, Winter Vol 87 No 1, 2005. NAACP 2007; Phi Kappa Phi Acad hon Soc 1995. Grauer Awd for Excellence in Preaching and Ch Ldrshp Eden TS 2008. pastorragland@gmail.com

RAGSDALE, James Lewis (Colo) 3143 S Nucla St, Aurora CO 80013 B Fort Smith AR 9/10/1939 s Elmer M Ragsdale & Fannie. AA Trinidad Jr Coll TT 1959; BA U of Nthrn Colorado 1962; MDiv Nash 1964. D 6/11/1964 P 12/1/1964 Bp Joseph Summerville Minnis. m 5/22/1965 Shirley Webb Miller. Supply/Int P Dio Colorado Denver CO 1993-2008; R Gr Epis Ch Chadron NE 1989-1992; S Paul's Epis Ch Lamar CO 1978-1989; Asst Chr Epis Ch Denver CO 1976-1978; R S Mk's Epis Ch Durango CO 1969-1976. shirlragsdale@juno.com

RAGSDALE, Katherine Hancock (Mass) 99 Brattle St, Cambridge MA 02138 **EDS Cambridge MA 2009-** B Richmond VA 11/22/1958 d Ambler Coleman Ragsdale & Ann. EDS; BA W&M 1980; MDiv VTS 1987. D 6/3/1993 Bp John Shelby Spong P 4/9/1994 Bp Jack Marston McKelvey. m 1/1/2011 Margaret Ewing. Vic S Dav's Epis Mssn Pepperell MA 1996-2009; Advocacy Coordntr Epis Ch Cntr New York NY 1990-1993. Auth, "Boundary Wars: Intimacy & Distance In Healing Relationships," 1996; Auth, "Rel Issues In Dom Violence," *Albany Law Revs*, 1994. EWC; Integrity. kragsdale@eds.edu

RAHAM, Roland Victor (Fla) 842 Se State Road 100, Keystone Heights FL 32656 B Niagara Falls NY 2/25/1940 s Victor Raham & Ann. BA Thiel Coll; USAF; Ya Berk 1965; MDiv GTS 1974. D 6/8/1974 Bp George E Rath P 12/1/1974 Bp George R Selway. m 6/26/1965 Carolyn Hays c 2. S Mk's Ch Starke FL 1993-2002; R S Anne's Epis Ch Keystone Heights FL 1992-2003; Supply P Dio Florida Jacksonville FL 1991-1992; S Geo's Epis Ch Warren MI 1984-1988; Cn Min Cathd Ch Of S Paul Detroit MI 1982-1984; R Chr Ch Pleasant Lake MI 1977-1982; Vic S Andr's Ch Jackson MI 1977-1982; Vic Trin Ch Mackinac Island MI 1974-1977. Auth, "We Need Only You (Mus)," 2001. Alpha Chi Rho. rahamr@bellsouth.net

RAHHAL, Michele Duff (Okla) 721 Franklin Dr, Ardmore OK 73401 B Saint Louis MO 2/10/1946 d Robert Thomas Duff & Jacquelin Ann. BS U of New Mex 1968. D 6/24/2000 Bp Robert Manning Moody. m 7/5/1969 William Rahhal c 3. Dio Oklahoma Oklahoma City OK 2002-2008; Oak Hall Epis Sch Ardmore OK 2000-2001.

RAHM, Kent David (Va) 6604 Willow Pond Dr, Fredericksburg VA 22407 **R Trin Ch Fredericksburg VA 1997-** B Riverhead NY 5/6/1956 s David Charles Rahm & Laura Winchester. BA Pr 1978; MDiv GTS 1983. D 6/7/1982 Bp Robert Campbell Witcher Sr P 5/28/1983 Bp Morgan Porteus. m 10/15/1988 Joanne T Tabacchi c 2. Dn Dio Long Island Garden City NY 1993-1997; R H Trin Epis Ch Vlly Stream NY 1990-1997; Vic Epis Ch Of S Mk The Evang No Bellmore NY 1986-1990; Cur Epis Ch Of S Thos Taunton MA 1982-1986. kentrahm@comcast.net

RAHN, Gaynell M (Va) 905 Princess Anne St, Fredericksburg VA 22401 **Assoc R S Geo's Ch Fredericksburg VA 2006-** B Savannah GA 2/10/1946 d Lawrence Joseph Martin & Myrtis Estelle. Dio Georgia Diac Trng GA; RN Graduatey Nrsng Sch; EFM STUSo. D 9/30/1989 Bp Harry Woolston Shipps P 2/5/2000 Bp Frank Kellogg Allan. m 10/9/1965 Thomas K Rahn c 3. S Steph's Ch Pittsfield MA 2002-2005; S Mk's Ch Dalton GA 1998-2002; Ch Of The Gd Shpd Jacksonville FL 1996-1998; D Calv Ch Memphis TN 1991-1996; D S Thos Ch Savannah GA 1989-1991. gemrahn1@juno.com

RAIH, Donald Roger (WVa) 250 N Marsham St, Romney WV 26757 B Freeport IL 8/29/1940 s Frederick Paul Raih & Ellen Marie. BA S Meinrad Coll 1963; MRE Loyola U 1973; Nash 1982. Rec from Roman Catholic 6/1/1982 as Deacon Bp William Cockburn Russell Sheridan. m 9/1/1978 Patricia Joan Broerman c 2. Hampshire Hardy Yoke Wardensville WV 1997-2000; Epis Shared Minist Of Nwohio Sherwood OH 1993-1997; Co-Pstr Gr Ch Defiance OH 1993-1997; Co-Pstr S Jn The Evang Ch Napoleon OH 1993-1997; Co-Pstr Trin Ch Bryan OH 1993-1997; Vic S Steph's Elwood IN 1986-1993; COM Dio Nthrn Indiana So Bend IN 1984-1987; R S Paul's Epis Ch Gas City IN 1983-1993. Auth, *Handbook for Indiana Luth-Epis Dialogue*, Pathways/Self, 1988.

RAILEY, Robert Macfarlane (NMich) 3029 N Lakeshore Blvd, Marquette MI 49855 B Berkeley CA 6/4/1940 s Isham Railey & Marie Louise. BS Stan 1962; PhD Stan 1976. D 5/9/2006 P 5/27/2007 Bp James Arthur Kelsey. m 12/29/2002 Nancy M Royce c 6. rmrailey@excite.com

RAINEY, Frank Cobb (SwFla) 2635 Cleveland Ave, Fort Myers FL 33901 **Died 12/9/2009** B Oakland CA 11/30/1926 s Phillip Wensler Rainey & Harriet Cobb. AA San Mateo Coll 1948. D 1/31/1971 Bp Sumner Walters. c 2.

RAINEY ENGLISH, Allison Rainey (Los) 18631 Chapel Ln, Huntington Beach CA 92646 **COM Dio Los Angeles Los Angeles CA 2010-; Assoc for Yth S Wilfrid Of York Epis Ch Huntington Bch CA 2008-** B Franklin IN 1/17/1982 d Phillip Martin Rainey & Judith Allen. BA Hanover Coll 2004; Mdiv Claremont TS 2008. D 6/7/2008 P 1/10/2009 Bp Joseph Jon Bruno. m 10/11/2008 Robert English. 76th GC Yth Prog- Asst Dir Ecusa / Mssn Personl New York NY 2008-2009; Stdt Mnstry Intern The Ch Of The Ascen Sierra Madre CA 2006-2008. allison.english@hotmail.com

R

RAINING, Hillary Dowling (Be) 763 S. Valley Forge Road, Wayne PA 19087 **Assoc S Dav's Ch Wayne PA 2011-** B Tunkhannock PA 10/8/1982 BA Moravian Coll Bethlehem PA 2005; MDiv Ya Berk 2008. D 2/2/2008 P 8/15/2008 Bp Paul Victor Marshall. m 7/9/2005 Kenneth Reinholz c 1. Cur Trin Ch Bethlehem PA 2008-2011. hillary.raining@gmail.com

RAINS JR, Harry James (WNC) 8 Nicole Lane, Weaverville NC 28787 **St. Paul's-Lake Jas, Morganton, NC S Paul's Epis Ch Morganton NC 2009-** B Larned KS 1/28/1940 s Harry James Rains & Dorothy Vera. BA Murray St U 1965; MDiv PDS 1968. D 4/20/1968 P 10/28/1968 Bp Alfred L Banyard. m 6/21/1980 Sharon Hawkins c 3. St. Jn's Epis Ch Wytheville, VA S Jn's Epis Ch Wytheville VA 2007; R S Andr's Ch La Mesa CA 1999-2005; R Ch Of S Mich The Archangel Colorado Sprg CO 1998-1999; R S Jas Ch Potomac MD 1994-1998; Chair Resolutns Com Dio Vermont Burlington VT 1987-1991; R S Jn's Chap Manchestr Ctr VT 1986-1994; R Zion Ch Manchester Cntr VT 1986-1994; Co-Chair Stwdshp & Evang Cmsn Dio Vermont Burlington VT 1983-1986; R S Jn's In The Mountains Stowe VT 1981-1986; R Trin Epis Ch Lewiston ME 1978-1981; R Ch Of The Gd Shpd Rangeley ME 1971-1978; Vic Chr Ch Magnolia NJ 1969-1971; Cur Gr Ch In Haddonfield Haddonfield NJ 1968-1969. hjrains1@gmail.com

RAISH, John Woodham (WLa) 211 Linden St, Shreveport LA 71104 B Denver CO 1/8/1945 s Donald Ridlington Raish & Elizabeth Grace. BA SW U Georgetown TX 1967; MDiv Nash 1980. D 6/28/1980 P 1/1/1981 Bp William Carl Frey. m 5/27/1972 Margaret Helen Sampson c 2. Dio Wstrn Louisiana Alexandria LA 2003; Exec Com Dio Wstrn Louisiana Alexandria LA 1998-2000; R S Mths Epis Ch Shreveport LA 1997-2006; R H Trin Epis Ch Sulphur LA 1985-1997; Vic S Andr's Epis Ch Ft Lupton CO 1980-1985; Vic S Eliz's Epis Ch Brighton CO 1980-1985; Dio Colorado Denver CO 1980. jwraish@yahoo.com

RAJ, Vincent S (ECR) 618 W Acacia St, Salinas CA 93901 B Madras India 4/16/1945 s Anthony S Raj & Monica. BD Pontificia Universitas Urbaniana Rome It 1965; PHL Pontificia Universitas Urbaniana Rome It 1967; BD Pontificia Universitas Urbaniana Rome It 1969; STL Pontificia Universitas Urbaniana Rome It 1971. Rec from Roman Catholic 1/25/2002 as Priest Bp Richard Lester Shimpfky. m 3/27/1993 Carol Ann Baker c 4. R S Geo's Ch Salinas CA 2002-2010. vincentraj@att.net

RAJAGOPAL, Doris Elizabeth (Pa) 763 Valley Forge Rd, Wayne PA 19087 **All SS Ch Collingdale PA 2010-** B Philadelphia PA 11/8/1961 d Henry Hunt & Doris. BA Tem 1983; PhD CUNY 2000; MDiv Luth TS 2009. D 6/14/2008 P 1/10/2009 Bp Edward Lewis Lee Jr. m 6/30/1989 Subrahmanyam Rajagopal c 2. Asst S Dav's Ch Wayne PA 2008-2009. sharada2000@verizon.net

RALPH, Harry (SO) 280 Walden Way #210, Dayton OH 45440 **Died 6/10/2010** B Laurel DE 10/28/1920 s Harry Longstreet Ralph & Fannie Ellen. BS Roa 1948; BD VTS 1951; U Of Delaware Newark 1955. D 6/8/1951 P 12/5/1951 Bp Arthur R Mc Kinstry. c 4.

RALPH, Michael Jay (LI) 28 Highland Rd, Glen Cove NY 11542 **S Paul's Ch Glen Cove NY 2009-** B Saratoga NY 12/7/1969 D 6/19/2004 P 4/11/2005 Bp Stacy F Sauls. m 7/1/2000 Aimee L Ralph c 2. Ch Of The Ascen Mt Sterling KY 2006-2009; Trin Ch Covington KY 2004-2006. majralh@msn.com

RALPH, S Lester (Mass) 88 King St, Reading MA 01867 B Lynn MA 7/9/1931 s Albert Ralph & Grace Amour. BA Bos 1954; BD VTS 1958; MA Bos 1959; LLB Bos 1963; DD VTS 1973. D 6/21/1958 Bp Frederic Cunningham Lawrence P 12/1/1958 Bp Anson Phelps Stokes Jr. m 6/29/1964 Joyce Caldwell Caldwell Palmer c 3. R Chr Ch Somerville MA 1964-1981; Asst Old No Chr Ch Boston MA 1964-1965; Asst Gr Epis Ch Medford MA 1960-1963; Cur Chr Ch Waltham MA 1958-1960. Auth, "Methods Of Law Pract In Ma," W Pub, 1965. slralph1@verizon.net

RALSTON, Betty Marie (Colo) Po Box 773627, Steamboat Springs CO 80477 B Greeley CO 9/28/1938 d Paul Borden Laws & Sybil Marie. Dio Colorado Diac Trng Prog CO; S Lk Sch Nrsng. D 11/2/1996 Bp William Jerry Winterrowd. m 3/17/1967 Robert Sanford Ralston. D S Paul's Epis Ch Steamboat Sprg CO 1999-2009. bmr@steamboatdsl.com

RALSTON, D Darwin (O) 711 College Ave, Lima OH 45805 B Bellefontaine OH 12/18/1945 s Delva Darwin Ralston & Ethyl Piccola. BA OH SU 1972; MDiv GTS 1975. D 5/31/1975 P 12/1/1975 Bp John Mc Gill Krumm. m 6/20/1970 Andrea Jane Alloway c 2. R Chr Ch Lima OH 1989-2005; Stndg Com Dio Indianapolis Indianapolis IN 1987-1989; Ch Of St Mich And All Ang Indianapolis IN 1986-1989; Mssn & Strtgy Com Dio Indianapolis Indianapolis IN 1980-1989; Bi Par Mnstry Addyston OH 1978-1986; Wrshp Cmsn Dio Indianapolis Indianapolis IN 1978-1982; LocTen S Jn's Ch Worthington OH 1977-1978; Assoc R S Jn's Ch Worthington OH 1975-1976.

RAMBO JR, Charles B (CFla) Po Box 46, Rutherfordton NC 28139 **Chr The King Epis Ch Orlando FL 2010-** B Mongomery AL 11/27/1960 s Charles Blake Rambo & Dorothy. BA Stetson U 1991; MDiv STUSo 1997. D 6/28/1997 P 12/1/1997 Bp John Wadsworth Howe. m 8/15/1987 Carol Harrison. S Paul's Epis Ch New Smyrna Bch FL 2006-2008; S Fran' Epis Ch Rutherfordton NC 1999-2002; D Shpd Of The Hills Epis Ch Lecanto FL 1997-1999. Ord S Lk The Physcn. fbjr06@yahoo.com

RAMBO, Thomas Birch (Spok) 323 Catherine St, Walla Walla WA 99362 **R S Paul's Ch Walla Walla WA 2008-** B Addis Ababa Ethiopia 5/10/1970 s Thomas Clough Rambo & Elinor Elisabeth. BA New Coll of Florida 1992; ABD U Of Kentucky 1998; MDiv STUSo 2001. D 6/9/2001 P 4/11/2002 Bp Stacy F Sauls. m 7/3/1992 Katherine Mary Clevenger c 2. P-in-c Epis Ch of Our Sav Richmond KY 2004-2008; Asst To The R Ch Of The Gd Shpd Lexington KY 2001-2004. fr.birch@gmail.com

RAMCHARAN, Carlisle John (SC) 719 Boulevard St, Orangeburg SC 29115 **Died 11/8/2010** B 1/3/1925 s John Ramcharan & Lily. BA Lon 1947; Lon 1949; MA Emory U 1967; Fllshp Coll of Preachers 1968. D 10/1/1949 P 4/1/1951 Bp The Bishop Of Trinidad. LADIESFITNESS@MSN.COM

RAMEY, Lloyd Francis (Ore) 1444 Liberty St Se, Salem OR 97302 B Ironton OH 8/9/1923 s John Wesly Ramey & Myrtle Mae. BS USC 1950. D 3/31/1965 Bp James Walmsley Frederic Carman. m 1/31/1953 Suzanne Huggins c 3. D /Asst S Paul's Epis Ch Salem OR 1965-2000.

RAMIREZ, Mark Lloyd (Chi) St Barnabas Episc Church, 22W415 Butterfield Rd, Glen Ellyn IL 60137 B San Pablo CA 1/7/1960 s Lloyd J Ramirez & Joyce N. BS Grand Canyon U 1986; MA Wheaton Coll 1988. D 1/19/2008 Bp Victor Alfonso Scantlebury. m 8/3/1996 Anne K Ramirez c 2. mark7029@sbcglobal.net

RAMIREZ-MILLER, Gerardo Carlos (NY) 351 W 24th St Apt 6-C, New York NY 10011 B New York NY 5/17/1945 s Leon Osias Miller & Belen. BA CUNY 1967; MDiv UTS 1986. D 1/12/1987 Bp Paul Moore Jr P 5/1/1988 Bp Jose Antonio Ramos. Supply P S Mary's Ch Carle Place NY 2001-2005; Supply P S Andr's So Fallsburg Woodbourne NY 2000-2001; Supply P S Jas Ch Callicoon NY 2000-2001; Diocn Msnry & Ch Extntn Socty New York NY 2000; Epis Soc Serv New York NY 1989-2001; Epis Mssn Soc New York NY 1989-1990. Epis Actors' Gld - Life Mem 2000; OHC 1985. rammil@juno.com

RAMIREZ-SEGARRA, Cesar (PR) PO Box 1967, Yauco PR 00698 Puerto Rico **Dio Puerto Rico S Just PR 2008-** B Puerto Rico 8/8/1968 s Cesar A Ramirez & Ana L. Rec from Roman Catholic 7/6/2008 Bp David Andres Alvarez-Velazquez. m 3/7/2009 Reinabelle Rosado-Gonzalez. ce_emil@hotmail.com

RAMNARAINE, Barbara Allen (Minn) St. Luke's Episcopal Church, 4557 Colfax Ave. 5, Minneapolis MN 55403 **D S Paul's Ch Minneapolis MN 1989-; Coordntr, Epis Disabil Ntwk Dio Minnesota Minneapolis MN 1985-; Coordntr, Epis Disabil Ntwk Dio Minnesota Minneapolis MN 1985-** B Minneapolis MN 6/6/1934 d Rudolf W Koucky & Ladene. BA Macalester Coll 1955; Dio Minnosota D Trng MN 1984. D 1/25/1984 Bp Robert Marshall Anderson. m 3/15/1955 Cecil Ramnaraine c 3. "Assessibility Guidelines for Epis Ch"; Auth, "AccessAbility: A Manual for Ch". Oblate Ord Of S Ben. disability99@earthlink.net

RAMOS, Mary Serena (Minn) 662 Goodrich Ave, Saint Paul MN 55105 B Duluth MN 7/23/1963 d Kenneth Moran & Jackie. BS U MN 1985; MS U MN 1989; MDiv CDSP 2006. D 6/8/2006 P 12/21/2006 Bp James Louis Jelinek. m 9/12/1987 Dean Arthur Ramos c 3. P S Steph The Mtyr Ch Minneapolis MN 2006-2009. marysramos@aol.com

RAMOS, Pablo (U) 1904 Dale Ridge Ave, Salt Lake City UT 84116 **Dio Utah Salt Lake City UT 2005-** B Guadalajara MX 1/23/1967 s Pablo Ramos-Suarez & Elizama. MDiv S Andr's Sem Mx 1996. D 5/26/1996 P 12/1/1996 Bp Sergio Carranza-Gomez. m 5/19/1989 Beatriz Rodriguez-Hernandez c 3. Cathd Ch Of S Mk Salt Lake City UT 1998-2005; Dio Mex 1996-1998. Auth, "Prot Theol 1900-60". Cmnty Of Hope S Lk Hosp Houston Tx. revpablo@comcast.net

✠ **RAMOS-ORENCH, Rt Rev Wilfrido** (Ct) 77 Linnmoore St, Hartford CT 06114 B 5/4/1940 s Francisco Ramos-Garcia & Maria. Caribbean Cntr for Advncd Stds; BA Pontifical Cath U of Puerto Rico 1962; MDiv ETSC 1966; GTS 1974; DMin Estrn Bapt TS 1992. D 5/29/1966 P 12/1/1966 Bp Francisco Reus-Froylan Con 1/1/2000 for Ct. m 8/17/1984 Marling Cotay-Colon. Provsnl Bp Cntrl Dio Ecuador EC 2006-2009; Bp Suffr Dio Connecticut Hartford CT 2000-2006; Cntrl Epis Dnry New Britain CT 1998-2000; Grtr Hartford Reg Mnstry E Hartford CT 1995-2000; S Lk's/S Paul's Ch Bridgeport CT 1984-1993; Dio Puerto Rico S Just PR 1978-1979; Cetym C A 1975-1977; Epis Sem Of The Caribbean Carolina PR 1968-1975. Auth, "Our Hist Cross Roads: Towards A New Orientation In Mssn"; Auth, "Out Of The Depths"; Auth, "Una Vision Del Ministerio Hispano En La Diocesis Epis De Ct". Aamft; Natl Hisp Cltn, The Consult, Urban Caucus. RAMOSWM@AOL.COM

RAMSAY, Allan Leavenworth (Mich) 14560 Lakeside Cir Apt 242, Sterling Heights MI 48313 **Died 5/17/2011** B Durand MI 1/20/1911 s Charles Leavenworth Ramsay & Clara Agnes. AA Jackson Jr Coll 1932; BA MI SU 1935; DS SWTS 1940; DD SWTS 1969. D 6/29/1940 P 1/11/1941 Bp Frank W Creighton. c 3. Bro of S Andr 1929; EvangES 1940; SIM 1940. RamsayJamesA@aol.com

RAMSAY, Frederick Jeffress (Md) 16027 W. Sandia Park Dr., Surprise AZ 85374 B Baltimore MD 2/28/1936 s Alfred Ogden Ramsay & Mette. BS W&L 1958; MS U IL 1960; PhD U IL 1962; MEd U IL 1969. D 3/12/1970 Bp Harry

Lee Doll P 2/28/1971 Bp David Keller Leighton Sr. m 12/17/1982 Susan Joanne Fennell c 6. R S Andr's Ch Pasadena MD 1991-2000; Vic S Andr's Epis Ch Glenwood MD 1987-1991; Assoc S Jn's Ch Reisterstown MD 1983-1987; Assoc The Ch Of The Nativ Cedarcroft Baltimore MD 1972-1977; D-In-Trng Trin Ch Towson MD 1970-1971. Auth, "BUFFALO Mtn," do, 2007; Auth, "JUDAS, The gospel of betrayal," AuthorHouse/ Perfect Niche Press, 2007; Auth, "IMPULSE," do, 2006; Auth, "SECRETS," do, 2005; Auth, "ARTSCAPE," Poisoned Pen Press, 2004; Auth, "Med & Rel"; Auth, "Effects Of Adjuvant & Antiserum On Tumor Growth"; Auth, "Investigation Of Virus-Like Material Assocd w C3 H/F9 Leukemia"; Auth, "The Baltimore Declaration". Curs. Bp'S Awd For Outstanding Ord Mnstry Dio Maryland 2000. fredramaz@cox.net

RAMSDEN, Charles Leslie (Cal) 1266 139th Ave, San Leandro CA 94578 B Saint Louis MO USA 2/5/1946 s Richard Hugh Ramsden & Cecelia Mary. U of Missouri 1966; BS Washington U 1971; MDiv CDSP 1974; Grad Theol Un 1985. D 6/22/1974 Bp George Leslie Cadigan P 12/28/1974 Bp Hanford Langdon King Jr. c 2. Ch Pension Fund New York NY 2000-2008; Int S Paul's Epis Ch Morris Plains NJ 1999-2001; Int S Jas Epis Ch Danbury CT 1998-1999; De GC Dio California San Francisco CA 1994-1997; Dioc Coun Dio California San Francisco CA 1993-1995; R S Fran' Epis Ch San Francisco CA 1991-1998; Dept of Missions Dio California San Francisco CA 1987-1991; Trst of Epis Chars Appeal Dio California San Francisco CA 1987-1990; R S Anselm's Epis Ch Lafayette CA 1986-1991; Stndg Com Dio El Camino Real Monterey CA 1980-1984; Dioc Coun Dio California San Francisco CA 1979-1980; R S Steph's Epis Ch San Luis Obispo CA 1977-1986; Chair of Bp's Cmsn on CE Dio Idaho Boise ID 1976-1977; Cn S Mich's Cathd Boise ID 1974-1977. Auth, *Dio California Par & Mssn Self-Study*, 1991. charles.ramsden@comcast.net

RAMSEY, Henry Elrod (WMass) 57 Loomis Dr Apt A1, West Hartford CT 06107 B Atlanta GA 3/19/1938 s William Little Ramsey & Farrar. BA U GA 1960; STB Ya Berk 1966. D 6/1/1966 Bp Randolph R Claiborne P 12/1/1966 Bp Robert McConnell Hatch. m 12/29/1960 Madge Mcleod Bowen. Asst To R S Jn's Ch Northampton MA 1967-1969; Cur S Paul's Ch Holyoke MA 1966-1967.

RAMSEY, Ronald Edward (Mass) 8 Meacham Rd, Cambridge MA 02140 **S Jn's Ch Arlington MA 1998-** B Lake Wales FL 12/10/1954 s Joe Ramsey & Viola. MDiv Morehouse Sch of Rel 1980; DMin Trin Luth Sem 1984; CAS EDS 1992; MPA Harv 1993. D 6/4/1994 Bp David Elliot Johnson P 12/1/1994 Bp M(arvil) Thomas Shaw III. m 7/17/2003 Jean Ramsey c 1. Trin Ch In The City Of Boston Boston MA 1994-1996. ramseylewis@earthlink.net

RAMSEY JONES, Beverly Jean (Alb) 7460 Se Concord Pl, Hobe Sound FL 33455 B Norwalk OH 9/8/1950 d Donald Byron Fish & Miriam Elizabeth. Florida Atlantic U; AA Palm Bch Cmnty Coll 1970; BA Barry U 1999. D 12/21/1991 Bp Calvin Onderdonk Schofield Jr. m 8/11/2004 Michael Jones. S Mary's Epis Ch Stuart FL 2000-2011; Assoc For Cmncatns The Epis Ch Of Beth-By-The-Sea Palm Bch FL 1993-1995; D S Dav's-In-The-Pines Epis Ch Wellington FL 1991-1995. revbevcreekside@aol.com

RAMSEY-MUSOLF, Michael Jeffrey (Los) Dept of Physics, Univ of Wisconsin-Madison, Chamberlin Hall, 1150 University Ave, Madison WI 53706 B Portland OR 12/13/1961 s Lyndon Musolf & Barbara. BA Pomona Coll 1984; MA Pr 1986; PhD Pr 1989; MDiv EDS 1993. D 6/12/1993 Bp George Phelps Mellick Belshaw P 1/29/1994 Bp Frank Harris Vest Jr. m 10/1/1996 Darrel Ramsey-Musolf. Asstg P All SS Par Los Angeles CA 2001-2008; Asstg P S Ptr's And S Andr's Epis Providence RI 1999-2000; Asst S Paul's Ch Seattle WA 1996-1998; Serv Chr and S Lk's Epis Ch Norfolk VA 1993-1995. Tertiary Of The Soc Of S Fran. Young Investigator Natl Sci Fndt 1993. mjrmlap@att.net

RAMSHAW, Lance Arthur (Del) 106 Alden Rd, Concord MA 01742 B Meriden CT 6/21/1953 s Walter Arthur Ramshaw & Ruth. BA Ob 1974; MDiv EDS 1977; MS U Of Delaware Newark 1983; PhD U Of Delaware Newark 1989. D 6/25/1977 Bp John Harris Burt P 2/25/1978 Bp William Hawley Clark. m 9/9/1989 Abigail G Wine. Int S Barn Ch Wilmington DE 1983-1985; Int Trin Ch Elkton MD 1982-1983; Int S Thos's Par Newark DE 1981-1982; Dio Delaware Wilmington DE 1980-1985; Int All SS Ch Rehoboth Bch DE 1980-1981; Co-R S Paul's Ch Camden DE 1977-1980. refused@refused.com

RAMSHAW, Lynn Cecelia Homeyer (Chi) 2941 Sunset Ave, Flossmoor IL 60422 B Orange NJ 9/2/1937 d Arthur Claus Homeyer & Cecelia Doris. BA Ohio Wesl 1959; MSW Barry U 1991; MA GTS 1997. D 5/8/1980 P 6/29/1996 Bp Calvin Onderdonk Schofield Jr. c 3. Assoc The Ch Of S Jn The Evang Flossmoor IL 1999-2002; Cn Trin Cathd Cleveland OH 1997-1999; Asst S Ptr's Ch New York NY 1995-1997; St Laurence Chap Pompano Bch FL 1991-1994; Asst S Benedicts Ch Plantation FL 1986-1990; COM Dio SE Florida Miami FL 1980-1986. Auth, "sev arts," *Luth Wmn Today*, Fortress Press, 2010. Benedictine Wmn of Madison 2005; OHC 1985-2004. grmlynn@sbcglobal.net

RAMSTAD, Philip Robert (Minn) 901 Como Boulevard East, #304, Osceda WI 54020 B Saint Paul MN 9/24/1944 s Robert L Ramstad & Marjorie. Pur; BA S Thos Coll Miami FL 1968; MDiv SWTS 1977. D 6/25/1977 P 2/1/1978 Bp Philip Frederick McNairy. Reserve P S Jn The Evang S Paul MN 2005-2007; Supply Dio Minnesota Minneapolis MN 2004-2007; R Ch Of The H Cross Dundas MN 1990-1993; All SS Ch Northfield MN 1990-1992; Cur All SS Ch New York NY 1985-1986; R Chr And S Steph's Ch New York NY 1980-1985; Chr Ch Totowa NJ 1980-1985; Vic Ch Of Our Sav Little Falls MN 1977-1980; Vic Ch Of The Gd Samar Sauk Cntr MN 1977-1980. ramstad3@aol.com

RANDALL, Anne Elizabeth (Dal) 421 Custer Rd, Richardson TX 75080 **Assoc Ch Of The Epiph Richardson TX 2009-** B Ft Worth 1/12/1967 d Edwin C Woodrift & Barbara B. BA U of Texas 1990; MDiv Perkins TS Sthrn Methodist 2009. D 6/20/2009 P 2/2/2010 Bp James Monte Stanton. m 4/6/1991 Gardner Randall c 2. randallcrew@sbcglobal.net

RANDALL, Catharine Louise (Ct) 91 Minortown Rd, Woodbury CT 06798 B Lafayette IN 4/14/1957 d Edward Randall & Sally Ashley. MA Boston Coll 1981; PhD U Pgh 1986; MA R Yale DS New Haven CT 2008. D 6/27/2007 Bp Jeffrey Neil Steenson P 11/10/2007 Bp William Carl Frey. m 1/23/1998 Randall Balmer c 4. Assoc S Jn's Ch Washington CT 2008-2009; S Paul's Ch Woodbury CT 2008. crandall@fordham.edu

RANDALL II, Chandler Corydon (SanD) Po Box 1137, Bloomfield Hills MI 48304 **Theol-in-Res Chr Ch Cranbrook Bloomfield Hills MI 2000-** B Ann Arbor MI 1/22/1935 s Frederick Stewart Randall & Leta Madeline. AB U MI 1957; STB Ya Berk 1960; PhD Hebr Un Coll-Jewish Inst of Rel 1969. D 6/29/1960 Bp Archie H Crowley P 6/27/1961 Bp Roger W Blanchard. m 7/2/1960 Marian Archias Montgomery c 3. R S Ptr's Epis Ch Del Mar CA 1988-2000; R Trin Ch Ft Wayne IN 1971-1988; R S Paul's Ch Richmond IN 1967-1971; Cur Gr Ch Cincinnati OH 1960-1964. Auth, "An Approach To Biblic Satire," Forw Pub, 1990; Auth, "Satire In Bible," U Microfilus, 1969; Auth, "Shaharith and Matins," *Variant*, Hebr Un Coll, 1963. Who's Who in Amer The Marquis Who's Who Pub Bd 1997; DD Ya Berk/New Haven, CT 1985. umpadre@aol.com

RANDALL, Elizabeth Penney (Colo) 735 S Vine St, Denver CO 80209 **S Andr's Ch Denver CO 2009-** B Buffalo NY 6/29/1957 d Harry Garfield Randall & Marian Clapp. BA Smith 1979; MDiv Ya Berk 1988. D 6/11/1994 P 12/1/1994 Bp William Jerry Winterrowd. m 6/8/1985 Alan Gottlieb c 1. S Jn's Cathd Denver CO 1994-2009. eprandall@gmail.com

RANDALL, Richard Alan (CPa) 222 N 6th St, Chambersburg PA 17201 B Detroit MI 3/27/1944 s Robert William Randall & Barbara May. BA Wayne 1967; MDiv SWTS 1970. D 6/29/1970 Bp Archie H Crowley P 1/23/1971 Bp Richard S M Emrich. m 7/10/1976 Martha Jean Aston c 2. R Trin Epis Ch Chambersburg PA 1987-2000; Dio Cntrl Pennsylvania Harrisburg PA 1985-2002; R H Trin Epis Ch Shamokin PA 1978-1987; Vic Gd Shpd Ch Clarion PA 1974-1977; Vic Ch Of The H Trin Brookville PA 1972-1978; Vic Chr Ch Punxsutawney PA 1972-1974; Cur All SS Ch E Lansing MI 1970-1972. ASSP 1973. rrandall41@comcast.net

RANDALL JR, Robert James (SVa) 716 Abbey Dr, Virginia Beach VA 23455 **R Old Donation Ch Virginia Bch VA 2004-** B Chandler AZ 12/20/1952 s Robert Randall & Anna. BS RPI 1974; ME RPI 1975; MDiv VTS 1997. D 5/31/1997 P 2/1/1998 Bp Charles Farmer Duvall. m 1/28/1984 Christine Lee Everitt c 2. Vic S Mary's Epis Ch Andalusia AL 1997-2004. Rotary Intl 1997. brandall@olddonation.org

RANDALL SSM, Sarah Archais (Mass) P.O. Box C, Duxbury MA 02331 **Soc Of St Marg Roxbury MA 2010-** B Cincinnati OH 1/28/1966 d Chandler Corydon Randall & Marian Archias. BA Ya 1988; MAT Van 1990; MDiv EDS 2010. D 6/5/2010 Bp Gayle Elizabeth Harris P 1/8/2011 Bp M(arvil) Thomas Shaw III. Asst S Lk's/San Lucas Epis Ch Chelsea MA 2010-2011. sarah@ssmbos.org

RANDLE, Cameron D (Los) 6125 Carlos Ave, Los Angeles CA 90028 B Mt View MO 5/6/1957 s James H Randle & Sandra C. BA Oral Roberts U 1980; Juris Doctorate U of Tulsa 1987; MDiv Ya Berk 2008. D 1/18/2009 P 9/26/2009 Bp Sergio Carranza-Gomez. m 3/20/1999 Angelica Garcia c 1. D S Steph's Par Los Angeles CA 2009-2011. crandle777@yahoo.com

RANDOLPH JR, Henry George (NI) 26824 CR 4, Elkhart IN 46514 **Vocations Dir Dio Nthrn Indiana So Bend IN 2002-; R S Dav's Epis Ch Elkhart IN 1991-** B Richmond VA 8/18/1950 s Henry George Randolph & Virginia. BA St Andr's U Laurinburg NC 1972; MDiv VTS 1977. D 12/6/1978 P 6/6/1979 Bp Robert Poland Atkinson. m 8/19/1972 Anita Adams c 1. Assoc R S Jas Epis Ch Baton Rouge LA 1986-1991; R S Mary's Ch Kinston NC 1984-1986. Auth, *Var Hymns & Bk Revs*. frhgrandolphjr@gmail.com

RANDOLPH, Michael Phillip Gibson Gantling (SO) 4969 Pershing Pl, Saint Louis MO 63108 B Brooklyn NY 11/27/1940 s Lewis Randolph & Juliette. S Paul's Coll Lawrenceville VA 1962; BS Tennessee St U 1968; MDiv EDS 1970. D 6/13/1970 P 12/1/1970 Bp Jonathan Goodhue Sherman. Chr Ch Cathd S Louis MO 2000-2002; Gr Ch Kirkwood MO 1999-2000; S Paul's Epis Ch Pittsburgh PA 1997-1999; S Mk's Epis Ch Dayton OH 1995-1996; Int The Ch Of Ascen And H Trin Cincinnati OH 1993-1994; Int Chr Ch Xenia OH 1991-1993; Int S Simon Of Cyrene Epis Ch Cincinnati OH 1988-1989; Int H

Trin Ch Cincinnati OH 1983-1985; Int S Jas Epis Ch Cincinnati OH 1982-1983; Epis Soc Of Chr Ch Cincinnati OH 1977-1982; Dio Atlanta Atlanta GA 1974-1977; Cur/Actg Vic Par of Trin Ch New York NY 1970-1974. Auth, "Fiction & Histo," *Fiction & Hist Biographies For Var Chld'S mag.* mrand87940@aol.com

RANEY III, A Raymond (RG) 04 Tano Road, Santa Fe NM 87506 **Cn for Dioc Life Dio The Rio Grande Albuquerque NM 2011-; R Ch Of The H Cross Edgewood NM 2007-** B Bedford Indiana 2/24/1947 s Arthur Raymond Raney & Maxine Whitted. BA Indiana U 1974; BFA U of New Mex 1992; BAFA U of New Mex 1992; MFA U of New Mex 1995; MDiv Iliff TS 2006. D 5/20/2006 P 12/17/2006 Bp Jeffrey Neil Steenson. m 10/31/1982 Linda Lewis. AAM 2007. raymondraney@usa.net

RANK SSP, Andrew Peter Robert (SanD) Po Box 34548, San Diego CA 92163 B Des Moines IA 9/8/1937 s William Phillip Rank & Bessie Marie. D 11/3/1983 P 5/5/1984 Bp Charles Brinkley Morton. Mutual Mnstry Revs Team Dio San Diego San Diego CA 2002-2003; Chapt Cathd Ch Of S Paul San Diego CA 2001-2010. Ed, *S Paul's Printer*, 1980; Ed, *Directory's Conf Rel Life*, 1975. Conf of Angl Rel Ord of Amer 1972; NECAD 1982; Soc of S Paul 1958. Hon Cn S Paul's Cathd San Diego CA 2000; Fell Amer Coll Healthcare Admin 1979. anbssp@earthlink.net

RANKIN, Deborah Truman (O) 1500A 17th St., Huntington WV 25701 **R S Jn's Epis Ch Cuyahoga Falls OH 2007-** B Victoria TX 12/31/1948 d Joseph Dean Truman & Frederike. Victoria Coll Victoria TX; BS Baylor U 1970; MA Rice U 1992; CAS Nash 1999. D 6/13/1998 P 6/12/1999 Bp John H(enry) Smith. c 2. The No Cntrl Cluster Elkins WV 2003-2004; R S Paul's Ch Weston WV 2001-2007; Intern Chr Ch Point Pleasant WV 1998-2002; D Gr Ch Ravenswood WV 1998-2002; D S Jn's Ripley WV 1998-2002; River Bend Cluster Point Pleasant WV 1998-2000. ACPE. revdrankin@sbcglobal.net

RANKIN, Edward H(arris) (Oly) 11510 NE 35th Ave, Vancouver WA 98686 B Berkeley CA 11/17/1936 s Sheldon Stevens Rankin & Marion Ivy. BA U Pac 1958; BD CDSP 1961; MA Oklahoma St U 1969; MA U of Oregon 1970; DMin SFTS 1989. D 6/25/1961 Bp James Albert Pike P 12/31/1961 Bp Leland Stark. m 3/23/1969 Kara Lynn Kinnick c 1. R S Lk's Epis Ch Vancouver WA 1980-2000; R S Steph's Epis Par Portland OR 1973-1980; Vic S Andr's Epis Ch Florence OR 1970-1973; Vic S Mary Ch Gardiner OR 1970-1973; Asst S Andr's Ch Stillwater OK 1962-1969; Cur S Andr And H Comm Ch So Orange NJ 1961-1962. Auth, "Pleasures Forevermore," *The Angl*, 1985. Angl Soc; Associated Parishes. Phi Kappa Phi. ehrankin@comcast.net

RANKIN, Glenn Edger (Ia) 2206 Frontier Rd, Denison IA 51442 **Trin Ch Denison IA 1974-** B Milwaukee WI 8/26/1945 s Edger David Rankin & Janice Louise. BA Carroll Coll 1967; MDiv Nash 1971. D 1/18/1971 P 7/27/1971 Bp Gordon V Smith. c 3. H Trin Ch Atlantic IA 1971-1975; S Paul's Ch Harlan IA 1971-1975; Dio Iowa Des Moines IA 1971-1974. Associated Parishes, HSEC, AGO. bach@frontiernet.net

RANKIN, Jerry Dean (Kan) 406 Hillside St, Abilene KS 67410 **P-in-c S Jn's Ch Abilene KS 2006-** B Manitou Springs CO 10/28/1954 s Jack Rankin & Sandra. BA Ft Hays St U 1981; MDiv CDSP 1984. D 6/30/1984 Bp John Forsythe Ashby P 1/23/1985 Bp Roger Howard Cilley. m 6/6/1981 Diana Facklam c 3. R S Matt's Ch Enid OK 1996-2004; R Ch Of The Epiph Sedan KS 1991-1996; Dio Kansas Topeka KS 1991-1996; Vic S Matt's Ch Cedar Vale KS 1991; Asst R S Mk's Epis Ch Casper WY 1988-1991; Assoc S Lk's Epis Ch Manchester MO 1986-1988; Cur The Ch of the Gd Shpd Austin TX 1984-1986. jdrankin406@yahoo.com

RANKIN II, William Wright (Cal) 13 Mara Vista Ct, Tiburon CA 94920 B Schenectady NY 10/10/1941 s John Gordon Rankin & Dorothy Bosher. BA Duke 1963; BD EDS 1966; PhD Duke 1977; MA Duke 1979. D 6/16/1966 Bp Walter M Higley P 6/16/1967 Bp Ned Cole. m 9/5/1964 Sally Katherine Heller c 2. Assoc Ch Of The Nativ San Rafael CA 1998-2005; Dio California San Francisco CA 1998-2002; Pres and Dn EDS Cambridge MA 1993-1998; R S Steph's Par Belvedere CA 1983-1993; Assoc R All SS Ch Pasadena CA 1980-1983; LocTen S Barth's Ch Pittsboro NC 1974-1980; Asst All SS Ch Pasadena CA 1967-1974; Cur Trin Ch Elmira NY 1966-1967. Auth, "Soc Ethics," *Cracking the Monolith*, Crossroads/Doubleday, 1994; Auth, "Profsnl Ethics," *Confidentiality and Cler*, Morehouse Pub, 1990; Auth, "Soc Ethics," *Countdown to Disaster*, Foreward Mvmt, 1982. Bd Overseers, Wellesley Coll Cntr for Wmn 1994-1998; Boston Theol Inst Chair 1996-1998; Intl Bioethics Inst 1990-1993; Renaissance Weekend 1993. Vstng Resrch Brocher Fndt, Geneva, CH 2012; Vstng Sci Swiss Tropical Inst, U. Basel, CH 2009; Schlr in Res Rockefeller Fndt, Bellagio, IT 2004. wrankingaia@gmail.com

RANKIN-WILLIAMS, Chris (Cal) Po Box 217, Ross CA 94957 **R St Johns Epis Ch Ross CA 2003-** B New York NY 3/22/1968 s Gregory Phillips Williams & Daphne. BA Reed Coll 1990; MDiv EDS 1996. D 5/25/1996 Bp George Edmonds Bates P 1/18/1997 Bp Chester Lovelle Talton. m 6/13/1993 Amy C Rankin-Williams c 2. Assoc All SS-By-The-Sea Par Santa Barbara CA 1996-2003. Soc of S Jn the Evang 1996. crw@stjohnsross.org

RANNENBERG, Pamela Lamb (RI) 442 Wickford Point Rd, North Kingstown RI 02852 B New London CT 3/20/1951 d Samuel Stillman Lamb & Anne LeGrande. BFA U of Connecticut 1972; MA Old Dominion U 1983; MDiv VTS 1995. D 6/3/1995 P 1/10/1996 Bp Peter James Lee. m 8/27/1972 John Elliot Rannenberg c 2. Cn Dio Rhode Island Providence RI 1999-2004; Asst S Jn's Ch Centreville VA 1995-1996. peterpan1379@netzero.net

RANSOM, Charles Wilfred (O) 716 Coshocton Ave, Mount Vernon OH 43050 B Mount Vernon OH 10/13/1938 s Robert Dale Ransom & Bess Louise. BA Muskingum Coll 1960; BD Bex 1966. D 6/11/1966 P 12/18/1966 Bp Nelson Marigold Burroughs. m 6/30/1962 Daryl Sobehart c 2. S Paul's Ch Mt Vernon OH 1992-1998; R Trin Ch Coshocton OH 1982-1992; S Mk's Epis Ch Wadsworth OH 1974-1978; R S Lk's Epis Ch Niles OH 1969-1973; Cur S Jn's Ch Youngstown OH 1966-1968. Auth, "The Seed Planters," Ransarts, 2000; Auth, "Farm Week: An Alternative To A Smelly Ch Basement," Ransarts, 1999. spiruralformation3@gmail.com

RANSOM, James Clifford (Md) PO Box 26, 41 Atwood Rd, Wilmot NH 03287 **P-in-c S Mk's Ch Ashland NH 2011-** B Norfolk NE 11/23/1944 s Clifford James Ransom & Carolyn Antoinette. BA U of Nebraska 1967; MDiv GTS 1970. D 6/21/1970 P 12/21/1970 Bp Russell T Rauscher. m 6/19/1976 Deborah Almy c 2. New Cong Mnstrs Dio Maryland Baltimore MD 2000-2005; Eccl Crt Dio Maryland Baltimore MD 1998-2002; R Trin Ch Towson MD 1997-2009; Trst The GTS New York NY 1995-2009; Cn for Congs & Cler Dio Maryland Baltimore MD 1990-1997; Cn for Congregations and Cler Dio Maryland Baltimore MD 1989-1997; R Ch Of The H Apos Wynnewood PA 1982-1989; Asst S Paul's Ch Philadelphia PA 1977-1982; Asst S Lk's Ch Scranton PA 1976-1977; R S Lk's Ch Plattsmouth NE 1970-1972. ransom.james.c@gmail.com

RANSOM, Lisa Michelle (Vt) 2016 Us Rr 2, Waterbury VT 05676 B Gunnison CO 7/9/1968 d Ward Clark Ransom & Mary Jane. BA U of Kansas 1991; MDiv Ya Berk 1995. D 6/24/1995 Bp William Edward Smalley P 1/19/1996 Bp Donald Purple Hart. m 1/14/1995 Scott Morgan Baughman c 2. S Jn's In The Mountains Stowe VT 2010; S Dunst's Epis Mssn Waitsfield VT 2002-2009; Dio Vermont Burlington VT 1999-2000; Cur S Matt's Epis Ch Wilton CT 1995-1997. lransom@together.net

RAPP, Phillip James (WK) 6529 Clifton Rd, Clifton VA 20124 B Toledo OH 7/22/1935 s Phillip Rapp & Margaret Marie. BEd U of Toledo 1957; MDiv Bex 1961; MA Bowling Green St U 1970; Untd States-Army War Coll Carlisle PA 1987; W&M Natl Planned Giving Institut 1991. D 6/10/1961 P 12/18/1961 Bp Nelson Marigold Burroughs. m 10/15/1966 Anne Louise Minsel c 3. S Fran Cmnty Serv Inc. Salina KS 1988-2002; Off Of Bsh For ArmdF New York NY 1984-1988; St Johns Hm Cleveland OH 1980-1984; Assoc S Andr's Epis Ch Toledo OH 1970-1978; Vic S Jn The Evang Ch Napoleon OH 1961-1970. Auth, "For Profit & Not for Profit Alliances," *Behavioral Hlth Mgmt*, 1998. Amer Coll of Healthcare Executives 1995-2002; Amer Hosp Assn 1994-2002. Who's Who Among Outstanding Americans 1996; Who's Who Worldwide 1994, 1995, 2000 1995; Legion of Merit US Army 1988; Presidential Awd Lions Intl 1980. p_rapp@yahoo.com

RARDIN, Thomas Michael (Tex) 332 Oklahoma Ave, Hewitt TX 76643 **Asstg P Epis Ch Of The H Sprt Waco TX 1999-** B Akron OH 4/9/1952 s Bernard Walter Rardin & Roberta Marie. U of Akron 1971; BA Kent St U 1974; MDiv VTS 1977; Res CPE 1985. D 6/25/1977 Bp John Harris Burt P 2/4/1978 Bp David Keller Leighton Sr. m 9/8/1973 Christine Marie Tostevin c 3. Vic for Deaf Mnstry Dio Cntrl Pennsylvania Harrisburg PA 1982-1985; Vic Ch Of The H Sprt Harrisburg PA 1981-1983; Vic for Deaf Mnstry Dio Maryland Baltimore MD 1979-1981; Asstg P S Tim's Ch Catonsville MD 1977-1981. trardin@grandecom.net

RASCHKE, Gerald Wesley (Spr) 2921 Haverford Rd, Springfield IL 62704 **D The Cathd Ch Of S Paul Springfield IL 1996-** B Omaha NE 8/28/1924 s Otto Theodore Raschke & Louise Marie. Indiana U; U of Notre Dame. D 12/17/1975 Bp William Cockburn Russell Sheridan. m 5/4/2002 Dorothy May Denton c 2. Archd Dio Dallas Dallas TX 1994-1996; D Ch Of The Annunc Lewisville TX 1992-1993; D Epis Ch Of The Redeem Irving TX 1976-1996; D The Cathd Ch Of S Jas So Bend IN 1975-1976. gwrddd@comp.net

RASCHKE, Vernon Joseph (SD) 625 W Main, Lead SD 57754 B Burke SD 3/30/1936 s Herman F Raschke & Rose C. BA S Jn's U Collegeville MN 1958; S Jn's Sem Collegeville MN 1962; PhD U MN 1972. Rec from Roman Catholic 5/26/1980 as Priest Bp Walter H Jones. m 3/27/1971 Helen Fieber c 2. R S Thos Epis Ch Sturgis SD 2002-2006; R Trin Epis Ch Winner SD 1999-2002; Dio So Dakota Sioux Falls SD 1999-2001; S Thos Epis Ch Sturgis SD 1999-2001; S Steph's Epis Ch Wichita Falls TX 1987-1999; P-in-c Trin Ch Henrietta TX 1981-1988; Dio Ft Worth Ft Worth TX 1981-1987. Auth, "Breaks in Adult Sibling Relatns," *Fam Perspective*; Auth, "Dogmatism & Committed & Consensual Religiosity," *Journ for Sci*; Auth, "Post Divorce Adjustment," *Journ of Mar & Fam*. AAMFT 1975-1999. raschke@rushmore.com

RASICCI, Michael Dominic (Chi) 222 S Batavia Ave, Batavia IL 60510 **R Calv Epis Ch Batavia IL 2002-** B Akron Ohio 2/1/1953 s Sylvester Eugene Rasicci & Dora Emma. AA Lehigh Carbon Cmnty Coll 1973; BA Allentown Coll of St. Fran de Sales 1975; MDiv Cath Theol Un 1980. Rec from Roman Catholic 10/24/2000 Bp William Dailey Persell. m 6/4/1994 Linda K

R

Waloszyk. Int Ch Of S Columba Of Iona Hanover Pk IL 2001-2002. CBS 2000; SocMary 2000; SSC 2002. michael.rasicci@sbcglobal.net

RASKE, L (Mo) 4916 Jamieson Ave., Apt.2A, Saint Louis MO 63109 B Alma MI 9/1/1950 s Phillip Dean Raske & Doris Maxine. BA Siena Heights Coll 1976; MDiv SWTS 1982. D 6/26/1982 Bp John Harris Burt P 3/1/1983 Bp Gerald Nicholas McAllister. m 2/4/1972 Sharon Scheub c 2. Trin Ch S Jas MO 1994-2003; Vic Ch Of The Ascen Pawnee OK 1982-1987; Vic S Alb's Ch Cushing OK 1982-1987.

RASKOPF, Roger William (LI) 1250 Newport Dr., Oconomowoc WI 53066 **Consulting Psychol Nash Nashotah WI 2006-** B Jamaica NY 9/17/1936 s William Frank Raskopf & Josephine. BA CUNY 1958; Nash 1961; MDiv GTS 1962; PhD St. Johns U 1975; Harv 1980. D 4/28/1962 P 12/21/1962 Bp James P De Wolfe. m 9/5/1959 Edythe J DellaCorte c 2. Int S Edmunds Ch Milwaukee WI 2006-2008; Int Dn S Paul's Cathd Peoria IL 2004-2005; Int Trin-St Jn's Ch Hewlett NY 2002-2003; Int Caroline Ch Of Brookhaven Setauket NY 2000-2002; Int Gr Ch Utica NY 1999-2000; Int S Andr's Ch Stamford CT 1997-1999; Int S Mary's Ch Lake Ronkonkoma NY 1996-1997; R S Paul's Ch Great Neck NY 1970-1979; First R S Jas The Just Franklin Sq NY 1963-1969; Cur S Mk's Ch Jackson Heights NY 1962-1963; D Ch Of The H Cross Brooklyn NY 1961-1962. Kappa Delta Pi 1975; Tchg Fllshp St. Jn's U, NYC 1968. rwraskopf@yahoo.com

RASMUS, John Edward (Eau) 502 County Road Uu, Hudson WI 54016 B Eau Claire WI 4/28/1947 s Vernon John Rasmus & Jean. BA U of Wisconsin 1971; MS U of Wisconsin 1978; Nash 1988. D 9/14/1983 P 6/29/1989 Bp William Charles Wantland. m 12/29/1968 Rose Carlson c 1. Int Zion Epis Ch Oconomowoc WI 2010-2011; R S Paul's Ch Hudson WI 1989-2007. hon Soc Phi Kappa Phi. j.r.rasmus@gmail.com

RASMUS, Paul A (SeFla) 3740 Holly Dr, Palm Beach Gardens FL 33410 **R S Andr's Ch Lake Worth FL 2006-** B Peekskill NY 7/13/1947 s Paul Joseph Rasmus & Lillian Grace. BA Florida Intl U 1973; MDiv STUSo 1977. D 4/17/1977 P 10/24/1977 Bp James Loughlin Duncan. m 11/15/1987 Brenda Nell Bedwell c 4. Archd - Dioc Deploy Off Dio SE Florida Miami FL 2002-2004; R S Paul's Ch Key W FL 1994-2002; Assoc S Mk's Ch Palm Bch Gardens FL 1988-1993; Asst The Epis Ch Of The Gd Shpd Tequesta FL 1987; Asst S Mk's Ch Palm Bch Gardens FL 1986; R H Sprt Epis Ch W Palm Bch FL 1979-1986; Cur S Andr's Epis Ch Palmetto Bay FL 1977-1979. parasmus@aol.com

RASMUSSEN, Cynthia M (Roch) 215 Parkview Dr, Rochester NY 14625 **Epis Catalyst for Urban Mnstry Dio Rochester Rochester NY 2011-; P-in-c S Mk's And S Jn's Epis Ch Rochester NY 2008-** B Honesdale PA 11/28/1971 d Robert Hugg Rasmussen & Helen Marie. BS Coll Misericordia Dallas PA 1993; MDiv Luth TS at Gettysburg 1997; PhD UTS and Presb Sch of Chr 2008. D 6/30/2007 P 4/22/2008 Bp Jack Marston McKelvey. m 8/30/2007 Mary Ellen Forszt. Cur S Thos Epis Ch Rochester NY 2007-2008. rasmussen.cynthia@gmail.com

RASMUSSEN, Jeanne Louise (Minn) 520 N Pokegama Ave, Grand Rapids MN 55744 **Assoc S Ptr's Ch Casa Grande AZ 2010-** B Grand Rapids MN 9/28/1950 d Jack Collins Kent & Sylvia Elsie. D 6/21/2009 P 12/20/2009 Bp James Louis Jelinek. m 8/26/1972 Ronald Lee Rasmussen. jrasmussen2010@gmail.com

RASNICK, Thomas (ETenn) 6804 Glenbrook Cir, Knoxville TN 37919 **Cn Pstr S Jn's Epis Cathd Knoxville TN 1998-** B Miami FL 1/31/1964 s James Edwin Rasnick & Marilyn. AA Palm Bch Jr Coll 1985; BS Florida St U 1987; MDiv VTS 1992. D 5/28/1992 Bp Calvin Onderdonk Schofield Jr P 12/1/1992 Bp Earl Nicholas McArthur Jr. m 6/17/1989 Cynthia Lee c 3. Assoc R S Mich And All Ang Ch Dallas TX 1994-1998; Asst R S Thos Epis Ch And Sch San Antonio TX 1992-1994.

RATCLIFF, Elizabeth Rogers (WLa) 6478 Old Baton Rouge Hwy, Alexandria LA 71302 **Calv Ch Bunkie LA 2009-** B Alexandria LA 11/10/1944 D 6/7/2003 P 3/16/2004 Bp D(avid) Bruce Mac Pherson. m 6/18/1966 Robert Theodore Ratcliff c 4. Trin Epis Ch Natchitoches LA 2004-2006. erratcliff@centurytel.net

RATHBONE, Cristine F (Mass) 138 Tremont St., Boston MA 02111 **The Cathd Ch Of S Paul Boston MA 2009-** B New York NY 1/14/1966 d John Rankin Rathbone & Margarita. MDiv Boston Univ Sch Of Theo 2009. D 6/6/2009 Bp M(arvil) Thomas Shaw III. c 2. Ecclesia Mnstrs Boston MA 2009. cristinarathbone@hotmail.com

RATHBUN JR, Arthur John (Kan) 138 S 8th St, Salina KS 67401 **R S Mk's Ch Blue Rapids KS 2009-** B Erie PA 4/11/1936 s Arthur John Rathbun & Bernice Frances. BS Penn 1959; STB GTS 1962. D 6/18/1962 P 6/1/1964 Bp William Crittenden. m 6/6/1987 Trudy Ann Grier c 2. Chr Cathd Salina KS 1979-1987; Dio Wstrn Kansas Hutchinson KS 1978-1979; Epis Ch Of The Incarn Salina KS 1977-1979; Vic S Ptr's Ch Waterford PA 1966-1970; Vic S Jn's Ch Kane PA 1964-1966; Vic S Marg's Epis Ch Mt Jewett PA 1964-1966; D Gr Ch Lake City PA 1962-1963.

RATHMAN, Scott Stephen (Ak) 319 North Avenue #7, Council Bluffs IA 51503 B Billings MT 7/14/1936 s Omer Charles Rathman & Alma Hardy. BA U So 1963; MDiv EDS 1967. D 6/18/1967 P 12/1/1967 Bp Chandler W Sterling. m 6/11/1963 Diane F Finney c 3. P-in-c S Jn's Epis Ch Valentine NE 1999-2004; P-in-c S Jos's Ch Mullen NE 1999-2004; R S Christophers Ch Anchorage AK 1995-1998; R S Fran By The Sea Ch Kenai AK 1990-1995; R S Paul's Ch Coun Bluffs IA 1978-1990; Ch Growth Com Dio Nebraska Omaha NE 1974-1978; P-in-c St Marks Ch Omaha NE 1974-1978; R S Jn's Ch Broken Bow NE 1972-1974; Vic Ch Of The Ascen Forsyth MT 1968-1969; Vic S Thos Ch Hardin MT 1967-1969. scodiaia@cox.net

RATHMAN, William (SO) 1924 S. Beachclub, Hilton Head Island SC 29928 B Middletown OH 1/10/1927 s Ernest Daniel Rathman & Marguerite. BA Ken 1948; JD OH SU 1951; Untd TS 1975. D 6/30/1975 Bp John Mc Gill Krumm. m 11/28/1958 Constance Schedler c 2. Cur The Epis Ch Of The Ascen Middletown OH 1978-1995; Cur Trin Ch Hamilton OH 1977-1978; Cur S Pat's Epis Ch Lebanon OH 1975-1977. crathman@aol.com

RAULERSON, Aaron D (Ala) 910 Kayla Drive, Trussville AL 35173 **R H Cross Trussville AL 2007-** B Augusta GA 9/6/1971 s James Daniel Raulerson & Marsha Dendler. BA Carson-Newman Coll 1993; MDiv Epis TS of The SW 2001. D 6/2/2001 P 5/18/2002 Bp Philip Menzie Duncan II. m 9/11/1993 Rebecca L Massingill c 3. R Trin Ch Demopolis AL 2006-2007; Cur All SS Epis Ch Mobile AL 2001-2003. fatheraaron@centurytel.net

RAUSCHER JR, William Vernon (NJ) 663 N Evergreen Ave, Woodbury NJ 08096 B Long Branch NJ 10/17/1932 s William Vermon Rauscher & Marie Elizabeth. BS Glassboro St 1954; BS PDS 1957. D 4/27/1957 P 11/2/1957 Bp Alfred L Banyard. Trst Dio New Jersey Trenton NJ 1976-1979; Hon Cn Trin Cathd Trenton NJ 1971; Com Dioc Journ Pub Dio New Jersey Trenton NJ 1968-1974; Me Dio New Jersey Trenton NJ 1964-1974; R Chr Ch In Woodbury Woodbury NJ 1960-1996; Vic S Steph's Ch Florence NJ 1957-1960. Auth, "Goebel: The Man w the Magical Mind," *Goebel: The Man w The Magical Mind*, Martinka & Co., 2010; Auth, "Pleasant Nightmares," *Pleasant Nightmares*, S. S. Adams, 2008; Auth, "Rel, Magic and The Supernatural," *Rel, Magic, and The Supernatural*, Mystic Light Press, 2006; Auth, "Magic In Rhyme," *Magic in Rhyme*, 1878 Press, 2003; Auth, "S. S. Adams," *S.S. Adams*, 1878 Press, 2002; Auth, "The Mind Readers: Masters of Deception," *The Mind Readers: Masters of Deception*, Mystic Light Press, 2002; Auth, "The Houdini Code: A Sprt Mystery Solved," *The Houdini Code Mystery: A Sprt Secret Solved*, Magic Words, 2000; Auth, "To Be or Not To Be," *To Be or Not to Be: A Pstr View of Suicide in Today's Wrld*, Xlibris, 2000; Auth, "Servais leRoy: Monarich of Mystery," *Servais LeRoy: Monarch of Mystery*, Magic Words, 1999; Auth, "The Great Raymond: Entertainer of Kings, King of Entertainers," *The Great Raymond: Entertainment of Kings-King of Entertainment*, Baldwin, 1996; Auth, "Jn Calvert: Magic & Adventures," *Jn Calvert: Magic & Adventures Around the Wrld*, Claitor, 1987; Auth, "The Case Against Suicide," *The Case Against Suicide*, St Martins, 1981; Auth, "Ch in Frenzy," *Ch In Frenzy*, St Martins, 1980; Auth, "Sprtl Frontier," *Sprtl Frontier*, Doubleday, 1975; Auth, "Arthur Ford: The Man Who Talked w the Dead," *Arthur Ford: The Man Who Talked w the Dead*, New Amer Libr, 1973. Hon Cn Trin Cathd Trenton NJ 1971. wvrauscher@snip.net

RAVEN, Margaret Hilary (NJ) 324 Edgewood Dr, Toms River NJ 08755 B Liverpool UK 5/3/1945 d William Fallows Davies & Ruth Hilary. BA U Of Durham Gb 1967; Med U of Manchester 1973; MDiv VTS 1995; MDiv Wesley TS 1995. D 6/15/1996 Bp Peter James Lee P 6/14/1997 Bp John H(enry) Smith. Assoc Chr Ch Toms River Toms River NJ 1999-2000; Trin Epis Ch Martinsburg WV 1996-1999. Auth, "Mangodwoman:Poems," 2000; Auth, "Cmnty Involvement In Hlth Dvlpmt," Wrld Hlth Orgnztn, 1990; Auth, "Strengthening Performance Cmnty Hlth Workers In Primary Hlth Care," Wrld Hlth Orgnztn, 1989; Auth, "Adult Educ Cmnty Proj & Planned Parenthood," Ippf, 1981. Amer Farmland Trust; Int Mnstry Ntwk.

R

RAVNDAL III, Eric (CFla) 1302 Country Club Oaks Cir, Orlando FL 32804 B Orlando FL 9/26/1939 s Eric Ravndal & Florence Ida. BA Harvard Coll 1961; MDiv Nash 1980. D 6/22/1980 P 1/11/1981 Bp William Hopkins Folwell. m 9/26/1964 Sarah B Belden c 4. Pres Stndg Com Dio Cntrl Florida Orlando FL 1996-1998; Stndg Com Dio Cntrl Florida Orlando FL 1994-1998; R Epis Ch Of The H Sprt Apopka FL 1987-1998; Nash Nashotah WI 1983-1987; Asst S Barn Ch Deland FL 1980-1982. revrav@aol.com

RAWLINS, Patrick Allister (LI) 744 Havemeyer Ave, Bronx NY 10473 **R S Geo's Ch Hempstead NY 1999-** B 7/8/1954 s Charles Rawlins & Mary. BA Codrington Coll 1980; MA Ford 1984. Trans from Church in the Province Of The West Indies 3/11/1991. m 12/27/1986 Juliette Charles Rawlins c 1. R S Andr's Ch Bronx NY 1991-1999; Asst to R S Mk's Ch Brooklyn NY 1986-1991; Asst S Lk's Epis Ch Bronx NY 1983-1984; Asst Cathd Of St Jn The Div New York NY 1980-1983.

RAWLINSON, John Edward (Cal) 891 Dowling Blvd, San Leandro CA 94577 **Sprtl Dir Curs Sec Dio California San Francisco CA 1989-; Hisp Cmsn Dio California San Francisco CA 1986-; Pstr S Jas Ch Oakland CA 1984-** B Berkeley CA 4/12/1940 s Albert Rawlinson & Iona Ferne. BA Humboldt St U 1963; BD CDSP 1970; MA Grad Theol Un 1970; PhD Grad Theol Un 1982. D 6/23/1973 Bp C Kilmer Myers P 9/1/1974 Bp George Richard Millard. m

8/25/1962 Milene Tackitt c 1. Coordntr Field Educ Epis Sch for Ds Dio California San Francisco CA 1991-1994; Archv Dio California San Francisco CA 1986-2006; Field Educ Supvsr CDSP Berkeley CA 1975-1993; Cmsn Liturg Renwl Dio California San Francisco CA 1974-1984; Asst to Vic S Cuth's Epis Ch Oakland CA 1972-1974. Auth, "Congrl Hist: Researching Writing and Enjoying It," 1999; Auth, "Par Archive: Principles Orgnztn & Methods," 1998; "Michellaneous arts," *LivCh*. jmrawlinson@compuserve.com

RAWSON, William Leighton (Nwk) 10960 Big Canoe, Jasper GA 30143 B Teaneck NJ 8/30/1940 s William James Rawson & Ida Marie. BA Montclair St U 1962; MDiv VTS 1967. D 6/10/1967 Bp Leland Stark P 12/14/1967 Bp George E Rath. m 9/15/1996 Rhonda Stock c 2. Vic S Andr's Epis Ch Lincoln Pk NJ 1969-1971; Cur S Ptr's Ch Mtn Lakes NJ 1967-1969. hubley12@aol.com

RAY, Alice Marie (WNC) 1917 3rd St, Napa CA 94559 **Asst S Mary's Epis Ch Napa CA 2010-** B Asheville NC 7/18/1958 d Robert Lee Ray & Mildred Anne Black. BS No Carolina St U 1980; MDiv The TS at The U So 2010. D 5/23/2010 Bp Granville Porter Taylor P 11/30/2010 Bp Barry Leigh Beisner. c 2. alicemarieray@gmail.com

RAY, Doug (Colo) 5601 Collins Ave Apt 1511, Miami Beach FL 33140 B Greenwich CT 3/16/1948 s Edward Tiusley Ray & Isabel. BA Wms 1973; Cert U of Cambridge 1974; Dip. Min. McGill U 1976; LTh Montreal Inst Montreal QC CA 1976. Trans from Anglican Church of Canada 9/1/1978 as Priest Bp Morgan Porteus. m 1/13/2007 Melissa Ray c 2. Dio Colorado Denver CO 1988-2008; Pres Dio Colorado Denver CO 1988-2003; S Lk's Par Darien CT 1978-1985. Auth, "Beacon in the Hills (producer, Dir)," 1993. Outstanding Clergyman Cnty Ch & Synagogues Stamford CT 1984. RayDE316@yahoo.com

RAY, G(eorge) William (EC) 202 Bretonshire Rd, Wilmington NC 28405 B High Point NC 8/30/1926 s George William Ray & Lottie Johnson. BS No Carolina St U 1950. D 1/4/1989 Bp Brice Sidney Sanders. m 9/4/1976 Dorothy Cole McLain c 3. D S Paul's Epis Ch Wilmington NC 1994-2002; D S Andr's On The Sound Ch Wilmington NC 1989-1994. Ord Of S Lk. bunbray@cs.com

RAY, Harvey H (Cal) 1998 Tolman Creek Rd, Ashland OR 97520 B Atlanta GA 3/9/1947 s Homer Head Ray & Bernice Marie. BS Valdosta St U 1969; MDiv EDS 1975. D 6/14/1975 Bp Lyman Cunningham Ogilby P 12/1/1975 Bp Jonathan Goodhue Sherman. P-in-c S Mart's Ch Shady Cove OR 2003-2011; P Trin Epis Ch Ashland Ashland OR 2002-2011; Asst S Lk's Ch San Francisco CA 1993-2002; Ethics Com Dio California San Francisco CA 1991-1993; Asst Chr Ch Sausalito CA 1988-1993; Asst Ch Of The H Innoc San Francisco CA 1980-1988; Vic All SS Ch Hamlet NC 1978-1979; Asst S Gabr's Ch Hollis NY 1975-1978; Chapl The Woodhull Schools Hollis NY 1975-1978; Chapl S Jos's Ch Queens Vill NY 1975-1977. hhrls@att.net

RAY, John Sewak (At) 4808 Glenwhite Dr, Duluth GA 30096 **Vic Dio Atlanta Atlanta GA 2005-** B Hyderabad(Sindh) PK 10/28/1946 s Chandu Ray & Sarah. BA U Of Cbury Chr Ch Nz 1970; Dplma C.S. Regent Coll Vancouver Bc CA 1973; MA Oxf 1976. D 8/22/2004 P 3/8/2005 Bp J(ohn) Neil Alexander. m 7/17/1976 Aqeela Rumal Shah c 1. johnsewakray@aol.com

RAY, Mauldin Alexander (Okla) 1763 E 56th St, Tulsa OK 74105 B Huffman AR 2/21/1924 s Thomas Ray & Ella. BA/MED/EDD; STUSo. P 11/1/1974 Bp Chilton Powell. m 8/7/1984 Janet A Ripper c 2. S Jn's Epis Ch Tulsa OK 1978-1992. Kappa Delta Pi; Phi Delta Kappa. mjaray@att.net

RAY, Michael Fleming (Ct) 830 Whitney Avenue, New Haven CT 06511 **R S Thos's Ch New Haven CT 1985-** B Corsicana TX 9/2/1943 s William Fleming Ray & Harriet Amelia. BS Steph F. Austin St U 1965; MDiv Ya Berk 1969. D 6/18/1969 Bp Charles A Mason P 12/20/1969 Bp Joseph Warren Hutchens. c 3. R S Geo's Ch Clifton Pk NY 1978-1985; R S Thos Ch Greenville RI 1971-1978; Asst S Jn's Ch W Hartford CT 1969-1971. flemingray@hotmail.com

RAY, Philip Carroll (NwT) 1608 Monte Vista St, Dalhart TX 79022 **S Jas' Epis Ch Dalhart TX 2009-** B Wichita KS 3/12/1943 s Marion Ray & Margaret. BS K SU 1965; DDS U Of Missouri Kansas City MO 1969; MS Angelo St U San Angelo TX 1991; CITS Epis TS of the SW 2006. D 11/12/2006 P 6/9/2007 Bp C(harles) Wallis Ohl. m 3/16/1995 Sarah Ray c 5. Angl Ord of Preachers, Dominican, Prior 2007. pray@xit.net

✠ **RAY, Rt Rev Rayford Jeffrey** (NMich) 9922 U 65 Lane, Rapid River MI 49878 **Bp Dio Nthrn Michigan Marquette MI 2011-** B Heidelberg DE 8/30/1956 s Corbitt Ray & Gertrude. BA Cameron U 1979; MDiv Nash 1986. D 6/21/1986 Bp Gerald Nicholas McAllister P 4/10/1987 Bp William Jackson Cox Con 5/21/2011 for NMich. m 8/2/1992 Suzanne Patricia Bloomer c 1. Mnstry Dvlpmt Coordntr Dio Nthrn Michigan Marquette MI 1999-2001; Dioc Camp Dir Dio Nthrn Michigan Marquette MI 1994-1995; Yth Cmsn Dio Nthrn Michigan Marquette MI 1992-1994; Mnstry Dvlp So Cntrl Reg Manistique MI 1990-2011; R Ch Of The Redeem Okmulgee OK 1988-1990. rayfordray@chartermi.net

RAY, Suzanne Patricia (NMich) 9922 U 65 Lane, Rapid River MI 49878 **D Dio Nthrn Michigan Marquette MI 1990-; D Trin Ch Gladstone MI 1990-** B Dearborn MI 4/23/1953 d Robert A Bloomer & Elizabeth Ann. Dio Nthrn Michigan D Trng MI; RN Bay De Noc Cmnty Coll 1993. D 9/30/1990 P 6/1/1997 Bp Thomas Kreider Ray. m 8/2/1992 Rayford Jeffrey Ray.

✠ **RAY, Rt Rev Thomas Kreider** (NMich) 250 Partridge Bay Trl, Marquette MI 49855 B Barberton OH 5/24/1934 s Donald Cook Ray & Hazel. BA U MI 1956; STB GTS 1959. D 6/20/1959 Bp Benjamin M Washburn P 12/1/1959 Bp Francis W Lickfield Con 8/21/1982 for NMich. m 6/27/1959 Brenda Lee Ackerman. Asstg Bp Dio Nthrn Michigan Marquette MI 2007-2011; Asstg Bp Dio Iowa Des Moines IA 2001-2003; Bp Dio Nthrn Michigan Marquette MI 1982-1999; R S Lk's Ch Evanston IL 1971-1982; R Geth Epis Ch Marion IN 1964-1971; Vic S Chris's Ch Crown Point IN 1961-1964; Cur S Mk's Ch Grand Rapids MI 1959-1961. Auth, "The Sm Ch: Radical Reformation and Renwl of Mnstry," *ATR*, 1996; "Creating Hospitable Environmnet for Mutual Mnstry," Pub. SPCK London; "Loc Mnstry," *Story Process and Meaning*. thomaskray@aol.com

RAY, Wanda Louise (O) 312 Park St, Huron OH 44839 **No Cntrl Mssn Area Coun Chair Dio Ohio Cleveland OH 2010-; R Chr Epis Ch Huron OH 2003-** B Gilbert WV 1/25/1946 d Alex Stanley & Imogene Rachel. BA Coll of Charleston 1992; MDiv VTS 1995. D 12/12/1999 P 7/23/2000 Bp Edwin Max Leidel Jr. m 8/27/1977 Robert J Ray c 2. Supt of Wee People Sch Dio Ohio Cleveland OH 2007-2010; Stndg Com Mem Dio Estrn Michigan Saginaw MI 2001-2003; Dvlpmt Mssnr Dio Estrn Michigan Saginaw MI 2000-2003; Dioc Acolyte Coordntr Dio Estrn Michigan Saginaw MI 2000-2003; S Jn the Bapt Otter Lake MI 2000-2003; S Jn's Epis Ch Dryden MI 1999-2003. wndray@yahoo.com

RAY, Wayne Allen (Miss) 705 Rayburn at Porter, Ocean Springs MS 39564 **R S Jn's Epis Ch Ocean Sprg MS 1999-** B Owensboro KY 6/7/1947 BA Wstrn Kentucky U 1969; MDiv CDSP 1972; PhD OH SU 1981. D 6/29/1972 P 1/1/1973 Bp Charles Gresham Marmion. m 12/21/1984 Susan Davis Coleman c 1. Univ. of Virginia S Paul's Memi Charlottesville VA 1992-1999; AZ St U Dio Arizona Phoenix AZ 1990-1992; All SS Ch Seymour IN 1988-1990; Epis Ch of Our Sav Richmond KY 1980-1984; Assoc Trin Ch Covington KY 1977-1980; Cn Chr Ch Cathd Louisville KY 1972-1974. wray@cableone.net

RAYBOURN JR, Fred Loren (Neb) 1204 Sunshine Blvd, Bellevue NE 68123 B Carbondale IL 12/3/1932 s Fred Loren Raybourn & Donatila Maria. No Illinois St Teachers Coll Dekalb IL 1953; AA Panama Canal Coll 1957; BS Bradley U 1959; DMagist ETSC 1964. D 5/22/1964 Bp Albert Ervine Swift P 12/8/1964 Bp Reginald Heber Gooden. m 5/31/1967 Susan Miller c 2. R S Mart Of Tours Ch Omaha NE 1994-2003; R S Lk's Ch Plattsmouth NE 1990-1992; Int Cathd Of St Lk Balboa PANAMA CITY 1980-1981; Int San Marcos Ch 1980; Dio Panama 1976-1982. GAS 1991; P Assoc, Shrine of Our Lady of Walsingham 1991; SocMary 1985; SSC 1991.

RAYBURG-ELLIOTT, Jason Alan (WNY) 128 Pearl St, Buffalo NY 14202 B St Petersburg FL 11/13/1980 s Alan George Elliott & Jacqueline Marie. BA U of Buffalo 2004; MA U of Masschusetts 2011. D 7/10/2010 Bp J Michael Garrison. m 5/8/2009 James Rayburg. jaselliott88@hotmail.com

RAYE, Janice Marie (Md) 32 Main St, Westernport MD 21562 B Keyser WV 9/22/1951 d Louie T Schoppert & Norma Bray. D 12/21/2007 Bp John Leslie Rabb. c 2. jmraye@yahoo.com

RAYLS, John William (WTex) PO Box 6885, San Antonio TX 78209 **S Bon Ch Comfort TX 2011-** B Kokomo IN 6/19/1952 s William A Rayls & Daisy M. BS Indiana U 1973; MS St Fran U 1975; MDiv Luther Rice Sem 1985; PhD Capella U 2003. D 4/7/2010 Bp Gary Richard Lillibridge P 10/11/2010 Bp David Mitchell Reed. m 7/20/1974 Susan Nussbaum c 3. Cn Mssnr for Strategic Dvlpmt Dio W Texas San Antonio TX 2010. jb@madfriar.com

RAYMOND, Patrick R (Chi) 647 Dundee Ave, Barrington IL 60010 **R S Mich's Ch Barrington IL 2011-** B Bakersfield CA 12/10/1959 s Robert Lee Raymond & Loisjean. BA Wheaton Coll 1981; MDiv GTS 1987. D 3/16/1987 P 9/21/1987 Bp James Winchester Montgomery. m 9/21/1991 Elizabeth W Ward c 3. Gr Ch Madison WI 2007-2009; R S Andr's Ch Madison WI 1997-2006; S Dunst's Ch Madison WI 1996-1997; Non-par Dio Chicago Chicago IL 1992-1997; S Andr's and Pentecostal Epis Ch Evanston IL 1992-1993; Asst Ch Of Our Sav Chicago IL 1988-1992; Cur S Mk's Barrington Hills IL 1987-1988. togracechurchrector@gmail.com

RAYMOND, Robert Martin (Me) Po Box 215, Hulls Cove ME 04644 B Somerville MA 5/6/1934 s Clifford Haskell Raymond & Gertrude Muriel. BA Colby Coll 1956; MS Stan 1965; Bp TS in the Dio Colorado 1981. D 6/29/1981 P 4/25/1982 Bp William Carl Frey. m 12/28/1957 Frances Alice Wren c 2. R Ch Of Our Fr Hulls Cove ME 1986-1998; Assoc S Paul's Epis Ch Lakewood CO 1982-1985. rraymond5@roadrunner.com

RAYMOND, Sue Ann (Ia) Lot 17A, 1771 Golf Course Blvd., Independence IA 50644 **D S Jas Epis Ch Independence IA 2007-** B Independence IA 9/1/1939 d Clarence Lionel Raymond & Arlene Josephine. BS TCU 1960; Med TCU 1963. D 11/6/1999 Bp William Jerry Winterrowd. sueannr@indytel.com

RAZEE, George Wells (Ct) 234 Essex Mdws, Essex CT 06426 B Milford CT 9/16/1924 s George Clarence Razee & Edith May. AB Dart 1949; STB Ya Berk 1956. D 6/14/1956 P 4/16/1957 Bp Walter H Gray. m 7/13/1957 Nancy G Griggs c 3. Dio Connecticut Hartford CT 1984-1989; S Jn's Epis Ch Bristol

CT 1967-1988; Consult Lymns Div Dept Yth & Lymns Wk Dio Connecticut Hartford CT 1966-1970; Com On Evang Dio Connecticut Hartford CT 1962-1964; Chairman Yth Coun Dio Connecticut Hartford CT 1959-1963; R S Ptr's-Trin Ch Thomaston CT 1958-1967; Cur Chr Ch Stratford CT 1956-1958. gwrazee@snet.net

RAZIM, Genevieve Turner (Tex) 4120 Tennyson St, Houston TX 77005 **Trin Epis Ch The Woodlands TX 2010-** B Freeport Texas 4/1/1969 d Michael Lucian Turner & Sharon Kay Richey. BFA U of No Texas 1992; MDiv Perkins TS 2006. D 6/23/2007 Bp Don Adger Wimberly. m 10/15/1994 Edward A Razim c 2. Palmer Memi Ch Houston TX 2007-2010. genrazim@gmail.com

RAZZINO, Robin G (WA) 703 Tennessee Ave Apt 102, Alexandria VA 22305 **Asst to the R The Ch Of The Redeem Beth MD 2008-** B Baltimore MD 4/29/1975 d Edwin Funsten Gulick & Barbara. BS Jas Madison U 1997; MS Geo Mason U 2002; MDiv The Prot Epis TS 2008. D 6/14/2008 P 1/24/2009 Bp John Chane. m 12/2/2010 Brian Edward Razzino. revrobingulick@verizon.net

REA, Robert Allen (NC) 1226 21st Ave, San Francisco CA 94122 B Lancaster PA 3/5/1943 s Ivan Ross Rea & Marie Violet. BA Franklin & Marshall Coll 1965; MDiv Harvard DS 1987. D 6/11/1988 P 5/29/1989 Bp David Elliot Johnson. Vic Ch Of The Trsfg No Bergen NJ 1994-1995; S Jn's Chap Cambridge MA 1992-1993; The Soc Of St Jn The Evang Durham NC 1989-1992; S Jn's Chap Cambridge MA 1978-1988. gapetard@stsams.org

READ, Allison (Ct) 300 Summit St, Hartford CT 06106 **Trin Chap Hartford CT 2008-** B Point Pleasant NY 6/5/1973 d Charles E Read & Mary Jo. BA U of Virginia 1995; MA Yale DS 1997; MDiv Ya Berk 2003. D 3/8/2003 P 9/20/2003 Bp Mark Sean Sisk. m 10/17/1998 James Douglas Ebert c 1. Asst Chr Ch Short Hills NJ 2005-2007; P S Jas Ch New York NY 2003-2005; D Chr Ch Bronxville NY 2003. allisonread@netscape.net

READ, David Glenn (WTex) 11 Saint Lukes Ln, San Antonio TX 78209 **S Lk's Epis Ch San Antonio TX 2009-** B Winston-Salem NC 5/18/1965 s William A Read & Doris M. BA SW Texas St U San Marcos 1988; MDiv VTS 1992. D 6/14/1992 Bp Earl Nicholas McArthur Jr P 12/16/1992 Bp John Herbert MacNaughton. m 6/29/1991 Jacqueline Cheeseman c 2. R S Helena's Epis Ch Boerne TX 1998-2009; R S Fran Epis Ch Victoria TX 1995-1998; R S Paul's Ch Brady TX 1992-1995. rector@stlukes-sa.net

READ, Nancy Ann (Nwk) 12 Northfield Ter, Clifton NJ 07013 **D Gr Ch Nutley NJ 2010-** B Long Island NY 1/18/1957 Dplma Mountainside Hosp Sch Of Nrsng Montclair NJ 1978; Montclair St U 1999; one unit level I Chr Hosp 2002; 4 yr Cert EFM 2003; Diac Stds Epis Dio Newark 2003. D 6/5/2004 Bp John Palmer Croneberger. m 11/17/1979 Philip M Read c 2. Archd Dio Newark Newark NJ 2008-2010; D Chr Ch Glen Ridge NJ 2004-2009. nread888@aol.com

READ II, Philip Daugherty (SwFla) 11698 Pointe Cir, Fort Myers FL 33908 **R S Lk's Ch Ft Myers FL 2002-** B New Smyrna Bch FL 4/13/1961 s Philip Daugherty Read & Lois Sylvia. Auburn U 1982; LTh Nash 1995. D 6/12/1995 P 12/21/1995 Bp Jack Leo Iker. R S Andr's Ch Farmers Branch TX 1998-2002; Cur S Alb's Epis Ch Arlington TX 1995-1998. Assn Of Our Lady Of Walsingham 1997; Assn Of The CHS; Bd Trst-Nash 2005; CCU 1995; CBS 1995; Oblate Benedictine Abbey Subiaco Ar 1997; Ord Of S Lk 1995; SocMary 1995; SSC 1998. frphilip@juno.com

REANS, Douglas J (NJ) 512 Sycamore Ter, Cinnaminson NJ 08077 B Wabasha MN 12/8/1946 s Aubrey C Reans & Bernice. BA U MN 1968; MDiv Bex 1973. D 6/29/1973 P 3/1/1974 Bp Philip Frederick McNairy. c 2. Int S Ptr's Ch Spotswood NJ 2008-2010; S Andr's Epis Ch Bridgeton NJ 2003-2008; Evergreens Chap Moorestown NJ 1999-2003; S Paul's Epis Ch Bound Brook NJ 1993-1994; Gr Epis Ch Plainfield NJ 1992-1993; Vic S Cyp's Epis Ch Hackensack NJ 1984-1988; Dio Minnesota Minneapolis MN 1973-1974. djreans@yahoo.com

REARDIN, Lois Arline (NC) 221 Union St, Cary NC 27511 **P S Paul's Epis Ch Cary NC 2004-; Assoc S Paul's Epis Ch Cary NC 2000-** B West Chester PA 4/3/1932 d John Hubertus Hutchinson & Emma Ethel. BS Wm Paterson U 1954; MDiv VTS 1987. D 6/12/1987 P 5/12/1988 Bp Charlie Fuller McNutt Jr. m 7/11/1953 Charles Richard Reardin c 2. Assoc S Paul's Epis Ch Cary NC 2000-2004; S Jn's Ch Bala Cynwyd PA 1995-1998; Ch Of S Mart-In-The-Fields Philadelphia PA 1995; Assoc R Ch Of The Redeem Bryn Mawr PA 1989-1991; Field Worker Dio Cntrl Pennsylvania Harrisburg PA 1987-1989; D-Intern S Jn's Ch Marietta PA 1987-1988. lreardin@mindspring.com

REASONER, Rand Lee (Los) 5700 Rudnick Ave, Woodland Hills CA 91367 **Dn of Tri Vlly Dnry Dio Los Angeles Los Angeles CA 2003-; R Prince Of Peace Epis Ch Woodland Hills CA 1989-** B Los Angeles CA 9/1/1954 s Lee Reasoner & Joy Nadine. BA USC 1976; MDiv CDSP 1980. D 6/21/1980 P 4/11/1981 Bp Robert C Rusack. m 11/29/1980 Kathryn Linderman c 2. R Trin Par Fillmore CA 1983-1989; Asst All SS-By-The-Sea Par Santa Barbara CA 1981-1983; Dio Los Angeles Los Angeles CA 1980-1981. rector@popwh.org

REAT, Lee Anne (SO) 2318 Collins Dr, Worthington OH 43085 **S Jn's Ch Columbus OH 2005-** B Columbus OH 9/3/1952 d Albert Preston Harness & Mary Alice. BS Ohio U 1974; MA MI SU 1977; EdD U of Missouri 1987; MDiv Aquinas Coll 1993. D 9/17/1994 Bp Hays H. Rockwell P 5/1/1995 Bp Herbert Thompson Jr. m 8/4/1979 John Bryan Reat c 1. Columbus Comm Mnstrs Columbus OH 1996-2005; Dio Sthrn Ohio Cincinnati OH 1996; Asst R S Pat's Epis Ch Dublin OH 1994-1996. revreat@aol.com

REBHOLTZ, Brian Lawrence (NH) 79 Denton Rd, Wellesley MA 02482 **Asst S Andr's Ch Wellesley MA 2011-** B Roseville CA 1/5/1984 s David Lawrence Rebholtz & Deborah Margaret. BA U of New Hampshire 2007; MDiv CDSP 2011; MA Grad Theol Un 2011. D 8/30/2011 Bp V Gene Robinson. m 6/5/2010 Catherine Anne Fiske. brian@standrewswellesley.org

RECHTER, Elizabeth I (Los) 2744 Peachtree Rd Nw, Atlanta GA 30305 **S Mary's Par Laguna Bch CA 2005-** B Ithaca NY 5/30/1960 d Donald Clark Irving & Joan. BS Rutgers-The St U 1982; MDiv VTS 1991. D 6/15/1991 Bp Ronald Hayward Haines P 12/1/1991 Bp George Phelps Mellick Belshaw. m 2/5/1983 Jay Rechter c 2. Cn Cathd Of S Phil Atlanta GA 1994-2005; Asst Trin Ch Princeton NJ 1991-1994. elizabethrechter@mindspring.com

RECTENWALD, Marion Bridget (SD) 371 New College Dr, Sewanee TN 37375 B Fairmont WV 4/13/1949 d James Michael Morrison & Helen Bridget. BS Wheeling Jesuit U 1971. D 12/27/2002 P 6/6/2003 Bp George Wayne Smith. c 2. Dio So Dakota Sioux Falls SD 2004-2010; S Paul's Epis Ch Sikeston MO 2003-2004.

REDDELL, Ronald Kirk (Oly) 910 Harris Ave Unit 408, Bellingham WA 98225 B Everett WA 4/30/1948 s Harold Paul Reddell & Charlotte Laurita. U of St. Andrews; AA Skagit Vlly Coll 1970; BA Wstrn Washington U 1972; MDiv Nash 1976. D 7/31/1976 P 6/1/1977 Bp Robert Hume Cochrane. Vic Chr Epis Ch Blaine WA 1988-1994; Assoc S Paul Epis Ch Bellingham WA 1986-1988; Chapl Off Of Bsh For ArmdF New York NY 1982-1985; R S Andr's Ch Seattle WA 1979-1981; Assoc Trin Epis Ch Everett WA 1976-1979. Auth, "Liberation Theol & Low Intensity Conflict 86," 1986; Auth, "Bk Revs," 1985; Auth, "Mltry Revs". r.k.reddell@gmail.com

REDDIG, Mike (Eas) 107 High St, Cambridge MD 21613 **R Chr Epis Ch Great Choptank Par Cambridge MD 2005-** B Harvey ND 1/8/1946 s Albert E Reddig & Freda Pauline. BA Jamestown Coll 1968; MEd GW 1998; MDiv VTS 2002. Trans 3/20/2003 Bp Peter James Lee. m 7/5/1975 Judith Farish c 2. Asst R S Ptr's Ch Salisbury MD 2002-2005. frmike1@mac.com

REDDIMALLA, Samuel Rajaratnam (NY) 4673 Flatlick Branch Drive, Chantilly VA 20151 B Thadoor IN 10/15/1946 s Rajaratnam Narsaiah Reddimalla & Mary Rose. BA Serampore Coll Calcutta IN 1971; BD Untd Theol Coll Bangalore IN 1971; MA Osmania U Hyderabad IN 1977; 1987; ThM Asbury TS 1987. Trans from Church of South India 10/9/1999 Bp Rogers Sanders Harris. m 10/23/1974 Dorcas Talari c 2. P-in-c S Andr's Ch Beacon NY 2002-2008; Ch Of The Nativ Maysville KY 1999-2001; P S Martins-In-Fields Summersville WV 1997-1999; Asst Chapl S Aug's Chap Lexington KY 1994-1996; Ch S Mich The Archangel Lexington KY 1993-1995. frreddi46@yahoo.com

REDDING, Pamela (Cal) 2925 Bonifacio Street, Concord CA 94519 **R S Mich And All Ang Concord CA 2008-** B Colorado Springs CO 1/24/1950 d Clinton Redding & Dorothy. BA MWC 1972; Cert Shalem Inst Washington DC 1995; MDiv SWTS 1999; DMIN 2006. D 7/5/1999 P 1/23/2000 Bp Richard Sui On Chang. R S Chris-S Paul Epis Ch Detroit MI 2002-2007; Campus Mssnr Dio Hawaii Honolulu HI 1999-2002; Assoc R The Par Of S Clem Honolulu HI 1999-2002; S Andr's Priory Sch Honolulu HI 1999-2001. momelap@aol.com

REDFIELD, William (CNY) 225 Pelham Rd, Syracuse NY 13214 B Syracuse NY 8/7/1948 s William Victor Redfield & Jean Louise. BA Trin Hartford CT 1970; MS Bos 1975; MDiv EDS 1976. D 7/11/1976 P 6/1/1978 Bp Ned Cole. m 6/1/1985 Cathy Dutch. Dio Cntrl New York Syracuse NY 2005; Trin Epis Ch Fayetteville NY 1994.

REDMAN, Nolan Bruce (Spok) 3020 E Flintlock Ct, Mead WA 99021 B Whittier CA 5/6/1939 s Edwin W Redman & Thelma H. BA Whitworth U 1968; MDiv CDSP 1972. D 12/26/1971 P 7/1/1972 Bp John Raymond Wyatt. m 11/8/2003 Elvira Melendez c 4. The Epis Ch In Almaden San Jose CA 1986-2002; Calv Ch Roslyn WA 1986; Vic Ch Of The Resurr (Chap) Roslyn WA 1980-1986; R Gr Ch Ellensburg WA 1975-1986; Vic H Sprt Epis Ch Sandpoint ID 1972-1975; Vic S Mary's Bonners Ferry Bonners Ferry ID 1972-1975. viramel@comcast.net

REDMON, Robert Neal (Tex) 20407 Beigewood Ln, Humble TX 77338 B Longview TX 8/24/1937 s George V Redmon & Louise. BA U of No Texas; MDiv VTS. D 7/16/1972 Bp Samuel B Chilton P 12/1/1973 Bp J Milton Richardson. S Mk's Epis Ch Cleveland TX 1996-2004; All SS Epis Ch Crockett TX 1981-1983; R S Jn's Epis Ch Austin TX 1973-1982; Calv Epis Ch Bastrop TX 1973-1981.

REDMON, William Jessie (Md) 1050 E Ramon Rd Unit 125, Palm Springs CA 92264 B Baltimore MD 7/7/1932 s John Thomas Redmon & Myrtle Roe. AA Baltimore Coll of Commerce 1957; BS U of Baltimore 1961; MDiv Bex 1963. D 6/5/1963 P 12/18/1963 Bp Wilburn Camrock Campbell. m 9/17/1999 Caroline Diamond c 3. Assoc Gr Ch Lawr MA 1999-2003; Assoc S Lk's Ch Baltimore MD 1998-1999; Assoc Ch Of S Kath Of Alexandria Baltimore MD

1993-1998; R S Jas' Epis Ch Baltimore MD 1984-1993; S Jas Ch Irvington Baltimore MD 1984-1992; Cur S Mich And All Ang Ch Baltimore MD 1975-1983; R Chr Ch Fairmont WV 1967-1975; Ch Of The Gd Shpd Follansbee WV 1963-1967; Vic Olde S Jn's Ch Colliers WV 1963-1967. psd8888@aol.com

RED OWL, Cordelia (SD) Po Box 354, Porcupine SD 57772 B Kyle SD 7/26/1936 d Levi Red Owl & Sadie Whirlwind. BS Black Hill St U 1958; MS Black Hill St U 1977. D 12/21/1998 P 6/26/2000 Bp Creighton Leland Robertson.

REDPATH, Valerie Tolocka (NJ) 329 Estate Point Rd, Toms River NJ 08753 **R S Jas Ch Long Branch NJ 2007-** B Brooklyn NY 4/13/1950 d Francis Joseph Tolocka & Blanche Margaret. BSN Seton Hall U 1972; MDiv GTS 2004. D 6/12/2004 P 1/15/2005 Bp George Edward Councell. m 4/18/1998 Michael Redpath c 2. Int Ch Of S Mary's By The Sea Point Pleasant Bch NJ 2005. valredpath@hotmail.com

REECE, Herbert Anderson (O) 9522 Lincolnwood Dr, Evanston IL 60203 B Elizabeth NJ 1/1/1930 s Herbert A Reece & Gladys. BA/BS Kent St U 1951; LLB U of Akron 1962; BD EDS 1965. D 6/12/1965 Bp Beverley D Tucker P 2/1/1966 Bp Nelson Marigold Burroughs. m 3/17/1951 Jo Anne Liptak. rhysherb@sbcglobal.net

REECE, Mark Spencer (SeFla) Iglesia Catedral del Redentor, Calle Beneficencia #18, Madrid 28004 Spain B Hartford CT 8/27/1963 s Richard Lcc Reece & Loretta Witkins. BA Wesl 1985; MA U of York 1987; MTS Harv 1990; MDiv Ya Berk 2011. D 1/26/2011 P 10/2/2011 Bp Leopold Frade. msrfl@aol.com

REECE, Nathaniel Treat (Mass) 60 Edward Rd, Raynham MA 02767 B Boston MA 3/22/1947 s John Brooks Reece & Charlotte. BA U of Pennsylvania 1969; MDiv VTS 1998. Trans from Anglican Church of Tanzania 5/7/2002 Bp M(arvil) Thomas Shaw III. Jacksonville Epis HS Jacksonville FL 2008-2009; R Trin Ch Bridgewater MA 2002-2007; Asst R S Ptr's Ch In The Great Vlly Malvern PA 2000-2002. nreece@comcast.net

REECE, Richard Douglas (WVa) Hc 64 Box 1030, Romney WV 26757 B Sacramento CA 8/30/1931 s Clarence Douglas Reece & Evelyn Elizabeth. BA U of Memphis 1961; MDiv STUSo 1964. D 6/24/1964 Bp John Vander Horst P 1/6/1965 Bp William Evan Sanders. m 4/26/1989 Linda M Bair. Estrn Deanry - Dn Dio W Virginia Charleston WV 1985-1989; S Steph's Ch Romney WV 1978-1990; Peterkin C&C Romney WV 1978-1984; P-in-c Chr Ch Pearisburg VA 1975-1978. Employee of the Year Appalachian Cmnty Hlth Cntr Elkins WV 1991; Psi Chi Memphis St U. pjm@citlink.net

REED, Allan William (Pa) 4270 Biddeford Cir, Doylestown PA 18902 B Swanton OH 1/19/1929 s John Herman Reed & Nora Elvira. BA U of Toledo 1952; MDiv Bex 1955; MA U MI 1961. D 6/18/1955 Bp Nelson Marigold Burroughs P 1/21/1956 Bp Beverley D Tucker. c 3. Assoc. Dir. Pstr Care C.P.E Supvsr S Lk's-Roosevelt Hosp Cntr New York NY 1989-1994; Dir. Pstr Care Supvsr Epis Cmnty Serv Philadelphia PA 1980-1989; St Lk's Epis Hosp Houston TX 1978-1979; CPE Assoc EDS Cambridge MA 1961-1978; Vic S Barn' Ch Chelsea MI 1958-1961; Cur Trin Ch Toledo OH 1955-1958. Auth, "Problems of Impending Death," *Concerns of the Dying Patient & His Fam.* Dplma Coll Chapl 1976; Life Mem ACPE 1975; NECA 1980. U MI Phi Kappa Phi 1961; U of Toledo Phi Gamma Mu 1952.

REED, Anne L(ouise) (SO) Diocese of Southern Ohio, 412 Sycamore St., Cincinnati OH 45202 **Cn for Mssn Dio Sthrn Ohio Cincinnati OH 2010-** B Neptune NJ 4/23/1956 d William Ross Reed & Ellen. BS Hood Coll 1978; Cert STUSo 1984; MTS SWTS 1998. D 6/17/1989 Bp A(lbert) Theodore Eastman. m 9/18/1982 Gifford Blaylock c 2. D S Lk's Par Kalamazoo MI 2007-2008; Bp's Asst. for Congrl Dev. & Transition Min. Dio Wstrn Michigan Kalamazoo MI 2003-2010; Campus Coordntr SWTS Evanston IL 1999-2002; D S Jas' Epis Ch Baltimore MD 1998-2002; D Cathd Of The Incarn Baltimore MD 1994-1998; Congrl Dvlpmt Dio Maryland Baltimore MD 1990-1996; D Imm Epis Ch Glencoe MD 1989-1993. Contrib, "Beginning Mnstry Together," Alb Inst, 2002. NAAD 1987-1996. blaylock@giffblaylockcpa.com

REED, Bobette P (O) Deer Hill Rr#1, East Hampton CT 06424 B Cleveland OH 9/30/1951 d Robert Eugene Reed & Mary Thepa. BA Wms 1973; MDiv Harvard DS 1976. D 1/6/1977 Bp John Harris Burt. m 8/22/1980 Jeffrey St.

REED, C Davies (Ind) St. Christopher's Church, 1402 W. Main Street, Carmel IN 46032 **S Fran In The Fields Zionsville IN 2011-** B Bloomington IN 1/27/1962 s William Cyrus Reed & Martha Boehne Heseman. BA Wabash Coll Crawfordsville IN 1986; MDiv SWTS Evanston IL 2007. D 6/23/2007 Bp Catherine Elizabeth Maples Waynick P 9/27/2008 Bp William Edward Smalley. m 6/17/2006 Carol Rogers. Assoc R S Chris's Epis Ch Carmel IN 2007-2010. daviesreed@comcast.net

REED, Charlotte Collins (SO) 409 E High St, Springfield OH 45505 **Bd Mem Bex Columbus OH 2010-; COM-Chair Dio Sthrn Ohio Cincinnati OH 2010-; COM Dio Sthrn Ohio Cincinnati OH 2005-; R Chr Epis Ch Of Springfield Springfield OH 2000-** B Dothan AL 4/3/1959 d Richard Lawrence Collins & Ann Terry. BA Hendrix Coll 1981; MA Van 1985; Trin Luth Sem 1995; MDiv SWTS 1997. D 6/21/1997 P 1/24/1998 Bp Herbert Thompson Jr. m 1/2/1982 Donald Collins Reed c 2. Pres of Stndg Com Dio Sthrn Ohio Cincinnati OH 2006-2007; Stndg Com Dio Sthrn Ohio Cincinnati OH 2003-2007; P S Jas Ch Piqua OH 1997-2000; P S Mk's Ch Sidney OH 1997-2000; P S Paul's Epis Ch Greenville OH 1997-2000. charlotte@christ-in-springfield.org

REED, Craig Andrew (Dal) 9714 Lanward Dr, Dallas TX 75238 **S Andr's Ch Farmers Branch TX 2004-** B Marshall MI 4/21/1960 s Clyde A Reed & Elizabeth Jean. MDiv Nash 1982; BS SW U Georgetown TX 1982. D 12/27/1989 P 6/28/1990 Bp Clarence Cullam Pope Jr. m 9/4/1982 Karen Ryan c 1. Dio Dallas Dallas TX 2006; Pension Fund Mltry New York NY 2006; Spec Mobilization Spprt Plan Washington DC 2006; Ch Of The Incarn Dallas TX 1998-2003; Dio Ft Worth Ft Worth TX 1997-1998; Vic S Anth's Ch Alvarado TX 1997-1998; Ch Of The H Cross Burleson TX 1995-1997; R S Andr's Ch Breckenridge TX 1992-1995; Cur Ch Of The H Apos Aledo TX 1990-1991. fr_reed@msn.com

✠ **REED, Rt Rev David** (Ky) 5226 Moccasin Trl, Louisville KY 40207 **Chapl to Ret Cler S Matt's Epis Ch Louisville KY 2000-** B Tulsa OK 2/16/1927 s Paul Spencer Reed & Bonnie Frances. MDiv VTS 1951; AB Harv 2048. D 7/3/1951 Bp Clinton Simon Quin P 2/14/1952 Bp Reginald Heber Gooden Con 4/25/1964 for Colom. c 5. Asst Bp Dio Connecticut Hartford CT 1994-1995; Chair, PBp's Advsry Comm on Interfaith Rel Epis Ch Cntr New York NY 1992-1997; Rgnt The TS at The U So Sewanee TN 1977-1981; Bp Dio Kentucky Louisville KY 1975-1994; Bp Coadj Dio Kentucky Louisville KY 1972-1974; Vic S Matt's Epis Ch Rapid City SD 1962-1964; Asst to Dir of Ovrs Dept Epis Ch Cntr New York NY 1958-1961. DD ETSKy Lexington KY 1982; DD U So Sewanee TN 1972; DD VTS Alexandria VA 1964. xbpofky@bellsouth.net

✠ **REED, Rt Rev David Mitchell** (WTex) P. O. Box 6885, San Antonio TX 78209 **Bp Suffr Dio W Texas San Antonio TX 2006-** B Brownsville TX 3/9/1957 s William Wesley Reed & Olive Helen. BA U of Texas 1978; MDiv Epis TS of The SW 1983. D 6/12/1983 Bp Stanley Fillmore Hauser P 1/13/1984 Bp Scott Field Bailey Con 8/26/2006 for WTex. m 6/18/1988 Patricia Kopec c 2. R S Alb's Ch Harlingen TX 1994-2006; R S Fran Epis Ch Victoria TX 1987-1994; Asst R S Alb's Ch Harlingen TX 1983-1987. DD Epis TS of the SW 2008. david.reed@dwtx.org

REED, Elizabeth Hoffman (Be) 108 N 5th St, Allentown PA 18102 **P-in-c Gr Epis Ch Allentown PA 2010-** B Allentown PA 5/9/1962 d Melvin J Hoffman & Dorothy M. BA De Sales U 1984; MA The CUA 1987; MDIV Virginial TS 2009. D 6/6/2009 Bp Peter James Lee P 12/6/2009 Bp Shannon Sherwood Johnston. m 4/20/1996 Jeffrey Reed c 2. elizabeth.hoffmanreed@gmail.com

REED, Glenna J (Md) Church of the Holy Nativity, 4238 Pimlico Rd, Baltimore MD 21215 **Dio Maryland Baltimore MD 2009-** B Tulsa OK 1/18/1975 d Lawrence A Reed & Jayne L. BA Spelman Coll 1997; MDiv GTS 2001. D 6/9/2001 Bp Robert Gould Tharp P. S Paul's Epis Ch Atlanta GA 2006-2008; H Innoc Ch Atlanta GA 2003-2006; S Mart In The Fields Ch Atlanta GA 2001-2003; S Mart's Epis Sch Atlanta GA 2001-2003. extrarev@gmail.com

REED, Harold Vincent (Alb) 1718 Guilderland Ave, Schenectady NY 12306 **R S Paul's Ch Schenectady NY 1999-** B Chicago IL 4/29/1958 s Harold Vincent Reed & Albina. AA Nthrn Virginia Cmnty Coll 1987; BA Geo Mason U 1988; VTS 1989; MDiv Nash 1992. D 12/19/1992 Bp William Charles Wantland P 6/19/1993 Bp Charles Thomas Gaskell. m 10/18/2008 Stephanie Annette Cornett. S Geo's Epis Ch Schenectady NY 1992-1999. CBS; ESA; Forw In Faith 1999; GAS; SocMary; SSC 1993. hvratstpls@aol.com

REED SR, James Arthur (WVa) 884 6th Street Hill, Newell WV 26050 **Assoc Chr Ch Wellsburg WV 1998-; Assoc Olde S Jn's Ch Colliers WV 1998-; Vic S Matt's Ch Chester WV 1986-** B Chester WV 10/4/1934 s Arthur Bernard Reed & Mary Ellen. TESM. D 6/5/1985 Bp Robert Poland Atkinson P 6/1/1986 Bp William Franklin Carr. m 8/8/1965 Phyllis Jean Carman c 1.

REED, James Farr (WLa) 400 Contour Dr, Lake Charles LA 70605 B Bolton MS 7/24/1931 s Stevenson Reed & Nettie Marguerite. BS LSU 1953; BD STUSo 1958; MS McNeese St U 1969; MA Rice U 1972; PhD Rice U 1974. D 6/19/1958 Bp Iveson Batchelor Noland P 5/1/1959 Bp Girault M Jones. m 5/1/1973 Susan Howard Boggess. Cur Epis Ch Of The Gd Shpd Lake Chas LA 1965-1969; P-in-c All SS Ch Dequincy LA 1961-1965; P-in-c Trin Epis Ch Deridder LA 1961-1965; Vic S Andr's Ch Theriot LA 1958-1960.

REED, James Gardner (Va) 6013 Hot Spring Ln, Fredericksburg VA 22407 **R Ch Of The Mssh Fredericksburg VA 1995-** B Topeka KS 12/3/1954 s Richard Alden Reed & Elizabeth Alice. BS MI SU 1977; MDiv Gordon-Conwell TS 1984. D 6/12/1993 P 12/15/1993 Bp Peter James Lee. m 4/28/1984 Stephanie M Mann c 3. Vic Ch of the Incarn Mineral VA 1993-1995. BSA. jreed49@comcast.net

REED, Jeffrey Bruce (Az) Po Box 42618, Tucson AZ 85733 B 12/4/1955 s Robert Reed & Anna Rae. BA New Coll of California; Tcjc Sch Of Nrsng Ft Worth TX 1981; MDiv CDSP 2002. D 6/1/2002 P 12/7/2002 Bp William Edwin Swing. Dio Arizona Phoenix AZ 2003-2006; The Edge Chr Campus Cntr San Francisco CA 2002-2003. jeffrey-reed@cox.net

REED JR, J(oseph) Wilson (Chi) 227 E Walton Pl Apt 4-E, Chicago IL 60611 **Died 11/12/2009** B Joliet IL 6/5/1930 s Joseph Wilson Reed & Agnes

R

Cunningham. BA NWU 1952; STB GTS 1955. D 6/18/1955 Bp Charles L Street P 12/21/1955 Bp Gerald Francis Burrill.

REED, Juan Y (Chi) 1617 E 50th Place, Apt 4D, Chicago IL 60615 **Vic S Mart's Ch Chicago IL 1990-** B Chicago IL 12/14/1947 s Earl Reed & Lula. BA H Redeem Coll 1972; MSW Loyola U Chi 1981; MDiv SWTS 1991; D. Min. Cath Theol Un at Chicago 2004. Rec from Roman Catholic 7/1/1991 as Priest Bp Frank Tracy Griswold III. S Mart's Ch Chicago IL 1991-2010. juanreed@att.net

REED, Kenneth Courter (NJ) 59 George St, Milltown NJ 08850 **D S Jn The Evang Ch New Brunswick NJ 1985-** B Highland Park NJ 4/21/1921 s Leroy Elsworth Reed & Mable Leona. D 4/13/1985 Bp George Phelps Mellick Belshaw. m 8/17/1946 Ruth Anne Rule c 2. Ord Of S Lk.

REED, Loreen Hayward Rogers (At) 355 Porter St, Madison GA 30650 B Jersey City NJ 9/8/1944 d Bernard George Rogers & Doris Loreen. Columbia TS; BA Connecticut Coll 1966; MDiv Candler TS Emory U 1997. D 6/7/1997 Bp Onell Asiselo Soto P 12/1/1997 Bp Frank Kellogg Allan. m 6/20/1964 Walter Logan Reed c 3. The Epis Ch Of The Adv Madison GA 2003-2010; Asst R H Innoc Ch Atlanta GA 2001-2003; S Julian's Epis Ch Douglasville GA 2000; Asst S Jos's Epis Ch McDonough GA 1997-1998. lreed@adventmadison.org

REED JR, Poulson Connell (Az) 6300 N Central Ave, Phoenix AZ 85012 **R All SS Ch Phoenix AZ 2009-** B Richmond VA 5/22/1970 s Poulson Connell Reed & Nancy Bullard. BA U of Virginia 1992; MFA U of Utah 1994; MDiv Yale DS 1997. D 6/8/2002 Bp Andrew Donnan Smith P 1/18/2003 Bp William Jerry Winterrowd. m 11/20/2004 Megan Tiedt c 2. Cn S Jn's Cathd Denver CO 2002-2009. preed@allsaints.org

REED, Richard Wayne (RG) Hc 31 Box 17-B, Las Vegas NM 87701 B Marshalltown IA 12/8/1938 s Wayne F Reed & Hazel M. BA New Mex Highlands U 1964; MS Florida St U 1969. D 8/27/1986 Bp Richard Mitchell Trelease Jr P 6/1/1988 Bp William Davidson. m 1/2/1965 Lucy M Everrett. R S Paul's/Peace Ch Las Vegas NM 2001-2010; P-in-c H Trin Epis Ch - Mssn Raton NM 1995-2001; P S Paul's/Peace Ch Las Vegas NM 1986-1995. rwlmreed@cybermesa

REED, Robert Cooper (NwPa) 119 Forrest Rd., New Castle PA 16105 **D Trin Ch Hermitage PA 1966-** B New Castle PA 6/30/1928 s Jay Leroy Reed & Jessie. BS Grove City Coll 1950; DDS U Pgh 1954; DMD U Pgh 1970. D 12/18/1966 Bp William Crittenden. m 6/28/1952 Esther Elizabeth Lindstrom c 4.

REED, Ronald Lind (Kan) 4810 W 67th St, Prairie Village KS 66208 B Ashland KS 6/26/1946 s Donald Gilbert Reed & Lydia Lind. BA w/hon U of Oklahoma 1968; BD cl EDS 1971. D 6/29/1971 P 9/16/1972 Bp Chilton Powell. m 6/15/1999 Catherine Crichton. Vic S Paul's Ch Kansas City KS 2003-2010; Bd Mem Epis Cmnty Serv Kansas City MO 2002-2010; Stwdshp Com Dio Kansas Topeka KS 1991-2002; R S Jas Ch Wichita KS 1991-2001; Dir of Stwdshp and Dvlpmt Epis Ch Cntr New York NY 1984-1991; R Chr Ch And S Mich's Philadelphia PA 1975-1982; Vice Chair of Stndg Cmsn on Salaries and Pensions Dio Pennsylvania Philadelphia PA 1975-1982; Yth Mnstry Com Chair Dio Pennsylvania Philadelphia PA 1972-1981; Asst S Thos' Ch Whitemarsh Ft Washington PA 1971-1974. Auth, "The Stewards' Count," The Epis Ch Cntr, 1985. Apos of Stwdshp The Epis Ntwk for Stwdshp at GC 2009. ronaldlreed@gmail.com

REED, Stephen Kim (Colo) 1722 Linden St, Longmont CO 80501 B Watertown NY 10/16/1966 s James Arthur Reed & Itha Lee. MDiv Epis TS of The SW; Icisf Baltimore MD; BS Utica Coll. D 6/9/2001 P 12/2/2001 Bp William Jerry Winterrowd. m 10/21/1995 Laura Jean Drake c 2. Vic Prince Of Peace Epis Ch Sterling CO 2003-2010; Cur S Steph's Ch Longmont CO 2001-2003. stephenkreed@hotmail.com

REED, Thomas Louis (Pa) 11 South St, Eastport ME 04631 B Tulsa OK 1/10/1947 s Thomas Edwin Reed & Faye Lorrain. U of Tulsa 1966; BA Oklahoma Bapt U 1969; MDiv SW Bapt TS 1973; Cert Virginia Commonwealth U 1975; Oxf 1976. D 5/22/1976 Bp John Alfred Baden P 6/25/1977 Bp Robert Bruce Hall. St Pauls Ch Philadelphia PA 1982-1992; R Chr Epis Ch Spotsylvania VA 1976-1981. Biblic Archeological Soc 1970. revrun48@yahoo.com

REED, Vincent Moon (NMich) 201 E Ridge St, Marquette MI 49855 B Lansing MI 4/4/1946 s Kenneth A Reed & Roberta I. no degree MI SU 1968; BS Nthrn Michigan U 1971. D 5/9/2006 Bp James Arthur Kelsey P 5/3/2009 Bp Thomas Kreider Ray. c 1. vincentreed@gmail.com

REEDER, Thomas Parnell (CPa) 220 Confer Lane, Muncy PA 17756 **Stndg Com Dio Cntrl Pennsylvania Harrisburg PA 2011-; R Chr Ch Williamsport PA 2005-** B Silver Spring MD 6/13/1969 BA U CA 2000; MDiv TS 2003. D 6/1/2003 Bp Jerry Alban Lamb P 12/7/2003 Bp Stephen Hays Jecko. m 8/11/1990 Deeann Marie Reeder c 2. Stndg Com Dio Cntrl Pennsylvania Harrisburg PA 2011; Coun of Trst Dio Cntrl Pennsylvania Harrisburg PA 2008-2011; P-in-c S Mk's Epis Ch Jacksonville FL 2005; Assoc R S Mk's Epis Ch Jacksonville FL 2003-2004; D Dio Nthrn California Sacramento CA 2003. FR.TOM@CHRISTCHURCH.WS

REES, Donald Joseph (EpisSanJ) 12358 Newport Rd, Ballico CA 95303 **D S Fran' Epis Ch Turlock CA 1996-** B 4/10/1925 s Joseph Freely Rees & Susan Barbara. D 6/8/1996 Bp John-David Mercer Schofield. m 2/13/1982 Mary Maddux c 1.

REES, Elizabeth (Va) 1501 River Farm Dr, Alexandria VA 22308 **Assoc R S Aid's Ch Alexandria VA 2007-** B Baltimore MD 10/9/1972 d Charles Arthur Rees & Patricia May. BA Wake Forest U Winston-Salem NC 1994; JD Emory U Atlanta GA 1997; MDiv VTS 2007. D 6/16/2007 Bp Peter James Lee P 12/17/2007 Bp David Colin Jones. m 9/2/2001 Holden Hoofnagle c 2. reeseliz@yahoo.com

REES, Emily Frances (At) Po Box 223, Braselton GA 30517 B Atlanta GA 4/15/1946 d Arthur Rees & Emily. D 8/6/2006 Bp J(ohn) Neil Alexander. c 2. frances_rees@msn.com

REESE, Carol Sue (Chi) 1900 W Polk St # 1300, Chicago IL 60612 B St Louis MO 8/27/1956 d William Harold Reese & Katharine Annabell. BA Georgetown Coll 1978; MDiv The Sthrn Bapt TS 1981; MSW U IL 1984; Angl Stds SWTS 2009. D 6/5/2010 P 12/3/2010 Bp Jeffrey Dean Lee. c 2. csreese56@gmail.com

REESE, Frederic William (Miss) 373 Edenbrook, Brookhaven MO 39601 B Pleasantville NJ 1/14/1933 s Franklin White Reese & Catherine Elizabeth. BA Merc 1960; MDiv Epis TS In Kentucky 1964. D 5/30/1964 P 12/13/1964 Bp William R Moody. c 2. Assoc Ch Of The Gd Shpd Tomball TX 1999-2003; Vic Ch Of The Redeem Brookhaven MS 1982-1993; Vic Calv Ch Ripley MS 1978-1982; R Chr Ch Holly Sprg MS 1978-1982; R Ch Of The Gd Samar Knoxville TN 1972-1978; R Trin Ch Lumberton NC 1967-1972; R S Thos Ch Beattyville KY 1964-1967. fwr@cableone.net

REESE, Jeannette (WNC) 45 Spooks Branch Extension, Asheville NC 28804 **D Gr Ch Asheville NC 2009-** B Charleston SC 5/8/1945 d Daniel Wordsworth Ellis & Anna. BA Queens Coll 1967. D 5/29/1993 Bp Harry Woolston Shipps. m 4/30/1994 Robert Emory Reese c 2. D S Thos Epis Ch Burnsville NC 2007-2008; D S Andr's Ch Darien GA 1999-2004; D S Mk's Ch Brunswick GA 1993-1998.

REESE, John (SwFla) 509 E Twiggs St, Tampa FL 33602 **R S Andr's Epis Ch Tampa FL 2005-** B Passaic NJ 8/6/1961 s Arthur Paul Reese & Rose Marie. BA U CO 1986; MDiv VTS 1997. D 6/7/1997 Bp William Jerry Winterrowd P 12/13/1997 Bp David Charles Bowman. m 11/1/1986 Jeanette M Reese c 1. R Trin Epis Ch Fredonia NY 1997-2005. jandjreese@verizon.net

REESE, Mary (EC) 404 E. New Hope Rd., Goldsboro NC 27534 **Disciplinary Bd Dio E Carolina Kinston NC 2011-; COM Dio E Carolina Kinston NC 2010-; Liturg Cmsn Dio E Carolina Kinston NC 2010-; P-in-c S Andr's Ch Goldsboro NC 2010-; Dominican Republic Comp Dio Cmsn Dio E Carolina Kinston NC 2009-; Anti-racism Cmsn Dio E Carolina Kinston NC 2008-** B Brooklyn NY 2/28/1946 d William Horten Whitley & Mary Lee H. BS Cor 1967; MS Syr 1969; MDiv VTS 2008. D 6/14/2008 P 2/21/2009 Bp Clifton Daniel III. c 6. Trin Cntr Bd Dir Dio E Carolina Kinston NC 2004-2007; Dominican Rep. Comp Dio. Cmsn Dio E Carolina Kinston NC 2001-2007. revmaryreese@gmail.com

REESE, Robert Emory (WNC) 45 Spooks Branch Ext, Asheville NC 28804 **Assoc Gr Ch Asheville NC 2010-** B Asheville,NC 9/20/1949 s Robert H Reese & Ora Sue. BA U So 1971; MDiv VTS 1974; CPE Intern Year Pstr Inst Ft. Benning GA 1984; DMin VTS 1998. D 6/22/1974 Bp Matthew G Henry P 6/21/1975 Bp William Gillette Weinhauer. m 4/30/1994 Jeannette Ellis c 2. Int S Thos Epis Ch Burnsville NC 2007-2008; Int S Jn's Ch Sylva NC 2005-2006; R S Andr's Ch Darien GA 1999-2004; S Cyp's Ch Darien GA 1999-2004; S Mk's Ch Brunswick GA 1990-1999; Off Of Bsh For ArmdF New York NY 1981-1989. ACPE 1989-1998. Paul Harris Fell Intl Rotary 2003. revsreese@mac.com

REESE, Thomas Francis (LI) 141 Ascan Ave, Forest Hills NY 11375 **R S Lk's Ch Forest Hills NY 2000-** B Bayshore NY 7/13/1953 s Thomas Francis Reese & Joan. BA Colg 1975; MDiv EDS 1979; MA The Grad Cntr of CUNY 2010. D 6/2/1979 P 10/18/1980 Bp Wilbur Emory Hogg Jr. m Yin-Wei Liao c 2. Chairperson of Comission on Mnstry Dio Long Island Garden City NY 2006-2008; R S Ann's Epis Ch Bridgehampton NY 1992-2000; R Ch Of The H Adv Clinton CT 1988-1992; Pres of Metropltn Dnry Dio Albany Albany NY 1985-1987; Assoc R S Paul's Epis Ch Albany NY 1982-1988; Chapl Doane Stuart Sch Albany NY 1980-1982. stlukestom@yahoo.com

REESON, Geoffrey Douglas (EcuC) Casilla 17-16-95, Quito Ecuador B Barranquilla CO 10/18/1948 s William Bateman Reeson & Marjory Edith. BS U of The W Indies 1972; MDiv ETSC 1976. D 10/17/1976 P 4/17/1977 Bp William Alfred Franklin. m 5/19/1974 Marta Lidia Reeson. Adv-S Nich Ch Quito EC 2002-2006; Iglesia Epis Del Ecuador Ecuador 1987-2002; Iglesia Epis En Colombia 1976-1987. asngeoff@ecuanex.net.ec

REESON, Marta Lidia (EcuC) Casilla 17-16-95, Quito Ecuador **Ecuador New York NY 2011-** B Ecuador 12/8/1947 d Segundo Revelo & Clementina. Universidad Cntrl del Ecuador; MDiv Seminario Epis del Caribe 1976. D 2/18/2011 Bp Luis Fernando Ruiz Restrepo. m 5/19/1974 Geoffrey Douglas Reeson. martareeson@yahoo.com

REEVE, Keith John (NC) 3613 Clifton Ct, Raleigh NC 27604 B Ipswich England UK 1/11/1930 s Wilfred John Reeve & Amy Ethel. Lic VTS 1967. D

R

6/29/1967 P 1/6/1968 Bp Thomas H Wright. m 6/5/1954 Carmen Gardner c 5. S Tim's Ch Wilson NC 1989-1990; Chr Ch Rocky Mt NC 1988-1989; Int Dio No Carolina Raleigh NC 1987-1990; Trin Ch Scotland Neck NC 1987-1988; S Mk's Epis Ch Raleigh NC 1970-1986; Asst H Trin Epis Ch Fayetteville NC 1967-1970. ckreeve@mac.com

REEVE, Susan Margaret (NCal) 146 Saint Gertrude Ave, Rio Vista CA 94571 **Dio California San Francisco CA 1999-** B Bishop's Stortford UK 12/8/1945 d Leonard Reeve & Nellie Margaret. BA U of Durham GB 1967; MLS U CA 1976; BA Sch for Deacons 1999. D 11/20/1999 Bp Jerry Alban Lamb. D S Paul's Epis Ch Benicia CA 1999-2004. NAAD 1997. riolibrarian@yahoo.com

REEVES JR, C(harles) Edward (Ala) 4015 Knollwood Dr., Birmingham AL 35243 B Sandersville GA 3/7/1926 s Charles Edward Reeves & Pauline. BA Emory U 1949; BD Candler TS Emory U 1952; U So 1961. D 6/11/1961 P 1/13/1962 Bp Randolph R Claiborne. m 3/11/1956 Darline Jackson Grace Darline Jackson c 2. Vice Dn The Cathd Ch Of The Adv Birmingham AL 1988-1995; Dn S Mary's Cathd Memphis TN 1974-1988; R S Paul's Ch Augusta GA 1963-1974; Cn Cathd Of S Phil Atlanta GA 1961-1963. dandereeves@bellsouth.net

REEVES, Diane Delafield (Fla) 13588 Northeast 247th Lane, Box 18, Orange Springs FL 32182 **Vic-unpaid S Andr's Ch Interlachen FL 2000-** B Newton MA 8/25/1944 d Gordon Rae MacLechlan & Barbara Delafield. D 12/1/1999 P 6/1/2000 Bp Stephen Hays Jecko. m 11/23/1968 Ralph Harold Reeves.

REEVES, Frank B (FtW) 2204 Collington Dr, Roanoke TX 76262 B Seattle WA 5/26/1942 s Hume Wixom Reeves & Virginia Ruth. BS Texas A&M U 1970; MS Texas A&M U 1971; LST Angl TS 1980. D 6/28/1980 Bp A Donald Davies P 11/28/1981 Bp Robert Elwin Terwilliger. m 4/25/1964 Susan Krumbein c 2. R S Mart In The Fields Ch Keller TX 1989-2007; Dio Ft Worth Ft Worth TX 1985-1989; Cur S Chris's Ch And Sch Ft Worth TX 1981-1985; Cur Chr The King Epis Ch Ft Worth TX 1980-1981. Auth, "Perceptual Narrowing as a Function of Peripheral Cue Relevance," *Journ of Peripheral & Motor Skille*, 1971. revfrankreeves@charter.net

✠ **REEVES, Rt Rev (George) Paul** (Ga) 10 Briar Knoll Ct, Asheville NC 28803 **Died 4/15/2010** B Roanoke VA 10/14/1918 s George Floyd Reeves & Hattie Faye. DD Nash; DD STUSo; BA Randolph-Macon Coll 1940; BD Yale DS 1943. D 5/6/1948 P 11/1/1948 Bp Frank A Juhan Con 9/30/1969 for Ga. c 2. crpond@bellsouth.net

REEVES, Jack William (LI) 23 Old Mamaroneck Rd Apt 5R, White Plains NY 10605 B Crawford NE 10/15/1940 s Harry William Reeves & Mildred Maxine. BA U of Missouri 1962; BD Nash 1965. D 2/6/1965 P 8/1/1965 Bp Edward Randolph Welles II. R Gr Epis Ch Whitestone NY 1984-2001; R All SS' Epis Ch Long Island City NY 1979-1983; Chr Ch Epis Hudson NY 1975-1979; Vic S Lk's Epis Ch Excelsior Sprg MO 1966-1976; Cur S Paul's Ch Kansas City MO 1965-1966. ESA.

REEVES JR, Jess (SeFla) 8619 North Liston Avenue, Kansas City MO 64154 **Ch Of The Redeem Kansas City MO 2009-** B Pine Bluff AR 12/20/1952 s Jess Leonidas Reeves & Elizabeth Anne. BA W&L 1975; MDiv TESM 1987. D 8/24/1987 P 3/1/1988 Bp Bob Gordon Jones. S Ptr's Ch Columbia TN 2007-2009; S Thos Epis Ch Orange VA 1999-2004; The Epis Ch Of Beth-By-The-Sea Palm Bch FL 1999-2004; S Jn's Epis Ch Niantic CT 1998-1999; S Fran Ch Potomac MD 1990-1998; R Ch Of The H Comm Rock Sprg WY 1989-1990; S Geo's Ch Lusk WY 1987-1989. IMN 1995. jessreevesjr@aol.com

REEVES, Robin K (Tex) 523 E 4th St, Tyler TX 75701 **S Geo's Epis Ch Texas City TX 2011-** B Lamesa TX 4/28/1962 d Billy Eugene Reeves & Patricia. BBA U of No Texas 1984; MDiv Sem Of The SW 2006. D 6/24/2006 Bp Don Adger Wimberly P 1/8/2007 Bp Rayford Baines High Jr. Dio Texas Houston TX 2011; S Jas The Apos Epis Ch Conroe TX 2009-2010; Asst Trin Epis Ch The Woodlands TX 2008-2009; Cur/Asst R Chr Epis Ch Tyler TX 2006-2008. rreevestrinity@gmail.com

REEVES JR, William (Va) The Collegiate Schools, Richmond VA 23229 B Southport CT 9/3/1934 s William Reeves & Elizabeth Lee. BA Ya 1956; MA Harv 1960; Ya Berk 1961; MDiv EDS 1963. D 6/11/1963 Bp Walter H Gray P 4/1/1964 Bp Harry S Kennedy. m 2/22/1963 Jane Anne Weisenbarger. S Thos' Ch Richmond VA 2000-2001; Ch Of The Creator Mechanicsville VA 1997-1998; S Jn's Ch Richmond VA 1996-1997; All SS Ch Richmond VA 1981-1993; Collgt Schools Richmond VA 1977-1980; Chatham Hall Chatham VA 1971-1977; P-in-c S Mk's Ch Honolulu HI 1969-1970; Assoc Vic Waikiki Chap Honolulu HI 1965-1968. Auth, "Sino-Amer Coopration In Med:The Origins Of Hsiang-Ya".

REGAN, Thomas Francis (SD) 708 Sawyer St, Lead SD 57754 **D Chr Epis Ch Lead SD 1991-** B Deadwood SD 1/19/1950 s Jack Thomas Regan & June Elizabeth. Black Hill St U 1975; EFM STUSo 1989; EFM STUSo 1995; Niobrara Sum Sem 2000. D 12/15/1991 Bp Craig Barry Anderson. m 8/24/1969 Diana Lynn Colvin c 2. NAAD. tregan@ecunent.org

REGAS, George Frank (Los) 807 Las Palmas Rd., Pasadena CA 91105 B Knoxville TN 10/1/1930 s Frank Regas & Edith. BA U of Tennessee 1953; MDiv EDS 1956; U of Cambridge 1957; Rel. D Claremont TS 1972; DD EDS 1992. D 7/25/1956 Bp Theodore N Barth P 6/1/1957 Bp John Vander Horst. m 1/16/1977 Mary McCaslin c 3. Chair - Com Dio Los Angeles Los Angeles CA 1987-1995; Chair - Com Dio Los Angeles Los Angeles CA 1973-1980; R All SS Ch Pasadena CA 1967-1995; Bp'S Advsry Com On Ch And Race Dio New York New York City NY 1963-1964; R Gr Epis Ch Nyack NY 1960-1967; P-in-c The Epis Ch Of The Mssh Pulaski TN 1957-1960. Auth, "Kiss Yourself & Hug The Wrld". Kilgore Awd & Lectrs For Creative Mnstry; Awd Soc Justice B'Nai B'Rith; Humanitarian Awd La Cnty Pyschol Assn. gregas@regasinstitute.org

REGEN, Catharine Louise Emmert (Tenn) 306 Broadview Dr, Dickson TN 37055 **Vic Calv Ch Epis Dickson TN 1992-; S Tim Epis Ch Dickson TN 1992-** B Indianapolis IN 9/13/1931 d James Allan Emmert & Bernice Louise. U So; BA Indiana U 1953; MA Van 1955; MDiv Van 1990. D 6/9/1991 Bp George Lazenby Reynolds Jr P 3/1/1992 Bp William Evan Sanders. m 11/26/1959 Barney Brooks Regen c 2. Co-Cnvnr, NW Convoc Dio Tennessee Nashville TN 1994-1996. Woodrow Wilson Fllshp Van Nashville TN 1959; Ford Fndt Fllshp Van Nashville TN 1955.

REGER, Timothy Scott (CNY) 210 E Genesee St # 3, Fayetteville NY 13066 **S Jas' Ch Clinton NY 2010-** B Rochester NY 3/13/1972 s Kenneth Scott Reger & Elizabeth Parham. BA Le Moyne Coll 1996; CAS SWTS 2002; MA Boston Coll 2003. D 12/15/2002 P 6/19/2003 Bp Gladstone Bailey Adams III. m 12/8/1997 Rahel Irene Elmer. Gr Ch Baldwinsville NY 2004-2010; D S Mk The Evang Syracuse NY 2003-2004. fathertim@mac.com

REGISFORD, Sylvanus Hermus Alonzo (SeFla) 7580 Derby Ln, Shakopee MN 55379 B 9/20/1941 s David Jeshuran Regisford & Myrtle. U Tor; BD Codrington Coll 1965; Nmin Intl Sem 1982; DMin Intl Sem 1983. Trans from Church in the Province Of The West Indies 1/7/1981 Bp Calvin Onderdonk Schofield Jr. Ch Of S Chris Ft Lauderdale FL 1981-1998; S Phil's Ch Pompano Bch FL 1981-1998. CBS.

REGIST, Antonio Alberto (WTex) 1310 Pecan Valley Dr, Antonio TX 78210 **R S Phil's Ch San Antonio TX 2009-** B 10/31/1954 s Ernel Patrick Regist & Doris E. Assoc in Tech Panama Canal/Canal Zone Coll 1980; BS Nova SE U 1982; Cert in Pstr Centro de Estudios Cristianos de la Iglesia Epis Panama 2000; Cert in Total Mnstry Centro de Estudios Cristianos de la Iglesia Epis Panama 2000; Cert Spec Stds Epis TS of the SW 2003; MDiv Oblate TS San Antonio TX 2005; Cert of Residency CPE 2006. Trans from Iglesia Anglicana de la Region Central de America 4/24/2008 Bp Gary Richard Lillibridge. m 7/3/1982 Felmina Regist c 3. Marine Engr- hon Panama Nautical Acad 2001; Fr of the year Altamira Club Panama, Panama 1999. aaregist@hotmail.com

REHAGEN, Gerald Anthony (EMich) PO Box 920, Gaylord MI 49734 B Jefferson City MO 11/10/1938 s Henry Edward Rehagen & Alma Marie. BA Cardinal Glennon Coll 1960; MA Kenrick-Glennon Sem 1964; Post Grad S Louis U 1976. Rec from Roman Catholic 3/14/1987 Bp Donald Maynard Hultstrand. m 5/22/1976 M Donnellan c 2. R S Andr's Epis Ch Gaylord MI 1999-2009; P Dio Springfield Springfield IL 1987-1998. grehagen@yahoo.com

REHBERG, Gloria Irene (RG) 7104 Montano Rd Nw, Albuquerque NM 87120 **D Dio The Rio Grande Albuquerque NM 1992-** B Albuquerque NM 3/23/1934 d Leonard Michael Tartaglia & Irene Alma. BA U of New Mex 1982. D 6/26/1985 Bp Richard Mitchell Trelease Jr. m 9/19/1953 Charles Ray Rehberg c 1. D All SS Ch Grants NM 1989-1992; D Dio The Rio Grande Albuquerque NM 1985-1989. Auth, "Faith & Obedience," Creative Designs, 1998.

REHBERG, Gretchen (Spok) 713 8th St., Lewiston ID 83501 **Presiding Mem, SE Reg Dio Spokane Spokane WA 2011-; Commitee on Sci, Tech and Faith Exec Coun Appointees New York NY 2009-; R Epis Ch of the Nativ Lewiston ID 2006-** B Pullman WA 7/7/1964 d Wallace Albert Rehberg & Margaret Ella. BS U So 1986; PhD U MN 1990; MDiv GTS 2002. D 6/8/2002 P 2/13/2003 Bp Michael Whittington Creighton. Asst The Epis Ch Of S Jn The Bapt York PA 2002-2005. rector@nativitylewiston.com

REHLING JR, Carl William (Md) 11701 Mira Lago Blvd Apt 2123, Dallas TX 75234 **Dioc Liaison for Justice & Peace Mnstrs Dio Maryland Baltimore MD 1997-** B Catonsville MD 5/13/1925 s Carl William Rehling & Mildred Elizabeth. BS U of Baltimore 1955. D 6/15/1991 Bp A(lbert) Theodore Eastman. m 9/25/1948 Patricia Ann Lemmon c 2. D S Jas' Par Lothian MD 1995-2000; D Chr Ch Port Republic MD 1991-1995. NAAD 1991. rev.carl.rehling@gmail.com

REHO, James Hughes (SeFla) The General Theological Seminary, 440 W 21 Street, New York NY 10011 **Chapl and Dir of Pstr Care, Deploy, and Formation; Dir of Theol Field Educ The GTS New York NY 2011-** B New York City NY 4/12/1969 s George Zigmond Reho & Barbara Madeline. BA St Jn's U 1990; BS Wag 1994; MA Pr 1996; PhD Pr 2000; MDiv The GTS 2008. D 6/14/2008 Bp Clifton Daniel III P 12/20/2008 Bp Leopold Frade. m 11/9/1996 Carolanne Scali. Asst Trin Cathd Miami FL 2008-2011. reho@gts.edu

REICH, Jeffrey Walker (Miss) 834 N. 5th Ave, laurel MS 39440 **R S Jn's Ch Laurel MS 2008-** B Rome CA 4/10/1972 BS Mississippi St U; Masters of Div SWTS 2004. D 6/19/2004 P 12/21/2004 Bp Duncan Montgomery Gray III. m 12/13/1997 Catharine Bennett c 3. Vic S Jn's Ch Aberdeen MS 2004-2008. fr.reich@gmail.com

REICH, Karl Frederick (ND) 4227 Se Nehalem St, Portland OR 97206 **Died 8/31/2009** B Chicago IL 8/26/1922 s Walter George Reich & Dorothy Rosalie. BS Clemson U 1947; MDiv Bex 1957. D 5/31/1957 P 12/8/1957 Bp Nelson Marigold Burroughs. c 4.

REICHARD, Bernice Dorothy (Be) P.O. Box 368, Trexlertown PA 18087 **D S Anne's Epis Ch Trexlertown PA 2008-** B Philadelphia PA 7/7/1942 d Robert James Romig & Dorothy Marie. RN Abington Hosp Sch of Nrsng 1963; BSPA S Jos Coll 1984. D 2/2/2008 Bp Paul Victor Marshall. m 9/18/2004 Ronald Reichard c 3. BDReichard@ptd.net

REICHERT, Elaine Starr Gilmer (Cal) 1605 Vendola Dr, San Rafael CA 94903 B San Jose CA 1/6/1948 d Ralph Albert Gilmer & Lorna Elizabeth. BA California St U 1969; MS California St U 1974; MDiv CDSP 1979. D 12/11/1982 P 12/1/1983 Bp William Edwin Swing. m 10/12/1991 Arthur G Reichert. Asst P S Steph's Par Belvedere CA 2009-2010; Asst R S Jn's Epis Ch Oakland CA 2007-2011; Assoc R S Fran Of Assisi Ch Novato CA 1984-1985; Vol The Epis Ch Of S Jn The Evang San Francisco CA 1984-1985; Pstr Assoc S Ptr's Epis Ch San Francisco CA 1979-1983. g.r-elaine@comcast.net

REICHMAN, Amy Linda (Ct) PO Box 698, Sharon CT 06069 **D S Jn's Ch New Milford CT 2010-** B 3/3/1953 D 9/17/2005 Bp Andrew Donnan Smith.

REICHMANN, Jeffrey Harold (At) 500 Riverside Pkwy NW, Atlanta GA 30328 B Jamaica NY 6/26/1951 s Charles Thomas Reichmann & Jean Elise. BA New Engl Coll 1973; MDiv Nash 1976. D 6/5/1976 P 12/18/1976 Bp Jonathan Goodhue Sherman. m 8/9/1975 Jeanne Abblett c 3. H Innoc Ch Atlanta GA 2002-2006; H Innoc' Epis Sch Atlanta GA 2001-2010; R Chr Ch Babylon NY 1995-2001; S Paul's By-The-Sea Epis Ch Jacksonville Bch FL 1991-1995; Chapl Chr Sch & Assoc R Chr Ch Covington LA 1990-1991; Trin Epis Sch New Orleans LA 1984-1990; Cur Chr Ch Manhasset NY 1976-1984. jreich101@comcast.net

REID, Brian S (NwPa) 415 4th Ave, Warren PA 16365 **Secy of Conv & Coun Dio NW Pennsylvania Erie PA 2006-; Dep to Gnrl Conveniton Dio NW Pennsylvania Erie PA 1991-; Ecum Com Dio NW Pennsylvania Erie PA 1980-; Dioc Coun Dio NW Pennsylvania Erie PA 1978-; Const & Cn Com Dio NW Pennsylvania Erie PA 1977-** B Detroit MI 8/19/1948 s Russell Phillips Reid & H(ulda) Aileen. BA Wayne 1970; MDiv Nash 1973. D 6/30/1973 Bp H Coleman McGehee Jr P 1/18/1974 Bp Archie H Crowley. Int Ch Of Our Sav DuBois PA 2009-2010; Int S Jn's Ch Franklin PA 2007-2008; Bp Search Com Dio NW Pennsylvania Erie PA 2006-2007; Int The Lawrencefield Chap Par Wheeling WV 2003-2005; R Trin Memi Ch Warren PA 1996-2004; Dioc Sprtl Dir Dio NW Pennsylvania Erie PA 1983-1986; COM Dio NW Pennsylvania Erie PA 1981-1985; R S Fran Of Assisi Epis Ch Youngsville PA 1980-1996; Vic Ch Of The H Trin Houtzdale PA 1976-1980; Vic S Lawr Ch Osceola Mills PA 1976-1980; Urban Affrs Com Dio Michigan Detroit MI 1974-1976. breid@westpa.net

REID, Catharine Brannan (Oly) 1123 19th Ave East, Seattle WA 98112 **D S Clem's Epis Ch Seattle WA 2011-; Fin Admin S Paul's Ch Seattle WA 2011-** B Bryn Mawr PA 9/11/1950 d George Eric Reid & Elsie Pendleton. AB Smith 1972; MSLS Villanova U 1975; Dplma HE Trin, Bristol, Engl 1981; MDiv GTS 1983. D 2/15/2011 P 10/19/2011 Bp Gregory Harold Rickel. CBREID50@COMCAST.NET

REID, Franklin Lionel (NY) 1064 E 219th St, Bronx NY 10469 B AI 1/29/1959 s Roderick Archibald Reid & Felicia. U of The W Indies; BA Codrington Coll 1982; BA Codrington Coll 1982. Trans from Church in the Province Of The West Indies 12/10/1990 Bp Walter Decoster Dennis Jr. m 12/29/1985 Sandra Reid c 2. S Lk's Epis Ch Bronx NY 1990-2010. OHC.

REID, Gordon (Pa) 2013 Appletree St, Philadelphia PA 19103 **S Clements Ch Philadelphia PA 2004-** B Hawick Scotland 1/28/1943 s William Albert Reid & Elizabeth Jean. MA U of Edinburgh Edinburgh UK 1963; Edinburgh Theol Coll 1964; Cuddesdon Coll 1966; BA Keble Coll,Oxford 1966; MA Keble Coll,Oxford 1972. Trans from Diocese in Europe 1/1/2004 Bp Charles Ellsworth Bennison Jr. "Every Comfort At Golgotha," Tufton Books, 1998; "The Wind from The Stars," Harper Collins, 1992. gordonrr@earthlink.net

REID, Jennie Lou Divine (SeFla) 3840 Alhambra Ct, Coral Gables FL 33134 **S Faith's Epis Ch Cutler Bay FL 2009-** B Norfolk VA 6/13/1945 d Hugh William Divine & Marlon Mae. BA Duke 1967; MA U NC 1969; EFM 1992; St. Geo's Coll Jerusalem IL 1998; MDiv VTS 1999. D 6/11/1999 P 1/15/2000 Bp Calvin Onderdonk Schofield Jr. m 12/19/1970 Ralph Benjamine Reid c 3. S Thos Epis Par Coral Gables FL 2004-2008; Trin Cathd Miami FL 2003-2004; Chair -- Comm On Mnstry Dio SE Florida Miami FL 2001-2003; Comm On Min Dio SE Florida Miami FL 2000-2006; Asst R S Phil's Ch Coral Gables FL 1999-2002; Comm On Min Dio SE Florida Miami FL 1990-1995; Exec Bd Dio SE Florida Miami FL 1983-1986. dean.jlreid@gmail.com

REID, Manney Carrington (USC) Po Box 991, Pawleys Island SC 29585 **R Emer Trin Ch Myrtle Bch SC 1988-** B Columbia SC 11/22/1922 s Howard Dunklin Reid & Sadie Lillian. BS U of So Carolina 1943; MS Col 1947; MDiv VTS 1951. D 2/4/1951 P 12/1/1951 Bp John J Gravatt. m 7/28/1987 Frances Reid. Bp's Coun Dio Arizona Phoenix AZ 1981-1985; Assoc S Phil's In The Hills Tucson AZ 1980-1987; Cn Pstr Trin Cathd Columbia SC 1974-1980; R S Steph's Epis Ch Oak Ridge TN 1968-1974; R Ch Of The H Comf Sumter SC 1964-1968; R S Mary's Ch Kinston NC 1959-1964; R Trin Ch Myrtle Bch SC 1954-1959; P-in-c Our Sav Epis Ch Trenton SC 1951-1954; R Trin Ch Edgefield SC 1951-1954. Auth, "Watched Over and Blessed," Custom Pub, 2002. rreid9@sc.rr.com

REID, Michael Edgar (ECR) 146 12th St, Pacific Grove CA 93950 **Assoc Ch of S Mary's by the Sea Pacific Grove CA 2010-** B Brooklyn NY 9/30/1953 s Rupert Reid & Daphne. BA Adeiphi U; MA NYU; EDD Tem; MDiv CDSP 2007. D 11/1/2008 P 7/2/2009 Bp Mary Gray-Reeves. m 9/6/2008 William Robnett c 1. reidcdsp@yahoo.com

REID, M Sue (Oly) 8152 15th Ave SW, Seattle WA 98106 B Louisville KY 3/6/1949 d Stephen Leach Reid & Margaret Louise. BM DePauw U 1970; SMM UTS 1972; MDiv VTS 1976. D 6/5/1976 P 6/18/1977 Bp David Reed. m 12/30/1989 Paul Buche. S Mk's Cathd Seattle WA 2004-2007; R S Alb's Ch Indianapolis IN 1996-2004; Cn to Ordnry Dio Indianapolis Indianapolis IN 1988-1997; R Ch Of S Edw Columbus OH 1983-1987; Assoc S Steph's Epis Ch And U Columbus OH 1979-1983; Int S Jn's Ch Louisville KY 1978-1979; Trin Epis Ch Owensboro KY 1977-1978; Dio Kentucky Louisville KY 1976-1977. Auth, "Bk Revs," *Chr Herald*, 1973. AAM 1985-2005; ADLM 1984-1999; EWC 1972. sreid3649@aol.com

REID, Paul DeWitt (Eas) 7809 Old York Rd, Elkins Park PA 19027 **P-in-c S Paul's Ch Elkins Pk PA 2011-** B Washington IL 7/14/1948 s Paul DeWitt Reid & Joan Gowan-Stobo. Penn St 1968; Edinburgh U 1976; MDiv Luth TS at Philadelphia 2009. D 6/13/2009 P 12/12/2009 Bp James Joseph Shand. m 12/30/1977 Anne Mitchell c 2. thechoir@verizon.net

REID JR, Raymond W (SeFla) 11852 Chaparral Dr, Frisco TX 75035 B Los Angeles CA 8/2/1936 s Raymond W Reid & Flory. BA Humboldt St U 1976; MA Epis TS of The SW 1980. D 8/2/1980 P 3/1/1981 Bp Victor Manuel Rivera. m 5/26/1956 Rosalind Schilling. R S Matt the Apos Epis Ch Miami FL 1990-2005; R Epis Ch Of Our Sav Placerville CA 1983-1990; Vic S Jas Ch Lindsay CA 1980-1983; Epis Dio San Joaquin Modesto CA 1980-1982. Amer Assn Chr Counslr. RWRJREID@SBCGLOBAL.NET

REID, Richard (Va) Po Box 353, Saunderstown RI 02874 B Providence RI 10/15/1928 s Richard Irving Reid & Florence Augusta. BA Harv 1950; MA Harv 1954; BD EDS 1955; ThD UTS 1964. D 6/24/1955 P 3/24/1956 Bp John S Higgins. m 8/12/1950 Helen Bradner c 3. Prof VTS Alexandria VA 1968-1994; Asst Prof Nt VTS Alexandria VA 1958-1964; Asst Cathd Of St Jn The Div New York NY 1956-1958. Auth, "The Necessity Of A Biblic Christology," *Who Do You Say That I Am*, 1999. Sead. DD U So 2005.

REID OSB, Richard P (NI) 44591 San Rafael Ave, Palm Desert CA 92260 B Denver CO 4/1/1921 s William Lyle Reid & Ethel Ida. BS Loyola U 1948; DD SWTS 1986. D 11/23/1953 P 7/29/1954 Bp James R Mallett. Auth, *Sprt Loose in the Wrld*, Harbor Hse Pu, 1993. S Greg's Abbey, OSB 1948. Hon DD Seabury Wstrn TS Evanston IL 1985.

REID, Richard William (Vt) Po Box 70070, North Dartmouth MA 02747 **Int S Mk's Epis Ch Fall River MA 2001-** B Fall River MA 11/26/1939 s William Bowden Reid & Francis Louise. BA U Roch 1961; MDiv PDS 1964. D 5/23/1964 Bp Allen Webster Brown P 11/28/1964 Bp Charles Bowen Persell Jr. m 12/6/1980 Sondra Manley Cox c 4. Int S Paul's Epis Ch Westfield NJ 1997-2000; Int S Paul's Ch Norfolk VA 1996-1997; Gr Ch No Attleborough MA 1995-1996; R Imm Ch Bellows Falls VT 1989-1995; Int Emm Ch W Roxbury MA 1988-1989; S Aug And S Mart Ch Boston MA 1979-1988; Dio Massachusetts Boston MA 1974-1980; R S Mk's Epis Ch Fall River MA 1969-1974; Asst Trin Ch Potsdam NY 1967-1969; Asst Zion Ch Colton NY 1967-1969. Acad Par Cler. rwreid2@aol.com

REID JR, Roddey (Ct) 122 Moorings Park Dr Apt G507, Naples FL 34105 **Died 9/14/2010** B Rock Hill SC 11/2/1918 s Roddey Reid & Elizabeth Carlisle. BA Duke 1939; BD STUSo 1944; Fllshp Coll of Preachers 1962; DD SWTS 1983; DD Ya Berk 1990. D 2/16/1944 P 2/14/1945 Bp John J Gravatt.

REID-LEVY, Schelly (Md) No address on file. B Morgantown WV 7/30/1953 d Roberts Reid & Betty. D 6/5/2004 Bp Robert Wilkes Ihloff. m 1/19/1982 Steven Levy.

REIDT, Donna Jane (Vt) PO Box 8, Chester VT 05143 **D S Lk's Ch Chester VT 2010-** B Howell MA 9/17/1948 d Harold George Waterhouse & Mary Rose Jeannette. BA Norwich U 2002; MDiv EDS 2008. D 12/19/2009 P 12/18/2010 Bp Thomas C Ely. m 6/26/1971 James Reidt c 3. doreidt@yahoo.com

REIF, George G (EMich) 107 W Midland St, Bay City MI 48706 B Bay City MI 10/18/1923 s George John Washington Reif & Emma Martha. BS MI SU 1952; Michigan TS 1968. D 4/1/1968 Bp Archie H Crowley. m 8/2/1952 Beverly Beatrice Nelson c 3. D S Albans Epis Ch Bay City MI 1968-2005. puzzle@concentric.net

REILEY, Jennifer B S (Mass) 48 Prospect St, North Andover MA 01845 B Hartford CT 12/9/1954 d William Stanley Reiley & Barbara J. Bos; BA Mt Holyoke Coll 1977; MDiv Yale DS 1981; PhD Bos 1986. D 6/13/1981 P 3/1/1982 Bp Arthur Edward Walmsley. m 6/17/1979 Raymond Brockill. Trin Epis Ch Haverhill MA 2007; Edw Hosp Chapl Fndtn Inc Naperville IL 1986-1987.

R

REIMER, Leslie Graff (Pgh) 5426 Wilkins Ave, Pittsburgh PA 15217 **Calv Ch Pittsburgh PA 1997-** B New Kensington PA 2/8/1952 d Charles Abram Reimer & Lucetta M. BA Dickinson Coll 1974; MDiv GTS 1977. D 10/29/1977 P 12/13/1980 Bp Robert Bracewell Appleyard. Liturg Asst S Paul's Epis Ch Pittsburgh PA 1986-1998; Sheldon Calv Camp Pittsburgh PA 1981; Chr Epis Ch Indiana PA 1979-1981; Sheldon Calv Camp Pittsburgh PA 1979-1980; D S Jas Epis Ch Pittsburgh PA 1977-1978. lreimer@calvarypgh.org

REIMER, Susan Elizabeth (FdL) 100 N Drew St, Appleton WI 54911 **D All SS Epis Ch Appleton WI 2011-** B Aurora CO 2/28/1952 d Donald Hopkins & Alberta. AS N Harris Cmnty Coll 1997; Dio Fond du Lac Deacons Sch 2010; BLS U of Wisconsin OshKosh 2010. D 5/7/2011 Bp Russell Edward Jacobus. m 12/18/1971 Robert Reimer c 2. sreimer2004@yahoo.com

REIN, Lily Anne Beggs (At) 1105-L Clairemont Ave, Decatur GA 30030 B Memphis TN 10/5/1926 d George William Beggs & Celeste. BA SW Coll At Memphis 1948; MA Georgia St U 1970. D 10/23/1993 Bp Frank Kellogg Allan. c 2. D Cathd Of S Phil Atlanta GA 1993-1998. lareins@mindspring.com

REINECKE, Roderick Laury (NC) 1505 Von Bora Ct, Burlington NC 27215 B Washington DC 10/8/1933 s Paul Sorg Reinecke & Esther Jean. BA U NC 1955; MDiv VTS 1958. D 6/29/1958 P 12/30/1958 Bp Edwin A Penick. m 7/9/1976 Ruthmary Wright c 4. Int S Paul's Epis Ch Winston Salem NC 1995-1997; R Ch Of The H Comf Burlington NC 1968-1983; R S Tim's Epis Ch Winston Salem NC 1963-1968; Vic S Paul's Epis Ch Cary NC 1958-1959. Auth, "Leaving the Pastorate:Staying in Town," *A.I. Monthly Nwsltr*, Alb Inst, 1984; Auth, "In Relatns Column," *City-Cnty mag 1985-1999*. R Emer H Comf, Burlington, NC Burlington NC 1998; Who's Who in Rel Who's Who 1985. rodr@netpath.net

REINERS JR, Alwin (Va) 1600 Westbrook Ave, Richmond VA 23227 **P-in-res Emm Ch At Brook Hill Richmond VA 1994-** B Arlington VA 2/4/1926 s Alwin Reiners & Elizabeth. CUA 1950; LTh VTS 1954. D 5/30/1954 Bp Frederick D Goodwin P 2/25/1955 Bp William J Gordon Jr. m 2/5/1955 Shirley Joanne McElman c 3. Exec Bd Dio Virginia Richmond VA 1988-1991; Dn of Reg XI Dio Virginia Richmond VA 1984-1987; R S Paul's Ch Hanover VA 1982-1993; Epis Hm For Chld St Louis MO 1979-1982; Natl Netwk Exec Com Cler Assn Dio No Carolina Raleigh NC 1977-1980; Natl Netwk Exec Com Cler Assn Dio No Carolina Raleigh NC 1977-1980; Dn Charlotte Cler Dio No Carolina Raleigh NC 1976-1978; Exec Bd NC Cler Assn Dio No Carolina Raleigh NC 1975-1977; ExCoun Dio No Carolina Raleigh NC 1972-1974; R Ch Of The H Comf Charlotte NC 1968-1979; Exec Com Mid-Atlantic Trng Inst Dio Virginia Richmond VA 1966-1971; Chair DeptCE Dio Virginia Richmond VA 1966-1967; P-in-c S Barth's Ch Richmond VA 1961-1968; Yth Advsr Dio Virginia Richmond VA 1958-1963; Asst S Jas' Ch Richmond VA 1957-1961; P-in-c S Geo In The Arctic Kotzebue AK 1954-1957. jmreiners15@gmail.com

REINERS, Diane (NY) 196 Clermont Avenue, Brooklyn NY 11205 **D Cathd Of St Jn The Div New York NY 2011-** B Miami FL 12/19/1961 d Al Reiners & JoAnn. Hmnts NYU 2006; MDiv The GTS 2011. D 3/5/2011 Bp Mark Sean Sisk. diane@dianereiners.com

REINHARD, Kathryn Louise (NY) Christ Church, 84 Broadway, New Haven CT 06511 B Oberlin OH 5/3/1979 d Donald Reinhard & Constance. BFA NYU 2001; MDiv Ya Berk 2008. D 3/15/2008 P 9/20/2008 Bp Mark Sean Sisk. Chr Ch New Haven CT 2008-2009. kathryn.reinhard@yahoo.com

REINHARDT, Constance (WA) 27 Broad St, Newburyport MA 01950 **S Geo's Ch Glenn Dale MD 2006-** B Long Beach CA 2/17/1969 d James Ogier Reinhardt & Geraldine. BA Wellesley Coll 1991; MDiv Ya Berk 1995. D 5/9/1998 P 12/5/1998 Bp Douglas Edwin Theuner. m 6/19/2006 Emma Hadley. S Paul's Ch Newburyport MA 2000-2006; Mt Calv Camp Hill PA 1998-1999. rectorstgeo@verizon.net

REINHART, Rodney Eugene (Chi) 2508 Walnut St, Blue Island IL 60406 **S Jos's And S Aid's Ch Blue Island IL 2011-; R S Clem's Ch Harvey IL 2004-** B Toledo 1/13/1949 s Ralph Emerson Reinhart & Pauline Susan. BA Oakland U 1972; MDiv Bex 1975; Cert Wayne 1978; Cert Int Mnstry Prog 1996. D 12/15/1984 Bp Henry Irving Mayson P 4/12/1986 Bp H Coleman McGehee Jr. m Alan Engle. S Martha's Ch Detroit MI 2002-2003; Gr Ch Detroit MI 2002; Nativ Epis Ch Bloomfield Township MI 2001; Trin Epis Ch Farmington Hills MI 1999-2001; Int Trin Epis Ch Monroe MI 1996; S Geo's Epis Ch Warren MI 1994-1995; Supply All SS Ch Detroit MI 1993-1994; Assoc Emm Ch Detroit MI 1988-1994; St Andrews Meml Ch Detroit MI 1985-1987; Asst Pstr S Cyp's Epis Ch Detroit MI 1983-1985; Cur S Mich And All Ang Epis Ch Lincoln Pk MI 1975-1976. "Faith on the Front Line," *A cable TV show*, Chicago St U, 2007; "Lift High The Cross," *A Cable TV show*, Comcast Cable, Plymouth MI, 1998; Auth, "Sprtl Aerobics for the 21st Century," Operation Dome Press, 1996; Auth, "Splinters on the Wind," Operation Dome Press, 1988; Auth, "Twilights of Anth Way Drive," Operation Dome Press, 1988. Bp's Assoc, Chicago 2006; EPF 1980; EUC 1977; People Who Care Mnstrs 1984-2005; The People Who Care Interfaith Fund 1998; Wrld Sabbath of Rel Recon 1998. Cmnty Luminary Awd Detroit Edison and MNA 2003; Gvnr's Publ Serv Awd St of Michigan 2003; Diversity Chanpion Awd Birmingham/Bloomfield Hills MI 2002; Mart Luther King Awd Archdiocese of Detroit 1989; Sprt of Detroit Awd Detroit City Coun 1986; Cert of Merit MI St 1978. revrod@comcast.net

REINHEIMER, John Jay (NH) 227 W 6th St, Port Clinton OH 43452 **Int Dio Ohio Cleveland OH 2007-** B Fremont OH 7/21/1936 s John Louis Reinheimer & Maragret. BA Hob 1958; BD Bex 1961. D 6/10/1961 Bp Nelson Marigold Burroughs P 12/21/1961 Bp Dudley S Stark. m 6/16/1958 Patricia Lee Craig c 4. Vic Ch Of The Mssh No Woodstock NH 1992-2002; Supply P Dio New Hampshire Concord NH 1990-1992; P-in-c S Judes Epis Ch Franklin NH 1982-1989; R S Jn's Ch Clifton Sprg NY 1964-1973; Asst S Thos Epis Ch Rochester NY 1963-1964; Cur S Thos Epis Ch Rochester NY 1961-1962. padrejohn@roadrunner.com

REINHEIMER, Philip Schuyler (NCal) 13948 Gold Country Drive, Penn Valley CA 95945 **S Jn's Epis Ch Marysville CA 2011-; P St Johns Epis Ch Roseville CA 2009-** B Rochester NY 9/19/1943 s Frederick Smith Reinheimer & Barbara. BA U Pac 1965; MPA California St U 1986. D 1/12/1975 Bp C Kilmer Myers P 11/20/1979 Bp John Raymond Wyatt. m 4/1/1967 Vicki R Reinheimer c 3. P Trin Ch Sutter Creek CA 2010; Int Emm Epis Ch Grass Vlly CA 2007-2008; Asst H Trin Ch NEVADA CITY CA 2000-2009; Asst All SS Epis Ch Redding CA 1990-2000; Int S Jn The Div Epis Ch Morgan Hill CA 1989-1990; Int S Jas' Ch Monterey CA 1984-1985; Int S Jn The Div Epis Ch Morgan Hill CA 1981-1982; Asst All SS Epis Ch Watsonville CA 1976-1990; D S Jas' Ch Monterey CA 1975-1979. p_rev@sbcglobal.net

REINKEN, Dirk Chrisian (NJ) 1628 Prospect St, Ewing NJ 08638 **R S Lk's Ch Ewing NJ 2002-** B Anderson SC 12/31/1964 s Louis Arthur Reinken & Mary Louise. BA U of So Carolina 1987; MDiv GTS 1998. D 6/12/1999 P 1/15/2000 Bp Geralyn Wolf. m 12/20/2010 Thomas J Hargrove. Cur S Lk's Ch Philadelphia PA 1999-2002. Auth, "Archbp Ussher's Proposal For Synodical Govt," *The Angl*, 1998; Auth, "PB For The 21st Century (Bk Revs)," *The Angl*, 1998. OHC, Assoc 1994. dcreinken@gmail.com

REIS JR, Harry Albert (NY) 4357 Union St Apt 5d, Flushing NY 11355 B Port Chester NY 3/19/1934 s Harry Albert Reis & Agnes Catherine. BA Wag 1955; MDiv Nash 1959; MS U of Bridgeport 1978. D 6/11/1959 P 12/19/1959 Bp Horace W B Donegan. m 11/7/2011 Margaret Fletcher c 3. S Mk's Ch Jackson Heights NY 1985-1999; R Gr Epis Ch Monroe NY 1972-1977; Dpt Of Missions Ny Income New York NY 1969-1977; P-in-c Ch Of The Gd Shpd Greenwood Lake NY 1960-1977; Diocn Msnry & Ch Extntn Socty New York NY 1960-1977; P-in-c S Jn's In The Wilderness Stony Point NY 1960-1961; Cur S Jn's Ch Larchmont NY 1959-1960. Contrib, *Selected Sermons*. har19@msn.com

REISCHMAN, Charles J (Spr) 4767 Redbud Ct, Decatur IL 62526 **S Jn's Epis Ch Decatur IL 2008-** B Westlake OH 3/22/1955 s Paul Lewis Reischman & Jean. S Mary RC Sem; Walsh U; BA U Of Akron 1980; MDiv Epis TS of The SW 1990. D 6/9/1990 Bp James Russell Moodey P 12/1/1990 Bp William Harvey Wolfrum. m 8/5/1989 Gina L Burney c 3. New Life Epis Ch Littleton CO 2003-2005; Assoc S Lk's Epis Ch Akron OH 1993-2000; Acts 29 Mnstrs Atlanta GA 1991-1993; Ch Of The Trsfg Evergreen CO 1990-1991; Yth Pstr S Mart's Epis Ch Monroeville PA 1983-1986. Auth, "Acts 29 Pub"; Auth, "Focus Renwl News"; Auth, "Charisma". ERM, Ord S Phil-Evang; Joshua Force. rector@saintjohnsdecatur.org

REISHUS, John William (WMich) 20611 Goshen Rd, Gaithersburg MD 20879 B Quincy IL 8/7/1934 s Harald Reishus & Lauretta. BS U of Arizona 1956; PhD Iowa St U 1960; MDiv Nash 1971. D 6/19/1971 Bp Gerald Francis Burrill P 12/20/1971 Bp James Winchester Montgomery. m 4/27/1957 Beverly Brown. P-in-c Chr Epis Ch Lucketts Leesburg VA 2001-2003; Int Truro Epis Ch Fairfax VA 1999-2001; Asst P-in-c S Jas Ch Potomac MD 1997-1998; Int Chr Ch W River MD 1996-1997; Asst Int R S Tim's Ch Catonsville MD 1995-1996; Int S Andr The Fisherman Epis Mayo MD 1994-1995; Int S Jas Ch Potomac MD 1992-1994; R S Alb's Mssn Muskegon MI 1976-1991; Vic Gr Ch Sterling IL 1971-1976; Vic The Ch Of S Anne Morrison IL 1971-1976. jbreishus@aol.com

REISNER, Terry Ralph (Dal) 118 Overhill Dr, Waxahachie TX 75165 **Vic S Paul's Epis Ch Waxahachie TX 2007-** B Toronto Canada 3/3/1965 D 6/4/2005 P 4/29/2006 Bp James Monte Stanton. m 4/8/1989 Glenna Clark Reisner c 3. S Phil's Epis Ch Frisco TX 2005-2007; Trin Ch Marshall TX 1992-1999. reisners@sbcglobal.net

REISS, Gerald Anthony (NJ) 1048 Detweiler Ave, Hellertown PA 18055 B Bethlehem PA 4/21/1932 s Elmer Jacob Reiss & Anna Marie. BA Leh 1954; MDiv Ya Berk 1960. D 6/1/1960 P 12/1/1960 Bp Frederick J Warnecke. m 7/10/1954 Dorothy Spisak c 2. R S Ptr's Ch Clarksboro NJ 1964-1994; Asst Min Trin Ch Bethlehem PA 1962-1964; Vic Chr Ch Frackville Frackville PA 1960-1962; Vic S Jas Ch Schuylkill Haven PA 1960-1962.

REJOUIS, Mary Kate (Colo) 2700 University Heights Ave, Boulder CO 80302 **R S Aid's Epis Ch Boulder CO 2005-** B Boulder CO 2/28/1970 d Jacob Dean Schroeder & Mary Nelson. BA Dart 1993; MDiv SWTS 1997. D 6/14/1997 P 12/20/1997 Bp Douglas Edwin Theuner. m 11/20/2009 Jean

Hilaire Rejouis. Vic S Ptr's Ch Basalt CO 2000-2005; P-in-c/Assoc R S Mich And All Ang Ch So Bend IN 1997-2000. mary.kate.92@alum.dartmouth.org

RELLER, Wilfred Herman (Colo) 71 Aspen Ln, Golden CO 80403 B Old Monroe MO 2/19/1939 s William Reller & Coletta. BA Div Word 1963; MDiv Div Word 1967; MA Loyola U 1969. Trans from Anglican Church of Canada 7/1/1988 Bp William Carl Frey. m 7/28/1984 Irene Frances Sullivan. Chap Of The Resurr Limon CO 1988-2004. ireneequin@aol.com

RELYEA, Michael Johl (NY) 10857 65th Rd #1, Forest Hills NY 11375 **Assoc S Mk's Ch In The Bowery New York NY 1974-** B Faribault MN 6/10/1942 s Kenneth Elam Relyea & Ruth Louise. BA Lawr 1964; MS USC 1968; MDiv GTS 1973. D 1/27/1974 P 2/15/1975 Bp Philip Frederick McNairy. m 3/21/1970 Maria Magdalena Lemmen c 2. "A Comprehensive Guide to the St Mk's Ch in the Bowery Historic Site," St Mk's Ch in the Bowery, 1999. NYC Labor-Rel Cltn 1986. marrevelyea@aol.com

REMBOLDT, Cherry Ann (SanD) 47535 State Highway 74, Palm Deset CA 92260 B Fargo North Dakota 3/8/1952 d William Robert Wedberg & Meredith Ann. MEd Azusa Pacific U 1994; MEd Azusa Pacific U 1996. D 6/7/2008 Bp James Robert Mathes. m 8/13/1972 Henry Remboldt c 1. cherryr@stmargarets.org

REMENTER, Nancy Sandra (CPa) 239 E Market St, Marietta PA 17547 B Medford MA 2/25/1944 d Stanley Nelson Hedin & Jessie Blackwood. N/A Bucks Cnty Cmnty Coll; N/A Tem; Cert Prog Dio Cntrl PA Sch of Chr Stds 2010. D 10/31/2010 Bp Nathan Dwight Baxter. m 2/8/1964 Francis Rementer c 3. deaconnancy@embarqumail.com

REMER, Douglas Errick (SwFla) Saint John's Church, 906 South Orleans Avenue, Tampa FL 33606 **R St Johns Epis Ch Tampa FL 2003-** B Trenton NJ 9/13/1948 s Donald Glenn Remer & Rose Marie. A.B. Rutgers Coll 1971; M.Div. GTS 1975. D 4/26/1975 Bp Albert Wiencke Van Duzer P 2/5/1976 Bp Ned Cole. m 9/25/1976 Sterling Hull c 3. R S Mart In The Fields Ch Atlanta GA 1991-2002; R Calv Ch Tarboro NC 1982-1990; Assoc R S Mich's Ch Raleigh NC 1977-1982; Cur Gr Ch Utica NY 1975-1977. deremer@mindspring.com

REMINGTON, Melissa E (WVa) 202 Cazenovia St, Buffalo Ny 14210 **St Christophers Epis Ch Charleston WV 2009-** B Bangor ME 5/26/1958 d Christopher Wolcott Remington & Judith Ellen. BA U of Massachusetts Amherst 1981; MAT Stan 1991; MDiv Bex 2007. D 8/17/2007 P 5/24/2008 Bp J Michael Garrison. m 5/29/2004 Ralph William Strohm c 3. S Ptr's Ch Westfield NY 2008-2009. misremky17@yahoo.com

REMPPEL, Paulette Evelynn (NY) 52 Brookside Pl, New Rochelle NY 10801 **D Par Of Chr The Redeem Pelham NY 1998-** B Providence RI 8/13/1947 d Patrick J Paquin & Alice May. GTS; Iona Coll 1984. D 5/16/1998 Bp Richard Frank Grein. m 9/4/1993 Alfred R Remppel c 2. lette813@aol.com

REMY, Joseph Michel Jean (Hai) 5935 Del Lago Circle, Sunrise FL 33313 B 3/18/1943 s Dormestoy Remy & Thernolia. BA Coll S Pierre Ht 1966; MDiv ETSC 1971. P 1/1/1972 Bp Luc Anatole Jacques Garnier. m 7/17/1980 Marie Carmelle Deler c 3. Dio Haiti Ft Lauderdale FL 1971-2008. Soc Of S Marg. RJOMJ@YAHOO.FR

RENCHER, Ollie (WTenn) 124 Price St, Oxford MS 38655 **Ch Of The H Comm Memphis TN 2008-** B Clarksdale MS 3/16/1969 BA Millsaps Coll. D 6/11/2003 P 1/13/2004 Bp Duncan Montgomery Gray III. m 12/18/2010 Ellen Rencher. Asst R/Chapl S Ptr's Ch Oxford MS 2003-2008. orencher@holycommunion.org

RENDON OSPINA, Gonzalo Antonio (Colom) Cra 80 No. 53a-78, Medelin Antioquia 99999 Colombia B Rionegro 9/20/1957 s Noe Rendon & Deyanira. Rec from Roman Catholic 7/5/1992. m 4/9/2005 Johana Reyes c 1. Iglesia Epis En Colombia 2006-2009. gonzaloantonio@epm.net.co

RENEGAR, Douglas McBane (Ga) 224 Lakefield Rd., Waterloo SC 29384 B Long Island,NY 10/28/1948 s Garland Renegar & Jeanne. BA Wake Forest U 1970; MA E Carolina U 1974; MDiv VTS 1984. D 6/9/1984 Bp Brice Sidney Sanders P 12/14/1984 Bp A(rthur) Heath Light. m 6/4/1989 Margaret Renegar. R Chr Ch Frederica St Simons Island GA 1992-2004; R S Matt's Epis Ch Darlington SC 1988-1992; The Tazewell Cnty Cluster Of Epis Parishes Tazewell VA 1984-1988; Trin Ch Richlands VA 1984-1988. dmrenegar@hotmail.com

RENFREW, William Finch (Mich) 2101 Wellesley Dr, Lansing MI 48911 B Detroit MI 11/16/1931 s Charles Warren Renfrew & Louise Mcguire. MI SU; AA Lansing Cmnty Coll 1975. D 6/13/1992 Bp R(aymond) Stewart Wood Jr. m 8/11/1981 Eleanor Nelson Swanson. D S Paul's Epis Ch Lansing MI 1992-2004. Mi & Intl Police Chapl Assns. wren1116@aol.com

RENGERS, Josiah Daniel (Ala) 109 Woodcrest Circle, Eutaw AL 35462 **Dio Alabama Birmingham AL 2011-; R S Steph's Ch Eutaw AL 2011-** B Fairmont WV 6/1/1983 s Kevin Joseph Rengers & Joann. BA W Virginia U; MDiv VTS 2011. D 12/4/2010 P 6/14/2011 Bp William Michie Klusmeyer. m 5/22/2010 Katherine Toshiko Nakamura. josiahrengers@gmail.com

RENICK, Van Taliaferro (SwVa) 170 Mountain Ave, Rocky Mount VA 24151 B Augusta GA 1/5/1930 s Frank Taliaferro Renick & Roberta. BS Oklahoma St U 1952; BD STUSo 1967. D 6/18/1967 P 1/1/1968 Bp Albert R Stuart. m 4/25/1952 Kathryn H Hopkins c 2. R Trin Epis Ch Rocky Mt VA 1971-1992; Cur Chr Ch Martinsville VA 1970-1971; D Chr Epis Ch Cordele GA 1967-1969. vanr@va.net

RENN, Wade Allan (Nwk) 558 Highland Ave, Upper Montclair NJ 07043 **Collegial Cn Trin And S Phil's Cathd Newark NJ 2008-; P Hse Of Pryr Epis Ch Newark NJ 2006-** B Freeport NY 1/7/1935 s Ralph Eugene Renn & Edith Julia. BS Leh 1956; MS Leh 1960; MDiv GTS 1964. D 6/27/1964 P 1/16/1965 Bp Paul Moore Jr. m 2/4/1970 Mary Ann Lewis c 2. Int S Andr's Epis Ch Lincoln Pk NJ 1999-2000; Int Gr Epis Ch Westwood NJ 1997-1999; R Gr Ch Nutley NJ 1973-1996; Gr Ch Newark NJ 1969-1970; Cur Gr Ch Newark NJ 1964-1966. wade@therenn.net

REPLOGLE, Jennifer (NJ) 33 Mercer Street, Princeton NJ 08540 **Cur Trin Ch Princeton NJ 2011-** B 12/31/1982 d David Clayton Replogle & Rosemary Leverette. BA Mississippi Coll 2005; MDiv PrTS 2010; Dplma in Angl Stds VTS 2011. D 6/18/2011 Bp George Edward Councell. jennyrep11@gmail.com

REPP, Daniel Steven (NI) St Pauls Episcopal Church, 312 E Main St, Plymouth WI 53073 **S Jn The Evang Ch Elkhart IN 2009-** B Yale MI 9/24/1976 s Timothy S Repp & Pamela J. BA Lake Suptricr St U Sault Ste Marie MI 1998; MDiv Nash 2007. D 12/16/2006 P 7/1/2007 Bp Russell Edward Jacobus. m 4/7/2001 Miranda A Miranda Skoglund c 3. Vic S Paul's Ch Plymouth WI 2007-2009. fr.repp@hotmail.com

REPP, Jeanette Marie (Los) 1648 W 9th St, San Pedro CA 90732 **R S Ptr's Par San Pedro CA 2010-** B Oakland CA 9/26/1961 d Gordon Wayne Repp & Nancy Lee. BA U CA 1983; MDiv SWTS 1988; MSW Loyola U 1998. D 12/3/1988 Bp William Edwin Swing P 8/17/1989 Bp Frank Tracy Griswold III. c 2. Assoc S Nich w the H Innoc Ch Elk Grove Vill IL 2008-2010; Vic Ch Of The Incarn Bloomingdale IL 2004-2008; Int S Giles' Ch Northbrook IL 2003-2004; Assoc S Greg's Epis Ch Deerfield IL 1997-2003; D Intern Ch Of The Adv Chicago IL 1988-1989. Natl Assoc of Soc Workers 1997-2010. jzlrepp@gmail.com

RESSLER, Richard Alan (SD) Emmanuel Episc Church, 717 Quincy St., Rapid City SD 57701 **Fr Emm Epis Par Rapid City SD 2008-** B Cokato MN 3/22/1952 s Harry Walter Ressler & Norma Irene. BS U of Wisconsin 1978; MDiv SWTS 1995. D 6/28/1995 Bp James Louis Jelinek P 1/20/1996 Bp Sanford Zangwill Kaye Hampton. m 6/14/1975 Gayle Ann Dickinson. Dio Oklahoma Oklahoma City OK 2004-2008; R S Jas Epis Ch Oklahoma City OK 2002-2004; Dio Minnesota Minneapolis MN 2001-2002; Chr Ch Austin MN 1995-2000. stjamesokc@coxinet.com

RESTREPO, Miguel Angel (SeFla) 143 67 Southwest 96th Lane, Miami FL 33186 B Fredonia Ant CO 5/20/1926 s Enrique Restrepo & Carlina. Ant. Univeristy 1940; BA/MA/MDiv S Bonaventure/U Colom 1946; St Bonaventuure U 1951. Rec from Roman Catholic 3/1/1971 as Priest Bp Philip Menzie Duncan II. m 10/4/1996 Maria Doris Mondragon c 6. R H Cross Epis Ch Miami FL 1986-1998; Ch Of The H Comf Miami FL 1977-1987; P-in-c of the Spanish Cong H Cross Epis Ch Miami FL 1976-1977; Asst H Cross Epis Ch Miami FL 1974-1977; Prchr & Lay Min Iglesia Epis De Todos Los Santos Miami FL 1969-1971. Auth, "How a Pstr, a Monk a Bp Can Encounter w God"; Auth, *God & the Sunday Wrshprs Sprtl Retreat for the Yth*; Auth, "Mentally Retarded & Soc," *Mod Soc & Rel*. restrepomiguel@comcast.net

RETAMAL, M Regina (Mass) 59 Lawrence St, Framingham MA 01702 B Parral Chile 12/1/1944 d Juan Retamal & Regina. Cert Universidad Tecnica del Estada 1977; MRE Gordon-Conwell TS 1988; Cert Instituto Pstr Hispano 1992. D 5/30/1992 P 4/1/1993 Bp David Elliot Johnson. c 2. Iglesia De San Juan Hyde Pk MA 2000-2006; Dio Massachusetts Boston MA 1994-1999; S Paul's Ch Brookline MA 1993-1999; Cltn For Hisp Mnstrs Pepperell MA 1992-1994. FVC; Soc of S Jn the Evang. fellowship2006@netzero.net

RETTGER, John Hubbard (Minn) 65 - 104th Avenue Northwest, Coon Rapids MN 55448 B Ann Arbor MI 2/12/1935 s James Frederick Rettger & Esther Elizabeth. BA U of Connecticut 1958; LTh S Chad's Coll Regina SK CA 1959; MDiv The Coll of Emm and St. Chad 1993; DD U of Emml 2008. Trans from Anglican Church of Canada 4/26/1964 as Priest Bp Hamilton Hyde Kellogg. m 7/28/1954 Eudora Stewart c 4. Cn Cathd Ch Of S Mk Minneapolis MN 2000-2001; P-in-c S Jas Ch Marshall MN 1999-2000; Int S Mary's Ch St Paul MN 1997-1998; Assoc Cathd Ch Of S Mk Minneapolis MN 1994-1997; Supply P S Paul's Ch Minneapolis MN 1992-1993; Vic Ch Of The Resurr Minneapolis MN 1968-1992; R S Lk's Ch Willmar MN 1963-1968. Hon Cn S Mk Cathd Minneapolis 1997. jrettger@comcast.net

RETZLAFF, Georg (USC) 1612 Goldfinch Ln, West Columbia SC 29169 B Cologne DE 4/13/1946 s Rudolf Retzlaff & Erika. MDiv equiv. U of Bonn 1972; Dr. theol. U of Berne Berne CH 1978. m 12/29/1977 Joy L Kosalko. All SS Ch Cayce SC 2004-2011; Ch Of The Redeem Orangeburg SC 2002-2004; The TS at The U So Sewanee TN 2001-2002; The U So (Sewanee) Sewanee TN 2001-2002; Exec Coun Appointees New York NY 1984-1991; R S Paul's And Resurr Ch Wood Ridge NJ 1980-1984; Asst S Ptr's Ch Beverly MA 1979-1980. Georg Retzlaff, "Why the Cross?," *Meditations for H Week*, Authorhouse, 2010; Georg Retzlaff, "What Jesus Taught and Why it Matters," *Towards a Chrsnty w no other Fndt but Chr*, Authorhouse, 2010; Georg Retzlaff, "The Other Side," *Hitherto Unpublished Letters bz Biblic Heroes*,

Authorhouse, 2009; Georg Retzlaff, "Ch Psalter," *The Bk of Psalms for Liturg and Priv Use*, Authorhouse, 2009; Georg Retzlaff, "Die Äussere Erscheinung des Geistlichen im Alltag," Jakob Stämpfli & Cie., Bern, 1978; Georg Retzlaff, "Vorgänge um die alt-katholische Gemeindegründung," *Gedenkschrift*, Kuttruff Publ. Konstanz, 1973. gretz46@yahoo.com

REUMAN, Eugene Frederic (CFla) 2915 W Henley Ln, Dunnellon FL 34433 **R S Marg's Ch Inverness FL 2001-** B Toledo OH 9/9/1950 s Carl Henry Reuman & Naomi Teresa. AA Cntrl Florida Cmnty Coll 1979; BA S Leo Coll 1997; MDiv STUSo 2001. D 12/8/1990 P 7/1/2001 Bp John Wadsworth Howe. m 9/3/1983 Paula Sue Ely. D H Faith Epis Ch Dunnellon FL 1990-1998. efreuman@bellsouth.net

REUSCHLING, Walter Edward (Eas) 108 Oak St, Cambridge MD 21613 B Baltimore MD 7/24/1931 s Walter Lester Reuschling & Ida. S Mary Sem; BEd Towson U 1957; Med Loyola U 1963. D 2/3/1971 P 11/1/1971 Bp Harry Lee Doll. m 4/25/1957 Kathryn W Wett c 3. All Hallow's Ch Snow Hill MD 1995-2002; R H Cross Epis Mssn Stockton CA 1994-2002; Int S Andr's Epis Ch Princess Anne MD 1994-1995; R S Paul's Ch Windsor VT 1988-1994; Int S Mary's Epis Ch Pocomoke City MD 1985-1986; DRE, Int P Ch Of S Paul's By The Sea Ocean City MD 1976-1982; Ch Of-Ascen & Prince-Peace Baltimore MD 1974-1977. walterreuschling@comcast.net

REUSS, Patricia Ann Osborne (WNC) 133 Liberty Ct, Oak Ridge TN 37830 **Assoc S Steph's Epis Ch Oak Ridge TN 2004-** B Elizabethton TN 12/8/1943 d Dana Worth Osborne & Georgia Kate. BS Tennessee Tech U 1965; MDiv Ya Berk 1986. D 6/21/1986 P 1/24/1987 Bp George Nelson Hunt III. m 6/15/1968 Robert Julius Reuss c 2. Augusta Discernment Com Dio Georgia Savannah GA 2000-2003; R S Mich's Ch Waynesboro GA 2000-2003; Pres, Stndg Com Dio Wstrn No Carolina Asheville NC 1999-2000; Stndg Com Dio Wstrn No Carolina Asheville NC 1998-2000; R Ch Of The Mssh Murphy NC 1993-2000; Dioc Coun Dio Rhode Island Providence RI 1990-1993; S Dav's On The Hill Epis Ch Cranston RI 1987-1993. bobpatreuss@bellsouth.net

REUSS, Robert Julius (WNC) 133 Liberty Ct, Oak Ridge TN 37830 **Assoc S Steph's Epis Ch Oak Ridge TN 2004-** B Brooklyn NY 6/13/1934 s Andrew Conrad Reuss & Jessie Young. BA SUNY 1957; MDiv Ya Berk 1960. D 4/23/1960 P 10/29/1960 Bp James P De Wolfe. m 6/15/1968 Patricia Ann Osborne c 2. Int Trin Ch Statesboro GA 2001-2002; Int Ch Of The Gd Shpd Hayesville NC 1996-1997; Int Ch Of The Incarn Highlands NC 1994-1995; Alum Coun Ya Berk New Haven CT 1984-1991; Par Consult Dio Rhode Island Providence RI 1982-1988; Stndg Com Dio Rhode Island Providence RI 1981-1985; COM Dio Rhode Island Providence RI 1981-1984; Coll Wk Cmsn Dio Rhode Island Providence RI 1974-1979; R S Dav's On The Hill Epis Ch Cranston RI 1971-1994; DeptCE Dio Rhode Island Providence RI 1965-1976; Asst Chr Ch Westerly RI 1962-1971; Cur S Jn's Ch Huntington NY 1960-1962. bobpatreuss@bellsouth.net

REVEL, Anna Carter (Ky) 5146 Sunnybrook Dr, Paducah KY 42001 **D/Asst Gr Ch Paducah KY 1995-** B Marion KY 6/26/1924 d Thomas Homer Carter & Ruth. BS U Of Kentucky 1948; MS U of Wisconsin 1973; Cert Nash 1980; U MN 1983. D 11/28/1981 Bp Charles Thomas Gaskell. D/Asst H Trin Epis Ch In Countryside Clearwater FL 1990-1995; D/Asst Trin Ch Janesville WI 1981-1990. Curs 1978; DAR 2002; Pi Lambda Theta Educ Hon Soc 2002. annrevel@att.com

REW, Lawrence Boyd (EO) 1232 Nw Johns Ave, Pendleton OR 97801 **Died 7/16/2009** B Eugene OR 6/22/1936 BA Whitman Coll 1958; JD Willamette U 1961. D 6/16/1999 Bp Rustin Ray Kimsey P 11/18/2007 Bp William Benjamin Spofford. c 2. lbrew01@yahoo.com

REX III, Charles Walton (Chi) 530 Fullerton Pkwy, Chicago IL 60614 B Orlando FL 5/22/1950 s Charles Walton Rex & Samueline Stilley. BA VMI 1972. D 2/7/2009 Bp Jeffrey Dean Lee. m 11/14/1992 Susan Motycka c 4. cwrexiii@rmimidwest.com

REXFORD, William Nelson (Mich) 7213 Meadow Wood Way, Clarksville MD 21029 B Painesville OH 4/16/1934 s Charles Warren Rexford & Corene. BA Wayne 1958; MDiv VTS 1969. D 6/28/1969 Bp Richard S M Emrich P 3/1/1970 Bp John Melville Burgess. m 3/12/1955 Karen Olson c 3. Vic S Matt's Epis Ch Rockwood MI 1979-1984; Assoc Min S Andr's Epis Ch Livonia MI 1978-1979; Asst Min S Jas Epis Ch Birmingham MI 1973-1974; Asst Min S Jn's Ch Royal Oak MI 1970-1973; Cur S Mary's Epis Ch Barnstable MA 1969-1970. Auth, "Lamplight". Natl Assn For The Self- Supporting Active Mnstry.

REYES, Jesus (ECR) P.O. Box 1903, Monterey CA 93942 **Dio Virginia Richmond VA 2008-; Cn Dio El Camino Real Monterey CA 2008-** B MX 9/24/1954 s Desiderio Reyes & Aurora. BA Seminario Diocesano De Tijuana Tijuana Mx 1976; BA Universidad Iberoamericana Mex City Mx 1982; DAS VTS 2002. Rec from Roman Catholic 6/29/2002 as Priest Bp David Colin Jones. c 1. Vic San Jose Ch Arlington VA 2002-2005. jesusreyes@edecr.org

REYNOLDS, Alan David (Oly) PO Box 771, Hoodsport WA 98548 **Died 8/9/2011** B Los Angeles CA 4/15/1945 s Alfred Skinner Reynolds & Maxine Velva. BS USC 1973; MDiv GTS 1984. D 6/16/1984 P 1/5/1985 Bp Robert C Rusack. c 3. reynoldsfac@yahoo.com

REYNOLDS, Bettye (NCal) 4706 Oakbough Way, Carmichael CA 95608 **D La Mision Hispana El Divino Salvador Sacramento CA 1995-; D St Johns Epis Ch Roseville CA 1992-** B Water Valley MS 1/8/1935 d Wayne Buford Williamson & Gertrude Adelia. Mississippi U For Wmn; BA U of Mississippi 1958; BA California Sch for Deacons 1989. D 9/12/1992 Bp Jerry Alban Lamb. m 2/25/1956 Kenneth Eugene Reynolds c 3.

REYNOLDS JR, Edward Charles (Mich) 2112 Melrose Road, Ann Arbor MI 48104 B Havre de Grace MD 2/1/1944 s Edward Charles Reynolds & Jean Rebecca. BA U MI 1968; MDiv EDS 1971; JD U of Detroit 1979. D 7/31/1971 Bp Archie H Crowley P 2/2/1972 Bp Richard S M Emrich. c 2. S Matt's Epis Ch Rockwood MI 1971-1978. ecrjr@umich.edu

REYNOLDS, Eleanor Francis (Nwk) PO Box 240, Mendham NJ 07945 B Santa Barbara CA 6/17/1948 d Henry Johanson & Martha. BA U CA 1970; MDiv Drew U 2006. D 6/7/2008 P 12/13/2008 Bp Mark M Beckwith. P Assoc All SS Ch Millington NJ 2008-2009. Cmnty of St. Jn Bapt 1998. sref@csjb.org

REYNOLDS V, Elsbery Washington (Haw) 60005 Riverbluff Trail, Bend CA 97702 B Pomona CA 5/13/1941 s Elsbery Washington Reynolds & Betty. SWTS; BS OR SU 1964; MDiv CDSP 1967; DMin Claremont TS 1977; Cert Mt. San Jacinto Coll 1998. D 6/10/1967 Bp Hal Raymond Gross P 12/10/1967 Bp Harry S Kennedy. c 2. Vic S Hugh Of Lincoln Mssn Idyllwild CA 2002-2008; R S Jas Epis Ch Kamuela HI 1981-1997; Vic Emm Epis Ch Kailua HI 1977-1981; Cur Ch Of The Epiph Honolulu HI 1970-1977; Vic Chr Memi Ch Kilauea HI 1969-1970; Vic St Thos Ch Hanalei HI 1969-1970; Vic S Mich And All Ang Ch Lihue HI 1968-1970; Vic S Lk's Epis Ch Honolulu HI 1967-1968. bendbroadband.com

REYNOLDS, Frederic William (Roch) 49 Shoreham Dr, Rochester NY 14618 **R S Paul's Ch Rochester NY 1995-** B New York NY 6/20/1950 s Robert Dwight Reynolds & Louise Helen. CPE; BA Hob 1973; MDiv EDS 1978. D 10/28/1978 P 6/1/1979 Bp Robert Rae Spears Jr. m 8/5/1978 Jane B Pratt c 3. R S Dav's Epis Ch Kennebunk ME 1986-1995; Assoc S Ptr's by-the-Sea Epis Ch Bay Shore NY 1983-1986; Cur Trin Epis Ch Watertown NY 1978-1981; Chr Ch Sackets Harbor NY 1978-1979. fred@stpaulsec.org

REYNOLDS, Gail Ann (Kan) 9119 Dearborn St, Overland Park KS 66207 **D S Paul's Ch Kansas City KS 2005-** B Painesville OH 3/29/1938 d Nicholas August Lorenzen & Edna Marie. BA OH SU 1960; MA U of Missouri 1972. D 9/9/2000 Bp William Edward Smalley. c 2. D S Thos The Apos Ch Overland Pk KS 2000-2005. Oblate, Ord Of Ben, Mt. St. Scholastica 1996. Archdeacons' Cross Dio Kansas 2010. morningstar66204@everestkc.net

REYNOLDS SR, Gordon (Me) 5740 Viau Way, Zephyrhills FL 33540 B Seattle WA 6/23/1925 D 4/15/1973 P 5/3/1975 Bp Frederick Barton Wolf. m 9/25/1981 Barbara Ann Reynolds. Ch Of The Mssh Dexter ME 1973-1978. greynolds9@tampabay.rr.com

REYNOLDS, James Ronald (FtW) 3717 Cook Ct, Fort Worth TX 76244 **R S Mart In The Fields Ch Keller TX 2008-** B New Martinsville WV 5/18/1949 s Edwin Ronald Reynolds & Janet Louise. BA Northwood U 1997; MDiv Nash 2002. D 6/8/2002 P 12/21/2002 Bp Jack Leo Iker. m 10/16/1969 Linda Lee Dey c 2. Cur S Mart In The Fields Ch Keller TX 2002-2008. frjim@stmartininthefields.org

REYNOLDS, Joe Douglas (Tex) 1117 Texas St, Houston TX 77002 **Dn Chr Ch Cathd Houston TX 2000-** B Atlanta GA 2/14/1946 s Arthur Cherign Reynolds & Phyllis. BA Georgia St U 1971; MDiv VTS 1974. D 6/15/1974 Bp Milton LeGrand Wood P 5/28/1975 Bp Bennett Jones Sims. m 12/26/1965 Elizabeth Childress c 3. Dio Atlanta Atlanta GA 1994-2000; R H Innoc Ch Atlanta GA 1990-2000; R Gr Ch Grand Rapids MI 1982-1990; Assoc S Fran Ch Potomac MD 1981-1982; R S Jas Ch Eufaula AL 1977-1981; Asst H Innoc Ch Atlanta GA 1974-1977. jdreynolds@christchurchcathedral.org

REYNOLDS, Katharine Sylvia (Minn) Loring Green East, 1201 Yale Place #610, Minneapolis MN 55403 B Texas City TX 11/28/1933 d Thomas George Reynolds & Edith May. BA Penn 1955; MDiv Untd TS PA 1980; Cert EDS 1981. D 12/14/1982 P 6/1/1983 Bp Robert Marshall Anderson. m 11/27/1999 Michael H Schwimmer. Reynolds Consulting Inc Minneapolis MN 1996-2002; Pstr Counslr Dio Minnesota Minneapolis MN 1987-2002; S Jn's Ch Of Hassan Rogers MN 1987-1988; Asst R S Alb's Epis Ch Edina MN 1982-1984. ladykaty@comcast.net

REYNOLDS, Kay (ETenn) 4017 Sherry Dr, Knoxville TN 37918 **Assoc S Lk's Ch Knoxville TN 2010-** B Shreveport LA 6/1/1939 d Irvin Richard Reynolds & Katherine Edwards. BA LSU 1962; MA OH SU 1967; PhD OH SU 1974; MDiv STUSo 1989. D 5/31/1989 P 5/1/1990 Bp Duncan Montgomery Gray Jr. S Thos Epis Ch Knoxville TN 2002-2009; Tyson Hse Stdt Fndt Knoxville TN 1995-2000; Dio E Tennessee Knoxville TN 1994-2002; P-in-c S Mich And All Ang Knoxville TN 1994-2002; Vic S Matt's Epis Ch Forest MS 1992-1994; Cur S Paul's Epis Ch Meridian MS 1989-1991. Comt,SCHC 1987. kayr38@gmail.net

REYNOLDS, Mary Lou Corbett (Neb) Po Box 921, Ogallala NE 69153 B Terrington WY 5/4/1936 d John Kingsley Corbett & Clarissa Marie. Nova U; BA U of Wyoming 1957; Med U of Wyoming 1966; MDiv Epis TS of The SW

R

1995. D 6/22/1995 Bp Bob Gordon Jones P 12/1/1995 Bp James Edward Krotz. Vic S Geo's Ch Sidney NE 1995-2008; Vic S Paul's Ch Ogallala NE 1995-2008.

REYNOLDS, Max Midgley (WTex) 4485 Medina Hwy, Kerrville TX 78028 B Groveton TX 11/15/1938 s Clem Branch Reynolds & Essie Brookshire. BS Texas A&M U 1961; MDiv STUSo 1986. D 2/27/1987 P 10/23/1987 Bp John Herbert MacNaughton. c 3. R S Paul's Ch Brady TX 1998-2002; S Andr's Ch Port Isabel TX 1993-1998; Vic Ch Of Our Sav Aransas Pass TX 1990-1993; Vic Ch Of The Ascen Refugio TX 1990-1993; Vic Epis Ch Of The Gd Shepard Geo W TX 1987-1990; S Mich's Ch Sandia TX 1987-1990; St Mich's Epis Ch Geo W TX 1987-1990. Julian of Norwich 1986. maxpadre@ktc.com

REYNOLDS, Richard Seaver (Los) 8524 W Gage Blvd #294, Kennewick WA 99336 B El Paso TX 4/12/1955 s Thompson Reynolds & Heather Irene. BA U of Mary Hardin-Baylor 1975; MDiv TCU 1979; CTh Epis TS of The SW 1983; DMin Evang Luth Sem Tacoma WA 1995. D 6/11/1983 Bp Robert Elwin Terwilliger P 6/10/1984 Bp Donis Dean Patterson. m 9/8/1978 Victoria Gail Vetter c 3. R S Mary's Par Lompoc CA 2000-2006; R Epis Ch Of S Anne Stockton CA 1996-2000; R S Fran Ch Heber Sprg AR 1988-1996; Vic S Paul's Epis Ch Waxahachie TX 1985-1988; Cur Epis Ch Of The Ascen Dallas TX 1983-1985. Auth, "Marital Violence: A Handbook For Ministers," 1991. Oblate Ord Of S Ben. fatherfuzz@juno.com

REYNOLDS, Robert Eugene (Cal) 6832 Treeridge Dr, Cincinnati OH 45244 B Prescott AZ 2/7/1937 s Fred Kilby Reynolds & Miriam Evelyn. BA Arizona St U 1963; MDiv CDSP 1966. D 6/22/1966 P 12/27/1966 Bp James Walmsley Frederic Carman. c 3. Int S Thos Epis Ch Terrace Pk OH 2008-2010; R S Paul's Epis Ch Walnut Creek CA 1989-2005; R Chr Ch Par Lake Oswego OR 1979-1989; R All SS Ch Richland WA 1971-1979; Assoc S Paul's Epis Ch Salem OR 1966-1971. NNECA 1987. R Emer St. Paul's Epis Ch - Walnut Creek 2006. rreynolds003@cinci.rr.com

REYNOLDS, Roger James (Ore) 18271 Sw Ewen Dr, Aloha OR 97006 **D S Barth's Ch Beaverton OR 1990-** B San Francisco CA 12/2/1951 s Robert Archer Reynolds & Olga Ruth. BD DeVry Inst of Techology 1972. D 10/12/1990 Bp Robert Louis Ladehoff. m 10/23/1982 Tammy Ellen Scott c 1. unkleroger@aol.com

REYNOLDS, Stanley Lawrence (Okla) 108 Morgan St, Oberlin OH 44074 B Philadelphia PA 10/22/1925 s Leonard Reynolds & Marian. BA U of Hawaii 1952; MA Tufts U 1953; 1957; Ya Berk 1989; Ya Berk 1989. D 6/22/1957 P 12/21/1957 Bp Anson Phelps Stokes Jr. c 4. R Ch Of The H Trin Marlborough MA 1957-1960.

REYNOLDS JR, Wallace Averal (CFla) 500 W Stuart St, Bartow FL 33830 B Huntington WV 2/7/1945 s Wallace Averal Reynolds & Betty. BBA Marshall U 1971; Cert VTS 1976; PhD U Of Kentucky 1992. D 5/24/1975 P 2/28/1976 Bp Robert Poland Atkinson. m 12/12/1964 Shelia Lee Woodrum c 2. R H Trin Epis Ch Bartow FL 2002-2010; Assoc S Ann's Ch Nashville TN 1992-2002; R S Jas' Epis Ch Lewisburg WV 1981-1987; Int S Ptr's Ch Huntington WV 1979-1981; Assoc Trin Ch Huntington WV 1977-1979; Vic Gr Ch Ravenswood WV 1975-1977. drwalreyn@hotmail.com

REYNOLDS, Wayne Lamar (NJ) P.O.Box 679, 37 Calle del Sol, Questa NM 87556 **Died 12/9/2009** B Whiting,NJ 10/21/1947 s Paul Reynolds & Golda. BS VCU 1970; MS PDS 1973. D 4/28/1973 Bp Alfred L Banyard P 10/27/1973 Bp Albert Wiencke Van Duzer. c 4. fatherwayne@comcast.net

REZACH, Karen Beverly (Nwk) 74 Edgewood Pl, Maywood NJ 07607 B Jersey City NJ 11/6/1959 d Eugene Rezach & Kyong. BA WPC Wayne NJ 1981; MDiv Yale DS 1996; EdD Seton Hall U So Orange NJ 2002. D 6/2/2007 Bp Mark M Beckwith. Chr Ch Short Hills NJ 2007-2011. krezach@yahoo.com

REZIN, Mary Ellen (Eau) 27042 State Highway 21, Tomah WI 54660 **D S Mary's Epis Ch Tomah WI 2004-** B Sparta WI 12/10/1950 d William Jacob Leis & Evelyn Louise. ADN Wstrn Tech Coll 1982; BSN U of New York 1994. D 2/7/2004 Bp Keith Bernard Whitmore. m 11/9/1976 John Leis. mrezin@centurytel.org

RHEA, Pamela Towery (Miss) 318 College St, Columbus MS 39701 B Columbus MS 12/5/1959 d Coley Wade Towery & Eltra Elgene. BS Mississippi U for Wmn 1992. D 1/9/2010 Bp Duncan Montgomery Gray III. m 11/26/1982 Clyde Rhea c 3. pamtrhea@yahoo.com

RHETT JR, William Paterson (SC) 2 Saint Michaels Aly, Charleston SC 29401 **COM Dio So Carolina Charleston SC 1984-; P Dio So Carolina Charleston SC 1968-** B Charleston SC 8/4/1931 s William Paterson Rhett & Margaret. GTS; MDiv VTS; MEd Tem 1968; DEd Auburn U 1973. D 1/25/1960 Bp Thomas N Carruthers P 5/14/1961 Bp Gray Temple. m 2/24/1968 Dorothy Irene Carson. The Amer Psychol Assn 1973. Lifetime Mem Chi Sigma Iota hon Soc 1995; The Meritorious Serv Medal The USA 1991.

RHOADES, Stephen James (CFla) 338 E Lyman Ave, Winter Park IL 32789 **Asst P All SS Ch Of Winter Pk Winter Pk FL 2008-** B Aurora IL 12/18/1967 BA U IL 1990; JD Chicago-Kent Coll of Law 2003; MDiv STUSo 2007. D 6/2/2007 Bp William Dailey Persell P 12/6/2007 Bp Mary Gray-Reeves. m 1/7/1995 Anna J Notation-Rhoades c 5. Cur All SS Epis Ch Palo Alto CA 2007-2008. fatherstephen@gmail.com

RHOADS, Robert Louis (Oly) 181 W Maple St, Sequim WA 98382 **R S Lk's Ch Sequim WA 1999-** B Bakersfield CA 10/13/1953 s John Rhoads & Florence. BS U CA 1975; MDiv CDSP 1979. D 6/14/1979 Bp Wesley Frensdorff P 12/1/1979 Bp John Lester Thompson III. m 4/25/1992 Patricia A Chabot. R S Matt's Ch San Andreas CA 1992-1999; S Jas Epis Mssn Lincoln CA 1981; St Johns Epis Ch Roseville CA 1979-1992. ERM, Ord Of S Lk. bobnpatr@gmail.com

RHOADS, Tommy L (WTenn) 309 E Baltimore St, Jackson TN 38301 B Memphis, TN 11/30/1954 s Carl Emerson Rhoads & Tommie Rankin. No Degree Memphis TS; BA Lambuth Coll 1976; BS Lambuth Coll 1984. D 6/26/2010 Bp Don Edward Johnson. m 5/30/1977 Janice R Janice Roxane Taylor c 1. tommyrhoads@yahoo.com

RHODENHISER, James Cousins (Mich) St. Clare of Assisi Episcopal Church, 2309 Packard Road, Ann Arbor MI 48104 **R S Clare Of Assisi Epis Ch Ann Arbor MI 2003-** B Richmond VA 4/15/1962 s Oscar William Rhodenhiser & Nancye. BA Duke 1984; MA U of Virginia 1991; MDiv Ya Berk 1992. D 6/13/1992 Bp Robert Poland Atkinson P 12/21/1992 Bp Gethin Benwil Hughes. m 7/31/1993 Jayin Lynn Wavrik c 5. R Epis Ch Of The Gd Shpd Salinas CA 1996-2003; Yth Mssnr Dio Maine Portland ME 1993-1996; Assoc R Trin Epis Ch Portland ME 1993-1996; Asst S Ptr's Epis Ch Del Mar CA 1992-1993. Co-Auth, "What Do We Want To Be?," *The Record*, The Epis Dio Michigan, 2006; Auth, "Mnstry w Yth," *The Outlook*, EvangES, 1996. EvangES. jamesrhodenhiser@msn.com

RHODES, D(avid) Joseph (La) 2280 Clematis Trl., Sumter SC 29150 B Ridgeland SC 9/28/1949 s Jeter Ernest Rhodes & Lucille Irene. BS Cit 1971; MDiv STUSo 1978. D 6/4/1978 P 12/23/1978 Bp Gray Temple. m 6/18/1971 Christine Topp c 5. Pres of Stndg Com Dio Louisiana Baton Rouge LA 2001-2002; Stndg Com Dio Louisiana Baton Rouge LA 1998-2002; Vic/R Epis Ch Of The H Sprt In Baton Rouge Baton Rouge LA 1986-2008; Vic/R S Chris's Ch Sumter SC 1978-1986. LAND 1984. Cn Dio Honduras 2005. joetina71@aol.com

RHODES, Diane Lynn (Nwk) 38 Lynn St, Harrington Park NJ 07940 B Pittsburgh 5/8/1949 d George Frederick Rhodes & Bety. BA U Chi 1971; MBA FD 1982; MDiv Drew U 2004. D 6/11/2005 P 12/17/2005 Bp John Palmer Croneberger. rhodesdiane@msn.com

RHODES, Erroll Franklin (Cal) 19 Comly Ave, Greenwich CT 06831 B Ibaraki-ken 3/29/1924 s Erroll Allen Rhodes & Bessie Moore. BA Pepperdine U 1943; PhD U Chi 1948; SWTS 1952; Ya Berk 1968. D 6/1/1953 P 12/8/1953 Bp Henry H Shires. m 6/9/1950 Martha Elizabeth Stowell c 3. Translations Dept ABS New York NY 1968-2003. Ed, "Gd News Study Bible," ABS, 2000; Co-Ed, "The Translators To The Rdr: The Original Preface Of The King Jas Version 1611 Revisted," ABS, 1997; Auth, "Translations From Engl To Japanese, And From German To Engl," *Of Var arts*, 1969; Auth, "arts in Biblic Scholarly Pub," *Quarterly Pub And Textbooks*, 1960; Auth, "Annotated List Of Armenian NT Manuscripts," Rikkyo (S Paul's) U, 1959. SBL, 1947; Studiorum Novi Testamenti Societas 1954. erhodes@americanbible.org

RHODES, Judith L (Ct) 661 Old Post Rd, Fairfield CT 06824 **R S Paul's Ch Fairfield CT 2010-** B Arlington MA 4/6/1952 d Robert Henry Butt & Bertha Louise. BA Regis Coll Weston MA 1974; MDiv Harvard DS 1991. D 6/5/1993 P 5/21/1994 Bp Don Edward Johnson. m Martha Ellen Hughes. R S Mary's Epis Ch Ardmore PA 2002-2010; R Emm Ch W Roxbury MA 1996-2002; Assoc Chr Ch Needham MA 1993-1996. Dominican Sis S Cathr; Fllshp Soc Of S Jn The Evang. revjudy139@verizon.net

RHODES, Margaret Diana Clark (Ia) 22 Dillman Dr, Council Bluffs IA 51503 **P S Paul's Ch Coun Bluffs IA 2009-** B Keokuk IA 5/2/1984 d John Howard Clark & Colette Jean Detwiler. BA Drury U 2006; MDiv SWTS 2009. D 12/20/2008 P 6/27/2009 Bp Alan Scarfe. m 8/11/2007 Eric Rhodes. revrhodes@gmail.com

RHODES, Robert Richard (Nwk) 9 Harrington Ave., Westwood NJ 07675 **R Gr Epis Ch Westwood NJ 2008-** B St Louis MO 7/5/1968 s Glen Allen Rhodes & Jude Elaine. BFA Fontbonne U 1990; MDiv GTS 2003. D 12/27/2002 P 6/6/2003 Bp George Wayne Smith. m 11/15/1997 Lisa Copland. R S Matt's Ch Bogalusa LA 2006-2008; Cur S Mart's Ch Ellisville MO 2003-2006. rob_r86@yahoo.com

RHODES, Robert Wayne (Oly) 300 W 8th Street Unit 314, Vancouver WA 98660 B Seattle WA 9/11/1942 s Jewell Wayne Rhodes & Wilma Adrienne. BA U of Washington 1971; MDiv CDSP 1974. D 7/17/1974 P 7/1/1975 Bp Ivol I Curtis. m 9/15/1962 Rita Tyhuis c 3. Ch Of The Gd Shpd Vancouver WA 1978-2006; S Anne's Epis Ch Washougal WA 1976-1979; Res-in-Trng S Lk's Epis Ch Vancouver WA 1974-1976. bobr42@gmail.com

RHODES, William Chester (Az) 7047 N 28th Dr, Phoenix AZ 85051 B Philadelphia PA 1/24/1948 s John Frederick Rhodes & Janis. BA Ya 1970; MDiv GTS 1976. D 8/7/1976 Bp Lloyd Edward Gressle P 6/1/1977 Bp Harold Louis Wright. P-in-c S Mary's Epis Ch Phoenix AZ 1999-2003; R Ch Of The Adv Of Chr The King San Francisco CA 1984-1999; Asst S Mk's Ch Mt Kisco NY 1978-1984; Asst S Jn's Ch Larchmont NY 1976-1978. Hon Cn Dio Arizona 2010. sedonarhodes@hotmail.com

RHYS, (John) Howard (ETenn) 75 Louisiana Cir, Sewanee TN 37375 B Montreal QC CA 10/25/1917 s John Gabriel Rhys & Margaret Maude. BA McGill U 1939; LTh Montreal TS 1941; STB GTS 1944; STM GTS 1949; ThD GTS 1953. Trans from Anglican Church of Canada 6/15/1944 as Priest Bp Robert E Gribbin. P-in-c Ch Of The H Comf Monteagle TN 1975-1984; P-in-c S Jn The Bapt Sewanee TN 1953-2006; Prof of NT The TS at The U So Sewanee TN 1953-1983; P-in-c S Paul's Rock Creek Washington DC 1952-1953; Cur Trin Cathd Trenton NJ 1949-1951; Asst Ch Of The Trsfg New York NY 1948-1949; Vic S Jas Ch Black Mtn NC 1944-1948; Vic Trin Epis Ch Asheville NC 1944-1948. Auth, "Hymnal Comp," 1982; Auth, "Hastings Dictionary Of The Bible," 1963; Auth, "Epistle To The Romans," 1961; Auth, "Angl RC"; Auth, "ATR"; Ed 1988-2004, "Synrthesis". Hon Cn Dio Estrn Tennessee TN 1997.

RICE, Charles Lynvel (Nwk) 618 Quaker Plain Rd, Bangor PA 18013 B Chandler OK 12/12/1936 s William Clyde Rice & Dorothy Alene. BA Baylor U 1959; BD Sthrn Bapt TS Louisville KY 1962; STM UTS 1963; PhD Duke 1967. D 1/16/1988 P 6/4/1988 Bp John Shelby Spong. Trin Epis Ch Mt Pocono PA 2008-2010; Int S Dunst's Epis Ch Succasunna NJ 2001-2003; Int Chr Ch Short Hills NJ 1998-1999; Int S Lk's Ch Hope NJ 1996-1998; Int S Ptr's Ch Morristown NJ 1996-1997; Assoc S Ptr's Ch Morristown NJ 1988-1996. Auth, *The Embodied Word*, 1990; Auth, *Preaching the Story*, 1980; Auth, *Interp & Imagination*, 1970. Acad Homil 1970. Prof Emer Drew U 2003. clrice@epix.net

RICE, Debra Harsh (WNC) 51 N View Cir, Hayesville NC 28904 **R S Jn's Epis Ch Franklin NC 2007-** B Columbus OH 1/19/1950 d George Elden Harsh & Elsie Ruth. BS Otterbein Coll 1971. D 9/22/1980 P 5/1/1981 Bp Robert Shaw Kerr. m 7/10/1971 John David Sayre Rice c 1. Ch Of The Gd Shpd Hayesville NC 2006-2007; S Jas Ch Black Mtn NC 1995-1999; S Mary's Ch Morganton NC 1993-1995; S Jn The Bapt Epis Hardwick VT 1990-1991; Stff The Ch Of The H Sprt Lake Forest IL 1986-1988; S Andr's Epis Ch Colchester VT 1984-1985; Dioc Rel Educ Consult Dio Vermont Burlington VT 1980-1983. debrarice@dnet.net

RICE, Edward G (Pa) 351 Main Street, Ridgefield CT 06877 **S Steph's Ch Ridgefield CT 2011-; Chr Ch Cranbrook Bloomfield Hills MI 1972-** B New York NY 6/21/1943 s Kurt David Rice & Dorothy Marianne. BA Trin Hartford CT 1966; MDiv EDS 1971. D 12/16/1972 P 6/17/1974 Bp H Coleman McGehee Jr. m 5/15/2010 Patricia A Stelz c 2. Trin Memi Ch Philadelphia PA 2008-2011; The Ch Of The H Trin W Chester PA 2005-2008; Dio Massachusetts Boston MA 1997-2000; R S Paul's Ch Dedham MA 1994-2004; Chair - Com On Compstn Dio Michigan Detroit MI 1990-1994; Dio Michigan Detroit MI 1987-1988; R All SS Ch E Lansing MI 1981-1994; Assoc R Chr Ch Dearborn MI 1976-1981; Mssnr to Yth Chr Ch Cranbrook Bloomfield Hills MI 1972-1975. Auth, "H Week Lrng Centers"; Auth, "Healthy Chr Communities". edwardgrice@gmail.com

RICE JR, Frank G(racey) (Tenn) 4901 Timberhill Dr, Nashville TN 37211 B Chattanooga TN 6/17/1925 s Frank Gracey Rice & Mabel. BA Baylor U 1948; BD STUSo 1951; DMin Van 1974. D 8/19/1951 Bp Gerald Francis Burrill P 2/20/1952 Bp Charles A Mason. m 12/30/1954 Isabel J McKay c 2. Epis Dvlpmt Corp Nashville TN 1958-1985; P-in-c S Anne's Ch Ft Worth TX 1954-1956; Min in charge S Mart Epis Ch New Boston TX 1951-1953.

RICE, Glenda Ann (Ak) PO Box 1130, Sitka AK 99835 B Scotia CA 5/30/1952 d Farrell Glenn Swain & Jo Ann. AA U of Alaska SE Sitka 2008. D 5/1/2011 Bp Mark A Lattime. c 3. glenda.sitka@gmail.com

R

RICE, John David Sayre (WNC) 51 North View Circle, Hayesville NC 28904 **Ch Of The Gd Shpd Hayesville NC 2003-** B Columbus OH 12/5/1949 s Earnest Rice & Eleanor Louise. BS U of Vermont 1976; MA U of Vermont 1978; MDiv SWTS 1988. D 6/15/1988 P 12/15/1988 Bp Daniel Lee Swenson. m 7/10/1971 Debra Harsh c 1. Centurion Hse Asheville NC 2001-2005; R S Jas Ch Black Mtn NC 1993-2001; R S Mk's Epis Ch Newport VT 1988-1993. Ord of S Lk 1998. johnrice@dnet.net

RICE JR, John Fay (Va) 240 Old Main St, South Yarmouth MA 02664 **Chapl Trin Ch Huntington WV 2011-** B Philadelphia PA 6/28/1941 s John Rice & Sonia. BA Rhodes Coll 1963; MDiv SWTS 1968; L.E.A.D. Consultants 1980; DMin McCormick TS 1980; Fllshp Coll of Preachers 1989. D 6/16/1968 Bp John Vander Horst P 5/1/1969 Bp William Evan Sanders. m 5/30/1964 Maxine Allen Mitchel c 2. Chapl Hse Of The Redeem New York NY 2011; R Trin Ch Arlington VA 1995-2000; Int S Dav's Epis Mssn Pepperell MA 1995; Cn to the Ordnry Dio Massachusetts Boston MA 1991-1995; R Trin Ch Huntington WV 1987-1991; Dio Massachusetts Boston MA 1986-1987; Dio Massachusetts Boston MA 1979-1985; Dio Massachusetts Boston MA 1978-1987; R S Dav's Epis Ch Nashville TN 1978-1987; Asst Ch Of The H Comm Memphis TN 1975-1978; Vic Ch of the H Apos Collierville TN 1971-1975; Asst Ch Of The Ascen Knoxville TN 1969-1971. Associated Parishes, Liturg Conf 1971-1987. deaconrest@aol.com

RICE, Lawrence Allen (NMich) 5526 S Baker Side Rd, Sault Sainte Marie MI 49783 **D S Jas Ch Of Sault S Marie Sault Ste Marie MI 2006-** B Ogdensburg NY 6/14/1938 s Clarence Edwin Rice & Violet Lu Lu. D 5/28/2006 Bp James Arthur Kelsey. m 7/2/1960 Catherine Newton c 2. larice@up.net

RICE, Marshall Turk (RI) 40 Boulder Ave, Charlestown RI 02813 B Orange NJ 1/19/1934 s James K Rice & Ann M. BA Pr 1956; MDiv GTS 1959. D 5/23/1959 Bp Leland Stark P 12/1/1959 Bp Donald MacAdie. m 6/13/1999 Elizabeth Minturn c 3. Trin Ch Newport RI 1999-2000; Deploy Off Dio Newark Newark NJ 1997-2000; Dio Rhode Island Providence RI 1997-2000; R Chr Ch Ridgewood NJ 1967-1976; Vic Ch Of The Atone Fair Lawn NJ 1961-1964; Cur Chr Ch Hackensack NJ 1959-1961. mtrice15@cox.net

RICE, Randolf James (ECR) 2534 Dumbarton Ave, San Jose CA 95124 **Cn Chncllr Dio El Camino Real Monterey CA 1998-** B San Jose CA 7/1/1947 s James Allen Rice & Bette Jean. BA U CA 1969; Harv 1970; BD CDSP 1972; JD Hastings Coll of Law 1978. D 6/24/1972 Bp George Richard Millard P 1/6/1973 Bp Clarence Rupert Haden Jr. Chancllr Dio El Camino Real Monterey CA 1993-1998; Trin Cathd San Jose CA 1978-1980; Vic Chr Epis Ch Sei Ko Kai San Francisco CA 1975-1978; Com Dio El Camino Real Monterey CA 1972-1978; Cur Calv Epis Ch Santa Cruz CA 1972-1975. Auth, "Var arts Law". mbatranch@sprintmail.com

RICE, Rodney Vincent (NY) 1906 Rambling Ridge Ln Apt T-2, Baltimore MD 21209 B Winston-Salem NC 12/6/1960 s William Jasper Rice & Willie Mae. MDiv Yale DS 1987; BA U NC 1993; EdM Harv 1996. D 9/12/1987 P 5/26/1988 Bp Peter James Lee. Assoc S Jas Ch New York NY 1993-1995; S Andr's Sch Chap Middletown DE 1991-1993; P S Jas' Epis Ch Baltimore MD 1989-1991; S Paul's Ch Richmond VA 1987-1989. ricerv2005@comcast.net

RICE, Sandra Kay (Md) All Saint's Episcopal Church, 106 W. Church St., Frederick MD 21701 **D Dio Maryland Baltimore MD 2000-** B Frederick MD 6/17/1945 d Henry Russell Eury & Alice Estella. BA Hood Coll 1995; STUSo 2000. D 6/3/2000 Bp Robert Wilkes Ihloff. m 7/21/1963 Wilbur Eugene Rice c 2. Dir of Outreach All SS Ch Frederick MD 2004-2011; Dir of Outreach The Gathering: A Fam Of Faith Epis Ch Buckeystown MD 2000-2004. Daugters of the King 2001. ricecrispy1@comcast.net

RICE, Spencer Morgan (Mass) 4345 Westover Pl Nw, Washington DC 20016 **Assoc S Jn's Ch Lafayette Sq Washington DC 1996-** B San Marino CA 9/11/1928 s William Anthony Rice & Gaylord Georgia. BA Occ 1952; BD CDSP 1955. D 6/14/1955 P 2/1/1956 Bp Francis E I Bloy. c 3. Trin Ch In The City Of Boston Boston MA 1982-1993; Chair Of The Dept Of Ch Ext Dio California San Francisco CA 1967-1982; S Lk's Ch San Francisco CA 1966-1982; Archd Of Ch Ext Dio California San Francisco CA 1965-1969; Chair Of The Dept Of Min Dio California San Francisco CA 1964-1967; Dept Of Coll Wk Dio California San Francisco CA 1962-1982; R S Mk's Epis Ch Palo Alto CA 1962-1965; Secy For The Dept Of Coll Wk Dio Los Angeles Los Angeles CA 1958-1962; R S Simon's Par San Fernando CA 1958-1962; Cur S Mths' Par Whittier CA 1955-1958.

RICE, Steven Christopher (NC) 2575 Parkway Dr, Winston Salem NC 27103 **R S Tim's Epis Ch Winston Salem NC 2008-** B Greenwood SC 4/13/1979 s Easton Rice & Eleanor. BA Erskine Coll 2000; MDiv Candler TS Emory U 2004; D.Min Nash 2012. D 2/5/2005 P 8/6/2005 Bp Henry Irving Louttit. m 10/20/2001 Cherilyn A Walker c 2. R S Mich's Ch Waynesboro GA 2005-2008. CBS 2007; Soc of Cath Priests 2009. frsteve@sttimothys.ws

RICE, Whitney Elizabeth (Ind) Christ Church Cathedral, 55 Monument Cir. Ste. 600, Indianapolis IN 46204 **S Dav's Ch Beanblossom Nashville IN 2011-** B Lee's Summit MO 11/15/1982 d Charles David Rice & Judith Kay. BA U of Kansas 2005; MDiv Ya Berk 2008. D 6/7/2008 Bp Barry Robert Howe P 1/17/2009 Bp Catherine Elizabeth Maples Waynick. Cur Chr Ch Cathd Indianapolis IN 2008-2011; Supervised Mnstry Stdt Chr Ch Redding Ridge CT 2007-2008; Supervised Mnstry Stdt S Jn's Ch Guilford CT 2006-2007. wrice@stdavidsbb.org

RICE, Winston E (La) 512 E Boston St, Covington LA 70433 **Asstg P Chr Ch Covington LA 2011-; Seamens Ch Inst Income New York NY 2011-; Chr Ch Covington LA 2009-** B Shreveport LA 2/22/1946 s Winston Churchill Rice & Margaret Coughlin. JD LSU 1971; Cert Sch for Mnstry - Dio Louisiana 2002; Cert The McFarland Inst 2002. D 12/29/2004 Bp Charles Edward Jenkins III P 6/29/2005 Bp James Barrow Brown. m 4/16/1977 Barbara G Gay c 3. Dio Louisiana Baton Rouge LA 2010; Assoc R Chr Ch Covington LA 2008-2009; Asst R Chr Ch Covington LA 2005-2007; P-in-c S Matt's Ch Bogalusa LA 2005; Transitional D Chr Ch Covington LA 2004-2005. rice@ricellc.com

RICH III, Edward Robins (SwFla) 11315 Linbanks Pl, Tampa FL 33617 B Baltimore MD 6/28/1947 s Edward Rich & Carolyn Donoho. BA Davis & Elkins Coll 1969; MDiv VTS 1972. D 5/25/1972 P 2/4/1973 Bp David Keller Leighton Sr. m 6/7/1969 Sherry Russell c 3. R S Cathr's Ch Temple Terrace FL 2000-2010; Asst S Mary's Par Tampa FL 1998-2000; R Gr Ch Grand Rapids MI 1991-1997; R Chr Epis Ch Of Springfield Springfield OH 1985-1991; P-in-c New Life Epis Ch Uniontown OH 1982-1984; R S Ptr's Ch Akron OH 1976-1985; Asst S Paul's Ch Canton OH 1974-1976. Auth, "The Pearl Of

Great Price: A Manual For Par Stwdshp"; Auth, "The Hidden Treasure: Journey In Stwdshp Of Time & Talent". errich60769@gmail.com

RICH JR, Ernest Albert (Az) 10625 W White Mountain Rd, Sun City AZ 85351 B Bluefield VA 1/31/1922 s Ernest Albert Rich & Alice Margaret. BA Ken 1949; VTS 1952. D 6/11/1952 P 12/10/1952 Bp John T Heistand. m 6/21/1952 Ruth W Watt c 5. R S Chris's Ch Sun City AZ 1981-1986; R S Jn's Ch Ellicott City MD 1956-1981; Vic/R S Jas Bedford PA 1952-1956; Archd S Lk's Epis Ch Altoona PA 1952-1956. Auth, *VTS Journ*. earich22@juno.com

RICH, Michael Glenn (Ala) 408 Church Ave SE, Jacksonville AL 36265 **R S Lk's Epis Ch Jacksonville AL 2006-** B Gadsden AL 10/17/1961 BD NWU 1984; MS NWU 1985; PhD U of Iowa 2001; MDiv The GTS 2006. D 5/31/2006 Bp Marc Handley Andrus P 12/12/2006 Bp Henry Nutt Parsley Jr. mgrichphd@yahoo.com

RICH, Nancy Willis (O) 2499 Kingston Rd, Cleveland Heights OH 44118 **Assoc Trin Cathd Cleveland OH 2002-** B Washington DC 11/17/1936 d Howard Mott Willis & Virginia Seagle. BA McDaniel Coll 1958; MS W Virginia U 1960; CAS GTS 1987; MDiv S Mary RC Sem 1989. D 6/11/1988 Bp James Russell Moodey P 6/3/1989 Bp Arthur Benjamin Williams Jr. m 8/22/1959 James Chandler Rich c 4. Asst Epis. Shared Mnstrs Nw Lakewood OH 2001-2002; P-in-c S Mk's Epis Ch Wadsworth OH 1997-2000; Int S Chris's By-The River Gates Mills OH 1996-1997; Int S Phil's Epis Ch Akron OH 1993-1995; S Mk's Ch Cleveland OH 1992; Asst S Paul's Ch Akron OH 1989-1991; Asst Ch Of The Incarn Cleveland OH 1988-1989. nancyw.rich@sbcglobal.net

RICH, Noel D. (Minn) 808 Eldo Ln SW, Alexandria MN 56308 B Seattle WA 12/23/1942 s Ralph A Rich & Lucille A. BS Penn 1966; MDiv VTS 1979. D 6/22/1979 Bp David Rea Cochran P 1/5/1980 Bp Samuel B Chilton. m 3/19/1966 Virginia L Smith c 1. R S Jas' Epis Ch Fergus Falls MN 2005-2006; R Emm Epis Ch Alexandria MN 1996-2006; R Chr Ch Madison IN 1987-1996; Asst R S Andr Epis Ch Mentor OH 1983-1987; S Fran By The Sea Ch Kenai AK 1981-1983; P-in-c S Ptr's Ch Seward AK 1980-1983; Truro Epis Ch Fairfax VA 1979-1980. Bd Trst SAMS 1988. ngrich@gctel.net

RICH, Susan Chandler (EMich) 316 Engle St, Imlay City MI 48444 **R Gr Epis Ch Lapeer MI 2010-; Mssnr Dio Estrn Michigan Saginaw MI 2009-; R S Jn's Epis Ch Dryden MI 2004-** B Cleveland OH 10/9/1960 d James Chandler Rich & Nancy Willis. BS Ohio U 1983; MDiv Epis TS of The SW 2004. D 6/5/2004 Bp Michael Gene Smith P 12/18/2004 Bp Edwin Max Leidel Jr. revsuerich@gmail.com

RICH, Timothy Thayer (NH) 63 Green St, Concord NH 03301 **Dio New Hampshire Concord NH 2004-** B Mount Kisco NY 4/16/1962 s Wesley Everett Rich & Joan. BS Geo 1984; U of Maryland 1987; MDiv SWTS 1993. D 6/12/1993 Bp Ronald Hayward Haines P 12/16/1993 Bp Jane Hart Holmes Dixon. m 7/3/1993 Meghan Leigh Sjurson c 2. R S Jn's Ch Portsmouth NH 1996-2004; Asst R Chr Epis Ch No Hills Pittsburgh PA 1993-1996; Assoc R Chr Epis Ch Pottstown PA 1993-1996. trich@nhepiscopal@hotmail.com

RICH, William Warwick (Mass) 29 Greenough Ave Unit 2, Jamaica Plain MA 02130 **Sr Assoc for Chr Formation Trin Ch In The City Of Boston Boston MA 2005-** B Fairmont WV 3/7/1953 s Adrian Warwick Rich & Marian. BA Wms 1975; MDiv Yale DS 1980; STM UTS 1995; MPhil UTS 2001; PhD UTS 2002. D 4/26/1980 P 5/9/1981 Bp David Keller Leighton Sr. m 11/25/2008 Donald Schiermer. Int S Paul's Ch Doylestown PA 2004-2005; Int Chr Ch Bronxville NY 2003-2004; Int S Dav's Ch Kinnelon NJ 2002-2003; The Ch Of S Lk In The Fields New York NY 2001-2002; Dir Post Ord Trng Dio Maryland Baltimore MD 1992-1994; Bp's Com on Chr-Jewish Relatns Dio Maryland Baltimore MD 1988-1998; Asst Memi Ch Baltimore MD 1987-1999; Dn Diac Formation Dio Maryland Baltimore MD 1985-1991; Liturg and Mus Com Dio Maryland Baltimore MD 1984-1994; R Gr Ch Elkridge MD 1983-1987; Asst S Jn's Ch Reisterstown MD 1980-1983. Auth, "Gr And Imagination," *Journ Of Rel And Hlth*, 2001; Auth, "Var Bk Revs," *Journ of Rel and Hlth*. AAR 2000-2006; SBL 2000-2006. Phi Beta Kappa 1975. wrich@trinitychurchboston.org

RICHARD, Helen Taylor (Ore) 123 Grove St, Lebanon OR 97355 **D S Mart's Ch Lebanon OR 1987-** B Ely NV 3/3/1931 d Enoch Taylor & Myrna. CDSP; BS Oregon Coll of Educ 1953; Med OR SU 1963. D 11/1/1987 Bp Robert Louis Ladehoff. m 8/4/1955 John Francis Richard c 2. CHS. hrichard@proaxis.com

RICHARD, Mary Brownfield (WLa) PO Box 1627, Shreveport LA 71165 **R Ch Of The H Cross Shreveport LA 2010-** B Fort Worth TX 6/9/1947 d Jack Dearing Brownfield & Mackey. BA U of Texas 1969; Dipl. in Theol The Angl TS 2005. D 6/7/2008 P 3/7/2009 Bp D(avid) Bruce Mac Pherson. m 1/24/1970 Herschel Richard c 3. mbrichard47@yahoo.com

RICHARDS, Anne Frances (NY) 117 Oenoke Ridge, New Canaan CT 06840 **Sr Asst S Mk's Ch New Canaan CT 2008-** B Worcester MA 1/4/1951 d John James Connor & Anne Frances. BA Smith 1973; MA NYU 1980; MDiv GTS 1988. D 12/4/1988 Bp Furman Stough P 6/4/1989 Bp Jose Antonio Ramos. m 5/28/2004 Richard Frank Grein c 2. Chapl Gr Ch Sch New York New York NY 2004-2008; Sr P Assoc Gr Epis Ch New York NY 2001-2004; Cn Ordnry Dio New York New York City NY 1995-2001; Asst Ch Of The Heav Rest New York NY 1991-1995; COM Chair Dio New York New York City NY 1990-1995. Auth, "Cler Sexual Misconduct: Epis & RC Cler," *Predatory Priests, Silenced Victims: The Sexual Abuse Crisis & the Cath Ch*, Analytic Press, 2007. Friends of Julian of Norwich 2001. Bp's Cross Dio New York 2001; Best Sermon Competition (Winner) Epis/Evang Fndt 1994. arichards@stmarksnewcanaan.org

RICHARDS, Anne Marie (RI) 107 Old Beach Rd Apt 2, Newport RI 02840 **Bp's Search Com Dio Rhode Island Providence RI 2011-; Dioc Coun Dio Rhode Island Providence RI 2010-; R Trin Ch Newport RI 2010-** B Olney MD 2/2/1966 d Thomas James Aylward & Mary Louise. BS Columbia Un Coll Takoma Pk MD 2000; MDiv VTS 2005. D 6/11/2005 P 1/21/2006 Bp John Chane. m 12/30/1989 Brook Richards c 2. Assoc R Trin Ch Princeton NJ 2005-2010. richards.annemarie@gmail.com

RICHARDS, Daniel Paul (WMich) 529 W 10th St, Traverse City MI 49684 **Dn - Grand Traverse Dnry Dio Wstrn Michigan Kalamazoo MI 2010-; R Gr Epis Ch Traverse City MI 2009-** B Cleveland MS 10/15/1975 BA Grand Canyon U 1997; MDiv CDSP 2003. D 5/24/2003 P 12/13/2003 Bp Robert Reed Shahan. m 2/17/2007 Amy Crowley c 3. Vic Epis Ch of the H Sprt Phoenix AZ 2008-2009; COM Dio Arizona Phoenix AZ 2004-2009; Cur Epis Par Of S Mich And All Ang Tucson AZ 2003-2004. Poet, "And We Drown . . .," *Ruah*, Ruah Dominican Soc, 2002. Excellence in Mnstry Schlrshp CDSP 2000. danieloftheway@gmail.com

✠ **RICHARDS, Rt Rev David Emrys** (SeFla) 625 N Greenway Dr, Coral Gables FL 33134 B Scranton PA 1/24/1921 s Emrys Richards & Ida May. BA Leh 1942; STB GTS 1945; STD GTS 1952. D 4/7/1945 Bp Frank W Sterrett P 10/1/1945 Bp Reginald Heber Gooden Con 7/19/1951 for Alb. m 6/15/1950 Helen Rice. Epis Ch Cntr New York NY 1978-1988; Off Of Pstr Dvlpmt Coral Gables FL 1969-1977; Suffr Bp Of Alb Dio Albany Albany NY 1951-1957; Archd Dio Albany Albany NY 1950-1951; Asst S Geo's Epis Ch Schenectady NY 1948-1950.

RICHARDS, Dennison S. (LI) 107-66 Merrick Blvd, Jamaica NY 11433 **R Ch Of S Jas The Less Jamaica NY 2009-; Dio Coun Dio Long Island Garden City NY 2008-** B Castries St Lucia WI 4/15/1965 s Quentin Joseph Richards & Amy Maria. BA Codrington Coll 1994; CPE Coll of Pstr Supervision and Psych 2000. Trans from Church in the Province Of The West Indies 6/26/2002 Bp Orris George Walker Jr. m 1/7/1995 Fay Moreen Sargusingh c 1. Bd Dir Epis Cmnty Serv Long Island 1927 Garden City NY 2008-2011; S Paul's Ch Roosevelt NY 2004-2008; Bd Dir Dio Long Island Garden City NY 2003-2006; Dir of Pstr Care/Chapl Bp Chas W Maclean Epis Nrsng Hm Far Rockaway NY 2001-2008; Dir of Pstr Care Epis Hlth Serv Bethpage NY 2001-2008. Black Cler Caucus 2002; CPSP Far Rockaway Chapt 2000. DD Masters Intl Sch of Div 2011; Res Chapl Awd Epis Hlth Serv 2000. churchofstjamestheless@yahoo.com

RICHARDS, Edward Thomas (CGC) PO Box 595, Wewahitchka FL 32465 B Providence RI 8/21/1944 s Earl Thomas Richards & Cathlene Bushnell. BS Cor 1966; MBA Butler U 1968. D 2/10/2011 Bp Philip Menzie Duncan II. c 4. riched@knology.net

RICHARDS, Emily Barr (Pa) 654 N Easton Rd, Glenside PA 19038 **R S Ptr's Ch Glenside PA 2009-** B Lexington KY 7/23/1971 d Garland Hale Barr & Donna. BA U So 1994; MDiv TS 2002. D 6/8/2002 P 5/20/2003 Bp Stacy F Sauls. m 12/28/1996 Luman Daniel Richards c 1. Asst S Steph's Ch Ridgefield CT 2005-2009; Vic All SS Epis Ch Richmond KY 2005; Vic S Alb's Ch Morehead KY 2002-2005. vicaremily@yahoo.com

RICHARDS, Fitzroy Ivan (Oly) 12499 Eagle Dr, Burlington WA 98233 B Carapichima Trinidad TT 11/6/1926 s Sylvanus Richards & Adora. Dalhousie U; LTh U of King's Coll Halifax NS CA 1962. Trans from Anglican Church of Canada 5/30/1988 Bp Robert Hume Cochrane. m 11/14/1964 Yuklin Clementine Wah Hon c 3. P-in-c Chr Epis Ch Anacortes WA 1992-1998; Vic S Jas Ch Sedro-Woolley WA 1988-1990. richards_2636@comcast.net

RICHARDS, F Lee (Pa) 7833 Winston Rd, Philadelphia PA 19118 **Died 2/2/2011** B Philadelphia PA 2/1/1918 s John T Richards & Gertrude. BA Leh 1948; MDiv VTS 1951; STM Tem 1954; Fllshp Coll of Preachers 1965. D 6/9/1951 P 12/12/1951 Bp Oliver J Hart. c 1. Contrib, "Spanning Four Centuries," 1997; Contrib, "Invisible Philadelphia: Cmnty Through Vol Orgnztn," 1995; Auth, "A Revolution That Led To A Ch," Forw Mvmt Press, 1990; Contrib, "Pages Of Par Hist Of Epis Dio Pa". rich100@comcast.net

RICHARDS JR, George Richard (Roch) 18 Haviland Dr, Scotia NY 12302 B Scranton PA 6/26/1936 s George Richard Richards & Olive. BA Wilkes Coll 1958; STB PDS 1961. D 6/21/1961 P 2/1/1962 Bp Frederick J Warnecke. m 12/20/1969 Mary Newell Nohis c 1. Vic S Mths Epis Ch E Rochester NY 1963-1969; Dio Rochester Rochester NY 1961-1968; P-in-c S Jas' Ch Drifton PA 1961-1963. VOLCEGEO@AOL.COM

RICHARDS, Gerald Wayne (Be) 265 Old Mine Rd, Lebanon PA 17042 B Philadelphia PA 4/29/1934 s Richard Nicholas Richards & Margaret Alice. BA Juniata Coll 1956; MDiv Crozer TS 1959; CAS PDS 1960. D 11/18/1961 Bp Andrew Tsu P 6/13/1962 Bp Conrad Gesner. m 10/10/1959 Sue Ann Wilkins c

R

3. PA Coun Chs - Del Dio Bethlehem Bethlehem PA 1988-1992; R S Lk's Ch Lebanon PA 1973-1996; ExCoun Dio Delaware Wilmington DE 1970-1973; R S Mk's Ch Millsboro DE 1966-1973; Vic Gr Epis Ch Madison SD 1961-1966; DeSmet, SD S Steph's Ch De Smet SD 1961-1966. Angl Soc. Citation for Serv to S Lk's and Lebanon PA Pennsylvania Hse of Representatives 1996. JERRYR12@COMCAST.NET

RICHARDS, Jeffery Martin (O) 2510 Olentangy Dr, Akron OH 44333 B Akron OH 10/15/1928 s Martin Wright Richards & Mona Edith. BS U of Akron 1951; BD Bex 1959; MA Kent St U 1969. D 6/13/1959 P 12/19/1959 Bp Nelson Marigold Burroughs. P-in-c S Jn's Epis Ch Cuyahoga Falls OH 1984-1985; P-in-c S Andr's Ch Akron OH 1982-1984; S Paul's Epis Ch Of E Cleveland Cleveland OH 1967-1968; P-in-c S Aug's Epis Ch Youngstown OH 1962-1967; Cur Ch Of Our Sav Akron OH 1961-1962; S Paul's Epis Ch Of E Cleveland Cleveland OH 1959-1961. JMR2510@roadrunner.com

RICHARDS, Michael Gregory (Los) Po Box 220383, Newhall CA 91322 **Hon Cn Cathd Cntr of St. Paul Dio Los Angeles Los Angeles CA 2002-** B Torrance CA 2/8/1947 s Michael James Richards & Vera Marie. BA California St U 1968; MDiv GTS 1971; Cert. Coll of Fin Plnng 1987; Ph.D. Un Inst & U 2011. D 9/11/1971 P 3/18/1972 Bp Francis E I Bloy. m 8/16/1969 Deborah Elizabeth Saville c 2. Pstr to the Cler Cathd Cntr Of S Paul Cong Los Angeles CA 2002-2010; Eductr-in Res S Alb's Epis Ch Los Angeles CA 1998-2002; Coordntr - Epis Relief And Dvlpmt Dio Los Angeles Los Angeles CA 1989-2002; Chapl Campbell Hall Vlly Vill CA 1988-2002; Dioc Coun Dio Los Angeles Los Angeles CA 1983-1985; R All SS Par Beverly Hills CA 1982-1988; Cler Senate Dio Los Angeles Los Angeles CA 1975-1977; Asst All SS Par Beverly Hills CA 1973-1975; Assoc R S Steph's Par Whittier CA 1971-1973. Auth, "When Someone You Know Is Hurting," ZondervanHarper, 1994. St Geo Awd ECUSA 1982. rmgr@sbcglobal.net

RICHARDS, Rosalie Neal (Ct) 536 Old Glen Avenue, Berlin NH 03570 **Receiving Disabil Ret 2011-** B North Platte NE 3/20/1949 d Mark Herbert Richards & Mary Jane. BA Baylor U 1971; MA U of Texas 1975; MDiv GTS 1981; MSW Col 1992; PhD Univ. TX Sch of Publ Hlth 1996. D 6/13/1981 P 3/14/1982 Bp Paul Moore Jr. c 1. Chr Ch Canaan CT 2006-2011; S Lk's Ch Charlestown NH 2004; Un Ch Claremont NH 2004; Ascen Ch New Haven CT 1984-1989; S Ann's Ch Of Morrisania Bronx NY 1982-1984; Gr Epis Ch Nyack NY 1981-1982. Auth, "Variables Associated w Ethnic Violence and Factors Associated w Nonviolent Response to Grievances Toward Members of Other Ethnic Groups," *Dissertation*, The U of Texas Sch of Publ Hlth, 1996; Chapt co-Auth, "Homeless Wmn and Feminist Soc Wk Pract.," *Feminist Pract in the 21st Century.*, NASW Press, 1995. Outstanding Wmn of New Haven 1987; Outstanding Wmn of Amer 1983. richards787@att.net

RICHARDS, Susan M (Pa) 1074 BROADMOOR RD, BRYN MAWR PA 19010 B Philadelphia PA 3/8/1945 d Donald MacCallum & Mary Jane. BFA Moore Coll Of Art & Design Philadelpia PA 1967; MS Neumann Coll Aston PA 1990; MDiv VTS 1994. D 11/12/1994 P 11/1/1995 Bp Allen Lyman Bartlett Jr. m 8/6/1967 John Hartwell Richards. Asst All SS Ch Norristown PA 1999-2004; Incarn H Sacr Epis Ch Drexel Hill PA 1996-1997; The Ch Of The Trin Coatesville PA 1994-1996. Soc Of S Marg.

RICHARDSON, Carolyn Garrett (SanD) 3515 Lomas Serenas Dr., Escondido CA 92029 **Supply Cler Dio San Diego San Diego CA 2007-** B Whittier CA 10/10/1951 d Owen Ben Garrett & Martha Ann. Alliant Intl. U; BA California Wstrn U 1973; Cert USIU San Diego CA 1974; MDiv Claremont TS 2001. D 6/12/1999 P 8/25/2002 Bp Gethin Benwil Hughes. m 5/25/1974 Kenneth Edward Richardson c 2. Long Term Supply S Anne's Epis Ch Oceanside CA 2011; Long Term Supply S Hugh Of Lincoln Mssn Idyllwild CA 2009-2010; Asst R S Barth's Epis Ch Poway CA 2001-2006; Par D Trin Ch Escondido CA 1999-2001. "People Can't Be Replaced," *LivCh*, 1996. AAMFT 2007. Dorothy M. Mulac Bk Awd ETS, Claremont 1998. ecottage@cox.net

RICHARDSON, Christopher Cyril (SO) 8101 Beechmont Ave, Cincinnati OH 45255 **S Andr's Ch Dayton OH 2011-** B Columbus OH 9/24/1984 s Deryck D'arcy Richardson & Nadya Wilson. BS DeVry U; MDiv VTS 2009. D 6/13/2009 P 6/19/2010 Bp Thomas Edward Breidenthal. S Tim's Epis Ch Cincinnati OH 2009-2011. CHRISTOPHERCRICHARDSON@GMAIL.COM

RICHARDSON, David Anthony (Az) 3111 Silver Saddle Dr, Lake Havasu City AZ 86406 **Gr Epis Ch Lake Havasu City AZ 2004-** B Upton Wirral UK 7/10/1941 s Cuthbert James Richardson & Clarice Adelaide. Gnrl Ord Soc of the Sacr Mssn 1966. Trans from Church Of England 10/5/2005 Bp Kirk Stevan Smith. m 9/3/1968 Mary Donnison c 2. david@grace-episcopal.net

RICHARDSON, Ellen Harris (Ga) 112 Island Creek Ln, Savannah GA 31410 B Jacksonville FL 1/5/1952 d John William Harris & Louise Robidere. MDiv EDS; BA Georgia St U 1974; MD Med Coll of Georgia 1987. D 2/9/2008 P 9/27/2008 Bp Henry Irving Louttit. m 8/2/1981 Mark Lewis Richardson c 2. Transitional D Chr Ch Epis Savannah GA 2008. docrichardson@bellsouth.net

RICHARDSON JR, Grady Wade (Ala) 605 Country Club Dr, Gadsden AL 35901 **Calv Ch Oneonta AL 2005-** B New York NY 10/25/1938 s Grady Wade Richardson & Josephine. BA Birmingham-Sthrn Coll 1961; BD VTS 1968. D 6/14/1968 P 5/18/1969 Bp George Mosley Murray. m 8/29/1964 Virginia G Gibbs c 1. S Phil's Ch Ft Payne AL 1998; R Ch Of The Epiph Tunica MS 1990-1998; S Martins-In-The-Pines Ret Comm Birmingham AL 1985-1990; Assoc S Mary's-On-The-Highlands Epis Ch Birmingham AL 1978-1985; R S Jas' Epis Ch Alexander City AL 1975-1978; R Gr Ch Cullman AL 1974-1975; Cur Chr Ch Tuscaloosa AL 1968-1970. Contrib, *Living Ch*, 1994; Contrib, *Selected Sermons*, 1990; Auth, *Congressional Record*, 1980; Auth, *Pulpit Dig*, 1974.

RICHARDSON, James David (Va) 1700 University Ave, Charlottesville VA 22903 **S Paul's Memi Charlottesville VA 2008-** B Berkley CA 8/7/1953 s David Cutting Richardson & Margaret Jean. BA U CA 1975; MDiv CDSP 2000. D 6/10/2000 P 1/13/2001 Bp Jerry Alban Lamb. m 5/20/1989 Lori Korleski. All Souls Par In Berkeley Berkeley CA 2007-2008; Asst Trin Cathd Sacramento CA 2000-2006. Auth, "The Mem'S Speaker: How Willie Brown Held Cntr Stage In California," *Racial & Ethnic Politics In California*, 1998; Auth, "Willie Brown: A Biography," U CA, 1996; Auth, "California Political Almanac," California Journ Press. Fllshp Of Reconcilliation 2002; Save Hetch Hetchy Soc 1998. richardson@trinitycathedral.org

RICHARDSON, Janet Beverly (Ind) 4746 N County Road 250 W, Connersville IN 47331 **P Dio Indianapolis Indianapolis IN 2008-** B Rochester NY 8/18/1946 d Robert Thomas Hudson & Betty June. BS SUNY 1968; AA Finger Lakes Cmnty Coll 1981; MDiv Earlham Sch of Rel 1993. D 6/24/1992 P 1/17/1993 Bp Edward Witker Jones. m 8/9/1975 Marcus Richardson c 1. Dio Indianapolis Indianapolis IN 1999-2008; P S Jas Ch New Castle IN 1999-2008; Trin Ch Connersville IN 1999-2003; P Trin Ch Connersville IN 1993-1998; P Trin Ch Connersville IN 1993-1998; D Trin Ch Connersville IN 1992-1993. pasterjrich@yahoo.com

RICHARDSON, Jeffrey Roy (SC) 113 E Church St, Kingstree SC 29556 **Vic S Alb's Ch Kingstree SC 2005-; Vic S Steph's Ch S Steph SC 2005-** B Bethesda MD 1/21/1955 BA Wofford Coll 1977; MDiv Nash 2005. D 6/11/2005 P 12/7/2005 Bp Edward Lloyd Salmon Jr. m 7/4/1981 Patricia C Corbett c 4. CBS 2004; SocMary 2003. prichardson29133@yahoo.com

RICHARDSON JR, John Dowland (CGC) 19 Gaywood Circle, Birmingham AL 35213 B Tampa FL 6/17/1962 s Harold Leroy Richardson & Betty Jean. BS U of Alabama 1983; MDiv STUSo 1993; DMin Trin Evang DS Deerfield IL 1999. D 6/5/1993 Bp Furman Stough P 12/11/1993 Bp Robert Oran Miller. m 12/19/2003 Kristen Jane Richardson c 2. H Nativ Epis Ch Panama City FL 1996-2003; Asst. R S Mk's Ch Geneva IL 1994-1996; Cur S Mary's-On-The-Highlands Epis Ch Birmingham AL 1993-1994. JOHNRICHARDSON@BELLSOUTH.NET

RICHARDSON, John Marshall (WMo) 23405 S Waverly Rd, Spring Hill KS 66083 **D S Ptr's Ch Harrisonville MO 1999-** B Little Rock AR 3/18/1949 s William Sims Richardson & Elizabeth Ann. BS Missouri Wstrn St U 1973. D 2/14/1998 Bp John Clark Buchanan. m 8/9/1970 Barbara Diane Richardson. Ord Of S Lk.

RICHARDSON, Jon Mark (Nwk) 200 Main St, Chatham NJ 07928 **S Paul's Ch In Bergen Jersey City NJ 2010-** B Lake Charles LA 10/11/1978 s Charles Gerald Richardson & Carolyn Ann D. BGS LSU 2004; MDiv Drew U 2007. D 6/6/2009 P 12/12/2009 Bp Mark M Beckwith. S Paul's Epis Ch Chatham NJ 2009-2010; Dir of Yth & Fam Mnstry S Ptr's Ch Morristown NJ 2007-2009. jon5191@yahoo.com

RICHARDSON, Kristin Earhart (Nev) 1696 Stony Ridge Road, Eugene OR 97405 **Died 5/7/2010** B Hollywood CA 10/31/1940 d Joseph S Earhart & Katherine S. BA U of Oregon 1962; MDiv SWTS 1990. D 6/24/1990 Bp Andrew Hedtler Fairfield P 2/2/1991 Bp Cabell Tennis.

RICHARDSON, Marcia Ann Kelley (Me) 6 Jewett Cove Rd, Westport Is ME 04578 **D S Phil's Ch Wiscasset ME 1998-** B Natick MA 2/7/1939 d Wingate Barnes Kelley & Marguerite. U of Connecticut 1958; AS Universit Of Maine Augusta ME 1989. D 8/29/1998 Bp Chilton Abbie Richardson Knudsen. m 6/6/1959 George Dewey Richardson c 4.

RICHARDSON, Mary (SanD) 5833 College Ave, San Diego CA 92120 **Cathd Ch Of S Paul San Diego CA 2009-; Chapl Dio Los Angeles Los Angeles CA 2001-** B Leon MX 1/4/1952 d Jose Luis Moreno & Yolanda. ETSBH 1999. D 4/26/2002 Bp Joseph Jon Bruno P 2/13/2005 Bp Gethin Benwil Hughes. m 7/11/1997 Scott Eric Richardson. Dio San Diego San Diego CA 2003-2008; Epis Chapl Los Angeles CA 2002-2003.

RICHARDSON, Melvin Ashley (Vt) 1010 Wintergreen Ln, Charlottesville VA 22903 **Died 7/19/2011** B Barre VT 11/19/1940 s Elwin Andrew Richardson & Elizabeth Louise. Cert Bangor TS 1977. D 6/9/1977 P 12/9/1977 Bp Robert Shaw Kerr. melrichardson@adelphia.net

RICHARDSON, Michael William (Colo) 16181 Parkside Dr, Parker CO 80134 **R S Matt's Parker CO 2005-** B Portales NM 3/5/1957 s William Richard Richardson & Bennie Ruth. Acadia U 1978; BA/NHS Metropltn St Coll of Denver 1994; MDiv Epis TS of The SW 1997. D 6/7/1997 P 12/27/1997 Bp William Jerry Winterrowd. m 6/15/1991 Jo Ellen R Randolph c 2. Ch Of Our Sav Colorado Sprg CO 1997-2004. michaelwmr@comcast.net

RICHARDSON, Saundra Denise (Mich) 8850 Woodward Ave, Detroit MI 48202 B Petersburg VA 11/11/1948 d James Peter Richardson & Louella

R

Jeanette. AA Morristown Coll Morristown TN 1968; BS Clark Atlanta U 1970; MDiv VTS 1989. D 6/18/1989 P 4/29/1990 Bp William Evan Sanders. Admin Asst Chr Ch Detroit MI 2007-2010; P-in-c S Matt's And S Jos's Detroit MI 2002-2006; Coordntr Corp Dio Michigan Detroit MI 1995-2002; Prog Assoc Cornerstone Epis Ch Cntr New York NY 1992-1995; Assoc S Jas Ch New York NY 1992-1995; ECF Inc New York NY 1992-1994; Dio E Tennessee Knoxville TN 1990-1991; Vic S Lk's Ch Knoxville TN 1990-1991; D-In-Trng S Jn's Epis Cathd Knoxville TN 1989-1990. Auth, "Theologies In Dialogue," *Va Sem Journ*, 1989; Auth, "Black Amer Theol," *Wit*, 1988. Scer. saundrarichardsn@aol.com

RICHARDSON, Scott Eric (SanD) 2728 6th Ave, San Diego CA 92103 **Dn Cathd Ch Of S Paul San Diego CA 2003-** B Berkeley CA 7/27/1955 s Douglas Kent Richardson & Gladys. BA U CA Santa Barbara 1977; MDiv GTS 1989. D 6/11/1989 P 1/13/1990 Bp Frederick Houk Borsch. m 7/11/1997 Mary Richardson. Assoc All SS Ch Pasadena CA 1998-2003; R S Mary's Par Lompoc CA 1992-1998; Assoc S Wilfrid Of York Epis Ch Huntington Bch CA 1989-1992. richardson@stpaulcathedral.org

RICHARDSON, Susan (NJ) 20 N American St, Philadelphia PA 19106 **Gr-S Paul's Ch Mercerville NJ 2010-** B Augusta GA 9/18/1961 PhD Indiana U 1997; MDiv PrTS 2004; CAS VTS 2006. D 6/3/2006 P 12/9/2006 Bp George Edward Councell. c 1. Asst Min Chr Ch Philadelphia Philadelphia PA 2006-2010. susan.richardson1@verizon.net

RICHARDSON, Warren Edward (CFla) 2202 Winnebago Trl, Fern Park FL 32730 B Evanston IL 1/5/1928 s Edward Wolf Richardson & Ethel Telfer. BS NWU 1950; MDiv SWTS 1961. D 6/24/1961 Bp Charles L Street P 12/23/1961 Bp Gerald Francis Burrill. m 4/5/1975 Pamela A Holly c 2. S Mich's Ch Orlando FL 1997-1998; Ch Of The Mssh Winter Garden FL 1996; S Eliz's Epis Ch Sebastian FL 1994-1995; The Ch Of S Lk And S Ptr S Cloud FL 1992-1993; Int Dio Ohio Cleveland OH 1973-1978; R H Trin Ch Skokie IL 1963-1967; P-in-c S Bon Ch Tinley Pk IL 1961-1963. Auth, "Orlando Sentinel". Cn Dio Cntrl Florida 2000. pwrich6978@aol.com

RICHARDSON, W(illiam) Ramsey (Va) 2150 Whippoorwill Rd, Charlottesville VA 22901 B Charleston WV 1/24/1931 s Jewell Burgess Richardson & Zelema Miriam. BA Hampden-Sydney Coll 1952; Med U of Virginia 1960; MDiv VTS 1963. D 6/20/1963 P 6/24/1964 Bp William Henry Marmion. m 5/27/1967 Emily Howard Tongue c 3. Int S Steph's Epis Ch Forest VA 1997-1998; Int Chr Epis Ch Gordonsville VA 1996-1997; Int S Jn's Epis Ch Waynesboro VA 1995-1996; Int S Thos Epis Ch Orange VA 1993-1994; R Chr Epis Ch Charlottesville VA 1978-1993; R Ch Of The Redeem Midlothian VA 1966-1978; Asst S Paul's Epis Ch Lynchburg VA 1963-1966. wramseyr@embarqmail.com

RICHARDSON, Winfield Walter (Pa) 253 W Beidler Rd, King Of Prussia PA 19406 **Died 10/9/2010** B New York NY 6/13/1930 s William Landstreet Richardson & Ruth Lucielle. BS VPI 1959; Dio NJ Trng 1985. D 4/13/1985 Bp George Phelps Mellick Belshaw. m 5/17/1952 Diana Dorothy Woodall c 3. Asst Sprtl Dir (Curs) 1997-1997; Curs 1997-2001; KAIROS 2002-2003; Ord of S Lk 1985. ussameb55@verizon.net

RICHARDSON, W Mark (Cal) 175 9th Ave, New York NY 10011 **CDSP Berkeley CA 2010-** B Eugene OR 5/28/1949 s William Judson Richardson & Audrey Marie. BA U of Oregon 1971; MDiv PrTS 1975; PhD Grad Theol Un 1990. D 6/3/1978 P 12/10/1978 Bp Paul Moore Jr. m 6/9/1984 Brenda L Lane c 2. The GTS New York NY 1999-2010; Trin Educ Fund New York NY 1986-1990; Assoc Trin Par Menlo Pk CA 1984-1986; Trin Par Menlo Pk CA 1982; Cur Ch Of The Ascen New York NY 1978-1981. Stetson Epis Ch Fell. Post-Doc Awd Sir Jn Templeton Fndt. blr256@nyu.edu

RICHAUD III, Reynold Hobson (Tenn) 206 Trahern Ln, Clarksville TN 37040 **Camp Gailor Maxon Bd Dio Tennessee Nashville TN 2011-; COM Dio Tennessee Nashville TN 2001-; R Trin Ch Clarksville TN 2001-** B Midland TX 4/28/1950 s Reynold Hobson Richaud & Elizabeth Rosebud. BA LSU/New Orleans 1985; MDiv STUSo 1993. D 6/12/1993 Bp Robert Jefferson Hargrove Jr P 4/1/1994 Bp Bertram Nelson Herlong. m 8/12/1972 Janet N Nettles c 1. Vic S Matt's Epis Ch McMinnville TN 1995-2001; S Mich's Epis Ch And U Cookeville TN 1995; D-in-Trng S Geo's Ch Nashville TN 1993-1994. mjrichaud@gmail.com

RICHEY, Donald Delose (Ct) 99 Willowbrook Rd, Cromwell CT 06416 **Chr Ch Millville NJ 2005-** B Greenwich CT 4/18/1961 s Donald D Richey & Diana R. D 12/9/2000 Bp Andrew Donnan Smith. m 7/5/1992 Gail McNeil c 3. Dio Connecticut Hartford CT 2005-2010. DONALD.RICHEY@SNAT.NET

RICHEY, Leon Eugene (O) 2727 Barrington Dr, Toledo OH 43606 B Dresden OH 9/1/1933 s George Henry Richey & Mabel Bell. BA Ohio Wesl 1955; BD Garrett Evang TS 1959; MDiv Garrett Evang TS 1972. D 6/17/1967 Bp Nelson Marigold Burroughs P 12/17/1967 Bp John Harris Burt. m 5/29/1955 Mona Jean Lusetti c 3. P-in-c S Paul's Ch Oregon OH 1996-2006; Pstrl Assoc Trin Ch Toledo OH 1993-1995; Int Gr Ch Defiance OH 1990-1992; Plnng Cmsn Dio Ohio Cleveland OH 1979-1982; R S Mk's Epis Ch Toledo OH 1976-1989; R Gr Ch Cleveland OH 1972-1976; Vic S Tim's Ch Macedonia OH 1969-1976. Assn S Barn Bro; Intl Ord of S Lk. DD Intl Bible Sem 1984. bookworm933@hotmail.com

RICHMOND III, Allen Pierce (Ak) 2602 Glacier St, Anchorage AK 99508 B Hanover NH 8/24/1921 s Allen P Richmond & Constance F. BS U of New Hampshire 1944; MS NYU 1955. D 6/24/1973 P 11/12/1972 Bp William J Gordon Jr. m 7/27/1944 Veva P Richmond. Asst S Matt's Epis Ch Fairbanks AK 1979-1989; Asst S Christophers Ch Anchorage AK 1974-1979.

RICHMOND, John David (Spr) 4105 S Lafayette Ave, Bartonville IL 61607 **Supply P Trin Ch Lincoln IL 2010-; Supply P Dio Springfield Springfield IL 2001-** B Lincoln NE 7/11/1952 s Robert William Richmond & Mary Belle. BA SMU 1974; MS U IL 1979; MDiv Nash 1985; U IL 1995. D 6/11/1985 P 12/13/1985 Bp Richard Frank Grein. m 8/1/1992 Barbara Ellen Bennett c 1. Supply P S Matt's Epis Ch Bloomington IL 2007-2009; Supply P All SS Ch Morton IL 2006-2007; Supply P S Paul's Epis Ch Pekin IL 2001-2002; Supply P Dio Texas Houston TX 1995-2001; Supply P Dio Springfield Springfield IL 1994-1995; R Chr The King Epis Ch Normal IL 1987-1993; Asst S Mich And All Ang Ch Mssn KS 1985-1986; Cur S Thos The Apos Ch Overland Pk KS 1985-1986. Auth, "Hard Times for These Times," *Publ Libraries*, Publ Libr Assn, 2003. jdr1952@gmail.com

RICHMOND, Seth Gunther (Colo) 460 Prospector Ln, Estes Park CO 80517 **R S Barth's Ch Estes Pk CO 2009-** B Des Moines IA 1/19/1960 s Thomas Edwin Richmond & Joanne. BS Trevecca Nazarene U 1985; Cert Nash 1990; MDiv Trin Evang DS Deerfield IL 1990. D 6/16/1990 P 12/1/1990 Bp Frank Tracy Griswold III. m 8/12/1989 Sally Carleton Mary Hughes c 1. S Anne's Ch De Pere WI 2001-2009; Ch Of The Gd Shpd Rangeley ME 1993-2000; Assoc Trin Epis Ch Oshkosh WI 1990-1993. Auth, "Living Ch". stannes@sbcglobal.net

RICHMOND, Susan Odenwald (Mass) 197 8th St Apt 801, Charlestown MA 02129 B Saint Paul MN 3/29/1949 d Harold Wesley Odenwald & Elaine Miller. BA U NC 1971; MDiv Ya Berk 1996. D 6/1/1996 P 12/7/1996 Bp Richard Frank Grein. m 8/26/1972 Christopher Richmond c 2. Int P S Jas' Epis Ch Cambridge MA 2007-2008; Int P S Andr's Ch Framingham MA 2004-2007; Int P Trin Ch Topsfield MA 2002-2003; Asst Old No Chr Ch Boston MA 2001-2002; Int P S Andr's Ch Brewster NY 1999-2000; Asst S Barn Ch Irvington on Hudson NY 1996-1999. sorichmond@comcast.net

RICHNOW, Douglas Wayne (Tex) 4014 Meadow Lake Ln, Houston TX 77027 **Sr. Assoc R S Jn The Div Houston TX 2003-** B Pasadena TX 11/18/1946 s James Douglas Richnow & Mary Elizabeth. BS U of Texas 1970; MDiv VTS 1992; DMin Austin Presb TS 1999. D 6/27/1992 Bp Maurice Manuel Benitez P 1/21/1993 Bp William Jackson Cox. m 8/23/1980 Angela E Epley c 3. R S Lk's Epis Ch Birmingham AL 2001-2002; Sr. Assoc R S Jn The Div Houston TX 1995-2001; Vic Chr Epis Ch Cedar Pk TX 1994-1995; Assoc R S Matt's Ch Austin TX 1992-1994. Ord of St. Lazarus of Jerusalem 2004. drichnow@sjd.org

RICHTER, Amy Elizabeth (Md) 4 E University Pkwy, Baltimore MD 21218 **R S Anne's Par Annapolis MD 2009-** B Scarborough ON CA 9/14/1966 d George John Richter & Patricia. BA Valparaiso U 1987; MTS Harvard DS 1989; MDiv PrTS 1993; CAS GTS 1994; PhD Marq 2010. D 6/4/1994 P 5/27/1995 Bp Allen Lyman Bartlett Jr. m 8/26/1990 Joseph Samuel Pagano. Mssnr for Lifelong Chr Formation Dio Maryland Baltimore MD 2006-2009; R S Paul's Ch Milwaukee WI 2000-2006; Asst R S Chrys's Ch Chicago IL 1995-2000; Asst Min The Epis Ch Of The Adv Kennett Sq PA 1994-1995. Auth, "Opening Our Eyes," *Creative Styles Of Preaching*, Westminster Jn Knox Press, 2000. SBL 2008. arichter@stannes-annapolis.org

RICHTER, William Thompson (Miss) 1110 Friar Tuck Road, Starkville MS 39759 **Died 3/10/2011** B Savannah GA 1/30/1924 s Arthur Hugo Richter & Margaret. BA U So 1949; LTh STUSo 1969. D 6/24/1969 P 5/7/1970 Bp John M Allin. m 3/16/2011 Sherley Jones Richter c 2. MS/LA Mnstrl Allnce - Natchez, MS; Starkville Mnstrl Assn; U Common Mnstry. sherleyr@bellsouth.net

RICHTER JR, William Thompson (Tex) 2929 Woodland Hills Dr, Kingwood TX 77339 **Ch Of The Gd Shpd Kingwood TX 2009-** B Greenwood MS 10/4/1957 s William Thompson Richter & Sherley. BA Millsaps Coll 1979, MS VPI 1986; MDiv STUSo 1995. D 6/17/1995 P 3/2/1996 Bp Alfred Clark Marble Jr. m 12/14/1979 Susan Thames c 1. R S Simon's On The Sound Ft Walton Bch FL 2004-2009; S Andr's Cathd Jackson MS 1995-2004. wtrstr@embarqmail.com

RICK II, John William (Ct) 625 S St Andrews Pl, Los Angeles CA 90005 B Saint Louis MO 6/15/1941 s John William Rick & M Arline. BA Washington U 1965; MBA U of Virginia 1967; MDiv Yale DS 1974. D 6/22/1974 Bp George Leslie Cadigan P 5/1/1975 Bp Joseph Warren Hutchens. Gr Epis Ch Alexandria VA 1996-1997; S Jas Par Los Angeles CA 1994-1995; The Epis Ch Of Beth-By-The-Sea Palm Bch FL 1994; Asst The Ch Of The Adv Boston MA 1979-1980; Cur Chr Ch Greenwich CT 1974-1975. Omicron Delta Kappa; Outstanding Young Men Amer; Who'S Who In Rel.

RICKARD, Robert Burney (At) 1228 Whitlock Ridge Dr Sw, Marietta GA 30064 B Memphis TN 4/22/1934 s Carroll Evan Rickard & Rubye Constance.

BD STUSo; BA SW At Memphis. D 6/24/1959 Bp Theodore N Barth P 6/1/1960 Bp John Vander Horst. m 3/4/1981 Ruth Ann Rickard. S Clem's Epis Ch Canton GA 1989-1996; Asst S Dunst's Epis Ch Atlanta GA 1983-1988; Assoc R Ch Of Our Sav Washington DC 1962-1965; Vic Chr Ch Brownsville TN 1960-1962; Cur Chr Ch Cathd Nashville TN 1959-1960. Key To City Washington 1965. frbob@mindspring.com

RICKARDS JR, Joseph A (Ind) Spring Mills, 109 Jamestown Dr, Falling Waters WV 25419 B Raleigh NC 5/12/1927 s Joseph Asher Rickards & Emily A. BS W Virginia U 1950; BD Bex 1959. D 6/11/1959 P 12/19/1959 Bp Wilburn Camrock Campbell. m 3/24/1951 Nancy Scott c 3. R S Steph's Ch Terre Haute IN 1972-1992; R S Steph's Epis Ch Beckley WV 1960-1972; Asst S Jn's Epis Ch Charleston WV 1959-1960. Fllshp Coll of Preachers 1973. rickardssm@aol.com

RICKARDS, Reese Stanley (Eas) 115 Nentego Dr, Fruitland MD 21826 B Johnstown NY 11/10/1930 s Harold D Rickards & Lyle. Chicago Deacons Sch; OH SU; SWTS; Worcester Jr Coll. D 9/16/1972 Bp James Winchester Montgomery. m 10/31/1953 Jean M Kilmer c 4. MC, GC, 2006 Ecusa / Mssn Personl New York NY 2011; Ass't to Bp Dio Easton Easton MD 2002-2005; Cmncatn Off Dio Easton Easton MD 1995-2002; Ret S Alb's Epis Ch Salisbury MD 1993-2000; Asst D Ch Of The H Comm Maywood IL 1989-1992; Asst D S Greg's Epis Ch Deerfield IL 1986-1988; Asst D S Mart's Ch Des Plaines IL 1975-1986; D Dio Chicago Chicago IL 1972-1974. ECom Assn 1999. reeserickards@gmail.com

✠ **RICKEL, Rt Rev Gregory Harold** (Oly) 3209 42nd Ave SW, Seattle WA 98116 **Bp Dio Olympia Seattle WA 2007-; Bd Trst Epis TS Of The SW Austin TX 2007-** B Omaha NE 6/27/1963 s Morris Edwin Rickel & Linda Mae. BA U of Arkansas 1984; MA U of Arkansas 1987; MA U of Arkansas 1993; MDiv Epis TS of The SW 1996; DMin STUSo 2002. D 7/8/1996 P 1/18/1997 Bp Larry Earl Maze Con 9/15/2007 for Oly. m 5/26/1984 Martha R Porter c 1. R S Jas Ch Austin TX 2001-2007; Vic S Ptr's Ch Conway AR 1996-2001. *Living w Money (included Essay)*, Morehouse, 2002. D.Div (Hon) Sem of the SW 2007. ghrickel@gmail.com

RICKENBAKER, Thomas Michele (EC) Box 548, Edenton NC 27932 **R S Paul's Epis Ch Edenton NC 1998-** B Cheyenne WY 1/26/1956 s Arthur Lloyd Rickenbaker & Julia Alice. BA U of So Carolina 1978; MDiv VTS 1983; Ldrshp Acad for New Directions 1984. D 6/11/1983 P 5/12/1984 Bp William Arthur Beckham. m 6/18/1994 Cynthia Gosnell c 3. Dn, Albemarle Dnry Dio E Carolina Kinston NC 2009-2011; COM Dio E Carolina Kinston NC 2000-2003; Police Chapl Dio E Carolina Kinston NC 1999-2010; Dio Upper So Carolina Columbia SC 1996-1998; Police Chapl Dio Upper So Carolina Columbia SC 1996-1998; Dioc Coun Dio Upper So Carolina Columbia SC 1995-1998; Dn Estrn Deanry Dio Upper So Carolina Columbia SC 1993-1998; Chair Com on Ords Dio Upper So Carolina Columbia SC 1993-1995; Trst Dio Upper So Carolina Columbia SC 1991-1992; Dio Upper So Carolina Columbia SC 1989-1990; Evang Consult Dio Upper So Carolina Columbia SC 1988-1998; Stndg Com Dio Upper So Carolina Columbia SC 1988-1995; S Marg's Epis Ch Boiling Sprg SC 1986-1998; New Ch Growth & Dvlpmt Cmsn Dio Upper So Carolina Columbia SC 1985-1998; COM Dio Upper So Carolina Columbia SC 1985-1995; COM Dio Upper So Carolina Columbia SC 1985-1995; Chair Dioc Yth Mnstrs Dio Upper So Carolina Columbia SC 1985-1987; Dioc Coun Dio Upper So Carolina Columbia SC 1985-1987; Dioc Coun Dio Upper So Carolina Columbia SC 1985-1987; No Spartanburg Epis Mssn Boiling Spgs SC 1984-1985; Asst S Chris's Ch Spartanburg SC 1983-1984. Police Chapl Assn 1994-2009. stpaulsedenton@embarqmail.com

RICKETT, Catherine Tatem (Miss) St. Stephen's Episcopal Church, P.O. Box 761, Columbia MS 39429 **Vic S Steph's Ch Columbia MS 2008-** B Pittsfield MA 4/15/1961 d William Arthur Tatem & Sandra Lou. BA Franklin & Marshall Coll 1983; MDiv STUSo 2008. D 6/7/2008 P 12/14/2008 Bp Duncan Montgomery Gray III. m 9/18/1993 David Rickett. P-in-c S Eliz's Mssn Collins MS 2008-2010. Auth, "Recon," *Recon and Healing*, The Epis Preaching Fndt, 2007; Bk Revs, "Ladies Aux," *Tuesday Morning*, Rev. Dr. Susanna Metz, 2007. Bp Leopoldo Alard Prize for Excellence in Liturg Readin U So TS 2008. revcat08@gmail.com

RICKETTS, Linda Harriet (Mass) 20211 Huebner Rd Unit 223, San Antonio TX 78258 B Haverhill MA 3/27/1948 d Kenneth Ross & Mary Anna. BSE U of Arkansas 1970; MDiv VTS 1988. D 6/11/1988 P 12/14/1988 Bp John Thomas Walker. c 1. Assoc Par Of Chr Ch Andover MA 1998-2004; Dio Wstrn Massachusetts Springfield MA 1988-1998; Vic S Andr's Ch Turners Falls MA 1988-1998; Assoc S Jas' Ch Greenfield MA 1988-1998. lindaricketts@juno.com

RICKETTS, Marcia Carole Couey (NwT) 133 Olivias Ct, Tuscola TX 79562 **D Ch Of The Heav Rest Abilene TX 2001-** B Mobile AL 12/27/1955 d Freddie Eugene Couey & Marion Mahone. BA Sam Houston St U 1976; BBA Agape Sem of Jesus Chr 1981. D 10/28/2001 Bp C(harles) Wallis Ohl. m 12/18/1976 Robert William Ricketts c 2.

RICKETTS, Nancy Lee (Tex) 1500 N Capital of Texas Hwy, Austin TX 78746 B Oklahoma City OK 7/11/1948 d Lee Allen Overman & Marian Bernice. BA Oklahoma St U 1970; JD U of Texas Sch of Law 1973; MDiv Epis TS Of The SW 2008. D 6/19/2010 Bp C(harles) Andrew Doyle. m 12/30/1972 Philip Ricketts c 1. noricketts@aol.com

RICKEY, David (Cal) 420 29th St, San Francisco CA 94131 **Chapl Epis Sr Communities Walnut Creek CA 1997-; R S Ptr's Epis Ch San Francisco CA 1997-** B Buffalo NY 7/29/1946 s John Wallace Rickey & Dorothy. BA Westminster Coll 1968; MDiv UTS 1972; Cert Blanton-Peale Grad Inst 1977. D 6/12/1971 Bp Leland Stark P 4/8/1972 Bp George E Rath. m 11/10/2009 Aldemar A Aglanao. P-in-c S Paul's And Trin Par Tivoli NY 1993-1995; Assoc The Ch of S Ign of Antioch New York NY 1984-1987; P-in-c S Steph's Ch Jersey City NJ 1975-1984; Cur Gr Ch Nutley NJ 1972-1974. davidrickey@comcast.net

RICO, Bayani Depra (NCal) 2420 Tuolumne St, Vallejo CA 94589 **Co-Chair, Cmsn For Intercultural Mnstry Dio Nthrn California Sacramento CA 2008-; R Ch Of The Ascen Vallejo CA 2007-** B Bacolod City Phil 11/24/1951 s Federico R Rico & Merenciana D. AA Trin 1969; BTh St Andr's TS 1973; MDiv St Andr's TS 1993. Trans from Philippine Independent Church 11/24/2009 Bp Barry Leigh Beisner. m 3/22/1977 Bethsaida Gregorio c 4. rector_ascension@sbcglobal.net

RIDDER, John W (RG) 820 Melinda Ln, Las Vegas NM 87701 **Died 1/16/2011** B Bayonne NJ 6/17/1923 s John Edward Ridder & Edith Medora. BA Syr 1944; MDiv Bex 1957. D 5/1/1957 P 12/15/1957 Bp Nelson Marigold Burroughs. c 3. ridderlv@cybermesa.com

RIDDICK, Daniel Howison (Vt) 240 Blackwater Ridge Ln, Glade Hill VA 24092 B Lynchburg VA 12/12/1941 s Joseph Henry Riddick & Nancy. BA Duke 1963; MD Duke 1967; PhD Duke 1969. D 11/16/1969 Bp Angus Dun P 11/1/1970 Bp William Foreman Creighton. m 6/9/1963 Louisa Riddick c 2. Assoc R Calv Ch Underhill VT 1994-1997; R S Jn's In The Mountains Stowe VT 1986-1991; Asst Trin Epis Ch Collinsville CT 1979-1985; Asst S Jos's Ch Durham NC 1971-1979. abbariddick@gmail.com

RIDDLE III, Charles Morton (SVa) 1321 Fearrington Post, Fearrington Village NC 27312 **Ch Of The Epiph Danville VA 2000-** B Danville VA 12/15/1934 s Charles Morton Riddle & Mildred Bethel. BA U of Virginia 1957; BD VTS 1963; Sch Cont Educ 1970; London TS 1982; S Geo's Coll Jerusalem IL 1982; S Geo's Coll Jerusalem IL 1985; DMin VTS 1985. D 6/24/1963 P 6/1/1964 Bp David Shepherd Rose. c 3. Int S Paul's Ch Wilkesboro NC 2003-2004; Int The Epis Ch Of Gd Shpd Asheboro NC 1999-2000; Int Ch Of The H Comf Charlotte NC 1997-1999; Int S Mich's Ch Raleigh NC 1995-1997; Int S Jn's Epis Ch Charlotte NC 1994-1995; Int S Paul's Epis Ch Winston Salem NC 1992-1994; Int Chr Ch New Bern NC 1991-1992; Chair - COM Dio W Tennessee Memphis TN 1990-1991; R Gr - S Lk's Ch Memphis TN 1986-1991; R Estrn Shore Chap Virginia Bch VA 1971-1986; R Calv Ch Tarboro NC 1966-1971; Cur Trin Ch Portsmouth VA 1963-1966. cmredr@earthlink.net

RIDDLE, Hill Carter (La) 1515 Robert St, New Orleans LA 70115 B Danville VA 6/29/1936 s Charles Morton Riddle & Mildred Hill. BA U of Virginia 1958; MDiv VTS 1964; DD VTS 1991. D 6/1/1964 Bp George P Gunn P 5/23/1965 Bp David Shepherd Rose. m 8/25/1962 Anne M Clement c 3. Int S Paul's Ch New Orleans LA 2008; Ch Of The Trsfg Silver Sprg MD 2000-2004; Dep GC Dio Louisiana Baton Rouge LA 1991-1994; R Trin Ch New Orleans LA 1984-2003; Dep GC Dio Louisiana Baton Rouge LA 1979-1982; Exec Bd Dio SW Virginia Roanoke VA 1976-1978; R Chr Epis Ch Roanoke VA 1974-1984; Exec Bd Dio Virginia Richmond VA 1971-1974; R Ch Of S Jas The Less Ashland VA 1968-1974; Asst to R S Jn's Ch Hampton VA 1964-1968. "Bloom in Your Season," *Bloom in Your Season*, self, 2004. Hon DD VTS Alexandria VA 1991. hillriddle@gmail.com

RIDDLE, Jennifer Lynne (Ala) 530 Hurst Rd, Odenville AL 35120 **Chapl S Martins-In-The-Pines Ret Comm Birmingham AL 2010-** B Pell City AL 2/26/1965 d Frank Hubert Riddle & Linda Lue. BS Judson Coll 1986; MDiv New Orleans Bapt TS 1990; DAS VTS 2001. D 5/20/2001 P 12/11/2001 Bp Henry Nutt Parsley Jr. Asst R Ch Of The Epiph Guntersville AL 2001-2010. mojenn93@gmail.com

RIDEOUT, Robert Blanchard (SO) 7121 Muirfield Dr., Dublin OH 43017 **D S Pat's Epis Ch Dublin OH 2009-** B Ithaca NY 5/14/1941 s Blanchard Livingstone Rideout & Anne Louise. BA Wesl 1963; MPA Pr 1969. D 6/13/2009 Bp Thomas Edward Breidenthal. m 5/9/1970 Martha S George c 2. robrideout@sbcglobal.net

RIDER, David M (NY) 11 Suzanne Ln, Chappaqua NY 10514 **Pres and Exec Dir Seamens Ch Inst Income New York NY 2007-** B South Bend IN 12/7/1954 s Jack Z Rider & Catherine V. BA Carleton Coll 1977; MDiv UTS 1980; Cert Advncd CPE 1982; Cert Washington Sch of Psych 1988; STM GTS 1989; Cert Harv 1999; STM UTS 2001. D 6/24/1980 P 3/25/1981 Bp Edward Witker Jones. m 5/31/1980 Jacqueline Haines c 2. S Mk's Ch New Canaan CT 2004-2007; P-in-c Gr Epis Ch New York NY 2001-2004; S Mk's Epis Ch Yonkers NY 2000; Ch Pension Fund New York NY 1992-2002; Sr VP The CPG New York NY 1992-2002; Pstr Counslg Cntr Richmond VA 1991; Int Ch Of The Ascen Gaithersburg MD 1989-1991; VTS Alexandria VA 1989; Int S Dunst's Epis Ch Beth MD 1988-1989; Assoc R S Jn's Ch Chevy Chase MD

1982-1987; Asst S Alb's Ch Indianapolis IN 1980-1981. AAPC. Hon Cn Cathd of S Jas Nthrn Indiana 1996. drider@seamenschurch.org

RIDER, Joseph Frank (CFla) 400 18th St, E 4, Vero Beach FL 32960 B Fort Worth TX 8/21/1948 s Joseph V Rider & Jean May. Cert GTS 1974; M.Ed. Florida Atlantic U 2000. D 6/5/1974 P 12/7/1974 Bp Theodore H McCrea. R S Jn The Div Epis Ch Burlington WI 1979-1986; Asst S Paul's Ch Milwaukee WI 1978-1979; Assoc Gr Ch Madison WI 1976-1977; Cur S Alb's Epis Ch Arlington TX 1975-1976; Asst S Andr's Ch Grand Prairie TX 1974-1975. joerider@ekit.com

RIDER, Mary Dawn (SC) 710 Main St, Conway SC 29526 B Drevel Hill PA 9/18/1960 d Lewis F Herring & Mary Judith. BS S Leo U 1993. D 9/8/2007 Bp Edward Lloyd Salmon Jr. m 2/21/1983 Lewis Rider c 2. emdee@sccoast.net

RIDER, Paul G (Minn) 401 S 1st St Unit 610, Minneapolis MN 55401 **S Jn's Epis Ch Mankato MN 2004-** B Tarrytown NY 8/12/1957 s Franklin Lee Rider & Polly Anna. BA U of Arkansas 1981; MA U of Arkansas 1985; MDiv Nash 1989. D 6/29/1989 P 2/1/1990 Bp Craig Barry Anderson. All SS Ch Minot ND 1993-2000; R S Jas Epis Ch Belle Fourche SD 1989-1993; R S Thos Epis Ch Sturgis SD 1989-1993.

RIDER, Wm Blake (NY) 20 Carroll St, Poughkeepsie NY 12601 **R Chr Ch Poughkeepsie NY 2006-** B Nowata OK 1/13/1955 s Will Rogers Rider & Norma Louise. BA/BS Oral Roberts U 1978; MDiv VTS 2004. D 6/12/2004 P 12/6/2004 Bp Don Adger Wimberly. Cn Chr Ch Cathd Houston TX 2004-2006. wmblakerider@gmail.com

RIDGE, Charles Searls (Oly) 2658 48th Ave SW, Seattle WA 98116 **P-in-c S Matt Ch Tacoma WA 2010-** B Okanogan WA 5/10/1936 s Raymond Herbert Ridge & Estelle. BA Colorado Coll 1958; STB GTS 1961; DMin SMU 1979. D 6/29/1961 Bp William F Lewis P 5/25/1962 Bp John Brooke Mosley. m 2/21/1983 Courtney Searls c 2. Assoc S Paul's Ch Seattle WA 2008-2011; Bd Dir Dio Olympia Seattle WA 1997-2001; Chap of S Martha and S Mary of Bethany Seattle WA 1993-1996; R Ch Of The Ascen Seattle WA 1990-2001; R Trin Ch Matawan NJ 1979-1990; Hisp Cmsn Dio New Jersey Trenton NJ 1979-1988; Dio The Dominican Republic (Iglesia Epis Dominicana) 100 Airport AvVenice FL 1970-1979; Vic Iglesia Epis Epifania Santo Domingo Di DO 1970-1977; R S Andr's Epis Ch Nogales AZ 1964-1970; Asst Chr Ch Dover DE 1961-1964. Auth, "Cultural Discernment As Imperative In Mssn: A Proposal," 1979. Benedictine Oblate 2001. charlesridge@gmail.com

RIDGILL, Michael Earl (SC) 1121 Pine Lake Dr, Hartsville SC 29550 **R S Barth's Epis Ch Hartsville SC 2006-** B Manning SC 1/26/1963 s Herman Marion Ridgill & Mary Ellen. BA U of So Carolina 1987; JD U of So Carolina 1992; MDiv TESM 2002. D 6/2/2002 P 12/17/2002 Bp Edward Lloyd Salmon Jr. m 8/1/1987 Devvy Turner c 1. Cur Trin Ch Myrtle Bch SC 2002-2005. Amer Friends of the Epis Dio Jerusalem 2008; Conf of St. Greg's Abbey 2005; OSL the Physcn 2008. Amer Jurisprudence Awd Univ Of So. Carolina Sch Of Law 1992; Cert Of Appreciation Untd States Senate 1987. rectorstbarts@aol.com

RIDGWAY, George Edward (NCal) 3371 Avington Way, Shasta Lake CA 96019 **Pstr Emer S Barn Ch Mt Shasta CA 2010-** B Detroit MI 7/1/1930 s George Wyndham Ridgway & Virginia Marshall. BA U CA 1956; MDiv CDSP 1959. D 6/1/1959 Bp James Albert Pike P 1/2/1960 Bp Henry H Shires. m 4/23/1955 Shirley D Newcomb c 3. P-in-c S Barn Ch Mt Shasta CA 2005-2010; Asst All SS Epis Ch Redding CA 2003-2005; Asst Ch Of The Incarn Santa Rosa CA 1996-2003; R S Steph's Epis Ch San Luis Obispo CA 1987-1995; R S Tim's Ch Danville CA 1970-1987; Vic S Jas' Ch Monterey CA 1962-1966; Vic S Mths Ch Seaside CA 1962-1963; P-in-c S Mk's Par Crockett CA 1960-1962. gesdridgway@att.net

RIDGWAY, Michael Wyndham (ECR) 365 Stowell Ave, Sunnyvale CA 94085 B Los Angeles CA 4/15/1964 s Robert Irving Ridgway & Lorelei Marie. BS California St U 1994; BDS Epis Sch For Deacons 2008. D 11/1/2008 Bp Mary Gray-Reeves. m 10/1/1994 Kari Hurlbut c 1. D S Steph's In-The-Field Epis Ch San Jose CA 2008-2009. mwridgway@earthlink.net

RIEBE, Norman William (SanD) 5633 Chalyce Ln, Charlotte NC 28270 B Michigan City IN 12/27/1929 s Norman J Riebe & Gwendolyn E. BS U of New Mex 1950; MDiv CDSP 1955; MS Utah St U 1968. D 7/13/1955 P 2/24/1956 Bp C J Kinsolving III. m 12/26/1953 Janice Marilyn Cooke c 3. Sprtl Advsr Angl Curs Dio Arizona Phoenix AZ 1984-1987; Assoc S Paul's Ch Yuma AZ 1968-2005; Vic S Jn's Epis Ch Logan UT 1962-1968; Prov Dept of Coll Wk Dio Utah Salt Lake City UT 1962-1966; Cur The Ch Of The Ascen Denver CO 1958-1962; Secy Bp & Coun Dio Colorado Denver CO 1958-1960; Vic H Trin Epis Ch - Mssn Raton NM 1956-1958; Vic S Jas Epis Ch Taos NM 1955-1958; Asst Ch of the H Faith Santa Fe NM 1955-1956. nwriebe@bellsouth.net

RIEDELL, William George (Cal) 3012 S Fox St, Englewood CO 80110 **D S Tim's Epis Ch Centennial CO 1998-** B East Orange NJ 8/13/1921 s John Andrew Riedell & Millicent Concordia. Duke 1942; U IL 1948; BA Sch for Deacons 1983. D 6/27/1981 Bp William Edwin Swing. m 6/9/1989 Barbara Anderson. D All SS Epis Ch San Leandro CA 1993-1998; Asst S Clare's Epis Ch Pleasanton CA 1991-1993; Asst Gd Shpd Epis Ch Centennial CO 1986-1990; D All SS Epis Ch San Leandro CA 1981-1986. wriedell@aol.com

RIEGEL, John Wilfred (Pa) Po Box 288, Bailey Island ME 04003 B Boston MA 3/23/1926 s John Wallace Riegel & Marguerite Diana. BBA U MI 1947; MA Harv 1957; PhD Harv 1960; STB Nash 1968. D 1/6/1962 Bp William S Thomas P 12/22/1962 Bp Austin Pardue. m 5/30/1970 Nicole Philippin c 2. Sr Cn All SS' Cathd Milwaukee WI 1966-1967; R Emm Ch Pittsburgh PA 1962-1965.

RIEGEL, Robert Gambrell (USC) 1100 Sumter St, Columbia SC 29201 B New York NY 5/20/1930 s Theodore Riegel & Mary. BA Wms 1952; STM VTS 1955; LHD Voorhees Coll 1981. D 6/5/1955 Bp Horace W B Donegan P 12/18/1955 Bp Randolph R Claiborne. m 10/30/1983 Keren Moore. Evang Com Dio Upper So Carolina Columbia SC 1989-1992; Cn Mssnr Trin Cathd Columbia SC 1987-1996; Dioc Coun Dio Upper So Carolina Columbia SC 1986-1988; Com Dio Upper So Carolina Columbia SC 1982-1992; Bp Cmsn On Aging Dio Upper So Carolina Columbia SC 1980-1983; Dioc Secy Dio Upper So Carolina Columbia SC 1976-1977; Dioc Trst Dio Upper So Carolina Columbia SC 1975-1983; Stndg Com Dio Upper So Carolina Columbia SC 1973-1975; Bp Coun Dio Upper So Carolina Columbia SC 1967-1970; S Jas Epis Ch Greenville SC 1959-1987; Assoc R S Lk's Epis Ch Atlanta GA 1955-1959. Auth, "The God Who Will Not Fail You," Trin Cathd, 2001. riegel@trinitysc.org

RIEK JR, Forest O (Los) 3722 Effingham Pl, Los Angeles CA 90027 **Died 8/15/2009** B Rhinelander WI 9/1/1928 s Forest Riek & Dorothea. BE USC 1951; CTh ETSBH 1972. D 9/9/1972 P 3/17/1973 Bp Francis E I Bloy. c 3. frostyr@adelphia.net

RIERDAN, Jill Elizabeth (WMass) 128 Main St, Easthampton MA 01027 B Boston MA 4/6/1945 d Walter Phillip Rierdan & Dorothy Mary. BA Clark U 1967; MA Clark U 1970; PHD Clark U 1974; MFA Bennington Coll 2000; MDiv Andover Newton TS 2010. D 4/10/2010 P 10/16/2010 Bp Gordon Paul Scruton. P-in-c S Phil's Ch Easthampton MA 2010-2011. jillrierdan@aol.com

RIETH, Sarah Melissa (NC) 115 W 7th St, Charlotte NC 28202 B Buffalo NY 10/14/1951 d William Leon Rieth & Martha. BA SUNY at Albany 1972; MDiv Bex 1977; DMin Bex 1994. D 6/4/1977 P 5/13/1978 Bp Harold B Robinson. m 8/29/2008 Barbara Brody. S Andr's Epis Ch Charlotte NC 2010; Pstr Counslr and Consult S Ptr's Epis Ch Charlotte NC 2002-2010; Clincl Consult to Pstr Response Team Dio No Carolina Raleigh NC 2001-2006; Dio Wstrn New York Tonawanda NY 1998-2001; Vic Ephphatha Epis Ch Of The Deaf Eggertsville NY 1998-2001; Healing Consult Serv Buffalo NY 1994-1995; Chair Dioc T/F on Sexual Abuse by Cler Dio Wstrn New York Tonawanda NY 1991-1994; Ch Mssn of Help Buffalo NY 1987-1994; Samar Pstr Counslg Cntr Buffalo NY 1981-1987; Asst S Ptr's Epis Ch Eggertsville NY 1978-1980. Auth, "My Bro's Keeper: Reflections on Chld Siblings Grief," *In Loss, Illness, and Death: A Dialogue w Theol and Psychol*, Paulist Press, 2010; Auth, "Telling About Brokenheartedness," *Journ of Sprtlty in Mntl Hlth*, 2008; Auth, "Differentiated Solidarity: A Theol of Pstr Supervision," *Journ of Supervision and Trng in Mnstry*, 2001; Auth, "Scriptural Reflections on Deafness and Muteness as Embodied," *Journ of Pstr Theol*, 1993; Auth, "Ignorance is Not a Victimless Crime: The Caring Tchr," *Pstr Psychol*, 1993; Auth, "Adult Survivors: Healed by Faith in Truth," *Action Info*, Alb Inst, 1991; Auth, "The Victimology Handbook," *A New Model for the Treatment of Survivors of Sexual Abuse*, Garland Press, 1990. AAPC 1981; Epis Conf of the Deaf 1998; EWC 1975; Fllshp of St. Jn the Evang 2006; Intl Soc for the Study of Dissociation 1987-2000; No Carolina Fee--Based Practicing Pstr Counslr 2002; Soc of Pstr Theologians 1991. Polly Bond Awd ECom 2000; Distinguished Contribution Awd AAPC, Estrn Reg 1998; Polly Bond Awd ECom 1989. sarahrieth@bellsouth.net

RIETMANN, Paul David (Oly) 3615 N Gove St, Tacoma WA 98407 **R S Lk's Ch Tacoma WA 1999-** B The Dalles OR 5/15/1953 s David J Rietmann & Ruth Anne. BA U CA 1977; MDiv Epis TS of The SW 1981. D 6/24/1981 Bp Leigh Wallace Jr P 6/1/1982 Bp A Donald Davies. m 5/4/2003 Sallie R Kanofsky Rietmann. Chapl Mntl Hlth Chapl: Submini Tacoma WA 1993-1999; R S Matthews Auburn WA 1989-1990; Int Ch Of The H Sprt Vashon WA 1988; Int Ch Of The Gd Shpd Fed Way WA 1987-1988; R S Lk's Ch Mineral Wells TX 1983-1987; Asst Chr Epis Ch Dallas TX 1981-1983. PRIETMANN@COMCAST.NET

RIFFEE, Charles Alexander (Alb) 1205 W Franklin St, Richmond VA 23220 **S Jas' Ch Richmond VA 2011-** B Charleston WV 1/16/1986 s Charles Amos Riffee & Deborah Jay. BA Cntr Coll 2008; MDiv Ya Berk 2011. D 6/4/2011 Bp William Howard Love. m 6/18/2011 Yinghao Long. ARIFFEE@DOERS.ORG

RIGGALL, Daniel John (Me) Po Box 165, Kennebunk ME 04043 **R S Dav's Epis Ch Kennebunk ME 1997-; Dio Maine Portland ME 1978-** B New York NY 6/30/1950 s John Riggall & Marianne. BA Houghton Coll 1972; MDiv GTS 1978. D 6/3/1978 Bp Albert Wiencke Van Duzer P 12/16/1978 Bp George Phelps Mellick Belshaw. m 12/27/1975 Frances B Butterfield. Dioc Coun Dio Vermont Burlington VT 1991-1997; Dn Cathd Ch Of S Paul

Burlington VT 1990-1997; Bp'S Coun Of Advice Dio Newark Newark NJ 1988-1990; Pres Wstrn Convoc Dio Newark Newark NJ 1988-1990; Cmsn Ce Dio Newark Newark NJ 1987-1990; R S Ptr's Ch Mtn Lakes NJ 1987-1990; Chair Dept Mssn Outreach Dio No Carolina Raleigh NC 1984-1987; S Paul's Ch Monroe NC 1982-1987; Com Dio No Carolina Raleigh NC 1982-1985; Educ Trng Cmsn Dio No Carolina Raleigh NC 1982-1984; Assoc Chap Of The Cross Chap Hill NC 1980-1982; Cur Chr Ch New Brunswick NJ 1978-1979. danielriggall@cybertours.com

RIGGALL, George Gordon (CGC) PO Box 2, Magnolia Springs AL 36555 **R S Paul's Chap Magnolia Sprg AL 2004-** B Hendricks KY 12/30/1942 s John Henry Riggall & Marianne. BA Gordon Coll 1966; MDiv SWTS 1978. D 6/17/1978 P 5/31/1979 Bp Lyman Cunningham Ogilby. m 12/14/1990 Marguerita C Riggall c 2. P-in-c Gr Ch Sprg Hill TN 1991-2004; Int S Jas The Less Madison TN 1989-1991; Int S Ann's Ch Nashville TN 1988-1989; R S Tim's Ch Signal Mtn TN 1984-1988; Asst S Geo's Ch Nashville TN 1980-1984; Cur S Jas (Old Swedes) Ch of Kingsessing Philadelphia PA 1978-1980. georgeriggall@gmail.com

RIGGIN, John Harris (CGC) 4051 Old Shell Rd, Mobile AL 36608 **R S Paul's Ch Mobile AL 1993-; D S Paul's Ch Mobile AL 1992-** B Little Rock AR 1/29/1956 s John Thomas Riggin & Claudia. Rhodes Coll 1976; BD U of Memphis 1979; MBA U So 1986; MDiv STUSo 1992. D 6/13/1992 P 5/1/1993 Bp Charles Farmer Duvall. m 8/16/1980 Lauree Shields c 3. JHRIGGIN@BELLSOUTH.NET

RIGGINS, Patricia Reardon (SanD) 201 E Nolte, Seguin TX 78155 **Assoc S Andr's Epis Ch Seguin TX 2011-** B Plattsburgh NY 11/27/1950 d James Jeremiah Reardon & Virginia Helen. AB Sweet Briar Coll 1972; MBA Tul 1975; MPH Tul 1975; MDiv Epis TS Of The SW 2009. D 5/29/2009 Bp James Robert Mathes P 1/13/2010 Bp Gary Richard Lillibridge. m 11/17/2001 Michael Riggins c 1. Int The Ch Of The Recon Corpus Christi TX 2010-2011; Asst S Fran By The Lake Canyon Lake TX 2010; D S Fran By The Lake Canyon Lake TX 2009-2010. prriggins@satx.rr.com

RIGGLE JR, John Field (SwFla) 9267 Sun Isle Dr Ne, Saint Petersburg FL 33702 B Atlanta GA 10/14/1934 s John Field Riggle & Louise. BS Georgia Sthrn U 1960; BS Nash 1967. D 6/21/1967 Bp Henry I Louttit P 12/22/1967 Bp William Loftin Hargrave. m 10/11/1975 Jo Ann Riggle c 2. Ch Of The H Cross St Petersburg FL 1974-1991; Cur Cathd Ch Of S Ptr St Petersburg FL 1967-1974. JOANRIGGLE@YAHOO.COM

RIGGS, Katherine Grace (WTex) 936 Canterbury Hill St, San Antonio TX 78209 B Oak Park IL 1/20/1925 d John Henry Grace & Frances Coates. BA Vas 1945; MA Col 1947; MDiv Epis TS of The SW 1981. D 6/24/1981 Bp Stanley Fillmore Hauser P 2/2/1982 Bp Scott Field Bailey. c 2. Chapl Wmn's Cbnt Dio W Texas San Antonio TX 1993-1997; Pres Cler Assn Dio W Texas San Antonio TX 1986-1987; Vic S Fran By The Lake Canyon Lake TX 1983-1989; Asst R S Dav's Epis Ch San Antonio TX 1981-1984. DOK 1977. Hal Brook Perry Awd Epis TS of the SW Austin TX 2001. kgriggs@webtv.net

✠ RIGHTER, Rt Rev Walter Cameron (Ia) 204 Williamsburg Ln, Export PA 15632 **Died 9/11/2011** B Philadelphia PA 10/23/1923 s Richard Righter & Dorothy Mae. BS U Pgh 1948; MDiv Ya Berk 1951; Fllshp Coll of Preachers 1965; DD Ya Berk 1972; DCL Iowa Wesleyan Coll 1982; DD SWTS 1985. D 4/8/1951 P 10/6/1951 Bp Austin Pardue Con 1/12/1972 for Ia. m 8/22/1992 Nancy R Tolbert c 2. Auth, "A Pilgrim's Way," *A Pilgrim's Way*, Knopf, 1998; Auth, "Var arts," *DesMoines Register*, 1971; Auth, "Var arts," *Epis Life*, 1954; Auth, "Var arts," *Nashua Telegraph*, 1954; Auth, *Of Men and Mills*, Soc. for Prom. of Ind. Mssn. RC Bp's Cmsn for Unity 1965-1972. Louie Crew Awd Integrity 1997; Courageous Resister Awd Refuse & Resist 1996; Pstr Care Awd Oasis 1990; Gd Guy Awd St of Iowa 1987; Cert of Serv Exec Coun of ECUSA 1985. wcrighter@alltel.net

RIGHTMYER, Thomas Nelson (WNC) 16 Salisbury Dr 7304, Asheville NC 28803 B Lewes DE 3/27/1939 s Nelson Waite Rightmyer & Elizabeth Anne. S Andr's Sch Middletown DE 1957; BA JHU 1961; MDiv GTS 1966; ThM S Mary's Sem Baltimore MD 1972; DMin GTF 1986. D 6/21/1966 P 6/14/1967 Bp Harry Lee Doll. m 9/10/1966 Lucy Oliver Coons c 2. Int Ch of the Advoc Asheville NC 2008; Vic Chap Of The Gd Shpd Ridgeway NC 1997-2001; Ecum Com Dio Wstrn No Carolina Asheville NC 1990-2009; Assoc S Phil's Ch Durham NC 1990-2003; R Ch Of The Redeem Shelby NC 1980-1989; Ecum Chair Dio Wstrn No Carolina Asheville NC 1980-1989; R The Epis Ch Of Gd Shpd Asheboro NC 1974-1980; Ecum Chair Dio Maryland Baltimore MD 1970-1974; Vic Copley Par: The Ch Of The Resurr Joppa MD 1968-1974; Asst S Anne's Par Annapolis MD 1966-1968. Auth, "Calendar of the Fulham Papers XLI & XLII," *Angl and Epis Hist 62*, 1993; Auth, "Amer Colonial Angl Cler," in preparation. EDEO 1976-2002. trightmy@juno.com

RIIS, Susan Hollis (Chi) 144884 Harbor Dr E, Thornville OH 43076 B Waterbury CT 11/7/1943 d Harold Dore Hollis & Hazel Elizabeth. BA U MI 1967; MA U MI 1967. D 2/2/2002 Bp William Dailey Persell. m 1/2/1984 Thomas Engeman c 1. Trin Ch Highland Pk IL 2002-2011. SUSANRIIS@GMAIL.COM

RIKER JR, William Chandler (Nwk) 249 Hartshorne Rd, Locust NJ 07760 B New York NY 11/20/1940 s William Chandler Riker & Mary Jackson. BA U of Oregon 1963; MDiv CDSP 1973. D 4/10/1974 P 11/23/1974 Bp C Kilmer Myers. m 4/5/1997 Barbara U Carton-Riker c 2. Coun Dio Newark Newark NJ 2001-2003; Int S Paul's Epis Ch Morris Plains NJ 2001-2003; Mem Dioc Coun Dio Newark Newark NJ 2000-2003; Int Chr Ch Glen Ridge NJ 1999-2001; Int S Paul's Ch In Bergen Jersey City NJ 1997-1999; Int S Dunst's Epis Ch Succasunna NJ 1996-1997; Vic S Ben Epis Ch Lacey WA 1989-1996; R Gr Ch Cincinnati OH 1984-1989; Mem, Comm. on Mnstry Dio Sthrn Ohio Cincinnati OH 1984-1988; Stwdshp Com Dio Olympia Seattle WA 1981-1984; Ch Of The H Sprt Vashon WA 1981-1983; Mem Comm. on Mssn Dio Olympia Seattle WA 1978-1983; P-in-c S Aid's Epis Ch Camano Island WA 1978-1979; S Ptr's Epis Ch Redwood City CA 1974-1977; Mem Comm. on Mnstry Dio California San Francisco CA 1974-1975. Photographer & Ed, "Needlepoint of All SS' Memi," *Needlepoint Proj 2004-2008*, Landmark Trust, 2009; Auth, *Var arts*. williamriker1@juno.com

RILEY, Diane Napolitano (Nwk) 337 Woodland Rd, Madison NJ 07940 B Queens NY 8/7/1957 D 5/21/2005 Bp John Palmer Croneberger. m 6/1/1985 Elven Riley c 3. dianenriley@yahoo.com

RILEY, George Daniel (NY) 39 Minnesota Ave, Long Beach NY 11561 B Cushing OK 8/3/1940 s George Daniel Riley & Anna Lorinda. BA Oklahoma Bapt U 1961; MDiv Nash 1968. D 6/7/1969 P 5/1/1971 Bp Horace W B Donegan.

RILEY, Gregg Les (WLa) P.O. Box 2031, Alexandria LA 71309 **Cn to the Ordnry Dio Wstrn Louisiana Alexandria LA 2011-** B Bessemer AL 1/15/1947 s Lester L Riley & Moselle M. AA Arkansas St U 1977; BS U of Kentucky 1979; MDiv Epis TS In Kentucky 1980; STM Nash 2005. D 5/11/1980 P 12/13/1980 Bp Addison Hosea. m 2/11/1969 Carlene M Merrick c 2. Bdgt and Fin Com Dio Wstrn Louisiana Alexandria LA 2004-2007; R Gr Epis Ch Monroe LA 2002-2010; Exec Coun Dio Dallas Dallas TX 1999-2002; R Ch Of The Gd Shpd Cedar Hill TX 1998-2002; Stdng Com Dio Wstrn Kansas Hutchinson KS 1995-1997; R Gr Epis Ch Hutchinson KS 1992-1998; R S Jn's Ch Keokuk IA 1986-1992; R All SS Epis Ch Russellville AR 1984-1986; Mssn Cmsn Dio Iowa Des Moines IA 1982-1984; Asst Trin Cathd Davenport IA 1982-1984; P-in-c Chr Ch Ironton OH 1981-1982; Asst Calv Epis Ch Ashland KY 1980-1982; Yth Bd Dio Lexington Lexington KY 1980-1982. Auth, "Chld's prayers," *Bedtime Pryr w Your Chld*, St Fran Acad, 1997. Cmnty of S Mary 1982. Hon Cn Chr Ch Cathd Salina KS 1997. canonwla@aol.com

RILEY JR, James Foster (Minn) 132 Maj Hornbrook Road, Christchurch Canterbury New Zealand (Aotearoa) B Monett MO 2/6/1934 s James Foster Riley & Helen. BA Ken 1956; STB GTS 1959; MDiv GTS 1973. D 9/18/1959 P 3/19/1960 Bp Edward Randolph Welles II. m 5/28/1959 Edith Sevy c 3. R S Nich Ch Richfield MN 1966-1975; Cur Chr Epis Ch S Jos MO 1962-1966; D S Paul's Epis Ch Clinton MO 1959-1960. jim.riley@xtra.co.nz

RILEY, John Clayton (EC) 1333 Jamestown Rd, Williamsburg VA 23185 **S Mart's Epis Ch Williamsburg VA 2011-** B Pinehurst NC 8/27/1969 s Wallace Theodore Riley & Suzanne. BS Appalachian St U 1992; MDiv VTS 2011. D 6/11/2011 Bp Clifton Daniel III. m 9/11/1999 Margaret K Margaret Kate Berry c 2. clay@stmartinswmbg.org

RILEY, Reese Milton (Los) 1414 East Grovemont, Santa Ana CA 92705 B Pampa TX 9/2/1945 s George Thomas Riley & Dorcas Regina. BA Westminster Coll 1968; Harv 1971. D 11/20/1971 P 9/30/1972 Bp Frederick Barton Wolf. m 6/29/1968 Judith V Van Cura c 2. R S Paul's Epis Ch Tustin CA 1987-2011; R S Paul's Par Lancaster CA 1980-1987; R S Jn's Epis Ch Randolph VT 1976-1980; Res Cn Cathd Ch Of S Lk Portland ME 1972-1976; Vic Chr Ch Gardiner ME 1971-1972. New Engl Trng Inst 1975-1980; OHC 1982. Billing Prize For Publ Spkng Harv 1971; Omicron Delta Kappa Westminster Coll Fulton MO 1968; Phi Alpha Theta Westminster Coll Fulton MO. reesemriley@me.com

RIMASSA, Paul Stephen (NJ) 215 Briner Ln, Hamilton Square NJ 08690 **Trin Ch Rocky Hill NJ 2006-** B Newark NJ 12/19/1947 s Joseph Rimassa & Claire. Rec from Roman Catholic 11/22/2005 Bp George Edward Councell. m 5/23/2004 Mary St-Amour-Rimassa. psrimassa@verizon.net

RIMER, Kathleen Pakos (Mass) 25 Orrin St Apt B, Cambridge MA 02138 B Hyannis MA 10/8/1970 d Paul Edward Pakos & Patricia Ann. BA Bow 1992; MDiv Harvard DS 1998. D 6/15/2002 P 5/31/2003 Bp M(arvil) Thomas Shaw III. m 6/24/2000 Edward S Rimmer. Int Par Of Chr Ch Andover MA 2003-2004.

RIMKUS, William Allen (Chi) 14755 Eagle Ridge Dr, Homer Glen IL 60491 **D Emm Epis Ch La Grange IL 2002-** B Evergreen Park IL 10/17/1942 s Vincent William Rimkus & Anna Ethyl. Illinois Inst of Tech 1961; U IL 1961; Cert Sch of Diac 1987. D 12/26/1987 Bp Frank Tracy Griswold III. m 11/22/1975 Rebekah Totts c 5. S Dunst's Epis Ch Westchester IL 1995-2001; S Dunst's Epis Ch Westchester IL 1987-1994. williamrimkus@yahoo.com

RINCON, Virginia M (Me) 121 Margaret St Apt C, South Portland ME 04106 B La Follette TN 10/2/1952 Lic Practical Nurse Houston Tech Inst (Form San Jacinto High) 1972; B.L.S. w a major in Soc Wk St Edw's U 1993; Mstr of

Div EDS 1997. D 12/8/2001 Bp M(arvil) Thomas Shaw III P 9/18/2005 Bp Chilton Abbie Richardson Knudsen. c 1. Dio Maine Portland ME 2006-2010; Chr Ch Biddeford ME 2003-2007. tengovoz@hotmail.com

RINEHART, James Arnold (Be) 1318 Howard Ave, Pottsville PA 17901 **Commision on Mnstry Dio Bethlehem Bethlehem PA 2007-; R Trin Epis Ch Pottsville PA 2007-** B Lima OH 5/11/1946 s Claude Junior Rinehart & Naomi Elizabeth. AA S Petersburg Jr Coll 1966; BA U of So Florida 1968; MDiv Bex 1993. D 6/3/1995 Bp Edward Cole Chalfant P 7/13/1996 Bp William George Burrill. m 8/1/1975 Nancy Carolyn Rupnow. Dept of Mnstry Dio Long Island Garden City NY 2005-2007; R S Paul's Ch Patchogue NY 2000-2007; Dioc Coun Dio Rochester Rochester NY 1998-2000; R S Ptr's Epis Ch Bloomfield NY 1996-2000; D S Lk's Ch Fairport NY 1995-1996. jmsrnhrt@aol.com

RINES, Charles T (NCal) 3641 Mari Dr, Lake Elsinore CA 92530 **S Clem's Ch Rancho Cordova CA 2000-** B Oakland CA 11/1/1933 s Charles Henry Rines & Susan Grace. BA California St U 1958; MDiv TS 1964. D 6/21/1964 P 12/26/1964 Bp James Albert Pike. m 7/7/1957 Amanda Helen Jones c 3. Int S Steph's Mssn Menifee CA 2009-2011; Assoc Vic S Thos Epis Ch Temecula CA 2002-2009; R Epis Ch Of Our Sav Placerville CA 1992-1998; R Trin Ch Escondido CA 1978-1992; Assoc Cathd Ch Of S Paul San Diego CA 1976-1978; Asst S Ptr's Epis Ch Del Mar CA 1975-1976; R Chr Ch Par Ontario CA 1971-1973; R S Mich The Archangel Par El Segundo CA 1968-1971; Cur All SS Par Los Angeles CA 1967-1968; R S Chris's Epis Ch Boulder City NV 1965-1966. charlest12@earthlink.net

RING, Bonnie (Cal) 2055 Carlos Street, Moss Beach CA 94038 **Assoc Ch Of The H Fam Half Moon Bay CA 2007-** B New York NY 4/22/1940 d Richard Isaac Kilstein & Rita Adrienne. Vas; BA NYU 1962; EdM Bos 1964; UCLA 1966; EdD Bos 1972; MDiv CDSP 1990. D 12/7/1991 P 12/5/1992 Bp William Edwin Swing. m 1/14/1993 Life Partner. Chr Epis Ch Los Altos CA 2004; S Ambr Epis Ch Foster City CA 2003; S Jn's Epis Ch Oakland CA 2002-2004; Gd Shpd Epis Ch Belmont CA 2002-2003; S Paul's Epis Ch Walnut Creek CA 2002; S Lk's Ch Walnut Creek CA 2001-2002; Assoc Trin Ch San Francisco CA 1995-1999; Assoc S Cuth's Epis Ch Oakland CA 1992-1993. Co-Auth & Co-Ed, "H Relationships And The Authority Of Scripture," Dio California, 2000. APA 1964; California Psychol Assn 1974; Spritiual Dir Intl 1989. Educ Hon Soc Pi Lamda Theta 1965. drbring@pacbell.net

RING, Tony (Eau) W10601 Pine Rd, Thorp WI 54771 B Eau Claire WI 3/17/1937 s Henry Ring & Elvira Adela. D 5/31/2003 Bp Keith Bernard Whitmore. m 10/18/1980 Hazel Louise Murrier c 3. Fllshp of S Jn. deacontony@hotmail.com

RINGLAND, Robin Lynn (Oly) 415 S 18th St, Mount Vernon WA 98274 B Twin Falls ID 6/13/1953 d Robert Lee Gilliam & Jacqueline Irene. BA U CA 1978; MA San Jose St U 1983. D 10/29/2010 Bp Gregory Harold Rickel. m 8/20/1977 Peter Ringland c 4. ringland@wildblue.net

RIOS, Austin Keith (WNC) Diocese of Western North Carolina, 900-B Centre Park Dr., Asheville NC 28805 **Cn for Spanish-Spkng Mnstrs Dio Wstrn No Carolina Asheville NC 2007-; R La Capilla De Santa Maria Hendersonville NC 2007-** B Webster TX 3/19/1977 s Ronald Alton Rios & Cyndy Keith. BA Davidson Coll 1999; MDiv Epis TS of The SW 2003. D 1/15/2005 P 7/16/2005 Bp Granville Porter Taylor. m 7/3/2004 Jill Drzewiwcki Drzewiecki c 1. Gr Ch Asheville NC 2005-2007. Transltr (w Gabriela Reyes R, "Spanish Ed of Comp in Transformation," *Comp in Transformation: The Epis Ch's Wrld Mssn in a New Century*, Ch Pub; Contrib, "Mutuality in Mssn: The Tchg of Don Ricardo and his Cats," *The Scripture of their Lives*, Morehouse. lacapilla@bellsouth.net

RIPSON, H(arry) Robert (NJ) 34473 Palmetto Drive, Pinellas Park FL 33781 **Died 8/11/2011** B Lancaster PA 2/9/1933 s Hugh Robert Ripson & Helen Mae. BS U of Maryland 1970; MDiv Nash 1979; MA U of Dallas 1982. D 8/26/1979 Bp A Donald Davies P 6/23/1980 Bp Robert Elwin Terwilliger. c 4. Soc of S Fran - Tertiary 1976. bobripson@superweb.ca

RISARD, Frederick William (EpisSanJ) 3526 San Francisco St, Merced CA 95348 **Dioc Jubilee Off Epis Dio San Joaquin Modesto CA 2011-** B Winnemucca NV 4/24/1951 s Martin Hector Risard & Alice. BS California St Polytechnic U, SLO 1978; MDiv Nash 2004; MSW California St U Stanislaus 2012. D 12/10/2005 P 6/11/2006 Bp John-David Mercer Schofield. Dioc Coun Epis Dio San Joaquin Modesto CA 2008-2011; Dep to GC Epis Dio San Joaquin Modesto CA 2008-2010; P-in-c St Nich Epis Ch Atwater CA 2008-2010; St. Nich Epis Ch, Atwater Ca Epis Ch Cntr New York NY 2008; Strng Com, Reconstitute Epis Dio San Joaquin Epis Dio San Joaquin Modesto CA 2007-2008; Vic St Nich Epis Ch Atwater CA 2006-2007. frisard@mac.com

RISARD JR, Martin Hector (EpisSanJ) P.O. Box 3657, Sonora CA 95370 **Vic S Mary's In The Mountains Wilmington VT 2008-** B Oakland CA 6/24/1925 s Martin Hector Risard & Margaret. AA Sierra Coll Rocklin CA 1949; Tc U of Nevada at Las Vegas 1950; CDSP 1957; BA California St U 1969; MA California St U 1977. D 7/14/1957 P 7/10/1958 Bp Chandler W Sterling. m 6/21/1947 Alice Williams c 6. P-in-c S Mich And All Ang' Epis Ch Standard CA 1999-2002; S Clare of Assisi Epis Ch Avery CA 1985-1988; Gr Ch Copperopolis CA 1985-1987; R S Andr's Ch Oakland CA 1973-1984; Vic S Andr's Ch Ben Lomond CA 1966-1969; Cur Emm Epis Par Rapid City SD 1964-1966; R Ch Of The H Innoc San Francisco CA 1962-1964; Vic Calv Epis Ch Red Lodge MT 1957-1960. Auth, "Geography In The Land Of The Long White Cloud," *California Geographer*, 1976. mrisard@mlode.com

RISK III, James L (Chi) 901 N Delphia Ave, Park Ridge IL 60068 **Exec Dir Bp Anderson Hse Chicago IL 2002-; Chapl Rush U Med Cntr Chicago IL 2002-** B New York NY 5/12/1948 s James Lightfoot Risk & Barbara. BA Hob 1970; MDiv GTS 1975. D 6/14/1975 Bp Quintin Ebenezer Primo Jr P 12/1/1975 Bp James Winchester Montgomery. m 6/21/2008 Paula Allen c 4. Chair, Dioc Strategic Plnng Com Dio Chicago Chicago IL 2003-2008; Int R S Mary's Ch Pk Ridge IL 2001-2003; R S Giles' Ch Northbrook IL 1982-2001; Assoc Chr Ch Winnetka IL 1978-1982; Asst S Mk's Barrington Hills IL 1975-1978. Auth, "Screening for Sprtl Struggle," Journ of Pstr Care and Counslg, 2009; Auth, "Sprtl Struggle," *Healing Sprt*, Assn of Profsnl Chapl, 2009; Auth, "Being God's Fam," *Being God's Fam*, Epis Fam Ntwk, 1996. Hon Cn St. Jas Cathd, Dio Chicago 2007. james_l_risk@rush.edu

RITCH JR, Paul Livingston (Fla) 101 Cranes Lake Dr, Ponte Vedra Beach FL 32082 B Columbia SC 8/29/1928 s Paul Livingston Ritch & Ruby Stroupe. BA U NC 1950; STB GTS 1953. D 5/30/1953 P 5/29/1954 Bp Matthew G Henry. c 2. Bd Rgnts Dio Florida Jacksonville FL 1980-1988; Assoc R S Mk's Epis Ch Jacksonville FL 1977-1993; Assoc R S Jn's Epis Ch Tallahassee FL 1971-1977; Assoc R S Matt's Ch Kenosha WI 1969-1970; ExCoun Dio Florida Jacksonville FL 1962-1964; Asst R S Paul's By-The-Sea Epis Ch Jacksonville Bch FL 1958-1960; R Calv Ch Americus GA 1954-1958; Vic Chr Epis Ch Cordele GA 1954-1955; Min in charge S Phil's Ch Brevard NC 1953-1954. plritch@bellsouth.net

RITCHIE, Anne Gavin (Va) 1002 Janney's Lane, Alexandria VA 22302 B Coral Gables FL 7/14/1949 d Peter Michael Gavin & Gertrude Anne. BA Adel 1971; MDiv (cl) VTS 1978; DMin SWTS 2005. D 6/24/1978 P 6/7/1979 Bp John Thomas Walker. c 1. R Ch Of The Resurr Alexandria VA 1995-2011; Assoc S Jn's Ch Lafayette Sq Washington DC 1989-1995; Assoc S Mk's Ch Washington DC 1978-1986. Co-Auth, "Discussion Plans for So You Think You're Not Rel," *Discussion Plans for So You Think You're Not Rel?*, Alb Inst, 2000; Co-Auth, "What Do I Have Offer?," *What Do I Have to Offer?*, Alb Inst, 1985; Co-Auth, "My Struggle to Be a Caring Person," *My Struggle to Be a Caring Person*, Alb Inst, 1984. agr1@comcast.net

RITCHIE, Harold L (Fla) 12013 SW 1st St, Micanopy FL 32667 **P-in-c S Alb's Epis Ch Chiefland FL 2009-; Cler Cont Educ Dio Florida Jacksonville FL 2003-; Nomin Com Dio Florida Jacksonville FL 2002-; Yth Cmsn Dio Florida Jacksonville FL 2002-** B Lancaster PA 6/3/1950 s Marion L Ritchie & Dorothea. BA S Leo U 1996; MHS U of Florida 2000; MDiv STUSo 2002. D 6/9/2002 P 12/8/2002 Bp Stephen Hays Jecko. m 6/23/1979 Melody Joan Wagner c 1. Int S Jos's Ch Newberry FL 2009; Chapl Ch Of The Incarn Gainesville FL 2006-2007; R S Anne's Epis Ch Keystone Heights FL 2004-2009; Asst S Jos's Ch Newberry FL 2002-2004. Ord of S Lk's Healing Mnstry 1991. fatherritchie@aol.com

RITCHIE, Patricia Ritter (Tex) 4090 Delaware St, Beaumont TX 77706 **The iona Sch Field Wk Coordntr Dio Texas Houston TX 2011-; Com for the Diac Dio Texas Houston TX 2010-; D S Steph's Ch Beaumont TX 2009-** B Beaumont TX 8/28/1950 d James Price Ritter & Betty Brown. BA LSU 1972; Grad The Iona Sch for Mnstry 2009. D 2/22/2009 Bp Don Adger Wimberly. m 4/28/1990 Maurice Ritchie c 1. Lay Mnstrs S Mk's Ch Beaumont TX 2000-2006. ritchie.pat@gmail.com

RITCHIE, Robert Joseph (Pa) 7712 Brous Ave, Philadelphia PA 19152 B Philadelphia PA 8/30/1948 s Robert Ritchie & Evelyn. 1996 Sch of the Diac, Dio PA; BA Tem 1987; Grad F.B.I. Acad 1993; MS St. Jos's U 1993. D 10/27/1996 Bp Allen Lyman Bartlett Jr. m 4/28/1973 Charleen Hughes c 2. D Memi Ch Of The H Nativ Rockledge PA 2003-2007; D Trin Ch Oxford Philadelphia PA 1996-2003. ritchieatphila@aol.com

RITCHIE, Sandra Lawrence (Pgh) 1808 Kent Rd, Pittsburgh PA 15241 B Steubenville OH 11/5/1938 RN Ohio Vlly Hosp Sch Of Nrsng Steubenville OH 1960; BS K SU 1977; Med Tem 1983. D 6/14/2003 Bp Robert William Duncan. m 7/11/1964 Richard H Ritchie c 2. S Paul's Epis Ch Pittsburgh PA 2006-2009. sritchie@stpaulspgh.org

RITCHINGS, Frances Anne (Pa) 50 Quail Meadow Rd, Placitas NM 87043 B Baltimore MD 6/26/1946 d Edward Peyton Ritchings & Frances Evangeline. BA Salisbury St U 1968; MA U of Virginia 1970; MLS CUA 1975; MDiv EDS 1987. D 7/11/1987 Bp Ronald Hayward Haines P 2/4/1988 Bp George Nelson Hunt III. Ch Of The H Sprt Harleysville PA 1998-2001; Dio Pennsylvania Philadelphia PA 1993-1997; Assoc R S Thos' Ch Whitemarsh Ft Washington PA 1989-1993; Assoc R S Steph's Ch Providence RI 1987-1989. "Establishing the Mssn Ch of the H Sprt," *Journ of the Assn of Angl Mus*, 2004; "Poems," *Windchimes*, 2001. Soc of S Jn the Evang, Soc of S Marg. Salmon Wheaton Prize EDS 1987. bearcuisinenm@comcast.net

RITONIA, Ann M (Va) 114 W. Boscawen St., Winchester VA 22601 **Ch Of The Gd Shpd Orange CT 2011-** B Boston MA 8/13/1957 d Malcolm

R

McKinnon & Catherine. BA New Engl Conservatory of Mus 1979; MA Webster U 1994; MDiv Wesley TS 2007. D 5/24/2008 P 12/6/2008 Bp Peter James Lee. m 8/16/1986 Michael Ritonia c 4. Asst Chr Epis Ch Winchester VA 2008-2011; Asst S Anne's Epis Ch Reston VA 2007-2008. revmajorann@gmail.com

RITSON, Veronica Merita (Az) 6556 N Villa Manana Dr, Phoenix AZ 85014 **Archd Trin Cathd Phoenix AZ 2000-; D Dio Arizona Phoenix AZ 1993-** B JP 12/10/1949 d George Ritson & Elizabeth. AA Gateway Cmnty Coll Phoenix AZ 1975; EFM STUSo 1993. D 6/5/1993 Bp Robert Reed Shahan. v. ritson@att.net

RITTER, Christine E (Pa) 1771 Sharpless Rd, Meadowbrook PA 19046 **Dio Pennsylvania Philadelphia PA 2007-; Asst to Bp Dio Pennsylvania Philadelphia PA 2006-** B NJ 8/17/1941 d Howard John Erb & Eleanor Marion. BA Trenton St Coll 1978; MSW Rutgers-The St U 1981; MDiv GTS 1996. D 6/21/1996 P 12/14/1996 Bp Joe Morris Doss. c 2. Gr Ch Pemberton NJ 2005-2006; Int Trin Ch Solebury PA 2003-2005; R Ch Of Our Sav Jenkintown PA 1998-2002; Asst S Ptr's Ch In The Great Vlly Malvern PA 1997-1998; Gr Ch Pemberton NJ 1996-1997. rev.chris1@verizon.net

RITTER, Cindy A (Okla) 1604 S Fir Ave, Broken Arrow OK 74012 B Mangum OK 8/19/1950 d Joe Mac Silk & Doris Nathalyn. RN NWTH Hosp Sch of Nrsng Amarillo TX 1971; BS Langston U 1990; MS U of Oklahoma 1995. D 6/18/2005 Bp Robert Manning Moody. m 4/21/1973 Gordon Jochen Ritter c 3. silkritter@cox.net

RITTER, Kenneth Phillip (La) 3501 Twelve Oaks Ave, Baton Rouge LA 70820 B New Orleans LA 9/12/1961 s Harold Frank Ritter & Jeanelle. BA S Jos Sem Coll S Ben LA 1983; MDiv Notre Dame Sem Grad TS 1987; MA S Louis U 1993. Rec from Roman Catholic 4/8/2004 Bp Charles Edward Jenkins III. m 4/21/1973 Juliana M Ritter c 2. R Trin Epis Ch Baton Rouge LA 2005-2011; S Jas Place Baton Rouge LA 2004-2005; P Asst S Jas Epis Ch Baton Rouge LA 2003-2004. fatherken@trinitybr.org

RITTER, Nathan (Mich) 950 Broad St, Newark NJ 07102 B St Louis MO 5/8/1977 s Alan Edward Ritter & Elizabeth Rose. BA Truman St U 2001; MAR Yale DS 2004; MDiv The GTS 2010. D 5/29/2010 P 12/3/2010 Bp Wendell Nathaniel Gibbs Jr. m 7/8/2006 Jessica Diane Lambert c 2. ritternathan@hotmail.com

RIVAS, Vidal (WA) Episcopal Church House, Mount Saint Alban, Washington DC 20016 **Latino Mssnr Dio Washington Washington DC 2008-; R S Matt's Epis Ch Hyattsville MD 2008-** B El Salvador 4/28/1964 s Antonio Castillo Rivas & Maria Ventura Lima. Rec from Roman Catholic 1/19/2008 Bp John Chane. m 11/11/2006 Maria D Delos Angeles Brenes c 3. vidalvid@aol.com

RIVERA, Aristotle (Cal) PO Box 101, Brentwood CA 94513 **Area Mssnr/ Vic S Alb's Epis Ch Brentwood CA 2008-** B Los Angeles CA 11/26/1977 s Efren Rivera & Asuncion. BS USMA at W Point 1999; MS U of Missouri Rolla 2004; Mdiv Ya Berk 2008. D 5/31/2008 Bp William Howard Love P 12/6/2008 Bp Marc Handley Andrus. m 5/6/2005 Roselle p Castro. arisrivera@gmail.com

✠ **RIVERA, Rt Rev Bavi** (Oly) PO Box 1548, The Dalles OR 97058 **Provsnl Bp of Estrn Oregon Dio Estrn Oregon The Dalles OR 2009-** B Visalia CA 3/24/1946 d Victor Manuel Rivera-Toro & Barbara Ross. BA Wheaton Coll at Norton 1968; MDiv CDSP 1976. D 6/28/1975 Bp Victor Manuel Rivera P 5/5/1979 Bp C Kilmer Myers Con 1/22/2005 for Oly. m 2/16/1979 Robert Byron Moore c 1. Bp Suffr Dio Olympia Seattle WA 2004-2010; R S Aid's Ch San Francisco CA 1994-2004; COM, Chrmn Mnstry Educ & Dvlpmnt, Stndg Com Dio El Camino Real Monterey CA 1985-1992; R S Geo's Ch Salinas CA 1984-1993; COM, Stndg, Yth Mnstry Acad Dio California San Francisco CA 1981-1984; Assoc St Johns Epis Ch Ross CA 1979-1984; Asst S Clare's Epis Ch Pleasanton CA 1977-1979; S Paul's Epis Ch San Rafael CA 1975-1977. Soc of S Fran. DD CDSP 2005. nrivera@episdioeo.org

RIVERA, Marcos Antonio (CFla) No address on file. **D H Cross Ch Winter Haven FL 1997-** B 9/5/1939 s Roberto Rivera & Pilar. D 3/2/1987 Bp William Hopkins Folwell. m 11/28/1974 Pamela Ann Wintgens c 2. Auth, "Touched By The Fr'S Hand". popanchor@aol.com

RIVERS, Barbara White Batzer (Pa) 378 Paoli Woods, Paoli PA 19301 B Elizabeth NJ 7/15/1947 d Reinhold Kirk Batzer & Marjorie Marian. BA Buc 1969; MS Drexel U 1972; MDiv Estrn Bapt TS 1986. D 6/15/1985 P 5/26/1986 Bp Lyman Cunningham Ogilby. c 2. P-in-c S Christophers Epis Ch Oxford PA 2008-2011; Int S Jas Epis Ch Bristol PA 2007-2008; Int S Jn's Ch Glen Mills PA 2004-2006; Int Memi Ch Of S Lk Philadelphia PA 2003-2004; Int Ch Of The Redeem Bryn Mawr PA 1999-2002; Int Ch Of S Asaph Bala Cynwyd PA 1997-1999; Int The Epis Ch Of The Adv Kennett Sq PA 1996-1997; Int Trin Ch Buckingham PA 1995-1996; Int S Dunstans Ch Blue Bell PA 1994-1995; Int S Jas' Epis Ch Downingtown PA 1992-1994; Int Gr Epiph Ch Philadelphia PA 1990; Asst Ch Of The Mssh Lower Gwynedd PA 1987-1990; Asst Trin Ch Gulph Mills King Of Prussia PA 1985-1987. Int Mnstry Ntwk. bbrivers22@comcast.net

RIVERS, David Buchanan (Pa) 148 Heacock Ln, Wyncote PA 19095 B New Haven CT 5/22/1937 s Burke Rivers & Phyllis McCausland. BA Hav 1959; BD EDS 1964. D 6/1/1964 P 3/1/1965 Bp Frederick J Warnecke. m 8/5/1961 Elizabeth Lee Zeller c 4. Int H Trin Ch Lansdale PA 2004-2010; R Gloria Dei Ch Philadelphia PA 1972-2004; Vic S Eliz's Ch Schnecksville PA 1964-1968. Auth, "LivCh," 2001. Swedish Colonial Soc 1973-2004. rivdav@aol.com

RIVERS, John (WNC) 55 Wingspread Dr, Black Mountain NC 28711 **Mssnr to Deaf Dio Wstrn No Carolina Asheville NC 1980-** B Charleston SC 8/19/1931 s Elias Lynch Rivers & Dorothy Hyers. BS Coll of Charleston 1953; BD EDS 1956. D 7/14/1956 P 7/20/1957 Bp Thomas N Carruthers. m 6/23/1956 Jean Cleveland c 5. Team Evang Consult Dio Wstrn No Carolina Asheville NC 1988-1991; Sprtl Advsr Curs Dio Wstrn No Carolina Asheville NC 1985-1989; Dio Wstrn No Carolina Asheville NC 1981-1994; S Dav's Ch Cullowhee NC 1967-1981; Asst to the R Chr Ch Cathd Lexington KY 1966-1967; P-in-c All SS Epis Ch Clinton SC 1960-1966; P-in-c All SS Epis Ch Hampton SC 1957-1960; P-in-c Ch Of The Heav Rest Estill SC 1957-1960; M-in-c Ch Of The H Comm Allendale SC 1956-1957. ECDEF, 1st VP ECD, Ord of S Lk. jjrivers@mindspring.com

RIVERS, John Charles (WA) 4820 Girard Ln Apt 714, Raleigh NC 27613 B Washington DC 3/3/1925 s John Lawrence Rivers & Annie. USNA 1946; BS U of Virginia 1950; MDiv EDS 1962; MA CUA 1975. D 6/22/1962 P 6/21/1963 Bp George P Gunn. m 9/11/1948 Gloria Irma C Garavaglia c 2. LocTen S Paul's Epis Ch Edenton NC 1997-1998; LocTen S Jn's Epis Ch Wilmington NC 1992-1993; LocTen S Paul's Epis Ch Edenton NC 1990-1991; Personl Com Dio Washington Washington DC 1987-1988; Ecum Off Dio Washington Washington DC 1973-1983; R S Dunst's Epis Ch Beth MD 1972-1988; Adj Prof Liturg VTS Alexandria VA 1972-1987; Cur Estrn Shore Chap Virginia Bch VA 1962-1965. Auth, "Revised Ambrosian Rite of Milan," *Unpublished*, 1980; Auth, "Function," *Angl Dig*; Auth, "Enabler," *Epis*. Societas Liturgica 1975-1988. riversjack@embarqmail.com

RIVERS III, Joseph Tracy (Pa) 2902 Monterey Ct, Springfield PA 19064 B Buffalo NY 12/28/1946 s Joseph Tracy Rivers & Maxim. BA Harv 1969; MDiv EDS 1975; PhD Duke 1983. D 6/14/1975 P 8/1/1976 Bp Lyman Cunningham Ogilby. S Jas Ch Wilmington DE 2001; Int The Ch Of The Ascen Claymont DE 1999-2001; Calv Ch Glen Riddle PA 1998-1999; S Jas Ch Greenridge Aston PA 1995-1997; R S Andr's Epis Ch Glenmoore PA 1985-1994; S Giles Ch Upper Darby PA 1978-1985; P-in-c S Mk's Epis Ch Roxboro NC 1976-1978; Asst S Jos's Ch Durham NC 1975-1976. Ed, "S Geo Coll Chronicle," 1994; Auth, "Pattern & Process In Early Chr Pilgrimage"; Auth, "Challenge Of Renwl In Inner Suburban Cong". AAR; Conf Angl Theol; SBL. jrivers@adelphia.net

RIVET, E J (Colo) 46 North Ridge Court, Parachute CO 81635 **Mssn Partnership Vic S Jn's Epis Ch New Castle CO 2009-; Vic All SS Epis Ch Battlement Mesa CO 2007-** B Providence RI 8/15/1946 s Robert Matthias Rivet & Marguerite Marie. BA Metropltn St Coll of Denver 1973; MA U CO, Denver 1979; MDiv SWTS 2004. D 6/12/2004 P 12/18/2004 Bp Robert John O'Neill. m 10/22/1983 Martha Jane Morris c 2. Cler Mem of Stndg Com Dio Colorado Denver CO 2008-2011; Mssn Strtgy Commitee Dio Colorado Denver CO 2007-2011; Assoc R Chr's Epis Ch Castle Rock CO 2004-2007. Contributing Writer, ""Labyrinths Across the St,"" *Colorado Epis*, Dio Colorado, 2011; Contributing Writer, ""Emerging Mssn Partnerships,"" *Colorado Epis*, Dio Coloorado, 2009. Certifcate Ch Dvlpmt Inst Dio Colorado 2008. ejmrivet@q.com

RIVETTI, Mary Elisabeth (Spok) 1500 Ne Stadium Way, Pullman WA 99163 **R S Jas Pullman WA 2003-** B Great Falls MT 3/11/1950 d David Gray McDavid & Ellen McClintock. BA U CA, Santa Barbara 1972; MA U CA, Santa Barbara 1974; C. Phil U CA, Berkeley 1982; MDiv CDSP 2000. D 6/1/2000 P 12/7/2000 Bp Carolyn Tanner Irish. m 8/27/2009 George Rivetti c 4. Assoc S Paul's Epis Ch Walnut Creek CA 2000-2003. Participant Preaching Excellence Prog 2000; Grant Rec Soc for the Increase of Mnstry 1999. merivetti@gmail.com

RIVOLTA, Agostino Cetrangolo (NJ) 69 Broad St, Eatontown NJ 07724 B Carate Italy 10/27/1942 s Mario Rivolta & Ganzi. STB Immac Concep 1970; MPhil Drew U 1978; MLS Rutgers U 1979. Rec from Roman Catholic 6/1/2010 as Priest Bp George Edward Councell. m 12/20/1975 Barbara Rivolta. agostino.rivolta@comcast.net

RIZNER, Andrew Robert (ETenn) 3669 Ivy Way, Sevierville TN 37876 **Int Ch Of The Resurr Loudon TN 2002-** B Middletown CT 12/11/1926 s Andrew Rizner & Georgina Elizabeth. BS U of Florida 1950; STB GTS 1962. D 6/29/1962 Bp Henry I Louttit P 12/29/1962 Bp James Loughlin Duncan. m 2/6/1971 Constance Bufkin. Int S Jos The Carpenter Sevierville TN 1999-2002; Dioc Bd Dio Cntrl Florida Orlando FL 1990-1992; Dioc Bd Dio Cntrl Florida Orlando FL 1990-1992; Stwdshp Chair Dio Cntrl Florida Orlando FL 1990-1991; Stwdshp Chair Dio Cntrl Florida Orlando FL 1990-1991; Chair C&C Dio Cntrl Florida Orlando FL 1989-1994; Dioc Bd Dio Cntrl Florida Orlando FL 1988; Dep GC Dio Cntrl Florida Orlando FL 1985-1994; Dep GC Dio Cntrl Florida Orlando FL 1985-1994; Liturg Cmsn Dio Cntrl Florida

R

Orlando FL 1985-1987; Chair Fin Cmsn Dio Cntrl Florida Orlando FL 1985-1986; Chair Campus Mnstry Bd Dio Cntrl Florida Orlando FL 1984-1988; Dioc Bd Dio Cntrl Florida Orlando FL 1982-1984; Stndg Com Dio Cntrl Florida Orlando FL 1978-1988; Stwdshp Chair Dio Cntrl Florida Orlando FL 1976-1983; R S Mary Of The Ang Epis Ch Orlando FL 1973-1995; Dioc Bd Dio Cntrl Florida Orlando FL 1973-1975; Cn Cathd Ch Of S Lk Orlando FL 1967-1973; Cur S Steph's Ch Coconut Grove Coconut Grove FL 1963-1967; Cur S Jn's Epis Ch Homestead FL 1962-1963. Auth, *Tale of Two Congregations*. Chapl Ord of S Lk 1971; Soc of S Jn the Evang, Assoc 1966. Hon Cn Dio CFla 1995.

RIZO, Hermogenes Raphael U (HB) 500 W Park Dr # 208, Miami FL 33172 **Died 1/2/2010** B Matagalpa NI 8/7/1942 s Miguel Ugarte & Mercedes. BA Coll San Luis 1965; Sem Cntrl Managua 1967; Med Escuela Normal De Jinotega 1970; U of Miami 1997. D 10/4/1979 P 5/24/1980 Bp Hugo Luis Pina-Lopez. c 2. La Ord De La Santa Cruz.

ROACH, James Lehr (Neb) 1000 O Street, #310, Lincoln NE 68508 B Lincoln NE 7/15/1942 s James Sidney Roach & Janet. BA U of Nebraska 1964; STB EDS 1967; PhD U of Nebraska 1990. D 7/18/1967 P 12/21/1967 Bp Russell T Rauscher. m 12/15/1961 Sandra Jean Weber c 2. Fin Com Dio Nebraska Omaha NE 1975-1983; Hosp Auth Dio Nebraska Omaha NE 1975-1983; Chair of the Dept of Missions Dio Nebraska Omaha NE 1974-1983; Pres of Mnstrl Assn Dio Nebraska Omaha NE 1974-1975; Dep GC Dio Nebraska Omaha NE 1973-1982; Bp & Trst Dio Nebraska Omaha NE 1973-1980; Chair of Ecum Relatns Dio Nebraska Omaha NE 1972-1973; R S Steph's Ch Grand Island NE 1970-1982; Bp Coun Dio Nebraska Omaha NE 1970-1978; BEC Dio Nebraska Omaha NE 1970-1971; Secy of the Dept of Missions Dio Nebraska Omaha NE 1969-1977; Vic S Eliz's Ch Holdrege NE 1967-1970; Vic S Pauls Epis Ch Arapahoe NE 1967-1969. Jamesroach60@aol.com

ROACH, Kenneth Merle (Fla) 13846 Atlantic Blvd Apt 617, Jacksonville FL 32225 B Jacksonville FL 2/7/1941 s William Merle Roach & Etheleen. Presb Coll Clinton SC 1966; Jacksonville U 1969; BA U of No Florida 1974; MDiv STUSo 1989. D 6/11/1989 P 12/10/1989 Bp Frank Stanley Cerveny. m 6/19/2007 Terri Jo Kennedy c 2. R S Lk's Epis Ch Jacksonville FL 1995-2005; R S Paul's Epis Ch Quincy FL 1990-1995; Cur San Jose Epis Ch Jacksonville FL 1989-1990. Acad of Par Cler; OHC. kroach2741@bellsouth.net

ROACH, Robert Eugene (Alb) 8 Brookwood Dr, Clifton Park NY 12065 **D S Geo's Ch Clifton Pk NY 2002-** B Barnsdall OK 7/21/1923 s Robert Eugene Roach & Ella Mabel. BS Oklahoma St U 1944. D 6/18/1983 Bp Wilbur Emory Hogg Jr. m 10/19/1979 Susan Rae Detweiler c 3. D Gr And H Innoc Albany NY 2000-2002; Dioc Sprtl Dir Curs Dio Albany Albany NY 1988-1990; D S Geo's Ch Clifton Pk NY 1983-2000. rroach1@nycap.rr.com

ROADMAN, Betsy Johns (NY) 91 Mystic Dr, Ossining NY 10562 B Ellwood City PA 2/28/1952 d Jay Sharp Johns & Sara Elizabeth. BA Clarion U of Pennsylvania 1973; RN Sewickley Vlly Hosp Sch of Nrsng 1980; MDiv UTS 2001. D 3/10/2001 Bp Richard Frank Grein P 9/15/2001 Bp Mark Sean Sisk. m 12/27/1980 Larry Roadman c 2. Int S Aug's Epis Ch Croton On Hudson NY 2005-2006; Coordntr for EFM, Dio New York The TS at The U So Sewanee TN 2004-2011; Assoc S Aug's Epis Ch Croton On Hudson NY 2004-2005; Cur Chr's Ch Rye NY 2001-2004. betsyroadman@gmail.com

ROAF, Phoebe Alison (Va) 2900 Hanes Ave, Richmond VA 23222 **R S Phil's Ch Richmond VA 2011-** B Lansing MI 3/8/1964 d Clifton Roaf & Andree. AB Harvard Coll 1986; MPA Pr 1989; JD WALR Bowen Sch of Law 1998; MDiv VTS 2008. D 12/29/2007 P 7/9/2008 Bp Charles Edward Jenkins III. Assoc R Trin Ch New Orleans LA 2008-2011. phoeberoaf@yahoo.com

ROANE, Wilson Kessner (FdL) E2382 Pebble Run Rd, Waupaca WI 54981 **Mem and Pres, Stndg Com Dio Fond du Lac Appleton WI 2009-; Mem, COM Dio Fond du Lac Appleton WI 2009-; Mem, Invstmt Com Dio Fond du Lac Appleton WI 2008-** B Evanston IL 8/11/1938 s Kearney Daniel Roane & C Josephine. BA Ken 1960; MBA U Chi 1964; MDiv Nash 1990. D 12/30/1989 P 7/11/1990 Bp William L Stevens. m 12/30/1960 Susan Montgomery c 3. Int R Ch Of The Intsn Stevens Point WI 2010-2011; Int R S Anne's Ch De Pere WI 2009-2010; Int R Ch Of The H Apos Oneida WI 2007-2008; Mem, Stndg Com Dio Fond du Lac Appleton WI 2004-2008; Mem, Stndg Com Dio Fond du Lac Appleton WI 1996-1998; Mem, Exec Bd Dio Fond du Lac Appleton WI 1994; Mem, Fin Com Dio Fond du Lac Appleton WI 1992; R S Mk's Ch Waupaca WI 1990-2004; D in Charge S Epis Olaf's Ch Amherst WI 1989-1990; D in Charge S Mk's Ch Waupaca WI 1989-1990. Sis Of The H Nativ 1990. wilson.roane@gmail.com

ROBAYO-HIDALGO, Daniel Dario (Va) Emmanuel Episcopal Church, 660 S. Main St., Harrisonburg VA 22801 **Exec Bd Dio Virginia Richmond VA 2011-; R Emm Ch Harrisonburg VA 2009-; Misión Latina/Latino Mnstry T/F Dio Virginia Richmond VA 2007-** B Maracaibo VE 1/13/1956 s Daniel Enrique Robayo-Quintero & Angela Bertha. BA Trin Deerfield IL 1983; MDiv VTS 1987. D 6/13/1987 P 4/21/1988 Bp Peter James Lee. m 10/23/1999 E(lizabeth) Ann Robayo c 6. Pres of Stndg Com Dio Virginia Richmond VA 2009-2010; Stndg Com Dio Virginia Richmond VA 2007-2009; Sprtl Discernment Fac Dio Virginia Richmond VA 2006-2010; Exec Bd Dio Virginia Richmond VA 2006-2007; R Chr Epis Ch Luray VA 2003-2009; Assoc R S Andr's Ch Burke VA 1999-2003; Exec Bd Dio Virginia Richmond VA 1998-1999; Bp's Dialogue Grp on Human Sxlty Dio Virginia Richmond VA 1997-2003; R Emm Epis Ch (Piedmont Par) Delaplane VA 1991-1999; COM Dio Virginia Richmond VA 1990-1999; Assoc R S Andr's Ch Burke VA 1988-1991; Asst Hisp Mssnr Dio Virginia Richmond VA 1987-1988; Com On Human Sxlty Dio Virginia Richmond VA 1983-1984. drobayo2@gmail.com

ROBB, George Kerry (SeFla) 521 Rhine Rd, Palm Beach Gardens FL 33410 **Int S Ptr's Ch Fernandina Bch FL 2011-** B Tampa FL 3/23/1936 s Charles Robb & Gladys C. BA Stetson U 1958; BD Candler TS Emory U 1961. D 7/28/1967 Bp William Loftin Hargrave P 11/30/1967 Bp Henry I Louttit. m 9/6/1957 Sally T Tait c 3. Int S Mary's Epis Ch Stuart FL 2009-2011; Int S Paul's Ch Key W FL 2008-2009; Int H Trin Ch Gainesville FL 2006-2007; Int Chr Ch Bradenton FL 2004-2007; Dioc Secy Dio SE Florida Miami FL 1980-1990; Stndg Com Pres Dio SE Florida Miami FL 1974-1976; GC Dep Dio SE Florida Miami FL 1973-1991; R S Mk's Ch Palm Bch Gardens FL 1968-2004; Cur S Andr's Ch Lake Worth FL 1967-1968. Hon Cn Trin Cathd Miami FL 2000. canonrobb@yahoo.com

ROBB, Philip (Los) 22641 Lark St, Grand Terrace CA 92313 B Philadelphia PA 6/6/1929 s Philip Fisher Robb & Eleanor Louise. BA Pr 1951; MDiv VTS 1956; MSW How 1958; JD U of La Verne La Verne CA 1976. D 6/20/1956 Bp Archie H Crowley P 4/11/1957 Bp Angus Dun. m 2/9/1985 Carol Irene Leonard c 2. Asst S Jn's Par San Bernardino CA 2005-2006; Assoc All SS Ch Pasadena CA 1999-2004; S Jn's Par San Bernardino CA 1980-1983; S Lk's Mssn Fontana CA 1978-1979; S Tim's Epis Ch Apple Vlly CA 1977-1978; S Columba's Epis Mssn Big Bear Lake CA 1975-1977; Trin Epis Ch Redlands CA 1967-1976. Epis League for Soc Action; ESCRU; Los Angeles Cler Assn 2006. Phi Beta Kappa Pr Chapt 1951. phrobb@aol.com

ROBBINS, Anne Wilson (SO) 10831 Crooked River Rd., #101, Bonita Springs FL 34135 B Chicago IL 1/13/1931 d Everett Broomall Wilson & Bernice. GTS; BA Wells Coll 1953; Med USC 1968; MDiv Untd TS Dayton OH 1982. D 6/10/1982 P 1/2/1983 Bp William Grant Black. m 6/13/1953 Richard Eugene Robbins c 2. Stndg Com Dio Sthrn Ohio Cincinnati OH 1997-2002; BEC Dio Sthrn Ohio Cincinnati OH 1991-1997; S Pat's Epis Ch Dublin OH 1989-2002; S Dav Vandalia OH 1983-1989; Asst S Mk's Epis Ch Dayton OH 1982-1983. Auth, *Welcome to Total Mnstry*. ESMA; EWC. annerobbins@comcast.net

ROBBINS, Buckley Howard (ETenn) 781 Shearer Cove Rd, Chattanooga TN 37405 B Philadelphia PA 12/25/1938 s Buckley Cutler Robbins & Esther Dickinson. BA U MI 1960; MA U MI 1965; MDiv STUSo 1983. D 6/26/1983 P 5/15/1984 Bp William Evan Sanders. m 6/23/1990 Janice Rothe Robbins c 5. Dio E Tennessee Knoxville TN 1991-2008; R S Fran Of Assisi Epis Ch Ooltewah TN 1991-2008; P-in-c S Mary Magd Ch Fayetteville TN 1984-1987; Gr Ch Chattanooga TN 1983-1991. Cmnty of S Mary 1983. b_robbins@comcast.net

ROBBINS, Charlotte Ann (ND) 3600 25th St. S., Fargo ND 58104 **D Geth Cathd Fargo ND 2007-** B Scottsbluff NE 5/27/1939 d Charles Blanchard Comstock & Vada Ardis Gatewood. BSN U of Nebraska Sch of Nrsng 1961. D 6/22/2007 Bp Michael Gene Smith. m 11/23/1962 James Robbins c 3. charlotte.robbins@hotmail.com

ROBBINS, Geoffrey Thayer (Me) 14 Liberty Ln, Apt 75, South Portland ME 04106 B Bryn Mawr PA 8/7/1943 s Geoffrey Wolcott Robbins & Virginia. BA Colby Coll 1965; MDiv Ya Berk 1968. D 6/8/1968 P 12/21/1968 Bp Horace W B Donegan. m 4/25/1981 Marlese Murphy c 3. Int S Steph's Ch Middlebury VT 2004-2005; All SS Epis Ch Skowhegan ME 1992-1994; Int All SS Epis Ch Skowhegan ME 1991-1992; Int S Barn Ch Augusta Augusta ME 1988-1989; Int Vic All SS Epis Ch Skowhegan ME 1985-1987; Int S Mk's Ch Augusta ME 1982-1983; Int Ch Of The Gd Shpd Rangeley ME 1978-1979; S Mk's Epis Ch Penn Yan NY 1972-1978; S Mk's And S Jn's Epis Ch Rochester NY 1972-1977; Asst Ch Of The Atone Westfield MA 1970-1972. geoff1221@maine.rr.com

R

ROBBINS, Herbert John (RG) HC 46 Box 667, Ruidoso Downs NM 88346 B Hempstead NY 2/14/1939 s Herbert Samuel Robbins & Katharine. BS W Virginia Wesleyan Coll 1969; MDiv S Paul TS 1972. D 9/15/1978 P 8/6/1979 Bp Richard Mitchell Trelease Jr. m 3/9/1973 Kelly Marie Robinson c 2. R S Paul's Ch Artesia NM 1988-2005; Dio The Rio Grande Albuquerque NM 1985-1988; R S Paul's Ch Artesia NM 1980-1985; Cur S Andr's Ch Roswell NM 1979-1980; Asst S Thos A Becket Ch Roswell NM 1978-1979. Auth, "Sem Ch Hist". handkrobbins@valornet.com

ROBBINS, Janice Rothe (ETenn) 3425 Alta Vista Dr, Chattanooga TN 37411 **S Nich Sch Chattanooga TN 2001-** B Chattanooga TN 6/29/1945 BA U Of Chattanooga 1967; MS Trevecca Nazarene U 1989. D 6/16/2001 Bp Charles Glenn VonRosenberg. m 6/23/1990 Buckley Howard Robbins c 4.

ROBBINS, Lance David (Roch) 1130 Webster Rd, Webster NY 14580 **R Ch Of The Gd Shpd Webster NY 1991-** B Chicago IL 9/12/1956 s Hiram Michael Robbins & Elizabeth Ann. BA Thiel Coll 1978; MDiv SWTS 1982. D 6/5/1982 P 12/18/1982 Bp Donald James Davis. m 11/9/2011 Karen Robbins c 1.

Asst R Calv Ch Columbia MO 1986-1991; Vic S Aug Of Cbury Ch Edinboro PA 1982-1985; Vic S Ptr's Ch Waterford PA 1982-1985; Dio NW Pennsylvania Erie PA 1982. ESMHE. LROBBINS3714@AOL.COM

ROBBINS-COLE, Adrian (NH) 49 Concord St, Peterborough NH 03458 **All SS Ch Peterborough NH 2004-** B London ENGLAND 4/6/1962 s Eric Cole & Pamela Alice. BS The London Sch of Econ and Political Sci 1984; MA Oxf 1992; CAS CDSP 1993; Ripon Coll Cuddesdon Oxford GB 1993; MA King's Coll, London - Lon 1996. Trans from Church Of England 9/2/2004 Bp V Gene Robinson. m 1/1/1994 Sarah Jane Robbins c 2. revrobbinscole@myfairpoint.net

ROBBINS-COLE, Sarah Jane (NH) 49 Concord St, Peterborough NH 03458 **All SS Ch Peterborough NH 2006-** B Des Moines IA 10/18/1968 d Henry Bellows Robbins & Karen Jane. BA U of Vermont 1990; CDSP 1993; BA/MA Oxf 1995; MA King's Coll, London 2000. Trans from Church Of England 9/2/2004 Bp V Gene Robinson. m 1/1/1994 Adrian Cole c 2. sarahrobbinscole@yahoo.com

ROBBINS-PENNIMAN, Becky (SwFla) Church of the Good Shepherd, 639 Edgewater Dr, Dunedin FL 34698 **P-in-c Ch Of The Gd Shpd Dunedin FL 2010-; Cmsn on Liturg and Mus Dio SW Florida Sarasota FL 2010-; Const and Cn Com Dio SW Florida Sarasota FL 2003-** B Orange County FL 6/22/1954 d Richard Eugene Robbins & Anne Wilson. BA Ken 1976; JD OH SU 1979; Cert of Angl Stds Bex 2000; MDiv Trin Luth Sem 2000. D 6/24/2000 P 1/6/2001 Bp Herbert Thompson Jr. m 5/29/1976 Gus Robbins-Penniman c 2. Resolutns Com Dio SW Florida Sarasota FL 2005-2010; R and Assoc Pstr Lamb Of God Epis Ch Ft Myers FL 2002-2010; Const and Cn Com Dio Sthrn Ohio Cincinnati OH 2001-2002; Faith in Life Cmsn Dio Sthrn Ohio Cincinnati OH 2001-2002; Intern All SS Epis Ch New Albany OH 2000-2002; Interfaith & Ecum Relatns Cmsn Dio Sthrn Ohio Cincinnati OH 1996-2002. HSEC 1999-2004. Seidler Awd for Excellence in Systematic Theol Trin Luth Sem 2000; Peters Awd for Ldrshp Trin Luth Sem 1999; Schaaf Awd for Excellence in Ch Hist Trin Luth Sem 1998. beckyrp@gmail.com

ROBERSON, Mary Moore Mills (USC) 3123 Oakview Rd, Columbia SC 29204 B Greenville SC 7/22/1939 d John Linton Roberson & Mary Mills. BA Furman U 1985; MDiv GTS 1998. D 6/13/1998 P 5/29/1999 Bp Dorsey Felix Henderson. Assoc S Jn's Epis Ch Columbia SC 2003-2010; Asst R S Ptr's Epis Ch Greenville SC 1999-2003; Chr Epis Ch Lancaster SC 1998-1999. mroberson5@sc.rr.com

ROBERSON, Whitney Wherrett (Cal) 641 47th Ave, San Francisco CA 94121 **P-in-c S Aid's Mssn Bolinas CA 2011-** B Glendale OH 4/26/1947 d Norman Lewis Wherrett & Evelyn Mae. BA Duke 1969; MA San Francisco St U 1972; MDiv CDSP 1996. D 12/6/1997 P 6/6/1998 Bp William Edwin Swing. c 3. Assoc Gr Cathd San Francisco CA 2002-2008; Asst For Fam Mnstrs S Bede's Epis Ch Menlo Pk CA 2001-2002; Assoc Ch Of The Epiph San Carlos CA 1998-2001. Auth, "Life and Livehood: A Handbook for Spiritualtiy at Wk," Morehouse Pub, 2004; Auth, "The Mass: Remembering Our Story," Franciscan Cmncatn, 1990. whitrober@att.net

ROBERT, Mary Christopher (CGC) 551 W Barksdale Dr, Mobile AL 36606 **Asst R All SS Epis Ch Mobile AL 2007-** B New Orleans LA 3/21/1954 d Frank Wall Robert & Donna. BA Peabody Coll 1975; MDiv TS 1979; A.D.N U of Mobile 1982. D 6/18/1979 Bp William F Gates Jr P 3/19/1983 Bp Charles Farmer Duvall. Asst S Paul's Epis Ch Daphne AL 1982-1986; D S Jn's Epis Cathd Knoxville TN 1979. asstrector@allsaintsmobile.org

ROBERTS, Alice (NH) 2 Moore Rd, Newport NH 03773 B Palo Alto CA 4/16/1941 d Herbert Edwin Hawkes & Frances Roberts. BA Smith 1962; MDiv EDS 1995. D 4/1/1995 P 5/1/1996 Bp Mary Adelia Rosamond McLeod. m 8/13/1995 Russell Berry c 4. aliceandruss@comcast.net

ROBERTS, C(harles) Jon (SwFla) Good Shepherd Episcopal Church, 1115 Center Rd, Venice FL 34292 **R The Epis Ch Of The Gd Shpd Venice FL 2007-** B North Carolina 10/7/1968 s Charles Winston Roberts & Louise Talmadge. BS Nc St U Raleigh NC 1990; MS Duke Durham NC 1998; MDiv Nash 2007. D 6/2/2007 Bp John Bailey Lipscomb P 12/5/2007 Bp Dabney Tyler Smith. m 4/4/1998 Lynne W Roberts c 2. Mich Ramsey Soc 2008. jrgoodshepherd@comcast.net

ROBERTS, George C (USC) 170 Saint Andrews Rd, Columbia SC 29210 **Cur S Mary's Ch Columbia SC 2009-** B Raleigh NC 8/26/1963 s Danny Lee Roberts & Barbara Jean. BS Campbell U 1986; MFA U of Mississippi 1997; MDiv VTS 2009. D 5/6/2009 P 12/4/2009 Bp Dorsey Felix Henderson. m 6/10/1995 Tracey Tracey June Roy c 4. george.actorpriest@gmail.com

ROBERTS, Harold Frederick (Miss) 7417 Falcon Cir., Ocean Springs MS 39564 B Oakville ON CA 3/8/1944 s Harold Ernest Roberts & Jessie Elizabeth. BA Richmond Coll Toronto ON CA 1970; MDiv U Tor 1973; Exec Dev. Prog. York U 1991; D.Min. SWTS 2008. Trans from Anglican Church of Canada 3/17/1997 Bp Alfred Clark Marble Jr. m 9/7/1968 Janice Mary Stewart. R The Epis Ch Of The Redeem Biloxi MS 1997-2011. P Assoc - The Sis of S Jn the Div - Toron 1973. A Grant of Arms Gvnr Gnrl of Can 1997; GCLJ(E) Ord of S Lazarus 1993; Can 125 Medal Govt of Can 1992; Hon Cn S Jas Cathd - Toronto Toronto Can 1992; Can Forces Decoration Govt of Can 1983; Queen's Silver Jubilee Medal Govt of Can 1978. hfroberts@cableone.net

ROBERTS III, Henry Pauling (EC) 260 Houser Road, Blacksburg SC 29702 B Fort Gordon GA 8/19/1944 s Henry Pauling Roberts & Winefred. BBA Georgia Coll GA 1973; MBA Georgia Coll GA 1975; MDiv STUSo 1987. D 6/5/1987 Bp Robert Oran Miller P 12/1/1987 Bp Furman Stough. m 8/30/1969 Sarah Roberts. R Chr Ch Eliz City NC 1997-1999; R S Jn's Ch Winnsboro SC 1992-1994; R S Mary's Epis Ch Jasper AL 1987-1992. Auth, "The Twilight's Last Gleaming On Publ Educ," Xlibris Corp, 2008.

ROBERTS, James Beauregard (Miss) 2441 S Shore Dr, Biloxi MS 39532 **R S Mk's Ch Gulfport MS 1969-** B Biloxi MS 11/4/1941 s Henry Hinsdale Roberts & Alma Lucille. BA Wm Carey U 1963; MDiv PDS 1966; DD Amer Bible Inst 1974. D 6/11/1966 P 5/20/1967 Bp John M Allin. m 1/26/1962 Pamela Mitchell c 3. Vic S Timothys Epis Ch Southaven MS 1968-1969; Cur H Cross Epis Ch Olive Branch MS 1966-1968; Cur H Innoc' Epis Ch Como MS 1966-1968. Outstanding Young Men of Amer; Personalities of the So. stmarks@cableone.net

ROBERTS, J(ames) Christopher (Mont) 515 N Park Ave, Helena MT 59601 B Hartford CT 5/10/1949 s Albert William Roberts & Audrey Catherine. BA Hampden-Sydney Coll 1971; MDiv VTS 1976; MA Duquesne U 1992. D 6/12/1976 P 12/15/1976 Bp David Shepherd Rose. m 9/25/1999 Linda Lee Secora c 3. R S Martha's Epis Ch Papillion NE 2003-2009; Dir Dioc Min Formation Prog Dio Montana Helena MT 1998-2000; R Ch Of The Incarn Great Falls MT 1996-2003; The Wheeling Cluster Wheeling WV 1996; Dio W Virginia Charleston WV 1993-1996; P-in-c S Paul's Ch Wheeling WV 1991-1996; R S Jas' Epis Ch Lewisburg WV 1988-1990; Chapl Boys Hm Covington VA 1986-1987; SCCM Dio Upper So Carolina Columbia SC 1981-1983; R Chr Epis Ch Lancaster SC 1980-1984; Asst S Martins-In-The-Field Columbia SC 1977-1980; Emm Ch Mears VA 1976-1977. mtcto@qwestoffice.net

ROBERTS, Jason Thomas (WTex) 8642 Cheviot Hts, San Antonio TX 78254 **Vic Ch Of The H Sprt San Antonio TX 2009-** B Richmond VA 4/7/1975 s James Orville Roberts & Nancy. BA Jas Madison U 1997; M.Ed. Jas Madison U 1999; MDiv VTS 2003; Grad Cert Virginia Commonwealth U 2006. D 6/14/2003 P 12/20/2003 Bp Peter James Lee. m 1/3/2009 Susannah E Nicholson c 1. Asst/Assoc R Gr & H Trin Epis Ch Richmond VA 2003-2008. jsntroberts@gmail.com

ROBERTS JR, John Bannister Gibson (CFla) 860 Ohlinger Rd, Babson Park FL 33827 B Charleroi PA 1/1/1928 s John Bannister Gibson Roberts & Christine Ament. BA Washington and Jefferson U 1950; MDiv PDS 1954. D 6/19/1954 P 12/18/1954 Bp William S Thomas. m 6/14/1952 Fay Kathryn Boord. S Ann's Epis Ch Wauchula FL 1984-1999; Off Of Bsh For ArmdF New York NY 1959-1969; All SS Ch Aliquippa PA 1954-1959; P-in-c S Lk's Epis Ch Georgetown PA 1954-1959. Legion of Merit USAF 1983; Bronze Star USAF 1970; Meritorious USAF.

ROBERTS III, John Marshall (Mass) No address on file. **Died 11/27/2009** B Norfolk VA 12/29/1932 D 6/22/1957 P 2/1/1958 Bp Anson Phelps Stokes Jr.

ROBERTS, Jose F (RI) 236 Central Ave, Pawtucket RI 02860 **Dio Rhode Island Providence RI 2004-** B 2/19/1955 s Jose Roberts & Carmen Lucia. Centro De Estudios Teologicas. D 8/15/1982 P 6/1/1984 Bp Telesforo A Isaac. m 2/20/1983 Dolores Rijo c 1. Dio Puerto Rico S Just PR 2000-2003; Dio The Dominican Republic (Iglesia Epis Dominicana) Santo Domingo DO 1995-2000; Dio Panama 1988-1990; Dio The Dominican Republic (Iglesia Epis Dominicana) Santo Domingo DO 1982-1988; Vic Iglesia Epis San Andres Santo Domingo DO 1982-1987.

ROBERTS, Judith Sims (Ind) 342 Red Ash Cir, Englewood FL 34223 **Asst Ch Of The Gd Shpd Punta Gorda FL 2007-** B Nantucket MA 7/22/1935 d Albert Randolph Sims & Nancy Chapman. SWTS; BA Br 1957; MDiv EDS 1957. D 6/23/1995 Bp Edward Witker Jones P 9/15/2002 Bp Catherine Elizabeth Maples Waynick. m 8/10/1957 Richard Fred Roberts c 4. Coordntr Dio SE Florida Miami FL 2005-2008; Asst S Dav's Epis Ch Englewood FL 2003-2007; Asst All SS Ch Seymour IN 2002-2003; Global Missions Com Dio Indianapolis Indianapolis IN 2000-2003; Stndg Com Dio Indianapolis Indianapolis IN 1999-2000; Com Dio Indianapolis Indianapolis IN 1996-1998; D S Paul's Ch Columbus IN 1995-2002. revjsr@cs.com

ROBERTS, Katherine Alexander (At) 18 Clarendon Ave, Avondale Estates GA 30002 B New York NY 6/28/1942 d Henry Herman Harjes & Joan. BA Marymount Manhattan Coll 1972; MDiv Candler TS Emory U 1991; CAS CDSP 1995. D 6/28/1995 Bp James Louis Jelinek P 2/1/1996 Bp Sanford Zangwill Kaye Hampton. c 1. S Anth's Epis Ch Winder GA 1998-2001; The Epis Ch Of The Nativ Fayetteville GA 1998. Co-Auth, "The Unhealed Wounders," *Restoring the Soul of a Ch*, Liturg Press, 1995.

ROBERTS, Linda Lee (Neb) 16404 72nd St, Plattsmouth NE 68048 **P, Ret (Assoc P) S Martha's Epis Ch Papillion NE 2007-** B Whitehall MT 8/5/1946 d Leo B Secora & Mary. Montana St U 1969. D 6/11/1991 P 2/1/1996 Bp Charles Jones III. m 9/25/1999 J(ames) Christopher Roberts c 2. S Mary's Epis Ch Blair NE 2004-2006; Dio Montana Helena MT 1997-1999; P Chr Ch

Sheridan MT 1996-1999; Mem, Stndg Cmsn Dio Montana Helena MT 1996-1999; Epis Mnstry Ennis MT 1995-1996; S Paul's Ch Virginia City MT 1994-1999; Mem, Cmsn Dio Montana Helena MT 1991-1996; Pstr Asst S Steph's Ch Billings MT 1991-1994. lsecora@hotmail.com

ROBERTS III BSG, Malcolm (EC) 520 Taberna Way, New Bern NC 28562 B Camp White OR 11/27/1943 s Malcolm Roberts & Nancy. AA Mitchell Coll 1964; BA Windham Coll 1966; MDiv VTS 1975. D 6/7/1975 P 12/13/1975 Bp Joseph Warren Hutchens. m 5/13/1972 Mary Lamar Simpson c 2. Peace Epis Ch New Bern NC 2006-2010; Off Of Bsh For ArmdF New York NY 1978-2004; Cur S Jn The Evang Yalesville CT 1975-1978; Cur S Paul's Ch Wallingford CT 1975-1978. Bro of S Greg 1999. mroberts12@hotmail.com

ROBERTS, Patricia E (At) 4748 Big Oak Bnd, Marietta GA 30062 **Died 12/5/2010** B Rochester NY 5/24/1949 d Clifford Coburn Scrivener & Nance Babcock. Indiana U 1969; BA Webster U 1973; Bex 1992; MDiv Candler TS Emory U 1998. D 6/5/1999 Bp Onell Asiselo Soto P 2/5/2000 Bp Frank Kellogg Allan. c 2. paxt2you@aol.com

ROBERTS, Patricia Joyce (Ia) 3226 S Clinton St, Sioux City IA 51106 **D Calv Epis Ch Sioux City IA 1995-** B Sioux City IA 9/14/1939 d John Henry Graham & Evelyn Jenett. Morningside Coll. D 12/17/1995 Bp Carl Christopher Epting. m 8/20/1960 Vernon Carl Roberts c 2. vproberts1@juno.com

ROBERTS, Patricia Kant (CFla) 35 Willow Dr, Orlando FL 32807 B Mineola NY 8/17/1939 d William Theodore Kant & Marion Shea. AD Florida Chr U 2005. D 12/9/2006 Bp John Wadsworth Howe. c 8. pkracts29@aol.com

ROBERTS, Paul Benjamin (At) 33 Cross Crk E, Dahlonega GA 30533 **P Assoc Ch of the Resurr Sautee Nacoochee GA 2008-** B Austin TX 1/1/1943 s Fowler Roberts & Frances Wray. U So 1961; BA SMU 1964; MDiv Ya Berk 1967; DMin Van 1991. D 6/15/1967 P 12/21/1967 Bp William Paul Barnds. m 11/28/1968 Florence Bright c 2. R S Eliz's Epis Ch Dahlonega GA 2002-2006; Int Ch of the Resurr Sautee Nacoochee GA 2000-2002; Archd Dio W Virginia Charleston WV 1994-1999; R Trin Ch Huntington WV 1993-2000; R S Mths Ch Nashville TN 1977-1993; Vic S Thos Epis Ch Knoxville TN 1974-1977; Vic Ch Of Our Sav Gallatin TN 1971-1974; Asst R Gr - S Lk's Ch Memphis TN 1968-1971. Grad Fllshp Berkely DS 1967; Bromberg Awd SMU Dallas TX 1963; Wilson Fell SMU Dallas TX 1961. paulmoonrush2@windstream.net

ROBERTS, Peter Francis (CFla) 5500 N Tropical Trl, Merritt Island FL 32953 **S Lk's Epis Ch Merritt Island FL 2003-** B Birmingham England 10/4/1959 s Jack Francis Roberts & Yvonne Jean. BS Nthrn Illinois U 1981; BA U of Leeds 1987; Coll of the Resurr 1988; Untd Coll of the Ascen Selly Oak W Midlands Eng 1991. Trans from Church Of England 9/11/2003 Bp John Wadsworth Howe. m 6/19/1987 Ann Elizabeth Roberts c 3. pfroberts@peoplepc.com

ROBERTS, Steven Michael (La) 1613 7th St, New Orleans LA 70115 **Cn Chr Ch Cathd New Orleans LA 2002-** B Glendale CA 8/9/1964 s Bryan Whitfield Roberts & Nancy Susan. BS Louisiana Tech U 1987; MDiv SWTS 1996. D 6/8/1996 P 1/12/1997 Bp Robert Jefferson Hargrove Jr. m 12/29/1990 Penny B Brown. Assoc R Epis Ch Of The Gd Shpd Lake Chas LA 1999-2002; R Trin Ch Crowley LA 1997-1999; Cur S Mich's Epis Ch Pineville LA 1996-1997. stevenroberts@cccnola.org

ROBERTS, William Allan (Ida) 1336 E Walker St, Blackfoot ID 83221 B Springfield OH 3/3/1933 s Arthur Roberts & Lydia Belle. BA Witt 1955; BD CDSP 1958. D 6/14/1958 P 12/9/1958 Bp Henry W Hobson. m 6/9/1957 Lorraine DeNicole c 3. Mtn Rivers Epis Cmnty Idaho Falls ID 1991-1995; R Chr Ch Xenia OH 1984-1991; R S Andr's Epis Ch Washington Crt Hse OH 1984-1989; R All SS Epis Ch Portsmouth OH 1977-1984; Assoc The Epis Ch Of The Ascen Middletown OH 1968-1977; Asst S Andr's Ch Meriden CT 1962-1968; Min in charge Gr Ch Pomeroy OH 1958-1962. war-lmr@q.com

ROBERTS, William D (Chi) 875 Wilmot Rd, Deerfield IL 60015 **R S Greg's Epis Ch Deerfield IL 1988-** B Evanston IL 5/5/1950 s James Huston Roberts & Charlotte Magie. AB Dart 1972; MDiv SWTS 1978. D 6/17/1978 Bp Quintin Ebenezer Primo Jr P 12/16/1978 Bp Walter Cameron Righter. m 3/30/1974 Ingrid C Carlson c 2. Asst S Barth's Ch New York NY 1981-1988; Asst Trin Cathd Davenport IA 1978-1981. Auth, "And the Word became Welsh," 2004; Auth, "The Angl Commitment to the Historic Episcopate," *Ecum Trends*, 2000; Auth, "Toward a Luth Anamnesis of the Historic Episcopate," *Ecum Trends*, 1998; Auth, "Two Kinds of Suffering," *LivCh*, 1998; Auth, "Response to the Significance of the ELCA's 1997 Ecum Agenda for the Wider Ch," *Ecum Trends*, 1997; Auth, "A Way to Pray Through the Ch Year Each Week Day by Day," *A Way to Pray Through the Ch Year Each Week Day by Day*, Forw Mvmt Press, 1986. williamsink@msn.com

ROBERTS, William Tudor (Mich) 584 E Walled Lake Dr, Walled Lake MI 48390 **Trst Dio Michigan Detroit MI 2011-; P/Pstr S Anne's Epis Ch Walled Lake MI 2011-; Cathd Chapt Dio Michigan Detroit MI 2010-; Cmsn on Const and Cn Dio Michigan Detroit MI 2010-** B Boston MA 12/7/1945 s O Tudor Roberts & Jeannette W B. D 11/3/2010 P 6/21/2011 Bp Wendell Nathaniel Gibbs Jr. m 4/11/1986 Alicia Alicia Grajales Droste c 2. D S Anne's Epis Ch Walled Lake MI 2010-2011. wroberts@walledlake.com

ROBERTSHAW III, Arthur Bentham (Ct) 88 Notch Hill Rd Apt 240, North Branford CT 06471 B Woonsocket RI 11/10/1927 s Arthur Bentham Robertshaw & Florence Eunice. BA Ya 1948; STB Ya Berk 1952. D 6/17/1952 P 12/19/1952 Bp Walter H Gray. R Ch Of The H Adv Clinton CT 1964-1987; Chair Yth Coun Dio Connecticut Hartford CT 1956-1966; P-in-c Ch Of S Jn By The Sea W Haven W Haven CT 1955-1964; Asst S Jn's Ch W Hartford CT 1954-1955.

ROBERTSHAW, Michelle Lyn (NC) 109 Celeste Circle, Chapel Hill NC 27517 **Asst R Ch Of The H Fam Chap Hill NC 2006-** B Tampa FL 8/30/1967 BA U of So Florida 1990; MDiv VTS 2003. D 6/14/2003 P 1/1/2004 Bp John Bailey Lipscomb. Vic S Mary Magd Lakewood Ranch FL 2005-2006; Asst S Bon Ch Sarasota FL 2003-2005. ixoye4u@aol.com

ROBERTSON, Ben G. (WTenn) 102 N 2nd St, Memphis TN 38103 **Calv Ch Memphis TN 2010-** B Louisville KY 1/23/1974 s Benjamin George Robertson & Else Sogaard. BA Ken 1996; MDiv VTS 2003. D 5/17/2003 P 12/6/2003 Bp Edwin Funsten Gulick Jr. m 5/25/2002 Ellen M Robertson c 2. R All SS' Epis Ch Gastonia NC 2006-2010; S Matt's Epis Ch Louisville KY 2004-2006. bengrobertsoniv@gmail.com

ROBERTSON, Bruce Edward (NMich) 452 Silver Creek Rd, Marquette MI 49855 B Marquette MI 8/29/1951 s Robert Bruce Roberton & Alberta Mary. D 4/1/1999 Bp Thomas Kreider Ray P 3/5/2000 Bp James Arthur Kelsey.

ROBERTSON, C(harles) K(evin) (Az) 815 2nd Avenue, New York NY 10017 **Rgstr Dom And Frgn Mssy Soc- Epis Ch Cntr New York NY 2009-** B El Paso TX 3/19/1964 s Francis Elmer Robertson & Virginia Marietta. BA VPI 1985; MDiv VTS 1993; PhD Dur 1999. D 6/19/1993 P 1/6/1994 Bp John Wadsworth Howe. m 5/18/1991 Deborah Ann Vinson c 3. Cn to the Ordnry Dio Arizona Phoenix AZ 2004-2007; R S Steph's Ch Milledgeville GA 1999-2004; P-in-c S Jn's Ch Melbourne FL 1993-1996. Auth, "A Dangerous Dozen," SkyLIght Paths, 2011; Auth, "Sorcerers and Supermen: Old Mythologies in New Guises," *Rel and Sci Fiction*, Pickwick Pub, 2011; Auth, "Conversations w Scripture: Acts," Morehouse, 2010; Co-Ed, "Global Perspectives on Jesus and Paul," T&T Clark, 2009; Auth, "Transforming Stwdshp," CPI, 2009; Auth, "To Make Room for the Sprt to Wk: Reflections from Lambeth Conferences on Theol Educ," *ATR*, ATR, 2008; Auth, "Courtroom Dramas: A Pauline Alternative for Conflict Mgmt," *ATR*, ATR, 2007; Ed, "Rel and Sxlty: Passionate Debates," Ptr Lang Pub, 2006; Auth, "The Limits of Ldrshp: Challenges to Apostolic Homeostasis in Lk-Acts," *ATR*, ATR, 2005; Auth, "The True Übermensch: Batman as Humanistic Myth," *The Gospel According to Superheroes*, Ptr Lang Publishin, 2005; Ed, "Rel and Alco: Sobering Thoughts," Ptr Lang Pub, 2004; Auth, "Barn: A Model For Holistic Stwdshp," TENS Pub, 2003; Ed, "Rel as Entertainment," Ptr Lang Pub, 2002; Auth, "Conflict In Corinth: Redefining The System," Ptr Lang Pub, 2001; Co-Ed, "New Dimensions for Theol in The Epis Ch," *ATR*, ATR. Angl Assn of Biblic Scholars 2009; Natl Coun of Ch Gvrng Bd 2011; SBL 1997. Bacclaureate Speaker GTS 2010; Commencement Speaker Sem of the SW 2009; Honoree The Epis Ntwk for Stwdshp 2007; Helping Amer's Yth Honoree White Hse 2005; Phi Kappa Phi hon Prof Georgia Coll & St U 2000; Hon Citizen of the City &Cnty of Durham Durham Cnty Coun 1999; ECF Fllshp ECF 1998; Bell-Woolfall Fllshp VTS 1996; Dudley Awd for Excellence in Reading of Liturg & Scripture VTS 1993. crobertson@episcopalchurch.org

ROBERTSON, Claude Richard (Ark) 1605 E Republican Rd, Jacksonville AR 72076 B Moberly MO 11/22/1942 BBA SMU 1964; MBA U Of Cntrl Arkansas 1975. D 6/3/2006 P 12/9/2006 Bp Larry Earl Maze. c 1. pthrsfarm@cs.com

✠ **ROBERTSON, Rt Rev Creighton Leland** (SD) 500 S Main Ave, Sioux Falls SD 57104 B Kansas City MO 3/6/1944 s Sylvester Thomas Robertson & Lana May. BS Black Hill St U 1971; JD U of So Dakota 1976; MDiv STUSo 1989. D 6/22/1989 P 5/6/1990 Bp Craig Barry Anderson Con 6/19/1994 for SD. m 6/3/1967 Ann Clare Robertson. Bp Dio So Dakota Sioux Falls SD 1994-2009; Bp Dio So Dakota Sioux Falls SD 1992-2009; Cmsn on Racism Dio So Dakota Sioux Falls SD 1992-1994; Evang Cmsn Dio So Dakota Sioux Falls SD 1989-1994. Bro of S Andr. DD U So TS 2001. bpcreighton.diocese@midconectwork.com

ROBERTSON JR, Edward Ray (La) 6249 Canal Blvd., New Orleans LA 70124 B New Orleans LA 9/11/1945 s Edward Ray Robertson & Marguerite. BA U of New Orleans 1967; MA U of New Orleans 1969; MDiv Nash 1981. Trans 11/1/2003 Bp Charles Edward Jenkins III. m 6/11/1966 Jeanne Edwards c 2. R S Jn's Epis Ch Thibodaux LA 2005-2011; R S Jude's Epis Ch Niceville FL 2003-2005; R S Mk's Epis Ch Harvey LA 1998-2003; Assoc S Geo's Epis Ch New Orleans LA 1993-1998; Chapl & Chair Dept Rel S Mart's Epis Sch Metairie LA 1990-1998; Assoc Gr Ch New Orleans LA 1990-1992; Cn Pstr Chr Ch Cathd New Orleans LA 1989-1990; Asst R S Jas Epis Ch Baton Rouge LA 1987-1989; R Trin Ch Tallulah LA 1984-1987; Cur S Jas Epis Ch Baton Rouge LA 1981-1984. fathered212@yahoo.com

ROBERTSON, Frederick W (Kan) 626 E Montclaor St Apt 1D, Springfield MO 65807 B Eureka UT 11/15/1937 s Stafford Francis Robertson & Rose Catherine. BA Drury U 1961; MDiv Nash 1974. D 6/24/1974 Bp Arthur Anton Vogel P 12/1/1974 Bp Charles Thomas Gaskell. m 11/23/1960 Charlotte

Robertson. Vic Ch Of The Ascen Neodesha KS 1974-1975; R Ch Of The Epiph Independence KS 1974-1975; Asst S Thos Of Cbury Ch Greendale WI 1974-1975. FRFWR@BLOOMBB.COM

ROBERTSON, James Bruce (Pa) 8327 Elliston Drive, Wyndmoor PA 19038 **Serv S Paul's Ch Philadelphia PA 2009-** B Hot Sprgs AR 3/10/1948 s Paul Robertson & Myrtle. BA U of Kansas 1970; MA U of Kansas 1972; Cert Pennsylvania Diac Sch 1991; AUD U of Florida 2000. D 10/9/1993 Bp Allen Lyman Bartlett Jr. m 7/8/2009 Dean L Ennis. Serv Gloria Dei Ch Philadelphia PA 1996-1998; Serv S Ptr's Ch Philadelphia PA 1994-1996; Serv Ch Of The H Apos Wynnewood PA 1993-1994. jasbrob@aol.com

ROBERTSON, John Brown (Az) Good Shepherd of the Hills, PO Box 110, Cave Creek AZ 85327 B Albuquerque NM 5/4/1939 s Alexander Johnson Robertson & Alice Catherine. Engr Colorado Sch of Mines 1961; U of Arizona 1966. D 1/26/2008 Bp Kirk Stevan Smith. m 3/31/1963 Diana Taff c 4. jeanjack@aaip.net

ROBERTSON, John Edward (Minn) 38378 Reservation Highway 101, PO Box 369, Morton MN 56270 **Dio Minnesota Minneapolis MN 2005-** B Sisseton SD 9/29/1952 s Walter Angus Robertson & Lorene Augusta. Macalester Coll 1977; Minnesota St U Mankato 1984; MDiv SWTS 1993. D 6/19/1993 Bp Robert Marshall Anderson P 12/21/1993 Bp James Louis Jelinek. m 1/15/1983 Deborah Kay Prescott c 4. Native Mnstrs Off Epis Ch Cntr New York NY 1999-2003; P-in-c Ch Of The Gd Shpd Windom MN 1995-1998; Cn Mssnr for Indn Wk Dio Minnesota Minneapolis MN 1995-1998; P-in-c S Jas Ch Marshall MN 1994-1995; Dio Minnesota Minneapolis MN 1993-1998. vicar@mchsi.com

ROBERTSON, Karen (Suzi) Sue (Oly) 1757 244th Ave NE, Sammamish WA 98074 **Resolutns Com Dio Olympia Seattle WA 2011-; Vic Gd Samar Epis Ch Sammamish WA 2009-** B Fort Worth TX 1/10/1952 d Kenneth Ray Robertson & Bertha Margaret. BD St. Edw's U Austin TX 1982; MA U of St. Thos 1984; MDiv Houston Grad TS 2000; DMin SMU 2001. D 10/27/2002 P 5/14/2003 Bp Don Adger Wimberly. m 6/4/1989 Nolen D Holcomb c 1. Chair, Cmsn on Schools Dio NW Texas Lubbock TX 2007-2009; St. Jn's Epis Sch Abilene TX 2007-2009; Cathd Chapt Dio Texas Houston TX 2006-2007; Dn, E Harris Convoc Dio Texas Houston TX 2006-2007; Exec Bd Dio Texas Houston TX 2006-2007; R S Lk The Evang Houston TX 2004-2007; Prof Exec Coun Appointees New York NY 2003; Assoc Trin Ch Galveston TX 2002-2003; Chr Ch Cathd Houston TX 1998-2000. Auth, "Windows Into The Sprtlty of Chld," Booksurge Pub, 2006; Auth, "Alexander's Pryr," *Ldr In The Ch Sch Today*, Meth Pub Hse, 2002; Auth, "Recruiting For The New Milennium," *Ldr In The Ch Sch Today*, Meth Pub Hse, 2000; Auth, "Ask, Don't Tell," *Ldr In The Ch Sch Today*, Meth Pub Hse, 2000; Auth, "Brandon's Story," *Ldr In The Ch Sch Today*, Meth Pub Hse, 1999; Auth, "Giving Chld the Light of Chr," *Ldr In The Ch Sch Today*, Meth Pub Hse, 1998; Auth, "The Post Schooling Sunday Sch," *Ldr In The Ch Sch Today*, Meth Pub Hse, 1995; Auth, "How to Chair a Successful Meeting," *Ldr In The Ch Sch Today*, Meth Pub Hse, 1994; Auth, "Latchkey Mnstry: Mssn and Educ," *Tchr mag*, Meth Pub Hse, 1993; Auth, "A Tchr Recruiting Cmpgn that Works," *Ldr In The Ch Sch Today*, Meth Pub Hse, 1992; Auth, "All God's People: A Prog for Persons who are Mentally Retarded," People to People, Carrollton TX, 1987; Auth, "Love Your Neighbor," Yth Mnstry Resource Exch, 1985. Chr Ch Cathd Chapt, Houston TX 2006. Grant Rec Dio Olympia 2011; Grant Rec Trin, Wall St 2005; Grant Rec Dio Texas 2003. suzirobertson2003@yahoo.com

R

ROBERTSON, Marilyn Sue (Okla) 127 NW 7th St, Oklahoma City OK 73102 **D S Paul's Cathd Oklahoma City OK 2008-** B Oklahoma City OK 7/2/1963 d Thomas Preston Robertson & Betty Ann. BSN Oklahoma Cntrl St U 1986. D 6/21/2008 Bp Edward Joseph Konieczny. horsewhsp2@aol.com

ROBERTSON, Patricia Rome (Me) PO Box 177, 3 Kimball Road, Northeast Harbor ME 04662 **Dioc Coun Dio Maine Portland ME 2009-; R The Par Of S Mary And S Jude NE Harbor ME 2008-** B Berwyn IL 6/2/1949 d Irvin Joseph Rome & Dorothy. BA SUNY 1974; MS U Pgh 1978; MDiv EDS 1986. D 6/13/1987 P 6/6/1988 Bp David Elliot Johnson. m 5/29/1982 George G Robertson c 2. Chair, Mssn Strtgy Study Grp Dio Maine Portland ME 2009-2011; Dioc Coun Dio Maine Portland ME 2009-2011; Pres, Stndg Com Dio Olympia Seattle WA 2004-2005; R S Steph's Epis Ch Seattle WA 1997-2007; sabbatical supply Chr Ch Tacoma WA 1996; Dioc Coun Dio California San Francisco CA 1993-1995; Vic/R S Ambr Epis Ch Foster City CA 1992-1996; COM Dio El Camino Real Monterey CA 1989-1992; Assoc S Thos Epis Ch Sunnyvale CA 1988-1992; Asst S Mich's Ch Marblehead MA 1987-1988. Auth, "Being Made New," *Congregations*, Alb Inst, 2008; Auth, "Contemplative Ldrshp - Discovering the Wisdom to Lead," *Seattle Theol and Mnstry Revs*, Seattle U, 2008. Contemplative Outreach 1998; EWC 1980; Sprtl Dir Intl 1994. revprome@hotmail.com

ROBESON, Terry A. Luzuk (Wyo) 665 Cedar St, Lander WY 82520 **P Trin Ch Lander WY 2006-** B Denver CO 9/29/1953 d Alex Lazuk & Florence Gertrude. BA U of Nthrn Colorado 1975. D 2/24/2006 P 9/2/2006 Bp Bruce Edward Caldwell. m 7/5/1980 Thomas Ann Robeson c 2. lighthouse_lady53@hotmail.com

ROBILLARD, Roger M (Va) 400 S Cedar Ave, Highland Springs VA 23075 B Woonsocket RI 3/20/1942 s Raymond G Robillard & Monique G. BTh McGill U 1978; DIT Montreal TS 1979. Trans from Anglican Church of Canada 11/1/1997 Bp Geralyn Wolf. m 7/6/1968 Lydia Sgroi. Vic Trin Ch Highland Sprg VA 2001-2008; R S Jas Epis Ch At Woonsocket Woonsocket RI 1997-2001. Kiwanis 2002-2006; Soc Of S Marg 1976. rev@cheerful.com

ROBINSON, Allen Florence (Md) 2729 Moores Valley Dr, Baltimore MD 21209 **R S Jas' Epis Ch Baltimore MD 2002-** B Galveston TX 2/8/1970 s Allen Florence & Patricia Ann. BA S Aug's Coll Raleigh NC 1992; MDiv VTS 1995; DMin Fuller TS 2007. D 6/17/1995 Bp Claude Edward Payne P 1/18/1996 Bp Leopoldo Jesus Alard. m 4/20/1996 Allison J Crawford c 3. Assoc Calv Ch Memphis TN 1999-2002; S Dunst's Epis Ch Houston TX 1998-1999; Ch Of The Resurr Houston TX 1995-1997; Asst S Jas Epis Ch Houston TX 1995-1997. a.robinson@verizon.net

ROBINSON, Alvin Errington (LI) 25 Westlawn Pl, Palm Coast FL 32164 B Canal Zone PA 3/28/1928 s Louis Charles Robinson & Ida Catherine. S Ptr's Theol Coll 1953; Oxf 1958; BA CUNY 1967; MA NYU 1968; DMin Bos 1982. Trans from Church in the Province Of The West Indies 9/1/1965. m 9/29/1962 Winsome E Davis. S Thos Flagler Cnty Palm Coast FL 1997; S Cyp's St Aug FL 1996; Ch Of The Resurr E Elmhurst NY 1986-1995; Dio Massachusetts Boston MA 1980-1996; Prov I Coun Dio Massachusetts Boston MA 1973-1979; R S Barth's Ch Cambridge MA 1971-1985; Personl Secy Dio New York New York City NY 1969-1971; Dep Csr Dio New York New York City NY 1968-1970; Vic S Fran Assisi And S Martha White Plains NY 1963-1968. Auth, "Faith Of Teenagers In Their Search For Freedom". Cn No Estrn Caribbean & Aruba 1995.

ROBINSON, Carla Lynn (Oly) 15220 Main St, Bellevue WA 98007 **All SS Ch Seattle WA 2010-** B Cleveland OH 10/21/1958 d Ferdinand M Robinson & Thelma Hall. BA Concordia Coll 1980; MDiv Concordia Sem 1984. D 1/15/2009 Bp Gregory Harold Rickel. Cler Dio Olympia Seattle WA 2009; Admin Asst Dio Olympia Seattle WA 2005-2009. crobinson_98@yahoo.com

ROBINSON III, Charles Alexander (At) 3750 Peachtree Rd Ne # 924, Atlanta GA 30319 **Died 12/1/2010** B Rock Hill SC 2/16/1930 s Charles Alexander Robinson & Dana. BA USC 1952; BD VTS 1957. D 7/16/1957 P 5/29/1958 Bp Clarence Alfred Cole.

ROBINSON, Charles Allen (SVa) 2124 Benomi Dr., Williamsburg VA 32185 **Alt Dep GC Dio Sthrn Virginia Norfolk VA 2011-; Vic Bruton Par Williamsburg VA 2007-** B Ponca City OK 3/15/1952 s Charles Arthur Robinson & Pauline Eithol. BBA Natl U 1980; MA Webster U 1982; MDiv Epis TS of The SW 2004. D 6/5/2004 P 12/8/2004 Bp David Conner Bane Jr. m 2/6/1971 Terry L Spaulding c 2. Chair, COM: Sem Formation Dio Sthrn Virginia Norfolk VA 2007-2010; R S Jn's Ch Suffolk VA 2004-2007. crobinson@brutonparish.org

ROBINSON, Charles Edward (U) PO Box 981208, Park City UT 84098 **Mutual Mnstry Revs Team Dio Utah Salt Lake City UT 2009-; R S Lk's Ch Pk City UT 2004-** B Houston TX 1/10/1955 s Edward D Robinson & Brenda Joyce. MA in process H Apos Sem & Coll; BS U of Texas 1978; MDiv Golden Gate Bapt TS 1985; MA San Francisco St U 1987; Cert CDSP 1988; MBA DeVry U 2004. D 12/3/1988 P 12/1/1989 Bp William Edwin Swing. m 6/1/1985 Bonnie Ann Brown c 1. Chair - Stwdshp Educ Team Dio Utah Salt Lake City UT 2008-2011; Chair - COM Dio Utah Salt Lake City UT 2007-2011; Chair - Cler Compstn T/F Dio Utah Salt Lake City UT 2007-2009; Dioc Coun Dio Utah Salt Lake City UT 2005-2008; R S Andr's Ch Glendale AZ 1991-1999; Assoc for Fam Mnstrs S Barn On The Desert Scottsdale AZ 1990-1991. AAPC 1998-2004. pastor@stlukespc.org

ROBINSON, Chris (Miss) PO Box 1001, McComb MS 39649 **Par Of The Medtr-Redeem McComb MS 2010-** B Tupelo MS 5/21/1984 s Joseph Oliver Robinson & Diane D. BA Millsaps Coll 2006; MDiv VTS 2010. D 6/27/2010 P 1/22/2011 Bp Duncan Montgomery Gray III. chrisrobinson84@gmail.com

ROBINSON, Constance Wiegmann (Eas) 5820 Haven Ct, Rock Hall MD 21661 B Philadelphia PA 11/30/1947 d Karl Henry Wiegmann & Constance Ethel. BS W Chester St Coll 1970; MEd W Chester St Coll 1976; MDiv PrTS 1984. D 7/16/2005 P 1/28/2006 Bp James Joseph Shand. m 9/20/1986 David Gordon Robinson. Chr Ch Worton MD 2006-2007; Emm Epis Ch Chestertown MD 2005-2006. cwrobinson@verizon.net

ROBINSON, Cristopher Allan (WTex) 1621 Santa Monica St, Kingsville TX 78363 **R Ch Of The Epiph Kingsville TX 2009-** B Houston TX 10/27/1970 s Allan D Robinson & Pauline R. BS Rice U 1993; MS U of Texas 1995; MDiv Epis TS of The SW 2005. D 7/9/2005 Bp Sylvestre Donato Romero P 1/11/2006 Bp Gary Richard Lillibridge. m 11/18/1995 Kristina Robinson c 2. Asst. R S Thos Epis Ch And Sch San Antonio TX 2005-2009. cristopherrobinson@sbcglobal.net

ROBINSON JR, David Gordon (NH) 430 Savage Road, Milford NH 03055 B Seaford DE 12/17/1953 s David Gordon Robinson & Erma Esther. BA Salisbury U 1975; MDiv VTS 1979. D 3/6/1982 Bp William Hawley Clark P 3/12/1983 Bp George E Rath. m 5/28/1979 Cynthia Lee Giviens. Ch Of The H Sprt Plymouth NH 2011; Int Ch Of The H Sprt Plymouth NH 2011; Chair, Cler

Compstn Com Dio New Hampshire Concord NH 2004-2010; R Ch Of Our Sav Milford NH 2000-2011; Mem, Dioc Coun Dio New Hampshire Concord NH 2000-2004; R Gr Ch Norwood MA 1986-2000; Asst The Ch Of The H Sprt Orleans MA 1982-1986. Auth, *w Grateful Hearts*, Gr Pub, 1997; Auth, *From Bounden Duty to a Joyful Thing*, Gr Pub, 1992. chiprobinson@aol.com

ROBINSON, David Gordon (Eas) 5820 Haven Ct, Rock Hall MD 21661 B Medford MA 10/25/1939 s Walter Franklin Robinson & Miriam Eunice. AB Dart 1961; MDiv EDS 1984. D 6/21/1986 P 5/14/1987 Bp George Nelson Hunt III. m 9/20/1986 Constance Wiegmann c 3. R Chr Ch Worton MD 2004-2007; Asstg P Chr Ch Cranbrook Bloomfield Hills MI 1987-1999. cdrobinson@verizon.net

ROBINSON, David Kerr (Me) Po Box 7554, Ocean Park ME 04063 **Trin Ch Saco ME 2006-; Dio Maine Portland ME 2000-** B New York NY 3/6/1952 s Irving Edward Robinson & Jean Phylis. BS St. Lawr Canton NY 1974; MDiv Nash 1977. D 6/4/1977 P 12/10/1977 Bp Wilbur Emory Hogg Jr. m 8/17/1974 Patricia Hobson Jakeman c 3. R S Lk's Ch Brockport NY 1986-2006; Vic S Jn's Ch Murray KY 1981-1986; Cur S Jas Ch Oneonta NY 1977-1981. dkr52@aol.com

ROBINSON, David Scott (Pa) 603 Misty Hollow Dr, Maple Glen PA 19002 **R S Matt's Ch Maple Glen PA 1985-** B Monterey CA 11/16/1953 s George Douglas Robinson & Virginia. BA Grove City Coll 1975; PrTS 1975; MDiv GTS 1978; STM GTS 1985; CSD Jesuit Cntr For Sprtl Growth Wernersville PA 2003. D 6/9/1978 P 1/25/1979 Bp Dean T Stevenson. m 6/11/1977 Lynn S Smith c 2. R S Jn's Epis Ch Bellefonte PA 1980-1985; Cur S Andr's Ch St Coll PA 1978-1979. dscotrobin@aol.com

ROBINSON, David Wendell (CPa) P O Box 235, 3913 Lincoln Street, Scotland PA 17254 **Trin Epis Ch Chambersburg PA 2000-** B Canton OH 8/14/1941 s Harvey Nelson Robinson & Mary Evangeline. BA Houghton Coll 1963; MDiv EDS 1968. D 6/12/1968 Bp Walter M Higley P 5/27/1969 Bp Ned Cole. c 2. Int S Lk's Epis Ch Altoona PA 1999-2000; R Gr Ch Manchester NH 1980-1999; Dio Cntrl New York Syracuse NY 1975-1980; Dio New Hampshire Concord NH 1971-1999; R Zion Epis Ch Greene NY 1971-1980; Cur Trin Memi Ch Binghamton NY 1968-1971. dawrobin@comcast.net

ROBINSON, Dorothy Linkous (Tex) 7700 Pleasant Meadow Cir, Austin TX 78731 B Blacksburg VA 1/27/1940 d Gilbert Franklin Linkous & Margaret Dorothy. BS VPI 1962; MDiv Epis TS of The SW 1992. D 3/21/1994 Bp Claude Edward Payne P 12/19/1994 Bp Maurice Manuel Benitez. m 8/23/1963 William Archie Robinson. Asstg P S Jn's Epis Ch Austin TX 1994-1998.

ROBINSON, Edward Geoffrey (NY) 6035 Verde Trl S Apt J216, Boca Raton FL 33433 **Died 5/9/2010** B Belmont Bolton England UK 2/23/1924 s Henry Robinson & Dora Gertrude. BS U of Wyoming 1950; MDiv VTS 1953. D 6/13/1953 P 12/9/1953 Bp James W Hunter. APHA; AEHC; Assn of Profsnl Chapl; HHC.

ROBINSON, Franklin Kenneth (Ct) 305 Golden Ginkgo Lane, Salisbury MD 21801 B Altadena CA 6/7/1929 s Frank D Robinson & Edna. BA Ya 1951; STM Ya Berk 1954; ThM PrTS 1966; MS The Amer Coll 1966. D 6/2/1954 P 4/1/1955 Bp Walter H Gray. m 9/10/1994 Emilie Wood c 5. Dir of Pstr Mnstry Chr Ch Greenwich CT 1966-1972; Loc Ten S Mths Epis Ch E Rochester NY 1964-1965; P-in-c S Andr's Epis Ch Caledonia NY 1963-1964; Cur S Jn's Ch Stamford CT 1954-1956. fkr1141@aol.com

ROBINSON, Fredrick Arthur (SwFla) 222 South Palm Avenue, Sarasota FL 34236 **R Ch Of The Redeem Sarasota FL 1994-** B Columbus OH 11/5/1951 s Richard Thompson Robinson & Fredna Marie. BA OH SU 1974; ThM SMU 1978; STM Nash 1982. D 6/26/1982 P 10/26/1982 Bp A Donald Davies. m 6/22/1974 Linda H Hartman c 2. Dioc Coun Dio SW Florida Sarasota FL 1994-2000; Dn Monroe Convoc Dio Wstrn Louisiana Alexandria LA 1990-1994; R Gr Epis Ch Monroe LA 1988-1994; R S Andr's Ch Grand Prairie TX 1984-1988; Cur S Mk's Ch Arlington TX 1982-1984. fredlindarobinson@comcast.net

ROBINSON, Grant Harris (Minn) 1840 University Ave W Apt 413, Saint Paul MN 55104 B Saint Paul MN 5/19/1925 s Donald Brandt Robinson & Alma Elizabeth. BME U MN 1949; MDiv VTS 1969. D 6/30/1969 P 4/4/1970 Bp Hamilton Hyde Kellogg. m 12/23/1946 Meredith Hatch c 4. P-in-c Ch Of The Redeem Cannon Falls MN 1974-1980; R Ch Of The Nativ Burnsville MN 1971-1990; Vic Ch Of Our Sav Little Falls MN 1969-1971. mlrob246@comcast.net

ROBINSON JR, H(enry) Jefferson (Fla) 314 Glen Ridge Ave, Temple Terrace FL 33617 **Assoc S Cathr's Ch Temple Terrace FL 2006-** B Plant City FL 8/1/1937 s Henry Jefferson Robinson & Gladys Margaret. BM Stetson U 1961; BA Sthrn Bapt TS Louisville KY 1963; MM U of So Florida 1969; MA U of So Florida 1979; EdD Nova U 1985; MDiv GTS 1989. D 6/11/1989 P 12/12/1989 Bp Frank Stanley Cerveny. m 4/26/1975 Patricia V Van Auken c 5. R S Jas' Epis Ch Lake City FL 1999-2005; Asst S Lk's Epis Ch Live Oak FL 1997-1999; R S Marg's Ch Inverness FL 1990-1993; Asst R S Mich's Ch Gainesville FL 1989-1990. jprobin1@verizon.net

ROBINSON, Janet Rohrbach (Ga) 3565 Bemiss Rd., Valdosta GA 31605 B Selins Grove PA 1/14/1924 d Thomas Nelson Rohrbach & Hannah F. BMusEd Susquehanna U 1946; MM LSU 1975. D 2/12/2009 Bp Henry Irving Louttit. m 3/29/1958 Lavan Robinson. robinsjanet@gmail.com

ROBINSON, Janice Marie (WA) 10200 Ridgemoor Dr, Silver Spring MD 20901 B Philadelphia PA 6/6/1943 d Calvin C Robinson & Leola O. BD U Of Bridgeport 1965; MA NYU 1970; MDiv Ya Berk 1988. D 6/11/1988 P 12/1/1988 Bp John Thomas Walker. m 10/27/2010 Berit Lakey. R Gr Epis Ch Silver Sprg MD 1997-2009; Cathd of St Ptr & St Paul Washington DC 1995-1997; S Jn's Ch Chevy Chase MD 1988-1995. Auth, "Grassroots & Nonprofit Ldrshp: Guide For Orgnztn In Changing Times+". revjan61@hotmail.com

ROBINSON, Joseph Oliver (Mass) Po Box 1366, Jackson MS 39215 **R Chr Ch Cambridge Cambridge MA 2006-** B Mendenhall MS 4/25/1956 s Ned Robinson & Willie. BA Delta St U 1978; MDiv STUSo 1982. D 5/19/1982 P 2/1/1983 Bp Duncan Montgomery Gray Jr. m 7/29/1978 Diane D Davion c 2. Dn S Andr's Cathd Jackson MS 1996-2005; Cn S Jn's Cathd Denver CO 1992-1996; R Trin Ch Yazoo City MS 1986-1992; P-in-c S Jn's Ch Aberdeen MS 1982-1986. Auth, "As We Gather To Pray," Ch Hymnal Corp; Auth, "Morning Star Press"; Auth, "Mary," *Jos Huddle Here*. Dio Liturg & Mus Cmsn. jor@cccambridge.org

ROBINSON, Katherine Sternberg (Wyo) 2350 S Poplar St, Casper WY 82601 B Philadelphia PA 10/30/1948 d Ralph Roy Sternberg & Marcella. BA U of New Mex 1970; MA U of New Mex 1973; MDiv Iliff TS 2002. D 3/8/2003 P 11/12/2003 Bp Bruce Edward Caldwell. m 11/29/1969 Donald Robinson c 2. wyomom50@gmail.com

ROBINSON, Kenneth Rupert (Ct) 1111 S Lakemont Ave Apt 634, Winter Park FL 32792 B New York NY 6/15/1916 s Rupert Talbert Robinson & Adelaide Delcina. BA Springfield Coll Springfield MA 1943; UTS 1945; MDiv EDS 1946; EdM Bos 1970. D 6/29/1946 P 3/8/1947 Bp William A Lawrence. m 9/7/1996 Roberta Fox Smith c 3. Asst Ch Of The Gd Shpd Orange CT 1967-1968; Assoc S Matt's Epis Ch Wilton CT 1958-1967; R Gr Epis Ch Trumbull CT 1953-1958; Vic Chr Ch Rochdale MA 1948-1953; Cur S Ptr's Ch Albany NY 1946-1948.

ROBINSON, Linda Gail Herring Hornbuckle (Ala) 6324 Woodlake Dr., Buford GA 30518 B Attalla AL 5/15/1940 d Leonard Winters Herring & Ethel Nmi. BS Howard Coll 1962; MDiv Yale DS 1984. D 12/11/1985 P 12/19/1986 Bp Furman Stough. m 8/30/1987 Claud Andrew Robinson. Ch Of H Fam Fresno CA 1998-2001; Int All SS Epis Ch Birmingham AL 1989-1990; The Epis Ch Of S Fran Of Assisi Indn Sprg Vill AL 1988-1989. crobj@yahoo.com

ROBINSON, Mark K J (Ct) 82 Shore Rd, Old Lyme CT 06371 **R S Ann's Epis Ch Old Lyme CT 2011-; COM Dio Connecticut Hartford CT 1996-** B Columbus OH 2/19/1958 s Jefferson Davis Robinson & Anne Kilbourne. Brooks Sch 1977; ABS Ken 1981; MDiv EDS 1988; Hartford Sem 2009. D 6/4/1988 P 12/3/1988 Bp Edward Cole Chalfant. m 6/27/1987 Eleanor Perkins c 3. Dio Ohio Cleveland OH 2009-2011; R Calv Ch Stonington CT 1993-2009; S Fran Ch Potomac MD 1990-1992; S Jn's Ch Georgetown Par Washington DC 1988-1989; Asst S Jn's Ch Lafayette Sq Washington DC 1988-1989. Ed, *Watch Hill Chap PB*, 1998. Exec Com of the Cbury Cathd's Friends in Am 1995; S.S.J.E. 1988; Uganda Chr U Friends Soc 1998-2003. revmkjr@aol.com

ROBINSON, Michael Eric (ETenn) 345 East Onwentsia Road, Lake Forest IL 60045 **Lake Forest Country Day Sch Lake Forest IL 2005-** B Williamstown MA 10/11/1964 s Arthur Edward Robinson & Nancy Farrell. BS U of Massachusetts 1986; MDiv VTS 1992. D 6/13/1992 Bp Andrew Frederick Wissemann P 12/1/1992 Bp Peter James Lee. m 10/3/1987 Frances Fox Merriman c 3. S Nich Sch Chattanooga TN 1999-2000; S Pat's Epis Day Sch Washington DC 1993-1999; Asst R S Pat's Ch Washington DC 1993-1995; Asst R S Mary's Epis Ch Arlington VA 1992-1993; Asst Convoc of Amer Ch in Europe Paris FR 1990-1991. Auth, *And a Chld Shall Lead Them: Reflection on the Gift of a Ch Sch*, 1994. Cmnty Cross of Nails; NAES 1994. robinson847@gmail.com

ROBINSON, Michael Kevin (Ark) 305 Pointer Trl W, Van Buren AR 72956 B Fort Smith AR 11/1/1955 s Jerry Dixon Robinson & Jolea. BA U of Arkansas 1977; MDiv Epis TS of The SW 1986. D 6/28/1986 P 5/23/1987 Bp Herbert Alcorn Donovan Jr. m 12/5/1981 Lisa Sass c 2. Vic Trin Ch Van Buren AR 1991-2010; Vic Gr Ch Siloam Sprg AR 1987-1990; Vic S Thos Ch Springdale AR 1987-1990; Cur Trin Ch Pine Bluff AR 1986-1987. trinityvanburen@aol.com

ROBINSON, Paula Patricia (Mo) 123 S 9th St, Columbia MO 65201 B Belfast IE 3/16/1950 d Walter Ernest Robinson & Enis Santina. Dip.Ed. U of Manchester 1981; MEd U of Manchester 1985; BTh Trin 1994. Trans from Church of Ireland 3/1/2000. c 1. R Calv Ch Columbia MO 2008-2009; R S Andr's Ch Leonardtown California MD 2000-2008. Auth, "Restorating Justice: Living The Jubilee," Natl Bible Soc Of Ireland, 1999; Auth, "Crossfire," Dublin And Glendalough Dioceses, 1993; Auth, "A Lent Study," Dublin And Glendalough Dioceses, 1993; Auth, "Guide For FA," Dublin And Glendalough Dioceses, 1993; Auth, "Physical Educ Within Spec Educational Provision- Equality And Entitlement, Equality, Educ," *And Physical Educ*,

Falmer Press London, 1993; Auth, "Distance Lrng Courses For Teachers Of Chld w Speech And Lang Disorders," U Of Birmingham Sch Of Educ, 1991; Auth, "Tchg Chld w Physical Disabil," Cassells London, 1989; Auth, "Incontinence," *Profound Rtrdtn And Multiple Impairment*, Chapman And Hall, 1989; Auth, "Spec Educ Spec Schools," *A Dictionary Of Rel Educ*, Scm Press London, 1984. Purser Shortt Liturg Ch Of Ireland Theol Coll 1994; Downes' Theol Ch Of Ireland Theol Coll 1994; Weir, Downes' Oration Ch Of Ireland Theol Coll 1992. revpaula@supanet.com

ROBINSON, Robert Nesbitt (At) 333 Nelson St SW Unit 416, Atlanta GA 30313 B Dallas TX 12/10/1936 s Luther William Robinson & Mamie. PhD Emory U; BA U So 1959; Cert Oxf 1963; BTh U Tor 1964. Trans from Anglican Church of Canada 1/1/1968 Bp Milton LeGrand Wood. m 10/3/1987 Katie Edwards c 1. S Mary Magd Ch Columbus GA 2001-2002; S Jos's Epis Ch McDonough GA 1998-2000; S Paul's Epis Ch Clinton NC 1994-1997; Cong Of St Ann Myrtle Bch SC 1983-1991; The Epis Ch Of The Resurr Surfside Bch SC 1980-1982; P-in-c S Paul's Epis Ch Conway SC 1972-1980. Auth, "Theme Of Joy In Thos Traherne"; Auth, "Hermetic Traherne Stds In Harmony & Joy"; Auth, "Trahernes Metaphors Of Joy". Trst Isaac Auld Trust.

ROBINSON, Sonja (EC) 1009 Midland Dr, Wilmington NC 28412 B 3/5/1939 Ohio Vlly Sch Of Nrsng Wheeling WV. D 6/14/2003 Bp Clifton Daniel III. c 2.

ROBINSON, Sybil Clara Frances (Mil) 8301 Old Sauk Rd Apt 321, Middleton WI 53562 **D S Dunst's Ch Madison WI 2002-** B ZA 11/8/1925 d Archibald Cecil Dee & Kathleen. PhD U of Wisconsin 1970. D 6/23/2002 Bp Roger John White.

✠ **ROBINSON, Rt Rev V Gene** (NH) Diocese Of New Hampshire, 63 Green St., Concord NH 03301 **Bp Dio New Hampshire Concord NH 2003-** B Lexington KY 5/29/1947 s Charles Victor Robinson & Imogene. BA U So 1969; MDiv GTS 1973. D 6/9/1973 Bp Leland Stark P 12/15/1973 Bp George E Rath. m 6/7/2008 Mark Andrew c 2. Nomin Com for PBp Dio New Hampshire Concord NH 2001-2003; Nomin Com for PBp Dio New Hampshire Concord NH 2001-2003; Nomin Com for PBp Prov I Middletown CT 2001-2003; Dep GC Dio New Hampshire Concord NH 2000-2003; Dio New Hampshire Concord NH 1998-2000; Exec Secy Epis Prov Of New Engl Dorset VT 1990-2003; Cn Dio New Hampshire Concord NH 1988-2003; Exec Secy Prov I Middletown CT 1983-2003; COM Dio New Hampshire Concord NH 1981-1987; Yth Coordntr Prov I Middletown CT 1978-1985; Cur Chr Ch Ridgewood NJ 1973-1975. Ed, *Fresh Start: A Resource for Cler and Congregations in Transition*, Epis Ch, 2000; Ed, *Epis Guide to Teens for AIDS Prevention*, Epis Ch, 1994; Ed, *Bearing Fruit: Resource Cler Self-Assessment*, Cornerstone Fndt, 1992; Auth, *Yth Mnstry in the Age of AIDS*, Epis Ch, 1989. DD EDS 2004; DD The GTS 2004. grinnh@aol.com

ROBINSON JR, Virgil Austin Anderson (Chi) 1527 Chapel Ct, Northbrook IL 60062 B New Orleans LA 3/31/1938 s Virgil Austin Anderson Robinson & Myrtle. BS SW U Lafayette LA 1961; Air War Coll 1975; MDiv Oxf 1980; S Geo's Coll Jerusalem IL 1981; MA Loyola U 1988. Trans from Church Of England 5/16/1986 Bp James Winchester Montgomery. m 1/24/1961 Marilynn Jones c 2. S Jn's Epis Ch Naperville IL 2004-2006; The Ch Of The H Sprt Lake Forest IL 2004; Int S Lk's Ch Evanston IL 2000-2003; Int S Paul's Ch Milwaukee WI 1998-2000; Int Ch Of S Paul And The Redeem Chicago IL 1996-1998; Int S Paul's Cathd Fond du Lac WI 1994-1996; Epis Coun At Nthrn Illinois U Evanston IL 1993-1994; S Giles' Ch Northbrook IL 1986-1990. varobinsonjr@aol.com

R

ROBINSON-COMO, Glenice Arlette (Tex) 1117 Texas St, Houston TX 77002 **Chf Admin Off Chr Ch Cathd Houston TX 2010-** B Petersburg VA 4/3/1959 d Theodore N Robinson & Ruby Lee Jackson. BS Virginia Commonwealth Unversity 1982; MDiv SMU-Perkins TS 2009; Dplma Theol Stds Epis TS Of The SW 2010. D 6/19/2010 P 1/13/2011 Bp C(harles) Andrew Doyle. m 11/2/1991 Paul L Como c 2. g2pc@msn.com

ROBISON, Bruce Monroe (Pgh) 5801 Hampton Street, Pittsburgh PA 15206 **First Alt Cler Dep, GC 2012 Dio Pittsburgh Monroeville PA 2010-; Stndg Com Dio Pittsburgh Monroeville PA 2010-; R St Andrews Epis Ch Pittsburgh PA 1994-** B Los Angeles CA 7/5/1953 s Richard Monroe Robison & Mary Ann. BA U CA 1975; MA U CA 1979; MDiv CDSP 1986; DMin Pittsburgh TS 2001. D 6/14/1986 Bp John Lester Thompson III P 1/26/1987 Bp Charlie Fuller McNutt Jr. m 5/23/1980 Susan M Johnson c 2. Stndg Com Dio Pittsburgh Monroeville PA 2010; Cler Dep, GC 2009 Dio Pittsburgh Monroeville PA 2008-2010; R S Paul's Ch Bloomsburg PA 1988-1994; Cur S Andr's Ch St Coll PA 1986-1988. Confr. OSB 2006. Phi Beta Kappa 1975. bmrobison@alum.calberkeley.org

ROBISON, Ronald Livingston (CFla) 331 Lake Avenue, Maitland FL 32751 B Providence RI 4/20/1938 s Reuel Francis Robison & Helen Luvinia. Cit; LTH, MDIV VTS 1992. D 6/20/1992 P 12/1/1992 Bp John Wadsworth Howe. m 11/1/1959 Margaret Robison c 3. Ch Of The Gd Shpd Maitland FL 2008-2009; H Cross Epis Ch Sanford FL 2007-2008; Aquia Ch Stafford VA 1999-2000; The Ch Of The H Sprt Ocean City MD 1996-1999; R H Fam Ch Orlando FL 1992-1996. rlr1205@aol.com

ROBISON, Sandra L(ee) (Spok) 1407 Thayer Dr, Richland WA 99354 **D All SS Ch Richland WA 1993-** B Seattle WA 1/10/1943 d Robert Eugene Haughee & Willa Mae. Arizona St U 1963. D 2/20/1993 Bp Frank Jeffrey Terry. m 6/8/1963 Thomas John Robison c 3. Mem, COM Dio Spokane Spokane WA 1994-2000. momrobi@frontier.com

ROBLES, Lawrence Arnold (ECR) 651 Broadway, Gilroy CA 95020 **Santa Maria Urban Mssn San Jose CA 2009-** B Bellflower CA 10/8/1956 s Arnold Diaz Robles & Rosa Guerrero. BA California St U 1995; MDiv Amer Bapt Sem of the W 1998. D 9/16/2007 Bp Sylvestre Donato Romero P 3/29/2008 Bp Mary Gray-Reeves. c 2. lrobles74@gmail.com

ROBLES-GARCIA, Daniel (DR) 12921 Valley Wood Dr, Silver Springs MD 12921 B Bonao DO 4/10/1939 s Dionisio Robles & Herminia. Doctor U Santa Domingo 1967; MDiv ETSC 1972; Mstr Universidad Pedro H.Ureña 1977. D 5/28/1972 P 12/14/1972 Bp Telesforo A Isaac. m 3/30/1968 Maria E Robles-Garcia c 2. Asst S Lk's Par Bladensburg MD 2001-2007; Dio Puerto Rico S Just PR 1992-1996; Hisp P Dio Washington Washington DC 1986-1999; Mssn San Juan Washington DC 1986-1990; Dio The Dominican Republic (Iglesia Epis Dominicana) Santo Domingo DO 1972-1981. Auth, "Vivencia del ministerio anglicano," 2001; Auth, "Ch & Rt In the Dom.Rep.," 1990; Auth, "Dominican Agrarian Rt," 1967. danierobles@gmail.com

ROBSON, David John (CPa) 2985 Raintree Rd, York PA 17404 **R S Andr's Epis Ch York PA 2005-** B Toronto ON CA 6/6/1955 s John David Robson & Brenda SW. B.A. U Tor 1978; M.Div. The Coll of Emm and St. Chad 1981; Th.M. Queens U 1986; M.Ed. Queens U 1996; D.Min. Luth TS at Gettysburg 2004. Trans from Anglican Church of Canada 9/1/1999 Bp Michael Whittington Creighton. m 4/28/1984 Dianna Lynn Vanner c 1. R Chap Of The Gd Shpd Hawk Run PA 1999-2005; R S Paul's Ch Philipsburg PA 1999-2005. Auth, "Thinking about Weddings," Angl Bk Cntr: Toronto, 1994. djr6@comcast.net

ROBSON, John Merritt (Neb) 1620 Atlas Ave, Lincoln NE 68521 **D S Dav Of Wales Epis Ch Lincoln NE 1991-** B Gordon NE 9/22/1930 s John Wesley Robson & Martha Mildred. BS U of Nebraska 1953; MA U Denv 1959; U MN 1966. D 4/26/1991 Bp James Edward Krotz. m 8/26/1951 Kathryn Mae Baker c 3. NAAD 1991. j2rob@yahoo.com

ROBY JR, Jesse (Mich) 1550 Cherboneau Pl Apt 202, Detroit MI 48207 B Austin TX 6/4/1918 s Jesse Roby & Lessie. BS Sam Huston Coll Austin TX 1942; Med Wayne 1949; Michigan TS 1979. D 6/26/1976 Bp H Coleman McGehee Jr. m 8/2/1944 Claudia Josephine Greene c 1. Asst S Jn's Ch Detroit MI 1984-1994; Cler All SS Ch Detroit MI 1976-1983. Sacr Ord Of Deacons. Cert Of Merit St Of Michigan 1977.

ROBYN, Richard J(ames) (Pa) 6901 Rising Sun Ave, Philadelphia PA 19111 **Trin Ch Oxford Philadelphia PA 2009-** B Kalamazoo MI 1/2/1974 s John Michael Robyn & Linda Marie. AA Kalamazoo Vlly Cmnty Coll 1995; BA Loyola U New Orleans LA 1997; MDiv The GTS 2007. D 7/1/2007 Bp Charles Edward Jenkins III P 6/11/2008 Bp E(gbert) Don Taylor. m 8/15/2010 Peter Datos. Hon Cur Ch Of The Resurr New York NY 2007-2009; Asst Ch Of The Trsfg New York NY 2005-2007. CBS 2008; US Friends of Walsingham 2008; US SocMary 2008. rjrobyn@gmail.com

ROCCOBERTON, Marjorie Ruth Smith (Ct) 82 Shoddy Mill Rd, Bolton CT 06043 **Cn to the Ordnry Dio Connecticut Hartford CT 2000-** B East Orange NJ 6/13/1953 d Edward Kensel Smith & Ruth Edith. Hartford Sem; Montclair St U 1973; BA Stockton St Coll 1975; MA U of Connecticut 1991; MA U of Hartford 1998. D 6/8/1996 Bp Clarence Nicholas Coleridge. m 12/1/1973 Bartolo Peter Roccoberton c 1. Pstr Response Coordntr Dio Connecticut Hartford CT 1999-2000; Pstr Response Coordntr Dio Connecticut Hartford CT 1999-2000; D S Mk's Chap Storrs CT 1996-2000. AAMFT 1990; CAMFT 1990; NAAD 1996. Kappa Delta Pi 1998. mroccoberton@ctdiocese.org

ROCK, Jean-Baptiste Kenol (NY) 3061 Bainbridge Ave, Bronx NY 10467 B Gressier Port-au-Prince HT 1/7/1958 s Samuel Rock & Vesta. BS Iteh 1985; Seteh Bt 1989. D 7/30/1989 P 2/1/1990 Bp Luc Anatole Jacques Garnier. m 5/23/1992 Thurin Rock c 3. Dio Haiti Ft Lauderdale FL 1989-2006. jr2629@columbia.edu

ROCK, J Konrad (WK) 706 E 74th Ave, Hutchinson KS 67502 **P Dio Wstrn Kansas Hutchinson KS 1996-** B McPherson KS 10/6/1940 s Clayton Russell Rock & Lucille Bernice. AA Hutchinson Cmnty Coll 1960; BA U of Kansas 1962; DDS U of Missouri 1966; Specialty Cert U of Missouri 1968. D 3/4/1989 Bp John Forsythe Ashby P 3/1/1996 Bp Vernon Edward Strickland. m 6/10/1962 Brenda Elaine Homman. Asst Gr Epis Ch Hutchinson KS 2000-2002.

ROCK, John Sloane (Minn) PO BOX 1178, Bemidji MN 56619 B White Earth MN 4/23/1938 s Reuben Rock & Anna. D 10/29/2005 P 1/20/2007 Bp James Louis Jelinek. c 3.

ROCKABRAND, Walter Ralph (Okla) Po Box 534, Mcalester OK 74502 B DeKalb IL 10/12/1943 s Charles William Rockabrand & Ethel Frank. BS Illinois St U 1965; SWTS 1970. D 6/13/1970 Bp James Winchester Montgomery P 12/1/1970 Bp George R Selway. c 1. All SS Ch McAlester OK 1992-1999; Ch Of The Adv S Louis MO 1991-1992; R S Paul's Epis Ch

Sikeston MO 1987-1991; Vic S Aug's Epis Ch Elkhorn NE 1980-1986. walrock@icok.net

ROCKMAN, Jane Linda (NJ) 559 Park Ave, Scotch Plains NJ 07076 **R All SS' Epis Ch Scotch Plains NJ 2000-** B Newark NJ 3/15/1944 d Joseph Rockman & Charlotte. BA Smith 1965; MA NYU 1969; MDiv UTS 1986. D 6/7/1986 P 11/17/1987 Bp Paul Moore Jr. Cur Ch Of The Ascen New York NY 1989-1999; Epis Ch Cntr New York NY 1986-1987. Ed, "Peace In Search Of Makers," 1979.

ROCKWELL, Cristine V (WMass) 51 Perkins St, Springfield MA 01118 B Johnson City NY 4/22/1948 d Donald Van Kirk Grey & Kathryn. U Neuchalel-Suisse 1969; BS SUNY at Geneseo 1970; MDiv Bex 1988. D 4/1/1990 P 10/1/1990 Bp William George Burrill. m 6/1/1974 Bruce A Rockwell c 1. R S Jn's Ch Clifton Sprg NY 1994-1998; Asst The Ch Of The Epiph Rochester NY 1992-1994; D Ch Of The Incarn Penfield NY 1990-1992. crockwelll@comcast.net

✠ **ROCKWELL, Rt Rev Hays H.** (Mo) Po Box 728, West Kingston RI 02892 B Detroit MI 8/17/1936 s Walter Francis Rockwell & Kathryn McElroy. Oxf; BA Br 1958; BD EDS 1961. D 6/29/1961 Bp Robert Lionne DeWitt P 4/1/1962 Bp John S Higgins Con 3/2/1991 for Mo. m 9/7/1957 Linda Hullinger c 4. Bp Dio Missouri S Louis MO 1991-2002; R S Jas Ch New York NY 1976-1991; Dn Bex Columbus OH 1971-1976; Chapl S Geo's Sch Newport RI 1961-1969. Auth, "Proclamation 2, H Week," *Series C*, Fortress Press, 1979; Auth, *arts, assorted-- The New York Times, The St. Louis Post Dispatch, The Chr Century, ATR, etc.*; Auth, "Steal Away," *Steal Away Hm*, Doubleday and Co. Soc of S Jn the Evang 1991. DD U So TS 2000; Doctor of Hmnts S Louis U 1994; DD Epis TS of the SW 1984; DD Ken 1974. retbish@aol.com

ROCKWELL, Melody Neustrom (Ia) 220 40th St NE, Cedar Rapids IA 52402 **D Chr Ch Cedar Rapids IA 2009-** B Kearney NE 9/25/1942 d Willys E Neustrom & Geraldine Slocum. BA U of Nebraska at Kearney 1964; MA U of Iowa 1980. D 2/21/2009 Bp Alan Scarfe. m 6/6/1964 Melvin Daniel Rockwell c 3. mrockwrite@netins.net

ROCKWELL III, Reuben (CGC) 4051 Old Shell Road, Mobile AL 36608 **Cur S Paul's Ch Mobile AL 2008-** B Augusta GA 12/20/1980 s Reuben Rockwell & Gail Scott. AB U GA 2003; MDiv VTS 2007. D 2/3/2007 P 8/18/2007 Bp Henry Irving Louttit. m 7/24/2004 Erin Carroll c 2. Vic S Barn Epis Ch Valdosta GA 2007-2008. reubenrockwell@gmail.com

ROCKWELL, Sarah (NH) 10 Pond Rd, Derry NH 03038 **COM Dio New Hampshire Concord NH 2009-; R S Ptr's Epis Ch Londonderry NH 2004-** B Geneva IL 2/11/1965 d Richard George Rockwell & Jane Foster. BA Smith 1987; MDiv Ya Berk 1993. D 12/1/1996 Bp Carl Christopher Epting P 6/14/1997 Bp Gordon Paul Scruton. m 1/25/2008 Hays M Junkin. Dioc Coun Mem Dio New Hampshire Concord NH 2006-2008; Assoc R Ch Of The Gd Shpd Burke VA 1999-2004; Cur S Andr's Ch Longmeadow MA 1997-1999. sarahrockwell@comcast.net

RODDAM, John William Richard (Oly) 724 North 182nd Street, Shoreline WA 98133 B Pictou NS CANADA 12/9/1954 s Keith Edgar William Roddam & Hazel Helen Kathleen. BSc Acadia U 1977; MDiv Acadia Div Coll 1981; Urban Min. Dplma Sem Consortium For Urban Pstr Ed Chicago IL 1982; DMin Fuller TS 1997. Trans from Anglican Church of Canada 11/18/2000 Bp Vincent Waydell Warner. m 5/4/1979 Holly Michelle White c 4. R S Lk's Epis Ch Seattle WA 2000-2010. john_roddam@hotmail.com

RODDY, Bonnie Joia (Ore) 266 4th Ave, #601, Salt Lake City UT 84103 B Salt Lake City UT 4/24/1933 d James Hodgson & Margaret Ann. AA Fullerton Coll; U of Utah; BA Chapman U 1962; MCSp Creighton U 1985; MDiv CDSP 1988. D 5/15/1988 P 5/31/1989 Bp George Edmonds Bates. m 6/16/1978 Jack Edward Roddy. Asst All SS Ch Salt Lake City UT 2005-2010; Dio Oregon Portland OR 1995-2000; Vic S Cathr Of Alexandria Manzanita OR 1995-2000; R S Steph's Baker City OR 1992-1995; Assoc R S Alb's Epis Ch Tucson AZ 1990-1992; Cur All SS Ch Salt Lake City UT 1988-1990; Dio Utah Salt Lake City UT 1988-1990. "w Death on My Shoulder," Infinity, 2005. bonniejoia@gmail.com

RODDY, Jack Edward (Ore) 266 4th Ave. Apt 601, Salt Lake City UT 84103 B Carrolton GA 7/3/1932 s Seaborn Edward Roddy & Julia Edna. D 5/21/1994 Bp Rustin Ray Kimsey. m 6/16/1978 Bonnie Joia Hodgson. D All SS Ch Salt Lake City UT 2005-2011; D S Cathr Of Alexandria Manzanita OR 1995-2000; D S Steph's Baker City OR 1994-2000. JRODDY3319@MSN.COM

RODERICK, Keith R (Spr) 402 West Mill St., Carbondale IL 62901 **R S Andr's Ch Carbondale IL 2009-** B Springfield IL 2/26/1953 s Donald E Roderick & A Joanne. BA U IL, Springfield 1976; MDiv U Of Dubuque 1980; Cert Nash 1986; DD Faith TS Gujranwala Pk 1996. D 6/5/1986 P 10/1/1986 Bp Donald Maynard Hultstrand. m 6/29/1974 Mary Hansen c 1. S Geo's Ch Macomb IL 1987-1998; P S Jas Epis Ch McLeansboro IL 1986-1987; P S Steph's Ch Harrisburg IL 1986-1987; Sthrn Dnry Team Mnstry Mc Leansboro IL 1986-1987. Gnrl Dir Soc S Steph, SSC, SocMary. father.roderick@gmail.com

RODGERS, Billy W(ilson) (CFla) 13465 SE 93rd Court Rd, Summerfield FL 34491 B Erick OK 10/17/1932 s Henry Wilson Rodgers & Thelma Louise. BA California St U 1954; MA California St U 1955; BD EDS 1958; ThD GTS 1965. D 6/16/1958 Bp Donald J Campbell P 4/1/1959 Bp Charles Francis Boynton. m 9/15/1951 Helen Irene Temple c 3. Asst, Spanish Wk S Aug's Ch New York NY 1960-1961; Asst S Lk's Epis Ch Metuchen NJ 1958-1960; Fell/Tutor The GTS New York NY 1958-1960. Auth, "Cristologia: Estudio de La Epistola a Los Hebreos," Centro de Reflexion Teologia, 1993; Auth, "Var arts & Bk Revs". erickborn.rodgers@gmail.com

RODGERS, Paul Benjamin (Mass) 359 Elm St, Dartmouth MA 02748 B Alexandria VA 5/20/1972 s John Hewitt Rodgers & Blanche K. BA Buc 1994; MDiv TESM 2003. D 6/14/2003 Bp Robert William Duncan P 1/21/2004 Bp Henry William Scriven. m 6/13/1998 Leigh Lauren Herlong c 1. R S Ptr's Ch Dartmouth MA 2006-2010; Trin Ch Tariffville CT 2003-2006; Dio Pittsburgh Monroeville PA 2003. paulbenjaminrodgers@gmail.com

RODGERS, Peter R (Ct) 400 Humphrey St, New Haven CT 06511 **P-in-c S Andr's In The Highlands Mssn Antelope CA 2009-** B Huntington,NY 9/14/1943 s Frederick Rodgers & Ruth Cleveland. BLitt Oxf; BA Hob 1966; STB GTS 1969. D 6/14/1969 Bp Jonathan Goodhue Sherman P 1/1/1970 Bp Donald J Campbell. m 7/19/1986 Katherine Gardiner. S Jn's Ch New Haven CT 1979-2003; R Ch Of The Recon Webster MA 1978-1979; Asst S Jn's Ch Williamstown MA 1969-1974. Auth, "Knowing Jesus". peterrodg@gmail.com

RODGERS, Richard Clark (Okla) 6791 E 4th St, Tucson AZ 85710 B Colorado Springs CO 1/1/1916 s Cecil Edwin Rodgers & Marion. BA Colorado Coll 1937; MDiv GTS 1959. D 6/9/1940 P 12/22/1940 Bp Fred Ingley. m 4/19/1941 Lilllian Quarles c 4. Assoc S Jn's Epis Ch Tulsa OK 1972-1978; Chair DeptCE Dio Oklahoma Oklahoma City OK 1972-1976; Secy Stndg Com Dio Oklahoma Oklahoma City OK 1962-1963; R S Lk's Epis Ch Bartlesville OK 1947-1966; Vic S Jn's Ch Shenandoah IA 1945-1946; R S Mary's Ch Nebraska City NE 1941-1947; Asst to Dn S Jn's Cathd Denver CO 1940-1941. lrrodgs@aol.com

RODGERS, Robert Allen (Eau) 618 N Summit St, Spooner WI 54801 **S Alb's Ch Spooner WI 2004-; S Lk's Ch Spooner WI 2004-** B Racine WI 6/16/1945 s Stanley John Rodgers & Esther Catherine. BA U of Wisconsin 1968; MS U of Wisconsin 1972; MDiv Nash 2003. D 2/8/2003 P 8/9/2003 Bp Keith Bernard Whitmore. c 2. vicarbob@charter.net

RODGERS, Stephen M (NY) 14160 SW Teal Blvd. 32 B, Beaverton OR 97008 **Ch Of The H Sprt Episco Battle Ground WA 2008-** B Spokane WA 12/9/1953 s Walter R Rodgers & Lynne. BA U of Washington 1976; MDiv EDS 1980; MA Portland St Universithy 2003; MA Geo Fox U 2011. D 6/24/1980 Bp Leigh Wallace Jr P 3/4/1981 Bp Paul Moore Jr. m 5/20/1978 Lesley Sepetoski. Assoc S Jas Epis Ch Tigard OR 2002-2006; Chr Ch Par Lake Oswego OR 1998-1999; Asst Ch Of The Heav Rest New York NY 1980-1984. revstever@comcast.net

RODMAN, Edward Willis (Mass) 62 W Central St, Natick MA 01760 B Indianapolis IN 8/6/1942 s Orland Worthington Rodman & Charllotte Jesse. BA Hampton U 1965; BD EDS 1967; LHD S Aug's Coll Raleigh NC 1990. D 6/1/1967 Bp Anson Phelps Stokes Jr P 5/1/1968 Bp Joseph Warren Hutchens. m 1/30/1964 Gladys Carroll c 2. EDS Cambridge MA 2001-2008; Dio Massachusetts Boston MA 1973-2001; Cn Mssnr For Minority Communities Dio Massachusetts Boston MA 1971-2002; Asst S Paul And S Jas New Haven CT 1967-1971. Auth, "Let There Be Peace Among Us". UBE, EUC, Black Leaders & Dioc Executives. erodman.eds.edu

RODMAN, Janet Laura (EC) 218 Fairway Drive, Washington DC 27889 **Dio E Carolina Kinston NC 2003-** B NY NY 10/31/1952 BA Heidelberg Coll. D 6/14/2003 Bp Clifton Daniel III. m 2/2/1991 John Douglas Rodman c 2.

RODMAN, Reginald Cary (Ore) 10434 Brackenwood Ln NE, Bainbridge Island WA 98110 B Cambridge MA 1/1/1935 s Oliver Hazard Perry Rodman & Dorothea. BA Marlboro Coll 1957; BD SWTS 1968. D 6/11/1968 Bp Joseph Summerville Minnis P 12/14/1968 Bp Edwin B Thayer. m 7/3/1980 Terrie Lynne Armstong c 3. Vic S Edw's Ch Silverton OR 2004-2008; Southcoast Mssnr Dio Oregon Portland OR 1999-2005; So Coast Mssnr Dio Oregon Portland OR 1999-2004; R Chr Ch Kealakekua HI 1987-1996; Vic S Ambr Epis Ch Boulder CO 1983-1987; Vic S Paul's Epis Ch Cntrl City CO 1980-1983; R Ch Of S Jn Chrys Golden CO 1971-1980, Chapl/Asst S Aid's Epis Ch Boulder CO 1970-1971; Cur S Paul's Epis Ch Lakewood CO 1968-1970. scomish6@yahoo.com

RODMAN III, Samuel Sewall (Mass) 112 Randolph Ave, Milton MA 02186 **Dio Massachusetts Boston MA 2010-** B Springfield MA 6/7/1959 s Samuel Sewall Rodman & Mary Jane. BA Bates Coll 1981; MDiv VTS 1987. D 8/22/1987 P 3/19/1988 Bp Andrew Frederick Wissemann. m 5/26/1985 Deborah Nedurian c 2. R S Mich's Ch Milton MA 1994-2010; Asst R Ch Of The Redeem Chestnut Hill MA 1989-1994; Cur S Thos' Ch Whitemarsh Ft Washington PA 1987-1989; Secy Epis Ch Cntr New York NY 1982-1984. rodmans4@aol.com

RODRIGUES, Theodore Earl (EO) P.O. Box 2206, Sisters OR 97759 **R Epis Ch Of The Trsfg Sis OR 2006-** B Cincinnati OH 6/12/1953 s Sherwood Theodore Rodrigues & Shirley Lee. BA California St U 1977; MDiv CDSP 1987. D 12/12/1987 P 6/14/1988 Bp David Bell Birney IV. m 5/26/1985 Gayle

R

Thelma Blank. Pres of Stndg Com Dio Estrn Oregon The Dalles OR 2007-2008; Dioc Coun & Stndg Com Dio Estrn Oregon The Dalles OR 2006-2008; Dioc Coun Dio Oregon Portland OR 2003-2005; Bd Trst Dio Oregon Portland OR 1996-1999; Dn of Sunset Convoc Dio Oregon Portland OR 1995-2000; R S Barn Par Portland OR 1993-2006; Bd Dir Epis Cmnty Servs Dio Nthrn California Sacramento CA 1988-1992; Vic S Tim's Ch Gridley CA 1987-1993. OHC 1987. therevted@bendbroadband.com

RODRIGUEZ, Albert R (Tex) 2503 Ware Rd, Austin TX 78741 **R S Jn's Epis Ch Austin TX 1999-** B San Antonio TX 12/16/1941 s Manuel Rodriguez & Francisca. BBA St. Mary's U San Antonio TX 1964; MA U Pgh 1969; MDiv Epis TS of The SW 1996. D 6/22/1996 Bp Claude Edward Payne P 1/12/1997 Bp Leopoldo Jesus Alard. m 4/3/1965 Helen LaVerne Calvin c 2. P-in-c Trin Ch Longview TX 1996-1999; Exec Dir El Buen Samaritano Epis Mssn Austin TX 1989-1995. padrealrod@aol.com

RODRIGUEZ, Christopher Michael (NJ) 65 W Front St, Red Bank NJ 07701 **Dioc Coun Dio New Jersey Trenton NJ 2011-; Chair, Congrl Dvlpmt Comm Dio New Jersey Trenton NJ 2009-; R Trin Epis Ch Red Bank NJ 2007-** B Yonkers NY 12/20/1968 s Anthony Rodriguez & Susan. BA Penn 1991; MS No Carolina St U 1996; MDiv TESM 2004. Trans from Church of the Province of Central Africa 1/10/2007 Bp George Edward Councell. m Kathleen M Faulkner c 3. Cur All SS Ch Wynnewood PA 2005-2007. Co-Auth, "The Measurement of Orgnztn Citizenship Behavior: Are we expecting too much?," *Journ of Applied Soc Psychol*, Wiley, 1997. crodriguez@trinityredbank.org

RODRIGUEZ, Hector Raul (Md) 6960 Sunfleck Row, Columbia MD 21045 **Latino Mssnr Dio Maryland Baltimore MD 2009-** B Eagle Pass TX 5/7/1945 s Salvador G Rodriguez & Elisa. Rec from Roman Catholic 10/4/2009 Bp John Leslie Rabb. m 9/25/1976 Camelia Ramirez c 3. hectorraul@verizon.net

RODRIGUEZ, Isaias Arguello (At) 3004 Mccully Dr NE, Atlanta GA 30345 **Hisp Mssnr Dio Atlanta Atlanta GA 1998-** B Leon ES 5/27/1941 s Erasmo Rodriguez & Felisia. Cert San Juan de la Cruz Burgo de Osma Soria ES 1962; Lic Pontifica Facultas Theol Teresianum Rome IT 1967; Candler TS Emory U 1984; Cert STUSo 1984. Rec from Roman Catholic 1/13/1985 as Deacon Bp Charles Judson Child Jr. m 11/23/1979 Mary Katherine Clawson c 3. Reg Assoc for Hispnaic Minstry Epis Ch Cntr New York NY 1986-1994; S Lk's Epis Ch Atlanta GA 1985-1998. Auth, *Temas de Orientación Prematrimonial*, Forw Mvmt Press, 2000; Auth, *Historia y Reforma de la Iglesia Anglicana*, Forw Mvmt, 1999; Auth, *Reflexiones sobre el Diezmo y la Mayordomía*, Forw Mvmt Press, 1998; Auth, "Temas de un Diario," *El Monte Carmelo*, 1993; Auth, "Yo Creo En El Amor," *Desclée De Brouwer*, 1974. irodriguez@episcopalatlanta.org

RODRIGUEZ, Katherine Renee (RG) 10A Bisbee Ct, Santa Fe NM 87508 B Davenport IA 11/16/1982 d Richard Alan Rodriguez & Amy L. BA TCU 2005; MAR Epis TS Of The SW 2010. D 9/18/2010 Bp William Carl Frey. katspetkat@yahoo.com

RODRIGUEZ, Luis Mario (EpisSanJ) 519 N Douty St, Hanford CA 93230 **R Epis Ch Of The Sav Hanford CA 2008-** B 1/19/1964 s Luis Rodriguez & Miriam. BA Occ 1986; MA California St U 1993; MTh Oxf (St Steph's Hse), UK 1999; MA Sch of Psych and Counselling Psychol, UK 2008. Trans from Church Of England 12/11/2008 Bp Jerry Alban Lamb. luis@smeltern.com

RODRIGUEZ, Ramiro Rodriguez (Los) 7540 Passons Blvd, Pico Rivera CA 90660 B MX 12/18/1959 s Manuel Rodriguez Mares & Maria Reyes. Gnrl Antonio Rosales 1985; Pacific Luth TS 1995. D 6/10/1995 P 1/1/1996 Bp Frederick Houk Borsch. m 9/10/1988 Maria Gloria Cazares Avila c 2. S Barth's Mssn Pico Rivera CA 1996.

RODRIGUEZ ESPINEL, Neptali (Minn) 1524 Summit Ave, Saint Paul MN 55105 **Asst Vic La Mision El Santo Nino Jesus S Paul MN 2010-** B Colombia 9/6/1979 s Gustavo Rodriguez Tellez & Ana Isabel. Theol Javeriana-ITE PAL 2002; Cn Rt Javeriana-ITE PAL 2002; Missionology Javeriana-Consolata 2003; Rel Life Marianum 2004. Rec from Roman Catholic 1/7/2010 as Priest Bp James Louis Jelinek. m 5/16/2007 Rebekah Taylor c 1. padreneptali@gmail.com

RODRIGUEZ-PADRON, Francisco M (LI) 418 50th St, Brooklyn NY 11220 **P-in-c S Andr's Ch Brooklyn NY 2004-** B Matanzas Cuba 5/17/1963 s Agustin Rodriguez & Santa. GTS; U of Matanzas 1985; MDiv Evang TS Matanzas 1993. D 3/13/2004 P 9/18/2004 Bp Mark Sean Sisk. All SS' Epis Ch Long Island City NY 2004. frfranciscor@hotmail.com

RODRIGUEZ-SANTOS, Carlos (Hond) Diocese of Honduras, Imc Sap #215, Miami FL 33152 **Dio Honduras Miami FL 2006-** B San Pedro Sula 11/3/1952 s Catividad Rodriguez & Ana Maria. D 10/28/2005 Bp Lloyd Emmanuel Allen. m 7/26/1971 Doris Mariela Megia c 2. charlescatrachosantosarron.com

RODRIGUEZ-SANTOS, Toribio (NJ) 38 W End Pl, Elizabeth NJ 07202 **Vic San Jose Epis Ch Eliz NJ 2010-** B Dominican Republic 9/15/1963 s Ramon Rodriguez & Esperanza. Lic in Theol St Thos Aquinas 1994; AA TCI Tech Career Insitute 2008. Rec from Roman Catholic 4/24/2010 Bp Sylvestre Donato Romero. m 5/9/2001 Tereza Carrion c 2. frtory94@yahoo.com.mx

RODRIGUEZ VALLECILLO, Digna Suyapa (Hond) Barrio Zaragoza, Calle De La Shell, Siguatepeque Honduras **Dio Honduras Miami FL 2006-; Iglesia Epis Hondurena San Pedro Sula 2006-** B Villanueva Cortes 4/13/1964 d Julio Cesar Rodriguez & Eva. Seminario Diocesano. D 10/30/2005 P 7/24/2010 Bp Lloyd Emmanuel Allen. c 3.

RODRIGUEZ-YEJO, Ruden (Del) 1005 Pleasant St, Wilmington DE 19805 **The Ch Of The Ascen Claymont DE 2007-** B Guayama PR 4/1/1934 s Luis Rodriguez & Ana Luisa. BA U of Puerto Rico; MDiv ETSC 1967. D 5/17/1967 P 12/1/1967 Bp Francisco Reus-Froylan. Chr Ch Greenville Wilmington DE 1988-1991; Capilla Santa Nombre De Jesus Bethlehem PA DO 1986-1988; Dio Puerto Rico S Just PR 1967-1979. rrodyejo@aol.com

ROECK, Gretchen Elizabeth (Minn) 322 2nd St, Excelsior MN 55331 **D Trin Ch Excelsior MN 2010-** B Chicago IL 5/16/1983 d James Michael Roeck & Kathryn Traas. BA Denison U 2005; MDiv UTS 2008; Angl Stds GTS 2009. D 6/5/2010 Bp Jeffrey Dean Lee P 2/17/2011 Bp Brian N Prior. m 5/23/2009 John Jelickman. gretchen@trinityexcelsior.org

ROEGER JR, William Donald (Mo) 419 N 6th St, Hannibal MO 63401 **P-in-c S Jas Epis Ch Griggsville IL 1999-** B Camden NJ 3/23/1931 s William Donald Roeger & Naomi Lillian. Drexel U 1952; PDS 1961. D 11/5/1960 P 6/29/1961 Bp Alfred L Banyard. m 5/17/1952 Gwyneth L Jones c 4. Asst S Jn's Epis Ch Peoria IL 1995-2002; Conv Plnng & Arrangements Com Dio Missouri S Louis MO 1993-1994; Conv Plnng & Arrangements Com Dio Missouri S Louis MO 1988-1989; Pres of the No Convoc Dio Missouri S Louis MO 1987-1995; R Trin Ch Hannibal MO 1986-1995; R Chr Ch Ironton OH 1982-1986; R All SS Ch Leonia NJ 1977-1982; Bd Missions Dio Newark Newark NJ 1972-1982; Chr Ch Glen Ridge NJ 1970-1977; Vic S Andr's Ch Lambertville NJ 1961-1963; Vic H Trin Ch Pennsauken NJ 1960-1961; Archit Cmsn Dio New Jersey Trenton NJ 1953-1969. wroeger@areatech.com

ROESCHLAUB, Robert Friedrich (Ind) 20 Pannatt Hill, Millom, Cumbria LA18 5DB Great Britain (UK) B Melrose Park IL 11/22/1939 s George Robert Roeschlaub & Elizabeth Gertrude. BS Pur 1963; STB Ya Berk 1966. D 6/11/1966 P 12/1/1966 Bp John P Craine. m 6/16/1967 Gail Mary Long c 2. Stndg Com Dio Indianapolis Indianapolis IN 1974-1976; R S Mk's Ch Plainfield IN 1970-1977; Cur Trin Ch Indianapolis IN 1966-1970. AAR 1963-1997; CBS 1963; SBL 1963-1997. hoosier@btconnect.com

ROESKE, Michael Jerome (Mass) 35 Bowdoin St, Boston MA 02114 **Trin Ch Houston TX 2011-** B Barstow CA 5/11/1961 s Jerome Darman Roeske & Bevra Anne. BA NWU 1983; MDiv Ya Berk 2000. D 5/27/2001 P 12/8/2001 Bp Keith Bernard Whitmore. Ch Of S Jn The Evang Boston MA 2003-2005; St Greg The Tchr Mssn Onalaska WI 2001-2002; Cn Mssnr Dio Eau Claire Eau Claire WI 2000-2002. mjroeske@yahoo.com

ROFINOT, Laurie Ann (Mass) 88 Lexington Ave # 2, Somerville MA 02144 B Cheyenne WY 7/20/1956 d N Ensley Rofinot & Beverly Faye. BA U MN 1979; MDiv EDS 1986. D 6/24/1986 P 12/15/1987 Bp Robert Marshall Anderson. m 8/23/1980 Patrick G Michaels c 1. Assoc All SS Par Brookline MA 2009-2011; Assoc P S Jas' Epis Ch Cambridge MA 2007-2009; Dio Massachusetts Boston MA 2005; Tufts U Epis Chap Medford MA 2005; Dio Massachusetts Boston MA 2003-2004; R S Jn's Ch Charlestown (Boston) Charlestown MA 1996-2003; Asst R S Anne's In The Fields Epis Ch Lincoln MA 1990-1995; Assoc P S Jas' Epis Ch Cambridge MA 1986-1989. Contrib, "Revolutionary Forgiveness: Feminist Reflections On Nic," Orbis, 1987. EPF 2000; EWC 1985; MECA Co-Pres 2006-08, Treas 2008-present; NNECA Bd 2007-08, Ed LEAVEN 2008-present. larofinot@aol.com

ROGAN, Donald Lynn (O) Kenyon College, Box 371, Gambier OH 43022 B Staunton VA 6/16/1930 s Charles Ernest Rogan & Jane. BA Morris Harvey Coll 1951; STB GTS 1954; Dplma S Aug's Coll Cbury 1960. D 6/7/1954 Bp Robert E L Strider P 12/15/1954 Bp Wilburn Camrock Campbell. m 8/25/1954 Sarah Larew c 4. Ken Gambier OH 1965-1999; R Trin Ch Morgantown WV 1956-1962; Vic All SS Ch Charleston WV 1954-1956. Auth, *Campus Apocalypse*, Seabury Press, 1969; Ed, *Spkng God's Word*, 1956. DD GTS 2000; DHL Ken/Gambier, OH 1999. donaldrogan5@aol.com

ROGERS, Allan Douglas (SwFla) 4352 Arrow Ave, Sarasota FL 34232 **D S Bon Ch Sarasota FL 2003-** B Summerville SC 9/1/1949 s Claude A Rogers & Pauline. MA U of So Florida 1976. D 1/18/2003 Bp John Bailey Lipscomb. m 7/23/1971 Holly B Carr c 1. ar9189@aol.com

ROGERS, David Beebe (SO) 3148 Gracefield Rd Apt 615, Silver Spring MD 20904 B Oak Park IL 8/25/1925 s H(arry) Barrett Rogers & Harriett Jean. BS NWU 1950; MDiv VTS 1965. D 6/26/1965 P 1/2/1966 Bp Roger W Blanchard. m 3/26/1983 Susan Margaret Rogers c 4. Assoc S Paul's Epis/Angl Ch Frederiksted VI VI 1981-1986; Asst S Jn's Ch Christiansted VI 1969-1980; R H Trin Ch Cincinnati OH 1966-1968; Cur Gr Ch Cincinnati OH 1965-1966. captdbr@aol.com

ROGERS, Diana (Minn) 318 E 25th St Apt D8, Minneapolis MN 55404 B Waynesboro PA 5/2/1948 d Gerald Campbell McKelvey & Mary Louise. BA Metro St U 2002; Untd TS 2007; MDiv The GTS 2008. D 1/25/2008 Bp Keith Bernard Whitmore P 10/6/2008 Bp James Louis Jelinek. c 2. Int R Chr Ch

Austin MN 2010-2011; Coordntr of Vocations Dio Minnesota Minneapolis MN 2002-2007. dianamrogers@gmail.com

ROGERS, Elizabeth Page (Ct) 99 Lee Farm Dr, Niantic CT 06357 **R S Jn's Epis Ch Niantic CT 1999-** B Kansas City MO 9/10/1953 d George Sterling Rogers & Suzanne. BA Wheaton Coll at Norton 1976; MDiv Ya Berk 1980. D 12/5/1981 P 6/10/1982 Bp Arthur Edward Walmsley. Com Chairman Dio Connecticut Hartford CT 1998-2002; Const And Cn Dio Connecticut Hartford CT 1998-1999; Excoun Dio Connecticut Hartford CT 1989-2009; Vic Chr Epis Ch Middle Haddam CT 1985-1999; Par Dvlpmt Consult Dio Connecticut Hartford CT 1984-1993; S Jas Epis Ch Farmington CT 1982-1985. Soc Of S Jn The Evang 1999. saltydog1021@snet.net

ROGERS III, George Michael Andrew (Alb) 325 East 80th Street, 1D, New York NY 10021 B New York NY 4/12/1969 s George Michael Rogers & Sylvia Emilia. B.S. Ya 1991; DAS Ya Berk 1995; MDiv Yale DS 1995. D 5/10/1999 P 11/13/1999 Bp Daniel William Herzog. m 7/19/2003 Yun Lee Too. Asst Par Of Chr The Redeem Pelham NY 2003-2010; Admin Vic The Ch of S Ign of Antioch New York NY 2002-2003; The GTS New York NY 2001-2003; Asst P S Thos Ch New York NY 2000-2003; Asst Mssns S Paul's Ch Brant Lake NY 1999-2000; Dio Albany Albany NY 1999. Dio Albany Theol Cmsn 1999-2004; Grand Lodge of NY - F. and A.M. 2000; Hobart Soc 1995-2003; Yale Club of NYC 1991. Mercer Schlrshp Dio Long Island 1998. george@christchurchpelham.org

ROGERS, Henry Stanley Fraser (Oly) 4770 116th Ave Se, Bellevue WA 98006 B Port Arthur ON CA 6/7/1927 s Henry James Rogers & Marjorie Adelaide. BA U Of British Columbia Vancouver Bc CA 1950; BCA U Of British Columbia Vancouver Bc CA 1952; U Of British Columbia Vancouver Bc CA 1952. D 9/29/1975 Bp Ivol I Curtis P 10/18/1979 Bp Robert Hume Cochrane. m 5/9/1953 Helen de Lotbiniere-Harwood. Assoc All SS Ch Bellevue WA 1997-2002; Vic Ch Of Our Sav Monroe WA 1991-1996; Supply Dio Olympia Seattle WA 1989-1991; P-in-c S Clare of Assisi Epis Ch Snoqualmie WA 1985-1989. hrogers@nwlink.com

ROGERS JR, Jack A (Ark) 2185 Aztec Dr, Dyersburg TN 38024 B Macon GA 8/24/1957 s Jack Rogers & Anne. BA Utc 1994; MDiv Epis TS of The SW 1998. D 6/13/1998 P 2/6/1999 Bp Robert Gould Tharp. m 6/15/1998 Lisa Toot c 2. S Ptr's Ch Conway AR 2006-2008; S Lk and S Jn's Caruthersville MO 2004-2006; S Mary's Epis Ch Dyersburg TN 2003-2006; Asst S Mart Of Tours Epis Ch Chattanooga TN 2000-2003; S Mart's Epis Sch Metairie LA 1999-2000; Asst Vic S Tim's Ch La Place LA 1999-2000; D All SS' Epis Ch Morristown TN 1998-1999. jackrogers@aol.com

ROGERS, James Arthur (FtW) 4302 Wynnwood Dr, Wichita Falls TX 76308 B Albuquerque NM 5/12/1943 s James Moracle Rogers & Suzanne Marion. BA U CO 1967; MDiv Nash 1975; AS Midwestern St U 1994. D 6/17/1975 P 12/17/1975 Bp A Donald Davies. m 6/15/1968 Susan M Murfee c 1. Chr's Hm Place Mnstrs Inc. Wichita Falls TX 2003-2004; Asst Ch Of S Jn The Div Burkburnett TX 2002-2004; S Pat's Ch Bowie TX 1999-2004; Trin Ch Henrietta TX 1999; Dio Ft Worth Ft Worth TX 1997-2001; Int Ch Of S Jn The Div Burkburnett TX 1997-1998; Int P Trin Ch Henrietta TX 1997-1998; P Dio Ft Worth Ft Worth TX 1992-1997; Ch Of The Gd Shpd Wichita Falls TX 1975-1992. smrogers@chpm-inc.org

ROGERS, James Luther (Tenn) 935 Mount Olivet Rd, Columbia TN 38401 **Int The Epis Ch Of The Mssh Pulaski TN 2009-** B Memphis TN 12/26/1946 s Luther Mckeown Rogers & Maggie Sue. BS Lambuth U 1968; MDiv Nash 1971. D 6/27/1971 Bp William F Gates Jr P 4/1/1972 Bp William Evan Sanders. m 6/17/2000 Linda Rogers. P S Mary Magd Ch Fayetteville TN 2002-2008; The Epis Ch Of The Resurr Franklin TN 1989-1995; Vic The Epis Ch Of The Resurr Franklin TN 1983-1988; R S Mart Of Tours Epis Ch Chattanooga TN 1975-1979; Vic S Columba's Epis Ch Bristol TN 1973-1975; D-In-Trng St Jas Epis Ch at Knoxville Knoxville TN 1971-1972.

ROGERS JR, John Albert (Ct) 69 Butternut Ln, Rocky Hill CT 06067 **Chapl S Eliz Chap Hartford CT 2001-** B New Haven CT 2/25/1939 s John Albert Rogers & Martha Elsa. BA Drew U 1960; MDiv GTS 1963; U of Connecticut 1971; VTS 1992. D 6/11/1963 P 2/29/1964 Bp Walter H Gray. m 4/28/1962 Faye Marie Locke c 2. P All SS' Epis Ch E Hartford CT 2003-2010; Chapl CDAG Dio Connecticut Hartford CT 1990-2001; Secy Ch Schlrshp Soc Dio Connecticut Hartford CT 1983-1986; Dn Hartford Deanry Dio Connecticut Hartford CT 1983-1984; R Trin Ch Wethersfield CT 1975-2001; Asst Trin Ch Wethersfield CT 1970-1975; P Chr Ch Oxford CT 1966-1970; P Trin Ch Wethersfield CT 1963-1966. rogloc69@msn.com

ROGERS, John Sanborn (RI) 106 Osprey Dr, Saint Marys GA 31558 B Portland ME 9/1/1937 s William Nathaniel Rogers & Margaret Belle. BA Mid 1960; MDiv EDS 1963. D 6/8/1963 P 12/15/1963 Bp Oliver L Loring. m 2/4/2005 Judith F Fry c 3. Int Chr Ch Frederica St Simons Island GA 2009-2010; Int S Mk's Ch Brunswick GA 2008-2011; S Mary's Ch Portsmouth RI 1993-1999; S Geo's Sch Newport RI 1976-1999; R S Alb's Ch Cape Eliz ME 1969-1976; R S Steph's Epis Ch Bloomfield CT 1965-1969; Chapl Chap Of S Andr Boca Raton FL 1964-1965; Cur S Paul's Ch Holyoke MA 1963-1964. Chapl Emer St. Geo's Sch 2006. jrfara@tbs.net

ROGERS, Joy Edith Stevenson (Chi) 65 E. Huron, Chicago IL 60611 **Cathd Of S Jas Chicago IL 2007-** B Philadlephia PA 9/29/1946 d James Edward Stevenson & Dolores Sally. BS Penn 1967; AD Lorain Cnty Cmnty Coll 1976; MDiv SWTS 1985; DMin SWTS 1993. D 5/31/1985 Bp James Winchester Montgomery P 11/1/1985 Bp Frank Tracy Griswold III. m 9/30/1967 Nathaniel Rogers c 2. R S Thos Epis Ch Battle Creek MI 1995-2007; P-in-c Ch Of The H Fam Lake Villa IL 1995; S Lk's Ch Evanston IL 1985-1995. Auth, "Rachel Weeping: Abortion and Jeremiah's God," *Sewanee Theol Revs*, TS, Univ of the So, 1993. Fell, Coll of Preachers Coll of Preachers 1993. joyrogers@comcast.net

ROGERS, Marcus (Ct) 5601 County Route 30, Granville NY 12832 B New York NY 3/4/1934 s Raymond Griffin Rogers & Marion Louise. BS Cor 1955; STB GTS 1966. D 6/4/1966 P 12/1/1966 Bp Horace W B Donegan. m 6/18/1955 June Q Quattrone. Trin Epis Ch Bristol CT 1975-1997. ERM, Curs, Epis Untd.

ROGERS, Martha C (Ia) 235 Partridge Ave, Marion IA 52302 **R Chr Ch Cedar Rapids IA 2009-** B Fall River MA 8/10/1954 d James William Crowley & Irene Blanche. BS Rhode Island Coll 1976; MS Wstrn Illinois U 1985; MDiv STUSo 1997. D 6/13/1997 Bp James Louis Jelinek P 12/15/1997 Bp Creighton Leland Robertson. m 2/13/1982 David G Rogers c 2. Vic The Epis Ch of the Resurr Broomfield CO 2007-2009; R S Alb's Ch Sprt Lake IA 2000-2006; Cn Calv Cathd Sioux Falls SD 1997-2000. Cmnty of S Mary 1996; DOK 2007. marthar@christepiscopal.org

ROGERS, Norma Jean (Az) PO Box 4567, Tubac AZ 85646 **Affiliated Cler S Phil's In The Hills Tucson AZ 2011-** B Gadsden AZ 3/29/1937 d Clifford John Prather & Ruth Willhelmina. BA Arizona St U 1971; MA Arizona St U 1974; MDiv VTS 1991. D 6/15/1991 P 12/18/1991 Bp Ronald Hayward Haines. m 7/21/1984 John Leo Rogers c 3. Int Epis Ch Of S Fran-In-The-Vlly Green Vlly AZ 2007-2008; Affiliated Cler Epis Ch Of S Fran-In-The-Vlly Green Vlly AZ 2003-2007; R S Andr's Epis Ch Nogales AZ 1994-2003; Dio Arizona Phoenix AZ 1994; Vic Ch Of S Mary The Vrgn Nixon NV 1992-1994; Dio Nevada Las Vegas NV 1992-1994; Vic S Mich And All Ang Ch Wadsworth NV 1992-1994; Asst to R S Pat's Ch Washington DC 1991-1992. DOK - Chapl 2003. reverendnjr@aol.com

ROGERS, Robert Gerald (La) Po Box 233, Clinton LA 70722 **Asst S Andr's Ch Theriot LA 1981-** B Baton Rouge LA 1/17/1936 s John Clarence Rogers & Henriette Marie. BA Notre Dame Sem 1960; BS Loyola U 1962; MS LSU 1968. Rec from Roman Catholic 6/1/1981 as Priest Bp James Barrow Brown. m 4/22/1995 Joy Rogers c 2. S Matt's Epis Ch Houma LA 2007-2008; S Andr's Ch Theriot LA 1996-2007.

ROGERS III, Sampson (FtW) 828-28 Avenue North #4, Menomonie WI 54751 B Rockford IL 8/26/1929 s Maurice Rogers & Jeannette. BA Beloit Coll 1953; LTh SWTS 1957. D 6/15/1957 Bp Charles L Street P 12/21/1957 Bp Gerald Francis Burrill. Asstg Gr Epis Ch Menomonie WI 2002-2011; S Andr's Ch Ashland WI 1987-1994; All SS Ch San Diego CA 1983; S Fran Ch Pauma Vlly CA 1982-1983; Bec Dio Fond du Lac Appleton WI 1975-1979; S Aug's Epis Ch Rhinelander WI 1969-1981; Vic S Bon Plymouth WI 1964-1969; R S Paul's Ch Plymouth WI 1964-1969; Cur S Andr's Ch Baltimore MD 1959-1964; Cur S Giles' Ch Northbrook IL 1957-1959. Oblate Cmnty Resurr 1968. frsr3@winbirte.net

ROGERS III, Thomas Sherman (Md) 600 N. Wolfe Street, Halsted 144, Baltimore MD 21287 **Dio Maryland Baltimore MD 2011-** B Oklahoma City OK 7/24/1978 s Thomas Sherman Rogers & Betty Mae. Oklahoma City U 1998; BA TCU 2000; MDiv SMU 2004. D 6/4/2005 P 3/25/2006 Bp James Monte Stanton. m Jason M Sutton. Assoc R All SS Ch Frederick MD 2006-2011; Cur S Jas Epis Ch Texarkana TX 2005-2006. rev.thomas.rogers@gmail.com

ROGERS, Timothy James (Mass) 65 Shild St. #2, Jamaica Plain MA 02130 B Cambridge MA 6/17/1964 s Ernest James Rogers & Marie Helen. BA Macalester Coll 1995; MDiv CDSP 1998. D 12/2/2000 P 6/2/2001 Bp William Edwin Swing. S Jn's Ch Newtonville MA 2006-2009; S Ptr's Ch Salem MA 2001-2006; D Trin Par Menlo Pk CA 2000-2001. padretim@hotmail.com

ROGERS, Victor (Ct) 111 Whalley Ave, New Haven CT 06511 B 10/2/1944 s Grafton Simmons & Violet. LTh Codrington Coll; MA Jackson St U; BA Laurentian U; PhD Mississippi St U 1987. m 2/4/1984 Gloria Buck c 3. R S Lk's Epis Ch New Haven CT 1983-2010; R S Mk's Ch Jackson MS 1974-1983. vicalvinrog@yahoo.com

ROGERS, William Pettit (WTex) 1209 Monroe Dr, Kerrville TX 78028 **Died 12/1/2010** B Pittsburg KS 12/5/1929 s James Leslie Rogers & Geraldine Prudence. U CO 1949; U Denv 1950; Epis TS of The SW 1978. D 6/16/1978 P 1/1/1979 Bp Scott Field Bailey. Fllshp S Alb & S Sergius. billprogers@yahoo.com

ROGERSON, George William (Ia) 11536 Wild Rose Dr, West Burlington IA 52655 **Par Of Chr The Redeem Pelham NY 2007-** B Eldon IA 12/8/1928 s Russell W Rogerson & Beatrice E. D 4/7/2001 Bp Carl Christopher Epting. m 1/5/1950 Rita Amelia Bugden. D Chr Epis Ch Burlington IA 2001-2008. deacongeorge@christchurchonline.com

ROGGE, Joel Jay (WA) 84 County Rd, Ipswich MA 01938 B New York NY 12/15/1934 s Leo Harrison & Mollie. JD Col 1958; MDiv EDS 1968; STM Andover Newton TS 1969; Fllshp ECF 1971; DMin Andover Newton TS 1975; EdD Harv 1976. D 6/29/1968 Bp William Foreman Creighton P 6/29/1969 Bp Frederic Cunningham Lawrence. m 12/27/1959 Maryellen Gongas c 3. Assoc Ascen Memi Ch Ipswich MA 1990-1992. Auth, "Publ Fed Agencies". Diplomate, AAPC, Natl Bd Gvnr; Fell ECF. jjrogge@bigfoot.com

ROGINA, Julius M (Nev) 1080 Del Webb Pkwy West, Reno NV 89523 **P Assoc Trin Epis Ch Reno NV 1988-** B Zagreb Croatia 12/10/1945 s Julius Rogina & Maria Mira. BA Filozofski Fakultet Druzbe Isusove, Zagreb Croatia 1969; MDiv Jesuit TS 1975; STM Jesuit TS 1976; PhD Grad Theol Un, UofCal Berkeley 1981. Rec from Roman Catholic 6/1/1988 as Priest Bp Stewart Clark Zabriskie. c 3. Stndg Commitee Dio Nevada Las Vegas NV 2003-2005. Auth, "Logotherapy Treatment of Com;icated Grief Syndrom," *Intl Forum of Logotherapy*, Viktor Frankl Inst of Logotherapy, 2010; Auth, "Logotherapy in Clincl Pract," *Psych: Theory & Resrch*, APA, 2008; Auth, "Avoidant Personality Disorders," *Intl Forum of Logotherapy*, Viktor Frankl Insitute of Logotherapy, 2007; Auth, "Gnrl Anxiety Disorders and Logotherapy," *Intl Forum For Logotherapy*, Viktor Frankl Inst of Logotherapy, 2005; Auth, "Treating Nacisistic Personality Disorders," *The Intl Forum for Logotherapy*, Viktor Frankl Inst of Logotherapy, 2004; Auth, "Treating Gnrl Anxiety Disorders," *Intl Forum of Logotherapy*, Viktor Frankl Inst of Logotherapy, 2002; Auth, "On Being Grounded in the Cmnty of Faith," *Desert Ch*, Dio Nevada, 1989; Auth, "Mssn Thoelogy Today," *The Jesuit*, Jesuit Sch fo Theol at Berkeley, 1974. The NNECA 2003. jmrogina@sbcglobal.net

ROHDE, Katherine M. (Wyo) 1326 East A St., Casper WY 82601 B Eureka CA 8/2/1950 d Harold Henry Rohde & Marylee Patricia. Humboldt St U 1970; BS California St Polytechnic U 1975. D 3/14/1993 P 10/3/1993 Bp Stewart Clark Zabriskie. c 1. Int R S Mk's Epis Ch Casper WY 2010-2011; Mssn Dvlp Dio Wyoming Casper WY 2007-2010; P S Chris's Epis Ch Boulder City NV 1993-2007. CT. kayrangerrev@gmail.com

ROHLEDER, Robert Arthur (Mil) 2409 10th Ave Apt 309, South Milwaukee WI 53172 **D S Mk's Ch So Milwaukee WI 1976-** B Milwaukee WI 2/14/1931 s Waldemar Gustav Rohleder & Meta Louise. Cert SUNY 1986. D 11/6/1976 Bp Charles Thomas Gaskell. m 2/24/1951 Jane Vernette Bolduan c 2. SUNY AS 1986. rarar@merr.com

ROHMAN, Suzannah Lynn (Ct) St. Paul's Episcopal Church, 145 Main St., Southington CT 06489 **R S Paul's Ch Southington CT 2009-** B Augusta ME 5/20/1973 d James Christopher Rohman & Marcia Chaplin. BA Dickinson Coll 1995; MDiv GTS 1999; DMin SWTS 2009. Trans 1/20/2004 Bp Wayne Parker Wright. Assoc R S Geo's Epis Ch Arlington VA 2003-2009; Asst R S Thos's Par Newark DE 2001-2003; Asst R S Paul's Ch Maumee OH 1999-2001. pastor@stpaulsouthington.org

ROHRER, Glenn E (CGC) 5636 Firestone Dr, Pace FL 32571 **Vic Ch Of The Epiph Crestview FL 2011-** B Columbus OH 12/5/1944 s Chester S Rohrer & Bertha L. BSW Ohio St 1966; MDiv Methodist TS in Ohio 1969; MSW Ohio St 1973; Phd Ohio St 1979. D 1/8/2011 P 8/20/2011 Bp Philip Menzie Duncan II. m 10/28/1995 Lois Collins c 4. Prof Emer E CArolina U 2006. grohrer@uwf.edu

ROHRER, Jane (Nev) Trinity Episcopal Church, 200 Island Ave., Reno NV 89501 **Assoc Ch Of The H Cross Redmond WA 2011-; Pstr Assoc Trin Epis Ch Reno NV 2008-** B Faribault MN 7/17/1940 d Christian A Rohrer & Lydia G. BS U MN 1962; MA U MN 1964; MA Boise St U 1976; PhD Kent St U 1992; MTS SWTS 2005. D 7/12/2008 P 2/21/2009 Bp Dan Thomas Edwards. c 3. Auth, "It's not that Simple.," *Sierra Nevada Coll Revs.*, 1999; Joint Auth w Sue Welsch, "The lake Tahoe Watershed Proj: lessons learned about middle Sch females encountering math and Sci," *Roeper Revs*, 1998; Auth, "We interrupt this Prog to show you a bombing: Chld and schools respond to televised war," *Childhood Educ*, 1996; Auth, "Primary Tchr conceptions of giftedness: image, evidence, and nonevidence," *Journ for the Educ of the Gifted*, 1995; Joint Auth, "The impact of portfolio assessment on Tchr classroom activities," *Journ of Tchr Educ*, 1992. Grant Awd Epis EvangES 2005. janerohrer2003@yahoo.com

ROHRS, John D (SVa) 1023 Graydon Ave, Norfolk VA 23507 **S Andr's Ch Norfolk VA 2009-** B Stillwater OK 12/9/1976 BA Duke Universtiy 1999; MDiv Ya Berk 2005. D 6/26/2005 P 2/12/2006 Bp Michael Bruce Curry. m 10/18/2003 Andrea Lynn Wigodsky c 3. Asst To The R Chr Epis Ch Raleigh NC 2005-2009. jrohrs.staec@verizon.net

ROJAS POVEDA, Jesus Antonio (EC) 737 Delma Grimes Rd, Coats NC 27521 B Columbia South America 1/9/1937 Divinidad Seminario Conciliar. Trans from Province IX 11/27/2000 Bp Clifton Daniel III. m 12/23/1995 Lucia Hincapie c 4. Epis Farmworker Mnstry Newton Grove NC 2001-2009. jrojas7@nc.rr.com

ROKOS, Michael George (Md) 2203 Mayfield Ave, Baltimore MD 21213 **S Marg's Epis Ch Baltimore MD 2004-** B Chicago IL 4/2/1946 s George Washington Rokos & Dorothea Juanita. BA Jn Hopkins U 1968; MDiv VTS 1972; Cert Chas U in Prague 2000. D 5/25/1972 P 2/22/1973 Bp David Keller Leighton Sr. Deer Creek Par Darlington MD 2003-2004; P-in-c Gr Epis Ch Darlington MD 1994-2003; Copley Par: The Ch Of The Resurr Joppa MD 1982-1990; Chr Ch Greenville Wilmington DE 1978-1981; Asst S Thos' Ch Garrison Forest Owings Mills MD 1974-1978; Asst Ch Of The Ascen Silver Sprg MD 1972-1974. Auth, *Cops & Cults*; Auth, *Cults & the Ch*; Auth, *Identifying & Treating Satanically/Ritually Involved*. mrokosbalt@aol.com

ROLAND, Carla Elena (NY) Church of St Matthew & St Timothy, 26 W 84th St, New York NY 10024 **R The Ch of S Matt And S Tim New York NY 2004-** B Amarillo TX 11/23/1971 d Robert C Roland & Gloria A. MDiv CDSP 2001; MA Grad Theol Un 2001; BS Cor 2004. D 10/13/2002 P 10/5/2003 Bp David Andres Alvarez-Velazquez. Fell ECF 2002. ceroland@yahoo.com

ROLDAN, Roman D (La) 11621 Ferdinand St, Saint Francisville LA 70775 **Sprtl Dir, Angola St Prison, Epis Mnstrs Dio Louisiana Baton Rouge LA 2011-2014; Exec Bd Dio Louisiana Baton Rouge LA 2010-2013; Partnr in Mssn Dio Louisiana Baton Rouge LA 2010-2012; R Gr Ch Of W Feliciana S Francisville LA 2009-** B Colubmia SA 2/26/1966 s Jose Isidoro Roldan & Rosa Angelica. BA St Jn Vianney Coll Sem, Miami, FL 1989; MSW Rutgers-The St U, NEwark, NJ 1995; MDiv TESM, Ambridge, PA 2007. D 6/2/2007 Bp John Wadsworth Howe P 12/15/2007 Bp Alan Scarfe. m 6/17/1993 Chris A Chris Anna Earon c 4. COM Dio Iowa Des Moines IA 2008-2009; Assoc Trin Cathd Davenport IA 2007-2009. frroldan@gmail.com

ROLES, Elizabeth Jane (At) 175 9th Ave # 123, New York NY 10011 **Emmaus Hse Epis Ch Atlanta GA 2009-** B Charleston WV 4/20/1970 d Forrest Hansberry Roles & Emily Mcphail. BA Tufts U 1992; MDiv Candler TS Emory U 1998; CAS GTS 2006. D 12/21/2005 P 6/25/2006 Bp J(ohn) Neil Alexander. m 8/7/2004 Jeremy R Mauldin c 1. S Mk's Ch Dalton GA 2006-2009. elizabeth.roles@gmail.com

ROLFE-BOUTWELL, Suzan Jane (Mass) 7588 N Meredith Blvd, Tucson AZ 85741 B New York NY 7/15/1945 d David Raynore Rolfe & Helen. BA Harv 1979; MS MIT 1982; MDiv EDS 1987. D 6/13/1987 P 6/4/1988 Bp David Elliot Johnson. m 7/27/1980 Jeffrey Hovd Boutwell. S Dav's Epis Mssn Pepperell MA 1991-1992; S Ptr's Ch Beverly MA 1987-1990. Auth, "Harvard Political Revs".

ROLLINS, Alfred Woodman (Ind) 2404 Daphne Lane, Alexandria VA 22306 B Houston TX 7/23/1926 s James Alpheus Rollins & Jane Bein. MS U of Texas; BS U of Texas 1950; BD Epis TS of The SW 1962. D 6/19/1962 Bp Frederick P Goddard P 6/18/1963 Bp John E Hines. m 5/15/1977 Dolores Hahn c 5. Epis Ch Cntr New York NY 1966-1976; D Ch Of The Ascen Houston TX 1962-1964. Auth, *Gender Considerations in Dvlpmt*, 1989; Ed/Basic Rdr, *Human Relatns Trng*, 1970. alrollins@cox.net

ROLLINS, Andrew Sloan (La) 3724 Octavia St, New Orleans LA 70125 **Dio Louisiana Baton Rouge LA 2004-** B OH 8/30/1963 s Robert Rollins & Betsy. BA U So 1987; MDiv VTS 1995. D 6/3/1995 P 1/13/1996 Bp Peter James Lee. m 1/2/1993 Jeanette Randolph c 5. Assoc R Trin Ch New Orleans LA 1995-2004. lsuchaplain@stalban.org

ROLLINS, Belle Frances (WLa) 1001 Berry St, Pineville LA 71360 **S Jas Epis Ch Alexandria LA 2004-** B Lexington MS 3/2/1943 d John Murphy Privette & Willie Carl. BA U of Mississippi; MA U of Virginia 1966; MS LSU 1984; MA Loyola U 1996. D 1/12/2002 Bp Robert Jefferson Hargrove Jr. m 8/26/1972 Justin J Rollins. D S Mich's Epis Ch Pineville LA 2007-2008. grollins@lsua.edu

ROLLINS, E(verette) Wayne (Me) 10 Alton St., Portland ME 04103 B South Charleston WV 2/9/1956 s Arnold Rollins & Janet. BS W Virginia St U 1978; MA Westminster Choir Coll of Rider U 1981; MDiv Methodist TS In Ohio 1997. D 5/26/2004 P 12/11/2004 Bp William Michie Klusmeyer. R S Ptr's Ch Portland ME 2008-2011; Int Ch Of The Gd Shpd Charleston WV 2005-2007. ewrollins@gmail.com

ROLLINS, John August (Nwk) 11 Fine Road, High Bridge NJ 08829 B Wabasha County MN 1/8/1942 s Leonard Henry Rollins & Louise Alice. BA Hamline U 1964; U MN 1965; MDiv Drew U 1968; GTS 1969. D 3/26/1969 P 8/3/1969 Bp George E Rath. c 2. Dioc Curs Sprtl Dir Dio Newark Newark NJ 1996-2004; ECUSA Website Ed Epis Ch Cntr New York NY 1996-2004; Dep GC Dio Newark Newark NJ 1982-1988; R Chr Ch Pompton Lakes NJ 1974-2007; Cur Gr Ch Madison NJ 1969-1974. Bp's Cbury Schlr Dio Newark 1997. jarollins@earthlink.net

ROLLINS, Roger Burton (Ia) 3170 E Stroop Rd Apt 114, Dayton OH 45440 B Lowell MI 12/16/1930 s Ellis William Rollins & Mary Belle. BA Olivet Nazarene Coll 1953; BD Garrett Evang TS 1956. D 10/8/1961 P 6/21/1962 Bp Charles Bennison. m 3/2/2003 Mary Esther Ritchey c 2. Ret Affilliate P S Geo's Epis Ch Dayton OH 1996-2010; Chr Ch Cedar Rapids IA 1986-1995; R S Andr's Ch Dayton OH 1967-1986; R S Jn's Epis Ch Cambridge OH 1963-1967; Cur S Lk's Par Kalamazoo MI 1960-1963. MRA1940@AOL.COM

ROLLINSON, John Thomas (RG) 1120 Gidding St, Clovis NM 88101 B Bayonne NJ 7/24/1938 s John Rollinson & Elizabeth Pierson. U of Vienna 1959; BA Br 1960; MA Geo 1971; US-A Russian Inst Garmisch-Partenkirchen 1973; MDiv TESM 1985. D 6/8/1985 Bp Alden Moinet Hathaway P 3/23/1986 Bp

R

Victor Manuel Rivera. m 10/15/1977 Shirley Morris. R Ch Of S Jas The Apos Clovis NM 1992-2006; High Plains Team Mnstry Clovis NM 1992-1993; Asst R S Thos Ch Houston TX 1990-1992; Vic Ch Of The Resurr Clovis Clovis CA 1985-1990; Asst To The Bp Epis Dio San Joaquin Modesto CA 1985-1988. ERM 1992; Forw In Faith/ No Amer 1989; NOEL 1985; SSC 1995. Soc Serv Medal Republic Of Vietnam 1971; Bronze Star US-A 1969; Phi Beta Kappa Br 1960. rollinsonrev@yahoo.com

ROMACK, Gay Harpster (Az) 609 N Old Litchfield Rd, Litchfield Park AZ 85340 B St. Louis MO 8/22/1947 d Rodney Melvin Harpster & Shirley Elizabeth. BA NWU 1969; MA Asu 2000; MATS Claremont TS 2007. D 10/14/2006 Bp Kirk Stevan Smith. m 7/5/1969 John Romack c 1. ghrstudy@aol.com

ROMAN, James Michael (NJ) Po Box 77356, West Trenton NJ 08628 B Brooklyn NY 3/21/1945 s James Roman & Dorothy Tillman. BA Rider Coll 1969. D 4/13/1985 Bp George Phelps Mellick Belshaw. m 10/19/1985 Julia A Steinmetz. D Trin Cathd Trenton NJ 1985-1993. Ord Of S Lk, SocMary.

ROMANIK, David Felton (Ct) 602 Meander St, Abilene TX 79602 **Ch Of The Heav Rest Abilene TX 2011-** B Hartford CT 8/3/1985 s Donald V Romanik & Margaret Felton. BA Bos 2007; MDiv VTS 2011. D 6/11/2011 Bp Laura Ahrens. m 10/9/2011 Sarah Y Sarah Beth Yoder. dfromanik@gmail.com

ROMANS, Nicholas J (Az) 514 S Mountain Road, Mesa AZ 85208 **P-in-c Epis Ch Of The Trsfg Mesa AZ 2007-** B Los Angeles CA 5/4/1955 s Marion Francis Fink & Mary. BA USC 1977; MDiv EDS 1982. Trans from Church Of England 9/21/2006 Bp Kirk Stevan Smith. m Rex Romans. Int S Steph's Ch Phoenix AZ 2006-2007. njromans@yahoo.com

ROMER, William Miller (NH) 128 AUDUBON DR, ACTON MA 01720 B Albany NY 4/20/1935 s Earle Frederick Romer & Helen Beatrice. BA Br 1957; MDiv EDS 1960. D 5/28/1960 Bp Frederick Lehrle Barry P 12/17/1960 Bp Allen Webster Brown. m 5/20/1983 Molly Hardy c 3. The Ch Of The Redeem Rochester NH 2001-2003; Dio New Hampshire Concord NH 1998-2000; S Jas Epis Ch At Woonsocket Woonsocket RI 1997; S Dav's On The Hill Epis Ch Cranston RI 1994-1997; Calv Epis Ch Burnt Hills NY 1992-1994; Ch Of Beth Saratoga Sprg NY 1989-1993; S Lk's Ch Catskill NY 1987-1989; Int Specl Dio Albany Albany NY 1971-1997; Dio Rhode Island Providence RI 1971-1997; Vic S Bon Ch Guilderland NY 1965-1970; Asst S Andr's Ch Hanover MA 1964-1965; P-in-c S Mary's Ch Lake Luzerne NY 1960-1964. molroms@aol.com

ROMERIL, Gwendolyn Jane (Be) 26 W Market St, Bethlehem PA 18018 B Cornwall NY 7/15/1932 d Daniel Heiter & Margaret. RN S Jn's Epis Hosp New York 1953; MDiv Moravian TS 1981; Cert GTS 1985. D 6/13/1981 P 6/11/1982 Bp Lloyd Edward Gressle. m 11/11/1953 Robert D Romeril c 5. S Andr's Epis Ch Allentown PA 1996-2002; Assoc Trin Ch Easton PA 1988-1995; Cn Pstr Cathd Ch Of The Nativ Bethlehem PA 1980-1988. "Var arts," *The Morning Call, Allentown PA*, 2005; "Womens Uncommon Prayers (Contrib)," Morehouse Pub, 2000. gjromeril@verizon.net

✠ **ROMERO, Rt Rev Sylvestre Donato** (NJ) 410 Auburn Way Apt 13, San Jose CA 95129 B Belize ND HN 12/31/1944 s Valentine Romero & Cleofa Palma. Bahiller en Teologia Sem Guatemala 1973; Mstr Theol CDSP 1988. Trans from Church in the Province Of The West Indies 1/13/2005 Bp Frank Tracy Griswold III. m 11/29/1968 Evangelina Leon Romero c 4. Asst Bp Dio New Jersey Trenton NJ 2007-2010; Int Bp Dio El Camino Real Monterey CA 2004-2007; Asst H Faith Par Inglewood CA 1993; S Phil's Ch San Jose CA 1987-1991; Dio Guatemala Guatemala City 1974-1987. DD CDSP 1998. sylvestreromero@yahoo.com

ROMERO-GUEVARA, Antonio N (EcuC) Dias De La Madrid 943, Quito Ecuador B 6/20/1954 s Antonio Vicente Romero & Olga Piedad. D 12/20/1992 Bp J Neptali Larrea-Moreno. m 10/1/1977 Maria Elena Zurita c 3. Ecuador New York NY 1996-2009.

ROMERO MARTE, Francisco Alfredo (DR) C/O Episcopal Church In Dominican Republic, Box 764, Dominican Republic Dominican Republic **Dio The Dominican Republic (Iglesia Epis Dominicana) Santo Domingo DO 2010-** B 10/8/1949 s Jose Romero & Tonasina. Lic Centro de Estudios Teologicos 2009. D 2/14/2010 P 2/20/2011 Bp Julio Cesar Holguin-Khoury. m 10/9/1983 Teresa Tavarez c 3. ronalfredo@hotmail.com

ROMULUS, Jean Michael (Hai) c/o Diocese of Haiti, Boite Postale 1309 Haiti **Died 12/15/2009** B 12/14/1964 s Emmanuel J Romulus & Marie Rolande. D 1/25/2006 P 2/18/2007 Bp Jean Zache Duracin. mromulus1412@yahoo.com

RONDEAU, Daniel James (SanD) 47535 State Highway 74, Palm Desert CA 92260 **Assoc S Marg's Epis Ch Palm Desert CA 1993-** B Mankato MN 7/10/1949 s Richard Francis Rondeau & Margery Ann. BS U of San Diego 1972; STB Pontificia Universitas Gregoriana Rome It 1975; MS San Diego St U 1983. Rec from Roman Catholic 2/17/1986 as Priest Bp Charles Brinkley Morton. m 8/6/1980 Carol Tripoli c 2. Vic S Mary's In The Vlly Ch Ramona CA 1988-1992; Cur S Dav's Epis Ch San Diego CA 1985-1988. drondeau22@dc.rr.com

RONKOWITZ, George R (SeFla) 145 NE 10th St, Homestead FL 33030 B Teaneck NJ 4/25/1946 s Rudolph Ronkowitz & Sophia. BA St. Bern's Sem Rochester NY 1967; MDiv St. Bern's Sem Rochester NY 1970; Med Ford 1976. Rec from Roman Catholic 12/11/1988 as Priest Bp Jeffery William Rowthorn. c 2. R and Sch Headmaster S Jn's Epis Ch Homestead FL 2003-2011; Vic Trin-S Mich's Ch Fairfield CT 1995-2003; Assoc S Ptr's Epis Ch Milford CT 1991-1995; Assoc S Andr's Ch Milford CT 1988-1991. grronk@aol.com

RONN, Denise Marie (Ga) 2600 Rolling Hill Dr, Valdosta GA 31602 **Dioc Coun Dio Georgia Savannah GA 2009-; SW Convoc Dn Dio Georgia Savannah GA 2009-; Vic S Barn Epis Ch Valdosta GA 2008-** B Washington DC 11/28/1952 d Robert James Collins & Cecilia. BA Pacific Luth U 1976; Masters Valdosta St U 1995; 24 credits TS 2004; Ph.D. Capella U 2009. D 2/7/2004 P 8/11/2004 Bp Henry Irving Louttit. m 11/13/1971 David Lee Ronn c 2. dmronn28@yahoo.com

RONTANI JR, William (NCal) 104 Main St., Wheatland CA 95692 **Vic S Jas Epis Mssn Lincoln CA 2006-** B San Francisco CA 7/12/1948 s William Thomas Rontani & Dorothy Elizabeth. VTS; BA San Jose St U 1971; MDiv CDSP 1974; AA Coll of San Mateo 1975. D 6/29/1974 P 5/1/1975 Bp C Kilmer Myers. c 1. P-in-c Gr Epis Ch Wheatland CA 2004-2006; Vic S Lk's Mssn Calistoga CA 1995-2006; Non-par Dio California San Francisco CA 1993-1994; R S Chris's Ch San Lorenzo CA 1985-1993; Vic S Chris's Ch San Lorenzo CA 1975-1984. Alum Preaching Prize CDSP 1974. fr.bill@sbcglobal.net

ROOD JR, Peter H (Los) 702 W Alegria Ave, Sierra Madre CA 91024 **R H Nativ Par Los Angeles CA 2002-** B San Francisco CA 7/29/1955 s Peter H Rood & Roberta A. Pacific Oaks Coll 1991; MDiv Epis TS of The SW 1994. D 6/19/1994 Bp Clarence Rupert Haden Jr P 1/1/1995 Bp Frederick Houk Borsch. m 9/2/1978 Martha Segner Rood. Ch Of Our Sav Par San Gabr CA 1994-1999.

ROOF SR, John Phillips (Ind) 620 N Washington St, 1896 N CR 100 E, Danville IN 46122 B Cincinnati OH 9/11/1937 s Harry Enos Roof & Mary Virginia. BA Hanover Coll 1959; BD Nash 1966. D 6/11/1966 P 12/14/1966 Bp John P Craine. m 6/18/1966 Margaret Gard c 3. R S Aug's Epis Ch Danville IN 1966-2009. augies@indy.net

ROOS, Carl A (Ind) 6920 Mohawk Ln, Indianapolis IN 46260 B Celestine IN 3/31/1942 s Harry P Roos & Veronica M. BS S Meinrad Coll 1964; ThM U Innsbruck At 1968; MS Indiana U 1977; MS Indiana U 1986; Cert SWTS 1990. Rec from Roman Catholic 7/1/1990 as Priest Bp Edward Witker Jones. m 10/17/1987 Michelle Kate Johnson c 1. R S Jas Ch Vincennes IN 1997-2005; S Thos' Epis Ch Falls City NE 1992-1997; Assoc Trin Ch Anderson IN 1990-1992. stjames@vincennes.inet

ROOS, Michelle Kate (Ind) 720 Dr. Martin Luther King Jr St., Indianapolis IN 46202 **Pstr S Phil's Ch Indianapolis IN 2007-** B Indianapolis IN 1/8/1955 d Richard Peter Johnson & Martha Sue. BS Pur 1980; MDiv S Paul TS Seabury-Wstrn Theol 1995; Masters St. Meinrad TS 2006. D 6/23/1995 P 1/6/1995 Bp Edward Witker Jones. m 10/17/1987 Carl A Roos c 1. Vic S Geo Epis Ch W Terre Haute IN 1997-2000; Dio Nebraska Omaha NE 1995-1997. 2csandmom@comcast.net

ROOS, Richard John (Ind) 2033 Paradise Oaks Ct, Atlantic Beach FL 32233 B Jasper IN 8/5/1945 s Harry Peter Roos & Veronica Madalena. BA S Meinrad Coll 1967; STB/STL Gregorian U 1971; MA Indiana U 1974. Rec from Roman Catholic 6/1/1976 as Deacon Bp John P Craine. m 8/15/2005 Jennifer Roos c 4. R S Phil's Ch Indianapolis IN 1977-2006; Assoc Pstr S Mk's Ch Plainfield IN 1976-1977. *Origines Adamantius*, No Amer Collage, 1971. rrockish@aol.com

ROOSEVELT, Nancy A (O) 17100 Van Aken Blvd, Shaker Heights OH 44120 B New York NY 7/7/1947 d W Emlen Roosevelt & Arlene Marion. Premiere Degree U Of Paris-Sorbonne Fr 1967; BA Hollins U 1969; MDiv GTS 1985. D 6/1/1985 Bp George Phelps Mellick Belshaw P 1/5/1986 Bp A(rthur) Heath Light. c 2. COM Dio Ohio Cleveland OH 2002-2004; R Chr Ch Shaker Heights OH 2000-2004; Trst The GTS New York NY 1995-1998; Cn Dio Rochester Rochester NY 1991-1999; Dioc Deploy Off Dio Rochester Rochester NY 1987-2000; Dep For Prog Dio SW Virginia Roanoke VA 1987-1991; Chair Com Dio SW Virginia Roanoke VA 1986-1987; R E Lee Memi Ch (Epis) Lexington VA 1985-1987. Soc Of S Jn The Evang 1995. naroosevelt@gmail.com

ROOT, Diane Eleanor (Vt) 316 Mission Farm Rd, Killington VT 05751 **Vic Ch of Our Sav Killington VT 2010-** B Bethesda MD 10/9/1953 d Lloyd Eugene Root & Dorothy Wilda. BA Colorado Coll 1975; MDiv Andover Newton TS 1982. D 6/5/1982 Bp John Bowen Coburn P 8/1/1983 Bp Morgan Porteus. Three Rivers Reg Mnstry Killington VT 1998-2010; Vic S Lk's Ch Lanesboro MA 1988-1998; Assoc S Steph's Memi Ch Lynn MA 1983-1988; Asst S Jn's Ch Winthrop MA 1982-1983. droottrrm@aol.com

ROPER, Charles Murray (At) 128 River Ridge Ln, Roswell GA 30075 B Atlanta GA 8/9/1929 s Robert Harold Roper & Clara Mae. Cert VTS; BS Davidson Coll 1952; MDiv Columbia TS 1955. D 6/1/1956 P 12/1/1956 Bp Randolph R Claiborne. m 8/9/1953 Elizabeth Mason c 6. Cn To Ordnry Dio Atlanta Atlanta GA 1994-1999; S Thos Epis Ch Columbus GA 1978-1995; Sprtl Dir Curs Mvmt Dio Atlanta Atlanta GA 1976-1984; Pres Stndg Com Dio Atlanta Atlanta GA 1975-1976; Stndg Com Dio Atlanta Atlanta GA 1974-1976;

Spec Asst To Bp In Dvlpmt Cltn Mnstry Dio Atlanta Atlanta GA 1973-1976; Chair Dept Stwdshp Dio Atlanta Atlanta GA 1966-1968; Vic/R Ch Of The H Cross Decatur GA 1963-1978; Exec Bd Dio Atlanta Atlanta GA 1962-1968; Assoc H Trin Par Decatur GA 1958-1963; Vic S Jn's W Point GA 1956-1958. Auth, "The Wrld, the Flesh and God," Self Pub, 2010. croper@mindspring.com

ROPER, Jeffrey Howard (Kan) 3750 E Douglas Ave, Wichita KS 67208 B Norman OK 10/24/1957 s John Dee Roper & Alice Suzanne. BA U of Kansas 1979; BA Wichita St U 1997; MA Wichita St U 2003; Kansas Sch for Mnstry 2010. D 1/8/2011 Bp Dean Elliott Wolfe. m 12/29/1979 Victoria Baker c 2. jroper@cox.net

ROPER, John Dee (Kan) 14802 E Willowbend Cir, Wichita KS 67230 **D S Andr's Ch Derby KS 2009-** B Oklahoma City OK 2/15/1935 s Clay M Roper & Hester Anne. BBA Oklahoma St U 1956; LLB Oklahoma St U 1958; MA SMU 1990. D 12/11/1981 Bp Richard Frank Grein. m 3/16/1957 Alice Suzanne Baldwin c 3. D S Jn's Ch Wichita KS 1981-2005. johndroper@sbcglobal.net

ROPER, Terence Chaus (Pa) 1815 John F Kennedy Blvd Apt 2308, Philadelphia PA 19103 B Portsmouth Hampshire UK 6/21/1935 s Charles Leonard Roper & Mabel Violet. Lon 1959; S Bon Coll Warminster GB 1960. D 6/1/1960 P 5/1/1961 Bp John Henry Lawrence Phillips. R The Ch Of The H Trin Rittenhouse Philadelphia PA 1999-2004; R The Epis Ch Of The Trsfg Dallas TX 1976-1999; R Epis Ch Of The Redeem Irving TX 1973-1976; Asst R The Epis Ch Of S Thos The Apos Dallas TX 1965-1967; Cur S Alb's Epis Ch Arlington TX 1963-1965. Bd Trst - EDS, Cambridge, MA` 1963-1998. Dallas AIDS Interfaith Awd 1998. ropertc@aol.com

ROQUE, Christopher Collin (WTex) 3500 N 10th St, Mcallen TX 78501 **S Jas Epis Ch Ft McKavett TX 2008-; S Jn's Epis Ch Sonora TX 2008-** B Corpus Christi TX 5/30/1970 s Felix Roque & Judy Ann. BA SW Texas St U San Marcos 1994; MDiv STUSo 2005. D 6/13/2005 Bp James Edward Folts P 1/6/2006 Bp Gary Richard Lillibridge. m 3/11/1995 Leticia Ann Perez c 2. Cur S Jn's Ch McAllen TX 2005-2008. fatherchrisroque@verizon.net

RORKE, Stephen Ernest (Roch) 6727 Royal Thomas Way, Alexandria VA 22315 **Lorton Cmnty Action Cntr Lorton VA 2002-** B Buffalo NY 5/7/1947 s Edward Cuningham Rorke & Alice. BA Trin Hartford CT 1970; MDiv EDS 1975. D 6/29/1975 Bp Robert Rae Spears Jr P 4/20/1977 Bp Harold B Robinson. m 12/16/1972 Jeanne Soderland c 1. Yth S Ptr's Epis Ch Arlington VA 1998-2002; Arlington Comm Temp Shltr Inc Arlington VA 1997-2001; St Fran Cntr Washington DC 1991; Acts Dumfries VA 1990-1991; S Fran Ch Potomac MD 1983-1985; Assoc Epis Ch Hm Buffalo NY 1975-1977. Ed, *Adolescent Abuse & Neglect: Model Progs*, Nat'l Cntr on Chld Abuse & Neglect, 1981; Ed, *Adolescent Maltreatment*, Nat'l Cntr on Chld Abuse and Neglect, 1981; Auth, *Preventing Yth from Running Away*, Dept. of Hlth & Human Serv, 1978; Auth, *Prevention: A Positive Process*, Dept. of Hlth & Human Serv, 1978; Auth, *Manuel for Yth Outreach Projects*; Auth, *Yth Outreach Mnstry*. steve@lortonaction.org

ROS, Salvador Patrick (NJ) 739 Seminary Ave, Rahway NJ 07065 **R Ch of the Gd Shpd Rahway NJ 2006-; Dio The Dominican Republic (Iglesia Epis Dominicana) Santo Domingo DO 2001-** B New York, NY 3/17/1956 s Ralph Osvaldo Ros & Maria. BA Cathd Coll of the Immac Concep 1979; MDiv St Jos's Sem 1982. Rec from Roman Catholic 8/18/2001 Bp Julio Cesar Holguin-Khoury. m 4/9/1994 Lissette Patrick Pappaterra c 1. R H Comf Ch Rahway NJ 2006-2008. padreros40@hotmail.com

ROSA, Thomas Phillip (Chi) 121 W Macomb St, Belvidere IL 61008 **Sunday Long Term Supply Trin Epis Ch Aurora IL 2011-; Ret/Affiliating Emm Epis Ch Rockford IL 2009-** B Chicago IL 12/19/1942 s Alex John Rosa & Wanda. U IL 1962; BA Sthrn Illinois U 1966; Ya Berk 1970; MDiv Nash 1971; Certification Int Mnstry Ntwk 2004. D 6/19/1971 Bp Gerald Francis Burrill P 12/18/1971 Bp James Winchester Montgomery. Int S Mk's Ch Evanston IL 2010-2011; Int Emm Epis Ch La Grange IL 2006-2008; Int S Lawr Epis Ch Libertyville IL 2005-2006; Int Epis Ch Of The Atone Chicago IL 2004-2005; Chapt Mem Cathd Of S Jas Chicago IL 1996-1999; Dioc Coun Dio Chicago Chicago IL 1977-1996; R The Epis Ch Of The H Trin Belvidere IL 1974-2001; Mus Cmsn Dio Chicago Chicago IL 1973-1976; Asst Ch Of The H Fam Pk Forest IL 1971-1974. AGO 2005. R Emertius H Trin Ch, Belvidere, IL 2008. thomasrosa@mac.com

ROSANAS, Louis Rosanas (Hai) Box 1309, Port-Au-Prince Haiti **Dio Haiti Ft Lauderdale FL 1991-** B Leogane HT 11/1/1958 s Lizamene Rosanas. Cert 1985; Cert Sem 1991. D 9/15/1991 P 4/1/1992 Bp Luc Anatole Jacques Garnier. m 2/23/1995 Erline Juste.

ROSARIO DE LA CRUZ, Juan Antonio (DR) Juan Antonio, Apartment 764, Santo Domingo Dominican Republic **Vic Iglesia Epis San Matias Baní DO 1996-; Dio The Dominican Republic (Iglesia Epis Dominicana) Santo Domingo DO 1992-** B 11/2/1964 s German Rosario & Maritza. Centro De Estudios Teologicas 1991. D 6/6/1992 P 12/1/1993 Bp Julio Cesar Holguin-Khoury. m 10/31/1994 Reyna Pina. guelmy@mailexcite.com

ROSE, Ann W (Ore) 7 Saint Johns Rd Apt 30, Cambridge MA 02138 **D S Mary's Epis Ch Eugene OR 1993-** B Portland OR 5/11/1943 d Carl W Wegener & Barbara C. BS U of Oregon 1965; BA Lake Erie Coll 1981. D 12/4/1993 Bp Robert Louis Ladehoff.

ROSE, Carol Benson (EO) 2133 N Cajeme Ave, Casa Grande AZ 85222 **Assoc S Ptr's Ch Casa Grande AZ 2005-** B Ontario OR 2/9/1932 s George Franklin Rose & Lillian Cecil. D 7/17/1977 P 9/28/1978 Bp William Benjamin Spofford. m 7/20/1967 Laura Lee Shank. P S Thos Ch Canyon City OR 1977-1995. cbll@webtv.net

ROSE, Christopher Lee (Ct) 30 Woodland Street Unit 10NP, Hartford CT 06106 B Hartford CT 10/7/1953 s Esmond Leon Rose & Anne Elizabeth. BA U of Connecticut 1975; MDiv GTS 1978; STM GTS 1986. D 6/10/1978 P 12/1/1978 Bp Morgan Porteus. m 1/2/2005 Deborah Lee Rose. Gr Epis Ch Hartford CT 1982-2002; S Jas Ch New London CT 1979-1982; Asst S Jn's Epis Par Waterbury CT 1978-1979. Auth, "The Hartford Courant". OHC. Natl Radio Broadcast Awd 88-92; Epis Fndt Top 10 Sermons 91-92; Polly Bond Awd. christopherlrose@yahoo.com

ROSE, David D (SwVa) 210 4th St., Radford VA 24141 **R Gr Ch Radford VA 2009-** B Winston-Salem NC 6/1/1950 s Norman Earl Rose & Josephine. VTS; BA Lenoir-Rhyne Coll 1974; MDiv Bangor TS 1984. D 6/15/1985 P 3/19/1986 Bp William Gillette Weinhauer. m 6/18/1983 Susan Cameron MacCuaig c 3. R S Paul's Ch Lancaster NH 2001-2008; Exec Coun Appointees New York NY 2000-2001; Trin Ch Spruce Pine NC 1985-2000. daviddrose2000@yahoo.com

ROSE, Edwin Sandford (WTex) Po Box 1943, Fulton TX 78358 B Ottawa ON CA 9/24/1933 s Edwin Maurice Rose & Beatrice Victoria. BS Trin Hartford CT 1955; BD VTS 1968. D 6/18/1968 P 3/13/1969 Bp Robert Raymond Brown. m 6/14/1955 Jane Ellis c 5. S Ptr's Epis Ch Rockport TX 1996-2002; R S Jn's Ch McAllen TX 1982-1996; R The Epis Ch Of The Adv Alice TX 1976-1982; Asst Ch Of The Gd Shpd Corpus Christi TX 1972-1976; R S Jn's Ch Camden AR 1970-1972; Cur Trin Ch Pine Bluff AR 1968-1970. esrjsrbr@gmail.com

ROSE, John Kreimer (SO) 7 Spring Hill Dr, Cincinnati OH 45227 **Died 9/29/2011** B Cincinnati OH 12/11/1929 s John Rose & Helen. Dio Angl Acad London OH; U Cinc 1953; JD Harv 1960. D 10/30/1999 Bp Herbert Thompson Jr. mjrose@fbtlaw.com

ROSE, Josefa (Josie) Rodriguez (NwT) 2907 Emerson Pl, Midland TX 79705 **Iglesia Epis de Santa Maria Midland TX 2005-** B Gonzales TX 3/29/1943 d Eugenio Alvarado Rodriguez & Santos Salinas. BA U of Texas 1989; MDiv Epis TS of The SW 2003. D 11/30/2002 P 6/7/2003 Bp C(harles) Wallis Ohl. m 5/30/1964 Roland Rose c 2. Dio NW Texas Lubbock TX 2005-2011; Asst R Ch Of The H Trin Midland TX 2003-2005. jrrose1204@gmail.com

ROSE, Joy Ann (WA) Saint Paul Episcopal Church, 4535 Piney Church Rd, Waldorf MD 20604 **Dioc Coun Dio Washington Washington DC 2009-; R S Paul's Epis Ch Piney Waldorf MD 2007-** B Norwalk CT 12/23/1944 d Vincent A Aquino & Anne B. BA Syr 1966; MA U Of Bridgeport 1980; MA Hartford Sem 1999; Ya Berk 2002; MDiv Ya Berk 2002; DMin VTS 2010. D 7/13/2002 P 1/18/2003 Bp Keith Bernard Whitmore. c 3. COM Dio Washington Washington DC 2007-2009; R Emm Ch Harrisonburg VA 2004-2007; Cn for CE Dio Eau Claire Eau Claire WI 2003-2004; Asst Chr Ch Cathd Eau Claire WI 2002-2004. Auth, "The Ch's Invisible Majority," *Doctoral Thesis*, VTS, 2010. The Soc Of S Fran, Third Ord 2000. revjoyrose@aol.com

ROSE, Leland Gerald (WNY) 602 Crescent Ave, East Aurora NY 14052 **D S Mk's Ch Orchard Pk NY 1998-** B Ithaca NY 9/21/1934 s Wayne Gerald Rose & Evelyn Mae. BA W Virginia U 1965; MA SUNY 1968. D 9/12/1998 Bp David Charles Bowman. m 8/21/1965 Martha Eileen Darnell c 2. "Gone w a Pryr," *Sharing mag*, OSL, 2003; "Anointing by Proxy," *Sharing mag*, Ord of St Lk, 2000. Bro of S Andr 1990; Diakoneo 1998; Ord of S Lk 1996. lmrose@verizon.net

ROSE, L(oran) A(nson) Paul (WA) 6101 Edsall Rd Apt 508, Alexandria VA 22304 B Cleveland OH 12/20/1945 s Jerry Rose & Dolores. BA Amer U 1967; MDiv GTS 1972; PhD NYU 1976. D 6/17/1972 Bp William Foreman Creighton P 3/1/1973 Bp Stephen F Bayne Jr. Calv Ch Washington DC 1979-1986; Asst S Paul's Rock Creek Washington DC 1977-1978; Assoc Chr Ch Prince Geo's Par Rockville MD 1974-1976; Asst Ch Of The Resurr E Elmhurst NY 1972-1973.

ROSE, Margaret Rollins (At) 531 E 72nd St Apt 3c, New York NY 10021 **Epis Ch Cntr New York NY 2003-; Dir Epis Ch Cntr New York NY 2003-** B CarrolltonGA 1/4/1954 d Frank Watson Rose & Ellen Radcliffe. BA Wellesley Coll 1976; Cert Geneva U Geneva NY 1978; MDiv Harvard DS 1979. D 5/30/1981 P 4/18/1982 Bp John Bowen Coburn. c 2. R S Dunst's Epis Ch Atlanta GA 1992-2003; Int S Barn Ch Falmouth MA 1991-1992; Chr Ch Hyde Pk MA 1989-1991; S Gabr's Epis Ch Marion MA 1988; Coordntr Feminist Liberation Theol Prog EDS Cambridge MA 1987-1989; Ch Of S Jn The Evang Hingham MA 1987; Asst Ch Of S Jn The Evang Boston MA 1983-1986; Stff The Cathd Ch Of S Paul Boston MA 1981-1983. revmrose@aol.com

ROSE, Roger Franklin (Los) 3 Pursuit Apt 109, Aliso Viejo CA 92656 **Asst S Thos' Mssn Hacienda Heights CA 2005-** B Chicago IL 8/21/1926 s Frank Rose & Vivian Mary. BA IL Wesl 1948; ThM Yale DS 1956. D 9/10/1964 P 3/1/1965 Bp Francis E I Bloy. m 2/15/1958 Shirley Jean Reece. Assoc S Gabr's Par Monterey Pk CA 2000-2005; Ch Of The H Trin and S Ben Alhambra CA 1994-1998; Vic Ch Of The Epiph Los Angeles CA 1992-1993; P-in-c Trin Epis Par Los Angeles CA 1989-1990; Asst S Steph's Par Whittier CA 1988-1989; Asst S Steph's Par Whittier CA 1984-1986; St Matthews Ch Baldwin Pk CA 1980-1981; Dio Los Angeles Los Angeles CA 1965-1992. Ord of Agape and Reconciliation 1973. Blue Key Hon Fraternity 1948. mushr1@juno.com

ROSE, Roland (NwT) 2907 Emerson Pl, Midland TX 79705 **Iglesia Epis de Santa Maria Midland TX 2005-** B Oklahoma City OK 10/1/1939 s Frank Albert Rose & Elena. BA U of No Texas 1962; Med U of No Texas 1963. D 10/28/2001 Bp C(harles) Wallis Ohl. m 5/30/1964 Josefa (Josie) Rodriguez c 2. D S Jn's Epis Ch Odessa TX 2001-2004. dnrose@suddenlink.net

ROSE, Shirley Jean (Los) 3 Pursuit # 109, Aliso Viejo CA 92656 B Inglewood CA 6/29/1928 d Paul Reece & Ruth Alza. BA U Pac 1951; UTS 1956; MA Claremont TS 1984; ETSBH 1986. D 6/20/1987 P 1/1/1988 Bp Oliver Bailey Garver Jr. m 2/15/1958 Roger Franklin Rose c 3. S Edm's Par San Marino CA 1998-1999; S Mths' Par Whittier CA 1988-1998; DRE S Mths' Par Whittier CA 1979-1987. Auth, "Focus On Galations," *Living The Gd News*, 1989; Auth, "Go In Peace Dio Peace Curric 91". Outstanding Alum Claremaont TS 1994; Hon Cn S Paul Cathd Cntr Los Angeles 1993. mushri@juno.com

ROSE, William Harrison (SC) 20 Riverview Dr, Beaufort SC 29907 **Vic Ch Of The Heav Rest Estill SC 1999-** B New Brunswick NJ 6/25/1931 s William Author Rose & Lucy Fern. U of Kentucky; LTh Epis TS In Kentucky 1963. D 6/1/1963 P 12/1/1963 Bp William R Moody. m 1/28/1961 Beatrice VanHorn. Dio So Carolina Charleston SC 1990-1995; The Ch Of The Cross Bluffton SC 1990-1995; R Ch Of The Gd Shpd Columbia SC 1978-1990; S Jn's Ch Winnsboro SC 1968-1978; R Emm Epis Ch Winchester KY 1963-1968. whrose@comcast.net

ROSE-CROSSLEY, Ramona (Vt) 68 Church St, Poultney VT 05764 B Philadelphia PA 12/18/1935 d William Alfred Seegers & Vinita Josephine. BA Barnard Coll of Col 1958; MS U of Maryland 1963; MDiv STUSo 1981. D 2/22/1986 P 4/11/1987 Bp Charles Judson Child Jr. m 2/20/1977 Remington Rose. S Mk's-S Lk's Epis Mssn Castleton VT 1999-2000; S Paul's Epis Ch Wells VT 1999-2000; Trin Epis Ch Poultney VT 1999-2000; Dio Micronesia Tumon Bay GU GU 1990-1998; Vic The Epis Ch of S Jn the Div Tamuning GU 1990-1998; Vic S Mary Magd Ch Columbus GA 1987-1989; Dio Atlanta Atlanta GA 1986-1987; D S Lk's Epis Ch Atlanta GA 1986-1987. Jn Hines Preaching Awd VTS Alexandria VA 1999. rrosec2@charter.net

ROSE-CROSSLEY, Remington (Vt) 327 University Ave, Sewanee TN 37375 B New Jersey 8/16/1937 s Donald Remington Rose & Maude Marie Irene. BA Trin Hartford CT 1958; MA Pr 1960; PhD Pr 1964; Cert of Theo Study TS 2005. D 7/16/2005 P 3/30/2006 Bp Thomas C Ely. m 2/20/1977 Ramona Seegers c 3. rrosec2@charter.net

ROSEN, Elisabeth Payne (Cal) Box 1306, 115 Lagunitas Road, Ross CA 94957 B Shreveport LA 5/4/1942 d Francis Cameron Payne & Ann. BA Hollins U 1964; BD Sch for Deacons 1993. D 6/4/1994 Bp William Edwin Swing. m 5/27/1967 Martin Gerald Rosen c 2. D Ch Of Our Sav Mill Vlly CA 2007-2010; D Chr Ch Sausalito CA 1995-2005; D The Epis Ch Of S Jn The Evang San Francisco CA 1994-1995. Auth, "Hallam's War," *novel*, Berkley Books, 2009. betsyrosen@comcast.net

ROSENBAUM, Richard Lemoine (Okla) 9804 Cisler Lane, Manassas VA 20111 **EFM Mentor Dio Oklahoma Oklahoma City OK 1995-** B Wellsville OH 9/27/1921 s Hazel Lemoine Rosenbaum & Anna Sabina. E Carolina U 1958; U of Maryland 1960; BA Tem 1963; Estrn New Mex U 1989. D 6/27/1992 Bp Terence Kelshaw P 6/23/2001 Bp Robert Manning Moody. m 9/10/1984 Mary Elizabeth Meyerhoff. D S Andr's Epis Ch Lawton OK 1995-2001; D S Andr's Ch Roswell NM 1992-1995. rosetree@netscape.com

ROSENBERG, Elizabeth Powell (Del) 2361 Elliott Island Rd, Vienna MD 21869 B Wilmington DE 1/30/1945 d Hans Reinhard Rosenberg & Rebecca Leigh. Mt Holyoke Coll 1965; BA U Of Delaware Newark 1967; MS U NC 1969; MDiv VTS 1972; DMin Bex 1975. D 6/22/1974 P 1/1/1977 Bp William Foreman Creighton. Chr Ch Sausalito CA 2000-2004; Asst R Gr Ch Washington DC 1977-1978. Wmn Ord, Now, EWC.

ROSENBERG, Elma Joy Van Fossen (SwFla) 7200 Sunshine Skyway Ln S Apt 15-G, Saint Petersburg FL 33711 B Northville MI 7/15/1948 d Walter Scott VanFossen & Rosemary Joy Miller. BA Albion Coll 1970; AD S Mary Jr Coll Minneapolis MN 1977. D 6/24/1989 Bp Gerald Francis Burrill. m 9/24/1972 Calvin Lee Ronald Rosenberg. D Cathd Ch Of S Ptr St Petersburg FL 2001-2006; D Dio SW Florida Sarasota FL 1999-2001; D Cathd Ch Of S Ptr St Petersburg FL 1989-1999. elmajoy@verizon.net

ROSENBLUM, Nancy Jo (Alb) 22 Buckingham Dr, Albany NY 12208 **D S Paul's Epis Ch Albany NY 2007-** B Arlington VA 7/21/1946 d Owen Dean Hoopes & Pat Louise. BA SUNY 1968; MA SUNY 1974. D 10/13/1980 Bp Wilbur Emory Hogg Jr. m 8/25/1967 David Alan Rosenblum. Asst S Paul's Ch Troy NY 1997-2006; Secy Dio Albany Albany NY 1989-1990; D Cathd Of All SS Albany NY 1988-1993; Com Lay Mnstry Dio Albany Albany NY 1987-1989; Ecum Comm Dio Albany Albany NY 1986-1999; Chair COM Dio Albany Albany NY 1982-1988; Asst S Andr's Epis Ch Albany NY 1980-1988. Amnesty Intl ; Bread for Wrld.

ROSENDAHL, Mary Alvarez (CFla) 1043 Genesee Avenue, Sebastian FL 32958 **R Epis Ch Of The Nativ Port S Lucie FL 2008-** B Camden NJ 5/19/1951 d Frank Raphael Alvarez & Celeste. BA Barry U 1994; MDiv STUSo 2001. D 5/26/2001 Bp John Wadsworth Howe P 12/9/2001 Bp Stephen Hays Jecko. m 6/17/1972 Michael Rosendahl. Asst R H Trin Epis Ch Melbourne FL 2004-2008; Asst S Andr's Epis Ch Ft Pierce FL 2003-2004; Assoc R S Mk's Epis Ch Jacksonville FL 2001-2003. maryrosendahl@yahoo.com

ROSENGREN, Linda W (Fla) 5054 Ripple Rush Dr N, Jacksonville FL 32257 B Charleston SC 6/17/1949 d Addie Weatherford & Ella. BS Winthrop U 1970; Med Coll of Charleston 1977; Inst for Chr Stds Dio Cntrl Florida 1997. D 12/13/1997 Bp John Wadsworth Howe. m 8/22/1970 Charles Rosengren c 2. Asst to the R Ch Of The Gd Shpd Jacksonville FL 2004-2010; Dir of Chr Formation S Mk's Epis Ch Jacksonville FL 2000-2004; Dir od Chr Formation All SS Ch Of Winter Pk Winter Pk FL 1998-2000; Dio Coordntr of CE Dio Cntrl Florida Orlando FL 1994-1999. lindarosengren@aol.com

ROSENLIEB, Carl Edward (SC) 237 Xavier Street, Charleston SC 29414 B Steubenville OH 9/1/1947 D 9/10/2005 Bp Edward Lloyd Salmon Jr. m 8/21/1999 Sarah Chapman. EDWARD629@LIVE.COM

ROSENZWEIG, Edward Charles (Md) Po Box 95, Brooklin ME 04616 B Newark NJ 10/24/1929 s Edward August Rosenzweig & Josephine Wilhelmina. BA Cntr Coll 1951; MS U of Maryland 1956; PhD U of Maryland 1959; MDiv VTS 1976. D 11/21/1976 Bp Harry Lee Doll P 6/1/1977 Bp David Keller Leighton Sr. m 7/30/1955 Carla H Heider c 2. Asst S Jn's Ch Mt Washington Baltimore MD 1976-1977.

ROSHEUVEL, Terrence Winst (NJ) 25 Sunset Ave E, Red Bank NJ 07701 B Charity GY 2/25/1944 s John Rosheuvel & Ruby. LTh Codrington Coll 1968; MDiv Drew U 1997. Trans from Church in the Province Of The West Indies 12/1/1981 Bp Albert Wiencke Van Duzer. m 9/18/1971 Maylene Rosheuvel c 3. R S Thos Epis Ch Red Bank NJ 1981-2010.

✠ ROSKAM, Rt Rev Catherine Scimeca (NY) 55 Cedar St, Dobbs Ferry NY 10522 **S Thos' Epis Ch Amagansett NY 2009-; Bp Suffr Of New York Dio New York New York City NY 1996-** B Hempstead NY 5/30/1943 d Frank Scimeca & Elvira Luisa. BA Mid 1965; MDiv GTS 1984. D 6/9/1984 Bp James Stuart Wetmore P 12/20/1984 Bp Paul Moore Jr Con 1/27/1996 for NY. m 9/3/1966 Philip Roskam. Dioc Mssnr Dio California San Francisco CA 1991-1995; P-in-c Ch Of The H Innoc San Francisco CA 1990-1991; Dio California San Francisco CA 1989-1991; Coordntr Cler-In-Trng Dio California San Francisco CA 1989-1991; Int Ch Of Our Sav Mill Vlly CA 1989-1990; Asst Ch Of The H Apos New York NY 1984-1988; Chapl The GTS New York NY 1984-1986. Soc Of S Jn The Evang 1981. DD GTS New York NY 1996. bproskam@dioceseny.org

ROSS, Anne Meigs (NY) 88 Ridge Rd, Valley Cottage NY 10989 B Star Lake NY 5/22/1957 d Kenneth Rodee Ross & Anne Bradley. BA Dickinson Coll 1979; MDiv UTS 1983; DAS GTS 1997; MSW NYU 2010. D 6/13/1998 P 12/19/1998 Bp Richard Frank Grein. c 2. COM Dio New York New York City NY 2003-2009; Dir of Educ The Healthcare Chapl Inc New York NY 1999-2008. ACPE 1994. Acpe Supvsr ACPE 1999. amr9033@gmail.com

ROSS, Cleon Marrion (SVa) 196 Homeport Ln, Danville VA 24540 **Dn of Convoc 9 Chr Epis Ch Danville VA 2005-** B Portsmouth NH 6/3/1946 s John Culbert Ross & Mabel Grace. Cert Douglas Hosp 1980; LTh McGill U 1980; Montreal TS 1980. Trans from Anglican Church of Canada 7/1/1983 Bp Frederick Barton Wolf. m 11/15/1969 Pauline T Gagnon c 2. Dn of Convoc 9 Chr Epis Ch Danville VA 2005-2011; Dio Sthrn Virginia Norfolk VA 2005-2006; Dept. of Missions Dio Sthrn Virginia Norfolk VA 1994-1996; R All SS Ch So Hill VA 1992-1999; Reg Coun Chair Dio Maine Portland ME 1984-1986; Vic S Aug's Epis Ch Dover Foxcroft ME 1983-1992. cleonross@comcast.net

ROSS, David Jeffrey (Cal) Po Box 774, Pinole CA 94564 B Pasadena CA 2/6/1954 s Robert Winston Ross & Elizabeth Murial. BA Sch for Deacons 2002. D 12/7/2002 Bp William Edwin Swing. D S Alb's Ch Albany CA 2002-2006.

ROSS, Donna Baldwin (ECR) 3291 Pickwick Ln, Cambria CA 93428 **Assoc S Ben's Par Los Osos CA 2008-** B Los Angeles CA 12/20/1940 d DeForest Baldwin & Mary Harriet. BA U CA 1962; MDiv CDSP 1984. D 6/9/1984 P 1/18/1985 Bp William Grant Black. m 6/9/1962 Robert Talman Ross. Stndg Com Dio El Camino Real Monterey CA 2002-2005; R S Paul's Ch Cambria CA 1995-2005; Stndg Com Dio Ohio Cleveland OH 1993-1995; R Chr Ch Oberlin OH 1986-1995; Cur S Ptr's Epis Ch Delaware OH 1984-1986. Phi Beta Kappa Ucla 1962. donnaross@charter.net

ROSS, Edmund Pitt (RG) 439 Dartmouth Dr Ne, Albuquerque NM 87106 **Died 8/20/2010** B Albuquerque NM 1/6/1926 s Edmund Ross & Evelyn. USNA Annapolis 1946; BS U of New Mex 1950; Cbury Coll 1974; Cert S Geo's Coll Jerusalem IL 1982. D 4/15/1958 Bp C J Kinsolving III P 8/6/1975 Bp Richard

R

Mitchell Trelease Jr. c 5. Bro of S Andr 1950; Ord of S Lk 1960; Soc of S Ben 1998. Cn Cathd Ch of S Jn 2005; The Ord of the Chalice Cathd Ch of S Jn 2001.

ROSS, Ellen Marie (Neb) 106 Robin Rd, Council Bluffs IA 51503 **D Trin Cathd Omaha NE 2001-** B Council Bluffs IA 5/12/1943 d Robert Erwin Reimer & Evelyn Marie. Cert STUSo 1988. D 5/7/1988 Bp James Daniel Warner. Secy Ch Of The Resurr Omaha NE 1988-1993. ereimerross@hotmail.com

ROSS, George Crawford Lauren (Cal) 1876 Buttner Rd, Pleasant Hill CA 94523 B Albany NY 12/22/1929 s George Gustav Ross & Noel Louise. BS NWU 1952; MDiv SWTS 1955. D 6/18/1955 Bp Charles L Street P 12/21/1955 Bp Gerald Francis Burrill. m 2/17/1979 Darlene Sharon Sanderson c 4. Asst S Paul's Epis Ch Walnut Creek CA 2008-2010; Int S Edm's Epis Ch Pacifica CA 2002-2003; Gr Ch Martinez CA 1978-2001; R Cathd Ch Of S Paul San Diego CA 1974-1978; R S Mk's Ch Milwaukee WI 1967-1974; R Gr Epis Ch Freeport IL 1964-1967; Vic S Richard's Ch Chicago IL 1955-1957. gclross@sbcglobal.net

ROSS, George Mark (Minn) Po Box 1231, Cass Lake MN 56633 B White Earth MN 8/3/1930 s Mark J Ross & Violet. Bemidji St U 1981; MDiv SWTS 1989. D 6/18/1989 P 12/1/1989 Bp Robert Marshall Anderson. Dio Minnesota Minneapolis MN 1989-2001.

ROSS, Harry Stewart Spencer (Oly) 1301 Grand Ave, Everett WA 98201 B Benton Harbor MI 8/6/1925 s Harry Ervin Ross & Helen May. LTh Nash 1946; BA Kalamazoo Coll 1948; Oxf 1954. D 5/2/1948 P 8/31/1949 Bp Lewis B Whittemore. c 4. Assoc Trin Epis Ch Everett WA 1973-1992; Chpl to Bp Dio Wstrn Michigan Kalamazoo MI 1968-1971; RurD Dio Wstrn Michigan Kalamazoo MI 1961-1963; R S Paul's Epis Ch S Jos MI 1950-1968; Asst D-in-c S Paul's Epis Ch S Jos MI 1948-1949. hstewartr@earthlink.net

ROSS, Jeffrey Austin (Del) 213 W Third St, Lewes DE 19958 **R S Ptr's Ch Lewes DE 2005-** B Chester PA 11/10/1965 s James William Ross & Janet Elizabeth. BA Millersville U of Pennsylvania 1987; MS Neumann U, Aston PA 1992; MDiv GTS 1998. D 6/20/1998 Bp Charles Ellsworth Bennison Jr P 5/29/1999 Bp Franklin Delton Turner. m 1/18/1992 Sheila M Bravo c 2. R Emm Ch Quakertown PA 2001-2005; Int Epis Ch At Cornell Ithaca NY 1999-2000; Asst R S Thos' Ch Whitemarsh Ft Washington PA 1998-1999; Yth Coordntr Dio Pennsylvania Philadelphia PA 1991-1995. Auth, "A Model For Dioc Yth Mnstry," *Resource Bk Mnstrs Yth & YA*, 1995; Auth, "Suicide: An Unspoken Fair," *Resource Bk Mnstrs Yth & YA*, 1995; Auth, "The Edge: Boundries And Norms For Yth Prog," *Resource Bk Mnstrs Yth & YA*, 1995. frjeffross@aol.com

ROSS, John (ETenn) 413 Cumberland Ave, Knoxville TN 37902 **Dn S Jn's Epis Cathd Knoxville TN 1986-; Asst S Jn's Epis Cathd Knoxville TN 1985-** B Kansas City MO 12/2/1954 s William Sidney Ross & Harriet Elizabeth. BS U of Memphis 1976; MDiv STUSo 1980. D 6/15/1980 Bp William Evan Sanders P 5/1/1981 Bp William F Gates Jr. m 8/26/1978 Lois Haws c 2. R Ch Of The Redeem Shelbyville TN 1981-1985; D-In-Trng Gr Ch Chattanooga TN 1980-1981. jross@stjohnscathedral.org

ROSS, Johnnie Edward (Lex) 283 S Arnold Ave, Prestonsburg KY 41653 **S Raphael's Ch Lexington KY 2008-; Chair - Min. In The Mountains T/F Dio Lexington Lexington KY 2000-** B Detroit MI 9/14/1957 s Edward Ross & Mary Annette. Berea Coll; EDS; Epis TS In Kentucky; Morehead St U; Prestonsburg Cmnty Coll. D 5/25/1995 P 12/21/1995 Bp Don Adger Wimberly. m 12/15/1991 Kay Hale c 4. Mssn Dvlp Dio Lexington Lexington KY 2003-2008; Dep Gc Dio Lexington Lexington KY 2000-2003; S Jas Epis Ch Prestonsburg KY 1999-2005; P-in-c S Davids Ch Pikeville KY 1998-2000. E Kentucky Sci Cntr - Treas/Mem Of The Bd Dir; Floyd Cnty Bd Educ - Chairman/Vice-Chairman/Mem 1998-2002. Big Sandy Reg'S Most Popular Cler Floyd Cnty Times 2003; Admiral Kentucky Natural Resources & Environ Protection Cbnt 2003; Outstanding Young Men Of Amer 1987; St. Geo'S Awd BSA 1987; Colonel Gvnr Off/Commonwealth Of Kentucky 1978; Fac Serv Awd Prestonsburg Cmnty Coll. jross@diolex.org

ROSS, Patricia Lynn (Cal) 215 10th Ave, San Francisco CA 94118 B Modesto CA 7/12/1951 d Robert Gilson Ross & Maxine Dorothy. BA Sch for Deacons 1995. D 7/22/1995 Bp Jerry Alban Lamb. m Mary Christie McManus c 3. D The Epis Ch Of S Jn The Evang San Francisco CA 1996-1998; D Trin Ch Folsom CA 1995-1996. NAAD.

ROSS, Robert Layne (Ala) 3764 Rockhill Rd, Birmingham AL 35223 B Covington KY 8/3/1928 s Robert Layne Ross & Ruth. BA Samford U 1963; MDiv STUSo 1966. D 6/18/1966 Bp Charles C J Carpenter P 4/1/1967 Bp George Mosley Murray. m 6/27/1998 Martha C Chafin c 4. Assoc S Mary's-On-The-Highlands Epis Ch Birmingham AL 1996-1998; Assoc The Cathd Ch Of The Adv Birmingham AL 1979-1995; R H Cross Trussville AL 1969-1979; R S Mich's Ch Faunsdale AL 1966-1968; R S Wilfrid's Ch Marion AL 1966-1968. Auth, "arts In Var mag". AAPC; Apha; SACEM. rross81@gmail.com

ROSS, Robert Murray (Ct) 91 Miry Brook Rd, Danbury CT 06810 **S Matt's Epis Ch Wilton CT 2009-; Wooster Sch Danbury CT 2005-** B Winchester MA 11/12/1950 s Clinton William Ross & Kathryn Ann. ALB Harv 1984; MDiv VTS 1992. D 5/30/1992 P 2/13/1993 Bp David Elliot Johnson. m 1/25/1986 Sarah Hallock Gleason c 2. Dio California San Francisco CA 2002-2006; Exec Coun Dio California San Francisco CA 2002-2003; Trin Par Menlo Pk CA 1999-2005; R S Ptr's Ch Osterville MA 1995-1999; Asst to R S Paul's Epis Ch Alexandria VA 1992-1995. "How to Create a Third Serv," *LivCh*, LivCh Fndt, 2007; Auth, "Bldg Up the Ch," *Foward Mvmt*, Forw Mvmt Press, 1996; Auth, "When Your Newcomers Don't Speak Engl," *Congregations*, The Alb Inst, 1994. NAES. robert.ross@woosterschool.org

ROSS, Robert William (LI) 225 Surinam St, Punta Gorda FL 33983 B Brooklyn NY 10/18/1954 s William Thomas Ross & Elizabeth. BA Nyack Coll 1981; MDiv STUSo 1986. D 6/30/1986 Bp Henry Boyd Hucles III P 2/12/1987 Bp Robert Campbell Witcher Sr. m 6/22/1996 Mary Stella c 1. R Ch Of Chr The King E Meadow NY 1996-2007; Cur Ch Of The Adv Westbury NY 1986-1996. Auth, *S Lk Journ of Theol*, 1987. rectorbobr@aim.com

ROSS, Rowena Jane (RG) P O Box 232, Albuquerque NM 87103 B San Antonio TX 4/4/1946 D 7/30/2005 Bp Jeffrey Neil Steenson. m 6/14/1969 Ronald E Ross c 2. ronandjaneross@aol.com

ROSS, Sue Ann (Dal) 1500 N Garrett Ave, Dallas TX 75206 **Exec Dir/Chapl Cathd Garden Apartments Dallas TX 2003-** B Dallas TX 3/11/1945 d Clarence Aubrey Fox & Emma Faye. Lic Angl TS 1999. D 6/3/2000 Bp James Monte Stanton. m 4/28/1971 Ross Lanny Ross c 2. sueannross6@gmail.com

ROSS JR, Victor Sheridan (Ct) 108 Seabury Drive, Bloomfield CT 06002 **Died 4/23/2011** B Baltimore MD 3/2/1925 s Victor Sheridan Ross & Anne Perry Claggett. BA U of Maryland 1950; MDiv VTS 1953. D 7/1/1953 P 5/31/1954 Bp Noble C Powell. c 3. victor.s.ross@snet.net

ROSSER SR, James Bernard (At) 2703 Sanibel Ln Se, Smyrna GA 30082 **Assoc S Jude's Ch Marietta GA 2007-** B Savannah GA 7/12/1946 s J C Rosser & Mildred. BS Florida A&M U 1970; Med Armstrong Atlantic St Coll 1980; MDiv GTS 1984. D 6/2/1984 Bp (George) Paul Reeves P 3/1/1985 Bp Harry Woolston Shipps. m 8/18/1980 Mary Natson c 2. P-in-c S Paul's Epis Ch Atlanta GA 2001-2002; Assoc R for Urban Mssn S Anne's Epis Ch Atlanta GA 1996-1998; Vic Ch Of The Gd Shpd Thomasville GA 1986-1996; Vic The Epis Ch Of S Jn And S Mk Albany GA 1986-1996; D Ch Of The Gd Shpd Thomasville GA 1984-1985. Co-Auth, "The Afr Frgn Plcy of Secy of St Henry Kissinger," 2007; Co-Auth, "Liberian Politics," *the Portrait by Amer Dplma J. Milton Turner*, 2002; Co-Auth, "Henry Highland Garnet Revisited," *The Journ of Negro Hist*, 1983. OHC 1983. jbernard07@yahoo.com

ROSSNER, John Leslie (Mass) President, Int'l Institute of Integral Human Sciences, & Emerit, 1974 de Maisonneuve West, Montreal, Quebec H3H 1K5 Canada B Norwood MA 9/8/1930 s Adolph Edward Rossner & Eleanor Louise. MDiv Nash 1958; MA Br 1960; STM McGill U 1967; PhD Heed U Montreal QC CA 1979; DSC Open Intl U for Complementary Med Col 1993. D 6/21/1958 Bp Frederic Cunningham Lawrence P 12/1/1958 Bp Anson Phelps Stokes Jr. m 7/15/1974 Marilyn Sylvia Zwaig. Cur Ch Of The Trsfg New York NY 1961-1962; Cur Trin Ch Newport RI 1960-1961. Auth, *Toward Recovery of the Primordial Tradition and the Cosmic Chr*, Lewlleyn, 1989; Auth, *Rel, Sci, and Sprtlty*, U Press of Amer - Lantham, MD, 1983; Auth, *From Ancient Magic to Future Tech (vol. 1)*, U Press of Amer - Lantham, MD, 1979; Auth, *From Ancient Rel to Future Sci (vol. 2)*, U Press of Amer - Lantham, MD, 1979. Ecum Ord of the Trsfg [Mem unit, ICCC/NCC/ 1988; Pres, Intl Inst of Integral Human Sciences (1975; Wrld Fllshp of Rel - New Delhi, India - Hon Co- 1980-1982. Paramatma Vidwan - Samsad Intellectual Awd Wrld Dvlpmt Parliament, India Pondicherry India 1989; Doctor of Lit Wrld U of Amer 1989. jrossner@iiihs.org

ROSSO, Tricia Anne (Cal) 716 Hensley Ave # 1, San Bruno CA 94066 B Oakland CA 5/9/1954 d Richard Anthony Rosso & Bernice Clare. BA San Francisco St U 1978; BA Sch for Deacons 1992. Rec from Roman Catholic 5/1/1983 Bp William Edwin Swing. DOK 2005. revtricia@hotmail.com

ROTH, Frank Alwin (Ala) 2310 Skyland Blvd E, Tuscaloosa AL 35405 **R S Mths Epis Ch Tuscaloosa AL 2008-** B Baton Rouge LA 10/16/1947 s Walter Alwin Roth & Ada Lillie. BSF LSU 1970; MS LSU 1972; DF Steph F. Austin St U 1983. D 4/25/2004 P 10/23/2004 Bp Larry Earl Maze. m 1/18/1969 Beverly Tye Roth c 3. stmathiaschurch@bellsouth.net

ROTH, Nancy Leone (O) 330 Morgan St, Oberlin OH 44074 **Assoc Chr Ch Oberlin OH 1999-; Credo Inst Inc. Memphis TN 1981-** B New York NY 3/30/1936 d Robert Foster Moore & Gertrude Elizabeth. BA Ob 1958; MDiv GTS 1981. D 6/13/1981 Bp Paul Moore Jr P 12/19/1981 Bp James Stuart Wetmore. m 6/21/1959 Robert N Roth c 2. Int S Andr's Epis Ch Elyria OH 1995-1996; Chr Ch Oberlin OH 1992-2001; H Sprt Sum Chap W Cornwall CT New York NY 1984-1991; The GTS New York NY 1981-1982. Auth, "Sprtlty," *Epis Life*, 2001; Auth, *Invitation to Chr Yoga*, Cowley, 2001; Auth, *New Every Morning: Meditation on Hymns*, Ch Pub Inc, 2000; Auth, *Meditations for Choir Members*, Morehouse Pub, 1999; Auth, "Awake," *My Soul: Meditations on Hymns*, Ch Pub Inc, 1999; Auth, *A Closer Walk: Meditating on Hymns*, Ch Pub Inc, 1998; Auth, *Organic Pryr*, Cowley Press, 1993; Auth, *Praise my Soul: Meditation on Hymns*, Ch Pub, 1991; Auth, *Praying: A Bk for Chld*, Ch Hymnal, 1991; Auth, *The Breath of God*, Cowley Press, 1990; Auth,

R

A New Chr Yoga, Cowley Press, 1989; Auth, *We Sing of God: A Hymnal for Chld*, Ch Hymnal, 1989. EPF 1980; Ord of S Helena, Assoc 1977. J Wilson Sutton Prize for hon thesis GTS New York NY 1981. revnancyroth@aol.com

ROTH JR, Ralph Carl (Be) Rr 5 Box 5096, Stroudsburg PA 18360 B Philadelphia PA 2/11/1936 s Ralph Carl Roth & Pauline Caroline. BA Tem 1962; BD TS Of The Reformed Epis Ch PA 1962; MDiv PDS 1965. D 6/12/1965 Bp Robert Lionne DeWitt P 12/18/1965 Bp Andrew Tsu. m 9/6/1958 Jean I Gibson c 3. Trin Epis Ch Mt Pocono PA 1967-1998; Cur S Phil's In The Field Oreland PA 1965-1967. R Emer Trin Epis Ch 2000; Sr Theol Awd Reformed Epis Sem 1962; OT Exegesis Awd Reformed Epis Sem 1962; Knights Of Pythias Awd Tem 1962.

ROTHAUGE, Arlin John (Ore) 2122 Sheridan Rd, Evanston IL 60201 B Eugene OR 4/27/1938 s Arvid John Rothauge & Mildred Deborah. BA U of Oregon 1961; BD Phillips U 1965; PhD U Of Glasgow Gb 1968; DD Ya Berk 1987. D 12/17/1973 Bp James Walmsley Frederic Carman P 12/1/1974 Bp Matthew Paul Bigliardi. m 10/7/1989 Earlene A Taplan c 2. Prof Of Congrl Stds S Jn The Div Chap Evanston IL 1995-2003; Prof Of Congrl Stds SWTS Evanston IL 1995-2000; Epis Ch Cntr New York NY 1981-1994; R All SS Ch Portland OR 1975-1980. Auth, "Catechism: The Outline Of The Faith We Profess"; Auth, "Sizing Up The Cong"; Auth, "Parallel Dvlpmt". rothauge@nwu.edu

ROTTGERS, Steven Robert (Tex) 122 Retama Dr., Georgetown TX 78626 B Fort Thomas KY 7/30/1954 s Robert Franklin Rottgers & Wanda June. BA No Kentucky St U 1975; MDiv Epis TS In Kentucky 1980; DMin SWTS 2007. D 5/11/1980 Bp Addison Hosea P 12/12/1980 Bp Gray Temple. m 8/2/1979 Mary G Hassenstein c 4. R Gr Epis Ch Georgetown TX 2007-2011; R H Cross Trussville AL 1997-2006; Dio Michigan Detroit MI 1994-1997; Chr The King Epis Ch Tabb VA 1987-1993; Dio Sthrn Virginia Norfolk VA 1985-1986; Assoc S Jn's Ch Hampton VA 1982-1985; Assoc S Jn's Ch Florence SC 1980-1981. Auth, "Ripe for the Harvest," 2007; Auth, "I am Yours!," *The Entheos Ldr*, 2006; Auth, "Rethinking Par Structures: The Quality Questions," 2005; Auth, "A Stwdshp Parable," *Outstanding In His Field*, Proctor Pub, 1995; Auth, "Shaping Our Future," *Shaping Our Future*, Cowley Pub, 1995; Auth, "The Entheos Ldr," *Ldrshp for New Apostolic Era*, 1993. srottgers1@aol.com

ROUFFY, Edward Albert (Colo) 950 Sw 21st Ave Apt 402, Portland OR 97205 B New York NY 12/10/1936 s Fernand Emanuel Rouffy & Deborah Margaret. BA U of So Carolina 1958; MDiv STUSo 1961. D 6/24/1961 Bp Clarence Alfred Cole P 7/14/1962 Bp Randolph R Claiborne. m 7/1/1961 Virginia Porcher c 3. R S Jos's Par Buena Pk CA 1992-1999; Int S Paul's Epis Ch Steamboat Sprg CO 1991-1992; R Chr's Epis Ch Castle Rock CO 1982-1991; R Ch Of The Ascen Salida CO 1969-1982; R Gr Ch Buena Vista CO 1969-1982; Vic S Andr's Ch Cripple Creek CO 1965-1969; Vic S Lk's Ch Westcliffe CO 1965-1969; Cur S Jn's Epis Ch Boulder CO 1963-1965; Cur Chr Ch Macon GA 1961-1963. FA! 1967; Schools of Pstr Care 1967-2007. evrouffy@comcast.net

ROULETTE, Philip Burwell (Md) 3738 Butler Road, Glyndon MD 21071 B Hagerstown MD 11/11/1940 s George Edward Roulette & Page Burwell. BA W&L 1964; MDiv VTS 1967. D 6/20/1967 P 5/1/1968 Bp Harry Lee Doll. m 6/8/1968 Clover Purvis. Bd Epis Soc Mnstrs Dio Maryland Baltimore MD 1976-2003; R S Jn's Ch Reisterstown MD 1974-2003; Vic S Chris Epis Ch Linthicum Heights MD 1970-1973; Asst The Ch Of The Redeem Baltimore MD 1967-1970. Auth, "The Baltimore Declaration Of Faith," 1991. Soc Of The Cincinatti, Chapl-Gnrl 1996. Awd Of Recognition Epis Soc Of Ministers Of Maryland. philiproulette@comcast.net

ROUMAS, Peisha Geneva (WMo) 913 E 100th Ter, Kansas City MO 64131 B Maywood CA 8/18/1942 D 2/7/2004 Bp Barry Robert Howe. m 9/1/1963 William Stephen Roumas c 3.

ROUNTREE, Philip (Cal) 60 Martinez Ct, Novato CA 94945 B Freeport NY 11/7/1952 s Philip Lyon Rountree & Mary Elizabeth. Phd Grad Theol Un; BA Ya 1974; MDiv EDS 1979. D 6/23/1979 P 2/18/1980 Bp John Harris Burt. m 6/24/2006 Jodi D Sama c 3. Instr CDSP Berkeley CA 1990-1998; R S Fran Of Assisi Ch Novato CA 1982-2010; Asst S Mich And All Ang Par Corona Del Mar CA 1979-1982. stphilofnovato@mac.com

ROUSE, Albertine Coney (Los) PO Box 456, Verdugo City CA 91046 B Laurel MS 8/4/1943 d Albert M Coney & Myrtle Catherine. DMin Fuller TS; BS Alcorn St U 1965; MDiv Duke 1996. D 1/27/2002 Bp Chester Lovelle Talton P 9/8/2002 Bp Joseph Jon Bruno. m 10/12/1990 Robert Milton Rouse. Ch Of The H Comm Gardena CA 2004-2011; Chr The Gd Shpd Par Los Angeles CA 2003-2004. REVACR@GMAIL.COM

ROUSSEAU, Sean Kenneth (Va) 114 W Boscawen St, Winchester VA 22601 **Montross & Washington Par Montross VA 2011-** B Riverside CA 12/12/1968 s Kenneth P Rousseau & Mary Catherine. BA St Chas Borromeo Sem 1991; MDiv St Chas Borromeo Sem 1994. Rec from Roman Catholic 4/3/2011 Bp Shannon Sherwood Johnston. Int Asst R Chr Epis Ch Winchester VA 2011. seankennethrousseau@gmail.com

ROWE, Gary Lee (Del) 2020 N Tatnall St, Wilmington DE 19802 **GC Alt Dep Dio Delaware Wilmington DE 2006-; Cn to the Ordnry Dio Delaware Wilmington DE 2005-; GC Dep Dio Delaware Wilmington DE 2003-; GC Alt Dep Dio Delaware Wilmington DE 2000-** B Newport News VA 5/15/1955 s Ernest Lee Rowe & Dorothy. AB Davidson Coll 1977; MM U Cinc 1979; MDiv EDS 1982. D 6/11/1982 Bp William Grant Black P 2/4/1983 Bp Lyman Cunningham Ogilby. m 10/2/1983 Leslie Acker c 2. Stndg Com, Pres Dio Delaware Wilmington DE 2003-2004; Dio Coun Dio Delaware Wilmington DE 1997-2000; R S Dav's Epis Ch Wilmington DE 1996-2005; Assoc R Estrn Shore Chap Virginia Bch VA 1989-1996; Exec Bd Dio Sthrn Virginia Norfolk VA 1987-1988; R Gr Ch Newport News VA 1984-1988; Asst S Anne's Ch Abington PA 1982-1984. garyrowe@verizon.net

ROWE, Jacquelyn Gilbert (CGC) PO Box 326, Pine Beach NJ 08741 **Ch Of S Clem Of Rome Belford NJ 2011-** B Miami FL 4/12/1947 d Albert Cato Gilbert & Ellen Victoria. Ottawa U; U of Nthrn Colorado; BA Pepperdine U 1978; MDiv GTS 1998. D 6/20/1998 Bp John Lewis Said P 12/1/1998 Bp Calvin Onderdonk Schofield Jr. c 2. Exec Dir of Mnstry Chr Ch Toms River Toms River NJ 2006-2009; R Ch Of The Gd Shpd Mobile AL 2002-2004; Wilmer Hall Mobile AL 2001-2002; R S Geo's Epis Ch Riviera Bch FL 1998-2001. revjrowe@yahoo.com

ROWE, Mary Stone (Mont) 608 Aqua Cir, Circle Pines MN 55014 B Richmond VA 12/21/1947 d James Stone & Elizabeth. D 12/2/1995 P 9/14/2000 Bp Charles Jones III. m 6/7/1969 Thomas Rowe c 2.

ROWE, Matthew Robert (Miss) Church of the Nativity, P.O. Box 1006, Greenwood MS 38930 **Duncan M. Gray Camp & Conf Cntr Bd Managers Dio Mississippi Jackson MS 2011-; Exec Com Dio Mississippi Jackson MS 2011-; GC Alt Dep Dio Mississippi Jackson MS 2011-; R Ch Of The Nativ Greenwood MS 2006-** B Bellflower CA 3/29/1963 s Robert Thomas Rowe & Catherine Mary. BS Biola U 1986; MDiv Epis TS of The SW 1993. D 6/12/1993 Bp Chester Lovelle Talton P 12/17/1993 Bp William Harvey Wolfrum. m 10/7/1995 Elizabeth E Brown c 2. Assoc R Trin Epis Ch Baton Rouge LA 2005-2006; R S Pat's Ch Zachary LA 2001-2005; R S Chris's Ch Bandera TX 2000-2001; Cur Gr Ch Of W Feliciana S Francisville LA 1997-2000; Cur S Jn Mssn Laurel Hill S Francisville LA 1997-2000; Assoc R Gr And S Steph's Epis Ch Colorado Sprg CO 1994-1997; Cur S Mk's Epis Ch Durango CO 1993-1994. frmatt@nativitygreenwood.org

ROWE, Michael Gordon (SwFla) 9213 Estero River Cir, Estero FL 33928 **R S Mary's Epis Ch Bonita Sprg FL 2005-** B Manning AB CA 4/20/1955 s Thomas Desmond Rowe & Elizabeth May. BA McGill U 1977; MA Oxf 1979; MDiv Montreal TS 1980; STM McGill U 1983; D. Min. TS 2005. Trans from Anglican Church of Canada 11/1/1992 as Priest Bp Edward Cole Chalfant. m 7/8/1978 Dianne Calista Beaulieu c 2. R Ch Of S Thos Camden ME 1992-2005. mgrowe@comcast.net

ROWE, Richard C(harles) (NwPa) 706 Wilhelm Rd, Hermitage PA 16148 **Dioc Coun Dio NW Pennsylvania Erie PA 2006-** B Sharon PA 4/19/1947 s Walter Richard Rowe & Ruth Arlene. BS Youngstown St U 1973; MS Youngstown St U 1974; Dioc Sch for Mnstry Titusville PA 2000. D 5/18/2002 P 11/17/2002 Bp Robert Deane Rowley Jr. m 7/6/1968 Patricia Meehan c 2. P-in-c Ch Of The Redeem Hermitage PA 2005-2010. Int Mnstry Ntwk 2002. rowerpsc@yahoo.com

ROWE, Richard Charles (WNY) 64 Oak Gate Dr, Hendersonville NC 28739 **Systems Coach, Dept Cong Vitality Dio Wstrn No Carolina Asheville NC 2011-; S Jn's Epis Ch Marion NC 2011-** B Oakland CA 7/18/1941 s Ralph Cornish Rowe & Mary. BA U CA 1963; MDiv EDS 1966; Urban Trng Cntr 1967. D 6/19/1966 Bp James Albert Pike P 10/1/1967 Bp George Richard Millard. m 12/30/1965 Katherine Whitney O'Neill. Int S Ptr's Par San Pedro CA 2009-2010; Int Ch Of The Redeem Shelby NC 2005-2009; Int Ch Of The Epiph Laurens SC 2005; Int S Fran of Assisi Chapin SC 2003-2004; Int S Alb's Ch Davidson NC 2002-2003; Cn Dev Mssn/Minstry Dio Wstrn New York Tonawanda NY 1991-2002; S Annes Ch Mililani HI 1991; Inst For Human Serv Inc Honolulu HI 1989-1991; Vic S Matt's Epis Ch Waimanalo HI 1989-1990; S Steph's Ch Wahiawa HI 1986-1989; R S Ptr's Ch Honolulu HI 1982-1985; S Ambr Epis Ch Foster City CA 1974-1982; Asst S Ptr's Epis Ch Redwood City CA 1971-1973; Vic The Epis Ch Of The Gd Shpd Berkeley CA 1967-1970. Auth, "Prevention Of Chld Abuse: A Manual For Epis Schools"; Auth, "Of Chld Abuse"; Auth, "The Role Of Educators & Caregivers In The Prevention," *Detection & Reporting*. korowe@juno.com

ROWE, Sandra Jeanne (CFla) PO Box 2206, Breckenridge CO 80424 B Arcadia FL 12/8/1946 d Raymond Guard & Ellen H. BA Stetson U Deland FL 1968; Med Stetson U Deland FL 1981; EdD U Of Cetnral Floriday Orlando FL 1997. D 12/8/1990 Bp John Wadsworth Howe. m 12/30/1967 Gary Robert Rowe c 1. Dir Of Fam Mnstry Epis Ch Of S Jn The Bapt Breckenridge CO 2005-2009. s2growe@aol.com

✠ **ROWE, Rt Rev Sean Walter** (NwPa) 1870 Henley Pl, Fairview PA 16415 **Bp Dio NW Pennsylvania Erie PA 2007-** B Sharon PA 2/16/1975 s Richard C(harles) Rowe & Patricia. BA Grove City Coll 1997; M.Div. VTS 2000. D

R

5/27/2000 P 12/2/2000 Bp Robert Deane Rowley Jr Con 9/8/2007 for NwPa. m Carly Rowe. R S Jn's Ch Franklin PA 2000-2007. seanwrowe@gmail.com

ROWE-GUIN, Kathy (Va) 5911 Fairview Woods Dr, Fairfax Station VA 22039 **S Peters-In-The-Woods Epis Ch Fairfax Sta VA 2011-** B Dallas TX 9/3/1959 d Joseph M Rowe & Elizabeth B. BA Texas Tech U 1981; Elem Teachers Cred Chapman Univerity 1999; MDiv VTS 2011. D 6/4/2011 Bp Shannon Sherwood Johnston. m 6/11/1988 David Guin c 2. revguin@gmail.com

ROWELL, Ernest Michael (USC) PO Box 847, Ocklawaha FL 32183 **Int H Trin Epis Ch Fruitland Pk FL 2008-** B Ocala FL 11/10/1944 s Ernest McCredie Rowell & Dot Guess. BS Florida St U; MDiv STUSo. D 6/13/1973 P 6/4/1974 Bp Edward Hamilton West. m 6/3/1972 Amy Sexton c 2. R S Monica's Epis Ch Naples FL 1999; R S Thad Epis Ch Aiken SC 1998; S Thad Epis Ch Aiken SC 1985-1997; R S Patricks Ch Albany GA 1978-1985; The Epis Ch Of The Annunc Vidalia GA 1976-1978; Ch Of The Gd Shpd Jacksonville FL 1973-1976. asremr@aol.com

ROWELL, Rebecca Earlene (Ga) 6329 Frederica Rd, St Simons Island GA 31522 B Moultrie GA 2/9/1954 d Lawrence George Rowell & Earlene Wilson. BS U GA 1976; MEd U GA 1977; MPA Georgia Sthrn U 1992. D 11/4/2009 Bp Henry Irving Louttit. m 5/25/1985 Charles Lamkin. browell221@earthlink.net

ROWINS, Charles Howard (Los) 1 Warrenton Rd, Baltimore MD 21210 B Pasadena CA 1/11/1942 s Edward Holton Rowins & Lucille. BA U CA 1963; MA GW 1966; MDiv GTS 1969; DMin PrTS 1987. D 6/22/1969 Bp William G Wright P 12/20/1969 Bp Horace W B Donegan. m 6/4/1983 Suzanne M Rowins c 2. P-in-c St Chris By The Sea Gibson Island MD 1997-2003; Headmaster S Jas' Sch Los Angeles CA 1982-1995; Headmaster S Steph's Epis Sch Austin TX 1980-1982; Chapl Kent Sch Kent CT 1971-1980; Asst S Thos Ch New York NY 1969-1971. Auth, *Holding Action: An Understanding of the Ch*, Forw Mvmt Press. rowins@jhu.edu

ROWLAND, Kenneth George (Ga) 6463 Cobbham Rd, Appling GA 30802 **P Chr Ch Augusta GA 2009-** B New York NY 8/17/1931 s Edwin Kenneth Rowland & Elizabeth Jane. BS SUNY 1956; MA NYU 1958. D 9/12/2006 P 3/24/2007 Bp Henry Irving Louttit. P H Cross Ch Thomson GA 2007-2008. kgrowland@bellsouth.net

ROWLAND, Richard William (La) 100 Christwood Blvd Apt 221, Covington LA 70433 B Waterbury CT 10/29/1922 s Eustis Thatcher Rowland & Gladys Louise. Cit 1943; U Cinc 1944; MDiv GTS 1949. D 6/16/1949 P 12/17/1949 Bp Wallace E Conkling. c 2. Trst The GTS New York NY 1980-1986; COM Dio Louisiana Baton Rouge LA 1973-1982; Dir Fam Serv Soc Dio Louisiana Baton Rouge LA 1970-1976; Liturg Cmsn Dio Louisiana Baton Rouge LA 1969-1973; Dep GC Dio Louisiana Baton Rouge LA 1967-1976; Chair DeptCE Dio Louisiana Baton Rouge LA 1965-1967; Dn Chr Ch Cathd New Orleans LA 1963-1985; R S Fran' Epis Ch San Francisco CA 1961-1963; Dn Cathd Ch Of S Mk Salt Lake City UT 1952-1961; Assoc Ch Of The H Comf Kenilworth IL 1950-1952; Cur S Ptr's Epis Ch Chicago IL 1949-1950. Ord of S Lazarus of Jerusalem - Sr Chapl 1980. deanrwr@gmail.com

ROWLES, S(tephen) (Va) 9750 Essex Hills Road, New Kent VA 23124 **R S Ptr's Par Ch New Kent VA 2006-** B Halifax VA 10/12/1953 s James Rayfield Rowles & Ruth Esther. BA U Rich 1984; MDiv SE Bapt TS Wake Forest NC 1986; DMin Estrn Bapt TS 1996. D 10/5/2002 P 4/5/2003 Bp Peter James Lee. m 8/8/1981 Cynthia Ann Kendrick. Beckford Par Woodstock VA 2002-2006; Emm Ch Woodstock VA 2002; S Andr's Ch Mt Jackson VA 2002. paul.rowles@gmail.com

R

ROWLEY, Angela (Ct) Yale New Haven Hospital, 20 York Street, New Haven CT 06510 **Asst S Ptr's Epis Ch Milford CT 2008-** B Glasgow Scotland 5/30/1946 d John Hargroves & Margaret Clark. MDiv Ya Berk 2005. D 6/11/2005 Bp Andrew Donnan Smith P 1/28/2006 Bp James Elliot Curry. c 4. P Trin Ch Branford CT 2006-2008; S Jn's Epis Ch Kula HI 2000-2001. ahrowley@yahoo.com

ROWLEY, Graham Thurston (Eas) 30140 Southampton Bridge Rd, Salisbury MD 21804 B Hartford CT 6/29/1932 s William Thurston Rowley & Alice. BA Duke 1954; MA U IL 1958; MDiv EDS 1968. D 6/11/1968 Bp Walter H Gray P 3/22/1969 Bp John Henry Esquirol. Int S Alb's Epis Ch Salisbury MD 2000-2001; R S Paul's Berlin MD 1993-1998; Int St Mich & Gr Ch Rumford RI 1992-1993; S Paul's Ch Portsmouth RI 1989-1992; Int Ch Of The H Comf Luthvle Timon MD 1988-1989; R Ch Of The Redemp Baltimore MD 1986-1988; Par Of The H Fam Pen Argyl PA 1981-1986; R S Jos's Ch Pen Argyl PA 1981-1986; R Trin Epis Ch Weymouth MA 1978-1981; R S Matt's Ch Goffstown NH 1970-1977; Cur Gr Epis Ch Norwalk CT 1968-1970.

ROWLEY, Jennifer Holder (NwT) 1318 Amarilla St, Abilene TX 79602 B Greensboro NC 2/21/1952 d Worthe Holder & Helen. BA U of Texas 1973; MA U NC 1991. D 6/8/2002 Bp James Monte Stanton P 1/16/2010 Bp James Scott Mayer. m 11/1/2004 Lyle Bishop Rowley c 3. S Anne's Epis Ch Desoto TX 2007-2008. Rowley.Jennifer@baylorhealth.edu

✠ ROWLEY JR, Rt Rev Robert Deane (NwPa) 1796 Stone Hill Dr., York PA 17402 **Died 1/18/2010** B Cumberland MD 7/6/1941 s Robert Deane Rowley & Alyce Wilson. BA U Pgh 1962; LLB U Pgh 1965; LLM GW 1970; MDiv Epis TS of The SW 1977; DD Epis TS of The SW 1989. D 6/22/1977 P 1/6/1978 Bp Edmond Lee Browning Con 5/13/1989 for NwPa. Auth, "A Proposal To Strengthen The Servanthood Mnstry Of The Ch," 1980; Auth, "Report On The Diac," 1979. Alum Of Dist S Vinc Latrobe PA 1989. rdrowleyjr@aol.com

✠ **ROWTHORN, Rt Rev Jeffery William** (Ct) 17 Woodland Dr, Salem CT 06420 **Ret Bp Suffr of Convoc of Ch in Europe Convoc of Amer Ch in Europe Paris FR 2002-** B Newport Monmouthshire UK 4/9/1934 s Eric William Rowthorn & Eileen. BA U of Cambridge 1957; BD UTS 1961; Cuddesdon Theolgical Coll 1962; MA U of Cambridge 1962; BLitt Oxf 1972; DD Ya Berk 1987. D 9/30/1962 P 9/29/1963 Bp Mervyn Stockwood Con 9/19/1987 for Ct. m 11/16/1963 Anne Wheeler c 3. Bp-in-Charge Convoc of Amer Ch in Europe Paris FR 1994-2001; Bp Suffr Dio Connecticut Hartford CT 1987-1993; Bp Godard Assoc Prof of Pstr Theol Ya Berk New Haven CT 1973-1987; Sum Vic S Mart's Epis Ch Fairlee VT 1969-1980. Auth, "Singing Songs of Expectation," Hope Pub Co, 2007; Auth, "The Wideness of God's Mercy," Morehouse Pub, 2007; Auth, "A New Hymnal for Colleges and Schools," Yale Univ. Press, 1992; Auth, "Laudamus," Yale DS, 1980. Bishops Working for a Just Wrld; Episcopalians for Global Recon 2003; Hymn Soc of No Amer; No Amer Acad of Liturg 1973; Societas Liturgica. Ya Tercentennial Medal Ya 2001; DD Ya Berk 1987. jefferyrowthorn@yahoo.com

ROY, Byron Willard (Roch) 19 Abbotswood Crescent, Penfield NY 14526 B Akron OH 3/11/1941 s Bruce Willard Roy & Florence Louise. BA Kent St U 1974; MDiv Bex 1977. D 7/3/1977 Bp Robert Rae Spears Jr P 1/1/1978 Bp John Harris Burt. S Geo's Ch Hilton NY 1978-1992; Cur S Lk And S Simon Cyrene Rochester NY 1978. bypaul@frontiernet.net

ROY JR, Derik Justin Hurd (Alb) 10 W High St, Ballston Spa NY 12020 **R Chr Epis Ch Ballston Spa NY 1994-** B Albany NY 10/3/1952 s Derik Justin Hurd Roy & Marilyn Grace. BA SUNY 1974; MDiv Nash 1977. D 6/4/1977 Bp Wilbur Emory Hogg Jr P 12/21/1977 Bp Charles Bowen Persell Jr. m 5/19/2007 Catherine Larosa-Roy c 7. Vic S Barth's Epis Ch Mio MI 1981-1994; Vic S Fran Epis Ch Grayling MI 1981-1994; Asst Chr/St Jn's Par Champlain NY 1979-1981; Asst S Steph's Ch Delmar NY 1977-1979. djroyjrcec@msn.com

ROY, Jeffrey (Minn) 8 Ambrose Lane, Holmdel NJ 07733 **Cur S Geo's-By-The-River Rumson NJ 2011-** B Omaha NE 1/27/1964 s Virgil E Roy & Darlene M. BA Bethel U 2006; MDiv The GTS 2011. D 7/29/2010 P 6/30/2011 Bp Brian N Prior. m 12/31/1989 Janine Renee Lamm c 2. jroy2@me.com

ROY, Robert Royden (Minn) 1289 Galtier St, Saint Paul MN 55117 **P All SS Epis Indn Mssn Minneapolis MN 2004-** B White Earth MN 8/8/1940 Untd TS Of The Twin Cities. D 8/24/1999 P 6/3/2000 Bp James Louis Jelinek. m 9/18/1993 Katherine Masquot c 2.

ROYALS, Deborah (Los) 7945 N Village Avenue, `, Tucson AZ 85704 **Dir of Dvlpmt Indigenous Theol Trng Inst Minneapolis MN 2011-** B Tucson AZ 5/8/1953 d Norman Royals & Artemisa. RN U of AZ 1973; BA Prescott Coll Tucson AZ 2002; MDiv CDSP Berkeley CA 2005; MA CDSP 2006. D 1/16/2005 P 7/16/2005 Bp Mark Lawrence Mac Donald. c 2. P In Charge S Mich's Epis Ch Riverside CA 2010-2011; Consult Indigenous Theol Trng Inst Minneapolis MN 2009-2010; Supply S Jos Of Arimathea Mssn Yucca Vlly CA 2008-2010; Supply S Mart-In-The-Fields Mssn Twentynine Palms CA 2008-2010; Mssnr for Native Amer Mnstry Dvlpmt Dio Los Angeles Los Angeles CA 2006-2009; Mssnr of Native Amer Mnstry Dvlpmt Dio Nthrn California Sacramento CA 2005-2007; Congrl Dvlp Four Winds Native Amer Cong Sacramento CA 2003-2006. Auth/Prod Ed, "How Red Is God?/God is Still Red," *First People's Theol Journ*, Indigenous Theol Trng Inst, 2010; Prod Ed/Auth, "Oklahoma IV 2010 Spec Ed/Recognition/Liturg," *First People's Theol Journ*, Indigenous Theol Trng Inst, 2010; Contrubuting Auth, "Prayers," *Lifting Wmn Voices*, Moorehouse Press, 2009; Contributing Auth, "Unity in Diversity," *Those Preaching Wmn*, Judson Press, 2008; Prod Ed, "The Gospel in Four Directions," *The Gospel in Four Directions*, Prov VIII Indigenous People's Mnstry Ntwk, 2007; Contributing Auth, "Angl Comm and Homosexuality," *Two Sprt*, Angl Comm, 2007; Auth, "Remembrance, Recognition and Recon," *First People's Theol Journ*, Indigenous Theol Trng Inst, 2006; Auth, "Transformation: Jesus Walked Among Us Too," *First People's Theol Journ*, Indigenous Theol Trng Inst, 2005; Auth, "Creation: The Talking Tree," *First People's Theol Journ*, Indigenous Theol Trng Inst, 2001. debroyals@yahoo.com

ROYALTY, Virginia B (Minn) 1599 Juliet Avenue, Saint Paul MN 55105 **R S Clem's Ch S Paul MN 2007-** B Boston MA 3/20/1958 d Robert Malcolm Royalty & Patricia. U So 1978; BS Georgia St U 1986; MDiv STUSo 1999. D 6/5/1999 P 2/5/2000 Bp Frank Kellogg Allan. c 1. All SS Epis Ch Atlanta GA 1999-2006; S Clem's Ch S Paul MN 1999-2006. broyalty@stclements-stp.org

ROYER, Christopher Scott (SC) PO Box 278, Bluffton SC 29910 **Asst R The Ch Of The Cross Bluffton SC 2008-** B Boulder CO 3/21/1967 s Galen Bruce Royer & Arlene Carol. Mdiv Denver Sem 2004; Dipl. in Angl Stds TESM 2007. D 6/7/2008 Bp Robert William Duncan P 1/11/2009 Bp Mark Joseph Lawrence. m 1/15/1994 Choonae Park c 2. c24tky@gmail.com

ROZENDAAL, Jay Calvin (Oly) 1134 Finnegan Way # 302, Bellingham WA 98225 **Assoc S Paul's Ch Seattle WA 2009-** B Holland MI 3/28/1962 s John Henry Rozendaal & Ardyce Jane. BMus Westminster Choir Coll of Rider U 1982; MM Cleveland Inst of Mus 1985; MDiv GTS 2002; STM GTS 2005. D 6/29/2002 Bp Sanford Zangwill Kaye Hampton P 1/25/2003 Bp Vincent Waydell Warner. m 10/9/1989 David Crile Kisling. Vic Chr Epis Ch Blaine WA 2007-2009; The GTS New York NY 2002-2006; The Ch of S Ign of Antioch New York NY 2002. CHS 2006; Ord of Julian of Norwich 1997-2002. fatherjayr@gmail.com

ROZENE, Wendy Anne (Me) 17 Fox Run Rd, Cumberland ME 04021 **D S Ann's Epis Ch Windham Windham ME 2007-; D Dio Maine Portland ME 1990-** B Lawrence MA 6/4/1950 d Alfred Bradstreet & Gladys. BS U of Maine 1973; MS in Ed U of New Engl 2004. D 9/13/1990 Bp Edward Cole Chalfant. m 12/22/1973 Richard Arthur Rozene c 3. NAAD.

ROZZELLE, Stephen Michael (Nwk) 400 Ramapo Avenue, Pompton Lakes NJ 07442 **P-in-c Chr Ch Pompton Lakes NJ 2010-** B Washington DC 6/16/1948 s Frederick Russell Rozzelle & Audrey Irene. MDiv PDS 1973; STM NYTS 1981. D 4/28/1973 Bp Alfred L Banyard P 10/27/1973 Bp Albert Wiencke Van Duzer. m 7/5/2008 Maureen Gallivan c 3. R S Mk's Ch Basking Ridge NJ 1978-2006; St Peters Ch Woodbury Heights NJ 1975-1976; H Trin Epis Ch Wenonah NJ 1973-1978. Cmnty Of S Jn The Bapt. Humanitarian Of The Year Partnr In Ending Hunger 2003. smrozzelle@hotmail.com

RUBEL, Christopher Scott (Los) 250 N Live Oak Ave, Glendora CA 91741 B Long Island NY 2/10/1933 s Henry Scott Rubel & Dorothy. AA San Bernardino Vlly Coll 1956; BA U of Redlands 1961; Rel. D. Claremont TS 1967. D 6/18/1977 P 1/14/1978 Bp Robert C Rusack. m 11/3/1985 Katherine Hauser c 2. Assoc H Trin Epis Ch Covina CA 2001-2005. Auth, *Authentic Being as Model for Mnstry*, 1967. AAMFT; Amer Psych Assn; ACPE; CAMFT; GPASC; Natl Assn for the Self- Supporting Active Mnstry. chrisrubel@rewells.net

RUBIANO-ALVARADO, Raul (CFla) 2851 Afton Cir, Orlando FL 32825 **P Iglesia Epis Jesus de Nazaret Orlando FL 2008-; P S Mary Of The Ang Epis Ch Orlando FL 2005-** B Macheta Cundinamarca CO 7/14/1952 s Lucindo Rubiano & Marelena. U Bogota. Rec from Roman Catholic 4/1/1984 as Priest Bp Bernardo Merino-Botero. m 3/13/1980 Maria Consuelo Garcia c 2. P Our Merc Sav Epis Ch Denver CO 2004-2005; P Ch Of S Phil And S Jas Denver CO 1998-2004; P Iglesia Epis En Colombia 1995-1998; P Dio The Dominican Republic (Iglesia Epis Dominicana) Santo Domingo DO 1990-1995; P Iglesia Epis En Colombia 1984-1989. raul_rubiano@hotmail.com

RUBIN, Richard Louis (Los) 163 W. 11th St., Claremont CA 91711 **R Chr Ch Par Ontario CA 1995-** B Pomona CA 10/7/1958 s Louis Alfred Rubin & Catherine Angeline. BA Cath U of Louvain 1980; BA U of San Diego 1980; MA/STB Cath U of Louvain 1983. Rec from Roman Catholic 7/1/1992 as Priest Bp Frederick Houk Borsch. m 4/5/1992 Lauriel Jean Cover c 2. S Geo's Ch Riverside CA 1995; Ch Of The Trsfg Arcadia CA 1994-1995. CHRISTCHURCHONT@VERIZON.NET

RUBINSON, Rhonda Joy (NY) 400 W 119th St Apt 11-L, New York NY 10027 **P-in-c S Phil's Ch New York NY 2007-** B Brooklyn NY 10/3/1958 d Jacob Joseph Rubinson & Arlene. BA Barnard Coll of Col 1980; MA Col 1981; MA UTS 1999. D 3/18/2000 P 9/16/2000 Bp Richard Frank Grein. Asst Ch Of The Heav Rest New York NY 2000-2007. rev.rhondarubinson@yahoo.com

RUBRIGHT, Elizabeth Alice Shemet (SwFla) D 6/29/1991 Bp Barbara Clementine Harris.

RUBY, Lorne Dale (Pa) 20 N 2nd St, Columbia PA 17512 B York PA 6/29/1937 s Sterling Henry Ruby & Martha Elizabeth. BS Millersville U 1959; MS Rutgers-The St U 1961; MDiv PDS 1971. D 6/19/1971 P 12/21/1971 Bp Robert Lionne DeWitt. m 9/4/2008 Ernest Dancil Barba. Int Ch Of The Annuniciation Philadelphia PA 2002-2003; Int S Thos The Apos Hollywood Los Angeles CA 2000-2002; P-in-c The Ch Of The Trin Coatesville PA 1999-2000; Int S Jn's Ch Gap PA 1998-1999. budruby@comcast.net

RUCKER, J(ames) Cliff(ord) (Tex) 2329 12th St, Port Neches TX 77651 **R H Trin Epis Ch Port Neches TX 2002-** B Ballinger TX 1/25/1952 s Harry Sidney Rucker & Dorothy Jean. BA Baylor U 1973; MA Baylor U 1976; MBA Georgia St U 1978; MDiv Nash 1997. D 6/14/1997 P 12/16/1997 Bp Robert Jefferson Hargrove Jr. m 10/5/1988 Judith Anne Hoover c 3. Assoc R Epis Ch Of The Gd Shpd Lake Chas LA 1999-2002; Cn & Dir Hardtner C&C Pollock LA 1998-1999; Cur S Alb's Epis Ch Monroe LA 1997-1998; Cur S Pat's Epis Ch W Monroe LA 1997-1998. abbacliff@ymail.com

RUDACILLE, Stephen Lee (SwFla) 2702 Saint Cloud Oaks Dr, Valrico FL 33594 B Winchester VA 6/24/1940 s Leonard Lee Rudacille & Carolyn Boguess. BA Lynchburg Coll 1961; BD VTS 1966. D 6/21/1966 P 5/31/1967 Bp Harry Lee Doll. m 6/23/1962 Gayle Paschal c 2. R H Innoc Epis Ch Valrico FL 1976-2005; Assoc R S Ptr's Epis Ch Charlotte NC 1975-1976; Asst R S Thos' Epis Ch St Petersburg FL 1971-1975; Vic Ch Of The Trsfg Braddock Heights MD 1967-1971; Asst S Barth's Ch Baltimore MD 1966-1971. sruda@tampabay.rr.com

RUDE, David B (Chi) 711 1st Ave, Sterling IL 61081 **Part Time Gr Ch Sterling IL 2007-** B Cooperstown NY 3/9/1942 s John Kendall Rude & Esther Amanda. LTh Epis TS In Kentucky 1976. D 5/16/1976 Bp Addison Hosea P 2/25/1977 Bp Morris Fairchild Arnold. m 1/16/1999 Elizabeth A Swopes c 4. Full Time S Clare Of Assisi Rancho Cucamonga CA 2000-2007; Part Time S Ptr's Par Rialto CA 1997-1998; Part Time S Jos Of Arimathea Mssn Yucca Vlly CA 1995-1997; Part time S Columba's Epis Mssn Big Bear Lake CA 1994-1995; Part Time S Hilary's Epis Ch Hesperia CA 1993-1994; Trin Epis Ch Redlands CA 1990-1993; Asst All SS Epis Ch Riverside CA 1982-1990; Full Time Ch Of S Jn The Evang Hingham MA 1976-1979. frdavidr@aol.com

RUDER, John Williams (Oly) 602 6th St., Castlegar BC V1N2G1 Canada B Albuquerque NM 9/29/1949 s John Herman Ruder & Mary Jane. BS U of Wisconsin 1971; MDiv Nash 1974. D 4/19/1974 Bp Charles Thomas Gaskell P 12/21/1974 Bp William Hampton Brady. m 5/18/1974 Karen Kraemer. Vic S Columba's Epis Ch And Chilren's Sch Kent WA 1996-2009; Dio Fond du Lac Appleton WI 1974-1977; Vic S Mk's Ch Oconto WI 1974-1977; Vic S Paul's Ch Suamico WI 1974-1977. Theta Alpha Phi. mjohnwr@aol.com

RUDINOFF, Jan Charles (Haw) 2775 Kanani St, Lihue HI 96766 B Philadelphia PA 3/31/1942 s Mortimer Rudinoff & Virginia. BA VMI 1964; MDiv VTS 1972. D 5/27/1972 Bp Robert Bruce Hall P 5/10/1973 Bp J(ohn) Joseph Meakins Harte. m 3/2/1976 Paula B Rudinoff. Vic Chr Memi Ch Kilauea HI 1982-1984; S Mich And All Ang Ch Lihue HI 1976-2004; Vic St Thos Ch Hanalei HI 1974-1982; Assoc S Phil's In The Hills Tucson AZ 1972-1974. Auth, "Mnstry in Resort Communities," *Alb*, 1988. rudinoff@aloha.net

RUDOLPH, Patrick Charles (FdL) 3130 Carney Ave, Marinette WI 54143 **D S Paul's Ch Marinette WI 1996-** B Marinette WI 6/27/1940 s Patrick Rudolph & Dorothy. BA U of Wisconsin 1978. D 9/12/1996 Bp Russell Edward Jacobus. m 1/16/1960 Jacqueline Rudolph c 1. deaconpcr@hotmail.com

RUEF, John Samuel (SVa) Po Box 1143, Chatham VA 24531 B Chicago IL 1/24/1927 s John Evangelist Ruef & Leota Alice. BA U Chi 1945; BD SWTS 1950; STM SWTS 1955; ThD Harvard DS 1960. D 5/1/1950 Bp Wallace E Conkling P 1/27/1951 Bp Charles L Street. m 10/11/1951 Jane Holt c 4. Emm Epis Ch Chatham VA 1993; Trin Ch Gretna VA 1993; Chatham Hall Chatham VA 1985-1993; Nash Nashotah WI 1974-1985; Assoc S Paul's Memi Charlottesville VA 1971-1972; Ya Berk New Haven CT 1960-1971; Asst S Anne's Ch Lowell MA 1959-1960; Asst Instr SWTS Evanston IL 1954-1956; Vic Ch Of The H Fam Pk Forest IL 1950-1954. Auth, "The NT and the Sacraments of the Ch," Self-Pub, 1973; Auth, "Paul's First Letter to Corinth," Penguin Books, 1971; Auth, "Understanding the Gospels," Seabury Press, 1963. Angl Assn of Biblic Sci. DD SWTS 1975. revruef@gamewood.net

RUEHLEN, Petroula Kephala (Tex) 3541 Adrienne Ln, Lake Charles LA 70605 **Int H Trin Epis Ch Sulphur LA 2007-** B Greece 5/7/1938 d Constantinos Kephalas & Athena. Epis TS of The SW; BA U Thessaliniki 1961; MA LSU 1965. D 5/23/1981 Bp Willis Ryan Henton P 1/19/1991 Bp Robert Jefferson Hargrove Jr. m 9/15/1962 Thomas Ruehlen. R H Trin Epis Ch Port Neches TX 1992-2001; Ecum Off Dio Wstrn Louisiana Alexandria LA 1991-1992; R Gr Ch Lake Providence LA 1991-1992; Lake Chas Convoc D Dio Wstrn Louisiana Alexandria LA 1981-1990. petroularuehlen@aol.com

RUFFINO, Russell Gabriel (Eur) Corso Cavour, 110, C.P. #81, Orvieto 05018 Italy B Jersey City NJ 7/2/1933 s Anthony Ruffino & Josephie Catherine. STL Gregorian U 1954; BA Seton Hall U/Immac Concep Sem 1954; PhD Gregorian U 1961. Rec from Roman Catholic 10/27/1990 as Priest Bp George Nelson Hunt III. m 8/1/1970 Barbara Ann Casey c 2. Chair, Cler Assn Dio Rhode Island Providence RI 1993-1997; R S Ptr's By The Sea Narragansett RI 1991-2005; Asst S Lk's Ch Pawtucket RI 1990-1991. Auth, *Analysis & Critique of BF Skinner*; Ed, *Responsibility of Dissent*. FVC 2003. russellruffino@yahoo.com

RUGGLES, Roxanne (USC) Saint James Episcopal Church, 301 Piney Mountain Rd, Greenville SC 29609 **Asst R S Jas Epis Ch Greenville SC 2010-** B Georgetown OH 11/19/1952 d Robert Elwood Ruggles & Shirley Grace. BA Asbury Coll 1975; MAR Asbury TS 1977; MDiv Epis TS of the SW 2009. D 1/18/2009 Bp Stacy F Sauls P 4/30/2010 Bp Rogers Sanders Harris. c 2. Stwdshp Dir S Dav's Ch Austin TX 2009-2010. butterflyrocks@juno.com

RUGH, Nathan (Los) 1227 4th St, Santa Monica CA 90401 **Cur Calv Ch Pittsburgh PA 2006-** B Bethlehem PA 9/27/1973 s Alex Rugh & Lucy. BA U CO 2000; MDiv VTS 2006. D 6/10/2006 P 12/14/2006 Bp Robert John O'Neill. m 6/17/2009 Rebecca Rugh c 3. nate.rugh@gmail.com

✠ **RUIZ RESTREPO, Rt Rev Luis Fernando** (EcuC) Carrera 80 #53 A 78, Medellin Colombia B Medellin CO 3/23/1956 s Edildo Octavio Ruiz & Isabel. Simon Bolivar U; Coast Corporetion U Tokyo Jp 1982; BTh S Thos U 1988. D 12/8/1988 P 10/21/1990 Bp Bernardo Merino-Botero Con 8/1/2009 for Central Ecu. m 9/7/1991 Tania Jaramillo. Bp Cntrl Dio Ecuador EC 2009-2011; Iglesia Epis En Colombia 2007-2008.

RUK, Michael Raymond (Pa) 89 Pinewood Dr, Levittown PA 19054 **All SS Epis Ch Fallsington PA 2007-; R S Paul Ch Levittown PA 2004-** B Natrona

Heights PA 2/4/1974 BA Alleg 1996; MA Duquesne U 1999; MDiv Nash 2003. D 6/14/2003 P 12/21/2003 Bp Robert William Duncan. Asst Trin Cathd Pittsburgh PA 2003-2004. stpaullevittown@hotmail.com

RULE, Alan R (CFla) 216 Orange Ave, Daytona Beach FL 32114 B Beloit WI 9/14/1942 s Richard S Rule & Gertrude A. Nash; U of Wisconsin; U of Wisconsin; U of Wisconsin; Rock Cnty Law Enforcement Acad 1966. D 4/28/1973 Bp Donald H V Hallock P 11/1/1973 Bp Charles Thomas Gaskell. m 7/20/1963 Beverly Walsh c 3. S Mary's Epis Ch Daytona Bch FL 1982-1998; St Mich & The Ang Ch Platteville WI 1977-1979; S Andr's Epis Ch Monroe WI 1974-1979. arule53@twcry.rr.com

RULE II, John Henry (Okla) 1122 E 20th St, Tulsa OK 74120 B Wichita KS 12/15/1951 s John Henry Rule & Carol May. BA Oklahoma City U 1972; JD U of Texas 1977; MDiv VTS 2005. D 6/25/2005 P 1/7/2006 Bp Robert Manning Moody. m 11/11/1995 Paula R Inman c 3. Cur S Jn's Epis Ch Tulsa OK 2005-2006. BroSA 1999. jhrule@gmail.com

RUMPLE, John Glenn (Ind) 550 University Blvd # 1410, Indianapolis IN 46202 **D S Mk's Ch Plainfield IN 2011-** B Danville IN 9/3/1969 s Robert B Rumple & Shirley Kay. MDiv Emm Sch of Rel 1995; Phd in N.T. U of Edinburgh 2009; Angl Dplma The GTS 2011. D 6/18/2011 Bp Catherine Elizabeth Maples Waynick. johnrumple@hotmail.com

RUNDLE, Gary Burrows (Mass) Po Box 633, Waldoboro ME 04572 B Meriden CT 6/27/1935 s Leslie Brice Rundle & Dorothy Baldwin. BA Wesl 1957; BD VTS 1962. D 6/23/1962 Bp Walter H Gray P 3/5/1964 Bp John Henry Esquirol. m 8/3/1979 Carol Richenburg c 2. R S Mary's Epis Ch Dorchester MA 1980-1988; S Jn's Ch Winthrop MA 1979-1980; R S Dunstans Epis Ch Dover MA 1968-1978; Asst S Jn's Ch Beverly Farms MA 1964-1968; Cur Chr And H Trin Ch Westport CT 1962-1964. rundlecargar@aol.com

RUNDLETT, Brad (Va) St Timothy's Episcopal Church, 432 Van Buren St, Herndon VA 20170 **R S Tim's Ch Herndon VA 1994-** B Atlanta GA 8/9/1949 s Brewster Rundlett & Prudence Ayers. BA U GA 1972; MDiv STUSo 1981. D 6/13/1981 P 5/15/1982 Bp William Arthur Beckham. m 10/7/1989 Cecile D DeOrnellas c 5. R S Andr The Fisherman Epis Mayo MD 1989-1993; Assoc R S Jas Ch Potomac MD 1984-1989; Vic Epiph Ch Spartanburg SC 1981-1984. bradr@saint-timothys.org

RUNGE, Phillip Diedrich (Ga) 338 Lakeview Dr, Baxley GA 31513 **D S Thos Aquinas Mssn Baxley GA 2009-** B Arrington England 11/17/1957 D 5/20/2001 Bp Roger John White. D S Matt's Ch Kenosha WI 2001-2009. phildrunge@aol.com

RUNGE, Thomas L (Lex) 7 Court Pl, Newport KY 41071 **D S Paul's Ch Newport KY 2009-** B Covington KY 5/3/1945 s Wilfred Charles Runge & Clara May. Coll of Mt. St. Jos 1995. Rec from Roman Catholic 8/22/2009 Bp Stacy F Sauls. m 10/2/1999 Shelia Dodd c 4. golftom@zoomtown.com

RUNKLE, John Ander (WA) Washington National Cathedral, 3101 Wisconsin Ave NW, Washington DC 20016 **Consulting Proj Mgr for the Reconstruction of H Trin Cathd in Port-au-Prince, Haiti Epis Ch Cntr New York NY 2011-; Asst to the R S Mary's Epis Ch Arlington VA 2010-** B Greenville NC 7/12/1957 s Charles David Runkle & Mary Stella. BA Mary Baldwin Coll 1981; BArch U of Tennessee 1984; MDiv STUSo 1999. D 6/2/1999 Bp A(rthur) Heath Light P 12/11/1999 Bp Frank Neff Powell. m 7/14/1984 Harriet B Barksdale c 1. Cathd Conservator Cathd of St Ptr & St Paul Washington DC 2005-2010; Int R Ch Of The Gd Shpd Rocky Mt NC 2003-2004; Assoc R Chr Epis Ch Roanoke VA 1999-2003. Auth, "The Gift," *Stone & Light: A Celebration of a H Place*, The SSJE, 2010; Auth, "Hidden Eternity: Marking A Sacr Space," *Living Stones: Washington Natl Cathd at 100*, Washington Natl Cathd, 2007; Auth, "Bldg and Renovating Ch: Pstr Dimensions of Sacr Space," *Sewanee Theol Revs 49:3*, U So TS, 2006; Ed/Auth, "Searching For Sacr Space," Ch Pub, 2002. Cathd Architects Assn, UK 2006; HSEC 2007. Fell-in-Res U So TS 2004. jrunkle9@verizon.net

RUNNELS, Rufus Stanley (WMo) 11 E 40th St, Kansas City MO 64111 **R S Paul's Ch Kansas City MO 2006-** B Hattiesburg MS 3/22/1952 s Jessie James Runnels & Florence Elaine. BS Millsaps Coll 1974; MDiv STUSo 1983; Merrill Fell Harvard DS 2002. D 5/25/1983 Bp Christoph Keller Jr P 2/2/1984 Bp Duncan Montgomery Gray Jr. m 2/16/1980 Mary Guyton Holley c 3. R S Jn's Ch Laurel MS 1989-2006; R S Steph's Epis Ch Indianola MS 1985-1989; Vic S Mary's Ch Enterprise MS 1983-1985; Cur S Paul's Epis Ch Meridian MS 1983-1985; Vic Trin Ch Newton MS 1983-1985. Chas Merrill Fllshp Harvard Div, Harv 2002. stan.runnels@gmail.com

RUNNER, Paul W (RI) 370 Main St, Wakefield RI 02879 **R Ch Of The Ascen Wakefield RI 2010-** B Camden NJ 7/3/1947 s Edward Joseph Runner & Elizabeth Marie. Trenton St Coll 1968; BS Athens St U 1970; MDiv STUSo 1988. D 6/11/1988 Bp George Phelps Mellick Belshaw P 1/1/1989 Bp Vincent King Pettit. m 2/8/1969 Karen E Kerr c 1. R Trin Ch Cranston RI 1996-2010; R Ch Of The Atone Stratford NJ 1991-1996; Asst Trin Ch Moorestown NJ 1988-1990. WRUNNER105@AOL.COM

RUNNING JR, Joseph Martin (EC) 3207 Notting Hill Rd, Fayetteville NC 28311 **P-in-c S Paul's Epis Ch Clinton NC 2011-** B Minneapolis MN 8/7/1945 s Joseph Martin Running & Jeanne Louise. BA Langston U 1987; MDiv GTS 2001. D 6/9/2001 Bp David Conner Bane Jr P 12/15/2001 Bp Edwin Max Leidel Jr. m 6/3/1988 Maureen Elizabeth Somers c 3. R All SS' Epis Ch Duncan OK 2005-2010; R S Jn's Epis Ch Alma MI 2001-2005. jrunning@att.net

RUNNION, Norman Ray (Vt) Po Box 415, Brookfield VT 05036 B Kansas City MO 10/14/1929 s Ray Runnion & Winifred. BD NWU 1951; MDiv VTS 1993. D 6/12/1993 Bp Daniel Lee Swenson P 12/5/1993 Bp Mary Adelia Rosamond McLeod. m 7/10/1993 Linda Wangsness Runnion c 1. R S Mart's Epis Ch Fairlee VT 1993-2001. Auth, "Up The Ivy Ladder"; Auth, "Gemini"; Auth, "Vt Odyssey". nrunnion@sover.net

RUOF, George Christian (EpisSanJ) 4147 East Dakota At Cedar, Fresno CA 93726 B Buffalo NY 5/29/1924 s Adolf Ruof & Minnie. BA SUNY 1949; MDiv PDS 1952. D 6/9/1952 P 5/1/1953 Bp Lauriston L Scaife. m 12/27/1948 Margaret McCullor. COM Epis Dio San Joaquin Modesto CA 1979-1992; S Jas Epis Cathd Fresno CA 1979-1992; Stndg Com Dio Wstrn New York Tonawanda NY 1976-1979; Cmsn For The Mnstry Dio Wstrn New York Tonawanda NY 1971-1979; Stndg Com Dio Wstrn New York Tonawanda NY 1970-1973; R Trin Epis Ch Hamburg NY 1958-1979; Vic S Paul's Epis Ch Angola NY 1954-1958; Cur S Simon's Ch Buffalo NY 1952-1954.

RUPP, Lawrence Dean (SO) 1 Balsam Acres, New London NH 03257 B Wauseon OH 7/14/1933 s Dewey Victorious Rupp & Alice Carrie. MDiv EDS 1961; Bos 1968; BA Coll of Wooster 1985. D 6/24/1961 Bp Anson Phelps Stokes Jr P 4/19/1962 Bp Roger W Blanchard. m 6/4/1982 Gail Skillings c 1. Asst Min Emm Epis Ch Wakefield MA 1965-1966; Asst Gr Epis Ch Medford MA 1963-1964; Asst S Paul And S Jas New Haven CT 1962-1963; Asst Emm Ch Boston MA 1961-1962. Faith & Sci Exch, Inst On Rel In An Age Of Sci. rlawrenc@tds.net

RUPP, Lloyd Gary (Nev) 43 West Pacific Ave, Henderson NV 89015 B Seattle WA 2/27/1935 s Lloyd Raymond Rupp & Beverly Doris. MA CDSP; SFTS; AA Antelope Vlly Coll 1956; BA California St U 1958; BD CDSP 1964; MS CPU 1985; PhD CPU 1987. D 7/22/1964 P 4/1/1965 Bp Clarence Rupert Haden Jr. c 2. R S Tim's Epis Ch Henderson NV 2001-2007; Gr And H Trin Cathd Kansas City MO 1987-2002; Off Of Bsh For ArmdF New York NY 1968-1986; Vic Ch Of The Gd Shpd Orland CA 1966-1968; Vic S Andr's Mssn Corning CA 1966-1968. OHC 1960. lgrvlr@aol.com

RUPPE, David Robert (SO) 25005 SR 26, New Matamoras OH 45767 **R S Lk's Ch Marietta OH 2009-** B Rutherfordton NC 7/9/1949 s James Avant Ruppe & Ruby Mae. BA Duke 1971; MDiv UTS 1975; PhM Col 1981; PhD Col 1988. D 6/11/1977 Bp Paul Moore Jr P 12/17/1977 Bp Harold Louis Wright. m 3/30/1975 Karen I Starling c 3. Bex Columbus OH 1999-2006; Dn of Angl Acad Dio Sthrn Ohio Cincinnati OH 1999-2004; R Trin Epis Ch Seneca Falls NY 1993-1999; Exec Coun Appointees New York NY 1991-1992; S Barth's Ch Pewaukee WI 1988-1991; Asst Prof NT Nash Nashotah WI 1985-1991; Secy Dio Cntrl New York Syracuse NY 1982-1983; R Ch Of The Sav Syracuse NY 1981-1983; P The Ch of S Matt And S Tim New York NY 1977-1980. davidruppe@gmail.com

RUPPE-MELNYK, Glyn Lorraine (Pa) 689 Sugartown Road, Malvern PA 19355 **R S Fran-In-The-Fields Malvern PA 2001-** B Camp Lejeune NC 2/21/1950 d James R Ruppe & Syble M. BA Old Dominion U 1970; MDiv TS 1992. D 6/27/1992 Bp Henry Irving Mayson P 6/27/1993 Bp R(aymond) Stewart Wood Jr. m 11/1/2011 W(alter) William Melnyk c 2. R Chr Epis Ch Tarrytown NY 1998-2001; R S Jas-In-The-Hills Epis Ch Hollywood FL 1994-1997; Asst R Chr Ch Detroit MI 1992-1994; Consult Sprtl Dir Dio Michigan Detroit MI 1990-1992. Contrib, "Wmn Uncommon Prayers," Morehouse, 2001; Auth, "Feminism Without Illusions," *Sewanee Theol Revs*, 1992. Cmnty Of S Mary. rectorstfrancisfields@verizon.net

RUSCHMEYER, Henry Cassell (NY) 2929 SE Ocean Blvd Apt M9, Stuart FL 34496 B New York NY 1/9/1944 s Henry Karl Ruschmeyer & Josephine Cecilia. BA Un Coll Schenectady, NY 1966; MS Educ Bank St Coll of Educ 1973; MDiv GTS 1978; MA NYU 1988. D 6/17/1978 Bp Robert Campbell Witcher Sr P 1/6/1979 Bp Wilbur Emory Hogg Jr. Asst Ch Of The Redeem Sarasota FL 2002-2003; Asst Ch Of The Gd Shpd New York NY 1983-1989; Cur Ch Of The Ascen New York NY 1981-1983; Asst S Geo's Ch Clifton Pk NY 1980-1981; Cur S Ptr's Ch Albany NY 1978-1980. Auth, "Chateaugay Lake: The Adirondack Resort Era, 1830-1917," Serbin, 2010. hruschmeyer@uw211manasota.net

RUSHTON, Joseph M (Md) P O BOX 602, Georgetown DE 19947 **R S Paul's Ch Georgetown DE 2011-** B Baltimore MD 4/2/1955 s John Rushton & Gertrude Lucille. BA Mt St. Mary's U 1977; MDiv U of Notre Dame 1980; MS U of Maryland 1989; Post-Grad Dip., Angl VTS 2007. Rec from Roman Catholic 1/7/2007 Bp Robert Wilkes Ihloff. m 5/27/2004 Francis Nicholas Codd. Int Ch Of The Gd Shpd Ruxton MD 2011; Int Ch Of The H Comf Luthvle Timon MD 2009-2011; Assoc Trin Ch Towson MD 2007-2009. joerushton@verizon.net

RUSLING, Julia Griswold (Roch) 432 Lockwood Ter., Decatur GA 30030 B Rochester NY 1/9/1969 d Thomas Griswold Rusling & Ellen. MDiv Ya Berk; BA Ob; BA Ob. D 9/24/2000 Bp David John Bena P 3/24/2001 Bp Daniel William Herzog. m 6/22/1996 Daniel Jin Lee. Chr Ch Pittsford NY 2005-2006; Calv Epis Ch Burnt Hills NY 2000-2001.

RUSS JR, Frank D (SC) 1159 Wyndham Rd, Charleston SC 29412 **Bp Gadsden Epis Cmnty Charleston SC 2007-** B Burgaw NC 10/2/1954 s Frank Dobinson Russ & Barbara Woodcock. BA U NC 1976; MDiv SE Bapt TS Wake Forest NC 1981; DAS VTS 1991; E Carolina U 2001. D 6/22/1991 P 12/27/1991 Bp Brice Sidney Sanders. The Ch of S Matt And S Tim New York NY 2004-2007; R S Fran Ch Goldsboro NC 1996-2004; Asst To The Bp For Prog & Mnstry Dio E Carolina Kinston NC 1994-1996; R S Christophers Ch Elizabethtown NC 1991-1994. frank.russ@bishopgadsden.org

RUSSELL, Ann Veronica (VI) Box 3066, Sea Cow's Bay, Tortola British Virgin Island VG 1110 British Virgin Islands B Fulham England 11/26/1935 d Charles Lansdell & Claire. BA Hull U; MA Wright St U; Tchr Trained Brentwood Teachers Trng Coll 1966. D 6/14/2008 Bp Edward Ambrose Gumbs. m 11/25/1960 Ronald Russell c 4. russellann73@hotmail.com

RUSSELL JR, Carl Asa (Me) 9 Perkins Rd, Boothbay Harbor ME 04538 **S Paul's Epis Ch Brighton MI 2006-; S Columba's Epis Ch Boothbay Harbor ME 1997-** B Portland ME 8/18/1936 s Carl Asa Russell & Ruth Elizabeth. BA Bow 1958; M.Div. GTS 1961; Fllshp Coll of Preachers 1971. D 5/27/1961 P 12/21/1961 Bp Oliver L Loring. m 6/14/1958 Margaret Ellen Street c 4. Chr Ch Shaker Heights OH 2003-2004; R S Paul's Ch Darien CT 1992-1996; R Chr Ch Fitchburg MA 1982-1992; Dio Wstrn Massachusetts Springfield MA 1981-1992; Trin Epis Ch Portland ME 1971-1981; R S Andr's Ch Millinocket ME 1963-1971; Vic S Thos Ch Winn ME 1961-1963. dulcenea59@yahoo.com

RUSSELL, Carlton Thrasher (Mass) 27 Abnaki Way, Stockton Springs ME 04981 **Mus Dir/Org S Fran By The Sea Blue Hill ME 2006-** B Keene NH 7/29/1938 s Jay Harold Russell & Nina Laura. BA Amh 1960; Cert AGO 1962; MFA Pr 1962; PhD Pr 1966; MA EDS 1983. D 6/2/1984 Bp John Bowen Coburn P 5/14/1985 Bp Roger W Blanchard. m 8/15/1964 Lorna Smithers Brookes. Assoc Trin Epis Ch Wrentham MA 1985-2005. Auth, *w Grateful Gladness: The Wheaton Organ at 30 CD Rcrdng*, Wheaton Coll, 1999; Auth, "sev arts(Ch Mus), anthems," *and Serv settings*. OHC, Assoc. crussell@wheatonma.edu

RUSSELL, D(aniel) Scott (SwVa) 202 Roanoke St E, Blacksburg VA 24060 **Assoc R Chr Ch Blacksburg VA 2003-; Campus Min at Virginia Tech Chr Ch Blacksburg VA 2003-** B Baltimore MD 1/21/1968 s Richard Wells Russell & Patricia Joann. BA Asbury U 1990; MDiv TESM 2001. D 6/15/2002 P 12/22/2002 Bp Robert William Duncan. Chair, COM in Higher Educ Dio SW Virginia Roanoke VA 2004-2007; Exec Bd Dio SW Virginia Roanoke VA 2004-2007. "Film Revs," *New Dictionary of Chr Apologetics*, InterVarsity Press, 2006. canterburyvt@yahoo.com

RUSSELL, Jack Dempsey (Tex) 800 E Hudson St, Tyler TX 75701 B Corsicana TX 9/6/1927 s Jeff Davis Russell & Donia Inez. BS Texas A&M U 1948; BD Epis TS of The SW 1956; MDiv Epis TS of The SW 1971. D 7/6/1956 P 6/29/1957 Bp John E Hines. c 3. Assoc Chr Epis Ch Tyler TX 2000-2003; Chair of the Div of Coll Dio Texas Houston TX 1989-1992; R S Geo's Epis Ch Port Arthur TX 1984-1992; Cn to the Ordnry Dio Dallas Dallas TX 1979-1984; R S Paul's Epis Ch Greenville TX 1969-1979; R S Mths Epis Ch Shreveport LA 1962-1969; R S Mary's Ch Bellville TX 1957-1962.

RUSSELL, John Alan (WNY) 768 Potomac Ave, Buffalo NY 14209 B Philadelphia PA 8/19/1932 s Steuart Frederick Russell & Mary Alice. LCSW St of New York; BA GW 1956; MDiv Ya Berk 1959; MSW St of New York 1970. D 4/25/1959 P 10/31/1959 Bp Alfred L Banyard. m 6/11/1982 Debra Lee Lefferts. Vic S Pat's Ch Cheektowaga NY 2006-2011; Int S Phil's Ch Buffalo NY 2001-2005; R S Jude's Ch Buffalo NY 1992-2000; Vic S Aid's Ch Alden NY 1987-1992; S Dav's Epis Ch W Seneca NY 1987; Assoc S Jn's Gr Ch Buffalo NY 1984-1987; S Mart In The Fields Grand Island NY 1969-1980; Assoc P Calv Epis Ch Williamsville NY 1967-1969; R S Andr's Epis Ch Lawton OK 1964-1967. Auth, "Var arts". cl Berkeley Div Sch At Yale 1959. johnar@iopener.net

RUSSELL, Kathleen Sams (SanD) 3112 James Street, San Diego CA 92106 **Epis TS Of The SW Austin TX 2005-** B Buffalo NY 2/25/1947 d Edward J Sams & Grace M. BA Daemen Coll 1968; MDiv SWTS 1989. D 6/17/1989 P 12/1/1989 Bp Frank Tracy Griswold III. m 7/15/1972 Michael Bennett Russell c 2. S Andr's By The Sea Epis Par San Diego CA 2000-2004. krussell@ssw.edu

RUSSELL, Kenneth P (Ore) 5311 Sw Wichita St, Tualatin OR 97062 B Seattle WA 5/28/1960 s Paul James Russell & Catherine Mae. BS OR SU 1982; JD Lewis & Clark Coll 1985. D 9/30/2000 Bp Robert Louis Ladehoff. m 8/14/1982 Cindra Helene Foote c 2. Chr Ch Par Lake Oswego OR 2000-2007. kenrus@comcast.net

RUSSELL, Margaret Ellen Street (Me) 9 Perkins Rd, Boothbay Harbor ME 04538 **Dio Maine Portland ME 1996-** B Portland ME USA 5/24/1937 d Nathanael Street & Margaret Christina. 3 years Mid; BA U of Sthrn Maine 1976; MA Lesley U 1986; MDiv Ya Berk 1995. D 6/8/1996 P 12/1/1996 Bp Clarence Nicholas Coleridge. m 6/14/1958 Carl Asa Russell c 4. Vic S Columba's Epis Ch Boothbay Harbor ME 1997-2006; S Paul's Ch Darien CT 1996-1997. grussell524@yahoo.com

RUSSELL, Michael Bennett (SanD) 3112 James St, San Diego CA 92106 **R All Souls' Epis Ch San Diego CA 1999-** B Baltimore MD 9/15/1949 s Harry Lawrence Russell & Avis Patricia. BA U of Virginia 1973; MA Chicago TS 1975; MDiv SWTS 1986. D 6/14/1986 Bp James Winchester Montgomery P 12/1/1986 Bp Frank Tracy Griswold III. m 7/15/1972 Kathleen Sams Russell c 2. R Gr Ch Elkridge MD 1989-1999; Ch Of S Paul And The Redeem Chicago IL 1986-1989. Auth, "Greenville: The Non-Un Culture: Sthrn Exposure"; Auth, "Via Media"; Auth, "Political Grief," *An Exploration Of Grieving*. michael.pointloma@gmail.com

RUSSELL, Patricia Griffith (NwT) 1802 Broadway, Lubbock TX 79401 **Cbury Epis Campus Mnstry at Texas Tech Lubbock TX 2010-; Chapl Dio NW Texas Lubbock TX 2010-** B San Angelo TX 10/14/1947 d Brandon H Griffith & Margaret Madden. BA U of Oklahoma 1971; ADN Hartnell Coll 1978; MPA U of Oklahoma 1983. D 9/20/2008 Bp C(harles) Wallis Ohl P 3/28/2009 Bp James Scott Mayer. m 7/30/1988 William F Russell c 4. patrussell@ransomcanyon.net

RUSSELL, Sherrill Ann (WMo) 7110 N State Route 9, Kansas City MO 64152 B Macon MO 1/15/1937 d Harold M Brush & Shirley Lee Thomas. No Degree Cntrl Bapt TS; BS Cntrl Missouri U 1960; MS K SU 1981. D 2/5/2011 Bp Barry Robert Howe. m 1/7/1961 Charles Edward Russell c 3. sherrill@kc.rr.com

RUSSELL, Susan Hayden (Mass) 72 Cavendish Circle, Salem MA 01970 B Newton MA 11/30/1943 d Jesse Lloyd Hayden & Alice Sarah. BA Ob 1965; MDiv SWTS 1998. D 6/20/1998 P 1/23/1999 Bp J Clark Grew II. m 8/3/1968 John Merrill Russell c 2. P-in-c Wyman Memi Ch of St Andr Marblehead MA 2008-2011; COM Dio Ohio Cleveland OH 2007-2008; R All SS Ch Parma OH 2000-2008; Asst R S Paul's Epis Ch Medina OH 1998-2000. Ord of S Helena 1971. revsusan54@gmail.com

RUSSELL, Susan Lynn Brown (Los) 680 Mountain View St, Altadena CA 91001 **Exec Dir All SS Ch Pasadena CA 2002-** B Los Angeles CA 6/10/1954 d William Comstock Brown & Betty. BA U CA 1976; MDiv Claremont TS 1996. D 6/1/1996 P 1/17/1998 Bp Frederick Houk Borsch. m 4/21/1979 Anthony Edwin Russell c 2. Asst S Ptr's Par San Pedro CA 1998-2002; Asst S Mk's Par Altadena CA 1996. revsusanrussell@earthlink.net

RUSSELL, Tracy Johnson (Ct) 89 Lenox St Unit N, New Haven CT 06513 **S Thos's Day Sch New Haven CT 2011-; S Andr's Ch New Haven CT 2003-** B Indianapolis IN 9/20/1969 BA Mia 1991; MDiv Ya Berk 1995; MA Quinnipiac U 1997. D 6/20/2003 P 7/24/2004 Bp Andrew Donnan Smith. m 3/21/2009 Fitzroy Russell. tlmjoh5683@global.net

RUSSELL, William Hamilton (LI) 101 Cambridge Trail Apt 193, Sun City Center FL 33573 B New York NY 7/10/1928 s William Hamilton Russell & Marie Gallard. BA U of Virginia 1951; Mercer TS 1981. D 6/1/1981 P 6/11/1988 Bp Robert Campbell Witcher Sr. m 9/6/1969 Elizabeth Buck Truslow c 1. P Assoc S Jn The Div Epis Ch Sun City Cntr FL 2002-2003; R S Paul's Ch Patchogue NY 1989-1998; Asst S Jn's Ch Huntington NY 1986-1989; D H Trin Epis Ch Hicksville NY 1983-1989; D S Marg's Ch Plainview NY 1982-1983. frgrazing@msn.com

RUSSELL, William LaBarre (Tex) 15015 Memorial Dr, Houston TX 77079 **Died 2/15/2010** B Palmerton PA 12/16/1931 s William Paul Shively Shively Russell & Margaret Labarre. BA Leh 1952; STB Ya Berk 1955; Dur 1960; MA Midwestern St U 1966; U of No Texas 1969. D 6/14/1955 P 12/17/1955 Bp Matthew G Henry. c 1.

RUTENBAR, C(harles) Mark (WTenn) 8238 Greengate Cove, Memphis TN 38018 **Bp & Coun Dio W Tennessee Memphis TN 2008-; R Ch Of The H Comm Memphis TN 2006-; Cmsn On Mnstry Dio Wstrn Michigan Kalamazoo MI 1994-** B New Haven CT 10/4/1953 s Howard Charles Rutenbar & Jeanne. Dplma Cranbrook Sch Bloomfield Hills MI 1972; BA SMU 1976; MDiv VTS 1980. D 6/11/1980 Bp Arthur Anton Vogel P 12/1/1980 Bp Addison Hosea. m 8/18/1979 Larae Jordan c 2. R S Lk's Par Kalamazoo MI 1994-2006; Stndg Comm Dio Atlanta Atlanta GA 1989-1992; R S Paul's Ch Macon GA 1988-1994; Asst Emm Epis Ch Athens GA 1982-1988; Sprtl Dir Dio Lexington Lexington KY 1980-1982; Cur Trin Ch Covington KY 1980-1981. mrutenbar@holycommunion.org

RUTENBAR, Larae Jordan (WMich) 8238 Greengate Cove, Cordova TN 38018 **COM Dio Wstrn Michigan Kalamazoo MI 2003-** B Loup City NE 5/29/1954 d Dale Briggs Jordan & Kathryn Marie. Pacific Luth U 1974; BA Rocky Mtn Coll 1976; MDiv VTS 1980. D 5/31/1980 Bp Jackson Earle Gilliam P 6/1/1982 Bp William Grant Black. m 8/18/1979 C(harles) Mark Rutenbar. Chr Ch Cathd Lexington KY 2010-2011; All SS' Epis Ch Tupelo MS 2007-2008; All SS Ch E Lansing MI 2005-2006; Emm Ch Petoskey MI 2004-2005; Int S Mart Of Tours Epis Ch Kalamazoo MI 2003-2004; P-in-c Epis Ch Of The Gd Shpd Allegan MI 2000-2003; Trin Epis Ch Marshall MI 1999-2000; Trin Ch Niles MI 1997-1999; Ch Of The Resurr Battle Creek MI 1997; S Jn's Epis Ch Charlotte MI 1996; Int Dio Wstrn Michigan Kalamazoo MI 1994-1996; S Thos Epis Ch Battle Creek MI 1994-1995; Comp of Dioc Com Dio Atlanta Atlanta GA 1993-1994; Asst R S Paul's Ch Macon GA 1988-1994; Comp of Dioc Com Dio Atlanta Atlanta GA 1988-1990; Int The Epis Ch Of The Adv

Madison GA 1986-1988; Supply P Dio Atlanta Atlanta GA 1982-1986; Asst Trin Ch Covington KY 1980-1981. molarae@rutenbar.com

RUTH, Margaret Foster (WMo) 402 West 50th #2 South, Kansas City MO 64112 B Denver CO 6/28/1928 d John McCullough Foster & Margaret. BA U of Kansas 1951. D 9/26/1978 Bp Arthur Anton Vogel. c 4. D S Paul's Ch Kansas City MO 1994-1996; S Andr's Ch Kansas City MO 1990-1993; S Paul's Ch Kansas City MO 1978-1993.

RUTH, Same (SwFla) 5210 Pale Moon Dr, Pensacola FL 32507 B New Britain CT 4/7/1938 BS USNA 1959; MS U of Washington 1964; MBA City U of Seattle 1982. D 1/18/2003 Bp John Bailey Lipscomb. m 6/3/1959 Ellen Marie Conner c 4. D S Jn's Ch Naples FL 2003-2006. allenrruth@hotmail.com

RUTH, Stuart Gillette (SwFla) 1763 Royal Oaks Dr., Bradbury CA 91010 B Alhambra CA 7/28/1923 s John Benton Ruth & Mary Alice. BA Br 1948; GTS 1950; BD CDSP 1951. D 5/19/1951 P 11/21/1951 Bp Frank A Rhea. c 3. Asst Ch Of Our Sav Par San Gabr CA 1978-1981; Vic S Cecilia's Ch Tampa FL 1971-1975; Asst S Mary's Par Tampa FL 1967-1971; R Ch Of The Ascen Wakefield RI 1959-1967; P-in-c All SS Ch No Granville NY 1953-1959; R Trin Ch Granville NY 1953-1959; Vic Emm Ch Hailey ID 1951-1953; Vic S Thos Epis Ch Sun Vlly ID 1951-1953.

RUTHERFORD, Allen Dale (Ind) 420 Locust Street, Mt. Vernon IN 47620 **R S Jn's Epis Ch Mt Vernon IN 2005-** B St Paul IN 3/11/1962 Cert SWTS 2004; MDiv Chr TS 2005. D 7/17/2004 P 5/22/2005 Bp Catherine Elizabeth Maples Waynick. m 6/25/1983 Lydia S Kuhn c 2. H Fam Epis Ch Fishers IN 2004-2007. rutherford317@sbcglobal.net

RUTHERFORD, Ellen Conger (NJ) 1115 New Pear Street, Vineland NJ 0836-4116 **P-in-c S Andr's Epis Ch Bridgeton NJ 2009-; P-in-c Trin Epis Ch Vineland NJ 2009-** B West Chester PA 10/8/1956 d Edwin Keatley Rutherford & Nona. BA Duke 1977; MA U Chi 1979; MDiv GTS 1989; MS Pratt Inst 2000. D 6/16/1989 P 12/17/1989 Bp Frank Tracy Griswold III. P-in-c Chr Ch Palmyra NJ 2000-2006; P-in-c Riverfront Epis Team Mnstry Riverside NJ 2000-2006; P-in-c S Steph's Ch Riverside NJ 2000-2006; Mssnr Chap Of S Jn The Div Tomkins Cove NY 1997-1999; Mssnr Chr Epis Ch Sparkill NY 1997-1999; Mssnr S Paul's Ch Sprg Vlly NY 1997-1999; Mssnr Trin Epis Ch Garnerville NY 1997-1999; R Thumb Epis Area Mnstry Deford MI 1991-1997; Assoc Paris Cluster Chadwicks NY 1989-1991. ecrutherford@juno.com

RUTHERFORD, Roy Calvert (Cal) 550 Battery St. Apt. 2210, San Francisco CA 94111 B Dallas TX 12/9/1922 s Roy Calvert Rutherford & Lillian. BS U of Texas 1948; MDiv Epis TS of The SW 1958. D 5/30/1958 Bp Everett H Jones P 6/1/1959 Bp Richard Earl Dicus. m Jean Rutherford c 3. Planned Giving Dio California San Francisco CA 1997-2000; Assoc S Fran Ch Houston TX 1967-1974; Vic Ch Of The Resurr San Antonio TX 1964-1966. Auth, "Dr. Kano's Question," lulu, 2008. Chit Chat Club of San Francisco 1992. calrutherford@aol.com

RUTHERFORD, Thomas Houston (CFla) 1260 Log Landing Drive, Ocoee FL 34761 **COM Dio Cntrl Florida Orlando FL 2003-; R Ch Of The Mssh Winter Garden FL 1996-** B Memphis TN 4/10/1955 s Oliver Houston Rutherford & Tommie Belle. Marq 1975; BS Middle Tennessee St U 1979; MDiv STUSo 1993. D 5/15/1993 Bp William Evan Sanders P 4/17/1994 Bp William Arthur Beckham. m 12/28/1980 Martha Anderson c 3. Stndg Com Dio Cntrl Florida Orlando FL 2008-2010; COM Dio Cntrl Florida Orlando FL 2003-2010; Int R S Chris's Ch Spartanburg SC 1995-1996; Asst R S Chris's Ch Spartanburg SC 1993-1995; Yth Pstr S Barth's Ch Bristol TN 1979-1990. tomrutherford@earthlink.net

R

RUTHVEN, Carol Lynn (Lex) St Andrew's Episcopal Church, 401 N Upper St, Lexington KY 40508 **S Agnes Hse Lexington KY 2008-** B Pembroke, Canada 8/20/1958 d Melvin Edwin Ruthven & Amy. BA U of Alberta Edmonton AB CA 1980; MA Queen's U Kingston ON CA 1981; PhD Queen's U Kingston ON CA 1986; MDiv U So TS 2007. D 6/9/2007 P 12/17/2007 Bp Stacy F Sauls. m 6/23/1990 Alan Fryar c 2. S Agnes Hse Lexington KY 2007-2008; S Andr's Ch Lexington KY 2007-2008. ruthvencarol@yahoo.com

RUTHVEN, Scott Alan (RG) 805 Lenox Ave., Las Cruces NM 88005 **R S Andr's Epis Ch Las Cruces NM 2003-** B Los Alamos NM 10/9/1955 s William James Ruthven & Lenora Mae. BA Rockmont Coll 1984; MDiv TESM 1988. D 6/11/1988 Bp William Carl Frey P 12/1/1988 Bp Jeffery William Rowthorn. m 7/14/1979 Mary Jo Moody c 3. R S Jn's Epis Ch Alamogordo NM 1992-2003; R Ch Of The Ascen High Rolls NM 1992; Asst Trin Ch Tariffville CT 1988-1992. SBL. frscott@zianet.com

RUTLAND, Edward Cumpston (Dal) 6106 Sagebrush Ave, Texarkana TX 75503 B Houston TX 2/10/1926 s James Walter Rutland & Margaret Douglas. U So 1947; U of Texas 1952; Epis TS of The SW 1955. D 7/1/1955 Bp Clinton Simon Quin P 7/3/1956 Bp Frederick P Goddard. m 6/1/1952 Laura Taylor c 3. Supply S Mk's Ch Hope AR 1995-2000; Int Trin NE Texas Epis Ch Mt Pleasant TX 1993-1995; Vic All SS Ch Atlanta TX 1991-1993; Vic S Mart Epis Ch New Boston TX 1991-1993; R S Mary's Epis Ch Texarkana TX 1986-1991; Exec Coun Dio Dallas Dallas TX 1984-1986; R S Dav's Ch Denton TX 1975-1986; Exec Coun Dio Dallas Dallas TX 1970-1972; R Chr The King Epis Ch Ft Worth TX 1968-1973; R Ch Of The Epiph Independence KS 1960-1968; Assoc S Geo's Epis Ch Arlington VA 1958-1960; Mssy S Mk's Ch Gladewater TX 1957-1958; Vic S Jn's Epis Ch Carthage TX 1955-1958; Asst Chr Ch San Aug TX 1955-1957. Auth, "Var arts," *LivCh*, 1995; Auth, *The H Mysteries*, Morehouse-Barlow, 1958; Auth, "Var arts," *Epis*. HSEC 1955. ecrtxktx@aol.com

RUTLEDGE, Fleming (NY) 38 Hillandale Rd, Rye Brook NY 10573 B Richmond VA 11/24/1937 d John Crump Parker & Alice Saunders. BA Sweet Briar Coll 1959; GTS 1975; MDiv UTS 1975. D 6/14/1975 Bp Paul Moore Jr P 1/21/1977 Bp James Stuart Wetmore. m 10/3/1959 Reginald Rutledge c 2. Int S Jn's Ch Salisbury CT 1996-1997; Assoc Gr Epis Ch New York NY 1981-1993; Chr's Ch Rye NY 1975-1981. "Not Ashamed of the Gospel," Eerdmans, 2007; "The Seven Last Words," Eerdmans, 2005; "The Battle for Middle-earth," Eerdmans, 2004; "The Undoing of Death," Eerdmans, 2002; "Help My Unbelief," Eerdmans, 2000; "The Bible and the New York Times," Eerdmans, 1998. DD VTS 1999; Fell Cntr of Theol Inquiry Princeton New Jersey 1997. frutledge@earthlink.net

RUTLEDGE JR, Frederick Alexander (WVa) Po Box 126, Oak Hill WV 25901 **The New River Epis Mnstry Hansford WV 2006-** B Marietta OH 3/27/1951 s Frederick Alexander Rutledge & Maryls. Bex; BSIE No Carolina St U 1973; Pstr Prep Equipping the SS 2006. D 12/16/2006 P 6/16/2007 Bp William Michie Klusmeyer. m 12/28/1972 Kathy Ann Young c 3. krutledge@peoplepc.com

RUTLEDGE, Lynn Vickery (Me) 13 Garnet Head Rd, Pembroke ME 04666 **D Chr Epis Ch Eastport ME 2004-** B Texarkana AR 11/11/1950 BA U Of Houston 1972; Cert Texas A&M U 1991. D 6/19/2004 Bp Chilton Abbie Richardson Knudsen. m 6/14/1991 Richard Rutledge c 1. rutledge6046@roadrunner.com

RUTLEDGE, Theodore Elsworth (RG) 170 Sunset Ln, Tillamook OR 97141 B Puyallup WA 1/20/1923 s Keizer Eugene Rutledge & Violet Ella. BA U of Texas 1979; Epis TS of The SW 1982. D 6/24/1982 P 2/1/1983 Bp Richard Mitchell Trelease Jr. c 3. Asst R All SS Epis Ch El Paso TX 1985-1988; Dio The Rio Grande Albuquerque NM 1983-1985; Asst All SS Epis Ch El Paso TX 1982-1984.

RUTTAN, Karl D (SO) 125 E Broad St, Columbus OH 43215 **Cn Dio Sthrn Ohio Cincinnati OH 2007-** B Detroit MI 8/8/1948 s Arden Ruttan & Marjorie. BA Ken 1970; MDiv Chicago TS 1975; Cert EDS 1975; Med Duquesne U 1988; PhD Duquesne U 1998. D 6/21/1975 P 5/1/1976 Bp John Harris Burt. m 8/14/1976 Mary Barkalow c 2. R S Jn's Epis Ch Charleston WV 1994-2006; R Chr Ch Greensburg PA 1984-1994; Exec Coun Appointees New York NY 1980-1983; Asst S Andr's Epis Ch Elyria OH 1976-1980; Mssnr to YA All SS Par Brookline MA 1975-1976. H Cross 2002. DeRoo Ecum Awd WV Coun of Ch 2006. kruttan@diosohio.org

RUTTER, Deborah Wood (Va) Po Box 1306, Front Royal VA 22630 **Chair, COM Dio Virginia Richmond VA 2011-; Bd Dir S Marg's Sch Tappahannock VA 1996-2012; COM Dio Virginia Richmond VA 1996-; R Calv Epis Ch Front Royal VA 1995-** B Washington DC 2/16/1948 d Jackson Clark Smith & Anne Mary Katherine. BA W&M 1970; MDiv Pittsburgh TS 1982. D 2/15/1983 Bp Alden Moinet Hathaway P 1/7/1984 Bp Robert Bruce Hall. m 9/15/1989 George W Rutter c 2. Shrine Mont Bd Dir Dio Virginia Richmond VA 1998-2011; Int R Gr Ch Kilmarnock VA 1994-1995; Asst Gr Ch Kilmarnock VA 1992-1994; Asst R Gr Ch Kilmarnock VA 1992-1994; Exec Bd Dio Virginia Richmond VA 1989-1992; R Ch Of The Sprt Alexandria VA 1986-1992; Peace Com Dio Virginia Richmond VA 1986-1992; R Kingston Par Epis Ch Mathews VA 1986-1992; Chapl S Marg's Sch Tappahannock VA 1983-1986. revdeb3@gmail.com

RUYAK, Mark Andrew (Cal) 5 Weatherly Drive Apt 109, Mill Valley CA 94941 B Pottstown PA 10/21/1955 s Joseph Thomas Ruyak & Joanne. Bachelor of Arts Penn 1978; Mstr of Educ Penn 1981; Mstr of Div CDSP 1999. D 4/17/1999 Bp Richard Mitchell Trelease Jr P 1/22/2000 Bp Paul Victor Marshall. Int S Fran' Epis Ch San Francisco CA 2009-2011; Int Ch Of The Redeem San Rafael CA 2008-2009; Assoc Gr Cathd San Francisco CA 2000-2007; Assoc Emm Ch Baltimore MD 1999-2000. mruyak2000@comcast.net

RUYLE, Everett Eugene (At) 1195 Terramont Dr, Roswell GA 30076 B Beatrice NE 9/15/1935 s Everett Herbert Ruyle & Naomi Margaret. BA U Of Florida 1959; BD VTS 1962; PhD Un Grad Sch 1977. D 6/27/1962 P 4/1/1963 Bp Edward Hamilton West. c 3. S Mart In The Fields Ch Atlanta GA 1992-2005; Asst R H Trin Ch Gainesville FL 1964-1969; Vic Ch Of The H Comf Cres City FL 1962-1964. Auth, "Making A Life"; Auth, "Team Kit: A Trng Prog For Sm Groups". Tillich Soc.

RYAN SSM, Adele Marie (Mass) 17 Highland Park St, Boston MA 02119 **Soc Of St Marg Roxbury MA 1960-** B New York NY 6/1/1938 d George William Ryan & Evelyn. BA FD 1960; MA Luth TS, Philadelphia 1980. D 6/14/1980 P 6/10/1981 Bp Lyman Cunningham Ogilby. Cmsn on the Mnstry Dio Massachusetts Boston MA 1992-1994; Chair, Sprtl Growth Com Dio Pennsylvania Philadelphia PA 1984-1987; Asst S Lk's Ch Philadelphia PA 1980-1985. "Rel

Ord And Congregations 4:Angl," Eerdmans-Brill Encyclopedia Of Chrsnty. adelemarie@ssmbos.org

RYAN, Bartholomew Grey (Ia) 15005 Orchard Dr., 15005 Orchard Dr., Burnsville MN 55306 B Chicago IL 11/4/1950 s Vernon Robert Ryan & Barbara. BS Indiana U 1972; MA S Mary 1993; CAS Nash 1995. D 3/22/1995 P 9/1/1995 Bp William Charles Wantland. m 11/4/1972 Barbara B Borlik c 2. Trin Ch Muscatine IA 2003-2005; Trin Ch River Falls WI 2000-2003; R S Alb's Ch Superior WI 1995-2000. SSC. frryanssc@comcast.net

RYAN, David Andrew (RI) 1663 Kensington Pl, The Villages FL 32162 B Providence RI 5/1/1934 s Edward James Ryan & Lillian. BA NEU 1957; STB Ya Berk 1960; S Geo's Coll Jerusalem IL 1980; Steph Mnstry 2007. D 6/18/1960 P 12/17/1960 Bp John S Higgins. m 6/22/1957 Constance Anita Blouin c 3. Dioc Coun Dio Rhode Island Providence RI 1968-1982; R The Epis Ch Of S Andr And S Phil Coventry RI 1965-1996; R Ch Of The H Trin Tiverton RI 1962-1965; Cur S Barn Ch Warwick RI 1960-1962. 10davidconnie@comcast.net

RYAN, Dennis L (Miss) 3507 Pine St, Pascagoula MS 39567 B Biloxi MS 12/27/1947 s Adrian Elbert Ryan & Opal. Mississippi Gulf Coast Cmnty Coll; LTh STUSo 1993. D 6/12/1993 Bp Duncan Montgomery Gray Jr P 3/1/1994 Bp Alfred Clark Marble Jr. m 12/23/1966 Eva Carolyn Ryan c 3. Assoc S Jn's Epis Ch Pascagoula MS 2000-2005; Trin Ch Hattiesburg MS 1993-2000. dryan@netdoor.com

RYAN III, Frances Isabel Sells (Az) 3150 N Winding Brook Rd, Flagstaff AZ 86001 B Weyburn Saskatchewan Canada 2/28/1922 d John Francis Charles Sells & Sarah Isabelle. BA NWU 1943; MS Pur 1970; JD U of Wisconsin 1975; Cert Inst for Chr Stds 1993. D 5/21/1994 Bp Roger John White. c 4. D Ch Of The Epiph Flagstaff AZ 2002-2009; D S Andr's Ch Madison WI 1998-2001; D S Andr's Ch Madison WI 1994-1995.

RYAN, John Prime (Okla) 3300 NW 61st St, Oklahoma City OK 73112 B Lincoln,NE 1/8/1932 s Claude Clinton Ryan & Ida Florence. BA Ken 1954; STB GTS 1957; ThM U Tor 1969; STD Anselmianum Rome IT 1985. D 4/25/1957 Bp Charles Francis Boynton P 10/25/1957 Bp Chilton Powell. R S Jn's Ch Oklahoma City OK 1988-2003; R Emm Epis Ch Shawnee OK 1982-1988; Exec Asst to Bp Dio Wyoming Casper WY 1980-1982; Chapl to Cler Dio Los Angeles Los Angeles CA 1977-1980; R S Geo's Epis Ch Holbrook AZ 1977; R S Paul's Epis Ch Winslow AZ 1977; Asst Gr S Paul's Epis Ch Tucson AZ 1975-1977; Cur S Lk's Epis Ch Bartlesville OK 1957-1959. Auth, *Supernatural Beatitude According to S Albert the Great*; Auth, "The Rational Creatures Natural Appetite for Natural & Supernatural Beatitude Accord," *The Rational Creatures Natural Appetite for Natural & Supernatura*. VP Oklahoma Conf of Ch. jryan111@cox.net

RYAN, Katherine Feltman (WNC) 1223 Sea Pines Dr, Aubrey TX 76227 B Dallas,TX 12/24/1958 d David Edward Feltman & Arden Daniel. BS Texas A&M U 1981; MA U of Texas 1984; MDiv STUSo 1993; DMin SMU 2000. D 6/12/1993 Bp Robert Jefferson Hargrove Jr P 12/18/1993 Bp James Monte Stanton. m 10/19/1991 William Wilson Feltman c 3. S Paul's Newport AR 2005; Ch Of The H Cross Tryon NC 2003-2004; S Lk's Epis Ch Anth NM 2001-2003; Assoc S Geo's Epis Ch Bradenton FL 2000-2001; S Thos' Epis Ch St Petersburg FL 1999-2000; S Dav's Epis Ch Englewood FL 1996-1999; S Jas Epis Ch Alexandria LA 1994-1995; Cur S Alb's Epis Ch Monroe LA 1993-1994. kfryan3@sbcglobal.net

RYAN, Kathryn McCrossen (Dal) 8787 Greenville Ave, Dallas TX 75243 **Bd Trst; Chair - Governance Epis TS Of The SW Austin TX 2004-; R Epis Ch Of The Ascen Dallas TX 1999-** B Raton NM 12/22/1964 d Eric Thor McCrossen & Patricia Ann. BA U So 1986; MDiv Epis TS of The SW 1992. D 6/27/1992 Bp Terence Kelshaw P 6/24/1993 Bp Scott Field Bailey. m 5/20/1989 Timothy David Ryan c 2. COM, Chair Dio Cntrl Gulf Coast Pensacola FL 1998-1999; Asst S Lk's Epis Ch Mobile AL 1993-1999; Yth Min All SS Epis Ch Austin TX 1992-1993. revkryan@ascensiondallas.org

RYAN, Matthew Wayne (NwPa) 136 East Fourth Steet, Emporium PA 15834 **P-in-c Emm Epis Ch Emporium PA 2004-** B Pittsburgh PA 8/13/1956 s Joseph Gibbs Ryan & Martha Marie. BA Columbia St U Metaire LA 1997. D 4/20/2002 P 11/17/2002 Bp Robert Deane Rowley Jr. m 6/25/1983 Barbara Jean Williams c 3. Vic S Marg's Epis Ch Mt Jewett PA 2002-2004; Vic S Matt's Epis Ch Eldred PA 2002-2004. APMI 1983; SAE 1995. mattwryan@yahoo.com

RYAN, Michael J (WMich) 410 Erie St, South Haven MI 49090 **R The Epis Ch Of The Epiph So Haven MI 2009-** B Grand Rapids MN 8/27/1962 s Edward Clement Ryan & Kathleen Ann. BA S Jn's U 1986; MDiv SWTS 2009. D 6/20/2009 Bp Stephen Taylor Lane P 12/20/2009 Bp Robert R Gepert. m 11/1/2011 Susan J Trabucchi. Recovery Mnstrs of the Epis Ch 2007. anglcan09@gmail.com

RYAN JR, Thomas Francis (SeFla) 1222 Jayhil Dr, Minneola FL 34715 **Assoc S Jas Epis Ch Leesburg FL 2011-; Chair - Cmsn on Soc Concerns Dio SE Florida Miami FL 1990-** B West Palm Beach FL 10/9/1936 s Thomas Ryan & Anice. BEd U of Miami 1960; MDiv Yale DS 1972; MA Estrn Illinois U 1977. D 9/11/1971 Bp James Loughlin Duncan P 6/29/1972 Bp Morgan Porteus. m 4/15/1974 Courtenay D De Saussure c 3. P-in-c Corpus Christi Epis Ch Okahumpka FL 2009-2010; Assoc Corpus Christi Epis Ch Okahumpka FL 2008-2010; Dioc Bdgt Cmsn Dio SE Florida Miami FL 1993-2004; Natl Jubilee Off Dio SE Florida Miami FL 1990-2004; Evang Cmsn Dio SE Florida Miami FL 1989-1990; R All SS Epis Ch Jensen Bch FL 1988-2004; Chair - Cmsn on Evang Dio SW Florida Sarasota FL 1984-1988; R S Barth's Ch St Petersburg FL 1984-1988; Outreach Com Dio Cntrl Pennsylvania Harrisburg PA 1982-1984; R Chr Ch Berwick PA 1981-1984; Chapl Berwick Hospita; Dio Cntrl Pennsylvania Harrisburg PA 1981-1984; Liturg Cmsn Dio Bethlehem Bethlehem PA 1979-1981; Assoc S Lk's Ch Lebanon PA 1978-1981; Cmsn of Higher Educ Dio Springfield Springfield IL 1976-1978; COM Dio Springfield Springfield IL 1976-1978; Chapl Estrn Illinois Univ. Dio Springfield Springfield IL 1975-1978; R Trin Epis Ch Mattoon IL 1975-1978; R S Mary Magd Epis Ch Coral Sprg FL 1972-1974; P-in-c S Phil's Ch Pompano Bch FL 1972-1973. Auth, "Dvlpmt Of Self-Death Awareness Scale," Estrn Illinois U; Auth, "arts," *SW Florida Dio Nwspr*; Auth, "Reach Out Column," *The Sthrn Cross*, Dio SW Florida. Who'S Who In Rel 1985. frryan@cfl.rr.com

RYAN, William Wilson (WTenn) 9233 Speerberry Ln, Cordova TN 38016 **S Matt's Ch Covington TN 2010-** B Monroe LA 11/5/1958 s Thaddeus Jere Ryan & Katherine. BBA SMU 1980; MDiv STUSo 1993. D 6/12/1993 P 12/11/1993 Bp Robert Jefferson Hargrove Jr. m 10/19/1991 Katherine Feltman Ryan c 3. H Trin Ch Memphis TN 2003-2009; S Mk's Epis Ch Venice FL 1995-2001; Asst R S Jas Epis Ch Alexandria LA 1994-1995; Cur Gr Epis Ch Monroe LA 1993-1994. timsloan@bellsouth.net

RYDER, Anne Elizabeth (WMass) PO Box 1294, Sheffield MA 01257 **Chr Epis Ch Sheffield MA 2004-** B Palo Alto CA 5/5/1950 d Oliver Allison Ryder & Elizabeth Semans. BS California St U 1982; MDiv VTS 1996; MS Wheelock Coll 1996. D 6/22/1996 P 12/30/1996 Bp Richard Lester Shimpfky. c 1. R S Pat's Epis Ch Pagosa Sprg CO 1998-2004; Assoc All SS Ch Carmel CA 1996-1998. Harris Awd VTS Alexandria VA 1996. anniepie50@hotmail.com

RYDER, Barbara Helen (SVa) 12 spring Street, Decatur Guanajuato 30030 B Flint MI 5/7/1937 d Orval Cecil Hendrickson & Helen Irene. BS Case Wstrn Reserve U 1960; MDiv VTS 1997. D 6/14/1997 Bp Frank Harris Vest Jr P 4/1/1998 Bp Peter James Lee. m 7/11/1959 Craig Anthony Ryder c 2. Washington Epis Sch Beth MD 2002-2006; Asst S Jn's Ch Centreville VA 1997-2001. bhwryder@bellsouth.net

RYERSON, Raymond Willcox (FdL) 1758 Le Brun Rd, De Pere WI 54115 B Detroit MI 8/24/1932 s Laverne Willcox Ryerson & Edith Ethel. BS Wayne 1955; MDiv Nash 1985. D 4/20/1985 P 10/19/1985 Bp William L Stevens. m 7/7/1990 Kathleen Diane Elder c 3. Int S Ptr's Epis Ch Sheboygan Falls WI 2002-2003; Exec Coun Dio Fond du Lac Appleton WI 2001-2006; Int S Jas Ch Manitowoc WI 2000-2001; Comm. on Congrl Dvlpmt Dio Fond du Lac Appleton WI 1998-2000; Chr Ch Green Bay WI 1995-1999; S Bon Plymouth WI 1991-1995; Vic S Paul's Ch Plymouth WI 1991-1995; Stndg Cmsn Dio Fond du Lac Appleton WI 1991-1993; Comm. on Congrl Dvlpmt Dio Fond du Lac Appleton WI 1989-1993; Sec Curs Mvmt Dio Fond du Lac Appleton WI 1989-1992; Com on Evang & Renwl Dio Fond du Lac Appleton WI 1986-1988; Vic S Jn's Ch Shawano WI 1985-1991; Vic S Jn's Epis Ch New London WI 1985-1991. NOEL 1988-1996. knr@netnet.net

RYMER, Lionel Simon (VI) Po Box 7335, St Thomas VI 00801 Virgin Islands (U.S.) B Road Town Tortola VI 10/26/1936 s Stewart A Rymer & Maria L. MDiv ETSC 1970; Med U of The Vrgn Islands 1988. D 7/2/1970 P 6/1/1971 Bp Cedric Earl Mills. m 6/29/1961 Riisa Todman. S Lk's Ch Charlotte Amalie VI VI 1978-2008; Vic S Ursula Ch St Jn VI 1971-1979. Auth, "S Lk Journ Theol". eastersert@yahoo.com

S

SAAGER, Rebecca Ann (Lex) 311 Washington St, Frankfort KY 40601 B Buffalo NY 5/30/1957 d Stan Gorsica & Sonia. BS Morehead St U 1979; MS Estrn Kentucky U 1992. D 6/5/2011 Bp Stacy F Sauls. m 5/16/1982 Donald Saager c 2. rsaager@live.com

SAAK, William (Okla) 6701 N Harvard Ave, Oklahoma City OK 73132 **Died 8/25/2010** B Sand Springs OK 10/23/1927 s York Saak & Frances. BBA U CA 1952; MS U CA 1954. D 12/10/1969 Bp Chilton Powell. c 5. Natl Coll of Chapl 1978-1992; Oklahoma Chapl Assn VP 1977-1988; OHC, 1976. Carnegie Hero Awd Andr Carnegie Assoc. 1979; Presidential Citation Pres Carter 1979; Valor Awd St of Oklahoma 1979.

SABETTI III, Henry Martin (Eas) 12822 Shrewsbury Church Rd, Kennedyville MD 21645 **Shrewsbury Par Ch Kennedyville MD 2010-** B Portland OR 12/9/1961 s Henry Martin Sabetti & Florence Carol-Agnes. BA Wabash Coll 1984; MSW Indiana U 1986; MDiv VTS 1998. D 6/13/1998 Bp Robert Wilkes Ihloff P 1/30/1999 Bp John Leslie Rabb. Ch Of The Trsfg Braddock Heights MD 2004-2010; S Fran Cmnty Serv Inc. Salina KS 2001-2004; S Nich Chap

Ellsworth KS 2000-2004; York Place Epis Ch Hm For Chld York SC 2000-2001; Cur Ch Of The H Comf Luthvle Timon MD 1998-2000. Acad of Cert Soc Workers (ACSW); Lic Cert Soc Worker - Clincl (LCSW-C) 1995; NASW 1984. shrewsbury@baybroadband.net

SABOM, Steve (At) 1143 Sanden Ferry Dr, Decatur GA 30033 B Houston TX 7/10/1942 s William Oscar Sabom & Felicia. BA Colorado Coll 1964; MDiv VTS 1970; ThM Duke 1974; STD SFTS 1980. D 6/23/1970 Bp Scott Field Bailey. m 11/23/1996 Sharon Ann Mathis c 1. Ed, "Healing a Generation," *J. Am Acad Psychotherapists*, Guiltford Press, 1991; Auth, "The Moral Trauma of the Vietnam Veteran," *Pstr Psychol*, 1990; Auth, "Judgment at Catecka," *Voices*, 1989; Auth, "The Gnostic Wrld of Anorexia Nervosa," *Journ of Psychol & Theol*, 1983; Auth, "Heresy and Pstr Counslg," *J. Pstr Care*, 1980; Auth, "Near-Death Experience: A Revs from Pstr Psychol," *J. Rel and Hlth*, 1979. AAPC 1976. ssabom@pilink.org

SABUNE, Petero Aggrey Nkurunziza (NY) 293 Highland Ave, Newark NJ 07104 **Epis Ch Cntr New York NY 2010-** B Bufumbira Kigezi UG 9/23/1952 s Andereya Nzabanita Sabune & Ayirini Mfikije. BA Vas 1977; MDiv UTS 1981. Trans 7/27/1984 Bp James Stuart Wetmore. m 9/4/1978 Maureen Fonseca c 4. Vic S Jas Ch New York NY 1998-2004; Dn Trin And S Phil's Cathd Newark NJ 1992-1998; Assoc For Grants Par of Trin Ch New York NY 1990-1992; R Ch Of The Incarn Jersey City NJ 1987-1990; Dio Newark Newark NJ 1987-1990; R Epis Ch Of SS Jn Paul And S Clem Mt Vernon NY 1982-1987; Cur Gr Ch White Plains NY 1981-1982. CHS; UBE. Cmnty Serv Awd Naacp 1989; Fr Of The Year Awd Newark NJ; Cmnty Serv Awd Mt Vernon NY; Mntl Hlth Awd Westchester Cnty NY. psabune@yahoo.com

SACCAROLA FAVARO, Flavio (EcuC) Apdo 08-01-404, Esmeraldas Ecuador **Dio El Salvador Ambato 18-01-525 Tu EC 1998-; P Iglesia San Alfonso Ambato EC 1998-** B 12/22/1946 s Giuseppe Saccarola & Luigia Favaro. BA U Theol & Philos de Latran Titolo Rome IT 1973. Rec from Roman Catholic 11/1/1997 as Priest Bp J Neptali Larrea-Moreno. m 10/16/1992 Catalina Saccarola. Ecuador New York NY 1998-2009. flacat@andinanet.net

SACCO, Ronald John (Ind) 1219 14th St, Bedford IN 47421 B Sewickley PA 8/27/1944 s John Floyd Sacco & Margret. MDiv TESM 1987. D 6/4/1988 P 12/1/1988 Bp Alden Moinet Hathaway. m 1/1/2003 Lisa Klein Sacco. S Jn's Epis Ch Bedford IN 1989-2001; S Mk's Ch Johnstown PA 1988-1989. Bro Of S Andr. sje@kiva.net

SACHERS, Calvin Stewart (Tex) 145 Lake View Dr, Boerne TX 78006 B Richmond VA 1/16/1926 s Gustave Eric Sachers & Wilhelmina Otey. BA U of Virginia 1950; MDiv Epis TS of The SW 1958. D 6/19/1958 Bp James Parker Clements P 12/1/1959 Bp John E Hines. m 2/2/1964 Hallie Frances Perry c 2. Asst R Chr Epis Ch Charlottesville VA 1975-1978; R Buck Mtn Epis Ch Earlysville VA 1970-1975; Cur S Dav's Ch Austin TX 1964-1967; R S Barth's Ch Hempstead TX 1963-1964; Cur S Mk's Ch Beaumont TX 1960-1961; M-in-c S Jn's Epis Ch Columbus TX 1958-1960.

SACHS, William Lewis (Va) 5 River Rd, Richmond VA 23226 B Richmond VA 8/22/1947 s Lewis S Sachs & Dorothy. BA Baylor U 1969; MDiv Van 1972; STM Yale DS 1973; PhD U Chi 1981. D 5/26/1973 P 5/31/1974 Bp Robert Bruce Hall. m 5/17/1986 Elizabeth Tucker c 1. ECF Inc New York NY 2000-2006; S Lk's Par Darien CT 2000; R S Matt's Epis Ch Wilton CT 1994-2000; Exam Chapl Dio Virginia Richmond VA 1982-1992; Asst S Steph's Ch Richmond VA 1980-1994; Asst S Chrys's Ch Chicago IL 1975-1980; Cur Emm Ch At Brook Hill Richmond VA 1973-1975. Auth, "Homosexuality and the Crisis of Anglicanism," Cambridge, 2009; Auth, "The Epis Ch in the Twentieth Century," *Encyclopedia of Rel in Amer*, 2009; Auth, "Plantations and Mssn," *Oxford Guide to the Bookf of Common Pryr*, Oxford, 2006; Auth, "Restoring The Ties That Bind," Ch Pub, 2003; Auth, "The Transformation Of Anglicansim," Cambridge, 1993; Auth, "Of One Body," Westminster/ Jn Knox, 1986. HSEC 1976. Polly Bond Awds For Rel Journalism 1991. wls@aol.com

S

SACQUETY JR, Charles William (Los) 8402 Castilian Dr, Huntington Beach CA 92646 B Detroit MI 11/20/1932 s Charles William Sacquety & Lorine. BA U MI 1954; MA U MI 1956; MDiv CDSP 1965. D 6/29/1965 Bp Archie H Crowley P 3/12/1966 Bp Richard S M Emrich. Pstr Care All SS Ch Pasadena CA 2001-2003; Archd Dio Los Angeles Los Angeles CA 1998-1999; R S Wilfrid Of York Epis Ch Huntington Bch CA 1978-1998; R The Angl/Epis Ch Of Chr The King Frankfurt am Main 60323 DE 1971-1977; Asst S Mk's Par Glendale CA 1969-1971; Vic Gr Epis Ch Southgate MI 1967-1969; Cur S Dav's Ch Southfield MI 1965-1967. Hon DD CDSP; Hon Cn Dio Los Angeles. sacquety@earthlink.net

SADLER, Alice Irene (SwFla) 553 Galleon Dr, Naples FL 34102 **Assoc R Trin By The Cove Naples FL 2001-** B Charlotte NC 9/25/1949 d James Charles Sadler & Florence Alice. BA Erskine Coll 1971; MA U NC 1975; MDiv TESM 2001. D 10/16/2001 P 4/20/2002 Bp John Bailey Lipscomb. ASADLER@TRINITYBYTHECOVE.COM

SAFFORD, Timothy Browning (Pa) 20 N American St, Philadelphia PA 19106 **R Chr Ch Philadelphia Philadelphia PA 1999-** B Pasadena CA 3/9/1959 s Henry Barnard Safford & Kathryn Greene. BA Claremont McKenna Coll 1981; Cert Ya Berk 1985; MDiv Yale DS 1985. D 6/15/1985 P 1/25/1986 Bp Robert C Rusack. m 5/4/1985 Lynn Annette Karoly c 2. Sr Assoc for Mssn & Outreach All SS Ch Pasadena CA 1988-1999; Cur S Jn's Ch Bridgeport CT 1985-1988. Pstr Theol Cntr for Rel Inquiry, Princeton. 2001; Mikkelsen Preaching Prize St. Jn's Ch, Capitola, CA 2000. tsafford@christchurchphila.org

SAFFRAN, Walter Thomas (Fla) 9 Lakeshore Dr, Saint Augustine FL 32080 **Died 6/9/2011** B Jacksonville FL 11/13/1928 s Harold Edward Saffran & Grace Caroline. BA U of Florida 1957; U So 1961. D 8/27/1961 P 4/19/1962 Bp Edward Hamilton West. c 3. msaffl3@aol.com

✠ **SAID, Rt Rev John Lewis** (SeFla) 6508 Nw Chugwater Cir, Port Saint Lucie FL 34983 **Ret Suffr Bp Dio SE Florida Miami FL 2002-** B Marion IN 8/29/1932 s Isaac Henry Said & Vivian Ethel. BA Wabash Coll 1955; STB Ya Berk 1958; DD Ya Berk 1996. D 6/21/1958 P 1/10/1959 Bp Richard Ainslie Kirchhoffer Con 2/25/1995 for SeFla. m 6/11/1955 Barbara Ann McCormack c 3. Bp Suffr Dio SE Florida Miami FL 1995-2002; R S Kevin's Epis Ch Opa Locka FL 1987-1994; Assoc S Bern De Clairvaux N Miami Bch FL 1978-1982; Cur Trin Ch Indianapolis IN 1964-1966; R S Mk's Ch Plainfield IN 1960-1964; Cur Gr Ch Muncie IN 1958-1960. Bro of St Andr 1987. Hon DD Berk New Haven CT 1996. nufsaid@bellsouth.net

SAIK, Ernest William (La) 14344 S. Harrells Ferry Road, Baton Rouge LA 70816 **R Epis Ch Of The H Sprt In Baton Rouge Baton Rouge LA 2011-** B Jackson MS 1/17/1950 s William Emile Saik & Luree Cross. BA Mississippi St U 1972; MDiv STUSo 1978. D 10/23/1978 P 10/18/1979 Bp Duncan Montgomery Gray Jr. m 9/28/1996 Brenda L Sullivan c 2. P-in-c Chr Ch Slidell LA 2008-2010; Assoc S Lk's Ch Baton Rouge LA 1999-2008; Vic S Jn's Ch Leland MS 1995-1999; Vic Ch Of The Redeem Greenville MS 1995; Vic S Paul's Ch Hollandale MS 1995; Vic All SS Ch Cameron TX 1993-1994; Vic S Thos' Epis Ch Rockdale TX 1993-1994; R Trin Ch Marshall TX 1988-1991; Assoc R Chr Epis Ch Tyler TX 1981-1988; Vic Gr S Bernards Ch Okolona MS 1980-1981; Vic S Jn's Ch Aberdeen MS 1978-1981. esaik79@yahoo.com

SAILER, David Walter (WNC) 3 Oak Leaf Ln, Arden NC 28704 B Wheeling WV 6/15/1941 s Walter Emil Sailer & Catherine Jane. BA W Liberty St Coll 1964; MDiv VTS 1967. D 6/12/1967 P 2/24/1968 Bp Wilburn Camrock Campbell. c 3. Int Ch Of The Gd Shpd Tryon NC 2002-2003; R Calv Epis Ch Fletcher NC 1984-1998; Assoc Trin Ch Huntington WV 1973-1984; Vic S Thos' Epis Ch Weirton WV 1969-1973; R Gr Epis Ch Elkins WV 1967-1969. Auth, "Hist of Calv, Fletcher, NC," *The Windows of Calv Ch*, 1999. Outstanding Young Men Amer 1976. davidsailer@att.net

SAINT-PIERRE, Nathanael L B (NY) Haitian Congregation of the Good Samaritan, 661 E 219th St, Bronx NY 10467 **P in charge Haitian Cong of the Gd Samar Bronx NY 2007-** B Port-au-Price, Haiti 8/25/1963 s Bernardin Saint-Pierre & Prophite Emmanuella. Dplma in Mechanic Cntr Pilote de Formation Propessionelle; Cert Epis TS 1992; Assoc in Computer Sci Institut Superieu d' Electronic 1997. Trans from Anglican Church of Canada 11/6/2007 Bp Mark Sean Sisk. m 9/27/1986 Karline Bernard c 2. nathou@optonline.net

SAINT ROMAIN, Brad (Tex) 8302 Whippoorwill Dr, Woodway TX 76712 **Assoc R S Paul's Ch Waco TX 2004-** B New Orleans LA 10/29/1958 s Joseph Bert Saint Romain & Patsy Selesia. BS LSU 1980; MDiv Epis TS of The SW 2003. D 12/28/2002 P 11/17/2003 Bp Charles Edward Jenkins III. m 11/21/1981 Lisa Carlin Terry c 3. Chr Epis Ch Cedar Pk TX 2004; The Ch of the Gd Shpd Austin TX 2003-2004. bradst.romain@gmail.com

SAJNA, Barbara Jean Reiser (FdL) 2100 Ridges Rd., Baileys Harbor WI 54202 **R S Lk's Sis Bay WI 2004-** B Rhinelander WI 8/28/1940 d Max Berthold Reiser & Dorothy Elizabeth. JD U of Wisconsin 1983; MDiv SMU 1997. D 6/27/1998 P 5/1/1999 Bp James Monte Stanton. c 3. Cur The Epis Ch Of The Trsfg Dallas TX 2000-2004; Chapl/Asst Ch Of The Gd Shpd Dallas TX 1998-2000. bsajna@dcwis.com

SAKIN, Charles Robert (NJ) 1812 Rue De La Port Drive, Wall NJ 07719 B Baltimore MD 5/11/1943 s Harold Sakin & Emma Louise. BA Ge 1965; STB PDS 1968; ThM PrTS 1970; MS Monmouth U 1977. D 4/20/1968 P 10/1/1968 Bp Alfred L Banyard. m 8/26/1967 Katherine Pawlikowski. Assoc Trin Epis Ch Red Bank NJ 1981-1997; P-in-c S Steph's Ch Whiting NJ 1974-1977; Cur S Jn's Ch Somerville NJ 1968-1969. Auth, "Its Worth A Laugh".

SAKRISON, David L (U) 280 E 300 S, Moab UT 84532 **Dio Utah Salt Lake City UT 2010-** B Salida CO 3/25/1946 s Linwood H Sakrison & Dorotha M. D 6/7/2003 P 5/30/2004 Bp Carolyn Tanner Irish. m 11/23/1974 Melody Lynn Sakrison c 2. sakrison@citlink.net

SALAMONE, Robert Emmitt (At) 1009 Pin Oak Trl, Hendersonville NC 28739 **R Emm Epis Ch Athens GA 2006-** B Jersey City NJ 3/16/1952 s Louis John Salamone & Eileen Margaret. BA Don Bosco Coll; M Div Immac Concep Sem 1979. Rec from Roman Catholic 12/21/1999 Bp Robert Hodges Johnson. m 8/25/1996 Karen C Salamone. S Jas Epis Ch Hendersonville NC 1997-1999. rector@emmanuelathens.org

SALAZAR, Fernando Herrera (RG) 201 Capri Arc, Las Cruces NM 88005 B San Antonio TX 12/26/1925 s Francisco Salazar & Francisca. BA Trin U 1950; SMU 1954. D 12/21/1967 P 7/13/1968 Bp C J Kinsolving III. m 4/22/

1961 Elizabeth Martinez c 3. S Jas' Epis Ch Mesilla Pk NM 1973-1994; Vic S Steph's Epis Ch Espanola NM 1969-1973; Asst S Paul's Ch Artesia NM 1967-1968.

SALAZAR-SOTILLO, Orlando Rafael (Ve) 49-143 Colinas De Bello Monte, Caracas 1042 Venezuela **Dio Venezuela Colinas De Bello Monte Caracas 10-42-A VE 2004-** B 2/16/1950 D 12/17/1992 P 6/24/1993 Bp Onell Asiselo Soto.

SALAZAR-VÁSQUEZ, José Francisco (Ve) No address on file. **Dio Venezuela Colinas De Bello Monte Caracas 10-42-A VE 2004-** B 4/19/1967 D 2/24/2005 Bp Orlando Jesus Guerrero. m 12/28/1990 Pragedes Coromoto Jimenez de Salazar.

SALBADOR, Gus William (Wyo) 2510 Stonebridge Way, Mount Vernon WA 98273 B Lake Charles LA 11/5/1929 s Gustave Salbador & Anna Mae. BS Steph F. Austin St U 1954; DVM Texas A&M U 1958; MDiv The Coll of Emm and St. Chad 1990. D 11/14/1992 Bp Leopold Frade P 9/14/1993 Bp Charles Jones III. m 6/7/1952 Jane Helpinstill c 2. Cn Dio Wyoming Casper WY 2001-2007; Int S Matt's Epis Cathd Laramie WY 2000-2001; Vic S Barn Epis Ch Saratoga WY 1998-2000; Vic Iglesia Epis San Geo Roatan Sandy Bay HN 1992-1998; Vic Iglesia Epis San Pedro de Mar Roatan Is HN 1992-1998; Dio Montana Helena MT 1992-1997. Cn Cathd El Buen Pstr Sps Honduras 1997. janesalbador@mac.com

SALIK, Lamuel Gill (NwT) 138 Liveoak St, Hereford TX 79045 B Sahiwal Punjab PK 3/5/1941 s Feroze Masih Gill & Fazal. LTh Gujranwala TS Pk 1970; BA U of Karachi 1973; GTS 1994; MDiv Faith TS Philadelphia PA 1997; Dre Faith TS Philadelphia PA 1998. Trans from Anglican Church Of Pakistan 11/1/1992 Bp George Phelps Mellick Belshaw. m 10/16/1981 Roseline W John c 2. R S Jas' Epis Ch Dalhart TX 2006-2009; P-in-c S Mk's Epis Ch Plainview TX 2000; R S Thos Epis Ch Hereford TX 1999-2005; Supply Dio New Jersey Trenton NJ 1993-1998; S Lk's Ch Woodstown NJ 1992-1993; Asst S Lk's Epis Ch Metuchen NJ 1989-1991; Asst S Andr's Astoria NY 1982-1989. Ed, "Outreach"; Transltr, "A Chr'S Handbook On Communism". stjames@xit.net

SALINARO, Katherine Ella Mae (Cal) 121 Sheffield, Hercules CA 94547 **D Ch Of The H Trin Richmond CA 2002-; D Ch Of The H Trin Richmond CA 2002-; Instr/D Epis Sch For Deacons Berkeley CA 1997-** B Saint Louis MO 11/28/1936 BA San Francisco St U 1958; BA Sch for Deacons 1984; MA H Name U 1991. D 12/7/1985 Bp William Edwin Swing. c 3. Assn of Epis Deacons 1984; Third Ord SSF 1981. deaconkl@comcast.net

SALLES, Stacy Dee (Mich) 67640 Van Dyke Rd # 10, Washington MI 48095 **R St Paul's Epis Romeo MI 2006-** B Owosso MI 9/9/1955 d John Albert Salles & Harriett Ann. BS Nthrn St U Aberdeen SD 1978; MDiv SWTS 1999. D 12/21/2002 P 6/25/2003 Bp Wendell Nathaniel Gibbs Jr. c 1. Asst Trin Ch Belleville MI 2003-2006; D Trin Ch Belleville MI 2002-2003. revsalles@juno.com

SALLEY JR, George Bull (Ga) 310 McLaws Street, Savannah GA 31405 **Hon. Assoc S Paul's Ch Savannah GA 2002-** B Orangeburg SC 1/10/1937 s George Bull Salley & Martha Helen. BS U of So Carolina 1959; MDiv TS 1973. D 6/26/1973 P 5/30/1974 Bp George Moyer Alexander. m 4/4/1976 Anne Bizzell c 2. Asst S Geo's Epis Ch Savannah GA 1999-2001; Dioc Coun Dio Georgia Savannah GA 1986-1989; R S Mich And All Ang Savannah GA 1985-1999; R All SS Ch Cayce SC 1978-1985; Vic S Alb's Ch Lexington SC 1974-1978; Cur All SS Ch Cayce SC 1973-1974. factoids@comcast.net

SALMON JR, Abraham Dickerson (Md) 7351 Willow Rd Apt 2, Frederick MD 21702 B Morristown NJ 8/28/1930 s Abraham Dickerson Salmon & Audrey Lucas. BA Franklin & Marshall Coll 1952; LTh SWTS 1957. D 6/21/1957 Bp Walter M Higley P 6/11/1958 Bp Malcolm E Peabody. m 9/8/1956 Jeannine T Toman c 4. R All SS Ch Frederick MD 1970-1992; R Gr Ch Brunswick MD 1963-1970; Chr Ch Guilford CT 1957-1962. ads1930@yahoo.com

SALMON, Alan Kent (NJ) 4 Tara Ln, Delran NJ 08075 B Moorestown NJ 4/15/1938 s Walter William Salmon & Marie Dorothy. U of Madrid 1959; BA Trin Hartford CT 1960; MA Trin Hartford CT 1961; MDiv GTS 1964; DMin Drew U 1989. D 4/25/1964 P 10/31/1964 Bp Alfred L Banyard. Dn - Burlington Convoc Dio New Jersey Trenton NJ 1978-1981; R Chr Ch Riverton NJ 1970-2003; Cur Trin Epis Ch Cranford NJ 1964-1966. Auth, "arts," *Word & Sacr*. Phi Beta Kappa Trin, Hartford, CT 1960. aks4taralane@comcast.net

✠ SALMON JR, Rt Rev Edward Lloyd (SC) 9 Westmoreland Place, Saint Louis MO 63108 **Int All SS' Epis Ch Chevy Chase MD 2010-; Ret Bp of SC Dio So Carolina Charleston SC 2007-** B Natchez MS 1/30/1934 s Edward Lloyd Salmon & Helen Bernice. BA U So 1956; BD VTS 1960. D 6/24/1960 P 3/1/1961 Bp Robert Raymond Brown Con 2/24/1990 for SC. m 1/26/1972 Louise Salmon c 2. Bp Of SC Dio So Carolina Charleston SC 1990-2007; Dio So Carolina Charleston SC 1990-2006; R S Mich & S Geo Clayton MO 1978-1990; S Paul's Ch Fayetteville AR 1967-1978; Vic S Andr's Ch Rogers AR 1960-1963; Vic S Jas Ch Eureka Sprg AR 1960-1963; Vic S Thos Ch Springdale AR 1960-1963. DD Nash Sem 2007; DD U of thr So 1991; DD VTS 1991. elsalmon@dioceseofsc.org

SALMON JR, John Frederick (Nwk) 752 York Rd, Mount Laurel NJ 08054 **Asst Trin Ch Moorestown NJ 1996-** B Camden NJ 12/2/1931 s John Frederick Salmon & Dorothy Croasdale. BS Rutgers-The St U 1953; LTh GTS 1956; MDiv GTS 1958; M Ed Rutgers-The St U 1965. D 4/28/1956 P 10/27/1956 Bp Alfred L Banyard. m 11/30/1957 Suzanne Virginia Sutphen c 2. Rgstr The GTS New York NY 1973-1974; R Ch Of The Adv Bloomfield NJ 1965-1996; R Ch Of S Andr The Apos Camden NJ 1957-1965; Vic Ch Of S Clem Of Rome Belford NJ 1957; Vic S Mk's Epis Ch Keansburg NJ 1957; Cur Trin Cathd Trenton NJ 1956-1957. suzannejacksalmon@earthlink.net

SALMON, Marilyn Jean (Minn) 1077 Laurel Ave, Saint Paul MN 55104 B Watertown SD 5/10/1948 d Guy Sumner Salmon & Marllys. BA Concordia Coll 1970; MDiv Luther TS 1977; PhD Hebr Un Coll 1986. D 5/30/1990 P 12/1/1990 Bp Robert Marshall Anderson. c 2. S Clem's Ch S Paul MN 1999-2008; Dio Minnesota Minneapolis MN 1991-1992; S Matt's Ch St Paul MN 1991-1992. "Preaching Without Contempt," Augsburg Fortress, 2006; Auth, "Insider or Outsider? Lk's Relatns w Judaism"; Auth, "Lk-Acts & the Jewish People".

SALMON, Walter Burley (At) 6640 Akers Mill Rd Se, Atlanta GA 30339 B Natchez MS 10/23/1971 s Walter Thomas Salmon & Myrtis Virginia. BA Millsaps Coll 1993; MDiv Ya Berk 1998. D 4/30/2011 Bp Keith Bernard Whitmore. wbss@aya.yale.edu

SALT, Alfred Lewis (Nwk) 4822 Martinique Way, Naples FL 34119 B Hackensack NJ 4/30/1927 s Alfred J Salt & Lillian. BA Bps 1949; MA Bps 1951; LST Bps 1954; BD Bps 1960; AMP Harv 1970; DMin GTF 1988. Trans from Anglican Church of Canada 2/2/1972 as Priest Bp Leland Stark. m 6/18/1949 Elizabeth M Loveland c 4. Dio Estrn Michigan Saginaw MI 1993-2002; R All SS Ch Millington NJ 1972-1993; Camp Com Chairman Dio Newark Newark NJ 1972-1974. Auth, "God's Healing Gr," *A COMPASSbook*, BRF, 1995; Auth, "Freedom in Chr Jesus," *Fellows Yearbook 1988*, Wyndham Hill Press, 1988; Auth, "The Nature, Scope," *and Hist of VMTC*, VMTC, 1983; Auth, "Var arts," *Sharing*, OSL. Chapl Ord of S Lk 1980; Comp WSHS/WBHS 2007; Dir VMTC 1981-1992. Who's Who in Amer 2012; Who's Who in the Wrld 2007; Fell GTF 1988; Hon Cn Dio Quebec 1970. alemsalt@comcast.net

SALTZGABER, Jan Mcminn (Ga) 225 W Point Dr, Saint Simons Island GA 31522 **D Chr Ch Frederica St Simons Island GA 2001-** B Harvey IL 7/27/1933 s Merrill Archer Saltzgaber & Anna Elizabeth. PhD Syr; BA Wayne 1959; MA Wayne 1965. D 12/19/2001 Bp Henry Irving Louttit. m 6/28/1988 Pauline Elizabeth Kull.

SALVATIERRA SERIAN, Juan E (EcuC) Apdo 17-11-6165, Quito Ecuador **Vic Catedral de "El Senor" Quito EC 1998-; Ecuador New Yorke NY 1998-** B Empalme Guayas 6/12/1966 s Enrique D Salvatierra & Humberta Victoria. BS Sem Mayor Cristo Sacerdote Colombia CO 1986. Rec from Roman Catholic 7/1/1996 as Priest Bp Alfredo Morante-España. m 2/16/2003 Zoraida Monserrate Muentes Mora.

SAM, Albert Abuid Samuel (WNY) 7469 Dysinger Rd, Lockport NY 14094 B Dunkirk NY 5/22/1938 s Samuel Albert Sam & Mary N. SUNY, Fredonia 1968; U of Buffalo 1968; MDiv Bex 1971. D 1/6/1972 P 7/8/1972 Bp Harold B Robinson. m 6/9/1957 Hannah F Sam c 4. S Jn's Ch Wilson NY 1999; Cn Mssnr Dio Wstrn New York Tonawanda NY 1992-1996; St Mk Epis Ch No Tonawanda NY 1978-1990; Vic S Pat's Ch Cheektowaga NY 1972-1978. papasamabuid@verizon.net

SAM, Helen (WNY) PO Box 14, Dunkirk NY 14048 B Pomfret NY 5/1/1932 d Albert Sam & Nacima Norman. BA U of Buffalo 1980. D 4/14/2009 P 11/8/2009 Bp J Michael Garrison. helen@dayoubinc.com

SAMMONS, Gregory P (O) 4684 Brittany Rd, Toledo OH 43615 **Dn, W Mssn Area Dio Ohio Cleveland OH 2001-; R S Michaels In The Hills Toledo OH 1993-** B Columbus OH 8/11/1950 s James Edward Sammons & Dorothy Elizabeth. BA Trin 1972; Harvard DS 1973; MDiv EDS 1976. D 9/25/1976 P 4/23/1977 Bp Alexander Doig Stewart. m 9/10/1977 Margaret Holt c 2. GC Alt Dep Dio Ohio Cleveland OH 2008-2009; Dioc Coun Dio Ohio Cleveland OH 2000-2002; Angl Partnerships Dio Ohio Cleveland OH 1997-1999; Assoc Chr Ch Grosse Pointe Grosse Pointe Farms MI 1983-1993; Dept of Admin and Fin Dio Wstrn Massachusetts Springfield MA 1980-1983; R S Phil's Ch Easthampton MA 1978-1983; Asst S Mich's-On-The-Heights Worcester MA 1976-1978. Rotary Intl of Toledo, Ohio 2008. Phi Beta Kappa Trin, Beta Chapet, Conn. 1971. sabbaticalsammons@yahoo.com

SAMMONS, Margaret Holt (O) 4684 Brittany Rd, Toledo OH 43615 **Co-R S Michaels In The Hills Toledo OH 2003-** B Chicago IL 12/24/1948 d James Craigie Holt & Joan Duncan. BA Wellesley Coll 1971; MDiv EDS 1977; Cert Worcester Pstr Counslg 1978. D 6/5/1977 P 5/19/1978 Bp Charles Bennison. m 9/10/1977 Gregory P Sammons c 2. Assoc S Michaels In The Hills Toledo OH 1994-2002; Assoc Chr Ch Grosse Pointe Grosse Pointe Farms MI 1983-1993; Cur & Coll Min. S Jn's Ch Northampton MA 1980-1983; Int S Lk's Ch Worcester MA 1977-1978. Auth, *Declare His Glory: Lenten Study Prog Mssn*, Dio Wstrn Mass., 1979. peg@saintmichaelsepiscopal.org

SAMPLES, Stephen Randolph (Okla) 1619 W Maine Ave, Enid OK 73703 **R S Matt's Ch Enid OK 2005-** B Evansville IN 4/12/1954 s Edmond Oral

Samples & Laura. BBA U of Texas 1985; MDiv TESM 1994. D 6/25/1994 Bp Maurice Manuel Benitez P 1/10/1995 Bp William Elwood Sterling. c 5. S Jas' Epis Ch Meeker CO 2001-2005; Stndg Com Dio Wyoming Casper WY 2000-2005; R S Lk's Epis Ch Buffalo WY 1998-2001; Stwdshp Com Dio Wyoming Casper WY 1995-2005; R S Andr's Ch Basin WY 1995-1997; Vic S Andr's Ch Meeteetse WY 1995-1997; Dio Wyoming Casper WY 1995; Environ Div Dio Texas Houston TX 1994-1995; Asst to R S Cyp's Ch Lufkin TX 1994-1995. Bro of S Andr; Ord of S Lk. steve.samples@sbcglobal.net

SAMPSON, Paula Kathryn (Ak) 4317 Birch Avenue, Terrace V8G 1X2 Canada **R S Phil's Ch Wrangell AK 2009-** B Ketchikan AK 10/23/1948 d Kenneth Paul Sampson & Beatrice Kathryn. BA U of Washington 1970; MA H Name U 1991; MDiv PSR 1994; PhD CDSP 2000. D 6/24/1994 P 4/1/1995 Bp Steven Charleston. m 8/3/1996 Venerable Ian MacKenzie. S Augustines' Epis Ch Homer AK 1995-1996; D The Epis Ch Of The Gd Shpd Berkeley CA 1994-2004; Pres of The Stndg Com Dio Alaska Fairbanks AK 1988-1989; Dn Dio Alaska Fairbanks AK 1986-1989; Dio Arkansas Little Rock AR 1986-1989. paula-sampson@ecunet.org

SAMPSON, Timothy Warren (WMass) Via Bagaro 65, Ferrara 44121 Italy B Williamsville NY 9/23/1949 s Joseph Warren Sampson & Sylvia. BA U Of Hartford 1971; MDiv VTS 1976. D 6/16/1976 Bp Alexander Doig Stewart P 1/26/1977 Bp Harold B Robinson. Asst R S Chris's Ch Chatham MA 1991-1993; Cur S Lk's Epis Ch Jamestown NY 1976-1978. dontim@libero.it

SAMRA, Gordon L (NI) 14823 Waterbrook Rd, Fort Wayne IN 46814 **D Trin Ch Ft Wayne IN 2004-** B Fort Wayne IN 3/17/1943 s Alfred Foad Samra & Gladys E. AA S Fran Coll Ft Wayne IN 1986. D 11/30/1995 Bp Francis Campbell Gray. m 7/15/1967 Patricia Anne Meyer c 2. D Trin Ch Ft Wayne IN 2001-2003; D Trin Ch Ft Wayne IN 1995-2001.

SAMS, David Lee (Minn) 203 Aspenwood Drive, Redwood Falls MN 56283 **D/Asst Bp Whipple Mssn Morton MN 1992-; Supply Cleric Dio Minnesota Minneapolis MN 1987-** B Sioux City IA 2/27/1951 s Leland Harold Sams & Doris Marilyn. D Formation Prog; BA SW St U Marshall MN 1973; MA Minnesota St U Mankato 1996. D 12/27/1984 Bp Robert Marshall Anderson. D S Jn's Epis Ch Mankato MN 2000-2002; D S Jn Worthington MN 1994-1998; D S Ptr's Ch New Ulm MN 1988-1991; Bp Whipple Mssn Morton MN 1985-1986; D Ch Of The Gd Shpd Windom MN 1984-1985; D S Jn Worthington MN 1984-1985. dsams@mchsi.com

SAMS, Jonathan Carter (Mich) 6402 Fredmoor Dr, Troy MI 48098 **Assoc Chr Ch Cranbrook Bloomfield Hills MI 2011-** B Charleston SC 6/1/1942 s Henry Whittington Sams & Carolyn. BA Ob 1963; MDiv Nash 1966. D 6/11/1966 Bp James Winchester Montgomery P 12/17/1966 Bp Gerald Francis Burrill. m 9/4/1999 Nancy Irey c 6. Dn Dio Michigan Detroit MI 2002-2005; R S Steph's Ch Troy MI 1991-2011; S Tim's Ch Griffith IN 1983-1991; S Paul's Epis Ch Munster IN 1977-1982; Assoc S Chris's Ch Crown Point IN 1977-1978; Yth Dir S Tim's Ch Griffith IN 1976-1982; Cur Ch Of The Ascen Chicago IL 1966-1967. Auth, "Fam Album (Poetry)," Bennett, 1993; Auth, "Rambling R (Column)," *Record (Dio Mi Nwspr)*, 1992; Auth, "(Var arts)," *Congregations*, Alb Inst, 1990; Auth, "Chickenbone Lake," Anadromous Press, 1988; Auth, "Reflections Of A Fishing Parson," Abingdon, 1972; Auth, "Angling Theologically," *Field & Stream*, 1970. Living Stones 1984-2000; Soc Of S Jn The Evang 1996. episcopal2@comcast.net

SAMUEL, Amjad John (Ct) 27 Church St, Stonington CT 06378 **Assoc S Paul's Ch Akron OH 2010-** B 7/17/1971 s John Victor Samuel & Shirin. BA Alma Coll Alma MI 1992; MTS Duke DS 1995. Trans from Anglican Church Of Pakistan 5/23/2008 Bp James Elliot Curry. m 11/21/2008 Maria Katherine Mitchell. Cur/Dir of Chr Formation Calv Ch Stonington CT 2008-2010. amji71@hotmail.com

SAMUEL, Daniel (DR) Aptd 764, Santo Domingo Dominican Republic **Vic Iglesia Epis San Jose Andrés Boca Chica DO 1995-; Vic Iglesia Epis San Marcos Haitiana 1995-; Vic Iglesia Epis San Tomas Santo Domingo DO 1995-; Dio The Dominican Republic (Iglesia Epis Dominicana) Santo Domingo DO 1992-** B Leogane HT 12/1/1956 s Mathurin Samuel & Imanie. BA Centro De Estudios Teologicas 1991. D 6/7/1992 P 12/1/1993 Bp Julio Cesar Holguin-Khoury. m 1/23/1982 Marie Aurianne Rosier.

SAMUEL, Jason Wade (Mo) 97 Rue de Paix, Lake Saint Louis MO 63367 **R Ch Of The Trsfg Lake S Louis MO 1997-** B Minden Louisiana 8/20/1963 s James Leon Samuel & Betty Jo. BA Oral Roberts U 1985; MDiv Nash 1990. D 11/28/1992 P 7/4/1993 Bp Roger John White. P-in Charge S Andr's Ch Milwaukee WI 1996; R S Dav Of Wales Ch New Berlin WI 1994-1996; Asst S Mk's Ch Milwaukee WI 1992-1993. Claiming the Blessing Bd 2002; EPF 2001; Integrity 1994; NEAC 1999; The Oasis Missouri 2000. jasonsamuel@earthlink.net

SAMUEL JR, Morris Vaughn (Los) 6917 Ranchito Ave, Van Nuys CA 91405 B Scranton PA 4/15/1928 s Morris Vaughn Samuel & Jeanette. BS Penn 1951; MDiv CDSP 1959; MS U CA 1969. D 6/22/1959 P 2/1/1960 Bp Francis E I Bloy. Dio El Camino Real Monterey CA 1987-1988; Dir Of The Counslg Cntr S Andr's Ch Saratoga CA 1986-1987; Dio Los Angeles Los Angeles CA 1985-1986; P-in-c Of CE S Mk's Par Altadena CA 1978-1979; Asst S Tim's Par Compton CA 1965-1966; Cur The Par Ch Of S Lk Long Bch CA 1959-1962. Auth, "The Housemeeting Approach To Cmnty Orgnztn". OHC.

SAMUELS, Robert Marshall (WNY) 320 High St, De Pere WI 54115 B Melrose MA 4/10/1945 s Robert James Samuels & Helen Corinne. AA Penn Behrend Coll Erie PA 1981; MDiv TESM 1988; ThD Slidell Bapt Sem 2000. D 11/30/1988 P 6/17/1989 Bp William L Stevens. m 12/14/1968 Sharon Louise Hopkins c 3. Vic S Mary's Ch Salamanca NY 2002-2005; S Mary's Ch Erie PA 2000-2005; R Gr Epis Ch Menomonie WI 2000-2001; H Trin Ch Conrath WI 1998-1999; Our Sav's Phillips WI 1995-1998; R S Kath's Ch Owen WI 1994-1999; S Alb's Epis Ch Marshfield WI 1993; Cur S Anne's Ch De Pere WI 1988-1992. revbob333@att.net

SAMUELSON, Kenneth Bernhard (NCal) P.O. Box 84, Loleta CA 95551 **Died 3/15/2011** B Alton CA 8/31/1914 s John Herman Samuelson & Harriet Christina. BA Humboldt St U 1938; MDiv CDSP 1949. D 5/28/1949 P 12/10/1949 Bp Archie W N Porter. Intl Ord Of S Lk 1964. Hon Cn (Lifetime) Trin Cathd Sacremento CA 1965.

SANBORN, Calvin Francis Lyon (Me) Po Box 823, York Harbor ME 03911 **Dio Maine Portland ME 2002-** B Bridgeton ME 5/31/1974 s Earl Joses Sanborn & Patricia Ann. BA S Jos's Coll Standish ME 1996; MDiv EDS 2002. D 6/1/2002 P 11/30/2002 Bp Chilton Abbie Richardson Knudsen. R S Matt's Epis Ch Hallowell ME 2005-2010; Dio New York New York City NY 2004-2005; Asst S Geo's Epis Ch York Harbor ME 2002-2004. calvin.sanborn@gmail.com

SANBORN, Marda Leigh Steedman (Oly) 720 E Guiberson St, Kent WA 98030 **R S Jas Epis Ch Kent WA 1997-** B Chelsea MA 9/16/1951 d Allen Bradley Steedman & Marguerite. Cert Olympia TS; BA U of Washington 1972; Med U of Washington 1974; EdD Seattle U 1991. D 1/27/1992 P 11/22/1996 Bp Vincent Waydell Warner. m 8/27/1988 Douglas Craig Sanborn c 1. P S Mk's Cathd Seattle WA 1992-1997. Auth, "Coping w Stress: The Kindergarten Fndt". msanborn@stjameskent.org

SANBORN, Victoria B M (NY) 3919 Pocahontas Ave, Cincinnati OH 45227 B Brooklyn NY 11/1/1939 d Frederic Rockwell Sanborn & Janet. BA Wellesley Coll 1961; BA Oxf 1964; MA Oxf 1969; MDiv GTS 1982. D 6/2/1979 P 5/1/1980 Bp Paul Moore Jr. Assoc S Jn's Ch New York NY 1997-2000; Dio Sthrn Ohio Cincinnati OH 1985-1989; Vic Chap Of The Nativ Cincinnati OH 1985-1988; Assoc S Barth's Ch New York NY 1979-1983; Seamens Ch Inst Income New York NY 1979-1981. vbmsanborn@gmail.com

SANCHEZ, Jose De Jesus (SeFla) 525 NE 15th St, Miami FL 33132 **Dio SE Florida Miami FL 2011-** B Mexico 9/12/1959 s Jesus Sanchez & Aurora. Bachelor Intercontinental U 1989; Bachelor Philos Universidad Intercontinental 2004. Rec from Roman Catholic 5/25/2011 Bp Leopold Frade. m 12/12/2004 Glenda Reoyo c 2. padrejose@latinportugueseministry.org

SANCHEZ NAVARRO, Aida Consuelo (Hond) Col.Lomas Iraflores, Sur 3 C11 Bd No. 4318, Tegucigalpa 21105 Honduras **Dio Honduras Miami FL 2006-; Iglesia Epis Hondurena San Pedro Sula 2006-** B Santa Rosa de Coxan 2/13/1963 d Sergio Sanchez Ruiz & Maria Consuelo. Universidad Nacional Autonama De Honduras 1988; Programa Diocesano De Educ Teologica 2003. D 10/29/2005 Bp Lloyd Emmanuel Allen. m 1/13/2001 Luis Gustavo Brenes Vaigas c 1. csanchezhn@yahoo.com

SANCHEZ PUJOL, Augusto Sandino (DR) Santiago #114, Santo Domingo Dominican Republic **Par P Dio The Dominican Republic (Iglesia Epis Dominicana) 100 Airport AvVenice FL 1997-** B Bani DO 8/14/1953 s Juan Sanchez & Juana Pujol. Coll Epis S Marcos 1975; Centro De Estudios Teologicas 1995. D 6/29/1996 Bp Julio Cesar Holguin-Khoury. m 3/13/1987 Isabel Lantigua.

SAND, David Allan (NMich) PO Box 805, Iron Mountain MI 49801 B Iron Mountain, MI 1/23/1949 s Bortel Oscar Sand & Ruth Marie. BS Nthrn Michigan U 1971; Mutual Mnstry 2010. D 3/29/2010 P 10/3/2010 Bp Thomas Kreider Ray. m 2/16/1974 Lynn Ann Larson c 2. dave@dickinsonhomes.com

SAND, Lynn Ann (NMich) PO Box 805, Iron Mountain MI 49801 B Iron Mountain MI 1/10/1949 d Robert F Larson & Lois Carlene. RN Illinois Masonic Hosp. Sch of Nrsng 1970; Mutual Mnstry 2010. D 3/29/2010 P 10/3/2010 Bp Thomas Kreider Ray. m 2/16/1974 David Allan Sand c 2. dave@dickinsonhomes.com

SANDERS, E(dwin) Benjamin (Ky) 3812 Burning Bush Rd, Louisville KY 40241 B Marion VA 8/20/1938 s Edwin Bradley Sanders & Elizabeth Deblois. BA U of Virginia 1959; BD Drew U 1962. D 12/18/1970 P 4/18/1971 Bp William Henry Marmion. m 12/16/1976 Mary H Hill. Vic Trin Ch Russellville KY 2005-2008; Sch Chapl/Assistint Ch Of The Gd Shpd Punta Gorda FL 2001-2003; R Calv Ch Louisville KY 1981-2000; Asst S Mary's Cathd Memphis TN 1979-1981; R S Eliz's Ch Roanoke VA 1971-1976. Phi Beta Kappa. msanders48@gmail.com

SANDERS, Harvel Ray (Mo) 110 Walnut Park Dr, Sedalia MO 65301 B Ava MO 8/29/1941 s Herbert Sanders & Stella. BA U of Missouri 1963; STB EDS 1966. D 6/25/1966 P 1/1/1967 Bp George Leslie Cadigan. m 6/28/2008 Susan Wehrle c 3. R Gr Ch Jefferson City MO 1970-2005; R S Paul's Ch S Louis MO 1969-1970; Cur Gr Ch Kirkwood MO 1966-1969. papaharv@gmail.com

S

SANDERS, Jack Eugene (WMass) 510 Park St, Miami OK 74354 **Asstg P All SS Epis Ch Miami OK 1996-** B Cardin OK Ottawa 4/11/1923 s Franklin Jefferson Sanders & Pearl Grace. BA Phillips U 1944; MA Phillips U 1948; BD Phillips U 1949; GTS 1965. D 6/14/1965 Bp John P Craine P 12/15/1965 Bp Robert McConnell Hatch. m 5/26/1944 Pauline Ann Gary c 3. Dn Franklin/Hampshire Deanry & Mem Fin Com Dio Wstrn Massachusetts Springfield MA 1971-1973; Chair COM Dio Wstrn Massachusetts Springfield MA 1970-1973; Assoc S Jas' Ch Greenfield MA 1965-1968.

SANDERS, Jaime Morrow Wrench (Ore) 2190 Crest Dr, Lake Oswego OR 97034 **S Jn The Evang Ch Milwaukie OR 2008-** B Eugene OR 7/16/1956 d David F Wrench & Barbara E. BA U Of Oregon Eugene OR 1978; JD Willamette Coll Of Law Salem OR 1985; MDiv CDSP 2007. D 6/30/2007 P 1/5/2008 Bp Johncy Itty. m 1/7/1984 Stephen Sanders c 2. D All SS Ch Portland OR 2007. jmwsanders@cartlink.net

SANDERS, James Lemuel (ETenn) 32968 Steelwood Ridge Rd, Loxley AL 36551 B Birmingham AL 12/9/1931 s Samuel Henry Sanders & Nettie Bell. BA Birmingham-Sthrn Coll 1956; VTS 1968. D 6/14/1968 P 3/1/1969 Bp George Mosley Murray. m 10/26/1952 Sara DeLay. Dn S Jn's Epis Cathd Knoxville TN 1980-1997; R S Paul's Ch Selma AL 1971-1980; Vic S Tim's Epis Ch Athens AL 1968-1971. Auth, "Alabama Stwdshp Plan," *Jesus Dollars and Sense*. vicar.stwd@gulftel.com

SANDERS, Joanne (Cal) Stanford Memorial Church, Stanford University, Stanford CA 94305 B Buffalo NY 4/16/1960 d David James Sanders & Patricia Ann. BS Grand Canyon U 1982; MS Seattle Pacific U 1990; MDiv CDSP 2000; Cert Seattle U 2010. D 6/3/2000 P 12/2/2000 Bp William Edwin Swing. COM Dio California San Francisco CA 2008-2009; Yth Dir Trin Par Menlo Pk CA 1995-1997. AAR 2008; Assn of Coll and U Rel Affrs 2001; Natl Assn of Coll and U Chapl 2003; Natl Assn of Stdt Personl Administrators 2009. REVJO@MAC.COM

SANDERS, John Clarke (At) 2744 Peachtree Rd Nw, Atlanta GA 30305 **Dn Cathd Of S Phil Atlanta GA 2001-** B Houston TX 3/21/1933 s Carroll Dean Sanders & Estelle Texas. BBA Texas 1955; BD Epis TS of The SW 1958; STM VTS 1969. D 6/19/1958 P 6/1/1959 Bp James Parker Clements. m 9/16/1955 Frances Jameson c 3. Cathd Of S Phil Atlanta GA 1986-1998; R Chr Ch Shaker Heights OH 1975-1986; Dn Cathd Ch Of S Jn Wilmington DE 1970-1975; R S Jas Epis Ch Houston TX 1963-1970; R H Trin Epis Ch Port Neches TX 1960-1963; M-in-c H Trin Epis Ch Port Neches TX 1958-1959. Cmnty of the Cross of Nails 1975-1995; Epis Soceity for Cultural and Racial Unity 1963-1972. DD Epis TS of The SW 1993. FJSANDERS55@SBCGLOBAL.NET

SANDERS, Lynn Coggins (NY) St. Bartholomew's Church, 325 Park Avenue, New York NY 10022 **Assoc R S Barth's Ch New York NY 2008-** B Greenville SC 9/1/1954 d Woodrow H Coggins & Ethlyn B. BS Furman U 1976; MBA Clemson U 1990; MDiv CDSP 2004. D 3/13/2004 P 9/18/2004 Bp Mark Sean Sisk. Congrl T/F Dio Texas Houston TX 2005-2007; Nomin Com Dio Texas Houston TX 2004-2007; Asst R The Ch of the Gd Shpd Austin TX 2004-2007. lmcsanders@gmail.com

SANDERS, Marilyn Mae (CNY) 841 Charlotte Creek Road, Oneonta NY 13820 **R S Ptr's Ch Bainbridge NY 2010-** B Detroit MI 6/21/1947 d Robert James Mauck & Natalie Maxine. BS NWU 1969; MDiv Duke 1994. D 6/16/2001 P 12/19/2001 Bp Wendell Nathaniel Gibbs Jr. m 7/4/1989 Francis David Sanders c 3. R S Paul's Epis Ch Albany NY 2006; Int Epis Ch Of The Trsfg Sis OR 2004-2005; Assoc R Ch Of The Adv Spartanburg SC 2002-2004; Asst to the Int R S Clare Of Assisi Epis Ch Ann Arbor MI 2001-2002. ladypriest.marilyn@gmail.com

SANDERS, Megan (Nwk) The Seamen's Church Institute of NY & NJ, 118 Export St., Newark NJ 07114 **Asstg P S Lk's Epis Ch Montclair NJ 2009-; Port Chapl and Tri St Ch Coordntr Seamens Ch Inst Income New York NY 2008-** B Washington DC 1/24/1977 d Frederick Jefferson Sanders & Irene Hanas. BA Flagler Coll St Aug FL 1998; MDiv GTS 2007. D 6/14/2007 Bp James Louis Jelinek P 1/12/2008 Bp Richard Lester Shimpfky. Asstg P S Mary's Ch Sparta NJ 2008-2009; Asst R for Yth and Fam Mnstrs S Ptr's Ch Essex Fells NJ 2007-2008. msanders77@gmail.com

SANDERS JR, Patrick Henry (Miss) 8873 Timber Lake Cir, Meridian MS 39305 B Atlanta GA 5/30/1921 s Patrick Henry Sanders & Norma Applewhite. MDiv VTS 1959; BIE Georgia Inst of Tech 2048. D 3/26/1959 P 9/29/1959 Bp Duncan Montgomery Gray. m 12/8/1943 Elaine Cole c 3. Int S Andr's Cathd Jackson MS 1995-1996; Int S Lk's Epis Ch Jackson TN 1989-1990; R S Jn's Ch Laurel MS 1984-1988; R Ch Of The Atone Sandy Sprg GA 1977-1984; Vic S Jn's Ch Leland MS 1975-1977; Vic S Paul's Ch Hollandale MS 1975-1977; Stwdshp Consult Dio Mississippi Jackson MS 1972-1994; R All SS Epis Ch Mobile AL 1968-1975; R S Jas Ch Greenville MS 1961-1968; Asst S Andr's Cathd Jackson MS 1959-1961. esan39305@bellsouth.net

SANDERS, Patrick W (Miss) 8245 Getwell Rd, Southaven MS 38672 **S Timothys Epis Ch Southaven MS 2009-; S Jas Ch Greenville MS 2006-** B Vicksburg MS 8/30/1975 s Larry Sanders & Pamela. U of Mississippi; BD U of Sthrn Mississippi 2003; MDiv Etss Austin 2006. D 5/24/2006 Bp Duncan Montgomery Gray Jr P 2/27/2007 Bp Duncan Montgomery Gray III. m 7/31/1999 Jennifer W Kirk c 1. Dio Mississippi Jackson MS 2009. patrick@sainttimothys.net

SANDERS, Richard Evan (Ga) 605 Reynolds St, Augusta GA 30901 **R S Paul's Ch Augusta GA 2002-** B Union City TN 1/19/1957 s Brice Sidney Sanders & Nancy Elizabeth. BS Centenary Coll 1979; MDiv VTS 1985; DD SWTS 2000. D 6/11/1985 P 5/28/1986 Bp Duncan Montgomery Gray Jr. m 8/11/1984 Margaret Juanita Oates. Assoc R S Geo's Ch Nashville TN 1992-2001; Vic S Jn's Ch Leland MS 1987-1991; Vic S Paul's Ch Hollandale MS 1987-1991; Cur S Paul's Epis Ch Meridian MS 1985-1987. rector@saintpauls.org

SANDERS, Wayne Francis Michael (SanD) 3563 Merrimac Ave, San Diego CA 92117 B Chicago IL 4/3/1940 s Edward Sanders & Irene. BA S Mary of the Lake Sem. Rec from Roman Catholic 12/1/1974 Bp Robert Munro Wolterstorff. m 4/15/1974 Kathleen Bracken c 2. R Ch Of The Gd Samar San Diego CA 1978-2005; All SS Ch San Diego CA 1974-1978. revwfs@hotmail.com

✠ **SANDERS, Rt Rev William Evan** (ETenn) 404 Charlesgate Ct, Nashville TN 37215 **Ret Bp Of E Tennesse Dio E Tennessee Knoxville TN 1992-** B Natchez MS 12/25/1919 s Walter Richard Sanders & Agnes M(ortimer). BA Van 1942; BD STUSo 1945; STM UTS 1946; DD U So 1959. D 2/18/1945 P 6/11/1946 Bp James M Maxon Con 4/4/1962 for Tenn. m 6/11/2005 Marlin Jones c 4. Bp Dio E Tennessee Knoxville TN 1985-1991; Bp Dio Tennessee Nashville TN 1977-1984; Bp Coadj Dio Tennessee Nashville TN 1962-1976; Dn S Mary's Cathd Memphis TN 1946-1962; Cur S Paul's Epis Ch Chattanooga TN 1945-1946. xwordyx@comcast.net

SANDERSON, Herbert (Alb) 468 Pinewoods Rd, Melrose NY 12121 **Asst Gr Ch Waterford NY 2002-** B Brattleboro VT 5/20/1931 s Herbert Warren Sanderson & Elizabeth. BA Bos 1953; MDiv Ya Berk 1959; EdM Bos 1970; PhD SUNY 1973. D 6/20/1959 Bp Anson Phelps Stokes Jr P 12/19/1959 Bp Vedder Van Dyck. m 6/17/2000 Anne Capron c 3. Int P Gr And H Innoc Albany NY 1998-2004; Trin Ch Watervliet NY 1996-1998; Ch Of The Ascen Troy NY 1993-1994; Samar Counslg Cntr Schenectady NY 1990; R Ch Of The H Cross Troy NY 1978-1990; Asst Chr Ch Schenectady NY 1972-1978; Asst S Ptr's Epis Ch Bennington VT 1965-1967; R S Paul's Epis Ch On The Green Vergennes VT 1961-1965; In-c Chr Ch Island Pond VT 1959-1961; In-c S Ptr's Mssn Lyndonville VT 1959-1961. Amer Assn of Chr Counselors. twosanders@earthlink.net

SANDERSON, Joseph Wesley (Ala) Po Box 116, Guntersville AL 35976 **P-in-c S Barn' Epis Ch Hartselle AL 2004-** B Town Creek AL 8/29/1934 s Lewis Wesley Sanderson & Etta Mary. LTh SWTS. D Bp Robert Munro Wolterstorff P 5/1/1964 Bp Hamilton Hyde Kellogg. m 9/7/1957 Jan H Harrelson. R Ch Of The Epiph Guntersville AL 1983-1999; S Lk's Epis Ch Jacksonville AL 1978-1983; Trin Ch Wetumpka AL 1976-1978; R S Andr's Ch Marianna AR 1969-1976; Yth Advsr Dio Arkansas Little Rock AR 1966-1967; Vic Trin Par Ch Epis Searcy AR 1965-1967; Vic Emm Epis Ch Alexandria MN 1963-1965.

SANDERSON, Marshall Dow (SC) 218 Ashley Avenue, Charleston SC 29403 **R Ch Of The H Comm Charleston SC 2001-** B Montgomery AL 1/30/1959 s Henry Lee Sanderson & Julia Gardner. BA Coll of Charleston 1981; MDiv VTS 1986. D 6/15/1986 P 5/10/1987 Bp C(hristopher) FitzSimons Allison. m 5/7/1983 Fiona Richardson c 2. Stndg Com (Pres) Dio So Carolina Charleston SC 2005-2008; R Ch Of The Redeem Orangeburg SC 1993-2001; Asst R Ch Of The H Comf Sumter SC 1990-1993; Exam Chapl Dio So Carolina Charleston SC 1990-1993; Asst R S Andr's Epis Ch Arlington VA 1989-1990; Vic S Alb's Ch Kingstree SC 1986-1989. holycomm@bellsouth.net

SANDERSON, Peter Oliver (Ia) 410 Brentwood Dr, Alamogordo NM 88310 B South Shields England UK 1/26/1929 s Harold Beckwith Sanderson & Doris Amelia. BA U of Durham GB 1952; DIT U of Durham GB 1954. Trans from Scottish Episcopal Church 11/1/1991 Bp Carl Christopher Epting. m 4/4/1956 Doreen Gibson c 3. Int Epis Ch In Lincoln Cnty Ruidoso NM 2007-2009; P-in-res Trin Ch Iowa City IA 2000-2002; Vic All SS Epis Ch Storm Lake IA 1991-2000. RSCM. frpeter.sanderson@gmail.com

SANDERSON, (Simmons) Holladay (Ida) All Saints Episcopal Church, 704 S Latah St, Boise ID 83705 **Chair, Liturg Cmsn Dio Idaho Boise ID 2011-; Chair, Sexual Ethics Com + Trnr Dio Idaho Boise ID 2010-; Dep, 2012 GC Dio Idaho Boise ID 2010-; R All SS Epis Ch Boise ID 2009-; COM, Mem Dio Idaho Boise ID 2009-** B Raleigh NC 5/17/1950 d Hal Venable Worth & Mary Simmons. BA U NC 1972; MM E Carolina U 1975; MDiv VTS 2001. D 6/2/2001 P 12/8/2001 Bp James Edward Waggoner. m 7/2/1984 Stanley McNaughton Sanderson. Vic S Andr's Ch Chelan WA 2009; Vic S Paul's Ch Cheney WA 2007-2009; T/F on Mnstry Dvlpmt, Chair Dio Spokane Spokane WA 2005-2006; Living Stones Coordntr Dio Spokane Spokane WA 2004-2009; Mssn and Bdgt Com Dio Spokane Spokane WA 2003-2005; COM, Mem Dio Spokane Spokane WA 2002-2009; Chair, Sexual Ethics Com + Trnr Dio Spokane Spokane WA 2001-2009; R S Mart's Ch Moses Lake WA 2001-2009; Dioc Coun, Mem Dio Spokane Spokane WA 2001-2003. hsanderson@qosi.net

S

SANDFORT, Candace Christine (NY) 19 Sandfort Ln, Warwick NY 10990 **S Paul's Ch Chester NY 2009-** B Newton MA 11/25/1951 d Glen Philip Bieging & Eldora McLaughlin. BA U of Virginia 1973; MDiv The GTS 2004; STM The GTS 2008. D 3/15/2008 P 9/20/2008 Bp Mark Sean Sisk. m 9/24/1972 John Sandfort c 4. sandfort@warwick.net

SANDLIN, Allan (At) 1881 Edinburgh Terrace NE, Atlanta GA 30307 **Vice Chair of the Nomin Com for the 10th Bp of Atlanta Dio Atlanta Atlanta GA 2011-2012; Vice Chair of the Nomin Com for the 10th Bp of Atlanta Dio Atlanta Atlanta GA 2011-; P-in-c S Paul's Epis Ch Newnan GA 2011-; COM Dio Atlanta Atlanta GA 2007-; Assoc R H Trin Par Decatur GA 2007-; Chair of the Deputation to GC Convoc of Amer Ch in Europe Paris FR 2006-; GC Dep Convoc of Amer Ch in Europe Paris FR 2003-** B Fort Worth TX 8/25/1952 s Bryce Sandlin & LaVerne. BA SUNY 1976; MMus Hardin-Simmons U 1978; MDiv Candler TS Emory U 1989. D 6/8/1991 P 1/25/1992 Bp Frank Kellogg Allan. m 3/21/1987 Gretchen Nagy c 2. Bd Frgn Parishes Convoc of Amer Ch in Europe Paris FR 1999-2007; R The Angl/Epis Ch Of Chr The King Frankfurt am Main 60323 DE 1999-2007; Coun of Advice Convoc of Amer Ch in Europe Paris FR 1999-2002; R S Fran By The Sea Blue Hill ME 1994-1999; S Lk's Epis Ch Atlanta GA 1991-1994. Fllshp of St. Jn the Evang 1997. Theta Pi Candler TS 1989; Omicron Delta Kappa Candler TS 1989; Robert W. Woodruff Fell Candler TS 1985. allansandlin@bellsouth.net

SANDOE, Deirdre Etheridge (WA) 400 Rouen Dr Apt H, Deland FL 32720 B Miami FL 6/23/1946 d Earl Dewitt Etheridge & Louise Featherston. BA U of Tennessee 1990; MDiv VTS 1995. D 6/5/1996 Bp M(arvil) Thomas Shaw III P 6/12/1999 Bp John Wadsworth Howe. Ch Of The H Comf Vienna VA 2002; S Barn Ch Deland FL 1999; D Ch Of The Ascen Silver Sprg MD 1997-2000; D Ch Of S Jn The Evang Boston MA 1995-1997.

SANDOVAL, Juan (At) 161 Church St NE, Marietta GA 30060 B Phoenix AZ 5/26/1947 s Porfino Ernesto Sandoval & Lillian. D 8/6/2011 Bp J(ohn) Neil Alexander. m 4/18/1994 Elizabeth Anne Sandoval c 4. elsapifico@gmail.com

SANDOVAL CROS, Carlos Juan (SeFla) 10950 Sw 34th St, Miami FL 33165 **R S Simons Ch Miami FL 1995-** B 6/12/1958 s Lester Sandoval & Mercedes B. Miami-Dade Cmnty Coll; Seminario Epis Teologico Del Ecuador; MD Universidad Catolica Madre Y Maestra 1983; U of Miami 1995. D 12/18/1988 P 5/1/1990 Bp Adrian Delio Caceres-Villavicencio. Int Epis Ch Of The H Fam Miami Gardens FL 1994-1995; Assoc Trin Cathd Miami FL 1991-2001; Iglesia Epis Del Ecuador Ecuador 1990-1991. Ed, "Himnos De Vida," 1988; Ed, "Dios Cuida A Su Pueblo," 1988. cjsandoval@bellsouth.net

SANDROCK, Hans Erwin (Cal) 2366 Carolyn Pl, Encinitas CA 92024 **Cn For Dvlmpt Cathd Ch Of S Paul San Diego CA 1998-; Hon Asst S Jas By The Sea La Jolla CA 1992-** B Waverly IA 10/11/1922 s Sigmund Herman Sandrock & Hilda Elizabeth. BA Wartburg Coll 1944; MDiv Wartburg TS 1946; MA Air U Maxwell AFB AL 1962; LLD Atlanta Law Sch Atlanta GA 1968; DD Wartburg TS 1978; DMin GTF 1986. D 12/5/1992 P 6/5/1993 Bp William Edwin Swing. m 9/30/1956 Eleanor K Stockwell. Cn To Ord Dio California San Francisco CA 1987-2001. Auth, "ArmdF Hymnal," 1972. Cn To Ordnry Dio Cal 1987.

SANDS, Fred W(illiam) (SeFla) 300 Sw 29th Ave, Fort Lauderdale FL 33312 **D Ch Of S Chris Ft Lauderdale FL 1995-; D S Ambr Epis Ch Ft Lauderdale FL 1995-** B Miami FL 2/27/1933 s Charles Malachi Sands & Maydon Charsetta. AA Edw Waters Coll Jacksonville FL 1953; BS Florida A&M U 1958. D 6/12/1995 Bp John Lewis Said. m 6/20/1964 Frances Frandessa Fair c 1. COM, Curs 1995-2000; Curs 1979. Chair, Mnstry On Aging St Chris'S Epis Ch 1994.

SANDWELL-WEISS, Rosa Leah (Az) 8502 N Deer Valley Dr, Tucson AZ 85742 **D S Phil's In The Hills Tucson AZ 2011-** B Columbia MO 2/23/1954 d Robert Lee Sandwell & Rosemary. BA U of Missouri 1975; MA U of Missouri 1977; JD U of Arizona 1984. D 1/29/2011 Bp Kirk Stevan Smith. m 7/5/1980 Karl Weiss c 1. lsandwellweiss@gmail.com

SANFORD, Carol Webb (WMo) 1914 W 50th Ter, Westwood Hills KS 66205 B Springfield MO 8/22/1950 GTS; BA Emory U 1972; MDiv CDSP 2005. D 6/4/2005 P 12/3/2005 Bp Barry Robert Howe. m 12/30/1972 Grady H Sanford. Assoc Gr And H Trin Cathd Kansas City MO 2005-2009; Campus Mnstry Coordntr Dio W Missouri Kansas City MO 2005-2006. cawsanford@yahoo.com

SANFORD, Gary L(ee) (NwT) 1801 Edmund Blvd, San Angelo TX 76901 **Exec Coun Dio NW Texas Lubbock TX 2011-; D Emm Epis Ch San Angelo TX 2006-** B St. John KS 6/30/1951 s Charles Mason Sanford & Sarah Lee. D 10/29/2006 Bp C(harles) Wallis Ohl. m 6/20/1981 Eldra Gibson c 1. NAAD / AED 2005; NCMA 2008. garysanford@emmanuel-sa.org

SANFORD JR, Paul Emery (Alb) PO Box 282, Chestertown NY 12817 B Potsdam NY 10/3/1928 s Paul Emery Sanford & Sarah Jane. BS SUNY 1951; MDiv PDS 1954. D 6/6/1954 P 12/18/1954 Bp Frederick Lehrle Barry. R S Jas Ch Delhi NY 1981-1990; Vic S Alb's Ch Spooner WI 1976-1981; Vic S Steph's Shell Lake WI 1976-1981; St Stephens Ch Spooner WI 1976-1981; R Ch Of The H Cross Warrensburg NY 1960-1972; Sr Asst Cathd Ch Of S Paul Burlington VT 1959-1960; R Par Of S Jas Ft Edw NY 1954-1959. psanford2@nycap.rr.com

SANON, Jean-Louis Felix (NY) 2757 Jacob Lane, Douglasville GA 30135 B Cazale HT 7/14/1940 s Pierre Mirabeau Normil Sanon & Quercina Benoit. Lic U of Ethnology Port-au-Prince HT 1966; Lic U of Law Port-au-Prince HT 1969; MDiv ETSC 1974; Cert Oxf 2001. D 4/28/1974 P 1/30/1975 Bp Luc Anatole Jacques Garnier. m 12/19/1978 Milorenne Normil c 3. P-in-c Haitian Cong of the Gd Samar Bronx NY 1997-2007; R, St Pierre, Mirebalais Dio Haiti Ft Lauderdale FL 1995-1996; R, St. Simeon, Croix-des-Bouquets Dio Haiti Ft Lauderdale FL 1990-1995; Cathd Admin, Port-au-Prince Dio Haiti Ft Lauderdale FL 1982-1990; P in charge Resurr, Gros-Morne Dio Haiti Ft Lauderdale FL 1975-1982; R, Resurr Ch, Gros-Nore Dio Haiti Ft Lauderdale FL 1975-1982; D, St Sauveur, Cayes Dio Haiti Ft Lauderdale FL 1974-1975. jlfelix14@aol.com

SANTANA, Carlos Enrique (DR) C/O Episcopal Church In Dominican Republic, Box 764, Dominican Republic Dominican Republic **Dio The Dominican Republic (Iglesia Epis Dominicana) Santo Domingo DO 2010-** B 8/7/1972 D 2/14/2010 P 2/20/2011 Bp Julio Cesar Holguin-Khoury. m Estefanie Garcia de Santana. santanaenrique@hotmail.com

SANTANA, Rosa M (DR) Apartado 128, San Pedro De Macoris Dominican Republic B 11/1/1962 d Severiano Santana & Eva. Universidad Autonoma Arquitecta 1987; LTh Centro De Estudios Teologicas 1991. D 3/10/1991 Bp Telesforo A Isaac P 6/1/1992 Bp Julio Cesar Holguin-Khoury. m 8/9/1991 Vincent Serge Pierre-Louis. Dio The Dominican Republic (Iglesia Epis Dominicana) Santo Domingo DO 1991-2010.

SANTANA-RUIZ, Benjamin (SwFla) 222 S Palm Ave, Sarasota FL 34236 B 12/4/1945 BA Wrld U. D 2/24/1978 P 1/14/1979 Bp Francisco Reus-Froylan. m 2/16/1990 Dielma Santana. Hisp Mnstry Ch Of The Redeem Sarasota FL 2008-2010; Dio Vrgn Islands St Thos VI VI 2006-2007; S Lk's Ch Brockport NY 2004-2009; All SS Epis Ch Meriden CT 2004-2006; Dio Puerto Rico S Just PR 2004; Dio Wstrn New York Tonawanda NY 2002-2004; Dio Puerto Rico S Just PR 2002-2003; Dio Puerto Rico S Just PR 1998-2000; Dio Puerto Rico S Just PR 1980-1988; Dio Puerto Rico S Just PR 1978-1979. benjamin.santana@gmail.com

SANTIAGO, Vicente C (Pgh) 132 Sherwood Drive, Greensburg PA 15601 **Dio Pittsburgh Monroeville PA 2011-** B San Juan PR 10/6/1944 MDiv TESM; BSEE U of Puerto Rico 1967. D 6/12/2004 Bp Robert William Duncan P 12/12/2004 Bp Henry William Scriven. m 8/2/2006 Gwen Santiago. S Mk's Ch Johnstown PA 2009-2011; D S Jas Epis Ch Pittsburgh PA 2004-2006. vicentecarlos@email.com

SANTIVIAGO-ESPINAL, Maria Isabel (NY) 2453 78th St # 2, East Elmhurst NY 11370 **S Ann's Ch For The Deaf New York NY 2007-** B Asuncion PARAGUAY 12/30/1941 d Felipe Santiviago & Isabel Mercedes. D 3/18/2000 P 9/16/2000 Bp Richard Frank Grein. m 12/18/1982 Miguel D Espinal. Mision San Juan Bautista Bronx NY 2000-2009. ICTUS41@RCN.COM

SANTOS-MONTES, Margarita (PR) PO Box 8453, Ponce PR 00732 Puerto Rico **Dio Puerto Rico S Just PR 2007-** B Ponce 8/28/1955 d Justino Santos & Zendoia. BA Pontificia Universidad Catilica 1976; Diacono Permanente Santisima Trinidad 1994. D 10/15/1995 P 2/11/2007 Bp David Andres Alvarez-Velazquez. m 12/18/1982 Rodriguez Echevarria Efrain. margaret7@coqui.net

SANTOS-RIVERA, Carlos (Pa) 3554 N 6th St, Philadelphia PA 19140 **Dio Pennsylvania Philadelphia PA 1991-** B 5/12/1942 Trans from Province IX 11/21/1986 Bp Lyman Cunningham Ogilby. c 3. Chr And S Ambr Ch Philadelphia PA 1986-1990; Dio Puerto Rico S Just PR 1975-1979.

SANTOSUOSSO, John Edward (SwFla) 3474 Christina Groves Ln, Lakeland FL 33813 B Camden NJ 2/21/1939 s John Blase Santosuosso & Mildred Irene. BA Ursinus Coll 1961; MA Clark U 1963; MDiv Louisville Presb TS 1968; PhD U Of Florida 1981. D 5/19/1981 Bp William Hopkins Folwell. m 6/15/1968 Janet Ann Beard. D All SS Epis Ch Lakeland FL 1994-1998; D S Ptr's Ch Plant City FL 1986-1994; D S Dav's Epis Ch Lakeland FL 1981-1986. Auth, "Can: An Intro for Americans," 2007; Auth, "Shostring Investing Made E-Z," 2000. Phi Beta Kappa 1981. jsantosuosso@flsouthern.edu

SANTUCCI, Mark (Ct) 166 Lambtown Rd, Ledyard CT 06339 **R S Mk's Ch Mystic CT 1993-** B Bristol CT 5/14/1947 s Albert Francis Santucci & Martha Stockdale. BA Lycoming Coll 1969; MS U of Scranton 1972; MDiv GTS 1982. D 6/5/1982 P 12/18/1982 Bp Charlie Fuller McNutt Jr. m 8/28/1971 Marlene Ann McGibbon c 2. R Chr Ch Williamsport PA 1986-1993; Asst S Andr's Ch Harrisburg PA 1982-1986. msantucci@sbcglobal.net

SANZO, Maria B (NJ) 318 Huxley Dr, Brick NJ 08723 **Com on the Diac Dio New Jersey Trenton NJ 2011-; R Trin Ch Matawan NJ 2011-** B Bayonne NJ 4/18/1956 d Salvatore Charles Sanzo & Rose Marie. BA Immaculata U 1978; MDiv GTS 2010. D 10/21/2000 Bp David B(ruce) Joslin P 6/19/2010 Bp George Edward Councell. c 1. Asst Ch Of S Mary's By The Sea Point Pleasant Bch NJ 2010-2011; D S Raphael The Archangel Brick NJ 2003-2009; D Trin Ch Asbury Pk NJ 2001-2003; D Chr Ch Toms River Toms River NJ 2000-2001. mariabsanzo@comcast.net

SARAI-CLARK, Wilhelmina Olivia (Spok) 503 E D St, Moscow ID 83843 **D S Jas Pullman WA 1992-** B Tuskegee Inst AL 1/25/1927 d William Arthur Clark & Olivia Stanford. PhD U of Wisconsin 1970; Cert Dio Spokane TS 1992. D 5/10/1992 Bp Frank Jeffrey Terry. Auth, "Philos Of Dance As Art For Non-Philosophers"; Auth, "Carnival: A Dance For Two"; Auth, "Isms & Power". NAAD, Sacr Dance Gld.

SARGENT, Arthur Lloyd (Dal) HC 78 Box 9119, Ranchos de Taos NM 87557 B Amarillo TX 8/31/1935 s William M Sargent & Chelsea B. BA U of No Texas 1957; STB GTS 1961; MA U of No Texas 1967. D 6/20/1961 Bp Charles A Mason P 12/21/1961 Bp J(ohn) Joseph Meakins Harte. m 2/9/1957 Jonnie Dell Braden c 5. Asst S Jas Epis Ch Taos NM 1999-2002; Cmnty Consult on Bp Stff Dio Dallas Dallas TX 1973-1975; Asst S Mich And All Ang Ch Dallas TX 1961-1963. Auth, "Memi Day," *Preaching Through H Days and Holidays*, Morehouse, 2003. asargent@centurytel.net

SARGENT GREEN, Nancy Hunnewell (EO) 18160 Cottonwood Rd Pmb 719, Sunriver OR 97707 B Boston MA 5/23/1947 d George Lee Sargent & Hester Lloyd. AA Bradford Jr Coll 1967; BA GW 1969; MDiv Andover Newton TS 1977. D 10/15/1977 Bp Morris Fairchild Arnold P 6/3/1978 Bp William J Gordon Jr. m 4/28/2007 Roy Donald Green c 2. Stndg Com Dio Estrn Oregon The Dalles OR 2007-2009; Pres, Eccl Crt Dio Estrn Oregon The Dalles OR 2004-2006; Trin Ch Bend OR 1997; All SS Of The Cascades Epis Ch Sunriver OR 1996; S Steph's Ch Troy MI 1984; Com Dio Michigan Detroit MI 1982-1986; Chr Ch Grosse Pointe Grosse Pointe Farms MI 1981-1982; Int S Jas Ch Grosse Ile MI 1981-1982; Chr Ch Detroit MI 1978-1980. nsm523@aol.com

SARKISSYIAN, Sabi Kamel (Mo) 524 Fox Run Estates Ct, Ballwin MO 63021 B Palestine 2/10/1937 s Kamel Sarkissyian & Najl. BD Cairo EG 1962. Trans from The Episcopal Church in Jerusalem and the Middle East 7/21/2001 Bp Hays H. Rockwell. m 7/5/1970 Firyal S Sarkissyian c 3. Arabic Min S Tim's Epis Ch Creve Coeur MO 2004-2011; Arabic Min Ch Of The Gd Shpd S Louis MO 1999-2004. Cn Emer The Epis Ch of Jerusalem and the M. E. 1997; Cn The Epis Ch of Jerusalem and the M. E. 1983. yara0582@yahoo.com

SARRAZIN, Victor Joseph (Az) 3880 Via De La Reina, Sierra Vista AZ 85650 **S Steph's Ch Sierra Vista AZ 2006-** B Montebello CA 8/25/1958 BA S Marys Sem 1984; MDiv S Thos Sem Denver CO 1990. Rec from Roman Catholic 6/4/2005 Bp Barry Robert Howe. m 8/9/2003 Rhonda R Sarrazin c 3. vsarrazin@cox.net

SARTIN, George Randall (Fla) 3480 Lakeshore Drive, Tallahassee FL 32312 **Chairman, COM Dio Florida Jacksonville FL 2011-; R Ch Of The Adv Tallahassee FL 2008-** B New Orleans LA 7/3/1955 s Jack Sartin & Billie Frances. BS Liberty U 1978; MDiv VTS 1986. D 6/30/1986 P 6/11/1987 Bp Duncan Montgomery Gray Jr. m 12/15/1984 Ute K Koehler c 1. R S Geo's Epis Ch Clarksdale MS 1998-2008; R Ascen Epis Ch Amherst VA 1988-1997; R S Mk's Ch Clifford VA 1988-1994; P-in-c Ch Of The Redeem Greenville MS 1986-1988; Cur S Jas Ch Greenville MS 1986-1988. grsartin@me.com

SARTIN, Nancy Avera (Ga) 1521 N Patterson St, Valdosta GA 31602 B Macon GA 7/21/1957 d Carol E Avera & Anne t. BSEd Valdosta St U 1979; Masters Valdosta St U 1983; EdSpec Valdosta St U 1984. D 9/11/2010 Bp Scott Anson Benhase. m 4/14/2007 Michael Lee Richardson c 1. nancysartin@att.net

SASAKI, Norio (Haw) 3252 Charles St, Honolulu HI 96816 B Waialua HI 11/18/1925 s Nobudane Sasaki & Yoshi. BA U of Hawaii 1951; MDiv CDSP 1958; Fllshp Procter Fllshp 1981. D 6/10/1958 Bp Henry W Hobson P 12/10/1958 Bp Harry S Kennedy. m 12/8/1951 Florence S Nakagawa c 4. Stff S Eliz's Ch Honolulu HI 1970-1971; Assoc The Par Of S Clem Honolulu HI 1966-1970; S Alb's Chap Honolulu HI 1958-1988. Hawaii Cler Assn. nsasaki@aloha.net

SASSER JR, Howell Crawford (NC) Saint Peter's Episcopal Church, 137 N Division St, Peekskill NY 10566 **Asst S Ptr's Epis Ch Peekskill NY 2009-** B Tacoma WA 9/4/1966 s Howell Sasser & Elaine. BA JHU 1988; MPH U of So Carolina 1995; PhD U Pgh 1999; BD Lon 2003; BD Lon 2003; STM Ya Berk 2009. D 6/13/2009 Bp Michael Bruce Curry P 4/28/2010 Bp Catherine Scimeca Roskam. howell.sasser@hotmail.com

SASSMAN, William Arthur (NCal) 5601 Natomas Blvd Apt 21301, Sacramento CA 95835 B Philadelphia PA 11/27/1936 s John Williams Sassman & Ruth Beatrice. BS Leh 1958; ThM ETSC 1967; MA Inter Amer U of Puerto Rico 1970; Cert CDSP 1981. D 5/17/1967 P 12/21/1967 Bp Francisco Reus-Froylan. m 7/22/2002 Elizabeth Cano c 3. S Fran Epis Ch Fair Oaks CA 1994-2002; Off Of Bsh For ArmdF New York NY 1973-1987. Auth, "arts," *Interchange*, U.S. AF. Mltry Chapl Assn 1973. wsassman@hotmail.com

SASSO-CRANDALL, Charles David (NJ) 206 Central Ave, Hammonton NJ 08037 B Boston MA 2/6/1937 s Willis Bollard Crandall & Dorothy Louzella. BS Boston Coll 1959; MDiv GTS 1979. D 6/2/1979 Bp Albert Wiencke Van Duzer P 12/1/1979 Bp George E Rath. m 6/11/1961 Rose Mary Sasso-Crandall c 1. Vic S Mk's Ch Hammonton NJ 1995-2004; Int S Aug's Ch Camden NJ 1993-1995; Chr Ch Collingswood NJ 1980-1990; Cur S Ptr's Ch Freehold NJ 1979-1980. sassocrandall@aol.com

SASSO-CRANDALL, Rose Mary (NJ) 206 Central Ave, Hammonton NJ 08037 B Boston MA 10/17/1938 d Louis Sasso & Josephine. Med Boston Coll 1960; MDiv GTS 1983; ThM New Brunswick TS 1986. D 6/4/1983 Bp George Phelps Mellick Belshaw P 2/4/1984 Bp Vincent King Pettit. m 6/11/1961 Charles David Crandall c 1. Vic S Jas Epis Ch Cape May NJ 1996-2004; Supply P Chr Ch Collingswood NJ 1989-1996; R Chr Ch Collingswood NJ 1984-1988. endicott163@aol.com

SASTRE, Iane Maria (Ga) 21268 US Highway 17, White Oak GA 31568 B Montevideo Uruguay 2/18/1953 s Renee Florentino Sastre & Nenetta Mafalda. BS Mercy Coll 1981; Mstr CSUSM 1999; MDiv The TS at The U So 2010. D 2/6/2010 Bp Scott Anson Benhase. m 11/16/1995 Lydia W Williams c 2. isastre@tds.net

SATO, Judith Ann (ECR) 7269 Santa Teresa Blvd, San Jose CA 95139 **Admin S Steph's In-The-Field Epis Ch San Jose CA 2008-** B Ventura CA 3/22/1951 d Thomas Edward Hanes & Bessie Mathilda. BS Colorado St U 1974; MDiv CDSP 2007. D 6/5/2010 P 1/18/2011 Bp Mary Gray-Reeves. m 9/4/1976 Rodney Sato c 3. j.sato@sbcglobal.net

SATORIUS, Joanna (Los) Po Box 512164, Los Angeles CA 90051 **For Cler Formation and Transitions Mnstry Dio Los Angeles Los Angeles CA 2003-** B Milwaukee WI 11/1/1948 d Edwin Cramer Roozen & Mary Louise. Illinois St U; BFA Stephens Coll 1971; MA U of Iowa 1974; MDiv Claremont TS 1994. D 6/18/1994 Bp Chester Lovelle Talton P 1/14/1995 Bp Frederick Houk Borsch. c 2. R S Geo's Ch Riverside CA 1996-2003. DOK; OHC, Assoc. jrspriest@hotmail.com

SATTERLY, Norris Jay (NMich) 132 Henford Ave, Kingsford MI 49802 **D H Trin Ch Iron Mtn MI 2004-** B Charlotte MI 12/23/1947 BSW Nthrn Michigan U 1992. D 2/29/2004 Bp James Arthur Kelsey. m 11/19/1967 Hazel Messer c 3. Bronze Star USAF 1968. normsatterly@sbcglobal.net

SATULA, John (Ct) 290 Weaver Street, Larchmont NY 10538 B New York, NY 3/17/1980 s Anthony Satula & Deborah. BA Elmira Coll; MDiv The GTS 2006; Mstr of Theol Duke 2007. D 11/30/2006 Bp Gladstone Bailey Adams III P 12/15/2007 Bp Andrew Donnan Smith. H Trin Ch Gainesville FL 2009-2011; Asst R S Matt's Epis Ch Wilton CT 2007-2009. john.satula@gmail.com

SAUCEDO-NAVA, Esteban (Dal) 1801 Keyes Ln, Aubrey TX 76227 **Died 10/24/2011** B Mexico City MX 11/24/1926 s Lorenzo Jostiniano Saucedo & Adela. CTh Epis TS of The SW 1957. D 8/6/1957 Bp Richard Earl Dicus P 2/26/1958 Bp Everett H Jones. m 10/28/2011 Yolanda Saucedo-Nava c 3.

SAUCEDO SICA, Susan Teresa (Nwk) 407 N Broad St, Lansdale PA 19446 **Vic S Greg's Epis Ch Parsippany NJ 2003-** B San Antonio TX 7/6/1955 d Melchor Saucedo Mendoza & Catherine B. BA Concordia U 1978; MDiv GTS 1999. D 5/22/1999 Bp Melchor Saucedo-Mendoza P 2/5/2000 Bp Herbert Alcorn Donovan Jr. m 6/17/1978 David R Sica c 2. Assoc Trin Ch Solebury PA 2002-2003; Assoc R H Trin Ch Lansdale PA 1999-2002. Cmnty Of S Jn The Bapt. padrecita@juno.com

✠ **SAULS, Rt Rev Stacy F** (Lex) 815 Second Ave., New York NY 10017 **Form Bp Dio Lexington Lexington KY 2011-; Chf Operating Off Epis Ch Cntr New York NY 2011-** B Atlanta GA 12/9/1955 s Kenneth Howard Sauls & Katie Joyce. BA Furman U 1977; JD U of Virginia 1980; MDiv GTS 1988; DD GTS 2001; DD STUSo 2002; LLM Cardiff U 2009. D 6/11/1988 P 4/6/1989 Bp Frank Kellogg Allan Con 9/30/2000 for Lex. m 8/11/1979 Ginger Lynn Malone c 2. Bp Dio Lexington Lexington KY 2000-2011; Stndg Cmsn on Const and Cn Epis Ch Cntr New York NY 2000-2006; R S Barth's Epis Ch Atlanta GA 1994-2000; R S Thos Ch Savannah GA 1990-1994; Assoc R S Geo's Epis Ch Griffin GA 1988-1990. *That We May Evermore Dwell in HIm and He in Us (w Chas Jenkins)*, Forw Mvmt, 2004. ssauls@episcopalchurch.org

SAULTERS, Elizabeth Boutwell (Miss) 6697 Bee Lake Rd, Tchula MS 39169 B Mobile AL 7/15/1957 d Charles C Boutwell & Mary Louis. U So 1977; BA Mississippi Coll 1979; MDiv SWTS 1990. D 5/31/1990 P 5/1/1991 Bp Duncan Montgomery Gray Jr. m 12/31/1983 Michael Foose c 1. S Jn's Cathd Denver CO 1992; S Jas Ch Jackson MS 1990-1992.

SAUNDERS, Cora Germaine (At) 607 River Run Dr, Sandy Springs GA 30350 B St Thomas VI 10/26/1959 d Clement Saunders & Esther. BA Carthage Coll 1982; JD Vermont Law Sch 1989; MDiv Candler TS Emory U 2003. D 11/2/2003 P 1/15/2006 Bp J(ohn) Neil Alexander. S Mich And All Ang Ch Stone Mtn GA 2006-2009. cgsaunders4@aol.com

SAUNDERS, Elizabeth Goodwin (NC) 3029 Mountainbrook Rd, Charlotte NC 28210 **Assoc R Chr Ch Charlotte NC 1988-** B Winston-Salem NC 5/8/1959 d Robert Flournoy Goodwin & Caroline Winter. BA U NC 1981; MDiv VTS 1984. D 6/8/1985 Bp Robert Whitridge Estill P 6/1/1986 Bp Calvin Onderdonk Schofield Jr. m 5/24/1981 Timothy Gray Saunders. Cur S Phil's Ch Coral Gables FL 1986-1987.

SAUNDERS, Ferdinand Davis (Cal) 2102 Tanglewood Dr, Sarasota FL 34239 **Died 12/31/2009** B Clinton SC 3/25/1918 s James Ishmal Saunders & Bertha. Priv Educ; Long Island Dioc TS 1959. D 4/10/1959 P 10/10/1959 Bp James P De Wolfe. padresaunders@msn.com

S

SAUNDERS, James (NJ) 8113 Rugby St, Philadelphia PA 19150 **Par Of Chr The King Willingboro NJ 2002-** B Grand Island TC 10/2/1945 s Thomas Benjamin Saunders & Catherine. Untd Theol Coll Of The W Indies Kingston Jm. D 12/12/1975 Bp The Bishop Of Barbados P 4/4/1976 Bp The Bishop Of Bahamas. m 7/31/1971 Hyacinth Leona. Dio Pennsylvania Philadelphia PA 1999; Hse Of Pryr Philadelphia PA 1982-1998. leroy.saundrs@ wwwchristtheking.org

SAUNDERS III, Kenneth H (Md) 120 Allegheny Ave, Towson MD 21204 **R Trin Ch Towson MD 2011-** B Portsmouth VA 3/7/1967 s Kenneth Hope Saunders & Nolie Lorraine. Cit Charleston SC 1989; BS U NC at Asheville 2003; MDiv TS The U So 2007. D 6/9/2007 Bp Granville Porter Taylor P 12/ 21/2007 Bp William O Gregg. m 10/6/1990 Kelly E Everitt c 3. R Chr Ch Cleveland NC 2007-2011. Soc of Cath Priests 2009. The Rev. Jeffrey Lowrance Citizenship Medal Sons of the Amer Revolution 2010. fr. kensaunders@gmail.com

SAUNDERS, Lisa Ann (WA) St John'S Church, Lafayette Square, 1525 H St Nw, Washington DC 20005 **Asst R S Jn's Ch Lafayette Sq Washington DC 2007-** B Madison WI 11/10/1979 d Richard Eugene Saunders & Susan Ann. BS U Of Wisconsin Oshkosh WI 2001; MDiv VTS 2007. D 6/2/2007 P 12/15/ 2007 Bp Steven Andrew Miller. lisaannsaunders@gmail.com

SAUNDERSON, Ann Marie (Oly) 3918 N 24th St, Tacoma WA 98406 B Seattle WA 10/22/1946 d Walter William Saunderson & Olive Marie. Linfield Coll 1989; MDiv Seattle U TS and Mnstry 2005. D 6/24/2006 Bp Vincent Waydell Warner P 2/2/2007 Bp Bavi Rivera. c 2. Assoc Chr Epis Ch Puyallup WA 2007-2010. annms@wamail.net

SAUNKEAH, Bobby Reed (Okla) 110 E 17th St, Ada OK 74820 B Oklahoma City, OK 4/24/1954 s Jasper Saunkeah & Dorothy Jean. Bach of Nrsng U of Oklahoma 1978. D 6/12/2010 Bp Edward Joseph Konieczny. m 5/24/1985 Peggy Peggy Grisso c 1. bobby.saunkeah@chickasaw.net

SAUSSY JR, Hugh (At) 4549 SW24th Ave, Dania FL 33312 B Atlanta GA 8/15/1927 s Hugh Saussy & Lillian Elese. U So 1947; BA Emory U 1949; ThB PDS 1952; MPA U GA 1970. D 6/11/1952 Bp John Buchman Walthour P 12/ 16/1952 Bp Edwin A Penick. c 4. R H Innoc Ch Atlanta GA 1957-1967; Cn Cathd Of S Phil Atlanta GA 1955-1957; Vic All SS Ch Warner Robins GA 1953-1955; R S Andr's Epis Ch Ft Vlly GA 1952-1955. Epis. Soc for Cultural and Racial Unity 1963-1968. hsaussy@gmail.com

SAVAGE JR, Arthur L (SO) 8800 Johnson Rd Apt 136, The Plains OH 45780 **Died 10/24/2010** B Meridian MS 8/7/1928 s Arthur Lafayette Savage & Mary Eleanor. BA U of Alabama 1950; MA MI SU 1971; PhD MI SU 1973. D 6/28/ 1978 Bp John Mc Gill Krumm. Auth, *Var Journ arts*. SocMary 1996-2003. absavage@eurekanet.com

SAVAGE, Harley Stewart (Tex) 180 CR 222, Bay City TX 77414 **committe Mem of bi-vocational Mnstry Dio Texas Houston TX 2005-** B Bay City TX 3/21/1931 s Francis Irving Savage & Frances. BBA St. Mary's U San Antonio TX 1953. D 12/19/1998 Bp Leopoldo Jesus Alard P 8/3/1999 Bp Claude Edward Payne. m 10/12/1951 Jane Kirby. Ret Chr Ch Matagorda TX 1998-2003. HARLEY_SAVAGE@YAHOO.COM

SAVAGE, Jack Laverne (Mich) 1157 E Buckhorn Cir, Sanford MI 48657 B Vassar MI 10/29/1935 s Warren T Savage & Thelma M. LTh Bex 1968; BA U Of Detroit 1972. D 6/29/1968 P 1/1/1969 Bp Archie H Crowley. m 9/17/1977 Sue Eleanor Hurst. S Matt's Epis Ch Rockwood MI 1984-1985; R S Marg's Ch Hazel Pk MI 1981-1984; Vic Ch Of The H Sprt Livonia MI 1969-1972; Asst S Andr's Epis Ch Livonia MI 1968-1969.

SAVIDGE, Karen Elizabeth Franklin (Mimi) (WMo) 207 N. 7th, St. Joseph MO 64501 B Marshall MO 9/4/1946 d Robert Enfield Franklin & Tralucia Frances. BS Missouri Wstrn St U 1992; MDiv Yale DS 1995. D 5/10/1995 P 5/1/1996 Bp John Clark Buchanan. m 1/14/1966 George Savidge c 3. R Chr Epis Ch S Jos MO 2007-2011; R All SS Ch Nevada MO 1999-2007; S Andr's Ch Kansas City MO 1998; Dio W Missouri Kansas City MO 1995-1997. mimisavidge@ yahoo.com

SAVILLE III, John K (Los) Po Box 152, Corona CA 92878 **R S Jn The Bapt Par Corona CA 1991-** B Los Angeles CA 5/25/1952 s John Kimball Saville & Nellie Ann. BA U of Redlands 1974; MDiv GTS 1982. D 6/19/1982 P 2/5/ 1983 Bp Robert C Rusack. m 5/1/1976 Kathleen Grace Bernier c 2. R S Mary's Par Lompoc CA 1990-1991; R S Jn The Bapt Par Corona CA 1985-1990; Cur Trin Epis Ch Redlands CA 1982-1985. stjohnrector@ sbcglobal.net

SAVILLE, Milton (SO) 3580 Shaw Avenue #323, Cincinnati OH 45208 B Kansas City MO 10/23/1925 s Virgil Saville & Willie May. BA Ken 1948; MDiv EDS 1951. D 6/8/1951 P 2/1/1952 Bp Norman B Nash. Int S Paul's Ch Akron OH 1990-1991; P-in-c S Ptr's Ch Glenside PA 1987; Int Epis Soc of Chr Ch Cincinnati OH 1984-1986; Epis Soc Of Chr Ch Cincinnati OH 1983-1987; Asst Epis Soc of Chr Ch Cincinnati OH 1983-1984; St Albans Ch 1977-1982; Exec Coun Appointees New York NY 1973-1982; S Jn's Epis Ch Westwood MA 1963-1973; R S Lk's Epis Ch Fall River MA 1958-1963; Asst Epis Soc of Chr Ch Cincinnati OH 1955-1958.

SAVINO, Bella Jean (Ak) Po Box 70786, Fairbanks AK 99707 **D S Matt's Epis Ch Fairbanks AK 2003-** B Fort Yukon AK 6/6/1945 d David Francis & Myra. D. m 6/11/1994 Donald Savino.

SAWICKY, Blake Andrew (Alb) 1350 Washington St, Denver CO 80203 **S Jn's Cathd Denver CO 2011-** B Marshfield WI 8/17/1984 s Jay Blake Sawicky & Deborah Ann. BA Wheaton Coll 2006; MA U Coll London 2007; MDiv Ya Berk 2011. D 6/4/2011 Bp William Howard Love. blakesawicky@ gmail.com

SAWTELLE, Gary Donald (Roch) 3 Genesee St E, Scottsville NY 14546 **Assoc S Thos Epis Ch Rochester NY 2006-** B Mineola NY 7/15/1947 s Donald Joseph Sawtelle & Dorothy. BA SUNY 1969; MDiv PDS 1972. D 6/8/1972 P 12/23/1972 Bp Jonathan Goodhue Sherman. m 8/23/1969 Barbara R Roff c 2. Chapl To Ret Cler Dio Rochester Rochester NY 2003-2005; Chair Of The Bdgt Com Dio Rochester Rochester NY 1994-1995; Com Dio Rochester Rochester NY 1989-1995; Chair Of Cont Educ Dio Rochester Rochester NY 1989-1994; CE Cmsn Dio Rochester Rochester NY 1984-1987; Evang Cmsn Dio Rochester Rochester NY 1982-1985; Gr Ch Lyons NY 1981-2002; Futures Cmsn Dio Rochester Rochester NY 1981-1983; CE Consult Dio Sthrn Virginia Norfolk VA 1980-1981; Stwdshp Cmsn Dio Sthrn Virginia Norfolk VA 1978-1981; Assoc Old Donation Ch Virginia Bch VA 1976-1981; Cur Gr Epis Ch Massapequa NY 1972-1976. gsawtell@rochester.rr.com

SAWYER, Anne M (Az) 737 N 6th Ave, Tucson AZ 85705 **Imago Dei Middle Sch Tucson AZ 2007-** B Tucson AZ 11/11/1964 d Chnelos H Sawyer & Jane A. BA U of Arizona 1987; MA U Chi 1993; MDiv Harvard DS 2004. D 2/19/ 2005 P 9/18/2005 Bp Kirk Stevan Smith. D, P, Asst. R S Andr's Epis Ch Tucson AZ 2005-2007; Dio Arizona Phoenix AZ 2005-2006. asimagodei@aol. com

SAWYER, Frank Denzil (Ga) 4459 Andover Drive, Evans GA 30809 **The Ch Of The Gd Shpd Augusta GA 2007-** B Brantford Canada 1/29/1971 s Denzil Brooks Sawyer & Catherine Louise. BA U Tor 1993; MDiv U Tor 1997; DMin CDSP 2004. Trans from Anglican Church of Canada 9/8/1999 Bp William Edwin Swing. m 9/19/1998 Ginnelle Margaret Elliot c 1. Gr Cathd San Francisco CA 1999. "The Sprtl Life of Boys in an Epis Sch (D.Min. Thesis)," Grad Theol Un Libr, Berkeley, CA, 2004. Coun for Sprtl and Ethical Educ 1999; NAES 1999. fsawyer@edsaugusta.com

SAWYER, Robert Claremont (NC) Po Box 28024, Raleigh NC 27611 **Ch Of The Gd Shpd Raleigh NC 1996-** B Norfolk VA 6/15/1949 s Julian Claremont Sawyer & Dorothy Frances. BA Randolph-Macon Coll 1971; MDiv VTS 1980. D 5/27/1980 P 12/1/1980 Bp C(laude) Charles Vache. m 4/29/1972 Linda B Barranger c 2. R S Andr's Ch Richmond VA 1986-1996; Asst Ch Of The Adv Spartanburg SC 1982-1986; R Gr Epis Ch Drakes Branch VA 1980-1982; R S Jn's Epis Ch Chase City VA 1980-1982; R S Tim's Epis Ch Clarksville VA 1980-1982. BOB.SAWYER@CGS-RALEIGH.ORG

SAWYER, Stanley Whitfield (SVa) 2200 Cape Arbor Dr, Virginia Beach VA 23451 **Bd Trst VTS Alexandria VA 2009-; Dn Of Convoc Dio Sthrn Virginia Norfolk VA 1986-; R All SS' Epis Ch Virginia Bch VA 1981-** B Norfolk VA 6/15/1949 s Julian Claremont Sawyer & Dorothy. BS Randolph-Macon Coll 1971; S Geo's Coll Jerusalem IL 1975; MDiv VTS 1976; DMin GTF 1993. D 5/26/1976 Bp David Shepherd Rose P 12/13/1976 Bp C(laude) Charles Vache. m 9/5/1970 Linda Louise Rawlings c 2. Pres of Stndg Com Dio Sthrn Virginia Norfolk VA 2008-2009; Stndg Com Dio Sthrn Virginia Norfolk VA 2006-2009; Exec Bd Dio Sthrn Virginia Norfolk VA 1985-1989; Asst Chr And Gr Ch Petersburg VA 1976-1981. stansawyer1@verizon.net

SAWYER, Susan Carter (Kan) 1640 Sunflower Rd, Clay Center KS 67432 **R S Paul's Epis Ch Clay Cntr KS 1992-** B Bethesda MD 3/12/1950 d William Thomas Sawyer & Mary Carter. AA Bard Coll 1970; MDiv EDS 1985. D 6/1/ 1985 Bp John Bowen Coburn P 4/29/1986 Bp Andrew Frederick Wissemann. m 11/3/1990 David George Verschelden. Dio Kansas Topeka KS 1991; Assoc S Paul's Ch Manhattan KS 1989-1990; Dio Wstrn Massachusetts Springfield MA 1985-1989; Cur S Jn's Ch Northampton MA 1985-1989. ssawyer@ kansas.net

SAWYER HARMON, Cecily Judith (Del) 262 S College Ave, Newark DE 19711 B Bronx, NY 9/3/1946 d Samuel Leon Sawyer & Estelle Josephine. MSW Adelphi Sch of Soical Wk 1976; BA Hampton U 1976. D 12/5/2009 Bp Wayne Parker Wright. c 3. csawhar@udel.edu

SAXE, Joshua Andrew (WVa) 430 Juliana Street, Parkersburg WV 26101 **Cur Trin Ch Parkersburg WV 2011-** B Fort Walton Beach FL 1/7/1983 s Timothy Saxe & Susan. BS W Virginia U 2005; MDiv The GTS 2011. D 12/4/ 2010 P 6/14/2011 Bp William Michie Klusmeyer. jsaxe83@gmail.com

SAXON, Mary-Margaret (Colo) 5527 Harrison Street, Kansas City MO 64110 B New Orleans LA 6/6/1941 d James Winfred Saxon & Mary Margaret. RN U of Mobile 1974; MDiv U So 1988. D 5/2/1988 Bp Leopold Frade P 12/1/1988 Bp Frank Stanley Cerveny. S Paul's Epis Ch Lakewood CO 1999-2001; S Jn's Epis Ch Tallahassee FL 1988-1994. mmsaxon.ms@gmail.com

SAXON, Miriam Scarsbrook (NC) 2214 Buck Quarter Farm Rd, Hillsborough NC 27278 **Assoc R Ch Of The Gd Shpd Raleigh NC 2008-** B Baton Rouge LA 8/22/1950 d Clarence Edwin Scarsbrook & Mildred Moore. BA Auburn U

Auburn AL 1972; MS Florida St U Tallahassee FL 1974; MA Duke Durham NC 1985; VTS 2006; MDiv Duke 2007. D 5/19/2007 P 12/19/2007 Bp Michael Bruce Curry. m 6/2/1973 John Saxon c 2. mss22@duke.edu

SAYLORS, Joann Leslie (Dal) 2700 Warren Cir, Irving TX 75062 **Cur Epis Ch Of The Redeem Irving TX 2010-** B Pittsburgh PA 9/24/1968 d Roy M Schriner & Beryl Keller. BBA U of Texas at Austin 1991; BA U of Texas at Austin 1991; MDiv Epis TS Of The SW 2010. D 6/5/2010 P 5/24/2011 Bp James Monte Stanton. m 4/30/2000 Lawrence C Saylors. joann.saylors@gmail.com

SCALES, Linda (Ga) 4344 Miller Dr, Evans GA 30809 B Concordia KS 5/27/1939 d Paul Metz & Ruth. BS K SU 1960; MS K SU 1978; Med Bos 1982; EdD Tem 1989. D 4/25/1990 Bp Charles Lovett Keyser. m 6/17/1978 Lou(ie) Grady Scales c 2. D Ch Of Our Sav Martinez GA 2002-2009; D S Alb's Epis Ch Augusta GA 2001-2002; D S Paul's Ch Augusta GA 2000-2001. Wmn of Excellence Girls Scouts 2006. lou.linda.scales@bellsouth.net

SCALES JR, Lou(ie) Grady (Ga) 4344 Miller Drive, Evans GA 30809 B Fayette AL 7/25/1947 s Louie Grady Scales & Ruth Carolyn. BA Birmingham-Sthrn Coll 1969; MDiv Candler TS Emory U 1972; Med Bos 1982; ThM PrTS 1985. D 10/20/1991 Bp John Mc Gill Krumm P 5/17/1992 Bp Charles Lovett Keyser. m 6/17/1978 Linda Metz c 2. R Ch Of Our Sav Martinez GA 2002-2009; Assoc S Paul's Ch Augusta GA 2000-2002; Off Of Bsh For ArmdF New York NY 1992-2000. Auth, "Poetry, Song & A Theol Tchg," *Mltry Chapl's Revs*, 1987. lou.scales@saintpauls.org

SCALES JR, Sherrill (Ct) 568 S Farms Ct, Southington CT 06489 B Louisville KY 9/22/1924 s Sherrill Scales & Ada Lee. AA U Cinc 1950; BFA Ohio U 1951; MDiv Bex 1957. D 6/2/1957 P 12/2/1957 Bp Henry W Hobson. m 11/8/1970 Joyce Marilyn Higgins c 1. S Barth's Ch New York NY 1975-1977; S Jn's Ch E Hartford CT 1968-1975; Gnrl Secy, Dept of Missions & Ch Ext Dio Connecticut Hartford CT 1962-1968; R Calv Ch Enfield CT 1959-1962; Asst S Jas Epis Ch Danbury CT 1958-1959; Asst S Paul's Ch Columbus OH 1957-1958. Auth, *Ch Site & Bldg*, 1982. Hon Cn Dio Connecticut 1967.

SCALIA, Deborah White (La) 10136 Walden Dr, River Ridge LA 70123 **S Mart's Epis Sch Metairie LA 1999-** B Wellsboro PA 1/23/1951 BA Loyola U 1974. D 9/13/2003 Bp Charles Edward Jenkins III. m 6/1/1974 Salvador S Scalia. deborah.scalia@stmsaints.com

SCALISE, Margaret M. (Ala) 8816 Old Greensboro Rd Apt 19103, Tuscaloosa AL 35405 **Counslg Mnstry Professionals Tuscaloosa AL 2008-** B Birmingham AL 8/20/1952 d Peter Paul Scalise & Frances. BS Birmingham-Sthrn Coll 1974; MD U of Alabama 1978; MDiv Ya Berk 2002. D 6/2/2002 P 12/3/2002 Bp Henry Nutt Parsley Jr. Assoc R Chr Ch Tuscaloosa AL 2002-2009. mscalise@earthlink.net

SCANLAN, Audrey (Ct) 22 Dyer Ave # 6019, Canton CT 06019 **Dio Connecticut Hartford CT 2011-; R St Gabr's Ch E Berlin CT 2006-** B Portchester NY 9/20/1958 BA Wheaton Coll at Norton 1980; Cert Cntrl Connecticut St U 1992; MDiv Ya Berk 2003; MDiv Ya Berk 2003. D 6/21/2003 P 1/24/2004 Bp Andrew Donnan Smith. m 8/11/1984 Glenn Scanlan c 3. R Ch of our Sav Plainville CT 2006-2011; Cur Trin Ch Torrington CT 2003-2006. scanlangc@aetna.com

SCANLON, Geoffrey Edward Leyshon (Spr) 1226 N Vermilion St, Danville IL 61832 **R Ch Of The H Trin Danville IL 1987-** B Dewsbury Yorkshire UK 12/30/1944 s John Edward Scanlon & Edith Anne. Coll Engr Leeds Gb; U Of Leeds Gb. D 6/1/1976 P 6/1/1977 Bp The Bishop Of Durham. Vic S Dav's Epis Ch Columbia SC 1985-1987; Vic Ch Of The Epiph Laurens SC 1981-1985. tcotholytrinity@comcast.net

SCANNELL, Alice Updike (Ore) 6735 NE Sacramento Street, Portland OR 97213 **Vic S Anne's Epis Ch Washougal WA 2004-** B New York NY 7/15/1938 d Godfrey Updike & Mary Alice. BA Smith 1960; MRE UTS 1963; Cert Windham Hse 1963; PhD Portland St U 1989. D 5/15/1998 P 12/12/1998 Bp Robert Louis Ladehoff. m 6/13/1964 John Scott Scannell c 2. Chapl S Aidens Place Portland OR 1998-2005; S Mich And All Ang Ch Portland OR 1998-2004. "Focus Groups Help Congregations Improve Its New Mem Mnstry," *Revs of Rel Resrch*, 2003. Amer Soc on Aging 1985; Assembly of Epis Healthcare Chapl 1999; Assn for Rel Resrch 1990; Assn of Profsnl Chapl 1998; Gerontological Soc of Amer 1985. Fell Coll of Preachers 2002; Woods Fllshp VTS 2002; Post-doctoral Fllshp in Applied Gerontology Gerontological Soc of Amer 1989. johns@easystreet.com

SCANNELL, John Scott (Ore) 6735 NE Sacramento St, Portland OR 97213 **Assoc Trin Epis Cathd Portland OR 2008-; S Mich And All Ang Ch Portland OR 2002-** B Mount Vernon NY 11/5/1939 s Nicholas Joseph Scannell & Enid Frances. BA Col 1961; MDiv PDS 1964. D 6/6/1964 P 12/19/1964 Bp Horace W B Donegan. m 6/13/1964 Alice Updike c 2. S Mich And All Ang Ch Portland OR 1979-2002; Ch Of S Thos Bethel CT 1975-1979; R Chr Ch Waterbury CT 1968-1975; Min in charge Chr Ch Sodus Point NY 1964-1968; Min in charge S Steph's Ch Wolcott NY 1964-1968. jsscannell@gmail.com

SCANTLEBURY, Cecil Alvin (NY) 61 Santuit Pond Rd., Mashpee MA 02649 B BB 9/14/1931 s Cecil Scantlebury & Elfreda. BA CUNY; DIT Codrington Coll 1955. D 3/1/1955 P 6/1/1955 Bp The Bishop Of Barbados. m 6/25/1960 Winifred Elizabeth Gay c 2. S Fran Assisi And S Martha White Plains NY 1976-1996; Diocn Msnry & Ch Extntn Socty New York NY 1969-1976; Dpt Of Missions Ny Income New York NY 1969-1976; Asst S Aug's Epis Ch Brooklyn NY 1967-1968; Cur S Andr's Ch New York NY 1963-1967. EBADOS@AOL.COM

✠ **SCANTLEBURY, Rt Rev Victor Alfonso** (Chi) 65 E Huron St, Chicago IL 60611 B Colon PA 3/31/1945 s Barclay Bynoe & Diana. EDS 1972; MDiv ETSC 1973. D 10/29/1973 P 8/6/1974 Bp Lemuel Barnett Shirley Con 3/15/1991 for RP. m 8/11/1973 Marcia Thomas c 2. Asst Bp Dio Chicago Chicago IL 2000-2011; S Mk's Ch Jackson MS 1995-2000; St Pauls Ch 1985-1991; Iglesia San Juan 1978-1985; Dio Panama 1973-1994. bpvictor864@aol.com

SCARBOROUGH, Anjel Lorraine (Md) 2711 Flintridge Ct, Myersville MD 21773 **Supply Cler Gr Ch Brunswick MD 2011-; Sprtl Advsr to MD Epis Curs Dio Maryland Baltimore MD 2010-** B San Diego CA 1/16/1964 d Robert Edwin Ayrer & Earlene Mae. AS Orange Coast Coll Costa Mesa CA 1985; BS California St U Long Bch CA 1987; MDiv Luth TS at Gettysburg 2007. D 6/16/2007 P 2/2/2008 Bp John Leslie Rabb. m 11/18/1988 Stuart Scarborough c 2. Asst. R S Mk's Ch Lappans Boonsboro MD 2009; Int S Lk's Ch Baltimore MD 2008-2009; R The Gathering: A Fam Of Faith Epis Ch Buckeystown MD 2008; D The Gathering: A Fam Of Faith Epis Ch Buckeystown MD 2007-2008. Auth, "We Look for the Resurr of the Dead," *Congregations mag*, The Alb Inst, 2010. DOK 2002. NT Schlrshp Luth TS at Gettysburg 2007. revscarborough@gmail.com

SCARCIA, Steven Angelo (Alb) Po Box 592, Little Falls NY 13365 **R Emm Ch Little Falls NY 1978-** B Peekskill NY 4/13/1948 s Angelo F Scarcia & Kathryn. BA Westminster Choir Coll of Rider U 1971; MDiv Nash 1973; DMin Luther Rice TS 1982. D 12/22/1973 Bp Allen Webster Brown P 11/1/1974 Bp Wilbur Emory Hogg Jr. Trst Dio Albany Albany NY 1985-1988.

✠ **SCARFE, Rt Rev Alan** (Ia) 225 37th St, Des Moines IA 50312 **Bp of Iowa Dio Iowa Des Moines IA 2003-** B Bradford Yorkshire UK 5/3/1950 s Norman Scarfe & Regina Golding. GTS; MA Oxf 1972; Romanian Orth Institiute Bucuresti RO 1974; Romanian Orth Inst Bucuresti RO 1975; STM GTS 1986. D 6/21/1986 Bp Robert C Rusack P 12/21/1986 Bp Oliver Bailey Garver Jr Con 3/11/2003 for Ia. m 8/23/1975 Donna Bryan c 4. Mnstry Dio Los Angeles Los Angeles CA 2000-2003; Ecum Off Dio Los Angeles Los Angeles CA 1995-1998; Cmsn on Ecum Dio Los Angeles Los Angeles CA 1991-1999; R S Barn' Epis Ch Los Angeles CA 1990-2003; Assoc R S Columba's Par Camarillo CA 1986-1989. Auth, *Call for Truth- Ch & S in Romania*; Ed/Contrib, *Chrsnty & Marxism*; Auth, "Romanian Orth Ch," *Orth Ch & Politics in 20th Century*. DD GTS 2003. ascarfe@iowaepiscopal.org

SCARIATO, Albert Fredrick (WA) 3909 Albemarle St Nw, Washington DC 20016 **S Jn's Ch Georgetown Par Washington DC 2004-** B Philadelphia PA 8/25/1955 s Albert Scariato & Rita Antoinette. D 6/15/1996 P 4/1/1997 Bp Ronald Hayward Haines.

SCARLETT, William George (Md) 44 Partridge Ln, Carlisle MA 01741 B 12/31/1944

SCHAAL, Richard (CNY) 1504 76th Rd, Berkshire NY 13736 **St Johns Epis Ch Berkshire NY 2010-** B Erie PA 5/28/1947 Formation Prog Dio Cntrl NY; BA Gannon U 1969. D 5/8/2010 P 12/4/2010 Bp Gladstone Bailey Adams III. rschaal@stny.rr.com

SCHACHT, Lawrence Arthur (NY) 525 W End Ave Apt 4-H, New York NY 10024 B Detroit MI 9/2/1927 s Edward Frederick Schacht & Anna Marie. D 5/30/1992 Bp Richard Frank Grein. D The Ch Of The Epiph New York NY 2000-2002; D S Mich's Ch New York NY 1992-1996. NAAD.

SCHADEWITZ, M Ramsey (Ore) 1811 Ne Schuyler St, Portland OR 97212 **Died 6/11/2011** B Moro OR 12/29/1925 s Melvin R Schadewitz & Lanora Mae. BA U of Oregon 1951; MDiv CDSP 1955. D 6/18/1954 P 12/1/1954 Bp Benjamin D Dagwell. c 4. hrothgar@cascadia.net

SCHADT, Stuart Everett (Va) 6070 Greenway Ct, Manassas VA 20111 **R Trin Ch Manassas VA 1990-** B La Marque TX 8/3/1955 s Michel C Schadt & Marian L. BA U of Texas 1976; MDiv VTS 1980. D 6/17/1980 P 3/1/1981 Bp Roger Howard Cilley. m 11/13/1976 Pamela L Oyston c 1. R Gr Epis Ch Houston TX 1983-1990; Asst Trin Ch Galveston TX 1980-1983. Auth, "A Time For Vision". seschadt@trinityepiscopalchurch.org

SCHAEFER, Jane (Chi) 417 N. Beck Road, Lindenhurst IL 60046 B Independence IA 5/29/1948 d James Kester & Eleanor. BA NE Illinois U 1990; MDiv SWTS 1994. D 6/18/1994 P 12/17/1994 Bp Frank Tracy Griswold III. m 2/27/1965 Craig Schaefer c 2. R The Epis Ch Of S Jas The Less Northfield IL 2003-2010; Assoc The Ch Of The H Sprt Lake Forest IL 1998-2003; Asst to R S Aug's Epis Ch Wilmette IL 1994-1998. cs.js@comcast.net

SCHAEFER III, John (Neb) 10206 Ohio St, Omaha NE 68134 **R S Andr's Ch Omaha NE 2009-** B Waynesburg PA 2/2/1957 s Otto John Schaefer & Rosemary Eleanor. BA/BS Nthrn Arizona U 1979; MDiv CDSP 1991; DMin SWTS 2004. D 6/15/1991 Bp Frederick Houk Borsch P 12/14/1991 Bp John Stuart Thornton. m 6/17/1989 Margaret Sutherland c 2. Cn Dio Nebraska Omaha NE 2005-2009; R Ch Of Our Sav No Platte NE 1998-2004; Vic Ch Of

H Nativ Meridian ID 1993-1995; D All SS Epis Ch Boise ID 1991-1993. jschaefer3@gmail.com

SCHAEFER, Lee Paul (Ind) 444 South Harbour Drive, Noblesville IN 46062 **R S Mich's Ch Noblesville IN 2007-** B Minneapolis MN 2/6/1956 s Philip Alois Schaefer & June Maria. S Thos Coll Miami FL; AA Normandale Cmnty Coll Bloomington MN 1976; BS St. Cloud St U 1978; MDiv VTS 1983; DMin VTS 2005. D 12/6/1983 P 6/1/1985 Bp Robert Marshall Anderson. m 8/18/1984 Alison Mahr c 2. R S Tim's Epis Ch Kingsport TN 1997-2007; Ch Of The Gd Shpd Sioux Falls SD 1992-1997; Cn Geth Cathd Fargo ND 1989-1992; Asst to R Ch Of The Gd Shpd Raleigh NC 1986-1989; Asst to R S Nich Ch Richfield MN 1983-1986. *Introducing New Cultures into a Par*, VTS, 2005. stmichaelsfrlee@yahoo.com

SCHAEFER, Lynette Ulumahiehie (Haw) PO Box 1233, Kaunakakai HI 96748 B San Mateo CA 4/23/1948 d Philip Sheridan Golderman & Florence Marjorie. U of New So Wales 1966; BEd U of Hawaii 1971; MDiv CDSP 1976. D 4/25/1977 P 6/29/1978 Bp Edmond Lee Browning. m 12/30/1977 Winthrop S Schaefer c 3. Vic Gr Ch Hoolehua HI 1978-2010; S Ptr's Ch Honolulu HI 1977-1978. HI 1st Lady Awd 1982; Outstanding Young Wmn of Amer 1979. lynette.schaefer@gmail.com

SCHAEFER, Philip David (Roch) 47 Brougham Dr, Penfield NY 14526 **Int Ch Of The Ascen Rochester NY 2000-; Supply P Dio Rochester Rochester NY 1995-** B Toledo OH 5/23/1935 s Philip William Schaefer & Helen B. BA Denison U 1957; MDiv Ya Berk 1960; ThM Bex 1973. D 6/11/1960 Bp Beverley D Tucker P 1/21/1961 Bp Nelson Marigold Burroughs. m 9/6/1958 Elsa Brumbaugh c 4. R Ch Of The Incarn Penfield NY 1974-1987; R Zion Ch Avon NY 1969-1974; R All SS Ch Aliquippa PA 1963-1969; P-in-c S Lk's Epis Ch Georgetown PA 1963-1969; Cur S Jas Ch Painesville OH 1960-1963. elsaphil@frontiernet.net

SCHAEFFER, John Grant (Oly) 1827 Southeast 18th Place, Renton WA 98055 **S Mich And All Ang Ch Issaquah WA 2002-** B Washington DC 10/28/1929 s William Peter Schaeffer & Lucy Virginia. BA U of Washington 1951; Nash 1952; MDiv SWTS 1954. D 6/29/1954 P 6/29/1955 Bp Stephen F Bayne Jr. m 3/4/1984 Lorrie M La Branche c 2. P-in-c Ch Of The H Cross Redmond WA 2001-2002; Int S Mich And All Ang Ch Issaquah WA 1999-2000; Secy Dioc Conv Dio Olympia Seattle WA 1989-1994; Dio Olympia Seattle WA 1968-1979; R S Lk's Epis Ch Renton WA 1959-1994; Vic Chr Epis Ch Anacortes WA 1956-1959; P St Steph's Epis Ch Oak Harbor WA 1956-1957; Cur Chr Ch Tacoma WA 1954-1956. Hon Cn St. Mk's Cathd Seattle Wa 2009. jgs1929@aol.com

SCHAEFFER, Phillip Negley (NMich) 1803 N Schaeffer Rd, N4244 Gladhaven Road, Moran MI 49760 B Columbus OH 12/17/1923 s Negley Schaeffer & Gladys. BS Pur 1948. D 8/4/1991 P 2/29/1992 Bp Thomas Kreider Ray. c 4. R Ch Of The Gd Shpd S Ignace MI 1992-2011. phill803@hotmail.com

SCHAEFFER, Susan Edwards (NY) 17 Perkins Ave, Northampton MA 01060 B Oakland CA 1/31/1946 d Clarence Henry Schaeffer & Louise. BA Lycoming Coll 1967; MDiv UTS 1980; PhD UTS 1991. D 6/7/1980 P 1/25/1981 Bp Paul Moore Jr. m 5/3/1980 BH Pete Schellenbach c 2. Dio New York New York City NY 1997-2004; Stndg Com Dio New York New York City NY 1992-1996; R S Ptr's Ch Port Chester NY 1992-1996; Liturg Cmsn Dio New York New York City NY 1986-1994; Assoc The Ch Of S Lk In The Fields New York NY 1980-1992. Auth, "Gospel Of Ptr," 1991; Auth, "SBL Seminar Papers," 1991; Auth, "The Guard At The Tomb". Angl Assn Of Biblic Scholars; SBL.

SCHAFFENBURG, Karl Christian (Miss) 1011 N. 7th St., 103 W. Broad Street, Sheboygan WI 53081 **R Gr Epis Ch Sheboygan WI 2011-; R Epis Ch Of The Incarn W Point MS 2006-** B Cleveland OH 11/24/1956 s Carlos Alfonso Schaffenburg & Lila Marie. BS U of Mississippi 1980; JD U of Mississippi 1984; MDiv Nash 2006. D 12/17/2005 P 6/24/2006 Bp Russell Edward Jacobus. m 12/23/1986 Elizabeth B Brewer c 2. Auth, "Irish Evolution and the Politics of Identity," *Orbis: A Journ of Frgn Affrs*, Frgn Plcy Resrch Inst, 2009; Auth, "Russkiy & Rossiiskiy: Russian Natl Identity after Putin," *Orbis: A Journ of Frgn Affrs*, Frgn Plcy Resrch Inst, 2007. k.schaffenburg@gmail.com

SCHAFFNER, Philip Perry (Minn) 2401 33rd Ave. S, Minneapolis MN 55406 B St Paul MN 5/17/1980 s Gregory K Schaffner & Patricia. BA Gri 2001; MPP Harvard Kennedy Sch of Govt 2009. D 6/18/2005 Bp James Louis Jelinek. No Amer Assn of the Diac 2003. philip.p.schaffner@gmail.com

SCHAFROTH, Stephen Louis (EO) 1107 Lewis St, The Dalles OR 97058 **GC Dep Dio Estrn Oregon The Dalles OR 2009-; GC Dep Dio Estrn Oregon The Dalles OR 2009-; Ecum Off Dio Estrn Oregon The Dalles OR 2001-** B Ames IA 7/3/1949 s Arthur Louis Schafroth & Alice Jeanette. D 9/29/1999 Bp Rustin Ray Kimsey. m 5/7/1983 Colleen Mangan c 1. schafroth@embarqmail.com

SCHAIBLE II, Donald J (Be) Christ and Trinity Parishes, 58 River St, Carbondale PA 18407 **R Trin Epis Ch Carbondale PA 2008-** B Warren NJ 7/24/1963 s Donald Joseph Schaible & Joan Marie. BA DeSales U Allentown PA 1985; MDiv St Chas 1988; MA St Chas 1990; MS U of Scranton 2000. Rec from Roman Catholic 6/29/2007 Bp Paul Victor Marshall. m 9/17/2005 Sharon Sharon Quinn c 1. dschaible2@hotmail.com

SCHAITBERGER, Stephen Harold (Minn) 1402 S 8th St, Brainerd MN 56401 B Camp Lejeune NC 5/17/1945 s Harold LeRoy Schaitberger & Betty Jean. BA U MN 1967; MDiv Nash 1970; Command and Gnrl Stff Coll 1980. D 6/29/1970 Bp Hamilton Hyde Kellogg P 2/21/1971 Bp Philip Frederick McNairy. S Jas' Epis Ch Fergus Falls MN 2002-2004; Cn Dio Minnesota Minneapolis MN 1995-2003; S Paul's Ch Brainerd MN 1980-1995; P-in-c S Jn's Ch Aitkin MN 1980-1986; R Ch Of The H Comm S Ptr MN 1973-1980; Dn SW Deanry Dio Minnesota Minneapolis MN 1972-1976; P-in-c S Jas Ch Marshall MN 1971-1973; P-in-c S Jn Worthington MN 1971-1973; P-in-c S Paul's Ch Pipestone MN 1971-1973. Soc of S Fran - Tertiary 1986. Bush Fllshp Awd 1994; Chapl, Minnesota Army NG; Commendation,Achievement Medals,Meritorious Serv Medals US-A. stephenschaitberger@charter.net

SCHALLER JR, Carleton (NH) 61 Fairview St, Littleton NH 03561 B New York NY 5/27/1923 s Carleton Otto Schaller & Katherine Dulcie. BA NYU 1954; VTS 1957; MDiv VTS 1970. D 6/17/1957 P 12/21/1957 Bp Horace W B Donegan. m 6/11/1948 Mary-Lu Stephenson c 2. Int S Steph's Ch Pittsfield NH 1990-1991; Nthrn Grafton Shared Mnstry Lyman NH 1982-1985; R All SS Epis Ch Littleton NH 1962-1989; Vic Ch Of The Mssh No Woodstock NH 1962-1989; Asst Calv and St Geo New York NY 1957-1962.

SCHALLER, Joseph G (Pa) 303 W. Lancaster Avenue, Suite 2C, Wayne PA 19087 **Asst S Mary's Epis Ch Ardmore PA 2007-; Asst S Gabr's Epis Ch Philadelphia PA 2006-** B Rochester NY 12/20/1954 s Joseph Anthony Schaller & Ruby Rose. BA Geo 1978; MDiv Weston Jesuit TS 1981; MA U of Notre Dame 1985; STL Weston Jesuit TS 1989; PsyD Widener U 1999. Rec from Roman Catholic 6/4/2006 Bp Charles Ellsworth Bennison Jr. m 8/20/2004 Phillip C Bennett. jgschaller@aol.com

SCHALLER JR, Warren August (Va) Po Box 712, Garrisonville VA 22463 B Syracuse NY 3/5/1937 s Warren August Schaller & Natalie. BA Ken 1959; MA U MN 1961; STM GTS 1964. D 6/27/1964 Bp Hamilton Hyde Kellogg P 4/1/1965 Bp Philip Frederick McNairy. m 2/11/1961 Patricia A Campbell c 4. P S Mary's Fleeton Reedville VA 2004-2007; Assoc Truro Epis Ch Fairfax VA 1975-1976; R S Andr's Ch Manchester NH 1971-1973; R Ch Of The H Apos S Paul MN 1967-1971; Vic Epiph Epis Ch S Paul MN 1964-1967. Auth, "Hist Of The Soc Policies Of The Epis Ch In The 20th Century". warrenschaller@hotmail.com

SCHANE, Clifford Edward (Tenn) 1616 Piedmont Ave Ne Apt O9, Atlanta GA 30324 B Wheeling WV 11/23/1937 s Samuel McKinley Schane & Helen. BS W Virginia U 1960; MDiv VTS 1964; Ldrshp Acad for New Directions 1977; VTS 1992. D 6/11/1964 P 12/17/1964 Bp Wilburn Camrock Campbell. c 1. R & Sprtl Dir Otey Memi Par Ch Sewanee TN 1979-1996; Dn of Reg #15 Dio Virginia Richmond VA 1975-1978; S Anne's Par Scottsville VA 1974-1979; R Chr Ch Point Pleasant WV 1968-1972; Vic S Jas' Epis Ch Lewisburg WV 1964-1968. OHC - Assoc P 1961. cliffschane@bellsouth.net

SCHAPER, Richard (Cal) 646 Ridgewood Avenue, Mill Valley CA 94941 **Dio California San Francisco CA 2003-** B Bayshore NY 1/8/1945 s Louis Arthur Schaper & Mary Amanda. BA Colg 1967; U Coll Oxford 1968; ThM U Chi 1970; Ya 1971; CFP Golden Gate U 1997; NonProfit Mgmt U of San Francisco 1997. Rec from Evangelical Lutheran Church in America 12/7/2002 Bp William Edwin Swing. m 6/18/1983 Anita Ruth Ostrom c 2. richards@diocal.org

SCHAPER, Robert Newell (Los) 1443 Glen Oaks Blvd, Pasadena CA 91105 B Indianapolis IN 2/4/1922 s Newell Ralph Schaper & Mary Irene. ThM Fuller TS 1964; ThD Claremont TS 1972. D 6/21/1980 P 11/2/1980 Bp Robert C Rusack. m 5/17/1944 Margaret Dick Smith. The ETS At Claremont Claremont CA 1982-1983; Asst Ch Of Our Sav Par San Gabr CA 1980-2004. Auth, "In His Presence"; Auth, "Why Me God". Acad Humiltics.

SCHARF, Douglas Frederick (SwFla) 3714 Cystal Dew St, Plant City FL 33567 **R H Innoc Epis Ch Valrico FL 2007-** B West Islip NY 9/21/1979 s Frederick Edward Scharf & Carol H. BA Florida Gulf Coast U 2001; MDiv VTS 2004. D 6/12/2004 Bp Rogers Sanders Harris P 12/19/2004 Bp John Bailey Lipscomb. m 11/20/1999 Shannon J Scharf c 3. Assoc Ch Of The H Sprt Osprey FL 2004-2007. dscharf@hiepiscopal.org

SCHARF JR, Frederick Edward (SwFla) 11644 Spindrift Loop, Hudson FL 34667 **Asst S Mart's Epis Ch Hudson FL 2007-** B Oswego NY 9/14/1939 s Frederick Edward Scharf & Ruth. BS SUNY 1962; MS SUNY 1972; MDiv VTS 1988. D 6/11/1988 P 12/22/1988 Bp Gerald Francis Burrill. m 4/21/2001 Vera G Scharf c 3. Int The Epis Ch Of The Gd Shpd Venice FL 2006-2011; Vic Lamb Of God Epis Ch Ft Myers FL 1990-1999; St Josephs Ch Ft Myers FL 1990-1999; Asst S Mary's Epis Ch Bonita Sprg FL 1988-1990. fred.scharf@verizon.net

SCHARK, Frederick J (EMich) 10 Nims St, Croswell MI 48422 **Trin Epis Ch Lexington MI 2005-** B Saginaw MI 9/13/1955 s Christian Schark & Flora. MDiv Hur; BA Trin IN. D 1/29/2005 P 8/14/2005 Bp Edwin Max Leidel Jr. m 9/22/1997 Kristi T Guzik c 1. rkschark@sbcglobal.net

S

SCHARON-GLASER, Anne Swiger (Mo) 420 N Florissant Rd, Saint Louis MO 63135 **P For Pstr Care S Steph's Ch Ferguson MO 2001-** B Clarksburg,WV 7/9/1919 d Ira Leslie Swiger & Maude Nicholson. BA Bridgewater Coll 1944; MDiv Eden TS 1977; Cert VTS 1978. D 8/26/1978 Bp Walter H Jones P 3/29/1979 Bp William Augustus Jones Jr. m 9/7/1940 Harry Leroy Scharon. Vic Prince of Peace S Louis MO 1981-1995. aec49@comcast.net

SCHATZ, Stefani S (Nev) 200 Island Ave, Reno NV 89501 **Mem, Stndg Com Dio Nevada Las Vegas NV 2009-; R Trin Epis Ch Reno NV 2008-** B Dallas TX 9/24/1962 d Lawrence D Schatz & Iva M. BA Mills Coll 1984; MDiv EDS 2001. D 6/30/2001 Bp Chester Lovelle Talton P 1/12/2002 Bp Frederick Houk Borsch. m 11/15/2003 Joe F Duggan. Dir Rel Educ All SS Par Brookline MA 2004-2006; Assoc S Cross By-The-Sea Ch Hermosa Bch CA 2001-2003. revstefani@gmail.com

SCHAUBLE, Jack L (Chi) Po Box 88, Compton IL 61318 B Barrington IL 5/13/1934 s Fredrick August Schauble & Neva Elaine. BA Elmhurst Coll 1956; MDiv SWTS 1959; MS U IL 1976; Cert Illinois Vlly Cmnty Coll 2005. D 6/20/1959 P 12/19/1959 Bp Charles L Street. m 5/11/1993 Sandra Jones c 3. P-in-c Emm Epis Ch Rockford IL 2006-2007; P-in-c The Epis Ch Of The H Trin Belvidere IL 2004-2005; Int Gr Epis Ch Freeport IL 2001-2003; Int Gr Epis Ch Galena IL 1999-2001; Int Gr Epis Ch New Lenox IL 1998-1999; Int Gr Epis Ch Sheboygan WI 1998; Int S Lk's Ch Dixon IL 1995-1997; Int All SS Epis Ch Appleton WI 1995; Luth Soc Serv Of Illinois Oregon IL 1990-1995; Vic S Jude's Epis Ch Rochelle IL 1986-1990; Chapl NW Mil & Nav Acad Lake Geneva WI 1976-1986; Vic S Ann's Ch Woodstock IL 1969-1975; R S Paul's Ch La Salle IL 1962-1969; Cur Ch Of The H Comf Kenilworth IL 1959-1962. woodspur@pcwildblue.com

SCHEEL, William Preston (Ark) 26 Cypress Point, Wimberley TX 78676 B Chicago IL 9/19/1936 s Harvey Andrew Scheel & Mildred Jeanette. BA U So 1959; BD SWTS 1962; EdD U of Massachusetts 1971. D 6/29/1962 Bp Hamilton Hyde Kellogg P 5/18/1963 Bp Philip Frederick McNairy. m 6/24/1989 Vivian Carol Rowe c 3. Pres of the Bd Shattuck-S Mary's Sch Faribault MN 1999-2003; Assoc Chr Epis Ch Plano TX 1995-2003; Dio NW Texas Lubbock TX 1988-1990; Exec Dir SW Assn Of Epis Schools Canyon TX 1986-1999; Dio New Jersey Trenton NJ 1977-1980; Asst The Epis Par Of S Dav Minnetonka MN 1964-1966; Yth Advsry Coun Dio Minnesota Minneapolis MN 1963-1969; Vic S Antipas Ch Redby MN 1962-1964; Vic S Jn-In-The-Wilderness Redlake MN 1962-1964. *Var Bk Revs & arts*, 2003. The Rev. A. Dn Calcote Awd SW Assn of Epis Schools 2007; Jn Verdery Awd Nat'l Assn of Epis Schools 2002; Hon Cn Cathd of Our Merc Sav Fairbault MN 1967. wscheel@s-sm.org

SCHEELER, Joseph Lester (Mont) 640 Mill Rd, Helena MT 59602 **Ch Of The Nativ/Elkhorn Cluster Helena MT 2001-** B Bryn Mawr PA 8/10/1950 BA La Salle U 1976; Mnstry Formation Prog 1999. D 11/10/2001 P 10/8/2002 Bp Charles Lovett Keyser. m 11/26/1983 Ramona Pocha c 2. joe.scheeler@ashgrove.com

SCHEELER, Richard Edward Gerhart (Mil) 1540 S 166th St, New Berlin WI 53151 **Bp D for Chr Formation Dio Milwaukee Milwaukee WI 2009-** B Milwaukee WI 1/25/1951 s Stanley Joseph Scheeler & Barbara Ann. BA U of Wisconsin-Whitewater 1973; Inst for Chr Stds Dio Sch at Nashotah Ho 1978. D 1/25/1979 Bp Charles Thomas Gaskell. m 6/11/1977 Patty Ann Cerny c 3. D S Thos Of Cbury Ch Greendale WI 2008-2009; D S Edmunds Ch Milwaukee WI 2000-2008; D S Jn Ch/Mision San Juan Milwaukee WI 1990-2000; D S Thos Of Cbury Ch Greendale WI 1985-1990; D S Edmunds Ch Milwaukee WI 1979-1985. Ord of S Vinc 1979. DNREGS@WI.RR.COM

SCHEIBLE, Anne Clare Elsworth (Minn) 21590 654th Ave, Darwin MN 55324 B Des Moines IA 9/4/1942 d John Nelson Elsworth & Katherine Vietta. BS Hamline U 1964. D 7/28/1996 Bp Sanford Zangwill Kaye Hampton P 2/15/1997 Bp James Louis Jelinek. m 10/2/1965 James William Scheible. P S Matt's Epis Ch Chatfield MN 1997-2003. Ascp 1964-2003. jascheib@aol.com

SCHEIBLE, Gordon Kenneth (SanD) 42110 Crest Dr, Hemet CA 92544 B San Diego CA 12/13/1948 s Walter Theodore Scheible & Charlotte (Davis) Scheible. BA U of San Diego 1971; MDiv CDSP 1974. D 7/7/1974 P 1/1/1975 Bp Robert Munro Wolterstorff. m 2/18/1978 Pamela Ferguson c 3. R The Epis Ch Of The Gd Shpd Hemet CA 1999-2008; Off Of Bsh For ArmdF New York NY 1977-1998; S Jas By The Sea La Jolla CA 1975-1976. CBS 1985; Ord of S Lk 1997; OHC - Assoc 1973; Soc of Cath Priests 2001. frscheible@msn.com

SCHEID, Daniel S (WMich) 1462 Colfax Ave, Benton Harbor MI 49022 **R S Aug Of Cbury Epis Ch Benton Harbor MI 2006-** B Greenville MI 12/2/1965 s Howard Scheid & Margaret. BA Aquinas Coll 1990; MDiv SWTS 2006. D 12/17/2005 P 6/24/2006 Bp Robert R Gepert. m 10/17/1986 Annette Scheid c 4. dsjscheid@gmail.com

SCHEIDER, David Max (CNY) No address on file. **Off Of Bsh For ArmdF New York NY 1999-** B Peoria IL 9/14/1957 s Max Burton Scheider & Joyce. BA Col 1980; MDiv Andrews U 1983; MS Wright St U 1988; MS K SU 1997. D 12/12/1998 P 6/12/1999 Bp David B(ruce) Joslin. m 8/9/1981 Beverley Alison Futcher c 3. Aamft; Fell AAPC. david.scheider@hotmail.com

SCHELB, Holly Greenman (NC) 1323 Irving St, Winston Salem NC 27103 B Cortland NY 8/2/1955 D 1/8/2005 Bp Michael Bruce Curry. c 2.

SCHELL, Anita Louise (RI) 42 Dearborn St, Newport RI 02840 **Emm Ch Newport RI 2010-; R Emm Ch Newport RI 2010-** B Lancaster PA 2/13/1957 d Theodore William Schell & Anne. BA Br 1979; MDiv GTS 1983; D Min EDS 2009. D 6/10/1983 P 6/14/1984 Bp Charlie Fuller McNutt Jr. c 2. R S Ptr's Epis Ch Bennington VT 2005-2010; Dio Pennsylvania Philadelphia PA 2001-2005; Assoc Ch Of The H Apos Wynnewood PA 1990-2001; S Paul's Ch Philadelphia PA 1985-2005; Dioc Ce Com Dio Pennsylvania Philadelphia PA 1985-1988; Trin Educ Fund New York NY 1984-1985; Stwrd Com Dio New York New York City NY 1983-1985; D-In-Trning Par of Trin Ch New York NY 1983-1984. Outsanding Young Wmn Awd 1985. rector@emmanuelnewport.org

SCHELL, Donald J (Cal) 555 De Haro St Ste 330, San Francisco CA 94107 **All SS Co Auburn CA 2007-** B San Jose CA 4/11/1947 s Harold Newton Schell & Nancy Emma. BA S Jn 1968; PrTS 1969; STB GTS 1971; MA U of San Francisco 1992; Fllshp Coll of Preachers 1999. D 10/11/1971 P 9/23/1972 Bp Stephen F Bayne Jr. m 5/10/1975 Ellen S Phelps c 4. Area Chair Sprtlty, Sch D Dio California San Francisco CA 1982-1986; R S Greg Of Nyssa Ch San Francisco CA 1980-2007; Dce Dio Idaho Boise ID 1977-1980; R S Dav's Epis Ch Caldwell ID 1976-1980. Auth, ",My Fr My Daughter: Pilgrims On The Road To Santiago," Ch Pub Inc, 2000; Founding Coordntr, "Presence," 1995; Ed, "Connections," 1994. Associated Parishes Coun 1998; Sprtl Dir Intl 1989-1995. Distingushed Alum The GTS 2004. donald@allsaintscompany.org

SCHELL, Peter G (WA) 1700 Powder Mill Rd, Silver Spring MD 20903 **Assoc Ch Of Our Sav Silver Sprg MD 2007-** B San Francisco 10/5/1980 s Donald J Schell & Ellen S. MDiv Yale DS 2002; MDiv CDSP 2006. D 6/3/2006 Bp William Edwin Swing P 12/2/2006 Bp Marc Handley Andrus. m 7/26/2006 Rondesia Jarrett. peterstgregoryschell@yahoo.com

SCHELL, Richardson Whitfield (Ct) Kent School, Kent CT 06757 **Sch Headmaster S Jos's Chap at the Kent Sch Kent CT 1981-; Kent Sch Kent CT 1980-** B Evanston IL 2/17/1951 s Frank Charles Schell & Carol Ely. BA Harv 1973; MDiv Ya Berk 1976. D 5/24/1976 P 11/1/1976 Bp James Winchester Montgomery. m 6/8/1974 Jennifer Almquist. The Ch Of The H Sprt Lake Forest IL 1976-1980. RWSCHELL@GMAIL.COM

SCHELLENBERG, Roger Thomas (Va) 5775 Barclay Drive Suite G, Kingstowne VA 22315 **Ch Of The Sprt Alexandria VA 1999-** B Winchester MA 9/16/1958 s Roland Charles Schellenberg & Lydia Lois. BA W&M 1980; MDiv GTS 1984; DMin VTS 2009. D 6/8/1984 P 5/26/1985 Bp C(laude) Charles Vache. m 10/26/1985 Virginia Scherrer c 2. Dio Virginia Richmond VA 1997-1999; Dio Wstrn Massachusetts Springfield MA 1993-1997; R S Matt's Ch Worcester MA 1993-1997; R The Par of S Mich's Auburn ME 1987-1993; Asst to the R S Mk's Ch Mt Kisco NY 1985-1987; Asst to the R S Andr's Ch Norfolk VA 1984-1985. Soc of S Jn the Evang 1987. rschllnbrg@cox.net

SCHELLING, Robert Louis (Colo) 393 Private Road 5730, Jefferson TX 75657 B 1/1/1937 s Lovere Victor Schelling & Marian Lee. B.A. Univ of Colorado 1960; MDiv SWTS 1976; B.S. Colo St Univ-Pueblo 1996. D 6/23/1976 P 12/23/1976 Bp William Carl Frey. m 12/3/1966 Lynda Layton c 3. Ch Of The Ascen Pueblo CO 1983-1995; S Tim's Epis Ch Rangely CO 1980-1983; S Paul's Ch Blackfoot ID 1978-1979; Interfaith T/F Loveland CO 1976-1977. roblou64@hotmail.com

SCHELLINGERHOUDT, Elizabeth Lewis (At) 450 Clairmont Ave, Atlanta GA 30030 **Assoc S Lk's Epis Ch Atlanta GA 2010-** B Cincinnati OH 10/15/1960 d Alvin Hayden Lewis & Lorton Lee. BA Converse Coll 1982; MDiv Candler TS Emory U 2009. D 12/20/2008 P 2/21/2010 Bp J(ohn) Neil Alexander. m 9/1/1990 Cornelis Schellingerhoudt c 2. S Marg's Ch Carrollton GA 2010; Ch Of The Epiph Atlanta GA 2008-2009. liz.schellingerhoudt@gmail.com

SCHELLKOPF, Julian Kurt (Alb) 820 Albany Shaker Rd, Albany NY 12211 B Schenectady NY 7/1/1936 s Sigmund Walter Schellkopf & Marion Elizabeth. BA Un Coll Schenectady NY 1958; MA SUNY 1959; STB PDS 1962. D 6/16/1962 P 12/1/1962 Bp Allen Webster Brown. c 2. R Par Of S Jas Ft Edw NY 1976-1977; Calv Epis Ch Cairo NY 1975-1976, Gloria Dei Epis Ch Palenville NY 1975-1976; Trin Ch Ashland Webster NY 1975-1976; Cur S Ptr's Ch Albany NY 1972-1975; Cur The Ch Of The Mssh Glens Falls NY 1964-1966. SBL, AAR 1962-1976.

SCHEMBS, Lois Jean (Nwk) 321 Lamberts Mill Rd, Westfield NJ 07090 B Oceanside NY 12/10/1952 d Carl George Meyer & Kay Irene. BA Wm Smith 1974; MA Suc 1978; MDiv VTS 1981. D 6/24/1981 P 3/1/1982 Bp Edward Witker Jones. m 4/24/1993 Douglas C Schembs. Int Gr-S Paul's Ch Mercerville NJ 2008-2010; R S Mart's Ch Maywood NJ 2000-2008; Int The Ch Of The Annunc Oradell NJ 1999-2000; Int S Andr's Ch Harrington Pk NJ 1998-1999; Int S Ptr's Ch Mtn Lakes NJ 1997-1998; Int S Alb's Ch Oakland NJ 1996-1997; Int S Mart's Ch Maywood NJ 1995-1996; Int All SS Memi Ch Navesink NJ 1993-1995; Assoc S Paul's Epis Ch Westfield NJ 1987-1993; S Jas Epis Ch Bowie MD 1984-1987; The Cathd Ch Of S Paul Des Moines IA 1983-1984; Gr Ch Muncie IN 1981-1983.

SCHENCK, Sister Judith A (Mont) 280 Idaho Hill Rd, Marion MT 59925 B Alva OK 5/15/1942 d Clifford Traverse & Trescinda. BA U of Montana 1986; MDiv Angl Coll 1990. D 6/3/1990 P 12/1/1990 Bp Charles Jones III. c 4. S Matt's Ch Glasgow MT 1991-1992; Dio Montana Helena MT 1990-1997. Franciscan Poor Clare Solitary (under SSF, CSF) 2007. sistermonk@bresnan.net

SCHENCK, Timothy E (Mass) 172 Main St, Hingham MA 02043 **Ch Of S Jn The Evang Hingham MA 2009-** B Milwaukee WI 10/30/1968 s Andrew C Schenck & Lois R. BA Tufts U 1991; MDiv SWTS 2000. D 6/10/2000 P 12/8/2000 Bp John Leslie Rabb. m 3/25/1995 Bryna Rogers c 2. Prov Coun Prov II 2007-2011; Bd Gvnr The Epis Life Ambler PA 2007-2011; Dn Epis Dio Of Ny Mid Hudson Regio Boiceville NY 2005-2007; R All SS' Epis Ch Briarcliff Manor NY 2002-2009; Cur S Paul's Par Baltimore MD 2000-2002. Auth, "In Gd Faith monthly column," *Syndicated Columnist*, GateHouse Media, 2011; Auth, "What Size Are God's Shoes: Kids, Chaos and the Sprtl Life," Morehouse, 2008; Auth, "From Sem to Par: Navigating Your First Cler Job Search," Self, 2001. ECom 2004. Polly Bond Awards ECom 2008. frtim1@gmail.com

SCHENEMAN, Mark Allan (CPa) 226 Acre Dr, Carlisle PA 17013 **R S Jn's Epis Ch Carlisle PA 1986-** B Washington DC 10/13/1948 s William A Scheneman & Jeanne K. BA Moravian TS 1970; MDiv GTS 1973; MA Tem 1976; DMin Estrn Bapt TS 1983. D 3/15/1974 P 1/25/1975 Bp Lloyd Edward Gressle. m 8/15/1970 Dorothy Hoshauer c 3. Dep Gc Dio Cntrl Pennsylvania Harrisburg PA 1997-2003; Stndg Com Dio Cntrl Pennsylvania Harrisburg PA 1993-2003; Jub Mnstry Off Dio Cntrl Pennsylvania Harrisburg PA 1991-1996; Chair Dio Cntrl Pennsylvania Harrisburg PA 1990-1999; Fin Com Dio Cntrl Pennsylvania Harrisburg PA 1987-1990; Chair Prog & Bdgt Com Dio Pennsylvania Philadelphia PA 1984-1986; Prog & Bdgt Com Dio Pennsylvania Philadelphia PA 1979-1981; R S Ptr's Epis Ch Broomall PA 1977-1986; Asst S Anne's Ch Abington PA 1975-1977; Asst S Mary's Epis Ch Ardmore PA 1974-1975. Auth, "Way Of The Cross," Forw Mvmt, 1983. OHC, Assoc 2001. Hon Cn St. Steph's Cathdral, Dio Cntrl PA 1995. d. scheneman@comcast.net

SCHENKEL JR, Robert Downes (Be) 1435 Colgate Dr, Bethlehem PA 18017 **P-in-c Dio Bethlehem Bethlehem PA 2005-** B Baltimore MD 11/21/1930 s Robert Downes Schenkel & Caryl Palen. BS W&L 1952; MDiv VTS 1960. D 7/8/1960 Bp Noble C Powell P 5/31/1961 Bp Harry Lee Doll. m 7/20/1957 Anne M Mathias c 4. Dioc Coun Dio Bethlehem Bethlehem PA 1987-1993; Dn Cathd Ch Of The Nativ Bethlehem PA 1984-1995; R Ch Of The Gd Shpd Nashua NH 1972-1984; Assoc S Andr's Ch Kansas City MO 1968-1972; R S Marg's Ch Annapolis MD 1963-1968; Chr Ch Columbia MD 1960-1963. Contrib, *Celebrate*. HSEC 1990. revrob@rcn.com

SCHERCK, Steven H (Alb) P.O. Box 397, Guilderland NY 12084 **Great Chapt Representitive Cathd Of All SS Albany NY 2010-; R S Bon Ch Guilderland NY 2009-** B Morristown NJ 4/1/1964 s Edwin Leslie Scherck & Joan K. Bachelor of Sci FD Madison 1987; MArts Fairfield U 1994; MArts Whitefield TS 2005; Lic in Theol S Andr's TS 2007; MST S Andr's TS 2008. D 5/31/2008 P 6/13/2009 Bp William Howard Love. m 9/19/1987 Robin L MacDonald c 3. D Cathd Of All SS Albany NY 2008-2009. sscherck@frontiernet.net

SCHERER, Anna Julia Katheryn Minor (SVa) 1830 Kirby Rd, McLean VA 22101 **Asst R S Dunst's McLean VA 2009-** B Austin TX 9/2/1982 d Charles Paul Minor & Mary Minor. BA Roa 2003; MDiv VTS 2009. D 6/13/2009 Bp Herman Hollerith IV P 1/9/2010 Bp David Colin Jones. m 1/24/2009 Dave Scherer. oneofgrace3@gmail.com

SCHERER-HOOCK, Joyce Lynn (Mass) Po Box 308, Topsfield MA 01983 **S Andr's Ch Ayer MA 2009-** B Lincoln NE 8/26/1954 d Michael Stuart Scherer & Betty Lynn. BA Asbury Coll 1976; MDiv Gordon-Conwell TS 1980. D 6/11/1988 Bp David Elliot Johnson P 9/17/1989 Bp Barbara Clementine Harris. m 6/21/1980 Robert F Scherer-Hoock. S Anne's In The Fields Epis Ch Lincoln MA 2007-2009; S Paul's Ch Peabody MA 2004-2007; Trin Ch Topsfield MA 1993-2004; Asst Trin Par Melrose MA 1989-1992; D Gr Ch Salem MA 1988-1989. "Sermon," *Sermons that Wk*. Catechesis of Gd Shpd. jshoock@comcast.net

SCHERM, Mary Cecelia (WMass) 14 Pine St, Northfield MA 01360 **R Chr Ch Rochdale MA 2010-; Dn Belmont Chap at S Mk's Sch Southborough MA 2000-** B Larchmont NY 2/12/1952 d Albert Elmer Scherm & Mary Jean. BA Goucher Coll 1974; MDiv EDS 1978; DMin EDS 1992. D 6/3/1978 Bp Paul Moore Jr P 12/31/1978 Bp James Stuart Wetmore. m 2/12/1978 Peter Blaine Martin. mollyscherm@stmarksschool.org

SCHEYER, Joyce Mack (Neb) 465 First Parish Road, Scituate MA 02066 **Min for Yth, Families, and Ch Sch S Lk's Epis Ch Scituate MA 2011-** B Fort Dix NJ 7/18/1956 d William Mack & Roberta. BA Harv 1978; MS OR SU 1986; PhD U of Nebraska 1998; MDiv EDS 2010. D 6/2/2010 P 1/19/2011 Bp Joe Goodwin Burnett. c 3. P Intern S Matt's Ch Lincoln NE 2010-2011. momscheyer@gmail.com

SCHIEFFELIN JR, John Jay (WMass) PO Box 60425, Florence MA 01062 **S Mich's-On-The-Heights Worcester MA 1971-** B New York NY 9/12/1936 s John Jay Schieffelin & Lois Lindon. MA U; BA Ya 1959; STB GTS 1962. D 6/22/1962 P 12/1/1962 Bp Robert McConnell Hatch. m 7/15/1973 Lois Shelly Tushman c 3. Stff Dio Wstrn Massachusetts Springfield MA 1970-1971; Vic Ch Of The Nativ Northborough MA 1965-1970; Asst Min S Jas' Ch Greenfield MA 1962-1965. JSCHIEFF@COMCAST.NET

SCHIEFFLER, Daniel Kent (Ark) 19 Woodberry Rd., Little Rock AR 77212 **R S Mk's Epis Ch Little Rock AR 2008-** B Victoria TX 5/15/1955 s Eugene Lester Schieffler & Lenita Pearl. BS U of Arkansas 1977; JD U of Arkansas 1980; MDiv STUSo 1999. D 7/10/1999 P 1/15/2000 Bp Larry Earl Maze. m 7/23/1977 Judith Ann Cracraft c 3. Cur S Jn's Epis Ch Ft Smith AR 1999-2008. dkschieffler@gmail.com

SCHIERING, Janet Christine (EO) P0 Box 1323, Hood River OR 97031 B Berea OH 4/23/1957 d Laird G Schiering & Eunice L. BA Witt 1979; BA Witt 1979; MA Seattle Pacific U 1982; Wstrn Sem 1991; MDiv Wstrn Evang Sem 1994. D 5/22/1994 Bp Rustin Ray Kimsey P 5/9/2006 Bp William O Gregg. m 10/10/1999 David J Hancock. Pstr Care Coordntr The Par Of S Mk The Evang Hood River OR 1990-1996. AAPC 1991; Gorge Ecum Mnstrs 1991-1998. jcsalpha@gorge.net

SCHIESLER, Robert Alan (WMich) 265 Paris Ave SE, Grand Rapids MI 49503 **Pres Stndg Com Dio Wstrn Michigan Kalamazoo MI 2011-; R S Mk's Ch Grand Rapids MI 2007-** B Lancaster PA 9/3/1949 s Robert Joseph Schiesler & Rita Marie. BA S Mary Baltimore MD 1971; MA S Mary Sem Baltimore MD 1975; MDiv InterMet Washington DC 1977; PhD Pacific Wstrn U Los Angeles 1992. Trans 2/2/2004 Bp John Palmer Croneberger. m 4/12/1997 Mary Elizabeth Novello. Exec Coun Dio Wstrn Michigan Kalamazoo MI 2008-2010; Dn The Cathd Ch Of S Paul Des Moines IA 2004-2007; Exec Coun Dio Newark Newark NJ 2000-2004; R S Lk's Epis Ch Montclair NJ 1997-2004; R Chr Ch Prince Geo's Par Rockville MD 1996-1997; GC Del Dio Delaware Wilmington DE 1991-1996; Pres Stndg Com Dio Delaware Wilmington DE 1990-1995; R Ch of St Andrews & St Matthews Wilmington DE 1988-1996; R S Andrews and S Matthews Mnstry Wilmington DE 1988-1996; Chair Anti-Racism Cmsn Dio Pennsylvania Philadelphia PA 1986-1988; R S Steph's Ch Philadelphia PA 1985-1988; Consult Dioc Dvlpmt Dio Michigan Detroit MI 1982-1985; Dioc Coun; Dioc Dn Dio Wstrn Michigan Kalamazoo MI 1981-1995; R Trin Ch Belleville MI 1980-1985. Cn of hon Dio Iowa 2006. roberts@stmarksgr.org

SCHIESS, Betty Bone (CNY) 6987 Van Antwerp Dr, Cicero NY 13039 B Cincinnati OH 4/2/1923 d Evan Paul Bone & Leah. BA U Cinc 1945; MA Syr 1947; MDiv CRDS 1972. D 6/25/1972 Bp Ned Cole P 7/29/1974 Bp Daniel Corrigan. m 8/28/1947 William A Schiess. Gr Ch Mex NY 1985-1987; Chapl Gr Epis Ch Syracuse NY 1976-1978. Who'S Who Rel; Inducted Natl Wmn'S Hall Fame 94; Who'S Who 98; Who'S Who Of Amer Wmn. dur1234e@aol.com

SCHIFF, Paulette Agnes (Az) 217 Tyler Ave, Miller Place NY 11764 B Rockville Centre NY 12/5/1946 d Arthur Charles Toppin & Sophy Margaret. BA Muhlenberg Coll 1968; MDiv GTS 1987. D 6/6/1987 Bp Edward Cole Chalfant P 5/14/1988 Bp Allen Lyman Bartlett Jr. m 6/7/1969 Walter Schiff c 1. S Paul's Ch Patchogue NY 2009-2011; S Jas Epis Ch S Jas NY 2005-2007; S Mary's Epis Ch Phoenix AZ 2003-2005; Assoc Gd Shpd Of The Hills Cave Creek AZ 2000-2001; Asstg P Ch Of S Mary The Vrgn New York NY 1997-1999; Int S Ptr's Ch Philadelphia PA 1997-1999; Asst S Mk's Ch Philadelphia PA 1990-1993; Dioc Ecum Coun Dio Pennsylvania Philadelphia PA 1989-1999; AIDS Com Dio Pennsylvania Philadelphia PA 1989-1992; Dioc Coun Dio Pennsylvania Philadelphia PA 1989-1991; EFM Mentor Dio Pennsylvania Philadelphia PA 1988-1994; D S Mk's Ch Philadelphia PA 1987-1988.

SCHIFFMAYER, Jeffrey Paul (Tex) 8739 Serenade Ln, Houston TX 77040 B Racine WI 11/9/1938 s George Francis Schiffmayer & Margaret Elizabeth. BA U of Wisconsin 1961; BD Nash 1964. D 2/22/1964 P 8/1/1964 Bp Donald H V Hallock. m 8/16/1969 Sylvia Sumner c 2. Cullen Memi Chap Houston TX 1997-2004; St Lk's Epis Hosp Houston TX 1997-2004; S Fran Epis Ch Coll Sta TX 1988-1997; R Ch Of The Redeem Houston TX 1968-1983. JEFFSCHIFFMAYER@YAHOO.COM

SCHILLING III, Walter Bailey (CFla) 1803 Crane Creek Blvd, Melbourne FL 32940 **The Centeburry Grp Dhahran 31311 2008-** B Chicago IL 4/8/1951 s Walter Bailey Schilling & Joan Winslow. U Freiburg W DE 1972; BA U of Wisconsin 1973; MDiv VTS 1988. D 6/11/1988 Bp James Russell Moodey P 2/1/1989 Bp John Herbert MacNaughton. m 11/12/2004 Kathleen A Schilling c 2. Hope Epis Ch Melbourne FL 1990-2008; Asst R S Geo Ch San Antonio TX 1988-1990. wallyschilling@mac.com

SCHILLREFF, Kathy (SwFla) 278 Sawgrass Ct, Naples FL 34110 **Dn, Naples Dnry Dio SW Florida Sarasota FL 2010-; Stndg Com Dio SW Florida Sarasota FL 2010-; R S Monica's Epis Ch Naples FL 2000-** B Ann Arbor MI 5/17/1946 d Joseph Louis Myrick & Barbara. Ball St U; Untd TS; BS Florida St U 1968; MDiv SWTS 1996. D 6/29/1996 P 5/3/1997 Bp Herbert Thompson Jr. m 8/19/1972 Harold Vincent Schillreff c 1. Int Chr Epis Ch Dayton OH 1996-1999. kschillreff@comcast.net

S

SCHINDLER, Gary Charles (WNY) 591 E Main St, Springville NY 14141 **Vic S Paul's Epis Ch Springville NY 1991-** B Bayshore NY 5/7/1956 s Charles Louis Schindler & Frances. BS SUNY 1978; MDiv EDS 1983. D 6/19/1983 Bp Harvey D Butterfield P 1/20/1984 Bp Wilbur Emory Hogg Jr. m 8/19/1978 Virginia Lynn McBride c 3. R Epis Untd Mnstry Nanticoke PA 1986-1991; R S Geo's Ch Nanticoke PA 1986-1991; R S Mart-In-The-Fields Mtn Top PA 1986-1991; Asst Chr Ch Pittsford NY 1983-1986. Soc of S Jn the Evang 1983. revschindler@yahoo.com

SCHINK, Susan Alma (Nwk) 481 Airmount Avenue, Ramsey NJ 07446 **S Clem's Ch Hawthorne NJ 2011-; P-in-c S Clem's Ch Hawthorne NJ 2011-** B Paterson NJ 10/11/1951 d William H Schink & Margaret Percy. BA Colby Coll 1973; MBA Rutgers-The St U 1980; MDiv UTS 2003. D 6/7/2003 Bp Rufus T Brome P 12/20/2003 Bp John Palmer Croneberger. Chr Ch Short Hills NJ 2010-2011; Int S Agnes Ch Little Falls NJ 2007-2010; H Trin Epis Ch Hillsdale NJ 2004-2007; S Eliz's Ch Ridgewood NJ 2003-2010. saschink@verizon.net

SCHIRMACHER, Michael Grayson (Md) 3202 Lake St Apt 2, Houston TX 77098 B Houston TX 8/19/1949 s Grayson Victor Schirmacher & Laura Angeline. Jn Hopkins U; BA Amer U 1971; MDiv EDS 1980. D 6/28/1980 P 1/1/1981 Bp David Keller Leighton Sr. S Jas Ch Austin TX 1999; Dio Maryland Baltimore MD 1989-1992; R S Mths' Epis Ch Baltimore MD 1985-1988; S Barn Kensington Philadelphia PA 1980-1982. Pstr Care Ntwk For Soc Responsibility; Supvsr ACPE, Fell Coll Of Chapl, AEHC. Robbins Fell 1989. mgschirm@mdanderson.org

SCHISLER, Richard Thomas (SO) 2210 Cleveland Ave, Portsmouth OH 45662 **D All SS Epis Ch Portsmouth OH 2002-** B Portsmouth OH 5/4/1939 BA Mia. D 10/26/2002 Bp Herbert Thompson Jr. m 5/16/1970 Sallie Chellis c 2. dickandsallie@adelphia.net

SCHISLER, Sallie Chellis (SO) 2210 Cleveland Ave, Portsmouth OH 45662 **P-in-c Chr Ch Ironton OH 2010-; Mem, Bd Bex Columbus OH 2009-; Mem, Procter Fund Dio Sthrn Ohio Cincinnati OH 1993-** B Huntington WV 4/15/1945 Cert Epis Dio Sthrn Ohio 2002; Cert Bex 2008. D 10/26/2002 Bp Herbert Thompson Jr P 6/28/2008 Bp Thomas Edward Breidenthal. m 5/16/1970 Richard Thomas Schisler c 2. Cur All SS Epis Ch Portsmouth OH 2008-2010. scschisler@aol.com

SCHISSER, Janet Elaine (Mo) 1203 Castle Bay Pl, Columbia MO 65203 B Childress 12/23/1943 d William Ralph Council & Mary Frances. BBA U of Oklahoma 1965. D 6/24/2006 Bp Robert Manning Moody. c 2. D Columbia Hope Ch Columbia MO 2009-2010; D S Mich's Epis Ch Norman OK 2006-2009. janetschisser@centurytel.net

SCHIVELY, John Alrik (NCal) 6901 New Creek Ln, Citrus Heights CA 95621 **Assoc St Johns Epis Ch Roseville CA 1998-** B San Francisco CA 1/21/1934 s Charles Stockley Schively & Kalmar Francisco. BS U of San Francisco 1956; MDiv CDSP 1960. D 6/26/1960 Bp James Albert Pike P 6/24/1961 Bp George Richard Millard. c 2. Assoc S Fran Epis Ch Fair Oaks CA 1998; R S Matt's Epis Ch Sacramento CA 1986-1998; Ch Of The Redeem Pendleton OR 1983-1986; S Edw The Confessor Epis Ch San Jose CA 1974-1983; R S Jn's Epis Ch Oakland CA 1968-1973; R S Steph's Ch Gilroy CA 1962-1968; Cur Chr Ch Alameda CA 1960-1962. Ord of S Lk. darev@surewest.net

SCHJONBERG, Mary Frances Frances (Nwk) 407 Seaview Circle, Neptune NJ 07753 **ENS Ed/reporter Epis Ch Cntr New York NY 2005-; Asstg P Trin Ch Asbury Pk NJ 2005-** B Madison WI 5/15/1954 d Conrad Emil Schjonberg & Mildred Lillian. BA U of Wisconsin 1975; Mstr of Div CDSP 2000; DD CDSP 2011. D 6/18/2000 P 1/18/2001 Bp Charles Jones III. Mem, Diac Ord Com Dio Newark Newark NJ 2005-2007; Asst to the R Chr Ch Short Hills NJ 2000-2005. Auth, "Theol column," *The Missoulian*, Lee Enterprises, 1997. ECom 2005; Epis Preaching Fndt 2002. DD, h.c. CDSP 2011. mfrances54@optonline.net

SCHLACHTER, Barbara Jeanne Hartley (SO) 7 Glenview Knl NE, Iowa City IA 52240 **Assoc Trin Ch Iowa City IA 2010-** B OH 8/10/1945 d Charles Beatty Hartley & Jeanne. BA Ohio Wesl 1967; MA Col 1970; MDiv UTS 1972; DMin Estrn Bapt TS 1988. D 6/9/1973 Bp Paul Moore Jr P 1/20/1977 Bp James Stuart Wetmore. m 8/24/1968 Melvin Harlan Schlachter c 2. Assoc R Chr Ch Cedar Rapids IA 2003-2010; EWC New Era MI 2002; Co-R Trin Epis Ch Troy OH 1987-2002; Co-R S Marg's Ch Staatsburg NY 1982-1987; Asst S Barth's Ch In The Highland White Plains NY 1977-1982. Auth, *How Many Loaves Have You?*. Ch Dvlpmt Bd 1972-1983; Com on Status of Wmn in the Ch 2000-2006; Fndr & 1st Pres EWC 1971-1975; Pres Natl Ntwk of Epis Cler Assn 1992-1998. Phi Beta Kappa Ohio Wesleyan 1967. b. schlachter@mchsi.com

SCHLACHTER, Melvin Harlan (Ia) 7 Glenview Knl NE, Iowa City IA 52240 **COM Dio Iowa Des Moines IA 2007-; R Trin Ch Iowa City IA 2002-** B San Pedro CA 2/2/1946 s Melvin Frederick Schlachter & Mildred. BA U of Nebraska 1967; MA U of Wisconsin 1968; DIT Oxf 1971; MDiv UTS 1972; Shalem Inst for Sprtl Formation Washington DC 1994. D 6/6/1972 Bp Robert Patrick Varley P 12/9/1972 Bp Paul Moore Jr. m 8/24/1968 Barbara Jeanne Hartley Schlachter c 2. Stndg Com Dio Sthrn Ohio Cincinnati OH 1998-2001; Dio Sthrn Ohio Cincinnati OH 1997; Co-Chair Cler Assn Dio Sthrn Ohio Cincinnati OH 1990-1995; COM Dio Sthrn Ohio Cincinnati OH 1988-1992; Co-R Trin Epis Ch Troy OH 1987-2002; Co-R S Marg's Ch Staatsburg NY 1982-1987; Bishops Advsry Com New York NY 1973-1976; Cluster Yonkers NY 1972-1973; Assoc Min San Andres Ch Yonkers NY 1972-1973. *Var newpaper/mag essays*. Clincl Cert Intl TA Assn 1976-1980; Fell, AAPC 1976; OHC-Assoc. mschlachter@trinityic.org

SCHLAFER, David John (Mil) 5213 Roosevelt Street, Bethesda MD 20814 **P Assoc (Vol) The Ch Of The Redeem Beth MD 2000-** B Louisville KY 10/21/1944 s Frederick George Schlafer & Billie Anne. BA Wheaton Coll 1966; MA Sthrn Illinois U 1969; PhD Sthrn Illinois U 1974; Cert Nash 1984. D 6/28/1980 P 3/1/1985 Bp James Winchester Montgomery. m 6/14/1997 Margaret A Tucker c 2. Cathd of St Ptr & St Paul Washington DC 2002-2003; Cathd of St Ptr & St Paul Washington DC 1993-1995; VTS Alexandria VA 1993-1995; The TS at The U So Sewanee TN 1991-1993; The U So (Sewanee) Sewanee TN 1991-1993; Nash Nashotah WI 1986-1991; P-in-c St Philips Epis Ch Waukesha WI 1986-1990; Dio Chicago Chicago IL 1984-1987; S Lk's Ch Racine WI 1984-1985. "What's the Shape of Narrative Preaching?," Chalice, 2007; Auth, "Preaching What We Pract: Proclamation and Moral Formation," Morehouse, 2007; "Sermons That Wk (Vol. 5 - 14)," Morehouse, 2006; Auth, "The Shattering Sound of Amazing Gr: Disquieting Tales from St. Jn's Gospel," Cowley, 2006; Auth, "Playing w Fire: Preaching Wk as Kindling Art," Cowley, 2004; Auth, "What Makes This Day Different?: Preaching Gr on Spec Occasions," Cowley, 1998; "Your Way w God's Word: Discovering Your Distinctive Preaching Voice," Cowley, 1995; "Surviving the Sermon: A Guide to Preaching for Those Who Have to Listen," Cowley, 1992. dschlafer@juno.com

SCHLEGEL, Stuart Allen (ECR) 3400 Paul Sweet Road, Apt. B-213, Santa Cruz CA 95065 B Sewickley PA 12/11/1932 s Glenn M Schlegel & Elizabeth W. BA U CA 1957; MDiv CDSP 1960; MA U Chi 1965; PhD U Chi 1969. D 5/31/1960 Bp Ivol I Curtis P 1/25/1961 Bp Lyman Cunningham Ogilby. c 2. Calv Epis Ch Santa Cruz CA 1992-1993; R S Lk's Ch Los Gatos CA 1984-1992; Asst R S Lk's Ch Los Gatos CA 1979-1984. Auth, *Wisdom From a Rainforest*, U GA Press, 1998; Auth, *Tiruray Subsistence*, Ateneo de Manilla U Press, 1979; Auth, *Tiruray-Engl Lexicion*, U CA Press, 1971; Auth, *Tiruray Justice*, U CA Press, 1970. Professed Tertiary of the Soc of S Fran 1997. schlegel@cruzio.com

SCHLEY JR, Joseph Hastings (FtW) 6015 Millie Pl, Amarillo TX 79119 B Dallas TX 4/13/1939 s Joseph Hastings Schley & Jane. U So 1958; BA SMU 1960; JD SMU 1963; S Geo's Coll Jerusalem IL 1973; MDiv VTS 1974. D 6/5/1974 P 12/18/1974 Bp Willis Ryan Henton. m 5/15/1964 Carolyn H Higginbotham c 2. Dn Dio Ft Worth Ft Worth TX 1993-1999; Our Lady Of The Lake Clifton TX 1993-1999; Dio Ft Worth Ft Worth TX 1989-1992; R Ch Of The H Comf Cleburne TX 1987-1989; Dn Dio NW Texas Lubbock TX 1985-1987; Eccl Crt Dio NW Texas Lubbock TX 1983-1987; R S Nich' Epis Ch Midland TX 1979-1987; R S Simons Ch Miami FL 1976-1979; Ch Of The Heav Rest Abilene TX 1974-1976; Dio NW Texas Lubbock TX 1974-1976. Auth, "arts," *Living Ch*. Amarillo "Medtr of the Year" Dispute Resolution Ctr. 2005; Midland "Boss of the Year" JCC 1985.

SCHLISMANN, Robert (Neb) 1309 R St, Lincoln NE 68508 B Chicago IL 6/19/1950 s William B Schlismann & Charlotte Cecilia. BS Illinois St U 1972; MDiv Reformed TS 1987; MDiv The TS at The U So 2009. D 10/28/2009 P 5/22/2010 Bp Joe Goodwin Burnett. m 9/19/1974 Carol A Cortes c 3. Cur S Mk's On The Campus Lincoln NE 2009-2010. rschlismann@hotmail.com

SCHLOSSBERG, Stephen K K (Alb) 2777 Mission Rd, Nashotah WI 53058 **Zion Epis Ch Oconomowoc WI 2008-; Cmncatn Dir Nash Nashotah WI 2007-** B Minneapolis MN 9/4/1963 s Herbert Schlossberg & Teresa Ann. BA Bethel Coll 1986; MDiv Nash 2007. D 12/7/2006 P 9/30/2007 Bp Keith Lynn Ackerman. m 10/3/1987 Angie K Schlossberg c 5. Truro Epis Ch Fairfax VA 1997-2004. sschlossberg@nashotah.edu

SCHLOTTERBECK, Marilou Jean (WMich) 12530 Cinder Rd, Beulah MI 49617 **D S Phil's Ch Beulah MI 1994-** B Detroit MI 10/11/1946 d Ernest Russell Ming & Mary Louise. EFM 1994. D 8/6/1994 Bp Edward Lewis Lee Jr. m 6/15/1968 Kurt Sand Schlotterbeck c 3. schlotterbeckm@michigan.gov

SCHMALING, Pamela J (Oly) 7913 W Golf Course Dr, Blaine WA 98230 **D S Paul Epis Ch Bellingham WA 2000-** B Pomeroy WA 8/7/1945 d Lowell Nelson Baker & Thelma May. Cert Vancouver TS 2002. D 8/8/1998 Bp Frank Jeffrey Terry. m 6/5/1990 Jan Schmaling c 1. S Mich's Epis Ch Yakima WA 1998-2000. pschmaling@attbi.com

SCHMIDT, Ann Welsh (Ark) 726 Davemar Dr, Saint Louis MO 63123 B Cincinnati OH 9/14/1942 d Allen Preston Welsh & Elizabeth Raymond. BA Mia 1968; MDiv Untd TS Dayton OH 1987. D 8/30/1987 Bp Don Adger Wimberly. m 10/1/1979 Robert Frederick Schmidt. Ecum Cmsn Dio Arkansas Little Rock AR 1997-1999; Asst S Matt's Epis Ch Benton AR 1996-1998; Asst S Lk's Ch Hot Sprg AR 1992-1995; Asst S Andr's Ch Ft Thos KY

S

1987-1991. Auth, *Tales of a Wanton Gospeller*, 1994. awschmidt42@sbcglobal.net

SCHMIDT, Carolyn Jean Decker (Minn) PO Box 278, 1633 Croftville Rd, Grand Marais MN 55604 **Asst Sprt of the Wilderness Grand Marais MN 2011-; Stndg Com Dio Minnesota Minneapolis MN 2009-** B Buffalo NY 3/11/1952 d James Eugene Decker & Marjorie Jean. BA Wells Coll 1974; MDiv VTS 1987. D 6/24/1987 P 12/1/1987 Bp Robert Marshall Anderson. m 9/23/1976 Milan C Schmidt c 2. Adv Ch Farmington MN 2009-2011; Assoc The Epis Cathd Of Our Merc Sav Faribault MN 1997-1998; R Ch Of The H Cross Dundas MN 1994-2005; Vic S Paul's Epis Le Cntr MN 1993-1994; Stndg Com Dio Minnesota Minneapolis MN 1989-1995; Vic S Andr's Epis Ch Waterville MN 1987-1989. RWF, Mn Epis Cleric Assn, Neca. madrecj@aol.com

SCHMIDT, David William (SD) 2013 Buffalo Street, Pierre SD 57501 B Reno NV 3/8/1942 s William Henry Schmidt & Oma. BS Westminster Coll 1965; MDiv GTS 1971; MSW Estrn Washington U 1985. D 6/24/1971 Bp Richard S Watson P 12/1/1971 Bp Otis Charles. m 6/27/1970 Norma Evans c 4. Chr Epis Ch Gettysburg SD 1998-2005; Stndg Com Dio So Dakota Sioux Falls SD 1993-1997; S Fran Cmnty Serv Inc. Salina KS 1992-1993; Stndg Com Dio So Dakota Sioux Falls SD 1988-1992; R Trin Epis Ch Pierre SD 1986-1990; P-in-c H Trin Epis Ch Wallace ID 1985-1986; Supply P Dio Spokane Spokane WA 1983-1985; R S Christophers Ch Anchorage AK 1978-1983; Bountiful Cmnty Ch Bountiful UT 1971-1978; Vic S Jn's Epis Ch Logan UT 1971-1974. v.bede@pie.midco.net

SCHMIDT, Edward William (Md) 1500 Hilton Ave # 21238, Catonsville MD 21228 B Staten Island NY 7/12/1939 s Edward Albert Schmidt & Martha Washington. BA Wag 1960; BD Nash 1963. D 6/11/1963 P 12/21/1963 Bp Horace W B Donegan. All SS Cnvnt Catonsville MD 1981-2004; R Gr Epis Ch Westwood NJ 1973-1978; Assoc San Andres Ch Yonkers NY 1969-1970; Vic S Greg's Epis Ch Woodstock NY 1966-1969; Cur Chr Ch Poughkeepsie NY 1964-1966; Cur Par Of Chr The Redeem Pelham NY 1963-1964. domedwosb@aol.com

SCHMIDT JR, Frederick William (WA) Po Box 750133, Dallas TX 75275 B Louisville KY 6/20/1953 s Frederick William Scmidt & Pauline Ruth. BA Asbury Coll 1975; MDiv Asbury TS 1978; PhD Oxf 1986. D 6/11/1993 P 12/1/1993 Bp Charlie Fuller McNutt Jr. c 1. Ch Of The Incarn Dallas TX 2004-2008; S Lk's Epis Ch Dallas TX 2003-2004; S Mich And All Ang Ch Dallas TX 2000; Cn Cathd of St Ptr & St Paul Washington DC 1997-2000; Assoc All SS' Epis Ch Hershey PA 1995-1996; Exec Coun Appointees New York NY 1994-1997; Intern S Andr's Ch Harrisburg PA 1993-1994. Ed/Contrib, "Conversations w Scripture," Morehouse Pub, 2005; Auth, "What God Wants for Your Life," Harper One, 2005; Auth, "Sofferenza, All ricerca di una riposta," Claudiana, 2004; Auth, "When Suffering Persists," Morehouse Pub, 2001; Auth, "The Changing Face of God," Morehouse Pub, 2000; Auth, "A Still Sm Voice," Syr Press, 1996; Contrib, "44 Minor Entries," *Anchor Bible Dictionary*, Doubleday, 1992. AAR; Angl Assn Biblic Scholars; Cath Biblic Assn; Natl Institutes of Hlth, Pulmonary DSMB (=Data Sfty Mon; New Engl Resrch Inst, Stop II DSMB (=Data Sfty Moni; Soc for the Sci Study of Rel; SBL; The Soc for the Study of Chr Sprtlty. Angus Dun Fellowowship Dio Washington 1999; Class XI, The Cler Ldrshp Proj (CLP) Trin Wallstreet, NY 1999; Serv Recognition Natl Institutes of Hlth 1998; Sr Fell WF Albright Inst of Archeol Resrch Jerusalem 1995; Who's Who in Biblic Stds and Archeol 1993; FW Dillstone Schlrshp Oriel Coll,Oxford 1984; Hall Houghton Schlrshp U of Oxford 1983; Fell Amer Coun on Educ (ACE); Ovrs Resrch Stdt Awd Com of Vice-Chancellors & Principals The Universities of the Untd Kingdom. fschmidt@mail.smu.edu

SCHMIDT, Julanne Best (Chi) 35131 Arboretum Road, Glen Ellyn IL 60137 **D S Barn' Epis Ch Glen Ellyn IL 1992-** B Rock Island IL 1/28/1930 d Henry Lambert Best & Alma Madeline. NWU 1949; BD Nthrn Illinois U 1969. D 12/2/1989 Bp Frank Tracy Griswold III. m 12/17/1949 Walter Leighton Schmidt c 4. Bd Natl Assn Catechesis Of Gd Shpd; Tertiary Of The Soc Of S Fran. julbs@aol.com

SCHMIDT, Kenneth L (Cal) 1350 Waller St, San Francisco CA 94117 **R All SS' Ch San Francisco CA 1988-** B Buffalo NY 10/26/1946 s Lorenzo Dow Schmidt & Violet Emma. BA Houghton Coll 1968; MDiv PrTS 1971; PhD PrTS 1980; DMin SFTS 2000. D 6/11/1977 P 3/7/1978 Bp Paul Moore Jr. m 5/31/1975 John H Roberts. S Lk's Ch Philadelphia PA 1985-1987; Trin Ch Princeton NJ 1980-1982; Chr Ch New Brunswick NJ 1980. SSM 1986. tfdrkls@gmail.com

SCHMIDT, Kevin Lynn (Kan) 15309 W 153rd St, Olathe KS 66062 **S Thos The Apos Ch Overland Pk KS 2009-; P-in-c H Apos Ch Ellsworth KS 2001-; P-in-c S Jn's Ch Great Bend KS 2001-; P-in-c S Mk's Ch Lyons KS 2001-; P-in-c SS Mary And Martha Of Bethany Larned KS 2001-** B Larned KS 9/27/1964 s Sandy Lynn Schmidt & Vera May. BS Sterling Coll 1996. D 1/20/2001 Bp John Forsythe Ashby P 9/15/2001 Bp Vernon Edward Strickland. m 1/14/1995 Lisa Ann Eberle c 2. klschmidt@comcast.net

SCHMIDT, Linda Marie (FdL) N2592 State Highway 17, Merrill WI 54452 **COM Dio Fond du Lac Appleton WI 2006-; D Ch of the Ascen Merrill WI 2003-** B Milwaukee WI 9/14/1945 Marq; U of Wisconsin; U of Wisconsin. D 8/30/2003 Bp Russell Edward Jacobus. m 4/20/1968 Earl Schmidt c 6.

SCHMIDT, Norma (Ct) 661 Old Post Rd, Fairfield CT 06824 B Gary IN 1/1/1958 d Norman Michalski & Phyllis. MA U Chi 1982; MDiv Luth TS 1986; MA Fairfield U 2001. Rec from Evangelical Lutheran Church in America 1/29/2010 Bp Andrew Donnan Smith. m 9/19/1982 David Schmidt c 2. Assoc S Paul's Ch Fairfield CT 2011. norma_3223@yahoo.com

SCHMIDT, Richard Hanna (CGC) 101 Fairwood Blvd., Fairhope AL 36532 B Louisville KY 9/26/1944 s Craig Richard Schmidt & Betsy Hanna. BA Ken 1966; MDiv Van 1970; DMin Wesley TS 1999. D 6/11/1970 P 12/16/1970 Bp Wilburn Camrock Campbell. m 8/17/1968 Pamela H Hegerberg c 3. Ed/Dir FMP Cincinnati OH 2005-2011; Dio Cntrl Gulf Coast Pensacola FL 1998-2000; Dep GC Dio Cntrl Gulf Coast Pensacola FL 1994; R S Paul's Epis Ch Daphne AL 1990-2000; Mng Ed The Epis Life Ambler PA 1988-1990; S Ptr's Epis Ch St Louis MO 1982-1988; R Chr Ch Fairmont WV 1975-1982; Assoc S Jn's Epis Ch Charleston WV 1971-1975; Vic Emm Ch Moorefield WV 1970-1971; Vic S Steph's Ch Romney WV 1970-1971. Auth, "God Seekers: Twenty Centuries of Chr Spiritualities," Wm B. Eerdmans, 2008; Auth, "A Gracious Rain: A Devotional Commentary on the Prayers of the Ch Year," Ch Pub, 2008; Auth, "Life Lessons from Alpha to Omega," Ch Pub, 2005; Auth, "Praises, Prayers & Curses: Conversations w the Psalms," Forw Mvmt, 2005; Auth, "Glorious Comp: Five Centuries of Angl Sprtlty," Wm. B. Eerdmans, 2002. rhsphs@gmail.com

SCHMIDT, Thomas Carson (WMass) 2 Larkspur Ln, Brunswick ME 04011 B York PA 10/15/1930 s George Small Schmidt & Josephine. BA Pr 1952; MDiv VTS 1955; PhD SUNY 1971. D 4/1/1955 Bp John T Heistand P 10/1/1955 Bp Reginald Heber Gooden. m 11/26/1983 Robin Bell Graham c 3. R S Andr's Ch Longmeadow MA 1961-1968; Asst S Jas Ch New London CT 1958-1961. Auth, "Chinas Schools In Flux," Sharpe, 1979; Auth, "Pediatric Med & Educ," *Rhode Island Med Journ*, 1973; Auth, "Planing & Info Exch Process," *Educ Planing Journ*, 1972. tschmidt1952@gmail.com

SCHMIDT, Wayne Roy (NY) 3 Ashley Dr, Newburgh NY 12550 B Brooklyn NY 2/20/1934 s Wainwright Paul Schmidt & Gertrude A. BA Hob 1956; MDiv GTS 1959. D 4/4/1959 P 10/10/1959 Bp James P De Wolfe. m 10/1/1988 Ann Devlin c 2. Asst Zion Epis Ch Wappingers Falls NY 2000-2003; Trst Cathd Of St Jn The Div New York NY 1988-1994; R S Geo's Epis Ch Newburgh NY 1975-1994; Vic S Paul's Ch Pleasant Vlly NY 1964-1973; Asst to the R Ch Of S Jas The Less Scarsdale NY 1960-1964; Cur S Steph's Ch Port Washington NY 1959-1960. wayneschmi@net

SCHMIDTETTER, Todd Thomas (SC) 415 Wilson Dr, Penn Hills PA 15235 B Pittsburgh PA 9/14/1977 s David William Schmidtetter & Shirley Ann. BS Charleston Sthrn U 2008; MDiv Trin Sch for Mnstry 2011. D 6/4/2011 Bp Mark Joseph Lawrence. m 4/14/2002 Michelle Hedlund c 1. theobrew@yahoo.com

SCHMITT, Barbara Joyce (SO) 115 N 6th St, Hamilton OH 45011 B Cincinnati OH 3/4/1960 d Robert Andrew Schmitt & Nancy Jean. D 6/14/2008 Bp Thomas Edward Breidenthal. c 1. FMP Cincinnati OH 1992-2008; Foward Mvmt Pub Cincinnati OH 1992-2003. barbara_schmitt2003@yahoo.com

SCHMITT, Geoffrey (WLa) 3910 Parkway Dr, 1605 Gray Lake Dr, Princeton LA 71067 B Phillipsburg PA 5/22/1949 s Robert Henry Schmitt & Eileen. BS SUNY 1971; MDiv Bex 1978; DMin Gordon-Conwell TS 1995. D 6/17/1978 P 12/18/1978 Bp Alexander Doig Stewart. m 3/17/2005 Brenda Morris. First Luth Ch ELCA Shreveport LA 2009-2010; R S Geo's Ch Bossier City LA 2000-2007; Vic Calv Epis Ch Jacksonville FL 1997-1999; Asst S Marg's Epis Ch Waxhaw NC 1995-1997; R S Chris's Ch Charlotte NC 1990-1995; Vic Ch Of The Resurr Tucson AZ 1985-1990; R Ch Of The Recon Webster MA 1980-1985. Assn Of Psychol Type. drgeoffrey@earthlink.net

SCHMITT, Jacqueline Mary (Mass) 31 Ely Dr., Fayetteville NY 13066 **R S Dav's Ch De Witt NY 2011-** B Syracuse NY 11/2/1953 d Francis Thomas Schmitt & Dorothy Elaine. BA Amer U 1975; MDiv UTS 1980. D 6/21/1980 P 4/11/1981 Bp Ned Cole. m 6/29/1985 Tim Stewart Hall c 4. Vic S Paul's Ch Boston MA 2005-2011; Assoc Trin Ch In The City Of Boston Boston MA 2005; Chapl Epis Chapl At Harvard & Radcliffe Cambridge MA 2004-2005; Harvard Radcliffe Ch Cambridge MA 2004-2005; Cn Precentor S Paul's Cathd Syracuse NY 1992-1994; Emm Ch E Syracuse NY 1990-1992; Chair Coll Wk Cmsn Dio Cntrl New York Syracuse NY 1988-1994; Paris Cluster Chadwicks NY 1986-1988; Int S Thos Ch Hamilton NY 1986-1988; Epis Ch Of SS Ptr And Jn Auburn NY 1985-1986; Dio No Carolina Raleigh NC 1982-1984; Dio Cntrl New York Syracuse NY 1980-1982; Assoc S Dav's Ch De Witt NY 1980-1982. Auth, "The Body and Liturg," *Liturg: Journ*, The Liturg Conf, 2009; Auth, "Sacrifical Adventure," *Deeper Joy*, Ch Pub Inc, 2005; Auth, "Vida Dutton Scudder," *A Heart for the Future*, Ch Pub Inc, 2004; Auth, "Coll Chapl And The Future Of Theol,A New Conversation," *A New Conversation*, Ch Pub Inc, 1999; Auth, "The Epis Ch Welcomes You?,Disorganized Rel," *Disorganized Rel*, Cowley Press, 1998; Auth, "Living Under And Above The

Law, Prophet Of Justice," *Prophet Of Life*, Ch Pub Inc, 1997; Ed Bd, "ATR," 1996. ESMHE, Epis W 1980-2004. jacqueline.schmitt@gmail.com

SCHMITZ, Barbara G (CNY) **Tpic (Int) Epis Ch Of S Mary The Vrgn Falmouth ME 2011-** D 6/24/1989 Bp H Coleman McGehee Jr P 3/11/1990 Bp R(aymond) Stewart Wood Jr.

SCHMOETZER, Jane Ellen (Mont) 1322 Kimball Ave., Richland WA 99354 **R All SS Ch Richland WA 2010-; Vic Our Sav Epis Joliet MT 2006-; Vic S Alb's Epis Ch Laurel MT 2006-; Vic S Paul's of the Stillwater Ch Absarokee MT 2006-** B Fort Bragg NC 8/24/1961 d James Foster Mayberry & Carolyn May. BS Pur 1983; MDiv SWTS 2005. D 4/15/2005 P 10/22/2005 Bp Edward Stuart Little II. m 5/28/1983 Bruce E Schmoetzer c 2. Dioc Coun Dio Spokane Spokane WA 2010-2011; Yellowstone Epis Mnstrs Red Lodge MT 2010; BEC Dio Montana Helena MT 2007-2010; VP, Dioc Coun Dio Montana Helena MT 2007-2010; Vic Calv Epis Ch Red Lodge MT 2006-2010; Dio Montana Helena MT 2006-2009; Cur S Andr's By The Lake Epis Ch Michigan City IN 2005-2006. jane@schmoetzer.com

SCHNAARE, Anne Elizabeth (Ga) 335 Tennessee Ave., Sewanee TN 37383 **R Trin Epis Ch Marshall MI 2011-; Calv Ch Americus GA 2009-** B Royal Oak MI 5/5/1978 d Dexter D Schassberger & Harriet Virginia. BA U of Wisconsin 2001; MDiv The U So (Sewanee) 2009. D 12/20/2008 P 6/27/2009 Bp Russell Edward Jacobus. m 7/14/2001 Matthew R Schnaare c 1. anneschnaare@yahoo.com

SCHNABEL, Charles Edward (LI) 143 Lakeside Trail, Ridge NY 11961 B Long Island NY 2/19/1936 s John J Schnabel & Gladys B. BA CUNY, Queens Coll 1958; MDiv Ya Berk 1961. D 4/8/1961 P 10/28/1961 Bp James P De Wolfe. c 3. Geo Mercer TS Garden City NY 1994-1995; Dio Long Island Garden City NY 1973-1977; R Ch Of The Nativ Mineola NY 1963-1998; Cur H Trin Epis Ch Vlly Stream NY 1961-1963. Angl Theol Conf 1972-1989. schnabelce@verizon.net

SCHNABL, Emily Jessica (Okla) 4036 Neptune Dr, Oklahoma City OK 73116 **Int S Chris's Ch Midwest City OK 2006-** B Chicago IL 3/18/1967 d Ernest Eric Schnabl & Carile Lucile. BA U IL 1988; MA U of Arizona 1991; MDiv SWTS 1999. D 6/11/2000 P 5/8/2001 Bp Peter Hess Beckwith. m 11/10/2001 David Robert Stock. Trin Ch Guthrie OK 2005-2006; Asst R S Geo's Ch Belleville IL 2000-2004. "Christmas Trees Preaching Through H Days & Holidays," Morehoouse, 2003. Phi Beta Kappa 1988. emilyjess_1999@yahoo.com

SCHNATTERLY, Michael Dean (USC) 5 Mountain Vista Rd, Taylors SC 29687 **Mem of Dioc Exec Coun Dio Upper So Carolina Columbia SC 2012-; R Ch Of The Gd Shpd Greer SC 2006-** B Hays KS 10/9/1955 s Harry Lee Schnatterly & Toya Ann. BA Furman U 1979; MDiv SWTS 1989. D 6/12/1989 Bp William Hopkins Folwell P 12/16/1989 Bp Elliott Lorenz Sorge. m 7/21/1984 Clare Lorelle Inman c 2. Dn, Reedy River Convoc Dio Upper So Carolina Columbia SC 2006-2008; P-in-c Ch Of The Gd Shpd Greer SC 2005-2006; Mem of Dioc Coun Dio No Carolina Raleigh NC 2003-2004; R S Fran Ch Greensboro NC 2001-2004; Sprtl Advsr to Curs Sec Dio Cntrl Florida Orlando FL 1999-2001; R S Edw The Confessor Mt Dora FL 1996-2001; R Emm Epis Ch Opelika AL 1992-1996; Exam Chaplin, Liturg Dio Easton Easton MD 1990-1992; Cur Chr Ch St Michaels MD 1989-1992. Assoc of Ord Of S Helena 1989. Cotton Memi Awd SWTS 1989; Mem in Mensa Mensa 1980. schnat@aol.com

SCHNAUFER, Dennis Eric (USC) 6 Del Norte Blvd, Greenville SC 29615 B Palestine TX 3/15/1945 s Frank Cleaver Schnaufer & Edith Errette. BA SW U Georgetown TX 1967; VTS 1968; MDiv Epis TS of The SW 1970. D 8/26/1970 Bp J Milton Richardson P 6/28/1971 Bp Scott Field Bailey. m 6/23/1973 Thiela Louise Falkenstrom c 1. R S Ptr's Epis Ch Greenville SC 1985-2010; R Chr Epis Ch Dublin GA 1978-1985; Assoc Trin Epis Ch Columbus GA 1974-1978; Vic Gr Epis Ch Georgetown TX 1973-1974; Actg R S Jas' Ch Taylor TX 1973-1974; Vic Ch Of The Gd Shpd Tomball TX 1970-1973. deschnaufer@charter.net

SCHNEIDER, Charles William (WK) 13702 Stoney Hill Dr, San Antonio TX 67401 **P-in-c S Andr's Epis Ch Liberal KS 2008-; Cn Chr Cathd Salina KS 2002-; Trin Epis Ch Norton KS 1998-; Cdo Dio Wstrn Kansas Hutchinson KS 1997-** B Lewistown IL 7/21/1938 s charles W Schneider & Hannah. Cert Great Bend Cmnty Coll 1974. D 5/16/1997 P 4/17/1999 Bp Vernon Edward Strickland. m 2/4/2005 LyLith Ann Heiss c 4. P-in-c Epis Ch Of The Incarn Salina KS 2007-2008; S Fran Cmnty Serv Inc. Salina KS 1998-2008; D Chr Cathd Salina KS 1997-1998. holysmoke@satx.rr.com

SCHNEIDER, Edward Nichols (EMich) 1216 N Cranbrook Rd, Bloomfield Village MI 48301 B Detroit MI 9/28/1926 s Louis John Schneider & Geraldine. BA U CA 1949; MDiv VTS 1962. D 6/29/1962 Bp Archie H Crowley P 2/1/1963 Bp Robert Lionne DeWitt. c 3. S Jas Epis Ch Birmingham MI 1970-1989; Asst R Trin Ch Swarthmore PA 1967-1970; Vic S Edw The Confessor Epis Ch Clinton Township MI 1962-1963.

SCHNEIDER, Gregg Alan (NC) 703 Milwaukee Road, Beloit WI 53511 **D S Paul's Epis Ch Beloit WI 2008-** B Green Bay WI 7/5/1956 D 6/13/2004 Bp Michael Bruce Curry. m 2/25/1995 Susan Elizabeth Adams c 2. schneider.gregg@gmail.com

SCHNEIDER, Judith Irene (Colo) 2187 Canyon Ct W, Grand Junction CO 81503 **Boec Dio Colorado Denver CO 2005-; D S Matt's Ch Grand Jct CO 2003-** B Omaha NE 1/28/1942 d Lawrence Allan Williams & Irene Lorraine. Macomb Cmnty Coll; Whitaker TS; AA Colorado Wmn Coll 1962; BS New Mex St U. 1982. D 6/11/1994 Bp R(aymond) Stewart Wood Jr. m 5/29/1962 Donald Kenneth Schneider c 3. D Dio Colorado Denver CO 2002-2003; D Ch Of The Nativ Grand Jct CO 1998-2002; Chapl S Matt's And S Jos's Detroit MI 1996-1998; D St Paul's Epis Romeo MI 1994-1998. jschneider60@cs.com

SCHNEIDER, Marian Schneider (Roch) 13 E Water St, Friendship NY 14739 **Vol S Andr's Ch Friendship NY 2004-** B Norwich NY 8/15/1943 d John Wallace & Clarissa. Mildred Elley Secretarial Coll Albany NY 1962; Bex 2002. D 12/6/2001 P 10/26/2002 Bp Jack Marston McKelvey. m 11/21/1983 James F Schneider.

SCHNEIDER, Marilyn Butler (Colo) 7900 E Dartmouth Ave Apt 58, Denver CO 80231 **S Gabr The Archangel Epis Ch Cherry Hills Vill CO 2006-** B Pueblo CO 6/12/1933 d Howard Eugene Butler & Stella Mae. BA Colo. St. Coll of Educ 1955; MA Indiana U 1966; MA S Thos TS 1988; MDiv S Thos TS 1993. D 6/11/1994 P 12/18/1994 Bp William Jerry Winterrowd. c 3. S Mart In The Fields Aurora CO 2003-2005; Asstg Chr Epis Ch Denver CO 2003; Int Epiph Epis Ch Denver CO 2001-2002; Int S Thos Epis Ch Denver CO 1999-2001; Assoc R Chr Epis Ch Denver CO 1995-1999. revmarilyns@yahoo.com

SCHNEIDER, Marni Jacqueline (Los) 2972 Cadence Way, Virginia Beach VA 23456 **Vic S Simon's-By-The-Sea Virginia Bch VA 2007-** B Lakewood OH 8/15/1942 d Jack Morton Schneider & Grace Katherine. Pur; BA Loyola U 1982; MDiv CDSP 1986. D 6/21/1986 Bp Robert C Rusack P 12/28/1986 Bp Oliver Bailey Garver Jr. Assoc R S Thos Epis Ch Chesapeake VA 2002-2007; Int S Chris's Epis Ch Portsmouth VA 2002; Int S Jn's Ch Hampton VA 2001; Int S Geo's Epis Ch Laguna Hills CA 1998-2000; Int S Aug By-The-Sea Par Santa Monica CA 1994-1997; Assoc R S Edm's Par San Marino CA 1986-1993. revmarni@gmail.com

SCHNEIDER, M P (Vt) 164 Milton Road, Warwick RI 02888 **R S Mary's Epis Par Northfield VT 2010-** B Glocester RI 2/14/1952 d Richard Knight Rhodes & Lois. BS Rhode Island Coll 1974; MA Rhode Island Coll 1980; MDiv GTS 2007. D 3/28/1992 Bp George Nelson Hunt III P 9/25/2010 Bp Geralyn Wolf. c 2. D S Steph's Ch Providence RI 1999-2004. revempy@cox.net

SCHNEIDER, Stephen Vance (Ore) 2427 Ne 17th Ave, Portland OR 97212 **R Gr Memi Portland OR 1994-** B Pasadena CA 5/29/1942 s Vance Wallace Schneider & Madeline Rebecca. BA Wheaton Coll 1964; MDiv PrTS 1967; CAS GTS 1989. D 7/6/1989 P 1/1/1990 Bp Robert Louis Ladehoff. m 11/14/1970 Ann Lee Herzog c 2. Epis Par Of S Jn The Bapt Portland OR 1989-1994. rector@gvale-memorial.org

SCHNEIDER, William John (Mass) 276 Riverside Dr Apt 4e, New York NY 10025 B Cleveland OH 4/4/1933 s William John Schneider & Grace Elizabeth. BA Ya 1955; STM EDS 1958. D 5/30/1958 P 1/1/1959 Bp Nelson Marigold Burroughs. c 3. Epis Chapl At Harvard & Radcliffe Cambridge MA 1963-1978; Asst R E Lee Memi Ch (Epis) Lexington VA 1961-1963; Asst Gr Epis Ch Sandusky OH 1958-1960. Auth, "The Jon Daniels Story". wschnei106@gmail.com

SCHNITZER, William Lawton (NY) 26 N Manheim Blvd, New Paltz NY 12561 B Newport RI 5/25/1933 s Robert Fern Schnitzer & Alice Lawton. BA U of Rhode Island 1958; STB Ya Berk 1962; STM UTS 1971. D 6/23/1962 P 12/22/1962 Bp John S Higgins. m 6/14/1958 Carol Ann Lowensohn c 3. S Paul's Ch Pleasant Vlly NY 1996-1997; S Greg's Epis Ch Woodstock NY 1992-1993; Supply P Dio New York New York City NY 1985-2003; P-in-c S Paul's Ch Chester NY 1977-1985; Cur S Geo's Epis Ch Newburgh NY 1972-1977; Cur S Paul's Epis Ch Paterson NJ 1968-1969; Cur Ch Of The Gd Shpd Pawtucket RI 1962-1963. npschnitz@hvc.rr.com

SCHOECH, Howard A (Neb) 3311 Highway 66, Plattsmouth NE 68048 B 10/30/1933 D 6/6/1979 P 12/21/1979 Bp James Daniel Warner. m 12/26/1983 Janet K Evers c 4. St Augustines Of Cbury Epis Mssn Elkhorn NE 1994; The Epis Cluster Of SS & Fam Papillion NE 1989-1994; S Lk's Ch Plattsmouth NE 1979-1989; Ch Of The H Sprt Bellevue NE 1979-1982.

SCHOENBRUN, Zoila Collier (Cal) 327 San Rafael Ave, Belvedere CA 94920 B Choloma HN 6/1/1935 d Zadik Collier & Opal Winona. BA USC 1957; MA CDSP 1980; MDiv CDSP 1985. D 12/7/1985 P 12/6/1986 Bp William Edwin Swing. m 12/18/1955 Richard Lee Schoenbrun c 3. Asst S Steph's Par Belvedere CA 1996-2004.

✠ **SCHOFIELD JR, Rt Rev Calvin Onderdonk** (SeFla) 8195 Sw 151st St, Palmetto Bay Miami FL 33158 B Delhi NY 1/6/1933 s Calvin Onderdonk Schofield & Mabel Ellen. BA Hob 1959; MDiv Ya Berk 1962; DD Ya Berk 1979; STD Hob 1980; DD STUSo 1984. D 6/30/1962 Bp James Loughlin Duncan P 12/31/1962 Bp William Loftin Hargrave Con 3/23/1979 for SeFla. m 8/3/1963 Elaine Fullerton c 2. Bp Dio SE Florida Miami FL 1979-2000; Dn So Dade Dnry Dio SE Florida Miami FL 1972-1976; Dn So Dade Dnry Dio SE Florida Miami FL 1972-1976; R S Andr's Epis Ch Palmetto Bay FL

S

1964-1978; Yth Advsr Miami Dnry Dio SE Florida Miami FL 1964-1972; Cur Cathd Ch Of S Ptr St Petersburg FL 1962-1964. OHC. DD U So 1984; S.T.B. Hob 1980; D.D. Berk 1979. calvinschofield@bellsouth.net

SCHOFIELD, Kathlyn Elizabeth (CNY) St Paul's Episcopal Church, 204 Genesee St, Chittenango NY 13037 **S Paul's Ch Chittenango NY 2007-** B Syracuse, NY 9/17/1948 d Robert L Ripple & Kathlyn S. BS - Nrsng D'Youville Coll 1970; Dioc Formation Prog CNY 2006. D 10/7/2006 P 6/6/2007 Bp Gladstone Bailey Adams III. m 8/31/1970 James Paul Schofield c 3. krschof@twcny.rr.com

SCHOFIELD, Peter (Alb) 39 Imperial Dr., Niskayuna NY 12309 **Chair, Cmsn on Minstry Dio Albany Albany NY 2006-; P Assoc Chr Ch Schenectady NY 2004-** B Ilford Essex UK 4/9/1944 s Thomas A Schofield & Lilian. BS Rugby, UK 1967; MS Rugby, UK 1968. D 10/13/1980 Bp Wilbur Emory Hogg Jr P 7/24/2004 Bp Daniel William Herzog. m 5/16/1970 Sylvia T Sullivan c 1. P's Asst Chr Ch Schenectady NY 1980-2004. frpetercc@aol.com

SCHOFIELD-BROADBENT, Carrie Kathlyn (CNY) 941 Euclid Ave., Syracuse NY 13210 **R S Matt's Epis Ch Liverpool NY 2006-** B Syracuse NY 11/12/1974 d James Paul Schofield & Kathlyn Elizabeth. BA Juniata Coll 1997; MDiv VTS 2003. D 6/28/2003 P 1/3/2004 Bp Gladstone Bailey Adams III. m 6/20/1998 Keith John Broadbent c 2. S Paul's Cathd Syracuse NY 2004-2006; S Paul's Ch Owego NY 2003-2004. mothercarrie@verizon.net

SCHOLER, Linda C. (NJ) P O Box 1206, Chincoteague Island VA 23336 B Titusville PA 11/12/1946 d John Albin Carlson & Marion Gertrude. MA Georgian Crt Coll 1980; MSS Bryn Mawr Grad Sch Soc Wk 1982; Luth TS 1986; ThM New Brunswick TS 2001. D 6/2/2001 P 1/12/2002 Bp David B(ruce) Joslin. m 11/29/1986 Frederick R Scholer c 1. S Dav's Ch Cranbury NJ 2007-2008; Calv Epis Ch Flemington NJ 2001-2005. Cmnty St. Jn Bapt-Assoc 1971. Summa Cum Laud New Brunswick Teological Sem 2001. lindamercy1982@Verizon.net

SCHOMAKER, Kenneth Elmer (Ind) 2030 Chester Blvd IH 7B, Richmond IN 47374 B Pittsburgh PA 1/31/1935 s Elmer Winfield Schomaker & Elizabeth Coleman. BA Wesl 1957; BD VTS 1960. D 6/13/1960 P 7/6/1961 Bp Walter H Gray. m 10/17/1987 Dianne Hill c 5. R S Andr's Epis Ch Greencastle IN 1983-1986; Assoc S Jas Ch Collegeville PA 1979-1982; R Gd Shpd Ch Hilltown PA 1974-1978; R Chr Ch And S Mich's Philadelphia PA 1970-1974; R Ch Of The Atone Carnegie PA 1963-1970; Cur S Jn's Ch E Hartford CT 1960-1963. dianneandken@comcast.net

SCHOOLER, William Thomas (Cal) 352 Bay Rd, Atherton CA 94027 B Georgetown SC 1/16/1935 s Benjamin Harrison Schooler & Marion Louise. BA U of So Carolina 1957; MS U of San Francisco 1980; BTS Sch for Deacons 1988. D 12/3/1988 Bp William Edwin Swing. m 3/29/1963 Ruth E Gracy c 1. D/Asst Trin Par Menlo Pk CA 1993-2006; Asst S Bede's Epis Ch Menlo Pk CA 1990-1993; Asst Chr Ch Portola Vlly CA 1988-1990. Assembly opf Epis Healthcare Chapl 2000-2009; Mltry Chapl of the US 2000-2009; Natl Assn of Veterans Affrs Chapl 2000-2009. ruthbill@pacbell.net

SCHOONMAKER, Daniel Holt (O) 18426 Winslow Rd, Shaker Heights OH 44122 **R S Hubert's Epis Ch Mentor OH 2000-** B Middletown NY 2/19/1959 s Robert Louis Schoonmaker & Dorothy. Thunderbird-Mgmt Glendale; BA Eisenhower Coll-Rochester Inst of Tech 1981; MA GW 1983; MBA Amer Grad Sch of Intl Mgmt Glendal 1988; MDiv VTS 1996. D Bp Ronald Hayward Haines P 12/14/1996 Bp Robert Reed Shahan. c 2. Int S Paul's Epis Ch Of E Cleveland Cleveland OH 1999-2000; Cur S Anth On The Desert Scottsdale AZ 1996-1998. Auth, "Evang (Chapt)," *Bldg Up The Ch*, Forw Mvmt Press, 1997. dignusus@aol.com

SCHOONMAKER, Lisa Katherine (CPa) 21 S Main St, Lewistown PA 17044 **All SS Epis Ch Riverside CA 2007-** B Schenectady NY 3/28/1952 d Harold Schoonmaker & Lucille. BMus S Olaf Coll 1975; JD Franklin Pierce Law Cntr 1987; MDiv Ya Berk 2004. D 2/12/2005 P 8/27/2005 Bp Keith Bernard Whitmore. P-in-c S Mk's Epis Ch Lewistown PA 2007-2010. revlks@gmail.com

SCHRAMM, George Thomas (WVa) Po Box 308, Shepherdstown WV 25443 **R Trin Ch Shepherdstown WV 1983-** B Wheeling WV 7/8/1952 s George Palmer Schramm & Jo Ann. BS Wheeling Jesuit U 1974; MDiv VTS 1977; DMin VTS 1997. D 6/8/1977 P 5/10/1978 Bp Robert Poland Atkinson. m 7/20/1979 Susan Cochran Bailey c 2. Archd Dio W Virginia Charleston WV 1990-1999; Dioc Coun Dio W Virginia Charleston WV 1980-1983; Dioc Coun Dio W Virginia Charleston WV 1980-1983; Com Ecum Rela Dio W Virginia Charleston WV 1978-1981; Asst Trin Ch Parkersburg WV 1977-1983. Vol of the Year Hospice of the Panhandle 1998; Outstanding Young Men in Amer 1985. trinityshep@citlink.net

SCHRAMM, John Eldon (NI) PO Box 421, Plymouth IN 46563 **R S Thos Epis Ch Plymouth IN 1982-** B Winona MN 6/18/1947 s Eldon LaVerne Schramm & Mary Winnifred. BA NW Nazarene Coll 1969; MDiv Nazarene TS 1972; ThM Harvard DS 1981. D 11/26/1978 P 6/5/1979 Bp James Winchester Montgomery. m 7/3/1971 Barbara Jean Stollngwa c 2. Liturg Com Dio Nthrn Indiana So Bend IN 1995-1996; Dio Nthrn Indiana So Bend IN 1985-1991; Cur Ch Of The Ascen Chicago IL 1978-1982. Hon Cn Diocesis de Honduras 2000. john@clerke.info

SCHRAPLAU, Frederick William (NY) 182 Nixon Avenue, Staten Island NY 10304 **P-in-c S Alb's Epis Ch Staten Island NY 2000-; R S Alb's Epis Ch Staten Island NY 2000-** B Macon GA 9/9/1943 s William Schraplau & Mabel Kathleen. GTS; BS High Point U 1965; New York Cathd Inst 1978. D 2/18/1978 Bp Harold Louis Wright P 10/25/1978 Bp Paul Moore Jr. Assoc S Mary's Castleton Staten Island NY 1990-2000; Assoc S Andr's Epis Ch Staten Island NY 1983-1990; S Paul's Ch Staten Island NY 1981-1983; Cur S Paul's Ch Staten Island NY 1978-1979. Soc of the Our Lady of Walsingham 1980. fvonschsi@aol.com

SCHREIBER, Mary Fiander (WMass) 6 Wall St, Shelburne Falls MA 01370 B Sudbury CA 8/15/1941 d Edgar Lincoln Fiander & Grace Merwin. RN Greenwich Hosp Sch of Nrsng 1962; BS New Sch for Soc Resrch 1988; MDiv Bex 1992. D 5/30/1992 P 9/18/1993 Bp David B(ruce) Joslin. c 5. Gr Ch Dalton MA 2000; S Lk's Ch Lanesboro MA 2000; R S Paul's Epis Ch Gardner MA 1998-1999; Cathd Of All SS Albany NY 1997-1998; Vic All SS Epis Ch Skowhegan ME 1994-1997; Vic Chr Ch Manlius NY 1993-1994. revmschreiber@yahoo.com

SCHREIBER, Michael Nelson (Cal) 162 Hickory St, San Francisco CA 94102 B St Louis MO 5/24/1939 s Dalton William Schreiber & Elizabeth. BFA Washington U 1964; AOS California Culinary Acad 1992; Bachelor of Deaconal Stds The Sch for Deacons 2008. D 6/6/2009 Bp Marc Handley Andrus. m 10/21/1978 Shelley A Wilson c 3. m_schreiber@sbcglobal.net

SCHREINER, Shawn Maureen (Chi) 5 North 047 Route 83, Bensenville IL 60106 **P-in-c Gr Ch Oak Pk IL 2004-** B Greensburg IN 5/25/1961 d John Anthony Schreiner & Jean Ann. BA Hanover Coll 1983; MDiv SWTS 1991. D 6/24/1991 P 3/20/1992 Bp Edward Witker Jones. Cn Cathd Of S Jas Chicago IL 2002-2004; R S Bede's Epis Ch Bensenville IL 1993-2002; Asst Gr Ch Muncie IN 1991-1993. shawnschreiner@sbcglobal.net

SCHRIDER, Jim (Los) 620 D Street, SE, Washington DC 20003 B Washington DC 10/6/1933 s James Edward Schrider & Helen Alice. BA Ford 1957; MA Ford 1958; PHL Ford 1959; ThB Wood 1964; ThL Wood 1965; MA U Chi 1968. Rec from Roman Catholic 5/1/1987 as Priest Bp Oliver Bailey Garver Jr. m 8/30/1971 Fredericka Cartwright c 3. Assoc R S Jas Par Los Angeles CA 1989-1991; Asst S Aug By-The-Sea Par Santa Monica CA 1987-1989. Alb Inst. jschrider@igc.org

SCHRIMSHER, Alyce Marie (Dal) 6132 Yellow Rock Trl, Dallas TX 75248 **D S Barn Ch Garland TX 2005-** B Hillsboro TX 7/4/1950 d John Franklin Schrimsher & Betty Gene. BA U of Texas-Arlington 1972; Lic in Mnstry Angl TS 2000. D 12/19/2001 Bp D(avid) Bruce Mac Pherson. D Ch Of The Epiph Richardson TX 2001-2005. OSL the Physcn 2006; Ord of the DOK 2004.

SCHRODER, Edward Amos (Fla) 15 Hickory Lane, Amelia Island FL 32034 B Hokitika NZ 6/11/1941 s Carl Francis Wakefield Schroder & Phyllis Maven. BA U of Cbury Christchurch NZ 1963; DTh U of Durham GB 1966. Trans from Church Of England 12/20/1973 Bp John Melville Burgess. m 3/28/1970 Antoinette B Bowie c 2. Amelia Plantation Chap Amelia Island FL 2000-2004; R Chr Epis Ch San Antonio TX 1986-2000; R Gr Epis Ch Orange Pk FL 1979-1986; Asst to Bp Dio Florida Jacksonville FL 1976-1979; Chr Ch So Hamilton MA 1974-1976. Auth, "Real Hope," Amelia Island Pub, 2011; Auth, "Solid Love," Amelia Island Pub, 2008; Auth, "Surviving Hurricanes," Amelia Island Pub, 2006; Auth, "Buried Treasure," Amelia Island Pub, 2005; Auth, "Inward Light," Amelia Island Pub, 2003; Auth, "I Will Fear No Evil," 2000; Auth, "Communicating the Gospel w Generation X," 2000; Auth, "The Armor of God," 1999; Auth, "A Vision for the Ch," 1992. tschroder@ameliachapel.com

SCHROEDER, Beverly Clarisse (WTenn) 2425 S. Germantown Rd., Germantown TN 38138 **Cur S Geo's Ch Germantown TN 2009-** B New York NY 10/6/1954 d John Gustav Schroeder & María Isabel. BMus Manhattan Sch of Mus 1980; MMus Manhattan Sch of Mus 1981; JD The Washington Coll of Law (of the Amer U) 1996; MDiv VTS 2009. D 6/7/2009 P 5/1/2010 Bp Don Edward Johnson. Asst Chapl S Mary's Epis Sch Memphis TN 2000-2006. OSL 2000; Ord of the DOK 2002. beatitudeiv@hotmail.com

SCHROEDER, Cecelia Carlile (Va) 14 Cornwall St NW, Leesburg VA 20176 **S Gabr's Epis Ch Leesburg VA 2010-** B Norfolk VA 2/20/1978 d John Harrison Goodman & Amanda Grantham. MDiv VTS 2004. D 6/19/2004 Bp Gethin Benwil Hughes P 12/19/2004 Bp Robert Wilkes Ihloff. m 7/21/2003 John Christopher Schroeder c 2. Asst S Lk's Ch Salisbury NC 2006-2010; Asst R Middleham & S Ptr's Par Lusby MD 2004-2006. cc-schroeder@hotmail.com

SCHROEDER, Donald John (Spr) 49 Ward Cir, Brunswick ME 04011 B Union City NJ 2/1/1927 s Carleton John Schroeder & Ethel Delphine. BS Rutgers-The St U 1951; MBA NYU 1955; MDiv PDS 1966. D 6/11/1966 Bp Leland Stark P 12/1/1966 Bp George E Rath. Dio Springfield Springfield IL 1982-1989; Trin Epis Ch Mattoon IL 1982-1989; S Lk's Ch Hope NJ 1981-1982; Secy For The Inter-Faith Com On Aging Dio Newark Newark NJ 1980-1981; Newark Epis Coop For Min & Miss Newark NJ 1980; Dept Of CSR Dio Newark Newark NJ 1978-1979; Dioc Coun Dio Newark Newark NJ

S

1975-1976; Dept Of Mssn Dio Newark Newark NJ 1973-1975; Evang Com Dio Newark Newark NJ 1973-1974; Mar Thoma Ch New Jersey Randolph NJ 1969-1980; P-in-c Calv Epis Ch Summit NJ 1966-1969.

SCHROETER, George H (CGC) 500 Spanish Fort Blvd Apt 29, Spanish Fort AL 36527 B Mobile AL 10/1/1932 s Herbert Frederick Schroeter & Julia Anita. BA U So 1953; MDiv VTS 1956; MA U of Sthrn Mississippi 1970. D 7/6/1956 Bp Charles C J Carpenter P 5/1/1957 Bp George Mosley Murray. Supply P S Matt's Ch Mobile AL 1980-1995; Vic S Ptr's Ch Jackson AL 1976-1979; Supply P Trin Epis Ch Mobile AL 1965-1975; Cur H Comf Ch Gadsden AL 1964-1965; Vic S Mths Epis Ch Tuscaloosa AL 1962-1964; Exam Chapl Dio Alabama Birmingham AL 1961-1964; Vic S Mich's Ch Ozark AL 1957-1962; M-in-c Ch Of The Epiph Enterprise AL 1956-1957; Cur The Epis Ch Of The Nativ Dothan AL 1956-1957. Auth, "The Ballad Of Les Mccater," Seabury Press, 1965; Auth, "Perfect Freedom," Seabury Press, 1965. gschroeter@wvsf.org

SCHUBERT, Kevin Lane Johnson (Tex) 3307 Garden Villa Ln, Austin TX 78704 **S Geo's Ch Austin TX 2010-** B Brenham TX 7/26/1976 s Charles Schubert & Pam. BA Texas St U San Marcos, TX 2000; MDiv Epis TS of The SW 2007. D 6/23/2007 Bp Don Adger Wimberly P 1/22/2008 Bp Dena Arnall Harrison. m 5/1/2004 Heather Schubert. Cur S Matt's Ch Austin TX 2007-2010. co-Auth, "Beyond Contemporary," *Episcorific Issue 2, Fall 2008*, Episcorific, 2008; co-Auth, "2000 Belize Vlly Archeol Field Report, Cayo Dist Belize," *TSU in SM, Anthropology Dept.*, Texas St U, 2001; co-Auth, "Site 41HY37 Excavation of Gnrl Edw Burlesons Cabin San Marcos, TX," *TSU in SM, Cntr for Archeol Stds*, Texas St U, 2001; co-Auth, "1999 Belize Vlly Archeol Field Report, Cayo Dist Belize TSU in SM, Anthropology Dept.," *TSU in SM, Anthropology Dept.*, Texas St U, 2000; co-Auth, illustrator, "1997 The Lower Paleolithic in Oman, Dhofar Reg, Oman Arabian Peninsula," *TSU in SM, Anthropology Dept.*, Texas St U, 1998. schubertkevin@hotmail.com

SCHUBERT, Rebecca Malcolm (WMo) 3700 West 83 Terrace, Prairie Village KS 66206 **D All SS Epis Ch Kansas City MO 2006-** B Bartlesville OK 1/21/1943 d Eugene Glynn Malcolm & Ferne Bingham-Malcom. BA U of Missouri 1994; MA U of Missouri 2003; Cert U of Missouri 2003. D 2/4/1995 Bp John Clark Buchanan. m 9/8/1973 Robert Edward Schubert c 4. Dio W Missouri Kansas City MO 1998-1999; Asst to Bp Dio W Missouri Kansas City MO 1997-1998. "Best Times," *Bi-Monthly Article*. Assn of Profsnl Chapl 1996; Bd Cert Coll Chapl 1996. beckschubert@kc.rr.com

SCHUEDDIG JR, Louis Charles (At) 345 9th St Ne, Atlanta GA 30309 **Epis Media Cntr Atlanta GA 1998-; Pres/Exec Dir Epis Media Cntr Inc Atlanta GA 1983-** B Saint Louis MO 4/23/1948 s Louis Charles Schueddig & Beth Adelle. BS NWU 1970; MDiv VTS 1973. D 6/9/1973 Bp George Leslie Cadigan P 12/8/1973 Bp James Winchester Montgomery. R S Mich's Ch Grand Rapids MI 1976-1983; Assoc S Aug's Epis Ch Wilmette IL 1973-1976. Auth, "On Being A Godparent," *Epis Life*, 2002; Auth, "No Longer Mainstream," *LivCh*, 2000. Hon Cn S Phil's Cathd Atlanta GA 1992. lschueddig@day1.org

SCHUETZ, Mary Joanne Rawlings (EMich) 3536 West River Road, Sanford MI 48657 B Flint MI 5/25/1945 d John Hamilton Rawlings & Virginia Emilie. MI SU 1964; Saginaw Vlly St U 1985; TS Whitaker TS 1992; Cert SWTS 1996. D 6/13/1992 Bp R(aymond) Stewart Wood Jr P 12/7/1996 Bp Edwin Max Leidel Jr. m 12/29/1978 James Schuetz c 1. R S Paul's Epis Ch Gladwin MI 2000-2010; Asst S Jn's Epis Ch Saginaw MI 1997-2000; Epis Tri Par Cluster Gladwin MI 1996-1997. mjschuetz@charter.net

SCHUILING, Alice Catherine (NMich) 1100 Sunview Dr Apt 201, Saint Johns MI 48879 B Grand Rapids MI 7/13/1927 D 10/12/2003 Bp James Arthur Kelsey. m 6/5/1948 Melvin James Schuiling c 3.

SCHULENBERG, George W (ND) 135 Skogmo Blvd, Fergus Falls MN 56537 B Red Wing MN 5/28/1938 s Willard G Schulenberg & Alta Adolphina. Macalester Coll 1958; BA Int'l Chr Univ. Mitaka-shi, Hodogaya-Ku, Japan 1962; BD EDS 1969; MDiv EDS 1972. D 6/30/1969 Bp Hamilton Hyde Kellogg P 3/8/1970 Bp Philip Frederick McNairy. m 7/22/1962 Etsuko O Ouchi c 2. Asst to the Bp Dio No Dakota Fargo ND 1990-1992; R Gr Epis Ch Jamestown ND 1988-2001; Minnesota Ldrshp Prog Dio Minnesota Minneapolis MN 1983 1988; R S Jas' Epis Ch Fergus Falls MN 1975-1983; Vic Trin Ch Wahpeton ND 1975-1983; Supervising P Breck Memi Mssn Naytahwaush MN 1970-1975; Supervising P S Columba White Earth MN 1970-1975; Vic S Phil Naytahwaush MN 1970-1975; Vic Samuel Memi Naytahwaush MN 1970-1975. Rural Worker's Fllshp 1983-1988. gschulen@prtel.com

SCHULENBERG, Michael A (Minn) 715 N High St, Lake City MN 55041 B Red Wing MN 2/14/1941 s Willard George Schulenberg & Alta Alberta. BA Trin Hartford CT 1963; BD EDS 1969. D 6/30/1969 Bp Philip Frederick McNairy P 1/9/1970 Bp Richard S M Emrich. m 9/2/1966 Karen Turk. R H Cross Ch Pensacola FL 1992-2002; R Chr Ch Red Wing MN 1989-1992; R S Mk's Epis Ch Aberdeen SD 1980-1989; S Paul's Epis Ch Flint MI 1969-1980. kschulenberg@hotmail.com

SCHULER, Rock Hal (WA) 415 Brighton Dam Rd, 415 Brighton Dam Rd, Brookeville MD 20833 B Casper WY 3/17/1965 s Harold D Schuler & De R. BS U of Wyoming 1987; MDiv SWTS 1990; DMin SWTS 2002. D 6/25/1990 P 5/30/1991 Bp Bob Gordon Jones. m 11/22/2004 Jennifer L Schuler c 2. R S Jn's Ch Olney MD 2006-2008; Chr Ch Norcross GA 2004-2006; Dioc Fin & Prop Com Dio Wyoming Casper WY 1998-2000; Dioc Coun Dio Pennsylvania Philadelphia PA 1997-2000; R H Trin Ch Lansdale PA 1994-2004; Asst S Mk's Epis Ch Casper WY 1991-1994; Stndg Com Dio Wyoming Casper WY 1991-1992; Vic S Andr's Ch Meeteetse WY 1990-1991. Auth, "A Living Ch Serving A Living Lord: Mssn And Mnstry In The 21st Century," *Gathering The Next Generation*, Morehouse Pub, 2000; Auth, "The Supplemental Liturg Texts: A Theol Inquiry," *ATR*, 1991. Sylvia Cohen Awd For Cmnty Serv JCRC 1997. rockschuler@comcast.net

SCHULLER, Christopher David (SwFla) 100 Bay Point Dr. NE, St. Petersburg FL 33704 B St Louis MO 3/12/1959 BA U MI 1983; MDiv EDS 2003. D 6/21/2003 Bp Leopold Frade P 1/16/2004 Bp Henry Irving Louttit. m 9/15/1989 Bettina D Schuller c 2. R S Thos' Epis Ch St Petersburg FL 2007-2011; R S Paul's Epis Ch Jesup GA 2003-2007. awoundedhealer@yahoo.com

SCHULTZ, Alison Morna (At) 5560 Chemin de Vie, Atlanta GA 30342 **Mem Cmsn of Educ Dio Atlanta Atlanta GA 2010-; Assoc H Innoc Ch Atlanta GA 2006-** B Akron OH 3/7/1958 d Robert Gardner Schultz & Carol Ann Wierath. BS U Of Akron 1981; MS U of W Florida 1983; MDiv GTS 2006. D 12/21/2005 P 6/25/2006 Bp J(ohn) Neil Alexander. m 12/31/1981 Todd A Broadbridge c 2. alto58@gmail.com

SCHULTZ, Gregory Allen (FdL) West 7145 County Road U, Plymouth WI 53073 **D S Ptr's Epis Ch Sheboygan Falls WI 1999-** B Sheboygan WI 5/6/1949 s Eugene Francis Schultz & Cora May. DeVry Inst of Techology 1969; Lakeshore Tech 1970. D 8/28/1996 Bp Russell Edward Jacobus. m 10/23/1971 Barbara Ann Susen. D S Paul's Ch Plymouth WI 1996-1999. NAAD. deacon.greg@excel.net

SCHULTZ OHC, Thomas Haines (Cal) St. Mary's Retreat House, 505 E. Los Olivos St., Santa Barbara CA 93105 **Prior Incarn Priory Dio Pittsburgh Monroeville PA 1995-** B Pittsburgh PA 10/7/1933 s William Robert Schultz & Marian Alice. BA U Pgh 1956; MDiv Nash 1959; Med Cit 1986. D 6/13/1959 Bp William S Thomas P 12/19/1959 Bp Austin Pardue. Incarn Priory Berkeley Dio California San Francisco CA 1990-2008; Non-par Dio Pittsburgh Monroeville PA 1959-1998; Non-par Dio Pittsburgh Monroeville PA 1959-1998. Auth, *Rosary for Episcopalians*, Incarn Priory Pr, 1992. Amer Counslg Assn 1986; So Carolina Counslg Assn 1986. DD CDSP 2006; MENSA 1984. ohcmonks@ohcmonks.org

SCHULZ, David Allen (Del) 224 N Bayshore Dr, Frederica DE 19946 B Saint Louis MO 4/17/1933 s John H Schulz & Bertha Stella. BA Pr 1954; MDiv VTS 1960; PhD Washington U 1968. D 6/28/1960 Bp Frederick D Goodwin P 3/1/1961 Bp George Leslie Cadigan. m Lieba Kaplan c 1. Aux P Cathd Ch Of S Jn Wilmington DE 1971-1980; Supply P Dio Cntrl Pennsylvania Harrisburg PA 1967-1970; Cur Gr Ch Kirkwood MO 1960-1962. Auth, "The Changing Fam: Its Function & Future"; Auth, "Mar," *The Fam & Personal Fulfillment*. david224@comcast.net

SCHULZE, Thomas R (Mass) 110 Carville Ct, Stevensville MD 21666 B PA 10/4/1944 s James Wallace Schulze & Margaret. BA U of Charleston 1968; MDiv Ya Berk 1971; STM Yale DS 1976. D 1/23/1972 Bp John S Higgins P 1/1/1973 Bp Joseph Warren Hutchens. m 8/22/1970 H Kay Gladwell. R Trin Epis Ch Stoughton MA 1976-1989; Assoc P S Jn's Ch No Haven CT 1975-1976. Auth, *hon Thesis Annointing of the Sick:*; Auth, *Some Tradition & Symbolisms of Chr Healing*. trschulze@aya.yale.edu

SCHUNEMAN, Steven Lawrence (Chi) 9300 S Pleasant Ave, Chicago IL 60643 **Ch Of The H Nativ Chicago IL 2010-** B Sterling IL 2/29/1956 s Robert Schunneman & Sarah. BA Nthrn Illinois U 1978; MDiv Nash 1982. D 6/19/1982 P 12/18/1982 Bp James Winchester Montgomery. m 9/17/1983 Annette W SW. P-in-c S Tim's Ch Griffith IN 2000-2010; R S Paul's Epis Ch Munster IN 1997-2000; R Trin Ch Niles MI 1987-1997; Asst Trin Ch Wauwatosa WI 1984-1987; Vic S Chad Epis Ch Loves Pk IL 1982-1984. Auth, "Epis Radio/Tv Video Welcoming The Newcomer". Dir Epis Radio/Tv Video "8th Commandment"; Dir Epis Radio/Tv Video "Earthen Vessels"; Dir Epis Radio/Tv Video "Welcoming The Newcomer". schuney@sbcglobal.net

SCHUNIOR, Rebecca Justice (At) 118 N Washington St, Alexandria VA 22314 **S Mk's Ch Washington DC 2011-** B Chapel Hill NC 5/28/1976 d Charles Edward Schunior & Claudia Anne. BA St Jn's Coll 1999; MDiv Candler TS 2009. D 12/20/2008 P 6/28/2008 Bp J(ohn) Neil Alexander. Cler Res Chr Ch Alexandria VA 2009-2011. justi.schunior@stmarks.net

SCHUSTER III, Franklin Phillip (RG) 28231 Pine Lake St, Edwardsburg MI 49112 **S Jas Epis Ch Taos NM 2007-** B Galveston TX 10/24/1954 s Franklin Phillip Schuster & Bettie. U of Texas; BBA TCU 1977; MDiv SWTS 1984. D 6/26/1984 P 3/5/1985 Bp Richard Mitchell Trelease Jr. m 11/25/1995 T J Patton. R Trin Ch Niles MI 1999-2007; R S Andr's Ch Derby KS 1992-1999; Sub-Dn Pro Cathd Epis Ch Of S Clem El Paso TX 1986-1992; S Jn's Cathd Albuquerque NM 1985-1986; Dio The Rio Grande Albuquerque NM 1984. Ord Of S Lk. rock@wintershope.com

SCHUSTER, Lawrence Arthur (WNY) 10348 2nd St, Dunkirk NY 14048 **P in charge Ch Of S Jn The Bapt Dunkirk NY 1998-** B Chicago IL 5/9/1927 s Lawrence Philip Schuster & Helen Agnes. BS U IL 1950; MDiv Ya Berk 1960. D 5/28/1960 Bp Frederick Lehrle Barry P 12/24/1960 Bp Allen Webster Brown. m 4/28/1951 Mary Patricia Reynolds c 6. R Trin Epis Ch Fredonia NY 1963-1995; Cur Ch Of Beth Saratoga Sprg NY 1960-1963. rev.schuster@yahoo.com

SCHUSTER, Richard L (Ct) 73 Harbor Dr # 414, Stamford CT 06902 **Died 8/29/2009** B Waterbury CT 4/5/1945 s Robert Bryan Schuster & Mabel Margaret. BA Nasson Coll 1968; MDiv Ya Berk 1971. D 6/12/1971 P 1/22/1972 Bp Joseph Warren Hutchens. c 3. Hometown Hero Bank of Amer 2008; Bp Awd for Cmnty Serv 1992. rschuster@stlukeslifeworks.org

SCHUSTER WELTNER, Alicia (At) 2744 Peachtree Rd NW, Atlanta GA 30305 **Dio Atlanta Atlanta GA 2004-** B Rahway NJ 1/8/1962 d Allan Denis Schuster & Gail Dorothy. BA Mt Holyoke Coll 1984; MDiv STUSo 1995. D 6/10/1995 Bp Frank Kellogg Allan P 12/16/1995 Bp Onell Asiselo Soto. m 8/19/1995 Philip Weltner c 1. Assoc R S Mart In The Fields Ch Atlanta GA 2001-2004; Assoc R & P-in-c H Trin Par Decatur GA 1999-2000; Asst R S Mich And All Ang Ch Stone Mtn GA 1995-1998. "Sermons That Wk Collection," *2003/Morehouse Barlowe*, 2003, 2003. alicia@iweltner.org

SCHUTZ, Christine Elizabeth (O) 843 Tarra Oaks Dr, Findlay OH 45840 **Trin Ch Findlay OH 2005-** B Omaha NE 8/24/1946 d William Robert Mueller & Elizabeth. BA U of Iowa 1968; MDiv STUSo 2000. D 6/11/2000 Bp Carl Christopher Epting P 7/26/2001 Bp J Clark Grew II. c 3. S Paul's Ch Maumee OH 2001-2005; Ch Of The H Comf Monteagle TN 2000-2001. chrisschutz@att.net

SCHUYLER, Janice MacFarland (Me) 6 Village Way, Rutland MA 01543 B Norwich CT 4/14/1942 d Arnold Hillman MacFarland & Lea Marie. Albertus Magnus Coll 1962; BA Ohio Dominican Coll 1967; MA U of Notre Dame 1977; MA Cath Theol Un 1982; Bangor TS 1992. D 12/18/1992 P 8/24/1993 Bp Edward Cole Chalfant. m 4/25/1986 William Kearns Schuyler. Dio Maine Portland ME 2000-2007; Vic S Steph The Mtyr Epis Ch E Waterboro ME 1994-2007; Assoc P S Dav's Epis Ch Kennebunk ME 1993-1995. norwichnewhaven@yahoo.com

SCHUYLER, Philip William (Az) 7535 Navigator Cir, Carlsbad CA 92011 B Los Angeles CA 11/11/1930 s Philip Clarence Schuyler & Helen Elizabeth. BA Stan 1952; BD CDSP 1955. D 6/1/1955 P 2/21/1956 Bp Francis E I Bloy. m 2/24/1957 Mary Ann Barton c 2. Pstr Asst S Lk's Ch San Diego CA 2000-2002; Sun Asst S Michaels By-The-Sea Ch Carlsbad CA 1998-1999; Asst to R S Lk's Ch San Diego CA 1996-1997; Pstr Asst S Lk's Ch San Diego CA 1995-1996; Asst to R Trin Ch Escondido CA 1993-1994; Asst to R The Epis Ch Of The Blessed Sacr Placentia CA 1992-1993; Vic Gr Epis Ch Lake Havasu City AZ 1988-1989; Fndr Dio Los Angeles Los Angeles CA 1983-1988; Pres Sw Dnry Dio Los Angeles Los Angeles CA 1977-1978; R Chr Ch Par Redondo Bch CA 1971-1988; Chapl Indonesian Refugees Dio Los Angeles Los Angeles CA 1963-1971; Vic S Mary's Par Lompoc CA 1957-1963; Cur Ch Of The Mssh Santa Ana CA 1955-1957. Forw In Faith; PB Soc. Bd Supervisot'S Citation Los Angeles Cnty 1988; Mayor'S Citation For Serv To Srs & Refugees Los Angeles Mayor Tom Bradley 1988; Mayor Barbara Doerr Redondo Bch 1988; Man Of Year Awd Redondo Bch 1978; California Lesgislature Awd California Legislature Gerald Felando. schuylerphilip@yahoo.com

SCHUYLER, William Kearns (Me) 19 Ridgeway Ave, Sanford ME 04073 B Richmond KY 1/2/1945 s Walter B Schuyler & Alene M. BA DePauw U 1967; STB GTS 1970. D 6/10/1970 P 12/28/1970 Bp John P Craine. m 4/25/1986 Janice MacFarland Schuyler. Dio Maine Portland ME 2000-2007; R S Geo's Epis Ch Sanford ME 1993-2007; R Ch Of The Gd Shpd Houlton ME 1990-1993; Assoc S Jn's Ch Worthington OH 1988-1990. norwichnewhaven@yahoo.com

SCHWAB, A(nthony) Wayne (Nwk) PO Box 294, Hinesburg VT 05461 **P Assoc, Vol Trin Ch Plattsburgh NY 2007-** B Washington DC 10/20/1928 s James Edward Schwab & Mary Elizabeth. BA Leh 1950; MDiv VTS 1953. D 4/10/1954 P 6/18/1955 Bp Angus Dun. m 10/22/2010 Renate B Parke c 4. P-in-c S Jn's Ch Essex NY 2000-2002; Epis Ch Cntr New York NY 1975-1993; Chr. Ldrshp Trng Comm.,Dept. of Chr. Ed. Epis Ch Cntr New York NY 1972-1975; CE Chair Dio Newark Newark NJ 1964-1975; R S Paul's Ch Montvale NJ 1956-1975; Asst S Paul's Par Washington DC 1954-1956. Auth, "Living the Gospel," Mem Mssn Press, 2010; Auth, "When the Members are the Missionaries," Mem Mssn Press, 2002; Auth, "Notebook," *E-Share 1-7, 1991-93*, Epis Ch Cntr, 1991; Auth, "Proclamation as Offering Story & Choice," Epis Ch Cntr, 1988; Auth, "Guidebook One for Evang, Renwl," *and Ch Growth: Getting Started and the First Three Years*, Epis Ch Cntr, 1980; Auth, "Handbook for Evang," Epis Ch Cntr, 1979; Auth, "Nwsltr," *Evang News 1975-1989*, Ep. Ch. Cntr, New York, NY; Ed, "Nwsltr," *Mem Mssn Nwsltr, 2003-2011*, Mem Mssn Ntwk, Inc. AAPC 1970-1980. aschwab525@aol.com

SCHWAB, Susan Mary Brophy (Mass) 96 Mechanic St Apt C, Foxboro MA 02035 **S Jn The Evang Taunton MA 2007-; co-Mssnr S Mk's Ch Taunton MA 2006-** B Urbana IL 4/22/1946 d William Reuben Brophy & Mary Edna. BA Ohio U 1967; MDiv EDS 1987. D 6/2/1990 Bp David Elliot Johnson P 6/7/1991 Bp David Bell Birney IV. Assoc Trin Epis Ch Rockland MA 1999-2001; Supply Dio Massachusetts Boston MA 1992-1999; Assoc S Eliz's Ch Sudbury MA 1992-1998; Asst S Paul's Ch Natick MA 1990-1992. REVSCHWAB@YAHOO.COM

SCHWAHN, Vincent Carl (Los) 117 Avenida San Jeronimo, San Angel, Mexico City 01000 Mexico **S Mk's Par Van Nuys CA 2011-** B Bismark ND 1/21/1959 s Leopold Schwahn & Geraldine. BTh U of St. Thos 1981; MDiv U of St. Thos 1987; GTS 1991. D 6/24/1991 P 12/28/1991 Bp Robert Marshall Anderson. S Clem's-By-The-Sea Par San Clemente CA 2010-2011; Chr Ch 2004-2010; Dio Mex 1997-2005; Vic Ch Of The Mssh Prairie Island Welch MN 1994-1996; Asst S Paul's On-The-Hill Epis Ch St Paul MN 1993-1996; Dio Minnesota Minneapolis MN 1991-1997. vincentcarlschwahn@gmail.com

SCHWARTZ, William Edward (Mil) PO Box 3210, Doha QATAR Qatar **Appointed Mssy Epis Ch Cntr New York NY 1993-; P Exec Coun Appointees New York NY 1993-** B Omaha NE 4/7/1952 s John Thomas Schwartz & Patricia Anne. BA Tarkio Coll 1975; Ord Salisbury & Wells Theol Coll Sem Gb 1993. Trans from The Episcopal Church in Jerusalem and the Middle East 8/12/1993 as Priest Bp Terence Kelshaw. m 8/21/1976 Edith Louise Schlei c 4. Dio The Rio Grande Albuquerque NM 1993. Off of the British Empire (Hon) Eliz II 2006; Off of the British Empire HH Queen Eliz II 2006; Cn, St Chris's Cathd Bahrain Rt Revd G Clive Handford 2006. epiphany@qatar.net.qa

SCHWARZ, Robert Carl (SD) 500 S Main Ave, Sioux Falls SD 57104 B Darby PA 1/3/1952 s Carl Robert Schwarz & Virginia Ann. Amer U; Penn; Tem; MDiv STUSo 1986. D 5/16/1986 P 11/1/1986 Bp William Cockburn Russell Sheridan. m 6/17/1972 Jeanne L Andrews c 4. Ch Of The Ascen Mt Vernon NY 2006-2007; The Ch of S Ign of Antioch New York NY 2006-2007; Int S Fran Assisi And S Martha White Plains NY 2004-2006; Dio So Dakota Sioux Falls SD 2002-2004; Int All Souls Ch New York NY 2001-2003; Diocn Msnry & Ch Extntn Socty New York NY 2000; Geo Mercer TS Garden City NY 2000; Diocn Msnry & Ch Extntn Socty New York NY 1999; Ch Of The Mssh Lower Gwynedd PA 1998; Exec Coun Appointees New York NY 1996-1997; S Lk's Epis Ch Milwaukee WI 1989-1996; Vic S Clem's Epis Ch Hermitage PA 1986-1989. Auth, "Var Poems & arts".

SCHWARZ, Robert Louis (LI) 5436 Rock Creek Ct, North Charleston SC 29420 B Jamaica NY 9/19/1932 s Louis Adam Schwarz & Irene Dorothy. BA Duke 1954; U of Virginia 1970; Cert Mercer TS 1977. D 12/19/1976 Bp Jonathan Goodhue Sherman P 12/17/1977 Bp Robert Campbell Witcher Sr. m 8/28/1954 Barbara Schwarz c 5. Geo Mercer TS Garden City NY 2000; R S Ann's Ch Sayville NY 1986-2004; Emm Epis Ch Great River NY 1985-1986; Asst S Ptr's by-the-Sea Epis Ch Bay Shore NY 1977-1979; Asst Chr Ch Babylon NY 1976-1977. FA. abbabob@aol.com

SCHWARZER, Margaret Katherine (Mass) 40 Prescott St, Brookline MA 02446 **Gr Ch Newton MA 2011-** B Syracuse NY 2/17/1963 d Franklin John Schwarzer & Harriet Elizabeth. NWU; BA Smith 1983; MA Smith 1985; MDiv Ya Berk 1991. D 6/11/1994 Bp Ronald Hayward Haines P 12/1/1994 Bp Joe Morris Doss. S Paul's Epis Ch Bedford MA 2010-2011; S Mary's Ch Newton Lower Falls MA 2009-2010; Par Of Chr Ch Andover MA 2009; Dio Massachusetts Boston MA 1997-2008; Trin Ch Princeton NJ 1994-1997. Auth, "Essays On The Formation And Mnstry Of Gen X Priests," *Gathering The Next Generation*, Morehouse Pub, 2000; Auth, "Series 1 Year A," *The Abingdon Wmn Priesting Annual*, Abingdon Press, 1998; Contrib, "Sermons That Wk Vi," Morehouse Pub, 1997. Best Sermon Competition (1 Of 10 Winners) Epis Evang Fndt 1996. margaret.schwarzer@gmail.com

SCHWEINSBURG JR, Richard Lyle (RI) 46 Fairway Dr, Washington Village, Coventry RI 02816 **Supply P Dio Rhode Island Providence RI 2009-; POC, Mltry Mnstrs Dio Rhode Island Providence RI 2001-** B Southampton NY 12/15/1951 s Richard Lyle Schweinsburg & Phyllis Louise. BA Ge 1974; MDiv VTS 1977; DMin GTF 1991. D 6/11/1977 Bp Jonathan Goodhue Sherman P 12/17/1977 Bp Robert Campbell Witcher Sr. m 9/3/1977 Jane Duberg. Assoc S Jos And S Jn Ch Steilacoom WA 2008-2009; Assoc S Mk's Ch Alexandria VA 2004-2005; Supply P S Mich's-On-The-Heights Worcester MA 2002-2003; R The Epis Ch Of S Andr And S Phil Coventry RI 1998-2001; VP Metropltn Dnry Dio Albany Albany NY 1993-1998; R S Paul's Ch Schenectady NY 1988-1998; R Chr Ch Denton MD 1986-1988; R S Paul's Ch Philipsburg PA 1979-1986; Cur S Jn's Epis Ch Lancaster PA 1977-1979. Auth, "D.Min Thesis," *A Manual for Acolytes on Video*, GTF, 1991. Angl Soc 1977; Epis Armed Serv Chapl Assn 1977; Mltry Chapl Assn 1977; Soc of S Fran 1977. Humanitarian of Year Animal Protective Fndt Schenectady Cnty 1995; Amer Red Cross Spec Citation for Exceptional Voluntar Moshannon Vlly Chapt 1986. frrich@webtv.net

SCHWENKE, Carol Flenniken (SwFla) 3000 S Schiller St, Tampa FL 33629 B Alexander City AL 7/2/1940 d Fred Gordon Flenniken & Lucille. BS U of Tennessee 1962; MS U of Tennessee 1975; MDiv STUSo 1985. D 6/22/1985

Bp Emerson Paul Haynes P 4/28/1990 Bp Rogers Sanders Harris. m 11/29/1980 Roger Dean Schwenke c 3. Ch Pension Fund Benefici New York NY 2005; Cler Ldrshp Proj Dio W Missouri Kansas City MO 1998-2001; Cn Gr And H Trin Cathd Kansas City MO 1997-2001; H Innoc Epis Ch Valrico FL 1988-1997; Chair Com on AIDS Mnstry Dio SW Florida Sarasota FL 1987-1997; D S Jn's Epis Ch Clearwater FL 1985-1988. cfschwenke@verizon.net

SCHWENZFEIER, Paul MacLeod (Mass) 32 Arlington Rd., Wareham MA 02571 B Lowell MA 7/19/1941 s Frederick Ernst Schwenzfeier & Christine. BA Ken 1963; MDiv EDS 1968. D 6/15/1968 P 3/8/1969 Bp John S Higgins. m 1/25/1964 Rita Maria Collar c 2. Ch Of Our Sav Somerset MA 1976-2000; R Ch Of The H Sprt Mattapan MA 1976-2000; R Trin Epis Ch Wrentham MA 1969-1976; Asst S Mk's Epis Ch Riverside RI 1968-1969. pmschwenzfeier@mac.com

SCHWERT, Douglas Peters (WTex) 433 Trojan St, Port Aransas TX 78373 **Vic Trin-By-The-Sea Port Aransas TX 2009-** B Wellsville NY 3/23/1946 s Edward Ehler Schwert & Virginia. AAS Paul Smith's Coll 1969; BS U Denv 1971; MDiv SWTS 1978. D 6/29/1978 Bp William Hopkins Folwell P 1/5/1979 Bp Charles Bennison. m 12/14/1999 Gerre L Leffler c 2. S Mary's Sewanee Sewanee TN 2002-2008; Incarn Cntr Ivoryton CT 1996-2002; R S Ptr's Epis Ch Kansas City MO 1995-1996; R S Lk's Epis Ch Bartlesville OK 1990-1995; R S Dav's Ch Glenview IL 1985-1990; S Ptr's By-The-Lake Ch Montague MI 1978-1985. dougschwert@gmail.com

SCHWOYER, Robin V (Pa) 4531 Solly Ave, Philadelphia PA 19136 B Philadelphia PA 7/8/1964 d David Joseph VanHorn & Shirley Edna. BS Drexel U 1987; Cert Pennsylvania Dioc Sch For The Diac 1996; Cert Cntr For Human Integration Philadelphia PA 2003. D 9/12/1998 Bp Charles Ellsworth Bennison Jr. m 10/26/1996 Ronald Joseph Schwoyer. D The Free Ch Of S Jn Philadelphia PA 1998-2001. NAAD 1998; The Assn For Humanistic Psychol 2003; The New Millennia Mystics Soc 2000. deaconrobin@yahoo.com

SCIAINO, Elizabeth Rauen (Nwk) 15 Basking Ridge Rd, Millington NJ 07946 **Cur All SS Ch Millington NJ 2011-** B Manchester NH 5/21/1977 d Paul Thomas Rauen & Jane Leahy. BA Wesl 1999; MDiv Drew U - Drew TS 2011. D 6/4/2011 Bp Mark M Beckwith. m 7/10/2004 Peter Loftus Sciaino c 1. bethrs@mac.com

SCIPIO, Clarence Tyrone (VI) PO Box 1148, St Thomas VI 00804 Virgin Islands (U.S.) B Trinidad 11/25/1931 s John Scipio & Matilda. D 3/5/2011 Bp Edward Ambrose Gumbs. m 1/18/1991 Francine Penn-Scipio c 4.

SCISSONS, Antoinette M (Ia) 3237 Jennings St, Sioux City IA 51104 B Rosebud SD 11/24/1944 d Willis Howard Scissons & Doris Mae. Portland Cmnty Coll; Cert Vancouver TS 2001; MDiv Vancouver TS 2002. D 6/24/2000 P 2/17/2001 Bp Robert Louis Ladehoff. c 3. Dio Iowa Des Moines IA 2007-2011; S Andr's Ch Burns OR 2004-2007; S Paul's Indn Mssn Sioux City IA 2004-2007; Dio Oregon Portland OR 2000-2003. ascisns4@live.com

SCOFIELD, Lawrence Frederick (NwPa) 24 W Frederick St, Corry PA 16407 B NY 11/22/1945 s William Archibald Scofield & Elisabeth. BA Carleton Coll 1967; NYU 1975; MDiv Ya Berk 1986; CAS Ya Berk 1986. D 6/14/1986 Bp Arthur Edward Walmsley P 12/22/1986 Bp Arthur Anton Vogel. m 7/1/1967 Susan M McMillion c 2. Exam Chapl Dio NW Pennsylvania Erie PA 2006-2010; R Emm Ch Corry PA 1996-2010; Sch For Mnstry Coordntr Dio NW Pennsylvania Erie PA 1996; Vic S Geo Epis Ch Camdenton MO 1988-1996; Cur Chr Epis Ch S Jos MO 1986-1988. Auth, "Asstg Victims: a Theol look at rationale and procedures," *Fire Chapl Inst Trng Manual*, Fed of Fire Chapl, 2004. Fed of Fire Chapl 1987; NNECA 2003-2010. larry.scofield@yahoo.com

SCOFIELD, Susan M (NwPa) Nonparochial, 24 W. Frederick St., Corry PA 16407 B St Charles IL 3/7/1945 d Harry H McMillion & Margaret Nelson. BA Carleton Coll 1967; U So 1985; Dio Sch for Mnstry 2001. D 11/17/2006 Bp Arthur Benjamin Williams Jr P 12/21/2007 Bp Sean Walter Rowe. m 7/1/1967 Lawrence Frederick Scofield c 2. Eccl Crt Dio NW Pennsylvania Erie PA 2008-2009; P-in-c S Fran Of Assisi Epis Ch Youngsville PA 2008-2009. suescofield@neo.rr.com

SCOTT JR, Benjamin Ives (Minn) 8429 55th St Sw, Byron MN 55920 B Rochester MN 10/15/1935 s Benjamin Ives Scott & Jennie Alice. BA NWU 1957; MDiv Nash 1960; NYU 1969. D 6/18/1960 P 5/22/1961 Bp Hamilton Hyde Kellogg. m 7/2/1960 Sarah E Welch c 2. The Epis Cathd Of Our Merc Sav Faribault MN 1997-2001; Dio Minnesota Minneapolis MN 1989-2001; Gr Memi Ch Wabasha MN 1989-2000; Trst SWTS Evanston IL 1989-1996; Trst Dio Minnesota Minneapolis MN 1978-1984; Rochester Area 6 Pnt Coord Cncl Rochester MN 1976-1989; P-in-c S Matt's Epis Ch Chatfield MN 1976-1989; P-in-c S Ptr's Epis Ch Kasson MN 1976-1989; R S Mary's Ch St Paul MN 1969-1976; S Jn's Ch New York NY 1968-1969; Gr Epis Ch Massapequa NY 1967-1968; Vic H Trin Epis Ch Luverne MN 1960-1964. Ed, "Hist of Calv Ch, Rochester," Davies Printing, 2009; Auth, "The 1st Cathd: An Epis Cmnty For Mssn," Mod Printing, 1987; Auth, "Hist of Gr Memi, Wabasha (pamphlet)"; Auth, "Episcopalians In Mn (pamphlet)". Hon Cn Cathd Of Our Merc Sav, Faribault 2000. sbscott@kmtel.com

SCOTT, Catherine F (Neb) 1903 Pleasantview Ln, Bellevue NE 68005 B Williamsport PA 5/27/1952 d Vincent Paris Fish & Hazel Mildred. BA Carthage Coll 1973; MDiv SWTS 1977. D 6/28/1977 Bp James Winchester Montgomery P 7/23/1979 Bp William Arthur Dimmick. m 12/14/1974 Robert W Scott c 3. Ch Of The H Trin Lincoln NE 2007-2010; Min Dev Coord Dio Nebraska Omaha NE 1997-2007; R S Lk's Ch Plattsmouth NE 1997-2007; S Matt's Ch Lincoln NE 1995-1997; Mutual Mnstry Spprt Stff Dio Nthrn Michigan Marquette MI 1988-1994; Dioc Coun Dio Nebraska Omaha NE 1985-1987; COM Dio Nthrn Michigan Marquette MI 1982-1993; Co-Vic Trin Ch Gladstone MI 1982-1988; Vic Zion Ch Gladstone MI 1982-1988; Dioc Coun Dio Nthrn Michigan Marquette MI 1979-1982; Vic S Pauls Ch Nahma MI 1978-1988; M-in-c S Jn's Ch Munising MI 1978-1980. Soc Of S Fran - Tertiary. catherinescott777@hotmail.com

SCOTT, David Allan (Va) 3543 SW Ida St, Seattle WA 98126 B Providence RI 6/27/1936 s Henry Scott & Nora May. BA Amh 1958; BD EDS 1961; MA Pr 1965; Fllshp Tubingen U Tubingen DE 1967; PhD Pr 1968. D 6/24/1961 Bp Robert McConnell Hatch P 12/31/1961 Bp Bravid W Harris. m 10/7/1966 Rosemarie Hildegaard Hogrebe c 2. Prof Theol & Ethics VTS Alexandria VA 1971-2001; Instr Theol EDS Cambridge MA 1967-1970. Auth, "Jeremy Taylor & Contemporary Chr Ethics," 1992; Auth, "A Chr Response To Human Sxlty," 1987. Conf Of Angl Theologians 1970-2001; Scholars Engaged w Angl Doctrine 1989-2001. davidscott1234@aol.com

SCOTT, David Thomas (NwT) Po Box 88, Perryton TX 79070 B Hazel TX 12/11/1958 s Boyce Thomas Scott & Wanda Cleo. W Texas A&M U; BA McMurry U 1980; JD Texas Tech U 1982. D 10/31/1993 P 5/1/1994 Bp Sam Byron Hulsey. m 8/4/1979 Denyce Elaine Baucum c 2. St. Geo (BSA) 2004.

SCOTT, Donna Jeanne (Tenn) 404 Siena Drive, Nashville TN 37205 B 3/16/1936 d Robert Oscar Hurt & Virginia Allie. BA SMU 1959; EDS Peabody Coll 1975; TS 1985; MDiv Van 1985; DMin Wesley Sem Washington DC 1995. D 7/7/1985 P 10/15/1986 Bp George Lazenby Reynolds Jr. m 5/30/2003 John W Eley c 3. Pstr Counslg (P-t) Ch Of The Adv Nashville TN 1990-1994. Auth, "Caregiver's Bible (NIV) (surrounding material)," Cokesbury, 2008; Co-Auth, "The Eranos Volumes (after C.G. Jung), w Chas E. Scott," *Journ of Rel Stds*, 1983; Ed Asst, "Plato Manuscripts IX-XIII Centuries: A Catalogue," Ya Press, 1960. revdjscott@comcast.net

SCOTT, Douglas Gordon (Pa) PO Box 1914, Ranchos De Taos NM 87557 B Philadelphia PA 1/14/1949 s Robert Allen Scott & Jean Hamilton. BA Muskingum Coll 1970; MDiv PDS 1974; STM GTS 1979; MA Penn Coun For Relationships Philadelphia PA 2002; PSY D GTF 2005. D 6/15/1974 P 12/1/1974 Bp Lyman Cunningham Ogilby. m 8/13/1977 Jane Elizabeth Kirkby c 3. R S Mart's Ch Radnor PA 1985-2004; R S Thos Of Cbury Ch Smithtown NY 1980-1984; R Ch Of S Jn The Div Hasbrouck Heights NJ 1977-1980; Cur Ch Of The Atone Tenafly NJ 1975-1977; Stff Assoc Dio Pennsylvania Philadelphia PA 1974-1975; Asst S Mary's Ch Wayne PA 1974-1975. Auth, "There's A War Going On In My Backyard," Ragged Edge Press, 1998; Auth, "Mastering Transitions," Multnomah, 1991. drdgscott@gmak.com

SCOTT, Edward Chisolm (NC) 525 Lake Concord Rd Ne, Concord NC 28025 **S Jas Ch Mooresville NC 2006-** B Waco TX 8/23/1957 s Charles Prioleau Scott & Ann. BA U NC 1979; MDiv VTS 1986. D 12/14/1986 Bp Robert Whitridge Estill P 12/1/1987 Bp Frank Harris Vest Jr. m 8/18/1984 Noel Elizabeth Rhodes. R All SS' Epis Ch Concord NC 1995-2000; R Trin Ch Mt Airy NC 1989-1995; Asst To The R S Paul's Epis Ch Winston Salem NC 1986-1989. edandnoelle@cetlink.net

SCOTT, George Michael (Ga) PO Box 294, Cochran GA 31014 B Raleigh NC 9/11/1948 s John Albert Sweat & Mary Bowen. BA No Carolina St U 1971; MS Georgia St U 1991. D 8/20/2010 Bp Scott Anson Benhase. m 2/20/1999 Nancy Scott c 2. bowwow99@windstream.net

SCOTT, Horton James (NY) 489 Saint Pauls Pl, Bronx NY 10456 **P-in-c S Paul's Ch Morrisania Bronx NY 2008-** B Freetown, Sierra Leone 9/15/1954 s Horton James Scott & Cleopatra. BA S Jos's Coll Standish ME 2002; MPS NYTS 2006; MA S Jos's Coll Standish ME 2007. Trans from Church of the Province of West Africa 5/1/2008. c 1. P-in-c S Paul's Ch Morrisania Bronx NY 2007-2008. hscott1052@aol.com

SCOTT JR, James Edward (Tex) 8407 Glenscott St., Houston TX 77061 B Bay City TX 6/13/1935 s James Edward Scott & Fannie. BA Rice U 1957; MDiv Epis TS of The SW 1961. D 7/25/1961 P 2/8/1962 Bp James W Hunter. m 6/2/1957 Carol Ford c 2. S Lk The Evang Houston TX 2001; All SS Epis Ch Hitchcock TX 1996-1999; R S Ptr's Epis Ch Brenham TX 1970-1972; Vic Chr Ch Matagorda TX 1967-1970; Vic S Jn's Epis Ch Palacios TX 1967-1970; R S Geo's Ch Lusk WY 1965-1967; Vic All Souls Ch Kaycee WY 1961-1965; Vic Chr Epis Ch Glenrock WY 1961-1965. Meritorius Serv Awd Houston Intl Seafarers Ctr. Houston TX 2001; Hal Perry Distinguished Alum Awd Epis TS of the SW Austin TX 1995. cross_s@hal-pc.org

SCOTT, Jean Pearson (NwT) 1101 Slide Rd., Lubbock TX 79416 B Washington DC 12/28/1950 d Ivan C Pearson & Christine E. BSHE U NC 1973; MS U NC 1975; PhD U NC 1979. D 9/20/2008 Bp C(harles) Wallis Ohl P 3/27/2009 Bp James Scott Mayer. m 8/12/1973 Gary C Scott c 2. jean.scott@ttu.edu

SCOTT, John Charles (SwVa) 150 Circle Dr, DeFuniak Springs FL 32435 B Panama City FL 7/16/1938 s E M Scott & Mildred Hill. BS U of Florida 1962; MDiv U So, St. Lk's Sem 1973. D 6/13/1973 P 5/1/1974 Bp Edward Hamilton West. m 9/5/1959 Sheila Leto c 3. Int R S Agatha's Epis Ch Defuniak Sprg FL 2007-2011; Int R S Lk's Ch Marianna FL 2006-2007; R S Barn Ch Lynchburg VA 2000-2003; R Trin Epis Ch Lynchburg VA 2000-2003; R S Nath Ch No Port FL 1990-2000; Cur S Paul's Ch Delray Bch FL 1985-1990; Asst Ch Of The Gd Shpd Jacksonville FL 1976-1979; Vic Ch Of The H Comm Hawthorne FL 1973-1976; Vic Trin Epis Ch Melrose FL 1973-1976. jsscott@comcast.net

SCOTT JR, John Franklin (SC) Po Box 9, Eutawville SC 29048 B Mobile AL 2/8/1936 s John Franklin Scott & Annie Mae. AA St. Bern's Sem Cullman AL 1956; BA S Mary U Baltimore MD 1958; CAS STUSo 1993. Rec from Roman Catholic 6/1/1993 as Priest Bp Charles Farmer Duvall. m 8/6/1985 Toni F Franco c 3. R The Ch Of The Epiph Eutawville SC 1993-2008.

SCOTT III, John Llewellyn (Alb) 86 Lake Hill Rd, Burnt Hills NY 12027 **R Calv Epis Ch Burnt Hills NY 2000-** B Springfield MA 10/18/1955 s John Llewellyn Scott & Barbara. BA Bethany Coll 1977; MDiv GTS 1983. D 8/20/1984 Bp A Donald Davies P 6/1/1985 Bp Clarence Cullam Pope Jr. c 4. Stndg Com Dio Albany Albany NY 1997; Chr And Zion Par Coun Gilbertsville NY 1996-2000; Dn Susquehanna Dio Albany Albany NY 1993-2000; Dioc Trst Dio Albany Albany NY 1992-1996; Dioc Coun Dio Albany Albany NY 1991-1993; Zion Ch Morris NY 1988-1996; Chr Ch Gilbertsville NY 1988-1993; Asst S Jn's Ch Ft Worth TX 1986-1988; Asst S Vinc's Cathd Bedford TX 1984-1986. rector@calvarybh.org

SCOTT JR, John Llewellyn (Me) 9440 Poinciana Pl Apt 410, Fort Lauderdale FL 33324 **Died 1/26/2010** B Lewiston ME 3/27/1923 s John Llewellyn Scott & Alice Maude. BA Bates Coll 1944; BD SWTS 1949; S Aug's Coll Cbury Gb 1959. D 3/25/1949 P 3/25/1950 Bp Oliver L Loring. c 1.

SCOTT, Keith Elden (RI) 103 Union Ave S, Delmar NY 12054 **S Andr's Epis Ch Albany NY 1961-** B Somerset NY 7/31/1933 s Ernest Fillmore Scott & Ruth Maria. BA U Roch 1955; MDiv EDS 1958. D 6/7/1958 Bp Dudley S Stark P 12/14/1958 Bp Roger W Blanchard. m 6/24/1967 Mary P White c 3. P-in-c Gr And H Innoc Albany NY 2003-2005; Int S Andr's Epis Ch Albany NY 2000-2002; Int Gr Epis Ch Norwalk CT 1999; Int Gr Ch Millbrook NY 1997-1999; Int S Paul's Ch Southington CT 1996-1997; P-in-c Chr Ch Coxsackie NY 1987-1991; R S Ptr's By The Sea Narragansett RI 1969-1978; Assoc Gr Ch In Providence Providence RI 1964-1969; M-in-c S Andr's Epis Ch Cincinnati OH 1961-1964; Asst Chr Epis Ch Of Springfield Springfield OH 1958-1961. kescott733@yahoo.com

SCOTT, Marshall Stuart (WMo) 1256 W 72nd Ter, Kansas City MO 64114 **St Lk's Chap Kansas City MO 2004-** B Knoxville TN 6/11/1955 s James Louis Scott & Nancy Jane. BA U of Tennessee 1976; MDiv STUSo 1980. D 3/25/1981 Bp William Evan Sanders P 10/11/1981 Bp William F Gates Jr. m 7/16/1988 Karen L Woods c 2. St Lk's Chap Kansas City MO 1994-2004; St Lk's So Chap Overland Pk KS 1994-2004; Henry Ford Cont Care Harper Woods MI 1992-1993; Dio Michigan Detroit MI 1989-1994; Advoc Hlth Care Oak Brook IL 1987-1988; Dio W Tennessee Memphis TN 1984-1987; Asst S Jn's Epis Ch Memphis TN 1981-1983. Auth, *Caregiver Journ*; Auth, *Journ of Pstr Care*; Auth, *S Lk's Journ of Theol*. Assembly of Epis Healthcare Chapl 1991; Assoc, OHC 1979. mscottsail@everestkc.net

SCOTT, Matthew Rhoades (NwPa) 5001 Olley Ln, Fairfax VA 22032 **P-in-c Trin Memi Ch Warren PA 2010-** B Sliver Spring MD 9/6/1975 s Jerry Stuart Scott & Brenda. BA U of Connecticut 1997; BS U of Connecticut 1999; MDiv VTS 2007. D 6/9/2007 Bp Andrew Donnan Smith P 12/17/2007 Bp David Colin Jones. m 6/22/2002 Nancy S Ouillette c 2. Assoc R Ch Of The Gd Shpd Burke VA 2007-2010. msrev2007@gmail.com

SCOTT, Nolie Edward (ETenn) 12026 Pine Cove Dr, Soddy Daisy TN 37379 B Blountsville AL 10/20/1939 s Lee B Scott & Alma E. BS U of Alabama 1962; PhD Pur 1968. D 6/16/2001 Bp Charles Glenn VonRosenberg. m 6/21/1969 Susan Elizabeth McGaghie c 2. D S Alb's Epis Ch Hixson TN 2001-2009. edscott@comcast.net

SCOTT, Norma J (Nev) Po Box 750, Hawthorne NV 89415 **S Philips-in-the-Desert Hawthorne NV 1992-** B Chico CA 8/30/1928 d William Lowery Montgomery & Ruth. D 12/15/1991 P 6/28/1992 Bp Stewart Clark Zabriskie. m 11/7/2011 James N Scott. circuitrdr@hotmail.com

SCOTT, Peggy King (La) 607 E Main St, New Roads LA 70760 **P-in-c S Mary's Ch New Roads LA 2010-; P-in-c S Paul's/H Trin New Roads LA 2010-** B Andalusia AL 9/30/1949 d William Hugh King & Johnnie Ruth Reeves. BA Samford U 1971; MA Florida St U 1974; MDiv Wycliffe Coll 2009. D 12/27/2008 Bp Charles Edward Jenkins III P 7/17/2010 Bp Morris King Thompson Jr. c 2. Dir, Pstr Care Gr Ch Of W Feliciana S Francisville LA 2010. peggykingscott@gmail.com

SCOTT, Rebecca Jean (Oly) 4534 Beckonridge Loop SE, Lacey WA 98513 B Long Beach CA 6/15/1943 D 6/25/2005 Bp Vincent Waydell Warner. deaconbscott@aol.com

SCOTT, Richard Hervey (Oly) 4885 NW Chad Ct, Silverdale WA 98383 B Seattle WA 2/20/1939 s Clayton Allen Scott & Virginia. BA Estrn Washington U 1990; MDiv CDSP 1993. D 5/29/1993 Bp Frank Jeffrey Terry P 1/4/1994 Bp Vincent Waydell Warner. m 7/27/1963 Margaret L Greene c 2. Dir Of Corp. Dio Olympia Seattle WA 1998-2004; Vic S Antony Of Egypt Silverdale WA 1993-2007; Dioc Coun Dio Spokane Spokane WA 1987-1988. Chart Property Casualty Underwriters 1989. tlbwy@telebyte.com

SCOTT, Robert W (Neb) 13054 Thomas Drive, Bellevue NE 68005 B Omaha NE 7/25/1950 s William H Scott & Jane. BS K SU 1972; MDiv SWTS 1977. D 6/15/1977 Bp James Daniel Warner P 1/1/1978 Bp James Winchester Montgomery. m 12/14/1974 Catherine F Scott c 3. Liturg Cmsn Dio Nebraska Omaha NE 1995-1996; Ch Of The H Sprt Bellevue NE 1994-2007; R Gr Ch Ishpeming MI 1989-1994; S Jn's Ch Negaunee MI 1989-1994; So Cntrl Reg Manistique MI 1989; Vic Trin Ch Gladstone MI 1982-1988; S Alb's Ch Manistique MI 1978-1982; Vic S Jude's Ch Edina MN 1978-1982; Asst S Andr's and Pentecostal Epis Ch Evanston IL 1977-1978. bobscottster@gmail.com

SCOTT, Roger Timothy (Az) **Ldrshp Formation Grp Dio Arizona Phoenix AZ 1996-** D 6/14/1968 P 5/25/1969 Bp John M Allin.

SCOTT, Sheila Maria (NwT) 301 W. Coventry Ct # 203, Milwaukee WI 53217 B Pankota Romania 2/9/1955 d Arpad Fekete & Aniko Maria. BSN Marian Coll 1993; MSN U of Phoenix 2007. D 8/28/2010 Bp James Scott Mayer. csillams@sbcglobal.net

SCOTT, Shelby Hudson (Okla) 9119 S 89th E Ave, Broken Arrow OK 74133 **S Pat's Epis Ch Broken Arrow OK 2000-** B Duncan OK 5/28/1963 s George Scott & Ellen. BS SW Oklahoma St U 1984; MDiv SWTS 1990. D 6/23/1990 Bp Robert Manning Moody P 12/23/1990 Bp Francis Campbell Gray. c 2. Dio Oklahoma Oklahoma City OK 1996-1999; S Jn Of The Cross Bristol IN 1990-1996. shelbysails@aol.com

SCOTT, Thomas Crawford Hunt (WMich) 1006 3rd St., Muskegon MI 49440 **R S Paul's Ch Muskegon MI 2008-** B Pittsburgh PA 1/29/1950 s Walter James Scott & Nancy Elizabeth. BA U Pgh 1976; MA MI SU 1978; MDiv EDS 1981; Cert Pittsburgh Pstr Inst Intern 1983; DMin Drew U 1990. D 6/11/1981 P 12/12/1981 Bp Robert Bracewell Appleyard. m 6/10/1978 Dorothy Jean Frantz c 2. R S Mk's Ch Evanston IL 1990-2008; R S Andr's Epis Ch Lincoln Pk NJ 1985-1989; Cur Calv Ch Pittsburgh PA 1981-1985. Soc Of S Jn The Evang. Cler Grant The Lilly Fndt 2002. tchscott@aol.com

SCOTT JR, William Tayloe (Cal) 1100 California St, San Francisco CA 94108 **Cathd Mssnr/P-in-c S Cyp's Ch San Francisco CA 2009-** B Harrisonburg VA 8/26/1979 s William T Scott & Rebecca. BA Simon's Rock Coll Of Bard 2002; MDiv VTS 2004. D 6/26/2004 P 1/10/2005 Bp Peter James Lee. m 11/23/2009 Matthew Chayt. Assoc Gr Cathd San Francisco CA 2006-2010; Assoc S Jn's Epis Ch McLean VA 2004-2006. wills@gracecathedral.org

SCOTT-HAMBLEN, Shane (NY) 1 Chestnut St, Cold Spring NY 10516 **R S Mary's Ch Cold Sprg NY 2002-** B Lawrenceburg IN 12/28/1966 s Jerry E Hamblen & Linda D. ThD GTS; B.M. Webster U 1989; St. Louis U 1991; STB Pontifical U Of St Thos Aquinas 1994; MA Pontifical U Of St Thos Aquinas 1995; STL Pontifical U Of St Thos Aquinas 1996. Rec from Roman Catholic 12/18/1999 Bp Catherine Elizabeth Maples Waynick. m 6/23/1996 Mary-Therese Robinson c 3. S Paul's Epis Ch Evansville IN 1999-2002. Auth, ",Martha's Old Mistake," *LivCh*, 2003. frshane@optonline.com

SCOTTO, Vincent Francis (SwFla) 23465 Harborview Rd Apt634, Port Charlotte FL 33980 B New York NY 3/12/1948 s Frank Vincent Scotto & Vivian R. BFA New York Inst of Tech 1970; LTh CDSP 1974. D 6/8/1974 Bp Paul Moore Jr P 12/21/1974 Bp Harold Louis Wright. m 10/15/2005 Kathleen Hicks c 2. Dn Dio SW Florida Sarasota FL 1995-2000; Dioc Coun Dio SW Florida Sarasota FL 1990-1994; Epis Nomntns Com Dio SW Florida Sarasota FL 1987-1989; R Ch Of The Gd Shpd Punta Gorda FL 1986-2010; R S Mk's Epis Ch Penn Yan NY 1979-1986; Vic S Lk's Ch Branchport NY 1979-1981; Asst Gr Epis Ch Nyack NY 1977-1979; Cur Zion Epis Ch Wappingers Falls NY 1974-1976. Amer. Soc on Aging 1998; ISL 1995; Int Mnstry Ntwk 1999; RWF 1979; Soc. for Study of Myth & Tradition 1998; Via Media 2004. vfscotto@gmail.com

SCOVELL, Dean Halcyon (Oly) 3091 Se Kamilche Point Rd, Shelton WA 98584 B Tacoma WA 6/13/1933 s Halsey Joel Scovell & Eva Jane. BS U Of Puget Sound 1955; BS U of Washington 1962. D 9/11/1971 Bp Ivol I Curtis P 10/18/1977 Bp Robert Hume Cochrane. m 8/17/1956 Dorothy J Flora. Int St Steph's Epis Ch Oak Harbor WA 1998-2000; Asst S Lk's Epis Ch Renton WA 1972-1995; Asst S Mich And All Ang Ch Issaquah WA 1971-1972. The Ord Of S Lk The Physcn 1983.

SCRANTON, Susan Lee (Los) 1420 E Foothill Blvd, Glendora CA 91741 **R Gr Epis Ch Glendora CA 1997-** B Monterey Park CA 3/25/1954 d James Monroe Scranton & Marilyn Blaine. BM USC 1976; MM USC 1978; Fuller TS 1992; MDiv VTS 1994. D 6/11/1994 Bp Chester Lovelle Talton P 1/1/1995 Bp Frederick Houk Borsch. Asst S Ptr's Par San Pedro CA 1994-1997. slscranton@verizon.net

SCRIBNER, The Rev. Chaplain Jean (Neb) 1725 Old Haywood Rd., Asheville NC 28806 B Appleton WI 9/8/1944 d Charles Woodrow Scribner & Mary Louise. B M U of Wisconsin 1969; M M U of Washington 1973; MDiv SWTS 1983. D 1/23/1987 P 11/24/1987 Bp Rustin Ray Kimsey. Beatrice Cmnty

Hosp Beatrice NE 1997-2006; Supply Dio Oregon Portland OR 1990-1995; Sr Stff Chapl Legacy Gd Samar Hosp Portland OR 1990-1995; R Ch Of The Medtr Harbert MI 1988-1990; R S Aug Of Cbury Epis Ch Benton Harbor MI 1988-1989. Auth, "Wmn Uncommon Prayers," Morehouse Pub, 2000. AAPC, Par Assoc 1992; Assembly Of Epis Healthcare Chapl, Past Pres 1992; Assn of Profsnl Chapl, Bd-Cert Chapl 1992. jmssouldr@charter.net

SCRIVEN, Elizabeth Amy (Mich) 2309 Packard St, Ann Arbor MI 48104 **Assoc S Clare Of Assisi Epis Ch Ann Arbor MI 2008-** B Cleveland OH 10/6/1980 d Peter Sperry Scriven & Laurel Beth Coffin. BA Smith Northampton MA 2003; MDiv SWTS 2007. D 6/9/2007 Bp Mark Hollingsworth Jr P 10/18/2008 Bp David Charles Bowman. indiyoda@gmail.com

SCRIVENER, William Eugene (SO) 7193 Foxview Dr, Cincinnati OH 45230 B Munich West Germany 8/1/1947 s Wayne Eston Scrivener & Helen. BA Leh 1969; MDiv EDS 1973. D 6/9/1973 Bp Joseph Warren Hutchens P 2/1/1974 Bp Morgan Porteus. m 6/14/1975 Susan Pace c 3. Com On Oversight & Exam Dio Connecticut Hartford CT 1984-1990; Chap of the H Chld at Chld's Hosp Cincinnati OH 1981-2006; Zion Epis Ch No Branford CT 1977-1981; Asst To Dir Ordinands Trng Prog Dio Connecticut Hartford CT 1977-1979; Asst Ch of the H Sprt W Haven CT 1975-1976; Cur Gr Epis Ch Norwalk CT 1973-1975. Contrib, "Bioethics Educ In A Pediatric Med Cntr". ACPE Supvsr 1980; Assn Of Profsnl Chapl, Bd Cert Chapl 1985. bill.scrivener@ccmcc.org

SCRUGGS JR, C(harles) Perry (ETenn) 540 Bryant Rd, Chattanooga TN 37405 B Jacksonville FL 6/15/1949 s Charles Perry Scruggs & Eleanor Law. BA Florida St U 1971; MDiv VTS 1974. D 6/4/1974 Bp Edward Hamilton West P 5/4/1975 Bp Frank Stanley Cerveny. m 5/23/1998 Sue E Hughes c 2. Assoc Ch Of The Gd Shpd Lookout Mtn TN 1994-2004; Ch Of The Gd Shpd Raleigh NC 1990-1993; Epis U Mnstry Johnson City TN 1987-1990; Vic S Mk's Epis Ch Troy AL 1983-1987; H Innoc Ch Atlanta GA 1977-1983; H Innoc' Epis Sch Atlanta GA 1977-1979; Asst Ch Of The Adv Tallahassee FL 1974-1977. sescps4@yahoo.com

SCRUTCHINS, Arthur Paul (Okla) 45 Cherokee, Shawnee OK 74801 B Oklahoma City OK 11/22/1956 s James Robert Scrutchins & Glenda Vern. BA Oklahoma Bapt U 1980; EFM STUSo 1987. D 7/1/1987 Bp William Jackson Cox. m 3/17/2005 Ramona Scrutchins c 2. Dio Oklahoma Oklahoma City OK 2010; Holland Hall Sch Tulsa OK 2009; Emm Epis Ch Shawnee OK 1999-2005. Auth, "Friend of Crime Fighters," *LivCh*. artscrutch@aol.com

✠ **SCRUTON, Rt Rev Gordon Paul** (WMass) 37 Chestnut St, Springfield MA 01103 **Bp of Wstrn Massachusetts Dio Wstrn Massachusetts Springfield MA 1996-** B Rochester NH 3/8/1947 s Paul Herbert Scruton & Marjorie Ellen. BA Barrington Coll 1968; ThM Bos 1971. D 6/5/1971 Bp John S Higgins P 1/30/1972 Bp Frederick Hesley Belden Con 10/12/1996 for WMass. m 6/15/1968 Rebecca Polley. Cong Dvlmnt Comm Dio Wstrn Massachusetts Springfield MA 1987-1990; R S Fran Ch Holden MA 1981-1996; Dio Wstrn Massachusetts Springfield MA 1981-1986; Chair Sp Life Comm Dio Wstrn Massachusetts Springfield MA 1979-1987; N Berkshire Dnry Dio Wstrn Massachusetts Springfield MA 1979-1981; R Gr Ch Dalton MA 1977-1981; Asst S Paul's Ch No Kingstown RI 1975-1977; COM Dio Rhode Island Providence RI 1974-1977; Evang Comm Dio Rhode Island Providence RI 1973-1976; Asst S Mk's Epis Ch Riverside RI 1971-1975. Auth, "Pstr's Sp Life," *New Engl Ch Resource Handbook*, 1980; Auth, "var arts," *Living Ch*. FVC 1973. gpscruton@gmail.com

SCULLY, Edward Anthony (SwFla) 311 Irwin Ave, Albion MI 49224 B San Francisco CA 11/13/1940 s Edward Anthony Scully & Bernice Henrietta. BA U of San Francisco 1973; MA U of San Francisco 1975; MDiv EDS 1987. Trans from Anglican Church of Canada 12/1/1989. m 11/21/1981 Susan Durrett c 2. Dio Wstrn Michigan Kalamazoo MI 1999-2002; R S Jas' Epis Ch Of Albion Albion MI 1994-2009; R S Jn's Ch Fremont MI 1989-1994; S Mk's Ch Newaygo MI 1989-1990. Acad Par Cleric; Amer Acad Mnstry; Associated Parishes; ADLMC; Conf Of S Ben; Life Mem Of Amer Assn For Respiratory Care; Liturg Conf; No Amer Catechumenal Con; No Amer Forum On Catechumenate; Ord Of S Lk. Outstanding Young Man Of Amer. padretampa@gmail.com

SCUPHOLME, Anne (SeFla) 1990 English Oaks Cir N, Charlottesville VA 22911 B Whitby UK 5/3/1942 d Albert Cooper Scupholme & Kathleen Mary Barbara. BA Florida Intl U 1986; MA U of Miami 1989. D 9/11/1998 Bp Calvin Onderdonk Schofield Jr. D Trin Cathd Miami FL 1998-2000. ACNM; ACOG; APHA; NAAD. ascupholme@aol.com

SEABORN, Sandra L (NY) 669 Albany Post Rd, #8805, Scarborough NY 10510 **P-in-c S Mary's Ch Of Scarborough Scarborough NY 2011-** B 7/18/1972 d Richard Seaborn & Catherine. BA U Tor 1995; MSW Wlfd Laurier U Waterloo ON CA 1997; MDiv VTS 2009. D 3/7/2009 P 9/12/2009 Bp Mark Sean Sisk. m 5/23/1998 Matthew Scott c 2. s.seaborn@gmail.com

SEABROOK, Alexander (Chi) PO Box 57, Lockport IL 60441 **Supply P Ch Of The Gd Shpd Momence IL 2008-; S Bon Ch Tinley Pk IL 1997-** B Vienna AT 6/10/1926 s Edward Seabrook & Josephine. BA OH SU 1949; MA OH SU 1951; STM EDS 1954; MSW U Pgh 1972. D 6/20/1954 P 12/19/1954 Bp Henry W Hobson. m 10/2/1994 Cecilia Gaynes c 2. Int S Paul's Epis Ch La Porte IN 1996-1997; P-in-c H Cross Epis Ch Wilkes Barre PA 1993-1996; Int S Paul's Epis Ch Westfield NJ 1992-1993; R Chr Ch Joliet IL 1982-1992; R S Mk Pittsburgh PA 1964-1982; Cur S Paul's Epis Ch Dayton OH 1954-1957. alexseabrook@aol.com

SEABURY, Scott Hamor (WMass) 10 Rawlings Brook Rd, Suffield CT 06078 **Chr Formation Mssnr Dio Wstrn Massachusetts Springfield MA 2008-; R S Chris's Ch Fairview Chicopee MA 2002-** B New York NY 5/30/1952 s Raymond Mumford Seabury & Helen Hamor. BA U of Massachusetts 1974; MDiv Ya Berk 1983. D 9/18/1983 P 4/1/1984 Bp Alexander Doig Stewart. m 4/10/1976 Linda Williams c 1. Asst R S Dav's Ch Feeding Hills MA 2000-2002; R All SS Ch So Hadley MA 1993-1999; R S Barn And All SS Ch Springfield MA 1986-1993; Asst S Paul's Ch Holyoke MA 1983-1986. seabs52@aol.com

SEADALE, Vincent Gerald (Mass) 10 Bold Meadow Rd, Edgartown MA 02539 **S Andr's Ch Edgartown MA 2009-** B Brooklyn NY 11/22/1960 s Vincent Seadale & Joyce. BA Colg 1982; JD U of Connecticut 1988; MDiv Ya Berk 2004. D 6/12/2004 Bp Andrew Donnan Smith P 2/24/2005 Bp Samuel Johnson Howard. m 5/28/1983 Colleen M Seadale c 3. R The Epis Ch of The Redeem Jacksonville FL 2007-2009; Chr Epis Ch Ponte Vedra Bch FL 2005-2007. fatherchip@standrewsmv.org

SEAGE, Brian Richard (Miss) 106 Vinson Cv, Madison MS 39110 **S Columb's Ch Ridgeland MS 2005-** B Thousand Oaks CA 7/30/1963 s Richard Miller Seage & Mary Ann. BA Pepperdine U 1986; MDiv Epis TS of The SW 1997. D 6/21/1997 Bp Chester Lovelle Talton P 1/18/1998 Bp Frederick Houk Borsch. m 10/14/1995 Kyle Dice c 2. S Thos Epis Ch Diamondhead MS 1997-2005; Dir Yth Mnstry S Patricks Ch And Day Sch Thousand Oaks CA 1990-1994. brseage@gmail.com

SEAGE, Kyle Dice (Miss) 106 Vinson Cv, Madison MS 39110 **Int S Phil's Ch Jackson MS 2010-** B Topeka KS 5/14/1966 d Joseph Spratley Dice & Patricia. BA U So 1988; MDiv Epis TS of The SW 1996. D 6/22/1996 P 4/22/1997 Bp Alfred Clark Marble Jr. m 10/14/1995 Brian Richard Seage c 2. All SS Ch Inverness MS 2009-2010; Dio Mississippi Jackson MS 2005-2008; Int Chr Ch Bay St Louis MS 2003-2005; S Fran Cmnty Serv Inc. Salina KS 2000-2002; Assoc R S Jn's Epis Ch Pascagoula MS 1997-2000. kseage@comcast.net

SEAGLE, Teresa Ryan (Fla) 5375 Ortega Farms Blvd, Unit 404, Jacksonville FL 32210 **S Paul's Epis Ch Jacksonville FL 2011-** B Decatur IL 11/21/1966 d Charles Edmund Ryan & Barbara Sue. BA U of No Florida 1994; MEd U of No Florida 1999; MDiv The U So (Sewanee) 2008. D 6/1/2008 Bp Samuel Johnson Howard. R S Fran Of Assisi Epis Ch Tallahassee FL 2008-2011. teresaseagle@gmail.com

SEAL, William Christopher Houston (NCal) 171 Grove St, Nevada City CA 95959 **Dioc Coun Dio Nthrn California Sacramento CA 2007-; R H Trin Ch NEVADA CITY CA 1994-** B Long Beach CA 5/26/1950 s William Seal & Betty. AB Occ 1972; MDiv CDSP 1981. D 6/21/1981 P 1/10/1982 Bp Robert C Rusack. m 1/7/1983 Gae Victoria Goodrich c 3. Stndg Com Pres Dio Nthrn California Sacramento CA 2000-2001; Chair, Congrl Dvlpmt T/F Dio Nthrn California Sacramento CA 2000; Dioc Coun Dio Nthrn California Sacramento CA 1996-1999; Vic Chr The King Quincy CA 1983-1988; Cur S Mk's Par Glendale CA 1981-1983. Auth, "Post Reformation Monuments," *Monuments in Cambridgeshire Ch 1530-1994*, Paul Watkins Pub., 1997. Assoc Alum Nash 1997; Oblate Benedictine Camaldolese Ord (RC) 1985. Hon Cn, St. Ptr's Cathd Dio Kinkiizi, Uganda 2008; Colonel Aide De Camp St of Tennessee 1992. wchseal@gmail.com

SEALE, James Richard (Md) 7583 Tred Avon Cir, Easton MD 21601 **Chr Ch S Ptr's Par Easton MD 2011-** B Elizabeth NJ 5/10/1946 s Alfred Seale & Dorothy. BS Penn 1968; MS Geo 1973; MS Loyola U 1983; MDiv VTS 1990. D 6/9/1990 P 1/19/1991 Bp Ronald Hayward Haines. m 1/14/1989 Pamela G Potter c 4. R All SS Ch Frederick MD 1994-2006; Assoc S Jas Ch Potomac MD 1990-1994. jamesseale@goeaston.net

SEALS, William Frederick (CFla) 23 Surrey Run, Hendersonville NC 28791 B Miami OK 5/24/1939 s Denver Frederick Seals & Louise. BS Oklahoma St U 1961. D 6/12/1995 Bp John Lewis Said. m 7/10/1983 Treva Lynn Sinclair c 2. D Gloria Dei Epis Ch Cocoa FL 1996-2003; D S Jas Epis Ch Hendersonville NC 1996-2002; D S Jas The Fisherman Islamorada FL 1995-1996. wfseals@juno.com

SEAMAN, Henry Frederick (Oly) 3115 Squalicom Pkwy Apt 237, Bellingham WA 98225 B Gadsden AL 3/22/1922 s Eugene Cecil Seaman & Henrietta Morgan. BA U So 1943; BD VTS 1949. D 6/1/1949 Bp Lloyd Rutherford Craighill P 12/19/1949 Bp George Henry Quarterman. c 2. Pres, NW Harvest Dio Olympia Seattle WA 1986-1994; Ecum Off Dio Olympia Seattle WA 1977-1987; Vic Ch Of The Gd Shpd Fed Way WA 1967-1987; Pres, N.M. Coun of Ch Dio The Rio Grande Albuquerque NM 1963-1964; R Ch of the H Faith Santa Fe NM 1954-1965; Vic S Mk's Epis Ch Plainview TX 1949-1954; Vic S Thos Epis Ch Hereford TX 1949-1953.

SEAMAN, Martha Lee (Az) 7419 E Palm Ln, Scottsdale AZ 85257 **D Epis Ch Of The Trsfg Mesa AZ 2007-** B Dearborn MI 5/30/1952 d Allen Seaman &

Janet. BA MI SU 1974; JD Wayne 1977. D 10/9/2004 Bp Robert Reed Shahan. c 2. martha.seaman1@cox.net

SEARFOSS, Vernon Francis (Be) 106 Echo Dr, Clarks Summit PA 18411 B Coalport PA 7/16/1931 s George Roosevelt Searfoss & Nora May. BA Leh 1955; MDiv GTS 1958; STB GTS 1958. D 5/12/1958 P 12/20/1958 Bp Frederick J Warnecke. m 6/7/1958 Dorothy Pondish c 3. Vic S Jas' Ch Drifton PA 1996-1998; R Ch Of The Gd Shpd Scranton PA 1969-1996; Excoun Dio Bethlehem Bethlehem PA 1963-1971; R S Mich's Epis Ch Bethlehem PA 1963-1967; Vic S Anne's Epis Ch Trexlertown PA 1957-1969. Outstanding Civic Participation Pa Legis & Gvnrs 1994; Outstanding Contrib Educ And Civic Wellbeing Pa Senate & Hse 1992.

SEARLE, Susan Elizabeth (Nwk) 200 W 79th St Apt 14-P, New York NY 10024 B Wichita KS 6/16/1947 d Oscar William Searle & Maxine. BA Wichita St U 1976; JD Harv 1979; MDiv EDS 1998. D 6/13/1998 P 12/19/1998 Bp Richard Frank Grein. Chr Ch Ridgewood NJ 2006-2010; S Jn's Ch New City NY 2004-2005; Assoc Chr Ch Bronxville NY 2000-2004; Asst R All SS Ch New York NY 1998-2000. lizesqe@mac.com

SEARS III, Albert Nelson (Mass) 98 Ridgewood Dr, Rocky Hill CT 06067 B Brockton MA 4/18/1941 s Albert Nelson Sears & Beulah Francis. BA Estrn Nazarene Coll 1964; MDiv Ya Berk 1969. D 5/26/1971 Bp John Melville Burgess P 5/1/1972 Bp Morris Fairchild Arnold. Ch Of Our Sav Middleboro MA 2001-2004; Dio Massachusetts Boston MA 1973-1976; Dio Massachusetts Boston MA 1972.

SEARS, Barbara (Md) 7030 Upland Ridge Dr, Adamstown MD 21710 **D S Jas Epis Ch Mt Airy MD 2009-** B Orange NJ 4/18/1925 d Ralf Lee Hartwell & Mary. Swarthmore Coll 1945; BS NYU 1949. D 6/3/1989 Bp Alden Moinet Hathaway. m 11/28/1953 Kenneth Avard Brown c 3. D/Asst Otey Memi Par Ch Sewanee TN 1990-1993; Asst S Thos' Epis Ch Canonsburg PA 1989-1990. Cmnty S Mary 96-; NAAD. mbrown@edurostream.com

SEARS, Barbara Anne (Md) 366 Doral Ct, Westminster MD 21158 **D S Geo Ch Hampstead MD 2001-** B Baltimore MD 3/9/1946 d Earl Melvin Schwartz & Margaret Eaton. BA Wstrn Maryland Coll 1966; MA Morgan St U 1971; EFM STUSo 1994. D 6/10/1995 Bp Charles Lindsay Longest. m 10/11/1969 William Norman Sears. D S Jas Ch Monkton MD 1998-2001; D Ch Of The Trsfg Braddock Heights MD 1995-1998. NAAD 1995. redrock2@verizon.net

SEARS, Gwen W (WMass) 235 Walker St. Apt. 162, Lenox MA 01240 **D S Steph's Ch Pittsfield MA 1981-** B Rhinebeck NY 1/9/1928 d Clarence A Watson & Helen Jane. AA Virginia Intermont Coll 1947. D 10/9/1982 Bp Alexander Doig Stewart. m 6/5/1948 Noel Sears c 4. cronelady@roadrunner.com

SEATON, Robert Deane (WK) 3118 N Brush Creek St, Wichita KS 67205 **D Chr Cathd Salina KS 2001-** B Iola KS 2/9/1949 s Deane Robert Seaton & Martha Hannah. BA U of Kansas 1971; MD U of Kansas 1978. D 11/30/2001 Bp Vernon Edward Strickland P 3/1/2003 Bp James Marshall Adams Jr. m 9/17/1998 Anne Christine Bergeson.

SEATVET, Lloyd Dayle (La) 3901 Montecito Dr Apt 126, Denton TX 76210 **Asst S Dav's Ch Denton TX 1993-** B Omaha NE 10/28/1930 s John Austin Seatvet & Fae Catherine. Austin Peay St Coll 1953; El Paso Cmnty Coll, Colorado Sprg 1971; LTh Nash 1974. D 12/22/1973 P 7/3/1974 Bp William Carl Frey. m 11/9/1951 Dana Keiser c 4. Dn Dio Louisiana Baton Rouge LA 1992-1993; R Trin Epis Ch Morgan City LA 1989-1992; R S Corn Epis Ch Dodge City KS 1978-1989; S Paul's Epis Ch Lamar CO 1975-1977; Cur The Ch Of The Ascen Denver CO 1974-1975. lstalwart@aol.com

SEAVER, Maurice Blanchard (WNC) 3500 Carmel Rd, Charlotte NC 28226 B Johnson City TN 7/25/1927 s Wiley Rex Seaver & Barbara Jeanette. Astc 1948; No Carolina St U 1949. D 6/12/1976 Bp William Gillette Weinhauer. m 2/4/1949 Bobbie Nell Brown c 2.

SEAVEY, SuZanne Elane (ETenn) 135 Fountainhead Ct, Lenoir City TN 37772 B Houston TX 12/13/1946 d Albert Leighton Shirley & Bernice. BA U GA 1968; MDiv SWTS 1990. D 6/16/1990 P 12/15/1990 Bp Frank Tracy Griswold III. m 11/5/2011 Jerome J Seavey. Ch Of The Resurr Loudon TN 2002-2006; Asst R Ch Of The Ascen Hickory NC 1999-2002; H Sprt Ch Indianapolis IN 1995-1999; Dio Indianapolis Indianapolis IN 1995; Int S Ambr Ch Chicago Heights IL 1993-1995; Int Gr Epis Ch New Lenox IL 1992; S Chas Ch S Chas IL 1990-1992. seseavey@charter.net

SEAY, Donald Robert (CFla) 247 N Main St #14, Dousman WI 53118 B Lebanon OH 6/11/1926 s Curtis D Seay & Anna M. BA U of Kentucky 1950; MDiv Nash 1976. D 5/15/1976 Bp Quintin Ebenezer Primo Jr P 11/1/1976 Bp James Winchester Montgomery. m 3/17/1948 Carol Powell c 3. R S Fran Of Assisi Epis Ch Lake Placid FL 1986-1991; Assoc R Gr Epis Ch Of Ocala Ocala FL 1983-1986; Vic Ch Of The Resurr Blue Sprg MO 1978-1983; Dio W Missouri Kansas City MO 1978-1983; Vic S Mich's Epis Ch Independence MO 1978-1982; Cur Gr Ch Sterling IL 1976-1978; Vic The Ch Of S Anne Morrison IL 1976-1978. CHS Ord of S Fran, Cath C.

SEBRO, Jacqueline Marie (ECR) 815 Sycamore Canyon Rd, Paso Robles CA 93446 **D-In-Res S Jas Ch Paso Robles CA 1994-** B San Bernardino CA 11/7/1956 d William Patrick Sebro & Barbara Jo Ann. BS California St Polytechnic U 1978; MA Epis TS of The SW 1993; Cert California Sch for Deacons 1994. D 7/9/1994 Bp Matthew Paul Bigliardi. jmsebro@tcsn.net

SECAUR, Stephen Charles (Mil) 803 Briar Ridge Rd, Woodville TX 75979 B Lincoln NE 10/14/1944 s Charles Harold Secaur & Frances Lenora. MDiv SWTS 1981. D 6/29/1981 P 12/29/1981 Bp Robert Marshall Anderson. m 3/15/1969 Nancy K Ball. P-in-c S Lk's Ch Whitewater WI 1999-2004; R Trin Ch Baraboo WI 1993-1999; Vic S Steph's Ch Mt Carmel PA 1990-1993; R H Trin Epis Ch Shamokin PA 1988-1993; Assoc Ch Of Our Sav Akron OH 1987-1988; R S Mk's Epis Ch Wadsworth OH 1984-1986; P-in-c Chr Ch Duluth MN 1981-1984; R S Andr's Ch Le Sueur MN 1981-1984. OHC. scsecaur@sbcglobal.net

SECOR, Neale A (Pa) 4 Appletree Ct, Philadelphia PA 19106 B Peekskill NY 7/3/1934 s Allen Burtis Secor & Edith Winifred. BA Drew U 1956; JD U Chi 1959; MDiv UTS 1966. D 6/11/1966 P 12/10/1966 Bp Horace W B Donegan. m 9/17/2011 Ricardo Linano c 4. Sum P in charge Ch Of The Redeem Longport NJ 1997-2000; Dir Seamens Ch Inst Philadelphia PA 1985-1996; Port Newark Dir Seamens Ch Inst Income New York NY 1980-1984; R S Mary's Manhattanville Epis Ch New York NY 1966-1980. Auth, "Brief for a Homosexual Ethic," *The Same Sex*, Pilgrim Press, 1967; Co-Auth, "Taxation of Ch Property," *Law and Rel*, Seabury Press, 1965. Man-of-the-Year Wrld Trade Assn 1996. nealcsccor@gmail.com

SEDDON, Anne Christine (Ct) 4 Maybury Rd, Suffield CT 06078 B Dorchester MA 3/10/1946 d Ejnar George Iversen & Anne Catherine. BA S Mary's Coll So Bend IN 1968; MDiv Maryknoll TS 1983. D 6/14/1986 P 12/27/1986 Bp Arthur Edward Walmsley. m 6/29/1968 John Seddon c 2. Receiving Disabil Ret 1997-2011; R Ch Of The Gd Shpd Shelton CT 1989-1997; H Cross Monstry W Pk NY 1986-1988. SBL, AAR.

SEDDON, Barbara Cynthia (Mont) 4328 Trailmaster Dr, Billings MT 59101 **D S Steph's Ch Billings MT 1999-** B Liverpool UK 11/9/1931 d Archibald Laurence Hughes & Frances Amy. Liverpool Coll Of Art Gb; MA Berean U 1975; EFM STUSo 2000. D 3/13/1999 Bp Charles Jones III. m 8/25/1951 Ernest Cragg Seddon.

SEDGWICK, R(oger) Stephen (O) 647 Reid Ave, Lorain OH 44052 **Ch Of The Gd Shpd Beachwood OH 2009-; Dio No Dakota Fargo ND 1974-; Dio Alaska Fairbanks AK 1970-** B Melrose Park IL 1/15/1946 s Roger Stanley Sedgwick & Virginia Mae. BA Lawr 1967; STB GTS 1970. D 6/13/1970 Bp James Winchester Montgomery P 12/17/1970 Bp William J Gordon Jr. m 8/30/1991 Carol Marie Irwin c 1. R Ch Of The Redeem Lorain OH 2000-2009; Epis. Shared Mnstrs Nw Lakewood OH 1994-2000; S Mk's Ch Cleveland OH 1994-1998; Int Trin Ch Excelsior MN 1992-1993; Int Trin Ch Anoka MN 1990-1992; Dio Minnesota Minneapolis MN 1987-1988; S Barth's Epis Ch Bemidji MN 1983-1990; Int Chr Ch Hackensack NJ 1982-1983; Vic SS Mary And Mk Epis Ch Oakes ND 1977-1980; St Marks Ch Guelph ND 1977-1980; Gd Shpd McVille ND 1975-1977; P-in-c S Mk's Ch Nenana AK 1970-1973. RWF Pres 1987-1990. frsteve@centurytel.net

SEDLACEK, Carol Westerberg (Ore) 2103 Desiree Pl, Lebanon OR 97355 **R S Mart's Ch Lebanon OR 2002-** B Astoria OR 10/16/1966 d Robert Charles Westerberg & Grace Aletha. BS OR SU 1990; MDiv VTS 1994. D 5/28/1994 P 11/29/1994 Bp Robert Louis Ladehoff. m 4/20/1996 Wes Sedlacek. Vic S Fran Ch Sweet Hm OR 2002-2007; Assoc R The Epis Ch Of The Gd Samar Corvallis OR 2002-2005; Assoc R The Ch of the Gd Shpd Austin TX 1999-2002; Assoc R S Barth's Ch Beaverton OR 1994-1999. carolrev@aol.com

SEDLACEK, Wes (Ore) 2103 Desiree Pl, Lebanon OR 97355 **Chapl Samar Albany Gnrl Hosp Albany OR 2005-** B Oregon City OR 7/3/1971 s Lawrence James Sedlacek & Janice Charlene. BA U of Portland 1993; MDiv Epis TS of The SW 2002. D 6/19/2002 P 12/28/2002 Bp Robert Louis Ladehoff. m 4/20/1996 Carol Westerberg. COM Dio Oregon Portland OR 2003-2008; Asst The Epis Ch Of The Gd Samar Corvallis OR 2002-2005. Bd Cert Chapl Assn of Profsnl Chapl 2010. wsedlacek@samhealth.org

SEDWICK, Katherine Langlitz (Minn) 5128 40th Avenue South, Minneapolis MN 55417 **S Lk's Ch Minneapolis MN 2006-** B St Louis MO 8/1/1961 d E(ldred) Langlitz & Ann. BA U of Washington 1998; MDiv Seattle U IETS 2002. D 6/28/2003 P 1/17/2004 Bp Sanford Zangwill Kaye Hampton. m 4/14/1984 John Michael Sedwick c 2. Trin Par Seattle WA 2003-2006. "Reporting on AAC in Plano," *The Voice*, Dio Olympia, 2003. ksedwick@aol.com

SEEBECK, William Bernard (NY) 91 Wolfpit Rd, Wilton CT 06897 **D Trin S Paul's Epis New Rochelle NY 1990-** B San Francisco CA 3/4/1950 s John William Seebeck & Margaret Mary. Manhattan Coll 1970; Ford 1972. D 6/29/1990 Bp Richard Frank Grein. m 10/5/1985 Joan Elizabeth Howard c 2. NAAD.

SEEBER, Laurian (Vt) 47 Shadow Lang Berlin, Barre VT 05641 B Cambridge MA 5/25/1938 d Robert Rex Seeber & Dorothea. BA U of Kansas 1959; MA U NC 1963; PhD U NC 1973; MA EDS 1978. D 11/16/1992 P 6/13/1993 Bp Daniel Lee Swenson. Asst to the R Chr Ch Montpelier VT 2000-2009; Pstr Assoc S Ptr's Ch Port Chester NY 1999-2000; Pstr Assoc S Barn Ch Ardsley NY 1996-1998; Loc P S Paul's Ch Canaan VT 1993-1996. srl@pshift.com

S

SEEFELDT, Scott Allen (Mil) 111 6th St, Baraboo WI 53913 **R Trin Ch Baraboo WI 2009-** B Wausau WI 1/6/1975 s Charles August Seefeldt & Ann Cynthia. BD U Of Wisconsin Madison WI 1999; MDiv Nash 2007. D 6/2/2007 P 12/8/2007 Bp Steven Andrew Miller. m 11/13/1999 Stephanie L Stephanie Martens c 4. Asst S Mich's Epis Ch Racine WI 2007-2009. skotallen@yahoo.com

SEEGER, Elisabeth Ann (Oly) 4467 S. 172nd St., SeaTac WA 98188 **R S Eliz's Ch Burien WA 2005-** B Buffalo NY 11/3/1945 d Willard Arthur Seeger & Patricia. BA U of Washington 1971; MDiv CDSP 1991. D 6/18/1991 P 2/1/1992 Bp Vincent Waydell Warner. Int Chr Epis Ch Puyallup WA 2005; R St Ptr's Epis Par Seattle WA 2002-2005; R S Paul's Epis Ch Sacramento CA 1994-2002; Vic H Fam of Jesus Epis Ch Tacoma WA 1992-1993; Assoc S Paul Epis Ch Bellingham WA 1991. Celtic Cross Soc. tikipaulatoo@msn.com

SEEGER, Sue Fisher (Mass) 28 Seagrave Rd, Cambridge MA 02140 **D S Jn's Ch Charlestown (Boston) Charlestown MA 2007-** B Natick MA 7/4/1939 BA Mid 1961; EdM Harv 1987; Massachusetts Diac Formation Prog 2005. D 6/3/2006 Bp M(arvil) Thomas Shaw III. D Chr Ch Cambridge Cambridge MA 2006-2007. fisherseeger@aol.com

SEELEY JR, Walter Duane (Wyo) 2024 Rolling Hills Road, Kemmerer WY 83101 **Dio Wyoming Casper WY 2010-; D/Cn 9 P S Jas Ch Kemmerer WY 2000-** B Charleston SC 11/7/1955 s Walter Duane Seeley & Alma Jean. BS U of Wyoming 1981. D 5/16/2000 P 12/6/2000 Bp Bruce Edward Caldwell. m 8/6/1977 Janet Lynne Pauli. seeley@hamsfork.net

SEELYE FOREST, Elizabeth Jane (Mich) 14191 Ivanhoe Dr Apt 3, Sterling Heights MI 48312 **D S Steph's Ch Troy MI 2001-** B 5/16/1948 D 6/20/2001 Bp Wendell Nathaniel Gibbs Jr. m 5/20/2001 Raymond Forest c 1.

SEFCHICK, Frank Stephen (Be) 1498 Quakake Rd, Weatherly PA 18255 B Chester PA 8/6/1949 s Frank S Sefchick & Justine A. BS Tem 1973; PharmD Broadmore U 2001. D 9/21/1994 P 9/19/1995 Bp James Michael Mark Dyer. c 2. S Mart-In-The-Fields Mtn Top PA 2003-2007. revsefc@pa.metrocast.net

SEGAL, D(anna) Joy (Pa) 916 South Swanson Street, Philadelphia PA 19147 **R Gloria Dei Ch Philadelphia PA 2006-** B Peru IN 12/14/1949 d Daniel John Welty & Erlene. BA Tem 1998; MDiv GTS 2001. D 6/23/2001 Bp Charles Bennison P 6/1/2002 Bp Charles Ellsworth Bennison Jr. m 9/11/1982 Alan Jacob Segal. Mem of Stndg Com Dio Pennsylvania Philadelphia PA 2007-2011; Dn of Southwark Dnry Dio Pennsylvania Philadelphia PA 2007-2010; R Trin Ch Buckingham PA 2003-2006; Asst R Ch Of The Mssh Lower Gwynedd PA 2001-2003. jsegal1214@aol.com

SEGER, David Lloyd (NI) 13259 Hisega Dr, Rapid City SD 57702 B Mason City IA 4/28/1938 s Joe EW Seger & Beulah Clara. BA U of Iowa 1960; MDiv Nash 1972; Med LSU 1983. D 8/8/1971 P 9/21/1972 Bp Walter H Jones. m 2/11/1961 Nancy Roberts c 3. Cn to theOrdinary Dio Nthrn Indiana So Bend IN 1991-2006; Dir of Admssns Nash Nashotah WI 1987-1991; Asst Dir - CDO Epis Ch Cntr New York NY 1984-1987; Exec & Secy Off New York NY 1983-1984; Asst P S Lk's Ch Baton Rouge LA 1976-1983; Chair of Dept. of Rel Epis HS Baton Rouge LA 1974-1983; P-in-c H Trin Epis Ch Luverne MN 1972-1974. CODE 1991-2007. dseger7@juno.com

SEGERBRECHT, Stephen Louis (Kan) 1715 Prestwick Dr, Lawrence KS 66047 **D Trin Ch Lawr KS 2006-** B 9/26/1955 s Brian Segerbrecht & Margaret. BA U of Kansas 1977; MD U of Kansas 1980. D 6/3/2006 Bp Dean Elliott Wolfe. m 5/3/1980 Lynn Segerbrecht c 2. loaseg@pol.net

SEIBEL, James William (O) 126 State St, Seneca Falls NY 13148 B Sandusky OH 9/30/1931 s George William Seibel & Rose Kathryn. BA Kent St U 1953; STB Ya Berk 1956; PhD Ya 1963. D 6/1/1956 Bp Nelson Marigold Burroughs P 1/1/1957 Bp Beverley D Tucker. R Ascen Ch New Haven CT 1961-1967; Asst Chr Ch New Haven CT 1959-1961; Asst S Andr's Ch Meriden CT 1956-1959.

SEIBERT, Joanna Johnson (Ark) 27 River Ridge Rd, Little Rock AR 72227 B Richmond VA 4/5/1942 d James Howe Johnson & Florence Elizabeth. BA U NC 1964; MD U of Tennessee 1968; Ia U of Iowa 1973. D 4/28/2001 Bp Larry Earl Maze. m 10/18/1969 Robert Walstrom Seibert c 3. D Trin Cathd Little Rock AR 2007-2011; D S Marg's Epis Ch Little Rock AR 2001-2005. Ed, "Surrounded By A Cloud Of Witnesses," Rose Pub, 1994; Auth, "Var arts, LivCh, Workbook Of ECW Of Arkansas," *And Arkansas Epis*, 1988. Recognition Of The Diac Mnstry In The Tradtiion Of St Steph Naad 2003. jjs@george.ach.uams.edu

SEIBERT, Thomas E (Colo) 145 W 5th St, Delta CO 81416 **R S Lk's Epis Ch Delta CO 2009-** B Chicago IL 5/2/1949 s John Henry Seibert & Mary Jane. St. Jn'Sem 1975; BA Psychol Marq Milwaukee 2006; Angl Stds SWTS 2008. Rec from Roman Catholic 5/1/2009 Bp Victor Alfonso Scantlebury. m 6/28/2006 Andrea Potaczek. biscuit5249@hotmail.com

SEIDLE, Betty Elaine (Me) Po Box 197, East Machias ME 04630 **D S Aidans Ch Machias ME 2004-** B Philadelphia PA 12/7/1938 d Charles Stanley Seidle & Hattie Elizabeth. BS Tem; MA Adams St Coll 1970. D 6/19/2004 Bp Chilton Abbie Richardson Knudsen. keyboard@midmaine.com

SEIDMAN, Kimberly Anne (NwT) 126 N Payne St, Alexandria VA 22314 **Vic Ch Of The H Comf Broomfield CO 2010-** B Austin, TX 7/4/1977 d Harry Jack Seidman & Sheila Ann. BA Abilene Chr U 1999; MDiv Emory U 2003; Dipl. in Angl Stds VTS 2008. D 1/8/2008 P 6/26/2008 Bp C(harles) Wallis Ohl. m 7/5/2003 Raj Chitikila. Cler Res Chr Ch Alexandria VA 2008-2010. seidwoman@yahoo.com

SEIFERT, Cynthia Lynne (Tenn) 5041 English Village Dr, Nashville TN 37211 **Asst Ch Of The Gd Shpd Brentwood TN 2007-** B Decatur GA 5/12/1971 d Clarence Fenton Seeliger & Gwendolyn Grace. BA Presb Coll Clinton SC 1993; MDiv TESM 2004. D 6/5/2005 P 4/29/2006 Bp Bertram Nelson Herlong. c 1. S Phil's Ch Nashville TN 2006-2007; Asst to R/Campus Min S Paul's Epis Ch Murfreesboro TN 2005-2006; S Barth's Ch Bristol TN 1996-2003. cynthiaseifert@gmail.com

SEIFERT, Robert Joseph (ECR) 161 Palo Verde Ter, Santa Cruz CA 95060 **Admin Vic S Lk's Ch Jolon CA 2009-** B Paris AR 8/29/1941 s Leonard Theodore Seifert & Mary Magdalena. BA San Jose St U 1967; MA San Jose St U 1968; BTS California Sch for Deacons 1982; Fllshp Coll of Preachers 1995; STM Jesuit TS 1996; Fllshp S Vladimir Orth Sem Crestwood NY 1997. D 9/23/1984 Bp Charles Shannon Mallory. c 2. S Tim's Epis Ch Mtn View CA 1997-2004; D S Lk's Ch Los Gatos CA 1992-1997; D S Geo's Ch Salinas CA 1989-1992; D S Lk's Ch Hollister CA 1988-1989; D Ch Of S Jn The Bapt Aptos CA 1985-1988; Dio El Camino Real Monterey CA 1985-1988; D S Jas' Ch Monterey CA 1984-1985; S Jn's Chap Monterey CA 1984-1985. robseifert@sbcglobal.net

SEILER, Jeffrey Hamilton (Va) 4003 St Erics Turn, Williamsburg VA 23185 B Boston MA 8/17/1950 s Peter Andrew Seiler & Marilyn Jane Twombly. AA Mitchell Coll 1971; BA Framingham St Coll 1979; MDiv Gordon-Conwell TS 1982; CAS VTS 1986. D 6/4/1986 Bp John Bowen Coburn P 10/4/1986 Bp Peter James Lee. m 6/18/1977 Jennie Delzell c 4. Chapl US Navy Off Of Bsh For ArmdF New York NY 1989-2011; Assoc R S Marg's Ch Woodbridge VA 1986-1989. AAPC 1981-1985; APA 2007; ACPE 1981. seiler1@cox.net

SEILER, Michael Scott (Los) 1031 Bienveneda Ave, Pacific Palisades CA 90272 **Assoc R The Par Of S Matt Pacific Palisades CA 2001-** B Redwood City California 5/23/1961 s Fred & Lorraine. BA Pepperdine U 1982; Cert Ya Berk 1997; MDiv Ya 1997. D 6/14/1997 P 1/11/1998 Bp Frederick Houk Borsch. Cur S Mk's Ch Philadelphia PA 1997-2001; All SS Par Beverly Hills CA 1991-1994. Affirming Catholicism 1999; Fllshp of S Jn 1997. mseiler@aya.yale.edu

SEILER, Robert Stuart (Va) 4810 Stuart Ave, Richmond VA 23226 B San Francisco CA 7/30/1919 s Charles Edwin Seiler & Louise. VTS 1952. D 6/6/1952 Bp Frederick D Goodwin P 6/1/1953 Bp Robert Fisher Gibson Jr. m 10/11/1952 Margaret Gordon c 3. Shepherds Cntr Richmond VA 1984; Dio Virginia Richmond VA 1983-1984.

SEILER-DUBAY, Noreen (WA) 5031 Laguna Rd, College Park MD 20740 **Supply P Dio Washington Washington DC 2011-; Transition Com in Bp's Election Dio Washington Washington DC 2010-** B New York NY 4/28/1956 d Carl Edward Buckley & Regis Marie. BA Villanova U 1978; MA CUA 1980; MDiv VTS 1990. D 6/9/1990 P 12/18/1990 Bp Ronald Hayward Haines. m 5/25/2002 Charles F Dubay c 2. R S Matt's Epis Ch Hyattsville MD 2001-2011; Int Chr Epis Ch Clinton MD 1999-2001; Int Nativ Epis Ch Temple Hills MD 1998-1999; Long Term Supply P Dio Washington Washington DC 1996-1998; Int S Dav's Par Washington DC 1995-1996; Assoc R Chr Ch Capitol Hill Washington DC 1990-1995. ACPE 1989-1993. revnoreen@aol.com

SEILS, Donald Davis (Colo) 5749 N Stetson Ct, Parker CO 80134 B Rochester NY 4/16/1948 s Edward Carl Seils & Arlene Winifred. BA U Of Houston 1974; MDiv VTS 1979. D 7/10/1979 P 8/6/1980 Bp Roger Howard Cilley. m 4/25/1987 Allison Kletke c 2. S Phil In-The-Field Sedalia CO 2010; Calv Ch Golden CO 2004; P-in-c Ch Of The H Sprt Cherry Hills Vill CO 2000; Ch Of The Trsfg Evergreen CO 1997-1998; Vic S Eliz's Epis Ch Brighton CO 1990-1996; S Andr's Epis Ch Ft Lupton CO 1990-1993; R S Matt's Parker CO 1989-1990; Asst R S Paul's Ch Leavenworth KS 1986-1989; R H Trin Carrizo Sprg TX 1984-1986; Gr Epis Ch Hutchinson KS 1980-1982; St Jas Ch Houston TX 1979-1980; St Matthews Ch Beaumont TX 1979-1980.

SEIPEL, James Russell (Los) 25769 Player Dr, Valencia CA 91355 **Assigned P Chr The King A Jubilee Mnstry Palmdale CA 2006-** B Buffalo NY 6/25/1942 s Edson W Seipel & Frances A. BA San Diego St Coll 1965; STB GTS 1968. D 9/7/1968 P 3/9/1969 Bp Francis E I Bloy. m 11/15/1986 Elizabeth Curwen c 2. Int S Paul's Par Lancaster CA 1993-1996; S Steph's Epis Ch Santa Clarita CA 1974-1984; Cur S Cross By-The-Sea Ch Hermosa Bch CA 1968-1974. mail4mrs@yahoo.com

SEIPP, Vivian (NY) 39 Cumberland Rd, Fishkill NY 12524 **D Trin Ch Fishkill NY 1992-** B New York NY 2/20/1928 d Peter Robertin & Ursula. AAS Dutchess Cmnty Coll Poughkeepsie NY 1985; EFM STUSo 1991. D 5/30/1992 Bp Richard Frank Grein. m 5/4/1952 Charles John Seipp c 4.

SEITER, Claudia D (U) 1100 S 2000 E Apt C323, Clearfield UT 84015 **P-in-c S Mich's Ch Brigham City UT 2007-; Strategic Plnng Com Dio Utah Salt Lake City UT 2003-** B Colorado Springs CO 5/16/1952 d Robert Casel Collier & Eloie Dare. BS/MED Weber St U 1980; Mcs Indiana U 1986; MA Harv 1991. D 11/30/2000 P 6/24/2001 Bp Carolyn Tanner Irish. m 6/24/1988 David

Michael Seiter. D Ch Of The Gd Shpd Ogden UT 2000-2001. davidseiter3026@msn.com

SEITZ, Christopher R (Dal) Wycliffe College, University Of Toronto, 5 Hoskin Avenue, Toronto ON M5S 1H7 Canada **Wycliffe Coll 2009-; P Assoc Ch Of The Incarn Dallas TX 2008-; Cn Theol Dio Dallas Dallas TX 2008-** B Blowing Rock NC 5/22/1954 s Thomas Comstock Seitz & Mary Janet. BA U NC 1976; MA VTS 1979; STM Yale DS 1981; MA Ya 1982; PhD Ya 1986. D 6/22/1980 P 1/1/1981 Bp William Hopkins Folwell. Com Dio Connecticut Hartford CT 1992-1993; Asst S Paul's Ch Fairfield CT 1991-1992; Assoc Ch Of Our Sav Jenkintown PA 1985-1986; Asst Chr Ch New Haven CT 1981-1984. Auth, "Prophecy and Hermeneutics," Baker Acad, 2007; Auth, "Figured Out," Westminster Jn Knox, 2001; Auth, "Seven Lasting Words," Westminster Jn Knox, 2001; Auth, "Word Without End," Eerdmans, 1998; Auth, "Isaiah 1-39," Westminster Jn Knox, 1993; Auth, "Zion'S Final Destiny," Fortress, 1991; Auth, "Theol In Conflict," Walter de Gruyter, 1989. Amer Theol Soc; Angl Comm Inst; SBL; Soc of OT Study. ECF Fell ECF 1983. christopher.seitz@utoronto.ca

SEITZ, Mark Ellis (WVa) Box 508, Wheeling WV 26003 **R S Matt's Ch Wheeling WV 1995-** B Huntington WV 10/29/1956 s Thomas Comstock Seitz & Mary Janet. BA U NC 1978; MDiv Epis TS of The SW 1983. D 6/11/1983 P 2/1/1984 Bp Emerson Paul Haynes. m 1/12/1985 Kathleen Bradley c 2. R S Andr's Ch Oak Hill WV 1990-1995; Mssnr The New River Epis Mnstry Hansford WV 1990-1995; Vic S Paul's Epis Ch Woodville TX 1986-1990; Asst Ch Of The Gd Shpd Tomball TX 1985-1986; Cur S Andr's Epis Ch Sprg Hill FL 1983-1985. mseitz@stmatts.com

SEITZ, Philip Allan (EMich) 3003 Mill Station Road, Hale MI 48739 **Stndg Com Dio Estrn Michigan Saginaw MI 2008-; Chair, Mssn T/F Dio Estrn Michigan Saginaw MI 2004-; GC Dep Dio Estrn Michigan Saginaw MI 2004-; R Trin Epis Ch W Branch MI 2003-** B Lima OH 8/21/1939 s Carl Nelson Seitz & Miriam Joyce. BS OH SU 1962; MS MI SU 1978; CTh SWTS 2002. D 11/2/2002 P 5/24/2003 Bp Edwin Max Leidel Jr. m 11/4/1960 Phyllis Irene Terrill c 3. R Gr Epis Ch Standish MI 2002-2007. seitzp@centurytel.net

SEITZ JR, Thomas Comstock (CFla) 221 S 4th St, Lake Wales FL 33853 **R The Epis Ch Of The Gd Shpd Lake Wales FL 1997-** B Blowing Rock NC 7/27/1952 s Thomas Comstock Seitz & Mary Janet. BA U NC 1974; MDiv VTS 1977. D 6/8/1977 P 6/15/1978 Bp Robert Poland Atkinson. m 5/20/1978 Anna P Page c 3. R S Paul's Epis Ch Lansing MI 1992-1997; Dn Monongahela Deanry Dio W Virginia Charleston WV 1984-1992; R Chr Ch Clarksburg WV 1981-1992; Ch Of The Gd Shpd Burke VA 1978-1981; S Steph's Epis Ch Beckley WV 1977-1978. tcseitzjr@gmail.com

SEITZ SR, Thomas Comstock (CFla) 2565 Salzburg Loop, Winter Haven FL 33884 B Springfield OH 3/5/1928 s William Clinton Seitz & Florence. BA Ken 1949; MDiv Bex 1951; MA Wstrn Carolina U 1971. D 6/27/1951 P 6/4/1952 Bp Matthew G Henry. m 6/16/1951 Janet Reese c 4. Stndg Com Dio W Virginia Charleston WV 1986-1989; R S Jn's Ch Huntington WV 1981-1993; S Mk's Cathd Shreveport LA 1978-1981; S Paul's Sch Clearwater FL 1976-1978; Chr Sch Arden NC 1967-1976; R Chr Ch Fairmont WV 1959-1967; Exec Coun Dio W Virginia Charleston WV 1957-1962; Dn Kanawha Convoc Dio W Virginia Charleston WV 1957-1958; R S Ptr's Ch Huntington WV 1955-1958; P-in-c S Lk's Ch Boone NC 1951-1955; P-in-c S Mary Of The Hills Epis Par Blowing Rock NC 1951-1955. tseitzsr@aol.com

SELDEN, Elizabeth Ann (Minn) 6212 Crest Ln, MN Edina 55436 B 7/5/1920 BA Mills Coll 1941. D 10/23/1978 Bp Robert Marshall Anderson. D/Asst S Steph The Mtyr Ch Minneapolis MN 1978-1988.

SELES, Deborah Galante (Ida) 1172 Woodriver Dr, Twin Falls ID 83301 **R Ch Of The Ascen Twin Falls ID 2010-; Dioc Coun, Cler at Lg Dio Idaho Boise ID 2010-; Mem, Paradise Point Com Dio Idaho Boise ID 2010-; S Phil's Epis Palatine IL 2009-** B Chicago IL 11/3/1951 d Sebastian Galante & Donna. BA Quincy Coll 1974; MSW U IL 1979; MDiv SWTS 2002. D 6/15/2002 P 12/21/2002 Bp William Dailey Persell. Int S Richard's Ch Chicago IL 2009-2010; Int S Phil's Epis Palatine IL 2008-2009; P-in-c S Hilary's Ch Prospect Hts IL 2008; Mem, Bp's T/F on Tentmaker Mnstrs Dio Chicago Chicago IL 2007-2010; Chapl Bp Anderson Hse Chicago IL 2006-2010; Long Term Supply Ch Of S Columba Of Iona Hanover Pk IL 2006-2007; L'‘Arche Chicago Cicero IL 2002-2005; Assoc S Chris's Epis Ch Oak Pk IL 2002. Auth, "2 Reasons," *101 Reasons To Be Epis*, Morehouse Pub, 2003; Auth, "The Risk Of Meeting Chr," *Living Pulpit*, 2002. W.T. Tayolr Stephenson Awd In Theol Seabury 2001; H.N. Moss Bk Awd Seabury 2001. revdeb2002@cableone.net

SELF, Deborah Davis (SeFla) 1021 Corallita Ct, Wellington FL 33414 **Chap Of S Andr Boca Raton FL 2010-** B Ann Arbor MI 8/31/1953 D 4/17/2004 P 11/20/2004 Bp Leopold Frade. m 4/3/1992 David L Self c 2. S Greg's Ch Boca Raton FL 2004-2010. dself@aol.com

SELFE-VERRONE, A(nne) (NY) Chapel of St. Francis, 3621 Brunswick Ave., Los Angeles CA 90039 **Dio Los Angeles Los Angeles CA 2007-; Supply P Epis Chap Of S Fran Los Angeles CA 2007-** B Lock Haven PA 10/22/1960 d John Walter Selfe & Catherine Ann. BA Gallaudet U; Spec Stds GTS 2004. D 6/12/2004 Bp Henry Nutt Parsley Jr P 12/18/2004 Bp Catherine Scimeca Roskam. m 9/16/2006 Alexander Joseph Verrone. Vic S Ann's Ch For The Deaf New York NY 2003-2007. christineverrone@yahoo.com

SELL, James William Henry (SVa) 239 Duke St Unit 207, Norfolk VA 23510 B Charleston,WV 10/1/1942 s James Nathaniel Sell & Helen Kathryn. BA W Virginia U 1964; MDiv VTS 1969. D 6/11/1969 P 12/19/1969 Bp Wilburn Camrock Campbell. m 8/31/1968 Ellen Dorothy Major. Int Trin Ch On The Green New Haven CT 2009-2011; Int Trin Ch Princeton NJ 2007-2009; Int St Martins-In-The-Field Ch Severna Pk MD 2006; R Chr and S Lk's Epis Ch Norfolk VA 1990-2005; Archd Dio Newark Newark NJ 1985-1990; R S Mary's Ch Sparta NJ 1980-1985; Vts Alum VTS Alexandria VA 1980-1983; S Jas' Epis Ch Lewisburg WV 1978-1980; S Thos Epis Ch White Sulphur Sprg WV 1972-1977; Vic Chr Memi Ch Williamstown WV 1970-1972; Vic S Martins-In-Fields Summersville WV 1969-1970. Auth, "Var arts". sell.jim@gmail.com

SELLERS, Robert Clayton (Tex) 1401 S PALMETTO AVE, APT 207, DAYTONA BEACH FL 32114 B Fayetteville AR 2/24/1937 s Robert Clayton Sellers & Mary Virginia. BA Ya 1958; MA Oxf 1962; MDiv CDSP 1963; Oxf 1998. D 6/19/1963 P 5/5/1964 Bp John E Hines. c 2. R Ch Of St Philips 0 1998-2002; R S Steph's Ch Liberty TX 1990-1997; R S Mk's Epis Ch Richmond TX 1981-1990; Hd of Hist Dept S Thos Ch Houston TX 1970-1979; R S Paul's Ch Kilgore TX 1965-1969; Asst S Jn The Div Houston TX 1963-1965. Auth, "Revs," *FIDES ET HISTORIA*. robertclaytonsellers@msn.com

SELLERY, David (LI) 290 Harbor Rd, Cold Spring Harbor NY 11724 **S Ptr's by-the-Sea Epis Ch Bay Shore NY 2007-** B Norwood MA 3/6/1966 s Stephen Edward Sellery & Priscilla Barton. BA U of Connecticut 1989; MDiv GTS 1992. D 6/13/1992 Bp Arthur Edward Walmsley P 1/9/1993 Bp Robert Gould Tharp. m 1/4/2003 Jane M Muir c 4. Asst S Jn's Ch Cold Sprg Harbor NY 2005-2007; Asst Chr Ch Bronxville NY 2001-2005; P-in-c S Barth's Ch In The Highland White Plains NY 1999-2001; Ecum Cmsn Dio New York New York City NY 1996-2002; Cur S Thos Ch New York NY 1995-1999; Ecum Off Dio E Tennessee Knoxville TN 1994-1995; Cur S Mart Of Tours Epis Ch Chattanooga TN 1993-1994; Cur S Paul's Epis Ch Kingsport TN 1992-1993. Auth, "The Challenge Of Evang," *Acts 29*, 1992; Auth, "The Hist Episcopate Obstacle & Opportunity For Ch Unity? 92," *Ecum Trends*, 1992; Auth, "Triadic Vs. Trinitarian: A Battle For The Gospel," *The Angl*, 1992. The Most Venerable Ord Of S Jn Of Jerusalem - Sub-Chapl 1996. Ord Of Civil Merit Hse Of Savoy 1998. frsellery@stpetersbayshore.org

SELL-LEE, William Merle (WA) 377 Osprey Glen Rd, Sequim WA 98382 B Santa Maria CA 4/30/1936 s Merle Jackson Lee & Vivian Annetta. Indep study CDSP; BS California St Polytechnic U 1962. D 2/26/1974 Bp C Kilmer Myers P 5/21/1975 Bp George Richard Millard. m 5/1/1979 Sandra Sell c 4. R S Lk's Ch Sequim WA 1989-1998; Int S Mich And All Ang Ch Issaquah WA 1987-1989; Int Ch Of The Epiph Seattle WA 1985-1986; Int Trin Par Seattle WA 1983-1984; Asstg P, Int R S Barn Epis Ch Bainbridge Island WA 1979-1983; Asstg D, P The Epis Ch In Almaden San Jose CA 1974-1979. bselllee@olypen.com

SELLS, Jeffery Edward (Oly) Po Box 3090, Salt Lake City UT 84110 B Pueblo CO 11/1/1945 s Bob Edward Sells & Pauline. BS U of New Mex 1967; MDiv CDSP 1972. D 8/31/1972 P 8/1/1973 Bp Richard Mitchell Trelease Jr. m 1/21/1995 Patricia Sells c 2. The Ch Of S Dav Of Wales Shelton WA 2003-2009; Cathd Ch Of S Mk Salt Lake City UT 1997-2003; Dio Utah Salt Lake City UT 1997-2001; R S Steph's Baker City OR 1976-1982; Trin Epis Ch Reno NV 1975-1976. jsells@hcc.net

SELLS, Patricia (Oly) PO Box 356, Shelton WA 98584 **jubilee Off Dio Olympia Seattle WA 2011-** B 9/6/1949 D 6/14/2001 Bp Carolyn Tanner Irish. m 1/21/1995 Jeffery Edward Sells c 1. Dio Olympia Seattle WA 2010-2011; The Ch Of S Dav Of Wales Shelton WA 2008-2010; Cathd Ch Of S Mk Salt Lake City UT 1996-2003. psells@hctc.com

SELNICK, Thomas Conrad (O) Po Box 519, Gates Mills OH 44040 **R S Chris's By-The River Gates Mills OH 2003-** B Bay Village OH 9/7/1957 s William Blake Selnick & Barbara Jane. BA Jn Hopkins U 1979; MDiv EDS 1983; MS Case Wstrn Reserve U 1997. D 6/11/1983 P 12/1/1983 Bp William Grant Black. m 6/16/1984 Elizabeth A Eaton c 2. GC Dep Dio Ohio Cleveland OH 2009; Int R S Paul's Epis Ch Medina OH 2001-2003; R S Ptr's Ch Ashtabula OH 1990-1999; Organizing Pstr S Andr's Ch Pickerington OH 1987-1990; Asst R S Alb's Epis Ch Of Bexley Columbus OH 1983-1986. Auth, "Hosting A 12 Step Grp In Your Ch". cselnick@suite224.net

SELVAGE, Daniel Lee (CPa) 120 W Lamb St, Bellefonte PA 16823 **Chair, Dioc BEC Dio Cntrl Pennsylvania Harrisburg PA 2010-; Penn St U Dio Cntrl Pennsylvania Harrisburg PA 2009-; Mem, Dioc Liturg and Mus Cmsn Dio Cntrl Pennsylvania Harrisburg PA 1993-** B Philipsburg PA 11/11/1949 s William Barns Selvage & Morrell Levoy. BA Mansfield U of Pennsylvania 1972; MDiv GTS 1975. D 6/14/1975 P 12/20/1975 Bp Donald James Davis. Mem, Dioc COM Dio Cntrl Pennsylvania Harrisburg PA 1994-2010; R S Jn's Epis Ch Bellefonte PA 1991-2009; Archd Dio NW Pennsylvania Erie PA 1984-1990; Vic S Mary's Ch Erie PA 1979-1982; Vic Ch Of The H Cross No E PA 1975-1984. CBS 1982; NNECA 1994. Cn St.

Steph's Cathd, Harrisburg, PA 2008; Archd (honoris causa) Dio NW Pennsylvania 1990. danselvage2@comcast.net

SELVEY, Mark F (Neb) 285 S 208th St, Omaha NE 68022 **R S Aug's Epis Ch Elkhorn NE 2008-** B Columbus NE 3/2/1955 s Richard Selvey & Janet. AS Coll of S Mary 1977; BA Chadron St Coll 1995; MDiv Iliff TS 2006. D 5/18/2006 P 2/15/2007 Bp Joe Goodwin Burnett. m 12/31/1991 Jill Forrest Ament c 5. Cur S Martha's Epis Ch Papillion NE 2006-2008. mjselvey@cox.net

SELZER, David O (WNY) 4 Phylis St, Ottawa ON K2J 1V2 Canada **Archd Dio Ottawa 2010-** B Portsmouth VA 9/13/1951 s Christian William Selzer & Betty Jean. BA U of Kentucky 1972; MDiv Nash 1976. D 6/5/1976 P 6/8/1977 Bp David Reed. m 11/24/1985 Ann Miller c 2. Dio Ottawa 2008-2010; Prof Bex Columbus OH 2001-2009; R The Epis Ch Of The Gd Shpd Buffalo NY 1995-2008; Chapl U Epis Cntr Minneapolis MN 1984-1995; Assoc S Matt's Epis Ch Louisville KY 1976-1984. EPF 1989; Ord of S Helena, Assoc 1988. doselzer@gmail.com

SEMES, Robert Louis (Ore) 1998 Tolman Creek Rd, Ashland OR 97520 **P S Marg's Epis Ch Palm Desert CA 2011-** B Miami FL 1/20/1941 BA Belhaven Coll 1962; Nash 1965; MA U of Virginia 1968; Rutgers-The St U 1971; MDiv EDS 1976. D 6/12/1976 P 12/21/1976 Bp William Gillette Weinhauer. P Trin Epis Ch Ashland Ashland OR 2004-2005; P Ch Of The Adv Of Chr The King San Francisco CA 1992-1996; Dn - San Francisco Dnry Dio California San Francisco CA 1992-1993; Prof Epis Sch For Deacons Berkeley CA 1991-1995; Int S Jn's Epis Ch Oakland CA 1991-1992; Mem - Cmsn 2000 Dio California San Francisco CA 1990-1995; Assoc S Matt's Epis Ch San Mateo CA 1989-1991; Mem - Resolutns Com - Dioc Conv Dio California San Francisco CA 1987-1995; Asst S Fran' Epis Ch San Francisco CA 1987-1989; P Chr Ch Sausalito CA 1983-1985; P S Lk's Ch San Francisco CA 1981-1982; P Trin Ch San Francisco CA 1980-1981; R Ch Of The Epiph Newton NC 1977-1979; Asst S Thos Ch Mamaroneck NY 1976-1977. Auth, "Hawai'i's H War: Engl Bp Staley Amer Congregationalists and the Hawaiian Monarchs 1860-1870," The Hawaiian Journ of Hist, 2000; Auth, "What is a D in the Epis Ch?," The Sch for Deacons (Dio California), 1993; Auth, "Of These Stones: A Hist Sketch of the Ch of S Matt San Mateo California 1865-1990," St. Matt's Epis Ch San Mateo California, 1990; Auth, "A Hse of Pryr for All People: A Short Hist of St. Fran' Epis Ch San Francisco California," St. Fran' Epis Ch San Francisco California, 1987. Resrch Grant HSEC 1998. hhrls@att.net

SEMON, Kenneth JG (RG) 311 E. Palace Avenue, Santa Fe NM 87501 **Bd of Exam Chapl Dio The Rio Grande Albuquerque NM 2011-; Stndg Com Dio The Rio Grande Albuquerque NM 2011-; R Ch of the H Faith Santa Fe NM 2007-** B Milwaukee WI 9/18/1945 s Milton K Semon & Joyce K. BA U of Wisconsin 1968; PhD U of Washington 1971; MDiv SWTS 1980. D 6/14/1980 Bp Quintin Ebenezer Primo Jr P 12/13/1980 Bp James Winchester Montgomery. m 12/7/1973 Caroline C Chinn c 3. Chr Ch Of The Ascen Paradise Vlly AZ 2003-2007; Stndg Com Dio Missouri S Louis MO 1994-1997; Com Dio Missouri S Louis MO 1992-1993; R S Mich & S Geo Clayton MO 1991-1997; Bd Dir Epis Chars Dio The Rio Grande Albuquerque NM 1987-1991; R S Fran On The Hill El Paso TX 1985-1991; Hospice Bd Dio Wstrn Michigan Kalamazoo MI 1982-1985; R St Jn's Epis Ch of Sturgis Sturgis MI 1981-1985; Cur The Ch Of The H Sprt Lake Forest IL 1980-1981. "Var arts & Revs In Living Ch Rg Epis Other Journ". Engl Spkng Un 2000-2004; OSB, Oblate 1989. kjsemon@gmail.com

SEMON-SCOTT, Deborah Anne (Mich) 3 N Broad St, Hillsdale MI 49242 **S Chris-S Paul Epis Ch Detroit MI 2009-** B Grand Rapids MI 12/25/1952 d Donald Glenn Semon & Virginia Margaret. AA Grand Rapids Cmnty Coll 1973; BS Grand Vlly St U 1975; MDiv SWTS 1979. D 6/16/1979 P 4/1/1980 Bp H Coleman McGehee Jr. m 8/9/1980 Leonard Harry Scott c 3. S Ptr's Epis Ch Hillsdale MI 2001-2006; S Mk's Ch Coldwater MI 1999-2001.

SENECHAL, Roger Edward (WMass) 7601 Harper Road, Joelton TN 37080 **P Assoc S Geo's Ch Nashville TN 2007-** B Leominster MA 4/11/1944 s Edward Bernard Senechal & Simonne Lorette. BA Marist Coll 1967; MDiv Weston Jesuit TS 1974; ThM Harvard DS 1980. Rec from Roman Catholic 7/1/1984 as Deacon Bp Philip Alan Smith. m 9/4/1978 Diana Sullivan c 1. R S Thos Epis Ch Auburn MA 1988-2007; Assoc Chr Ch Exeter NH 1985-1988. Fllshp of the Way of the Cross 1991. jrsenechal@gmail.com

SENETTE JR, D(ouglas) John (La) 9839 Royal Street, St. Francisville LA 70775 B Franklin LA 6/14/1945 s Douglas John Senette & Shirley Elizabeth. BA U So 1967; MA Tul 1968; MDiv Nash 1971; PhD Tul 1991. D 6/21/1971 P 1/6/1972 Bp Iveson Batchelor Noland. m 7/6/2002 Felicia Guerra c 3. Chapl Bd Trst The CPG New York NY 2003-2009; Assoc All SS Prot Epis Ch Ft Lauderdale FL 2000-2002; Dn Chr Ch Cathd New Orleans LA 1991-2000; Assoc S Lk's Ch Baton Rouge LA 1986-1991; P-in-c S Andr's Paradis Luling LA 1984-1986; R Gr Ch Of W Feliciana S Francisville LA 1976-1984; Asst S Paul's Ch Albany GA 1972-1975; Cur Chap Of The H Comf New Orleans LA 1971-1972. Phi Beta Kappa U So 1966. jjohnsenette@yahoo.com

SENEY, Robert William (Miss) 892 2nd Ave, Mancos CO 81328 **P-in-c S Paul's Ch Mancos CO 2009-** B Springfield MO 5/17/1938 s Alvia Paul Seney & I(nez). BA U of Missouri 1960; MDiv Nash 1965; Cert Texas Tech U 1974; EdD U of Houston 1987. D 6/20/1965 P 12/21/1965 Bp Chilton Powell. m 6/1/1972 Judith A Stockton c 1. Visting P Ch Of The Ascen Brooksville MS 1996-2006; Vstng P Ch Of The Nativ Macon MS 1996-2006; Headmaster Bp Noland Epis Day Sch Lake Chas LA 1973-1976; Headmaster Epis Ch Of The Gd Shpd Lake Chas LA 1973-1976; Headmaster S Chris's Epis Ch Lubbock TX 1970-1973; Cur Gr Epis Ch Ponca City OK 1968-1970; Cur S Paul's Ch Clinton OK 1965-1966. Auth, "Plnng the Lrng Environ," *Methods and Materials for Tchg the Gifted (2001)*, Prufrock Press, 2005; Auth, "The Process Skills and the Gifted Chld," *Methods and Materials for Tchg the Gifted (2001)*", Prufrock Press, 2005; "Var arts in educational Journ and mag"; "Revs for Young Readers," *Columbus Comercial Dispatch*, Comercial Dispatch; "Books, Books, More Books," *Tchg for High Potential*, Natl Assn for Gifted Chld; "About Books," *Twice Exceptional Nwsltr*, 2ENewsletter. Colorado Assn for Gifted and Talented 2006; MS Assn for Gifted Chld 1992-2006; Natl Assn of Gifted Chld 1982; Natl Conf for Gvnr's Schools 1992; Phi Delta Kappa; Texas Assn for Gifted Chld 1978; Wrld Coun for Gifted Chld 1985. Prof Emer Mississippi U for Wmn 2006; Jim Brey and Lil Press Awd for Life Time Contribution to Gift Natl Conf of Gvnr's Schools 2006; Pres's Awd Texas Assn for Gifted and Talented 1996; Who's Who in Amer Educ; Heritage Who's Who. bseney@muw.edu

SENUTA, Lisa Ann (Kan) 4301 Acropolis Ct Apt D, Austin TX 78759 **Assoc S Mich And All Ang Ch Mssn KS 2003-** B Kansas City MO 11/23/1972 d Glen Jr Lester Burrington & Carol Ann. MDiv Epis TS of The SW; BA K SU. D 3/17/2001 P 10/16/2001 Bp William Edward Smalley. m 7/31/1994 Chad K Senuta. Cur S Thos The Apos Ch Overland Pk KS 2001-2003.

SERACUSE, Linda Kay (Tex) Po Box 559, Conroe TX 77305 B Denver CO 1/29/1945 d Frebert Otto Wangerin & Addie Mae. BA Colorado Coll 1966; Cert Epis TS of The SW 1991; MDiv Iliff TS 1991. D 6/15/1991 P 1/25/1992 Bp William Jerry Winterrowd. m 5/23/1981 Jerome Seracuse c 3. S Jas The Apos Epis Ch Conroe TX 2001-2009; Gr And S Steph's Epis Ch Colorado Sprg CO 1992-2001; Dir CE Consult S Paul's Epis Ch Lakewood CO 1991-2001. lindaseracuse@gmail.com

SERAS, Barbara J (Md) 67 River Bend Park, Lancaster PA 17602 **R S Mary's Epis Ch Woodlawn Baltimore MD 2005-; Prov III Chester Sprg PA 2004-** B Carlisle PA 4/18/1951 d Peter William Seras & Anna Eleanor. BA Chatham Coll 1973; JD Penn St Dickinson Sch of Law 1978; MDiv SWTS 1992. D 6/13/1992 P 5/19/1993 Bp A(lbert) Theodore Eastman. R S Mk's Ch Highland MD 1997-2002; Asst to R Chr Ch Columbia MD 1992-1997. Ord of S Helena. Fell Coll of Preachers Washington DC 2002. maxthecat1@earthlink.net

SERDAHL, Dennis Lee (Ark) 831 Northpointe Dr, Mountain Home AR 72653 B Des Moines IA 7/8/1933 s Emil Adolph Serdahl & Frances. BS U IL 1956; MDiv Ken 1964. D 6/13/1964 P 12/1/1964 Bp Nelson Marigold Burroughs. m 10/19/1958 Margot Horn c 3. Vic S Andr's Ch Mtn Hm AR 1992-1998; Cn Mssnr Dio The Rio Grande Albuquerque NM 1991-1992; Ch Of The Redeem Pendleton OR 1987-1990; S Paul's Epis Ch Salinas CA 1976-1987; Mem, Exec Coun Dio El Camino Real Monterey CA 1975-1976; Par Contracts Consult Dio El Camino Real Monterey CA 1969-1974; Dn, Deanry VII Dio El Camino Real Monterey CA 1966-1976; Cur S Jn's Ch Youngstown OH 1964-1966. dennis33@suddenlink.net

SERFES, Patricia May (Me) 2524 Casa Dr, New Port Richey FL 34655 **D All SS Ch Tarpon Sprg FL 1996-** B Lapeer MI 5/26/1933 d Dewey Alonza Van Wagnen & Helen Mary. Maine Diac Formation Prog 1983. D 1/7/1984 Bp Frederick Barton Wolf. m 3/4/1955 Harry Frank Serfes c 3. D S Lk's Ch Land O Lakes FL 1993-1995; D H Trin Epis Ch In Countryside Clearwater FL 1992-1993; D S Mart's Epis Ch Hudson FL 1991-1992; D, Cleric-in-Charge Ch Of The H Sprt Portland ME 1989-1990; D S Steph The Mtyr Epis Ch E Waterboro ME 1987-1989; D Chr Ch Biddeford ME 1984-1987. DOK 1996; ECW 1996; Sis of Charity 1984. pserfes@verizon.net

SERFLING, Robert Allan (Chi) 618 N Central Ave Rm 941, C/O Westword Ho Associates, Phoenix AZ 85004 **Died 9/1/2010** B Pueblo CO 5/23/1930 s William Orvill Serfling & Ruby Constance. BA U CO 1953. D 6/1/1957 Bp Charles L Street P 12/1/1957 Bp Gerald Francis Burrill. pserfling@q.com

SERMON, William Todd (Colo) 1612 E Custer St, Laramie WY 82070 **R Gr Epis Ch Chadron NE 2006-; R S Andr's Ch Cripple Creek CO 2000-** B Kansas City MO 2/15/1933 s William Harry Sermon & Martha Elizabeth. BA Colorado Coll 1955; The Coll of Emm and St. Chad 1999. D 4/17/1995 P 11/17/1995 Bp Bob Gordon Jones. m 6/29/1980 Kristine Utterback. EFM Mentor. wsermon@aol.com

SERPA-ORDONEZ, Pedro Abel (EcuC) Casilla Postal 533, Riobamba Ecuador B Canar EC 3/22/1932 s Abel Serpa & Mercedes. Sem 1987. D 3/14/1987 P 12/1/1988 Bp Adrian Delio Caceres-Villavicencio. Iglesia Epis Del Ecuador Ecuador 1993-2004; Iglesia San Gabr Riobamba 1988-2004.

SERRA-LIMA, Federico (Alb) 28 Harrington Lane, Old Chatham NY 12136 B Buenos Aires AR 7/17/1929 s Federico Alberto Serra Lima & Elena. BS Col 1963; MA NYU 1965; PhD NYU 1971; Cert GTS 1981. D 6/19/1982 P 12/21/1982 Bp Wilbur Emory Hogg Jr. m 3/17/1974 Margaret Nordberg. Trin Ch Ashland Webster NY 1996-1997; S Jn's Ch Cohoes NY 1994-1996; S Lk's Ch

Chatham NY 1987-1992; COM Dio Albany Albany NY 1982-1988; S Paul's Ch Franklin NY 1982-1986. Auth, "The Buddhist Influence," *LivCh*, 2009; Auth, "PB Revs in Theory and Reality," *LivCh*, 2006; Auth, "Beyond Christmas Day," *LivCh*, 1988. SSC 2000. Fell NEH 1979; Founders' Day Awd NYU 1972; Woodrow Wilson Fell 1963; Phi Beta Kappa 1963. fs232@columbia.edu

SERVELLON, Maria Filomena (NY) 948 E. 156 Street, Bronx NY 10455 **Vic Mision San Juan Bautista Bronx NY 2011-** B El Progreso Honduras 1/15/1949 d Alfonso Servellon & Julia. BA Autonomous U 1978; MDiv The GTS 2006. D 3/11/2006 P 9/15/2007 Bp Mark Sean Sisk. c 1. Asst Ch Of The Medtr Bronx NY 2008. menaserve@aol.com

SERVETAS, Linda Anne (Alb) 16 Dean St, Deposit NY 13754 **D Chr Ch Deposit NY 2002-** B Miami FL 11/13/1943 d William Albert Erbeck & Evelyn Anne. Bangor TS; Paterson St Teachers Coll; Rutgers-The St U. D 6/1/2002 Bp David John Bena. m 1/6/1973 Nickolas Servetas. 1servatas@tds.net

SERVETAS, Nickolas (Alb) 16 Dean St, Deposit NY 13754 **Chr Ch Deposit NY 1995-** B South Berwick ME 6/20/1941 s Nickolas Servetas & Mildred. Dplma, Ma Bangor TS 1992. D 7/8/1992 Bp Edward Cole Chalfant P 5/1/1993 Bp David Standish Ball. m 1/6/1973 Linda Anne Erbeck c 1. S Paul's Ch Bloomville NY 1995-1998; Chr Ch Walton NY 1993-1998. NSERVETAS@TDS.NET

SESSIONS, Judy Karen (WTex) 2910 Treasure Hills Blvd Apt B, Harlingen TX 78550 B Idabel OK 7/15/1944 d Joseph Sessions & Alene. BA Colorado Coll 1966; GTS 1990; MDiv Epis TS of The SW 1991; Grad Theol Un 1994. D 6/22/1991 P 1/4/1992 Bp Robert Manning Moody. Assoc R S Alb's Ch Harlingen TX 2000-2009; Assoc S Lk's Epis Ch Anth NM 1998-2000; Assoc Gr S Paul's Epis Ch Tucson AZ 1994-1997. Phi Beta Kappa The Colorado Coll 1966. jksessions@live.com

SESSIONS, Marcia Andrews (RI) 15 Hattie Ave, Greenville RI 02828 B Providence RI 6/27/1953 d Henry Marchant Sessions & Carolyn Edwards. BS Barrington Coll 1975; MLS U of Rhode Island 1982; MDiv VTS 1991. D 6/22/1991 P 1/4/1992 Bp George Nelson Hunt III. R S Thos Ch Greenville RI 1994-1995; Pohick Epis Ch Lorton VA 1991-1994. Epis Ntwk for Animal Welf 2006. sessions3@mac.com

SESSUM, Robert Lee (Lex) 101 South Hanover Ave Suite 6 L, Lexington KY 40502 B Memphis TN 2/17/1943 s William Calvin Sessum & Elaine Holt. BA Rhodes Coll 1965; MDiv VTS 1970. D 7/5/1970 Bp John Vander Horst P 4/24/1971 Bp William F Gates Jr. m 7/8/1967 Donna Snyder c 1. R Ch Of The Gd Shpd Lexington KY 1994-2010; R All SS' Epis Ch Concord NC 1979-1993; Assoc R Chr Epis Ch Raleigh NC 1974-1979; Vican Ch Of The Nativ Ft Oglethorpe GA 1972-1974; D; Asistant to the R S Paul's Epis Ch Chattanooga TN 1970-1972. Paul Harris Fell Concord Rotary 1993; Sr Man of the Year Concord Jaycees 1984; Outstanding Young Citizen ChmbrCom GA 1973. bsessum@iglou.com

SETMEYER, Robert Charles (Chi) 711 S River Rd Apt 508, Des Plaines IL 60016 B Hammond IN 10/8/1946 s Charles F Setmeyer & Eleanore. BS DePaul U 1972; BS Nash 1975. D 6/14/1975 P 12/13/1975 Bp James Winchester Montgomery. m 11/26/1983 Joyce A Setmeyer c 2. R S Mart's Ch Des Plaines IL 1978-2007; Ch Of The Redeem Elgin IL 1975-1978; Advsr Yth Elgin Dnry Dio Chicago Chicago IL 1974-1978. Graduated on Dn's List DePaul U 1972. father_bobs@hotmail.com

SETTLES, Russell Lee (NC) 9118 Kings Canyon Dr, Charlotte NC 28210 **D S Andr's Epis Ch Charlotte NC 1998-** B Cheyanne WY 4/21/1954 s George W Settles & Ruth. Brenau U; Spartanburg Methodist Coll; U GA; Cert No Carolina Diac Prog 1999. D 6/12/1999 Bp J(ames) Gary Gloster. m 5/20/1995 Tammy Maria Helms. D S Jn's Epis Ch Charlotte NC 1999-2000.

S

SETZER, Eleanor Scott Johnson (RG) No address on file. **Yth Min S Jn's Ch Farmington NM 1986-** B Atlanta GA 7/31/1949 d Kenneth Elvin Johnson & Eleanor. Cert Prchr Lewis Sch Of Mnstry 1987. D 2/29/1988 P 9/1/1988 Bp William Davidson. m 3/17/1978 Ronnie Lamar Setzer.

SEUFERT, Carmen Rae (Roch) 103 Williams St, Newark NY 14513 **Gr Ch Lyons NY 2009-; S Jn's Ch Sodus NY 2004-; S Mk's Ch Newark NY 2004-** B Kansas City MO 1/10/1946 d George Richard Cheney & Carmen Jacks. BS SUNY 1986; MDiv Bex 1994. D 12/9/1995 P 9/14/1996 Bp David Charles Bowman. m 5/22/1965 Dwight Robert Seufert. R S Pat's Ch Cheektowaga NY 2000-2004; P-in-c S Paul's Ch Holley NY 1996-2000. crseufert@prodigy.net

SEVAYEGA, Reginald Delano (HB) 3804 Forbes Ave, Pittsburgh PA 15260 B Harrisburg PA 7/4/1937 s William Silverington Dockens & Thelma Mae. BD JCU 1962; MDiv/STM Evang Luth TS 1970; MA/PhD U Pgh 1971. D 6/19/1968 P 12/1/1968 Bp John Harris Burt. m 1/16/1965 Dina De La Garza. Auth, "Mobility & Rigid Body Transport"; Auth, "La Filosofia De La Vida Capitalista Y La Lucha Para Libertad".

SEVER, Cynthia Jean Anthony (WNY) 3390 Lyell Rd, Rochester NY 14606 **Chr Ch Albion NY 2009-** B Blue Island IL 2/10/1959 d Raymond Edgar Anthony & Marilyn Ruth. BA U IL 1981; AAS Parkland Coll Champaign IL 1983; MDiv Bex 2000. D 6/1/2002 P 12/14/2002 Bp Jack Marston McKelvey. m 5/29/1982 Byron Ross Sever c 1. Asst R Chr Ch Pittsford NY 2007-2008; Yth Mssnr Dio Rochester Rochester NY 2004-2007; Cur S Mk's And S Jn's Epis Ch Rochester NY 2002-2004. csever2@rochester.rr.com

SEVICK, Gerald (Tex) 3901 S. Panther Creek, The Woodlands TX 77381 **R Trin Epis Ch The Woodlands TX 2007-** B Bryan TX 6/24/1954 s Thomas L Sevick & Doris A. BA Baylor U 1977; Grad Sch Of Soc Wk-Arlington Arlington TX 1982; MDiv SWTS 1987; D.Min Sem of the So 2009. D 7/25/1987 Bp Clarence Cullam Pope Jr P 5/21/1988 Bp Donis Dean Patterson. m 7/24/1982 Donna K Boyd-Robertson c 4. R S Anne's Epis Ch Desoto TX 1989-2007; Asst P Epis Ch Of The Ascen Dallas TX 1987-1989. Auth, "Sacrificial Servnt," *LivCh (September 30)*, 2001; Auth, "Embracing The Cntr," *LivCh (February 14)*, 1999; Auth, "A Season Of Pryr For The Healing Of Hunger & Pvrty"; Auth, "Meditation On Matt 5:42," *Roots Of Hope*. Professed Tertiary Of The Soc Of S Fran 1983. gsevick@trinitywoodlands.org

SEVILLE, John C (Chi) 802 Foxdale Ave, Winnetka IL 60093 **Int S Paul's Ch Ivy VA 2011-** B Pittsburgh PA 11/15/1943 s David Walter Seville & Katherine. BA Ups 1967; MDiv PDS 1970. D 6/28/1970 P 3/1/1971 Bp Dean T Stevenson. m 8/18/1984 Cindee Ruth Scott c 1. Int R The Memi Ch Of The Gd Shpd Parkersburg WV 2008-2010; Dio W Virginia Charleston WV 2008-2009; S Jas' Epis Ch Lewisburg WV 2008; S Ptr's Ch Salisbury MD 2007-2008; Chr Epis Ch Winchester VA 2006-2007; Int Trin Ch Highland Pk IL 2004-2005; S Geo's Ch Fredericksburg VA 2003-2004; Int Ch Of The Trsfg Palos Pk IL 2001-2003; Int S Hilary's Ch Prospect Hts IL 1999-2001; S Jn's Epis Ch Mt Prospect IL 1997-1999; S Paul's Ch Hamilton MT 1997-1999; Int Ch Of Our Sav Chicago IL 1995-1997; Int Gr Epis Ch Freeport IL 1994-1995; S Mk's Ch Geneva IL 1993-1994; P-in-c S Chrys's Ch Chicago IL 1993; Int S Mk's Barrington Hills IL 1991-1993; Int Chr Ch Waukegan IL 1989-1991; Int Gr Ch Oak Pk IL 1988-1989; Dn Dio Connecticut Hartford CT 1980-1981; Exec Coun Dio Connecticut Hartford CT 1979-1980; Sub-Dn of New Haven Dnry Dio Connecticut Hartford CT 1978-1979; R Ch of the H Sprt W Haven CT 1977-1981; Vic St Jas Epis Ch Muncy PA 1972-1977; R S Jas Ch Muncy PA 1971-1977; D-Intern S Jas Ch Lancaster PA 1970-1971; D-Intern S Thos Ch Lancaster PA 1970-1971. Auth, *Be of Gd Cheer*. SPIVYSEVILLE@AOL.COM

SEVILLE, Joseph (CPa) 1405 Wedgewood Way, Mechanicsburg PA 17050 **Assoc The Epis Ch Of S Jn The Bapt York PA 2010-** B Pittsburgh PA 10/2/1948 s David Walter Saville & Katharine. BA Tem 1970; MDiv Yale DS 1973; MPA Penn 1981. D 6/8/1973 P 3/23/1974 Bp Dean T Stevenson. m 8/21/1971 Linda Turnbaugh. S Andr's Ch Harrisburg PA 2002-2010; Cn Ordnry Dio Cntrl Pennsylvania Harrisburg PA 1996-2010; Asst Ecum Off Dio Kansas Topeka KS 1991-1996; R S Thos The Apos Ch Overland Pk KS 1989-1996; Stwdshp Dept Dio Easton Easton MD 1984-1989; R Chr Epis Ch Great Choptank Par Cambridge MD 1983-1989; R S Lk's Epis Ch Mt Joy PA 1979-1983; Yth Cmsn Dio Cntrl Pennsylvania Harrisburg PA 1975-1983; R S Jn's Epis Ch Bellefonte PA 1974-1979; Intrn S Lk's Epis Ch Altoona PA 1973-1974. Auth, "The Epis Dio Cntrl Pennsylvania As A Systems Model: A Case Study". JSEVILLE03@GMAIL.COM

SEWELL, Edith (Haw) 1212 Punahou #2504, Honolulu HI 96826 B Atlanta GA 6/24/1931 d Frank Anderson Sewell & Margaret Clarkson. Agnes Scott Coll; BA U NC 1953; MA U of Hawaii 1974; Dio Hawaii Diac Prog Ord HI 1985. D 7/18/1985 Bp Edmond Lee Browning. m 4/8/1989 Robert Barr Husselrath. D- in - Res-Vol S Barth's Epis Ch Poway CA 1998-2004; D S Eliz's Ch Honolulu HI 1985-1990. Hawaii Epis Cleric Assn.

SEWELL, John Wayne (WTenn) 53 Shepherd Ln, Memphis TN 38117 **Cmsn on Liturg & Mus Dio W Tennessee Memphis TN 2011-; Stndg Com Dio W Tennessee Memphis TN 2011-; R S Jn's Epis Ch Memphis TN 2002-** B Lester AL 11/8/1951 s Neil Richard Sewell & Doris Nell. BS U of No Alabama 1974; MDiv Asbury TS 1979; Cert SWTS 1981. D 5/30/1981 P 12/1/1981 Bp Furman Stough. m 5/23/1987 Marilyn Purcell. R The Chap Of The Cross Madison MS 1989-2001; Assoc R S Lk's Epis Ch Birmingham AL 1987-1989; R Chr Epis Ch Albertville AL 1981-1987; D S Phil's Ch Ft Payne AL 1981-1982. mpsewell@att.net

SEXTON JR, Lewis Roper (Nwk) 431 Diekema Ave. Apt. 209, Holland MI 49423 B Bay City TX 1/28/1926 s Lewis Roper Sexton & Edith. BA Roosevelt U 1948; MA NWU 1949; STB PDS 1957. D 6/21/1957 Bp Charles L Street P 12/1/1957 Bp Joseph Thomas Heistand. c 1. Cur Ch Of The Medtr Chicago IL 1967-1970; Vic Ch Of The Trsfg No Bergen NJ 1963-1966; Cur S Jn's Ch Passaic NJ 1961-1963; Cur Ch Of The Trsfg New York NY 1960-1961; Vic Chr Ch Harvard IL 1958-1960; Cur The Epis Ch Of S Jn The Bapt York PA 1957-1958.

SEXTON, Timothy Wayne (Haw) 650 Pecos Ave, Raton NM 87740 **part time H Trin Epis Ch - Mssn Raton NM 2011-** B South Charleston WV 9/19/1948 s Buford Sexton & Wanda Lou. U of So Florida 1970; BS U of Cntrl Florida 1978; MDiv Nash 1983. D 3/1/1976 P 6/21/1983 Bp William Hopkins Folwell. m 8/1/1997 Barbara Jean Metzker c 6. Provost S Andr's Cathd Honolulu HI 2007-2010; Cn S Andr's Cathd Honolulu HI 2004-2007; Cn Chr Epis Ch Anacortes WA 2000-2004; Cn S Jas Ch Sedro-Woolley WA 1999-2004; R/Cn Mssnr S Paul's Epis Ch Mt Vernon WA 1997-2004; Cn Dio Utah Salt Lake

City UT 1989-1996; R Ch Of Our Sav No Platte NE 1986-1989; P-in-c S Aidans Ch Hartford WI 1984-1986; Yth Dir Dio Milwaukee Milwaukee WI 1983-1986; Asst S Mart's Ch Brown Deer WI 1983-1984; In-c S Aidans Ch Hartford WI 1982-1983; D-in-c S Aidans Ch Hartford WI 1980-1981; D S Mary Of The Ang Epis Ch Orlando FL 1978-1980; D S Chris's Ch Orlando FL 1976-1978. twsexton@gmail.com

SEY, Reginald Franklyn (Chi) 11219 S Peoria St, Chicago IL 60643 B Sekondi GH 1/30/1960 s Gabriel Augustus Sey & Johannah E. DIT Trin TS Legon Gh 1986; BA U Of Ghana Legon Gh 1989; MA Wheaton Coll 1994; PhD Trin Evang DS Deerfield IL 2002. Trans 5/23/2002 Bp William Dailey Persell. m 12/27/1986 Hilda Micah c 2. Ch Of The H Cross Chicago IL 2002-2011; Vic S Ambr Ch Chicago Heights IL 2002-2005; R Ch Of The H Cross Chicago IL 1997-2001. hcepis@juno.com

SEYMOUR, John (Jack) David (Chi) 946 W Hubbard St, Chicago IL 60642 **Cathd Shltr Chicago IL 2010-; Dir, Sch for Deacons Dio Chicago Chicago IL 2009-; D Ch Of S Paul And The Redeem Chicago IL 2004-** B Springfield IL 1/9/1952 s John Milford Seymour & Loretta Margaret. IL Wesl 1972; BA U IL 1975; M.Div. Chicago TS 2011. D 9/19/1994 Bp Peter Hess Beckwith. m 9/4/1976 Janis Joy Gomien c 2. D The Cathd Ch Of S Paul Springfield IL 1994-2002. jack_seymour2000@yahoo.com

SEYMOUR, Marlyne Joyce (Mil) 862 No. Sandy Lane, Elkhorn WI 53121 **Asst Chr Epis Ch Of Delavan Delavan WI 1991-** B Madison WI 5/16/1932 d Arthur Henry Schantz & Agnes Opal. U of Wisconsin 1952. D 10/21/1989 Bp Roger John White. m 7/13/1957 William Lester Seymour. DOK 1986; NAAD 1989; Ord of Julian of Norwich 1988. firtree@elknet.net

SHACKELFORD III, Edwin Telpha (NCal) 2667 9th Ct Se, Salem OR 97302 B Colonial Hgts VA 9/7/1928 s Edwin Telpha Shackelford & Willie Lee. BA/MCL Pk Coll Parkville MO 1973; MDiv Epis TS In Kentucky 1978; Coll of Preachers 1982. D 5/14/1978 Bp Addison Hosea P 12/17/1978 Bp Victor Manuel Rivera. m 5/12/1990 Sally R Morris c 1. Int S Mary's Ch Woodburn OR 2001-2003; Evan & Ch Growth Dio Nthrn California Sacramento CA 1988-1992; VP, Dioc Coun Dio Nthrn California Sacramento CA 1988-1989; St Marys Ch Elk Grove Sacramento CA 1985-1992; Dioc Coun Dio Nthrn California Sacramento CA 1985-1988; Cmsn Outreach Epis Dio San Joaquin Modesto CA 1980-1981; R S Mths Ch Oakdale CA 1980; Epis Dio San Joaquin Modesto CA 1979-1981; Dir Dioc LayR Cmsn Epis Dio San Joaquin Modesto CA 1979-1981; Int H Trin Epis Ch Madera CA 1979-1980; Vic Ch Of The Epiph Corcoran CA 1978-1979; Epis Dio San Joaquin Modesto CA 1978; Vic S Thos Ch Avenal CA 1978. Auth, *The H Euch: Notes for Newcomers & Bewildered Oldtimers*. e.t.shackelford@att.net

SHACKELFORD, L(ynn) Clark (Okla) 37 Mojave Dr, Shawnee OK 74801 **Chair, BEC Dio Oklahoma Oklahoma City OK 2009-; BEC - Exam in H Scripture Dio Oklahoma Oklahoma City OK 1995-** B Nashville TN 10/14/1946 s Clarence Odis Shackelford & Grace Lurine. BA Van 1967; JD Nashville Sch of Law 1977; MDiv Epis TS of The SW 1994. D 6/24/1994 Bp Edward Witker Jones P 12/23/1994 Bp John Forsythe Ashby. m 4/20/1974 Jane Sullivan c 4. R Emm Epis Ch Shawnee OK 2004-2010; Dioc Coun Dio Oklahoma Oklahoma City OK 2003-2004; Dn, Tulsa Reg Dio Oklahoma Oklahoma City OK 2000-2003; Tulsa Cler and Reg Dio Oklahoma Oklahoma City OK 2000-2003; Justice, Eccl Crt Dio Oklahoma Oklahoma City OK 1999-2003; Justice Dio Oklahoma Oklahoma City OK 1997-2003; R S Matt's Ch Sand Sprg OK 1995-2004; R S Lk's Epis Ch Scott City KS 1994-1995. Auth, "Var," *Countrywide News & Shawnee Sun, Tecumseh, OK*, 2009; Auth, "Var," *Shawnee News-Star, Shawnee, OK*, 2005; Auth, "Var," *Sand Sprg Ldr, Sand Sprg, OK*, 1997. Affirming Angl Catholicism 1999; CHS 1997; Ecum Soc of BVM 2008. csshackelford@allegiance.tv

SHACKLEFORD, Richard Neal (LI) Timber Ridge, 711 John Green Rd, Jonesborough TN 37659 **Int Dio E Tennessee Knoxville TN 2008-; Int S Tim's Epis Ch Kingsport TN 2008-** B LaGrange MO 7/1/1940 s Benjamin Samuel Shackleford & Oma Anice. BA U Denv 1964; MA U of Nthrn Colorado 1974; Oxf 1985. Trans from Church Of England 2/1/1989 Bp William Carl Frey. m Belen H Kendall. R S Bon Epis Ch Lindenhurst NY 2005; S Bon Epis Ch Lindenhurst NY 1996 2005; S Jn's Cathd Denver CO 1988 1992. crvpftn@charter.net

SHACKLETT JR, Richard Lee (Kan) 6535 Maple Dr, Mission KS 66202 B Wichita KS 11/8/1927 s Richard Lee Shacklett & Kay Margaret. BA Friends U 1950; BD EDS 1954; MS U of Utah 1973. D 6/11/1954 Bp Goodrich R Fenner P 6/20/1960 Bp James W Hunter. m 10/12/1957 Ela Erica Oudheusden. Assoc Gr And H Trin Cathd Kansas City MO 1964-1966; R All SS Ch Wheatland WY 1962-1964; R S Paul's Epis Ch Dixon WY 1960-1961.

SHADDEN JR, Harry Spencer (Tenn) 736 E Ash St, Fayetteville AR 72703 B 8/7/1931 Tennessee Tech U; Cert U So. D 6/25/1961 P 5/14/1962 Bp John Vander Horst. m 6/9/1955 Barbara B Shadden. Auth, "Coping w Comunication Disorders In Aging"; Auth, "Aids In The Wkplace". bshadde@uark.edu

SHADOW, Burton Alexander (FtW) 3540 Manderly Place, Fort Worth TX 76109 B Fort Lauderdale FL 8/5/1963 s Roger Edmund Shadow & Waltraut. BA Ramapo St Coll 1986; MS Ford 1988; MDiv NYTS 1998; STM Nash 2000. D 4/24/2000 P 11/18/2000 Bp Jack Leo Iker. m 4/24/1993 Ingrid L Taveras c 2. Asst S Jn's Ch Ft Worth TX 2000-2006; Cur Dio Ft Worth Ft Worth TX 2000-2002. Auth, "The Dio Responds to the Changing Nbrhd," *Forw in Mssn*, 2001; Auth, "Hisp Ordinands Need Cmnty," *LivCh*, 2001. CCU 2001. burtonshadow@hotmail.com

SHAEFER III, Harry Frederick (Mich) 407 Highland Ave., Johnson City TN 37604 B Brooklyn NY 8/8/1939 s H(arry) Frederick Shaefer & Dorothea Reynolds. BA Ob 1961; GTS 1963; BD UTS 1964; DMin Ecum TS 1992. D 6/13/1964 P 12/14/1964 Bp Nelson Marigold Burroughs. m 3/17/1974 Marjorie Moore Shaefer c 4. Cathd Ch Of S Paul Detroit MI 1998-1999; R S Jas' Epis Ch Dexter MI 1978-1991; Assoc S Clem's Epis Ch Inkster MI 1969-1977; Cur Par Of S Jas Ch Keene NH 1966-1969; Vic S Jn's Ch Walpole NH 1966-1969; Cur Ch Of The Ascen Mt Vernon NY 1964-1966. harry@eaglesolutions.com

SHAEFER, Susan Adelaide Hernandez (Mich) 1605 E. Stadium Blvd., Ann Arbor MI 48104 B Ann Arbor MI 10/1/1978 d Jeanne B. BA U MI 2000; MDiv SWTS 2005. D 12/18/2004 P 7/2/2005 Bp Wendell Nathaniel Gibbs Jr. m 6/8/2002 Harry Luke Shaefer c 1. S Jn's Ch Plymouth MI 2009-2011; Dio Michigan Detroit MI 2007-2008; S Paul's Epis Ch Lansing MI 2005-2007. susie_shaefer@yahoo.com

SHAFER, Jean Lankford (NwT) 4902 43rd St, Lubbock TX 79414 B Cuero TX 4/7/1926 d Jack Walton Lankford & Maryjo Elva. BA U of Texas 1985. D 11/1/1992 Bp Sam Byron Hulsey. m 1/12/1946 James Edman Shafer. D S Paul's On The Plains Epis Ch Lubbock TX 1997-2000; D-In-C S Jn's Ch Lamesa TX 1991-1994. NAAD. stpauls@juno.com

SHAFER, Lee Franklin (Ala) 5 Booger Holw, Anniston AL 36207 **R Gr Ch Anniston AL 2008-** B Gasden AL 6/8/1961 d Denson Nauls Franklin & Virginia Lee. BS U of Alabama 1984; STM Nash 2003; Doctor of Mnstry STUSo 2012. D 9/18/2001 P 4/17/2002 Bp Henry Irving Louttit. m 8/26/2004 Thomas Shafer c 2. S Jn's Epis Ch Tallahassee FL 2006-2008; Chr Ch Valdosta GA 2003-2006. leefshafer@aol.com

SHAFER, Michael Gales (NY) 21 Decker Road, Stanfordville NY 12581 **P-in-c Ch Of The Regeneration Pine Plains NY 2000-** B New York NY 3/12/1941 s Judson Bell Shafer & Helene. BA Bard Coll 1966; STB Ya Berk 1969. D 6/7/1969 P 12/1/1969 Bp Horace W B Donegan. m 6/17/1967 Johanna M Bauby c 2. P-in-c S Lk's Ch Chatham NY 1995-1999; Trin Ch Watervliet NY 1989-1995; Assoc S Ptr's Ch Albany NY 1986-1988; S Jn's Ch So Salem NY 1971-1986; Cur H Trin Epis Ch Vlly Stream NY 1969-1971. *Old Values for a New Generation*, Vantage Press, 2002. jmshafer@earthlink.net

SHAFER, Samuel Harvey (RG) 630 66th St, Oakland CA 94609 B Denver CO 7/17/1939 s Samuel H Shafer & Fern A. BA U CO 1963; MDiv Iliff TS 1982. D 9/1/2001 P 9/5/2002 Bp Terence Kelshaw. m 12/11/1965 Joanna Magers c 3. Asst R Chr The King Epis Ch Santa Barbara CA 2002-2004; Asst for Mssn & Outreach S Jas' Epis Ch Los Angeles CA 1982-1989. sjshafer@sbcglobal.net

SHAFFER, Charles Omer (Md) 7200 3rd Ave # B118, Sykesville MD 21784 B Madisonville KY 11/19/1933 s Marion Omer Shaffer & Nannie Love. BA Transylvania U 1956; MDiv Epis TS In Kentucky 1971. D 5/29/1971 Bp William R Moody P 6/23/1972 Bp Addison Hosea. m 6/18/1963 Barbara S Scanlon. Int Ch Of The Mssh Baltimore MD 1993; R Harriet Chap Catoctin Epis Par Thurmont MD 1975-1991; Asst to R S Tim's Ch Catonsville MD 1972-1975. Elected to Mem Maryland Sr Citizens Hall of Fame 2008. c111933@comcast.net

SHAFFER, Dallas Bertrand (WVa) 1415 Cornell St, Keyser WV 26726 B Northfork WV 6/9/1933 s Carl Denton Shaffer & Hazel Lucy. VTS; BA U Rich 1954; MA W Virginia U 1961; PhD W Virginia U 1966. D 6/14/1997 P 6/13/1998 Bp John H(enry) Smith. m 10/15/1960 Jennie Mae Lininger. ptcoo571@mail.wvnet.edu

SHAFFER, Dee (Ga) 299 Ga Episcopal Conference Ctr Rd, Waverly GA 31565 **Chr Ch Frederica St Simons Island GA 2011-; Vic Ch of Our Sav at Honey Creek Waverly GA 2008-** B Pittsburgh PA 5/21/1954 d Richard Henry Stock & Jean Sabal. BA Queens U 1976; Tchr Cert Armstrong St Coll 1995; MDiv Asbury TS Orlando FL 2007. D 9/25/2008 P 6/18/2009 Bp Henry Irving Louttit. m 9/3/1987 Michael Richard Shaffer c 2. Georgia Epis Conf Cntr At H Waverly GA 2009-2010. dee@revdeeshaffer.com

SHAFFER, Harold Franklin (Nwk) Po Box 3, North Chatham MA 02650 B Washington DC 8/14/1926 s Harold Shaffer & Hazel Francis. BA U So 1950; STB GTS 1954; Grad Clincl Pstr Counslg Hdi Dover NJ 1976; DMin Drew U 1980; Albert Einstein Coll of Med 1995; Harv 1996. D 6/12/1954 Bp Angus Dun P 12/13/1954 Bp Benjamin M Washburn. Deptce Dio Newark Newark NJ 1957-1977; S Mary's Ch Sparta NJ 1954-1979. "For The Pstr Counslr," Doctoral Thesis, 1980; "Transcendence: A Synthesis," Drew U, 1980. AAPC 1978-2002; Fell Amer Orthopedic-Psych Assn 1979-2002; Massachusetts Mntl Hlth Couselors Assn` 1993-2003; Ord Of H Cross - Assoc 1950-2002; SE Ma Psych Assn - Affiliate 2002. achefs@verizon.net

SHAFFER, John Alfred (CNY) 162 W 3rd St, Oswego NY 13126 B York PA 7/25/1951 s Lester Wolz Shaffer & Mildred Webster. BA W Virginia

S

Wesleyan Coll 1973; MA U of Wisconsin 1975; MDiv Nash 1992. D 6/13/1992 P 6/11/1993 Bp John H(enry) Smith. m 8/5/1972 Barbara Ammerman. R Gr Ch Baldwinsville NY 1996-2003; Cur S Matt's Ch Wheeling WV 1992-1996. john.shaffer@oswego.edu

✠ **SHAHAN, Rt Rev Robert Reed** (Az) 10175 S North Lake Ave, Olathe KS 66061 B Elkhart KS 10/18/1939 s John Arlin Shahan & Freda Elizabeth. BS U of Kansas 1961; MBA MI SU 1967; MDiv Nash 1973; PhD NWU 1979; DD SWTS 1994. D 5/19/1973 P 11/24/1973 Bp Charles Bennison Con 10/3/1992 for Az. m 8/11/1963 Mary Carol Stephenson. Bp Dio Arizona Phoenix AZ 1992-2004; Dn Gr Cathd Topeka KS 1985-1992; Dn Gr Cathd Topeka KS 1984-1992; R S Thad Epis Ch Aiken SC 1981-1984; Vic S Fran Epis Ch Chicago IL 1976-1981; Prof of Preaching & Sm Ch Mnstry SWTS Evanston IL 1975-1981; Vic S Alb's Mssn Muskegon MI 1973-1975. Hon DD SWTS Evanston IL. rrsfal@comcast.net

SHAHEEN, Leonard N (NCal) 5780 Stillmeadow Drive, Reno NV 89502 **Died 3/2/2010** B Los Angeles CA 8/24/1935 s Elias Nicholas Shaheen & Ileen Sadi. BA San Fernando Vlly St Coll 1963; MDiv CDSP 1966; CDSP 1974; MS CDSP 1992. D 9/10/1966 P 3/4/1967 Bp Francis E I Bloy. c 4. Cn Bp Jerry A Lamb 2006; St Vol of the Year 1987. leonard13@charter.net

SHAIN-HENDRICKS, Christy Ann (Colo) Po Box 10000, Silverthorne CO 80498 **R Epis Ch Of S Jn The Bapt Breckenridge CO 2006-; Dio Colorado Denver CO 2005-** B Waco TX 2/6/1956 d Rox Shain & Nancy L. BA U CO 1995; MDiv Iliff TS 1999. D 6/5/1999 P 12/11/1999 Bp William Jerry Winterrowd. m 7/21/1979 Glenn Arthur Hendricks c 3. P-in-c Ch Of The H Sprt Colorado Sprg CO 2004-2006; S Ben Epis Ch La Veta CO 2002-2004; Ch Of S Ptr The Apos Pueblo CO 1999-2001. Dok. J Spangler Awd For Excellence In Rel And Psychol Iliff TS 1999. c.a.shain-hendricks@comcast.net

SHAKESPEARE, Lyndon (NJ) 1922 N. Madison Street, Arlington VA 22205 **Cathd of St Ptr & St Paul Washington DC 2011-; R All SS Memi Ch Navesink NJ 2006-** B Gosford New South Wales AU 7/30/1972 s Leslie Henry Shakespeare & Rosslyn. BA Wheaton Coll 1995; MDiv VTS 2002. D 6/8/2002 Bp Barry Robert Howe P 12/8/2002 Bp James Winchester Montgomery. m 1/4/1997 Amie Charles Flowers c 3. Asst to R Chr Ch Georgetown Washington DC 2002-2006. Pstr Study Proj Louisville Inst 2010; Promising Schlr ECF 2005. lshakespeare@cathedral.org

SHALLCROSS, Lexa Herries (Be) 150 Elm St, Emmaus PA 18049 B Philadelphia PA 8/9/1946 d Herbert Lex Shallcross & Elizabeth Olive. BA Douglass 1968; MS Rutgers-The St U 1971; MDiv GTS 1987. D 5/30/1987 P 2/7/1988 Bp James Michael Mark Dyer. m 11/23/1968 Domenick J Billera c 1. R S Marg's Ch Emmaus PA 1989-2010; P-in-c Chr Ch Forest City PA 1987-1989; P-in-c Trin Epis Ch Carbondale PA 1987-1989. canonlex@ptd.net

SHAMBAUGH, Benjamin Albert (Me) 143 State St, Portland ME 04101 **GC Dep Dio Maine Portland ME 2009-; Dn Cathd Ch Of S Lk Portland ME 2005-** B Washington DC 9/20/1963 s George Elmer Shambaugh & Katherine. BA (hon) NWU 1985; Codrington Coll 1987; MDiv GTS 1988; DMin SWTS 2005. D 6/18/1988 P 12/16/1988 Bp Frank Tracy Griswold III. m 8/19/1989 Shari Goddard c 2. R S Jn's Ch Olney MD 1995-2005; Cn The Amer Cathd of the H Trin Paris 75008 FR 1991-1995; Cur The Ch Of The H Sprt Lake Forest IL 1988-1991. Auth, "The Epis Ch Is Or The Epis Ch Are," *LivCh*, 2002; Auth, "A Call To Curacy," *Gathering The Next Generation*, 2000; Auth, "Are We An Epis Or A Congrl Ch?," *LivCh*, 1999. Washington Epis Cler Assn 1995-2005. Who'S Who Top Exec 1998. shambaugh@gwi.net

SHAMEL, Andrew Thompson (Ind) 55 Monument Cir Ste 600, Indianapolis IN 46204 **Chr Ch Cathd Indianapolis IN 2011-** B Abington PA 10/17/1982 s Louis B Shamel & Cynthia Marie Liebold. AB Dart 2005; MDiv CDSP 2010; MA CDSP/GTU 2011. D 6/19/2010 P 4/9/2011 Bp James Robert Mathes. shamel@gmail.com

SHAMHART, Lewis Roper (LI) 510 W 46th St Apt 621, New York NY 10036 B Johnson City TN 1/29/1926 s Paul Bolton Shamhart & Emily Woods. BA W&L 1948; MDiv VTS 1951; Fllshp GTS 1957. P 12/21/1951 Bp Henry D Phillips. Archd for Multicultural Ministers Dio Long Island Garden City NY 1994-1998; Liturg Cmsn Dio Long Island Garden City NY 1967-1984; BEC Dio Long Island Garden City NY 1962-1980; Pres of Epis Assn Dio Long Island Garden City NY 1961-1963; R S Mk's Ch Jackson Heights NY 1960-1991; Assoc Ch Of The Heav Rest New York NY 1957-1960; Asst Chr And S Steph's Ch New York NY 1956-1957; Asst Gr Ch Madison NJ 1955-1956; Asst S Jn's Epis Ch Wytheville VA 1953-1955; R S Thos Epis Christiansburg VA 1951-1953. Oblate Ord of S Ben 1998. Hon Cn Cathd of the Incarn LI 1998. none@invalid.com

SHAMO, Vincent Agoe (Los) 3225 Hollypark Dr Apt 4, Inglewood CA 90305 B Teshie Accra 10/1/1954 LTh S Nich Theol Coll Cape Coast Gh. Trans from Church of the Province of West Africa 4/27/2004 Bp Joseph Jon Bruno. m 9/21/1991 Florence Shamo c 3. Dio Los Angeles Los Angeles CA 2004-2010; S Jas Par Los Angeles CA 2003-2004. vshamo@yahoo.com

SHAN, Becky King-Chu (ECR) 604 San Conrado Ter Unit 7, Sunnyvale CA 94085 B CN 4/16/1937 d Luen-Li Shan & Pui-Chun. Cert Grantham Teachers' Trng Coll 1958; Evening Sch of High Chinese Stds 1965; UTS Hong Kong 1968. D 3/27/1993 P 11/6/1993 Bp Richard Lester Shimpfky. Dio El Camino Real Monterey CA 2000-2007; Vic H Light Chinese Cong Campbell CA 1995-2003; S Thos Epis Ch Sunnyvale CA 1993-1994.

SHANAHAN, Thomazine Weinstein (CPa) 4426 Reservoir Rd Nw, Washington DC 20007 B Miami Beach FL 3/11/1944 d Jerome Weinstein & Thomazine Harris. BA Penn 1965; MA GW 1978; MDiv VTS 1990. D 6/9/1990 P 1/1/1991 Bp Ronald Hayward Haines. c 1. Asst S Pat's Ch Washington DC 1996-1998; Asst Chr Ch Georgetown Washington DC 1990-1996.

✠ **SHAND, Rt Rev James Joseph** (Eas) 208 Somerset Ct, Queenstown MD 21658 **Chairman VTS Alexandria VA 2009-; Bp Dio Easton Easton MD 2003-** B New York NY 8/21/1946 s Jean Valentine Shand & Mary Katherine. BA Canaan Coll 1969; MDiv PDS 1972; MA VTS 1999. D 4/22/1972 P 10/28/1972 Bp Alfred L Banyard Con 1/25/2003 for Eas. m 8/3/1974 Lynne Stevens c 2. Trst VTS Alexandria VA 2003-2009; Stndg Com, Pres Dio Easton Easton MD 1998-2001; R Chr Ch Par Kent Island Stevensville MD 1989-2002; Dep GC Dio Easton Easton MD 1982-1994; Camp Com Dio Easton Easton MD 1979-1991; Dioc Coun Dio Easton Easton MD 1978-1997; CE Com Dio Easton Easton MD 1977-1987; Stndg Com Dio Easton Easton MD 1976-1985; R S Mary Anne's Epis Ch No E MD 1975-1989; Asst Gr Ch Merchantville NJ 1972-1975. DD VTS 2003. budlynne83@yahoo.com

SHAND III, William Munro (WA) 10033 River Rd, Potomac MD 20854 **R S Fran Ch Potomac MD 1987-** B Columbia SC 5/16/1950 s William Munro Shand & Evelyn Roberta. BA U of So Carolina 1971; MA U of So Carolina 1977; MDiv VTS 1981. D 6/13/1981 Bp William Arthur Beckham P 5/15/1982 Bp Maurice Manuel Benitez. m 5/26/1979 Jennifer Benitez c 2. COM Dio Washington Washington DC 2000-2006; R S Paul's Epis Ch Prince Frederick MD 1983-1987; Vic Calv Ch Pauline SC 1981-1983. Auth, "arts," *Angl Dig*, Angl Dig, 2011; Auth, "From There He Will Come To Judge," *Exploring & Proclaiming The Apos' Creed*, Eerdman's, 2004; Auth, "Sing Praise to God," *Hymns from Amer*, Oxf Press, 2003. AAM 1988. wshand@stfrancispotomac.org

SHANDS III, Alfred Rives (Ky) 8915 Highway 329, Crestwood KY 40014 B Washington DC 12/19/1928 s Alfred Rives Shands & Elizabeth Sheffer. BA Pr 1950; BD VTS 1954. D 6/20/1954 Bp Arthur R Mc Kinstry P 5/1/1955 Bp John Brooke Mosley. m 9/1/1967 Mary Dulaney. Vic S Jn's Ch Harbor Sprg MI 1985-1999; Vic S Clem's Ch Louisville KY 1976-1991; Vic S Aug's Epis Ch Washington DC 1960-1969; Assoc Ch Of The Adv Louisville KY 1958-1960; Rep Study Liturg Mvmt In Eur Cathd Cathd Of St Jn The Div New York NY 1956-1957; Cur Calv Epis Ch Hillcrest Wilmington DE 1954-1956. Auth, "Liturg Mvmt & Loc Ch," *How & Why*.

SHANDS, Harriet Goodrich (Mil) 21 Chestnut Ridge Road, Pisgah Forest NC 28768 **P-in-c S Paul's Ch Edneyville NC 2009-** B Madison WI 12/30/1940 d Ruebush George Shands & Elizabeth. Cottey Coll 1960; BA U of Wisconsin 1963; Nash 1987; MDiv SWTS 1989; Dplma in SWTS 1997; Dplma in Congrl Dvlpmt SWTS 2011. D 8/12/1989 Bp Thomas Kreider Ray P 5/19/1990 Bp Roger John White. m 5/4/2006 Francis Sheahan. Stndg Com Dio Milwaukee Milwaukee WI 2000-2002; Vic S Andr's Epis Ch Monroe WI 1997; R S Paul's Epis Ch Beloit WI 1996-2002; Vic Ch Of The Epiph Centerville IA 1993-1995; Vic Gr Ch Albia IA 1993-1995; Vic S Andr's Ch Chariton IA 1993-1995; Dio Iowa Des Moines IA 1990-1995; Chapl Mision San Miguel Madison WI 1989-1990; Asst S Dunst's Ch Madison WI 1989-1990. Professed OA 1994. hgshands@citcom.net

SHANE, Johnnette (Cal) 412 E Harrison St, Kirksville MO 63501 **Vic Trin Epis Ch Kirksville MO 2010-** B Louisville KY 9/22/1954 BA Rhodes Coll 1976; JD Wm Mitchell Coll of Law 1987; MDiv CDSP 2006. D 6/13/2008 P 12/6/2008 Bp Marc Handley Andrus. Assoc S Anne's Ch Fremont CA 2008-2010. jshane922@yahoo.com

SHANK, Michael Joseph (Alb) 87 E Main St, Sidney NY 13838 **Vic S Marg's Ch Sidney NY 2006-; Vic S Mary's Ch Downsville NY 2006-** B Abington PA 12/14/1940 s Charles A Shank & Mildred Elizabeth. BA W&L 1963; MDiv PDS 1966. D 6/11/1966 P 12/20/1966 Bp Robert Lionne DeWitt. m 8/5/2000 Carol E Waverly. Chr Ch Gilbertsville NY 2004-2006; Vic S Paul's Ch Franklin NY 2000-2004; S Paul's Ch Sidney NY 2000-2004; R Gr Ch Waterford NY 1994-1999; Bdgt Com Dio New Jersey Trenton NJ 1992-1993; Vic S Lk's Ch Westville NJ 1987-1994; Vic H Sprt Bellmawr NJ 1987-1993; Dn, Camden Convoc Dio New Jersey Trenton NJ 1986-1989; R H Trin Ch Collingswood NJ 1982-1987; Dept of CE Dio New Jersey Trenton NJ 1980-1984; Cur Gr Ch Merchantville NJ 1979-1982; Asst S Mary's Epis Ch Philadelphia PA 1976-1979; Asst Calv Ch Glen Riddle PA 1975-1978; Com on Democratic Process Dio Pennsylvania Philadelphia PA 1970-1977; R S Aidans Ch Cheltenham PA 1969-1975; Ch Of Our Sav Jenkintown PA 1967-1969; Cantar Ch Of S Asaph Bala Cynwyd PA 1967-1969; Cur Trin Ch Oxford Philadelphia PA 1966-1967. cwaverly@stny.rr.com

SHANK, Nancy (Kan) 111 Pine St, Danville PA 17821 **Chr Memi Epis Ch Danville PA 2009-** B South Bend IN 5/5/1955 d Donald Vance Shank & Rosemary. BS Nyack Coll 1978; MDiv SWTS 1987. Trans 9/9/1991 Bp Frank Tracy Griswold III. R Gr Ch Chanute KS 2003-2009; Vic All Ang Ch Red

Oak IA 1995-2003; Dio Iowa Des Moines IA 1995-2003; Vic S Jn's Ch Shenandoah IA 1995-2003; Vic S Jn's Epis Ch Glenwood IA 1995-2003; R Trin Epis Par Waterloo IA 1993-1995; Neosho Vlly Epis Cluster Chanute KS 1991-1993; S Barth's Ch Wichita KS 1990-1991; S Jas Ch Wichita KS 1990-1991; Int Emm Epis Ch Rockford IL 1989-1990; Dio Chicago Chicago IL 1988-1989; S Paul's Ch Kankakee IL 1987. nshank5@yahoo.com

SHANK JR, Robert Sylvester (Mich) 951 W Orange Grove Rd Apt 54204, Tucson AZ 85704 B Easton OH 10/30/1934 s Robert S Shank & Mary L. MDiv Bex 1959; BA Heidelberg U 1959. D 6/13/1959 Bp Nelson Marigold Burroughs P 12/17/1959 Bp William J Gordon Jr. S Jn's Ch Plymouth MI 1966-1994; Asst S Jn's Ch Detroit MI 1964-1966; Asst S Jas Ch Grosse Ile MI 1962-1964; P-in-c S Andr's Ch Stevens Vill AK 1959-1962. Intl Enneagram Assn 1995. rsshaz@gmail.com

SHANKLES, Jeffrey Scott (Va) 2302 Sanford St, Alexandria VA 22301 **Asst R S Alb's Epis Ch Annandale VA 2005-; D S Steph's Boise ID 1988-** B Anchorage AK 11/10/1960 s Troy Edward Shankles & Velta Ann. BA Geo Fox U 2002; MDiv VTS 2005. D 1/31/1998 Bp John Stuart Thornton P 9/28/2005 Bp Harry Brown Bainbridge III. m 10/28/1983 Katheryn Wettstein c 2. jeff_shankles@stalbansva.org

SHANKS, Estelle (Nev) PO Box 98, Austin NV 89310 **Assoc S Geo's Ch Austin NV 1988-** B Reno NV 2/19/1924 d Matthew H Bertrand & Charlotte. D 4/5/1988 P 10/1/1988 Bp Stewart Clark Zabriskie. m 2/15/1986 John Shanks c 3.

SHANKS, Margaret Ruth (Lex) 367 Stratford Dr, Lexington KY 40503 **Dio Lexington Lexington KY 2010-** B Ashland KY 12/23/1952 d George Shanks & Jean. BD U Of Kentucky 1976; BS U Of Kentucky 1990. D 6/9/2001 Bp Stacy F Sauls. S Agnes Hse Lexington KY 2005-2008. MSHANKS@IGLOU.COM

SHANKS OHC, Stephen Ray (Ala) 112-C King Valley Rd, Pelham AL 35124 B San Antonio TX 11/1/1956 s Leroy Shanks & Jane Adams. D 10/30/2004 Bp Marc Handley Andrus. m 8/6/1977 Vickie Lynn Morrow c 1. EPF 1975; OHC 2002. srshanks@gmail.com

SHANLEY-ROBERTS, Eileen M (Chi) 326 N Martin Luther King Jr Ave, Waukegan IL 60085 **Dn, Waukegan Dnry Dio Chicago Chicago IL 2011-; Hlth Ins sub-Com Dio Chicago Chicago IL 2009-; R Chr Ch Waukegan IL 2007-** B Freemont NB 1/22/1967 d Donald Philip Shanley & Helen Marie. BA U of Notre Dame 1989; MA U of Notre Dame 1994; MDiv EDS 2004. Rec from Roman Catholic 1/1/1997 Bp Kenneth Lester Price. m 2/2/1991 Ross Alan Roberts c 2. Dioc Coun Representatve Dio Chicago Chicago IL 2008-2011; Asst The Ch Of Ascen And H Trin Cincinnati OH 2004-2007. Epis Environ Ntwk 2006; Natl Epis Historians and Archivists 2009; SCHC 2005. Mnstry Fell Fund for Theol Educ 2001. shanleyroberts@gmail.com

SHANNON JR, Carl Steen (Tex) 102 Pecan Grv Apt 121, Houston TX 77077 B Wharton TX 12/16/1932 s Carl Steen Shannon & Leonora. BA SMU 1955; MDiv Epis TS of The SW 1958. D 6/27/1958 Bp James Parker Clements P 6/25/1959 Bp John E Hines. m 6/6/1956 Carolyn Jo Staton. S Ptr's Epis Ch Brenham TX 1993-1996; Chr Ch 1985-1993; S Andr's Epis Ch Pearland TX 1982-1985; R Chr Ch Dearborn MI 1970-1976; R Ch Of The Ascen Houston TX 1966-1970; P-in-c H Trin Epis Ch Austin TX 1965-1966; P-in-c S Mk's Ch Austin TX 1965-1966; Vic S Steph's Ch Huntsville TX 1960-1962. carlshannon@sbcglobal.net

SHANNON, Carolyn Louise (Nev) 2366 Aqua Vista Ave, Henderson NV 89014 **D S Matt's Ch Las Vegas NV 1992-** B Portland OR 9/29/1941 d Isaac Edward Van Van Winkle & Ellen Dow. BS Linfield Coll 1964. D 10/25/1992 Bp Stewart Clark Zabriskie. m 7/2/1971 Jack Vernon Shannon. D Dio Nevada Las Vegas NV 1992-2011. NAAD.

SHANNON SR, Himie-Budu (O) 425 E 17th St, Charlotte NC 28206 **S Andr's Ch Cleveland OH 2009-** B Monrovia Liberia 3/26/1954 s Jonathan Himie-Budu Shannon & Albertha R. Cert Natl Police Acad 1974; BA S Aug's Coll Raleigh NC 1980; MDiv VTS 1984; MSW UCONN, Connecticut 2003. Trans from Lib 12/2/1993 Bp Frank Harris Vest Jr. m 11/23/2009 Madia-Garga Richardson c 3. Chap Of Chr The King Charlotte NC 2005-2009; R S Monica's Ch Hartford CT 1994-2005; Vic Chr Epis Ch Halifax VA 1991-1994; Vic S Lk's Ch Richmond VA 1991-1994. Bro Of S Andr 1984. bertas5c@bellsouth.net

SHANNON, James L (Pa) 112 Lansdowne Ct, Lansdowne PA 19050 B Easton PA 5/14/1946 s Thomas Shannon & Marjorie Ruth. BA FD 1968; MDiv PDS 1973. D 6/9/1973 Bp Leland Stark P 12/16/1973 Bp Robert Lionne DeWitt. Int Ch Of The Epiph Royersford PA 2007-2009; EDS Cambridge MA 2007-2008; Cn Residentiayr / Sub Dn Philadelphia Cathd Philadelphia PA 2003-2007; Cathd Chap Dio Pennsylvania Philadelphia PA 2001-2003; R Chr Epis Ch Bensalem PA 1992-2003; Trin Ch Princeton NJ 1992; R St Pauls Ch Philadelphia PA 1978-1981; Asst Chr Ch Philadelphia Philadelphia PA 1973-1977. Assoc Sis S Margeret 1998; S Geo Soc 1975. lowell46@comcast.net

SHANNON, James Michael (ND) 319 S 5th St, Grand Forks ND 58201 **R S Paul's Epis Ch Grand Forks ND 2003-** B Winfield KS 1/17/1950 s Donald Wille Shannon & Helen May. Cov Coll Lookout Mtn GA; BA LeTourneau U 1972; MDiv Cov TS S Louis MO 1976; DMin Grad Theol Un 1982. D 9/18/1998 P 3/19/1999 Bp Andrew Hedtler Fairfield. m 8/3/1970 Ruth L Lawton c 5. Com Dio Wstrn Kansas Hutchinson KS 2000-2003; R S Andr's Epis Ch Liberal KS 1999-2003. frshannon@msn.com

SHANNON, Marvin Boyd (FtW) Po Box 5555, Laguna Park TX 76644 **All SS' Epis Ch Ft Worth TX 2008-** B Fort Worth TX 7/30/1948 s Marvin Boyd Shannon & Martha Elbertine. ABS Dallas Inst Of Mortuary Sci Dallas TX 1971; BBA TCU 1974; MDiv Nash 1998. D 6/27/1998 P 1/6/1999 Bp Jack Leo Iker. m 6/27/1969 Mary E Hood c 2. All SS' Epis Ch Ft Worth TX 2004-2008; Dio Ft Worth Ft Worth TX 2004-2008; Vic Our Lady Of The Lake Clifton TX 2002-2003; S Alb's Epis Ch Arlington TX 1998-2002. frshannon@allsaintsfortworth.org

SHANNON II, Robert Lloyd (Roch) 17 Uncle Bens Way, Orleans MA 02653 **The Cmnty Of Jesus Inc Orleans MA 1991-** B JP 11/11/1953 s Robert Lloyd Shannon & Norma M. BA Hob 1974; MDiv Gordon-Conwell TS 1977; Cert EDS 1988; PhD CUA 2004. D 1/6/1988 P 6/29/1988 Bp William George Burrill. m 8/24/1974 Mary Jane Anderson c 4. shannon@c4.net

SHAON, Gerald E (Cal) 3811 Somerset Drive #206, Prairie Village KS 66208 B Kansas City MO 12/7/1940 s Claude L Shaon & Rosa Mae. BSBA Cntrl Missouri St U 1964; BA California Sch for Deacons 1994. D 12/3/1994 Bp William Edwin Swing. Gr Cathd San Francisco CA 1994-2005. St. Stehpen's Awd NAAD 2000; St. Steph's Awd Dio California Sch for Deacons 1994. gerrys1207@yahoo.com

SHAPTON, Eleanor Louise (Spok) 240 Maringo Rd, Ephrata WA 98823 B Los Angeles CA 12/6/1948 d Edward William Schrader & Aileen. BA U CA 1971; MLS USC 1973; MDiv CDSP 1982. D 11/4/1984 P 5/1/1985 Bp Wesley Frensdorff. Dio Spokane Spokane WA 2001-2005; Dioc Coun Dio Spokane Spokane WA 1991-1994; Vic S Dunst's Epis Ch Grand Coulee WA 1990-2000; Vic S Jn The Bapt Epis Ch Ephrata WA 1990-2000; St Dunstans Ch Electric City WA 1990-2000; All SS Epis Ch Las Vegas NV 1988-1990; Dio Nevada Las Vegas NV 1988-1990; Assoc S Chris's Epis Ch Boulder City NV 1987-1990; Assoc S Matt's Ch Las Vegas NV 1985-1990. Rev Ellie Shapton Day Nv S 1988.

SHARP, Carolyn Jackson (Ct) Yale Divinity School, 409 Prospect St., New Haven CT 06511 **S Andr's Ch New Haven CT 2011-; Ya New Haven CT 2000-** B Hartford CT 11/5/1963 d Thomas Farrell Sharp & Sarah Dallam. BA Wesl 1985; MAR Yale DS 1994; PhD Yale DS 2000. D 6/11/2011 Bp Laura Ahrens. m 6/10/1989 Leo Lensing c 2. carolyn.sharp@yale.edu

SHARP, Charles Edward (EC) 3526 Canterbury Rd, New Bern NC 28562 **Died 1/14/2010** B Harrellsville NC 7/10/1924 s Starkey Sharp & Eutha. U NC 1943; BA Wake Forest U 1948; BD Yale DS 1951; VTS 1952. D 6/23/1952 P 12/23/1952 Bp Thomas H Wright. c 3.

SHARP, James Leonard (ETenn) 4016 White Wood Cir, Morristown TN 37814 B Helena AR 7/25/1947 s Homer Stroud Sharp & Helen Hazel. E Tennessee St U; EFM STUSo; AS Columbia St Cmnty Coll Columbia TN 1972; BS U of Memphis 1974. D 6/14/1997 Bp Robert Gould Tharp. m 6/27/1969 Carolyn Gayle Hughes.

SHARP, Kenneth Jay (WA) 128 Yellow Pine Rd, Aiken SC 29803 **Died 9/15/2010** B Reamstown PA 10/13/1927 s Paul L Sharp & Elizabeth. BA Franklin & Marshall Coll 1947; BD Luth TS 1950; GTS 1958. D 4/26/1956 P 11/1/1956 Bp Frederick Lehrle Barry. c 2. Auth, *Chrsnty Today*.

SHARP CSF, Lynne (Cal) Community of St. Francis, 3743 Cesar Chavez, San Francisco CA 94131 **Assoc S Paul's Epis Ch Burlingame CA 2011-** B Rochester NY 1/24/1954 d James Edward Hunt & Alice Ann. BA SUNY Brockport 1982; MSEd SUNY Brockport 1984; MDiv CDSP 2008. D 6/13/2008 P 12/6/2008 Bp Marc Handley Andrus. c 2. Asst Gr Cathd San Francisco CA 2010-2011; Asst S Aid's Ch San Francisco CA 2008-2010. lynnesharp@yahoo.com

SHARP, Robert Elven (Kan) 1007 Central St, Leavenworth KS 66048 B Eagle Grove IA 9/30/1923 s George Elven Sharp & Marian Edna. Cert Oxf; JD U of Missouri 1949. D 3/13/1965 P 9/26/1965 Bp Edward Clark Turner. c 4. Int Ch Of The Ascen Epis Springfield MO 1991-2000; Dio W Missouri Kansas City MO 1990; Int S Mk's Epis Ch Kimberling City MO 1989-1990; S Mart-In-The-Fields Edwardsville KS 1968-1977; St Raphaels Ch 1967-1980. BSA - Dist Cmssnr; RWF 1960; YMCA of Kansas City, MO - Pres, Bd Managers. Pres of Alpha Chapt of Pi Kappa Alpha U of Missouri 1946; Hon German Fraternity U of Iowa 1943; Pi Kappa Alpha 1941. rsharp@dialnet.net

SHARP, Wesley Eric (CFla) 700 Rinehart Rd, Lake Mary FL 32746 **S Ptr's Epis Ch Lake Mary FL 2011-** B Ft Payne AL 5/11/1979 s William D Sharp & Darleen C. MDiv Reformed TS 2007; Angl Cert Nash Sem 2010. D 6/11/2011 Bp Hugo Luis Pina-Lopez. m 8/9/2003 Alison Kittrell c 2. sharpwes@gmail.com

SHARPE, Sheila Gast (Del) 65 East Stephen Drive, Newark DE 19713 **Coun Prov III Chester Sprg PA 2011-; D Imm Ch Highlands Wilmington DE 2010-** B Glen Ridge, NJ 2/4/1941 d Raymond Wallace Gast & Helen Boddington. BA U of Delaware 1964; MS Neumann U 2001; Dplma Luth Theol at

Phila 2009. D 12/5/2009 Bp Wayne Parker Wright. m 8/6/1966 Richard Arden Sharpe c 3. D S Alb's Wilmington DE 2009-2010. sgsharpe@comcast.net

SHARPTON, Larry (Ala) 8501 Olde Gate, Montgomery AL 36116 **P-in-c Epis Ch Of The Epiph Montgomery AL 2007-** B Denver CO 9/12/1943 s Clarence Talmadge Sharpton & Barbara Lucille. BA U of Alabama 1965; MDiv STUSo 1982. D 6/5/1982 P 12/1/1982 Bp Furman Stough. m 7/22/1967 Patricia Cagle c 5. Supply P S Matthews In The Pines Seale AL 1999-2007; P-in-c Trin Un Spgs Montgomery AL 1996-1998; Assoc Ch Of The H Comf Montgomery AL 1990-1999; Dio Alabama Birmingham AL 1989-1999; R H Cross Trussville AL 1987-1989; Birmingham Epis Campus Mnstrs Birmingham AL 1984-1986; R S Jn's Ch Birmingham AL 1984-1986; Cur Chr Ch Tuscaloosa AL 1982-1984. larry_sharpton@yahoo.com

SHARROW, Chuck (WTex) 960 Toledo Dr, Brownsville TX 78526 B Saint Paul MN 4/26/1950 s Clarence Sharrow & Lucille. Minnesota St U Mankato; Stout St U; MDiv Epis TS of The SW 1994. D 6/29/1994 Bp James Louis Jelinek P 1/1/1995 Bp James Edward Folts. m 5/11/1973 Ruthanne Harrison c 3. Asst R Ch Of The Adv Brownsville TX 1994-2004; Asst to the Vic S Paul's Epis Ch Brownsville TX 1994-2004. chucksharrow@gmail.com

SHATAGIN, Theodore Ivan (Vt) Po Box 1807, Ardmore OK 73402 B Detroit MI 5/22/1939 s John Theodore Shatagin & Helen. BA Earlham Coll 1960; U MI 1961; BD Yale DS 1964. D 12/14/1966 Bp Wilburn Camrock Campbell P 11/1/1967 Bp Harvey D Butterfield. m 6/28/1969 Betsy Bucklin Walsh c 1. Asst To The R & Prog Dir S Ptr's Epis Ch Bennington VT 1967-1969; Asst S Andr's Ch Mullens WV 1966-1967; Asst S Steph's Epis Ch Beckley WV 1966-1967.

SHATTUCK JR, Gardiner H (RI) 190 North St, Warwick RI 02886 **P-in-c Ch Of The Gd Shpd Pawtucket RI 2009-** B Boston MA 12/21/1947 s Gardiner Humphrey Shattuck & Mary Pickering. BA Br 1970; MDiv GTS 1975; MA Harv 1981; PhD Harv 1985. D 6/10/1975 P 12/20/1975 Bp John Melville Burgess. m 1/8/1983 Cynthia L Logan c 1. P Assoc S Steph's Ch Providence RI 2004-2009; Supply P Dio Rhode Island Providence RI 1990-2004; R Ch Of The Ascen Cranston RI 1986-1990; Int Epiph Par Walpole MA 1985-1986; Supply P Dio Massachusetts Boston MA 1978-1985; Asst All SS' Epis Ch Belmont MA 1975-1978. Auth, "Weeping over Jerusalem: Anglicans and Refugee Relief in the Middle E," *Angl and Epis Hist*, 2011; Auth, "True Israelites: Chas Thorley Bridgeman and Angl Missions in Palestine," *Angl and Epis Hist*, 2008; Auth, "The Episcopalians," Praeger, 2004; Auth, "The Episcopalians (pbk)," Ch Publ, 2004; Auth, "Episcopalians & Race," Univ Press Ky, 2000; Auth, "Encyclopedia of Amer Relig Hist," Facts on File, 1996; Auth, "A Shield & Hiding Place," Mercer Univ Pr, 1987. HSEC Bd 2004-2009; Strng Comm, AAEHC 2004. ghshattuck@cox.net

SHAUBACH, Sheila Kathryn (EpisSanJ) Po Box 164, Raymond CA 93653 B Bakersfield CA 1/29/1935 San Joaquin Schools For Mnstry. D 12/13/2003 Bp John-David Mercer Schofield. c 4.

SHAVER, Ellen M (Me) 139 High Head Rd, Harpswell ME 04079 B Detroit MI 5/16/1941 d Lawrence Stannard Martz & Jean Lee. BD Pace U 1978; MDiv Yale DS 1981. D 6/16/1981 P 2/1/1982 Bp Paul Moore Jr. m 2/1/1961 Alan M Shaver. Assoc S Paul's Ch Brunswick ME 1998-2003; Job Number One New York NY 1996-1998; Int S Paul's Ch Brunswick ME 1996-1997; Dio New York New York City NY 1994-1995; Cn To The Ordnry For Deploy Dio New York New York City NY 1990-1995; Diocn Msnry & Ch Extntn Socty New York NY 1990-1994; Dpt Of Missions Ny Income New York NY 1990-1994; R S Jn's Ch Tuckahoe Yonkers NY 1983-1989; Cur S Jn's Ch Larchmont NY 1981-1983. ellenshaver@comcast.net

SHAVER, John (Minn) 3448 Rum River Dr, Anoka MN 55303 **Assoc Mssh Epis Ch S Paul MN 2002-** B 1/4/1939 s John Howard Shaver & Caroline. BA U MN 1962; MA U MN 1967; MDiv Nash 1975. D 4/26/1975 P 11/1/1975 Bp Charles Thomas Gaskell. m 7/11/1962 Virginia Ann Fry. P-in-c S Mary's Basswood Grove Hastings MN 1995-2000; S Jn's Epis Ch Mankato MN 1994-1995; The Epis Par Of S Dav Minnetonka MN 1990-1992; Trin Ch Anoka MN 1982-1990; Crt Chapl Dio Milwaukee Milwaukee WI 1978-1982; Cur S Jas Epis Ch Milwaukee WI 1975-1977.

SHAVER, Stephen Richard (Oly) 1400 E Mercer St Apt 12, Seattle WA 98112 **Mem, Liturg and Arts Cmsn Dio Olympia Seattle WA 2010-; Cur S Steph's Epis Ch Seattle WA 2010-** B Denison TX 12/23/1981 s Mark Daniel Shaver & Sara Hurdis. BA Emory U 2003; MDiv GTS 2007. D 12/21/2006 P 7/1/2007 Bp J(ohn) Neil Alexander. m 5/27/2007 Julia Shaver. Epis Ch Of The Ascen Dallas TX 2007-2009. stephenshaver@gmail.com

SHAVER, Thomas Ronald (SO) 25 State Rd 13 Apt H8, Saint Johns FL 32259 **P Assoc St Pat's Epis Ch S Johns Fl 2011-** B Evanston IL 6/25/1934 s Clarence Huston Shaver & Hazel Eleanor. BA Mia 1955; JD Stan 1960; MDiv CDSP 1986. D 6/21/1986 Bp Robert C Rusack P 1/10/1987 Bp Oliver Bailey Garver Jr. m 9/5/1959 Marylin Ann Austin c 3. Permanent Supply P S Lk Ch Cincinnati OH 2003-2010; Int S Andr's Epis Ch Cincinnati OH 2000-2001; S Mk's Epis Ch Columbus OH 1998-1999; Calv Ch Cincinnati OH 1998; R All SS Ch Cincinnati OH 1989-1997; Assoc S Mich and All Ang Epis Ch Studio City CA 1988-1989; Assoc Trin Epis Ch Orange CA 1986-1988. OHC 1987. Meritorious hon Awd Untd States St Dept 1965; Phi Beta Kappa Iota of Ohio, Miami Uniiversity 1955. gyrenets@yahoo.com

SHAW III, Chauncey L (SeFla) 4445 Pine Forest Drive, Lake Worth FL 33463 B New Bedford MA 12/27/1932 s Roland Shaw & Ruth. Epis TS In Kentucky. D 5/30/1970 P 12/18/1970 Bp William R Moody. S Jn's Ch Hollywood FL 1994-1995; H Sacr Pembroke Pines FL 1987-1988; Asst The Epis Ch Of Beth-By-The-Sea Palm Bch FL 1982; P-in-c S Paul's Ch Edneyville NC 1975-1976.

SHAW, Gerald Keith Gregg (CNY) 2503 Nw 52nd Ave, Gainesville FL 32605 B Victoria British Columbia CA 12/22/1932 s John Gregg Shaw & Doris Nellie. Can Inst of Chart Acctg 1957; MDiv St. Johns U 1968. Trans from Anglican Church of Canada 8/1/1980. m 8/5/1978 Margaret Elizabeth Hutchon. Asst Ch Of The Incarn Gainesville FL 2000-2003; St. Anth's Par 0 1991-1992; R S Alb's Ch Syracuse NY 1988-1990; Asst S Greg's Ch Boca Raton FL 1983-1988; R Ch Of The Trsfg Bat Cave NC 1980-1983. SHAWMARGARET@BELLSOUTH.NET

SHAW, Jane Alison (Cal) 110 California St, San Francisco CA 94111 **Dn Gr Cathd San Francisco CA 2010-** B Peterborough England 4/28/1963 d Jack Davies Shaw & Joyce. BA Oxf 1985; MDiv Harvard DS 1988; PhD U CA 1994. Trans from Church Of England 10/19/2010 as Priest Bp Marc Handley Andrus. m 10/27/2010 Sarah Ogilvie. JANES@GRACECATHEDRAL.ORG

SHAW, Joan Elizabeth (EMich) 120 Grandview Blvd, Gaylord MI 49735 **D S Andr's Epis Ch Gaylord MI 1999-** B Flint MI 11/17/1933 d Herbert Winter Wroll & Margaret. D 10/9/1999 Bp Edwin Max Leidel Jr.

SHAW, Margaret Elizabeth (Alb) 10215 Carriage Dr, Plymouth IN 46563 **S Jn's Ch Essex NY 2009-** B Albert Lea MN 4/12/1947 d Richard Emery & Alice. Associated Mennonite Biblic Sem; Associated Mennonite Biblic Sem; BA Cornell Coll 1969; MS Indiana U 1985. D 6/9/2006 P 1/12/2007 Bp Edward Stuart Little II. m 12/28/1968 Terrance D Shaw c 2. S Eliz's Epis Ch Culver IN 2007-2009. tmshaw36@comcast.net

SHAW, Martini (Pa) 6361 Lancaster Ave, Philadelphia PA 19151 **R The Afr Epis Ch Of S Thos Philadelphia PA 2003-** B Detroit MI 11/6/1959 s Melton Shaw & Joyce. BA Wayne 1983; BS Wayne 1983; MDiv McCormick TS 1988; CAS SWTS 1988; DMin GTF 2008. D 6/18/1988 P 12/18/1988 Bp Frank Tracy Griswold III. R Ch Of S Thos Chicago IL 1990-2003; Cur The Ch Of S Jn The Evang Flossmoor IL 1988-1989. frmartinishaw@aol.com

✠ **SHAW III SSJE, Rt Rev M(arvil) Thomas** (Mass) 980 Memorial Dr, Cambridge MA 02138 **Bp Dio Massachusetts Boston MA 1994-** B Battle Creek MI 8/28/1945 s Marvil Shaw & Wilma Sylvia. BA Alma Coll 1967; MDiv GTS 1970; MA CUA 1976; DD SWTS 1992; DD GTS 1993. D 7/2/1970 Bp Charles Bennison P 6/1/1971 Bp The Bishop Of Peterborough Con 9/24/1994 for Mass. S Jn's Chap Cambridge MA 1977-1994; Asst S Jas Epis Ch Milwaukee WI 1972-1974. Auth, "Conversations w Scripture and w Each Other," Rowan and Littlefield, 2006. Soc of S Jn the Evang 1974-1994. jdrapeau@diomass.org

SHAW, Philip Algie (Az) Trinity Episcopal Church, P.O. Box 590, Kingman AZ 86402 **Vic Dio Arizona Phoenix AZ 2010-** B Camden SC 12/19/1950 s Algie P Shaw & Vera N. BLA Mississippi St U 1977; DAS Epis Theol Semary of SW 2007. D 6/23/2007 P 2/2/2008 Bp Kirk Stevan Smith. m 7/4/1970 Beverly Clark c 1. Trin Epis Ch Kingman AZ 2007-2009. pascla55@aol.com

SHAW, Robert Clyde (Mil) 46 New Cross N, Asheville NC 28805 B Saint Louis IL 8/29/1932 s Clyde W Shaw & Eugenia Ray. BA U of Wisconsin 1954; BD Nash 1957; STM Nash 1960; MA U of Wisconsin 1962; PhD U of Wisconsin 1967; MS U of Wisconsin 1980. D 4/27/1957 P 11/1/1957 Bp Donald H V Hallock. m 9/7/1977 Janet Nadina Fowler. R S Andr's Ch Madison WI 1960-1977; Vic S Fran Ch Menomonee Falls WI 1957-1960. clydebar29@hotmail.com

SHAW, Samuel Gates (Ala) 4112 Abingdon Ln, Birmingham AL 35243 **Chr Ch Fairfield AL 1999-** B Birmingham AL 11/17/1946 s Samuel R Shaw & Anne Wescott. BA W&L 1968; MDiv GTS 1981. D 3/24/1981 P 10/1/1981 Bp Furman Stough. m 5/22/1994 Margot Rafield c 2. Assoc The Cathd Ch Of The Adv Birmingham AL 1995-1997; S Andr's Ch Montevallo AL 1991-1993; S Andrews's Epis Ch Birmingham AL 1981-1983; Gr Ch Birmingham AL 1981-1982.

SHAW, Timothy Joel (CFla) 901 Thompson Cir Nw, Winter Haven FL 33881 B Springfield OH 1/18/1945 s Delmas Lee Shaw & Rheba Ivaloe. BA S Leo Coll 1980; MDiv SWTS 1983. D 6/24/1983 Bp William Hopkins Folwell P 1/10/1984 Bp Calvin Onderdonk Schofield Jr. m 12/3/1971 Arlene Hamlin c 2. R S Paul's Ch Winter Haven FL 1998-2011; R Ch Of Our Sav Okeechobee FL 1985-1998; Cur All SS Epis Ch Jensen Bch FL 1983-1985. Soc H Cross 1993; SocMary 1993. Hon Cn Dioceses Negros Oriental 1994. ashaw002@tampabay.rr.com

SHAW, Warren Ervin (Pa) 361 Harper Drive, Orange VA 22960 B Philadelphia PA 5/24/1933 s Ervin Shaw & Esther. BA Tem 1955; MDiv Tem 1958. D 6/9/1962 P 12/15/1962 Bp Joseph Gillespie Armstrong. m 10/13/1956 Shirley Christ c 3. Int Emm Ch Rapidan VA 2002-2003; S Paul's Ch Chester PA 1962-1998. Forw in Faith 1994. warrenandshirley@verizon.net

SHAW, W. Lee (U) 4887 S 1710 E, Salt Lake City UT 84117 **R S Steph's Ch W Vlly City UT 2003-** B Helena MT 5/20/1948 s Winston Luther Shaw & LaRue. BS U of Utah 1972; BS U of Utah 1973; MDiv CDSP 1992. D 5/31/1992 P 12/5/1992 Bp George Edmonds Bates. c 1. Assoc S Jas Epis Ch Midvale UT 1996-2003; Vic S Mich's Ch Brigham City UT 1992-1996. Auth, "A Thoughtful & Rational Alternative-The Epis Ch In Utah"; Auth, "When A Mormon Inquires About Your Ch: Pstr & Theol Considerations"; Contrib, "Sermons That Wk Iii". Cmnty of the Cross of Nails 2008. winstonls@aol.com

SHAWHAN JR, Benjamin Harrison (Tex) 11819 Southlake Dr, Houston TX 77077 B Memphis TN 1/17/1930 s Benjamin Harrison Shawhan & Helen. BA Rhodes Coll 1952; MDiv STUSo 1960. D 6/29/1960 Bp Theodore N Barth P 1/24/1961 Bp John Vander Horst. m 9/5/1958 Diana Brown c 3. R S Paul's Ch Navasota TX 1987-1993; Assoc S Steph's Ch Beaumont TX 1979-1987; St Lk's Epis Hosp Houston TX 1978-1979; R Calv Epis Ch Richmond TX 1969-1978; Assoc S Mk's Ch Beaumont TX 1967-1969; Dept of Missions Dio Tennessee Nashville TN 1963-1966; P-in-c The Epis Ch Of The Mssh Pulaski TN 1962-1966; In-charge S Thos Ch Somerville TN 1960-1962; In-charge Trin Ch Mason TN 1960-1962. Ord of S Lk, Flying Ang.

SHEARER, Donald Robert (Nwk) 156 Mountain Dr, Greentown PA 18426 B Sydney NSW AU 10/19/1938 s Robert Colins Shearer & Enid Flora. S Jn's Coll Morpeth NSW 1962. Trans from Anglican Church Of Australia 4/1/1970 as Priest Bp Robert Lionne DeWitt. Cathd Chapt Trin And S Phil's Cathd Newark NJ 1996-1998; Dept of Missions Dio Newark Newark NJ 1990-1996; Cathd Chapt Trin And S Phil's Cathd Newark NJ 1986-1989; Pres So Essex Convoc Dio Newark Newark NJ 1983-1985; R All SS Ch Orange NJ 1982-2002; R Ch Of The H Comm Paterson NJ 1975-1982; Dioc Liturg Cmsn Dio Pennsylvania Philadelphia PA 1973-1975; Asst S Anne's Ch Abington PA 1971-1975; Cur S Clements Ch Philadelphia PA 1968-1970. CBS 1963; GAS 1963; P Assoc C.S.J.B. 1986; P Assoc O.L.W. 1964. Cbury Schlolarship Awd Dio Newark 1986. donald1938@earthlink.net

SHEARER, Robert L (RI) 15620 Riverside Dr W Apt 13-I, New York NY 10032 **P-in-c S Paul's Ch Englewood NJ 2009-; Chr Epis Ch Tarrytown NY 2006-; Int Chr Ch So Amboy NJ 2004-** B Sunnyside WA 10/8/1936 s Maynard Grady Shearer & Aileen. CDSP; AB Whitman Coll; MDiv GTS 1960. D 6/20/1960 Bp J(ohn) Joseph Meakins Harte P 12/1/1960 Bp Charles A Mason. c 3. Int S Ptr's Ch Morristown NJ 2007-2009; Chr Ch New Brunswick NJ 2004-2006; S Ptr's Ch Medford NJ 2003-2004; Chr Ch Toms River Toms River NJ 2001-2002; Gr Epis Ch Plainfield NJ 1999-2001; Int S Ambr Epis Ch New York NY 1997-1998; Int S Phil's Ch New York NY 1996-1998; Ch Of The H Trin Pawling NY 1989-1995; Dio Rhode Island Providence RI 1981-1986; Dio California San Francisco CA 1980-1981; Vic S Mich's Ch Anderson CA 1965-1969; Asst S Jas Ch Pewee Vlly KY 1962-1965; Asst S Lk's Ch Anchorage KY 1962-1965; Vic Ch Of The Epiph Dallas TX 1960-1961; Cur Ch Of The Incarn Dallas TX 1960-1961. Auth, *One-Minute Liturg*, H Trin Press, 1995; Auth, *Affirmative Action Bk*; Auth, *Mysticism & Rel*. Mastery Fndt Trst 1983-1993. rshearer@att.net

SHEARS, S(idney) Herbert (SanD) 4166 Clubhouse Rd, Lompoc CA 93436 **Pstr Asst S Mary's Par Lompoc CA 1975-** B Rochester NY 2/14/1913 s S(idney) N Shears & Florence Mae. BA Syr 1938; MDiv CRDS 1942; MA Col 1950; CDSP 1964. D 9/10/1964 P 3/10/1965 Bp Francis E I Bloy. m 4/17/1972 Ethna Miller. R S Paul In The Desert Palm Sprg CA 1968-1975; Asst Min Ch Of Our Sav Par San Gabr CA 1964-1968. herbnkelly@gmail.com

SHEAY, Virginia M (NJ) 12 Glenwood Ln, Stockton NJ 08559 **Assoc Trin Ch Solebury PA 2002-** B Whitehouse NJ 5/16/1939 d George Anderson Space & Edna Martha. BM Westminster Choir Coll of Rider U 1962; MDiv GTS 1975; PrTS 1975; STM NYTS 1983; DMin Drew U 1992. D 4/26/1975 Bp Albert Wiencke Van Duzer P 4/30/1977 Bp George Phelps Mellick Belshaw. m 5/25/2005 Ronald Joseph Sheay c 3. H Trin Epis Ch Hollidaysburg PA 2000-2001; Evang Consult Dio New Jersey Trenton NJ 1989-2001; Stwdshp Consult Dio New Jersey Trenton NJ 1985-1992; COM Dio New Jersey Trenton NJ 1985-1988; R S Lk's Ch Ewing NJ 1983-2001; Asst S Matt's Ch Pennington NJ 1975-1983. Auth, "Developing a Mnstry of Evang Through Hosp at S Lk's". revdrvirginias@aol.com

SHECTER, Teri Ann (Colo) 2939 El Torro Rd, Grand Junction CO 81503 **D Ch Of The Nativ Grand Jct CO 2004-; Reg D Dio Colorado Denver CO 2002-** B New Haven CT 9/26/1955 d Frederick Shecter & Majorie Hazel. MA U CO. D 11/9/2002 Bp William Jerry Winterrowd. m 6/27/1998 William Dale Page.

SHEEHAN JR, David (Del) 614 Loveville Road D2H, 3401 Greenbriar Ln., West Grove PA 19390 B Philadelphia PA 1/12/1931 s David Sheehan & Mary Gilligan. BS U of Delaware Newark 1954; BD VTS 1959. D 10/3/1959 P 10/8/1960 Bp John Brooke Mosley. m 8/20/1960 Charlotte Rode c 2. R Calv Epis Ch Hillcrest Wilmington DE 1975-1995; Vic S Nich' Epis Ch Newark DE 1964-1974; Cur Ch of St Andrews & St Matthews Wilmington DE 1959-1963; Vic Chr Ch Delaware City DE 1959-1961. sdavid202@aol.com

SHEEHAN, John Thomas (Va) 512 Duff Rd Ne, Leesburg VA 20176 **D Ch Of Our Redeem Aldie VA 2001-** B Springfield MA 5/8/1947 s John James Sheehan & Irene Mary. BS La Salle U; MDiv TESM 2001. D 6/23/2001 P 12/29/2001 Bp Peter James Lee. m 6/23/1979 Denise Ann Larroca c 3. Evang Fllshp - USA 1999. sheehanvicar@aol.com

SHEERIN JR, Charles Wilford (Va) 250 Pantops Mountain Rd. #15, Charlottesville VA 22911 **Died 10/4/2011** B Richmond VA 1/9/1926 s Charles Sheerin & Maria Ward. BA U of Virginia 1950; BD VTS 1955. D 6/3/1955 P 6/1/1956 Bp Frederick D Goodwin. c 3. snnycrst@aol.com

SHEETZ, David Allan (Cal) 250 Baldwin Ave Apt 303, San Mateo CA 94401 **Assoc Chr Ch Portola Vlly CA 2010-; Assoc S Bede's Epis Ch Menlo Pk CA 2007-** B Detroit MI 6/15/1946 s Harold Jacob Sheetz & Doris Ruth. Ripon Coll Cuddesdon Oxford GB; BA Wayne 1971; MA Stan 1974; MDiv CDSP 1993. D 6/3/1995 P 6/1/1996 Bp William Edwin Swing. Dir Mus & Lit Chr Ch Portola Vlly CA 1999-2006; Dir Mus All SS Epis Ch Palo Alto CA 1997-1998; Int S Paul's Epis Ch Burlingame CA 1997; Int S Fran' Epis Ch San Francisco CA 1996; Assoc Chr Epis Ch Los Altos CA 1995-2008; Int S Bede's Epis Ch Menlo Pk CA 1995. dasheetz@comcast.net

SHEFFER, Richard Stanley (WNC) 5 Norwich Dr, Asheville NC 28803 **Died 9/21/2010** B Schenectady NY 1/14/1936 s Lloyd Ellis Sheffer & Anna Catherine. BA Florida St U 1958; MS Florida St U 1960; STB GTS 1965. D 6/1/1965 Bp William Loftin Hargrave P 1/1/1966 Bp Philip Menzie Duncan II. Phi Mu Alpha. sheffer55037@bellsouth.net

SHEFFIELD III, Earl J (Tex) 325 Apache Run Road, Wallisville TX 77597 B Galveston TX 6/4/1939 s Earl J Sheffield & Madelyne Elizabeth. AA Alvin Coll 1958; BA U of Texas 1961; MDiv Epis TS of The SW 1968; BS Lamar U 1979. D 6/12/1968 Bp J Milton Richardson P 5/1/1969 Bp Frederick P Goddard. m 6/20/1964 Renee F Fowler c 3. Trin Ch Anahuac TX 2001-2005; Chapl Cullen Memi Chap Houston TX 1999-2000; Asst R S Jas Epis Ch Houston TX 1999-2000; St Lk's Epis Hosp Houston TX 1999-2000; Vic Chr Ch San Aug TX 1994-1999; P-in-c S Jn's Epis Ch Cntr TX 1994-1999; R S Mk's Epis Ch Richmond TX 1990-1994; Asst S Mk's Epis Ch Richmond TX 1983-1990; Asst Ch Of The H Trin Midland TX 1976-1977; St Matthews Ch Beaumont TX 1971-1976; S Mk's Ch Gladewater TX 1968-1971; Vic S Mich And All Ang' Epis Ch Longview TX 1968-1971. tutuejs@hotmail.com

SHEFFIELD, Jack (Tex) PO Box 12615, San Antonio TX 78212 B Albuquerque NM 12/17/1949 s Bordeau Elwood Sheffield & Mary Alice. BA U Of Houston 1976; ThM SMU 1981; CTh Epis TS of The SW 1992; DMin. SWTS 2001. D 6/27/1992 Bp Maurice Manuel Benitez P 1/1/1993 Bp William Jackson Cox. m 7/13/1974 Anna Marie Oftelie c 2. S Chris's Epis Ch Austin TX 1992-2001. "The Genesis Seed," Imago Pub, 2008; "Under Healing Wings," Imago Pub, 2005; "God's healing River," Imago Pub, 2003. deepriver_4@yahoo.com

SHEHANE, Mary Kathryn (Oly) 9416 1st Ave Ne Apt 408, Seattle WA 98115 **D Ch Of The Ascen Seattle WA 2011-; Dio Olympia Seattle WA 2001-** B Shreveport LA 3/25/1947 d Guy James Shehane & Kathryn Anne. Cntrl Washington U; Cert Dioc TS 1993. D 6/24/1995 Bp Vincent Waydell Warner. c 2. D S Mk's Cathd Seattle WA 2001-2011; Chr Ch SEATTLE WA 1997-2000. NAAD. shehane@drizzle.com

SHELBY, F Stuart (Tex) 9004 Mountain Mist Ln, Round Rock TX 78681 **S Richard's Of Round Rock Round Rock TX 2011-** B 4/15/1975 s Franck A Shelby & Glenda B. B.A. Samford U 1997; M.Div. VTS 2005. D 6/4/2005 P 6/10/2006 Bp Philip Menzie Duncan II. m 7/17/2003 Crista J McKinney c 3. Assoc S Mart's Epis Ch Houston TX 2007-2011; Cur S Jas Ch Fairhope AL 2005-2007; Ch Planter Dio Cntrl Gulf Coast Pensacola FL 1999-2002; Epis Ch Of The Apos Daphne AL 1998-2002; Dir of Chld's and Yth Mnstry S Jn's Ch Monroeville AL 1998-1999. stushelby@bellsouth.net

SHELBY, Jason B (Miss) 106 Sharkey Ave, Clarksdale MS 38614 **S Geo's Epis Ch Clarksdale MS 2010-** B Fort Wayne IN 3/1/1977 s Stephen Charles Shelby & Barbara. BA Indiana U 2003; MDiv U So 2007. D 12/21/2006 P 9/11/2007 Bp Edward Stuart Little II. S Columb's Ch Ridgeland MS 2008-2010; S Mart's Epis Sch Metairie LA 2007-2008. jason.shelby7@gmail.com

SHELDON, Jaclyn Struff (Ct) 85 Holmes Rd, East Lyme CT 06333 **S Paul's Epis Ch Willimantic CT 2009-** B Manchester CT 10/10/1952 d John James Struff & Barbara Ann. BS U Of Bridgeport 1977; MDiv Ya Berk 1996. D 6/14/1997 P 5/1/1998 Bp Clarence Nicholas Coleridge. m 7/29/1978 William Phelps Sheldon c 2. Vic S Jas Ch Preston CT 2000-2008; Vic All SS Ch Ivoryton CT 1998-2000; Incarn Cntr Ivoryton CT 1997-2000.

SHELDON III, J(oseph) Victor (Spr) 1220 Uss Daniel Boone Ave, Kings Bay GA 31547 **Baltimore Intl Seafarers' Cntr Inc Baltimore MD 2007-; Spec Mobilization Spprt Plan Washington DC 2007-** B Charlotte NC 7/5/1960 s Joseph Victor Sheldon & Martha Elizabeth. BS LSU 1982; MDiv TESM 1989. D 6/10/1989 P 4/1/1990 Bp Herbert Alcorn Donovan Jr. Pension Fund Mltry New York NY 2007-2008; R S Marg's Epis Ch Baton Rouge LA 1995-2007; Cn Pstr Chr Ch Cathd New Orleans LA 1992-1995; Asst to R Chr Epis Ch Little Rock AR 1990-1992; Dio Arkansas Little Rock AR 1990; Intern/Cur Trin Ch Van Buren AR 1989. Evang Fllshp In The Angl Comm 1989; Mustard Seed Orphanage - Bd Mem 1992. joseph.sheldon@navy.mil

S

SHELDON, Karen Sears (Vt) 86 S Main St, Hanover NH 03755 B Grand Rapids MI 5/29/1937 d Philip Henry Sears & Esther Ryden. BA U MI 1960; MA U MI 1964. D 7/11/1979 P 5/24/1980 Bp Robert Shaw Kerr. m 2/8/1964 Richard Robert Sheldon c 4. R S Jn The Bapt Epis Hardwick VT 1992-1999; Assoc S Thos Ch Hanover NH 1988-1991; S Mart's Epis Ch Fairlee VT 1984-1987; Asst S Paul's Epis Ch White River Jct VT 1981-1983; Instr Dio Vermont Burlington VT 1980-1994. Auth, "Navigating In The DivineMilieu," *Teilhard Revs*. karenssheldon@gmail.com

SHELDON, Patricia Lu (Neb) 3818 N 211th St, Elkhorn NE 68022 **D S Aug's Epis Ch Elkhorn NE 1997-** B Washington DC 5/15/1940 d Frank Lynn Carter & Lucille Milne. BS U of Maryland 1962; BS San Jose Chr Coll 1989; AAS Metropltn Cmnty Coll Omaha NE 1993. D 12/1/1997 Bp James Edward Krotz. m 5/20/1967 Laurence Francis Sheldon c 3. DOK 2000; OSL 2008. Wmn Mnstry Honored Wmn Dio Nebraska 2009. patsheldon@cox.net

SHELDON, Peggy Ann (SeFla) 2000 Sw Racquet Club Dr, Palm City FL 34990 **S Mary's Epis Ch Stuart FL 1999-; Sprtl Dir Dio SE Florida Miami FL 1995-** B Webster NY 8/21/1927 d Carroll McLean Roberts & Dorothy. Michigan TS 1975; GTS 1977; Shalem Inst for Sprtl Formation Washington DC 1994. D 8/20/1977 Bp Henry Irving Mayson P 9/29/1978 Bp H Coleman McGehee Jr. m 9/11/1947 Howard Walter Sheldon c 5. P-in-c S Monica's Ch Stuart FL 1994-1996; Asst S Lk's Epis Ch Port Salerno FL 1988-1991; Asst S Mich's Ch Grand Rapids MI 1978-1980. peggyasheldon@yahoo.com

SHELDON, Raymond S (Oly) 1075 Alexander Pl Ne, Bainbridge Island WA 98110 **D Admin Faith Ch Kingston WA 2004-** B Glendale AZ 11/30/1944 s Edward W Sheldon & Nina T. BA NYU 1969; MBA Loyola Coll 1975. D 6/26/2004 Bp Vincent Waydell Warner P 7/25/2009 Bp Gregory Harold Rickel. m 11/28/1969 Jere J Allen. rssjas@worldnet.att.net

SHELDON, Terry Lynn (CNY) 21 White St, Clark Mills NY 13321 **Supply All SS Ch Utica NY 2009-; R S Mk's Ch Clark Mills NY 2002-; R S Geo's Epis Ch Chadwicks NY 1995-** B Hudson NY 6/25/1937 s Gerald Wilson Sheldon & Mildred Ruth. BS Syr 1959; STUSo 1983. D 6/8/1985 P 5/20/1986 Bp O'Kelley Whitaker. m 9/5/1959 Mary Anne Seeger c 3. Assoc All SS Ch Utica NY 1985-1999. Chapl, "Var arts 2006-2011," *The Empire St Patriot*, Sons of the Amer Revolution. OHC 1984. Chapl of the Year New York St CAP 1991. tlmas@roadrunner.com

SHELL, Lawrence S (NMich) 201 E. Ridge St., Marquette MI 49855 B De Kalb IL 4/29/1963 s Lawrence S Shell & Leona J. BA NWU 1987. D 5/27/2007 Bp James Arthur Kelsey. larry@shell-family.com

SHELLY, Marshall Keith (NJ) 505 Main St, Spotswood NJ 08884 **R S Ptr's Ch Spotswood NJ 2010-** B East Lansing MI 7/7/1967 s Robert Keith Shelly & Ann Converse. U of Aberdeen Aberdeen GB 1988; BA Ken 1989; MDiv GTS 1994; cert. Int Mnstry Ntwk 2004. D 6/17/1994 P 6/17/1995 Bp Herbert Thompson Jr. m 10/28/2000 Laura B Bares. Int R Trin Ch Matawan NJ 2009-2010; R/Hd of Sch Trin Ch Solebury PA 2005-2009; Int R S Andr's Epis Ch New Providence NJ 2003-2005; Assoc R Gr Ch Madison NJ 1998-2003; Assoc R Trin Ch Newport RI 1995-1998; Assoc R S Steph's Epis Ch And U Columbus OH 1994-1995. marshallshelly1@gmail.com

SHELTON, Benson Eldridge (SwVa) 9220 Georgetown Pike, Great Falls VA 22066 **Asst R S Fran Epis Ch Great Falls VA 2010-** B Langley VA 4/6/1981 s Matthew Benson Shelton & Susan Diane. AAS Pat Henry Cmnty Coll 2003; BS Radford U 2005; MDiv VTS 2010. D 9/29/2010 P 4/2/2011 Bp Frank Neff Powell. D-in-c S Paul's Ch Martinsville VA 2010. asstrector@stfrancisgreatfalls.org

SHELTON, Edna S (Mich) 18270 Northlawn St, Detroit MI 48221 B Tyrone PA 7/7/1937 d James Benjamin Martin & Edna May. RN Lewistown Hosp Sch 1958; Siena Coll 1988; Whitaker TS 1993. D 6/12/1993 Bp R(aymond) Stewart Wood Jr. m 10/27/1962 Bobby Leonard Shelton c 3. D S Pat's Epis Ch Madison Heights MI 2000-2010; D S Martha's Ch Detroit MI 1993-2000.

SHELTON, Joan Adams (CNY) 2126 Connecticut Ave Nw Apt 49, Washington DC 20008 B Ithaca NY 9/21/1932 d John Cranford Adams & Alice. BA Vas 1954; Med Leh 1979; MDiv Moravian TS 1979. D 6/17/1976 P 3/29/1979 Bp Lloyd Edward Gressle. Supply Dio Long Island Garden City NY 1999-2002; Fac Dio Haiti Ft Lauderdale FL 1996-1999; Vic S Jas Ch Cleveland NY 1991-1996; Vic S Paul's Ch Chittenango NY 1991-1996; Calv Ch Syracuse NY 1989-1990; R S Paul's Ch Portsmouth RI 1986-1989; Chr Ch Stroudsburg PA 1985-1986; S Mk's Epis Ch Moscow PA 1985; S Dunstans Ch Blue Bell PA 1983-1984; Int Dio Bethlehem Bethlehem PA 1982-1986; S Alb's Epis Ch Reading PA 1981-1983. Auth, "Stone Turning Into Star," Panlist, 1986. Tertiary Of The Soc Of S Fran. scl Moravian TS 1979; Phi Beta Kappa 1954. joanshelton@rcn.com

SHELTON, Linda Shelton (Tex) 3507 Plumb St, Houston TX 77005 **D Palmer Memi Ch Houston TX 2007-** B Bartlesville OK 9/12/1952 d Jack Holly Ross & Charlotte Louise. BA U of Texas 1973; Iona Sch for Mnstry--Dio Texas 2007. D 2/9/2007 Bp Don Adger Wimberly. m 11/9/1974 Thomas Shelton c 2. lshelton@palmerchurch.org

SHEMATEK, Jon Paul (Md) 9120 Frederick Rd, Ellicott City MD 21042 B Sewickley PA 11/24/1946 s Matthew Shematek & Ann. BA Bos 1968; MD U Pgh 1972. D 6/17/1989 Bp A(lbert) Theodore Eastman. m 7/5/1969 Eleanor Ann Mullins c 2.

SHEMAYEV, Roman Aelred (Mil) 3528 Valley Ridge Rd, Middleton WI 53562 B Saint Petersburg Russia 6/5/1972 s Vyacheslav Schekin & Tatyana. Herzen St Pedagogical U of Russia 1993; MDiv; MA Aquinas Inst of Theol 2000. Rec from Roman Catholic 9/11/2005 Bp Steven Andrew Miller. m 4/12/2002 Kara McCarty. Assoc R Gr Ch Madison WI 2005-2007. Comp of St. Lk-OSB 2007. rs4501h@hotmail.com

SHEPARD, Alfred Hugh (Colo) 6891 W Eldorado Pl, Lakewood CO 80227 B Denver CO 10/6/1932 s John Henry Shepard & Marg Elizabeth. BA U CO 1957; Dio Colorado Bp's TS CO 1982; Cert Nash 1984. D 6/2/1982 Bp William Carl Frey P 6/17/1984 Bp William Harvey Wolfrum. m 9/11/1956 Merta Margaret Bowers c 4. The Epis Par of S Greg Littleton CO 1996-2004; Vic S Mths Epis Ch Monument CO 1991-1993; S Marks Ch Eau Claire WI 1988-1991; S Phil's Ch Eau Claire WI 1988-1991; Coun On Mssn Strtgy Dio Eau Claire Eau Claire WI 1988-1990; S Barn Ch Clear Lake WI 1984-1991; Ch Of S Thos And S Jn New Richmond WI 1984-1988; Asst Ch Of S Phil And S Jas Denver CO 1982-1984. Ed, "Herald". mentasheperd@inzl.com

SHEPARD, Diane Elise Rucker (Pgh) 1155 Brintell St, Pittsburgh PA 15201 **P Calv Ch Pittsburgh PA 2007-** B Washington DC 9/9/1941 d Leslie Clary Rucker & Doris. BA W&M 1963; MA U CA 1972; MDiv Pittsburgh TS 1984; MS Chatham U 2011. D 6/2/1984 P 12/13/1984 Bp Alden Moinet Hathaway. m 8/24/1963 Paul Fenton Shepard c 2. R S Steph's Epis Ch Wilkinsburg PA 1992-2006; Assoc R St Andrews Epis Ch Pittsburgh PA 1984-1991. shepard1@mac.com

SHEPARD, John Holland (Spok) 5416 S Garfield St, Spokane WA 99223 **Died 8/24/2009** B Spencer IA 8/3/1944 s Thomas Ball Merrick Shepard & Leota Mae. BA U of So Dakota 1966; JD U of So Dakota 1971; MDiv CDSP 1991. D 11/1/1986 P 8/1/1991 Bp Craig Barry Anderson. c 2. john-shepard@ecunet.org

SHEPARD, Kenneth Reis (Neb) 811 Colony Ln, Lincoln NE 68505 B Evanston IL 11/8/1952 s Kenneth Sihler Shepard & Helen. BA DePauw U 1974; MA Estrn New Mex U 1976; MDiv Epis TS of The SW 1979; U of Nebraska 1996. D 8/6/1979 P 5/9/1980 Bp Richard Mitchell Trelease Jr. m 5/17/1974 Natalie Joann Brown c 1. R Trin Epis Ch Norfolk NE 2001-2003; P-in-c Trin Memi Epis Ch Crete NE 1999-2001; P-in-c S Mary's Ch Nebraska City NE 1997-1999; S Matt's Ch Lincoln NE 1994-1995; S Mk's On The Campus Lincoln NE 1992-1997; P-in-c S Jn's Epis Ch Vinita OK 1991; R S Basil's Epis Ch Tahlequah OK 1989-1990; Asst Emm Epis Ch Mercer Island WA 1987-1988; Chr Ch Sidney NE 1985-1987; R Ch Of The Gd Shpd Bridgeport NE 1985-1987; Ch of the H Faith Santa Fe NM 1982-1985; P-in-c S Mich's Ch Tucumcari NM 1980-1982; P-in-c S Jn's Ch Ft Sumner NM 1979-1982; P-in-c Trin Ch Portales NM 1979-1982. Outstanding Young Rel Ldr 1987. kshepard@unl.edu

SHEPARD, Margaret S (CGC) 1608 Baker Ct, Panama City FL 32401 **R S Andr's Epis Ch Panama City FL 2011-** B Birmingham AL 11/14/1940 d Robert E Smith & Jimmie. BA Birmingham-Sthrn Coll 1962; Cert U of Alabama 1964; MDiv STUSo 1994; DMin Wesley TS 2009. D 5/21/1994 P 12/3/1994 Bp Robert Oran Miller. m 8/21/1964 William Scott Shepard c 2. R S Jn The Evang Robertsdale AL 2006-2009; Int R H Sprt Epis Ch Gulf Shores AL 2005-2006; R Gr Epis Ch Mt Meigs AL 2002-2004; R All SS' Ch Sthrn Shores NC 1997-2001; Stndg COM Dio E Carolina Kinston NC 1997-2001; R S Andr's Ch Montevallo AL 1994-1996. Auth, "Called to Serve in Cmnty; Transforming a Par Vitality Through Intentionality and Pract," 2009; Auth, "Birmingham, Oh Birmingham," *Tracings*, STUSo, 1994. Dn of the Albemarle Dio E Carolina 1998; Biblia Hebrica STUSo Sewanee TN 1994. revshepard@gulftel.com

SHEPHERD, Angela F. (Md) Episcopal Diocese of Maryland, 4 E University Pkwy, Baltimore MD 21218 **GC - Disciplinary Bd for Bishops Dio Maryland Baltimore MD 2011-; Baltimore Intl Seafarers' Cntr Dio Maryland Baltimore MD 2010-; Camp Amazing Gr Dio Maryland Baltimore MD 2010-; Cn for Mssn and Outreach Dio Maryland Baltimore MD 2010-; Educ T/F Dio Maryland Baltimore MD 2010-; Epis Cmnty Serv of Maryland Dio Maryland Baltimore MD 2010-; Epis Serv Corps Dio Maryland Baltimore MD 2010-; Anti-Racism Dio Maryland Baltimore MD 2002-** B Louisville KY 5/1/1960 d Thomas Eugene Shepherd & Anna Mae. BBA Austin Peay St U 1983; MA Webster U 1988; MDiv SWTS 1996. D 6/22/1996 Bp Edwin Funsten Gulick Jr P 12/21/1996 Bp Arthur Benjamin Williams Jr. c 1. Stndg Com, Pres 2006-07 Dio Maryland Baltimore MD 2003-2007; GC Dep, 2003, 2006, 2009 Dio Maryland Baltimore MD 2002-2011; COM Dio Maryland Baltimore MD 2001-2006; R S Phil's Ch Annapolis MD 1999-2010; Dioc Coun Dio Ohio Cleveland OH 1997-1999; Vic S Aug's Epis Ch Youngstown OH 1996-1999. Auth, "Sharing the Cup," *Maryland Ch News*, Dio Maryland, 2006; Auth, "At A Vigil for Dom Violence," *Wmn Uncommon Prayers*, Morehouse Pub, 2000. DOK 1994. ML King Peace Maker Awd Anne Arundel Co. Black Cler Assoc. 2003; Field Prize for Homil SWTS 1996. afsmystic@msn.com

S

SHEPHERD, Burton Hale (WTex) 185 Towerview Dr Apt 1101, Saint Augustine FL 32092 B Kansas City KS 11/11/1927 s Orin Alfred Shepherd & Mary Ellen. BA Wstrn St Coll of Colorado 1952; MDiv Epis TS of The SW 1981. D 6/23/1981 Bp Scott Field Bailey P 1/20/1982 Bp Stanley Fillmore Hauser. m 7/9/1950 Mildred Krneta c 2. Exec Coun Dio W Texas San Antonio TX 1983-1990; R Ch Of The Epiph Kingsville TX 1983-1989; P-in-c S Fran By The Lake Canyon Lake TX 1982; Asst S Mk's Ch San Marcos TX 1981-1982. b_shepherd@bellsouth.net

SHEPHERD, Karlyn Ann (RG) 22 Bowersville Rd, Algodones NM 87001 B Washington DC 3/17/1944 d Henry King Nourse & Barbara Kristine. BA California St U. D 7/31/1990 Bp Charles Jones III. m 4/4/1974 Gordon Shepherd c 3. D S Mich And All Ang Ch Albuquerque NM 1999-2004.

SHEPHERD, Nancy DeLane (At) 1100 Pine Valley Road, Griffin GA 30224 **R S Geo's Epis Ch Griffin GA 2005-** B McKinney TX 8/29/1953 d Richard DeLane Layton & Velta Lee. BA Austin Coll 1974; MA Austin Coll 1975; MDiv SMU 1989; DAS VTS 1993. D 6/5/1993 P 12/15/1993 Bp A(rthur) Heath Light. m 6/30/1995 William Henry Shepherd c 1. R S Andr's Ch Milford CT 1996-2005; Assoc R S Matt's Ch Maple Glen PA 1993-1996; S Jn's Ch Lynchburg VA 1989-1992. revnancy@gmail.com

SHEPHERD, Nancy Hamilton (Mass) 172 Harvard Rd, Stow MA 01775 B Brooklyn NY 4/7/1931 d Peter Hamilton & Nancy Spalding. BA Mid 1953; Med Bos 1975; MDiv Bex 1981. D 5/30/1981 Bp John Bowen Coburn P 6/1/1982 Bp Roger W Blanchard. m 8/15/1953 Thomas R Shepherd c 4. Dn Of Concord River Dnry Dio Massachusetts Boston MA 1996-1999; Chair - Prison Min Comm Dio Massachusetts Boston MA 1990-1999; Co-Chair Of Pstr Outreach Cmsn Dio Massachusetts Boston MA 1987-1990; R Trin Chap Shirley MA 1984-2001; Co-Chair Of Par Dvlpmt Com Dio Massachusetts Boston MA 1983-1987; Asst Trin Chap Shirley MA 1981-1982. Ma Epis Cleric Assn.

SHEPHERD, Richard Golder (NY) 39 Crockett Point Road, Bernard ME 04612 B Syracuse NY 7/29/1927 s Thomas Dudley Shepherd & Elsbeth Ellerby. BFA Cor 1949; STB Ya Berk 1956; STM Yale DS 1957. D 6/1/1956 P 12/18/1956 Bp Horace W B Donegan. m 9/3/1955 Ruth Adams c 2. Liturg Cmsn Dio New York New York City NY 1973-1983; R Trin Ch Saugerties NY 1960-1992; P-in-c Ch Of The Epiph Southbury CT 1956-1960. rgshepherd@roadrunner.com

SHEPHERD, Stephen Gregory (Va) 6019 Hibbling Ave, Springfield VA 22150 **R S Dunst's McLean VA 2005-** B Denville NJ 7/12/1960 s Dennis Shepherd & Ivy. BS NYU 1982; MDiv VTS 2002. D 6/15/2002 P 12/18/2002 Bp Peter James Lee. m 7/18/1987 Tami Shepherd. Asst S Barn Ch Annandale VA 2002-2005.

SHEPHERD, Thomas Charles (Mass) 6600 Ne 22nd Way Apt 2323, Fort Lauderdale FL 33308 B Toledo OH 5/8/1938 s Wayne George Shepherd & Virginia. MDiv Bex 1960; BA U of Toledo 1960. D 6/15/1963 P 12/21/1963 Bp Nelson Marigold Burroughs. R Chr Ch Epis Harwich Port MA 1982-2000; Dioc Coun Dio New York New York City NY 1979-1981; R S Andr's Ch Walden NY 1973-1982; Asst S Andr's Epis Ch Toledo OH 1963-1965. Auth, "Ministering to Ex-Offenders," *Wit*, 1985. tmshepr@aol.com

SHEPHERD, Thomas Eugene (WMo) 1107 Saratoga Drive, Euless TX 76040 B Jackson TN 8/9/1936 s Earle Frank Shepherd & Loaraine Alberta. BS U of Louisville 1969; MS U of Louisville 1973; MDiv STUSo 1980. D 6/21/1980 P 1/10/1982 Bp David Reed. m 12/30/1958 Anna Young c 4. Stndg Com; Dio W Missouri Kansas City MO 2003-2004; R S Aug's Ch Kansas City MO 1999-2004; COM; Soc Concerns Commision; Dioc Nwsltr Bd; Bd Truistees, St. Andr's Sch, Boca Raton Dio SE Florida Miami FL 1992-1998; R S Matt's Epis Ch Delray Bch FL 1990-1999; Bp & Coun Bd; Cmsn on Evang & Racism; Emm Epis Cntr Bd; Sprtl Dir for Curs Dio W Tennessee Memphis TN 1985-2000; R Emm Ch Memphis TN 1985-1990; Exec Coun Dio Kentucky Louisville KY 1985; R Ch Of Our Merc Sav Louisville KY 1981-1985; Dio Kentucky Louisville KY 1980-1981; D S Geo's Epis Ch Louisville KY 1980-1981. EUC 1980-1990; OHC 1980; UBE 1980-2004. Bp's Shield Bp of W Missouri 2004; Annual Awd for Meritorious & Faithful Serv for Establis UBE 1993. thomaseshep@sbcglobal.net

SHEPHERD JR, William Henry (At) 1100 Pine Valley Rd, Griffin GA 30224 B Indianapolis IN 9/20/1957 s William H Shepherd & Joycelyn D. BA U GA 1979; MDiv Ya Berk 1982; PhD Emory U 1994; MLIS Valdosta St U 2008. D 10/28/1982 P 5/25/1983 Bp Edward Witker Jones. m 6/30/1995 Nancy DeLane Layton. Int S Jn's Ch Bridgeport CT 2003-2005; Int S Ptr's Epis Ch Cheshire CT 2002-2003; Int Gr And S Ptr's Epis Ch Hamden CT 1999-2001; Int Chr Ch Avon CT 1998-1999; Prof Geo Mercer TS Garden City NY 1996-2000; Int S Lk's Ch Katonah NY 1996-1998; Int Emm Ch Quakertown PA 1995-1996; Int S Geo's Ch Pennsville NJ 1994-1995; Asst Prof Homil VTS Alexandria VA 1991-1993; Asst S Cathr's Epis Ch Marietta GA 1989-1990; Assoc S Paul's Epis Ch Indianapolis IN 1984-1986; Asst S Chris's Epis Ch Carmel IN 1982-1983. Auth, "Without a Net," CSS, 2004; Auth, "If a Sermon Falls in The Forest: Preaching Resurection Texts," CSS, 2003; Auth, "No Deed Grtr than a Word," CSS, 1998; Auth, "Narrative Function of H Sprt in Lk-Acts," Scholars Press, 1994. whshep@gmail.com

SHEPHERD, William John (Pa) 110 W Johnson St, Philadelphia PA 19144 B Philadelphia PA 7/29/1929 s John Shepherd & May. BS Tem 1957; STM PDS 1960. D 5/14/1960 Bp Joseph Gillespie Armstrong P 11/1/1960 Bp Albert Ervine Swift. m 2/18/1969 Dolores R Kelly. Philadelphia Cathd Philadelphia PA 1997-1999; Int S Lk's Ch Philadelphia PA 1995-1997; Asst S Lk's Ch Philadelphia PA 1984-1994; Vic S Geo S Barn Ch Philadelphia PA 1960-1961. jack.shepherd@verizon.net

SHEPIC, Charlotte Louise (Colo) 14031 W Exposition Dr, Lakewood CO 80228 B Elkhart KS 12/31/1954 d Robert Norman Thomas & Ida May. BA Knox Coll 1976; Cert Barnes Bus Coll 1985; D Formation Prog 1997; Cert Sursum Corda 2005. D 11/8/1997 Bp William Jerry Winterrowd. m 9/20/1980 John Anthony Shepic c 1. D S Paul's Epis Ch Lakewood CO 2001-2006; Dio Colorado Denver CO 1998-2005; Admin - H Ord Dio Colorado Denver CO 1998-2004; D S Martha's Epis Ch Westminster CO 1998-2000. clshepic@q.com

SHEPLEY, Joseph (Ct) 65 Grey Rock Road, Southbury CT 06488 **P-in-c S Paul's Ch Brookfield CT 2009-** B Saint Louis MO 9/28/1970 s Joseph Edmund Griesedieck & Carolyn Rhett. BS Bradley U 1992; MDiv TESM 1996. D 6/8/1996 Bp John Clark Buchanan P 12/14/1996 Bp Sanford Zangwill Kaye Hampton. m 8/20/1994 Tara DeCristoforo c 3. Asst S Paul's Ch Brookfield CT 2006-2009; Cur S Thos Ch New York NY 1999-2002; Cur S Mary's Ch Lakewood WA 1996-1999. shepley.j@gmail.com

SHEPPARD, Dale Eugene (WVa) 1051 Walker Road, Follansbee WV 26037 **Brooke-Hancock Cluster Wellsburg WV 2006-** B Parkersburg WV 7/10/1948 BS Ohio Vlly Coll 2001; MDiv Bex 2006. D 12/10/2005 P 6/10/2006 Bp William Michie Klusmeyer. m 10/29/1968 Janice Janice Kay Richards c 3. DALESHEPPARD@COMCAST.NET

SHEPPARD, Edward Lee (Minn) 1365 Iowa Ave W, Saint Paul MN 55108 B Kennewick WA 10/26/1924 s Edward Sheppard & Viola. MA U IL 1943; BA U of Washington 1945; MDiv U Chi 1952; MS U MN 1976. D 6/20/1959 Bp Philip Frederick McNairy P 12/1/1959 Bp Hamilton Hyde Kellogg. m 8/20/1980 Betty Sheppard. P-in-c Bp Whipple Mssn Morton MN 1978-1985; Vic Our Fr's Hse Ft Washakie WY 1976-1978; St Michaels Ch - Ethete Laramie WY 1976-1977; Dio Minnesota Minneapolis MN 1972-1984; R S Mart's Epis Ch Fairmont MN 1970-1972; Cur S Jn In The Wilderness White Bear Lake MN 1967-1970; In-C Adv Ch Farmington MN 1964-1966; R Ascen Ch St Paul MN 1963-1967; P-in-c S Paul's Ch Pipestone MN 1961-1963; Vic Emm Ch Rushford MN 1959-1961; Vic S Matt's Epis Ch Chatfield MN 1959-1961. Auth, "Second 50 Years". Phil Beta Kappa. BPSHEPPARD25@MSN.COM

SHEPPARD, Patricia K (Fla) 919 San Fernando St., Fernandina Beach FL 32034 **S Fran Of Assisi Epis Ch Tallahassee FL 2011-** B Cleveland OH 9/26/1949 d Irvin Kofsky & Margaret M. MDiv CDSP 2001. Trans 2/29/2004 Bp J Clark Grew II. m 9/11/2005 Don A Robbins c 1. Bethany Ch Hilliard FL 2007-2008; Ch Of The H Sprt Charlestown RI 2004-2005; S Jn's Epis Ch Bowling Green OH 2002-2004. therevpatricia@aol.com

SHERARD, Susan (NC) 235 W Hedgelawn Way, Southern Pines NC 28387 B Vicksburg MS 7/30/1949 d James Gorman Sherard & Florence Elizabeth. BA Lake Forest Coll 1971; MA Sangamon St U 1974; MDiv GTS 1985. D 6/15/1985 P 1/18/1986 Bp William Gillette Weinhauer. m 11/11/2000 Thomas J Panek. S Dav's Epis Ch Laurinburg NC 2004-2005; Chair COM Dio Wstrn No Carolina Asheville NC 1995-2000; Dn Asheville Deanry Dio Wstrn No Carolina Asheville NC 1990-1993; COM Dio Wstrn No Carolina Asheville NC 1987-1995; Dio Wstrn No Carolina Asheville NC 1987-1993; Epis Ch Of The H Sprt Mars Hill NC 1985-2000.

SHERFICK, Kenneth L (WMich) 1517 Emoriland Blvd, Knoxville TN 37917 B Washington IN 3/8/1936 s Kenneth Lyle Sherfick & Edith May. BA Franklin Coll 1962; BD ETSBH 1965. D 6/14/1965 P 12/20/1965 Bp John P Craine. m 8/16/1983 Kathleen English c 5. Assoc S Thos Epis Ch Knoxville TN 1999-2008; Stndg Com Dio Wstrn Michigan Kalamazoo MI 1990-1998; Bps Search Com Dio Wstrn Michigan Kalamazoo MI 1988; R S Mk's Ch Coldwater MI 1984-1998; Dep Gc Dio Indianapolis Indianapolis IN 1979-1982; R Gr Ch Muncie IN 1968-1984; Cur Chr Ch Cathd Indianapolis IN 1965-1968. ksherfick@knology.net

SHERIDAN-CAMPBELL, Laura M (SanD) 6540 Ambrosia Ln Apt 1128, Carlsbad CA 92011 **COM Dio San Diego San Diego CA 2011-; Vic H Cross Mssn Carlsbad CA 2010-** B Des Moines IA 5/9/1964 d Harold H Sellner & Patricia A. Wartburg Coll 1984; BA U of Iowa 1987; MS Iowa St U 1990; MDiv Ya Berk 1993; D. Min. CDSP 2010. D 5/19/1993 P 3/1/1994 Bp Carl Christopher Epting. m 1/28/2011 Jerry L Campbell. Tchg Asst CDSP Berkeley CA 2008-2010; Stndg Com Dio NW Texas Lubbock TX 2006-2008; GC Cler Dep Dio NW Texas Lubbock TX 2004-2006; GC Cler Dep Alt. Dio NW Texas Lubbock TX 2001-2003; S Jn's Epis Ch Odessa TX 1996-2008; Chapl S Jn's Epis Ch Odessa TX 1996-2008; Chapl S Jn's Epis Ch Odessa TX 1996-2008; Cur The Cathd Ch Of S Paul Des Moines IA 1993-1996. lsheridancampbell@att.net

SHERK JR, Grant Rhoads (Va) 2307 Devonshire Way, Palm Beach Gardens FL 33418 **Died 4/9/2010** B West Norfolk VA 4/3/1920 s Grant Rhoads Sherk &

S

Madie Lee. BA U of Virginia 1948; MA U of Virginia 1950; MDiv VTS 1957. D 9/1/1957 P 6/1/1958 Bp Frederick D Goodwin. c 3.

SHERMAN, Andrew James (SeFla) 245 NE 2nd St., Boca Raton FL 33432 **Bd, St. Andr's Sch Dio SE Florida Miami FL 2010-; Bd, Epis Chars Dio SE Florida Miami FL 2008-; R S Greg's Ch Boca Raton FL 2005-** B Rockville Center NY 6/30/1962 s Harry Benjamin Sherman & Joan Marie. BA Amer U 1984; MA U of Virginia 1992; MDiv VTS 1992. D 6/23/1992 Bp John Wadsworth Howe P 2/20/1993 Bp Charlie Fuller McNutt Jr. m 8/18/2005 Anita Sarah Cherian c 2. Dn, So Palm Bch Dnry Dio SE Florida Miami FL 2006-2009; R The Memi Ch Of The Prince Of Peace Gettysburg PA 1995-2005; S Jn's Epis Ch Carlisle PA 1992-1995. co-Auth, "I Believe," *Cnfrmtn Prog*, Ldr Resources, 2006. asherman@st-gregorys.com

SHERMAN, Clark Michael (Mont) 5 W Olive St, Bozeman MT 59715 **Reg Cn Dio Montana Helena MT 2005-; Yth & Coll Comm Dio Montana Helena MT 2004-; R S Jas Ch Bozeman MT 1997-** B Ancon PA 1/18/1957 s Louis Leroy Sherman & Mildred Mozelle. BD How 1979; MA Steph F. Austin St U 1984; MDiv Iliff TS 1991; S Thos Sem Denver CO 1992; DPS Evang Chr U Monroe LA 2001. D 6/12/1993 P 12/18/1993 Bp William Jerry Winterrowd. m 12/29/1978 Jamie D Douglas c 3. Fndt Bd Dio Montana Helena MT 2002-2006; Eccl Crt Dio Montana Helena MT 1999-2006; Chairman Dio Montana Helena MT 1999-2001; Stndg Com Dio Montana Helena MT 1998-2001; BEC Dio Colorado Denver CO 1996-1997; Exec Coun Dio Colorado Denver CO 1995-1997; Dir Dio Colorado Denver CO 1993-1997; Vic S Pat's Epis Ch Pagosa Sprg CO 1993-1997; Dio Colorado Denver CO 1993-1996. The Ord of S Lk the Physcn 1984. paran97@gmail.com

SHERMAN, Elizabeth Ann (Cal) St. Francis Episcopal Church, San Francisco CA 94127 **R S Fran' Epis Ch San Francisco CA 2011-** B Dallas TX 11/21/1955 d Wilbur Brown Sherman & Virginia. BA U of Texas 1977; MDiv GTS 1981. D 6/7/1982 Bp Brice Sidney Sanders P 4/9/1983 Bp John Shelby Spong. P-in-c S Dav's On The Hill Epis Ch Cranston RI 2008-2011; Brown and RISD Dio Rhode Island Providence RI 1998-2008; Vic St Fran Epis Ch Coventry RI 1998-2008; Asst For Ce Par of Trin Ch New York NY 1985-1990; Cur Chr Ch Ridgewood NJ 1982-1985. potopos2@gmail.com

SHERMAN, Guy Charles (Oly) 12527 Roosevelt Way Ne Apt 404, Seattle WA 98125 B Tenino WA 5/6/1940 s Robert Holland Sherman & Elsie Nelline. BA U of Puget Sound 1964; MDiv CDSP 1973. D 11/10/1973 Bp Ivol I Curtis P 5/9/1980 Bp Robert Hume Cochrane. c 2. Int S Paul's Epis Ch Bremerton WA 2009-2010; Int Chr Epis Ch Puyallup WA 2005-2007; Int St Jn's Epis Ch of Sturgis Sturgis MI 2003-2004; Int Ch Of The H Trin Midland TX 2002-2003; Int Chr Ch Eureka CA 2000-2002; Vic S Aid's Epis Ch Camano Island WA 1988-1998; Dio Olympia Seattle WA 1987-1988; Dio Olympia Seattle WA 1980-1983; Assoc Trin Epis Ch Everett WA 1976-1988; Asst Chr Ch SEATTLE WA 1973-1974. guycs@comcast.net

SHERMAN JR, Levering Bartine (Me) 86 Hawk La, Hartland ME 04943 **S Mart's Epis Ch Pittsfield ME 2006-; Dio Maine Portland ME 2000-; Vic All SS Epis Ch Skowhegan ME 1997-** B Charlotte NC 2/10/1946 s L(evering) Bartine Sherman & Elizabeth Davidson. BA U NC 1969; Pr 1971; MDiv EDS 1973; MA U NC 1984. D 11/4/1973 P 6/8/1974 Bp Matthew G Henry. m 3/14/1986 Adrianna Paliyenko c 3. Vic S Barn Ch Augusta Augusta ME 1989-1997; P Ch Of S Mths Asheville NC 1973-1975. Auth, *Like an Ever-Rolling Stream: Sm Ch in Maine*, Maine PBS, 1991; Auth, *Pokin' Fun: The Tradition of Maine Humor*, Maine PBS, 1991. Maine Broadcasters Assn Awd of Excellence 1990; "Who's Who in Amer Colleges and Universities" 1972. lbsherma@yahoo.com

SHERMAN, Russell E (WTex) 510 Belknap Pl, San Antonio TX 78212 B Oceanside NY 10/23/1949 s Robert Emmett Sherman & Martha Elsa. BA Ken 1972; MDiv STUSo 1985. D 6/16/1985 Bp Frank Stanley Cerveny P 5/1/1986 Bp Allen Lyman Bartlett Jr. m 12/27/1975 Kathleen Schert c 3. Chr Epis Ch San Antonio TX 1997-2003; R S Jn's Ch Speedway IN 1995-1997; Asst Ch Of The Gd Samar Paoli PA 1985-1995. ERM; Episcopalians Untd; Ord Of S Lk; Ord Of S Mary. russell.sherman@gmail.com

SHERRER, Wayne Calvin (Be) 150 Elm Street, Emmaus PA 18049 **P-in-c S Marg's Ch Emmaus PA 2010-** B Phillipsburg NJ 10/8/1951 s August Calvin Sherrer & Lois Alva. BA Immac Heart Coll 1980; MDiv McCormick TS 1986. D 2/2/2009 Bp John Palmer Croneberger P 9/29/2009 Bp Paul Victor Marshall. m 4/9/1994 Mildred Evangeline Brooks c 2. Assoc Trin Ch Easton PA 2009-2010; D S Geo's Epis Ch Hellertown PA 2009. wayneshrrr@gmail.com

SHERRILL, Christopher Ralph (NJ) P.O. Box 45, Southport ME 04576 B Warm Sprgs GA 1/11/1935 s Ralph Lumpkin Sherrill & Edith Marvin. BA Geneva Coll 1960; BD Yale DS 1965. D 6/19/1965 Bp William S Thomas P 12/18/1965 Bp Austin Pardue. m 8/13/1960 H Leigh Davidson c 3. Assoc Trin Ch Princeton NJ 1992-2001; Assoc The Ch Of The Epiph Washington DC 1988-1992; R Chr Ch Wm And Mary Newburg MD 1986-1988; Asst All Souls Memi Epis Ch Washington DC 1984-1986; St Matthews Ch Mitchellville MD 1979-1980; S Pat's Ch Washington DC 1972-1979; R S Alb's Ch Danielson CT 1969-1972; Assoc Chr Epis Ch S Jos MO 1966-1969. EvangES 1995-2001. kitleigh@gwi.net

SHERRILL II, Edmund Knox (NH) St. Mark's School, 25 Marlboro Rd, Southborough MA 01772 **CFS The Sch At Ch Farm Exton PA 2009-** B Dickinson ND 9/9/1956 s Franklin Goldthwaite Sherrill & Mary Chamberlain. BA Macalester Coll 1979; MDiv Ya Berk 1983. D 6/28/1985 P 5/1/1986 Bp Philip Alan Smith. m 8/18/1979 Elizabeth Roberts Evans c 2. St. Mk's Sch of Southborough Inc. Southborough MA 2003-2009; S Andr's-In-The-Vlly Tamworth NH 2002-2003; Dio Micronesia Tumon Bay GU GU 1998-2002; COM Dio New Hampshire Concord NH 1992-1998; S Paul's Sch Concord NH 1991-1998; Wooster Sch Danbury CT 1986-1990; S Paul's Sch Concord NH 1985-1986; Assoc H Cross Epis Ch Weare NH 1984-1986. esherrill@gocfs.net

SHERRILL II, Franklin Goldthwaite (NH) High Haith Rd, Box 2, Center Harbor NH 02/01/3226 B Boston MA 5/5/1928 s Henry Knox Sherrill & Barbara. BA Ya 1949; UTS 1950; BD EDS 1953. D 6/6/1953 P 12/11/1953 Bp Henry Knox Sherrill. m 6/12/1953 Mary Chamberlain Taylor c 3. P-in-c S Mk's Ch Ashland NH 2000-2006; Int Gr Epis Ch Concord NH 1998-2001; Int The Ch Of The Redeem Rochester NH 1996-1997; Int S Jn's Ch Portsmouth NH 1995-1996; Int S Thos Ch Hanover NH 1993-1994; R Gr Ch Brooklyn NY 1967-1993; R Ascen Memi Ch Ipswich MA 1958-1967; R S Jn's Epis Ch Dickinson ND 1953-1958.

SHERRILL JR, George (WVa) 603 Hawthorne Ln, Hurricane WV 25526 **R Chr Ch Clarksburg WV 2008-; S Tim's In The Vlly Hurricane WV 2008-** B Atlanta GA 2/15/1966 s George Sherrill & Claire. BA Wofford Coll 1989; MDiv VTS Alexandria VA 2006. D 12/10/2005 P 6/10/2006 Bp William Michie Klusmeyer. m 6/22/1991 Sara Sherrill c 3.

SHERROUSE, Wanda Gail (CFla) 121 W 18th St, Sanford FL 32771 B Toledo OH 10/2/1952 AS Valencia Cmnty Coll. D 12/13/2003 Bp John Wadsworth Howe. c 2. D H Cross Epis Ch Sanford FL 2003-2004.

SHERWIN, Lawrence Alan (Vt) 54 E State St, Montpelier VT 05602 B Bennington VT 3/30/1939 s Leo J Sherwin & Margaret Isabelle. BA U of Vermont 1962; MA EDS 1968. D 6/15/1968 P 12/1/1968 Bp Harvey D Butterfield. c 3. R S Jas Epis Ch Arlington VT 1970-1974; Cur Cathd Ch Of S Pàul Burlington VT 1968-1970. larrys1411@yahoo.com

SHERWOOD, Zalmon Omar (Mich) PO Box 1342, Arcadia FL 34265 B Geneva OH 11/3/1956 s Zalmon Omar Sherwood & Janet Ann. BA Hiram Coll 1979; MDiv EDS 1981; MA New Engl Conservatory of Mus 1984. D 6/30/1984 Bp James Russell Moodey P 6/22/1985 Bp Robert Whitridge Estill. Exec Dir S Jas Epis Mssn Beaver Island MI 1990-1993; Cur S Paul's Epis Ch Jackson MI 1986-1990; Cur Emm Par Epis Ch And Day Sch Sthrn Pines NC 1984-1985. Auth, "Equal Rites: Liberating Wrshp For Lesbians & Gay Men," Westminster, 1990; Auth, "Kairos- Confessions Of A Gay P," Alyson, 1986. zalmon@centurylink.net

SHETTERS, Lucy Lee (Tenn) Saint Marys Convent, Sewanee TN 37375 **Sis-In-Charge Sis of St Mary Sewanee TN 1972-** B Cowan TN 12/18/1933 d James Henry Shetters & Ruby Katherine. MDiv STUSo 1979. D 6/29/1979 P 5/1/1980 Bp William Evan Sanders.

SHEVLIN, James Charles (Alb) Saint Paul's Church, 25 River St, Sidney NY 13838 **P S Paul's Ch Sidney NY 2003-** B Johnson City NY 6/24/1949 s John Andrew Shevlin & Margaret Dorthea. DAS TESM 2008. D 1/12/2003 Bp David John Bena P 12/15/2007 Bp William Howard Love. m 1/26/1991 Jean M Russell c 7. jjshevlin@msn.com

SHEW, Debra Ann (At) 3627 Shadowood Pkwy Se, Atlanta GA 30339 **Dio Atlanta Atlanta GA 1999-** B Fort Dix NJ 9/26/1960 d Richard Joseph Metzgar & Martha Ann. BA Davidson Coll 1982; Med Georgia St U 1985; Pyschological Stds Inst For Chr Counslg 1985; MDiv GTS 1994. D 6/4/1994 P 12/1/1994 Bp Frank Kellogg Allan. m 7/17/2003 David Shew c 1. H Innoc Ch Atlanta GA 1994-1999. dshew@episcopalatlanta.org

SHEWMAKER, David Paul (NCal) St Francis Episcopal Ch, 568 16th St, Fortuna CA 95540 **S Paul's Mssn Cres City CA 2008-** B St Joseph MO 1/18/1945 s Marion Francis Shewmaker & Carolyn Joy. BA U of Missouri 1969; MA U of Missouri 1971; CAS CDSP 2007. D 9/7/2007 P 4/12/2008 Bp Barry Leigh Beisner. m 11/29/1986 Alicia Shewmaker c 4. shew1@suddenlink.net

SHIELD, Catherine Ann (Kan) 13420 E Harry St, Wichita KS 67230 **D S Jude's Ch Wellington KS 2007-; D S Jas Ch Wichita KS 2000-** B Abilene TX 8/29/1946 d Dixon Putnam Griffith & Mary Elizabeth. BS U of Oklahoma 1968. D 10/26/1990 Bp William Edward Smalley. m 8/31/1966 Charles Franklin Shield c 3. NAAD.

SHIELDS, James Mark (Md) 6153 Waiting Spg, Columbia MD 21045 B Pittsburgh PA 11/30/1931 s James Mark Shields & Mary Randolph. BA U of Maryland 1965; BD ETS 1968. D 6/29/1968 Bp William S Thomas P 12/21/1968 Bp Robert Bracewell Appleyard. m 12/22/1955 Seiko Hattori c 1. R Chr Ch Columbia MD 1979-1999; R Ch Of The Adv Pittsburgh PA 1970-1979; D-in-c Ch Of The Gd Shpd Pittsburgh PA 1968-1969. jms1931@verizon.net

SHIELDS, John Edward (NC) 520 Summit St, Winston Salem NC 27101 B Winston-Salem NC 8/13/1938 s John Oliver Shields & Myrtle Pearl. U NC; VTS; Wake Forest U; BA Guilford Coll 1960. D 4/25/1985 P 4/25/1986 Bp Robert Whitridge Estill. m 8/29/1958 Kay W Watts c 3. Int Ch Of The H Comf Charlotte NC 2009-2010; S Paul's Epis Ch Winston Salem NC 1997-2009;

S

Vic Chr Ch Walnut Cove NC 1986-1996; Vic S Eliz Epis Ch King NC 1986-1996; Asst S Tim's Epis Ch Winston Salem NC 1985-1986. jeshields@stpauls-ws.org

SHIELDS, John Wesley (Me) 2508 Amity Ave, Gastonia NC 28054 B Asheville NC 4/6/1977 BS No Carolina St U 1999; MDiv STUSo 2003. D 5/31/2003 P 12/4/2003 Bp Robert Hodges Johnson. m 12/30/2000 Laura Goodson Shields c 2. S Columba's Epis Ch Boothbay Harbor ME 2009-2011; Ch Of S Andr's In The Pines Pinedale WY 2004-2009; S Mk's Ch Gastonia NC 2003-2004. shields.laura@rocketmail.com

SHIELDS, Richard E (Haw) 1330 1st Ave Apt 424, New York NY 10021 **Supply P Dio Hawaii Honolulu HI 2005-** B Beacon NY 12/11/1952 s Roger Douglas Shields & Kathleen Mary. BS Creighton U 1974; LTh SWTS 1979; MA U of Nebraska 1983; PharmD U IL 1996. D 5/21/1979 Bp Quintin Ebenezer Primo Jr P 11/30/1979 Bp James Daniel Warner. Supply P Dio Hawaii Honolulu HI 2006-2011; Supply P Dio Georgia Savannah GA 2003-2005; Supply P Dio W Virginia Charleston WV 1997-2003; Novc, SSJE S Jn's Chap Cambridge MA 1989-1990; Int All SS Epis Ch Boise ID 1988-1989; Mssy Exec Coun Appointees New York NY 1986-1988; Supply P Dio Nebraska Omaha NE 1983-1986; R Chr Ch Cntrl City NE 1981-1983; Vic S Johns Ch Albion NE 1981-1983; Cur S Andr's Ch Omaha NE 1979-1980. Soc of St Jn the Evang 1989-1990. pharmer@nyc.rr.com

SHIER, Marshall Wayne (Los) 1348 E Wilshire Ave, Fullerton, 92831-3927 CA B Port Angeles WA 3/8/1944 s Lloyd Ellis Owen & Frances Earle. BA Seattle U 1966; MLS U CA 1969; Cert U CA 1970; ETSBH 1975; Rel M Claremont TS 1976. D 6/19/1976 P 1/15/1977 Bp Robert C Rusack. S Andr's Par Fullerton CA 1976-2009. blackturtle@bearturtle.us

SHIER, Nancy Katherine (Los) 224 Bradbury Dr, San Gabriel CA 91775 B Pasadena CA 5/31/1938 d Cyril Winfred Shier & Katherine Esther. BA Stan 1960; MA California St U 1974; MA California St U 1987; MDiv Claremont TS 2000. D 10/21/2001 Bp Frederick Houk Borsch P 11/23/2002 Bp Chester Lovelle Talton. c 2. Ch Of Our Sav Par San Gabr CA 2003-2010; Imm Mssn El Monte CA 2001-2003. nkas@charter.net

SHIER, Pamela Cottrell (WVa) 164 Mason Ridge Rd, Mount Morris PA 15349 **P-in-c Prince Of Peace Salem Salem WV 1999-** B Plainfield NJ 1/16/1952 d Leon Wilfred Cottrell & Joan Cottrell. BS Cor 1975; MDiv EDS 1979. D 6/23/1979 P 6/24/1980 Bp Ned Cole. m 6/12/1983 Michael R Johnson. COM Dio W Virginia Charleston WV 1982-1990; Dio W Virginia Charleston WV 1980-1990; Assoc S Thos a Becket Epis Ch Morgantown WV 1980-1988; D S Andr's Ch Ann Arbor MI 1979-1980. Prof Serv Awd Coll of Chapl 1990. pamelashier@hotmail.com

SHIFLET JR, William Ray (Md) 4520 Cornflower Ct, Ellicott City MD 21043 B Roanoke VA 5/3/1947 s William Ray Shiflet & Rachel. AA Ferrum Coll 1967; BS VPI 1969; MDiv VTS 1972; DMin Hartford Sem 1980. D 6/9/1972 Bp William Henry Marmion P 12/13/1972 Bp Philip Alan Smith. m 8/26/1967 Mary Milton Larner c 2. VTS Alexandria VA 2006; R S Jn's Ch Ellicott City MD 1987-2005; R Trin Ch Branford CT 1980-1987; Assoc Trin Epis Ch Southport CT 1976-1980; Asst Chr Epis Ch Roanoke VA 1972-1976. Branford Citizen Of The Year 1986. drwshiflet@verizon.net

SHIGAKI, Jerry M (Oly) 6963 California Ave Sw Unit 102, Seattle WA 98136 B Seattle WA 10/21/1946 s George Shigaki & Yasuko. BA U of Washington 1968; MSW U of Washington 1975; MDiv SWTS 2000. D 6/24/2000 P 1/13/2001 Bp Sanford Zangwill Kaye Hampton. c 1. Mssnr for Ethnic Mnstry Dio Olympia Seattle WA 2000-2010; Assoc S Ben Epis Ch Lacey WA 2000-2002. jershigaki@hotmail.com

SHIKE, Charles Wesley (Nwk) 2600 Netherland Ave Apt 2117, Bronx NY 10463 B Hope NJ 11/17/1924 s Charles Edward Shike & Virginia. BA Swarthmore Coll 1948; MDiv VTS 1951; Robbins Fell 1963; Cert Natl Psychol Assn For Psychoanalysis 1967; DMin Andover Newton TS 1974. D 6/16/1951 P 6/1/1952 Bp Angus Dun. m 7/17/2003 Soomintra Rai Shike c 2. The Ch of S Matt And S Tim New York NY 1994-1998; S Paul's Ch Montvale NJ 1963-1965; Dio Newark Newark NJ 1960-1961; Dept Of Chr Soc Relatns Dio Newark Newark NJ 1960-1961; Advsr For The Newark Archdnry Dio Newark Newark NJ 1958-1960; Bd Yth Consulting Serv Dio Newark Newark NJ 1957-1962; Dept Of Missions Dio Newark Newark NJ 1957-1958; Dept Of CE Dio Newark Newark NJ 1954-1958; R S Thos Ch Lyndhurst NJ 1953-1960; Advsr Of NW Chr Yth Coun Dio Washington Washington DC 1952-1953; Dept Of CE Dio Washington Washington DC 1951-1953; Asst S Alb's Par Washington DC 1951-1953. AAPC, AAMFC; Amer Assn Play Ther; Chair Bd Exam Natl Assn Advancement Psychol 1996. Robbins Fell 1960; Dip Aapc. cwshike@aol.com

SHILEY, Edward (Pa) 145 West Springfield Road, Springfield PA 19064 **Ch Fndt Bd Dio Pennsylvania Philadelphia PA 2009-2012; Shiley, E. Edw Ch Of The Redeem Springfield PA 2004-** B Winchester VA 8/21/1944 s Earl White Shiley & Vada. BA Westminster Choir Coll of Rider U 1966; MDiv EDS 1997. D 7/12/1997 Bp Arthur Benjamin Williams Jr P 1/1/1998 Bp J Clark Grew II. m 8/21/1976 Kim A Martinelli c 2. Dioc Mssn Plnng Cmsn Dio Pennsylvania Philadelphia PA 2009-2011; Dn of Delaware Dnry Dio Pennsylvania Philadelphia PA 2008-2011; Salaries and Pennsions Dio Pennsylvania Philadelphia PA 2007-2008; Dioc Coun Dio Pennsylvania Philadelphia PA 2002-2011; R S Ptr's Epis Ch Broomall PA 2000-2004; R S Jas Epis Ch Boardman OH 1997-2000.

✠ SHIMPFKY, Rt Rev Richard Lester (ECR) 10 Liberty St Apt 25G, New York NY 10005 **Died 2/28/2011** B Albuquerque NM 10/18/1940 s Henry Lester Shimpfky & Thelma Louise. BA U CO 1963; MDiv VTS 1970; DD VTS 1991. D 6/20/1970 P 6/1/1971 Bp Philip Alan Smith Con 9/8/1990 for ECR. c 3. Auth, "The Par Eucharistic Ch," 1990. DD VTS 1991. richardshimpfky@gmail.com

SHIN, Allen Kunho (LI) 12 Prospect St, Huntington NY 11743 **R S Jn's Ch Huntington NY 2010-** B Seoul KR 6/26/1956 s Kyung Joon Shin & Chu Young. SWTS 1995; MDiv GTS 1996; STM GTS 2001; Oxf 2001. D 6/15/1996 Bp Frank Tracy Griswold III P 12/7/1996 Bp Richard Frank Grein. m 5/25/1991 Clara H Mun. Cur Ch Of S Mary The Vrgn New York NY 1999-2001; Asst Ch Of S Mary The Vrgn New York NY 1996-1999; Asst Congreg Mnstrs Epis Ch Cntr New York NY 1996-1999. ashinox@gmail.com

SHINN, Richard Emerson (Mich) 6710 Little Hemlock St, Stanwood MI 49346 B Brooklyn MI 11/22/1927 s Emerson Leroy Shinn & Marian Corah. BA MI SU 1951; BD Bex 1962. D 7/1/1962 Bp Archie H Crowley P 1/24/1963 Bp Robert Lionne DeWitt. m 6/25/1966 Marlene Edna Pollock c 3. Supply P S Jn's Ch Mt Pleasant MI 1999-2000; P-in-c Chr The King Epis Ch Taylor MI 1993-1996; R S Thos Ch Trenton MI 1975-1991; Asst to Bp for Admin and Fin Dio Michigan Detroit MI 1973-1975; Asst Exec Dir Admin Dio Michigan Detroit MI 1968-1973; Asst Exec Dir of Admin Dio Michigan Detroit MI 1968-1973; Vic Gr Epis Ch Southgate MI 1965-1968; D in Charge S Paul's Epis Ch Bad Axe MI 1962-1963. mardickshinn@centurytel.net

SHIPLEY, Wayne Sanford (Spr) 326 N High St, Carlinville IL 62626 B Olney IL 9/19/1930 s Everett Clifton Shipley & Hannah Jane. BA Indiana Cntrl U 1952; GTS 1955. D 6/4/1955 P 12/1/1955 Bp Richard Ainslie Kirchhoffer. R S Paul's Epis Ch Carlinville IL 1966-1995; S Ptr's Ch Carlinville IL 1966-1991; Cur S Jn's Epis Ch Decatur IL 1963-1965; Cur S Paul's Epis Ch Evansville IN 1955-1957. shipout@frontiernet.net

SHIPMAN, Bruce MacDonald (Ct) 241 Monument St Apt 6, Groton CT 06340 **VP of the Bd Epis Ch At Yale New Haven CT 2000-** B Minneapolis MN 11/8/1941 s Harold Richmond Shipman & Lois Helen. BA Carleton Coll 1963; BA Oxf 1965; MDiv GTS 1968. D 6/8/1968 P 12/21/1968 Bp Horace W B Donegan. Vic Ch Of The H Adv Clinton CT 2006-2011; Bd Mem, Chld's Mssn S Paul And S Jas New Haven CT 2000-2008; All SS Ch Ivoryton CT 2000; Mem COM Dio Connecticut Hartford CT 1992-1999; Mem Dioc Exec Com Dio Connecticut Hartford CT 1990-1999; Mem, Camp Washington Bd Dir Dio Connecticut Hartford CT 1990-1999; R Chr Ch Roxbury CT 1981-2000; Assoc Chr And H Trin Ch Westport CT 1973-1981; Asst All SS Ch Bayside NY 1970-1972; Cur S Ptr's Ch Port Chester NY 1968-1970. "Misc. arts," *The Day*, New London Day Trust, 2006; Auth, "Why I Am Going To Hebron," *Gd News*, Dio CT Nwspr, 2002; "Misc. Bk Revs," *Gd News*, Dio CT Nwspr, 2001; "Misc. arts," *LivCh*, Living Ch Fndt, 1999. Assoc Alum of GTS 1968. bruceshipman@sbcgloal.net

SHIPP, Mary Jane McCoy (Mont) St. James' Episcopal Church, PO Box 1374, Dillon MT 59725 B Greenville SC 3/13/1939 d Henry Hubert McCoy & Lucile. BA Furman U 1961; SMMus UTS 1963; GTS 1984. D 6/7/1992 P 12/21/1992 Bp Charles Jones III. m 5/31/1967 Clifford M Shipp c 3. R St Jas Epis Ch Dillon MT 2003-2009; Dio Montana Helena MT 2003-2008; Supply P Dio Montana Helena MT 2002-2003; Asst S Jas Ch Bozeman MT 1992-2001. Assoc: OSH 1979. revmjs@gmail.com

SHIPPEE, Richard Cook (RI) 3330 E Main St Lot 109, Mesa AZ 85213 **S Mk's Epis Ch Riverside RI 2009-** B Pawtucket RI 1/6/1949 s Elmer Robinson Shippee & Virginia Francis. BA Colby Coll 1971; MDiv UTS 1974; STM Nash 1978; CG Jung Inst 1982. D 6/14/1975 P 1/1/1977 Bp Frederick Hesley Belden. m 8/16/1969 Cathy Lynn Pagano c 2. S Ptr's By The Sea Narragansett RI 2007-2008; S Mart's Ch Pawtucket RI 2006; S Jn's Ch Cumberland RI 2005-2006; S Paul's Ch Pawtucket RI 1979-1984; Cur S Paul's Ch Pawtucket RI 1976-1979. Auth, "The Cloud Of Unknowing".

SHIPPEN II, Joseph Jenkins (At) PO Box 1213, Griffin GA 30224 **R S Jas Ch Macon GA 2009-** B Atlanta GA 12/2/1977 s Benjamin S Shippen & Josephine S. BSE Merc 2002; BS Presb Coll 2002; MDiv GTS 2006. D 12/21/2005 P 7/29/2006 Bp J(ohn) Neil Alexander. m 7/20/2003 Suzanne Elizabeth Hobby c 1. Int S Fran Ch Macon GA 2009; Asst S Jas Epis Ch Marietta GA 2006-2008. frjs@me.com

SHIPPEN, Sallie Elliot (Cal) 756 14th Way Sw, Edmonds WA 98020 B Philadelphia PA 2/24/1935 d Robert Dunn & Frances Toby. BA Portland St U 1978; MDiv CDSP 1982. D 6/23/1982 Bp Matthew Paul Bigliardi P 6/29/1983 Bp Rustin Ray Kimsey. c 2. R S Jn's Epis Ch Oakland CA 1992-1995; R Gr Epis Ch Astoria OR 1984-1992; Asst Epis Par Of S Jn The Bapt Portland OR 1982-1984. sallie.shippen@gmail.com

SHIPPEY, Edgar Elijah (Ore) 940 N Dean St, Coquille OR 97423 B Pateau OK 6/6/1937 s WL Shippey & Marie. BA U of Arkansas 1959; BD Epis TS of

The SW 1962. D 6/14/1962 P 6/1/1963 Bp Robert Raymond Brown. m 7/18/1987 Christina Swerrie c 3. Dio Oregon Portland OR 1996-2009; R H Trin Epis Ch Ukiah CA 1987-1996; The California Wind Chld Novato CA 1979-1981; Asst S Fran Of Assisi Ch Novato CA 1977-1979; Asst Trin Cathd Little Rock AR 1964-1970; Vic S Jas Ch Eureka Sprg AR 1962-1964; Vic S Thos Ch Springdale AR 1962-1964. Auth, "The Flower & The Flag," 1978; Auth, "A Sprtl Drama," 1976; Auth, "A Folksong Life Of Chr," 1966. etshippey@mycomspan.com

✠ **SHIPPS, Rt Rev Harry Woolston** (Ga) 95 Skidaway Island Park Rd Unit 20, Savannah GA 31411 **Bp in Res S Paul's Ch Savannah GA 2000-; Ret Bp of Ga Dio Georgia Savannah GA 1995-** B Trenton NJ 1/28/1926 s Harry Longstreet Shipps & Ruth. New York St Maritime Acad Ft Schuyler NY 1946; GD STUSo 1958. D 5/20/1958 Bp Albert R Stuart P 1/17/1959 Bp Alfred L Banyard Con 1/6/1984 for Ga. m 5/16/1953 Louise Rosenberger c 4. Asst Dio Dallas Dallas TX 1995-1999; SCER Dio Georgia Savannah GA 1991-1994; Bp of Ga Dio Georgia Savannah GA 1985-1995; SCER Dio Georgia Savannah GA 1985-1988; Bp Coadj of Ga Dio Georgia Savannah GA 1984-1985; Chair COM Dio Georgia Savannah GA 1977-1983; Dn Augusta Convoc Dio Georgia Savannah GA 1977-1983; Dn Augusta Convoc Dio Georgia Savannah GA 1977-1983; Dioc Coun Dio Georgia Savannah GA 1974-1977; Pres, Stndg Com Dio Georgia Savannah GA 1974-1976; Dep GC Dio Georgia Savannah GA 1973-1982; R S Alb's Epis Ch Augusta GA 1970-1983; Chair Ecum Cmsn Dio Georgia Savannah GA 1970-1978; Stndg Com Dio Georgia Savannah GA 1967-1971; Liturg Cmsn Dio Georgia Savannah GA 1966-1971; Secy Dio Georgia Savannah GA 1963-1970; The Epis Ch Of S Jn And S Mk Albany GA 1958-1963. *arts in Ecum and Hist Journ*, 2003. Compas Rose Soc 1997; Ord of S Jn of Jerusalem 1996; OHC (Assoc) 1956. Hon DD STUSo Sewanee TN 1986. lhshipps@aol.com

SHIRES, Robert A (SeFla) 10860 Tamoron Ln, Boca Raton FL 33498 **P-in-c Epis Ch Of The Adv Palm City FL 2009-** B Ronceverte WY 4/13/1944 s Charles Clinton Shires & Birdie Mae. BA W Virginia U 1966; MDiv Gordon-Conwell TS 1969; DMin PrTS 1983. D 9/19/2004 P 4/23/2005 Bp James Hamilton Ottley. m 12/31/1993 Beth L Duggar c 1. Zion Evang Luth Ch Deerfield Bch FL 2008-2009; S Mk The Evang Ft Lauderdale FL 2005-2008. boshires413@aol.com

SHIREY, William Carrol (Colo) 277 Old Man Mountain Ln, Estes Park CO 80517 **Asstg P S Barth's Ch Estes Pk CO 2001-** B Chickasha OK 7/18/1929 s George Jeremiah Shirey & Lovell Louise. BA U of Oklahoma 1954; JD U of Oklahoma 1956; MDiv SWTS 1964. D 6/18/1964 P 12/18/1964 Bp Theodore H McCrea. m 6/24/1956 Shirley Louise Flippen c 2. Int S Barth's Ch Estes Pk CO 1996-1997; Dept Of Missions Dallas TX 1986-1990; Vic S Chas The Mtyr DAINGERFIELD TX 1986-1990; Vic S Dav's Ch Gilmer TX 1986-1990; Vic Trin NE Texas Epis Ch Mt Pleasant TX 1986-1990; Chair Prov VII Mssn Cler Conf Dio Oklahoma Oklahoma City OK 1972-1989; R S Andr's Epis Ch Lawton OK 1971-1986. eppadre1@msn.com

SHIRLEY, David Edward (ETenn) 140 Confederacy Way, Knoxville TN 37934 **Died 2/7/2011** B New York NY 11/24/1924 s Kenneth Walter Shirley & Addie. Carson-Newman Coll; Mia; U of Tennessee. D 3/7/1982 P 2/1/1983 Bp William Evan Sanders.

SHIRLEY, Diana Frangoulis (SO) 664 Glacier Pass, Westerville OH 43081 B Newton MA 2/14/1944 d John Frangoulis & Florence. BS Bos Boston MA 1966; Med Rivier Coll Nashua NH 1991. D 5/13/2006 Bp Kenneth Lester Price. m 4/15/1966 Fred Shirley c 2. dianashirley@columbus.rr.com

SHIRLEY, Fred (SO) 664 Glacier Pass, Westerville OH 43081 B Boston MA 5/20/1941 s Fredric T Shirley & Ethel Frances. Angl Acad; BD Bentley Coll 1966; MS SUNY 1970. D 5/13/2006 Bp Kenneth Lester Price. m 4/15/1966 Diana Frangoulis c 2. D S Matt's Ch Westerville OH 2008-2011; D for 3 Ch cluster Ch Of The Epiph Urbana OH 2006-2008; Field P lacement S Jn's Ch Columbus OH 2005-2006. fredshirleyoh@gmail.com

SHIRLEY, Michael Olenius (Mass) 28 Amherst St, Lawrence MA 01843 B New London NH 10/25/1941 s Morison Potter Shirley & Lillian Catherine. BA Bos 1963; STB Ya Berk 1966. D 6/25/1966 Bp Anson Phelps Stokes Jr P 5/25/1967 Bp Frederic Cunningham Lawrence. m 10/27/1988 Edna Marie Gosselin c 2. R S Jas Ch Amesbury MA 1986-2006; Int S Jn's Ch Winthrop MA 1985-1986; R S Andr's Ch Belmont MA 1975-1985; Asst Par Of The Mssh Auburndale MA 1972-1975; Asst S Jn's Ch Newtonville MA 1972-1975; Asst Chr Ch Manhasset NY 1968-1971; Cur S Paul's Ch Boston MA 1966-1968. Mng Ed, *Issues*, The Consult, 2000. EPF 1982; Heifer Intl 1967; Merrimack Vlly Proj 1995; Rotary Intl 1969. Paul Harris Fllw. michaelshirley@peoplepc.com

SHIRLEY, Sarah A (WA) 88005 Overseas Hwy #9-361, Islamorada FL 33036 B Cambridge MA 1/20/1960 d Robert Lloyd Shirley & Mary Coe. BA Webster U 1991; MDiv Claremont TS 1997. D 4/20/1997 P 12/29/1997 Bp Stewart Clark Zabriskie. m 4/21/2006 Robert Branham. Spec Mobilization Spprt Plan Washington DC 2008-2010; Pension Fund Mltry New York NY 2008-2009; S Mary's Epis Ch Andalusia AL 2008; Off Of Bsh For ArmdF New York NY 2001-2006; St Teresa Of Avila Desert Cathd Flagstaff AZ 1997-2001. EPF; Epis Publ Plcy Ntwk; EWC. sarahshirley@gmail.com

SHIRLEY, Sylvia Kirkland (Okla) St John's Episcopal Church, 5201 N Brookline Ave, Oklahoma City OK 73112 B Glasgow Scotland 2/25/1948 d Thomas Kirkland & Margaret Jane. BSRN Oklahoma Bapt U 1971; MDiv Epis TS of the SW 2005. D 6/23/2007 Bp Robert Manning Moody P 6/28/2011 Bp Edward Joseph Konieczny. c 1. kirkland16@aol.com

SHIROTA, Kunihito Andrew (Oly) 800 Abbot Rd, East Lansing MI 48823 **Cur All SS Ch E Lansing MI 2011-** B 11/12/1973 s Kunihiko Shirota & Kimiko. BS City of U of Seattle 2001; MDiv SWTS 2009. D 4/17/2009 Bp Gregory Harold Rickel P 11/17/2009 Bp Bavi Rivera. Assoc S Ben Epis Ch Lacey WA 2009-2010. andrew.k.shirota@gmail.com

SHISLER, Sara Lynn (Md) 4 E University Pkwy, Baltimore MD 21218 **Asst P Cathd Of The Incarn Baltimore MD 2010-** B Calvert County MD 12/16/1982 d Michael C Shisler & Joan R B. BA Elon U 2004; MDiv Ya Berk 2008; STM Ya Berk 2009. D 6/19/2010 Bp John Leslie Rabb P 1/29/2011 Bp Eugene Sutton. sara.shisler2@gmail.com

SHIVELY, William Delbert (O) 99 Birdsong Way Apt D308, Hilton Head Island SC 29926 **Died 10/2/2011** B Cleveland OH 7/29/1925 s Arthur Morris Shively & Vida Fay. BA Baldwin-Wallace Coll 1945; MDiv UTS 1949. D 3/8/1956 P 9/16/1956 Bp Nelson Marigold Burroughs. c 2.

SHIVES, Beverly Mason (SeFla) 159 Biscayne Ave, Tampa FL 33606 **Serv Dio SE Florida Miami FL 1990-** B Winston-Salem NC 7/12/1929 s Raymond Mason Shives & Ruby Lucille. Sthrn Tech Inst Orlando FL 1951; BFA Art Inst of Atlanta 1960; Georgia Inst of Tech 1962; Dio SE Florida Sch For Mnstry FL 1990; CPE Tampa Gnrl Hosp 1998. D 2/11/1990 Bp Calvin Onderdonk Schofield Jr. m 11/12/1983 Pamela Maurine Von Stroh Shives c 5. Dioc Convnt Dio SW Florida Sarasota FL 1999-2000; St Johns Epis Ch Tampa FL 1996-2002; Dio Property & Loan Com Dio SE Florida Miami FL 1991-1994; Dioc Stwshp Cmsn Dio SE Florida Miami FL 1987-1988. Epis Conf Of The Deaf Of The Epis Ch In The 1990. Fell Ecdec. bshives159@aol.com

SHOBE, Melody Wilson (RI) 2407 Cranston St., Cranston RI 02920 **Assoc Emm Epis Ch Cumberland RI 2011-** B Little Rock AR 1/30/1981 d Robert G Wilson & Mary Winburn. BA Tufts U 2003; MDiv VTS 2006. D 6/24/2006 Bp Peter James Lee P 1/18/2007 Bp Don Adger Wimberly. m 5/21/2005 Robert Casey Shobe. Assoc Chr Ch In Lonsdale Lincoln RI 2008-2011; Asst S Thos The Apos Epis Ch Houston TX 2006-2008. melody.shobe@gmail.com

SHOBE, Robert Casey (RI) 2407 Cranston St., Cranston RI 02920 **Mem of Bp Search Transition Com Dio Rhode Island Providence RI 2011-; Chair of 2015 Strategic Needs T/F Dio Rhode Island Providence RI 2010-; Chair of Congrl Dvlpmt Cmsn Dio Rhode Island Providence RI 2010-; S Ptr's By The Sea Narragansett RI 2006-** B Richmond VA 7/15/1978 s Michael Leroy Shobe & Susan Casey. The U Of Texas Sch Of Law; BA U of Texas 2000; M.Div. VTS 2006. D 6/24/2006 P 1/18/2007 Bp Don Adger Wimberly. m 5/21/2005 Melody Wilson c 1. Cur Chr Ch Cathd Houston TX 2006-2008. shobewon@gmail.com

SHOBERG, Warren E (SD) 3316 E 28th St, Sioux Falls SD 57103 B Rapid City SD 5/28/1941 s Walfred Ephraim Shoberg & Ethel Evelyn. BA Augustana Coll 1963; MM U of So Dakota 1983. D 9/29/1981 P 9/29/1982 Bp Walter H Jones. Vic Ch Of The H Apos Sioux Falls SD 1983-2007; H Trin Epis Ch Luverne MN 1982-1985. CBS 1984; FIF/NA 1990; GAS 1987; P Assoc Shrine Our Lady of Walsingham 1995; SocMary 1988; SSC 1987. wshoberg@sio.midco.net

SHOCKLEY, Stephanie Elizabeth (NJ) 316 E 88th St, New York NY 10128 B Stratford, NJ 12/19/1974 d Thomas John O'Connor & Elizabeth Carolyn. BA MWC 1997; MDiv The GTS 2009. D 5/16/2009 Bp Sylvestre Donato Romero P 6/19/2010 Bp George Edward Councell. m 11/30/2002 Daniel Aaron Shockley. shockley.stephanie@yahoo.com

SHOEMAKER, Adam James (NC) The Episcopal Church of the Holy Comforter, 320 East Davis Street, Burlington NC 27215 **R Ch Of The H Comf Burlington NC 2011-** B 7/12/1979 s Thomas Johns Shoemaker & Jamie Stanforth. BS Bos 2001; MDiv Harv 2005; Cert. in Angl Stds Gnrl Sem 2007. D 6/2/2007 P 1/12/2008 Bp M(arvil) Thomas Shaw III. m 5/31/2008 Courtney Elizabeth Davis. Asst R Par Of Chr Ch Andover MA 2007-2011. adam712@gmail.com

SHOEMAKER, Eric Wayne (WA) 8795 Lowell Road, Pomfret MD 20675 **D Chr Ch Port Tobacco Paris La Plata MD 2003-** B Muncy PA 7/10/1947 s Clyde Bryant Shoemaker & Edith Melida. BA W&M 1972; MS Virginia Commonwealth U 1978; Spec Stdt VTS 2003. D 9/1/2001 Bp Leopold Frade. m 9/15/1979 Joan Louise Anderson c 1. D Chr Ch Durham Par Nanjemoy MD 2002-2003; D S Jn's Epis Ch Homestead FL 2001-2002. S Greg'S Abbey - Confrator 2003. Mem Phi Kappa Phi 1978. jjackoe@comcast.net

SHOEMAKER, H(etty) Stephanie Condon (RI) 96 Washington St, Newport RI 02840 B Fulton NY 12/26/1940 d Donald William Condon & Hetty Semple. BA Bryn 1962; MDiv EDS 1996. D 3/16/1991 Bp George Nelson Hunt III P 6/15/1996 Bp Geralyn Wolf. m 6/30/1962 Charles Padley Shoemaker c 3. Int Emm Ch Newport RI 2008-2010; R S Jn The Div Ch Saunderstown RI

S

2001-2007; Assoc S Columba's Chap Middletown RI 1996-2000; D S Matt's Par Of Jamestown Jamestown RI 1991-1994. revshoe@aol.com

SHOEMAKER, Jack G (Haw) 3045 Fir Tree Dr Se, Salem OR 97317 B Lancaster PA 7/6/1929 s Allison William Shoemaker & Florence Lillian. MDiv VTS 1954; BA Washington Coll 1954. D 12/18/1954 Bp Angus Dun P 12/5/1955 Bp Charles F Hall. m 3/18/1983 Roxanne Hutchison c 4. Emm Epis Ch Kailua HI 1981-1994; Ashville Sch Inc Asheville NC 1977-1980; Chr Sch Arden NC 1976-1977; Chapl Belmont Chap at S Mk's Sch Southborough MA 1965-1974; R S Lk's Epis Ch Seaford DE 1962-1965; Assoc Cn Cathd of St Ptr & St Paul Washington DC 1961-1962; Chair NH BEC Dio New Hampshire Concord NH 1959-1961; Mstr Sacr Stds S Paul's Ch Concord NH 1954-1956. Auth, *For Heaven's Sake! (Collection of Poems)*, 2007. roxanne@viser.net

SHOEMAKER, Patricia Ross Pittman (NC) 22 Mayflower Ln, Lexington NC 27295 **D Dio No Carolina Raleigh NC 1988-** B Southampton County VA 2/17/1939 d Robert Waverly Pittman & Frances Catherine. BD Med Coll of Virginia 1961; MS U NC 1979. D 10/2/1988 Bp Robert Whitridge Estill. m 8/1/1964 John Bruce Shoemaker c 2. NAAD.

SHOFSTALL, Sarah Jane (WMass) 37 Chestnut Street, Springfield MA 01103 **Cn Dio Wstrn Massachusetts Springfield MA 1997-** B Presque Isle ME 5/22/1951 d Jack E Shofstall & Iris. BS U of Nebraska 1973; JD U of Nebraska 1979; GTS 1990. D 5/7/1988 Bp James Daniel Warner P 8/11/1990 Bp James Edward Krotz. R Gr Ch Amherst MA 1997-2000; Dio Iowa Des Moines IA 1994-1997; Assoc S Lk's Ch Kearney NE 1988-1999. The SCHC 1987. canon@diocesewma.org

SHOLANDER, Mark (CFla) 907 Oakway Dr, Auburndale FL 33823 B Detroit MI 2/13/1954 s Carl John Sholander & Beatrice Margaret. BA U MI 1974; MPA U MI 1985; MDiv TESM 2000. D 5/27/2000 P 12/9/2000 Bp John Wadsworth Howe. m 6/30/1979 Cyntahia Mae Shumaker c 3. R S Alb's Epis Ch Auburndale FL 2002-2006; Asst All SS Ch Of Winter Pk Winter Pk FL 2000-2002. marksholander@hotmail.com

SHOLTY JR, Henry Edward (Dal) 5942 Abrams Rd # 209, Dallas TX 75231 B Dallas TX 6/18/1942 s Henry Edward Sholty & Melba Ann. BA U of No Texas 1964; U Of Dallas Dallas 1966; BD Nash 1970. D 6/18/1970 Bp Theodore H McCrea P 1/1/1971 Bp Stanley Hamilton Atkins. m 1/25/1964 Mary Janet Poindexter c 2. Asst To The Dn S Matt's Cathd Dallas TX 1982-1987; LocTen Ch Of The H Cross Dallas TX 1982; Cur S Dav's Ch Garland TX 1979-1981; BEC Dio Eau Claire Eau Claire WI 1971-1973; Our Sav's Phillips WI 1970-1976; Vic S Marg's Pk Falls WI 1970-1976; Exec Coun Dio Eau Claire Eau Claire WI 1970-1973. Ed, "Convocare 88-". NNECA.

SHOOK, Janis Helen (WVa) PO Box 692, Moorefield WV 26836 **D Emm Ch Moorefield WV 2010-** B Oceanside NY 2/1/1951 d Eugene Ellsworth Torborg & Florence Elizabeth. Springfield Coll 1980; MTS Wesley TS 2002; DMin Wesley TS 2005; Angl Stds VTS 2010. D 10/10/2010 Bp William Michie Klusmeyer. m 4/6/1974 Stephen Shook c 2. shookjanis10@gmail.com

SHORT, James Healy (Colo) 797 Tower Hill Rd., Appomattox VA 24522 B Pittsburgh PA 3/31/1933 s Leo Napolean Short & Elizabeth Anena. BA U Of Dayton 1955; Ord to the priesthood U Of Fribourg Ch 1963; MA Ford 1964; Rel Educ certification Lumen Vitae Brussels 1964. Rec from Roman Catholic 2/1/1978 as Priest Bp William Carl Frey. m 6/28/1970 Barbara Gumm c 5. Asst S Jn's Ch Portsmouth VA 2002-2005; R The Ch Of The Ascen Denver CO 1980-2001; Dio Colorado Denver CO 1978-1979. Dir of Prod, "Living the Gd News Curric," 1977. SocMary 1950-1970. shortapp@gmail.com

SHORT, James Ritchie (EpisSanJ) 6276 N 1st St, Fresno CA 93710 B 5/16/1951 s Margaret Duncan. MDiv CDSP; BA Lebanon Vlly Coll; Nasd Series 6-80; Series 7 63-98 Lutcf 94; Cert Wycliffe Hall of Oxf. D 6/4/1977 P 6/16/1978 Bp Victor Manuel Rivera. m 8/24/1974 Cynthia Short c 1. Ch Of The Epiph Corcoran CA 1997-2000; S Phil's Ch Coalinga CA 1997-2000; Epis Dio San Joaquin Modesto CA 1979-1981; S Columba Ch Fresno CA 1977-1979. Auth, "Is Universal Life A Plan For All Seasons?," 1990; Auth, "Less Thunder More Lightning," 1989. Natl Assn For The Self- Supporting Active Mnstry. Yakoboshort@yahoo.com

SHORTELL, Bruce Mallard (At) PO Box 1293, Flowery Branch GA 30542 B Pittsburgh PA 2/13/1934 s John Edward Shortell & Lillian. BS Moravian TS 1956; MDiv VTS 1964. D 6/20/1964 P 3/27/1965 Bp Frederick J Warnecke. m 7/10/2006 Carolyn P Pitts c 3. Cn Pstr Cathd Of S Phil Atlanta GA 1981-1998; P-in-c S Steph's Ch Harrington DE 1973-1981; P-in-c S Ptr's Epis Ch Tunkhannock PA 1964-1973. EvangES. BRUCESHOR@AOL.COM

SHORTES, Stephen Edward (NCal) 2883 Coloma St, Placerville CA 95667 **D Epis Ch Of Our Sav Placerville CA 1999-** B Fort Worth TX 9/20/1944 s Louis Edward Shortes & Betty Jean. BS Sacramento St Coll 1967; BA Sch for Deacons 1999. D 7/24/1999 Bp Jerry Alban Lamb. m 9/5/1980 Leslyn Marlene Meyers.

SHORTRIDGE, Delores J (Nev) 973 S. Fulton St., Denver CO 80247 B Oklahoma City OK 10/25/1944 d Leon William Harman & Mary Kathern. BS U of Cntrl Oklahoma 1967; MDiv Iliff TS 2005. D 1/9/2005 P 1/7/2006 Bp Katharine Jefferts Schori. m 11/26/1968 Earl Wade Shortridge c 5. Ch Of S Ptr The Apos Pueblo CO 2010-2011; Our Merc Sav Epis Ch Denver CO 2008-2010. deloresshortridge@yahoo.com

SHORTT, Mary J (EMich) P.O. Box 151, West Branch MI 48661 **S Barth's Epis Ch Mio MI 2011-** B West Branch 2/1/1960 d Lee Adelbert Shortt & Beverly Ann. BA Saginaw Vlly St U 1983; MDiv VTS 1989; BSW Saginaw Vlly St U 1997. D 10/16/1999 P 7/22/2000 Bp Edwin Max Leidel Jr. R S Paul's Ch Fremont OH 2004-2006; Gr Epis Ch Lachine MI 2001-2008; R Calv Epis Ch Hillman MI 2001-2004; Chr Epis Ch E Tawas MI 1999-2008; Lakeshore Epis Area Parishes Oscoda MI 1999-2001. fathermary@hotmail.com

SHOUCAIR, James Douglas (Pgh) 130 Westchester Dr, Pittsburgh PA 15215 **BEC for the Priesthood Dio Pittsburgh Monroeville PA 2003-; R Chr Epis Ch No Hills Pittsburgh PA 2002-** B Kingston Jamaica West Indies 2/3/1958 s Elias S Shoucair & Nellie A. BA Bos 1979; JD Ford Sch of Law 1982; MDiv TESM 1998. D 6/20/1998 P 1/8/1999 Bp Robert William Duncan. m 2/22/1980 Sandra Leigh Horne c 4. Com on Const and Cn Dio Pittsburgh Monroeville PA 2008-2010; Ecum Off Dio Pittsburgh Monroeville PA 2007-2008; Cn Pstr/P-in-c Trin Cathd Pittsburgh PA 1999-2002; Asst Ch Of The Nativ Crafton PA 1998-1999. thegoodcanon@gmail.com

SHOULAK, James Eugene (Minn) 20475 County Road 10, Corcoran MN 55340 B Manitowoc WI 9/6/1958 s Eugene Paul Shoulak & Margaret Mary. AA Anoka-Ramsey Cmnty Coll 2007; MARL Untd TS 2010. D 7/29/2010 Bp Brian N Prior. m 9/14/1984 Judith Shoulak c 3. jimmacmn@earthlink.net

SHOULDERS, David Ira (Ind) 3415 Windham Lake Place, Indianapolis IN 46214 B Detroit MI 2/25/1941 s Charles Denver Shoulders & Frances Meta. BA Indiana U 1969; MS Penn 1970; MDiv VTS 1975. D 6/6/1975 P 3/1/1976 Bp Dean T Stevenson. m 9/6/1969 Ruth Colter c 2. Cn Pstr Chr Ch Cathd Indianapolis IN 2000-2006; S Paul's Epis Ch Indianapolis IN 1996-2001; R Chr Ch Waukegan IL 1991-1996; Cn to the Ordnry Dio Indianapolis Indianapolis IN 1986-1991; Vic S Jn's Ch Speedway IN 1979-1986; Gd Shpd Montoursville PA 1976-1979; Ch Of Our Sav Montoursville PA 1976-1978; Dio Cntrl Pennsylvania Harrisburg PA 1976-1977; Asst R S Jn's Epis Ch Lancaster PA 1975-1976. Listening Hearts Mnstrs 1994-2008. Cn Emer Chr Ch Cathd, Indianapolis 2006; Mayor's Awd 96 Mayor of Waukegan, Illinois Waukegan 1996; Phi Beta Kappa Indiana U 1969. PresterD@sbcglobal.net

SHOWERS, David Gordon (Md) Middleham & St. Peter Ep. Parish, PO Box 277, Lusby MD 20657 **R Middleham & S Ptr's Par Lusby MD 2008-** B Battle Creek MI 1/23/1949 s Gordon Showers & Luella. MA Asbury Coll 1971; MDiv Asbury TS 1974; GTS 2005. D 10/29/2005 Bp Robert Wilkes Ihloff P 5/7/2006 Bp John Leslie Rabb. S Lk's Ch Baltimore MD 2008; R S Lk's Ch Baltimore MD 2006-2008; Vic Ch Of S Paul The Apos Baltimore MD 2005-2007. davidmsp@comcast.net

SHOWS, W(illiam) Derek (NC) 12 Upchurch Cir, Durham NC 27705 **P Assoc S Steph's Ch Durham NC 1992-** B Soso MS 7/3/1936 s William Orion Shows & Mitchell Rea. BA U IL 1957; MA U IL 1958; U of Heidelberg DE 1960; PhD Duke 1967; CAS GTS 1982. D 6/29/1982 P 6/24/1983 Bp Robert Whitridge Estill. m 5/18/1974 Priscilla Grahame Walker c 4. Sabbatical Prof The GTS New York NY 1999-2000; Int S Steph's Ch Durham NC 1989-1990; Int S Steph's Ch Durham NC 1985-1986; Asst S Mk's Epis Ch Raleigh NC 1982-1984. Auth, "A Psychol Theory of Later Years-CG Jung," *GeroPsychology*, 1977; Auth, "Psychol Differentiation & the A-B Dimension:A Dyadic Interaction Hypothesis," *Genetic Psychol Monographs*. Amer Psychoanalytical Assn 1988-2008; APA 1968; CG Jung Soc 1983; NC Psychoanalytical Soc; NC Psychol Assn 1968. wdj@duke.edu

SHOWS CAFFEY, Elizabeth Kristen (At) 634 W Peachtree St NW, Atlanta GA 30308 **Assoc R All SS Epis Ch Atlanta GA 2007-** B Zurich Switzerland 1/13/1976 d W(illiam) Derek Shows. Bow 1996; BA Duke 1998; MDiv GTS 2005. D 6/26/2005 P 3/11/2006 Bp Michael Bruce Curry. m 9/17/2005 Ian Scott Caffey c 1. Ch Of The Advoc Philadelphia PA 2004-2006; Ch Of The H Trin New York NY 2004-2006; Chap Of The Cross Chap Hill NC 1999-2002. elizabethshows@yahoo.com

SHRINER, Brian Gerald (CFla) 140 W Panama Rd, Winter Springs FL 32708 B Akron OH 12/7/1965 s Robert Shriner & Marilyn. BA Florida Sthrn Coll 1988; MDiv TESM 1997. D 1/11/1998 P 8/15/1998 Bp John Wadsworth Howe. m 7/23/1988 Leslie E Hannon c 4. Epiph Epis Ch Orlando FL 2003-2005; Ch Of The New Cov Winter Sprg FL 2002-2003; Asst All SS Ch Of Winter Pk Winter Pk FL 1998-2002. bgshriner@msn.com

SHRIVER, Domingo F (NY) 182 Route 376, Hopewell Junction NY 12533 **R Ch Of The Resurr Hopewell Jct NY 2007-** B York PA 6/27/1965 s Joseph Lee Shriver & Frances Carmen. BA Sprg Arbor U 2001; MDiv VTS 2005. D 1/29/2005 P 10/15/2005 Bp Robert R Gepert. m 5/9/1997 Paula Marie Gray c 6. Assoc P S Mk's Ch Grand Rapids MI 2005-2007. fathermic@gmail.com

SHRIVER JR, Frederick Hardman (NY) 37 W. 12th Street, Apt. 4K, New York NY 10011 B Parkersburg WV 10/21/1932 s Frederick Hardman Shriver & Evelyn Louise. BA Harv 1954; STB GTS 1960; PhD U of Cambridge 1967. D 6/10/1960 P 12/1/1960 Bp Wilburn Camrock Campbell. m 9/23/1961 Susan Hubbard Courtney c 2. Prof The GTS New York NY 1971-1998; Tutor The

GTS New York NY 1962-1964; Asst Trin Ch Morgantown WV 1960-1962. Auth, "Engl Hist Revs"; Auth, "The Study Of Anglicanism". fhshriver@verizon.net

SHUART, R(obert) Stephen (NwPa) Po Box 368, South Harwich MA 02661 B Englewood NJ 12/26/1943 s Herman Robert Shuart & Audrey Patricia. BA CL Thiel Coll 1966; Westminster Coll 1966; M.Div Ya Berk 1969. D 6/23/1969 P 12/19/1970 Bp William Crittenden. m 8/17/1968 Trina Dubowick c 3. R S Lk's Epis Ch Smethport PA 2003-2004; R S Jn's Ch Kane PA 1995-2004; Vic S Jn's Ch Kane PA 1969-1977; Vic S Marg's Epis Ch Mt Jewett PA 1969-1976. stephen.shuart@verizon.net

SHUCKER II, Courtney A (U) 203 Palmer St, Salida CO 81201 B Fort Lauderdale FL 4/7/1946 s Courtney Albert Shucker & Geraldine May. U of Redlands 1968; MDiv CDSP 1996. D 11/21/1996 P 5/18/1997 Bp Stewart Clark Zabriskie. P-in-c Ascen S Matt's Ch Price UT 1998-2006; Vic Ch Of The H Trin Price UT 1998-2006; P Dio Utah Salt Lake City UT 1998-2006; D Dio Nevada Las Vegas NV 1996-1998; P-in-c Gr-St Fran Cmnty Ch Lovelock NV 1996-1998. Assn of Angl Mus 1976-1997. cashucker2@netscape.net

SHUFORD, Carlton L (Ga) 131 Avondale Dr, Augusta GA 30907 B Atlanta GA 6/25/1948 s Charles Robert Shuford & Louise Eleanor. BD U GA 1974; M. Div Erskine TS 2008. D 3/1/1990 Bp Harry Woolston Shipps P 4/3/2008 Bp Henry Irving Louttit. m 9/12/1970 Kathleen Mackaye Metzger c 3. Ch Of Our Sav Martinez GA 1990-2010. cshuford3@knology.net

SHUFORD, Sheila Cathcart (Nwk) 12 Sorman Ter, Randolph NJ 07869 B NYC NY 3/6/1935 d James Provost Smith & Elizabeth. D 6/3/2006 Bp John Palmer Croneberger. m 8/27/1960 Sydney Shuford c 1. scshuford@optonline.net

SHULDA, David Leroy (Ore) 2139 Berwin Ln, Eugene OR 97404 B New Britain CT 5/19/1927 s Charles W Shulda & Elizabeth M. Teachers Coll Of Connecticut. D 2/1/1984 Bp Matthew Paul Bigliardi. m 4/24/1954 Anne Laura Lutynski c 1. D Ch Of S Jn The Div Springfield OR 1984-2010.

SHUMAKER, John Hilton (EpisSanJ) 1317 Gold Hunter Rd, San Andreas CA 95249 **Gold Country Mssnr Epis Dio San Joaquin Modesto CA 2011-; Stndg Com Epis Dio San Joaquin Modesto CA 2008-** B Pittsburgh PA 4/27/1947 s John Hopkins Shumaker & Laverne Hilton. Dplma The Salvation Army Sch for Off' Trng 1967; AA Cmnty Coll of Allegheny Cnty Pittsburgh PA 1970; BA U Pgh 1971; MDiv Nash 1975. D 10/25/1975 Bp Robert Bracewell Appleyard P 6/2/1976 Bp James Winchester Montgomery. RurD of the Delta Dnry Epis Dio San Joaquin Modesto CA 2009-2010; Stndg Com Epis Dio San Joaquin Modesto CA 2008-2010; R S Matt's Ch San Andreas CA 2001-2005; Dioc Coun Dio Ohio Cleveland OH 1995-1996; R S Paul's Ch Steubenville OH 1993-2001; R S Rocco's Ch Youngstown OH 1986-1993; Dioc Coun Dio Pittsburgh Monroeville PA 1982-1983; R The Ch Of The Adv Jeannette PA 1980-1985; Vic Ch Of S Agnes By The Lake Algoma WI 1977-1980; Vic Ch Of The Precious Blood Gar Algoma WI 1977-1980; Chair, T&C Cmsn Dio Fond du Lac Appleton WI 1977-1980; Sec., Ad Hoc Hisp Cmsn Dio Chicago Chicago IL 1976-1977; Cur Gr Ch Oak Pk IL 1975-1977. CBS; GAS; Lions Club; SocOLW. fathershumaker@hotmail.com

SHUMARD, Jim (Ga) 21 Mary Musgrove Dr, Savannah GA 31410 **R S Mich's Ch Waynesboro GA 2010-** B Fort Belvoir VA 9/6/1951 s Gordon Hughes Shumard & Mary. BA Rhodes Coll 1974; MDiv Candler TS Emory U 1985; D Min EDS 2010. D 6/7/1997 Bp Onell Asiselo Soto P 12/13/1997 Bp Frank Kellogg Allan. m 4/5/1986 Maureen Elizabeth Horgan c 2. All SS Epis Ch Thomasville GA 2010; S Ptr's Epis Ch Savannah GA 2009; R S Fran Of The Islands Epis Ch Savannah GA 2001-2009; R S Alb's Ch Elberton GA 1998-2001; R S Andr's Ch Hartwell GA 1998-2001; Asst R Gr Epis Ch Gainesville GA 1997-1998. jshumie@aol.com

SIBLEY, David C (USC) 9818 Fort Hamilton Pkwy, Brooklyn NY 11209 **Cler-in-Charge S Jn's Epis Ch Ft Hamilton Brooklyn NY 2011-** B Camden SC 6/13/1985 s Mark D Sibley & Deni L. BS Furman U 2007; MS Furman U 2008; MDiv The GTS 2011. D 6/4/2011 Bp W(illiam) Andrew Waldo. dsibley@saintjohns1834.org

SICKELS, Peter L (Ia) 4814 Amesbury Ct, Davenport IA 52807 **Chr Epis Ch Clinton IA 2011-** B Dayton OH 7/3/1946 s William Herbert Sickels & Shirley Ellen. Golden Gate Bapt TS; BA Denison U 1968; MDiv Nash 1984. D 6/7/1986 P 10/1/1987 Bp William Edwin Swing. m 10/25/1985 Alison Katharine Bates-Sickels c 2. Zion Luth Ch Princeton IA 2003-2011; Shpd Of The Cross Luth Ch Muscatine IA 2002; First Luth Ch Moline IL 2001-2002; Trin Cathd Davenport IA 1990-1999; Vic S Paul's Ch Durant IA 1986-1990. Curs Amer Farmland Trust. SICKELSALL@MSN.COM

SICKLER, Brenda Pamela (WMo) 5 E 337th Rd, Humansville MO 65674 **D S Alb's In The Ozarks Ch Bolivar MO 1999-** B Hove Sussex UK 10/27/1935 d Basil Peter Jackson & Laura. D 2/13/1999 Bp Barry Robert Howe. m 3/2/1958 Kenneth Lynch Sickler.

SICKLES, Clarence William (Nwk) 68 Heath Village, Hackettstown NJ 07840 B Harrison NJ 2/11/1921 s John Joseph Sickles & Mary Lois. BA Col 1945; STB GTS 1951; Med Col 1972; MDiv GTS 1976. D 5/23/1948 P 11/30/1948 Bp Benjamin M Washburn. m 2/11/1950 Jean Stover c 8. Asst Pstr S Jn's Ch Dover NJ 1993-1995; Assoc Chr Ch Short Hills NJ 1990-1991; Heath Vill Ret Cmnty Hackettstown NJ 1965-1983; Vic S Jas' Epis Ch Hackettstown NJ 1953-1965; Vic S Ptr's Ch Mt Arlington NJ 1953-1955; Cur Chr Ch New Brunswick NJ 1951-1953; Vic Ch Of The Atone Fair Lawn NJ 1949-1951; Cur S Mary's Ch Sparta NJ 1948-1949. Pres ESMA 1974-1976. DD GTS New York NY 1976. csickles@goes.com

SIDEBOTHAM, John Nelson (Chi) 400 E Westminster Rd, Lake Forest IL 60045 **R The Ch Of The H Sprt Lake Forest IL 2004-** B Bronxville NY 4/15/1954 s John Arthur Sidebotham & Grace Mildred. BA Trin 1976; MDiv UTS 1989. D 12/10/1989 P 6/24/1990 Bp George Nelson Hunt III. m 4/20/1985 Frances D Murchison c 2. Vic S Barth's Ch New York NY 1999-2004; S Lk's Epis Ch Durham NC 1995-1998; Assoc S Columba's Ch Washington DC 1991-1995; Asst S Mart's Ch Providence RI 1989-1991. jsidebotham@sbcglobal.net

SIDERIUS, Donna-Mae Amy (SVa) 3 Mizzen Cir, Hampton VA 23664 B Winnipeg MT CA 7/9/1948 d Stewart Douglas Arthur Beatty & Donna Lorraine. BTh McGill U 1981; STM GTS 1997. Trans from Anglican Church of Canada 2/1/1990 Bp C(laude) Charles Vache. m 7/5/1969 John Siderius c 2. R S Jn's Ch Hampton VA 2003-2011; Cn Dio Sthrn Virginia Norfolk VA 1995-2002; Asst R S Jn's Ch Hampton VA 1990-1995. dmsiderius@aol.com

SIEFFERMAN, Norman Clyde (Va) 609 Shaw Ct, Fredericksburg VA 22405 B Cincinnati OH 2/27/1934 s Floyd Earl Siefferman & Phyllis Violet. BA Merc 1958; MDiv Epis TS of The SW 1961; Emory U 1982. D 6/1/1961 P 7/1/1962 Bp Randolph R Claiborne. m 6/20/1954 Sara Mote c 2. R Emm Ch King Geo VA 1984-2000; The Epis Ch-King Geo Co King Geo VA 1982-1998; Trin Epis Ch Columbus GA 1964-1979; Vic St Mary's Atlanta GA 1961-1964. Auth, *A Study of Prospon in Nestorius' Bazaar of Heracleides*; Auth, *O Felix Culpa*; Auth, *Reason in Rel*; Auth, *Sci & Rel: Reply to Jn F Miller*. Intl Herder Soc. nsieffer@earthlink.net

SIEGEL II, Carl De Haven (WMo) 1405 Boyce Ave, Baltimore MD 21204 B Kansas City MO 4/16/1955 s Carl De Haven Siegel & Ruth. BA U So 1978; MDiv GTS 1982; PhD California Sch of Profsnl Psychol 1990. D 6/21/1982 P 12/1/1982 Bp Arthur Anton Vogel. m 5/26/1984 Katherine Tucker Smith. Gr And H Trin Cathd Kansas City MO 1982-1986.

SIEGENTHALER, David John (Mass) 54 Concord Ave Apt 102, Cambridge MA 02138 B Buffalo NY 11/1/1926 s Gottlieb Siegenthaler & Agatha Leblanc. BA Franklin & Marshall Coll 1947; BD Yale DS 1950; MA Ya 1952; DD EDS 1995. D 6/25/1955 P 1/21/1956 Bp Norman B Nash. c 4. Tutor Hist EDS Cambridge MA 1969-1995; R Ch Of S Jn The Evang Duxbury MA 1957-1968; Cur Emm Ch Boston MA 1955-1957.

SIEGFRIEDT, Karen Faye (NCal) 835 Argonaut Drive, Jackson CA 95642 **R Trin Ch Sutter Creek CA 2010-** B Boston MA 3/28/1954 d Karle Frances Siegfriedt & Faye Norberta. AS U of Indianapolis 1973; BA U of Massachusetts 1977; MS U of San Francisco 1986; MDiv CDSP 1992. D 6/6/1992 P 6/5/1993 Bp William Edwin Swing. R Ch Of S Jude The Apos Cupertino CA 1998-2010; Assoc S Lk's Ch Los Gatos CA 1994-1998; P-in-c S Barth's Epis Ch Livermore CA 1993; Assoc Ch Of The H Innoc San Francisco CA 1992-1993. Auth, "Prize Sermon," *Sermons That Wk*, 1995. rectororders@yahoo.com

SIEGMUND, Mary Kay (Kan) 3 Ne 83rd Ter, Kansas City MO 64118 **P-in-c S Matt's Epis Ch Newton KS 2010-** B Kansas City MO 8/18/1953 d John Thompson & Agnes. MDiv MidWestern Bapt TS 1995; Cert Epis TS of The SW 1998. D 6/6/1998 Bp Barry Robert Howe P 12/1/1998 Bp John Clark Buchanan. m 12/27/1979 Mark Steven Siegmund c 2. Dio Kansas Topeka KS 2006-2009; Asst Ch Of The Gd Shpd Nashua NH 2001-2006; Vic S Jn's Ch Kansas City MO 1998-2001. mk.siegmaud@gmail.com

SIEMSEN, David P (CPa) 5400 Roland Ave, Baltimore MD 21210 B Northumberland PA 10/31/1939 s Fred P Siemsen & Mary L. BA Pontifical Coll Josephinum 1961; MLS Syr 1964. D 6/12/1981 Bp Dean T Stevenson. m 10/14/1967 Lois E Siemson c 2.

SIENER, George Richard (NH) 6 Whippoorwill Ln, Exeter NH 03833 **Asst S Jn's Ch Portsmouth NH 2002-** B New York NY 11/15/1937 s George Siener & Frances. BA U of Bridgeport 1959; MDiv Ya Berk 1962; Fllshp VTS 1982; DD Ya Berk 1996. D 6/1/1962 Bp Walter H Gray P 3/16/1963 Bp Joseph Warren Hutchens. m 6/10/1961 Sheila Day. Asst Ch Of The Gd Shpd Nashua NH 1998-2002; R Chr Ch Exeter NH 1975-1997; Vic S Dav's Ch Gales Ferry CT 1964-1975; Cur S Jn's Ch Stamford CT 1962-1964. Fllshp of the Way of the Cross 1966. grsiener@myfairpoint.net

SIERACKI, Emily K (NY) 101 Earl Hall # 2008, New York NY 10027 **Asst to the R Gr Epis Ch Nyack NY 2007-** B Washington DC 4/24/1981 d Paul Stanley Sieracki & Connie. BA Barnard Coll of Col 2003; MDiv UTS 2007. D 3/10/2007 P 9/15/2007 Bp Mark Sean Sisk. emily_sieracki@yahoo.com

SIERRA, Frank (WMo) 2718 Alabama Ct, Joplin MO 64804 **R S Phil's Ch Joplin MO 2005-** B Morenci AZ 12/17/1955 s Demecio Lopez Sierra & Natalia Cervantez. U of Arizona 1974; AA Phoenix Coll Phoenix AZ 1976; MDiv Nash 1990. D 6/9/1990 Bp William Harvey Wolfrum P 12/14/1990 Bp John Herbert MacNaughton. m 9/12/1980 Deborah Stewart c 2. Cn Ch Of The H Cross San Antonio TX 2003-2004; Cn Trin Ch San Antonio TX 2003-2004;

R S Steph's Epis Ch San Antonio TX 1992-2004; R Gr Ch Weslaco TX 1990-1992. stphiliprector@aol.com

SIERRA-COLADO, Federico (Los) 1021 W Roses Rd, San Gabriel CA 91775 **S Mk's Par Van Nuys CA 2008-** B Mexico 7/8/1951 Trans from La Iglesia Anglicana de Mex 1/7/2005 Bp Joseph Jon Bruno. Ch Of The Ascen Tujunga CA 2005-2008; Dio Cuernavaca 2004; Dio Mex 2000-2004. ascension.episcopal.church@verizon.net

SIERRA ECHEVERRY, Gabriel Alcides (Colom) Parroquia La Anunciacion, El Bagre, Apartado Aereo 52964, Bogota Colombia B Caracoli Antioquia CO 11/24/1950 s Pedro Jose Sierra Garcia & Maria Bertha. Lic 1984. D 2/28/1986 P 1/1/1987 Bp Bernardo Merino-Botero. m 4/17/1986 Luz Marina Ramirez Terrez. Iglesia Epis En Colombia 1986-2005. LUZMABOGADA@HOTMAIL.COM

SIFERS, Julianne (Kan) 12673 W. 116th St., Overland Park KS 66210 **GC Dep Dio Kansas Topeka KS 2010-2013; Cmsn for Ch Growth and Dvlp Dio Kansas Topeka KS 2009-2013; Cmsn for Liturg and Arts Dio Kansas Topeka KS 2007-2013; Dioc Coun Dio Kansas Topeka KS 2007-2013; P-in-c S Aid's Ch Olathe KS 2005-** B Belleville KS 9/4/1941 d Samuel Edwin Elyea & Hazel Celeste. Johnson Cnty Cmnty Coll; BA Ottawa U 1992; MDiv Epis TS of The SW 1996. D 6/8/1996 P 12/14/1996 Bp John Clark Buchanan. m 4/7/1978 Russell S Sifers c 4. GC Dep Dio Kansas Topeka KS 2007-2010; Bd Mem Epis Cmnty Serv Kansas City MO 2005-2010; Convoc Dn Dio W Missouri Kansas City MO 2003-2005; Stndg Com Pres Dio W Missouri Kansas City MO 2002-2003; Bp Spencer Place Inc Kansas City MO 2001-2004; Dioc Coun Dio W Missouri Kansas City MO 2000-2003; Dio W Missouri Kansas City MO 1998-2001; Crittenton Kansas City MO 1996-1997. motherjuli@staidansolathe.org

SIFFORD, Thomas Andrew (Ark) 74 Sierra Dr, Hot Springs Village AR 71909 B Benbrook TX 8/1/1929 s Thomas Andrew Sifford & Novice Beatrice. BA U of Texas 1968; Angl TS 1975. D 9/15/1975 Bp A Donald Davies P 9/29/1976 Bp Robert Elwin Terwilliger. m 2/1/1952 Rita Nichols c 3. Vic H H Trin Epis Ch Hot Sprg Vill AR 1986-1997; S Alb's Epis Ch Arlington TX 1985; Dio Ft Worth Ft Worth TX 1984; S Greg's Epis Ch Mansfield TX 1983; Cur S Mich's Ch Richland Hills Richland Hills TX 1975-1982.

SIGAFOOS, Richard Vaughn (Colo) 131 31 Rd, Grand Junction CO 81503 B Omaha NE 5/13/1940 s Rolland B Sigafoos & Mary Agnes. BA U CO 1967. D 12/29/1991 Bp William Harvey Wolfrum P 6/1/1992 Bp William Jerry Winterrowd. m 8/7/1965 Gretchen O Lamb c 2. Stndg Com Dio Colorado Denver CO 2000-2005; COM Dio Colorado Denver CO 1995-1999; R Ch Of The Nativ Grand Jct CO 1993-2005. rsigafoos@acsol.net

SIGAMONEY, Christopher (LI) 88 27 216 Street, Queens Village NY 11427 **P Ch Of Chr The King E Meadow NY 2009-; P S Bede's Epis Ch Syosset NY 2009-** B 12/1/1952 BACHELOR OF Div UNITEED Theol Coll, BANGALORE, INDIA 1981; DOCTOR OF Mnstry NYTS 2002. m 5/28/1982 Freeda Sigamoney. Chapl Interfaith Med Cntr Brooklyn NY 2004-2011; Chapl Epis Hlth Serv Bethpage NY 2001-2004. chrissigamoney@gmail.com

SIGLER, James Markham (NCal) P.O. Box 467, Wimberley TX 78676 B Corpus Christi TX 3/30/1941 s Robert James Sigler & Myrtle Hortense. BA U So 1963; MDiv VTS 1967. D 6/23/1967 Bp Everett H Jones P 1/4/1968 Bp Richard Earl Dicus. m 1/1/1991 Shelley Garvin c 2. Dioc Coun Dio Nthrn California Sacramento CA 1994-1996; Pres Cler Assn Dio Nthrn California Sacramento CA 1992-1996; R Emm Epis Ch Grass Vlly CA 1991-2006; Dioc Coun Dio Oklahoma Oklahoma City OK 1988-1991; R All SS' Epis Ch Duncan OK 1986-1991; Assoc S Geo's Epis Ch Schenectady NY 1985-1986; Dn Sthrn Deanry Dio Dallas Dallas TX 1976-1985; Vic Vol S Alb's Ch Hubbard TX 1975-1983; S Jn's Epis Ch Corsicana TX 1972-1985; Assoc S Dav's Epis Ch San Antonio TX 1968-1972; Assoc S Thos And S Mart's Ch Corpus Christi TX 1967-1968. jmsigler@hughes.net

SIGLOH, Jane Engleby (SwVa) 4068 Garth Rd, Crozet VA 22932 B Houston TX 4/14/1934 d Thomas Slack & Kate. BA Sweet Briar Coll 1956; MA Hollins U 1975; MDiv Ya Berk 1987. D 6/10/1989 Bp Arthur Edward Walmsley P 3/31/1990 Bp Jeffery William Rowthorn. m 4/14/1979 Dennis Boyde Sigloh. COM Dio SW Virginia Roanoke VA 1995-1996; R Emm Ch Staunton VA 1992-1998; Cur S Matt's Epis Ch Wilton CT 1989-1991. "Like Trees Walking," Cowley, 2007; Contrib, *Sermons that Wk*, 1991; Auth, *More Sermons That Wk 1992 & 1995*. OSH 1988. Prchng Excellence Awd Epis Evang Fndt 1991. jsigldh@cstone.net

SIGNORE, Richard Scott (Mass) 19 Briggs Ave., Bourne MA 02532 B Newton MA 8/28/1952 s Frank Signore & Ethel. BA Boston Coll 1974; MDiv GTS 1977; ThM New Brunswick TS 1986. D 6/4/1977 Bp Albert Wiencke Van Duzer P 12/11/1977 Bp George Phelps Mellick Belshaw. m 7/25/1977 Nina C Signore c 2. S Ptr's Ch On The Canal Buzzards Bay MA 1988-2004; R S Mths Ch Hamilton NJ 1982-1988; Dio New Jersey Trenton NJ 1978-1981; Vic Trin Epis Ch Stratford NJ 1978-1981; Asst Trin Epis Ch Stratford NJ 1977. richardsignore@comcast.net

SIGNORELLI, Barry Michael (NY) 278 Monmouth St Apt 4-L, Jersey City NJ 07302 B 4/17/1958 s John Michael Signorelli & Lois Beverly. BFA Webster U 1981; MDiv GTS 1987. D 6/13/1987 Bp Paul Moore Jr P 12/1/1987 Bp Richard Beamon Martin. m 3/4/2004 Bruce E Parker. Ch Of The H Apos New York NY 1999-2009; Asst S Jn's Ch Brooklyn NY 1988-1990; The Ch Hymnal Corp New York NY 1987. Auth, "The Dream Realized," *Washington Dc Natl Cathd*, 1990; Auth, "Our Journey," *GC*, 1988. Integrity. bsignorelli@mindspring.com

SIGUENCIA VELECELA, Angel Serafin (EcuC) Av. Real Audiencia N 63-47, Y Sabanilla Quito Ecuador Ecuador B Azogues, Canar 6/25/1968 s Paulino Siguencia & Maria. D 11/30/2003 P 5/20/2004 Bp J Neptali Larrea-Moreno. Ecuador New York NY 2006-2009; Iglesia Epis Del Ecuador Ecuador 2006-2009. assiguencia@puce.edu.eu

SILAS, Berkman (Ak) Saint Barnabas Church, Minto AK 99758 B Old Minto AK 12/23/1922 s Louis Silas & Susan. D 5/13/1972 P 1/1/1974 Bp William J Gordon Jr. m 3/24/1944 Sarah Frank.

SILBAUGH, Morgan Collins (Cal) 914 Mountain Meadows Cir, Ashland OR 97520 B Lancaster OH 2/21/1935 s Hugh Reber Silbaugh & Charlotte Mary. BA Amh 1957; MA Cor 1958; BD EDS 1963. D 6/8/1963 P 6/13/1964 Bp Walter M Higley. m 2/12/1977 Charlotte V Van Auken c 3. Assoc Trin Epis Ch Ashland Ashland OR 2005-2009; Stndg Com Dio California San Francisco CA 1996-1998; R Chr Epis Ch Los Altos CA 1990-2000; Stndg Com Dio Cntrl New York Syracuse NY 1989-1990; VIM Funding Com Chair Dio Cntrl New York Syracuse NY 1985-1990; R Trin Epis Ch Watertown NY 1985-1990; R Chr Ch Manlius NY 1968-1984; Assoc S Thos' Epis Ch Syracuse NY 1966-1968; Mssy-in-c St. Jn'sPhoenix, New York Dio Cntrl New York Syracuse NY 1963-1966. Fayetteville-Manlius Rotary Citizen of Dist Rotary 1984; Vill of Manlius Citizen Recogniton Awd Vill of Manlius New York 1979. morgansilbaugh@earthlink.net

SILBEREIS, Richard (Ct) 155 Wyllys St, Hartford CT 06106 B Dayton OH 1/12/1951 s Charles Henry Silbereis & Julie Ann. BA The Athenaeum of Ohio 1973; BA U Cinc 1980; MDiv CDSP 1987. D 6/27/1987 P 1/1/1988 Bp Oliver Bailey Garver Jr. m 6/29/1980 Helen Elaine Scalzo c 2. Serv Ch Of The Gd Shpd Hartford CT 1995-2008; S Clare's Ch Matthews NC 1991-1995; Asst Min S Andr's Ch Saratoga CA 1988-1991; Chr Ch Alameda CA 1988; Chr Ch Alameda CA 1987-1988. esilbereis@hotmail.com

SILCOX JR, James Heyward (SeFla) 3684 Inverness Way, Augusta GA 30907 **Cur S Paul's Ch Augusta GA 2005-** B Charleston SC 11/22/1950 BS USMA at W Point 1972; MA U of Wisconsin 1980; MDiv STUSo 2005. D 4/17/2005 Bp Leopold Frade P 10/18/2005 Bp Henry Irving Louttit. m 11/18/1972 Jane Anne Thornley c 3. elisalive@aol.com

SILIDES JR, George Constantine (Ak) 411 Gold St, Juneau AK 99801 **The Ch Of The H Trin Juneau AK 2004-** B Fairbanks AK 9/18/1955 s George Constantine Silides & Mary Ruth. BEd U of Arizona 1977; MDiv GTS 1986. D 6/14/1986 Bp George Phelps Mellick Belshaw P 6/1/1987 Bp William Edwin Swing. m 12/21/1997 Hunter Pearson c 4. Exec Coun Appointees New York NY 2002-2008; Dvlpmt Off Dio Alaska Fairbanks AK 2002-2007; Dio Alaska Fairbanks AK 1998-2004; Co-Vic S Steph's Ch Ft Yukon AK 1998-2002; S Paul's Day Sch Of Oakland Oakland CA 1989-1998; Chair of the Dept of Yth Mnstry Dio California San Francisco CA 1987-1996; Cur S Matt's Epis Ch San Mateo CA 1986-1989; COM Dio California San Francisco CA 1986-1988. revsilides@gci.net

SILIDES, Hunter Pearson (Ak) 411 Gold St, Juneau AK 99801 B New York NY 9/19/1963 d John Haskew Pearson & Sarah Margaret. BA Wesl 1968; MDiv CDSP 1992. D 12/5/1992 P 12/1/1993 Bp William Edwin Swing. m 12/21/1997 George Constantine Silides c 4. The Ch Of The H Trin Juneau AK 2008-2009; Exec Coun Appointees New York NY 2002-2008; Fairbanks Luth Ch Fairbanks AK 2002-2003; Vic S Mk's Ch Nenana AK 2001-2004; Dio Alaska Fairbanks AK 1998-2002; Co-Vic/Appointed Mssy S Steph's Ch Ft Yukon AK 1998-2001; Trin Par Menlo Pk CA 1993. hsilides@aol.com

SILK-WRIGHT, Margaret (Marnie) (CFla) 1813 Palo Alto Ave, Lady Lake FL 32159 **P-in-c S Steph's Epis Ch Ocala FL 2011-; P-in-c Ch Of The Adv Dunnellon FL 2008-** B Pontiac MI 6/10/1938 d Albert Edward Silk & Margaret Priscilla. AA Dupage Glen Ellyn IL 1978; BS Geo Wms of Aurora U 1980; MDiv SWTS 1985. D 9/21/1985 Bp James Winchester Montgomery P 4/1/1986 Bp Frank Tracy Griswold III. c 5. Vic S Fran Of Assisi Ch Bushnell FL 2003; Assoc S Geo Epis Ch The Villages FL 1997-2003; Vic Calv Epis Ch Sioux City IA 1990-1996; Dio So Dakota Sioux Falls SD 1990-1996; Vic S Geo's Epis Ch Le Mars IA 1990-1996; Vic S Paul's Epis Ch Vermillion SD 1990-1996; Assoc S Jn's Ch Plymouth MI 1987-1990; Emm Ch Petoskey MI 1986-1987. Int Mnstry Ntwk. wright4u@comcast.net

SILLA, SuzeAnne Marie (NI) Diocese of Northern Indiana, 117 N Lafayette Blvd, South Bend IN 46601 **Cn to the Ordnry Dio Nthrn Indiana So Bend IN 2007-** B Roscoe NY 4/24/1943 d Harold Steeves & Iola Donaldson. BA Miami-Dade Cmnty Coll 1981; Cert U So 1998. D 5/8/1984 P 7/11/1998 Bp Calvin Onderdonk Schofield Jr. c 4. Dio Milwaukee Milwaukee WI 2003-2007; S Mary Magd Epis Ch Coral Sprg FL 2003; Asst S Margarets Epis Ch Miami Lakes FL 1992-2003; Dio SE Florida Miami FL 1992-2002; Chair -

S

Com Dio SE Florida Miami FL 1986-1988; Asst Epis Ch Of The H Fam Miami Gardens FL 1984-1992. canon@ednin.org

SILLERS, Ernest Dwyer (Los) 23701 Colima Bay, Dana Point CA 92629 **Died 10/16/2009** B River John NS CA 10/2/1910 s Sherman L Sillers & Amanda L. ThB Gordon Coll 1935; MA U of New Hampshire 1940. D 6/12/1941 P 12/1/1941 Bp John T Dal. c 1. Auth, "Story of A Visionary," Cathd Cntr Press, 2007. alexbratcher@gmail.com

SILTON, Margaret Kanze (NC) 304 East Franklin St., Chapel Hill NC 27514 **D Chap Of The Cross Chap Hill NC 2010-** B White Plains NY 11/16/1954 d Edward Joseph Kanze & Joyce Brownell. BA Binghamton U 1976; MA Duke 1977; MDiv Duke DS 2005. D 6/14/2008 Bp Michael Bruce Curry. m 3/12/1977 Andrew Silton c 3. D S Jos's Ch Durham NC 2008-2010. mksilton@gmail.com

SILVER, Deborah Lee (At) 3005 St James Pl, Grovetown GA 30813 B Aberdeen WA 11/19/1953 BS Manchester Coll. D 12/19/1998 P 6/23/1999 Bp Henry Irving Louttit. m 1/27/1990 William Thomas Deneke. Asst H Trin Par Decatur GA 2000-2010. Auth, "A Feminist," *Trinitarian Model Of Pstr Care & Counslg w Wmn*. AAPC.

SILVER, Gayanne Miller (Fla) 14557 Basilham Ln, Jacksonville FL 32258 B New York NY 3/4/1942 d Charles Roderick Miller & Emma Antoinette. BA Mercy Coll 1967; MDiv GTS 1997. D 6/21/1997 P 6/20/1998 Bp Robert Carroll Johnson Jr. c 2. Dio Florida Jacksonville FL 2004-2009; Assoc Par of Trin Ch New York NY 2000-2004; Asst Vic S Pat's Mssn Mooresville NC 1997-2000. gaysilver@bellsouth.net

SILVERSTRIM, Elaine Margaret (CPa) 110 Dry Run Rd., Coudersport PA 16915 **Lead Supply Ch Of Our Sav Montoursville PA 2009-** B Sidney NY 2/21/1946 d John M Sheldon & Ruby. BS Albany St U 1976; MA U of Scranton 1988; MDiv GTS 1991. D 6/8/1991 P 2/5/1992 Bp James Michael Mark Dyer. m 2/8/1969 Leland E Silverstrim c 5. R Chr Ch Coudersport PA 2002-2006; Vic Trin Ch Renovo PA 1996-2002; Vic Trin Ch Boothwyn PA 1993-1995; P-in-res Cathd Ch Of The Nativ Bethlehem PA 1992-1993; Dio Bethlehem Bethlehem PA 1991-1993. Sis of St. Marg 1995. silverstrim@zitomedia.net

SILVINSKAS, Peter Paul (Pa) 156 Sweet Gum Ln, Aiken SC 29803 B Philadelphia PA 5/12/1933 s Casimir Silvinskas & Emily. BA S Chas Sem Overbrook PA 1954; STD Pontifical Gregorian U Rome IT 1961. Rec from Roman Catholic 11/1/1982 as Priest Bp Lyman Cunningham Ogilby. m 8/25/1979 Mary B Farrelly. Assoc S Paul Ch Exton PA 1999-2000; Assoc R Washington Meml Chap Vlly Forge PA 1997-1999; Ch Of The Gd Samar Paoli PA 1983-1997. Auth, *Prot Concepts of Unity & Diversity in Faith & Ord Mvmt*. silvinskas@aol.com

SILVIUS III, Herman Theodore (Mass) 1128 SE 17th Ter, Cape Coral FL 33990 B Sacramento CA 6/8/1926 s Herman Theodore Silvius & Jessie. BA U CA 1948; BD PrTS 1951; EDS 1952; ETSC 1975. D 6/7/1952 Bp Norman B Nash P 12/16/1952 Bp George Ashton Oldham. m 11/9/1952 Jean Richardson c 3. BEC Dio Massachusetts Boston MA 1969-1988; Cmsn Mssn (Chair, 1972-1974) Dio Massachusetts Boston MA 1967-1988; R Trin Ch Topsfield MA 1957-1989; Cur Trin Par Melrose MA 1952-1954.

SIMEONE, Richard John (Mass) 203 Pemberton St Unit 3, Cambridge MA 02140 **EFM Co-Coordntr Dio Massachusetts Boston MA 2009-** B Harrisburg PA 8/7/1941 s Ernest John Simeone & Frances (N)ettie. AB Br 1963; MDiv GTS 1966. D 6/15/1966 Bp John T Heistand P 12/17/1966 Bp Thaddeus F Zielinski. m 11/23/1986 Lyn G Gillespie c 3. R S Jn's Epis Ch Gloucester MA 1997-2010; Eccl Trial Crt Judge Dio Massachusetts Boston MA 1997-2003; Dioc Mus Cmsn Dio Connecticut Hartford CT 1994-1997; R Trin Epis Ch Collinsville CT 1978-1997; Liturg Cmsn Dio Maine Portland ME 1970-1978; Vic All SS Epis Ch Skowhegan ME 1968-1978; Vic S Mart's Epis Ch Pittsfield ME 1968-1978; Cur S Mths Epis Ch E Aurora NY 1966-1968. Assoc of the OHC 1990. rjs4166@earthlink.net

SIMMONDS, Richard Frank (Ak) Po Box 58041, Minto AK 99758 B Troy NY 11/25/1931 s Raymond F Simmonds & Charlotte Ruth. BA Ken 1953; STB Ya Berk 1956. D 5/27/1956 Bp Frederick Lehrle Barry P 12/1/1956 Bp William J Gordon Jr. m 6/1/1962 Pauline Joyce Charlie c 2. Dio Alaska Fairbanks AK 1992; R S Matt's Epis Ch Fairbanks AK 1990-1991; S Fran By The Sea Ch Kenai AK 1985-1988; P S Matt's Epis Ch Fairbanks AK 1970-1987; Asst S Jn's Epis Ch Troy NY 1967-1970; P-in-c S Matt's Ch Beaver AK 1962-1967; P-in-c S Barn Ch Minto AK 1956-1962.

SIMMONITE JR, Thomas Francis (SC) 2220 Atlantic Ave, Sullivans Island SC 29482 B 1/2/1943 s Thomas Francis Simmonite & Margaret Skinner. D 9/10/2005 Bp Edward Lloyd Salmon Jr. m 6/23/2001 Elizabeth Tezza c 2.

SIMMONS, C Douglas (Ark) 1558 N Stable Ave, Fayetteville AR 72703 B Ypsilanti MI 8/21/1937 s Carl J Simmons & Dortha Marie. BS Estrn Michigan U 1960; MDiv VTS 1965; DMin VTS 1984. D 6/29/1965 Bp C Kilmer Myers P 2/5/1966 Bp Archie H Crowley. m 6/27/1959 Nina Seddon. Dio Arkansas Little Rock AR 1995-2001; Assoc R S Paul's Ch Fayetteville AR 1995-2000; P Gd Shpd Epis Ch Silver Sprg MD 1991-1995; Int Dio Washington Washington DC 1986-1990; R Trin Epis Ch Asheville NC 1984-1991; Chair of Cont Ed. Com for Cler Dio Wstrn No Carolina Asheville NC 1982-1991; R Chr Epis Ch Of Springfield Springfield OH 1976-1984; Assoc S Paul's Ch Kansas City MO 1972-1976; Asst S Steph The Mtyr Ch Minneapolis MN 1970-1972. Auth, "Bk-The Joshua Chronicles," Red Lead Press, 2010; Auth, "Bk-The Joshua Chronicles," Red Lead Press, 2010. dougsimmons13@sbcglobal.net

SIMMONS, David Clark (NMich) 5976 Whitney 19.8 Blvd, Gladstone MI 49837 **Non-par S Steph's Ch Escanaba MI 1992-** B Minneapolis MN 7/2/1941 s Bert Hoff Simmons & Dortha Naomi. BBA U of Iowa 1964. D 8/21/1992 P 2/21/1993 Bp Thomas Kreider Ray. m 9/24/1966 Mary Rose Krasean. simmons@chartermi.net

SIMMONS, David Todd (Mil) 808 S East Ave, Waukesha WI 63186 **Bd Mem EDEO Ft Meyers FL 2011-; Dep to Gnrl Assembly Natl Coun Of Ch New York NY 2010-; Ecum Off Dio Milwaukee Milwaukee WI 2008-; R St Mths Epis Ch Waukesha WI 2008-** B Lawrence KY 7/15/1970 s Herbert Nelson Simmons & Judy Christine. BA Wstrn Kentucky U 1992; MDiv VTS 2001. D 6/3/2001 P 1/12/2002 Bp Edwin Funsten Gulick Jr. m 6/27/1992 Dawn M Bewley c 2. R S Jn's Ch Murray KY 2003-2007; Cur S Matt's Epis Ch Louisville KY 2001-2003. Ord of Julian of Norwich 2006. dsimmons@mac.com

SIMMONS, Elizabeth H (Mil) 614 Main St, Racine WI 53403 **S Lk's Ch Racine WI 2009-** B Tokyo Japan Japan 12/26/1957 d Ronald Franklin Huskey & Helene. BA U NC 1980; MDiv GTS 1994. D 6/18/1994 Bp Brice Sidney Sanders P 1/18/1995 Bp David Charles Bowman. Asst S Jn's Epis Ch Boulder CO 2008-2009; Ch Of The Apos Oro Vlly AZ 2006-2008; R S Steph's Ch Phoenix AZ 1999-2006; Assoc S Phil's In The Hills Tucson AZ 1996-1999; Asst R Trin Epis Ch Buffalo NY 1994-1996. madreliz@gmail.com

SIMMONS, Harriet Phillips (Miss) 4911 Country Club Dr, Meridian MS 39305 B Yazoo City MS 12/24/1947 d Darrington Phillips & Werdna Crawford. Millsaps Coll 1966; BA U of Mississippi 1968; MA Mississippi Coll 1973; New Orleans Bapt TS 1989. D 2/22/1992 Bp Duncan Montgomery Gray Jr P 5/21/2000 Bp Alfred Clark Marble Jr. m 3/23/1968 William Simmons. Vic S Fran Of Assisi Ch Philadelphia MS 2001-2011; S Mary's Ch Enterprise MS 2001-2011; P S Mary's Ch Enterprise MS 2000-2001; D S Paul's Epis Ch Meridian MS 1992-2000. NAAD. billsimm@comcast.net

SIMMONS, Harriette J (At) Saint Paul'S Church, 605 Reynolds Street On The Riverwalk, Augusta GA 30901 **Int R Chr Ch Macon GA 2008-; S Jas Epis Ch Port Gibson MS 2008-** B Macon GA 10/2/1942 d Russell James & Elizabeth Coates. BA Wesleyan Coll 1964; MDiv Candler TS Emory U 1994. D 6/10/1995 P 12/16/1995 Bp Frank Kellogg Allan. m 2/27/1965 James W Simmons c 3. S Aug Of Cbury Ch Augusta GA 2005-2008; S Paul's Ch Augusta GA 2002-2004; Chr Ch Macon GA 1995-2002. Rotary Club 1996-2003. Outstanding Alum Wesleyan Coll 1996. harriette@christchurchmacon.com

SIMMONS, Kenneth William (Minn) 11 Kellogg Blvd E Apt 715, Saint Paul MN 55101 B Ponca City OK 8/7/1935 s Lyle Cole Simmons & Karolyn Frances. BA U of Tulsa 1958; MDiv Epis TS of The SW 1963. D 6/29/1963 P 5/20/1964 Bp Hamilton Hyde Kellogg. m 6/29/1975 Barbara Ann Langer c 2. S Anne's Epis Ch Sunfish Lake MN 1966-1983.

SIMMONS, Mary Rose (NMich) 5976 Whitney 19.8 Blvd, Gladstone MI 49837 **D S Steph's Ch Escanaba MI 2001-** B South Bend IN 11/8/1942 d William Henry Krasean & Rose Ercelia. BA Marygrove Coll 1964. D 5/27/2001 Bp James Arthur Kelsey. m 9/24/1966 David Clark Simmons.

SIMMONS, Ned Allen (Ga) 109 Flint River Circle, Quitman GA 31643 **D S Jas Epis Ch Quitman GA 1992-** B Ambrose GA 6/13/1923 s Charlie Reuben Simmons & Maggie Estelle. BS U GA 1945; MS Florida St U 1950. D 3/4/1990 Bp Harry Woolston Shipps. c 2.

SIMMONS IV, Thomas William (Va) 1807 Hungary Rd, Richmond VA 23228 **R S Ptr's Epis Ch Purcellville VA 2002-** B Denver CO 9/2/1967 s Thomas Simmons & Blair. BA Jas Madison U 1989; MDiv Westminster TS 1993; VTS 1998. D 6/13/1998 P 4/20/1999 Bp Peter James Lee. m 2/25/1995 Tait N Simmons c 5. All SS Ch Richmond VA 1998-2002. deovivere@aol.com

SIMMONS, Walter C(lippinger) (Md) 514 Limerick Cir. Unit 201, Lutherville Timonium MD 21093 B Cincinnati OH 4/29/1940 s Benjamin Coleman Simmons & Virginia Clippinger. BA Mia 1964; MA U Pac 1967; MDiv EDS 1972. D 7/16/1972 P 6/3/1973 Bp John Raymond Wyatt. R S Marg's Epis Ch Baltimore MD 1994-2003; Vic S Steph's Elwood IN 1993-1994; COM Dio Indianapolis Indianapolis IN 1991-1993; Assoc S Paul's Epis Ch Indianapolis IN 1991-1993; Jub Off Dio Rhode Island Providence RI 1987-1990; R Ch Of The Mssh Providence RI 1981-1990; Chr Epis Ch Anacortes WA 1980-1981; Assoc S Lk's Ch Tacoma WA 1975-1980; Cur S Dav's Ch Spokane WA 1972-1973. *Var arts*, 2003. Providence 1 in 350 Ldrshp Awards City of Providence 1986.

SIMON JR, Kenneth A (SanD) 6556 Park Ridge Boulevard, San Diego CA 92120 **P S Dunst's Epis Ch San Diego CA 2009-** B Paterson NJ 4/12/1974 s Kenneth Augusto Simon & Daisy Anayansi. BA U of San Diego 1996; MDIV Fuller TS 2004; CAS CDSP 2009. D 6/27/2009 Bp James Robert Mathes. D Chr Ch Coronado CA 2009. ksimonj316@yahoo.com

S

SIMON, Michael Gerard (WVa) Po Box 692, Augusta WV 26704 **Died 6/7/2011** B Wheeling WV 1/22/1946 s Michael Simon & Betty. BA W Liberty St Coll 1987; MA VTS 1995; DMin GTF 2004. D 6/14/1997 P 6/13/1998 Bp John H(enry) Smith. mgsimon1@frontier.com

SIMONIAN, Marlene Jenny (RI) 1346 Creek Nine Dr, North Port FL 34290 B Providence RI 3/22/1942 d Pasquale J Cesino & Anastasia. Rhode Island Sch for Deacons 1988. D 6/23/1990 Bp George Nelson Hunt III. m 2/29/1972 Robert Martin Simonian c 2. D Ch Of The Gd Shpd Punta Gorda FL 1998-2003; D St Mich & Gr Ch Rumford RI 1994-1998; D S Mk's Ch Warren RI 1990-1994; Stndg Com Dio Rhode Island Providence RI 1984-1988. robert_simonian@verizon.net

SIMONS, Daniel J (NY) 74 Trinity Pl, New York NY 10006 **P for Liturg, Hosp & Pilgrimage Trin Par New York NY 2008-** B Land O'Lakes WI 9/29/1964 s James John Simons & Lois Ruth. BA Wheaton Coll 1987; MDiv VTS 1994. D 6/18/1994 Bp Frank Tracy Griswold III P 12/18/1994 Bp John Clark Buchanan. m 11/20/2010 Javier Galito-Cava. Cn Pstr Cathd Ch Of S Steph Harrisburg PA 1995-1998; P S Paul's Ch Leavenworth KS 1994-1995. dnl.smns@gmail.com

SIMONS, Harrison Thayer (NC) 512 Harris St, Oxford NC 27565 **Died 8/31/2011** B Melrose MA 2/6/1934 s Webster Little Simons & Dorothy Ballard. BA Randolph-Macon Coll 1959; MDiv Bex 1962. D 6/9/1962 Bp Robert Fisher Gibson Jr P 6/8/1963 Bp Samuel B Chilton. c 2. Auth, "The Present Generation," *Hist of S Steph's Epis Ch 1823-1998*, Roble Pub., 1998; Auth, *Booknotes*. Epis Booksellers Associaton 2001; NC Cleric Assn 1973-1978. DD (honoris causa) VTS 2007; Distinguished Alum Awd Randolph-Macon Coll 1998; Nancy Susan Reynolds Racism Awd Reynolds Fndt 1997. hgkjelr@gloryroad.net

SIMONS, James Burdette (Pgh) 731 Laurel Dr, Ligonier PA 15658 **Dio Pittsburgh Monroeville PA 2000-; R S Michaels Of The Vlly Epis Ch Ligonier PA 1988-** B Sewickley PA 7/8/1957 s Stephen Jewette Simons & Dolly Lee. BS Alleg 1980; MDiv TESM 1985; D.Min. TESM 2007. D 6/8/1985 P 12/19/1985 Bp Alden Moinet Hathaway. m 6/14/1980 Lisa Marie Grabowski c 2. Cathd Dn Search Com Dio Pittsburgh Monroeville PA 1999-2000; Chair - Com Dio Pittsburgh Monroeville PA 1997-2000; Gc Cmncatn Com Dio Pittsburgh Monroeville PA 1991-1994; Asst R S Mart's Epis Ch Monroeville PA 1985-1988. jsimons@stmichaelsligonier.org

SIMONSEN, Douglas C (Oly) P.O. Box 1974, Anacortes WA 98221 **R S Dav's Epis Ch Friday Harbor WA 2010-** B Flint MI 11/22/1949 BS Michigan Tech U 1977; MTS Seattle U 1994; CAS CDSP 1996. D 6/28/1997 P 6/20/1998 Bp Vincent Waydell Warner. m 10/6/1978 Cynthia Shoop c 2. P-in-c S Dav's Epis Ch Friday Harbor WA 2008-2010; Reg Mssnr Dio Spokane Spokane WA 2004-2005; P-in-c H Trin Epis Ch Sunnyside WA 2004-2005; Vic S Hilda's - S Pat's Epis Ch Edmonds WA 2000-2002; Assoc P Gr Ch Bainbridge Island WA 1997-2000. DCSIMONSEN@COMCAST.NET

SIMOPOULOS, Nicole Martha (WA) 3202 Wellington Road, Alexandria VA 22302 **Lower Sch Chapl Cathd of St Ptr & St Paul Washington DC 2009-** B San Francisco CA 2/23/1973 BA Stan 1995; MDiv Amer Bapt Sem of the W 2000; MA Grad Theol Un 2002. D 5/27/2003 Bp Robert Louis Ladehoff P 1/3/2004 Bp Johncy Itty. c 1. Asst to the R Gr Memi Portland OR 2005-2008; Cur Epis Par Of S Jn The Bapt Portland OR 2003-2005; Chapl Oregon Epis Sch Portland OR 2002-2009. nsimopoulos@cathedral.org

SIMPSON, Cynthia (WA) Christ Episcopal School, 107 S Washington St, Rockville MD 20850 **Asst to the R Chr Ch Prince Geo's Par Rockville MD 2007-; Chr Epis Sch Rockville MD 2007-** B Alexandria, VA 2/25/1958 d Omer Clayton Simpson & Mary Adelle Chapman. BA Baylor U 1981; MDiv Sthrn Bapt TS Louisville KY 1985; Stds Dplma VTS 2005. D 6/9/2007 P 1/19/2008 Bp John Chane. c 1. S Ptr's Ch Poolesville MD 1999-2007. csimpson@cesstaff.org

SIMPSON, Dawn Simpson (Colo) Po Box 291, Monte Vista CO 81144 **San Luis Vlly Epis Mssn Monte Vista CO 2008-; P-t S Thos The Apos Epis Ch Alamosa CO 2003-** B Pekin IL 8/23/1961 d William W Davis & MaryLou. BS Adams St Coll 1989; MA in Theol Trin TS 2009. D 7/19/2003 Bp William Jerry Winterrowd P 1/29/2004 Bp Robert John O'Neill. m 5/1/1990 Grant Patrick Simpson c 3. priestdawn@gmail.com

SIMPSON, Geoffrey Sedgwick (Mil) The Laurels, Queen Street, Yetminster, Dorset DT9 6LLGB Great Britain (UK) B South Milwaukee WI 8/20/1932 s Alexander Mcbeth Simpson & Helen Rhoda. BA Ham 1954; STB GTS 1957; MA U of Wisconsin 1966; PhD U of Cambridge 1973. D 6/1/1957 P 12/1/1957 Bp Donald H V Hallock. m 8/18/1971 Mary McCarthy c 2. Asst Chapl S Steph's Ch Racine WI 1963-1966; Vic S Barth's Ch Pewaukee WI 1958-1962; Cur Chr Ch Whitefish Bay WI 1957-1958.

SIMPSON, Geoffrey Stewart (Va) 212 W Lancaster Ave, Paoli PA 19301 **Assoc Cler Ch Of The Gd Samar Paoli PA 2010-** B Norfolk VA 5/29/1964 s John P(atrick) Simpson & Gret P. Coll of Wooster; BA Trin 1987; MDiv TESM 1993. D 6/12/1993 Bp Arthur Edward Walmsley P 12/15/1993 Bp Peter James Lee. Yth Mnstry Gr Epis Ch Trumbull CT 1985-1990. geoff@good-samaritan.org

SIMPSON JR, John P(atrick) (Pa) 244 Woodbine Ave, Narberth PA 19072 B Philadelphia PA 4/9/1939 s John Patrick Simpson & Charlotte. BS Tem 1961; MDiv VTS 1968. D 6/8/1968 P 3/8/1969 Bp Robert Lionne DeWitt. m 7/29/1999 Robert E Crook c 3. Long-term Supply S Barth's Ch Philadelphia PA 1992-2002; S Mths Ch Philadelphia PA 1977-1980; S Fran Cmnty Serv Inc. Salina KS 1970-1977; H Apos Ch Ellsworth KS 1970-1975; Cur Ch Of The Gd Samar Paoli PA 1968-1970. AAPC; Coll of Chapl.

SIMPSON OSH, Mary Michael (NY) 151 E 31st St Apt 8-H, New York NY 10016 **Died 7/20/2011** B Evansville IN 12/1/1925 d Link Wilson Simpson & Mary Garrett. BS Texas Wmn's U-Denton 1946; BA Texas Wmn's U-Denton 1946; New York Trng Sch for Dss 1949; CUNY 1972; Cert Westchester Inst 1976; STM GTS 1982. D 12/14/1974 Bp James Stuart Wetmore P 1/7/1977 Bp Paul Moore Jr. Auth, *Yes To Wmn Priests*. Dio Cler Wmn Assn; EWC; Gld of Pstr Psychol; NAAP; NYSAPP. mmsimpsonosh@gmail.com

SIMPSON, Richard Edmund (LI) 754 Main St, Islip NY 11751 **R S Mk's Ch Islip NY 2001-** B Port Huron MI 6/3/1954 s Jorma C Simpson & Lois B. BA MI SU 1976; MDiv Epis TS of The SW 1981. D 6/30/1981 Bp Henry Irving Mayson P 5/1/1982 Bp H Coleman McGehee Jr. m 7/26/1980 Janet Robertson c 1. R Trin Ch Muscatine IA 1988-2001; Cn Trin Cathd Davenport IA 1985-1988; Vic S Paul's Ch Durant IA 1983-1985; Asst S Phil's Epis Ch Rochester MI 1981-1983. CBS; Tertiary of the Soc of S Fran 1991; Treas Gnrl C.B.S. 1993. ricktssf@optonline.net

SIMPSON, Richard Michael (WMass) 88 Highland St, Holden MA 01520 **Search Com for IX Bp (Chair) Dio Wstrn Massachusetts Springfield MA 2011-; R S Fran Ch Holden MA 1998-** B Honesdale PA 3/17/1963 s Ernest Richard Simpson & Margaret Ann. Jr Year Abroad U of St. Andrews 1984; BA Geo 1985; MDiv Drew U 1988; ThM PrTS 1990; DMin Columbia TS 2005. D 6/12/1993 Bp Arthur Edward Walmsley P 2/5/1994 Bp Clarence Nicholas Coleridge. m 5/25/1986 Elizabeth Hatheway MacMahon c 2. COM (Chair) Dio Wstrn Massachusetts Springfield MA 2006-2011; Mem of Dioc Coun Dio Wstrn Massachusetts Springfield MA 2004-2007; Asst Chr And H Trin Ch Westport CT 1993-1998. Contrib, "Homiletical Notes (in two volumes)," *Feasting on the Word*, Westminister/Jn Knox Press, 2011. richsimpson.317@gmail.com

SIMPSON, Richard Roy (RI) 277 High St., Westerly RI 02891 B Seattle WA 1/24/1943 s Floyd Thurston Simpson & Elsie Rosyland. BA U of Hawaii 1966; BD CDSP 1969. D 6/10/1969 P 12/1/1969 Bp Edwin Lani Hanchett. m 8/28/1965 Cynthia Chandler. R S Dav's On The Hill Epis Ch Cranston RI 1997-2001; S Fran Cmnty Serv Inc. Salina KS 1994-1997; R Trin Ch Sonoma CA 1987-1994; S Pauls Epis Ch The Dalles OR 1981-1987; S Jn's Ch Hermiston OR 1977-1981; R S Andr's Epis Ch McCall ID 1976-1977; Ch Of H Nativ Meridian ID 1975-1977; R Ch Of The Redeem Salmon ID 1973-1975; Vic S Andr's Cathd Honolulu HI 1971-1972; Asst Ch Of The Epiph Honolulu HI 1969-1970. simpson7833@comcast.net

SIMPSON, Ward Howard (SD) 500 South Main Ave, Sioux Falls SD 57104 **GC Dep Dio So Dakota Sioux Falls SD 2012-; Chair, BEC Dio So Dakota Sioux Falls SD 2010-; Dn Calv Cathd Sioux Falls SD 2009-** B Faribault MN 3/30/1962 s Charles Van Simpson & Alma Patricia. BS Minnesota St U Mankato 1984; MDiv Nash 1991. D 6/24/1991 Bp Robert Marshall Anderson P 12/27/1991 Bp William Charles Wantland. m 12/10/1983 Barbara Annette Peach c 3. GC Dep Dio Eau Claire Eau Claire WI 2009; GC Dep Dio Eau Claire Eau Claire WI 2006; GC Dep Dio Eau Claire Eau Claire WI 2003; GC Dep Dio Eau Claire Eau Claire WI 1997; R S Andr's Ch Ashland WI 1995-2009; Vic S Alb's Ch Spooner WI 1991-1995; Vic S Steph's Shell Lake WI 1991-1995. ward.simpson@gmail.com

SIMRILL, Spenser Davenport (Minn) 4945 Dupont Ave S, Minneapolis MN 55419 **Dn Cathd Ch Of S Mk Minneapolis MN 2002-; Com Dio Sthrn Ohio Cincinnati OH 1988-** B Charlotte NC 3/14/1948 s Frank Preston Simrill & Francis Simmons. BA Hampden-Sydney Coll 1970; MA U of Louisiana 1974; MDiv Louisville Presb TS 1978; Cert GTS 1979; DMin Louisville Presb TS 1989. D 6/25/1979 P 6/1/1980 Bp David Reed. m 9/2/1972 Susan Davenport c 2. R S Lk's Epis Ch Atlanta GA 1992-2002; R The Ch Of Ascen And H Trin Cincinnati OH 1986-1992; P-in-c Chr Ch Cathd Louisville KY 1986; Com Dio Kentucky Louisville KY 1985-1986; D-In-Res Chr Ch Cathd Louisville KY 1979-1980; Dio Kentucky Louisville KY 1979-1980. Advsry Bd, Angl Observer To The Untd Nations 2003; Bd Mem, Endowed Parishes Consortium Of The Epis Ch 2001-2004. Prchr Awd Gnrl Theolgical Sem 1979; Mayors Distinguished Citizens Awd 85; Archdio Louisville Peace & Justice Awd 85. SPENSERS@OURCATHEDRAL.ORG

SIMS, Carol Carruthers (SVa) 3929 Ocean Cut Lane, Virginia Beach VA 23451 B Charlottesville VA 8/31/1938 d Thomas Moore Carruthers & Mabel Olivia. BA U NC 1972; Med U of Virginia 1975; EDS U of Virginia 1979; Mnstry Formation Prog 1997. D 6/21/1997 P 12/20/1997 Bp Charles Jones III. c 3. Pstr Asst Ch Of The Epiph Norfolk VA 2008-2010; Assoc Galilee Epis Ch Virginia Bch VA 2007-2009; Upper Yellowstone Epis Ch Livingston MT 2007; All SS in Big Sky Big Sky MT 2004-2007; Dio Montana Helena MT 2001-2002; R S Jas Ch Lewistown MT 1997-2001. Auth, "Emotional

Responses Of Cancer Diagnosis," *Coping*, 1995; Auth, "Travesty In Palestine," *The Middle E Journ*, 1990. cmcsims@aol.com

SIMS, Edward Raymond (SO) 8 Calebs Ln, Rockport MA 01966 B Davenport IA 8/14/1923 s Lewis Raymond Sims & Sarah Cosette. BS U of Kansas 1946; BD CDSP 1949. D 6/22/1949 P 12/23/1949 Bp Robert N Spencer. m 8/2/1947 Elizabeth Jane Jordan c 4. Pstr Affiliate S Jn's Ch Beverly Farms MA 2000-2004; All SS in Big Sky Big Sky MT 2000-2002; Min Emm Chap Manchester MA 2000-2002; Pstr Affiliate S Jn's Ch Beverly Farms MA 1995-1999; Epis Soc Of Chr Ch Cincinnati OH 1972-1985; R Calv Epis Ch Sedalia MO 1951-1959. Auth, *A Season w the Sav*, Seabury Press, 1978; Auth, "arts," *Epis Life*; Auth, "arts," *Pstr Psychol mag*. DD CDSP 1976.

SIMS, Edward Raymond (Mil) 519 S Michigan St, Prairie Du Chien WI 53821 **Died 1/8/2010** B Brazil IN 4/20/1920 s George Sims & Flossie May. BA U of Memphis 1955; MDiv Nash 1963. D 6/15/1963 Bp James Winchester Montgomery P 12/21/1963 Bp Gerald Francis Burrill. m 10/15/2007 E Raymond Sims. Assoc, Julian of Norwich; SocMary. Hon Cn All SS Cathd Milwaukee WI 1997.

SIMS, Gregory Brian (Chi) 412 N Church St, Rockford IL 61103 B Linton IN 5/19/1947 s George Bernard Sims & Marjory Ann. BA U IL 1969; MDiv Nash 1972. D 5/20/1972 Bp Albert A Chambers P 12/2/1972 Bp Albert William Hillestad. R Emm Epis Ch Rockford IL 1990-2002; Cn Res S Jn's Cathd Albuquerque NM 1987-1990; R The Epis Ch Of The Adv W Bloomfield MI 1982-1986; R S Thos Epis Ch Plymouth IN 1976-1981; R S Ptr's By-The-Lake Ch Montague MI 1973-1976; Cur Emm Memi Epis Ch Champaign IL 1972-1973. Cn Res St. Jn's Cathd, Albuquerque, NM 1988. gsims@mac.com

SIMS, Gregory Knox (Cal) Po Box 1, Boonville CA 95415 B Moline IL 8/6/1933 s Wilbert Gremmels & Naomi Ann. BA U CA 1955; BD CDSP 1960; MA Stan 1964; PhD Stan 1971. D 6/13/1960 P 3/3/1961 Bp Francis E I Bloy. m 8/27/1995 Clarissa Schaeffer c 4. Assoc All SS Epis Ch Palo Alto CA 1962-1964; Asst S Ptr's Par San Pedro CA 1960-1962. Co-Auth, "Treating Sprtl Disorders: Promoting Sprtl Recovery," Hlth Acc Pr, 2001. Commencement Speaker U Ca-Berk Berkeley CA 1973. clarissa@saber.net

SIMS, Kenneth Harry (SeFla) 3970 Nw 188th St, Opa Locka FL 33055 B Miami FL 12/30/1942 s James Rollins Sims & Leola. EdD Nova SE U; BS Florida A&M U 1966; MS Florida Atlantic U 1980. D 6/16/2001 Bp John Lewis Said. m 6/21/1986 Gwendolyn Tynes.

SIMS, Mark Howard (SeFla) 1165 Ne 105th St, Miami Shores FL 33138 **S Mary Magd Epis Ch Coral Sprg FL 2003-** B Lakeland FL 9/17/1957 s Howard W Sims & Violet Alice. BA U Of Florida 1979; MDiv Epis TS of The SW 2000. D 6/14/2000 Bp John Lewis Said P 12/15/2000 Bp Leopold Frade. m 9/10/2003 Gail Haldeman Sims c 1. Trin Cathd Miami FL 2000-2003. Comission On Mnstry. revmarksims@mac.com

SIMS, Richard Osborn (Nev) 24 Elysium Dr, Ely NV 89301 **P S Barth's Ch Ely NV 2000-** B Ely NV 2/26/1952 s Philip A Sims & Marilyn G. Educ Dynamics Inst; Utah Tech Coll. D 4/2/2000 Bp John Stuart Thornton P 11/18/2000 Bp George Nelson Hunt III. m 1/7/1975 Shelba-Kay Costa. red@stbartholomewnevada.com

SIMS, Ronald Frank (Wyo) 2037 Thornburgh Dr, Laramie WY 82070 B Ogden UT 7/27/1929 s Frank J Sims & Elna Marie. BA U of Wyoming 1963; BD CDSP 1966. P 12/1/1966 Bp James W Hunter. m 8/12/1949 Shirley D Frodsham c 3. S Matt's Epis Cathd Laramie WY 1986-1992; R Ch Of S Thos Rawlins WY 1977-1986; R All SS Epis Ch Torrington WY 1968-1976; R Ch Of Our Sav Hartville WY 1968-1975; Vic S Barn Epis Ch Saratoga WY 1966-1968; Vic S Jas Ch Rawlins WY 1966-1968. simsdynasty@aol.com

SIMSON, John Everett (Mass) 4773 Abargo St, Woodland Hills CA 91364 B Hamilton OH 4/28/1958 s Everett D(avis) Simson & Mimi. BA U CA 1984; MDiv GTS 1993; DMin CDSP 2008. D 6/26/1993 P 5/14/1994 Bp Richard Lester Shimpfky. m 9/13/1986 Suzanne M Simson c 1. R S Anne's Ch Lowell MA 1996-2003; Cur Ch Of S Jn The Evang Hingham MA 1994-1996. Dioc Coun 2001-2002; Exec Com Epis City Mssn 1997-2003. johnesimson@yahoo.com

S

SINCLAIR, Gregory Lynn (NwT) 402 W Maple St, Fort Gibson OK 74434 **D Gr Ch Muskogee OK 2007-** B Geneva IL 12/14/1944 s Edward Harvey Sinclair & Virginia Anderson. BAS Abilene Chr U 1995; Med Hardin-Simmons U 2003. D 11/6/1988 Bp Sam Byron Hulsey. m 8/28/1968 Mary-Margaret Russell c 1. D S Mk's Epis Ch Abilene TX 2000-2007; D S Steph's Ch Sweetwater TX 1996-1999; D S Mk's Epis Ch Abilene TX 1988-1994. Ord Of S Lk The Physcn 2001. gsinclair111@cox.net

SINCLAIR, Nancy Park (Los) 502 Hawk Ln, Fountain Valley CA 92708 **Vic S Theo Of Cbury Par Seal Bch CA 2006-** B New Orleans LA 3/23/1945 D 1/31/2004 P 1/22/2005 Bp Joseph Jon Bruno. m 6/10/1967 Donald Sinclair c 2. S Mk's Par Downey CA 2004-2005. nsinclair@surfside.net

SINCLAIR, Roderick Doig (SwVa) Wcbr 250 Pantops Mountain Rd, Apt. 131, Charlottesville VA 22911 B Nassau BS 2/8/1931 s Thomas Doig Sinclair & Dorothy. BA U of Virginia 1953; LLB U of Virginia 1958; MDiv VTS 1966. D 6/11/1966 Bp Robert Fisher Gibson Jr P 12/10/1966 Bp David Shepherd Rose. m 2/27/1954 Louise Minor c 3. Chapl Chr Ch Blacksburg VA 1992-1996; U Chapl Dio SW Virginia Roanoke VA 1988-1991; Chapl Hollins Coll Hollins Clg VA 1981-1987; Chapl S Dunst's: The Epis Ch at Auburn U Auburn AL 1971-1981; Co-Chapl S Paul's Memi Charlottesville VA 1968-1971; Assoc Min S Geo's Epis Ch Arlington VA 1966-1968. Auth, "Epis Life, Jubilee," *Plumline*. Cltn For Justice 1970; Cuba Proj 1980-1988; Fllshp Recon 1980-1988; Virginia Inter-Faith Cntr For Publ Plcy 1996-2005. rodlusin@comcast.net

SINCLAIR, Scott Gambrill (Cal) 663 Coventry Rd, Kensington CA 94707 B Baltimore MD 3/29/1950 s James Edward Sinclair & Pauline Louise. BA Jn Hopkins U 1971; MA Jn Hopkins U 1972; MDiv CDSP 1976; PhD Grad Theol Un 1986. D 6/26/1976 Bp C Kilmer Myers P 5/19/1977 Bp Chilton Powell. Ch Of The Ascen Burlingame CA 1977-1978; S Andr's Epis Ch San Bruno CA 1976-1977. Auth, "A Saintudy Guide To S Paul'S Letter To The Romans," Bibal Press, 2000; Auth, "A Study Guide To Mk'S Gospel," Bibal Press, 1996; Auth, "The Road And The Truth: The Ed Of Jn'S Gospel," Bibal, 1994; Auth, "Revelation: A Bk For The Rest Of Us," Bibal Press, 1992; Auth, "Jesus Chr According To S Paul," Bibal Press, 1988. scottgsinclair@hotmail.com

SINGER, A(llen) Michael (EC) 800 Rountree St., Kinston NC 28501 **R S Mary's Ch Kinston NC 1999-** B Waynesboro PA 9/21/1955 s Edward Ervin Singer & Barbara. BA Morris Harvey Coll 1977; MDiv Nash 1980. D 6/13/1980 P 12/20/1980 Bp Dean T Stevenson. m 8/26/1978 Teresa Belcher c 1. R S Lk's Epis Ch Altoona PA 1984-1999; Dept Ch Growth Dio Cntrl Pennsylvania Harrisburg PA 1981-1995; Trin Ch Jersey Shore PA 1981; P-in-c All SS Epis Ch Williamsport PA 1980-1984. amsinger@suddenlink.net

SINGER, Susanna Jane (Cal) 268 Wawona Street, San Francisco CA 94127 **Assoc Prof of Mnstry Dvlpmt CDSP Berkeley CA 2005-** B London England UK 3/29/1957 d Kenneth Kent & Doris. MA U of Cambridge 1979; MDiv CDSP 1989; PhD Boston Coll 2008. D 12/8/1990 P 12/7/1991 Bp William Edwin Swing. m 9/19/1981 David William Singer c 1. Asst All SS Par Brookline MA 2002-2005; Asst All SS' Ch San Francisco CA 1997-2002; Educ Crdntr Dio California San Francisco CA 1997-2002; Cn Liturg Gr Cathd San Francisco CA 1991-1996. ssinger@cdsp.edu

SINGER-HEDLUND, Sylvia Marly (EpisSanJ) 416 S Regent St, Stockton CA 95204 B Cambridge MA 11/26/1933 d Bauer Edwin Kramer & Eleanor. BA U CA 1955; MA U CA 1960; MDiv CDSP 1983; DMin SFTS 1992. D 7/17/1983 Bp Victor Manuel Rivera. m 5/27/1989 Richard James Hedlund c 2. Int Epis Ch Of S Anne Stockton CA 1995-1996; St Laurences Ch Stockton CA 1984-1989; Epis Dio San Joaquin Modesto CA 1983-1989. OHC.

✠ **SINGH, Rt Rev Prince Grenville** (Roch) 4 Cathedral Oaks, Fairport NY 14450 **Bp Dio Rochester Rochester NY 2008-** B Nergercoil Jamil Nadu IN 4/16/1962 s Yesudian Wise Blessed Singh & Ida Jessy Flora. PhD Candidate Drew U; BD Un Biblic Sem Pune Mr IN 1989; ThM UTS Richmond VA 1994; ThM PrTS 1995. Trans from Church of South India 4/18/2000 Bp John Palmer Croneberger Con 5/31/2008 for Roch. m 10/18/1991 Jegaroja Ponuthai Satayasatachi c 2. R S Alb's Ch Oakland NJ 2000-2008. prince@rochesterepiscopaldiocese.com

SINGH, Simon Peter (Chi) 261 W Army Trail Rd, Bloomingdale IL 60108 **First Asian Ch Bloomingdale IL 2009-** B Allahabad, India 7/4/1950 s Khushal Singh & Indira. G.Th Allahabad Bible Sem 1973; MA Narmada Mahavidayla 1976. Trans from Church of North India 11/20/2009 Bp Jeffrey Dean Lee. m 5/14/1980 Deepa Jonah c 4. simjuly4@aol.com

SINGLETON, Lester Brian (Fla) 18120 Southeast 59 Street, Micanopy FL 32667 **Vic Ch Of The H Comm Hawthorne FL 1998-; Vic Ch Of The Medtr Micanopy FL 1983-** B Miami FL 6/23/1942 s Jack Irby Singleton & Edith Marie. STM Candidate Luth TS at Chicago; BA U Chi 1964; BD SWTS 1967. D 6/17/1967 Bp James Winchester Montgomery P 12/16/1967 Bp Gerald Francis Burrill. m 6/25/1983 Addie L Singleton. S Matthews Ch Mayo FL 1989-1990; Vic S Barn Epis Ch Williston FL 1988-1996; Pryr and Praise Com Dio Milwaukee Milwaukee WI 1975-1979; R S Steph's Ch Racine WI 1970-1979; Cur Emm Epis Ch La Grange IL 1967-1970. Auth, "Bk Revs," *Living Ch*. Cmnty of S Mary, SBL 1966. lsinglet@atlantic.net

SINGLETON, Richard Oliver (Mich) 1520 W River Rd, Scottsville VA 24590 **Vic S Jn's Columbia Columbia VA 2008-** B Pontiac MI 3/14/1939 s William Wesley Singleton & Lydia DeNise. BA MI SU 1961; MA MI SU 1962; MDiv EDS 1965. D 6/29/1965 P 4/1/1966 Bp Richard S M Emrich. m 6/18/1960 Sharron Loretta Daley c 2. Dn Cathd Of S Jn Providence RI 1986-1998; Dn Dio Rhode Island Providence RI 1986-1998; Ecum Off Dio Rhode Island Providence RI 1986-1998; Ecum Off Dio Michigan Detroit MI 1976-1986; R S Aid's Ch Ann Arbor MI 1968-1986; Asst Min S Andr's Ch Ann Arbor MI 1966-1976; Cur S Mich And All Ang Epis Ch Lincoln Pk MI 1965-1966. Auth, *Last Words of Resurrected Chr*, S Mary's Press, 1998; Auth, *One Person Exhibit-Photographs*; Auth, *The Radiant Call-Folk Hymns*. Coll of Preachers; Ord of S Lk 1995. rosingleton39@gmail.com

SINISI, Gabriel Arcangelo (Az) 17025 W Aberdeen Dr, Surprise AZ 85374 **R Ch Of The Adv Sun City W AZ 2006-** B Englewood NJ 10/10/1947 s Joseph Henry Sinisi & Marie Elizabeth. Cert Seton Hall NYU Fairleigh Dickinson

Univ. 1970; MD U of Guadalajara Guadalajara Jalisco MX 1974; MDiv TS 1997. D 5/31/1997 Bp Jack Marston McKelvey P 12/6/1997 Bp John Shelby Spong. m 3/1/1990 Mary B Rankin c 3. S Chris's By-The-Sea Epis Ch Key Biscayne FL 1999-2005; R Ch Of The H Sprt Verona NJ 1997-1999. Third Ord, Soc of S Fran 1995. Stdt Body Pres The STUSo 1996. marysinisi@msn.com

SINK, Thomas Leslie (NJ) No address on file. B Philadelphia PA 1/5/1944 s Thomas Leslie Sink & Eleanor Mae. MA FD; BA Eliz 1965; STB PDS 1968; PrTS 1969. D 4/20/1968 P 10/1/1968 Bp Alfred L Banyard. m 8/19/1968 Carol Ann. P-in-c S Elis's Ortley Bch Lavallette NJ 1988-1992; P-in-c S Raphael The Archangel Brick NJ 1982-1983; Asst Chr Ch Toms River Toms River NJ 1968-1969.

SINNING, Thomas John (Minn) 1517 Rosewood Cir, Alexandria MN 56308 **D Dio Minnesota Minneapolis MN 1987-; D Emm Epis Ch Alexandria MN 1987-** B Canton SD 12/3/1949 s Thomas Edward Sinning & Leona Josephine. U of So Dakota. D 10/25/1987 Bp Robert Marshall Anderson. m 8/14/1971 Mary Ann Protivinsky c 3.

SINNOTT, Lynn D (Roch) 2842 Hawks Rd, Wellsville NY 14895 **P-in-c Chr Ch Xenia OH 2011-** B Philadelphia PA 1/13/1947 d C William Doll & Stella E. BD Elizabethtown Coll 1997; MDiv GTS 2000; DMin Drew U 2008. D 6/9/2000 P 1/10/2001 Bp Michael Whittington Creighton. m 12/19/1970 Peter S Sinnott c 3. Int Ch Of The Ascen Bradford PA 2008-2009; Zion Epis Ch Palmyra NY 2002-2008; Chr Soc Mnstry Harrisburg PA 2001. revlynn@rhtns.com

SINTIM, Hector (NC) 2607 Pebble Meadow Ln, Raleigh NC 27601 B Ghana 2/4/1962 s George Sintim & Olivia. LTh St. Nich Bon 1989; MDiv Shaw DS 2001; PhD Trin Sem 2005. Trans from Church of the Province of West Africa 10/4/2005 Bp Michael Bruce Curry. m 5/1/1989 Nana Biney c 3. S Steph's Epis Ch Winston Salem NC 2009; Asst R S Ambroses Ch Raleigh NC 2006-2008. revsintim@hotmail.com

SIPE, Robert B (Ore) 59048 Whitetail Ave., Saint Helens OR 97051 **Vic Chr Ch S Helens OR 2001-** B Weiser ID 6/25/1948 s Billie Sipe & Margaret Louise. BS U of Idaho Moscow 1976; MDiv CDSP 2001. D 5/20/2001 P 12/14/2001 Bp Harry Brown Bainbridge III. m 6/8/1968 Martha Winifred Rice c 2. christch@christchurch-sth.org

SIPES, David Sheldon (O) 446 Shepard Rd, Mansfield OH 44907 B Shelby OH 11/1/1935 s Irvin Ross Sipes & Eleanor Lucille. BA Bowling Green St U 1958; BD Bex 1961. D 6/1/1960 P 12/10/1961 Bp Nelson Marigold Burroughs. m 9/27/1960 Margaret Lillian Close c 4. Gr Epis Ch Mansfield OH 1961-1998. ohbeach1@aol.com

SIPPLE, Peter Warren (Pa) 45 Bay View Avenue, Cornwall on Hudson NY 12520 B Cleveland OH 4/10/1939 s Elmer Peter Sipple & Alice. BA Ya 1962; MA Harv 1964; PhD U CA 1968; MA Grad Theol Un 1969. D 6/9/1973 P 6/1/1974 Bp John Melville Burgess. m 7/18/1964 Margaret Elsemore c 2. R Ch Of The Redeem Bryn Mawr PA 2005-2009; S Paul's Ch Philadelphia PA 2004; Epis Cmnty Serv Philadelphia PA 2001-2002; Int R Ch Of The Redeem Bryn Mawr PA 2000-2001; Ya Berk New Haven CT 1999-2000; Oregon Epis Sch Portland OR 1975-1982. Auth, "Separatism, Assimilation & Interaction: Case of Urban Schools," *NAES Journ*; Auth, "Another Look at Stdt Freedom," *NAES Journ*. Pres, NAES 1981-1984. DD CDSP 2006. sipplemp@gmail.com

SIROTA, Victoria R (NY) Cathedral Church of St John the Divine, 1047 Amsterdam Ave, New York NY 10025 **Chair, Com for a Solitary Dio New York New York City NY 2010-; Cn Pstr and Vic Cathd Of St Jn The Div New York NY 2007-** B Oceanside NY 7/5/1949 d Henry Francis Ressmeyer & Ruth Marie. BMus Ob 1971; MMus Bos 1975; DMA Bos 1981; MDiv Harvard DS 1992. D 6/5/1993 P 9/17/1994 Bp David Elliot Johnson. m 12/21/1969 Robert Sirota c 2. Mssn Strtgy Com Dio Maryland Baltimore MD 2001-2005; Chair, Liturg and Mus Com Dio Maryland Baltimore MD 1998-2002; Dioc Coun Dio Maryland Baltimore MD 1997-2000; Vic Ch Of The H Nativ Baltimore MD 1995-2005; Asst. Prof of Ch Mus Ya Berk New Haven CT 1992-1995. Auth, "Preaching to the Choir: Claiming the Role of Sacr Mus," Ch Pub, 2006; Auth, "Four Sermons," *The Journ of the AAM*, AAM, 2005; Auth, "From the Chapl (Columns)," *The Amer Org*, AGO, 2000; Auth, "An Exploration of Mus as Theol," *Sacr Imagination: The Arts and Theol Educ*, Theol Educ, 1994. Ord of Urban Missioners 2000; Soc of S Marg 1996. Ecum Serv Awd Cntrl MD Ecum Coun 2002; Excellence in Arts Newington-Cropsey Fndt 2002; Outstanding Ord Mnstry Bp's Awd, Dio MD 2001; Excellence in Tchg Ecum Inst of Theol 1999. vgrsirota@aol.com

SISK JR, Edwin Kerr (Ark) 9649 Reeder Pl, Overland Park KS 66214 B Detroit MI 1/7/1930 s Edwin Kerr Sisk & Grace Pearl. BA MI SU 1955; MDiv Bex 1969. D 6/28/1969 Bp Richard S M Emrich P 1/3/1970 Bp Archie H Crowley. m 3/26/1955 Barbara Baker c 3. Int S Thos Ch Springdale AR 2002-2004; Int S Jn's Epis Ch Alma MI 2000-2001; Div Of Evang And Ch Growth Dio Arkansas Little Rock AR 1988-1990; S Theo's Epis Ch Bella Vista AR 1986-1996; St Lk's So Chap Overland Pk KS 1981-1982; Dio W Missouri Kansas City MO 1980-1986; Vic S Mich's Epis Ch Independence MO 1980-1986; R Chr Ch Lima OH 1976-1980; Stndg Com Dio So Dakota Sioux Falls SD 1973-1974; Cn Calv Cathd Sioux Falls SD 1970-1976; Asst Min All SS Epis Ch Pontiac MI 1969-1970. sisko2@everestkc.net

✠ **SISK, Rt Rev Mark Sean** (NY) 1047 Amsterdam Ave, New York NY 10025 **Bp Dio New York New York City NY 1998-** B Takoma Park MD 8/18/1942 s Robert James Sisk & Alma Irene. BS U of Maryland 1964; STB GTS 1967; DCL SWTS 1998. D 6/24/1967 Bp William Foreman Creighton P 12/24/1967 Bp Alfred L Banyard Con 4/25/1998 for NY. m 8/31/1963 Karen Womack c 3. Dn SWTS Evanston IL 1984-1998; Archd Dio New York New York City NY 1977-1984; Diocn Msnry & Ch Extntn Socty New York NY 1977-1984; Dpt Of Missions Ny Income New York NY 1977-1984; R S Jn's Epis Ch Kingston NY 1973-1977; Asst Chr Ch Bronxville NY 1969-1973; Cur Chr Ch New Brunswick NJ 1967-1969. Soc of S Fran 1967. DL Seabury- Wstrn TS 1998; DD The GTS 1985; Hon Cn Cathd S Jn Div NYC 1977. marksisk@att.net

SISK, Robert Buchanan (Mont) Rr 1 Box 241, Wilsall MT 59086 B Waterloo IA 9/6/1943 s Clyde G Sisk & Matilda Clara. BA U of Iowa 1965; BD CDSP 1969. D 6/28/1969 P 1/29/1970 Bp Gordon V Smith. m 2/6/1981 Carol K Sisk c 1. Dio Iowa Des Moines IA 1972; Cur S Andr's Ch Des Moines IA 1969-1971.

SISSON, Duane (Cal) 2973 California St, Oakland CA 94602 **Asst S Alb's Ch Albany CA 2011-** B Waterloo IA 10/14/1938 s Ralph Fletcher Sisson & Cheryl Isabel. BA Sioux Falls Coll 1960; MDiv Amer Bapt Sem of The W 1965; Cert California St U 1986; CDSP 1987. D 6/3/1989 P 6/5/1990 Bp William Edwin Swing. m 11/19/2009 Burt Kessler c 2. R S Giles Ch Moraga CA 2001-2010; The Epis Ch Of S Jn The Evang San Francisco CA 2000-2001; Int Ch Of The H Fam Half Moon Bay CA 1999-2000; Int S Fran' Epis Ch San Francisco CA 1999; S Anselm's Epis Ch Lafayette CA 1997-1998; Chr Ch Alameda CA 1995-1997; P-in-c S Jn's Epis Ch Oakland CA 1990. duanesisson@gmail.com

SISSON, Penny Ray (Miss) 414 Turnberry Cir, Oxford MS 38655 **D S Ptr's Ch Oxford MS 2001-** B Alexandria LA 11/26/1942 d Henry Ray & Fern. BA U of Mississippi 1964; MA U of Mississippi 1980. D 1/6/2001 Bp Alfred Clark Marble Jr. m 12/27/1964 Edward Brewer Sisson. psisson@olemiss.edu

SISSON, Rick L (Ia) 820 N Adams St, Carroll IA 51401 B Munising MI 11/15/1946 s Jack R Sisson & Mary Lois. Trans 1/7/1983 Bp Paul Moore Jr. m 2/2/1991 Anita Rene Batta. D Trin Ch Carroll IA 1997-2000. NAAD.

SITES, William Kilmer (CNY) 5801 Saint Peters Rd, Emmaus PA 18049 B Dayton VA 7/24/1920 s Isaac Dice Sites & Carrie Bell. BS W Virginia U 1942; BD UTS 1949. D 6/7/1954 Bp William A Lawrence P 12/15/1954 Bp John S Higgins. m 10/18/1952 Elizabeth Riley c 3. S Andr's Ch Vestal NY 1956-1986; Vic S Jn The Div Ch Saunderstown RI 1954-1956. Auth, "Ethics In Perspective & Pract"; Auth, "Sex In Perspective". wksepr1524@enter.net

SITTON, Gary William (Colo) 7695 Quitman St, Westminster CO 80030 **P-in-c S Andr's Epis Ch Ft Lupton CO 1995-** B Los Angeles CA 8/26/1938 s Boyd Tyzzer Sitton & Wilhelmina Amelia. AA Pierce Jr Coll 1958; BA California St U at Los Angeles 1961; MDiv CDSP 1964. D 9/10/1964 P 3/1/1965 Bp Francis E I Bloy. m 11/12/1977 Karen Elizabeth Foster c 4. Assoc S Thos Epis Ch Denver CO 1992; Dio Colorado Denver CO 1987-1992; Vic S Martha's Epis Ch Westminster CO 1983-1987; P Intsn Epis Ch Thornton CO 1981-1982; R S Mk's-In-The-Vlly Epis Los Olivos CA 1966-1976; Cur Gr Epis Ch Glendora CA 1965-1966; Cur S Jude's Epis Par Burbank CA 1964-1965. grsttn7@gmail.com

SITTS, Joseph (CFla) 271 New Waterford Pl, Longwood FL 32779 B Ilion NY 11/5/1942 s Clifton A Sitts & Alice C. BA Syr 1964; STM Ya Berk 1968. D 6/1/1968 P 12/7/1968 Bp Charles Bowen Persell Jr. m 9/7/1968 Margaret L Jones c 3. Dio Cntrl Florida Orlando FL 1999-2008; Sheriff Chapl Dio Cntrl Florida Orlando FL 1994-2009; R Epis Ch Of The Resurr Longwood FL 1992-2008; Com Dio Cntrl Florida Orlando FL 1986-1989; Dir Dio Cntrl Florida Orlando FL 1984-1992; Dio Cntrl Florida Orlando FL 1982-1992; Police Chapl Dio Ohio Cleveland OH 1982-1992; Chair Dio Cntrl Florida Orlando FL 1980-1983; Chair Dio Cntrl Florida Orlando FL 1980-1983; Chr Epis Ch Warren OH 1977-1993; R S Steph's Ch Schenectady NY 1970-1977; P Ch Of The H Sprt Schenevus NY 1968-1970; Cur S Jas Ch Oneonta NY 1968-1970. Auth, "Var Article". cjsitts@gmail.com

SIVLEY, John Stephen (CPa) 869E Rhue Haus Ln, Hummelstown PA 17036 **Asstg P Cathd Ch Of S Steph Harrisburg PA 2011-; Partnr In Mssn Commision Dio Cntrl Pennsylvania Harrisburg PA 2006-** B Memphis TN 11/30/1953 s John Harrison Sivley & Martha Jane. BA Jas Madison U 1974; MDiv STUSo 1981; MSW Norfolk St U Norfolk VA 1990. D 6/27/1981 P 4/24/1982 Bp David Keller Leighton Sr. c 1. Stannding Com Dio Cntrl Pennsylvania Harrisburg PA 2008-2011; Sprtlty Cmsn Dio Cntrl Pennsylvania Harrisburg PA 2003-2007; P Assoc All SS' Epis Ch Hershey PA 1999-2010; P Assoc Chr and S Lk's Epis Ch Norfolk VA 1990-1995; Asst R Ch Of The Gd Shpd Norfolk VA 1982-1987; Cur S Anne's Par Annapolis MD 1981-1982. Auth, *Confirmed to Serve*. jsivley869@comcast.net

SIVRET, David Otis (Me) 46 Oak Lane, Alexander ME 04694 B Augusta ME 5/20/1955 s Robert Joseph Sivret & Hope Lillian. BA Bangor TS 1988; MDiv Bangor TS 1998; BD SUNY 1998. D 6/4/1988 P 12/17/1988 Bp Edward Cole

Chalfant. m 9/28/1982 Sherry Brooks c 5. Off Of Bsh For ArmdF New York NY 2005; Pension Fund Mltry New York NY 2004-2005; Chr Epis Ch Eastport ME 2003-2004; R S Anne's Ch Calais ME 2003-2004; Dio Maine Portland ME 2000-2010; Asst R S Matt's Epis Ch Hallowell ME 1998-2003; R Chr Ch Coxsackie NY 1995-1998; S Judes Epis Ch Franklin NH 1989-1995; R Trin Epis Ch Tilton NH 1989-1995; Asst S Matt's Epis Ch Hallowell ME 1988-1989. SocMary 1989. chsivret@yahoo.com

SIWEK, Peter Christopher (Chi) 733 Hayes Ave, Oak Park IL 60302 **Ch Of The Adv Chicago IL 2009-** B Jersey City NJ 3/10/1972 s Christopher Siwek & Barbara. MDiv SWTS; BA U of Notre Dame. D 6/15/2002 P 12/21/2002 Bp William Dailey Persell. m 1/1/2000 Juan A Perez c 2. Vic Cathd Of S Jas Chicago IL 2002-2008. psiwek@saintjamescathedral.org

SIX, George (Los) PO Box 235, Horse Shoe NC 28742 B Lyons KS 11/22/1934 s Henderson Elmer Six & Helen Roberta. BS U of Kansas 1964; MDiv Bex 1967; Cert Cbury Ecum Sch 1983; Cert Amer Mgmt Assn. NY 1986. D 7/1/1967 P 12/1/1967 Bp Gordon V Smith. m 6/10/1955 Irene Ethel Coonfer c 3. Int and Supply Duties Dio Wstrn No Carolina Asheville NC 1999-2009; Vic Chr The King A Jubilee Mnstry Palmdale CA 1995-1999; Int Ch Of The Epiph Oak Pk CA 1994; Mssnr Dio Los Angeles Los Angeles CA 1993-1994; R The Par Of S Matt Pacific Palisades CA 1991-1992; Trst Bex Columbus OH 1986-1997; R and Hd Mstr S Phil's Ch Coral Gables FL 1984-1991; Archd Dio Arizona Phoenix AZ 1980-1983; Mem, Dioc Coun Dio Arizona Phoenix AZ 1980-1983; R S Paul's Ch Yuma AZ 1977-1980; Dep, GC Dio Iowa Des Moines IA 1976; Mem, Dioc Coun Dio Iowa Des Moines IA 1973-1976; Dep, GC Dio Iowa Des Moines IA 1973; R Trin Ch Muscatine IA 1969-1977; P-in-c S Alb's Ch Sprt Lake IA 1967-1969. sixgeorge@bellsouth.net

SIZE, Patricia Barrett (Mil) 2215 Commonwealth Ave, Madison WI 53726 B Camden New Jersey 4/26/1945 d John Anthony Barrett & Mary Crowell. BS U of Pennsylvania 1970; MS U of Wisconsin 1978; MDiv SWTS 2000. D 5/20/2000 P 12/2/2000 Bp Roger John White. m 12/30/1972 Timothy Size c 4. Gr Ch Madison WI 2004-2010; Assoc R S Andr's Ch Madison WI 2000-2003. patsize@charter.net

SKAGGS, Richard Lee (WVa) 1410 Chapline St, Wheeling WV 26003 **Chair of Cmsn on Sprtlty Dio W Virginia Charleston WV 2008-; Asst S Matt's Ch Wheeling WV 2007-** B Wheeling WV 8/19/1947 s William Earl Skaggs & Dorothy Lee. BA W Liberty St Coll 1970; MAAT Wheeling Jesuit U 1990. D 6/11/1991 Bp John H(enry) Smith P 9/14/2004 Bp William Michie Klusmeyer. Dn Of Study Prog Dio W Virginia Charleston WV 1991-1993. rskaggs@stmatts.com

SKALA, Kira B (Va) 241 Signal Ridge Ln, Winchester VA 22603 B Middletown NY 10/12/1963 d Robert Carl Skala & Elizabeth Jeanne. BS Shenandoah U 1985; MDiv VTS 2001. D 6/23/2001 P 12/28/2001 Bp Peter James Lee. m 7/29/2006 Timothy Skinner c 1. R Emm Epis Ch (Piedmont Par) Delaplane VA 2003-2009; Asst R Emm Ch Middleburg VA 2001-2003. kira@emmanuel-delaplane.org

SKALESKI, Elizabeth Harris (Ct) 102 Ward St, Norwalk CT 06851 **S Jn's Ch Stamford CT 2009-** B Norwalk CT 6/24/1956 d Arthur B Harris & Norine Pickett. BM Wstrn Connecticut St U 1985. D 9/12/2009 Bp Andrew Donnan Smith. m 9/21/1985 Robert A Skaleski c 3. deaconliz624@gmail.com

SKAU, Laurie Jean (Minn) 6727 France Ave N, Brooklyn Center MN 55429 B Duluth MN 7/10/1953 d Vernon Leland Skau & Ethel Lera. S Lk Sch 1977; BA S Scholastica 1980; MDiv Bex 1985. D 6/24/1985 P 7/1/1986 Bp Robert Marshall Anderson. Presb Hm Of Minnesota Arden Hills MN 1992-1995; Coordntr Of The Aids Mnstry Dio Minnesota Minneapolis MN 1990-1991; R H Trin Intl Falls MN 1986-1989. ACPE. lauriejskau@msn.com

SKELLEN, Bonnie Jean (NwPa) 425 E Main St, Ridgway PA 15853 **D Gr Epis Ch Ridgway PA 1996-** B Rochester NY 11/5/1946 d Robert Charles Larnder & Shirley Marguerite. D 1/27/1996 Bp Robert Deane Rowley Jr. c 2. Gr Epis Ch Ridgway PA 2006-2007. bskellen@windstream.net

SKELLY, Herbert Cope (Mass) 40 Woodland Way, Eastham MA 02642 B Dover NH 11/20/1935 s Alexander Skelly & Mary Cope. BA U of New Hampshire 1957; MDiv EDS 1961. D 6/15/1961 P 12/16/1961 Bp Charles F Hall. m 8/26/1961 Margaret Conant Sheldon c 3. The Ch Of The H Sprt Orleans MA 1987-1993; Int Ch Of The Gd Shpd Clinton MA 1986-1988; Asst S Jn's Ch Worcester MA 1984-1986; Supply P Dio Wstrn Massachusetts Springfield MA 1971-1984; Vic Trin Ch N Scituate RI 1964-1970; Cur Ch Of The Gd Shpd Nashua NH 1961-1963. Auth, "An Adv Event," Morehouse-Barlow. amskel@comcast.net

SKELTON, Melissa Maxine (Oly) P.O. Box 9070, Seattle WA 98109 **Cn Dio Olympia Seattle WA 2008-; R S Paul's Ch Seattle WA 2005-** B Columbus GA 3/14/1951 d Lawrence Rye Skelton & Dorothy Evelyn. BA U GA 1973; MA U of So Carolina 1977; MBA U Chi 1989; MDiv VTS 1990. D 7/25/1992 P 5/1/1993 Bp Herbert Thompson Jr. c 1. R Trin Ch Castine ME 2002-2005; Assoc S Andr's Ch Trenton NJ 1996-1997; Vice-Pres for Admin The GTS New York NY 1994-1997; Assoc Par of Trin Ch New York NY 1994-1996; Cur All SS Ch Cincinnati OH 1992-1993. melissaskelton@comcast.net

SKIDMORE, Joanne Louise (Mil) 24845 Runyard Way E, Trevor WI 53179 **Chair, Cmsn on Missions and Develoment Dio Milwaukee Milwaukee WI 2009-; P-in-c S Jn The Div Epis Ch Burlington WI 2001-** B Schenectady NY 9/6/1950 d Burton Miller Hardie & Marjorie Louise. Montana St U; San Jose St U; SWTS; BA WA SU 1973; MA Chapman U 1976; MDiv SWTS 1998. D 6/27/1998 Bp Charles Jones III P 1/17/1999 Bp Frank Tracy Griswold III. m 7/8/1972 david Paul Skidmore. Asst P St Mths Epis Ch Waukesha WI 1998-2000. joanneskidmore@prodigy.net

SKILLICORN, Gerald Amos (WMo) 2207 Conrad Way, Somerset NJ 08873 B Watsonville CA 1/11/1930 s Walter Amos Skillicorn & Thelma Gertrude. STB GTS 1956. D 7/1/1956 P 1/12/1957 Bp Karl M Block. m 5/16/1969 Melisande Magers. S Paul's Epis Ch Lees Summit MO 1990-1995; R Ch Of The Epiph Kirkwood S Louis MO 1987-1989; R S Paul's Epis Ch S Jos MI 1981-1987; Asst S Hilary's Ch Prospect Hts IL 1976-1980; Asst All SS Epis Ch San Leandro CA 1962-1965; R S Fran' Epis Ch Turlock CA 1958-1962; Cur The Epis Ch Of S Mary The Vrgn San Francisco CA 1956-1958. meskillicorn@yahoo.com

SKILLINGS, Thomas (Cal) 1104 Mills Ave, Burlingame CA 94010 **R S Paul's Epis Ch Burlingame CA 2002-** B Greenbrae CA 7/18/1959 s Thomas James Skillings & Helen Jeneatte. Diablo Vlly Coll 1983; BA California St U 1986; MDiv Ya Berk 1989. D 6/3/1989 P 6/9/1990 Bp William Edwin Swing. m 1/1/2001 Julie Ann Graham c 1. S Mich And All Ang Concord CA 1993-2002; Assoc R S Paul's Epis Ch Walnut Creek CA 1989-1993. revtskillings@gmail.com

✠ **SKILTON, Rt Rev William Jones** (DR) 4969 Parkside Dr, North Charleston SC 29405 B Havana CU 8/16/1940 s William Edward Skilton & Blandina Springs. BS Cit 1962; LTh STUSo 1965; U So 1999. D 7/10/1965 Bp Gray Temple P 1/26/1966 Bp Paul Axtell Kellogg Con 3/2/1996 for SC. m 8/26/1963 Lynda Skilton c 2. Bp Suffr Dio So Carolina Charleston SC 1996-2006; Bp Coun Dio So Carolina Charleston SC 1991-1994; Mem, Dioc Coun Dio So Carolina Charleston SC 1991-1994; R S Thos Epis Ch No Charleston SC 1988-1996; Mem, Stndg Com Dio So Carolina Charleston SC 1988-1991; Stndg Com Dio So Carolina Charleston SC 1988-1991; Mem, Exec Coun Dio The Dominican Republic (Iglesia Epis Dominicana) Santo Domingo DO 1985-1988; Bp Coun Dio So Carolina Charleston SC 1982-1985; Bp Coun Dio So Carolina Charleston SC 1978-1980; R H Trin Epis Ch Charleston SC 1976-1985; Bp Coun Dio So Carolina Charleston SC 1973-1976; Campus Min Dio So Carolina Charleston SC 1972-1976; P-in-c The Ch Of The Cross Bluffton SC 1972-1973; Mem, Exec Coun Dio The Dominican Republic (Iglesia Epis Dominicana) Santo Domingo DO 1965-1972. DD Cit, the Mltry Coll of SC 2006; Doctor in Div U So, Sewanee, Tenn. 2001. skiltonw@bellsouth.net

SKINNER, Beatrice (SD) PO Box 534, Mclaughlin SD 57642 B Bullhead SD 9/12/1936 d Michael Hollow & Olivia. D 6/22/2007 Bp Creighton Leland Robertson.

SKINNER, Jean Mary (CNY) 40 Faxton St, Utica NY 13501 B 3/6/1945 d Ralph J Skinner & Virginia R. BS SUNY 1977. D 11/19/2005 Bp Gladstone Bailey Adams III. buttons79@msn.com

SKINNER, John Emory (Kan) 10 Crestwood Dr, Arkansas City KS 67005 **Died 8/22/2009** B Arkansas City KS 9/21/1925 s John William Skinner & Viola Edna. Iliff TS 1949; BA U Denv 1949; MA U Denv 1950; PDS 1952; STB Tem 1954; STD Tem 1956. D 5/7/1951 Bp Goodrich R Fenner P 3/29/1952 Bp William P Roberts. Auth, *The Chr Disciple*, 1984; Auth, *Meaning of Authority*, 1983; Auth, *Self and Wrld*, 1962. Amer Theol Soc 1963; Metaphysical Soc of Amer 1963. jskinner6@cox.net

SKINNER, Susan (Mo) 400 Mark Dr, Saint Louis MO 63122 B Lexington KY 3/30/1941 AB Transylvania U 1962; Med U of Missouri 1976; MDiv Eden TS 1979. D 6/7/1980 Bp Morris Fairchild Arnold P 6/11/1981 Bp John Bowen Coburn. c 1. Int S Mart's Ch Ellisville MO 2007-2010; S Matt's Epis Ch Warson Warson Woods MO 2005-2006; Chr Ch Cathd S Louis MO 2004-2005; Epis City Mssn St Louis MO 2002-2006; S Jn's Ch W Point VA 2001-2002; Emm Epis Ch Webster Groves MO 1981-2001.

SKIPPER, James Louis Dean (Ala) 1426 Gilmer Ave, Montgomery AL 36104 B Dothan AL 11/5/1950 s Louie Otis Skipper & Geraldine. BA U of Alabama 1973; MA Hollins U 1974; MFA U of Iowa 1976; MDiv Epis TS of The SW 1998. D 5/26/1998 Bp Henry Nutt Parsley Jr P 12/2/1998 Bp Robert Oran Miller. m 6/1/2001 Susan Williams c 2. St. Matt's Epis Ch Madison AL 2010-2011; S Paul's (Carlowville) Minter AL 2006-2010; Dio Alabama Birmingham AL 2004-2010; S Steph's Epis Ch Birmingham AL 2000-2004; Ch Of The Epiph Guntersville AL 1998-2000. "The Wk Ethic of the Common Fly," Settlement Hse Press, 2007; "The Fourth Watch of the Night," Swan Scythe Press, 2001; Auth, "Deaths That Travel w the Weather," Orchesis Press, 1992; Auth, "Sm Song of the New Moon," Bellwether Press, 1977. fatherskipper@gmail.com

SKIRVEN JR, James French (WA) 403 Tarpon Ave Apt 102, Fernandina Beach FL 32034 B Miami FL 7/11/1935 s James French Skirven & Lillian. BA U Of Florida 1957; MDiv STUSo 1968. D 6/26/1968 P 6/24/1969 Bp Edward

S

Hamilton West. m 8/14/1965 Martha Virginia Kinsey. Asst S Jas Ch Potomac MD 1973-1974; P-in-c S Andr's Ch Interlachen FL 1970-1973; P-in-c S Paul's Fed Point Hastings FL 1970-1973; Asst All SS Epis Ch Jacksonville FL 1968-1969. jimmar@netmagic.net

SKIRVING, Robert Stuart (EMich) St. John's Episcopal Church, 405 N. Saginaw Road, Midland MI 48640 **Dn Dio Estrn Michigan Saginaw MI 2011-; R S Jn's Epis Ch Midland MI 2004-** B Windsor Ontario Canada 8/28/1960 s Archibald Howard Skirving & Anne Margaret. Advncd Cert SWTS; B.A. U of Waterloo 1982; M.Div. Hur, Can 1986. Trans from Anglican Church of Canada 1/1/2005 Bp Edwin Max Leidel Jr. m 10/4/1986 Sandra J Brenneman c 2. rskirving@sjec-midland.org

SKRAMSTAD, Dawn Marie (Alb) St. Mary's Church, P.O. Box 211, Lake Luzerne NY 12846 B Corinth NY 9/1/1956 D 6/11/2005 Bp Daniel William Herzog. m 10/8/2004 Lawrence Skramstad c 2. dmwptl@yahoo.com

SKUTCH, Patrick John (Miss) 333 Demontluzin St, Mississippi MS 39520 **Chr Ch Bay St Louis MS 2009-** B Savannah GA 11/19/1979 s Janison Skutch & Marie. BA U GA 2002; MDiv GTS 2005. D 12/21/2004 P 7/31/2005 Bp J(ohn) Neil Alexander. m 6/8/2002 Bonny Elizabeth Skutch c 2. S Mart In The Fields Ch Atlanta GA 2005-2009. frskutch@yahoo.com

SKYLES, Benjamin Henry (Tex) 2110 Canyon Lake Dr, Deer Park TX 77536 B Des Moines IA 1/21/1934 s Jack Lane Skyles & Bernice. BA U of Texas 1955; BD Epis TS of The SW 1958; MA U of Houston 1974. D 6/1/1958 Bp Frederick P Goddard P 6/10/1959 Bp James Parker Clements. m 8/5/2006 Mary Jamison c 5. Stndg Com Dio Texas Houston TX 1983-1986; ExCoun Dio Texas Houston TX 1969-1972; S Ptr's Ch Pasadena TX 1964-1999; Assoc S Mk's Ch Beaumont TX 1961-1964; Min in charge S Thos' Epis Ch Rockdale TX 1958-1961. Auth, *Alive Now*; Auth, "arts," *Epis*; Auth, *From the Belly of the Great Fish*; Auth, *Tell Us of the Morning*. Distinguished Alum Awd Epis Sem of the SW 2006; DD Epis TS of the SW Austin TX 1983; Rel Serv Awd Natl Conf Ch & Jews Houston TX. bskyles1@comcast.net

SLACK, James Cooper Simmons (Dal) 1019 Sassafras Lane, Niles MO 49120 **R Trin NE Texas Epis Ch Mt Pleasant TX 1998-** B St Louis MO 2/23/1937 s Morris Cooper Slack & Dorthy Eleanor. BA Earlham Coll 1959; LTh SWTS 1964. D 6/27/1964 Bp Hamilton Hyde Kellogg P 4/9/1965 Bp Philip Frederick McNairy. m 8/31/1963 Karen M Fricke c 3. R S Chas The Mtyr DAINGERFIELD TX 1998; R S Dav's Ch Gilmer TX 1998; Trin NE Texas Epis Ch Mt Pleasant TX 1997-2007; S Phil's Ch Circleville OH 1977-1994; Bi Par Mnstry Addyston OH 1972-1976; Vic S Jn Hutchinson MN 1966-1972; Vic S Columba White Earth MN 1964-1966. jkslack37@comcast.net

SLADE, Debra Katherine Ann (Ct) 503 Old Long Ridge Rd, Stamford CT 06903 **S Fran Ch Stamford CT 2008-** B 3/29/1957 d Donald Worrell Slade & Evelyn Patricia. BA U of Manitoba 1978; MA U of Manitoba 1981; BA Oxf 1983; MA Oxf 1998; MDiv Ya Berk 2008. D 6/13/2009 Bp Andrew Donnan Smith P 1/2/2010 Bp James Elliot Curry. m 3/14/1986 Peter Kent c 2. debra.slade@gmail.com

SLADE, Tyler J (Alb) 68 S Swan St, Albany NY 12210 **Yth Dir Dio Albany Albany NY 2010-** B Red Bank, NJ 10/14/1980 s David Raymond Slade & Marilyn V. BA Dartmouth 2003; ODM Wycliffe Hall - Oxford 2009. D 12/12/2010 P 12/4/2010 Bp William Howard Love. m 9/5/2010 Audrey H Headland. tslade@infocus.org

SLAGLE, William C (ECR) 13543 Debbie Ln, Saratoga CA 95070 **Assoc S Andr's Ch Saratoga CA 1969-** B Austin TX 2/8/1928 s William Mackey Slagle & Frankie Mae. BS Texas Tech U 1951; MS Texas Tech U 1952; Case Wstrn Reserve U 1965; MDiv CDSP 1973; MBA Santa Clara U 1978. D 3/23/1969 P 6/17/1973 Bp George Richard Millard. m 7/24/1950 Virginia Sue Smith c 2. w.slagle@worldnet.att.net

SLAKEY, Anne-Elisa Margaret (Ida) 110 N. 10th St., Payette ID 83661 **D St Marys Ch Elk Grove Sacramento CA 2002-** B Annapolis MD 3/1/1964 d Thomas John Slakey & Marion Isabel. BA S Jn's Coll Santa Fe NM 1988; MA Iowa St U 1993; MDiv CDSP 2002. D 11/16/2002 Bp Roger John White P 9/29/2003 Bp Gethin Benwil Hughes. S Jas Ch Payette ID 2008-2010; S Thos Ch Canyon City OR 2006; S Matt's Epis Ch Ontario OR 2005-2008. madreanne@live.com

SLANGER, George C (ND) 8435 207th St. W., Lakeville MN 55044 B Big Timber MT 10/16/1937 s Benjamin Slanger & Josephine C. BS Montana St U 1959; MA San Francisco St Coll 1965; PhD U of Washington 1976. D 10/8/2000 P 5/21/2001 Bp Andrew Hedtler Fairfield. m 11/28/1980 Joanne Mary Kalcevic c 4. farfox@me.com

SLATER, Joan (NMich) PO Box100, Mackinac Island MI 49757 B 2/17/1955 D 2/7/2001 P 8/12/2001 Bp James Arthur Kelsey.

SLATER, JoAnn Kennedy (Mich) 301 Scio Village Ct Unit 153, Ann Arbor MI 48103 **Trst Dio Michigan Detroit MI 2010-; R S Lk's Epis Ch Ypsilanti MI 2006-** B Indianapolis IN 2/13/1953 d John Slater & Mary Jo. BA Pur 1974; MA DePaul U 1975; DMin Chicago TS 1990; JD U MI 2001. D 6/19/1993 P 12/18/1994 Bp R(aymond) Stewart Wood Jr. P-in-c S Lk's Epis Ch Ypsilanti MI 2001-2006; Asst S Andr's Ch Ann Arbor MI 1995-1998; Asst Dio Michigan Detroit MI 1993-1994; Asst Dio Michigan Detroit MI 1992-1993. AAR; ABA; Coll for Theol Soc; SBL. slaterj@umich.edu

SLATER, Michael (Nev) 7900 Pueblo Drive, Stagecoach NV 89429 **Ad Hoc Ecum & Interreligious Off Dio Nevada Las Vegas NV 2009-** B Romford England 4/21/1942 City of London Coll 1970; DIT ETSBH 2003; MDiv Claremont TS 2006. D 7/16/2005 Bp Joseph Jon Bruno. m 4/12/1986 Barbara Slater. D S Paul's Ch Virginia City NV 2009; D S Jn The Div Epis Ch Costa Mesa CA 2005-2007. dekmichael@aol.com

SLATER, Scott Gerald (Md) 4 East University Parkway, Baltimore MD 21218 **Cn to the Ordnry Dio Maryland Baltimore MD 2010-** B Long Beach CA 4/18/1960 s Gerald Martin Slater & Helen Phyllis. BLA U Of Florida 1981; MACE VTS 1992; MDiv VTS 1992; DMin Columbia TS 2000. D 6/20/1992 Bp John Wadsworth Howe P 1/7/1993 Bp James Barrow Brown. m 10/12/1985 Rebecca M Miller c 2. R Ch Of The Gd Shpd Ruxton MD 2001-2010; Assoc S Columba's Ch Washington DC 1996-2001; Assoc S Lk's Epis Ch Birmingham AL 1993-1996; Chapl S Mart's Epis Sch Metairie LA 1992-1993; Yth Min H Trin Epis Ch Melbourne FL 1985-1989; Root Grp Coordntr Dio Cntrl Florida Orlando FL 1983-1985. Contributing Ed, "Epis Curric for Yth," Morehouse, 1996; Auth, "Shopping for the Rt Ch," *Living Ch*, Living Ch, 1995; Auth, "Antique Bible Proves Popular Among Chld...," *Epis Tchr*, VTS, 1993; Contrib, "Epis Chld Curric," Morehouse, 1992. Maryland Epis Cler Assn 2003-2009; Washington Epis Cler Assn 1996-2000. sslater@episcopalmaryland.org

SLAUGHTER, Susan Emmert (FtW) 1612 Boardwalk Ct, Arlington TX 76011 **D S Lk's In The Meadow Epis Ch Ft Worth TX 2002-** B St. Louis MO 8/22/1942 d Max Emmert & Inez. BA Sam Houston St U 1975; MEd U of No Texas 1981; Cert Angl TS 2002. D 10/12/2002 Bp Jack Leo Iker P 11/15/2009 Bp Edwin Funsten Gulick Jr. m 8/11/1978 Jerry Slaughter c 5. sslaughter22@att.net

SLAUSON II, Holley B (NY) 41 Wolfpit Ave Apt 3-N, Norwalk CT 06851 **Par of St Paul's Ch Norwalk Norwalk CT 1998-** B Norwalk CT 9/14/1942 s Holley Irving Slauson & Frances. BA Wstrn Connecticut St U 1971; MDiv GTS 1977. D 3/19/1977 P 5/19/1978 Bp Morgan Porteus. R S Anne's Ch Washingtonville NY 1982-1987; Epis. Comm Of Cntrl Orange Goshen NY 1979-1983; Vic S Dav's Ch Highland Mills NY 1979-1982; Vic S Anne's Ch Washingtonville NY 1977-1982; Cur S Jn's Ch W Hartford CT 1977-1979. rs3_hb@sbcglobal.net

SLAWNWHITE, Virginia Ann (NH) Po Box 433, Portsmouth NH 03802 B Lynn MA 5/11/1941 d Clifford R Billows & Vera May. D 11/1/1997 Bp Douglas Edwin Theuner. m 5/7/1961 Stephen C Slawnwhite. D The Ch Of The Redeem Rochester NH 1998-2000.

SLAWSON III, H Thomas (Miss) 5400 Old Canton Rd, Jackson MS 39211 **R S Phil's Ch Jackson MS 1996-** B Memphis TN 7/7/1955 s Henry Thomas Slawson & Marion Louise. BA U of Tennessee 1978; MDiv SWTS 1985. D 6/30/1985 P 5/11/1986 Bp William Evan Sanders. m 10/25/2010 Linda Smith c 2. S Phil's Ch Jackson MS 1996-2010; S Paul's Epis Ch Meridian MS 1991-1996; Assoc R S Paul's Epis Ch Meridian MS 1991-1995; Vic H Innoc' Epis Ch Como MS 1986-1991; R Ch Of The Epiph Tunica MS 1986-1989; D-In-Trng Gr Ch Chattanooga TN 1985-1986. tomslawson@ymail.com

SLAYMAKER, Lorraine P (Ark) 1112 Alcoa Rd, Benton AR 72015 **Vic S Matt's Epis Ch Benton AR 2003-** B Hartford CT 1/24/1956 d Fred John Pistel & Phyllis Adarie. BS U of Connecticut 1978; BS Montana St U 1990; MDiv Epis TS of The SW 1999. D 5/29/1999 Bp Charles Jones III P 2/2/2000 Bp Larry Earl Maze. m 5/16/1981 William D Slaymaker c 2. Cur S Lk's Ch Hot Sprg AR 1999-2003. lorslaymaker@sbcglobal.net

SLAYTER, Malcolm Franklin (NwT) 2809 Moss Ave, Midland TX 79705 B Boston MA 12/9/1920 s John Theodore Harding Slayter & Helen Margaret. BGE Omaha U 1957; MA Omaha U 1959; MA S Mary's Sem and U Baltimore MD 1973; DMin GTF 1988. D 1/15/1975 Bp Paul Saneaki Nakamura P 12/1/1976 Bp Benito C Cabanban. m 9/3/1962 Fumiko Okada c 4. S Nich' Epis Ch Midland TX 1980-1983; Dio Micronesia Tumon Bay GU GU 1977-1980. Auth, "The Role of an AF Tactical Hosp in Med Air Evacuation," *ArmdF Med Journ*. mslayter@sbcglobal.net

SLEMP, Dennett Clinton (SVa) 11001 Ashburn Rd, Richmond VA 23235 B Washington DC 3/7/1932 s Patton Wise Slemp & Dorothy Dixon. BA Jn Hopkins U 1957; MDiv VTS 1961; Inst of Rel Houston TX 1967; STM Epis TS of The SW 1968. D 6/26/1961 P 6/27/1962 Bp William Henry Marmion. m 6/22/1957 Mary Clarke c 2. Virginia Inst Of Pstr Care Richmond VA 1973-1991; Vic Epis Ch Of Our Sav Midlothian VA 1968-1973. Diplomate AAPC 1970. dcslemp@verizon.net

SLENSKI, Mary Lynn (SO) 2388 Meadow Green Dr, Beavercreek OH 45431 **Asst Chr Epis Ch Dayton OH 2010-; Int S Paul's Epis Ch New Albany IN 2010-** B Detroit MI 9/8/1958 d Joseph Jankowski & Judith Ann. BSE U of Florida 1980; MBA Wright St U 1990; MDiv EDS 2008. D 6/14/2008 P 6/20/2009 Bp Thomas Edward Breidenthal. m 11/8/1980 George Slenski c 2. Asst Chr Epis Ch Dayton OH 2010; Monthly supply P S Paul's Epis Ch Greenville

OH 2009-2010; Asst S Mk's Epis Ch Dayton OH 2008-2010. m_slenski@ameritech.net

SLIGH, John Lewis (SeFla) 2422 W Stroud Ave, Tampa FL 33629 B Washington DC 9/16/1951 s John Hilary Sligh & Norma Elaine. Juilliard Sch 1970; BA U GA 1974; MDiv Nash 1977. D 2/14/1977 Bp (George) Paul Reeves P 10/1/1978 Bp William Carl Frey. Cur S Benedicts Ch Plantation FL 1985-1987; P-in-c S Lk's Epis Ch Ft Collins CO 1980-1983; Cur S Lk's Epis Ch Ft Collins CO 1978-1979; Nash Nashotah WI 1977-1978. lewsligh@aol.com

SLOAN III OJN, Carey Erastus (O) 2390 N Orchard Rd NE, Bolivar OH 44612 B Atlanta GA 3/30/1940 s Carey E Sloan & Mildred. BA Duke 1962; MDiv VTS 1965; DMin IAPS 1984. D 6/29/1965 P 6/29/1966 Bp Thomas Augustus Fraser Jr. m 9/26/1981 Katherine L Danner c 2. R S Mk's Ch Canton OH 1976-2007; R S Paul's Ch Henderson KY 1967-1976; Vic S Lk's Ch Salisbury NC 1966-1967; R S Matt Ch Salisbury NC 1966-1967; D-in-C S Jn's Ch Battleboro NC 1965-1966; D-in-C S Mich's Ch Tarboro NC 1965-1966. Auth, *The Secret of the Rose*, St Marks, 1993; Auth, *The Meaning of a Secular Soc*, St Marks, 1992; Auth, *If We Could Talk to the Animals*, St Marks, 1991; Auth, *How to Improve Your Score*, St Marks, 1989; Auth, *Use of Humor in Par Ch*, 1985. Ord of Julian of Norwich 1988. R Emer St Marks Epis Ch, Canton OH 2008. dutchsloan@aol.com

SLOAN JR, Charles Frederick (Md) 2 Saint Peters Pl, Lonaconing MD 21539 **Died 12/4/2009** B Lonaconing MD 6/1/1945 s Charles Frederick Sloan & Marcella Allen. Doctorate of Ed U of Maryland; BS Frostburg St U 1970; MA Frostburg St U 1972. D 9/7/2008 P 5/9/2009 Bp John Leslie Rabb. c 3.

SLOAN, Ellen Margaret (SwFla) 2304 Periwinkle Way, Sanibel FL 33957 **R Ch Of S Mich And All Ang Sanibel FL 2009-** B New Bedford MA 10/15/1950 d William Gerard Smith & Rosemary. BS Plymouth St U 1972; MA Dart 1977; PhD U of Connecticut 1996; MDiv GTS 2002. D 6/1/2002 Bp Rufus T Brome P 12/7/2002 Bp John Palmer Croneberger. m 12/26/1993 Ralph Edward Sloan. The GTS New York NY 2005-2009; Assoc Chr Ch Ridgewood NJ 2002-2004. Auth, "Strategies for Fostering Partnerships Between Educators and Hlth Professionals," *Boundary Crossings*, Jossey-Bass, 1997; Auth, "Interns as legitimate Participants in the Cmnty of Pract," *Journ of Sch Ldrshp*, Technomic, 1996. Cmsn on Wmn 2000; Soc of St. Blandina 2006. rector@saintmichaels-sanibel.org

✠ **SLOAN, Rt Rev John McKee** (Ala) 521 North 20th Street, Birmingham AL 35203 B Vicksburg MS 11/13/1955 s Richard Crofton Sloan & Mary Bayer. BA Mississippi St U 1976; MDiv STUSo 1981. D 5/16/1981 P 5/29/1982 Bp Duncan Montgomery Gray Jr Con 1/12/2008 for Ala. m 10/3/1987 Tina B Brown c 2. Stndg Com Dio Alabama Birmingham AL 1999-2003; Dioc Coun Dio Alabama Birmingham AL 1995-1998; R St Thos Epis Ch Huntsville AL 1993-2007; Stndg Com Dio Mississippi Jackson MS 1990-1993; Asst S Ptr's Ch Oxford MS 1990-1993; All SS Epis Ch Grenada MS 1987-1990; Exec Com Dio Mississippi Jackson MS 1985-1989; Vic Epis Ch Of The Incarn W Point MS 1983-1986; Cur H Cross Epis Ch Olive Branch MS 1981-1983; Gray Cntr Bd Dio Mississippi Jackson MS 1973-1977. sloans745@charter.net

SLOAN, Richard Drake (NY) 90 Gilbert Road, Ho-Ho-Kus NJ 07423 **Col Dio New York New York City NY 2008-; Stwdshp Off Dio New York New York City NY 1993-; Coordntr, CSP Diocn Msnry & Ch Extntn Socty New York NY 1993-** B South Weymouth MA 11/11/1948 s Walter F Sloan & Ruth Chantler. BA Rutgers-The St U 1970; MDiv PDS 1973; JD Pace U 1979. D 5/11/1974 Bp Frederick Hesley Belden P 11/16/1974 Bp George E Rath. m 9/7/1974 Carolyn M Kennedy c 2. R Gr Epis Ch Monroe NY 1988-1994; R S Elis's Epis Ch Floral Pk NY 1981-1986; St Elizabeths Meml Chap Sloatsburg NY 1981-1986; Asst S Eliz's Ch Ridgewood NJ 1977-1981; Cur S Paul's Ch Pawtucket RI 1974-1976. Gld of S Ives 1997; Soc of the Magi 2000. Bp's Cross Dio New York 2001. rsloan@dioceseny.org

SLOAN, Stan Jude (Chi) 2313 N Kedzie Blvd # 2, Chicago IL 60647 B Guthrie OK 7/25/1963 s Bob Ray Sloan & Mary Jane. BS Oklahoma St U 1985; MDiv U Of S Mary Of The Lake 1991; MA Weston Jesuit TS 1992. Rec from Roman Catholic 6/1/1997 as Priest Bp Frank Tracy Griswold III. Cathd Shltr Chicago IL 1998-2000; Vic S Geo/S Mths Ch Chicago IL 1997-1999; Epis Chars And Cmnty Serv (Eccs) Chicago IL 1997-1998. Chicago Cltn For The Homeless Bd; Ecum Coun; Westhaven Dvlpmt Bd. SSLOAN@CHICAGOHOUSE.ORG

SLOAN, Susan (Ala) 821 Baylor Drive, Huntsville AL 35802 **Stndg Com, Pres Dio Alabama Birmingham AL 2008-; R S Steph's Epis Ch Huntsville AL 2005-** B Mobile AL 7/21/1949 d Milton Sebastian Cabot Pullen & Ernestine Shearer. BS U of Alabama 1989; MDiv STUSo 1996. D 1/13/1996 P 7/20/1996 Bp Robert Oran Miller. m 3/22/1969 Thomas D Sloan c 2. S Mk's Ch Birmingham AL 2004; Int Gd Shpd Decatur AL 2002-2003; Assoc R S Lk's Epis Ch Birmingham AL 1999-2002; Cn The Cathd Ch Of The Adv Birmingham AL 1996-1999. "Epis Chld's Curric," Morehouse. Dioc Coun 2002-2004; Prog Com Kanuga Conf Cntr 2001-2004; SOT Alum Com 2000-2008; Sewanee Alum Coun 2000-2004; Stndg Com 2005; Stndg Com of Dio 1997-2000; Trst, U So 2009. Lowery Serv Awd SOT Sewanee 1996. ssloanpr@knology.net

SLOANE, Andrew (WA) 2430 K St Nw, Washington DC 20037 **R S Paul's Par Washington DC 1998-** B Liverpool England UK 4/27/1953 s Leslie James Sloane & Averill. Ripon Coll Cuddesdon; BA Oxf 1975; MA Oxf 1977; MA Nash 1978. Trans from Church Of England 1/7/1983 Bp Paul Moore Jr. R Gr Epis Ch Sheboygan WI 1989-1998; Ch Of S Mary The Vrgn New York NY 1982-1989; Cur S Geo's Epis Ch Schenectady NY 1978-1981. Cmnty of S Mary, New York; CBS; Coun GAS; SHN; SocMary; SocOLW. DD Nash 2005; Guardian Shrine of Our Lady of Walsingham 2003. sloane@stpauls-kst.com

SLOCOMBE, Iris Ruth (Mich) APDO Postal 673, Ajijic Jalisco 45920 Mexico B Goodmayes UK 10/20/1928 d John Gomes Rocha & Milla. SRN Poole Gnrl Sch of Nrsng Poole GB 1958; SCM Neath U Sch of Nrsng 1960; MA U of Oklahoma 1962; MDiv STUSo 1983. D 5/15/1983 Bp Furman Stough P 5/10/1984 Bp C(laude) Charles Vache. m 3/27/1948 Albert E Slocombe c 3. R Gr Ch Mt Clemens MI 1989-1995; Assoc R S Jn's Epis Ch Memphis TN 1987-1989; Asst R Estrn Shore Chap Virginia Bch VA 1983-1987. Auth, "Adam's Song," *S Lk Journ*, 1983. Altrusa Wmn of the Year - Memphis Altrusa Intl Memphis TN 1989. slocomberector@live.com

SLOCUM, Robert Boak (Lex) PO Box 2505, Danville KY 40423 B Macon GA 5/21/1952 s James Robert Slocum & Sara Lila. BA Van 1974; JD Van 1977; MDiv Nash 1986; DMin STUSo 1992; PhD Marq 1997. D 6/21/1986 P 5/2/1987 Bp James Barrow Brown. m 4/22/2007 Victoria S Charnetski c 3. Ecum Off Dio Lexington Lexington KY 2009-2011; R Trin Epis Ch Danville KY 2007-2010; Ch Of The H Comm Lake Geneva WI 1993-2002; R St Philips Epis Ch Waukesha WI 1991-1992; Vic S Andr's Ch Clinton LA 1987-1991; Vic S Pat's Ch Zachary LA 1987-1991; D-in-Trng Trin Ch New Orleans LA 1986-1987. Auth, "Light in a Burning-Glass, A Systematic Presentation of the Theol of Austin Farrer," Un.of So. Carolina Press, 2007; Ed, "A Heart for the Future, Writings on the Chr Hope," Ch Publising, Inc, 2004; Co-Ed, "Discovering Common Mssn; Lutherns & Episcopalians together," Ch Publising, Inc, 2003; Co-Ed, "To Hear Celestial Harmonies, Essays on Wit of Jas DeKoven and The DeKoven Cntr," Forw Mvmt, 2002; Ed, "Engaging the Sprt, Essays on the Life and Theol of the H Sprt," Ch Pub, Inc, 2001; Co-Ed, "An Epis Dictionary of the Ch," Ch Pub, Inc, 2000; Auth, "The Theol of Wm Porcher DuBose: Life, Mvmt, and Being," Un. of So. Carolina Press, 2000; Ed, "A New Conversation, Essays on the Future of Theol and the Epis Ch," Ch Pub, Inc, 1999; Ed, "Prophet of Justice, Prophet of Life, Essays on Wm Stringfellow," Ch Pub, Inc, 1997; Co-Ed, "Documents of Witness, A Hist of the Epis Ch, 1782-1985," Ch Pub, Inc, 1994. rbslocum@genevaonline.com

SLOVAK, Anita M (Okla) All Saints' Episcopal Church, 809 West Cedar Ave, Duncan OK 73533 **R All SS' Epis Ch Duncan OK 2011-** B Johnstown PA 6/22/1958 d George Martinec & Anna Lita. BA U Pgh 1979; MS U of Texas 1983; MDiv Perkins TS, SMU 2006. D 1/26/2008 P 10/11/2008 Bp James Monte Stanton. m 6/27/1998 Johnny V Slovak c 2. Chapl Cbury Epis Sch Desoto TX 2010-2011; Asst S Nich Ch Flower Mound TX 2010-2011; Cur Ch Of The Gd Shpd Dallas TX 2008-2010; Chair - Chr Formation Cmsn Dio Dallas Dallas TX 2006-2011; DCE Ch Of The Epiph Richardson TX 2004-2008; Par Mgr S Phil's Epis Ch Frisco TX 2002-2003. amslovak@gmail.com

SLUSHER, Montie Bearl (Ak) 1133 Park Dr., Fairbanks AK 99709 **D S Matt's Epis Ch Fairbanks AK 1990-** B Billings MT 3/18/1935 s Earl Slusher & Myrtle. BS Rocky Mtn Coll 1962; N/A Iliff TS 1964; MAT Lewis & Clark Coll 1978. D 6/4/1985 Bp Barbara Clementine Harris. m 11/22/1975 Lynn Locke c 4. slusher@alaska.net

SLUSS, Mark Duane (Mo) 2918 Victor St, Saint Louis MO 63104 B Columbus OH 4/5/1965 s Roger Hugh Sluss & Barbara Lee. AA Jefferson Coll 1985; BS Missouri St U 1988. D 2/7/2007 Bp George Wayne Smith. sluss@sbcglobal.net

SMALL, Timothy Keesey (CPa) 370 Spring Hill Ln, Columbia PA 17512 **Hope Epis Ch Manheim PA 2009-** B York PA 9/7/1955 s George Augustus Small & Catherine Elizabeth. BA Juniata Coll 1977; MDiv VTS 1982. D 6/5/1982 P 12/17/1982 Bp Charlie Fuller McNutt Jr. m 8/20/1977 Betsy Righter Mastran. S Lk's Epis Ch Mechanicsburg PA 2008; Int H Trin Epis Ch Shamokin PA 1999-2000; R S Paul's Ch Manheim PA 1989-1998; S Edw's Epis Ch Lancaster PA 1983-1989. wigwamlbi@aol.com

SMALL, William David (Alb) 451 State Route 86, Paul Smiths NY 12970 B Albany NY 5/9/1934 s William Charles Small & Helen Blendina. BA SUNY 1957; MDiv Ya Berk 1960. D 5/28/1960 Bp Frederick Lehrle Barry P 12/18/1960 Bp Allen Webster Brown. m 11/11/2007 Darleen Ellen Mills c 3. S Jn's Ch Johnstown NY 1977-1996; Doane Stuart Sch Albany NY 1964-1977; Vic S Bon Ch Guilderland NY 1962-1965; Cur S Andr's Epis Ch Albany NY 1960-1962. wmsmall2@aol.com

SMALLEY, H Bud (Ida) 5170 Leonard Rd, Pocatello ID 83204 B Ashland OH 11/15/1951 s Harold Henry Smalley & Florence Veronica. Cert Idaho St U 1986. D 12/8/1996 P 6/14/1997 Bp John Stuart Thornton. m 5/26/1976 Ann Debra Flatt. S Jn's Epis Ch Amer Falls ID 1997-2009; Asst Trin Epis Ch Pocatello ID 1997-2002. hbsmalley@aol.com

SMALLEY, Nancy T (Dal) 416 Victorian Dr, Waxahachie TX 75165 B Ardmore OK 12/28/1949 d John Moulton Tuttle & Jane. BFA SMU 1971; MA U of Texas 1975; STL 1989; MS Texas A&M U 1990; CTh Epis TS of the SW 1996. D 4/2/1997 P 5/5/1998 Bp James Monte Stanton. m 5/19/1973 Tom Edward Smalley c 2. Int S Anne's Epis Ch Desoto TX 2008-2009; Int Epis Ch Of The Redeem Irving TX 2002-2004; Supply S Mart's Ch Lancaster TX 2001-2002; Cur S Lk's Epis Ch Dallas TX 1997-2001. CT. smallnance@aol.com

SMALLEY, Richard Craig (Ala) 2017 6th Avenue North, Birmingham AL 35203 **Cn Mssnr and Day Sch Chapl The Cathd Ch Of The Adv Birmingham AL 2011-** B Orlando FL 2/3/1968 s Richard Laye Smalley & Barbara Ann. BA Cit 1990; MDiv VTS 1995. D 5/28/1995 P 12/16/1995 Bp Edward Lloyd Salmon Jr. m 5/28/1992 Paula Swartz c 3. Cn for CE The Cathd Ch Of The Adv Birmingham AL 2006-2011; R Epis Ch Of The Ascen Birmingham AL 2001-2006; LocTen Trin Epis Ch The Woodlands TX 2000-2001; Assoc Ch Of The H Cross Sullivans Island SC 1997-2000; Cur Cathd Of S Lk And S Paul Charleston SC 1995-1997. Chairman Dept Coll Mnstry; Dioc Eccl Crt; Sprtl Dir, Happ Of So Carolina. craig@cathedraladvent.com

SMALLEY, Stephen Mark (Pgh) 989 Morgan Street, Brackenridge PA 15014 B Washington DC 9/11/1953 s Robert Fields Smalley & Ruth Elizabeth. BA McDaniel Coll 1975; MDiv Garrett Evang TS 1978; DMin Drew U 2005. D 1/25/1992 P 8/1/1992 Bp John-David Mercer Schofield. m 6/28/1975 Kristin P Peterson c 2. R S Barn Ch Brackenridge PA 1999-2011; Dioc Coun Dio Easton Easton MD 1996-1999; R Aug Par Chesapeake City MD 1995-1999; Off Of Bsh For ArmdF New York NY 1992-1995. smsmalley@gmail.com

✠ **SMALLEY OSB, Rt Rev William Edward** (Kan) 13809 E 186th St, Noblesville IN 46060 **Ret Bp of Kansas Trin Ch Anderson IN 2007-** B New Brunswick NJ 4/8/1940 s August Harold Smalley & Emma May. BA Leh 1962; STM EDS 1965; MS Tem 1970; DMin Wesley TS 1987. D 6/26/1965 P 3/5/1966 Bp Frederick J Warnecke Con 12/8/1989 for Kan. m 9/12/1964 Carole Kuhns c 2. Int S Paul's Ch Columbus IN 2005-2006; Ret Bp of Kansas Dio Kansas Topeka KS 1989-2003; COM Dio Washington Washington DC 1988-1989; R Ch Of The Ascen Gaithersburg MD 1980-1989; Dep GC Dio Bethlehem Bethlehem PA 1976-1979; S Jn's Epis Ch Palmerton PA 1975-1980; ExCoun Dio Bethlehem Bethlehem PA 1969-1971; R All SS Epis Ch Lehighton PA 1967-1975; Vic S Mart-In-The-Fields Mtn Top PA 1965-1967; Vic S Ptr's Epis Ch Hazleton PA 1965-1967. Auth, "Reg Mnstrs," *The Sm Ch Nwsltr*, 1994. Oblate Ord of S Ben 1998. Omicron Delta Kappa Leh 1962. hob851@aol.com

SMART, Clifford Edward James (Mo) 6045 Glennaire Dr, Saint Louis MO 63129 B Bedford England 5/31/1928 s Archdale Charles Smart & Nellie. Kelham Theol Coll 1953. Trans from Church Of England 5/4/2001 Bp Hays H. Rockwell. m 5/16/1974 Judith Kay Thiele. Trin Ch De Soto MO 2001-2005. clifford.smart@sbcglobal.net

SMART SR, E(lton) Dennis (Dal) 1407 Ficklin Ave, Corsicana TX 75110 **Died 12/3/2010** B Pine Bluff AR 6/11/1927 s Elton Dallas Smart & Azelle Lulu. Texas A&M U 1945; SMU 1948; LTh Epis TS In Kentucky 1963. D 9/21/1963 P 3/21/1964 Bp Theodore H McCrea. c 1. CBS 1957. denden@airmail.net

SMART JR, Frank Fogwill (Va) Po Box 83, White Stone VA 22578 **Died 8/23/2011** B Dorchester MA 5/7/1914 s Frank Fogwill Smart & Florence Isobel. BS USNA 1937; MDiv VTS 1941. D 9/1/1941 P 3/10/1942 Bp William Scarlett. c 2.

SMART JR, James Hudson (NwT) 1826 Elmwood Dr, Abilene TX 79605 **Assoc S Mk's Epis Ch Abilene TX 2011-** B Abilene TX 3/3/1948 s Hudson Smart & Martha. BS McMurry U 1970; JD Texas Tech U 1973. D 5/8/2004 P 11/20/2004 Bp C(harles) Wallis Ohl. m 10/8/1977 Patricia Elliott.

SMART, John A (Pa) 5100 N Northridge Cir, Tucson AZ 85718 B McKeesport PA 9/15/1934 s William Henry Smart & Jean Caroline. BA Indiana St U 1957; STB Ya Berk 1961. D 7/17/1961 Bp Austin Pardue P 12/9/1961 Bp William S Thomas. m 6/22/1963 Marie Everson c 1. R S Mich's Ch Coolidge AZ 2003-2006; R S Alb's Epis Ch Wickenburg AZ 1996-2000; Dio Pennsylvania Philadelphia PA 1985-1986; R The Ch Of The H Trin Rittenhouse Philadelphia PA 1984-1996; R S Mart's Ch Radnor PA 1977-1984; R Trin Ch Solebury PA 1968-1977; Cur Ch Of The Redeem Springfield PA 1963-1968; Cur S Paul's Epis Ch Westfield NJ 1961-1963. smartsaz@netzero.com

SMART, J(ohn) Dennis (At) 442 Euclid Terrace N.E., Atlanta GA 30307 **Assoc R Ch Of The H Cross Decatur GA 1991-** B Waco TX 11/2/1940 s Noble Carleton Smart & Ruth. BA Baylor U 1963; MA U of Texas 1972; MDiv VTS 1978. D 6/13/1978 Bp Roger Howard Cilley P 6/1/1979 Bp J Milton Richardson. m 4/9/1966 Susan Harrell c 2. Ch Of The H Cross Decatur GA 1994-2002; Gd Shpd Epis Ch Austell GA 1992-1993; Dio Atlanta Atlanta GA 1991; Dn of Macon Dnry Dio Atlanta Atlanta GA 1986-1990; R All SS Ch Warner Robins GA 1984-1991; Assoc Trin Ch Longview TX 1980-1984; R Chr Ch Jefferson TX 1978-1980; S Paul's Ch Jefferson TX 1978-1980; St Pauls Ch 1978-1980. john.smart@comcast.net

SMART, Lula Grace (Pa) 147 7th Ave, Folsom PA 19033 **R Calv Ch Germantown Philadelphia PA 1998-** B Limon CR 5/20/1951 d Rudolph Morris & Adina. BA Universidad Autonomus De Centro Amererica 1987; MDiv GTS 1997. D 6/21/1997 Bp Allen Lyman Bartlett Jr P 5/30/1998 Bp Franklin Delton Turner. The Afr Epis Ch Of S Thos Philadelphia PA 1997-1998. lugsmart@comcast.net

SMEDLEY IV, Walter (Va) The Church of the Holy Cross, 2455 Gallows Road, Dunn Loring VA 22027 **Stndg Com Dio Virginia Richmond VA 2011-; R Ch Of The H Cross Dunn Loring VA 2005-** B Pennsylvania 8/12/1974 s Walter Smedley & Kathleen. BA Wms 1996; Earlham Sch of Rel 1999; MDiv Ya Berk 2002. D 6/22/2002 P 5/31/2003 Bp Charles Ellsworth Bennison Jr. m 10/17/2004 Loraine Smedley c 1. Asst Chr Ch Philadelphia Philadelphia PA 2002-2005. wes.smedley@holycrossepiscopal.org

SMELLIE, Larry Gene (SwFla) 15051 Sterling Oaks Dr, Naples FL 34110 **Dio SW Florida Sarasota FL 2000-** B Defiance OH 10/1/1940 s Walter Haven Smellie & Francis. BA Defiance Coll 1962; MDiv Bex 1965. D 6/12/1965 Bp Beverley D Tucker P 2/1/1966 Bp William Crittenden. m 5/31/1964 Susan Joy. Dep GC Dio SW Florida Sarasota FL 1991-1997; Dn Ft Myers Deanry Dio SW Florida Sarasota FL 1988-1994; R S Paul's Ch Naples FL 1971-1999; Vic S Alb's Epis Ch Ft Wayne IN 1967-1971; Cur Cathd Of S Paul Erie PA 1965-1967. frlry@aol.com

SMELSER, Todd Dudley (At) 1358 E Rock Springs Rd Ne, Atlanta GA 30306 **Pstr Care Assoc Cathd Of S Phil Atlanta GA 2008-** B Richmond IN 5/10/1948 s Wayne Harold Smelser & Marie Porter. BA Earlham Coll 1970; MDiv Andover Newton TS 1974. D 6/8/1974 P 11/30/1974 Bp John P Craine. Cn for Pstr Care & Wrshp Cathd Of S Phil Atlanta GA 2002-2008; Assoc S Pat's Epis Ch Atlanta GA 2002; Int S Geo's Epis Ch Maplewood NJ 1999-2001; Dn Cathd Of S Jas Chicago IL 1992-1999; R S Jn The Bapt Epis Ch Minneapolis MN 1983-1992; Litur Cmsn Dio Minnesota Minneapolis MN 1983-1989; Regent 2 Of New York Pleasantville NY 1981-1983; S Alb's Epis Ch Ft Wayne IN 1980-1981; Trin Ch Ft Wayne IN 1974-1979. jgandts@att.net

SMERCINA, Eugene Edward (O) 4307 Cleveland Rd E, Huron OH 44839 B Cleveland OH 4/19/1933 s Edward Joseph Smercina & Helen Anna. BA Kent St U 1955; BD Bex 1959; MA Bowling Green St U 1969; GTS 1985. D 6/13/1959 P 12/21/1959 Bp Nelson Marigold Burroughs. m 5/23/1981 Susanne Biehl. Chr Epis Ch Huron OH 1966-2001; Vic S Matt's Ch Ashland OH 1959-1966. whimsy2@msn.com

SMIRAGLIA, Richard Paul (Pa) 340 Fitzwater Street, Philadelphia PA 19147 **Assoc The Ch Of The H Trin Rittenhouse Philadelphia PA 2007-** B New York NY 3/18/1952 s Sylvio Carl Smiraglia & Marcia Jane. BA Lewis & Clark Coll 1973; MLS Indiana U 1974; PhD U Chi 1992; MDiv GTS 1997. D 6/21/1997 Bp Allen Lyman Bartlett Jr P 6/13/1998 Bp Charles Ellsworth Bennison Jr. m 5/31/2008 James Bradford Young. R S Phil Memi Ch Philadelphia PA 2002-2006; S Mk's Ch Philadelphia PA 2000-2001; Asst S Mary's Ch Hamilton Vill Philadelphia PA 1999-2000; Asst Trin Memi Ch Philadelphia PA 1997-1998. rsmiraglia@htrit.org

SMITH, A(lan) Bruce (SO) 99 Indian Springs Dr, Columbus OH 43214 **Affirmative Aging Cmsn Dio Sthrn Ohio Cincinnati OH 2009-; Assoc S Mk's Epis Ch Columbus OH 2000-** B Newark NJ 6/30/1951 s Alan Leslie Smith & Emilie Lawrence. BA Ithaca Coll 1973; MDiv Drew U 1996; MTS Methodist TS In Ohio 1999. D 6/24/2000 P 1/6/2001 Bp Herbert Thompson Jr. m 6/26/1982 Susan Warrener c 3. The Epis Ntwk for Stwdshp 1999. abssws@att.net

SMITH JR, Alfred Hersey (Los) 9566 Vervain St, San Diego CA 92129 B San Rafael CA 1/6/1934 s Alfred Hersey Smith & Susie. BA U So 1956; BD CDSP 1959; DMin VTS 1988. D 7/30/1959 P 2/29/1960 Bp William J Gordon Jr. m 6/3/1961 Stephaine S Harms c 2. P in Res - Vol S Barth's Epis Ch Poway CA 2006; S Columba's Par Camarillo CA 1970-1999; R S Tim's Epis Ch Apple Vlly CA 1966-1970; Asst S Fran' Par Palos Verdes Estates CA 1964-1966; Vic S Tim's Ch Tok AK 1962-1964; Vic S Matt's Ch Beaver AK 1960-1962; Vic S Andr's Ch Stevens Vill AK 1959-1960. Auth, "Call To Excellence," Foward Mvmt Pub, 1992; Auth, "Dvlpmt Of The Vstry Of S Columba'S Ch," 1988. OHC. alsteph@san.rr.com

SMITH, Aloha Lee (Los) 5848 Tower Rd, Riverside CA 92506 B Spokane WA 8/19/1942 d Edward Herman von Glan & Chloe Gertrude. BA U CO 1964; Cert Rutgers-The St U 1982; BTh McGill U 1986; STM McGill U 1987; MDiv Montreal TS 1988; DMin STUSo 1997. D 10/1/1988 P 5/14/1989 Bp Reginald Hollis. m 12/26/1972 Roberts Smith c 2. S Mich's Epis Ch Riverside CA 2007-2008; P-in-c S Fran Of Assisi Par San Bernardino CA 2002-2006; Assoc Trin Epis Ch Redlands CA 1998-2002. Chapl Ord of S Lk - Co-Dir Reg VII 1990; EFM Mentor 1994; Ord of S Helena 1980. revs2smith@earthlink.net

SMITH, Andrea (Ct) 16 Clam Shell Alley, P.O. Box 412, Vinalhaven ME 04863 B Greenwich CT 10/15/1943 d Andrew William Smith & Gail. BA Syr 1970; MDiv EDS 1980. D 6/13/1981 P 3/17/1982 Bp Arthur Edward Walmsley. m 8/19/1972 John Hale c 2. Asst S Jas Ch Hartford CT 1981-1984; S Jas's Ch W Hartford CT 1981-1984. AAPC 1994; Assocation of Profsnl Chapl

1988. Proclamation of Dedicated Efforts in Response to September 11th Gvnr Jn Rowland Connecticut 2002. agua1015@gmail.com

✠ **SMITH, Rt Rev Andrew Donnan** (Ct) 27 Rillbank Ter, West Hartford CT 06107 **Ret Bp of Connecticut All SS Chap Hartford CT 1999-; Bp Dio Connecticut Hartford CT 1999-** B Albany NY 1/20/1944 s Frederick Anderson Smith & Grace Irma. BA Trin Hartford CT 1965; BD EDS 1968; DD Ya Berk 2000. D 6/11/1968 P 3/22/1969 Bp Walter H Gray Con 5/4/1996 for Ct. m 6/12/1971 Kate Carroll Smith c 2. Suffr Bp Of Connecticut Dio Connecticut Hartford CT 1996-2010; Dn Hartford Dnry Dio Connecticut Hartford CT 1987-1991; Stndg Com Dio Connecticut Hartford CT 1986-1991; R S Mary's Epis Ch Manchester CT 1985-1996; R S Mich's Ch Naugatuck CT 1976-1985; Asst S Jn's Epis Par Waterbury CT 1971-1976; Cur Trin Epis Ch Hartford CT 1968-1971. Chapl Hartford Chapt Comp H Cross 1993-1995; Soc For The Increase Of Mnstry 1989. ktadsmith@comcast.net

SMITH, Anne (EpisSanJ) 1055 S Lower Sacramento Rd, Lodi CA 95242 **Asst S Jn The Bapt Lodi CA 2011-** B Pennsylvania 6/1/1975 d Jorg Richard Largent & Elizabeth Jackson. non earned U of Maryland; BA Pepperdine U 1997; MDiv CDSP 2010. D 6/5/2010 Bp Marc Handley Andrus P 12/11/2010 Bp Jerry Alban Lamb. m 1/3/1998 Keith Smith c 3. katesma@gmail.com

SMITH, Ann-Lining (Cal) 7261 Mesa Dr, Aptos CA 95003 B Florence AL 8/5/1949 d Lewis King Smith & Nancy Camille. CDSP; Intl Ministers Ntwk; BA U of Alabama 1971; MDiv Amer Bapt Sem of The W 1976. D 1/6/1980 Bp C Kilmer Myers P 3/1/1981 Bp William Edwin Swing. All SS Epis Ch Watsonville CA 1997-1999; S Mths Ch Seaside CA 1996-1997; Int Epis Ch Of The Gd Shpd Salinas CA 1995-1996; Dio California San Francisco CA 1992-1993; Vic Ch Of The H Fam Half Moon Bay CA 1984-1992; Dep Vic S Clare's Epis Ch Pleasanton CA 1983-1984; Int Ch Of The Incarn San Francisco CA 1982-1983; Cur Ch Of The Incarn San Francisco CA 1980-1982. Auth, "Reverend Ms Evelyn Morgan Jones," *I Love You*. mightoftheloon@yahoo.com

SMITH, Ann Robb (Pa) 816 Castlefinn Ln, Bryn Mawr PA 19010 B Philadelphia PA 3/9/1928 d Henry Burnett Robb & Gertrude Ann. BA U of Pennsylvania 1950; MDiv Luth TS at Gettysburg 1991. D 6/16/1990 Bp Allen Lyman Bartlett Jr P 6/15/1991 Bp Barbara Clementine Harris. m 7/1/1950 Kaighn Smith c 3. Dn Wissahickon Deanry Dio Pennsylvania Philadelphia PA 1995-1998; Ch Of The Advoc Philadelphia PA 1991-1997. Auth, "El Salvador: A People Crucified," *Wit mag*, 1988; Auth, "Nicaragua: A People Longing for Peace," *Wit mag*, 1988. Quality of Life Awd Founders Bank 2002; Marg Bailey Speer Awd The Shipley Sch 2001. revannsmith@aol.com

SMITH, Barbara Joan (U) P.O. Box 849, Cordova AK 99574 B Vancouver CA 9/27/1935 d Clair Curtis Smith & Wanda. BA U Of British Columbia Vancouver BC CA 1957; MDiv Vancouver TS 1988. D 6/13/1987 Bp Arthur Edward Walmsley P 3/17/1989 Bp George Edmonds Bates. P-in-c S Geo's Ch Cordova AK 2002; R S Paul's Epis Ch Vernal UT 1996-1998; Dio Utah Salt Lake City UT 1993-2002; S Fran Ch Moab UT 1989-1992. bstgeorges@ctcak.net

SMITH, Bardwell Leith (Minn) 104 Maple St, Northfield MN 55057 B Springfield MA 7/28/1925 s Winthrop Hiram Smith & Gertrude Ingram. BA Ya 1950; BD Yale DS 1953; MA Ya 1957; PhD Ya 1964; Harv 1965; London U 1972; Kyoto U 1986. D 6/13/1954 P 12/1/1954 Bp Horace W B Donegan. m 8/19/1961 Charlotte McCorkingdale McCorkindale c 5. Cur Trin Ch Highland Pk IL 1954-1956. Auth, *The City as a Sacr Cntr: Essays on 6 Asian Contexts*, E.J. Brill (Netherlands), 1987; Auth, *Essays on Gupta Culture*, Motilal Banarsidass, 1983; Co-Ed/Contrib, "Warlords," *Artists, Warlords & Commoners: Japan in 16th Century*, U Press of Hawaii, 1981; Auth/Ed, *Rel and Legitimation of Power in Sri Lanka*, Anima Press, 1978; Ed/Contrib, *Hinduism: New Essays in Hist of Rel*, E.J. Brill, 1976; Auth/Ed, *Unsui: Diary of Zen Monastic Life*, U Press of Hawaii, 1973. AAR 1960; Amer Soc for the Study of Rel 1982; Assn for Asian Stds 1962. Pres Amer Soc for the Study of Rel 1996; Resrch Grant Natl Endowmt for the Hmnts (NEH) 1991; Fulbright Resrch Grant (Japan) Fulbright 1986; Resrch Fllshp Amer Coun Learned Socs 1972. bsmith@carleton.edu

SMITH JR, Ben Huddleston (Md) 1401 Carrollton Ave, Baltimore MD 21204 B Richmond VA 2/5/1932 s Ben Huddleston Smith & Katherine Randolph. PhD U NC 1962; Cert GTS 1982. D 5/21/1982 P 5/1/1983 Bp A(rthur) Heath Light. Assoc Cathd Of The Incarn Baltimore MD 2000-2001; R Ch Of The Gd Shpd Ruxton MD 1985-1999; Asst Chr Ch Alexandria VA 1982-1984. ruddyben@aol.com

SMITH, Benjamin Bosworth (SC) 420 Church St, Mount Pleasant SC 29464 **Died 10/21/2010** B Montgomery,AL 12/6/1929 s Frederick Rutledge Smith & Mary Burton. BA U of Alabama 1951; VTS 1954; Inst Advncd Pstr Stds 1962; U So 1964; Fllshp Coll of Preachers 1967; LHD Coll of Charleston 1991. D 6/24/1954 P 5/26/1955 Bp Charles C J Carpenter. c 4. benchassc@comcast.net

SMITH, Bert Orville (At) 841 Kings Grant Dr NW, Atlanta GA 30318 **D Ch Of The H Comf Atlanta GA 2006-** B Atlanta GA 3/29/1948 s Bert O Smith & Yancey. D 8/6/2006 Bp J(ohn) Neil Alexander. m 5/15/2007 Patricia Smith. bertsmithatl@aol.com

SMITH, Betty Lorraine (NMich) 8114 Trout Lake Rd, Naubinway MI 49762 B Epoufette MI 6/9/1933 d Mack Mccoy Alexander & Mary Isabelle. D 10/13/2002 Bp James Arthur Kelsey. c 2. bettylsmith@lighthouse.net

SMITH, Bradford Ray (NC) 116 S Church St, PO Box 293, Monroe NC 28111 **COM Dio No Carolina Raleigh NC 2011-; Bd Trst (Univ. of the So) The TS at The U So Sewanee TN 2011-; R S Paul's Ch Monroe NC 2009-** B Lexington KY 5/31/1970 s Donald Ray Smith & Faith Wilford. BA W&M 1992; PhD U of Tennessee 1998; MDiv STUSo 2003. D 5/31/2003 P 1/31/2004 Bp Charles Glenn VonRosenberg. m 12/30/1994 Deborah Ann Gold. New Beginnings, Sprtl Dir Dio Atlanta Atlanta GA 2008; Bp's Congrl Consult Com Dio Atlanta Atlanta GA 2007-2009; Cmsn on Educ Dio Atlanta Atlanta GA 2005-2009; Cmsn on Stwdshp Dio Atlanta Atlanta GA 2005-2009; Assoc R The Ch Of S Matt Snellville GA 2005-2009; Supply S Fran' Ch Norris TN 2005; Co-Fndr/Co-Dir, Cmsn on Bioethics Dio E Tennessee Knoxville TN 2004-2005; Bp and Coun Dio E Tennessee Knoxville TN 2003-2005; Asst R S Andr's Ch Maryville TN 2003-2005. "Rel Elements in Healing," *The Hlth Care Profsnl as Friend and Healer: Bldg on the Wk of Edm D. Pellegrino*, Geo Press, 2000; "Re-establishing Connections Between Bioethics and Chrsnty: Narratives and Virtues in Caring for a Chr Patient," U of Tennessee, Knoxville, 1998. CSB (St. Greg's Abbey) 2005; Fllshp of S Jn 2002-2005. Woods Ldrshp Awd U So TS 2002. revbrads@gmail.com

SMITH, Brian E (Fla) 5507 Winford Court, Fairfax VA 22032 B Michigan City IN 10/15/1978 s Timothy Vangorder Smith & Barbara Martin. BS U of New Hampshire 2001; MDiv VTS 2007. D 12/20/2006 P 6/29/2007 Bp George Wayne Smith. Asst R Trin Epis Ch St Aug FL 2007-2009. brians@minister.com

SMITH, Bruce (Cal) 14 Ardmore Ct, Pleasant Hill CA 94523 **R Ch Of The Resurr Pleasant Hill CA 1987-** B Washington DC 9/23/1950 s Richard Harrison Smith & Mary Louise. BA U CA 1972; MDiv PSR 1979. D 6/28/1980 P 7/1/1981 Bp William Edwin Swing. m 4/27/1980 Deborah Dee Holderness. S Steph's Epis Ch Orinda CA 1982-1987; S Andr's Ch St Coll PA 1980-1982. bsmith@resurrectionph.org

SMITH, Carol Coke (Minn) 1211 Jackson Ave, Detroit Lakes MN 56501 **D S Columba White Earth MN 2005-** B Cass Lake MN 4/3/1958 d Harold O Annette & Joyce O. D 10/29/2005 P 1/20/2007 Bp James Louis Jelinek. m 8/6/1976 Richard Smith c 2. ECCIM 2003; MCIW 1997. rsmith@arvig.net

SMITH, Carol Kay Huston (Mil) 4522 Aztec Trail, Fitchburg WI 53711 **D Gr Ch Madison WI 2008-; D S Lk's Ch Racine WI 2000-** B Washington DC 2/19/1942 d Carl Adam Huston & Lucy Jeanette. BA Florida St U 1964; MA Florida St U 1970. D 3/28/1987 Bp Roger John White. m 8/16/1965 Stephen Wesley Smith. D S Mich's Epis Ch Racine WI 1987-2000.

SMITH, Cecilia Mary Babcock (Tex) PO Box 2247, Austin TX 78768 **Dio Texas Houston TX 2008-; Safe Ch Min Dio Texas Houston TX 2008-; Coun Mgmt Dio Texas Houston TX 2007-** B Buffalo NY 3/10/1942 d Donald Wight Babcock & Mary. BA Vas 1964; MA U of Texas 1970; MDiv Epis TS of The SW 1990; ThM S Mary U San Antonio TX 1990. D 6/16/1990 Bp Maurice Manuel Benitez P 1/1/1991 Bp Anselmo Carral-Solar. m 10/30/1964 Virgil Raymond Smith c 3. Supply P S Andr's Ch Bryan TX 2007; GC Dep Dio Texas Houston TX 2005-2010; Stndg Com Dio Texas Houston TX 2004-2007; Exec Bd Dio Texas Houston TX 1999-2002; R S Ptr's Epis Ch Brenham TX 1997-2007; Assoc R S Dav's Ch Austin TX 1994-1996; Asst S Dav's Ch Austin TX 1990-1991. csmith@epicenter.org

SMITH, Channing (ECR) 13601 Saratoga Avenue, Saratoga CA 95070 **R S Andr's Ch Saratoga CA 2009-** B Niskayuna NY 5/23/1966 s Channing Sylvester Smith & Elizabeth Harper. BA Ken 1988; MDiv GTS 1992. D 7/25/1992 P 5/15/1993 Bp Herbert Thompson Jr. m 5/25/1991 Mary Richards. Stndg Com Pres Dio California San Francisco CA 2006-2007; R Trsfg Epis Ch San Mateo CA 1997-2009; Treas/Secy of Alum The GTS New York NY 1995-1996; The Ch of the Redeem Cincinnati OH 1992-1997. channing@st-andrews-saratoga.org

SMITH, Charles Howard (Az) 807 W Toledo St, Chandler AZ 85225 B Detroit MI 8/3/1932 s Charles I Smith & Ethel. BBA SMU 1954; MDiv CDSP 1964. D 6/20/1964 Bp J(ohn) Joseph Meakins Harte P 12/1/1964 Bp Harry S Kennedy. m 10/29/1955 Betty Hoover. Dioc Coun Dio Arizona Phoenix AZ 1981-1984; S Matt's Ch Chandler AZ 1980-1997; S Matt's Ch Chandler AZ 1975-1979; R S Jn's Epis Ch Stockton CA 1970-1975; R S Tim's Ch Aiea HI 1969-1970; Dioc Coun Dio Hawaii Honolulu HI 1968-1970; Vic H Innoc' Epis Ch Lahaina HI 1964-1968. kanakachas@earthlink.net

SMITH, Charles Jeremy (SVa) 101 Saint Matthews Ln, Spartanburg SC 29301 **D S Matt's Epis Ch Spartanburg SC 2011-** B Roanoke VA 11/18/1982 s Andre Marcel Smith & Pammy Christine. BA Hampden Sydney Coll 2005; MDiv VTS 2011. D 6/18/2011 Bp Herman Hollerith IV. m 7/15/2006 Christina R Kennedy. CHARLES.JEREMY.SMITH@GMAIL.COM

SMITH, Charles L (NwT) PO Box 3346, Odessa TX 79760 B Fort Worth TX 9/18/1950 s James William Smith & Francis. BA Auston Coll 1973; MDiv Nash 1979. D 5/13/1979 Bp Addison Hosea P 12/1/1979 Bp Emerson Paul Haynes. m 5/19/1978 Casey Carruth. S Jn's Epis Ch Odessa TX 2009-2010; S

Fran Ch Tampa FL 1981-1983; S Chris's Ch TAMPA FL 1980-1981; Cur S Steph's Ch New Port Richey FL 1979-1980. LAYNE48@HOTMAIL.COM

SMITH, Charles Stuart (Alb) 45 Pierrepont Ave., Potsdam NY 13676 B Boston MA 2/25/1955 s David Orchard Smith & Janet Rowe. BA Coll of Wooster 1979; MDiv GTS 1990. D 6/9/1990 Bp Arthur Edward Walmsley P 5/1/1991 Bp Clarence Nicholas Coleridge. m 12/27/1986 Elaina Marie Wadeka c 2. P-in-c The St Lawr Team Ministr Waddington NY 1998-2001; R Ch Of The H Trin Greenport NY 1993-1997; Asst S Mk's Ch Islip NY 1991-1993; Asst Gr Epis Ch Norwalk CT 1990-1991. csmit41@twcny.rr.com

SMITH, Christopher Atkins (Alb) 12 Main St., Hagaman NY 12086 B Waterbury CT 5/3/1947 s James Leonard Smith & Julie. BA U of Connecticut 1969; MDiv GTS 1979. D 7/18/1979 P 6/7/1980 Bp Morgan Porteus. m 9/15/1973 Maria Guimaraes c 1. R S Ann's Ch Amsterdam NY 1990-2011; Vic S Paul's Ch Plainfield CT 1983-1990; Cur Chr Ch Stratford CT 1979-1983. adeodatus@mac.com

SMITH, Claude Archibald (Mass) 160 River Street, Norwell MA 02061 B Boston MA 2/1/1933 s Claude Taylor Smith & Elizabeth Archibald. BA Pr 1954; Yale DS 1954; STB EDS 1957; PhD Harv 1964. D 6/22/1957 Bp Anson Phelps Stokes Jr P 12/21/1957 Bp Donald B Aldrich. m 9/7/1957 Elizabeth Scoville c 4. The Par Of S Chrys's Quincy MA 1999-2002; Assoc S Andr's Ch Hanover MA 1993-1997; Assoc S Mk's Barrington Hills IL 1986-1993; R S Andr's Epis Ch Hopkinton NH 1962-1964; Asst S Andr's Ch Wellesley MA 1961-1962; P-in-c S Paul's Epis Ch Bedford MA 1959-1960; Cur S Andr's Ch Wellesley MA 1957-1959. Auth, "Jonathan Edwards & the Way of Ideas," *Harvard Theol Revs*, Harv Press Vol. 59, #2., 1966. 1954. bcsmith57@verizon.net

SMITH, Claudia L (Me) 1150 Morgan Bay Rd, Blue Hill ME 04614 **Grants Revs Com Dio Maine Portland ME 2011-; Chair, Cmsn on Congrl Life Dio Maine Portland ME 2010-; Dioc Coun Dio Maine Portland ME 2010-; R S Fran By The Sea Blue Hill ME 2007-; Dio Maine Portland ME 2005-** B New York NY 10/26/1949 d John Francis Wyatt & Florence R. AA Chr Coll 1970; BS SE Oklahoma St U 1973; MDiv STUSo 2005. D 6/11/2005 P 12/17/2005 Bp Robert John O'Neill. c 1. S Ben Epis Ch La Veta CO 2005-2007. revclaudiainmaine@gmail.com

SMITH, Coleen Haas (Mil) 2145 N 90th St, Wauwatosa WI 53226 **D S Paul's Ch Milwaukee WI 2008-** B 8/17/1948 BA DePaul U 2003; MA Loyola U 2006. D 2/4/2005 Bp Victor Alfonso Scantlebury. m 3/14/1999 James Haas Smith c 1. bri0817@aol.com

SMITH III, Colton Mumford (SC) 1 Bishop Gadsden Way A-346, Charleston SC 29412 B Vicksburg MS 3/12/1935 s Colton Mumford Smith & Alice Powers. BA U So 1958; STB GTS 1961; DMin STUSo 1980. D 6/17/1961 Bp Duncan Montgomery Gray P 12/20/1961 Bp John M Allin. m 11/11/1961 Angela P K Keyser c 3. R Ch Of Our Sav Johns Island SC 1991-2001; Cn Dio Mississippi Jackson MS 1984-1991; R S Phil's Ch Jackson MS 1981-1984; R All SS Ch Jackson MS 1969-1981; Vic Ch Of The Ascen Hattiesburg MS 1965-1969; Vic S Steph's Ch Columbia MS 1965-1969; Vic Par Of The Medtr-Redeem McComb MS 1962-1965; Cur S Jas Ch Jackson MS 1961-1962. Auth, *A Period of Adjustment & Growth: A Study of the Epis Dio Mississippi*; Auth, *A Position Paper on Ord of Wmn to the Priesthood & the Epis Ch*; Auth, *Intrnernship for Deacons & 1st Year P*. colton35@att.net

SMITH, Craig Faulkner (Vt) 5167 Shelburne Road, Shelburne VT 05482 **R Trin Ch Shelburne VT 1998-** B Springfield VT 7/17/1954 s Alexander Jessup Smith & Janet Loring. BA U of Vermont 1980; MDiv GTS 1983. D 5/21/1983 P 11/1/1983 Bp Robert Shaw Kerr. m 12/29/1979 Candace R Smith c 1. Ch Of The Gd Shpd Barre VT 1984-1998; Cur Chr Ch Montpelier VT 1983-1984. craig@trinityshelburne.org

SMITH JR, C(urruth) Russell (WNC) 670 Run Away Rdg, Clyde NC 28721 **D S Andr's Epis Ch Canton NC 1996-** B Birmingham AL 10/23/1931 s Curruth Russell Smith & Cecile Grey. BS U of Alabama 1953; MD U of Alabama Sch of Med 1956; Dio Cntrl Florida Inst Chr Stds FL 1992. D 11/7/1992 Bp John Wadsworth Howe. m 6/27/1953 Barbara Bates Brotherton c 3. D S Dav's Epis Ch Lakeland FL 1992-1995.

✠ **SMITH, Rt Rev Dabney Tyler** (SwFla) 7313 Merchant Ct, Sarasota FL 34240 **Bp Dio SW Florida Sarasota FL 2007-** B Brownwood TX 12/7/1953 s Dorsey Green Smith & Dorothy Hazel. AA Santa Fe Cmnty Coll 1975; BA U of So Florida 1980; MDiv Nash 1987; DMin SWTS 1999. D 6/23/1987 P 12/28/1987 Bp William Hopkins Folwell Con 3/10/2007 for SwFla. m 10/11/1975 Mary Ellen Krieg c 3. R Trin Ch New Orleans LA 2005-2007; R H Trin Epis Ch Melbourne FL 1998-2005; R S Mich And All Ang Ch So Bend IN 1989-1998; Asst Gr Epis Ch Inc Port Orange FL 1987-1989. DD Seabury-Wstrn 2008; DD Sewanee 2008; DD Nash 2007. dabneyt@aol.com

SMITH, Dale Leroy (Los) 1427 Lyndon St, South Pasadena CA 91030 B Glendale CA 10/25/1942 s Carlyle Wilbur Smith & Beryl. BA Los Angeles Pacific Los Angeles CA 1964; MDiv SWTS 1971. D 7/11/1971 P 7/1/1972 Bp J(ohn) Joseph Meakins Harte. m 8/24/1985 Janet Elizabeth Meyer c 3. All SS Par Los Angeles CA 2003-2004; S Barth's Mssn Pico Rivera CA 1999-2003; P-in-c Imm Mssn El Monte CA 1997-1998; Assoc S Steph's Par Los Angeles CA 1985-1995; Assoc S Jas' Par So Pasadena CA 1980-1984; St Elizabeths Mssn Phoenix AZ 1976-1979; St Elizabeths Mssn Phoenix AZ 1972. dalejan@earthlin.net

SMITH, David Emerson (Mass) 76 Middle St, Bath ME 04530 **Died 5/4/2011** B Norwood MA 8/9/1931 s Hubert Lyman Smith & Fannie Ruth. BA Bos 1954; BD EDS 1957; MA Syr 1970. D 6/22/1957 P 12/21/1957 Bp Anson Phelps Stokes Jr. c 5. riversmith@clinic.net

SMITH, David Grant (Roch) St. Mark's Episcopal Church, P.O. Box 424, Penn Yan NY 14527 **P-in-c S Mk's Epis Ch Penn Yan NY 2008-** B Saginaw MI 1/27/1962 s Robert Grant Smith & Doris Dean. BA Olivet Nazarene Coll 1983; MDiv CRDS / Bex / Crozer The 1999. D 6/30/2007 P 4/12/2008 Bp Jack Marston McKelvey. D S Lk's Ch Fairport NY 2007-2008. davidstmarks@verizon.net

SMITH, David Hayes (Va) 800 Chatham Hall Cir., Chatham VA 24531 B Roanoke VA 4/15/1952 s W R Smith & Helen. BA S Andr's Presb Coll Laurinburg NC 1974; DMin UTS 1979. D 11/14/2008 Bp John Clark Buchanan P 6/2/2009 Bp Herman Hollerith IV. m 7/19/1990 Jane Smith c 2. Chatham Hall Chatham VA 2009-2010; Emm Epis Ch Chatham VA 2009-2010. david.smith@woodberry.org

SMITH, Dennis Lee (USC) Retired SC 29301 B Chester SC 8/13/1936 s John L Smith & Beulah. BA U of So Carolina 1963; MDiv VTS 1963; PhD U of So Carolina 1978. D 6/29/1966 P 7/2/1967 Bp John Adams Pinckney. m 3/18/1978 Shirley Ann Hanson c 1. S Matt's Epis Ch Spartanburg SC 1993-2001; Asst To Bp Dio Wstrn No Carolina Asheville NC 1986-1989; Cn To Ordnry Dio Upper So Carolina Columbia SC 1979-1982; P-in-c S Fran of Assisi Chapin SC 1979-1980; Dio Upper So Carolina Columbia SC 1971-1982; Dce Chr Ch Greenville SC 1967-1971; Cur Gr Epis Ch And Kindergarten Camden SC 1966-1967. dlssah@aol.com

SMITH, Donald Hedges (Roch) 2492 Keystone Lake Drive, Cape Coral FL 33909 B Cambridge NY 11/20/1925 s Richard Woodworth Smith & Margaret Elizabeth. BA Ya 1949; MDiv Bex 1971. D 6/19/1971 Bp John Mc Gill Krumm P 12/18/1971 Bp Robert Rae Spears Jr. c 4. S Thos Epis Ch Rochester NY 1975-1980; Asst Ch Of The Incarn Penfield NY 1971-1972. donaldsmith09@comcast.net

SMITH III, Donald M (CGC) 860 N Section St, Fairhope AL 36532 **S Jas Ch Fairhope AL 2008-** B Memphis TN 2/18/1969 s Donald Meredith Smith & Martha Rives. BBA U of Mississippi 1991; MDiv Epis Sem of the SW 2007. D 6/2/2007 P 12/8/2007 Bp Don Edward Johnson. m 12/28/1991 Lloyd E Early c 2. All SS Epis Ch Memphis TN 2007-2008. dsmith@allsaintsmem.org

SMITH, Don Leland (Oly) 8989 S Pine Dr, Beulah CO 81023 B Portland OR 4/11/1935 s Clarence Charles Smith & Ola Maude. BTh NW Chr Coll Eugene OR 1958; BA U of Oregon 1958; BD PSR 1963. D 6/23/1963 Bp James Albert Pike P 6/1/1964 Bp George Richard Millard. m 6/29/1963 Patricia June Hart c 2. S Paul's Epis Ch Mt Vernon WA 1982-1995; R S Fran Of Assisi Ch Novato CA 1972-1982; Vic S Edm's Epis Ch Pacifica CA 1966-1972; Cur Trin Par Menlo Pk CA 1963-1966. cityfolk@comcast.net

SMITH, Doris Graf (At) 11210 Wooten Lake Rd, Kennesaw GA 30144 **R Chr Epis Ch Kennesaw GA 2002-** B Atlanta GA 7/24/1946 d George Graf & Jennie Doris. BS U GA 1968; MDiv Candler TS Emory U 1984. D 6/9/1984 P 5/1/1985 Bp Charles Judson Child Jr. m 6/4/1967 Archer D Smith c 2. Asst H Innoc Ch Atlanta GA 2000-2001; COM Dio Atlanta Atlanta GA 1997-2002; Cn for Adult Educ Cathd Of S Phil Atlanta GA 1994-1999; S Mich And All Ang Ch Stone Mtn GA 1993-1994; Ch Of The Ascen Cartersville GA 1989-1993; S Cathr's Epis Ch Marietta GA 1984-1989.

SMITH, Douglas Cameron (CPa) 21 Cornell Dr, Hanover PA 17331 **All SS Ch Hanover PA 2004-** B Providence RI 2/28/1951 s Donald Stephen Smith & Gladys Mae. BA Br 1974; MDiv Andover Newton TS 1987. D 6/13/1987 P 5/1/1988 Bp Don Edward Johnson. m 8/9/1975 Beth Ann Smith c 4. R Chr Ch Cooperstown NY 1989-2004; Asst R Gr Ch No Attleborough MA 1987-1989. smith06@aol.com

SMITH, Duane Andre (Lex) 110 Chestnut Ct, Berea KY 40403 **Dio Lexington Lexington KY 2010-** B Cherokee OK 4/18/1957 s Norval Duane Smith & Nedra Jane. BA Wm Penn Coll 1980; MDiv Earlham Sch of Rel 1983; PhD Harv 1994. D 1/18/2009 P 8/19/2009 Bp Stacy F Sauls. c 2. duane_smith@berea.edu

SMITH, Edward Daniel (Mo) 1210 Locust St, Saint Louis MO 63103 **Cn to the Ordnry Dio Missouri S Louis MO 2003-** B Jacksonville FL 1/23/1956 s Willard Tonkin Smith & Gertrude Agnes. BA U of Cntrl Florida 1978; MDiv Nash 1981; DMin SWTS 2001. D 6/21/1981 P 1/1/1982 Bp William Hopkins Folwell. m 7/1/1978 Evelyn M Hallecks c 2. R S Tim's Epis Ch W Des Moines IA 1996-2002; R S Chris's Ch Kailua HI 1988-1996; S Matt's Epis Ch Orlando FL 1987-1988; Emm Ch Orlando FL 1982-1986; Cur S Sebastian's By The Sea Melbourne Bch FL 1981-1982. edsmith@diocesemo.org

SMITH, Edwin Ball (FdL) 1060 S Westhaven Dr, Oshkosh WI 54904 **Int R S Thos Ch Menasha WI 2009-; Dioc Yth Dir Dio Fond du Lac Appleton WI 1984-** B Milwaukee WI 8/17/1937 s Alanson Follansbee Smith & Mary Lois. BS Carroll Coll 1961; Indiana U 1961; PhD Kent St U 1965; DMin GTF 2000;

S

EdD GTF 2007. D 10/18/1983 Bp William L Stevens P 9/1/1996 Bp Russell Edward Jacobus. m 8/27/1960 Joan Williamson. Int S Thos Ch Menasha WI 2001-2002; Int S Anne's Ch De Pere WI 2000-2001; Int Trin Epis Ch Oshkosh WI 1997-1998; Asst All SS Epis Ch Appleton WI 1986-1996; Asst Trin Epis Ch Oshkosh WI 1983-1986. smithed@vbe.com

SMITH, Edwin Earl St Clair (Pa) 154 Locksley Rd, Glen Mills PA 19342 B Chicago IL 4/4/1930 s Neal Dow Smith & Mary Ella. BS U IL 1953; BD SWTS 1956; MA Marq 1970; STM SWTS 1970. D 6/18/1956 Bp Charles L Street P 12/21/1956 Bp Gerald Francis Burrill. m 1/25/1958 Alma Franze. P-in-c Calv Epis Ch Nthrn Liberty Philadelphia PA 1997; R S Mk's Ch Wilmington NC 1991-1997; S Mary Epis Ch Chester PA 1989-1990; S Andr's Ch Bronx NY 1986-1988; Assoc R The Afr Epis Ch Of S Thos Philadelphia PA 1984-1986; Dio Pennsylvania Philadelphia PA 1979-1984; Vic S Monica's Ch Stuart FL 1974-1978; Cn/Urban Vic All SS' Cathd Milwaukee WI 1969-1972; R S Cyp's Ch San Francisco CA 1966-1969; Cur S Jas' Epis Ch Baltimore MD 1957-1958; Cur Ch Of S Thos Chicago IL 1956-1957. Auth, "Living Ch". Soc Of S Jn The Evang. frsmith1@aol.com

SMITH JR, Elton Osman (WNY) 4101 Cathedral Ave Nw Apt 817, Washington DC 20016 B Springfield MO 6/13/1929 s Elton Osman Smith & Mary Elizabeth. BA Drury U 1950; Bossey Ecum Inst 1955; MDiv GTS 1956; STUSo 1961; VTS 1982. D 6/21/1956 P 12/22/1956 Bp Edward Randolph Welles II. Asst S Jas Ch Potomac MD 2005-2011; Cathd of St Ptr & St Paul Washington DC 1994; Dn S Paul's Cathd Buffalo NY 1968-1994; R S Paul's Epis Ch Lees Summit MO 1959-1962; Vic S Paul's Epis Ch Lees Summit MO 1956-1958. Co-Ed, *Manual for Everymem Canvasses*. Doctor of Div inity D.D. Drury U 1999; Doctor of Laws LL.D D'Youville Coll, Buffalo, N.Y. 1994; DD D.D. GTS 1981. eosmithdc@aol.com

SMITH, Eugene Glass (CPa) Po Box 3227, Lancaster PA 17604 B Lancaster PA 10/4/1931 s I(ra) Eugene Smith & Helen. BA Franklin & Marshall Coll 1955; EDS 1958. D 6/14/1958 Bp Earl M Honaman P 12/1/1958 Bp John T Heistand. Asst S Thos Ch Lancaster PA 1966-1968; Vic Chr Ch Milton PA 1962-1965; Vic St Jas Epis Ch Muncy PA 1962-1965; Trin Ch Renovo PA 1959-1962. Hon Asst R S Thos' Lancaster PA 1966. eugenegs@msn.com

SMITH, Frank Arnold (SeFla) 1123 Sandbar Ct, Chapin SC 29036 **Died 9/20/2009** B Flint,MI 6/16/1931 s George Dewey Smith & Grace. BA Bob Jones U 1953; BD Berkeley Bapt TS 1960; CDSP 1962. D 10/1/1961 P 12/1/1961 Bp George Richard Millard. c 3. fsmith57@sc.rr.com

SMITH JR, Frank Warner (Neb) 2303 Elk, Beatrice NE 68310 **D Chr Ch Epis Beatrice NE 1999-** B Omaha NE 5/5/1922 s Frank Warner Smith & Donna. BS U of Nebraska 1948. D 8/10/1999 Bp James Edward Krotz. m 12/2/1946 Verna Julene Vickers. fwsmith@beatricene.com

SMITH, Gail Sampson (Mass) 35 Skyline drive, Chatham MA 02633 **Asst S Chris's Ch Chatham MA 2007-** B Buffalo NY 1/11/1949 d Elmer Bailey Sampson & Mary Lucille. BA Towson U 1985; MDiv VTS 1993. D 6/12/1993 Bp A(lbert) Theodore Eastman P 5/14/1994 Bp Charles Lindsay Longest. m 6/1/1968 David Martin Smith c 2. S Jn's Ch Ellicott City MD 1993-1999. caperev@aol.com

SMITH, Gary Miles (WNC) 321 N. Cedar St., Lincolnton NC 28092 **R S Lk's Epis Ch Lincolnton NC 2008-** B Charlotte NC 3/14/1956 s Herman Miles Smith & Connie Ruth. BA Duke 1978; MDiv Duke DS 1981. D 6/4/2001 P 4/27/2002 Bp Robert Hodges Johnson. c 1. Cur S Mary's Ch Asheville NC 2002-2003. gmilessmith@charter.net

SMITH, Geoffrey T (Mass) 1 Old Colony Road, Hull MA 02045 **Archd Dio Massachusetts Boston MA 2011-; Archd, Deploy and Pstr Care Dio Massachusetts Boston MA 2011-; D Old No Chr Ch Boston MA 2008-** B New Britain CT 8/4/1956 s Leander Willis Smith & Beverly Ann. BA U of Connecticut 1978; MBA DePaul U 1981; Sch for Deacons 1996. D 2/3/1996 Bp Frank Tracy Griswold III. m 10/6/1979 Gerri Lynn Hibbard c 2. D Trin Epis Ch Portland ME 2003-2008; D Cathd Of S Jas Chicago IL 2000-2002; D S Greg's Epis Ch Deerfield IL 1996-2000. Recognition in the Tradition of St. Steph No Amer Assn of the Diac 2007. geoffrey.smith@ironmountain.com

SMITH III, George Dresser (Chi) 792 Forest Ave, Glen Ellyn IL 60137 **Bd Dir Epis Chars And Cmnty Serv (Eccs) Chicago IL 2009-; COM Dio Chicago Chicago IL 2008-; S Mk's Epis Ch Glen Ellyn IL 2006-** B Chicago IL 4/4/1963 s George Dresser Smith & Rosemarie Knuti. BA Wesl 1985; MBA NWU 1992; MDiv SWTS 2003. D 6/21/2003 P 12/20/2003 Bp William Dailey Persell. m 6/29/1991 Cecilia L Smith c 3. Chr Ch Winnetka IL 2003-2006. georgedsmith@yahoo.com

SMITH, George Joel (SVa) 76 Wilson Farm Rd, Keysville VA 23947 **Died 12/15/2010** B Denver CO 2/21/1929 s Carl E Smith & Gertrude F. BA Colorado Coll 1951; CDSP 1954. D 6/12/1954 P 12/12/1954 Bp Arthur Kinsolving. c 3. smisimp@msinets.com

✠ **SMITH, Rt Rev George Wayne** (Mo) 823 Carillon Ct, Saint Louis MO 63141 **Bp Dio Missouri S Louis MO 2002-** B Abilene TX 1/29/1955 s George Taylor Smith & Hilda. BA Baylor U 1975; MA Baylor U 1978; MDiv Nash 1981; MDiv STUSo 1993. D 6/12/1981 P 6/11/1982 Bp Sam Byron Hulsey Con 3/2/2002 for Mo. m 5/21/1977 Debra Lynn Morris c 3. R S Andr's Ch Des Moines IA 1989-2002; R Emm Ch Hastings MI 1983-1989; Vic The Epis Ch Of The Gd Shpd Brownfield TX 1981-1983; Dio NW Texas Lubbock TX 1981; S Chris's Epis Ch Lubbock TX 1981. Auth, "Admirable Simplicity," Ch Pub Inc, 1996. dlmsmith@gmail.com

SMITH, Glenn Colyer (Chi) 754 Main St, Islip NY 11751 B Oak Park IL 9/12/1924 s Frank Earnest Smith & Ada Maryann. AA Evanston Coll Inst Evanston IL 1948; BD Loyola U 1951; MS CUA 1955; MDiv CUA 1955; DMin Trin Evang DS Deerfield IL 1981. D 6/18/1971 Bp Gerald Francis Burrill P 2/15/1972 Bp James Winchester Montgomery. Asst Emm Epis Ch Rockford IL 1986-1994; R Ch Of S Jn Chrys Delafield WI 1972-1978; Cur S Dav's Epis Ch Aurora IL 1971-1972. Auth, "Cath Pastors Manual For Evang," Tyndall Hse; Auth, "Evang In The 80s," Tyndall Hse; Auth, "Evangelizing Adults," Tyndall Hse; Auth, "Evangelizing Yth," Tyndall Hse; Auth, "Evangelizing Blacks," Tyndall Hse; Ed, "Cath Living Bible," Tyndall Hse; Auth, "11 Manuals For Evang," Apostolic Mininstries.

SMITH, Graham Michael (Chi) 1105 Shermer Rd, Glenview IL 60025 B Winnipeg MT CA 5/24/1948 s Norman Obed Smith & Ann Marie. BA Ford 1970; MDiv EDS 1974; DMin VTS 1997. D 6/8/1974 Bp Paul Moore Jr P 1/25/1975 Bp Harold Louis Wright. m 5/5/1973 Sharon Lee c 1. R S Dav's Ch Glenview IL 1992-2011; R Ch Of The Gd Shpd Beachwood OH 1977-1992; Asst S Ptr's Epis Ch Lakewood OH 1974-1977. sherryngraham@gmail.com

SMITH, Gregory (Pa) 5421 Germantown Ave, Philadelphia PA 19144 **S Lk's Ch Philadelphia PA 1997-** B Chicago IL 12/7/1951 s Harold Smith & Mable Lee. BS Bradley U 1974. D 6/14/1980 Bp Quintin Ebenezer Primo Jr P 12/1/1980 Bp James Winchester Montgomery. R Ch Of The H Redeem Denver CO 1993-1997; Vic S Tim's Decatur GA 1990-1993; R S Lk And S Simon Cyrene Rochester NY 1985-1990; Ch Of The H Cross Chicago IL 1981-1985; Asst S Edm's Epis Ch Chicago IL 1980. sacerdos1@aol.com

SMITH, Gregory Louis (SC) 314 Grove Street, Charleston SC 29403 **D S Steph's Epis Ch Charleston SC 2007-** B Denver CO 5/1/1947 s Robert Smith & Janet. BS Colorado St U 1970. D 9/4/1999 Bp Edward Lloyd Salmon Jr. m 5/14/2011 Marilyn Smith c 2. D Old S Andr's Par Ch Charleston SC 2004-2007; D Epis Ch of the Gd Shpd Charleston SC 1999-2004. gregorylouissmith@yahoo.com

SMITH, Gregory Michael (SC) 171 Moultrie St, MSC #3, Charleston SC 29409 **Ch Of The H Cross Sullivans Island SC 2008-** B Dayton OH 1/12/1972 s Franklin Smith & Freda Marlaine. BMus Wheaton Coll 1995; MDiv TESM 2000. Trans from L'Eglise Episcopal au Rwanda 8/14/2008 as Deacon Bp Mark Joseph Lawrence. m 5/13/1995 Anna Goodwin. Lead Pstr Cmnty At The Well Dio Colorado Denver CO 2000-2008. greg@ionanet.org

SMITH, H Alan (CNY) 2891 Oran Delphi Rd, Manlius NY 13104 B 6/10/1940 BA Hob 1964; STB PDS 1969. D 6/7/1969 Bp William Elwood Sterling P 12/1/1969 Bp John Harris Burt. m 6/28/1969 Louise Harrington Smith. Archd And Cn To The Ordnry Dio Cntrl New York Syracuse NY 1988-2004; S Paul's Ch Watertown NY 1979-1987; S Andr's Ch New Berlin NY 1971-1979; S Matt's Ch So New Berlin NY 1971-1979; Cur S Chris's By-The River Gates Mills OH 1969-1971. hsmith@twcny.rr.com

SMITH JR, Harmon Lee (NC) 3510 Randolph Rd, Durham NC 27705 **Vic S Mk's Epis Ch Roxboro NC 1992-; P Assoc S Phil's Ch Durham NC 1985-** B Ellisville MS 8/23/1930 s Harmon L Smith & Mary Magdalen. BA Millsaps Coll 1952; BD Duke 1955; PhD Duke 1962. D 2/24/1972 P 6/24/1972 Bp Thomas Augustus Fraser Jr. m 8/21/1951 Bettye Joan Watkins. Int S Tit Epis Ch Durham NC 1991-1992; Int S Tit Epis Ch Durham NC 1987-1989; LocTen S Paul's Epis Ch Smithfield NC 1983-1984; LocTen S Tit Epis Ch Durham NC 1979-1980; LocTen S Tit Epis Ch Durham NC 1974-1975. Auth, *Where Two or Three are Gathered: Liturg & the Moral Life*, Pilgrim, 1995; Auth, *Profsnl Ethics and Primary Care Med*, Duke, 1986; Auth, *The Promiscuous Teenager*, Chas C. Thos, 1974; Auth, *Ethics and the New Med*, Abingdon, 1970; Auth, *The Chr and his Decisions*, Abingdon, 1969; Auth, *Var arts*. Amer Assn of Theol Schools - Fell 1968; Cooper Fndt for Neurologic Resrch and Educ - Fello 1968; Gurney Harris Kearns Fndt - Fell 1961; Lilly Fndt - Fell 1959; Mary Duke Biddle Fndt - Fell 1967; Natl Hmnts Cntr - Fell 1982; S Barn' Hosp - The Bronx, NY - Resrch Fell 1973. DSA of Merit Amer Heart Assn 1980. orare@aol.com

SMITH, Harold Vaughn (Ind) 8328 Hawes Ct, Indianapolis IN 46256 B Muncie IN 2/25/1935 s Norman Henry Smith & Beatrice Evelyn. BD Ball St U Teachers Coll 1962; MA Ball St U 1966; Estrn Kentucky U 1979; DMus Ball St U 1981; MDiv Epis TS In Kentucky 1987. D 7/13/1988 P 2/18/1989 Bp James Daniel Warner. m 6/26/1976 Christine M Moore c 2. P-in-c Trin Ch Connersville IN 2004-2008; Vic S Ptr's Ch Lebanon IN 1995-2003; R All SS Epis Ch Torrington WY 1991-1995; Vic S Mk's Ch Creighton NE 1988-1991; Vic S Ptr's Ch Neligh NE 1988-1991. Bd Trsts Hse of Trsfg Bayard NE 1992-1995; Lions Intl 1998-2007; Mssn Strtgy Com 1998-2009; Proj Help 1995-2003. episcoman@comcast.net

SMITH, Hilary Borbon (Va) 213 Banbury Ter, Winchester VA 22601 **R S Paul's On-The-Hill Winchester VA 2003-** B Washington DC 2/21/1968 d David Henry Smith & Rosemary. BA U Rich 1990; MA U of Leicester 1993;

S

PhD U of Virginia 1997; MDiv VTS 2000. D 6/24/2000 P 2/6/2001 Bp Peter James Lee. Assoc R Ch Of S Jas The Less Ashland VA 2002-2003; Asst R S Paul's Ch Richmond VA 2000-2002. hilary@spoth.org

SMITH, H Mark (Mass) 10 Linda Lane, #2-8, Dorchester MA 02125 **D S Jn's Epis Ch Holbrook MA 2011-; D, Yth Mnstrs Off Dio Massachusetts Boston MA 2010-** B Bellefonte PA 7/18/1956 s Mearle Smith & Trudie. BA Buc 1978; MA Emerson Coll 1985. D 6/3/2006 Bp M(arvil) Thomas Shaw III. D, Boston Chinese Mnstry Dio Massachusetts Boston MA 2006-2010. mark@hmarksmith.com

SMITH, Howard Louis (Alb) 970 State St., Schenectady NY 12307 **D Chr Ch Schenectady NY 2008-** B Derby CT 11/10/1972 s Leroy Smith & Beverly Rose. AA Hudson Vlly Cmnty Coll 1992. D 5/10/2008 Bp William Howard Love. m 10/4/1997 Sheila Ellison c 3. smith4jc@yahoo.com

SMITH, Jacob Andrew (NY) St Georges Episcopal Church, 209 E 16th St, New York NY 10003 **Calv and St Geo New York NY 2007-** B Monument UT 5/8/1976 s David Claire Smith & Mary Jo. BA U of Arizona 2000; MDiv TESM 2006. D 6/4/2006 Bp James Robert Mathes P 12/2/2006 Bp E(gbert) Don Taylor. m 8/4/2001 Melina Luna Smith c 2. revjacob@gmail.com

SMITH, Jacqueline Kay (Oly) 6208 83rd St Sw, Lakewood WA 98499 B Hemet CA 9/20/1933 d Raymond Selvester Smith & Ruby Olive. California St U; Heritage U; U of Puget Sound; U of San Diego; BA USC 1954; MA USC 1961; Spec Ed Credentia U CA 1976. D 6/25/2005 Bp Vincent Waydell Warner. c 3. jacqsmith@comcast.net

SMITH, James Albert (Az) 29305 N 146th St, Scottsdale AZ 85262 B 11/17/1925 D 10/5/2002 Bp Robert Reed Shahan. m 12/29/1995 Laura Lang c 2.

SMITH, James Clare (Be) 302 Pine St, Ashland PA 17921 **R H Apos Frackville PA 2000-; P No Par Epis Ch Frackville PA 1999-** B Reading PA 9/15/1932 s Dorothy Keebs. D 9/25/1999 P 3/15/2000 Bp Paul Victor Marshall. m 11/11/1955 Lois Joan Batdorf.

SMITH, James Drinard (SVa) 3235 Sherwood Ridge Dr, Powhatan VA 23139 **Consult COM Dio SW Virginia Roanoke VA 1992-; Happ Sprtl Advsr Dio SW Virginia Roanoke VA 1992-; Chair Evang Cmsn Dio SW Virginia Roanoke VA 1990-; Curs Sprtl Advsr Dio SW Virginia Roanoke VA 1990-; Cmsn Alco & Drug Abuse Dio SW Virginia Roanoke VA 1989-; Educ Consortium Dio SW Virginia Roanoke VA 1989-; Media Consult Dio SW Virginia Roanoke VA 1986-** B Richmond VA 9/5/1936 s George Wilson Smith & Elizabeth Virginia. BA U Rich 1959; BD VTS 1962; MDiv VTS 1970; Fell Coll of Preachers, Natl Cathd 1971; VTS 1984; EFM STUSo 2001. D 6/9/1962 P 6/1/1963 Bp Robert Fisher Gibson Jr. m 6/9/1959 Geraldine Hoffman c 1. R Chr Ch Amelia Crt Hse VA 1997-2003; R Emm Epis Ch Powhatan VA 1997-2003; R S Jas Ch Cartersville VA 1997-2003; Dn So Richmond Convoc Dio Sthrn Virginia Norfolk VA 1997-1999; Dio SW Virginia Roanoke VA 1992-1996; Prog Com Dio SW Virginia Roanoke VA 1990-1995; Exec Bd Dio SW Virginia Roanoke VA 1990-1994; R S Eliz's Ch Roanoke VA 1989-1997; Int S Steph's Epis Ch Forest VA 1989; Int S Thos' Epis Ch Abingdon VA 1987-1989; Yth Task Grp Dio SW Virginia Roanoke VA 1986-1988; Int S Jas Ch Roanoke VA 1986-1987; Int Gr Ch Lewiston Woodville NC 1985-1986; Int S Mk's Ch Rich Sq NC 1985-1986; Dn Dio Sthrn Virginia Norfolk VA 1984-1985; ExCoun Dio SW Virginia Roanoke VA 1984-1985; Prog Design Team Dio Sthrn Virginia Norfolk VA 1981-1985; Cmsn on Alco Use and Abuse Dio Sthrn Virginia Norfolk VA 1980-1985; Cmsn on Alco Use and Abuse Dio Sthrn Virginia Norfolk VA 1980-1985; Curs Sprtl Advsr Dio Sthrn Virginia Norfolk VA 1976-1979; Inst Ldr Dio Sthrn Virginia Norfolk VA 1975-1976; R S Chris's Epis Ch Portsmouth VA 1974-1985; Cn Asst Cathd Of S Paul Erie PA 1970-1974; Yth Cmsn Dio NW Pennsylvania Erie PA 1970-1974; Assoc Trin Ch Manassas VA 1968-1970; DeptCE Dio Virginia Richmond VA 1966-1970; R Chr Epis Ch Luray VA 1962-1968. SWECA 1989-1990. Personalities of the So 1975; Who's Who in Rel 1975. jdpsmith@worldnet.att.net

SMITH JR, James Owen (EC) 113 S Woodlawn Ave, Greenville NC 27858 B Bessemer AL 11/21/1949 s James Owen Smith & Mary Jo. Auburn U 1970; BS U of Alabama 1973; MA U of Mississippi 1975; PhD U of Mississippi 1980. D 2/11/1988 Bp Brice Sidney Sanders. m 8/10/1974 Sylvia Dianne Hughes c 1.

SMITH, James Ross (NY) 145 W 46th St #4, New York NY 10036 **Cur Ch Of S Mary The Vrgn New York NY 2007-** B North Tonawanda NY 1/31/1951 s William Marion Smith & Ann Winifred. BA Cor 1973; MFA Cor 1977; MDiv UTS 1987; STM Ya Berk 1989; M.Phil. Ya 1993. D 6/10/1989 Bp Paul Moore Jr P 12/9/1989 Bp Richard Frank Grein. m Jose Vidal. Asstg P Ch Of S Mary The Vrgn New York NY 2004-2007; Asst Ch Of S Mary The Vrgn New York NY 2001-2003; Asstg P Ch Of S Mary The Vrgn New York NY 1998-1999; Asstg P Chr Ch New Haven CT 1989-1996. ECF Fllshp. Fell ECF 1989. jrs451@gmail.com

SMITH, Jane Carol (Mont) 412 10th Ave N, Lewistown MT 59457 **Died 11/28/2010** B Kansas City MO 6/21/1944 d Allen Dale Smith & Beverly Jane. BA U of Missouri 1982; MDiv SWTS 2001. Trans 8/29/2003 Bp William Edward Smalley. c 4. the4wind@gmail.com

SMITH, Jane Gravlee (WNC) 40 Wildwood Ave., Asheville NC 28804 B Birmingham AL 12/23/1936 d William Lafayette Gravlee & Lula Bronson. BS Wstrn Carolina U 1977; MDiv STUSo 1994. D 6/5/1994 P 12/10/1994 Bp Robert Hodges Johnson. c 1. Int S Jn's Ch Asheville NC 2006-2007; Cn to the Ordnry Dio Wstrn No Carolina Asheville NC 2001-2005; The TS at The U So Sewanee TN 1998-2000; Dio Wstrn No Carolina Asheville NC 1994-2005; Gr Ch Asheville NC 1994-2001. S Mary's Cnvnt Sewanee. therevsmith@charter.net

SMITH, Jean (NJ) 58 Jenny Ln, Brattleboro VT 05301 **Assoc S Mich's Epis Ch Brattleboro VT 2008-** B Saint Louis MO 12/23/1942 d John Bryant Reinhart & Helen Elizabeth. BS NWU 1964; MDiv CDSP 1980; Doctor of Div. CDSP 1995. D 6/28/1980 Bp William Edwin Swing P 5/1/1981 Bp George Phelps Mellick Belshaw. m 6/15/1964 Peter T Smith c 2. Exec Dir Seamens Ch Inst Income New York NY 2003-2007; Dir Of Seafarers' Serv Seamens Ch Inst Income New York NY 1990-1995; Trin Ch Princeton NJ 1980-1990. DD CDSP 1998. revjrsmith@comcast.net

SMITH, Jean Ann (Ind) 6033 Gladden Dr, Indianapolis IN 46220 **P S Alb's Ch Indianapolis IN 1998-** B Indianapolis IN 9/14/1943 d William Eugene McAnulty & Ann Lyde. BA Butler U 1965; MDiv Chr TS 1999. D 6/24/1997 Bp Edward Witker Jones P 7/5/1998 Bp Catherine Elizabeth Maples Waynick. Theta Phi Chr TS 1997. smithj@lei.org

SMITH, Jeffry Bradford (EpisSanJ) 10 St Theresa'S Avenue, W Roxbury MA 02132 Great Britain (UK) B Inglewood CA 1/15/1956 s Roger Lewis Smith & Marguerite Elizabeth. Ripon Coll Cuddesdon Oxford Gb; BA Pitzer Coll 1982; MDiv CDSP 1985. D 2/22/1986 P 4/1/1987 Bp Victor Manuel Rivera. m 12/10/1977 Barbara H Smith. S Paul's Epis Ch Visalia CA 1986.

SMITH, Jerry W (Tenn) 4800 Belmont Park Ter, Nashville TN 37215 **R S Barth's Ch Bristol TN 2005-** B Bracebridge Ontario CA 9/22/1951 s Clarence Smith & Elaine. BA U of Wstrn Ontario 1973; MDiv Hur 1976; DMin Trin Evang DS Deerfield IL 1995; Med Nipissing U No Bay ON CA 2002. Trans from Anglican Church of Canada 1/1/2005 Bp Bertram Nelson Herlong. m 8/18/1973 Marjorie Ellen Aldom c 3. jerrysmith@stbs.net

SMITH, Jesse George (FtW) 2825 Winterhaven Dr, Hurst TX 76054 **Chapl Baylor All SS Med Cntr Ft Worth TX 2005-** B Poolville TX 1/3/1932 s Burcus Edward Smith & Stella. BA Baylor U 1953; BS U of New Mex 1960; MDiv Nash 1987. D 12/23/1987 P 6/23/1988 Bp Clarence Cullam Pope Jr. m 5/30/1953 Betty Jean Stuart c 3. Int S Mich's Ch Richland Hills Richland Hills TX 2000-2001; Asst S Mart In The Fields Ch Keller TX 1997-2000; R S Lk's In The Meadow Epis Ch Ft Worth TX 1995-1997; S Anth's Ch Alvarado TX 1993-1995; Dio Ft Worth Ft Worth TX 1992; Assoc R S Steph's Epis Ch Hurst TX 1988-1991; St Stephens Ch Hurst TX 1988-1991. jsmith1056@aol.com

SMITH IV, Jess Wayne (Nev) 33 Wind Ridge Rd, Laramie WY 82070 **P S Mary's Ch Winnemucca NV 1997-** B Denver CO 3/10/1947 s Jess Wayne Smith & Virginia Olive. Colorado Sch of Mines 1970. D 6/3/1997 P 12/1/1997 Bp Stewart Clark Zabriskie. m 7/26/1969 Leigh Ann Wailes.

SMITH, Jethro Larrie (At) 46 S Main St, Wadley GA 30477 B Millen GA 1/12/1944 s Elder Edgar Cecil Smith & Ethel Pauline. BBA Georgia St U 1969; MDiv VTS 1973; Franciscan U of Steubenville 1981; U So 1981; Sch Pstr Care 1983. D 12/19/1973 Bp Bennett Jones Sims P 6/1/1974 Bp R(aymond) Stewart Wood Jr. m 11/8/2003 Janet Clifon c 2. R S Jn's W Point GA 1977-2006; S Jn's W Point GA 1975-2006; Asst S Mich And All Ang Ch Stone Mtn GA 1974-1975. jlarrie@mindspring.com

SMITH JR, J Hamilton (SC) c/o Church of the Holy Comforter, PO Box 338, Sumter SC 29151 **Ch Of The H Comf Sumter SC 2009-; S Mich's Epis Ch Charleston SC 2009-** B Charleston SC 10/16/1975 s John Hamilton Smith & Ellen Walker. BA Coll of Charleston 1998; JD U of So Carolina 2001; BTh Oxf 2006. D 7/1/2006 P 1/27/2007 Bp Edward Lloyd Salmon Jr. m 5/18/2001 Elizabeth Oakes c 2. hamandlizzie@aol.com

SMITH, J Harmon (SVa) 2228 Karen Dr, Salem VA 24153 **Cur S Paul's Epis Ch Salem VA 2003-** B Newport News VA 11/9/1924 s Charles Christian Smith & Susie Harmon. BS VPI 1948; BD Epis TS In Kentucky 1960. D 6/8/1960 P 12/17/1960 Bp William R Moody. c 2. Trin Ch Shepherdstown WV 1999-2006; Emm Ch Glenmore Buckingham VA 1986-1989; Emm Ch Scottsville VA 1976-1989; R S Anne's Ch Appomattox VA 1976-1989; Dio Sthrn Virginia Norfolk VA 1976-1978; Vic Hickory Neck Ch Toano VA 1969-1975; Vic Dio SE Florida Miami FL 1966-1967; Vic Iglesia Epis Espiritu Santo Tela HN 1962-1965; Vic Ch S Mich The Archangel Lexington KY 1960-1962. hsmith1018@aol.com

SMITH, Joan Addison (Ky) 3232 Running Deer Cir, Louisville KY 40241 **Cn to the Ordnry Dio Kentucky Louisville KY 2007-** B Beckley WV 9/18/1948 d John Wesley Smith & Dorothy Claire. BA Randolph-Macon Wmn's Coll 1971; MDiv VTS 1971. D 6/2/1982 P 6/1/1983 Bp Robert Poland Atkinson. S Paul's Ch Henderson KY 2006-2007; S Phil's Ch Harrodsburg KY 2004-2005; Ch Of The Adv Louisville KY 2003-2004; Int S Paul's Ch Louisville KY 2002-2003; Int S Raphael's Ch Lexington KY 2000-2002; Int Ch Of The Gd Shpd Lexington KY 1999-2000; Trin Epis Ch Danville KY 1999; Int Ch Of

The Nativ Maysville KY 1998-1999; Ch S Mich The Archangel Lexington KY 1998-1999; Assoc The Ch of the Redeem Cincinnati OH 1990-1995; P-in-c S Pat's Epis Ch Lebanon OH 1987-1990; Epis Soc Of Chr Ch Cincinnati OH 1983-1987; Asst Epis Soc of Chr Ch Cincinnati OH 1983-1987; Dio W Virginia Charleston WV 1982-1983; D Trin Ch Huntington WV 1982-1983; Trst VTS Alexandria VA 1981-1985. jasmith2@ix.netcom.com

SMITH, Joan Barr (Chi) St Mark's Episcopal Church, 1509 Ridge Ave, Evanston IL 60201 B Chicago IL 9/22/1939 d James Carson Worthy & Mildred Leritz. BA Syr 1961; MM Kellogg Grad Sch of Mgmt 1996; D Sch of Dio Chicago 2007. D 1/19/2008 Bp Victor Alfonso Scantlebury. m 10/9/2005 Wayne Smith c 2. joanbarr@aol.com

SMITH, John Cutrer (NY) 45 E 85th St, New York NY 10028 B Clarksdale MS 1/13/1924 s Edward White Smith & Blanche. U of Virginia 1948; STB GTS 1954; Cert Amer Fndt of Rel & Psych 1958; STM UTS 1962. D 6/4/1954 Bp Frederick D Goodwin P 12/18/1954 Bp James P De Wolfe. Asst S Ann And The H Trin Brooklyn NY 1958-1959; Cur S Ann And The H Trin Brooklyn NY 1954-1957. AAPC.

SMITH JR, J(ohn) Elton (Mont) 3400 S Hillcrest Dr, Butte MT 59701 **R S Jn's Ch Butte MT 2005-** B Savannah GA 6/12/1960 s John Elton Smith & Gussie Mae. BA scl Troy St U-Troy AL 1981; JD U of Alabama 1985; MA Tul 1987; MDiv cl Nash 1994. D 9/30/1994 Bp Russell Edward Jacobus P 4/8/1995 Bp Dorsey Felix Henderson. m 4/29/1995 Sutton Cecil c 1. Cmsn On Dom Violence Dio Newark Newark NJ 2001-2005; C & C Com Dio Newark Newark NJ 2000-2005; Dio Newark Newark NJ 2000; R Gr Epis Ch Westwood NJ 1999-2005; R All SS Epis Ch Clinton SC 1995-1999. "Wm of Occam," "encyclopedia article," *Encyclopedia of Theologians*, Blackwell's, 2009; "Congregationalists," "encyclopedia article," *Encyclopedia of the Early Republic and Antebellum Amer*, M.E. Sharpe, 2009; "Quakers," "encyclopedia article," *Encyclopedia of the Early Republic and Antebellum Amer*, M.E. Sharpe, 2009; "Episcopalians," "encyclopedia article," *Encyclopedia of the Early Republic and Antebellum Amer*, M.E. Sharpe, 2009; "Temperance Mvmt in Great, "encyclopedia article," *Wrld Hist Encyclopedia*, ABC-CLIO (electronic Pub first), 2009. fatherelton@qwestoffice.net

SMITH, John Ferris (Mass) Box 3064, Wellfleet MA 02667 **P-in-c Chap Of S Jas The Fisherman Wellfleet MA 2000-** B Flint MI 11/20/1934 s Joseph Smith & Agnes. BA U MI 1956; MDiv EDS 1959. D 6/27/1959 Bp Archie H Crowley P 1/21/1960 Bp Richard S M Emrich. c 2. Chapl S Jn's Chap Groton MA 1978-2000; Chapl Dio Massachusetts Boston MA 1961-1978; Cur S Chris-S Paul Epis Ch Detroit MI 1959-1961. Auth, "Cycle of Pryr for Epis Schools, 2nd Ed," NAES, 2008; Auth, *Living Forw: Reflections on Reaching A Certain Age*, Sorin Books, 2003; Auth, *Raising a Gd Kid*, Sorin Books, 2002; Auth, "Cycle of Pryr," *NAES*, NAES, 1991; Auth, *The Bush Still Burns*, Sheed Andrews and McMeel, 1978. jacksmith7@comcast.net

✠ **SMITH, Rt Rev John H(enry)** (Me) 42 Signature Drive, Brunswick ME 04011 B Panama City PA 9/11/1939 s John Robert Smith & Elsie Bertha. BA Cor 1961; STB GTS 1964; DMin Hartford Sem 1980. D 6/20/1964 Bp Anson Phelps Stokes Jr P 6/18/1965 Bp Oliver L Loring Con 6/24/1989 for WVa. m 5/30/1964 Victoria Wainright Dawley c 2. R S Ptr's Epis Ch Bridgton ME 2006-2011; The GTS New York NY 1990-1993; Bp Dio W Virginia Charleston WV 1989-1999; Trst VTS Alexandria VA 1989-1999; R Trin Ch Rutland VT 1974-1989; Dio Vermont Burlington VT 1974-1984; R S Steph's Ch Middlebury VT 1969-1974; Chapl, Hd Dept Bible Stds Natl Cathd Sch Cathd of St Ptr & St Paul Washington DC 1967-1969; Vic All SS Epis Ch Skowhegan ME 1966-1967; Vic S Mart's Epis Ch Pittsfield ME 1966-1967; Cur Epis Ch Of S Mary The Vrgn Falmouth ME 1964-1966. Auth, "Cluster Mnstry: A Faithful Response To Change," Fox Press, 1996. Hon DD GTS New York NY 1990; Hon DD VTS Alexandria VA 1990. jhsme1@aol.com

SMITH, John Moffett (Va) 1103 Fearrington Post, Pittsboro NC 27312 B Bluefield WV 4/30/1936 s Clyde Bryan Smith & Margaret. BA Duke 1959; MDiv VTS 1982. D 6/13/1962 P 12/1/1962 Bp Wilburn Camrock Campbell. m 8/18/1962 Eleanor Harrison Boothe c 3. R S Jas' Epis Ch Leesburg VA 1975-1998; Assoc Chr Ch Charlotte NC 1974-1975; Assoc Chr Ch Exeter NH 1964-1968; Asst Trin Ch Morgantown WV 1962-1964. Auth, *Upholding Mar*, 1988. eleajohn@earthlink.net

SMITH, John P (Fla) 256 E Church St, Jacksonville FL 32202 **Cn S Jn's Cathd Jacksonville FL 2008-** B Knoxville TN 10/21/1944 s John Milton Smith & Yuma Frances. BA GW 1971; MA U of Oklahoma 1977; STM VTS 2003. D 2/29/1988 Bp William Davidson P 6/25/2002 Bp Robert Wilkes Ihloff. m 12/7/1968 Eloise Penny Smith c 2. Ch Of S Marks On The Hill Pikesville MD 2004; Emm Ch Baltimore MD 2002-2004; D Cathd Of The Incarn Baltimore MD 1999-2001; Assoc S Ptr's Epis Ch Ellicott City MD 1995-1996; Int Ch Of The Ascen And S Agnes Washington DC 1993-1994; Assoc Cathd Ch Of S Mk Minneapolis MN 1989-1993; Assoc SS Martha And Mary Epis Ch Eagan MN 1988-1989. psmith@saintjohnscathedral.org

SMITH, John Peterson (WLa) 1904 Jasmine Dr, Opelousas LA 70570 **R Ch Of The Epiph Opelousas LA 1990-** B Carlsbad NM 3/3/1943 s Joe Purser Smith & Helen. BA TCU 1966; MDiv SWTS 1969. D 6/18/1969 Bp Charles A Mason P 1/1/1970 Bp William Paul Barnds. m 7/3/1966 Janice McKillop. R Gr Ch Lake Providence LA 1987-1990; R Emm Ch Lake Vill AR 870-2652230or8 1976-1987; R S Thos Ch Ennis TX 1971-1976; Cur All SS' Epis Ch Ft Worth TX 1969-1971. petesmi2000@yahoo.com

SMITH JR, John Robert (Az) 602 N Wilmot Rd, Tucson AZ 85711 **R Epis Par Of S Mich And All Ang Tucson AZ 1995-** B National City CA 1/12/1949 s John Robert Smith & Florence. BA S Thos 1971; STB Gregorian U 1974. Rec from Roman Catholic 11/1/1983 as Priest Bp Robert Hume Cochrane. m 6/26/2010 Teresa Smith c 3. COM Dio Arizona Phoenix AZ 1989-1994; R S Mich's Ch Coolidge AZ 1987-1995; Assoc S Paul's Ch Seattle WA 1983-1987. EPF; SocMary. jrsmith49@aol.com

SMITH, John Thomas (Md) 1204 Maple Ave, Annapolis MD 21401 **P-in-c S Jas Ch Payette ID 1997-** B Philadelphia PA 4/29/1942 s Arthur Smith & Laura E. BS Penn 1972; MDiv Epis TS of The SW 1996. D 12/15/1996 P 7/11/1997 Bp John Stuart Thornton. m 8/21/2010 Sue Smith c 2. R S Lk's Ch Annapolis MD 2002-2010; S Jas Ch Payette ID 1996-2002. eastportjts@gmail.com

SMITH, Joseph (USC) 101 Shelton Dr, Spartanburg SC 29307 **Dioc Exec Com Dio Upper So Carolina Columbia SC 2009-; Vic S Chris's Ch Spartanburg SC 2009-** B Columbia SC 5/18/1965 s Robert Mccurdy Smith & Margaret Lang. BA Coll of Charleston 1987; MDiv TS 2007. D 5/26/2007 P 2/2/2008 Bp Dorsey Felix Henderson. m 7/2/1998 Sharon B Baer c 3. Bp's Transiton Com Dio Upper So Carolina Columbia SC 2009-2010; Eccl Crt Dio Upper So Carolina Columbia SC 2008-2009; Asst S Matt's Epis Ch Spartanburg SC 2007-2008; Yth Dir S Jn's Epis Ch Columbia SC 1993-2004. jks@stchrisonline.org

SMITH III, J(oseph) Wesley (At) 210 Willie Six Road, Sewanee TN 37375 B Savannah GA 3/29/1953 s Joseph Wallace Smith & Velma. BA Trevecca Nazarene U 1975; MDiv Van 1985; DMin STUSo 2004. D 12/19/1998 Bp Vincent Waydell Warner P 6/19/1999 Bp Sanford Zangwill Kaye Hampton. m 6/21/1996 Shirley Kristina Lanz c 3. S Mk's Epis Ch Lagrange GA 2009; Chr Ch Macon GA 2003-2009; S Dav's Epis Ch Topeka KS 2000-2003; Off Of Bsh For ArmdF New York NY 1999-2000. OSL the Physcn 2000. Bronze Star US Army. weschat@gmail.com

SMITH, Kent Clarke (Ct) 112 Sconset Ln, Guilford CT 06437 **P Affiliate Chr Ch New Haven CT 2004-; Mem, Bd Managers, Ch Missions Pub Corpo Dio Connecticut Hartford CT 2004-; Archv Com Dio Connecticut Hartford CT 1995-** B Teaneck NJ 8/18/1937 s William Hewlett Smith & Dorothy Elizabeth. AB Pr 1959; MA Ya 1961; PhD Ya 1970; Cert EDS 1982. D 6/9/1984 P 4/13/1985 Bp Arthur Edward Walmsley. m 3/21/1970 Margaret Charlotte ZLouise Williams c 2. Coordntr, D Trng Prog Dio Connecticut Hartford CT 1999-2005; Com Pstr Oversight & Exam Of Dioc Com Dio Connecticut Hartford CT 1989-1995; Exec Coun Dio Connecticut Hartford CT 1989-1992; R Chr Ch Redding Ridge CT 1986-2003; Excoun Dio Connecticut Hartford CT 1986-1992; Cur Trin Ch Newtown CT 1984-1986. Auth, "arts & Revs In Chinese Hist". The Fllshp of S Jn 1985. Phi Beta Kappa 1959. kcsp59@att.net

SMITH, Kermit Wade (WMo) Po Box 634, Kimberling City MO 65686 B Bedford OH 5/28/1932 s Reuben Caven Smith & Blanche Marie. BA SMU 1953; MTh SMU 1956. D 12/18/1966 P 7/3/1968 Bp Chilton Powell. m 6/2/1979 Lilly Mae Louise Bruno c 2. Vic S Mk's Epis Ch Kimberling City MO 2000-2007; Chapl Samar Hlth Serv Corvallis OR 1987-1997; Chapl Resrch & Med Cntr Kansas City MO 1970-1980; Asst S Andr's Epis Ch Lawton OK 1966-1968. (Clergycompanion) Worker Sis/Brothers Of The H Sprt 1975; Assn Of Profsnl Chapl 1969. The Bp's Shield Dio W Missouri 2009. padrek@centurytel.net

SMITH, Kerry Jon (Md) 6097 Franklin Gibson Rd, Tracys Landing MD 20779 **Archd S Jas' Par Lothian MD 2011-; Archd Dio Maryland Baltimore MD 2006-** B Brockton MA 7/15/1948 s John Arthur Smith & Lorraine Catherine. BS USNA 1970; MBA Geo Mason U 1982; EFM STUSo 2000. D 6/10/2000 Bp Robert Wilkes Ihloff. m 12/6/1980 Arlinda Richard. D All SS Epis Par Sunderland MD 2003-2008; D Chr Ch W River MD 2000-2003. ksmith9913@aol.com

SMITH, Kevin Corbin (Oly) 507 Mcgraw St, Seattle WA 98109 B Yonkers NY 4/12/1956 s Vernard Blair Smith & Helen Marie. BA Pacific Luth U 1979; MDiv GTS 1991. D 6/27/1992 P 4/1/1993 Bp Vincent Waydell Warner. S Geo Epis Ch Maple Vlly WA 2009-2010; S Andr's Ch Seattle WA 2004-2006; S Catherines Ch Enumclaw WA 1995-2003.

SMITH, Kirby Marvin (Los) 25 E Laurel Ave, Sierra Madre CA 91024 **Vic Faith Epis Ch Laguna Niguel CA 2011-** B Mt Clemens MI 8/22/1954 s Wayne Smith & Evelyn Nadine. BA Van 1976; MBA U of San Diego 1983. D 6/7/2008 P 1/10/2009 Bp Joseph Jon Bruno. m 9/19/2008 Clifford Chally. S Lk's Of The Mountains La Crescenta CA 2009-2011; Asst The Ch Of The Ascen Sierra Madre CA 2008-2009; The Gooden Cntr Pasadena CA 1998-2005. kirbymsmith@sbcglobal.net

✠ **SMITH, Rt Rev Kirk Stevan** (Az) 114 W Roosevelt St, Phoenix AZ 85003 **Bp Dio Arizona Phoenix AZ 2004-** B Soap Lake WA 6/6/1951 s Richard K Smith & Harriet. BA Lewis & Clark Coll 1973; MDiv Ya Berk 1979; MA Cor

1983; PhD Cor 1983. D 6/23/1979 Bp Joseph Thomas Heistand P 1/1/1980 Bp Morgan Porteus Con 4/24/2004 for Az. m 5/23/1998 Laura Fisher Hilstrom. R S Jas Par Los Angeles CA 1991-2004; R S Ann's Epis Ch Old Lyme CT 1984-1991; Assoc R S Jn's Ch W Hartford CT 1979-1984. Auth, *Foundations of Chr Faith*; Auth, "Pope," *Teachers & Canonists*; Auth, *Thos Netter of Walden An Engl Conciliarist*. DD Berkely DS 2006. bishop@azdiocese.org

SMITH, Kristy K (Ia) 4220 Holland Dr, Des Moines IA 50310 B Davenport IA 9/12/1950 d Robert Theodore Lindsay & Mary Lea. BFA U of Iowa 1973; MDiv SWTS 1986. D 5/30/1986 P 12/3/1986 Bp Walter Cameron Righter. m 6/1/1974 David Edwin Smigh c 2. S Andr's Ch Des Moines IA 2002-2003; Reg Vic S Matt's-By-The-Bridge Epis Ch Iowa Falls IA 1998-1999; Stndg Com Dio Iowa Des Moines IA 1992-1995; Cler Fam Cmsn Dio Iowa Des Moines IA 1990-1993; R S Mk's Epis Ch Des Moines IA 1989-1996; Bd Dir Dio Dio Iowa Des Moines IA 1986-1991; Asst to R The Cathd Ch Of S Paul Des Moines IA 1986-1989. kristyks@juno.com

SMITH, Larry Phillip (Dal) 17236 Lechlade Lane, Dallas TX 75252 B Columbus OH 8/27/1941 s Phillip Devol Smith & Joanna. Mar 1968; BA W Liberty St Coll 1974; MDiv cl Nash 1977. D 6/8/1977 P 4/10/1978 Bp Robert Poland Atkinson. m 7/8/1967 Patricia Smith c 2. Ch Of The Incarn Dallas TX 1997-2007; R Trin Ch Wauwatosa WI 1982-1997; R Trin Ch Arkansas City KS 1978-1981; D-In-Trng Chr Ch Fairmont WV 1977-1978. lpsmithtx@gmail.com

SMITH, Leslie Carl (NJ) 98 Nassau St. #2, Princeton NJ 08542 **Int S Lk's Par Darien CT 2011-** B Montague MA 5/22/1939 s Leslie Whitman Smith & Janis Elizabeth. BA Suffolk U 1961; Bos 1965; MDiv, cl VTS 1969. D 6/21/1969 Bp Anson Phelps Stokes Jr P 5/1/1970 Bp John Melville Burgess. m 8/13/1960 Lois Kathleen Dougherty c 5. Int Calv Ch Stonington CT 2009-2010; Int Chr Ch Short Hills NJ 2007-2008; R Trin Ch Princeton NJ 1991-2006; Archd Dio Newark Newark NJ 1986-1990; R Chr Ch Glen Ridge NJ 1979-1986; Assoc R The Ch Of The Epiph Washington DC 1972-1979; Asst Min All SS' Epis Ch Belmont MA 1969-1972. DD VTS 2005; Polly Bond Journalism Awds Epis Pub 1990; Polly Bond Journalism Awds Epis Pub 1988. smithlois1@comcast.net

SMITH, Letitia Lee (NC) 2725 Wilshire Ave. S.W., Roanoke VA 24015 B Washington DC 10/29/1952 d Henry Lee Smith & Virginia Jane. BA Mid 1975; MA Iliff TS 1978; MDiv Iliff TS 1981; Syr 1997; CAS Epis TS of The SW 1999; Int Mnstry Prog 2000. D 6/7/1999 P 12/18/1999 Bp Robert Jefferson Hargrove Jr. m 3/22/1994 R(alph) Bradley Laycock. Vic S Barn' Ch Greensboro NC 2003-2004; Ch of the Epiph Rumford RI 2001; St Mich & Gr Ch Rumford RI 2001; Int S Alb's Wilmington DE 2000; The Ch Of The H Trin Rittenhouse Philadelphia PA 1999-2000. Auth, "Wmn and Adult Educ: An Analysis of Perspectives in Major Journ," *Adult Educ Quarterly*, 1994. letitiasmith@laycock.uscom

SMITH, Lilly Mae Louise (WMo) Po Box 634, Kimberling City MO 65686 B Saint Louis MO 5/18/1936 d Robert Eugene Bruno & Anita Martha. Cert Shalom Pryr Cntr Mt Ang OR; BEd Washington U 1984; Cntr for Diac Mnstry 1995. D 12/30/1995 Bp Robert Louis Ladehoff. m 6/2/1979 Kermit Wade Smith c 3. D S Mk's Epis Ch Kimberling City MO 2000-2008; D S Anselm Cbury Ch Corvallis OR 1995-2000; Stff & Cmnty Instr Samar Hlth Serv Corvallis OR 1995-2000; D The Epis Ch Of The Gd Samar Corvallis OR 1995-2000; Pstr Care Asst S Paul's Epis Ch Salem OR 1995-1996. NAAD. angoralil@centurytel.net

SMITH, Lisa White (Minn) Po Box 8, Naytahwaush MN 56566 **Vic Breck Memi Mssn Naytahwaush MN 2004-; Vic S Columba White Earth MN 2004-; Dio Minnesota Minneapolis MN 1997-; Vic S Phil Naytahwaush MN 1994-** B Ardmore OK 6/11/1957 d Otis Peyton White & Nita Wilhelmina. Oklahoma St U; BS Marymount Coll 1979; MDiv SWTS 1992. D 6/13/1992 P 1/6/1993 Bp Robert Manning Moody. m 5/24/1980 Michael Gene Smith c 3. Vic Samuel Memi Naytahwaush MN 1994-1997; Cur St Phil's Epis Ch Ardmore OK 1992-1994. lwsmith@tvutel.com

SMITH, Lizabeth Patterson (Nwk) 275 Lafayette Ave, Hawthorne NJ 07506 B Bellefonte PA 5/4/1946 BA Maryville Coll 1968; MSW SUNY at Buffalo 1996. D 1/11/2003 Bp J Michael Garrison. m 4/6/1969 Stuart Hardie Smith c 3. The Epis Acad Newtown Sq PA 2003-2005. lizabethsmith@gmail.com

SMITH, Lora Alison (Alb) 531 County Route 59, Potsdam NY 13676 **D Trin Ch Potsdam NY 2003-** B Warren OH 9/26/1959 D 6/29/2003 Bp Daniel William Herzog. m 8/25/1984 David Alan Smith c 3. smithda@potsdam.edu

SMITH III, L(ouis) Murdock (NC) St. Martin's Church, 1510 E. Seventh Street, Charlotte NC 28204 **Dn Dio No Carolina Raleigh NC 2009-; R S Mart's Epis Ch Charlotte NC 1999-** B Raleigh NC 12/1/1948 s Louis Murdock Smith & Susanne Griswold. BA Swarthmore Coll 1972; MDiv Epis TS of The SW 1982; MS U of Tennessee 1989; STM GTS 1990; PhD U of Tennessee 1994. D 6/16/1982 P 6/11/1983 Bp Robert Whitridge Estill. m 2/1/1975 Linda V Van Tassel c 3. COM Dio No Carolina Raleigh NC 2001-2008; Par Of S Jas Ch Keene NH 1995-1999; Int Trin Epis Ch Gatlinburg TN 1992-1993; Asst Ch Of The Ascen Knoxville TN 1986-1988; R S Alb's Epis Ch Hixson TN 1984-1986; Asst S Mary's Epis Ch High Point NC 1982-1983. Auth, "Var Theol & Counslg arts". AAMFT 1992; Ord Of S Lk 1986-1994; OHC 1982. lms3nc@bellsouth.net

SMITH, Manning Lee (Md) PO Box 2157, Mountain Lake Park MD 21550 B Winston-Salem NC 1/7/1943 s Charles Manning Smith & Martha Myers. BA Wake Forest U 1964; MDiv VTS 1968; MA Marshall U 1977; EdD U of Maryland 1989. D 6/11/1968 P 12/18/1968 Bp Wilburn Camrock Campbell. m 6/14/1969 Katharine L Squibb c 2. R S Jas Epis Ch Westernport MD 2000-2007; R S Matt's Par Oakland MD 1996-2008; R S Matt's Par Oakland MD 1974-1986; Vic S Jas Ch Charleston WV 1971-1974; St Christophers Epis Ch Charleston WV 1971-1974; Asst Calv Epis Ch Ashland KY 1970-1971; Min in charge Emm Ch Moorefield WV 1968-1970. ACA 1977; NBCC 1983. thegablespoolman@verizon.net

SMITH, Marc David (Mo) 4520 Lucas and Hunt Rd, Saint Louis MO 63121 **Mem, Denominational Hlth Plan Subcommittee Dio Missouri S Louis MO 2011-** B Cody WY 10/24/1949 s Albert Keene Smith & Eddyth Jean. BS U of Missouri 1971; MDiv Luth TS 1975; PhD S Louis U 1979; Cert CDSP 2010. D 12/23/2010 P 6/24/2011 Bp George Wayne Smith. m 12/17/1977 Mary Lee c 1. Auth, "For the Common Gd," *Trst mag*, Amer Hosp Assn, 2010; Co-Auth, "Best Practices in Hosp and Hlth System Governance," Missouri Hosp Assn, 2005; Auth, "Resrch: Reflection on Achilles' Heel, Magic Bullets and Routine Complications," *Anatomy of a Merger: BJC Hlth System*, Hlth Admin Press, 1997; Auth, "Missions, Margins and the Multitudes," *Anatomy of a Merger: BJC Hlth System*, Hlth Admin Press, 1997; Auth, "Creating a Clincl Resrch Framework for the Latvian Partnership," *Commonwealth*, 1996; Auth, "Cert of Need Regulation: Seeking Common Ground," *Hlth Systems Revs*, 1996; Ed, "BJC Hlth System: Anatomy of a Merger," Hosp Resrch and Educational Trust, 1995; Co-Auth, "Governance in Integrated Delivery Systems: Serving the Publ's Interest," *Frontiers of Hlth Serv Mgmt*, 1995; Co-Auth, "Transplantation and the Medicare End-Stage Renal Disease Prog," *New Engl Journ of Med*, 1988; Co-Auth, "The Hlth Ins Experience and Status of Missouri Renal Transplant Recipients," *Missouri Med*, 1987; Co-Auth, "Depressive Symptomatology and Treatment in Patients w End-Stage Renal Disease," *Psychol Med*, 1987; Co-Auth, "Living-Related Kidney Donors: A Multicenter Study of Donor Educ, Socioeconomic Status and Rehab," *Amer Journ of Kidney Diseases*, 1986; Co-Auth, "An Assessment of the Soc Networks of Patients Receiving Maintenance Ther for End-Stage Renal Disease," *Perspectives*, 1986; Auth, "An Integrated Thanatology Curric for a Grad Prog in Hlth Serv Admin," *The Thanatology Curric for Schools of Med, Nrsng, and Related Hlth Professions*, Col Press, 1986; Co-Auth, "Does Soc Spprt Determine the Treatment Setting for Hemodialysis Patients?," *Amer Journ of Kidney Diseases*, 1985; Co-Auth, "Geographic Access to Hlth Care Serv: The Case of Maintenance Hemodialysis," *Amer Journ of Kidney Diseases*, 1985; Co-Auth, "Diagnosis of Depression in Patients w End-Stage Renal Disease: Comparative Analysis," *The Amer Journ of Med*, 1985; Co-Auth, "Treatment Bias in the Mgmt of End-Stage Renal Disease," *Amer Journ of Kidney Diseases*, 1983; Co-Auth, "The Quality of Maintenance Ther for End-Stage Renal Disease: A Revs of Soc Adjustment and Rehab," *Evaltn & the Hlth Professions*, 1983; Co-Auth, "Pretreatment Intervention in the Mgmt of End-Stage Renal Disease," *Dialysis & Transplantation*, 1982; Co-Auth, "Pretreatment Depression in End-Stage Renal Disease," *The Lancet*, 1982; Co-Auth, "Instrn in Ethics in Schools of Pharmacy," *Amer Journ of Pharmaceutical Educ*, 1981; Auth, "Mediating Structures in the Regionalization of an Inpatient Pediatric System," *System Sci in Hlth Care*, Pergamon Press, 1981; Co-Auth, "Characteristics of Death Educ Curric in Amer Med Schools," *Journ of Med Educ*, 1980. cotterboatworks@aol.com

SMITH, Martin L (WA) St Columbas Church, 4201 Albemarle St NW, Washington DC 20016 **Assoc S Columba's Ch Washington DC 2007-** B Bury Lancashire UK 7/13/1947 s Edward Alfred Smith & Pamela Jenifer. BA Oxf 1968; Ripon Coll Cuddesdon 1970; MA Oxf 1971. Trans from Church Of England 11/5/1981 Bp Morris Fairchild Arnold. S Jn's Chap Cambridge MA 1981-2002. Auth, "Compass and Stars," Ch Pub, 2007; Auth, "A Season for the Sprt," Cowley Pub, 1991; Auth, "The Word Is Very Near You," Cowley Pub, 1989; Auth, "Recon: Preparing for Confession in the Epis Ch," Cowley Pub, 1985. martinsmith47@verizon.net

SMITH, Mary Jo (Vt) 973 Route 106, Reading VT 05062 B Fort Monmouth NJ 11/2/1943 d John Valmore LePage & Constance Elizabeth. BA S Norbert Coll De Pere WI 1970. D 4/13/1985 Bp George Phelps Mellick Belshaw. m 6/27/1970 Channing Leslie Smith c 2. D S Barth's Ch Cherry Hill NJ 1985-2000. smith9mj@yahoo.com

SMITH, Melissa M (NC) 84 Broadway, New Haven CT 06511 **S Aug's Chap Nashville TN 2010-** B Nashville TN 6/11/1973 d Gilbert N Smith & Mary Jane. BA Trin 1995; MDiv UTS 2003; CAS CDSP 2008. D 6/28/2008 Bp Alfred Clark Marble Jr P 5/15/2009 Bp Michael Bruce Curry. m 10/12/2002 Edwin D Williamson c 2. D Chr Ch New Haven CT 2008-2010. smith_melissa_@hotmail.com

S

SMITH JR, Merle Edwin (Ia) 715 W 7th St S, Newton IA 50208 **Vocational D S Steph's Ch Newton IA 2001-** B Des Moines IA 8/3/1955 D 4/7/2001 Bp Carl Christopher Epting. m 4/6/1991 Jana Illingworth. msmith@skiffmed.com

SMITH, Michael Allen (Az) 2800 W Ina Rd, Tucson AZ 85741 **R Chr The King Ch Tucson AZ 2004-** B Las Cruces NM 2/15/1963 s William Edgar Smith & Martha Jean. Van 1982; BA U of Texas 1984; MDiv VTS 1994. D 6/25/1994 Bp James Monte Stanton P 2/25/1995 Bp Sam Byron Hulsey. m 8/13/1994 Tamara Kim Hainline c 1. Dio NW Texas Lubbock TX 1994-2004; Emm Epis Ch San Angelo TX 1994-2003. Auth, "Burning Questions for God," *Sermons That Wk IX*, Morehouse Pub, 2000; Auth, "Creation's Praise of God: A Reading of Aug's Cosmology," *hon Thesis*, VTS, 1994. smith.hainline@gmail.com

✠ **SMITH, Rt Rev Michael Gene** (ND) Po Box 8, Naytahwaush MN 56566 **Dn Geth Cathd Fargo ND 2011-; Bp Dio No Dakota Fargo ND 2004-** B Purcell OK 9/5/1955 s Harold Gene Smith & Nora Jane. BS Oklahoma St U 1977; BA Marymount Coll 1980; MSK U of Oklahoma 1985; MDiv SWTS 1991. D 6/22/1991 P 1/18/1992 Bp Robert Manning Moody Con 5/8/2004 for ND. m 5/24/1980 Lisa White Smith c 3. Vic S Columba White Earth MN 1997-2004; Vic Breck Memi Mssn Naytahwaush MN 1994-1997; Vic Samuel Memi Naytahwaush MN 1994-1997; Cur St Phil's Epis Ch Ardmore OK 1991-1994. bpnodak@aol.com

SMITH, Michael Wayne (SC) 218 Ashley Ave., Charleston SC 29403 **D Ch Of The H Comm Charleston SC 2006-** B Charleston SC 10/11/1949 s Vernon Smith & Gwendolyn. AS Trident Tech Coll 1972; MAR Luth Theol Sthrn Sem 2006; STM Luth Theol Sthrn Sem 2012. D 10/12/2006 Bp Edward Lloyd Salmon Jr. m 3/24/1996 Eleanor Gray c 2. mwssr123@aol.com

SMITH, Mitchell Tonkin (Ia) 237 W Orange Rd, Waterloo IA 50701 **Trin Ch New Orleans LA 2011-** B Oconomowoc WI 5/25/1981 s Edward Daniel Smith & Evelyn Hallects. BA Wstrn Illinois U 2003; SWTS 2006. D 12/17/2005 Bp Alan Scarfe. m 6/21/2003 Denise T Smith c 1. Trin Epis Par Waterloo IA 2006-2011. rev.mitchell@gmail.com

SMITH, Molly Dale (NJ) 805 Timber Ln., Nashville TN 37215 **P S Dav's Epis Ch Nashville TN 2009-** B Rochester NY 11/2/1945 d William Andrew Dale & Corinne. BA Hollins U 1967; MA Candler TS Emory U 1990; MDiv SWTS 1993; DMin S Paul TS 2000. D 6/5/1993 P 12/6/1993 Bp John Clark Buchanan. m 3/18/1967 Richard Smith c 3. S Ptr's Epis Ch Peekskill NY 2006; Int R All SS Epis Ch Jacksonville FL 2003-2006; Int R All SS Ch Millington NJ 2003; Chr Ch Three Bridges NJ 2002; Int R All SS Ch Millington NJ 2000-2002; Int S Thos Ch Alexandria Pittstown NJ 2000; Int Chr Ch Ridgewood NJ 1999-2000; Asstg P S Lk's Ch Gladstone NJ 1999; Int S Paul's Epis Ch Morris Plains NJ 1998-1999; Dio W Missouri Kansas City MO 1994-1998. Ed, "Transitional Mnstry: Time of Opportunity," Ch Pub, 2009. mollydsmith@yahoo.com

SMITH, Myrl Elden (O) 5707 Corey Cv, Sylvania OH 43560 B Circleville OH 10/21/1938 s Myrl E Smith & Helen G. BS Witt 1960; MDiv EDS 1964. D 6/13/1964 P 12/19/1964 Bp Roger W Blanchard. c 4. R Trin Ch Findlay OH 1979-2004; R S Paul Epis Ch Norwalk OH 1972-1979; Vic S Matt's Ch Ashland OH 1966-1972; Asst S Phil's Ch Columbus OH 1964-1966. esm1021a@aol.com

SMITH, Nancy Metze (SwFla) 13011 Sandy Key Bend, Apt 1, North Fort Myers FL 33903 **D All Souls Epis Ch No Ft Myers FL 2010-; D Ch Of The Epiph Cape Coral FL 2005-** B Charleston SC 3/1/1939 d Hugo William Metze & Irene Webber. D 6/18/2005 Bp John Bailey Lipscomb. c 2. "UN's Millennium Dvlpmt Goal," *The Sthrn Cross*, Dio SW FL, 2006; "A Pryr from the Beacon of H.O.P.E.," *Pine Island Eagle*, The Breeze Pub., 2005. OSL 2008; Steph Min Ldr 2008. artistnsmith@yahoo.com

SMITH, Nancy Spencer (Mass) 29 W Cedar St, Boston MA 02108 B Boston MA 8/21/1941 d Carlton Wentworth Spencer & Helen Collier. BA Connecticut Coll 1963; JD Bos 1966; MDiv EDS 1991. D 6/5/1993 P 6/1/1994 Bp Don Edward Johnson. m 3/10/1984 Geoffrey Welles Smith. The Epis Ch Of S Jn The Bapt Sanbornville NH 1993-1994.

SMITH, Nora (NY) 11 N. Broadway, Irvington NY 10533 **R S Barn Ch Irvington on Hudson NY 2009-; Diocn Msnry & Ch Extntn Socty New York NY 2007-** B New York NY 9/23/1957 d Robert Smith & Jean Mary. BA Brandeis U 1981; MDiv Ya Berk 2007. D 3/10/2007 P 9/15/2007 Bp Mark Sean Sisk. m 9/2/2000 Peter Nyikos. Assoc Ch Of The Intsn New York NY 2007-2009; Dio New York New York City NY 2007-2009. revnorasmith@gmail.com

SMITH, Patrick (Tenn) 2661 Ashland City Rd., Clarksville TN 37043 **Vic S Jn's Epis Mssn Clarksville TN 2005-** B Dallas TX 2/1/1968 s Josephus Murray Smith & Patricia. BA U of Texas 1990; Nash 1994. D 12/28/1993 P 7/3/1994 Bp Clarence Cullam Pope Jr. m 6/19/1993 Catherine Elizabeth King c 1. Dio Tennessee Nashville TN 2005-2010; Chapl S Alb's Chap & Epis U Cntr Baton Rouge LA 1997-2005; Dio Louisiana Baton Rouge LA 1997-2004; S Lk's Ch Baton Rouge LA 1994-1997. frpatricksmith@yahoo.com

SMITH, Patsy Ann (NC) 229 E New York Ave, Southern Pines NC 28387 **The Bp Edwin A Penick Vill Sthrn Pines NC 2004-** B Winona MS 1/21/1947 d Clinton Barth Smith & Hoyte. BS Mississippi U For Wmn 1969; Med Auburn U Montgomery 1980; MDiv STUSo 2000. D 6/10/2000 Bp Robert Carroll Johnson Jr P 1/27/2001 Bp J(ames) Gary Gloster. Assoc R S Mich's Ch Raleigh NC 2000-2004. psmith130@nc.rr.com

SMITH, Paul Bruce (Ak) 9631 Noaya, Eagle River AK 99577 **H Sprt Epis Ch Eagle River AK 2010-; P-in-c S Jas The Fisherman Kodiak AK 2008-** B Wheeling WV 4/27/1947 s Charles E Smith & Catherine Ann. BA W Liberty St Coll 1980; MDiv VTS 1984. D 6/6/1984 P 4/15/1985 Bp Robert Poland Atkinson. R S Jas The Fisherman Kodiak AK 1993-1998; S Mk's Epis Ch Berkeley Sprg WV 1985-1993; Cur Trin Ch Huntington WV 1984-1985. Natl Inst Of Ethics 2001. padrepbs@yahoo.com

SMITH, Paul Robert Gundar (NI) 632 Marquette Ave, South Bend IN 46617 B Wrightsville PA 7/19/1927 s Paul Charles James Smith & Daisy Mae. BA Wabash Coll 1952; MA U of Notre Dame 1962; PhD U of Notre Dame 1968. D 12/15/1978 P 5/1/1983 Bp William Cockburn Russell Sheridan. m 8/19/1961 Doris Ellen Bowser. Mltry Chapl Assn.

SMITH, Paul Weeghman (Ky) 3724 Hillsdale Rd, Louisville KY 40222 B Richmond IN 7/23/1935 s Paul Leslie Smith & Dessolyn Weeghman. BA MI SU 1957. D 11/19/1976 P 4/25/1978 Bp William Cockburn Russell Sheridan. m 6/25/1961 Susan Porter c 4. Non-Stipendiary S Mk's Epis Ch Louisville KY 1994-2000; R S Ptr's Epis Ch Louisville KY 1986-1994; Non-stip S Geo Ch Berne IN 1983-1985; Assoc Trin Ch Ft Wayne IN 1982-1985. wasppws1@insightbb.com

SMITH, Perry Michael (WA) 15 Charles Plz Apt 2307, Baltimore MD 21201 B Springfield MO 9/1/1937 s Perry Edmund Smith & Marian Beverly. BA Harv 1959; STB Ya Berk 1962; U Chi 1966. D 4/24/1962 P 11/8/1962 Bp Edward Randolph Welles II. Com Dio Washington Washington DC 1987-1992; R Ch Of The Ascen And S Agnes Washington DC 1985-1994; Vic Ch of the H Name Dolton IL 1977-1985; Dir - Coll Wk Dept Dio Wstrn New York Tonawanda NY 1966-1972; Asst S Lk's Ch Evanston IL 1963-1966; Vic Trin Epis Ch Marshall MO 1962-1963. Auth, "Cfm:A Confrontation"; Auth, "Last Rites," Scribners; Auth, "For Jeff," Dell. CCU; ECM. prysmith@verizon.net

✠ SMITH, Rt Rev Philip Alan (NH) 4800 Fillmore Ave Apt 810, Alexandria VA 22311 **Died 10/10/2010** B Belmont MA 4/2/1920 s Herbert Leonard Smith & Elizabeth Jane. BA Harv 1942; DMin VTS 1949; S Aug's Coll Cbury GB 1958. D 6/3/1949 Bp Norman B Nash P 12/18/1949 Bp John M Walker Jr Con 1/28/1970 for NH. c 3. DD VTS Alexandria VA 1970.

SMITH, P(hilip) Kingsley (Md) 8339 Carrbridge Cir, Towson MD 21204 **R Imm Epis Ch Glencoe MD 2008-; Hstgr Dio Maryland Baltimore MD 1996-** B Toronto CA 5/14/1929 s Frank Hinman Smith & Amy. BA Amh 1950; MDiv VTS 1956; Fllshp Coll of Preachers 1984. D 7/5/1956 P 4/12/1957 Bp Noble C Powell. m 11/17/1951 Mary Lee Evans c 4. Int Ch Of The Redemp Baltimore MD 2002-2003; Int Sherwood Epis Ch Cockeysville MD 1999-2001; Int S Geo's Ch Perryman MD 1996-1998; Dio Maryland Baltimore MD 1988-1989; Trin Ch Towson MD 1956-1995. Auth, *Towson Under God*, Baltimore Cnty Libr, 1976. Natl Epis Historians & Archivists 1996; SBL 1957. pksmi@comcast.net

SMITH, Ralph Eugene (NY) 219 Old Franklin Grove Dr Apt 6-A, Chapel Hill NC 27514 **S Paul's Ch Morrisania Bronx NY 2003-** B Inman SC 6/7/1932 s Hubert Dixon Smith & Hulda Cornelia. BA CUNY 1966; MDiv GTS 1969; STM NYTS 1976. D 6/7/1969 P 12/20/1969 Bp Horace W B Donegan. m 9/7/1991 Susannah Rankin c 3. Int Ch Of S Jn The Div Hasbrouck Heights NJ 1994-1996; S Ptr's Ch Newark NJ 1994; Chr Ch Hackensack NJ 1993-1994; Vic Ch Of The Trsfg No Bergen NJ 1990-1993; Ch Of The H Comm Paterson NJ 1990; S Mart Ch Detroit MI 1987-1990; Chr Ch Marlboro NY 1977-1987; R S Thos Epis Ch New Windsor NY 1971-1985; Ch Of St Thos Detroit MI 1971-1984; Diocn Msnry & Ch Extntn Socty New York NY 1969-1976; Dpt Of Missions Ny Income New York NY 1969-1976. susannahralph@mindspring.com

SMITH JR, Ralph Wood (ETenn) Po Box 476, Mountain Home TN 37684 B Bluefield WV 5/14/1926 s Ralph Wood Smith & Gladys Erwin. BS Davidson Coll 1947; MDiv VTS 1950. D 7/25/1950 Bp Robert E L Strider P 7/21/1951 Bp Wilburn Camrock Campbell. m 5/28/1977 Jeanne B Burton c 1. Vic S Jn's Ch Mart TN 1985-1989; Dio W Tennessee Memphis TN 1985-1988; R S Anne's Ch Millington TN 1980-1984; R Ch Of The Ascen Lafayette LA 1966-1967; R S Tim's Epis Ch Kingsport TN 1960-1966; R S Andr's On The Sound Ch Wilmington NC 1953-1956; R Chr Ch Wellsburg WV 1951-1953. CH. Soc for Coll Wk 1955-1960.

SMITH, Raymond Robert (Colo) 8148 S Algonquian Cir, Aurora CO 80016 B Columbus OH 8/6/1921 s Raymond Robert Smith & Clara Louise. Carnegie Inst of Tech 1944; FD 1964; BA/BS U CO 1968; MDiv Nash 1978. D 6/29/1978 P 2/14/1979 Bp William Carl Frey. m 10/22/2006 Maryan Stratman c 2. Assoc S Lk's Ch Denver CO 1996-1997; Int S Lk's Ch Denver CO 1991-1992; The Epis Par of S Greg Littleton CO 1979-1989; Dio Colorado Denver CO 1978-1979; Cur H Apos Epis Ch Englewood CO 1978-1979. frrobertsmith@att.net

SMITH, Richard Byron (NC) 6 Natchez Court, Greensboro NC 27455 B Newport News VA 7/28/1927 s Charles Christian Smith & Susie Everette. U of Tennessee 1956; Epis TS In Kentucky 1961; CR Lang Sch 1965. D 6/11/1961 P 12/17/1961 Bp William R Moody. m 9/5/1953 Mary B Boon c 3. Asst S Jn's Ch Hampton VA 1987-1989; R Ch Of The Adv Enfield NC 1984-1987; P-in-c S Jn's Ch Battleboro NC 1984-1987; R S Geo's Epis Ch Newport News VA 1968-1984; Asst Chr Epis Ch Warren OH 1963-1965. mlbs6@juno.com

SMITH, Richard Keene (Minn) 13810 Community Dr Apt 215, Burnsville MN 55337 **Died 7/30/2011** B Fort Sheridan IL 9/12/1923 s Richard Keene Smith & Josephine Otelia. BA Carleton Coll 1949; MDiv SWTS 1952; DD SWTS 1983. D 7/21/1952 P 12/23/1952 Bp Stephen E Keeler. c 2. Auth, *Ministering to Sick Chld*. Wrdn CBS. Hon Sioux & Chippewa Indn; Outstanding Young Man of Year JCC. rksmrs103@aol.com

SMITH, Richard Leslie (Cal) 226 Clinton Park, San Francisco CA 94103 **P Assoc The Epis Ch Of S Jn The Evang San Francisco CA 2001-** B Seattle WA 2/10/1950 s Leslie B Smith & Margaret M. MDiv Loyola U 1979; PhD Greaduate Theol Un Berkeley CA 1993. Rec from Roman Catholic 6/2/2001 Bp William Edwin Swing. m 6/17/2000 Robby C K Tan.

SMITH JR, Richard Winton (Pa) 305 E 83rd St Apt 4g, New York NY 10028 B Wyandotte MI 8/9/1939 s Richard Winton Smith & Alicia. MDiv EDS; BA MI SU 1961. D 6/29/1965 Bp C Kilmer Myers P 1/1/1966 Bp Richard S M Emrich. m 6/24/1978 Mildred Borkoski c 3. H Innoc S Paul's Ch Philadelphia PA 1994-1999; Evang Stff Dio Michigan Detroit MI 1990-2002; Dio Michigan Detroit MI 1987-1994; R Gr Ch Mt Clemens MI 1977-1987; R S Lk's Epis Ch Allen Pk MI 1971-1977; Cur S Paul's Epis Ch Flint MI 1965-1969. smim123@aol.com

SMITH JR, Robert Adrian (Me) 35 Prospect St, Caribou ME 04736 **Dio Maine Portland ME 2000-; R Aroostook Epis Cluster Caribou ME 1991-; Vic S Anne's Ch Mars Hill ME 1991-** B Augusta ME 6/22/1945 s Robert Adrian Smith & Barbara Louise. BS Aroostook St Teachers Coll 1967; MA U of Maine 1968; MDiv Bangor TS 1991; DMin Bangor TS 1997. D 6/10/1991 P 12/14/1991 Bp Edward Cole Chalfant. m 10/4/1969 Thelma Love c 2. Vic Ch Of The Adv Caribou ME 1991; R S Jn's Ch Presque Isle ME 1991; R S Lk's Ch Caribou ME 1991; R S Paul's Ch Ft Fairfield ME 1991. rsmith19@maine.rr.com

SMITH, Robert Angus (WMich) 212 Courtland St, Dowagiac MI 49047 B Chicago IL 9/17/1933 s James Robert Smith & Lora Maud. BA Lawr 1955; BD Nash 1958; MA U of Wisconsin 1975; STM Nash 1979; Ldrshp Acad for New Directions 1983; DMin GTF 1986. D 3/22/1958 P 10/4/1958 Bp William Hampton Brady. Com on Wrshp Dio Wstrn Michigan Kalamazoo MI 1992-2004; Ecum Rela Com Dio Wstrn Michigan Kalamazoo MI 1991; R S Paul's Epis Ch Dowagiac MI 1988-1998; Dioc Coun Dio Nthrn Michigan Marquette MI 1981-1984; Chair Ecum Rel Com Dio Nthrn Michigan Marquette MI 1979-1987; COM Dio Nthrn Michigan Marquette MI 1978-1988; Chair Com Memis & Resolutns Dio Nthrn Michigan Marquette MI 1978-1987; Del Prov Vic Syn Dio Nthrn Michigan Marquette MI 1978-1986; Hunger Cmsn Dio Nthrn Michigan Marquette MI 1978-1981; Human Sxlty Com Dio Nthrn Michigan Marquette MI 1977-1980; Human Sxlty Com Dio Nthrn Michigan Marquette MI 1977-1980; R Gr Epis Ch Menominee MI 1976-1988; Gr Ch Madison WI 1974-1976; ExCoun Dio Fond du Lac Appleton WI 1972-1974; ExCoun Dio Fond du Lac Appleton WI 1965-1969; Vic S Paul's Ch Suamico WI 1960-1974; Asst S Paul's Ch Plymouth WI 1958-1960.

SMITH, Robert Clarke (Pa) 3826 The Oak Rd, Philadelphia PA 19129 **R Ch Of The Gd Shpd Philadelphia PA 2004-** B Sioux Center IA 3/12/1940 s Alfred William Smith & Elizabeth. BA U of Iowa 1962; MA U Chi 1963; Luth TS at Philadelphia 2000; MDiv GTS 2001. D 6/23/2001 Bp Charles Bennison P 6/1/2002 Bp Charles Ellsworth Bennison Jr. m 8/27/1983 Lorene Cary c 3. Dn Dio Pennsylvania Philadelphia PA 2008-2010; Asst S Paul's Ch Doylestown PA 2001-2004. revbobsmith@mac.com

SMITH, Robert Edward (Mich) 22326 Cherry Hill St, Dearborn MI 48124 **D Trin Ch Detroit MI 1996-** B Detroit MI 1/6/1944 s Edward Glen Smith & Marion Salina. BA Wayne 1973; Cert Whitaker TS 1994. D 9/28/1996 Bp R(aymond) Stewart Wood Jr. m 8/24/1968 Sharon Lightner c 3. Chr Ch Dearborn MI 2001-2011; D Chr Ch Detroit MI 1996-2000. NAAD 1997. Meritorious Serv Medal U.S. AF 1995. ccawifey@comcast.net

SMITH, Robert Kennedy (CFla) 3224 Carleton Circle East, Lakeland FL 33803 **R S Dav's Epis Ch Lakeland FL 1999-** B Clarksburg WV 10/6/1949 s Gerald N Smith & Betty Jane. DMin RTS Orlando in Progress; BA W Virginia U 1975; MDiv VTS 1988. D 6/1/1988 Bp Robert Poland Atkinson P 6/1/1989 Bp William Franklin Carr. m 11/8/1968 Deborah Gerau c 2. Trin Ch Vero Bch FL 1990-1998; Assoc S Jn Wheeling WV 1990-1991; Assoc S Lk's Ch Wheeling WV 1990-1991; Assoc S Paul's Ch Wheeling WV 1990-1991; The Wheeling Cluster Wheeling WV 1989-1990; D-in-Trng S Matt's Ch Wheeling WV 1988-1989. Amer Assn Chr Counslrs. frbubba@hotmail.com

SMITH, Robert Macleod (Del) 726 Loveville Rd Apt 107, Hockessin DE 19707 B Wilmington NC 8/31/1924 s Robert Macleod Smith & Charlotte. Duke; VTS; Wake Forest U. D 5/31/1950 Bp Thomas H Wright P 12/1/1952 Bp PJ Machijima. c 3. R Trin Par Wilmington DE 1968-1986; R S Paul's Epis Ch Lynchburg VA 1966-1968. Screen Actors Gld 1988. Hon DD VTS. robmacleod@comcast.net

SMITH, Robert Nelson (FdL) 217 Houston St, Ripon WI 54971 B Cocoa Beach FL 12/17/1971 s Richard Smith & Julia Sheridan. BA Estrn Illinois U 1994; MA Webster U 2003; MA Nash 2009. D 6/29/2010 P 1/15/2011 Bp Russell Edward Jacobus. m 11/19/1994 Angela Odom c 4. robertsmith@theenlacegroup.com

SMITH, Robert Russell (Eas) 175 Saint Mark's Church Rd, PO BOX 337, Perryville MD 21903 B Englewood NJ 7/13/1947 s James Joseph Smith & Viola Valerie. BA Amer U in Cairo 1970; MDiv GTS 1976. D 6/5/1975 P 12/11/1976 Bp George E Rath. m 5/24/1975 Susan D'Antonio. R S Mk's Epis Ch Perryville MD 2006-2010; R Ch Of The H Comm Norwood NJ 1995-2006; Chr Edu Com Dio Newark Newark NJ 1995-1998; R S Jas' Ch Indn Hd MD 1981-1994; Dio Arizona Phoenix AZ 1981; Gr Ch Tucson AZ 1980-1981; Asst Gr S Paul's Epis Ch Tucson AZ 1980-1981; Cur Par Of Chr The Redeem Pelham NY 1976-1979. Auth, "Full length Drama," *The Inquiry: A New Look at the Death of Jesus*, 2011; Auth, "Chancel Comedies," *Bad Ideas About God*, 2002; Auth, "Chancel Comedies," *Talent Show*, 1996; Auth, "Tomb KV5: Is Underground Tomb for Sons of Ramses II a Coptic Monstry?," *Coptic Ch Revs*, 1995; Auth, "Chancel Drama," *Kiss of Peace*, 1985; Auth, "Chancel Comedies, All In The One Fam (Adam and Eve," *Cain and Abel)*; Auth, "Chancel Comedies," *I Dissed My Boss w His Own Dough- A Chancel Comedy on Stwdshp*; Auth, "Chancel Comedies, Henry VIII vs Mart Luther," *Next on Theologically Incorrect*; Auth, "Chancel Comedies," *Parents Who Forgive Prodigals for Anything Next on Horrendo*; Auth, "Chancel Comedies," *The Temptation Zone*. Fllshp Of Merry Christians 2002; WECA 1981-1994. voxbobandsusan@atlanticbb.net

SMITH, Roberts (Los) 5848 Tower Rd, Riverside CA 92506 B Charlotte NC 12/28/1941 s David Benjamin Smith & Carol May. BA U of Vermont 1968; MDiv CDSP 1972; DMin STUSo 1997. D 11/1/1974 Bp Harvey D Butterfield P 5/23/1975 Bp Robert Shaw Kerr. m 12/26/1972 Aloha Lee Smith c 2. Curs Sec Mem Dio Los Angeles Los Angeles CA 2001-2005; R S Mich's Epis Ch Riverside CA 1998-2008; Cmsn on Lay Mnstry Dio New Jersey Trenton NJ 1980-1982; R S Jn The Evang Ch New Brunswick NJ 1979-1982; Curs Sec Mem Dio New Jersey Trenton NJ 1979-1981; Asst/Assoc S Lk's Ch Gladstone NJ 1976-1979; Curs Sec Mem Dio Vermont Burlington VT 1975-1976; Vic H Trin Epis Ch Swanton VT 1975-1976. OSL the Physcn 1976. revs2smith@earthlink.net

SMITH, Robin (Oly) 504 Tecumseh Rd, Clinton MI 49236 **S Andr's Ch Clawson MI 2008-; S Jn's Ch Clinton MI 2008-; S Ptr's Ch Tecumseh MI 2008-** B Vancouver WA 9/6/1951 d Bernard Luman Smith & Elaine. BA Rosary Coll River Forest IL 1973; MDiv GTS 1982; STM GTS 1983. D 6/5/1982 Bp Albert Wiencke Van Duzer P 12/21/1982 Bp George Phelps Mellick Belshaw. c 2. R S Andr's Ch Walden NY 1992-2000; St Fran of Assisi Montgomery NY 1992-1996; P-in-c Ch Of S Clem Of Rome Belford NJ 1991-1992; Vic Ch Of The Trsfg Rome GA 1986-1990; The GTS New York NY 1982. rsmith12jm@msn.com

SMITH, Robin Penman (Dal) 2712 E Aspen CT, Plano TX 75075 **P-in-c Trin Epis Ch Dallas TX 2010-** B Hamilton ON CA 7/31/1939 s Harold Penman Smith & Ruth. BA Gordon Coll 1965; MDiv Ya Berk 1969; DMin Fuller TS 1989. D 6/21/1969 Bp Anson Phelps Stokes Jr P 5/31/1970 Bp John Melville Burgess. m 8/26/1965 Diana McNatt c 2. Int S Ptr's Ch McKinney TX 2009-2010; R Ch Of The Apos Coppell TX 1990-2009; Vic Dept Of Missions Dallas TX 1989-1990; R Trin Ch Covington KY 1983-1989; R S Steph's Epis Ch Mckeesport PA 1980-1983; Assoc S Barth's Ch Bristol TN 1977-1979; R Ch Of The Gd Shpd Watertown MA 1971-1977; Cur The Par Of S Chrys's Quincy MA 1969-1971. Auth, "7 Keys to a Working Faith," *Chr Life mag*, 1993; Auth, "Leading Christians To Chr: Evangelizing The Ch," Morehouse, 1989. CBS; Oblate Ord Of S Ben 1997. domanselm@hotmail.com

SMITH, Rod (Tex) 1738 Ridgeway Road, Memphis TN 38119 B 4/1/1938 s William Charles Smith & Elsa Maria. BS Tusculum Coll 1960; MEd Mississippi Coll 1967, MDiv STUSo 1971. D 5/30/1971 P 5/1/1972 Bp John M Allin. m 12/26/1993 Annette C Cacioppo c 3. H Sprt Epis Sch Houston TX 1996-2000; H Sprt Epis Ch Houston TX 1994-1996; Cbury Epis Sch Desoto TX 1992-1994; S Clem's Epis Par Sch El Paso TX 1981-1992; Assoc Pro Cathd Epis Ch Of S Clem El Paso TX 1981-1991; Epis Sch Of Acadiana Inc. Cade LA 1976-1981; Trin Epis Sch New Orleans LA 1973-1976. Auth, "Sci arts". crodneysmith@gmail.com

SMITH, Roger Stilman (Me) 70 Country Club Rd, Manchester ME 04351 B Norwood MA 11/30/1928 s Edward Lewis Smith & Gladys May. BA Colg 1950; MDiv Ya Berk 1953; DMin Hartford Sem 1985. D 6/15/1953 P 3/30/1954 Bp Oliver L Loring. m 6/6/1953 Edna Newell c 2. Int S Jas Ch Old Town ME 1992-1993; Int Ch Of S Jas The Less Scarsdale NY 1991; Vic S Andr's Ch Readfield ME 1986-1990; St Andrews Mssn Augusta ME 1986-1990; Cathd Ch Of S Lk Portland ME 1977-1982; S Mk's Ch Augusta ME

1965-1977; Vic Ch Of The Gd Shpd Rangeley ME 1953-1955. Contrib, *Ecology & Chr Responsibility*, 1975. Comp CCN. rogersmith@myfairpoint.net

SMITH, Roger William (SC) 15 Newpoint Rd, Beaufort SC 29907 B Jackson MI 2/21/1928 s Hugh Thompson Smith & Genevieve. BA U MI 1949; STB EDS 1954; Fllshp Coll of Preachers 1965; Oxf 1971; MA Trin Hartford CT 1972. D 6/20/1954 P 12/21/1954 Bp Albert Ervine Swift. m 5/30/1953 Headley Hall Mills c 4. Assoc All SS Ch Hilton Hd Island SC 1995-2003; R Par Ch of St. Helena Beaufort SC 1984-1993; R Ch Of The H Sprt Wayland MA 1976-1984; Dio Wstrn Michigan Kalamazoo MI 1975-1976; R S Jas Epis Ch Farmington CT 1961-1975; R S Jn's Ch Christiansted VI 1957-1960; Vic S Andr's Ch Charlotte Amalie VI VI 1956-1957; All SS Epis Sch S Thos VI 1954-1957. OHC 1964. revrws@embarqmail.com

SMITH, Ronald Nelson (Tex) 1403 Preston Ave, Austin TX 78703 **S Dav's Ch Austin TX 1992-** B Kansas City MO 6/14/1947 s J Neil Smith & Frances. BA U of Kansas 1970; MA U of Kansas 1974; MDiv Epis TS of The SW 1975; MBA U of Texas 1983; MA U of Texas 1992. D 7/13/1986 P 6/15/1988 Bp Thomas Kreider Ray. m 6/1/1969 Anna Cummings c 1. Assoc Dio Nthrn Michigan Marquette MI 1986-2001. ron.s@stdave.org

SMITH, Rose Ann Ann (NwT) 3500 Barclay Dr, Amarillo TX 79109 B Santa Fe NM 6/4/1938 d William Edward McAtee & Rosaamond. Dplma NW Texas Hosp Nrsng Sch 1973; Cert U of Texas 1979; BSN W Texas St U 1983; MSN W Texas A & M U 1993. D 11/6/1988 Bp Sam Byron Hulsey. m 11/18/1968 William Burnam Smith c 3. D S Ptr's Epis Ch Amarillo TX 1993-2003; D S Thos Epis Ch Hereford TX 1988-1993. rabsmith@sbcglobal.net

SMITH, Samuel Earl (Cal) 2673 Alder St, Eugene OR 97405 B Long Beach CA 8/15/1936 s Samuel Sterling Smith & Myrtle Sophia. BA U CA 1959; MDiv GTS 1962; MS U of Oregon 1971. D 6/24/1962 Bp James Albert Pike P 3/1/1963 Bp George Richard Millard. m 9/5/1966 Elizabeth Seccombe c 2. Cur S Paul's Epis Ch Walnut Creek CA 1962-1964. sambetsy@mindspring.com

SMITH, Samuel Jay (NY) 1047 Amsterdam Ave, New York NY 10025 **Epis Chars New York NY 2011-** B Corpus Christi TX 3/4/1962 s Jerry Jay Smith & Betty Christine. BM SW U 1985; MS Indiana U 1987; MDiv The GTS 2009. D 6/20/2009 P 2/4/2010 Bp Catherine Elizabeth Maples Waynick. m Donald R Temples. Asstg P Cathd Of St Jn The Div New York NY 2010-2011; D Cathd Of St Jn The Div New York NY 2009-2010; Dio New York New York City NY 2009-2010; Dir of Cmncatn Trin Ch Indianapolis IN 2002-2006. samueljsmith@yahoo.com

SMITH JR, Sherrill Bronson (Mass) Po Box 218, Orleans MA 02653 **S Andr By The Sea Hyannis Port MA 1997-** B Norwood MA 9/17/1929 s Sherrill Bronson Smith & Gertrude. BS Springfield 1951; MDiv Ya Berk 1954. D 6/2/1954 P 12/18/1954 Bp William A Lawrence. m 10/15/2007 Jean Ida Monson c 4. S Dav's Epis Ch So Yarmouth MA 1973-1994; R S Jas Ch Glastonbury CT 1963-1970; R Chr Ch Easton CT 1956-1962; Asst S Paul's Ch Holyoke MA 1954-1956. *Var Commercial Fishing arts*. sherrill.smith2@verizon.net

SMITH, Sidney Thomas (WMass) 475 Central St, Boylston MA 01505 **Died 6/20/2011** B Winnipeg MT CA 9/16/1932 s Harold A Smith & Josephine Ann. BS Vlly City St Teachers Coll 1954; BD Bex 1957; DMin Andover Newton TS 1973. D 6/14/1957 P 3/1/1958 Bp Richard R Emery. c 8. AAMFC; Clincl Mem Aamft; Clincl Mem Agpa; Inactive Clincl Supvsr Aacpe; Mar & Fam Ther.

SMITH, Stanley James (O) 249 E 7th St, New York NY 10009 B Memphis TN 4/14/1943 s Stanley James Smith & Grayson S. BA U of Tennessee 1965; BD EDS 1970. D 9/23/1970 P 5/31/1971 Bp John Harris Burt.

SMITH JR, Stanley Joe (Ky) Po Box 23336, Anchorage KY 40223 **Dn of NE Dnry of the Dio Kentucky Dio Kentucky Louisville KY 2011-; R S Lk's Ch Anchorage KY 2002-** B Bonham TX 4/24/1961 s Stanley Joe Smith & Dolores Ann. BA Austin Coll 1983; MDiv Sthrn Bapt TS Louisville KY 1988; STD Loyola U 1998; DMin SWTS 1998. D 2/23/1992 P 2/21/1993 Bp David Reed. m 8/6/1983 Kella Lucretia Pyle. R S Ptr's Epis Ch Louisville KY 1995-2002; R Ch Of Our Merc Sav Louisville KY 1993-1995; Dio Kentucky Louisville KY 1992-1993. stlukesrector@insightbb.com

SMITH, Stephen (Tex) 3310 Nathanael Rd., Greensboro NC 27408 **Ch Of The H Sprt Greensboro NC 2009-; Supply P/Int R Dio No Carolina Raleigh NC 2009-** B Belville IL 10/18/1951 s Sanford Hale Smith & Ann Love. BA Campbell U 1974; MDiv TESM 1979; Post Grad. Dplma St. Jn's Coll, Nottingham Engl 1980. D 11/30/1980 P 8/1/1981 Bp Robert Bracewell Appleyard. m 4/19/1974 Harriette Smith. S Paul's Par Oregon City OR 2004-2005; Transitional Consult/Int R Dio Oregon Portland OR 1997-2005; Int R/Supply Dio Olympia Seattle WA 1995-1998; Dio Oregon Portland OR 1995-1997; Asst S Jn The Div Houston TX 1986-1992; Dio Florida Jacksonville FL 1983-1986. Natl Assn of Christians in Recovery 1989; NECAD 1989-1997. thecoach@spiritone.com

SMITH, Stephen Bradley (SO) 7121 Muirfield Dr., Dublin OH 43017 **R S Pat's Epis Ch Dublin OH 2003-** B Lansing MI 9/25/1957 s Wallace Smith & Anna Lee. BS Ohio U 1979; Untd TS 1984; MDiv STUSo 1988. D 6/18/1988 P 4/25/1989 Bp William Grant Black. m 7/11/1981 Jan Sargent c 2. R Chr Ch Epis Hudson OH 1996-2003; R Ch Of The Redeem Lorain OH 1990-1996; Asst Epis Soc of Chr Ch Cincinnati OH 1988-1990. Auth, "Saving Salvation: the Amazing Evolution of Gr," Morehouse, 2005; Auth, "When Scandal Strikes," *Living Ch*, 1993; Auth, "From Outreach Proj to Cmnty Action Agcy," *The Wk You Give Us to Do*, Seabury, 1985. CT 1992. Best Sermon Competition: 2nd Place Epis Evang Fndt 1991; Woods Ldrshp Awd TS Sewanee 1986. revd.up@att.net

SMITH, Stephen John Stanyon (WNY) 100 Beard Ave, Buffalo NY 14214 **P Assoc S Andr's Ch Buffalo NY 2008-** B London UK 10/4/1949 s Peter Alexander Smith & Margaret. BA U of Sussex 1981; MS U Of Birmingham Birmingham Gb 1983; CTh Westcott Hse Cambridge 1985. Trans from Church Of England 3/1/1994 Bp Creighton Leland Robertson. m 6/25/1994 Sarah Wallace Buxton. Ecum Interfaith Off Dio Wstrn New York Tonawanda NY 2000-2004; Cn Pstr S Paul's Cathd Buffalo NY 1998-2004; Asst All SS Ch Ivoryton CT 1995-1998; Assoc S Jn's Epis Ch Essex CT 1995-1998; Mssnr Rosebud Epis Mssn Mssn SD 1991-1994. Auth, "One Sunday In January," *Epis Life*, 1998. sjsmith6@buffalo.edu

SMITH, Stephen Vaughn (Mass) 32 Popponesset Ave, Mashpee MA 02649 **R S Mary's Epis Ch Barnstable MA 2004-** B Dayton OH 3/5/1954 s Burton S Smith & Audrey T. BA Macalester Coll 1976; PrTS 1978; MDiv EDS 1981. D 6/29/1981 P 1/6/1982 Bp Robert Marshall Anderson. m 8/25/1979 Jeannette Anne Hanlon c 3. R S Jn's Epis Ch Westwood MA 1989-2004; Ch Of The Redeem Chestnut Hill MA 1984-1989; Asst S Chris's Epis Ch Roseville MN 1981-1984. Auth, "Blinding Glory," *Desert Call*, Sprtl Life Inst, 2008. Soc Of S Jn The Evang, Epis Soc For Min. svs@cape.com

SMITH, Steven Ronald (Eur) Church of the Ascension, Seybothstrasse 4, 81545 Munich Germany **R Ch of the Ascen Munich 81545 DE 2009-** B Salt Lake City UT 12/31/1961 s Ronald Harding Smith & Ellen. BA U of Utah 1985; JD Bos 1989; STM GTS 2003; MDiv Yale DS 2003. D 6/29/2002 Bp Chester Lovelle Talton P 1/11/2003 Bp Joseph John Bruno. c 2. Mssn Consult Trin Par New York NY 2007-2009; Assoc R for Mssn S Jas Ch New York NY 2004-2007; Ch Of The H Trin New York NY 2002-2004. revstevesmith@ascension-munich.com

SMITH, Stuart Hardie (Nwk) 653 Courtney Hollow Ln, Madison VA 22727 B Miami FL 2/12/1948 s William Harrison Smith & Helen. BA Maryville Coll 1971; MDiv VTS 1986. D 6/14/1986 P 3/21/1987 Bp William Gillette Weinhauer. m 4/6/1969 Lizabeth Patterson c 3. R S Clem's Ch Hawthorne NJ 2003-2011; Fin Com Dio Wstrn New York Tonawanda NY 2000-2002; Vic S Aid's Ch Alden NY 1996-2000; Int Ch Of S Jn The Bapt Dunkirk NY 1994-1996; R St Mk Epis Ch No Tonawanda NY 1991-1993; Dept Mssn Dio E Tennessee Knoxville TN 1989-1991; R Ch Of The Resurr Loudon TN 1989-1990; Cmsn on Mssns Dio Virginia Richmond VA 1988-1989; R Farnham Ch No Farnham Par Warsaw VA 1986-1989; R S Jn's Ch Warsaw VA 1986-1989. shsmiths@gmail.com

SMITH, Susan Marie (WMo) 5123 E Truman Rd, Kansas City MO 64127 B Fort Benning GA 10/30/1947 d Richard Jean Smith & Ruth Elizabeth. U of Notre Dame; BA Wake Forest U 1969; MA Candler TS Emory U 1985; PhD Theol Un 2002. D 8/12/1995 Bp Steven Charleston P 5/1/1996 Bp Herbert Thompson Jr. S Paul TS Kansas City MO 2007-2010; S Paul's Ch Kansas City MO 2004-2010; S Andr's Sch Saratoga CA 2001-2003; S Mary's Ch Anchorage AK 1995-1996. "Healing Rituals," *Liturg*, 2007; Auth, "Stranger at The Table," *Benedictines*, 2005; Auth, "Mnstry Dvlpmt Journ," *SS Today*. Acad of Homil; No Amer Acad of Liturg; Oblate Ord of S Ben 1992; Societes Liturg. ammasusan.smith@gmail.com

SMITH, Susannah Rankin (NY) 219 Old Franklin Grove Dr, Chapel Hill NC 27514 B Atlanta GA 5/1/1939 d James King Rankin & Margaret Mather. BA Van 1961; MDiv UTS 1989. D 6/3/1989 P 12/16/1989 Bp John Shelby Spong. m 9/7/1991 Ralph Eugene Smith c 2. CREDO Fac The CPG New York NY 2005-2011; Assoc R S Jas Ch New York NY 1997-2004; Cler Ethics Com Dio Newark Newark NJ 1995-1997; ACTS/Vim Com Dio Newark Newark NJ 1994-1997; R S Ptr's Ch Clifton NJ 1992-1997; Int The Ch Of The Sav Denville NJ 1992; Mem, Cmsn on Mssn Dio Newark Newark NJ 1990-1997; Int Ch Of The Incarn Jersey City NJ 1990-1991; Int S Jn Jersey City NJ 1990-1991; Bergen Hill Mssnr Dio Newark Newark NJ 1989-1991. Pub, "monthly pub. since 2005," *'Inspirited Ldrshp*, self. sr-smith@mindspring.com

SMITH, Susan Sims (Ark) 1809 Canal Pointe, Little Rock AR 72202 B Jonesboro AR 10/12/1950 d Charles Sims & Kakie. BA Rhodes Coll 1972; MS U of Arkansas 1974; CTh Epis TS of The SW 1998. D 8/29/1998 P 3/13/1999 Bp Larry Earl Maze. m 10/29/1971 George Smith c 2. Dio Arkansas Little Rock AR 2001-2007; Dir of Off of Tchg & Evang Dio Arkansas Little Rock AR 2000-2007; Cur Trin Cathd Little Rock AR 1998-2000. sss96@sbcglobal.net

SMITH, Taylor Magavern (Md) 3608 Horned Owl Ct, Ellicott City MD 21042 **R Gr Ch Elkridge MD 2000-** B Buffalo NY 2/10/1965 s Philip Taylor Smith & Julie Magavern. BA Duke 1987; MDiv VTS 1996. D 5/29/1996 P 12/7/1996 Bp Robert Hodges Johnson. m 6/22/1996 Katherine Phillips c 2. Assoc R S Alb's Ch Hickory NC 1997-2000; Bp's Asst for Yth Mnstry Dio Wstrn No Carolina Asheville NC 1996-1998; Asst for Mnstry w Chld and Yth Trin Epis Ch Asheville NC 1996-1997. taylorsemail@gmail.com

S

SMITH, Ted William (Tex) PO Box 10357, Liberty TX 77575 **R S Steph's Ch Liberty TX 2010-** B Zanesville OH 11/30/1955 s William Earnest Smith & Margaret Lillian. BTS St. Mich's Coll 2005; MDiv St. Mich's Coll 2008. D 6/19/2010 P 12/21/2010 Bp C(harles) Andrew Doyle. m 9/11/1975 Kathryn F Fletcher c 2. tedwsmith@att.net

SMITH, Theophus Harold (At) 460 Euclid Ter Ne, Atlanta GA 30307 **P Assoc Cathd Of S Phil Atlanta GA 2001-** B Athens GA 1/24/1951 s Willie Harold Smith & Josephine Josette. BA St. Jn's Coll Annapolis MD 1975; MA VTS 1977; PhD Grad Theol Un 1987. D 6/9/2001 Bp Robert Gould Tharp. "Vengeance Is Never Enough: Alternative Visions Of Justice In Roads To Recon: Conflict And Dialogue In The Twenty-First Century," M.E. Sharpe, 2005; "Conjuring Culture: Biblic Formations Of Black Amer," Oxf Press, 1994; "Curing Violence," Polebridge Press, 1994; "From Cure Of Souls To Curing Culture: The Prospect For Ritual Ldrshp In The Black Rel Tradition," Virginia Sem Journ, 1993. thee.smith@emory.edu

SMITH, Thomas Eugene (EMich) P.O. Box 86, Dryden MI 48428 B Dennison OH 9/7/1955 s Dwane Henry Smith & Norma Jean. BS Ohio St 1978; MS Michigan St 1995. D 9/13/2008 Bp S(teven) Todd Ousley. m 11/20/1982 Marie MacDiarmid c 2. tomandmarie55@yahoo.com

SMITH, Thomas Gibson (Chi) 118 Tanglewood Dr, Elk Grove Village IL 60007 **Mem Dioc Audit Com Dio Chicago Chicago IL 2000-** B Columbus OH 4/5/1939 s Ralph Gibson Smith & Frances Allamae. BS OH SU 1961; SWTS 1973. D 1/12/1974 Bp James Winchester Montgomery. m 8/18/1962 Hope Bell c 3. D Asst Calv Ch Lombard IL 2003-2011; Mem Dioc Audit Com Dio Chicago Chicago IL 2000-2002; Asst Ch Of Our Sav Elmhurst IL 1999-2002; Asst One In Chr Ch Prospect Heights IL 1997-1999; Trst-Bp & Trst Dio Chicago Chicago IL 1990-2005; D Asst S Nich w the H Innoc Ch Elk Grove Vill IL 1974-2002. NASSAM; NAAD. thomasgsmith@email.com

SMITH JR, Thomas Parshall (NY) 225 W 99th St, New York NY 10025 B Tallahassee FL 11/23/1955 s Thomas Parshall Smith & Jean Keith. BS Florida St U 1979; MDiv SWTS 1996. D 8/24/1996 P 4/19/1997 Bp Frank Tracy Griswold III. Asst Pstr S Mich's Ch New York NY 1997-2000.

SMITH JR, Thomas Richard (Va) 1500 Westbrook Ct Apt 3142, Richmond VA 23227 B Quincy FL 4/21/1932 s Thomas Richard Smith & Christine Elizabeth. BA U Of Florida 1954; BD VTS 1957; UTS 1963. D 7/1/1957 P 3/1/1958 Bp Edward Hamilton West. R The Fork Ch Doswell VA 1987-1992; Asst S Jas' Ch Richmond VA 1983-1987; Par Ch of St. Helena Beaufort SC 1982-1983; R S Aug's Epis Ch Washington DC 1973-1977; Cn Res Cathd Ch Of S Lk Portland ME 1969-1973; Asst S Barth's Ch New York NY 1964-1968; Asst S Thos Epis Ch Terrace Pk OH 1960-1962. smithtr44@gmail.com

SMITH, Travis K (NC) St. Michael's Episcopal Church, 1520 Canterbury Rd., Raleigh NC 27608 **All SS Ch Loveland CO 2010-** B Edmonds WA 7/13/1977 s Kerry Wayne Smith & Sharon Louise. MDiv, cl GTS 2005. D 6/25/2005 P 1/14/2006 Bp Vincent Waydell Warner. m 8/11/2002 Aleta Skaanland c 3. Assoc R of Emerging Mnstrs S Mich's Ch Raleigh NC 2007-2010; Ch of the Apos Seattle WA 2006-2007; Chapl S Alb's Ch Edmonds WA 2003-2004; S Alb's Ch Edmonds WA 2000-2003. traviskerrysmith@gmail.com

SMITH, Vicki Lovely (NC) 10104 Sorrills Creek Lane, Raleigh NC 27614 **S Johns Epis Ch Wake Forest NC 2011-** B Portland ME 8/24/1957 d Thurber Almon Lovely & Carla. BA U of Maine 1979; MDiv Ya Berk 1984; DMin McCormick TS 2002. D 6/2/1984 P 12/8/1984 Bp Frederick Barton Wolf. m 8/28/1983 Kevin Smith. R S Thos Epis Ch Reidsville NC 2008-2011; Int S Phil's Ch Durham NC 2006-2007; R S Mk's Epis Ch Columbus OH 1999-2006; R S Jn's Epis Ch Cuyahoga Falls OH 1993-1999; Assoc S Dav's Ch Wayne PA 1990-1993; Assoc S Ptr's Epis Ch Amarillo TX 1988-1990; Int Ch Of The Annunc Bridgeview IL 1986-1988. saintmarksrector@ameritech.net

SMITH, Walter E (At) 3750 Peachtree Rd.NE, Atlanta GA 30319 **All SS Epis Ch Atlanta GA 2007-** B Jacksonville,FL 9/3/1932 s Walter Evans Smith & Elizabeth Jane. Emory U; Georgia St U; BA W&L 1954; MDiv VTS 1957. D 6/27/1957 P 4/1/1958 Bp Edward Hamilton West. c 3. COM Dio Atlanta Atlanta GA 1972-1982; Pstr Ther Dio Atlanta Atlanta GA 1969-2002; Exec Coun Dio Atlanta Atlanta GA 1965-1967; Asst All SS Epis Ch Atlanta GA 1964-1969; Asst H Trin Ch Gainesville FL 1961-1964; P-in-c: Vic S Fran Of Assisi Gulf Breeze FL 1957-1961. "Bk Revs," *Int'l Journ Grp Psych*, AGPA, 1983; Auth, *Portrait of Atlanta*, Seabury Press, 1969; Auth, *Yth Mnstry Notebook*, Seabury Press, 1969. Amer Assn for Mar and Fam Ther 1972; Amer Grp Psych Assn 1971. Fell Amer Grp Psych Ass 1983. wsmith1925@aol.com

SMITH III, Walter Frederick (RG) 10328 Rempas Ct Nw, Albuquerque NM 87114 B Trenton NJ 8/24/1943 s Walter Frederick Smith & Marion. BA MacMurray Coll 1966; MDiv PDS 1970. D 4/11/1970 P 10/1/1970 Bp Alfred L Banyard. m 11/13/1971 Elizabeth Dodge c 2. R S Fran Ch Rio Rancho NM 1994-2005; Pres Nm Chapl Assn Dio The Rio Grande Albuquerque NM 1990-1992; Dio The Rio Grande Albuquerque NM 1989; R S Jn's Epis Ch Alamogordo NM 1980-1984; R Ch Of The H Sprt Lebanon NJ 1973-1980; Cur S Jn's Ch Somerville NJ 1970-1973. Fell Coll of Chapl 1989. frwaltalbq@msn.com

SMITH, Wayne Lamarr (NJ) 10 Redstone Rdg, Voorhees NJ 08043 **Died 5/14/2011** B Lancaster PA 12/25/1934 s Warren Russell Smith & Bevlah Caroline. BA Franklin & Marshall Coll 1957; BD Lancaster TS 1961; U Chi 1965; Nash 1966; DMin Drew U 1989. D 6/11/1966 Bp James Winchester Montgomery P 12/17/1966 Bp Austin Pardue. c 3. Auth, "Ch arts". Mercersberg Soc. P Awd Dio Milwaukee 1980. ridgrun10@verizon.net

SMITH, Wendy M (ECR) 4061 Sutherland Dr, Palo Alto CA 94303 **Exam Chapl Dio El Camino Real Monterey CA 1997-; R S Thos Epis Ch Sunnyvale CA 1996-** B Bloomington IL 7/8/1946 d Martin John Smith & Joan. BA Scripps Coll 1968; MTS Harvard DS 1970; PhD U of Washington 1977. D 5/10/1975 Bp James Walmsley Frederic Carman P 2/9/1977 Bp Robert Hume Cochrane. m 6/7/1981 Troy W Barbee c 1. Assoc R Chr Epis Ch Los Altos CA 1990-1996; Asst All SS Epis Ch Palo Alto CA 1989-1990; Int Trin Par Menlo Pk CA 1987-1988; Int Ch Of S Jude The Apos Cupertino CA 1986-1987; Int S Clare's Epis Ch Pleasanton CA 1986. wsmithca@earthlink.net

SMITH, Wesley Hugh (Va) 30 Macopin Ave, Montclair NJ 07043 **P Assoc S Barth's Ch Cherry Hill NJ 2002-** B New York NY 5/28/1933 s Irving Hugh Smith & Phyllis Ball. BA Dart 1956; MDiv GTS 1959; MS Col, Grad Sch of Bus 1974. D 5/23/1959 P 12/17/1959 Bp Donald MacAdie. c 2. Asst S Ptr's Ch Clifton NJ 2004-2009; Epis Ch Of The H Fam Santa Fe NM 1998-2001; Epis Ch Of The H Fam Santa Fe NM 1993-1995; Int S Jn's Epis Ch McLean VA 1993-1994; St Martins-In-The-Field Ch Severna Pk MD 1991-1992; Int S Lk's Ch Alexandria VA 1989-1991; S Andr's-On-The-Mt Harpers Ferry WV 1988; Asst P S Paul's Rock Creek Washington DC 1986-1989; Int R S Andr's-On-The-Mt Harpers Ferry WV 1986-1988; Ch Of St Thos Of Cantebury Kent CT 1976-1977; Asstg P Ch Of The H Trin New York NY 1969-1972; P-in-c Chr Ch Patterson NY 1963-1969; R Ch Of The H Trin Pawling NY 1963-1969; Assoc, Int R Ch Of The Heav Rest New York NY 1961-1963; Cur Gr Epis Ch Rutherford NJ 1959-1961. Ed, "Nature Of The Mnstry We Seek," Natl Coun Of Ch, 1958.

SMITH, William Alfred (Ore) 5255 Columbia Rd, Columbia MD 21044 B Paterson NJ 11/19/1933 s Edward Turner Smith & Lilliam Emma. CDSP; BS NEU 1956; MS U of Vermont 1964; Con Ed VTS 1980. D 9/20/1970 Bp George Richard Millard P 11/6/1972 Bp C Kilmer Myers. m 8/25/1956 Janet M Jellison c 4. S Tim's Ch Brookings OR 2000-2003; Vic S Tim's Ch San Diego CA 1988-1995; Vic S Anth Of The Desert Desert Hot Sprg CA 1987-1988; S Jn's Ch Indio CA 1985-1988; S Clare's Epis Ch Pleasanton CA 1975-1985. wasmith8@live.com

SMITH, William Herbert (WMich) 2073 SE North Blackwell Dr, Port St Lucie FL 34952 **P-in-c H Faith Epis Ch Port S Lucie FL 2008-** B Surrey England 11/5/1934 s Donald Herbert Telford Smith & Muriel Leslie. S Aid's, Birkenhead Engl 1964; Dplma Lon 1964. Rec 4/5/1997 Bp Edward Lewis Lee Jr Trans from Church Of England 4/5/1997. m 6/2/1972 Paula Ann Marie Russell c 7. Int H Faith Epis Ch Port S Lucie FL 2002-2004; Int S Mary's Epis Ch Cadillac MI 1995-2000.

SMITH, William Herman (Cal) 3001 Veazey Ter Nw, Washington DC 20008 B Centerville IA 5/17/1930 s Herman J Smith & Mildred Elizabeth. BA Wesl 1952; BD SMU 1955. D 3/12/1960 Bp Gordon V Smith P 10/29/1960 Bp George Richard Millard. m 6/18/1950 Mary Lou Ladd c 3. Assoc R S Ptr's Epis Ch Redwood City CA 1960-1962. no

SMITH, William Louis (Md) 24 Lake Drive, Bel Air MD 21014 B Baltimore MD 9/27/1943 s William Sudler Smith & Grace Elizabeth. BS Cit 1965; STM PDS 1968. D 6/18/1968 P 6/3/1969 Bp Harry Lee Doll. m 5/15/1970 Patricia Parks. R S Mary's Ch Abingdon MD 1972-2011; Asst All SS Ch Frederick MD 1970-1972; Asst Epiph Ch Dulaney Vlly Timonium MD 1968-1970. billonlake@verizon.net

SMITH, William Loyd (WTenn) PO Box 702632, Dallas TX 75370 B 11/19/1947 B.A. Sewanee: The U So 1969; M. Div. TS 1976; M.P.A. The U of No Texas 1991; D. Min. GTF 1992; M.S. The U of No Texas 1996. D 6/27/1976 Bp William F Gates Jr P 4/12/1977 Bp William Evan Sanders. m 12/29/1986 Jo Betsy Bush. S Andr's Epis Ch Amarillo TX 1986-1987; S Jn's Cathd Albuquerque NM 1985; Bd Dir All SS' Epis Sch Vicksburg MS 1981-1984; S Geo's Epis Ch Clarksdale MS 1980-1984; Chr Ch Cathd Nashville TN 1977-1980; S Jn's Epis Cathd Knoxville TN 1976-1977. DALDRWLS@GMAIL.COM

SMITH III, William Paul (Fla) PO Box 1005, Hilliard FL 32046 B 5/12/1944 s William Paul Smith & Gereldina Roberta. MDiv Iliff TS; ABS Pfeiffer. D 6/2/1982 P 10/18/1982 Bp William Carl Frey. m 3/23/1968 Martha Josephine Mills c 1. Dio Florida Jacksonville FL 2010-2011; P-in-c Gr Epis Ch Florence KY 2004-2007; S Alb's Ch Superior WI 2001-2003; S Paul's Epis Ch Goodland KS 1992-2000. Auth, "Older Elem"; Auth, "Fllshp Times". frpaul3@me.com

SMITH, Willie James (Nwk) 1795 Riverside Dr Apt 4L, New York NY 10034 **P-in-c Trin Ch Cliffside Pk NJ 2005-** B New York NY 11/29/1953 s Jessie

Smith & Sarah Margaret. BA St. Jos's Coll 1976; MS Ford 1986; Cert Natl Psychol Assn For Psychoanalysis 1999; MDiv GTS 2004. D 6/12/2004 Bp Martin Gough Townsend P 1/8/2005 Bp John Palmer Croneberger. Who'S Who In Amer Colleges 1976. willeschutze@erols.com

SMITH, Zachary (CPa) 8 E. Keller St., Mechanicsburg PA 17055 **R S Lk's Epis Ch Mechanicsburg PA 2008-** B Newton, MA 8/5/1965 BA The Curtis Inst of Mus 1987; BA U of Pennsylvania 1988; MDiv Candler TS Emory U 2006. D 12/21/2005 P 6/28/2006 Bp J(ohn) Neil Alexander. m 6/4/1994 Wendy Wood c 2. S Paul's Ch Macon GA 2006-2008. rector.st.luke@verizon.net

SMITH-ALLEN, Serita Verner (EO) Po Box 186, Union OR 97883 B Jefferson City MO 8/9/1948 d Henry Charles Verner & Louise Beatrice. AA Mesa Cmnty Coll 1985; BA Arizona St U 1987; MDiv CDSP 1992. D 6/3/1995 P 6/4/1996 Bp William Edwin Swing. m 8/1/1997 John F Allen c 7. S Ptr's Ch La Grande OR 1999-2003; St Johns Epis Ch Ross CA 1996-1999; S Steph's Epis Ch Orinda CA 1995-1996.

SMITH-CRIDDLE, Linda C (O) 19 Pent Road, Madison CT 06443 **Supply Dio Connecticut Hartford CT 2000-** B Philadelphia PA 8/18/1936 d Joseph Timothy Corcoran & Kathryn Veronica. BA Colby Coll 1958; MDiv Winebrenner TS 1980; MA Bowling Green St U 1996; DMin GTF 1996; PhD GTF 2000. D 6/28/1980 P 1/26/1981 Bp John Harris Burt. m 12/25/1987 Arthur Hawthorne Criddle c 4. Assoc S Paul's Ch Oregon OH 1981-1984; Dep GC Dio Ohio Cleveland OH 1979-1982. Auth, *Shaping Access to Hosp Ethics Committees*. APC 1980; APC Bioethics Com 1998-2001; AEHC 1980; ACPE 1980. smithcriddle@snet.net

SMITHDEAL JR, Foss Tyra (NC) 8050 Ravenwood Ln, Stanley NC 28164 **D S Mart's Epis Ch Charlotte NC 2004-** B Winston-Salem NC 4/7/1943 s Foss T Smithdeal & Lucia Sloan. High Point U. D 6/13/2004 Bp Michael Bruce Curry. m 3/18/1989 Debra Lavern Jacobs c 6. tsmithdeal@stmartins-charlotte.org

SMITHER, Gertrude Gaston (Dal) 7900 Lovers Ln, Dallas TX 75225 **Stndg Com Dio Dallas Dallas TX 2000-; Mssnr Dio Dallas Dallas TX 1997-** B Dallas TX 10/6/1937 d John Nelson Jackson & Sallie Bell. Sweet Briar Coll 1957; BA U of Texas 1959; MDiv Epis TS of The SW 1985. D 10/13/1990 P 4/28/1991 Bp William Elwood Sterling. c 4. Assoc S Chris's Ch Dallas TX 2004-2007; Asst S Chris's Ch Dallas TX 1997-2002; Excoun Dio Dallas Dallas TX 1997-2000; S Matt's Cathd Dallas TX 1992-1997; Dir Hosp Chapl Dio Dallas Dallas TX 1992-1994; Wm Temple Epis Ctr Galveston TX 1990-1992. Assembly Of Epis Hospitals Chapl 1987; Assn Of Profsnl Chapl 1987; Dok 1994; Ord Of S Lk 1988. smither8@aol.com

SMITHERMAN, Gene (ETenn) 211 Brookwood Dr, Chattanooga TN 37411 B Birmingham AL 12/7/1947 s Erskine Ramsey Smitherman & Eva Jean. BA Van 1970; JD U of Alabama 1974; MDiv STUSo 1996. D 6/29/1996 P 3/15/1997 Bp Robert Gould Tharp. m 12/19/1971 Suzanne Smitherman c 2. Gr Ch Chattanooga TN 2002-2010; S Chris's Ch Kingsport TN 1997-2002; All SS' Epis Ch Morristown TN 1996-1997. DRGEOFFEREY@EARTHLINK.NET

SMITHERMAN, Suzanne (ETenn) 1108 Meadow Ln, Kingsport TN 37663 **Assoc R S Paul's Epis Ch Chattanooga TN 2005-** B Chattanooga TN 5/14/1952 d Nicholas Richardson Nichols & Caroline. BD U of Alabama 1974; MDiv STUSo 1996. P 3/1/1997 Bp Robert Gould Tharp. m 12/19/1971 Gene Smitherman c 2. Chr Ch Epis So Pittsburg TN 2003-2004; S Paul's Epis Ch Kingsport TN 1997-2002; All SS' Epis Ch Morristown TN 1996-1997. smitherman@stpaulschatt.org

SMITHERS, Charles William (WNC) 311 Lakeside Ct, Kernersville NC 27284 B Fond du Lac WI 9/21/1942 s Edwin Charles Smithers & Marion Jeanette. U of Wisconsin 1967; BS U of Wisconsin 1970; MS U of Wisconsin 1980; MDiv STUSo 1992. D 4/22/1992 P 10/25/1992 Bp Roger John White. m 5/19/1974 Joyce Carol Dzielak c 2. S Steph's Ch Oxford NC 2007-2008; All SS' Epis Ch Gastonia NC 2005-2006; Bp's Com on the Diac Dio No Carolina Raleigh NC 1998; S Matt's Epis Ch Kernersville NC 1997-2005; Ecum Cmsn Dio Sthrn Virginia Norfolk VA 1996-1997; Co-Pstr Ch Of H Apos Virginia Bch VA 1992-1997. jncsmithers@triad.rr.com

SMITH-GATLIN, Vickie Mitchell (Ark) 601 Brookside Dr Apt 12, Little Rock AR 72205 B Decatur IN 3/21/1958 BA LSU. Trans 2/1/2004 Bp Charles Edward Jenkins III. c 2. Cur S Mk's Epis Ch Little Rock AR 2003-2005. vickiegatlin@hotmail.com

SMITH GRAHAM, Shirley Elizabeth (SVa) 118 N Washington St, Alexandria VA 22314 **R S Mart's Epis Ch Williamsburg VA 2007-** B Mountain View CA 10/28/1968 BA California St U 1989; MDiv VTS 2002. D 6/1/2002 P 12/18/2002 Bp Jerry Alban Lamb. m 8/5/2001 Earnest Newt Graham c 1. Chr Ch Alexandria VA 2002-2007. The Chas And Janet Harris Awd Virginia Sem 2002. sgraham@historicchristchurch.org

SMITH GRAYBEAL, Felicia Marie (Colo) 236 Bowen St, Longmont CO 80501 **St Brigit Epis Ch Frederick CO 2009-** B Ruston LA 5/30/1967 d Charles Robert Carver Smith & Karen Dean. BA U Of Cntrl Florida 1989; MDiv VTS 2002. D 6/8/2002 P 1/11/2003 Bp William Jerry Winterrowd. m 3/15/1997 Lyle Graybeal. Cur S Mary Magd Ch Boulder CO 2002-2008. fsmithgray@msn.com

SMITH-KURTZ, Mary Bonnagean (WMich) 7280 Deepwater Point Rd, Williamsburg MI 49690 **D Dio Wstrn Michigan Kalamazoo MI 1992-** B Laredo TX 3/17/1944 d Richard Pha Smith & Mary Lenora. Pediatric Nurse Practioner; AS NW Michigan Coll 1964; RN NW Michigan Coll 1966; MI SU 1967. D 5/2/1992 Bp Edward Lewis Lee Jr. m 11/4/1967 William Kurtz c 3. Auth, "Post-Traumatic Therap," *Post-Traumatic Ther & Victims Of Violence*. Fllshp Merry Christmas, Associated Parishes, Diakoneo.

SMITH-MORAN, Barbara Putney (Mass) 93 Anson Road, Concord MA 01742 **P-in-c Gr Ch Everett MA 2007-** B Richmond VA 7/15/1945 d Maynard Putney Smith & Mary Helen. BA Randolph-Macon Wmn's Coll 1967; MAT JHU 1969; MA Harv 1974; MDiv EDS 1989; DMin CDSP 2009. D 6/3/1989 P 5/8/1990 Bp David Elliot Johnson. m 11/30/1974 James Michael Moran c 2. Int P Chr Ch Cambridge Cambridge MA 2004-2005; Int Trin Chap Shirley MA 2002-2003; Asst Grad Theol Un Berkeley CA 2000-2002; Asst The Ch Of The Gd Shpd Acton MA 2000-2001; Int S Jn's Epis Ch Westwood MA 1996; Int S Andr's Ch Framingham MA 1992-1995; Asst S Andr's Ch Framingham MA 1991-1992; Asst Boston Theol Inst Newton Cntr MA 1990-2000. Auth, "Preformationist Theory: Its persistent influence," *Bulletin*, Soc of Ord Scientists, 2006; Auth, "Bldg Victim Awareness into Ch Websites," *Wit*, 2006; contributing Auth, "A Catechism of Creation: An Epis Understanding," ECUSA, 2005; Prncpl Auth, "The Sci of Sexual Behavior in Humans and Other Animals: A Resource for the Ch," Dioc. of Massachusetts, 2005; Auth, "Strategies for Bldg a Ch Based Allnce," *Reshape*, Sexual Assault Cltn, 2005; Auth, "The Evolutionary Past & Future of God," *God for the 21st Century*, Templeton Press, 2000; Auth, "Soul at Wk: Reflections on Sprtlty of Working," St. Mary's Press, 1999; co-Ed, "Consumption, Population & Sustanability," Island Press, 1999; Ed, "Proceedings of Forum on Human Genetic Enhancement," Dioc. of Massachusetts, 1998; Ed, "Journ of Faith & Sci Exch, 1997-2001," Boston Theol Inst., 1997. Dio Mass EWC 1986-1993; Epis Ch Ntwk for Sci, Tech & Faith 1994; ECom 2000-2006; EPF 2003; Mass. Cler Assn 1989; Soc of Ord Scientists 1992. The Genesis Awd for Sci and Rel Episc. Ch. Ntwk for Sci, Tech & Faith 2007; Polly Bond Awd ECom 2006; Polly Bond Awd ECom 2001; Team Tchg Grant Louisville Inst 1996. smithmoran@earthlink.net

SMITS, Hilary Jerome (CPa) 631 Colonial Ave, York PA 17403 B DePere WI 8/15/1931 s Irvin Aloysius Smits & Agnes Elizabeth. BA S Norbert Coll De Pere WI 1953; MA U of Notre Dame 1961. Rec from Roman Catholic 4/1/1983 as Priest Bp Emerson Paul Haynes. m 7/16/1975 Doris Lerew. S Lk's Epis Ch Mt Joy PA 1996-2000; R S Jn's Ch Marietta PA 1995-1999; Chr Ch Coudersport PA 1994-1996; R S Jas Bedford PA 1990-1993; R Chr Epis Ch Pulaski VA 1985-1990; S Wlfd's Epis Ch Sarasota FL 1983-1984. Auth, "The Mass In Progress," S Norbert Abbey Press, 1965. dorismits@comcast.net

SMODELL, George (CFla) 2394 Lakes of Melbourne Dr, Melbourne FL 32904 **D S Sebastian's By The Sea Melbourne Bch FL 1989-** B Albany NY 1/23/1928 s John Henry Smodell & Thelma Alberta. Brevard Cmnty Coll; Inst for Chr Stds. D 10/28/1989 Bp John Wadsworth Howe. m 9/24/1956 Donna Tillapaugh. NAAD.

SMOKE, Joan C(laire) (Mil) 731 Sunset Blvd #67, Wisconsin Dellsq WI 53965 **R H Cross Epis Ch Wisconsin Dells WI 2007-** B Boston MA 9/30/1944 d Edwin E Tuttle & Mary S. U of Wisconsin; BS Indiana St U 1966; Garrett Evang TS 1968; MEPD U of Wisconsin 1980; D Formation Prog 1998. D 6/27/1998 Bp Russell Edward Jacobus P 2/11/2006 Bp Steven Andrew Miller. m 12/27/1967 Jay Smoke. NAAD; Oblate Ord Of S Ben. hlysmk@gmail.com

SMUCKER III, John Reed (Mich) 108 N Quaker Ln, Alexandria VA 22304 B Kansas City MO 4/20/1928 s John Reed Smucker & Dorothy. BS Swarthmore Coll 1952; MDiv VTS 1958. D 6/13/1958 Bp Frederick D Goodwin P 5/29/1959 Bp Richard S M Emrich. m 6/28/1958 Louisa Smucker c 2. Vic S Barn' Ch Chelsea MI 1962-1966; S Columba Ch Detroit MI 1958-1961. Soc of the Anchor Cross (BPFWR). jonjam3@msn.com

SMULLEN, Thema Alice (Md) 15708 Bradford Drive, Laurel MD 20707 **Transition Consult Dio Maryland Baltimore MD 2007-; Cler Assoc S Barth's Ch Baltimore MD 2007-; Fresh Start Team Dio Maryland Baltimore MD 2006-** B Baltimore MD 5/1/1943 d Oswald von Behren & Marion Mildred. BA Washington Coll 1964; MDiv VTS 1984. D 6/9/1984 P 12/15/1984 Bp John Thomas Walker. m 6/12/1965 John Alfred Smullen c 2. Int S Geo's Ch Glenn Dale MD 2004-2006; Int Chr Ch Par Kent Island Stevensville MD 2003-2004; Int S Marg's Ch Annapolis MD 2002; Int The Ch Of The Redeem Baltimore MD 2000-2001; Dioc Coun Dio Maryland Baltimore MD 1992-1995; R The Ch Of The H Apos Halethorpe MD 1989-2000; Int Gr Ch Washington DC 1988-1989; Int The Ch Of The Ascen Lexington Pk MD 1987-1988; Dioc Coun Dio Washington Washington DC 1986-1989; Int Ch Of The Ascen Silver Sprg MD 1986-1987; CE Cmsn, Chair Dio Washington Washington DC 1985-1987; Asst Ch Of The Ascen Silver Sprg MD 1984-1986. Fell Coll of Preachers 1994. tasmullen@gmail.com

SMYITHE, Frederick Kitchener (Minn) 1700 Norton Ave NW Apt 107, Bemidji MN 56601 B Minneapolis MN 7/18/1919 s Charles Edward Smyithe & Celeste May. BA U MN 1942; MDiv SWTS 1945; DD SWTS 1973. D 6/18/1945 P 12/21/1945 Bp Stephen E Keeler. m 12/6/2002 Betty Christensen c 4. Int H Trin Intl Falls MN 1985-1986; Int S Andr's Epis Ch Nogales AZ 1984-1985; Int S Matt's Epis Ch Fairbanks AK 1983-1984; Dio Minnesota Minneapolis MN 1979-1983; S Jn's Ch Aitkin MN 1976-1980; R S Paul's Ch Brainerd MN 1976-1979; S Ptr's Ch Warroad MN 1974-1976; R H Trin Intl Falls MN 1969-1976; Vic Our Fr's Hse Ft Washakie WY 1966-1969; CnMssny Dio No Dakota Fargo ND 1960-1966; Supr Presb Dio No Dakota Fargo ND 1955-1966; R All SS Ch Vlly City ND 1955-1960; R Trin Epis Ch Pk Rapids MN 1953-1955; Archd Dio Minnesota Minneapolis MN 1952-1955; Vic S Ptr's Ch Warroad MN 1948-1952; Vic Emm Epis Ch Alexandria MN 1945-1948. RWF 1943. fredabet@paulbunyan.net

✠ **SMYLIE, Rt Rev John Sheridan** (Wyo) 123 S Durbin St, Casper WY 82601 **Bp Dio Wyoming Casper WY 2010-** B Baltimore MD 12/31/1952 s Charles Albert Smylie & Marguerette. BA Syr 1975; MDiv EDS 1981. D 6/12/1982 P 12/15/1982 Bp John Shelby Spong Con 7/31/2010 for Wyo. m 1/25/2003 Jill L Smylie c 4. R S Mk's Epis Ch Casper WY 2007-2010; Dn Cathd Of S Jn The Evang Spokane WA 1998-2005; R Trin Epis Ch Hamburg NY 1989-1998; Assoc Calv Epis Ch Summit NJ 1987-1989; Assoc Chr Ch Ridgewood NJ 1985-1986; R S Lk's Ch Hope NJ 1982-1984. Auth, "Chr Parenting"; Auth, "Treasure," *Audio Rcrdng*; Auth, "Forw In Faith," *Audio Rcrdng*; Auth, "Stretching The Truth," *Bk On Tape*; Auth, "The Other Side Of Day," *Record Album*. Soc Of S Jn The Evang. jssmylie@yahoo.com

SMYTH, Margaret Emma Ferrell (NJ) 53 Mulberry St, Medford NJ 08055 **D S Mart-In-The-Fields Lumberton NJ 1998-** B Camden NJ 4/19/1943 d Robert William Ferrell & Elizabeth. Burlington Cnty Coll 1995; D Formation Prog 1998. D 10/31/1998 Bp Joe Morris Doss. m 4/20/1963 Tyson Robert Smyth. Oblate OHF.

SMYTH, William E (NC) PO Box 615, Columbia NC 27925 **P-in-c S Andr's Ch Columbia NC 2011-** B Greensboro NC 2/17/1947 s Thomas James Campbell Smyth & Julia. BA Davidson Coll 1969; MA Mid 1973; MDiv GTS 1980. D 6/7/1980 Bp Paul Moore Jr P 12/21/1980 Bp Thomas Augustus Fraser Jr. m 12/28/1991 Frances Wilson c 3. Vic S Lk's Ch Tarboro NC 1994-2010; R Calv Ch Tarboro NC 1992-2010; R All SS Ch Roanoke Rapids NC 1983-1992; Cmnty Worker S Jas Ch New York NY 1980-1982. williamesmyth@gmail.com

SMYTHE JR, Colville Nathaniel (Los) 2103 Hill Ave, Altadena CA 91001 B Los Angeles CA 1/12/1943 s Colville Nathaniel Smythe & Pauline Healey. BA U CA, Riverside 1965; Cert U CA, Riverside 1967; STB GTS 1971. D 9/11/1971 P 5/27/1972 Bp Francis E I Bloy. m 1/14/1989 Sylvia Smythe. R S Mk's Par Altadena CA 1995-2007; R S Andr's Ch Ben Lomond CA 1988-1995; Assoc R Ch Of The Mssh Santa Ana CA 1984-1988; Assoc S Mths' Par Whittier CA 1978-1984; Cur S Lk's Of The Mountains La Crescenta CA 1972-1974; Cur S Steph's Ch Phoenix AZ 1971-1972. cssmythe@charter.net

SMYTHE, Sally Lee (ND) 301 Main St S, Minot ND 58701 B Monterey CA 7/4/1945 d Burwell Barton Smythe & Mildred Hannah. BS U of Maryland 1983. D 7/23/2010 Bp Michael Gene Smith. c 2. sallyleesmythe@yahoo.com

SMYTHE, William (Neb) 16811 Burdette St Apt 203, Omaha NE 68116 B Reading PA 12/14/1925 s Thomas Smythe & Marguerite. MDiv PDS 1956; Ft Hays St U 1970; BA Moravian Coll 2046. D 5/26/1956 Bp Frederick J Warnecke P 12/14/1956 Bp Harry S Kennedy. m 8/9/1947 Ann R Rosenau c 4. Assoc S Paul's Epis Ch Ft Collins CO 1992-2002; Cur S Andr's Ch Omaha NE 1989-1991; Exec Com Dio Nebraska Omaha NE 1980-1983; Vic Gd Shpd Of The Plains Harrisburg NE 1973-1989; Vic S Hildas Ch Kimball NE 1973-1989; Vic S Eliz's Ch Russell KS 1968-1973; Vic Ascen-On-The-Prairie Epis Ch Colby KS 1966-1968; Chr Soc Relatns Dio Wstrn Kansas Hutchinson KS 1966-1968; Vic S Paul's Epis Ch Goodland KS 1966-1968; Asst to Dn Chr Cathd Salina KS 1963-1965; Vic H Apos Ch Ellsworth KS 1962-1963; Vic S Eliz's Ch Russell KS 1962-1963; Vic S Mk's Ch Lyons KS 1962-1963; Vic Gr Ch Hoolehua HI 1959-1962; Vic Chr Ch Kealakekua HI 1956-1959. wsmythe@aol.com

SNAPP, J(ames) Russell (Ark) 1702 S Spring St, Little Rock AR 72206 **Trin Cathd Little Rock AR 2010-** B Newport AR 3/31/1959 BA U So 1981; AA Harv 1982; PhD Harv 1988; MDiv GTS 2004. D 12/27/2003 P 6/29/2004 Bp Larry Earl Maze. R S Paul's Newport AR 2006-2010; Gr Ch Siloam Sprg AR 2004-2006. "Jn Stuart And The Struggle For Empire On The Sthrn Frontier," LSU Press, 1996. rsnapp@trinitylittlerock.org

SNARE, Pamela Porter (Tenn) Episcopal Diocese of Tennessee, 50 Vantage Way, Suite 107, Nashville TN 37228 **Cn to the Ordnry Dio Tennessee Nashville TN 2007-** B Winston-Salem NC 1/21/1953 d Ivil Lawson Porter & Leona Esther. BA U NC 1975; MDiv Duke 1979; Cert. Angl Studi GTS 1983. D 5/28/1983 P 6/9/1984 Bp Robert Whitridge Estill. m 6/5/1999 Gerald Snare. Cur Chr Ch Covington LA 1997-2007; Int H Trin Epis Ch Greensboro NC 1995-1997; Int Chr Ch Cleveland NC 1992-1993; Int Ch Of The Nativ Raleigh NC 1991; Asst to R S Tim's Epis Ch Winston Salem NC 1983-1987. geraldsnare@comcast.net

SNEARY, Jerry Mack (WTex) Po Box 2031, Canyon Lake TX 78133 B Hardtner KS 5/5/1943 s Edward Leslie Sneary & Alice Pearl. BA Oklahoma City U 1965; BD SMU 1968. D 6/25/1983 P 1/7/1984 Bp Gerald Nicholas McAllister. m 6/17/1995 Martha Pierce c 3. R S Fran By The Lake Canyon Lake TX 2002-2009; R S Jas' Epis Ch Dalhart TX 1995-2001; Vic S Jn's Epis Ch Woodward OK 1991-1995. martha.sneary@gmail.com

SNELL, Carol Burkey (CPa) 182D Dew Drop Rd, York PA 17402 **Archd Emer Dio Cntrl Pennsylvania Harrisburg PA 2011-; D S Andr's Epis Ch York PA 1988-** B Old Washington OH 3/15/1942 d John William Burkey & Evelyn Ilene. OH SU; Sch of Chr Stds 1988. D 6/10/1988 Bp Charlie Fuller McNutt Jr. m 1/6/1962 Harry Howard Snell c 3. Archd Dio Cntrl Pennsylvania Harrisburg PA 1997-2004. NAAD 1988. snellhc@comcast.net

SNEVE, Paul Marshall (SD) 2408 Central Blvd, Rapid City SD 57702 **Archd Dio So Dakota Sioux Falls SD 2010-; Vic S Matt's Epis Ch Rapid City SD 1999-** B Cedar Rapids IA 1/20/1961 s Vance Marshall Sneve & Virginia Rose. BFA U of So Dakota 1983; MDiv Vancouver TS 1999. D 12/21/1998 P 6/27/1999 Bp Creighton Leland Robertson. m 1/1/1994 Tally K Salisbury c 3. paul1@rushmore.com

SNICKENBERGER, Patricia Wolcott (Chi) 179 School Street, Libertyville IL 60048 **Bd Trst Epis Chars And Cmnty Serv (Eccs) Chicago IL 2011-; R S Lawr Epis Ch Libertyville IL 2007-** B Geneva IL 6/11/1953 d Oliver Manley Wolcott & Leota. BA Drake U 1974; MSW U IL 1976; MDiv SWTS 1999. D 6/12/1999 Bp David B(ruce) Joslin P 2/2/2000 Bp William Dailey Persell. m 5/14/1983 Thomas Warren Snickenberger c 3. COM Dio Chicago Chicago IL 2004-2010; Chr Ch Winnetka IL 1999-2006. Auth, "Where do you Stand?," *Sermons That Wk XIII*, Morehouse, 2005; Auth, "All SS' Day," *The Chorister*, 2002. Henry Benjamin Whipple Schlr Seabury Wstrn TS Evanston IL 1999. pws611@aol.com

SNIDER II, Michael Ellsworth (WVa) Christ Episcopal Church, 200 Duhring St, Bluefield WV 24701 **R Chr Ch Bluefield WV 2007-** B Canton OH 12/19/1974 s Michael Ellsworth Snider & Carol Jo. BA Mt Un Coll 1998; MDiv St Lk's TS 2005; STM St Lk's TS 2006. D 9/27/2006 Bp Granville Porter Taylor P 10/23/2007 Bp William Michie Klusmeyer. m 9/23/2000 Penelope Jane Beachy c 4. mikesnider@onebox.com

SNIDER, Stephen B (Pa) 254 Crosshill Rd, Wynnewood PA 19096 **Int All SS Ch Philadelphia PA 2010-** B Iowa City IA 1/14/1948 s John Morton Snider & Wilma Lee. BA U So 1970; MDiv SWTS 1974. D 6/17/1974 P 12/20/1974 Bp Walter Cameron Righter. m 6/14/1974 Irene C Kale c 2. Int Nevil Memi Ch Of S Geo Ardmore PA 2008-2009; Int The Ch Of The H Comf Drexel Hill PA 2007-2008; P-t Asst Ch Of The Redeem Bryn Mawr PA 2006-2007; R Ch Of The H Apos Wynnewood PA 1991-2006; R S Ptr's Ch Bettendorf IA 1983-1990; R S Johns Ch Cedar Rapids IA 1978-1983; Cur S Tim's Epis Ch W Des Moines IA 1975-1978; Asst S Mk's Epis Ch Ft Dodge IA 1974-1975. Integrity 1994. sbsnider@verizon.net

SNIECIENSKI, Edward Thomas (Los) PO Box 26688, Los angeles CA 90026 B New York NY 12/21/1948 s Thomas B Sniecienski & Maria. California St U; ETSBH; BA St. Fran Coll Brooklyn NY 1971. D 1/14/2005 Bp Joseph Jon Bruno. Dio Los Angeles Los Angeles CA 2005-2011. No Amer Assn of Deacons 2003. deaconed@gmail.com

SNIFFEN, E(rnest) Timothy (Me) P0 Box 368, Readfield ME 04355 B Newport News VA 10/31/1944 s Harold Scott Sniffen & Anna Elizabeth. BA Trin Hartford CT 1966; MDiv EDS 1971; BS U of New Engl Biddeford 1986. D 6/19/1971 P 6/1/1972 Bp David Shepherd Rose. m 4/21/1972 Luvia McGehee c 3. Int S Andr's Ch Readfield ME 1991-1992; R S Paul's Ch Ft Fairfield ME 1979-1984; P-in-c S Anne's Ch Mars Hill ME 1979-1980; Asst All SS Ch Richmond VA 1978-1979; P-in-c S Jas Ch Tanana AK 1972-1977; D-in-trng Galilee Epis Ch Virginia Bch VA 1971-1972. sniffen@mint.net

SNIFFEN, Michael Thomas (LI) 520 Clinton Ave, Brooklyn NY 11238 **P-in-c The Ch Of S Lk and S Matt Brooklyn NY 2010-** B Glen Cove NY 10/20/1980 s Robert D Sniffen & Diane D. BA W Virginia Wesleyan Coll 2002; MDiv Drew TS 2005; PhD Drew U 2013. D 9/15/2007 P 3/29/2008 Bp Mark M Beckwith. m 10/14/2010 Joanna M Yoho. Cur S Jn's Of Lattingtown Locust Vlly NY 2007-2010; Asst S Ptr's Ch Essex Fells NJ 2006-2007; Yth Dir S Ptr's Ch Mtn Lakes NJ 2005-2006. Epis Preaching Excellence Prog 2005-2005; No Amer Acad of Liturg 2008; The Amer Acad of Homil 2011; The AAR 2006. michaelsniffen@gmail.com

SNIVELY, Candy (NC) 103 Cibola Dr, Cary NC 27513 **D S Paul's Epis Ch Cary NC 2005-** B Boston MA 11/27/1945 d Paul Gordon Foley & Helen Louise. Penn 1965; Barry U 1990; BA Meredith Coll 2001. D 5/16/2005 Bp Michael Bruce Curry. m 6/25/1965 Craig Snively c 2. candy.snively@att.net

SNODGRASS, Cynthia (SO) 5146 SW 9th Lane, Gainesville FL 32607 B Iowa City Iowa 7/15/1950 d William Dewitt Snodgrass & Lila J. BA Syr 1976; MA Syr 1979; MDiv Bex 1985; PhD Univ. of Stirling - Scotland 2008. D 12/17/1988 P 7/20/1989 Bp William Grant Black. m 6/22/1985 Patrick Leroy Scully. Cbury Crt W Carrollton OH 1991-1993; Asst P S Geo's Epis Ch Dayton OH 1990-1992. Auth, "The Sonic Thread," *The Sonic Thread*,

Paraview Press, 2000. AAR 2005-2013; Assn of Pstr Care 1984-2013. cynthia@sacredsoundinstitute.org

SNODGRASS, Galen David (WMo) 1125 S Main St, Carthage MO 64836 **D Gr Ch Carthage MO 2004-** B St. Joseph MO 2/8/1957 s David Loren Snodgrass & Effie Ernestine. BS U of Missouri; MS Pittsburg St U 2001. D 2/7/2004 Bp Barry Robert Howe. m 9/1/1979 Kimberly Ann Surber c 4.

SNODGRASS JR, Samuel Lea (NY) 4 Truman Dr, Stony Point NY 10980 B Brooklyn NY 2/1/1921 s Samuel Lea Snodgrass & Mary. BA CUNY 1949; STM GTS 1952; NYU 1971. D 4/19/1952 P 10/25/1952 Bp James P De Wolfe. m 9/7/1957 Adeline Tinder c 2. Dpt Of Missions Ny Income New York NY 1969-1976; Vic S Jn's In The Wilderness Stony Point NY 1964-1993; R Trin Epis Ch Garnerville NY 1964-1993; Diocn Msnry & Ch Extntn Socty New York NY 1964-1976; Vic S Paul's Ch Morrisania Bronx NY 1958-1964; Cur S Aug's Ch New York NY 1955-1958; Cur S Steph's Ch Port Washington NY 1952-1955.

SNODGRASS, T(homas) James (PR) Po Box 612, AibonitoOlean PR 00705 Puerto Rico B Chicago IL 1/14/1947 s Thomas Joseph Snodgrass & Jeanne Bowie. BA Lawr 1970; Cert GTS 1976; MDiv UTS 1977. D 10/4/1975 Bp Paul Moore Jr P 5/28/1976 Bp Harold Louis Wright. m 7/1/1995 Patricia E Parsley c 7. Chr Ch Binghamton NY 1999-2006; R S Steph's Ch Olean NY 1990-2006; Epis Soc Of Chr Ch Cincinnati OH 1986-1990; R Epis Soc of Chr Ch Cincinnati OH 1986-1989; Hse Of Pryr Epis Ch Newark NJ 1984-1986; Newark Epis Coop For Min & Miss Newark NJ 1980-1983; Assoc S Ann's Ch Of Morrisania Bronx NY 1978-1980; Cur Gr Ch White Plains NY 1976-1978; D Chr Ch Bronxville NY 1975-1976. The Soc of S Jn the Evang 1974. Ecum Awd OLEAN Assn of Ch 2005; Intl Fell Col 1974. peparsley1@juno.com

SNOOK, Susan Brown (Az) 15657 E Golden Eagle Blvd, Fountain Hills AZ 85268 **Vic Epis Ch of the Nativ Phoenix AZ 2010-** B Newbrucke Germany 4/24/1962 d James Brown & Glenda. BA Rice U 1983; MA Rice U 1985; MBA Rice U 1985; MDiv CDSP 2003. D 5/24/2003 P 12/13/2003 Bp Robert Reed Shahan. m 12/24/1983 Thomas Dykes Snook c 2. Dio Arizona Phoenix AZ 2006-2009; S Anth On The Desert Scottsdale AZ 2004-2006; Cur S Ptr's Ch Litchfield Pk AZ 2003-2004. snook.susan@gmail.com

SNOW, George Richard (Wyo) 151 Washakie Dr, Evanston WY 82930 **P S Paul's Epis Ch Evanston WY 2002-** B Evanston WY 2/27/1969 s George Lindy Snow & Sharyl Graham. BS U of Wyoming 1993. D 11/7/2001 P 5/9/2002 Bp Bruce Edward Caldwell. m 4/22/1995 Nikki Lyn Ballinger c 5. georgesnowconstruction@yahoo.com

SNOW, Peter D (Oly) 927 36th Ave, Seattle WA 98122 B Chadwell Heath Essex UK 12/3/1937 s Arther William Snow & Ena May. BA U of Cambridge 1962; MA U of Cambridge 1965. Trans from Church Of England 1/1/1968. m 11/30/1991 Elizabeth Spencer Robertson c 3. P-in-c S Hilda's - S Pat's Epis Ch Edmonds WA 2002-2003; R Ch Of The H Cross Redmond WA 1991-2001; P-in-c Ch Of The H Cross Redmond WA 1988-1990; Asst R Ch Of The Resurr Bellevue WA 1983-1986; R S Jn's Epis Ch Jackson WY 1975-1981; Yth Cn Mssnr Dio Los Angeles Los Angeles CA 1971-1975; Asst All SS-By-The-Sea Par Santa Barbara CA 1967-1971. Auth, "Jesus: Man, Not Myth," *Bk*, Bk Pub's Ntwk, 2010. peterorlisa@comcast.net

SNOW, Robert Gerald (DR) Po Box 407052, Fort Lauderdale FL 33340 **Dio Nebraska Omaha NE 1999-** B Great Falls MT 1/4/1943 s Gerald Snow & Alice Marie. BA U of Nebraska 1966. D 11/8/1985 Bp James Daniel Warner. m 9/22/1963 Ellen Fay McKenzie. SAMS Ambridge PA 1994-1999. bob_snow.parti@ecunet.org

SNOW II, William Josiah (SC) 1115 Pruitt Dr, Orangeburg SC 29118 **Died 5/13/2011** B Washington DC 9/22/1923 s William Arthur Snow & Margaret. BS USMA At W Point 1945; BD VTS 1963; DMin Ibis 1980. D 6/1/1963 P 4/29/1964 Bp Gray Temple. c 4. DD Ibis 1981.

SNYDER, Albert Eric (Be) 290 Conklin St, Farmingdale NY 11735 B Glendale CA 3/15/1925 s Roy Highland Snyder & Margaret Houston. BA Occ 1945; BD UTS 1949; MS Col 1957. D 10/9/1957 P 6/24/1958 Bp Horace W B Donegan. m 1/24/1953 Jean Swerdfeger c 5. R Calv Ch Tamaqua PA 1987-1994; R S Jas' Ch Drifton PA 1987-1994; Int Chr Ch Towanda PA 1985-1987; Int Chr Ch Forest City PA 1983-1985; Int Trin Epis Ch Carbondale PA 1983-1985; Asst Gr Ch White Plains NY 1959-1963; Cur S Mich's Ch New York NY 1957-1959. ersnie@gmail.com

SNYDER, Albert Llwyd (WTex) 527 Sonnet Dr, San Antonio TX 78216 B Muskogee OK 6/16/1938 s Llwyd Christian Snyder & Helen Genevive. Wichita St U; BD U of Nebraska 1975; MDiv Epis TS of The SW 1984. D 1/22/1985 P 7/22/1985 Bp Stanley Fillmore Hauser. Dio W Texas San Antonio TX 1987-2003; Vic Ch Of The H Cross San Antonio TX 1985-2003; Vic Santa Fe Epis Mssn San Antonio TX 1985-1987. asnyder1@satx.rr.com

SNYDER, Bindy Ann Wright (WTenn) 539 Cherry Rd, Memphis TN 38117 **All SS Epis Ch Memphis TN 2009-; P Chr Epis Ch Forrest City AR 2002-; P Ch Of The Gd Shpd Forrest City AR 2002-; P Gr Ch Wynne AR 2002-** B Saint Louis MO 3/18/1947 d Horace Wright & Audrey. BA U of Tennessee 1969; MA U of Memphis 1972; MA Memphis TS 1996; MDiv Memphis TS 1998; post grad U of Wales at Lampeter 1998; -- GTS 2000; DMin Sewanee 2012. D 3/15/2002 P 9/10/2002 Bp Larry Earl Maze. c 3. Dio Arkansas Little Rock AR 2003-2009; P- in-Charge, Mssy Chapl Calv Epis Ch Osceola AR 2002-2003; S Steph's Ch Blytheville AR 2002-2003; Cmncatn Off Dio W Tennessee Memphis TN 1986-1990. Assoc - Cmnty of S Mary, Sewanee 1995; Coun for Wmn Mnstrs 1986; DOK 1997; ECom 1986-1991; HSEC 2001; Natl Epis Historians and Archivists (NEHA) 2001. MHE Bd Dio W Tennessee 2007; Bd Trst Natl Epis Historians and Archivists 2007; Chair, Transition Com Dio Arkansas 2006; Chapl DOK Dio W Tennessee 2006; Natl Pres EWHP 2005. revbindy@bellsouth.net

SNYDER, David L (NJ) St. Andrew's Episcopal Church, 121 High Street, Mt. Holly NJ 08060 B Lansdale PA 8/11/1950 s Richard Snyder & Margaret Schwartz. BS Lock Haven U Lock Haven PA 1972; MDiv Sthrn Bapt TS Louisville KY 1985; DMin Bangor TS 1997. Rec from Evangelical Lutheran Church in America 2/24/2008 Bp George Edward Councell. m 8/18/1973 Susan Rosenberry c 4. Assoc S Lk's Ch Gladstone NJ 2011; P-in-c Ch Of The Atone Stratford NJ 2010-2011; The Evergreens Moorestown NJ 2010. deweysnyder1@comcast.net

SNYDER, George Lewis (SO) 1105 Scenic Ct, Troy OH 45373 **D S Mk's Epis Ch Dayton OH 2011-; D's Coun Dio Sthrn Ohio Cincinnati OH 2009-** B Troy OH 2/11/1947 s Clarence Leroy Snyder & Isabelle Gross. Sch for the Deaconate; BA Wilmington Coll 1969; MEd Wright St U 1981. D 10/20/2001 Bp Herbert Thompson Jr. c 1. snyder.gl.47@gmail.com

SNYDER, Gregory Alan (SC) 1990 Bohicket Rd, Johns Island SC 29455 **Asst R S Jn's Epis Par Johns Island SC 2002-** B Palo Alto CA 6/29/1960 s Raymond Henry Snyder & Anita Sue. BS U of Tennessee 1982; MS Colorado Sch of Mines 1986; PhD Colorado Sch of Mines 1990; MDiv TESM 2002. D 5/25/2002 P 12/14/2002 Bp Edward Lloyd Salmon Jr. m 12/27/1982 Elizabeth Rebecca Breland c 2. "Critical Cath: The Intellectual Life And Times Of Eric Lionell Mascall," ATR, 2006; "Bk Revs - Race And The Cosmos," ATR 86, 2004; "Is The Preaching In Your Par Of Any Use To Anyone," Epis Evang Journ No.4, 2002; "Planetary Petrology And Geochemistry," Geological Soc Of Amer/Bellwether, 1999. Systematic Theol Awd Trin Sch Of Mnstry 2002; Gk Schlrshp Awd Trin Sch Of Mnstry 2001. rgreg@stjohnsparish.net

SNYDER, Judith Urso (Be) 4621 Ashley Ln, Bethlehem PA 18017 **Assoc S Anne's Epis Ch Trexlertown PA 2005-; S Anne's Epis Ch Trexlertown PA 2004-** B Reading PA 8/25/1948 d Frank Charles Urso & Martha. BS Bloomsburg U of Pennsylvania 1970; Moravian TS 1991; MDiv GTS 1992. D 3/8/1992 P 11/23/1992 Bp James Michael Mark Dyer. c 1. Vic S Brigid's Ch Nazareth PA 1999-2003; Asst R H Trin Ch Lansdale PA 1998-1999; The Epis Acad Newtown Sq PA 1996-1998; Trin Ch Bethlehem PA 1996; Int S Ptr's Epis Ch Hazleton PA 1993-1995; Dio Bethlehem Bethlehem PA 1992-1993; D / Intern S Anne's Epis Ch Trexlertown PA 1992-1993. judith.snyder@stannesepiscopal.net

SNYDER, Kenneth McClellan (Oly) 3200 Wailea Alanui Dr Apt 304, Kihei HI 96753 B Elmira NY 7/14/1930 s Kenneth McClellan Snyder & Alice Estelle. AA Wesley Coll 1950; BA U of Delaware Newark 1952; STB Tem 1955. D 6/15/1957 Bp John Brooke Mosley P 12/1/1957 Bp Russell S Hubbard. m 6/3/1950 Charlesta Davis c 4. Int S Jn's Epis Ch Olympia WA 1992-1993; Natl Ntwk Of Epis Cler Assn Lynnwood WA 1988-1993; S Columba's Epis Ch And Chilren's Sch Kent WA 1983-1992; Int S Matthews Auburn WA 1982-1983; Dio Olympia Seattle WA 1980-1993; Int S Mich And All Ang Ch Issaquah WA 1979-1980; Dio Olympia Seattle WA 1979; S Andr's Ch Seattle WA 1978-1979; Int S Andr's Epis Ch Tacoma WA 1977-1978; Consult to Bp of Olympia Dio Olympia Seattle WA 1967-1968; Exec Dir Stwdshp Dio Olympia Seattle WA 1964-1968; Exec Dir Stwdshp Dio Dallas Dallas TX 1961-1964; Vic S Steph's Epis Ch Spokane WA 1958-1961; Asst Min Cathd Of S Jn The Evang Spokane WA 1957-1958. kscd11@aloha.net

SNYDER, Larry Alan (Q) 100 Washington Ave, Newtown PA 18940 B York PA 8/29/1947 s Earl Eugene Snyder & Marjorie Elizabeth. BS Millersville U 1968; MDiv PDS 1972. D 6/24/1972 Bp Robert Lionne DeWitt P 1/20/1973 Bp Lyman Cunningham Ogilby. m 5/25/1968 Karen L Snyder c 1. R S Lk's Ch In The Cnty Of Buck Newtown PA 1986-2007; Asst R Washington Memi Chap Vlly Forge PA 1982-1986; R Trin Ch Coshocton OH 1975-1977; Asst Chr Ch Epis Hudson OH 1972-1975. ASSP, Our Lady Of Walsingham & Soc Mary; SSC, Soc King Chas Mtyr. larryasnyder@gmail.com

SNYDER, Paul Leech (Okla) PO Box 10722, Midwest City OK 73140 B Oklahoma City OK 10/3/1949 s Byron R Snyder & Kathrine A. D 6/19/2010 Bp Edward Joseph Konieczny. m 8/5/1978 Marry Summers c 2. sopausny@oklahomacounty.com

SNYDER, Philip L (Dal) 2220 Susan Cir, Plano TX 75074 **D Trin Epis Ch Dallas TX 2010-** B Maysville CA 2/13/1962 s Albert L Snyder & Karen. BS U of Texas 1990; LM Angl TS 2004. D 6/5/2004 Bp James Monte Stanton. m 9/25/1987 Beverly Poindexter c 2. D S Jas Ch Dallas TX 2004-2010. philip_l_snyder@yahoo.com

SNYDER, Philip Wiseman (CNY) 1 Eagleshead Rd, Ithaca NY 14850 **R S Jn's Ch Ithaca NY 1988-** B Albany NY 3/4/1947 s Willis Embry Snyder & Margaret. BA Franklin & Marshall Coll 1968; BD EDS 1971. D 6/5/1971 Bp

S

Allen Webster Brown P 12/4/1971 Bp Charles Bowen Persell Jr. m 9/18/1971 Kluane Baier c 3. Stndg Com Dio Cntrl New York Syracuse NY 1993-2000; R Chr Epis Ch Burlington IA 1985-1988; Trst Dio Albany Albany NY 1978-1984; R The Ch of St Lk The Beloved Physcn Saranac Lake NY 1974-1984; Cur S Geo's Epis Ch Schenectady NY 1971-1974. Auth, "River Trips, Revelations, and Old Trees," Morehouse- Barlow, 2000. psnyder1@twcny.rr.com

SNYDER, Richard Henry (NAM) 400 S Saliman Rd Apt 134, Carson City NV 89701 **Stndg Cmsn on Cmncatn and Info Tech Epis Ch Cntr New York NY 2009-; San Juan Mssn Farmington NM 2008-** B Bakersfield CA 11/22/1946 s David Henry Snyder & Margaret Louise. AA Bakersfield Cmnty Coll 1966; BA San Jose St U 1968; MDiv CDSP 2004. D 1/9/2005 Bp Katharine Jefferts Schori P 9/1/2005 Bp Carolyn Tanner Irish. m 10/4/1997 Debra D McDonald. Treas and Admin Navajoland Area Mssn Farmington NM 2008-2011; Reg Mnstry Dvlp S Chris's Ch Bluff UT 2008-2009; Vic S Jn The Baptizer Bluff UT 2008-2009; Vic S Mary Of-The-Moonlight Bluff UT 2008-2009; Mnstry Dvlp; Vic Utah Reg Bluff UT 2008-2009; Dio Utah Salt Lake City UT 2005-2007. "Another Bethlehem," *Epis Life*, Epis Ch, 2008; "Rhythm and Balance," FMP, 2007; "Poor Richard's Almanac," *Dioc Dialogue*, Dio Utah, 2007. ECom 1978; NAAD 2008. rhsnyder12@aol.com

SNYDER, Robert Paul (Ind) 3221 - 29th, Bedford IN 47421 B Princeton IN 1/1/1923 s Charles H Snyder & Della. MA Indiana St U; BA Wabash Coll 1946; EDS Indiana U 1956. D 12/19/1970 Bp John P Craine. c 4. D-in-c S Jn's Ch Washington IN 1981-1983; Cur S Jn's Epis Ch Bedford IN 1970-1988.

SNYDER, Roger Charles (Nwk) 13 Partlow St, Staunton VA 24401 **Assoc Trin Ch Staunton VA 1993-** B Springfield OH 8/28/1927 s Roger Henry Snyder & Doris Frances. BA Witt 1953; STB Wesley TS 1956; Cert VTS 1961; MA Wesley TS 1971. D 10/17/1961 P 6/22/1962 Bp George P Gunn. m 6/27/1953 Rhoda Baker c 2. R S Ptr's Ch Mt Arlington NJ 1981-1991; R S Andr's Ch Norfolk VA 1969-1981; Assoc S Andr's Ch Norfolk VA 1966-1969; Asst Trin Ch Bethlehem PA 1964-1966; Cur S Andr's Ch Norfolk VA 1961-1964. Auth, "Poetry," *Natl Congr of Poetry*, 1996. chaucile@ntelos.net

SNYDER, Susanna Jane (Mass) 99 Brattle St, Cambridge MA 02138 **EDS Cambridge MA 2011-** B Hertford UK 9/9/1978 d Michael Snyder & Mary. BA Emml 2000; Theol Stds Queen's Fndt 2004; MA Emml 2005; PhD U of Birminghan 2009. Trans from Church Of England 8/24/2011 Bp M(arvil) Thomas Shaw III. susanna.snyder@bt@internet.com

SNYDER, William Delpharo (O) 4920 Woodview Rd, Ravenna OH 44266 **D Gr Ch Ravenna OH 1997-; D Dio Ohio Cleveland OH 1992-** B Charlestown WV 7/20/1943 s Oliver D Snyder & Merlin. D 11/13/1992 Bp James Russell Moodey. m 5/16/1965 Marsha Ann Luther c 2.

SO, Alistair (Md) All Hallows' Parish, P.O.Box 235, Davidsonville MD 21035 **R All Hallows Par So River Davidsonville MD 2008-** B Shijiazhuang China 4/7/1976 s Sze-Man So & Monica Kam-Ying. BS Amer U 1998; MS Geo 2000; MDiv VTS 2005. D 6/11/2005 P 1/21/2006 Bp John Chane. S Mart's-In-The-Field Day Sch Severna Pk MD 2005-2008; Assoc R St Martins-In-The-Field Ch Severna Pk MD 2005-2008. alistairso@gmail.com

SOARD, John Robert (Tex) 5010 N Main St, Baytown TX 77521 **Trin Epis Ch Baytown TX 2011-** B Houston TX 3/17/1980 s Robert Soard & Susan. BA Baylor U 2002; MDiv Epis TS Of The SW 2011. D 6/18/2011 Bp C(harles) Andrew Doyle. m 3/8/2003 Claire B Brockman c 2. johnsoard@gmail.com

SOBOL, Walter (O) 4627 Indian Ridge Rd, Sylvania OH 43560 B Malden MA 10/24/1935 s Demasus Joseph Sobol & Margaret May. BA Tufts U 1957; BD EDS 1960. D 6/18/1960 Bp Anson Phelps Stokes Jr P 12/1/1960 Bp Frederick J Warnecke. R Trin Ch Toledo OH 1987-1993; R S Lk's Epis Ch Montclair NJ 1981-1987; R All SS Ch Chelmsford MA 1975-1981; R S Mk's Ch Foxborough MA 1968-1974; R Trin Epis Ch Weymouth MA 1963-1968; Asst S Steph's Epis Ch Wilkes Barre PA 1960-1963. Auth, "Chr Century". kwsobol@accesstoledo.com

SODERGREN, Oscar Frederick (Alb) 9 Pinewood Dr, Scotia NY 12302 **P Asst Calv Epis Ch Burnt Hills NY 2000-** B Whitefield NH 10/10/1922 s Oscar Frederick John Sodergren & Hazel Viola. BA RPI 1956; MS Un Coll Schenectady NY 1971. D 10/13/1980 Bp Wilbur Emory Hogg Jr P 7/1/1998 Bp Daniel William Herzog. m 8/12/1944 Doris Edna Best. P-in-c All SS Ch Round Lake NY 1998-2002; Asst Treas Dio Albany Albany NY 1991-1998; D-In-C All SS Ch Round Lake NY 1990-1993; Admin Trsts Dio Albany Albany NY 1987-1998; Asst All SS Ch Round Lake NY 1986-1990; Asst Ch Of Beth Saratoga Sprg NY 1980-1986. osodergr@nycap.rr.com

SOJWAL, Imlijungla (NY) 201 W 72nd St Apt 15e, New York NY 10023 **All Souls Ch New York NY 2011-** B Mokokchung India 10/6/1965 d Limatemjen Ao & Lanlila. BD Un Biblic Sem 1990; MS Ford 2001; STM The GTS 2005. D 3/11/2006 P 9/23/2006 Bp Mark Sean Sisk. m 1/5/1990 Milind Sojwal c 2. Epis Ch Of Our Sav New York NY 2007-2009. ajungla@aol.com

SOJWAL, Milind (NY) 16 All Saints Rd, Princeton NJ 08540 **R All Ang' Ch New York NY 2000-** B Nagpur Maharashtra IN 8/18/1960 s Bhaskar Sojwal & Manorama. BA Madras Chr Coll 1982; Symbiosis Inst 1984; BD Un Biblic Sem Pune Mr IN 1989; ThM PrTS 1995. Trans from Church of North India 7/1/1998 Bp Joe Morris Doss. m 1/5/1990 Imlijungla Lima c 2. Asst R Ch Of The Redeem Bryn Mawr PA 1999-2000; All SS Ch Princeton NJ 1998-1999. msojwal@aol.com

SOLA, Geri Ely (NMich) 6579 W Center Dr, Hurley WI 54534 **R Ch Of The Trsfg Ironwood MI 1998-** B South Haven MI 7/17/1944 d Peter Franklin Ely & Cleone Margeret. MS Wstrn Michigan U 1971. D 11/12/1997 P 5/1/1998 Bp Thomas Kreider Ray. m 7/21/1972 John Raymond Sola.

SOLAK, Ketlen Adrien (Va) 8009 Fort Hunt Rd, Alexandria VA 22308 **Assoc R S Lk's Ch Alexandria VA 2005-** B Haiti 12/5/1961 BA CUA 1983; MA CUA 1988; MDiv VTS 2005. D 6/18/2005 P 12/21/2005 Bp Peter James Lee. m 4/23/1988 Scott J Solak. D S Mary's Epis Ch Arlington VA 2005. ksolak6@gmail.com

SOLBAK, Mary Martha (CPa) 719 Jake Landis Rd, Lititz PA 17543 **COM Dio Cntrl Pennsylvania Harrisburg PA 2008-** B Lancaster PA 7/1/1941 d Robert Charles Batchelder & Catherine. BA Lake Erie Coll 1963; Cert U of Pennsylvania 1964; Cert Dioc Sch Of Chr Stds Harrisburg PA 1987; Cert Pennsylvania U Hosp Chapl 1988; MAR Lancaster TS 2002. D 6/16/1989 Bp Charlie Fuller McNutt Jr. m 2/4/1967 Arne Solbak c 3. Stndg Com Dio Cntrl Pennsylvania Harrisburg PA 2002-2004; Cur S Jas Ch Lancaster PA 1989-2006. Bd, Dioc Sch of Chr Stds 2003; Bd, Epis Gardens, Thompsontown 1993-2000; Bd, Epis Hm, Shippensburg 1990; Cmsn on Liturg and Ch Mus 1996; NAAD, Life Mem 1990; VP ESMA 1993-2001. knitnpray@aol.com

SOLDWEDEL, Erik Gustav (Nwk) 176 Palisades Ave, Jersey City NJ 07306 **Dio New Jersey Trenton NJ 2010-; Dio Newark Newark NJ 2010-; D of the Hosp Chr Hosp Jersey City NJ 2009-** B Ridgewood NJ 6/30/1958 s Warren Nicholas Soldwedel & Solveig Casper. Newark TS; Ramapo Coll of NJ. D 12/15/2007 Bp Mark M Beckwith. m 12/30/1989 Linda Aprile. esoldwedel@aol.com

SOLLER, Robin (NH) 23 Old Bristol Rd, New Hampton NH 03256 **R Trin Ch Meredith NH 1995-** B Cambridge MA 2/13/1958 d Julian Thomas & Gisela Elisabeth (Martens). BA Wm Smith 1980; MEd U of Maine 1985; MDiv VTS 1989. D 6/10/1989 P 1/30/1990 Bp Edward Cole Chalfant. m 11/4/2000 Jon Mark Soller. Cur Trin Ch Ft Wayne IN 1992-1995; Cur Zion Epis Ch Wappingers Falls NY 1989-1992. robin.soller@trinitymeredith.org

SOLOMON SR, Mardon (Ak) 1/2 Mile Base Road, Fort Yukon AK 99740 **Died 1/20/2010** B Fort Yukon AK 8/8/1927 s Paul Solomon & Hannah. D 9/2/2000 Bp Mark Lawrence Mac Donald.

SOLOMON, Mildred Jeanne (Nwk) 5 Lincoln St, New Bedford MA 02740 B Argentina/New Bedford MA 11/9/1950 d Antone F Pina & Eloise Victoria. BA Birmingham-Sthrn Coll 1978; MDiv CRDS 1986. D 9/12/1987 P 10/1/1988 Bp Don Edward Johnson. R Hse Of Pryr Epis Ch Newark NJ 1998-2004; R S Barn Ch Newark NJ 1998-2004; Newark Reg Mnstry Newark NJ 1998-2003; Dio Wstrn Massachusetts Springfield MA 1994-1997; S Lk's Epis Ch Malden MA 1991-1993; Asst S Steph's Memi Ch Lynn MA 1988-1990; Asst S Steph's Epis Ch Boston MA 1987-1988. ECA. bethsolo@aol.com

SOLON JR, Robert Francis (Nwk) 307 Route 94, Vernon NJ 07462 **Vic S Thos Ch Vernon NJ 2008-** B Grand Rapids MI 3/16/1967 s Robert Solon & Joanie. BA Capital U 1988; MBA Anderson U 1999; MDiv, hon GTS 2006. D 6/24/2006 P 2/3/2007 Bp Catherine Elizabeth Maples Waynick. Cur Trin Ch Bayonne NJ 2006-2008; Windmill Allnce Inc. Bayonne NJ 2006-2007. Fllshp of St. Jn 2002. rsfc@earthlink.net

SOLON, T(erry) Tim (Wyo) 3251 Acacia Dr, Cheyenne WY 82001 B Elyria OH 8/25/1934 s Howard Francis Johnson Solon & Marjorie Clarissa. BA Hiram Coll 1956; BD Bex 1959; MDiv Bex 1971. P 3/1/1961 Bp William Crittenden. c 4. R S Chris's Ch Cheyenne WY 1987-2000; S Steph's Ch Casper WY 1967-1981; Vic Chr Ch - Epis Newcastle WY 1963-1967; Vic Ch Of The Epiph Grove City PA 1960-1963. Auth, "Pre-Marital Inventory And Related Materials," Bess Assoc., 1972. Soc Justice Advoc Wyoming Assn Of Ch 2003. timsolon@msn.com

SOMERS, David Wayne (CFla) 5873 N Dean Rd, Orlando FL 32817 **S Matt's Epis Ch Orlando FL 2010-** B Fremont MI 4/20/1959 s Wayne Keith Somers & Susan Jane. degree not complete yet Nash; BA Oral Roberts U 1981; None U of Cntrl Florida 1993. D 12/11/2010 Bp John Wadsworth Howe. m 4/25/1987 Patricia Patricia Susan Louree c 3. somerda@yahoo.com

SOMERS, Faye Veronica (SeFla) 2707 NW 37th St, Boca Raton FL 33434 B Jamaica West Indies 11/7/1953 d John Grizzle & Edna I. BSC York U 1974; MA Natl U 1991; Dioc Sch for Chr Stds 2009. D 4/8/2011 Bp Leopold Frade. c 3. fada4@comcast.net

SOMERVILLE II, Ben Leonidas (Az) 542 Raymond Dr, Sierra Vista AZ 85635 B Savannah GA 5/15/1940 s Ben Leonidas Somerville & Edna Vergie. BS W Virginia U 1962; MDiv STUSo 1968. D 6/29/1968 Bp Milton LeGrand Wood P 5/17/1969 Bp Randolph R Claiborne. m 8/15/1959 Mary Anne Somerville c 2. R S Steph's Ch Sierra Vista AZ 1999-2005; R Gr Epis Ch Canton NY 1989-1999; Trin Chap Morley Canton NY 1989-1999; Dio Maryland Baltimore MD 1988-1989; Ch Of The H Cov Baltimore MD 1987-1989; Ch Of-Ascen & Prince-Peace Baltimore MD 1986-1987; Ch Of The Ascen Baltimore MD 1986-1987; Dio Wyoming Casper WY 1983-1985; Trin Epis

S

Ch Hartford CT 1980-1983; S Lk's Ch Annapolis MD 1979-1980; EFM Mentor ; EFM Trnr The TS at The U So Sewanee TN 1976-1996; Dio Maryland Baltimore MD 1975-1980; Vic S Andr The Fisherman Epis Mayo MD 1975-1980; Asst St Martins-In-The-Field Ch Severna Pk MD 1970-1973; Gr-Calv Epis Ch Clarkesville GA 1968-1970. Auth, *Var Journ arts.* bensomerville@cox.net

SOMERVILLE, David James (Ga) 128 King Cotton Rd, Brunswick GA 31525 B Yonkers NY 5/11/1943 s Robert Lynn Somerville & Elizabeth. MS LIU; BA Bos 1967; STB PDS 1969. D 4/19/1969 P 10/1/1969 Bp Alfred L Banyard. m 6/22/1996 Sherry Somerville c 1. Int S Paul's Epis Ch Jesup GA 2002-2003; Chr Ch Middletown NJ 1995-2008; Off Of Bsh For ArmdF New York NY 1976-1995; S Barth's Ch Cherry Hill NJ 1972-1976; Vic The Ch Of The Gd Shpd Berlin NJ 1969-1973. summerdave@aol.com

SOMES, Norman Frederick (ECR) 85 Anna Laura Rd., 85 Anna Laura Drive, Jacksonville OR 97530 B Romford Essex England 1/28/1936 s Norman Henry Somes & Mary Rosina. BS Lon 1957; MS Lon 1962; PhD Lon 1964; PMD Harv 1976; MDiv CDSP 1988. D 6/4/1988 P 6/3/1989 Bp William Edwin Swing. m 3/8/1958 Patricia Cotter c 3. Chair Cler Dio El Camino Real Monterey CA 1993-1994; R S Barn Ch Arroyo Grande CA 1992-2005; Dioc Coun Dio El Camino Real Monterey CA 1992-1994; Assoc Ch of S Mary's by the Sea Pacific Grove CA 1988-1992. Auth, "So, you really want Ch growth. A handbook for Epis Ch rectors.," Jacksonville Press, 2011. somes@charter.net

SOMMER, Susan Lemmon (WMo) 4508 NW 64th Ter, Kansas City MO 64151 **Gr And H Trin Cathd Kansas City MO 2005-** B Ann Arbor MI 10/3/1956 d Robert Lewis Lemmon & Kay Betty. BA Cntrl Michigan U 1977; MDiv SWTS 1993. D 6/24/1993 Bp Robert Marshall Anderson P 1/6/1994 Bp William Walter Wiedrich. m 1/14/1979 Rick Sommer c 1. Vic Gr Epis Ch New Lenox IL 1999-2005; Asst R Emm Epis Ch La Grange IL 1994-1999; Dir Stdts Servs SWTS Evanston IL 1993-1994; Asst R The Annunc Of Our Lady Gurnee IL 1993-1994. "Actg ourselves into Thinking Rt," Preaching as Prophetic calling Sermons that Wk XII, 2004. ssommer@ghtc-kc.org

SOMODEVILLA, Rene Francisco (WTenn) 4018 S Lakewood Dr, Memphis TN 38128 **S Andr's Epis Ch Collierville TN 2010-** B Havana CU 4/14/1946 s Santiago Urbano Somodevilla & Elvira. BA Midwestern U 1969; MSSW U of Texas 1972; LST Angl TS 1984. D 6/16/1984 P 1/23/1985 Bp Donis Dean Patterson. m 5/9/1992 Nancy Ann Arko c 4. Dio W Tennessee Memphis TN 2004-2010; S Elis's Epis Ch Memphis TN 1997-2004; R S Barn Ch Garland TX 1986-1997; Cur Epis Ch Of The Ascen Dallas TX 1984-1986. renesomodevilla@yahoo.com

SONDEREGGER, Kathrine Ann (Va) 669 Weybridge St # 5753, Middlebury VT 05753 **Prof Of Theol VTS Alexandria VA 2002-** B Marquette MI 8/18/1950 d Richard Paul Sonderegger & Marion. D 8/13/2000 Bp Mary Adelia Rosamond McLeod. D S Steph's Ch Middlebury VT 2000-2002.

SONGY, Benedict Gaston (Tex) 375 Arthur Ave, Shreveport LA 71105 **Asst S Mths Epis Ch Shreveport LA 1999-; P Assoc S Mths Epis Ch Shreveport LA 1999-** B New Orleans LA 7/28/1929 s Gaston Joseph Songy & Magda Ann. BS S Jos Sem 1957; MA S Louis U 1958; PhD S Louis U 1968. Rec from Roman Catholic 5/1/1982 as Priest Bp Willis Ryan Henton. m 12/18/1976 Jacklyn S Shelton. Vic S Jn's Epis Ch Carthage TX 1986-1997; Asst Ch Of The H Cross Shreveport LA 1982-1986. Auth, "Alexis De Tocqueville & Slavery". jbsongy@sport.rr.com

SONNEN, Jon Anton (Tex) 4403 Seneca St, Pasadena TX 77504 B Houston TX 11/19/1936 s Louis Carl Sonnen & Waldene Burdette. BA SMU 1959; MA SMU 1965; MDiv Epis TS of The SW 1974. D 6/16/1974 Bp J Milton Richardson P 6/1/1975 Bp Scott Field Bailey. m 12/28/1957 Marilyn Braly c 3. S Barn Epis Ch Houston TX 1990-1999; Vic S Jn's Epis Ch Silsbee TX 1988-1990; S Thos Ch Houston TX 1987-1988; R S Barth's Ch Hempstead TX 1978-1987; All SS Epis Ch Stafford TX 1974-1978. Auth, "Concept Of Duty In Plato & Kant," 1964. CBS, ECM; NOEL. sonnenja@aol.com

SONNESYN, Roger Earl (Minn) 12908 Hideaway Trl, Hopkins MN 55305 **Supply P S Andr's Epis Ch Minneapolis MN 2008-** B 4/30/1949 D 6/24/1980 Bp Robert Marshall Anderson. m 2/3/1979 Patricia Sonnesyn. S Catherines Ch Enumclaw WA 1987-1989; S Jas Epis Ch Kent WA 1984-1986; Exec Coun Appointees New York NY 1980-1984. sonnesyn@msn.com

SOPER JR, Leroy Dilmore (At) 514 E. NewJersey Ave Apt. 5125, Southern Pines NC 28387 **Assoc Gr And S Steph's Epis Ch Colorado Sprg CO 2009-** B Brownsville TX 10/30/1921 s Leroy Dilmore Soper & Valentine Evelyn. BA Cit 1943; MDiv STUSo 1959. D 6/1/1959 Bp William Francis Moses P 12/24/1959 Bp Henry I Louttit. m 12/31/1995 Imogene Lewis c 4. Chapl Gr And S Steph's Epis Ch Colorado Sprg CO 1998-2002; Int Ch Of S Mich The Archangel Colorado Sprg CO 1997-1998; Int Ch Of The Ascen Pueblo CO 1996-1997; Int The Par Of S Clem Honolulu HI 1993-1994; R The Epis Ch Of The Adv Madison GA 1987-1989; Dio SE Florida Miami FL 1968-1970; R H Cross Epis Ch Sanford FL 1964-1986; R S Mary Of The Ang Epis Ch Orlando FL 1959-1964. roysoper@aol.com

SOPER, Robert Arthur (WTex) 300 Hollywood Dr, Edinburg TX 78539 B Fort Benning GA 3/22/1940 s Leroy Dilmore Soper & Jeanette Cecil. BS Georgia Inst of Tech 1963; MDiv Epis TS of The SW 1968; Med Pan Amer U 1975; U of Texas 1980. D 7/25/1968 P 1/29/1969 Bp Richard Earl Dicus. m 6/8/1982 Julia Ava Niehaus c 2. S Steph's Epis Sch Austin TX 1978-1980; Vic S Matt's Ch Edinburg TX 1968-1974. soperbob11@swbell.net

SORENSEN, Harry Roy (NJ) 1312 Braken Ave, Wilmington DE 19808 B Astoria OR 9/13/1928 s Magnus Sorensen & Lena Kirstine. BA U of Oregon 1950; Br 1952; BD CDSP 1959; GTS 1969. D 6/19/1959 P 12/19/1959 Bp Clarence Rupert Haden Jr. c 2. Dio New Jersey Trenton NJ 1971-1986; Dept of Missions Dio New Jersey Trenton NJ 1964-1969; R All SS Memi Ch Navesink NJ 1962-1993; Exec Coun Dio Nthrn California Sacramento CA 1960-1962; Vic S Lk's Ch Galt CA 1959-1962; Vic Trin Ch Sutter Creek CA 1959-1962.

SORENSEN, John Thomas (Pa) 576 Concord Road, Glen Mills PA 19342 **Dioc Mssn Plnng Cmsn Dio Pennsylvania Philadelphia PA 2009-; R S Jn's Ch Glen Mills PA 2006-** B East Orange NJ 9/4/1952 s William Thornbury Sorensen & Julanne. AA Cape Cod Cmnty Coll 1978; AB Boston Coll 1982; MDiv VTS 1985; DMin SWTS 2004. D 6/4/1986 Bp John Bowen Coburn P 6/1/1987 Bp Ronald Hayward Haines. m 5/19/1984 Jeannine Maher c 2. RurD, Nthrn Adirondacks Dio Albany Albany NY 1998-2005; COM Dio NW Texas Lubbock TX 1998-1999; R Trin Ch Plattsburgh NY 1991-2006; Assoc R Ch Of The H Trin Midland TX 1987-1990; Chapl Trin Sch Of Midland Midland TX 1987-1990; Ass't Chapl St Steph Sch Alexandria VA 1986-1987. Auth, "Bk Revs/arts," 2003. Albany Via Media 2003-2006; Fndr Alexandria Christmas In April 1985-1987. Dn, Nthrn Adirondack Dnry Dio Albany 1999. jsorensen576@comcast.net

SORENSEN, Lael (WA) 1607 Grace Church Rd, Silver Spring MD 20910 **Asst Gr Epis Ch Silver Sprg MD 2010-; Chapl Gr Epis Day Sch Silver Sprg MD 2010-** B Berkeley, CA 1/7/1957 d Harry Roy Sorensen & Barbara. BA Rutgers U 1979; MA U MI 1984; MDiv Ya Berk 2010. D 6/19/2010 Bp Stephen Taylor Lane P 1/22/2011 Bp John Chane. lael.sorensen@gmail.com

SORENSEN, Richard Todd (Nev) 1580 G St, Sparks NV 89431 **P S Steph's Epis Ch Reno NV 1997-** B Reno NV 6/14/1950 s Alfred John Sorensen & JoAnn. BA U of Nevada at Reno 1979. D 9/6/1996 P 5/17/1997 Bp Stewart Clark Zabriskie. m 1/12/1980 Ellen Kathleen Easton. ricktsorensen@msn.com

SORENSEN, Todd Wallace (Colo) 6653 W Chatfield Ave, Littleton CO 80128 **R The Epis Par of S Greg Littleton CO 1990-** B Minneapolis MN 12/25/1951 s Neil Thomas Sorensen & Nancy Ruth. BA Arizona St U 1974; MDiv CDSP 1975. D 6/24/1979 Bp Joseph Thomas Heistand P 5/25/1980 Bp George R Selway. m 11/8/2011 Barbara J Hartmann c 3. Eccl Crt Dio Colorado Denver CO 2009-2011; Cler Wellness Cmsn (Chair final year) Dio Colorado Denver CO 1992-1998; Vic S Thos Epis Ch Temecula CA 1985-1990; Assoc The Epis Ch Of The Gd Shpd Hemet CA 1985-1988; Asst S Jas' Epis Ch Los Angeles CA 1982-1985; Camps & Conferences (Chair final year) Dio Arizona Phoenix AZ 1980-1982; COM Dio Arizona Phoenix AZ 1980-1982; Cur Chr Ch Of The Ascen Paradise Vlly AZ 1979-1982. frdrummer@msn.com

SORENSON, James Ronald (EMich) 226 W Nicolet Blvd, Marquette MI 49855 B Marquette MI 4/29/1940 s Leslie Oren Sorenson & Eva Luella. Bex; TS Dio Michigan; BA Alma Coll 1962; SWTS 1972. D 7/24/1972 Bp H Coleman McGehee Jr P 11/24/1973 Bp Archie H Crowley. m 5/22/2004 Suzanne Marie Lynn c 3. Reg Mssnr S Jn's Epis Ch Caseville MI 2002-2005; COM Dio Estrn Michigan Saginaw MI 1996-2000; Stndg Com Dio Estrn Michigan Saginaw MI 1994-1996; R S Matt's Epis Ch Saginaw MI 1993-2005; P-in-c S Andrews-By-The-Lake Epis Ch Harrisville MI 1992-1993; Dn Dio Michigan Detroit MI 1988-1992; R Chr Epis Ch E Tawas MI 1985-1993; COM Dio Michigan Detroit MI 1985-1989; P-in-c S Jn's Epis Ch Caseville MI 1977-1985; P-in-c S Paul's Epis Ch Bad Axe MI 1977-1985; P-in-c The Epis Ch In Huron Cnty Bad Axe MI 1977-1985; SW Convoc Dio Michigan Detroit MI 1975-1977; Vic S Andr's Ch Jackson MI 1974-1985; R Chr Ch Pleasant Lake MI 1974-1977; Cur S Andrews-By-The-Lake Epis Ch Harrisville MI 1972-1973; Cur S Lk's Epis Ch Rogers City MI 1972-1973; Cur Trin Epis Ch Alpena MI 1972-1973. R Emer St. Matt's Saginaw, MI 2005. jimsorenson@sbcglobal.net

SOREY, Gene Christine (Fla) 4304 Redtail Hawk Dr, Jacksonville FL 32257 B Washington DC 9/11/1946 d Daniel George Klein & Gene Stratton. Cert STUSo 1995; BS Jacksonville U 2000. D 9/17/1995 Bp Stephen Hays Jecko. m 12/11/1976 Robert Sorey. San Jose Epis Ch Jacksonville FL 1999-2010; COM Dio Florida Jacksonville FL 1999-2003; D San Jose Epis Ch Jacksonville FL 1995. Chapl, Ord Of S Lukes; NAES; NCA; Natl hon Soc; NAAD; SocMary. revchris@comcast.net

✠ **SORGE, Rt Rev Elliott Lorenz** (Eas) 5500 E. Peakview Ave. Apt. 2215, Centennial CO 80121 **Ret Bp Dio Easton Easton MD 1993-** B Michigan City IN 1/31/1929 s Charles Bryan Sorge & June Violet. BA DePauw U 1951; LTh SWTS 1954; MDiv SWTS 1956. Trans from Igreja Episcopal Anglicana do Brasil 5/1/1977 Con 1/31/1971 for Diocese of Southern Brazil. m 9/4/1959 Marjorie Romine c 3. Exec. Coun Dio Easton Easton MD 1988-1994; Bp Dio

S

Easton Easton MD 1983-1993; Field Off For Dvlpmt of Mnstry Epis Ch Cntr New York NY 1977-1980; P-in-c S Steph's Ch Fargo ND 1960-1964; P-in-c SS Mary And Mk Epis Ch Oakes ND 1954-1960. Hon DD VTS Alexandria VA 1984; Depauw U Alumnini Citation 1982. esorge@comcast.net

SORGE, Norman Murdoch Moses (Pa) 2700 Chestnut St Unit 905, Chester PA 19013 **Died 3/11/2010** B River Hebert Cumb County CA 6/1/1913 s Moses Abraham Sorge & Rose. Cert Illinois/Pennsylvania; Nova Scotia Normal Sch 1932; Toronto Grad Sch Of Journalism Toronto CA 1935; LST U Of King's Coll Halifax Ns CA 1948; Med Siue 1969; Cert Temporary Spec Educ 1972. Trans from Anglican Church of Canada 10/1/1957. m 9/16/1942 Effie Sorge c 2. Auth, "Numerous arts & Sermons".

SORVILLO, August Louis (CFla) 90 Bridgewater Ln, Ormond Beach FL 32174 B Youngstown OH 1/15/1938 s August Sorvillo & Louise. Youngstown St U 1958; LTh Nash 1973; DMin Pittsburgh TS 1992. D 5/26/1973 P 12/7/1973 Bp William Hopkins Folwell. m 6/23/1962 Shirley Hodges c 3. R S Jas Epis Ch Ormond Bch FL 1982-2003; Vic Gloria Dei Epis Ch Cocoa FL 1975-1982; Cur S Barn Ch Deland FL 1973-1975. als62shs@bellsouth.net

SORVILLO SR, James August (CFla) 9101 Palm Tree Dr., Windermere FL 34786 **R Epis Ch Of The Ascen Orlando FL 2003-** B Miami FL 2/18/1963 s August Louis Sorvillo & Shirley Joan. AA Daytona Bch Cmnty Coll 1985; BA U Of Cntrl Florida 1987; MDiv STUSo 2000. D 5/27/2000 P 12/9/2000 Bp John Wadsworth Howe. m 6/25/1988 Debra J Apicella c 2. Asst H Trin Epis Ch Melbourne FL 2000-2003. jsorvillo@cfl.rr.com

SOSA, Gary Rafael (NAM) Po Box 216, Bluff UT 84512 B San Francisco CA 4/30/1954 s Hugo Rafael Sosa & Marie Leona. BS Bethany Bible Coll 1976. D 6/16/1991 Bp Steven Tsosie Plummer Sr. m 8/24/1974 Linda Ann Higley.

SOSNOWSKI, Frederick Skinner (SC) 2426 Sea Island Yacht Club Rd, Wadmalaw Island SC 29487 B Charleston SC 9/1/1925 s John Ferrars Sosnowski & Eliza. BA U of So Carolina 1951; MDiv VTS 1955. D 6/16/1955 P 7/1/1956 Bp Thomas N Carruthers. m 5/29/1982 Polly B Sanford. Asst Epis Ch of the Gd Shpd Charleston SC 1994-1997; S Jas Ch Charleston SC 1990-1994; Dir: Pstr Counslg Ctr Dio So Carolina Charleston SC 1977-1994; P-in-c Atone Ch Walterboro SC 1975-1977; R S Jude's Epis Ch Walterboro SC 1975-1977; Dio Coun Dio So Carolina Charleston SC 1971-1974; Asst S Phil's Ch Charleston SC 1968-1975; R S Matt's Ch Henderson TX 1957-1959; Asst Trin Cathd Columbia SC 1955-1957. polly.sosnowski@gmail.com

SOSNOWSKI, John William (NJ) 310 95th St, Stone Harbor NJ 08247 **R S Mary's Epis Ch Stone Harbor NJ 1997-** B Torrington CT 12/10/1954 s Edward Stephen Sosnowski & Mary Ann. AA S Thos Coll 1974; BA S Mary Seminar Coll 1976; MDiv S Mary Seminar & U 1979; MA Sthrn Connecticut St U 1986. Rec from Roman Catholic 6/1/1995 as Priest Bp Clarence Nicholas Coleridge. m 9/16/1989 Cynthia L Barrall c 2. Dn of Atlantic Convoc Dio New Jersey Trenton NJ 2006-2009; Dioc Visioning Com Dio New Jersey Trenton NJ 2005-2007; Supply Dio Connecticut Hartford CT 1995-1997. Connecticut Lic Mar & Fam Ther. frjohnstmsh@verizon.net

SOTELO, George Salinas (Az) 13685 N Balancing Rock Dr, Oro Valley AZ 85755 B Adrian MI 7/25/1949 s Jose Sotelo & Marta. Sch for Deacons; BD Wm Tyndale Coll 1975; CAS CDSP 1993. D 6/5/1993 P 12/1/1993 Bp William Edwin Swing. m 3/7/2006 Stephen L McElroy. R S Andr's Epis Ch Tucson AZ 2006-2011; Dio Arizona Phoenix AZ 2006-2009; Dio California San Francisco CA 1994-2005; Ch Of The H Trin Richmond CA 1993-2003; S Aid's Ch San Francisco CA 1993-1994; The Epis Ch Of S Jn The Evang San Francisco CA 1993-1994. padregeo@aol.com

SOTO, Luis Fernando (DR) No address on file. B San Jose Costa R CA 7/1/1950 s Enrique Soto & Maria Teresa. Cert Cntrl Sem Cr 1976; Cert Gregorian U 1978; Cert Angelicum U 1980. Rec from Roman Catholic 7/1/1985. m 3/19/1985 Guiselle Sterloff. Dio The Dominican Republic (Iglesia Epis Dominicana) Santo Domingo DO 1986-1988. Soc Recon & Agape.

✠ **SOTO, Rt Rev Onell Asiselo** (Ala) 3350 Torremolinos Ave, Doral FL 33178 B 11/17/1932 s Juan Aurelio Soto & Maria. BA U of Havana Havana CU 1956; STM STUSo 1964. D 6/29/1964 Bp George Mosley Murray P 8/18/1965 Bp David Reed Con 7/11/1987 for Ve. m 7/4/1960 Nina Ulloa. Asst Bp Dio Alabama Birmingham AL 1999-2001; Asst Bp Dio Atlanta Atlanta GA 1995-1999; Mssn Info & Educ Off ECEC Epis Ch Cntr New York NY 1978-1987; Exec Secy Prov IX New York NY 1971-1977; Asst S Steph's Epis Ch San Antonio TX 1964-1965. ECom. DD TS U So 1988; Ord of Simon Bolivar Pres of Venezuela Venezuela. obisposoto@aol.com

SOTO, Pedro S (RG) 505 Bryce Dr, Horizon City TX 79928 B Ciudad Juarez Chihuahua MX 8/7/1954 s Pedro Soto Sanchez & Carmen Sanchez. Centro Educacional Remington Contador Privado 1979. D 12/19/1977 P 2/1/1983 Bp Leonardo Romero-Rivera. m 7/31/1982 Elvira Jaquez c 2. S Chris's Epis Ch El Paso TX 1997-2005; H Faith Par Inglewood CA 1994-1995; Ch Of The Epiph Los Angeles CA 1994; Dio Nthrn Mex 1991-1993; Dio Mex 1984-1990. pedsoto@juno.com

SOTOMAYOR, Ricardo (Tex) 12815 Paleo Ct, Sugar Land TX 77478 B 6/12/1942 s Antonio S Sotomayor & Maria. M Div Lateranensis U (Roma) 1969. Rec from Roman Catholic 6/14/1995 Bp Claude Edward Payne. m 7/17/2003 Angelina Sotomayor c 2. S Paul's Ch Houston TX 1997-2002; Vic Mssn De La Santa Cruz Houston TX 1995-2006. Angl Stds The TS/The U So 1995.

SOUCEK, Paul (Nwk) 111 Harding St, Trenton NJ 08611 B 12/10/1939 D 7/1/1973 P 6/8/1974 Bp George E Rath.

SOUDER, Diane J (Az) Po Box 1077, Winter Park FL 32790 **Supply P & Sprtl Dir Dio Cntrl Florida Orlando FL 2004-** B Miami FL 12/29/1941 d H Lloyd Jordan & Frances R. BA U of Florida 1963; MDiv GTS 1992. D 6/29/1992 Bp Calvin Onderdonk Schofield Jr P 1/1/1993 Bp Jane Hart Holmes Dixon. c 1. Cong Ahwatukee Foothills Phoenix AZ 1999-2000; RTA Hospice Phoenix AZ 1999; Assoc Ch Of The Epiph Tempe AZ 1996-1998; S Lk's At The Mtn Phoenix AZ 1995-1996; S Pat's Ch Washington DC 1992-1993. dianesouder@yahoo.com

SOUGHERS, Tara Kathleen (Mass) 23 Horseshoe Dr., Plainville MA 02762 B Indianapolis IN 8/21/1961 d Richard Keith Soughers & Peggy Sue. BS New Mex Tech 1981; MA Rice U 1985; MDiv VTS 1990. D 6/17/1990 P 1/9/1991 Bp Don Adger Wimberly. m 7/18/1981 Michael Hans Helmuth Dehn c 2. R Trin Epis Ch Wrentham MA 2005-2009; Bp's Coun, Exec Coun Dio Connecticut Hartford CT 2001-2003; R Trin Ch Portland CT 2000-2004; Dioc Counc Dio Cntrl New York Syracuse NY 1994-2000; R Calv Ch Homer NY 1992-2000; R S Matt's Ch Moravia NY 1992-2000; Tri-Cnty Cluster Glen Aubrey NY 1992-2000; All SS Ch Salt Lake City UT 1991-1992; Dio Utah Salt Lake City UT 1990-1991. Auth, "Treasures of Darkness: Finding God When Hope Is Hidden," Abingdon Press, 2009; Auth, "Fleeing God: Fear, Call and the Bk of Jonah," Cowley/Rowman & Littlefield, 2007; Auth, "Falling In Love w God: Passion, Pryr and the Song of Songs," Cowley, 2005; Auth, "To Equip the SS (Curric)," Privately distributed. tksoughers@comcast.net

SOUKUP, Patricia Marie (RG) 3700 Parsifal St NE, Albuquerque NM 87111 **D S Jn's Cathd Albuquerque NM 2007-** B Albuquerque NM 10/7/1963 d Richard Earl Hardy & Carol Marie. BA U of New Mex 1986; MA U of New Mex 1994; Ext Prog of TESM 2006. D 10/21/2006 Bp Jeffrey Neil Steenson. m 5/2/1987 Michael Soukup. psoukup2@earthlink.net

SOULE, Patrick R (WTex) 13026 Leopard St, Corpus Christi TX 78410 **Vic S Andr's Epis Ch Corpus Christi TX 2009-** B Pontiac MI 9/13/1974 s Douglas Ross Soule & Sandra Lee. BS Tennessee Tech U Cookeville TN 1997; MDiv TESM 2007. D 6/2/2007 P 4/12/2008 Bp John Crawford Bauerschmidt. m 6/19/1999 Cassandra B Cassandra Gail Blackburn c 3. S Phil's Ch Nashville TN 2008-2009. soulepr@yahoo.com

SOUTHERLAND, Ronald Bruce (Ga) 625 Will Scarlet Way, Macon GA 31220 **Died 10/8/2010** B Palatka FL 10/19/1942 s William Floyd Southerland & Dorothy Louise. BSF U GA 1965; MDiv STUSo 1972. D 7/9/1972 Bp William Evan Sanders P 6/2/1973 Bp William F Gates Jr. c 1. epis_ch@planttel.net

SOUTHERLAND, Thomas Rudolph (SO) 10555 Montgomery Rd., Apt 32, Cincinnati OH 45242 B Stonega VA 9/16/1937 s James Ason & Thelma Kate. Sthrn Ohio D Acad London OH; U Cinc OH. D 6/23/2007 Bp Thomas Edward Breidenthal. m 9/16/1937 Barbara Barbara Brown c 4. thomas_southerland@yahoo.com

SOUTHERN JR, John Carlton (WNC) 42 Alclare Ct, Asheville NC 28804 **Dio Wstrn No Carolina Asheville NC 2004-** B Winston-Salem NC 12/14/1946 s John Carlton Southern & Mary Elizabeth. GTS 1972; BA U NC 1973. D 6/8/1974 P 6/14/1975 Bp William Gillette Weinhauer. S Lk's Epis Ch Lincolnton NC 2006-2008; S Mk's Ch Gastonia NC 2004-2005; Ch Of The Gd Shpd Rocky Mt NC 2004; Int S Lk's Ch Boone NC 2002-2004; Ch Of The Gd Shpd Cashiers NC 2001-2002; S Lk's Ch Salisbury NC 1999-2000; Par Of The H Comm Glendale Sprg NC 1998-1999; Trin Epis Ch Asheville NC 1992-1998; P Dio Wstrn No Carolina Asheville NC 1986-1990; Ch Of The Redeem Asheville NC 1981-1986; Asst R S Mary's Ch Asheville NC 1977-1980; Vic S Mich's Ch Baton Rouge LA 1975-1977; Vic Trin Ch Kings Mtn NC 1974-1975. j28804anc@aol.com

SOUTHWORTH, Richard Louis (Cal) PO Box 710, Leander TX 78646 B Cincinnati OH 2/21/1940 s Constant Williams Southworth & Ruth Margaret. BA Butler U 1964; VTS 1966; Cert ETSC 1968; MSW U of Maryland 1970; MA Nthrn Arizona U 1979. D 4/22/1969 Bp Paul Moore Jr P 1/1/1971 Bp George Edward Haynsworth. Dir of Soc Serv S Fran Hse Little Rock AR 1996-1997; Mississippi Dir S Fran Cmnty Serv Inc. Salina KS 1995-1996; Co-Dir of Native Amer Com Dio Arizona Phoenix AZ 1989-1991; Dir of Hisp Com Dio Arizona Phoenix AZ 1989-1991; San Pablo Mssn Dio Arizona Phoenix AZ 1989-1991; Sch Chapl Gr Cathd San Francisco CA 1983-1984; Vic S Chris's Ch Bluff UT 1981-1983; Asst (Ft. Defiance, AZ) Ch Of The Gd Shpd Ft Defiance AZ 1975-1976; Assoc S Steph's Ch Phoenix AZ 1973-1974; St. Fran Epis Ch, Managua, Nicaragua Iglesia Anglicana de la Reg Cntrl de Amer 274 San Salvador 1971-1972. ESCRU 1964-1969. rlsouthworth@sbcglobal.net

SOUZA, Raymond Manuel (EC) 846 Wide Waters, Bath NC 27808 B Richmond VA 4/20/1955 s Raymond Souzo & Violet Marie. BA W&M 1979; MDiv Epis TS of The SW 1998. D 6/13/1998 Bp Frank Harris Vest Jr P 12/12/1998 Bp Joe Morris Doss. m 12/19/1992 Heidi E Eger. R S Thos' Epis Ch

Bath NC 2001-2009; Asst Trin Ch Moorestown NJ 1998-2001. Batsouza@aol.com

SOWAN, Michael George (Alb) Box 1185, Street Sacrement Lane, Bolton Landing NY 12814 B Potsdam NY 7/22/1939 s George Sowan & Rose. BA Hob 1961; STB PDS 1966. D 6/11/1966 P 12/19/1966 Bp Allen Webster Brown. m 7/22/1973 Nancy Jutiva Abrahamson c 1. R Ch Of S Sacrement Bolton Landing NY 1995-2003; R S Paul's Ch Kansas City KS 1980-1995; Stndg Com Dio Montana Helena MT 1973-1980; R S Steph's Ch Billings MT 1973-1980; Cur S Ptr's Par Helena MT 1970-1973; P The Ch Of The Gd Shpd Canajoharie NY 1967-1970.

SOWARDS, William Michael (Fla) Chapel of the Resurrection, 655 W Jefferson St, Tallahassee FL 32304 **P-in-c S Paul's Epis Ch Quincy FL 2008-** B Portsmouth VA 10/29/1960 s Billy Lee Sowards & Ina Shirleen. BA U of No Flordia 1997; MEd U of No Florida 2000; MDiv Virginia Theol 2007. D 5/27/2007 P 12/9/2007 Bp Samuel Johnson Howard. m 6/20/1981 Sonya K Sonya Kay Nutter c 2. msowards1@comcast.net

SOWERS, Susan R (Va) 3200 N 12th Ave, Pensacola FL 32503 **Assoc R S Chris's Ch Pensacola FL 2010-** B Frankfurt, Germany 3/7/1960 d William Risque Sowers & Mary Johnson. BS USMA 1982; MS U of Washington 1991; MS US Army War Coll 2003; MDiv VTS 2010. D 6/5/2010 Bp Shannon Sherwood Johnston P 12/18/2010 Bp Philip Menzie Duncan II. susan@scpen.org

SOX, Harold David (Cal) 20 The Vineyard, Richmond, Surrey TW 10 6 AN Great Britain (UK) B Hickory NC 4/24/1936 s Samuel L Sox & Nellie Vye. BA U NC 1958; MDiv UTS 1960; VTS 1961. D 6/10/1961 P 12/1/1961 Bp Leland Stark. Campbell Hall Vlly Vill CA 1981-1982; Minor Cn Gr Cathd San Francisco CA 1971-1974; Asst S Jas Ch Upper Montclair NJ 1961-1963. Auth, "Pere Dav," *Pere Dav*, Sessions of York, 2009; Auth, "Jn Woolman," *Jn Woolman*, Sessions of York, 2003; Auth, "Quaker Plant Hunters," *Quaker Plant Hunters*, Sessions of York, 2003; Auth, "Bachelors of Art," *Bachelors of Art*, Fourth Estate, 1991; Auth, "Unmasking the Forger," *Unmasking the Forger*, Geo Allen and Unwin, 1987; Auth, "Relics and Shrines," *Relics and Shrines*, Geo Allen and Unwin, 1985; Auth, "Gospel of Barn," *Gospel of Barn*, Geo Allen and Unwin, 1984; Auth, "Image on the Shroud," *Image on the Shroud*, Geo Allen and Unwin, 1981; Auth, "File on the Shroud," *File on the Shroud*, Hodder and Stoughton, 1978. Rel Soc of Friends 1996. THEVINEYARD20@AOL.CO.UK

SPACCARELLI, Cara Elizabeth (WA) 620 G St SE, Washington DC 20003 **R Chr Ch Capitol Hill Washington DC 2010-** B Cincinnati OH 5/27/1980 d John Spaccarelli & Janeth. BA Carleton Coll 2002; MDiv Epis TS of The SW 2006. D 6/8/2006 P 12/21/2006 Bp James Louis Jelinek. m 1/3/2004 Michael Christopher Lawyer c 3. Cn Cathd Ch Of S Mk Minneapolis MN 2006-2010. caraspaccarelli@gmail.com

SPAETH, Colleen Grayce (NJ) 247 Merion Ave, Haddonfield NJ 08033 **D S Barth's Ch Cherry Hill NJ 1998-** B Trenton NJ 12/14/1950 d Jos Donald Moore & Margaret. Rutgers-The St U; AA Burlington Cnty Coll 1985. D 10/31/1998 Bp Joe Morris Doss. m 10/10/1992 David Charles Spaeth.

SPAFFORD, Donald Wick (Dal) 5903 Bonnard Dr, Dallas TX 75230 **Assoc S Lk's Epis Ch Dallas TX 2005-** B Pampa TX 5/13/1935 s Perry Parker Spafford & Ebba Wick. D 8/26/1972 P 3/15/1973 Bp William J Gordon Jr. m 1/31/1959 Nancy Spafford c 2. Assoc S Mich And All Ang Ch Dallas TX 1997-2005. dws3536@aol.com

SPAID, William John (WMich) 2008 Hudson Ave, Kalamazoo MI 49008 **Cn To The Ordnry Dio Wstrn Michigan Kalamazoo MI 2003-; Assoc The Par Ch Of Chr The King Portage MI 2002-** B Lorain OH 11/29/1953 s John William Spaid & Phyllis Marion. BS Frostburg St U 1975; MEd Frostburg St U 1977; MDiv Nash 1986. D 9/6/1986 Bp A(lbert) Theodore Eastman P 3/21/1987 Bp Howard Samuel Meeks. c 2. R S Mart Of Tours Epis Ch Kalamazoo MI 1986-2002; Org/Chrmstr S Thos Of Cbury Ch Greendale WI 1983-1986. william.spaid@sbcglobal.net

SPAINHOUR, J(ohn) Robert (EC) 745 Cromartie Road, Elizabethtown NC 28337 **S Jas Par Wilmington NC 2009-** B Morganton NC 9/11/1956 s William Robert Spainhour & Mary Eleanor. BA The Coll of Charleston 1978; Med Cit 1984; MDiv TESM 1992. D 6/4/1992 P 12/1/1992 Bp Edward Lloyd Salmon Jr. c 2. S Christophers Ch Elizabethtown NC 2006-2009; Cler Mem and Chair of CE Dio So Carolina Charleston SC 1993-2002; Dio So Carolina Charleston SC 1992-2006; Stwdshp Consult Dio So Carolina Charleston SC 1992-2002; S Jn's Ch Charleston SC 1992-2001; Lay vestryman-in-charge of CE Trin Epis Ch Pinopolis SC 1984-1986. Cursillos in Chrsnty 1981; Kairos 1986; The Bro of S Andr 1989; The OSL 1987. jrspainhour@bladen.k12.nc.us

SPANGENBERG, Carol Anne (WMich) 1612 Stoney Point Dr, Lansing MI 48917 B Detroit MI 3/24/1941 d William Aubrey Thomas Harvey Corner & Mary Alice. BA MI SU 1964; MA MI SU 1974; EDS MI SU 1978; DMin Gnrl Theol Fndt-Notre Dame U 1989. D 9/12/1983 Bp William J Gordon Jr P 6/1/1990 Bp Henry Irving Mayson. m 7/27/1963 David Spangenberg c 3. R S Jn's Epis Ch Charlotte MI 1997-2010; D S Paul's Epis Ch Lansing MI 1983-1990. Auth, *Cultural Journalism*; Auth, *Fells Yearbk*. revcarol1941@sbcglobal.net

SPANGENBERG, Ronald Wesley (SVa) 6085 River Crest, Norfolk VA 23505 B Washington DC 9/12/1931 s Wesley Spangenberg & Jessie Helen. BS U of Maryland 1954; MDiv Epis TS of The SW 1960; EdD Indiana U 1970. D 7/7/1960 Bp Everett H Jones P 1/25/1961 Bp Richard Earl Dicus. m 5/30/1958 Dorothy Breslin c 1. Chr The King Epis Ch Tabb VA 1997-2000; P-in-c S Steph's Epis Ch Jacksonville AR 1964-1966; Cur Chr Epis Ch Little Rock AR 1962-1966; Vic Ch Of The Ascen Refugio TX 1960-1962. Auth, "Human Factors in Design of Carrels"; Auth, "Structural Coherence in Pictorial & Verbal Displays," *Journ of Educational Psychol*. Ch Hisorical Soc 1964; Ord of S Lk 1965. frrons@aol.com

SPANGLER, Haywood B (Va) 1205 Swan Lake Dr Apt 303, Charlottesville VA 22902 **Bd Mem/Governance Chair Ptr Paul Dvlpmt Cntr Of The Epis Ch Richmond VA 2006-** B Danville VA 5/19/1971 s John Barringer Spangler & Bes. BA U NC 1993; MDiv Yale DS 1996; PhD U of Virginia 2003. D 9/6/1997 P 3/14/1998 Bp Robert Hodges Johnson. R S Barth's Ch Richmond VA 2004-2011; P-in-c Ch Of The Gd Shpd Charlottesville VA 2001-2003; Int Chr Epis Ch Luray VA 2000-2001; Int S Paul's Memi Charlottesville VA 1999; D S Lk's Epis Ch Asheville NC 1997-1998. Inventor, "Spangler Ethical Reasoning Assessment," *Self-scoring preference survey*, Auth holds the copyright, 2009. hspangler@lmronline.org

SPANGLER, N(ancy) DeLiza (WNY) 128 Pearl St, Buffalo NY 14202 **Dn S Paul's Cathd Buffalo NY 2006-** B Clinton MO 10/8/1953 d Robert Wallace Spangler & Nancy Elizabeth. BA Lindenwood U 1975; PrTS 1976; MDiv GTS 1978; JD Willamette U 1985. D 5/21/1978 P 5/18/1979 Bp William Augustus Jones Jr. m 1/30/2009 Luanne Bauer. Dioc Wrshp Cmsn. Chair Dio Wstrn Michigan Kalamazoo MI 1996-2002; Cler Comp Cmsn Dio Wstrn Michigan Kalamazoo MI 1996-1997; R S Paul's Epis Ch S Jos MI 1995-2005; Dioc Coun Dio Alaska Fairbanks AK 1993-1994; S Phil's Ch Wrangell AK 1989; Assoc S Phil's Ch Wrangell AK 1985-1988; Asst S Paul's Epis Ch Salem OR 1982-1985; Dio Alaska Fairbanks AK 1979-1982; Co-R S Andr's Epis Ch Petersburg AK 1979-1982; Co-R S Phil's Ch Wrangell AK 1979-1982; Asst Gr Ch Jamaica NY 1978-1979. mtrliza@yahoo.com

SPANGLER, Robert Joseph (Okla) 7 Strathmore Dr, Arden NC 28704 B Ash Grove MO 7/7/1927 s John Albert Spangler & Vada. BA U of Kansas 1950; U of Missouri 1952; MA Ft Hays St U 1962; MDiv CDSP 1968. D 4/25/1968 P 12/21/1968 Bp William Davidson. m 9/3/1950 Linda Sanborn c 3. Chair Dept CE Dio Oklahoma Oklahoma City OK 1988-1991; Curs Strng Com Dio Oklahoma Oklahoma City OK 1986-1989; Curs Strng Com Dio Oklahoma Oklahoma City OK 1986-1989; Assoc S Jn's Epis Ch Tulsa OK 1980-1992; Bd VOOM Dio Oklahoma Oklahoma City OK 1979-1984; Chair DeptCE Dio Oklahoma Oklahoma City OK 1976-1978; Bp Coun Dio Oklahoma Oklahoma City OK 1976-1977; R S Mary's Ch Edmond OK 1974-1980; Asst Gr Epis Ch Hutchinson KS 1973-1975; Dep GC Dio Oklahoma Oklahoma City OK 1970-1973; P-in-c S Steph's Ch Guymon OK 1969-1973; P-in-c S Tim's Epis Ch Hugoton KS 1969-1973; Vic S Jn's Ch Ulysses KS 1968-1973. Auth, "Hist of the Hays Daily News," *Ft Hays Stds*, Ft Hays St Coll, 1962. Preaching Awd CDSP Berkeley CA 1968; Sigma Delta Chi 1951. spnglr@bellsouth.net

SPANN, Paul Ronald (Mich) 2971 Iroquois Avenue, Detroit MI 48214 **Dir, Sprtlty Cntr Chr Ch Grosse Pointe Grosse Pointe Farms MI 2003-; Sprtlty Fac Credo Inst Inc. Memphis TN 2002-** B Ann Arbor MI 11/7/1943 s Paul Leon Spann & Ruth Ann. BA Kalamazoo Coll 1965; U Roch 1966; MDiv EDS 1970; Emory U 1987; Cert PRH-Inst Intl Poitiers FR 1998. D 6/29/1970 Bp Archie H Crowley P 1/16/1971 Bp Richard S M Emrich. m 1/4/1976 Jacqueline Graves c 2. Assoc R Chr Ch Cranbrook Bloomfield Hills MI 1998-2002; Econ Justice Cmsn Dio Michigan Detroit MI 1993-2005; Stndg Com Dio Michigan Detroit MI 1992-1995; Exam Chapl in Issues in Contemporary Soc Dio Michigan Detroit MI 1988-1992; R Ch Of The Mssh Detroit MI 1971-1996; Asst S Tim's Ch Detroit MI 1970-1971. Auth, "Chapt 11: Mustard Tree Co-op," *Making Hsng Happen*, Chalice Press, 2006; Auth, "Another Point of View," *Sermons That Wk XIII*, Morehouse, 2005; Auth, "Preaching Jesus to Urban Teens," *Wit*, Wit, 1996; Auth, "Recon and Race," *Sojourners*, Sojourners, 1990; Auth, "Cmnty and Identity," *Sojourners*, Sojourners, 1990; Auth, "Liturg and Justice," *Liturg*, No Amer Liturg Conf, 1989. Chr Cmnty Dvlpmt Assn, Un of Black Epi 1989; Inst Personnalite et Relatns Humaines 1998; Sprtl Dir Intl 2007; UBE 1973. Thompson Lecture in Rel Kalamazoo Coll 2001; Alum of the Year Kalamazoo Coll 1999; Hon Cn Cathd S Paul Detroit MI 1993; 1st McGehee Fund Cmnty Builder of Year 93 Schiffman Fndt and Econ. Justice Cmsn, Dio. of Mich 1993. rspann@prh-usa.org

SPANNAGEL JR, Lawrence Elden (NwT) 676 E Willowbrook Dr, Meridian ID 83646 B Memphis TX 4/10/1943 s Lawrence Elden Spannagel & Sula Faye. D 4/23/1972 P 11/26/1972 Bp William J Gordon Jr. c 3. Int S Ptr's Epis Ch Amarillo TX 2007-2008; Dio NW Texas Lubbock TX 2004-2008; S Ptr's Epis Ch Borger TX 2000-2003; R S Lk's Epis Ch Wenatchee WA 1997-2000; R Chr Ch Anchorage AK 1994-1996; Int H Sprt Epis Ch Eagle River AK 1992-1993; S Dunst's Epis Ch Carmel Vlly CA 1989-1990; S Mary's Ch Anchorage AK 1974-1989. larryspan@msn.com

SPANUTIUS, Warren Frederick (WTex) 505 Coral Pl, Corpus Christi TX 78411 B Bethlehem PA 6/30/1928 s Edward Ramsey Spanutius & Marion Adalena. BS U of Alabama 1952. D 8/19/1967 Bp Milton LeGrand Wood P 11/3/1974 Bp Harold Cornelius Gosnell. m 3/29/1947 Audrey Mae Sandlin. Int Gr Ch Port Lavaca TX 1994-1995; Vic S Thos And S Mart's Ch Corpus Christi TX 1986-1993; Asst All SS Epis Ch Corpus Christi TX 1982-1987; EME Dio W Texas San Antonio TX 1976-1982; D All SS Epis Ch Corpus Christi TX 1967-1974. bradpart@callerinfi.net

SPARKS, Douglas Everett (Minn) 1809 Baihly Hills Dr Sw, Rochester MN 55902 **R S Lk's Epis Ch Rochester MN 2004-** B Saint Louis MO 1/8/1956 s Lenn Jewell Sparks & Myrtress. BA S Mary Sem Coll Leavenworth KS 1980; MDiv DeAndreis Sem 1984; CAS SWTS 1989; DMin SWTS 1993; Cert SWTS 2003. Rec from Roman Catholic 6/4/1989 as Priest Bp William Augustus Jones Jr. m 12/28/1988 Dana Wirth c 3. R St Mths Epis Ch Waukesha WI 1995-2002; R S Lk's Ch Whitewater WI 1990-1994; Asst S Greg's Epis Ch Deerfield IL 1989-1990. douglas_sparks@earthlink.net

SPAULDING, Mark (Cal) 19179 Center St, Castro Valley CA 94546 **R H Cross Epis Ch Castro Vlly CA 2003-; Off Of Bsh For ArmdF New York NY 1998-** B Richmond CA 2/9/1958 s Glenn F Spaulding & Mary Ann. BA California St U 1987; MDiv Yale DS 1990. D 6/9/1990 P 6/8/1991 Bp William Edwin Swing. m 11/16/2009 Susan T Spaulding c 2. Assoc S Tim's Ch Danville CA 1990-1998; Dir Of Yth Mnstrs S Paul's Epis Ch Walnut Creek CA 1980-1985. mark@garageshop.org

SPEAKS, John Thomas (SO) 632 Clearview Rd, Birmingham AL 35226 **Died 2/8/2010** B LaGrange GA 8/25/1920 s Luther Alvin Speaks & Elsie Lavada. BA Emory U 1946; MDiv STUSo 1949; Oxf 1967; S Aug's Coll Cbury GB 1970; U of Cambridge 1973. D 5/25/1949 Bp Charles C J Carpenter P 11/30/1949 Bp Randolph R Claiborne. c 2. Auth, *Love Story of the Bible Chinese & Engl*, Forw Mvmt Pub, 1992. ESMA; Royal Geographical Soc London, Fell 1984. jtspeaks1@aol.com

SPEAR, Les Edward (WTex) 4222 State Hwy. 7 West, Crockett TX 75835 B Corpus Christi TX 8/30/1947 s Everett General Spear & Dorothy Mildred. Angl TS 1985; BA Steph F. Austin St U 1989; MDiv Epis TS of The SW 1993. Trans 1/1/2004 Bp Creighton Leland Robertson. m 3/26/2004 Tanya Y Bartlett c 5. S Lk's Ch Cypress Mill TX 2007-2008; Gr Ch Weslaco TX 2004-2006; Mnisose Cluster Sioux Falls SD 2002-2003; Chr Ch Chamberlain SD 2001-2004; Chr Epis Ch Ft Thompson SD 2001-2004; H Comf Ch Lower Brule SD 2001-2004; S Alb's Epis Ch Porcupine SD 2001-2004; S Jn's Ch Chamberlain SD 2001-2004. les_n_tanya@yahoo.com

SPEARE-HARDY II, Benjamin E K (SO) 5301 Free Pike, Trotwood OH 45426 **R S Marg's Ch Trotwood OH 2000-** B Monrovia LR 5/31/1958 s Benjamin E K Speare-Hardy & Theresa Evelyn. BS S Aug's Coll Raleigh NC 1983; MDiv VTS 1990. D 6/13/1992 Bp Robert Poland Atkinson P 12/16/1992 Bp Peter James Lee. S Mary Magd Ch Columbus GA 1994-1999; Christchurch Sch Christchurch VA 1992-1994. Auth, "Epis Chld Curric"; Auth, "Out From The Shameful Past," *Pstr Forum*. Prince Hall Free And Accepted Masons. Cmnty Serv Awd Negro Bus & Profsnl Wmn Club, Inc 1998; Resolution For Cmnty Serv Relatns City Coun Of Columbus Ga Columbus GA 1997. bspearehar@aol.com

SPEAR-JONES, Michael William (SVa) 1305 Dutchess of York Quay, Chesapeake VA 23320 **Dio Sthrn Virginia Norfolk VA 2010-** B Muncie IN 3/18/1952 s William Wendell Jones & Dorothy. BA U So 1974; MDiv Nash 1978. D 6/4/1978 P 12/12/1978 Bp James Loughlin Duncan. m 10/12/2003 Gwen Spear-Jones. R S Thos Epis Ch Chesapeake VA 1995-2010; Bruton Par Williamsburg VA 1988-1995; Dio SE Florida Miami FL 1981-1988; Cur H Trin Epis Ch W Palm Bch FL 1978-1981. Auth, "Personal Reflections," *Nashotah Revs*, 1978; Auth, "Selected Poetry," *Mtn Sum (Anthology)*, Sewanee Press, 1974; Auth, "A Living Hope (Hymn text)," *People'S Mass Bk (RC)*. AP. mspear.jones@gmail.com

SPEARS, Melanie Lea (Minn) 3543 22nd Ave S, Minneapolis MN 55407 B Minneapolis MN 7/23/1957 d James O Morgan & Phyllis A. BA Macalester Coll 1980; MDiv SWTS 1991. D 12/16/1992 P 6/1/1993 Bp Robert Marshall Anderson. m 8/14/1976 George L Spears. P-in-c All SS Epis Indn Mssn Minneapolis MN 1992-2003; Dio Minnesota Minneapolis MN 1992-2003.

SPECK-EWER, Nathan Stewart (Ct) 42 N Eagleville Rd, Storrs Mansfield CT 06268 **S Mk's Chap Storrs CT 2010-** B Memphis TN 9/6/1975 s Keith Stewart Ewer & Helen. BA U So 1997; MDiv Ya Berk 2000. D 6/8/2002 Bp Andrew Donnan Smith P 2/22/2003 Bp Wilfrido Ramos-Orench. m 9/9/1995 April Lorraine Speck-Ewer c 2. R S Tim's Epis Ch Mtn View CA 2006-2010; Assoc R Trin Ch On The Green New Haven CT 2002-2006; Asst. to the R Trin Ch On The Green New Haven CT 2000-2002. nathanse@gmail.com

SPEEKS, Mark William (NY) 23 Bunhill Row, London EC1Y 8LP Great Britain (UK) B Northampton UK 11/14/1962 s John Louis Speeks & Rita Kathleen. BA U Of Exeter Gb 1982; MS Oxf 1983; MDiv Yale DS 2002. D 3/16/2002 P 9/21/2002 Bp Mark Sean Sisk. Asst S Alb's Epis Ch Los Angeles CA 2002-2003. MSPEEKS@HOTMAIL.COM

SPEER, James D (Ct) 63 Clyde Ave, Waterbury CT 06708 **S Ptr's Epis Ch Oxford CT 2009-; P-in-c Chr Ch Bethlehem CT 2008-** B Pasadena CA 7/21/1950 s Donald Livingstone Speer & Barbara. Westchester Inst; BA U Of Puget Sound 1973; MDiv Vancouver TS 1979; CG Jung Inst 2001. Trans from Anglican Church of Canada 12/15/1993 Bp William Charles Wantland. m 5/19/1990 Mary Jane M MacInnis c 2. R S Paul's Ch Camden DE 2005-2006; Dio Minnesota Minneapolis MN 2002-2005; S Antipas Ch Redby MN 2002; Vic S Jn-In-The-Wilderness Redlake MN 2002; The Epis Ch In Navajoland Coun Farmington NM 1993-1994. Minnesota Jung Assn 2002-2004; N.A.A.P. 2007. stpeters4210oxford@yahoo.com

SPEER, Richard T (WTex) 800 S. Inediana Ave, 800 S. Indiana Ave, Weslaco TX 78596 **R Gr Ch Weslaco TX 2008-** B New York NY 12/10/1945 s James Ramsey Speer & Irene. BA U of Texas 1968; MDiv Epis TS of The SW 1986. D 6/15/1986 P 6/13/1987 Bp Donis Dean Patterson. m 8/20/1972 Laura Dexter c 3. Ch Of The Epiph Kingsville TX 1999-2008; Vic S Andr's Epis Ch Corpus Christi TX 1993-1999; R The Epis Ch Of The Adv Alice TX 1989-1993; Asst R For Yth Ch Of The Epiph Richardson TX 1987-1989; Cur H Trin Epis Ch Garland TX 1986-1987. rtspeer@yahoo.com

SPEER, Robert Hazlett (Md) 5732 Cross Country Blvd, Baltimore MD 21209 B Kalispell MT 5/31/1939 s Robert Hazlett Speer & Mary Irene. BA Montana St U 1961; MDiv SWTS 1964; MS Ford 1977; MA CUA 1990. D 6/21/1964 P 1/25/1965 Bp Chandler W Sterling. m 2/10/1985 Donna Kirshbaum c 3. Gr And S Ptr's Ch Baltimore MD 1998-2011; S Paul's Par Baltimore MD 1991-1993; Ch Of S Paul The Apos Baltimore MD 1990; Vic S Tim's Ch Walkersville MD 1987-1989; Off Of Bsh For ArmdF New York NY 1967-1987; Kent Sch Kent CT 1966-1967; Asst S Jos's Chap at the Kent Sch Kent CT 1966-1967; Cur Chr Ch Las Vegas NV 1964-1966. Auth, *Letters from Jim*.

SPEER, William Roth (NJ) 2000 Miller Ave #12, Millville NJ 08332 B Baltimore MD 6/27/1936 s William Speer & Josephine Virginia. BA U Rich 1959; STM PDS 1962; MSW Rutgers-The St U 1990. D 6/26/1962 Bp Noble C Powell P 4/1/1963 Bp Harry Lee Doll. c 2. Assoc Trin Epis Ch Vineland NJ 1988-2001; Assoc Par Of Chr The King Willingboro NJ 1980-1983; Trin Ch Riverside NJ 1974-1977; Asst S Jas Ch New London CT 1968-1970; Asst Chr And H Trin Ch Westport CT 1967-1968; Vic Ch Of The Trsfg Braddock Heights MD 1963-1967; R S Anne's Epis Ch Smithsburg MD 1963-1966; Asst Vic Ch Of The Resurr Baltimore MD 1962-1963. Mercy of God Cmnty 1999. wilrspeer@msn.com

SPEIR, Susan Elizabeth (Ida) 2009 Alan St, Idaho Falls ID 83404 **COM Dio Idaho Boise ID 2009-; R S Lk's Epis Ch Idaho Falls ID 2008-** B Los Angeles CA 8/14/1950 d Maxwell Oliver Schramm & Dorothy Kristen. BS U of Oregon 1983; MDiv Epis TS of The SW 2000. D 6/10/2000 Bp William Jerry Winterrowd P 12/9/2000 Bp J(ames) Gary Gloster. m 11/29/2003 Edmund Speir c 2. P Gr Epis Ch Lapeer MI 2005-2007; R S Fran' Ch Norris TN 2003-2005; Assoc Ch Of The H Comf Charlotte NC 2000-2003. susan.e.speir@gmail.com

SPELLER, Lydia Agnew (Mo) Saint Mark's Church, 4714 Clifton Ave, Saint Louis MO 63109 B New York NY 11/28/1954 d Seth Marshall Agnew & Mary Elisabeth. BA Bryn 1975; PhD Oxf 1980; STM GTS 1987. D 10/31/1987 P 5/1/1988 Bp James Michael Mark Dyer. m 8/20/1977 John Speller c 2. Int Ch Of The H Sprt Missoula MT 2010-2011; Chair - COM Dio Missouri S Louis MO 2001-2006; R S Mk's Ch S Louis MO 1993-2010; Assoc R Chr Ch Reading PA 1988-1993; Chr Ch Reading PA 1987-1988. Auth, "The Empty Womb," *The C Mnstry*, 1993; Auth, "A Note on Eusebius of Vercelli," *JTS*, 1985; Auth, "New Light on the Photinians," *JTS*, 1983. lydia.speller@gmail.com

SPELLERS, Stephanie (Mass) 82 Commonwealth Ave Apt 2, Boston MA 02116 **Ch Pension Fund New York NY 2010-; Cox Fell & Radical Welcome Mssnr The Cathd Ch Of S Paul Boston MA 2005-** B Frankfort KY 12/15/1971 BA Wake Forest U 1993; MA Harvard DS 1996; MDiv EDS 2004. D 6/4/2005 P 1/7/2006 Bp M(arvil) Thomas Shaw III. sspellers@post.harvard.edu

SPELLMAN, Lynne (Ark) 1219 W Lakeridge Dr, Fayetteville AR 72703 **P S Paul's Ch Fayetteville AR 2000-; Prof Dio Arkansas Little Rock AR 1977-** B Omaha NE 2/15/1948 d Robert Lyndon McBain & Marjorie Helen. BA Sthrn Illinois U 1969; MA U IL 1973; PhD U IL 1977; DAS GTS 1999. D 4/24/1999 P 12/11/1999 Bp Larry Earl Maze. m 3/20/1973 James Spellman. Auth, "Unbolting the Dark, a Memoir: On Turning Inward in Search of God," Hamilton Books (Rowman & Littlefield), 2011; Auth, "Origen On The Images And Mediating Activities Of The Logos," *Journ Of Neoplatonic Stds*, 1999; Auth, "Substance And Separation In Aristotle," Cambridge U Press, 1995. Amer Philos Assn 1977; No Amer Patristics Soc 2001-2002; Soc Of Ancient Gk Philos 1977; Soc Of Chr Philosophers 1987. Vstng Fell, Lucy Cavendish Coll, Camb Engl 1990. spellman@uark.edu

SPELLMAN, Robert Garland Windsor (Ct) 281 Ridge Rd Apt 2-B, Wethersfield CT 06109 B Cleveland OH 9/21/1921 s Frank Arthur Mangold & Agnes Marie. Case Wstrn Reserve U 1942; LTh U of Emml Saskatoon CA

1946; BA U Sask 1946; Case Wstrn Reserve U 1948. Trans from Anglican Church of Canada 6/16/1950 as Priest Bp Frederick G Budlong. S Thos's Day Sch New Haven CT 1983-1986; S Thos's Ch New Haven CT 1975-1986; S Ptr's Ch Plymouth CT 1974-1975; Trin Ch Torrington CT 1972-1975; Vic All SS Epis Ch Oakville CT 1972-1974; Cur Ch Of The Mssh Baltimore MD 1970-1972; Cur S Thos's Ch New Haven CT 1960-1970; R Ch of the Ascen Munich 81545 DE 1956-1960; Cur S Steph's Ch Pittsfield MA 1951-1956; Cur Ch Of The H Trin Middletown CT 1948-1951. Auth, "Ebenezer Landon & Some of His Descendants". rgws0921@aol.com

SPELMAN, Harold James (HB) No address on file. B Chicago IL 8/12/1923 s William Edward Spelman & Helen Irene. BA U Chi 1946; JD U Chi 1948. D 5/23/1970 Bp James Winchester Montgomery. m 6/14/1947 Joanne Adams c 2. Auth, "Var Legal Journ".

SPELMAN, Katherine Collingwood (Chi) 20 N American St, Philadelphia PA 19106 **Chr Ch Philadelphia Philadelphia PA 2011-** B New York NY 4/23/1984 d John Spelman & Rosalie. BA The U Chi 2006; Angl Dplma Berk 2011; MDiv Ya 2011. D 6/4/2011 Bp Jeffrey Dean Lee. KSPELMAN@CHRISTCHURCHPHILA.ORG

SPENCE, Douglas Morcom (Chi) Po Box 988, Ashland OR 97520 **Died 8/1/2010** B Pasadena CA 6/23/1928 s Harold Gerald Spence & Robina Jean. BA Occ 1956; MDiv CDSP 1959; U of Pennsylvania 1963; VTS 1980. D 6/10/1959 Bp Francis E I Bloy P 5/14/1960 Bp Andrew Tsu. c 3. Co-Auth, "Winery,Defenses & Soundings at Gibeon," *Museum Monographs*, U Museum (U. of Pennsylvania), 1964. NNECA 1971-1993. dougdi@jeffnet.org

SPENCER, Allison D (LI) 12706 Se Pinehurst Ct, Hobe Sound FL 33455 **Supply P S Monica's Ch Stuart FL 1996-** B Glen Cove NY 12/7/1931 d Nelson Edward Disbrow & Mary Catherine. AA SUNY 1980; Mercer TS 1982; BS Clayton U 1989. D 6/13/1983 Bp Robert Campbell Witcher Sr P 6/13/1989 Bp Orris George Walker Jr. m 4/18/1953 Arthur James Spencer c 3. R Chr Ch Babylon NY 1989-1994; D Chr Ch Babylon NY 1983-1989. twospencers@comcast.net

SPENCER JR, Arthur James (LI) 12706 Se Pinehurst Ct, Hobe Sound FL 33455 **Supply P S Monica's Ch Stuart FL 1996-** B Floral Park NY 3/24/1927 s Arthur J Spencer & Mildred Augusta. BA Adel 1949; Mercer TS 1981. D 6/1/1981 Bp Robert Campbell Witcher Sr P 6/1/1988 Bp Orris George Walker Jr. m 4/18/1953 Allison D Disbrow c 3. D/Asst S Thos Of Cbury Ch Smithtown NY 1981-1988. twospencers@comcast.net

SPENCER, Bonnie Sarah (Colo) 130 N. Mack St., Fort Collins CO 80521 **R S Paul's Epis Ch Ft Collins CO 2009-** B New York NY 6/8/1961 d Peter Harvey Spencer & Carol. BA U CO 1983; MDiv GTS 1999. D 6/5/1999 P 12/12/1999 Bp William Jerry Winterrowd. R Ch Of Our Sav Somerset MA 2005-2009; Asst R Gd Shpd Epis Ch Centennial CO 1999-2005. bonspen@yahoo.com

SPENCER, Carol (Miss) 1623 Acadia Ct., Jackson MS 39211 **D S Andr's Cathd Jackson MS 2009-; D Gr Epis Ch Canton MS 2000-** B New Orleans LA 11/5/1947 d Clayton Borne & Doris. BA Centenary Coll 1969; MA Loyola U 1994. D 1/4/1997 Bp Alfred Clark Marble Jr. m 6/12/2000 Robert Frank Spencer c 3. D S Ptr's By The Sea Gulfport MS 2006-2008; Dio Mississippi Jackson MS 2004-2008; D The Chap Of The Cross Madison MS 1997-1998. Trin Cleric Ldrshp Proj; Alpha Sigma Nu; Fndr's Awd MS Rel Ldrshp Conf. cbstew@bellsouth.net

SPENCER, Cynthia Margaret (Az) 15163 N Cutler Dr, Tucson AZ 85739 **Ch Of The Apos Oro Vlly AZ 2010-** B Minneapolis MN 3/15/1939 d John Boyd Spencer & Dorothy Donnelly. BA U MN 1964; MBA Golden Gate U 1986; MDiv GTS 1990. D 6/2/1990 Bp Charles Shannon Mallory P 4/13/1991 Bp Robert Deane Rowley Jr. Int S Mich's Ch Coolidge AZ 2010; R S Paul's Epis Ch Elk Rapids MI 2002-2003; Int Gr Epis Ch Kingston PA 2001-2002; Int S Jas Ch Paso Robles CA 2000; P-in-c S Paul's Ch Cambria CA 2000; COM Dio El Camino Real Monterey CA 1994-1998; Vic Ch Of S Jos Milpitas CA 1993-1999; BEC Dio NW Pennsylvania Erie PA 1991-1993; R S Jn's Ch Kane PA 1990-1993; Chair of Cmsn on Hisp Mnstry Dio El Camino Real Monterey CA 1985-1987. cms614@mac.com

SPENCER, James Scott (CFla) 28 Miracle Strip Pkwy Sw, Fort Walton Beach FL 32548 **R S Ptr The Fisherman Epis Ch New Smyrna Bch FL 2003-** B Glenridge NJ 3/21/1950 s William T Spencer & Barbara. BS Davis & Elkins Coll 1973; ThM Gordon-Conwell TS 1978; MDiv PrTS 1980. D 5/14/1989 P 11/1/1989 Bp William Hopkins Folwell. m 2/28/1995 Sally Wells c 1. R S Simon's On The Sound Ft Walton Bch FL 1998-2003; Assoc R All SS Ch Of Winter Pk Winter Pk FL 1989-1998; All SS Ch Of Winter Pk Winter Pk FL 1982-1989. stsimon@adisfwb.com

SPENCER, Leon P (NC) 6005 Starboard Dr, Greensboro NC 27410 **BEC Dio No Carolina Raleigh NC 2009-** B Roanoke Rapids NC 10/10/1943 s Leon Pharr Spencer & Jane. BA Wake Forest U 1965; MA Indiana U 1967; PhD Syr 1975; MDiv VTS 1989. D 6/6/1989 P 12/8/1989 Bp Robert Oran Miller. m 8/8/1998 Karen O Olson c 2. Dio No Carolina Raleigh NC 2004-2009; Washington Off On Afr Washington DC 1998-2004; Grtr Birmingham Mnstrs Birmingham AL 1997-1998; Assoc S Lk's Epis Ch Birmingham AL 1997-1998; Exec Coun Appointees New York NY 1994-1996; R S Lk's Ch Brighton Brookeville MD 1991-1992; Washington Off Of The Epis Ch Washington DC 1989-1990. Auth, "Not Yet There: Seminaries and the Challenge of Partnership," *Intl Bulletin of Mssy Resrch*, 2010; Producer, "Toward a Mssy Dio," *Sch of Mnstry Par DVDs*, Dio No Carolina, 2009; Producer, "Toward a Theol of partnership," *Sch of Mnstry Par DVDs*, Dio No Carolina, 2008; Interviewee and producer, "Reflections on Chr formation," *Sch of Mnstry Par DVDs*, Dio No Carolina, 2008; Producer, "Conversations about the Kingdom of God," *Sch of Mnstry Par DVDs*, Dio No Carolina, 2008; Auth, "Mssn and Mnstry through the Millennium Dvlpmt Goals," *Sch of Mnstry Par Stds*, Dio No Carolina, 2006; Auth, "Strengthening Chr ethical discourse: Conversations about societal issues," *Sch of Mnstry Par Stds*, Dio No Carolina, 2006; Auth, "Toward Solidarity w the Struggle in So Afr: A Congregregational Resource for Understanding the Ch's Witness," Epis Ch Cntr, 1990; Auth, "Ch and St in Colonial Afr," *Journ of Ch and St*, 1989; Auth, "Sthrn Afr in `Context: The Challenge of Grassroots Theol Educ," *Virginia Sem Journ*, 1989; Auth, "Radical Discipleship and the Afr Ch," *Communities of Faith and Radical Discipleship*, Merc Press, 1986; Auth, "Chrsnty and Colonial Protest," *Journ of Rel in Afr*, 1982. DD VTS 2005. lpspencer@triad.rr.com

SPENCER, Michael Edwin (NH) 325 Pleasant Street, Concord NH 03301 **P-in-c S Jn's Epis Ch Fishers Island NY 2008-; Dn of Chap and Rel Life S Paul's Sch Concord NH 2007-** B New Bedford MA 10/20/1971 s Edwin Fermino Spencer & Izabel. STM Ya Berk; BA Coll of the H Cross 1993; MDiv Yale DS 1998; Cert. Angl. Stds Ya Berk 2004. D 6/12/2004 P 1/16/2005 Bp Andrew Donnan Smith. m 7/22/1995 Amy Cofone c 2. Asst P S Jn's Epis Par Waterbury CT 2004-2007. Auth, "A New Penteost: Epis Schools and the Future of Anglicanism," *NAES Connections*, NAES, 2009; Auth, "Morning has Broken," *Alum Horae*, St. Paul's Sch, 2008; Auth, "To the No and to the So: Tayeb Salih and encounters w the other," *Wrld Rel Nwsltr*, Coun for Sprtl and Ethical Educ, 2007; Auth, "Taft: Rel and Sprtl Life," *Taft Alum Bulletin*, The Taft Sch, 2003; co-Auth, "Applied Ethics," *Applied Ethics*, Coun for Sprtl and Ethical Educ, 1999; Auth, "The Price," *Theol Today*, Theol Today, 1998. Forw Mvmt 2007; NAES 2007. mspencer@sps.edu

SPENCER, Orval James (Neb) 6700 Tamerson Ct, Raleigh NC 27612 B Virden MT CA 1/31/1929 s Edward Ingle Spencer & Edith Hazel. BA U of Manitoba 1950; LTh S Jn CA 1954. Trans from Anglican Church of Canada 6/1/1957. c 2. R S Matt's Ch Allnce NE 1961-1991; Ex Coun Dio Nebraska Omaha NE 1959-1973; P-in-c S Jn's Ch Valentine NE 1957-1961.

SPENCER, Patricia Ann (CFla) 851 Village Lake Dr S, Deland FL 32724 **D The Ch Of The H Presence Deland FL 2008-; D S Barn Ch Deland FL 2002-** B Tallahassee FL 1/31/1948 Wesleyan Coll. D 12/14/2002 Bp John Wadsworth Howe. c 1.

SPENCER, Peter Levalley (RI) 107 Green Hill Ave, Wakefield RI 02879 B Providence RI 11/18/1938 s Lee Valley Spencer & Mary Josephine. BA Br 1960; STB GTS 1965; Cert EDS 1994. D 6/1/1965 P 2/12/1966 Bp John S Higgins. m 5/4/1961 Mary Louise Bruno. Pres Stndg Com Dio Rhode Island Providence RI 1998-1999; Stndg Com Dio Rhode Island Providence RI 1995-1999; Chair Evang Com Dio Rhode Island Providence RI 1992-1997; Evang Com Dio Rhode Island Providence RI 1990-1997; Pres Stndg Com Dio Rhode Island Providence RI 1989-1990; Stndg Com Dio Rhode Island Providence RI 1986-1990; Dn Narragansett Deanry Dio Rhode Island Providence RI 1982-1985; Sprtl Dir Intern Dio Rhode Island Providence RI 1980-1984; Chair Evang Com Dio Rhode Island Providence RI 1978-1980; Dioc Coun Dio Rhode Island Providence RI 1976-1979; Cn Cathd Of S Jn Providence RI 1972-2001; Evang Com Dio Rhode Island Providence RI 1971-1978; Dioc Coun Dio Rhode Island Providence RI 1971-1974; Deptce Dio Rhode Island Providence RI 1969-1972; S Paul's Ch No Kingstown RI 1967-2001; Dept Mssn Dio Rhode Island Providence RI 1967-1969; Cur S Paul's Ch Pawtucket RI 1965-1967. PLSPENCERSR@AOL.COM

SPENCER, Richard William (NY) 4 Hemlock Rd, Hartsdale NY 10530 **D S Barn Ch Ardsley NY 1999-** B Yonkers NY 6/27/1952 s Thomas Albert Spencer & Evelyn. BS Emerson Coll 1974. D 5/16/1998 Bp Richard Frank Grein. m 9/11/1982 Susan Anne Reed c 2. D S Andr's Epis Ch Hartsdale NY 1998-2006. "Epis New Yorker Advsry Bd," 2006. Deacon880@optonline.net

SPENCER, Robert Dennis (Wyo) 4508 Cottage Ln, Cheyenne WY 82001 B Warren PA 3/20/1939 s Robert Mead Spencer & Marguerite. Mar 1962; VTS 1972; Dplma Acad for Pstr Ed 1996. D 1/29/1972 Bp Robert Bruce Hall P 9/9/1972 Bp Gray Temple. m R Gaye c 2. S Mk's Ch Cheyenne WY 1997; Ch Of The Redeem Salmon ID 1988-1991; Dio Idaho Boise ID 1988-1989; R Trin Epis Ch Pocatello ID 1981-1985; Ch Of The Adv Spartanburg SC 1978-1981; Coordntr Yth Mnstrs Dio Upper So Carolina Columbia SC 1978-1981; Asst Ch Of The H Comf Sumter SC 1974-1999; R Ch Of The Cross Columbia SC 1974-1978. Auth, "Aids- The Pstr Perspective"; Auth, "Trng Manual For Hosp Chapl". AEHC. densob748@msn.com

SPENCER, Robert Frank (Miss) 1623 Acadia Court, Jackson MS 39211 **Exec Dir Stewpot Cmnty Serv Jackson MS 2003-; D The Chap Of The Cross Madison MS 2003-** B Greenwood MS 5/1/1947 s Benjamin Franklin Spencer

S

& Mary Winifred. BA U of Mississippi 1970; JD U of Mississippi 1974. D 1/4/2003 Bp Alfred Clark Marble Jr. m 6/12/2000 Carol Borne c 2. NAAD 2002. fspencer@stewpot.org

SPENCER, Ronald (WMo) Po Box 197, Angel Fire NM 87710 B Oakland CA 12/24/1934 s Dwight Thompson Spencer & Aubrey Claire. BA U CA 1958; MDiv CDSP 1963. D 1/26/1963 Bp George Richard Millard P 7/27/1963 Bp Richard Ainslie Kirchhoffer. c 2. Comp, Worker Sis And Worker Brothers Of The H Spiri 1993. N/A

SPENCER, Warren Dove (NJ) 68 Hull Ave, Freehold NJ 07728 B Brooklyn NY 11/28/1941 s Samuel Dove Spencer & Marion. D 4/13/1985 Bp George Phelps Mellick Belshaw. m 8/19/1967 Susan Lewis. wds4818@msn.com

SPERRY, Rebecca Lynne (Chi) 2056 Vermont St, Blue Island IL 60406 **D S Jos's And S Aid's Ch Blue Island IL 1991-** B Blue Island IL 11/11/1953 d Thomas Lynne Sperry & Margaret Carroll. Moraine Vlly Cmnty Coll Palos Hills IL 1975; U IL 1981; Chicago Deacons Sch 1991. D 12/7/1991 Bp Frank Tracy Griswold III. Liturg Cmsn Dio Chicago Chicago IL 1994-2000. becky.sperry@gmail.com

SPICER JR, C(lyde) Allen (Md) 724 Morningside Dr, Towson MD 21204 **Chapl to Cler and Cler Families (FOCUS) Dio Maryland Baltimore MD 2010-; Chairman of the Bd Trst Bp Clagget Cntr Buckeystown MD 1999-** B Baltimore MD 3/14/1937 s Clyde Allen Spicer & Mildred Eleanor. BA McDaniel Coll 1959; BD VTS 1962; STD McDaniel Coll 1981. D 6/1/1962 Bp Harry Lee Doll P 4/1/1963 Bp Noble C Powell. m 6/13/1964 Gwendolyn N Narbeth. Assoc R Ch Of The H Comf Luthvle Timon MD 1998-2010; R S Geo's Ch Perryman MD 1998-2000; R The Ch Of The Nativ Cedarcroft Baltimore MD 1984-1998; Secy of the Dioc Coun Dio Easton Easton MD 1972-1983; Dn Trin Cathd Easton MD 1972-1983; R Emm Epis Ch Chestertown MD 1968-1972; Dir of Camp Wright Dio Easton Easton MD 1965-1983; R Chr Ch Denton MD 1965-1968; Asst R Emm Ch Baltimore MD 1963-1965. S.T.D Dr. Of Sacr Theol Wstrn Maryland Coll 1982. ALLENANDGWEN@COMCAST.NET

SPICER, John M (WMo) St. Andrews Episcopal Church, 6401 Wornall Terrace, Kansas City MO 64113 **Assoc, Missions S Andr's Ch Kansas City MO 2005-** B Springfield MO 1/10/1965 s Holt V Spicer & Marion A. BA SW Missouri St U 1986; MDiv Epis TS of The SW 2002. D 6/8/2002 P 12/7/2002 Bp Barry Robert Howe. m 8/11/1990 Ann E Farmer c 2. Vic Ch Of The Gd Shpd Springfield MO 2002-2005; Dio W Missouri Kansas City MO 2002-2005. frjohn@standrewkc.org

SPICER, John Tildsley (Fla) 25 Eyrie Dr, Crawfordville FL 32327 B Washington DC 4/24/1952 s Donald Worthington Spicer & Mary Helen. Earlham Coll 1971; BA W&L 1974; MDiv GTS 1978. D 6/16/1978 P 2/24/1979 Bp William Henry Marmion. c 1. R S Teresa Of Avila Crawfordville FL 2003-2008; Vic All SS Epis Ch Brighton Heights Pittsburgh PA 2000-2003; Int S Chris's Epis Ch Cranberry Twp PA 1999-2000; Chr Epis Ch Indiana PA 1998-1999; S Thos Ch In The Fields Gibsonia PA 1985-1998; Reg Dir Dio Wstrn No Carolina Asheville NC 1983-1985; S Andr Ch Mt Holly NC 1983-1985; Cur Chr Ch Blacksburg VA 1978-1983. jspicer99@comcast.net

SPICER-SMITH, Robert Saunders (Los) 910 Patterson Ave, Glendale CA 91202 B Toledo OH 3/20/1924 s Robert Gideon Smith & Elsie Beth. BA USC 1945; LTh SWTS 1948; Cert U CA 1956. D 2/22/1948 Bp Richard T Loring Jr P 10/24/1948 Bp Charles A Clough. Asst R Ch Of Our Sav Par San Gabr CA 1954-1958; Asst R S Paul's Cathd Peoria IL 1949-1951. robertglendale@gmail.com

SPIEGEL, Phyllis Ann (SwVa) 120 Cherry Ln, Christiansburg VA 24073 **Search Com for Diocesean Yth Coordntr Dio SW Virginia Roanoke VA 2011-; T/F for Same Gender Blessing Materials Dio SW Virginia Roanoke VA 2011-; R S Thos Epis Christiansburg VA 2006-; P-in-c S Thos Epis Christiansburg VA 2004-** B Roanoke VA 9/22/1966 BA Emory & Henry Coll 1984; MDiv VTS 2004. D 4/13/2004 P 10/15/2004 Bp Frank Neff Powell. c 1. GC Dep Dio SW Virginia Roanoke VA 2009-2011; Provencial Syn Del Dio SW Virginia Roanoke VA 2009-2010; Trst Bd for Diocesean Grants Dio SW Virginia Roanoke VA 2005-2010; Dn of Convoc Dio SW Virginia Roanoke VA 2005-2008; Exec Bd Dio SW Virginia Roanoke VA 2005-2008. rev.spiegel@verizon.net

SPIELMANN, Richard Morisse (Roch) 2126 E Alameda Dr, Tempe AZ 85282 B Flushing NY 2/24/1930 s Frank Aloysius Spielmann & Lillian Louise. BA CUNY 1953; STB GTS 1956; ThD GTS 1964. D 4/7/1956 Bp James P De Wolfe P 10/20/1956 Bp Jonathan Goodhue Sherman. m 6/20/1953 Janet Wilson Cherry c 2. Dioc Liturg Cmsn Chairman Dio Rochester Rochester NY 1971-1978; Bex Columbus OH 1968-1992; R Ch Of The Gd Shpd Barre VT 1959-1963; BEC Dio Vermont Burlington VT 1959-1963; P-t Asst Chr And S Steph's Ch New York NY 1958-1959; Par Of Chr The Redeem Pelham NY 1957-1958; Fell & Tutor The GTS New York NY 1956-1959; P-t Asst Ch Of The Redeem Morristown NJ 1956-1957. Auth, "Bex: 150 Years: a Brief Hist," *Bex: 150 Years: a Brief Hist*, 1974; Auth, "Westminster Dictionary of Ch Hist," *Westminster Dictionary of Ch Hist*, Westminster Pr, 1971; Auth, "Hist of Chr Wrshp," *Hist of Chr Wrshp*, Seabury Press, 1966. Amer Soc of Ch Hist 1959-2006; Ed Bd Angl & Epis Hist 1977-2007; HSEC 1963. jrspiel@cox.net

SPIERS, Linda Mitchell (Ct) 3 Whirling Drive, Canton CT 06019 **Bd Mem Soc For The Increase Of Mnstry W Hartford CT 2011-; Dep to GC Dio Connecticut Hartford CT 2010-; Title IV Disciplinary Bd Dio Connecticut Hartford CT 2010-; R Trin Epis Ch Collinsville CT 2004-** B Washington DC 6/17/1945 d Carl Cooper Mitchell & Margaret. BS MWC 1966; MBA U Rich 1990; MDiv Ya Berk 2000. D 6/10/2000 Bp Andrew Donnan Smith P 1/20/2001 Bp James Elliot Curry. Pres of Stndg Com Dio Connecticut Hartford CT 2007-2009; Assoc Chr Ch Cathd Hartford CT 2000-2004. lindaspiers@aol.com

SPIGNER, Carol H (Va) 10730 Scott Dr, Fairfax VA 22030 **Ch Of The Resurr Alexandria VA 2011-** B Ridgewood NJ 11/11/1954 d Bayard Hancock & Phyllis Anne. BA Keene St Coll 1976; MDiv VTS 1985. D 9/28/1985 Bp Philip Alan Smith P 5/10/1986 Bp William Arthur Beckham. c 2. Int S Chris's Ch Springfield VA 2009-2011; Int Ch Of The H Comf Vienna VA 2008-2009; S Jn's Epis Ch McLean VA 2007-2008; S Mk's Ch Alexandria VA 2005-2007; S Dunst's McLean VA 2004-2005; Assoc All SS' Epis Ch Chevy Chase MD 1997-2003; Asst S Martins-In-The-Field Columbia SC 1989-1995; Dio Upper So Carolina Columbia SC 1988-1996; Trin Cathd Columbia SC 1988-1996; S Phil's Epis Ch Greenville SC 1988; D Epis Ch Of The Redeem Greenville SC 1985-1986. cjhspigner@aol.com

SPIGNER, Charles Bailey (Va) 2310 Military Road, Arlington VA 22207 B Columbia SC 1/13/1951 s Adolphus Fletcher Spigner & Henrietta Geddes (Bailey) Spigner. U So; BA U of So Carolina 1977; MDiv VTS 1985. D 6/8/1985 P 5/10/1986 Bp William Arthur Beckham. c 2. S Andr's Epis Ch Arlington VA 2004-2006; S Barn Ch Annandale VA 1999-2000; The Epis Ch-King Geo Co King Geo VA 1998-1999; Assoc R Ch Of The H Comf Vienna VA 1996-1998; Int S Mary's Ch Columbia SC 1995-1996; Assoc R S Martins-In-The-Field Columbia SC 1987-1995; Vic Ch Of The Epiph Laurens SC 1985-1987; DCE S Mich And All Ang' Columbia SC 1980-1982. cbspigner@comcast.net

SPINA, Frank Anthony (Oly) 414 W Newell St, Seattle WA 98119 **Assoc S Marg's Epis Ch Bellevue WA 1998-** B Long Beach CA 9/30/1943 s Frank Spina & Mary. BA Greenville Coll 1965; MDiv Asbury TS 1968; MA U MI 1970; PhD U MI 1977. D 6/26/1999 P 1/23/2000 Bp Vincent Waydell Warner. m 12/17/1994 Jo-Ellen Watson.

SPITLER, Joseph Campbell (Tex) 1305 Travis St, Columbus TX 78934 **Died 2/11/2011** B Lufkin TX 11/13/1941 s William Marion Spitler & Dorothy. BBA TCU 1967; MDiv VTS 1982. D 6/17/1982 Bp Maurice Manuel Benitez P 1/1/1983 Bp Roger Howard Cilley. joseph@trinitybaytown.org

SPLINTER, John Theodore (FdL) 23 Lilac Lane, Edgerton WI 53534 **Cn S Paul's Cathd Fond du Lac WI 2005-** B Watertown WI 10/10/1941 s Herbert H Splinter & Irene E. BS U of Wisconsin 1963; BD Nash 1966. D 3/5/1966 P 9/13/1966 Bp Donald H V Hallock. m 6/25/1966 Barbara Ann Schaefer c 2. Vic S Jn's Epis Ch Sparta WI 2000-2004; Vic Ch Of The H Apos Oneida WI 1994-1998; Ch Of S Jn The Bapt Wausau WI 1993-1994; R S Alb's Epis Ch Marshfield WI 1976-1993; Vic S Barn Epis Ch Tomahawk WI 1972-1976; Vic St Ambr Epis Ch Antigo WI 1972-1976. bjsplint@charter.net

✠ **SPOFFORD, Rt Rev William Benjamin** (WA) 2425 Sw 6th Ave # 358, Portland OR 97201 B Brooklyn NY 1/28/1921 s William Benjamin Spofford & Dorothy Grace. BA Antioch Coll 1942; BD EDS 1945; Advncd CPE 1953; DD CDSP 1968; STD The Coll of Idaho 1973. D 11/30/1944 P 6/1/1945 Bp William A Lawrence Con 1/25/1969 for EO. VTS Alexandria VA 1983-1984; Asst Bp Dio Washington Washington DC 1980-1984; Asstg Bp Of Washington Dio Washington Washington DC 1979-1984; Bp Dio Estrn Oregon The Dalles OR 1969-1980; Bp Of Estrn Oregon Dio Estrn Oregon The Dalles OR 1969-1979; Dn S Mich's Cathd Boise ID 1960-1969; Vic S Jas Ch Payette ID 1953-1956; Vic S Lk's Ch Weiser ID 1953-1956; Min in charge Ch Of The Gd Shpd Waban MA 1946-1947. Auth, "Pilgrim In Transition Brainstorming w A Bp". ACPE, RWF, EPF. DD CDSP 1973. wbish@tplaza.org

✠ **SPONG, Rt Rev John Shelby** (Nwk) 24 Puddingstone Rd, Morris Plains NJ 07950 B Charlotte NC 6/16/1931 s John Shelby Spong & Doolie Boyce. BA U NC 1952; MDiv VTS 1955. D 6/24/1955 Bp Richard Henry Baker P 12/28/1955 Bp Edwin A Penick Con 6/12/1976 for Nwk. m 1/1/1990 Christine M Bridger c 3. Bp Dio Newark Newark NJ 1978-2000; Bp of Newark Dio Newark Newark NJ 1978-2000; Bp Coadj Dio Newark Newark NJ 1976-1978; Mem, Stndg Com Dio Virginia Richmond VA 1973-1976; R S Paul's Ch Richmond VA 1969-1976; Dep to GC Dio Virginia Richmond VA 1969-1973; Pres, Stndg Com Dio SW Virginia Roanoke VA 1966-1969; R S Jn's Ch Lynchburg VA 1965-1969; Mem, Exec Coun Dio No Carolina Raleigh NC 1959-1962; Chair, Evang Cmsn Dio No Carolina Raleigh NC 1958-1959; R Calv Ch Tarboro NC 1957-1965; P-in-c St Marys Epis Ch Speed NC 1957-1965; R S Jos's Ch Durham NC 1955-1957. "Jesus for the Non-Rel," 2007; "The Sins of Scripture: Exposing the Bible's Texts of Hate to Reveal the God of Love," 2005; Columnist, "Columnist," *WaterfrontMedia.com*, 2002; Auth, "A New Chrsnty For a New Wrld," 2001; Auth, "Columnist,"

S

BeliefNet.com, 2000; Auth, "Here I Stand: My Struggle for a Chrsnty of Integrity," *Love and Equality*, 2000; Auth, "The Bp's Voice: Essays Compiled and Edited by Christine Mary Spong," 1999; Auth, "Why Chrsnty Must Change or Die: A Bp Speaks to Believers in Exile," 1998; Auth, "Liberating the Gospels: Reading the Bible w Jewish Eyes," 1996; Auth, "Ressurrection: Myth or Reality," 1994; Auth, "b of A Wmn," 1992; Auth, "Rescuing the Bible from Fundamentalism," 1991; Auth, "Living in Sin? A Bp Rethinks Human Sxlty," 1988; Auth, "Beyond Moralism," 1985; Auth, "Into the Whirwind, The Future of The Ch," 1983; Auth, "The Easter Moment," 1980; Auth, "The Living Commandment," 1977; Auth, "Life Approaches Death," 1976; Auth, "Dialogue In Search of Jewish Chr Understanding," 1975; Auth, "Churchpower," 1975; Auth, "This Hebr Lord," 1974; Auth, "Honest Pryr," 1973. Dav Friedrich Strauss Soc; Jesus Seminar. DHL Leh 2006; DHL U NC 2006; DHL Holmes Inst 2002; DHL Muhlenberg Coll 1998; Quarter Centenary Schlr Camb 1992; Awd ACLU of NJ 1988; DD VTS 1977; DD S Paul's Coll Lawrenceville VA 1976; Phi Beta Kappa 1952; Jn A T Robinson Awd for Theol Integrity Jesus Seminar. cmsctm@aol.com

SPOOR, Cornelia Paradise (NJ) Po Box 624, Roosevelt NJ 08555 B Niagara Falls NY 10/31/1952 d K Franklin Spoor & Margaret. BA Rutgers-The St U 1987; MS Rutgers-The St U 1993; Cert New Jersey Cntr For Fam Stds 1999. D 9/21/2001 Bp David B(ruce) Joslin. c 2. D Trin Ch Princeton NJ 2002-2004.

SPRAGUE, James Wilson (Los) PO Box 303, Santa Barbara CA 93102 **S Paul's Epis Ch Ventura CA 2011-** B Aurora IL 3/15/1948 s Theodore Smith Sprague & Janet. BA Hob 1970; MDiv GTS 1979. D 6/23/1979 P 12/21/1979 Bp Frederick Barton Wolf. m 6/21/2008 Ann Bradbury. S Mths' Par Whittier CA 2009-2011; S Mart's Epis Sch Metairie LA 1998-2005; S Jas Sch St Jas MD 1994-1998; S Lk's Ch Hudson MA 1992-1993; St. Mk's Sch of Southborough Inc. Southborough MA 1988-1990; S Marks Sch Of Texas Dallas TX 1984-1988; Vic S Mart's Epis Ch Pittsfield ME 1979-1982; Vic All SS Epis Ch Skowhegan ME 1979-1980. popssprague@hotmail.com

SPRAGUE, Minka Shura (Miss) 1815 Piedmont St, Jackson MS 39202 **Assoc R S Jas Ch Jackson MS 2003-; D S Jas Ch Jackson MS 2003-** B Kansas City MO 11/19/1944 d Daniel Charles Shura & Mary Francis. BA U MN 1966; MA GTS 1978; ThD GTS 1985. D 12/8/1986 Bp Paul Moore Jr P 5/1/2006 Bp Duncan Montgomery Gray III. c 2. D Cathd Of St Jn The Div New York NY 1988-1997; D for Educ Ch Of The H Trin New York NY 1985-1988; Asst Dir Cont Educ The GTS New York NY 1977-1980. Auth, "One to Watch, One to Pray," *One to Watch, One to Pray*, Ch Pub, 2004; Auth, "Praying from the Free Throw Line - For Now," *Praying from the Free-Throw Line -- For Now*, Ch Pub, 1999. msprague@stjjax.org

SPRATT, George Clifford (Kan) 828 Center St, Fulton MO 65251 B Los Angeles CA 3/14/1929 s George Spratt & Jean H. BA Macalester Coll 1952; MDiv Bec 1955. D 6/29/1955 Bp Hamilton Hyde Kellogg P 12/21/1955 Bp Stephen E Keeler. m 8/3/1957 Mary L Sommers c 3. Asst S Mich And All Ang Ch Mssn KS 1983-1991; Asst S Andr's Ch Kansas City MO 1974-1983; R Gr Memi Ch Wabasha MN 1963-1967; P-in-c All SS Ch Northfield MN 1957-1958; P-in-c Ch Of The H Cross Dundas MN 1956-1958; In-charge Gilfillan Memi Chap Squaw Lake MN 1955-1956. g.spratt@sbcglobal.net

SPRINGER, Alice Elizabeth Ballard (Dal) 22-M Smith Rd, Rockwall TX 75087 B Beeville TX 2/27/1937 d James Franklin Ballard & Jewel. BS U of Texas 1961; MA SWTS 1968. D 6/23/1968 Bp Charles A Mason. m 9/27/1969 Robert Harris Springer c 2. Stff S Jas Epis Ch Texarkana TX 1968-1970.

SPRINGER, David Richard (Alb) 12 Shannon Ct, West Sand Lake NY 12196 B Baltimore MD 6/15/1946 Amh 1968; PDS 1973. D 6/9/1973 Bp Paul Moore Jr P 12/15/1973 Bp William Henry Mead. c 2. Ch Of The H Cross Troy NY 1991-1999; Vic Ch Of The H Trin Brookville PA 1985-1991; S Barn Ch Bay Vill OH 1981-1984; Dio Bethlehem Bethlehem PA 1981; The Epis Ch Of The Medtr Allentown PA 1976-1980; Dio Delaware Wilmington DE 1975-1976; Asst Imm Ch Highlands Wilmington DE 1974-1975.

SPRINGER, Lloyd Livingstone (NY) 740 E 242nd St, Bronx NY 10470 B BB 4/28/1930 s Oscar Gill & Olive. Cert Acad Of Gerontology Educ & Dvlpmt; GOE Codrington Coll 1963; STM NYTS 1975; MA NYU 1982. D 1/6/1971 P 12/8/1971 Bp Horace W B Donegan. m 5/2/1970 Ottoria Philips c 1. R S Edm's Ch Bronx NY 1973-2000; Asst S Mart's Ch New York NY 1971-1972. S Edm'S Appreciation Awd From Vstry And Servers 1983; Bronx Borough Pres Cmnty Serv Awd; Mt Hope Cmnty Awd For Cmnty Serv; Honoraryored Citizen Of The St Of New York; Citation From City Of New York, Borough Of The Bronx For Excellent Cmnty Wk; Cert Of Merit From Dio New York; Aliens Citizen Awd Emmigrant Bank.

SPRINGER, Susan Woodward (U) 85 E. 100 N., Logan UT **Dio Utah Salt Lake City UT 2009-** B Ridgewood NJ 5/20/1958 d William Stevenson Hawkey & Edith Sognier. Mid 1977; U of Sthrn Maine-Portland 1978; MDiv The TS at The U So 2009. D 3/21/2009 Bp Brian James Thom P 12/1/2009 Bp Carolyn Tanner Irish. S Thos Epis Ch Sun Vlly ID 2003-2006. susanatseminary@gmail.com

SPROAT, Jim (WTex) PO Box 3, Junction TX 76849 **Trin Ch Jct TX 2006-; Vic Calv Ch Menard TX 2005-** B Grand Rapids MI 3/24/1947 s Robert Gregory Sproat & Jeanne Louise. BS Tarleton St Coll 1970; MEd Texas A&M U 1974; MDiv Epis TS of The SW 1979. D 7/3/1979 P 6/3/1980 Bp Roger Howard Cilley. c 4. R S Steph's Epis Ch Sherman TX 1999-2004; H Innoc' Epis Ch Madisonville TX 1990-1991; Dioc Com On Scouting Dio Texas Houston TX 1987-1999; Cler Pstr Care Com Dio Texas Houston TX 1984-1999; Dioc Stwdshp Com Dio Texas Houston TX 1984-1990; All SS Ch Baytown TX 1983-1990; Vic S Fran Of Assisi Epis Prairie View TX 1979-1983. CBS 1965; ESA 1988; The Loyal Ord of the Purple Suspender 1993. Silver Beaver SHAC - BSA 1999; Vigil hon OA - BSA 1995; St Geo Awd - BSA PECUSA 1987. jlsproat@cebridge.net

SPROUL, J(ames) Renfro (EC) Po Box 586, Salter Path NC 28575 **S Fran by the Sea Bogue Banks Salter Path NC 1998-** B Williamsburg,KY 1/30/1935 s Harvey Lafayette Sproul & Ruth. BA U of Tennessee 1957; MDiv Ya Berk 1960; DMin Van 1973. D 2/16/1978 P 6/9/1979 Bp William Gillette Weinhauer. c 2. Int Chr Ch Eliz City NC 1995-1997; Int S Fran Ch Goldsboro NC 1994-1995; Int S Jas Par Wilmington NC 1993-1994; Int Trin Epis Ch Seneca Falls NY 1990-1992; Int Sis of St Mary Sewanee TN 1988-1990; Int S Paul's Ch Franklin TN 1987-1988; Assoc S Andr's Epis Ch Tampa FL 1985-1987; R Ch Of The Epiph Newton NC 1980-1985; Calv Epis Ch Fletcher NC 1979-1980. Auth, "A New Ecum Mnstry," *Campus Mnstry Bulletin (Winter)*, 1971; Auth, "The New Creation," *The Pulpit (September)*, 1966. Danforth Fllshp Grant Danforth Fndt 1966. jrenfro@lpmonline.net

SPROUSE, Herbert Warren (NH) 21 Centre St, Concord NH 03301 **Cur S Paul's Ch Concord NH 2010-** B Charlottesville VA 8/27/1954 s William Warren Sprouse & Catharine Ratzburg. BMus Ithaca Coll 1976; MBA Yale Sch of Mgmt 1979; MMus Yale Sch of Mus 1979; MDiv EDS 2009. D 10/31/2009 P 5/11/2010 Bp V Gene Robinson. hsprouse@aol.com

SPRUHAN, John (SD) Po Box 257, Rosebud SD 57570 **Supervising P Ch Of The H Sprt Winner SD 2008-; Supervising P Calv Epis Ch Greg SD 2006-; Supervising P/Vic Rosebud Epis Mssn Mssn SD 2004-; Supervising P/Vic Trin Epis Ch Mssn SD 2004-; Vic/Supervisory P Ch Of Jesus Mssn SD 1997-; Supervising P/Vic H Innoc Epis Ch Mssn SD 1997-** B Detroit MI 9/13/1950 s John Galey Spruhan & Beatrice Teresa. BS U MI 1972; MDiv No Pk TS 1978; Cert SWTS 1980. D 6/14/1980 Bp Quintin Ebenezer Primo Jr P 12/13/1980 Bp James Winchester Montgomery. m 5/20/1972 Judy Bennett Judd c 2. Ecum Off Dio So Dakota Sioux Falls SD 2001-2010; Chair Call to Common Mssn Com Dio So Dakota Sioux Falls SD 2000-2010; Chair Jubilee Com Dio So Dakota Sioux Falls SD 1999-2010; Dio So Dakota Sioux Falls SD 1997-2010; Rosebud Epis Mssn Mssn SD 1997-1999; Vic S Paul's Ch Mssn SD 1997-1998; Vic S Thos Ch Mssn SD 1997-1998; Dn Chi W Deanry Dio Chicago Chicago IL 1994-1997; Chair Hunger Cmsn Dio Chicago Chicago IL 1985-1997; Vic St Cyprians Ch Chicago IL 1981-1997. Phil Marquard Hunger Awd 1996; Hunger Fighter of the Year 1992; Outstanding Young Citizen Chicago Jr ChmbrCom & Industry 1984. revdrwho@aol.com

SPRUHAN, Judy Bennett (SD) Po Box 257, Rosebud SD 57570 B Northville MI 1/23/1951 d William Andrew Bennett & Helen Onedia. Judson Coll 1970; Dplma Cook Cnty Sch of Nrsng Chicago IL 1976; BS No Pk U 1986; MS No Pk U 1996. D 12/2/1989 Bp Frank Tracy Griswold III P 6/25/2000 Bp Creighton Leland Robertson. m 5/20/1972 John Spruhan c 2. P Ch Of Jesus Mssn SD 2000-2010; P Dio So Dakota Sioux Falls SD 2000-2010; P H Innoc Epis Ch Mssn SD 2000-2010; D Ch Of Jesus Mssn SD 1997-2000; D H Innoc Epis Ch Mssn SD 1997-2000; D Rosebud Epis Mssn Mssn SD 1997-2000; D S Paul's Ch Mssn SD 1997-2000; D S Thos Ch Mssn SD 1997-2000; D St Cyprians Ch Chicago IL 1989-1997. dcnfrodo@aol.com

SPRUILL, Robert Leigh (Tenn) 5825 Robert E Lee Dr, Nashville TN 37215 **R S Geo's Ch Nashville TN 2005-** B Richmond VA 11/29/1963 s Joseph Elna Spruill & Cora Sue. BA U NC 1988; MDiv STUSo 1996. D 6/15/1996 P 1/7/1997 Bp Peter James Lee. m 10/28/1989 Susalee C Spruill c 3. R S Mk's Epis Ch Jacksonville FL 2001-2005; S Lk's Epis Ch Birmingham AL 1998-2001; Asst R S Jas' Ch Richmond VA 1996-1998. leigh@stgeorgesnashville.org

SPRUILL JR, William Arthur (Fla) 4107 Marquette Ave, Jacksonville FL 32210 **Cn Dio Florida Jacksonville FL 1995-** B Miami FL 11/15/1931 s William Arthur Spruill & Elizabeth May. BA U So 1953; MA Col 1956; BD VTS 1968. D 6/26/1968 Bp C J Kinsolving III P 12/27/1968 Bp Albert Ervine Swift. m 2/27/1960 Charlotte Slight c 3. Rep Fl Coun Chs Dio Florida Jacksonville FL 1976-1983; Asst To Bp Dio Florida Jacksonville FL 1975-1994; Asst Min S Paul's Ch Delray Bch FL 1968-1975. Ccn. Dsa 1995. charttespruill@sprintmail.com

SPULNIK, Frederick Joseph (RI) 4873 Collwood Blvd unit B, San Diego CA 92115 B Boise ID 9/23/1941 s Joseph Bernard Spulnik & Helen Irere. AA Boise St U 1961; BA U of Portland 1963; MDiv GTS 1966. D 6/26/1966 Bp Norman L Foote P 1/6/1967 Bp Charles Waldo MacLean. R S Matt's Par Of Jamestown Jamestown RI 1983-2004; R S Andr's Ch New Bedford MA 1973-1983; Assoc Ascen Memi Ch Ipswich MA 1968-1973; Cur S Lk's Ch E Hampton NY 1966-1968. fspulnik@cox.net

SPURLOCK, Michael Douglas (Tenn) Saint Thomas Church, 1 W. 53rd St., New York NY 10019 **Cur S Thos Ch New York NY 2010-** B Knoxville TN

5/5/1968 s Michael Louis Spurlock & Edna Jean. BFA U of Tennessee 1993; MDiv Nash 2007. D 6/2/2007 P 12/8/2007 Bp John Crawford Bauerschmidt. m 12/18/1997 Aimee M Marcoux c 3. Vic All SS Epis Ch Smyrna TN 2007-2010. vicar@all-saints-smyrna.org

SPURLOCK, Paul Allan (Colo) 10000 E Yale Ave Apt 4, 10000 E. Yale Ave Apt43, Denver CO 80231 B Denver CO 2/18/1940 s Granderson Spurlock & Addie E. BS Metropltn St Coll of Denver 1975; MDiv Iliff TS 1989. D 2/2/2002 P 8/6/2002 Bp William Jerry Winterrowd. m 7/20/2001 Saundra Nicholls c 2. S Thos Epis Ch Denver CO 2001-2007. psspurlo@msn.com

SQUIER, Timothy John (Chi) 500 East Depot Street, Antioch IL 60002 **R S Ign Of Antioch Ch Antioch IL 2008-** B Indianapolis IN 1/4/1971 s Larry Dean Squier & Susan Elizabeth. BA TCU 1993; MDiv Chr TS 1996; BA Briar Cliff U 2003; CAS SWTS 2004; MTS SWTS 2005. D 12/18/2004 P 10/2/2005 Bp Alan Scarfe. m 1/11/2003 Kristal J Aukland c 4. Asstg P S Mk's Ch Evanston IL 2006-2007. ignatius5@mac.com

SQUIRE, James Richard (Pa) Episcopal Academy, 1785 Bishop White Dr, Newtown Square PA 19073 **The Epis Acad Newtown Sq PA 1978-** B Conshohocken PA 3/30/1945 s Walter Hunter Squire & Harryanna. BS W Chester St Coll 1967; MDiv Ya Berk 1970; ThM Duke 1971. D 6/6/1970 P 1/30/1971 Bp Robert Lionne DeWitt. m 12/20/1969 Vicki Alice Gauthier c 4. H Apos And Medtr Philadelphia PA 1980; Asst Trin Ch Swarthmore PA 1971-1978. squire@ea1785.org

SQUIRE JR, Willard Searle (ETenn) 748 Hammond Pl, The Villages FL 32162 **Assoc S Geo Epis Ch The Villages FL 2008-** B Detroit MI 1/11/1938 s Willard Searle Squire & Mary Moore. BS U of Nebraska 1972; MAJ Wichita St U 1978; MDiv TS 1985. D 6/29/1985 Bp George Lazenby Reynolds Jr P 1/6/1986 Bp William Evan Sanders. m 9/17/1959 Margaret Vincent Bregenzer c 6. P-in-c Chr Epis Ch Tracy City TN 2001-2002; Int R S Lk's Ch Cleveland TN 2001-2002; R Ch Of The Adv Nashville TN 1997-2000; Ch Of The Ascen Hickory NC 1997; Partnr for Dvlpmt Dio Haiti Ft Lauderdale FL 1993-1996; Dio E Tennessee Knoxville TN 1991-1996; R S Tim's Epis Ch Kingsport TN 1987-1991; S Lk's Ch Cleveland TN 1985-1987. SSM 1994. billsquire@embarqmail.com

SRAMEK JR, Tom (ECR) St. Edward's Episcopal Church, 15040 Union Ave., San Jose CA 95124 **Mem, Stndg Com Dio El Camino Real Monterey CA 2010-; P-in-c S Edw The Confessor Epis Ch San Jose CA 2009-** B Pittsburgh PA 2/28/1968 s Thomas Frederick Sramek & Suzanne. BA Humboldt St U 1990; MDiv VTS 1995. D 12/2/1995 Bp William Edwin Swing P 12/21/1996 Bp Franklin Delton Turner. m 8/1/1992 Elizabeth Anne Bell c 2. Vic S Alb's Epis Ch Albany OR 2002-2009; P Assoc for Yth S Ambr Epis Ch Foster City CA 2001-2002; Int Vic S Chris's Ch San Lorenzo CA 2000-2001; Assoc R S Paul's Epis Ch Burlingame CA 1997-2000; Asst/Cur The Ch Of The H Trin W Chester PA 1995-1997. "Out of the Darkness," *LivCh*, Living Ch Fndt, 2007; "PB Profile - Jefferts Schori," *LivCh*, Living Ch Fndt, 2006; "PB Profile - Parsley," *LivCh*, Living Ch Fndt, 2006; "The Quadrilateral: Our Only Unity?," *LivCh*, Living Ch Fndt, 2002. Gathering the Next Generation (GTNG) 1998; Pi Gamma Mu 1990; Psy Chi (Psychol) 1990. frtom@stedwards.org

SRINIVAS, Patricia Wing (Ala) 142 Elm Dr, Columbus MS 39701 B Decatur GA 7/11/1929 d Morris Clay Wing & Minnie. BA Wesl 1950; BFA Wesl 1951; MDiv STUSo 1981. D 2/2/1984 P 12/1/1984 Bp Furman Stough. m 11/26/1952 Kandala Srinivas c 3. Int H Cross-St Chris's Huntsville AL 1987; S Barn' Epis Ch Hartselle AL 1986. AAPC, ACPE.

SSERWADDA, Emmanuel (NY) 69 Georgia Ave, Bronxville NY 10708 B Masaka UG 4/2/1956 s Issachar Baliruno Sserwadda & Margaret. BA Buwalasi Teachers Inst 1976; Cert Bp Tucker Theol Coll Mukono Ug 1979; BD Bp Tucker Theol Coll Mukono Ug 1981; Cert Mercer TS 1991. Trans from Church of the Province of Uganda 5/1/1989 Bp Orris George Walker Jr. m 12/3/1983 Harriet Nakaye c 3. Epis Ch Cntr New York NY 2005-2010; Dio New York New York City NY 2000-2002; R Ch Of The Ascen Mt Vernon NY 1998-2007; R Ch Of The Mssh Cntrl Islip NY 1993-1998; Asst S Phil's Ch Brooklyn NY 1989-1992. Li Curs; UBE. emmanuel.sserwadda@yahoo.com

STAAB, J Thomas (Ore) 2722 Rainier Pl, West Linn OR 97068 **Ret Asst P S Paul's Par Oregon City OR 2007-** B Chicago IL 4/1/1938 s John Leonard Staab & Ruth Blennershassett. BA Denison U 1962; MDiv Bex 1966; Eden TS 1974. D 6/25/1966 Bp Roger W Blanchard P 12/29/1966 Bp Edward Hamilton West. m 8/19/1961 Linda Marie Patecek c 3. Retied Asst P Chr Ch Par Lake Oswego OR 1999-2007; Dioc Coun Dio Oregon Portland OR 1997-1998; R S Paul's Par Oregon City OR 1994-1999; Int P Gr Epis Ch Astoria OR 1993-1994; Chapl S Fran Cmnty Serv Inc. Salina KS 1991-1992; Spc Asst to Bp Off Of Bsh For ArmdF New York NY 1991; LocTen P S Augustines Ch S Louis MO 1974; P-in-c Ch Of The Nativ Jacksonville FL 1969-1971; R S Mk's Ch Starke FL 1968-1969; Cur S Mk's Epis Ch Jacksonville FL 1966-1968. twostaab@gmail.com

STACEY, Caroline Mary (NY) 487 Hudson St, New York NY 10014 **R The Ch Of S Lk In The Fields New York NY 2005-** B Chelmsford England UK 9/24/1963 d Michael Claud Stacey & Barbara Mary. MA U of St. Andrews 1986; MDiv Ya Berk 1990. D 6/9/1990 P 2/17/1991 Bp Arthur Edward Walmsley. m 6/4/2007 Scott Askegard. R All SS Ch E Lansing MI 1996-2005; Assoc R Trin Ch On The Green New Haven CT 1992-1996; Asst Par of Trin Ch New York NY 1990-1992. Auth, "Justification by Faith in the 2 Books of Homilies," *ATR*, 2001; Auth, "Bloy As Mentor," *Journ of Rel & Intellectual Life*, 1985. Rdr. Gnrl Ord Examinations 2000; Fell, Coll of Preachers 1999. cstacey@stlukeinthefields.org

STACKHOUSE, Marcia K (Colo) 3432 Vallejo St, Denver CO 80211 **Our Merc Sav Epis Ch Denver CO 2006-** B Kalamazoo MI 7/13/1940 d Gordon A McDowell & Helen M. BA Loretto Heights Coll 1988. D 6/29/1988 Bp William Carl Frey. m 6/4/1960 Robert Arnold Stackhouse c 3. Asst Epis Ch Of S Ptr And S Mary Denver CO 2003-2005; S Lk's Ch Denver CO 1994-2006; Dir Of Diac Formation Dio Colorado Denver CO 1990-2006; Pstr Asst The Ch Of The Ascen Denver CO 1988-1990. NAAD 1987; NAAD, Bd Mem 2001-2003. marcia.stackhouse@yahoo.com

STACY, Charles Herrick (Los) 1509 Eucalyptus Dr, Solvang CA 93463 B Berkeley CA 1/4/1944 s Clarence Herrick Stacy & Eleanor Margaret. BA U CA 1966; BD CDSP 1969; MS California St U 1973. D 6/28/1969 Bp C Kilmer Myers P 1/10/1970 Bp George Richard Millard. m 6/15/1968 Shirley M Stacy c 2. R S Mk's-In-The-Vlly Epis Los Olivos CA 1976-2008; Asst All SS Ch Carmel CA 1973-1976; Vic S Barn Ch San Francisco CA 1971-1973; Cur S Fran' Epis Ch San Francisco CA 1969-1971. charleshstacy@verizon.net

STADEL, Jerold Russell (SwFla) 1014 Pinegrove Dr, Brandon FL 33511 **Asst S Andr's Epis Ch Tampa FL 2008-; Cn Pstr to the Ret Dio SW Florida Sarasota FL 1999-; Chapl Dio SW Florida Sarasota FL 1971-** B Buffalo NY 5/7/1943 s Russell Frederick Stadel & Kathryn Lee. BA St. Lawr Canton NY 1965; STB Ya Berk 1968. D 6/22/1968 Bp Harold B Robinson P 12/22/1968 Bp Dudley B McNeil. m 8/19/1967 Anne Saunders c 1. Dir Dio SW Florida Sarasota FL 1985-1992; Chair Pstr Care Cmsn Dio SW Florida Sarasota FL 1982-1987; Chair of Fam Com Dio SW Florida Sarasota FL 1980-1982; Secy of Aging Com Dio SW Florida Sarasota FL 1974-1978; S Cathr's Ch Temple Terrace FL 1970-1993; Cur S Mths Epis Ch E Aurora NY 1968-1970. ESMA 1974-1992. jstadel@aol.com

STAFFORD, Gil Wade (Az) 14611 W Avalon Dr, Goodyear AZ 85395 **Vic S Aug's Epis Ch Tempe AZ 2006-; Coll Chapl Dio Arizona Phoenix AZ 2005-** B Cheyenne OK 10/31/1953 s Finis Newton Stafford & Loretta. BS Arizona St U 1976; MA Arizona St U 1979; PhD Trin Theol 1998; DMin SWTS 2005. D 6/18/2005 P 12/17/2005 Bp Kirk Stevan Smith. m 11/22/1971 Catherine Ann Hearne c 2. Contrib, "The Coll Campus as a Web of Sociality," *Transforming Campus Life*, Ptr Lang. OHC 2007. gstafford3@gmail.com

STAFFORD, Joseph Garld (Az) 25018 Arrow Rdg, San Antonio TX 78258 B Clinton OK 11/4/1934 s Earsel Glenn Stafford & Inez. BBA U of Texas 1960; MDiv SWTS 1970; MS Loyola U 1975. D 6/17/1970 Bp William Paul Barnds P 12/1/1970 Bp Gerald Francis Burrill. S Andr's Ch Glendale AZ 1983-1985; Asst S Andr's Ch Glendale AZ 1982; S Aug's Cntr - Chicago IL 1975-1978; Cur S Ptr's Epis Ch Chicago IL 1971-1973.

STAFFORD, Robert Holmes (NY) 401 S El Cielo Rd Apt 71, Palm Springs CA 92262 B Minneapolis MN 6/30/1947 s Edward Raymond Stafford & Betty Dibble. BA U MN 1968; MDiv Nash 1971; Cert U MN 1978; STM GTS 1979. D 6/29/1971 P 3/12/1972 Bp Philip Frederick McNairy. Pstr S Thos Ch New York NY 2004-2010; Dir MP AIDS Proj Manhattan Plaza Assoc New York NY 1994-2004; Asst S Thos Ch New York NY 1985-1991; Adj Prof The GTS New York NY 1985-1991; Chapl Morningside Hse Nrsng Hm Bronx NY 1982-1984; R S Paul's Epis Ch Owatonna MN 1980-1982; Cur S Mich's All Ang Ch Monticello MN 1971-1973. staffordrobert@live.com

STAFFORD, William Sutherland (Va) 125 Louisiana Cir, Sewanee TN 37375 **The TS at The U So Sewanee TN 2005-** B San Francisco CA 11/9/1947 s Chase Hutchinson Stafford & Harriette Grace. BA Stan 1969; MA Ya 1972; PhD Ya 1975. D 5/2/1981 P 1/17/1982 Bp Robert Bruce Hall. m 6/7/1969 Barbara Marie Vail c 3. Assoc Dn VTS Alexandria VA 1997-2004; S Chris's Ch Springfield VA 1981; Asst Prof Ch Hist VTS Alexandria VA 1976-1982. Auth, "Disordered Loves: Healing the Seven Deadly Sins," Cowley, 1994; Auth, "The Eve of the Reformation: Bp Jn Fisher 1509," *Hist mag of the Prot Epis Ch of the USA*, 1985; Auth, "Domesticating the Cler:The Inception of the Reformation in Strasbourg," Scholars Press, 1976. Amer Soc of Ch Hist 1976; Cath Hist Soc 1982. DD VTS 2005; Phi Beta Kappa Stan 1969. wsstaffor@sewanee.edu

STAHL, Daryl Wayne (RI) 91 Pratt St, providence RI 02906 B Huron SD 7/5/1935 s Edward H Stahl & Gwendolyn Amelia. BA Hur 1957; BD EDS 1960. D 6/24/1960 P 12/28/1960 Bp Conrad Gesner. m 9/2/1960 Elizabeth Ann Wetlaufer c 3. R S Jn's Ch Barrington RI 1990-2000; R S Thos' Epis Ch Sioux City IA 1976-1990; Asst S Mk's Ch New Britain CT 1969-1976; Vic Ch Of The Incarn Greg SD 1960-1969; Vic S Andr's Ch Greg SD 1960-1969. darylstahl@yahoo.com

STAIR, Adrian (Mass) 100 Myrtle Ave Apt 208, Whitman MA 02382 **Bristol Cluster Taunton MA 2004-** B Rye NY 7/29/1944 d Gobin Stair & Julia. BA Antioch Coll 1967; MS CUNY 1990; MDiv EDS 2003. D 6/7/2003 P 6/5/2004

S

Bp M(arvil) Thomas Shaw III. Emm Ch Braintree MA 2005-2008; S Jn The Evang Taunton MA 2004-2005. revadrian@comcast.net

STALEY, John Howard (Cal) 925 Divisadero St, San Francisco CA 94115 B Omaha NE 7/2/1937 s John Fenton Staley & Helen. BA U of Redlands 1959; BD CDSP 1962; MDiv CDSP 1972. D 9/6/1962 P 3/1/1963 Bp Francis E I Bloy. All SS' Ch San Francisco CA 1982-1991; Assoc S Mich's Mssn Anaheim CA 1968-1970; R Trin Epis Par Los Angeles CA 1966-1968; Assoc Urban Wk S Mary's Epis Ch Los Angeles CA 1964-1966; Cur S Mk's Par Glendale CA 1962-1963.

STALEY, Mary Linda (Va) PO Box 482, Put In Bay OH 43456 **P-in-c S Paul's Epis Ch Put-In-Bay OH 2010-** B 6/14/1955 d H(arlow) Staley & V Lorene. BA Iowa St U 1977; MA Webster U 1995; MDiv VTS 2005. D 6/18/2005 Bp Peter James Lee P 12/21/2005 Bp David Colin Jones. Asst R Ch Of Our Sav Charlottesville VA 2006-2010; Asst Vic S Patricks Ch Falls Ch VA 2005. revmlstaley@aol.com

STALLER, Margaretmary Boyer (Cal) 4821 Wolf Way, Concord CA 94521 B Buffalo NY 3/1/1933 d George E Boyer & Kathleen R. AA Burlington Cnty Coll 1981; BA Sch for Deacons 1984. D 12/7/1985 Bp William Edwin Swing. m 6/26/1954 Thomas Owen Staller. Gr Ch Martinez CA 2003-2004; S Lk's Ch Walnut Creek CA 1999-2000; D Trin Epis Ch Vineland NJ 1994-1997; Liturg D Gr Cathd San Francisco CA 1986-1992. NAAD, ACPE, AEHC. mbs@astound.net

STALLINGS, Floyd Monroe (Buddy) (NY) 10 Liberty St, Apt 28A, New York NY 10005 **P-in-c S Barth's Ch New York NY 2011-; Vic S Barth's Ch New York NY 2008-** B Houston MS 5/17/1953 s Floyd M Stallings & Christine. BA Mississippi Coll 1975; MA U of Tennessee 1976; MDIV GTS 1992. D 5/30/1992 P 5/1/1993 Bp Alfred Clark Marble Jr. c 1. R Ch Of The Ascen Staten Island NY 2002-2008; S Jas Ch Jackson MS 1992-2001. stallings@stbarts.org

STAMBAUGH, Doran Bartlett (SanD) PO Box 127, Carlsbad CA 92018 **P-in-c S Michaels By-The-Sea Ch Carlsbad CA 2011-; P-in-c S Michaels By-The-Sea Ch Carlsbad CA 2005-** B Cooperstown NY 9/14/1974 BA Wheaton Coll 1996; MDiv Nash 2005. D 1/25/2005 P 8/6/2005 Bp Keith Lynn Ackerman. m 8/23/1997 Therese M Stambaugh c 3. SSC 2006. frdoran@stmichaelsbythesea.org

STAMM, George William (Eau) 624 Bay St., Chippewa Falls WI 54729 B Syracuse NY 11/11/1942 s George Woodrow Stamm & Roberta. Advncd CPE; BA Waynesburg Coll 1966; MDiv Nash 1970; Cert 1981. D 2/28/1970 P 11/1/1970 Bp Stanley Hamilton Atkins. m 10/7/1995 Cynthia Stamm c 5. Chr Ch Chippewa Falls WI 2000-2008; S Simeon's Ch Stanley WI 2000-2008; S Barn Ch Clear Lake WI 1970-1977; S Phil's Ch Eau Claire WI 1970-1977. frgccss@sbcglobal.net

ST AMOUR III, Frank Shalvey (Be) 63 Covington Pl, Catasauqua PA 18032 **COM Dio Bethlehem Bethlehem PA 2010-; R S Steph's Ch Whitehall PA 2008-** B Philadelphia PA 12/24/1958 s Frank Shalvey Santamour & Doris Marie. BA St. Jn's Coll Annapolis MD 1980; BD U of Wales 1983. Trans from Church in Wales 4/8/1988 Bp John Thomas Walker. m 6/1/1985 Susan Pound. R S Steph's Epis Ch Hurst TX 2002-2008; Assoc R All SS Epis Ch Lakeland FL 1997-2002; Asst Ch Of S Mich And All Ang Berwyn IL 1996-1997; R Chr Ch Joliet IL 1994-1996; R Ch Of S Jn The Bapt Dunkirk NY 1989-1994; R S Alb's Ch Silver Creek NY 1989-1994; Asst Chr Ch Par Kensington MD 1987-1989. SocMary 1990; SSC 1998. fstamour@gate.net

STANDIFORD, Sarah Euphemia (Md) 1209 Anderson Ln, Darlington MD 21034 B 9/6/1929

STANFORD, David DeWitt (Chi) 6105 S. Michigan Ave., Chicago IL 60637 **Asst S Edm's Epis Ch Chicago IL 2010-; Asstg Cler Cathd Of S Jas Chicago IL 2008-** B Battle Creek MI 1/4/1949 s Freeman DeWitt Stanford & Nelle. BA JHU 1971; MDiv VTS 1980. D 6/21/1980 Bp John Thomas Walker P 1/4/1981 Bp A(rthur) Heath Light. c 1. Lawr Hall Sch Chicago IL 1996-2010; R Ch Of S Paul And The Redeem Chicago IL 1989-1996; Assoc for Campus Mnstry Chap Of The Cross Chap Hill NC 1983-1989; Asst Chr Epis Ch Roanoke VA 1980-1983. AEHC 1997; Assn of Profsnl Chapl 1998. dstanford4900@yahoo.com

STANFORD, Theresa Brice (At) 1424 N Dearborn St, Chicago IL 60610 **Emm Epis Ch La Grange IL 2008-** B Sumter SC 9/27/1948 BA Georgia St U 1995; MBA Merc 1997; MDiv GTS 2004. D 6/5/2004 P 12/11/2004 Bp J(ohn) Neil Alexander. c 2. Assoc R S Chrys's Ch Chicago IL 2004-2008. rector@eeclg.org

STANFORD, Virginia Francene (Md) 10901 Farrier Rd, Frederick MD 21701 **R Trin Ch Glen Arm MD 2007-** B Memphis TN 4/12/1953 d Carl Cooper Stanford & Jean Elizabeth. BS U of Memphis 1973; MD U of Tennessee 1976; MDiv VTS 1993; CAS Ecumencial Inst, St. Mary's Sem, Baltimore, MD 2007. D 6/19/1993 P 5/21/1994 Bp Don Adger Wimberly. Int Trin Ch Glen Arm MD 2005-2006; COM Dio Maryland Baltimore MD 2004-2010; Dioc Coun Dio Maryland Baltimore MD 1998-2001; R Harriet Chap Catoctin Epis Par Thurmont MD 1997-2005; Assoc S Jn's Ch Lynchburg VA 1993-1997. Alpha Omega Alpha Honoraryor Soc 1974. vfstanford@comcast.net

STANFORD, William Ted (FtW) 5509 Odessa Ave, Fort Worth TX 76133 **S Chris's Ch And Sch Ft Worth TX 2000-** B Houston TX 7/5/1954 s Wilbur Stanford & Ruth Gervaise. BA Tarleton St U 1980; MDiv Nash 1987. D 7/25/1987 P 2/2/1988 Bp Clarence Cullam Pope Jr. m 6/20/1998 Carla Kristine Stanford c 3. Gd Shpd Granbury TX 1998-2000; P-in-c S Jos's Epis Ch Grand Prairie TX 1997-1999; Cur/Co-Admin Of Sch S Andr's Ch Grand Prairie TX 1994-1997; Dio Ft Worth Ft Worth TX 1989-1992; Vic Trin Ch Henrietta TX 1989-1992; Cur S Andr's Ch Grand Prairie TX 1987-1989. Auth, "Unthrown Stone (Poem)," *Living Ch*, 1990. frbill54@att.net

STANGER, Mark E. (Cal) 124 Panorama Dr, San Francisco CA 94131 **Assoc Pstr Gr Cathd San Francisco CA 1997-** B Berwyn IL 5/31/1951 s Edward F Stanger & Dolores H. BA St. Johns U 1973; MDiv S Jn's U TS 1978; Patristic Inst Augustinianum 1984. Rec from Roman Catholic 6/6/1992 Bp William Edwin Swing. m 11/11/2009 Mark A Johnson. non-stipendiary Cler Ch Of The Adv Of Chr The King San Francisco CA 1992-1997. Contrib, "Lent responsorial psalm exegetical commentaries," *Feasting on the Word, Year B vol 2*, Westminster Jn Knox, 2008; Contrib, "Pictures," *Preaching as Pstr Caring: Sermons that Wk XIII*, Morehouse, 2005. marks@gracecathedral.org

STANLEY, Anne Grant (Me) Po Box 63, Paris ME 04271 **Dio Maine Portland ME 2000-** B Newton MA 6/20/1941 d George Richard Grant & Jane. BA Wellesley Coll 1963; MA Oakland U 1988; MDiv EDS 1994. D 6/11/1994 P 12/21/1994 Bp Douglas Edwin Theuner. m 11/26/1965 David Stanley c 3. R Chr Ch Norway ME 1998-2011; Asst Gr Ch Manchester NH 1994-1998. anne.stanley@roadrunner.com

STANLEY, Arthur Patrick (Ia) 10 Knights Ct, Frome Somerset BA 11 1JD England Great Britain (UK) B Kilmacthomas Ireland 6/24/1932 s Charles Geoffrey Nason Stanley & Violet Claire. ThD Trin, Dublin 1954; BA Trin, Dublin 1954; MA Trin, Dublin 1963. Trans from Church of Ireland 12/1/1988 Bp Walter Cameron Righter. m 8/15/1983 Jessie Fisher c 2. P-in-c All Ang Ch Red Oak IA 1988-1994; P-in-c S Jn's Ch Shenandoah IA 1988-1994. Auth, "Var arts," *Royal Army Chapl Dept Journ*, 1981; Auth, *Var Arts Royal Army Chapl Dept Journ 71-81*. Hon Chapl Britannic Majesty's Forces 1983. patnpaddy@hotmail.com

STANLEY, E(dward) Bevan (Ct) 36 Cleveland Rd, New Haven CT 06515 **Int Chr Ch Bethany CT 2011-; Conciliator Dio Connecticut Hartford CT 2011-** B Abington PA 5/20/1951 s Edward Livingston Stanley & Alice Kutzner. BA Chart Oak St Coll 1981; MDiv Ya Berk 1983; DMin Hartford Sem 2003. D 6/11/1983 P 2/7/1984 Bp Arthur Edward Walmsley. m 11/25/1972 Alinda Cronin c 2. Int Ch Of The Gd Shpd Orange CT 2008-2011; Dioc Coun Dio Newark Newark NJ 2001-2005; R Chr Ch Short Hills NJ 1999-2007; R Gr And S Ptr's Epis Ch Hamden CT 1995-1999; Vic Gr And S Ptr's Epis Ch Hamden CT 1990-1995; Dioc Coun Dio Connecticut Hartford CT 1986-1992; Vic S Ptr's Ch Hamden CT 1984-1990; Cur Chr Ch New Haven CT 1983-1984. Auth, "Organizing the Cong: The Use of Communityt Organizing Techniques in the Trng of Congrl Leaders," UMI Dissertaion Serv, 2003. CDI Trainers 1999. ebevanstanley@gmail.com

STANLEY BSG, Gordon John (Chi) 340 W Diversey Pkwy, Chicago IL 60657 **D S Ptr's Epis Ch Chicago IL 2000-** B Indianapolis IN 4/24/1946 s George John Stanley & Doris Dhia. BA Pur 1972; MA U of San Diego 1976. D 2/5/2000 Bp William Dailey Persell. gstanley0@gmail.com

STANLEY JR, John Hiram (FtW) 4105 Hartwood Dr, Fort Worth TX 76109 B Chicago IL 4/2/1938 s John Hiram Stanley & Pauline. BA Denison U 1960; BD SWTS 1963. D 6/15/1963 Bp James Winchester Montgomery P 12/1/1963 Bp Gerald Francis Burrill. m 8/13/1960 Lynne Simmons. Trin Epis Ch Ft Worth TX 1975-1998; Exec Asst To The Bp Of Nebraska Dio Nebraska Omaha NE 1973-1975; Cn Trin Cathd Omaha NE 1970-1972; Vic S Mich's Ch Grand Rapids MI 1966-1970; Cur S Aug's Epis Ch Wilmette IL 1963-1966. nicholsmyra@yahoo.com

STANLEY, Lauren Regina (Va) c/o Heffner, 3820 Acosta Rd., Fairfax VA 22031 B Kirkwood MO 11/4/1960 d James Gordon Zack & Marione Mildred. AA S Petersburg Jr Coll 1980; BA Marq 1982; MDiv VTS 1997; DMin VTS 2013. D 6/14/1997 P 4/21/1998 Bp Peter James Lee. Mssy, Haiti Exec Coun Appointees New York NY 2009-2010; Mssy, Sudan Exec Coun Appointees New York NY 2005-2009; Assoc S Alb's Epis Ch Annandale VA 2001-2005; R Gr Epis Ch Allentown PA 2000-2001; Assoc Trin Ch Arlington VA 1999-2000; Assoc Ch Of The Gd Shpd Burke VA 1997-1998. "Handbook for Short-Term Mssn," Dio Virginia, 2003; *Nwspr Column*, McClatchey/Tribune News Serv, 1994. merelaurens@gmail.com

STANLEY, Marjorie Jean (Spok) 255 W Shore Ln, Sandpoint ID 83864 **Supply P S Mary's Bonners Ferry Bonners Ferry ID 2008-; Asstg P H Sprt Epis Ch Sandpoint ID 2002-** B Ashland WI 2/20/1928 d Harold Wallace Thines & Ruth Helen. BA U of Wisconsin 1949; MA Indiana U 1950; PhD Indiana U 1953; Brite DS 1986; MDiv SWTS 1988. D 12/13/1997 P 7/11/1998 Bp Frank Jeffrey Terry. c 2. Assoc S Dav's Ch Spokane WA 1998-2002. Auth, "The Irwin Guide To Investing In Emerging Markets," Irwin, 1995; Auth, "Ethical Issues In Emerging Fin Markets," *Emerging Global Bus Ethics*, Quorum, 1994; Auth, "Multinational Capital Budgemultinational Capital Bdgt,

Emerging Markets & Mng Agcy: A Proposal For Ethically Constrain," 1993; Auth, "Capital Bdgt In Countries w Less Developed Capital Markets: Fin & Ethical Issues," *Bus Fin In Less Deveioped Capital Markets*, Greenwood, 1992; Auth, "Ethical Perspective On The Frgn Direct Invstmt Decisions," *Journ Of Bus Ethics Volume 9 #1*, 1990; Auth, "The Frgn Direct Invstmt Decisions & Job Export As Ethical Dilemma For Multinational Corp," *Ethics And The Multinational Enterprise*, U Press, 1986. Beta Gamma Sigma; Sigma Delta Pi; Theta Phi. Phi Kappa Phi 1949. mtstan@gotsky.com

STANLEY, Mark Andrew (Md) Old St. Paul's Church, 309 Cathedral Street, Baltimore MD 21201 **R S Paul's Par Baltimore MD 2004-** B Evanston IL 7/13/1964 s John Hiram Stanley & Lynne. MA U of Texas 1986; MDiv CDSP 1990. D 6/9/1990 P 6/8/1991 Bp William Edwin Swing. m 7/22/1989 Mary Luck c 2. R Chr Ch Sausalito CA 1994-2004; Cur All SS Epis Ch Palo Alto CA 1990-1994. Phi Beta Kappa 1986. mark@osp1692.org

STANLEY, Mary Luck (Md) Old St. Paul's Church, 309 Cathedral St., Baltimore MD 21201 **Assoc R S Paul's Par Baltimore MD 2006-** B Houston TX 6/22/1964 d George Edmund Luck & Jane Amantha. BS Texas A&M U 1987; MDiv CDSP 1997. D 6/7/1997 P 12/1/1997 Bp William Edwin Swing. m 7/22/1989 Mark Andrew Stanley c 2. Ch Of Our Sav Mill Vlly CA 2002; Asst Ch Of The Resurr Pleasant Hill CA 1997-1999. Auth, "Yth Mnstry Acad Manual". Stanleyhome@verizon.net

STANLEY, Stephen Ranson (SwVa) St. Mark's Episcopaql Church, 111 South Roanoke St. P.O. Box 277, Fincastle VA 24090 **P Mssnr S Mk's Ch Fincastle VA 2011-** B Asheville NC 11/4/1949 s Sherburn Moore Stanley & Helen. AA Gulf Coast Cmnty Coll 1970; BS U of W Florida 1972; Mstr Of Hlth Sci U Of Florida 1978; MDiv VTS 1982. D 6/26/1982 Bp Clarence Edward Hobgood P 2/1/1983 Bp Maurice Manuel Benitez. m 6/20/1981 Jacqueline Hamilton c 1. Assoc R Chr Epis Ch Roanoke VA 2003-2011; Assoc for Campus Mnstry Chap Of The Cross Chap Hill NC 1990-2003; R All SS' Epis Ch Gastonia NC 1987-1990; Assoc R S Paul's Ch Waco TX 1982-1987. Auth, "Discovering Genesis 25-50," *Guideposts Hm Biblic Stds*, 1988; Auth, "Discovering Lk," *Guideposts Hm Biblic Stds*, 1985. Cross Of Nails 1990; Iona Cmnty 2010. srstanley@cox.net

STANSBERY, Marylen Wilkins (Mo) 2 Warson Ln, Saint Louis MO 63124 B Kansas City MO 6/22/1935 D 4/30/1998 Bp Hays H. Rockwell. m 12/24/1987 Gary Lee Stansbery c 3. MSTANSBERY@SBCGLOBAL.NET

STANTON JR, Barclay Reynolds (Oly) 24447 94th St S, Kent WA 98030 B Primos PA 7/21/1938 s Barclay Reynolds Stanton & Louise Pomeroy. BA Wms 1961; MDiv VTS 1966. D 6/29/1966 Bp Allen J Miller P 6/1/1967 Bp George Alfred Taylor. m 6/19/1971 Barbara L Jones c 2. S Matt Ch Tacoma WA 1990-2001; R All SS Ch Wstrn Sprg IL 1985-1989; R All SS Ch Coudersport PA 1976-1984; R Chr Ch Coudersport PA 1976-1984; Asst Chr Ch S Ptr's Par Easton MD 1975-1976; Asst Chr Epis Ch Great Choptank Par Cambridge MD 1967-1969; Cur Emm Epis Ch Chestertown MD 1966-1967. barbar6114@comcast.net

✠ **STANTON, Rt Rev James Monte** (Dal) 1630 N Garrett Ave, Dallas TX 75206 **Bp Dio Dallas Dallas TX 1993-** B Atchison KS 10/29/1946 s Jewell E Stanton & Dorothy Marie. BA Chapman U 1968; DMin Sthrn California TS 1975; Cert CDSP 1977; DD STUSo 1994; DD Nash 1996; DD CDSP 2009. D 6/18/1977 Bp Robert C Rusack P 10/23/1977 Bp Victor Manuel Rivera Con 3/6/1993 for Dal. m 12/29/1968 Diane Hanson. R S Mk's Par Glendale CA 1987-1992; R S Lk's Epis Ch Cedar Falls IA 1982-1987; Chair of Wrld Mssn Cmsn Epis Dio San Joaquin Modesto CA 1979-1981; Vic S Steph's Ch Stockton CA 1977-1981. jmsdallas@edod.org

STANTON, John Frank (Nwk) 1625 Kennedy Causeway PH4, North Bay Village FL 33141 **Assoc Trin Cathd Miami FL 2011-** B Orange,NJ 7/20/1936 s Vernon Frank Stanton & Emily. BA Ham 1958; MDiv GTS 1962; MBA Wag 1976. D 10/6/1962 Bp Leland Stark P 4/6/1963 Bp Donald MacAdie. m 5/20/2006 Nora Stanton c 3. Int R S Jas The Fisherman Islamorada FL 2008-2011; Vic S Matt's Ch Paramus NJ 1998-2004; Int R Chr Ch Teaneck NJ 1997-1998; Int R Ch Of The H Sprt Verona NJ 1996; P S Matt's Ch Paramus NJ 1994-1996; Int R Chr Ch Belleville NJ 1991-1992; Supply P Dio Newark Newark NJ 1985-1986; Cur Chr Ch Hackensack NJ 1971-1985; Asst Chr Ch Hackensack NJ 1962-1965. stantonjf@atlanticbb.net

STANTON, John Robert (At) 4906 Sulky Dr Apt 204, Richmond VA 23228 B Macon GA 7/15/1923 s Clarence Hayden Stanton & Florence Uldine. BA Merc 1949; MDiv VTS 1953. D 6/24/1953 P 1/6/1954 Bp Henry D Phillips. c 1. Int Trin Ch Highland Sprg VA 1999-2001; R S Aug Of Cbury Morrow GA 1983-1993; S Barth's Epis Ch Atlanta GA 1982-1983; S Steph's Ch Newport News VA 1961-1981; R Trin Epis Ch Rocky Mt VA 1953-1956. AFP 1975-1990. stanjstnt3@aol.com

STANTON, Sarah Morningstar (EO) 1503 4th St, La Grande OR 97850 B Abilene KS 1/8/1945 d Fillepe Ricardo Lusk & Shirley Ena. BA Mt Mary Coll 1966; Med U of New Hampshire 1972; MDiv CDSP 1987. D 12/5/1987 P 12/3/1988 Bp William Edwin Swing. c 2. R S Ptr's Ch La Grande OR 2003-2009; R S Steph's Epis Ch Covington KY 1993-2003; Asst S Jas Ch Bozeman MT 1989-1992; Cur S Jn's Epis Ch Oakland CA 1988-1989. Auth, "Two Bk Revs," *ATR*, 2002. Soc Of S Fran - Tertiary 1984-2002. mssarahm@comcast.net

STANWISE, Ralph Joseph Francis (Q) 2608 N Kingston Dr, Peoria IL 61604 **Dio Quincy Peoria IL 1994-** B Brooklyn NY 8/12/1943 s Ralph John Joseph Stanwise & Dorothy Mae. BA U Denv 1965; MDiv Nash 1969; MA U of Wisconsin 1972. D 6/14/1969 P 12/20/1969 Bp Jonathan Goodhue Sherman. m 6/23/1973 Lynda J Seplavy c 1. Cn S Paul's Cathd Peoria IL 1994-2011; R S Jn's Ch Ogdensburg NY 1990-1993; Stndg Com Dio Eau Claire Eau Claire WI 1979-1990; R Gr Epis Ch Menomonie WI 1977-1990; P-in-c S Aidans Ch Hartford WI 1973-1977; P-in-c S Ptr's Ch No Lake WI 1973-1977; Cur Chr Ch Babylon NY 1969-1973. Mem Phi Alpha Theta 1965; Mem Phi Beta Kappa 1965. frstanwise@stpaulspeoria.com

STANWOOD, Thomas Reid (Ore) 1638 Boca Ratan Dr, Lake Oswego OR 97034 **D Chr Ch Par Lake Oswego OR 2003-** B Boston MA 4/24/1939 s William Reid Stanwood & Elisabeth. BA Un Coll Schenectady NY 1961. D 10/4/2003 Bp Johncy Itty. deacontoms@comcast.net

STAPLES, Ann McDonald (Pgh) Po Box 1, Marion Center PA 15759 **D Ch of SS Thos and Lk Patton PA 1993-; D S Thos Ch No Cambria PA 1993-** B San Antonio TX 8/9/1931 d Aubrey Henry McDonald & Doris. PhD Indiana U; BA SMU 1952; MA SMU 1953. D 6/22/1984 Bp Alden Moinet Hathaway. m 8/27/1967 James G Staples c 6. D All SS Epis Ch Verona PA 1989-1991; D S Alb's Epis Ch Murrysville PA 1984-1993.

STAPLETON JR, Jack W (Colo) 4222 W. 22nd Street Road, Greeley CO 80634 **R Trin Ch Greeley CO 2008-** B Lexington KY 12/29/1952 s Jack W Stapleton & Freda Ellen. BA Transylvania U 1974; MDiv Epis TS In Kentucky 1978. D 5/14/1978 P 12/17/1978 Bp Addison Hosea. m 6/23/1979 Dorie Ann Hucal. P-in-c Trin Ch Greeley CO 2003-2007; Assoc Chr Epis Ch Denver CO 2001-2003; Asst Epiph Epis Ch Denver CO 1999-2001; R Ch Of The Trsfg Evergreen CO 1989-1997; Assoc S Thos's Par Newark DE 1983-1989; Asst Ch Of The Gd Shpd Lexington KY 1981-1983; Vic S Alb's Ch Morehead KY 1979-1981. Cmnty of Aid and Hilda 1994; Third Ord, SSF 1974-1994. frjack@trinitygreeley.org

STARBUCK, Betsy D (Ct) 88 N Main St, PO Box 983, Kent CT 06757 B Orange NJ 3/10/1958 d Leroy Frederick Dackerman & Elizabeth Christian. BA Pepperdine U 1981; MDiv Fuller TS 1985; CTh Epis TS of The SW 1993. D 6/23/1993 Bp William Elwood Sterling P 3/1/1994 Bp Claude Edward Payne. m 7/20/2002 Peter Shepard Starbuck c 2. S Paul's Epis Ch Bantam CT 2006-2008; Kent Sch Kent CT 2001-2004; Chapl S Jos's Chap at the Kent Sch Kent CT 2001-2004; Chapl S Andr's Chap S Andrews TN 1999-2001; S Andr's-Sewanee Sch Sewanee TN 1999-2001; Assoc R H Sprt Epis Ch Houston TX 1994-1999; Asst to R S Fran Ch Houston TX 1993-1994. elizabeth.starbuck@ynhh.org

STARKES, Lionel Alfonso (Nev) Po Box 50763, Henderson NV 89016 **P S Matt's Ch Las Vegas NV 1993-** B Greenville FL 3/25/1945 s Lester Ward & Katie Mae. BA Sthrn Illinois U 1975; MS Sthrn Illinois U 1984. D 4/4/1993 P 11/23/1998 Bp Stewart Clark Zabriskie. Stndg Com Dio Nevada Las Vegas NV 1993-1998.

STARKEY, William Grover (SVa) 4929 Shallowford Cir, Virginia Beach VA 23462 **Died 6/3/2011** B Clarsburg WV 7/20/1926 BS W Virginia Wesleyan Coll 1950. D 6/4/1980 P 6/1/1981 Bp Robert Poland Atkinson.

STARKWEATHER, Betty (ND) 679 Lehigh Dr., Merced CA 95348 B Gardenville PA 8/8/1932 d Franklin Roy Bickhart & Elsie. BA Wheaton Coll 1954; MS New York St U 1957. D 10/8/1999 P 4/23/2000 Bp Andrew Hedtler Fairfield. m 8/20/1955 David Starkweather c 4. bettystarkweather@yahoo.com

STARR, Charles Christopher (Chris) (At) Church of the Atonement (Episcopal), 4945 High Point Road, Sandy Springs GA 30342 **R Ch Of The Atone Sandy Sprg GA 2008-** B Atlanta GA 1/15/1952 s David Homer Starr & Margaret. S Mary's Sem & U Baltimore; BA S Mary Baltimore MD 1975; MDiv S Vinc de Paul Sem Boynton Bch FL 1980. Rec from Roman Catholic 12/12/1993 as Priest Bp Frank Kellogg Allan. m 12/15/1984 Cecilia Kathy Wright c 1. Assoc Ch Of The Atone Sandy Sprg GA 1993-2000. cstarr1215@comcast.net

STARR, David H (Los) St. John's Church, 1407 N. Arrowhead Ave., San Bernardino CA 92405 **Dioc Coun Mem Dio Los Angeles Los Angeles CA 2009-; Vic S Jn's Par San Bernardino CA 2006-** B Atlanta GA 12/5/1944 s David Homer Starr & Margaret Mary. BS Georgia Inst of Tech 1968; MBA USC 1973; MDiv CDSP 2005. D 6/4/2005 P 12/3/2005 Bp William Edwin Swing. m 10/4/2008 Shelley Booth c 2. Assoc R S Steph's Par Los Angeles CA 2006. Fran Toy Multicultural Mnstry Awd CDSP 2005. dhs@starrnet.com

STARR, James Michael (Pgh) 4048 Circle Dr, Bakerstown PA 15007 B Syracuse NY 3/6/1951 s Nicholas John Starr & Florence. BA Wadhams Hall Sem Coll 1973; MA CUA 1976; DMin Pittsburgh TS 1996. Rec from Roman Catholic 10/1/1984 as Priest Bp Walter Cameron Righter. m 12/9/1990 Paulette Miriam Baer. Auth, "Dio Pittsburgh Bk Of Daily Pryr 90". Coll Chapl Pa Soc, Chapl Hosp Assn, AEHC, ACPE. starrcm@upmc.edu

STARR, Mark Lowell (CGC) 4666 Pinewood Dr N, Mobile AL 36618 B Long Beach CA 7/21/1946 s Perry Martin Starr & Gayle Lorraine. BA San Diego St

U 1969; MDiv PrTS 1972; MA U CA 1976; CPh U CA 1978; PhD U CA 1988. D 6/11/1981 P 12/1/1981 Bp Robert Munro Wolterstorff. m 3/25/1996 Barbara Brummit c 2. S Matt's Ch Mobile AL 2004-2008; R Ch Of S Mart Davis CA 1983-1988; Cur S Ptr's Epis Ch Del Mar CA 1981-1983. Dawson Tchr of the Year Sprg Hill Coll 1996; Vstng Fell Epis TS of the SW 1987; Dissertation Fllshp U of CA 1979; Fllshp Natl Endwmt for Hmnts 1975. starr@shc.edu

STARR, Nancy Barnard (Mil) 76 Grange Road, Mount Eden, Auckland NZ 1024 New Zealand (Aotearoa) B Baton Rouge LA 3/3/1953 d John Hunt Barnard & Doris Sara. BA U Roch 1975; MA U of Iowa 1978; MDiv Duke 1993; CAS CDSP 1994. D 1/14/1995 P 7/16/1995 Bp Roger John White. m 5/10/1976 Richard Granville Starr c 3. S Ambr Epis Ch Foster City CA 1995. rev.nancy@xtra.co.nz

STARR, Therese Ann (Okla) PO Box 759, Eufaula OK 74432 **D Trin Ch Eufaula OK 2011-** B St. Louis MO 1/6/1963 d John Leroy Hiller & Mary Ann. BS St Louis U 1984. D 6/18/2011 Bp Edward Joseph Konieczny. m 4/18/1998 Morris Starr. lpcstarr@yahoo.com

STARR, William Frederic (NY) 36 South Rd, Chilmark MA 02535 B New Haven CT 5/17/1933 s William Dean Starr & Janet. BA Ya 1955; STB GTS 1958; STM GTS 1965; PhD Col 1983. D 6/11/1958 P 1/1/1960 Bp Walter H Gray. m 12/14/1974 Susan Lee Strane. Diocn Msnry & Ch Extntn Socty New York NY 1983-1994; Dpt Of Missions Ny Income New York NY 1983-1994; Bishops Advsry Com New York NY 1973-1982; R Gr Ch Dalton MA 1960-1964; Trin Ch On The Green New Haven CT 1958-1960. Auth, *Never Trust a God Over 30*. ESMHE, Epis U. williamstarr@mac.com

STASSER, Nina Louise (U) 7718 W. Silver Nugget St, Tucson AZ 85735 **Affiliate, Ret Chr The King Ch Tucson AZ 2010-** B Goodland KS 1/1/1942 d Cecil Ivan Chilson & Phyllis Louise. BA Colorado St U 1963; Metropltn St Coll of Denver 1982; Loretto Heights Coll 1983; U of Nthrn Colorado 1985; Adams St Coll 1991; MDiv Iliff TS 1998. D 6/6/1998 P 12/12/1998 Bp William Jerry Winterrowd. m 12/16/1962 Richard Victor Stasser c 3. Mssn Partnership Dvlpmt and Trng Dio Colorado Denver CO 2007-2010; Assoc S Gabr The Archangel Epis Ch Cherry Hills Vill CO 2007-2009; Dio Utah Salt Lake City UT 2004-2008; R S Paul's Epis Ch Vernal UT 2004-2007; S Barn Ch Glenwood Sprg CO 1999-2004; Coordntr Of Mutual Mnstry Dio Colorado Denver CO 1999-2003; Cur Epis Ch Of S Jn The Bapt Granby CO 1998-1999. The Ord of the DOK 2003. revgma@q.com

STATER, Catherine J (CFla) 319 W Wisconsin Ave, Deland FL 32720 B Sparta IL 6/18/1938 d John Wayne Max Stater & Nina Wanda. BGS U of Maryland 1980. D 12/11/2010 Bp John Wadsworth Howe. m 1/4/1995 Dennis L Weir. denmn@aol.com

STATEZNI, Gregory George (EpisSanJ) 7000 College Ave Apt 21, Bakersfield CA 93306 **D Quest- Real People- Real Answers- Real Ch Bakersfield CA 1997-** B Schenectady NY 1/3/1947 s George Earl Statezni & Lenamae. BA Sonoma St U Rohnert Pk 1977; Cert Untd States Intl U San Diego CA 1985. D 6/14/1997 Bp John-David Mercer Schofield. m 1/19/1980 Deborah Lee Foran c 4. greggstate@aol.com

STATHERS JR, Birk Smith (SeFla) 208 N Lee St, Lewisburg WV 24901 B Clarksburg WV 3/4/1936 s Birk Smith Stathers & Margaret Ann. BS U of Pennsylvania 1958; MDiv GTS 1963. D 6/5/1963 P 12/18/1963 Bp Wilburn Camrock Campbell. m 2/6/1965 Martha B Battle c 2. Int S Greg's Ch Boca Raton FL 2004-2005; Int S Thos Epis Ch White Sulphur Sprg WV 2002-2004; Int Trin Ch Huntington WV 2000-2001; Int S Thad Epis Ch Aiken SC 1997-1998; Int Chr Ch Greenville SC 1995-1997; Int S Jn's Ch Ogdensburg NY 1994-1995; Int S Jn's Epis Ch Clearwater FL 1993-1994; Int Chr Ch Clarksburg WV 1992-1993; Int S Paul's Ch Wilkesboro NC 1990-1992; Exec Bd Dio SE Florida Miami FL 1983-1986; R S Matt the Apos Epis Ch Miami FL 1977-1989; Assoc Ch Of The Resurr Biscayne Pk FL 1973-1977; Supply P Dio W Virginia Charleston WV 1965-1969. Soc of S Jn the Evang 1990. frbirk@yahoo.com

STATON, Stephen Douglas (Okla) 4809 Nw 29th St, Oklahoma City OK 73127 **Died 5/12/2010** B Amarillo TX 7/1/1943 s Robert Victor Staton & Nawassa Agatha. BA Oklahoma Bapt U 1968. D 6/27/1992 Bp Robert Manning Moody. c 2. NAAD.

STAUFFER, Donald Gilbert (WMass) 555 Couch Ave #455, Aberdeen Heights, Saint Louis MO 63122 B Montclair NJ 3/30/1926 s Milton Theobald Stauffer & Marjorie Williams. BA Pr 1948; U of Edinburgh GB 1952; MDiv VTS 1954. D 6/13/1954 Bp James P De Wolfe P 12/1/1954 Bp Arthur C Lichtenberger. m 6/15/1956 Lynn Giessow c 4. Baystate Med Cntr Springfield MA 1984-1985; The Macduffie Sch Springfield MA 1981-1984; A-RC Consult Dio Connecticut Hartford CT 1977-1980; R S Paul's Ch Riverside CT 1974-1980; Mssns Dio Washington Washington DC 1965-1966; R S Andr's Epis Ch Coll Pk MD 1964-1968; Stwdshp Dio California San Francisco CA 1958-1962; S Chris's Ch San Lorenzo CA 1957-1964; Asst S Mich & S Geo Clayton MO 1954-1957. Auth, "Cup of Trembling Study Guide," *Seabury Press*, 1958; "arts & Bk Revs," *LivCh*. lynndon77@aol.com

STAUP, Thomas Peter (Md) 1024 Dulaney Mill Dr, Frederick MD 21702 B Lonaconing MD 5/31/1927 s Roland Clinton Staup & Grace Adaline. BA U of Maryland 1951; STB GTS 1959. D 6/21/1959 Bp Noble C Powell P 4/7/1960 Bp Harry Lee Doll. m 8/22/1959 Alysann B Bradburn c 2. Int Ch Of The Trsfg Braddock Heights MD 2000-2004; Int S Jn's Ch Frostburg MD 1997-2000; Int Harriet Chap Catoctin Epis Par Thurmont MD 1996-1997; Int S Geo's Epis Ch Mt Savage MD 1994-1996; R Gr Ch Brunswick MD 1970-1993. "Adv Greetings," *The Angl Dig - Adv 2006*, 2006. bstuaup@aol.com

STAYNER, David (Ct) 28 Myra Rd, Hamden CT 06517 **The Rev Dr S Ptr's Epis Ch Cheshire CT 2006-** B 6/14/1951 Ya Berk; BA Duquesne U Pittsburgh PA 1988; MS Mumbai U New York City 1993; PhD Mumbai U New York City 1994. D 6/21/2003 P 12/20/2003 Bp Andrew Donnan Smith. m 8/15/1987 Sandra Hardyman Stayner c 1. Gr And S Ptr's Epis Ch Hamden CT 2005.

STAYNER, Sandra Hardyman (Pgh) 28 Myra Rd, Hamden CT 06517 **The Rev S Ptr's Epis Ch Cheshire CT 2003-** B Bristol England UK 1/18/1953 d William Hardyman & Sheila Doreen. Cert Bedford Coll 1974; Yale DS 1988; MDiv Ya Berk 1990. D 6/2/1990 P 1/26/1991 Bp Alden Moinet Hathaway. m 8/15/1987 David Stayner c 1. Ya Berk New Haven CT 1999-2003; Chr Ch Greenwich CT 1990-1999. sandra.stayner@stpeterschesire.org

STAYTON, Darrell Lynn (Ark) PO Box 726, Stuttgart AR 72160 **Vic S Alb's Ch Stuttgart AR 2008-** B Pine Bluff AR 8/2/1952 s Max Thomas Stayton & Rosa Mae Stone. BA U of Arkansas 1978; JD U of Arkansas Sch of Law 1982; Nash 2007; The Prot Epis TS 2008. D 6/7/2008 P 12/7/2008 Bp Larry R Benfield. m 2/17/1979 Roberta Susan Stayton c 4. dls5920@yahoo.com

ST CLAIR, Melinda Lee (Spok) PO Box 2944, 120 Madisen Lane, Chelan WA 98816 **All SS Epis Ch El Paso TX 2010-** B Worland WY 5/23/1958 d Darrell Gates St Clair & Molly Lee. BS U of Wyoming 1985; MS U of Wyoming 1988; MDiv VTS 2001. D 6/2/2001 P 12/12/2001 Bp James Edward Waggoner. D S Andr's Ch Chelan WA 2001-2008; S Jas Epis Ch Brewster WA 2001-2008. melindaleestc@live.com

ST CLAIRE JR, Elbert Kyle (Pa) 1650 Franklin Dr, Furlong PA 18925 B Bryn Mawr PA 5/4/1945 s Elbert Kyle St Claire & Barbara. BA Hav 1968; MDiv EDS 1971; STM Yale DS 1974; MBA Tem 1982. D 6/18/1971 P 1/14/1972 Bp Robert Lionne DeWitt. m 3/24/1973 Teresa A M Whidden c 2. P-in-c Ch Of The Incarn Morrisville PA 2010-2011; Vic S Phil's Ch New Hope PA 1983-2005; Chr Ch And S Mich's Philadelphia PA 1982; Dio Pennsylvania Philadelphia PA 1981-1998; St Pauls Ch Philadelphia PA 1981; R H Trin Ch Lansdale PA 1976-1980; Stff Cler S Mk's Ch New Canaan CT 1974-1976; P-in-c S Jn's Ch New Haven CT 1973-1974; Asst The Epis Acad Newtown Sq PA 1971-1973. Soc of S Jn the Evang (Fllshp Mem). ekstclaire@verizon.net

STEADMAN, David Wilton (NCal) 756 Robinson Rd, Sebastopol CA 95472 B Honolulu HI 10/24/1936 s Alva Edgar Steadman & Martha Love. BA Harv 1960; MA Harv 1961; MA U CA 1966; PhD Pr 1974; MA CDSP 2002; Cert Sch for Deacons 2003. D 10/16/2004 Bp Jerry Alban Lamb. m 8/1/1964 Kathleen Carroll Reilly c 2. punto31157@aol.com

STEADMAN, Larry Kenneth (WK) 705 W 31st Ave, Hutchinson KS 67502 **Assoc Gr Epis Ch Hutchinson KS 2006-** B Hays KS 10/12/1936 s Charles Marion Steadman & Vivian Davis. AA Los Angeles Vlly Coll 1961. D 2/24/2001 Bp Vernon Edward Strickland P 12/21/2002 Bp James Marshall Adams Jr. m 7/14/1973 Diane M Steadman c 5. Vic S Thos Ch Garden City KS 2001-2006. ldsteadman@cox.net

STEADMAN, Marguerite Alexandra (Me) 3116 O St Nw, Washington DC 20007 **S Jn's Ch Bangor ME 2007-** B Toronto ON CA 5/30/1969 d Richard Glanville Henninger & Mary Sherbourne. BA Br 1991; MDiv GTS 1997. Trans 10/7/2003 Bp Mark Sean Sisk. m 6/24/2001 Eric Steadman c 2. Asst Chr Ch Georgetown Washington DC 1997-2007. rector@stjohnsbangor.org

STEARNS, Fellow Clair (ECR) Po Box 2789, Saratoga CA 95070 **Assoc S Andr's Ch Saratoga CA 1974-** B San Jose CA 10/14/1939 s Elwin Clair Stearns & Bertha Charlotte. U CA 1964. D 1/2/1972 P 5/1/1975 Bp C Kilmer Myers. m 9/21/1963 Molly Mattewson Wool.

STEARNS, Joanne (SO) 401 Alisha Ln, Fairborn OH 45324 B Detroit MI 12/13/1938 d John Warren Kaines & Kathryn. BA Aquinas Coll 1984; MDiv CDSP 1984. D 6/8/1985 P 6/7/1986 Bp William Edwin Swing. c 1. Ret Affilliate P S Geo's Epis Ch Dayton OH 2006-2010; Dioc Coun Dio Sthrn Ohio Cincinnati OH 1995-1998; R S Chris's Ch Fairborn OH 1993-2005; Asst to R S Phil's Ch Durham NC 1989-1993; Assoc R Ch Of The H Nativ Honolulu HI 1986-1989; D Ch Of The Resurr Pleasant Hill CA 1985-1986. joannes332@aol.com

STEARNS, Samuel D (RG) 3705 Utah St Ne, Albuquerque NM 87110 **D Epis Ch Of The Epiph Socorro NM 1998-; D S Mary's Epis Ch Albuquerque NM 1997-** B Seattle WA 6/18/1930 s Samuel D Stearns & Constance E. BS Stan 1953; MS U of New Mex 1962; Ds U of New Mex 1962. D 11/21/1997 Bp Terence Kelshaw. m 6/19/1993 Mary Esther Stearns.

STEBBINS JR, George Griswold (CFla) 1219 Augustine Dr, The Villages-Lady Lake FL 32159 **S Geo Epis Ch The Villages FL 1998-** B Madison WI 2/25/1930 s George Griswold Stebbins & Berenice Elizabeth. BA U of Wisconsin

1952; MD U of Wisconsin 1955; Amer Bd Surgery 1965; FACS Amer Coll of Surgeons 1967; Amer Coll of Emergency Physicians 1988. D 6/15/1975 Bp William Hopkins Folwell. m 8/3/1951 Alice Ruth Gustavson c 4. Asst Ch of the Resurr Sautee Nacoochee GA 1997-1998; Asst Gr-Calv Epis Ch Clarkesville GA 1988-1997; Asst H Cross Ch Winter Haven FL 1975-1988. Auth, "Med arts". Assn Mltry Surgeons; Chr Med Soc; FGBMFI; NAAD; Ord of S Lk. srev@comcast.net

STEBBINS, Marty (NC) 906 Treemont Rd NW, Wilson NC 27896 **Dioc Chr Formation Com Dio No Carolina Raleigh NC 2011-; R S Tim's Ch Wilson NC 2010-; Dioc Liturg Cmsn Secy Dio No Carolina Raleigh NC 2006-** B Fort Belvoir VA 9/9/1960 DVM No Carolina St U Coll of Veterinary Medici 1987; MPH U NC Sch of Publ Hlth 1991; PhD No Carolina St U Coll of Veterinary Medici 1994; M.Div. Epis TS of the SW 2005. D 6/26/2005 P 12/28/2005 Bp Michael Bruce Curry. m 7/2/1993 Robert W Grudier c 1. Dioc Coun Mem Dio No Carolina Raleigh NC 2008-2011; Dioc Liturg Cmsn Secy Dio No Carolina Raleigh NC 2006-2011; Mssn Resource Spprt Team Dio No Carolina Raleigh NC 2006-2008; P All SS Ch Hamlet NC 2005-2010; P S Dav's Epis Ch Laurinburg NC 2005-2010; Cluster Mssnr Sandhills Cluster Hamlet NC 2005-2010. marty_stebbins@hotmail.com

STEBER, Gary David (NC) 406 Lorimer Road, Box 970, Davidson NC 28036 B Mobile AL 1/29/1937 s David Nelson Steber & Sydney. BS U So 1959; MA Ya 1964; MDiv STUSo 1979. D 6/6/1979 P 4/27/1980 Bp George Mosley Murray. m 7/24/1982 Linda Gay Taylor c 2. Int S Paul's Ch Monroe NC 2009-2010; S Alb's Ch Davidson NC 1994-2002; S Lk's Ch Salisbury NC 1992-1994; Par Dvlpmt Com Dio Alabama Birmingham AL 1990-1992; R S Mths Epis Ch Tuscaloosa AL 1987-1992; Stndg Com Dio Cntrl Gulf Coast Pensacola FL 1985-1987; Vic The Ch Of The Redeem MOBILE AL 1982-1987; Cur All SS Epis Ch Mobile AL 1980-1982; Cur The Epis Ch Of The Nativ Dothan AL 1979-1980; Cur S Paul's Ch Mobile AL 1979. gdsteber@bellsouth.net

STEBINGER, Katharine E (SD) 3140 30th Ave S, Minneapolis MN 55406 B New Haven CT 3/19/1981 d Peter Arnold Robichaud Stebinger & Caron. BA Wellesley Coll 2003; MDiv EDS 2006. D 11/1/2005 P 7/22/2006 Bp Creighton Leland Robertson. Asst S Barn Ch Falmouth MA 2006-2009. kate.stebinger@gmail.com

STEBINGER, Peter Arnold Robichaud (Ct) 526 Amity Rd, Bethany CT 06524 B London England UK 10/14/1954 s Arnold Stebinger & Jean. BA Bow 1976; MDiv Ya Berk 1980; MA U of Connecticut 1997. D 6/14/1980 Bp Morgan Porteus P 2/26/1981 Bp Arthur Edward Walmsley. m 6/5/1976 Caron Robichaud c 2. Adj Fac, D. Min. Prog SWTS Evanston IL 2002-2007; Consult: Par Dvlpmt Dio Connecticut Hartford CT 1988-1993; Dio Connecticut Hartford CT 1986-1993; R Chr Ch Bethany CT 1982-2011; Cur S Jn's Epis Par Waterbury CT 1980-1982. Auth, *Congrl Paths to Holiness*, Forw Mvmt, 2000; Auth, *Faith, Focus & Ldrshp*, Forw Mvmt, 1990; "Var arts". ICISF. Hon Cn Schlr Chr Ch Cathd Hartford CT 1998; Resrch Grant ECF 1994. peterstebinger@gmail.com

STECH, Bill (Mich) 20500 W Old US Highway 12, Chelsea MI 48118 **P S Barn' Ch Chelsea MI 2010-** B Denver CO 11/26/1961 s Ernest L Stech & Cynthia Reed. BS Ferris St U 1983; MS Estrn Michigan U 2004. D 1/30/2010 P 11/20/2010 Bp Wendell Nathaniel Gibbs Jr. m 11/8/1986 Margaret Stech c 2. bill@mc-kelgardens.com

STECKER IV, Frederick (NH) Box 293, New London NH 03257 B Fairmont WV 8/18/1946 s Frederick Stecker & Virginia Marcella. BA U So 1968; MDiv VTS 1972; Fllshp EDS 1984; DMin Bangor TS 1994; Fllshp Ya 2007; Psy.D. Boston Grad Sch of Psychoanalysis 2008; Fllshp TS 2008. D 6/17/1972 Bp John Mc Gill Krumm P 12/18/1972 Bp Lyman Cunningham Ogilby. m 8/28/1971 Ann Page Blair c 1. R S Andr's Ch New London NH 1979-2002; Emm Par Epis Ch And Day Sch Sthrn Pines NC 1977-1979; Asst All SS Ch Wynnewood PA 1972-1977. Auth, "The Podium, the Pulpit, and the Republicans: How Presidential Candidates Use Rel Lang in Amer Political Debate," Praeger, 2011; Auth, "Var arts," *Epis, Living Ch, Cornerstone Proj.* fstecker@tds.net

STECKLINE, Donna Louise (Alb) P.O. Box 345, Gilbertsville NY 13776 B Norwich NY 6/9/1961 d John Emerick Howard & Ann Arlette. AAS SUNY - Cobleskill. D 5/10/2008 Bp William Howard Love. m 7/14/1990 Kevin Steckline c 2. S Steph's Ch Delmar NY 2002-2004. Steckline@frontiernet.net

STEDMAN, David Algernon (WNY) Po Box 7488, St Thomas VI 00801 B Mandeville JM 7/22/1941 s Algernon Stedman & Enid. S Peters Theol Coll 1965. Trans 8/1/1988 Bp E(gbert) Don Taylor. St Pauls Ch-Sea Cow Bay Tortola BV VG 1998-2006. fatherstedman@yahoo.com

STEED, John Griffith (NJ) 11b Portsmouth St, Whiting NJ 08759 B Dayton OH 5/30/1942 s James G Steed & Marion Griffith. BA OH SU 1964; MA OH SU 1965; MDiv GTS 1971; BA No Carolina Wesleyan Coll 1987; MA No Carolina Cntrl U 1993. D 6/26/1971 P 5/30/1972 Bp Robert Fisher Gibson Jr. m 12/19/1965 Mary Lou Widmer c 1. R S Steph's Ch Whiting NJ 1999-2004; R Trin Ch Scotland Neck NC 1993-1998; Supply P Ch Of The Epiph Rocky Mt NC 1991-1993; Chr Ch Rocky Mt NC 1989-1993; R S Jos's Ch Durham NC 1975-1989; Assoc S Tim's Ch Wilson NC 1972-1975; Cur S Steph's Epis Ch Culpeper VA 1971-1972. CT. jgsteed@yahoo.com

STEELE, Christopher Candace (Oly) 7747 31st Ave Sw, Seattle WA 98126 B Meeker CO 5/23/1952 d Volney Wagoner Steele & Joan Myrl. CRDS; GTS; U So 1975; CDSP 1979. D 7/22/1979 P 1/1/1980 Bp Jackson Earle Gilliam. S Clem's Epis Ch Seattle WA 2005-2008; S Catherines Ch Enumclaw WA 2004-2005; S Andr's Epis Ch Tacoma WA 2002; Trin Ch Houston TX 2000-2001; S Fran Ch Houston TX 1999-2000; St Lk's Epis Hosp Houston TX 1986-1989; Assoc R Palmer Memi Ch Houston TX 1986; Palmer Memi Ch Houston TX 1984-1985; The Epis Ch Of The Gd Shpd Berkeley CA 1983-1984; Ch Of The H Sprt Missoula MT 1979-1980. Auth, "Aids In Tx: Facing The Crisis". Associated Parishes, Cmnty Of Cross Nails Coventry Engl. Arthur Lichtenberger Fllshp 1976; Assoc Dir Legis & Plcy, Hlth Law Plcy Inst U Houston 95; Helen Farabee Fell 90-93; No Amer Mnstrl Fell 76-79. THEREVMS@COMCAST.NET

STEELE, Gary Ross (Ak) 2708 W 65th Ave, Anchorage AK 99502 **Supply P Dio Alaska Fairbanks AK 2002-** B Anchorage AK 8/16/1962 s Ira Wesley Steele & Ione Edna. BA Mid Amer Chr U 1984; MDiv The Sthrn Bapt TS Louisville KY 1991. D 10/18/1999 P 3/26/2000 Bp Mark Lawrence Mac Donald. m 4/30/1988 Treva Rene Laukhuf c 2. P-in-c Chr Ch Anchorage AK 2000-2002; Asst S Mary's Ch Anchorage AK 2000-2001. garysteele@ak.net

STEELE, James Logan (Chi) 317 Goold Park Dr, Morris IL 60450 **R S Thos Ch Morris IL 1971-** B Chicago IL 11/5/1944 s Fred Harold Steele & Edith. BA U Chi 1965; MDiv GTS 1968. D 6/15/1968 Bp James Winchester Montgomery P 12/21/1968 Bp Gerald Francis Burrill. Dioc Coun Dio Chicago Chicago IL 2000-2003; Dioc Coun Dio Chicago Chicago IL 1990-1996; COM Dio Chicago Chicago IL 1976-1982; BACAM Dio Chicago Chicago IL 1973-1986; Dioc Coun Dio Chicago Chicago IL 1972-1978; Cur Gr Ch Sterling IL 1968-1971; Vic The Ch Of S Anne Morrison IL 1968-1971. Auth, *arts Ch Pub.* CCU; CBS; SOM; SSC. sthomor@hotmail.com

STEELE, Lawrence Jay (Los) 490 E Indian School Ln, Banning CA 92220 **S Alb's Epis Ch Yucaipa CA 2007-** B Kansas City KS 12/27/1939 s John Milner Steele & Ruth. MS USC 1972; ETSBH 1998. D 10/30/1999 Bp Chester Lovelle Talton. c 2. Asstg S Agnes Mssn Banning CA 1989-2002. chaplain1b@yahoo.com

STEELE, Nancy Jo (EMich) 111 S Shiawassee St, Corunna MI 48817 B Flint MI 1/18/1947 d Keith Nicholas Schoch & Victoria Louise Wlosek. BS MI SU 1969. D 8/17/2007 P 2/23/2008 Bp S(teven) Todd Ousley. m 11/22/1969 Jonathan Steele c 2. nsteele@centruytel.net

STEELE, Robert Emanuel (Nwk) Psychology Dept Of, College Park MD 20742 B Mobile AL 7/2/1943 s Rollie Dee Steele & Minnie Belle. BA Morehouse Coll 1965; MDiv EDS 1968; MA Ya 1971; MS Ya 1974; PhD Ya 1975. D 11/30/1968 Bp George E Rath. m 6/6/1967 Jean Elizabeth Acker. Auth, "Suicide In The Black Cmnty". Soc Of Sci Study Of Rel And Rel Resrch Assn, NAAD.

STEEN JR, S(idney) James (Chi) 65 E. Huron St., Chicago IL 60611 **Dir of Mnstrs Dio Chicago Chicago IL 2011-** B Tulsa OK 1/15/1944 s Sidney James Steen & Flora Fola. BA W&L 1966; MDiv GTS 1969. D 6/29/1969 Bp Chilton Powell P 12/27/1969 Bp Frederick Warren Putnam. m 1/1/1988 Thomas E Chesrown c 1. Bp's Dep for Congregations and Admin Dio Chicago Chicago IL 2011; R Ch Of S Paul And The Redeem Chicago IL 1998-2010; P-in-c S Mk's Ch Washington DC 1996-1998; Exec Dir Prism Parishes Inc Washington DC 1994-1996; Pres Gts Alum The GTS New York NY 1992-1996; R S Pat's Ch Washington DC 1979-1993; S Dunst's Ch Tulsa OK 1976-1979; Assoc The Ch Of S Lk In The Fields New York NY 1975-1979; Assoc Trin Ch Princeton NJ 1972-1975; Cur S Thos Ch Medina WA 1970-1972. jimsteen@me.com

STEEVER JR, Raymond George Edward (Los) Route 1, Box 109, Pullman WA 99163 B Dallas TX 6/11/1943 s Raymond George Edward Steever & Ruth Hazel. BS WA SU 1965. D 12/13/1980 Bp Leigh Wallace Jr. m 7/6/1968 F Rebecca Cohen c 2.

STEEVES, Joan Altpeter (Colo) 6337 Deframe Way, Arvada CO 80004 B Plymouth MA 5/29/1935 d Leland Stanford Altpeter & Mabel Henrietta. BA U of Massachusetts 1957; Bp's Inst for Diac Formation 1992. D 10/24/1992 Bp William Jerry Winterrowd. m 9/8/1956 Carl Richard Steeves c 3. D The Ch Of Chr The King (Epis) Arvada CO 1992-2010. NAAD 1992. jd_steeves@comcast.net

STEEVES, Timothy (Pa) 409 E Lancaster Ave, Downingtown PA 19335 **R S Jas' Epis Ch Downingtown PA 2005-** B Chelsea MA 2/15/1945 s Frederick Steeves & Zona. MA Bos; MS Col; New York Psychoanalytic Soc and Inst; BA U of Massachusetts; MDiv VTS. D 6/9/1973 Bp John Melville Burgess P 12/1/1973 Bp William Hopkins Folwell. m 7/21/1984 Deborah Lou Morgan c 4. Assoc R S Thos' Ch Whitemarsh Ft Washington PA 2000-2005; Bdgt Com Dio Virginia Richmond VA 1995-1997; T/F on Sexual Misconduct in Pstr Care Dio Virginia Richmond VA 1994-2000; Ecum Cmsn Dio Virginia Richmond VA 1993-1995; Montross & Washington Par Montross VA 1990-2000; R S Jas Ch Montross VA 1990-2000; R S Ptr's Ch Oak Grove Montross VA 1990-2000; Asst R Trin Ch Branford CT 1984-1985; R S Jas' Ch New Haven

CT 1983-1984; Trin Ch On The Green New Haven CT 1978-1981; Cur S Jas Epis Ch Ormond Bch FL 1973-1975. Auth, "arts & Bk Revs," 2003. ACSW; Mltry Chapl Assn. timsteeves@verizon.net

STEFANIK, Alfred Thomas (Vt) 1475 Mud City Loop, Morrisville VT 05661 B Copaigue NY 7/5/1939 s Alfred Francis Stefanik & Julia Anna. BA Cathd Coll of the Immac Concep 1961; STB CUA 1965; MA S Mich's Coll Colchester VT 1970. Rec from Roman Catholic 8/15/1977 as Deacon Bp Robert Shaw Kerr. m 10/3/1969 Claire Helene Affourtit c 2. S Jn's In The Mountains Stowe VT 2009-2010; Chapl to Ret Cler and Spouses/Partnr Dio Vermont Burlington VT 2008-2010; S Jn The Bapt Epis Hardwick VT 2007-2009; Int H Innoc' Epis Ch Lahaina HI 2002-2004; R Trin Epis Ch Roslyn NY 1996-2002; R Trin Ch Shelburne VT 1988-1996; Campus Min Dio Vermont Burlington VT 1987-1988; Vic Trin Milton VT 1984-1987; Campus Min Cathd Ch Of S Paul Burlington VT 1983-1987. Auth, "Short Changing Our Yth," *Epis Life*, 1988; Auth, "Copycat Sam: Developing Ties w A Spec Chld," Human Sciences Press NYC, 1982; Auth, "Grandma'S Halloween," Burlington Free Press VT, 1978; Auth, "Bread Making On The Rise," *New York Times*, 1975; Auth, "Striped Bass Out Back," *E Coast Fisherman*, 1970. alstefanik@myfairpoint.net

STEFFENHAGEN, Leverne Richard (WNY) 9705 Niagara Falls Blvd Apt 19, Niagara Falls NY 14304 B Cheektowaga NY 12/21/1932 s Louis H Steffenhagen & Regina B. D 6/9/1984 Bp Harold B Robinson. Asst to R St Mk Epis Ch No Tonawanda NY 1984-1989.

STEGELMANN, Dawn Marie (Ct) 651 Pequot Ave, Southport CT 06890 **Cur Trin Epis Ch Southport CT 2008-** B Moline IL 6/14/1961 d Larry Harlan Requet & Julie Connell. BA Hillsdale Coll 1983; MDiv Ya Berk 2008. D 6/14/2008 Bp Andrew Donnan Smith P 2/7/2009 Bp James Elliot Curry. m 11/23/1984 Murry Stegelmann c 3. DarienDawn@aol.com

STEIDEMANN, Arthur Richard (Mo) 1 Mcknight Pl Apt G-45, Saint Louis MO 63124 **Died 9/17/2010** B Saint Louis MO 5/16/1915 s Arthur Otto Steidemann & Hazel. BD Washington U 1936; Cert Eden TS 1953; MDiv Eden TS 1971. D 6/1/1952 Bp Arthur C Lichtenberger P 12/1/1952 Bp William Scarlett. c 2. Ed, "The Deaf Epis 80-83". Epis Conf Of The Deaf 1975; Registry Of Interpreters For The Deaf 1976. Anne Sullivan Awd Epis Conf Of The Deaf 2001; Thos Gallaudet Awd Epis Conf Of The Deaf 1995; Traveling Fell To Dio Natal Soafr Bp Of Mo 1972. revsteidmn@att.net

STEIDL, Gerald S. (CFla) 127 E Cottesmore Cir, Longwood FL 32779 **D Epis Ch Of The H Sprt Apopka FL 1997-** B Cincinnati OH 4/4/1942 s Nelson Melish Steidl & Alice Loiuse. Mia; U Cinc; AA Seminole Cmnty Coll 1996; Inst for Chr Stds, Dio Cntrl Florida 1997. D 12/13/1997 Bp John Wadsworth Howe. m 7/16/1966 Susan Richter Nau c 3. HabHum- Pres; Honduras Med Missions; Prison Mnstry, Chapl & Kairos. hsdeak@aol.com

STEIG, George Terrance (Oly) 5241 12th Ave Ne, Seattle WA 98105 **Asst S Andr's Ch Seattle WA 2000-** B Longview MA 2/24/1948 s George G Steig & Margaret Marie. BA S Thos Coll Kenmore WA 1970; STB Angelicum U 1973; MA Gregorian U 1974; Med U Of Puget Sound 1983. Rec from Roman Catholic 6/22/1989 as Priest Bp Robert Hume Cochrane. m 8/16/1980 Theresa Lee Forhan c 2.

STEILBERG, Isabel Fourqurean (SVa) 221 34th St, Newport News VA 23607 **Stndg Commitee Dio Sthrn Virginia Norfolk VA 2000-; Mssn & Mnstry Fndt Dio Sthrn Virginia Norfolk VA 1998-; R S Paul's Ch Newport News VA 1996-** B 9/3/1941 d Henry Jordan Fourqurean & Lightfoot. Duke 1960; BA U NC 1962; MA Virginia Commonwealth U 1981; MDiv VTS 1992. D 6/7/1992 P 12/19/1992 Bp Frank Harris Vest Jr. Dio Sthrn Virginia Norfolk VA 1994-1997; Chair Dept Outreach Mnstrs Dio Sthrn Virginia Norfolk VA 1994-1997; Chair Dept Outreach Mnstrs Dio Sthrn Virginia Norfolk VA 1994-1997; Chr The King Epis Ch Tabb VA 1994-1996; S Andr's Epis Ch Newport News VA 1992-1994. isteilberg@infionline.net

S

STEIN, Edward Lee (Tex) 717 Sage Rd, Houston TX 77056 **Cn Precentor Chr Ch Cathd Houston TX 2000-** B Houston TX 6/30/1947 s Edward C Stein & Laura. BA U So 1969; MDiv VTS 1972. D 6/28/1972 Bp Frederick P Goddard P 6/1/1973 Bp J Milton Richardson. Asst S Bede Epis Ch Houston TX 1972-1999; S Mart's Epis Ch Houston TX 1972-1996. edstein@christchurchcathedral.org

STEIN, Orville John (Lex) 206 College St, Somerset KY 42501 **Dir Of S Lk'S Clnc Dio Lexington Lexington KY 1980-** B Black River Falls WI 10/27/1928 s George Frederick Stein & Ida Annette. BS Geo 1958; MD U of Louisiana 1962. D 3/15/1975 Bp Addison Hosea. m 8/1/1959 Sue Yantis Conkwright c 4. Asst S Pat Ch Somerset KY 1982-2000.

STEINER IV, John (Md) 7474 Washington Blvd, Elkridge MD 21075 **R Trin Ch Waterloo Elkridge MD 1993-** B Washington DC 12/20/1947 s John Steiner & Blanche Elizabeth. BS VMI 1969; MS U Of Florida 1977; MDiv GTS 1988. D 5/28/1988 P 12/1/1988 Bp James Michael Mark Dyer. m 9/3/1972 Carolyn Lemkau c 2. Asst R Ch Of The Gd Shpd Ruxton MD 1990-1993; P Gr Epis Ch Allentown PA 1988-1990. jsteineriv@comcast.net

STEINFELD, John Wilfred (Nev) 915 Gear St, Reno NV 89503 B Philadelphia PA 4/16/1933 s Hans Karl Steinfeld & Irma. BA U CO 1955; MDiv SWTS 1967. D 6/5/1967 P 12/21/1967 Bp Joseph Summerville Minnis. c 2. Trin Epis Ch Reno NV 1993-2000; Chr The King Quincy CA 1991-2001; Vic S Cuth's Epis Ch Oakland CA 1971-1974; Assoc S Mk's Epis Ch Palo Alto CA 1969-1971; Vic S Andr's Epis Ch Ft Lupton CO 1967-1969; Vic S Eliz's Epis Ch Brighton CO 1967-1969. frjohn67@gmail.com

STEINHAUER, Roger Kent (Roch) 25 Chadbourne Rd, Rochester NY 14618 B 7/11/1935 s William H Steinhauer & Charlotte Edith. BA Amh 1956; BD UTS 1959. D 6/13/1959 P 3/1/1960 Bp Nelson Marigold Burroughs. c 2. P-in-c The Epis Ch of The Redeem Jacksonville FL 1962-1967; Resurr Chap Tallahassee FL 1959-1962.

STEINHAUSER, Elizabeth (Mass) 419 Shawmut Ave., Boston MA 02118 B New York, NY 10/22/1967 d Richard Steinhauser & Elizabeth Settle. BA Colg 1989; MDiv Harvard DS 1996; Angl Cert EDS 2007. D 6/7/2008 Bp M(arvil) Thomas Shaw III P 1/10/2009 Bp Roy Frederick Cederholm Jr. m 6/3/2004 Cora Roelofs c 1. Yth Dir S Steph's Epis Ch Boston MA 2008. lizsteinh@netzero.net

STELK, Lincoln Frank (NY) 241 Bluff Rd, Yarmouth ME 04096 B Chicago IL 7/20/1934 s Lincoln Rentner Stelk & Anna Martha. BA Ohio Wesl 1956; BD EDS 1964. D 6/27/1964 Bp Paul Moore Jr P 1/16/1965 Bp William Foreman Creighton. m 6/17/1960 Virginia Horn c 3. R S Mary's Ch Mohegan Lake NY 1987-1998; Int S Tim's Ch Macedonia OH 1986-1987; Dept CSR Dio Ohio Cleveland OH 1978-1984; R Harcourt Par Gambier OH 1977-1986; Ken Gambier OH 1977-1984; Dio Sthrn Ohio Cincinnati OH 1976-1977; Dio Ohio Cleveland OH 1971-1977; Mem, Liturg Cmsn Dio Sthrn Ohio Cincinnati OH 1967-1974; R S Ptr's Epis Ch Delaware OH 1966-1977. BD Bex 1982. stelk2@aol.com

STELLE, Eric Arthur (Ala) 110 W Hawthorne Rd, Homewood AL 35209 **S Jn's Epis Ch Gig Harbor WA 2011-** B Vallejo CA 1/14/1971 s David Lee Stelle & Rosalind Troxell. BA U CA Los Angeles 1994; MDiv Regent Coll 2002; DAS The U So (Sewanee) 2009. D 5/19/2009 P 12/18/2009 Bp Henry Nutt Parsley Jr. m 8/18/2001 Cynthia Tidwell c 3. Reverend All SS Epis Ch Birmingham AL 2009-2011. cynthiastelle@gmail.com

STELZ, Patricia A (NH) 466 Summit House, West Chester PA 19382 **Int All SS Epis Ch Oakville CT 2011-** B Mt Vernon NY 10/9/1948 d Ernest William Stelz & Catherine Elizabeth Kelly. BA U of New Hampshire 1991; MDiv Bos 1997; MSw Bos 1997; CTh EDS 2004. D 6/11/2005 P 12/17/2005 Bp V Gene Robinson. m 5/15/2010 Edward G Rice c 2. Anti-Racism Cmsn Dio Pennsylvania Philadelphia PA 2006-2010; Assoc The Ch Of The H Trin W Chester PA 2005-2011; Yth Dir Dio New Hampshire Concord NH 1997-2005. patstelz1217@gmail.com

STEN, Pamela V (WMich) 2512 Bristol Terr, St Joseph MI 49085 **R S Paul's Epis Ch S Jos MI 2007-** B Towanda PA 1/2/1951 d Michael Vancko & Mary. BS Penn 1972; MDiv SWTS 2002. D 6/8/2002 Bp Edward Lewis Lee Jr P 12/21/2002 Bp William Dailey Persell. c 2. Asst R S Dav's Ch Glenview IL 2002-2007. pamsten@ameritech.net

STENNER, David Anthony (Md) 203 E Chatsworth Ave, Reisterstown MD 21136 **R All SS Epis Ch Reisterstown MD 1998-** B Oakland CA 7/10/1949 s Donald Wier Stenner & Evelyn Regina. AA Chabot Coll 1969; BA S Mary's Coll Moraga CA 1984; MDiv TESM 1988; DMin SWTS 2005. D 9/17/1988 P 3/17/1989 Bp John Lester Thompson III. m 6/17/1972 Janet Christine Howard c 3. Exec Com Capital Funds Cmpgn Dio Nthrn California Sacramento CA 1995-1997; Bp's Search Com Dio Nthrn California Sacramento CA 1990-1991; Vic S Fran Ch Fortuna CA 1988-1998. dastenner1@gmail.com

STENNETTE, Lloyd Roland (SeFla) Apartado Postal Box 288-1000, San Jose Costa Rica B Limon 1/6/1936 s Ridley Stennette & Emeline. BA Colegio Nocturno De Limon Cr 1964; Centro De Estudios Teologicas 1967; Epis TS of The SW 1983. D 7/10/1966 P 7/1/1968 Bp David Emrys Richards. m 1/25/1969 Doris Ritchie Watts Williams. Ch Of S Andr The Apos Camden NJ 1990-1997; Dpt Of Missions Ny Income New York NY 1986-1989; Mision San Pablo E Elmhurst NY 1986-1989; S Ann's Ch Of Morrisania Bronx NY 1986; Dio Costa Rica New York NY 1966-1976. Auth, "Stations Of The Cross In Spanish". rev.stennette@hotmail.com

STENNING, Gordon John (RI) 36 Brant Rd, Portsmouth RI 02871 B Providence RI 7/9/1930 s John Albert Stenning & Ethel. BA Br 1952; STB ETSBH 1955. D 6/24/1955 P 3/24/1956 Bp John S Higgins. m 6/28/1952 Barbara Luther c 2. Ch Pension Fund New York NY 1988-1995; VP and Secy The CPG New York NY 1988-1991; Chair Exec Com Ovrs Mssns Dio Rhode Island Providence RI 1983-1988; Dioc Coun Dio Rhode Island Providence RI 1970-1989; Dn Aquidnock Deanry Dio Rhode Island Providence RI 1969-1979; ExCoun Dio Rhode Island Providence RI 1958-1968; R S Mary's Ch Portsmouth RI 1957-1988; Cur S Paul's Ch Pawtucket RI 1955-1957. Portsmouth Citizen of the Year 1980. brantlight@juno.com

STEPHENS JR, Jefferson Chandler (Los) 480S Orange Grove Blvd Apt 12, Pasadena CA 91105 B Los Angeles CA 3/25/1933 s Jefferson Chandler Stephens & Sallie Gibson. BA California St U 1955; MDiv CDSP 1958; MA U of San Francisco 1978. D 6/2/1958 Bp Francis E I Bloy P 12/1/1958 Bp Harry S Kennedy. m 6/10/1989 Peggy Ann Neate c 3. Exec Dir Cmsn on Schools Dio

Los Angeles Los Angeles CA 2001-2009; Assoc S Geo's Par La Can CA 1995-1999; Cur Trin Par Menlo Pk CA 1962-1966. revjeff1@earthlink.net

STEPHENS, Paul Jeffery (Miss) P. O. Box 1358, Tupelo MS 38802 **R All SS' Epis Ch Tupelo MS 2009-** B Starkville MS 4/9/1956 s Caril V Stephens & Lois V. BS Mississippi St U 1978; JD U of Mississippi 1983; MDiv STUSo 2002. D 6/15/2002 Bp Alfred Clark Marble Jr P 1/5/2003 Bp Duncan Montgomery Gray III. m 6/23/1979 Martha Jane Randall c 2. Int Ch of the H Apos Collierville TN 2008; Int S Jn's Ch Laurel MS 2007-2008; Coast Epis Schools Inc Long Bch MS 2004-2007; Cur/Sch Chapl Trin Ch Natchez MS 2002-2004. revpaulstephens@gmail.com

STEPHENS, Thomas Lee (Okla) 1560 SE Pecan Place, Bartlesville OK 74003 **R S Lk's Epis Ch Bartlesville OK 1997-** B Boca Raton FL 1/14/1945 s Thomas J Stephens & Rose Mary. BA Oklahoma Bapt U 1969; MDiv MidWestern Bapt TS 1972; DMin MidWestern Bapt TS 1976. D 6/27/1992 Bp Maurice Manuel Benitez P 2/2/1993 Bp William Jackson Cox. m 12/17/1988 Lynda D Narron c 3. Dioc Coun Dio Oklahoma Oklahoma City OK 2002-2003; T/F On Recon Dio Oklahoma Oklahoma City OK 2002-2003; Dioc Coun Dio Oklahoma Oklahoma City OK 1997-1998; Asst Chr Epis Ch Tyler TX 1991-1996. leestephens@episcopalbartlesville.org

STEPHENS, Wyatt E (Mil) 1538 N 58th St, Milwaukee WI 53208 **Ret Dio Milwaukee Milwaukee WI 1996-** B Sulphur OK 12/15/1933 s Ira Wyatt Stephens & Julia Dorene. BA U of Oklahoma 1958; MS U of Oklahoma 1960; PhD U of Oklahoma 1963; MA Nash 1979. D 9/1/1979 P 3/1/1980 Bp Albert William Hillestad. m 8/23/1953 DixieLee Stumpff c 4. Cn for Parishes Dio Milwaukee Milwaukee WI 1988-1996; R Ch Of The H Comm Lake Geneva WI 1980-1988; Asst Trin Ch Wauwatosa WI 1979-1980. wstephens3@wi.rr.com

STEPHENSON, John William (Kan) Rr 1 Box 190, Riverton KS 66770 B 6/7/1946 s John Oliver Stephenson & Thelma Louise. AS Missouri Sthrn St U 1974; BA Missouri Sthrn St U 1975. D 5/12/1988 P 11/1/1988 Bp Richard Frank Grein. m 8/15/1965 Norma Geraldine Edwards c 2. P S Epis Mary's Ch Inc Galena KS 1988-2004; SE Convoc Bd Ft Scott KS 1988-1991.

STEPHENSON, Michael Perdue (Okla) 3427 N Harding Ave, Chicago IL 60618 **Int R S Andr's Ch Stillwater OK 2011-; Int R S Andr's Ch Stillwater OK 2011-** B Joplin MO 6/15/1952 s Clyde Edwin Stephenson & Dorothy Perdue. BA Tul 1974; MBA Washington U 1979; MDiv Chicago TS 2008. D 6/23/2007 Bp Robert Manning Moody P 1/26/2008 Bp William Dailey Persell. c 2. Cn for Dvlpmt Dio Chicago Chicago IL 2007-2011; Asstg P S Andr Ch Grayslake IL 2005-2011. mikestep@att.net

STEPHENSON JR, Randolph (WA) 4 Jeb Stuart Ct, Rockville MD 20854 **Middleham & S Ptr's Par Lusby MD 2008-; Int Chr Ch Accokeek MD 1998-** B Savannah GA 10/21/1946 s Randolph Robert Stephenson & Kathleen Helen. Geo; Armstrong Atlantic St Coll 1966; BA U GA 1968; Hofstra U 1973; MDiv VTS 1975. D 6/5/1976 Bp Jonathan Goodhue Sherman P 4/1/1977 Bp Reginald Heber Gooden. m 7/6/1976 Sally H Hill c 2. Int Chr Ch S Jn's Par Accokeek MD 1998-2001; P-in-c Trin Epis Par Hughesville MD 1995-1998; P-in-c S Mary's Chap Ridge St Marys City MD 1993-1994; St Marys Par St Marys City MD 1993-1994; Vic S Geo's Ch Glenn Dale MD 1982-1988; Asst Chapl S Alb's Chap & Epis U Cntr Baton Rouge LA 1978-1982; Asst S Mk's Cathd Shreveport LA 1976-1978. Washington Epis Cleric Assn.

STEPHENSON-DIAZ, Lark (SanD) 1023 Iris Ct, Carlsbad CA 92011 B Vallejo CA 4/1/1962 d John Arthur Stephenson & Katherine Jean Languedoc. BA U of Portland 1984; MDiv Ya Berk 1988. D 6/22/1988 P 1/5/1989 Bp Robert Louis Ladehoff. m 5/27/1995 Roberto Domingo Diaz. S Ptr's Epis Ch Del Mar CA 2005-2010; S Marg Of Scotland Par San Juan Capistrano CA 1995-2005; Asst S Tim's Ch San Diego CA 1995-1998; Assoc S Jas Par Los Angeles CA 1991-1994; Assoc S Jn The Evang Ch Milwaukie OR 1988-1991. larkdiaz@aol.com

STER, David (CPa) No address on file. **D S Lk's Epis Ch Mechanicsburg PA 1999-** B Cleveland OH 2/13/1953 s August Ster & Lona. AA U of Maryland 1981. D 6/11/1999 Bp Michael Whittington Creighton. m 2/26/1977 Patricia Pearce.

STERCHI, Margaret (NJ) 1704 Old Black Horse Pike, Blackwood NJ 08012 **R S Jn The Evang Ch Blackwood NJ 2006-** B Silver City NM 5/15/1951 d Robert Nichol Sterchi & Louise. BS U of New Mex 1974; MDiv Epis TS of The SW 2001. D 6/9/2001 Bp D(avid) Bruce Mac Pherson P 5/11/2002 Bp James Monte Stanton. Asst All SS Ch Rehoboth Bch DE 2003-2006; Cn Cathd Ch Of S Jn Wilmington DE 2001-2003. marsterchi@aol.com

STERKEN, Janet Leigh (Eau) 322 N. Water St., Sparta WI 54656 B Harvard IL 8/1/1968 d Wayne Sterken & Linda. BS Mt Senario Coll 1990; MA Bridgewater St Coll 2000. D 11/21/2008 Bp Mark Lawrence Mac Donald. sterkjl@charter.net

STERLING III, Edward Arthur (Oly) 3762 Palisades Pl W, University Place WA 98466 B Grandfield OK 3/10/1921 s Edward Arthur Sterling & Mary Louise. BS Texas A&M U 1942; MDiv Epis TS of The SW 1957. D 6/19/1957 Bp John E Hines P 6/18/1958 Bp Frederick P Goddard. c 4. Dioc Coun Dio Olympia Seattle WA 2004-2007; Asst S Andr's Epis Ch Tacoma WA 1986-1999; Stwdshp Cmsn Dio Olympia Seattle WA 1981-1983; P S Catherines Ch Enumclaw WA 1980-1983; LocTen Chr Epis Ch Puyallup WA 1978-1979; Off Of Bsh For ArmdF New York NY 1959-1975; M-in-c S Mary's Ch W Columbia TX 1957-1959.

STERLING, Franklin Mills (Cal) 1707 Gouldin Rd., Oakland CA 94611 **D S Jn's Epis Ch Oakland CA 2008-** B Ridley Park PA 11/4/1932 s Allan Charles Sterling & Mary Lapatesky. BSEE Ohio U 1960; MBA Golden Gate U 1981; Theol Stds Epis Sch For Deacons 2007. D 12/1/2007 Bp Marc Handley Andrus. m 5/28/1977 Marion Coles Sterling c 3. fms425@comcast.net

STERLING, John Campbell (WTenn) 3100 Stonecrest Cir, Lakeland TN 38002 **Died 3/21/2011** B Maryville TN 5/7/1926 s Campbell Henry Sterling & Mary Alexander. VTS 1968. D 6/24/1968 Bp William Evan Sanders P 12/24/1968 Bp John Vander Horst. c 2.

STERLING, Leslie Katherin (Mass) St. Bartholomew's Church, 239 Harvard Street, Cambridge MA 02139 **P-in-c S Barth's Ch Cambridge MA 2009-** B Washington DC 6/15/1957 d Mack Freeman & Barbarajean Washington. ABS Harv 1979; Cert St. Eliz's Med Cntr 1999; MDiv EDS 2001. D 6/2/2001 Bp Barbara Clementine Harris P 6/8/2002 Bp M(arvil) Thomas Shaw III. Assoc R All SS Par Brookline MA 2001-2009. UBE 2000. ammaleslie@gmail.com

STERNE, Martha Packer (At) 805 Mount Vernon Hwy NW, Atlanta GA 30327 **Assoc H Innoc Ch Atlanta GA 2007-** B Alexandria LA 12/1/1947 d James Malcolm Packer & Anna Milbury. BA Van 1970; Med Georgia St U 1983; MDiv Candler TS Emory U 1988. D 6/11/1988 P 4/1/1989 Bp Frank Kellogg Allan. m 6/20/1970 Carroll Payne Sterne c 2. S Andr's Ch Maryville TN 1997-2007; All SS Epis Ch Atlanta GA 1988-1997. "Earthly Gd," OSL, 2003. Theta Pi. cpsterne@gmail.com

STERRY, Steven Chapin (Los) 1314 N. Angelina Dr., Placentia CA 92870 **Dioc Coun Alt Dio Los Angeles Los Angeles CA 2011-** B Los Angeles CA 12/5/1942 s Charles Sterry & Eva. Cont Stds Biola U Sch of Apologetics; BS U CA 1965; MBA U CA 1972; Completion of course Talbot TS 2009. D 1/24/2009 Bp Chester Lovelle Talton. c 1. Natl Bus Sch hon Beta Gamma Sigma 1972. steve.sterry@gmail.com

STEUER, Lawrence William (Alb) 343 Pettis Rd, Gansevoort NY 12831 B Portland OR 1/18/1926 s Lawrence Arthur Steuer & Beneatha Dorothy. BA U of Washington 1949. D 12/19/1981 Bp Wilbur Emory Hogg Jr. m 12/23/1945 Mary Elizabeth McAllister c 2. D The Ch Of The Mssh Glens Falls NY 1995-2005; D /Asst S Tim's Ch Westford NY 1989-1995; D /Asst Ch Of Beth Saratoga Sprg NY 1981-1989. lwsteuer@aol.com

STEUP, Harold Wilbur (HB) 440 4th Ave N Apt 1510, Saint Petersburg FL 33701 B Fort Wayne IN 7/26/1920 s Carl Simon Steup & Wilhelmina Augusta. BA Ob 1942; MDiv GTS 1954. D 6/29/1954 P 6/1/1955 Bp Stephen F Bayne Jr. Vic Chr Epis Ch Anacortes WA 1964-1968; Asst Chr Ch Oyster Bay NY 1961-1964; Asst S Thos Ch Medina WA 1954-1956.

STEVENS JR, Arthur Grant (WMass) 904B West Victoria St, Santa Barbara CA 93101 B Washington DC 9/8/1941 s Arthur Grant Stevens & Frances. BA Cntr Coll 1963; MA U Of Kentucky 1965; PhD U MI 1970; MDiv CDSP 1987. D 6/6/1987 Bp Don Adger Wimberly P 6/3/1988 Bp Charles Shannon Mallory. m 6/11/1983 Judith Parris Heimlich. Int S Jas Ch Paso Robles CA 1992-1993; Asstg Cler S Ben's Par Los Osos CA 1989-1999; Dioc Sprtl Dir Dio El Camino Real Monterey CA 1988-1991; S Tim's Epis Ch Mtn View CA 1988. "Abundant Living For Christians: Making Decisions In Ch And Fam," Xulon Press, 2005. Ord Of H Cross. playforgod@msn.com

STEVENS JR, Ernest Lee (Az) 5109 Bunn Ave, Cheyenne WY 82009 B Contoocook NH 12/21/1925 s Ernest Lee Stevens & Marguarita Veronica. BA U of New Hampshire 1950; MDiv EDS 1957; US-A Chapl Sch 1970; AAS Rio Salado Coll 1990; MA Ottawa U 2002. D 6/29/1957 Bp Charles F Hall P 5/27/1960 Bp Richard S M Emrich. m 8/26/1989 Dorothy Barnett. Asst Chr Ch Of The Ascen Paradise Vlly AZ 1993-1997; P-in-c S Paul's Ch Phoenix AZ 1993; Vic Epiph On The Desert Gila Bend AZ 1992-1994; Int S Jn The Bapt Globe AZ 1990; Asst S Steph's Ch Phoenix AZ 1987-1990; Vic All SS Epis Ch Safford AZ 1980-1982; R SS Phil And Jas Morenci AZ 1977-1987; Off Of Bsh For ArmdF New York NY 1962-1969; R S Steph's Epis Ch Douglas AZ 1960-1962; Cathd Ch Of S Paul Detroit MI 1959-1960; Cur Chr Ch Dearborn MI 1957-1959. leedor135@yahoo.com

STEVENS, George (Mass) St. John's Church, P.O. Box 5610, Beverly MA 01915 **S Mary's Ch Newton Lower Falls MA 2010-** B NC 8/17/1976 s Hugh Stevens & Marilyn. BA U Rich 1999; MDiv GTS 2006. D 6/3/2006 Bp Michael Bruce Curry P 1/12/2008 Bp M(arvil) Thomas Shaw III. m 10/12/2002 Margaret Stevens c 2. Yth Min S Paul's Epis Ch Winston Salem NC 2000-2003; S Jn's Ch Beverly Farms MA 1996-2010. georgestevens3@gmail.com

STEVENS III, Halsey (Ct) 63 Route 81, Killingworth CT 06419 **P-in-c Chr Ch Avon CT 2008-** B Hartford CT 12/18/1939 s Halsey Stevens & Margaret. BA Nasson Coll 1962; MDiv Ya Berk 1965. D 6/14/1965 Bp Walter H Gray P 12/18/1965 Bp Joseph Warren Hutchens. m 6/13/1964 Betsey Burr Nash c 2. Ch of the H Sprt W Haven CT 2000; R S Paul's Ch Pawtucket RI 1993-2000; R S Mary's Ch Portsmouth RI 1990-1993; R Trin Ch Upper Marlboro MD

1982-1990; Vic S Andr The Apos Rocky Hill CT 1969-1982; Vic Ch Of The Epiph Southbury CT 1965-1969.

STEVENS, Judith Parris (WMass) 904B W Victoria St, Santa Barbara CA 93101 **Nonstipendiary P Trin Epis Ch Santa Barbara CA 2005-** B Columbus OH 6/5/1939 d William Friel Heimlich & Mary Eitel. BA w hon Smith 1961; MA Col 1963; PhD Col 1967; MDiv w hon CDSP 1987. D 6/6/1987 Bp Don Adger Wimberly P 6/3/1988 Bp Charles Shannon Mallory. m 6/11/1983 Arthur Grant Stevens. Dio Wstrn Massachusetts Springfield MA 1999-2004; R S Jn's Ch Northampton MA 1999-2004; S Ben's Par Los Osos CA 1989-1999; Cur All SS Epis Ch Palo Alto CA 1987-1989. Auth, *Conv Decisions and Voting Records*, Brookings, 1973; Auth, *The Conventional Problem*, Brookings, 1972; Auth, *Voting for Pres*, Brookings, 1970; Auth, *Congr and Urban Problems*, Brookings, 1969. Assoc of the H Cross 1983. Bp's Excellence Awd Dioc Conv 1992. playforgod@msn.com

STEVENS, Karl Peter (O) 201 W. Brooklyn St., Gambier OH 43022 **P-in-c S Paul's Ch Mt Vernon OH 2009-** B Albion MI 12/24/1971 BA Ken. D 6/12/2003 P 1/19/2004 Bp James Louis Jelinek. m 8/17/1997 Amy Elizabeth Stevens c 1. Dio Ohio Cleveland OH 2003-2010. karlstevens@me.com

STEVENS, M(errill) Richard (NAM) Saint Christopher's Mission, PO Box 28, Bluff UT 84512 **Pres, Stndg Com The Epis Ch In Navajoland Coun Farmington NM 2011-; Mnstry Coordntr S Chris's Ch Bluff UT 2009-; Vic S Jn The Baptizer Bluff UT 2009-; Vic S Mary Of-The-Moonlight Bluff UT 2009-; Ch Of The Gd Shpd Ft Defiance AZ 2007-** B Sewanee TN 9/2/1947 s Merrill Arthur Stevens & Walli. BA St. Jn's Coll Annapolis MD 1969; JD U of Arizona 1985; MDiv CDSP 1995; PhD Grad Theol Un 2003. D 10/13/2001 P 5/16/2004 Bp Mark Lawrence Mac Donald. m 7/4/1983 Willie Hulce c 1. Cler Assoc The Epis Ch Of The Gd Shpd Berkeley CA 2001-2007. Auth, "Burning for the Other," *Bk*, VDM Verlag Dr Mueller, 2009. redstevensgsm@gmail.com

STEVENS, Nancy Dunbar (Roch) The Church of the Epiphany, 3285 Buffalo Rd, Rochester NY 14624 **R The Ch Of The Epiph Rochester NY 1999-** B Rochester NY 2/21/1950 d Robert Croll Stevens & Jane Knauss. Beloit Coll 1971; BSN Case Wstrn Reserve U 1973; U of Dallas Irving 1989; MDiv Bex 1993. D 11/22/1993 P 5/28/1994 Bp William George Burrill. m 9/1/1995 David Lee Williams c 4. Asst to the R S Jas' Ch Batavia NY 1993-1999. Assoc, OSH 1991. coerector@frontier.com

STEVENS, Patricia D (At) P.O. Box 155, Johnston SC 29832 B Cincinnati OH 11/12/1949 d Andrew P Denuzze & Marguerite M. BA Manhattanville Coll 1971; JD U of Connecticut 1974; MDiv Ya Berk 1989. D 6/10/1989 P 12/1/1989 Bp Arthur Edward Walmsley. Ch Of The Ridge Trenton SC 2009-2010; S Pat's Epis Ch Atlanta GA 2003-2007; Ch Of The Epiph Atlanta GA 2001-2003; Pstr Asst Chr Ch Cathd Hartford CT 1995-1996; Chr Ch Cathd Houston TX 1994-1995; Vic Zion Epis Ch No Branford CT 1991-1993; Asst R S Jas's Ch W Hartford CT 1989-1991. ps261181@gmail.com

STEVENS, Robert (Ak) 4017 Spruce Ln, Juneau AK 99801 **Died 8/11/2011** B Detroit MI 6/16/1947 s Matt Starsinich & Mary. Vancouver TS; BA U of Puget Sound 1972; MA U of Puget Sound 1976. D 8/1/2004 P 7/7/2005 Bp Mark Lawrence Mac Donald. c 2. frbob@uk.net

STEVENS JR, Robert E (NH) 1113 Macon Ave, Pittsburgh PA 15218 **R S Jn's Ch Portsmouth NH 2005-** B Orlando FL 12/26/1968 s Robert Ellsworth Stevens. BS Florida St U 1991; MDiv SWTS 2001. Cur Calv Ch Pittsburgh PA 2001-2005.

STEVENS, Robert Ellsworth (CFla) 2346 Colfax Ter., Evanston IL 60201 B Baltimore MD 11/6/1937 s O Ellsworth Stevens & Lillian Carolyn. U Of Baltimore 1956; BA Maryville Coll 1959; MDiv Columbia TS 1972. D 9/5/1976 P 3/1/1978 Bp William Hopkins Folwell. m 9/7/1962 Elizabeth Jane Haught c 2. Chapl SWTS Evanston IL 1993-2001; Emm Ch Orlando FL 1987-1998; R S Steph's Ch Lakeland FL 1978-1987; S Lk The Evang Ch Mulberry FL 1978. resjhs@gmail.com

S

STEVENS, Scott J (Ct) Main Street, Box 151, Hampton CT 06247 **D S Paul's Ch Plainfield CT 2005-** B Concord NH 1/24/1955 s Robert Douglas Stevens & Patricia Ann. BA U of New Hampshire 1977; MA U of Connecticut 1980. D 12/1/1990 Bp Arthur Edward Walmsley. m 6/16/1979 Jodie Vail Griffin c 2. D S Paul's Ch Windham CT 1990-2005. Auth, "Pstr Care of Sexual Offenders," *Diakoneo*, NAAD, 2002. NAAD. dcnscott@gmail.com

STEVENS III, Walter Alexander (Haw) 1650 Kanunu St Apt 608, Honolulu HI 96814 **Vic S Aug's Epis Chap Kapaau HI 2002-** B Petersburg VA 12/25/1946 s Walter Alexander Stevens & Ida Richardson. BA Col 1967; MDiv EDS 2000. D 6/22/2000 P 3/25/2001 Bp Richard Sui On Chang. m 7/26/1998 Kathleen Kagimoto c 1. S Steph's Ch Wahiawa HI 2007-2011; S Paul's Ch Kohala Mssn Kapaau HI 2002-2004; Assoc R For Chld & Yth Calv Epis Ch Kaneohe HI 2001; S Phil's Ch Maili Waianae HI 2000-2001. revwastevens@gmail.com

STEVENS, Weaver L (Los) 477 London Ln, Severna Park MD 21146 **Died 12/13/2009** B 11/14/1929 D 6/14/1955 P 2/13/1956 Bp Francis E I Bloy.

STEVENS, William Clair (PR) Ingrams Cottage, Hardam, Pulborough, W Sussex Great Britain (UK) B 4/5/1935

STEVENS-HUMMON, Rebecca M (Tenn) 2902 Overlook Dr, Nashville TN 37212 **S Aug's Chap Nashville TN 2010-** B Milford CT 4/1/1963 d Gladstone Hudson Stevens & Anne. BA U So 1985; MDiv Van 1990; Cert STUSo 1991. D 6/9/1991 Bp George Lazenby Reynolds Jr. m 10/8/1988 Marcus S Hummon c 4. The Epis Ch Of The Resurr Franklin TN 1993-1994; D-In-Trng Dio Tennessee Nashville TN 1991-1995. Narpm. BECCA.M.STEVENS@VANDERBILT.EDU

STEVENSON, Anne Broad (Tenn) 216 chestnut hill, Nashville TN 37215 B Jackson MS 3/15/1939 d Charles Manton Broad & Octavia Mclean. BA Agnes Scott Coll 1961; BA U of Louvain 1982; MA U of Louvain 1983; STB U of Louvain 1983. D 6/24/1983 Bp John Mc Gill Krumm P 9/1/1984 Bp Robert Bracewell Appleyard. c 3. Cn Chr Ch Cathd Nashville TN 1989-2011; S Jas Ch Jackson MS 1985-1989. abstevenson@me.com

STEVENSON, Ann W (NH) 18 High St, North Berwick ME 03906 B Edinburgh Scotland GB 1/26/1948 d Ivar P Wevling & Ann. BA Champlain Coll 1967; MDiv Louisville Presb TS 1987; GTS 1990. D 6/3/1990 P 5/1/1991 Bp David Reed. m 1/1/1995 Wendel William Meyer c 2. Min Emm Chap Manchester MA 2003-2009; Pstr Affiliate S Jn's Ch Beverly Farms MA 2003-2008; Assoc R S Jn's Ch Portsmouth NH 2000-2003; Assoc R of Pstr Care Trin Ch In The City Of Boston Boston MA 1997-2000; Sr Assoc Ch Of The Redeem Bryn Mawr PA 1991-1997; D S Phil's Ch Garrison NY 1990-1991. SCHC (ME), Chapl 2002. awstevenson10@hotmail.com

STEVENSON, Carolyn Eve (NH) 231 Main St, Salem NH 03079 **COM Dio New Hampshire Concord NH 2009-; Cler Dvlpmt Dio New Hampshire Concord NH 2007-; Cnvnr of Sthrn Convoc Dio New Hampshire Concord NH 2007-; R S Dav's Ch Salem NH 2005-** B Youngstown OH 5/8/1954 d James Stewart Stevenson & Joan Marie. BS Kent St U 1976; MDiv Ya Berk 1987. D 2/14/1987 Bp Arthur Edward Walmsley P 12/22/2001 Bp Douglas Edwin Theuner. Asst S Matt's Ch Goffstown NH 2001-2004; Asst S Mk's Ch Mystic CT 1987. Tertiary Of The Soc Of S Fran 1992. cspaddler@myfairpoint.net

STEVENSON, E(dward) Mark (La) PO Box 5026, Baton Rouge LA 70821 **Cn to the Ordnry Dio Louisiana Baton Rouge LA 2005-** B Savannah GA 9/15/1964 s Philip John Stevenson & Helen. BS U IL 1986; MDiv Nash 2000. D 12/29/1999 P 8/5/2000 Bp Charles Edward Jenkins III. m 1/14/1995 Joyce O Owen. Ch Of The Gd Shpd Maitland FL 2004-2005; R The Ch Of The Annunc New Orleans LA 2000-2004. mstevenson@edola.org

STEVENSON, Frank Beaumont (SO) School Lane, Stanton Saint John, Oxford OX33 1ET Great Britain (UK) B Cincinnati OH 8/5/1939 s Howard Newell Stevenson & Laura Lindsay. BA Duke 1961; BD EDS 1964. D 6/13/1964 P 12/1/1964 Bp Roger W Blanchard. Ch Of S Edw Columbus OH 1970-2009; Epis Ch Cntr New York NY 1966-1968; Ch Of S Edw Columbus OH 1964-1966. Auth, "Dementia & Rel," *Degenerative Neurological Disease in the Elderly*; Auth, "An Application of Grp Analytic Principals in Pstr Trng for Cler," *Groeps Psychol*. Hon Cn Chr Ch Cathd, Oxford Oxford Engl 1998. beaumont.stevenson@bt.internet.com

STEVENSON, Frederic George (CPa) 890 Mccosh St, Hanover PA 17331 B Bethlehem PA 6/30/1947 s Dean T Stevenson & Doris. BA Leh 1969; MDiv PDS 1972. D 5/27/1972 P 2/1/1973 Bp Dean T Stevenson. m 8/22/1970 Mary Elizabeth c 1. Dio Cntrl Pennsylvania Harrisburg PA 2008-2010; Assoc S Andr's Epis Ch York PA 1998-2009; The Epis Ch Of S Jn The Bapt York PA 1974-1997; R All SS Ch Hanover PA 1974-1994.

STEVENSON, James Paul (Be) 11 Luzerne Ave, West Pittston PA 18643 B Bethlehem PA 9/14/1943 s Dean T Stevenson & Doris M. BA Leh 1965; MDiv GTS 1968; MS Marywood U 1982. D 5/29/1968 Bp Dean T Stevenson P 5/1/1969 Bp Frederick J Warnecke. m 7/14/1972 Judy M Moss c 1. Trin Epis Ch W Pittston PA 1988-2000; H Cross Epis Ch Wilkes Barre PA 1974-1988; Asst S Steph's Epis Ch Wilkes Barre PA 1968-1970. JPSTEVENSONWP@GMAIL.COM

STEVENSON, Janis Jordan (Mich) 430 Nicolet St, Walled Lake MI 48390 **S Anne's Epis Ch Walled Lake MI 2011-** B Sebring FL 7/2/1934 d Harold Erwin Jordan & Leona. D 11/3/2010 P 6/21/2011 Bp Wendell Nathaniel Gibbs Jr. c 3. jjstevenson34@comcast.net

STEVENSON JR, Phillip Marion (WTex) 1100 Grand Blvd., Apt 227, Boerne TX 78006 B Groveton TX 1/28/1928 s Phillip Marion Stevenson & Alma Dorman. BA U of Texas 1949; JD U of Texas 1952; MDiv CDSP 1968. D 6/23/1968 Bp J Milton Richardson P 5/1/1969 Bp Frederick P Goddard. m 8/5/1950 Evelyn James c 2. Chair- Resolutns Dio W Texas San Antonio TX 2006-2009; S Bon Ch Comfort TX 1995-1999; BEC Dio W Texas San Antonio TX 1990-1993; BEC Dio W Texas San Antonio TX 1979-1988; S Andr's Epis Ch San Antonio TX 1970-1995; Vic S Chris's Ch Killeen TX 1968-1969. stevensonphillip@gmail.com

STEVENSON, R(ichard) Hugh (NCal) Po Box 247, Kenwood CA 95452 **R S Patricks Ch Kenwood CA 1991-** B London UK 11/1/1945 s Arthur John Stevenson & Olivia Diana. BA U of Exeter GB 1968; Westcott Hse Cambridge 1970; DMin Bex 1984. Trans from Church Of England 10/1/1980 as Priest Bp Robert Rae Spears Jr. m 11/18/1972 Angela Bea Hunt c 2. Dist Dn

Dio Nthrn California Sacramento CA 1998-1999; COM Dio Rochester Rochester NY 1985-1991; R S Lk's Ch Fairport NY 1981-1991. info@stpatskenwood.org

STEVENSON, Robert Murrell (NY) 405 Hilgard Avenue, Los Angeles CA 90024 B Melrose NM 7/3/1916 s Robert Emory Stevenson & Ada. PhD U Roch 1942; STB Harvard DS 1943; ThM PrTS 1949; BLitt Oxf 1954; DMus CUA 1991; LHD IL Wesl 1992; DLitt Universidade Nova De Lisboa Lisbon Pt 1993. D 6/12/1949 Bp Charles K Gilbert P 12/1/1949 Bp Robert E Campbell. Asst S Alb's Epis Ch Los Angeles CA 1950-1951; Asst S Jas' Par So Pasadena CA 1949-1950. Auth, "24 Books, Titles In Who'S Who In The Wrld," *Who'S Who In Amer*, 1952. 5 Other Profsnl Societies; Amer Musicological Soc 1950; Hon Mem 2001. Who'S Who Rel; Who'S Who Wrld; Who'S Who In Amer.

STEVENSON, Thomas Edward (EO) Po Box 29, Alsea OR 97324 B Antioch CA 2/15/1940 s John S Stevenson & Marian F. BA U of Oregon 1963; MDiv GTS 1967. D 7/21/1967 P 2/13/1968 Bp William J Gordon Jr. m 4/4/1964 Gwendolyn Frances Walls c 2. R S Matt's Epis Ch Ontario OR 1973-1988; P-in-c Gd Shpd Huslia AK 1969-1973; Assoc R S Ptr's By-The-Sea Sitka AK 1967-1969. gwens@peak.org

STEVENS-TAYLOR, Sally Hodges (Az) PO Box 65840, Tucson AZ 85728 B Tucson AZ 10/17/1952 d Paul Arthur Hodges & Mary Louise Sawyer. BSc U of Arizona 1980. D 1/23/2010 Bp Kirk Stevan Smith. c 3. sally.stevens@gmail.com

STEVICK, Daniel Bush (Pa) 600 E Cathedral Rd Apt D203, Philadelphia PA 19128 B Elyria OH 9/17/1927 s Harlie G Stevick & Lois. BA Wheaton Coll 1950; STB Tem 1953; STM Tem 1956; U of Cambridge 1965; Fell Inst Ecuminical & Cultural Resrch 1970. D 6/13/1953 P 12/1/1953 Bp Joseph Gillespie Armstrong. c 2. EDS Cambridge MA 1974-1989; All SS Epis Ch Fallsington PA 1953-1959; Gr Epis Ch Hulmeville PA 1953-1954. Auth, "The Altar's Fire: An Intro to Chas Wesley's Hymns on the Lord's Supper," Epworth, Engl, 2005; "By Water and the Word: The Scriptures of Baptism," Ch Pub, 1997; "To Confirm or To Receive?," *Baptism and Mnstry: Liturg Stds I*, Ch Hymnal Corp., 1994; "The Crafting of Liturg: A Guide for Preparers," Ch Hymnal Corp., 1990; "A Matter of Taste: 1 Ptr 2:3," *Revs for Rel, Vol. 47, No.4.*, 1988; "Baptismal Moments: Baptismal Meanings," Ch Hymnal Corp., 1987; "The Sprtlty of BCP," *Angl Sprtlty*, Morehouse-Barlow, 1982; "Lang in Wrshp: Reflections on a Crisis," Seabury Press, 1970; "Civil Disobedience and the Chr," Seabury Press, 1965; "Cn Law: A Handbook," Seabury Press, 1965; "Beyond Fundamentalism," Jn Knox Press, 1964. Pres No Amer Acad of Liturg 1976; STD Gnrl Sem, NY 1971; Mem Drafting Com on Chr Initiation SLC 1970. danstevick203@aol.com

STEWART, Barbara Rindge (Los) 183 E Bay St, Costa Mesa CA 92627 **R S Jn The Div Epis Ch Costa Mesa CA 2001-** B Berkeley CA 8/23/1946 d Frederick Hastings Rindge & Phyllis Jane. BA U CA 1968; PhD U CA 1973; MDiv ETSBH 1992. D 6/13/1992 Bp Chester Lovelle Talton P 1/9/1993 Bp Frederick Houk Borsch. c 2. P-in-c S Jn The Div Epis Ch Costa Mesa CA 2001-2002; Assoc S Fran' Par Palos Verdes Estates CA 1995-2001; Asst S Aug By-The-Sea Par Santa Monica CA 1992-1995. bstewart@stjohncm.org

STEWART, Caroline Rinehart (Md) 4024 Stewart Rd, Stevenson MD 21153 B Charlottesville VA 3/11/1948 Post Grad. Dplma In Angl Stds V.T.S.; BA Converse Coll 1970; Med U of Virginia 1971; MA Loyola Coll 2002. D 6/24/2006 Bp John Leslie Rabb P 1/6/2007 Bp Robert Wilkes Ihloff. m 10/20/1973 William Stewart c 2. S Jn's Ch Reisterstown MD 2010; The Ch Of The Redeem Baltimore MD 2009-2010; Asst R S Andr's Epis Ch Glenwood MD 2006-2008. carolinestewart@comcast.net

STEWART, Carol Wendt (Roch) 3074 O'Donnell Rd, Wellsville NY 14895 B 2/13/1949 BS Clarkson Coll of Tech 1971; MSEd Canisius Coll 1985. D 2/14/2009 P 10/10/2009 Bp Prince Grenville Singh. m 12/19/1970 Gilbert Stewart. stewarcw@alfredstate.edu

STEWART JR, Claude York (WNC) 409-D Cane Creek Rd, Sylva NC 28779 **Int S Agnes Epis Ch Franklin NC 2002-** B Knoxville TN 7/19/1940 s Claude York Stewart & Anne Mae. BS Carson-Newman Coll 1962; STB Harvard DS 1966; ThD Harvard DS 1980; CAS GTS 1987. D 7/11/1987 P 1/1/1988 Bp William Gillette Weinhauer. m 7/3/1961 Elinor Christine Dowis c 2. S Alb's Epis Ch Hixson TN 2007-2008; S Fran' Ch Norris TN 2005-2006; Ch Of The Mssh Murphy NC 2004-2005; Epis Ch Of The H Sprt Mars Hill NC 2002; Ch Of The Mssh Murphy NC 2000-2001; S Jn's Epis Ch Marion NC 1999-2000; Epis Ch Of S Ptr's By The Lake Denver NC 1991-1995; S Jn's Ch Sylva NC 1988-1998; Cur Ch Of The H Cross Tryon NC 1987. AAR, Centr For Ethics & Soc Plcy. ZORAKSSHACK@AOL.COM

STEWART, Clifford Thomas (Ore) Po Box 447, Lake Oswego OR 97034 B Edmonton AB CA 6/30/1920 s Clifford Mills Stewart & Florence Henrieta. BA Willamette U 1947; Cntr for Diac Mnstry 1989. D 7/18/1989 Bp Hal Raymond Gross. m 9/14/1963 Eleanor Mae Turk c 2. D Chr Ch Par Lake Oswego OR 1999-2000; D S Fran Of Assisi Epis Wilsonville OR 1989-1998. NAAD. Gave Opening Pryr On 10/4/1994 Untd States Senate 1994.

STEWART, Daniel R (Oly) 322 Aoloa St Apt 1101, Kailua HI 96734 B Seattle WA 12/29/1943 s Daniel Robert Stewart & Margaret Elizabeth. BA U of Washington 1965; STB ATC 1969; MA Salve Regina U 1988; MA U of Hawaii 1995. D 8/6/1969 P 5/16/1970 Bp Ivol I Curtis. m 4/29/1967 Maryanne J Hayes. S Alb's Chap Honolulu HI 1988-2008; Off Of Bsh For ArmdF New York NY 1980-1988; Assoc S Lk's Epis Ch Seattle WA 1969-1980. Auth, "S Andr'S Cross". stewartd002@gmail.com

STEWART, Duke Summerlin (Ga) 701 Gaskin Ave N, Douglas GA 31533 B Columbus GA 10/30/1955 s Jack Stewart & Virginia. Emory U 1975; BS U GA 1977; MDiv Sthrn Sem 1980; CAS VTS 1998. D 7/1/1998 P 1/9/1999 Bp Henry Irving Louttit. c 3. Pstr S Andr's Epis Ch Douglas GA 1998-2002. dsstewart@alltel.net

STEWART, Jane Louise (Ia) 912 20th Ave., Coralville IA 52241 B Searcy AR 12/13/1956 d Robert Jean Stewart & Louise Wade. BA Rhodes Coll 1979; MDiv UTS Richmond VA 1982. D 7/26/2009 Bp Alan Scarfe. m 6/5/2009 Linda Kroon c 2. jane.stewart@mchsi.com

STEWART, Jeanne Leinbach (Chi) 1105 Princeton Pl, Wilmette IL 60091 **Chr Ch Winnetka IL 2007-** B Hartford CT 11/9/1960 d Russell Leinbach & Jacqueline. BA Mt Holyoke Coll 1982; MBA Cor 1986; MDiv SWTS 2007. D 6/2/2007 Bp William Dailey Persell P 12/15/2007 Bp Victor Alfonso Scantlebury. m 8/9/1986 Scott Stewart c 2. jeanne@christchurchwinnetka.org

STEWART, J(ohn) Bruce (Va) 4327 Ravensworth Rd Apt 210, Annandale VA 22003 **Goodwin Hse Incorporated Alexandria VA 2007-; Com on Mnstrs in Higher Educ Dio Virginia Richmond VA 1994-; Cntr For Liturg And The Arts Annandale VA 1981-** B Schenectady NY 10/23/1951 s James Arthur Stewart & Rose Kathryn. BA Hobart and Wm Smith Colleges 1973; MDiv VTS 1978. D 6/10/1978 Bp John Shelby Spong P 6/22/1979 Bp Robert Bruce Hall. Encounter Mus & Sprtl Dir Dio Sthrn Virginia Norfolk VA 1982-2000; Encounter Mus & Sprtl Dir Dio SW Virginia Roanoke VA 1982-2000; Liturg Cmsn Dio Virginia Richmond VA 1982-1987; Cur S Alb's Epis Ch Annandale VA 1978-1980. "Hope for the Future," 2005; "Living the Image," 1983; "Never Give Up," 1981. ADLMC; CE Ntwk; EPF; OHC CCL. bstewart@goodwinhouse.org

STEWART, Kevin P. (Mil) 4722 N 104th St, Wauwatosa WI 53225 **D Trin Ch Wauwatosa WI 2007-** B Akron OH 3/2/1957 s Paul Stewart & Betty. D 6/2/2007 Bp Steven Andrew Miller. m 7/6/1991 Melanie Stewart. Ord of Julian of Norwich 2009. kevinstewart@wi.rr.com

STEWART, Matthew Wellington (Mass) 11 W. Grove St., Middleboro MA 02346 **Ch of the H Sprt Fall River MA 2008-** B Boston MA 3/1/1974 D 6/4/2005 P 1/7/2006 Bp M(arvil) Thomas Shaw III. m 9/14/2005 Natasha Staatz c 1. Ch Of The Ascen Fall River MA 2008; S Steph's Memi Ch Lynn MA 2005-2008. matt.hsfr@verizon.net

STEWART, Natalie Ann (ECR) PO Box 515, Aromas CA 95004 B Carmel CA 4/12/1945 d Hampton Smith Stewart & Margaret Natalie. BA USC 1967; BTS Sch for Deacons 1995. D 6/11/1996 Bp Richard Lester Shimpfky. D All SS Ch Carmel CA 1998-2005; D S Mths Ch Seaside CA 1996-1998. nataliestewart@earthlink.net

STEWART, Natasha (Mass) 407 Rochester St, Fall River MA 02720 **R Trin Ch Bridgewater MA 2011-** B Milwaukee WI 12/11/1978 d William Dumont Staatz & Christina Gisela. BA U NC 2001; MDiv GTS 2005. D 5/28/2005 Bp Granville Porter Taylor P 1/7/2006 Bp Roy Frederick Cederholm Jr. m 9/14/2005 Matthew Wellington Stewart c 1. P-in-c Trin Ch Bridgewater MA 2008-2011; Asst R Par Of The Epiph Winchester MA 2006-2008; Asst for Chld, Yth and Families S Mich's Ch Marblehead MA 2005-2006. trinitypriest@gmail.com

STEWART, Ralph Roderick (Oly) 23 Turtle Rock Ct, New Paltz NY 12561 B Huron SD 1/9/1933 s Clarence Roland Stewart & Julia Etta. BA Carleton Coll 1954; STB GTS 1957; STM SWTS 1962. D 6/19/1957 P 12/21/1957 Bp Conrad Gesner. c 3. Dioc Counc Dio Olympia Seattle WA 1995-1998; Chapl Loc Chapt Integrity Dio Olympia Seattle WA 1987-1988; Cathd Chapt Dio Olympia Seattle WA 1986-1989; Ex Chapt Dio Olympia Seattle WA 1985-1988; Ecum Com on Bp Dio Olympia Seattle WA 1984-1986; Bd Cler Assn Dio Olympia Seattle WA 1983-1986; Bd Dir TS Dio Olympia Seattle WA 1981-1987; Archit Com Dio Olympia Seattle WA 1981-1986; Bp Com CE Dio Olympia Seattle WA 1981-1984; R S Jn The Bapt Epis Ch Seattle WA 1980-1995; ExCoun Dio Fond du Lac Appleton WI 1973-1974; R All SS Epis Ch Appleton WI 1970-1980; Chair Com Ch Mus Dio Milwaukee Milwaukee WI 1963-1970; P-in-c S Fran Ch Menomonee Falls WI 1962-1970; Assoc S Lk's Ch Evanston IL 1961-1962; Asst Cathd Of S Jas Chicago IL 1960-1962; Vic H Trin Epis Ch Peoria IL 1957-1960; Vic S Mary's Epis Ch Roslyn SD 1957-1960. Auth, "A Christological Experiment," *The Amer Ch Quarterly*, 1963.

STEWART JR, William Owen (Ga) PO Box 1171, Leesburg GA 31763 **The Epis Ch Of S Jn And S Mk Albany GA 2009-; Assoc Chr Epis Ch Cordele GA 2003-** B Americus GA 6/11/1948 s William Owen Stewart & Patsy Elizabeth Dodge. Florida St U; U Of The So Sch Of Theo Sewanee; BA Valdosta St U 1995. D 11/29/2001 P 6/29/2004 Bp Henry Irving Louttit. m 7/16/1976 Ann

Costello c 3. Int The Epis Ch Of The Annunc Vidalia GA 2008-2009; S Steph's Lee Cnty Leesburg GA 2005-2007. stew6637@bellsouth.net

STEWART-SICKING, Joseph (Md) 6196 Little Valley Way, Alexandria VA 22310 **Adj Fac VTS Alexandria VA 2003-** B Cincinnati OH 9/5/1973 s James Sicking & Angela. BS Xavier U 1995; EdD U Cinc 2002; CAS VTS 2003; MTS VTS 2008. D 6/23/2007 Bp Kenneth Lester Price P 6/28/2008 Bp Thomas Edward Breidenthal. m 5/10/1997 Megan Elizabeth Stewart c 1. Auth, "Joy that is complete," *All shall be well: Stories from CREDO*, Ch, 2009; Auth, "Resrch Methodology," *Chrsnty for the rest of us: How the Nbrhd Ch is revitalizing the faith*, HarperOne, 2006. jastewartsicking@loyola.edu

STEWART-SICKING, Megan Elizabeth (Md) 6196 Little Valley Way, Alexandria VA 22310 **Imm Epis Ch Glencoe MD 2010-** B Cincinnati OH 10/22/1975 BA Xavier U 1998; MDiv VTS 2003. D 10/26/2002 P 6/21/2003 Bp Herbert Thompson Jr. m 5/10/1997 Joseph Sicking c 1. Assoc R Ch Of The Gd Shpd Burke VA 2004-2009; Asst R Trin Ch Columbus OH 2003-2004; Dir of Yth Mnstrs Dio Sthrn Ohio Cincinnati OH 1998-2000. revmegss@gmail.com

STEWMAN, Kerry J (O) Po Box 366274, Bonita Springs FL 34136 B Springfield OH 5/9/1948 d Joe Dan Stewman & Martha Joan. U of Memphis 1969; BA Middle Tennessee St U 1981; MDiv Ya Berk 1988. D 6/1/1988 Bp Robert Poland Atkinson P 6/1/1989 Bp William Franklin Carr. m 11/26/1982 Zev William David Rosenberg c 3. New Life Epis Ch Uniontown OH 1995-1997; S Ptr's Ch Akron OH 1992-1995; Asst Ch Of The Gd Shpd Dallas TX 1990-1991; Cur S Jn's Epis Ch Charleston WV 1988-1989. KMoStew@aol.com

ST GEORGE, David (Nwk) 8 Binney Rd, Old Lyme CT 06371 B Montclair NJ 6/23/1925 s Lee E St St George & Pattie Watkins. DMin Drew U; BA U of Pennsylvania 1952; BD EDS 1955; Fllshp Coll of Preachers 1960; STM PrTS 1968. D 7/1/1955 Bp Benjamin M Washburn P 2/1/1956 Bp Lane W Barton. m 6/5/1954 Judith Alexander c 4. Supply Dio Connecticut Hartford CT 1994-2003; Int S Jas Ch Upper Montclair NJ 1993-1994; Int S Geo's Epis Ch Maplewood NJ 1992-1993; Int Chr Ch Short Hills NJ 1991-1992; R S Ptr's Ch Essex Fells NJ 1971-1990; R All SS Ch Millington NJ 1964-1971; P-in-c S Simon By-The-Sea Mantoloking NJ 1958-1978; Asst Chr Ch Short Hills NJ 1958-1964; P-in-c Ch of Our Sav Sum Lake OR 1955-1958; R S Lk's Ch Lakeview OR 1955-1958. Auth, "Pulpit Dig". st.george8@comcast.net

ST GERMAIN, Beverly Anne Lavallee (Vt) Three Cathedral Square 3A, Burlington VT 05401 B Burlington VT 9/21/1933 d Romeo Napolean Lavallee & Eva Marie. D 9/21/1988 Bp Daniel Lee Swenson. m 3/17/1952 Kenneth Paul St Germain c 1. D Cathd Ch Of S Paul Burlington VT 1988-1998.

ST GERMAIN JR, Kenneth Paul (SO) 2151 Dorset Rd, Columbus OH 43221 **S Mk's Epis Ch Columbus OH 2007-** B Burlington VT 3/17/1965 s Kenneth Paul St Germain & Beverly Anne Lavallee. BA U of Vermont 1987; MDiv Yale DS 1990. D 8/24/1990 Bp Daniel Lee Swenson P 6/21/1991 Bp John H(enry) Smith. Assoc R S Geo's Epis Ch Dayton OH 1993-2007; Cur S Jn's Ch Huntington WV 1990-1993. Wilcott Calkins Prchng Awd. rector@saintmarkscolumbus.org

ST GERMAIN-ILER III, Rob B (Ala) 283 Sutton Rd Se, Owens Cross Roads AL 35763 **R S Columba-In-The-Cove Owens Cross Roads AL 2006-** B Glendale CA 6/8/1957 s Robert St Germain-Iler & Lorraine. AA Snead St Coll 2001; BA Athens St U 2003; MDiv TS 2006. D 5/24/2006 Bp Marc Handley Andrus P 12/12/2006 Bp Henry Nutt Parsley Jr. m 11/30/2009 Elizabeth A St Germain-Iler c 3. eagleeyeler@yahoo.com

STICHWEH, Michael Terry (CFla) 410 Meridian Street, Apt 604, Indianapolis IN 46204 B Dayton OH 5/21/1940 s Carl Frederick Stichweh & Catherine Doris. BD EDS; BS Mia 1962. D 6/4/1966 P 12/17/1966 Bp Horace W B Donegan. S Mths Epis Ch Clermont FL 1996-1997; S Mary Of The Ang Epis Ch Orlando FL 1995-1996; R S Gabr's Ch Hollis NY 1973-1995; The Woodhull Schools Hollis NY 1973-1995; Asst Min Ch Of The Incarn New York NY 1966-1972. Phi Beta Kappa. sturdevant@mindspring.com

STICKLEY, David Charles (Cal) 101 Gold Mine Dr, San Francisco CA 94131 **Ch Of The H Innoc San Francisco CA 2009-; D S Aid's Ch San Francisco CA 2009-** B Binghamton, NY 6/29/1963 s Karl B Stickley & Jean C. BS Ithaca Coll 1985; Bachelor of Diac Stds Sch for Deacons 2005. D 6/6/2009 Bp Marc Handley Andrus. stickley_david@gmail.com

STICKNEY, Jane Burr (Ct) 14 Lone Pine Trl, Higganum CT 06441 B Bridgeport CT 2/5/1947 d Horace F Shipman & Rita Corsa. BA Drew U 1968; Cert Moray Hse Coll Of Educ Edinburgh Gb 1969; Med Andover Newton TS 1971; STM GTS 1987. D 6/13/1987 P 11/17/1987 Bp Arthur Edward Walmsley. m 5/23/1970 David Stickney. Vic S Jn's Ch Guilford CT 1997-2009; Ch Of The H Trin Middletown CT 1987-1996; Middlesex Area Cluster Mnstry Higganum CT 1987-1989. JBSTICKNEY@JUNO.COM

STICKNEY, Jim (Cal) 1324 Devonshire Ct, El Cerrito CA 94530 B San Francisco CA 12/1/1945 s Robert Floyd Stickney & Mary Jane. BA Gonzaga U 1969; MDiv Jesuit TS 1975; STM Jesuit TS 1976. Rec from Roman Catholic 10/1/1982 as Priest Bp William Edwin Swing. m 10/4/1997 Joni Jennings. P-in-c S Paul's Epis Ch Modesto CA 2009-2011; P-in-c S Paul's Epis Ch Modesto CA 2009-2010; Int Ch Of H Fam Fresno CA 2008-2009; Int Epis Ch Of The Sav Hanford CA 2008; Dioc Coun Dio California San Francisco CA 1999-2003; R S Alb's Ch Albany CA 1986-2006; Asst S Mk's Epis Ch Palo Alto CA 1984-1986; Asst Gd Shpd Epis Ch Belmont CA 1982-1984. Auth, "Splitting Your Dio: Can You Afford It?," *LivCh*, LivCh, 2008; Auth, "A Hist of Camp Galilee, Nevada: 1920 - 2000," Camp Galilee Fndt, 2001. jimstickney@mac.com

STICKNEY, Joyce Erwin (Los) 28211 Pacific Coast Hwy, Malibu CA 90265 **R S Aid's Epis Ch Malibu CA 2005-** B Boston MA 4/16/1970 d Robert Erwin Stickney & Nanette Jacquelyn. BA Ob 1992; MDiv Fuller TS 1995; CAS CDSP 1998. D 6/6/1998 Bp Chester Lovelle Talton P 9/9/1999 Bp Frederick Houk Borsch. m 12/31/1994 Calvin Gregory Prakasim c 2. Assoc S Aug By-The-Sea Par Santa Monica CA 2000-2005; Assoc S Edm's Par San Marino CA 1998-2000; Assoc For Yth And Fam Mnstrs S Geo's Par La Can CA 1992-1995. joyce@staidanschurch.org

STIEFEL, Jennifer Haynes (NH) 54 Silver St, Dover NH 03820 B Boston MA 7/18/1944 d Kilby Page Smith & Elizabeth. BA Rad 1966; MDiv Nash 1978; MA UTS 1993; PhD UTS 2000. D 5/29/1985 Bp William Carl Frey. m 12/6/1969 Robert Earl Stiefel. Dioc Coun Dio New Hampshire Concord NH 1994-1995; D Chr Ch Portsmouth NH 1991-2002; COM Dio Colorado Denver CO 1981-1987; Dir Epis Inst Dio Colorado Denver CO 1980-1987. Auth, "Wmn Deacons in 1 Tim: a Linguistic & Literary look at 'Wmn likewise' (1 Tim 3:11)," *NT Stds Volume 41*, 1995. AAR 1992-2002; NAACP 1993; No Amer Assn for Diac 1985; SBL 1988-2002. Rel Schlr SBL 1996; Fellowowship ECF 1987. jhstiefel@aol.com

STIEFEL, Robert Earl (NH) 54 Silver Street, Dover NH 03820 **Ret; Supply P. Dio New Hampshire Concord NH 2002-** B Baltimore MD 6/21/1941 s Earl Robert Stiefel & Gertrude Rea. BA Ob 1963; PhD Harv 1970; MDiv Nash 1978. D 6/17/1978 Bp Lyman Cunningham Ogilby P 2/26/1979 Bp William Carl Frey. m 12/6/1969 Jennifer Haynes Stiefel. Chair, Cler Cont Educ Comm. Dio New Hampshire Concord NH 1998-2002; Del, GC Dio New Hampshire Concord NH 1994-1997; R Chr Ch Portsmouth NH 1991-2001; R Trin Ch Asbury Pk NJ 1988-1991; R The Ch Of Chr The King (Epis) Arvada CO 1980-1988; Asst to Bp Dio Colorado Denver CO 1978-1980. Auth, "At the Loss of a Pet of Other Animal: A Serv of Grieving and Thanksgiving," *nhepiscopal.org*, 1997; Auth, "Preaching to All the People," *ATR*, 1991; Auth, "Transfiguraton and Transformation in Dante's Div Comedy," *Nashotah Revs*, 1976; Auth, "Heine's Ballet Scenarios," *Germanic Revs*, 1969. Amer Assn for Psychol Type 1984-2001; AAPC 1985-2011; Integrity, USA 1994; OSB - Confrator 1963-1984; OSB - Life Oblate 1984. Awd for Racial and Rel Harmony B'nai B'rith and Temple Israel, Portsmouth, NH 2000; Fell Coll of Preachers 1986. renstiefel@aol.com

STIEGLER, Mark Ashton (Roch) 3835 Oneill Rd, Lima NY 14485 **R Zion Ch Avon NY 2003-** B Flushing NY 2/26/1941 s George Ebdon Exley-Stiegler & Edna Marie. BFA SUNY 1966; MDiv Bex 2002. D 6/1/2002 P 3/22/2003 Bp Jack Marston McKelvey. m 9/19/2002 Shirley Chelton Cordell c 2. Dio Rochester Rochester NY 2002-2003; Cur Gr Ch Lyons NY 2002-2003.

STIEPER, John Richard (Chi) 7 Fernwood Dr, Barrington IL 60010 B Chicago IL 1/21/1935 s Elmer George Stieper & Margaret. BA DePauw U 1957; Cert U of Montpelier Montpelier FR 1958; MDiv Ya Berk 1961. D 10/20/1961 Bp Gerald Francis Burrill P 4/1/1962 Bp Charles L Street. c 2. Dioc Coun Dio Chicago Chicago IL 1979-1984; R Ch Of S Columba Of Iona Hanover Pk IL 1964-2000; Admin. Dir S Leonards Oratory Chicago IL 1963-1964; Cur Ch Of S Paul And The Redeem Chicago IL 1961-1963. SSC 1972. john@stieper.net

STIESS, Edward William (Mass) 9 Rexford St, Norwich NY 13815 B Philadelphia PA 11/28/1924 s Ernest William Stiess & Margaret Florence. BA Tem 1950; STB Tem 1952; CAS Harv 1980. D 10/15/1953 P 4/15/1954 Bp Angus Dun. m 8/5/1950 Ruth H Hampp c 4. Prof EDS Cambridge MA 1974-1987; Archd Dio Bethlehem Bethlehem PA 1967-1970; DCE Dio Bethlehem Bethlehem PA 1961-1966; Assoc Gr Epis Ch Silver Sprg MD 1956-1961; D-in-c /R All Faith Epis Ch Charlotte Hall MD 1953-1956. DD Berkeley TS 1968. ewstiess@frontiernet.net

STILES, Katherine Mitchell (Me) 74 Lexington Ave, Cambridge MA 02138 B Salem MA 2/4/1952 D 6/14/2003 P 12/20/2003 Bp Chilton Abbie Richardson Knudsen. c 1.

STILES, Susan (RI) Peace Dale Estates, 1223 Saugatucket Rd Apt A102, Peace Dale RI 02879 B Chicago IL 4/10/1940 d Arthur Simon Randak & Mary Frances. Salem Coll Winston Salem NC 1960; Providence Coll 1988; MDiv Andover Newton TS 1992. D 1/27/1996 Bp Morgan Porteus P 5/24/1997 Bp Geralyn Wolf. c 1. Int Ch Of The Ascen Wakefield RI 2009-2010; Int Vic Ch Of The H Sprt Charlestown RI 2005-2008; Int Emm Epis Ch Cumberland RI 2003-2005; P-in-c Chr Epis Ch Tarrytown NY 2001-2003; Ch Of The Ascen Wakefield RI 2000-2009; Int S Thos Ch Hanover NH 2000-2001; Int Ch Of The H Sprt Plymouth NH 1999-2000; Int S Jn The Evang Yalesville CT 1998-1999; Int S Mart's Ch Providence RI 1997-1998; Ch Of The H Sprt Charlestown RI 1996-1997; D S Jn The Div Ch Saunderstown RI 1996-1997; S Paul's Ch No Kingstown RI 1996. sstiles222@aol.com

STILL, Kimberly L (Fla) 919 San Fernando St, Fernandina Beach FL 32034 **S Marg's-Hibernia Epis Ch Fleming Island FL 2009-** B Springfield IL 4/22/1960 d James S Stilwell & Rosita A. BD OR SU 1985; MBA Loyola Coll 1995; MDiv U So 2007. D 5/27/2007 P 12/9/2007 Bp Samuel Johnson Howard. S Ptr's Ch Fernandina Bch FL 2007-2009. klstill@att.net

STILLINGS, Eugene Nelson (Eau) 1220 East St, Baraboo WI 53913 B London OH 11/15/1919 s Carl Raymond Stillings & Cora Louise. BS OH SU 1942; MS OH SU 1947; Cert Bex 1957. D 6/15/1957 Bp John P Craine P 12/21/1957 Bp Richard Ainslie Kirchhoffer. c 4. Int Dio Eau Claire Eau Claire WI 1984-2002; Int Dio Fond du Lac Appleton WI 1984-2002; Int Dio Milwaukee Milwaukee WI 1984-2002; Cn-Mssy Dio Eau Claire Eau Claire WI 1976-1984; Cn-Mssy Our Sav's Phillips WI 1976-1984; Cn-Mssy S Kath's Ch Owen WI 1976-1984; Cn-Mssy S Marg's Pk Falls WI 1976-1984; Cn-Mssy St Marys Ch Medford WI 1976-1984; R S Jas Epis Ch Milwaukee WI 1969-1976; Assoc R Gr Ch Madison WI 1965-1969; R S Andr's Epis Ch Greencastle IN 1959-1965; Vic S Lk's Epis Ch Shelbyville IN 1957-1959.

STILLINGS, Kyle David (Tex) William Temple Center, 427 Market St, Galveston TX 77550 **The Wm Temple Fndt Galveston TX 2008-; Exec Dir Wm Temple Epis Ctr Galveston TX 2008-** B Seattle WA 3/29/1979 s David R Stillings & Donna. BA U of Washington 2001; MDiv VTS 2007. D 1/26/2008 P 12/11/2008 Bp Gregory Harold Rickel. kylestillings@gmail.com

STILLMAN, Ann Allen (CNY) 2239 Gridley Paige Rd, Deansboro NY 13328 **D Gr Epis Ch Waterville NY 2006-** B Utica NY 6/10/1931 d Albert Edward Allen & Lillian Elizabeth. BS NWU 1953; MS U of Wisconsin 1979; Bex 2005. D 10/7/2006 P 6/27/2007 Bp Gladstone Bailey Adams III. c 4. aastillman@frontiernet.net

STIMPSON, Peter K (NJ) 510 Bergen St, Lawrenceville NJ 08648 **Coordntr, Pstr Response Team Dio New Jersey Trenton NJ 2005-; P-in-c H Trin Ch Sprg Lake NJ 2005-** B White Plains NY 5/16/1946 s Charles Henry Stimpson & Ina Elizabeth. AA Mater Christi Sem Albany NY 1966; BA U S Paul Ottawa ON CA 1968; BA U of Ottawa 1968; STB U S Paul Ottawa ON CA 1971; BTh U of Ottawa 1971; ThM S Paul U Ottawa ON CA 1972; MSW SUNY 1977. Rec from Roman Catholic 6/2/1983 as Priest Bp Wilbur Emory Hogg Jr. m 8/14/2005 Laurene Orcutt. Candidate for Bp Dio New Jersey Trenton NJ 2003; Mem, Anti-Racism Cmsn Dio New Jersey Trenton NJ 2002-2008; Chair, Deputation to GC Dio New Jersey Trenton NJ 2001-2004; Pres, Stndg Com Dio New Jersey Trenton NJ 2000-2001; Chair, Deputation to GC Dio New Jersey Trenton NJ 1998-2003; Mem of Stndg Com Dio New Jersey Trenton NJ 1998-2001; Mem, Dioc Coun Dio New Jersey Trenton NJ 1994-1997; Chair of Wellness Com Dio New Jersey Trenton NJ 1993-1998; Mem, T/F of Cler Ethics Dio New Jersey Trenton NJ 1992-1993; Chair, Com on Mar and the Fam Dio Albany Albany NY 1986-1989; Dep, Deputation to GC Dio Albany Albany NY 1986-1989; Mem, Stndg Com Dio Albany Albany NY 1986-1989; All SS Ch Round Lake NY 1985-1987; Mem, Major Cathd Chapt Dio Albany Albany NY 1983-1985. Auth, "Personal Advice Column," *US 1*, 2011; Auth, "MAP TO HAPPINESS: Straightforward Advice on Everyday Issues," *Self-Help Bk*, iUniverse, 2008; Auth, "Personal Advice Column," *Town Topic*, 1996; Auth, "Personal Advice Column," *Via Media*, Dio New Jersey, 1990; Auth, "Sectarian Agencies," *Encyclopedia of Soc Wk*, 1986; Auth, "Personal Advice Column," *The Albany Epis*, Dio Albany, 1983. AAMFT 1981; Dplma Amer Bd Exams in Clincl Soc Wk 1988; Dplma NASW 1987. Soc Worker of the Year Awd SUNY Albany 1992; Bp's Awd for Distinguished Serv Dio Albany Dioc Conv 1989. pks_tcs@msn.com

STINE, Stephen Blaine (Tex) 1220 Quirby Lane, Tyler TX 75701 **D Chr Epis Ch Tyler TX 1998-** B Midland TX 3/30/1951 s Edward Vernell Stine & Katherine. BS Texas Tech U 1972; Rutgers-The St U 1980; CTh Prchr Lewis Sch of Mnstry 1985; EFM STUSo 1990; MA The U of Memphis 1996; PhD The U of Memphis 2007. D 8/24/1986 Bp Richard Mitchell Trelease Jr. m 2/4/1999 Laurie Margaret Dowell c 1. Chr Ch Memphis TN 1992-1998; D Ch of the H Apos Collierville TN 1990-1992; D Calv Ch Memphis TN 1987-1990; D Imm Epis Ch La Grange TN 1987-1990; D S Lk's Epis Ch Anth NM 1986-1987. Auth, "Hist of WHER Radio in Memphis," *Papers of W Tennessee Hist Soc*, W Tennessee Hist Soc, 2000. dowellstine@suddenlink.net

STINGLEY, Elizabeth Anne (Los) 12880 Riverview Drive, 8821 SVL Box, Victorville CA 92395 B Los Angeles CA 6/1/1938 d Harry Ernest Jones & Mary Marjorie. BS Lebanon Vlly Coll 1976; MDiv CDSP 1990. D 6/16/1990 P 1/12/1991 Bp Frederick Houk Borsch. c 2. Vic S Hilary's Epis Ch Hesperia CA 1992-2009; Assoc S Paul's Par Lancaster CA 1991-1992. estingley@verizon.net

STINSON, Marian (Ct) 84 Ledgewood Dr, Glastonbury CT 06033 **P-in-c S Lk's Ch So Glastonbury CT 2006-** B Minneapolis MN 8/20/1951 d Malcolm Beard Stinson & Loraine Thomas. BSW USC 1973; MS USC 1974; MDiv CDSP 1991. D 6/15/1991 Bp Frederick Houk Borsch P 2/16/1992 Bp William Edwin Swing. m 5/25/1991 William Hardwick c 2. St Gabr's Ch E Berlin CT 2004-2006; P-in-c Trin Epis Ch Collinsville CT 2000-2004; S Columba's Epis Mssn Big Bear Lake CA 1995-2000; S Paul's Epis Ch San Rafael CA 1993-1995; S Steph's Par Belvedere CA 1991. pictrinity@aol.com

STINSON, Richard Lyon (Pgh) Twin Chimneys, 375 Country Club Rd, Indiana PA 15701 B New York NY 4/22/1938 s Dwight Elliot Stinson & Doris Lyon. BA Hob 1960; MDiv EDS 1963; STM STUSo 1969; Cert Amer U 1974; DMin How 1976. D 6/8/1963 P 12/21/1963 Bp Leland Stark. m 12/28/1960 Anne Melanie Freudenberg c 3. Vic Ch of SS Thos and Lk Patton PA 2007-2009; Asst St Pauls Epis Ch Oaks PA 2001-2005; R Washington Meml Chap Vlly Forge PA 1992-2000; Adj Prof VTS Alexandria VA 1983; R S Jas' Epis Ch Alexandria VA 1970-1991; VTS Alexandria VA 1970-1978; R S Lk's Ch Hope NJ 1963-1966. Assoc, Cmnty of St. Jn Bapt 1965; Assoc, OHC 1965; Fllshp Contemplative Pryr 1970-2004; Intl Conf Of Police Chapl 1981; Ord S Lazarus Of Jerusalem 1984; Sub-Chapl Ord S Jn 1996. Silver Pat Henry Awd For Patriotic Serv Mltry Ord Of The Wrld Wars 1998; Brigadier Gnrl St Of Virginia 1992; Lj Mcconnel Awd For Outstanding Serv As Police Chapl Inst Of Indstrl And Commercial Mnstrs 1983; Life Saving Awd Of Merit Amer Red Cross 1969. annestinson@comcast.net

STIPE, Nickie Maxine (Ak) 280 Northern Ave Apt 10-A, Avondale Estates GA 30002 B Hereford TX 2/12/1960 d Paul Max Lee Stipe & Frances Juanita. Emory U; BS Oklahoma Panhandle St U 1983; MDiv Ya Berk 1993; STM Ya Berk 1994. D 8/24/1993 Bp Sam Byron Hulsey. AAR; SBL.

STISCIA, Alfred Ronald (CPa) 1852 Market St, Harrisburg PA 17103 B Upland PA 6/2/1942 s Alfred V Stiscia & Elizabeth D. BA Dickinson Coll 1964; STB GTS 1967. D 6/1/1967 P 12/1/1967 Bp Dean T Stevenson. R S Andr's Ch Harrisburg PA 1973-2007; Vic S Mich And All Ang Ch Middletown PA 1968-1973; Cur S Jn's Epis Ch Carlisle PA 1967-1968. RSTISCIA@GMAIL.COM

STITT, David Watson (WLa) 1904 W 4th St, Hastings NE 68901 B Hastings NE 9/25/1938 s William Detlor Stitt & Agnes Thomasina. BA/BS U of Nebraska 1960; MDiv Trin TS-Singapore SG 1985; D Missions TESM 2005. Trans 9/1/1989 as Priest Bp William Carl Frey. m 4/18/1958 Darlene G Hemphill. Epis Ch Of The H Sprt Lafayette LA 1999-2000; R Gr Epis Ch Chadron NE 1993-1999; R Epis Ch Of The Trsfg Vail CO 1989-1993. Auth, "Cov - Martoma Ch," *India - Kerala St*, 1989. meanddee@inetnebr.com

STIVERS, Donald Austin (Los) 5023 Calle Tania, Santa Barbara CA 93111 B Geneva NY 5/10/1924 s Clinton Frederick Stivers & Laura Grace. BA Hob 1948; BD SWTS 1951; S Aug's Coll Cbury GB 1967; ThM CRDS 1972. D 6/11/1951 P 12/21/1951 Bp Dudley S Stark. m 9/10/1960 Florence Tryon c 2. Vic Chr The King Epis Ch Santa Barbara CA 1983-1991; R S Chris's Epis Ch Boulder City NV 1979-1982; All SS Angl Ch Rochester NY 1953-1979; Cur S Thos Epis Ch Rochester NY 1951-1953. Henry Benjamin Whipple Schlr Seabury-Wstrn, Evanston, IL 1951; Challes Palmerston Anderson Schlr Seabury-Wstrn, Evanston, IL 1950. dfstivers@verizon.net

ST JOHN, Andrew Reginald (NY) 1 E 29th St, New York NY 10016 **R Ch Of The Trsfg New York NY 2005-** B Melbourne Australia 2/16/1944 s Reginald Arctic St John & Lillian Edith. LLB U of Melbourne 1966; Th Schol Australian Coll of Theol 1971; STM GTS 1984. Trans from Anglican Church Of Australia 2/2/2006 Bp Mark Sean Sisk. Int Ch Of The H Trin New York NY 2003-2005. DD GTS, New York 1995. andrewstjohn@yahoo.com

ST JOHNS, Ernest Keys (RG) 6057 Rye Lane SE, Grand Rapids MI 49508 **Ret Assoc S Chad's Epis Ch Albuquerque NM 2001-; Ret Assoc S Mary's Epis Ch Albuquerque NM 2001-** B Pontiac MI 1/20/1927 s Harrison Keys St Johns & Bessie. Ya Berk; GW; BA Grand Vlly St U; Wayne. D 6/28/1959 P 6/29/1960 Bp Richard S M Emrich. m 12/24/1969 Rosemary E St Johns c 2. Supply P Dio Wstrn Michigan Kalamazoo MI 1993-1997; Int Dio Wstrn Michigan Kalamazoo MI 1986-1990; R S Andr's Ch Big Rapids MI 1980-1985; Vic Ch Of The Medtr Harbert MI 1977-1980; Cur S Paul's Epis Ch S Jos MI 1962-1965; Vic S Paul's Epis Ch Elk Rapids MI 1960-1962; Cur S Tim's Ch Detroit MI 1959-1960. semper0144mc@comcast.net

ST LOUIS, J. Allison (Ct) Christ Church Cathedral, 45 Church Street, Hartford CT 06103 **VTS Alexandria VA 2010-** B Trinidad WEST INDIES 9/26/1959 d Lawrence StLouis & Ivy. BA How 1985; MS How 1988; PhD How 1991; MDiv VTS 2000. D 6/10/2000 Bp Ronald Hayward Haines P 1/13/2001 Bp Jane Hart Holmes Dixon. Vic Chr Ch Cathd Hartford CT 2005-2010; Asst to R Ch Of Our Sav Silver Sprg MD 2000-2004. Prof Nissim Levy Undergraduate Resrch Awd How 1984; Phi Beta Kappa How 1984. astlouis@cccathedral.org

ST LOUIS, Leslie (WA) 13106 Annapolis Rd, Bowie MD 20720 **H Trin Epis Ch Bowie MD 2008-** B Wiesbaden Germany 4/26/1960 d Terence St Louis & Lydia. BS U of New Mex 1985; MDiv STUSo 2004. D 5/29/2004 P 1/8/2005 Bp Charles Glenn VonRosenberg. S Paul's Ch Rochester NY 2004-2008. lstlouis@htrinity.org

ST LOUIS, Samuel (Hai) PO Box 407139, C/O Lynx Air, Fort Lauderdale FL 33340 **Dio Haiti Ft Lauderdale FL 1999-** B 10/21/1966 D.

STOCK, David Robert (Okla) 4036 Neptune Dr, Oklahoma City OK 73116 **R S Jn's Ch Oklahoma City OK 2005-** B Logan UT 10/9/1964 s Reed Clark Stock & Janet Velois. BS Utah St U 1988; MDiv CDSP 2000. D 6/1/2000 P 1/25/2001 Bp Carolyn Tanner Irish. m 11/10/2001 Emily Jessica Schnabl. Asst S Ptr's Epis Ch St Louis MO 2000-2005. dstock@st-john.k12.ok.us

S

STOCKARD, Matthew Easter (EC) Po Box 1336, Kinston NC 28503 **Cn Ordnry Dio E Carolina Kinston NC 2000-** B Greensboro NC 4/9/1955 s Ben Bryan Stockard & Elizabeth Campbell. BA U NC 1977; MA U NC 1980; MDiv STUSo 1986. D 12/7/1986 Bp Robert Whitridge Estill P 12/13/1987 Bp Frank Harris Vest Jr. m 2/28/1981 Lisa Pegg. R S Paul's Ch Beaufort NC 1989-1999; S Tim's Ch Wilson NC 1987-1989. mattstockard@suddenlink.net

STOCKSDALE, Robert (Ct) 183 Pin Oak Dr, Southington CT 06489 **R S Andr's Ch Meriden CT 2003-** B Jacksonville FL 12/13/1942 s William Glocker Stocksdale & Ena Loretta. PhD Arizona Pharmaceutical Assn 1986; MDiv Bex 1991. D 6/8/1991 Bp Joseph Thomas Heistand P 12/1/1991 Bp William George Burrill. m 6/14/2003 Roberta Stocksdale c 3. R Ch Of The Gd Shpd Sioux Falls SD 1998-2003; R St Mk Epis Ch No Tonawanda NY 1994-1998; Asst Ch Of The Ascen Buffalo NY 1992-1994; Dio Wstrn New York Tonawanda NY 1992-1994; Asst St Mk Epis Ch No Tonawanda NY 1991-1992. ACPE 1998; Emiss 1993. rstocksdale@cox.net

STOCKTON, James Vernon (Tex) 16306 Ascent Cove, Pflugerville TX 78660 **R Ch Of The Resurr Austin TX 2001-** B Saint Louis MO 2/25/1958 s Vernon Ferdinand Stockton & Martha Lee. BA Abilene Chr U 1992; MDiv Harvard DS 1996; CITS Epis TS of The SW 1999. D 8/28/1999 Bp Claude Edward Payne P 8/30/2000 Bp Don Adger Wimberly. m 6/26/1988 Lee Elena Mathis c 3. Asst R S Steph's Epis Ch Houston TX 1999-2001. jstockton@sbcglobal.net

STOCKTON, Marietta Grace (WK) 406 W. Kingman Ave., Lakin KS 67860 B Cherokee OK 5/30/1939 d Nora Belle Oringderff. D 11/9/2002 P 10/11/2003 Bp James Marshall Adams Jr.

STOCKWELL-TANGEMAN, Carolyn Lee (WMo) No address on file. B Elmhurst IL 7/31/1945 d Clifford Henry Stockwell & Helen Marie. U of Missouri 1968; U of Pennsylvania 1968; W Missouri Sch of Mnstry 1993. D 1/23/1993 Bp John Clark Buchanan. m 6/4/1987 John Theodore Tangeman c 1. D Gr And H Trin Cathd Kansas City MO 1993-2000.

STODDART, David Michael (Va) Church of Our Saviour, 1165 Rio Road East, Charlottesville VA 22901 **R Ch Of Our Sav Charlottesville VA 2005-** B Port Chester NY 1/8/1961 s James Stevens Stoddart & Deborah Hinde. BA Harv 1983; MDiv GTS 1989. D 7/1/1989 P 1/27/1990 Bp George Nelson Hunt III. m 6/19/1993 Lori Ann Dion c 2. R S Lk's Ch Worcester MA 1994-2005; Assoc Chr Ch Westerly RI 1989-1994. Fllshp of S Jn. dstoddart@cooschv.org

STODGHILL, Dawnell Smith (WLa) St Thomas Episcopal Church, 3706 Bon Aire Drive, Monroe LA 71203 **P in Res S Thos' Ch Monroe LA 2007-** B Butte MT 11/19/1966 d Donald Nelson Smith & Ruth Clemow. BA U of Montana 1989; MDiv CDSP 1996. D 4/28/2007 P 12/1/2007 Bp D(avid) Bruce Mac Pherson. m 1/7/1995 Thomas Whitfield Stodghill c 2. dawnells@aol.com

STODGHILL, Marion Whitbread (Ky) Norton Hospital, Chaplain, 200 E. Chesnut Street, Louisville KY 40202 **Norton Healthcare Louisville KY 2001-** B Baltimore MD 10/7/1959 d William Bailey Stodghill & Susan. BA U MI 1981; MDiv Ya Berk 1984. D 6/10/1984 P 5/1/1985 Bp David Reed. m 9/30/2000 Marion Soards c 1. Resurr Ch Louisville KY 2010; H Trin Ch Brandenburg KY 2006-2007; S Jas Ch Shelbyville KY 2005-2006; S Paul's Epis Ch New Albany IN 2005; S Andr's Ch Louisville KY 1997-2001; The Epis Par Of S Dav Minnetonka MN 1993-1996; Cathd Ch Of S Mk Minneapolis MN 1989-1990; Asst R S Pat's Ch Washington DC 1987-1989; Cur S Paul's Ch Kansas City MO 1985-1987; D-In-Res S Fran In The Fields Harrods Creek KY 1984-1985. whit.stodghill@nortonhealthcare.org

STODGHILL III, Thomas Whitfield (WLa) Po Box 65, Mer Rouge LA 71261 **S Alb's Epis Ch Monroe LA 2011-; Vic Ch Of The Redeem Oak Ridge LA 2000-; R S Andr's Epis Ch Mer Rouge LA 2000-** B Winnsboro LA 4/24/1958 s Thomas Whitfield Stodghill & Mary Evelyn. BA LSU 1982; MDiv CDSP 1996. D 6/1/1996 P 6/7/1997 Bp William Edwin Swing. m 1/7/1995 Dawnell Smith c 2. Asst S Paul's Epis Ch Walnut Creek CA 1998-2000; Asst S Paul's Epis Ch Benicia CA 1996-1998. wstodghill@aol.com

STOESSEL, Andrew James (Mass) 36 Cornell St, Roslindale MA 02131 **P-in-c S Mich's Ch Marblehead MA 2002-** B Santa Monica CA 11/29/1954 s James Huston Stuessel & Deborah Anne. BA U of Massachusetts 1980; MDiv EDS 1998. D 6/2/2001 Bp Barbara Clementine Harris P 6/8/2002 Bp M(arvil) Thomas Shaw III. m 8/30/1997 Susan Mary Wythe. Asst R S Steph's Ch Cohasset MA 2001-2002. astoessel@verizon.net

STOFFREGEN, Diana Jacobson (Spok) 5609 S Custer Street, Spokane WA 99223 B Colfax WA 3/14/1946 d Edward Eugene Jacobson & Afton Bybee. Gonzaga U; BA Estrn Washington U 1991; MDiv CDSP 1994. D 1/14/1995 P 6/4/1995 Bp Frank Jeffrey Terry. m 3/8/1969 Robert Eric Stoffregen c 3. CDSP Berkeley CA 1999-2000; Cathd Of S Jn The Evang Spokane WA 1997-1998. Angl Wrld; EWHP; Soc for Study of Chr Sprtlty. springwork@comcast.net

STOFFREGEN, Megan Amy (Spok) 5609 S Custer Rd, Spokane WA 99223 B Spokane WA 6/13/1971 d Robert Eric Stoffregen & Diana Jacobson. BA U Of Puget Sound 1993; MA Gonzaga U 1994; MDiv CDSP 1999. D 5/29/1999 Bp Leigh Wallace Jr P 12/18/1999 Bp Douglas Edwin Theuner. CDSP Berkeley CA 2002; Asst Ch Of The Gd Shpd Nashua NH 1999-2001.

STOKES JR, George Ellis (Del) 1200 Carlos Dr Apt 501, Raleigh NC 27609 **Died 6/27/2011** B Norfolk VA 7/23/1921 s George Ellis Stokes & Rosina Karcher. BA U So 1947; MDiv VTS 1950. D 6/9/1950 Bp George P Gunn P 4/15/1952 Bp Robert Fisher Gibson Jr. c 3. HSEC, NCA. Phi Beta Kappa 1947.

STOKES, William Hallock (SeFla) 4830 S, Lee Rd., Delray Beach FL 33445 **R S Paul's Ch Delray Bch FL 1999-; Cmsn on Educ Dio SE Florida Miami FL 1996-** B Manhassett NY 2/18/1957 s Richard Hallock Stokes & Jean Audrey. BA Manhattan Coll 1987; MDiv GTS 1990. D 6/22/1990 P 4/27/1991 Bp Orris George Walker Jr. m 4/3/1976 Susan Martin c 4. Assoc The Epis Ch Of Beth-By-The-Sea Palm Bch FL 1995-1998; Cur Gr Epis Ch Massapequa NY 1990-1994. Bp of Newark Preaching Prize GTS 1990; Seymour Prize Best Extemporaneous Preaching 90 GTS. chipper141@aol.com

STOLZ JR, Clarence Frederick (Tex) 1501 Inverness Dr Apt 330, Lawrence KS 66047 B Saint Louis MO 11/8/1924 s Clarence Frederick Stolz & Alice May. BA Denison U 1949; BD Epis TS of The SW 1955. D 6/18/1955 P 12/21/1955 Bp Arthur C Lichtenberger. m 6/7/1952 Jeanne Shelford c 3. Assoc S Dav's Ch Austin TX 1982-1989; Cn Gr Cathd Topeka KS 1973-1982; Ecum Relatns Com Dio Kansas Topeka KS 1965-1967; Exec Com, Prov VII Dio Kansas Topeka KS 1962-1964; R Trin Ch Atchison KS 1959-1969; Vic S Augustines Ch S Louis MO 1955-1956.

STOMSKI, William L (SeFla) 3300B S Seacrest Blvd, Boynton Beach FL 33435 **Vol P S Jos's Epis Ch Boynton Bch FL 2005-; Chapl S Jos's Epis Sch Inc. Boynton Bch FL 2005-** B Pittsfield MA 1/29/1952 s Bernard Stanley Stomski & Helen Stomski. BS Arizona St U 1974; MDiv Luth TS 1978; MA U of Notre Dame 1986; DMin VTS 2012. Rec from Evangelical Lutheran Church in America 8/15/2005 as Priest Bp Leopold Frade. stomskiw@aol.com

STONE, Carey Don (Ark) 112 Traveler Ln, Maumelle AR 72113 **R S Lk's Epis Ch No Little Rock AR 2011-; Bd Mem for The Arkansas Hse of Pryr Dio Arkansas Little Rock AR 2010-; Pres of Stndg Com Dio Arkansas Little Rock AR 2009-** B 8/26/1963 s Lero Herman Stone & Wilma Lee. BM Arkansas St U 1986; MRC Arkansas St U 1992; MDiv VTS 2005. D 12/21/2004 P 7/22/2005 Bp Larry Earl Maze. Assoc. R S Mk's Epis Ch Little Rock AR 2005-2011. Geo Herbert Soc 2003-2005; Phillips Brooks Soc 2008; Sem Hill Soc 2010. Fell of Engl Poets Many Rivers Pub 2011. stonefoundation8@gmail.com

STONE, David Lynn (HB) 940 Channing Way, Berkeley CA 94710 **non-stipendiary P Assoc All Souls Par In Berkeley Berkeley CA 2007-** B Santa Monica CA 7/4/1930 s Stanley Stone & Ruth Jeannette. BA Reed Coll Portland OR 1957; BD CDSP 1960. D 6/22/1960 P 2/1/1961 Bp James Walmsley Frederic Carman. m 1/9/1960 Carol Christopher Kelton Drake c 4. Vic S Lk's Epis Ch Idaho Falls ID 1965-1967; Vic S Lk's Ch Weiser ID 1961-1965; Asst All SS Ch Portland OR 1960-1961. dstone940@yahoo.com

STONE, Dean P (Kan) 9201 West 82nd Street, Overland Park KS 66204 B Chicago IL 1/5/1923 s George Putnam Stone & Mildred Franklin. BS California Inst of Tech 1946. D 12/19/1976 P 6/24/1977 Bp Otis Charles. m 9/1/1951 Harriet Marie Maddock c 4. Asst S Ptr's Epis Ch Kansas City MO 1986-1990; Associated P S Mich And All Ang Ch Mssn KS 1977-2008; Sac D Cathd Ch Of S Mk Salt Lake City UT 1976-1977. frdeanstone@gmail.com

STONE, Glenn (EMich) 1608 Colorado St, Marysville MI 48040 **R S Paul's Epis Ch St. Clair MI 2002-** B Toronto Ontario CA 11/20/1955 s James Harvey Stone & Jean Gertrude. BA Mt Allison U 1978; MDiv Queens U 1984. Trans from Anglican Church of Canada 12/28/2001 Bp Edwin Max Leidel Jr. Dio Estrn Michigan Saginaw MI 2006-2009. ghstone9@mac.com

STONE, John Curtis (NJ) 40-B Center St, Highlands NJ 07732 B Jacksonville FL 9/7/1938 s Pebble Curtis Stone & Mildred. BA Davidson Coll 1960; STB GTS 1963; STM GTS 1993. D 6/29/1963 P 6/29/1964 Bp Richard Henry Baker. m 6/5/1965 Mary Ruth Long c 2. Vic S Jas Ch Long Branch NJ 1998-2001; Int Ch Of The H Sprt Tuckerton NJ 1995-1998; Int Dio New Jersey Trenton NJ 1995-1998; Int S Aug's Epis Ch Asbury Pk NJ 1995-1998; Int S Mk's Epis Ch Keansburg NJ 1995-1998; S Lk's Ch Gladstone NJ 1994-1995; Vic Ch Of The Incarn W Milford NJ 1986-1992; Mineral Area Reg Coun De Soto MO 1981-1986; Com Const & Cns Dio Sthrn Virginia Norfolk VA 1976-1981; R Emm Epis Ch Chatham VA 1975-1981; R S Jn's Ch Gretna VA 1975-1981; Trin Ch Gretna VA 1975-1981; P-in-c All SS Ch Hamlet NC 1968-1972; P-in-c S Dav's Epis Ch Laurinburg NC 1968-1972; Vic All SS Epis Ch Charlotte NC 1965-1968. Auth, "Pryr In Post-Mod Theol". Intgerim Mnstrs Ntwk; RWF. jomarst1@aol.com

STONE JR, Lewis Seymour (NH) 11 Governor Sq, Peterborough NH 03458 B Danbury CT 1/6/1937 s Lewis Seymour Stone & Elaine Hurlbutt. BBA Texas Tech U 1959; STB Ya Berk 1962; DMin Bos 1988. D 6/23/1962 P 12/23/1962 Bp John S Higgins. m 4/26/1980 Eve Stone. R All SS Ch Peterborough NH 1971-2002; R S Dav's On The Hill Epis Ch Cranston RI 1964-1971; Cur All SS' Memi Ch Providence RI 1962-1964. lewevestone@myfairpoint.net

STONE, Mary Ruth (NJ) 40 - B Center St, Highlands NJ 07732 B Winston-Salem NC 1/6/1936 d Paul Bruce Long & Mary Constance. BA U NC 1958; MSW U NC 1961; MDiv GTS 1990. D 10/27/1990 Bp John Shelby Spong P 5/1/1991 Bp Jack Marston McKelvey. m 6/5/1965 John Curtis Stone c 2. Int Ch of the Gd Shpd Rahway NJ 1999-2001; Int All SS Epis Ch Lakewood NJ 1998-1999; Asst S Paul's Epis Ch Paterson NJ 1990-1991. Assn Of Profsnl Chapl; Cert Grief Ther In Assn For Death Educ &; Coll Of Chapl. marusto@comcast.net

STONE, Michael Lee (SVa) 985 Huguenot Trail, Midlothian VA 23113 **Dioc Property T/F Dio Sthrn Virginia Norfolk VA 2011-; Chair Dispatch of Bus Com Dio Sthrn Virginia Norfolk VA 2006-; R Manakin Epis Ch Midlothian VA 2004-** B Texarkana AR 11/6/1951 s Hilliard Madison Stone & Peggy Jeane. BA U of Texas 1974; AKC King's Coll, Lon 1977; MDiv Epis TS of The SW 1978. D 6/25/1978 Bp Robert Elwin Terwilliger P 6/22/1979 Bp A Donald Davies. m 5/31/1982 Virginia Ayoub c 1. Dioc Executive Bd Dio Sthrn Virginia Norfolk VA 2005-2009; Chair Compstn & Benefits Com Dio Maryland Baltimore MD 1995-2004; Sr Assoc The Ch Of The Redeem Baltimore MD 1990-2004; Assoc R S Mk's On The Mesa Epis Ch Albuquerque NM 1981-1982; Cur S Lk's Epis Ch Anth NM 1978-1980. michaelstone51@verizon.net

STONE, Sandra Elizabeth (Lex) 3416 Crooked Creek Rd, Carlisle KY 40311 B Charleston WV 12/23/1956 d Richard Arlen Stone & Evelyn Gertrude. BA Morehead St U 1978; MDiv GTS 1999. D 2/28/1999 Bp Don Adger Wimberly P 8/29/1999 Bp Edwin Funsten Gulick Jr. m 6/13/1981 Timothy Terrell Durbin c 1. Stndg Com Dio Lexington Lexington KY 2008-2011; Bdgt Com Dio Lexington Lexington KY 2006-2007; Adv Ch Cynthiana KY 2005-2010; long range Plnng Com for Dio Dio Lexington Lexington KY 2003; camps & Conf Bd (chair) Dio Lexington Lexington KY 2000-2003; Exec Coun Dio Lexington Lexington KY 2000-2003; Assoc R Ch S Mich The Archangel Lexington KY 1999-2005. sndestn@aol.com

STONE, Thomas Michael (Q) 3601 N North St, Peoria IL 61604 **Cn to the Ordnry Dio Quincy Peoria IL 2010-** B Peoria IL 8/10/1948 s Virgil Stone & Opal Faye. MDiv Luth TS 2006. D 6/14/2008 Bp Keith Lynn Ackerman P 8/21/2009 Bp John Clark Buchanan. m 8/8/1970 Penelope Jane Stone c 1. fatherstone@att.net

STONER, D Scott (Mil) 2017 E. Olive St., Milwaukee WI 53211 B Pittsburgh PA 8/22/1955 s David Stoner & Muriel Dorothy. BA U of Wisconsin 1977; MDiv SWTS 1981; DMin Chicago TS 1985. D 5/30/1981 P 12/1/1981 Bp Charles Thomas Gaskell. m 8/6/1977 Holly H Hughes c 3. R S Chris's Ch River Hills WI 2001-2008; Int Zion Epis Ch Oconomowoc WI 2000-2001; Int Chr Ch Whitefish Bay WI 2000; Int S Chris's Ch River Hills WI 2000; Int S Mk's Ch Milwaukee WI 1998-1999; Int Trin Ch Wauwatosa WI 1997-1998; Asst S Matt's Ch Evanston IL 1981-1983. Creator, "Living Compass Faith & Wellness Prog," *Faith & Wellness*, Living Compass Mnstry, 2010. Amer. Assoc. Mar & Fam Ther 2008; AAPC 1985. dscottstoner@mac.com

STONER, Suzanne (Ark) 830 N Park Ave, Fayetteville AR 72701 **Cur S Paul's Ch Fayetteville AR 2006-** B McKeesport PA 3/26/1955 d Robert Stoner & Jacquelynn. Cert ETS At Claremont CA 2004; Cert SWTS 2005. D 1/8/2006 P 6/10/2006 Bp Larry Earl Maze. m 11/23/1983 William West c 5. suzannestoner@sbcglobal.net

STONESIFER, John DeWitt (WA) 5 Ingleside Ct, Rockville MD 20850 **Int R Imm Ch On The Green New Castle DE 2011-** B Alexandria VA 5/26/1958 s Joseph Novak Stonesifer & Jean. BA Clemson U 1980; MDiv VTS 1984; MBA Theol Coll of the Bahamas Nassau BS 1995. D 6/23/1984 Bp Peter James Lee P 12/21/1984 Bp Emerson Paul Haynes. m 6/2/1984 Susan Lee Meachum c 2. Int R Gr Ch Utica NY 2010-2011; Int R Trin Ch Morgantown WV 2008-2010; Int R S Jn's Ch Huntington WV 2007-2008; Int R S Barth's Ch Laytonsville MD 2004-2005; Int R S Mary's Epis Ch Woodlawn Baltimore MD 2004-2005; Int Dir PC Buckingham's Choice Adamstown MD 2003-2004; Bp Search Com Dio Washington Washington DC 2000-2001; Vic H Sprt Epis Ch Gaithersburg MD 1999-2003; Chapl Trin-Pawling Sch Pawling NY 1998-1999; Assoc All SS' Epis Ch Chevy Chase MD 1997-2003; Chapl Washington Epis Sch Beth MD 1990-1997; Assoc R S Fran Ch Potomac MD 1988-1990; R S Andr's Epis Ch Princess Anne MD 1986-1988; Asst S Jn's Ch Naples FL 1984-1986. Auth, "Chld of Abraham," Rockshire Press, 1998; Auth, "Putting a Sm Indep Sch on the Map," Thesis, 1995. Transition Mnstrs in the Epis Ch 2007. Templeton Fell Theol Coll of the Bahamas 1995. jdstonesifer@gmail.com

STOPFEL, Barry Lee (Nwk) RD1 Box 146, Mifflinburg PA 17844 B Harrisburg PA 10/10/1947 s Marlin E Stopfel & Carolyn L. BS Bos 1969; MA Col 1972; MDiv UTS 1988. D 9/30/1990 Bp Walter Cameron Righter P 9/1/1991 Bp John Shelby Spong. Unitarian/Universalist Cong Northumberland PA 2000-2002; S Geo's Epis Ch Maplewood NJ 1993-1999; Ch Of The Atone Tenafly NJ 1990-1993; Dir Of Bp Anand'S Chr Resource Cntr Dio Newark Newark NJ 1988-1989.

STOPPEL, Gerald Corwin (WMich) PO Box 65, Saugatuck MI 49453 **R All SS Ch Saugatuck MI 1990-** B Rochester MN 8/17/1952 s Fabian Englebritzen Stoppel & Eleanore Anne. BA Morningside Coll 1973; MDiv Duke 1976; Cert Nash 1985; PhD Columbia Pacific U 1993. Trans 1/1/1990 Bp Edward Lewis Lee Jr. m 8/19/2000 Patricia Dewey. Vic S Jn's Ch Marlinton WV 1988-1990. "Living Words," *Cowley*, 2004; Auth, "Road to Resurr," *Cowley*, 2003. Soc of S Jn the Evang. gstoppel@iserv.net

STOREY, Wayne Alton (CNY) 311 S Massey St, Watertown NY 13601 **Supply S Jn's Ch Black River NY 2011-** B Potsdam NY 8/25/1938 s Burton Roy Storey & Beatrice Cornelius. Cntrl New York Dio Formation Prog w Bex 2007. D 10/7/2006 P 6/16/2007 Bp Gladstone Bailey Adams III. m 6/25/1960 Elizabeth C Caswell c 2. Asst All SS Ch Tarpon Sprg FL 2010-2011; Asst S Jn's Ch Black River NY 2010; Asst All SS Ch Tarpon Sprg FL 2009-2010; Asst S Jn's Ch Black River NY 2009; Asst All SS Ch Tarpon Sprg FL 2008-2009; Asst S Jn's Ch Black River NY 2008; Asst All SS Ch Tarpon Sprg FL 2007-2008; Assoc S Paul's Ch Watertown NY 2007. wstorey1@mac.com

STORM, Astrid J (NY) 251 West 122nd St., #4, New York NY 10027 **COM Dio New York New York City NY 2011-; Vic Ch Of S Nich On The Hudson New Hamburg NY 2007-** B Fort Riley KS 2/5/1975 d Roger Lee Storm & Sarah Elizabeth. BA Wheaton Coll 1997; MDiv Ya Berk 2001. D 10/28/2000 P 6/23/2001 Bp Herbert Thompson Jr. m Andrew R Wood c 1. Ed Bd Epis New Yorker Dio New York New York City NY 2007-2011; Ecum Cmsn Dio New York New York City NY 2007-2010; Cur Gr Epis Ch New York NY 2004-2006; S Lk's Par Darien CT 2004; Asst S Jn's Ch Worthington OH 2001-2004. "Blogger," *Huffington Post*; "Contrib," *Slate mag.* astridstorm@gmail.com

STORM, David Anderson (Oly) 2611 Broadway E, Seattle WA 98102 **Asstg P S Steph's Epis Ch Seattle WA 1995-; All SS' Epis Ch Hershey PA 1993-** B Seattle WA 2/3/1928 s Jerome Richard Storm & Dorothy Rachel. BA Whitman Coll 1950; MDiv VTS 1965. D 6/20/1965 P 6/24/1966 Bp Russell S Hubbard. Dioc Coun Dio Olympia Seattle WA 1978-1982; Trng And Constation Serv Dio Olympia Seattle WA 1974-1990; Dioc Evaltn Com Dio Olympia Seattle WA 1974-1980; R S Andrews Epis Ch Port Angeles WA 1972-1993; Dioc Ce Cmsn Dio Olympia Seattle WA 1968-1978; Vic S Hilda's - S Pat's Epis Ch Edmonds WA 1967-1972; Asst/Cur S Steph's Epis Ch Spokane WA 1965-1967.

STORMENT, J(ohn) Douglas (WTex) 1635 Thrush Court Cir, San Antonio TX 78248 B Bartlesville OK 8/22/1942 s Joseph Edgar Storment & Waltha Reba. BS U of Tulsa 1964; MDiv Melodyland TS 1978; CTh Epis TS of The SW 1986. D 6/17/1986 Bp Stanley Fillmore Hauser P 12/20/1986 Bp Scott Field Bailey. m 12/18/1965 Marilyn McKinney c 2. R St Fran Epis Ch San Antonio TX 1998-2006; S Mk's Ch Corpus Christi TX 1987-1998; Dio W Texas San Antonio TX 1986. muffindump@sbcglobal.net

STORMER, Eugene Allen (Spr) 825 Lorraine Ave, Springfield IL 62704 **Part Time S Thos Epis Ch Glen Carbon IL 2005-; Cn Pstr Dio Springfield Springfield IL 2004-; Dioc Coun Dio Springfield Springfield IL 2002-** B Alton IL 3/30/1942 s Walter Henry Stormer & Helen Josephine. Dioc Sem of the Immac Concep; BA S Mary of the Lake Sem 1964; MA/STB S Mary of the Lake Sem 1968; MSW S Louis U 1973. Rec from Roman Catholic 2/9/1986 as Priest Bp Donald James Parsons. m 5/8/1972 Janet Miller c 1. Dio Springfield Springfield IL 2005-2010; S Barn Ch Havana IL 2003-2004; S Andr's Ch Carbondale IL 2001-2002; Int S Jn's Epis Ch Decatur IL 1999-2001; Asst P S Lk's Ch Springfield IL 1998-1999; Dio Quincy Peoria IL 1996-2000; Int S Matt's Epis Ch Bloomington IL 1996-1998; P-in-c S Jas Epis Ch Griggsville IL 1986-1990. e.stormer@comcast.net

STORY, Mark Denslow (Okla) 1701 Mission Rd, Edmond OK 73034 **R S Mary's Ch Edmond OK 2002-** B Dallas TX 11/29/1955 s William DeRone Story & Verda Angeline. BA Augustana Coll 1978; MDiv SWTS 1983; DMin SMU 2005. D 6/4/1983 Bp Conrad Gesner P 12/11/1983 Bp Charles Bennison. m 6/21/1980 Susan H Hill c 3. R/Hdmstr Epis Ch Of The Redeem Irving TX 1992-2002; R Gr Epis Ch Traverse City MI 1986-1991; Asst S Lk's Par Kalamazoo MI 1983-1986. mdsplus@cox.net

STOUDEMIRE, Stewart Mcbryde (WNC) 950 - 36th Avenue Circle Northeast, Hickory NC 28601 B Rock Hill SC 11/3/1941 s George Asbury Stoudemire & Margaret Louise. BS No Carolina St U 1965. D 5/25/1986 Bp William Gillette Weinhauer. m 8/8/1964 Cornelia Mcaulay Wood c 2. D S Alb's Ch Hickory NC 1986-2009.

STOUT, A(rla) Jeanne (Eau) 204 Sunnyside Ave, Cameron WI 54822 B Bisbee ND 7/15/1934 d C W Sibert & Florence Helen. S Lk's Hosp Sch Of Nrsng Fargo ND 1953; Bismarck St Coll 1986. D 6/29/1995 Bp William Charles Wantland. m 1/14/1956 James Stout c 3. Dioc Admnstr Dio Eau Claire Eau Claire WI 1995-2006; D Gr Ch Rice Lake WI 1995. NAAD 1995. jstout@chibardun.net

STOUT, David Alan (NJ) St. James' Church, PO Box 278, Kamuela HI 96743 **P-in-c S Jas Epis Ch Kamuela HI 2011-** B Kendallville IN 4/4/1967 s Jerry DeWayne Stout & Linda Ellen. AS Vincennes U 1987; BS Ball St U 1989; Cbury Cathd 1995; MDiv Duke DS 1996. D 4/9/1997 P 10/18/1997 Bp Clifton Daniel III. m 7/17/2003 Bobby Greer Clement. R Trin Ch Asbury Pk NJ 2004-2011; Assoc R S Barth's Ch New York NY 2000-2004; Cur S Paul's Ch

Beaufort NC 1997-2000; Sem Intern S Fran Ch Goldsboro NC 1994-1995. SSJE - Assoc 1990. frdavid@stjameshawaii.org

STOUTE, Barclay Lenardo (LI) 28 Fallon Ct, Elmont NY 11003 B BB 7/4/1954 s Seth Othneil Stoute & Clarice Victorine. DIT Codrington Coll 1978; GTS 1980; BA U of The W Indies 1980. Trans from Church in the Province Of The West Indies 4/25/1989 Bp Drexel Gomez. m 7/20/1985 Marcia W c 1. R Ch Of SS Steph And Mart Brooklyn NY 1988-2006; Asst P Ch Of S Thos Brooklyn NY 1986-1988. Black Cleric Caucus, OHC.

STOUT-KOPP OJN, Ronnie Thompson (Nwk) 50 Brams Hill Dr, Mahwah NJ 07430 **LocTen Ch Of The Gd Shpd Ringwood NJ 2007-** B Jersey City NJ 10/21/1958 d Edward Stout & Veronica. BA Montclair St U 1980; MDiv GTS 2000; STM GTS 2002; Doctor of Letters Drew U 2010. D 6/12/2004 Bp John Leslie Rabb P 12/18/2004 Bp John Palmer Croneberger. m 4/25/1986 David A Kopp. P in Charge All SS Ch Bergenfield NJ 2010-2011; Chair: Sprtl Formation Cmsn Dio Newark Newark NJ 2007-2009; Asst to R Chr Ch Pompton Lakes NJ 2004-2006. revrts@dakopp.com

STOWE, Barbara Elaine (Mass) 33 Washington St, Topsfield MA 01983 B Lynn MA 1/6/1942 d Chester Leonard Dodge & Margaret Stilman. RN Beverly Hosp Sch Of Nrsng 1963; BS Emml 1987. D 10/6/2001 Bp M(arvil) Thomas Shaw III. c 4. D S Ptr's Ch Beverly MA 2001-2006. deaconbarb2003@yahoo.com

STOWE, David Andrew (NJ) 28 Pine Valley Rd, Doylestown PA 18901 B New Brunswick NJ 11/1/1930 s Walter Herbert Stowe & K(atherine) Marguerite. BA Dart 1953; STB GTS 1956. D 4/28/1956 P 10/27/1956 Bp Alfred L Banyard. m 9/6/1956 Priscilla Lynn c 2. R S Jn's Ch Somerville NJ 1965-1996; Cn Cathd Of All SS Albany NY 1959-1965; Vic The Ch Of The Gd Shpd Acton MA 1958-1959; Cur H Trin Ch Collingswood NJ 1956-1958. Epis Ch Hist Soc 2005. plstowe3@aol.com

STOWE, Howard Timothy Wheeler (NY) 79 Ne 93rd St, Miami Shores FL 33138 B Danbury CT 10/14/1943 s Howard Wheeler Stowe & Marjorie. BA W Virginia Wesleyan Coll 1966; STM Ya Berk 1969; CSD GTS 1974. D 6/6/1970 P 12/19/1970 Bp Horace W B Donegan. m 4/15/1995 Anthony P Lee Loy. S Steph's Epis Day Sch Coconut Grove FL 1996-2002; S Steph's Ch Coconut Grove Coconut Grove FL 1996-2001; R The Ch of S Ign of Antioch New York NY 1977-1995; Bp's Asst Cathd Of St Jn The Div New York NY 1971-1973; Ed "The Epis New Yorker" Dio New York New York City NY 1970-1971. CHS - P Assoc 1995; CBS 1970; GAS 1970. Knights' Chapl Ord of S Jn of Jerusalem 1979. shores0703@hotmail.com

STOWE JR, Richard Henry (Mass) 33 Washington St, Topsfield MA 01983 **Died 1/14/2010** B Salem MA 8/27/1941 s Richard Stowe & Yvette. BS Salem St Coll Salem MA 1963; MALS Wesl 1968; MDiv EDS 1986. D 6/13/1987 Bp David Elliot Johnson P 5/14/1988 Bp Roger W Blanchard. c 4. richardhstowe@aol.com

STOWELL, Philip W (NJ) 207 W Main St, Moorestown NJ 08057 **Chair Ins Com Dio New Jersey Trenton NJ 2009-; Dn, Burlington Convoc Dio New Jersey Trenton NJ 2009-; Vice Chair Proctor Fndt Dio New Jersey Trenton NJ 2000-; Chair Pension Com Dio New Jersey Trenton NJ 1996-; R Trin Ch Moorestown NJ 1995-** B Chicago IL 9/17/1945 s Frank Henry Stowell & Marie. AB Pr 1967; MDiv, cl EDS 1970. D 6/10/1970 Bp John Henry Esquirol P 2/27/1971 Bp Joseph Warren Hutchens. m 11/8/1986 Susan Mann c 1. Chair Bdgt Com Dio New York New York City NY 1993-1995; R S Barth's Ch In The Highland White Plains NY 1990-1995; Assoc R S Phil's In The Hills Tucson AZ 1988-1990; Assoc S Mary's Epis Ch Manchester CT 1986-1988; Chair Com on Chr Initiation Dio Maryland Baltimore MD 1983-1985; R S Jn's Ch Ellicott City MD 1983-1985; R Chr Ch Avon CT 1972-1983; Asst to R S Ptr's Epis Ch Cheshire CT 1970-1972. trinitystow@aim.com

STOY, Carol Berry (NJ) 221 Herrontown Rd, Princeton NJ 08540 B New York NY 11/3/1922 d Samuel Winston Berry & Carolyn Rose. BS CUNY 1943; Polytech Inst of Brooklyn 1945; D Formation Prog 1980. D 4/13/1985 Bp George Phelps Mellick Belshaw. m 4/2/1949 William S Stoy c 2. Archd Dio New Jersey Trenton NJ 1999-2005; Cler Asst Trin Ch Princeton NJ 1985-2006. S Steph's Awd NAAD 1997. stoycaro@verizon.net

ST PIERRE, Joanne Madelyn (EMich) PO Box 217, Otter Lake MI 48464 B Warren MI 3/5/1940 d Robert Albrecht & Cecilia. D 3/21/2009 Bp S(teven) Todd Ousley. m 6/11/1971 Joseph Jean Denis St Pierre c 3. dandjsaint@charter.net

STRADER, James William (SO) 3207 Montana Ave, Cincinnati OH 45211 **R S Jas Epis Ch Cincinnati OH 2011-** B Tucson AZ 9/11/1957 s William Leo Strader & Bette Louise. BA U of Arizona 1980; MA GW 1997; MDiv EDS 2003. D 5/27/2006 P 12/2/2006 Bp Kirk Stevan Smith. Cur S Geo's-By-The-River Rumson NJ 2008-2011; Chapl Epis Campus Mnstry - U of Arizona Tucson AZ 2006-2008. edsjim@gmail.com

STRAHAN, Linda Carol (RI) 103 Kay St, Newport RI 02840 B Council Bluffs IA 12/13/1945 d Charles Daniel Strahan & Helen Esther. BA Stan 1967; MA U CA 1968; PhD U CA 1976; MDiv VTS 1979. D 6/23/1979 P 5/1/1980 Bp Robert Bruce Hall. Asst Emm Ch Newport RI 1988-1991; Int S Dav's Ch Gales Ferry CT 1987-1988; Int St Mich & Gr Ch Rumford RI 1986; Asst S Mart's Ch Providence RI 1983-1985; Asst Ch Of The Redeem Chestnut Hill MA 1979-1983. Auth, "Intro To Alan Of Lille'S Bk On The Plaint Of Nature". EvangES, OHC.

STRAIN, William Henry (Nwk) 4 Acacia Dr, Boynton Beach FL 33436 B East Orange NJ 8/10/1928 s William Caldwell Strain & Ethel Bennett. BA Hob 1953; Pr 1954; MDiv GTS 1957. D 6/15/1957 P 12/21/1957 Bp Benjamin M Washburn. m 5/17/1997 Phyllis Lloyd Smith c 2. Stndg Com Dio Newark Newark NJ 1971-1979; R Calv Epis Ch Summit NJ 1968-1993; Vic S Mich's Epis Ch Wayne NJ 1957-1968. Phi Beta Kappa Hob 1953. strainbill@comcast.net

STRAINGE JR, Roy Thomas (SeFla) No address on file. B New Haven CT 5/12/1924 s Roy Thomas Strainge & Cornelia May. BA U So 1945; STB GTS 1948. D 6/11/1948 Bp Henry I Louttit P 5/14/1949 Bp Wallace J Gardner. Int S Jas-In-The-Hills Epis Ch Hollywood FL 1998-1999; Asst S Jn's Ch Hollywood FL 1968-1986; Cur H Trin Epis Ch W Palm Bch FL 1948-1949; Cur S Geo's Epis Ch Riviera Bch FL 1948-1949.

STRAND, Jon Carl (Mass) Po Box 238, Natick MA 01760 **P-in-c S Paul's Ch Natick MA 1998-** B Winfield KS 11/8/1964 s James Harold Strand & Carolyn E. BA Wichita St U 1988; MDiv Ya Berk 1992; Cert Ya 1992. D 8/20/1992 Bp William Edward Smalley P 6/1/1993 Bp Edward Cole Chalfant. m 6/18/1994 Elizabeth Anderson c 2. Cathd Ch Of S Lk Portland ME 1992-1998. joncstrand@gmail.com

STRAND, Tyler (NCal) 319 North St. Apt. 3, Healdsburg CA 95448 **R S Paul's Ch Healdsburg CA 2008-** B Champaign IL 4/29/1951 s Alan Lawrence Strand & Barbara Maria. Uppsala U 1972; BA Augustana Coll 1973; St Steph's Hse Theol Coll, Oxford UK 1974; MDiv GTS 1978; H Cross Gk Orth TS 1995; Centro Bilingual Cuernavaca Mx 1997; TESOL Cert Sonoma St U 2011. D 10/29/1977 Bp Quintin Ebenezer Primo Jr P 4/29/1978 Bp James Winchester Montgomery. Int Ch Of The Epiph Chicago IL 1999-2000; The Ch Of The H Innoc Hoffman Schaumburg IL 1995-1999; Cur Ch Of The Ascen Chicago IL 1993-1994; R The Angl/Epis Ch Of Chr The King Frankfurt am Main 60323 DE 1985-1990; Ecum Off Dio Milwaukee Milwaukee WI 1983-1984; R S Lk's Ch Whitewater WI 1980-1985; Cur S Mich's Ch Barrington IL 1977-1980. Contrib, "The Min'S Manual 2001". Soc Of SS Alb & Sergius 1974-1985; SSC 1999-2000. tylerastrand@yahoo.co.uk

STRANE, Steven Roberts (Cal) 4489 Caminito Cuarzo, San Diego CA 92117 **Assoc S Jas By The Sea La Jolla CA 2011-** B Bethesda MD 10/14/1949 s John Roberts Strane & Doris Marie. BA California St U 1971; Tchg Cred San Diego St U 1974; MDiv VTS 1978. D 6/12/1978 P 12/16/1978 Bp Robert Munro Wolterstorff. m 4/14/1973 Jane H Smith c 1. R S Tim's Ch Danville CA 1988-2010; All Souls' Epis Ch San Diego CA 1979-1987; Cur S Paul In The Desert Palm Sprg CA 1978-1979. srstrane@gmail.com

STRANG, Ruth Hancock (Mich) 504 Prospect St, Howell MI 48843 B Bridgeport CT 3/11/1923 d Robert Hallock Wright Strang & Ruth. BA Wellesley Coll 1944; MD New York Med Coll 1949; Ecum TS 1992; MDiv SWTS 1993. D 6/19/1993 P 9/14/1994 Bp R(aymond) Stewart Wood Jr. P-in-c S Jn's Ch Howell MI 1994-2009; Asstg D S Aid's Ch Ann Arbor MI 1993-1994. SCHC 1984. stjohns@saintjohnsepiscopalhowell.org

STRANGE, Phillip Ross (Los) PO Box 3144, Wrightwood CA 92397 **Dio Los Angeles Los Angeles CA 2004-; Dio Los Angeles Los Angeles CA 1998-** B Ardmore OK 7/20/1941 s Oscar Alloway Strange & Laura Evelyn. BA Rice U 1962; MDiv GTS 1965; SMU 1973; U of New Mex 1990. D 6/18/1965 P 12/21/1965 Bp Charles A Mason. m 5/27/1967 Susan G Green c 3. R S Paul's Par Lancaster CA 1996-2004; R S Mich's Epis Ch Riverside CA 1990-1996; Int S Thos Of Cbury Epis Ch Albuquerque NM 1988-1990; Vic S Chad's Epis Ch Albuquerque NM 1980-1988; Sub-Dn Dallas Dnry E Dio Dallas Dallas TX 1974-1978; R S Jas Ch Dallas TX 1973-1980; Dir Stds Cathd Cntr for Cont Educ S Matt's Cathd Dallas TX 1971-1973; Asst S Mk's Ch Irving TX 1968-1971; Asst to Dn S Matt's Cathd Dallas TX 1966-1968; Vic S Barn Ch Garland TX 1965-1966. phil@strangelaw.net

STRASBURGER, Frank C (NJ) 27 Tidal Run Lane, Brunswick ME 04011 B Baltimore MD 8/14/1945 s Charles M Strasburger & Janet Kaufman. BA Pr 1967; MA Jn Hopkins U 1971; MDiv EDS 1980. D 4/26/1980 P 11/1/1980 Bp David Keller Leighton Sr. m 11/27/1982 Caroline Coleman c 3. Int S Andr's Ch Newcastle ME 2008-2010; Assoc Trin Ch Princeton NJ 1999-2007; Chapl Epis Ch at Pr Princeton NJ 1986-1997; Cn The Amer Cathd of the H Trin Paris 75008 FR 1984-1986; Asst S Mk's Ch New Canaan CT 1981-1984; D S Lk's Ch Katonah NY 1980-1981. Auth, "Why the Angl Comm Matters," Forw Mvmt, 2008; Auth, "Honoring hon," *Princeton Alum Weekly*, 1995; Auth, "Can Princeton Act Morally?," *The Nassau Weekly*, 1991; Auth, "Qui Est L'Etranger?," *Sens*, 1985; Auth, "Keeping the Faith: The Challenge of the Ch Sch," *NAES Journ*, 1980. fstras@gmail.com

STRASBURGER, Roy William (ECR) 89 Alpine Ave, Los Gatos CA 95030 B Temple TX 8/26/1928 s Roy Strasburger & Aileen. BS SW Texas St U San Marcos 1949; MDiv VTS 1952; DMin VTS 1977. D 7/1/1952 P 1/25/1953 Bp Everett H Jones. m 12/27/1954 Patricia McGovern c 2. VTS Alexandria VA

S

1985-1988; Stndg Com Dio El Camino Real Monterey CA 1983-1988; Trst CDSP Berkeley CA 1983-1987; Dep, GC Dio El Camino Real Monterey CA 1982-1988; Election Process Com Dio El Camino Real Monterey CA 1979-1980; R S Andr's Ch Saratoga CA 1957-1991; Cur S Mk's Epis Ch San Antonio TX 1952-1955.

STRASSER, Gabor (Va) 18525 Bear Creek Ter, Leesburg VA 20176 B Budapest HU 5/22/1929 s Rezso Strasser & Theresa. BD SUNY 1953; MS SUNY 1959; PMD Harv 1968; MDiv VTS 1992. D 6/13/1992 Bp Robert Poland Atkinson P 12/1/1992 Bp Peter James Lee. m 2/2/1978 Joka Verhoeff c 2. S Marg's Ch Woodbridge VA 1992-1993.

STRAUB, Gregory Stephen (Eas) Episcopal Church Center, 815 Second Avenue, New York NY 10017 **Exec Off and Secy of the GC Epis Ch Cntr New York NY 2005-** B Irvington NJ 10/18/1948 s Stephen Joseph Straub & Dorothy Mary. BA Dickinson Coll 1970; MDiv PDS 1973; DMin Drew U 1990. D 6/8/1973 P 3/30/1974 Bp Dean T Stevenson. Trst EDS Cambridge MA 2004-2010; Stndg Comm Dio Easton Easton MD 2001-2005; Stndg Com Dio Easton Easton MD 2001-2005; Bp Search Com Chair Dio Easton Easton MD 2001-2002; Chair, Bp Search Com Dio Easton Easton MD 2001-2002; Comp Dio Chair Dio Easton Easton MD 1988-1990; Dep to GC Dio Easton Easton MD 1985-2003; GC Dep Dio Easton Easton MD 1985-2003; Exec Coun Dio Easton Easton MD 1985-1993; Secy of Dioc Conv Dio Easton Easton MD 1983-2006; Secy of Dioc Conv Dio Easton Easton MD 1983-2006; R Emm Epis Ch Chestertown MD 1976-2005; Int Emm Epis Ch Chestertown MD 1975-1976; Int Emm Epis Ch Chestertown MD 1975-1976; Int S Thos Ch Lancaster PA 1974-1975; Int S Thos Ch Lancaster PA 1974-1975; Cur S Thos Ch Lancaster PA 1973-1974. HSEC 2003; NEHA 1983. gstraub@episcopalchurch.org

STRAUGHN, Richard Daniel (SwFla) 373 Corson Ln, Cape May NJ 08204 B Sea Isle City NJ 5/12/1947 s Richard Claude Straughn & Lina Margaret. BA Lycoming Coll 1969; MDiv PDS 1972. D 4/22/1972 P 10/28/1972 Bp Alfred L Banyard. c 2. Vic S Chad's Ch Tampa FL 1989-1996; Ch Of The H Sprt Tuckerton NJ 1988-1989; Assoc The Ch Of S Uriel The Archangel Sea Girt NJ 1983-1988; Vic Ch Of S Jn-In-The-Wilderness Gibbsboro NJ 1972-1983. frrick47@yahoo.com

STRAUKAMP, James Edward (NCal) 2140 Mission Ave., Carmichael CA 95608 B Chicago IL 6/23/1927 s Albert Straukamp & Josephine. Rec from Roman Catholic 10/22/1983 as Priest Bp John Lester Thompson III. hmk96@sbcglobal.net

STRAUSS, A(rlen) Richard (CNY) 109 Glenside Rd, Ithaca NY 14850 **Supply P Chr Epis Ch Willard NY 2003-; Assoc S Jn's Ch Ithaca NY 1980-** B Canton PA 10/20/1933 s James Vincent Strauss & Helen Louise. BA Ithaca Coll 1955. D 6/23/1979 P 6/7/1980 Bp Ned Cole.

STRAVERS, Cynthia A (Ct) 60 East Ave, Norwalk CT 06851 **Asst to the P Par of St Paul's Ch Norwalk Norwalk CT 2009-** B Grand Rapids MI 1/11/1956 d Gordon Lee Kauffman & Jeanne K. BS Wstrn Michigan U 1992; MA Wstrn Michigan U 1995; MDiv The GTS 2009. D 6/20/2009 Bp Wendell Nathaniel Gibbs Jr P 1/9/2010 Bp Laura Ahrens. c 3. S Lk's Par Kalamazoo MI 1997-2007. stravers@stpaulsnorwalk.org

STRAVERS, Richard Lee (WMich) 2118 N Westnedge Ave, Kalamazoo MI 49007 B Grand Rapids MI 12/21/1952 s Dick Merle Stravers & Ruth. BA Calvin Coll 1976; M.Div GTS 1987. D 12/6/1986 P 6/11/1987 Bp Howard Samuel Meeks. c 3. S Tim Ch Richland MI 1988-1999; S Lk's Par Kalamazoo MI 1986-1988. rstravers@charter.net

STRAWBRIDGE, Jennifer Ruth (Va) Keble College, Parks Road, Oxford OX13PG Great Britain (UK) B Pittsburgh PA 9/7/1978 d Craig M Strawbridge & Susan M. PhD Oxf; BA W&L 2001; MST Oxf 2002; DAS Ya Berk 2004; MDiv Yale DS 2004. D 6/11/2004 P 12/15/2004 Bp Frank Neff Powell. Assoc R S Mary's Epis Ch Arlington VA 2005-2009; Chapl Res Bridgeport Hosp Dept Of Pstr Care Bridgeport CT 2004-2005; Asst P Chr Ch New Haven CT 2004-2005. Auth, "How present is Romans in early Chr Sch exercises: Is P.Lond.Lit 207 mislabelled?," *Oxford Resrch Archive Journ*, Oxf Press, 2011; Auth, "The Word of the Cross: Mssn, Power, and the Theol of Ldrshp," *The ATR*, Winter, 91.1, 2009. Gathering of Leaders 2006. Omicron Delta Kappa 2001; Phi Beta Kappa 2000. jennifer_strawbridge@yahoo.com

STREEPY, Robert Shawn (Kan) 10700 W 53rd St, Shawnee KS 66203 **D S Lk's Epis Ch Shawnee KS 2011-** B Cheyenne WY 12/13/1952 BA U of Kansas 1973; JD U of Kansas 1976; Kansas Sch of Mnstry 2003. D 9/27/2003 Bp William Edward Smalley P 6/6/2009 Bp Dean Elliott Wolfe. m 4/25/1982 Marcia Kathleen Potucek c 2. Gr Ch Chanute KS 2009-2011. shawn@stlukes.net

STREET III, Claude Parke (Colo) 35 KILDEER Rd, Hamden CT 06517 B Nashville TN 12/3/1934 s Claude Parke Street & Elisabeth. BA Van 1952; BD Yale DS 1960; U So 1962; Fllshp Coll of Preachers 1976; S Geo's Coll Jerusalem IL 1982; DMin PrTS 1986. D 3/3/1963 P 7/3/1963 Bp Charles Gresham Marmion. m 7/30/2000 Eleanor Lee McGee-Street c 3. Vic Bad Wound's Sta Porcupine SD 1991-1996; R Ch Of The Adv Mart SD 1991-1996; R Ch Of The Epiph Pine Ridge SD 1991-1996; Vic Ch Of The Mssh Wounded Knee SD 1991-1996; Dio So Dakota Sioux Falls SD 1991-1996; Vic H Cross Epis Ch Mart SD 1991-1996; Vic S Alb's Epis Ch Porcupine SD 1991-1996; R S Andr's Epis Ch Pine Ridge SD 1991-1996; R S Jn's Epis Ch Pine Ridge SD 1991-1996; Vic S Julia's Epis Ch Mart SD 1991-1996; Vic S Katharine's Ch Mart SD 1991-1996; Vic S Mich's Ch Kyle SD 1991-1996; Vic S Ptr's Epis Ch Pine Ridge SD 1991-1996; Vic S Thos Ch Porcupine SD 1991-1996; Weca Bd Dio Washington Washington DC 1984-1988; Chair Par Intrnshp Prog Dio Washington Washington DC 1979-1982; R S Aug's Epis Ch Washington DC 1978-1991; Weca Bd Dio Washington Washington DC 1973-1975; Assoc S Marg's Ch Washington DC 1966-1978; Cn Chr Ch Cathd Louisville KY 1963-1966. cpstreet@aya.yale.edu

STREET, Terry Terriell (WTenn) 210 Walnut Trace Dr, Cordova TN 38018 **Bp and Coun Dio W Tennessee Memphis TN 2008-; R S Phil Ch Bartlett TN 2008-** B Memphis TN 12/18/1955 s Conway Terriell Street & Elois Johnson. BA U of Memphis 1978; MA U of Memphis 1984; MDiv STUSo 2006. D 8/5/2006 Bp Don Edward Johnson. m 7/16/1983 Edith Brown Street c 2. S Jn's Epis Ch Memphis TN 2006-2008. tstreet@stjohnsmemphis.org

STREETER, Christopher Michael (Roch) 36 S Main St, Pittsford NY 14534 **Chr Ch Pittsford NY 2009-** B Newton NJ 10/25/1980 s Michael Edward Streeter & Denise Jane. BMus Eastman Sch of Mus 2003; MDiv VTS 2009. D 6/6/2009 Bp Prince Grenville Singh P 12/12/2009 Bp Jack Marston McKelvey. m 7/9/2011 Jennifer Castle. chris@christchurchpittsford.com

STREIFF, Suzanne (Oly) 305 Burma Rd, Castle Rock WA 98611 **D S Matt Ch Castle Rock WA 2004-** B Kelso WA 12/24/1937 d Stanley Harold Lowe & Mina V Elizabeth. D 2/28/2004 Bp Sanford Zangwill Kaye Hampton. m 6/9/1960 Donald Edward Streiff c 3.

STREIT JR, John Paul (Mass) 41 Ackers Ave Apt 2, Brookline MA 02445 **The Cathd Ch Of S Paul Boston MA 2001-; Dn The Cathd Ch Of S Paul Boston MA 1995-** B Washington DC 9/21/1951 s John Paul Streit & Ann Thomas. BA Dickinson Coll 1973; MDiv EDS 1978. D 6/18/1978 Bp Morris Fairchild Arnold P 5/13/1979 Bp John Bowen Coburn. m 7/17/2004 Susan M Knight c 3. U Chapl- Bos Dio Massachusetts Boston MA 1984-1995; Asst The Ch Of Our Redeem Lexington MA 1978-1984. "Big Questions Worthy Dreams," *ATR*, 2002. ESMHE; Soc of S Jn the Evang. jepstreit@verizon.net

STRIBLING, Anna Jones (Va) 4540 Carrington Rd, Markham VA 22643 B Winchester VA 10/24/1939 d James R Jones & Anna Rudik. BS U Rich 1961; MDiv VTS 1982. D 6/9/1982 Bp David Henry Lewis Jr P 5/28/1983 Bp Robert Bruce Hall. m 7/1/1961 William C Stribling c 3. Dn, Reg III Dio Virginia Richmond VA 1994-1998; Trnr and Field Supvsr VTS Alexandria VA 1993-1998; Nomin Com for Bp Suffr Dio Virginia Richmond VA 1992-1993; Chair, CE Com Dio Virginia Richmond VA 1991-1992; R S Jn's Epis Ch Arlington VA 1989-2000; Compstn Com Dio Virginia Richmond VA 1986-1993; Pres, Stndg Com Dio Virginia Richmond VA 1986-1988; Assoc Ch Of The H Comf Vienna VA 1985-1989; Peace Cmsn Dio Virginia Richmond VA 1983-1993; Asst S Jas' Epis Ch Warrenton VA 1982-1984. annstribling@gmail.com

STRIBLING, Emily B (WA) 4621 Laverock Pl NW, WASHINGTON DC 20007 B Washington DC 1/9/1947 d E Taylor Chewning & Mary Wallach Mitchell. BA Sarah Lawr Coll Bronxville NY 1968; MDiv The Gnrl Sem 2002. D 6/9/2007 P 1/19/2008 Bp John Chane. m 9/13/2002 Robert M Stribling c 2. Cathd of St Ptr & St Paul Washington DC 2007-2009; The Ch Of The Epiph New York NY 1992-1994. twob1@aol.com

STRIBLING JR, Jess Hawkins (Va) 112 Marina Reach, Chesapeake VA 23320 B Chicago IL 12/18/1937 s Jess Hawkins Stribling & Antoinette Lauria. BA U NC 1959; BD VTS 1962; STM VTS 1973; JD GW 1974. D 6/16/1962 P 12/22/1962 Bp William Foreman Creighton. m 6/6/1959 Miriam Love McLaughlin c 1. Asst S Geo's Epis Ch Arlington VA 1986-2001; Assoc S Mich's Epis Ch Arlington VA 1974-1986; R S Ptr's Epis Ch Arlington VA 1967-1974; R Ch Of The Ascen Silver Sprg MD 1964-1966; Asst The Ch Of The Epiph Washington DC 1962-1964. j.stribling@cox.net

STRICKER, David Walter (USC) 12000 Turnmeyer Dr SE Apt 1120, Redstone Village, Huntsville AL 35803 B Pittsburgh PA 11/13/1939 s Joseph Hayhurst Stricker & Margaret Elizabeth. BA Otterbein Coll 1965; MDiv PDS 1968. D 5/25/1968 Bp William S Thomas P 12/21/1968 Bp Robert Bracewell Appleyard. m 10/30/1965 Gaye R Rowswell c 3. Vic S Barn Ch Dillon SC 2001-2007; Off Of Bsh For ArmdF New York NY 1982-2001; Cntrl Sussex Cltn Georgetown DE 1975-1982; R S Mk's Ch Millsboro DE 1975-1982; P-in-c Ch Of The Gd Samar Mc Keesport PA 1968-1975; P-in-c Ch Of The Trsfg Clairton PA 1968-1975. ddavstr@hotmail.com

STRICKLAND, Harold Somerset (Ark) 610 Northwest K, Bentonville AR 72712 B Kansas City MO 12/25/1921 s Frank Strickland & Edith Isobel. BA U of Kansas 1947; BD STUSo 1950. D 6/18/1950 P 12/18/1950 Bp Edward Randolph Welles II. m 6/18/1950 Mary Ellen Yeakey. Vic Gr Ch Siloam Sprg AR 1981-1985; Vic S Theo's Epis Ch Bella Vista AR 1981-1985; Coll Field Des Moines IA 1972-1980; S Lk's Epis Ch Cedar Falls IA 1970-1981; R S Paul's Ch Leavenworth KS 1962-1970; Vic S Mart-In-The-Fields Edwardsville KS 1957-1962; P-in-c S Lk's Epis Ch Excelsior Sprg MO 1950-1956.

✠ **STRICKLAND, Rt Rev Vernon Edward** (WK) 665 N Desmet Ave, Buffalo WY 82834 **Asstg Bp Dio Wyoming Casper WY 2002-** B Holopaw FL 11/26/1938 s Vernon Strickland & Edna. BA Carson-Newman Coll 1967; Candler TS Emory U 1969; MDiv VTS 1970. D 6/24/1970 Bp Edward Hamilton West P 4/16/1971 Bp George Mosley Murray Con 10/25/1994 for WK. m 5/22/1965 Mary Joyce Bishop c 1. Bp Dio Wstrn Kansas Hutchinson KS 1995-2002; Archd Dio Wyoming Casper WY 1990-1995; Chair Com Dio Wyoming Casper WY 1987-1989; R S Lk's Epis Ch Buffalo WY 1985-1989; Ch Of S Jas The Apos Clovis NM 1983-1985; St Jas Epis Ch Dillon MT 1982-1983; Archd Dio The Rio Grande Albuquerque NM 1980-1982; R S Dav's Epis Ch Lakeland FL 1977-1979; Chair Prog Cmsn Dio Cntrl Florida Orlando FL 1973-1977; Asst S Mich's Ch Orlando FL 1973-1977; R S Lk's Epis Ch Live Oak FL 1971-1973; Vic S Agatha's Epis Ch Defuniak Sprg FL 1970-1971.

STRICKLAND, Virginia Lisbeth (Eur) 209 Madison Ave, New York NY 10016 **Asst Ch Of The Incarn New York NY 2011-** B Houston TX 10/12/1978 d Larry Alvie Strickland & Kristin Virginia. BA U NC 2001; MDiv Yale DS 2006. D 6/4/2011 Bp Pierre W Whalon. GINGER@CHURCHOFTHEINCARNATION.ORG

STRICKLAND JR, William Earl (Alb) 4 Avery Place, Clifton Park NY 12065 **Cur Gr Ch Waterford NY 2008-** B Oxford MS 8/11/1958 s William Earl Strickland & Jane Ann. BA U of Mississippi 1980; MA U of Texas at Austin 1982; JD Amer U 1988; MA Nash 2008. D 5/31/2008 P 12/6/2008 Bp William Howard Love. m 7/12/2003 Elizabeth McFarland c 2. strcklnd@nycap.rr.com

STRICKLIN, Paul E (USC) 6408 Bridgewood Rd., Columbia SC 29206 **R S Mich And All Ang' Columbia SC 2008-** B Birmingham AL 3/25/1952 s Elmer Riley Stricklin & Marcella Ring. Cert Walker Coll 1972; BS U of Alabama 1974; MDiv VTS 1978. D 6/12/1978 P 12/12/1978 Bp Furman Stough. m 5/14/1977 Katherine Morgan Komenak c 2. R Calv Epis Ch Cleveland MS 2004-2008; Asst R Ch Of The Gd Shpd Dallas TX 1992-1997; Chr Sch Arden NC 1989-1992; R S Geo's Epis Ch Summerville SC 1986-1989; Chapl S Ptr's Ch Oxford MS 1984-1986; Dio Alabama Birmingham AL 1983-1984; Asst R All SS Epis Ch Birmingham AL 1980-1984; Cur S Paul's Ch Selma AL 1978-1980. Cris 1989-2004; NAES 1989-2004; Saes 1992-2004. rector@stmichaelepiscopal.com

STRID, Paul E. (Cal) 3115 W Meadow Dr SW, Albuquerque NM 87121 **Assoc S Mich And All Ang Ch Albuquerque NM 2007-** B Fresno CA 5/8/1946 s Paul Victor Strid & Hallie Belle. BA Pomona Coll 1968; MDiv Amer Bapt Sem of The W 1972; U CA 1974; CDSP 1988; CDSP 2006. D 12/2/1989 P 12/1/1990 Bp William Edwin Swing. Vic S Cuth's Epis Ch Oakland CA 1995-2006; Int S Aid's Ch San Francisco CA 1993-1994; Int S Ptr's Epis Ch Redwood City CA 1992-1993; D S Alb's Ch Albany CA 1989-1990. Associated Parishes, OHC, No Amer As. pstrid505@mac.com

STRIDIRON, Andrea Renee (Roch) 2000 Highland Ave, Rochester NY 14618 B Philadelphia PA 8/18/1953 d Clifton Thomas Stridiron & Theresa Smith. D 5/2/2009 Bp Prince Grenville Singh. stritz@frontiernet.net

STRIMER, Peter McCoy (Oly) 1551 10th Ave E, Seattle WA 98102 **S Andr's Ch Seattle WA 2006-** B Delaware OH 2/14/1954 s Robert Merrill Strimer & Jane Rose. BA Duke 1976; MS U of Connecticut 1980; MDiv Yale DS 1980; PhD OH SU 1994. D 9/7/1980 P 3/15/1981 Bp William Grant Black. m 7/29/1995 El Mcfarland. Cmncatn Mssnr Dio Olympia Seattle WA 2003-2006; Cn for Urban Wk S Mk's Cathd Seattle WA 1995-2003; Third Av Cmnty Churc Columbus OH 1994-1995; Vic S Jn's Ch Columbus OH 1991-1995; Dio Sthrn Ohio Cincinnati OH 1989-1993; The Hunger Ntwk Columbus OH 1984-1988; Trin Ch Columbus OH 1981-1985. pstrimer@comcast.net

STRING, Jansen Edward (Md) 2900 Dunleer Rd, Baltimore MD 21222 **R S Geo's And S Matthews Ch Baltimore MD 1994-** B Cleveland OH 8/15/1952 s Ralph Edward String & Barbara Elaine. BA U of Wisconsin 1974; MDiv EDS 1983; MS Loyola Coll 2000. D 6/25/1983 Bp John Harris Burt P 6/1/1984 Bp Frank Stanley Cerveny. m 5/27/1995 Constance Labbe c 4. R Gd Samar Epis Ch Orange Pk FL 1991-1994; S Eliz's Epis Ch Jacksonville FL 1986-1991; Cur Ch Of The Gd Shpd Jacksonville FL 1983-1985; Cur Ch Of The H Cross Tryon NC 1983. jansenstring@usa.net

STRINGER, Pamela (EC) 111 N King St, Bath NC 27808 **R H Trin Epis Ch Hampstead NC 2000-** B Oak Park IL 8/3/1947 d Warner Stringer & Barara. BD U Of Florida 1969; MA U of Alabama 1973; MDiv SWTS 1984. D 6/24/1984 Bp William F Gates Jr P 4/21/1985 Bp William Evan Sanders. Int S Thos' Epis Ch Bath NC 1999-2000; S Paul's Epis Ch Clinton NC 1997-1999; Cn Mssnr Chr Ch Cathd Indianapolis IN 1991-1996; P Chr Ch Cathd Indianapolis IN 1985-1986; S Steph's Epis Ch Oak Ridge TN 1984-1991. mtrpamela@yahoo.com

STRINGER, Stacy Bussy (Tex) 4613 Highway 3, Dickinson TX 77539 **Dn of Galveston Convoc Dio Texas Houston TX 2011-; Nomin Com Dio Texas Houston TX 2010-; R H Trin Epis Ch Dickinson TX 2010-** B New York 2/20/1958 d Francis Clark Bussy & Patricia Kelly. BA SUNY Plattsburgh; MDiv Epis TS Of The SW 2008. D 6/28/2008 Bp Don Adger Wimberly P 2/7/2009 Bp C(harles) Andrew Doyle. m 11/2/2011 Stephen Stringer. Chair of Sprtl Formation Cmsn Dio Texas Houston TX 2009-2011; Cur Trin Ch Houston TX 2008-2010. sbstringer@att.net

STRINGFELLOW, Howard (Be) 333 Wyandotte St., Bethlehem PA 18015 **Archd Dio Bethlehem Bethlehem PA 2005-** B Fort Huachuca AZ 8/9/1952 s Howard W Stringfellow & Jean. BA Van 1974; MA Wake Forest U 1976; MDiv GTS 1986. D 10/4/1986 Bp William Arthur Beckham P 5/31/1987 Bp McAlister Crutchfield Marshall. m 5/19/1984 Carolyne Lyles Ellison. R S Lk's Ch Scranton PA 1993-2004; Ecum Cmsn Dio New York New York City NY 1990-1993; Cur S Thos Ch New York NY 1986-1993. archdeacon@diobeth.org

STROBEL JR, Henry Willis (Tex) 2701 Bellefontaine St Apt B32, Houston TX 77025 **Asst S Bede Epis Ch Houston TX 2000-; P Assoc Palmer Memi Ch Houston TX 1972-** B Charleston SC 2/19/1943 s Henry Willis Strobel & Madge Ruth. BS Coll of Charleston 1964; PhD U NC 1968; Michigan TS 1972. D 2/20/1971 Bp Richard S M Emrich P 6/9/1979 Bp J Milton Richardson. Cur S Aid's Ch Ann Arbor MI 1971-1972. Auth, "Recombinant Dna Tech & The Relatns Of Humanity To God"; Auth, "S Lk Journ Of Theol". ESMHE. Sigma Xi.

STROBEL, Pamela Owen (Ct) 254 E Putnam Ave, Greenwich CT 06830 **Exec Coun Appointees New York NY 2011-** B Chicago IL 12/20/1949 d Alfred Wallace Owen & Marjorie Dolsen. Grad Sch of Rel, Ford; Syr 1968; NEU 1969; CUNY 1984; BA SUNY 1995; MDiv GTS 1998. D 6/13/1998 P 12/19/1998 Bp Richard Frank Grein. c 1. Sr Assoc to the R Chr Ch Greenwich CT 2000-2011; Gr Epis Ch Port Jervis NY 2000; Cur S Jas' Ch Goshen NY 1998-2000. postrobel@yahoo.com

STROH, Nancy Marshall (Pa) 3440 Norwood Pl, Holland PA 18966 B Wilmington DE 10/17/1938 d Alva Woodland Marshall & Jessie Travers. BA Drew U 1960; Med Goucher Coll 1961; GTS 1987; MA Luth TS at Philadelphia 1988. D 6/11/1988 P 5/27/1989 Bp Allen Lyman Bartlett Jr. c 2. P-in-c Ch Of The Redemp Southampton PA 2007-2010; Cathd Chapt Dio Pennsylvania Philadelphia PA 1995-2001; Vic Ch Of The H Nativ Wrightstown PA 1991-2006; Mem, Chair of Stwdshp Com Dio Pennsylvania Philadelphia PA 1991-1997; Int Trin Ch Gulph Mills King Of Prussia PA 1990-1991; Asst R S Andr's Ch Yardley PA 1988-1990. nancy3810@verizon.net

STROHL, Patrick Francis (CPa) 113 S Broad St, Mechanicsburg PA 17055 **D Cathd Ch Of S Steph Harrisburg PA 2010-; Chair-Prison Mnstry Cmsn Dio Cntrl Pennsylvania Harrisburg PA 2004-** B Chicago IL 1/3/1943 s Peter Paul Strohl & Pearl Madeline. BSBA U Of Cntrl Florida 1975; Cert Dioc Sch Of Chr Stds 2005. D 11/19/2005 Bp Michael Whittington Creighton. m 6/1/1996 Sandra Loy c 2. Chapl to the Bp Dio Cntrl Pennsylvania Harrisburg PA 2007-2010; D S Benedicts Epis Ch New Freedom PA 2005-2007. Assoc. of Epis Deacons 2005; Cler Assoc. of Cntrl PA- 2005; Cler Assoc. of Cntrl PA-Sec'y 2005-2010; NNECA Bd Dir 2008; NNECA Bd Dir-Past Pres 2011; NNECA Bd Dir-Pres 2010-2011. deaconpat@aol.com

STROHM, Ralph William (WVa) 2248 Adams Ave, Huntington WV 25704 **S Ptr's Ch Huntington WV 2009-; R S Simon's Ch Buffalo NY 2000-** B Muscatine IA 5/11/1944 s Ralph Clarence Strohm & Ferris Marie. BBA U of Iowa 1967; Cert U of Iowa 1969; MA Nthrn Arizona U 1975; JD U of Iowa 1978; MDiv Bex 1990. D 1/30/1991 P 10/1/1991 Bp William George Burrill. m 5/29/2004 Melissa E Remington c 3. Gr Ch Lockport NY 1999-2000; Ch Of The Incarn Penfield NY 1992-1999; The Ch Of The Epiph Rochester NY 1991-1992. Bex Soc 1987-1990; Soc of S Jn the Evang 2004. rwstrohm@gmail.com

STROM, Aune Juanita (Mo) St Andrew's By the Lake Episcopal, PO Box 8766, Michigan City IN 46361 **R Chr Ch Rolla MO 2009-** B Renton Washington 11/17/1952 d Erick Rinert Strom & Elsi Jarvi. BA Whitworth Coll 1975; MA Fuller TS 1979; PhD Fuller TS 1981; SWTS 2005. D 10/7/2007 P 4/9/2008 Bp Edward Stuart Little II. m 8/7/1987 Jon E Threlkeld. S Andr's By The Lake Epis Ch Michigan City IN 2007-2009. aunejs@hotmail.com

STROMWELL, Gloria Regina (Md) 126 E. Liberty St., Oakland MD 21550 **D S Matt's Par Oakland MD 2008-** B Minneapolis MN 12/18/1939 d Charles Joseph Little & Esther Lillian. D 7/5/2008 P 6/27/2009 Bp John Leslie Rabb. m 12/26/1959 Stephen W Stromwell c 2. gstromwell@gmail.com

STRONG, Anne Lorraine (Az) PO Box 65840, Tucson AZ 85728 B Chicago IL 9/15/1945 d Langdon Davenport Strong & Lorraine G. D 1/23/2010 Bp Kirk Stevan Smith. c 3. annes@qwestoffice.net

STRONG, Daniel Robert (WMass) 17 Exeter Dr, Auburn MA 01501 B Winthrop MA 3/19/1949 s William Melvin Strong & Roberta. BA Wstrn Connecticut St U 1979; MDiv GTS 1982. D 6/5/1982 Bp Paul Moore Jr P 3/25/1983 Bp James Stuart Wetmore. m 11/14/1981 Nancy Baillie c 1. P-in-c S Jn's Ch Worcester MA 2002-2006; Dio Wstrn Massachusetts Springfield MA 2000-2005; Int Trin Epis Ch Milford MA 2000-2002; P-in-c S Dav's Ch Highland Mills NY 1985-2000; P-in-c S Paul's Ch Chester NY 1985-2000; Epis. Comm Of Cntrl Orange Goshen NY 1985-1995; Cur Chr Ch Of Ramapo Suffern NY 1982-1984; Vic Chr Epis Ch Sparkill NY 1982-1984. Ord Of S Lk. frdan319@msn.com

STRONG III, Maurice Leroy (Chi) 26 E Stonegate Dr, Prospect Heights IL 60070 **P-in-c Ch Of The Incarn Bloomingdale IL 2009-** B Washington DC 10/3/1960 s Maurice Leroy Strong & Nancy Ann. BS Pur 1987; MDiv SWTS 1992; MS NWU 2006. D 6/13/1992 Bp Joseph Thomas Heistand P 12/1/1992 Bp Frank Tracy Griswold III. m 6/16/1984 Kimberly Paffett c 2. Asst S Lawr Epis Ch Libertyville IL 2001-2004; S Greg's Epis Ch Deerfield IL 1993. maurice.strong@ngc.com

STRONG, Nancy Baillie (WMass) 17 Exeter Dr, Auburn MA 01501 **Chair, COM Dio Wstrn Massachusetts Springfield MA 2010-; R S Matt's Ch Worcester MA 2000-** B Chester PA 5/3/1954 d Craig Baillie & Nancy Anne. BA Lebanon Vlly Coll 1976; MDiv GTS 1983. D 6/11/1983 Bp Lyman Cunningham Ogilby P 11/10/1984 Bp Walter Decoster Dennis Jr. m 11/14/1981 Daniel Robert Strong c 3. Chair, COM Dio Wstrn Massachusetts Springfield MA 2010; Mem, BEC Dio Wstrn Massachusetts Springfield MA 2003-2010; Pstr Ch Of The Gd Shpd Newburgh NY 1993-2000; Hudson Vlly Mnstrs New Windsor NY 1990-2000; P-in-c Ch Of The Gd Shpd Greenwood Lake NY 1988-1989; Asst S Steph's Ch Pearl River NY 1983-1985. Auth, "Poetry," *Wmn Uncommon Prayers*, Morehouse Pub, 2000. nbs5354@msn.com

STROTHEIDE, Cassandra Jo (Colo) 19210 E Stanford Dr, Aurora CO 80015 **Asst The Ch Of The Ascen Denver CO 2010-; Exec Com- High Plains Reg Dio Colorado Denver CO 2009-** B Ossining NY 9/19/1949 d Charles Burton Acker & Patricia Lantz. BS Colorado St U 1971; MDiv Epis TS of The SW 2005. D 6/11/2005 P 12/17/2005 Bp Robert John O'Neill. m 4/7/1972 Larry L Strotheide c 2. P-in-c All SS Epis Ch Denver CO 2007-2008; Asst S Matt's Parker CO 2005-2007. cass@strotheide.com

STROUD, Nancy Webb (WMass) 64 Westwood Dr, Westfield MA 01085 **R Ch Of The Atone Westfield MA 2009-** B Bryn Mawr PA 4/6/1957 d Stuart Bates Webb & Julia Nelson. BA U of Virginia 1979; Luth TS at Philadelphia 2004; MDiv GTS 2005. D 6/4/2005 P 12/17/2005 Bp Charles Ellsworth Bennison Jr. m 8/20/1983 William D Stroud c 3. S Ptr's Ch In The Great Vlly Malvern PA 2006-2009; S Paul's Ch Philadelphia PA 2005-2006. nwstroud@gmail.com

STROUD, Robert L (WNC) PO Box 38, Rutherfordton NC 28139 B 1/18/1940 D.

STROUP, Susan Louise (Oly) No address on file. **D S Paul's Epis Ch Bremerton WA 2004-** B Kellogg ID 11/10/1962 BA Evergreen St Coll 2002. D 6/26/2004 Bp Sanford Zangwill Kaye Hampton.

STRUBEL, Gary Francis (Alb) 457 3rd St, Troy NY 12180 B Troy NY 6/1/1968 BA SUNY 1993; MLS SUNY 1996; MA St. Bernards TS And Mnstry Rochester NY 2004. D 6/12/2004 Bp Daniel William Herzog P 1/15/2005 Bp David John Bena. m 9/14/1996 Tina Krstine Bruce c 2. All SS Ch Hoosick NY 2005-2008; D S Paul's Ch Troy NY 2004-2005. fatherstrubel@yahoo.com

STRUBLE, Kenneth Charles (At) 4076 Riverdale Rd., Toccoa GA 30577 **Dio Atlanta Atlanta GA 2002-** B Toccoa GA 6/7/1962 s Robert Bryan Struble & Peggy Joe. BA U GA 1987; MDiv GTS 1993; MA Georgia Sch Of Profsnl Psychol Atlanta GA 2000. D 6/5/1993 P 12/1/1993 Bp Frank Kellogg Allan. m 12/30/1989 Melanie Gearing c 3. Asst R S Dav's Ch Roswell GA 1993-2002. kstruble@windstream.net

STUART JR, Calvin Truesdale Biddison (Mo) 5008 Bischoff Ave, Saint Louis MO 63110 B Saint Louis MO 1/6/1937 s Calvin Biddison Stuart & Cynthia Jane. BS Washington U 1961; MDiv EDS 1964. D 6/1/1964 P 12/4/1964 Bp George Leslie Cadigan. m 9/3/1960 Georgiana Bernice Baier c 3. Asst Ch Of The Ascen S Louis MO 1964-1965. stuanhill@sbcglobal.net

STUART, Charles Moore (EMich) 821 Adams St, Saginaw MI 48602 B Grand Rapids MI 5/6/1928 s James Victor Stuart & Margaret Lee. BA Ya 1950; BD EDS 1956; Fllshp Coll of Preachers 1970; DMin VTS 1983. D 6/23/1956 P 12/23/1956 Bp Dudley B McNeil. m 6/28/1958 Judith A Anderson c 4. Archd Reg I Dio Estrn Michigan Saginaw MI 1986-1992; R S Jn's Epis Ch Saginaw MI 1967-1993; Cathd Chapt Dio Michigan Detroit MI 1966-1969; Chair, Fin Com Dio Michigan Detroit MI 1966-1967; Exec Coun Dio Michigan Detroit MI 1965-1967; R Trin Epis Ch Monroe MI 1962-1967; Chair, Dept CSR Dio Wstrn Michigan Kalamazoo MI 1958-1962; R S Jn's Ch Mt Pleasant MI 1958-1962; Asst Gr Epis Ch Traverse City MI 1956-1958. cjkbaca@aol.com

STUART, Judith L (Mass) PO Box 789, Chatham MA 02633 **P Dio Massachusetts Boston MA 2006-** B Boston MA 3/1/1955 d Robert Butler & Carol. BS NEU 1981; M.Ed. Boston Coll 1982; MDiv EDS 2001. D 5/9/2002 P 11/3/2002 Bp Edwin Max Leidel Jr. m 6/7/1975 William J Stuart c 2. Assoc Ch Of The Redeem Chestnut Hill MA 2003-2006; Asst S Christophers Epis Ch Grand Blanc MI 2002-2003. JLBSTUART@GMAIL.COM

STUART, Lawrence Earl (Mich) 3901 Cheyenne Rd, Richmond VA 23235 **Vic S Jn's Ch Chesaning MI 1969-; Cur Calv Memi Epis Ch Saginaw MI 1968-** B Schenectady NY 8/31/1931 s Clifford Ward Stuart & Thelma Irene. Michigan TS 1968. D 3/28/1968 Bp Archie H Crowley P 9/1/1976 Bp H Coleman McGehee Jr. m 12/27/1949 Lilia Elizabeth Tipaldi. Asst Ch Of The Gd Shpd Richmond VA 1995-2006. lestuart@erols.com

STUART, Marianne D(esmarais) (Ala) 249 Arch St, Philadelphia PA 19106 **S Jn's Epis Deaf Ch Birmingham AL 2006-** B Springfield MA 10/9/1951 d Camille L Desmarais & Marjorie A. U of Alabama; NW Connecticut Cmnty Coll Winsted CT 1971; MacMurray Coll 1973; Bp St 1976. D 5/26/1994 Bp Calvin Onderdonk Schofield Jr P 10/1/1995 Bp John Lewis Said. m 9/16/2010 Peter F Stuart c 8. Dio Pennsylvania Philadelphia PA 2001-2006; All Souls Ch For The Deaf Philadelphia PA 2001; Mssnr w The Deaf Dio Wstrn No Carolina Asheville NC 1997-2001. Epis Conf Of The Deaf Of The Epis Ch In The USA. mariannestuart@juno.com

STUART, Mark Donald (Los) 2260 N Cahuenga Blvd # 507, Los Angeles CA 90068 **Int Ch Of The Mssh Santa Ana CA 2011-; Chair, Stwdshp and Dvlpmt Dio Los Angeles Los Angeles CA 2007-** B Hutchinson KS 5/19/1951 s Donald Edward Stuart & Eunice Catherine. BA San Francisco St U 1974; MDiv Nash 1979. D 6/30/1979 Bp C Kilmer Myers P 4/12/1980 Bp William Edwin Swing. Int S Aug By-The-Sea Par Santa Monica CA 2010-2011; Assoc S Thos The Apos Hollywood Los Angeles CA 2002-2010; Assoc Trin Epis Ch Mobile AL 1993-2000; Wilmer Hall Mobile AL 1990-2001; Assoc R Trin Ch Atchison KS 1989-1990; Vic Ch Of The Trsfg Bennington KS 1986-1989; Com Dio Wstrn Kansas Hutchinson KS 1982-1984; S Fran Cmnty Serv Inc. Salina KS 1981-1990; Cur Calv Epis Ch Santa Cruz CA 1979-1981; Com Dio California San Francisco CA 1979-1980. Auth, "Grief Transformed," Paige Press, 2010. markdstuart@sbcglobal.net

STUART, Robert Allen (Fla) 28 Burning Bush Dr, Palm Coast FL 32137 **Died 9/25/2011** B Canonsburg PA 7/11/1940 s Malcolm Henry Stuart & Ethel Elaine. BS Florida St U 1962; MDiv VTS 1965; VTS 1971. D 6/22/1965 P 3/31/1966 Bp Edward Hamilton West. c 4. Cn Dio FL 2008. stuart@pcfl.net

STUART, Toni Freeman (NCal) 4881 8th St, Carpinteria CA 93013 **Asst S Mich's U Mssn Island Isla Vista CA 2005-** B Bakersfield CA 11/27/1937 d Jack R B Freeman & Elinor. BA Stan 1959; MA Claremont TS 1989. D 6/10/1989 P 1/13/1990 Bp Frederick Houk Borsch. c 3. R S Matt's Epis Ch Sacramento CA 2000-2005; Vic Epis Chap Of S Fran Los Angeles CA 1993-2000; Int S Thos' Mssn Hacienda Heights CA 1993; Asst S Paul's Pomona Pomona CA 1991-1993; Assoc All SS Par Los Angeles CA 1989-1991. Co-Ed, "The Last Great Bch Town Revs," Lulu, 2009; Auth, "Adventures Of The Soul," 2000. Immac Heart Cmnty 1998. Polly Bond Awd Epis Cmncatn 1995. tonistuart@cox.net

STUBBS, John Derek (NY) 33 Linwood Avenue, Whitinsville MA 01588 **P-in-c Trin Epis Ch Whitinsville MA 2011-** B Johannesburg ZA 9/3/1952 s Derek Duncan Stubbs & Margaret Helen. BTh U of So Afr ZA 1980; MDiv GTS 1983; STM UTS 1984; Organisational Dvlpmt 1988; Microsoft Access Visual Basic 1995; Myers Briggs Type Indicator 1995; ThD U of So Afr ZA 1999. Trans from Church of the Province of Southern Africa 4/1/1985 as Deacon Bp Paul Moore Jr. m 5/28/2009 Barbara Stubbs c 3. Int S Mary's Castleton Staten Island NY 2008-2010; Dio Grahamstown 1999-2008; Dio Cape Town 1995-1999; Exec Coun Appointees New York NY 1991-1995; Ch Of The Heav Rest New York NY 1986-1991; Chr Ch Of Ramapo Suffern NY 1985-1986. "Dinazade: Tell Me Your Story," Unpublished, 2007; "Origin of the Sources of Mk's Gospel," Unpublished, 2005; Auth, "A Certain Wmn Raised Her Voice: The Use of Grammatical Structure and the Origins of Texts.," *Neotestamentica 36(1-2) 2002, page 21 37. Festschrift for Prof Jn Suggit*, U of Kwa-Zulu Natal, 2002; Auth, "Synoptic Hist and Style Through Syntax," *Doctoral Dissertation*, U of So Afr, 1999; Auth, *The Ord Process in the Dio Capetown*, The Angl Dio Cape Town, 1998; Auth, "Popo Molefe," *Witness mag*, 1990; Auth, *Prov Yth Mnstry Manual*, The Angl Ch of So Afr, 1978. NT Soc of So Afr; SBL. Hon Cn Dio Grahamstown, So Afr 2006; Citation of Mnstry So Afr Cmnty in the USA 1991. johnderekstubbs@gmail.com

STUBBS JR, Thomas M (At) 1190 Monroe Dr Ne, Atlanta GA 30306 **Cler Assoc All SS Epis Ch Atlanta GA 2007-; Part time Dio Atlanta Atlanta GA 2002-** B Atlanta GA 8/9/1925 s Thomas M Stubbs & Beatrice Whitney. BA Harv 1948; JD U GA 1952; MDiv STUSo 1965. D 7/18/1965 P 3/1/1966 Bp Randolph R Claiborne. m 6/17/1967 Elmira Jane Poff c 3. Int S Tim's Decatur GA 1996-1997; S Aug Of Cbury Morrow GA 1974-1982; Vic S Steph's Epis Ch Smiths Sta AL 1967-1974; Vic S Mary Magd Ch Columbus GA 1965-1974. Auth, "Assault and Battery," *Encyclopedia of Georgia Law Vol. 2*, Harrison Co., 1961; Auth, *Georgia Bar Revs*, Georgia St Bar, 1950. Bro of S Andr. myraandtom@gmail.com

STUBE, Peter Brownell (EC) 1013 Basil Dr., New Bern NC 28562 **R Chr Ch New Bern NC 2003-** B Gloucester MA 1/23/1951 s Edwin Brownell Stube & Barbara Cecilia. U NC 1971; BA Columbia Intl U 1973; Estrn Nazarene Coll 1975; MDiv VTS 1979; DMin VTS 1990. D 6/30/1979 Bp David Keller Leighton Sr P 1/6/1980 Bp Jackson Earle Gilliam. m 6/22/1974 Rachael O Oram c 3. Pres of the Stndg Com Dio E Carolina Kinston NC 2009-2010; Dn Dio Pennsylvania Philadelphia PA 1999-2003; Liturg Cmsn Dio Pennsylvania Philadelphia PA 1992-1998; Ch Of The Redeem Springfield PA 1990-2003; S Jude's Ch Marietta GA 1986-1990; R Ch Of The Gd Shpd Forrest City AR 1983-1986; Vic Ch Of The H Cross Owasso OK 1981-1982; Cur S Lk's Ch Billings MT 1979-1981. Auth, *Preparing a Grp for Servnt Ldrshp: An Experiment in Mssn/ Cov*. Soc of S Fran - Tertiary 1983. Liberty hon Awd Craven Cnty NAACP 2007. peterstube@christchurchnewbern.com

STUBER, Richard Leonard (Wyo) 1320 Landon Ave, Yakima WA 98902 B Wapato WA 12/27/1933 s Leonard Adolph Stuber & Fern Lorene. Lic Vancouver TS 1971. Trans from Anglican Church of Canada 8/27/1978 Bp Bob Gordon Jones. m 4/18/1958 Mary Ann Tillmanc c 4. S Mk's Epis Ch Casper WY 1978-1980.

STUCKEY, Ross Woods (WMo) 1654 E Cardinal St, Springfield MO 65804 B Monticello AR 11/21/1938 s Monroe Frank Stuckey & Helen. Arkansas A&M Coll; SW-at-Memphis; BA U of Arkansas 1962; MDiv VTS 1976. D 5/22/1976 Bp John Alfred Baden P 3/12/1977 Bp Christoph Keller Jr. m 6/1/1996 Paula B Breazeale c 3. R S Jas' Ch Springfield MO 1990-2008; Assoc Gr Ch Carthage MO 1986-1989; R S Jn's Ch Harrison AR 1982-1985; R Ch Of The Gd Shpd Forrest City AR 1978-1982; Vic Gr Ch Wynne AR 1978-1982; Vic S Jas Ch Magnolia AR 1976-1978; Cur S Mary's Epis Ch El Dorado AR 1976-1978. rwstuckey@yahoo.com

STUDDIFORD, Linton Hervey (Me) 124 Bunganuc Rd, Brunswick ME 04011 **Dep, GC Dio Maine Portland ME 2009-** B New York NY 11/11/1941 s Andrew Douglass Studdiford & Marjorie Harkness. BA Pr 1963; MA U of Pennsylvania 1966; MDiv Bangor TS 1985; DMin Bangor TS 1997. D 6/29/1980 P 3/1/1985 Bp Frederick Barton Wolf. m 4/3/1963 Bonnie Bingham c 2. P-in-c S Phil's Ch Wiscasset ME 2009-2011; Dep, GC Dio Maine Portland ME 2006-2008; Dep, GC Dio Maine Portland ME 2003-2005; Dep, GC Dio Maine Portland ME 2000-2002; Cn to the Ordnry Dio Maine Portland ME 1999-2008; Dep, GC Dio Maine Portland ME 1997-1999; Pres, Stndg Com Dio Maine Portland ME 1994-1997; Dep, GC Dio Maine Portland ME 1994-1996; R S Alb's Ch Cape Eliz ME 1992-1999; R S Geo's Epis Ch Sanford ME 1985-1992; Vic All SS Epis Ch Skowhegan ME 1985; Asst All SS Epis Ch Skowhegan ME 1980-1982. Soc of S Jn the Evang. lintonstuddiford@gmail.com

STUDLEY, Carolyn Mary (Minn) 614 N Old Litchfield Rd, Litchfield Park AZ 85340 **D Dio Minnesota Minneapolis MN 1987-** B Duluth MN 3/22/1931 d Orien Russell Anderson & Helen Marie. S Lk's Sch of Nrsng 1953; BS Bemidji St U 1983; Cert Kino Inst Phoenix AZ 2002. D 10/25/1987 Bp Robert Marshall Anderson. c 3. staykudley@cox.net

STUDLEY, Richard E (Minn) 9817 W. Pinecrest Dr, Sun City AZ 85351 **D Ch Of The Adv Sun City W AZ 2010-** B Brockton MA 4/6/1932 s John Benjamin Studley & Sarah Isabelle. BS Bryant U 1957; MA U of San Francisco 2004. D 10/25/1987 Bp Robert Marshall Anderson. m 12/27/1955 Carolyn Mary Anderson. D S Paul's Epis Ch Duluth MN 1987-2000. Ord of S Lk.

STUHLMAN, Byron David (CNY) PO Box 74, Round Pond ME 04564 B Dayton OH 6/8/1941 s Byron C Stuhlman & Margaret Evelyn. BA (mcl) Ya 1963; STB (cl) GTS 1966; PhD Duke 1991. D 6/11/1966 Bp Walter H Gray P 3/1/1967 Bp John Henry Esquirol. m 6/28/1968 Hester K Krusen c 1. Chair, Dioceasn Cmsn on Liturg & Mus Dio Cntrl New York Syracuse NY 1998-2007; R Gr Epis Ch Waterville NY 1997-2007; Int Emm Ch Norwich NY 1996-1997; Chenango Cluster Norwich NY 1996; Assoc S Jas' Ch Clinton NY 1992-2001; Chair, Liturg Cmsn Dio Connecticut Hartford CT 1972-1985; R S Mk's Ch Bridgewater CT 1971-1988; Cur Chr Ch Cathd Hartford CT 1966-1971. Auth, "The Initiatory Process in the Byzantine Tradition," Gorgias Press, 2009; Auth, ",A Gd and Joyful Thing," Ch Pub, Inc, 2000; Auth, ",Occasions of Gr," Ch Publshing, Inc, 1995; Auth, ",Redeeming the Time," Ch Pub, Inc, 1992; Auth, "Eucharistic Celebration 1789-1979," Ch Pub, 1988; Auth, ",PB Rubrics Expanded," Ch Pub, Inc, 1987. Associated Parishes, ADLMC, Societas Liturgica 1976-1992. bstuhl@tidewater.net

STUHLMANN, Robert (Ct) 2000 Main St, Stratford CT 06615 B Boston MA 11/14/1943 s Robert K Stuhlmann & Phyllis E. BA Hob 1966; MDiv ETS 1970. D 11/6/1971 Bp John Melville Burgess P 12/14/1976 Bp John Bowen Coburn. m 5/31/2003 Jean Guenther c 2. Chr Ch Stratford CT 1996-2010; Philadelphia Cathd Philadelphia PA 1995-1996; Urban Coordntr Dio Connecticut Hartford CT 1987-1996; S Jn's Ch Jamaica Plain MA 1984-1986. Auth, "Dorchester Argus Citizen". Nj Epis Cleric Assn. bobstuhlmann@gmail.com

STUMP, Celeste Smith (Los) 330 E 16th St, Upland CA 91784 B New Orlens LA 6/2/1956 d James L Smith & Armantine. BA Loyola - New Orleans 1978; MPA U of Arizona 1984; Cert in Deaconal Stds ETS Claremont 2010. D 5/23/2010 Bp Chester Lovelle Talton. m 9/28/1990 Scott Stump c 3. csstump@fastmail.com

STUMP, Derald William (CPa) 106 S Outer Dr, State College PA 16801 B Des Moines IA 11/5/1930 s Joseph V Stump & Leah. Cert Unniversity of Pennsylvania; BA Drake U 1953; MDiv EDS 1959; Harv 1959; U So 1963; Med Penn 1968; EdD Penn 1979. D 6/29/1959 P 5/28/1960 Bp Gordon V Smith. m 6/5/1957 Jean Conway. S Mk's Epis Ch Lewistown PA 1999-2001; Cnvnr Altoona Convoc Dio Cntrl Pennsylvania Harrisburg PA 1997-1999; Assoc R S Andr's Ch St Coll PA 1997-1999; Dio Cntrl Pennsylvania Harrisburg PA 1989-1991; Mem Eccl Trial Crt Dio Cntrl Pennsylvania Harrisburg PA 1989-1991; CFS The Sch At Ch Farm Exton PA 1982-1983; Chair Dept MHE Dio Cntrl Pennsylvania Harrisburg PA 1974-1982; Secy Dio Cntrl Pennsylvania Harrisburg PA 1973-1982; COM Dio Cntrl Pennsylvania Harrisburg PA 1971-1976; Bd Profnl Dvlpmt Mnstry Dio Cntrl Pennsylvania Harrisburg PA 1970-1982; ExCoun Dio Cntrl Pennsylvania Harrisburg PA 1967-1971; S Andr's Ch St Coll PA 1963-1965; Dioc Mssy Dio Iowa Des Moines IA 1960-1963; Cur The Cathd Ch Of S Paul Des Moines IA 1959-1960. Contrib, *The Gospel According to ESPN: Saviours and Sinners*, 2003; Auth, *Nile Kinnick: The Man & The Legend*, Univ of iowa press, 1975. ESMHE 1969-1982. jcs18jcs18@gmail.com

STURDY, Robert Charles (SC) 5717 Porcher Dr, Myrtle Beach SC 29577 **R Trin Ch Myrtle Bch SC 2006-** B Atlanta GA 4/26/1981 s John Oliver & Cheryl Gene. BA Cit 2003; BTh Wycliffe Hall of Oxf 2006. D 7/1/2003 P 1/8/2007 Bp Edward Lloyd Salmon Jr. m 6/21/2003 Stephanie McLaughlin. robert.sturdy@hotmail.com

STURGEON, Mary Sue (Neb) 5176 S 149th Ct, Omaha NE 68137 B Bedford IN 8/7/1940 d Grant Marion Coover & Maxine Mildred. D 11/8/1985 Bp James Daniel Warner. m 9/4/1993 William John Kouth c 3. D All SS Epis Ch Omaha NE 1985-2007. msturgeon@tconl.com

STURGEON, Stephen C (U) 85 E 100 N, Logan UT 84321 **Epis Cmnty Serv Inc Salt Lake City UT 2011-** B Berkeley, CA 10/30/1967 s Jack Dean. BA Gri 1990; PhD U CO 1998; Cert Utah Mnstry Formation Progran 2009. D 6/12/2010 Bp Carolyn Tanner Irish. m 7/25/1998 Stacy Stacy Louck c 1. scsturgeon67@gmail.com

STURGES, Harriette Horsey (WA) 3001 Wisconsin Ave NW, Washington DC 20016 **D Sprtl Dir Dio No Carolina Raleigh NC 1990-** B Savannah GA 12/19/1944 d Richard Henry Horsey & Harriette Augusta. BA Sweet Briar Coll 1966; MTS Duke 1989; Sch for Deacons in NC 1990. D 6/9/1990 Bp Robert Whitridge Estill. m 9/3/1966 Conrad Sturges c 2. S Alb's Par Washington DC 2007-2011; D S Phil's Ch Durham NC 1995-2007; D S Paul's Ch Louisburg NC 1990-1993. NAAD 1990; Soc Comp of the H Cross 1986. hsturges@st-albans-parish.org

STURGES, Kathleen McAuliffe (Va) 446 White Cedar Road, Barboursville VA 22923 **Vic Ch Of S Jn The Bapt Ivy VA 2001-; Dio Virginia Richmond VA 2001-** B Walnut Creek CA 6/16/1968 d John Gary McAuliffe & Kathryn Ann. BA Seattle Pacific U 1991; MDiv Ya Berk 1996. D 6/22/1996 Bp Vincent Waydell Warner P 1/7/1997 Bp Peter James Lee. m 8/24/1991 Michael Eliot Sturges c 3. Asst Ch Of Our Sav Charlottesville VA 1996-2000. kmsturges@hotmail.com

STURGESS, Amber (Cal) 6208 Sutter Ave, Richmond CA 94804 **S Geo's Epis Ch Antioch CA 2007-** B Tulia TX 5/5/1962 d Larry Bradford Sturgess & Phyllis June. BA Texas Tech U 1984; MA Texas Tech U 1989; MA Perkins TS 1996; CAS Cdsp Berkeley 2005. D 10/16/2004 P 9/7/2005 Bp C(harles) Wallis Ohl. CDSP Berkeley CA 2006-2007; Asst S Cuth's Epis Ch Oakland CA 2005-2006. asturgess@msn.com

STURGIS, Janet Elizabeth (Neb) Po Box 2285, Kearney NE 68848 B Mount Holly NJ 3/12/1943 d Malcolm Baker Sturgis & Ann Louise. BA U of Missouri 1965; MDiv VTS 1984. D 5/26/1984 Bp Walter Cameron Righter P 12/18/1984 Bp William Foreman Creighton. m 10/28/1967 Terry Elsberry c 2. Chapl Epis Ch At Cornell Ithaca NY 2001-2003; R S Lk's Ch Kearney NE 1999-2001; Int Chr Ch Fairmont WV 1997-1999; S Jas The Apos Epis Ch Tempe AZ 1993-1995; Int S Mich's Ch Naugatuck CT 1992-1993; Chr Ch Oxford CT 1990-1992; Int S Jn's Epis Ch Bristol CT 1989-1990; Chr Ch Greenwich CT 1986-1989; S Fran Ch Potomac MD 1986; Zion Epis Ch Chas Town WV 1985-1986; Asst S Fran Ch Potomac MD 1985. Ees. jes4319@yahoo.com

STURM, Charles Edwin (Mich) 219 Saint Awdry St, Summerville SC 29485 **Asst Ch Of The H Fam Moncks Corner SC 2003-** B Detroit MI 9/30/1927 s Max Carl Sturm & Nina Marion. BA Wayne 1960; MDiv Bex 1961. D 6/29/1961 Bp Robert Lionne DeWitt P 1/6/1962 Bp Archie H Crowley. m 5/25/1974 Barbara Ann Brown c 3. R S Paul's Epis Ch Brighton MI 1982-1992; Emrich Retreat Cntr Detroit MI 1973-1982; R S Jn's Ch Howell MI 1970-1973; Vic H Faith Ch Saline MI 1966-1970; Vic S Jn's Ch Clinton MI 1966-1970; Asst All SS Epis Ch Pontiac MI 1964-1966; Vic S Andr's Epis Ch Rose City MI 1961-1964; Vic Trin Epis Ch W Branch MI 1961-1964. sturm@utm.net

STURNI, Gary K (WTenn) 1853 Miller Farms Rd, Germantown TN 38138 **R S Geo's Ch Germantown TN 2004-** B Newark NJ 1/24/1946 s Albert Christian Sturni & Kathryn Brisley. BA Sacramento St U 1967; BD CDSP 1970; MA Grad Theol Un 1970; DMin SFTS 1987; Cert W&M 2000. D 6/29/1970 Bp Clarence Rupert Haden Jr P 5/1/1971 Bp Edward McNair. m 12/28/1976 Cynthia Chrysler White c 3. Ch Of The Mssh Lower Gwynedd PA 2003-2004; The Ch Of Ascen And H Trin Cincinnati OH 2001-2003; H Trin Epis Ch Oxford OH 1997; S Fran Cmnty Serv Inc. Salina KS 1993-2003; Chair of the Funding Com Dio Sthrn Ohio Cincinnati OH 1988-2003; Trin Ch Hamilton OH 1988-1993; Sr Assoc S Andr's Ch Saratoga CA 1985-1988; Founding P-in-c Chr The King Quincy CA 1978-1980; R S Jn The Evang Ch Chico CA 1974-1985; Vic S Lk's Mssn Calistoga CA 1972-1974; Cur Chr Ch Eureka CA 1970-1972. Auth, "Producer Hisp Mnstry in Prov VIII," *Hisp Mnstry in ECR videos*. gsturni@gmail.com

STURTEVANT, Henry Hobson (NY) 484 W 43rd St Apt 33-H, New York NY 10036 B Portland ME 1/25/1945 s Peter Mann Sturtevant & Katharine Bryan. BFA Bos 1967; BD EDS 1971. D 7/24/1971 P 4/27/1972 Bp Henry W Hobson. S Andr's Ch Oceanside NY 1995-2010; S Clem's Ch New York NY 1975-1980; Asst Indn Hill Ch Cincinnati OH 1971-1975.

STUTLER, James Boyd (At) 2124 Summerchase Dr, Woodstock GA 30189 **R S Clem's Epis Ch Canton GA 2004-** B Charleston SC 8/10/1956 s Warren Harding Stutler & Joan Roberta. GW 1975; BA U So 1979; JD Mississippi Coll 1986; MDiv STUSo 1999. D 6/6/1999 P 12/12/1999 Bp Edward Lloyd Salmon Jr. c 2. Vic S Alb's Ch Kingstree SC 1999-2004; Vic S Steph's Ch S Steph SC 1999-2004. frjamie@stclementscanton.org

SUAREZ, Shanna Neff (Tex) 906 Padon St, Longview TX 75601 **Trin Ch Longview TX 2009-** B Cleveland TX 7/17/1963 d Louis E Neff & Barbara. BA U of St. Thos 1985; MDiv VTS 1991. D 6/22/1991 Bp Maurice Manuel Benitez P 3/1/1992 Bp William Elwood Sterling. m 6/29/1991 Stephen Suarez c 2. Dio Oklahoma Oklahoma City OK 2002-2008; S Aug Of Cbury Oklahoma City OK 2001-2002; H Sprt Epis Ch Houston TX 2000-2001; R S Jn's Epis Ch Silsbee TX 1995-2000; All SS Epis Ch Hitchcock TX 1993-1995; S Fran Epis Day Sch Houston TX 1993; S Mk's Epis Sch Houston TX 1993; S Cyp's Ch Lufkin TX 1991-1992. revshanna@aol.com

SUAREZ ELLES, Jose Armando (Colom) Cr 3 Sur # 11-A-02, Malambo ATLANTICO Colombia B Cartagena Bolivar 2/12/1968 s Jose Suarez & Acela. Lic Pontificio Universidad Jaucnana; Teologia-Filosofia Seminario Mal De Cristo; Teologia Filosofia Seminario Prov. De Cartogena. D 10/14/2006 Bp Francisco Jose Duque-Gomez. c 1. padresjosvell@hotmail.com

SUCRE-CORDOVA, Guillermo Antonio (Ve) 49-143 Colinas de Bello Monte, Caracas 1042 Venezuela **Dio Venezuela Colinas De Bello Monte Caracas 10-42-A VE 2004-** B 11/29/1941 D 7/24/1997 Bp Orlando Jesus Guerrero. GISELASUCREH@HOTMAIL.COM

SUELLAU, David Irving (CFla) 8614 Heartwood Ct, Tallahassee FL 32312 B Port Chester NY 5/6/1930 s Irving Chester Suellau & Selina. BA Stetson U 1976; MDiv STUSo 1978; DD Honolulu U 1994. D 6/21/1965 Bp William Loftin Hargrave P 12/21/1965 Bp Henry I Louttit. m 1/3/1998 Nancy Shebs Leigh. Int Ch Of The Ascen Carrabelle FL 2003-2004; Int S Mich And All Ang Ch Tallahassee FL 2000; Epis Ch Of The H Sprt Tallahassee FL 1999-2000; Cur Epis Ch Of The H Sprt Tallahassee FL 1998-1999; Int Ch Of The Gd Shpd Jacksonville FL 1997-1998; S Barn Ch Deland FL 1975-1994; R Ch Of The Gd Shpd Maitland FL 1968-1975; Cur Emm Ch Orlando FL 1965-1968. shebbers@aol.com

SUELLAU, Nancy Shebs (Fla) St Catherines Episcopal Church, 4758 Shelby Ave, Jacksonville FL 32210 **Chair of Dispatch of Bus, Dioc Conv 2012 Dio Florida Jacksonville FL 2012-; Alt Deligate to Natl Conv 2012 Dio Florida Jacksonville FL 2011-; Mem of the Eccl Crt Dio Florida Jacksonville FL 2010-2012; Dioc Congreational Emergency Response Team Mem Dio Florida Jacksonville FL 2009-; ECW Chapl Dio Florida Jacksonville FL 2009-; Congrl Dvlpmt Com Dio Florida Jacksonville FL 2008-2013; R S Cathr's Ch Jacksonville FL 2007-** B Tallahassee FL 6/22/1954 d Robert Townes Leigh & Mary J. BA Florida St U 1975; MS Flordia St U 1976; BSN Florida St U 1983; MDiv TESM 2007. D 5/27/2007 P 12/9/2007 Bp Samuel Johnson Howard. m 1/3/1998 David Irving Suellau c 2. d the King 2000. mtrnancy@gmail.com

SUGENO, David Senkichi (Tex) PO Box 89, Round Mountain TX 78663 **Trin Epis Ch Marble Falls TX 2009-** B 6/2/1965 s Frank Eiji Sugeno. BA Connecticut Coll New London CT 1987; MA Texas A&M U Coll Sta TX 2000; MDiv Epis TS of The SW 2006. D 6/24/2006 Bp Don Adger Wimberly P 1/20/2007 Bp Dena Arnall Harrison. m 4/17/1999 Amy S Sugeno c 1. Asst S Jas The Apos Epis Ch Conroe TX 2006-2009. DAVID@TRINITYMARBLEFALLS.ORG

SUHAR, John Charles (SwFla) 771 34th Ave N, Saint Petersburg FL 33704 **P-in-c S Thos' Epis Ch St Petersburg FL 2011-; P-in-c S Thos' Epis Ch St Petersburg FL 2011-; Assoc R S Thos' Epis Ch St Petersburg FL 2005-** B Weisbaden GERMANY 4/23/1950 s Walter Suhar & Yvonne. U Of Missouri Columbia Whiteman Afb MO; BS USAF Acad 1972; JD U of Miami 1978; MA Pepperdine U Homstead Afb FL 1981; MDiv VTS 2005. D 6/18/2005 P 12/18/2005 Bp John Bailey Lipscomb. m 6/23/1973 Barbara Lynn Van Eaton c 2. jsuhar@tampabay.rr.com

SUHR, Esther J (Mont) 2584 Mt Hwy 284, Townsend MT 59644 **Cn 9 P S Jn's Ch/Elkhorn Cluster Townsend MT 2006-** B Billings MT 3/12/1960 d Louis William Suhr & Olive Jean. D 9/18/2005 P 7/29/2006 Bp Charles Franklin Brookhart Jr. esuhr@mt.net

SUIT, Marvin Wilson (Lex) 440 Fountain Avenue, Flemingsburg KY 41041 B Maysville KY 7/13/1933 s Perry Wilson Grover Suit & Mary Nelson. BS U of Kentucky 1955; LLB/JD U of Kentucky 1957; Lic Epis TS In Kentucky 1988. D 6/12/1988 P 4/1/1992 Bp Don Adger Wimberly. m 6/8/1956 Nancy Calhoun Wilder. P-in-c S Alb's Ch Morehead KY 2000-2004; Vic S Fran' Epis Ch Flemingsburg KY 1992-2000. NAAD; Tertiary of the Soc of S Fran.

SULERUD, Mary Catherine (WA) Washington National Cathedral, Mount Saint Alban, Washington DC 20016 **Cathd of St Ptr & St Paul Washington DC 2011-** B Richmond VA 2/14/1951 d Leo James Miller & Gene Eldridge. BS St. Cloud St U 1973; MDiv VTS 1988. D 6/23/1988 Bp Robert Marshall Anderson P 5/5/1989 Bp Peter James Lee. m 12/6/1975 Peder Anders Sulerud c 1. Dio Washington Washington DC 2003-2011; VTS Alexandria VA 1997-2001; Dio Washington Washington DC 1996-1998; R Ch Of The Ascen Silver Sprg MD 1995-2002; Dio Virginia Richmond VA 1989-1991; Gr Epis Ch Alexandria VA 1988-1995. EDOW Coun 1998-2002; EDOW Fin Com Chair 1999-2002; GBEC 2002-2009; WECA Bd Mem 1999-2003. msulerud@cathedral.org

SULLIVAN, Ann Mary (NCal) 99 E Middlefield Rd Apt 25, Mountain View CA 94043 **R Ch Of S Nich Paradise CA 2006-** B San Jose CA 10/23/1957 d Eugene Farrell Sullivan & Yvonne Margaret. California St U; BS San Diego St U 1980; MS Santa Clara U 1987; MDiv CDSP 1997. D 6/27/1998 P 2/1/1999 Bp Richard Lester Shimpfky. m 10/6/2001 Linn J Brownmiller c 3. S Edw The Confessor Epis Ch San Jose CA 2001-2006; S Mk's Epis Ch Santa Clara CA 1999-2000. REVANNSTNICK@GMAIL.COM

SULLIVAN, Bernadette Marie (LI) Po Box 243, Hampton Bays NY 11946 **R S Mary's Ch Hampton Bays NY 2000-** B Bronx NY 2/20/1948 d John Patrick O'Rourke & Helen Elizabeth. BA SUNY 1992; MDiv GTS 1997. D 6/28/1997 Bp Rodney Rae Michel P 3/1/1998 Bp Orris George Walker Jr. m 10/20/1973 Charles Moffitt Sullivan c 4. Asst S Jn's Of Lattingtown Locust Vlly NY 1997-2000. bmsullivan220@yahoo.com

SULLIVAN JR, Bob Sullivan (SeFla) 8144 Bridgewater Ct Apt C, West Palm Beach FL 33406 B 5/2/1945 D 6/3/2006 Bp Leopold Frade. m 6/18/1966 Linda Robert Sullivan c 3. bob@sullivanelectric-pump.com

SULLIVAN, Bradley Joseph (Tex) 3003 Memorial Ct Apt 2405, Houston TX 77007 **Asst To The R Emm Ch Houston TX 2005-** B 4/6/1978 BS U of Texas 2000; MDiv VTS 2005. D 6/11/2005 P 12/17/2005 Bp Don Adger Wimberly. m 5/22/2004 Kristin Louise Sullivan. bradaa23@hotmail.com

SULLIVAN, Brian Christopher (At) 207 E 10th St Sw # A, Rome GA 30161 **St Ben's Epis Ch Smyrna GA 2010-** B White Plains NY 5/28/1971 s Gary B Sullivan & Margaret Stahlmann. BFA U GA 1993; MDiv GTS 1997. D 6/7/1997 Bp Onell Asiselo Soto P 12/1/1997 Bp Frank Kellogg Allan. m 5/20/2000 Mindy Sullivan c 3. R Ch Of The Incarn Highlands NC 2004-2010; Assoc S Anne's Epis Ch Atlanta GA 2000-2004; Asst S Ptr's Ch Rome GA 1997-2000. fr.bsully@gmail.com

SULLIVAN, Charles Moffitt (LI) PO Box 243, Hampton Bays NY 11946 B Brooklyn NY 3/31/1932 s William M Sullivan & Mary T. BA Cathd Coll of the Immac Concep 1953; Immac Concep Sem 1957; Mercer TS 1977. Rec from Roman Catholic 9/1/1978 as Priest Bp Robert Campbell Witcher Sr. m 10/20/1973 Bernadette Marie O'Rourke c 4. Trst, Estate of the Dio Dio Long Island Garden City NY 1996-2001; S Thos Of Cbury Ch Smithtown NY 1985-2002; S Thos Ch Malverne NY 1983-1985; Epis Ch Of S Mk The Evang No Bellmore NY 1978-1983. Rotary of Smithtown 1988. Paul Harris Fell Rotary 1995. BMSULLIVAN220@YAHOO.COM

SULLIVAN, Daniel Kilmer (Pa) Po Box 334, Bear Creek PA 18602 **Died 9/3/2009** B St Stephen New Brunswick CA 3/2/1928 s Edward Vincent Sullivan & Marie Louise. BA Trin Hartford CT 1953; MDiv Ya Berk 1956. D 5/26/1956 P 11/30/1956 Bp Oliver L Loring. c 3.

SULLIVAN, David Andrew (Alb) P.O. Box 146, Elizabethtown NY 12932 B Plattsburgh NY 1/9/1949 s Francis Sullivan & Virginia. D 5/10/2008 P 12/19/2010 Bp William Howard Love. m 7/8/1972 Roberta Sullivan c 1. dsullivan@gmail.com

SULLIVAN, Donald Parks (SeFla) 800 Center Street, Key West FL 33040 **Dn of the Keys Dio SE Florida Miami FL 2008-; Vic S Ptr's Epis Ch Key W FL 2007-** B Minneapolis MN 6/20/1937 s Joseph Albert Sullivan & Mary. AA Orange Coast Jr Coll Costa Mesa CA 1960; CTh GTS 1986. D 6/6/1987 Bp William Edwin Swing P 10/28/1988 Bp Robert Campbell Witcher Sr. R S Faith's Epis Ch Cutler Bay FL 2000-2007; Vic S Chris's Ch San Lorenzo CA 1993-2000; Int Ch Of The H Fam Half Moon Bay CA 1992; Chapl Epis Mssn Soc New York NY 1990-1992; Asst S Mary's Ch Lake Ronkonkoma NY 1986-1989. Soc Of S Fran 1975-1992. donsullivan37@bellsouth.net

SULLIVAN, Elmer Lindsley (NJ) 13 Llanfair Ln, Ewing NJ 08618 B Philadelphia PA 11/3/1930 s Robert Edmund Sullivan & Marion Florence. AB Dart 1952; STB GTS 1955; ThM PrTS 1978. D 4/30/1955 P 11/5/1955 Bp Alfred L Banyard. m 2/4/1967 Jean Carhart c 2. Int S Mich's Ch Trenton NJ 1991-1994; Dio New Jersey Trenton NJ 1990; Admin Asst to the Bp Dio New Jersey Trenton NJ 1983-1989; Urban Coordntr Dio New Jersey Trenton NJ 1978-1981; R S Lk's Ch Ewing NJ 1974-1983; R S Lk's Ch Ewing NJ 1962-1967; Dept Mssns Dio New Jersey Trenton NJ 1962-1966; BEC Dio New Jersey Trenton NJ 1957-1969; Vic S Lk's Ch Ewing NJ 1955-1962. Phi Beta Kappa 1951.

SULLIVAN, Herbert Patrick (Mich) 1400 Northwood Rd, Austin TX 78703 B Detroit MI 5/27/1932 s Herbert L Sullivan & Gertrude L. BD/MA U Chi 1956; MLitt Banares Hindu U 1959; PhD U Of Durham Gb 1960; JD U of Tx 1990.

D 6/25/1955 Bp Richard S M Emrich P 6/17/1956 Bp Archie H Crowley. m 6/24/1960 Joyce Ann Robinson c 2. Asst S Tit Epis Ch Durham NC 1967-1970; P-in-c S Tit Epis Ch Durham NC 1960-1963; Asst Ch Of The H Cross Chicago IL 1955-1956. Auth, "Numeroud books, monographs & arts". Life Fell, Royal Asiatic Soc 1964. ACLS Fell 1976; Guggenheim Fell 1974; D. Litt. U of Delhi 1972; Ford Fnd Fellowow 1971; Ford Fnd Fell 1968; Fulbright Fell 1965; Fulbright Fell 1962.

SULLIVAN, James Stanley (FtW) 1960 CR 158, Evant TX 78525 **Died 3/28/2011** B Lubbock TX 9/12/1937 s Vernie Rose. BBA SMU 1963; BA U of Wyoming 1981; MA U of Wyoming 1982; Med Drury U 1989. D 6/5/1980 P 6/24/1981 Bp Bob Gordon Jones. c 2. Ord of S Lk 1980. dunbroke@centex.net

SULLIVAN, Judith A (Pa) Philadelphia Episcopal Cathedral, 3723 Chestnut Street, Philadelphia PA 19104 **Dn Philadelphia Cathd Philadelphia PA 2010-; Bd Mem Epis Cmnty Serv Kansas City MO 2009-** B New Haven CT 9/10/1956 d William Wynne Sullivan & Muriel Cordett. BA Wellesley Coll 1978; MDiv GTS 2004. D 6/19/2004 P 12/18/2004 Bp Charles Ellsworth Bennison Jr. m 5/1/1984 Gilbert A Rosenthal c 2. Assoc Ch Of The Redeem Bryn Mawr PA 2007-2010; Cn Res Philadelphia Cathd Philadelphia PA 2004-2007. sullivan910@gmail.com

SULLIVAN, Karen Sue Racer (Ind) 5619 Lowell Ave., Indianapolis IN 46219 **COM Dio Indianapolis Indianapolis IN 2011-; Dir of LEV Trng Dio Indianapolis Indianapolis IN 2008-; D S Phil's Ch Indianapolis IN 2008-; Coun on the Diac Dio Indianapolis Indianapolis IN 2005-** B Hartford City IN 8/28/1955 d Donald Edward Racer & Joan Dixie. Chld Dvlpmt U of Nevada at Las Vegas 1979; D Formation Prog 2005; Bachelor of Arts St. Mary-of-the-Woods Coll 2009. D 6/18/2005 Bp Catherine Elizabeth Maples Waynick. m 6/9/1975 Sean Kevin Sullivan c 3. Assn of Epis Deacons 2005. indydoodle@sbcglobal.net

SULLIVAN, Kristin Louise (Tex) 5207 Four Rivers Ct, Houston TX 77091 **Ch Of The Epiph Houston TX 2010-; Asst S Paul's Par Lancaster CA 2005-** B PA 2/4/1978 d Roger Barkerding & Sandra. BA Jas Madison U; MDiv VTS. D 6/26/2004 P 1/10/2005 Bp Peter James Lee. m 5/22/2004 Bradley Joseph Sullivan c 2. Palmer Memi Ch Houston TX 2005-2010; Asst S Mary's Epis Ch Arlington VA 2004-2005. ksullivan@palmerchurch.org

SULLIVAN, Margaret Peggy (NY) P.O. Box 708, Walden NY 12586 **S Andr's Ch Walden NY 2009-** B Highland Park, IL 10/3/1953 BA Natl Coll of Educ 1976; MA Hartford Sem 2000; ThM EDS 2005. D 6/11/2005 P 1/14/2006 Bp Andrew Donnan Smith. m 6/26/1976 Peter Sullivan c 2. Int S Paul's Ch Woodbury CT 2008-2009; Asst S Jas Ch Glastonbury CT 2005-2008. peggysullivan2@sbcglobal.net

SULLIVAN, Mark C (Del) 463 Nicole Ct, Smyrna DE 19977 B Springfield MA 6/27/1949 s Edward B Sullivan & Dorothy Ann. AB Ken 1971; MDiv VTS 1974. D 6/16/1974 P 1/1/1975 Bp Alexander Doig Stewart. m 2/16/1985 Jane Sullivan. R S Ptr's Ch Smyrna DE 1999-2011; Assoc S Ptr's Ch Salisbury MD 1997-1999; Cn for Mnstry Dvlpmt Dio Easton Easton MD 1994-1997; Dn Trin Cathd Easton MD 1984-1994; Int Gr Epis Ch Trumbull CT 1983-1984; Co-R S Andr's Epis Ch Lincoln Pk NJ 1981-1982; Emm Epis Ch Stamford CT 1979-1981; Asst S Paul's Ch Riverside CT 1975-1979; Asst S Jn's Ch Williamstown MA 1974-1975. Auth, "Contributing Ed," *Mnstry Dvlpmt Journ*. marksulliva@gmail.com

SULLIVAN, Maryalice (Mass) 104 N Washington St, North Attleboro MA 02760 **Gr Ch No Attleborough MA 1997-** B Bronx NY 7/16/1947 d Robert John Terrell & Mary. Cert Manchester Cmnty Coll 1984; BA Estrn Connecticut St U 1986; MDiv Ya Berk 1990. D 9/23/1990 P 10/10/1991 Bp Arthur Edward Walmsley. m 7/22/1967 John Sullivan c 4. No Cntrl Reg Mnstry Enfield CT 1993-1997; Asst Calv Epis Ch Summit NJ 1991-1992. Auth, "Chld Advoc Awareness 1995," *Cltn Chld*. Soc of St Jn the Evang 1991. revmas@aol.com

SULLIVAN, Michael Radford (At) 805 Mount Vernon Highway NW, Atlanta GA 30328 **Regent The U So (Sewanee) Sewanee TN 2011-; Bd Trst The U So (Sewanee) Sewanee TN 2010-; R H Innoc Ch Atlanta GA 2009-; R H Innoc' Epis Sch Atlanta GA 2009-** B Seneca SC 11/20/1966 s Leland Radford Sullivan & Patricia A. BA Wofford Coll 1989; JD U of So Carolina 1995; MDiv STUSo 2000. D 9/23/2000 P 6/8/2001 Bp Dorsey Felix Henderson. m 5/18/1991 Page Poston c 2. Exec Coun Dio SW Virginia Roanoke VA 2008-2009; R S Jn's Ch Lynchburg VA 2005-2009; Stndg Com and Exec Coun Dio Upper So Carolina Columbia SC 2003-2005; Cn For Mssn Trin Cathd Columbia SC 2002-2005; Asst R Ch Of The Adv Spartanburg SC 2000-2002. Auth, "Windows into the Light," Morehouse, 2008; Auth, "Windows into the Soul," Morehouse, 2006. Woods Ldrshp Awd U So 1998; Ord Of The Coif U Of SC 1994; Law Revs U Of SC 1993; AmL Awd Wofford Coll 1989; Phi Beta Kappa Wofford Coll 1988. msullivan@holyinnocents.org

SULLIVAN, P David (Mass) 138 Tremont St., Boston MA 02111 **D Ch Of The Adv Medfield MA 2009-2012** B Waltham MA 11/13/1946 s Paul Ambrose Sullivan & Margaret Frary. BS Boston St Coll 1974. D 6/6/2009 Bp M(arvil) Thomas Shaw III. m 4/8/1972 Patricia Murphy c 3. ltcrtd@gmail.com

SULLIVAN JR, Robert Edmund (NJ) 3450 Wild Oak Bay Blvd, Apt 138, Bradenton FL 34210 **Asst Ch Of The Redeem Sarasota FL 1999-** B Philadelphia PA 5/3/1925 s Robert Edmund Sullivan & Marion Florence. BA Pr 1949; MDIV/THB PDS 1952; Institut Catholique De Paris 1959. D 6/14/1952 Bp Alfred L Banyard P 12/20/1952 Bp Wallace J Gardner. P-in-res Chr Ch In Woodbury Woodbury NJ 1998-2009; Pres Camden-Woodbury Cler Dio New Jersey Trenton NJ 1979-1981; Missions Bd Dio New Jersey Trenton NJ 1974-1977; R S Jn The Evang Ch Blackwood NJ 1972-1997; Vic S Jas Epis Ch Cape May NJ 1952-1958.

SULLIVAN, Rosemari G(aughan) (WA) 402 Virginia Avenue, Alexandria VA 22302 **Spec Asst to PB for Haiti Epis Ch Cntr New York NY 2010-; R S Paul's Rock Creek Washington DC 2006-** B ScrantonPA 8/3/1946 d John Robert Gaughan & Margaret Mary. BA CUA 1973; MS CUA 1974; MDiv VTS 1985; D. Min. Wesley TS 2009. D 6/22/1985 P 3/29/1986 Bp Peter James Lee. m 11/24/1973 Edmund Sullivan c 2. Exec Off-Secy of GC Epis Ch Cntr New York NY 1998-2005; R The Ch of S Clem Alexandria VA 1987-1998; Assoc R Gr Epis Ch Alexandria VA 1985-1987. "Web Homilies," *Natl Cath Reporter Online*, Natl Cath Reporter, 1998; Auth, "No Ordnry Time: The Season After Pentecost at S Clem," *Liturg*, 1996. Oblate Ord of S Ben 1997. DD VTS 2005; Untd Way Serv Awd Untd Way Alexandria 1996. rsullivan@episcopalchurch.org

SULLIVAN CLIFTON, Sonia (Ga) 3137 Denham Ct, Orlando FL 32825 **R S Matt's Epis Ch Orlando FL 2010-** B Savannah GA 6/5/1963 d George Washington Tutan & Carole. BBA Valdosta St U 1984; MBA Valdosta St U 1988; MDiv STUSo 1993. D 5/29/1993 P 12/19/1993 Bp Harry Woolston Shipps. m 6/14/2003 Steve Clifton c 2. Sum Camp Dir Georgia Epis Conf Cntr At H Waverly GA 2010-2011; Chapl Trin Preparatory Sch Of Florida Winter Pk FL 2003-2011; Assoc R Chr The King Epis Ch Orlando FL 2003-2010; Stndg Com Dio Georgia Savannah GA 1999-2003; Diocesean Coun Dio Georgia Savannah GA 1996-1999; Vic Ch Of The Gd Shpd Swainsboro GA 1993-2003; Vic Epis Ch Of S Mary Magd Louisville GA 1993-1995. soniasullivanclifton@gmail.com

SUMMERFIELD, LeRoy James (WNC) 5365 Pine Ridge Dr, Connellys Springs NC 28612 B Akron OH 1/20/1933 s LeRoy M Summerfield & Emily M. BA Bob Jones U 1956; MDiv New Orleans Bapt TS 1962; Advncd CPE 1970; BSW Livingstone Coll 1979; DMin NYTS 1989. D 12/23/1978 P 6/1/1979 Bp William Gillette Weinhauer. m 6/17/1960 Joan Patten. P-in-c S Steph's Epis Ch Morganton NC 1998-1999; S Ptr's Ch Millbrook NY 1983-1984; M-in-c S Steph's Epis Ch Morganton NC 1978-1981. Assn Mntl Hlth Chapl, Assembly of Epis Hospi 1972; New York Counsel of Ch 1981-1995. rjsummerfield@bellsouth.net

SUMMEROUR, William W (WNC) 233 Deep Ford Fls, Lake Toxaway NC 28747 **Assoc R Ch Of The Gd Shpd Cashiers NC 2007-** B Jackson MS 2/28/1950 s Tom Wisdom Summerour & Margaret Reagan. MDiv STUSo 2007. D 12/30/2006 Bp Charles Edward Jenkins III P 7/25/2007 Bp Granville Porter Taylor. m 6/9/1973 Carroll Summerour c 4. sheptoby@frontier.com

SUMMERS, Charles Raymond (Ia) 936 Grayson Dr. Apt. 329, Springfield MA 01119 **P-in-c S Barn And All SS Ch Springfield MA 2000-** B Philadelphia PA 3/15/1930 s Clifford Raymond Summers & Rose. BA Ursinus Coll 1952; ThB PDS 1955; MDiv EDS 1980; Med U of Pennsylvania 1981. D 5/21/1955 P 12/3/1955 Bp Oliver J Hart. c 1. Int S Jas' Ch Greenfield MA 1998-1999; Int Ch Of The Atone Westfield MA 1997-1998; Int Trin Epis Par Waterloo IA 1996; Int Ch Of The Intsn Stevens Point WI 1995-1996; Liturg & Mus Com Dio Iowa Des Moines IA 1990-1995; Educ Cmsn Dio Iowa Des Moines IA 1988-1995; R S Paul's Ch Marshalltown IA 1988-1995; S Mk's Ch Hammonton NJ 1984-1987; S Mary's Ch Burlington NJ 1982-1983; S Mart's Ch Bridgewater NJ 1981-1982; Dioc Fndt Dio New Jersey Trenton NJ 1978-1981; Csr Dio New Jersey Trenton NJ 1977-1987; Corp Relief Of Widows & Orphans Dio New Jersey Trenton NJ 1975-1987; R Gr Ch Pemberton NJ 1966-1980; Asst S Chrys's Ch Chicago IL 1955-1958.

SUMMERS, Joseph Holmes (Mich) 1435 South Blvd, Ann Arbor MI 48104 **Dio Michigan Detroit MI 2008-; Oasis Mnstry Ann Arbor MI 2008-; Vic Ch Of The Incarn Pittsfield Twp Ann Arbor MI 1987-** B Hartford CT 4/19/1955 s Joseph Holmes Summers & U T. BA U MI 1977; MDiv Ya Berk 1987; MA U MI 1994. D 6/27/1987 P 6/27/1988 Bp H Coleman McGehee Jr. m 4/28/1990 Donna Susan Ainsworth. "Peace In Israel," Wit, 1998; "Unpacking Anti-Racism," Wit, 1998; "The End Of The Age Of The U.S.," Wit, 1992; "The Lessons Of Counter Terroism," Wit, 1986. Distinguished Cmnty Serv Awd St Of Michigan Allnce For The Mentally Ill 1993; Distinguished Cmnty Serv Awd Washtenaw Cnty Allnce For Mentally Ill 1992; Cmnty Serv Recognition Awd Washtenaw Cmnty Coll 1991. jsummers@umich.edu

SUMMERS, Ronald (Lex) Box 27, Fort Thomas KY 41075 B Lexington KY 8/18/1937 s Horace Lee Summers & Geneva. BA U of Kentucky 1962; MDiv Epis TS In Kentucky 1975; DD Evang Bible Coll 1975; DMin Lexington TS 1986. D 3/19/1976 P 8/15/1976 Bp Addison Hosea. m 6/2/1957 Mary Sadler c 1. R S Andr's Ch Ft Thos KY 1984-2009; R S Raphael's Ch Lexington KY 1976-1984. Auth, *Daily Guide to Devotions*, Standard Pub. Assn ComT; Ord of S Lk. standrews@nkol.net

SUMMERSON, Stephen Lyn (Me) PO Box 8, Presque Isle ME 04769 **D Aroostook Epis Cluster Caribou ME 2007-; D S Jn's Ch Presque Isle ME 2007-** B Millinocket ME 3/2/1951 s Frank Summerson & Katherine. AS Nthrn Maine Cmnty Coll 1972; BA Husson U 1974. D 8/4/2007 Bp Chilton Abbie Richardson Knudsen. m 4/16/1994 Teresa Summerson c 1. ssummerson@ainop.com

SUMMERVILLE, Stephen Claude (HB) No address on file. B Wichita KS 3/27/1941 s Herbert Charles Summerville & Beulah Elaine. LTh SWTS; BA Wichita St U. D 1/18/1968 Bp George R Selway. Asst R S Paul's Ch Marquette MI 1968-1969.

SUMNER JR, Edwin Roberts (NJ) 8 Heath Vlg, Hackettstown NJ 07840 B Moorestown NJ 1/11/1931 s Edwin Roberts Sumner & Margaret. BA Dart 1952; STB GTS 1957; MDiv GTS 1972; ThM PrTS 1985. D 4/27/1957 P 11/2/1957 Bp Alfred L Banyard. m 12/30/1995 Carol A Lucas c 3. Chair, Evang Cmsn Dio New Jersey Trenton NJ 1983-1986; R Calv Epis Ch Flemington NJ 1969-1996; Secy, Cmsn on Mus Dio New Jersey Trenton NJ 1964-1969; R S Lk's Ch Woodstown NJ 1963-1969; Vic S Lk's Ch Woodstown NJ 1959-1962; Vic S Steph's Ch Mullica Hill NJ 1959-1962; Cur Trin Cathd Trenton NJ 1957-1958. Chapl 1975; Ord of S Lk 1975; OHC 1957. candesumner@comcast.net

SUMNERS III, Charles Abram (WTex) 4055 Bercket Dr., Colorado Springs CO 80906 B Austin TX 11/1/1941 s Charles Abram Sumners & Virginia Ruth. BA SW U Georgetown TX 1964; M. Div. VTS 1967. D 6/27/1967 Bp Scott Field Bailey P 5/1/1968 Bp John E Hines. m 3/17/2000 Robin Funnell c 2. Dio W Texas San Antonio TX 1987-2000; R S Phil's Ch Beeville TX 1983-1999; S Helena's Epis Ch Boerne TX 1983; Dir of Cmncatn S Barth's Ch New York NY 1978-1980; S Lk's Epis Ch Atlanta GA 1972-1978; Cur S Pat's Ch Washington DC 1967-1970. charlie@pvco.net

SUMNERS, Cristina Jordan (WTex) South Haven, Woolmer Hill Road, Haslemere GU27 1LT Great Britain (UK) B Brady TX 5/8/1947 d Thomas David Sumners & Mary Joan. BA Vas 1973; MDiv GTS 1976; MA Oxf 1985. D 12/13/1978 Bp George E Rath P 12/1/1982 Bp John Shelby Spong. m 12/29/1985 Colin Ian Nicholls. Asst R S Dav's Epis Ch San Antonio TX 1980-1990. Auth, "Reconsider: Response To Issues In Human Sxlty". Affirming Catholicism; Lesbian & Gay Chr Mvmt.

SUNDERLAND, Douglas Clark (Wyo) 18 Manning Rd, Cody WY 82414 **Assoc Cler Chr Ch Cody WY 2002-** B Morristown NJ 5/12/1953 d Hovey Charles Clark & Aline Wise. BA Trin Hartford CT 1975; MSW U of Washington 1980. D 9/17/2001 P 4/26/2002 Bp Bruce Edward Caldwell. m 6/23/1984 Gale Wayne Sunderland c 2. dsunder@tctwest.net

SUNDERLAND, Edward (Az) 225 West 99th Street, New York NY 10025 **S Barth's Ch New York NY 2010-** B Pittsburgh PA 12/20/1957 s James Edward Sunderland & Margaret Jacqueline. BA Grove City Coll 1978; MDiv SWTS 1985; MSW Arizona St U 1998. D 6/29/1985 Bp Donald James Davis P 1/25/1986 Bp Wesley Frensdorff. Cathd Of St Jn The Div New York NY 2009-2010; Gr Ch White Plains NY 2008-2009; Gr Ch White Plains NY 2006-2007; Dio Arizona Phoenix AZ 1991-1998; Vic Iglesia Epis De San Pablo Phoenix AZ 1991-1998; R Ch Of The Epiph Los Angeles CA 1988-1991; Epis Cbury Fllshp Phoenix AZ 1988; S Aug's Epis Ch Tempe AZ 1985-1988. sunderland@stbarts.org

SUNDERLAND JR, Edwin Sherwood Stowell (Me) 115 Williams St, Providence RI 02906 B New York NY 2/11/1926 s Edwin Sherwood Stowell Sunderland & Dorothy. BA Harv 1949; JD Harv 1952; MDiv CDSP 1957; U of Cambridge 1960; CUA 1982. D 6/30/1957 P 1/11/1958 Bp Karl M Block. m 7/28/1991 Phyllis Choumenkovitch c 2. VTS Alexandria VA 1995-1996; VTS Alexandria VA 1983-1988; Cn The Cathd Ch Of S Paul Boston MA 1975-1979; Lectr Cn Law The GTS New York NY 1972-1980; R S Jn's Ch Newtonville MA 1968-1971; Asst S Ptr's Epis Ch Cambridge MA 1966-1968; Asst S Paul's Ch Dedham MA 1965-1966; Ch Of The Gd Shpd Dedham MA 1964-1965; R S Eliz's Ch Sudbury MA 1961-1964; Cur S Lk's Ch San Francisco CA 1957-1958. Auth, *Dibdin & the Engl Establishment*, 1995; Auth, "arts," *Angl & Epis Hist*. SEAD 1994-2006.

SUNDERLAND, Melanie Jane (O) 1103 Castleton Rd, Cleveland Heights OH 44121 **P Chr Ch Shaker Heights OH 2010-** B Salt Lake City UT 11/28/1956 d John Frederic Sunderland & Jean. BS U IL 1984; MA NYU 1992; MDiv VTS 2001. D 7/11/2002 P 5/15/2003 Bp Carolyn Tanner Irish. m 10/1/2006 Christina L Rouse c 2. Luth Chapl Serv Cleveland OH 2003-2007; Dio Utah Salt Lake City UT 2002-2003. melanie@sunderlandclan.org

SUNTKEN, Brian Scott (O) 21 Aurora Street, Hudson OH 44236 **Chr Ch Epis Hudson OH 2005-** B New Brunswick NJ 5/29/1961 s Larry Gordon Suntken & W(ilma) Jane. BA Manhattan Sch of Mus 1983; MDiv GTS 1989. D 6/13/1989 Bp William Gillette Weinhauer P 6/14/1990 Bp Robert Hodges Johnson. m 4/9/1989 Kathy Ann Holbrook c 1. S Pat's Mssn Mooresville NC 1996-2005; Assoc R Chr Ch Charlotte NC 1991-1996; Assoc R Ch Of The Ascen Hickory NC 1989-1991; Sem Asst Convoc of Amer Ch in Europe Paris FR 1985-1986. kathysuntken@windstream.net

SUPIN, Charles Robert (Nev) 554 East Landing Ridge Circle, Jefferson NC 28640 B Brooklyn NY 1/31/1933 s Louis Supin & Eleanor Wisdom. BA Adel 1955; STB Ya Berk 1960; MFA U of Nevada at Las Vegas 1993. D 4/23/1960 P 10/1/1960 Bp James P De Wolfe. m 12/26/1959 Benita Pearl Percik. All SS Epis Ch Las Vegas NV 1974-1979; Gr Epis Ch Massapequa NY 1960-1962. Auth, "Beyond Pledging"; Auth, "Dennis"; Auth, "Undertow". csupin@skybest.com

SURFACE JR, H(enry) Howard (Ky) 719 Cottonwood Dr, Bowling Green KY 42103 **Died 6/1/2011** B Washington DC 10/19/1926 s Henry Howard Surface & Marion Gessford. BA U of Virginia 1948; MDiv VTS 1951. D 6/16/1951 P 6/1/1952 Bp Angus Dun. c 2.

SURGEON, Ornoldo A (SeFla) 20011 Nw 39th Ct, Miami Gardens FL 33055 **D Ch Of The Atone Lauderdale Lakes FL 2002-; D Ch Of The H Comf Miami FL 2002-** B Panama City PA 7/23/1937 s Pete Surgeon & Rosalia. Miami-Dade Cmnty Coll; Our Lady Of Carmen 1954. D 6/12/1995 Bp John Lewis Said P 9/30/2006 Bp Leopold Frade. m 2/3/1960 Diana E Brown c 2.

SURINER, Noreen P (WMass) PO Box 464, Middlefield MA 01243 B Northampton MA 9/13/1947 d Wayne Alden Suriner & Priscilla Packard. BA Berkshire Chr Coll 1969; Med Amer Intl Coll 1974; MDiv VTS 1976; S Geo's Coll Jerusalem IL 1988; Cert STUSo 2004. D 6/13/1976 P 3/12/1977 Bp Alexander Doig Stewart. Dio Cntrl New York Syracuse NY 2005; Trin Memi Ch Binghamton NY 1995-2007; Alum Bd VTS Alexandria VA 1988-1991; Dioc Coun Dio Maryland Baltimore MD 1986-1988; Epis Ch Of Chr The King Windsor Mill MD 1982-1995; Assoc The Ch Of The Redeem Baltimore MD 1980-1982; P-in-c S Columba's Ch Washington DC 1979-1980; Yth Min S Columba's Ch Washington DC 1976-1977. Auth, "Surviving Mnstry From Wmn Perspective," *Surviving Mnstry*, 1990. NNECA 1989; Paul Harris Fndt 1999-2007; Rotary 1998-2007. noreen.suriner@gmail.com

SURREY, Peter John (Chi) 2100 Freeport Rd Apt 419-D, Sterling IL 61081 **Died 2/13/2011** B Timmins Ontario Canada 6/12/1928 s Herbert R Surrey & Annie M. BA U Tor 1951; STB U Tor 1954; Med Nthrn Illinois U 1973. Trans from Anglican Church of Canada 6/17/1954 Bp Gerald Francis Burrill. m 10/15/2007 Jane Morford c 4. Auth, "Sm Town Ch," Abingdon Press, 1981. survey@essex1.com

SURUDA, Teresa Ann (NJ) 58 Ravine Dr, Matawan NJ 07747 B Jersey City NJ 12/16/1941 d John Aloysius Suruda & Helen. BA Caldwell Coll 1968; MA Trenton St Coll 1974. D 10/21/2000 Bp David B(ruce) Joslin. D Trin Ch Matawan NJ 2000-2010.

SUTCLIFFE, David Kenneth (Alb) 75 Willett St. Apt. 41, Albany NY 12210 **Int S Lk's Ch Catskill NY 2008-** B Pawtucket RI 3/28/1948 s Kenneth Walsh Sutcliffe & Thelma Mae. BA Hob 1970; MDiv GTS 1975. D 5/15/1976 Bp Morris Fairchild Arnold P 11/1/1977 Bp Robert Poland Atkinson. m 6/29/1974 Paula Harriet Sutcliffe c 3. Int The Ch of St Lk The Beloved Physcn Saranac Lake NY 2005-2007; Int S Christophers Ch Haverhill FL 2004-2005; Int Ch Of The H Redeem Lake Worth FL 2003; R Gr Ch New Orleans LA 2000-2003; Vic Ch Of The Gd Shpd Ft Defiance AZ 1996-2007; R S Fran Ch Menomonee Falls WI 1985-1996; Vic S Dav Of Wales Ch New Berlin WI 1980-1985; Vic St Philips Epis Ch Waukesha WI 1980-1985; Vic All Souls' Epis Ch Daniels WV 1977-1980; Asst S Matt's Ch Wheeling WV 1976-1977. Auth, "Var arts on Chr Iniation and Formation," *Var*, Var, 1990. Assoc, Ord of St Mary 2007; Int Mnstry Ntwk 2004; The Cmnty of the Cross of Nails 1996. frsutcliffe@gmail.com

SUTER, Vernon Lewis (SanD) 30329 Keith Ave, Cathedral City CA 92234 **Assoc S Paul In The Desert Palm Sprg CA 1990-** B Phoenix AZ 12/1/1931 s Harold Moody Suter & Nellie Louise. Cert The Wm Glasser Inst.; Arizona St U 1950; CPE 1979; MDiv Untd TS 1981; BA California Coast U 2000. D 4/13/1980 Bp Robert Marshall Anderson P 5/9/1983 Bp Charles Brinkley Morton. m 6/16/1973 Bonnie Louise Lucas. Assoc S Marg's Epis Ch Palm Desert CA 1985-1989. vsuter@earthlink.net

SUTHERLAND, Alan (Okla) 18417 Black Bear Trail, Norman OK 73072 **R S Mich's Epis Ch Norman OK 2010-** B 8/12/1955 s Donald Sutherland & Alma. Greystoke Coll; CTh Salisbury & Wells Theol Coll Sem GB 1980. Trans from Church Of England 9/13/1984 Bp Charles Judson Child Jr. m 4/29/2006 Judith Sutherland c 2. R S Jn's Ch Versailles KY 2004-2009; R Emm Epis Ch Winchester KY 1995-2004; R All SS Epis Ch Russellville AR 1987-1995; Asst R S Mart In The Fields Ch Atlanta GA 1983-1987. fr.alan@stmichaelsok.com

SUTHERLAND, Linda Ann (FtW) 830 County Road 109, Hamilton TX 76531 **D S Mary's Ch Hamilton TX 2009-** B Fresno CA 7/11/1941 d Milton Edward Lawrence & Muriel Alice. BA San Francisco St U 1966; Dplma St Lk's Sch of Nrsng 1966; Cert St Andr's Coll for Diac 1983. D 11/11/1983 Bp Edmond Lee Browning. m 6/17/1988 Neal Sutherland. sutherlandsauce@aol.com

SUTHERLAND, Mark Robert (Az) 100 W Roosevelt St, Phoenix AZ 85003 **Cn Pstr Trin Cathd Phoenix AZ 2010-** B Christchurch New Zealand 3/18/1955 s Frank Robert Sutherland & Ann Isabella. LLB U of Cbury 1977; Cert Theol Ripon Coll, Cuddesdon 1985; MA Lon 1995; MA U of E London 2004.

Trans from Church Of England 11/23/2010 as Priest Bp Kirk Stevan Smith. Pstr Counslg Trin Cathd Phoenix AZ 2009-2010. mark@azcathedral.org

SUTHERLAND, Melody (Eas) 219 Somerset Rd, Stevensville MD 21666 **D Chr Ch Par Kent Island Stevensville MD 2001-** B Kalamazoo MI 1/19/1948 d Harold Milton Cessna & Charlotte Dorrell. Cert Dio Easton Sch For Total Mnstry Easton MD. D 9/15/2001 Bp Martin Gough Townsend. m 1/24/1970 Donald K Sutherland c 3. Assn CPE 2000. msuth@verizon.net

SUTHERS, Derwent Albert (At) 1178 Circulo Canario, Rio Rico AZ 85648 **Asstg P S Andr's Epis Ch Nogales AZ 2011-** B Columbus OH 10/3/1931 s Albert Edward Suthers & Ruth Marie. BD CDSP 1955; BA Ob 1955. D 6/25/1955 P 12/24/1955 Bp Richard S M Emrich. m 8/29/1969 Maria P Tarbutt. Assoc R S Mart In The Fields Ch Atlanta GA 1998-2010; S Dav's Barneveld NY 1989-1997; Utica Area Coop Mnstry Whitesboro NY 1988; Assoc Gr Ch Utica NY 1986-1989; R S Kath's Ch Williamston MI 1962-1965; Vic S Kath's Ch Williamston MI 1955-1961. suthers@stmartins.org

SUTOR, Jack Thomas (Va) Po Box 271, Hanover VA 23069 **R S Paul's Ch Hanover VA 2004-** B Lynchburg VA 10/3/1945 s Jack Thomas Sutor & Jane Anne. BA U of Virginia 1969; JD U Rich 1978; MDiv VTS 1990. D 6/2/1990 P 2/6/1991 Bp Peter James Lee. c 1. Int Emm Ch Harrisonburg VA 2003-2004; Trst/Dir, Bloomfield Fndt Dio Virginia Richmond VA 1993-2011; R Trin Epis Ch Martinsburg WV 1993-2003; Asst to R S Geo's Ch Fredericksburg VA 1990-1993. Gvnr's Awd, Virginia 1987; Acad of Amer Poets 1969. stpaulshanover@comcast.net

SUTTON, Christine Marie PO Box 198, Lehman PA 18627 B Kingston PA 7/24/1950 d Emery G Havrilla & Cornelia F. Dplma RN Mercy Hosp Sch for Nrsng 1971. D 12/21/2009 Bp Paul Victor Marshall. m 4/3/1971 David Sutton c 3. suttonchris50@yahoo.com

✠ **SUTTON, Rt Rev Eugene** (Md) 611 W University Pkwy, Baltimore MD 21210 **Bp Dio Maryland Baltimore MD 2008-** B Washington DC 1/9/1954 s James Melchor Sutton & Aleen. PhD Candidate PrTS; BA Hope Coll 1976; MDiv Wstrn TS 1981. D 10/19/1995 P 4/27/1996 Bp Joe Morris Doss. m 6/19/1999 Sonya Sutton c 4. Cn Cathd of St Ptr & St Paul Washington DC 2000-2008; Assoc R S Columba's Ch Washington DC 1998-2000; Int S Mary's Epis Ch Foggy Bottom Washington DC 1997-1998; P-in-c S Marg's Ch Washington DC 1996-1997; Asst To Bp Dio New Jersey Trenton NJ 1995-1996; Vic S Mich's Ch Trenton NJ 1995-1996. Auth, "Afr Amer Sprtlty," *The Diversity Of Centering Pryr*, Continuum, 1999; Auth, "More Will Be Given," *Sermons That Wk*; Auth, "Nobodies," *Sermons That Wk*. Epis EvangES; Epis Homil Consult; Fndr Contemplative Outreach Metropltn Washington; Global Epis Mssn Ntwk. Distinguished Alum Awd Hope Coll 2003. esutton@ang-md.org

SUTTON, John (Cal) 1045 Neilson St, Albany CA 94706 **R S Anselm's Epis Ch Lafayette CA 1998-** B Oakland CA 11/28/1956 s Charles Zook Fitzalan Sutton & Anne Catherine. BA U CA 1979; MBA Golden Gate U 1986; MS Golden Gate U 1987; MDiv CDSP 1995. D 6/3/1995 P 6/1/1996 Bp William Edwin Swing. m 4/8/1989 Elizabeth Ann Partee c 1. Assoc S Paul's Epis Ch Walnut Creek CA 1995-1998. suttonj@comcast.net

SUTTON, Norma Sarah (Chi) 5218 N Sawyer Ave, Chicago IL 60625 **Asst S Ptr's Epis Ch Chicago IL 2007-** B Three Rivers MI 4/22/1946 d Elmore Sutton & Wilma Amelia. BS Goshen Coll 1968; MDiv Associated Mennonite Biblic Sem 1976; MA U of Notre Dame 1978; MA Emory U 1979; Cert. SWTS 2004. D 6/18/2005 P 12/17/2005 Bp William Dailey Persell. D S Mart's Ch Chicago IL 2005; Intern S Jn's Epis Ch Chicago IL 2003-2004. Sutton, Norma, "Arise for it is Day: The Jn Day Imprints and the Engl Reformation, 1545-1559," *Journ of Rel & Theol Info*, 1993; Sutton, Norma, "A Gift ot the Ch," *The Mennonite*, 1991; Sutton, Norma, "God's Gr in My Life," *Cov Comp*, 1984; Sutton, Norma, "Simplicity: The Call and the Challenge," *Cov Comp*, 1983; Sutton, Norma, "To the Glory of God," *Cov Quarterly*, 1982; Sutton, Norma, "The Influence of Radical Pietism on Russian Mennonites," *Cov Quarterly*, 1980; Auth, "Var arts". nsutton@northpark.edu

SUTTON, Sharon Laverne (NJ) St Stephen's Episcopal Church, 324 Bridgeboro St, Riverside NJ 08075 **D S Steph's Ch Riverside NJ 2008-** B Charleston SC 7/25/1952 d Roy Benjamin Sutton & Isabelle Cobbs. BA New Jersey City U 1995. D 6/9/2007 Bp George Edward Councell. suts16@verizon.net

SVOBODA-BARBER, Helen (O) 4 Arden Ln, Mount Vernon OH 43050 **Harcourt Par Gambier OH 2004-** B Abiline KS 4/1/1969 d Charles Raymond Svoboda & Betty Florita. BA U of Kansas 1991; MDiv Epis TS of the SW 1998. D 2/9/1998 P 9/12/1998 Bp William Edward Smalley. m 11/25/2000 Shawn R A Svoboda-Barber c 2. H Cross Luth Ch Overland Pk KS 2001-2004; Gr Cathd Topeka KS 1998-2001. HOD Pres's Coun of Advice 2000-2006. hsvobodabarber@gmail.com

SWAIN, Allen Whitcomb (Mass) PO Box 541, Pocasset MA 02559 **Died 8/12/2010** B Boston MA 12/5/1940 s Laurence Randolph Swain & Emma Mae. BA Hob 1962; MA Ya Berk 1966. D 6/25/1966 Bp Anson Phelps Stokes Jr P 5/1/1967 Bp John Melville Burgess. c 3. swain@gis.net

SWAIN, Barry Edward Bailey (NY) Church of the Resurrection, 119 East 74th Street, New York NY 10021 **R Ch Of The Resurr New York NY 2001-** B New York NY 1/27/1959 s Francis M Swain & Nancy. BA Alleg 1981; MA McMaster U 1982; MDiv GTS 1986. D 12/16/1987 P 6/29/1988 Bp Robert Campbell Witcher Sr. S Clements Ch Philadelphia PA 1993-2001; Cur S Clements Ch Philadelphia PA 1988-1992; Ch Of S Mary The Vrgn New York NY 1986-1988. rector@resurrectionnyc.org

SWAIN, Storm Kirsten (NY) 7301 Germantown Ave, Lutheran Seminary, Philadelphia PA 19119 **Assist. Prof. of Pstr Care & Theol; Dir of Angl Stds The Luth TS Philadelphia PA 2009-** B 12/3/1965 d Roger Kenneth Swain & Rhondda Janet. B.Theol. U of Otago/Knox Theol Hall 1992; Cert. Theory of Psych Ashburn Hall Educ and Resrch Fndt 1996; STM UTS 1999; Cert. Psychonalysis Blanton Peale Grad Inst 2004; Cert. Pstr Psych Blanton Peale Grad Inst 2004; MPhil UTS 2004; PhD UTS 2009. Trans from Anglican Church in Aotearoa, New Zealand and Polynesia 7/31/2004 Bp Mark Sean Sisk. m 9/18/2004 Stephen Riker Harding c 1. Asst P Gr Ch Bronx NY 2007-2010; Assoc P The Ch of S Ign of Antioch New York NY 2007-2009; Cn Pstr Cathd Of St Jn The Div New York NY 2002-2007; Asst P Cathd Of St Jn The Div New York NY 2000-2002. Bk, "Trauma & Transformation at Ground Zero: A Pstr Theol," Fortress Press, 2011; Article, "The T. Mort. Chapl at Ground Zero: Presence and Privilege on H Ground," *Journ of Rel and Hlth: Volume 50, Issue 3*, 2011; Article, "From Ground Zero to Ground Zero: Looking at One Disaster in the Light of Another," *Plainviews*, The Healthcare Chapl, NY, 2011; Article, "Ten Days Before Christmas 2001," *Journ of Rel and Hlth: Volume 41, Issue 1*, 2002. AAR 2009. Cmnty Serv Awd Blanton Peale Grad Inst 2003; Wmn Awd U of Otago, New Zealand 1992; U Bookshop Prize in Theol U of Otago, New Zealand 1991. sswain@ltsp.edu

SWAN, Clinton E (Ak) Po Box 50037, Kivalina AK 99750 B Kivalina AK 1/21/1914 s David Swan & Regina Llagiaq. D 4/23/1972 P 12/1/1972 Bp William J Gordon Jr. m 1/21/1935 Charlotte Swan.

SWAN, Craig R (CNY) St Luke's Epicopal Church, 5402 W Genesse St, Camillus NY 13031 **R S Lk's Epis Ch Camillus NY 2003-** B Hartford CT 8/24/1962 s Leslie Burnham Swan & Beverly Margaret. BS St. Lawr Canton NY 1984; MDiv Ya Berk 1988. Trans 10/23/2003 Bp M(arvil) Thomas Shaw III. m 6/28/1986 Maureen Ellen Winters c 2. Asst R Ch Of The Redeem Chestnut Hill MA 2000-2003. Niles Awd St. Lawr 1984. frcraig1@yahoo.com

SWAN, Richard A (Spr) P.O. Box 1513, Decatur IL 62525 **P-in-c S Jn's Epis Ch Decatur IL 2011-** B Cleveland OH 9/16/1948 s Harold Richard Swan & Dorothy Ragnhild. BBA U Cinc 1971; MBA U of Dayton 1986; MDiv Nash 1995. Trans 3/10/2004 Bp J Clark Grew II. m 1/4/1969 Mary Ann Varhola c 2. Cn Mssnr Dio Springfield Springfield IL 2004-2011; Prison Chapl Dio Ohio Cleveland OH 1998-2004; Assoc Dio Springfield Springfield IL 1996-1998. Blessed Sacr 1994; SocMary 96 1996. padre.swan@comcast.net

SWAN JR, William Orr (Ore) 115 Starling Circle, Grass Valley CA 95945 B Memphis TN 6/29/1927 s William Orr Swan & Mary Louise. MDiv VTS; BS U Of Chattanooga 1949; MS Emory U 1950; BD VTS 1957. D 6/30/1957 P 1/1/1958 Bp Richard S M Emrich. m 12/15/1970 Marian Schwartz c 3. Ch Of S Jn The Div Springfield OR 2000-2006; Vic S Edw's Ch Silverton OR 1993-2000; R S Andr's Ch Taft CA 1989-1991; Asst S Chris's Ch San Lorenzo CA 1987-1989; Asst Ch Of S Jos Milpitas CA 1985-1987; Asst S Tim's Epis Ch Mtn View CA 1983-1984; S Jude's Ch Wellington KS 1980; Vic S Andr's Ch Derby KS 1979-1982; Vic S Jude's Ch Wellington KS 1976-1979; Vic S Jn The Div Epis Ch Morgan Hill CA 1972-1975; Vic S Andr's Ch Clawson MI 1958-1959. Ord Of S Lk, Physcn. bswan9@comcast.net

SWANLUND, Callie Estelle (Chi) 8000 Saint Martins Ln, Philadelphia PA 19118 **Assoc for Formation & Fam Mnstry Ch Of S Mart-In-The-Fields Philadelphia PA 2011-; Liturg Cmsn Dio Pennsylvania Philadelphia PA 2011-; Yth Bd Dio Pennsylvania Philadelphia PA 2011-** B Normal IL 11/19/1982 d Randall Lee Swanlund & Courtenay de Saussure. BS Illinois St U 2005; MDiv CDSP 2008. D 6/5/2010 Bp Jeffrey Dean Lee P 1/22/2011 Bp Charles Ellsworth Bennison Jr. m 9/4/2005 Phillip Joseph Augustine Fackler. Int Asst. Min Chr Ch Philadelphia Philadelphia PA 2010-2011; Com on the Status of Wmn Exec Coun Appointees New York NY 2006-2009. callieswan@gmail.com

SWANN, Albert Henry (ETenn) 4515 Glennora Drive, Walland TN 37886 B Dandridge TN 12/12/1936 s Henry Frederick Swann & Irene. BS Carson-Newman Coll 1958; MS U of Mississippi 1963; EdD U of Mississippi 1967; Emmanual Sch of Rel Johnson City TN 1983; U So 1985. D 7/7/1985 P 6/8/1986 Bp William Evan Sanders. m 4/7/1979 Sharon Undine Guinn c 4. R Ch Of The Gd Shpd Knoxville TN 1988-2006; Asst S Jn's Epis Ch Johnson City TN 1987-1988; LocTen S Tim's Epis Ch Kingsport TN 1986-1987; D S Jn's Epis Ch Johnson City TN 1985-1986. hswann1549@yahoo.com

SWANN, Catherine Williams (Va) P.O. Box 245, Kinsale VA 22488 **Fresh Start Facillitator Dio Virginia Richmond VA 2006-; R Cople Par Hague VA 2005-** B Nashville TN 9/18/1945 d Peyton Randolph Williams & Elbert Goodwin. BA Converse Coll 1967; Cert STUSo 1992; MDiv VTS 1999. D 6/12/1999 Bp David Conner Bane Jr P 12/11/1999 Bp Donald Purple Hart. m 8/5/1967 Robert Rudd Swann c 2. Transition Com for Bp. Coadj Dio Virginia Richmond VA 2006-2008; Fresh Start Facillitator Dio Sthrn Virginia Norfolk

VA 2002-2004; Stndg Com, Secy 2002-03 Dio Sthrn Virginia Norfolk VA 2000-2003; Liturg Cmsn Dio Sthrn Virginia Norfolk VA 1999-2004; Assoc S Andr's Ch Norfolk VA 1999-2004. NECA 2001-2004; SoVECA 2001-2004. kakiswan@gmail.com

SWANN, Stephen Barham (Dal) 4223 Ridge Rd, Dallas TX 75229 B Longview TX 10/13/1944 s Robert Carroll Swann & Jane. BA NE St U 1967; SMU 1968; BD CDSP 1970. D 6/18/1970 Bp Theodore H McCrea P 12/20/1970 Bp A Donald Davies. m 4/7/1998 Carolyn Campbell c 2. Epis Sch Of Dallas Dallas TX 1975-1995; Asst S Mich And All Ang Ch Dallas TX 1971-1974. Ord of S Jn of Jerusalem. swanns@esdallas.org

SWANN, Stuart Alan (SwFla) 1560 S Fredrica Ave, Clearwater FL 33756 **S Alb's Epis Ch St Pete Bch FL 2010-; P-in-c S Dunst's Epis Ch Largo FL 2010-** B Atlanta GA 11/30/1953 s Conon Doyle Swann & Nancy Loving. BS Florida St U 1975; MSW U NC 1979; MDiv VTS 1992. D 6/13/1992 Bp Robert Poland Atkinson P 12/1/1992 Bp Peter James Lee. m 5/19/2001 Michelle Swann c 2. R S Jn's Epis Ch Brooksville FL 2008-2010; Vic S Matt's Epis Ch Sterling VA 1995-1999; Asst S Anne's Epis Ch Reston VA 1992-1995. stuswann@tampabay.rr.com

SWANN JR, Sydney Chaille (Va) 5500 Williamsburg Landing Dr, Apt 120, Williamsburg VA 23185 **Died 2/16/2010** B Salisbury NC 11/26/1913 s Sydney Chaille Swann & Nina. BS U Rich 1935; BD VTS 1941; DD VTS 1974. D 6/6/1941 P 3/1/1942 Bp Henry St George Tucker. c 3.

SWANNER-MONTGOMERY, Rhoda J (Tex) Saint Thomas Episcopal Church, 906 George Bush Dr, College Station TX 77840 **S Thos Epis Ch Coll Sta TX 2010-** B Washington DC 8/27/1962 d Joe Bailey Swanner & Regina. BA Baylor U 1983; MDiv Epis TS of The SW 2001; D.Min. SWTS 2009. D 6/16/2001 P 6/20/2002 Bp Claude Edward Payne. m 4/6/2002 Robert H Montgomery. Cn Chr Ch Cathd Houston TX 2008-2010; Asst The Ch of the Gd Shpd Austin TX 2001-2008. rhoda@stthomasbcs.org

SWANSON, Donel Gustavus (Eau) 3856 20th Ave S, Minneapolis MN 55407 B Minneapolis MN 3/7/1931 s Carl Ludvic Swanson & Amelia (Emily) Katrina. AA U MN 1956. D 10/14/1995 Bp Sanford Zangwill Kaye Hampton. D S Paul's Ch Hudson WI 1996-2002. Ord Of H Cross.

SWANSON, George Gaines (Nwk) 349 Seawall Rd, Southwest Harbor ME 04679 B San Francisco CA 6/26/1933 s Walter Gaines Swanson & Leta Pauline. BA Harv 1955; STB GTS 1958. D 6/29/1958 Bp Henry H Shires P 6/11/1959 Bp James Albert Pike. Heights Hudson Proj Hoboken NJ 1979-1984; Ch of the Ascen Jersey City NJ 1977-1993; Geo Swanson New York NY 1977-1979; St Georges Ch Kansas City MO 1968-1977; R S Phil's Ch Coalinga CA 1960-1968; Cur Trin Par Menlo Pk CA 1958-1960. Auth, "Setswana Through Pictures"; Auth, "Wmn & H Ord"; Auth, "The Propers". Oblate Of Concep Abbey; Sis Of The Trsfg. george@gsbanjo.com

SWANSON, Geraldine Ann (NY) 250 Greeley Ave, Staten Island NY 10306 **D Chr Ch New Brighton Staten Island NY 2010-; Diocesean ERD Rep Dio New York New York City NY 2007-** B Bronx NY 4/30/1949 d John Michael Redden & Florence Mary. BA Hunter Coll CUNY 1971; MS Ed Richmond Coll CUNY 1975; Mstr of Arts GTS 2008. D 4/26/1997 Bp Richard Frank Grein. m 12/9/1972 Robert Steven Swanson c 4. D Ch Of The Ascen Staten Island NY 2007-2010; D S Clem's Ch New York NY 2001-2006; D The Ch Of S Steph Staten Island NY 1999-2000; D S Andr's Epis Ch Staten Island NY 1997-1999. Auth, "Dss Susan Trevor Knapp," *Epis New Yorker*, Dio NY, 2011; Auth, "Reflections on a Flawed Past," *The Epis New Yorker*, Dio NY, 2010; Auth, ""Be Thour my Vision..."A Reflection," *Diakoneo*, NAAD, 2005; Auth, "Feetwashing/Servanthood/Boarders," *Diakoneo*, 2002; Auth, "Deacons And The Mssn Field," *Diakoneo*, 2001; Auth, "Dss," *Diakoneo*, 2000. Cmnty Serv Awd New York St Untd Teachers 1998. deakswan@aol.com

SWANSON OJN, John-Julian (Mil) 450 Sunnyslope Dr Apt 305, Hartland WI 53029 B Green Bay WI 10/13/1932 s Clifford Douglas Swanson & Mildred Marie. BA Carleton Coll 1954; MDiv Nash 1957. D 2/2/1957 P 8/9/1957 Bp William Hampton Brady. Ch Of The Resurr Norwich CT 1981-1988. Auth, *A Lesson of Love: The Revelations of Julian of Norwich*, Walker, 1989; Auth, *People w People*, NETI, 1974. The Ord of Julian of Norwich 1982. johnjulianojn@sbcglobal.net

SWANSON, Karen (ECR) Saint Andrew's Episcopal Church, 1600 Santa Lucia Ave, San Bruno CA 94066 **S Andr's Ch Saratoga CA 2010-** B Fairbault MN 1/26/1956 d Henning Wilhelm Albert Swanson & Ruth Evelyn. BA S Olaf Coll 1978; MDiv CDSP 1983. D 6/29/1983 Bp Robert Marshall Anderson P 6/1/1984 Bp Edmond Lee Browning. m 2/4/1984 David Yasuhide Ota c 1. Int S Andr's Epis Ch San Bruno CA 1999-2010; S Matt's Epis Ch San Mateo CA 1997-1998; Cn Pstr S Andr's Cathd Honolulu HI 1992-1997; Cnvnr Cler Dio Hawaii Honolulu HI 1990-1992; Dioc Coun Dio Hawaii Honolulu HI 1988-1990; R Ch Of The Epiph Honolulu HI 1986-1991; S Andr's Priory Sch Honolulu HI 1985-1986; Yth Mnstry S Andr's Cathd Honolulu HI 1984-1985. revkarenswanson@sanbrunocable.com

SWANSON, Kenneth Banford (At) 1015 Old Roswell Rd, Roswell GA 30076 **R S Dav's Ch Roswell GA 2010-** B Minneapolis MN 5/10/1948 s Neil H Swanson & Helen. BA U of Wisconsin 1972; MDiv Fuller TS 1976; PhD U Of Edinburgh Gb 1979. D 6/13/1981 Bp James Stuart Wetmore P 12/18/1981 Bp Walter Decoster Dennis Jr. c 1. Dn Chr Ch Cathd Nashville TN 1997-2007; R Gr Ch Millbrook NY 1987-1997; Sr Cur Gr Ch Millbrook NY 1982-1987; S Barth's Ch New York NY 1981-1982. Auth, "Uncommon Pryr: Approaching Intimacy w God". swanson510@gmail.com

SWANSON, Richard Alden (Cal) Po Box 670, Bodega Bay CA 94923 B Saint Paul MN 5/21/1939 s John Alex Swanson & Ruth Alden. BBA U MI 1961; BD EDS 1964; MA Ball St U 1974; EdD USC 1980. D 6/29/1964 Bp Archie H Crowley P 1/25/1965 Bp Richard S M Emrich. m 6/8/1963 Janice Rae Mainwaring c 2. R All SS Epis Ch San Leandro CA 1987-2001; Chapl Off Of Bsh For ArmdF New York NY 1966-1987. Auth, "Sexual Knowledge & Attitudes of Theol Students". bodegafog@gmail.com

SWANSON, Richard Reif (Vt) PO Box 1175, Stowe VT 05672 **R S Jn's In The Mountains Stowe VT 2010-** B Saint Paul MN 9/4/1970 s William Roy Swanson & Helen Carolyn. AA U of Montana 1993; BA California St U 1995; MDiv SWTS 2000. D 6/24/2000 P 1/6/2001 Bp Frederick Houk Borsch. R S Paul's Epis Ch Dowagiac MI 2006-2010; Assoc For Yth And Fam Mnstrs S Ptr's Ch Morristown NJ 2002-2006; Cur S Mk's-In-The-Vlly Epis Los Olivos CA 2000-2001. rick@stjohnsinthemountains.org

SWARR, James P (WMass) 37 Chestnut St, Springfield MA 01103 **R S Mk's Epis Ch E Longmeadow MA 2009-** B Biddeford Maine 10/3/1979 s James Howard Swarr & Martha Ann. BA Wheaton Coll 2002; MDiv VTS 2006. D 6/25/2006 P 2/24/2007 Bp Chilton Abbie Richardson Knudsen. m 6/21/2002 Angela Tully-Young. Assoc R S Jn's Ch Plymouth MI 2006-2009. Harris Awd VTS 2006. padre.peter.swarr@gmail.com

SWARTHOUT, James Edward (Chi) 10275 N. River Rd, Barrington Hills IL 60102 **Int S Paul's Ch McHenry IL 2007-** B HIghland Park IL 6/19/1954 s James Elmer Warthout & Theresa. BA Wstrn Illinois U 1980; MDiv S Mary Sem Baltimore MD 1986; MS Loyola U 1996. Rec from Roman Catholic 1/17/2002 as Priest Bp William Dailey Persell. m 7/11/1998 Claudia Koselke. S Jas Ch W Dundee IL 2003-2006. "Keeping the Faith," *NW Herald*. frjim5254@sbcglobal.net

SWARTSFAGER, Ames Kent (LI) 1022 Marine Dr Ne Unit 2, Olympia WA 98501 **Died 3/14/2010** B New York NY 3/26/1938 s Vernon Arlington Swartsfager & Grace Irene. BA San Francisco St Coll 1961; BD CDSP 1964; Advncd CPE and Actg CPE Supervis 1977. D 6/21/1964 Bp James Albert Pike P 12/22/1964 Bp David Emrys Richards. m 7/26/1958 Judith Ann Thrasher c 3. Auth, "Involving Fam & Cmnty In Rehabilitating Offenders". Chapl Of The Year U.S. Bureau Of Prisons 1989. ames11111@aol.com

SWARTZENTRUBER, A Orley (NJ) 5433 Crestlake Blvd, Sarasota FL 34233 **Schlr in Res Ch Of The Redeem Sarasota FL 1994-** B Buenos Aires AR 6/13/1926 s Amos Swartzentruber & Edna. BA Goshen Coll 1948; BD Goshen Biblic Sem 1951; MA Pr 1963; PhD Pr 1970. D 5/14/1963 P 9/1/1963 Bp Allen Webster Brown. m 9/8/1950 Jane Willey c 4. R All SS Ch Princeton NJ 1968-1993. orleyswartzentruber@comcast.net

SWAYZE, Marie Zealor (Pa) 641 Pickering Lane, Phoenixville PA 19460 **Asstg P S Mk's Ch Philadelphia PA 2008-** B Bryn Mawr PA 2/28/1943 d Murray Philip Zealor & Marie. BS Trin Washington DC 1965; MS W Chester U of Pennsylvania 1985; MDiv Luth TS at Philadelphi 1993. Rec from Roman Catholic 5/18/1978 Bp Lyman Cunningham Ogilby. m 2/27/1971 Richard Allen Swayze c 2. PreSchool Dir Chr Ch Media PA 2004-2006; R S Ptr's Ch Phoenixville PA 1998-2004; Int S Andr's Ch Yardley PA 1997-1998; Int S Mk's Ch Philadelphia PA 1996-1997; Int St Pauls Epis Ch Oaks PA 1994-1995; Ch Sch Dir. S Mary's Epis Ch Ardmore PA 1993; Trans D S Jas' Epis Ch Downingtown PA 1992-1993. AAUW. Sem Awd ABS 1989. revmarieswayze@verizon.net

SWEARINGEN, James Donald (NCal) 601 Van Ness Ave #222, San Francisco CA 94102 **Assoc Ch Of The Adv Of Chr The King San Francisco CA 1998-** B Cooper TX 10/19/1935 s Donald Lee Swearingen & Lenora Bernice. BA California St U 1959; MDiv GTS 1962; Clu The Amer Coll 1977; Rel Educ Sch 1982; CH Natl Gld of Hypnotists 2006. D 9/1/1962 P 3/1/1963 Bp Francis E I Bloy. m 12/24/1983 Lynn Corbin. Receiving Disabil Ret 1990-2000; R S Mich And All Ang Ch Ft Bragg CA 1988-1990; Gr Epis Ch Nampa ID 1986-1988; The Epis Ch In Almaden San Jose CA 1985-1986; Assoc S Thos Of Cbury Par Long Bch CA 1982-1983; Vic Gr Ch Broad Brook CT 1980-1982; Assoc S Paul's Epis Ch Bantam CT 1972-1974; P-in-c S Paul's Schoharie NY 1965-1967; P-in-c S Paul's Ch Bloomville NY 1963-1965; P-in-c S Ptr's Ch Hobart NY 1963-1965; Cur S Edm's Par San Marino CA 1962-1963. OHC, Ord Of S Lk. frjim3653@gmail.com

SWEENEY, Craig Chandler (Be) 14014 Church Hill Rd, Clarks Summit PA 18411 **R Ch Of The Epiph Glenburn Clarks Summit PA 2006-** B Baltimore MD 4/7/1951 s John Easter Sweeney & Virginia Lee. BA U Denv 1973; MBA/JD U Denv 1978; MDiv VTS 2001. D 3/17/2001 P 9/29/2001 Bp William Edward Smalley. m 8/25/1973 Robin Jo Roy c 3. R Gr Epis Ch Winfield KS 2001-2006; R Trin Ch Arkansas City KS 2001-2006. frcraig1@mac.com

SWEENEY, David Cameron (Ore) 503 N Holladay Dr, Seaside OR 97138 **Dn Columbia Convoc Dio Oregon Portland OR 2000-; Calv Ch Seaside OR**

1992- B Seattle WA 10/26/1956 s Donald Lebosquet Sweeney & Margaret Anne. BS NWU 1979; MDiv VTS 1984. D 6/16/1984 Bp Quintin Ebenezer Primo Jr P 6/24/1985 Bp James Winchester Montgomery. Stndg Com Dio Oregon Portland OR 1996-1999; Dn So Coast Convoc Dio Oregon Portland OR 1993-1999; Dio Oregon Portland OR 1992-1999; Vic S Chris's Ch Port Orford OR 1992-1999; Vic S Jn-By-The-Sea Epis Ch Bandon OR 1992-1999; Vic All SS Ch Hamlet NC 1987-1992; R Ch Of The Mssh Rockingham NC 1987-1992; Asst S Mary's Epis Ch High Point NC 1984-1987. dcsweeney@msn.com

SWEENEY, Joseph Francis (NJ) 43 Elizabeth St., Pemberton NJ 08068 B Flushing NY 9/2/1939 s Joseph Francis Sweeney & Clara Bridget. D 5/16/2009 Bp Sylvestre Donato Romero. m 5/11/1985 Lynn Tibus c 3. D Gr Ch Pemberton NJ 2009-2010. sweeneyj25@comcast.net

SWEENEY, Peter Harry (Alb) 2497 Antonia Dr, Niskayuna NY 12309 **D Calv Epis Ch Burnt Hills NY 2002-** B Lyons NY 5/6/1959 s Bernard Thomas Sweeney & Marion Wagner. BS Clarkson U; MS RPI 1986. D 6/16/2002 Bp David John Bena. m 10/14/1989 Stacey Ranae Arnold.

SWEENEY, Sylvia A (Los) Bloy House The Episcopal Theological School At Claremont, 1325 N College Ave, Claremont CA 91711 **Dn and Pres The ETS At Claremont Claremont CA 2009-** B Fort Sill OK 12/22/1955 d James T Sweeney & Lieselotte. BS Florida St U 1975; MS Florida St U 1980; MDiv SWTS 1985; PhD CDSP 2007. D 6/15/1985 Bp Frank Stanley Cerveny P 2/1/1986 Bp Charles Jones III. m 3/10/1985 J(ohn) Robert Honeychurch. Dioc BEC Dio California San Francisco CA 2006-2008; Assoc R S Jas Ch Fremont CA 2005-2008; Mentor P Dept Of Missions San Francisco CA 2001-2003; Chair of COM Dio Idaho Boise ID 1997-2001; Co-R S Lk's Epis Ch Idaho Falls ID 1992-2001; Vic H Trin Epis Ch Troy MT 1988-1992; Co-Vic S Lk's Ch Libby MT 1987-1992; Dioc Yth Circuit Rider Dio Montana Helena MT 1985-1986. Auth, ""Baptism as the Gateway to Epis Liturg Renwl,"" *Liturg: The St of Liturg Renwl*, The Liturg Conf, 2011; Auth, ""Discussion Guide,"" *Chr Holiness and HumanSexuality*, Chicago Consult, 2009; Auth, "An Ecofeminist Perspective on Ash Wednesday and Lent," *Ptr Lang Amer U Stds Series*, Ptr Lang Pub, 2009. No Amer Acad of Liturg 2007. Bogard Fell CDSP 2006. ssweeney@cst.edu

SWEENEY, W Terry (Md) 2147 Timber Mdws, Charlottesville VA 22911 **R S Tim's Ch Catonsville MD 2006-** B Tranquility OH 10/12/1946 s Raymond Edward Sweeney & Ruth. BSW Estrn Michigan U 1984; MDiv SWTS 1988. D 6/25/1988 Bp Henry Irving Mayson P 3/9/1989 Bp H Coleman McGehee Jr. m 8/10/1979 Olivia Latigo c 4. Dio Louisiana Baton Rouge LA 2003-2006; Ch Of The Cross Charlottesville VA 1999-2002; Dio Virginia Richmond VA 1997-1998; S Mk's Epis Ch Peoria IL 1994-1997; S Jn's Epis Ch Peoria IL 1994-1995; S Lk's Epis Ch Bartlesville OK 1991-1992; R S Andr's Ch Big Rapids MI 1989-1991; Cur S Jn's Epis Ch Midland MI 1988-1989. Auth, "Lenten Meditations-Journey Through The Word". Chapl For The Ord Of S Lk The Physcn. terrylivsweeney@gmail.com

SWEENY, Thomas Edward (NJ) 102 New St, Egg Harbor Township NJ 08234 **D Ch Of S Mk And All SS Absecon Galloway NJ 2002-** B New Rochell NY 9/27/1942 D 9/21/2002 Bp David B(ruce) Joslin. m 8/6/1960 Bari Colleen Green c 3. tomsweenyineht@aol.com

SWEET, Fran (Cal) Po Box 1384, Alameda CA 94501 B Tucson AZ 1/15/1940 d Robert Willard MacIver & Clemence Marie-Agnes. San Francisco City Coll 1960; Foothill Coll 1970; BA San Francisco St U 1977; BTh California Sch for Deacons 1989. D 6/8/1991 Bp William Edwin Swing. m 7/12/1980 Allen Alexander Sweet c 4. D Chr Ch Alameda CA 2002-2004; D H Cross Epis Ch Castro Vlly CA 1998-2002; Dir Chld'S Mnstrs All SS Epis Ch Palo Alto CA 1996-1998; S Patricks Ch And Day Sch Thousand Oaks CA 1993-1995; D S Anne's Ch Fremont CA 1991-1992. NAAD 1984. dcnfran@aol.com

SWEIGERT, Cynthia Bronson (Pgh) 5700 Forbes Ave, Pittsburgh PA 15217 **R The Ch Of The Redeem Pittsburgh PA 1995-** B Minneapolis MN 6/16/1952 d Edgerton Bronson & Roxanne Dickerson. BA U MN 1975; MDiv GTS 1978. D 6/24/1978 Bp Robert Marshall Anderson P 12/1/1980 Bp Philip Frederick McNairy. m 11/12/1994 Dan Sweigert. Buffalo Area Metro Mnstrs Inc Buffalo NY 1993-1994; Cn S Paul's Cathd Buffalo NY 1989-1992; S Jn's Ch Youngstown OH 1985-1989; Assoc Chr And S Steph's Ch New York NY 1980-1986; Trin Epis Ch Roslyn NY 1978-1979. revcynthia2000@aol.com

SWENSEN, Oscar Warren (Mass) 38 Munnick Point Rd, Lyman ME 04002 B Stoneham MA 10/24/1931 s Oscar Walter Swensen & Gunhild Jensene. BA Harv 1953; STM EDS 1959. D 6/20/1959 Bp Anson Phelps Stokes Jr P 12/21/1959 Bp Charles F Hall. m 6/27/1958 Constance E Speedie c 3. Dioc Counc Dio Massachusetts Boston MA 1970-1978; R Calv Ch Danvers MA 1968-1993; R Ch Of The Trsfg Derry NH 1964-1968; Cur Ch Of The Gd Shpd Nashua NH 1959-1960. Phillips Brooks Clerics Club of Boston: Pres 1971; Phillips Brooks Clerics Club of Boston: Rcrdng Secy 196 1959-1994. Legion of hon Kiwanis Intl 2001. coswensen@roadrunner.com

✠ **SWENSON, Rt Rev Daniel Lee** (Minn) 1211 Sunset Ct, Northfield MN 55057 B Oklahoma City OK 2/2/1928 s Daniel Swenson & Lillian. BA U MN 1950; Minnesota Tutorial Prog MN 1961. D 6/18/1960 P 6/29/1961 Bp Hamilton Hyde Kellogg Con 5/17/1986 for Vt. m 6/9/1951 Sally Mason c 3. Asstg Bp Dio Minnesota Minneapolis MN 1997-2009; Bp Dio Vermont Burlington VT 1986-1993; Trst SWTS Evanston IL 1979-1988; R S Jn In The Wilderness White Bear Lake MN 1978-1986; Stndg Com Dio Minnesota Minneapolis MN 1976-1981; Dn The Epis Cathd Of Our Merc Sav Faribault MN 1975-1978; P-in-c S Jn's Ch Eveleth MN 1966-1975; R S Paul's Ch Virginia MN 1966-1975; Vic S Edw The Confessor Wayzata MN 1962-1965; DCE S Mart's By The Lake Epis Minnetonka Bch MN 1959-1962. DD SWTS Evanston TN 1987.

SWENSON, Richard Clive (Neb) 305 Ridgeway Dr, Glenwood IA 51534 **P-in-c Gr Ch Tecumseh Nebraska City NE 2006-** B Ann Arbor MI 9/5/1947 JD Creighton U 1978; MA Creighton U 2004. D 5/20/2004 P 12/16/2004 Bp Joe Goodwin Burnett. rcswenson@msn.com

SWESEY, Jean Elizabeth (Minn) 1008 Transit Ave, Roseville MN 55113 B Minneapolis MN 7/2/1935 d Thomas Prentis Sawyer & Marjorie Elizabeth. BA U MN 1958; BA U MN 1978. D 1/25/1984 Bp Robert Marshall Anderson. m 11/22/1958 John Frank Swesey c 2. D S Nich Ch Richfield MN 1992-2001; S Mk's Ch S Cloud MN 1985-1992; D S Chris's Epis Ch Roseville MN 1984-1985. swese001@tc.umn.edu

SWETMAN, Margarita (Nwk) 2528 Palmer Ave, New Orleans LA 70118 B Sucre BO 6/10/1938 d Maximo Ortiz & Concpcion Mattos. BA U of Sthrn Mississippi 1966; MA Tul 1971; MDiv CDSP 1997. D 6/21/1997 P 1/1/1998 Bp Frederick Houk Borsch. Gr Ch Un City NJ 2002-2004; Epis Chapl Los Angeles CA 2000-2001; Asst St Johns Pro-Cathd Los Angeles CA 1997-1999. Curs. maroswet@yahoo.com

SWIEDLER, Anne Elizabeth (At) 5625 Mill Glen Ct, Atlanta GA 30338 **Asst to R Pstr Care S Dav's Ch Roswell GA 2002-** B 3/22/1950 d William Ernest McBurney & Eleanor. MDiv Candler TS Emory U 2001. D 6/8/2002 P 1/25/2003 Bp J(ohn) Neil Alexander. m 3/14/1970 Edward A Swieder c 2. anne@swiedler.com

SWIFT, Daniel Willard (Los) 24874 Olive Tree Ln, Los Altos CA 94024 B Long Beach CA 5/28/1940 s Howard Newman Swift & Jessella Gregg. BA U CA 1965; MDiv Nash 1970. D 9/12/1970 Bp Francis E I Bloy P 3/27/1971 Bp Victor Manuel Rivera. S Matt's Epis Ch San Mateo CA 1984-1985; Corp Of The Cathd Ch Of St Paul Los Angeles CA 1973; Trin Epis Ch Santa Barbara CA 1973; Asst All SS Par Los Angeles CA 1970-1972.

SWIFT, John Kohler (WMo) 6 Hunter Dr, Guilford CT 06437 B Hartford CT 3/26/1939 s Donald David Swift & Marion. BA Hav 1961; RelD TS at Claremong CA 1969. Trans from Anglican Church of Canada 6/1/1985. m 11/24/1983 Elizabeth A Kennedy. Chapl St Lk's Chap Kansas City MO 1999-2005. ACPE, Coll Chapl A. jkswift@gmail.com

SWIFT, Stephen A (Md) 913 Sylvan Ave, Fairmont WV 26554 B Dennison TX 7/30/1946 s Robert C Swift & Mary. BA Kansas U 1968; MDiv GTS 1972. D 6/18/1972 Bp Albert Ervine Swift P 6/1/1973 Bp Stephen F Bayne Jr. m 9/2/1985 Amy Panek c 2. Ch Of The Mssh Baltimore MD 2008-2009; Chr Ch Fairmont WV 2003-2008; Ch Of The Gd Shpd Dunedin FL 2002-2003; Int S Chris's Epis Ch Carmel IN 2000-2002; S Andr Epis Ch Kokomo IN 1999-2000; R Gr Ch Brunswick MD 1996-1999; Chapl S Pat's Ch Washington DC 1995-1996; Int S Aid's Epis Ch Boulder CO 1991-1992; Vic S Mary Magd Ch Boulder CO 1990-1991; Vic H Cross Epis Mssn Sterling CO 1985-1987; Assoc Calv Ch Columbia MO 1978-1985; R S Jn's Ch Durant OK 1977-1978; Cur Chr Epis Ch Denver CO 1974-1977; The Ch Of Chr The King (Epis) Arvada CO 1974-1977; Cur Holyrood Ch New York NY 1972-1974. Phi Beta Kappa; Phi Beta Kappa. iggy1968@comcast.net

SWINDELL, Kay Howard (EC) 1514 Clifton Rd, Jacksonville NC 28540 **D S Phil's Ch Holly Ridge NC 2011-** B Rocky Mount NC 1/27/1951 d Walter Hardy Howard & Maxine. AA Louisburg Coll 1971. D 6/20/1992 Bp Huntington Williams Jr. m 2/16/1985 Robert Temple Swindell c 2. S Anne's Epis Ch Jacksonville NC 2010; Dir of Lay Mnstry S Anne's Epis Ch Jacksonville NC 2003-2009; D S Anne's Epis Ch Jacksonville NC 1992-2002. bob_kayswindell@coastalnet.com

SWINDLE, Frank Moody (NwT) 155 Rainbow Drive #5521, Livingston TX 77399 B Bastrop LA 1/23/1943 s Moody Swindle & Elaine. BA NE Louisiana U 1965; MDiv STUSo 1973; DMin STUSo 1996. D 6/18/1973 P 5/12/1974 Bp Robert B Gooden. m 11/29/1963 Gloria Folds c 1. Int S Phil's Ch Joplin MO 2001-2003; Int S Paul's Par Kent Chestertown MD 2001; Int Chr Epis Ch Little Rock AR 1999-2000; Int S Ptr's Epis Ch Amarillo TX 1996-1999; Vic All SS Ch Colorado City TX 1986-1996; Vic S Steph's Ch Sweetwater TX 1986-1996; R Tri SS Cluster Sweetwater TX 1986-1996; Cur Gr Epis Ch Monroe LA 1981-1986; Cur Epis Ch Of The Gd Shpd Lake Chas LA 1978-1980; Vic Leonidas Polk Memi Epis Mssn Leesville LA 1976-1978; R Trin Epis Ch Deridder LA 1976-1978; Cur S Paul's Ch New Orleans LA 1973-1976. fngswindle@aol.com

SWINEHART, Bruce Howard (Lex) 206 W Columbia St, Somerset KY 42501 **P-in-c S Pat Ch Somerset KY 2009-** B Berkeley CA 9/28/1957 s Howard Luther Swinehart & Elizabeth F. BA Bow 1980; MA U CO 1984; MDiv

S

CDSP 2009. D 6/6/2009 Bp Robert John O'Neill P 12/21/2009 Bp Stacy F Sauls. m 8/22/1987 Daphne Chellos. BRUCE.SWINEHART@GMAIL.COM

SWINEHART JR, Charles Henry (Mich) 1615 Ridgewood Dr, East Lansing MI 48823 **Vic S Andr's Ch Jackson MI 1995-** B Cleveland OH 9/8/1940 s Charles Henry Swinehart & Rosemary Lucille. BA U So 1962; MDiv VTS 1965. D 6/29/1965 Bp C Kilmer Myers P 1/3/1966 Bp George R Selway. m 4/30/1966 Carol Y Young c 3. R S Steph's Ch Hamburg MI 1988-1992; Asst Trin Epis Ch Bay City MI 1974-1976; Vic S Alb's Ch Manistique MI 1969-1973; Vic S Pauls Ch Nahma MI 1969-1973; Vic Ch Of The Ascen Ontonagon MI 1965-1969; Vic S Mk's Ch Ewen MI 1965-1969. Advoc of the Year Epilepsy Fndt of Amer 1997. chsjr1@sbcglobal.net

SWINEHART, Howard Luther (ECR) 591 Saint Claire Dr, Palo Alto CA 94306 **D All SS Epis Ch Palo Alto CA 1967-** B Sandpoint ID 4/11/1927 s Luther Oswald Swinehart & Judith Eleanor. BS U CA 1952. D 12/30/1967 Bp George Richard Millard. m 1/8/2000 Dorothy G Hall c 3. howdot@aol.com

✠ **SWING, Rt Rev William Edwin** (Cal) 105 Pepper Ave., Burlingame CA 94010 B Huntington WV 8/26/1936 s William Lee Swing & Elsie Bell. BA Ken 1958; BD VTS 1961; DD VTS 1980; DD Ken 1981; LHD U of San Francisco 2005; DD Churc h DS of the Pacific 2008; LHD U of Palo Alto 2009. D 6/11/1961 P 12/1/1961 Bp Wilburn Camrock Campbell Con 9/29/1979 for Cal. m 10/7/1961 Mary Willis Taylor c 2. Bp Dio California San Francisco CA 1979-2006; R S Columba's Ch Washington DC 1969-1979; Vic S Matt's Ch Chester WV 1963-1968; Vic S Thos' Epis Ch Weirton WV 1963-1968; Asst S Matt's Ch Wheeling WV 1961-1963. "A Swing w A Crosier," Epis Dio California, 1999; "The Coming Untd Rel," Conexus Press, 1998; "Bldg Wisdom'S Hse (Co-Authored w Rabbi Steph Pearce Jn Schlegel S.J. And Bonnie Menes Kahn," Addison Wesley Longman, 1997. DD Ch Div. Sch of the Pacific 2007; Doctor of Humane Letters U of San Francisco 2005; DD Ken 1980; DD VTS 1980. pluswes@aol.com

SWINNEA, Stephanie Lavenia Bethard (Okla) 510 S 15th St, Mcalester OK 74501 **R All SS Ch McAlester OK 2007-; Dio Oklahoma Oklahoma City OK 2005-** B Oklahoma 7/26/1951 d Myron Grant Bethard & Stella Eugenia. BS Texas Wmn's U-Denton 1973; MDiv Epis TS of The SW 2005. D 6/25/2005 P 1/7/2006 Bp Robert Manning Moody. m 2/23/1973 Sam Swinnea c 4. Cur S Lk's Epis Ch Bartlesville OK 2005-2007. "I, Pat, A Sinner," Aaron Allgood Books, 1999. DOK 2005. swinnea@sbcglobal.net

SWITZ, Robert William (Cal) 1189 W Park View Pl, Mount Pleasant SC 29466 B Upper Darby PA 9/16/1936 s Louis Joseph Switz & Margaret. BS Villanova U 1960; BD VTS 1968. D 6/21/1968 Bp James Loughlin Duncan P 1/1/1969 Bp William Loftin Hargrave. m 7/1/1981 Cheryl D Winter c 3. The Ch Of The Epiph Summerville SC 1999; Trin Ch San Francisco CA 1997-1999; Indn Epis Mnstry San Francisco CA 1982-1983; Assoc Gr Cathd San Francisco CA 1980-1982; R S Greg's Ch Boca Raton FL 1974-1980; Asst Trin Cathd Miami FL 1968-1970. the1padre@hotmail.com

SWONGER, Timothy Lee (Nev) 1560 Jamielinn Ln Unit 103, Las Vegas NV 89110 **P S Thos Ch Las Vegas NV 1997-** B Los Vegas NV 11/10/1955 s Verna Swonger. D 6/22/1997 P 12/1/1997 Bp Stewart Clark Zabriskie. tlswonger@aol.com

SWOPE, Bob (Ak) D 9/12/1973 Bp Matthew G Henry P 4/1/1974 Bp William Gillette Weinhauer.

SWORD OHC, Carl Richard (NY) 200 East 33rd St, Apt # 14-J, New York NY 10016 **P H Cross Monstry W Pk NY 1973-** B Bath PA 3/6/1931 s Rodgelio Sword & Hilda Valerie. BS Penn 1958; MDiv EDS 1962; MC Arizona St U 1972; Cert Westchester Inst 1982. D 6/16/1962 Bp William S Thomas P 12/22/1962 Bp Austin Pardue. Asst Trin Epis Ch Washington PA 1963-1964; In-c S Thos' Epis Ch Canonsburg PA 1962-1964; In-c S Geo's Ch Waynesburg PA 1962-1963. Dio Gld Pstr Psychologists 1983; OHC: Life Professed 1973.

SY, Jonathan Jimenez (Los) 21202 Spurney Ln, Huntington Beach CA 92646 **Assoc S Jn The Div Epis Ch Costa Mesa CA 2010-** B Cebu, Philippines 11/24/1956 s Priscilo F Sy & Maria Corazon J. BS U of San Carlos; MDiv SWTS 2010. D 6/12/2010 Bp Diane M Jardine Bruce P 1/8/2011 Bp Mary Douglas Glasspool. jonjsy@yahoo.com

SYDNOR JR, Charles Raymond (Va) 67 Scenic Dr, Montross VA 22520 B Kinsale VA 2/4/1944 s Charles Raymond Sydnor & Mary Frances. BA U Rich 1966; MDiv VTS 1970. D 6/20/1970 P 5/15/1971 Bp Philip Alan Smith. c 1. S Geo's Ch Fredericksburg VA 1973-2003; D S Matt's Epis Ch Sterling VA 1970-1973. frsydnor@nnwifi.com

SYEDULLAH, Masud Ibn (RG) 311 E Palace Ave, Santa Fe NM 87501 **Assoc R for Adult Chr Formation, and Liturg Ch of the H Faith Santa Fe NM 2011-** B Saint Louis MO 10/11/1948 s Masud Syedullah & Alice Marie. B.M.E. Oral Roberts U 1971; M.Mus. U CO 1974; MDiv SWTS 1979. D 6/16/1979 P 4/14/1980 Bp Gerald Nicholas McAllister. m 7/16/1971 Janice Taylor c 2. Chair, Epis-Muslim Relatns Com Dio New York New York City NY 2008-2011; Sprtl Dir, Happ Dio New York New York City NY 2006-2008; Pres of the Stndg Com Dio New York New York City NY 2005-2006; Vic Ch Of The Atone Bronx NY 1998-2011; Cmsn on Liturg and Mus Dio New York New York City NY 1992-2002; P-in-c Corp Of Trin Ch New York NY 1992-1993; Assoc for Wrshp and Educ Mnstrs Par of Trin Ch New York NY 1990-1993; Assoc for Adult Educ and Liturg Epis Soc Of Chr Ch Cincinnati OH 1988-1990; Vic S Aid's Epis Ch Tulsa OK 1981-1988; Sprtl Dir, Happ Dio Oklahoma Oklahoma City OK 1981-1986; Cmsn on Mus Dio Oklahoma Oklahoma City OK 1980-1988; Chapl & Hd of Rel and Psychol Holland Hall Sch Tulsa OK 1979-1981; Assoc S Aid's Epis Ch Tulsa OK 1979-1981. Third Ord, Soc of S Fran 1979; UBE 1988. misyedullah@att.net

SYKES, Robert James (Pa) 102 Woodland Dr, Lansdale PA 19446 B Philadelphia PA 9/11/1931 s Joseph Pennington Sykes & Rebecca Hamilton. BS Tem 1954; STB PDS 1957; MA U of Pennsylvania 1980; Cert Montgomery Cnty Cmnty Coll 1983; AA Montgomery Cnty Cmnty Coll 1984. D 4/27/1957 P 11/1/1957 Bp Alfred L Banyard. m 9/11/1954 Mary Katherine Hoehn c 4. R Memi Ch Of The H Nativ Rockledge PA 1969-1979; Vic The Ch Of The Gd Shpd Berlin NJ 1960-1969; Cur Chr Ch In Woodbury Woodbury NJ 1957-1960.

SYLER, Gregory Charles (WA) St George Church, PO Box 30, Valley Lee MD 20692 **R S Geo's Wm And Mary Vlly Lee MD 2007-** B Chicago IL 9/8/1975 s Earl Gordon Syler & Dorothy Mae. BA S Xavier U Chicago IL 1993; MDiv U Chi 2000; DAS VTS 2005. D 6/18/2005 P 12/17/2005 Bp William Dailey Persell. m 9/3/2006 Meredith Meredith Carter c 1. Cur Ch Of Our Sav Chicago IL 2005-2007. gregsyler@yahoo.com

SYLER, Meredith (WA) Trinity Parish, PO Box 178, Hughesville MD 20637 **R Old Fields Chap Hughesville MD 2007-** B Washington DC 12/19/1980 d Jimmy Maxwell Carter & Carolyn. BA Appalachian St U Boone NC 2003; MDiv SWTS 2007. D 6/9/2007 Bp Granville Porter Taylor P 1/19/2008 Bp John Chane. m 9/3/2006 Gregory Charles Syler c 1. S Paul's Epis Ch Piney Waldorf MD 2010-2011; P-in-c Trin Epis Par Hughesville MD 2007-2010. meredithsyler@yahoo.com

SYLVESTER, Kathleen Dillon (Los) 1548 San Rafael Dr, Corona CA 92882 **Prog Dir S Paul's Epis Ch Tustin CA 2005-; D Ch Of The H Innoc San Francisco CA 2004-; Every Voice Ntwk San Francisco CA 2004-** B Durango CO 4/12/1959 d John Desbrisay Sylvester & Roma Lucile. BA Ft Lewis Coll 1981; MDiv CDSP 2003. D 6/19/2004 Bp Chester Lovelle Talton P 1/22/2005 Bp Joseph Jon Bruno. katydillon@yahoo.com

SYMINGTON, Ann Pritzlaff (Los) No address on file. **D S Barn On The Desert Scottsdale AZ 2002-** B Milwaukee WI 1/5/1952 d John Charles Pritzlaff & Mary Dell. BA Scripps Coll 1974; Cert San Francisco St U 1975. D 10/5/2002 Bp Robert Reed Shahan. m 2/7/1976 J Fife Symington c 3. aops99@aol.com

SYMINGTON, Sidney S (Roch) 68 Second St, Geneseo NY 14454 **Assoc S Ptr's Epis Ch Henrietta NY 2009-** B St Louis MO 12/17/1956 s Stuart Symington & Janey Studt. BA Yale Coll 1978; MFA NYU 1984; MDiv Yale DS 2004. D 6/6/2009 P 2/13/2010 Bp Prince Grenville Singh. m 8/13/2005 Martha Wadsworth c 4. sssymington@yahoo.com

SYMONDS, John W (Neb) 321 W Chestnut St, Lancaster PA 17603 **P-in-c S Mary's Epis Ch Blair NE 2010-** B Lancaster PA 8/22/1967 s Gordon Symonds & Carole Ann. BS Rutgers U New Brunswick 1990; MDiv Lancaster TS 2007; DAS Epis TS of the SW 2008. D 6/7/2008 P 2/18/2009 Bp Nathan Dwight Baxter. S Jas Ch Lancaster PA 2009-2010. johnsymonds20@yahoo.com

SYMONS, Frederic Russell (NCal) 5301 Whitney Ave, Carmichael CA 95608 B Sussex NJ 1/18/1947 s Harold Frederick Symons & Mary. BA San Diego St U 1971; MDiv CDSP 1974. D 7/25/1974 P 5/31/1975 Bp Wesley Frensdorff. c 1. Vic S Andr's In The Highlands Mssn Antelope CA 1995-2003; Supply Dio El Camino Real Monterey CA 1990-1995; Dio El Camino Real Monterey CA 1990-1993; Cur S Matt's Epis Ch San Mateo CA 1980-1985; Ch Mus Cmsn Epis Dio San Joaquin Modesto CA 1978-1980; Ch Growth Cmsn Epis Dio San Joaquin Modesto CA 1977-1980; S Phil's Ch Coalinga CA 1976-1980; Cur Chr Ch Alameda CA 1974-1975. Dn SE Dnry 2000-2003; Eccl Crt 1997-2000.

SYMONS, Harold Frederick (ECR) 75 Camino Arroyo S, Palm Desert CA 92260 B Wilkes-Barre PA 10/14/1917 s Harold Symons & Alberta Mae. BA Syr 1940; MDiv Drew U 1947. D 7/25/1981 P 11/30/1981 Bp Charles Shannon Mallory. m 8/25/1938 Alberta Emeline Bunker c 1. Asst S Jn's Ch Indio CA 1989-1999; Assoc S Barn Ch Arroyo Grande CA 1981-1988.

SYNAN, Thomas Norbert Justin (NY) 115 E 82nd St Apt 5d, New York NY 10028 **Assoc P Ch Of The Heav Rest New York NY 2000-** B New York NY 4/14/1961 s William Edmund Synan & Catherine Irene. BS U of Pennsylvania 1983; JD Geo 1989; MDiv Ya Berk 2000. D 3/18/2000 P 9/16/2000 Bp Richard Frank Grein. Ord of St.Jn of Jerusalem 1990. tsynan@heavenlyrest.org

SZACHARA, Joell Beth (CNY) 3415 Havenbrook Dr Apt 104, Kingwood TX 77339 **S Steph's Ch New Hartford NY 2007-** B Binghamton NY 4/5/1967 d Bernard Szachara & Shea. AA SUNY 1987; BA St. Jn Fisher Coll 1990; MDiv VTS 1997. D 6/11/1997 Bp David B(ruce) Joslin P 5/1/1998 Bp Claude Edward Payne. Dio Cntrl New York Syracuse NY 2007-2008; S Jn's Ch Marcellus NY 2006; S Thos' Epis Ch Syracuse NY 2005-2006; All SS Ch Frederick

MD 1999-2005; Ch Of The Gd Shpd Kingwood TX 1997-1999. revjoell@allsaintsmd.org

SZOBOTA, Nicholas Stephen (Md) 3497 N. Chatham Road, Ellicott City MD 21042 **Chr Ch W River MD 2011-** B Bridgeport CT 3/7/1979 s Stephen Andrew Szobota & Heidi Wynn. BA Drew U 2001; MDiv GTS 2005. D 6/11/2005 P 12/21/2005 Bp John Palmer Croneberger. Assoc R S Jn's Ch Ellicott City MD 2007-2011; Cler Res Chr Ch Alexandria VA 2005-2007. ccwrnick@comcast.net

SZOKE, Robyn J (CPa) 6 Kitszell Dr, Carlisle PA 17015 **Dio Cntrl Pennsylvania Harrisburg PA 2010-** B SyracuseNY 10/20/1950 d Robert Anthony Grigonis & Lela Adell. BA Austin Coll; BS W Chester St Coll 1972; Med Leh 1984; MDiv Moravian TS 1988; STM GTS 1989. D 5/28/1988 P 1/17/1989 Bp James Michael Mark Dyer. S Jn's Epis Ch Carlisle PA 2004-2011; Sff Off For Chldrn'S Mnstrys And Chrstn Ed Epis Ch Cntr New York NY 1999-2001; Dio Pennsylvania Philadelphia PA 1995-1999; Asst Chr Epis Ch Pottstown PA 1990-1995; Trin Epis Ch Pottsville PA 1990-1995; Assoc S Steph's Epis Ch Wilkes Barre PA 1989-1990; Asst The Epis Ch Of The Medtr Allentown PA 1988-1989. Jn Hus Awd Moravian TS. rszoke@stjohnscarlisle.org

SZOST, Lois Anne Whitcomb (NY) 57 Goodwin Rd, Stanfordville NY 12581 **D S Thos Ch Amenia Un Amenia NY 1998-** B Wilton NH 5/1/1930 d Leon Edwin Whitcomb & Nancy Farnum. D 5/16/1998 Bp Richard Frank Grein.

SZYMANSKI, Michael Stephen (WNY) 21 Modern Ave, Lackawanna NY 14218 **D S Paul's Cathd Buffalo NY 2000-** B Buffalo NY 10/14/1949 s Stanley Robert Szymanski & Irene Frances. D 12/11/1999 Bp J Michael Garrison. m 12/9/1972 Jane Wall.

SZYMANSKI SSF, Walter (Roch) 334 Main St, Pittsburgh PA 15201 B Pittsburgh PA 11/23/1939 s Walter Szymanski & Helen. Dplma U.S. Army Signal Corp. 1958; BA S Vinc Sem Latrobe PA 1964; MDiv St. Bern's Sem Rochester NY 1970; ThM St. Bern's Sem Rochester NY 1971; DMin CRDS 1979; Dplma Alleg 1998. Rec from Roman Catholic 6/1/1973 as Priest Bp Robert Rae Spears Jr. m 1/1/1984 Paul Marrocco. S Paul's Ch Monongahela PA 1994-1995; Dio Rochester Rochester NY 1984-1993; Calv/St Andr's Par Rochester NY 1979-1993; Asst S Lk And S Simon Cyrene Rochester NY 1976-1979; Asst S Thos Epis Ch Rochester NY 1972-1975. Auth, "Blessings of Same Gender Relationshps," Integrity Pub, 1982; Auth, "As We Believe God," Integrity Pub, 1982; Auth, "Clincl Implications in Human Relatns," Integrity Pub, 1979; Auth, "Fam Mnstry & the Homophile Cmnty," Integrity Pub. Angl Soc Of S Fran 2002; Intl Assn of Cert Chem Addiction Couns 2001; Life Mem, Amer Assn for Mar and Fam Thera 1973. LifeTime Serv to The Gay and Lesbian Cmnty Interfaith Alliances For Gay Lesbian and Bisexual Persons 1995; Cn for Spec Mnstrs Epis Dio Rochester 1979. stfrancis33@yahoo.com

T

TABB, Stewart Mason (At) 6725 Knollwood Cir, Douglasville GA 30135 **S Julian's Epis Ch Douglasville GA 2003-** B Charlottesville VA 12/27/1959 d Waller Crockett Tabb & Anthony Mason. BA Davidson Coll 1982; MDiv CDSP 1999. D 12/5/1998 P 6/5/1999 Bp Stewart Clark Zabriskie. Asst R S Tim's Ch Herndon VA 2000-2003; Reg Vic Dio Nevada Las Vegas NV 1999-2000. stewarttabb@yahoo.com

TABER II, Kenneth William (WMich) 200 College Ave NE, Grand Rapids MI 49503 B Pasadena CA 7/4/1938 s Kenneth William Taber & Alice. BA Dart 1960; MDiv VTS 1963; Virginia Commonwealth U 1972; MSW Wstrn Michigan U 1992. D 7/15/1963 Bp Noble C Powell P 6/12/1964 Bp Harry Lee Doll. m 12/30/1988 Cornelia M Taber c 3. S Phil's Epis Ch Grand Rapids MI 2008-2009; R S Mich's Ch Grand Rapids MI 2002-2007; Ch of the H Sprt Belmont MI 1995-2000; Int S Andr's Ch Big Rapids MI 1992-1994; ExCoun Dio Connecticut Hartford CT 1980-1985; R Chr Ch Stratford CT 1974-1985; Vic Ch Of The Creator Mechanicsville VA 1967-1974; Asst H Trin Epis Ch Greensboro NC 1965-1967. "Sacrifice of Praise and Thanksgiving," *St. Mich's Ch*, 2007; Auth, "Outplacement: An Idea Whose Time Has Come," *Connections - WMU*, 1995; Auth, "ISMS: Use of Narrative in Healing Racism," *Institutes For Healing Racism Trng*, 1994. Intl TA Assn 1965; NASW 1962; USATransactional Analysis Assoc. 2006. Counslr Natl Bd Cert Counselors 1996; Career Counslr Natl Bd Cert Counselors 1996; Lic Clincl Soc Worker St of Michigan 1996; Career Mgmt Fell Intl Career Certification Inst 1995; Developmenr Spec NTL 1965. kta4careers@hotmail.com

TABER-HAMILTON, Nigel John (Oly) 5217 S. Honeymoon Bay Road, Freeland WA 98249 **Bd Mem, Faith Action Ntwk Dio Olympia Seattle WA 2009-; Interfaith Off Dio Olympia Seattle WA 2008-; R S Augustines In-The-Woods Epis Par Freeland WA 2000-** B London UK 4/7/1953 s Kenneth William Harris & Kathleen Patricia. BA(MCL) U of Wales, Bangor 1975; B.A. U of Birmingham GB 1976; MDiv Queens Coll 1977; Cert of one year's study CDSP 1978; D. Min. SFTS 2012. Trans from Church Of England 8/29/1979 Bp William Edwin Swing. m 5/1/1993 Rachel K Taber. GC Dep Dio Olympia Seattle WA 2006; Cler Assn Dio Olympia Seattle WA 2005-2007; Cmsn on Mssn Strtgy Dio Indianapolis Indianapolis IN 1997-2000; Cmsn on Stwdshp Dio Indianapolis Indianapolis IN 1997-2000; Vic All SS Ch Seymour IN 1994-2000; Assoc Trin Epis Ch Bloomington IN 1992-1994; Cmsn on Liturg & Mus Dio Indianapolis Indianapolis IN 1991-1994; Int R S Steph's Epis Ch New Harmony IN 1991-1992; Int R S Jn's Epis Ch Crawfordsville IN 1990-1991; Int R S Jn's Epis Ch Bedford IN 1988-1989; COM Dio Indianapolis Indianapolis IN 1984-1999; Assoc S Mk's Par Berkeley CA 1979-1981. writer, "The Reformation Continues," *Epis Voice*, Dio Olympia, 2005; writer, "The Windsor Report: a critical Revs," *Epis Voice*, Dio Olympia, 2004. Associated Parishes 1997. Polly Bond Awd of Merit, ECom/The Reformation Continues 2006; Polly Bond Awd of Excellence, ECom/The Windsor Report 2005; WCC Ecum Fell WCC 1977. rector@whidbey.com

TABER-HAMILTON, Rachel K (Oly) 333 High St, Freeland WA 98249 **Stndg Com Dio Olympia Seattle WA 2011-; R Trin Epis Ch Everett WA 2011-; Com on Indigenous Mnstrs Exec Coun Appointees New York NY 2009-** B Cleveland Heights OH 3/15/1963 BA SUNY; MA U Alaska Fairbanks 1988; PhD Indiana U 1991; MDiv Loyola U Chicago 1994. D 6/28/2003 P 2/14/2004 Bp Vincent Waydell Warner. m 5/1/1993 Nigel John Taber-hamilton. St Steph's Epis Ch Oak Harbor WA 2007-2008; Dioc Coun Dio Olympia Seattle WA 2006-2008; First Nations Com, Chair Dio Olympia Seattle WA 2004-2008. Auth, "The Necessity of Native Amer Autonomy for Successful Partnerships," *ATR*, Seabury Wstrn, 2010. Assn of Profsnl Chapl (APC) 2000. Polly Bond Awd ECom 2004; Bd Cert Chapl Assn of Profsnl Chapl 2001. chaplain@whidbey.com

TACHAU, Charles Brandeis (Ky) 1080 Baxter Ave Apt 1, Louisville KY 40204 B Louisville KY 5/1/1922 s Charles Gabriel Tachau & Jean Brandeis. Swarthmore Coll 1942; MDiv VTS 1963; JD U of Louisville 2048. D 6/18/1963 P 1/27/1964 Bp Charles Gresham Marmion. Archd Dio Kentucky Louisville KY 1986-1989; BEC Dio Kentucky Louisville KY 1968-1972; Vic S Geo's Epis Ch Louisville KY 1965-1985; Vic S Andr's Ch Glasgow KY 1963-1965.

TACKETT, Thomas Tolbert (RG) 7017 Majorca Ct, El Paso TX 79912 B Waco TX 9/1/1934 s Tolbert Preston Tackett & Dorothy. BBA Texas Tech U 1960. D 6/27/1992 Bp Terence Kelshaw. D S Fran On The Hill El Paso TX 1992-2000. tttackett@aol.com

TACKKETT, Antoinette Vance (Kan) 613 Elm St, Coffeyville KS 67337 **Vic S Paul's Epis Ch Coffeyville KS 2012-** B Kansas City MO 1/7/1947 d Roy Vance Finnell & June. BA U of Missouri, Columbia, MO 1968; MS Pittsburg St U, Pittsburg, KS 1990; Cert Kansas Sch For Mnstry, Topeka, KS 2011. D 6/5/2010 P 1/8/2011 Bp Dean Elliott Wolfe. m 5/15/1990 Dale Tackkett c 8. Assoc S Paul's Epis Ch Coffeyville KS 2011. oomomma@yahoo.com

TADKEN, Neil Alan (Los) 914 N Kings Rd Apt 1, West Hollywood CA 90069 **Prog Grp on GLBT Mnstrs Dio Los Angeles Los Angeles CA 2011-; Dnry 3 Treas Dio Los Angeles Los Angeles CA 2005-; Assoc R for Pstr Care S Jas Par Los Angeles CA 2005-** B New York NY 4/25/1960 s Donavan Lee Tadken & Ellen Kay. BA Occ 1983; MFA Cor 1985; MDiv ETSBH 2004. D 6/11/2005 Bp Chester Lovelle Talton P 1/14/2006 Bp Joseph Jon Bruno. m 7/11/2008 Frank Slesinski. Bd Dir Epis Urban Intern Prog Los Angeles CA 2006-2010; Dnry 3 Treas Dio Los Angeles Los Angeles CA 2005-2011; Prog Grp on HIV/AIDS Mnstrs Dio Los Angeles Los Angeles CA 2005-2011; Assoc R for Pstr Care S Jas Par Los Angeles CA 2004-2005. Presidents Awd for Acad Excellence Claremont TS 2004; Ribbon of Hope Awd Acad of Television Art and Sciences 1997. ntadken@sbcglobal.net

TAFLINGER, Mary Jeanine (Ind) 5553 Leumas Rd, Cincinnati OH 45239 **Vic Trin Ch Lawrenceburg IN 1996-** B Findlay OH 7/29/1958 d Donald Jean Taflinger & Bette Mae. BA Mia 1980; MDiv Harvard DS 1986. D 6/20/1987 P 5/1/1988 Bp William Grant Black. m 9/7/1991 Christopher Meshot c 1. R S Jn's Epis Ch Crawfordsville IN 1990-1995; S Alb's Epis Ch Of Bexley Columbus OH 1987-1990. mtaflinger1@juno.com

TAFOYA, Stacey Timothy (Colo) 315 Leyden St, Denver CO 80220 **R Epiph Epis Ch Denver CO 2002-** B Denver CO 5/10/1970 s Timothy Tafoya & Martha. BA Colorado Chr U 1992; MDiv Epis TS of The SW 2000. D 6/10/2000 P 12/10/2000 Bp William Jerry Winterrowd. m 7/11/1998 Sarah E Robinette c 3. Cur The Ch Of Chr The King (Epis) Arvada CO 2000-2002. SS Alb & Sergius 2001; Soc Of S Mary 2001. stace_tafoya@yahoo.com

TAFT JR, Paul Eberhart (Tex) 5504 Andover Dr, Tyler TX 75707 B Houston TX 12/5/1939 s Paul Eberhart Taft & Harriet. BA Van 1961; MDiv VTS 1967. D 6/27/1967 Bp J Milton Richardson P 5/30/1968 Bp Scott Field Bailey. m 9/10/1960 Lucy Akerman. All SS Epis Sch Tyler TX 2003-2007; R S Steph's Ch Liberty TX 1998-2003; R S Jn's Epis Ch Austin TX 1992-1998; R S Alb's Epis Ch Waco TX 1979-1992; R H Trin Epis Ch Dickinson TX 1972-1979; Vic Chr Epis Ch Mexia Mexia TX 1968-1972; Cur Chr Ch Cathd Houston TX 1967-1968. palu.taft@sbcglobal.net

TAIT, Charles William Stuart (WA) PO Box 25541, Seattle WA 98165 B Boston MA 9/8/1923 s Charles Herman Avis Tait & Jennie. BA Harv 1947; BD VTS 1961. D 6/17/1961 Bp William Foreman Creighton P 6/9/1962 Bp Stephen F Bayne Jr. Salisbury Sch Dio Connecticut Hartford CT 1968-1987; Asst S Andr's Ch Wellesley MA 1964-1966.

TAKACS, Erika L (Va) Saint Mark's Church, 1625 Locust St, Philadelphia PA 19103 **S Mk's Ch Philadelphia PA 2011-** B West Chester PA 10/30/1973 d Frank Takacs & Norma Cary. BS W Chester U of Pennsylvania 1995; MM Westminster Choir Coll Princeton NJ 1998; MDiv VTS 2007. D 12/15/2007 Bp Franklin Delton Turner. Cler Res Chr Ch Alexandria VA 2007-2009. etakacs@saintmarksphiladelphia.org

TAKES WAR BONNETT, Ray Lee (SD) No address on file. B Pine Ridge SD 7/22/1955 s Leo Lee Takes War Bonnett & Sophia. MDiv STUSo 1988. D 6/19/1988 Bp Craig Barry Anderson. m 1/4/1975 Delores Annette Broken Rope.

TALBERT, Thomas Keith (CGC) 701 N Pine St, Foley AL 36535 **R S Paul's Ch Foley AL 2001-** B Columbus GA 4/24/1955 s Thomas Sidney Talbert & Joyce Ann. BS U of Alabama 1977; MDiv STUSo 1994. D 6/4/1994 P 2/1/1995 Bp Charles Farmer Duvall. m 3/12/1978 Carol Lynn Talbert c 2. R S Paul's Epis Ch Daphne AL 2000-2001; Assoc S Paul's Epis Ch Daphne AL 1994-2000. frtkt1@gmail.com

TALBIRD JR, John D (ETenn) 3184 Waterfront Drive, Chattanooga TN 37419 B Macon GA 4/18/1940 s John Talbird & Sara Lucile. BA U GA 1962; MDiv VTS 1965. D 6/26/1965 P 3/19/1966 Bp Randolph R Claiborne. m 6/26/1976 Mary Talbird c 5. Ch Of The Gd Shpd Lookout Mtn TN 1982-2006; Ch Of The Incarn Gainesville FL 1967-1982; Dio Florida Jacksonville FL 1967-1982; Assoc Chapl Resurr Chap Tallahassee FL 1967-1969; Asst S Lk's Epis Ch Atlanta GA 1965-1967. Auth, "The In Hse Critic," *Living Ch*, LivCh Fndt, Inc., 1977. johntalbird@hotmail.com

TALBOT, John Stiles (NY) No address on file. B 2/3/1928 D 6/11/1958 P 12/22/1958 Bp Horace W B Donegan.

TALBOTT, John Thayer (WA) 8 Ledge Road, Old Saybrook CT 06475 B New York NY 2/21/1939 s Harold Elstner Talbott & Margaret Borland. AS Odessa Coll 1964; BA U of Alabama 1983; MDiv Van 1985; CAS STUSo 1986. D 6/28/1986 P 2/8/1987 Bp George Lazenby Reynolds Jr. m 6/26/1965 Anne Washington Kinsolving c 3. Assoc S Ann's Epis Ch Old Lyme CT 2000-2010; R S Aug's Epis Ch Washington DC 1992-2004; R Ch Of The Redeem Shelbyville TN 1986-1992. Auth, *Chr Wrshp: A Study Guide for Disciples*. Jttalbott@comcast.net

TALBOTT, Lucy Brady (EC) 1257 Government St, Murray House #213, Mobile AL 36604 B Fall River MA 6/1/1946 d Francis I Brady & Sue Schenck. BA Duke 1968; MDiv VTS 1981; Fllshp EDS 1992. D 6/20/1981 P 1/9/1982 Bp John Thomas Walker. c 1. Dep GC Dio E Carolina Kinston NC 1994-1997; R S Paul's In The Pines Epis Ch Fayetteville NC 1983-2001; Assoc The Ch of S Clem Alexandria VA 1981-1983. "Peace, Lucy," Lulu.com, 2007; Auth, "Journey Through the Vlly Called AIDS," *Journ of the Alb Inst*, 1988. Proctor Fell EDS 1992; Giraffe Awd Wmn Soc of Fayetteville 1985. amandatalbott@yahoo.com

TALCOTT, Barbara Geer (NH) St. Mark's School, 25 Marlboro Rd., Southborough MA 01772 **S Paul's Sch Concord NH 2008-** B Boston MA 6/9/1961 d Hooker Talcott & Jane. BA Pr 1983; MBA Stan 1988; MTS Harvard DS 2003. D 6/25/2008 P 2/4/2009 Bp V Gene Robinson. m 12/3/1983 Douglas C Borchard c 3. barbaratalcott@stmarksschool.org

TALIAFERRO, Robert Davis (NwT) P.O. Box 3751, Amarillo TX 79116 **R S Ptr's Epis Ch Amarillo TX 2009-** B Greensboro NC 10/9/1956 s Richard McCullough Taliaferro & Esther Talley-Davis. AAS Oklahoma St U 1994; BA U Of Cntrl Oklahoma 1996; MDiv Epis TS of The SW 1999. D 6/26/1999 P 12/21/1999 Bp Robert Manning Moody. m 11/3/1984 Margaret Anne Wycherley c 3. R S Ptr's Ch Tulsa OK 2001-2009; S Jn's Ch Norman OK 1999-2001; Cur S Jn's Ch Oklahoma City OK 1999-2000. frbobt@aol.com

TALK IV, John Gordon (Mich) 960 E. Jefferson Ave., Detroit MI 48207 **Chr Ch Detroit MI 2009-; Epis Ch Of The Epiph Wilbraham MA 2006-; Epis Ret HmInc. Cincinnati OH 2003-** B Dallas TX 8/23/1964 BA Centenary Coll. D 10/26/2002 P 6/21/2003 Bp Herbert Thompson Jr. m 8/30/2006 Shelly Talk c 5. Dio Wstrn Massachusetts Springfield MA 2006-2009; Cbury Crt W Carrollton OH 2003-2006. johngtalk@gmail.com

TALLANT, Greg (At) 13 Castlewood Dr. S.W., Rome GA 30165 **COM Dio Atlanta Atlanta GA 2009-; Assoc R S Ptr's Ch Rome GA 2007-** B Cumming GA 5/1/1969 s Jimmy Leland Tallant & Constance Barnett. BA Presb Coll 1991; No Georgia Coll and St U 1993; MDiv GTS 2007. D 12/21/2006 P 7/14/2007 Bp J(ohn) Neil Alexander. m 11/16/1996 Emily George c 2. gregorytallant@yahoo.com

TALLEVAST, William Dalton (CPa) University Med Ctr Dept of Pastoral Care, 1501 N Campbell Ave, Tucson AZ 85724 B Asheville NC 10/25/1941 s William Dalton Tallevast & Irene Constance. BA U NC 1965; BD VTS 1968; Duke 1970. D 6/17/1968 P 12/1/1968 Bp Matthew G Henry. c 1. P-in-c S Lk's Ch Mineral Wells TX 1971-1972; Asst S Phil's Ch Durham NC 1970-1971; D S Andr's Ch Mt Holly NJ 1968-1970. Auth, "Eschatolgoy & Self-Integratn". AAPC, ACPE.

TALMAGE, John Philip (Mil) 12310 N Golf Dr, Mequon WI 53092 **Died 9/10/2010** B Brooklyn NY 3/31/1928 s George Edwin Talmage & Evelyn. BA U of Virginia 1950; MDiv Nash 1953; MALS U of Wisconsin 1965. D 4/11/1953 P 10/31/1953 Bp James P De Wolfe. c 2. Auth, "Uscc Pub In Print - A Descriptive Index," Natl Conf Of Cathd Bishops, 1991; Auth, "Marq Index To Pub Of The Nccb/Uscc," U.S. Cath Conf, 1991; Auth, "Personl Libr Bibliography," Amer Soc for Personal Mgmt, 1970. sorptalmage@aol.com

✠ **TALTON, Rt Rev Chester Lovelle** (Los) 1528 Oakdale Road, Modesto CA 95355 **Provsnl Bp Epis Dio San Joaquin Modesto CA 2011-** B Eldorado AR 9/22/1941 s Chester Talton & Mae Ola. BS California St U 1965; BD CDSP 1970. D 6/27/1970 P 2/1/1971 Bp C Kilmer Myers Con 1/26/1991 for Los. m 5/25/2007 April Greyson. Bp Suffr Dio Los Angeles Los Angeles CA 1990-2010; R S Phil's Ch New York NY 1985-1990; Mssn Off Par of Trin Ch New York NY 1981-1985; Trin Educ Fund New York NY 1981-1985; Dio Minnesota Minneapolis MN 1980-1981; R S Phil's Ch S Paul MN 1976-1981; Vic Ch Of The H Cross Chicago IL 1973-1976; Cur All SS Ch Carmel CA 1971-1973; Dio Los Angeles Los Angeles CA 1971-1973; Vic The Epis Ch Of The Gd Shpd Berkeley CA 1970-1971. DD CDSP 1992. cktalton@sbcglobal.net

TAMMEARU, Deborah Gibson (NY) 125 Teresa Ln, Mamaroneck NY 10543 **Dioc Trng Cntr New York NY 1998-; R S Thos Ch Mamaroneck NY 1994-** B Passaic NJ 6/13/1947 d Charles Christian Gibson & Sophia. BS FD 1970; MDiv GTS 1982. D 6/24/1982 Bp Richard Mitchell Trelease Jr P 2/1/1983 Bp Walter Decoster Dennis Jr. Wstrn Dutchess Mnstry New Hamburg NY 1985-1994; P-in-c Of Wstrn Dutchess Mnstry Dio New York New York City NY 1984-1994; Cur Zion Epis Ch Wappingers Falls NY 1982-1984. rector@saintthomasmmrk.org

TAMPA, John Grey (NC) 265 Fairway Dr, Southern Pines NC 28387 **Emm Par Epis Ch And Day Sch Sthrn Pines NC 2006-** B Rochester NY 10/6/1951 s Nicholas James Tampa & Anne Grey. BA Le Moyne Coll 1974; MDiv VTS 1998. D 6/13/1998 Bp Peter James Lee P 4/14/1999 Bp Robert Poland Atkinson. m 12/30/1988 Julia Kathryn Tampa c 3. S Ptr's Ch In The Great Vlly Malvern PA 1999-2006; S Dav's Ch Wayne PA 1998-1999. jtampa@nc.rr.com

TAN, Wee Chung (Minn) L B Pearson College Of The Pacific, 650 Pearson College Drive Canada B 1/6/1930 Trans from Church Of England 4/9/1973 Bp Philip Frederick McNairy.

TANABE, Irene (Oly) 4533 52nd Ave S, Seattle WA 98118 **Cur S Mk's Cathd Seattle WA 2011-** B Tokyo Japan 4/21/1951 d Shinichiro Tanabe & Toshiko. BA Wstrn Washington U 1977; JD U CO Sch of Law 1985; PhDiv CDSP 2011. D 2/15/2011 Bp Gregory Harold Rickel. m 7/7/2001 Michael Burnap c 1. irene.tanabe@gmail.com

TAN CRETI, Michael James (Neb) 2051 N 94th St, Omaha NE 68134 B Carroll IA 8/5/1940 s Marcus Ralph Tan Creti & Irene Luey. BA Dart 1962; MDiv Ya Berk 1967; MA Candidate Aquinas Inst of Theol 1980. D 6/22/1967 P 12/1/1967 Bp Gordon V Smith. m 6/3/1967 Jane Warnecke. All SS Epis Ch Omaha NE 1977-2005; S Jn's Epis Ch Dubuque IA 1974-1977; S Paul's Epis Ch Grinnell IA 1969-1973. janetancred@msn.com

TANG, Christopher Douglas (Md) 3118 Cape Hill Ct, Hampstead MD 21074 **R Ch Of The H Comf Luthvle Timon MD 2011-** B Washington DC 5/2/1966 s Douglas Brayton Tang & Karen Mildred. BA U of Maryland 1989; MDiv VTS 1996. D 6/15/1996 P 1/1/1997 Bp Robert Wilkes Ihloff. m 11/13/1993 Kara Marie McDowell. R S Geo Ch Hampstead MD 1998-2011; Cur Ch Of The H Comf Luthvle Timon MD 1996-1998. tangchris@comcast.net

TANNER, Michael Abbott (Ga) 63 1st Ave SE, Atlanta GA 30317 **Vic Ch Of The H Comf Atlanta GA 2006-; Dio Atlanta Atlanta GA 2006-** B Pascagoula MS 4/27/1948 s Abbott Hoover Tanner & Mary Frances. Candidate D.Min TS; AA Florida Coll 1968; AB U of Alabama 1973; JD U of Alabama Sch of Law 1976; none 2003; MDiv Candler TS Emory U 2005. D 12/21/2005 P 7/26/2006 Bp J(ohn) Neil Alexander. m 6/2/1970 Carol Cozette Tanner c 5. mtanner@bellsouth.net

TANNO, Lewis Oliver (SwFla) 37421 Meridian Ave, Dade City FL 33525 B Cleveland OH 3/2/1931 s Dan A Tanno & Filomena. Epis TS In Kentucky 1969; BA Morehaed St U 1974; MA Morehaed St U 1975; MA Morehaed St U 1976. D 12/15/1968 P 11/21/1969 Bp William R Moody. m 7/26/1952 Kathryn Naomi Farquhar. R S Mary's Ch Dade City FL 1986-2003; R Ch Of The Ascen Mt Sterling KY 1973-1986; Asst Chr Ch Cathd Louisville KY 1969-1970. OHC 1979.

TANTIMONACO, Daniel Frank (Az) 307 N Mogollon Trail, Payson AZ 85541 **Dioc Coun VP Dio Arizona Phoenix AZ 2011-; R S Paul's Ch Payson AZ 2006-** B Bridgeport CT 1/16/1953 s Anthony Paul Tantimonaco & Florence Pearl. Dplma Epis TS of The SW 2005. D 4/17/2005 Bp Leopold Frade P 11/5/2005 Bp Kirk Stevan Smith. m 9/25/1993 Roberta H Tantimonaco c 2. Cn Assoc. - Trin Cathd Dio Arizona Phoenix AZ 2005-2006. rev.dan@msn.com

TAPLEY, William Clark (WTex) 1604 W Kansas Ave, Midland TX 79701 B Rochester NY 8/5/1930 s Iaian Cameron Gordon-Tapley & Ethel Dorothea. BA U Roch 1955; MA Col 1957; MDiv Bex 1971; Ldrshp Acad for New Directions 1984; CPE 1986. D 6/12/1971 P 12/1/1971 Bp Harold B Robinson. m 6/26/1961 Joyce E Smith c 2. R Ch Of The Redeem Eagle Pass TX 1994-1996; Vic H Trin Carrizo Sprg TX 1994-1996; Vic S Jas Ch Monahans TX 1987-1994; R Ch Of The Epiph Sedan KS 1980-1985; Dio Kansas Topeka KS 1980-1985; S Matt's Ch Cedar Vale KS 1980-1985; Com Dio Wstrn Kansas Hutchinson KS 1977-1980; Vic SS Mary And Martha Of Bethany Larned KS 1977-1980; R All SS Ch Aliquippa PA 1975-1977; P-in-c Ch of SS Thos and Lk Patton PA 1972-1975; Asst S Mk's Ch Johnstown PA 1972-1974. Auth, "Happily Ever After Is No Accident: Premarital & Mar Counslg Prog"; Auth, "Finding Serenity: Sprtlty For Recovery". ERM. Rossiter Schlr 1981.

TAPPE, Elizabeth or Ibba Peden (Fla) 2935 Tidewater St, Fernandina Beach FL 32034 B Hickory NC 4/29/1951 d James Gwyn Peden & Ann. Assoc Arts S Mary's Jr. Coll, Raleigh, NC 1971; BA U NC Chap Hill 1973; MDiv VTS 1977. D 6/25/1977 P 5/6/1978 Bp William Gillette Weinhauer. c 2. R S Ptr's Ch Fernandina Bch FL 1998-2005; Stndg Com, Stndg Com Chair; Exec Coun (ex officio) Dio Florida Jacksonville FL 1998-2002; R S Cathr's Ch Jacksonville FL 1997-1998; Int Assoc, Epis HS in Jacksonville, FL Dio Florida Jacksonville FL 1996-1997; R Ch Of The Gd Shpd Jacksonville FL 1990-1996; Com on St of the Ch, and Chair; Com on Mnstry, Eccl Crt Dio Florida Jacksonville FL 1989-1995; Stndg Com, Bp Coadj Search Com, Com Trans Episcopate Dio Wstrn No Carolina Asheville NC 1987-1989; R S Jn's Ch Asheville NC 1983-1989; COM, Eccles Crt Dio Wstrn No Carolina Asheville NC 1983-1986; Exec Coun Dio Connecticut Hartford CT 1981-1982; R S Mich's Ch Naugatuck CT 1980-1982; Asst S Andr's Ch Meriden CT 1979-1980; R S Andr's Ch Meriden CT 1979-1980; Supvsr Yale Div Students Ya Berk New Haven CT 1978-1980; R S Andr's Ch Meriden CT 1978; Deacons' Trng Prog; Epis Soc Serv, Com V COM Dio Connecticut Hartford CT 1977-1980; Cur S Andr's Ch Meriden CT 1977-1978. epedentappe@aol.com

TARBELL, Albert Weatherbee (RG) 500 Aliso Dr Se, Albuquerque NM 87108 B Bangor ME 12/27/1909 s Lester Fairfield Tarbell & Florence Lilian. BA Bow 1932; Ya 1935; MDiv GTS 1959. D 7/1/1959 P 1/10/1960 Bp C J Kinsolving III. S Mary's Epis Ch Albuquerque NM 1964-1978; Cn S Jn's Cathd Albuquerque NM 1959-1964. OHC 1959. Hon Cn S Jn's Cathd, Albuquerque NM Albuquerque NM.

TARBET JR, Bob (Tex) 121 Goliad St., Mc Gregor TX 76657 B Dallas TX 11/30/1938 s Robert Tarbet & Lula Edith. BS USMA at W Point 1962; MDiv Epis TS of The SW 1973; MBA SMU 1984. D 1/3/1974 Bp J Milton Richardson P 12/14/1974 Bp Scott Field Bailey. m 7/28/1962 Beverly Bragg Tarbet c 2. R Trin Epis Ch Marble Falls TX 1993-1997; Vic S Lk's Epis Ch Lindale TX 1992-1993; Chapl Off Of Bsh For ArmdF New York NY 1977-1991; Vic Chr Ch Matagorda TX 1974-1976; Vic S Jn's Epis Ch Palacios TX 1974-1976. 11usma62@sbcglobal.net

TARBET, David Blalock (Tex) 3926 Roseland St, Houston TX 77006 **Died 3/4/2010** B Fort Worth TX 3/6/1941 s Robert Morgan Tarbet & Edith. BA U of Texas 1963; MDiv GTS 1966; MA U Of Houston 1979. D 6/15/1966 Bp Charles A Mason P 12/21/1966 Bp Theodore H McCrea. Angl Soc 1966; Associated Parishes 1973; ADLMC 1983-2000; Fndt Contemporary Theol 1998; Integrity 1975. dtarbet@flash.net

TARBOX, Janet Ellen (USC) 207 Country Club Road, Edgefield SC 29824 B Lafayette IN 8/25/1953 d Gurdon Lucius Tarbox & Milver Ann. BA U of So Carolina 1975; MEd U of So Carolina 1978; MDiv VTS 1992. D 12/12/1992 P 6/12/1993 Bp William Arthur Beckham. m 8/18/1990 Talmadge Moore LeGrand. Vic Ch Of The Ridge Trenton SC 2001-2008; Assoc S Thos' Ch Whitemarsh Ft Washington PA 1997-2000; Dio E Carolina Kinston NC 1996-1997; Asst S Jas Par Wilmington NC 1995-1997; Asst Gr Epis Ch And Kindergarten Camden SC 1992-1995. tarboxje@bellsouth.net

TARDIFF, Richard A (Haw) PO Box 545, Kealakekua HI 96750 **Chr Ch Kealakekua HI 2010-** B Bangor ME 3/19/1952 s Raymond Libby Tardiff & Eleanor Frances. MDiv CDSP 2005; EdD U Of Sarasota Orange CA 2005; Med U of Hawaii 2005. D 11/27/2004 P 6/18/2005 Bp Mark Lawrence Mac Donald. m 6/30/1979 Pamela VanWechel. R S Andr And S Jn Epis Ch SW Harbor ME 2006-2010. fathertardiff@me.com

TARPLEE JR, Cornelius (Nwk) 1405 Duncan St., Key West FL 33040 B Charles Town WV 11/29/1944 s Cornelius Caleb Tarplee & Priscilla Adams. BA Ob 1967; MA U of Wisconsin 1968; MDiv VTS 1980. D 6/14/1980 Bp Arnold M Lewis P 12/17/1980 Bp Ned Cole. m 2/1/1987 Judith McConnell c 3. R S Steph's Ch Millburn NJ 1992-2009; Vic Ch Of S Jn The Evang Dunbarton NH 1986-1992; Vic H Cross Epis Ch Weare NH 1986-1992; R S Thos Ch Hamilton NY 1980-1986. ctarplee@gmail.com

TARPLEY, Kent W (SwVa) 375 East Pine St, Wytheville VA 24382 **Exec Bd Dio SW Virginia Roanoke VA 2011-; R S Jn's Epis Ch Wytheville VA 2008-** B Elgin IL 7/31/1949 s Kenneth Jackson Tarpley & Vera Louise. BA Trin Hartford CT 1971; MDiv SWTS 1974; MSW Loyola U 1981; Cert Shalem Sprtl Gdnc Prog 1996; Cert Ch Dvlpmt Inst 2003. D 6/8/1974 Bp Quintin Ebenezer Primo Jr P 12/21/1974 Bp James Winchester Montgomery. m 5/12/1979 Laura J Jabbusch c 2. Curs Sprtl Advsr Dio Maine Portland ME 2004-2007; R S Marg's Ch Belfast ME 1997-2008; Chapl Deacons Sch Dio Chicago Chicago IL 1995-1997; R S Paul's Ch Kankakee IL 1992-1997; Dn Lakeshore Deanry Dio Fond du Lac Appleton WI 1987-1991; R S Ptr's Epis Ch Sheboygan Falls WI 1985-1992; Asst S Lk's Ch Evanston IL 1978-1985; Asst The Epis Ch Of S Jas The Less Northfield IL 1974-1976. Comp Of Cmnty Of Celebration, Aliquippa, Pa 1994-2007; Conf Of S Ben 1978; Soc Of S Jn The Evang 1998. tarpley375@embarqmail.com

✠ **TARRANT, Rt Rev John Thomas** (SD) 500 South Main Ave, Sioux Falls SD 57104 **Bp Dio So Dakota Sioux Falls SD 2009-** B Kansas City MO 2/17/1952 s Robert Claire D'Newton Tarrant & Leticia Marie. BA MI SU 1974; MDiv VTS 1983. D 6/11/1983 Bp Charles Bennison P 2/11/1984 Bp Alexander Doig Stewart Con 10/31/2009 for SD. m 6/29/1990 Patricia J Donaldson c 2. R Trin Epis Ch Pierre SD 2005-2009; R S Paul's Epis Ch Stockbridge MA 1996-2005; P Grtr Waterbury Mnstry Middlebury CT 1991-1996; Asst S Paul's Ch Holyoke MA 1989-1991; R S Paul's Epis Ch Gardner MA 1985-1989; Asst Ch Of The Atone Westfield MA 1983-1985. Way Of The Cross 1998-2005. bishop.diocese@midconetwork.com

TARRANT, Paul John (RI) 39 Jeffrey Street, Edinburgh EH1 1DH Great Britain (UK) B Barton-on-Sea UK 3/17/1957 BA U Of Birmingham Birmingham Gb 1981; Chichester Theol Coll 1982. Trans from Church Of England 3/1/1990. Vic S Andr's By The Sea Little Compton RI 1995-1996; Liturg & Mus Com Dio Massachusetts Boston MA 1991-1994; R Epis Ch Of S Thos Taunton MA 1990-1994. PJTARRANT@AOL.COM

TARSIS, George Michael (O) 399 Jefferson Ave, Barberton OH 44203 **R S Andr's Ch Barberton OH 2000-** B Chicago IL 3/16/1949 s George Josef Tarsis & Agnus Louise. BBA U Of Kentucky 1972; MBA U Of Kentucky 1973; MDiv Epis TS In Kentucky 1985. D 6/1/1985 Bp Addison Hosea P 3/16/1986 Bp Don Adger Wimberly. m 1/8/1972 Mary Kathryn Ponchot c 2. R Trin Epis Ch Norfolk NE 1993-2000; Adv Ch Cynthiana KY 1985-1993. gtar23@yahoo.com

TARTT JR, Jo C (WA) 2727 34th Pl Nw, Washington DC 20007 B Birmingham AL 10/9/1941 s Jo Cowin Tartt & Dorothy Helen. BA W&L 1965; MDiv VTS 1969. D 6/6/1969 Bp George Mosley Murray P 6/1/1970 Bp William Foreman Creighton. m 1/11/1993 Judith W Tartt c 2. Gr Ch Washington DC 1971-1981; Asst Min S Mk's Ch Washington DC 1969-1971. JCTJR@EARTHLINK.NET

TARWATER, Thomas William (ECR) 610 Le Point St, Arroyo Grande CA 93420 **D S Steph's Epis Ch San Luis Obispo CA 1992-** B Pasadena CA 12/14/1928 s Thomas Myro Tarwater & Alice Elizabeth. AA Pasadena City Coll 1955; BA California Sch for Deacons 1992. D 6/27/1992 Bp Richard Lester Shimpfky. m 6/5/2004 Patricia Myers c 4. San Luis Obispo Cnty Publ Sfty Chapl Assn 1992.

TASY, Beverly Ann Moore (O) 38580 Glenwood Rd, Westland MI 48186 **All SS Epis Ch Toledo OH 2006-** B Utica NY 12/9/1956 BA Keuka Coll 1978; MDiv VTS 1985. D 6/8/1985 P 5/1/1989 Bp O'Kelley Whitaker. m 7/10/1982 Alexander Stephen Tasy. Gr In The Desert Epis Ch Las Vegas NV 2004; R S Clem's Epis Ch Inkster MI 1996-2004; Dir Of Campus Mnstry Dio Wstrn New York Tonawanda NY 1994-1996; Asst R All SS Epis Ch Pontiac MI 1990-1993. BATASY@COMCAST.NET

TATA, Suzanne Walker (SC) 3000 Hwy 17 North, Myrtle Beach SC 27572 B Charleston SC 2/23/1953 D 9/14/2002 Bp Edward Lloyd Salmon Jr. m 9/18/1971 Rohinton Hoshang Tata c 3.

TATE, Donald Steven (At) 201 Ellen Ct, Warner Robins GA 31088 **R S Andr's Epis Ch Ft Vlly GA 2003-; Vic S Mary's Epis Ch Montezuma GA 2003-** B Chicago IL 8/13/1956 s Byron Day Tate & Mildred Lorraine. BA No Cntrl Coll 1979; MS Geo Wms Downers Grove IL 1982; PhD U IL 1988; MDiv STUSo 2002. D 4/5/2002 P 11/1/2002 Bp Creighton Leland Robertson. m 7/16/1994 Ruth Newman c 1. Asst S Jas Sewanee TN 2002-2003. Ord of Julian of Norwich 1990. donaldtate@windstream.net

TATE, Katherine T (Del) PO Box 464, Lewes DE 19958 **S Ptr's Ch Lewes DE 2010-; Yth/YA/Higher Ed Dir Dio SW Florida Sarasota FL 2002-** B New York NY 9/6/1961 d Edward French Tate & Lucretia Howe. Luth TS at Gettysburg; BA Emory & Henry Coll 1983; Med U of So Florida 1987. D 6/23/2001 Bp Charles Ellsworth Bennison Jr. m 5/24/2011 Sandra White c 1. Dio SW Florida Sarasota FL 2003-2009; The Epis Ch Of The Adv Kennett Sq PA 2001-2002; The Epis Ch Of The Adv Kennett Sq PA 1996-2001. ktate@stpeterslewes.org

TATE, Robert Lee (Pa) 7209 Lincoln Dr., Philadelphia PA 19119 **Assoc Philadelphia Cathd Philadelphia PA 2010-** B New York NY 9/26/1950 s Robert T Tate & Constance M. BA Pr 1972; MDiv Ya Berk 1976. D 6/9/1979 P 3/29/1980 Bp Morgan Porteus. m 8/7/1977 Ann Greene c 2. R Ch Of S Mart-In-The-Fields Philadelphia PA 1995-2009; R Chr Ch Capitol Hill Washington DC 1984-1995; Asst Cathd Ch Of The Nativ Bethlehem PA 1980-1984; Chapl Wooster Sch Danbury CT 1979-1980. Epis Cler Assoc. of PA 1995; EPF 1980; Int Mnstry Ntwk 2007; NNECA 1995. rlt19119@aol.com

T

TATE, Ruth Newman (At) 201 Ellen Ct, Warner Robins GA 31088 **Assoc R S Andr's Epis Ch Ft Vlly GA 2003-; Vic S Mary's Epis Ch Montezuma GA 2003-** B Shattuck OK 10/26/1954 BA Oklahoma City U 1976; MS U of Oklahoma 1978; PhD U of Oklahoma 1984; MDiv STUSo 2003. D 4/25/2003 Bp Creighton Leland Robertson P 2/29/2004 Bp J(ohn) Neil Alexander. m 7/16/1994 Donald Steven Tate c 1. DOK 2002. ruthtate@alltel.net

TATE, Stanton Davis (Spok) 8060 Stewart Rd, Meridian ID 83642 B Boise ID 12/5/1932 s John Patton Tate & Marjorie. BA U of Idaho Moscow 1955; MDiv PrTS 1958; DMin SFTS 1990. D 2/17/1963 P 6/1/1963 Bp Norman L Foote. m 6/10/1954 Lynn C Campbell. S Mk's Epis Ch Moscow ID 1981-1987; Assoc The Epis Ch Of The Gd Samar Corvallis OR 1978-1981; Vic S Andr's Epis Ch McCall ID 1963-1971. Auth, *Jumping Skyward*. Who's Who Rel 75; Outstanding Young Idahonian. standtate@gmail.com

TATEM JR, Francis Clelland (SwVa) 1552 Park Rd, Harrisonburg VA 22802 B Westbury NY 11/9/1924 s Francis Clelland Tatem & Margaret Dorothy. BA Leh 1948; BD SWTS 1951; MDiv SWTS 1952; Fllshp SWTS 1969. D 3/1/1951 P 11/3/1951 Bp James P De Wolfe. m 7/14/1953 Ann Haldeman c 5. Dn New River Convoc Dio SW Virginia Roanoke VA 1984-1986; R S Thos Epis Christiansburg VA 1981-1989; Bd APSO Dio Albany Albany NY 1974-1981; S Jas Ch Delhi NY 1971-1981; Assoc S Thos Epis Ch Rochester NY 1966-1971; Assoc H Trin Epis Ch Hicksville NY 1963-1966; Asst S Andr's Ch Louisville KY 1962-1963. RWF 1950; SSJE - Mem, Fllshp of the Soc of S Jn the Evan 1949. fctatem@myvmrc.net

TATEM, Sandra Lou (Alb) 39 Greyledge Dr, Loudonville NY 12211 B Johnson City NY 6/8/1936 d Charles Foote & Ella. AA SUNY 1955. D 6/10/2006 Bp Daniel William Herzog. m 2/4/1956 William Arthur Tatem c 3. statem@nycap.rr.com

TATEM, William Arthur (Alb) 39 Graystone Rd, Loudonville NY 12211 **Admin S Andr's Epis Ch Albany NY 2000-** B 11/5/1932 s Frank Tatem & Margaret. BS Alfred U 1954; MS Alfred U 1962. D 6/10/2006 Bp Daniel William Herzog. m 2/4/1956 Sandra Lou Foote c 3. wtatem@nycap.rr.com

TATLOCK, Alan Ralph (Alb) 2938 Birchton Rd, Ballston Spa NY 12020 **D Asst Calv Epis Ch Burnt Hills NY 1994-** B Amsterdam NY 12/18/1939 s Ralph Harold Tatlock & Irene Frances. BS USNA 1964; MS Un Coll Schenectady NY 1974. D 10/10/1994 Bp David Standish Ball. m 1/18/1986 Jane Elizabeth Young c 4.

TATTERSALL, Elizabeth Ann (Nev) Po Box 3388, Stateline NV 89449 B Palo Alto CA 12/28/1961 d Richard Russell & Ann. BA Stan 1984; PhD U of Nevada at Reno 2006. D 9/6/1996 P 3/15/1997 Bp Stewart Clark Zabriskie. m 4/3/1993 Stewart Graham Tattersall. P S Jn's In The Wilderness Ch Glenbrook NV 1996-2010. Mltry Chapl Assn 2003. eat@unr.nevada.edu

TAVAREZ TEJEDA, Luis Bienvenido (DR) Proyeceo #6, Apartado 301, Puerto Plata Dominican Republic B Bayaguana DO 11/22/1955 s Bienvenido Agustin Tavarez Vasquez & Elia Edelmira. Universidad Autonoma De Santo Domingo; Lic Centro De Estudios Teologicas 1988. D 12/20/1987 P 7/1/1988 Bp Telesforo A Isaac. m 12/19/1978 Loyda Maria De Los Santos Travieso. Exec Coun Appointees New York NY 1999-2001; Dio The Dominican Republic (Iglesia Epis Dominicana) Santo Domingo DO 1987-1999. Tertiary Of The Soc Of S Fran.

TAVERNETTI, Suzanne (ECR) 7021 Timber Trail Loop, El Dorado Hills CA 95762 B Salinas CA 10/24/1938 d Loran Atillio Giacomazzi & Olga Mae. BA California Sch for Deacons 1989. D 6/24/1989 Bp Charles Shannon Mallory. m 6/6/1964 David E Tavernetti c 3. D In Charge S Lk's Ch Jolon CA 1993-2003; D In Charge S Matt's Ch San Ardo CA 1993-1997; Asst S Mk's Ch KING CITY CA 1989-1992. NAAD 1989. suetavernetti@sbcglobal.net

TAYLOR, A(lice) Susan (NY) 85 Coachlight Sq, Montrose NY 10548 B Great Barrington MA 3/4/1938 d Bernherd H Berning & Irma Burdett. D 4/13/1985 Bp George Phelps Mellick Belshaw. m 9/10/1960 Wilber Nelson Taylor c 3. D Ch Of The Div Love Montrose NY 1993-2004; Gr Ch In Haddonfield Haddonfield NJ 1990-1992; Par Secy Gr Ch In Haddonfield Haddonfield NJ 1967-1969. sue414bill@aol.com

TAYLOR, Alton Holmes (Nwk) 25 Nairn Pl, Nutley NJ 07110 **Died 1/14/2010** B Passaic NJ 9/7/1931 s Alton Parker Taylor & Christine Elizabeth. BA W Virginia Wesleyan Coll 1957; STB PDS 1962. D 6/9/1962 Bp Leland Stark P 12/1/1962 Bp Donald MacAdie.

TAYLOR, Andrea Maija (Mass) 146 Wachusett Ave, Arlington MA 02476 **Assoc S Bon Ch Sarasota FL 2007-** B Milwaukee WI 6/19/1967 d John Gunther Suess & Bettie Davenport. BA Pr 1988; MDiv Harvard DS 1994. D 6/4/1994 P 4/1/1995 Bp J Clark Grew II. m 6/16/1990 Jonathan B Taylor c 2. DCE The Ch Of Our Redeem Lexington MA 1998-2007; Asst To The R S Ptr's Ch Beverly MA 1997-1998; Asst Min All SS' Epis Ch Belmont MA 1994-1997. ataylor@bonifacechurch.org

TAYLOR, Arnold Godfrey (WA) 507 3rd St SE, Washington DC 20003 **R Emer Chr Ch Durham Par Nanjemoy MD 2000-** B Providence RI 8/24/1925 s Leander Filmore Taylor & Viola May. BA Pacific U 1951; MDiv VTS 1968. D 6/29/1968 P 6/5/1969 Bp William Foreman Creighton. m 7/3/1954 Lilian Baskerville Bedinger c 3. Dioc Coun Dio Washington Washington DC 1981-1983; Dioc Coun Dio Washington Washington DC 1975-1977; R Chr Ch Durham Par Nanjemoy MD 1971-1993; Asst Chr Epis Ch Clinton MD 1968-1971. Washington DC Epis Cler Assn 1968. ahnoldt@aol.com

TAYLOR, Barbara Ann (SwVa) 20 Frontier Ridge Ct Apt 4205, Staunton VA 24401 B Berkeley CA 11/6/1935 d Arthur Bayles McGlade & Edith Beatrice. U CA 1954; U CA 1955; BA U of Nevada at Reno 1968; MA U of Nevada at Reno 1970; PhD Brigham Young U 1975. D 8/15/1981 Bp Wesley Frensdorff P 5/9/1991 Bp A(rthur) Heath Light. c 2. S Mart In The Fields Ch Atlanta GA 1998-2001; Aug Par Chesapeake City MD 1994-1995; Asst R R E Lee Memi Ch (Epis) Lexington VA 1990-1994; S Jn's Ch Roanoke VA 1990; St Christophers Epis Ch Charleston WV 1988-1990; Coordntr Mnstrs W Epis Ch Cntr New York NY 1986-1988. Auth, *Nevada St Drug Abuse Curric*, 1974; Auth, "Morning Pryr," *A Reflection*; Auth, *Evaltn: 3 Year Study of a Drug Abuse Prevention Prog*. 3rd Ord Fransican (TSSF) 1980; Ord of S Helena. goodsheperd@comcast.net

TAYLOR, Barbara Brown (At) PO Box 1030, Clarkesville GA 30523 B Lafayette IN 9/21/1951 d Earl Clement Brown & Rebecca Grace. BA Emory U 1973; MDiv Ya Berk 1976. D 6/11/1983 P 5/1/1984 Bp Charles Judson Child Jr. m 11/20/1982 Ernest Edward Taylor c 2. R Gr-Calv Epis Ch Clarkesville GA 1992-1997; All SS Epis Ch Atlanta GA 1983-1992. Auth, *Leaving Ch*, HarperSanFrancisco, 2006; Auth, *The Seeds of Heaven*, Westminster Jn Knox, 2004. Hon DD U So 2005; Hon DD SWTS 2002; Hon DD VTS 2001; Hon DD Berk 1997. btaylor@piedmont.edu

TAYLOR, Barry Robert (Los) 504 N Camden Dr, Beverly Hills CA 90210 **Assoc R All SS Par Beverly Hills CA 2010-** B Woking, Surrey UK 2/10/1956 s Dennis James Taylor & Ruth Marjorie. MA Fuller TS 1999; PhD Fuller TS 2005. D 12/13/2009 Bp Chester Lovelle Talton P 6/13/2010 Bp Joseph Jon Bruno. btaylor@allsaintsbh.org

TAYLOR, Brenda Marie (CFla) 5200 Berryleaf Grv, Columbus OH 43231 **Epis Ch Of The Resurr Longwood FL 2004-; D S Phil's Ch Columbus OH 1995-** B Harrisburg PA 9/27/1942 d Patrick H Taylor & Beulah M. D 10/28/1995 Bp Herbert Thompson Jr. m 11/22/2002 Antonio Kelly. bmtaylor@att.net

TAYLOR, Brian Clark (RG) 1401 Los Arboles Avenue Northwest, Albuquerque NM 87107 **R S Mich And All Ang Ch Albuquerque NM 1983-** B Sacramento CA 4/13/1951 s William Frederick Taylor & Marylou McClure. BA Goddard Coll 1973; MA Goddard Coll 1975; MDiv CDSP 1981. D 6/27/1981 P 5/30/1982 Bp William Edwin Swing. m 12/30/1978 Susanna Hackett c 2. Asst Gr Cathd San Francisco CA 1981-1983. Auth, "Becoming Human," Cowley Pub, 2005; Auth, "Becoming Chr," Cowley Pub, 2002; Auth, "Setting the Gospel Free," Continuum Pub, 1996; Auth, "Sprtlty for Everyday Living," Liturg Press, 1989. Hon Doctorate of Div CDSP 2004. brian@all-angels.com

TAYLOR, Bruce Willard (VI) The Valley, Box 65, Virgin Gorda VI B McKinney TX 3/15/1947 s Willard Taylor & Nadia Christine. BA Wstrn St Coll of Colorado 1969; MS Our Lady Of The Lake U San Antonio TX 1974; MDiv Epis TS of The SW 1985. D 6/13/1985 Bp Donis Dean Patterson P 2/24/1986 Bp John Herbert MacNaughton. m 9/27/1991 Brenda Gayle Harper c 6. St Marys Ch Vrgn Gorda BV VG 1995-1998; Ch Of The Resurr San Antonio TX 1990-1991; Gr Ch Cuero TX 1989; Chr Epis Ch San Antonio TX 1985-1988. Associated Parishes. WATCHMEN_BRUCE@YAHOO.COM

TAYLOR JR, Charles Arville (Ala) 122 Lenox Dr, Birmingham AL 35242 B Atlanta GA 6/21/1934 s Charles Taylor & Katherine. BA Emory U 1955; MDiv CDSP 1959; Fell Menninger Clnc 1967; STM Dubuque TS 1971. D 6/16/1959 P 12/19/1959 Bp Randolph R Claiborne. m 1/21/1995 Margaret Anne Hanson c 3. S Mary's-On-The-Highlands Epis Ch Birmingham AL 1994; Cn to Ordnry Dio Wstrn No Carolina Asheville NC 1990-1994; ExCoun Dio Wstrn No Carolina Asheville NC 1988-1990; Asst S Jas Epis Ch Hendersonville NC 1982-1990; Assoc S Paul's Epis Ch Winston Salem NC 1972-1981; R S Thaddaeus' Epis Ch Chattanooga TN 1967-1970; Asst S Dav's Epis Ch Topeka KS 1966-1967; P-in-c Ch Of The Resurr Loudon TN 1965-1966; P-in-c S Alb's Epis Ch Hixson TN 1965-1966; Cur H Innoc Ch Atlanta GA 1963-1965; Vic S Jas Epis Ch Clayton GA 1960-1963; Cur S Mths Epis Ch Toccoa GA 1959-1963. Natl Cmsn on Soc and Spec Mnstrs 1983-1988; Soc of S Jn the Evang 1986. ellivra@aol.com

TAYLOR, Charles Dean (At) 1600 Southmont Dr, Dalton GA 30720 **Int S Bon Ch Sarasota FL 2011-** B Auburn AL 10/25/1955 s Bobby Paul Taylor & Celia. BA U So 1978; MDiv VTS 1984. D 7/8/1984 Bp William Evan Sanders P 4/1/1985 Bp William F Gates Jr. m 8/9/1980 Jane Sample c 3. S Jas Epis Ch Marietta GA 2010-2011; R S Mk's Ch Dalton GA 1990-2010; Assoc S Fran In The Fields Harrods Creek KY 1987-1990; D Ch Of The Adv Nashville TN 1984-1987. DEANTAYLOR1955@GMAIL.COM

TAYLOR, Charles Gary (CNY) South Main, Box 370, New Berlin NY 13411 **Emm Ch Norwich NY 2009-; S Andr's Ch New Berlin NY 1985-; S Matt's Ch So New Berlin NY 1985-** B Barnesboro PA 10/12/1951 s Charles Harry Taylor & Lois Delphine. BA U Pgh 1972; MDiv Bex 1979. D 6/9/1979 P 12/1/1979 Bp Robert Bracewell Appleyard. m 1/1/1972 Donna Lee Abrams. S Mk's

T

Ch Johnstown PA 1981; S Thos Ch No Cambria PA 1980-1985; Ch of SS Thos and Lk Patton PA 1980-1981. FRCHUCKT@FRONTIERNET.NET

TAYLOR, Charles Henry (WNC) 84 Keasler Rd, Asheville NC 28805 B Lockport NY 11/17/1939 s Henry Taylor & Mildred. BS SUNY 1962; STM PDS 1967; MA S Thos U Miami FL 1990. D 6/17/1967 P 12/21/1967 Bp Lauriston L Scaife. m 1/7/1990 Sheila Sharkey c 2. R S Jn's Ch Asheville NC 1990-2005; Vic S Mich's Ch Miami FL 1987-1990; R Ch Of The H Redeem Lake Worth FL 1984-1987; R Zion Epis Ch Palmyra NY 1975-1984; R St Johns Epis Youngstown NY 1969-1975; Cur Gr Ch Merchantville NJ 1967-1969. cht39@charter.net

TAYLOR, Charles Wellington (Cal) 2451 Ridge Rd, Berkeley CA 94709 B Dayton OH 5/3/1937 s Georgia Lucille. BA W Virginia U 1958; MDiv Bex 1967; DMin Wesley TS 1979. D 6/17/1967 P 12/1/1967 Bp Roger W Blanchard. c 3. Asst S Steph's Par Belvedere CA 1998; S Clare's Epis Ch Pleasanton CA 1985; Prof CDSP Berkeley CA 1978-1998; R Ch Of The H Comf Washington DC 1971-1978; Asst S Steph's Epis Ch And U Columbus OH 1967-1968. Auth, "Premarital Gdnc," Fortress Press, 1999; Auth, "The Skilled Pstr," Fortress Press, 1991.

TAYLOR, Cynthia nan (Ga) 973 Hunting Horn Way W, Evans GA 30809 **H Comf Ch Martinez GA 2006-; Alt Dep GC Dio Georgia Savannah GA 1997-** B Indianapolis IN 10/27/1955 d Robert Floyd Taylor & Janice. BA U of So Carolina 1977; MDiv VTS 1986; DMin STUSo 2007. D 6/15/1986 P 5/15/1987 Bp C(hristopher) FitzSimons Allison. S Paul's Ch Augusta GA 1991-2006; Cn The Amer Cathd of the H Trin Paris 75008 FR 1988-1991; All SS Ch Florence SC 1986-1988. cntzilla@aol.com

TAYLOR, David Edwin (Spr) 617 Main Street, Lancaster NH 03584 **R S Paul's Ch Lancaster NH 2011-** B Carbondale IL 12/26/1965 s Robert Edwin Taylor & Ruby Ann. BA Sthrn Illinois U 1988; MDiv Midwestern TS 1998; Nash 1999. D 2/27/1999 P 10/18/1999 Bp Keith Lynn Ackerman. m 7/16/1988 Angela D Bruzan c 4. R S Andr's Ch Carbondale IL 2003-2008; R S Barn Ch Havana IL 2000-2003; Cur S Lk's Ch In The Cnty Of Buck Newtown PA 1999-2000. detaylor65@aol.com

TAYLOR, David G (USC) 301 Piney Mountain Rd., Greenville SC 29609 **R S Jas Epis Ch Greenville SC 2009-** B Montreal QC Canada 4/16/1961 BA No Carolina Sch Of The Arts. D 6/7/2003 P 12/17/2003 Bp J(ohn) Neil Alexander. m 7/31/1993 Judy Armandroff c 2. R Ch Of The Redeem Greensboro GA 2003-2008. d.geoffreytaylor@gmail.com

TAYLOR, David Kenneth (Nwk) 124 Franklin Ct, Flemington NJ 08822 B Trenton NJ 2/9/1942 s Earl Kenneth Taylor & Anne Lillian. BA W Maryland Coll 1964; MDiv PDS 1967. D 4/22/1967 P 10/1/1967 Bp Alfred L Banyard. m 12/30/1995 S Christine Jochem. Assoc P Trin Cathd Trenton NJ 1987-1996; R S Geo's Ch Pennsville NJ 1974-1976; R S Steph's Ch Florence NJ 1970-1974; Cur S Jas Ch Trenton Yardville NJ 1967-1970. Auth, *God & Being in Thought of Austin Farrer*, 1991. Cath Theol Soc of Amer 1994; Soc of Chr Philosophers 1986. Phi Beta Kappa; Hon Cn 93 Trin Cathd Trenton NJ. frdavid_1999@yahoo.com

TAYLOR, Edgar Garland (Ct) 211 Silver Lake Rd, Middletown DE 19709 **S Anne's Epis Sch Middletown DE 2011-** B Pittsburgh PA 10/30/1965 s Edgar Rives Taylor & Guion Trau. BA Yale Coll 1987; EdM Harvard Grad Sch of Educ 1991; MDiv VTS 2011. D 6/11/2011 Bp Laura Ahrens. m 8/10/1991 Karen Shipley c 3. garyofpgh@gmail.com

TAYLOR, Edward Norman (Mich) 80 Wellesley Street East #904, Toronto M4Y 2B5 Canada B Hamilton ON CA 10/1/1943 s Russell Stanley Taylor & Joan Irene. LTh U Tor 1972. D 5/1/1972 P 1/1/1973 Bp The Bishop Of Saskatoon. m 8/27/1966 Beverley Dawn Rowley c 3. All SS Ch Prudenville MI 1979-1982; Trin Ch Emmetsburg IA 1976-1979.

✠ **TAYLOR, Rt Rev E(gbert) Don** (NY) 1047 Amsterdam Ave, New York NY 10025 B Kingston JM 9/2/1937 s Gilbert Taylor & Elma. Kingston Coll Kingston JM; BA U of The W Indies; MA U Tor; STM U Tor. Trans from Church in the Province Of The West Indies 3/1/1974 Con 2/28/1987 for VI. c 1. Bp in Res S Martha's Ch Bronx NY 2002-2009; Vic Bp for New York City Dio New York New York City NY 1994-2009; Ny Income New York NY 1994; Bp Dio Vrgn Islands St Thos VI VI 1987-1994; R Ch Of The H Cross Decatur GA 1982-1986; R S Phil's Ch Buffalo NY 1974-1978. Auth, *Living in Today's Wrld Without Chr*, 1981. OHC. Hon DD U Tor Toronto Can. bpedont@yahoo.com

TAYLOR, Gloria Atkinson (NI) 1809 Holly Ln, Munster IN 46321 B New York NY 10/25/1929 d Walter Hedland Atkinson & Margaret Rose. Dioc Sch of Faith & Mnstry So Bend IN 1989. D 6/12/1989 Bp Francis Campbell Gray. m 2/23/1947 Frederic Edward Taylor. D Trin Ch Michigan City IN 1989-2011; AIDS Coordntr Dio Nthrn Indiana So Bend IN 1989-1999; D S Paul's Epis Ch Munster IN 1989-1993. NAAD; Sacr Ord of Deacons. gataylor89@aol.com

TAYLOR, Gordon A (CPa) 12381 State 64 SW, Motley MN 56466 B 7/31/1925 D 6/2/1954 Bp Oliver L Loring P 12/18/1954 Bp Robert McConnell Hatch. All SS Ch Spokane WA 1971-1976.

TAYLOR, G(ordon) Kevin (Los) 6503 Stone Crest Way, Whittier CA 90601 B Dublin IE 11/22/1938 s Benjamin Taylor & Florence W. GOE Ch of Ireland Theol 1973. Trans from Church of Ireland 8/1/1982. Asst S Marg's Epis Ch So Gate CA 2004-2011; P-in-c S Geo's Mssn Hawthorne CA 1999-2001; R S Mich The Archangel Par El Segundo CA 1994-2004; P-in-c S Jn's Mssn La Verne CA 1994; R S Mk's Par Downey CA 1984-1993; Asst S Wilfrid Of York Epis Ch Huntington Bch CA 1982-1984.

✠ **TAYLOR, Rt Rev Granville Porter** (WNC) 44 Ravenwood Dr, Fletcher NC 28732 **Bp Dio Wstrn No Carolina Asheville NC 2004-** B Rock Hill SC 9/17/1950 s Richard Mccrary Taylor & Sarah Richardson. BA U NC 1972; MA U of So Carolina 1974; PhD Emory U 1983; MDiv STUSo 1993. D 6/6/1993 Bp William Evan Sanders P 4/13/1994 Bp Bertram Nelson Herlong Con 9/18/2004 for WNC. m 5/13/1972 Jo Abbott c 2. R S Greg The Great Athens GA 1996-2004; Asst S Paul's Ch Franklin TN 1993-1996. Auth, "To Dream As God Dreams," Green Berry Press, 2000. ptaylor@diocesewnc.org

TAYLOR, Gregory Blackwell (Va) 250 Pantops Mountain Rd. Apt. 5407, Charlottesville VA 22911 B Cleveland OH 8/13/1930 s S Blackwell Taylor & Helen. BA Ya 1952; JD Harv 1957; MDiv VTS 1963. D 6/15/1963 P 12/1/1963 Bp Nelson Marigold Burroughs. m 9/8/1956 Anne Barbour Doak c 2. Sead.

TAYLOR, Harold Edwin (Ind) Po Box 302, Nashville IN 47448 B Moline IL 12/4/1918 s John Henry Taylor & Agnes Emma. BA U IL 1947; BD EDS 1949; PhD Indiana St U 1974. D 6/8/1949 P 12/1/1949 Bp Norman B Nash. m 6/28/1952 Gladys Eleanor Gillman c 3. S Dav's Ch Beanblossom Nashville IN 1983-1990; R S Steph's Ch Terre Haute IN 1960-1970; Assoc S Fran In The Fields Harrods Creek KY 1956-1960; Dierctor Of CE Dio Wstrn Massachusetts Springfield MA 1953-1955; R Trin Epis Ch Whitinsville MA 1951-1955; Vic S Jn's Ch Millville MA 1951-1953; Asst Chr Ch Cambridge Cambridge MA 1949-1951. Auth, "Taylor Behavioral Value Indicator & Mgmt Cmncatn Workbook".

TAYLOR, James Delane (CFla) 10 Fox Cliff Way, Ormond Beach FL 32174 **R S Mary's Epis Ch Daytona Bch FL 2001-** B Nashville GA 6/11/1946 s John Leonard Taylor & Mary Louise. BS Florida St U 1969; MDiv Nash 1983. D 6/24/1983 P 1/10/1984 Bp William Hopkins Folwell. m 3/12/1969 Glenda Maxine Rule c 1. R S Steph's Ch Lakeland FL 1988-2000; Cur/Assoc S Jas Epis Ch Ormond Bch FL 1983-1988. Life Mem Bro of S Andr, Ord of S Lk 1998; Life Mem OSL 1999. jimglendataylor@earthlink.net

TAYLOR JR, James Edward (SC) 1150 East Montague Ave., North Charleston SC 29405 **Stwdshp Chair Dio So Carolina Charleston SC 2011-; Dioc Coun Dio So Carolina Charleston SC 2007-; R S Thos Epis Ch No Charleston SC 2003-** B Wilmington NC 12/16/1960 s James E Taylor & Ellen Veronica. BA U NC At Wilmington 1988; MDiv. VTS 1992. D 6/20/1992 Bp Huntington Williams Jr. Dioc Coun Dio So Carolina Charleston SC 2007; Conv Wrshp Coordntr Dio So Carolina Charleston SC 2004-2007; Assoc R S Jn's Epis Ch Fayetteville NC 1999-2003; R Gr Ch Whiteville NC 1996-1999; R Emm Ch Farmville NC 1992-1996. REVJIMTAYLOR@GMAIL.COM

TAYLOR OHC, James K (CNY) 6112 Cobblestone Dr Apt A12, Cicero NY 13039 B Terre Haute IN 10/31/1935 s Kenneth Wallace Taylor & Rebekah May. BS Indiana St U 1957; MA Indiana St U 1958; STB Ya Berk 1961; MDiv Yale DS 1961. D 6/24/1961 P 12/17/1961 Bp John P Craine. Permanent Supply S Dav's Barneveld NY 2005-2010; R Gr Epis Ch Syracuse NY 1995-1999; Chapl Dio Cntrl New York Syracuse NY 1987-1999; Com of Homosexual Persons Dio Michigan Detroit MI 1986-1987; Chapl Trin Epis Ch Bloomington IN 1973-1986; R S Matt's Ch Indianapolis IN 1966-1973; Vic All SS Ch Seymour IN 1963-1966. Chart Mem, Integrity 1973; Oblates of Mt Calv, OHC, Associated Pari 1956; Rel & Intellectual Life, Natl Epis Aids Coali 1961. Dictionary of Intl Biography Intl Biographical Cntr 1977; Who's Who Rel Marquis Who's Who 1977; Fell Royal Soc Arts Royal Soc of Arts 1969. frjimt@verizon.net

TAYLOR, James Maurice (Pa) 160 Marvin Rd, Elkins Park PA 19027 B Washington DC 2/28/1966 s Volney Maurice Taylor & Janise Clair. BA Emory & Henry Coll 1988; MDiv VTS 1994; MA La Salle U 2007; Certification La Salle U 2011. D 6/11/1994 P 12/14/1994 Bp Peter James Lee. m 8/31/2002 Douglas K Alderfer. R Gr Epiph Ch Philadelphia PA 1998-2005; Asst Chr Ch Philadelphia Philadelphia PA 1994-1998. jamestaylor66@comcast.net

TAYLOR, John Harvey (Los) 19968 Paseo Luis, Yorba Linda CA 92886 **S Jn Chrys Ch And Sch Rancho Santa Margarita CA 2009-** B Detroit MI 10/26/1954 s Harvey Hileman Taylor & Jean Taylor. BA U CA 1980; MDiv Claremont TS 2003. D 6/7/2003 P 1/24/2004 Bp Joseph Jon Bruno. m 7/6/2002 Kathleen Hannigan O'Connor c 2. Asst S Andr's Par Fullerton CA 2003-2004. "Patterns Of Abuse," Wynwood Press, 1989. Hon Cn Dio Los Angeles 2008. revjht@msn.com

TAYLOR, LeBaron Thomas (SwVa) P.O. Box 709, Covington VA 24426 **R Emm Ch Covington VA 2008-** B Mobile AL 9/23/1939 s Herbert Lee Taylor & Lucielle. BS Alabama St U 1961; MDiv Claremont TS 1990; CAS VTS 1995. D 6/3/1995 P 12/9/1995 Bp Robert Jefferson Hargrove Jr. S Steph's Epis Ch Winston Salem NC 2003-2007; S Eliz Epis Ch King NC 2003-2005; S Aug's Coll Raleigh NC 2001-2003; S Thos Ch Minneapolis MN 1997-2001; D Ch Of The H Cross Shreveport LA 1995-1997. lebaronttaylor@hotmail.com

TAYLOR JR, Lewis Jerome (SVa) 1200 Atlantic Shores Drive, #3 HarbourWay, Virginia Beach VA 23454 **Died 2/21/2011** B Norfolk VA 2/22/1923 s Lewis Jerome Taylor & Roberta Page. BS USNA 1944; BD SWTS 1961; PhD Duke 1972. D 6/29/1961 P 5/1/1962 Bp George P Gunn. Auth, *ATR*; Auth, *In Search of Self: Life Death & Walker Percy*. Who's Who Rel.

TAYLOR, Linda Sue (ECR) 1809 Palo Santo Dr, Campbell CA 95008 **R S Mk's Epis Ch Santa Clara CA 2001-** B Fort Worth TX 11/23/1943 d Elmo Mason McCaleb & Irma Marie. BD San Jose St U 1977; MS U CA 1981; MBA San Jose St U 1991; MDiv CDSP 1999. D 6/26/1999 P 11/22/2000 Bp Richard Lester Shimpfky. Assoc Trin Cathd San Jose CA 2000-2001; D S Andr's Ch Saratoga CA 1999-2000. lindastay@aol.com

TAYLOR, Lloyd Gregory (Ala) 1265 Old Us 231 North, Wetumpka AL 36092 B Canton OH 3/18/1930 s Lloyd Hannis Taylor & Kathleen. Emory U 1950; MS NWU 1955; MDiv VTS 1970. D 6/24/1970 P 5/1/1971 Bp James Loughlin Duncan. m 6/22/1953 Martha Ann Bennington. R S Paul's Epis Ch Lowndesboro AL 1980-1986; All SS Epis Ch Aliceville AL 1975-1978; R S Mich's Epis Ch Fayette AL 1975-1978; Asst All SS Epis Ch Birmingham AL 1972-1975; M-in-c S Phil's Ch Pompano Bch FL 1970-1972. Auth, "Writer," *& Pub Gd News For You Letters*.

TAYLOR, Lloyd Hopeton (LI) 13304 109th Ave, South Ozone Park NY 11420 **R S Jn's Ch S Ozone Pk NY 1983-** B 7/22/1942 s Isaac Taylor & Henrietta Amanda. DIT Untd Theol Coll Of The W Indies Kingston Jm 1974; BA U of The W Indies 1974; BBA CUNY 1989. D 6/29/1974 P 1/1/1975 Bp The Bishop Of Belize. c 1.

TAYLOR, Margaret Anne (Ala) Po Box 361352, Birmingham AL 35236 **COM, Chair Dio Alabama Birmingham AL 1999-** B Pasadena CA 10/29/1945 d James Romero & Luada. BA Colorado Coll 1967; MA Fairfield U 1982; MDiv GTS 1990. D 6/23/1990 P 1/2/1991 Bp George Nelson Hunt III. m 1/21/1995 Charles Arville Taylor. Alum Exec Com The GTS New York NY 1998-2003; Alt Dep Gc Dio Alabama Birmingham AL 1997; H Apos Ch Birmingham AL 1995-2011; Par Dvlpmt Dio Alabama Birmingham AL 1994-1998; Dio Alabama Birmingham AL 1994-1995; Evang Com Dio Alabama Birmingham AL 1991-1994; Chair T/F Human Sxlty Dio Alabama Birmingham AL 1991-1993; Asst R Ch Of The Nativ Epis Huntsville AL 1990-1994. mtaylor944@aol.com

TAYLOR, Marjorie Beth (Colo) 470 Church Rd, Bloomfield Hills MI 48304 **Chr Ch Cranbrook Bloomfield Hills MI 2010-** B Buckhannon WV 12/16/1965 d John E Taylor & Martha R. BA Nthrn Arizona U 1989; MDiv SWTS 2010. D 6/5/2010 Bp Robert John O'Neill. m 8/13/1994 Mark A Miliotto c 2. bethtaylor65@gmail.com

TAYLOR, Mary Ann (Me) 83 Indian Hill Ln, Frankfort ME 04438 B Newark NY 5/16/1936 d Achiel Joseph DeMetsenaere & Emma Jane. BA Coll of New Rochelle 1958; S Bonaventure U 1966; U Roch 1974; MDiv Bex 1987. D 11/17/1988 P 5/18/1989 Bp William George Burrill. m 9/16/1978 F Carter Taylor. S Jas Ch Old Town ME 2005; R S Jn's Epis Ch Honeoye Falls NY 1989-1994; Cmncatn Off Dio Rochester Rochester NY 1988-1989. EWC, ADLMC, Associated Parishes. maryanntay@aol.com

TAYLOR, M(ary) Josephine A (SVa) 3100 Shore Dr Apt 625, Virginia Beach VA 23451 **Assoc Chr and S Lk's Epis Ch Norfolk VA 2008-; S Aid's Ch Virginia Bch VA 2005-** B Richmond VA 3/11/1933 d Robert Bacon Arnold & Josephine Alsey. BA U Rich 1954; MA Tul 1965; MDiv VTS 1982. D 6/23/1984 Bp Peter James Lee P 5/11/1985 Bp David Henry Lewis Jr. c 1. Int Hungars Par Eastville VA 2002-2004; Int Abingdon Epis Ch White Marsh VA 2001-2002; Ch Of The Epiph Norfolk VA 2000-2001; Int The Epis Ch Of The Adv Norfolk VA 1999-2000; Int S Geo's Epis Ch Newport News VA 1998-1999; Int All SS Epis Ch Reisterstown MD 1996-1998; COM Dio Maryland Baltimore MD 1995-1997; Dioc Coun Dio Maryland Baltimore MD 1990-1993; S Geo Ch Hampstead MD 1987-1996; Asst R S Paul's Ch Wallingford CT 1984-1987. tayjoa@wcbeach.com

TAYLOR, Marylou McClure (Cal) 501 Portola Rd # 8072, Portola Valley CA 94028 **D Chr Ch Portola Vlly CA 2006-** B Oakland CA 12/26/1923 d Lowe Abeel McClure & Mary. BA Stan 1946; BTh California Sch for Deacons 1985. D 12/7/1985 Bp William Edwin Swing. m 9/2/1959 William Frederick Taylor c 2. D Trin Par Menlo Pk CA 1986-1992; D S Mk's Epis Ch Palo Alto CA 1985-1986.

TAYLOR, Norman Dennis (Oly) 4218 Montgomery Place, Mount Vernon WA 98274 B Evanston IL 2/20/1948 s Bernard Zachary Taylor & Joy Lawson. ADN Everett Cmnty Coll 1977; Assoc Skagit Vlly Coll 1977; Cert Dioc TS 1994. D 7/7/2001 Bp Vincent Waydell Warner. m 3/13/1971 Mary Ann Krahe c 1. Steph Mnstry Awd NAAD 2007. small1@mac.com

TAYLOR, Patricia Lois (Oly) 75 E Lynn St Apt 104, Seattle WA 98102 B Vancouver BC CA 9/8/1932 d William John Mooney & Winifred Daisy. EdD U Of British Columbia Vancouver Bc CA 1953; A.D.N Shoreline Cmnty Coll 1975; Cert Olympia TS 1977. D 6/30/1984 Bp Robert Hume Cochrane P 11/22/1996 Bp Vincent Waydell Warner. m 3/27/1953 James Vinton Taylor. Ch In The Wrld Cmsn Dio Olympia Seattle WA 2000-2001; All SS Ch Seattle WA 1996-2001; Bd Dio Olympia Seattle WA 1993-1995; D S Geo's Ch Seattle WA 1992-1995; Cath Chapt S Mk's Cathd Seattle WA 1991-1994; Hosp Chapl Coordntr Dio Olympia Seattle WA 1986-1991; Cur Trin Par Seattle WA 1986-1991; Cler Res Ch Of The Epiph Seattle WA 1984-1986. Wmn Of Light Awd Homeless Wmn Cltn, Seattle 2000. patguggy@gmail.com

TAYLOR, Paul N. (WMass) 34 Boylston Cir., Shrewsbury MA 01545 B Brighton MA 10/6/1943 s David Edwin Taylor & Erna Francette. BA MacMurray Coll 1965; BD Yale DS 1968; STM Yale DS 1970; Doctoral Fell Tubingen Universitat 1974; PhD U of Iowa 1979. D 6/22/1968 Bp Anson Phelps Stokes Jr P 5/1/1969 Bp Joseph Warren Hutchens. m 6/29/1987 Andrea Taylor c 2. R Trin Epis Ch Shrewsbury MA 1988-2007; Ch Of S Jn The Evang Duxbury MA 1984-1987; Asst S Jn's Ch No Haven CT 1968-1970. pntaylor@townisp.com

TAYLOR JR, Philip Justice (WTex) 139 W Resaca Rd, Los Frenos TX 78566 B Philadelphia PA 10/1/1945 s Philip Justice Taylor & Jeanette. Leh 1964; BS Parsons Coll 1967; MDiv PDS 1972; DMin McCormick TS 1987. D 6/6/1970 Bp Robert Lionne DeWitt P 6/23/1971 Bp Harold Cornelius Gosnell. m 6/20/1970 Helen Eddy c 1. R S Andr's Ch Port Isabel TX 1999-2010; Vic Calv Ch Menard TX 1994-1999; Vic Trin Ch Jct TX 1994-1999; Vic All SS Epis Ch Pleasanton TX 1993-1994; Vic S Mths Devine TX 1993-1994; Assoc S Dav's Epis Ch San Antonio TX 1978-1993; P-in-c Ch Of Our Sav Aransas Pass TX 1974-1978; P-in-c Trin-By-The-Sea Port Aransas TX 1974-1978; Asst S Lk's Epis Ch San Antonio TX 1971-1974. pandh@flash.net

TAYLOR, Phyllis Gertrude (Pa) 401 Central Ave, Cheltenham PA 19012 B Fort Erie ON CA 5/24/1944 d Garnet John Painter & Beatrice. BA U Tor 1967; BD Melbourne Coll of Div 1971. D 6/15/1985 P 5/31/1986 Bp Lyman Cunningham Ogilby. m 9/10/1966 John M Taylor. Trin Ch Oxford Philadelphia PA 1995-2007; Int S Thos' Ch Whitemarsh Ft Washington PA 1993-1995; Int S Ptr's Ch Glenside PA 1992-1993; P-Intern Ch Of The Mssh Lower Gwynedd PA 1985-1987. Auth, "Epis Evang Fndt Best Sermon Competition Winner 93," *Grand Winner 94*. Soc of S Jn the Div. Best Sermon Competion Grand Winner Epis Evang Fndt 1994; Best Sermon Competition Winner, 1993 Epis Evang Fndt 1993. phyllis.taylor1@verizon.net

TAYLOR, Ralph Douglas (Az) St Philips in the Hills, PO Box 65840, Tucson AZ 85728 B Niagra Fall NY 2/14/1945 s Ralph D Taylor & Ruth Ann. BSPA U of Arizona 1978. D 1/26/2008 Bp Kirk Stevan Smith. c 9. rtaylor625@comcast.net

TAYLOR JR, Raymond George (NC) 461 Pemaquid Harbor Rd, Pemaquid ME 04558 B New Brighton PA 3/2/1939 s Raymond George Taylor & Florence Lydia. BS Buc 1959; BD EDS 1962; MS U of Pennsylvania 1964; EdD U of Pennsylvania 1966; MPA Penn 1977; MBA U of Sthrn Maine 1986; PhD GTF 1996. D 6/9/1962 Bp Joseph Gillespie Armstrong P 3/2/1963 Bp Andrew Tsu. m 6/1/1959 Christine Mary Morton c 2. S Thos Ch Oriental NC 1997-1999; Assoc S Paul's Epis Ch Smithfield NC 1987-1990; Vic S Mary's Ch Warwick RI 1970-1977. Edelman Laureate Internat'l Forum Oprtns Resrch and Mgmt Sciences 2007. ray.taylor@ncsu.edu

TAYLOR, Richard Louis (WLa) 108 Jason Ln, Natchitoches LA 71457 **LocTen S Paul's Ch Winnfield LA 2002-** B Corbin KY 8/30/1933 s Bryan J Taylor & Sarah K. BA Piedmont Coll Demorest GA 1959; MA E Carolina U 1962; MDiv STUSo 1975. D 6/11/1975 P 12/22/1975 Bp Christoph Keller Jr. m 1/28/1966 Marilyn Hedges c 5. Int Chr Memi Ch Mansfield LA 2000-2001; Int S Tim's Ch Alexandria LA 1998-1999; R Trin Epis Ch Natchitoches LA 1982-1998; R Ch Of The H Comf Angleton TX 1980-1982; R S Andr's Ch Marianna AR 1975-1980. haleakela@msn.com

TAYLOR, Roberta Renee (Md) PO Box 293, Kiiauea HI 96754 **Vic Chr Memi Ch Kilauea HI 2011-** B Havre de Grace MD 11/28/1955 d Brady Bert Caudill & Mabel Marie. BS JHU 1977; MDiv VTS 2011. D 6/4/2011 Bp Eugene Sutton. m 4/21/1979 David Taylor c 3. rev.robin2011@gmail.com

TAYLOR, Robert C (USC) 511 Roper Mtn Rd, Greenville SC 29615 **Dio Upper So Carolina Columbia SC 2007-** B Brooklyn NY 8/18/1945 s Mortimer John Downing & Constance. LTh Gregorian U; MS Rutgers-The St U. Rec from Roman Catholic 2/5/1981 Bp Robert Campbell Witcher Sr. m 12/21/1974 Anita Segue. Trin Ch Paterson NJ 1986; Exec Coun Appointees New York NY 1981-1984. frtaylor@aol.com

TAYLOR, Robert Charles (Chi) 200 Wyndemere Cir, Wheaton IL 60187 **Died 10/31/2010** B 1/20/1919 s Fred R Taylor & Jessie S. BS U IL 1940. D 1/12/1974 Bp James Winchester Montgomery. c 3. Auth, *Maintenance for Ch Buildings*. deaconrtaylor@gmail.com

TAYLOR, Robert E (Ct) 4 Harbor View Drive, Essex CT 06426 B Bridgeport CT 7/13/1943 s Lewis Edward Taylor & Anna Leniah. BA U Of Bridgeport 1966; MDiv Ya Berk 1969. D 6/11/1969 P 12/12/1969 Bp John Henry Esquirol. m 6/15/1968 Judith Douville. R S Paul's Ch Riverside CT 1992-2007; R S Mk's Ch Mystic CT 1983-1992; Vic S Mk's Chap Storrs CT 1974-1983; Vic S Jas' Ch New Haven CT 1971-1974; Cur S Andr's Ch Meriden CT 1969-1971. retaylor@snet.net

TAYLOR, Robert Jemonde (Dal) 8011 Douglas Ave, Dallas TX 75225 **Mssnr S Mich And All Ang Ch Dallas TX 2009-** B Henderson NC 12/12/1977 s Robert Taylor & Levonia Richardson. BS No Carolina St U 2000; MS Stan

2002; MDiv The GTS 2009. D 5/6/2009 Bp Dorsey Felix Henderson P 11/21/2009 Bp James Monte Stanton. jtaylor@saintmichael.org

TAYLOR, Robert Martin (NI) 3825 N Ridge Ct, Marion IN 46952 B Atlanta GA 4/26/1952 s Dillard Taylor & Dollie. AA Emory U 1972; BA Emory U 1972; MS U MI 1988. D 11/16/1984 Bp William Cockburn Russell Sheridan. D Geth Epis Ch Marion IN 1984-2009. CBS, SocMary, Conf Of S Ben, GAS, NAAD.

TAYLOR, Robert Stuart (SeFla) 400 Seabrook Rd, Tequesta FL 33469 **R The Epis Ch Of The Gd Shpd Tequesta FL 1989-** B Providence RI 6/10/1950 s James David Taylor & Elizabeth. BA U of Rhode Island 1972; MDiv EDS 1976. D 6/11/1976 P 12/16/1976 Bp Frederick Hesley Belden. m 10/7/1978 Marlene J Clough c 3. Dn No Palm Bch Deanry Dio SE Florida Miami FL 1993-1996; R Trin Epis Ch Wrentham MA 1983-1989; Asst S Mart's Ch Providence RI 1979-1983; Cur S Jn's Ch Barrington RI 1976-1979. rstaylor50@yahoo.com

TAYLOR, Robert Vincent (Oly) 10707 W Acord Rd, Benton City WA 99320 B Cape Town ZA 4/24/1958 s Donald Vincent Taylor & Elizabeth May. BA Rhodes U Grahamstown Za 1979; MDiv UTS 1984. D 12/18/1983 Bp Paul Moore Jr P 6/18/1984 Bp Walter Decoster Dennis Jr. Dn S Mk's Cathd Seattle WA 1999-2009; Mem Bd Dio New York New York City NY 1996-1999; R S Ptr's Epis Ch Peekskill NY 1988-1999; Comp Dioc Com Dio New York New York City NY 1987-1994; Int Trin S Paul's Epis New Rochelle NY 1987-1988; Int Ch Of S Mary The Vrgn Chappaqua NY 1986-1987; Gr Ch White Plains NY 1983-1986. Auth, "arts," *Chicago Tribune*; Auth, "arts," *Epis Life*; Auth, "arts," *Gannett Nwspr*; Auth, "arts," *Ny Newsday*. robert.taylor@spherefoods.com

TAYLOR, Ronald Brent (WNC) 7545 Sarah Dr., Denver NC 28037 **R Epis Ch Of S Ptr's By The Lake Denver NC 1996-** B Gastonia NC 10/9/1958 s Ray Charles Taylor & Mima Ruth. BA Wingate U 1980; MDiv STUSo 1992; DMin STUSo 2006. D 6/6/1992 P 5/1/1993 Bp Robert Hodges Johnson. m 6/2/1984 Karen Fairbanks c 2. Asst S Jn's Epis Ch Columbia SC 1992-1996. CANISMAJORM41@YAHOO.COM

TAYLOR, Stanley Richard (HB) 157 Patrick Crescent, Essex N8M 1X2 Canada B Windsor ON CA 9/13/1940 s Stanley Taylor & Margaret. Electronics Inst Detroit MI 1962; LTh Hur 1968; BA U of Windsor 1976; BEd U of Windsor 1977. D 5/1/1968 Bp The Bishop Of Huron. m 6/1/1968 Karen Eileen Bachand. Auth, "Neither Bond Nor Free".

TAYLOR, Stefanie Elizabeth (WNC) 906 S Orleans Ave, Tampa FL 33606 **Cur St Johns Epis Ch Tampa FL 2011-** B Denver CO 4/29/1983 d Erich Conroy Pearson & Lizabeth Ann. BA U of So Carolina 2007; MDiv The GTS 2011. D 12/18/2010 Bp Granville Porter Taylor. m 8/15/2009 Arthur Taylor. staylor@stjohnstampa.org

TAYLOR, Sylvester O'Neale (LI) 485 Linwood St, Brooklyn NY 11208 **P in charge S Barn Epis Ch Brooklyn NY 2000-** B BB 8/12/1959 s Vernon Leon Taylor & Alicia. BS SUNY 1994; MDiv GTS 1996. D 9/15/1997 Bp Orris George Walker Jr P 5/2/1998 Bp Rodney Rae Michel. m 5/26/1990 Jocelyn G Richards c 1. S Phil's Ch Brooklyn NY 1997-2000. syljoyce526@aol.com

TAYLOR, Terrence Alexander (SeFla) 20822 San Simeon Way Apt. 109, Miami FL 33179 **P-in-c Ch Of The Trsfg Opa Locka FL 2010-; Par Mssnr S Agnes Ch Miami FL 2010-; P-in-c S Kevin's Epis Ch Opa Locka FL 2010-** B Miami FL 11/29/1966 s Hilton Alexander Taylor & Mary Elizabeth. BS Florida St U 1988; MPA Florida Intl U 1992; Angl Stds Dip Ya Berk 2003; MDiv Ya 2003. D 6/21/2003 P 12/20/2003 Bp Leopold Frade. P-in-c S Christophers Ch Haverhill FL 2006-2009; Cn for Yth and YA Mnstry Dio SE Florida Miami FL 2003-2006. terrence.taylor@aya.yale.edu

TAYLOR, Terry Ray (O) 1108 Secretariat Dr W, Danville KY 40422 B Evansville IN 8/12/1940 s William Robertson Taylor & Violet Hester. BA Kentucky Wesleyan Coll 1963; MDiv Epis TS In Kentucky 1968. D 5/25/1968 P 12/1/1968 Bp William R Moody. m 5/29/1965 Mary Linda Jeffers. P Trin Epis Ch Danville KY 2001; R S Barth's Ch Mayfield Vill OH 1984-2001; All Souls Ch Wadesboro NC 1974-1982; Calv Ch Wadesboro NC 1974-1982; P-in-c Ch Of The Mssh Mayodan NC 1970-1974; Vic S Alb's Ch Morehead KY 1968-1970. terryrtaylor@bellsouth.net

TAYLOR, Thomas Herbert (NCal) 14234 N Newcastle Dr, Sun City AZ 85351 B Salem OR 8/12/1939 s James Herbert Taylor & Lois Irene. California St U 1959; BA U of Oregon 1962; DMD U of Oregon 1967; Cert California Sch for Deacons 1980. D 6/19/1982 Bp William Edwin Swing P 2/1/1984 Bp George Clinton Harris. m 9/23/1978 Gloria Irene Cunha. Vic S Paul's Mssn Cres City CA 2000-2004; Dio Nthrn California Sacramento CA 1999-2004; R Ch Of The H Apos Hilo HI 1989-1999; Vic S Augustines' Epis Ch Homer AK 1984-1989. Auth, "Healed From Depression," *Sharing mag*, 1985. Ord Of S Lk 1986. aztom812@cox.net

TAYLOR JR, Timus Gayle (Tenn) 4715 Harding Pike, Nashville TN 37205 **P Assoc S Geo's Ch Nashville TN 1998-** B Paducah KY 12/16/1935 s Timus Gayle Taylor & Virginia. BA Van 1956; Cntrl Coll of Ang. Comm, Cbury, Engl 1957; Yale DS 1958; U of Louisville, KY 1960; DMin VTS 1963. D 6/27/1964 P 1/9/1965 Bp Paul Moore Jr. m 2/9/1957 Mary Ready Parrent c 2. S Geo's Ch Nashville TN 1993-1997; Sthrn Dnry Team Dio Springfield Springfield IL 1988-1990; P S Mart's-In-The-Fields Mayfield KY 1986-1987; P S Paul's Ch Hickman KY 1986-1987; P S Ptr's of the Lakes Gilbertsville KY 1986-1987; P Trin Epis Ch Fulton KY 1986-1987; P S Jas Epis Ch McLeansboro IL 1980-1981; P S Steph's Ch Harrisburg IL 1980-1981; Paducah Coop Mnstry Paducah KY 1975-1976; Int Gr Epis Ch Paris TN 1975; Gr Ch Paducah KY 1973-1985; Int Gr Ch Hopkinsville KY 1972; Int Gr Epis Ch Paris TN 1971; Asst All SS Par Beverly Hills CA 1967-1970; Dioc Mssnr Dio Washington Washington DC 1964-1967. "Selected Sermons and Occasional Writings," 2001. Natioanl Cathd Assn; NOEL.

TAYLOR, Walter Hamilton (Tex) Po Box 2126, Lenox MA 01240 B Cincinnati OH 1/27/1938 s Robert Willey Taylor & Margaret. BA Ken 1960; MDiv VTS 1963; DD Ya Berk 1988. D 6/15/1963 P 12/1/1963 Bp Roger W Blanchard. m 6/18/1960 Mary Wilson c 2. Dn Chr Ch Cathd Houston TX 1992-1998; R S Lk's Par Darien CT 1977-1992; R Trin Ch Columbus OH 1969-1977; P-in-c H Trin Epis Ch Oxford OH 1966-1969; Asst Epis Soc of Chr Ch Cincinnati OH 1963-1966. Auth, "Faces," *Voices & the Lord*, 1986. Ord of S Lk. whtmwt@aol.com

TAYLOR JR, Willard Seymour (EC) 245 Mcdonald Church Rd, Rockingham NC 28379 B Charlotte NC 10/9/1936 s Willard Seymour Taylor & Frances Jean. BA U NC 1959; BD VTS 1962. D 4/29/1963 Bp Richard Henry Baker P 2/1/1964 Bp Thomas H Wright. m 5/4/1997 Margaret R Nicholl. Int Chr Ch Albemarle NC 1998-1999; S Steph's Epis Ch Erwin NC 1992-1997; P-in-c S Jas The Fisherman Epis Ch Shallotte NC 1969-1998; P-in-c S Phil's Ch Southport NC 1969-1998; D Emm Ch Farmville NC 1963-1964. tomtay@intrstar.net

TAYLOR JR, William Brown (SVa) 4025 Reese Dr S, Portsmouth VA 23703 **S Jn's Ch Hopewell VA 2007-** B Wheeling WV 4/9/1957 s William Brown Taylor & Susan Elizabeth. BA Old Dominion U 1981; MDiv VTS 1986. D 6/6/1987 P 4/30/1988 Bp C(laude) Charles Vache. m 12/18/2004 Kathryn Taylor c 1. Exec Dir Dio Sthrn Virginia Norfolk VA 2002-2007; Dir Yth Mnstrs Dio Sthrn Virginia Norfolk VA 1992-2002; R Ch Of The Epiph Norfolk VA 1989-1992; Dio Sthrn Virginia Norfolk VA 1988-1989; Asst Ch Of The Ascen Norfolk VA 1987-1989. chanco1@aol.com

TAYLOR III, William John (FtW) 2814 Waterford Dr, Irving TX 75063 B Cleveland OH 2/6/1943 s William John Taylor & Mildred. BA Cor 1964; JD U of Virginia 1967; MDiv UTS 1984; Cert GTS 1985. D 8/9/1986 Bp Quintin Ebenezer Primo Jr P 4/1/1988 Bp Donis Dean Patterson. m 10/7/1989 Jillian Smith. Trin Epis Ch Ft Worth TX 2004-2009; Epis Ch Of The Ascen Dallas TX 2002-2004; Epis Cntr For Renwl Dallas TX 2001-2002; R S Steph's Epis Ch Hurst TX 1992-2001; St Stephens Ch Hurst TX 1992-2001; Cur S Alb's Epis Ch Arlington TX 1988-1992; Cur S Lk's Epis Ch Dallas TX 1987. Travelling Fllshp Uts. billjt3@sbcglobal.net

TAYLOR, Williamson Sylvanus (NY) 3102 Hollywood Blvd, Hollywood FL 33021 **Cn For Congrl Dvlpmt Dio New York New York City NY 2002-; S Jos's Ch Bronx NY 2002-; R S Andr's Epis Ch Of Hollywood Dania Bch FL 1994-** B Freetown LK 9/9/1942 s George Taylor & Marie. BA Forah Bay Coll Of Dur 1969; Med How 1975; MA How 1977; STM Bos 1984; ThD Bos 1989. Trans from Church of the Province of West Africa 3/1/1994 Bp Calvin Onderdonk Schofield Jr. m 11/7/1970 Monica B Doherty. S Anne's Epis Ch Hallandale Bch FL 1994-2002; Assoc P The Cathd Ch Of S Paul Boston MA 1990-1993; Supply P Dio Massachusetts Boston MA 1983-1993. AAR; Hallandale Ministral Allnce; SBL. w.s.taylor@att.net

TAYLOR LYMAN, Susan May (SD) 325 N Plum St, Vermillion SD 57069 **D S Paul's Epis Ch Vermillion SD 2007-** B Siouy Falls SD 7/1/1943 d Harry Higbee Smith & Pauline Clarissa Mary. Heidelberg TS, Vermillion SD; MDiv Niobrara Sum Sem; No Amer Bapt Sem; BD U Of So Dakota Vermillion SD 1989. D 6/22/2007 Bp Creighton Leland Robertson. m 11/21/1998 Samuel Kenneth Lyman c 4.

TAYLOR-WEISS, Douglas (CNY) 169 Genesee St, Auburn NY 13021 **R Epis Ch Of SS Ptr And Jn Auburn NY 1998-** B Grand Rapids MI 6/1/1956 s Warren Henry Schut & Esther. BA Wheaton Coll 1977; MA SWTS 1981; DMin SWTS 1996. D 6/11/1983 Bp Quintin Ebenezer Primo Jr P 12/17/1983 Bp James Winchester Montgomery. m 11/10/1984 Debra Sue Dedie c 2. R S Andr's Ch Dayton OH 1987-1998; Cur S Marg's Ch Chicago IL 1983-1987. taylorweisses@verizon.net

TCHAMALA, Theodore K (Md) 6515 Loch Raven Blvd., Baltimore MD 21239 **S Andr's Ch Baltimore MD 2007-** B 6/18/1945 s Moise MBenga & Madeleine. BTh Jn XXIII Sem 1972; MA Sorbonne 1976; PhD U of Montreal 1986. Trans from Anglican Church of Canada 3/20/2008 Bp John Leslie Rabb. m 8/30/1979 Anne Mukajimuenji c 3. ttchamala@yahoo.com

TEAGUE JR, Addison Dawson (NY) Po Box 748, Augusta GA 30903 B Augusta GA 2/22/1930 s Addison Dawson Teague & Eleanor. BA U GA 1951; MDiv VTS 1956. D 6/20/1959 P 5/1/1960 Bp Albert R Stuart. R Zion Ch Dobbs Ferry NY 1977-1987; Chr Epis Ch Tarrytown NY 1976-1977; Gr Epis Ch New York NY 1976; Seamans Inst Bonus 4 Per Cent New York NY 1973-1974. Contrib, "Epis Ch In Georgia Nwspr". Acad Of Amer Poets;

Augusta Authors Club; Soc Of Colonial Works In The St Of Georgia. Who'S Who Of Amer Pulpits 1978.

TEAGUE, C(harles) Steven (Mil) ST PAUL'S EPISCOPAL CHURCH, 914 E KNAPP ST, MILWAUKEE WI 53202 **Pres, Stndg Com Dio Milwaukee Milwaukee WI 2011-; Dn, Metro Milwaukee Convoc Dio Milwaukee Milwaukee WI 2009-; R S Paul's Ch Milwaukee WI 2007-** B Hickory NC 4/20/1950 s Charles Vandiver Teague & Adelaide Shuford. BA U NC 1972; MDiv Sthrn Bapt TS Louisville KY 1975; Cert Wake Forest U 1982; DMin SE Bapt TS Wake Forest NC 1983; DAS VTS 2000. D 6/24/2000 P 12/30/2000 Bp Clifton Daniel III. m 5/28/1988 Karen Wolfe c 2. R Ch S Mich The Archangel Lexington KY 2004-2007; Dn, Lower Cape Fear Dnry Dio E Carolina Kinston NC 2001-2003; Assoc S Jas Par Wilmington NC 2000-2004. Writer, "Re-imaging the Ch's Image," *Doctor of Mnstry Dissertation*, SEBTS, 1983. DD Hampden Sydney Coll, Hampden Sydney, VA 1986. steve.teague@sbcglobal.net

TEASLEY, Robin Tredway (SVa) 11406 Glenmont Rd, Richmond VA 23236 **D Ch Of The Redeem Midlothian VA 2011-** B Richmond VA 6/1/1958 d Robinet Whitmore Tredway & Jane Cole. BS Catawba Coll 1979; MDiv Un - PSCE 2010; Angl Stds Dplma VTS 2011. D 6/18/2011 Bp Herman Hollerith IV. m 11/24/1979 Paul Wirt Teasley c 3. robintteasley@gmail.com

TEDERSTROM, John Patton (Ky) 1007 Hess Ln, Louisville KY 40217 B Pittsburgh PA 11/23/1938 s Albert Harlow Tederstrom & Roberta Ernestine. BA Pr 1960; MDiv CDSP 1964. D 6/20/1964 Bp Conrad Gesner P 12/19/1964 Bp Austin Pardue. c 5. Int S Geo's Epis Ch Louisville KY 1999-2000; Supply P Dio Kentucky Louisville KY 1996-1999; Int Ch Of Our Merc Sav Louisville KY 1995-1996; Supply P Dio Kentucky Louisville KY 1992-1995; Int Ch Of The Adv Louisville KY 1991-1992; Supply P Dio Kentucky Louisville KY 1989-1991; Int S Geo's Epis Ch Louisville KY 1987-1989; Supply P Dio Kentucky Louisville KY 1983-1985; R S Jn's Ch Louisville KY 1980-1983; Int Ch Of Our Sav Middleboro MA 1979-1980; Dep GC Convoc of Amer Ch in Europe Paris FR 1979; Alt Dep GC Convoc of Amer Ch in Europe Paris FR 1976; P-in-c Amer Mnstry In The Riviera 1975-1979; Dep GC Convoc of Amer Ch in Europe Paris FR 1973; R Ch of S Aug of Cbury 65189 Wiesbaden DE 1972-1975; Secy 1971-1979 Convoc of Amer Ch in Europe Paris FR 1971-1979; R S Jas Epis Ch Firenze IA IT 1967-1972; Reserv Mnstrs Dio So Dakota Sioux Falls SD 1964-1967. Hon Mem Royal British Legion 1979; Phi Beta Kappa 1960. JOHNTEDERSTROM@ATT.NET

TEDESCO, Robert Lincoln (Va) 407 Russell Ave Apt 605, Gaithersburg MD 20877 **P Olivet Epis Ch Franconia VA 1992-** B Hartford CT 2/12/1927 s Nicholas John Tedesco & Mary Anna. BA U of Connecticut 1951; MS Trin Hartford CT 1959; MDiv VTS 1985. D 8/30/1985 Bp David Henry Lewis Jr P 5/31/1986 Bp Peter James Lee. m 11/7/1953 Dorothy Gladys Calabro c 4. Par Assoc Olivet Epis Ch Franconia VA 1992-2000; Int Olivet Epis Ch Franconia VA 1990-1992; Dio Virginia Richmond VA 1989-1990; Assoc S Tim's Ch Herndon VA 1986-1989; Cur Olivet Epis Ch Franconia VA 1985-1986. "Tech arts on Nuclear Power," 1957. ANS 1972-1982. dbted.tedesco7@gmail.com

TEDESCO, William Nicholas (Ct) 20 Erickson Way, South Yarmouth MA 02664 B Hartford CT 1/25/1924 s Nicholas John Tedesco & Mary S. MA Trin Hartford CT; AA/BA U of Hartford; MDiv VTS. D 6/8/1974 P 12/21/1974 Bp Joseph Warren Hutchens. m 8/30/1947 Rose Mancuso c 4. R Trin Ch Seymour CT 1977-1988; Cur All SS Epis Ch Oakville CT 1974-1977; Chr Ch Par Epis Watertown CT 1974-1977. amted@earthlink.net

TEED, Lee Barbara (SanD) 4860 Circle Dr, San Diego CA 92116 B Mount Kisco NY 12/23/1940 d George Allan Teed & Phyllis Josephine. BA U CA 1967; MA Untd States Intl U 1975; MDiv CDSP 1990. D 6/16/1990 P 12/15/1990 Bp Charles Brinkley Morton. subdean Cathd Ch Of S Paul San Diego CA 1994-2005; Cur The Epis Ch Of S Andr Encinitas CA 1990-1992. Ord Of H Cross. lteed@sbcglobal.net

TEETER, Barbara Hutchinson (CNY) 535 Mount Hope Ave, Apt 205, Rochester NY 14620 **Supply P Emm Ch Elmira NY 1998-** B Evanston IL 1/3/1926 d Paul Hutchinson & Agnes. BS NWU 1946; MDiv Bex 1980. D 6/1/1980 Bp Ned Cole P 5/1/1981 Bp O'Kelley Whitaker. m 12/29/1945 John Hursh Teeter c 5. Supply P Gr Ch Waverly NY 1998-2008; Supply P Chr Ch Wellsburg NY 1998-2005; Supply P S Jn's Epis Ch Elmira Heights NY 1998-2005; Int Gr Ch Cortland NY 1995-1996; Int Calv Ch Homer NY 1990-1992; Int S Matt's Ch Moravia NY 1990-1992; Tri-Cnty Cluster Glen Aubrey NY 1990-1992; Dio Cntrl New York Syracuse NY 1980-1990; Cn S Paul's Cathd Syracuse NY 1980-1982. jbtreysa@twcny.rr.com

TEETER, John Hursh (CNY) 535 Mount Hope Ave. Apt. 205, Rochester NY 14620 B Ashland OH 3/23/1925 s Everett Hale Teeter & Wilma Jeanette. BS NWU 1946; MDiv SWTS 1957. D 6/15/1957 Bp Charles L Street P 3/22/1958 Bp William Henry Marmion. m 12/29/1945 Barbara Hutchinson c 5. Int S Paul's Ch Endicott NY 2001-2003; Int S Matt's Ch Moravia NY 1999-2001; Int S Andr's Ch Vestal NY 1996-1998; Int Zion Epis Ch Greene NY 1994-1996; Int S Thos' Epis Ch Syracuse NY 1989-1991; Int All SS Epis Ch Johnson City NY 1988-1989; Int All SS Ch Syracuse IN 1986-1987; R S Jame's Ch Skaneateles NY 1963-1985; Vic Trin Epis Ch Rocky Mt VA 1957-1959. jbtrevs@twrochester.com

TELLARI, Stephen Stefani (Oly) 1501 32nd Ave S, Seattle WA 98144 B Rugby CO 3/30/1941 s Steve Tellari & Pamela Inez. BEd Cntrl Washington U WA 1962; MED U of Puget Sound 1971. D 10/17/2009 Bp Gregory Harold Rickel. m 8/1/1998 Shirley C Hickey c 2. stellari@harbornet.com

TELMAN, Hilbert Leslie (SwFla) 18535 Gentle Breeze Ct, Hudson FL 34667 **D S Steph's Ch New Port Richey FL 2003-** B Demerara GUYANA 10/5/1935 s Julius Telman. BS/MS/GUD LIU 1989. D 6/14/2003 Bp John Bailey Lipscomb. m 4/20/1957 Baird Telman c 3.

TEMBECKJIAN, Renee Melanie (CNY) 4782 Hyde Rd, Manlius NY 13104 **Dio Cntrl New York Syracuse NY 2011-** B New York NY 7/6/1955 d Edward Tembeckjian & Arpine. MS,CAS SUNY Coll at Oswego 1983; PhD Syr 1992; Dioc Formation Prog 2009. D 6/29/2009 P 1/9/2010 Bp Gladstone Bailey Adams III. m 7/10/1988 Thomas Zino c 2. rmtphd@aol.com

TEMME, Louis H (Pa) c/o Trinity Church, N. Chester Road & College Ave, Swarthmore PA 19081 B Philadelphia PA 3/16/1944 s Louis Charles Temme & Rose. BS Drexel U 1967; CPE St. Lk's Hosp Houston Texas 1969; MDiv PDS 1970; MS St. Johns U 1972; Cert Credo Conf Roslyn VA 2004. D 6/6/1970 P 12/1/1970 Bp Robert Lionne DeWitt. m 4/5/1975 Kathryn M Rosse c 2. Int R Ch Of S Mart-In-The-Fields Philadelphia PA 2009-2011; Int R Washington Memi Chap Vlly Forge PA 2007-2009; Int R Trin Ch Swarthmore PA 2005-2007; R Trin Memi Ch Philadelphia PA 1972-2005; Asst R Chr Ch Oyster Bay NY 1970-1972. Achievement Awd Dio Pennsylvania Oyster Bay NY 2000; Fllshp Cont Educ VTS 1986. loutemme@att.net

TEMPLE, Charles S (NY) 1 E 29th St, New York NY 10016 B Indianapolis IN 8/10/1950 s Charles Sloan Temple & Mary Ann. BA Rhode Island Coll 1976; MDiv GTS 1979. D 6/2/1979 Bp Frederick Hesley Belden P 12/13/1979 Bp John S Higgins. Ch Of The Trsfg New York NY 1982-1997; Cur S Jn's Ch Barrington RI 1979-1982. charlestemple@webtv.net

TEMPLE, Edith Sue (WMo) 5809 Harrison St, Kansas City MO 64110 B Kansas City MO 11/22/1915 d George Vaughan Dameron & Laura Marie. Rockhurst Coll; S Paul TS. D 9/29/1981 Bp Arthur Anton Vogel. m 9/2/1940 Paul Temple c 2. Asst S Mary's Epis Ch Kansas City MO 1981-1992.

TEMPLE, Gordon Clarence (ETenn) 6808 Levi Rd, Hixson TN 37343 B Knoxville TN 7/11/1934 s Clarence Vardaman Temple & Julia Adele. BD U of Tennessee 1954; BD Auburn U 1959; MDiv STUSo 1986; VTS 1995. D 6/22/1986 P 5/1/1987 Bp William Evan Sanders. m 6/6/1958 Helen Haven Jones. Int S Mart Of Tours Epis Ch Chattanooga TN 2003-2011; Int S Tim's Ch Signal Mtn TN 2002-2003; Int Gr Ch Chattanooga TN 2001-2002; Int All SS Epis Ch Whitefish MT 1999-2001; Asst R Ch Of The Ascen Knoxville TN 1998-1999; Int Ch Of The Ascen Knoxville TN 1996-1998; R S Matt's Ch Columbia Falls MT 1993-1996; R All SS Epis Ch Whitefish MT 1992-1996; Assoc Ch Of The Ascen Knoxville TN 1986-1987. Prov Coordntr, ESMA, Chapl Ord Of S Lk. ghtemple1934@bellsouth.net

TEMPLE JR, Gray (At) 10685 Bell Rd, Duluth GA 30097 B Washington DC 9/25/1941 s Gray Temple & Maria. Schlr Gottingen U DE 1964; BA U NC 1965; BD VTS 1968. D 6/17/1968 P 12/18/1968 Bp Matthew G Henry. m 8/28/1966 Jean Dillin c 2. R S Pat's Epis Ch Atlanta GA 1975-2006; Vic S Lk's Ch Boone NC 1968-1975. Auth, "The Molten Soul," Ch Pub Inc, 2001; Auth, "When God Happens," Ch Pub Inc, 2001; Auth, "52 Ways To Help Homeless People," 1991; Auth, "5 Sermons," *Selected Sermons*. Hon Cn S Lk Cathd Butere Kenya 1985. jeanhdt@mindspring.com

TEMPLE, Palmer Collier (At) 1883 Wycliff Rd Nw, Atlanta GA 30309 B Nashville TN 12/14/1934 s Thomas Hudson Temple & Margaret. BA Van 1957; MDiv Candler TS Emory U 1960. D 2/18/1976 Bp James Winchester Montgomery P 6/1/1976 Bp Quintin Ebenezer Primo Jr. m 12/21/1968 Helen Elizabeth Harris c 2. Serv, Trng and Counslg Cntr S Lk's Epis Ch Atlanta GA 1981-1994; St Lukes Trng & Coun.Ctr Atlanta GA 1981-1994; S Tim's Decatur GA 1978-1980. Auth, "Chld in Hospitals: A Matter of Life, Death and Lrng," *Chicago Tribune mag*, 1975; Auth, "Var arts," *Journ on Pstr Care*.

TEMPLEMAN, Mark Alan (Mass) 60 Monument Avenue, Swampscott MA 01907 **Dio Estrn Michigan Saginaw MI 2008-; R The Ch Of The H Name Swampscott MA 2006-** B Fayetteville NC 1/25/1968 s Bruce Alan Templeman & Jane Elizabeth. BA Wright St U 1999; MA TESM 2002. D 10/20/2001 P 6/1/2002 Bp Herbert Thompson Jr. m 10/22/1995 Jennifer M Murray c 3. Chr Ch Frederica St Simons Island GA 2004-2006; Cur S Lk's Ch Marietta OH 2002-2003. Auth, "A Distant Shore," *A Distant Shore*, Idyllwood Press, 2002; Auth, "Candle in an Ocean," *Candle in an Ocean*, Idyllwood Press, 1999. St. Lk the Physcn 2004. Mike Henning Preaching Prize Mike Henning Memi Preaching Schlrshp 2000. templeman4@comcast.net

TEMPLETON, Gary Lynn (Okla) 903 N Primrose St, Duncan OK 73533 **D All SS' Epis Ch Duncan OK 1987-** B Bartlesville OK 2/20/1947 s Henry Clay Templeton & Catherine Irene. BS Oklahoma St U 1974. D 8/24/1987 Bp Gerald Nicholas McAllister. m 9/30/1978 Ellen Louise Drought. garellen@ableone.net

T

TEMPLETON, John (At) 274 Hershey Lane, Clayton GA 30525 B Memphis TN 10/20/1938 s Loyd Clayton Templeton & Virginia Ellen. BA Rhodes Coll 1962; MDiv STUSo 1969; MSW U GA 1989. D 6/29/1969 P 6/1/1970 Bp John Adams Pinckney. m 4/22/1988 John M Siegel c 3. R S Paul's Ch Macon GA 1977-1988; R Chr the King Pawleys Island SC 1971-1977; Asst S Jn's Epis Ch Columbia SC 1969-1971. jht1938@windstream.net

TEMPLETON, Patricia Dale (At) 4393 Garmon Road NW, Atlanta GA 30327 **R S Dunst's Epis Ch Atlanta GA 2004-** B Houston TX 3/1/1956 d Robert Parker Templeton & Lena Dot. BA U GA 1978; MDiv STUSo 1994. D 5/29/1994 Bp Bertram Nelson Herlong P 5/25/1995 Bp Robert Gould Tharp. m 12/29/1996 Joseph Monti c 1. Assoc R S Tim's Ch Signal Mtn TN 1995-2002; Assoc R Ch Of The Ascen Knoxville TN 1994-1995. Auth, "Runaway Bunnies -- and Believers," *Sermons That Wk XIV*, Morehouse, 2006; Auth, "Sanctifying What Has Been Desecrated," *Sermons That Wk XIII*, Morehouse, 2005; Auth, "A Reason For Wounds In A Risen Body," *Sermons That Wk IX*, Morehouse, 2000. Pres, Stndg Com Dio Atlanta 2010; Pres, Stndg Com Dio E Tennessee 2000. stdunstans@juno.com

TENCH, Jack M. (Oly) 1919 NE Ridgewood Ct, Poulsbo WA 98370 B Chicago IL 1/7/1938 s Marvin Edward Tench & Ruth Elaine. BA Colorado Coll 1960; STB GTS 1964. D 6/13/1964 Bp James Winchester Montgomery P 12/19/1964 Bp Gerald Francis Burrill. m 4/3/1970 Joan Berdean Dunham c 3. R S Lk's Epis Ch Seattle WA 1991-2000; R St Steph's Epis Ch Oak Harbor WA 1981-1991; Exec Coun Appointees New York NY 1979-1981; Ch Of The Resurr Bellevue WA 1971-1979; Cur S Jn's Epis Ch Mt Prospect IL 1964-1966. jmtench1@comcast.net

TENDICK, James Ross (U) 1780 Plateau Cir, Moab UT 84532 **Vic Mision de San Francisco Moab UT 2007-; Dio Utah Salt Lake City UT 1996-** B Long Beach CA 7/19/1948 s Cullen Bryce Tendick & Sylvia Woodward. CDSP 1988; MDiv CDSP 2000. D 6/4/1988 Bp William Edwin Swing P 5/13/1989 Bp George Edmonds Bates. m 8/5/1978 Marcia Moeller c 3. R S Fran Ch Moab UT 1996-2006; S Jas Epis Ch Midvale UT 1989-1996. jrossten@msn.com

✠ **TENNIS, Rt Rev Cabell** (Del) 841 33rd Ave E, Seattle WA 98112 **Ret Bp of Delaware Dio Delaware Wilmington DE 1998-** B Hampton VA 10/24/1932 s Calvin Tennis & Francis. BA W&M 1954; JD W&M 1956; MDiv VTS 1964. D 6/1/1964 P 12/19/1964 Bp George P Gunn Con 11/8/1986 for Del. m 8/21/1954 Hyde Southall Jones c 4. Bp Dio Delaware Wilmington DE 1986-1997; Dn S Mk's Cathd Seattle WA 1972-1986; ExCoun Dio Olympia Seattle WA 1972-1975; ExCoun Dio Wstrn New York Tonawanda NY 1969-1972; Assoc Trin Epis Ch Buffalo NY 1965-1969; Asst S Jn's Ch Portsmouth VA 1964-1965. Assn For Conflict Resolution. Hon DD VTS Alexandria VA 1987. cabell-hyde@msn.com

TENNISON, G(eorge) (La) 10 Colony Trail Dr, Mandeville LA 70448 **P-in-c S Matt's Ch Bogalusa LA 2011-** B New Orleans LA 12/30/1944 s George Tennison & Elise. U of New Orleans; BS Lamar U 1967; Sch for Mnstry Dio Louisiana 2003. D 12/30/2006 P 6/30/2007 Bp Charles Edward Jenkins III. m 6/10/1977 Martha Ann North c 1. S Mich's Epis Ch Mandeville LA 2006-2011. ntennison@charter.net

TENNY, Claire Mary (Chi) Po Box 426, Vails Gate NY 12584 B New York NY 11/17/1959 d Fred Tenny & Claire. MD Albany Med Coll 1983; BS Un Coll Schenectady NY 1983; MDiv STUSo 2002. D 6/8/2002 P 12/8/2002 Bp William Jerry Winterrowd. Cathd Of St Jn The Div New York NY 2007-2009; S Andr Ch Grayslake IL 2003-2006; Assoc for Campus Mnstry S Alb's Ch Davidson NC 2002-2003. tennycm@gmail.com

TEPAVCHEVICH, Kathie Elaine (Chi) 6588 Shabbona Rd, Indian Head Park IL 60525 **D Ch Of The H Nativ Clarendon Hills IL 2001-** B Springfield IL 10/1/1953 d Harvey Dale Bergman & Nancy Jean. Natl-Louis U; BA Quincy Coll 1975. D 2/15/1997 Bp Frank Tracy Griswold III. m 11/23/1974 Thomas Tepavchevich. D Emm Epis Ch La Grange IL 1997-2002. dkt1001@aol.com

TEPE, Donald James (EMich) 3226 Meadowview Ln, Saginaw MI 48601 B Chicago IL 6/2/1929 s James Henderson Tepe & Ruth. BS NWU 1954; BD Garrett Evang TS 1957; SWTS 1961; MSW U MI 1973. D 6/20/1961 P 12/26/1961 Bp Charles Bennison. c 2. P in charge Calv Memi Epis Ch Saginaw MI 1995-2010; P-in-c Calv Memi Epis Ch Saginaw MI 1976-1988; R S Jas' Epis Ch Of Albion Albion MI 1969-1973; Vic S Alb's Mssn Muskegon MI 1966-1969; Cur Gr Ch Grand Rapids MI 1961-1966. dontepe@concentric.net

TERHUNE JR, Robert Dawbarn (SeFla) 2605A Spring Ln, Austin TX 78703 B New Haven CT 3/28/1932 s Robert Dawbarn Terhune & Josephine. BA Ya 1953; STB Ya Berk 1958; MA U of Houston 1976. D 6/22/1958 Bp Henry I Louttit P 12/22/1958 Bp William Francis Moses. m 4/16/1955 Lorna MacLean c 4. Vic S Mk's Ch Palm Bch Gardens FL 1963-1968; Cur Ch Of The Resurr Biscayne Pk FL 1961-1963; Vic S Dunst's Epis Ch Largo FL 1958-1961; P-in-c S Giles Ch Pinellas Pk FL 1958-1960. SocMary 1998. lrterhune@austin.rr.com

TERRILL, Robert Allen (Kan) 3524 Sw Willow Brook Ln, Topeka KS 66614 B Brookfield MO 12/18/1936 s Curtis Alber Terrill & Esther Lucille. BS U of Kansas 1958; MDiv SWTS 1961. D 6/11/1961 P 12/1/1961 Bp Edward Clark Turner. m 6/10/1989 Judith Ann Coates. Provost Gr Cathd Topeka KS 1997-2000; R Chr Epis Ch S Jos MO 1988-1997; Vic Ch Of The Resurr Blue Sprg MO 1984-1988; Dio W Missouri Kansas City MO 1984-1988; Ch Of Our Sav Colorado Sprg CO 1982-1983; P-in-c S Lk's Ch Westcliffe CO 1978-1982; P-in-c Trin Ch Trinidad CO 1978-1982; R S Mk's Epis Ch Glen Ellyn IL 1972-1978; Vic S Barth's Ch Wichita KS 1971-1972; R S Chris's Epis Ch Wichita KS 1968-1972; R Trin Ch Arkansas City KS 1964-1968; Vic S Lk's Ch Wamego KS 1961-1964. Epis Cleric Assn. robertterrill472@gmail.com

TERRY, Eleanor Applewhite (Ct) 27 Senexet Village Road, Woodstock CT 06281 **Secy of Conv Dio Connecticut Hartford CT 2007-; Vic S Paul's Ch Plainfield CT 2005-** B New Haven CT 7/23/1969 d Philip B Applewhite & Harriet V. BA Smith 1991; MDiv Ya Berk 1997. D 6/8/2002 P 5/24/2003 Bp Andrew Donnan Smith. m 7/3/1999 Bronson E Terry c 2. Assoc R S Ptr And Paul Epis Ch Portland OR 2002-2005; Min Of Sprtlty And Aging S Paul And S Jas New Haven CT 1998-2002. reveaterry@yahoo.com

TERRY, Mildred Carlson (SwFla) 4071 Center Pointe Pl, Sarasota FL 34233 B Chicago IL 4/16/1925 d Svenn John Carlson & Esther Adalia. BA U Chi 1945; Chicago St U 1954; MA S Xavier Coll 1969; Cert Inst for Chr Stds 1987. D 9/2/1987 Bp William Hopkins Folwell. m 7/16/1945 Joseph Garside Terry c 3. D S Marg Of Scotland Epis Ch Sarasota FL 1989-2000; D S Alb's Epis Ch Auburndale FL 1987-1989. Dok.

TERRY, Susan Preston (Kan) 3209 W 25th St, Lawrence KS 66047 **Dio Kansas Topeka KS 2007-** B Fort Benning GA 8/16/1947 d James Kyle Terry & Wilma. BA S Mary 1971; MDiv Epis TS In Kentucky 1986. D 11/8/1986 Bp Don Adger Wimberly P 5/23/1987 Bp Joseph Thomas Heistand. c 3. H Cross Ch Thomson GA 2001-2003; Chapl The Ch Of The Gd Shpd Augusta GA 1988-2007; S Greg HS Tucson AZ 1987-1988. susanpterry@cs.com

TERRY, William Hutchinson (La) 626 Congress St., New Orleans LA 70117 **P-in-c Gr Ch New Orleans LA 2008-; R S Anna's Ch New Orleans LA 2003-** B New Orleans LA 7/4/1951 s Arthur H Terry & Betty. BA Tul 1978; MPS Loyola U 2002; MDiv Nash 2003. D 12/28/2002 P 7/20/2003 Bp Charles Edward Jenkins III. m 7/30/1983 Victoria L Rosich c 3. wterry2217@aol.com

TESCHNER, David Hall (SVa) 31 Belmead St, Petersburg VA 23805 **R Chr And Gr Ch Petersburg VA 1990-** B Natick MA 11/1/1951 s Douglass Paul Teschner & Mary Elizabeth. BA U of Rhode Island 1977; MDiv VTS 1986. D 6/21/1986 P 3/22/1987 Bp George Nelson Hunt III. m 11/13/2009 Juanita Watts Bouser. Asst to R S Steph's Ch Richmond VA 1986-1990. dtesch@christandgrace.us

TESI, Elizabeth A B (Ct) PO Box 50428, Eugene OR 97405 **Asst S Mary's Epis Ch Eugene OR 2011-** B Hartford CT 3/17/1979 d Robert Peter Bagioni & Kathleen Marie. BA Wells Coll 2001; MDiv VTS 2004; MS Virginia Commonwealth U 2007. D 6/12/2004 P 4/14/2005 Bp Andrew Donnan Smith. m 5/11/2007 Martin G Tesi. P-in-c Ch Of The Epiph Southbury CT 2007-2010; Int Vic Ch Of Our Sav Montpelier VA 2006-2007; Asst R Trin Ch Arlington VA 2004-2006. betsytesi@gmail.com

TESKA, William Jay (Minn) 940 Franklin Terrace, Apt. 409, Minneapolis MN B Minneapolis MN 10/2/1942 s Roy J Teska & Alice Anabel. BA Dart 1964; STB Ya Berk 1968. D 10/7/1968 Bp Hamilton Hyde Kellogg P 6/1/1969 Bp Philip Frederick McNairy. The OTCG Tucson AZ 2000-2003; Dio Minnesota Minneapolis MN 1999; R S Paul's On-The-Hill Epis Ch St Paul MN 1991-1999; R Par Of The H Trin And S Anskar Minneapolis MN 1984-1989; P-in-c Epiph Epis Ch S Paul MN 1981-1984; Epis Par Of S Mich And All Ang Tucson AZ 1980-1981. billteska@gmail.com

TESS, Michael Patrick (Mil) 124 Dewey St, Sun Prairie WI 53590 **Vic Ch Of The Gd Shpd Sun Prairie WI 2007-** B Manitowoc WI 8/17/1964 s Clayton Patrick Tess & Nancy Lee. BA St. Johns U 1987; MDiv St. Mary Of The Lake Sem Mundelein IL 1991; Iliff TS 1998. Rec from Roman Catholic 5/9/1998 as Priest Bp William Jerry Winterrowd. m 5/9/1998 Heidi A Oehmen c 4. Dio Milwaukee Milwaukee WI 2007-2009; P-in-c S Aidans Ch Hartford WI 2001-2007. mhtess@frontier.com

TESSMAN, Michael J R (Ct) 289 Balsam Rd, Wakefield RI 02879 **P-in-c Ch Of The H Sprt Charlestown RI 2008-** B Saint Paul MN 7/1/1948 s Roger Herman Tessman & Jean Margaret. BA U Chi 1970; MDiv Yale DS 1973; Cert WCC-Geneva 1987; Cert GTS 1997; DMin GTF 1998. D 6/12/1976 P 4/3/1977 Bp Joseph Warren Hutchens. m 7/21/1974 Carol Davidson c 2. Int S Jn's Ch Washington CT 2007-2008; Int S Monica's Ch Hartford CT 2006-2007; Int S Jn's Ch New Haven CT 2003-2005; Ecum Off Dio Milwaukee Milwaukee WI 1999-2002; Pstr Theol Nash Nashotah WI 1997-2003; R Imm S Jas Par Derby CT 1991-1997; Stndg Com Dio Connecticut Hartford CT 1989-1992; Vic S Mk's Ch Waterbury CT 1988-1991; Vic Trin Ch Litchfield CT 1988-1991; R Trin Epis Ch Trumbull CT 1981-1988; Vic S Jn The Evang Yalesville CT 1979-1981; Asst S Paul's Ch Wallingford CT 1979-1981; Cur Ch Of The H Trin Middletown CT 1976-1979. Auth, "Bk Revs," *LivCh*, LivCh, 2001; Auth, "Remembering Henri Nouwen," *LivCh*, LivCh, 2000; Auth, "The Legacy of Roland Allen," *Missiology for the 21st Century*, GTF, 1998; Auth, "Getting Little at Christmas," *LivCh*, LivCh, 1998; Auth, "The

Ch's Responsibility to Homosexual Persons," *Karatana Papers*, Karatana, Inc, 1981. ACPE 1998-2003; Karatana Cmnty 1972; Theol of Institutions Proj (STW) 1998-2008. Fell GTF 1998; Fell Rockefeller Brothers Fndt 1970. mandctessman@aol.com

TESTA, Dennis Arthur (Md) 302 Homewood Rd, Linthicum MD 21090 B Laurelton,NY 1/4/1945 s Vincent Joseph Testa & Rosalie. BA Adams St Coll 1969; MDiv GTS 1973. D 6/16/1973 P 9/22/1973 Bp Jonathan Goodhue Sherman. m 8/23/1969 Margaret Friberg c 2. S Alb's Epis Ch Glen Burnie MD 1981-2004; Copley Par: The Ch Of The Resurr Joppa MD 1978-1981; S Alb's Ch Manistique MI 1974-1977; S Jn's Ch Munising MI 1974-1977. longdeb2003@yahoo.com

TESTER, Helen Whitener (Miss) 4400 King Road, Meridian MS 39305 **R The Epis Ch Of The Medtr Meridian MS 2007-** B Hickory NC 5/6/1950 d Thomas Manly Whitener & Sophie Bonham. BA Lenoir-Rhyne Coll 1973; MA Appalachian St U 1983; Doctor of Mnstry VTS 2011. D 1/15/2000 Bp Alfred Clark Marble Jr P 1/22/2005 Bp Duncan Montgomery Gray III. m 6/1/1996 Charles K(amper) Floyd c 2. D H Trin Ch Crystal Sprg MS 2002-2006. Mississippi Soc For Lic Mar & Fam Therapists 2000. Included In "50 Leading Bus Wmn For 2000" Mississippi Bus Intl 2000. helentester@msn.org

TESTIN, Joan M (Eas) 101 N Cross St, Chestertown MD 21620 **Cur Emm Epis Ch Chestertown MD 2010-** B Pittsburgh PA 8/14/1961 d Robert F Testin & Jeanette R. BA W&M 1983; Cert VTS 2009; MDiv Luth TS 2010. D 6/12/2010 P 12/18/2010 Bp James Joseph Shand. vicarjoan@aol.com

TETER, Jane Esther (Be) 1728 Butztown Rd Apt A4, Bethlehem PA 18017 B Schenectady NY 10/20/1937 d Thomas James Ballantyne & Esther Emma. Wm Smith 1956; Cert Moravian TS 1983; Cert Moravian TS 1985. D 9/7/1983 P 11/1/1984 Bp James Michael Mark Dyer. c 3. Vic S Brigid's Ch Nazareth PA 1995-2001; Cn Dio Bethlehem Bethlehem PA 1994-2009; The Welcome Place Bethlehem PA 1993; Int Chr Ch Stroudsburg PA 1991-1992; Asst Trin Ch Bethlehem PA 1987-1990; Int S Marg's Ch Emmaus PA 1984-1985; Asst S Marg's Ch Emmaus PA 1983-1984. jteter@diobeth.org

TETRAULT, David Joseph (SVa) 22501 Cypress Point Road, Williamsburg VA 23185 B Kankakee IL 3/19/1941 s Omer Frederick Tetrault & Eloise Emma. BA S Jos Rensselaer IN 1962; DMin S Mary U Baltimore MD 1986. D 6/23/1973 Bp William Foreman Creighton P 12/23/1973 Bp David Shepherd Rose. m 10/11/1977 Georgian Ann Prescott c 2. Volntr Pstr Care Mnstry Advsr Bruton Par Williamsburg VA 1987-1996; Dio Virginia Richmond VA 1983-1987; Gr Ch Newport News VA 1982; S Paul's Ch Richmond VA 1977-1980; Asst Bruton Par Williamsburg VA 1973-1977. Epis Conf of the Deaf of the Epis Ch in the 1977-1987. bigshowrev@aol.com

TETZ, William Edward (Mich) No address on file. B Pittsburgh PA 8/1/1944 s Edward Tetz & Elizabeth Tez. BA Hillsdale Coll; MDiv Hur. D 6/15/1974 P 3/15/1975 Bp H Coleman McGehee Jr. m 6/26/1964 Kathleen Tetz c 2.

THABET, David George (Va) 1305 15th St, Huntington WV 25701 B Spencer WV 1/14/1938 s George Nimmer Thabet & Martha Columbia. LTh Epis TS In Kentucky 1968. D 6/11/1968 P 12/18/1968 Bp Wilburn Camrock Campbell. m 11/17/1957 Edna L Diamond c 3. All SS Ch Charleston WV 2001-2006; R Chr Epis Ch Spotsylvania VA 1991-1999; R S Ptr's Ch Huntington WV 1986-1991; R Trin Ch Moundsville WV 1973-1985; R H Trin Ch Logan WV 1968-1973. "Nueden," Xulon Press, 2008. nueden1@yahoo.com

THACKER II, James Robert (SwVa) 207 Lookout Point Dr., Osprey FL 34229 B Buckhannon WV 11/15/1940 s James Robert Thacker & Katherine Roberta. BA W Virginia St U 1963; BD Nash 1966; MSW CUA 1976. D 6/3/1966 P 12/1/1966 Bp Wilburn Camrock Campbell. m 8/15/1970 Maria Martin c 2. Chr Epis Ch Roanoke VA 1985-1992; R Gr Memi Ch Lynchburg VA 1979-1985; S Mk's Ch Westhampton Bch NY 1977-1978; S Andr's-On-The-Mt Harpers Ferry WV 1972-1977; R S Lk's Ch Wheeling WV 1968-1971; R S Paul's Ch Martins Ferry OH 1968-1971; R Trin Ch Bellaire OH 1968-1971. robertthacker@ymail.com

THADEN, Timothy Robert (Colo) 780 Devinney Ct, Golden CO 80401 **Ecum Off Dio Colorado Denver CO 2009-; Exec Com, Colorado Coun of Ch Dio Colorado Denver CO 2009-; R Ch Of S Jn Chrys Golden CO 2006-** B Denver CO 10/31/1952 s Robert T Thaden & Imogene I. AA Front Range Cmnty Coll 1997; BA Metropltn St Coll of Denver 1999; MDiv Epis TS of The SW 2004. D 6/12/2004 P 12/18/2004 Bp Robert John O'Neill. m 9/17/1983 Katherine H Hawkins c 3. Vic Trin Ch Kremmling CO 2004-2006. trthaden@msn.com

THAMES, David Blake (Tex) 4419 Taney Ave No 202, Alexandria VA 22304 B San Antonio TX 11/15/1962 s Clendon Horton Thames & Mary Nell. BS U of Texas 1985; MDiv VTS 1992; MS Duquesne U 2011. D 6/27/1992 P 2/1/1993 Bp Maurice Manuel Benitez. m 6/1/1984 Elizabeth Louise Frank. R S Mk's Ch Beaumont TX 2000-2002; S Mary's Epis Ch Cypress TX 1994-1996; Asst R S Paul's Ch Waco TX 1992-1994. Sead. DTHAMES2009@YAHOO.COM

THARAKAN, Angeline H (Ark) 501 S Phoenix Ave, Russellville AR 72801 B IL 1/11/1967 d Leslie G Bramley & Alice Joy. Sewanee TS; BS IL St U 1989; MDiv Estrn Bapt TS 1996. D 10/16/2010 P 5/7/2011 Bp Larry R Benfield. m 6/8/2003 Jos Tharakan c 2. angi@thanku.org

THARAKAN, Jos (Ark) 158 Dawn Cir., Russellville AR 72802 **Mem of Exec Coun Dio Arkansas Little Rock AR 2009-2012; Mem of COM Dio Arkansas Little Rock AR 2008-2014; R All SS Epis Ch Russellville AR 2007-** B Nemmini India 5/30/1964 s Chakkunni Tharakan & Rosy. BA U Of Delhi 1988; BA Calv Philos Coll 1991; MDiv St Fran Theol 1995; BEd U Of Bhopal 1996. Rec from Roman Catholic 7/18/2006 Bp Larry Earl Maze. m 6/8/2003 Angeline H Bramley c 2. Chapl Chr Ch Mena AR 2006-2007; Dio Arkansas Little Rock AR 2006-2007. fatherjos@gmail.com

THAYER, Andrew Richard (WTex) 446 Irvington Dr, San Antonio TX 78209 B Austin TX 11/4/1968 s Gilbert Richard Thayer & Ann E. BFA U of Texas; MDiv STUSo 2004. D 6/26/2004 P 1/6/2005 Bp James Edward Folts. m 6/4/1994 Kelsey Elaine Thayer c 2. S Barth's Ch Corpus Christi TX 2006-2009; S Mk's Epis Ch San Antonio TX 2004-2006. Optime Merens Sewanee 2004. kelsey2422@me.com

THAYER JR, Charles Cleveland (FdL) 1409 W Dow Rummel St, Apt 114, Sioux Falls SD 57104 B Abingdon VA 7/12/1931 s Charles Cleveland Thayer & Margaret Lee. BA Emory & Henry Coll 1953; MDiv Drew U 1956; Nash 1964; U MN 1971. D 12/17/1958 P 12/21/1959 Bp William Henry Marmion. m 6/29/1956 Evelyn Brush c 1. R S Aug's Epis Ch Rhinelander WI 1981-1987; R S Mart's Epis Ch Fairmont MN 1972-1981; Gd Shpd Blue Earth MN 1972-1976; Chapl The Epis Cathd Of Our Merc Sav Faribault MN 1969-1972; Sub-Dn Cathd Ch Of S Mk Minneapolis MN 1965-1969; S Mk's Ch St Paul VA 1961-1965; Cur S Jn's Ch Roanoke VA 1957-1961. Angl Soc; Anglicans for Life; Assoc. Sis of H Nativ; CCU; Confraternal Ord of S Ben; CBS; Curs; Ord of St. Vinc; P Assoc. Shrine of Our Lady; Soc. King Chas Mtyr; SocMary. Who's Who Rel 1977. ettoo@fio.midco.net

THAYER, Evan Lynch (Mass) 15 Elko St # 2135, Brighton MA 02135 **S Aug And S Mart Ch Boston MA 2005-** B Baton Rouge LA 4/12/1961 BA LSU. D 6/7/2003 P 6/5/2004 Bp M(arvil) Thomas Shaw III.

THAYER II, Frederick William (SanD) 16275 Pomerado Rd, Poway CA 92064 **Mem Corp of EDSD Dio San Diego San Diego CA 2010-; R S Barth's Epis Ch Poway CA 2006-** B Quincy MA 8/16/1949 s Donald William Thayer & Corinne Pratt. BA Colg 1971; MDiv EDS 1975. D 6/10/1975 Bp John Melville Burgess P 5/2/1976 Bp Robert Rae Spears Jr. m 8/31/1974 Ann Marie Furtek. Mem Epis Cmnty Serv Bd Dio San Diego San Diego CA 2008-2010; Pres Stndg Com Dio Missouri S Louis MO 2004-2005; Dep to GC Dio Missouri S Louis MO 2001-2004; VP Corp of EDMO Dio Missouri S Louis MO 2001-2004; R Calv Ch Columbia MO 1998-2006; Mem Epis Hlth Serv Bd Dio Long Island Garden City NY 1988-1998; R S Lk's Ch Forest Hills NY 1986-1998; R S Lk's Ch Sea Cliff NY 1980-1986; S Ann's Ch Sayville NY 1977-1980; Asst The Ch Of The Epiph Rochester NY 1975-1977. fthayer2@earthlink.net

THAYER, Steven Allen (NJ) Po Box 440, Jamison PA 18929 B Berlin NH 12/4/1948 s Wendall Carroll Thayer & Mary Elizabeth. BA Iowa Wesleyan Coll 1970; MDiv PDS 1973. D 4/28/1973 Bp Alfred L Banyard P 10/27/1973 Bp Albert Wiencke Van Duzer. Cur S Jn's Ch Somerville NJ 1973-1975.

THEBEAU, Duane Howard (NCal) 468 Winding Wood Way, Sebastopol CA 95472 B San Pedro CA 1/24/1934 s Howard Louis Thebeau & Blanche Arlene. BA Pacific CA 1955; MDiv CDSP 1959; PhD Cg TS 1971. D 6/22/1959 P 2/1/1960 Bp Francis E I Bloy. m 11/15/1986 Anne Gray c 1. Asst S Paul's Ch Healdsburg CA 1999; S Steph's Epis Ch Sebastopol CA 1990-1999; R S Lk's Ch Bakersfield CA 1987-1990; R S Anne's Epis Ch Oceanside CA 1968-1986; Vic S Jn's Ch Indio CA 1961-1966. Auth, "Chrsnty Today". ANNEG@pacbell.net

THEODORE, Margaret Bessie (Alb) P.O. BOX 446, Potsdam NY 13676 **D S Phil's Ch Norwood NY 2007-; D Trin Ch Potsdam NY 2003-** B Watertown NY 4/7/1941 d Peter John Boyesen & Bessie. BS SUNY at Oswego 1966. D 6/29/2003 Bp Daniel William Herzog. m 6/25/1966 Chris James Theodore c 4. DOK 2003; OSL'S 1991. omorphia@twcny.rr.com

THEODORE, Pamela Hillis (Dal) 6055 Walnut Hill Cir, Dallas TX 75230 **S Mich And All Ang Ch Dallas TX 2009-** B Little Rock AR 6/29/1946 d Charles Raymond Hillis & Polly. BS SMU 1978; MDiv SMU 1997. D 6/27/1998 P 5/23/1999 Bp James Monte Stanton. m 7/3/1973 Douglas Brent Theodore. Asst R S Mich And All Ang Ch Dallas TX 1999-2004. ptheo@airmail.net

✠ **THEUNER, Rt Rev Douglas Edwin** (NH) 5 Wildemere Ter, Concord NH 03301 B New York NY 11/15/1938 s Alfred Edwin Kipp Theuner & Grace Elizabeth. BA Coll of Wooster 1960; BD Bex 1962; MA U of Connecticut 1968. D 6/9/1962 P 12/22/1962 Bp Nelson Marigold Burroughs Con 4/19/1986 for NH. m 5/16/1959 Jane Lois Szuhany. Bp Dio New Hampshire Concord NH 1986-2004; R S Jn's Ch Stamford CT 1974-1986; R S Paul's Epis Ch Willimantic CT 1968-1974; Vic S Geo's Ch Bolton CT 1965-1968; Cur S Ptr's Ch Ashtabula OH 1962-1965. AEC, Bd 1993-2008; Colleges & Universities of the Angligan Cmnty, Bd 1993-2008. DD Bex 2003; Doctor of Human Letters Cuttington Coll 2002. corvusg@gmail.com

THEUS SR, James Graves (WLa) 6291 Old Baton Rouge Hwy, Alexandria LA 71302 B Monroe LA 5/7/1944 s John Crawford Theus & Louise Graves. BA LSU; MDiv STUSo 1967. D 6/23/1970 P 4/1/1971 Bp Iveson Batchelor Noland. m 12/29/1982 Caroline Theus c 3. Ch Of The Gd Shpd Cashiers NC 2006; Ch Of The Gd Shpd Cashiers NC 2005; Ch Of The Incarn Highlands NC 2005; Ch Of The Gd Shpd Cashiers NC 2004; Ch Of The Incarn Highlands NC 2002-2004; Ch Of The Gd Shpd Cashiers NC 1998-2003; Ch Of The Incarn Highlands NC 1998-2002; Calv Ch Bunkie LA 1991-2007; S Jn's Ch Oakdale LA 1983-1986; R S Tim's Ch Alexandria LA 1974-1983; Vic Ch Of The Incarn Amite LA 1971-1974; Cur Ch Of The Redeem Ruston LA 1970-1971. jgtheus@att.net

THEW, Richard H (EO) Po Box 125, Cove OR 97824 B Long Beach CA 4/25/1940 s Henry Prior Thew & Imogene. Oregon Tech Inst 1959; BA E Oregon U 1965; MDiv EDS 1970. D 8/12/1970 P 8/1/1971 Bp William Benjamin Spofford. m 8/31/1968 Kathy Jane Jones c 1. Asst S Ptr's Ch La Grande OR 1981-2002; Dio Estrn Oregon The Dalles OR 1970-1982; Vic S Thos Ch Canyon City OR 1970-1975. thewre@coveoregon.com

THEW FORRESTER, Kevin G (NMich) 402 Harrison St, Marquette MI 49855 **Mnstry Dvlp S Jn's Ch Negaunee MI 2008-; S Paul's Ch Marquette MI 2007-; S Andr's Ch Lexington KY 2000-** B Monroe MI 12/12/1957 s Joseph Lee Forrester & Patricia Agnes. BA U of St. Thos 1980; MA CUA 1984; PhD CUA 1992; MA CDSP 1993. D 6/19/1993 Bp R(aymond) Stewart Wood Jr P 5/27/1994 Bp Robert Louis Ladehoff. m 11/5/1984 Rise Fay Thew c 2. Coord. Min. Dev. Dio Nthrn Michigan Marquette MI 2001-2006; Dio Estrn Oregon The Dalles OR 1997-2001; Co Mssnr S Alb's Epis Ch Redmond OR 1997-2001; Co Mssnr S Andr's Epis Ch Prineville OR 1997-2001; Cleric S Mk's Epis and Gd Shpd Luth Madras OR 1997-2001; Dio Oregon Portland OR 1996-1997; Vic Four Winds Cmnty Portland OR 1995-1998; S Mich And All Ang Ch Portland OR 1993-1997. Auth, "My Heart is a Raging Volcano of Love for You," LeaderResources, 2011; Auth, "Holding Beauty in My Soul's Arms," LeaderResources, 2011; Auth, "I Have Called You Friends," Ch Pub, 2003; Auth, "Ldrshp And Mnstry Within A Cmnty Of Equals," InterCultural Mnstry Dvlpmt, 1997. kevingtf@gmail.com

THEW FORRESTER, Rise Fay (NMich) 402 Harrison St, Marquette MI 49855 **Mnstry Dvlp So Cntrl Reg Manistique MI 2011-** B Hillsboro OR 4/6/1964 d Henry William Thew & Ann Louise. BS U of Oregon 1986; MDiv CDSP 1993. D 6/10/1993 P 1/22/1994 Bp Robert Louis Ladehoff. m 11/5/1984 Kevin G Thew Forrester c 2. Mssnr Ch Of S Jas The Less Harvey MI 2001-2003; Mssnr S Thos Ch Canyon City OR 2000-2001; Mssnr Dio Estrn Oregon The Dalles OR 1997-2001; Co-Mssnr S Alb's Epis Ch Redmond OR 1997-2001; Co-Mssnr S Andr's Epis Ch Prineville OR 1997-2001; Co-Mssnr S Mk's Epis and Gd Shpd Luth Madras OR 1997-2001; Dio Oregon Portland OR 1994-1997; Vic S Andr's Ch Portland OR 1994-1997; Chapl Legacy Gd Samar Hosp Portland OR 1993-1994; Assoc S Jn The Evang Ch Milwaukie OR 1993-1994. risetf@gmail.com

THIBODAUX, Louise Ruprecht (Ala) 4261 Old Leeds Rd, Mountain Brk AL 35213 **D Dio Alabama Birmingham AL 2005-** B New York NY 9/22/1944 BA Mt Holyoke Coll 1966; MA USC 1969; PhD U of Alabama 2002. D 11/2/2002 Bp Marc Handley Andrus. m 6/23/1973 Paul Thibodaux. yellowboots@charter.net

THIBODEAUX, James Lawrence (Oly) 1610 S King St, Washington MD 98144 **R St Ptr's Epis Par Seattle WA 2008-** B Los Gatos CA 5/21/1977 s James Delano Thibodeaux & Judy Dawn. BA Westmont Coll 2000; MDiv The Luth TS at Philadelphia 2006; STM The GTS 2007. D 3/25/2007 Bp Paul Victor Marshall P 5/18/2008 Bp Bavi Rivera. m 7/28/2001 Annaka Gustafson Gustafson Annaka Alane. jthibodo@yahoo.com

THIEL, Spencer Edwin (Chi) 12407 S 82nd Ave, Palos Park IL 60464 **P-in-c S Chris's Ch Crown Point IN 2002-** B Oak Park IL 10/16/1940 s Edwin Jacob Oscar Thiel & Margaret Hilma. BA NWU 1962; STM GTS 1965; STM SWTS 1970. D 6/12/1965 Bp Gerald Francis Burrill P 12/18/1965 Bp James Winchester Montgomery. S Jos's And S Aid's Ch Blue Island IL 1970-2001; Cur Trin Ch Highland Pk IL 1967-1970; Cur S Greg's Epis Ch Deerfield IL 1965-1967. Hisp Affrs Cmsn; Int Mnstry Ntwk 2000; Spanish-Spkng Priests Assn.

THIELE, William Charles (Nwk) 215 Lafayette Ave., Passaic NJ 07055 **P-in-c S Jn's Ch Passaic NJ 2007-** B Detroit MI 3/21/1942 s Richard Robert Thiele & Clara. BS Pur 1965; MDiv GTS 2004. D 6/12/2004 P 12/19/2004 Bp George Edward Councell. m 4/26/1986 Marilyn M Schaefer c 3. Cur S Paul's Epis Ch Westfield NJ 2004-2006. frthiele@gmail.com

THIERING, Barry Bernard (WTex) 2404 W Riviera Dr, Cedar Park TX 78613 B Sydney NSW AU 10/1/1930 s Bernard Lawrence Thiering & Pearl Victoria. ThL Moore Theol Coll, Sydney 1954; BA U of Sydney 1954; Dplma RE Melbourne Coll of Div 1956; MA U of Sydney 1967; DMin SFTS 1983. Trans from Anglican Church Of Australia 12/1/1991 Bp John Herbert MacNaughton. m 9/5/1981 Linda Carol Wukasch c 5. Emm Epis Ch Lockhart TX 1992-2000; S Eliz's Epis Ch Buda TX 1992-1994. Auth, *The Bk of Howlers*, Kangaroo Press, 1985; Auth, *Australian Ch*, Ure Smith, 1979; Auth and Co-Ed, *Towards Understanding (series of textbooks)*, Westbooks, 1974; Co-Auth, *Some Trust in Chariots*, Westbooks, 1973; Auth, *A Guide to Me & You*, Fam Life Mvmt of Australia, 1967. Mem of the Australian Coll of Educ 1988; Mem of the Australian Coll of Educ 1968. thiering@sbcglobal.net

THIGPEN III, William McCord (At) 5152 Patriot Dr, Stone Mountain GA 30087 **R S Barth's Epis Ch Atlanta GA 2002-** B Atlanta GA 8/16/1955 s William McCord Thigpen & Doris Mae. BS Oral Roberts U 1978; BA Oral Roberts U 1978; MDiv GTS 1983. D 6/25/1983 Bp Gerald Nicholas McAllister P 5/26/1984 Bp William Jackson Cox. m 5/26/1979 John Lavier c 3. R Trin Epis Par Los Angeles CA 1990-2002; S Jas' Sch Los Angeles CA 1990-1991; Asst R S Jas Par Los Angeles CA 1988-1990; Trin Ch Tulsa OK 1983-1988. Auth, "Let your heart sing!," *Pathways*, Dio Atlanta, 2008; Auth, "Out in Sprt," *Edge Sprtlty Column*, Edge mag, 1994. mac@stbartsatlanta.org

THIM, Paul Russell (At) 697 Densley Dr., Decatur GA 30033 B New Haven CT 12/30/1946 s John Raymond Thim & Mary Antoinette. BA Swarthmore Coll 1968; MDiv Candler TS Emory U 1972. D 10/23/1974 P 6/2/1975 Bp Bennett Jones Sims. m 1/24/1981 Alexandra V Thim c 2. Cov Cmnty Inc Atlanta GA 2004-2006; Assoc R - Chr Soc Mnstrs All SS Epis Ch Atlanta GA 1997-2004; S Barth's Epis Ch Atlanta GA 1996-2007; S Lk's Epis Ch Atlanta GA 1995-1997; St Lukes Trng & Coun.Ctr Atlanta GA 1995-1997; Epis Ch Of The H Fam Jasper GA 1994; Ch Of The Ascen Cartersville GA 1992-1994; Dio Wstrn Massachusetts Springfield MA 1987-1992; R S Jn's Ch Worcester MA 1987-1992; P S Augustines Ch S Louis MO 1981-1987; R S Paul's Ch S Louis MO 1981-1987; Dio Missouri S Louis MO 1981-1982; Asst All SS Epis Ch Atlanta GA 1974-1981. pthim@comcast.net

THOBER, Ellie Thober (Neb) 4718 18th St, Columbus NE 68601 **Ins Com Dio Nebraska Omaha NE 2010-; R Gr Ch Par -Epis Columbus NE 2010-; Safeguarding God's Chld Trnr Dio Nebraska Omaha NE 2004-** B San Pedro CA 11/28/1948 d Melvin F Schlachter & Mildred C. Dplma in Nrsng Bp Clarkson Sch Of Nrsng 1969; BA Doane Coll 1990; MDiv VTS 2004. D 6/18/2004 P 12/19/2004 Bp Joe Goodwin Burnett. m 9/19/1970 Robert Thober c 3. New Bp Transition Com Dio Nebraska Omaha NE 2010-2011; Exec Cmsn Dio Nebraska Omaha NE 2007-2010; R Ch Of Our Sav No Platte NE 2006-2010; Cur S Andr's Ch Omaha NE 2004-2006; Safe Chld Guidelines T/F Dio Nebraska Omaha NE 2004-2005. rthober@neb.rr.com

THOENI, Thomas Andrew (SwFla) 302 Carey St, Plant City FL 33563 **R S Ptr's Ch Plant City FL 2003-** B Ocala FL 7/4/1962 s John Paul Thoeni & Martha JoAnn. BD U of Florida 1988; MDiv SWTS 1994. D 6/18/1994 P 12/21/1994 Bp Stephen Hays Jecko. m 12/28/1996 Quincey B Thoeni c 2. Asst Chr Ch Par Pensacola FL 1997-2003; S Paul's Ch Albany GA 1994-1997. therector@verizon.net

THOM, Ashley Jane Squier (Chi) 1938 W Farwell Ave, Chicago IL 60626 B Burlington VT 8/14/1965 d Kenley Dean Squier & Susan. BA Stan 1988; MDiv Harvard DS 1993; CAS Nash 1998. D 6/10/1998 P 12/17/1998 Bp Roger John White. m 7/31/1993 Winfield Scott Thom. P All SS Epis Ch Chicago IL 2000-2002; Dio Milwaukee Milwaukee WI 1998; Cur Trin Ch Janesville WI 1998. 4thoms@sbcglobal.net

✠ **THOM, Rt Rev Brian James** (Ida) 1858 W. Judith Lane, Boise ID 83705 **Bp Dio Idaho Boise ID 2008-** B Portland OR 12/1/1955 s Arnold Kirk Thom & Rose Marie. BS OR SU 1980; MDiv CDSP 1987. D 6/24/1987 P 3/25/1988 Bp Robert Louis Ladehoff Con 10/11/2008 for Ida. m 1/30/2010 Ardele Hanson c 2. R Ch Of The Ascen Twin Falls ID 1991-2008; Asst R S Marg's Epis Ch Palm Desert CA 1989-1991; Cur Epis Par Of S Jn The Bapt Portland OR 1987-1989. bthom@idahodiocese.org

THOM, David Lewis (Az) 540 Atchison Lane, Wickenburg AZ 85390 B Chicago IL 9/25/1944 s Franklin William Thom & Annabelle Elizabeth. Maryknoll TS 1965; BA Seattle U 1966; Arizona St U 1982; CAS STUSo 1999; STM STUSo 2004. Rec from Roman Catholic 11/24/1996 as Deacon Bp Bertram Nelson Herlong. m 4/1/1991 Mary Gadarowski c 4. S Alb's Epis Ch Wickenburg AZ 2006-2008; Ch Of The Adv Sun City W AZ 2005; R Ch Of The Epiph Tunica MS 1999-2004; D S Clem's Epis Ch Clemmons NC 1998-1999; S Jn's Epis Ch Mt Juliet TN 1997-1998; The Ch Of The Epiph Lebanon TN 1997-1998; S Phil's Ch Nashville TN 1997. dlthom@att.net

THOM, Kenneth Stow (Eas) 3849 Sirman Dr, Snow Hill MD 21863 B Philadelphia PA 7/28/1937 s William John Angus Thom & Catherine Stow. BSEE Drexel U 1960; MDiv VTS 2001. D 5/19/2001 Bp Martin Gough Townsend P 11/18/2001 Bp Charles Lindsay Longest. m 7/4/1958 Arlene McElhaney c 2. P-in-c All Hallow's Ch Snow Hill MD 2003-2009; Asst R Ch Of S Paul's By The Sea Ocean City MD 2001-2002. ksthom@gmail.com

THOMAS, Adam Parsons (Mass) 16 Highland Ave, Cohasset MA 02025 **Asst S Steph's Ch Cohasset MA 2010-** B Portland ME 1/12/1983 s William Carl Thomas & Edna Marie. BA U So 2005; MDiv The Prot Epis TS 2008. D 12/15/2007 P 6/14/2008 Bp William Michie Klusmeyer. m 2/12/2011 Leah Thomas. Trin Epis Ch Martinsburg WV 2008-2010. Auth, "Digital Disciple," Abingdon Press, 2011. therev.adamthomas@gmail.com

THOMAS, Allisyn (SanD) St. Paul's Cathedral, 2728 Sixth Avenue, San Diego CA 92103 **Cn Cathd Ch Of S Paul San Diego CA 2002-** B Berkeley CA 12/

T

7/1953 d Geoffrey Hyde Thomas & Lorna Jean. BA Wstrn St U Coll of Law 1982; JD Wstrn St U Coll of Law 1982; ETSBH 1996; MDiv GTS 2000. D 6/10/2000 P 12/14/2000 Bp Gethin Benwil Hughes. m 12/22/1999 John A Thomas. Assoc Pstr S Jn's Epis Ch Chula Vista CA 2000-2002. Juris Prudence Awd Wstrn St U Coll of Law. thomasa@saintpaulcathedral.org

THOMAS JR, A(rthur) Robert (Ak) Po Box 1872, Seward AK 99664 B Seattle WA 4/7/1957 s Arthur R Thomas & Joanne. BA Chapman U 1993; MA Salve Regina U 2000; MDiv Vancouver TS 2006. D 12/21/1999 Bp Drexel Gomez P 8/6/2000 Bp Mark Lawrence Mac Donald. R S Ptr's Ch Seward AK 2000-2008. episcopalpadre@gmail.com

THOMAS, Benjamin Randall (WK) 175 9th Ave Apt 225, New York NY 10011 **Chr Cathd Salina KS 2010-** B 9/13/1974 s Bobby Lee Thomas & Rhonda Jo. BA/BS U of Oklahoma 1997; MA Cu- Boulder Boulder CO 2000; MDiv GTS NY NY 2007. D 6/9/2007 P 12/8/2007 Bp Robert John O'Neill. m 3/22/2002 Holly Krech c 4. Gr Epis Ch New York NY 2008-2010. fatherbenjamin@christcathedral.net

THOMAS, Bethany Ann (Colo) 1221 Illinois St. Apt 2A, Golden CO 80401 **D Calv Ch Golden CO 1989-** B Lansing MI 8/13/1950 d William Curtis Baker & Beverly Rose. AA Grand Rapids Cmnty Coll 1970; BA Wstrn Michigan U 1972; U MI 1975; S Thos Sem 1987. D 9/21/1988 Bp William Harvey Wolfrum P. m 2/23/1974 Steven Rowe Thomas c 4. deacon.bethany@calvarygolden.net

THOMAS, Cheeramattathu John (Tex) 301 Eagle Lakes Dr, Friendswood TX 77546 **Asst R S Chris's Ch League City TX 1998-** B Punnaveli Kerala IN 8/25/1925 s Cheeramattathu John Itty & Mariam Abraham. BA S Berchmans Coll Changanacherry IN 1946; BD Govt Tchr's Coll 1949; BD Untd Theol Coll Bangalore IN 1955; MA Andover Newton TS 1966. Trans from Church Of England 8/1/1996 Bp Claude Edward Payne. m 6/9/1955 Mary Abraham. Mssy S Steph's Ch Liberty TX 1997-1998; P S Thos Ch Houston TX 1988-1989. Auth, "The Mssy Task Of Our Csi Members In No Amer," Csi Coun Of No Amer, 1998; Auth, "A Short Hist Of The First Hundred Years Of The Par Ch Of S Jn The Evang Great Sutton 1879-1979," Dio Chester, 1979; Auth, "Some Thoughts On Adv And Christmas," Eastham Par Ch, 1972.

THOMAS, David Powers (Pa) 38 Penns Greene Dr, West Grove PA 19390 **Died 12/16/2009** B Brattleboro VT 5/2/1941 s Edger Gordon Thomas & Lucile E. BA Amer Intl Coll 1963; LTh SWTS 1967. D 6/10/1967 Bp Harvey D Butterfield P 12/21/1967 Bp Russell T Rauscher. c 2. Ed, *Handbook for Ch Growth*, Dio PA. Hon Cn S Stephens Cathd Harrisburg PA 1991; Preaching Awd SWTS Evanston IL 1967. tdpt1227@aol.com

THOMAS, David R (Nwk) 7740 LIGUTHOUSE COVE DR., PORT HOPE MI 48468 **P-in-c S Paul's Epis Ch Bad Axe MI 2010-** B Highland Park MI 5/16/1942 s Evan Rhys Thomas & Monima Isabel. BA Detroit Inst of Tech 1965; S Dav's Coll Lampeter GB 1966; MDiv CDSP 1968; MA Montclair St U 1981; EDS Seton Hall U 1984. D 6/29/1968 Bp Archie H Crowley P 3/1/1969 Bp Richard S M Emrich. m 7/28/1979 Daphne Florence Naparlo c 4. Supply P Chr Ch Harrison NJ 2000-2010; R Calv Ch Tamaqua PA 1970-1972; R Trin And S Phil's Epis Ch Lansford PA 1970-1972; Vic S Anne's Epis Ch Trexlertown PA 1969-1970; Cur The Ch Of The Redeem Southfield MI 1968-1969. frdave571@comcast.net

THOMAS, Douglas Earl (WTex) 2722 Old Ranch Rd, San Antonio TX 78217 B Corpus Christi TX 9/5/1944 s Jesse Earl Thomas & Gertrude Ellen. BA Texas A&M U, Kingsville 1971; MDiv Epis TS of The SW 1974. D 6/6/1974 Bp Richard Earl Dicus P 12/7/1974 Bp Harold Cornelius Gosnell. m 2/14/1970 Pamela Van Winkle c 1. Epis Ch Of The Mssh Gonzales TX 1993-1995; Gr Ch Port Lavaca TX 1988-1993; S Geo Ch San Antonio TX 1985-1988; S Chris's By The Sea Portland TX 1978-1985; H Comf Sinton TX 1978-1980; S Lk's Epis Ch San Antonio TX 1976-1978; Ch Of The Annunc Luling TX 1974-1976. dthomas1225@hotmail.com

THOMAS JR, Frederick S (Md) 707 Park Ave, Baltimore MD 21201 **Asst Gr And S Ptr's Ch Baltimore MD 1977-** B Erwin NC 8/25/1948 s Fredrick Shepherd Thomas & Elizabeth Whitney. MDiv GTS; BA U So. D 5/31/1973 Bp Addison Hosea P 12/1/1973 Bp David Keller Leighton Sr. Asst S Mich's Ch New York NY 1975-1976; Asst Mt Calv Ch Baltimore MD 1973-1975. CCU, ECM, Cath League, Epis Syn Amer.

THOMAS, Howard Francis (O) 9640 Sylvania Metamora Rd, Sylvania OH 43560 **Died 12/9/2009** B Marion OH 11/13/1921 s James Nelson Thomas & Barbara. BA Baldwin-Wallace Coll 1954; Bex 1957; Med Bowling Green St U 1971. D 5/31/1957 Bp Nelson Marigold Burroughs P 12/15/1957 Bp Beverley D Tucker. c 1.

THOMAS, Humbert Anderson (WMass) 556 Central St Lot 160, Leominster MA 01453 **Asst S Mk's Ch Leominster MA 2002-** B Dracut MA 12/22/1919 s Harry Washburn Thomas & Beulah Isabelle. Bos 1944; Boston Coll 1950; U So 1974; Assumption Coll 1990. D 6/28/1976 Bp Alexander Doig Stewart. m 4/19/1940 Dorothy Nolan c 3. Asst Ch Of The Gd Shpd Fitchburg MA 1998-2000; Vic Chr Ch So Barre MA 1982-1995. Ord of S Lk 1977-1992. Vol of the Year Nature Coast Vol Cntr 2001.

THOMAS, Jaime Alfredo (Dal) P.O. Box 15, Fort Ord CA 93941 B Consuelo DO 7/23/1943 s John R Thomas & Helena. BA Inter Amer U of Puerto Rico 1969; MDiv ETSC 1974. D 8/18/1974 Bp Telesforo A Isaac P 6/1/1977 Bp Francisco Reus-Froylan. c 2. Asst S Paul's Epis Ch Salinas CA 1999-2003; Off Of Bsh For ArmdF New York NY 1978-1993; Dio The Dominican Republic (Iglesia Epis Dominicana) Santo Domingo DO 1974-1976.

THOMAS JR, James Morris (ECR) 18402 Yale Court, Somoma CA 95476 B Sedalia MO 9/12/1940 s James Morris Thomas & Thelma Juanita. BS Drury U 1963; MS Estrn Washington U 1970; PhD Oklahoma St U 1973; MDiv VTS 2001. D 6/23/2001 Bp Robert Manning Moody P 1/31/2002 Bp Richard Lester Shimpfky. m 1/1/1981 Seara Elizabeth Sheppard c 2. S Andr's Ch Saratoga CA 2004-2010; Dio El Camino Real Monterey CA 2002-2003; S Tim's Epis Ch Mtn View CA 2001. "The Seven Steps to Personal Power: Creating Opportunities Within," Hlth Cmncatn, Inc., 1993; "arts & Bk chapters re. Mntl Hlth issues". jmthomasca@yahoo.com

THOMAS, John Alfred (Va) 3800 Powell Ln Apt 813, Falls Church VA 22041 B Dubuque IA 7/4/1933 s Gailen Peter Thomas & Martha. MA Aquinas Inst of Theol 1959; MA Aquinas Inst of Theol 1960; STD U Of S Thos Rome It 1962. Rec from Roman Catholic 5/13/1976 as Deacon Bp Robert Bruce Hall. m 9/7/1968 Helene C Garrett. Int Ch Of The H Cross Dunn Loring VA 1999-2001; Asst S Jas' Epis Ch Warrenton VA 1991-1997; Asst S Alb's Epis Ch Annandale VA 1976-1991. Ed, "Reconsiderations". CHS 1983. angelicum@aol.com

THOMAS, John Harvey (Mass) Po Box 536, Sandwich MA 02563 B Camden ME 10/12/1928 s George Harvey Thomas & Frances Carolyn. BS U of Maine 1950; MDiv EDS 1959; DMin VTS 1987. D 6/1/1959 Bp Anson Phelps Stokes Jr P 1/17/1960 Bp Frederic Cunningham Lawrence. m 4/14/1951 Frances Graham Mary Frances Graham c 5. R S Jn's Ch Sandwich MA 1993; M-in-c S Jn's Ch Sandwich MA 1959-1968. Auth, *Thesis Mnstry w Men in a Sm Town*. jhthomas@cape.com

THOMAS, John Patterson (O) 752 Somerville Dr, Pittsburgh PA 15243 **Assoc S Paul's Epis Ch Pittsburgh PA 1999-** B Pittsburgh PA 12/24/1934 s William S Thomas & Janet Clutter. BA U Pgh 1958; MDiv PDS 1961. D 6/1/1961 P 12/23/1961 Bp William S Thomas. m 9/7/1957 Janet Wissinger c 2. Int S Andr Epis Ch Mentor OH 1997-1998; Int Calv Ch Pittsburgh PA 1991-1992; Sheldon Calv Camp Pittsburgh PA 1985-1996; R Chr Epis Ch Geneva OH 1985-1991; R S Ptr's Ch Ashtabula OH 1977-1985; R S Jas Epis Ch Pittsburgh PA 1966-1977; P-in-c S Fran In The Fields Somerset PA 1961-1966. thomjj4@aol.com

THOMAS, John Paul (Dal) 635 N. Story Rd, Irving TX 75061 **Catechesis Cmsn Dio Dallas Dallas TX 2011-; Par D S Mk's Ch Irving TX 2011-; Latino Cler Cmsn Dio Dallas Dallas TX 2010-** B Seattle WA 9/3/1952 s Robert John Thomas & Aileen Virginia. BS U of Washington 1974; MDiv Gordon-Conwell TS 1982; MA U of No Dakota 1992. D 10/18/2008 Bp James Monte Stanton. m 12/19/1981 Barbara Perch c 2. paul_thomas@sil.org

THOMAS, John Taliaferro (Tenn) 290 Quintard Rd, Sewanee TN 37375 **S Andr's-Sewanee Sch Sewanee TN 2008-** B Wilmington OH 8/1/1966 s Emory Morton Thomas & Frances Craddock. BA U So 1988; MDiv VTS 1993. D 6/12/1993 Bp Peter James Lee P 2/10/1994 Bp Charles Farmer Duvall. m 2/20/1993 Janice Marie Thimons c 2. S Andr's Epis Sch Potomac MD 2002-2008; S Columba's Ch Washington DC 2002-2007; Assoc R S Lk's Epis Ch Atlanta GA 1996-1999; Asst R Chr Ch Par Pensacola FL 1993-1996. jthomas@sasweb.org

THOMAS, John Walter Riddle (ETenn) 4530 Joack Ln, Hixson TN 37343 B Richard City TN 8/20/1929 s Walter Russell Thomas & Bennie Lee. BM U Of Chattanooga 1951; STB PDS 1960. D 7/3/1960 P 4/25/1961 Bp John Vander Horst. m 4/25/1962 Elizabeth Carleton Etter c 1. Assoc S Ptr's Ch Chattanooga TN 1998-2010; Vic S Mk's Ch Copperhill TN 1992-1995; R Trin Epis Ch Gatlinburg TN 1986-1992; R Ch Of The H Cross Sullivans Island SC 1984-1986; R S Paul's Ch Bennettsville SC 1972-1984; Vic S Lk's Epis Ch Honolulu HI 1970-1971; R S Barn Ch Tullahoma TN 1962-1967; P-in-c S Bede's Epis Ch Manchester TN 1962-1965; Vic S Elis's Epis Ch Memphis TN 1960-1962. fatherwalt@verizon.net

THOMAS, Jonathan Ryan (NJ) 1864 Post Rd, Darien CT 06820 **S Lk's Par Darien CT 2011-** B Fredericksburg VA 10/3/1981 s Janes Anthony Thomas & Robin Brooks. BA U of Virginia 2004; MDiv PrTS 2010; Dplma Angl Stds VTS 2011. D 6/18/2011 Bp George Edward Councell. m 8/12/2005 Elizabeth A Elizabeth Allison Jackson. jonathan.ryan.thomas@gmail.com

THOMAS, Joshua M (Oly) 1551 10th Ave E, Seattle WA 98102 **Dio Olympia Seattle WA 2011-** B Kingston PA 10/24/1977 s Jay Garfield Thomas & Dorothy Jane Phillips. AB Dart 2000; MDiv UTS 2005; PhD (cand.) Candler TS Emory U 2012. D 6/1/2007 P 1/20/2008 Bp V Gene Robinson. Dio Massachusetts Boston MA 2009-2010; Campus & YA Mssnr Dio New Hampshire Concord NH 2008-2010; S Barth's Epis Ch Atlanta GA 2007-2008. joshthomas00@gmail.com

THOMAS, Kathryn L (NI) 10010 Aurora Pl, Fort Wayne IN 46804 **R Gr Epis Ch Ft Wayne IN 2008-** B Lakewood OH 4/16/1951 Bachelor of Sci Kent St U

1973; Mstr of Rel Educ St. Meinrad TS 1988; Mstr of Div Chr TS 2001. D 2/15/2004 P 10/3/2004 Bp Catherine Elizabeth Maples Waynick. m 10/14/ 1972 David S Thomas c 3. Assoc R S Paul's Epis Ch Indianapolis IN 2004-2008; Dir. of CE S Chris's Epis Ch Carmel IN 1992-2003. kthomasatgracechurchfortwayne@frontier.com

THOMAS, Kenneth Dana (Ct) 5 Bassett St Apt B10, West Haven CT 06516 **Atndg P Chr Ch New Haven CT 1991-** B Bridgeport CT 1/29/1927 s Kenneth Augustine Thomas & Bessie Mae. BA Trin Hartford CT 1952; STB GTS 1955. D 6/14/1955 P 5/26/1956 Bp Walter H Gray. R S Jn's Epis Ch Essex CT 1964-1991; St Pauls Mssn of the Deaf W Hartford CT 1958-1964; Cur Trin Epis Ch Hartford CT 1955-1958.

THOMAS, Laughton Dennis (Fla) 113 W 6th Ave, Lawrenceville VA 23868 **S Mich And All Ang Ch Tallahassee FL 2003-; Vic S Paul's Meml Chap Lawrenceville VA 1989-** B Buffalo NY 7/27/1945 s Laughton Fowler Thomas & Ormah Elena. BS SUNY 1973; MDiv GTS 1978. D 6/3/1978 P 12/1/1978 Bp Albert Wiencke Van Duzer. S Paul's Coll Lawrenceville VA 1993-2002; S Alb's Epis Ch New Brunswick NJ 1979-1989; Asst S Mk's Ch Plainfield NJ 1978. laughtondt@yahoo.com

THOMAS, Leonard Everett (EC) 916 Lord Granville Dr., Morehead City NC 28557 B Gastonia NC 4/19/1943 s Leonard Monroe Thomas & Thelma Roberson. MDiv SE Bapt TS Wake Forest NC 1968; ThM SE Bapt TS Wake Forest NC 1975; DMin SE Bapt TS Wake Forest NC 1977; BA Mars Hill Coll 1995; PhD GTF 2000. D 1/27/1978 P 5/30/1978 Bp Hunley Agee Elebash. m 8/25/ 1963 Phyllis Thomas. R The Epis Ch Of Gd Shpd Asheboro NC 2000-2008; R S Lk's Epis Ch Lincolnton NC 1983-2000; S Jn's Epis Ch Fayetteville NC 1978-1982. AAMFC; AAPC; Natl Allnce Of Familly Life Incorporated. ethomas256@aol.com

THOMAS JR, Lester B(rooks) (WMich) 1037 Northwood St NE, Grand Rapids MI 49505 **Died 2/10/2011** B Grand Rapids MI 9/20/1920 s Lester Brooks Thomas & Lillian Bertha. BA Cntrl Michigan U 1948; BD Bex 1951; MDiv CRDS 1952. D 6/1/1951 Bp Beverley D Tucker P 12/15/1951 Bp Lewis B Whittemore. c 3. LBCT@SBCGLOBAL.NET

THOMAS, Margaret Lucie (Az) 1084 Paseo Guebabi, Rio Rico AZ 85648 **R S Andr's Epis Ch Nogales AZ 2003-** B Sonora CA 2/3/1947 d Leon Richards Thomas & Catherine Richardson. BA Bryn 1968; Cert Universidad de San Cristobal de Huamanga Ayacucho PE 1969; MA Washington U 1972; MDiv CDSP 1995. D 6/9/1995 Bp Robert Louis Ladehoff P 12/20/1995 Bp James Louis Jelinek. Assoc R S Paul's Epis Ch Duluth MN 1995-2003. "The Legacy of Enmegahbowh," *The Great Minnesota Welcome, 74th GC*, The Epis Dio Minnesota, 2003. MinnECA 1996-2003; NNECA 1996. Louise Hunderup Awd/Rel Educ Ecum Mnstrs of Oregon OR 1993. mlthomas@dakotacom.net

THOMAS, Margaret (Peg) (Me) 297 Wardwell Point Rd, Penobscot ME 04476 **P-in-c Trin Ch Castine ME 2011-; P Assoc Trin Ch Castine ME 2003-** B Cleveland OH 6/2/1945 d Frank Robert Wiesenberger & Marie. BA Albion Coll 1967; MA MI SU 1969; PhD MI SU 1981; Bangor TS 1995; MDiv GTS 1997. D 8/16/1997 Bp Frederick Barton Wolf P 6/6/1998 Bp Chilton Abbie Richardson Knudsen. m 9/14/1978 James Blake Thomas. Coordntr of D Formation Prog Dio Maine Portland ME 1999-2010; Cur S Fran By The Sea Blue Hill ME 1997-1999. SSM / Assoc 2002. pegthomasmaine@gmail.com

THOMAS, Margaret Warren (Minn) 9426 Congdon Blvd, Duluth MN 55804 B Ann Arbor MI 8/9/1936 d Edward Seymour Warren & Wava Mary. SWTS; BA U MI 1958; MA U MI 1982; MDiv Untd TS Of The Twin Cities 1997. D 6/13/1997 P 12/15/1997 Bp James Louis Jelinek. m 11/29/1958 Nelson Allen Thomas c 3. Asst S Paul's Epis Ch Duluth MN 2006-2009; S Edw's Ch Duluth MN 2004-2006. tmsnelmw@cpinternet.com

THOMAS, Michael Jon (WNY) 703 W Ferry St Apt C9, Buffalo NY 14222 B Auburn NY 10/15/1939 s Joseph Franklin Thomas & Janice. BA Cntrl Wesleyan Coll Cntrl SC 1966; Bex 1968; CDSP 1969. D 6/21/1969 P 1/3/1970 Bp Lauriston L Scaife. m 2/12/2011 Katrina Austin. P-in-c S Mich's Epis Ch Oakfield NY 1984-1992; Cur Gr Ch Lockport NY 1969-1971.

THOMAS, Micki-Ann (Alb) 232 Main St, Hudson Falls NY 12839 B Barton VT 8/14/1948 d Thomas Emmerson & Alice Gertrude. LPN Sthrn Adirondack Ed. Ctr. 1983; AAS-Nrsng Adirondack Cmnty Coll 1989. D 5/10/2008 Bp William Howard Love. m 7/2/1966 Ronald Lucien Thomas c 3. rmthom@netzero.com

THOMAS, Owen Clark (Mass) 1402 Glendale Ave, Berkeley CA 94708 B New York NY 10/11/1922 s Harrison Cook Thomas & Frances Arnold. BA Ham 1944; BD EDS 1949; PhD Col 1956. D 6/14/1949 P 6/14/1950 Bp Angus Dun. m 6/6/1981 Margaret R Miles c 3. Emm Ch Jaffrey NH 1968-1980; Assoc Prof EDS Cambridge MA 1962-1965; Chair Dept coll Wk Dio Massachusetts Boston MA 1956-1959; Instr Theol EDS Cambridge MA 1952-1956; Chapl dept Coll Wk Dio New York New York City NY 1951-1952. Auth, *Intro to Theol, 3rd Ed*, Morehouse Pub, 2002; Auth, *God's Activity in the Wrld*, Scholars, 1983; Auth, *Theol Questions: Analysis & Argument*, Morehouse, 1983; Auth, *The Sprt of Anglicanism*, Morehouse Pub, 1979; Auth, *Attitudes Toward Other Rel*, Harper & SCM, 1969; Auth, *Sci Challenges Faith*, Seabury Press, 1967; Auth, *Wm Temples Philos of Rel*, SPCK & Seabury, 1961. ot75@aol.com

THOMAS, Patricia Menne (EC) 136 Saint Andrews Cir, New Bern NC 28562 B Evanston IL 10/6/1936 d Wilbur Louis Menne & Kathryn Helen. BA U CA 1958; MDiv VTS 1979; DMin VTS 1988. D 6/15/1979 P 4/13/1980 Bp Dean T Stevenson. m 8/16/1958 Hoben Thomas c 2. Asst S Paul's Epis Ch Greenville NC 2003-2005; R Chr Ch New Bern NC 1999-2002; Cn Precentor Cathd of St Ptr & St Paul Washington DC 1996-1999; Cn to Ordnry Dio Washington Washington DC 1992-1996; Liturg Instr VTS Alexandria VA 1989-1994; Assoc R S Columba's Ch Washington DC 1984-1992; Field Wkr Dio Cntrl Pennsylvania Harrisburg PA 1980-1984; Vic S Jn's Epis Ch Huntingdon PA 1980-1984. Auth, *Identification & Trng of Baptismal Sponsors in a Par Setting*, 1988. Fllshp Contemplative Pryr, WECA 1980-1986. pmthomas@embarqmail.com

THOMAS, Peter (Tex) 832 Fearrington Post, Pittsboro NC 27312 B Detroit MI 10/11/1938 s Glyn Arvon Thomas & Marion Jean. BA U So 1960; MDiv VTS 1963; DMin Candler TS Emory U 1993. D 6/29/1963 P 6/29/1964 Bp Richard Henry Baker. m 11/28/1964 Carolyn M McLoud c 2. Dir Pstr Care and Mssn Outreach S Mart's Epis Ch Houston TX 1996-2004; Cn Dir Pstr Care & Prog The Cathd Ch Of The Adv Birmingham AL 1989-1996; Bd Trst The U So (Sewanee) Sewanee TN 1986-1988; R S Paul's Ch Augusta GA 1981-1989; Assoc S Lk's Epis Ch Atlanta GA 1976-1981; Dir St Lukes Trng & Coun.Ctr Atlanta GA 1976-1981; Asst S Lk's Epis Ch Atlanta GA 1970-1976; Assoc Ch Of The H Comm Memphis TN 1966-1970; Cur Ch Of The H Comf Charlotte NC 1963-1966. Cert Supvsr, Assoc. of CPE 1976-2004; Clincl Mem For AAMFT 1976-2004; Ldrshp, Georgia 1981-1987. cpthomas@embarqmail.com

THOMAS JR, Phillip Langston (La) 1318 Washington Ave, New Orleans LA 70130 B Erwin NC 1/29/1934 s Phillip Langston Thomas & Rose. U NC 1957; LTh Epis TS In Kentucky 1968; MS Estrn Kentucky U 1971; MDiv Epis TS In Kentucky 1971. D 5/25/1968 P 12/15/1968 Bp William R Moody. m 8/16/ 1957 Ann C Thomas c 2. S Mary's Ch Franklin LA 1985-1988; Pres Dio Cler Dio Lexington Lexington KY 1982-1984; Chair Dept Coll Wk Dio Lexington Lexington KY 1981-1985; S Aug's Chap Lexington KY 1981-1983; R Chr Ch Slidell LA 1975-1981; R S Phil's Ch Brevard NC 1971-1975; Pres Dio Cler Dio Lexington Lexington KY 1969-1971; Vic S Phil's Ch Harrodsburg KY 1967-1970. pthomas@datastar.net

THOMAS, Rachel Woodall (Ct) 155 Essex St, Deep River CT 06417 **R S Steph's Ch E Haddam CT 1996-** B Atlanta GA 8/5/1955 d Robert Baugh Woodall & Matilda Hammond. BA W&M 1977; MA Wheaton Coll 1981; MA Ya Berk 1991; DMin Hartford Sem 2007. D 6/8/1991 P 12/1/1991 Bp Arthur Edward Walmsley. m 1/6/2001 Eric J Thomas. S Steph's Ch E Haddam CT 2006-2010; Mssnr Middlesex Area Cluster Mnstry Higganum CT 1991-1996. rwthomas55@att.net

THOMAS, Robert Leroy (WVa) 401 11th Ave, Huntington WV 25701 **Chr Ch Ironton OH 1988-** B Williamsburg VA 6/6/1925 s Minor Wine Thomas & Grace Lee. BA Bridgewater Coll 1947; MDiv VTS 1950. D 6/29/1950 P 4/25/ 1951 Bp Henry D Phillips. c 3. R Trin Ch Huntington WV 1965-1987; Dce Dio SW Virginia Roanoke VA 1960-1965; R Chr Ch Blacksburg VA 1955-1960. rthomas@marshall.edu

THOMAS, Robert William (NC) 413 Dogwood Creek Pl, Fuquay Varina NC 27526 **D S Mk's Epis Ch Raleigh NC 2010-** B Philadelphia PA 4/11/1950 s Harold Gomer Thomas & Rosemarie Caroline. BA Rutgers-The St U 1972; MA Rutgers-The St U 1986; Dio NJ D Formation Prog 1998. D 10/31/1998 Bp Joe Morris Doss. m 8/6/1983 Cynthia Grace Scott c 2. D S Paul's Epis Ch Smithfield NC 2008-2010; D The Epis Ch Of The H Comm Fair Haven NJ 2006-2008; D S Dav's Ch Cranbury NJ 2001-2006; D Coun Dio New Jersey Trenton NJ 1999-2001; D Trin Cathd Trenton NJ 1998-2001. Auth, "Prov II: New Jersey," *Diakoneo*, NAAD, 2002; Auth, "Deacons Search Hidden Windows," *Via Media*, Dio NJ, 2002; Auth, "Liturg Crown Fest," *Via Media*, Dio NJ, 2002. Assn for Epis Deacons 1996; NAECED 2004. RWTeagle1@aol.com

THOMAS, Roz Pickering (NwT) 1241 Sayles Blvd, Abilene TX 79605 **Vic Trin Ch Albany TX 2005-** B Syracuse NY 2/2/1945 d Henry Pickering Thomas & Virginia. BA Winthrop U 1966; JD Atlanta Law Sch Atlanta GA 1978; CTh Epis TS of The SW 1990. D 2/3/1991 P 4/27/1992 Bp James Hamilton Ottley. Assoc R Ch Of The Heav Rest Abilene TX 1996-2006; P-in-c Dio Panama 1991-1994. padreroz@suddenlink.net

THOMAS, Samuel Sutter (SeFla) 135 W Crescent Dr, Clewiston FL 33440 B Philadelphia PA 6/16/1941 s Samuel Sutter Thomas & Cecile Adele. LTh SWTS 1966; Med Florida Atlantic U 1971; MDiv SWTS 1975; PhD U of Miami 1975; Cert U of Paris-Sorbonne FR 1985; Cert Universite de Strassbourg 1986. D 6/29/1966 Bp James Loughlin Duncan P 1/5/1967 Bp William Loftin Hargrave. m 9/11/1967 Eddie Lue Hutto. R S Mart's Ch Clewiston FL 2000-2006; Int Ch Of S Chris Ft Lauderdale FL 1998-2000; Int S Phil's Ch Pompano Bch FL 1998-2000; Int Ch Of The Atone Lauderdale Lakes FL 1994-1998; S Fran Cmnty Serv Inc. Salina KS 1993; LocTen S Mart's Ch Clewiston FL 1976-1977; Asst S Matt the Apos Epis Ch Miami FL

1972-1975; Cur All SS Epis Ch Lakeland FL 1966-1969. Auth, "arts," *Clewiston News*, 2000-present, 2000; Auth, "Val d'Or Star," *Northland mag*, (1980-1989), 1980; Auth, "Denial as Psychol Mechanism among Alcoholics"; Auth, "Authoritarianism and Emotional Independence in a Grp of Clergymen Counselors and Their Effects on Perceived Counslg Effect," *(dissertation)*. Amer Orthopsychiatic Assn; Amer Psychol Assoc; AEHC; Can Register of Hlth Serv Providers in Psychol; Florida Psychol Assoc; Intl Conf of Police Chapl; St and Prov Boards of Examiners in Psychol. Pres Rotary Club Clewiston FL 2003; Fell Amer Orthopsychiatric Assn 1988. smec1@embarqmail.com

THOMAS, Sherry Hardwick (Va) 386 N Anna Dr, Louisa VA 23093 B Cincinnati OH 5/25/1949 d Coy Hardwick & Louise. Vas 1968; BA U Cinc 1971; MDiv VTS 1989. D 6/10/1989 P 3/24/1990 Bp Peter James Lee. c 3. Int Trin Epis Ch Charlottesville VA 2008-2009; R S Jas Epis Ch Louisa VA 1998-2005; Assoc R Ch Of The Gd Shpd Burke VA 1994-1998; S Phil's Ch Cincinnati OH 1994; Dir Yth Mnstrs Dio Sthrn Ohio Cincinnati OH 1991-1993; S Dav's Par Washington DC 1989-1991; Gr Epis Ch Silver Sprg MD 1989-1990. hardwickthomas@yahoo.com

THOMAS, Teresa Ann Collingwood (Ak) PO Box 76, Fort Yukon AK 99740 **D S Steph's Ch Ft Yukon AK 1990-** B Newton Abbot Devon UK 5/31/1936 d Ivan Theodore Barling & Mary Fredrica. U of Alaska; U NC; MA S Andr's U 1960. D 6/29/1990 Bp George Clinton Harris. m 9/1/1967 John Thomas c 2. Cler-in-Charge S Jn's Epis Ch Eagle AK 2001-2005. tacthomas@hotmail.com

THOMAS, Timothy Bosworth (SeFla) 3434 N Oceanshore Blvd, Flagler Beach FL 32136 B Portland IN 5/25/1950 s William Bosworth Thomas & Marjorie Lou. BA Indiana U 1972; MDiv SWTS 1980. D 5/25/1980 Bp Charles Ellsworth Bennison Jr P 12/1/1980 Bp James Winchester Montgomery. m 5/31/1980 Marguerite Alderman c 1. Chair, Cler Assistance Prog Dio SE Florida Miami FL 2007-2011; COM Chair, Screening and Revs Dio SE Florida Miami FL 2000-2005; Mnstry Discernment Assoc Dio SE Florida Miami FL 1998-2011; COM Dio SE Florida Miami FL 1995-2005; R Ch Of S Nich Pompano Bch FL 1993-2011; Assoc R Trin Ch New Orleans LA 1985-1993; Assoc R S Fran Ch Potomac MD 1983-1984; Cur Ch Of Our Sav Chicago IL 1980-1983. st.nicholasepis@att.net

THOMAS, Trevor E. G. (Nwk) 90 Rossini Road, Westerly RI 02891 **R Emer Ch Of The H Innoc W Orange NJ 1989-** B Cardiff Wales GB 12/23/1925 s Philip Thomas & Sarah Beatrice. BA S Dav's Coll Lampeter GB 1948; GOE S Dav's Coll Lampeter GB 1950. D 3/24/1951 P 10/27/1951 Bp Benjamin M Washburn. c 3. Archd Dio Newark Newark NJ 1969-1974; R Ch Of The H Innoc W Orange NJ 1952-1989; Vic Ch Of The H Innoc W Orange NJ 1951-1952. tegthomas@cox.net

THOMAS, Valerie Bricker (Fla) 244 Ashley Lake Dr, Melrose FL 32666 B Olswinford Worchester UK 3/11/1944 d Gerald Neville Nash & Audrey Kathleen. D 9/14/1997 Bp Stephen Hays Jecko. m 2/15/1986 Wallace Fitzgerald Thomas. D S Mk's Ch Palatka FL 2000-2002; D S Mich's Ch Gainesville FL 1998-2000; D Ch Of The Medtr Micanopy FL 1997-1998. krippiesmom1@hotmail.com

THOMAS, Victor J (Tex) 3129 Southmore Blvd, Houston TX 77004 **S Jas Epis Ch Houston TX 2009-** B Oakland CA 11/1/1966 s Albert Sylvester Thomas & Rachel Alice. BA New Coll of California 1994; MDiv CDSP 1997. D 6/21/1997 Bp Richard Lester Shimpfky P 5/1/1998 Bp Michael Whittington Creighton. m 12/17/1994 Nicole Jessica Hudson c 2. R S Paul's Epis Ch Harrisburg PA 2002-2008; Assoc R S Jas Ch Lancaster PA 1997-2002. victorstph@comcast.net

THOMAS, Virginia Campbell (Vt) 3140 Route 108 S, East Fairfield VT 05448 **Died 4/30/2011** B Utica NY 11/22/1917 d Daniel Randle Campbell & Bessie Ormiston. BA Cor 1939; MA Luther TS 1978. D 6/11/1978 Bp Lyman Cunningham Ogilby. Auth, "Clipped Wings," *Mnstry Dvlpmt Journ*, 1985; Auth, "You'Re A What? What'S A Dolphin?," *Geriatric Nrsng*, 1982. vcthomas@sovet.net

THOMAS JR, Warren Garfield (NJ) 10950 Temple Ter Apt W401, Seminole FL 33772 B Philadelphia PA 10/19/1910 s Warren Garfield Thomas & Ruth Miller. BA U of the Arts Philadelphia PA 1932. D 10/27/1962 Bp Alfred L Banyard. m 5/22/1999 Bonnie Lee Kachel. D S Matt's Ch St Petersburg FL 1996-2011; D S Ptr's Epis Ch Greenville SC 1992-1996; S Steph's Ch Whiting NJ 1990-1992; Chr Ch Toms River Toms River NJ 1962-1990. "Mischief Passion Keepsakes," Random Hse. Purchase Awd Ocean Cnty Coll 1974; Silver Medal (Indstrl Design) Natl Art Dir Assn 1956.

THOMAS, Wayland Eugene (Md) 55 Brooklyn Hts Rd, Thomaston ME 04861 B Peckville PA 6/16/1940 s Wayland Thomas & Mildred. BS Acctg Tem 1965; MDiv Yale DS 1972. D 6/24/1972 P 1/1/1973 Bp Harold B Robinson. m 6/18/1988 Judith E Larabee c 3. Asstg P Memi Ch Baltimore MD 1989-1994; R S Barn Ch Rumford ME 1984-1988; R S Andr's Ch Millinocket ME 1982-1984; R St Mk Epis Ch No Tonawanda NY 1974-1978; Cur S Mk's Ch Orchard Pk NY 1972-1974. thomas3331@roadrunner.com

THOMAS, William Carl (WVa) 1974 Parkwood Rd., Charleston WV 25314 **R S Matt's Ch Charleston WV 2003-** B Mount Kisco NY 8/13/1952 s Samuel LeRoy Thomas & Dorothy Jean. BS Bos 1985; MDiv Nash 1989. D 6/17/1989 Bp Orris George Walker Jr P 12/20/1989 Bp Robert Campbell Witcher Sr. m 10/13/1973 Edna Marie Parsons c 2. R S Mths Epis Ch Tuscaloosa AL 1995-2003; R S Mk's Ch Warren RI 1991-1994; Assoc S Ann's Ch Sayville NY 1989-1991. Auth, "Deep Ch," *LivCh*, LivCh Fndt, 2002; Auth, *Giving the Increase:Supporting God's Wk in the Wrld*, Dio Long Island, 1994; Auth, *Putting Powerful Prchng in the Pulpit*, Preaching Excellency Fndt, 1989; Auth, "Living Our Baptismal Cov-The Milwaukee Process," *Video Producer & Workbook Ed / Dio Milwaukee*, 1989. williamcarlthomas@gmail.com

THOMAS, William Steven (SeFla) 14445 Horseshoe Trce, Wellington FL 33414 **R S Dav's-In-The-Pines Epis Ch Wellington FL 1991-** B Augusta GA 11/3/1955 s William Bradley Thomas & Jean. BA Transylvania U 1976; BTh Chichester Theol Coll 1981; STM STUSo 1990. D 6/13/1981 P 3/28/1982 Bp Addison Hosea. m 5/28/2005 Erin Burke c 4. Inst Dio SE Florida Miami FL 1988-1990; Chapl Chap Of S Andr Boca Raton FL 1986-1991; S Andew's Sch Boca Raton FL 1986-1991; Cur S Mk The Evang Ft Lauderdale FL 1984-1986; Mus Cmsn Dio Rhode Island Providence RI 1982-1984; Cur S Mich's Ch Bristol RI 1981-1984. AAM. fatherthomas@comcast.net

THOMAS, William Tuley (Mo) 7846 Gannon Ave, Saint Louis MO 63130 B Louisville KY 1/1/1931 s Vincent Cox Thomas & Mary Speed. BA U of Louisiana 1954; BD VTS 1957; DMin Eden TS 1971. D 6/20/1957 P 12/1/1957 Bp Charles Gresham Marmion. m 2/12/1970 Helen Marie Wall. P-in-c S Jn's Ch Murray KY 1957-1961; P-in-c S Mart's-In-The-Fields Mayfield KY 1957-1961.

THOMASON, Clayton Leslie (Chi) 42 Ashland Ave, River Forest IL 60305 **Assoc Gr Ch Oak Pk IL 2009-; Chapl Rush U Med Cntr Chicago IL 2006-** B Los Angeles CA 11/25/1959 s James Clayton Thomason & Lois Arlein. AA Simon's Rock Coll Of Bard 1979; BA U CA 1980; JD USC 1987; MDiv Ya Berk 1994. D 6/15/1994 Bp Oliver Bailey Garver Jr P 1/14/1995 Bp Frederick Houk Borsch. Assoc All SS Ch E Lansing MI 2000-2003; P-in-c S Paul's Epis Ch Lansing MI 1999; Assoc S Jas Par Los Angeles CA 1994-1998. Auth, "Contrib To Withdrawal Of Treatment & Active Euthanasia In"; Auth, "Ethical Issues In Hiv Care". Ascpe, EFM, Epis Evang Fndt. Preaching Excellence Prog Epis Evang Fndt 1993. thomascl@comcast.net

THOMASON, Steve (Ark) 224 N. East Avenue, PO Box 1190, Fayetteville AR 72701 **P Assoc S Paul's Ch Fayetteville AR 2009-** B Little Rock AR 2/13/1965 s Robert H Thomason & Mary H. BS U So 1987; MD U of Arkansas 1991; MDiv Epis TS of The SW 2004. D 12/27/2003 P 6/26/2004 Bp Larry Earl Maze. m 8/3/1985 Katherine M Prunty c 2. Cn Mssnr Dio Arkansas Little Rock AR 2005-2008; S Thos Ch Springdale AR 2004-2008. "A Peaceful Death," *Med Econ*, Med Econ, 2003; "We Can take Care Of Ourselves," *Med Econ*, Med Econ, 2002. steve.thomason@sbcglobal.net

THOMPSON, Barkley Stuart (SwVa) PO Box 257, Roanoke VA 24002 **R S Jn's Ch Roanoke VA 2007-** B Paragould AR 11/17/1972 BA Hendrix Coll 1995; MA U Chi 1998; MDiv Epis TS of The SW 2003. D 6/28/2003 P 1/10/2004 Bp Don Edward Johnson. m 6/10/1995 Jill B Thompson c 2. R Ch of the H Apos Collierville TN 2003-2007. *Conciliar Authority*, LivCh, 2004; *The Barber Shop and Sabbath Time*, Ratherview, 2001; *The Melting Pot Overturned: Preparing the Ch for a Multicultural Soc*, Ratherview, 2001; *Toward a Christology of Purpose: The Early Royce and the Incarn*, Amer Journ of Philos and Theol, 2000. bthompson@stjohnsroanoke.org

THOMPSON, Carla Eva (Va) 322 N Alfred St, Alexandria VA 22314 B Kenosha WI 3/20/1948 d Carl Robert Thompson & Olga. BA U of Wisconsin 1970; MDiv VTS 1997. D 6/14/1997 P 3/11/1998 Bp Peter James Lee. Ch Of The Trsfg Silver Sprg MD 1999-2006; Vic Meade Memi Epis Ch Alexandria VA 1999-2006; Asst Trin Ch Arlington VA 1997-1998. emptytomb123321@verizon.net

THOMPSON, Catherine M (WLa) 148 Touline St, Natchitoches LA 71457 **R Trin Epis Ch Natchitoches LA 2006-** B Dallas TX 7/4/1971 d Michael Neil Hedrick & Donna Whitmarsh. BA Vas 1993; MDiv VTS 2000. D 6/3/2000 P 5/23/2001 Bp D(avid) Bruce Mac Pherson. m 10/23/1993 Mark Anthony Thompson c 2. Assoc S Phil's Epis Ch Frisco TX 2002-2006; Cur S Anne's Epis Ch Desoto TX 2000-2002. rector@trinityparish.info

THOMPSON, C(harles) Christopher (WVa) Greenbrier Episcopal Ministry, PO Box 148, White Sulphur Springs WV 34901 **Vic Greenbrier Monroe Epis Mnstry White Sulphur Sprg WV 2011-** B Portsmouth OH 2/10/1953 s Charles Raymond Thompson & Judith Clayton. CREDO I; CREDO II; BA W Liberty St Coll 1975; MDiv VTS 1979; Fllshp VTS 1995. D 6/6/1979 P 6/4/1980 Bp Robert Poland Atkinson. m 11/22/1980 Mary Brown c 1. Int S Steph's Epis Ch Beckley WV 2010-2011; R Estrn Shore Chap Virginia Bch VA 2005-2010; R S Thos' Epis Ch St Petersburg FL 1996-2005; R All SS Epis Ch Portsmouth OH 1986-1996; Yth Coordntr Dio W Virginia Charleston WV 1981-1985; Vic S Jn's Ripley WV 1980-1986; D S Jn's Ch Huntington WV 1979-1980. NNECA 2003-2010. Distinguished Serv Medallion Bp Suffr of Chaplaincies 2004. cthompson5151@gmail.com

THOMPSON, Claud Adelbert (Mil) 5030 Vista View Crescent, Nanaimo BC V9V 1L6 Canada B Milwaukee WI 9/15/1933 s Claud Adelbert Thompson & Emily Jane. BA, cl Ripon Coll Ripon WI 1955; MA, hon Col 1960; BD, cl

SWTS 1964; PhD U of Wisconsin 1970. D 6/1/1964 P 12/1/1964 Bp William Hampton Brady. m 8/31/1968 Phyllis Ann Kuhn c 1. Asst S Fran Ch Madison WI 1966-1968; Asst All SS Epis Ch Appleton WI 1964-1966. Auth, "Doctrine and Discipline of Divorce, A Bibliographical Study," *Transactions of the Cambridge Bibliographical Soc*, Camb Libr, 1977; Auth, "Trinities in Piers Plowman," *Mosaic*, U of Manitoba Press, 1976; Auth, "'Coded' Signatures: A Printer's Clue...," *Papers of the Bibliographical Soc of Amer*, The Soc, 1974; Auth, "Spenser's 'Many Faire Pourtraicts, and Many a Faire Feate," *Stds in Engl Lit*, Jn Hopkins Press, 1972; Auth, "Rhetorical Madness: An Ideal in the 'Phaedrus,'" *Quarterly Journ of Speech*, Speech Assn of Amer, 1969; Auth, "'That Two-Handed Engine' Will Smite: Time Will Have a Stop," *Stds in Philology*, U NC Press, 1962. cathom@telus.net

THOMPSON, Danielle Lee (Tenn) 1424 N Dearborn St, Chicago IL 60610 **Cur S Chrys's Ch Chicago IL 2010-** B Iowa City IA 4/22/1980 d Steven Wayne Thompson & Barbara B. BA Lipscomb U 2001; MDiv Vanderbilt DS 2006; Angl Stds The TS at The U So 2010; STM The TS at The U So 2011. D 6/5/2010 P 12/13/2010 Bp John Crawford Bauerschmidt. m 6/21/2003 Joshua B Davis c 1. thomdl80@gmail.com

THOMPSON, Daniel R (EO) 215 NE 97th Ave, Portland OR 97220 **Died 2/23/2011** B Klamath Falls OR 8/4/1938 s Rollin Elmer Thompson & Leola Grace. BD EDS; BS Sthrn Oregon Coll 1960. D 11/6/1966 P 11/6/1967 Bp Lane W Barton. c 1. CHS 1965. foxholedon2002@yahoo.com

THOMPSON, David Frank Ora (USC) 723 Arrow Wood Dr, North Augusta SC 29841 **R S Barth's Ch No Augusta SC 1985-** B Cumberland MD 4/3/1951 s Guy Ora Thompson & Audrey. BA Salisbury St U 1973; MDiv GTS 1976; STM GTS 1985. D 6/4/1976 P 4/16/1977 Bp David Keller Leighton Sr. m 8/16/1975 Virginia Gaiser c 4. Tutor The GTS New York NY 1983-1985; R S Mths' Epis Ch Baltimore MD 1978-1983; Cur S Marg's Ch Annapolis MD 1976-1978. rector@saintbart.org

THOMPSON, David Joel (Colo) 360 Scrub Oak Cir, Monument CO 80132 **Prince Of Peace Epis Ch Sterling CO 2011-** B Waterloo IA 9/24/1950 s Wayne Charles Thompson & Carol. BA Colorado St U 1974; MDiv GTS 1979; MA U Denv 1984; U CO 1996. D 10/28/1982 P 1/1/1985 Bp William Harvey Wolfrum. Vic S Paul's Epis Ch Lamar CO 2000-2006; Int Ch Of The Ascen Salida CO 1997-1999; Int S Barn Ch Glenwood Sprg CO 1991-1992; Vic S Dav Of The Hills Epis Ch Woodland Pk CO 1988-1991; Cur Gr And S Steph's Epis Ch Colorado Sprg CO 1986-1988; P-in-c Ch Of S Mich The Archangel Colorado Sprg CO 1985-1986. ESMA.

THOMPSON, Donald Frederick (Ct) 11 Lenox Ave, Norwalk CT 06854 B Winnipeg Manitoba CA 7/10/1944 s Donald Alexander Thompson & Lillian Ruby. BA U of Manitoba 1965; MA Harvard DS 1968; PhD McGill U 1981; DD S Jn's Coll Winnipeg Mn CA 1996; DD Montreal TS 2001. Trans from Anglican Church of Canada 4/19/2002 Bp Andrew Donnan Smith. m 6/15/1968 Susan Smith. AEC- Epis Ch Cntr Norwalk CT 2001-2011. Co-Auth, "Reply Of The Angl-RC Dialogue Of Can To The Vatican Response To The Final Report Of The Angl-RC Intl Comm," 1993; Co-Auth, "Initiation Into Chr: Ecum Reflections And Common Tchg On Preparation For Baptism," Wood Lake Books/ Novallis, 1992; Auth, "Ch And Culture: An Analytic Structure For The Relatns," *Arc: The Journ Of The Fac Of Rel Stds*, Mcgill U, 1991; Auth, "Whose Chld Is This?," Toronto, 1990; Auth, "Lonergan And Educating For Mnstry: A Construction, Method: A Journ Of Lonergan Stds, Vol. 8," *No. 12*, 1990; Auth, "A Theol Reflection On Chr Values And 'Surrogacy,'" *Surrogacy: The Report Of Angl T/F On Surrogate Motherhood*, Angl Ch Of Can, 1989; Auth, "Pstr Care Of Interchurch Families, One In Chr, Vol. 24," *No.3*, 1988; Ed/ Co-Auth, "Violence Against Wmn: Taskforce Report To Gnrl Syn 1986 Of The Angl Ch Of Can," Toronto, Angl Bk Cntr, 1987; Auth, "Coalitions As Vehicles For Unity: The Can Experience.," *Oecumenisme/ Ecum #86*, 1987; Auth, "Experiential Theol: Fad Or Fndt?," *Justice As Mssn: An Agenda For The Ch*, Toronto, Trin Press, 1984. Amer Assn Of Rel 1980; Can Theol Soc 1980. thompsondft@gmail.com

T

THOMPSON, E(dgar) A(ndrew) (Colo) 971 E Lone Pine Road, Pahrump NV 89048 B White Plains NY 4/16/1930 s Herbert Andrew Thompson & Vera Lucie. BA U CO 1956; BD Nash 1959; MDiv Nash 1960; Beth Hosp 1983. D 6/29/1959 P 2/2/1960 Bp Joseph Summerville Minnis. m 8/31/1979 Roberta R McCusker c 3. Rgnl P Mssnr Ch Of The H Sprt Bullhead City AZ 1996-1999; R All SS Epis Ch Torrington WY 1980-1982; Cur All SS Epis Ch Denver CO 1979; Vic S Andr's Ch La Junta CO 1978; R S Steph's Ch Longmont CO 1965-1977; Cur S Paul's Epis Ch Lakewood CO 1961-1965; Vic/R S Andr's Ch Manitou Sprg CO 1959-1961. Auth, "Chapl in Corrections," *Corrections Today*, 1989; Auth, "Jennifer Wants to Speak, Lord," *Beth Bulletin*, 1983. Amer Correctional Assn 1985-1995; RACA 1997. fr.thomnbobbie@hotmail.com

THOMPSON, Edward (Cal) 1714 Santa Clara Ave, Alameda CA 94501 B Bethesda MD 1/11/1963 s Edward Ivins Bradbridge Thompson & Lynn Taylor. BA Wms 1985; U MI 1992; MDiv CDSP 1995. D 6/8/1996 Bp R(aymond) Stewart Wood Jr P 6/1/1997 Bp William Edwin Swing. m 10/2/2004 Mary Ann Kimura. Long-Term Int R Chr Ch Alameda CA 2002-2009; Chr Epis Ch Sei Ko Kai San Francisco CA 1997-2002; Asst to R Trin Par Menlo Pk CA 1996-1997; Trin Par Menlo Pk CA 1995-1996. marykimura@yahoo.com

THOMPSON, Edward Hnebe (VI) PO Box 745, Frederiksted VI 00841 Virgin Islands (U.S.) **R S Paul's Epis/Angl Ch Frederiksted VI VI 2004-** B Maryland County Liberia 3/21/1962 s John Yede Thompson & Blaa-Hedoo. A.Sc. Tubman Coll Of Tech 1984; BATh Cuttington U Coll 1988; Cert of Proficiency Intl Sch of Evang 1992; MDiv Nash 2000. Trans from Church of the Province of West Africa 11/27/2002 Bp Roger John White. m 5/7/1994 Vashti Collins c 4. COM Dio Milwaukee Milwaukee WI 2003-2004; P-in-c S Mart's Ch Brown Deer WI 2002-2004; Chapl Dio Liberia 1000 Monrovia 10 Liberia 2000-2001. Rotary Intl 1997-2004. Stdt Ldrshp Awd Cuttington U Coll 1988. wudabo62@aol.com

THOMPSON, Elena (Ga) PO Box 1167, Baxley GA 31515 **Asst S Paul's Ch Savannah GA 2010-** B Glen Ridge NJ 2/7/1952 d Stuart M Thompson & Dorothy J. BA Duke 1974; MA U of Florida 1975; MDiv STUSo 1982; PhD U of Texas 1988. D 8/3/2002 P 2/24/2003 Bp Henry Irving Louttit. S Paul's Epis Ch Jesup GA 2007-2008; Ch Of The H Nativ St Simons Island GA 2003-2006; S Aug Of Cbury Ch Augusta GA 2002-2003. sisterelena@msn.com

THOMPSON JR, Fred Edward (SC) 2138 Allandale Plantation Rd, Wadmalaw Island SC 29487 **S Mich's Epis Ch Charleston SC 2005-** B Charleston SC 7/31/1966 s Fred Edward Thompson & Lois Ann Mathewes. BA Newberry Coll 1988; MA Luth TS 1995. D 9/10/2005 Bp Edward Lloyd Salmon Jr. m 7/1/1989 Alicia Anderson Thompson. thompsfe@musc.edu

THOMPSON, Fred Leonard (NC) 135 Broadmeade Dr, Southern Pines NC 28387 **Assoc S Mary Magd Ch W End NC 2008-** B Charlotte NC 12/20/1928 s Leonard Bernard Thompson & Amelia Caroline. BS Cit 1951; Cert VTS 1984. D 6/16/1984 P 6/30/1985 Bp Robert Whitridge Estill. m 6/16/1951 Lena Miller c 2. Vic All Souls Ch Wadesboro NC 1990-1995; R Calv Ch Wadesboro NC 1990-1995; Asst Emm Par Epis Ch And Day Sch Sthrn Pines NC 1984-1990. frfred@nc.rr.com

THOMPSON, Helen Plemmons (At) 91 Wylde Wood Dr, McDonough GA 30253 **D Gr Ch Robbinsville NC 2009-** B Buncome County NC 12/22/1937 d Merlin Plemmons & Ruby Justice. D 8/6/2006 Bp J(ohn) Neil Alexander. c 3.

THOMPSON III, H (enry) (SC) 2310 Meadow Vue Dr, Moon Township PA 15108 B Toledo OH 1/12/1953 s Henry Lawrence Thompson & Charlotte. BA Denison U 1975; BA Trin Bristol GB 1978; MDiv GTS 1979; Cert Estrn Bapt TS 1984; DMin TESM 2001. D 6/23/1979 P 5/24/1980 Bp John Harris Burt. m 6/28/1975 Mary Willis c 3. TESM Ambridge PA 1997-2009; Dio Connecticut Hartford CT 1986-1993; Reg Dn Dio Connecticut Hartford CT 1986-1989; Gr Epis Ch Trumbull CT 1985-1997; Asst R Ch Of The Gd Samar Paoli PA 1979-1985. Auth, "Sprtl Journeys," *MV Alum mag*, 2007; Auth, "Common Wrshp Lectionary," *ATR*, 2002; Auth, "Feast of the Wrld's Redemp," *Living Ch*, 2001; Auth, "Personality Type & Evang," *New Engl Ch Life*, 1987. Assn of Psychol Type 1987; FOCUS, Bd 1994-1996; Fllshp of Witness / EFAC USA Bd 1985; St Mk's Day Care Bd 1995-1997. lthompson@tsm.edu

THOMPSON SR, Howard (Alb) 140 Foster Rd, North Lawrence VA 12967 **Chr Ch Morristown NY 2005-** B Salem OR 12/19/1941 s Robert Ernest Thompson & Grace Elizabeth. D 6/11/2005 Bp Daniel William Herzog. m 2/2/1963 Geraldine Vina Bissell-Thompson c 6. dcntn@hotmail.com

THOMPSON, James Calvin (SVa) 2003 Camelia Cir, Midlothian VA 23112 B South San Gabriel CA 1/12/1932 s John Benson Thompson & Mary Victoria. BA U of Redlands 1953; MA USC 1956; ThM Claremont TS 1959; Cert GTS 1964. D 9/10/1964 P 3/11/1965 Bp Francis E I Bloy. m 8/28/1954 Lois A Uecker c 2. Asst Ch Of The Redeem Midlothian VA 1998-2008; R S Jn's Par Porterville CA 1977-1992; Epis Dio San Joaquin Modesto CA 1969-1977; Vic S Tim's Ch Bp CA 1969-1977; Vic Trin Memi Epis Ch Lone Pine CA 1969-1970; Vic S Geo's Ch Riverside CA 1964-1969. Auth, *Notes on Catechism*, Morehouse, 1979. oldrev@aol.com

THOMPSON, James Edwin (EpisSanJ) 3930 SE 162nd Ave Spc 22, Portland OR 97236 B Roseburg OR 7/15/1947 s Wilbur Raymond Thompson & Louise Frances. NW Chr Coll Eugene OR 1974. D 11/16/1975 Bp Matthew Paul Bigliardi P 6/1/1994 Bp Robert Louis Ladehoff. m 9/16/1968 Patricia Ann Browning c 3. S Lk's Epis Ch Gresham OR 2002-2007; Dio Oregon Portland OR 2002-2004; Cn Ordnry Epis Dio San Joaquin Modesto CA 1998-2002; S Jas Epis Cathd Fresno CA 1994-1998; Admin S Steph's Epis Par Portland OR 1987-1990; Asst S Matt's Epis Ch Portland OR 1981-1983; Asst to Bp of Ore Dio Oregon Portland OR 1979-1987; Asst S Ptr And Paul Epis Ch Portland OR 1979-1981; Asst S Mk's Ch Myrtle Point OR 1977-1979; Mus Cmsn Dio Oregon Portland OR 1975-1978. Cmnty of Chr Fam Mnstry 2004. Hon Cn Dio Oregon 1987. anchorhold@frontier.com

THOMPSON, Jerry A. (Neb) St. Mark's on the Campus Episcopal Church, Lincoln NE 68508 **R S Mk's On The Campus Lincoln NE 2005-** B Warren OH 10/25/1960 s Dean Vernor Thompson & Mary Lou. BA Coll of Wooster 1982; MA Indiana U 1985; MDiv Chr TS 1989; CAS SWTS 1990; DMin SWTS 1994. D 6/24/1990 P 5/1/1991 Bp Edward Witker Jones. m 6/26/1982 Carol Lynn Thompson c 2. Int S Jn's Ch Speedway IN 2004-2005; S Tim's Ch Indianapolis IN 2004-2005; Cn Chr Ch Cathd Indianapolis IN 1998-2004; R S

Matt's Epis Ch Brecksville OH 1992-1997; Trin Epis Ch Bloomington IN 1990-1991. Theta Phi 1988. Alumnini Awd Chr TS Indianapolis IN 1989; Theta Phi Chr TS Indianapolis TN 1988; Fac Awd Chr TS Indianapolis IN 1988; Shelton Awd Chr TS Indianapolis IN 1987; Phi Beta Kappa Coll Of Wooster Wooster OH 1982; Eta Sigma Phi Coll Of Wooster Wooster OH 1980. smoc.rector@stmarks-episcopal.org

THOMPSON, John E (At) 2732 Chapel Hill Rd, Clarksville TN 37040 **Assoc S Jas' Epis Ch Warrenton VA 2009-** B Sumter SC 7/16/1977 s E Thompson & Lula. D 12/21/2004 P 8/20/2005 Bp J(ohn) Neil Alexander. rev.jet@gmail.com

THOMPSON, John Francis (CFla) 90 E Jinnita St, Hernando FL 34442 **D S Marg's Ch Inverness FL 1997-** B Chaptico MD 11/24/1933 s Alton Eugene Thompson & Margaret Pearl. BS U of Maryland 1960; MS U of Maryland 1964; PhD MI SU 1966. D 8/25/1984 Bp Charles Thomas Gaskell. m 8/19/1967 Janet M Morton c 2. D Chr Ch Epis Madison WI 1994-1996; D S Andr's Ch Madison WI 1990-1993; D Gr Ch Madison WI 1984-1990. jthomp30@embarqmail.com

THOMPSON, John Kell (Oly) PO Box 508, Vashon WA 98070 B Pittsburgh PA 1/20/1943 s Gordon Kell Thompson & Ruth Ester. BA Muskingum Coll 1966; MS San Diego St U 1970; PhD U of Arizona 1972; CDSP 1991. D 6/18/1991 P 12/21/1991 Bp Vincent Waydell Warner. m 6/13/1965 Joan W Thompson c 2. R Ch Of The H Sprt Vashon WA 1994-2008; Stndg Com Dio Olympia Seattle WA 1993-1996; Assoc to Prog Dvlpmt S Thos Ch Medina WA 1991-1994. john.thompson30@comcast.com

THOMPSON, John Paul (Alb) PO Box 180, Copake Falls NY 12517 B Milwaukee WI 4/5/1958 BA Cardinal Stritch U 1982; MA Franciscan U of Steubenville 1987; MDiv STUSo 2005. D 6/5/2005 Bp Samuel Johnson Howard P 12/13/2005 Bp Henry Nutt Parsley Jr. R S Jn In-The-Wilderness Copake Falls NY 2008; S Mths Epis Ch Tuscaloosa AL 2006-2008; Chr The Redeem Ch Montgomery AL 2005-2006. johnpthom@netzero.net

THOMPSON JR, John Wesley Bell (CGC) 4542 Thomas Road, Sebastopol CA 95472 **Died 1/8/2011** B Franklin VA 1/2/1932 s John Wesley Bell Thompson & Patricia. BA Harv 1954; STB GTS 1957. D 6/22/1957 P 12/1/1957 Bp Anson Phelps Stokes Jr. wrosevines@aol.com

THOMPSON, Karen Elizabeth (EMich) 18890 Fireside Hwy, Presque Isle MI 49777 **D Asst Trin Epis Ch Alpena MI 2001-** B Detroit MI 9/5/1950 d Rudolph Johann Schneider & Eugenia Elizabeth. BA Oakland U 1972; CTh Whitaker TS 1989. D 6/24/1989 Bp H Coleman McGehee Jr. m 6/2/1979 Jack Thompson c 2. Asst S Ptr's Ch Detroit MI 1997-2000; Asst S Gabr's Epis Ch Eastpointe MI 1989-1997. Auth, "Reflections On Jail Mnstry," *Diakoneo*, Naad, 1999; Auth, "Day w Dad," *The Record*, 1999. Epis Cler Assn Of Michigan 1991; Michigan Chapl Assn 1999; NAAD 1989. hfhaai@freeway.net

THOMPSON, Kenneth David (Ky) 1768 Plum Ridge Rd, Taylorsville KY 40071 B Lexington KY 8/14/1926 s Elmer Ira Thompson & Beulah Logan. D 12/21/1963 P 3/2/1969 Bp Charles Gresham Marmion. m 9/27/1947 Phyllis Burton Valleau. Int S Jas Ch Shelbyville KY 1999-2002; Int Ch Of The Ascen Bardstown KY 1986-1998; Int S Alb's Epis Ch Fern Creek Louisville KY 1980-1986; Int S Thos Epis Ch Louisville KY 1980-1986; Cn Chr Ch Cathd Louisville KY 1974-1984; Vic S Ptr's Epis Ch Louisville KY 1971-1974; Asst S Paul's Ch Louisville KY 1965-1971; Stff Chr Ch Cathd Louisville KY 1963-1966. Auth, *Beyond the Double Night*, Buggy Whip Press, 1996; Auth, *Bless This Desk*, Abingdon Press, 1976. emmausfarm@aol.com

THOMPSON, Marisa Tabizon (Ore) 1329 E 19th Ave, Eugene OR 97403 **S Mary's Epis Ch Eugene OR 2010-; Chapl Epis Campus Mnstry Eugene OR 2008-** B Albany OR 1/8/1976 d Daniel Albert Tobizon & Marjorie Joyce. BA U of Oregon Clark hon Coll 1998; Cert of Angl Stds Ya Berk 2004; Mstr of Div Yale DS 2004. D 5/30/2009 P 1/16/2010 Bp Sanford Zangwill Kaye Hampton. m 7/4/2005 Joseph Thompson c 1. D S Mary's Epis Ch Eugene OR 2009-2010. marisatabizonthompson@gmail.com

THOMPSON, Mark A (Minn) 700 Douglas Ave Apt 907, Minneapolis MN 55403 **S Paul's On-The-Hill Epis Ch St Paul MN 2005-** B Anaheim CA 9/25/1961 s Elliot Raymond Thompson & Betty Lou. BA Castleton St Coll 1989; MDiv SWTS 1992. D 6/11/1992 P 12/21/1992 Bp Daniel Lee Swenson. P-in-c SS Martha And Mary Epis Ch Eagan MN 2000-2005; Int Ch Of The Epiph Epis Plymouth MN 1999-2000; Int S Geo's Ch St Louis Pk MN 1997-1999; Liturg Cmsn Dio Indianapolis Indianapolis IN 1994-1997; Stwdshp Com Dio Indianapolis Indianapolis IN 1994-1996; Dioc Coun Dio Indianapolis Indianapolis IN 1994-1995; S Anne's Epis Ch Warsaw IN 1992-1997; Vic All SS Ch Syracuse IN 1992-1995. Associated Parishes; Int Mnstry Ntwk. Presidential Schlrshp Castleton St Coll 1988; Steel Fllshp 88. markthompson@stpaulsonthehillmn.org

THOMPSON, M Dion (Md) 1208 John St, Baltimore MD 21217 **R Ch Of The H Cov Baltimore MD 2007-** B Los Angeles CA 9/2/1956 AA California St U 1979; MFA USC 1982; MDiv GTS 2007. D 6/16/2007 P 1/26/2008 Bp John Leslie Rabb. m 2/15/1986 Jean E Thompson c 1. slidin88d6@aol.com

THOMPSON, Michael B (EC) Dashwood House, Sidgwick Avenue, Cambridge CB3 9DA Great Britain (UK) B Goldsboro NC 10/1/1953 No Carolina St U 1973; BA U NC 1975; ThM Dallas TS 1979; VTS 1980; PhD U of Cambridge 1988. D 8/16/1980 Bp Hunley Agee Elebash P 2/1/1981 Bp Brice Sidney Sanders. Asst R Chr Ch New Bern NC 1980-1983. Co-Ed, "Arianism: Is Jesus Chr Div and Eternal or Was He Created?," *Heresies and How to Avoid Them, ed B Quash and M Ward*, SPCK, 2007; Auth, "When Should We Divide?," Grove Books Ltd, 2004; Auth, "The New Perspective on Paul," Grove Books Ltd, 2002; "Transforming Gr: A Study of 2 Corinthians," Bible Reading Fllshp, 1998; "A Vision for the Ch," T & T Clark, 1997; "The H Internet: Cmncatn Between Ch in the First Chr Generation," *The Gospels for All Christians, ed R Bauckham*, Eerdmans, 1997; "Stumbling Block, Strong and Weak, Tchg/Paraenesis, Tradition," *Dictionary of Paul & His Letters, ed R P Mart et al*, InterVarsity Press, 1993; "Clothed w Chr: The Example & Tchg of Jesus in Romans 12-15.13," JSOT Press, 1991. Inst for Biblic Resrch 1991; SBL 1983; Tyndale Fllshp 1985. mbt2@cam.ac.uk

THOMPSON, Michael King (NC) 103 Sheffield Rd, Williamsburg VA 23188 B Staten Island NY 2/21/1942 s William Lyall Thompson & Beatrice. BA Randolph-Macon Coll 1964; MDiv VTS 1967; Fllshp VTS 1977; Coll of Preachers 1984; Cert Int Mnstry Prog 1993; MS Radford U 1993. D 6/10/1967 P 6/15/1968 Bp Robert Fisher Gibson Jr. m 1/27/1968 Elizabeth Johanna Van Wert c 3. Assoc S Jn's Epis Ch Charlotte NC 1996-1999; Supply P Dio SW Virginia Roanoke VA 1994-1995; P-in-c Chr Ch Blacksburg VA 1992-1994; Gr Ch Radford VA 1972-1991; Asst Chr Epis Ch Winchester VA 1968-1972; Asst S Chris's Ch Springfield VA 1967-1968. michaeljo2000@verizon.net

✠ **THOMPSON JR, Rt Rev Morris King** (La) 1623 7th Street, New Orleans LA 70115 **Bp Dio Louisiana Baton Rouge LA 2010-** B Cleveland MS 10/2/1955 s Morris King Thompson & Jean. BS Mississippi St U 1980; MDiv Sthrn Bapt TS Louisville KY 1983. D 12/2/1990 P 6/9/1991 Bp Don Adger Wimberly Con 5/10/2010 for La. m 6/5/1982 Rebecca Roper c 2. Dn & R Chr Ch Cathd Lexington KY 1997-2010; Assoc S Jas Ch Jackson MS 1992-1997; Assoc Calv Epis Ch Ashland KY 1991-1992. DD U So, Sewanee 2010. mthompson@edola.org

THOMPSON, Owen Chuhwuma (LI) 22 Roe Ct, Islip NY 11751 **Cur S Lk's Ch Trin Par Beth MD 2005-; Trin-St Jn's Ch Hewlett NY 2005-** B Brooklyn NY 1/26/1971 s Herbert Thompson. BA Hob. D 10/26/2002 P 6/21/2003 Bp Herbert Thompson Jr. m 8/6/2000 Jonna Morales c 2. Cur S Mk's Ch Islip NY 2003-2005. OCTTRINITY@OPTONLINE.NET

THOMPSON, Paul Mason (Vt) 4323 Main Street, Rt 6A, Cummaquid MA 02637 **Int Assoc S Ptr's Ch Osterville MA 2002-** B Spartanburg SC 3/8/1935 s Paul Mason Thompson & Byrd. BA Rhodes Coll 1958; STB EDS 1962; Oxf 1967. D 7/2/1962 P 5/1/1963 Bp Duncan Montgomery Gray. m 2/9/1963 Sallie Hews McClenahan c 2. R S Mich's Epis Ch Brattleboro VT 1974-1998; Vic S Jas Epis Ch Bowie MD 1968-1974; Vic Ch Of The Redeem Greenville MS 1963-1966; Vic S Jn's Ch Leland MS 1963-1966; Cur S Jas Ch Greenville MS 1963-1965; P-in-c S Steph's Ch Columbia MS 1962-1963. pmtsmt@verizon.net

THOMPSON, Peggy Reid (ECR) 451 Vivienne Dr, Watsonville CA 95076 B Washington DC 12/4/1938 d Vernon Ford Reid & Lillian Margaret. BA Sch for Deacons 1987. D 6/26/1987 Bp Charles Shannon Mallory. m 12/28/1966 Gene E Thompson. D S Geo's Ch Salinas CA 1999-2001; D Calv Epis Ch Santa Cruz CA 1992-1999; D S Phil The Apos Scotts Vlly CA 1987-1992. NAAD. getpeg@got.net

THOMPSON, Robert Gaston (Colo) 9987 W Oregon Pl, Lakewood CO 80232 B Powell WY 5/11/1938 s Herbert Orr Thompson & Dorritt Dicy. BA U of Nthrn Colorado 1960; US-A Chapl Sch 1966; MDiv CDSP 1967. D 6/21/1967 P 12/21/1967 Bp James W Hunter. m 6/30/1960 Ivajean Day c 2. S Anne's Epis Sch Denver CO 1995-2005; R H Apos Epis Ch Englewood CO 1994-1995; R S Jos's Ch Lakewood CO 1982-1991; S Fran Of Assisi Colorado Sprg CO 1977-1982; Gr And S Steph's Epis Ch Colorado Sprg CO 1971-1976; R S Andr's Ch Basin WY 1967-1971. Who's Who in Rel 1975. ivabob@msn.com

THOMPSON, Robert Wildan (Ky) 1206 Maple Ln, Anchorage KY 40223 **Asst S Lk's Ch Anchorage KY 2010-** B Salem OR 12/9/1951 s George Button Thompson & Marjorie Hargis. MDiv Emm Chr Sem 1983; MS Abilene Chr U 1993; ThM Brite DS 2008; DMin Brite DS 2011. D 5/29/2010 P 2/5/2011 Bp William Michie Klusmeyer. m 5/27/2000 Pamala Pamala Kay Poston c 3. Amer Assn for Mar & Fam Ther 1995; AAPC 2000. robert.w.thompson2@us.army

THOMPSON, Roderick James Marcellus (Cal) 140 Dolores St Apt 108, San Francisco CA 94103 **Assoc Ch Of The Adv Of Chr The King San Francisco CA 2002-** B Twickenham UK 12/2/1957 s James Edward Thompson & Nina. BS Lon 1978; MS Portland St U 1982; MDiv CDSP 1993. D 7/4/1993 P 6/25/1994 Bp William George Burrill. Vic S Cyp's Ch San Francisco CA 1999-2002; Ch Of The H Innoc San Francisco CA 1994-2002; Assoc S Steph's Epis Par Portland OR 1993-1994. "Liber Precum Publicarum: The 1979 Bk of Common Pryr in Latin," The Laud Liturg Press, 2008. anglorod@comcast.net

THOMPSON, Scott A (Tex) Holy Cross Episc Church, 5653 W. River Park Dr., Sugar Land TX 77479 **H Cross Epis Ch Sugar Land TX 2008-** B Richmond CA 3/23/1963 s Harry Maurice Thompson & Carole Alene. BA Gr TS Pleasant Hill CA 1986; ThM Dallas TS 1991; Cert Nash 1999. D 6/5/1999 P 10/24/1999 Bp Russell Edward Jacobus. m 3/13/2008 Linda S Thompson c 1. Vic St Jas Epis Ch Mosinee WI 1999-2008. sathompsonintx@comcast.net

THOMPSON SR, Stephen Lafoia (ETenn) 134 Iris Pl, Newport TN 37821 **D / Dir - Chr Formation Ch Of The Gd Shpd Knoxville TN 2002-** B Kingsport TN 4/20/1950 s Lafoia Adolphus Thompson & Edith. BS E Tennessee St U 1972; MA E Tennessee St U 1976; EDS E Tennessee St U 1986. D 6/24/1991 Bp Robert Gould Tharp. c 2.

THOMPSON, Sue (Cal) St Edmund's Episcopal Church, PO Box 688, Pacifica CA 94044 **Dept of Mnstry Dvlpmt, Chair Dio California San Francisco CA 2008-; Vic S Edm's Epis Ch Pacifica CA 2003-** B New Haven CT 4/28/1951 d Lawrence Earl Thompson & Patricia Marie. BS U GA 1973; Med U GA 1974; Candler TS Emory U 1996; MDiv CDSP 1999. D 5/13/2000 P 11/28/2000 Bp Richard Lester Shimpfky. m 7/8/2001 Kristin (Stina) Pope c 2. Int Dio California San Francisco CA 2002-2003; S Thos Epis Ch Sunnyvale CA 2002; Chr Ch Alameda CA 2000-2002. stedmundsvicar@gmail.com

THOMPSON, W(alter) Douglas (NCal) 1431 S St, Eureka CA 95501 **Mus & Liturg Dio Nthrn California Sacramento CA 1987-** B Pine Ridge OR 7/11/1939 s Walter Lewis Thompson & Alta Fay. BS Sthrn Oregon Coll 1961; MDiv CDSP 1964; Fllshp VTS 1990. D 6/29/1964 P 1/25/1965 Bp James Walmsley Frederic Carman. m 1/21/1962 Hannell Rippee c 3. Dn NW Deanry Dio Nthrn California Sacramento CA 1997-2002; R Chr Ch Eureka CA 1982-2000; R S Paul's Ch Klamath Falls OR 1976-1982; R Epis Ch Of S Anne Stockton CA 1972-1976; Cur Calv Epis Ch Santa Cruz CA 1970-1972; Vic S Andr's Epis Ch Florence OR 1966-1970; Vic S Mary Ch Gardiner OR 1966-1970; Cur S Matt's Epis Ch Portland OR 1964-1966. ComT; NNECA; NoCCA, Pres 1999-2000. frdougl957@sbcglobal.net

THOMPSON, Wanda Jean (Me) 1375 Forest Ave. Apt. H14, Portland ME 04103 **D Aroostook Epis Cluster Caribou ME 2002-; D S Paul's Ch Ft Fairfield ME 2002-** B Jeffersonville IN 2/14/1938 d Frank Anderson Smith & Dorothy Edna. Luth Hosp Sch Of Nrsng Moline IL 1959; BS Unity Coll Unity ME 1978. D 4/13/2002 Bp Chilton Abbie Richardson Knudsen. c 1. D Cathd Ch Of S Lk Portland ME 2007-2009. wjt1939@myfairpoint.net

THOMPSON, Warren Norvell (CFla) Po Box 1606, Winter Haven FL 33882 **P S Lk The Evang Ch Mulberry FL 2004-** B Ladysmith WI 4/5/1922 s Eben Calvin Thompson & Lydia Caroline. BS U of Wisconsin 1947; MDiv Nash 1964. D 4/25/1964 P 12/21/1964 Bp Donald H V Hallock. P-in-c S Fran Of Assisi Epis Ch Lake Placid FL 1998; Int S Paul's Ch Winter Haven FL 1990-1991; Cur S Paul's Ch Winter Haven FL 1978-1989; Vic Chr Ch Longwood FL 1966-1976; S Barn Ch Deland FL 1965-1966; S Matt's Epis Ch Minneapolis MN 1964-1965. ftbird22@gate.net

THOMPSON JR, William Early (USC) 16 Bernwood Dr, Taylors SC 29687 B Macon GA 3/30/1952 s William Early Thompson & Neva Koontz. BA Furman U 1974; MS Virginia Commonwealth U 1979; MDiv EDS 1983. Trans 11/17/2003 Bp Chilton Abbie Richardson Knudsen. m 2/2/2002 Nicki P Thompson c 5. S Mich's Epis Ch Easley SC 2003-2004; S Matt's Epis Ch Spartanburg SC 2002-2003; Olivet Epis Ch Franconia VA 2000-2002; Int The Ch of S Clem Alexandria VA 1999-2000; S Mk's Ch Washington DC 1997-1999; Downeast Epis Cluster Deer Isle ME 1985-1986; Cur Trin Ch Torrington CT 1984-1985. "The Power of Play: The ABC's of Living w Wonder and Exuberance," Auth Hse, 2006. coachwill@charter.net

THOMPSON, Zachary Robert (At) 634 W Peachtree St NW, Atlanta GA 30308 **S Jas Ch Cedartown GA 2011-** B Cincinnati OH 9/19/1982 s Michael Trent Thompson & Carmen Maria. BA Piedmont Coll 2006; MDiv Candler TS at Emory U 2011. D 12/18/2010 P 6/26/2011 Bp J(ohn) Neil Alexander. m 5/31/2009 Amy Rine. zachary42@gmail.com

T

THOMPSON DE MEJIA, Kara Ann (Hond) Spring Garden, Islas De La Bahia, Roatan Honduras **Dio Honduras Miami FL 2006-; Iglesia Epis Hondurena San Pedro Sula 2006-** B New Brunswick Canada 8/24/1974 d Gordon Thompson & Bell. BA St. Steph's U. D 10/29/2005 Bp Lloyd Emmanuel Allen. m 1/19/2002 Nelson Yovany Mejia c 2.

THOMPSON-QUARTEY, C John (NJ) 622 Forman Avenue, Point Pleasant Beach NJ 08742 **R Ch Of S Mary's By The Sea Point Pleasant Bch NJ 2005-** B Ghana W. Africa 9/8/1961 s George Thompson-Quartey & Beatrice. Montclair St U 1990; BS Rutgers-The St U 1993; MDiv GTS 1997. D 5/31/1997 Bp John Shelby Spong P 12/13/1997 Bp Jack Marston McKelvey. m 6/21/2005 Jerlyn Paula Thompson-Quartey c 3. Asst Chr Ch Ridgewood NJ 1997-1999. EvangES 2007-2010; SSM 1987; UBE 1997. jthompsonq@gmail.com

THOMSEN, William Robert (WNC) No address on file. B Greenwich CT 5/14/1933 s William Thomsen & Elizabeth Lucille. Asme Norwalk St Tech Coll 1963. D 10/27/1990 Bp David Elliot Johnson. c 4. D Epis Ch Of The H Sprt Mars Hill NC 2002-2011; S Thos Epis Ch Burnsville NC 1994-2006.

THOMSON, Jacqueline Clark (Va) 9405 Shouse Dr, Vienna VA 22182 **Stndg Com Dio Virginia Richmond VA 2011-; Sr Assoc R S Anne's Epis Ch Reston VA 2007-; Chair, Cmsn for the Prevention of Sexual Misconduct Dio Virginia Richmond VA 2000-; Asst R S Anne's Epis Ch Reston VA 2000-; Colloquy Mentor VTS Alexandria VA 2000-** B Boston MA 4/7/1948 d Charles Clark & Carolyn Pelland. BA Simmons Coll 1970; U of Maryland 1971; MDiv VTS 1998. D 6/13/1998 P 4/15/1999 Bp Peter James Lee. m 5/16/1970 Bernard Melchoir Thomson c 4. Exec Bd Dio Virginia Richmond VA 2008-2011; Chair, Cmsn for the Prevention of Sexual Misconduct Dio Virginia Richmond VA 2000-2011; Cur S Alb's Epis Ch Annandale VA 1998-2000. contributer, "sermon for 9/11," *Gd Prchr - online*, Lectionary Homil, 2011. jackiethomson@verizon.net

THOMSON, James Vestal (Okla) 501 S Cincinnati Ave, Tulsa OK 74103 B Methil Fife Scotland 1/16/1939 s Walter Foster Thomson & Agnes. LTh S Andr's Coll Melrose Gb 1963; CTh Epis TS of The SW 1989. Rec from Roman Catholic 6/1/1989 as Priest Bp James Russell Moodey. c 1. Assoc Trin Ch Tulsa OK 1995-2005; R S Matt's Ch Enid OK 1990-1995; Cur All Souls Epis Ch Oklahoma City OK 1989-1990. jtumilty@hotmail.com

THOMSON, Malcolm Davis (WMich) Church Pension Group, 445 5th Ave, New York NY 10016 B 11/26/1929 D 6/4/1955 P 12/8/1955 Bp Dudley B McNeil.

THOMSON, Richard Dwight (Los) 714 Osprey Ct, Mount Pleasant SC 29464 B Minneapolis MN 10/1/1928 s Dwight O Thomson & Katheryn. AMS U MN 1948; Cert CDSP 1962. D 6/29/1962 P 12/19/1962 Bp Richard S Watson. m 4/18/1982 Mary Lou Cocherell c 4. Vic S Jas Santee Ch McClellanville SC 1993-2006; R H Trin Epis Ch Covina CA 1974-1992; R S Paul's Epis Ch Tustin CA 1971-1974; Assoc Cathd Ch Of S Paul San Diego CA 1966-1971; Cur Ch of S Mary's by the Sea Pacific Grove CA 1964-1965; Vic S Paul's Epis Ch Vernal UT 1962-1964. dickthomson@msn.com

THOMSON, Ronald Reed (RG) 733 Lakeway Dr, El Paso TX 79932 **Supply P Dio Texas Houston TX 1997-; Supply P Dio The Rio Grande Albuquerque NM 1997-; Supply P Dio W Texas San Antonio TX 1997-** B Coffeyville KS 10/24/1932 s Samuel Eugene Thomson & Lena Matys. BBA Texas A&I U 1954; BD Epis TS of The SW 1963. D 6/28/1963 Bp Richard Earl Dicus P 1/5/1964 Bp Everett H Jones. m 12/20/1952 Doris Lovorn c 3. Int S Mk's On The Mesa Epis Ch Albuquerque NM 2001-2002; Int S Thos A Becket Ch Roswell NM 1997-1998; GC Dep Dio The Rio Grande Albuquerque NM 1978-2003; Stndg Com Dio The Rio Grande Albuquerque NM 1974-1981; R/Provost Pro Cathd Epis Ch Of S Clem El Paso TX 1972-1996; R S Jn's Ch New Braunfels TX 1966-1972; Asst Ch Of The Gd Shpd Corpus Christi TX 1963-1966. ron_thomson@swbell.net

THON, Susan Cecelia (WA) 5998 Benalder Dr, Bethesda MD 20816 **R The Ch Of The Redeem Beth MD 1994-** B Baltimore MD 2/9/1947 d Robert William Thon & Evelyn Ellen. BA Cor 1969; JD Cor 1975; MDiv GTS 1989. D 6/10/1989 Bp Paul Moore Jr P 12/9/1989 Bp Richard Frank Grein. m 10/22/2011 Peter Magrath c 3. Asst The Ch Of The Redeem Baltimore MD 1989-1994. "Signs," *Preaching from Psalms, Oracles, and Parables*, Morehouse Pub, 2006; "Risks in Spkng Out--or Not," *Preaching as Prophetic Calling*, Morehouse Pub, 2004. EvangES 2003. revsusanburns@verizon.net

THORN, Jack Horace (Nwk) 209 Chestnut St, Boonton NJ 07005 **P S Paul's Ch No Arlington NJ 2008-; Ret Assoc S Paul's Epis Ch Morris Plains NJ 1996-** B Beacon NY 3/19/1930 s Walter Thorn & Helen. BA Hob 1952; MDiv PDS 1955. D 6/5/1955 P 12/16/1955 Bp Horace W B Donegan. c 4. R S Jn's Epis Ch Boonton NJ 1963-1995; R S Paul's And Trin Par Tivoli NY 1958-1963; Vic Ch Of Our Sav Okeechobee FL 1957-1958; Vic H Nativ Pahokee FL 1957-1958; Cur Gr Ch Middletown NY 1955-1957. Hon Alum GTS. jackthorn@optonline.net

THORNBERG, Anne (NH) 43 Pine St, Exeter NH 03833 **Cur Chr Ch Exeter NH 2010-** B Des Moines IA 12/10/1981 d David Allen Stoller & Nancy Leachman. BA The U NC at Chap Hill 2004; MDiv The GTS 2010. D 6/12/2010 Bp Clifton Daniel III P 12/16/2010 Bp V Gene Robinson. m 5/23/2009 Jeffrey Douglas Thornberg. annethornberg@gmail.com

THORNBERG, Jeffrey Douglas (NH) 101 Chapel St., Portsmouth NH 03801 **S Jn's Ch Portsmouth NH 2008-** B Phoenix AZ 10/23/1982 s Douglas Allen Thornberg & Susan Marie. MDiv GTS; BA U of Texas 2005. D 6/3/2008 P 12/12/2008 Bp V Gene Robinson. m 5/23/2009 Anne Thornberg. curate@stjohnsnh.org

THORNE, Joyce Terrill (RI) 670 Weeden Street, Pawtucket RI 02860 **D S Lk's Ch Pawtucket RI 2011-** B Cambridge MA 1/16/1942 d George Quinton Brathwaite & Virginia Terrill. D 5/22/2010 Bp Geralyn Wolf. c 1. 1bmp@verizon.net

THORNELL, Kwasi (WA) 1525 Casino Cir, Silver Spring MD 20906 B Tuskegee AL 7/27/1944 s Harold Thornell & Mabel. BA Alma Coll 1967; MDiv EDS 1972; DMin EDS 2004. D 6/29/1972 Bp Richard S M Emrich P 3/31/1973 Bp John Thomas Walker. m 5/11/1996 Linda B Cross. Epis Soc Of Chr Ch Cincinnati OH 2000-2004; Cn Vic Epis Soc of Chr Ch Cincinnati OH 2000-2004; R S Phil's Ch Columbus OH 1996-2000; Asst R Calv Ch

Washington DC 1993-1995; Cathd of St Ptr & St Paul Washington DC 1985-1993; Epis Soc of Chr Ch Cincinnati OH 1985-1993; S Steph's Ch S Louis MO 1983-1985; Dio Missouri S Louis MO 1978-1983; S Matt's And S Jos's Detroit MI 1974-1976; Asst Ch Of The Intsn New York NY 1973-1974; Assoc Gr Ch Detroit MI 1972-1973. Auth, *Encore*. katimani@aol.com

THORNTON, Daniel Ingram (Ala) 1402 Prier Dr, Marion AL 36756 **S Wilfrid's Ch Marion AL 2006-** B Florence AL 8/22/1943 s Melton Delano Thornton & Mabel Pearl. BA U So 1965; MA U of Alabama 1967; PhD U of Alabama 1975; DMin STUSo 2004. D 12/21/1993 P 6/24/1994 Bp Robert Oran Miller. c 2. Epis Black Belt Mnstry Demopolis AL 1997-2005; Pstr S Wilfrid's Ch Marion AL 1994-1996; Pstr Trin Ch Demopolis AL 1993-2000; Pstr S Paul's Ch Greensboro AL 1993-1999. thor2741@bellsouth.net

✠ **THORNTON, Rt Rev John Stuart** (Ida) 323 W Jefferson St Apt 204, Boise ID 83702 B Somonauk IL 10/2/1932 s Andrew Robertson Thornton & Gertrude Mae. BA Indiana U 1954; MDiv SFTS 1962; DD CDSP 1995; DD Albertson Coll 1996. D 6/19/1962 P 12/19/1962 Bp James W Hunter Con 9/1/1990 for Ida. m 6/9/1978 Janylee DeBoer. Asst to the R S Mary's Epis Ch Eugene OR 2005-2010; Transitional R S Barn On The Desert Scottsdale AZ 2002-2005; Asstg Bp Dio Spokane Spokane WA 1999-2000; Bp Dio Idaho Boise ID 1990-1998; Vic Ch Of Chr The King On The Santiam Stayton OR 1982-1990; R S Steph's Par Belvedere CA 1969-1982; R Chr Ch Sausalito CA 1964-1968; Asst S Ptr's Epis Ch Sheridan WY 1962-1964. DD Albertson Coll Caldwell ID 1996; DD CDSP Berkeley 1995; Phi Beta Kappa Indiana U 1954. jsthornton32@gmail.com

THORNTON, Norman Edward (Del) Box 2805, Northfield MA 01360 B Winchester MA 3/15/1948 s Norman Miles Thornton & Ruth. BA Hob 1970; MDiv Harvard DS 1977; Cert Amer U in Cairo 1987; MA U of Massachusetts 2000. D 6/18/1977 P 12/20/1978 Bp William Hawley Clark. m 9/16/1972 Mary Patterson Field.

THORNTON, Theresa Joan (SO) 10345 Montgomery Rd, Cincinnati OH 45242 **H Trin Ch Cincinnati OH 2011-** B Brooklyn NY 4/20/1950 d Pasquale D Amendolari & Elodia. U Cinc; BFA SUNY Albany 1972; MDiv Bex 2008. D 6/14/2008 P 6/20/2009 Bp Thomas Edward Breidenthal. m 8/23/1980 James L Thornton c 2. S Barn Epis Ch Montgomery OH 2008-2011. revtjthornton@gmail.com

THORP, Steven Tanner (Spr) 1717 Park Haven Dr, Champaign IL 61820 **P-in-c S Andr's Ch Paris IL 2000-; D Ch Of S Chris Rantoul IL 1997-** B Westerly RI 7/10/1948 s Ira Thorp & Audrey. BA U of Rhode Island 1970; MDiv SWTS 1978; BS NWU 1982. D 6/1/1997 Bp Peter Hess Beckwith. m 7/12/1980 Jael Ruth Cronk.

THORPE, John Andrew (Ia) 2117 North 4th Ave East, Newton IA 50208 **R S Steph's Ch Newton IA 2008-** B Tulsa OK 10/25/1977 s Robert Samuel Thorpe & Christine Leigh. BMUC Oral Roberts U 2002; BA Oral Roberts Universtiy 2002; MDiv Ya Berk 2005. D 6/11/2005 Bp Daniel William Herzog P 12/21/2005 Bp David John Bena. m 12/29/2001 Beth Noelle Thorpe c 1. Assoc R S Ptr's Ch Albany NY 2007-2008; Cur S Ptr's Ch Albany NY 2005-2008; Sem Intern S Ptr's Epis Ch Milford CT 2004-2005. fr_john@iowatelecom.net

THORPE, Mary Brennan (Va) 14 Cornwall St. N.W., Leesburg VA 20176 **Epiph Epis Ch Richmond VA 2010-** B Elizabeth NJ 8/12/1952 d Joseph Owen Brennan & Ann Burgess. BA New Jersey City St U; MME U of Hartford; MDiv VTS. D 6/6/2009 Bp Peter James Lee P 12/6/2009 Bp Shannon Sherwood Johnston. m 10/12/1997 Douglas M Thorpe c 3. Int S Gabr's Epis Ch Leesburg VA 2009-2010. mbthorpe52@gmail.com

THORSTAD, Anita Fortino (SeFla) 951 De Soto Rd Apt 330, Boca Raton FL 33432 **D S Greg's Ch Boca Raton FL 2006-** B Norristown PA 2/16/1941 Dioc Sch For Chr Stds Dio SE F 2005. D 1/21/2006 Bp Leopold Frade. c 2. aspire312@comcast.net

THORWALDSEN, Roland Warren Thor (Los) 1330 Bush St Apt 9m, San Francisco CA 94109 **Died 12/14/2009** B Monmouth IL 9/29/1923 s Adam Martin Thorwaldsen & Albertina Sigrid. BA Monmouth Coll 1947; MA U CA 1949; MDiv CDSP 1952; Fllshp Harv 1965. D 8/9/1952 Bp Karl M Block P 2/15/1953 Bp Henry H Shires.

THRALL, Barbara Judith (WMass) 475 Appleton St, Holyoke MA 01040 **R S Paul's Ch Holyoke MA 2007-** B Chicago IL 5/23/1951 d Frederick Machesney Thrall & Catherine. BA Loyola U 1974; MRE Loyola U 1979; MDiv GTS 1986. D 6/7/1986 P 12/14/1986 Bp Paul Moore Jr. m 6/29/1974 Edward Anthony Farrell c 1. R All SS Epis Ch Littleton NH 1990-2007; Asst Chr And S Steph's Ch New York NY 1986-1990. efbt@comcast.net

THRASHER, Lester Arnold (Tex) 1022 Marine Dr NE Unit 2, C/O Judy Swartsfager - POA, Olympia WA 98501 **Died 3/14/2010** B Saint Elmo IL 6/19/1910 s Jacob Thrasher & Minnie Melissa. BS U IL 1938; MA IL Wesl 1942; Peabody Coll 1950; CDSP 1966. D 5/21/1967 P 6/1/1968 Bp James W Hunter. c 3.

THREADGILL, Nancy Lee (CGC) 5477 White Pine Ct, Mobile AL 36693 **R Ch Of The Gd Shpd Mobile AL 2008-** B Honolulu HI 2/23/1950 d Walter Lee Threadgill & Selena Mary. BS MI SU E Lansing MI 1972; MS MI SU E Lansing MI 1978; BSN U Of Wisconsin Madison WI 1987; MDiv SWTS 2006. D 6/3/2006 P 4/28/2007 Bp Philip Menzie Duncan II. Cur S Lk's Epis Ch Mobile AL 2006-2008. nlthread@comcast.net

THROOP, John Robert (SVa) 500 Court St., Portsmouth VA 23704 **P-in-c Trin Ch Portsmouth VA 2009-** B Evanston IL 6/10/1956 s Robert Smith Throop & Catherine Anne. BA U Chi 1978; MDiv STUSo 1981; DMin Fuller TS 1995. D 6/3/1981 Bp Quintin Ebenezer Primo Jr P 12/4/1981 Bp James Winchester Montgomery. m 12/31/1993 Cindy Jane Ford c 2. Asst Lasalle Cnty Epis Mnstry La Salle IL 2007-2009; Int S Geo's Ch Macomb IL 2006; Vic Chr Ch (Limestone) Peoria IL 1996-2008; Vic S Fran Epis Ch Dunlap IL 1989-1996; Asst S Paul's Ch Akron OH 1987-1989; Assoc Chr Ch Shaker Heights OH 1986-1987; R Ch Of The Medtr Chicago IL 1983-1985; Cur S Simons Ch Arlington Heights IL 1981-1983. Auth, "Shape Up From The Inside Out," Tyndale Hse, 1986; Auth, "Your Ch"; Auth, "Dealing w Suicide," Dav C Cook Pub Co; Auth, "Wrshp Leaders"; Auth, "arts," *Chrsnty Today*; Auth, "Bk Revs," *Living Ch*; Auth, "Bk Revs," *Pub Weekly*. Amer Red Cross Bd Mem 1993-2000; Bd Source 1998-2007; CMA 1996; Cntrl IL Friends of People w AIDS 1994-2002; City Cler Fllshp 1981; City of Portsmouth VA/ADA Cmsn 2010; Grtr Peoria Mass Transit Dist/Trst 2000-2004; Jubilee Coll St Historic Site 1994-2004. drthroop@yahoo.com

THRUMSTON, Richard Emmons (SanD) 3642 Armstrong St, San Diego CA 92111 B Chicago IL 7/27/1922 s Richard Lull Thrumston & Patience Childs. BA Ripon Coll Ripon WI 1947; LTh SWTS 1950; U MN 1958. D 4/11/1950 P 10/28/1950 Bp Harwood Sturtevant. c 3. R Calv Ch Hyannis NE 1981-1984; P S Jos's Ch Mullen NE 1981-1984; Int S Jn's Ch Broken Bow NE 1981; R S Andr's By The Sea Epis Par San Diego CA 1969-1978; R Chr Ch Cn City CO 1962-1969; Cn Chancllr Gr And H Trin Cathd Kansas City MO 1959-1962; R S Matt's Ch St Paul MN 1955-1959; R S Aug's Epis Ch Rhinelander WI 1952-1955; R S Paul's Ch Plymouth WI 1950-1952. Auth, "arts," *Chr Challenge*; Auth, "arts," *Living Ch*.

THULLBERY, Marion F (NC) VA Medical Center, 508 Fulton Street, Durham NC 27705 **Dio No Carolina Raleigh NC 2002-** B Lake Wales FL 11/22/1954 d Alfred Charles Thullbery & Betty Frances. BA Erskine Coll 1976; MDiv TESM 1984; PhD GTF 2008. D 12/21/1985 P 9/15/1986 Bp William Hopkins Folwell. S Paul's Epis Ch Smithfield NC 1998-2000; Asst All SS Epis Ch Enterprise FL 1990-1992; S Richard's Ch Winter Pk FL 1986-1987. marion.thullbery@va.gov

THURLOW, David William Tackaberry (SC) 30 S Dukes St, Summerton SC 29148 **R S Mths Epis Ch Summerton SC 2001-** B Ottowa Ontario CA 7/12/1967 s William John Thurlow & Catherine Therese. BA Carleton U 1990; MDiv U Tor 1995. Trans from Anglican Church of Canada 10/16/2001 Bp Edward Lloyd Salmon Jr. m 3/2/1996 Catherine Cashman.

THURSTON, Anthony Charles (Ore) 39 Greenridge Ct, Lake Oswego OR 97035 **P-in-c S Jn The Evang Ch Milwaukie OR 2009-** B Holland MI 11/26/1940 s Lyman Clifford Thurston & Kathryn Belyou. BA Butler U 1966; STM Ya Berk 1969; New Sch for Soc Resrch 1969; NYU 1969. D 6/13/1969 Bp John P Craine P 12/1/1969 Bp Horace W B Donegan. m 1/30/1965 Christine Anne Olsen c 2. Int S Matt's Epis Ch Eugene OR 2007-2008; Int Dn Trin Cathd Sacramento CA 2005-2006; S Jn The Evang Ch Milwaukie OR 2003-2004; Trin Epis Cathd Portland OR 1991-2003; Cn Dio Milwaukee Milwaukee WI 1986-1991; Epis Hm Mgt Milwaukee WI 1986-1991; R S Paul's Ch Milwaukee WI 1981-1986; R Chr Ch Rochester NY 1977-1981; Cn Cathd Ch Of S Mk Minneapolis MN 1974-1977; Assoc Chr Ch Cathd Indianapolis IN 1971-1972. Chas Berwind Awd Big Brothers/Big Sis 1971; Watson Fllshp Berk 1969. thurstonanthony7@gmail.com

THWEATT III, Richmond Fitzgerald (WLa) 7109 Woodridge Ave, Oklahoma City OK 73132 B Norman OK 6/29/1939 s Richmond F Thweatt & Viola Juanita. BA U of Oklahoma 1961; MDiv SWTS 1964; VTS 1985. D 6/20/1964 P 2/2/1965 Bp Chilton Powell. m 6/27/1964 Josephine E Edwards c 2. Vic Leonidas Polk Memi Epis Mssn Leesville LA 1998-2006; R Trin Epis Ch Deridder LA 1998-2006; Supply P Chr Epis Ch S Jos MO 1997-1998; Int S Paul's Epis Ch Lees Summit MO 1995-1996; Asst S Mich's Epis Ch Independence MO 1994-1998; Trin Epis Ch Marshall MO 1992; Dio W Missouri Kansas City MO 1987-1991; Vic S Mary's Epis Ch Kansas City MO 1987-1990; Int Chr Epis Ch Charlevoix MI 1986-1987; Sec Dioc Conv Dio Wstrn Michigan Kalamazoo MI 1986-1987; Sprtl Dir Happ Dio Wstrn Michigan Kalamazoo MI 1979-1984; Dio Wstrn Michigan Kalamazoo MI 1977; R Trin Epis Ch Grand Ledge MI 1969-1986; Supply P S Jas Ch Antlers OK 1968; Supply P S Mk's Ch Hugo OK 1968; Supply P S Barn Ch Foreman AR 1966; Vic S Lk The Beloved Physcn Idabel OK 1965-1969; Cur Gr Ch Muskogee OK 1964-1965. Auth, *40 Days and 40 Nights- The Flood of '93*. rftiii@aol.com

THWING, Robert C (Ak) Po Box 91943, Anchorage AK 99509 **Asst S Mary's Ch Anchorage AK 1973-** B Seattle WA 3/14/1934 s Samuel Prentice Thwing & Marianne Alice. BA U of Washington. D 11/26/1972 P 5/1/1973 Bp William J Gordon Jr. Assoc S Geo's Ch Cordova AK 1974-1980. Who'S Who In Rel 1977.

TIAPULA, Imo Siufanua (Haw) Po Box 2030, Pago Pago AS 96799 B Laulii 9/13/1938 s Mamea Taiau Tiapula & Salavao. BA Simpson Bible Coll 1970; Med Brigham Young U 1975. D 7/27/1971 Bp C Kilmer Myers P 1/1/1974 Bp Edwin Lani Hanchett. m 7/27/1970 Aliitia T Tuliau c 1. Evang Tchr Trng Assn.

TIBBETT, William Kirkham (NJ) 6481 Midday Ln., Mechanicsville VA 23111 **Died 3/6/2011** B Chippewa Falls WI 2/17/1924 s William Richard Tibbett & Bonnie Jean. BA Westminster Coll 1947; STB (M Div.) EDS 1951. D 6/20/1951 P 12/16/1951 Bp Arthur C Lichtenberger. c 2. Auth, "Lenten Meditations For Students," Luth Ch Of Amer, 1963. Bp'S Medal Of hon Dio NJ Trenton, NJ 1982.

TIBBETTS, Catherine Johnson (Va) The Falls Chruch Episcopal, 225 E. Broad Street, Falls Church VA 22046 **Int P-in-c The Falls Ch Epis Falls Ch VA 2011-; Co-Chair Cmte. on Prevention of Sexual Misconduct Dio Virginia Richmond VA 2010-; Asst P The Falls Ch Epis Falls Ch VA 2009-; Asst The Falls Ch Epis Falls Ch VA 2008-** B Jacksonville FL 3/17/1951 d James E Johnson & Elizabeth E. BS U NC 1973; MPH U Pgh 1977; MDiv VTS 2008. D 5/24/2008 P 12/14/2008 Bp Peter James Lee. m 4/7/1984 Clark Tibbetts c 2. Co-Chair Cmte. on Prevention of Sexual Misconduct Dio Virginia Richmond VA 2010; Mntl Hlth Com Dio Virginia Richmond VA 2006-2010. cathytibbetts@gmail.com

TIBBETTS, Ronald Creighton (Mass) 9 Cooney Ave, Plainville MA 02762 **D All SS Epis Ch Attleboro MA 2010-** B Newton MA 9/22/1953 s Harmon Tibbetts & Carol. D 10/6/2001 Bp M(arvil) Thomas Shaw III. m 2/22/1974 Victoria A Bonollo c 1. Nbrhd Action Inc Boston MA 2002-2009. RONTIBBETTS@YAHOO.COM

TICKNOR, Patricia Horan (WMo) 12270 N New Dawn Ave, Oro Valley AZ 85755 B Indianapolis IN 10/8/1939 d Frederick Charles Horan & Mary Ellen. Ottawa U; U of Kansas; W Missouri Sch of Mnstry. D 1/18/1992 Bp John Clark Buchanan. m 2/7/1958 Brian L Ticknor. S Andr's Ch Kansas City MO 1993-2007. pticknor@mac.com

TICKNOR, William Howard Correa (Md) 5757 Solomons Island Rd, Lothian MD 20711 **R S Jas' Par Lothian MD 1973-; R S Mk's Chap Deale Lothian MD 1973-** B Baltimore MD 4/29/1946 s William Ephraim Ticknor & Elizabeth. BS Towson U 1968; MDiv PDS 1971. D 6/22/1971 Bp Harry Lee Doll P 2/5/1972 Bp David Keller Leighton Sr. m 4/20/1979 Pamela Crandell c 4. Asst Epiph Ch Dulaney Vlly Timonium MD 1971-1973. ticknor@stjameslothian.com

TIDWELL, Janet Ruth (At) 582 Walnut St, Macon GA 31201 B Detroit MI 10/21/1942 d George Stanley Strachan & Erma Lucille. BS Wayne 1965. D 8/6/2011 Bp J(ohn) Neil Alexander. c 2. jtid46@aol.com

TIDY, John Hylton (SeFla) 4025 Pine Tree Dr, Miami Beach FL 33140 **R All Souls' Epis Ch Miami Bch FL 2006-** B Chatham UK 9/7/1948 s Derek H C Tidy & Helen N. AKC King's Coll, London 1971. Trans from The Episcopal Church in Jerusalem and the Middle East 6/26/2007 Bp Leopold Frade. m 4/12/2008 Jill Louise Baker c 3. jtidy@atlanticbb.net

TIEDERMAN, Nancy Jo Copass (Oly) 920 Cherry Ave NE, Bainbridge IS WA 98110 **Asstg P S Barn Epis Ch Bainbridge Island WA 2011-** B Seattle WA 7/18/1940 d Mike Keys Copass & Lucile Dean. BA Stan 1962; MDiv Chr TS 1990. D 9/21/1982 P 7/11/1992 Bp Edward Witker Jones. m 6/29/1963 William G Tiederman c 3. R S Dav's Epis Ch Friday Harbor WA 2002-2008; Chapl Ch Of The Incarn Gainesville FL 1996-2002; Dio Florida Jacksonville FL 1996-2002; Vic S Mary's Ch Palatka FL 1995-1996. Theta Phi. Theta Phi Hon Soc. nancytiederman10@gmail.com

TIEGS, Karen Sara Bretl (Ore) All Saints' Episcopal Church, 3847 Terracina Dr., Riverside CA 92506 **All SS Ch Hillsboro OR 2010-** B Portland OR 9/6/1976 d Robert Francis Bretl & Diana Kathleen. BA Linfield Coll 1999; MDiv CDSP 2007. D 6/30/2007 Bp Johncy Itty P 3/29/2008 Bp Sergio Carranza-Gomez. m 7/7/2007 Peter Greg Tiegs. Cur All SS Epis Ch Riverside CA 2007-2009. revkarentiegs@gmail.com

TIELKING, Claudia Gould (WA) 6533 Mulroy Street, Mc Lean VA 22101 **Beauvoir Sch Cathd of St Ptr & St Paul Washington DC 2003-; Bd Mem S Andr's Epis Sch Potomac MD 2001-** B Manhassett NY 6/3/1961 d Gerald Bernhard Gould & Sue McAdoo. BA Connecticut Coll 1983; MDiv VTS 1990. D 6/9/1990 P 12/15/1990 Bp Ronald Hayward Haines. m 9/21/2002 Nathan Tielking c 2. S Albans Sch Prot Epis Cathd Fndt Washington DC 1992-2003; Asst R Ch Of Our Sav Silver Sprg MD 1990-1992. ctielking@cathedral.org

TIERNEY, Bridget Katherine (Chi) 114 N Pine St, New Lenox IL 60451 B Geneva IL 12/31/1948 d Lawrence Clifford Tierney & Dorothy Mabe. BS Xavier U; MDiv SWTS 2003. D 10/26/2002 P 6/21/2003 Bp Herbert Thompson Jr. m 11/28/2009 John Joseph Nicastro c 3. Gr Epis Ch New Lenox IL 2007-2010; S Jn's Ch Worthington OH 2006; S Jas Epis Ch Columbus OH 2005-2006; P-in-c Trin Epis Ch Troy OH 2003-2005. firefan17@gmail.com

TIERNEY, Dennis Stanley (Oly) 6973 Island Center Rd NE, Bainbridge Island WA 98110 **P S Barn Epis Ch Bainbridge Island WA 2007-** B Los Angeles CA 9/23/1946 s Stanley Edwin Tierney & Laurel. BA U IL 1968; MA NE Illinois U 1974; PhD Claremont Grad Schl 1979; MDiv CDSP 2002. D 6/1/2002 P 12/7/2002 Bp William Edwin Swing. m 11/24/1978 Grace Elinor Grant. S Bede's Epis Ch Menlo Pk CA 2002-2007. dennis@grant-tierney.us

TIERNEY III, Peter George (RI) PO Box 491, Little Compton RI 02837 **R S Andr's By The Sea Little Compton RI 2010-** B Geneva NY 6/4/1977 s Peter George Tierney & Susan Pola. MDiv Ya Berk 2006; STM Ya Berk 2007; BA Hob 2007. D 6/30/2007 P 2/25/2008 Bp Jack Marston McKelvey. m 8/11/2007 Veronica Mary Carlsen. Cur Chr Ch Needham MA 2007-2010. pgtiii@aya.yale.edu

TIERNEY, Philip Joseph (RI) 1412 Providence Rd, Charlotte NC 28207 B Boston MA 11/8/1950 s John Paul Tierney & Ethel B. DMin Bos; BA Gordon Coll 1972; S Jn Coll Gb 1974; MDiv VTS 1976. D 6/9/1976 Bp Morris Fairchild Arnold P 5/11/1977 Bp William Henry Marmion. m 7/9/1988 Sandra T Tsouprake. S Paul's Ch No Kingstown RI 2004-2010; R Chr Ch Charlotte NC 1998-2004; Chair - Com Dio California San Francisco CA 1989-1998; R Trin Par Menlo Pk CA 1988-1998; The Par Of S Chrys's Quincy MA 1987-1988; Chair - Com Dio Pittsburgh Monroeville PA 1982-1984; Ch Of The Ascen Pittsburgh PA 1980-1984; Assoc S Chris's Ch Springfield VA 1978-1980; Chr Ch Blacksburg VA 1976-1978. Clincal Theol Assn. pjtierney@cox.net

TIERNEY, Veronica Mary (Los) St. George's School, PO Box 1910, Newport RI 02840 **Asst Chapl S Geo's Sch Newport RI 2010-** B Victoria BC Canada 9/11/1973 d Barrie Carlsen & Rosemary Ruth. BA Clark U 1995; MDiv Ya Berk 2007. D 6/9/2007 P 5/31/2008 Bp Joseph Jon Bruno. m 8/11/2007 Peter George Tierney. P Assoc Trin Ch Newton Cntr MA 2007-2010. veronicamtierney@gmail.com

TIFF II, Richard Olin (Los) Po Box 2083, Yountville CA 94599 B Arcadia CA 4/10/1969 D 6/11/2005 Bp Chester Lovelle Talton P 1/14/2006 Bp Joseph Jon Bruno. Off Of Bsh For ArmdF New York NY 2005-2008; S Marg Of Scotland Par San Juan Capistrano CA 2005-2008; S Mary's Par Lompoc CA 1998-2004; Ch Of The Epiph San Carlos CA 1998-2002. rtiff@gts.edu

TIFFANY, Roger Lyman (Mich) 941 Damon Dr, Medina OH 44256 B Hartford CT 8/22/1923 s Wallace Case Tiffany & Marjorie Rose. BA Br 1948; BD EDS 1951; MLS Kent St U 1975. D 5/30/1951 Bp William A Lawrence P 6/1/1952 Bp Granville G Bennett. c 3. Vic S Mk's Epis Ch Marine City MI 1977-1984; R S Thos' Epis Ch Port Clinton OH 1958-1975; R Trin Epis Ch Collinsville CT 1955-1958; Asst Gr Ch In Providence Providence RI 1951-1955.

TIGHE, Maureen (Ore) 1001 B-Ne 90th Ave, Portland OR 97220 **P Assoc Trin Epis Cathd Portland OR 1997-** B Minneapolis MN 11/3/1933 d William Michael Tighe & Josephine. BA U MN 1957; MFA Mills Coll 1978; MDiv CDSP 1996. D 6/30/1996 P 4/6/1997 Bp Robert Louis Ladehoff. c 2. Chapl Legacy Gd Samar Hosp Portland OR 1997-2005. Assembly Of Epis Hosp Chapl 1996; Assn Of Profsnl Chapl 1996-2007. reenyfoof@msn.com

TILDEN, George Bruce (NCal) No address on file. B 11/24/1939 D 6/23/1963 Bp James Albert Pike P 12/19/1970 Bp Clarence Rupert Haden Jr.

TILDEN, Roger (Md) 8089 Harmony Rd, Denton MD 21629 B Brooklyn NY 11/27/1940 s Earle Ray Tilden & Margaret Catherine. BA Hob 1962; STB Ya Berk 1965; STM UTS 1968; DMin S Mary Seminarysaint Mary Sem/U Baltimore 1982. D 6/19/1965 P 12/1/1965 Bp Jonathan Goodhue Sherman. c 2. R S Paul's Ch Trappe MD 2001-2004; R S Mich And All Ang Ch Baltimore MD 2000-2001; R S Jas Epis Ch Birmingham MI 1986-1999; R S Lk's Ch Alexandria VA 1983-1986; R S Paul's Ch Petersburg VA 1978-1983; R Ch Of S Marks On The Hill Pikesville MD 1975-1978; Assoc S Lk's Ch E Hampton NY 1968-1970; Asst S Mk's Ch Islip NY 1965-1967. Fell Coll Of Preachers. rogertilden@comcast.net

TILING, Robert Henry (Q) 386 Perthshire Dr, C/O Sarah Coffey, Orange Park FL 32073 Philippines B Saint Paul,MN 12/5/1945 s Henry Charles Tiling & Elizabeth. BA U MN 1968; MA Penn 1971; MDiv Nash 1985. D 6/24/1985 Bp Robert Marshall Anderson P 1/1/1986 Bp William Charles Wantland. m 6/7/1969 Carla Gwen Tiling. Brent Intl Sch 2000-2006; Cathd Of The H Trin 1996-2000; R Gr Epis Ch Galesburg IL 1992-1996; Our Sav's Phillips WI 1989-1992; S Marg's Pk Falls WI 1989-1992; S Kath's Ch Owen WI 1985-1992. Auth, "7 Hist arts For Mn Hist Soc". bobtiling@yahoo.com

TILLER, Monte Jackson (SeFla) 6409 Lantana Pines Dr, Lantana FL 33462 B Louisville KY 11/4/1942 s Armand A Tiller & Mona. MDiv Louisville Presb TS 1982; SWTS 1982; Sfcts 1993. D 8/30/1979 P 11/4/1980 Bp David Reed. m 5/21/1994 Susan A Tiller c 1. R Ch Of The H Redeem Lake Worth FL 1994-2002; Int S Mary Magd Epis Ch Coral Sprg FL 1992-1994; Vic Ch Of The Resurr W Chicago IL 1982-1985; S Lk's Ch Anchorage KY 1980-1982; D S Andr's Ch Louisville KY 1979-1980.

TILLER JR, Thomas E(lton) (Miss) 1428 Kimwood Dr, Jackson MS 39211 B Memphis TN 12/7/1925 s Thomas Elton Tiller & Ruby Catherine. CTh Epis TS of The SW 1958. D 6/11/1958 P 12/11/1958 Bp Duncan Montgomery Gray. m 1/8/1949 Frances Aurand c 4. Cn S Andr's Cathd Jackson MS 1992-1995; Mississippi Rel Ldrshp Conf Jackson MS 1985-1990; The Chap Of The Cross Madison MS 1980-1985; S Chris's Ch Jackson MS 1978-1990;

Ecum Off Dio Mississippi Jackson MS 1972-1994; In-c S Mk's Ch Jackson MS 1963-1974; Vic All SS Ch Inverness MS 1958-1963; Vic S Thos Ch Belzoni MS 1958-1963. EDEO Epis/Jewish Relatio 1972-1994. TILLER_T@bellsouth.net

TILLEY, David James (La) 12636 E Robin Hood Dr, Baton Rouge LA 70815 B Jersey City NJ 11/3/1939 s Louis N Tilley & Mary. BA LSU 1961; MDiv STUSo 1970. D 6/25/1970 P 4/1/1971 Bp Iveson Batchelor Noland. m 9/1/1962 Carole Ann Lemoine c 3. Vic S Tim's Ch La Place LA 1981-1984; S Aug's Ch Baton Rouge LA 1971-1979; Cur Epis Ch Of The Gd Shpd Lake Chas LA 1970-1971. ERM, Curs, Fa. songbird600@aol.com

TILLITT, Jay Lanning (LI) 1021 N University St, Redlands CA 92374 B San Bernardino CA 6/23/1941 s Harley E Tillitt & Sylvia. BA U of Redlands 1963; Nash 1967. D 7/25/1968 Bp Joseph Summerville Minnis P 12/1/1969 Bp Jonathan Goodhue Sherman. R All SS' Epis Ch Long Island City NY 1975-1978; Cur Chr Ch Epis Hudson NY 1973-1975; Cur S Jn's Ch Brooklyn NY 1969-1973; Cur S Andr's Ch Stamford CT 1968-1969. Cltn Of The Apolistic Mnstry; Tertiary Of The Soc Of S Fran.

TILLMAN, Ann Marie (CNY) Caroline Church of Brookhaven, 1 Dyke Road, Setauket NY 11733 **Cur Caroline Ch Of Brookhaven Setauket NY 2008-** B Fairbanks AK 4/20/1959 d Perry Lynn Dedrick & Jean Westbrook. BS Cor 1998; MDiv GTS 2008. D 6/14/2008 Bp Gladstone Bailey Adams III P 2/21/2009 Bp E(gbert) Don Taylor. m 10/20/1990 Jason Tillman c 2. Pstr Assoc Ch Of The Atone Bronx NY 2008. ann.tillman@gmail.com

TILLMAN, Christine Wylie (WMich) 3826 Wedgewood Dr Sw, Wyoming MI 49519 B Grand Rapids MI 6/7/1951 d Robert Milton Wylie & Peggyann Dorothy. BA Wstrn Michigan U 1974. D 5/3/1986 Bp Howard Samuel Meeks. c 2. Stff H Trin Epis Ch Wyoming MI 1986-2002. NAAD.

TILLOTSON, Ellen Louise (Ct) 220 Prospect St, Torrington CT 06790 **Bd Trst The GTS New York NY 2011-; COM Dio Connecticut Hartford CT 2008-** B Bismarck ND 6/11/1957 d William Wolcott Tillotson & Doris Carol. BA-cl U of No Dakota 1979; MDiv GTS 1983. D 7/10/1983 P 2/14/1984 Bp Harold Anthony Hopkins Jr. m 8/7/1999 Frank Miller Turner. COM Dio Connecticut Hartford CT 2008-2011; Stndg Com Dio Connecticut Hartford CT 2006-2011; Alum/ae Exec Commitee Pres The GTS New York NY 2006-2009; R Trin Ch Torrington CT 1992-2011; Trin Ch On The Green New Haven CT 1983-1992. Auth, "The H Sprt," *The Epis*. Paul Harris Fell Rotary Intl 2006. revelt01@aol.com

TILSON, Alan Russell (Kan) 2020 W 49th St, Shawnee Mission KS 66205 B Maryville MO 6/10/1949 s Billy French Tilson & Clarice Jean. BA Washburn U 1975; MDiv Nash 1984. D 6/29/1984 P 1/1/1985 Bp John Forsythe Ashby. c 3. R S Paul's Ch Kansas City KS 1997-2003; Ch Of The Cov Jct City KS 1997; Ch Of The Nativ Burnsville MN 1992-1996; R Ch Of The H Comm S Ptr MN 1986-1991; P-in-c S Ptr's Ch New Ulm MN 1986-1991; P-in-c Ch Of The Trsfg Bennington KS 1984-1986; S Fran Cmnty Serv Inc. Salina KS 1984-1986. altilson@swbell.net

TILSON JR, Hugh Arvil (NC) 3819 Jones Ferry Rd, Chapel Hill NC 27516 B Plainview TX 7/24/1946 BS Texas Tech U 1968; PhD U MN 1972. D 6/3/2006 Bp Michael Bruce Curry. m 9/4/1981 Gaylia Harry. tilsm.hugh@epa.gov

TIMBERLAKE, George Philip (WA) 5 Walnutwood Ct, Germantown MD 20874 **P-in-c S Barn Epis Ch Temple Hills MD 2009-** B Steubenville OH 12/23/1923 s Richard Henry Timberlake & Margaret Elizabeth. AB Ken 1947; BD Bex 1950; ThM Holland-Wstrn TS, Mich. 1969. D 6/13/1950 P 12/16/1950 Bp Beverley D Tucker. m 6/25/1977 Patricia Timberlake c 5. Pstr Visitor S Columba's Ch Washington DC 2002-2008; H Sprt Epis Ch Gaithersburg MD 1980-1982; P-in-c Chr Ch Towanda PA 1978-1979; P-in-c S Paul's Ch Troy PA 1978-1979; R Trin Ch Athens PA 1977-1979; Asst S Phil's Epis Ch Laurel MD 1975-1977; R Chr Ch Par La Crosse WI 1970-1972; R S Jn's Epis Ch Grand Haven MI 1958-1970; R Trin Ch Findlay OH 1951-1958. Auth, "Hm Characteristics of Faith that Help Us..."; Auth, "Make End-of-Life Decisions"; Auth, "Bk Revs on Med Ethics," *Reformed Revs*. Angl Working Grp in Bioethics 2002; Metro Washington Bioethics Ntwk 2002; WECA 2002. timbergeo@aol.com

TIMBERLAKE, Roland Ashley (Tex) 8609 Appalachian Dr, Austin TX 78759 B Hebbronville TX 11/28/1932 s Roland Henry Timberlake & Elmora. BBA U of Texas 1959; MDiv Epis TS of The SW 1972. D 6/8/1972 Bp Harold Cornelius Gosnell P 12/10/1972 Bp Richard Earl Dicus. m 6/11/1955 Alice Magruder. Alt Dep, GC Dio Texas Houston TX 1997-2002; Exec Coun Dio Texas Houston TX 1989-1992; Trst Dio Texas Houston TX 1983-1986; R S Lk's On The Lake Epis Ch Austin TX 1982-2002; Sprtl Dir, Curs Dio Texas Houston TX 1979-1980; Dio Texas Houston TX 1976-1978; R S Chris's Ch League City TX 1975-1982; Assoc S Mk's Epis Ch San Antonio TX 1972-1975; Dir, Stwdshp Cont Dio W Texas San Antonio TX 1967-1968. Auth, *Our Chr Times*; Auth, *Texas Epis*. Chapl OSL-Physcn 1992. Outstanding Young Men in Amer 1966. rolandt@sbcglobal.net

TIMMERMAN, Melissa Roen (Md) 484 Lymington Rd, Severna Park MD 21146 **D H Cross Faith Memi Epis Ch Pawleys Island SC 2008-; S Bede's Ch Atlanta GA 2005-** B Los Angeles CA 7/2/1957 d John Roen & Patricia. D 6/5/2004 Bp Robert Wilkes Ihloff. m 5/21/1983 Robert Timmerman c 2. D Gr Ch Elkridge MD 2005-2008; S Mary's Outreach Cntr Baltimore MD 2004-2005. mrtalt@msn.com

TIMMONS III, Thomas Jefferson (SO) 163 E High St # B, London OH 43140 **Died 8/6/2011** B Middletown OH 4/8/1933 s Charles Bennett Timmons & Marguerite. BA Ohio Wesl 1955; MDiv EDS 1958. D 6/4/1958 P 1/4/1959 Bp Henry W Hobson. m 8/10/2011 Sarah S Timmons c 3.

TINDALL, Byron Cheney (SC) 102 Fir Court Unit 1260, Waleska GA 30183 **P Assoc Epis Ch Of The H Fam Jasper GA 2008-** B Atlanta GA 5/18/1941 s James Francis Tindall & Gladys Shaw. W&M 1961; BA Emory & Henry Coll 1965; TEE Cert TS 1979. D 6/17/1978 P 6/1/1979 Bp Ned Cole. m 3/16/1963 Anne Lee Talbot c 3. Chr Ch Denmark SC 1992-2006. bctindall@hotmail.com

TINKLEPAUGH, John R (Pa) 400 Walnut Lane, North East MD 21901 **S Paul's Ch Plymouth WI 2007-** B Binghamton NY 11/20/1936 s Joseph David Tinklepaugh & Pearl Angeline. BA The Kings Coll Briarcliff Manor NY 1960; MDiv Denver Sem 1964; VTS 1974; DMin Lancaster TS 1995. D 6/23/1974 P 11/10/1974 Bp Robert Rae Spears Jr. m 1/2/1981 Carole Nunamaker c 4. R Ch Of S Jude And The Nativ Lafayette Hill PA 1985-2006; Ch Of Our Sav Jenkintown PA 1985; Int Dio Pennsylvania Philadelphia PA 1983-1985; R Ch Of S Andr And S Monica Philadelphia PA 1982-1983; Ch Of The Gd Shpd Savona NY 1980-1981; R S Jas Ch Hammondsport NY 1980-1981; L'Eglise Epis au Rwanda New York NY 1978-1980; Asst Min S Paul's Ch Rochester NY 1974-1978. elkboh@aol.com

TINNING, Herbert Peter (Nwk) 93 Sagamore Rd, Millburn NJ 07041 **Died 11/7/2010** B Hoboken NJ 4/17/1928 s Peter Christian Tinning & Emmy Asta. ME Stevens Inst of Tech 1952. D 12/15/1974 Bp James Winchester Montgomery. c 2. herbt@qwestinternet.net

TINNON, Becky Vollicks (CGC) 909 Santa Rosa Blvd Unit 256, Fort Walton Beach FL 32548 B New Castle PA 11/1/1961 d Edward Vollick & Mardelle. BA Olivet Nazarene U 1984; MRE Nazarene TS Kansas City MO 1987; MDiv Nazarene TS Kansas City MO 1997. D 1/6/2008 P 6/28/2008 Bp Philip Menzie Duncan II. m 10/26/1985 Michael Scott Tinnon c 2. Ch Of The Epiph Crestview FL 2011; Cur S Simon's On The Sound Ft Walton Bch FL 2008-2011. mbtinnon@bellsouth.net

TINNON, Michael Scott (CGC) U S. Air Force Chaplain, 210 Cody Ave., Hurlburt Field FL 32544 B Lexington KY 3/7/1950 s Lloyd Earl Tinnon & Carlyn Vermillion. BA U of Kentucky 1982; MDiv/MRE Nazarene TS Kansas City MO 1987; DMin Asbury TS Wilmore KY 2001. D 1/6/2008 P 6/28/2008 Bp Philip Menzie Duncan II. m 10/26/1985 Becky Vollicks Tinnon c 3. mbtinnon@bellsouth.net

TINSLEY JR, Fred Haley (WLa) 1252 Canterbury Dr, Alexandria LA 71303 **R S Jas Epis Ch Alexandria LA 2003-** B Pampa TX 1/27/1948 s Fred Haley Tinsley & Juanita Maureen. BS U of Oklahoma 1972; MDiv STUSo 1982. D 6/24/1982 P 2/21/1983 Bp Sam Byron Hulsey. m 6/6/1969 Judy K Watkins c 2. R S Matt's Epis Ch Houma LA 1996-2003; R Ch Of The H Cross W Memphis AR 1992-1996; Asst S Andr's Epis Ch Amarillo TX 1988-1992; All SS Epis Sch Lubbock TX 1987-1988; H Cross Lubbock TX 1987-1988; Vic Gr Ch Vernon TX 1984-1987; Vic Trin Ch Quanah TX 1984-1987; Cur Ch Of The H Trin Midland TX 1982-1984. OHC 1979. fht3127@gmail.com

TIPPETT, Michael R (Minn) 2202 Lexington Parkway South, Saint Paul MN 55105 **P-in-c S Paul's Epis Ch Owatonna MN 2002-** B Kilwinning Scotland GB 1/15/1954 s Ronald George Tippett & Jessie Alexina. Oxf 1976; BA Royal Mltry Acad 1978; Psc British Army Stff Coll 1985; MDiv Ya Berk 1994. D 6/11/1994 Bp Clarence Nicholas Coleridge P 3/1/1995 Bp Sanford Zangwill Kaye Hampton. m 5/28/1989 Krista Tippett c 2. Geth Ch Minneapolis MN 2000-2001; Int S Jn The Evang S Paul MN 1996-2000; Assoc S Jn The Evang S Paul MN 1994-1995. michaeltippett@earthlink.net

TIPTON, Harry Steadman (CGC) 129 Camellot Ct, Crestview FL 32539 B Knoxville TN 8/10/1937 s Harry Britt Tipton & Henrietta Marcelle. BS LSU 1960; ThM SWTS 1965. D 6/26/1965 Bp Iveson Batchelor Noland P 5/1/1966 Bp Girault M Jones. m 9/1/1962 Maureen May Maxwell. Ch Of The Epiph Crestview FL 1991-1998; P-in-c S Monica's Cantonment FL 1990-1991; Off Of Bsh For ArmdF New York NY 1969-1990; Vic Calv Ch Bunkie LA 1965-1969. ECM, ERM, Bro Of S Andr. Commendation Medal 3rd Oak Leaf Cluster; Meritorious Serv Medal Af. REVAROAMIN@YAHOO.COM

TIPTON, Tommy Hicks (USC) 1029 Old Plantation Dr, Pawleys Island SC 29585 **Dio Upper So Carolina Columbia SC 2011-** B Rutherforton NC 4/14/1952 s Alvin Hicks Tipton & Edith Marie. AA S Leo Coll 1988; MDiv STUSo 1991. D 6/24/1991 P 6/1/1992 Bp Edward Lloyd Salmon Jr. m 3/6/1970 Betty Faye Cole c 1. R H Cross Faith Memi Epis Ch Pawleys Island SC 1999-2011; Prince Geo Winyah Epis Preschool Georgetown SC 1991-1999; Asst to R Prince Geo Winyah Epis Ch Georgetown SC 1991-1999. tht414@gmail.com

TIPTON-ZILE, Cynthia (Md) 4500 C Dunton Ter, Perry Hall MD 21128 **R S Alb's Epis Ch Glen Burnie MD 2006-** B Rome GA 8/12/1950 d James Burton Tipton & Ethel Marie. EFM 1995; Maryland TS 1995. D 6/10/1995 Bp Charles Lindsay Longest P 12/20/2003 Bp Robert Wilkes Ihloff. m 1/10/2009 ERic Neil Zile. Prog and Bdgt Com Dio Maryland Baltimore MD 2005-2011;

R Ch Of The Ascen Baltimore MD 1999-2006; Dioc Coun Dio Maryland Baltimore MD 1999-2003; Cathd Of The Incarn Baltimore MD 1999-2000; Bp's Search Com Dio Maryland Baltimore MD 1997-1998; Eccl Crt Dio Maryland Baltimore MD 1996-1998; D H Cross Ch St MD 1995-1998. tipmain@verizon.net

TIRADO, Hernan (Colom) Apartado Aereo 52, Cartagena Colombia B 7/17/1930 D 9/7/1974 P 2/13/1976 Bp William Alfred Franklin. m 9/8/1971 Amparo Cardon. Iglesia Epis En Colombia 1974-1980.

TIRADO, Vincent (SeFla) 18601 Sw 210th St, Miami FL 33187 B Puerto Rico 1/22/1943 s Vincent Tirado & Recci. D 7/25/2003 Bp Leopold Frade. m 5/3/1964 Delia Tirado c 3.

TIRRELL, Charles David (Tex) 9701 Meyer Forest Dr Apt 12112, Houston TX 77096 B Phillipsburg NJ 12/13/1935 s Matthew Vincent Tirrell & Ruth Katherine. BA Villanova U 1958; ThM Augustinian Coll 1962; MA CUA 1966. Rec from Roman Catholic 12/1/1998 as Priest Bp Claude Edward Payne. m 9/2/1978 Brenda P Peabody c 2. S Mk's Ch Houston TX 2002-2005; S Steph's Epis Ch Houston TX 2002; Asst Emm Ch Houston TX 2000-2003; Vic Lord Of The St Epis Mssn Ch Houston TX 1999-2000. Cert Pstr Addictions Counslr; Lic Psychol. ctirrell@tds.net

TIRRELL, John Alden (Cal) No address on file. B Chicago IL 11/12/1932 s Henry Stanley Tirrell & Dorothy Elliot. BA Stan 1955; BTh VTS 1958; Phillips U 1959. D 6/24/1958 P 6/1/1961 Bp James Albert Pike.

TISDALE JR, William Alfred (Ct) 27 Church St, Stonington CT 06378 B Sumter SC 1/10/1953 s William Alfred Tisdale & Lottie Ethel Yates. BA Wofford Coll 1975; DMin The UTS 1979; STM The GTS 1999. D 6/13/2009 Bp Andrew Donnan Smith P 1/16/2010 Bp James Elliot Curry. m 12/28/1974 Leonora Tubbs Leonora Muldrow Tubbs c 2. R Calv Ch Stonington CT 2010; Ya Berk New Haven CT 2009-2010; Chr Ch New Haven CT 2009-2010. william.tisdale@yale.edu

TISDELLE, Celeste Richardson (Fla) St. Mary's Episcopal Church, 400 St. Johns Ave, Green Cove Springs FL 32043 **R S Mary's Epis Ch Green Cove Sprg FL 2010-** B Key West FL 9/11/1951 BA U Of Florida 1974; MDiv STUSo 2003. D 6/8/2003 P 12/7/2003 Bp Stephen Hays Jecko. m 5/14/1977 Achille Carlisle Tisdelle c 3. P-in-c S Mary's Epis Ch Green Cove Sprg FL 2009-2010; Chapl to Day Sch Gr Epis Ch Orange Pk FL 2006-2009; Cn for Pstr Care & Chapl to Cathd Fndt S Jn's Cathd Jacksonville FL 2004-2006; Chapl to Day Sch S Andr's Ch Jacksonville FL 2003-2004. ctisdelle@stmarysgreencovesprings.com

TITCOMB, Cecily Johnson (SeFla) 295 Bahama Ln, Palm Beach FL 33480 B Saint Paul MN 7/5/1947 d Donald Johnson & Marjorie. BS Barry U; Briarcliffe Coll; Wms. D 11/7/2004 Bp Leopold Frade. m 8/16/1969 E Rodman Titcomb c 4. D The Epis Ch Of Beth-By-The-Sea Palm Bch FL 2005-2010. cecie295@yahoo.com

TITTLE, Darlene Anne Duryea (Nwk) 11 Overhill Dr, Budd Lake NJ 07828 B Orange NJ 3/25/1943 d Norman Earl Duryea & Viola Emma. BA Glassboro St U 1966; MA Virginia Tech U 1973; MDiv VTS 1981; DMin Wesley Sem 1993. D 6/13/1981 P 12/1/1981 Bp Robert Bruce Hall. m 7/18/1976 Richard L Tittle. R Chr Ch Budd Lake NJ 2004-2008; P-in-c S Steph's Ch S Louis MO 1999-2003; H Sprt Epis Ch Gaithersburg MD 1986-1999; All SS' Epis Ch Chevy Chase MD 1981-1986; Asst S Chris's Ch Springfield VA 1980-1981; Asst Chr Ch Columbia MD 1976-1979. Auth, "A Handful Of Quiet"; Auth, "The Sprtl Ldrshp Of The Epis Ch"; Auth, "We Are One In The Sprt". revdarlenetittle@aol.com

TITUS, Bessie Charlotte (Ak) Po Box 75357, Fairbanks AK 99707 B Fairbanks AK 4/8/1955 D 9/3/2000 P 4/8/2001 Bp Mark Lawrence Mac Donald.

TITUS, Fred David (Ia) St. Thomas' Episcopal Church, 710 N. Main St., Garden City KS 67846 B North Platte NE 4/29/1942 s Fred Bruce Titus & Kathleen Mable. LTh Epis TS In Kentucky 1978. D 5/26/1978 P 3/1/1979 Bp Walter Cameron Righter. m 11/13/1967 Ilis Charleen Telitz. Calv Epis Ch Sioux City IA 1984-1988; S Geo's Epis Ch Le Mars IA 1984-1985; Dio Iowa Des Moines IA 1978-2007; S Andr's Ch Des Moines IA 1978-1984.

TITUS, John Clark (At) 5428 Park Cir, Stone Mountain GA 30083 **D S Mich And All Ang Ch Stone Mtn GA 1992-** B Philadelphia PA 10/14/1940 s George Samuel Titus & Clare. BA Pr 1962; MA GW 1972. D 10/23/1993 Bp Frank Kellogg Allan. mojotitus@mindspring.com

TITUS, John Liscomb (Neb) 1722 East Avenue Drive, Holdrege NE 68949 **Dept Of Congrl Dvlpmt Dio Nebraska Omaha NE 1998-; D S Eliz's Ch Holdrege NE 1985-** B Holdrege NE 9/30/1941 s Liscomb Johnson Titus & Jane. EFM; BA Hastings Coll of Law 1964. D 11/8/1985 Bp James Daniel Warner. m 7/8/1991 Suzanne R Titus. Evang Cmsn Dio Nebraska Omaha NE 1987-1989; Exec Coun Dio Nebraska Omaha NE 1983-1986. jltitus947@msn.com

TITUS, Luke (Ak) Saint Barnabas Mission, Minto AK 99758 B Tenana AK 7/9/1941 s Robert Titus & Elsie Titus. Cook Chr Trng Sch. D 7/14/1971 P 1/1/1972 Bp William J Gordon Jr. c 1. Navajoland Area Mssn Farmington NM 1978-1979; Dio Alaska Fairbanks AK 1971-1978. Auth, "Epis".

TITUS, Nancy Espenshade (NC) 1739 Berwickshire Cir, Raleigh NC 27615 **D Epis Campus Mnstry No Carolina St U Raleigh NC 2010-** B Washington DC 8/6/1940 d Paul Slaymaker Espenshade & Irene Barlow. BSN Duke 1962; MS Boston Coll 1964; Dio No Carolina 1995; Cert Haden Inst 2009. D 1/6/1996 Bp Huntington Williams Jr. c 3. D Ch Of The Nativ Raleigh NC 2000-2009; D S Paul's Epis Ch Smithfield NC 1996-1999. DOK 1984. DEACON_NANCY@EARTHLINK.NET

TJELTVEIT, Maria Washington Eddy (Be) 124 S Madison St, Allentown PA 18102 **R The Epis Ch Of The Medtr Allentown PA 1999-** B Sapporo JP 12/24/1959 d Elizabeth Toole. BA Swarthmore Coll 1981; MDiv Ya Berk 1986. D 6/11/1986 P 6/12/1987 Bp Robert Poland Atkinson. R S Andr's Ch Harrington Pk NJ 1994-1998; Asst R S Jn's Epis Ch Tappahannock VA 1988-1994; S Paul's Epis Ch Alexandria VA 1988-1994; Asst R S Matt's Ch Charleston WV 1986-1988. revmariat@verizon.net

TJOFLAT, Marie Elizabeth (Fla) 895 Palm Valley Rd, Ponte Vedra FL 32081 **St Fran in the Field Ponte Vedra FL 2011-** B Jacksonville FL 11/29/1960 d Gerald Bard Tjoflat & Sarah Marie Pfohl. BA Jacksonville U 1984; MA USC 1993; MDiv Ya Berk 2011. D 12/5/2010 P 6/19/2011 Bp Samuel Johnson Howard. marie.tjoflat@yale.edu

TLUCEK, Laddie Raymond (Okla) 1509 Nw 198th St, Edmond OK 73003 B Nampa ID 2/2/1945 s Louis Joseph Tlucek & Helen Marie. BA U Of Idaho Moscow 1966; U of Utah 1968; MDiv CDSP 1971; Med Albertson Coll 1979. D 6/25/1971 P 12/28/1971 Bp J(ohn) Joseph Meakins Harte. m 7/7/1973 Andrea Beatty c 2. Assoc All Souls Epis Ch Oklahoma City OK 2000-2010; R S Paul's Epis Ch Grand Forks ND 1996-2000; R S Lk's Epis Ch Wenatchee WA 1982-1996; Vic S Geo's Ch Seattle WA 1979-1982; R S Jas Epis Ch Midvale UT 1974-1979; R S Mary's Ch Emmett ID 1972-1974; Cur Gd Shpd Of The Hills Cave Creek AZ 1971-1972; Cur S Steph's Ch Phoenix AZ 1971-1972. laddiet@gmail.com

TO, Albany Shiu-Kin (NY) 69 Coachman Dr, Rising Sun MD 21911 B HK 10/31/1931 s Herbert Wai-Ting To & Alice Shui-Tung. BS Hong Kong Tech Hk 1954; BTh Trin 1961; MBA Pace Coll 1976. P 9/1/1962 Bp The Bishop of Singapore. m 4/7/1958 Patsy Lye-Hwa Ngoi c 4. All SS' Epis Ch Briarcliff Manor NY 1993; R Epis Ch Of Our Sav New York NY 1993; Consult To Asian Mnstry Calv and St Geo New York NY 1976-1978; Vic Epis Ch Of Our Sav New York NY 1973-1988; Diocn Msnry & Ch Extntn Socty New York NY 1973-1976; Dpt Of Missions Ny Income New York NY 1973-1976. Auth, "Clergyman As Effective Mgr"; Auth, "Computer Registration," *Computer Secy Ch Acctounting & Register Computer Software For Par.* Resrch Fell Coventry Cathd 1969; Bp Cross Dio Ny 91; Fell 69 Wcc. atoonline@zoominternet.net

TOBERMAN, Harold Frederick (Ark) 1809 Dew Drop Dr, Marion IL 62959 **D S Jas Epis Ch Marion IL 2011-** B Chicago IL 7/6/1950 s Harold Francis Toberman & Lorraine Mary. BA No Cntrl Coll 1972; MBA Loyola U 1978; Cert 1987. D 12/26/1987 Bp Frank Tracy Griswold III. m 7/3/1971 Linda Marie Cavanaugh c 3. D Emm Ch Lake Vill AR 870-2652230or8 1999-2006; D Ch Of The Incarn Bloomingdale IL 1987-1999. NAAD 1988. hal.toberman@gmail.com

TOBIAS, Gwendolyn Warnke (SeFla) 3300A S. Seacrest Blvd., Boynton Beach FL 33435 **Assoc P S Jos's Epis Ch Boynton Bch FL 2011-** B Milwaukee WI 11/5/1954 d James R Warnke & Beverley A. M.Div. VTS 2008. D 12/22/2007 P 7/1/2008 Bp Leopold Frade. m 5/12/1990 Scott Tobias c 3. Dir of Wrshp Cathd of St Ptr & St Paul Washington DC 2008-2011. revwendy@stjoesweb.org

TOBIAS, Susan (Vt) 115 Tebbetts Rd, Marshfield VT 05658 B New York NY 3/6/1943 d James Kenneth Lindsay & Priscilla. BA Ob 1965; UTS 1966; MS U Chi 1968; MDiv Claremont TS 1986. D 6/14/1986 P 12/21/1986 Bp Charles Brinkley Morton. c 2. S Jn The Bapt Epis Hardwick VT 2000-2007; R S Dav's Epis Ch San Diego CA 1991-2000; Asst to the R S Jas By The Sea La Jolla CA 1988-1991; Dio San Diego San Diego CA 1986-1988; Asst to the R S Mk's Ch San Diego CA 1986-1988. Auth, "Seasons of Friendship: Leaders Guide (co-Auth)," Innisfree Press, 1990. sltob@fairpoint.net

TOBIN, Florence Kit (Roch) PO Box 304, Corning NY 14830 **Apportnmt T/F Dio Rochester Rochester NY 2011-; GC Alt Dep Dio Rochester Rochester NY 2011-; Safe Ch Trnr Dio Rochester Rochester NY 2011-; Long Term Supply S Matt's Epis Ch Horseheads NY 2011-; Anti Racism Com Trnr Dio Rochester Rochester NY 2008-; Dioc Coun Dio Rochester Rochester NY 2008-; Oasis Rochester Dio Rochester Rochester NY 2008-** B Oak Bluffs MA 8/5/1939 d Elizabeth Lane Lovell. BA Bennington Coll 1961; MA GTS 2002; Providence Coll Grad Rel Stds 2003; CPE St Anne's Hosp 2003. D 4/20/2008 Bp Jack Marston McKelvey P 11/22/2008 Bp Prince Grenville Singh. c 2. P in Charge Chr Ch Corning NY 2009; Asst P Chr Ch Corning NY 2008-2011; Transitional D Chr Ch Corning NY 2008. Integrity USA 2007; Integrity USA Dioc Organizer 2011; Ord of St Lk the Physcn 1990; Recovery Mnstrs Natl Bd 2004-2010; Recovery Mnstrs of the Epis Ch 2003. kitt_789@yahoo.com

T

TOBIN, Robert Benjamin (Mass) 2 Garden St., Cambridge MA 02138 B Washington DC 9/28/1970 s Robert W(allace) Tobin & Maurine M. Trans from Church Of England 8/27/2009 Bp M(arvil) Thomas Shaw III. Epis Chapl At Harvard & Radcliffe Cambridge MA 2009-2010. rtobin@cantab.net

TOBIN JR, Robert W(allace) (Mass) Po Box 113, Sunset ME 04683 B Austin TX 1/12/1936 s Robert Wallace Tobin & Frances Louise. BA U of Texas 1957; MDiv Epis TS of The SW 1960; CAS Harv 1977; EdD Harv 1980. D 6/13/1960 P 12/21/1960 Bp George Henry Quarterman. m 6/3/1958 Maurine M Motter c 5. R Chr Ch Cambridge Cambridge MA 1987-2004; All SS Epis Sch Lubbock TX 1981-1987; Int Gr Ch Salem MA 1978-1979; Int S Mk's Ch Westford MA 1976-1977; Vic S Ptr's Epis Ch Borger TX 1960-1966. "How Long O Lord," Cowley, 2003. Morris Arnold Awd Epis City Mssn-Boston 2005. rwtobin@verizon.net

TOBIN, Roger Martin (SeFla) 5690 N Kendall Dr, Miami FL 33156 B Minneapolis MN 1/4/1951 s John Dudley Tobin & Barbara. BA Hob 1972; MDiv EDS 1977; MS Barry U 1998. D 7/3/1977 P 6/3/1978 Bp Robert Rae Spears Jr. m 9/11/1971 Janis Tobin. S Thos Epis Par Sch Miami FL 1987-2003; R S Thos Epis Par Coral Gables FL 1986-2009; R S Steph's Epis Ch Wilkinsburg PA 1981-1986; Asst S Thos Epis Ch Rochester NY 1977-1981. Auth, "Eds Quarterly"; Auth, "Living Ch". revrmt@gmail.com

TOBOLA, Cynthia Pruet (Tex) PO Box 895, Palacios TX 77465 B San Angelo TX 6/19/1947 d Royce Pruet & Mary Fay. Texas Tech U 1969; MBA U of Houston 1987; Iona Sch for Mnstry 2009. D 6/20/2009 Bp C(harles) Andrew Doyle P 12/21/2009 Bp Rayford Baines High Jr. m 8/4/1984 Logic Tobola c 4. cynthiatobola2@yahoo.com

TODD, Christopher Howard (SeFla) 30243 Coconut Hwy, Big Pine Key FL 33043 **R S Fran-In-The-Keys Episcop Big Pine Key FL 2002-** B St. Louis MO 10/17/1954 s William Howard Todd & Phyllis Jacqueline. BA Wheaton Coll 1977. D 6/16/2002 P 12/21/2002 Bp Leopold Frade. m 10/7/1978 Julia Elaine Buryn c 2. "Superheroes of the Faith," *The Net*, Epis Dio SE Florida, 2007; "Sherlock Holmes as Literary Chr Figure," *The Baker St Journ*, Ford Press, 1985. revchristodd@aol.com

TODD, Edward Pearson (Eur) 18 Hall Pond Lane, Copake NY 11516 Afghanistan B Cleveland OH 6/22/1945 s Donald Pearson Todd & Marjorie Patricia. BA Harv 1967; MDiv GTS 1970. D 6/21/1970 P 12/1/1970 Bp Frederick Barton Wolf. m 5/24/2004 Charles B Matlock c 3. R S Paul's Within the Walls Rome 00184 IT 1986-1991; Int The Ch Of Our Redeem Lexington MA 1984-1985; Exec Coun Appointees New York NY 1972-1984; All SS Epis Ch Skowhegan ME 1970-1972; M-in-c S Hugh Lincoln ME 1970-1972; M-in-c S Thos Ch Winn ME 1970-1972. thadeusfrosch@mac.com

TODD, Eugene Fredrick (Wyo) 6345 Osage Ave, Cheyenne WY 82009 B Sheridan WY 7/1/1928 s Fred Johnston Todd & Gladys Gertrude. BA U Denv 1951; ThM Iliff TS 1954; MA U of So Dakota 1960; VTS 1961. D 7/25/1961 P 2/6/1962 Bp James W Hunter. m 12/31/1975 Rosemary F Fleming c 3. Int Chr Epis Ch Aspen CO 1998-2000; Int S Gabr The Archangel Epis Ch Cherry Hills Vill CO 1997-1998; Int Epis Ch Of S Jn The Bapt Breckenridge CO 1996-1997; Int S Phil In-The-Field Sedalia CO 1993-1996; Dep GC Dio Wyoming Casper WY 1982-1985; Prov VI Del Dio Wyoming Casper WY 1977-1979; R S Mk's Ch Cheyenne WY 1965-1992; R S Jn's Ch Green River WY 1961-1965. Auth, *Tales & Irreverencies of a Country Parson*, Wstrn Americana, 1997; Auth, *Todd Legacy*, 1985; Auth, *R's Journ*, 1978; Auth, *Recollections of a Piney Creek Rancher*, 1967. EUGENETODD@AOL.COM

TODD, Michael P (SanD) 1460 W Arroyo Dr, Yuma AZ 85364 **R Ch Of The H Sprt Osprey FL 2011-** B Lake Wales FL 8/4/1974 s Russell Todd & Carol Ann. B.S. U of So Flordia 1997; MDiv. TESM 2004. D 5/22/2004 Bp John Wadsworth Howe P 2/13/2005 Bp Gethin Benwil Hughes. S Paul's Ch Yuma AZ 2008-2011. OSL 2005. namaste187@yahoo.com

TODD, Richard Alfred (Minn) 38378 Glacier Dr, North Branch MN 55056 B Duluth MN 4/14/1960 s Richard Eaton Todd & Carol Ion. BA U MN 1982; MA U MN 1992. D 6/12/2003 Bp James Louis Jelinek. m 6/7/1986 Jill Wobbe c 2. jrtodd@nsatel.net

TODD JR, Samuel Rutherford (Tex) 2423 Mcclendon St, Houston TX 77030 B Columbia SC 7/5/1940 s Samuel Rutherford Todd & Beverley. BA Harv 1962; MDiv UTS 1966. D 12/27/1965 Bp Horace W B Donegan P 7/9/1966 Bp Charles Francis Boynton. m 6/28/1975 Sara Sanborn c 4. Assoc R Palmer Memi Ch Houston TX 1996-2002; Ch Of Recon San Antonio TX 1979-1996; Assoc Chr Epis Ch San Antonio TX 1976-1979; S Steph's Epis Sch Austin TX 1972-1976; Asst Calv and St Geo New York NY 1966-1971. Auth, *An Intro to Chrsnty: a First Millennium Fndt for Third Millennium Thinkers*, Brocton Pub Co, 2000; Contributing Ed, *Dio W Texas News*; Contributing Ed, *The Texas Epis*. stodd2423@att.net

TODD, William Marion (WNC) 615 Spring Forest Rd, Raleigh NC 27609 **Died 9/19/2009** B Wilmington NC 11/4/1927 s Leon Mccoy Todd & Nancy Catherine. Conf 70; Natl Trng Lab Key Exec; BA U NC 1950; U of Texas 1963; MDiv Epis TS of The SW 1966; Ldrshp Trng Inst 1968. D 6/16/1966 P 4/1/1967 Bp George Mosley Murray. c 1.

TOELLER-NOVAK, Thomas Leo (WMich) 555 Michigan Ave, Holland MI 49423 **Epis Ch Of The Gd Shpd Allegan MI 2011-** B Muskegon MI 3/27/1940 s Leo L Novak & Mary Katherine. BA Athenaeum 1961; STB Pontificia U Gregoriana Rome It 1963; STL Pontificia U Gregoriana Rome It 1965. Rec from Roman Catholic 11/1/1984 as Priest Bp Howard Samuel Meeks. m 6/30/1976 Deirdre Toeller-Novak. Int S Paul's Epis Ch S Jos MI 2006-2007; R Gr Ch Holland MI 1990-2005; Int Gr Ch Grand Rapids MI 1990-1991; Asst R Gr Ch Grand Rapids MI 1985-1987; Res P S Mk's Ch Grand Rapids MI 1984-1985. ttn76@sbcglobal.net

TOEPFER, Laura (Cal) 724 Valle Vista Avenue, Vallejo CA 94590 B Berkeley CA 10/9/1968 d Louis Eugene Toepfer & Janet May. BA Ob 1990; AAS Rochester Inst of Tech 1993; MDiv CDSP 2001. D 6/23/2001 P 5/4/2002 Bp Jack Marston McKelvey. Sabbatical Int All SS Epis Ch San Leandro CA 2010; Assoc R Chr Ch Alameda CA 2003-2008; Asst R & Chapl to Ken Dio Ohio Cleveland OH 2001-2002. toepferblue@gmail.com

TOFANI, Ann Lael (Spr) 427 W 4th St, Mount Carmel IL 62863 **D S Mary's Ch Robinson IL 2010-; D Ch Of S Jn The Bapt Mt Carmel IL 2000-** B Milwaukee WI 10/3/1939 d Halsey Hubbard & Lois Elizabeth. BA U Of Evansville 1973. D 6/11/2000 Bp Peter Hess Beckwith. aht19@frontier.com

TOFFEY, Judith E (Ct) 41 Cannon Ridge Dr, Watertown CT 06795 **S Mich's Ch Naugatuck CT 2011-; R All SS Epis Ch Oakville CT 1993-** B Waterbury CT 5/6/1946 d Herbert Toffey & Julie. BA U of Massachusetts 1972; MS Bos 1976; MDiv EDS 1987. D 6/11/1988 Bp David Elliot Johnson P 5/1/1989 Bp Barbara Clementine Harris. Chr Ch Waterbury CT 2009-2011; S Paul's Ch Southington CT 2007-2009; S Mary's Epis Ch Manchester CT 2006; Trin Epis Ch Trumbull CT 2002-2005; Exec Coun Appointees New York NY 2002; All SS Epis Ch Oakville CT 1992-2000; Cur Gr Ch New Bedford MA 1988-1992. revjetct@yahoo.com

TOIA, Frank Phillip (Pa) 2127 Kriebel Rd, Lansdale PA 19446 B Sewickley PA 4/25/1937 s Thomas John Toia & Helen Katherine. BA Duke 1959; MDiv PDS 1962; U of Pennsylvania 1971; Estrn Pennsylvania Psych Inst 1972. D 6/16/1962 Bp William S Thomas P 12/16/1962 Bp Harry S Kennedy. m 11/17/1985 Linda Ann Latosek c 3. Asstg P Ch Of S Mart-In-The-Fields Philadelphia PA 1999; Gd Shpd Ch Hilltown PA 1979-1999; Ch Of The Mssh Lower Gwynedd PA 1972-1979; Vic Ch Of S Jn The Evang Philadelphia PA 1971-1972. franktoia@comcast.net

TOLAND JR, William Leslie (Spr) Po Box 3161, Springfield IL 62708 B Macomb IL 4/12/1928 s William Leslie Toland & Winifred Josephine. BS Wstrn Illinois U 1950; LTh Bex 1955; MA Bradley U 1957. D 6/2/1955 P 12/6/1955 Bp William L Essex. S Laurence Epis Ch Effingham IL 1987-1990; Assoc Chr Ch Springfield IL 1965-1970; Chair Dio Springfield Springfield IL 1963-2000; Vic Trin Epis Ch Mattoon IL 1960-1965; Asst S Jn's Epis Ch Decatur IL 1958-1960; Chair Dio Springfield Springfield IL 1957-1958; Assoc S Jas Epis Ch Lewistown IL 1955-1958; Assoc S Ptr's Ch Peoria IL 1955-1958. Mltry Chapl Assn; OHC.

TOLEN, Richard George (RG) 2319 L St, Ord NE 68862 **Died 10/3/2010** B Ord NE 3/2/1931 s Mark Dwight Tolen & Lucile George. BA Hastings Coll of Law 1953; MA U of Nthrn Colorado 1958. D 8/27/1986 Bp Richard Mitchell Trelease Jr. c 4. rtolenl@aol.com

TOLES, John Forest (Mont) 400 Maple St, Anaconda MT 59711 **S Marks Pintler Cluster Anaconda MT 2010-** B Bastrop LA 12/21/1964 s Donal Wayne Toles. BBA Steph F. Austin St U 1989; MDiv Nash 2004. D 9/14/2004 P 5/5/2005 Bp Charles Franklin Brookhart Jr. m 6/14/2001 Robyn Lynn Wiley. D Dio Montana Helena MT 2004-2009. reverend@pintlercluster.com

TOLL, Richard Kellogg (Ore) 1707 Se Courtney Rd, P.O. Box 220112, Milwaukie OR 97269 B Pecos TX 4/14/1939 s Richard Leon Toll & Francis. BBA Texas Tech U 1962; MDiv CDSP 1967; DMin VTS 1985. D 6/29/1967 Bp C J Kinsolving III P 1/10/1968 Bp James Walmsley Frederic Carman. m 9/1/1962 Wanda Elaine Toll c 2. Pres Cler Assn Dio Olympia Seattle WA 1990-1992; R S Jn The Evang Ch Milwaukie OR 1984-2003; Dio Olympia Seattle WA 1981-2003; Pres Cler Assn Dio Olympia Seattle WA 1981-1983; Bd Trst CDSP Berkeley CA 1979-1991; Cn Pstr S Mk's Cathd Seattle WA 1976-1984; Pres Stndg Com Dio Estrn Oregon The Dalles OR 1973-1976; Dioc Coun Dio Estrn Oregon The Dalles OR 1972-1976; R S Steph's Baker City OR 1971-1976; Assoc Gr Memi Portland OR 1967-1970. DD CDSP 2001; Hon Cn Dio Olympia 1984. etoll2@aol.com

TOLLEFSON, Jane (Jill) Carol (Minn) 2700 Canby Ct, Northfield MN 55057 **D All SS Ch Northfield MN 2007-** B Weymouth MA 1/13/1946 d Arthur S Dwyer & Ruth Paelford. Emerson Coll. D 6/17/2001 Bp James Louis Jelinek. m 6/26/1965 Rolf H Tollefson c 4. D La Mision El Santo Nino Jesus S Paul MN 2004-2007; D The Epis Cathd Of Our Merc Sav Faribault MN 2001-2003. Third Ord Franciscan 2000. jill.tollefson@yahoo.com

TOLLEFSON, Walter Jerome (Minn) PO Box 868, Detroit Lakes MN 56502 **Total Mnstry P S Lk's Ch Detroit Lakes MN 2008-** B Pelicah Rapids MN 6/26/1939 s Walter Leonard Tollefson & Helen Christine. BA Moorhead St U Moorhead MN 1981. D 12/8/2007 Bp Daniel Lee Swenson P 9/13/2008 Bp

James Louis Jelinek. m 7/30/1983 Doreen Tollefson c 2. tollefson@lakesnet.net

TOLLEY, John Charles (Cal) 594 Los Altos Drive, Chula Vista CA 91914 B Cleveland OH 5/20/1935 s James Joseph Tolley & May. BBA Baldwin-Wallace Coll, Berea, Ohio 1961; Cert Dio of California Dioc Sch for Mnstrs San Fran 1980; BA California Sch for Deacons-Dio California 1983; Cert CDSP, Berkeley, CA 1988. D 4/12/1981 P 12/3/1988 Bp William Edwin Swing. m 6/15/1959 Sarah Jane Birch c 2. Pstr Assoc S Paul's Epis Ch Walnut Creek CA 1995-2001; S Clem's Ch Berkeley CA 1991-1992; Pstr Assoc S Jn's Epis Ch Clayton CA 1989-1991; Bay Area Seafarers' Serv Oakland CA 1988-1992; S Paul's Epis Ch Walnut Creek CA 1986-1987; Field Educ Supvsr CDSP Berkeley CA 1985-1986. Cmnty Serv Awd Contra Costa Cnty, CA Contra Costa Cnty California 1986. JTOLLEYSR@AOL.COM

TOLLISON JR, Henry Ernest (USC) 105 Freeport Dr, Greenville SC 29615 B Greenville SC 2/28/1937 s Henry Ernest Tollison & Mary Elizabeth. BS Clemson U 1959; MDiv STUSo 1969. D 6/29/1969 P 6/24/1970 Bp John Adams Pinckney. m 9/4/1959 Elisabeth McAfee. R S Fran Ch Greenville SC 1977-2001; Vic Ch Of The Incarn Gaffney SC 1972-1977; Dio Upper So Carolina Columbia SC 1972-1977; Asst S Martins-In-The-Field Columbia SC 1970-1972; Asst Gr Epis Ch Anderson SC 1969-1970.

TOLLIVER, Lisa Anne (Lex) 145 E 5th St, Morehead KY 40351 **S Alb's Ch Morehead KY 2010-** B Bristol TN 2/16/1967 d L Earl Tolliver & Edwinna R. MS U of Kentucky; Angl Courses Seabury Wstrn Sem 2010; MDiv Lexington TS 2011. D 6/19/2010 P 12/20/2010 Bp Stacy F Sauls. LTTW@INSIGHTBB.COM

TOLLIVER, Richard Lamar (Chi) 4729 S. Drexel Blvd, Chicago IL 60615 **Gilead Mgmt Co Chicago IL 2004-; S Edm's Redevelopment Corp Chicago IL 1993-; R S Edm's Epis Ch Chicago IL 1989-** B Springfield OH 6/26/1945 s Kenneth Brown & Evelyn Marie. BA Mia 1967; MA Bos 1971; MDiv EDS 1971; PhD How 1983; MA Bos 1986. D 6/5/1971 P 12/18/1971 Bp Horace W B Donegan. R S Tim's Epis Ch Washington DC 1977-1984; R S Cyp's Ch Roxbury MA 1972-1976; Asst S Phil's Ch New York NY 1971-1972. DD SWTS 1997; Distinguished Achievement Medal Miami 1996. rick2251@aol.com

TOLZMANN, Lee Ann (Ct) St. Paul's Church, 200 Riverside Ave, Riverside CT 06878 **R S Paul's Ch Riverside CT 2008-** B New York NY 11/27/1955 d Leslie B Disharoon & Ann. BA Dart 1977; MDiv GTS 2001. D 6/9/2001 Bp Robert Wilkes Ihloff P 12/9/2001 Bp John Leslie Rabb. m 6/19/1976 David C Tolzmann c 2. R Ch Of The Mssh Baltimore MD 2003-2008; Asst to the R S Andr's Epis Ch Glenwood MD 2001-2003. latolzmann@optimum.net

TOMAINE, Jane A (Nwk) 349 Short Dr, Mountainside NJ 07092 B Milwaukee WI 5/15/1947 d Stanley Woodard Thomas & Cecelia Zentner. BA Cornell Coll 1969; MA OH SU 1971; MDiv Drew U 1995; DMin Drew U 2004. D 6/3/1995 Bp Jack Marston McKelvey P 12/9/1995 Bp John Shelby Spong. m 7/27/1991 John Tomaine. R S Ptr's Epis Ch Livingston NJ 1995-2008. *St. Ben's Toolbox: The Nuts and Bolts of Everyday Benedictine Living*, Morehouse Pub, 2005. SCHS - Chapl New York Chapt 2006-2008. jtomaine1685@verizon.net

TOMAS, Bernardo Diomedes (Mo) 10970 Sw 179th St, Miami FL 33157 B Panama City PA 10/27/1923 s Gamaliel Christopher Thomas & Madelda K. Long Island Dioc TS. D 4/12/1958 P 10/1/1958 Bp James P De Wolfe. m 8/2/1953 Edith Louise Chambers. Ch Of The Ascen S Louis MO 1983-1988; Dio Missouri S Louis MO 1981-1982; Asst P All SS Ch S Louis MO 1974; Cur All SS Ch S Louis MO 1966-1968; R Ch Of S Jas The Less Jamaica NY 1959-1965; Cur S Aug's Epis Ch Brooklyn NY 1958-1959.

TOMBAUGH, Richard Franklin (Ct) 58 Terry Rd, Hartford CT 06105 B Syracuse NY 8/18/1932 s John Richard Tombaugh & Mary Louise. BA Pr 1954; MA Col 1956; STB GTS 1958; ThD GTS 1964. D 6/14/1958 Bp Charles L Street P 12/14/1958 Bp Gerald Francis Burrill. m 1/31/1959 Sandra Clarke c 3. Cn to he Ordnry Dio Connecticut Hartford CT 1986-1998; Exectuive Dir Arts And Educ Coun Of St Louis St Louis MO 1978-1982; Chapl to Colleges and Universities in S Louis Dio Missouri S Louis MO 1970-1976; Team Mnstry Trin Ch S Louis MO 1969-1970; P-in-c Trin Ch S Louis MO 1967-1968; Asst The Ch of S Ign of Antioch New York NY 1960-1964; Cur Gr Epis Ch Hinsdale IL 1958-1960. "Ecclesial Impatience: A Response to the Windsor Report," *Conversations in Rel and Theol*, Blackwell, 2005. ESCRU 1964-1980; ESMHE 1964-1986; The Epis Majority 2006. The Bp's Awd for Ch and Cmnty Dio Connecticut 1998. rftombaugh@yahoo.com

TOMBERLIN, JoAnn (WNC) 419 Turnpike Rd, Mills River NC 28759 B Minden LA 2/5/1931 d Frank Alsey Tomberlin & Etolee Morgan. BS Texas Wmn U 1952; Cert Grady Vaughn Sch of Physical Ther 1953; MA Stan 1960; Diac Iona Sch of Mnstry 2009. D 2/22/2009 Bp Don Adger Wimberly. jate2531@gmail.com

TOMCZAK, Beth Lynn (WMich) 321 N Main St, Three Rivers MI 49093 B Three Rivers MI 2/7/1959 d Elwin Donald Ruggles & Beverly Joyce. Grad Dav Oakahater Sch for Deacons 2008. D 6/21/2008 Bp Robert Alexander Gepert Jr. c 2. bethers7@comcast.net

TOMEI, Gail R (SwFla) 936 Cambridge Dr, Manheim PA 17545 **Asst S Jn's Ch Marietta PA 2009-** B Minneapolis MN 12/31/1946 d Orem Olford Robbins & Jean. B.A. Denver U 1968; MTS VTS 1995; MDIV VTS 2004. D 6/12/2004 P 1/8/2005 Bp Rogers Sanders Harris. m 6/11/1988 Anthony J Tomei. Assoc S Mary's Epis Ch Bonita Sprg FL 2006-2009; Dir of Pstr Care S Jn's Ch Naples FL 2000-2003. GTOMEI@PTD.NET

TOMKINS, James Patrick (La) 71429 Seeger Rd, Covington LA 70433 B Lake Charles LA 9/30/1960 D 9/13/2003 Bp Charles Edward Jenkins III. m 12/24/1987 Allyson Jones. jamestomkins@netscape.net

TOMLIN, Billy Frank (Tex) Po Box 5193, Tyler TX 75712 B Tyler TX 9/20/1926 s Herbert Henry Tomlin & Sarah Francis. BA U of Texas 1966; MDiv VTS 1969; MA U of Texas 1983. D 7/1/1969 Bp J Milton Richardson P 6/1/1970 Bp Frederick P Goddard. m 8/18/1946 Orla Broward c 3. St Lukes Ch Rusk TX 1978-1983; Vic Trin Ch Jacksonville TX 1978-1983; R Gr Ch Galveston TX 1977-1978; R S Ptr's Epis Ch Brenham TX 1972-1977; Vic All SS Ch Cameron TX 1969-1972; Vic S Thos' Epis Ch Rockdale TX 1969-1972.

TOMLIN, Kyle R (Pa) 6769 Ridge Ave # A, Philadelphia PA 19128 **R S Alb's Ch Roxborough Philadelphia PA 2010-** B Elmer NJ 9/26/1975 s Earl Kyle Tomlin & Sharon Marie. BA (Psych) Richard Stockton Coll 1997; MDiv TESM 2009. D 12/12/2009 P 6/21/2010 Bp William Howard Love. m 4/12/2003 Holly R Regina. krtomlin75@yahoo.com

TOMLINSON, Diane B (Mich) 5299 Hatchery Rd, Waterford MI 48329 **R S Andr's Ch Waterford MI 2010-** B Royal Oak Michigan 11/9/1960 BBA Walsh Coll 2002; MDiv Huron U Coll 2006. D 6/6/2006 P 12/9/2006 Bp Wendell Nathaniel Gibbs Jr. m 8/18/1984 Mark Charles Tomlinson c 1. Assoc Emm Ch Baltimore MD 2008-2010; Cur Nativ Epis Ch Bloomfield Township MI 2006-2007. dtomlinson1109@gmail.com

TOMLINSON, Ruth Marie (Neb) 5704 N. 159th St., Omaha NE 68116 **S Dav Of Wales Epis Ch Lincoln NE 2011-** B Culver City CA 5/5/1948 d Kenneth LeRoy Burr & Rosemary. BA California St U 1970; MA California St U 1973; MDiv Claremont TS 2000. D 6/3/2000 Bp Joseph Jon Bruno P 1/6/2001 Bp Frederick Houk Borsch. c 2. R Trin Epis Ch Norfolk NE 2004-2010; Assoc Vic S Jn Chrys Ch And Sch Rancho Santa Margarita CA 2000-2004. DOK 2006. Participant, Sum Collegium VTS 2007; Pres's Awd, Highest Grade Point Average Claremont TS Claremont CA 2000. rmtomlinson@yahoo.com

TOMLINSON III, Samuel Alexander (Miss) 28 Homochitto St, Natchez MS 39120 B Natchez MS 9/8/1935 s Samuel Alexander Tomlinson & Jane Elizabeth. BA Millsaps Coll 1958; MDiv GTS 1961. D 6/9/1961 Bp Duncan Montgomery Gray Jr P 12/20/1961 Bp John M Allin. m 6/24/1989 Susanne Kirk Smith c 1. Asstg P Trin Ch Natchez MS 1998-2002; Vic S Jas Epis Ch Port Gibson MS 1988-1997; Vic S Fran Of Assisi Ch Philadelphia MS 1986-1988; Vic S Matt's Epis Ch Kosciusko MS 1986-1988; Vic S Eliz's Mssn Collins MS 1976-1986; Cur Trin Ch Pine Bluff AR 1970-1974; Vic The Chap Of The Cross Madison MS 1965-1969; R Gr Epis Ch Canton MS 1964-1969; P-in-c S Paul's Epis Ch Corinth MS 1961-1964. suskirk@aol.com

TOMPKIN, William Frederick (O) 307 Portage Trail East, Cuyahoga Falls OH 44221 **S Jn's Epis Ch Cuyahoga Falls OH 2000-** B Cuyahoga Falls OH 11/14/1932 s James Tompkin & Winifred. U of Akron. D 11/13/1992 Bp James Russell Moodey. c 5. S Paul's Ch Canton OH 1995-2000; D S Jn's Epis Ch Cuyahoga Falls OH 1992-1994. snkndcn1@sbcglobal.net

TOMPKINS JR, Douglas Gordon (Pa) 310 S Chester Rd, Swarthmore PA 19081 **R Chr Ch Epis Ridley Pk PA 2000-** B Newport RI 2/20/1954 s Douglas Gordon Tompkins & Nancy Jane. BA U of Wisconsin 1977; MDiv GTS 1981; Dipl C.G. Jung Inst of NY 2007. D 6/12/1981 P 12/16/1981 Bp William Charles Wantland. m 12/27/1980 Joyce Laura Ulrich c 3. R Chr Ch Whitefish Bay WI 1992-2000; R S Paul's Ch In Nantucket Nantucket MA 1986-1992; Asst Chr Ch Short Hills NJ 1982-1986; Cur S Mary's Ch Pk Ridge IL 1981-1982. dg.tompkins@verizon.net

TOMPKINS III, George Johnson (SC) 90 Fieldfare Way, Charleston SC 29414 B Lexington VA 7/17/1951 s George Johnson Tompkins & Jeanne Willann. U of Edinburgh GB 1972; BA U of Virginia 1973; MA Yale DS 1975; MDiv GTS 1976; DMin STUSo 1990. D 6/12/1976 P 3/12/1977 Bp Joseph Warren Hutchens. m 1/1/1985 Elizabeth Porcher Jones c 2. R Old S Andr's Par Ch Charleston SC 1987-2006; R S Thos' Ch Windsor NC 1982-1987; Cur Bruton Par Williamsburg VA 1978-1981; Cur S Jas Ch New London CT 1976-1978.

TOMPKINS, Joyce Laura Ulrich (Pa) 310 S Chester Rd, Swarthmore PA 19081 **Assoc Trin Ch Swarthmore PA 2000-** B Morristown NJ 4/4/1955 d Henry Theodore Ulrich & Ada Blanche. BA Cor 1977; Ds Ya Berk 1980; MDiv GTS 1982. D 6/12/1982 P 12/14/1982 Bp John Shelby Spong. m 12/27/1980 Douglas Gordon Tompkins. Chr Ch Whitefish Bay WI 1992-1999; S Paul's Ch In Nantucket Nantucket MA 1988-1992; Asst Chr Ch Short Hills NJ 1985-1986; Assoc R S Paul's Epis Ch Morris Plains NJ 1982-1985. jtompki1@swarthmore.edu

TOMTER, Patrick Austin (Oly) PO Box 10785, Portland OR 97296 **Hon Cn Trin Epis Cathd Portland OR 1995-** B Long Beach CA 9/11/1938 s Austin Tomter & J(essie) Marie. BA Occ 1960; MDiv CDSP 1964; Cert U of So

T

Florida 1986. D 9/10/1964 P 3/11/1965 Bp Francis E I Bloy. m 7/7/1961 Evelyn J Tomter c 3. Alum/ae Coun CDSP Berkeley CA 2003-2009; Chair, COM Dio Oregon Portland OR 1997-2001; Dir Sprtl Care Legacy Gd Samar Hosp Portland OR 1994-2010; Archd Dio Olympia Seattle WA 1990-1994; Dep to GC (4) Dio Olympia Seattle WA 1982-1990; Stndg Com (Pres, 1982) Dio Olympia Seattle WA 1979-1983; R Chr Ch Tacoma WA 1976-1990; R S Eliz's Ch Burien WA 1972-1976; U of W Campus Min Dio Olympia Seattle WA 1969-1972; Assoc S Steph's Epis Ch Longview WA 1968-1969; Cur S Mk's Par Altadena CA 1964-1966. patomter@gmail.com

TONGE, Samuel Davis (Ga) 1023 Woods Road, Waycross GA 31501 B Macon GA 11/30/1947 s Jack Stephens Tonge & Eloise. Furman U 1965; U GA 1968; OD Sthrn Coll of Optometry Memphis TN 1972; MDiv Epis TS 1985; MRE S Meinrad TS 1985; DMin SWTS 2000. D 4/27/1985 P 1/24/1986 Bp Harry Woolston Shipps. m 8/2/1975 Sharon Varner c 5. Pres, Stndg Com Dio Georgia Savannah GA 2006-2007; Stndg Com Dio Georgia Savannah GA 2004-2007; Dep to GC Dio Georgia Savannah GA 1997; Dioc Curs Sp. Dir Dio Georgia Savannah GA 1996-1999; Convoc Dn Dio Georgia Savannah GA 1994-2010; Pres, Stndg Com Dio Georgia Savannah GA 1994-1995; Stndg Com Dio Georgia Savannah GA 1992-1995; R Gr Ch Waycross GA 1988-2011; Vic S Matt's Epis Ch Fitzgerald GA 1985-1987. *Var arts*, Angl Dig, 2004. grace-episcopal@wayxcable.com

TONGUE, Mary Jane (Md) 203 Star Pointe Ct Unit 3d, Abingdon MD 21009 B Baltimore MD 9/19/1937 d Paul V Kraft & Mary Catherine. Bon Secours Sch of Nrsng 1958; MD D Formation Prog 1997. D 6/14/1997 Bp Charles Lindsay Longest. mjtongue@aol.com

TONSMEIRE SR, Louis Edward (At) 224 Trammell St, Calhoun GA 30701 B Mobile AL 7/18/1933 s Arthur Clarence Tonsmeire & Marie Louise. BA Sprg Hill Coll 1954; MDiv STUSo 1957. D 7/17/1957 P 5/1/1958 Bp Charles C J Carpenter. m 12/5/1957 Sarah B Bond c 2. R S Tim's Epis Ch Calhoun GA 1994; R S Thaddaeus' Epis Ch Chattanooga TN 1990-1994; R The Epis Ch Of S Ptr And S Paul Marietta GA 1981-1989; R Ch Of The Ascen Cartersville GA 1965-1981; R S Andr's Epis Ch Sylacauga AL 1960-1965; Vic S Mary's Epis Ch Childersburg AL 1960-1965; Cur All SS Epis Ch Birmingham AL 1957-1960. letons@adelphia.net

TONTONOZ, David Costa (Eas) 5211 Dove Point Ln, Salisbury MD 21801 B Saint Louis MO 7/13/1939 s John Costa Tontonoz & Nellie. BS Coll H Cross 1961; BD EDS 1966; DMin Andover Newton TS 1973. D 6/22/1966 P 12/21/1966 Bp Robert McConnell Hatch. c 3. Dn of Sthrn Convoc Dio Easton Dio Easton Easton MD 1996-2008; Pres of Stndg Com Dio Easton Dio Easton Easton MD 1992-1995; R S Ptr's Ch Salisbury MD 1988-2007; Asst Gr Ch Lawr MA 1984-1988; R S Dav's Epis Ch Wilmington DE 1975-1983; R Trin Epis Ch Milford MA 1967-1975; Cur H Trin Epis Ch Southbridge MA 1966-1967. Auth, "arts," *Bro Of S Andr*; Auth, "arts," *New Life*. AAPC 1973. tontonoz@comcast.net

TOOF, Jan Jarred (CNY) 2006 Manchester Rd, Wheaton IL 60187 B Highland Park IL 1/6/1938 s Frederick Olmsted Toof & Yvonne. BA Lake Forest Coll 1960; MDiv SWTS 1963; MBA Keller Chicago IL 1983. D 6/15/1963 Bp James Winchester Montgomery P 12/14/1963 Bp Gerald Francis Burrill. m 6/23/1962 Norma Toof c 1. S Jn's Epis Ch Chicago IL 1995-1996; Asstg S Jn's Epis Ch Chicago IL 1993-1994; Chr Ch Gilbertsville NY 1965-1968; Cur Gr Ch Oak Pk IL 1963-1965. Soc of S Mary 1963.

TOOKEY, Carol Ruth (NAM) Po Box 720, Farmington NM 87499 B Rangely CO 12/16/1955 d George F Tookey & Carol Louise. AD San Juan Coll Farmington NM 1984; Cert Prchr Lewis Sch of Mnstry 1985; BSW New Mex St U. 1992; MS New Mex Highlands U 1994; MDiv Vancouver TS 2007. D 2/29/1988 Bp William Davidson P 5/1/1999 Bp Carl Christopher Epting. m 8/23/1975 Leslie Spencer Lundquist. N.M.R. Vic, Admin Navajoland Area Mssn Farmington NM 2001-2008; All SS Farmington NM 2001-2007; D S Paul's/Peace Ch Las Vegas NM 1992-1994; D S Andr's Epis Ch Las Cruces NM 1990-1992; D S Jn's Ch Farmington NM 1988-1990. Tertiary of the Soc of S Fran 1979. ctookeytssf@yahoo.com

TOOMEY, David C (NY) PO Box 1467, Norwich VT 05055 B New York NY 8/1/1950 s Arthur Reynolds Toomey & Ruth Althea. BA Bos 1972; MDiv Bex 1976; PhD Rhodes U 1998. D 6/8/1976 P 4/1/1977 Bp Morris Fairchild Arnold. m 8/19/1978 Lindsey Toomey c 3. Exec Coun Appointees New York NY 1996-2000; Spprt Com Poughkeepsie NY 1993-1996; R Chr Ch Poughkeepsie NY 1985-1993; R S Jn's Ch Winthrop MA 1980-1985; All SS Ch Chelmsford MA 1979-1980; S Anne's Ch Lowell MA 1977-1978; Asst S Matt And The Redeem Epis Ch So Boston MA 1976-1977. Auth, "Bus Dvlpmt through Interfirm Linkages," *Econ Revs*, USAID, 1994; Auth, "Litany In Memi Of Dr Ml King Jr," Rossiter Schlr, 1983; Auth, "So Afr At The Crossroads," *Economical Devolpment Linkages In So Afr*. dtoomey@sover.net

TORNQUIST, Frances (Cal) 2748 Wemberly Dr, Belmont CA 94002 B Shawnee OK 12/29/1942 d Jack P Cromwell & Frances Mae. BA Westminster Coll 1964; MDiv CDSP 1989. D 6/3/1989 P 6/1/1990 Bp William Edwin Swing. m 9/7/1963 John W Tornquist c 1. Vice-Dn and Cn Pstr Gr Cathd San Francisco CA 1990-2006; Asst S Bede's Epis Ch Menlo Pk CA 1989-1990. DD CDSP 2007. ftornquist@sbcglobal.net

TORO, Suzanne Frances Rosemary (NY) 296 Ninth Ave, New York NY 10001 **Assoc P Ch Of The H Apos New York NY 2010-** B Miami, FL 7/14/1962 d Anthony Albert Toro & Shirlie June. BMus U Tor 1986; Dplma Amer Mus & Dramatic Acad 1989; MDiv The GTS 2010. D 3/13/2010 P 9/25/2010 Bp Mark Sean Sisk. zanne.toro@gmail.com

TORRES, Julio Orlando (NY) 232 E 11th St # 3, New York NY 10003 B San Salvador El Salvador EC 4/30/1946 s Julio Torres & Margoth. Baldwin-Wallace Coll; Cntrl Amer U; BA SUNY 1978; MDiv EDS 1982; MA Drew U 1996. D 10/4/1982 P 6/25/1983 Bp John Harris Burt. m 10/2/1999 Maria Cruz c 4. S Mk's Ch In The Bowery New York NY 2000-2006; The Ch of S Matt And S Tim New York NY 1996-2000; R Gr Ch White Plains NY 1994-1999; Int The Ch of S Edw The Mtyr New York NY 1985-1986; Hisp Epis Cntr San Andres Ch Yonkers NY 1985; Assoc S Ann's Ch Of Morrisania Bronx NY 1984-1985. Auth, "Face To Face w A Crucified People"; Auth, "La Eucaristia". jtorresphd@yahoo.com

TORRES, Michele Angier (Mass) 103 Harvard Ave, Medford MA 02155 B La Jolla CA 10/2/1966 d John Alfred Torres & Carolyn Angier. BA Stan 1989; MDiv EDS 1995; MA Lesley U 1996. D 6/24/1995 P 6/1/1996 Bp Richard Lester Shimpfky. Gr Ch Everett MA 2004-2006; S Jn's Epis Ch Westwood MA 1998-2007; Asst S Steph's Epis Ch Boston MA 1996-1998. em_michele@verizon.net

TORRES BAYAS, Jose Javier (Cal) Guerrero #589, Tuxtepec Mexico **Dio California San Francisco CA 2010-** B Bolivar EC 3/24/1964 s Jorge Torres & Libia. Pontifical Cath U of Ecuador 1990; Epis TS 1995. Rec from Roman Catholic 5/28/1995 as Priest Bp J Neptali Larrea-Moreno. m 5/28/1991 Laura Dahik c 1. Ch Of The H Trin Richmond CA 2005-2009; Dio SE Mex 2002; Iglesia Epis Del Ecuador Ecuador 1996-2001. unoenchristo@hotmail.com

TORRES FUENTES, Pascual Pedro (Hond) Apdo 16, Puerto Cortes Honduras **Vic Iglesia Epis San Juan Bautista Puerto Cortes HN 1991-; Dio Honduras Miami FL 1989-** B San Pedro Sula Cortes HN 8/10/1959 s Carlos Alberto Torres & Ziola Concepcion. Lic Universidad Nacional Autonoma De Honduras 1981; TS 1987; MA Epis TS of The SW 1989. D 10/6/1989 P 3/1/1991 Bp Leopold Frade. m 12/19/1992 Elizabeth Torres Fuentes.

TORRES MARTINEZ, Wilfrido Oswaldo (EcuC) Convencion Y Solanda 056, Guaranda Ecuador B Pelileo Tuagurahua 11/3/1946 s Abel Torres & Maria. Teolog Universidad Catolica; Sem Mayor San Jose 1977. Trans 12/1/1992 Bp J Neptali Larrea-Moreno. m 11/6/2002 Irma Pilar Salazar Ramos c 4. Ecuador New York NY 2003-2009. TORRES_WILFRIDO@YAHOO.COM

TORREY, Bruce N (Ct) 96 Main St, East Windsor CT 06088 **S Jn's Ch E Windsor CT 1998-; R Trin Ch Canaseraga NY 1989-** B Mineola NY 1/27/1956 s Robert James Torrey & Barbara Ann. BA SUNY 1978; MDiv SWTS 1981. D 6/1/1981 P 12/6/1981 Bp Robert Campbell Witcher Sr. m 1/30/2008 Kathleen Torrey c 3. R Chr Epis Ch Hornell NY 1989-1998; R S Ptr's Ch Dansville NY 1989-1998; Tri-Par Mnstry Hornell NY 1989-1998; R H Trin Epis Ch Vlly Stream NY 1984-1989; Cur S Ann's Ch Sayville NY 1981-1984. bntorrey@gmail.com

TORREY, Dorothy Ellen (NCal) 901 Lincoln Rd Apt 40, Yuba City CA 95991 **S Aug Of Cbury Rocklin CA 2011-** B Buffalo NY 12/3/1947 d Henry Schierstein & Dorothy. MS San Francisco St U 1992; BS Wstrn Connecticut St U 1992; MDiv CDSP 2001. D 6/23/2001 P 2/16/2002 Bp Richard Lester Shimpfky. R S Jn's Epis Ch Marysville CA 2006-2010; Asst S Mich's Epis Ch Carmichael CA 2001-2006. dori.torrey@gmail.com

TORVEND, Samuel Edward (Oly) 15 Roy St, Seattle WA 98109 **Assoc for Adult Educ S Paul's Ch Seattle WA 2009-** B Longview WA 6/9/1951 s Elmer Silas Torvend & Alice K. MDiv Wartburg Sem 1975; MA Aquinas Inst 1980; PhD S Louis U 1990; AB Pacific Luth U 1993. Rec from Roman Catholic 2/15/2009 Bp Gregory Harold Rickel. torvensa@plu.edu

TOTHILL, Marlene Grey (NwT) No address on file. B Birmingham AL 11/2/1930 d Aaron Leo Grey & Florence. BS W Chester U of Pennsylvania 1952; MA U of Texas 1979; MDiv Epis TS of The SW 1985. D 6/15/1985 P 5/1/1986 Bp Gerald Nicholas McAllister. c 2. Asst S Chad's Epis Ch Albuquerque NM 2002-2004; Int S Chris's Epis Ch El Paso TX 1991; Asst R S Chris's Epis Ch El Paso TX 1987-1989; Cur S Jn's Epis Ch Tulsa OK 1985-1986.

TOTMAN, Glenn Parker (CGC) 122 County Road 268, Enterprise AL 36330 B Apalachicola FL 7/20/1937 s Donald Parker Totman & Sybil Bernell. BA U So 1960; VTS 1963; MBA U of So Alabama 1981. D 6/24/1963 P 3/1/1964 Bp Edward Hamilton West. m 6/1/1979 Nancy Sides. Ch Of The Epiph Enterprise AL 1997-2003; S Mk's Ch Chattahoochee FL 1989-1991; S Paul's Epis Ch Quincy FL 1983-1989; S Paul's Ch Foley AL 1973-1978; Asst Chr Ch Par Pensacola FL 1969-1973; Vic Ch Of The Ascen Carrabelle FL 1965-1966; Vic Bethany Ch Hilliard FL 1963-1965; Vic S Jas Ch Macclenny FL 1963-1965. GLENN004@CENTURYTEL.NET

TOTTEN, Julia Kay (Ore) PO Box 15, Florence OR 97439 B Columbia MS 12/15/1945 d Kenneth Keith Slade & Sarach Louise. Bachelor in Nsg Lewis &

Clark Coll 1985; Mstr in Nsg Whitworth Coll 1988. D 5/23/2009 Bp Bavi Rivera. m 9/29/1984 William Robert Totten c 3. bktotten@msn.com

TOTTEN, William Robert (Ore) PO Box 15, Florence OR 97439 **Vic S Andr's Epis Ch Florence OR 2009-** B Helena MT 6/18/1949 s William R Totten & Shirley Ann. BS U of Idaho 1971; MBA U of Idaho 1972; MDiv CDSP 2009. D 5/23/2009 Bp Bavi Rivera P 12/15/2009 Bp Sanford Zangwill Kaye Hampton. m 9/29/1984 Julia Kay Linn c 2. bktotten@msn.com

TOTTEY JR, Alfred George (CNY) 7385 Norton Ave, Clinton NY 13323 B Ithaca NY 1/25/1938 s Alfred George Tottey & Edna Lorraine. BA Duke 1959; CPE 1961; MDiv EDS 1962; Fllshp Coll of Preachers 1970. D 6/18/1962 P 6/22/1963 Bp Walter M Higley. c 2. Calv Ch Homer NY 1975-1984; Mem, Dioc Coun Dio Cntrl New York Syracuse NY 1975-1977; Assoc Zion Ch Rome NY 1968-1971; Chair Of The Yth Cmsn Dio Cntrl New York Syracuse NY 1967-1969; D S Paul's Ch Chittenango NY 1962-1963. ttottey@hotmail.com

TOUCHSTONE, G(rady) Russell (Los) 1069 S Gramercy Pl, Los Angeles CA 90019 **Int S Fran Mssn Norwalk CA 2004-** B Los Angeles CA 11/13/1932 s Grady Russell Touchstone & Geraldine Alice. USC 1954; Wells Theol Coll 1965. Trans from Church Of England 1/1/1970 as Priest Bp Horace W B Donegan. m 6/4/1964 Terri Lavonne Mosley c 1. Int S Marg's Epis Ch So Gate CA 2002-2004; S Marg's Epis Ch So Gate CA 2002-2003; Int Epis Chap Of S Fran Los Angeles CA 2001; Int Cong Of S Athan Los Angeles CA 2000; Int S Marg's Epis Ch So Gate CA 1995-1998; Asst S Thos The Apos Hollywood Los Angeles CA 1990-1994; Int S Clem's Mssn Huntington Pk CA 1988; Asst Trin Epis Par Los Angeles CA 1986-1988; Assoc H Fam Mssn No Hollywood CA 1985; Assoc Iglesia Epis De La Magdalena Mssn Glendale CA 1985; Cmsn on Racism and Discrimination Dio Los Angeles Los Angeles CA 1984-1988; Int Gr Epis Ch Glendora CA 1984; Asst All SS Par Beverly Hills CA 1980-1983; Asst Chr The Gd Shpd Par Los Angeles CA 1974-1976; Asst Cong Of S Athan Los Angeles CA 1973. Cmnty of the Servnt of the Will of God; SSC. daddyrussell@juno.com

TOURANGEAU, Edward J (Ind) 4443 Doe Path Ln, Lafayette IN 47905 B Syracuse NY 11/19/1945 s Donald John Tourangeau & Ruth Melrose. BA U of Utah 1967; MDiv Nash 1970. D 6/24/1970 Bp Richard S Watson P 12/21/1970 Bp Donald H V Hallock. m 7/14/1967 Patricia Searle c 1. R St Johns Epis Ch Lafayette IN 1991-2010; R Emm Epis Ch Great River NY 1987-1990; Cn S Paul's Cathd Peoria IL 1980-1987; Vic H Trin Epis Ch Peoria IL 1977-1979; Vic S Mk's Epis Ch Peoria IL 1975-1979; Vic Ch Of S Chris Rantoul IL 1972-1975; Cur S Mk's Ch Milwaukee WI 1970-1972. nelliesgrampa@gmail.com

TOURNOUX, Gregory Allen (Spr) 2056 Cherry Road, Springfield IL 62704 **Chr Ch Springfield IL 2005-** B Canton OH 10/2/1958 s Richard B Tournoux & Marilyn Kay. Trin TS IN; BS Slippery Rock U 1982; MDiv VTS 1988; DMin Trin TS IN 1997. D 6/11/1988 Bp James Russell Moodey P 5/9/1989 Bp Peter James Lee. m 8/30/1986 Nada Divic c 4. R Chr Epis Ch Owosso MI 1991-2004; Assoc S Paul's Epis Ch Winston Salem NC 1989-1991; Cur S Paul's Ch Haymarket VA 1988-1989. Auth, "What Will the Thriving Epis Ch of the Future Look Like?," *LivCh*, 1999; Auth, "A Modest Proposal," *Pro Fide*. Consult in ""Natural Ch Dvlpmt""; Fllshp of Chr Athletes 1977; NOEL; SEAD 1994. n.tournoux@comcast.net

TOVEN, Kenneth H (Minn) 1505 13th Street N., Princeton MN 55371 **Total Mnstry Advsr Chr Epis Ch Grand Rapids MN 2007-** B Grand Rapids MN 9/12/1951 s Harold A Toven & Marion. BA S Scholastica 1976; MDiv SWTS 1980. D 6/24/1980 P 12/1/1980 Bp Robert Marshall Anderson. m 1/15/1972 Pamula Jean Johnson. P-in-c S Jas Ch Marshall MN 2003-2006; R Ch Of The Resurr Minneapolis MN 1992-2001; Int Ch Of The Nativ Burnsville MN 1990-1991; Int S Chris's Epis Ch Roseville MN 1989-1990; Asst Ch Of The Ascen Stillwater MN 1980-1984. kentoven1@mac.com

TOWERS, Arlen Reginald (Cal) 43 Wildwood Pl, El Cerrito CA 94530 B San Antonio TX 7/24/1929 s Harold Emil Towers & Bonnie Marie. BA S Mary U 1960; MDiv CDSP 1964; Med U of Texas 1971. D 6/30/1964 Bp Richard Earl Dicus P 1/1/1965 Bp Everett H Jones. m 4/10/1953 Dione Darling Rockey c 1. Supply P Dio California San Francisco CA 1971-1993; Vol Assoc S Mk's Par Berkeley CA 1971-1993; Vic Ch Of The Resurr San Antonio TX 1968-1970; R S Andr's Epis Ch Seguin TX 1966-1968; Vic S Chris's Ch Bandera TX 1964-1965. arlentowers@comcast.net

TOWERS, Paul Wayne (CPa) 2309 Richmond Rd., Endwell NY 13760 **Supply P Dio Bethlehem Bethlehem PA 2011-; Supply P Dio Cntrl New York Syracuse NY 2011-** B 8/28/1948 BS Vlly Forge Chr Coll Pheonixville PA 1978; MDiv Drew U 1983; DMin VTS 2001. D 7/3/2007 P 1/16/2010 Bp Gladstone Bailey Adams III. m 7/2/1977 Marian L Towers. R S Lk's Epis Ch Altoona PA 2010-2011. ptowers@stny.rr.com

TOWERS, Richard Allen (Chi) Anglican Cathedral Seoul, Seoul 11004 Korea (South) B Rochester NY 12/22/1969 s Sherwood Richard Towers & Terry Rose. BA Houghton Coll 1992; MDiv Bex 1997. D 10/9/1999 Bp William George Burrill P 6/26/2000 Bp Jack Marston McKelvey. m 8/28/1993 Rupa Barbara Kanakarai. S Marks Sch Of Texas Dallas TX 2008-2011; SWTS Evanston IL 2005-2008; The Epis Ch of S Jn the Div Tamuning GU 2003-2005; S Paul's Ch Rochester NY 2001-2002. richtowers@hotmail.com

TOWLER, Lewis Wilson (Mich) 1711 Pontiac Trl, Ann Arbor MI 48105 **Asst S Andr's Ch Ann Arbor MI 2008-** B Cincinnati OH 7/21/1925 s John Willard Towler & Dorothy May. BA U MI 1950; U of Heidelberg DE 1951; UTS 1952; MA U MI 1952; BD VTS 1955; STM GTS 1966. D 7/17/1955 P 1/24/1956 Bp Richard S M Emrich. c 3. Asst S Jn's Ch Plymouth MI 2000-2005; Assoc S Paul's Ch No Kingstown RI 1989-1997; Asst S Aug's Ch New York NY 1987-1989; Assoc R All Ang' Ch New York NY 1984-1987; Vic S Jn's Ch Chesaning MI 1980-1984; Cbury MI SU E Lansing MI 1978-1980; Assoc R Chr Ch Cranbrook Bloomfield Hills MI 1973-1978; Asst Cathd Of St Jn The Div New York NY 1964-1971; Fac The GTS New York NY 1963-1973; Asst Chr Ch Bronxville NY 1963-1964; R 62-63 S Matt's Epis Ch Saginaw MI 1957-1962; Cur All SS Epis Ch Pontiac MI 1955-1957. Auth, "arts," *Living Ch*; Auth, "Bk," *Planned Cont CE for Cler & Laity*. ActorsEquity Asscn. 1987. lewtowler@live.com

TOWNE, Jane Clapp (ND) 1111 N 1st St Apt 10, Bismarck ND 58501 **D S Geo's Epis Ch Bismarck ND 2002-** B Detroit MI 2/2/1927 d Frederick William Clapp & Hazel. Wstrn Coll of Mia in Ohio 1945; BA Carleton Coll 1948. D 11/23/2001 Bp Andrew Hedtler Fairfield. m 6/27/1953 Roy Towne c 3. janeroytbis@midco.net

TOWNER, Paul Eugene (Nev) 1090 War Eagle Dr N, Colorado Springs CO 80919 B Denver CO 5/20/1932 s Reginald Vincent Towner & Lorraine Rosalie. BA Colorado Coll 1954; STB Ya Berk 1957. D 6/24/1957 P 1/6/1958 Bp Joseph Summerville Minnis. Stndg Com Dio Nevada Las Vegas NV 1971-1991; Chair - COM Dio Nevada Las Vegas NV 1968-1996; DioCoun Dio Nevada Las Vegas NV 1967-1990; S Paul's Epis Ch Sparks NV 1966-1997; Vic H Trin Epis Ch Fallon NV 1964-1966; S Philips-in-the-Desert Hawthorne NV 1964-1966; Vic Gr And S Steph's Epis Ch Colorado Sprg CO 1957-1964.

TOWNER, Robert Arthur (Mo) 38 N Fountain St, Cape Girardeau MO 63701 **R Chr Ch Cape Girardeau MO 2001-** B Portsmouth VA 8/18/1949 s Robert Vincent Towner & Nancy Pfieffer. BA Trin Hartford CT 1973; MDiv SWTS 1977. D 6/18/1977 Bp Quintin Ebenezer Primo Jr P 12/1/1977 Bp James Winchester Montgomery. m 8/19/1973 Helen Illich c 1. S Jn's Ch Mason City IA 1987-2001; Vic S Paul's Epis Ch Grinnell IA 1980-1987; Cur S Giles' Ch Northbrook IL 1977-1980. LAND 1986; Mssnr to Sudan 2006; NECAD 1980; RACA, Past Pres & Direct 1979. btowner@charter.net

TOWNES III, Henry C (Chi) 12219 S 86th Ave, Palos Park IL 60464 B Beech Grove IN 9/5/1937 s Henry C Townes & Ruth A. BA Indiana U 1960. D 12/26/1987 Bp Frank Tracy Griswold III. m 11/12/1964 Margaret G Box c 2.

TOWNLEY JR, Richard Woodruff (NJ) 43 Delaware Ave, Lambertville NJ 08530 **S Andr's Ch Lambertville NJ 1989-** B Elizabeth NJ 7/18/1948 s Richard W Townley & Eleanor R. BA Drew U 1970; MDiv VTS 1973. D 6/9/1973 P 1/1/1974 Bp Leland Stark. Vic S Thos Ch Alexandria Pittstown NJ 1976-1983; Chap Of St Thos Of Alexandria Annandale NJ 1976-1982; Cur S Lk's Epis Ch Metuchen NJ 1973-1975. Auth, "Final Report Progress Report"; Auth, "Food For The Journey"; Auth, "Who In The Wrld?". rickt@snip.net

TOWNSEND, Bowman (Tex) 2205 Matterhorn Ln, Austin TX 78704 **R S Chris's Epis Ch Austin TX 2006-** B Knoxville TN 1/29/1956 BS U of Tennessee 1979; MDiv Epis TS of The SW 2003; MAC St. Edwards U 2008. D 5/31/2003 Bp Charles Glenn VonRosenberg P 1/17/2004 Bp Don Adger Wimberly. m 10/27/1984 Elizabeth Lee Adair c 2. R S Richard's Of Round Rock Round Rock TX 2004-2006; R S Richard's Of Round Rock Round Rock TX 2003-2004. botownsend@austin.rr.com

TOWNSEND, Craig Devine (NY) 445 Degraw St, Brooklyn NY 11217 **Vic S Jas Ch New York NY 1997-** B Syracuse NY 9/25/1955 s Terry Monk Townsend & Sara. BA Br 1978; MDiv EDS 1982; PhD Harv 1998. D 6/19/1982 Bp O'Kelley Whitaker P 5/26/1983 Bp Ned Cole. m 8/21/1982 Catherine N Fuerst c 2. Asstg P S Phil's Ch New York NY 1994-1997; Trin Preschool New York NY 1987-1990; Asst S Ann And The H Trin Brooklyn NY 1984-1987; Chr Ch Cranbrook Bloomfield Hills MI 1982-1984. Auth, "Faith in Their Own Color: Black Episcopalians in Antebellum New York City," Col Press, 2005; Auth, "Episcopalians and Race in New York City's Anti-Abolitionist Riots of 1834: The Case of Ptr Williams and Benjamin Onderdonk," *Angl and Epis Hist*, 2003. HSEC. Fllshp ECF 1991. cdt@craigdtownsend.com

TOWNSEND, Jerrald Lynn (O) Po Box 567, Gambier OH 43022 **Died 2/26/2011** B Wilmington NC 8/2/1941 s Earl Cleveland Townsend & Katherine Memory. BA U NC 1963; MA Washington U 1966; MDiv Ya Berk 1981; MEd U of Dayton 1996. D 6/27/1981 Bp John Harris Burt P 2/20/1982 Bp William Davidson. Alb Inst; Int Mnstry Ntwk. Phi Beta Kappa. townsendj@kenyon.edu

TOWNSEND, John Tolson (Mass) 40 Washington St, Newton MA 02458 **Prof EDS Cambridge MA 1994-** B Halifax NS CA 7/25/1927 s William Thomas Townsend & Olley. AB Br 1949; LTh U Tor (Wycliffe Coll 1952; STM Harvard DS 1953; ThD Harvard DS 1959. D 6/14/1952 P 12/21/1952 Bp Granville G Bennett. m 6/13/1956 Mary Van Zandt Rust c 2. EDS Cambridge

T

MA 1974-1993; P-in-c Ch Of The Gd Shpd Fairhaven MA 1955-1957; Cur Ch Of The Mssh Providence RI 1953-1954. Auth, "Midrash Tanhuma (Buber)," *vol. 3*, KTAV, 2003; Auth, "Midrash Tanhuma (Buber)," *vol. 2*, KTAV, 1991; Auth, "Midrash Tanhuma (Buber)," *vol. 1*, KTAV, 1989; Auth, *A Liturg Interp of the Passion of Jesus Chr in Narrative Formation (2nd ed.)*, NCCJ, 1985; Contrib, *Antisemitism & the Foundations of Chrsnty*; Auth, *Date of Lk-Acts*; Auth, *Study of Judaism I & II*; Auth, *The Gospel of Jn & the Jews*. Assn Jewish Stds 1978; Chr Schlrshp Grp on Chr-Jewish Relatns 1969; Chr Schlrshp Grp on Chr-Jewish Relatns, Chai 1983-1984; Natl Assn of Professors of Hebr 1995; SBL 1956. jhntwnsnd0@gmail.com

✠ **TOWNSEND, Rt Rev Martin Gough** (Eas) HC 86 Box 48 C-1, Springfield WV 26763 B Cambridge England UK 8/7/1943 s Frederick Henry Townsend & Beatrice Nora. BA Hob 1965; MDiv VTS 1968; DMin VTS 2000; DD VTS 2003. D 6/20/1968 P 5/26/1969 Bp Ned Cole Con 11/23/1992 for Eas. m 8/22/1964 Barbara Gunderman. P-in-c Emm Ch Keyser WV 2008-2011; Int R Trin Ch Upperville VA 2005-2007; Asst Bp Dio Newark Newark NJ 2004; Int The Ch of the Redeem Cincinnati OH 2001-2003; Bd Trst VTS Alexandria VA 1993-2001; Bp Dio Easton Easton MD 1992-2001; R Chr Ch Blacksburg VA 1987-1992; R St Marys Par St Marys City MD 1977-1987; R S Chris's Ch New Carrollton MD 1971-1977; Bec Dio Cntrl New York Syracuse NY 1969-1971; Asst S Paul's Cathd Syracuse NY 1968-1971. DD VTS Alexandria VA 1993. martintownsend@mac.com

TOWSON, Louis Albert (CFla) 348 Sherwood Ave, Satellite Beach FL 32937 **Vic S Jas Ch Macclenny FL 2008-** B Miami,FL 6/27/1947 s Harry Norman Towson & Julia. BS Florida St U 1969; MDiv VTS 1973. D 6/13/1973 P 5/9/1974 Bp Edward Hamilton West. m 2/4/1995 Susan Ann Towson. R Epis Ch Of The H Apos Satellite Bch FL 1980-2005; Asst H Trin Epis Ch Melbourne FL 1977-1979; Bethany Ch Hilliard FL 1976-1977; S Geo's Epis Ch Jacksonville FL 1975-1977; S Ptr's Ch Fernandina Bch FL 1975-1977; P-in-c Ch Of The Medtr Micanopy FL 1974-1976; P-in-c S Barn Epis Ch Williston FL 1974-1976. Auth, "How To Run A Com Or Orgnztn: A Manual For Ch Leaders," Resource Pub, Inc., 2000; Auth, "The Effective Ch Com: A Mem'S Handbook," Resource Pub, Inc., 2000. ltowson47@aol.com

TOY, Fran Y (Cal) 4151 Laguna Ave, Oakland CA 94602 **Credo Inst Inc. Memphis TN 2000-** B Oakland CA 8/9/1934 d Joe Yee & Bertha. BA U CA 1956; MA U of San Francisco 1977; MDiv CDSP 1984; DD CDSP 1996. D 6/9/1984 P 6/8/1985 Bp William Edwin Swing. m 8/5/1956 Arthur Chun Toy c 2. Dir Of Alum/ae and Stdt Affrs CDSP Berkeley CA 1991-1996; AlumCoordinator CDSP Berkeley CA 1987-1990; Ch Of The Resurr Pleasant Hill CA 1986-1987; Int Chr Ch Alameda CA 1986; Epis Ch Of Our Sav Oakland CA 1985-1996; Intrim R True Sunshine Par San Francisco CA 1984-1985. Auth, "Cutting Through the Double Blind," *Daughters of Sarah*, 1989. Bd Dir EWC 1985-1987; EAM Advocates 1997; Epis Asiamerica Mnstry 1973; Exec Bd EWHP 1985-1988; Fdr Coun of Wmn Mnstrs 1983-2003. DD CDSP Berkeley CA 1996. frantoy@att.net

TRACHE, Robert G (SeFla) 5100 N Ocean Blvd Apt 604, Lauderdale By The Sea FL 33308 B Newburgh NY 8/20/1947 s Gustave Trache & Ida. BA GW 1969; MA GW 1973; MDiv Harvard DS 1977. D 6/4/1977 Bp Robert Bruce Hall P 1/1/1978 Bp Hunley Agee Elebash. m 4/6/2002 Eliza Ragsdale c 2. Par Of The Epiph Winchester MA 2005-2008; S Mk The Evang Ft Lauderdale FL 2005-2008; Dio Atlanta Atlanta GA 2000; R S Jas' Ch Richmond VA 1994-2000; Imm Ch-On-The-Hill Alexandria VA 1984-1994; S Eliz's Ch Sudbury MA 1980-1984; Asst S Jn's Epis Ch Wilmington NC 1977-1979. Auth, *Opening Day*. rgtrache@comcast.net

TRACHMAN, Mike David (Okla) 2213 Galaxy Dr, Altus OK 73521 **D S Paul's Ch Altus OK 2004-** B Malden MA 1/3/1940 AA Wstrn Oklahoma St Coll. D 6/19/2004 Bp Robert Manning Moody. m 7/6/1979 Linda Long c 4. abet1940@gmail.com

TRACY, Dick Blaylock (Kan) 3020 Oxford Cir, Lawrence KS 66049 **D Trin Ch Lawr KS 2000-** B Bushton KS 10/9/1936 s Henry Franklin Tracy & Lucy Irene. BS U of Kansas 1958; MS U of Kansas 1965; PhD U of Kansas 1966. D 9/9/2000 Bp William Edward Smalley. m 5/29/1964 Rita Vanessa Tracy.

TRACY, Edward J. (SVa) 600 Talbot Hall Rd, Norfolk VA 23505 **Cn for Admin Dio Sthrn Virginia Norfolk VA 2011-** B Manhattan NY 5/27/1952 s Edward Joseph Tracy & Clare Marie. BA U Of Albuquerque 1974; MDiv VTS 1995. D 7/1/1995 Bp Terence Kelshaw P 1/25/1996 Bp David Charles Bowman. m 6/29/1985 Lee Ann Lewis. R Ch Of S Jas The Less Ashland VA 2007-2011; R Johns Memi Epis Ch Farmville VA 1998-2007; Asst Calv Epis Ch Williamsville NY 1995-1998. etracy@diosova.org

TRACY, Paul John (NI) 1025 Park Pl Apt 159, Mishawaka IN 46545 B Caldwell ID 8/8/1932 s Walter Frank Tracy & Lottie. BA U Of Idaho Moscow 1958; BD CDSP 1961; MA U of Notre Dame 1985. D 6/12/1961 P 12/16/1961 Bp Norman L Foote. Asst S Dav's Epis Ch Elkhart IN 1995-1996; R S Paul's Ch Mishawaka IN 1986-1995; P-in-c S Ptr's Ch Rensselaer IN 1981-1986; S Lk's Ch Weiser ID 1979-1981; R S Jas Ch Payette ID 1971-1981; Cn S Mich's Cathd Boise ID 1969-1971; P-in-c Ch Of The Epiph Arco ID 1964-1969; Vic Ch Of The Redeem Salmon ID 1964-1969; Vic Gd Shpd Ft Hall ID 1961-1964. Auth, "Chr Initiation Complete In Baptism? A Cont Question For Anglicans"; Auth, "The 4th Day". Angl Soc, SocMary. pjtracy369@cs.com

TRACY, Rita Vanessa (Kan) 3020 Oxford Cir, Lawrence KS 66049 **D Trin Ch Lawr KS 2000-** B Leavenworth KS 9/10/1938 d Wilbert Gottlieb Schreiber & Evelyn Vanessa. BD U of Kansas 1960; MS Ohio U 1972; MS U of Kansas 1982. D 9/9/2000 Bp William Edward Smalley. m 5/29/1964 Dick Blaylock Tracy.

TRAFFORD, Edward John (RI) 45 Rotary Dr, West Warwick RI 02893 B Providence RI 3/6/1944 s Harold Lawrence Trafford & Catherine. BS Bryant U 1978; MA Rhode Island Coll 1993. D 4/5/1986 Bp George Nelson Hunt III. m 10/29/1966 Susanne Oliviera c 2. D All SS' Memi Ch Providence RI 2001-2008; Serv Gr Ch In Providence Providence RI 1993-2000; D Dio Rhode Island Providence RI 1986-1991. deacon3644@cox.net

TRAFTON, Clark Wright (Cal) 875 S Nueva Vista Dr, Palm Springs CA 92264 **Asst S Marg's Epis Ch Palm Desert CA 2005-** B Marathon IA 3/28/1935 s Rex B Trafton & Myrtle May. BS Iowa St U 1955; MS Iowa St U 1957; BD CDSP 1960; Cert Westchester Inst 1978. D 6/15/1960 P 12/17/1960 Bp Gordon V Smith. m 6/20/2008 Lewis Kerman. Int S Mk's Ch Jackson Heights NY 2003-2005; Int S Geo's Epis Ch Maplewood NJ 2001-2002; S Mk's Ch In The Bowery New York NY 1997-2000; S Jn's Ch New York NY 1996-2000; Vic Trin Ch Winterset IA 1963-1965; Vic S Paul Epis Ch Des Moines IA 1960-1965. Amer Psych Assn, Diplomate 2000-2006; Natl Assn for the Advancement of Psychoanalysis 1979-2006; OHC 1965-1992. DD CDSP 1984. expedition@ix.netcom.com

TRAGER, Jane (O) 222 Eastern Heights Blvd, Elyria OH 44035 B New Haven CT 11/14/1943 d George L Trager & Sadie. BA/MA St U of NY Buffalo. D 11/12/2010 Bp Mark Hollingsworth Jr. jtinhouse@gmail.com

TRAIL, Shirley Ethel (WNY) 42 Haller Ave, Buffalo NY 14211 B Buffalo NY 7/26/1945 BA SUNY. D 3/1/1986 Bp Harold B Robinson.

TRAINOR, Helen Chase (WA) Legal Aid & Justice Center, 1000 Preston Ave. Ste A, Charlottesville VA 22903 B Boston MA 7/20/1949 d Irving Hanson Chase & Anne. BA Smith 1971; JD Suffolk U 1976. D 6/16/2002 Bp Leopold Frade. S Columba's Ch Washington DC 2004-2007; D Chr Ch Prince Geo's Par Rockville MD 2002-2008. trainor.helen142@gmail.com

TRAINOR, Mary Patricia (Los) 10925 Valley Home Ave, Whittier CA 90603 **Vic S Steph's Par Whittier CA 2007-; D S Steph's Par Whittier CA 2005-** B Bell CA 12/3/1945 d Robert James Trainor & Della Mae. BS California St Polytechnic U 1969; MDiv Epis TS 2005. D 6/11/2005 P 1/14/2006 Bp Joseph Jon Bruno. revmary@aol.com

TRAINOR, Mary Stoddard (FdL) E942 Whispering Pines Rd, Waupaca WI 54981 **S Jn's Ch Shawano WI 2011-; Chair, Deputation to GC 2012 Dio Fond du Lac Appleton WI 2010-; Dioc Coordntr, EFM Dio Fond du Lac Appleton WI 2006-; Vic S Steph's Par Whittier CA 2005-** B Milwaukee WI 6/26/1950 d Frederick Jackson Stoddard & Annette. BS U IL 1972; MS U IL 1974; PhD U CA 1979; TESM 2000; TESM 2006. D 2/21/1998 Bp Terence Kelshaw P 5/23/2009 Bp Russell Edward Jacobus. m 2/21/1987 Robert James Trainor c 3. Asst Ch Of The Intsn Stevens Point WI 2004-2011; D S Fran On The Hill El Paso TX 2002-2004; D Trin On The Hill Epis Ch Los Alamos NM 1998-1999. Auth, "Var arts," *Profsnl Journ in Educ, biology, educational Tech*. Bp's Cross Dio Fond du Lac 2010. pastormaryt@aol.com

TRAINOR, Robert James (FdL) E942 Whispering Pines Rd, Waupaca WI 54981 **Dep, GC 2012 Dio Fond du Lac Appleton WI 2011-; VP, Exec Coun Dio Fond du Lac Appleton WI 2009-; Dn, Wisconsin River Dnry Dio Fond du Lac Appleton WI 2006-** B Bell CA 6/15/1944 s Robert James Trainor & Della Mae. BS California St Polytechnic U 1966; MS U CA 1970; PhD U CA 1974; TESM 2002; MDiv Trin Sem Newburgh IN 2002. D 2/21/1998 P 3/16/1999 Bp Terence Kelshaw. m 2/21/1987 Mary Stoddard c 1. COM Dio Fond du Lac Appleton WI 2007-2011; R Ch Of The Intsn Stevens Point WI 2004-2010; R S Fran On The Hill El Paso TX 2002-2004; Assoc R S Mk's On The Mesa Epis Ch Albuquerque NM 1999-2002; D Trin On The Hill Epis Ch Los Alamos NM 1997-1999. Auth, "Grasp: Making Sense of Sci and Sprtlty," UpNorth Press, 2010; Auth, "Var arts," *Profsnl Physics Journ*. trainors3@gmail.com

TRAKEL, Debra Lynn (Mil) N81 W13442 Golfway Drive, Menomonee Falls WI 53051 **R S Chris's Ch River Hills WI 2010-** B Madison WI 3/18/1953 d Donald Charles Trakel & Arlene Hansena. BA Mt Mary Coll 1975; MSW U of Wisconsin 1981; MDiv SWTS 1995. D 2/2/1995 P 9/9/1995 Bp Roger John White. Exec Coun Dio Milwaukee Milwaukee WI 2004-2007; Stndg Com Dio Milwaukee Milwaukee WI 2002-2004; Com on Sexual Exploitation Dom And Frgn Mssy Soc- Epis Ch Cntr New York NY 2000-2003; R S Jas Epis Ch Milwaukee WI 1999-2010; P-in-c H Cross Epis Ch Wisconsin Dells WI 1997-1999; Asst to Bp for Pstr Care Dio Milwaukee Milwaukee WI 1996-1999; Cler Misconduct Case Mgr Dio Milwaukee Milwaukee WI 1995-2007; Assoc Chapl S Fran Ch Madison WI 1995-1996. EWC 1995; Mem Natl Com on Sexual Exploitation 2000-2003; Nathan Ntwk 2002; OSH--Assoc Mem 1995. Jonathan Myrick Daniels Fell EDS 1994; Natl Fell Fund for Theol Educ 1992. revdebra@aol.com

TRAMBLEY, Adam Thomas (NwPa) 343 Forker Blvd, Sharon PA 16146 **Fac, Strategic Plnng Process Dio NW Pennsylvania Erie PA 2011-; Pres, Stndg Com Dio NW Pennsylvania Erie PA 2010-; S Jn's Epis Ch Sharon PA 2009-** B Erie PA 3/30/1971 s Gerald Patrick Trambley & Marlene Clara. A.B. Harv 1994; M.Div VTS 2004. D 10/25/2003 P 6/12/2004 Bp Robert Deane Rowley Jr. m 12/21/1996 Jane Huey c 2. Dep to GC Dio NW Pennsylvania Erie PA 2006-2009; R Trin Memi Ch Warren PA 2004-2009. Soc for Biblic Lit 2003. atrambley@gmail.com

TRAMEL, Stephanie MG (Ia) 2300 Bancroft Way, Berkeley CA 94704 B Davenport IO 5/16/1967 d Frederick Claremont Green & Ann Janette. AB Bryn 1989; MA U of Iowa 1994; MDiv CDSP 2000. D 6/10/2000 P 1/7/2001 Bp Carl Christopher Epting. m 6/30/2006 James Russell Tramel c 1. Sabbatical Int Assoc R Trsfg Epis Ch San Mateo CA 2008. greenfigs@earthlink.net

TRAMMELL, Robert William (Okla) St. Augustine Of Canterbury, 14700 N. May Ave., Oklahoma City OK 73134 **Vol D S Aug Of Cbury Oklahoma City OK 2007-** B Siloam Springs AR 9/17/1952 s Bobby Lee Trammell & Edna Ruth. BA Cntrl St U 1979; MA U of Oklahoma 1986. D 6/16/2007 Bp Robert Manning Moody. m 4/19/1974 Linda Trammell c 3. rtrammell@oklahoman.com

TRAN, Catherine Caroline (Colo) 6556 High Dr., Morrison CO 80465 **Gd Shpd Epis Ch Centennial CO 2011-** B North Babylon NY 5/23/1959 d Louis Stephan Conover & Caroline. U CO 1979; MDiv S Thos Sem 1994; MA S Thos Sem 1995; Cert Sprtl Direction Shalem Inst Washington DC 1998. D 6/11/1994 P 1/14/1995 Bp William Jerry Winterrowd. m 8/18/1979 Tam Tran c 2. R Ch Of The Trsfg Evergreen CO 1998-2009; Assoc R S Gabr The Archangel Epis Ch Cherry Hills Vill CO 1994-1998. cathctran@gmail.com

TRAPANI, Kathleen M (Cal) 30 Greenridge Pl, Danville CA 94506 **Int S Tim's Ch Danville CA 2002-** B San Jose CA 2/18/1957 d Joseph Ribardo & Alice. BA U CA 1979; MBA U CA 1987; MDiv CDSP 2001. D 12/2/2000 P 6/2/2001 Bp William Edwin Swing. m 5/31/1980 Thomas A Trapani c 4. Phi Beta Kappa 1979. kmtrapani@gmail.com

TRAPP, Grace J. (SwVa) PO Box 328, Harpswell ME 04079 B Milwaukee WI 2/5/1950 d Eugene Trapp & Grace Carol. BS U of Wisconsin 1973; MDiv SWTS 1976; MEd Natl-Louis U 1996. D 5/1/1976 Bp Charles Thomas Gaskell P 12/19/1979 Bp A(rthur) Heath Light. Dir Pstr Care S Lk's Hosp Racine WI 1986-1987; Asstg P S Lk's Ch Evanston IL 1983-2003; COM Dio SW Virginia Roanoke VA 1979-1981; Asstg P Emm Ch Staunton VA 1979-1981; Stuart Hall Staunton VA 1979-1981; Spec Mnstry Com Dio Milwaukee Milwaukee WI 1976-1979. Rec Wmn's Bd Prize SWTS 1976.

TRAPP, James E. (NY) PO Box 40697, Portland OR 97240 B Paducah KY 10/30/1946 s Ralph Carl Trapp & Mary Louise. B.Mus.Ed NWU 1968; MDiv Nash 1971. D 6/19/1971 Bp Gerald Francis Burrill P 12/18/1971 Bp James Winchester Montgomery. m 9/16/2005 John Lynn Keating c 1. Assoc R Ch Of The Intsn New York NY 1979-1984; Asst Chr Ch Fitchburg MA 1977-1979; Yth Dir Dio Sthrn Ohio Cincinnati OH 1974-1977; Cur Trin Epis Ch Wheaton IL 1971-1974. jbo.4900@yahoo.com

TRAQUAIR, Megan McClure (Az) 11460 N Quicksilver Trl, Tucson AZ 85737 **Vic Ch Of The Apos Oro Vlly AZ 2008-** B Pasadena CA 12/19/1962 d Malcolm Traquair McClure & Patricia Diane. BA Pomona Coll 1985; MDiv SWTS 1991. D 6/15/1991 P 1/1/1992 Bp Frederick Houk Borsch. m 8/24/1985 Philip S Smittle c 2. S Phil's In The Hills Tucson AZ 2002-2009; R Geth Epis Ch Marion IN 1997-2002; S Jn Of The Cross Bristol IN 1994-1996; Asst to R S Mich And All Ang Par Corona Del Mar CA 1991-1993. traquair@mac.com

TRASK, Richard Edward (NJ) 2816 Havasupai Ave Apt 4, San Diego CA 92117 B Concord NH 6/23/1924 s Edward Prankard Trask & Helen Almina. BA Carroll Coll 1949; MDiv PDS 1953; STM NYTS 1981. D 6/6/1953 Bp Norman B Nash P 12/12/1953 Bp Wallace J Gardner. c 2. Int H Trin Ch Collingswood NJ 1987-1989; S Jas Ch Trenton Yardville NJ 1986-1987; S Mary's Ch Sparta NJ 1985-1986; S Mary's Ch Haledon NJ 1984-1985; S Bern's Ch Bernardsville NJ 1984; Int S Jn's Ch Salem NJ 1983-1984; S Mary's Epis Ch Pleasantville NJ 1982-1983; Ch Of S Mk And All SS Absecon Galloway NJ 1969-1983; Historic Ch of Ascen Atlantic City NJ 1969-1982; Vic S Mary's Ch Clementon NJ 1956-1968; R Trin Epis Ch Houghton MI 1954-1956; Asst to Dn Trin Cathd Trenton NJ 1953-1954. richedwtrask@juno.com

TRASK III, Robert Palmer (EMich) 4111 James Ct, Fort Gratiot MI 48059 **R Gr Epis Ch Port Huron MI 1998-** B Boston MA 9/13/1947 s Robert Palmer Trask & Hazel Christine. BA Gordon Coll 1969; MDiv TESM 1983. D 6/19/1983 P 5/20/1984 Bp John Forsythe Ashby. m 2/17/1973 Margaret S Schoenherr c 5. COM Dio Nebraska Omaha NE 1989-1998; R S Alb's Epis Ch McCook NE 1987-1998; Vic S Eliz's Ch Russell KS 1985-1987; Vic H Apos Ch Ellsworth KS 1983-1987; Dio Wstrn Kansas Hutchinson KS 1983-1985; Vic S Mk's Ch Lyons KS 1983-1985. bob_trask@hotmail.com

TRAVERSE, Alfred (CPa) 9212 Standing Stone Rd., Huntingdon PA 16652 B P.E.I. Canada 9/7/1925 s Alfred Freeman Traverse & Pearle. SB Harv 1946; AM Harv 1948; PhD Harv 1951; MDiv Epis TS of The SW 1965. D 6/1/1965 Bp J Milton Richardson P 5/1/1966 Bp Scott Field Bailey. m 6/30/1951 Elizabeth Jane Insley c 4. Vic S Jn's Epis Ch Huntingdon PA 1976-1980; Cur S Paul's Ch Philipsburg PA 1966-1975; Cur S Matt's Ch Austin TX 1965-1966. "Paleopalynology," *Second Ed (Topics in Geobiology)*, Springer; 2nd Ed, 2008; Auth, "Sci Books," *arts*, 1950. CBS. Hon Mem Awd Amer Assn Stuart Thynologistic 2005; Excellence in Educ Medal Amer Assn Stuart Thynologistic 2002; Phi Beta Kappa 1950; Indn Int Gold Medal In Palaeobotany 91-92. atraverse@comcast.net

TRAVIS, Douglas Brooks (Tex) Seminary of the Southwest, 501 East 32nd Street, Austin TX 78705 **Dn & Pres Epis TS Of The SW Austin TX 2007-** B San Antonio TX 8/5/1953 s Murray William Travis & Jane Ellen. BA Trin U 1975; MATS McCormick TS 1977; M.A. U Chi 1980; STM GTS 1994; DMin SMU 2000. D 6/13/1987 P 5/1/1988 Bp Donis Dean Patterson. m 8/16/1975 Pamela Jean Coleman c 2. R Trin Epis Ch The Woodlands TX 2001-2006; R S Jas Ch Dallas TX 1992-2001; Exec Coun Dio Dallas Dallas TX 1992-1995; Cn S Matt's Cathd Dallas TX 1989-1991; Cur Epis Ch Of The Redeem Irving TX 1987-1989. DD GTS 2008; Phi Beta Kappa. dtravis@ssw.edu

TRAVIS, Michelle Halsall (Mont) 1821 Westlake Dr Apt 124, Austin TX 78746 B Jackson MS 8/18/1947 d Archibald Conway Halsall & Amy Patricia. BA Rice U 1971; MS Rice U 1977; MDiv Epis TS of The SW 1985. D 5/23/1985 P 12/1/1985 Bp Jackson Earle Gilliam. m 11/16/1984 Arthur Edwin Travis. Asst R S Mk's Ch Austin TX 1987-1989; Asst R S Dav's Epis Ch San Antonio TX 1985-1986.

TRAVIS, R(obert) (CFla) 2103 Indian River Dr, Cocoa FL 32922 B Williamson WV 10/29/1940 s Robert Haskel Travis & Nell May. BA Col 1962; STB GTS 1967; MA Rhode Island Coll 1984. D 6/17/1967 P 12/21/1967 Bp Jonathan Goodhue Sherman. m 12/28/1968 Karen M Mathis c 3. R Ch Of S Dav's By The Sea Cocoa Bch FL 1998-2008; R Trin Ch Rochester NY 1983-1998; R All SS Epis Ch Attleboro MA 1978-1983; R Gr Ch In The Mountains Waynesville NC 1970-1978; Cur S Steph's Ch Port Washington NY 1967-1970. "Cmnty Meitationss On The Stations Of The Cross," Ldr Resources Inc., 2003. rcarrolltravis@hotmail.com

TRAVIS, Robert P. (ETenn) 800 Northshore Dr, Knoxville TN 37919 B Waynesville NC 5/14/1976 s R(obert) Travis & Karen. BA Col 1998; MDiv STUSo 2006. D 5/27/2006 P 12/16/2006 Bp John Wadsworth Howe. m 2/8/2003 Jacqueline C Camm c 3. Ch Of The Ascen Knoxville TN 2007-2008; Asst R S Mich's Ch Orlando FL 2006-2007; Dir of Yth Mnstry S Steph's Ch Port Washington NY 1999-2003. Ch Club of New York 2001-2004. ABS CE Prize STUSo 2006. frrob@knoxvilleascension.org

TRAVIS, Sherry Margaret (Miss) 314 Mayfield Ln Ne, Jacksonville AL 36265 **R S Andr's Cathd Jackson MS 2006-** B Jackson MS 7/16/1948 d Loyd Kelley Travis & Margaret Jean. LSU 1968; BA Belhaven Coll 1971; Med Mississippi St U 1978; MDiv VTS 1992. D 6/20/1992 Bp Duncan Montgomery Gray Jr P 11/30/1993 Bp Alfred Clark Marble Jr. R S Lk's Epis Ch Jacksonville AL 1999-2006; Assoc R St Thos Epis Ch Huntsville AL 1996-1999; P All SS Epis Ch Memphis TN 1993-1996; Ch of the H Trin Vicksburg MS 1992-1996. Cler Ldrshp Proj 2001; HabHum - Bd Mem 1997-1999. s.m.travis@comcast.net

TRAYLOR, Thomas Wallace (Cal) 1801 Jackson St Apt 4, San Francisco CA 94109 **Pstr Assoc All SS' Ch San Francisco CA 2003-** B Atlanta GA 1/8/1950 BA Emory U 1972; MDiv Sthrn Bapt TS Louisville KY 1975; MSSW U of Louisville 1986. D 12/6/2003 P 6/5/2004 Bp William Edwin Swing. thomas.traylor@kp.org

TRAYNHAM, Warner Raymond (Los) 6125 Alviso Ave, Los Angeles CA 90043 B Baltimore MD 9/9/1936 s Hezekiah Elando Traynham & Virginia Valeria. BA Dart 1957; Oxf 1958; BD VTS 1961. D 7/6/1961 P 4/4/1962 Bp Noble C Powell. m 1/23/1965 Jocelyn Phyllis Dawson c 4. Dep GC Dio Los Angeles Los Angeles CA 1988-2000; R St Johns Pro-Cathd Los Angeles CA 1983-2001; R S Cyp's Ch Roxbury MA 1967-1972; Vic S Phil's Ch Annapolis MD 1962-1965; Asst S Jas' Epis Ch Baltimore MD 1961-1962. Auth, "Chr Faith in Black & White," Parameter Press. Phi Beta Kappa Dartmouth Phi Beta Kappa 1957. warnerrtray@aol.com

TREADWELL II, Richard Allen (Ore) 1916 NE Gibbs Circle, Mcminnville OR 97128 B Portland OR 7/22/1938 s Richard Allen Treadwell I & Eva Mary. BS OR SU 1961; MDiv CDSP 1964. D 6/29/1964 Bp James Walmsley Frederic Carman P 12/30/1964 Bp William J Gordon Jr. m 3/24/1962 Shirley Vaughan Shepard c 3. Dio Oregon Portland OR 2000-2006; Epis Chars Bd Dio Oregon Portland OR 1991-1994; R S Barn Par McMinnville OR 1976-2005; S Jas Epis Ch Taos NM 1970-1976; P-in-c S Andr's Ch Stevens Vill AK 1966-1970; P-in-c S Matt's Ch Beaver AK 1966-1970; S Jn's Epis Ch Eagle AK 1964-1966; P-in-c H Trin Ch Cir AK 1964-1965; Cur S Steph's Ch Ft Yukon AK 1964-1965. OHC 1960. dickt22@verizon.net

TREADWELL III, William Charles (Tex) 515 Columbus Ave, Waco TX 76701 **S Paul's Ch Waco TX 2004-** B Rock Hill SC 5/20/1960 s William Charles Treadwell & Louise. BA Geo 1983; MDiv STUSo 1989. D 6/17/1989 P 5/31/1990 Bp Donis Dean Patterson. m 6/8/1985 Christine Lynn Chapman c 3. R S Paul's Ch Waco TX 2004-2011; R S Ptr's Ch McKinney TX 1993-2004; Cur S Mich And All Ang Ch Dallas TX 1989-1991. Auth, "Earth Lent"; Auth, "Adoption". chuck@stpaulswaco.org

T

TREBILCOX, Donna J (WMass) 19 Pleasant St, Chicopee MA 01013 **P-in-c Gr Ch Chicopee MA 2011-; R Gr Ch Chicopee MA 2011-; Bement/Waterfield Schlrshp Comm. Dio Wstrn Massachusetts Springfield MA 2007-; S Geo's Ch Lee MA 2006-** B Panama City FL 8/17/1944 d Arthur Randolph Larson & Alice Theresa. BS SUNY 1972; M Ed Leh 1976; MDiv GTS 2004. D 4/17/2004 P 10/31/2004 Bp Paul Victor Marshall. m 12/30/1975 Harry Gilbert Trebilcox c 3. Dicocesan Coun Dio Wstrn Massachusetts Springfield MA 2007-2010; Trin Ch Easton PA 2004-2006. St. Matt's Soc 1998. dtrebilcox@verizon.net

TREES, Thomas Heino (WLa) 1030 Johnston St, Lafayette LA 70501 **Assoc Ch Of The Ascen Lafayette LA 2009-** B Washington DC 10/8/1968 BA U of Virginia 1991; MDiv Regent U 1997; STM Cranmer Theol Hse 2000. D 11/30/2002 Bp David John Bena P 5/31/2003 Bp Daniel William Herzog. m 3/23/1997 Kathleen Margaret Quinn c 3. COM Dio Albany Albany NY 2008-2009; Dioc Coun Dio Albany Albany NY 2003-2009; R St Augustines Ch Ilion NY 2002-2009. ascensiontrees@yahoo.com

TREFTS, Todd Hubbard (Spok) 339 S 4th Ave, Sandpoint ID 83864 **Died 10/5/2009** B Buffalo NY 1/29/1933 s John Chilion Trefts & Frances Lynette. BA Trin 1955; BD VTS 1961. D 6/23/1961 Bp Lauriston L Scaife P. c 4.

TREGARTHEN, Doran Woodrow (Los) 27625 Summerfield Ln, San Juan Capistrano CA 92675 **Asst S Marg Of Scotland Par San Juan Capistrano CA 1988-** B San Pedro CA 2/19/1919 s Harold Shepherd Tregarthen & Alice. BA U CA 1942; Med U CA 1954; MA Claremont TS 1988. D 6/25/1988 Bp Frederick Houk Borsch P 1/7/1989 Bp Oliver Bailey Garver Jr. m 12/26/1942 Ethel Mae Geabhart. Auth, *Tchg in the Elem Sch*; Auth, *Who Are the Poor?*. church@smeg.org

TREGO, Randall (Tex) 3106 Heritage Creek Oaks, Houston TX 77008 **Dio Texas Houston TX 2011-; Chapl Cullen Memi Chap Houston TX 2002-** B Lancaster PA 5/19/1953 s Earl Martin Trego & Elsie Mae. BA Gordon Coll 1976; MDiv VTS 1987. D 6/13/1987 Bp David Elliot Johnson P 5/6/1988 Bp Cabell Tennis. m 5/20/1978 Lois Anne Cleveland c 2. Assoc S Jn The Div Houston TX 1989-2001; Cur Chr Ch Greenville Wilmington DE 1987-1989. rtrego@mac.com

TREHERNE-THOMAS, Rhoda Margaret (NY) 10 Bay Street Lndg Apt 6l, Staten Island NY 10301 **Assoc S Jn's Ch Staten Island NY 2003-** B Mumbles Wales GB 11/6/1927 d Francis Hugh Treherne-Thomas & Margaret Edwards. BA Smith 1948; MA Col 1951; MDiv UTS 1980. D 6/7/1980 P 12/7/1980 Bp Paul Moore Jr. P-in-c S Simon's Ch Staten Island NY 1994-2003; Asst S Ptr's Ch Bronx NY 1993-1997; Asst Par Of Chr The Redeem Pelham NY 1992-1993; Int Chr Epis Ch Tarrytown NY 1989-1991; Consult Epis Ch Cntr New York NY 1988; Par Of Chr The Redeem Pelham NY 1988; P-in-c S Jos's Ch Bronx NY 1986-1988; Consult Epis Ch Cntr New York NY 1985-1986; Asst S Ptr's Ch Bronx NY 1980-1984. CSM 1982.

TREI, Rosemary Randall (Dal) 5923 Royal Ln, Dallas TX 75230 **Jubilee Mnstry Off Dio Dallas Dallas TX 2009-; D S Lk's Epis Ch Dallas TX 2009-; Rgstr of Stanton Cntr S Matt's Cathd Dallas TX 2009-** B Long Beach CA 12/18/1944 d Ralph Barnett Randall & Julia Helen. BA H Names U 1966; CA Teachers Cred San Diego St U 1967; Dplma Stanton Cntr for Mnstry Formation 2008. D 6/6/2009 Bp James Monte Stanton. m 6/24/1967 Charles A Trei c 3. crtrei@sbcglobal.net

TREJO-BARAHOMA, Oscar (Hond) C/O Igelsia Episcopal, PO Box 523900, Miami FL 33135 **Dio Honduras Miami FL 1998-** B 7/10/1961 P 3/5/2005 Bp Lloyd Emmanuel Allen. m 4/16/1993 Filomena Chicas Romero c 2.

TRELEASE, Murray Lincoln (Oly) 343 Eagles Roost Ln, Lopez Island WA 98261 B Kansas City MO 11/7/1929 s Richard Mitchell Trelease & Ruth Benjamin. BA U of Kansas 1952; MDiv CDSP 1959. D 6/1/1959 Bp John Brooke Mosley P 12/9/1959 Bp William J Gordon Jr. m 4/8/1961 Mariette Pauline Gaspar. Vic Gr Ch Lopez Island WA 2000-2002; Dio Olympia Seattle WA 1993-1994; P-in-c Gr Ch Lopez Island WA 1992-1993; R/ Headmaster S Paul's Ch Kansas City MO 1980-1992; R S Paul's Ch Milwaukee WI 1972-1980; Cn P S Mk's Cathd Seattle WA 1967-1971; Archd Dio Alaska Fairbanks AK 1964-1967; Vic S Steph's Ch Ft Yukon AK 1964-1967; Yukon Vlly Mssnr Dio Alaska Fairbanks AK 1959-1963. Auth, "Dying Among Alaskan Indians"; Auth, "Death The Final Stage Of Growth"; Auth, "Dioc Nwspr Series Aunt Clara's Famous Ironing Bd Lectures". murraylt@rockisland.com

TREMAINE, Gordon Hyde (Fla) 100 Ne 1st St, Gainesville FL 32601 B New York NY 12/27/1954 s A Robert Tremaine & Shirley Ann. BA Dickinson Coll 1976; MDiv VTS 1981. D 6/13/1981 P 12/1/1981 Bp John Shelby Spong. c 2. R H Trin Ch Gainesville FL 2002-2006; R S Ptr's Ch Essex Fells NJ 1991-2002; R S Steph's Ch Millburn NJ 1984-1991; Cur Calv Epis Ch Summit NJ 1981-1984.

TREMBATH, Jack Graham (Mich) 939 Chippewa St, Mount Clemens MI 48043 **Chair Com Affirmative Aging Dio Michigan Detroit MI 1998-; D S Mich's Ch Grosse Pointe Woods MI 1987-** B Windsor ON CA 4/13/1922 s John Trembath & Theresa. Amer Coll of Life Underwriters 1969; Whitaker TS 1976. D 12/10/1976 Bp Henry Irving Mayson. m 4/27/1946 Redina Josephine Conrow c 3. Pres D Coun Dio Michigan Detroit MI 1995-1997; S Edw The Confessor Epis Ch Clinton Township MI 1986-1987; Gr Ch Mt Clemens MI 1976-1986. jaret01@juno.com

TREMMEL, Marcia Ann (SwFla) 11588 57th Street Cir. E., Parrish FL 34219 **D S Mary Magd Lakewood Ranch FL 2007-** B Orlando FL 1/10/1948 d Louis Livingston & Sylvia. BA U of So Florida 1969; MBA U of So Florida 1992; BS U of So Florida 1996. D 6/12/2004 Bp Rogers Sanders Harris. m 4/13/1968 Allan Michael Tremmel c 2. D S Mary's Epis Ch Palmetto FL 2005-2006; D S Wlfd's Epis Ch Sarasota FL 2004-2005. matremmel@tampabay.rr.com

TREPPA, Joyce Lynn (Mich) 18610 San Quentin, Lathrup Village MI 48076 **D All SS Epis Ch Pontiac MI 2011-** B Detroit MI 5/6/1949 d Elmer William Treppa & Marjorie. BS Estrn Michigan U 1988; Whitaker TS 2001. D 6/16/2001 Bp Wendell Nathaniel Gibbs Jr. m 8/8/1981 Jonathan Carl Campbell. D Chr Ch Detroit MI 2001-2009. joyceandjon@aol.com

TREVATHAN, W(illiam) Andre (Ky) 1 Franklin Town Blvd Apt 1515, Philadelphia PA 19103 B Little Rock AR 11/6/1931 s William Alford Trevathan & Martha Esther. BA U So 1953; STB GTS 1956; U of Puerto Rico 1983. D 6/17/1956 Bp Charles Gresham Marmion P 12/1/1956 Bp Horace W B Donegan. m 6/2/1985 Carol A Altland c 3. Dept Of CSR Dio Kentucky Louisville KY 1987-2002; Vic S Jn's Ch Murray KY 1986-1996; Int Dio Kentucky Louisville KY 1985-1986; Purhas Coun Epis Ch Paducah KY 1985-1986; Asst Par of Trin Ch New York NY 1958-1962; Asst Chapl Ch Of The Incarn New York NY 1956-1958. Iglesia Epis Puertorrique, "Ritos Autorizados," *Ritos Autorizados*, Iglesia Epis Puertorriqueña, 1983. Cmnty Of S Mary 1986-2006. trevathans@comcast.net

TREWHELLA, Charles Keith (Ore) 19691 Nw Meadow Lake Rd, Yamhill OR 97148 B Eureka CA 4/5/1928 s William A Trewhella & Erlene M. BA U of Portland 1953; ATC 1969. D 6/24/1969 P 3/7/1970 Bp James Walmsley Frederic Carman. Bp of Oregon Fndt Portland OR 1989-1993; Legacy Gd Samar Hosp Portland OR 1969-1989. AEHC 1969.

TREZEVANT, Margaret Anne (Cal) 1350 Waller St, San Francisco CA 94117 B Travis A.F.B., CA 6/12/1950 d Lee Delsworth Shillingberg & Mayme. BA San Francisco St U 1985; MS U CA - San Francisco 1994; BDS Sch for Deacons 2009. D 6/6/2009 Bp Marc Handley Andrus. m 3/26/1983 Richard Gray Trezevant c 1. Sojourn Multifaith Chapl San Francisco CA 2010-2011. trez3@mindspring.com

TRIGG, Joseph (WA) Po Box 760, La Plata MD 20646 **R Chr Ch Port Tobacco Paris La Plata MD 1993-** B Henderson KY 10/25/1949 s George Foster Trigg & Jean Ashby. VTS; BA Rice U 1971; MA U Chi 1974; PhD U Chi 1978. D 6/15/1984 P 5/1/1985 Bp David Reed. m 6/12/1983 Joy E Scheidt c 2. VTS Alexandria VA 1991-1992; VTS Alexandria VA 1987-1989; S Patricks Ch Falls Ch VA 1986-1993; Gr Ch Paducah KY 1984-1986. Auth, "Message of the Fathers of the Ch: Volume 9," *Biblic Interp*; Auth, *Of One Body: Renwl Movements in the Ch*; Auth, *Origen (Early Chr Fathers)*. No Amer Patristic Soc. Phi Beta Kappa Rice U 1971. jtrigg@olg.com

TRIGLETH, John Paul (Mil) S3919A Highway 12, Baraboo WI 53913 B Vandalia IL 11/8/1941 s Irwin Lonzo Trigleth & Mary Ethel. BD U of Wisconsin 1986. D 1/13/2001 Bp Roger John White. m 11/2/1963 Margaret Bertha Vander. D Trin Ch Baraboo WI 2001-2009. mptrigleth@yahoo.com

TRIMBLE, James Armstrong (Pa) 326 S Third St, Philadelphia PA 19106 B Philadelphia PA 6/13/1931 s James Armstrong Trimble & Ella May. BA U of Pennsylvania 1953; BD VTS 1956. D 6/1/1956 Bp Joseph Gillespie Armstrong P 1/25/1957 Bp Oliver J Hart. m 12/26/1996 Gail H Hutchison c 3. R Chr Ch Philadelphia Philadelphia PA 1978-1998; July R S Chris Sum Chap Winter Harbor ME 1961-2010; Vic Ch Of The Redemp Southampton PA 1958-1960. Auth, "Var arts," *Var Epis Pub*. DD VTS 1989. jat3261@verizon.net

TRIMBLE, James Edward Richard (Ky) 5303 Old Herring Pl, Crestwood KY 40014 **R S Jas Ch Pewee Vlly KY 2009-** B Louisville KY 10/30/1967 s Robert Lucien Trimble & Ursula Ann. BS Murray St U 1990; MDiv Epis TS of The SW 2005. D 6/4/2005 P 12/10/2005 Bp Edwin Funsten Gulick Jr. m 9/18/1999 Sarah Peoples c 1. S Matt's Epis Ch Louisville KY 2007-2009; S Mary's Ch Madisonville KY 2005-2007. "Jump...Or You'll Get Pushed," *Place Gives Rise to Sprt: Writers on Louisville*, Fleur de Lis Press, 2001. jim.trimble@gmail.com

TRIMBLE, Sarah M (Va) 3401 Chantarene Dr, Pensacola FL 32507 B Saint Paul BR 9/6/1940 d Prudencio Moure & Sarah Holmes. BA Florida St U 1962; MDiv VTS 1989. D 6/10/1989 Bp Edward Lewis Lee Jr P 3/1/1990 Bp Robert Poland Atkinson. m 6/26/1965 Henry Leland Trimble c 2. R The Fork Ch Doswell VA 1993-1997; Int R Epis Ch Of Leeds Par Markham VA 1992-1993; Asst R S Jas' Epis Ch Warrenton VA 1989-1991. SMTRIM@ATT.NET

TRIMMER, Thomas Edward (EMich) 3532 W Monroe Rd, Alma MI 48801 B Lansing MI 7/6/1941 s Theodore Roosevelt Trimmer & Clarabelle Dorothy. Bethel Coll 1972; Epis TS In Kentucky 1974. D 2/4/1979 Bp William J Gordon Jr. m 8/7/1965 Margaret J Harper c 3. Asst S Jn's Epis Ch Alma MI 1979-1990. Natl Coun- Fllshp of Recon; Natl Exec Coun, EPF.

TRIMPE, Herbert William (NY) 26 Van Demark Ln, Kerhonkson NY 12446 **D Dio New York New York City NY 1992-** B Peekskill NY 5/26/1939 s Herbert Trimpe & Anna Mae. D 5/30/1992 Bp Richard Frank Grein. m 9/9/1972 Linda Ann Fite c 3. "The Power Of Ang," Big Apple Vision, 2005. trimpdog@hotmail.com

TRIPP, Arthur D (RG) Po Box 398, Raton NM 87740 B San Antonio TX 9/1/1932 s Arthur Lee Tripp & Anna Jo. BS NE St U 1955; MDiv Epis TS of The SW 1959. D 5/20/1959 P 11/30/1959 Bp Chilton Powell. m 1/21/1977 Nilah Richardson c 3. Vic H Trin Epis Ch - Mssn Raton NM 2001-2009; R S Chris's Epis Ch El Paso TX 1992-1996; Exec Coun Appointees New York NY 1977-1992; R S Aid's Epis Ch Tulsa OK 1967-1976; Chair Dept Mssn Dio Oklahoma Oklahoma City OK 1963-1976. tripp@zianet.com

TRIPP, Roy (Mass) 12 Brandywine Blvd, Wilmington DE 19809 **Ch Of S Jn The Evang Duxbury MA 2007-** B Bangor ME 11/24/1954 s Claivoy A Tripp & Lillian H. MDiv CDSP 1996. D 6/22/1996 P 5/1/1997 Bp Vincent Waydell Warner. m 9/16/1982 Lizbeth Ann Devoir. R S Alb's Wilmington DE 2001-2007; S Clare of Assisi Epis Ch Snoqualmie WA 1998-2001; Trin Epis Ch Everett WA 1997-1998. OHC. roytripp@mac.com

TRIPP, Thomas Norman (WNY) 354 Burroughs Dr, Amherst NY 14226 B Buffalo NY 1/6/1947 s Norman Sidney Tripp & Betty Irene. BS St Coll at Buffalo 1968; MS St Coll at Buffalo 1973. D 11/17/2007 Bp J Michael Garrison. m 1/23/1971 Lois Jean Tripp c 3. tntljt@roadrunner.com

TRIPPE, George Edward (Md) 43 Valerie Street, Dianella WA 6059 Australia B Jamaica NY 4/14/1942 s John Jacob Trzpis & Beatrice May. BA USC 1963; MDiv PDS 1967; PhD Edith Cowan U Perth AU 2000. D 9/9/1967 P 3/1/1968 Bp Francis E I Bloy. m 1/18/1964 Shirley Unger c 3. Bp Claggett Cntr Buckeystown MD 1990-1992; R S Mich's Mssn Anaheim CA 1980-1985; Asst R All SS Par Beverly Hills CA 1976-1980; S Andr's Epis Ch Ojai CA 1971-1976; Cur S Steph's Par Los Angeles CA 1967-1968. gtrippe@hotmail.com

TRIPSES, Kathleen R (Ia) 2844 NW Northcreek Circle, Ankeny IA 50023 **D S Anne's By The Fields Ankeny IA 2001-** B Eagle Grove IA 9/19/1932 d C Leroy McDowell & M Helene. BS Iowa St U 1954; Med Tech Drake U 1972. D 4/7/2001 Bp Carl Christopher Epting. m 6/20/1954 Richard Tripses c 4. OSL the Physcn 2001; Third Ord, SSF 1985. ktripses@msn.com

TRISKA, Patricia Ilene (Ia) 1009 Parkway Dr Apt 7, Boone IA 50036 **D Gr Ch Boone IA 1995-** B Prescott AZ 10/10/1931 d John William Moxley & Thelma Agnes. RN Des Moines Cmnty Coll Des Moines IA 1989; EFM STUSo 1993. D 5/25/1995 Bp Carl Christopher Epting. c 2. gracechurch707@msn.com

TRISTRAM SSJE, Geoffrey Robert (Mass) 980 Memorial Dr, Cambridge MA 02138 **S Jn's Chap Cambridge MA 2008-** B Cardiff UK 9/27/1953 s Frank Tristram & Patricia. BA U of Cambridge 1978; Westcott Hse Cambridge 1979; MA U of Cambridge 1981. Trans from Church Of England 3/13/2002 Bp M(arvil) Thomas Shaw III. geoffrey@ssje.org

TRIVELY, Timothy Churchill (SwFla) 2404 Amberside Way, Wesley Chapel FL 33544 B Lincoln NE 7/17/1937 s Ilo Allely Trively & Maxine Elliot. BS Clemson U 1960; MDiv STUSo 1963. D 6/29/1963 P 6/1/1964 Bp Richard Henry Baker. m 8/26/1961 Elizabeth Anne Wells c 2. Acts Of The Apos Mssn S Petersburg FL 1990-1997; Dio SW Florida Sarasota FL 1988-1989; S Andr's Epis Ch Tampa FL 1983-1988; R S Jas Epis Ch Lenoir NC 1967-1983; R Trin Ch Scotland Neck NC 1964-1967; M-in-c Ch Of The Gd Shpd Rocky Mt NC 1963-1964. heytimanne@gmail.com

TROEGER, Thomas Henry (Colo) 56 Hickory Rd, Woodbridge CT 06525 B Suffern NY 1/30/1945 s Henry Troger & Lorena. BA Ya 1967; BD CRDS 1970; STD Dickinson Coll 1993. D 6/5/1999 P 12/5/1999 Bp William Jerry Winterrowd. m 6/25/1967 Merle Marie Butler.

TROGDON, Denise (Va) 1700 Wainwright Dr, Reston VA 20190 **Assoc R Fam Mnstrs S Anne's Epis Ch Reston VA 2008-** B England 8/30/1959 d Floyd Harnson Trogdon & Berenice McManus. BA The W&M 1980; MSW Virginia Commonwealth U 1988; MDiv VTS 2008. D 5/24/2008 P 12/14/2008 Bp Peter James Lee. c 2. Revneesie@stabbes-Reston.org

TRONCALE, John Emanuel (NJ) 301 Meadows Dr, Forest VA 24551 B Elizabeth NJ 9/29/1946 s Pellegrino Troncale & Ninfa. BA Kean U 1980; MDiv GTS 1983. D 6/4/1983 P 12/1/1983 Bp George Phelps Mellick Belshaw. m 3/2/1974 Patricia D Silvey c 4. Vic Chr Ch Millville NJ 1991-1994; S Lk's Ch Woodstown NJ 1987-1990; S Paul's Ch Camden NJ 1984-1987; Ch Of Our Sav Camden NJ 1983-1987; S Wilfrid's Ch Camden NJ 1983. "His Mysterious Ways," *Guideposts*.

TROST, James Biggs (CPa) 3079 Sheffield Dr, State College PA 16801 **Died 3/6/2010** B Lancaster PA 2/17/1928 s Clarence Adam Trost & Frances. BA Franklin & Marshall Coll 1950; BD EDS 1953. D 6/30/1953 P 1/16/1954 Bp John T Heistand. c 7. Auth, "Bk Revs".

TROTTER, John Scott (Ark) 1121 W Pecan, Blytheville AR 72315 **S Steph's Ch Blytheville AR 2010-** B Atlanta GA 2/3/1953 s John Trotter & Carolyn. BA Emory U 1972; BA Emory U 1975; MDiv STUSo 1994. D 6/4/1994 P 12/10/1994 Bp Frank Kellogg Allan. m 7/18/1980 Angela M Michelli c 2. S Ptr's Epis Ch Bon Secour AL 2008-2010; R Ch Of The H Cross W Memphis AR 2001-2007; Vic Epis Ch Of The H Fam Jasper GA 1994-1996. amjshome80@gmail.com

TROTTIER, Francois Edward (Mass) St Barnabas Anglican Church, 838 Massachusetts Ave, Deep River ON K0J 1P01P0 Canada B Ottawa Ontario CA 4/26/1955 s Gerald Mathew Trottier & Irma. Trans from Anglican Church of Canada 1/26/2004 Bp M(arvil) Thomas Shaw III. m 12/28/2001 Nancy Anderson Mortensen c 4. S Ptr's Epis Ch Cambridge MA 2006-2010. ftrottier347@gmail.com

TROWBRIDGE, Dustin E (Del) 1108 N. Adams St., Wilmington DE 19801 **Assoc R Trin Par Wilmington DE 2009-** B Glen Dale WV 5/14/1976 s Ronald Gene Trowbridge & Patricia Ann. BA Ya 1998; MPA and MA Indiana U 2005; MDiv The GTS 2009. D 6/20/2009 Bp Catherine Elizabeth Maples Waynick P 1/9/2010 Bp Wayne Parker Wright. dustintrowbridge@hotmail.com

TRUAX, Heidi M (Ct) 31 Hilltop Rd, Sharon CT 06069 **Trin Ch Lakeville CT 2009-** B Santa Ana CA 12/3/1955 MDiv Ya Berk 2004. D 6/11/2005 P 1/28/2006 Bp Andrew Donnan Smith. m 6/23/1974 Philip S Truax c 4. Cur Trin Epis Ch Southport CT 2005-2008. heidi@heiditruax.com

TRUBINA, John Francis (Cal) 3350 Hopyard Road, Pleasanton CA 94588 **D S Clare's Epis Ch Pleasanton CA 2011-** B Wilmington DE 4/6/1952 s Francis John Trubina & Mary Agnes. Cert Sch for Deacons, Berkeley CA 2011. D 6/4/2011 Bp Marc Handley Andrus. c 1. An Epis Mnstry to Convalescent Hm - Bd Mem/Treas 2009-2011. deaconjt0604@comcast.net

TRUBY, Laura C(hristine) (Ore) 14221 Livesay Rd, Oregon City OR 97045 B Evanston IL 11/19/1947 d Keith Eugene Hamilton & Marilynn Laverne. BA Cornell Coll 1969; MDiv S Paul TS, Kansas City MO 1972. D 6/10/2000 P 12/9/2000 Bp Edward Lewis Lee Jr. m 5/16/1971 Thomas L Truby c 2. S Jas Ch Lincoln City OR 2010-2011; Chr Epis Ch Owosso MI 2004-2006; Trin Epis Ch Flushing MI 2004; Ch Of The Redeem Elgin IL 2003; S Thos Epis Ch Battle Creek MI 2000-2001. lauratruby@comcast.net

TRUE, Jerry Erwin (WNY) 2612 Brightside Ct, Cape Coral FL 33991 B Fulton NY 10/21/1939 s Lisle Edwin True & Marjorie Mae. BLS Amer Intl Coll 1976; MDiv GTS 1979. D 6/1/1979 P 12/8/1979 Bp Alexander Doig Stewart. m 11/3/2011 David C Melrose. P-in-c Gr Ch Chicopee MA 2007-2011; Pres Stndg Com Dio Wstrn New York Tonawanda NY 2000-2002; Dioc Coun Dio Wstrn New York Tonawanda NY 1987-1994; R S Lk's Epis Ch Attica NY 1983-2005; Asst S Mich's-On-The-Heights Worcester MA 1979-1983; Yth Cmsn Dio Wstrn Massachusetts Springfield MA 1979-1982. Affirming Angl Catholism Of No Amer 1995. jerry5185@aol.com

TRUELOVE, Kenneth Elwood (WA) 508 S Mckinley Ave, Champaign IL 61821 **Trin Epis Ch Mattoon IL 2004-; Supply S Laurence Epis Ch Effingham IL 2000-; Int S Mary's Ch Robinson IL 2000-** B Terre Haute IN 11/29/1939 s Herman F Truelove & Flora A. BA DePauw U 1961; BD SMU 1964; PDS 1970. D 6/6/1970 P 3/31/1971 Bp Robert Lionne DeWitt. m 5/29/1963 Theresa W Truelove. S Andr's Ch Paris IL 2005-2006; S Andr's Ch Livingston MT 2002-2003; Chr Ch Cape Girardeau MO 1998-1999; Dio Springfield Springfield IL 1995-1998; Trin Epis Ch Mattoon IL 1995-1998; Trin Ch St Chas MO 1994-1995. kentruelove@hotmail.com

TRUIETT SR, Melvin Edward (Md) 2322 Ivy Ave, Baltimore MD 21214 B Baltimore MD 10/22/1936 s Melvin Edward Truiett & Edna. U Of Baltimore. D 6/26/1983 Bp David Keller Leighton Sr P 6/1/1994 Bp Robert Manning Moody. m 7/20/1963 Alice G Ford c 3. Int Ch Of The H Cov Baltimore MD 2002-2007; R Epis Ch Of The Redeem Oklahoma City OK 1994-2001; Asst S Paul's Cathd Oklahoma City OK 1991-1993; P-in-c H Fam Ch Langston OK 1989-1994; Asst Epis Ch Of The Redeem Oklahoma City OK 1988-1990; Asst S Steph's Epis Ch Winston Salem NC 1986-1988; D Gr And S Ptr's Ch Baltimore MD 1983-1984. m.truiettsr@comcast.net

TRULL, C scott (NJ) 327 s juniper st, Philadelphia PA 19107 B New Brunswick NJ 7/4/1941 s George Irvine Trull & Sarah Elizabeth. BA U NC 1965; MDiv UTS 1977. D 6/11/1977 Bp Paul Moore Jr P 12/1/1977 Bp Harold Louis Wright. c 3. Chr Ch Riverton NJ 2003-2005; Ch Of S Mary's By The Sea Point Pleasant Bch NJ 1979-2003; Cur Ch Of The Atone Tenafly NJ 1977-1979. Soc of S Jn the Evang 1977. cstrull@verizon.net

TRUMBLE JR, John Louis (O) 51 Walnut St, Tiffin OH 44883 B Martin SD 9/30/1950 s John Louis Trumble & Florence Yeaton. BA W Virginia Wesleyan Coll 1980; MDiv VTS 1983. D 6/1/1983 P 4/1/1984 Bp Robert Poland Atkinson. m 5/26/1979 Rebecca Short c 2. Old Trin Epis Ch Tiffin OH 2000-2007; Trin Epis Shared Mnstry Tiffin OH 1995-2007; Gr Epis Ch Elkins WV 1986-1990; S Martins-In-Fields Summersville WV 1983-1986. sunny.s.koilparampil@ampf.com

TRUMBORE, Frederick Rhue (Va) 322 Eagle St, Woodstock VA 22664 **Emm Ch Woodstock VA 2001-; S Andr's Ch Mt Jackson VA 2001-** B Wilkes-Barre PA 12/17/1934 s Frederick William Trumbore & Leah Grace. BA Leh 1956; MDiv PDS 1960; Cert Ldrshp Acad for New Directions 1987. D 6/16/1960 P 12/1/1960 Bp Frederick J Warnecke. m 11/5/1960 Jean Killam c 2. Dio Virginia Richmond VA 1996-1999; Chr Epis Ch Luray VA 1984-1999; Ch Of Our Sav Okeechobee FL 1969-1984; Vic Ch Of The H Chld

T

Ormond Bch FL 1964-1969; Vic Ch Of The Intsn Ft Lauderdale FL 1962-1964; S Jas-S Geo Epis Ch Jermyn PA 1960-1962; S Lk's Ch Scranton PA 1960-1962. LAND, RWF; Phi Alpha Theta (Natl Hist Soc) 1956. FRITZJ@NTELOS.NET

TRUMBORE, William Wilson (Del) 302 Spring Dr, Easton MD 21601 B Fitchburg MA 2/12/1932 s Clarke Richard Trumbore & Marion Minerva. BA Leh 1954; MDiv GTS 1957. D 6/15/1957 P 12/21/1957 Bp Frederick J Warnecke. m 12/10/1960 Catherine A Cooney c 4. P-in-c All Faith Chap Miles River Par Easton MD 1996-2004; R St Annes Epis Ch Middletown DE 1985-1995; Ch Of The Gd Shpd Ruxton MD 1970-1985; Dn Nw Convoc Dio W Virginia Charleston WV 1966-1969; R S Paul's Ch Wheeling WV 1964-1970; R S Geo's Ch Nanticoke PA 1960-1964; Vic S Jas Ch Schuylkill Haven PA 1957-1960; Cur Trin Epis Ch Pottsville PA 1957-1960. Phi Beta Kappa 1984. BILLT@GOEASTERN.NET

TRUSCOTT, Nancy (Alb) 10 Orchard Street, Delhi NY 13753 **D S Jn's Ch Delhi NY 2003-** B Rockville Centre NY 3/11/1945 d Raymond Francis Baldwin & Jean Gladys. SUNY; BS SUNY 1968. D 1/18/2003 Bp David John Bena. m 7/20/1968 David Winston Truscott c 3. Ord of the DOK 2004. ntruscott@dmcom.net

TRUTNER, Thomas Kirk (Cal) 245 La Espiral, Orinda CA 94563 B Oakland CA 5/25/1935 s Herman Cameron Trutner & Everlyn Valesta. BA U CA 1958; MDiv PrTS 1961. D 6/19/1982 P 12/1/1982 Bp William Edwin Swing. m 4/5/2002 Roxanna Smith Trutner c 3. S Steph's Epis Ch Orinda CA 1991-2004.

TRYGAR SR, Earl Paul (Be) RR 2, Box 2229, Moscow PA 18444 **S Mk's Epis Ch Moscow PA 2003-** B Scranton PA 3/18/1951 s Walter Paul Trygar & Beverly Christine. Kutztown U; Penn. D 4/6/2002 P 10/6/2002 Bp Paul Victor Marshall. m 12/19/1970 Mary Helen Shorten c 2. Asst S Lk's Ch Scranton PA 2002-2003. tryac@verizon.net

TRYTTEN, Patricia Shoemaker (Oly) 310 N K St, Tacoma WA 98403 B Philadelphia PA 11/25/1943 d William Mercer Shoemaker & Elizabeth Jane. BA Parsons Coll Fairfield IA 1964; MDiv CDSP 1995. D 6/24/1995 P 1/1/1996 Bp Richard Lester Shimpfky. P-in-c Chr Ch Tacoma WA 1997-2008; Int S Andr's Ch Ben Lomond CA 1995-1997. patshoe@aol.com

TUAZA CASTRO, Luis Alberto (EcuC) Calle Hernando Sarmiento, N 39-54 Y Portete Ecuador B Ecuador 11/19/1974 s Segundo Andres Tuaza & Segunda Josefina. Presbitero San Leon Magno 2000; Licenciado en teologia Universidad del Azuay 2000. Rec from Roman Catholic 2/18/2011 Bp Luis Fernando Ruiz Restrepo. m 7/29/2009 Fanny Yolanda Munoz c 2.

TUBBS, James Collin (Tenn) 5256 Village Trce, Nashville TN 37211 B Chattanooga TN 6/16/1940 s Eugene William Tubbs & Delphi. BS U of Tennessee 1976; MDiv STUSo 1981. D 6/21/1981 Bp William F Gates Jr P 4/21/1982 Bp William Evan Sanders. m 4/22/1960 Carole Elizabeth Steiner c 2. R S Mths Ch Nashville TN 1998-2004; Dio E Tennessee Knoxville TN 1986-1998; Vic S Jos The Carpenter Sevierville TN 1986-1998; S Jn's Epis Cathd Knoxville TN 1981-1985. jimtubbs@aol.com

TUBBS, Suzanne Freeman (Tex) 604 Tryon Ct, Tyler TX 75703 B Dallas TX 12/26/1944 d Linton Hughes Freeman & Martha Sue. BA SMU 1966; Med U of No Texas 1982; MDiv STUSo 1999. D 10/6/1991 Bp Joseph Thomas Heistand P 6/18/1999 Bp Henry Irving Louttit. m 8/6/1977 Michael Tubbs c 4. S Fran Epis Ch Tyler TX 2005-2010; S Paul's Ch Macon GA 2003-2004; Assoc R S Pat's Epis Ch Atlanta GA 2002-2003; Vic S Jn's Epis Ch Bainbridge GA 1999-2002; Dir Of Sprtl Dio Arizona Phoenix AZ 1994-1996; D Gr S Paul's Epis Ch Tucson AZ 1991-1996. priest2@att.net

TUCK, Michael G (RI) 114 George St, Providence RI 02906 **Brown/RISD Chapl Dio Rhode Island Providence RI 2009-; Acct S Steph's Ch Providence RI 2009-** B Bryn Mawr PA 1/14/1977 s R(alph) Michael Tuck & Mary P. AB Br 1999; MA Coll of the Resurr 2009. D 7/4/2009 Bp Stephen Platten. m 8/20/2005 Annemarie Haftl c 2. curate@sstephens.necoxmail.com

TUCKER, Alice Elizabeth (Tex) 2900 Bunny Run, Austin TX 78746 B Bomi Hills LR 5/13/1958 d James Lydell Tucker & Marjory K. BA Swarthmore Coll 1980; MDiv VTS 1987. D 6/11/1987 Bp Gordon Taliaferro Charlton P 6/1/1988 Bp Anselmo Carral-Solar. c 1. S Steph's Epis Sch Austin TX 1993-2008; Assoc R S Thos The Apos Epis Ch Houston TX 1988-1993; DRE S Steph's Epis Ch Houston TX 1982-1984. atuckeratx@yahoo.com

TUCKER JR, Beverley (SVa) 901 Poquoson Cir, Virginia Beach VA 23452 **Old Donation Ch Virginia Bch VA 1998-** B Charlottesville VA 11/26/1918 s Beverly Dandridge Tucker & Eleanor Lile. BA U of Virginia 1942; MDiv VTS 1948. D 6/4/1948 Bp Frederick D Goodwin P 6/8/1949 Bp Henry St George Tucker. m 4/7/1956 Julia Moore c 3. Pstr Assoc Chr and S Lk's Epis Ch Norfolk VA 1984-1990; Excoun Dio Sthrn Virginia Norfolk VA 1962-1965; Excoun Dio Sthrn Virginia Norfolk VA 1956-1959; Chair Dept Mssns Dio Sthrn Virginia Norfolk VA 1956-1958; R Old Donation Ch Virginia Bch VA 1953-1984; D-In-C S Anne's Par Scottsville VA 1948-1949.

TUCKER, Douglas Jon (Tex) 2 Barque Ln., Galveston TX 77554 **Int Gr Ch Galveston TX 2011-** B Cedar Rapids IA 9/6/1942 s Robert John Tucker & Dorothy Ann. BS U of Nebraska 1965; MS GW 1976; MDiv STUSo 1980. D 6/7/1980 Bp Walter Cameron Righter P 6/25/1981 Bp Maurice Manuel Benitez. m 4/13/1968 Cheryl Allee c 3. Int S Geo's Epis Ch Texas City TX 2011; Int H Trin Epis Ch Dickinson TX 2008-2010; R S Cyp's Ch Lufkin TX 2004-2008; Assoc S Jn The Div Houston TX 2001-2004; Dio Texas Houston TX 1999-2008; R S Alb's Epis Ch Waco TX 1993-2001; Epis Fndt Dio Texas Houston TX 1990-1994; R Chr Ch Nacogdoches TX 1983-1992; Asst S Chris's Ch League City TX 1981-1983; Asst Chapl The TS at The U So Sewanee TN 1980-1981. dctucker2@comcast.net

TUCKER, Elizabeth Spier (CFla) 1020 Keyes Ave, Winter Park FL 32789 **D All SS Ch Of Winter Pk Winter Pk FL 2006-** B Teaneck NJ 10/30/1956 d Peter W Spier & Jean M. D 12/9/2006 Bp John Wadsworth Howe. m 11/22/1980 John W Tucker c 2. liztuck99@aol.com

TUCKER, Gene Richard (Spr) 1100 Harrison, Mt. Vernon IL 62864 **P-in-c S Jn's Ch Centralia IL 2008-; R Trin Ch Mt Vernon IL 2007-; Secy Dio Springfield Springfield IL 2005-** B David City NE 3/26/1947 s Jesse Morgan Tucker & Clara Christine. BA Eastman Sch of Mus 1969; MDiv VTS 2004. D 6/29/2004 P 3/12/2005 Bp Peter Hess Beckwith. m 10/17/1981 Deborah K Kinney c 2. friartuck3@yahoo.com

TUCKER, James M (NJ) 130 Prince St., Bordentown NJ 08505 **D-in-c Chr Ch Bordentown NJ 2008-** B Long Branch NJ 9/4/1974 s James Henry Tucker & Caroline Katherine. BA Elon U 1997; MDiv The Prot Epis TS 2008. D 6/7/2008 Bp George Edward Councell P 12/7/2008 Bp Sylvestre Donato Romero. m 7/2/2010 Doan H Tucker. jmtucker37@hotmail.com

TUCKER, James Thomas (Tex) 3708 Underwood St, Houston TX 77025 **R Ch Of The Epiph Houston TX 1996-** B Alexandria VA 3/4/1952 BA U of Texas 1974; M. Div. VTS 1981. D 6/18/1981 P 2/1/1982 Bp Maurice Manuel Benitez. m 6/10/1978 Virginia Moyer. St Lk's Epis Hosp Houston TX 1996; Palmer Memi Ch Houston TX 1986-1995; S Ptr's Ch Pasadena TX 1982-1986. jttucker@epiphany-hou.org

TUCKER, Jared Horton (Los) 3227 N Rancho La Carlota Rd, Covina CA 91724 **D H Trin Epis Ch Covina CA 1999-** B San Francisco CA 8/18/1930 s Hyman Tucker & Gertrude. BA Whittier Coll 1953; MD U CA 1958. D 11/1/1995 Bp Chester Lovelle Talton. m 1/28/1956 Marilyn Elaine Bim c 2. Assoc S Barn' Par Pasadena CA 2011; D S Jn's Mssn La Verne CA 1997-2000.

TUCKER, John Westervelt (SeFla) 1516 S Lakeside Dr Apt 114S, Lake Worth FL 33460 **Died 3/27/2010** B Sola Camaguey CU 11/7/1925 s Frank Lovering Tucker & Martha Brown. Brevard Cmnty Coll 1950; BA Catawba Coll 1952; Bex 1957. D 6/1/1957 P 5/1/1958 Bp Matthew G Henry. c 3.

TUCKER, Julia Moore (SVa) 901 Poquoson Cir, Virginia Beach VA 23452 B Norfolk VA 9/7/1931 d William Hugh Moore & Nell. BA Salem Coll Winston Salem NC 1953; MA Oklahoma St U 1980. D 1/18/1997 Bp Frank Harris Vest Jr. m 4/7/1956 Beverley Tucker Jr. D S Fran Ch Virginia Bch VA 1997-2002.

TUCKER, Kenneth Merrill (USC) 1502 Greenville Street, Abbeville SC 29620 **Actg Vic Trin Ch Abbeville SC 2010-** B Arlington MA 1/23/1931 s William Merrill Tucker & Doris Lovrin. BS Franklin & Marshall Coll 1953; MDiv Ya Berk 1969. D 6/10/1969 Bp Charles F Hall P 12/19/1969 Bp William Henry Marmion. m 2/5/1977 Mary E Martin c 3. Int S Jn's Epis Ch Wilmington NC 2007-2008; Vic Trin Ch Abbeville SC 1994-1997; Vic S Mich And All Ang' Epis Ch Standard CA 1990-1994; Vic Episcpoal Ch Of Groveland Groveland CA 1990-1992; P-in-c S Andr's Epis Ch Greenville SC 1988-1989; R Ch Of The Mssh Murphy NC 1986-1988; Vic Gr Ch Mohawk NY 1980-1984; R S Jas Epis Ch Westernport MD 1978-1979; Asst S Tim's Ch Catonsville MD 1975-1977; R S Geo's Ch Maynard MA 1972-1975; Cur S Mths Epis Ch E Aurora NY 1971-1972; Vic S Mk's Ch St Paul VA 1969-1971. kmtucker@wctel.net

TUCKER, Ralph Lewis (Mass) Po Box 306, Georgetown ME 04548 **Died 3/28/2010** B Winthrop MA 5/29/1921 s Sidvin Tucker & Ruby. BA Tufts U 1944; MS EDS 1947; CPE 1970. D 3/30/1947 P 10/1/1947 Bp Norman B Nash. c 4.

TUCKER PARSONS, Martha L (ETenn) 6 Rock Crest Dr, Signal Mountain TN 37377 **S Fran Of Assisi Epis Ch Ooltewah TN 2009-; R Dio E Tennessee Knoxville TN 2006-** B Knoxville TN 6/10/1955 BA U So. D 5/25/2002 P 1/23/2003 Bp Charles Glenn VonRosenberg. m 12/29/1979 Mark K Parsons c 2. Gr Ch Chattanooga TN 2006-2009; Cur St Jas Epis Ch at Knoxville Knoxville TN 2002-2004. louisatp@aol.com

TUDELA, Mary Elizabeth (Chi) 647 Dundee Ave, Barrington IL 60010 B Ponce Puerto Rico 4/13/1954 MDiv SWTS 2004; Cert Interfaith Stds FaithBridge 2010. D 6/19/2004 Bp William Dailey Persell P 1/19/2005 Bp Victor Alfonso Scantlebury. c 2. Int S Ann's Ch Woodstock IL 2011; Int S Mk's Barrington Hills IL 2008; Assoc S Mich's Ch Barrington IL 2004-2007. Auth, "Walking My Faith," Trafford, 2011. Wmn of Achievement Honoree Anti-Defamation League 1999. maryt@sccnw.org

TUDOR, Richard Beresford (Mo) 3106 Aberdeen Dr, Florissant MO 63033 B Little Rock AR 8/29/1942 s Robert Bruce Tudor & Emily June. BA U of Kansas 1966; MDiv CDSP 1971; DMin Eden 1996. D 6/24/1971 Bp George Theodore Masuda P 5/3/1972 Bp John Harris Burt. m 6/22/1974 Elizabeth A Thornton c 4. Plnng Com Dio Missouri S Louis MO 1997-2000; Dept Congrl Dev. Dio Missouri S Louis MO 1990-1995; R S Barn Ch Florissant MO 1989-2008; Chair COM Dio Missouri S Louis MO 1980-1985; S Mich's and

T

All Ang' Ch Fairview MT 1976-1989; Vic S Ptr's Epis Ch Williston ND 1974-1989; Cur S Paul's Ch Akron OH 1971-1973. Auth, "The Challenge of Change," *Living Ch*, 2009; Auth, "The Empty Stocking," *Angl Dig*, 2008; Auth, "Feeling the Sqeeze," *Living Ch*, 2007; Auth, "A Long Series of Revolutions," *Angl Dig*, 2005; Auth, "How Firm a Fndt," *Living Ch*, 2005; Auth, "Mar in the Wrong Aisle," *Living Ch*, 2003; Auth, "The Flow Goes On," *Living Ch*, 1990. Unit Mnstry Team of the Year US-A 1989. richtudor@sbcglobal.net

TUDOR, William Ellis (Ind) 3021 94th Ave E, Edgewood WA 98371 B Iowa City IA 10/24/1931 s Hugh Jones Tudor & Eugenie Marie. BA U of Puget Sound 1955; MA U of Iowa 1956; BD CDSP 1959. D 6/29/1959 Bp Stephen F Bayne Jr P 6/11/1960 Bp William F Lewis. m 6/9/1956 Jean Cameron c 2. Cn Pstr Chr Ch Cathd Indianapolis IN 1983-1996; Assoc R Chr Ch Grosse Pointe Grosse Pointe Farms MI 1978-1983; R Gr Ch Newport News VA 1969-1978; Cur S Mk's Cathd Seattle WA 1959-1962. jwtudor@aol.com

TUDOR-FOLEY, Hugh W (Ct) 3168 Dona Sofia Dr, Studio City CA 91604 **Other Cler Position Dio Los Angeles Los Angeles CA 2011-; Mem, Cler Educ Com Dio San Diego San Diego CA 2007-; Mem, Com on Chem Dependency Educ and Spprt Dio New Jersey Trenton NJ 2005-; Chair, Com on Chem Dependency Educ and Spprt Dio Vermont Burlington VT 2002-; Mem, Caribbean Relatns Com Dio Connecticut Hartford CT 2001-; Mem, Fin Com Dio Connecticut Hartford CT 1997-** B Wharton TX 8/25/1940 s Edred Hugo Foley & Aileen. BA U of Houston 1972; MA Fairfield U 1988; MDiv Ya Berk 1991. D 2/23/1992 P 10/31/1992 Bp Clarence Nicholas Coleridge. m 3/5/1978 Rebecca Tudor. Int R The Epis Ch Of The Gd Shpd Hemet CA 2008-2010; Int R S Paul's Ch Yuma AZ 2007-2008; Int R S Jn's Ch Stamford CT 2006-2007; Int R All SS Memi Ch Navesink NJ 2004-2005; Int R Trin Ch Rutland VT 2002-2004; Asst R Chr Ch Greenwich CT 1995-2002; Assoc R S Barth's Ch New York NY 1993-1995; Cur Gr Epis Ch Norwalk CT 1992-1993; DRE S Lk's Par Darien CT 1990-1991. Auth, "Video," *A Gift of Hope*, Miami Proj to Cure Paralysis; Auth, "Video," *Formation in Cmnty*, Berkeley at Yale; Auth, "Video Inst of Bp Andr Smith," *Video Consecration of Bp Jas Curry & Wilfredo Ramos-Orenz*, Dio Connecticut. Assn of Profsnl Chapl 2006; Inerim Mnstry Ntwk 2002; Int Mnstry Ntwk 2001; NAEMS 2006; OHC 1998; Pres Greenwich Fllshp Cler 1999-2002; RACA 2001. Peer Evaltn AIBS SPARS 2011; Peer Evaltn SAMHSA 2011. htudorfoley@mac.com

TUFF, Roy Wynn (SwFla) 401 W. Henry St, Punta Gorda FL 33950 **Ch Of The Gd Shpd Punta Gorda FL 2010-** B Hays KS 5/18/1962 s Robert Wayne Tuff & Judy Lea. BA Florida Gulf Coast U 2000; MDiv STUSo 2003. D 6/14/2003 P 12/20/2003 Bp John Bailey Lipscomb. m 7/13/1985 Maria Renee Mikolai c 3. S Steph's Epis Sch Bradenton FL 2003-2010. Preaching Excellence Prog The Epis Evang Fndt 2002. royria@aol.com

TULIS, Edward (CNY) No address on file. B 3/6/1931 D 6/22/1957 Bp Anson Phelps Stokes Jr P 1/18/1958 Bp Frederic Cunningham Lawrence.

TULK, John Fowlow (Minn) 4643 W 139th St, Savage MN 55378 **Supply P Dio Minnesota Minneapolis MN 2000-** B New York NY 12/8/1934 s Reginald Gilbert Tulk & Arabella Sophie. BA Trin Hartford CT 1956; MDiv GTS 1959. D 4/4/1959 Bp James P De Wolfe P 11/8/1959 Bp Norman L Foote. m 1/6/1968 Sylvia Stone c 3. Vic S Helen's Ch Wadena MN 1984-1987; Coun Dio Kansas Topeka KS 1982-1984; R S Andr's Ch Ft Scott KS 1981-1984; R Trin Epis Ch Pocatello ID 1970-1980; Mem, Dioc Coun Dio Idaho Boise ID 1970-1973; Chairperson, Liturg Cmsn Dio Idaho Boise ID 1969-1973; Dn, Cntrl Rural Dnry Dio Idaho Boise ID 1966-1968; Vic Calv Epis Ch Jerome ID 1959-1969; Vic Chr Ch Shoshone ID 1959-1969; Vic Trin Ch Buhl ID 1959-1969; Vic Trin Ch Gooding ID 1959-1969. Associated Parishes 1960-1975; EPF 1965-1980; RWF 1959-1980. jftulk@msn.com

TULL, Alan Condie (U) 753 N 480 W, Orem UT 84057 **Died 11/4/2009** B Salt Lake City UT 7/7/1933 s Alan White Tull & Verna Condie. BA Stan 1955; STB GTS 1958; ThD GTS 1968; Fell Jewish TS 1979. D 6/10/1958 P 12/13/1958 Bp Richard S Watson. ESMHE 1964-1990; NACUC 1964-1990. a.c.tull@usa.net

TULL, Sandra Ann (Fla) 1021 Oxford Dr, Saint Augustine FL 32084 **Asst Ch Of The Nativ Jacksonville FL 2008-; P-in-c Ch Of The Epiph Jacksonville FL 2007-** B Plattsburg NY 7/26/1943 d Henry Cole Tallmadge & Dorothy Louise. RN U of Miami 1965; BS St. Jos's Coll No Windham ME 1985; MA Norwich U 1987. D 11/9/2004 P 5/10/2005 Bp Samuel Johnson Howard. m 1/28/1967 John Tull c 2. czarinat26@msn.com

TULLER, Stuart Sidney (Va) 2132 Owls Cove Ln, Reston VA 20191 B Great Barrington MA 10/22/1935 s Stuart Sidney Tuller & Mary Ethel. BA Amh 1957; MDiv VTS 1960. D 6/4/1960 P 6/1/1961 Bp Robert McConnell Hatch. m 6/20/1959 Ann Worthington Howard c 2. R S Chris's Ch Springfield VA 1965-1971; Vic All SS Ch Hanover PA 1963-1965; Cur S Matt's Ch Bedford NY 1960-1963.

TULLY, Coleen (Minn) 101 N 5th St, Marshall MN 56258 B Menomonie WI 8/5/1957 d James Haley Tully & Sally Rae Schill. Rehabilitative Counslg U of WI 1989. D 6/12/2005 Bp Daniel Lee Swenson P 12/11/2005 Bp James Louis Jelinek. m 4/12/1990 Steven Thomsen c 4. coleenandsober@yahoo.com

TULLY, William M (NY) St. Bartholomew's Church, 109 E 50th Street, New York NY 10022 **R S Barth's Ch New York NY 1994-** B Glendale CA 1/21/1947 s Andrew McDonald Tully & Leah Sara. BA Occ 1968; MS Col 1969; MDiv GTS 1974. D 3/24/1974 Bp Harold Louis Wright P 9/29/1974 Bp Paul Moore Jr. m 6/16/1968 Jane W Williams c 2. R S Columba's Ch Washington DC 1980-1994; Assoc S Fran Ch Potomac MD 1976-1980; Cur The Ch Of The Epiph New York NY 1974-1976. wmcdtully@mac.com

TUMA, George Wood (Mich) 482 Gilbert Ave, Menlo Park CA 94025 B 2/25/1938 D 6/29/1962 P 2/8/1963 Bp Archie H Crowley.

TUMILTY, Richard Chapman (NCal) 21349 Leslie Dr, Grass Valley CA 95945 **Assoc (Chrmstr/Org) Emm Epis Ch Grass Vlly CA 1993-** B Oklahoma City OK 10/31/1928 s Howard Tinsley Tumilty & Louise Elizabeth. BA Rhodes Coll 1950; MA Bos 1951; STB GTS 1958. D 6/21/1958 P 1/17/1959 Bp Clarence Rupert Haden Jr. m 6/11/1966 Joan Fay c 3. Dioc Coun Dio Nthrn California Sacramento CA 1989-1991; Stndg Com Dio Nthrn California Sacramento CA 1978-1982; Dioc Coun Dio Nthrn California Sacramento CA 1974-1976; Dn, Sonoma Convoc Dio Nthrn California Sacramento CA 1973-1974; Gr Ch S Helena CA 1969-1992; Chr Ch Tacoma WA 1963-1968; S Andr's Of The Redwoods Redway CA 1960-1962; Cur Chr Ch Eureka CA 1958-1960; Cur Ch Of The Ascen Vallejo CA 1958-1960. rctumilty@yahoo.com

TUMMINIO, Danielle Elizabeth (Ct) 12 Quincy Ave, Quincy MA 02169 **Chr Ch Quincy MA 2011-** B Manhattan NY 1/2/1981 d Gregory Tumminio & Marguerite. BA Ya 2003; MDiv Yale Berkeley 2006; STM Yale Berkeley 2008; PhD Bos 2012. D 6/12/2010 Bp Ian Theodore Douglas P 1/15/2011 Bp Laura Ahrens. m 9/4/2010 Eric Hansen. danielle.tumminio@aya.yale.edu

TUNKLE, Paul Dennis (Md) 134 W Lanvale St, Baltimore MD 21217 **R The Ch Of The Redeem Baltimore MD 2001-** B New York NY 2/6/1950 s Samuel Tunkle & Sophie. BS U of Maine 1981; MDiv GTS 1984; DMin Drew U 1993. D 6/2/1984 Bp Frederick Barton Wolf P 6/1/1985 Bp Robert Whitridge Estill. m 2/28/1972 Judith Elaine Cox. Stndg Com Dio Wstrn Louisiana Alexandria LA 1998-2000; Pres - Com Dio Wstrn Louisiana Alexandria LA 1995-1997; R S Jas Epis Ch Alexandria LA 1993-2001; R H Trin Ch So River NJ 1988-1993; Asst S Lk's Ch Salisbury NC 1984-1987. OHC. paul@tunkle.com

TUNNEY, Elisabeth Ellerich (WMass) 31 Rider Avenue, Patrchogue NY 11772 B New York NY 9/23/1956 d Joseph John Tunney & Lillian E. BA Smith 1978; MBA Wstrn New Engl Coll 1990; MDiv The GTS 2011. D 3/19/2011 Bp Gordon Paul Scruton. liz.tunney@gmail.com

TUOHY, James Fidelis (Ala) 3842 11th Ave S, Birmingham AL 35222 B Thurles IE 4/17/1937 s Denis J Tuohy & Bridget. MDiv All Hallows Coll 1961; BA U of Alabama 1971; DMin Van 1978. Rec from Roman Catholic 12/1/1980 as Priest Bp Furman Stough. m 10/16/1970 Elizabeth Mary Hannon c 2. R S Andr's Ch Montevallo AL 1999; S Mich And All Ang Anniston AL 1992-1999; Assoc S Andrews's Epis Ch Birmingham AL 1980-1992. jf_tuohy@yahoo.com

TURBERG, Judith E (Az) 100 S Laura Ln, Casa Grande AZ 85194 **Vic S Ptr's Ch Casa Grande AZ 2011-** B Glen Cove NY 12/1/1945 d Joseph Richard Turberg & Evelyn Pelcher. BA NWU 1967; MS Adel 1975; USC 1977; MDiv ETSBH 1998. D 6/13/1998 Bp Robert Marshall Anderson P 1/9/1999 Bp Frederick Houk Borsch. The ETS At Claremont Claremont CA 2002-2011; Asst/Assoc S Ambr Par Claremont CA 2000-2002; S Thos' Mssn Hacienda Heights CA 1999; D S Mich And All Ang Par Corona Del Mar CA 1998-1999. judy.turberg@gmail.com

TURBEVILLE JR, Norman McKeithan (WTex) P.O. Box 292, Buda TX 78610 **Assoc Chr Ch Greenville SC 2011-; D-in-c S Eliz's Epis Ch Buda TX 2008-** B Charleston SC 7/31/1966 s Norman McKeithan Turbeville & Sandra Dupree. BS SUNY 1991; Theol Stds The Prot Epis TS 2005; MDiv Epis TS of the SW 2008. D 5/24/2008 Bp Peter James Lee P 12/4/2008 Bp Gary Richard Lillibridge. m 4/27/1991 Karen Cope c 3. S Jas' Epis Ch Leesburg VA 2002-2005. kturbeville2008@gmail.com

TURCZYN, Jeffrey Robert (NY) 4 Surf Rd, Cape Elizabeth ME 04107 B Bronx NY 8/28/1945 s Steve Turczyn & Maria. BA Villanova U 1968; STB CUA 1971; STL CUA 1972; MS Col 1988. Rec 6/24/1995 as Priest Bp Walter Decoster Dennis Jr. m 10/10/1987 Kathleen Scott. P-in-c Trin Ch Saugerties NY 1997-2008; Asstg P S Mich's Ch New York NY 1995-1997. jturczyn@gmail.com

TURK, Davette Lois (Fla) 8256 Wallingford Hills Ln, Jacksonville FL 32256 B Asbury Park NJ 8/27/1935 d David Louis Ryan & Regina Victoria. GTS; BA Villanova U 1960; MA La Salle U 1985. D 6/16/1985 P 12/15/1985 Bp Frank Stanley Cerveny. m 9/12/1975 Richard Martin Turk. Int R The Epis Ch of The Redeem Jacksonville FL 2007; Fresh Mnstrs Jacksonville FL 1998-2004; Assoc R All SS Epis Ch Jacksonville FL 1989-1997; Asst R The Epis Ch of The Redeem Jacksonville FL 1986-1989.

TURK, Richard Martin (Fla) 8256 Wallingford Hills Ln, Jacksonville FL 32256 B Perth Amboy NJ 8/5/1939 s Martin Stephen Turk & Mary Elizabeth. ThM PrTS 1963; BA S Mary Baltimore MD 1963; DMin Columbia TS 2002. Rec from Roman Catholic 12/1/1978 as Priest Bp Lyman Cunningham Ogilby. m 9/12/1975 Davette Lois Ryan. R S Andr's Ch Jacksonville FL 1986-2005; Cn Dio Florida Jacksonville FL 1980-1986; S Thos' Ch Whitemarsh Ft Washington PA 1978-1980. Dsa Florida Coun On Crime & Delinquency. rturk58645@aol.com

TURMO, Joel Lee (SeFla) PO Box 1503, Boca Raton FL 33429 **S Greg's Ch Boca Raton FL 2008-** B Stanton MI 4/4/1969 s David James Turmo & Hazel Louise. BS Cntrl Michigan U 1995; MS Wstrn Michigan U 1998; MDiv U So TS 2008. D 12/22/2007 Bp Russell Edward Jacobus. m 5/7/1995 Melissa Balgenorth Melissa Ann Balgenorth c 2. jturmo@gmail.com

TURNAGE, Benjamin Whitfield (Md) 1124 Lakeview Crescent, Birmingham AL 35205 B Charleston,SC 5/19/1945 s Benjamin Otto Turnage & Adelaide Plumb. BS Charleston Sthrn U 1971; MS Clemson U 1973; MDiv VTS 1976. D 6/18/1976 P 1/1/1977 Bp Gray Temple. m 9/13/1968 Melissa R Robertson c 2. R Trin Ch Glen Arm MD 1988-2004; Chr Ch Macon GA 1985-1988; R Ch Of The Epiph Atlanta GA 1980-1984; Asst S Phil's Ch Charleston SC 1977-1980; Asst S Lk's Epis Ch Hilton Hd SC 1976-1977. benjamint035@gmail.com

TURNAGE, Richard Wentworth (SC) 1920 Rimsdale Dr, Myrtle Beach SC 29575 B Hartsville SC 10/23/1929 s Louis Alexander Turnage & Vivian White. BS Davidson Coll 1950. D 9/14/1997 Bp Edward Lloyd Salmon Jr. m 3/22/1952 Joan Mclver Malone. The Epis Ch Of The Resurr Surfside Bch SC 1999. dickt97@aol.com

TURNBULL, Henry George (RI) 6465 River Birchfield Rd, Jamesville NY 13078 B Providence RI 6/7/1931 s Henry John Mansie Turnbull & Esther Victoria. BA Br 1953; BD Nash 1960. D 6/23/1956 P 3/1/1957 Bp John S Higgins. R S Jn The Evang Ch Newport RI 1960-1991; Cur Trin Ch Newport RI 1957-1960; Cur S Jn's Ch Barrington RI 1956-1957.

TURNBULL, Joseph William (Haw) 2825 S King St Apt 902, Honolulu HI 96826 **Died 5/25/2011** B Terry MT 8/14/1920 s Joseph William Turnbull & Anna Ottilie. BA S Olaf Coll 1942; SWTS 1945. D 1/6/1945 P 2/24/1946 Bp Henry Hean Daniels. c 4.

TURNBULL, Malcolm Edward (Va) 8700 Rockcrest Court, Bon Air VA 23235 B Asheville NC 2/11/1937 s Arthur Robert Turnbull & Betty. BA U of Virginia 1958; MDiv VTS 1970. D 5/28/1970 Bp Philip Alan Smith P 12/13/1970 Bp Edwin Lani Hanchett. m 7/1/1960 Nell J Jones c 2. Dn, Reg XII Dio Virginia Richmond VA 1980-1984; R S Barth's Ch Richmond VA 1977-2002; Chapl Virginia Epis Sch Lynchburg VA 1976-1977; Asst R Bruton Par Williamsburg VA 1973-1976; Vic Emm Epis Ch Kailua HI 1971-1973; Asst R Ch Of The H Nativ Honolulu HI 1970-1971. AAPC 1989. meturnbull@gmail.com

TURNER, Alice Camp (WNY) 90 South Dr, Lackawanna NY 14218 B Buffalo NY 9/27/1940 d Russell Claude Hughes & Grace Lillian. AAS Erie Cmnty Coll 1960. D 6/11/1983 Bp Harold B Robinson. m 10/1/1960 Richard Howard Turner c 4. D S Dav's Epis Ch W Seneca NY 1989-2006.

TURNER, Alicia Beth (WNC) 900 Centre Park Dr # B, Asheville NC 28805 **Mssnr for Adult Vocation Dio Wstrn No Carolina Asheville NC 2010-** B Raleigh NC 9/11/1962 d George F Turner & Alice Fay. BA Carson - Newman Coll 1984; MDiv SE Bapt TS 1989. D 5/29/2004 Bp Robert Carroll Johnson Jr P 5/15/2005 Bp Granville Porter Taylor. Assoc Ch Of The H Cross Valle Crucis NC 2005-2009; Dio Wstrn No Carolina Asheville NC 2004-2005. asucampusminister@gmail.com

TURNER, Amy Porterfield (WVa) 1100 Sam Perry Blvd, Fredericksburg VA 22401 B Winchester VA 4/16/1982 d Philip Terrill Porterfield & Barbara Pharr. AB Washington U 2004; MDiv VTS 2010; MEd U of Mary Washington 2012. D 1/9/2010 P 1/8/2011 Bp William Michie Klusmeyer. m 7/10/2010 Brian William Turner. Auth, "Nurturing a Fragile Faith: An Intersection of Rel Communities and the Mentally Handicapped," VTS, 2010; Auth, "Nurturing a Fragile Faith: An Intersection of Rel Communities and the Mentally Handicapped". amyporterfieldturner@gmail.com

TURNER, Anne Michele (Va) 14 Boltwood Walk, Amherst MA 01002 **S Mary's Epis Ch Arlington VA 2009-** B Springfield OH 12/14/1971 d Michael Van Turner & Linnea Summers. BA W&M 1993; MA Shakespeare Inst, U of Birgmingham 1996; M. Div. Ya Berk 2003. D 6/14/2003 Bp John Chane P 12/22/2003 Bp Allen Lyman Bartlett Jr. m 5/30/1998 Stephen Baldwin Watts c 2. Assoc Gr Ch Amherst MA 2008-2009; Asst R Gr Epis Ch Alexandria VA 2003-2007. annemturner@yahoo.com

TURNER, Arlie Raymond (RG) 213 TWP RD 1057, Proctorville OH 25669 B Huntington WV 12/24/1939 s Carl Raymond Turner & Pauline Louise. BA Marshall U 1967; MA Marshall U 1971; MDiv VTS 1985. D 6/5/1985 Bp Robert Poland Atkinson P 12/19/1985 Bp William Franklin Carr. m 8/2/1963 Cora Dean Pruitt c 2. P-in-c Ch Of The H Sprt Gallup NM 2005-2007; R H Sprt Epis Ch El Paso TX 1996-2005; Assoc S Matt's Ch Charleston WV 1992-1996; R S Tim's In The Vlly Hurricane WV 1985-1991. aturner123@msn.com

TURNER, Bonnie L (NMich) 510 E Park Dr, Peshtigo WI 54157 **Gr Epis Ch Menominee MI 1994-** B Escanaba MI 5/29/1947 BS U of Wisconsin 1973; MA Viterbo Coll 1994. D 3/17/1994 P 10/1/1994 Bp Thomas Kreider Ray. m 6/10/1967 John R Turner.

TURNER, Brian William (SO) 825 College Ave, Fredericksburg VA 22401 **Asst R Trin Ch Fredericksburg VA 2010-** B Worthington OH 11/21/1980 s James W Turner & Victoria W. BA The OH SU 2003; MDiv VTS 2010. D 6/12/2010 Bp Thomas Edward Breidenthal P 1/8/2011 Bp William Michie Klusmeyer. m 7/10/2010 Amy Porterfield. Auth, "Pro Christo Per Ecclesiam: A Hist of Coll Mnstry in the Epis Ch," 2010. janus532@gmail.com

TURNER, Carlton Barry (ECR) 891 Vista Del Brisa, San Luis Obispo CA 93405 **R S Steph's Epis Ch San Luis Obispo CA 1996-** B Sutherland NE 9/8/1947 s Roy Delbert Turner & Joyce Enid. BA U CA, San Diego 1970; MDiv Fuller TS 1979; Cert of One Year Study CDSP 1980. D 10/23/1980 P 4/27/1981 Bp John Lester Thompson III. m 8/16/1980 Ruth Whitney c 2. Stwdshp Chair Dio Nthrn California Sacramento CA 1986-1996; R S Paul's Epis Ch Oroville CA 1985-1996; P-in-c Emm Ch Coos Bay OR 1984-1985; Assoc Chr Ch Par Lake Oswego OR 1983-1984; Asst S Mary's Epis Ch Napa CA 1980-1982. carltonba@msn.com

TURNER JR, Claude Sylvester (SVa) 118 Little John Rd, Williamsburg VA 23185 B Martinsville VA 12/13/1932 s Claude Sylvester Turner & Amy Lucile. BS Georgia Inst of Tech 1956; MDiv STUSo 1969. D 6/24/1969 P 6/29/1970 Bp George P Gunn. m 2/6/2005 Mary LaRoche Douglas c 2. Vstng Com The TS at The U So Sewanee TN 2007-2010; Int S Jas Epis Ch Portsmouth VA 1991-1992; Int Emm Ch Franklin VA 1989-1991; Assoc Chr and S Lk's Epis Ch Norfolk VA 1988-1989; R Gr Ch Yorktown Yorktown VA 1976-1988; P S Paul's Ch Petersburg VA 1974-1976; R S Jn's Ch Petersburg VA 1971-1976; Asst S Mich's Ch Bon Air VA 1969-1971. csturner2@aol.com

TURNER, David Michael (Md) 218 Shaw St., Frostburg MD 21532 **Died 2/15/2010** B Cumberland MD 12/24/1946 s James Richard Turner & Laura Durst. BA Wstrn Maryland Coll 1968; MBA Frostburg St U 1982. D 9/7/2008 P 5/9/2009 Bp John Leslie Rabb. c 1. dave_turner@goodyear.com

TURNER, Diana Serene (NCal) 9031 Tuolumne Dr, Sacramento CA 95826 **Assoc S Andr's In The Highlands Mssn Antelope CA 2006-** B Sacramento CA 5/20/1960 d Robert Edward Peterson & Gail Doris. AS Umpqua Cmnty Coll 1982. D 11/9/1997 P 10/1/1998 Bp Stewart Clark Zabriskie. m 9/20/1991 Teddy Nathan Turner. Assoc S Geo's Ch Carmichael CA 2001-2006; P S Alb's Epis Ch Yerington NV 1997-2002. tedsgal99@yahoo.com

TURNER, Donald Lee (CNY) PO Box 865, Barnegat Light NJ 08006 **Vic S Ptr's At The Light Epis Barnegat Light NJ 2005-** B Indianapolis IN 12/2/1938 s Vance Lee Turner & Thelma sadler. Georgetown Coll 1957; BA Butler U 1961; MDiv CRDS 1965; CTh SWTS 1984. D 6/16/1985 Bp Frank Tracy Griswold III P 10/18/1985 Bp Allen Webster Brown. m 4/21/1978 Candace Calvert c 4. Pres, Dioc Coun, Dio CNY Dio Cntrl New York Syracuse NY 1999-2001; Mem, Thornfield Discernment Com Dio Cntrl New York Syracuse NY 1999-2000; Mem, Long Range Plnng, Dio CNY Dio Cntrl New York Syracuse NY 1997-2004; Mem, Dioc Bd Dio Cntrl New York Syracuse NY 1997-2001; Dn, No Country Dist Dio Cntrl New York Syracuse NY 1994-2004; R Trin Epis Ch Watertown NY 1991-2004; Dn, Star Prairie Dnry, Dio Eau Claire Dio Eau Claire Eau Claire WI 1988-1991; Vic Trin Ch River Falls WI 1987-1991; P-in-c S Mich's Ch Barrington IL 1986-1987; Cur S Mich's Ch Barrington IL 1985. Ed, "Wrshp," *A Bk of Wrshp for the Healing Mnstry*, Orrville Press, 1971; Ed, "Wrshp," *A Bk of Wrshp: Comm and Ante-communion*, Orrville Press, 1970. Cath Fllshp Epis Ch 1985; Ord of S Lk 1969-1977; SocMary 1987. frdltpadre1@yahoo.com

TURNER, Elizabeth Holder (Del) 125 Gull Pt, Millsboro DE 19966 B Wilmington DE 6/27/1930 d William Purvis Holder & Eleanor Elizabeth. D 1/12/1980 Bp John Mc Gill Krumm. m 10/11/1958 Arthur W Turner c 3. D All SS Ch Rehoboth Bch DE 1996-2001; Asst S Geo's Chap Rehoboth Bch DE 1996-2001; All SS Ch Rehoboth Bch DE 1995-1999; Dio Delaware Wilmington DE 1988-2001; Asst S Mk's Ch Millsboro DE 1988-1990. turnereht1@aol.com

T

TURNER, Elizabeth Zarelli (Tex) 9520 Anchusa TRL, Austin TX 78736 **R S Mk's Ch Austin TX 2008-** B Tacoma WA 9/19/1953 d Albert Anthony Zarelli & Georgina Elizabeth. BA Seattle Pacific U 1976; MA Ya Berk 1978; MDiv GTS 1984. D 6/30/1984 Bp Robert Hume Cochrane P 2/2/1985 Bp William Grant Black. m 5/25/1986 Philip Williams Turner III c 1. Asst R S Mk's Ch Austin TX 1999-2004; All SS Ch Atlanta TX 1997-1999; Assoc All SS Epis Ch Austin TX 1997-1999; Ya Berk New Haven CT 1994-1997; Assoc S Jas Ch New York NY 1988-1991; Asst Ecum Off Epis Ch Cntr New York NY 1986-1988; All Ang' Ch New York NY 1986-1987; Asst to R The Ch of the Redeem Cincinnati OH 1984-1986. Auth, "Men & Wmn: Sexual Ethics In Turbulent Times"; Auth, "Implications Of The Gospel"; Auth, "Study Guide For Luth- Epis Dialogue Document"; Auth, "Love," *Mar & Friendship*. eztpwt3@yahoo.com

TURNER SR, Eric Wood (CFla) 4581 Bellaluna Dr., West Melbourne FL 32904 **Stndg Com Dio Cntrl Florida Orlando FL 2010-; Chair, Chr**

Formation Cmsn Dio Cntrl Florida Orlando FL 2009-; R S Jn's Ch Melbourne FL 2004- B Pittsburgh PA 12/9/1958 s Russell Wood Turner & Frances. W Virginia U 1977; BS Alleg 1980; MDiv TESM 1988. D 6/4/1988 P 4/1/1989 Bp Alden Moinet Hathaway. m 12/15/1984 Charlene S Sherbondy c 2. Stndg Com Dio Cntrl Florida Orlando FL 2010; Dn of SE Dnry Dio Cntrl Florida Orlando FL 2007-2010; R S Paul's Epis Ch Shelton CT 2001-2004; Asst R S Matt's Ch Richmond VA 1988-1994. Ord of S Lk. Phi Beta Kappa. eric@stjohnsmlb.org

✠ **TURNER, Rt Rev Franklin Delton** (Pa) 825 Spring Ave, Elkins Park PA 19027 **Ret Bp Suffr of PA Dio Pennsylvania Philadelphia PA 2000-** B Norwood NC 7/19/1933 s James Thomas Turner & Dora Streater. BA Livingstone Coll 1956; MDiv Ya Berk 1965; DD Ya Berk 1978; DD Livingstone Coll 1979. D 6/12/1965 Bp Leland Stark P 12/21/1965 Bp Charles A Mason Con 10/7/1988 for Pa. m 7/6/1963 Barbara Jean Dickerson. Bp Suffr Dio Pennsylvania Philadelphia PA 1983-2000; Asst to Bp for Congregations Dio Pennsylvania Philadelphia PA 1983-1988; Trst Ya Berk New Haven CT 1982; Epis Ch Cntr New York NY 1972-1983; Assoc Trin And S Phil's Cathd Newark NJ 1972-1983; Pres/Fndr Epis Cler Assn Dio Washington Washington DC 1967-1969; R S Geo's Ch Washington DC 1966-1972; Mnstry Higher Educ Com Dio Washington Washington DC 1966-1969; Vic Ch Of The Epiph Dallas TX 1965-1966.

TURNER, (Irvin) Doyle (Minn) 37688 Tulaby Lake Rd, Waubun MN 56589 B White Earth MN 10/20/1943 s Robert Irvin Turner & Blanche May. 1982; BS Minnesota St U Moorehead 1982; MDiv SWTS 1985. D 8/3/1985 P 2/13/1986 Bp Robert Marshall Anderson. m 2/27/1965 Mary M Olsen c 3. Chapl Epis Cmnty Serv Benidji MN 2005-2006; Indigenous Theol Trng Inst Oklahoma City OK 1999-2000; Vic Dio Minnesota Minneapolis MN 1985-1998; D Breck Memi Mssn Naytahwaush MN 1985-1994; D Samuel Memi Naytahwaush MN 1985-1994. Auth, "Blood, Bone & Sprt," *First Peoples Theol Journ*, ITTI, 2010; Auth, "I Put My Back To It," *First Peoples Theol Journ*, ITTI, 2006; Auth, "The Way (Poem)," *First Peoples Theol Journ*, ITTI, 2006; Auth, "Meeting Jesus Again," *First Peoples Theol Journ*, ITTI, 2005; Auth, "Native Sprtl Realities (Poem)," *First Peoples Theol Journ*, ITTI, 2005; Auth, "Traditional Native Amer And Chr Sprtlty: A Dialogue," *First Peoples Theol Journ*, ITTI, 2002; Auth, "Creation," *First Peoples Theol Journ*, Indigenous Theol Trng Inst (ITTI), 2001; Auth, "A Warrior w A Pen," *Stories Migrating Hm*, Loon Feather Press, 1999. 2006 Chld's Ldrshp Awd The Sheltering Arms Fndt 2006. dmturn@tvutel.com

TURNER, Jane Carver (Los) 4865 Garnet Street, Eugene OR 97405 B Los Angeles CA 4/28/1924 d Hugo Cowell Carver & Agnes Maud. BA U CA 1948; MDiv CDSP 1983. D 10/10/1982 Bp Robert C Rusack P 5/8/1983 Bp George West Barrett. c 4. Asst St Johns Pro-Cathd Los Angeles CA 1988-1995; Asst S Alb's Epis Ch Los Angeles CA 1982-1988. garnetwoods@gmail.com

TURNER, John Edward (Haw) 19446 N. 110th Lane, Sun City AZ 85373 B Tulsa OK 7/18/1952 s William Joseph Turner & Dixie Alice. D 3/4/2000 P 7/14/2001 Bp Richard Sui On Chang. S Jude's Hawaiian Ocean View Ocean View HI 2004-2006; P S Jude's Hawaiian Ocean View Ocean View HI 2001-2003. rev.jet@hotmail.com

TURNER, J Scott (Colo) St. Paul's Episcopal Church, P.O. Box 770722, Steamboat Springs CO 80477 **P-in-c S Paul's Epis Ch Steamboat Sprg CO 2009-** B Lubbock TX 3/5/1954 s Kenneth Lanse Turner & Golda Glynn. B.A. Texas Tech U 1976; M.Div TS 1980. D 6/21/1980 Bp Willis Ryan Henton P 6/20/1981 Bp Sam Byron Hulsey. m 11/1/1996 JoAnne Modesitt Grace c 2. Assoc All SS Ch Loveland CO 2007-2009; P-in-c S Alb's Ch Windsor CO 2004-2007; Assoc All SS Ch Loveland CO 2000-2003; R The Ch Of Chr The King (Epis) Arvada CO 1988-1994; Assoc Trin Ch Galveston TX 1984-1988; Vic S Jn The Bapt Epis Clarendon TX 1980-1984; Dio NW Texas Lubbock TX 1980-1981; P-in-c S Matt's Ch Pampa TX 1980-1981. EPF 1979. jsturner@frii.com

TURNER, Linnea Summers (Va) 5701 Hunton Wood Dr, Broad Run VA 20137 **COM Dio Virginia Richmond VA 2000-** B Washington DC 7/24/1946 d George Clyde Summers & Lucille Eleanor. BA Duke 1968; MA Wright St U 1975; MDiv VTS 1989. D 6/10/1989 Bp Peter James Lee P 3/15/1990 Bp Robert Poland Atkinson. m 9/2/1967 Michael V Turner c 2. Chair, Cmsn on Wrld Mssn Dio Virginia Richmond VA 2000-2003; Chair, Com on CE Dio Virginia Richmond VA 1995-1999; R Epis Ch Of Leeds Par Markham VA 1993-2010; Assoc All SS' Epis Ch Chevy Chase MD 1992-1993; Int Epis Ch Of Leeds Par Markham VA 1991-2002; Asst S Patricks Ch Falls Ch VA 1989-1991. Busmn of the Year in the Area of Serv Fauquier Cnty Bus & Profsnl Wmn Club 2000. linnea@hughes.net

TURNER, Mary LaRoche Douglas (SVa) 118 Little John Road, Williamsburg VA 23187 B Ticonderoga NY 7/29/1948 d Benjamin Henry Douglas & Mary La Roche. BA Agnes Scott Coll 1970; MDiv Candler TS Emory U 1994. D 6/4/1994 P 12/10/1994 Bp Frank Kellogg Allan. m 2/6/2005 Claude Sylvester Turner c 3. P-in-c Bruton Par Williamsburg VA 2008-2009; Stndg Com Dio Sthrn Virginia Norfolk VA 2007-2010; Exec Bd & Dn of Jamestown Convoc Dio Sthrn Virginia Norfolk VA 2002-2005; Assoc R Bruton Par Williamsburg VA 2000-2010; Trst The U So (Sewanee) Sewanee TN 1998-2000; Congrl Dvlpmt T/F Dio Atlanta Atlanta GA 1997-2000; Vic S Jas Epis Ch Clayton GA 1996-2000; Exec Bd Dio Atlanta Atlanta GA 1995-1997; Asst R Gr Epis Ch Gainesville GA 1994-1996. Contrib, "Commentaries on Psalms," *Feasting on the Word (Year B, Vol. 3)*, Westminster Jn Knox, 2009. Theta Phi hon Fraternity Candler TS 1994. claudeandmollie@yahoo.com

TURNER, Maurice Edgar (Cal) 4222 Churchill Drive, Pleasanton CA 94588 B Manchester England UK 6/29/1932 s Edward Hodgson Pratt Turner & Emily Florence. BS Royal Tech Coll Salford Gb 1956; MDiv CDSP 1973. D 6/24/1972 Bp C Kilmer Myers P 12/1/1972 Bp Sumner Walters. c 3. S Clare's Epis Ch Pleasanton CA 1986-2003; Assoc R S Steph's Epis Ch Orinda CA 1979-1986; R Redeem And Hope Epis Ch Delano CA 1976-1978; S Mich And All Ang Concord CA 1974-1976; Asst Ch Of The H Trin Richmond CA 1972-1973. friartuck72@comcast.net

TURNER, Melvin Eugene (Minn) 4759 Shellbark Rd, Owings Mills MD 21117 **Assoc All SS Epis Ch Reisterstown MD 2004-** B Grimes County TX 4/21/1936 s Oliver Turner & Essie L. Nthrn Bapt TS 1959; VTS 1977. D 6/24/1978 P 3/18/1979 Bp John Thomas Walker. m 1/10/1959 Margaret Alois Humphrey c 3. S Phil's Ch S Paul MN 1990-2001; S Phil's Chap Baden Brandywine MD 1978-1990. Outstanding Cler of thc Ycar 1988. eugtur@comcast.net

TURNER, Peter Knight (NJ) PO Box 1134, Hillburn NY 10931 **Extended Supply Ch Of The Gd Shpd Greenwood Lake NY 2008-** B Rockford IL 5/5/1935 s William Andrew Turner & Marion Gertrude. BA Wms 1957; MBA NYU 1971; Cert Merc 1978. D 6/3/1978 P 12/1/1978 Bp Albert Wiencke Van Duzer. m 9/7/1996 Georgine Sargent c 2. S Lk's Ch Beacon NY 2006; S Mk's Epis Ch Yonkers NY 2004; Gr Epis Ch Monroe NY 2001-2007; S Andr's Ch Scotia NY 2000; S Paul's Epis Ch Greenwich NY 1999-2000; P-in-c S Lk's Ch Catskill NY 1998-1999; S Steph's Ch Schenectady NY 1998; S Jn In-The-Wilderness Copake Falls NY 1997-1998; Gr Epis Ch Port Jervis NY 1995-1996; Team Monticello NY 1995; Assoc Gr Ch Middletown NY 1990-1994; Assoc S Mary's-In-Tuxedo Tuxedo Pk NY 1989-1990; S Mk's Ch Hammonton NJ 1988-1989; Cur All SS' Epis Ch Scotch Plains NJ 1978-1981.

TURNER, Philippa Anne (NY) 2 E 90th St, New York NY 10128 **Assoc Ch Of The Heav Rest New York NY 1995-** B London UK 7/17/1964 d Amedee Edward Turner & Deborah Owen. BA U of Durham GB 1986; MDiv Ya Berk 1988. D 7/9/1994 P 2/16/1995 Bp Richard Frank Grein. Ch Of The Heav Rest New York NY 1994; Chapl S Jas Ch New York NY 1992-1995. Coll of Chapl 1991; Secy AEHC 1991. Hon Doctorate Ursinus Coll 2002. pipturn@gmail.com

TURNER III, Philip Williams (Tex) 9520 Anchusa Trl, Austin TX 78736 B Winchester VA 6/3/1935 s Philip Williams Turner & Constance Virginia. BA W&L 1958; BD VTS 1961; Oxon 1965; MA Pr 1973; PhD Pr 1978. D 6/17/1961 P 12/1/1961 Bp Angus Dun. m 5/25/1986 Elizabeth Zarelli c 4. Int Ch Of The Incarn Dallas TX 2007-2008; Int Dn Epis TS Of The SW Austin TX 2005-2007; All Ang' Ch New York NY 1986-1987; Fac The GTS New York NY 1980-1991; Epis TS Of The SW Austin TX 1974-1979. Auth, "The Fate of Comm"; Auth, "Sex Money and Power"; Auth, "Crossroads Ave For Meeting"; Auth, "Men & Wmn: Sexual Ethics In Turbulent Times"; Auth, "The Crisis Of Moral Tchg In The Epis Ch". Hon Doctorate Ya Berk; Hon Doctorate Epis TS of the SW; Hon Doctorate VTS. eztpwt3@yahoo.com

TURNER, Reverend Clay H (USC) 2285 Armstrong Creek Road, Marion NC 28752 B Mobile AL 11/26/1938 s Henry Clay Turner & Mary Louise. BA SMU 1961; MDiv Duke 1964; ThM Duke 1965; Angl Stds EDS 1966; DMin PrTS 1992. D 6/29/1966 P 6/1/1967 Bp Thomas Augustus Fraser Jr. m 9/1/1961 Jane Rollins c 3. R Ch Of The Adv Spartanburg SC 1990-2004; Chair of Exam Chapl Dio SW Virginia Roanoke VA 1981-1990; R S Jn's Ch Roanoke VA 1975-1990; R Trin Epis Ch Statesville NC 1969-1975; Chr Ch Rocky Mt NC 1966-1969; D S Jn's Ch Battleboro NC 1966-1969. "The Potter's Wheel," *Selected Sermons through the Cycle of the Liturg Year*, The Reprint Co, 2006. Amer Assn for Mariage and Fam Ther 1973; AAPC 1970; Assn for Couples in Mar Enrichment. claymarion@aol.com

TURNER, Robert (NJ) 525 Pleasant Ave, Piscataway NJ 08854 **Congrl Dvlpmt Dio New Jersey Trenton NJ 2006-; D Dio New Jersey Trenton NJ 2002-; D S Mk's Ch Plainfield NJ 2002-** B Newark NJ 11/19/1938 s Major Turner & Ruth. BS Bloomfield Coll 1979. D 1/25/1975 Bp George E Rath. m 5/28/1965 Dolores Letitia Grant c 4. D Ch Of The H Trin New York NY 1999-2002; Com on Diac Dio New Jersey Trenton NJ 1994-2002; D S Mk's Ch Plainfield NJ 1992-1999; Dio New Jersey Trenton NJ 1985-1988; Asst S Fran Ch Dunellen NJ 1982-1992. bobt525@verizon.net

TURNER, Saundra Lee (Ga) 2104 Amberley Pass, Evans GA 30809 **D Ch Of Our Sav Martinez GA 2006-** B Milford DE 4/3/1947 d James Turner & Elsie. BA Amer U 1972; MS Cath Univ 1974; EdD U GA 1990. D 5/31/2006 Bp Henry Irving Louttit. sturner99@comcast.net

TURNER, Sharon Richey (Dal) 6728 Mayer Road, La Grange TX 78945 **P-in-c S Jn's Epis Ch Columbus TX 2009-** B Beaumont TX 8/17/1942 d James

Wilburn Richey & Emma Mae. B.F.A. U of Texas 1964; M.Ed. U of Houston 1975; M.Div. Epis TS of The SW 1987; D.Min. Austin Presb TS 2007. D 6/8/1987 Bp Anselmo Carral-Solar P 5/11/1988 Bp Maurice Manuel Benitez. m 9/4/1965 Michael Lucian Turner c 2. Assoc R S Mich And All Ang Ch Dallas TX 1994-2002; Assoc R H Sprt Epis Ch Houston TX 1987-1994; Asst Ch Of The Gd Shpd Tomball TX 1987. Auth, "The Lesson and the Arts," *Lectionary*, 2000. sharonkayturner@yahoo.com

TURNER, Stanley Eugene (SwFla) 230 Normandy Circle, Palm Harbor FL 33563 **Died 8/8/2010** B Greenville TX 9/3/1926 s Carl Eugene Turner & Novie Lucile. Georgia Inst of Tech 1947; BS U of So Carolina 1947; PhD U of Texas 1951. D 11/1/1978 Bp Emerson Paul Haynes. c 2. stanturner@aol.com

TURNER, Stephen Deree (EC) 16 Gregg Way, Fort Rucker AL 36362 B Atlanta GA 5/5/1953 s Trevor Deree Turner & Lois Grey. BA U of Virginia 1975; MDiv Candler TS Emory U 1978; DMin Candler TS Emory U 1988. D 9/12/1993 Bp Charles Lovett Keyser P 3/1/1994 Bp C(laude) Charles Vache. m 6/6/1982 Loura Dale Hardesty c 1. Off Of Bsh For ArmdF New York NY 1994-2001. sdturner6706@hotmail.com

TURNER III, Thomas Selma (WTex) 200 N. Wright Streed, Alice TX 78332 **The Epis Ch Of The Adv Alice TX 2011-** B Norfolk VA 4/22/1945 s Thomas Selma Turner & Maudine Long. BA Emory and Henry Coll 1974; JD St Mary's and U Sch of Law 1978; Cert Iona Sch for Mnstry 2010. D 6/24/2010 Bp Gary Richard Lillibridge. m 10/8/1966 Darlene Berger c 2. D S Mk's Ch Corpus Christi TX 2010-2011. tturner2692@sbcglobal.net

TURNER, Timothy Jay (WTex) 120 Herweck Dr, San Antonio TX 78213 B San Antonio TX 10/2/1950 s Marion Orville Turner & Margaret Ann. BA U of Houston 1972; MDiv Oblate TS 1979; CTh Epis TS of The SW 1991; MBA U of Texas at San Antonio 1999. Rec from Roman Catholic 6/10/1991 as Priest Bp John Herbert MacNaughton. m 8/2/1986 Elizabeth Kimmell. R Trin Ch San Antonio TX 1993-1997; Asst S Jn's Ch McAllen TX 1991-1993. Auth, "Loc Govt e-Disclosure & Comparisons: Equipping Deliberative Democracy for the 21st Century," U Press of Amer, 2005; Auth, "Welcoming the Baptized: Angl Hosp within the Ecum Enterprise," Grove Books Ltd., 1996. Texas Bus Hall of Fame Schlrshp Texas Bus Hall of Fame 1999. tjturner@satx.rr.com

TURNER JR, William Joseph (CNY) 2 Ridgefield Pl, Biltmore Forest NC 28803 B Milwaukee WI 6/22/1926 s William Joseph Turner & Dorothy Maud. BA Carroll Coll 1947; MA U of Wisconsin 1950; STB Ya Berk 1956. D 6/3/1956 P 12/1/1956 Bp Horace W B Donegan. m 6/30/1954 Barbara Addison c 2. Vic Gr Ch Mex NY 1991-1994; R S Matt's Epis Ch Liverpool NY 1983-1991; R S Jn's Epis Ch Gloucester MA 1975-1983; Assoc S Andr's Ch Wellesley MA 1966-1975; Cn Chncllr S Paul's Cathd Buffalo NY 1962-1966; Cur S Simon's Ch Buffalo NY 1956-1958. beejeegolf@gmail.com

TURNER-JONES, Nancy Marie (SO) 318 E. 4th St., Cincinnati OH 45202 **Cn Epis Soc Of Chr Ch Cincinnati OH 2008-** B 12/12/1954 d Theodore F Wehr & Gertrude M. BA Mia 1988; MA Cincinnati Conservatory of Mus Cincinnati 1991; MDiv Lexington TS 1995; DMin STUSo 1999. D 12/16/2000 P 9/6/2001 Bp Stacy F Sauls. m 7/21/2001 Larry Paul Jones. Int The Epis Ch Of The Ascen Middletown OH 2007-2008; R S Dav's Ch Southfield MI 2004-2007; Asst S Jas Epis Ch Birmingham MI 2002-2004; Prof The TS at The U So Sewanee TN 2002; Asst Ch Of The Ascen Frankfort KY 2001-2002; D Chr Ch Cathd Lexington KY 2000-2001. njones@cccath.org

TURNEY, Anthony Brian (Cal) 3545 Market St. Apt. A, San Francisco CA 94131 B UK 12/23/1937 s Sidney James Turney & Ida Mary. BA Sch for Deacons 1996. D 6/1/1996 Bp William Edwin Swing. The Epis Ch Of S Jn The Evang San Francisco CA 2001-2002; D The Epis Ch Of S Jn The Evang San Francisco CA 2000-2001; Gr Cathd San Francisco CA 1998-2004; D Gr Cathd San Francisco CA 1996-1998. sfdeacon@comcast.net

TURNEY, Harper McAdoo (O) 13704 Lake Shore Blvd, Cleveland OH 44110 **Gd Shpd Ch Hilltown PA 2006-** B Carlsbad NM 9/30/1944 d Hardin A McAdoo & Ina. BA W&M 1966; MA New Mex Highlands U 1971; MFA U Denv 1973; MDiv SWTS 1993. D 6/5/1993 Bp James Russell Moodey P 1/18/1994 Bp Arthur Benjamin Williams Jr. m 5/29/1977 Wayne Scott Turney c 1. R S Andr Epis Ch Mentor OH 1998-2006; S Paul's Epis Ch Cleveland Heights OH 1996-1998; Com Dio Ohio Cleveland OH 1995-2000; S Ptr's Epis Ch Lakewood OH 1993-1996.

TURRELL, James Fielding (Be) School of Theology, U. of the South, 335 Tennessee Ave, Sewanee TN 37383 **assoc. prof. & assoc. Dn The TS at The U So Sewanee TN 2008-** B Tunkhannock PA 4/20/1970 s James Joel Turrell & Susan. BA Ya 1991; MDiv Ya Berk 1996; MA Van 1999; PhD Van 2002. D 6/8/1996 Bp James Michael Mark Dyer P 12/21/1996 Bp Paul Victor Marshall. m 5/1/2004 Jennie Goodrum c 1. asst. prof. The TS at The U So Sewanee TN 2002-2008; stated supply P Trin Ch Clarksville TN 2000-2001; stated supply P S Jn's Epis Ch Mt Juliet TN 1999-2000; Res Intern The Cathd Ch Of S Jas So Bend IN 1996-1998. Auth, "Richard Baxter's Attempt to Rehabilitate Cnfrmtn," *Studia Liturgica*, 2011; Auth, "A Dim Mirror: Archbp Rowan Williams's Reflections on the 2009 GC," *ATR*, 2010; Auth, "Uniformity and Common Pryr," *Comp to Richard Hooker*, Brill, 2008; Auth, "P and People in the Angl Tradition," *Sewanee Theol Revs*, 2008; Auth, "Muddying the Waters of Baptism: Theol Com's Report on Baptism, Cnfrmtn, and Chr Initiation," *ATR*, 2006; Auth, "Catechisms," *Oxford Guide to BCP*, Oxford Univ. Press, 2006; Auth, "Until Such Time as He Be Confirmed: Laudians and Cnfrmtn," *Seventeenth Century*, 2005; Auth, "The Ritual Of Royal Healing: Scrofula, Liturg And Politics," *Angl And Epis Hist*, 1999. Amer Hist Assn 2001; Amer Soc Of Ch Hist 2000; No Amer Acad of Liturg 2005; No Amer Conf On British Stds 2002. Colloquium Prize Sewanee Mediaeval Colloquium 2002; Doctoral Fell ECF 2001; Grad Fell Van 1998. jturrell@sewanee.edu

TURRIE, Anne Elizabeth (RG) PO Box 2427, Mesilla Park NM 88047 **D S Jas' Epis Ch Mesilla Pk NM 2009-** B Marion IN 6/27/1946 d William Shirley Coffman & Carolyn Ruth. BA U CO 1970; MA Ball St U 1972; Dplma Trin Sem 2009. D 9/19/2009 Bp William Carl Frey. m 6/5/1971 Stephen Turrie. turrienewmex@aol.com

TURTON, Neil Christopher (NJ) 509 Lake Ave, Bay Head NJ 08742 **Vic All SS Ch Bay Hd NJ 2002-** B Manchester GB 12/29/1945 s Alan Ingham Turton & Helen Christine. Oxf 1979. Trans from Church Of England 3/14/2002 Bp David B(ruce) Joslin. m 7/7/1979 Wendy W Turton c 2. neilturton@exit109.com

TUSKEN, Mark Anthony (Chi) 327 S 4th St, Geneva IL 60134 **R S Mk's Ch Geneva IL 1994-** B Lansing MI 2/1/1956 s Roger Anthony Tusken & Margaret June. BA Van 1978; MDiv TESM 1981; DMin GTF 1999. D 10/11/1981 P 5/4/1982 Bp Bob Gordon Jones. m 2/3/2007 Peggy Tusken c 1. R Chr The Redeem Ch Montgomery AL 1986-1994; Asst R S Jn's Ch Huntingdon Vlly PA 1983-1986; Cur S Mk's Epis Ch Casper WY 1981-1983. marktusken@hotmail.com

TUTON, Daniel Joseph (RG) 201 E Chatsworth Ave, Reisterstown MD 21136 **Hope in the Desert Eps Ch Albuquerque NM 2007-** B Nebraska City NE 8/5/1955 BS U CA 1978; MS Sacramento St U 1986; MDiv TESM 2003. D 6/21/2003 P 1/24/2004 Bp Terence Kelshaw. m 6/7/1986 Michele Lynn Hathaway Tuton c 3. Cur All SS Epis Ch Reisterstown MD 2003-2007. tutons@verizon.net

TUTTLE, Margaret Constance (Nwk) 19 Oberlin St, Maplewood NJ 07040 B Brooklyn NY 1/30/1954 d Edward Darnowski & Josephine. BS NYU 1975; MA NYU 1978; MDiv Drew U 1999. D 6/1/2002 P 12/14/2002 Bp John Palmer Croneberger. margaret.tuttle@verizon.net

TUTTLE, Peggy Elaine Wills (Minn) 1660 Riverton Pt, Eagan MN 55122 B Fort Worth TX 7/10/1940 d Marvin Elton Wills & Mabel Vida. MDiv VTS 1995; BS Natl-Louis U 1996. D 10/16/1996 P 5/1/1997 Bp James Louis Jelinek. m 1/24/1976 Jon F Tuttle c 2. S Jn The Evang S Paul MN 2010-2011; S Mart's By The Lake Epis Minnetonka Bch MN 2009-2010; Asstg P S Mart's By The Lake Epis Minnetonka Bch MN 2008; S Paul's Epis Ch Duluth MN 2005-2006; The Epis Par Of S Dav Minnetonka MN 2004; Dio Minnesota Minneapolis MN 1999-2003; Adv Ch Farmington MN 1998; Asst S Jos's Ch Lakewood CO 1997-1998. pegtuttle@aol.com

TUTU, Mpho Andrea (WA) 3001 Park Center Dr Apt 1119, Alexandria VA 22302 B London England 11/30/1963 d DM Tutu. D 6/7/2003 Bp Gordon Paul Scruton P 1/17/2004 Bp DM Tutu. m 12/31/1993 Joseph Charles Burris c 1. Chr Ch Alexandria VA 2003-2006.

TUZROYLUKE SR, Seymour (Ak) Po Box 171, Point Hope AK 99766 **Supply P Chr Ch Anchorage AK 2002-** B Pt Hope AK 8/4/1924 s Bob Tuzroyluke & Helen. D 6/10/1983 P 6/8/1984 Bp George Clinton Harris. m 6/8/1950 Claudia Hank.

TWEEDALE, David Lee (Colo) 423 E Thunderbird Dr, Fort Collins CO 80525 **Assoc Pstr S Alb's Ch Windsor CO 2002-** B Denver CO 4/8/1946 s Gilbert Morris Tweedale & Evelyn Pearl. BA Minnesota St U Moorehead 1989. D 7/31/2002 P 2/26/2003 Bp William Jerry Winterrowd. m 2/4/1996 Weltha Ann McGraw. d.tweedale@comcast.net

TWEEDIE, Billy (Tex) 301 E 8th St, Austin TX 78701 **S Dav's Ch Austin TX 2011-** B Milford CT 12/15/1976 s William Duane Tweedie & Andrea Jean. Texas St U 2001; MDiv Epis TS Of The SW 2009. D 6/20/2009 Bp Joseph Doyle P 1/5/2010 Bp C(harles) Andrew Doyle. m 10/19/2002 Laura Jayne Houlden c 2. S Paul's Ch Waco TX 2010-2011; Cur Dio Texas Houston TX 2009; Yth Dir Chr Ch Cathd Houston TX 2004-2006; Yth Dir S Mk's Ch Houston TX 2002-2004. billytweedie@gmail.com

TWEEDY, Jeanette E(lizabeth) (NY) PO Box 172, Peacham VT 05862 B Kingston NY 10/19/1950 d Oliver Tweedy & Helen. Eisenhower Coll 1970; BS Green Mtn Coll 1981; MDiv Bex 1991. D 6/22/1991 Bp O'Kelley Whitaker P 5/5/1992 Bp David B(ruce) Joslin. c 2. Cn Dio Vermont Burlington VT 2002-2010; S Andr's Epis Ch St Johnsbury VT 1999-2001; R S Mary's Epis Ch Hillsboro OH 1993-1998; D Intern Of The Chenango Cluster Of Ch Dio Cntrl New York Syracuse NY 1991-1993. PRIESTTWEEDY@GMAIL.COM

TWEEL, Esber Naif (WVa) 3709 Washington Ave Se, Charleston WV 25304 B Huntington WV 7/15/1941 s Naif Esber Tweel & Margaret. BS Marshall U 1965; MDiv VTS 1972. D 6/5/1972 P 2/1/1973 Bp Wilburn Camrock Campbell. m 6/19/1965 Carol Lynn Fields. R Ch Of The Gd Shpd Charleston WV 1974-2004; Vic S Steph's Ch Romney WV 1972-1974. "One People, Three

Faces," *An Allegory*, M and D Ink, Lulu Online, Inc. goodshepherdch@aol.com

TWELVES, Paul Douglass (RI) 341 Spinnaker Lane, Bristol RI 02809 B Philadelphia PA 2/1/1929 s John Wesley Twelves & Rachel Gilchrist. BS Tem 1951; MDiv EDS 1954. D 5/29/1954 Bp Oliver J Hart P 12/7/1954 Bp Norman B Nash. m 9/30/1989 Joy Wassell c 3. S Mich's Ch Bristol RI 2008-2009; Int Ch Of The Mssh Providence RI 2000-2002; Int S Paul's Ch Portsmouth RI 1998-2000; Int S Mart's Ch Providence RI 1997-1998; Int S Alb's Ch No Providence RI 1995-1997; Int Gr Ch Amherst MA 1994-1995; Int S Matt's Ch Bedford NY 1993-1994; Int S Paul's Ch Kansas City MO 1992-1993; Int S Jn's Ch Lynchburg VA 1991-1992; Int S Geo's Epis Ch Dayton OH 1989-1991; Int S Steph's Epis Ch And U Columbus OH 1988-1989; Int S Alb's Ch Syracuse NY 1987-1988; R S Ptr's Ch Glenside PA 1975-1986; R All SS Ch Chelmsford MA 1954-1975. ptwelves@fullchannel.net

TWENTYMAN JR, Donald Graham (Ia) 107 24th St, Spirit Lake IA 51360 **D S Mk's Epis Ch Mesa AZ 2010-; D S Alb's Ch Sprt Lake IA 1998-** B Rochester MN 12/16/1941 s Donald Graham Twentyman & Gwendolyn. AB U Chi 1964; Epis Dio Minnesota 1982. D 12/2/1982 Bp William Arthur Dimmick. m 6/27/1998 Mary B Hermansen c 2. D Gr Memi Ch Wabasha MN 1996-1998; D/Mentor S Matt's Epis Ch Chatfield MN 1993-1996; D Calv Ch Rochester MN 1982-1993. Assn for Epis Deacons 1980. d-twentyman-7@alumni.uchicago.edu

TWIGGS, Frances R (NY) 28 Wendell St, Apt. 9, Cambridge MA 02138 B Kingsport TN 7/22/1960 d Henry Cumming Twiggs & Joan Mary. BSW E Tennessee St U 1982; MDiv GTS 2002. D 10/20/2001 P 6/1/2002 Bp Herbert Thompson Jr. R S Jn's Ch New City NY 2005-2011; S Anne Epis Ch W Chester OH 2005; Ch Of The Gd Samar Amelia OH 2004-2005; Cur The Ch of the Redeem Cincinnati OH 2002-2004. frank.twiggs@gmail.com

TWINAMAANI, Benjamin B (SwFla) 9533 Pebble Glen Ave, Tampa FL 33647 **R Gr Ch Tampa FL 2005-** B Kabale Uganda 6/26/1961 s Faith N. U of So Florida; BD Bp Tucker Theol Coll Mukono Ug 1990; ThM Dallas TS 2000. Trans from Church of the Province of Uganda 11/18/2004 Bp John Bailey Lipscomb. m 8/22/1998 Camilla Judith Twinamaani c 3. Auth, "Faithful Locally, Prayerful Globally: Par Mnstry in the new Angl Disorder," *Fulcrum: Renewing the Evang Cntr UK*, LivCh mag, 2010; Auth, "Preparing for Lambeth 2008: Praying, Hoping and Working for Angl Faith and Ord," *Angl Comm Inst Website*, Angl Comm Inst, 2007; Auth, "How Amer Anglicans Think and Act: A Primer for the Global So.," *Angl Comm Inst Website*, Angl Comm Inst, 2007; Auth, "Let's Keep It Real," *LivCh mag*, LivCh mag, 1999; Auth, "The Hermeneutical Aspects of Proper Biblic Names and their Impact on Bible Translation for Afr," *unpublished Masters Thesis*, Dallas TS, 1999. Angl Comm Partnr Cler 2010; Angl Evang Soc 2005. Honorable Mem The Natl Scholars hon Soc 2007. canontwin@yahoo.com

TWISS, Ian Reed (Mich) Holy Faith Church, 6299 Saline Ann Arbor Rd, Saline MI 48176 **Dn of the Huron Vlly Dnry Dio Michigan Detroit MI 2009-; Pstr H Faith Ch Saline MI 2007-** B Canberra Australia 1/10/1971 s Robert John Twiss & Helen Walker Stuart. AB in Engl Pr 1994; MFA in Creative Writing U MI 1997; MDiv SWTS 2007. D 12/16/2006 P 6/23/2007 Bp Wendell Nathaniel Gibbs Jr. m 8/13/1994 Nancy R Reed c 3. ian@holy-faith-church.org

TWO BEARS, Neil V (ND) Po Box 685, Fort Yates ND 58538 **D S Jas Ch Ft Yates ND 2003-; Asst S Lk's Ch Ft Yates ND 2003-** B Cannon Ball ND 12/9/1929 D 6/12/2003 P 12/13/2003 Bp Andrew Hedtler Fairfield.

TWO BULLS, Robert G (U) Po Box 168, Hermosa SD 57744 B Pine Ridge SD 4/4/1934 s Peter Two Bulls & Marth. Dakota Ldrshp Prog; DLP Niobrara Sum Sem. D 6/25/1978 P 6/1/1980 Bp Walter H Jones. c 5. P Dio Utah Salt Lake City UT 1996-1998; P S Eliz's Ch Whiterocks UT 1996-1998; P Dio So Dakota Sioux Falls SD 1995-1996; P Dio So Dakota Sioux Falls SD 1995; P Dio Utah Salt Lake City UT 1993-1995; R S Matt's Epis Ch Rapid City SD 1986-1993; P Dio So Dakota Sioux Falls SD 1983-1993.

TWO BULLS, Robert W (Los) 3317 33rd Ave S, Minneapolis MN 55406 **Vic All SS Epis Indn Mssn Minneapolis MN 2006-; Dir, Dept Of Indn Mnstrs Dio Minnesota Minneapolis MN 2006-** B Rapid City SD 3/16/1963 s Robert G Two Bulls & Delores L. BS U of Maryland 1996; MDiv GTS 2000. D 6/1/2000 Bp Carolyn Tanner Irish P 1/6/2001 Bp Frederick Houk Borsch. m 6/26/1990 Ritchie R Robertson c 2. Prog Off For Native Amer Mnstrs Dio Los Angeles Los Angeles CA 2003-2006; Assoc R S Geo's Par La Can CA 2000-2003. rtwobulls@hotmail.com

TWO HAWK, Webster Aaron (SD) 604 East Missouri Avenue, Fort Pierre SD 57532 **Vic (non-stipendiary) S Ptr's Epis Ch Ft Pierre SD 1982-** B White River SD 2/4/1930 s Albert H Two Hawk & Annie Nelliw. BS U of So Dakota 1952; BD Bex 1957. D 6/29/1957 P 2/3/1958 Bp Conrad Gesner. m 8/29/1996 Marjorie F Grant c 1. P-in-c S Ptr's Ch Wagner SD 1957-1962. DD Hur Can 1972. adam57501@msn.com

TWOMEY, Patrick Timothy (FdL) 415 E Spring St, Appleton WI 54911 **All SS Epis Ch Appleton WI 1995-** B Saint Clair Shores MI 1/7/1960 s James Francis Twomey & Irene Betty. BA Albion Coll 1981; MDiv SWTS 1986. D 6/28/1986 Bp Henry Irving Mayson P 1/6/1987 Bp H Coleman McGehee Jr. m 7/18/1981 Mary Catherine Henry c 2. S Lk's Ch Dixon IL 1990-1995; Asst Trin Epis Ch Oshkosh WI 1986-1990. ptwomey@tds.net

TWYMAN, Thomas Wellwirth (CNY) 122 Metropolitan Ave, Ashland MA 01721 B Jackson MI 9/14/1938 s Wilford Page Twyman & Karolina. BA Mia 1960; BD VTS 1965; MS Bos 1978; Cert Boston Grad Sch of Psychoanalysis 1992. D 6/12/1965 Bp Leland Stark P 2/1/1966 Bp John S Higgins. m 8/22/1964 Jean Marie Twyman c 1. R Emm Ch E Syracuse NY 1967-1971; Cur S Jn's Ch Barrington RI 1965-1967. tw.twyman@comcast.net

TYLER, Lera Patrick (WTex) 1416 N Loop 1604 E, San Antonio TX 78232 **Asst R S Thos Epis Ch And Sch San Antonio TX 2009-** B Henderson TX 12/3/1948 d Clifton Maxwell Tyler & Cecile Betty. BA SW U 1971; MA U of New Orleans 1986; MA Sem of SW 2004. D 1/14/2009 Bp Gary Richard Lillibridge P 8/6/2009 Bp David Mitchell Reed. c 2. lera@plumgreen.com

TYLER, Pamela Hawes (Los) 1101 Witt Road, Taos NM 87471 B Ankara TURKEY 11/19/1948 d Morgan Seymour Tyler & Norma Louise. BA Florida St U 1970; JD U Of Florida 1986; MDiv Ya Berk 1995. D 6/10/2000 Bp Joseph Jon Bruno P 1/6/2001 Bp Frederick Houk Borsch. Dio Los Angeles Los Angeles CA 2005-2009; S Geo's Epis Ch Laguna Hills CA 2000-2005. Vice Chncllr Of Dio Dio Los Angeles 2004. phtyler@pacbell.net

TYNDALL, Constance Flanigan (WMo) 4239 E Valley Rd, Springfield MO 65809 B Carthage MO 11/24/1936 d John Hagar Flanigan & Minerva. W Missouri Sch for Mnstry; U of Missouri 1957; SW Missouri St U 1990. D 5/12/1991 Bp John Clark Buchanan. m 8/23/1957 Brent Vincent Tyndall c 3. Chair - Cmnty of Deacons Dio W Missouri Kansas City MO 1995-1997; D S Jas' Ch Springfield MO 1991-2011. Bp's Shield Dio W Missouri 2010; Steph Awd NAAD 2010; Omicron Delta Kappa 1989. vnctyndall@sbcglobal.net

TYNDALL, Jeremy Hamilton (Ore) 2150 Birchwood Ave, Eugene OR 97401 B Sutton Surrey UK 3/29/1955 s Francis Tyndall & Peggy. BTH/LTH U of Nottingham 1981; Fndt Yale DS 1998; MA U of Birmingham GB 2001. Trans from Church Of England 10/1/2001 Bp Robert Louis Ladehoff. m 3/5/1994 Susan Marie Knight c 4. S Thos' Epis Ch Eugene OR 2001. jeremytyndall@hotmail.com

TYO JR, Charles Hart (Roch) 16 Elmwood Ave, Friendship NY 14739 B Potsdam NY 2/20/1944 D 12/8/2001 P 10/26/2002 Bp Jack Marston McKelvey. m 8/14/1965 Bonnie Pratt c 3.

TYON, Agnes Lucille (SD) Po Box 282, Pine Ridge SD 57770 **P S Katharine's Ch Mart SD 2001-** B Pine Ridge SD 1/11/1933 d William Benjamin Gibbons & Elsie (NMN). Black Hill St U; TS - Native Sch Of Mnstrs Vancouver B. D 10/12/1993 Bp Harold Stephen Jones P 10/17/1997 Bp Creighton Leland Robertson. m 4/25/1952 Eugene G Tyon.

TYON, Benjamin Ruben (SD) Po Box 14, Pine Ridge SD 57770 B Pine Ridge SD 7/8/1934 s George Tyon & Sarah. BS Chadron St Coll 1957; MS Black Hill St U 1976. D 6/29/1980 Bp William Augustus Jones Jr P 11/1/1984 Bp Craig Barry Anderson. m 6/3/1957 Clementine E Brewer c 1. Dio So Dakota Sioux Falls SD 1987-2004.

TYREE, Richard (SwVa) 132 Lincoln St, Holyoke MA 01040 B Lynch Sta VA 1/9/1925 s Charles Terrell Tyrell & Anne Minor. VPI 1947; LTh VTS 1961. D 6/1/1961 P 6/3/1992 Bp William Henry Marmion. m 7/11/1980 Linda E Eggleston. Int S Lk's Ch Springfield MA 1998-2000; Exec Coun Appointees New York NY 1983-1990; Archd Dio SW Virginia Roanoke VA 1969-1983; R Gr Memi Ch Lynchburg VA 1964-1969; Vic Trin Ch Arlington VA 1961-1964. tyree132@comcast.net

TYREE-CUEVAS, Susan McCorkle (Oly) 1804 Pointe Woodworth Dr NE, Tacoma WA 98422 B Lexington VA 10/3/1949 d William Bradley Tyree & Lula Virginia. BFA Virginia Commonwealth U 1971; MDiv VTS 1986. D 6/18/1988 P 4/18/1989 Bp Peter James Lee. m 9/13/1992 Charles Cuevas. R S Matt Ch Tacoma WA 2003-2010; Int Ch Of The Ascen Seattle WA 2002; Dio Virginia Richmond VA 1999-2001; Assoc R S Dunst's McLean VA 1988-1999. cuev33@comcast.net

TYRIVER, Marcia Rivenburg (Mil) 255 Ba Wood Ln, Janesville WI 53545 **Trin Ch Janesville WI 2007-** B 8/13/1940 d Charles Henry Rivenburg & Esther Mariana. BA Lawr Appleton WI 1962; MA U IL Champaign-Urbana IL 1965. D 6/2/2007 Bp Steven Andrew Miller. c 2. marciatyriver@sbcglobal.net

TYRRELL JR, Robert G (NY) 3716 80th St Apt B52, Jackson Heights NY 11372 **Died 11/15/2010** B Torrington CT 12/20/1940 s Robert Grattan Tyrrell & Helena Elizabeth. BA Br 1963; STB GTS 1966. D 6/4/1966 P 12/17/1966 Bp Horace W B Donegan. Auth, "Hist Of Ch Of Chemung Cnty Ny," *Bicentennial Hist Of Chemung Cnty*, 1976; Auth, "Chemung Cnty". rgtyrrell@aol.com

TYSON, Alfred Stephen (Ore) 5320 Fox Hollow Road Apt D-5, Eugene OR 97405 B Eugene OR 8/22/1915 s Alan Hugh Tyson & Carrie. BS U of Oregon 1937; MA U of Oregon 1939; BD CDSP 1947; Cbury Cathd 1976. D 8/19/1946 P 7/25/1947 Bp Benjamin D Dagwell. m 10/15/2007 L c 2. P-in-c S Dav's Ch Drain OR 1987-2002; Com Ch Mus Dio Oregon Portland OR 1983-1985; P-in-c Ch Of The H Sprt Sutherlin OR 1971-1978; Com Ch Mus Dio Oregon Portland OR 1956-1959; P-in-c Ch Of The Ascen Riddle OR

T

1949-1978; R S Geo's Epis Ch Roseburg OR 1949-1978; Vic Chr Ch S Helens OR 1947-1949. Auth, "Mem Scriptural Index Com," *The Hymnal 1982*, 1979. Phi Beta Kappa U of Oregon 1936. tyzell@comcast.net

TYSON, Lynda (Ct) 12 Parsons Hill Rd, Wenham MA 01984 **Assoc R S Jn's Ch Beverly Farms MA 2011-** B Lorain OH 3/7/1955 BS The OH SU 1977; MDiv Ya Berk 2005. D 6/11/2005 P 12/17/2005 Bp Chilton Abbie Richardson Knudsen. m 2/14/1986 Charles R Tyson. Sr. Assoc R S Lk's Par Darien CT 2007-2010; PLSE Mssnr Epis Ch Cntr New York NY 2006-2007; Epis PLSE Coordntr The AEC New York NY 2005-2006. revtyson@gmail.com

TYSON, Stephen Alfred (Ore) 370 Market Ave., Coos Bay OR 97420 **Dn Sthrn Convoc Dio Oregon Portland OR 2010-; R Emm Ch Coos Bay OR 2001-** B Portland OR 9/3/1949 s Alfred Stephen Tyson & Caroline Porter. BA Dart 1971; GTS 1972; MDiv CDSP 1974. D 7/26/1974 P 6/8/1975 Bp Matthew Paul Bigliardi. m 6/26/1971 Celeste Anne Kaye. R S Jn's Epis Ch Marysville CA 1989-2001; S Thos Epis Ch Dallas OR 1977-1988; Vic S Hilda's Ch Monmouth OR 1977-1981; Cur Emm Ch Coos Bay OR 1974-1977. coastcatsat@frontier.com

TZENG, Wen-Bin (Tai) No. 7 Lane 105, Section 1, Hang Chow South Road, Taipei Taiwan B Zhanghua TW 11/27/1974 s Tzeng Qing Xun & Guo Lai. MA Inst of Rel Sci; BA Fu-Jen Cath U 2001. D 1/25/2002 P 8/24/2002 Bp Jung-Hsin Lai. m 11/30/2002 Ming-Chin Ming Yang c 1. ashta_leotzeng@hotmail.com

U

UBIERA, Jose Ramon (DR) Calle Santiago # 114, Santo Domingo Dominican Republic **P Iglesia Epis San Felipe Apostol Santo Domingo Norte DO 2000-** B San Pedro de Macoris DO 6/2/1973 s Ramon Ubiera & Maribel. BA S Steph's Sch 1993; Cntr For Theol Educ 1998. D 4/10/1999 P 5/13/2000 Bp Julio Cesar Holguin-Khoury. m 8/28/1999 Candida Maria de los Santos. Dio The Dominican Republic (Iglesia Epis Dominicana) Santo Domingo DO 1999-2010. ramonubiera@yahoo.com

UDELL, C(arlton) (Vt) 293 Collamer Cir, Shelburne VT 05482 B Brooklyn NY 10/29/1930 s Carlton Granger Udell & Martha Christina. BA Hob 1952; MDiv UTS 1957; GTS 1958. D 11/9/1960 P 5/25/1961 Bp Horace W B Donegan. m 4/30/1960 Susanne Schiller c 2. COM Dio Vermont Burlington VT 1992-1994; Fletcher Allen Healthcare Burlington VT 1971-1996; Asst Ch Of The Resurr New York NY 1960-1966. Auth, "Hosp Chapl as Vehicle for Gods Healing," *Coll Chapl*, 1985; Auth, "Patient Rts, CBS TV,NY," *NY (nationwide broadcast)*, 1971. APC (Assn of Profsnl Chapl); AEHC; ACPE. Phi Beta Kappa Hob Geneva NY 1952. clelandudell@comcast.net

UDELL, George Morris Edson (Tex) 1436 Daventry Dr, DeSoto TX 75115 **P S Anne's Epis Ch Desoto TX 2005-** B Providence RI 2/16/1931 s George Udell & Alice Louise. BA U of New Mex 1957; CDSP 1960. D 6/1/1960 P 12/1/1960 Bp C J Kinsolving III. m 12/18/1955 Rosemary Heldt c 3. Asst Ch Of The Gd Shpd Cedar Hill TX 2002-2004; R Chr Ch Jefferson TX 1998-2001; R S Fran Par Temple TX 1977-1996; Assoc S Paul's Ch Waco TX 1969-1977; Asst Pro Cathd Epis Ch Of S Clem El Paso TX 1966-1969; Vic S Mich's Ch Tucumcari NM 1963-1966. gmeu@aol.com

UEDA, Ajuko Lois Kaleikea (Haw) Rikkyo University, 1-2-26, Kitano, Niizashi, Saitama Japan B Kawasaki JP 1/10/1956 d Ryoji Takagi & Teruko. BA Musashino Musica Academia Tokyo JP 1978; BD Tokyo Cntrl TS 1985; MDiv EDS 1994. D 5/31/2001 P 5/25/2002 Bp Richard Sui On Chang. m 11/3/1986 Noviaki Ueda. D/P S Jn's By The Sea Kaneohe HI 2001-2003; CE Dir S Mk's Ch Honolulu HI 1996-1999; Japanese Lang Mssnr Dio Hawaii Honolulu HI 1994-2003. aju@aloha.net

UFFELMAN, Stephen Paul (EO) 915 Ne Crest Dr, Prineville OR 97754 **P S Andr's Epis Ch Prineville OR 1996-** B Portland OR 2/15/1946 s Richard Victor Uffelman & Rae. BS OR SU 1969. D 4/22/1995 P 8/1/1996 Bp Rustin Ray Kimsey. m 6/15/1968 Janet Marie Fuller c 1. stephenu@crestviewcable.com

UFFMAN, Craig David (NI) 2000 Highland Avenue, Rochester NY 14618 **R S Thos Epis Ch Rochester NY 2010-** B Baton Rouge LA 4/27/1960 s Kenneth E Uffman & Grace. BS USNA 1982; MDiv Duke DS 2008. D 8/28/2009 P 2/28/2010 Bp Edward Stuart Little II. m 8/21/1982 Claudia Schaedel c 3. Asst-to-the-R S Anne's Epis Ch Warsaw IN 2008-2010. uffmanc@gmail.com

UHLIK, Charles R (WMo) 1902 Twin Bluff Rd, Red Wing MN 55066 **S Jas' Ch Springfield MO 2010-** B 8/12/1963 BA U of St. Thos 1987; MDiv U Of S Mary Of The Lake 1991. Rec from Roman Catholic 6/4/2005 Bp Barry Robert Howe. m 5/26/2000 Susan K Heavican c 2. Chr Ch Red Wing MN 2006-2010. revcu@sbcglobal.net

UITTI, Aaron Leopold (At) 124 Commercial Ave, East Palatka FL 32131 **R S Paul's Fed Point Hastings FL 2011-** B Hancock MI 7/21/1937 s William Leopold Uitti & Julia Margaret. BA NW Coll 1959; MDiv Concordia TS 1965; STM Concordia TS 1972. D 6/16/1985 P 12/15/1985 Bp Frank Stanley Cerveny. m 12/18/1983 Penelope Wertz c. R The Epis Ch Of S Ptr And S Paul Marietta GA 1993-2007; Cn S Jn's Cathd Jacksonville FL 1988-1993; Assoc All SS Epis Ch Jacksonville FL 1985-1988. SBL 1964. auitti@yahoo.com

ULLMAN, Richard Leo (O) 342 S 5th St, Philadelphia PA 19106 B Wilmington DE 10/14/1939 s Emanuel Ullman & Jacqueline Ambler. BA Amh 1961; BD EDS 1966. D 9/17/1966 Bp John Brooke Mosley P 3/18/1967 Bp Frederick J Warnecke. m 10/18/1980 Margaret Rose Epsenschied c 3. R Trin Ch Toledo OH 1993-2001; Int Galilee Epis Ch Virginia Bch VA 1992-1993; Int Ch Of The Gd Shpd Raleigh NC 1992; Archd Dio Sthrn Ohio Cincinnati OH 1987-1991; Reg Exec Miami Vlly Epis Coun Dayton OH 1980-1986; R Ch Of The Redeem Springfield PA 1971-1980; R S Paul's Ch Camden DE 1968-1971; Asst S Lk's Ch Scranton PA 1966-1968. Auth, "Choosing to Serve," CDO, 1991; Auth, "Called to Wk Together," Off for Mnstry Dvlpmt, 1983; Auth, "Var arts," *Action Info*, Alb Institue; Auth, "Var arts," *Leaven*, NNECA; Auth, "Var sermons," *Selected Sermons*. Fell Alb Inst 1983. ullmanshome@verizon.net

ULMER, B(enjamin) Sanford (Ga) 12 E 63rd St, Savannah GA 31405 **Died 10/27/2011** B Savannah GA 6/30/1930 s Roy Sanford Ulmer & Aleene Mae. BS Georgia Inst of Tech 1952. D 1/31/1992 Bp Harry Woolston Shipps P 12/5/1997 Bp Henry Irving Louttit. CODE. sanfordu@att.net

ULRICH, S(amuel) Burtner (NY) 1 Hudson, Yonkers NY 10701 B New Haven CT 9/24/1939 s William Wyndham Ulrich & Helen Sarah. BA Dart 1963; MDiv Ya Berk 1967. D 6/6/1967 P 12/1/1967 Bp Horace W B Donegan. S Jn's Ch Getty Sq Yonkers NY 1967-2006. Ven Ord Of Hospitals S Jn Of Jerusalem (Amer Chapt) 1985. sbu@stjohnsgettysquare.org

ULRICH, Stephanie Lyn (Neb) 9302 Blondo St., Omaha NE 68134 **Hlth Min All SS Epis Ch Omaha NE 1989-** B Ortonville MN 9/24/1951 d Donald Eugene Hintz & Terrel Dian. Dplma Bp Clarkson Sch of Nrsng 1972; Dio Nebraska Sprtl Direction 2005. D 6/22/2008 Bp Joe Goodwin Burnett. m 7/15/1972 Frederick Joseph Ulrich c 1. Auth, "Natl Epis Hlth Minisries," *Hlth Mnstry in the Loc Cong*, 815- Natl Ch, 2011. stephulrich@tconl.com

UMEOFIA, Christian Chinedu (NC) Po Box 1333, Goldsboro NC 27533 B Nnewi NG 6/5/1958 s Edwin O Umeofia & Jannet N. Jackson St U; Langston U; BA Cntrl St U 1984; MA Epis TS of The SW 1987. Rec 5/1/1996 Bp Brice Sidney Sanders. m 8/1/1984 Faith C Igwilo c 3. S Andr's Ch Goldsboro NC 1995-1998.

UMPHLETT, David Alton (NC) 108 Madison St, Plymouth NC 27962 **S Mary's Epis Ch High Point NC 2009-** B Norfolk VA 10/27/1977 s Mack M Umphlett & Martha. BMus U NC 2000; MDiv VTS 2004. D 6/19/2004 P 12/21/2004 Bp Clifton Daniel III. m 6/28/2003 Lorinda H Holderness c 2. R Gr Epis Ch Plymouth NC 2004-2009. AP 2004. davidumphlett@yahoo.com

UNDERHILL, Robin (Los) Tigh Ban, Hightae, Lockerbie DG-11 1JN Great Britain (UK) B Birmingham UK 5/10/1931 s Walter Underhill & Mabel. DIT ETSBH 1987; BS Woodbury U 1991; MA ETSBH 1992. D 6/12/1993 Bp Chester Lovelle Talton P 1/15/1994 Bp Frederick Houk Borsch. Int S Simon's Par San Fernando CA 1998-2000; Seamens Ch Inst Of Los Angeles San Pedro CA 1993-1998; Pstr Care Asst All SS Par Beverly Hills CA 1992-1994. Mssn to Seafarers 1993; No Amer Maritime Ministers Assn 1993-1998. mts_scotland@onetel.com

UNDERHILL, Scott A (Alb) 912 Route 146, Clifton Park NY 12065 **D S Geo's Ch Clifton Pk NY 2009-** B Schenectady NY 3/7/1969 s Jack Harry Underhill & Martha Jane. BS SUNY at Buffalo 1991; MS SUNY at Buffalo 1993. D 5/30/2009 Bp William Howard Love. m 2/5/1994 Lynne M Kalle c 3. saulmu@nylap.rr.com

UNDERHILL, William Dudley (WA) 25 Nottingham Dr, Kingston MA 02364 B Boston MA 12/10/1931 s Frank Hopewell Underhill & Marion Louise. BA Wesl 1953; BD UTS 1956; Cert EDS 1963; Cert S Geo's Coll Jerusalem IL 1986. D 6/23/1956 P 1/13/1957 Bp Norman B Nash. m 7/20/1991 Sandra Ruth Dahlgren c 2. Int Trin Ch Bridgewater MA 2001-2002; R Chr Epis Ch Clinton MD 1991-1998; Int S Andr's Ch Ayer MA 1989-1991; Int S Jn's Ch Stamford CT 1988-1989; S Dav's Epis Mssn Pepperell MA 1987-1988; Sem Field Educ Supvsr EDS Cambridge MA 1974-1978; R The Par Of S Chrys's Quincy MA 1969-1987; R Trin Epis Ch Wrentham MA 1959-1969; Cur Trin Par Melrose MA 1956-1959. Co-Auth, "Alco," *I Can Take It or Lv It*, Foreward Mvmt Press. Alb Inst 1990-1998; Washington DC Epis Cleric Assn 1991-1998; Washington DC Fllshp of St. Jn 1998. Norman B Nash Fell Dio Massachusetts 1985. exrector@aol.com

UNDERWOOD, Arthur Hugh (Ct) 253 Wyionewood Circle, Apt. A-1, Griffin GA 30224 **Died 12/21/2009** B Paris France 6/1/1921 s Pierson Underwood & Elizabeth. BA Ya 1943; STB Ya Berk 1950; Cert. S Aug's Coll Cbury GB 1965; STM STUSo 1969. D 6/14/1950 Bp Angus Dun P 12/1/1950 Bp Joseph Gillespie Armstrong. c 1. Ord Of S Lk, EUC. ahun@starpower.net

UNDERWOOD, Deborah Ann (Okla) 501 S. Cincinnati Ave., Tulsa OK 74103 B Hollywood CA 8/31/1957 d Norman Ward & Betty. D 6/21/2008 Bp Edward Joseph Konieczny. m 3/20/1981 Michael Underwood c 4. deborahu@att.net

UNDERWOOD, Robert Franklin (CPa) 396 Hollingsworth Ln., Lexington SC 29072 B Mount Carmel PA 7/21/1929 s Lewis Percy Underwood & Florence Mary. BA Dickinson Coll 1951; MDiv GTS 1961. D 6/13/1961 P 2/24/1962 Bp Frederick J Warnecke. m 5/12/1962 Lois Ann Jenkins c 3. Assoc All SS' Epis Ch Hershey PA 1987-1989; Vic All SS Ch Selinsgrove PA 1969-1973; Vic S Mk's Epis Ch Northumberland PA 1969-1973; R Chr Ch New Brighton PA 1966-1969.

UNTERSEHER, Cody Carlton (ND) 17 Sagamore Rd, Bronxville NY 10708 **P Assoc Chr Ch Bronxville NY 2009-** B Bismarck ND 2/23/1976 s Kim D Unterseher & Carla M. BA U of Mary 2003; MA S Jn's TS/Seminay 2007; STM The GTS 2008. D 3/30/2007 P 9/29/2007 Bp Michael Gene Smith. Supply P S Thos Ch New York NY 2008-2009; Assoc Chr Ch Bronxville NY 2007-2008. codyunterseher@gmail.com

UPCHURCH, Stan (Okla) 617 Leaning Elm Dr, Norman OK 73071 **D S Tim's Epis Ch Pauls Vlly OK 2001-; Archv Dio Oklahoma Oklahoma City OK 1992-; D S Jn's Ch Norman OK 1990-** B Ardmore OK 9/15/1946 s Stanley Benjamin Upchurch & Eva Elizabeth. BS U of Oklahoma 1979. D 6/30/1990 Bp Robert Manning Moody. m 5/2/1969 Carol Jo Wages c 1. Dio Oklahoma Oklahoma City OK 2007-2008. Natl Epis Historians and Archv 1990. Cn Jn Davis Awd Natl Epis Historians and Archv 2000. supchurch@episcopaloklahoma.org

UPHAM, Judith Elizabeth (FtW) 9805 Livingston Rd, Fort Washington MD 20744 B Tulsa OK 8/16/1942 d John Dale Upham & Marion Beatrice. BA Rad 1964; MDiv EDS 1967; MS Washington U 1972. D 12/6/1975 P 1/1/1977 Bp William Augustus Jones Jr. S Mk's Ch Candor NY 2004-2007; St Johns Epis Ch Berkshire NY 2004-2007; All SS Ch Fulton NY 2002-2003; Int S Phil's Ch San Jose CA 1999-2002; S Barth's Ch Laytonsville MD 1997-1998; Int S Jas' Ch Indn Hd MD 1995-1996; Int Chr Ch Durham Par Nanjemoy MD 1993-1995; Syracuse Urban Cluster Syracuse NY 1989-1990; Gr Epis Ch Syracuse NY 1979-1989; LocTen S Steph's Ch S Louis MO 1977-1978; Dio Missouri S Louis MO 1975-1978; D S Mk's Ch S Louis MO 1975-1977. revjudy@aol.com

UPTON, David Hugh (USC) 206 W Prentiss Ave, Greenville SC 29605 B Fayetteville NC 4/28/1947 s Richard Upton & Hazel. BA U NC 1969; MDiv VTS 1973. D 6/23/1973 Bp Thomas Augustus Fraser Jr P 3/1/1974 Bp Philip Frederick McNairy. R S Andr's Epis Ch Greenville SC 1997-2007; Chr Ch And Sch Greenville SC 1996-1997; Int R S Andr's Epis Ch Greenville SC 1996-1997; Virginia Epis Sch Lynchburg VA 1987-1996; Ch Of The Gd Shpd Greer SC 1981-1987; Chr Ch Greenville SC 1975-1981. Hon Cn Cathd Of Our Merc Sav Dio Minnesota 1975. du@charter.net

UPTON, Thomas Lee (Neb) 14017 Washington St, Omaha NE 68137 **D S Andr's Ch Omaha NE 2005-; Mem, Bdgt Com Dio Nebraska Omaha NE 2004-** B Omaha NE 3/25/1944 s Carl Murral Upton & Nancy Marie. BSBA U of Nebraska 1967; MBA Creighton U at Omaha 1974. D 4/8/1989 Bp James Daniel Warner. m 11/18/1966 Jane Evelyn Treutler c 2. D H Fam Epis Ch Omaha NE 2002-2005; D S Andr's Ch Omaha NE 1989-2002. tlupton@tconl.com

URANG, Gunnar (Vt) Po Box 306, Norwich VT 05055 B Staten Island NY 5/2/1929 s Olai Urang & Anna. MA U Chi 1951; PhD U Chi 1969. D 6/9/1984 P 12/1/1984 Bp Robert Shaw Kerr. m 6/21/1971 Sarah Catherine Horton c 2. R Geth Ch Proctorsville VT 1986-1994; R S Mk's Ch Springfield VT 1986-1994; Asst Trin Ch Rutland VT 1984-1986. "An Inquirer's Guide to Chr Believing," Wilf and Stock, 2005; "Chas Williams & JRRTolkien," SCM Press, 1971; Auth, "Shadows Of Heaven, Rel & Fantasy In The Writings Of Cs Lewis," Pilgrim Press, 1970. gunnar.urang@valley.net

URBAN JR, Percy Linwood (Pa) The Quadrangle # 2301, 3300 Darby Road, Haverford PA 19041 B Philadelphia PA 4/12/1924 s Percy Linwood Urban & Mary. BA Pr 1946; STB GTS 1948; STM GTS 1954; ThD GTS 1959. D 5/28/1948 P 12/16/1948 Bp Frederick G Budlong. m 6/16/1951 Ann C Coward c 3. Assoc S Ptr's Ch New York NY 1950-1951; Stff Chr Ch Cathd Hartford CT 1948-1950. Auth, "A Short Hist Of Chr Thought (Revised & Enlarged)," Oxf Press, 1995; Auth, "Willam Of Ockams Theol Ethics," *Franciscan Stds*, Annual, 1973; Auth, "Was Luther A Thoroughgoing Determinist?," *Journ Of Theol Stds (April)*, 1971. AAR; Amer Philos Assn; Conf Angl Theologians. Phi Beta Kappa 1946. purban1@swarthmore.edu

URBANEK, Virgina (Me) P.O. Box 455, Houlton ME 04730 **Ch Of The Gd Shpd Houlton ME 2011-** B Merrill WI 3/12/1946 d Gerard Elmer Kohn & Arline Mae. AA Concordia Jr Coll 1966; BA Valparaiso U 1969. D 6/29/2008 Bp Chilton Abbie Richardson Knudsen P 3/21/2009 Bp Stephen Taylor Lane. c 2. S Thos Ch Winn ME 2009-2011. mainebrat@hotmail.com

URE III, Lincoln Richard (U) 80 S 300 E, Salt Lake City UT 84111 **Epis Cmnty Serv Inc Salt Lake City UT 1991-** B Salt Lake City UT 10/4/1947 s Lincoln R Ure & Betty. BA U of Utah 1970; MDiv GTS 1974. D 6/16/1974 P 12/1/1974 Bp Otis Charles. m 8/30/1969 Maureen O'Hara c 1. P-in-c S Lk's Ch Pk City UT 1980-1990; St Marks Hosp Salt Lake City UT 1976-1991; D-In-Trng Ch Of The Gd Shpd Ogden UT 1974-1975. ACPE 1983. maureen.oharaure@utah.edu

URMSON-TAYLOR, Ralph (Okla) 47a Via Porta Perlici PG, Assisi OK 06081 Italy B Rochdale England 1/26/1928 s Ralph Urmson Taylor & Lucy. BD Kelham Theol Coll 1956; MA U of Tulsa 1972; Manchester Coll 1974. Trans from Church Of England 5/1/1967 as Priest Bp Chilton Powell. Holland Hall Sch Tulsa OK 1980-1993; Trin Ch Tulsa OK 1977-1993; P-in-c S Bede's Ch Cleveland OK 1971-1973; Asst P Trin Ch Tulsa OK 1962-1965.

USHER JR, Guy Randolph (Eau) 303 S Hollybrook Dr, Chillicothe IL 61523 **Int R S Paul's Ch Hudson WI 2007-** B Hayward WI 3/29/1971 s Guy Randolph Usher & Evelyn Ann. MDiv Nash; BA Estrn Illinois U 1993; MA Estrn Illinois U 1994. D 12/21/1996 P 6/1/1997 Bp William Charles Wantland. S Kath's Ch Owen WI 2000-2007; Vic S Fran Epis Ch Dunlap IL 1997-2000. guyusher@tds.net

UTLEY, Lathrop Palmer (USC) 2273 Whippoorwill Ln, Elgin SC 29045 B Poughkeepsie NY 2/21/1927 s Romeyn Lathrop Utley & Portia. BA U of Maryland 1951; GTS 1954; MA LIU 1973. D 6/12/1954 P 12/18/1954 Bp Benjamin M Washburn. m 6/14/1958 Florence Ellen Hambley c 1. Off Of Bsh For ArmdF New York NY 1967-1969; R S Ptr's Ch Medford NJ 1964-1967; R Ch Of The Ascen Gloucester City NJ 1958-1964. lathropu@peoplepc.com

UZUETA JR, Luis (Ak) 1392 Benshoof Dr, North Pole AK 99705 **S Jude's Epis Ch No Pole AK 2004-** B Deming NM 9/7/1947 s Luis Uzueta & Anita. BA New Mex Highlands U 1970; MDiv Nash 1977. D 6/4/1977 P 12/1/1977 Bp James Daniel Warner. m 3/19/1970 Lona C Uzueta. Dio Alaska Fairbanks AK 1991-2000; Vic S Mk's Ch Gordon NE 1980-1991; Vic S Mary's Ch: Holly Rushville NE 1980-1991; Asst S Matt's Ch Lincoln NE 1977-1980; P-in-c Trin Memi Epis Ch Crete NE 1977-1980. Auth, "Soup in the Sandhills," *Jubilee Journ*, Jub. SocMary 1976. POCO@ACSALASKA.NET

V

✠ VACHE, Rt Rev C(laude) Charles (SVa) 216 Swimming Point Walk, Portsmouth VA 23704 **Died 11/1/2009** B New Bern,NC 8/4/1926 s Jean Andre Vache & Edith Virginia. BA U NC 1949; MDiv SWTS 1952; Fllshp Coll of Preachers 1961; DD SWTS 1976; DD VTS 1976; DD S Paul Coll 1977. D 6/11/1952 P 6/11/1953 Bp George P Gunn Con 5/29/1976 for SVa. Auth, *Portsmouth Par*. Hon DD S Paul's Coll Lawrenceville Va; Hon DD SWTS Evanston IL; Phi Beta Kappa U NC; Hon DD VTS. cvache@surfree.com

VAFIS, John Symon (NCal) PO Box 1044, Colusa CA 95932 B Detroit MI 12/29/1938 s Symon Vafis & Annie. BA Stan 1960; MA U Pgh 1965. D 5/15/2005 P 11/20/2005 Bp Jerry Alban Lamb. m 3/28/1960 Patricia Vafis c 1. revjohn@ststephens-colusa.org

VAGGIONE OHC, Richard Paul (Cal) 1601 Oxford St, Berkeley CA 94709 B San Jose CA 1/19/1945 s Roger Cesar Vaggione & Evelyn Howell. BA Santa Clara U 1966; BA Cath U of Louvain 1969; STB GTS 1970; STM GTS 1970; PhD Oxf 1976. D 6/27/1970 Bp C Kilmer Myers P 2/1/1971 Bp Jonathan Goodhue Sherman. All Souls Par In Berkeley Berkeley CA 1992-1993; Int S Ambr Epis Ch Foster City CA 1991-1992; Int S Clem's Ch Berkeley CA 1989-1990; Ch Of The Epiph Corcoran CA 1979-1980; Asst P S Jas Epis Ch Scarborough ME 1977-1978; Int S Jn's Epis Ch Clayton CA 1976-1977; Lectr In Medieval Latin The GTS New York NY 1971-1972; Cur S Lk's Ch E Hampton NY 1970-1971. Auth, "Over All Asia?"; Auth, "Journ Of Biblic Lit"; Auth, "Theo Of Mapsuestia'S Contra Eunomium". SBL. vaggione@rogers.com

VAGUENER, Martha (SwFla) 3105 Short Leaf St, Zephyrhills FL 33543 B Boston MA 9/11/1945 d Hugo Norden & Mary Frances. BA Bos 1967; M.Ed. Salem St Coll Salem MA 1971; MA Providence Coll 1978; MDiv EDS 1985; CAES Boston Coll 2004. D 7/13/1985 P 1/26/1986 Bp George Nelson Hunt III. m 6/28/1969 Raymond Vaguener. S Eliz's Epis Ch Zephyrhills FL 2004-2010; R S Paul's Ch Peabody MA 1998-2004; Vic S Jn's Ch Millville MA 1988-1998; Asst Chr Ch In Lonsdale Lincoln RI 1987-1988; Dio Rhode Island Providence RI 1985-1987. AAUW 1990; Assn of Psychol Type 1984-2010; Catechesis of the Gd Shpd 2007; MECA 1999; NECCA 1999. mvaguener@aol.com

VAIL, Jean Parker (Chi) 305 Sutherland Ct, Durham NC 27712 **Assoc S Matt's Epis Ch Hillsborough NC 1999-** B Santa Barbara CA 9/24/1932 d Henry Burr Parker & Emily Theresa. BA Wellesley Coll 1954; MDiv SWTS 1985; DMin SWTS 1993. D 9/20/1985 Bp James Winchester Montgomery P 5/24/1986 Bp Frank Tracy Griswold III. m 12/29/1956 Thomas Peale Vail c 3. Int S Mart's By The Lake Epis Minnetonka Bch MN 1996-1998; SWTS Evanston IL 1994-1998; Cathd Ch Of S Mk Minneapolis MN 1994-1996; Int S Helena's Ch Willowbrook IL 1993; Provost Cathd Of S Jas Chicago IL 1990-1991; Int S Elis's Ch Glencoe IL 1989-1990; Assoc S Andr's Ch Downers Grove IL 1987-1989; D All SS Ch Wstrn Sprg IL 1985-1986. Auth, "In the Name of GOD," Chap Hill Press, 2004. BEC- Dioc Of NC 2004; Chapl: Soc. of Comp of H Cross 2000. Hon Cn Cathd of S Jas Chicago Chicago 1998. jeanvail@att.net

VALADEZ-JAIME, Agustin (Az) 2025 W Indian School Rd Apt 907, Phoenix AZ 85015 **Dio Mex 2007-** B 11/6/1975 D 6/19/2004 Bp Kirk Stevan Smith. JAIMEPHO@HOTMAIL.COM

VALANDRA, Linda Beth (SD) 410 University Ave, Hot Springs SD 57747 **S Lk's Ch Hot Sprg SD 2005-** B Burnet TX 1/5/1953 d Thomas Willard Massey & Marion Roselee. D 6/11/2005 Bp Creighton Leland Robertson. c 1.

VALANTASIS, Richard (Mo) 17 Wildflower Way, Santa Fe NM 87506 **Cn Theol Dio The Rio Grande Albuquerque NM 2011-** B Canton OH 12/6/1946 s Louis Valantasis & Irene. BA Hope Coll 1968; EDS 1972; ThM Harvard DS 1982; ThD Harvard DS 1988. D 6/9/1973 P 3/1/1974 Bp John Melville Burgess. m 6/10/1973 Janet Carlson. Ch Of S Jn The Evang Boston MA 1987-1992; R S Jn's Ch Winthrop MA 1975-1978; Cur S Paul's Ch Natick MA 1974-1975. "Beliefnet Guide to Gnosticism and Other Vanished Christianities," Doubleday, 2006; "The New Q: Translation and Commentary," T & T Clark, 2005; "Centuries of Holiness," Continuum, 2005; "Rel of Late Antiquity in Pract," Pr Press, 2000; "The Gospel of Thos," *NT Readings*, Routledge, 1997; Auth, "Asceticism," Oxf Press, 1995; Auth, "Third Century Sprtl Guides," *Harvard Dissertations in Rel*, Fortress Perss, 1991. AAR; SBL. Woodrow Wilson Fell 1968. rvalantasis@usa.net

VALCOURT, Theodore Philippe-Francois (CGC) 401 Live Oak Ave, Pensacola FL 32507 **Off Of Bsh For ArmdF New York NY 2007-** B Savannah GA 3/9/1965 s Arthur Felix Valcourt & Dorothy S. BA Morris Brown Coll 1989; MPH Savannah St U 1991; MDiv Interdenominational Theol Cntr Atlanta GA 1995; MS Troy St U 2004. D 2/17/2007 P 7/28/2007 Bp Philip Menzie Duncan II. m 5/20/1995 Rosalyn Warren c 3. theodore.valcourt@us.army.mil

VALDEMA, Pierre-Henry Fritz (Hai) Eglise Sainte Trinite, Rue Mgr Guilloux, Box 1309, Port-Au-Prince Haiti **Dio Haiti Ft Lauderdale FL 1979-** B 7/11/1951 s Charles Dorcal & Alda Desvarieux. Coll Philadelphie Degre Secondary 73; Theol Etude Theologique. D 7/29/1979 P 5/1/1980 Bp Luc Anatole Jacques Garnier. m 9/6/1984 Marie Carmel Germain.

VALDES, Paul Anthony (NC) 8105 Summit Springs Ct, Browns Summit NC 27214 B New York NY 1/27/1939 s Paul Valdes & Roslyn. BA Greensboro Coll. D 6/26/2005 Bp Michael Bruce Curry. m 5/4/1974 June Swanston-Valdes c 6.

VALDEZ, Pedro Antonio (Micr) 826 Howard St, Carthage MO 64836 B Guatemala City GT 10/1/1943 s Pedro Valdez Garcia & Clotilde. Esciela De Comercio Guatemala; U Mariano Galvez De Guatemala Gt; BA Sem Santotomas Apostol Gt 1980; Lic Theol U Luteran Of The El Salvador C.A. Sv 1997. D 7/4/1980 P 10/1/1981 Bp Anselmo Carral-Solar. m 8/8/1968 Lilia Salazar. Dio W Missouri Kansas City MO 2000-2008; Dio Guatemala Guatemala City 1980-1999. pedroantvaldez@hotmail.com

VALENTINE III, A(llen) Wilson (Ak) 924 C St, Juneau AK 99801 **S Phil's Ch Wrangell AK 2011-** B Richmond VA 2/4/1952 s Allen Wilson Valentine & Dora Jane. Chris Newport U 1972; BA U of Alaska 1977; MDiv Bex 1991. D 5/9/1991 Bp George Clinton Harris P 8/1/1992 Bp Steven Charleston. m 6/2/1982 Priscilla Harris. Presiding Judge Eccl Crt Dio Alaska Fairbanks AK 1995-2001; R S Brendan's Epis Ch Juneau AK 1993-2000; Asst Trin Ch Rochester NY 1991-1992. Gvnr'S Awd For Heroism St Of Alaska 1984. awv431@netscape.net

VALENTINE JR, John Carney (WVa) 206 E 2nd St, Weston WV 26452 **R S Paul's Ch Weston WV 2008-** B Logan WV 7/1/1955 s John Carney Valentine & Norma Jean. MDiv St Marys Sem 1985. Rec from Roman Catholic 5/3/2008 Bp William Michie Klusmeyer. m 12/30/2000 Bertha Valentine c 2. bigjohnwvu@yahoo.com

VALENTINE VI, Mann Satterwhite (Lex) PO Box 109, Ashland KY 41105 **Died 12/29/2010** B Richmond VA 10/19/1947 s Mann Satterwhite Valentine & Dorothy. Cert Int Mnstry Prog; BA Ohio U; MDiv VTS. D 5/26/1973 Bp Robert Bruce Hall P 12/23/1973 Bp David Shepherd Rose. c 3. msv101947@gmail.com

VALENTINE, Peggy Lee (NwT) St Mark's Episcopal Church, 3150 Vogel St, Abilene TX 79603 **D S Mk's Epis Ch Abilene TX 2007-** B Corning NY 11/13/1946 d Robert Frank Lawrence & Florence Irene. BS Fredonia St Univ. of NY 1968; Masters Hardin-Simmons U 1985. D 10/31/2007 Bp C(harles) Wallis Ohl. m 4/7/1973 Gary Valentine c 2. DOK 2006. pegleeval123@yahoo.com

VALENTINE, Ronald Andrew (Chi) St James the Less Episcopal Church, 550 Sunset Ridge Rd, Northfield IL 60093 **Chapl The Epis Ch Of S Jas The Less Northfield IL 2000-** B Chicago IL 1/30/1942 s Andrew Lincold Valentine & Dorothy Roltsch. BS NWU 1965; MBA NWU 1968. D 1/19/2008 Bp Victor Alfonso Scantlebury. m 11/21/1980 Deborah Valentine c 4. chaplainronvalentine@yahoo.com

VALIATH, Abraham J (Be) 365 Lafayette Ave., Palmerton PA 18071 **R S Jn's Epis Ch Palmerton PA 2008-** B Mylapra India 7/24/1944 s Thomas Abraham & Sarah. BD Leonard Theol Coll 1969; MA Mysore U 1989; M. Th Serampore U 1997. Trans from Mar Thoma Syrian Church of Malabar 6/1/2008 Bp Paul Victor Marshall. c 2. Assoc S Andr's Epis Ch Allentown PA 2007-2008. abraham_valiath@yahoo.com

VALLE, Valerie Ann (ECR) 170 Seacliff Dr, Pismo Beach CA 93449 **Dio El Camino Real Monterey CA 2006-; R S Barn Ch Arroyo Grande CA 2006-** B Lakewood OH 2/19/1948 d Ralph Albert Hart & Lorna Mary. BA Carnegie Mellon U 1970; MS U Pgh 1973; PhD U Pgh 1974; MDiv CDSP 1991. D 6/8/1991 P 6/7/1992 Bp William Edwin Swing. m 6/7/1969 Ronald Stephen Valle c 3. Vic S Alb's Epis Ch Brentwood CA 1994-2006; S Anne's Ch Fremont CA 1991-1992. Auth, "Var arts". revvalerie@charter.net

VALLE-PLAZA, Juan Nelson (EcuC) No address on file. B Penipe EC 3/19/1963 s Carlos Valle & Rosa. U of Loja; Epis TS 1997. D 7/14/1996 P 3/1/1998 Bp Alfredo Morante-España. m 1/6/1993 Mireya Pinto. Litoral Dio Ecuador Guayaquil EQ EC 1997-2001.

VAN, Maron Ines (Ore) 4435 Fox Hollow Rd, Eugene OR 97405 **D Ch Of The Resurr Eugene OR 1988-** B North Bend OR 9/7/1936 d Earl Raymond Lyons & Evelyn Leona. U of Oregon. D 1/9/1988 Bp Robert Louis Ladehoff. m 6/22/1957 Maurice Allen Van c 4. maronvan@ix.netcom.com

VAN ANTWERPEN, Alanna Mary (NH) 214 Main St, Nashua NH 03060 **Asst Ch Of The Gd Shpd Nashua NH 2010-** B Danbury CT 6/3/1975 d Thomas Francis Ryan & Maureen Patricia. BA S Anselm Coll 1997; MDiv Jesuit TS at Berkeley 2007; Cert of Angl Stds CDSP 2008. D 7/1/2010 P 1/6/2011 Bp V Gene Robinson. m 6/23/2007 Franklin Van Antwerpen c 1. alanna@cgsnashua.org

VAN ATTA, Ralph Sherwood (Pa) 6505 Tabor Ave Apt 5116, Philadelphia PA 19111 B Binghamton NY 8/24/1919 s Ralph Oscar Van Atta & Jessie Birdsall. BS SUNY 1944; BD Ya Berk 1949. D 6/18/1949 Bp Walter M Higley P 11/1/1950 Bp Malcolm E Peabody. Int All SS Ch Rhawnhurst Philadelphia PA 1984-1985; The Ch Of Emm And The Gd Shpd Philadelphia PA 1980-1981; H Apos And Medtr Philadelphia PA 1978-1979; Dn Convoc Dio Pennsylvania Philadelphia PA 1962-1964; R S Paul's Ch Philadelphia PA 1957-1975; Asst S Barth's Ch Baltimore MD 1955-1957; Mssnr Chr Epis Ch Willard NY 1951-1954; Mssnr Ch Of The Epiph Trumansburg NY 1951-1954.

VANAUKER, Margaret Elizabeth (Md) 225 Bowie Trl, Lusby MD 20657 B Youngstown OH 7/13/1945 d Earl Hudson Young & Gladys Margaret. BA Youngstown St U 1968; MLa Jn Hopkins U 1977; MA S Mary Sem Ecuminical Inst Baltimore MD 1994. D 6/12/1993 Bp A(lbert) Theodore Eastman. m 12/20/1968 Joseph William Van Auker c 2. D Middleham & S Ptr's Par Lusby MD 2001-2008; D Chr Ch Columbia MD 1999-2001; D S Andr's Ch Pasadena MD 1993-1995. NAAD. mvanauker@direcway.com

VANBAARS, Sven Layne (Va) PO Box 146, Gloucester VA 23061 **R Abingdon Epis Ch White Marsh VA 2010-** B Portsmouth VA 5/25/1962 s Frans L vanBaars & Jacquelyn Kelley. Un-PSCE; AA Craven Cmnty Coll 1983; BA E Carolina U 1985; MPA E Carolina U 1988; MDiv The Prot Epis TS 2008. D 5/24/2008 P 12/6/2008 Bp Peter James Lee. m 8/3/1991 Jennifer W Warfel. Asst S Mart's Epis Ch Williamsburg VA 2008-2010; Dio Virginia Richmond VA 2000-2006. svanbaars@yahoo.com

VAN BEVEREN, Eugene Charles (Neb) 3041 SW Isaac Ave, Pendleton OR 97801 **Lic Dio Estrn Oregon The Dalles OR 2008-; Lic Dio Estrn Oregon The Dalles OR 2008-** B Hood River OR 4/20/1935 s Henry Van Beveren & Mary. BA Mt Ang Abbey 1958; BS E Oregon St La Grande OR 1973. Rec from Roman Catholic 6/1/1981 as Priest Bp Rustin Ray Kimsey. m 7/28/1973 Charlanne E Meyrovich c 3. Vic Ch Of The Incarn Greg SD 2002-2003; Vic Ch Of The Resurr (Chap) Roslyn WA 1991-2002; R Gr Ch Ellensburg WA 1991-2002; Dio Oregon Portland OR 1988-1991; S Chris's Ch Port Orford OR 1984-1988; S Jn-By-The-Sea Epis Ch Bandon OR 1984-1988; S Matt's Epis Ch Gold Bch OR 1984-1988; P-in-c S Andr's Epis Ch Prineville OR 1980-1983.

VAN BRUNT, Thomas Harvey (SO) 534 Chapel Road, Amelia OH 45102 B Willard OH USA 12/5/1943 s Percy Irving Van Brunt & Emma Lou. BA OH SU; MA OH SU 1968; PhD Indiana U 1976; MDiv STUSo 1986. D 6/7/1986 P 12/7/1986 Bp Don Adger Wimberly. m 6/14/1969 Nancye Eileen Knowles c 2. Int S Aug's Epis Ch Danville IN 2009-2011; Vic Ch Of The Gd Samar Amelia OH 2006-2008; R S Ptr's Epis Ch Delaware OH 1996-2005; Dn Wstrn Convoc Dio Upper So Carolina Columbia SC 1993-1996; R Ch Of The Resurr Greenwood SC 1990-1996; Dio Lexington Lexington KY 1986-1990; Vic S Alb's Ch Morehead KY 1986-1990; Vic S Fran' Epis Ch Flemingsburg KY 1986-1990. CT 1986. Fell in Res Univ of the So 2008; Fllshp Coll Of Preachers Coll of Preachers 1996. philippiansfoursix@roadrunner.com

VAN BUREN, Robert Barrett (Los) 15524 Pintura Dr, Hacienda Heights CA 91745 **D Asstg S Jn's Mssn La Verne CA 2008-** B Norwalk CA 1/25/1960 s Robert Van Buren & Muriel. BA California St U 1989; MDiv GTS 2005. D 11/1/2005 Bp Joseph Jon Bruno. m 11/19/1988 Penelope Barrett Van Buren c 2. D/Cur S Jas' Par So Pasadena CA 2007-2008; D Dio Los Angeles Los Angeles CA 2006-2007; D/Cur The Ch Of The Ascen Sierra Madre CA 2005-2006. rbvanburen@msn.com

VANCE, Bill (CFla) 26 Willow Dr, Orlando FL 32807 **Chr The King Epis Ch Orlando FL 2010-** B Goshen NY 10/1/1951 s Walter William Vance & Vivian Constance. MA Amer Grad U; BS Excelsior U 1989. D 12/11/2010 Bp John Wadsworth Howe. m 10/23/1971 Sue Vesper c 2. wvance51@gmail.com

VANCE, Christina Marie (Alb) 2331 15th St, Troy NY 12180 B Athens OH 7/6/1978 d Lowell Earl Vance & Margaret Rosina. BS Ohio U 1999; MDiv TESM 2010. D 6/5/2010 P 12/18/2010 Bp William Howard Love. asongofascents@yahoo.com

VANCE, Marc(us) Patrick (Ind) 2651 California St., Columubus IN 47201 **R S Paul's Ch Columbus IN 2006-** B Versailles KY 7/1/1962 s Henry Moss Vance & Patricia Ann. BS Estrn Kentucky U 1986; BS Estrn Kentucky U 1987; MDiv STUSo 1997. D 8/23/1997 P 3/20/1998 Bp Don Adger Wimberly. m 5/8/1993 Leticia Lynn Christison c 3. Assoc R H Trin Epis Ch Melbourne FL 1999-2006; Cn Assoc Gr And H Trin Cathd Kansas City MO 1997-1999; Yth Dir S Jn's Ch Versailles KY 1990-1993. makersmarc@gmail.com

VANCE, Timothy Keith (SwVa) PO Box 344, Sewanee TN 37375 B Norwalk CA 10/31/1958 s Dennis Keith Vance & Donna Kay. BA OR SU 1981; MDiv Yale DS 1986; STUSo 1997; U So 2008. D 5/25/1989 Bp William Hopkins Folwell P 11/30/1989 Bp Charles Jones III. m 9/1/2010 Sherry Vance c 2. R S Paul's Epis Ch Salem VA 1999-2006; R S Matthews Auburn WA 1992-1999; Vic S Jas Ch Lewistown MT 1989-1992. Auth, "Fly Fishing And Par Mnstry," *LivCh*, 2003; Auth, "Advice For Search Committees," *LivCh*. frvance@earthlink.net

VAN CULIN JR, Samuel (WA) 3900 Watson Place, NW #5D-B, Washington DC 20016 B Honolulu HI 9/20/1930 s Samuel Van Culin & Susie. DD VTS; BA Pr 1952; BD VTS 1955. D 6/3/1955 Bp Frederick D Goodwin P 11/30/1955 Bp Harry S Kennedy. Wrld Mssn Off Epis Ch Cntr New York NY 1961-1982; Asst R S Jn's Ch Georgetown Par Washington DC 1958-1960; Cur S Andr's Cathd Honolulu HI 1955-1956. Hon Cn Cbury Cathd Engl; Hon Cn Ibadan Cathd Nigeria; Hon Cn Prov Of So Afr; Hon Cn S Andrews Cathd, Hawaii; Res Cn Washington Natl Cathd.

VAN CULIN, T(homas) Andrew K. (Colo) 1350 Washington St, Denver CO 80203 **P-in-c S Chris Sum Chap Winter Harbor ME 2011-; S Jn's Cathd Denver CO 2009-** B Honolulu HI 2/22/1973 s Thomas Meyers Van Culin & Sarah Anne. BA Davidson Coll 1995; MDiv EDS 1999. D 7/18/1999 P 3/5/2000 Bp Richard Sui On Chang. m 1/9/2004 Jessica Lohr Van Culin c 1. The Epis Ch Of Beth-By-The-Sea Palm Bch FL 2005-2009; R S Dav Of The Hills Epis Ch Woodland Pk CO 2003-2005; P-in-c S Dav Of The Hills Epis Ch Woodland Pk CO 2001-2002; S Jas Epis Ch Kamuela HI 1999-2002; Yth Min Chr Ch Kealakekua HI 1999-2001; Yth Min S Aug's Epis Chap Kapaau HI 1999-2001; W Hawaii Yth Mnstry Kamuela HI 1999-2001. andrew.vanculin@me.com

VAN CULIN, Thomas Meyers (Haw) 2578-F Pacific Heights Rd, Honolulu HI 96813 **Vic S Matt's Epis Ch Waimanalo HI 1992-** B Honolulu HI 3/6/1938 s Samuel Van Culin & Susie Ellen. AA Barstow Cmnty Coll 1964; BS California St U 1966; MDiv CDSP 1990. D 9/1/1991 P 3/15/1992 Bp Donald Purple Hart. m 12/20/1992 Ernestina Williams c 1. S Lk's Epis Ch Honolulu HI 2007-2010; Dn Winward Deanry Dio Hawaii Honolulu HI 1996-1998; S Matt's Epis Ch Waimanalo HI 1993-2007. Ka Papa Anaina Hawaii, O Kristo. kahutom.vanculin@hawaiiantel.net

VANDAGRIFF, Mary Cordelia (Ala) 220 S Wood Rd, Homewood AL 35209 B Manhattan KS 11/19/1931 d William Brackett & Tacy. MA U of Alabama. D 10/30/2004 Bp Henry Nutt Parsley Jr. c 4. mavanda@bellsouth.net

VAN DEN BLINK, A(rie) J(ohannes) (CNY) 315 W Washington Ave, Elmira NY 14901 **P-in-c S Paul's Ch Troy PA 2010-** B Mojowarno Java ID 4/30/1934 s Jan van den Blink & Tine. BA Trin Hartford CT 1955; BD Yale DS 1962; PhD PrTS 1972. D 7/19/1993 P 1/22/1994 Bp William George Burrill. m 6/30/1956 Katherine Nelson Mooers c 3. Int Gr Epis Ch Elmira NY 2000-2009; Prof of Ascetical & Pstr Theol Bex Columbus OH 1993-2000. "Alle malen zal ik wenen: traumaverwerking en spiritualiteit," *Psyche en Geloof*, Boekencentrum Uitgevers, 2005; "Late Vocation: A Personal Reflection," *The Angl Cath*, Affirming Angl Catholicism, 2004; "Grp Sprtl Direction in Sem," *The Lived Experience of Grp Sprtl Direction*, Paulist Press, 2003; "Thoughts on the Trsfg," *The Angl Cath*, Affirming Angl Catholicism, 2002; Auth, "Reflections on Sprtlty in Angl Theol Educ," *ATR*, ATR, 1999; Auth, "Trauma Reactivation in Pstr Counslg," *Amer Journ of Pstr Counslg*, Haworth Press, 1998; Auth, "Seeking God: The Way of the Sprt: Some Reflections on Sprtlty and Pstr," *Journ of Pstr Theol*, Soc of Pstr Theol, 1995. Affirming Angl Catholicism 1996; AAPC 1972; Soc Pstr Theol 1990. Pres AAPC 1998; Sr Choice Awd/Outstanding Fac Mem Bex and CRDS 1998; Distingushed Contribution Awd AAPC Estrn Reg 1997. ajvdblink@stny.rr.com

VANDERAU JR, Robert Julian (RI) 2305 Edgewater Drive, Apt 1718, Orlando FL 32804 B Columbus OH 12/7/1945 s Robert Julian Vanderau & Margaret Jeanne. BS OH SU 1968; MDiv VTS 1976. D 6/10/1976 P 12/17/1976 Bp John Mc Gill Krumm. P-in-c S Richard's Ch Winter Pk FL 2010-2011; Cn to the Ordnry Dio Rhode Island Providence RI 2005-2007; R Ch Of The Ascen Cranston RI 1994-2005; Cn Precentor Cathd Ch Of S Lk Orlando FL 1982-1994; Asst to the R Ch Of The Gd Shpd Jacksonville FL 1980-1982; Cur Chr Ch Prince Geo's Par Rockville MD 1976-1980. AAM 1997; ADLMC 1986-2001; CODE 2005. robertvanderau@gmail.com

VANDERCOOK, Peter John (Chi) 208 Nesheim Trl, Mount Horeb WI 53572 B Derby CT 7/25/1935 s Willard Elmer Vandercook & Margaret Anne. BA Ya 1956; STB Berkley DS 1959. D 6/11/1959 P 5/27/1960 Bp Walter H Gray. Vic The Ch Of The H Innoc Hoffman Schaumburg IL 1970-1995; Vic S Chad Epis Ch Loves Pk IL 1964-1970; Cur S Lk's Ch Evanston IL 1962-1964; Cur S Jn's Ch Stamford CT 1959-1962.

VANDERCOOK, Ross Allan (Mich) 9900 N Meridian Rd, Pleasant Lake MI 49272 B Detroit MI 2/21/1949 s Edsall Vandercook & Naomi. EdS Cntrl Michigan U; MA Wayne. D 11/11/2010 P 7/2/2011 Bp Wendell Nathaniel Gibbs Jr. m 6/16/1973 Susan Elizabeth Hanson c 2. rsvandercook@att.net

VANDERCOOK, Susan Elizabeth (Mich) 9900 N Meridian Rd, Pleasant Lake MI 49272 B Tucson AZ 10/6/1949 d Raymond Hanson & Betty. BA MI SU 1970; JD Wayne 1975. D 11/11/2010 P 7/2/2011 Bp Wendell Nathaniel Gibbs Jr. m 6/16/1973 Ross Allan Vandercook c 2. rsvandercook@att.net

VAN DER HIEL, Rudolph J (CPa) 156 Jones Road, RR 1, Comp 5, Parry Sound ON P2A 2W7 Canada B Philadelphia PA 1/25/1940 s Peter C van der Hiel & Johanna J. BA Susquahanna U 1963; JD Tem 1966; MDiv Bex 1984. D 6/8/1984 P 5/1/1985 Bp Charlie Fuller McNutt Jr. m 6/6/1964 Mary Lynne Copestick c 4. R Trin Wellsboro PA 1991-2005; R S Jas Ch Mansfield PA 1985-2005. Auth, "Rudolph J. van der Hiel," *A Night in the Tioga Cnty Jail*. Mansfield Min, PA Coun Ch 1984-2005; W Muskoka Mnstrl Assn 2005. Pearl Jones Awd for Serv to Appalachia Cmsn on Rel in Appalachian. 1994; 1993 Outstanding Citizen Mansfield Area ChmbrCom 1993; Outstanding Serv to Law Enforcement Awd Tioga Cnty Law Enforcement Off Assn 1979. rjvdh@quik.com

VANDERMARK, Fayetta (Alb) 825 Covered Bridge Rd, Unadilla NY 13849 B Walton NY 5/22/1949 d Hilton William Shackelton & Dorothy Jean. D 9/9/2001 Bp Daniel William Herzog. m 9/3/1967 Roy James VanDermark c 3. D Chr Ch Gilbertsville NY 2001-2005. The Jas C. Earl Achivement Awd Unatego Bd Educ 2002; Gd Neighbor Unadilla ChmbrCom 1999; Employee Of The Year Unatego Jr/Sr HS. royvandermark@frontiernet.net

VANDERMARK, Roy James (Alb) 825 Covered Bridge Rd, Unadilla NY 13849 **D Vic in Charge S Tim's Ch Westford NY 2008-** B Sidney NY 5/28/1947 s Fredrick Raymond VanDermark & Pauline. D 6/12/2004 Bp Daniel William Herzog. m 9/3/1967 Fayetta VanDermark c 3. D S Matt's Ch Unadilla NY 2004-2008. Gd Neighbor Awd Unadilla Chamber if Commerce 1999; Fireman of the year Otsego Cnty 1998.

VANDERMEER, Leigh Anne (Chi) 1081 Westfield Way, Mundelein IL 60060 **Int Cbury NW Evanston IL 2009-** B Harvard IL 8/15/1958 d Matthew Michael Schalz & Beverley Joanne. BS Wstrn Illinois U 1981; MDiv SWTS 2005. D 6/18/2005 P 12/17/2005 Bp William Dailey Persell. c 2. Assoc S Mich's Ch Barrington IL 2005-2009. lvmeer@sbcglobal.net

VANDERPOEL, Frederick Thomas (Del) 300 Saint Mark Ave Apt 2232, Lititz PA 17543 B La Romana DO 3/17/1925 s Denton Robinson VanderPoel & Elizabeth. BA Cor 1950; PDS 1957. D 6/29/1957 Bp Austin Pardue P 12/21/1957 Bp William S Thomas. m 9/8/1951 Martha Biemesderfer c 4. Assoc S Phil's Ch Laurel DE 1992-1997; Bp's Asst Congreg Dvlpmt Dio Delaware Wilmington DE 1989-1992; Vic S Steph's Ch Harrington DE 1989-1992; Int Gr Epis Ch Alexandria VA 1988-1989; Int S Ptr's Ch Salisbury MD 1987-1988; Int S Paul's Epis Ch Alexandria VA 1985-1987; Chr Ch Cedar Rapids IA 1984-1985; Chair Strng Com Dio W Missouri Kansas City MO 1979-1981; Exec Com VIM Dio W Missouri Kansas City MO 1979-1980; R S Andr's Ch Kansas City MO 1978-1984; Dioc Coun Dio W Missouri Kansas City MO 1978-1982; Stndg Com Dio Maryland Baltimore MD 1971-1975; R St Martins-In-The-Field Ch Severna Pk MD 1966-1977; Chapt Pgh Trin Cathd Pittsburgh PA 1960-1964; Min in charge S Jas Epis Ch Pittsburgh PA 1957-1958. fvanderpoel@dejazzd.com

VANDERSLICE, Thomas Arthur (NH) 22 Stratham Grn, Stratham NH 03885 B Chicago IL 6/18/1928 s Thomas Henry Vanderslice & Maria. BA Ripon Coll Ripon WI 1951; MDiv GTS 1954. D 6/2/1954 P 12/21/1954 Bp Gerald Francis Burrill. m 2/23/1957 Marion McMurray c 2. Int Trin Ch Hampton NH 2008-2009; Int S Andr's Ch Manchester NH 2000-2004; Int Ch Of The Trsfg Derry NH 2000-2002; Int S Geo's Epis Ch York Harbor ME 1999-2000; Int S Geo's Ch Durham NH 1995-1998; R The Ch Of S Jn The Evang Flossmoor IL 1978-1993; R S Mk's Ch Geneva IL 1966-1978; Vic S Ann's Ch Woodstock IL 1961-1966; Assoc Trin Epis Ch Cranford NJ 1960-1961; R S Mart's Ch Chicago IL 1957-1959; Cur The Ch Of S Jn The Evang Flossmoor IL 1954-1957. tsavan@comcast.net

VANDERVEEN, Peter Todd (Pa) 230 Pennswood Rd, Bryn Mawr PA 19010 **R Ch Of The Redeem Bryn Mawr PA 2009-** B Detroit MI 7/6/1961 s Edward John Vanderveen & Dawn. BA Calvin Coll 1983; MDiv Ya Berk 1986. D 6/10/1989 P 2/24/1990 Bp Arthur Edward Walmsley. m 1/30/2008 Patricia Houston Powell. R S Ann's Epis Ch Old Lyme CT 1995-2009; Assoc S Chris's Ch Chatham MA 1993-1995; Cur Trin Ch Branford CT 1989-1993. "Ethics and the Ch," *New Engl Watershed*, 2006. Assoc of Angl Musicians 2002. ptvanderveen@verizon.net

VAN DERVOORT, V(irginia) (Tenn) 1106 Chickering Park Dr, Nashville TN 37215 **Assoc S Paul's Ch Franklin TN 1998-** B Indianapolis IN 1/4/1941 d Edward Tillman Baumgart & Virginia Helen. U of Wisconsin 1959; RN Jas Ward Thorne Sch of Nrsng 1963; BA Stephens Coll 1975; MDiv Van 1983; Cert Epis TS of The SW 1995. D 6/24/1995 Bp Chester Lovelle Talton P 1/13/1996 Bp Frederick Houk Borsch. m 3/27/1965 Robert Lordner Van Dervoort c 2. D Epis Ch Of The Redeem Irving TX 1995-1996. Cross Wind Retreat Cntr (Bd) 2000-2004; ECW; EWC Bd Mem 1985; Pstr Counslg Cntr of TN (Bd Mem) 1999. hon in Ethics Vanderbilt DS 1983; hon in the field Educ Vanderbilt DS 1983. ann@stpaulsfranklin.com

VANDER WEL, Brian Lee (WA) Christ Church, 600 Farmington Rd W, Accokeek MD 20607 **R Chr Ch S Jn's Par Accokeek MD 2007-** B Battlecreek MI 11/21/1967 s Norman Charles Vander Wel & Lois Annette. BA Calvin Coll 1990; MDiv w hon TESM 1999. D 6/12/1999 P 12/1/1999 Bp Robert William Duncan. m 12/17/1993 Elizabeth Page Bogard. Asst Chr Epis Ch Charlottesville VA 2001-2006; Exam Chapl in Ch Hist for Deaconal Ord Dio Pittsburgh Monroeville PA 2000-2001; Int S Chris's Epis Ch Cranberry Twp PA 2000; Asst Ch Of The Nativ Crafton PA 1999-2000. brianvanderwel@gmail.com

VAN DE STEEG, Franklin Exford (Minn) PO Box 155, Hastings MN 55033 **P S Lk's Epis Ch Hastings MN 2010-** B Sauk Centre, MN 6/8/1942 s Marenius Franklin & Lorrayne Marie. D 6/24/2009 P 1/9/2010 Bp James Louis Jelinek. m 4/24/1965 Lynette Slaughter c 1. fvandesteeg@msn.com

VAN DEUSEN, Robert Reed (CPa) 205 King St, Northumberland PA 17857 **R Chr Ch Milton PA 2009-; R S Mk's Epis Ch Northumberland PA 2004-** B Scranton PA 4/30/1947 s Lawrence Reed VanDeusen & Louise. Thiel Coll 1968; BA Franklin Coll 1971; MDiv STUSo 1997. D 6/14/1997 Bp Rogers Sanders Harris P 6/12/1999 Bp John Bailey Lipscomb. m 7/14/2001 Mary Van Deusen c 2. R S Matt's Epis Ch Sunbury PA 2004-2007; R Chr Ch River Forest IL 2001-2004; Assoc Ch Of The Redeem Cairo IL 1999-2001; Team Min Dio Springfield Springfield IL 1999-2001; Assoc S Jas Epis Ch Marion IL 1999-2001; Assoc S Mk's Ch W Frankfort IL 1999-2001; Assoc P S Steph's Ch Harrisburg IL 1999-2001. onefrbobvand@yahoo.com

VAN DEUSEN, R(obert) Wayne (Mil) 9360 West Terra Court, Milwaukee WI 53224 B Goshen NY 7/7/1951 s Robert Marvin Van Deusen & Jeanne Elizabeth. BA Hartwick Coll 1973; MDiv Nash 1976. D 8/5/1977 Bp Albert William Hillestad P 6/7/1978 Bp James Winchester Montgomery. R S Ptr's Ch W Allis WI 1991-2009; R S Andr's Ch Kenosha WI 1985-1991; Vic S Mary's Epis Ch Cadillac MI 1981-1985; Lawr Hall Sch Chicago IL 1979-1981. alphege@hotmail.com

VANDEVELDER, Frank Radcliff (Va) 5 Carson Drive, Fredericksburg VA 22406 B Jackson MI 8/3/1928 s Peter Emil VanDevelder & Myra Louise. BA Pasadena Coll 1951; MA Pasadena Coll 1953; MDiv VTS 1963; PhD Drew U 1967; Fllshp Ecumencial Inst, Tantur 1977. D 6/15/1963 Bp Robert Fisher Gibson Jr P 12/21/1963 Bp Leland Stark. m 5/26/1950 Mary B Bryant c 4. P Assoc S Steph's Epis Ch Oak Ridge TN 1998-2003; Prof Biblic Languages & Theol VTS Alexandria VA 1974-1994; Assoc Prof, OT VTS Alexandria VA 1969-1974; Asst to the R Chr Epis Ch E Orange NJ 1963-1966. Auth, "The Biblic Journey of Faith," *Biblic Journey of Faith: The Road of the Sojourner*, Fortress Press, 1988. SBL 1969. Fell ECF ECF 1967. frankvan28@comcast.net

VAN DEVENTER, (Arthur) Reed (Minn) 53 Winding Rd, Rochester NY 14618 B Rochester NY 2/16/1934 s Philip Milton Van Deventer & Emily Reed. BA Hob 1955; BD Bex 1958; MDiv Bex 1974; CTh VTS 1978; Cert Ldrshp Acad for New Directions 1985. D 6/7/1958 P 12/19/1958 Bp Dudley S Stark. m 6/20/1959 Abigail B Brown c 3. R S Jas Epis Ch Hibbing MN 1973-1988; Assoc S Ptr's Ch Ashtabula OH 1969-1973; R Chr Epis Ch Huron OH 1960-1965; Cur S Mk's And S Jn's Epis Ch Rochester NY 1958-1960. SSC 1999. R Emer S Jas' Ch, Hibbing, MN 1995. abarv@frontiernet.net

VANDEVENTER, Heather Ann (Chi) 3737 Seminary Road, House #30, Alexandria VI 22304 **Chr Ch Alexandria VA 2011-** B Hazelton PA 7/7/1972 d James E VanDeventer & Joan P. BA Ya 1994; MDiv SWTS 1998. D 3/25/1998 Bp Carolyn Tanner Irish P 10/21/1998 Bp Herbert Alcorn Donovan Jr. m 10/16/1999 David Timothy Gortner c 2. Epis HS Alexandria VA 2008-2011; Assoc R S Aug's Epis Ch Wilmette IL 2003-2004; Asst R S Aug's Epis Ch Wilmette IL 1998-2002. revheath@juno.com

VAN DINE JR, Howard Arthur (Vt) 384 Oakland Station Rd, Saint Albans VT 05478 B Mineola NY 2/25/1921 s Howard Arthur Van Dine & Anna. BS Buc 1949; U of Vermont 1963; Cert Bangor TS 2000; M Div Vision Intl Educ Ntwk 2005; D Min Vision Intl Educ Ntwk 2009. D 6/11/1963 P 12/17/1965 Bp Harvey D Butterfield. m 2/25/1995 Janice H Peck c 4. Supply P Dio Vermont Burlington VT 2000-2006; P-in-c S Thos Ch Winn ME 1997-2000; Int S Paul's Ch Windsor VT 1994-1997; Int S Andr's Epis Ch St Johnsbury VT 1991-1994; R S Paul's Epis Ch On The Green Vergennes VT 1981-1989; St Pauls Ch Bristol VT 1981-1988; Cn to Ordnry Dio Vermont Burlington VT 1977-1987; Dio Vermont Burlington VT 1975-1987; Cn Cathd Ch Of S Paul Burlington VT 1974-1981; Mssnr Calv Ch Underhill VT 1971-1974; Asst Cathd Ch Of S Paul Burlington VT 1963-1971. Hon Cn, S Paul Cathd Igreja Lusitana Lisbon Potugal 1992; Cn S Paul Cathd/Vermont Vermont 1977. howardvandine@aol.com

VANDIVORT JR, Paul Marshall (Mo) 12366 Federal Dr, Des Peres MO 63131 B Cape Girardeau MO 5/11/1940 s Paul Marshall Vandivort & Ida Marie. Gri 1960; BA SE Missouri St U 1963; MDiv VTS 1968; MD U of Missouri 1977. D 6/22/1968 P 5/1/1974 Bp George Leslie Cadigan. m 5/20/1971 Linda Minna Kilsheimer.

VAN DOOREN, John David (Chi) 5749 N Kenmore Ave, Chicago IL 60660 **R Epis Ch Of The Atone Chicago IL 2005-** B Hendersonville NC 9/18/1959 s Peter van Dooren & Sarah. BA U NC 1982; MDiv VTS 1987. D 11/1/1989 Bp Brice Sidney Sanders P 5/31/1990 Bp James Winchester Montgomery. R All Souls Memi Epis Ch Washington DC 1992-2005; St Martins-In-The-Field Ch Severna Pk MD 1991-1992; Cur All Souls Memi Epis Ch Washington DC 1989-1990. GAS; SocMary. johnvandooren@aol.com

VANDOREN JR, Robert Lawson (WTenn) 5097 Greenway Cv, Memphis TN 38117 **S Jn's Epis Ch Memphis TN 2002-** B Columbia SC 2/18/1944 s Robert Lawson Van Doren & Elizabeth Gaines. BA U So 1966; MDiv Memphis TS 2007. D 10/28/2000 Bp James Malone Coleman P 5/22/2004 Bp Don Edward Johnson. m 12/29/2007 Pamela VanDoren. rvandoren@stjohnsmemphis.org

VANDORT, Herbert John (CGC) 3819 N 12th Ave, Pensacola FL 32503 **Vic St Aug of Cbury Navarre FL 1990-** B Grand Rapids MI 12/8/1920 s Herman A Vandort & Mary C. MDiv Bex; AA Grand Rapids Cmnty Coll; BA Wstrn Michigan U 1943; BD Bex 1950; MA U MI 1953; PhD U MI 1963. D 6/13/1950 P 12/1/1950 Bp Lewis B Whittemore. S Cyp's Epis Ch Pensacola FL 1977-1986; Vic Protem S Steph's Ch Brewton AL 1970-1971; Assoc S Alb's Ch Superior WI 1963-1969; Assoc Chr Ch Shaker Heights OH 1961-1962; Chapl To Bp Of NW Pa Dio NW Pennsylvania Erie PA 1954-1961; Vic S Ptr's Ch Waterford PA 1954-1961; Cur Epis Ch Of The Gd Shpd Allegan MI 1950-1954. Auth, "Our Common Vocation Tchr Of The Year U Of Wi".

VAN DUSEN, David Buick (Mass) Po Box 301, Brooksville ME 04617 B Detroit MI 6/2/1929 s Charles Theron Van Dusan & Catherine Elizabeth. BA Pr 1951; BD/STM VTS 1957; STM Bos 1964. D 6/30/1957 P 1/1/1958 Bp Richard S M Emrich. m 11/17/2006 Margaret MCE Barton c 6. P-in-c S Brendan's Epis Ch Stonington ME 1991-1993; Dioc Coun Dio Massachusetts Boston MA 1981-1984; R S Ptr's Ch Weston MA 1976-1991; R Chr Ch Greensburg PA 1972-1976; Assoc Ch Of The Redeem Bryn Mawr PA 1968-1972; Asst Trin Ch In The City Of Boston Boston MA 1963-1967; Asst S Jas Epis Ch Birmingham MI 1960-1963; Vic S Dunst's Epis Ch Davison MI 1957-1959. davd@acadia.net

VAN DYKE, Bude (Tenn) Po Box 824, Sewanee TN 37375 **Vic S Matt's Epis Ch McMinnville TN 2011-; Chapl S Andr's-Sewanee Sch Sewanee TN 2001-; Sprtl Dir The TS at The U So Sewanee TN 2001-** B Jackson TN 10/7/1953 s Robert Hinton VanDyke & Clara Nelle. MDiv TS 1999; DMIn TS 2003. D 2/24/2000 P 9/10/2000 Bp Henry Nutt Parsley Jr. m 6/15/1974 Pamela Kay Abernathy. Auth, "Paul's Letter to Philemon: and appeal above and beyond the law," *Sewanee Theol Revs*, The TS, 1998. Fire Keeper Oklahom IV Consult 2010. budevandyke@gmail.com

VAN EENWYK, John Richter (Roch) P. O. Box 1961, Olympia WA 98507 B Sodus NY 3/11/1946 s John Franklin Van Eenwyk & Dorothy Marie. BA Colg 1967; STB EDS 1970; Propadeuticum CG Jung Inst Zurich 1977; Dplma CG Jung Inst Chicago 1981; PhD U Chi 1981. D 6/19/1970 Bp Archie H Crowley P 12/19/1970 Bp Robert Rae Spears Jr. m 6/5/1970 Juliet Schneller c 2. Assoc S Jn's Epis Ch Olympia WA 1992-1999; Assoc Ch Of Our Sav Chicago IL 1977-1992; Assoc Epis Ch Of The Atone Chicago IL 1977-1992. Auth, "Archetypes and Strange Attractors: The Chaotic Wrld of Symbols," Inner City Books, 1997; "Journ arts". NASSAM 1985. Alum Humanitarian Awd Colg 2009; Lifetime Acievement Awd Thurston Cnty Human Rts Cmsn 2008; Soc Issues Awd Washington St Psychol Assn 2008; Serval Awd Long Island Inst of Mntl Hlth 1985; Robbins Fllshp EDS 1974; Tchg Fllshp Harvard 1970. jrv@u.washington.edu

VAN ES, Kenneth (Eau) 2603 Yorktown Ct, Eau Claire WI 54703 **D Chr Ch Cathd Eau Claire WI 1998-** B Milwaukee WI 4/22/1950 s Kenneth Van Es & June Elizabeth. BA U of Wisconsin 1972. D 4/18/1998 Bp William Charles Wantland. m 7/31/1982 Rebecca Olivia Laverne Haltner.

VANG, Marshall Jacob (Alb) 5 Washington Pl. Apt. 2, Troy NY 12180 **Int Ch Of Beth Saratoga Sprg NY 2012-; Trst Nash Nashotah WI 1988-** B Corning NY 12/9/1947 s Norman John Vang & Lucretia Katherine. BA Ken 1970; MDiv GTS 1974. D 4/25/1974 P 10/28/1974 Bp Robert Rae Spears Jr. P-in-c Ch Of The H Cross Warrensburg NY 2011; Dn Cathd Of All SS Albany NY 1998-2010; R S Geo's Epis Ch Schenectady NY 1987-1998; R S Anth Of Padua Ch Hackensack NJ 1977-1986; Cur Gr Epis Ch Westwood NJ 1974-1977. CBS 1974; GAS 1977; SocMary 1977. deano192010@gmail.com

VAN GORDEN SR, Schuyler Humphrey (Eau) 120 10th Ave, Eau Claire WI 54703 B Osseo WI 7/30/1918 s Clyde Schuyler Van Gorden & Elsie Charlotte. BS U of Wisconsin; MS U of Wisconsin 1972. D 8/10/1982 Bp William

Charles Wantland. m 9/18/1937 Eileen Henrietta LaMay c 4. D Chr Ch Cathd Eau Claire WI 1982-1993.

VAN HOOK, Peter James (U) PO Box 17972, Salt Lake City UT 84117 **P-in-c S Mary's Ch Provo UT 2011-; Mutual Mnstry Revs Team, Consult Dio Utah Salt Lake City UT 2010-; Stndg Com; Pres, 2011-12 Dio Utah Salt Lake City UT 2010-; Transitioinal Mnstrs in The Epis Ch, Bd Dio Utah Salt Lake City UT 2010-; Fresh Start, Fac & Mentor Dio Utah Salt Lake City UT 2009-** B Los Angeles CA 5/5/1947 s James Thomas Van Hook & Elizabeth Virginia. BS Lewis & Clark Coll 1969; MDiv CDSP 1972; PhD U of Utah 1995. D 7/16/1972 P 2/1/1973 Bp Victor Manuel Rivera. m 3/8/1969 Carole Marie Van Hook c 3. Int R Ch Of The Gd Shpd Ogden UT 2009-2011; Int R S Jn's Epis Ch Logan UT 2008-2010; Int Gr Epis Ch St Geo UT 2005-2006; Supply Dio Utah Salt Lake City UT 2003-2006; Disaster Response Consult Ch Wrld Serv Elkhart IN 2002-2003; Dioc Coordntr, PBFWR Dio Utah Salt Lake City UT 1995-2002; Supply Dio Utah Salt Lake City UT 1995; COM Dio Utah Salt Lake City UT 1992-1995; Dio Utah Salt Lake City UT 1988-1990; R All SS Ch Salt Lake City UT 1981-1992; Ecum Off Dio Idaho Boise ID 1979-1981; Stndg Com, Secy Dio Idaho Boise ID 1977-1981; R S Mary's Ch Emmett ID 1975-1981; Chair of Aided Par Cltn Dio Idaho Boise ID 1975-1978; Vic St Raphael Epis Ch Oakhurst CA 1974-1975; Asst to Bp of San Joaquin Epis Dio San Joaquin Modesto CA 1972-1975; Assoc R S Paul's Ch Bakersfield CA 1972-1974. Auth, "[Var]," *Intl Encyclopedia of Publ Plcy & Admin*, 1985; Auth, "Using an Ethics Matrix in an MPA Prog," *Journ of Publ Admin*, 1985. Amer Soc for Publ Admin 1985; Int Mnstry Ntwk (IMN) 2005; Natl Assn for the Self- Supporting Active Mnstry 1992; Stonefly Soc of the Wasatch 1995; Transitional Mnstrs in The Epis Ch (TMEC) 2005. Mem Pi Alpha Alpha 1993. pjvanhook@msn.com

VAN HOOSER, Jack Boyd (WMich) 801 Vanosdale Rd Apt 511, Knoxville TN 37909 B Chattanooga TN 7/6/1928 s Hoskins Van Hooser & Ruth Naomi. BBA U of Tennessee 1950; BD CDSP 1958; ThD Harvard DS 1963. D 6/22/1958 Bp John Vander Horst P 4/25/1959 Bp Theodore N Barth. m 8/19/1955 Phyllis Taliaferro Mary Phyllis Taliaferro. Gnrl Bd Examning Chapl Dio Wstrn Michigan Kalamazoo MI 1989-1994; Stwdshp Dio Wstrn Michigan Kalamazoo MI 1985-1987; Com Dio Wstrn Michigan Kalamazoo MI 1984-1988; Resolutns Com Dio Wstrn Michigan Kalamazoo MI 1983-1987; Search Com For Bp Coadj Dio Wstrn Michigan Kalamazoo MI 1983-1984; R S Thos Epis Ch Battle Creek MI 1982-1993; Chair Com For Diac Dio Wstrn Michigan Kalamazoo MI 1982-1986; Chair Com For Diac Dio Wstrn Michigan Kalamazoo MI 1982-1986; Evang & Renwl Cmsn Dio Chicago Chicago IL 1981-1982; P-in-c S Elis's Ch Glencoe IL 1977-1978; Sub-Dn SWTS Evanston IL 1975-1978; Actg Dn SWTS Evanston IL 1974; Prof SWTS Evanston IL 1973-1982; Asst Prof Ot SWTS Evanston IL 1966-1969; Asst Instr Ot EDS Cambridge MA 1960-1962; Asst The Ch Of Our Redeem Lexington MA 1959-1962. Auth, "arts & Revs". OHC 1974. jackbvh@comcast.net

VAN HORN, Richard Scott (Los) 3050 Motor Ave, Los Angeles CA 90064 B Monrovia CA 9/24/1939 s Harlan Summers Van Horn & Evelyn Marie. BA Harv 1961; M. Div GTS 1965. D 9/16/1965 P 3/1/1966 Bp Francis E I Bloy. m 2/2/1986 Carolyn Jean Ferber c 1. MHA Long Bch CA 1980-1997; Cn Mssnr For Plnng Dio Los Angeles Los Angeles CA 1974-1980; Sch Dir The Par Ch Of S Lk Long Bch CA 1971-1974; R S Barn' Epis Ch Los Angeles CA 1968-1970; S Mary's Epis Ch Los Angeles CA 1967-1998; Cur S Mk's Par Van Nuys CA 1965-1967. Cn of the Dio Dio Los Angeles 1980. richard.vanhorn@sbcglobal.net

VAN HORNE, Beverly (Mo) 8425 Craighill Drive, Saint Louis MO 63123 B Columbia SC 4/7/1947 d George Dew & Barbara. Dioc Sch for Mnstry; BA Randolph-Macon Wmn's Coll 1969; CDSP 1970. D 12/22/2004 P 6/24/2005 Bp George Wayne Smith. m 6/12/1970 Peter Eric Van Horne c 2. P-in-c Trin Ch De Soto MO 2005-2010. beverlyvanhorne@global.net

VAN HORNE, Peter Eric (Mo) 8425 Craighill Dr, St. Louis MO 63123 **Int R S Mk's Ch S Louis MO 2011-** B Caldwell ID 12/28/1944 s Robert Negley Van Horne & Elizabeth Louise. BA U of Idaho Moscow 1967; MDiv CDSP 1970; MA Grad Theol Un 1970; DMin SWTS 2001. D 6/24/1970 P 12/19/1970 Bp Norman L Foote. m 6/12/1970 Beverly Dew c 2. Int R Trin Epis Ch Kirksville MO 2009-2010; Vic All SS Epis Ch Farmington MO 2001-2009; Stwdshp Com Dio Hawaii Honolulu HI 1995-2001; Vic Emm Epis Ch Kailua HI 1995-2001; Cn Dio Hawaii Honolulu HI 1986-1995; Cn to the Ordnry Dio Hawaii Honolulu HI 1986-1995; Exec Off Dio Hawaii Honolulu HI 1986-1995; Ch Hist Instr Diac Prog Dio Hawaii Honolulu HI 1983-1994; Ch Hist Instr Diac Prog Dio Hawaii Honolulu HI 1983-1994; Dioc Coun Dio Hawaii Honolulu HI 1981-1984; R Ch Of The Epiph Honolulu HI 1978-1986; Dioc Coun Dio Hawaii Honolulu HI 1977-1979; R S Jn's Epis Ch Kula HI 1976-1978; Cur All SS Epis Ch Boise ID 1970-1971. Auth, *ATR*. CODE - Pres 1987-1996. beverlyvanhorne@sbcglobal.net

VANI, Benedict Sele (CFla) 2341 Port Malabar Blvd Ne, Palm Bay FL 32905 B Glima LR 9/14/1932 s Baysama Vani & Christian Kpana Sowo. Cert Cuttington U Coll 1967; Cert Bird S. Coler Memi Hosp 1975; Lic Epis TS In Kentucky 1975. D 1/6/1976 P 1/6/1977 Bp George Daniel Browne. c 4. Dio Liberia 1000 Monrovia 10 Liberia 1976-1982.

VAN KIRK, Andrew Dela Ronde (Dal) 8787 Greenville Ave, Dallas TX 75243 **Cur Epis Ch Of The Ascen Dallas TX 2010-** B Chicago IL 2/22/1982 s Mark Van Kirk & Natalie Beam. BA Duke 2004; MDiv PrTS 2008; ThM PrTS 2009. D 5/2/2010 Bp George Edward Councell P 1/6/2011 Bp James Monte Stanton. m 1/3/2009 Stephanie Cox c 1. avankirk@gmail.com

VAN KIRK, Natalie Beam (Dal) Cathedral Church of Saint Matthew, 5700 Ross Ave, Dallas TX 75206 **Vic Ch Of The Gd Samar Dallas TX 2010-** B Baltimore MD 9/5/1956 d Roger E Beam & Joanna. BS Duke 1978; MA Perkins TS SMU 2000. D 5/24/2003 P 11/29/2003 Bp James Monte Stanton. c 3. Dio Dallas Dallas TX 2004-2006; S Matt's Cathd Dallas TX 2003-2008. "The Logic of Cncl Theism (co-Ed)," Eerdmans, 2008; "Finding One's Way Through the Maze of Lang," *Cistercian Stds Quarterly*, Gethsemani Abbey, Trappist KY, 2007; "Catching Butterflies and the Mysteries of God," *Preaching from Psalms, Oracles and Parables: Sermons That Wk XIV*, Morehouse Pub, 2006. nbvankirk@gmail.com

VAN KLAVEREN, Dina Els (Md) 1216 Seminole Dr, Arnold MD 21012 B Pomona, CA 3/19/1973 BA Whittier Coll 1995; MS U of Rhode Island 1997; MDiv CDSP 2006. D 6/24/2006 Bp John Leslie Rabb P 1/6/2007 Bp Robert Wilkes Ihloff. m 6/27/1998 David Stimler c 2. S Andr's Epis Ch Glenwood MD 2009; S Marg's Ch Annapolis MD 2006-2009. dinavk@gmail.com

VAN LIEW, Christina (LI) 85 Center St, Williston Park NY 11596 **P-in-c Epis Ch of The Resurr Williston Pk NY 2006-** B Glen Ridge NJ 9/1/1950 d Willard Randolph vanLiew & Vicki A. BS Bos 1975; MDiv GTS 2004. D 9/28/2004 P 2/5/2005 Bp Johncy Itty. c 2. Cur S Jn's Ch Cold Sprg Harbor NY 2004-2005. revxina@yahoo.com

VAN METER, Dale Lee (Mass) 66 Summit Ave, Sharon MA 02067 **S Steph's Ch Fall River MA 1996-** B Racine OH 9/28/1919 s Carl Lee Van Meter & Laura Ella. BA Ohio U 1944; STB Bos 1947; MS Boston Coll 1965. D 12/1/1951 P 6/14/1952 Bp William A Lawrence. m 6/22/1957 Elizabeth Codman Lawrence c 3. Assoc S Jn's/S Steph's Ch Fall River MA 1996-2004; S Paul's Epis Ch Hopkinton MA 1989-1991; Int Emm Ch Braintree MA 1987-1989; Int Trin Ch Marshfield Hills MA 1986-1987; Int S Mk's Ch Taunton MA 1984-1986; All SS Ch Whitman MA 1983-1984; S Dunstans Epis Ch Dover MA 1982-1983; Int R S Dunstans Epis Ch Dover MA 1981-1982; Vic S Steph's Ch Westborough MA 1956-1963; Vic Chr Ch So Barre MA 1951-1956; Vic Chr Memi Ch No Brookfield MA 1951-1956. EPF.

VANN, Deborah Louise (CFla) 380 Royal Palm Dr, Melbourne FL 32935 **R Hope Epis Ch Melbourne FL 2009-** B Melbourne FL 2/8/1954 d Russell Vann & Charlotte. MS Florida St U 1982; MDiv STUSo 2004. D 5/22/2004 P 1/30/2005 Bp John Wadsworth Howe. m 2/2/1985 John M Campbell c 2. S Aug Of Cbury Epis Ch Vero Bch FL 2007-2008; Asst Ch Of Our Sav Palm Bay FL 2005-2007. dvann2@cfl.rr.com

VANN, Tim E (Ia) 710 Matthies Dr, Papillion NE 68046 B Mitchell SD 2/25/1949 s Walter Wells Vann & Phyllis Barbara. BA U of Texas 1974; MDiv STUSo 1977; MBA U of So Dakota 1989. D 6/26/1977 P 1/6/1978 Bp Walter H Jones. m 5/31/1980 Cindy Schlosser. Dio Iowa Des Moines IA 2004-2008; S Martha's Epis Ch Papillion NE 2002-2003; S Lk's Ch Plattsmouth NE 1996-1997; Cn Dio Nebraska Omaha NE 1991-2004; Int Trin Cathd Omaha NE 1990-1991; Int Calv Epis Ch Sioux City IA 1989-1990; Int S Geo's Epis Ch Le Mars IA 1989-1990; Dio So Dakota Sioux Falls SD 1988-1990; Int Ch Of Our Most Merc Sav Wagner SD 1988-1989; Int S Paul's Epis Ch Vermillion SD 1988-1989; Int S Paul's Ch Brookings SD 1987-1988; R Ch Of The Gd Shpd Sioux Falls SD 1983-1986; Asst Emm Epis Par Rapid City SD 1980-1983; Vic Chr Epis Ch Gettysburg SD 1977-1980; R S Jas Epis Ch Mobridge SD 1977-1980. tvann@cox.net

VANNORSDALL, Albert Oliver (EC) 504 Kent Rd, Greenville NC 27858 **P-in-c Peace Epis Ch New Bern NC 2011-** B Columbus OH 1/6/1937 s Albert Dean Vannorsdall & Emma. BA DePauw U 1958; STM Bos 1961; PhD Bos 1968; MA Amberton U 1995. D 6/4/1980 P 6/1/1982 Bp James Daniel Warner. c 2. P-in-c S Fran Ch Goldsboro NC 2005-2009; Int Ch Of The H Trin Lincoln NE 1981-1984. vannors@swbell.net

VANO, Mary Foster (Tex) 14615 Brown Bear Dr., Little Rock AR 72223 **R S Marg's Epis Ch Little Rock AR 2011-** B Andrews Air Force Base 10/20/1976 d Robert Glenn Certain & Robbie L. BA TCU 1999; MDiv Epis TS of the SW 2003. D 5/18/2003 P 11/15/2003 Bp Gethin Benwil Hughes. m 8/7/1999 Stephen Thomas Vano c 2. Assoc P S Dav's Ch Austin TX 2003-2011. mfvano@gmail.com

VAN OSS SR, Earl T (U) 737 East Center, Orem UT 84057 B Sherwood ND 2/14/1913 s Ingbrighd Oss & Magli. BS U of Montana 1934. D 6/13/1976 Bp Otis Charles. m 6/18/1975 Nadine Johnson. Asst The Epis Ch Of The Gd Shpd Hemet CA 1976-1982.

VAN OSS, William Joseph (Minn) 1710 E Superior St, Duluth MN 55812 **R S Paul's Epis Ch Duluth MN 2006-** B Green Bay WI 3/29/1964 s Arnold Van Oss & Jean. BA U of St. Thos 1986; MDiv Mundelein Sem 1991; CAS SWTS 2000. Rec from Roman Catholic 5/1/2000 as Priest Bp James Louis Jelinek. m

6/24/1996 Susan Mary Brault c 1. R All SS Ch Northfield MN 2000-2006. billvanoss@stpaulsduluth.org

VANOVER, Debra A (Ore) 25 Hiatt St, Lebanon OR 97355 **Samar Lebanon Hosp Lebanon OR 2003-** B La Grande OR 5/5/1952 d Ralph Vanover & Arbelyn Belva. BA Victoria U Wellington Nz 1973; MA Fuller TS 1983; Vancouver TS 1995. D 7/22/1996 Bp George Clinton Harris P 1/1/1998 Bp Mark Lawrence Mac Donald. c 2. R S Jas The Fisherman Kodiak AK 1998-2002; Asst S Ptr's By-The-Sea Sitka AK 1997-1998. Assn of Epis Chapl 2002. debvann@gmail.com

VAN PARYS, Cynthia Leigh (NI) 1464 Glenlake Dr, South Bend IN 46614 **D S Mich And All Ang Ch So Bend IN 1996-** B Dowagiac MI 7/22/1957 d Timothy Gerald Welsh & Susan Ryan. D 10/16/1996 Bp Francis Campbell Gray. m 5/6/1978 Randy Michael VanParys.

VAN PLETZEN-RANDS BSG, Blane Frederik (U) 128 Pearl St, Buffalo NY 14202 B 2/18/1960 s George Harold van Pletzen & Helen Kay. BA Weber St U 1985; MA Utah St U 1988; MDiv The GTS 2010. D 6/12/2010 Bp Carolyn Tanner Irish P 12/18/2010 Bp J Michael Garrison. m 7/21/2007 Scott Edward Rands c 1. Cn S Paul's Cathd Buffalo NY 2010-2011. bvpr@mac.com

VAN SANT, Mark R (NJ) 295 Little Silver Point Road, Little Silver NJ 07739 **R S Jn's Epis Ch Little Silver NJ 1987-** B Elizabeth NJ 7/11/1956 s John Albion Van Sant & Lovey Grace. BA Glassboro St U 1979; MDiv Nash 1983. D 6/4/1983 Bp George Phelps Mellick Belshaw P 12/6/1983 Bp Albert Wiencke Van Duzer. m 9/27/1997 Sandra Segrest c 3. Cur S Mary's Ch Haddon Heights NJ 1983-1987. stjohnslittlesilver@verizon.net

VAN SANT, Paul Albion (NJ) 38 Anne Dr, Tabernacle NJ 08088 **R S Steph's Ch Whiting NJ 2006-; Dio New Jersey Trenton NJ 2005-** B Philadelphia PA 3/30/1954 s John Albion Van Sant & Lovey Grace. BA Rutgers-The St U 1984; MDiv Nash 1988; ThM New Brunswick TS 1995. D 6/11/1988 Bp George Phelps Mellick Belshaw P 2/24/1989 Bp Vincent King Pettit. m 9/29/1979 Priscilla Lee Renelt c 5. Fin & Bdgt Com Dio New Jersey Trenton NJ 1996-1999; The Ch Of The Gd Shpd Berlin NJ 1990-2006; S Paul's Ch Camden NJ 1988-1990. Auth, "The Person Concept In Monkeys"; Auth, "Journ Of Experimental Psychol: Animal Behaviour Processes". CBS, GAS; Dioconate Chapl Dok. pvansant@gmail.com

VAN SCOYOC, Gardner Warren (Va) 5928 Lomack Ct, Alexandria VA 22312 B Portland OR 12/2/1930 s Melwood Wertz Van Scoyoc & Beth Jonnie. Lic in Nrsng Hm Administor Virginia 71; AA Keystone Jr Coll 1952; BA Leh 1954; STM VTS 1958; GW 1966; Cert VCU 1971. D 6/13/1958 Bp Frederick D Goodwin P 6/27/1959 Bp Robert Fisher Gibson Jr. m 6/26/1954 Nancy Jean Kerns c 4. Exec Dir Dio Va Hms Dio Virginia Richmond VA 1970-1973; Westminster-Cbury Richmond VA 1965-1978; Exec Secy Dept CSR Dio Virginia Richmond VA 1963-1965; D-in-c Emm Ch Rapidan VA 1958-1959. Auth, "Life Care: A Long Term Solution?," Amer Assoc of Hm for Aging, 1977. ESMA 1967. DSA Amer Assn Hms & Serv for the Aging 1992.

VAN SICKLE, Kathleen (Cal) 555 Pierce St Apt 340e, Albany CA 94706 B Grayling MI 8/11/1952 d Chester L Van Sickle & Marion Ruth. BA Oakland U 1975; MDiv CDSP 1986; MS U CA 1992. D 6/10/1986 Bp John Lester Thompson III. CDSP Berkeley CA 2004; The Epis Ch Of The Gd Shpd Berkeley CA 1997-2007; D The Epis Ch Of The Gd Shpd Berkeley CA 1987-1991; Events Coordntr Gr Cathd San Francisco CA 1987-1990; D S Paul's Epis Ch Sacramento CA 1986-1987. deaconkvs@comcast.net

VAN SICLEN, John Remsen (Me) PO Box 101, Walpole ME 04573 B New York NY 7/31/1949 s John Wyckoff Van Siclen & Mary. BA Hob 1973; MDiv EDS 1977; DMin Bangor TS 1994. D 6/11/1977 Bp Jonathan Goodhue Sherman P 1/24/1978 Bp John Harris Burt. m 7/5/1980 Pamela Shakley c 1. P-in-c S Giles Ch Jefferson ME 2008-2011; Int Chr Ch In Lonsdale Lincoln RI 2005-2006; R S Mich's Ch Bristol RI 1999-2005; R S Paul's Epis Ch White River Jct VT 1990-1999; Int All SS Epis Ch Littleton NH 1990; R S Eliz's Ch Sudbury MA 1986-1990; R Ch Of The Adv Pittsburgh PA 1980-1986; Cur S Ptr's Epis Ch Lakewood OH 1977-1980. Fllshp of St. Jn 2007. Hon Cn S Jn's Cathd Providence RI 1999. johnvs@tidewater.net

VANUCCI, Anthony Joseph (Pa) 9700 Entrada Pl. N.W., Albuquerque NM 87114 B Philadelphia PA 10/10/1941 s Anthony Vanucci & Blanche. STL S Mary U Baltimore MD; STB S Mary U Baltimore MD 1968; MEd Coll of New Jersey 1979. Rec from Roman Catholic 1/1/1997 as Priest Bp Allen Lyman Bartlett Jr. m 8/12/1972 Anna Dewey c 1. R S Jas Epis Ch Bristol PA 2000-2007; R Ch Of Our Sav Somerset MA 1997-2000; Vic Ch Of The Redeem Andalusia PA 1994-1997. apadrevanucci@hotmail.com

VAN VALKENBURGH, William Burton (WMich) 6632 W. South Lake Gage Dr., Angola IN 46703 B Deer Creek OK 1/10/1926 s Alvin Milford Van Valkenburgh & Osie Blanche. BS U of Oklahoma 1950; MS Garrett Biblic Inst 1953; NWU 1954; Drew U 1963. D 11/28/1962 Bp Donald MacAdie P 4/1/1963 Bp Leland Stark. m 9/9/1950 Marilyn Joan Wilson c 3. P-in-c S Ptr's Ch Clifton NJ 1966-1969; Cur Ch Of The Redeem Morristown NJ 1963-1966. Wmich Epis Cleric Assn 1970. Danforth Grant 1963. WMVANV@AOL.COM

VAN WALTEROP, Norman Phillip (EpisSanJ) 2716 C Sherwood Ave, Modesto CA 95350 B Davenport IA 10/6/1928 s William Theodore Van Walterop & Adeline. BS U of Iowa 1954; MA U of Iowa 1958; MDiv CDSP 1963. D 6/22/1963 P 12/21/1963 Bp Sumner Walters. P S Paul's Epis Ch Modesto CA 1963-2001; Vic S Dunstans Epis Ch Modesto CA 1963-1966. normhawkeye@bigvalley.net

VAN WASSENHOVE, Mark Steven (Ind) 10202 Winlee Court, Indianapolis IN 46236 **R S Matt's Ch Indianapolis IN 2005-** B Kewanee IL 7/30/1958 s Leonard Van Wassenhove & Betty J. BA U of Notre Dame 1980; MDiv Jesuit TS 1988; MC U of Phoenix 1997. Rec from Roman Catholic 10/25/2000 as Priest Bp Robert Reed Shahan. m 3/5/1994 Kimberly A Ciani c 2. Assoc S Barn On The Desert Scottsdale AZ 2000-2005. stmattsrector@comcast.net

VAN WELY, Richard Francis (Ct) 215 Old Church Rd, Greenwich CT 06830 B Albany NY 8/15/1936 s Richard Christian VanWely & Myrtle Viola. BA Siena Coll 1960; STB Ya Berk 1962; STM Yale DS 1972. D 6/16/1962 P 12/16/1962 Bp Allen Webster Brown. m 12/14/1957 Judith L Van Patten c 4. R S Barn Epis Ch Greenwich CT 1976-2002; Vic S Andr's Ch Northford CT 1971-1976; Vic Zion Epis Ch No Branford CT 1969-1976; R Gr Epis Ch Canton NY 1965-1969; R S Andr's Epis Ch Albany NY 1962-1965. rvanwely@aol.com

VAN ZANDT, Jane Whitbeck (NH) 58 Hanson Rd, Chester NH 03036 **Nonstip Gr Ch Manchester NH 2000-** B Boston MA 4/17/1942 d Earl Burton Van Zandt & Genevieve. BSN Bos 1963; MDiv EDS 1981. D 6/5/1982 Bp John Bowen Coburn P 9/24/1983 Bp Edward Randolph Welles II. m 9/19/1987 W(illiam) Allan Knight. Assoc Cathd Of The Incarn Baltimore MD 1995-1999; Chair, AIDS Mnstry Dio Maryland Baltimore MD 1991-1999; Asst All SS Par Brookline MA 1985-1986; AIDS Mnstry Dio Massachusetts Boston MA 1984-1991. Auth, "Revolutionary Forgiveness," Orbis, 1987; Auth, "Close-up: Corys Legacy," *Wit*, 1986. EPF Exec Bd 1994-1997; EWC 1979; Integrity 1979; NEAC 1990. episrev@comcast.net

VAN ZANDT, Polk (Tenn) Saint Paul's Episcopal Church, 116 N Academy St, Murfreesboro TN 37130 **R S Paul's Epis Ch Murfreesboro TN 2008-** B Greenville MS 11/17/1952 s Thomas Kelly Van Zandt & Virginia Knox. BA U So 1974; MDiv STUSo 1994. D 5/21/1994 P 12/3/1994 Bp Alfred Clark Marble Jr. m 5/31/1975 Mary Josephine Pratt c 3. R S Paul's Ch Selma AL 2000-2008; R Epis Ch Of The Incarn W Point MS 1994-2000. rector@stpaulsmboro.org

VAN ZANTEN JR, Peter Eric (Oly) 2333 Lakemoor Dr Sw, Olympia WA 98512 B Minneapolis MN 12/27/1932 s Peter Van Zanten & Hilda. BA U MN 1961; MDiv SWTS 1963. D 6/27/1964 Bp Hamilton Hyde Kellogg P 4/1/1965 Bp Philip Frederick McNairy. m 3/5/2000 Lorinda Black. Vic S Chris's Epis Ch Olympia WA 1992-1999; S Matthews Auburn WA 1990-1991; S Paul's Epis Ch Lees Summit MO 1988-1989; Ch Of The Redeem Kansas City MO 1988; S Mich & S Geo Clayton MO 1978-1981; Asst Chr Epis Ch S Jos MO 1976-1978; Gr Ch Carthage MO 1972-1976; Vic S Jn Worthington MN 1968-1973; H Trin Epis Ch Luverne MN 1968-1970; Vic S Paul's Ch Pipestone MN 1968-1970; Epis Cmnty Servs Bd Dio Minnesota Minneapolis MN 1965-1968; Vic S Lk's Ch Detroit Lakes MN 1964-1968. eric2333@aol.com

VARAS, Dwayne Anthony (SwFla) 3901 Davis Blvd, Naples FL 34104 **Asst R S Paul's Ch Naples FL 2009-** B Tampa FL 8/2/1966 s Antonio Varas & Rose Marie Tamborello. Rec from Roman Catholic 6/6/2009 as Priest Bp Dabney Tyler Smith. dvaras@juno.com

VARDEMANN, Brady Jodoka (Mont) 556 S Rodney St, Helena MT 59601 **Dioc Deploy Off Dio Montana Helena MT 1999-** B Breckenridge TX 6/29/1943 d Armour Gamel Vardemann & Midge Mell. D 2/27/1999 P 9/4/1999 Bp Charles Jones III. Montana Assn of Ch Helena MT 2005-2008; Dio Montana Helena MT 2000-2005; Int S Fran Epis Ch Great Falls MT 1999-2000.

VARELA SOLORZANO, Marco Antonio (Hond) Colonia La Sabana, Samparo Sula Honduras **Dio Honduras Miami FL 2006-** B Yuscaran el Paraiso 8/20/1974 s Maximo Varela & Catalina. D 10/28/2005 P 10/16/2010 Bp Lloyd Emmanuel Allen. m 10/18/1997 Suyapa Marisala Ardon c 3.

VARELA ZUNIGA, Nery Yolanda (Hond) Colonia Los Robles, Atlantida, Ceiba 31105 Honduras **Dio Honduras Miami FL 2006-; Iglesia Epis Hondurena San Pedro Sula 2006-** B Tegucigalpa M.D.C. 4/9/1979 d Ramon Heriberto Vanela & Albertina. Programa Diocesano Educ. Teologica 2003. D 10/29/2005 Bp Lloyd Emmanuel Allen. m 9/4/2002 Sierra Javier Armando. neryun79@yahoo.com

VARGHESE, Winnie Sara (NY) 464 Riverside Drive. Apt. 41, New York NY 10027 **P-in-c S Mk's Ch In The Bowery New York NY 2009-** B Dallas TX 5/28/1972 d Cherian Varghese & Leela. BA SMU 1994; MDiv UTS 1999. D 6/19/1999 Bp Chester Lovelle Talton P 1/8/2000 Bp Frederick Houk Borsch. m Elizabeth Anne Toledo c 2. Chapl Dio Los Angeles Los Angeles CA 2002-2009; Columbia Univ Chapl Dio New York New York City NY 2002-2009; Cbury Westwood Fndt Los Angeles CA 1999-2002; Asst to the R S Alb's Epis Ch Los Angeles CA 1999-2002. wsvarghese@gmail.com

VARNER, Joshua H (NC) Holy Trinity Episcopal Church, 607 N Greene St, Greensboro NC 27401 **H Trin Epis Ch Greensboro NC 2004-** B Durham NC

7/13/1975 s Grant Bernard Varner & Vivian. BA U So 1997; MTS Harvard DS 1999; MDiv VTS 2001. D 6/23/2001 Bp Michael Bruce Curry P 5/18/2002 Bp J(ames) Gary Gloster. m 6/19/1999 Elizabeth A Ariail c 2. Asst to the R S Lk's Epis Ch Durham NC 2001-2004. varnerpublic@earthlink.net

VASQUEZ, Jaime Armando (Hond) IMS SAP Dept 215. PO Box 523900, Miami FL 33152 Honduras B 3/21/1972 s Amelia. D 3/11/2007 Bp Lloyd Emmanuel Allen. c 3. jaarva29@yahoo.com

VASQUEZ, Martha Sylvia (Cal) 345 Pimlico Dr., Walnut Creek CA 94597 **R S Paul's Epis Ch Walnut Creek CA 2006-** B San Antonio TX 11/19/1952 d Joe Fuentes Vasquez & Celia Ovalle. MTS Oblate TS 1991; MDiv Epis TS of The SW 1995. Rec from Roman Catholic 11/10/1990 Bp Earl Nicholas McArthur Jr. m 5/18/2001 Bill Marcus Ennis c 1. Cn for Congrl Dvlpmt Dio New York New York City NY 2003-2006; Vic S Dav's Ch Highland Mills NY 2003-2006; Assoc R Trin Par Wilmington DE 2000-2003; Vic All SS Epis Ch Pleasanton TX 1997-2000; Vic Epis Ch Of The Gd Shepard Geo W TX 1997-2000; Asst R S Paul's Epis Ch San Antonio TX 1995-1996. "Spkng the Word," *Sermons that Wk XII*, Morehouse Pub, 2004; Auth, "A Bean Taco and a Cup of Coffee," *Sermons that Wk*, Morehouse Pub, 1997. DOK 1995; EHWP 1992; EWC 1995. svasquez@stpaulswc.org

VASQUEZ, Martir (Los) 1736 Loma Drive, Hermosa Beach CA 90254 **Vic S Geo's Mssn Hawthorne CA 2001-** B Guatemala 5/30/1964 s Prudencio Vasquez & Lugarda. BA St, Thos (PETED) Guatemala 1986; Theol Lawyer St. Andr's Sem Mex City 1992; BA Jacob Arbens Sch Guatemala 1995. D 6/6/1986 P 11/1/1988 Bp Armando Roman Guerra Soria. m 4/28/1984 Marie Romero c 3. Dio Guatemala Guatemala City 1990-1995. The OSL 2007. martir07@verizon.net

VASQUEZ, Oscar Arturo (SwFla) 2153 46th Ter SW Apt B, Naples FL 34116 B Jocotan Chiquimula GT 5/18/1932 s Manuel De Jesus Vasquez & Gloria Ernestina. San Jose Inter-Dioconate Sem 1957; BA Pstr Inst Rome It 1964. Rec from Roman Catholic 11/1/1980 as Priest Bp Hugo Luis Pina-Lopez. m 2/28/1970 Rosani Caraccioli c 2. St Barn Bookstore Immokalee FL 1987-1991; Dio Cntrl Florida Orlando FL 1984-1985; Dio Honduras Miami FL 1980-1981.

VASQUEZ-JUAREZ, Patricia Ellen (Tex) 1534 Milam St, Columbus TX 78934 B Philadelphia PA 10/7/1954 d Thomas James Gleason & Margaret Jane. BA Neumann Coll Aston PA 1995; MDiv VTS 1997. D 10/11/1997 Bp Charles Bennison P 6/13/1998 Bp John H(enry) Smith. m 6/26/2009 Jose Luis Vasquez-Juarez c 3. S Jn's Epis Ch Columbus TX 2004-2008; S Matt's Ch Wheeling WV 2000-2004; S Ptr's Ch Huntington WV 1999-2000; Cur S Matt's Ch Charleston WV 1997-1999. zpew02@sleh.com

VASQUEZ-VERA, Gladis Elisa (EcuC) Ulloa 213 Y Carriba Apdo 17-02-5304, Quito Ecuador **Iglesia Epis Del Ecuador Ecuador 2004-; Vic Iglesia del Buen Pstr Quito 17-11-353 EC 1988-** B Guayaquil EC 4/26/1958 d Alfonso T Vasquez & Elisa T. Colegio Bachiller; Seminario-Bachiller En Teologia (4 Yrs); Teologia Anglicana. D 12/18/1988 P 12/1/1992 Bp J Neptali Larrea-Moreno. m 12/16/1994 Felicisimo Navas c 1. Dio SE Mex 2001-2004; Iglesia Epis Del Ecuador Ecuador 1996-2001. IGLESIAEPISCOPALADM@GMAIL.COM

VAUGHAN, Jesse L (NCal) 2140 Mission Ave, Carmichael CA 95608 **P-in-c S Mich's Epis Day Sch Carmichael CA 1993-; Trin Cathd Sacramento CA 1991-** B Emporia VA 9/18/1947 s Douglas Vaughan & Elizabeth. BS Hampton U 1969; MDiv EDS 1973; CAS Harv 1976. D 6/23/1973 Bp Robert Lionne DeWitt P 3/2/1974 Bp Morris Fairchild Arnold. S Mich's Epis Day Sch Carmichael CA 1981-1989; All SS' Epis Day Sch Carmel CA 1979-1981; S Dunst's Epis Ch Carmel Vlly CA 1979-1980; S Mths Ch Seaside CA 1977-1979; Par Of Chr Ch Andover MA 1975-1977. Auth, *Sprtl Crisis & The Young*. fathervaughan@smeds.net

VAUGHAN, John (CFla) 3295 Timucua Cir, Orlando FL 32837 B IE 2/22/1957 s John Vaughn & Eileen Angela. BA S Jn Waterford 1981; ThM S Jn Waterford 1984. D 2/18/1996 P 6/1/1996 Bp John Wadsworth Howe. m 6/22/1991 Rebecca Vaughan. S Jos Epis Ch Orlando FL 1998-2005; S Paul's Ch Winter Haven FL 1996-1998; Dio Cntrl Florida Orlando FL 1996-1997. jvaughan9097@yahoo.com

VAUGHN, Denise C (WMo) 4116 Paint Rock Dr, Austin TX 78731 **R Gr Epis Ch Chillicothe MO 2010-** B Utica NY 6/7/1954 d Daniel J Coe & Florence. BA U of So Florida 1976; MDIV Epis TS of the SW 2008. D 6/14/1997 Bp Rogers Sanders Harris P 2/22/2009 Bp Dena Arnall Harrison. c 1. The Ch of the Gd Shpd Austin TX 2008-2010; D S Dav's Epis Ch Englewood FL 2003-2005; D S Jas Epis Ch Port Charlotte FL 2000-2002; D S Nath Ch No Port FL 1997-2000. gracechurchchilli@att.net

VAUGHN, James Barry (Ala) Saint Alban's Church, 429 Cloudland Dr, Birmingham AL 35226 **S Alb's Ch Birmingham AL 2007-; R S Jn's In The Prairies Ch Eutaw AL 2000-; R S Steph's Ch Eutaw AL 2000-** B Mobile AL 10/29/1955 s Henry Clay Vaughn & Vera Nell. BA Harv 1978; MDiv Yale DS 1982; PhD U of St. Andrews 1990. D 10/14/1992 P 4/1/1993 Bp Robert Oran Miller. S Lk's Epis Ch Jacksonville AL 2006; R S Ptr's Ch Germantown Philadelphia PA 2000-2004; S Matt's Epis Ch San Mateo CA 1999-2000; S Ptr's Epis Ch Redwood City CA 1998-1999; Pstr S Wilfrid's Ch Marion AL 1997-1998; Epis Black Belt Mnstry Demopolis AL 1993-1998; Asst Epis Ch Of The Epiph Leeds AL 1992-1993. Auth, "In A New Light," *Sermon In Libr Of Distinctive Preaching*, 1996. AAM. Best Sermon Competition Runner-Up Epis Evang Fndt. anglcan@aol.com

VAUGHN, Jessie Harriet (NwT) 3303 Bacon St, Vernon TX 76384 **D Gr Ch Vernon TX 2002-** B Waterloo NY 1/19/1941 d Thomas Francis Sanpietro & Jessie Louise Harriet Elizabeth. Wm Smith. D 10/27/2002 Bp C(harles) Wallis Ohl. c 4. "The D's Charge (a poem)," *Invoking the Muse*, Watermark Press, 2004. jessievaughn@sbcglobal.net

VAUGHN, Peter Hancock (Ct) 36 Main St, Ellington CT 06029 **D H Trin Epis Ch Enfield CT 2008-; D Dio Connecticut Hartford CT 1990-** B Los Angeles CA 1/30/1937 s Milton Hancock Vaughn & Gladys Mary. BA U Of Hartford 1965; MBA U of Connecticut 1973. D 6/9/1990 Bp Arthur Edward Walmsley. m 11/23/1957 Sally Anne Locke c 3. D S Andr's Epis Ch Enfield CT 1996-2008; D S Jn's Epis Ch Vernon Rock Vernon CT 1990-1997. phvaughn@aol.com

VAUGHN, S. Chadwick (At) St. Francis Episcopal Church, 432 Forest Hill Rd., Macon GA 31210 **Exec Bd Dio Atlanta Atlanta GA 2011-; Pres of the Alum Strng Com Epis TS Of The SW Austin TX 2011-; Dn of the Macon Convoc Dio Atlanta Atlanta GA 2010-; Dioc Cmncatn Cmsn Dio Atlanta Atlanta GA 2010-; R S Fran Ch Macon GA 2009-** B Atlanta GA 9/16/1973 s Steven Douglas Vaughn & Alice Gibson. BA Oglethorpe U 1997; MDiv Epis TS of The SW 2006. D 12/21/2005 P 6/25/2006 Bp J(ohn) Neil Alexander. m 7/22/2000 Amanda Elizabeth Vaughn. Dioc Liturg Cmsn Dio Texas Houston TX 2008-2009; Assoc S Dav's Ch Austin TX 2006-2009; Exec Asst to the Dn Cathd Of S Phil Atlanta GA 2000-2003. Gathering of Leaders 2008. chadwickvaughn@yahoo.com

VAUGHN SR, Thomas Wade (Los) 10344 Wystone Ave, Northridge CA 91326 **Died 3/4/2011** B Benton KY 10/14/1936 s James Robert Vaughn & Elizabeth. BA Eureka Coll 1961; BD Yale DS 1964; MDiv Yale DS 1989. D 6/29/1964 Bp Archie H Crowley P 2/1/1965 Bp Richard S M Emrich. c 3. Auth, "The Encyclopedia Of Jazz By Leonard Feather," *Quincy Jones*.

VAZQUEZ-GELI, Jose R (PR) 912 Calle Zaragoza, Urb. La Rambla, Ponce PR 00730 B 6/12/1928 D P. m 7/28/1951 Zenaida Busigo. Dio Puerto Rico S Just PR 1997-2002.

VEACH, Deborah Joan (Ind) 215 N. 7th St., Terre Haute IN 47807 B Terre Haute IN 1/14/1953 d Jack Norman Vicars & Joanna. Assoc Nrsng Indiana St U 1989. D 10/26/2008 Bp Catherine Elizabeth Maples Waynick. m 6/19/1987 Alan Veach c 4. dveach53@yahoo.com

VEAL, David Lee (NwT) 2519 55th St, Lubbock TX 79413 **Vic S Lk's Epis Ch Levelland TX 2008-; Dep to GC Dio NW Texas Lubbock TX 2000-; Del to WCC Assembly, Harare, Zimbabwe Dom And Frgn Mssy Soc- Epis Ch Cntr New York NY 1998-; Dep to GC Dio NW Texas Lubbock TX 1997-; Dep to GC Dio NW Texas Lubbock TX 1994-; Dep to GC Dio NW Texas Lubbock TX 1991-; Dep to GC Dio NW Texas Lubbock TX 1988-; Dep to GC Dio W Texas San Antonio TX 1982-; Dep to GC Dio W Texas San Antonio TX 1979-** B Knoxville TN 3/10/1938 s Edward DeKalb Veal & Mae. BA U of Alabama 1960; MDiv STUSo 1971; DMin PrTS 1988. D 6/10/1971 P 12/15/1971 Bp Furman Stough. m 8/11/1967 Sue E McGough c 2. Pres EDEO Ft Meyers FL 2007-2010; Int S Chris's Epis Ch Lubbock TX 2005-2008; Int S Barn' Epis Ch Of Odessa Odessa TX 2002-2003; Dep to GC Dio NW Texas Lubbock TX 2000-2001; Moravian - Epis Dialogue Mem Dom And Frgn Mssy Soc- Epis Ch Cntr New York NY 1997-2011; SCER Dom And Frgn Mssy Soc- Epis Ch Cntr New York NY 1994-2000; The TS at The U So Sewanee TN 1994-1997; Trst The U So (Sewanee) Sewanee TN 1994-1997; Angl - RC Dialogue USA Dom And Frgn Mssy Soc- Epis Ch Cntr New York NY 1992-1998; Cn Dio NW Texas Lubbock TX 1987-2001; The TS at The U So Sewanee TN 1983-1986; Trst The U So (Sewanee) Sewanee TN 1983-1986; Dep to GC Dio W Texas San Antonio TX 1982-1983; R Ch Of The Resurr San Antonio TX 1980-1987; Trst Epis TS Of The SW Austin TX 1976-1978; COM Dio W Texas San Antonio TX 1973-1983; Ecum Off Dio Alabama Birmingham AL 1971-1973; R S Steph's Ch Eutaw AL 1971-1973. Auth, "Calendar of SS," Forw Mvmt Press, 2004; Auth, "The Moravians," Forw Mvmt Press, 1999; Auth, "An Esssential Unity," Morehouse Pub, 1997; Contrib, "Contrib," *Lesser Feasts and Fasts*, Ch Pub, Inc, 1980; Auth, "SS Galore," Forw Mvmt Press, 1971. CODE 1975-2001; EDEO 1976-2011; No Amer Acad of Eumenists 1988-2000. DuBose Awd for Serv U So TS 2006. veald@sbcglobal.net

VEALE, David Scott (Vt) 8 Bishop St, Saint Albans VT 05478 **S Lk's Ch S Albans VT 2010-** B Ridgefield NJ 1/12/1962 s Stewart V Veale & Nancy Lee. BA The Coll of New Jersey 1984; BTS Epis Sch for Deacons 2000; MTS Nash 2006. D 12/16/2000 Bp Richard Lester Shimpfky P 9/2/2006 Bp Keith Lynn Ackerman. m 11/21/1999 Donna Lynne Ford c 2. Gr Ch Un City NJ 2006-2010. SSC 2007. davidv@heavymettle.com

VEALE, Donald Meier (Ore) 5346 Don Miguel Dr, Carlsbad CA 92010 B Saint Louis MO 12/17/1931 s Donald Ernest Veale & Emma Georgiana. BA U Pgh

1954; MDiv PDS 1958. D 6/30/1958 Bp Thaddeus F Zielinski P 6/17/1959 Bp Lauriston L Scaife. m 8/20/1973 Barbara M Smith c 2. S Matt's Epis Ch Gold Bch OR 1994-2003; Dio Oregon Portland OR 1991-1993; Vic S Matt's Epis Ch Gold Bch OR 1991-1993; Vic S Tim's Ch Brookings OR 1991-1993; Int S Cross By-The-Sea Ch Hermosa Bch CA 1990-1991; Int H Faith Par Inglewood CA 1989-1990; Int S Fran' Par Palos Verdes Estates CA 1987-1988; All SS Epis Ch Verona PA 1978-1987; S Paul's Ch Monongahela PA 1977; Vic Ch Of The H Sprt Erie PA 1972-1974; Vic S Ptr's Ch Waterford PA 1962-1966; Vic Calv Epis Ch Williamsville NY 1958-1962.

VEALE JR, Erwin Olin (Ga) 3120 Exeter Rd, Augusta GA 30909 B Savannah GA 5/18/1958 s Erwin Olin Veale & Gloria Ann. BS U GA 1980; MDiv Sthrn Bapt TS Louisville KY 1985; DAS STUSo 1995. D 6/1/1994 Bp Harry Woolston Shipps P 3/14/1996 Bp Henry Irving Louttit. m 12/28/1991 Virginia Corinne Kilmer c 2. S Paul's Ch Augusta GA 1998-2004; Vic H Cross Ch Thomson GA 1995-1997. eveale@mail.mcg.edu

VEINOT, William (Ct) 327 Orchard St, Rocky Hill CT 06067 **R S Andr The Apos Rocky Hill CT 1991-** B Winchester MA 12/3/1954 s Richard Paul Veinot & Ellen Marie. AAS Paul Smith's Coll 1975; MDiv Bangor TS 1987; BS SUNY 1987; STM Yale DS 1988; DMin Gordon-Conwell TS 2003. D 6/4/1988 P 5/1/1989 Bp Edward Cole Chalfant. m 8/26/1989 Wendy Jeane c 3. Cur S Jn's Ch Larchmont NY 1988-1991. fatherjoyful@aol.com

VEINTIMILLA, Carlos (EcuC) P.O. Box 0901-5250, Guayaquil Ecuador B Guayaquil EC 3/8/1938 s Luis Veintimilla & Maria V. Seminario De San Andres Mex City Df Mx 1973. D 10/22/1972 Bp Jose Guadalupe Saucedo P 6/1/1973 Bp Adrian Delio Caceres-Villavicencio. m 3/3/1984 Juanita Quezada c 2. P-in-c Iglesia Cristo Rey Guayaquil EC 2000-2003; P-in-c Iglesia de la Transfiguracion Guayaquil EC 1995-2003; Litoral Dio Ecuador Guayaquil EQ EC 1986-2003; Iglesia Epis Del Ecuador Ecuador 1973-1994. Scroll Of Friendship Miami 1962. carlosvein@hotmail.com

VEIT JR, Richard Fred (Wyo) 7711 Hawthorne Dr, Cheyenne WY 82009 **R S Mk's Ch Cheyenne WY 2005-** B Bronxville NY 8/14/1967 s Richard Fred Veit & Betty Catherine. BA U CO 1989; MDiv VTS 1998. D 6/5/1999 P 12/1/1999 Bp William Jerry Winterrowd. m 2/23/2002 Caroline C Weidenkeller c 2. Asst S Marg's Ch Woodbridge VA 2000-2005; Asst All SS Ch Loveland CO 1999-2000. Young Men's Literary Club of Cheyenne 2007. rickfveit@aol.com

VELASQUEZ BORJAS, Gladis Margarita (Hond) Aldea Santa Cruz, Tegucigalpa, Tegucigalpa M.D.C. FM 15023 Honduras **Dio Honduras Miami FL 2006-; Iglesia Epis Hondurena San Pedro Sula 2006-** B Villa de San Francisco F.M. 2/27/1961 d Carlos Humberto Velasquez & Margarita. DIT Seminario Diocesano. D 10/29/2005 Bp Lloyd Emmanuel Allen. c 3.

VELEZ-RIVERA, Daniel (Mass) 11 Vinal St Apt 7, Brighton MA 02135 **P-in-c S Ptr's Ch Salem MA 2009-** B New York NY 10/27/1960 s Máximo Vélez Roman & Socorro. BD NEU 1983; MS Bos 2005; MDiv Bos 2006. D 6/3/2006 Bp M(arvil) Thomas Shaw III P 1/6/2007 Bp Gayle Elizabeth Harris. m 5/20/2004 Theodore P Gallagher. Gr Ch Salem MA 2006-2009. Auth, "Transforming Lives, Transforming Communities:The Mnstry of Presence," *ATR*, ATR, 2011; Auth, "Lay Wmn and Dss in Puerto Rico: The Legacy of Catalina Olivieri Rivera," *Deeper Joy: Lay Wmn & Vocation in the 20th Century Epis Ch*, Ch Pub, Inc., 2005. Distinguished Alum Awd Bos TS 2009; Transformational Mnstry Fell ECF 2007. danielvr1@verizon.net

VELLA, Joan Christine (WNC) 147 Sourwood Road, State Road NC 28676 **Int Gr Ch In The Mountains Waynesville NC 2007-** B New York NY 10/25/1936 d Vincent Paul Vella & Catherine Geraldine. BA Meredith Coll 1986; MA Washington Theol Un 1988; MDiv STUSo 1997; DMin Hood TS 2007. D 6/21/1997 P 6/20/1998 Bp Robert Carroll Johnson Jr. Int R S Tim's Ch Wilson NC 2008-2010; Int Ch Of The Epiph Newton NC 2005-2007; R Yadkin Vlly Cluster Salisbury NC 2004-2005; Vic Galloway Memi Chap Elkin NC 2000-2003; Asst P S Mk's Ch Wilson NC 1997-2000; Asst S Tim's Ch Wilson NC 1997-2000. vella54@gmail.com

VELLA JR, Joseph Agius (SwFla) 125 Lamara Way Ne, Saint Petersburg FL 33704 B Beaufort SC 1/27/1948 s Joseph Agius Vella & Mary Florine. U Grenoble Fr 1967; U So 1970; BA U of So Carolina 1984; MDiv TESM 1988. P 5/1/1989 Bp Plinio L Simoes. m 9/9/1978 Judith Rentiers. St Josephs Ch Ft Myers FL 1999-2000; Ch Of The H Cross St Petersburg FL 1998-1999; Dio Arkansas Little Rock AR 1995-1997; Ch Of The Annunc Cordova TN 1994-1995; R All SS Ch Cayce SC 1992-1994; D S Jn's Ch Charleston SC 1988-1989.

VELLOM, Lee Sherwin (Az) 1741 North Camino Rebecca, Nogales AZ 85621 **D S Andr's Epis Ch Nogales AZ 1996-** B Pasadena CA 9/21/1932 s Ralph Cauble Vellom & Dorothy Mildred. BA U CA 1954; BA Sch for Deacons 1984. D 12/3/1988 Bp William Edwin Swing. m 4/11/1953 James Fitzsimmons c 1. D S Jn's Epis Ch Oakland CA 1994-1996; D All SS Epis Ch San Leandro CA 1989-1993. NAAD 1983. Life Regent Natl Eagle Scout Assn 1980. skipvell@mchsi.com

VELLOM, Timothy John (WTex) 15919 Colton Wl, San Antonio TX 78247 **R S Matt's Epis Ch Universal City TX 1999-** B New London CT 1/22/1958 s Lee Sherwin Vellom & James. BA U So 1980; MDiv TESM 1985. D 6/20/1985 Bp Scott Field Bailey P 1/1/1986 Bp Stanley Fillmore Hauser. m 1/3/1981 Ann Vellom c 2. S Jas Epis Ch Del Rio TX 1993-1999; R Trin Epis Ch Edna TX 1992-1993; Vic Trin Epis Ch Edna TX 1988-1991; Asst All SS Epis Ch Corpus Christi TX 1985-1988. tjvellom@gmail.com

VELTHUIZEN, Teunisje (NI) 608 Cushing St, South Bend IN 46616 B Ermelo NL 3/18/1944 d Teunis Velthuizen & Aartje. BA Hope Coll 1966; MRE Wstrn TS 1977; MDiv GTS 1985; CSD GTS 1996. D 6/8/1985 P 12/1/1985 Bp Howard Samuel Meeks. R Ch Of The H Trin So Bend IN 1991-2007; Int S Paul's Epis Ch Jackson MI 1991; Int Ch Of The Resurr Battle Creek MI 1989-1990; Vic S Steph's Epis Ch Plainwell MI 1985-1989. Ord Of Julian Of Norwich, Oblate 1998. teunisje@aol.com

VENEZIA, Deborah Lynn (CFla) 7725 Indian Ridge Trail South, Kissimmee FL 34747 **Vic S Jos Epis Ch Orlando FL 2007-** B Morristown NJ 12/21/1956 d Michael Joseph Skibic & Alice May. BS FD 1979; MA Rutgers-The St U 1992; MDiv Drew U 2004. D 6/12/2004 Bp Martin Gough Townsend P 12/18/2004 Bp John Palmer Croneberger. m 7/31/1982 Ralph Venezia. Int S Jn's Epis Ch Boonton NJ 2005-2007; D S Geo's Epis Ch Maplewood NJ 2004-2005. revdvenezia@aol.com

VENKATESH, Catherine Richardson (WMass) 281 Renfrew St, Arlington MA 02476 **Lic Supply P Dio Massachusetts Boston MA 2007-; Lic supply P Dio Massachusetts Boston MA 2007-** B Lancaster PA 11/22/1966 d Jonathan Lynde Richardson & Alice Elmore. BA Wms 1988; Dplma U of Warwick 1989; MS U of Washington 1993; MDiv CDSP 1998. D 6/20/1998 Bp Vincent Waydell Warner P 1/9/1999 Bp Edward Lewis Lee Jr. m 11/11/2006 Venkatesh Natarajan c 1. P S Jn's Ch Newtonville MA 2009; Dn of So Berkshires Dio Wstrn Massachusetts Springfield MA 2003-2006; Mem, Congrl Dvlpmt Grants Team Dio Wstrn Massachusetts Springfield MA 2002-2006; R S Jas Ch Great Barrington MA 2002-2006; Int S Paul's Epis Ch Elk Rapids MI 2001-2002; Assoc R Gr Epis Ch Traverse City MI 1998-2001. Auth, "Jos'S Cross," *Preaching Through The Year Of Matt: Sermons That Wk X*, Morehouse, 2001; Auth, "The Wounds Of The Risen Chr," *Preaching Through The Year Of Mk: Sermons That Wk Viii*, Morehouse Pub, 1999; Auth, "Hope For All Creation: Seeds For A Chr Enviromental Ethic," *Millenium 3*, 1997. Phi Beta Kappa Wms 1988. cwoodsr@verizon.net

VENTRIS, Margaret Pyre (Los) 72348 Larrea Ave, Twentynine Palms CA 92277 **S Mart-In-The-Fields Mssn Twentynine Palms CA 2011-** B Tucson AZ 9/4/1949 d Jackman Pyre & Jane Wyndham Martin. Bloy Hse/CST; BS San Diego St U. D 6/4/2011 Bp Joseph Jon Bruno. m 4/27/1968 Kenneth Ventris c 2. kenandpeggy3@msn.com

VERBECK III, Guido Fridolin (WLa) 4741 Crescent Dr, Shreveport LA 71106 **Dep, GC Dio Wstrn Louisiana Alexandria LA 2000-2012; R S Paul's Epis Ch Shreveport LA 1996-** B Syracuse NY 12/30/1940 s Guido Fridolin Verbeck & Dorothea. BA Marq 1965; MDiv VTS 1983; Cont Educ Fllshp VTS 1994. D 6/10/1983 P 5/18/1984 Bp Charles Farmer Duvall. Chair Camp Hardtner Cmsn Dio Wstrn Louisiana Alexandria LA 1996-2005; R S Alb's Epis Ch Monroe LA 1992-1996; Dio Cntrl Gulf Coast Pensacola FL 1985-1992; Cur S Paul's Ch Mobile AL 1983-1990. Auth, "Funny Things Happen On The Way To The Altar". Ord of St. Geo BSA 2004. frguido@bellsouth.net

VERBER, James Leonard (RI) 146 Chatworth Rd, North Kingstown RI 02852 B De Pere WI 9/2/1925 s Peter John Verber & Marie Leona. BS U of Wisconsin 1949; MS U of Wisconsin 1950; MDiv EDS 1988. D 7/13/1985 P 6/25/1988 Bp George Nelson Hunt III. m 11/19/1960 Ruth Geraldine Beatty c 5. Int S Mk's Epis Ch Riverside RI 1994-1995; Int Ch Of The Gd Shpd Pawtucket RI 1993-1994; Int Chr Ch In Lonsdale Lincoln RI 1991-1992; Int S Jn's Ch Barrington RI 1989-1990; Int Ch Of The Epiph Providence RI 1989; Asst S Matt's Ch Barrington RI 1987-1988; Asst S Mths Ch Coventry RI 1985-1986. vgverberger@aol.com

VERDAASDONK, Henry Joseph (Alb) 34 Spencer Blvd, Coxsackie NY 12051 **D S Lk's Ch Catskill NY 2003-** B Coxsackie NY 8/18/1935 s Jacobus Jan Verdaasdonk & Maria. D 1/25/2003 Bp David John Bena. m 4/13/1958 Joyce Danetta Flansburg c 3.

VERDI, Barry Ellis (Los) 11551 Arminta St, North Hollywood CA 91605 B Los Angeles CA 10/9/1937 s Vaughn Linton Verdi & Edith. BA San Jose St U 1959; MDiv CDSP 1962; MA San Jose St U 1969. D 6/29/1962 P 1/1/1963 Bp Gordon V Smith. m 7/9/1986 Vicenta Villarreal. Asst S Nich Par Encino CA 2002; H Fam Mssn No Hollywood CA 1987-2002; Assoc S Simon's Par San Fernando CA 1983-1986; R S Jn's Epis Ch Clayton CA 1977-1981; Urban Assoc Trin Cathd San Jose CA 1973-1976; P-in-c All SS Epis Ch Palo Alto CA 1969-1970; Urban Assoc Trin Cathd San Jose CA 1966-1968; Vic Trin Ch Denison IA 1962-1965. Auth, "The Pk". Melchizidek Assn. Nosotros Pres Awd For Contrib To Hisp Cause 1990.

VERELL, Gary Archer (SeFla) 917 E Ridge Village Dr, Miami FL 33157 B Richmond VA 11/16/1933 s Emmett Archer Verell & Nena. BA Catawba Coll 1956; MDiv PDS 1959; Ctp U NC 1983. D 9/19/1959 P 3/26/1960 Bp Richard Henry Baker. m 12/28/1959 Phyllis Mead Roseman c 2. Stndg Com Dio SE

Florida Miami FL 1996-1998; S Faith's Epis Ch Cutler Bay FL 1989-1998; Stndg Com Dio Wstrn Kansas Hutchinson KS 1984-1989; Vic H Apos Ch Ellsworth KS 1982-1989; S Fran Cmnty Serv Inc. Salina KS 1982-1989; Chapl & Prog Dir S Nich Chap Ellsworth KS 1982-1989; Ch Of S Andr And S Monica Philadelphia PA 1980-1981; R All SS Ch Norristown PA 1976-1978; Stndg Com Dio SW Virginia Roanoke VA 1971-1976; R Emm Ch Covington VA 1969-1976; R S Thos Epis Ch Reidsville NC 1962-1969; Min in charge S Andr's Ch Haw River NC 1959-1962. GARYVERELLRP@GMAIL.COM

VERGARA, Winfred B (LI) 4011 68th Street #2, Woodside NY 11377 **Asian Mssnr Epis Ch Cntr New York NY 2004-; Mssnr, Asiamerica Mnstrs Epis Ch Cntr New York NY 2004-** B Pili Ajuy Iloilo PH 12/25/1950 s Aureo Pelias Vergara & Clarita Bagao. BA Trin U of Asia, PH 1973; MDiv S Andr's TS Manila Ph 1978; ThM SE Asia Grad Sch Sg 1983; DMin SFTS 1990; D.D. Honoris Causa CDSP 2007. Rec 1/1/1993 as Priest Bp Richard Lester Shimpfky. m 1/27/1979 Angela Cornel Vergara. Cn Dio El Camino Real Monterey CA 1993-2004; Founding Vic H Chld Epis Ch San Jose CA 1991-2004; Assoc S Phil's Ch San Jose CA 1988-1991. Auth, "Being Epis," The Epis Ch, 2011; Auth, "Catholicity and Brief Hist of the Epis Ch in the Philippines," The Epis Ch, 2010; Auth, "Evang, Mssn, Globalization," The Epis Ch, 2009; Auth, "Mainstreaming: Asians in ECUSA," *Epis Books & Resources*, The Epis Ch, 2006; Auth, "Milkfish In Brackish Water," *Filipino Mnstry In Amer Context*, Sunrise Pub, 1992; Auth, "Filipino Immigration And Theol Of Versatility," *Pacific Theol Revs*, SFTS, San Anselmo, California, 1990; Auth, "The Contextual Theol Of Kosuke Koyama," SEAGST, Singapore, 1989; Auth, "Dynamics Of Rel Revolution," SFTS, San Anselmo, California, 1989; Auth, "Theol Of The People:Aglipayan Challenge," SATS, Quezon City, Philippines, 1972. Alpha Phi Omega 1970; Epis Asiamerica Mnstry 1990; Filipino Amer Coun 1986-1995. Oustanding Alum Trin U of Asia 2009; DD, honoris causa CDSP 2007; Cn To Asian Cultures Epis Dio El Camino Real 2000. wvergara@episcopalchurch.org

VERGARA GRUESO, Edison (Colom) Carrera 6 No 49-85, Piso 2, Bogota Colombia B Buenaventura Colombia 6/11/1960 s Jesus M Vergara & Anatilde. Teologia Cristo Sacerdote 1994; DD.HH U.T. choco 2003. D 6/16/2007 P 10/18/2008 Bp Francisco Jose Duque-Gomez. m 9/9/1995 Ambrosina Cordona-Renteria c 2. edverg7@hotmail.com

VERNON, Valerie Veronica (SeFla) No address on file. B Montego Bay Jamaica 2/4/1951 AA Northwood U. D 7/26/2003 Bp Leopold Frade. c 2.

VERRET, Joan Claire (CFla) 220 E Palm Dr, Lakeland FL 33803 **Bd Dir Camp Wingmann Avon Pk FL 1995-** B Youngstown OH 9/22/1935 d Frederick Russell Verret & Ida Florence. S Jos's Hosp of Nrsng Reading PA 1956; BA S Leo Coll 1979; Cert Inst for Chr Stds Florida 1989. D 12/8/1990 Bp John Wadsworth Howe. c 4. D S Steph's Ch Lakeland FL 1997-2002; Dir Pstr Care All SS Epis Ch Lakeland FL 1990-1996. Anglical Fllshp of Pryr; NAAD. Rec of Steph Awd Dio Cntrl Florida 1999. joanclairev@aol.com

VERRETTE, Sallie Cheavens (Ia) St. Paul's Episcopal Church, 6th & State., Grinnell IA 50112 B El Paso TX 7/27/1932 d John H Cheavens & Erid Morgan. BA Willamette U 1954; MSW U of Iowa 1982. D 12/16/2006 P 6/16/2007 Bp Alan Scarfe. m 1/14/1956 Victor Verrette c 3. verrette@iowatelecom.net

VERSHURE, Claude Edward (SD) 25413 He Sapa Trail, Custer SD 57730 **D S Lk's Ch Hot Sprg SD 2000-** B Bemidji MN 9/3/1946 s Clarence A Vershure & Arlotte Anne. AA Hibbing Cmnty Coll 1972; BS Minnesota St U Moorehead 1976. D 6/12/2000 P 7/23/2005 Bp Creighton Leland Robertson. m 6/12/1971 Dorothy Susan Kangas c 2. cdvershure@gwtc.net

VERVYNCK, Jennifer R (SanD) 5002 Nighthawk Way, Oceanside CA 92056 **Cn S Jn's Epis Ch Chula Vista CA 2010-; Cn Congrl Dev., Deploy, and Formation Dio San Diego San Diego CA 1996-** B Honolulu HI 7/6/1947 d George William Renn & Anna Margaret. Wstrn Washington U 1967; BA U of Washington 1968; Cert ETSBH 1988. D 6/4/1988 Bp Charles Brinkley Morton. m 7/20/1968 Brian D Vervynck c 3. Dio San Diego San Diego CA 2010-2011; D S Barth's Epis Ch Poway CA 1996-1997; Epis Cmnty Serv San Diego CA 1995; D S Anne's Epis Ch Oceanside CA 1995; All SS Ch Vista CA 1988-1994. jennyvervynck@gmail.com

VESGA-ARDILA, Ramon (Ve) Ave. Caroni, Casa No. 100, Barquimeno 3001 Venezuela **Dio Venezuela Colinas De Bello Monte Caracas 10-42-A VE 2004-** B 10/26/1950 D 5/17/2002 Bp Orlando Jesus Guerrero.

VEST, Douglas C (Los) 1688 W. Placita Canoa Azul, Green Valley AZ 85614 B Covington KY 6/15/1920 s Hugh Finley Vest & Geraldine. ChE U Cinc 1942; MS USNA 1945; MS Jn Hopkins U 1953; MDiv EDS 1966; MA Duquesne U 1982. D 9/1/1966 P 3/11/1967 Bp Francis E I Bloy. m 12/11/1982 Norvene Foster c 2. Asst Epis Ch Of S Fran-In-The-Vlly Green Vlly AZ 2007-2010; Asst S Mk's Par Altadena CA 2002-2007; Asst Ch Of The Ang Pasadena CA 1997-2001; Asst Gr Epis Ch Glendora CA 1990-1997; Cn Mssnr for Mnstry Dio Los Angeles Los Angeles CA 1982-1989; Assoc All SS Ch Pasadena CA 1975-1981; Vic Epis Ch Of S Andr And S Chas Granada Hills CA 1968-1975; Asst S Andr's Par Fullerton CA 1966-1968. Auth, "A Second Helping," Cedar Creek Books, 2010; Auth, "Churchianity Lite," Xulon Press, 2007; Auth, "Entering the Mystery," Xulon Press, 2006; Auth, "Hm for the Heart," Xulon Press, 2005; Auth, "Deep Treasures from Retreat," Source Books, 2003; Contrib, "Sprtl formation Bible (4 Books)," Zonderven, 1999; Auth, "On Pilgrimage," Cowley Press, 1998; Auth, "Luminous Island," Source Books, 1996; Auth, "Sauntering into Holiness," Source books, 1995; Auth, "Why Stress Keeps Returning," Loyola, 1991. Oblate Ord of S Ben 1989. vest@composury.com

VETTEL-BECKER, Richard Arthur (Cal) 706 Tabriz Dr, Billings MT 59105 B Fort Belvoir VA 10/23/1955 s Arthur Andrew Becker & June Virginia. GTS; BA Evangel U 1977; MDiv Gordon-Conwell TS 1981. D 6/1/1992 P 7/1/1993 Bp Charles Jones III. m 12/16/1978 Cynthia Dawne Hutchinson. Trin Ch San Francisco CA 2003-2004; P Calv Epis Ch Roundup MT 1994-2006. ACPE. eschaton7@msn.com

VIA, John Albert (At) 8340 Main St., Port Republic VA 24471 B Gorman TX 10/13/1937 s Albert Hoyt Via & Hallie Mae. BA Baylor U 1959; MA Mississippi St U 1961; PhD U IL 1968. D 5/16/1976 P 6/1/1977 Bp Addison Hosea. m 9/9/1989 Alison Hardwick c 2. Ch Of The Medtr Washington GA 1990-2003; R Ch Of The Redeem Greensboro GA 1990-2003; Assoc H Trin Par Decatur GA 1982-1986; D S Bede's Ch Atlanta GA 1976-1982. Auth, *Milton's Antiprelatical Tracts: The Poet Speaks in Prose*, Milton Stds V; Auth, *Milton's The Passion: A Successful Failure*, Milton Quarterly; Auth, *The Rhythm of Regenerate Experience*, Renaissance Papers. ja37via@yahoo.com

VICENS, Leigh Christiana (Mil) 1833 Regent St, Madison WI 53726 **P S Andr's Ch Madison WI 2010-; D S Andr's Ch Madison WI 2009-** B Boston MA 9/11/1981 d Guillermo J Vicens & Martha Jean. BA Dart 2004; MA U of Wisconsin 2006; MDiv VTS 2009. D 6/6/2009 Bp Steven Andrew Miller. lvicens41@gmail.com

VICKERS, David Lee (EMich) 8119 M 68, Indian River MI 49749 **R S Jn's Epis Ch Ouray CO 2011-; S Andr's Epis Ch Gaylord MI 2010-; Dio Estrn Michigan Saginaw MI 2002-; Dn-Nthrn Convoc Dio Estrn Michigan Saginaw MI 2000-** B Detroit MI 4/10/1947 s Robert Lee Vickers & Dorothy Vernon. AA Macomb Cmnty Coll 1968; BA Estrn Michigan U 1971; MA Estrn Michigan U 1971; DMA U CO 1979; MDiv Epis TS of The SW 1999. D 6/5/1999 P 12/18/1999 Bp William Jerry Winterrowd. m 7/1/1981 Barbara Ruth Aumiller. Trsfg Epis Ch Indn River MI 2000-2011; The Ch Of Chr The King (Epis) Arvada CO 1999-2000.

VICKERY JR, Robert (Tex) St. Michael's Episcopal Church, 1500 N. Capital of Texas Highway, Austin TX 78746 **R S Mich's Ch Austin TX 1990-** B Lubbock TX 3/14/1951 s Robert Vickery & Norma Jean. BS Rice U 1973; MDiv VTS 1976. D 6/17/1976 P 6/22/1977 Bp Roger Howard Cilley. m 5/25/1973 Debra Ann Gill c 3. P-in-c S Mart's Epis Ch Copperas Cove TX 1983-1988; R S Chris's Ch Killeen TX 1979-1990; Chr Ch Cathd Houston TX 1979; Asst S Mart's Epis Ch Houston TX 1976-1979. EvangES 1977. rvickery1@austin.rr.com

VIDAL, Gene Vance (Az) Po Box 13647, Phoenix AZ 85002 B Washington DC 3/18/1942 s Eugene Luther Vidal & Katherine Amar. BA U of Arizona 1963; BD VTS 1966; MA U of Arizona 1971. D 6/22/1966 P 12/1/1966 Bp J(ohn) Joseph Meakins Harte. m 6/7/1966 Mary Vidal. Dio Maryland Baltimore MD 2003-2004; Asst S Mich's Ch Coolidge AZ 1978-1981; Vic All SS Epis Ch Stafford TX 1974-1978; Vic SS Phil And Jas Morenci AZ 1974-1978; Int S Andr's Epis Ch Nogales AZ 1971-1974; Asst Gr S Paul's Epis Ch Tucson AZ 1968-1969; Asst S Phil's In The Hills Tucson AZ 1967-1968; Vic Chr Ch Florence AZ 1966-1967.

VIDMAR, Mary Burton (WMass) 133 N, Main St, North Brookfield MA 01535 B Toledo OH 7/6/1938 d Burton Stewart Floraday & Florence. BA Mary Manse Coll 1966; MDiv U of Notre Dame 1987; CATS SWTS 2000. D 6/24/2000 P 1/6/2001 Bp Herbert Thompson Jr. c 2. R Chr Memi Ch No Brookfield MA 2004-2010; Dio Wstrn Massachusetts Springfield MA 2004-2010; P Dvlp H Fam Episc Fllshp Harrison OH 2000-2004; P-in-c S Lk Ch Cincinnati OH 2000-2004. Fllshp of the Way of the Cross 2005. mbcfv11@hotmail.com

VIE, Diane E (SwVa) 3536 Willow Lawn, Lynchburg VA 24503 **Asst to the R S Jn's Ch Lynchburg VA 2007-** B Pittsburgh PA 8/10/1966 d David Edwards & Barbara. BS Estrn Illinois U 1988; MDiv VTS 2007. D 6/2/2007 Bp William Dailey Persell P 12/8/2007 Bp William Michie Klusmeyer. m 6/19/1993 Todd M Vie c 1. diane@stjohnslynchburg.org

VIE, Todd M (SwVa) 3536 Willow Lawn Dr, Lynchburg VA 24503 **Assoc S Paul's Epis Ch Lynchburg VA 2007-** B St Louis MO 11/15/1963 s Richard Vie & Joan. U of Missouri; BD No Cntrl Coll 1987; MDiv VTS 2007. D 6/2/2007 Bp William Dailey Persell P 12/8/2007 Bp William Michie Klusmeyer. m 6/19/1993 Diane E Diane E Edwards c 1. stpaultodd@yahoo.com

VIEL, Brian John (WK) 800 W. 32nd Ave., Hutchinson KS 67502 **Assoc Gr Epis Ch Hutchinson KS 2011-** B Los Angeles CA 9/23/1949 s Andrew Sargent Viel & Lynne Margaret. AA Ft Scott Cmnty Coll 1980; BS Wichita St U 1982; MS Pittsburgh St U 1989; Ed.S. Pittsburgh St U 1992. D 3/15/2008 P 1/10/2009 Bp James Marshall Adams Jr. m 5/1/1987 Mary June Grant c 2.

Chapl S Jn's Mltry Sch Salina KS 2009-2011; P S Mk's Ch Lyons KS 2008-2009. bviel@cox.net

VIERECK, Alexis (Mass) No address on file. B 7/7/1946 D 12/1/1974 Bp John Melville Burgess P 12/6/1975 Bp Morris Fairchild Arnold.

VIGGERS, Jack Trenchard (Oly) Po Box 834, Prairie City OR 97869 **Died 10/10/2009** B Springfield MO 4/12/1924 s Gerald Henry Viggers & Mildred Shaw. USMMA 1943; CDSP 1958. D 6/17/1958 P 12/18/1958 Bp Norman L Foote. c 4. CADO 1986; NNECA; Rural Workers Ntwk 1950. Hon Life Mem Untd Way Untd Way of Booneville Cnty, ID ID Falls & Bonneville Cnty 1982. viggers@ortelco.net

VIGGIANO, Robert Peter (Tex) 139 Green Grv, Georgetown TX 78633 B Ridgewood NJ 6/22/1958 s Victor Viggiano & Dorothy. BA Alleg 1980; MA Shippensburg U 1993; MDiv Epis TS of The SW 1999. D 6/11/1999 P 1/15/2000 Bp Michael Whittington Creighton. m 12/27/1997 Karen Cecil c 1. Gr Epis Ch Georgetown TX 2005-2006; R S Jas' Epis Ch La Grange TX 2001-2005; Cur The Epis Ch Of S Jn The Bapt York PA 1999-2001. rpviggiano@yahoo.com

VIL, Jean Madoché (Hai) PO Box 407139, C/O Lynx Air, Fort Lauderdale FL 33340 Haiti **P in charge of Ascen Par, Bainet Dio Haiti Ft Lauderdale FL 2008-; P-in-c Dio Haiti Ft Lauderdale FL 2002-** B Port-au-Prince Haiti 8/24/1974 s Jean Vil & Josélia. Dplma Epis U Of Haiti 1999. D P 7/28/2002 Bp Jean Zache Duracin. m 12/18/2008 ketia Dorvilas.

VILAR-SANTIAGO, Miguel E (Md) PO Box 264, Brooklanville MD 21022 B Juana Diaz PR 10/18/1940 s Jose M Vilar & Irene. BA U of Puerto Rico 1964; MDiv ETSC 1967; STM Centro Estudios Caribbean 1973. Trans 6/1/1990 Bp A(lbert) Theodore Eastman. m 10/24/1970 Barbara Reed c 3. Dio Puerto Rico S Just PR 2004; Dio Puerto Rico S Just PR 1996-2003; Dio Maryland Baltimore MD 1990-1995; Hisp Mssn Baltimore MD 1990-1995; Hisp Mssnr Dio Maryland Baltimore MD 1989-1995; Dio Puerto Rico S Just PR 1980-1988; Dio Puerto Rico S Just PR 1971-1979.

VILAS, Franklin Edward (Nwk) 18 Greylawn Dr, Lakewood NJ 08701 B New York NY 11/21/1934 s Franklin Edward Vilas & Georgette. BA Ya 1956; BD VTS 1959; STM Andover Newton TS 1971; DMin NYTS 1978. D 6/11/1959 Bp Walter H Gray P 3/19/1960 Bp John Henry Esquirol. m 6/3/1958 Joyce H Hoinacki c 2. R S Paul's Epis Ch Chatham NJ 1991-2000; Wainwright Hse Rye NY 1985-1991; Dio Connecticut Hartford CT 1981-1985; S Ann And The H Trin Brooklyn NY 1976-1981; P-in-c Par of Trin Ch New York NY 1973-1976; R S Jn's Ch Beverly Farms MA 1964-1973; Cur S Mk's Ch New Canaan CT 1959-1964. Auth, "Teilhard and Jung: A Cosmic and Psychic Convergence," *Teilhard Stds Number 56*, Amer Teilhard Assn, 2008. revfvilas@optonline.net

VILLAGOMEZA, Christian G (SwFla) 1119 Dockside Dr, Lutz FL 33559 **Vic S Chad's Ch Tampa FL 2003-; Chapl Intl Seafarers Mssn of Tampa Bay Tampa FL 2000-** B Cotabato Philippines 4/5/1958 AA Trin Of Quezon City Ph 1978; BTh St. Andr's TS Quezon City Ph 1982; MDiv St. Andr's TS Quezon City Ph 1990. Trans from Episcopal Church in the Philippines 12/21/2005 Bp John Bailey Lipscomb. m 10/26/1983 Liwliwa S Reyes c 3. father@villagomeza.com

VILLAMARIN-GUTIERREZ, Washington Rigoberto (EcuC) Calle Hernando Sarmiento, N 39-54 Y Portete Ecuador **Ecuador New York NY 2009-; Iglesia Epis Del Ecuador Ecuador 2009-** B Quito Ecuador 7/22/1959 s Angel Benigno Villamarin & Rosa Elvira. D 5/30/2009 Bp Wilfrido Ramos-Orench. m 11/20/1990 Angelica Ortiz c 3. washo_v_g@hotmail.com

VILLEMUER, Lauren Anne (Lex) 809 Palomino Ln, Lexington KY 40503 **D Ch Of The Gd Shpd Lexington KY 2006-** B Inglewood CA 10/16/1961 d Philip Villemuer & Nancy. AAS U of Houston 1988; RN Alvin Coll 1991; Formation Prog Cntrl New York w Bex 2005. D 11/19/2005 Bp Gladstone Bailey Adams III. c 3. lauren@goodshepherdlex.org

VILORD, Charles Louis (SwFla) No address on file. **D Dio SW Florida Sarasota FL 1974-** B Suffern NY 7/2/1932 s Charles C Vilord & Evelyn I. D 12/21/1974 Bp Emerson Paul Haynes. m 8/4/1955 Elizabeth A Russell.

VINAL, K N (CFla) 5700 Trinity Prep Ln, Winter Park FL 32792 B Jacksonville FL 7/1/1960 s Nelson Corrie Vinal & Doris Edna. D 6/11/1995 Bp Stephen Hays Jecko P 12/16/1995 Bp Don Adger Wimberly. m 10/21/1989 Laura Borden c 2. vinalk@trinityprep.org

VINAS-PLASENCIA, Aquilino Manuel (CFla) 31 S Forsyth Rd, Orlando FL 32807 **Hisp Mssnr S Chris's Ch Orlando FL 2002-** B 1/4/1928 s Felix Pedro Vinas-Barrios & Victoria. Epis TS of The SW; BTh Los Pinos Nuevos Sem, Cuba 1954; BD Instituto de Segunda Ensenanza 1960; BD UTS 1960; Contador Institucion Nacional de Comercio 1964; Nova U 1979. Trans from Iglesia Episcopal de Cuba 8/25/1967 as Priest Bp Walter C Klein. c 5. Assoc Hisp Mssnr Chr The King Epis Ch Orlando FL 1997-2001; Assoc Cathd Ch Of S Lk Orlando FL 1984-1995; Dio Cntrl Florida Orlando FL 1974-1989; Cur Chr The King Epis Ch Orlando FL 1967-1978. "Obras y Promesas de Dios"; "Senderos de Fe"; Auth, "Mi Vida in El Campo"; Auth, "Albores De La Esperanza". hon a Quien hon merece Iglesia Santa Maria de los Angeles 2004; Reconocimento por labor Iglesia San Cristobal 2003; Honoring por Job in Hisp Mssn Cristo el Rey, Jerusalem 2001; Certificado de Apreciasin Cristo el Rey, Jerusalem.

VINCE, Gail Lynne (EMich) 449 Irons Park Dr, West Branch MI 48661 **P-in-c S Andr's Epis Ch Rose City MI 2004-** B Detroit MI 3/15/1935 d George Howard Glover & Kathryne Ann. BA U MI 1956; Cert U CA 1959; MDiv SWTS 1991. D 6/21/1991 Bp Henry Irving Mayson P 9/12/1992 Bp R(aymond) Stewart Wood Jr. m 2/12/1966 Robert E Godlewski c 1. Dio Estrn Michigan Saginaw MI 2003; R Trin Epis Ch W Branch MI 1994-2002; Asst Journey of Faith Epis Ch Detroit MI 1993-1995; Dio Michigan Detroit MI 1991-1992; Asst S Andr's Ch Waterford MI 1991-1992. Evang Educational Soc; OCCA. gvince@voyager.net

VINCENT, Janet (WA) 4974 Sentinel Dr Apt 304, Bethesda MD 20816 **R S Columba's Ch Washington DC 2006-** B Yonkers NY 2/18/1955 d Frederick Moore Vincent & Louise. BA Manhattanville Coll 1978; MDiv GTS 1983. D 6/4/1983 P 1/8/1984 Bp Paul Moore Jr. m 9/16/1978 Carl Vincent. R Santa Rosa Mssn at Gr Ch White Plains NY 1999-2006; Gr Ch White Plains NY 1997-2006; P Santa Rosa Mssn at Gr Ch White Plains NY 1997-1998; R S Jn's Epis Ch Kingston NY 1988-1997; Stff, Cntr for Xian Sprtlty The GTS New York NY 1986-1990; Assoc R Gr Epis Ch Nyack NY 1983-1988. Auth, "Voice Of The Shepherdess," 1996. jvs40@aol.com

VINCENT-ALEXANDER, Samantha Ann (SVa) 431 Massachusetts Ave., Norfolk VA 23508 **Asst to the R Ch Of The Ascen Norfolk VA 2005-** B Bethesda MD 2/9/1977 d William Vincent & Jan. BA Ge 1999; MDiv PrTS 2004; Post Grad Diplom VTS 2005. D 12/3/2005 P 6/24/2006 Bp Gladstone Bailey Adams III. m 5/20/2006 Conor Matthew Alexander. samanthavincent@hotmail.com

VINE, Walter James (Mil) 2655 N Grant Blvd, Milwaukee WI 53210 B Milwaukee WI 1/24/1946 s Pembroke Carleton Vine & Mabel Lydia. MA Chicago Med Sch Chicago IL; AS/RN Milwaukee Area Tech Coll; BS U of St. Fran. D 5/9/1998 Bp Roger John White. m 8/29/1970 Sharon Rae Carlson c 4. WALLYVINE@YAHOO.COM

VINSON, Donald Keith (WVa) 1701 Crestmont Dr, Huntington WV 25701 **Cn for Cong Dvlpmt Dio W Virginia Charleston WV 2007-** B Gadsden AL 9/29/1949 s Laurence Duncan Vinson & Opha G. BA U of Alabama 1971; MA U of Alabama 1978; MDiv GTS 1987. D 6/11/1987 P 12/17/1987 Bp Furman Stough. m 8/21/1971 Linda F Frost c 1. R S Jn's Ch Huntington WV 1994-2007; R S Mk's Epis Ch Perryville MD 1990-1994; Asst S Lk's Epis Ch Birmingham AL 1987-1990. dvinson@wvdiocese.org

VINSON, Richard Lee (Haw) Holy Nativity Church, 5286 Kalanianaole Highway, Honolulu HI 96821 **R Ch Of The H Nativ Honolulu HI 2006-** B Winchester VA 9/12/1955 s Freeland Vinson & Elizabeth. BA W Virginia Wesleyan Coll 1978; MDiv Wesley TS 1981; Cert VTS 1986; Cert VTS 1986. D 6/14/1986 P 12/1/1986 Bp John Thomas Walker. m 11/19/1983 Ellen Mar Levy. Dn Calv Cathd Sioux Falls SD 2002-2006; Int Pstr S Andr's Cathd Honolulu HI 2001-2002; Int S Jn's Ch Hampton VA 1999-2000; R Emm Epis Ch Hampton VA 1994-1999; Asst Chr Ch Prince Geo's Par Rockville MD 1986-1989. richkahuna@gmail.com

VIOLA, Carmen Joseph (NJ) 51 N Main St, Mullica Hill NJ 08062 B Philadelphia PA 9/18/1960 s Carmen J Viola & Mary A. BA Tem 1982; MS St Joe's U 1995; The Sch For Deacons 2009. D 5/16/2009 Bp Sylvestre Donato Romero. m 12/13/2003 Rachelle DeSha Viener c 2. carmen.viola@dla.mil

VIOLA, Harry Alexander (WNC) Po Box 1046, Hendersonville NC 28793 **Assoc Ch Of S Jn In The Wilderness Flat Rock NC 2005-** B Concord NC 2/17/1940 s George Viola & Blanche Arnita. BA Lenoir-Rhyne Coll 1962; STB GTS 1965; DD Lenoir-Rhyne Coll 1993. D 6/24/1965 P 6/18/1966 Bp Matthew G Henry. m 4/25/1970 Anne Ridenhour c 1. R S Jas Epis Ch Hendersonville NC 1974-2002; Assoc The Cathd Of All Souls Asheville NC 1968-1974; P-in-c S Steph's Epis Ch Morganton NC 1966-1967; M-in-c S Gabr's Ch Rutherfordton NC 1965-1966. Dd Lenior Rhyne Coll 1993.

VISCONTI, Richard Dennis (LI) 1 Dyke Rd, Setauket NY 11733 **Ecum Off Dio Long Island Garden City NY 2003-; R Caroline Ch Of Brookhaven Setauket NY 2002-** B New York NY 10/16/1954 s Michael Visconti & Mimi Alma. SUNY 1974; BS CUNY 1976; MDiv Sacr Heart TS Hales Corners WI 1980; CTh Epis TS of the SW 1985; DMin Pittsburgh TS 1994. Rec from Roman Catholic 10/27/1985 as Priest Bp Joseph Thomas Heistand. m 12/31/1985 Janna Schwartz c 2. Ecum Off Dio Nthrn California Sacramento CA 1996-2002; R S Mich's Epis Ch Carmichael CA 1995-2002; Chair Nomin Com Dio Pittsburgh Monroeville PA 1991-1995; R S Mary's Ch Charleroi PA 1990-1995; Asst S Matt's Ch Bedford NY 1985-1990. Auth, "Grief Mnstry: A Ch's Response To Those Who Mourn," Pittsburgh TS Press, 1994. ACPE 1980; Ord of S Lk - Chapl 1992; Ord of St. Vinc 1990. rvisconti@carolinechurch.net

VISGER, James Robert (Neb) 610 Sycamore Dr, Lincoln NE 68510 **D Ch Of The H Trin Lincoln NE 1992-** B Minneapolis MN 5/9/1940 s Harry Auther Leslie Visger & Mina Josephine. D 11/8/1985 Bp James Daniel Warner. m 7/16/1960 Merry Rue Lindgren c 2. D S Dav Of Wales Epis Ch Lincoln NE 1985-1992.

VISMINAS, Christine Elizabeth (Pgh) 70 Dennison Ave, Framingham MA 01702 B Summit NJ 11/22/1953 d Anthony Visminas & Roberta Jean. BA Duquesne U 1977; MA Pittsburgh TS 1988. D 12/11/1982 Bp Robert Bracewell Appleyard P 9/1/1983 Bp Alden Moinet Hathaway. m 5/1/1974 Steven Debolt Clark. Pstr Assoc The Ch Of The Redeem Pittsburgh PA 1982-1986. cevisminas@juno.com

VITET, Kino Germaine Lockheart (Alb) 1417 Union St, Brooklyn NY 11213 **S Mk's Ch Brooklyn NY 2011-** B 8/29/1977 s Samuel Vitet & Sybil. BS Leligh U 1999; MA Ford 2002; MDiv Ya Berk 2011. D 6/4/2011 Bp William Howard Love. m 9/16/2006 Elsie Poisson-Vitet c 3. kvitet@yahoo.com

VIVIAN, Tim (EpisSanJ) 10105 Mountaingate Ln, Bakersfield CA 93311 **Vic Gr Epis Ch Bakersfield CA 2008-** B Austin TX 7/28/1951 s Jerrold Morris Vivian & Louise. BA U CA 1973; MA California St Polytechnic U 1974; MA U CA 1981; PhD U CA 1985; MDiv CDSP 1988; Yale DS 1988. D 6/25/1988 Bp Frederick Houk Borsch P 12/1/1988 Bp Edward Witker Jones. m 7/20/1985 Miriam Lynn Raub. Int S Andr's Epis Ch Ojai CA 1994-1995; Cur S Andr's Ch Meriden CT 1988-2000. Co-Auth, "The H Workshop of Virtue: The Life of S Jn the Little," Cistercian, 2010; Co-Auth, "Mk the Monk: Counsels on the Sprtl Life," St. Vladimir's, 2009; Ed, "Becoming Fire: Through the Year w the Desert Fathers and Mothers," Cistercian, 2009; Co-Auth, "Witness to Holiness: Abba Daniel of Scetis," Cistercian, 2008; Auth, "Words to Live By: Journeys in Ancient and Mod Monasticism," Cistercian, 2005; Auth, "S Macarius the Spiritbearer," St. Vladimir's, 2004; Auth, "Four Desert Fathers," St. Vladimir's, 2004; Co-Auth, "The Life of Antony," Cistercian, 2003; Co-Auth, "The Life of the Jura Fathers," Cistercian, 2000; Auth, "Paphnutius: Histories of the Monks of Upper Egypt and the Life of Onnophrius," *rev.ed.*, Cistercian, 2000; Auth, "Journeying into God: Seven Early Monastic Lives," Fortress, 1996; Co-Auth, "The Life of S Geo of Choziba and The Miracles of the Most H Mo of God at Choziba," ISP, 1994; Auth, "Paphnutius: Histories of the Monks of Upper Egypt and the Life of Onnophrius," Cistercian, 1993; Co-Auth, "Two Coptic Homilies Attributed to S Ptr of Alexandria," Opus dei Copti manoscritti litterari, 1993; Auth, "S Ptr Of Alexandria: Bp & Mtyr," Fortress Press, 1988. Fac Resrch Awd CSU Bakersfield 2008; Annual Awaard S Shenouda the Archimandrite Coptic Soc 2005.

VIZCAINO, Roberto (EcuC) Jose Herboso 271, Cdla, La Flo, Quito Ecuador B Guayaquil EC 1/12/1933 s German Vizcaino & Amanda. D 5/18/1975 Bp Adrian Delio Caceres-Villavicencio. m 3/8/1951 Abigail Vargas. Iglesia Epis Del Ecuador Ecuador 1975-1977. Auth, "Rebeldia Juvenil".

✠ **VOGEL, Rt Rev Arthur Anton** (WMo) 720 W 44th St Apt 2005, Kansas City MO 64111 B Milwaukee WI 2/24/1924 s Arthur Louis Vogel & Gladys Eirene. BD Nash 1946; MA U Chi 1948; PhD Harv 1952; STD GTS 1969; Nash 1969; DD STUSo 1971; DD Epis TS of The SW 1995. D 2/24/1946 P 2/24/1948 Bp Benjamin F P Ivins Con 5/25/1971 for WMo. m 12/29/1947 Katharine Louise Nunn c 3. Bp Dio W Missouri Kansas City MO 1989; Bp of WMo Dio W Missouri Kansas City MO 1973-1989; V Bp of W Missouri (Ret) Dio W Missouri Kansas City MO 1973-1989; Bp Coadj Dio W Missouri Kansas City MO 1971-1973; R Ch Of S Jn Chrys Delafield WI 1953-1957. Auth, "God," *Pryr & Healing*, 1995; Auth, *Radical Chr & the Flesh of Jesus*, 1995; Auth, *Chr In His Time & Ours*, Sheed+Ward, 1992; Auth, *I Know God Better Than I Know Myself*, Morehouse-Barlow, 1989; Ed, *Theol in Anglicanism*, Morehouse-Barlow, 1984; Auth, *Jesus Pryr for Today*, Paulist, 1982; Auth, *Gift of Gr*, 1980; Auth, *Proclamation 2: Easter*, Fortress Press, 1980; Auth, *Power of His Resurr*, 1976; Auth, *Body Theol*, 1973; Auth, *Is the Last Supper Finished?*, 1968; Auth, *Next Chr Epoch*, 1966; Auth, *Chr Person*, 1963; Auth, "Reality," *Reason & Rel*, Morehouse-Gorham, 1957. Amer Philos Assn; Cath Theol Soc of Amer; Conf Angl Theologians; Metaphysical Soc of Amer. Hon DD Epis TS of the SW Austin TX 1995; Hon DD U So Sewanee TN 1971. akvogel@swbell.net

VOGEL, Caroline Carother (ETenn) 425 N Cedar Bluff Rd, Knoxville TN 37923 **D Ch Of The Gd Samar Knoxville TN 2011-** B Knoxville TN 2/12/1976 d Howard H Vogel & Lynn Massey. MA and MS U of Tennessee; BA DePauw U 1998; MDiv Harvard DS 2007. D 1/15/2011 Bp Charles Glenn VonRosenberg. m 7/9/2005 Charles Brown c 2. carolinevogel@gmail.com

VOGELE, Nancy AG (Vt) 97 Victory Cir, White River Junction VT 05001 **R S Paul's Epis Ch White River Jct VT 2001-** B Hinsdale IL 11/15/1963 d Robert Ernest Vogele & Ruth. BA Dart 1985; MDiv Ya Berk 1993; DMin EDS 1999. D 8/6/1993 P 2/12/1994 Bp Douglas Edwin Theuner. S Matt's Ch Goffstown NH 1998-2001; Asst S Paul's Ch Concord NH 1993-1997. Auth, "Conversion And Cmnty," *Gathering The Next Generation: Essays On The Formation And Mnstry Of Generation X Priests*, Morehouse Pub, 2000. Ord Of S Helena, Assoc 1998. nvogele@gmail.com

V

VOGT JR, Charles Melvin (Minn) 5216 Meadow Rdg, Edina MN 55439 B Tiffin OH 11/14/1932 s Charles Melvin Vogt & Mabel Elizabeth. BA Ken 1955; MDiv Bex 1958; Coll of Preachers 1960; Ya Berk 1964; Coventry Cathd & Epis TS Edinburg 1964; Coll of Preachers 1966; Study USSR 1986; U MN 1990. D 5/30/1958 Bp Nelson Marigold Burroughs P 12/6/1958 Bp Beverley D Tucker. m 6/13/1955 Jean F Feintuch c 3. Hon Cn Cathd Ch Of S Mk Minneapolis MN 1997-1998; R S Alb's Epis Ch Edina MN 1973-1997; R Ch Of The Incarn Great Falls MT 1968-1973; R Emm Epis Ch Stamford CT 1965-1968; R S Jas' Ch New Haven CT 1961-1965; Asst S Ptr's Ch Ashtabula OH 1958-1961. Auth, "Covenent Document, Epis & RC Ch in Mnstry," 1996; Auth, "Natl Proj - Gd Life in Light of the Chr Gospel".

VOIEN, Lucinda Hurst (Los) 1645 W 9th St # 2, San Pedro CA 90732 **S Ptr's Par San Pedro CA 2009-** B Whittier CA 7/28/1954 d James Arnold Hurst & Guelda Elwaine. AB U CA, Los Angeles 1976; CPhil U CA, Los Angeles 1985; MDiv CDSP 2009. D 6/6/2009 Bp Sergio Carranza-Gomez P 1/9/2010 Bp Chester Lovelle Talton. m 10/17/1975 Chris Steven Voien c 2. lvoien@whittier.edu

VOLKMANN, Jan Elizabeth (NY) 60 Pine Hill Park, Valatie NY 12184 B Peekskill NY 10/23/1942 d Edward Wilson Murden & Marjorie Estelle. D 5/15/1999 Bp Richard Frank Grein. m 9/22/1962 Peter Francis Volkmann c 1. D S Ptr's Epis Ch Peekskill NY 2000-2006. japevolkmann@aol.com

VOLLAND, Mary Catherine (Colo) 2201 Dexter St, Denver CO 80207 **Asst R S Thos Epis Ch Denver CO 2009-** B Buffalo NY 9/13/1954 d Edward Volland & Lucy Novo. MDiv The Iliff TS 2006. D 7/8/2008 Bp James Louis Jelinek P 1/10/2009 Bp Robert John O'Neill. m 8/19/2000 Margaret M Thompson. D S Bede Epis Ch Denver CO 2008-2009. mcvolland@aol.com

VOLPE, Gina (Chi) 4919 W Kamerling Ave, Chicago IL 60651 **Int R Ch Of The H Fam Pk Forest IL 2011-** B Chicago IL 9/22/1963 d Micheal Anthony Volpe & Mary Regenie. BA S Mary of the Woods Coll S Mary of the Woods IN 1985; MA Illinois St U 1989; MDiv SWTS 1993; Post-grad Certificat Rush U 2004. D 6/17/1995 P 12/16/1995 Bp Frank Tracy Griswold III. Ch Of The Redeem Elgin IL 2000-2003; Ch Of The H Comm Maywood IL 1996-1998; Asst Ch Of The H Nativ Clarendon Hills IL 1995-1996. Assembly of Epis Healthcare Chapl; Natl Hospice and Palliative Care Orgnztn; Soc of S Jn the Evang. Fndr's Awd - Hospice Chapl of the Year Vitas Healthcare Corp 2001; Loc Awd - Chapl of the Year - Chicago NW Vitas Healthcare Corp 2000. revgina@sbcglobal.net

VON DREELE, James Davison (Pa) 11 Dogwood Dr, Harbeson DE 19951 **Cn for Seafarer Mnstry Dio Pennsylvania Philadelphia PA 2010-; P Assoc S Dav's Epis Ch Wilmington DE 1997-; Exec Dir Seamens Ch Inst Philadelphia PA 1996-** B Minneapolis MN 11/20/1946 s Carl Von Dreele & Helen. BA Drew U 1968; MDiv Ya Berk 1971. D 6/12/1971 Bp Leland Stark P 12/18/1971 Bp George E Rath. m 11/3/2011 Elizabeth Allyn c 2. R S Matt's Epis Ch Homestead PA 1976-1996; R Ch Of S Jn The Div Hasbrouck Heights NJ 1973-1976; Asst Trin And S Phil's Cathd Newark NJ 1971-1973. No Amer Maritime Mnstry Assn - Pres 2002-2006. vondreele@sciphiladelphia.org

VON GONTEN, Kevin P (LI) 33 Railroad Avenue, P O Box 602, Center Moriches NY 11934 **R Ch Of S Jn The Bapt Cntr Moriches NY 2009-** B Brooklyn NY 3/21/1949 s Joseph William Von Gonten & Marion Geraldine. BA St. Fran Coll Brooklyn NY 1979; AM Ford 1982; STM GTS 1987. D 6/8/1987 P 12/19/1987 Bp Robert Campbell Witcher Sr. m 12/11/2010 Christine Marie Federico. Vic Ch Of S Jn The Bapt Cntr Moriches NY 2004-2009; Dio Long Island Garden City NY 1999-2001; Chair, Dept of Mssn Dio Long Island Garden City NY 1996-2000; VP, Bd Managers Camp DeWolfe Dio Long Island Garden City NY 1996-1998; Pres Bd Mgr Camp DeWolfe Dio Long Island Garden City NY 1995-1998; Trst of the Estate Belonging to the Dio Long Island Dio Long Island Garden City NY 1995-1998; Prof of Liturg Geo Mercer TS Garden City NY 1994-2000; Chair, Dioc Conv Arrangements Com Dio Long Island Garden City NY 1994-1997; Dioc Epis AIDS Cmsn Dio Long Island Garden City NY 1992-1996; Dept of Bdgt Dio Long Island Garden City NY 1992-1995; Dioc Coun Dio Long Island Garden City NY 1991-1999; Secy of the Conv Dio Long Island Garden City NY 1991-1999; Chair, Dioc Cmsn on Liturg and Mus Dio Long Island Garden City NY 1990-1999; Dio Long Island Garden City NY 1990-1993; Vic All Souls Ch Stony Brook NY 1989-2001; Dir, Exploration of Mnstry Prog Dio Long Island Garden City NY 1989-1999; Assoc R S Steph's Ch Port Washington NY 1987-1989; Asst to the R S Greg's Epis Ch Parsippany NJ 1985-1987. Auth, "The Great Vigil of Easter," *Tidings mag*, Dio Long Island, 1988. AAR 1980; Associated Parishes 1994; Coll Theol Soc 1980; FASNY 1997; New York Assn of Fire Chapl 1995; No Amer Assn for Catechumenate 1995. Franciscan Sprt Awd St. Fran Coll 1987; Theta Alpha Kappa Theta Alpha Kappa 1984. frkpv@optonline.net

VON GRABOW, Richard Henri (NCal) 580 Cooper Dr, Benicia CA 94510 **D Ch Of The Ascen Vallejo CA 2008-** B Oak Park IL 6/26/1932 s Henri Rudolph von Grabow & May Kathleen. BA Ball St U 1955; MA Ball St U 1958; DMA USC 1972; B ThS Sch for Deacons 2000. D 3/3/2002 Bp Jerry Alban Lamb. m 6/4/1955 Joan Flegal c 2. D H Fam Epis Ch Rohnert Pk CA 2007-2008; D Ch Of The Ascen Vallejo CA 2002-2004. Pub/Ed, *Mus Pub (Carillon)*, Amer Carillon Mus Editions, 1984. Gld Of Carillonners in No Amer 1973; Ord of S Lk 2001. Pi Kappa Lambda (Natl Mus hon Soc) Ball St U, Muncie IN 1955. rvongrabow@yahoo.com

VONGSANIT, Sam Chanpheng (EpisSanJ) 709 N Jackson Ave, Fresno CA 93702 **S Mart Of Tours Epis Ch Fresno CA 1998-** B Sayaburi Laos 3/7/1964 s Bounthan Vongsanit & Khong. BA GTS 2005. D 12/20/1997 P 6/1/

1998 Bp John-David Mercer Schofield. m 5/10/1986 Phong Tankhai c 4. vongsanit@juno.com

VON HAAREN, Barbara Elizabeth (Minn) 1862 W 6th St, Red Wing MN 55066 B Saint Petersburg FL 1/28/1941 d Weldon J Hulse & Verla Mae. U MN. D 4/3/1986 Bp Robert Marshall Anderson. m 2/27/1971 Peter Wolfgang Von Haaren c 2. D S Mk's Ch Lake City MN 1986-1988. gkraut@win.bright.net

VON HAAREN, Erika Shivers (Minn) 6715 N Mockingbird Ln, Scottsdale AZ 85253 **Stndg Com Dio Arizona Phoenix AZ 2008-; Assoc R S Barn On The Desert Scottsdale AZ 2006-** B Wabasha MN 1/17/1977 d Peter Wolfgang Von Haaren & Barbara Elizabeth. BA U MN 2001; MDiv The GTS 2006. D 6/8/2006 Bp James Louis Jelinek P 12/9/2006 Bp Kirk Stevan Smith. erika@saintbarnabas.org

VON NESSEN, Wayne Howard (HB) PO Box 35, Manchester VT 05254 B New York NY 4/4/1942 s Howard Charles Von Nessen & Dorothy Margaret. BA Muhlenberg Coll 1964; MDiv PDS 1968. D 5/25/1968 Bp Frederick J Warnecke P 12/1/1968 Bp John Harris Burt. m 6/20/1964 Barbara Horn Dilcher c 2. R Gr Epis Ch Of Ludington Michigan Ludington MI 1969-1970; Cur Chr Epis Ch Warren OH 1968-1970.

✠ **VONO, Rt Rev Michael Louis** (RG) Saint Pauls Within-The-Walls, Via Napoli, Rome Italy **Bp Dio The Rio Grande Albuquerque NM 2010-** B Providence RI 9/15/1948 s Anthony Vono & Lucy Carmella. BA Our Lady Of Providence 1972; MA CUA 1974; VTS 1976; DMin Hartford Sem 1986. D 6/26/1976 Bp William Foreman Creighton P 2/12/1977 Bp Alexander Doig Stewart Con 10/22/2010 for RG. R S Paul's Within the Walls Rome 00184 IT 1992-2010; R Chr Ch Rochdale MA 1980-1992; Cur All SS Ch Worcester MA 1976-1980. bp.michael@dioceserg.org

VON RAUTENKRANZ, Linda Sue (FdL) 1118B Aspen Court, Kohler WI 53044 **D S Paul's Ch Plymouth WI 2011-** B Evanston,IL 5/21/1956 d Carter von Rautenkranz & Patricia Grace. BS Marian Coll 1978; Dio Minnesota D Trng 1992; U MN 1997; Certification PrTS 2006. D 11/14/1992 Bp Sanford Zangwill Kaye Hampton. Bd Trst Heathwood Hall Epis Sch Columbia SC 2006-2010; The Bp Gravatt Cntr Bd Dio Upper So Carolina Columbia SC 2003-2010; D Trin Cathd Columbia SC 2002-2009; Yth Mnstry S Anne's Epis Ch Sunfish Lake MN 1995-1997; D For Yth Mnstry S Clem's Ch S Paul MN 1995-1997; Bp's Advsry Com for Litug & Mus Dio Minnesota Minneapolis MN 1992-1997; Min To Chld And Yth S Jn In The Wilderness White Bear Lake MN 1985-1995; Yth Bd Dio Minnesota Minneapolis MN 1985-1993; DRE Ch Of The Ascen Stillwater MN 1985-1986; Yth Mnstry Advsry Bd Dio Fond du Lac Appleton WI 1980-1985; Yth Min Gr Epis Ch Sheboygan WI 1978-1985. Auth, "Epis Yth Event Develops Leaders Among Yth," *The Epis Tchr*, Cntr for the Mnstry of Tchg, VTS, 2011; Auth, "Giving Your Heart Away: Some Thoughts on the Baptismal Cov," *Crosswalk*, Dio Upper So Carolina, 2008. NACED 2010. rev.suevon@gmail.com

VON ROESCHLAUB, W Kurt (LI) 4 Cornwall Ln, Port Washington NY 11050 B Mineola NY 11/13/1938 s Warren Nesbitt Von Roeschlaub & Elsbeth Ritchie. BA LIU 1974; Cert The Geo Mercer Jr. TS Garden City NY 1978; STM GTS 1991. D 6/11/1977 Bp Jonathan Goodhue Sherman P 12/17/1977 Bp Robert Campbell Witcher Sr. m 4/2/1962 Priscilla Anne Frank. S Steph's Ch Port Washington NY 1978-2010. Auth, "arts," *Ch of Ireland Gazette*; Auth, "arts," *Living Ch*; Auth, "arts," *Port Washington News*; Auth, "arts," *Tidings*. Compass Rose Soc 2000; Port Washington Cler Assn 1980. kurt@vonroeschlaub.com

✠ **VONROSENBERG, Rt Rev Charles Glenn** (ETenn) 132 Beresford Creek St., Daniel Island SC 29492 **Bp of E Tennessee Dio E Tennessee Knoxville TN 1999-** B Fayetteville NC 7/11/1947 s Charles Herman VonRosenberg & Frances. U So; BA U NC 1969; MDiv VTS 1974. D 6/29/1974 P 3/20/1975 Bp Hunley Agee Elebash Con 2/27/1999 for ETenn. m 6/2/1973 Ann Jones c 2. R S Jas Par Wilmington NC 1994-1999; Cn to the Ordnry Dio Upper So Carolina Columbia SC 1989-1994; COM Dio Upper So Carolina Columbia SC 1984-1986; R Ch Of The Resurr Greenwood SC 1983-1989; Exec Coun Dio E Carolina Kinston NC 1980-1983; R S Paul's Ch Beaufort NC 1979-1983; Assoc S Jas Par Wilmington NC 1977-1979; Exec Coun Dio Atlanta Atlanta GA 1976-1977; Asst S Jas Epis Ch Marietta GA 1976-1977; R S Jas Epis Ch Belhaven NC 1974-1976; Vic S Jn's Ch Scranton NC 1974-1976; Vic S Mary's Ch Belhaven NC 1974-1976. Auth, *Journ of Pstr Care*. DD U So TS Sewanee TN 2000; DD VTS Alexandria VA 1999. aandcvonr@gmail.com

VON WRANGEL, Carola (Eur) 55 Hudson St, Oneonta NY 13820 **The Angl/Epis Ch Of Chr The King Frankfurt am Main 60323 DE 2008-** B Feldkirch AT 2/2/1948 d Claus von Wrangel & Margaret. JD Seattle U 1979; MDiv Fuller TS 1989; DAS TESM 1999. D 3/24/2000 P 9/30/2000 Bp Daniel William Herzog. S Mary's Ch Lakewood WA 2007-2008; Dio Albany Albany NY 2005-2007; Gr Ch Waterford NY 2001-2007; S Jas Ch Oneonta NY 2001. CAROLAVW@HOTMAIL.COM

VOORHEES, Cindy Evans (Los) 5912 Edmonds Cir, Huntington Beach CA 92649 **Nonstipendiary Asstg St Johns Pro-Cathd Los Angeles CA 2006-** B Youngston OH 9/27/1954 d Elwyn Hugh Evans & Elizabeth. BA California St U 1978; CTh ETSBH 2002. Rec 5/1/1996 Bp Chester Lovelle Talton. m 3/21/1987 Jason Voorhees c 1. Asst S Mich And All Ang Par Corona Del Mar CA 2004-2005. Soc of Cath Priests 2010. cindy@voorheesdesign.com

VOORHEES JR, Edwin H (O) 170 M. l. King Ave., St. Augustine FL 32084 **Vic S Cyp's St Aug FL 2008-** B Montreal QC CA 6/22/1944 s Edwin Henderson Voorhees & Mildred Bradsher. BS Methodist Coll 1966; MA DePauw U 1968; MDiv VTS 1975. D 6/24/1975 Bp Hunley Agee Elebash P 6/12/1976 Bp Thomas Augustus Fraser Jr. m 9/1/1990 Caren S Goldman c 2. P-in-c S Jn's Ch Northampton MA 2004-2007; R S Mk's Epis Ch Toledo OH 1989-2004; S Johns Epis Ch Wake Forest NC 1983-1989; R All SS Ch Alexandria VA 1978-1983; Asst S Fran Ch Greensboro NC 1975-1978. Co-Auth, "Across The Threshold, Into the Questions," Morehouse Pub, 2008. berkanated@aol.com

VOORHEES, James Martin (SD) HC 30 Box 151, Belle Fourche SD 57717 B Sturgis SD 1/10/1934 s James Arthur Voorhees & Bertha Emma. EFM. D 10/2/1994 Bp Creighton Leland Robertson. m 8/31/1952 Myrtle Alice Moses.

VOORHEES, Jonathan Andrew (Va) 1700 University Ave, Charlottesville VA 22903 **Kent Sch Kent CT 2004-** B Turlock CA 8/12/1966 s Albert Edwin Voorhees & Nedra Irene. USMA At W Point 1984; BA U CA 1989; GTS 1990; MDiv CDSP 1992; Chapl Off Basic Course 1994. D 6/27/1992 Bp Richard Lester Shimpfky P 5/1/1993 Bp George Edmonds Bates. m 6/27/1998 Amy Meyer Caper. Assoc R S Paul's Memi Charlottesville VA 1999-2004; Dio Utah Salt Lake City UT 1994-1996; St Marks Sch Salt Lake City UT 1993-1994; Assoc P Cathd Ch Of S Mk Salt Lake City UT 1992-1994. chaplain@cstone.net

VORKINK II, Peter (NH) 20 Main St, Exeter NH 03833 B Plainfield NJ 12/10/1943 s Francois Nancen Vorkink & Janice Ruth. BA Ya 1965; BD UTS 1968; MA Harv 1978. D 6/24/1972 Bp Robert Lionne DeWitt P 4/15/1973 Bp Charles F Hall. m 6/8/1968 Gaye Vorkink c 1. Ed, "Bonhoeffer In A Wrld Come Of Age," Fortress Press, 1968.

VOSBURGH, Linda Ann (Colo) PO Box 1023, Broomfield CO 80038 B Baltimore MD 8/4/1945 d Gilbert J Vosburgh & Barbara S. BS Mia Oxford OH 1964; MAT U Denv 1977. D 11/17/2007 Bp Robert John O'Neill. m 6/24/1995 Arthur L Douglas. linda.vosburgh@colorado.edu

VOSSLER, Thomas Elmer (WNC) 304 Oklawaha Cir, Hendersonville NC 28739 **Died 8/31/2009** B Akron OH 7/27/1923 s Elmer William Vossler & Bernice May. BA Ken 1950; BD Bex 1951. D 6/12/1951 P 12/22/1951 Bp Beverley D Tucker. c 4.

VOTAW, Verling Alastair (Ct) 657 Wampler Dr, Charleston SC 29412 B Newcastle-upon-Tyne England 7/14/1939 s Verling Milton Votaw & Elizabeth. W&L 1959; BS Indiana U 1961; MDiv VTS 1964. D 6/13/1964 P 12/12/1964 Bp Roger W Blanchard. m 6/5/1971 Rhoda Rippey c 3. R Trin Epis Ch Southport CT 1989-2003; Assoc Chr Ch Greenwich CT 1983-1989; S Jn's Ch Portsmouth NH 1982; Trin Ch Hampton NH 1980-1982; Dio New Hampshire Concord NH 1975-1982; Chr Ch Exeter NH 1975-1980; Asst S Thos Epis Ch Terrace Pk OH 1964-1967. Beta Gamma Sigma 1961. al.votaw@gmail.com

VOTH, Murray Howard (SeFla) 14920 David Dr, Fort Myers FL 33908 B Fort Pierce FL 8/14/1928 s Gilbert Allen Voth & Marghuerita Hall. BS Florida St U 1949; MS Florida St U 1951; MDiv TS 1954. D 6/24/1954 Bp Henry I Louttit P 12/24/1954 Bp Martin J Bram. c 3. Off Of Bsh For ArmdF New York NY 1961-1969; R S Jn's Epis Ch Homestead FL 1956-1961; Organizer/Vic Gd Samar Epis Ch Clearwater FL 1955-1956; Vic Ch Of The H Sprt Sfty Harbor FL 1954-1956. Gold Key, Florida St U 1948-1949; Red Ribbon Soc, U So 1953-1954. Purple Heart (2 Awds) US Navy; Meritorious Serv Medal (3 Awds) US Navy; Legion Merit (2 Awds) US Navy.

VOUGA, Anne Fontaine (Ky) St Thomas Episcopal Church, 9616 Westport Road, Louisville KY 40241 **R S Thos Epis Ch Louisville KY 2011-; COM Dio Kentucky Louisville KY 2008-** B Houston TX 2/5/1961 d William Richard Downs & Anne Otter. BA The U So, Sewanee, TN 1982; Theol Stds L'Institut Prot de Theologie, Montpellier, France 1986; MA The U of Louisville 1997; Angl Stds VTS 2007; MDiv Louisville Presb Theol 2008. D 12/21/2007 P 6/21/2008 Bp Edwin Funsten Gulick Jr. c 3. S Paul's Ch Henderson KY 2010-2011; Eccl Crt Dio Kentucky Louisville KY 2008-2011; Asst S Mk's Epis Ch Louisville KY 2008-2010. Auth, "L'eglise Reformee de France," *The Presb Outlook, Vol. 173, No. 40*, 1991; Auth, "Presb Missions& Louisville Blacks: The Early Years," *Filson Club Hist Quarterly, Vol 58, No. 3*, 1984. avouga@gmail.com

VOYLE, Robert John (Ore) 24965 Nw Pederson Rd, Hillsboro OR 97124 B Hamilton NZ 12/28/1952 s Wilfred Victor Voyle & Margaret Mary. BS U Of Auckland Nz 1976; BD S Jn Theol Coll 1980; MS California St U 1988; Psyd Fuller TS 1994. Trans 8/1/1986 Bp Oliver Bailey Garver Jr. m 1/24/1987 Kim M Kempton. Trin Epis Cathd Portland OR 2002-2004; All SS-By-The-Sea Par Santa Barbara CA 2001-2002; S Paul's Epis Ch Santa Paula CA 2000-2001; All SS Par Beverly Hills CA 1996-1997; P-in-c S Nich Par Encino CA 1993-1995; P-in-c All SS Epis Ch Oxnard CA 1991-1992; S Mich's U Mssn Island Isla Vista CA 1990-1991; Assoc R S Jos's Par Buena Pk CA 1986-1988; Pstr'S Asst S Jos's Par Buena Pk CA 1984-1986. Auth, "Assessing Skills & Discerning Calls". Int Mnstry Ntwk. rob@voyle.com

VOYSEY, Stephen Otte (Mass) 1 Colpitts Road, Weston MA **R S Ptr's Ch Weston MA 2006-** B Evanston IL 10/3/1950 s Frank Ernest Voysey & Betty. BA U of Pennsylvania 1972; MA Rutgers-The St U 1973; MDiv EDS 1977. D 6/4/1977 Bp Quintin Ebenezer Primo Jr P 12/3/1977 Bp James Winchester Montgomery. m 1/19/2001 Amanda F Barnum c 2. R S Mk's Ch Mt Kisco NY 1996-2006; Dio New York New York City NY 1990-1996; R S Paul's Ch Pleasant Vlly NY 1983-1996; Dio New York New York City NY 1982-1986; Cur S Andr's Epis Ch Staten Island NY 1980-1983; Cur Trin Epis Ch Wheaton IL 1977-1979. Jas Arthur Muller Prize Hist EDS Cambridge CA 1977; Pi Gamma Mu 1972. sovoysey@comcast.net

VROON, Daron Jon (At) 939 James Burgess Road, Suwanee GA 30024 **Mem of Cmsn on Liturg Dio Atlanta Atlanta GA 2011-; Cur S Columba Epis Ch Suwanee GA 2010-** B East Lansing MI 3/26/1979 s Anton John Vroon & June Otten. Bachelor of Sci Hope Coll 2001; PhD Georgia Inst of Tech 2007; Mstr of Div GTS 2010. D 12/19/2009 Bp J(ohn) Neil Alexander. m 9/11/2004 Julie Williamson c 2. daron.vroon@gmail.com

VRYHOF SSJE, David B (Mass) 980 Memorial Dr, Cambridge MA 02138 **S Jn's Chap Cambridge MA 1995-** B Grand Rapids MI 11/12/1951 s Wesley Vryhof & Frances Mae. BA Calvin Coll 1973; MA Gallaudet U 1975; Duke 1992; MDiv GTS 1993. D 5/30/1993 Bp Huntington Williams Jr P 8/20/1994 Bp R(aymond) Stewart Wood Jr. Dio Michigan Detroit MI 1993-1994; D S Columba Ch Detroit MI 1993-1994. davidv@ssje.org

VUKICH, Dawn Elizabeth (Los) 26391 Bodega Ln, Mission Viejo CA 92691 B Burbank CA 3/24/1960 d Martin Laurence Vukich & Carol Ann. BA Biola U 1992; MDiv Talbot TS 2004. Trans from Church of the Province of Uganda 4/27/2010 Bp Joseph Jon Bruno. dvukich@gmail.com

VUKMANIC, Paula Jo Claret (Los) 2200 Via Rosa, Palos Verdes Estates CA 90274 **Assoc R S Fran' Par Palos Verdes Estates CA 2010-** B Torrance CA 9/30/1949 d Frank William Vukmanic & Mary Rocklyn. BFA Mt St Mary's Coll Los Angeles CA 1976; Mstr of Mnstry Seattle U 1987; JT.MDiv The ETS At Claremont 2009. D 6/6/2009 P 1/9/2010 Bp Sergio Carranza-Gomez. paulaart1@cox.net

VUONO, Dorothy Irene (Del) PO Box 191, DE Milford 19963 B Bayonne NJ 6/12/1945 d Vincent Boyle & Irene. AA Brookdale CC. D 12/5/2009 Bp Wayne Parker Wright. m 8/19/1978 Joseph Vuono c 3. christ.church.milford@verizon.net

W

WACASTER, David C (WA) 2711 Parkway Pl, Cheverly MD 20785 **Dioc Coun, Reg 4 Cler Mem Dio Washington Washington DC 2011-; R Gd Shpd Epis Ch Silver Sprg MD 2010-; 1st Alt, Cler Dep to GC Dio Washington Washington DC 2009-** B Eugene OR 11/13/1970 s C Thompson Wacaster & H Jane. BA U So 1992; MDiv VTS 2004. D 6/12/2004 P 1/22/2005 Bp John Chane. m 10/25/2003 Michael Robert Fraser. Asst S Lk's Ch Trin Par Beth MD 2005-2010; Cur S Thos' Par Washington DC 2004-2005. rector@gsecmd.org

WACOME, Karen Ann Halvorsen (Ia) 415 3rd St Nw, Orange City IA 51041 **Ch of the Sav Orange City IA 2007-** B Elizabeth NJ 9/7/1952 d Henry J Halvorsen & Blanche. BA King's Coll Wilkes-Barre PA 1974; MA Ya Berk 1991; CAS CDSP 1994; PhD Grad Theol Un 2005. D 3/23/1996 P 12/7/1996 Bp Carl Christopher Epting. m 8/24/1974 Donald Henry Wacome. Dio Iowa Des Moines IA 2006-2007; Dio Iowa Des Moines IA 1998-2005; Vic S Geo's Epis Ch Le Mars IA 1998-2005. Aabs; SBL. Schlrshp: Excellence In Mnstry CDSP 1994. wacome@frontiernet.net

WADDELL, Clayton Burbank (SeFla) 141 S County Rd, Palm Beach FL 33480 **D The Epis Ch Of Beth-By-The-Sea Palm Bch FL 2007-** B Sarasota FL 5/27/1961 s Wallace Waddell & Harriett. BA U Of Florida 1983. D 5/6/2007 Bp Leopold Frade. m 8/11/1990 Jacqueline Fisher c 2. waddellcb@adelphia.net

WADDELL, Jonathan H (Ala) 5014 Lakeshore Dr, Pell City AL 35128 **D Gr Ch Birmingham AL 2000-** B Centerville MS 8/30/1941 s Howard Waddell & Annie Josephine. BA Wm Carey U 1963; ThM New Orleans Bapt TS 1967; MRE New Orleans Bapt TS 1968; DEd New Orleans Bapt TS 1972. D 4/17/1991 P 9/1/1991 Bp Robert Oran Miller. m 11/24/1995 Lexa Magnus. Auth, "The Use Of Rel Lang In Pstr Counslg". ACPE; Dplma AAPC. Who'S Who In The So And SW 1993; Who'S Who In Rel 1975; Outstanding Young Men Of Amer 1972. jhwadd@aol.com

WADDELL, Thomas Robert (Va) 5911 Edsall Rd Ph 5, Alexandria VA 22304 B Wheeling WV 12/28/1940 s Robert Delano Waddell & Geneva Thelma. BA Bethany Coll 1962; BD Bex 1965; CRDS 1974; MS Syr 1981; Cert GW 1990. D 11/27/1965 P 11/27/1966 Bp Nelson Marigold Burroughs. Supply P Dio Virginia Richmond VA 1981-2001; R S Mary's Epis Ch Gowanda NY 1974-1979; Vic S Barn Akron NY 1973-1974; R S Jas Ch Painesville OH 1967-1973. twaddell@lga.att.com

WADDINGHAM, Gary Brian (Mont) 119 N 33rd St, Billings MT 59101 **COM Dio Montana Helena MT 1996-; R S Lk's Ch Billings MT 1994-** B Helena MT 5/3/1950 s Marvin Bailey Waddingham & Betty Kline. BS Montana St U 1972; MDiv Epis TS of The SW 1975; Emory U 1981. D 6/30/1975 P 7/3/1976 Bp Jackson Earle Gilliam. c 3. Vic S Andr's Ch Meeteetse WY 1992-1994; Pres Stndg Com Dio Wyoming Casper WY 1987-1988; R S Andr's Ch Basin WY 1981-1994; P/Cn Cathd Of S Phil Atlanta GA 1976-1981. Auth, "Literary Sources Reveal Buying Power of Drachma," *Celator*; Auth, "Numismatic Evidence of a Benevolent Semitic Goddess," *Celator*. waddingham@bresnan.net

WADDLE, Helen Ann (Okla) PO Box 12402, Oklahoma City OK 73157 B Oklahoma City 11/19/1950 D 6/19/1999 Bp Robert Manning Moody. c 2. Ch Of The Sav Yukon OK 2004-2007. deacongranny@cox.net

WADDY, lawrence heber (SanD) 5910 Camino De La Costa, La Jolla CA 92037 **Died 3/21/2010** B Parramatta AU 10/5/1914 s Percival Stacy Waddy & Etheldred. BA Oxf 1937; MA Oxf 1945. Trans from Church Of England 1/6/1963 as Priest Bp Francis E I Bloy. c 3. Auth, *Bible Drama*, Mtn-n-air books, 2004; Auth, *Pax Romana & Wrld Peace*, Chapman & Hall, 1950. Hon Cn Dio San Diego 1999; Hon Assist S Jas by the Sea La Jolla CA 1975. lawrencewaddy@yahoo.com

WADE, Carol Lynn (Los) Christ Church Cathedral, 166 Market St, Lexington KY 40507 **Chr Ch Cathd Lexington KY 2011-** B 12/14/1955 MDiv Ya Berk. D 6/7/2003 P 1/24/2004 Bp Chester Lovelle Talton. Cathd of St Ptr & St Paul Washington DC 2004-2010; Assoc Chr Ch New Haven CT 2003-2004. revcarolwade@gmail.com

WADE, Elizabeth Ann Till (Ky) 175 Ridgewood Ave, Paducah KY 42001 **R Gr Ch Paducah KY 2005-** B Montgomery AL 12/16/1947 d David Caffey Till & Dorothy Mae. BA Huntingdon Coll 1969; Auburn U 1971; Louisville Presb TS 1997; MDiv GTS 1998. D 5/31/1998 P 1/9/1999 Bp Edwin Funsten Gulick Jr. m 6/19/1971 James Calhoun Wade. Trst & Coun Dio Kentucky Louisville KY 2009-2011; GC Dep Dio Kentucky Louisville KY 2005-2011; R Ch Of Our Merc Sav Louisville KY 2000-2005; P-in-c S Mk's Epis Ch Louisville KY 1998-2000; Asst Chr Ch Cathd Louisville KY 1998-1999. Auth, "God Of The Night," *Wmn Uncommon Prayers*, Morehouse Pub, 2000; Auth, "Pryr For A Vstry," *Wmn Uncommon Prayers*, Morehouse Pub, 2000. Bell Awd For Excellence In Biblic Stds Louisville Presb Sem Louisville KY 1996; Presidential Schlr Louisville Presb Sem Louisville KY 1995. libby_wade@yahoo.com

WADE, Francis Howard (WA) 4836 Alton Place NW, Washington DC 20016 B Clarksburg WV 6/13/1941 s William Carlisle Wade & Eleann. BA Cit 1963; BD VTS 1966; DMin VTS 1981. D 6/3/1966 P 12/21/1966 Bp Wilburn Camrock Campbell. m 8/18/1963 Mary Jane Criss c 2. R S Alb's Par Washington DC 1983-2005; R The Memi Ch Of The Gd Shpd Parkersburg WV 1972-1983; R St Christophers Epis Ch Charleston WV 1968-1972; Vic S Andr's-On-The-Mt Harpers Ferry WV 1966-1968; Vic S Jn's Ch Harpers Ferry WV 1966-1968; Cur Zion Epis Ch Chas Town WV 1966-1968. Auth, "Transforming Scripture," Ch Pub, 2008; Auth, "Rites of Our Passage," Posterity Press, 2002; Auth, "Comp Along the Way," Posterity Press, 1996; Auth, "Beyond the Ordnry in the Kingdom of God," Forw Mvmt, 1991. fhmjwade@verizon.net

WADE, J Merrill (Tex) 11561 Cedarcliffe Dr, Austin TX 78750 **R S Matt's Ch Austin TX 2002-** B Tampa FL 1/4/1954 s John Aubrey Wade & Charlotte Patricia. BBA U of Texas 1976; MDiv GTS 1989. D 5/12/1989 P 4/18/1990 Bp Duncan Montgomery Gray Jr. m 6/2/1990 Crystal Kirkpatrick c 2. R S Paul's Epis Ch Meridian MS 1997-2002; Vic S Patricks Epis Ch Long Bch MS 1992-1997; Cur Ch of the H Trin Vicksburg MS 1989-1992. jmwade@austin.rr.com

WADE SR, Joseph Alfred (NY) 108 Horsley Dr, Hampton VA 23666 B Port Limon Province Limon CR 7/15/1927 s Ishmael Wade & Matilda. BA SUNY; S Aug Coll Cbury Gb 1964; CUNY 1969; Col 1969. D 9/29/1953 P 9/1/1954 Bp Robert B Gooden. c 1. S Johns Epis Hosp Far Rockaway NY 1986-1992; S Lk's Cnvnt Av New York NY 1979-1992; S Lk's-Roosevelt Hosp Cntr New York NY 1975-1986; Dpt Of Missions Ny Income New York NY 1969-1986; Vic Gr Epis Ch New York NY 1967-1982; Asst S Ann's Ch Of Morrisania Bronx NY 1964-1967; Asst S Aug's Ch Oakland CA 1952-1953. AEHC.

WADE, Karin Elizabeth (Mass) Po Box 372, Rockport MA 01966 **R S Mary's Epis Ch Rockport MA 1994-** B North Kingstown RI 3/10/1951 d Carl Donivan Wade & Bertha Frances. BA Amer U 1974; MDiv Nash 1989. D 6/14/1989 Bp Charles Lee Burgreen P 12/6/1989 Bp Bob Gordon Jones. Cathd Chapt Dio Massachusetts Boston MA 1996-1999; Dioc Coun Dio Massachusetts Boston MA 1995-1999; Exec Comm Dio Massachusetts Boston MA 1995-1999; Stndg Com Dio Wyoming Casper WY 1990-1994; R All SS Ch Wheatland WY 1989-1994; Vic Ch Of Our Sav Hartville WY 1989-1994. Soc for the Increase of Mnstry - Exec Com 1999; Third Ord of the Soc of S Fran 1988. revkew@verizon.net

WADE, Mary (Miss) 2681 Lake Cir, Jackson MS 39211 B Watertown NY 4/26/1951 d Richard Rollin MacSherry & Mary Alice. BA Skidmore Coll 1975;

MDiv EDS 1979. D 6/23/1979 P 5/1/1980 Bp Ned Cole. S Phil's Ch Jackson MS 2005; S Andr's Cathd Jackson MS 1980-1997; D-In-Trng All SS Par Brookline MA 1979-1980. Inst Servnt Leadrship. Humanitarian Of Year 95; City & Canonty Spec Serv Hon Citation; Rel Ldrshp Wmns Awd.

WADE, Stephen Hamel (Va) 19195 Sweig Terrace, Leesburg VA 20176 B Saint Louis MO 7/4/1945 s Leo Joseph Wade & Hermoine. BA Denison U 1967; MDiv Ya Berk 1970; MA Col 1974; CSD Weston Jesuit TS 1993; Cert Loyola Hse, Guelph, Ontario 2002; Cert Oxf 2002. D 6/10/1970 Bp John Henry Esquirol P 1/25/1971 Bp Joseph Warren Hutchens. m 9/4/1993 Mary Starr Huske c 3. R Imm Ch-On-The-Hill Alexandria VA 1995-2006; Sr Assoc R S Chrys's Ch Chicago IL 1994-1995; Assoc R Trin Ch In The City Of Boston Boston MA 1985-1994; R Trin Ch Torrington CT 1977-1985; Assoc R Chr Ch Greenwich CT 1975-1977; Asst R S Mich's Ch New York NY 1970-1975. Auth, "Some Reflections on Retreats in the Ignatian Tradition," *Bridges*, Bon Secours Sprtl Cntr, 2007; Auth, "Ask The Fundraising Profsnl In Your Cong To Help," *The Ch Fundraising Nwsltr*, Stevenson Pub, Inc., 2000; Auth, "Look Before Leaping Into That Next Real Estate Gift," *The Major Gifts Report*, Stevenson Pub, 1999; Auth, "Bk Revs: A Practical Guide To Cmnty Mnstry," *VTS Journ*, 1996; Auth, "Sprtl And Moral Educ: Grappling w Diversity," *Choate Rosemary Hall mag*, 1993; Auth, "Epistemology And Models In Rel Tchg," *The Journ Of The Rel Educ Assn US & Can*, 1975. stephenwade@smartneighborhood.net

WADE, Suzanne (Mass) 75 Cold Spring Rd, Westford MA 01886 **S Mk's Ch Westford MA 2011-** B Beverly MA 6/28/1969 d Richard Wesley Burnham & Marian Elsa. BA NEU 1991; MDiv EDS 2010. D 6/25/2011 Bp M(arvil) Thomas Shaw III. m 9/7/1991 Richard Wade c 2. suzanne@rswade.net

WADE III, Thomas Magruder (WLa) Po Box 802, Saint Joseph LA 71366 B Saint Joseph LA 5/3/1914 s Thomas Magruder Wade & Kate. BA LSU 1935; LLM LSU 1937; BD STUSo 1957. D 7/1/1957 Bp Girault M Jones P 5/1/1958 Bp Iveson Batchelor Noland. m 12/8/1946 Alma Fluitt c 2. Secy Dio Louisiana Baton Rouge LA 1973-1978; Stndg Com Dio Louisiana Baton Rouge LA 1973-1974; Dn Convoc Alexandria Dio Louisiana Baton Rouge LA 1971-1979; R S Mich's Epis Ch Pineville LA 1971-1979; Dn Convoc Baton Rouge Dio Louisiana Baton Rouge LA 1967-1971; Chair Div C&C DeptCE Dio Louisiana Baton Rouge LA 1966-1971; Assoc S Jas Epis Ch Baton Rouge LA 1966-1971; R S Jn's Epis Ch Minden LA 1960-1966; In-c All SS Ch Dequincy LA 1957-1960; In-c Leonidas Polk Memi Epis Mssn Leesville LA 1957-1960; In-c Trin Epis Ch Deridder LA 1957-1960.

WADE, William St Clair (Tenn) 81 Oklahoma Ave, Sewanee TN 37375 B Brooklyn NY 5/15/1943 s David Carl Wade & Ann. BA U So 1965; MDiv VTS 1968. D 6/29/1968 Bp Thomas H Wright P 1/6/1969 Bp Hunley Agee Elebash. m 6/23/1973 Joan Widman c 2. S Andr's-Sewanee Sch Sewanee TN 1981-2008; Cathd of St Ptr & St Paul Washington DC 1977-1981; Sch Mstr S Paul's Ch Concord NH 1973-1977; S Paul's Sch Concord NH 1973-1977; Asst Chr Ch Exeter NH 1971-1973; Asst S Jn's Epis Ch Fayetteville NC 1968-1971. "No Srings Attached," 2008; Auth, "What is Rel?," 1979. Ruth Jenkins Awd Natl Association of Epis Schools 2000; DD U So 1989. bwade@bellsouth.net

WAFER-CROSS, Melissa Lee (NwT) 3502 47th St, Lubbock TX 79413 **D S Chris's Epis Ch Lubbock TX 1999-** B El Paso TX 6/9/1948 d William Clyde Wafer & Katherine Amelia. BA Texas Tech U 1970; MA Texas Tech U 1996. D 10/29/1999 Bp C(harles) Wallis Ohl. m 8/3/1979 David Dyer Cross c 1. m/wcr.cross@yahoo.com

WAFF, Kay Childers (SwVa) 314 N Bridge St, Bedford VA 24523 B Oklahoma City OK 2/2/1943 d Clem Albert Childers & Cathryn Terry. AA St. Mary's JR. Coll 1963; BA U NC 1965. D 2/14/2003 Bp Frank Neff Powell. m 7/29/1966 John Waff c 4. kaywaff@msn.com

WAFF, William DuBard Razz (Mil) 2443 Lawson Blvd., Gurnee IL 60031 **P Assoc S Lk's Ch Evanston IL 1984-** B Memphis TN 10/8/1954 s William Thomas Waff & Dorothy Rebecca. BMus U of Mississippi 1976; MDiv SWTS 1983; DMin GTF 1997; MSS US-A War Coll 2001. D 6/11/1983 P 5/13/1984 Bp William Arthur Beckham. m 5/23/1992 Kathleen Busby. Dir of Pstr Care & Ethics S Lk's Hosp Racine WI 1985-2002; Columbia Epis Inst Mnstry Ch Of The Gd Shpd Columbia SC 1983; CPE Res NW Memi Hosp Chicago IL 1983. AEHC 1986; Assn of Prof Chapl 1987; ACPE 1983; Chapl S Jn Bapt SMOTJ 1997; Natl Chapl- SMOTJ 2000-2002; OHC 1980; Ord of St. Lazarus 2001. DSA Assn of Prof Chapl 1998; Awd for Outstanding Serv Bp for Chaplaincies 1998; Distinguished Chapl Awd Wis Chapl Comm Wisconsin 1998; Citation of Achievement Amer Prot Hlth Assn 1991. razzw@aol.com

WAFLER, Donald Samuel (Minn) 628 1st St Se, Faribault MN 55021 B Alliance OH 1/14/1916 s William Arnold Wafler & Ida Rose. Manchester Coll 1936; BA No Cntrl Coll 1939; U MN 1968. D 1/29/1979 Bp Robert Marshall Anderson. m 4/16/1943 Helen Margaret Hoyt c 2. Assoc The Epis Cathd Of Our Merc Sav Faribault MN 1979-1990. Auth, "Relatns Of Speech To The Rdr". Sr Citizens Of Faribault.

WAGAR, L A Catherine (Los) St. Stephen's Episcopal Church, 6128 Yucca St, Los Angeles CA 90028 B Saginaw MI 5/4/1948 d Wayne Bergey Wagar & Lorene Hirt. AB Br 1970; CPhil Wright Inst Los Angeles 1985; Cert. of Theol Stds ETS at Claremont 2008. D 1/24/2009 Bp Chester Lovelle Talton. m 5/19/1991 Bruce Rankin. Interfaith Refugee & Immigration Serv (IRIS) Dio Los Angeles Los Angeles CA 2009. ctswagar2@aol.com

WAGEMAN, Carole Allcroft (Vt) Trinity Episcopal Church, 5171 Shelburne Rd, Shelburne VT 05482 **Asst R Trin Ch Shelburne VT 2003-** B Paterson NJ 6/26/1948 d Harry Allcroft & Vera Mae. BA Jas Madison U 1970; Two years of study New Brunswick TS, NJ 1972; MAETS UTS 1974; Advncd Cert EDS 2003. D 5/29/2003 P 12/20/2003 Bp Thomas C Ely. m 5/17/1975 Edwin Joseph Wageman c 3. "Baptismal Mnstry in Vermont," Dioc Report, 2003. revmomvt@gmail.com

WAGENSEIL JR, Robert Arthur (SwFla) 1700 Patlin Cir S, Largo FL 33770 **P Calv Ch Indn Rocks Bch FL 1995-** B Jamaica NY 4/18/1954 s Robert Arthur Wagenseil & Marie Julian. BA Leh 1976; MDiv Nash 1980. D 6/7/1980 P 5/2/1981 Bp Robert Campbell Witcher Sr. m 8/12/1978 Patricia Torrey. Archd Dio Long Island Garden City NY 1992-1995; R All SS' Epis Ch Long Island City NY 1984-1995; Cur S Mary's Ch Lake Ronkonkoma NY 1983-1984; Cur S Lk's Ch Forest Hills NY 1981-1983. Citizen of the Year Rotary Club of Indn Rocks Bch 2011; Vol Fireman of the Year Pinellas Suncoast Fire and Rescue 2005. frbob.wagenseil@gmail.com

WAGENSELLER, Joseph Paul (Ct) 6 Clifford Ln, Westport CT 06880 B Portage WI 4/4/1939 s Wayne Macveagh Wagenseller & Mary Mason. BA Elizabethtown Coll 1961; MDiv GTS 1964; DMin Andover Newton TS 1975; CG Jung Inst 1975. D 6/22/1964 Bp John T Heistand P 11/5/1965 Bp Robert Fisher Gibson Jr. m 10/3/1970 Virginia F Fox c 3. S Andr's Ch Stamford CT 1973; Asst S Mk's Ch New Canaan CT 1966-1970; Asst S Paul's Ch Richmond VA 1964-1966. Auth, "The Archetype of Vocation," *Protestantism and Jungian Psychol*, New Falcon Pub, Tempe, AZ, 1995; Auth, "Sprtl Renwl at Midlife," *Journ of Rel and Hlth*. jwagensell@aol.com

✠ **WAGGONER, Rt Rev James Edward** (Spok) 245 E 13th Ave, Spokane WA 99202 **Bp Dio Spokane Spokane WA 2000-** B Ironton OH 12/26/1947 s James Edward Waggoner & Vera Jean. BA Marshall U 1973; MDiv VTS 1979; Fllshp VTS 1985; DMin VTS 1999. D 6/6/1979 P 6/4/1980 Bp Robert Poland Atkinson Con 10/21/2000 for Spok. m 6/22/1967 Gloria Waggoner c 2. Cn to the Ordnry Dio W Virginia Charleston WV 1992-2000; R Trin Epis Ch Martinsburg WV 1985-1991; R S Ptr's Ch Huntington WV 1981-1985; R Calv Ch Montgomery WV 1979-1981; R Ch Of The Gd Shpd Hansford WV 1979-1981. DD VTS 2001. jimw@spokanediocese.org

WAGGONER, Janet Cuff (Ct) 31 Church Street, Shelton CT 06484 **B&D Exec Coun Dio Connecticut Hartford CT 2009-; R S Paul's Epis Ch Shelton CT 2006-** B The Dalles OR 3/22/1967 d Thomas A Cuff & Peggy A. BA Willamette U 1989; MDiv Ya Berk 2001. D 6/17/2001 Bp Robert Louis Ladehoff P 2/2/2002 Bp Andrew Donnan Smith. m 10/12/1996 Edward Waggoner c 2. Asst R S Matt's Epis Ch Wilton CT 2003-2006; Assoc R S Lk's Par Darien CT 2001-2003. ConnECA 2008; Nneca 2002; SCHC 1998. mcl Yale DS 2001. revjanet@stpaulsct.org

WAGGONER, Leigh Farley (Eau) 110 W. North St., Cortez CO 81321 **R S Barn Of The Vlly Cortez CO 2011-** B Huntington WV 8/3/1946 d James Allen Farley & Phyllis. BS TCU 1968; MDiv SWTS 2003; DMin SWTS 2010. D 8/15/1997 Bp William Charles Wantland P 5/10/2003 Bp Keith Bernard Whitmore. m 9/28/1991 Wesley Robert Waggoner. P-in-c S Jn's Epis Ch Sparta WI 2004-2010; D S Alb's Ch Spooner WI 1997-2000. rector@stbarnabascortez.org

WAGNER, Barbara Jean (WMich) 2430 Greenbriar, Harbor Springs MI 49740 **D Chr Epis Ch Charlevoix MI 2002-** B Allegan MI 8/31/1941 d James Harvey Brian & Laura Margaret. BA MI SU 1967; MA Cntrl Michigan U 1975; CTh Whitaker TS 1988. D 4/29/1989 Bp H Coleman McGehee Jr. m 3/22/1969 Richard F Wagner c 3. D Emm Ch Petoskey MI 1999-2002; D S Jn's Epis Ch Alma MI 1989-1998. bwagner@netonecom.net

WAGNER, Beau (Me) St Matthew's Episcopal Church, PO Box 879, Lisbon ME 04250 **R S Matt's Epis Ch Lisbon ME 2007-** B Flushing NY 12/29/1955 s William Wagner & Janet Wagner. BA Bos 1976; JD Geo 1980; MS Geo 1984; MDiv Allnce TS 2007. D 6/9/2007 P 12/10/2007 Bp William Howard Love. m 11/25/1995 Debra Wagner c 2. pastorbeau@gwi.net

WAGNER, Beth Anne (CFla) 8455 Via Bella Notte, Orlando FL 32836 **D Epis Ch Of The Ascen Orlando FL 2001-** B Watertown NY 5/10/1955 d David Graham Chalk & Gail Dianne. BA SUNY 1977; AOS Mohawk Vlly Cmnty Coll 1983; Cert Inst For Choral Stds 1992. D 12/18/1993 Bp John Wadsworth Howe. m 8/23/1975 David Francis Wagner c 2. D Epis Ch Of The Ascen Orlando FL 1993-1998. bdwag19@idt.net

WAGNER, David William (At) 5220 Clemson Ave, Columbia SC 29206 **S Martins-In-The-Field Columbia SC 2011-** B Atlanta GA 5/12/1981 s Jack William Wagner & Nancy Smith. BA Presb Coll 2003; MDiv The GTS 2011. D 12/18/2010 P 6/26/2011 Bp J(ohn) Neil Alexander. m 8/14/2010 Kathleen Varner. davidwagner43@gmail.com

WAGNER, John Carr (Be) 6344 Opossum Lane, Slatington PA 18080 B Lewistown PA 2/6/1947 s Max Leroy Wagner & Betty. Ts Mary Immac Sem; BS

Penn 1974; MS Villanova U 1976. D 6/1/1986 P 12/10/1988 Bp James Michael Mark Dyer. m 12/20/1969 Nancy Elizabeth Dodd c 3. S Mk's Epis Ch Moscow PA 2002-2003; Asst S Steph's Ch Whitehall PA 1986-2005. Intl Ord Of S Lk. frjohn@enter.net

WAGNER, Mary Scott (Mass) 54 Robert Rd, Marblehead MA 01945 **C&C Bd Pres Dio Massachusetts Boston MA 2011-; R Ch Of The Gd Shpd Reading MA 2010-; Const and Cn Com Chair Dio Massachusetts Boston MA 2009-** B Bristol TN 10/9/1963 d Michael Jones Miller & Carole Ann. BA Carson-Newman Coll 1985; JD Van 1989; MDiv Harvard DS 1999. D 12/19/1998 P 12/4/1999 Bp M(arvil) Thomas Shaw III. m 8/5/1989 James Gray Wagner. R Wyman Memi Ch of St Andr Marblehead MA 2006-2008; Dioc Coun Dio Massachusetts Boston MA 2004-2007; COM Dio Massachusetts Boston MA 2003-2007; Rectir Calv Ch Danvers MA 2000-2006; Asst Par Of The Epiph Winchester MA 1999-2000. scottiewag@aol.com

WAGNER, Ralph Fellows (Ak) Po Box 1502, Palmer AK 99645 B Pittsburgh PA 10/24/1928 s Frank Newton Wagner & Ruth Edna. BA Penn 1950; MDiv Nash 1957; Duquesne U 1970. D 6/1/1957 Bp Austin Pardue P 12/1/1957 Bp William S Thomas. m 8/13/1949 Dorothy Marie Riley c 4. Vic S Barth's Ch Palmer AK 1991-1994; All SS' Epis Ch Anchorage AK 1990; New Life Epis Ch Uniontown OH 1989; Bp Of ArmdF- Epis Ch Cntr New York NY 1971-1988; R S Thos Memi Epis Ch Oakmont PA 1970-1971; Cn Trin Cathd Pittsburgh PA 1966-1970; R The Ch Of The Adv Jeannette PA 1957-1963. drwagner@worldnet.att.net

WAGNER, Richard Alden (Los) 40562 Via Amapola, Murrieta CA 92562 **Vic S Alb's Epis Ch Yucaipa CA 2001-** B Fitchburg Massachusetts 12/9/1937 s Herbert Constantine Wagner & Sigrid Marion. BA Tufts U 1959; MA Auburn U at Montgomery 1971; MDiv SWTS 1984. D 5/11/1984 Bp Richard Frank Grein P 11/18/1984 Bp James Winchester Montgomery. m 9/9/1959 Joan Lillian Watt c 3. R All SS Ch Vista CA 1996-2000; R The Annunc Of Our Lady Gurnee IL 1990-1996; Vic S Hugh Of Lincoln Epis Ch Elgin IL 1987-1990; Cur Trin Epis Ch Wheaton IL 1984-1986. dickydaddy@yahoo.com

WAGNER, Robert T (SD) 24497 Playhouse Rd, Keystone SD 57751 **Died 1/17/2011** B Sioux Falls,SD 10/30/1932 s Hans Herman Wagner & Helen Emily. BA Augustana Coll 1954; MDiv SWTS 1957; Coll of Preachers 1960; STM SWTS 1970; PhD So Dakota St U 1971. D 6/23/1957 P 1/1/1958 Bp Conrad Gesner. c 2. *Numerous Pub on Rural Dvlpmt & Cmnty*, JD St U, 1972. Alpha Kappa Delta 1972; Alpha Lamba Delta 1979; Gamma Sigma Delta 1970; Phi Kappa Phi 1978; Pi Gamma Mu 1971; Sigma Alpha Epsilon; Wm Given Fell, Epis Fndt 1969-1972. L.H.D. U of So Dakota 2001; D.D. SWTS 2000; Distinguished Regental Prof and Pres Emer So Dakota St Bd Rgnts 1998; Dr Pub. Serv. SD Dakota St Bd Rgnts 1997; L.H.D. Augustana Coll 1994. drswagnerrtmk@aol.com

WAGNER, Sharon Lavonne (Cal) 1921 Hemlock Dr, Oakley CA 94561 B San Francisco CA 6/13/1946 d Howard Prater & Elizabeth. BA California St U 1968; BA Sch for Deacons 1986. D 12/3/1988 Bp William Edwin Swing. m 6/12/1971 Fred Jay Wagner c 3. D S Geo's Epis Ch Antioch CA 1988-2002.

WAGNER JR, William Henry (Ore) 308 Dunmore St, Norfolk VA 23510 **Chr and S Lk's Epis Ch Norfolk VA 1992-** B Sioux City IA 5/30/1921 s William Henry Wagner & Ola. BA Drury U 1947; BD SWTS 1950. D 5/13/1950 P 12/2/1950 Bp Wallace E Conkling. m 5/23/1964 Cordelia Ruffin c 2. R Trin Epis Cathd Portland OR 1977-1990; R S Mk's Ch Islip NY 1964-1977; DRE S Barth's Ch New York NY 1959-1964; Cur S Steph's Ch Providence RI 1952-1954; Cur S Lk's Ch Evanston IL 1951-1952; Cur Emm Epis Ch La Grange IL 1950-1951. wllwgn@aol.com

WAGNER-PIZZA, Ken E (CPa) 1206 Faxon Parkway, Williamsport PA 17701 **R Trin Epis Ch Williamsport PA 2008-** B West Rockhill PA 11/7/1969 s Kenneth Eugene Pizza & Martha Viola. BS Elizabethtown Coll 1991; Luth TS at Gettysburg 1999; MDiv VTS 2002. D 6/21/2003 P 12/20/2003 Bp Charles Ellsworth Bennison Jr. m 10/16/1993 Rebecca J Wagner c 2. P-in-c Ch Of S Jn The Evang Essington PA 2003-2008. trinityrector@comcast.net

WAGNER SHERER, Kara Marie (Chi) 3857 N. Kostner Ave, Chicago IL 60641 **Dn of Chicago W Dnry Dio Chicago Chicago IL 2009-; S Jn's Epis Ch Chicago IL 2005-; S Mich's Ch La Marque TX 2005-** B Ellensburg WA 5/6/1969 d Curtis Arthur Wagner & Margaret Ann. BA S Olaf Coll 1991; M. Div SWTS 2003. D 6/21/2003 P 12/20/2003 Bp William Dailey Persell. m 6/12/1993 John Wagner Sherer c 2. Asst R Ch Of S Paul And The Redeem Chicago IL 2003-2005. rector@stjohnschicago.com

WAGNON, William S (WA) 9225 Crestview Dr, Indianapolis IN 46240 B Birmingham AL 11/4/1963 s William Macbeth Wagnon & Nancy Carolyn. BA Amer U 1985; MDiv Ya Berk 1993. D 6/12/1993 Bp Ronald Hayward Haines P 1/1/1994 Bp Morgan Porteus. m 5/29/1993 Verity Jones c 1. Affiliate/Supply S Geo Epis Ch W Terre Haute IN 1999-2000; Affiliate/Supply S Steph's Ch Terre Haute IN 1998-1999; P-in-c S Andr's Ch Paris IL 1997-1998; Assoc S Jn's Ch W Hartford CT 1993-1997. William@truewill.us

WAHL, Eugene Richard (Colo) 11684 Eldorado St Nw, Coon Rapids MN 55433 B National City CA 4/30/1954 s John Victor Wahl & Lillian Stacia. BA San Diego St U 1977; MA San Diego St U 1982; MDiv CDSP 1988; PhD Candidate U MN 2001. D 6/4/1988 Bp Charles Brinkley Morton P 11/1/1989 Bp William Edwin Swing. m 9/17/1988 Barbara A Dumke. Trin Ch Anoka MN 1997-2004; Supply S Mich's All Ang Ch Monticello MN 1993-1997; Chair Dio Minnesota Minneapolis MN 1993-1996; Asst St Johns Epis Ch Ross CA 1989-1992; D S Tim's Ch Danville CA 1988-1989. Auth, "Holocene Paleoecology Of Sthrn Ca : Methods, Results & Relation To Climate Models," *Geological Soc Of Amer Abstracts & Prog*, 2000; Auth, "A Late Paleoecological Record From Torrey Pines St Reserve Ca," *Quaternary Resrch (May)*, 2000; Auth, "Frontier Econ: Steady St Econ: Sustainable Dvlpmt," *Environ Encyclopedia*, Gale Resrch, 1994; Auth, "Country Cur'S Diary Gives Clues To An Environmntl Sprtly," *Soundings*, Epis Dio Minn, 1994; Auth, "The Rel Value Of Biodiversity," *Ecojustice Quarterly*, 1993. Ecological Soc Of Amer; EPF; No Amer Conf Chrsnty & Ecology. Best Stdt Resrch Proposal Geological Soc Of Amer 1998; Dissertation Improvement Awd Natl Sci Fndt 1998; Phi Kappa Phi; Phi Beta Kappa. generwahl@yahoo.com

WAHL, Hughes Edward (Md) 4010 Band Shell Ct, Chesapeake Beach MD 20732 B Pittsburgh PA 4/20/1942 s Carl Emert Wahl & Margaret Aneitha. BS Alderson-Broaddus Coll 1964; MDiv How 1995. D 6/17/1989 Bp A(lbert) Theodore Eastman. m 11/26/1977 Deborah Fallon Whetstone c 3. D S Andr The Fisherman Epis Mayo MD 1991-1996; D S Jas' Par Lothian MD 1989-1991. Untd States Naval Reserves - Lieutenant 1964; Eagle Scout BSA 1957.

WAID, Anna Neil Magruder (Del) 301 Woodlawn Rd, Wilmington DE 19803 B Greenwood MS 3/1/1945 d Douglas Neil Magruder & Marjorie Jane. BA LSU 1966; MA Jacksonville U 1972; MA Luth TS 1984. D 6/16/1984 P 6/11/1985 Bp Lyman Cunningham Ogilby. m 4/30/1968 William Waid c 2. R Gr Epis Ch Wilmington DE 1999-2010; Vic The Ch Of The Trin Coatesville PA 1994-1999; Int The Ch Of The H Comf Drexel Hill PA 1994; S Mary's Ch Hamilton Vill Philadelphia PA 1993-1994; Int S Mary's Epis Ch Philadelphia PA 1993-1994; Int Trin Ch Boothwyn PA 1990-1992; Asst The Ch Of The H Trin W Chester PA 1984-1990. rev.docwaid@yahoo.com

WAINWRIGHT, Philip (Pgh) 1025 Jancey St, Pittsburgh PA 15206 **Co-ordinator for Campus Mnstry Dio Pittsburgh Monroeville PA 2011-; Assoc St Andrews Epis Ch Pittsburgh PA 2011-** B Hastings England UK 3/26/1945 s Charles Edwin Wainwright & Doris Evelyn. BD U of New Mex 1981; ThM Lon 1984; PhD U of Kent at Cbury 2011. D 1/27/1986 P 2/12/1987 Bp Richard Mitchell Trelease Jr. m 8/27/1988 Thekla S Stark c 4. R S Ptr's Epis Ch Brentwood Pittsburgh PA 1999-2010; Cople Par Hague VA 1996-1999; R Nomini Ch Mt Holly Hague VA 1996-1999; R S Jas Ch Tidwells Hague VA 1996-1999; R Yeocomico Ch Tucker Hill Hague VA 1996-1999; S Jn's Epis Par Johns Island SC 1995-1996; R Ch of the H Faith Santa Fe NM 1988-1994; D-In-Trng Ch of the H Faith Santa Fe NM 1986-1987. Ed, "Epis Evang Journ," 1994. Alcuin Club 1989; Barn Proj 2008; EFAC USA 1994; Ecclesiological Soc 1990. pw35@kent.ac.uk

WAIT III, Benjamin Wofford (CFla) 962 Ocean Blvd, Atlantic Beach FL 32233 B Tampa FL 10/17/1934 s Benjamin Wofford Wait & Martha Elizabeth. BS U of Florida 1957; MA STUSo 1997; DMin STUSo 2006. D 6/15/1975 Bp William Hopkins Folwell P 5/1/1997 Bp Stephen Hays Jecko. m 8/24/1957 Shirleen Sasser. Cn Dio Florida Jacksonville FL 1997-2006; Asst Epis Ch Of The H Sprt Tallahassee FL 1990-1995; Asst Resurr Chap Tallahassee FL 1982-1990; Asst Gr Epis Ch Inc Port Orange FL 1981-1982; Asst S Paul's Epis Ch New Smyrna Bch FL 1976-1980; Asst S Mary Of The Ang Epis Ch Orlando FL 1975-1976. Angl Frontier Missions 2000; FA Natl Bd; Five Talents Intl 2001.

WAIT, Curtis Clark (Colo) 228 S Jefferson Ave, Louisville CO 80027 **Intsn Epis Ch Thornton CO 2007-** B Ann Arbor MI 8/22/1963 BS U CO 1998; MDiv STUSo 2004. D 6/12/2004 P 12/18/2004 Bp Robert John O'Neill. m 6/9/1984 Anne Margaret Wait c 2. The Epis Ch of the Resurr Broomfield CO 2004-2006. curtiswait@yahoo.com

WAIT, Roger Lee (Neb) 3711 A St, Lincoln NE 68510 B Comstock NE 8/26/1934 s Elvin Orland Wait & Marian Elizabeth. BA U of Nebraska 1964; Cert EFM 1989; CDTP SE Cmnty Coll Lincoln NE 1992. D 11/8/1985 Bp James Daniel Warner. m 5/9/1987 Phyllis Ann Wait. JPIC Team Dio Nebraska Omaha NE 1997-2000; D S Mk's On The Campus Lincoln NE 1985-2006; Bp's Com S Mk's On The Campus Lincoln NE 1981-1984. ACLU 2003; NAAD 1986; The Planetary Soc 2002-2003. valedictoriam Teachers Coll HS Lincoln NE 1952. rw00332@alltel.net

WAITS II, Emmett Moore (Dal) 9645 Cloister Dr, Dallas TX 75228 B Indianopolis IN 4/6/1923 s Emmett Moore Waits & Marie Church. BA Transylvania U 1945; BD STUSo 1949; S Aug's Coll Cbury Gb 1955; STM SMU 1961; DMin SMU 1980. D 12/1/1948 P 6/24/1949 Bp William R Moody. Asst P S Jn's Epis Ch Dallas TX 1989-2002; Dio Dallas Dallas TX 1974-1988; R S Barn Epis Ch Denton TX 1963-1973; R Ch Of The Ascen Mt Sterling KY 1949-1952. Apha Coll Of Chapl; Fllshp Soc Of S Jn The Evang; SSC.

WAJDA, Kathryn Annemarie Reardon (Md) 1505 Sherbrook Rd, Timonium MD 21093 **R Epiph Ch Dulaney Vlly Timonium MD 1998-** B Methuen MA 11/17/1945 d William Frank Reardon & Bertha Lilliam. BS U of New Hampshire 1967; MS U of Maine 1982; MDiv EDS 1984; DMin SWTS 2004. D

5/21/1985 Bp Philip Alan Smith P 3/9/1986 Bp A(lbert) Theodore Eastman. m 9/16/1967 Michael Wajda. Pres Reg Coun Dio Maryland Baltimore MD 1998-2000; Int Epiph Ch Dulaney Vlly Timonium MD 1996-1997; S Jn's Ch Ellicott City MD 1985-1996. EWC. kawajda@comcast.net

WAJNERT, Theresa Altmix (Nwk) Po Box 7560, Garden City NY 11530 B Denver CO 6/4/1948 d Richard H Altmix & Harriet. Drew U; BA Albertus Magnus Coll 1970; MDiv Yale DS 1974; Grad Theol Un 1983; Drew U 1988. D 6/29/1974 P 2/1/1977 Bp C Kilmer Myers. m 1/2/1982 Thomas C Wajnert c 4. Ch Of The Redeem Morristown NJ 1990-2004; Asst Ch of S Jn on the Mtn Bernardsville NJ 1984-1990; Asst S Bern's Ch Bernardsville NJ 1984-1990; S Aid's Ch San Francisco CA 1980-1984; S Aid's Ch San Francisco CA 1977-1979; Asst Trin Cathd San Jose CA 1975-1976; Asst S Andr's Ch Saratoga CA 1974-1975. theresa@twaj.com

WAKELEE-LYNCH, Julia (Cal) 1501 Washington Avenue, Albany CA 94706 **R S Alb's Ch Albany CA 2009-** B Ventura CA 1/21/1965 BA Occ 1983; MDiv CDSP 2003; MA Grad Theol Un 2004. D 6/28/2003 P 1/24/2004 Bp Joseph Jon Bruno. c 1. Int R Ch Of The Epiph San Carlos CA 2008-2009; Assoc The Par Ch Of S Lk Long Bch CA 2004-2008; D/Asstg P S Jas Epis Ch San Francisco CA 2003-2004. EPF 2000. jwakelee@gmail.com

WAKELY, Nancy Kay (Okla) PO Box 2088, Norman OK 73070 B Norman OK 1/4/1949 d Vernon Lee Lamirand & Betty Jo. D 6/16/2007 Bp Robert Manning Moody. m 11/4/1983 Thomas Martin Wakely c 2. wakely11@swbell.net

WAKEMAN, Nancy Ann (Md) 2120 Western Shores Blvd, Port Republic MD 20676 B Ephrata PA 3/9/1955 d Robert Ernest Johnson & Lorraine Yvonne. D 6/4/2011 Bp Eugene Sutton. m 6/18/1994 Timothy Wakeman c 4. rekstornan@comcast.net

WALBERG, Elsa Phyllis (Mass) Po Box 245 - B Weehawken NJ 8/2/1925 d George Phillip Walberg & Sophie Marie. BA CUNY 1949; MA NYU 1956; MDiv EDS 1962. D 2/19/1972 P 2/19/1977 Bp John Melville Burgess. Sprtl Direction Com Dio Vermont Burlington VT 1999-2001; Assoc S Andr's Epis Ch St Johnsbury VT 1995-2004; Supply P Dio Vermont Burlington VT 1992-2004; Assoc S Ptr's Mssn Lyndonville VT 1992-1994; T/F on Environ Dio Massachusetts Boston MA 1988-1991; R S Paul's Epis Ch Bedford MA 1983-1991; Assoc R S Andr's Ch Wellesley MA 1977-1983; Ecum Mnstry To Older Persons Brookline MA 1974-1977; Asst Trin Par Melrose MA 1962-1973. Ed, *Voices*, 2006; Auth, "Consider the Heavens," *NorthStar Monthly*, 1991; Auth, "Consider the Heavens," *monthly column*, 1991. EWC 1975-1990; SCHC 1974. Procter Fllshp EDS 1973. joelagain@comcast.net

WALCOTT, Robert (O) 2173 W 7th St, Cleveland OH 44113 B Boston MA 7/31/1942 s Robert Walcott & Rosamond. BA Coll of Wooster 1964; MDiv CDSP 1967; MA OH SU 1972. D 6/19/1968 P 12/24/1968 Bp John Harris Burt. m 9/3/1966 Diane Palmer c 1. H Trin Ch Lisbon OH 2005; S Aug's Epis Ch Youngstown OH 1993-1996; S Rocco's Ch Youngstown OH 1993-1995; Vic New Life Epis Ch Uniontown OH 1991-1993; R Ch Of The Trsfg Buffalo NY 1988-1991; P-in-c S Mart In The Fields Grand Island NY 1986-1987; Assoc S Lk's Ch Brockport NY 1981-1985; Assoc Chr Ch Oberlin OH 1979-1981; Assoc Chr Ch Oberlin OH 1975-1976; P-in-c S Jas Epis Ch Wooster OH 1972-1973; Cur S Mart's Ch Chagrin Falls OH 1968-1970. EPF 1968-2009. Marquis Who's Who in Amer; Marquis Who's Who in Healthcure; Marquis Who's Who in the Midwest. bobwal31@aol.com

WALCUTT, Gerald Gene (SanD) 1910 Royalty Dr, Pomona CA 91767 **Died 4/4/2010** B Crawford County OH 3/16/1924 s Rollie Mason Walcutt & Blanche Margaret. Heidelberg Coll 1948; BA Mt Un Coll 1949; MDiv Drew U 1952; ETSBH 1969. D 5/1/1969 P 10/1/1969 Bp Robert C Rusack.

WALDEN, Janice Marie (Mass) 110 Dean St., Unit #37, Taunton MA 02780 **Area Mssnr Bristol Cluster Taunton MA 2006-; Area Mssnr S Jn The Evang Taunton MA 2006-; Area Mssnr S Mk's Ch Taunton MA 2006-; Area Mssnr St Johns Ch Taunton MA 2006-** B New London CT 11/9/1956 d David Deland Walden & Cynthia Latham. BA Chart Oak St Coll 1991; MDiv Ya Berk 1995; STM Ya Berk 1996. D 6/8/1996 Bp Clarence Nicholas Coleridge P 1/25/1997 Bp Andrew Donnan Smith. Co-Mssnr Ch Of The Epiph Durham CT 1996-2006; Co-Mssnr Emm Ch Killingworth CT 1996-2006; Co-Mssnr Middlesex Area Cluster Mnstry Higganum CT 1996-2006; Co-Mssnr S Andr's Ch Northford CT 1996-2006; Co-Mssnr S Jas Epis Ch Higganum CT 1996-2006; Co-Mssnr S Paul's Ch Westbrook CT 1996-2006. janwalden1@gmail.com

WALDEN, Robert Eugene (Haw) 46-290 Ikiiki St, Kaneohe HI 96744 B Paragould AR 1/11/1938 s Clifton Eugene Walden & Vivian Juanita. BA Hendrix Coll 1959; MS USC 1972; MDiv CDSP 1977. D 8/31/1977 P 4/4/1978 Bp Edmond Lee Browning. m 6/9/1979 Ramona Redenbaugh c 4. R Dio Okinawa 1997-2003; Dioc Coun Dio Hawaii Honolulu HI 1981-2010; R All SS Ch Kapaa HI 1979-1997; Vic Chr Memi Ch Kilauea HI 1979-1981; Assoc Ch Of The H Nativ Honolulu HI 1977-1979. Auth, "Impact Of Asian-Amer Culture On Chr Wrshp," 1976. SSF 1976-1988. walden33@hotmail.com

WALDIE, Nanette Marie (Oly) 4228 Factoria Blvd SE, Bellevue WA 98006 B Denver CO 9/17/1956 d Donald E Hamilton & Therese I. MPM Seattle U 1990; AS CDSP 2006; MDiv Seattle U 2007. D 1/15/2009 P 7/31/2009 Bp Gregory Harold Rickel. m 9/1/1979 Ian Spencer Waldie c 2. nwaldie@gmail.com

WALDO JR, Mark E (Ala) 311 Lindsey Road, Coosada AL 36020 **R S Mich And All Ang Millbrook AL 2005-** B Houston TX 11/17/1956 s Mark Edward Waldo & Anne Ferris. BA Transylvania U 1979; MDiv VTS 1988. D 6/18/1988 P 4/25/1989 Bp Peter James Lee. m 5/16/2009 Mitzi Chesser c 4. Asst S Patricks Ch Falls Ch VA 2001-2005; R S Alb's Epis Ch Murrysville PA 1993-1998; Asst to R S Geo's Epis Ch Arlington VA 1988-1993. mark@stmichaelandallangels.com

WALDO SR, Mark Edward (Ala) 2046 Hazel Hedge Ln, Montgomery AL 36106 **R Emer Ch Of The Ascen Montgomery AL 2007-** B Fort Monroe VA 11/27/1926 s George Edward Waldo & Annie Tremaine. BA W&M 1948; MDiv VTS 1951; VTS 1969; DD Hampden-Sydney Coll 1983. D 6/24/1951 P 3/25/1952 Bp Middleton S Barnwell. m 6/5/1950 Anne Beekley c 6. Locten Gd Shpd Ch Montgomery AL 1989-1996; Locten S Paul's (Carlowville) Minter AL 1989-1996; Locten S Paul's Epis Ch Lowndesboro AL 1989-1996; Pres Dio Alabama Birmingham AL 1982-1984; Stndg Com Dio Alabama Birmingham AL 1980-1984; Chair Deptce Dio Alabama Birmingham AL 1978-1980; Excoun Dio Alabama Birmingham AL 1972-1973; Com Dio Alabama Birmingham AL 1971-1974; Dep Gc Dio Alabama Birmingham AL 1969-1973; Chair Dept Stwdshp & Evang Dio Alabama Birmingham AL 1966-1968; Excoun Dio Alabama Birmingham AL 1964-1967; Ch Of The Ascen Montgomery AL 1961-1989; Cn Pstr Chr Ch Cathd Houston TX 1956-1961; Exec Coun Dio Georgia Savannah GA 1954-1956; Asst Secy Dio Georgia Savannah GA 1953-1955; Vic S Andr's Epis Ch Douglas GA 1951-1956; Vic S Matt's Epis Ch Fitzgerald GA 1951-1956. Omicron Delta Kappa 1948; Phi Beta Kappa 1947. beauwaldo@gmail.com

✠ **WALDO, Rt Rev W(illiam) Andrew** (USC) 847 Kilbourne Rd, Columbia SC 29205 **Bp Dio Upper So Carolina Columbia SC 2010-** B Douglas GA 7/17/1953 s Mark Edward Waldo & Anne. BA Whittier Coll 1975; MA New Engl Conservatory of Mus 1980; MDiv STUSo 1988. D 6/25/1988 P 4/19/1989 Bp Douglas Edwin Theuner Con 5/22/2010 for USC. m 6/13/1981 Mary H Halverson c 3. Dio Minnesota Minneapolis MN 1999-2003; R Trin Ch Excelsior MN 1994-2010; R S Mk's Epis Ch Lagrange GA 1990-1994; Chair Bp's T/F on Econ Justice Dio New Hampshire Concord NH 1989-1990; Cur Gr Ch Manchester NH 1988-1990. Auth, "Baptism and Euch: Challenges," *OPEN*, Associated Parishes, 2000. D.Div. Hon. STUSo 2011. andrewwaldo1574@gmail.com

WALDON, Mark Wayne (Nwk) 39 Boyle Ave, Totowa NJ 07512 **R Chr Ch Totowa NJ 1985-** B Ocala FL 9/10/1944 s Albert Overall Waldon & (Mildren) Alice. BA Davidson Coll 1966; MDiv Candler TS Emory U 1969; Cert VTS 1970. D 6/24/1970 P 9/29/1971 Bp Edward Hamilton West. Chair Evang Consults Dio Newark Newark NJ 1987-2002; Vic Bethany Ch Hilliard FL 1980-1984; S Eliz's Epis Ch Jacksonville FL 1980; S Mary's Epis Ch Madison FL 1979; Locten Ch Of The H Comf Tallahassee FL 1971-1972; Vic Chr Ch Monticello FL 1970-1979. Auth, "Article," *The Epis*, 1983. Theta Phi. Theta Phi. mark.business@verizon.net

WALDON JR, Ray (U) 412 Shelby Springs Farms, Calera AL 35040 **Dn Cathd Ch Of S Mk Salt Lake City UT 2011-** B Shreveport LA 1/30/1956 s Raymond Joe Waldon & Marilyn Adams. BA Engl/Ba Journ Louisiana Tech U 1978; Lousiana St U Law Sch 1982; MDiv VTS 1995; audited Trin Newbury 2003. D 6/3/1995 P 12/3/1995 Bp Robert Jefferson Hargrove Jr. m 9/9/1978 Lisa F Waldon c 2. P-in-c S Ptr's Epis Ch Talladega AL 2008-2011; H Cross Ch Pensacola FL 2003-2007; R Gr Epis Ch And Kindergarten Camden SC 1998-2003; R/ Yoked- added 1998 S Alb's Epis Ch Monroe LA 1997-1998; R S Pat's Epis Ch W Monroe LA 1995-1998. Interview, "Ch," *Pensacola Journal*, Pensacola Journ, 2003; Auth, "What Christmas Means," *Camden Chronicle*, Camden Chronicle, 2001; Ed, "Dio Upper So Carolina Customary," *Bp's Customary*, Dio, 2000; Interview, "NBC Nightly Newiths w Tom Brokaw," *NBC*, NBC, 2000; Auth, "Stories On Rel And Ethics," *KNOE-TV*, KNOE TV 1995-1998, 1998; Rel Correspondence, "Nightly News," *KNOE-TV 1995-1998*, KNOE-TV 1995-1998, 1998; Auth, "Assisted Suicide," *Epis Life*, 1996. Bd Mem Birdell Fund 1999-2003; Bd Mem Hospice 1999-2003; Bd Mem Mnstrl Assn 1998-2003; Servnt Of Chr Priory- Oblate 2001; York Place Advsry 2001-2003. raywaldon@gmail.com

WALDRON, Susan Gail (Alb) 107 State St., Albany NY 12207 **S Mary's Ch Lake Luzerne NY 2011-; S Ptr's Ch Albany NY 2008-** B Albany NY 10/25/1966 d George C Pitsas & Carol A. AS SUNY Empire St Coll Saratoga 2002; BS SUNY Empire St Coll Saratoga 2003; MDiv Nash 2008. D 5/31/2008 Bp William David Smith Lovell P 12/21/2008 Bp William Howard Love. c 1. suewaldron@juno.com

WALDROP, Charlotte Macon Egerton (USC) 137 Summerwood Way, Aiken SC 29803 B Louisburg NC 8/4/1937 d Frank Nicholas Egerton & Pattie. BA U NC Asheville 1976; MDiv Duke 1986; Cert VTS 1986. D 6/14/1986 P 12/17/1986 Bp William Gillette Weinhauer. c 2. P Asstg S Thad Epis Ch Aiken SC 2006-2007; Vic All SS Ch Beech Island SC 2002-2010; Assoc R S Martins-In-The-Field Columbia SC 1999-2002; P-in-c S Martins-In-The-Field Columbia

SC 1998-1999; Del, Prov IV Wmn Conf Dio Wstrn No Carolina Asheville NC 1998; Assoc R S Martins-In-The-Field Columbia SC 1995-1997; Mem Stwdshp Dio Wstrn No Carolina Asheville NC 1990-1995; Mem Liturg Cmsn Dio Wstrn No Carolina Asheville NC 1989-1995; R Ch Of The Gd Shpd Hayesville NC 1986-1995; Int D Trin Ch Arlington VA 1986. revcharlot@aol.com

WALDROP JR, (John) Herbert (USC) 137 Summerwood Way, Aiken SC 29803 **Died 3/28/2010** B Greenville,NC 3/4/1927 s John Herbert Waldrop & Lois Zeigler. BA High Point U 1949; MDiv Duke 1952; CPE Duke 1969. D 5/15/1986 P 9/10/1986 Bp William Gillette Weinhauer. c 3.

WALK, Everett Prichard (SwFla) 8700 State Road 72, Sarasota FL 34241 **R S Marg Of Scotland Epis Ch Sarasota FL 1991-** B Washington DC 9/28/1949 s Everett Germond Walk & Sybil Agnus. BA Laf 1972; MDiv VTS 1977. D 6/2/1977 Bp Lloyd Edward Gressle P 12/18/1977 Bp Frank Stanley Cerveny. m 7/16/1977 Deborah W Wood c 1. Cn Pstr Cathd Ch Of S Lk Orlando FL 1986-1991; S Jn's Epis Ch Tallahassee FL 1977-1985. Ord Of S Lk. ewalk10704@aol.com

WALKER, Aurilla Kay (Neb) 712 W 18th St Apt 7, Cozad NE 69130 B Alliance NE 2/28/1949 D 12/13/2004 P 6/13/2005 Bp Joe Goodwin Burnett. c 2. aurilla@cozadtel.net

WALKER, Charles Henry (SD) 304 1st St, Wilmot SD 57279 **D Trin Epis Ch Pierre SD 1988-** B Pierre SD 9/13/1946 s William Henry Walker & Marjorie Maxine. DeVry Inst of Techology; So Dakota St U; U of So Dakota; Presentation Coll Aberdeen SD 2002. D 11/5/1988 Bp Craig Barry Anderson. m 11/9/1965 Betty Anne Koan c 3. Presentation Coll Bus Club. Pres'S List Presentation Coll; Deans List Presentation Coll. chwmedic@yahoo.com

WALKER, David Bruce (Spok) 127 E 12th Ave, Spokane WA 99202 B Sacramento CA 4/27/1956 s Samuel Campbell Walker & Elizabeth Ellen. BS Natl U 1991. D 6/11/2005 Bp James Edward Waggoner. m 4/18/1981 Julia L Julia Lee Akins c 2. dbwalk56@yahoo.com

WALKER, David Charles (Los) 6072 Avenida De Castillo, Long Beach CA 90803 B Washington DC 3/17/1938 s Edwin Stuart Walker & Frances Elizabeth. BA IL Wesl 1960; SMM UTS 1965; MDiv GTS 1973. D 6/9/1973 Bp Paul Moore Jr P 5/9/1974 Bp Ned Cole. Gd Samar Hosp Los Angeles CA 1991-2003; Int S Lk's Par Monrovia CA 1990; All SS Par Beverly Hills CA 1985-1990; Assoc All Souls' Epis Ch San Diego CA 1980-1985; R S Phil's Ch Brooklyn NY 1976-1980; Fac The GTS New York NY 1973-1976. Auth, "Hymn tune: Gnrl Sem," *The Hymnal 1982*, Ch Pub, 1982; Auth, "Hymn tune: Point Loma," *The Hymnal 1982*, Ch Pub, 1982. d.c.walker@mac.com

WALKER, Edwin Montague (SwFla) 1532 Vantage Pointe, Mount Pleasant SC 29464 B Yonkers NY 4/24/1933 s Harold Mitchell Walker & Gladys Mae. BEE RPI 1954; MSEE Georgia Inst of Tech 1956; MDiv VTS 1961; MA Van 1973. D 7/6/1961 Bp Noble C Powell P 6/22/1962 Bp Harry Lee Doll. m 6/29/1957 Margaret Blackman c 3. LocTen Ch Of The Redeem Pineville SC 2001-2008; S Dav's Epis Ch Englewood FL 1991-1999; S Mk's Epis Ch Charleston SC 1982-1991; Asst S Mich's Epis Ch Charleston SC 1980-1981; Assoc Chr Epis Ch Mt Pleasant SC 1978-1980; Supply P Dio So Carolina Charleston SC 1973-1978; P-in-c S Andr's Epis Ch New Johnsonville TN 1971-1972; Cur S Dav's Ch Baltimore MD 1961-1963. edmeg@bellsouth.net

WALKER, Elizabeth Ann (WVa) 3343 Davis Stuart Road, Fairlea WV 24902 **Off Of Bsh For ArmdF New York NY 1996-** B Clifton Forge VA 1/16/1957 d Weymouth Dove Walker & Betty. BD Concord U 1979; MDiv VTS 1987. D 5/30/1987 Bp Robert Poland Atkinson P 5/21/1988 Bp William Franklin Carr. Dio W Virginia Charleston WV 1996-2010; Vic Gr Ch Ravenswood WV 1993-1996; Stndg Com Dio W Virginia Charleston WV 1992-1997; R S Jn's Ripley WV 1988-1996; D-in-Trng Chr Ch Bluefield WV 1987-1988. dayspring@inetone.net

WALKER, Frederick Wyclif (SVa) 140 Tynes St, Suffolk VA 23434 **R S Mk's Ch Suffolk VA 2010-** B 11/21/1961 s Frederick Walker & Maggie. INC Cuttington U 1990; LTh St Nich Theol, Cape Coast, Ghana 1993; B.D. S Jn's Coll of theo 1995; M.Th. U Cape Coast 1998; Dplma Virginia Sem 2006; Biblic Stds Wesley TS 2007. Trans from Church of the Province of West Africa 4/26/2010 as Priest Bp Herman Hollerith IV. m 5/30/1992 Salome Nosegbe c 4. Hon Cn Dio Cape Coast, Ghana 2011. rectorstmarksuffolk@gmail.com

WALKER, Hugie Bermice (At) 108 Scarborough Rd, Centerville GA 31028 B Roberta GA 4/21/1919 s Gustavus Freeman Walker & Annie Willie. BS Ft Vlly St U 1942; MDiv VTS 1945. D 8/5/1945 P 7/1/1946 Bp John Thomas Walker. c 4. R S Jas Hse Of Pryr Tampa FL 1976-1983.

WALKER JR, H William (SeFla) St Thomas Episcopal Parish, 5690 N Kendall Dr, Coral Gables FL 33156 **Asstg P S Thos Epis Par Coral Gables FL 2011-** B Cincinnati OH 7/11/1946 s Harold William Walker & Claire W. BA W&L 1968; JD W&L 1971; MDiv Florida Cntr for Theol Stds 2009. D 12/21/2010 Bp Leopold Frade. m 6/29/1968 Laura C Campbell c 3. wwalker@whitecase.com

WALKER, (James) LEE (Los) 4114 South Norton Ave, Los Angeles CA 90008 B Houston TX 3/22/1948 s James Leander Walker & Myrtle Inez. BA U of Texas 1971; MDiv GTS 1973. D 6/11/1973 P 12/13/1973 Bp Theodore H McCrea. R Chr The Gd Shpd Par Los Angeles CA 1999-2003; Chr Ch Greenwich CT 1989-1999; Dio Ft Worth Ft Worth TX 1982-1985; Vic S Mart In The Fields Ch Keller TX 1982-1985; S Elis Ch Ft Worth TX 1976-1980; Cur S Chris's Ch And Sch Ft Worth TX 1974-1976; Intern Trin Ch Easton PA 1973-1974. shamanlee@ca.rr.com

WALKER, Janice Ficke (WNC) 6 Firestone Dr, Arden NC 28704 B Davenport IA 11/1/1935 d Parker Henry Ficke & Lucile Taylor. BA Carleton Coll 1957; MDiv SWTS 1979. D 6/16/1980 Bp James Winchester Montgomery P 2/24/1981 Bp Quintin Ebenezer Primo Jr. m 11/12/1983 James T Walker c 1. Int The Cathd Of All Souls Asheville NC 1998-1999; Assoc R S Mary Epis Ch Crystal Lake IL 1992-1995; Assoc R S Mk's Barrington Hills IL 1988-1991; Advoc Hlth Care Oak Brook IL 1982-1984; Asst S Mk's Barrington Hills IL 1979-1982. janwalker@ioa.com

WALKER, Jeffrey Hartwell (Ct) 4124 Berkman Dr, Austin TX 78723 B Houston TX 12/25/1944 s Jack Gardner Walker & Mary Taylor. BA U So 1972; MDiv STUSo 1975. D 6/16/1975 P 6/9/1976 Bp J Milton Richardson. m 7/30/1965 Elizabeth H Hall c 3. Int S Jas Ch Austin TX 2007-2009; R Chr Ch Greenwich CT 1993-2007; Assoc Palmer Memi Ch Houston TX 1979-1980; Cn Chr Ch Cathd Houston TX 1978-1979; Ass to Dn Chr Ch Cathd Houston TX 1975-1977. Sr Chapl Ord of S Lazarus of Jerusalem. Founders Awd Fndt for Interfaith Resrch and Mnstry. jhwehw@mac.com

WALKER III, John Edward (LI) 64 S Country Rd, Bellport NY 11713 **Stndg Com Dio Long Island Garden City NY 2006-; Hstgr Dio Long Island Garden City NY 2003-; Chr Ch Bellport NY 1995-** B New York NY 3/16/1948 s Edward F G Walker & Jane E. AA Queensborough Cmnty Coll 1969; BA CUNY 1971; MDiv Nash 1974. D 6/15/1974 P 12/1/1974 Bp Jonathan Goodhue Sherman. m 5/6/1978 Judith Durking c 1. Mercer Bd Mem Dio Long Island Garden City NY 2000-2005; Stwdshp Com Chair Dio Long Island Garden City NY 1998-2002; Deploy Advsry Grp Dio Pennsylvania Philadelphia PA 1994-1995; Stwdshp Com Dio Pennsylvania Philadelphia PA 1992-1994; S Jas Ch Greenridge Aston PA 1991-1994; R S Jas Epis Ch S Jas NY 1991-1994; Epis Hlth Serv Dio Long Island Garden City NY 1988-1991; Dioc Coun Dio Long Island Garden City NY 1988-1989; Peace Com Dio Long Island Garden City NY 1985-1986; Cler Conf Com Dio Long Island Garden City NY 1981-1991; Ecum Relatns Com Dio Long Island Garden City NY 1981-1986; R Ch Of The H Trin Greenport NY 1980-1991; Asst S Mk's Ch Islip NY 1978-1980; Cur Ch Of The Trsfg Freeport NY 1977-1978; S Geo's Par Flushing NY 1976; Asst Ch Of The H Apos Oneida WI 1974-1975. Rotarian Of The Year 1982. xchurchbellport@verizon.net

WALKER, John Francis (Oly) 509 S 2nd St, PO Box 116, La Conner WA 98257 **Supply P Dio Olympia Seattle WA 2000-** B Philadelphia PA 7/13/1929 s Francis Aloysious Walker & Blanche Estell. BS Tem 1957; STM PDS 1960. D 4/30/1960 P 11/5/1960 Bp Alfred L Banyard. m 4/23/1981 Jean Ann Wharton. Chapl Off Of Bsh For ArmdF New York NY 1962-1981; R Chr Ch Millville NJ 1960-1962. Third Ord SSF 1972. Chap 4 Chapl Legion of hon Tem Philadelphia PA 1970; Commendation Medal (Rec twice) USN 1968; Cross Gallantry Govt of Viet Nam Vietnam 1965; Korean Conflict Medal The Untd Nations 1953. tjww@wavecable.com

WALKER, Lynell Elizabeth (NCal) 2380 Wyda Way, Sacramento CA 95825 **S Paul's Epis Ch Sacramento CA 2005-; S Mich's Epis Day Sch Carmichael CA 2004-; Cn for Sprtl Formation Trin Cathd Sacramento CA 1999-** B Whttier CA 10/22/1948 d Edgar Lynell Esterwold & Francella Maurine. MDiv CDSP 1996. D 10/11/1998 P 5/25/1999 Bp Jerry Alban Lamb. m Patricia A Mitchell c 3. S Mich's Epis Ch Carmichael CA 2001-2003. lwalker259@aol.com

WALKER, Mary Lucia (Okla) 620 E Logan Ave, Guthrie OK 73044 B Berlin NH 8/30/1934 d Richard Gunsaules Urban & Lucia Clementine. BA Hood Coll 1956; MA U of Texas 1971; MA U of Texas 1974; MDiv Epis TS of The SW 1987. D 5/26/1996 Bp Sam Byron Hulsey P 11/25/1996 Bp Robert Manning Moody. m 10/23/1999 Thomas Tanner Walker c 2. Trin Ch Guthrie OK 2003-2005; Dio Oklahoma Oklahoma City OK 1996-2002; Vic Trin Ch Guthrie OK 1996-2002; Ch Of The Resurr Austin TX 1987-1994. mltwalker@cox.net

WALKER, Noble Ray (WTenn) 6855 Branch Rd, Olive Branch MS 38654 B Milan/Atwood TN 11/30/1940 s John Harice Walker & Frances Carnell. BA SW At Memphis (Rhodes Coll) 1962; MA U of Iowa 1963; STB (STM) GTS 1968; MS U of Memphis 1981. D 6/15/1968 Bp John Vander Horst P 5/6/1969 Bp William F Gates Jr. c 1. H Cross Epis Ch Olive Branch MS 1989-2007; Dio W Tennessee Memphis TN 1983-1985; Vic Bp Otey Memi Ch Memphis TN 1980-1986; Assoc S Jn's Epis Ch Memphis TN 1975-1980; P-in-c S Jas The Less Madison TN 1971-1975; Asst Gr Ch Chattanooga TN 1969-1971. Auth, "Washington Journ," *The Unicorn*, Gts_Ny, 1969; Auth, "O Tempus O Mores," *The Unicorn*, Gts-Ny, 1968; Auth, "Versos Del Sendero," *The Unicorn*, Gts-Ny, 1968. nrwalker@centurytel.net

✠ **WALKER JR, Rt Rev Orris George** (LI) PO Box 7334, Garden City NY 11530 **Bp of Long Island Dio Long Island Garden City NY 1991-** B Baltimore MD 11/5/1942 s Orris George Walker & Llewellyn Elizabeth. BA U of Maryland 1964; STB GTS 1968; U So 1970; DMin Drew U 1980; MA U of

Windsor 1984; MBA GTF 1993. D 6/18/1968 Bp Harry Lee Doll P 5/1/1969 Bp Edward Randolph Welles II Con 4/9/1988 for LI. m 6/12/1971 Norma Eloy McKinney c 1. Trst The CPG New York NY 1991-1997; Bp Dio Long Island Garden City NY 1988-2009; Dio Michigan Detroit MI 1986-1988; Trst The GTS New York NY 1982-1995; BEC Dio Michigan Detroit MI 1977-1980; Chair, Urban Affrs Com Dio Michigan Detroit MI 1975-1977; Trst Dio Michigan Detroit MI 1974-1977; Instr at TS Dio Michigan Detroit MI 1973-1988; S Matt's And S Jos's Detroit MI 1971-1988; Cur Ch Of The H Nativ Baltimore MD 1968-1969. Auth, *Lk Journ.* DHL St. Paul's Coll, Lawrenceville, VA 2000; DCL Ya Berk, New Haven, CT 1988; DD GTS, New York, NY 1988. owalker@dioceseli.org

WALKER, Paul Edward (Be) 276 Church St, Montrose PA 18801 **R S Paul's Ch Montrose PA 2009-** B Taylor PA 9/18/1951 s Harold William Walker & Doris Dora. BA Marywood U 1978; MS Marywood U 1981; MDiv Bex 1986. D 6/1/1986 P 1/24/1987 Bp James Michael Mark Dyer. m 3/6/2007 Randy Lee Webster c 2. Dioc Coun Dio Newark Newark NJ 2000-2004; Vic Chr Ch Belleville NJ 1999-2009; RurD Dio Rochester Rochester NY 1993-1999; Chair of the Dept for Soc Mnstry Dio Rochester Rochester NY 1990-1992; R Gr Ch Scottsville NY 1988-1999; R S Andr's Epis Ch Caledonia NY 1988-1999; Dio Wstrn Massachusetts Springfield MA 1986-1988; Cur S Matt's Ch Worcester MA 1986-1988. ChmbrCom (Vice-Pres) 1999; Rotary (Past-Pres) 1999. walkerpe51@aol.com

WALKER, Paul Nelson (Va) 100 W Jefferson St, Charlottesville VA 22902 **R Chr Epis Ch Charlottesville VA 2004-** B Richmond VA 7/8/1964 s Randolph H Walker & Lovey Jane. BA U of Virginia 1986; MDiv VTS 1995. D 6/3/1995 P 1/1/1996 Bp Peter James Lee. m 6/14/1986 Christie Lynn Robertson c 3. The Cathd Ch Of The Adv Birmingham AL 2001-2004. *Sermons For Chr Ch*, Legacy Word Pub, 2001. paul@christchurchcville.org

WALKER, Paul Shields (ETenn) 8632 Charles Towne Ct, Knoxville TN 37923 **Died 9/29/2010** B Newport TN 6/30/1929 s Edward Raymond Walker & Pauline Loutyna. BA U So 1950; MDiv STUSo 1956. D 6/30/1956 Bp John Vander Horst P 1/1/1957 Bp Theodore N Barth. c 4.

WALKER, Peggy (WNC) 824 Arabella St, New Orleans LA 70115 B Alexandria LA 6/15/1951 d William Foster Walker & Jane Yvonne. BA LSU 1973; MA Tul 1982; MA Tul 1983; MDiv STUSo 1992. D 6/13/1992 P 12/19/1992 Bp James Barrow Brown. m 8/30/1997 Francis Marion Covington King c 1. S Jn's Epis Ch Marion NC 2010-2011; Dio Louisiana Baton Rouge LA 2005-2008; R Prtem S Paul's Ch New Orleans LA 2001-2002; Assoc R S Paul's Ch New Orleans LA 1995-1998; Assoc R Chr Ch Covington LA 1994-1995; Asst R S Paul's Ch New Orleans LA 1992-1994. peggwalker@gmail.com

WALKER, Ralph Thomas (Colo) 1400 S University Blvd, Denver CO 80210 **Bd Trst Nash Nashotah WI 1976-; R S Mich And All Ang' Ch Denver CO 1975-** B Denver CO 6/14/1944 s Edward Lee Walker & Evelyn Rose. BA U of Nthrn Colorado 1966; MDiv Nash 1969; Coll of Preachers 1974; St. Geo's Coll Jerusalem 2001. D 6/24/1969 P 12/26/1969 Bp Edwin B Thayer. m 6/28/1969 Claudia Quealy c 2. R S Andr's Ch La Junta CO 1970-1975; Cur S Steph's Epis Ch Aurora CO 1969-1970. CCU 1970; CBS 1969; GAS 1966; SocMary 1969; SSC 1975. Doctory of Div Nash 1992. smaacrector@gmail.com

WALKER, Robert Howard (Colo) 3379 Mill Vista Rd. Unit 4309, Highlands Ranch CO 80129 **Asst The Epis Par of S Greg Littleton CO 2006-** B Bowling Green OH 8/31/1935 s Howard Kenneth Walker & Maxine Rose. BS California St U 1969; MDiv S Thos TS Denver CO 1995. D 6/10/1995 P 12/10/1995 Bp William Jerry Winterrowd. m 11/10/1956 Dorothy B Bruner c 1. R S Phil In-The-Field Sedalia CO 1996-2005; Asst S Ambr Epis Ch Boulder CO 1995-1996.

WALKER, Robert Lynn (NY) 120 W 69th St, New York NY 10023 B Anna IL 9/1/1929 D 6/11/1958 P 12/17/1958 Bp Gordon V Smith.

WALKER, Roger Dale (Mich) 4800 Woodward Ave, Detroit Mi 48201 **Dio Michigan Detroit MI 2011-; S Paul's Epis Ch Brighton MI 2011-** B Henderson KY 12/10/1947 s Leonard Earl Walker & Mary Frances. BA U of Evansville 1969; MSSW U of Louisville 1985; MDiv SWTS 2009. D 6/11/2011 Bp Wendell Nathaniel Gibbs Jr. rwalkerlcsw@gmail.com

WALKER, Samuel Clevenger (WA) Zach Fowler Road, Box 8, Chaptico MD 20621 B Bryn Mawr PA 9/26/1943 s Danforth Supplee Walker & Dorothy. BA Ups 1965; MDiv PDS 1968; STM Yale DS 1977; DMin GTF 1993. D 6/8/1968 Bp Robert Lionne DeWitt P 12/1/1968 Bp Jonathan Goodhue Sherman. m 8/24/1968 Alice Elizabeth Roswell c 2. P-in-c Chr Ch Chaptico MD 1991-2002; R Emm Par Epis Ch And Day Sch Sthrn Pines NC 1983-1991; R S Jn's Ch Bridgeport CT 1978-1983; Asst Chr Ch Greenwich CT 1973-1978; Cur All SS Ch Great Neck NY 1968-1969. Auth, "Natl Observer". Tosf, AAPC, ACPE, CHS. Outstanding Young Men Amer 1977; Who'S Who Rel Amer 78; Polly Bond Awd Excellence Rel Jornalism 94 Epis Cmncatns Assn.

WALKER, Scott Douglas (Alb) 3-6-25 Shiba-Koen, Minato-ku, Tokyo Japan 105-0011 Japan **S Albans Angl-Epis Ch Minato-ku Tokyo 2010-** B Memphis TN 3/4/1967 s Tolbert H Walker & Jerri L. BA SMU 1989; MS,MBA Baylor U 2002; MA Nash 2008. D 10/28/2008 P 6/29/2009 Bp William Howard Love. m 3/8/1994 Akemi Sato. mbamsis@aim.com

WALKER, Stephen Bruce (WNC) 303 S King St, Morganton NC 28655 **R Gr Ch Morganton NC 2002-** B Spartanburg SC 7/7/1953 s Lemuel Harrall Walker & Betty. BS U of So Carolina 1975; DMD Med U of So Carolina 1981; MDiv STUSo 1997. D 6/14/1997 P 5/9/1998 Bp Dorsey Felix Henderson. m 8/25/1979 Susie Young c 3. Assoc R S Paul's Ch Augusta GA 1999-2002; Asst R S Barth's Ch No Augusta SC 1997-1999. rector@gracemorganton.org

WALKER, Terrence Alaric (SVa) PO Box 753, Lawrenceville VA 23868 B Pittsburgh PA 5/22/1966 s Edwin Thurston Walker & Annie Louise. BS Jas Madison U 1988; MA Norfolk St U Norfolk VA 1990; MDiv Epis TS of The SW 1993; EdD GTF 2000. D 6/5/1993 Bp O'Kelley Whitaker P 5/21/1994 Bp William Elwood Sterling. Trin Ch So Hill VA 2007-2009; S Lk The Evang Houston TX 1993-2000. Auth, "The Educational Theol of Jas Solomon Russell," *Proceedings of the Midwest Philos of Educ Soc*, MPES, 1997. twalker@saintpauls.edu

WALKER, Thomas Cecil (NC) 2933 Wycliffe Rd, Raleigh NC 27607 B McCaysville GA 9/5/1939 s Henry Cecil Walker & Laura Jeanette. BA U NC 1962; MDiv EDS 1965; PGCS U NC 1976; PGCS U of Tennessee 1979. D 6/29/1965 Bp Thomas Augustus Fraser Jr P 12/1/1967 Bp William Moultrie Moore Jr. Asst R S Mich's Ch Raleigh NC 1965-1971. tostan1@juno.com

WALKER, William Delany (Mil) 907 Green St, Durham NC 27701 B Dallas TX 11/23/1923 s William Delany Walker & Mildred. GTS; U So; BA Rice U 1944; PhD Cor 1949. D 9/22/1964 Bp Donald H V Hallock. m 12/22/1946 Constance Kalbach c 3. Asst S Fran Ch Madison WI 1964-1971. Auth, "Sci arts".

WALKER, William Ray (CPa) St. Paul's Episcopal Church, P.O. Box 170, Philipsburg PA 16866 B Hawk Run PA 3/12/1939 s Raymond William Walker & Sarah M. BS Lock Haven U 1961; Med U of Pennsylvania 1965; Cert Sch Chr Stds PA 1996. D 11/9/1996 P 2/17/2002 Bp Michael Whittington Creighton. m 11/24/1974 Alice Hilderbrand c 1. S Paul's Ch Philipsburg PA 2006-2011; D S Lawr Ch Osceola Mills PA 1999-2002. deaconwm@hotmail.com

WALKER, William Royce (Wyo) 157 Pleasant Valley Rd, Hartville WY 82215 **P Ch Of Our Sav Hartville WY 2004-** B Hartville WY 1/23/1938 D 3/12/2004 P 12/18/2004 Bp Bruce Edward Caldwell. m 10/11/1959 Nina Mae Millikia c 3. valleywalk@scottsbluff.net

WALKER-FRONTJES, Stacy Ann (Chi) 910 Normal Road, DeKalb IL 60115 **R S Paul's Ch Dekalb IL 2010-** B Kansas City MO 11/18/1974 d Grover Walker & Janet. BS MI SU 1997; MDiv Epis TS of The SW 2006. D 12/18/2005 P 8/5/2006 Bp Edwin Max Leidel Jr. m 7/29/2000 Richard Andrew Frontjes c 2. Asst S Edm's Epis Ch Chicago IL 2009-2010; R S Albans Epis Ch Bay City MI 2006-2009. walkerfrontjes@yahoo.com

WALKER-SPRAGUE, Patricia Shields (Cal) 5653 Merriewood Dr, Oakland CA 94611 **non-stipendiary P Assoc All Souls Par In Berkeley Berkeley CA 1998-; P S Mk's Par Berkeley CA 1997-** B San Jose CA 1/17/1934 d Kenneth Rombout Shields & Elizabeth. Rad 1952; BA U CA 1955; MBA City U of Seattle 1984; MDiv CDSP 1997. D 10/28/1989 Bp Robert Hume Cochrane P 12/6/1997 Bp William Edwin Swing. m 8/3/1974 Willard Ford Sprague. D S Paul's Ch Seattle WA 1989-1994. NAAD. walkerrevp@aol.com

WALKLEY, Richard Nelson (Ga) 2016 Se 27th Dr, Homestead FL 33035 B Chattanooga TN 6/1/1929 s Richard Loope Walkley & Dorothy May. BS U of Memphis 1952; GD STUSo 1955. D 7/2/1955 P 6/29/1956 Bp John Vander Horst. c 1. Receiving Disabil Ret 1991-1994; Int S Jn's Epis Ch Homestead FL 1990-1992; Int Emm Epis Ch Hampton VA 1989-1990; Int S Steph's Ch Coconut Grove Coconut Grove FL 1987-1989; Int S Jn's Epis Ch Homestead FL 1986-1987; S Lk's Epis Hawkinsville GA 1982-1986; Asst S Thos Epis Ch Thomasville GA 1972-1977; Asst S Jas Epis Ch Baton Rouge LA 1969-1972; Vic Ch Of The Incarn Amite LA 1967-1969; Vic S Fran Ch Denham Sprg LA 1967-1969; R Trin Ch Demopolis AL 1962-1967; Vic S Tim's Ch Tok AK 1959-1962; Min in charge S Mary Magd Ch Fayetteville TN 1955-1959.

WALL, Anne Fuller (ECR) 535 Torrey Pine Pl, Arroyo Grande CA 93420 B Chicago IL 6/10/1946 d Douglas Raymond Fuller & Ruth. BA Stan 1969; BA Sch for Deacons 1998. D 6/3/2000 Bp William Edwin Swing. m 7/8/1967 James Curtis Wall c 2. S Mk's Epis Ch Palo Alto CA 2004-2006; S Bede's Epis Ch Menlo Pk CA 2000-2008. annefwall@aol.com

WALL JR, John Furman (Spr) 507 Hanover St, Fredericksburg VA 22401 B Boise ID 10/19/1931 s John Furman Wall & Helen Eulalie. BS USMA At W Point 1956; MS Pr 1961; PhD Cor 1973; JD GW 1982; MA VTS 1995. D 9/19/1994 P 4/25/1995 Bp Peter Hess Beckwith. m 6/30/1956 Suzanne McHenry Jones c 3. P-in-c S Ptr's Port Royal Port Royal VA 2005-2009; P-in-c Cople Par Hague VA 1999-2003; P-in-c Nomini Ch Mt Holly Hague VA 1999-2003; P-in-c S Jas Ch Tidwells Hague VA 1999-2003; P-in-c Yeocomico Ch Tucker Hill Hague VA 1999-2003; P-in-c S Alb's Epis Ch Olney IL 1994-1999; P-in-c S Mary's Ch Robinson IL 1994-1999. "Numerous Sci And Engr Treatises," 2003. Asce 1975; Crawford Cnty Ministral Assn 1994-1999;

Dc Bar Assn 1985; Richland Cnty Ministral Assn 1994-1999; Soc Of The Cicinnati 1975. Fell Asce; Fell Same.

WALL, John N (NC) English Dept Of Box 8105, NC State University, Raleigh NC 27695 B Wadesboro NC 8/24/1945 s John Nelson Wall & Frances Smith. BA U NC 1967; MA Duke 1969; MDiv EDS 1972; PhD Harv 1973. D 6/24/1972 P 6/1/1974 Bp Thomas Augustus Fraser Jr. m 8/22/1970 Terry Cobb c 2. Res Cler S Mk's Epis Ch Raleigh NC 1973-2004; Cur S Jn's Chap Cambridge MA 1972-1973. Auth, "A Dictionary for Episcopalians," Cowley, 2000; Auth, "A New Dictionary for Episcopalians," HarperCollins, 1990; Auth, "Transformations of the Word," Univ of Georgia Press, 1988; Auth, "Geo Herbert: Engl Works," Paulist Press, 1980. Phi Beta Kappa 1966. Digital Hmnts Grant Natuional Endwmt for the Hmnts 2011; Vstng Fell Wolfson Coll, Cambridge Cambridge Engl 2003; Fell Natl Hmnts Cntr 1980; Fell Mellon Fndt 1975. jnwall@ncsu.edu

WALL, Richard David (CPa) 208 W Foster Ave, State College PA 16801 **R S Andr's Ch St Coll PA 2009-** B Wordsley England 7/19/1978 s Richard Wall & Shirley. BA Oxf 1999; DipThTG St Steph's Hse Oxford 2002; MA Oxf 2004. Trans from Church Of England 7/24/2006 Bp Charles Ellsworth Bennison Jr. Cur S Clements Ch Philadelphia PA 2005-2009. revrichardwall@gmail.com

WALLACE, Gene Richard (Los) 1042 N Mountain Ave B554, Upland CA 91786 B Fall River MA 12/7/1948 s Irving Francis Wallace & Dolores. BA Bridgewater Coll 1970; MA EDS 1984; PsyD California Grad Inst 2008. D 5/28/1983 Bp John Bowen Coburn P 5/1/1984 Bp John Melville Burgess. m 4/16/1988 Carol H Wallace. R Ch Of The Trsfg Arcadia CA 1995-2008; R S Geo's Ch Riverside CA 1986-1995; Assoc R S Mich And All Ang Par Corona Del Mar CA 1984-1986; D S Paul's Ch Boston MA 1983-1984. wallace.gene48@gmail.com

WALLACE, Hugh Jefferson (SC) 10172 Ocean Hwy, Pawleys Island SC 29585 **P Assoc Chr the King Pawleys Island SC 2009-** B Albany GA 9/24/1956 s William McKinley Wallace & Lucy. BA Lenoir-Rhyne Coll 1979; MDiv Luth Theo Sthrn Sem 1984. D 6/7/2007 P 12/13/2007 Bp Edward Lloyd Salmon Jr. m 6/3/1978 Stephanie Stout Stephanie Jo Stout c 4. jwallace0101@aol.com

WALLACE JR, James Edward (ETenn) Po Box 3073, Montgomery AL 36109 **R S Mart Of Tours Epis Ch Chattanooga TN 2011-** B Pittsburgh PA 11/17/1953 s James Edward Wallace & Marian Lee. BA SUNY 1975; MDiv VTS 1981. D 6/10/1981 Bp Harold B Robinson P 12/1/1981 Bp Furman Stough. R All SS Ch Montgomery AL 1996-2011; S Paul's Ch Kansas City MO 1995-1996; Assoc S Jn's Ch Montgomery AL 1991-1994; Ch Of The Resurr Rainbow City AL 1983-1991; Cur S Lk's Epis Ch Birmingham AL 1981-1983. EDEO 1998. jwallace2845@charter.net

WALLACE, John Bruce (EMich) 7010 Brudy Road Box 790, Indian River MI 49749 **D Trsfg Epis Ch Indn River MI 1995-** B MI 10/29/1934 s John Benjamin Wallace & Cecilia. Lawr Tech U; U MI; EFM STUSo 1996; BSW Madonna U 2003. D 10/1/1995 Bp H Coleman McGehee Jr. m 8/10/1996 Mary Lynn Kraywinkel. john.wallace@cheboyganhospital.org

WALLACE, John Robert (CGC) 6841 Oak St, Milton FL 32570 B Wilmington DE 4/10/1953 s William Wallace & Frances Margaret. BA U of W Florida 1976; MDiv Epis TS of The SW 2003. D 1/18/2003 P 9/9/2004 Bp Wayne Parker Wright. m 7/4/1992 Patricia Ann Librandi c 2. Memi Ch Of The H Nativ Rockledge PA 2009-2011; S Mary's Epis Ch Milton FL 2004-2009. Assoc SHN 2002. bfbjrw@aol.com

WALLACE, Lance Stephen (SwFla) 222 S Palm Ave, Sarasota FL 34236 **D Ch Of The Redeem Sarasota FL 2010-** B Minneapolis MN 12/18/1953 s Benjamin B Wallace & Ilene A. MTS Reformed TS 2007; Angl Stds Nash 2010. D 6/5/2010 P 12/7/2010 Bp John Wadsworth Howe. m 5/23/2003 Diane Smith. wallace.lance@gmail.com

✠ WALLACE JR, Rt Rev Leigh (Spok) 2 Lower Lincoln Hills Dr, Missoula MT 59802 **Died 10/7/2010** B Norman OK 2/5/1927 s Leigh Allen Wallace & Nellie Elizabeth. BA U of Montana 1950; MDiv VTS 1962. D 7/1/1962 P 1/2/1963 Bp Chandler W Sterling Con 1/25/1979 for Spok. c 3. Hon DD VTS Alexandria VA 1979. plwall9249@aol.com

WALLACE, Martha Ellen (WA) 1350 Quincy St NW, Washington DC 20011 **Emm Epis Ch Alexandria MN 2011-** B Steubenville OH 12/29/1948 d John Lester Wallace & Ona Louise. BA VPI 1971; JD Suffolk Law Sch 1976; MS MIT 1983; MDiv SWTS 1999. D 6/26/1999 P 6/22/2000 Bp R(aymond) Stewart Wood Jr. m 1/4/1986 Dennis Craig White. Gr Ch Washington DC 2011; Int Chr Ch Capitol Hill Washington DC 2008-2010; Int S Andr's Epis Ch Coll Pk MD 2007-2008; Assoc R S Clare Of Assisi Epis Ch Ann Arbor MI 2004-2006; S Paul's Epis Ch Piney Waldorf MD 2004-2006; Asst Chr Ch Grosse Pointe Grosse Pointe Farms MI 2002-2004; All SS Epis Ch Pontiac MI 2000-2002. Alfred P Sloan Fell MIT 1982. girlpriest@comcast.net

WALLACE, Robert Edgar (FdL) Po Box 936, Minocqua WI 54548 **R S Mths Minocqua WI 1993-; R S Mths' Manitowish Waters Cong Minocqua WI 1993-; Vic S Mths Minocqua WI 1990-** B Osceola IA 12/25/1957 s Robert Marvin Wallace & Betty Elaine. BA Morningside Coll 1980; MDiv SWTS 1984. D 5/21/1984 Bp Walter Cameron Righter P 3/29/1985 Bp Gerald Nicholas McAllister. Trst SWTS Evanston IL 1994-1996; Asst To Dn S Paul's Cathd Fond du Lac WI 1986-1989; Cur S Lk's Epis Ch Ada OK 1984-1986; Vic S Tim's Epis Ch Pauls Vlly OK 1984-1986. Conf Of The Blessed Sacrement - Gnrl Secy 1983; SHN - Assoc 1983. edgarwallace@charter.net

WALLACE, Sean Michael (La) 119 E 74th St, New York NY 10021 **Cur Ch Of The Resurr New York NY 2009-** B Ft Smith AR 3/29/1966 s James Ward & Martha Sue. BM Jn Br 1989; MM Eastman Sch of Mus 1993; DMA/MAM MI SU 2000; MDiv The GTS 2009. D 12/27/2008 Bp Charles Edward Jenkins III P 7/24/2009 Bp Herbert Alcorn Donovan Jr. m 8/5/1989 Marcia Whitmore c 2. wallacesean@msn.com

WALLACE, Tanya Rebecca (WMass) 37 Chestnut St, Springfield MA 01103 **R All SS Ch So Hadley MA 2009-** B Montague MA 2/21/1972 BA Mt Holyoke Coll 1994; MDiv UTS 2000. D 6/10/2000 P 12/16/2000 Bp John Palmer Croneberger. m Kathleen West c 1. Cn Cathd Ch Of S Paul Burlington VT 2002-2009; Ch Of The Ascen New York NY 2000-2002. "Abraham and Isaac Revisited," Out in the Mountains, 2003; "The Face in the Mirror," St. Lk's Revs, 1999. EWC 1996; OSH - Assoc 1997. trwallace72@gmail.com

WALLACE, Thomas A (Tex) 407 E 22nd Ave, Belton TX 76513 B Houston TX 9/14/1946 s Howard Maldon Wallace & Lois Bertha. BA U of Texas 1969; MDiv VTS 1972. D 6/28/1972 Bp Frederick P Goddard P 6/20/1973 Bp J Milton Richardson. m 11/26/1970 Patricia Ann Skutca c 2. S Lk's Epis Ch Belton TX 1998-2006; Dioc Depatment of Cmncatn Mem Dio Texas Houston TX 1992-1995; R S Mary's Ch Bellville TX 1981-1998; Assoc R S Mk's Ch Beaumont TX 1974-1981; Vic S Lk's Ch Livingston TX 1972-1974; Vic S Paul's Epis Ch Woodville TX 1972-1974. tawallace69ut@att.net

WALLACE, William Lewis (Los) 1448 15th St Ste 203, Santa Monica CA 90404 **Asst The Par Of S Matt Pacific Palisades CA 1983-** B Santa Monica CA 7/17/1939 s Maurice Gower Wallace & Deane. BA San Fernando St Coll 1962; MDiv CDSP 1965; MA Peabody Coll 1972; PhD Peabody Coll 1978. D 9/1/1965 Bp Robert C Rusack P 6/15/1966 Bp Francis E I Bloy. m 7/23/1960 Sarah Lee Milstead. Asst S Phil's Epis Ch Laurel MD 2002-2003; Asst S Geo's Ch Nashville TN 1973-1975; P-in-c Ch Of The H Trin Nashville TN 1971-1973; Asst S Mart-In-The-Fields Par Winnetka CA 1966-1968; Cur S Mk's Par Glendale CA 1965-1966. APA 1978; California Psychol Assn 1976; Los Angeles Cnty Psychol Assn 1992. Hlth Plcy Fell APA 2002; Pres Ca Psych Assn 1999; Pres Los Angeles Cnty Psych Assn 1995. williamlwallace@attglobal.net

WALLENS, Michael Gary (Tex) 6500 St Stephens Dr, Austin TX 78746 **S Steph's Epis Sch Austin TX 2009-** B Chicago IL 8/6/1950 s Richard Louis Wallens & Barbara. BS U So 1972; MDiv GTS 1978. D 6/17/1978 Bp Quintin Ebenezer Primo Jr P 12/16/1978 Bp James Winchester Montgomery. m 1/20/1973 Susan M Merrill c 2. Int S Thos' Ch Garrison Forest Owings Mills MD 2007-2009; S Paul's Sch Brooklandville MD 2007; Trin Ch Towson MD 2004-2005; S Paul's Par Baltimore MD 2002-2004; H Innoc Ch Atlanta GA 1994-1998; H Innoc' Epis Sch Atlanta GA 1994-1998; S Marg Of Scotland Par San Juan Capistrano CA 1991-1994; S Mich And All Ang Ch Dallas TX 1982-1991; Dio Chicago Chicago IL 1981-1982; St Cyprians Ch Chicago IL 1980-1981. mwallens@sstx.org

WALLER, Clifford Scott (WTex) Po Box 12349, San Antonio TX 78212 **Asstg P S Mk's Epis Ch San Antonio TX 2002-** B El Paso TX 8/23/1935 s Clifford Wellington Waller & Ona. BA Trin U 1957; MDiv EDS 1960. D 7/7/1960 Bp Everett H Jones P 1/25/1961 Bp Donald J Campbell. m 8/25/1956 Elizabeth S Semmes c 2. Int S Dav's Epis Ch San Antonio TX 1997-1998; Assoc R S Phil's Ch San Antonio TX 1990-1996; Dio W Texas San Antonio TX 1987-1989; Headmaster, Texas Mltry Inst Dio W Texas San Antonio TX 1987-1989; Epis Ch Cntr New York NY 1983-1985; Ch Of The H Sprt San Antonio TX 1981-1983; Dio W Texas San Antonio TX 1980-1983; P-in-c Santa Fe Epis Mssn San Antonio TX 1966-1979; Instnl Chapl Of W Texas Dio W Texas San Antonio TX 1962-1966; Asst Min S Mk's Epis Ch San Antonio TX 1962-1966. Auth, "Human Sxlty: A Chr Perspective". Worker Sis/Brothers Of The H Sprt, Comp; Wtex Cleric Assn. DD Epis Sem of the SW 1986. cliffwaller@sbcglobal.net

WALLER, Stephen Jay (Dal) 6525 Inwood Rd, Dallas TX 75209 **R The Epis Ch Of S Thos The Apos Dallas TX 1989-** B Shreveport LA 11/25/1946 s Morgan Howard Waller & Elizabeth. W&L 1969; GTS 1972. D 6/9/1972 Bp Reginald Heber Gooden P 2/24/1973 Bp Iveson Batchelor Noland. R S Tim's Ch Milwaukee WI 1981-1989; Vic S Alb's Epis Ch Monroe LA 1977-1981; Cur Trin Epis Ch Baton Rouge LA 1973-1977; Cur Ch Of The Redeem Ruston LA 1972-1973; Cur S Lk's Chap Grambling LA 1972-1973. Bk, "Our Souls in Silence Wait," PDQ Press, Dallas. Soc of S Fran - Tertiary 1983. doubtertom@aol.com

WALLEY, Kent R (NJ) 182 Main St, P.O. Box 605, Gladstone NJ 07934 **R S Lk's Ch Gladstone NJ 2008-** B Pittsburgh PA 6/15/1961 s Richard Lee Walley & Mary. BD U MI 1983; MDiv TESM 1999. D 6/12/1999 Bp Robert William Duncan P 1/30/2000 Bp Edward Lloyd Salmon Jr. m 6/6/1987 Joy Brandt c 2. Assoc R S Lk's Epis Ch Hilton Hd SC 1999-2007. walley3@aol.com

WALLEY, Seth Martin (Miss) 113 S 9th St, Oxford MS 38655 **S Ptr's Ch Oxford MS 2011-** B Ocean Springs MS 3/19/1986 s Glennis Martin Walley & Sally Jo. BBA The U of Mississippi 2008; MDiv VTS 2011. D 6/4/2011 Bp Duncan Montgomery Gray III. smwalley@gmail.com

WALLING II, Albert Clinton (Tex) 8406 Lofty Ln, Round Rock TX 78681 B Fort Lauderdale FL 9/24/1925 s Jacob Biffle Walling & Nora Maurine. U San Luis Potosi Mx 1945; BA Trin U 1948; MDiv EDS 1953; Harv 1963; SMU 1972; STM STUSo 1973; Van 1975; DMin STUSo 1977. D 7/15/1953 P 1/25/1954 Bp Everett H Jones. m 12/26/1964 Carroll W Wicher c 2. H Sprt Epis Ch Houston TX 1982; R S Alb's Ch Houston TX 1977-1982; Assoc R S Mk's Ch Houston TX 1974-1977; R Epis Ch Of The Ascen Dallas TX 1971-1974; R Ch Of The Gd Shpd Terrell TX 1966-1971; Assoc S Jn's Ch Ft Worth TX 1964-1966; Asst R S Dav's Ch Austin TX 1954-1960; D All SS Epis Ch Pleasanton TX 1953-1954; D Epis Ch Of The Gd Shepard Geo W TX 1953-1954. Auth, "Battle Memories in the Lone Star Star St," *Clan Chisholm Journ*, 1975; Auth, "The Puritan Concept of God in Cov w Engl as Seen in the Founding of Jamestowne VA," *Thesis*, U So, 1973. Ch Hist Soc; Rel Speech Assn. Dep to Prov Syn Dio Dallas 1970; Trst U So Dio Dallas 1968. acw2cww@sbcglobal.net

WALLING, Ann Boult (Tenn) 6501 Pennywell Dr, Nashville TN 37205 B Nashville TN 12/25/1939 d Reber Fielding Boult & Olivia. BA Van 1962; MA Scaritt Coll 1977; Diac Trng SC 1997; STUSo 2000. D 9/14/1997 Bp Edward Lloyd Salmon Jr P 10/4/2000 Bp Bertram Nelson Herlong. m 7/19/1975 Clarence Dallas Walling c 4. Asst S Dav's Epis Ch Nashville TN 2000-2009; D All SS Ch Hilton Hd Island SC 1997-2000. EWC; Interfaith Allnce; NAAD. Bp Gray Temple Human Relatns Awd Dio So Carolina 1998. annwalling@bellsouth.net

WALLING, Carolyn M (U) BOX 5579 (DO NOT SEND MAIL), Aramco Mail Center Saudi Arabia B London UK 2/24/1947 d Alfred John Hayfield & Kathleen Mary. Dartington 1968; Rolle Coll U 1969; MDiv EDS 1987. D 12/14/1986 P 6/1/1987 Bp Otis Charles. m 8/4/1972 Brian Sidney Walling.

WALLING, Charles Edward (Miss) 4394 E Falcon Dr, Fayetteville AR 72701 B West Keansburg NJ 2/8/1937 s Alfred D Walling & Edna Pauline. ThM PDS 1962; BA U of Nthrn Colorado 1962. D 4/28/1962 P 10/27/1962 Bp Alfred L Banyard. m 12/21/1958 Mary Freeman c 3. R S Jn's Ch Aberdeen MS 1995-2000; R S Jn's Ch Harrison AR 1987-1995; Epis Campus Mnstry Dio W Missouri Kansas City MO 1984-1987; R S Barn Epis Ch Denton TX 1975-1984; R S Mths Ch Hamilton NJ 1969-1975; R S Lk's Ch Westville NJ 1965-1969. cwalling1@sbcglobal.net.com

WALLINGFORD, Katharine Tapers (Tex) 6221 Main St, Houston TX 77030 **Asstg P Palmer Memi Ch Houston TX 2006-** B Tallahassee FL 7/14/1940 d John Martin Tapers & Alma. BA, mcl Randolph-Macon Wmn's Coll 1962; LL.B. (J.D.) Harv 1965; PhD Rice U 1984. D 6/21/2003 P 1/21/2004 Bp Don Adger Wimberly. m 7/22/1966 John Rufus Wallingford c 2. Assoc Palmer Memi Ch Houston TX 2003-2006. Auth, "Robert Lowell's Lang of the Self," Univ. of No Carolina Press, 1988. kwallingford@palmerchurch.org

WALLIS, Hugh W (Colo) 1005 S Gilpin St, Denver CO 80209 B Denver CO 9/15/1942 s Hugh Ambrose Wallis & Clarissa Belle. BA U of Pennsylvania 1965; BD Nash 1968. D 6/11/1968 Bp Joseph Summerville Minnis P 12/1/1968 Bp Edwin B Thayer. Dio Colorado Denver CO 1973-1980; P-in-c S Andr's Epis Ch Ft Lupton CO 1973-1980; P-in-c S Eliz's Epis Ch Brighton CO 1973-1980; Cur Epis Ch Of S Ptr And S Mary Denver CO 1971-1973; Cur The Ch Of The Ascen Denver CO 1969-1971.

WALLIS, James Howard (Nev) 2528 Silverton Drive, Las Vegas NV 89134 **Mnstry Dvlpmt Cmsn, Mem Dio Nevada Las Vegas NV 2011-2014; Assoc Gr In The Desert Epis Ch Las Vegas NV 2002-** B Pontiac MI 10/20/1943 s Olis Wallis & Opal. BA Wayne 1968; MA Wayne 1976; MDiv EDS 1981; MA Claremont Grad U 1988; PhD Claremont Grad U 1993. D 6/13/1981 P 6/13/1982 Bp H Coleman McGehee Jr. Supply P Dio Nevada Las Vegas NV 1998-2002; R S Mk's Ch Detroit MI 1989-1994; Asstg S Mk's Epis Ch Upland CA 1985-1989; Asst R S Chris-S Paul Epis Ch Detroit MI 1982-1985; Asst Ch Of The Resurr Ecorse MI 1981-1982. Auth, "The Interfaith Coun of Sthrn Nevada and the Interreligious Dialogue," *Far-W Amer Culture Assn*, 2010; Auth, "Irving Greenberg's Contribution to Holocaust Stds," *Far-W Amer Culture Asso.*, 2005; Auth, "L.L. Langer's Contribution to Holocaust Stds," *Far-W Amer Culture Asso.*, 2004; Auth, "The Holocaust: Theodicy and Anti-Theodicy," *Far-W Amer Culture Assn*, 2003; Auth, "Rel Responses to the Holocaust," *Far-W Amer Culture Assn*, 2001; Auth, "Rel in Amer Today," *Far-W Amer Culture Assn*, 2000; Auth, "Post-Holocaust Chrsnty," U Press of Amer, Inc, 1997. AAR 1985; Amer Philos Assn 1985; Cntr for Process Stds 1985; Interfaith Coun of Sthrn Nevada 2002; SBL 1985. Fllshp - Seminar in Jeruselam Natl Conf of Chr and Jews, (NY,NY) 1987; Gr Schlrshp Claremont Grad U 1986. wallisj@unlv.nevada.edu

WALLNER, Frank (Pa) 404 Levering Mill Rd., Bala Cynwyd PA 19004 **R S Jn's Ch Bala Cynwyd PA 2008-** B New York NY 11/3/1946 s Frank Joseph Wallner & Jean Agnes. SWTS; BS U Of Scranton 1968; EdM Col 1972; MS SUNY 1972; MDiv GTS 1986. D 6/7/1986 P 1/1/1987 Bp Paul Moore Jr. c 1. R Ch Of The H Cross Kingston NY 1990-2008; Cur Gr Ch Middletown NY 1986-1990. ruahleb@aol.com

WALLNER, Ludwig (John) (Alb) 12 Killarney Ct, Saratoga Springs NY 12866 **Vol S Andr's Epis Ch Sprg Hill FL 2008-** B New York NY 9/14/1941 s Ludwig Wallner & Antonette. AAS Orange Cnty Cmnty Coll 1961; BS SUNY 1964; MS SUNY 1967; CAS SUNY 1972; EdD Highland U Athens TN 1982. D 1/4/2003 Bp Daniel William Herzog. m 12/19/1964 Carolyn Elizabeth Holzer c 2. D The Ch Of The Mssh Glens Falls NY 2003-2005.

WALLS, Alfonso (Los) No address on file. B Mexico City MX 9/25/1975 s Lourdes. BA S Ambr U Davenport IA 2000; MDiv SWTS 2006. D 6/3/2006 Bp Joseph Jon Bruno. Asst S Clem's-By-The-Sea Par San Clemente CA 2006. awnorthstar@gmail.com

WALMER, Robert Timothy (Me) 368 Knowlton Corner Rd, Farmington ME 04938 **Dio Maine Portland ME 1997-; S Lk's Ch Farmington ME 1997-** B Beloit KS 7/12/1950 s Paul Milton Walmer & Crystal Irene. BA U of Sthrn Colorado 1972; MDiv VTS 1984. D 6/16/1984 P 12/1/1984 Bp William Carl Frey. m 7/9/1980 Corey A Griffith c 2. S Alb's Ch Worland WY 1986-1997; S Alb's Ch Windsor CO 1986-1996; Vic S Mk's Ch Craig CO 1984-1986. twalmer@beeline-online.net

WALMISLEY, Andrew John (Haw) Po Box 625, Point Reyes Station CA 94956 **Assoc S Jn's Epis Ch Kula HI 2007-; Seabury Hall Makawao HI 2007-** B Fareham Hants UK 2/22/1955 s Raymond Eric Atherstone Walmisley & Elaine Rosa. BA U Of Exeter Gb 1975; Bourguiba Sch 1976; U of Cambridge 1978; MA San Francisco St U 1990. Trans from Church Of England 11/1/1981. R All Souls Par In Berkeley Berkeley CA 1997-2007; R S Ptr's Epis Ch Redwood City CA 1993-1997; Chapl Par of Trin Ch New York NY 1990-1993; Trin Sch New York NY 1990-1993; Chapl S Matt's Epis Ch San Mateo CA 1986-1990; Asst The Epis Ch Of S Mary The Vrgn San Francisco CA 1983-1986; Asst Chr Ch Portola Vlly CA 1981-1983. frandreww@aol.com

✠ **WALMSLEY, Rt Rev Arthur Edward** (Ct) 644 Old County Rd, Deering NH 03244 **Ret Bp of Connecticut S Mk's Epis Ch Haines City FL CA 2003-** B New Bedford MA 5/4/1928 s Harry Barlow Walmsley & Elizabeth Doris. BA Trin Hartford CT 1948; MDiv EDS 1951; DHum New Engl Coll 1972; DD Ya Berk 1980; DD Trin Hartford CT 1982. D 6/8/1951 Bp Norman B Nash P 5/1/1952 Bp Arthur C Lichtenberger Con 10/27/1979 for Ct. m 12/29/1954 Roberta Brownell Chapin c 2. Bp Dio Connecticut Hartford CT 1993; Bp of CT Dio Connecticut Hartford CT 1981-1993; Bp Coadj Dio Connecticut Hartford CT 1979-1981; R S Paul And S Jas New Haven CT 1974-1979; Dep to R Par of Trin Ch New York NY 1972-1974; P-in-c Gr Ch Amherst MA 1968-1969; BEC Dio Missouri S Louis MO 1953-1958; Assoc Ch Of The Ascen S Louis MO 1953-1955; P-in-c Trin Ch S Louis MO 1953-1955. Auth, *Ch In a Soc of Abundance*. Pi Gamma Mu; Phi Beta Kappa. a_walmsley@mcttelecom.com

WALMSLEY, John W (CFla) 966 Lombardy St, Kingston ON K7M8M7 Canada B England 3/29/1937 s George Walmsley & Kathleen. BA Wycliffe Hall Oxford 1968; MA Hiju U 1972; Pld Hiju U 1980. Trans from Church Of England 4/23/2007 Bp John Wadsworth Howe. m 6/27/1997 Patricia Ann Walmsley c 2. S Mk's Epis Ch Haines City FL CA 2007-2009. johnwwalmsley@hotmail.com

WALRATH, Harry Rienzi (Nev) 4822 Ramcreek Trl, Reno NV 89519 B Alameda CA 3/7/1926 s Frank Rienzi Walrath & Cathren Louise. BA U CA 1952; MDiv CDSP 1959. D 9/23/1959 Bp James Albert Pike P 9/1/1960 Bp George Richard Millard. m 6/24/1961 Dorothy Marshall Baxter c 1. Bp Of ArmdF- Epis Ch Cntr New York NY 1983-1986; Asst Trin Epis Ch Reno NV 1969-1972; Vic S Ptr's Ch Litchfield Pk AZ 1967-1969; Assoc Ch Of The H Sprt Missoula MT 1965-1967; Cur All Souls Par In Berkeley Berkeley CA 1959-1961. Natl Assn Veta Chapl; OHC. S Geo Awd Bsa & Epis Ch; Silver Beaver Awd BSA; Distr Awd Of Merit BSA. v7t11@aol.com

WALSER, Gay Craggs (WNY) 119 N Ellicott St, Williamsville NY 14221 B Colon Panama 1/17/1937 d Hugh Craggs & Gay Robertson. Dioc Prog; Katharine Gibbs Sch. D 6/9/1984 Bp Harold B Robinson. c 5. D Calv Epis Ch Williamsville NY 1993-2003; Pstr's Asst S Mk's Ch Buffalo NY 1984-1990.

WALSH, Eileen Patricia (SVa) 519 W 20th St Apt 303, Norfolk VA 23517 **R S Chris's Epis Ch Portsmouth VA 2005-** B Bristol PA 5/19/1959 d William Joseph Walsh & Virginia Martha. BS Bloomsburg U of Pennsylvania 1981; MDiv GTS 2002. D 6/15/2002 P 1/6/2003 Bp David Conner Bane Jr. Ch Of The Ascen Norfolk VA 2002-2005. ewalsh143@aol.com

WALSH JR, Harry Joseph (Mil) 420 Betzer #1, Delavan WI 53115 B Chicago IL 11/1/1935 s Harry J Walsh & Gladys. FBI Natl Acad; Ocso; Abbey Geth 1962; BA NE Illinois U 1974. Rec from Roman Catholic 12/1/1978 as Priest Bp James Winchester Montgomery. m 12/10/1977 Phyllis Drazine c 1. Chr Epis Ch Of Delavan Delavan WI 1987-1997; S Andr's Ch Peoria IL 1985-1987; R Gr Ch Pontiac IL 1982-1987; Asst S Phil's Epis Palatine IL 1980-1982; Asst S Hilary's Ch Prospect Hts IL 1978-1980. Oblate Ord Of S Ben; S Aug Hse Oxford Mi. sagart@charter.net

WALSH, Lora Jean (Chi) 65 E Huron St, Chicago IL 60611 **Epis Chars And Cmnty Serv (Eccs) Chicago IL 2011-** B 10/15/1978 d James John Walsh & Carol Lantz. BA Pepperdine U 2000; Cert Seabury-Wstrn 2009; PhD NWU 2010. D 6/4/2011 Bp Jeffrey Dean Lee. m 5/30/2009 Joshua Smith. LORAWALSH@GMAIL.COM

WALSH, Paul David (Ida) 1565 E 10th N, Mountain Home ID 83647 **D S Jas Ch Mtn Hm ID 1998-** B Saint Paul MN 1/10/1964 s Gregory Eugene Walsh & Carolyn Louise. D 10/31/1998 Bp John Stuart Thornton. m 8/28/1987 Dale Cheryl Skeen.

WALSH, Peter F (Ct) 111 Oenoke Rdg, New Canaan CT 06840 **S Mk's Ch New Canaan CT 2008-** B Buffalo NY 5/2/1959 s Frederick Rall Walsh & Breffny Ann. BA Harv 1983; MDiv Ya Berk 1992. D 6/11/1994 P 12/10/1994 Bp Richard Frank Grein. m 10/4/1986 Jennifer W White c 5. R All SS Ch Phoenix AZ 2003-2008; Assoc S Paul's Epis Ch Cleveland Heights OH 1996-2003; Kent Sch Kent CT 1994-1996. Assoc, SSJE 1992. pwalsh@stmarksnewcanaan.org

WALSH, Ruth Dimock (Va) 16640 Harwood Oaks Ct Apt 101, Dumfries VA 22026 B Greenwich CT 5/23/1941 d Thomas James Boniface Walsh & Mabel Ruth. BA Amer U 1980; MDiv VTS 1991. D 12/10/1991 Bp Peter James Lee P 6/1/1992 Bp Robert Poland Atkinson. Goodwin Hse Incorporated Alexandria VA 1998-2008; Int All SS Ch Alexandria VA 1996-1998; S Jas' Epis Ch Alexandria VA 1995-1996; Assoc R S Mk's Ch Alexandria VA 1991-1992. Dok. rdwalsh74@aol.com

WALSH-MINOR, Gina (NJ) 1A Hamilton Avenue, Cranford NJ 07016 **R Trin Epis Ch Cranford NJ 2008-** B Manhattan NY 9/3/1950 d Albert Joseph Walsh & Marguerite Mary. BA Florida Atlantic U 1974; Med U of Miami 1976; EdD U of Miami 1997; MDiv GTS 2003. D 6/21/2003 Bp Leopold Frade P 1/17/2004 Bp George Edward Councell. m 5/8/1976 Thomas F Minor c 4. Int S Jas Ch Long Branch NJ 2007; Vic Ch Of S Clem Of Rome Belford NJ 2004-2007; Vic S Mary's Ch Keyport NJ 2004-2006. gwalshminor@comcast.net

WALSTED, John Howard (NY) 1 Pendleton Pl, Staten Island NY 10301 **R Emer Chr Ch New Brighton Staten Island NY 1999-** B Cambridge MA 2/5/1932 s John Walsted & Ruth. BS U of Oregon 1956; MDiv CDSP 1959. D 6/17/1959 P 12/18/1959 Bp James Walmsley Frederic Carman. m 7/18/2003 Gerald Werner Otto Keucher. Assoc S Jn's Ch Getty Sq Yonkers NY 1994; R Chr Ch New Brighton Staten Island NY 1983-1994; P-in-c Chr Ch New Brighton Staten Island NY 1982-1983; Assoc S Paul's Ch Staten Island NY 1978-1982; Vic S Andr's Ch Portland OR 1961-1963; Cur S Paul's Epis Ch Salem OR 1959-1961. Epis Ch Visual Artists (ECVA) 2001; OHC (OHC) 1963-1978.

WALSTER, Don Bernard (Ore) 1133 1st St Unit 320, Coronado CA 92118 B Vallejo CA 1/12/1914 s George Bernard Walster & Mabelle Vivian. Oxf 1955; Fllshp Coll of Preachers 1960. D 6/23/1951 P 12/1/1951 Bp Benjamin D Dagwell. m 11/20/1994 Miriam C Ziegler. Dio Oregon Portland OR 1972-1977; Vic S Hilda's Ch Monmouth OR 1972-1977; Vic S Thos Epis Ch Dallas OR 1972-1977; R S Mary's Epis Ch Eugene OR 1964-1972; R Ch Of The Redeem Pendleton OR 1958-1964; R S Jas' Epis Ch Coquille OR 1956-1968; Assoc S Mary's Epis Ch Eugene OR 1955-1956; Vic S Jn's Epis Ch Toledo OR 1952-1954; Vic S Lk's Ch Waldport OR 1952-1954; Asst S Mk's Par Berkeley CA 1950-1951.

WALSTON, Gerald Wayne (Fla) 1718 Oakbreeze Ln, Jacksonville Beach FL 32250 **R Resurr Epis Ch Jacksonville FL 2005-** B Sasakwa OK 9/9/1938 s Kenneth Gerald Walston & Eunice Katherine. AA Jacksonville Jr Coll Jackson TN 1976; LTh STUSo 1979. D 6/5/1979 P 12/18/1979 Bp Frank Stanley Cerveny. c 2. Assoc Chr Epis Ch Ponte Vedra Bch FL 1987-2004; R S Lk's Epis Ch Jacksonville FL 1981-1987; Asst Chr Epis Ch Ponte Vedra Bch FL 1979-1981. Cmnty Of S Mary 1979. gwalston@comcast.net

WALTER, Andrew W (WA) Grace Episcopal Church, 1607 Grace Church Rd, Silver Spring MD 20910 **R Gr Epis Ch Silver Sprg MD 2011-** B Tarrytown NY 8/22/1963 s John Gordon Walter & Christine Wallace. BA Buc 1986; MDiv GTS 2007. D 3/10/2007 P 9/15/2007 Bp Mark Sean Sisk. m 9/6/1986 Susan Walter c 3. Assoc R S Lk's Par Darien CT 2007-2011. awalter@graceepiscopalchurch.org

WALTER, Cynthia Byers (WVa) PO Box 4063, Table Rock Lane, Wheeling WV 26003 **COM Dio W Virginia Charleston WV 2011-; Dn, Nthrn Reg Dio W Virginia Charleston WV 2011-; Chair, BEC Dio W Virginia Charleston WV 2010-; Sandscrest Bd Dio W Virginia Charleston WV 2010-; R The Lawrencefield Chap Par Wheeling WV 2006-** B Winchester MA 7/12/1955 d William Franklin Byers & Dorothy Rhoda. BA U of Virginia 1977; MDiv VTS 2003. D 6/14/2003 P 12/20/2003 Bp Peter James Lee. m 5/21/1977 Richard William Walter c 2. Chair, Cmsn on Evang Dio W Virginia Charleston WV 2006-2009; Asst R/Dre Chr Ch Par Kensington MD 2003-2006. Dudley Prize VTS 2003; Phi Beta Kappa U of Virginia 1977. cbwalter@comcast.net

WALTER, Francis Xavier (Ala) 100 Rattlesnake Spring Ln, Sewanee TN 37375 B Mobile AL 12/22/1932 s Francis Xavier Walter & Martha Josephine. BA Sprg Hill Coll 1954; MDiv STUSo 1957. D 7/17/1957 Bp Charles C J Carpenter P 6/24/1958 Bp George Mosley Murray. m 6/11/1977 Elizabeth Michell c 2. Assoc The Epis Ch Of S Fran Of Assisi Indn Sprg Vill AL 2000-2003; R S Andrews's Epis Ch Birmingham AL 1985-1999; Assoc S Andrews's Epis Ch Birmingham AL 1974-1985; P-in-c Gr Ch Van Vorst Jersey City NJ 1963-1965; R S Jas Ch Eufaula AL 1959-1961; Fell & Tutor The GTS New York NY 1957-1959. Auth, *The Naval Battle of Mobile Bay*, Prester Meridian Press, 1993; Auth, "Une Presence en Alabama," *Periodique Trimestriel: Publie par la Communante de Taize*. fxwalter@cafes.net

WALTER II, George Avery (EO) 77287 S Ash Rd, Stanfield OR 97875 **R S Andr's Epis Ch Polson MT 2008-** B Wenatchee WA 8/31/1948 s Willard Avery Walker & Lois June. BA Wstrn Washington U 1971; MDiv STUSo 2001. D 5/12/2001 Bp William Harvey Wolfrum P 11/13/2001 Bp Mark Lawrence Mac Donald. R S Jn's Ch Hermiston OR 2004-2008; R S Brendan's Epis Ch Juneau AK 2001-2004. gwalter315@gmail.com

WALTER, James Ian (Ala) 909 S Dean Rd, Auburn AL 36830 B Montgomery AL 1/24/1928 s John Adkin Walter & Marjorie. BA Huntingdon Coll 1951; BD VTS 1959; MS Auburn U 1967; EdD Auburn U 1968. D 6/12/1959 Bp Charles C J Carpenter P 7/1/1960 Bp George Mosley Murray. m 4/7/1961 Katharine Bunting Massengale c 2. S Jn's Ch Montgomery AL 1995-2000; S Barn Epis Ch Roanoke AL 1986-1992; Cur Ch Of The Nativ Epis Huntsville AL 1963-1964. "Moments of Forever".

WALTER, Kathleen Marie (Pa) 1819 Loney St, Philadelphia PA 19111 **R Ch Of S Jude And The Nativ Lafayette Hill PA 2007-** B Philadelphia PA 7/24/1955 d Lothar John Walter & Rose Marie. BA La Salle U Philadelphia PA 1977; MEd Tem Philadelphia PA 1982; MDiv GTS 2007. D 6/9/2007 Bp Charles Ellsworth Bennison Jr P 12/15/2007 Bp Franklin Delton Turner. m 8/16/1975 Gerard M Boone c 3. st.juderector@verizon.net

WALTER, Verne Leroy (FdL) 2209 S Wallonnie Dr, Marshfield WI 54449 B San Francisco CA 5/7/1945 s Verne Albert Walter & Mary Rose. AA Modesto Jr Coll 1966; BS Chapman U 1996; MDiv Nash 1999. D 6/19/1999 P 12/21/1999 Bp John-David Mercer Schofield. m 5/22/1966 Ruth Elaine Foster c 2. R S Alb's Epis Ch Marshfield WI 2005-2009; Cur S Michaels By-The-Sea Ch Carlsbad CA 1999-2005. vernelwalter@yahoo.com

WALTERS, David Lloyd (Vt) 43 Imperial Dr, South Burlington VT 05403 **Died 5/29/2011** B Philadelphia PA 1/16/1933 s Kenneth Lloyd Walters & Helen. BS Colorado St U 1958. D 7/31/1971 P 12/6/1973 Bp Harvey D Butterfield. dlwalters.printer@gmail.com

WALTERS, Delores Marie (ND) PO Box 214, Fort Yates ND 58538 B Wakpala SD 1/30/1941 d John C Cadotte & Sophia Iron Horn. D 6/9/2007 Bp Michael Gene Smith. m 8/22/1959 Ronald Walters c 6.

WALTERS, Fred Ashmore (USC) 1001 12th St, Cayce SC 29033 B Greenville SC 4/1/1951 s James David Walters & Mary Frances Ashmore. BS U of So Carolina 1975; JD U of So Carolina 1978. D 1/31/2009 Bp Dorsey Felix Henderson. m 11/8/1975 Connie B Walters c 1. faw@fawlawfirm.com

WALTERS, James (Ark) 109 Crystal Ct, Little Rock AR 72205 **R Chr Epis Ch Little Rock AR 2005-** B Norwalk CT 4/7/1967 s James Calvin Walters & Lynda Loy. BA Jn Br 1990; MDiv VTS 2005. D 1/18/2005 P 7/16/2005 Bp Larry Earl Maze. m 12/18/1993 R Ardelle Pote c 2. Harris Awd VTS 2005. swalters@christchurchlr.org

WALTERS, Jennifer Louise (Mich) 100 Laurel Hill Rd, Westhampton MA 01027 B Buffalo NY 9/24/1960 d Terrence William Walters & Sonia Cecilia. BA Marq 1982; MA Boston Coll 1985; DMin EDS 1990; MA MI SU 1994. D 6/19/1993 P 8/18/1994 Bp R(aymond) Stewart Wood Jr. m 2/19/2010 Celeste E Whiting c 3. Vic Ch Of The Incarn Pittsfield Twp Ann Arbor MI 1993-2000. "The job we have now been given," *J Walters (2002) The job we have now been given, Smith Alum Quarterly*, Smith Alum Assn, 2002; "Stdt Rel Orgnztn and the Publ U," *The Transformation of Campus Life: Sprtlty and Rel Pluralism in Stdt Affrs*, Ptr Lang Pub, 2001; "Evaluating the use of culture in HIV/AIDS educational materials," *AIDS Educ and Prevention*, 1994; "HIV Risk Assessment and Pre- and Post-Test Counslg: A Primary Care Approach," *Curric*, MI SU, 1994; "psychosocial care of HIV-infected persons," *Mntl Hlth Aspects of HIV/AIDS: Curric Modules*, U MI, 1992. AAR 1989; Assn for Conflict Resolution 1999. jwalters@smith.edu

WALTERS, Joshua David (LI) 23 Cedar Shore Dr, Massapequa NY 11758 **R Gr Epis Ch Massapequa NY 2009-** B Evansville IN 9/14/1976 s David Paul Walters & Betty Jo. BA Indiana U 1999; MDiv GTS 2006. D 6/24/2006 P 1/20/2007 Bp Catherine Elizabeth Maples Waynick. m 5/24/2003 Emily M Blecksmith c 2. Assoc R Chr Ch Winnetka IL 2006-2009. Alum/Alum Awd for Hist GTS 2006. joshuadavidwalters@gmail.com

WALTERS, Karen Graf (SVa) 716 Egret Walk Ln, Venice FL 34292 B Pensacola FL 11/11/1945 d Edward Wayne Graf & Elouise Alice. BFA Nthrn Illinois U 1979; MDiv VTS 1982; MS Loyola U 1985. D 1/4/1986 P 9/1/1986 Bp Barry Valentine. m 6/11/1972 William Albert Walters. R S Dav's Ch Baltimore MD 1991-1996; S Dav's Epis Ch Richmond VA 1991-1996; S Mary's Ch Baltimore MD 1989-1991; Int The Ch Of The H Apos Halethorpe MD 1988-1989; Asst R Emm Ch Baltimore MD 1986-1988. kaig@aol.com

WALTERS, Kerry Stephen (CPa) 207 S 13th St, Lewisburg PA 17837 **S Andr's Epis Ch Lewisburg PA 2005-** B Newfoundland CA 4/26/1954 BA U NC 1976; MA Marq 1980; PhD U Cinc 1985. D 6/11/2005 Bp Michael Whittington Creighton. c 1. "Merc Meekness," Paulist, 2005; "Jacob's Hip," Orbis, 2003; "Soul Wilderness," Paulist, 2002; "Finding Perfect Happiness w St. Fran," St. Anth Mssngr Press, 2001; "Praying Ceaselessly," St. Anth Mssngr Press, 2000. kwalters@gettysburg.edu

WALTERS, Lawrence Robert (Mich) 309 S Jackson St, Jackson MI 49201 **R S Paul's Epis Ch Jackson MI 2000-** B Newton KS 7/17/1948 s Cecil John Walters & Volneese Martha. U of Kansas 1971; BA Boise St U 1989; MDiv STUSo 1992; DMin SWTS 2006. D 2/2/1992 P 8/2/1992 Bp John Stuart Thornton. m 8/5/1972 Teresa A Daniels c 1. Assoc S Andr's Ch Kansas City MO 1998-2000; R S Mary's Ch W Columbia TX 1994-1998; Assoc & Org/ Choir S Chris's Ch Houston TX 1992-1994. frlarry@comcast.net

WALTERS, Robert Carroll (WMass) 4 Amherst St, Worcester MA 01602 B Indianapolis IN 4/8/1935 s Wallace Wendell Walters & Carol Elizabeth. BA Butler U 1956; STB Harvard DS 1959; GTS 1960; MA U of Massachusetts 1970; CAGS Clark U 1992. D 6/11/1960 P 12/1/1960 Bp John P Craine. m 11/ 10/1961 Nancy J Murphy c 1. S Mich's Ch Marblehead MA 1998; Asst S Mich's-On-The-Heights Worcester MA 1986-1998; Vic Chr Ch Rochdale MA 1966-1967; Vic S Paul's Ch Ft Benton MT 1961-1966; Cur Ch Of Our Sav Akron OH 1960-1961. None. rcwezis@aol.com

WALTERS, Roxanne (Cal) 1217 Skycrest Dr Apt 3, Walnut Creek CA 94595 B Morristown NJ 2/12/1943 d Walter Atmore Smith & Laura Tarbell. BS Sacramento St U 1975; BTh Sch for Deacons 1985. D 12/7/1985 Bp William Edwin Swing. m 6/28/1992 Sumner Francis Dudley Walters c 2.

WALTERS JR, Sumner Francis Dudley (Cal) 1217 Skycrest Dr Apt 3, Walnut Creek CA 94595 **Ecum Off Dio California San Francisco CA 2000-** B Fort Scott KS 12/24/1924 s Sumner Francis Dudley Walters & Evelyn Turpin. MA Stan 1949; BA Stan 1949; PhD Oxf 1956. D 6/8/1952 Bp The Bishop Of Croydon P 12/26/1952 Bp Sumner Walters. m 6/28/1992 Roxanne Smith c 4. S Andr's Ch Oakland CA 1991-1995; Exam Chapl Dio California San Francisco CA 1982-1995; Vic S Ambr Epis Ch Foster City CA 1982-1991; Stndg Comm. Dio Olympia Seattle WA 1975-1979; Dio Olympia Seattle WA 1966-1979; R S Lk's Epis Ch Vancouver WA 1966-1979; Exec Coun Dio Olympia Seattle WA 1966-1975; Ldrshp Trnr - Dept. of Chr Ed. Epis Ch Cntr New York NY 1956-1961; R The Par Of S Mk The Evang Hood River OR 1952-1956. Auth, *The Dvlpmt of Theol Educ C of E and ECUSA 1900-1950.* sumnerwalters@comcast.net

WALTERS, William Harry (USC) 1109 W Woodmont Dr, Lancaster SC 29720 B Indianapolis IN 8/5/1941 s Harry Frank Walters & Alice Mae. BA Milligan Coll 1965; GTS 1968; MDiv Chr TS 1969. D 8/23/1969 Bp Henry I Louttit P 5/23/1970 Bp William Hopkins Folwell. m 1/23/1968 Dana Burdeshaw c 2. Dioc Curs Coun Dio Upper So Carolina Columbia SC 1995-1997; R Chr Epis Ch Lancaster SC 1985-2006; R H Trin Epis Ch Fruitland Pk FL 1982-1985; Vic S Fran Of Assisi Epis Ch Lake Placid FL 1976-1982; Ch Of The Gd Shpd Maitland FL 1976; Cur Ch Of The Gd Shpd Maitland FL 1975-1976; Asst Chr The King Epis Ch Orlando FL 1972-1975; Cur All SS Epis Ch Lakeland FL 1969-1972.

WALTHALL, Charles Leroy (Eas) 3103 11th St NW, Washington DC 20010 **R All Faith Chap Miles River Par Easton MD 2005-; Cath Chpl Cathd of St Ptr & St Paul Washington DC 2004-** B Kansas City MO 9/27/1943 s Albert Charles Walthall & Naomi Agatha. BA SUNY 1965; MM CUA 1969; DMA CUA 1981; MDiv VTS 2001; DMin TS 2010. D 6/29/2002 P 6/8/2003 Bp Peter Hess Beckwith. Dio Springfield Springfield IL 2002-2004; D/Assoc P S Jas Epis Ch Marion IL 2002-2004; P S Steph's Ch Harrisburg IL 2001-2004. Auth, "Portraits of Johann Joachim Quantz," *Early Mus*, Oxf Press, 1986. Cmnty of St Mary Assoc 2006; SSJE friends of 1995. Magan cl SUNY Buffalo Buffalo NY 1965. dominusvobiscum@juno.com

WALTHER, Aileen Dianne Pallister (CFla) 753 Creekwater Ter Apt 101, Lake Mary FL 32746 B London England UK 10/7/1950 d Mervyn Victor Pallister & Ellen Rose. AA Lansing Cmnty Coll 1971; BA MI SU 1976; CTh Whitaker TS 1990; CAS TESM 2000. D 6/21/1991 Bp Henry Irving Mayson. m 8/23/ 1986 Patrick Bogart Walther. D Epis Ch Of The Resurr Longwood FL 1992-1994. Auth, "Writing Your Life Story w God As Your Guide," 2003; Auth, "Journ Writing," *LivCh*, 1997. awbigtree@hotmail.com

WALTON, Albert Connard (NJ) 71 Sunset Lake Rd, Bridgeton NJ 08302 **Died 10/19/2011** B Philadelphia PA 6/30/1925 s Albert Welsh Walton & Lillie Gladys. PDS; BA U of Vermont 1950; MS SUNY 1975. D 4/20/1968 P 10/1/ 1968 Bp Alfred L Banyard. m 10/28/2011 Edith Claire Walton c 1. OHC, Ord of S Lk 1962. CG Jung Soc 1996.

WALTON, Carol Leighann (Nev) 351 S Deer Run Rd, Carson City NV 89701 B Bellefonte PA 1/10/1954 D 10/10/2003 P 10/30/2004 Bp Katharine Jefferts Schori. c 1.

WALTON JR, Charles Friend (SC) 20 Tucson Dr, Sumter SC 29150 B Raleigh NC 11/15/1944 s Charles Friend Walton & Iva Myrtle. BA Wofford Coll 1967; MDiv VTS 1975. D 6/7/1975 Bp William Gillette Weinhauer P 4/1/1976 Bp Gray Temple. m 7/1/1967 Anne B Bartlett. R S Jn's Epis Par Johns Island SC 1997-2005; R S Lk's Ch Scottsboro AL 1994-1997; R Ch Of The H Comf Sumter SC 1985-1994; Dio So Carolina Charleston SC 1985-1992; R Chr Ch Eliz City NC 1981-1985; Dio E Carolina Kinston NC 1978-1981; R Gr Ch Whiteville NC 1977-1981; Cur S Jn's Ch Florence SC 1975-1977.

WALTON SSF, Dunstan (LI) Po Box 399, Mount Sinai NY 11766 B Winchendon MA 10/4/1922 s Wendell Herbert Walton & Dorothy Mildred. BA S Anselm Coll Manchester NH 1947; Mercer TS 1955. D 11/5/1955 P 7/7/1956 Bp James P De Wolfe. Asst Ch Of S Thos Brooklyn NY 1990-1994; Int Ch Of The Trsfg Freeport NY 1987-1988; Int S Ann's Ch Sayville NY 1985-1986. Auth, *Little Chronicle*; Auth, *St. Anns Correspondent*; Auth, *Trsfgs New Life*; Auth, *W Indies Fran News*. Curs; Ord of S Lk. mtsinaifriary@s-s-f.org

WALTON, Hugh (Ind) 8480 Craig St Apt 5, Indianapolis IN 46250 **Assoc Ch Of The Nativ Indianapolis IN 1993-** B Birmingham England UK 12/11/1925 s Harry Walter Walton & Elinor. Lon 1948; PE Indiana Soc of Profsnl Engr 1964. D 4/16/1978 P 12/1/1978 Bp Edward Witker Jones. m 9/3/1949 Kathleen Mary London c 3. R Trin Ch Connersville IN 1978-1993. Natl Epis Curs 1981. waltonh1@aol.com

WALTON, Joy Burnette Edemy (Del) 2550 Kensington Gdns Unit 103, Ellicott City MD 21043 B Baltimore MD 9/30/1943 d J(ames) Bruce Edemy & Ella Jeanetta. Morgan St U - Baltimore, MD 1963; BA Untd States Intl U San Diego CA 1964; MS Old Dominion U - Norfolk, VA 1979; MDiv GTS 1994. D 5/28/1994 P 3/11/1995 Bp Frank Harris Vest Jr. c 2. Chapl S Andr's Sch Chap Middletown DE 2005-2010; R S Cyp's Epis Ch Hampton VA 1998-2005; Old Donation Ch Virginia Bch VA 1994-1997. Amer Associtiion of Pstr Counselors 2004; Mem of Sthrn Virginia Cler Assn 2005; Ord of S Helena (Assoc) 1995. jwalton@standrews-de.org

WALTON, Lori Ann (Cal) 1905b Henry St, Berkeley CA 94704 **R S Jas Ch Fremont CA 2010-** B San Francisco CA 1/25/1967 d Richard Louis Lindelli & Patricia Ann. BA New Coll of California 1999; MDiv CDSP 2004. D 6/5/ 2004 P 12/4/2004 Bp William Edwin Swing. m 5/28/2011 Ronald Larson c 1. Assoc R S Mk's Epis Ch Palo Alto CA 2007-2010; All SS Epis Ch Palo Alto CA 2006-2007; S Alb's Epis Ch Brentwood CA 2005. lorilindelli@comcast.net

WALTON, Macon Brantley (SVa) 202 Ridgeland Dr, Smithfield VA 23430 **Vic Brandon Epis Ch Disputanta VA 1996-; Vic Chr Ch Waverly VA 1996-** B Richmond VA 4/16/1932 s Percy Brantley Walton & Anne Macon. BA VMI 1955; MDiv VTS 1958. D 6/1/1958 P 6/1/1959 Bp Frederick D Goodwin. Int The Epis Ch Of The Adv Norfolk VA 1992-1995; Cntrl Mecklenburg Cure Boydton VA 1990-1992; Int S Tim's Epis Ch Clarksville VA 1990-1991; Int H Trin Prot Epis Ch Onancock VA 1989-1990; R Chr Epis Ch Smithfield VA 1967-1988; Assoc Ch Of The Ascen Norfolk VA 1966-1967; Asst Galilee Epis Ch Virginia Bch VA 1962-1966; R S Asaph's Par Ch Bowling Green VA 1958-1962; R S Ptr's Port Royal Port Royal VA 1958-1962.

WALTON, Mary Fish (Okla) 1810 Park Ave, Richmond VA 23220 **D S Paul's Par Baltimore MD 2000-** B Birmingham AL 2/26/1948 d Bruce Baker Fish & Virginia Maron. VPI; BA Colorado Wmn Coll 1969. D 7/9/1994 Bp Robert Manning Moody. m 6/8/1969 Daniel Robert Walton c 2. SCHC.

WALTON, Regina Laba (Mass) 98 Oxford St. #1, Somerville MA 02143 **Cur Ch Of The Gd Shpd Waban MA 2007-** B Pompton Plains NJ 8/3/1978 d Michael Laba & Jacqueline. PhD Bos; BA Hampshire Coll Amherst MA 2000; MDiv Harvard DS 2003. D 6/2/2007 P 1/12/2008 Bp M(arvil) Thomas Shaw III. m 7/12/2003 Christopher L Walton c 1. Dir of Chld's Mnstrs Trin Ch Concord MA 2003-2006. Bk reviewer, "Bk Revs: The Web of Friendship: Nich Ferrar and Little Gidding by Joyce Ransome," *ATR vol. 93 no. 4*, 2011. Fllshp of St. Jn (SSJE) 2004; Massachusetts Epis Cler Assn 2009. Doctoral Fell ECF 2005. reginawalton@post.harvard.edu

WALTON, R(ichard) Lindsley Dixon (WNC) PO Box 1866, Sparta NC 28675 **Reverend Chr Epis Ch Sparta NC 2010-** B Washington DC 7/10/1966 s Richard Lindsley Walton & Sally. BA Gordon Coll 1991; MTS Duke 1997; MDiv VTS 1999. D 12/17/1999 Bp Peter James Lee P 6/17/2000 Bp Martin Gough Townsend. m 8/17/1996 Nancy Dixon c 2. Asst S Jn's Epis Ch Tallahassee FL 2008-2009; Exec Coun Appointees New York NY 2002-2006; Asst R S Ptr's Ch Salisbury MD 1999-2002. "Witness in Sudan," *The Chr Century*, 2008; "Fear of God and Darwin," *newsweek.washingtonpost.com*, 2008; "Liberating Mssn," *Epis Life*, 2007; "Div Can Make Faith Stronger," *Tallahassee Democrat*, 2007. frlinwalton@gmail.com

WALTON, Robert Harris (WMich) 2186 Tamarack Dr, Okemos MI 48864 B Bay City MI 9/26/1933 s John Magnay Walton & Gladys Marguerite. BA Cntrl Michigan U 1955; MDiv Bex 1958; MA MI SU 1973. D 6/29/1958 Bp Archie H Crowley P 5/25/1960 Bp Lane W Barton. m 6/25/1960 Julia Ann Hollyer c 3. Trin Epis Ch Grand Ledge MI 1986-1988; Supply P Dio Wstrn Michigan Kalamazoo MI 1984-2002; S Jn's Epis Ch Charlotte MI 1975-1984; Asst Min S Mich's Epis Ch Lansing MI 1970-1974; Asst S Paul's Epis Ch Lansing MI 1968-1970; Min in charge Trin Ch Tiffin OH 1963-1968. rhwalton33@comcast.net

WALTON, Sandra Lee (Colo) No address on file. B Milwaukee WI 5/2/1950 d Gerhardt Earl Nelson & Lillian Mae. AA Front Range Cmnty Coll 1984; BA Metropltn St Coll of Denver 1995. D 5/27/1987 Bp William Harvey Wolfrum. m 10/19/1968 Ray Allen Walton c 3.

WALTZ, William Lynn (Colo) 207 Rainbow Acres Lane, PO Box 21, Gunnison CO 81230 **Linked Mnstry w Gd Samar in Gunnison, CO All SS Of The Mtn Epis Chap Crested Butte CO 2007-; Vic Ch Of The Gd Samar Gunnison CO 2007-; Dio Iowa Des Moines IA 1974-** B Decatur IL 6/12/1947 s Harry Lynn Waltz & Lazora Stallard. BA U of Iowa 1969; MDiv CDSP 1973. D 10/23/1973 P 1/1/1976 Bp Walter Cameron Righter. m 3/6/1982 Rhonda Renee Knoche c 2. Int S Barn Ch Glenwood Sprg CO 2006-2007; S Barn Par Portland OR 1988-1991; Gr Epis Ch Glenns Ferry ID 1982-1984; R S Jas Ch Mtn Hm ID 1981-1987; Vic Gr Epis Ch Chas City IA 1973-1974; Vic S Andr's Epis Ch Waverly IA 1973-1974. bill.waltz@gmail.com

WALWORTH, Diana Lynn (Mich) PO Box 287, Onsted MI 49265 B Toledo OH 12/29/1962 d Ervin Charles Clark & Bonnie Lou. N/A U of Toledo; Total Mnstry Whitaker TS Dio Michigan. D 10/27/2010 P 5/24/2011 Bp Wendell Nathaniel Gibbs Jr. c 3. Other Lay Position S Mich And All Ang Onsted MI 2004-2010. dwalworth1@juno.com

WALWORTH, James Curtis (LI) 3118 Monroe Vlg, Monroe Township NJ 08831 B Wilmette IL 12/11/1926 s Jesse Johnson Walworth & Lela Maud. BA Ripon Coll Ripon WI 1948; Lic GTS 1956. D 6/18/1956 Bp Charles L Street P 12/17/1956 Bp Horace W B Donegan. m 7/9/1960 Dorothy E Campbell c 3. Asst S Paul's Epis Ch Willimantic CT 1995-2002; S Johns Epis Hosp Far Rockaway NY 1985-1991; Baylor All SS Med Cntr Ft Worth TX 1968-1985; Cur S Ptr's Epis Ch Peekskill NY 1957-1959; Cur Chr's Ch Rye NY 1956-1957. Auth, "A Way to Light a Ch," *LivCh*, 1989; Auth, "arts," *LivCh*. AEHC 1961; Assn of Profsnl Chapl 1965. jadow1930@yahoo.com

WALWORTH, Roy Chancellor (Wyo) 216 Southridge Rd, Evanston WY 82930 B Bremerton WA 3/29/1941 s Chancellor Reuben Walworth & Frieda Cecelia. U of Puget Sound 1965; BS WA SU 1980; MDiv The Coll of Emm and St. Chad 1992. D 5/4/1992 P 1/25/1993 Bp Bob Gordon Jones. m 5/19/1973 Antoinette M Sommer c 2. Mnstry Dvlp Dio Wyoming Casper WY 1992-2008; Vic S Paul's Epis Ch Evanston WY 1992-1997. rwalw@allwest.net

WAMPLER, D Delos (Alb) 5 Union St Apt 3, Schenectady NY 12305 **Asst P S Geo's Epis Ch Schenectady NY 1993-** B Chanute KS 2/2/1923 s Charles Leonard Wampler & Lillys Ruth. BS U of Kansas 1947; LTh SWTS 1953; MDiv SWTS 1954. D 6/14/1953 Bp Frederick Lehrle Barry P 12/21/1953 Bp David Emrys Richards. Dep to GC Dio Albany Albany NY 1973-1985; Exec Coun Dio Albany Albany NY 1960-1987; P S Paul's Ch Brant Lake NY 1959-1991; P-in-c S Paul's Ch Bloomville NY 1953-1959; P-in-c S Ptr's Ch Hobart NY 1953-1959. Oblate Soc of S Jn the Evang. Hon Cn All SS Cathd Albany NY 1975.

WAN, Sze Kar (Mass) 87 Herrick Rd, Newton Center MA 02459 B 4/23/1954 s Chai-Lai Wan & Chiu-Ying. MDiv Gordon-Conwell TS 1982; ThD Harvard DS 1992. D 6/4/2005 Bp M(arvil) Thomas Shaw III P 1/6/2007 Bp Gayle Elizabeth Harris. m 8/24/1996 Maria Mak. skekarwan@post.harvard.edu

WANCURA, Paul Forsyth (LI) Po Box 641, Shelter Island Heights NY 11965 B Brooklyn NY 6/22/1930 s Frank Edward Wancura & Mary Elizabeth. BA CUNY 1952; MBA Col 1954; MDiv GTS 1960. D 4/23/1960 P 10/28/1960 Bp James P De Wolfe. R Caroline Ch Of Brookhaven Setauket NY 1974-2000; Hon Cn Cathd Of The Incarn Garden City NY 1968; Archd Dio Long Island Garden City NY 1966-1974; R Ch Of The Ascen Greenpoint Brooklyn NY 1960-1966. wancuras@aol.com

WAND, Thomas C. (Pa) 31 Kleyona Ave, Phoenixville PA 19460 **Int R S Mary's Epis Ch Ardmore PA 2011-; Cler Salaries and Pensions Cmsn Dio Pennsylvania Philadelphia PA 1992-** B Denver CO 10/6/1948 s Robert Carney Wand & Lois Irene. BA Col 1970; MDiv EDS 1973; MBA RPI 1982; Fllshp Coll of Preachers 1987; Int Mnstry Trng 1996. D 6/9/1973 Bp Paul Moore Jr P 12/9/1973 Bp William J Gordon Jr. m 10/8/1977 Marlene Haines c 2. Fin and Property Com Dio Pennsylvania Philadelphia PA 2006-2011; Dio Pennsylvania Philadelphia PA 2002-2003; Int S Paul's Epis Ch Indianapolis IN 2000-2002; S Mk's Ch Philadelphia PA 1999-2000; Int S Mk's Ch Philadelphia PA 1999-2000; Int Trin Cathd Trenton NJ 1997-1999; Dio Pennsylvania Philadelphia PA 1995-1997; R S Ptr's Ch Phoenixville PA 1991-1997; R S Mary's Epis Ch Albuquerque NM 1989-1991; Chair Liturg & Mus Cmsn Dio The Rio Grande Albuquerque NM 1987-1989; R S Jas Ch Hartford CT 1978-1984; Dio New Hampshire Concord NH 1976-1978; Assoc Gr Ch Manchester NH 1976-1978; Dio Alaska Fairbanks AK 1973-1976; P-in-c Gd Shpd Huslia AK 1973-1976. Natl Treas Natl Epis Cler Assn 1986-1992. tcw18@columbia.edu

WANDALL, Frederick Summerson (Va) 4460 Forest Glen Ct, Annandale VA 22003 **Cler Assoc Truro Epis Ch Fairfax VA 1992-** B Camden NJ 6/8/1930 s Frederick Griffith Wandall & Thelma Elizabeth. BA Wesl 1953; MDiv GTS 1956; U of Pennsylvania 1958; MLitt Oxf 1961. D 4/28/1956 P 10/27/1956 Bp Alfred L Banyard. m 6/16/1962 Virginia H Smith c 2. Int S Andr's Epis Ch Arlington VA 1990-1991; Ch Of The Gd Shpd Burke VA 1977-1978; Asst Gr Epis Ch Alexandria VA 1972-1975; P-in-c S Mary's Epis Ch Arlington VA 1971-1972; St Steph Sch Alexandria VA 1969-1989; Vic S Andr's Epis Ch New Paltz NY 1963-1967; Asst Gr Epis Ch Nyack NY 1961-1963. Auth, "Chas Williams," *Minor British Novelists*. Phi Beta Kappa.

WANG, Kit (Me) PO Box 158, East Waterboro ME 04030 **Mem of Com on H Ord Dio Maine Portland ME 2011-; Vic S Steph The Mtyr Epis Ch E Waterboro ME 2008-** B Taipei Taiwan ROC 7/16/1960 d Jesse Wang & Meda Marie A. AB Smith 1981; MDiv Ya Berk 1984. D 6/14/2008 Bp Chilton Abbie Richardson Knudsen P 12/14/2008 Bp Stephen Taylor Lane. m 6/5/2004 Susan Elizabeth Tennant c 1. DCE S Jn's Ch Beverly Farms MA 1999-2002. kiturgy@yahoo.com

WANG, Tabitha Hsin Ching (SC) 63 Nicks Rock Rd, Plymouth MA 02360 **S Mich's Epis Ch Charleston SC 2008-; Mssy Dio So Carolina Charleston SC 2003-; Mssy Dio So Carolina Charleston SC 2003-** B China 2/16/1946 d FengYun Chao & Chin Hwa. MDiv EDS 1995; DMin Andover Newton TS 2003; PhD Yunnan U, Yunnan, China 2011. D 5/31/2003 P 12/4/2003 Bp Edward Lloyd Salmon Jr. c 2. Angl Frontier Missions Richmond VA 2003-2008. tabithawang@hotmail.com

WANSTALL, Donald Penton (CFla) 719 Cobblestone Drive, Ormond Beach FL 32174 **D S Mary's Epis Ch Daytona Bch FL 2000-** B Wilmington DE 7/18/1930 s James Stanley Wanstall & Anne Marie. Inst for Chr Stds; U of Delaware Newark. D 6/29/1983 Bp William Hopkins Folwell. m 11/16/1948 Nancy Ruth Parkhill c 4. S Jas Epis Ch Ormond Bch FL 1983-2000. BroSA; OSL; Steph Mnstry. wanstalld@bellsouth.net

WAPLE, Gary (WVa) RR 2 Box 243, Lewisburg WV 24901 B Arlington VA 3/9/1946 s George Henry Waple & Catherine Elizabeth. Hagerstown Jr Coll 1967; Riverview Hosp Sch Red Bank NJ 1971; Epis TS In Kentucky 1990. D 6/11/1991 Bp John H(enry) Smith. m 9/11/1980 Carol Ann Southern c 1. D Ch Of The Incarn Ronceverte WV 1995-2000; D Emm Ch Wht Sphr Spgs WV 1995-2000; D S Jn's Ch Marlinton WV 1995-2000; D S Thos Epis Ch White Sulphur Sprg WV 1995-2000; D S Jas' Epis Ch Lewisburg WV 1991-1994. NAAD 1990. S Steph's Awd NAAD 1997. gary_waple@yahoo.com

WAPPLER, Harry Vail (Oly) Po Box 21326, Seattle WA 98111 **Died 4/21/2010** B Chicago IL 12/21/1936 s Edwin G Wappler & Martha E. BS NWU 1958; MDiv Ya Berk 1961. D 6/24/1961 Bp Charles L Street P 12/1/1961 Bp Gerald Francis Burrill. c 2. Silver Cir Nat'L Acad Of Television Arts And Sciences.

WARD, Barbara Pyle (Ida) 450 W Highway 30, Burley ID 83318 **D S Jas Ch Burley ID 1997-** B Chicago IL 6/30/1947 d Ronald E Pyle & Beatrice Spotvold. BA DePauw U 1969; Med Indiana U 1974; Sped Indiana U 1975. D 2/2/1997 Bp John Stuart Thornton. m 8/8/1985 Thomas Charles Ward. bltw@pmt.org

WARD, Edwin Michael (Va) 8 Governors Ln, Hilton Head SC 29928 B Richmond VA 10/13/1927 s Varney Stuart Ward & Virginia. BA Emory U 1950; MDiv VTS 1955. D 6/3/1955 Bp Frederick D Goodwin P 12/15/1955 Bp George Mosley Murray. m 12/29/1954 Allein White c 2. Assoc R S Lk's Epis Ch Hilton Hd SC 1993-2001; Salisbury Sch Salisbury CT 1965-1981; Vic S Mk's Epis Ch Troy AL 1955-1959. Pres NAES 1973.

WARD, Elizabeth Howe (Chi) 79 Meadow Hill Rd, Barrington IL 60010 B Oak Park IL 9/21/1940 d John Bell Howe & Marion Elizabeth. IL Wesl 1960; BA Lake Forest Coll 1984; MDiv SWTS 1993. D 3/21/1996 P 9/21/1996 Bp William Walter Wiedrich. m 9/7/1963 John Arthur Ward c 3. Asst S Mk's Barrington Hills IL 2000-2004; S Giles' Ch Northbrook IL 1996-1999. fathermomehw@aol.com

WARD, Eugene Lee (Ky) 6877 Green Meadow Cir, Louisville KY 40207 **P-in-c S Andr's Ch Glasgow KY 2001-** B Detroit MI 5/11/1934 s Stewart James Ward & Anna Marie. S Jos Rensselaer IN 1953; BA S Meinrad Coll 1956; STB S Meinrad Sem 1961. Rec from Roman Catholic 6/3/1988 as Priest Bp James Daniel Warner. m 6/28/1968 Jan W Wiest c 2. Dio Kentucky Louisville KY 1993-1999; Asst Calv Ch Louisville KY 1993-1997; Asst S Andr's Ch Louisville KY 1993-1997; Barren River Area Coun Louisville KY 1991-1993; Int S Andr's Ch Glasgow KY 1989-1992; Int Trin Ch Russellville KY 1989-1992; S Lk's Ch Kearney NE 1988-1989.

WARD, Geoffrey Fremont (Ct) 29 Foothills Way, Bloomfield CT 06002 **Assoc Chr Ch Cathd Hartford CT 2007-** B Utica NY 11/9/1960 s Roger Caryl Ward & Haroldbelle June. BA Viterbo Coll 1982; MFA Trin U San Antonio TX 1984; MTS SWTS 2006. D 12/22/2007 P 1/3/2009 Bp Russell Edward Jacobus. c 5. fr.geoff@yahoo.com

WARD JR, George (Md) 3125 Starboard Dr, Annapolis MD 21403 B 7/28/1935 GEOWARDJR218@GMAIL.COM

WARD JR, Herbert Arthur (Nev) 112 Wyoming St, Boulder City NV 89005 B Jackson MS 3/30/1937 s Herbert Arthur Ward & Frances Florence. BA Millsaps Coll 1958; STM GTS 1961; DD Nash 1990. D 6/16/1961 Bp Duncan Montgomery Gray P 12/1/1961 Bp John M Allin. m 3/28/1978 Nancy Ruth Miles. Cur S Geo's Epis Ch New Orleans LA 1965-1970; Vic S Patricks Epis Ch Long Bch MS 1962-1965; Vic S Mk's Ch Gulfport MS 1961-1965; Cur S Ptr's By The Sea Gulfport MS 1961-1963.

WARD, Horace David (SeFla) 18501 Nw 7th Ave, Miami FL 33169 **R Epis Ch Of The H Fam Miami Gardens FL 1995-** B Kingston JM 1/1/1955 s Horace Donald Ward & Myrtle Joyce. MDiv Luth Theol Sthrn Sem; LTh Untd Theol Coll Of The W Indies Kingston Jm 1977; Untd Theol Coll Of The W Indies Kingston Jm 1977. D 6/19/1977 P 4/1/1978 Bp The Bishop Of Jamaica. m 12/16/1978 Marcia Radway c 3. Vic Ch Of The Gd Shpd Sumter SC 1990-1995; Cn In Res Trin And S Phil's Cathd Newark NJ 1984-1990; Asst R Chr Ch Shaker Heights OH 1981-1984. horace.ward@gmail.com

WARD, James (Cal) 3 Azalea Dr, Mill Valley CA 94941 B San Francisco CA 8/20/1947 s Herbert E Ward & Margery. BA Ya 1969; MDiv Yale DS 1974. D 6/29/1974 P 5/1/1975 Bp C Kilmer Myers. m 10/20/1979 Janet Erikson c 2. R S Steph's Par Belvedere CA 1994-2010; CDSP Berkeley CA 1985-1986; S Cuth's Epis Ch Oakland CA 1981-1994; Assoc S Steph's Epis Ch Orinda CA 1977-1981; Assoc S Andr's Ch Saratoga CA 1974-1977. Auth, "The Lay Acad". NNECA. jimward2@mac.com

WARD, Jeremiah (Tex) 43 N High Oaks Cir, Spring TX 77380 **Asstg R S Jas The Apos Epis Ch Conroe TX 2002-** B Wharton TX 4/22/1948 s Jeremiah Ward & Lucie Barker. BS Lamar U 1970; MDiv VTS 1978. D 6/23/1978 Bp J Milton Richardson P 7/1/1979 Bp Roger Howard Cilley. m 12/11/1992 Linda Cornuaud c 3. Assoc Cleric Trin Epis Ch The Woodlands TX 1999-2002; Dn Of Cntrl Convoc Dio Texas Houston TX 1988-1999; Dept Of CE Dio Texas Houston TX 1985-1999; Int S Dunst's Epis Ch Houston TX 1984; Asst Palmer Memi Ch Houston TX 1980-1984; Dio Texas Houston TX 1978-1980; Vic S Cuth's Epis Ch Houston TX 1978-1980. jeremiahward@att.net

WARD, Karen Marie (Oly) 4272 Fremont Ave N, Seattle WA 98103 B Cleveland OH 7/16/1961 d James A Ward & Barbara A. Rec from Evangelical Lutheran Church in America 8/22/2009 Bp Gregory Harold Rickel. Ch of the Apos Seattle WA 2009-2011. deskjockee@gmail.com

WARD, Katherine Lydia (Cal) 10370 Greenview Dr, Oakland CA 94605 B New Orleans LA 9/29/1934 d Johnny Neal Black & Corella Orelia. BA Jackson St U 1956; MA California St U 1969; EdD Nova U 1981; MDiv CDSP 1994; DDiv CDSP 2005. D 6/4/1994 P 6/1/1995 Bp William Edwin Swing. c 4. R S Aug's Ch Oakland CA 1996-2004; Chapl Dio California San Francisco CA 1996-2001; Asst S Fran' Epis Ch San Francisco CA 1996; Asst S Steph's Par Belvedere CA 1995. Auth, "...and A Heaping Cup of God's Love," *Mod Profiles of an Ancient Faith*, Epis Dio California, 2001; Auth, "Begin w The Tchr," *The Montclarian*, 1981. Epis Mnstry To Convalescent Hosps 1990; UBE 1994. revdrklw@aol.com

WARD, Mary Christine Mollie (Spr) 1104 N Roosevelt Ave, Bloomington IL 61701 **ECW Bd Chapl Dio Springfield Springfield IL 2004-** B Stuttgart Germany 3/6/1967 d Curtis Gene Ward & Christine Amalie. BA U of Oklahoma 1989; MDiv SWTS 2002. D 6/15/2002 P 12/21/2002 Bp William Dailey Persell. m 6/17/1989 Gregory Martin Shaw c 2. S Matt's Epis Ch Bloomington IL 2002-2007. CHS (Assoc) 1998; EPF 1989. ACPE Theory Paper of the Year Journ of Reflective Pract 2009. wardandshaw@gmail.com

WARD, Meredyth Wessman (WMass) 35 Somerset St, Worcester MA 01609 **Stndg Com Pres Dio Wstrn Massachusetts Springfield MA 2009-2013; P-in-c Epis Ch Of The Epiph Wilbraham MA 2009-; GC Dep Dio Wstrn Massachusetts Springfield MA 2006-2012** B Springfield MA 8/30/1955 d Robert Flagg Wessman & Jeanne Marie. BA Coll of the H Cross 1977; MDiv Jesuit TS 1981; CAS CDSP 2001. D 6/16/2001 P 12/15/2001 Bp Gordon Paul Scruton. m 9/17/1983 Matthew Oliver Ward c 2. R Chr Ch Rochdale MA 2001-2009. meredyth_ward@hotmail.com

WARD, Patrick Carroll (Mass) 147 Concord Rd, Lincoln MA 01773 **Asst R S Anne's In The Fields Epis Ch Lincoln MA 2008-** B Stoneham MA 11/4/1964 s Henry Joseph Ward & Theresa Anne. BA Br 1987; MDiv/Cert. in Angl Stds Ya Berk 2008. D 6/7/2008 Bp M(arvil) Thomas Shaw III. patrickcarrollward@gmail.com

WARD JR, Patrick John (NY) 168 Willow Dr, Briarcliff Manor NY 10510 **Int S Mk's Ch Westhampton Bch NY 2010-** B Philadelphia PA 2/21/1951 s Patrick John Ward & Rosemary Elizabeth. BA Wheaton Coll 1977; MDiv Nash 1980; MFT Sthrn Connecticut St U 1989. D 6/14/1980 Bp Quintin Ebenezer Primo Jr P 12/21/1980 Bp Edward Clark Turner. m 8/11/1979 Barbara Todisco c 2. Int Ch Of The Gd Shpd Granite Sprg NY 2008-2009; R S Mary's Ch Of Scarborough Scarborough NY 2006-2008; Int S Jas' Epis Ch Parkton MD 2005-2006; Int Chr Ch Forest Hill MD 2003-2004; R Ch Of The Gd Shpd Dunedin FL 1999-2002; Vic S Steph's Ch W Vlly City UT 1995-1999; Vic S Peters-In-The-Woods Epis Ch Fairfax Sta VA 1990-1995; R Chr Ch Oxford CT 1983-1990; Cur S Dav's Epis Ch Topeka KS 1980-1983. pward51@hotmail.com

WARD, Richard Philip (Spok) 1699 N Terry St Spc 46, Eugene OR 97402 B Medford OR 6/25/1945 s Lloyd Vernon Ward & Elise Martha. BS Pacific U 1967; MDiv CDSP 1982. D 7/15/1982 P 3/20/1983 Bp Edmond Lee Browning. m 4/2/1966 Dona Reaves c 2. R S Tim's Epis Ch Yakima WA 1999-2009; R The Ch Of The H Trin Juneau AK 1995-1999; Asst R Chr Ch Coronado CA 1990-1995; Yth Coordntr Dio NW Texas Lubbock TX 1985-1990; Assoc R S Chris's Epis Ch Lubbock TX 1984-1990; Dio Hawaii Honolulu HI 1982-1984; S Andr's Cathd Honolulu HI 1982-1984. dandrward@aol.com

WARD IV, Samuel Mortimer (Los) 2524 Chapala St, Santa Barbara CA 93105 **Dioc Transition Spec Dio Los Angeles Los Angeles CA 2003-** B New York NY 9/29/1937 s Samuel Mortimer Ward & Marion. BA Heidelberg Coll 1961; MDiv CDSP 1964. D 6/21/1964 Bp James Albert Pike P 3/11/1965 Bp Francis E I Bloy. m 2/7/1981 Alessandra H T Frees c 4. Int S Jas' Par So Pasadena CA 2001-2002; Int S Patricks Ch And Day Sch Thousand Oaks CA 1998-2001; Int S Tim's Epis Ch Creve Coeur MO 1998; Int S Ptr's Epis Ch St Louis MO 1997-1998; Int S Mart-In-The-Fields Par Winnetka CA 1995-1996; Int Chr The King A Jubilee Mnstry Palmdale CA 1994-1995; R Trin Epis Ch Santa Barbara CA 1986-1994; Transition Spec Dio Los Angeles Los Angeles CA 1981-2002; Vic S Fran Of Assisi Epis Ch Simi Vlly CA 1980-1986; Comm. Liturg & Mus (chair) Dio Los Angeles Los Angeles CA 1976-1988; Dioc Coun, Comm. Liturg & Mus Dio San Diego San Diego CA 1974-1976; R S Barth's Epis Ch Poway CA 1967-1980; Asst R H Trin Epis Ch Covina CA 1966-1967; Cur S Mary's Par Laguna Bch CA 1964-1966. Alb Inst 2002; Conf. Ord of S Ben 1965; Fresh Start Fac 2009; Int Mnstry Ntwk Fac 2002; TMEC 1997. mort@priest.com

WARD, Suzanne Lynn (EpisSanJ) 1934 S Santa Fe Ave, Visalia CA 93292 **P-in-c S Paul's Epis Ch Visalia CA 2009-** B Weiser ID 3/4/1952 d Thomas Chamberlin & Lois. Cert California St U 1977; BA U of Montana 1995; M. Div. Mennonite Brethren Biblic Sem 2009. D 6/14/1997 Bp John-David Mercer Schofield P 6/27/2009 Bp Jerry Alban Lamb. m 9/2/1978 Jonathan L J Ward c 2. D S Paul's Epis Ch Visalia CA 1997-2008. sward1978@sbcglobal.net

WARD JR, Thomas Reid (Tenn) Po Box 3270, Sewanee TN 37375 B Meridian MS 8/2/1945 s Thomas Reid Ward & Carolyn. BA U So 1967; MA Oxf 1969; MDiv VTS 1975. D 5/31/1975 P 5/31/1976 Bp Duncan Montgomery Gray Jr. m 5/19/1974 Margaret Nagley c 1. Chapl The TS at The U So Sewanee TN 1994-2005; R Chr Ch Cathd Nashville TN 1981-1994; R All SS Epis Ch Grenada MS 1977-1981; Asst Trin Ch Hattiesburg MS 1975-1977. tward@sewanee.edu

WARDER, Oran Edward (Va) 228 S Pitt St, Alexandria VA 22314 **R S Paul's Epis Ch Alexandria VA 1999-** B Philippi WV 9/18/1961 s Joseph Arthur Warder & Mary Kathryn. BA Marshall U 1984; MA Marshall U 1985; MDiv VTS 1988. D 6/1/1988 Bp Robert Poland Atkinson P 6/1/1989 Bp William Franklin Carr. m 6/21/1986 Amy Elizabeth Leatherberry c 3. Cn To Ordnry Dio Delaware Wilmington DE 1993-1999; Assoc S Phil's Epis Ch Laurel MD 1990-1993; Asst Trin Ch Huntington WV 1988-1990. oran@stpaulsalexandria.com

WARE, David James (NY) 1670 Route 25A, Saint John's Church, Cold Spring Harbor NY 11724 **R S Jn's Ch Cold Sprg Harbor NY 2007-** B Oak Ridge TN 1/9/1962 s Kenneth Ware & Mary Mcguyre. BA Ya 1984; MA S Jn's Coll Santa Fe NM 1991; MDiv GTS 1995. D 6/17/1995 Bp Jane Hart Holmes Dixon P 1/1/1996 Bp Ronald Hayward Haines. m 10/7/1989 Sarah Adams Hoover c 1. Hd of Upper Sch Cathd of St Ptr & St Paul Washington DC 2001-2007; Assoc Trin Par Wilmington DE 1997-2001; Assoc Chr Ch Ridgewood NJ 1995-1997. dware@stjcsh.org

WARE, Mary Jane Casper (Kan) 915 S Denver St, El Dorado KS 67042 **D Trin Epis Ch El Dorado KS 1996-** B Topeka KS 2/14/1930 d Joseph Taylor Casper & Marian Sara. AA Cottey Coll 1950; BS U of Missouri 1952; Med Wichita St U 1973. D 10/23/1996 Bp William Edward Smalley. m 12/29/1952 Joe Fred.

WAREHAM, George Ludwig (NwPa) 3111 Pearl Dr, New Castle PA 16105 B Furstenfeldbrook W. Germany 4/12/1956 s Samuel Anderson Wareham & Clara Bertha. BA Thiel Coll 1989; MDiv TESM 1993. D 10/30/1993 P 5/1/1994 Bp Robert Deane Rowley Jr. m Agatha S Littlefield c 1. R Trin Ch Hermitage PA 2001-2003; Dir - Yth Comm. Assoc Dio NW Pennsylvania Erie PA 1994-2001; S Jn's Epis Ch Sharon PA 1994-2001. Ord Of S Lk.

WAREING, Robert Edgar (Tex) 3122 Red Maple Dr, Friendswood TX 77546 B Corsicana TX 2/8/1947 s Edgar Charles Wareing & Betty Jo. BS Texas A&M U 1969; MDiv VTS 1981. D 6/17/1981 Bp Roger Howard Cilley P 2/25/1982 Bp Maurice Manuel Benitez. m 8/15/1970 Patricia Riley. Vic All SS Epis Ch Stafford TX 1999-2008; R Ch Of The Gd Shpd Friendswood TX 1990-1999; Chr Epis Ch Cedar Pk TX 1986-1990; Cur S Matt's Ch Austin TX 1981-1985. r.wareing@pobox.com

WARFEL, John B (NY) 17 Crescent Pl, Middletown NY 10940 **R Gr Ch Middletown NY 1998-** B Cheverly MD 6/25/1958 s George Lester Warfel & Patricia. BS Geo 1980; MDiv CDSP 1993. D 6/5/1993 P 12/4/1993 Bp William Edwin Swing. m 6/17/2010 Thomas Peter Mollicone. Chr Ch Las Vegas NV 1993-1998. "The Ultimate Conclusion to Every Question," *Sermons That Wk XIV*, Morehouse, 2006. gracemdt@warwick.net

WARFIELD JR, Edward Snowden (Md) 1802 Kenway Rd, Baltimore MD 21209 B Baltimore MD 1/26/1933 s Edward Snowden Warfield & Betty Byrd. BA Jn Hopkins U 1956; MDiv VTS 1962. D 6/26/1962 Bp Harry Lee Doll P 4/1/1963 Bp Noble C Powell. m 10/19/1973 Mary Rex Keener c 4. Assoc S

Barth's Ch Baltimore MD 1996; Ch Of S Marks On The Hill Pikesville MD 1987-1991; P Ch Of The Mssh Baltimore MD 1969-1986. edandmarywarfield@yahoo.com

WARFUEL, Ronald Lee (SC) 1458 Fort Lamar Rd., Charleston SC 29412 B Huntington WV 10/9/1953 D 9/10/2005 Bp Edward Lloyd Salmon Jr. m 8/16/2003 Kathryn Mary Heider c 2. warfuelr@yahoo.com

WARING, J(ames) Donald (NY) 802 Broadway, New York NY 10003 **Trst Gr Ch Sch New York New York NY 2004-; R Gr Epis Ch New York NY 2004-** B Orange NJ 1/11/1962 s James Henry Waring & Virginia. BA U of Sioux Falls 1984; MDiv GTS 1989. D 6/24/1989 Bp H Coleman McGehee Jr P 4/21/1990 Bp R(aymond) Stewart Wood Jr. m 12/30/1995 Stacie Anne Soule c 2. Dn Dio Sthrn Ohio Cincinnati OH 1998-2004; R S Thos Epis Ch Terrace Pk OH 1995-2004; Int R Chr Ch Cranbrook Bloomfield Hills MI 1993-1995; Assoc R Chr Ch Cranbrook Bloomfield Hills MI 1989-1993. Auth, "Best Sermons 4"; Auth, "Sermons That Wk Iii"; Auth, "Sermons That Wk Vi". dwaring@gracechurchnyc.org

WARING, William Davis (Oly) 747 N 135th St Apt 737, Seattle WA 98133 B 8/27/1925 s William Stanley Waring & Edna Mae. BA Wstrn Washington U 1955; MA U of Washington 1966; MDiv CDSP 1977. D 10/30/1977 P 2/1/1979 Bp Jose Guadalupe Saucedo. S Geo Epis Ch Maple Vlly WA 1987-1990; Exec Coun Appointees New York NY 1982-1985; Dio Wstrn Mex Zapopan Jalisco CP 45150 1977-1981. Angl Chmn's Soc.

WARLEY, Dianne (Ct) 73 Ayers Point Rd, Old Saybrook CT 06475 **S Jn's Epis Ch Niantic CT 2000-** B Milton MA 12/22/1943 D 12/9/2000 Bp Andrew Donnan Smith. m 5/23/1964 Edward Rogers Warley c 2. dwarley@comcast.net

WARNE III, Tom (Oly) 2915 SE 173rd Ct, Vancouver WA 98683 **R Ch Of The Gd Shpd Vancouver WA 2008-** B Wilkes-Barre PA 5/9/1967 s William Thomas Warne & Frances Louise. Dplma U of Kent, Cbury, UK 1988; BA Hobart and Wm Smith Colleges 1989; Con. Ed. California St U, Northridge 1992; MDiv STUSo 1997; DMin SWTS 2003. D 6/6/1997 P 2/21/1998 Bp Michael Whittington Creighton. m 6/24/1994 Saran Ruth Ball c 3. R S Jn's Epis Ch Huntingdon PA 1997-2008. Druid Soc of Hob 1988; Soc of S Jn the Evang 1997. revdrtomwarne@msn.com

WARNE II, William Thomas (CPa) 217 Urie Ave., Lake Winola PA 18625 B Scranton,PA 12/27/1941 s Thomas Abram Warne & Edna Mae. BA Hob 1963; STB (M. Div.) PDS 1966; Cert VTS 1979. D 6/18/1966 P 3/18/1967 Bp Frederick J Warnecke. m 5/23/1964 Frances Louise DeMartino c 3. P in Res Ch Of The Gd Shpd Scranton PA 2005-2009; Supply P Ch Of The Gd Shpd Scranton PA 2005; Chair Of Plnng Com Dio Cntrl Pennsylvania Harrisburg PA 1977-1983; Ch of the Nativ-St Steph Newport PA 1974-2004; St Stephens Epis Ch Thompsontown PA 1974-2004. Cntrl Pennsylvania Cleric Assn, Perry Cnty Mnstry 2004. Hon Cn S Steph's Cathd Harrisburg PA 1991; Eleanor Henschen Memi Awd For Vol Serv Tri-Cnty MHA 1981. cnwtw2@epix.net

WARNECKE JR, Frederick John (NC) 3017 Lake Forest Dr, Greensboro NC 27408 **Int Vic S Paul's Epis Ch Thomasville NC 2002-** B Ridgewood NJ 9/8/1933 s Frederick J Warnecke & Edith Grace. BA Leh 1955; MDiv VTS 1958. D 5/30/1958 Bp Benjamin M Washburn P 5/1/1959 Bp Frederick J Warnecke. m 6/21/1958 Abigail B Warnecke c 2. S Fran Ch Greensboro NC 1985-1999; R S Jas Ch Upper Montclair NJ 1971-1985; R Emm Ch At Brook Hill Richmond VA 1961-1971; In-Charge S Ptr's Par Ch New Kent VA 1958-1961. Confrerie De La Chaine Des Rotisseurs 2001; Confrerie Des Chevaliers Du Tastevin 1981. Commandeur Confrerie Des Chevaliers Du Tastevin 2003; Chevalier Confrerie Des Chevaliers Du Tastevin 1981; Phi Beta Kappa 1955; Chevalier Du Taste Vin. fwarnecke@aol.com

WARNER, Anthony Francis (Md) 2434 Cape Horn Rd, Hampstead MD 21074 **S Geo Ch Hampstead MD 2011-** B Danville PA 3/31/1933 s Anthony Warakomski & Theophilia. Cath U; Geo Washington Unversity; BSIE Penn St U 1954. Rec from Roman Catholic 6/7/2011 as Deacon Bp Eugene Sutton. m 11/23/1957 Sheila Warner c 3. aswarner1@comcast.net

WARNER, Christopher Scott (At) 1315 Cove Ave, Sullivans Island SC 29482 B Pueblo CO 12/21/1969 s Donald Gordon Warner & Ellen Marie. BA U NC 1991; MDiv TESM 2000. D 6/10/2000 Bp Robert William Duncan P 1/16/2001 Bp Robert Gould Tharp. m 10/23/1993 Catherine Dixon DeVane c 3. Assoc Ch Of The H Cross Sullivans Island SC 2002-2007; Cur Trin Epis Ch Columbus GA 2000-2002. cwarner320@gmail.com

WARNER, Dale Alford (Fla) 2736 NW 77th Blvd Apt #152, Gainesville FL 32606 **P-in-c S Mich's Ch Gainesville FL 2007-** B Toledo OH 4/11/1927 s Charles Ray Warner & Alma. BS U of Florida 1949; PhD U of Florida 1953; MDiv STUSo 1987. D 6/14/1987 Bp Frank Stanley Cerveny P 2/2/1988 Bp William Hopkins Folwell. m 8/15/1948 Lempi Fredericka van der Laan c 4. Vic Trin Epis Ch Melrose FL 1990-1997; Asst Epis Ch Of The Resurr Longwood FL 1987-1990. Phi Beta Kappa U of Florida 1952. dalewarner@bellsouth.net

WARNER, David Maxwell (Va) 8206 Chamberlayne Rd, Richmond VA 23227 B Denver CO 2/12/1931 s Maxwell Elanson Warner & Ethel. BA U Denv 1952; LTh SWTS 1955. D 6/29/1955 P 1/25/1956 Bp Joseph Summerville Minnis. m 11/26/1994 Penelope G Patton c 5. Int S Paul's Owens King Geo VA 2002-2004; Int S Dav's Ch Aylett VA 2000-2001; Int Aquia Ch Stafford VA 1996-1998; P-in-c Emm Ch At Brook Hill Richmond VA 1994; R Chr Ascen Ch Richmond VA 1974-1994; R Ch Of The Gd Shpd Ogden UT 1959-1971; Vic S Paul's Epis Ch Vernal UT 1957-1959; Vic S Tim's Epis Ch Rangely CO 1957-1959; The Ch Of Chr The King (Epis) Arvada CO 1956-1957; Vic S Martha's Epis Ch Westminster CO 1955-1957. dwpadre@aol.com

WARNER, Deborah Morris (Mass) Church of the Messiah, 13 Church St, Woods Hole MA 02543 **P-in-c Ch Of The Mssh Woods Hole MA 2005-** B New York NY 12/23/1951 d Wolcott Morris Warner & Eloise. BA Salem Coll Winston -Salem NC 1974; MDiv UTS 1980. D 6/5/1982 Bp Paul Moore Jr P 4/16/1983 Bp Walter Decoster Dennis Jr. Dn Dio Massachusetts Boston MA 1996-2005; R S Dunstans Epis Ch Dover MA 1990-2005; Co-Chair Cler Fam Ntwk Dio Massachusetts Boston MA 1990-1993; Epis Ch Of S Thos Taunton MA 1987-1990; COM Dio Massachusetts Boston MA 1986-1992; Ch Of S Jn The Evang Hingham MA 1984-1987; Asst Chr Ch Riverdale Bronx NY 1982-1984. Auth, "Bk Revs," *ATR*. Massachusetts Epis Cler Assiciation 1984. dwarner74@aol.com

WARNER, Donald Emil (Neb) 422 W 2nd St # 1026, Grand Island NE 68801 **D S Steph's Ch Grand Island NE 1985-** B Waverly NE 2/8/1922 s Arthur Emil Warner & Ruth. BS U of Nebraska 1947. D 11/8/1985 Bp James Daniel Warner. m 4/5/1947 Elizabeth Ann Kouanda c 3. D Epis Ch Of S Fran-In-The-Vlly Green Vlly AZ 1991-1992.

WARNER, Donald Nelson (Colo) 6961 S. Cherokee St., Littleton CO 80120 B Dallas TX 8/1/1935 s Nelson Warner & Margaret Virginia. BA Tarkio Coll-Tarkio MO 1957; MSM Sthrn Bapt TS Louisville KY 1960; MDiv Nash 1973. D 3/19/1973 Bp William Hopkins Folwell P 9/21/1973 Bp William Carl Frey. m 9/9/1961 Anne Sherer c 2. Inerim Min of Mus S Jn's Cathd Jacksonville FL 2006-2007; R S Tim's Epis Ch Centennial CO 1988-2003; Ex Coun & Stndg Com Dio Colorado Denver CO 1980-1988; R S Mk's Epis Ch Durango CO 1977-1988; Assoc S Tim's Epis Ch Centennial CO 1976-1977; Cur S Tim's Epis Ch Centennial CO 1973-1976. Compsr, "3 Mus Settings Of Rite 2". AGO 2007; Integrity 1995. dnwarner57@msn.com

✠ WARNER, Rt Rev James Daniel (Neb) 64 Shaker Pl, Valley NE 68064 **Died 9/10/2009** B Sheridan WY 5/1/1924 s Stephen Daniel Warner & Grace Margaret. SWTS; BS NWU 1950. D 3/21/1953 Bp William Hampton Brady P 11/3/1953 Bp Harwood Sturtevant Con 11/30/1976 for Neb. Soc Of S Jn The Evang. Doctor Of Humanitarian Serv Bp Clarkson Coll 1989; DD SWTS Evanston IL 1977.

WARNER, Janet Avery (EO) 444 NW Apollo Rd, Prineville OR 97754 **D, Non-Stipendiary S Andr's Epis Ch Prineville OR 2002-** B Washington DC 12/25/1955 d Edward Avery & Mary Jane. Estrn Oregon U 1975. D 5/1/2002 Bp William O Gregg. m 9/21/1975 Daniel Warner c 2. janetwarner247@yahoo.com

WARNER, John Seawright (Ga) 2211 Dartmouth Rd, Augusta GA 30904 B New Haven CT 7/8/1952 s George Edwin Warner & Patricia Elizabeth. BA NE Louisiana U 1974; MS NE Louisiana U 1977; MBA Augusta St U 1989. D 7/9/2002 Bp Henry Irving Louttit. m 3/31/1979 Marsha Sue Lord c 1. jwarner6@comcast.net

WARNER, Katherine Wakefield (SwFla) PO Box 272, Boca Grande FL 33921 **S Andr's Ch Boca Grande FL 2004-** B Louisville KY 2/14/1941 d George Cohn & Gladys Mary. BA Sarah Lawr Coll 1966; MDiv GTS 1986. D 6/24/1986 P 10/1/1987 Bp David Reed. m 4/27/1974 Lawrence Askew Warner c 4. S Lk's Chap Louisville KY 1994-1997; D-In-Res S Andr's Ch Louisville KY 1986-1987.

WARNER, Keithly R S (At) P.O. Box 468, Christiansted VI 00821 B 6/16/1937 s Rufus Oliver Warner & Ruby Delores. ETSC; Inter Amer U of Puerto Rico. D 6/11/1971 P 5/1/1972 Bp Dean T Stevenson. R S Jn's Ch Christiansted VI 1996-2000; S Aug's Epis Ch St Petersburg FL 1989-1994; Ch Of Beth Saratoga Sprg NY 1986-1988; Ch Of The Incarn Jersey City NJ 1977-1985; Calv Ch Charleston SC 1976; R Ch Of S Simon The Cyrenian New Rochelle NY 1972-1976. SSC. frkrswarner@hotmail.com

WARNER, Kevin Collins (SanD) 6556 Park Ridge Blvd, San Diego CA 92120 **R S Dunst's Epis Ch San Diego CA 2009-** B Fort Wayne IN 10/29/1957 s Roger Milton Warner & Carol Jean. BA Olivet Coll 1980; MDiv VTS 1985. D 6/29/1985 Bp H Coleman McGehee Jr P 2/1/1986 Bp William Arthur Beckham. m 8/9/1980 Susan E Ridley c 4. R The Epis Ch Of The Adv W Bloomfield MI 1994-2009; R S Kath's Ch Williamston MI 1988-1994; Asst R Gr Epis Ch Anderson SC 1985-1988. 4onhillandale@gmail.com

WARNER JR, Richard Wright (EC) 835 Calabash Rd. NW, Calabash NC 28467 B New Castle PA 11/10/1938 s Richard Wright Warner & Emily Ruth. BA Westminster Coll 1961; Med SUNY 1966; EdD SUNY 1969; Postdoc Auburn U 1978; CTh VTS 1984. D 5/29/1984 P 12/5/1984 Bp Brice Sidney Sanders. m 10/15/1989 Frances B Warner c 3. R S Jas The Fisherman Epis Ch Shallotte NC 1989-2003; R S Paul's Epis Ch Wilmington NC 1988-1989; R S Thos' Epis Ch Ahoskie NC 1985-1988; Asst S Steph's Ch Goldsboro NC 1984-1985.

Auth, "Grp Counslg: Theory And Process," Rand Mcnally, 1976; Auth, "Counslg: Theory & Process," Allyn And Bacon/Houghton/Mifflin. DSA Amer Personl And Gdnc 1980; Alum Prof Auburn U 1978. fbwrww@atmc.net

WARNER, Suzanne McCarroll (Ky) 1265 Bassett Ave, Louisville KY 40204 B Little Rock AR 3/28/1936 d John Ramsey McCarroll & Willma Louise. BA Rhoder Coll 1957; JD U of Louisville 1977; MA Presb TS 2008; MA The U So (Sewanee) 2010. D 12/21/2009 Bp Edwin Funsten Gulick Jr. c 3. smw40204@bellsouth.com

✠ WARNER, Rt Rev Vincent Waydell (Oly) Po Box 12126, Seattle WA 98102 **Ret Bp of Olympia Dio Olympia Seattle WA 2007-** B Roanoke VA 12/27/1940 s Vincent Waydell Warner & Virginia. Lic VTS 1971; DD VTS 1990. D 6/4/1971 P 12/1/1971 Bp William Henry Marmion Con 7/8/1989 for Oly. m 2/8/2004 Chen Warner c 1. Dio Olympia Seattle WA 1989-2007; R S Andr's Ch Wellesley MA 1983-1989; Archd Dio Maine Portland ME 1980-1983; R S Ptr's Ch Osterville MA 1976-1980; Asst Chr Ch Grosse Pointe Grosse Pointe Farms MI 1974-1976; Asst S Jn's Ch Roanoke VA 1971-1974. vwarner615@aol.com

WARNICK, Jeremy Matthew (Az) 1811 Loney Street, Philadelphia PA 19111 B Philadelphia PA 8/3/1972 s Ira Albert Warnick & Joan Elizabeth. BA Muhlenberg Coll 1994; MDiv GTS 1998. D 6/20/1998 P 5/29/1999 Bp Charles Ellsworth Bennison Jr. m 8/24/1996 Jennifer J Salvatori c 1. P-in-c All SS Ch Rhawnhurst Philadelphia PA 2009-2011; S Mk's Epis Ch Mesa AZ 2007-2009; Chr Ch New Bern NC 2003-2007; S Mk's Epis Ch Yonkers NY 2000-2003; Chapl Gr Epis Ch New York NY 1999-2000; Cur S Tim's Ch Roxborough Philadelphia PA 1998-1999; Intern/Asst - Off Of Ecum Relatns Epis Ch Cntr New York NY 1995-1998. The Angl Soc 2002-2004. frjwarnick@aol.com

WARNKE, James William (Nwk) 680 Albin St, Teaneck NJ 07666 **Sprtl Dir The GTS New York NY 2009-** B Plattsburg NY 12/13/1947 s Ernest W Warnke & Ruth Turnesa. BA Ford 1969; MA Manhattan Coll 1974; MS Ford 1978; DAS GTS 1996. D 6/1/1996 Bp John Shelby Spong P 12/1/1997 Bp Jack Marston McKelvey. m 12/28/1969 Marie Theresa Jones c 2. Assoc S Paul's Ch Englewood NJ 1999-2009. Auth, "Becoming An Everyday Mystic," Abbey Press, 1990. jwarnke@worldnet.att.net

WARNOCK, James Howard (NI) 2365 N Miller Ave, Marion IN 46952 **Secy, Dioc Coun Dio Nthrn Indiana So Bend IN 2010-; R Geth Epis Ch Marion IN 2002-** B San Francisco CA 11/10/1951 s Howard Samuel Warnock & Dorothy Margaret. Mcs Regent Coll, Vancouver, BC 1984; PhD U of Washington 1989; DAS Nash 1998. D 9/6/1998 P 3/13/1999 Bp Keith Lynn Ackerman. m 9/10/1976 Kresha Richman c 2. Stndg Com Dio Nthrn Indiana So Bend IN 2005-2011; Asst All SS Par Los Angeles CA 1999-2002. Amer Hist Assn; Conf On Faith & Hist. frjimwarnock@gmail.com

WARREN III, Allan Bevier (Mass) 30 Brimmer St, Boston MA 02108 **The Ch Of The Adv Boston MA 2005-** B Charlottsville VA 1/14/1947 s Allan Bevier Warren & Claudia Wyclif. STB GTS; BA Pr. D 6/25/1972 Bp John Adams Pinckney P 3/31/1973 Bp George Moyer Alexander. Ch Of The Resurr New York NY 1993-1999; Asst to the R The Ch Of The Adv Boston MA 1990-1993; R Ch Of The Gd Shpd Waban MA 1984-1990; The Amer Cathd of the H Trin Paris 75008 FR 1981-1984; Cur Ch Of The Trsfg New York NY 1974-1981; Vic All SS Epis Ch Clinton SC 1972-1974; Vic Ch Of The Epiph Laurens SC 1972-1974. rector@theadvent.org

WARREN, Annika Laurin (Ct) 31 Woodland St, Hartford CT 06105 B Hartford CT 12/8/1959 d Hubbard Hoover Warren & Annie Lee. BS S Aug's Coll Raleigh NC 1981; MDiv VTS 1984. D 6/9/1984 Bp Arthur Edward Walmsley P 2/1/1985 Bp Clarence Nicholas Coleridge. m 7/11/1987 Mozallen McFadden. S Monica's Ch Hartford CT 1990-1993; Chr Ch Cathd Hartford CT 1984-1987.

WARREN, Daniel (Me) 730 Mere Point Rd, Brunswick ME 04011 B New York NY 2/4/1948 s George Warren & Dorothy. BA Ya 1970; MDiv EDS 1977. D 6/11/1977 Bp Paul Moore Jr P 6/7/1978 Bp John Harris Burt. m 9/18/1976 Margaret Little c 2. S Paul's Ch Brunswick ME 1998-2011; R Gr Ch In Providence Providence RI 1982-1998; Dio Rhode Island Providence RI 1982-1985; Ch Of The H Trin New York NY 1979-1982; Assoc H Trin Epis Ch Inwood New York NY 1979-1982; S Michaels In The Hills Toledo OH 1977-1979. Auth, "Var arts," 2003. Fellowowship, Coll Of Preachers 1995. dwarren@suscom-maine.net

WARREN, Donna Lea (WMo) 301 N Withers Rd Apt G, Liberty MO 64068 B Lead SD 4/19/1934 d Earl Warren & Ivy. BS Black Hill St U 1956; W Missouri Sch of Mnstry 1991. D 5/30/1992 Bp John Clark Buchanan. D S Mary's Epis Ch Kansas City MO 1996-2000. Assn ComT 1964; NAAD 1992-2000. dimlitwit@aol.com

WARREN, Douglas G. (Cal) 18231 Glen Lake Ct., Reno NV 89508 B Alameda CA 1/27/1946 s George Arthur Warren & Ada. BA Occ 1967; STB Harvard DS 1970; PhD CDSP 1979. D 1/10/1976 Bp J(ohn) Joseph Meakins Harte P 1/6/1977 Bp Joseph Thomas Heistand. m 4/16/1977 Leslie Freezer c 3. R S Steph's Epis Ch Orinda CA 1986-2003; R S Paul's Ch Phoenix AZ 1980-1986; Asst S Phil's In The Hills Tucson AZ 1975-1980. oedfan@yahoo.com

WARREN, George Henry (RI) 12 Walnut Hill Rd, Pascoag RI 02859 B Pawtucket RI 7/21/1945 s James Henry Warren & Anna Olga. BA U of Rhode Island 1967; MDiv PDS 1971. D 6/5/1971 P 12/1/1971 Bp John S Higgins. m 12/9/2010 Annette Remington-Klein. P-in-c S Mk's Ch Warwick RI 2003-2008; P-in-c S Jn's Ch Millville MA 1998-2003; P-in-c S Jn's Epis Ch Sutton MA 1992-1995; Dio Wstrn Massachusetts Springfield MA 1975-2003; R Trin Epis Ch Milford MA 1975-1992; Cur S Barn Ch Warwick RI 1971-1974. Ord Of S Camillus (RC) 2001. FRGEORGEWARREN@AOL.COM

WARREN JR, Hallie (ETenn) 1021 Meadow Lake Rd, Chattanooga TN 37415 B Camden SC 4/21/1928 s Hallie Delesslin Warren & Elnora. BA U of So Carolina 1950; MDiv TS 1953; Ssas Ya 1959. D 6/25/1953 P 3/1/1954 Bp Thomas N Carruthers. m 7/16/1949 Martha C Dicks c 4. Int Ch Of The Nativ Ft Oglethorpe GA 1996-1998; R S Ptr's Ch Chattanooga TN 1964-1993; R Gr Ch Waycross GA 1957-1964; Asst R S Paul's Epis Ch Chattanooga TN 1956-1957; Min In Charge S Alb's Ch Kingstree SC 1953-1956; Min In Charge S Steph's Ch S Steph SC 1953-1956. halliew1@comcast.net

WARREN, Harold Robert (Colo) 2000 Stover St, Fort Collins CO 80525 B Needham MA 1/22/1948 s Robert Harold Warren & Agnes. BA U of So Florida 1970; MA U of So Florida 1972; MDiv STUSo 1975; DMin Columbia TS 1990. D 6/11/1975 Bp William Loftin Hargrave P 12/19/1975 Bp Emerson Paul Haynes. m 6/5/1971 Judith M Ackerman c 2. R S Lk's Epis Ch Ft Collins CO 2000-2011; R S Tim's Epis Ch Lake Jackson TX 1996-2000; The Epis Ch Of The Gd Shpd Lake Wales FL 1989-1996; R S Sebastian's By The Sea Melbourne Bch FL 1983-1988; R S Mary's Epis Ch Palmetto FL 1977-1983; Cur S Bede's Ch St Petersburg FL 1975-1977. Auth, *Personality Factors & Sprtl Styles (Thesis)*. Faithful Alum Awd Univ of the So Sewanee TN 1999. juhawarren@gmail.com

WARREN, Heather Anne (NC) 170 Reas Ford Rd, Earlysville VA 22936 B Bellshill, Scotland 8/22/1959 d James Warren & Marjorie Anne Logie. BA Cor 1981; BA Oxf 1984; MDiv Candler, Emory U 1985; PhD The JHU 1992. D 12/19/2009 P 6/26/2010 Bp Michael Bruce Curry. c 2. hwarren@virginia.edu

WARREN, J Lewis (Neb) Po Box 1201, Scottsbluff NE 69363 B Texas City TX 12/16/1941 s James Lewis Warren & Sidney Florence. BA SMU 1964; MA U of Oregon 1966; MA SWTS 1977; PhD OH SU 1979; DMin GTF 1994. D 6/14/1977 P 12/21/1977 Bp Charles Thomas Gaskell. m 8/29/1964 Rose Lee Christe c 1. Eccl Crt Dio Nebraska Omaha NE 1990-1992; R S Fran Epis Ch Scottsbluff NE 1983-2001; Stndg Com Dio Fond du Lac Appleton WI 1980-1982; R St Johns Epis Ch Wisconsin Rapids WI 1979-1982; Asst Trin Ch Wauwatosa WI 1977-1979. Auth, "Var arts". Dplma APA; Ocampr; Ordo Constantini Magni; SHN. elias1941@gmail.com

WARREN, John Wells (Ala) 1347 Shelton Mill Rd, Auburn AL 36830 **Dio Alabama Birmingham AL 1999-; Chapl Dio Alabama Birmingham AL 1999-; Chapl S Dunst's: The Epis Ch at Auburn U Auburn AL 1999-** B Bryan TX 10/4/1952 s William Michael Warren & Carolyn Glass. BA Auburn U 1974; Med Auburn U 1979; ABD U of Alabama 1986; Cert STUSo 1992; DMin STUSo 2004. D 1/13/1996 P 7/20/1996 Bp Robert Oran Miller. m 11/17/2009 Leigh W Williamson c 2. S Matthews In The Pines Seale AL 2009-2010; Emm Epis Ch Opelika AL 2005-2006; Vic S Mich's Epis Ch Fayette AL 1996-1999. The HSEC 2004. Phi Kappa Phi hon Soc Auburn U 1989; Phi Delta Kappa Educ Hon Auburn U 1980; Sigma Tau Delta Engl Hon Auburn U 1974. wellswarren@msn.com

WARREN, Joseph Palmer (Ala) 2017 6th Ave N, Birmingham AL 35203 **Dir Pstr Care The Cathd Ch Of The Adv Birmingham AL 1996-** B Mobile AL 11/21/1946 s Claude Morris Warren & Esther. BA U of Alabama 1970; MDiv VTS 1990. D 6/2/1990 P 4/10/1991 Bp Charles Farmer Duvall. m 9/7/1968 Susan L Lingo. R S Mary's Fleeton Reedville VA 1991-1996; R S Steph's Ch Heathsville VA 1991-1996; D The Epis Ch Of The Nativ Dothan AL 1990-1991. Auth, *Restoring the Broken Image*, 2001. Dioc Coun of Alabama 2000. joe@cathedraladvent.com

WARREN, Lindsay Dune (Ore) 20 SE 103rd Ave Apt 503, Portland OR 97216 **Died 1/14/2010** B Portland OR 12/5/1928 s Frederick Joseph Mullen & Eunice Gertrude. BA Reed Coll 1951; BD Bex 1955. D 6/18/1955 Bp Nelson Marigold Burroughs P 12/17/1955 Bp Alfred L Banyard. c 3. Tertiary of the Soc of S Fran Professed 1989. ldunw@msn.com

WARREN, Penelope Sandra Muehl (Minn) 3124 Utah Ave N, Crystal MN 55427 B Milwaukee WI 7/31/1946 d Earl W Muehl & Luella May. BS U of Wisconsin 1969; MS Illinois St U 1974; PhD Pur 1978; MDiv CDSP 1986. D 6/4/1988 P 6/1/1989 Bp William Edwin Swing. m 9/21/1968 Richard Lynn Warren. Assoc Ch Of The H Innoc San Francisco CA 2000-2004; Sr P Assoc The Epis Ch Of S Jn The Evang San Francisco CA 1994-2000; The Epis Ch Of S Jn The Evang San Francisco CA 1991-1993; Asst R Ch Of The Incarn San Francisco CA 1988-1990. pmwarren@comcast.net

WARREN JR, Ralph Ray (SeFla) 223 East Tall Oaks Circle, Palm Beach Gardens FL 33410 **August R S Chris Sum Chap Winter Harbor ME 2009-** B New York NY 3/10/1940 s Ralph Ray Warren & Virginia Sheridan. BA Trin 1962; STM Ya Berk 1965; Dplma in Pas Stu U of Birmingham GB 1966; DD Ya Berk 1989. D 6/12/1965 P 12/17/1966 Bp Horace W B Donegan. m 12/5/1998 Roselle Bettelley c 2. R The Epis Ch Of Beth-By-The-Sea Palm Bch FL 1982-2009; R S Paul's Epis Ch Pittsburgh PA 1977-1982; P-in-c S Jas Ch New York NY 1976; Asst S Jas Ch New York NY 1966-1977. Chapl Most Venerable Ord Hosp of S Jn in Jerusal 1978. Chapl Most Venerable Ord Hosp of S Jn 1983. hapwarren@priest.com

WARREN, Randall R (Chi) 65 E Huron St, Chicago IL 60611 **S Lk's Par Kalamazoo MI 2011-; Dir, Off of Pstr Care Dio Chicago Chicago IL 1998-** B Fort Lauderdale FL 8/24/1961 s Richard Earle Warren & Veneta Elizabeth. BA Milligan Coll 1983; MDiv SWTS 1986; ACPE Chr Hosp Oak Lawn IL 1987; CG Jung Inst 1992; DMin GTF 1997. D 6/17/1989 P 12/16/1989 Bp Frank Tracy Griswold III. Chr The King Ch Lansing IL 1999-2007; Trin Epis Ch Lansing IL 1996-1998; Ch Of The H Comm Maywood IL 1995-1996; Cler Team Mem Gr Ch Oak Pk IL 1992-1994; P-in-c H Trin Ch Skokie IL 1991-1992; Cur Ch Of Our Sav Elmhurst IL 1989-1990. Auth, "Incarnating Ch: The Liturg Redesign of a Sm Mssn Cong," *God's Friends*, St. Greg of Nyssa, 2004; Auth, "Contrib to," *Enriching Our Wrshp 2*, Ch Pub, 2000; Auth, "Connecting Themes through Liturg Seasons," *Open*, Associated Parishes, 1999; Auth, "Trsfg after the Bomb," *Pilgrimage mag*, Pilgrimage Press, 1998. The Nathan Newtork 2004. rrwolf1989@sbcglobal.net

WARREN, Robert Harold (SwFla) 2828-40th Avenue North, Saint Petersburg FL 33714 B Needham MA 4/26/1920 s Harold Warren & Annie. AA S Petersburg Jr Coll 1975; Dio Diac Prog 1978. D 10/18/1978 Bp Emerson Paul Haynes. m 8/2/1941 Agnes Wyllie Allardyce c 2. Asst S Bede's Ch St Petersburg FL 1980-1981; Asst S Mary's Epis Ch Palmetto FL 1979-1980; Asst Cathd Ch Of S Ptr St Petersburg FL 1978-1980. CBS.

WARREN, Thomas Paine Hopfengardner (EC) 800 Rountree Ave, Kinston NC 28501 **S Mary's Ch Kinston NC 2011-** B Cheverly MD 9/11/1981 s George Francis Warren & Sandra Hopfengardner. BS U.S. Coast Guard Acad 2003; MDiv Duke DS 2011. D 6/11/2011 Bp Clifton Daniel III. m 5/30/2004 Holly Alisha Carraway c 1. tom-ph-warren@hotmail.com

WARREN, Victoria Daniel (Nev) 305 N Minnesota St, Carson City NV 89703 **S Jn's In The Wilderness Ch Glenbrook NV 2011-** B Monroe OK 7/5/1947 d Robert E Daniel & Bonnie Vinson. BA Notre Dame Coll Belmont CA 1971; CTS CDSP 2005. D 10/24/2008 P 6/27/2009 Bp Dan Thomas Edwards. c 3. S Ptr's Epis Ch Carson City NV 2009-2011. vrwarren@pyramid.net

WARRINGTON, James Malcolm (Nwk) 2849 Meadow Ln, Falls Church VA 22042 B Boston MA 9/19/1926 s Lester Bowen Warrington & Helen Louise. BA VMI 1950; BD STUSo 1960; MBA FD 1966. D 6/28/1960 Bp Frederick D Goodwin P 7/1/1961 Bp Samuel B Chilton. Off Of Bsh For ArmdF New York NY 1966-1977; Asst Ch Of The Atone Tenafly NJ 1963-1964; Cur S Jn's Epis Ch McLean VA 1960-1963.

WARTER, Mark Wilkinson (RI) 155 Wickford Point Rd, Providence RI 02903 B New York NY 1/5/1948 s John Pennington Warter & Rosemary Crandall. BA Curry Coll Milton MA 1970; MEd Boston Coll 1976. D 6/14/2008 Bp Geralyn Wolf. m 8/16/1969 Edith Alfieri Edith Alfieri c 2. D Cathd Of S Jn Providence RI 2008-2010. mwarter@frontiersearch.com

WARTHAN, Frank Avery (Chi) 298 S Harrison Ave, Kankakee IL 60901 B Dinwiddie County VA 4/7/1938 s Linwood Riichard Warthan & Elizabeth. BS Marymount Coll 1972. D 10/5/1975 P 4/10/1976 Bp William Davidson. m 7/5/1980 Toni Disque. R S Paul's Ch Kankakee IL 1999-2009; St Philips Epis Ch Waukesha WI 1995-1998; Non-par Dio Milwaukee Milwaukee WI 1988-1999; Vic Chr Ch Kingman KS 1983-1988; Dio Wstrn Kansas Hutchinson KS 1983-1988; Vic Gr Ch Anth KS 1983-1988; Vic S Mk's Ch Pratt KS 1983-1988; Assoc S Thos Ch Garden City KS 1981-1982; Assoc Chr Ch Kingman KS 1979-1982; Assoc Gr Ch Anth KS 1979-1982; Assoc S Mk's Ch Pratt KS 1979-1982; S Fran Cmnty Serv Inc. Salina KS 1975-1977. frankrwarthan1731@comcast.net

WARWICK, Eilene R (Miss) 25 Twelve Oaks Dr, Madison MS 39110 B Jackson MS 12/16/1931 d Carroll Robinson & Jane Percy. BA Belhaven Coll 1956; MA Mississippi Coll 1973; EFM STUSo 1997. D 1/15/2000 Bp Alfred Clark Marble Jr. m 1/10/1953 Charles Warwick c 3. Recovery Mnstrs of the Epis Ch 1998. eilenewarwick@aol.com

WARWICK-SABINO, Debra Ann (NCal) 1405 Kentucky St, Fairfield CA 94533 **Title IV Coordntr Dio Nthrn California Sacramento CA 2010-; R Gr Epis Ch Fairfield CA 2004-; Safe Ch Coordntr Dio Nthrn California Sacramento CA 2003-** B Detroit MI 8/30/1952 d William Edward Dunne & Nancy Virginia. BS Estrn Michigan U; MA PSR; MDiv PSR 1993; MA PSR 1994. D 10/18/1998 P 5/16/1999 Bp Jerry Alban Lamb. m 11/12/1993 Robert Lewis Sabino c 5. Chr Formation Dir Dio Nthrn California Sacramento CA 2000-2007; Asst R Ch Of S Mart Davis CA 1999-2004; Asst Cur Trin Epis Ch Reno NV 1998-1999. Coll of Chapl. revdeb3@mac.com

WAS, Brent Gavin (Mass) 120 Main St, Amesbury MA 01913 **Cur S Jas Ch Amesbury MA 2011-** B Bad Kreuznach Germany 6/30/1971 s Robert Allan Was & Barbara Elizabeth. BA Carnegie Mellon U 1993; MDiv Harvard DS 2005; DMin EDS 2010. D 1/8/2011 P 6/25/2011 Bp M(arvil) Thomas Shaw III. m 8/26/2006 Windy Marie Dayton c 3. S Jn's Chap Cambridge MA 2006-2011. bwas@riseup.net

WASDYKE, Wesley Roger (NH) 6569 The Masters Ave, Lakewood Ranch FL 34202 **Gr Ch Manchester NH 1980-** B Passaic NJ 7/19/1942 s Bernard Tunas Wasdyke & Cecelia Anne. Intern 76-77 Res 77-79 Burlington VT; BA Hope Coll 1964; MDiv EDS 1969; MD Washington U 1976; Cert Amer Bd Anesth 1981. D 6/21/1969 Bp Anson Phelps Stokes Jr P 1/5/1970 Bp Roger W Blanchard. m 7/20/1968 Cynthia Spinney c 2. Asst S Bon Ch Sarasota FL 2006-2010; S Mary Magd Lakewood Ranch FL 2003-2005; Asst S Mich & S Geo Clayton MO 1975-1976; Asst Ch Of The H Comm U City MO 1972-1973; Asst Epis Soc of Chr Ch Cincinnati OH 1969-1972. wwasdyke@verizon.net

WASHAM JR, Charles W (Lex) 695 Windings Lane, Cincinnati OH 45220 **Psych Epis Cnslng Serv Dio Lexington Lexington KY 1994-** B Oceanside CA 7/9/1952 s Charles W Washam & Sherry L. BA Albertson Coll 1974; Duke 1975; MDiv VTS 1977; CPE Epis TS of The SW 1978; Advncd CPE 1981; Emory U 1983; M. Ed. Georgia St U 1984; DMin GTF 1989; MSW U of Kentucky 1998. D 6/18/1977 Bp Hunley Agee Elebash P 1/15/1978 Bp John Harris Burt. m 7/6/1989 Constance J Jordan c 1. Ch Of The H Trin Georgetown KY 2005-2006; Ch Of The Gd Shpd Lexington KY 1994; Gr And S Steph's Epis Ch Colorado Sprg CO 1992-1993; Dio Lexington Lexington KY 1991-2008; Heathwood Hall Epis Sch Columbia SC 1989-1991; Psych S Anne's Epis Ch Atlanta GA 1984-1989; Pace Acad Atlanta GA 1983-1984; Chap Of S Andr Boca Raton FL 1980-1982; S Andew's Sch Boca Raton FL 1980-1982; S Tim's Epis Ch Massillon OH 1979-1980; S Steph's Epis Sch Austin TX 1978-1979; Cur S Jn's Ch Youngstown OH 1977-1978. ACPE 1983. charleswwasham@aol.com

WASHINGTON, Derek Wayne (Eau) 931 Leroy Ct, River Falls WI 54022 B Sumter SC 11/14/1960 s Will E Washington & Mary E. BD/RN U of No Florida 1990; MDiv TESM 1996. D 6/13/1996 P 12/8/1996 Bp Stephen Hays Jecko. m 11/12/1994 Dorothy A McGinnis c 3. S Paul's Ch Hudson WI 2005-2007; Angl Frontier Missions Richmond VA 2000-2005; Asst Ch Of The Adv Tallahassee FL 1996-2000. Auth, "Album: Passion In The Dark," In-To-Me-See Mus, 2003; Auth, "Album: The Shpd'S Heart," In-To-Me-See Mus, 2000; Auth, "We Shall Be Like Him (Album)," In-To-Me-See Mus. Soc For The Preservation And Encouragement Of The Barbershop Quartet 1973. derekwashington@barnabas.org

WASHINGTON SR, Emery (Mo) 1267 Mohave Dr, Saint Louis MO 63132 B Palestine AR 2/27/1935 s Booker Taliafero Washington & Fannie Mae. BA Philander Smith 1957; MDiv VTS 1961; DD Eden TS 2002. D 7/20/1961 P 6/14/1962 Bp Robert Raymond Brown. m 10/1/1965 Alice Marie Bogard c 3. R All SS Ch S Louis MO 1983-2001; Emm Ch Memphis TN 1977-1983; S Mich's Epis Ch Little Rock AR 1972-1976; Ecum Off & Cn Mssn Dio Arkansas Little Rock AR 1971-1976; P-in-c Chr Epis Ch Forrest City AR 1962-1971. Congregations Allied for Cmnty Dvlpmt 1999; Dep to Six Gnrl Conventions 1969; Metropltn Ch Untd 1999; NAACP 1965; Natl Concerns Cmsn 2000-2003; Natl Coun on Soc & Spec Mnstrs 1985-1991; UBE 1965; Urban League 1988. Bp's Awd for Outstanding Serv Dio Missouri 2001; Citizen's Awd Human Serv Corp 2001; A Salute to Black Men Alpha Kappa Alpha-Alpha Nu Cp. 1996; Publ Serv Awd- Ldrshp Alpha Phi Alpha 1996; Serv Awd Mart Luther King, Jr. St Com 1995; Literacy Awd Alpha Kappa Alpha-Gamma Cp. 1990; Serv Awd S Louis Black Pages 1985; Amer Outstanding Cleric Dio Ark Ldrshp Dio Arkansas 1970. ewash@sbcglobal.net

WASHINGTON, Joyce D (NY) 657 E 222nd St, Bronx NY 10467 **D S Phil's Ch New York NY 1998-** B Norfolk VA 12/3/1927 d Amos Dodson & Mattie Montella. Bank St Coll of Educ; BA VTS 1950; MA Hampton U 1963. D 5/16/1998 Bp Richard Frank Grein. m 12/22/1967 Booker T Washington. NAAD.

WASHINGTON, Lynne Eaton (Va) 8076 Crown Colony Pkwy, Mechanicsville VA 23116 **Ptr Paul Dvlpmt Cntr Of The Epis Ch Richmond VA 2006-** B Washington DC 5/18/1962 d John Eaton & Margaret Elizabeth. Franklin U 1984; MDiv GTS 1997; BS S Paul Coll 1997. D 3/18/1997 Bp Frank Harris Vest Jr P 9/27/1997 Bp David Conner Bane Jr. m 8/27/1995 Larry Hancock Washington c 3. Dio Virginia Richmond VA 1999-2006; Asst to Bp for Outreach & Witness Dio Virginia Richmond VA 1998-2006; S Mich's Ch Bon Air VA 1996-1998. jnwashington09@gmail.com

WASINGER, Douglas Edward (Wyo) 710 13th St, Rawlins WY 82301 **Mnstry Dvlp Dio Wyoming Casper WY 2003-** B San Francisco CA 4/9/1969 s Harold Edwin Wasinger & Anita Jill. BA Ft Lewis Coll 1992; MDiv Epis TS of The SW 2003. D 6/26/2003 P 1/13/2004 Bp Bruce Edward Caldwell. m 1/1/2000 Kellie Marie Snell c 3. d9568wasinger@gmail.com

WASTLER, Mark William (Md) 12 Lockhart Ln, Bentonville VA 22610 **S Paul's Ch Sharpsburg MD 2010-** B Gettysburg PA 1/5/1967 s Clarence

William Wastler & Frances Elizabeth. BA Mssh Coll 1992; MDiv EDS 1999. D 6/12/1999 P 12/4/1999 Bp Robert Wilkes Ihloff. S Marg's Ch Annapolis MD 2003-2008; Par Of The Epiph Winchester MA 1999-2003. markwastler@hotmail.com

WATAN, Jay Sapaen (Cal) 900 Edgewater Blvd, Foster City CA 94404 **Exec Coun Mem Dio California San Francisco CA 2009-; Yth Min & Chapl S Ambr Epis Ch Foster City CA 2006-** B San Francisco CA 6/28/1971 s Pedro Puclay Watan & Dolores Sapaen. BA San Francisco St U 1996; MDiv CDSP 2007. D 6/3/2006 Bp William Edwin Swing P 6/2/2007 Bp Marc Handley Andrus. m 7/8/2000 Lilian Bulahao-Watan c 1. Yth Min Ch Of The Epiph San Carlos CA 2002-2005; Yth Min H Chld At S Mart Epis Ch Daly City CA 1993-1996. igorothighlander@hotmail.com

WATERS, Elliott Michael (Pa) 325 Cameron Station Blvd, Alexandria VA 22304 **Ch Of The Annuniciation Philadelphia PA 2004-** B Crisfield MD 4/30/1947 s Grover Harrison Waters & Ella Mae. BS Morgan St U 1969; MS USC 1980; MDiv VTS 2001. D 6/23/2001 P 12/29/2001 Bp Peter James Lee. m 8/31/1968 Barbara H Horton-Savory. Ch Of The H Cross Dunn Loring VA 2003-2004; S Paul's Epis Ch Alexandria VA 2001-2003. emwaters@earthlink.net

WATERS, Margaret Hunkin (Tex) 4902 Ridge Oak Dr, Austin TX 78731 **R S Alb's Epis Ch Austin Manchaca TX 2005-** B Cleveland OH 8/21/1946 BA Stan; MDiv Epis TS of The SW 2000. D 10/19/2002 P 7/5/2003 Bp Don Adger Wimberly. m 12/22/1991 John Bennet Waters c 4. Assoc S Dav's Ch Austin TX 2002-2005. mwaters821@gmail.com

WATERS, Sonia E (Nwk) 369 Sand Shore Rd, Budd Lake NJ 07828 **Chr Ch Budd Lake NJ 2009-** B Sussex 2/3/1972 d Anthony Waters & Marilyn. BA Wheaton Coll 1994; MDiv GTS 2005. D 6/11/2005 Bp Chester Lovelle Talton P 4/1/2006 Bp Joseph Jon Bruno. m John A Mennell. Asst Gr Ch Brooklyn NY 2005-2008. swaters@gracebrooklyn.org

WATKINS, Gilbert (WVa) 2721 Riverside Dr, Saint Albans WV 25177 B Birmingham England UK 1/1/1930 s Herbert H Watkins & Belle. Mercer TS 1973; Ya Berk 1974. D 6/10/1974 Bp Robert Poland Atkinson P 12/1/1974 Bp Wilburn Camrock Campbell. m 8/18/1951 Monica A c 4. Part Time S Ptr's Ch Huntington WV 1999-2009; Archd Dio W Virginia Charleston WV 1991-1994; R S Mk's Epis Ch S Albans WV 1978-1993; R S Pauls Epis Ch Williamson WV 1974-1978. FrGil@suddenlink.net

WATKINS, James William (SanD) 750 State St Unit 203, San Diego CA 92116 **Died 1/14/2010** B Bellefontaine OH 2/21/1934 s John Firman Watkins & Ethel May. BA OH SU 1956; MDiv Bex 1959. D 6/11/1959 P 12/1/1959 Bp John P Craine. c 2. jwatkipr@cox.net

WATKINS, Jane Hill (CGC) 8332 Bocowood Dr, Dallas TX 75228 **H Trin Epis Ch Pensacola FL 2003-** B Kansas City MO 9/2/1946 d Ralph Emerson Hill & Jane. BA SMU 1964; STL GTS 1986; CTh Epis TS of The SW 1989. D 6/17/1989 P 5/19/1990 Bp Donis Dean Patterson. m 6/27/1970 John Kenneth Watkins c 2. S Matt's Cathd Dallas TX 1999-2003; Int S Mary's Epis Ch Texarkana TX 1997-1998; Vic S Ptr's By The Lake Ch The Colony TX 1993-1997; Epis Sch Of Dallas Dallas TX 1991-1993. Tertiary Of The Soc Of S Fran 1994. jandy4@cox.net

WATKINS, LeeAnne Ingeborg (Minn) 1895 Laurel Ave, Saint Paul MN 55104 **R S Mary's Ch St Paul MN 1998-** B Great Falls MT 7/16/1966 d Bruce Lincoln Watkins & Ardelle Carleen. BA U of Montana 1990; MDiv CDSP 1993. D 7/19/1993 Bp Charles Jones III P 1/29/1994 Bp Sanford Zangwill Kaye Hampton. m 7/8/2009 David Harold Dorn c 1. Assoc R Ch Of The Ascen Stillwater MN 1993-1998. rector@saintmarysepiscopal.org

WATKINS, Linda King (CPa) 407 Greenwood St, Mont Alto PA 17237 **R S Mary's Epis Ch Waynesboro PA 2006-** B Dayton OH 11/25/1956 d Cameron Wesley King & Jeanne. BA SUNY 1979; MA MI SU 1981; MDiv GTS 1997. D 6/21/1997 Bp Frank Tracy Griswold III P 1/7/1998 Bp David B(ruce) Joslin. m 9/3/2000 Kenneth G Watkins. Vic S Ann's Ch Afton NY 1999-2006; Vic S Ptr's Ch Bainbridge NY 1999-2006. Third Ord Soc of S Fran 1994. rileydude607@hotmail.com

WATKINS, Lucien Alexander (SwFla) 1545 54th Ave S, Saint Petersburg FL 33705 **Archd S Thos' Epis Ch St Petersburg FL 1999-** B AG 3/28/1938 s Lissue Watkins & Doreen. D 6/12/1999 Bp John Bailey Lipscomb. m 11/19/1983 Barbara Dianne Wiltshire. lwatk94736@aol.com

WATROUS, Janet Couper (NC) 415 S Boylan Ave, Raleigh NC 27603 **Chr Ch Binghamton NY 2011-** B New York NY 2/17/1950 d Joseph Bert Watrous & Katharine. Kirkland Coll 1970; BA U Of E Anglia Norwich Gb 1972; MDiv EDS 1977. D 6/16/1977 P 6/22/1978 Bp Ned Cole. m 5/14/1977 Robert Charles Kochersberger Jr c 2. S Paul's Ch Montrose PA 2009; St Elizabeths Epis Ch Apex NC 2007-2008; R St Elizabeths Epis Ch Apex NC 2006-2007; All SS Ch Frederick MD 2006; Int Emm Par Epis Ch And Day Sch Sthrn Pines NC 2005-2006; Assoc R St Elizabeths Epis Ch Apex NC 2004-2005; Dio No Carolina Raleigh NC 2001-2003; Dir New Congrl Dvlpmt Dio No Carolina Raleigh NC 2001-2002; Int S Andr's Ch Greensboro NC 1999-2000; R S Mart's Epis Ch Charlotte NC 1998-1999; Ch Of The Gd Shpd Raleigh NC 1994-1998; P-in-c Gr Epis Ch Elmira NY 1984-1985; S Fran' Ch Norris TN 1984; P-in-c S Fran' Ch Norris TN 1983-1984; P-in-c Chr Ch Wellsburg NY 1981-1983; P-in-c Gr Ch Waverly NY 1981-1983; P-in-c Gr Ch Cortland NY 1979-1980. Bd Nceca 1994; Bd/ Pres EWHP 1992-1998. Wmn Of Achievement Awd 1978. revjanw@earthlink.net

WATSON, Charles Evan (RG) 535 Monte Vista Ave, Las Cruces NM 88005 **Died 7/20/2009** B Pampa TX 4/9/1936 s Herbert Hadley Watson & Verna Jo. BFA New Mex St U. 1966; MA New Mex St U. 1968; TESM 2001. D 7/28/2001 Bp Terence Kelshaw. m 8/8/1958 Betty Louise Watson c 2.

WATSON, Chester Franklin (Cal) 3104 Claudia Dr, Concord CA 94519 **Asst S Mich And All Ang Concord CA 1996-** B Crenshaw MS 7/12/1927 s Benjamin Franklin Watson & Mary Thersa (sic). Cert California Sch for Deacons 1978; BA Sch for Deacons 1983; Cert CDSP 1990. D 2/16/1980 P 6/8/1991 Bp William Edwin Swing. m 6/3/1950 Doris Eileen Parks. Asst S Giles Ch Moraga CA 1991-1996; D/Asst S Mich And All Ang Concord CA 1980-1981. watsoncord@aol.com

WATSON, Faith Elizabeth (Spok) 8735 Colgin Rd, Howard OH 43028 B Waymart PA 12/12/1923 d Alexis K Revera & Emelia Joanne. MT U MI 1945. D 6/11/1980 Bp Leigh Wallace Jr. c 5. Assoc Gr Ch Ellensburg WA 1980-1985.

WATSON, George Stennis (WTenn) 600 Bellevue Ave E Apt 103, Seattle WA 98102 **Assoc Chr Ch SEATTLE WA 2007-** B Tupelo MS 12/2/1953 s George Barrett Watson & Ethel Jeannette. BA Millsaps Coll 1975; MDiv Harvard DS 1979; Cert GTS 1980; MA U of Mississippi 1996; PhD U of Mississippi 1999. D 6/7/1980 P 5/1/1981 Bp Duncan Montgomery Gray Jr. Ch Of The H Comm Memphis TN 1988-1989; Vic The Epis Ch Of The Gd Shpd Columbus MS 1982-1988; Cur Ch of the H Trin Vicksburg MS 1980-1982. gstenniswatson@aol.com

WATSON, Jack Lee (Fla) Po Box 788, Cedar Key FL 32625 **Chr Ch Cedar Key FL 2000-** B Cedar Key FL 6/14/1935 s Joseph Emory Watson & Verona Mildred. BS Florida St U 1957; U So 1961. D 6/14/1961 P 4/1/1962 Bp Edward Hamilton West. m 7/29/1972 Tari B Watson c 1. S Alb's Epis Ch Chiefland FL 1990-1997; R S Paul's Ch Edneyville NC 1980-1989; Vic Ch Of The Epiph Laurens SC 1975-1980; P-in-c Ch Of The Gd Shpd Hayesville NC 1967-1975; P-in-c Ch Of The Mssh Murphy NC 1967-1975; M-in-c S Mk's Ch Chattahoochee FL 1961-1967. watson32625@aol.com

WATSON, James Darrell (Tex) 1101 Tiffany Ln, Longview TX 75604 B Vancouver WA 8/31/1945 s Boyd Jasper Watson & Frances Irene. BA U of Texas 1972; ThM Dallas TS 1977; EdD Texas A&M U 1981. D 6/24/2006 Bp Don Adger Wimberly P 1/27/2007 Bp Rayford Baines High Jr. m 8/24/1968 Sarah Cheney c 4. jimwatson@letu.edu

WATSON, Joan Ruth (NJ) 7 N Wendover Ave, Medford NJ 08055 B Runnemede NJ 3/7/1936 d Charles Edward Watson & Isabel. BA Rider Coll 1978; MSW U of Pennsylvania 1980; MDiv GTS 1984. D 3/30/1985 P 10/1/1985 Bp Vincent King Pettit. Int R Gr Ch Merchantville NJ 2008-2009; R Gr Ch Pemberton NJ 1989-2005; Asst P S Barth's Ch Cherry Hill NJ 1985-1989. revjoanwatson@earthlink.net

WATSON III, John R (NwT) 2700 W 16th Ave Apt 314, Amarillo TX 79102 B Haskell TX 11/5/1942 s John R Watson & Rosa Lucille. BA U of Texas 1970; MDiv Epis TS of The SW 1987. D 6/17/1987 Bp Anselmo Carral-Solar P 4/1/1988 Bp Gordon Taliaferro Charlton. m 11/26/1966 Lesley Schumacher. Dio NW Texas Lubbock TX 2007; S Ptr's Epis Ch Amarillo TX 1999-2007; Trin Ch Potsdam NY 1995-1999; R H Trin Epis Ch Thermopolis WY 1990-1995; Asst Calv Epis Ch Richmond TX 1987-1989.

WATSON, Karen Elizabeth (Neb) 925 S. 84th St., Omaha NE 68114 B Omaha NE 11/5/1946 d Louis Wells & Elizabeth. BS U of Nebraska Lincoln 1971; MA Creighton U 2005; CAS CDSP 2009. D 10/28/2009 P 5/6/2010 Bp Joe Goodwin Burnett. c 3. Cur S Andr's Ch Omaha NE 2009-2010. krnwtsn78@gmail.com

WATSON, Margaret (Va) 3216 Kensington Avenue, Richmond VA 23221 **R S Mk's Ch Richmond VA 2005-** B Berkeley CA 3/14/1956 d Alvin Sargent Hambly & Joan. BA Sonoma St U Rohnert Pk 1991; MA U Of Delaware, Winterthur 1993; MDiv CDSP 2003. D 4/26/2003 Bp Robert Louis Ladehoff P 11/15/2003 Bp Gethin Benwil Hughes. m 9/5/1981 S B Joel Watson. Asst R For CE & Formation S Marg's Epis Ch Palm Desert CA 2003-2005. Scholarships Soc For The Increase Of Mnstry 2001. rector@stmarksrichmond.org

WATSON, Richard Avery (SVa) 9 Westwood Drive, East Haddam CT 06469 B Hartford CT 3/17/1937 s Arthur Avery Watson & Helen M. BA Dart 1959; MDiv Gordon-Conwell TS 1983; DMin Wesley TS 1999. P 1/22/1989 Bp Douglas Edwin Theuner. m 12/13/1986 Susan Lovejoy c 3. Int Calv Ch Bath Par Dinwiddie VA 2000-2003; Int Ch Of The Gd Shpd Bath Par Mc Kenney VA 2000-2003; R Chr Ch Xenia OH 1993-2000; Par Of S Jas Ch Keene NH 1992. shamwari@comcast.net

WATSON, Robert William (Ct) 52 Missionary Rd # 22, Cromwell CT 06416 **Assoc St Gabr's Ch E Berlin CT 2001-** B Greenwich CT 6/27/1930 s Robert William Watson & Jessie Pearl. BA U of New Hampshire 1953; MDiv Ya Berk 1956; DMin S Mary Sem & U Baltimore MD 1986. D 6/14/1956 P 6/14/1957 Bp Walter H Gray. c 3. R S Chris Epis Ch Linthicum Heights MD 1974-1994; R Bp Seabury Ch Groton CT 1965-1974; R H Trin Epis Ch

Enfield CT 1958-1965; Cur S Jn's Ch Stamford CT 1956-1958; Vic S Lk's Par Darien CT 1956-1958. RMacWat@aol.com

WATSON JR, S B Joel (LI) 3216 Kensington Ave, Richmond VA 23221 B Toronto ON CA 11/16/1944 s Shelley Burch Watson & Alice Wingfield. Randolph-Macon Coll 1963; BA Frederick Coll Portsmouth VA 1967; Mercer TS 1973. D 6/26/1976 Bp C Kilmer Myers P 6/11/1977 Bp Chilton Powell. m 9/5/1981 Margaret Hambly. Dio Oregon Portland OR 2000-2002; Vic S Mart's Ch Shady Cove OR 1996-2003; Assoc Ch Of The Incarn Santa Rosa CA 1989-1990; R Ch Of The Ascen Greenpoint Brooklyn NY 1981-1982; Tutor The GTS New York NY 1979-1983; Asst Ch Of The H Innoc San Francisco CA 1976-1977. Auth, "The Reverend Geo Young & His Descendents 1749-1962". jwatson@jeffnet.org

WATSON, Suzanne Elizabeth (SanD) 2135 Coast Blvd, Del Mar CA 92014 **Corp Dio San Diego San Diego CA 2011-; First Alt to GC Dio San Diego San Diego CA 2011-; P-in-c S Dav's Epis Ch San Diego CA 2010-** B Burbank CA 2/28/1962 d Park Willoughby Richardson & Maureen. BS U CA 1985; MA California St Polytechnic U 1991; MDiv CDSP 2002. D 6/22/2002 P 3/29/2003 Bp Richard Lester Shimpfky. c 4. Epis Ch Cntr New York NY 2006-2010; Stff Off For Congr Dvlpmt-Sm Mem Ch Epis Ch Cntr New York NY 2005-2008; Assoc S Dunst's Epis Ch Carmel Vlly CA 2003-2004. Auth, "Article," *ATR*, 2009; Auth, "Creative Models of Sacramental Ldrshp," Epis Books & Resources, 2008; Auth, "Sm Ch Growth Strtgy Handbook," Epis Books & Resources, 2007. Seal of the Angl Dio the Waikato Angl Dio the Waikato, New Zealand 2004. revsuzannewatson@gmail.com

WATSON, Wendy (NCal) 990 Mee Lane, St Helena CA 94574 B Berkeley CA 3/5/1948 d James Bagby Watson & Margaret. BA U CA 1970; MDiv VTS 1983. D 6/25/1983 Bp William Edwin Swing P 5/11/1984 Bp Lyman Cunningham Ogilby. S Lk's Ch Woodland CA 2006-2007; Int S Paul's Epis Ch Walnut Creek CA 2005-2006; Int S Paul's Epis Ch Benicia CA 2003-2005; Int H Faith Par Inglewood CA 2001-2003; Assoc S Wilfrid Of York Epis Ch Huntington Bch CA 1997-2001; Ch Of The Mssh Santa Ana CA 1993-1997; Dio Los Angeles Los Angeles CA 1992; Ch Of The Ascen Tujunga CA 1990-1991; Asst Chr Ch Philadelphia Philadelphia PA 1989; Asst to R Ch Of The Redeem Bryn Mawr PA 1983-1988. rector@stlukewoodland.org

WATSON, William Breese (Ore) 3721 Hillview Dr Se, Salem OR 97302 **Died 6/15/2011** B Louisville KY 8/2/1924 s William Albert Watson & Rachel Breese. BA U So 1950; LTh Bex 1953. D 6/9/1953 Bp Nelson Marigold Burroughs P 12/1/1953 Bp James W Hunter. c 2. Chapl Ord of S Lk 1969-1998. WATB@CHEMEKETA.EDU

WATSON III, William John (SwVa) PO Box 3123, Lynchburg VA 24503 **S Jn's Ch Lynchburg VA 2010-** B Woodbury NJ 5/16/1951 s William John Watson & Elisabeth Marie. BA U of Virginia 1973; Med U of Virginia 1975; MD Estrn Virginia Med Sch Norfolk VA 1979; MDiv VTS 2003. D 2/15/2003 P 8/15/2003 Bp Edwin Funsten Gulick Jr. m 5/25/1974 Sally Turner c 3. R Gr Ch Hopkinsville KY 2003-2010. Harris Awd VTS 2003. bill@stjohnslynchburg.org

WATSON EPTING, Susanne K (Ia) 3026 Middle Road, Davenport IA 52803 B Muscatine IA 8/25/1949 d Stanley Leon Freyermuth & Bettie Louise. U of Iowa 1970; BS U MN 1975; MA U of Iowa 1989. D 11/4/1989 Bp Carl Christopher Epting. m 11/9/2001 Carl Christopher Epting c 2. Proclaiming Educ for All Exec & Secy Off New York NY 2004-2008; Primates T/F on Theol Educ Dio Cbury London 2004-2007; Cn to the Ordnry Dio Iowa Des Moines IA 1996-2001; Dir Inst for Chr Stds Dio Iowa Des Moines IA 1991-1996. Auth, "Beijing Circles," *Resource Guide*, Epis Ch Cntr, 2006; Auth, "Hannah Rose," *Wmn Uncommon Prayers*, Morehouse Pub, 2000; Auth, "Formation of Ministering Christians," *(monograph)*, NAAD, 1999. Convenor, Living Stories Dioc Partnership 1998-2000; NAAD 1995; Pres, NAAD 1999-2001. Isabel Turner Human Rts Awd 1996. skwatsonepting@aol.com

WATT, Gilbert Merwin (Pgh) 396 Woodlands Dr, Verona PA 15147 B IN 3/7/1921 s James Watt & Shirley. BA Washington and Jefferson U 1942; Wstrn TS 1948; Bex 1949. D 6/15/1949 P 12/1/1949 Bp Austin Pardue. c 2. S Paul's Ch Monongahela PA 1984-1985; S Dav's Epis Ch Venetia PA 1951-1984.

WATT, Jackie (At) 605 Dunwoody Chace Ne, Atlanta GA 30328 B Asheville NC 12/5/1935 d Bill Green Tyndale & Katherine. Candler TS Emory U; BS STUSo; BS U GA 1957. D 10/23/1993 Bp J(ohn) Neil Alexander. m 9/14/1957 John F Watt c 4. H Innoc Ch Atlanta GA 2007-2008; D H Innoc Ch Atlanta GA 1993-2009. Apc; Assn Death Educ & Counslg; ACPE. jackiewatt1@bellsouth.net

WATT, Jim (Tex) Rr 6 Box 88-E, Mission TX 78574 B Houston TX 3/29/1935 s James Henry Silas Watt & Eleanor. BA Rice U 1957; BD Epis TS of The SW 1960. D 6/28/1960 P 5/1/1961 Bp Frederick P Goddard. R S Jn's Epis Ch Columbus TX 1963-1978; Vic S Jas' Epis Ch La Grange TX 1963-1968; R Calv Epis Ch Bastrop TX 1960-1963; Vic S Jas' Epis Ch La Grange TX 1960-1961. Auth, "Sacrifice Of Glory". JHW10@EARTH-COMM.COM

WATTON, Sharon Louise (Mich) PoBox 80643, Rochester MI 48308 **D Cathd Ch Of S Paul Detroit MI 2010-; D The Epis Ch Of The Adv W Bloomfield MI 2001-** B Detroit MI 8/9/1945 d Richard Thomas Murphy & Jeanne Marie. Whitaker TS 2000. D 6/16/2001 Bp Wendell Nathaniel Gibbs Jr. c 3. D S Phil's Epis Ch Rochester MI 2006-2009; Dio Michigan Detroit MI 1997-2009. N.A.A.D. 2001; OHC 2001. sharonwatton@comcast.net

WATTS, Charles Melvin (O) 4113 West State Street, Route 73, Wilmington OH 45177 **Chr Epis Ch Dayton OH 2006-** B Mattoon IL 12/29/1948 s Garland Leon Watts & Betty Lou. BS Mississippi St U 1972; MDiv STUSo 1977; Securities Exch Cmsn 1990; AAM Coll for Fin Plnng 2002; CRPC Coll for Fin Plnng 2004. D 6/4/1978 P 1/4/1980 Bp Duncan Montgomery Gray Jr. m 5/29/1969 Mary Ogles c 1. S Fran Epis Ch Springboro OH 1990-2009; R S Paul Epis Ch Norwalk OH 1983-1990; Vic S Lk and S Jn's Caruthersville MO 1981-1983; Asst S Lk's Ch Brandon MS 1979-1981; Vic S Ptr's By The Lake Brandon MS 1979-1981; D S Jas Ch Jackson MS 1978-1979. Rotary Intl Paul Harris Fell. bananasplit@cinci.rr.com

WATTS, Janice Diane (Az) 4370 Woodland Ave, Western Springs IL 60558 **All SS Of The Desert Epis Ch Sun City AZ 2010-** B Oakland CA 11/24/1950 d Richard Alden Hoffman & Mary Louise. BA U of W Florida; MDiv SWTS 2007. D 12/12/2009 P 6/13/2010 Bp Jeffrey Dean Lee. m 6/10/1971 Patrick Watts c 2. Reverend All SS Ch Wstrn Sprg IL 2009-2010. jdw1124@gmail.com

WATTS, Marilyn Ruth (Haw) No address on file. **Vic S Phil's Ch Maili Waianae HI 1988-** B Denver CO 1/26/1946 d Charles Alfred Watts & Carolyn. BA Col 1971; Med U of Hawaii 1975; MDiv SFTS 1977. D 2/14/1988 P 6/1/1988 Bp Donald Purple Hart. m 12/21/1974 John Totten Norris. CHS.

WATTS, Robert William (Dal) 113 Summer View Ln, Pottsboro TX 75076 B Pontiac MI 1/31/1937 s Joseph Bernard Watts & Dorothy Laura. AA Oakland Cmnty Coll MI 1975; Whitaker TS 1993. D 10/27/1993 Bp James Monte Stanton. m 9/22/1956 Judith Ann Crawford c 3. D S Lk's Ch Denison TX 1993-2000.

WATTS, Timothy Joe (At) 3252 Green Farm Trl, Dacula GA 30019 **R S Mary And S Martha Ch Buford GA 2007-** B Munich FRG 6/29/1960 BS Troy St U 1984; MPA U of W Florida 1994; MDiv Epis TS of the SW 2004. D 6/12/2004 P 5/14/2005 Bp Philip Menzie Duncan II. m 11/1/1991 Alyce Stansill Watts c 2. Int S Jude's Epis Ch Niceville FL 2005-2006; S Jn The Evang Robertsdale AL 2004-2005. clergyofmm@bellsouth.net

WATTS JR, William Joseph (WMass) 19 Pleasant St, Chicopee MA 01013 **P-in-c S Lk's Ch Woodsville NH 2007-** B Boston MA 8/21/1943 s William Joseph Watts & Berthe Emma. BA U of Virginia 1965; MDiv EDS 1976. Trans from Anglican Church of Canada 4/1/1981 Bp John Bowen Coburn. m 6/8/1967 Noreen Coyne. R Gr Ch Chicopee MA 1988-2007; R Ch Of The H Trin Marlborough MA 1981-1987.

WAUTERS JR, John William (Los) 2449 Sichel Street, Los Angeles CA 90031 B Long Branch NJ 4/9/1949 s John William Wauters & Mary Elizabeth. BA Stan 1971; MDiv CDSP 1980. D 6/28/1980 P 5/29/1981 Bp William Edwin Swing. m 6/26/1976 Anna Guerra c 2. Dn , Dnry 4 Dio Los Angeles Los Angeles CA 2005-2009; Asst Trin Cathd Trenton NJ 1997-2003; Dio W Texas San Antonio TX 1991-1996; Vic Santa Fe Epis Mssn San Antonio TX 1991-1996; Ch Of The Gd Samar San Francisco CA 1985-1991; Vic Iglesia Epis Del Buen Samaritano San Francisco CA 1985-1991; ACTS/VIM Newark NJ 1983-1984; S Jn Jersey City NJ 1982-1984; St Stephens Ch Newark NJ 1982-1983; Ch Of The Epiph Los Angeles CA 1980-1981. Contrib, *Shocking Violence*, 2000. willwauters@yahoo.com

WAVE, John E (CGC) 3615 Phillips Ln, Panama City FL 32404 B Manistee MI 9/6/1934 s Hjalmar Conrad Wave & Bessie Marie. BS Florida St U 1957; MS Florida St U 1963; MDiv STUSo 1967. D 6/29/1967 P 6/26/1968 Bp Edward Hamilton West. m 8/31/1955 Mary J Williams c 3. Int P for Pstr Care H Nativ Epis Ch Panama City FL 2004-2005; Int S Jas' Epis Ch Port S Joe FL 2001-2002; Supply P Trin Ch Apalachicola FL 1999-2000; S Andr's Epis Ch Panama City FL 1994-1998; Supply P Ch Of The Epiph Crestview FL 1986-1989; Supply P S Agatha's Epis Ch Defuniak Sprg FL 1986-1989; R S Agnes Epis Ch Franklin NC 1980-1984; S Jude's Epis Ch Niceville FL 1968-1980; D-in-trng S Paul's By-The-Sea Epis Ch Jacksonville Bch FL 1967-1968. maryjohn728@aol.com

WAWERU, Christine G (LI) 215 Forward Support Battalion, Battalion & 74th St, Fort Hood TX 76544 B 11/24/1965 m 12/3/1988 David Waweru c 2. Off Of Bsh For ArmdF New York NY 2003-2011. christine.g.waweru@us.army.mil

WAWERU, David (LI) 2142 Modoc Dr, Harker Heights TX 76548 **Off Of Bsh For ArmdF New York NY 1994-** B Kiambu KE 6/30/1959 s Francis Waweru & Esther. Cert Bp Kariuki Bible Coll/U Nairobi Rel & T 1987; BD S Paul Theol Coll 1989; ThM PrTS 1993. Trans 9/27/1994 Bp Orris George Walker Jr. m 12/3/1988 Christine G Muchuuthi. P-in-c S Steph's Ch Jersey City NJ 1993-1994; Asst to R S Mk's Ch W Orange NJ 1992-1994.

WAY, Harry Lauren (Az) 4102 W Union Hills Dr, Glendale AZ 85308 **R S Jn The Bapt Epis Ch Glendale AZ 2001-** B Long Beach CA 9/2/1948 s Wallace J Way & Mary G. BA Phillips U 1970; MDiv Epis TS of The SW 1973. D 6/16/1973 Bp Chilton Powell P 12/1/1973 Bp Frederick Warren Putnam. m 12/26/1970 Patricia Totten c 2. R Ch Of S Thos Rawlins WY 1993-2001; R S

Andr's Ch La Junta CO 1986-1993; R S Jas' Epis Ch Fergus Falls MN 1984-1985; Trin Ch Wahpeton ND 1984-1985; Dio Montana Helena MT 1980-1984; Trin Ch Guthrie OK 1974-1976; S Jn The Bapt Epis Ch Glendale AZ 1973-1974; St Georges Ch Oklahoma City OK 1973-1974. wayfamwy@yahoo.com

WAY, Jacob Edson (NwT) 2807 42nd St., Lubbock TX 79413 **Dn, Llano Estacado Dnry Dio NW Texas Lubbock TX 2008-; R S Chris's Epis Ch Lubbock TX 2008-** B Chicago IL 5/18/1947 s Jacob Edson Way & Amelia Evans. BA Beloit Coll 1968; MA U Tor ON CA 1971; PhD U Tor ON CA 1978; MDiv Epis TS of the SW 2008. D 1/8/2008 P 6/28/2008 Bp C(harles) Wallis Ohl. m 9/6/1969 Jean Chappell Jean Ellwood Chappell c 3. jeway@earthlink.net

WAY, Michael (SO) 409 E. High St., Springfield OH 45505 **All SS Epis Ch New Albany OH 2010-** B Chillicothe OH 9/15/1959 s David Earl Way & Wanda Mae. BA Mia 1981; MDiv Bex 2010. D 6/13/2009 P 6/19/2010 Bp Thomas Edward Breidenthal. revway@gmail.com

WAY, Peter Trosdal (Va) Po Box 58, Keene VA 22946 **Assoc R S Anne's Par Scottsville VA 2002-** B Jacksonville FL 8/15/1936 s Thomas K Fitzpatrick & Beverley. Gri; U of Virginia; VTS. D 5/27/1972 Bp Robert Bruce Hall P 5/1/1973 Bp Robert Fisher Gibson Jr. m 1/25/1964 Elizabeth Crockett c 4. R Gr Ch Bremo Bluff VA 1977-1978; S Anne's Par Scottsville VA 1973-1977.

WAY SSJE, Russell (Mass) 6969 11 Mile Rd NE, Rockford MI 49341 B Sydney Mines Nova Scotia CA. 1/12/1924 s Rachel Mae. BA U Tor 1951; LTh U Tor 1953; U Tor 1953; BD Gnrl Syn of Can Wycliffe Coll Toronto ON CA 1955; STM Bos 1956. Trans from Anglican Church of Canada 6/1/1957 as Priest Bp Norman B Nash. m 6/23/2001 Linda Lee Ide c 3. Assoc Old No Chr Ch Boston MA 1982-1985; R S Jas' Epis Ch Cambridge MA 1961-1982; R All SS Ch Stoneham MA 1957-1961; R Trin Epis Ch Weymouth MA 1955-1956. Phillips Brooks Club 1957-1986. lindaide9@aol.com

WAYLAND, David Carlton (WVa) 46 Fishhook Ln, Hedgesville WV 25427 B Parkersburg WV 9/7/1940 s Walter A Wayland & Idris Arlene. BA W Liberty St Coll 1965; MDiv 1968. D 6/11/1968 P 12/1/1968 Bp Wilburn Camrock Campbell. m 4/11/1992 Rose Herr Wayland c 2. Asst S Jn's Par Hagerstown MD 1971-1972; Vic S Phil's Ch Chas Town WV 1969-1971; Vic S Andr's-On-The-Mt Harpers Ferry WV 1968-1971; Vic S Jn's Ch Harpers Ferry WV 1968-1971; Cur Zion Epis Ch Chas Town WV 1968-1969. Auth, "Depression-A First Step In Personal Growth (3 Part Series)," *The Counslr*, 1979; Auth, "Travels In Wonderland," *Pilgrimage*, 1973. Amer Acad Of Psych 1979-1998; AAPC 1979. davidw7358@gmail.com

WAYLAND, David Frazee (Va) 6474 Apple Green Ln, Crozet VA 22932 **Ch Of Our Sav Charlottesville VA 1962-** B Charlottesville VA 10/6/1935 s George Bourne Wayland & Norman. BA U of Virginia 1959; MDiv VTS 1962; Fllshp Coll of Preachers 1991. D 6/9/1962 Bp Robert Fisher Gibson Jr P 6/1/1963 Bp Samuel B Chilton. m 7/4/1964 Virginia Ruth Peck c 4. Vic Ch Of S Jn The Bapt Ivy VA 1997-2000; Dio Virginia Richmond VA 1997-2000; Vic H Cross Ch Batesville VA 1997-2000; Int S Jas Epis Ch Louisa VA 1996-1997; Int Cople Par Hague VA 1995-1996; Int Gr Ch Keswick VA 1993-1995; S Mich's Ch Colonial Heights VA 1993; Int R S Mich's Ch Colonial Heights VA 1992-1993; Vic S Paul's Ch Martins Ferry OH 1988-1992; R S Cathr's Epis Ch Marietta GA 1977-1988; Assoc R Trin Ch Covington KY 1971-1977; R Trin Epis Ch Rocky Mt VA 1968-1971; R Buck Mtn Epis Ch Earlysville VA 1963-1968. Auth, "Making A Difference: Effective Preaching For Soc Change," *Fell Coll Of Preachers*, 1991; Auth, "Plnng For Liturg," *Aware*, 1979. dfwayl@embarqmail.com

WAYMAN, Teresa Lachmann (WVa) Box 957-P Mineral Road, Glenville WV 26351 **P S Mk's Ch Glenville WV 2001-** B Cincinnati OH 5/4/1954 d Francis Joseph Lachmann & (Vella) Ruth. Dio W Virginia. D 9/9/1999 Bp John H(enry) Smith P 9/20/2001 Bp C(laude) Charles Vache. m 6/10/1978 Paul Charles Hartmann c 2. D S Mk's Ch Glenville WV 1999-2000. hartway78@verizon.net

WAYNE, David Boyd (NY) Po Box 271, Rowe MA 01367 B Burbank CA 12/17/1931 s John Boyd Wayne & Grace. BA U Pac 1953; STB GTS 1961. D 6/11/1961 P 12/16/1961 Bp Horace W B Donegan. c 2. R S Aug's Epis Ch Croton On Hudson NY 1976-1992; Diocn Msnry & Ch Extntn Socty New York NY 1973-1976; Dpt Of Missions Ny Income New York NY 1973-1976; Calv Hosp Bronx NY 1970-1973; R S Simeon's Ch Bronx NY 1967-1976; R S Edm's Ch Bronx NY 1964-1970; Cur The Ch Of The Epiph New York NY 1961-1964. Auth, "Behind Cranmer's Offertory Rubrics: The Offering of the People in the Mass Before the Reformation," *ATR*, 1969. R Emer S Aug's Epis Ch, Croton-on-Hudson, NY 1997.

✠ WAYNICK, Rt Rev Catherine Elizabeth Maples (Ind) 1100 W 42nd St, Indianapolis IN 46208 **Bp Of Ind Dio Indianapolis Indianapolis IN 1998-; Bp of Indianapolis Dio Indianapolis Indianapolis IN 1997-** B Jackson MI 11/13/1948 d Sevedus Allister Maples & Janet Ellen. Cntrl Michigan U; BA Madonna U 1981; MDiv St. Jn's Prov Sem Plymouth MI 1985. D 6/29/1985 P 10/19/1986 Bp H Coleman McGehee Jr Con 6/7/1997 for Ind. m 11/28/1968 Larry Wade Waynick. Stndg Com Pres Dio Indianapolis Indianapolis IN 1994-1995; R All SS Epis Ch Pontiac MI 1993-1997; Stndg Com Dio Indianapolis Indianapolis IN 1992-1994; Assoc R Chr Ch Cranbrook Bloomfield Hills MI 1985-1993; Admin & Fin Com Dio Michigan Detroit MI 1985-1989. Contrib, "Pryr Included In," *Uncommon Pryr*, 2000. DD GTS New York NY 1998; Frances Willard Awd For Outstanding Accomplishment Alpha Phi. bishop@indydio.org

WAYWELL, Roy Edmund (LI) 9725 Lefferts Blvd, South Richmond Hill NY 11419 **Died 8/31/2009** B UK 4/21/1944 s Herbert Waywell & Vera. Kelham Theol Coll 1972; GTS 1973. D 6/9/1973 Bp Paul Moore Jr P 12/9/1973 Bp Robert E Campbell. Our Lady of Walsingham, P Assoc 1974. royewaywell@hotmail.com

WEAD, Sean Scott Cornell (Ga) 9 Ridgeview Drive, Belle Mead NJ 08502 **Assoc All SS Ch Princeton NJ 2011-; Chapl Off Of Bsh For ArmdF New York NY 2000-** B JP 7/22/1967 s James Kenneth Wead & Joyce Ann. BS Estrn Kentucky U 1989; BS Georgia Sthrn U 1993; MDiv VTS 1998; DMin VTS 2010. D 6/11/1998 P 12/12/1998 Bp Henry Irving Louttit. m 7/23/1988 Kimberly Ann Hunt c 1. Assoc Trin Epis Ch Watertown NY 2005-2009; Assoc Trin Epis Ch Watertown NY 2000-2003; Vic S Steph's Lee Cnty Leesburg GA 1999-2000; Asst S Patricks Ch Albany GA 1998-2000. US-A Chapl Corps. seanwead@msn.com

WEATHERFORD, David William (SanD) 10835 Gabacho Dr, San Diego CA 92124 B Los Angeles CA 10/12/1928 s David Mims Weatherford & Clara Evelyn. BA Occ 1950; PrTS 1952; STB GTS 1959; Cert Chicago Urban Trng Cntr 1967; USC 1970. D 6/16/1958 Bp Donald J Campbell P 2/1/1959 Bp Francis E I Bloy. m 6/27/1959 Regina K Kunzel c 5. Asst S Eliz's Epis Ch San Diego CA 1976-1988; Asst Cathd Ch Of S Paul San Diego CA 1971-1976; Vic S Andr's Epis Ch Ojai CA 1960-1967; Cur Cathd Ch Of S Paul San Diego CA 1958-1960.

WEATHERHOLT, Anne Orwig (Md) 19 West High Street, Hancock MD 21750 **Secy of Conv Dio Maryland Baltimore MD 2011-; R S Mk's Ch Lappans Boonsboro MD 1994-** B Lansing MI 11/11/1952 d James Preston Orwig & Katharine. Berea Coll 1970; BA S Olaf Coll 1973; MDiv VTS 1978. D 5/14/1978 Bp Addison Hosea P 2/3/1980 Bp David Keller Leighton Sr. m 12/27/1980 F(loyd) Allan Weatherholt, Jr. c 2. Asst All SS Ch Frederick MD 1983-1993; Chapl S Aug's Chap Lexington KY 1978-1979. Contributig Auth, "Wisdom Found: Stories of Wmn Transfigured by Faith," Forw Mvmt, 2011; Auth, "Breaking the Silence: The Ch Responds to Dom Violence," Ch Pub, 2008; Auth, "Eleven Little Lies," *Tract*, Forw Mvmt, 2007; Auth, "Pregnancy and Priesthood," *Alb Inst*, Alb Inst, 1985; Auth, "Epis Chld's Curric," *Intermediate Level*, Living the Gd News, 1983; Auth, "New Approaches to Counslg Battered Wmn," *Nwsltr*, Alb Inst, 1979. DOK 2003. rector@stmarkslappans.org

WEATHERHOLT JR, F(loyd) Allan (Md) 2 E High Street, Hancock MD 21750 **COM Dio Maryland Baltimore MD 2011-; R S Thos' Par Hancock MD 1980-** B Cumberland MD 6/29/1948 s Floyd Allan Weatherholt & Elizabeth. AA Allegany Coll of Maryland 1969; BA Frostburg St U 1972; MDiv VTS 1975; Coll of Preachers 1982. D 5/28/1975 P 2/15/1976 Bp David Keller Leighton Sr. m 12/27/1980 Anne Orwig c 2. Dioc Coun Dio Maryland Baltimore MD 1984-1987; S Jn's Par Hagerstown MD 1977-1979; Epiph Ch Dulaney Vlly Timonium MD 1975-1977. BroSA 2000. Bp's Awd for Outstanding Ord Mnstry Epis Dio Maryland 2005; Outstanding Young Man Of Amer 1980. revfaweatherholt@aol.com

WEATHERLY, Beverly Kay Hill (WA) 44078 Saint Andrews Church Rd, California MD 20619 **S Andr's Ch Leonardtown California MD 2010-** B Indiana PA 8/29/1950 d Hal Howard Hill & Mildred Marie. Drew U; BS OH SU 1972; MDiv PrTS 1984; Cert GTS 1985. D 6/14/1986 Bp George Phelps Mellick Belshaw P 1/1/1987 Bp Vincent King Pettit. m 4/12/1986 John Weatherly. S Andr's Epis Ch Arlington VA 2005-2009; S Marg's Ch Woodbridge VA 2005; Chr Ch Alexandria VA 1995-2005; Assoc S Lk's Par Darien CT 1993-1995; Gr Epis Ch Norwalk CT 1993; S Andr's On The Sound Ch Wilmington NC 1991-1992; Exec Coun Appointees New York NY 1987-1990; Chr Ch Trenton NJ 1986-1987; Cur S Matt's Ch Pennington NJ 1986-1987. saintandrewsrector@verizon.net

WEATHERLY, Joe Edward (Tenn) 640 N Washington Ave, Cookeville TN 38501 **R S Mich's Epis Ch And U Cookeville TN 2003-** B Selma AL 11/24/1949 s Joseph Addison Weatherly & Elizabeth Harper. BS Georgia Inst of Tech 1972; MDiv STUSo 1996. D 6/8/1996 P 5/17/1997 Bp Dorsey Felix Henderson. m 3/1/1975 Louise M Millner c 5. Asst S Jn's Epis Ch Columbia SC 2000-2003; Cur S Mich And All Ang' Columbia SC 1996-2000. joe.weatherly7@gmail.com

WEATHERLY, John (Va) 8441 Porter Ln, Alexandria VA 22308 **S Mk's Ch Alexandria VA 2007-** B Bethlehem PA 9/10/1951 s Bruce Armfield Weatherly & Margaret Brooks. BA U So 1973; MA Duke 1974; MDiv Yale DS 1981; ThM New Brunswick TS 1995. D 6/6/1981 Bp Albert Wiencke Van Duzer P 12/10/1981 Bp George Phelps Mellick Belshaw. m 4/12/1986 Beverly Kay Hill c 3. Spec Mobilization Spprt Plan Washington DC 2007; Pension Fund Mltry New York NY 2006; P-in-c S Barn Epis Ch Temple Hills MD

1995-1997; Assoc S Lk's Par Darien CT 1993-1995; ExCoun/Farmwkrs Mnstry/COM Dio E Carolina Kinston NC 1989-1992; R H Trin Epis Ch Hampstead NC 1989-1992; Mssy to Brasilia, Brasil Epis Ch Cntr New York NY 1987-1989; Exec Coun Appointees New York NY 1987-1989; S Andr's Ch Trenton NJ 1982-1987; Vic Chr Ch Trenton NJ 1981-1987. EUC 2004; NECA 1997. jweathe951@aol.com

WEATHERLY, Robert H (Miss) 1414 Chambers St, Vicksburg MS 39180 **All SS' Epis Sch Vicksburg MS 2003-** B Ripley MS 7/22/1946 s Ernest Weatherly & Grace E. BS Mississippi St U 1968. D 1/4/2003 Bp Alfred Clark Marble Jr. m 12/27/1969 Danella C Compton c 2. bobby4wco@bellsouth.net

WEATHERWAX, Elizabeth May (Pgh) 402 Royal Ct, Pittsburgh PA 15234 B Pittsburgh PA 8/24/1935 d Nicholas Hugo Krayer & Joy. BS Chatham Coll 1957; VTS 1981. D 6/4/1980 P 6/1/1981 Bp Robert Poland Atkinson. m 6/28/1958 David Eugene Weatherwax. Par Visitor S Paul's Epis Ch Pittsburgh PA 1987-2011; Vic Prince Of Peace Salem Salem WV 1981-1987; Asst S Barn Bridgeport WV 1980-1981.

WEAVER III, David England (Chi) 3835 Johnson Ave, Western Springs IL 60558 B Chicago IL 1/2/1940 s David England Weaver & Phyllis. BA Ripon Coll Ripon WI 1962; MDiv GTS 1965; MA NWU 1969; DMin Chicago TS 1996; MS Natl-Louis U 1999. D 6/12/1965 Bp James Winchester Montgomery P 12/18/1965 Bp Gerald Francis Burrill. m 7/2/1966 Sally Bodmer c 3. R Emm Epis Ch La Grange IL 1987-2006; S Paul's On-The-Hill Epis Ch St Paul MN 1986-1987; S Paul's Ch Minneapolis MN 1986; Int R S Paul's Ch Minneapolis MN 1983-1985; Int S Phil's Ch S Paul MN 1981-1983; S Pat Minneapolis MN 1979-1981; Ch Of The H Nativ Clarendon Hills IL 1975-1979; Asst to R S Mart's Ch Des Plaines IL 1970-1975; Cur Gr Epis Ch Hinsdale IL 1965-1966. APA 1999; Natl Fire Chapl Assn 1990-2000. wellcare@aol.com

WEAVER, Eric James (LI) 8 Oceanside Ct, Northport NY 11768 B Purley Surrey UK 5/14/1938 s Edward Arthur Weaver & Cecily Amelia. AB Pr 1958; MDiv GTS 1961; MS CUNY 1968; PD Hofstra U 1973; EdD Hofstra U 1980. D 4/8/1961 P 5/19/1962 Bp James P De Wolfe. m 8/19/1973 Joyce Lynn McKean c 4. Int R Trin Ch Northport NY 1999-2009; Asst R Trin Ch Northport NY 1966-1999; Asst to the R Ch Of S Jas The Less Jamaica NY 1963; Vic Ch Of The Mssh Cntrl Islip NY 1961-1963; S Mich And All Ang Seaford NY 1961-1963; St Mich And All Ang Ch Gordon Heights NY 1961-1963. Auth, "Ocular," *Manual & Pediatric Dominance In Severely Retarded Older Adolescent Population Monograph*, U Pub, 1968; Auth, "Rudolf Bultmann & Mod Biblic Study Monograph," GTS, 1961; Auth, "Adolescent Population," *Monographs Phi Delta Kappa*. Ord Of H Cross P Assoc 1956. Proclamation Northport Ecum Lay Coun 2010; R Emer Trin Ch 2009; Trin Cross Trin Ch 2009; Proclamation New York St Senate 1998; Proclamation Suffolk Cnty Legislature 1998; Proclamation New York St Senate 1986; Fell AAMD 1979; Phi Delta Kappa 1973. eweaver@optonline.net

WEAVER, Evelyn Jean (SD) 2018 13th Ave, Belle Fourche SD 57717 **P S Jas Epis Ch Belle Fourche SD 2005-** B 1/26/1945 D 6/11/2005 P 2/12/2006 Bp Creighton Leland Robertson. m 7/19/1963 Ivan Michael Weaver c 2.

WEAVER, Ivan Michael (SD) 2018 13th Ave, Belle Fourche SD 57717 **D S Jas Epis Ch Belle Fourche SD 2005-** B 7/10/1942 D 6/11/2005 Bp Creighton Leland Robertson. m 7/19/1963 Evelyn Jean Evelyn Jean Erickson c 2.

WEAVER, Joseph Clyde (WA) 703 Winged Foot Drive, Aiken SC 29803 B Irwin PA 1/2/1928 s Clyde Clark Weaver & Retta. BD Epis TS In Kentucky 1967; MA Duquesne U 1971; MDiv Epis TS In Kentucky 1971; PhD Walden U Naples FL 1984. D 6/10/1967 Bp William S Thomas P 12/17/1967 Bp Austin Pardue. m 2/26/1983 Louise D Day c 2. S Andr's Ch Leonardtown California MD 1984-1992; R S Mk's Ch Marco Island FL 1973-1983; Assoc Ch Of The Gd Shpd Dunedin FL 1971-1973. jcw703@gmail.com

WEAVER, Lorne Edward (Los) 27910 Via De Costa, San Juan Capistrano CA 92675 B Lancaster PA 12/22/1944 s Lester M Weaver & Mary. BA Gordon Coll 1969; STM Gordon-Conwell TS 1972; MA U of Washington 1974; MDiv Fuller TS 1976; Claremont TS 1979. D 6/23/1979 P 1/12/1980 Bp Robert C Rusack. m 6/3/2001 Alessandra Licardo c 3. S Alb's Epis Ch Los Angeles CA 2002-2004; Int S Ptr's Par Santa Maria CA 1999-2001; Int Trin Epis Ch Orange CA 1997-1999; Int S Geo's Mssn Hawthorne CA 1994-1997; S Lk's Par Monrovia CA 1990-1993; S Geo's Epis Ch Laguna Hills CA 1988-1990; Vic S Andr's Epis Ch Irvine CA 1981-1987; Asst S Patricks Ch And Day Sch Thousand Oaks CA 1979-1981; Asst All SS Ch Pasadena CA 1975-1979. lewaml@asis.com

WEAVER, Robert Crew (O) 2553 Derbyshire Rd, Cleveland Heights OH 44106 B Clarksburg WV 2/20/1938 s Karl Bethel Weaver & Marian Crew. BA Denison U 1960; MDiv SWTS 1965. D 6/12/1965 Bp James Winchester Montgomery P 12/18/1965 Bp Gerald Francis Burrill. m 5/23/1992 Gertrude Bauer c 2. Dn - Cleveland E Dnry Dio Ohio Cleveland OH 1989-1990; R S Alb Epis Ch Cleveland Heights OH 1987-2003; Dioc Coun Dio Ohio Cleveland OH 1986-1989; Ch Of The Incarn Cleveland OH 1982-1987; Urban Vic of Chicago Dio Chicago Chicago IL 1967-1968; Urban Vic - Taylor Hm / Stateway Gardens Dio Chicago Chicago IL 1965-1967. robert.weaver.60@denison.edu

WEAVER, Roger Warren (Minn) Po Box 820, Tower MN 55790 B Muskegon MI 1/1/1940 s Chester Frank Weaver & Leona Mae. BS U of Wisconsin 1962; Chicago Urban Trng Cntr 1967; MDiv SWTS 1967. D 6/1/1967 Bp Richard S M Emrich P 3/8/1968 Bp Archie H Crowley. m 8/11/1962 Kathleen Patti Burns c 1. R S Mary's Ch Ely MN 1980-2001; R S Paul's Ch Virginia MN 1980-2001; S Jn's Ch Eveleth MN 1980-1981; R Chr Ch Frontenac MN 1973-1980; R Gr Memi Ch Wabasha MN 1973-1980; R S Mk's Ch Lake City MN 1973-1980; Asst Trin Cathd Davenport IA 1970-1973; P-in-c S Mich And All Ang Onsted MI 1967-1970. rogkathyw@frontiernet.net

WEAVER, Sally Sykes (Mo) 2575 Sunrise Dr, Eureka MO 63025 **Vic S Fran Epis Ch Eureka MO 2010-** B Saint Louis MO 2/4/1953 d William Graham Martin & Winifred Hamilton. BA Washington U 1975; MLA Washington U 1993; MDiv Eden TS 2005. D 12/22/2004 P 6/24/2005 Bp George Wayne Smith. m 1/3/2004 Anthony Weaver. Int S Jn The Evang Ch Elkhart IN 2008-2009; Assoc S Mart's Ch Ellisville MO 2006-2008; Epis City Mssn St Louis MO 2006-2007; Gr Ch Kirkwood MO 2005-2006; Epis City Mssn St Louis MO 2005. sallysweaver@yahoo.com

WEBB, Alexander Henderson (WMass) 40 Arundel Road, Peterborough NH 03458 B Mount Kisco NY 10/19/1951 s Jean Francis Webb & Nancy. BA Amh 1973; Gordon-Conwell TS 1977; MDiv GTS 1978; MA Antioch Coll 1993; DMin Gordon-Conwell TS 2011. D 6/17/1978 P 3/31/1979 Bp Alexander Doig Stewart. m 7/1/2006 Elizabeth Webb c 3. Supply The Chap Of All SS Leominster MA 2007-2011; supply Dio Wstrn Massachusetts Springfield MA 2004-2007; Assoc Chr Ch Fitchburg MA 2000-2004; Int Chr Ch Fitchburg MA 1998-1999; Int S Anne's Ch No Billerica MA 1994-1995; Int S Lk's Ch Hudson MA 1991-1994; Int Gr Ch Lawr MA 1990; R S Paul's Ch Lynnfield MA 1987-1989; Int Ch Of Our Sav Milford NH 1986-1987; Assoc Ch Of The Atone Westfield MA 1985-1986; Ch Of The Nativ Northborough MA 1980-1985; Asst S Thos Ch Hanover NH 1978-1980. Auth, "Selected Sermons," CPG. Bro of S Andr 1986; FVC 1982. ahwebb@aol.com

WEBB II, Alexander Henderson (NY) PO Box 257, Roanoke VA 24002 **Cur S Jn's Ch Roanoke VA 2010-; Liturg Consult for the GC Epis Ch Cntr New York NY 2008-2012** B Framingham MA 4/26/1983 s Alexander Henderson Webb & Ruth Poole. AB Ham 2010; MDiv VTS 2010. D 3/13/2010 P 9/25/2010 Bp Mark Sean Sisk. GC Off Epis Ch Cntr New York NY 2005-2007. Auth, "Stndg Commissions in the Twenty-First Century: A Case for Reform," *Journ of Epis Ch Cn Law*, VTS, 2010. Phi Beta Kappa 2010. sandywebb@gmail.com

WEBB, Anne Slade Newbegin (Vt) 43 Thorndike Pond Rd., Jaffrey NH 03452 **P in Charge S Fran Chap Marlborough Marlborough NH 2011-** B Ciudad Trujillo DO 5/19/1944 d Robert Newbegin & Katharine. BA Hollins U 1966; MDiv EDS 1969. D 7/17/1976 P 3/12/1977 Bp Philip Alan Smith. m 6/7/1969 Richard Cassius Lee Webb c 2. R S Mk's Ch Springfield VT 1994-2003; Co-R Ch Of The H Sprt Wayland MA 1985-1992; Int S Matt's Ch Goffstown NH 1983-1985; Vic St Michaels Ch Suncook NH 1979-1982; Asst Gr Ch Manchester NH 1976-1979. annesnwebb@myfairpoint.net

WEBB, Benjamin S (Ia) 511 W 12th St, Cedar Falls IA 50613 B Davenport IA 5/29/1954 s William Henry Webb & Mary Ellen. BS Iowa St U 1978; MDiv CDSP 1993; MA Grad Theol Un 1993. D 3/30/1993 P 1/6/1996 Bp Carl Christopher Epting. m 6/9/1979 Sarah Marilyn Paulos c 3. Int S Lk's Ch Des Moines IA 2011; Dio Iowa Des Moines IA 2009-2010; R S Lk's Epis Ch Cedar Falls IA 1996-2009. Auth, "Fugitive Faith:Conversations Sprtlty, Environ," *& Cmnty Renwl*, Orbis Books, 1998. benjaminswebb@gmail.com

WEBB SR, Donald Ray (NwT) 2147 Vine St, Colorado City TX 79512 **Chair Prsn Mnstry Com Dio NW Texas Lubbock TX 2000-** B Eastland TX 6/1/1936 s James Raymond Webb & Bertha. BA Angelo St U 1972. D 10/29/1999 Bp C(harles) Wallis Ohl. m 8/12/1956 Lola Clovis Williams. D All SS Ch Colorado City TX 2000-2002. NAAD. drwebb@nwol.net

WEBB, Estelle C (Ct) 615 Clay Ave Apt 1, Scranton PA 18510 B Philadelphia PA 6/26/1945 d S Raymond Webb & Doris M. MDiv GTS 2000; Cert Cntr for Sprtlty and Justice (CSPJ) 2001; STM GTS 2001. D 10/18/1996 P 5/30/1997 Bp Paul Victor Marshall. c 2. Assoc Trin Ch On The Green New Haven CT 2001-2010; Admin Vic The Ch of S Ign of Antioch New York NY 2000-2001. Soc of Cath Priests 2009-2011. ewebb615@comcast.net

WEBB, Fain Murphey (Nwk) P.O. Box 336, Columbia NJ 07832 B Chattanooga TN 9/30/1946 d Reid Stone Murphey & Valeria Gott. BA Van 1968; MDiv GTS 1992; STM GTS 1993. D 6/12/1993 Bp George Phelps Mellick Belshaw P 12/1/1993 Bp Joe Morris Doss. m 7/6/1968 John Webb III c 4. Vic Ch Of The Gd Shpd Sussex NJ 1996-2011; S Paul's Epis Ch Bound Brook NJ 1993-1996; Gr Epis Ch Plainfield NJ 1993-1994. CSJB 2006; OHC. fainwebb@aol.com

WEBB, Frieda Van Baalen (WNY) 3360 McKinley Parkway, Buffalo NY 14219 **Vic Ch Of The H Comm Lakeview NY 2010-; S Mths Epis Ch E Aurora NY 2008-** B Buffalo NY 7/21/1943 d Joseph Marcus Van Baalen & Sheila Virginia. BA Wm Smith 1975; Mstr of Div Bex 2006. D 12/20/2003 P 4/15/2007 Bp J Michael Garrison. m 12/23/1976 William Charles Webb c 2. S

Dav's Epis Ch W Seneca NY 2003-2008; S Mths Epis Ch E Aurora NY 1985-1989. gldn721@verizon.net

WEBB, James Kent (Dal) 4500 Roland Ave. #607, Dallas TX 75219 **Archd Dio Dallas Dallas TX 2011-** B Tyler TX 5/22/1951 s William Calvin Webb & Helen. BA SMU 1973; MBA Pepperdine U 1981; MTS SMU 1997. D 12/2/2006 Bp James Monte Stanton. m 10/17/1987 Connie S Webb c 2. jwebb@webbfinancial.net

WEBB JR, James Wilson (Miss) 309 E Parkway Dr, Indianola MS 38751 **S Steph's Epis Ch Indianola MS 2005-** B Durham NC 5/13/1946 s James Wilson Webb & Anna Bertha. BA U of Mississippi 1968; STUSo 2000; MDiv STUSo 2000. D 8/30/2000 P 3/18/2001 Bp Duncan Montgomery Gray III. m 8/25/1968 Marsha C Cole. Vic S Jas Epis Ch Port Gibson MS 2000-2005. Griffin Awd for Study in the H Land 2000.

WEBB III, Joseph Baxtar (Eau) 104 Nolan Drive, Georgetown TX 78633 B Sturgeon Bay WI 9/24/1945 s Joseph Baxtar Webb & Gloria L. Adv.Stdg. ACPE ACPE; BA Milton Coll 1969; MDiv NWU 1973; MA U of Wisconsin 1987; Nash 1988; DMin GTF 1991; CGSC/USArmy Command and Gnrl Stff Coll 1998. D 3/19/1988 P 9/24/1988 Bp William Charles Wantland. m 5/29/1998 Victoria S Summy c 2. Pstr Assoc Gr Epis Ch Georgetown TX 2005-2010; Chr Ch Par La Crosse WI 2003-2005; Gr Epis Ch Menomonie WI 2001-2002; Trin Ch Baraboo WI 2000; S Jn's Epis Ch Sparta WI 1991-1994; Luth Hosp La Crosse WI 1988-1999; Asst Chr Ch Par La Crosse WI 1988-1991. Auth, *PTSD: Diagnosis & Treatment*, US Army, 1991; Auth, *Creative Use of Loneliness & Separation*, Gundersen Luth.Med.Ctr, 1986; Auth, "Calling in the Hosp," *Rel and Sprtlty*, Gundersen Luth.Med.Ctr., 1982. Var U.S.Army Medals/Awards U.S. Army/DOD 2004. jbwvsshome@yahoo.com

WEBB III, Joseph Tarpley (Va) 4074 Thorngate Dr, Williamsburg VA 23188 B Bryn Mawr PA 12/24/1938 s Vernon Era Webb & Emily. BA Valdosta St U 1961; MDiv VTS 1964; Fllshp Coll of Preachers 1981. D 6/13/1964 Bp Robert Lionne DeWitt P 3/20/1965 Bp Randolph R Claiborne. m 9/2/1961 Toni Anne Steele c 3. R S Dunst's McLean VA 1988-2004; Ch Of The H Comf Luthvle Timon MD 1977-1988; Trin Ch Towson MD 1969-1976; Cur Chr Ch Macon GA 1964-1969. R Emer St. Dunst's Ch, McLean VA 2005. jtwebb@cox.net

WEBB, Pamela Connor (Va) 8221 Old Mill Lane, Williamsburg VA 23188 **Int Emm Ch At Brook Hill Richmond VA 2011-** B New Orleans LA 1/21/1948 d John Proudfit Connor & Jane. BEd U of Mississippi 1970; MDiv VTS 1994. D 5/28/1994 P 12/3/1994 Bp Frank Harris Vest Jr. m 6/8/1996 Robert Daniel Webb c 3. Int Ch Of The H Comf Burlington NC 2010-2011; Int S Paul's Ch Wilkesboro NC 2009-2010; R S Jn's Epis Ch Tappahannock VA 2000-2006; R Chr Epis Ch Smithfield VA 1996-2000; Vic S Lk's Historic Shrine Smithfield VA 1996-2000; Asst S Andr's Epis Ch Newport News VA 1994-1996. pamwebb@hotmail.com

WEBB, Richard Cassius Lee (NH) 43 Thorndike Pond Rd., Jaffrey NH 03452 **P-in-c S Fran Chap Marlborough Marlborough NH 2010-** B Concord NH 4/12/1945 s Charles Thomas Webb & Ann Carter. AB Harv 1967; BD EDS 1970. D 6/24/1970 P 1/16/1971 Bp Charles F Hall. m 6/7/1969 Anne Slade Newbegin c 2. S Lk's Ch Charlestown NH 1993-2003; Un Ch Claremont NH 1993-2003; Co-R Ch Of The H Sprt Wayland MA 1985-1992; S Chris's Ch Hampstead NH 1974-1985; Chair Dioc Liturg Cmsn Dio New Hampshire Concord NH 1974-1980; Cur S Thos Ch Hanover NH 1970-1974. rclwebb@myfairpoint.net

WEBB, Robert Joseph (Ind) 721 W Main St, Madison IN 47250 B Franklin PA 10/13/1937 s W Robert Webb & Elinor Elizabeth. ABS Wabash Coll 1959; MDiv VTS 1962. D 6/16/1962 P 12/1/1962 Bp John P Craine. m 11/10/1987 Marjorie Ann Kelley c 3. Asst S Ptr's Ch Lebanon IN 1976-1978; Asst S Mich's Ch Noblesville IN 1972-1975; Asst All SS Ch Seymour IN 1970-1972; R S Jn's Epis Ch Crawfordsville IN 1967-1969; Cur Chap Of The Gd Shpd W Lafayette IN 1962-1963. rwebb50@adelphia.net

WEBB, Ross Allan (USC) 2534 Shiland Dr, Rock Hill SC 29732 **Asst Chr Epis Ch Lancaster SC 1979-** B Westchester NS CA 7/22/1923 s William Oswald Webb & Permilla Madge. BA Acadia U 1949; MA U Pgh 1951; PhD U Pgh 1956. D 11/26/1961 Bp William R Moody P 12/19/1981 Bp William Arthur Beckham. m 6/19/1954 Ruth Evangeline Keil. Asst S Paul's Epis Ch Ft Mill SC 1973-1979; Asst Ch Of The Gd Shpd York SC 1971-1973; Asst Ch Of Our Sav Rock Hill SC 1967-1971; Asst Chr Ch Cathd Lexington KY 1961-1967. Auth, "The Torch Is Passed," Baak, 2002; Auth, "Var Works". Distinguished Prof 1977; Omicron Delta Kappa; Phi Beta Kappa.

WEBB, William Charles (WNY) 29 Grove St, Angola NY 14006 B Norwich NY 10/1/1950 s Charles Arthur Webb & Doris Edith. BA U Roch 1973; MDiv Bex 1976. D 7/3/1977 P 9/10/1979 Bp Robert Rae Spears Jr. m 12/23/1976 Frieda Van Baalen. S Paul's Ch Holley NY 2007-2009; S Jude's Ch Buffalo NY 2001-2006; Int S Pat's Ch Cheektowaga NY 2000; Int S Phil's Ch Buffalo NY 1995-1998; Dio Wstrn New York Tonawanda NY 1993-1994; S Paul's Epis Ch Lewiston NY 1993; P-in-c S Paul's Epis Ch Lewiston NY 1992-1993; P-in-c S Jn's Ch Wilson NY 1991-1992; S Mary's Epis Ch Gowanda NY 1990-1991; Int S Mary's Epis Ch Gowanda NY 1989-1990; Int S Ptr's Ch Westfield NY 1989-1990; Assoc Team Mnstrs Ch Of The H Comm Lakeview NY 1984-1989; Trin Epis Ch Hamburg NY 1984-1989; Epis Tri-Par Mnstry Dansville NY 1984; S Jn's Ch Canandaigua NY 1977-1979. Kairos; New Directions Ne; Ny Assn Firefighters Chapl. bfdf75@gmail.com

WEBBER, Bruce Milton (NJ) 19105 35th Avenue, Apt. J, Flushing NY 11358 B Woodbury NJ 1/11/1953 s Edward Sharp Webber & Doris May. BM U Roch 1975; MDiv GTS 1978; ThM PrTS 1986; MSW Ford 1997; NCPsyA Inst for Mod Psychoanalysis 2002. D 6/3/1978 Bp Albert Wiencke Van Duzer P 12/1/1978 Bp George Phelps Mellick Belshaw. S Jas Ch New York NY 1997; Int S Clem's Ch New York NY 1995-1996; Int S Andr's Epis Ch Staten Island NY 1994-1995; Int The Ch Of S Lk In The Fields New York NY 1992-1993; Asst Trin Ch Princeton NJ 1986-1992; R S Jas Ch Trenton Yardville NJ 1982-1986; Cur Gr Ch Madison NJ 1980-1982; Cur Ch Of S Mary's By The Sea Point Pleasant Bch NJ 1978-1979. bmw646@aol.com

WEBBER, Christopher L (Ct) Box 1724, 80 Herb Rd., Sharon CT 06069 **Vic S Paul's Epis Ch Bantam CT 2009-** B Cuba NY 1/5/1932 s Roy Lawrence Webber & Hortense Marie. Coll of Preachers; AB Pr 1953; STB GTS 1956; STM GTS 1963; DD GTS 2009. D 4/7/1956 Bp James P De Wolfe P 10/20/1956 Bp Jonathan Goodhue Sherman. m 4/7/1958 Margaret Elizabeth Rose c 4. Vic Chr Ch Canaan CT 1995-2006; Trst The GTS New York NY 1984-1987; Trst Cathd Of St Jn The Div New York NY 1978-1987; R Chr Ch Bronxville NY 1972-1994; R Chr Epis Ch Lynbrook NY 1960-1966; R Ch Of The Ascen Greenpoint Brooklyn NY 1957-1960. Auth, "Amer to the Backbone," Pegasus, 2011; Auth, "Welcome to Chr Faith," Morehouse, 2011; Auth, "Beyond Beowulf," iUniverse, 2008; Auth, "A Bk of Vigils," Ch Pub, 2002; Auth, "Hymns from the Bible 2000," Gemini Press, 2000; Auth, "Welcome to the Epis Ch," Morehouse, 1999; Auth, "Finding Hm," Cowley, 1997; Auth, "Re-inventing Mar," Morehouse, 1994; Auth, "A Vstry Handbook," Morehouse, 1991; Auth, "A New Metrical Psalter," Ch Pub, 1987. DD GTS 2006. clw@clwebber.com

WEBBER, Elizabeth Ann (Mich) 850 Timberline Dr, Rochester Hills MI 48309 **Ch Of The H Cross Novi MI 2010-** B St. Andrews Jamaica 2/1/1949 D 12/20/2003 P 6/26/2004 Bp Wendell Nathaniel Gibbs Jr. m 7/11/1970 Paul Webber c 3. S Jn's Ch Westland MI 2008-2009; S Phil And S Steph Epis Ch Detroit MI 2008; Trin Ch Toledo OH 2006; S Jn's Ch Royal Oak MI 2004-2006. etawebber@aol.com

WEBBER, Michael Basquin (NY) Po Box 121, Paradox NY 12858 **Asst Chr Ch Pottersville NY 1996-; Asst Ch Of The Gd Shpd Brant Lake NY 1996-; Asst S Andr's Ch Brant Lake NY 1996-; Asst S Barbara's Ch Brant Lake NY 1996-; Asst S Chris's Ch Brant Lake NY 1996-; Asst S Paul's Ch Brant Lake NY 1996-** B Cuba NY 7/6/1934 s Roy Lawrence Webber & Hortense Marie. BA Trin Hartford CT 1956; GTS 1961; STB PDS 1962. D 4/28/1962 Bp James P De Wolfe P 11/3/1962 Bp Charles Waldo MacLean. m 9/9/1961 Katherine L Ritt c 3. R Zion Epis Ch Wappingers Falls NY 1978-1996; R S Ptr's Ch Port Chester NY 1975-1978; Vic S Cuth's Epis Ch Selden NY 1968-1975; Cur S Ptr's Ch Port Chester NY 1967-1968. webberparadox@gmail.com

WEBER, Claudia Jo (ECR) 2931 Cottage Ln., Paso Robles CA 93446 **D S Lk's Ch Atascadero CA 2008-; Fac, Dn of Chap Epis Sch For Deacons Berkeley CA 2005-** B Crestline OH 5/30/1939 d Merl Claud Weber & Anne Dorothea. AB Vas 1961; MA California St U 1976; CTh CDSP 2000; BA Sch for Deacons 2002. D 5/31/2003 Bp Richard Lester Shimpfky. m 7/15/2008 Mary K Morrison c 2. D S Lk's Ch Los Gatos CA 2003-2008. Assn for Epis Deacons, Life Mem 1985. joweber@alum.vassar.edu

WEBER, Dean A. (Nwk) 81 Highwood Ave, Tenafly NJ 07670 B Chicago IL 5/1/1952 s William T Weber & Patricia. BA Col 1974; JD Rutgers-The St U 1987; MDiv UTS 2002. D 6/1/2002 P 12/1/2002 Bp John Palmer Croneberger. m 5/31/1986 Lynne Bleich Weber. D All SS Ch Leonia NJ 2002-2004; Chncllr Dio Newark Newark NJ 2002-2004. dweber81@optonline.net

WEBER, Lynne Bleich (Nwk) 81 Highwood Ave, Tenafly NJ 07670 **Dioc Coun Dio Newark Newark NJ 2008-; R Ch Of The Atone Tenafly NJ 2000-** B Jersey City NJ 11/23/1957 d Theodore Leopold Bleich & Dorothy. BA Houghton Coll 1979; MDiv UTS 1993. D 6/5/1993 Bp John Shelby Spong P 5/21/1994 Bp Jack Marston McKelvey. m 5/31/1986 Dean A. Weber. Prov Syn Dio Newark Newark NJ 1998-2000; Chair Womens Cmsn Dio Newark Newark NJ 1996-1998; Assoc S Eliz's Ch Ridgewood NJ 1993-2000. CHS 1991. lynne.weber@verizon.net

WEBER-JOHNSON, Jered Paul (Minn) 3001 Wisconsin Ave NW, Washington DC 20016 **S Jn The Evang S Paul MN 2011-** B Bemidji MN 4/25/1980 s David Johnson & Pauline. BS Greenville Coll 2002; MDiv The GTS 2009. D 4/17/2009 Bp Gregory Harold Rickel. m 5/31/2002 Erin R Weber c 1. S Alb's Par Washington DC 2009-2011. JERED_WEBERJOHNSON@YAHOO.COM

WEBNER, Marie Louise (Az) 455 S Irving Ave Apt 104, Tucson AZ 85711 **Asst S Andr's Epis Ch Tucson AZ 1989-** B Washington DC 8/18/1928 d Paul Egeriis Hansen & Gerda. BS Wilson Teachers Coll 1950; EFM STUSo 1989. D 10/21/1989 Bp Joseph Thomas Heistand. c 2. Auth, "In Mary's Arms," *Wmn Uncommon Prayers*, Morehouse, 2000; Auth, "Listening at the

Altar of Repose," *Wmn Uncommon Prayers*, Morehouse, 2000; Auth, "Wilderness: A Journey Through Grief, Sprtl Life (vol45," *#2) Sum*, 1999. Assoc, SSF 2003; Soc of Our Lady of Isles, Shetland 1999-2003; Third Ord, SSF 1953-1998. mlwebner@theriver.com

WEBSTER, Alan Kim (SwVa) 229 Lee Dr, Waynesboro VA 22980 **R S Jn's Epis Ch Waynesboro VA 2003-** B Alamance NC 8/27/1956 s Jessie Lee Webster & Bessie Mae. BA Lynchburg Coll 1978; RN Lynchburg Gnrl Hosp Sch of Nrsng 1991; MDiv VTS 1998. D 6/12/1998 P 12/7/1998 Bp Frank Neff Powell. m 11/29/1980 Carol J Weidner c 2. Vic S Ptr's Ch Altavista VA 1999-2003; Chapl Westminster-Cbury Of Lynchburg Lynchburg VA 1998-2003. awebs4@aol.com

WEBSTER, Daniel J (Md) 3900 N. Charles St. Apt 1014, Baltimore MD 21218 **Cn for Evang & Mnstry Dvlpmt Dio Maryland Baltimore MD 2010-** B Grand Island NE 5/5/1948 s James Laverne Webster & Lillian Lajeanne. Creighton U 1967; BA U of San Diego 1970; MS Col 1973; MDiv Epis TS of The SW 1996. D 5/25/1996 Bp George Edmonds Bates P 2/8/1997 Bp Carolyn Tanner Irish. m 11/5/2011 Meredith Gould c 2. Cn Dio New York New York City NY 2008-2009; Vic St Fran of Assisi Montgomery NY 2008-2009; Dir of Cmncatn Dio Utah Salt Lake City UT 2001-2006; R Chr Ch Alameda CA 1999-2001; Int Vic S Jn's Epis Ch Logan UT 1998-2011; Media Advsr Dio California San Francisco CA 1998-1999; Cur All SS Ch Salt Lake City UT 1996-1998; Media Advsr Dio Utah Salt Lake City UT 1996-1998. Auth, "Barack Obama - Powered by Hope," *Search/A Ch of Ireland Journ*, Ch of Ireland, 2009; Auth, "Media shun mainstream Ch' message," *Rel News Serv*, 2006; Auth, "Honoring Young Peacemakers," *Wit*, Epis Ch Pub Co., 2005; Auth, "Power, Money, Control...It's the Ch," *Search/A Ch of Ireland Journ*, Ch of Ireland, 2004; Auth, "Praying your labels: One response to globalization," *Wit*, Epis Ch Pub Co., 2004; Auth, "Preaching Peace In Wartime," *Epis News Serv*, The Epis Ch, 2003; Auth, "Terry Waite Urges Ch To Be Voice For Peace," *Epis News Serv*, The Epis Ch, 2003; Auth, "Hard Hearts, Minds On Faith's Frontline," *Salt Lake Tribune*, Media News Grp, 2002; Auth, "Get Facts Straight Before Calling U.S. Chr Nation," *Salt Lake Tribune*, Media News Grp, 2002; Auth, "Challenge Voices For War," *Wit*, Epis Ch Pub Co., 2002. ECom 1996; EPF 2002; Fllshp of Recon 2004. Acp Awd Of Merit Nwspr Design Spread Or Story Associated Ch Press 2002; Polly Bond Awd Of Excellence-Ed, In Depth Coverage ECom 2002; Polly Bond Awd Of Excellence-Ed, Nwspr Below 12000 Ci ECom 2002; Polly Bond Awd Of Excellence - ECom 2001; Silver Awd, Summit Creative Awards 2001; Polly Bond Awd Of Merit - "A New Epis Bp" Live Telev ECom 1996; Polly Bond Awd Of Merit - "Sem Of The SW" Video ECom 1994. dwebster@episcopalmaryland.org

WEBSTER, Donald A(ndrew) (LI) 29 Centennial St, Peaks Island ME 04108 **Died 4/11/2011** B Evansville IN 5/24/1924 s Andrew Thomas Webster & Marcia Harriet. BCE RPI 1948; VTS 1973; GTS 1981. D 6/11/1954 P 4/7/1955 Bp Vedder Van Dyck. c 4. OHC (Assoc) 1954. dwebster@gwi.net

WEBSTER, Edwin Crowe (La) 895 Will Brown Rd, Eros LA 71238 B Fond du Lac WI 11/29/1925 s Edwin White Webster & MaryEva Wood. BA Ripon Coll Ripon WI 1949; MA U of Wisconsin 1950; BD Nash 1953. D 2/8/1953 Bp Harwood Sturtevant P 10/4/1953 Bp Reginald Heber Gooden. m 6/15/1948 Carol J Thrumston c 6. R S Jn's Ch Kenner LA 1982-1988; R Chr Ch S Jos LA 1977-1982; P Gr Ch Waterproof LA 1977-1982; D Cathd Of St Lk Balboa PANAMA CITY 1969-1977. Auth, "A Rhetorical Study of Isaiah 66," *JSOT*, 1986; Auth, "Strophic Patterns in Job," *JSOT*, 1983; Auth, "Pattern in the Fourth Gospel," *Art & Meaning*, Sheffield U., 1982; Auth, "Defense of Portobelo," *FSU*, 1970. SBL 1951. nedcweb@hotmail.com

WEBSTER, Kiah S (Dal) 11540 Ferguson Rd, Dallas TX 75228 **Dio Dallas Dallas TX 2010-** B Grand Prairie TX 11/3/1980 d Toni Anita. BA Van 2003; MDiv Epis TS of The SW 2006. D 5/14/2005 Bp Herbert Thompson Jr P 6/24/2006 Bp Kenneth Lester Price. m 8/21/2004 Phillip Webster c 4. Assoc S Paul's On The Plains Epis Ch Lubbock TX 2009-2010; Asst R S Geo's Epis Ch Dayton OH 2007-2009; P-in-c S Paul's Ch Chillicothe OH 2006-2007. kshannon33@yahoo.com

WEBSTER, Pamela Ball (Minn) 435 Sunset Rd, Ely MN 55731 B Toronto Canada 6/29/1931 d Allen Servos Ball & Mary Josephine. BA Wellesley Coll 1954; EdM Harv 1955. D 10/12/2009 Bp James Louis Jelinek P 6/27/2010 Bp Brian N Prior. m 8/27/1978 Peter W Davis c 4. whiteironlake@mac.com

WEBSTER II, Phillip (Dal) 1802 Broadway, Lubbock TX 79401 B Chillicothe OH 9/2/1971 s Phillip Louis Webster & Elsie Marlene. BA The Pontifical Coll Josephinum Columbus OH 1993; MA The Pontifical Coll Josephinum Columbus OH 1995; JCL The CUA Washington DC 2001; MDiv Bex Columbus OH 2008. D 6/23/2007 P 6/28/2008 Bp Thomas Edward Breidenthal. m 8/21/2004 Kiah S Dennis c 3. Dio NW Texas Lubbock TX 2009-2010; Asst R S Fran Epis Ch Springboro OH 2008-2009; Asst R S Geo's Epis Ch Dayton OH 2007-2008. rev.phil.webster@gmail.com

WEBSTER, Randy Lee (Be) 393 Washington Ave, Belleville NJ 07109 **P Chr Ch Susquehanna PA 2110-** B Burlington IA 1/25/1957 s Shirley Lee Webster & Shirley Lea. BA Coe Coll 1982; MDiv Bex 1996. D 10/15/2005 P 4/22/2006 Bp John Palmer Croneberger. m 3/6/2007 Paul Edward Walker. P S Mk's New Milford PA 2010-2011; Cur Chr Ch Belleville NJ 2006-2009; Gr Ch Newark NJ 2000-2009. websterrl@aol.com

WEBSTER, Richmond Rudolphus (Ala) 202 Gordon Dr Se, Decatur AL 35601 **S Lk's Epis Ch Birmingham AL 2004-** B Clanton AL 9/26/1962 s Rufus Richmond Webster & Barbara Kay. U of Montevallo 1981; Huntingdon Coll 1983; BA Auburn U Montgomery 1993; MDiv VTS 1997. D 6/11/1997 Bp Robert Oran Miller P 12/17/1997 Bp Henry Nutt Parsley Jr. m 8/12/1988 Ellen Copeland c 2. R S Jn's Ch Decatur AL 1999-2004; Cur S Jn's Ch Montgomery AL 1997-1999. "Snapshots Of Hope," Morehouse, 2005. rwebster@saint-lukes.com

WEBSTER, Thomas Forbes (O) 1336 Ramblewood Trl, South Euclid OH 44121 B Cincinnati OH 7/23/1931 s Donald Clarence Webster & Jeannette Elenor. BS Bowling Green St U 1953; Med Kent St U 1958; BD Bex 1962. D 6/1/1962 P 12/1/1962 Bp Nelson Marigold Burroughs. m 9/6/1952 Olive M Eldred c 4. R Ch Of The Epiph Euclid OH 1992-1996; R Chr Epis Ch Kent OH 1980-1992; R S Tim's Epis Ch Cincinnati OH 1972-1980; S Paul's Epis Ch Of E Cleveland Cleveland OH 1968-1972; R Ch Of Our Sav Salem OH 1964-1968; P-in-c H Trin Ch Lisbon OH 1964-1968; Cur Ch Of Our Sav Akron OH 1962-1964. ttweb@sbcglobal.net

WEBSTER, Thomas Herbert (NC) 2906 Ridge Rd Nw, Wilson NC 27896 **Ch Of The Epiph Rocky Mt NC 2011-; St Marys Epis Ch Speed NC 2010-** B Minneapolis MN 5/4/1949 s Herbert Francis Webster & Patricia Joan. BS University of Pittsburgh 1971; BSW York Unniversity-Toronto 1974; MBA U of Manitoba 1990; LTh Montreal Dioc Theol Coll 1993. Trans from Anglican Church of Canada 2/1/2001 Bp Michael Bruce Curry. m 8/31/1974 Jane Suzanne Soules c 2. Ch Of The Adv Enfield NC 2006-2010; San Jose Mssn Smithfield NC 2006; Int All SS Ch Roanoke Rapids NC 2004-2005; E Reg Mnstry Tarboro NC 2002-2004; P Mssnr, E Reg Mnstry Dio No Carolina Raleigh NC 2001-2004; Dio No Carolina Raleigh NC 2001-2002. thwebster146@yahoo.com

WEBSTER, Valerie Minton (Mont) 311 S 3rd Ave, Bozeman MT 59715 B New Haven CT 3/27/1958 d Dwight Church Minton & Marian Haven. BA Mid 1982; Montana Mnstry Formation Prog 2004; Cert Epis TS of The SW 2005. D 9/18/2005 P 6/10/2006 Bp Charles Franklin Brookhart Jr. m 6/24/1986 James G Webster c 3. S Jas Ch Bozeman MT 2008-2009; P-in-c Geth Ch Manhattan MT 2006-2008; D-in-c Geth Ch Manhattan MT 2005-2006. Ord of S Lk 2003. VWEBSTER587@GMAIL.COM

WEBSTER II, Warren Raymond (Chi) 1424 N Dearborn St, Chicago IL 60610 **R S Chrys's Ch Chicago IL 1993-** B Chelsea MA 9/6/1945 s Warren Raymond Webster & Mildred. BA Pr 1967; BD EDS 1970. D 6/20/1970 P 12/15/1970 Bp John Melville Burgess. m 6/30/1970 Eve C Cabaniss c 2. R S Ptr's Ch Osterville MA 1981-1993; Assoc S Jas Ch New York NY 1977-1981; Supplement Accounts Boston MA 1976; R Trin Epis Ch Weymouth MA 1972-1977; Asst Chr Ch Needham MA 1970-1972. Dio Chicago Stndg Com 1997-2000; Stndg Com, Pres 2000-2000. wwebs16518@aol.com

WEDDERBURN, Derrick Hexford (NJ) Broadway & Royden, Cadmen NJ 08104 B Westmoreland Jama CA 5/11/1950 s Chester Arthur Wedderburn & Myrtle May. Untd Theol Coll Of The W Indies Kingston Jm; BA U of The W Indies 1980. D 7/6/1980 P 7/26/1981 Bp The Bishop Of Jamaica. m 12/29/1972 Madge Simmister c 1. S Mary's Epis Ch Pleasantville NJ 2008-2011; S Aug's Ch Camden NJ 1995-2005; S Mary's Epis Ch Phoenix AZ 1993-1995. Auth, "Fest Of The Palms Brochure". derrick3243@aol.com

WEDDLE, Karl Gilmore (ETenn) 313 Twinbrook Dr, Danville KY 40422 B Lincoln County KY 10/26/1936 s Carl Tilford Weddle & Helen Wood. BA Estrn Kentucky U 1960; MDiv SWTS 1968; MS U of Tennessee 1976; PhD U of Tennessee 1981. D 6/15/1968 Bp William F Gates Jr P 5/1/1969 Bp John Vander Horst. c 3. Ch Of The Gd Shpd Knoxville TN 1971-1983; D-In-Trng Calv Ch Memphis TN 1968-1969. weddle@knology.net

WEDGWOOD-GREENHOW, Stephen John Francis (NwT) 1412 W Illinois Ave, Midland TX 79701 **Ch Of The H Trin Midland TX 2010-** B Maryport England UK 5/30/1957 s Colin Wedgwood-Greenhow & Jean Hewitt. MA U of Cambridge 1978; BA U of Manchester 1982; ThM U of Edinburgh Edinburgh GB 1984. Trans from Church Of England 1/1/1991 as Priest Bp John Lester Thompson III. m 5/10/2010 Myrna Wedgwood-Greenhow. S Jas Of Jerusalem Epis Ch Yuba City CA 2004-2005; Dio Nthrn California Sacramento CA 1998-2003; Dio Nthrn California Sacramento CA 1995-1996; Int Trin Ch Sonoma CA 1994-1995; Int S Paul's Epis Ch Sacramento CA 1992-1994; S Mich's Epis Ch Carmichael CA 1990-1992. frjohngreenhow@yahoo.com

WEEKES, Jonathan Everton Walcott (CFla) 1604 Avenue Q, Fort Pierce FL 34950 **R Ch Of S Simon The Cyrenian Ft Pierce FL 1995-** B 4/5/1951 s Sydney Weekes & Veronica. THS Codrington Coll 1977; BA U of The W Indies 1977. m 7/8/1978 Judy Jennifer Keizer c 2.

WEEKS, Ann Gammon (ETenn) 305 N Forrest Ave, Lookout Mountain TN 37350 B Chattanooga TN 4/27/1946 d Wirt Henry Gammon & Brooke Younger. Interior Design U of Tennessee 1968. D 12/8/2007 Bp Charles Glenn

VonRosenberg. m 1/21/1978 WIlliam Bradley Weeks c 2. weeks305@gmail.com

WEEKS, Arianne R (NC) 1405 Boyce Ave, Towson MD 21204 **R Ch Of The Gd Shpd Ruxton MD 2011-** B New Yok City NY 8/5/1970 d John Raymond Rice & Dianne Gleason. BM New Engl Conservatory of Mus 1992; MDiv GTS 2008. D 3/15/2008 P 9/20/2008 Bp Mark Sean Sisk. m 11/23/2009 Khristian G Weeks c 1. Cler Disciplinary Bd Dio No Carolina Raleigh NC 2011; Assoc S Phil's Ch Durham NC 2008-2011. avrweeks@gmail.com

WEEKS, Jo Ann (Los) 23446 Swan St, Moreno Valley CA 92557 B Vernon TX 7/1/1939 d Thomas Winston Cole & Eva Mae. BA Wiley Coll 1960; MA Atlanta U Atlanta GA 1964; ETSBH 1988; MDiv CDSP 1990. D 6/16/1990 P 1/12/1991 Bp Frederick Houk Borsch. m 5/25/1963 Stanton Allen Weeks c 2. Vic Gr Mssn Moreno Vlly CA 1992-2011; Assoc All SS Epis Ch Riverside CA 1990-1992. Chapl OSL the Physcn 2003; Dioc Chapl Ord of the DOK 1994; Ord of DOK 1976; OSL the Physcn 2003. weeksj@msn.com

WEEKS, Lawrence Biddle (Me) 12 Catherine St, Portland ME 04102 **R Trin Epis Ch Portland ME 2002-; Dio Maine Portland ME 1996-** B Houston TX 9/3/1948 s William Preston Weeks & Thelma Biddle. BA Harv 1972; JD U of Arizona 1975; MDiv CDSP 1996. D 6/15/1996 P 12/1/1996 Bp Robert Reed Shahan. m 12/19/1997 Marcia Abbott Weeks c 2. R Chr Ch Florence AZ 1996-2002; Reg Mssnr Dio Arizona Phoenix AZ 1996-2002; R S Mich's Ch Coolidge AZ 1996-2002; R S Ptr's Ch Casa Grande AZ 1996-2002. rector@trinitychurchportland.org

WEEKS, Robert Oliver (Fla) 12825 Julington Rd, Jacksonville FL 32258 B New York NY 3/11/1926 s Carnes Weeks & Margaret. BA Ya 1949; GTS 1958; MDiv UTS 1959; MS NYTS 1976. D 6/11/1959 P 5/1/1960 Bp Horace W B Donegan. m 6/7/1958 Ann Holland c 3. Vic Bethany Ch Hilliard FL 1986-1989; Vic St Pat's Epis Ch S Johns Fl 1985-1986; Asst S Paul's Ch Darien CT 1975-1985; R Ch Of The H Apos New York NY 1968-1975; Asst Min Calv and St Geo New York NY 1967-1968. rowahw@aol.com

WEEKS, WIlliam Bradley (ETenn) Grace Episcopal Church, 20 Belvoir Ave, Chattanooga TN 37411 B Chattanooga TN 6/27/1949 s William Rawle Weeks & Elizabeth Bradley. BA U So 1971; JD U of Tennessee 1975. D 12/8/2007 Bp Charles Glenn VonRosenberg. m 1/21/1978 Ann Gammon Weeks c 2. bradw@wagnernelsonweeks.com

WEEKS WULF, Marta Joan Sutton (SeFla) 7350 SW 162nd Street, Palmetto Bay FL 33157 B Buenos Aires AR 5/24/1930 d Frederick Albert Sutton & Anne Loumina. Beloit Coll 1949; BA Stan 1951; MDiv Epis TS of The SW 1991. D 11/30/1991 P 6/5/1992 Bp Calvin Onderdonk Schofield Jr. m 9/1/2008 Karleton B Wulf c 3. Asst S Andr's Epis Ch Palmetto Bay FL 2007-2010; Asst S Andr's Epis Ch Palmetto Bay FL 2000-2002; Asst S Jas Epis Ch Midvale UT 1994-1995; P-at-Lg Dio SE Florida Miami FL 1992-2007; Dio SE Florida Miami FL 1992-1993. Auth, "Our Lord was Baptized, You Know," iuniverse, 2007. Dame, Ord S Jn of Jerusalem 1994. Hon Cn Trin Cathd, Miami Fl 2008; Hon DD Episc. Theol Sem. of the SW 2006. msweeks24@bellsouth.net

WEGER, Rohani Ann (SeFla) 1225 Texas St, Houston TX 77002 **Dio Texas Houston TX 2011-; S Simons Ch Miami FL 2000-** B Tanjung Indonesia 8/15/1965 d Dale Franklin Walker & Alice Francis. BA Wheaton Coll 1987; MDiv Epis TS Of The SW 2007. D 12/27/2008 Bp Leopold Frade P 1/23/2010 Bp Dena Arnall Harrison. m 7/11/1993 Hans Thomas Weger c 1. rohani2@sbcglobal.net

WEGLARZ, Eileen Eckert (NY) St. Mark's Episcopal Church, 85 E Main St, Mount Kisco NY 10549 **R S Mk's Ch Mt Kisco NY 2008-** B Reading PA 3/22/1948 d Ralph Edward Eckert & Fannie Ellen. Penn; Lic VTS 2002. D 6/8/2002 Bp Michael Whittington Creighton P 12/8/2002 Bp David John Bena. Missions Coordntr Dio Albany Albany NY 2003-2008; S Jn's Ch Essex NY 2002-2008. mothereileen@optonline.net

WEGMAN, Jay Daniel (NY) Cathedral Station, Box 1111, New York NY 10025 B Estherville IA 4/19/1964 s Jerry Merle Wegman & Rochelle Ann. BA U MN 1989; MDiv GTS 1993; STM Yale DS 1995; Cert Col 2002. D 6/24/1993 Bp Robert Marshall Anderson P 2/5/1994 Bp James Louis Jelinek. m 8/23/2005 Stephen A Facey. Lectr The GTS New York NY 2002-2003; Com Dio New York New York City NY 1997-2003; Cathd Of St Jn The Div New York NY 1993-2003. AAR 1995. Vilar Fell The Kennedy Cntr Washington DC 2003.

WEHMILLER, Paula Lawrence (Pa) 612 Ogden Ave., Swarthmore PA 19081 B Nashville TN 1/15/1946 d Charles Radford Lawrence & Margaret Morgan. BA Swarthmore Coll 1967; MS Bank St Coll of Educ 1971; MDiv GTS 1997. D 6/21/1997 Bp Allen Lyman Bartlett Jr P 6/27/1998 Bp Charles Ellsworth Bennison Jr. m 9/2/1967 John Frederick Wehmiller c 2. Pstr Bp'S Stff Dio Pennsylvania Philadelphia PA 1998-1999; Dio Pennsylvania Philadelphia PA 1997-1999; Asst To Bp Coadj Dio Pennsylvania Philadelphia PA 1997-1998. Auth, "A Gathering Of Gifts: A Journey Bk," Ch Pub, Inc., 2002; Auth, "Mister Rogers: Keeper of the Dream(Chapt)," *Mister Rogers Nbrhd: Chld, Television and Fred Rogers*, U Pgh Press, 1996; Auth, "When the Walls Come Tumbling Down (Chapt)," *Shifting Histories: Transforming Schools for Soc Change*, Harvard Educ Revs, 1995; Auth, "Face To Face: Lessons Learned On The Tchg Journey," *A Tyson-Mason Occasional Paper*, Friends' Coun On Educ, 1992; Auth, "When The Walls Come Tumbling Down," *Harvard Educational Revs*, Harvard Educational Revs, 1992; Auth, "The Miracle of the Bread Dough Rising," *A Tyson-Mason Occasional Paper*, Friends' Coun on Educ, 1986; Auth, "The Miracle Of The Bread Dough Rising," *Indep Sch Journ*, Natl Assn of Indep Schools, 1986. Benedictine Wmn Of Madison - Ecum Bd 1999-2006; EPF 1997; SSM - Assoc 1999; UBE 1997. Ecum Awd Benedictine Wmn of Madison 2007. revpaula@comcast.net

WEHNER, Paul B. (Tex) 2529 Avenue O, Galveston TX 77550 **Calv Epis Ch Richmond TX 2011-** B Austin TX 1/20/1948 s Sterling S Wehner & Elizabeth. Epis TS of the SW; BD U of Texas 1971; MBA SMU 1972; MDiv Epis TS of The SW 2001. D 6/16/2001 Bp Claude Edward Payne P 6/18/2002 Bp Don Adger Wimberly. m 9/6/1969 Sherry S Smith c 2. Gr Ch Galveston TX 2003-2011; Locum Tenons S Steph's Ch Beaumont TX 2001-2003. wehnerpb@prodigy.net

WEHRS SR, Jack Martin (Jack) (SanD) 4062 Varona St, San Diego CA 92106 B Chicago IL 5/12/1940 s Raymond F Wehrs & Florence G. BA U of St. Thos 1962; CTh ETSBH 1988; MDiv CDSP 1990. D 7/7/1991 Bp John Lester Thompson III P 12/11/1993 Bp Jerry Alban Lamb. m 6/2/1980 Shirley Kay Schiltz c 4. Dio San Diego San Diego CA 2003-2005; S Columba's Epis Ch Santee CA 1999-2001; Corp Dir Dio San Diego San Diego CA 1998-2009; Dioc Coun Dio San Diego San Diego CA 1996-1998; Vic S Anth Of The Desert Desert Hot Sprg CA 1996-1998; All SS Epis Ch Brawley CA 1994-1996; Asst S Steph's Epis Ch Sebastopol CA 1992-1993; Asst Ch Of The Incarn Santa Rosa CA 1991-1992. jackandshirley1@att.net

WEI, Fei-Jan Elizabeth (Tai) 114 Fuhe Rd 6FL, Yunghe City Taipei 23449 Taiwan B 9/7/1947 d Chao-Chun Wei & Jui-Lan. BA Fu-Jen Cath U 1997. D 5/30/1993 P 9/1/1997 Bp John Chih-Tsung Chien. m 12/25/1966 Te-Pei Chen c 2. weifeijan@yahoo.com.tw

WEICKER, Harold Hastings (Cal) 220 N Zapata Hwy #11-1014, Laredo TX 78043 **S Paul's Epis Ch San Rafael CA 2003-** B New York NY 9/24/1934 s Lowell Palmer Weicker & Mary Bickford. CDSP; BA Ya 1956; MDiv CDSP 1965; DMin U of Creation Sprtlty 2000. D 6/20/1965 Bp James Albert Pike P 12/1/1965 Bp Horace W B Donegan. m 1/24/1975 Carolyn M Morrison c 5. Chr Ch Santa Rosa CA 1988-1992; Dio Nthrn California Sacramento CA 1987; Asst S Aug's Epis Ch Tempe AZ 1984-1987; S Jn's Cathd Albuquerque NM 1973-1975; Asst The Ch of S Edw The Mtyr New York NY 1968-1972; R S Ptr's Epis Ch Monroe CT 1967-1968; Cn Mssnr Trin Cathd Phoenix AZ 1966-1967; Asst S Clem's Ch Berkeley CA 1965-1966. The Soc of the Anchor The PBp 1992. hhweicker@yahoo.com

WEIDMAN, Hal Joseph (At) 725 College St, Macon GA 31201 **Bd Gvnr, Appleton Fam Mnstrs Dio Atlanta Atlanta GA 2011-; Mem, Dioc Cmsn on Environ Stwdshp Dio Atlanta Atlanta GA 2011-; P-in-c S Paul's Ch Macon GA 2010-** B Birmingham AL 11/8/1957 s Frank Joseph Weidman & Loyette Rita. BS Auburn U 1980; MPH U of Alabama at Birmingham 1987; MDiv STUSo 2002. D 6/8/2002 Bp Jerry Alban Lamb P 12/15/2002 Bp Henry Nutt Parsley Jr. m 8/26/2010 Sara Mixon Weidman c 2. R S Jn's W Point GA 2007-2010; Assoc S Ptr's Epis Ch Talladega AL 2002-2003. hjweidman@aol.com

WEIDNER, David Jeffery (Fla) 128 Bilbao Dr, Saint Augustine FL 32086 **R Trin Epis Ch St Aug FL 2004-** B Canonsburg PA 9/1/1959 s Thomas John Weidner & Ora Louise. BS U Pgh 1981; MDiv TESM 1986; DMin Gordon-Conwell TS 1998. D 6/8/1986 Bp Alden Moinet Hathaway P 4/9/1987 Bp C(laude) Charles Vache. m 7/25/1981 Susan Henderson c 2. R S Chris's By The Sea Portland TX 1996-2004; Mssn Com Dio W Texas San Antonio TX 1996-2002; R Epis Ch Of Our Sav Midlothian VA 1989-1996; Assoc The Epis Ch Of The Mssh Chesapeake VA 1986-1989. Bro of S Andr 2004; Ord of S Lk 1996. weidner1234@bellsouth.net

WEIERBACH, Cornelia Miller (Va) 5613 23rd St N, Arlington VA 22205 B Bad Cannstatt, Germany 5/16/1955 d Robert Lee Miller & Cornelia vanden Toorn. BA St. Jn's Coll 1977; MA GW 1983; MDiv VTS 2010. D 6/5/2010 P 12/11/2010 Bp Shannon Sherwood Johnston. m 11/10/1990 Robert Weierbach c 2. Imm Ch-On-The-Hill Alexandria VA 2011; Trin Ch Arlington VA 2011. corry@weierbach.com

WEIHER, Joie Muir Clee (Va) 7057 Blackwell Rd, Warrenton VA 20187 **Ch Of The H Cross Dunn Loring VA 2011-** B Houston TX 10/19/1976 BA U Of Houston 1999; MDiv VTS 2005. D 6/11/2005 Bp Don Adger Wimberly P 12/21/2005 Bp Peter James Lee. m 1/8/2000 Jesse C Weiher. R S Lk's Ch Remington VA 2007-2011; Cur Trin Ch Upperville VA 2005-2006. joiemuir@gmail.com

WEIKERT, Robert Curtis (Mich) No address on file. B Rochester NY 4/5/1943 s Raymond Oscar Weikart & Ruth Leverne. AA Concordia Jr Coll 1963; BA Concordia Sr Coll 1965; MDiv Concordia TS 1969. P 2/1/1977 Bp H Coleman McGehee Jr. m 8/9/1969 Joanne Kay Bolinski.

WEIL, Louis (Cal) 2451 Ridge Rd, Berkeley CA 94709 B Houston TX 5/10/1935 s Ralph Weil & Alma Larue. Std 72; BA SMU 1956; MA Harv 1958;

STB GTS 1961; Cath U of Paris 1966. D 6/20/1961 Bp Charles A Mason P 1/1/1962 Bp J(ohn) Joseph Meakins Harte. CDSP Berkeley CA 1988-2007; Nash Nashotah WI 1971-1988. Auth, "Liturg For Living"; Auth, "Sacraments & Liturg". lweil@cdsp.edu

WEILER, Matthew Gordon Beck (CFla) 3538 Lenox Rd, Birmingham AL 35213 B Milwaukee WI 11/26/1970 s Gordon Harold Weiler & Lois Mary. BS U Of Cntrl Florida 1992; MA U Of Florida 1995; DAS Ya Berk 2001; MDiv Yale DS 2001. D 5/26/2001 Bp John Wadsworth Howe P 11/30/2001 Bp Frank Tracy Griswold III. m 12/17/1995 Janna Granger. Asst The Cathd Ch Of The Adv Birmingham AL 2004-2005; Int Ch Of The Resurr Hopewell Jct NY 2003-2004; Cur Ch Of S Mary The Vrgn New York NY 2001-2003. fatherweiler@hotmail.com

WEILER, William Leon (Va) 5908 9th St N, Arlington VA 22205 B Philadelphia PA 5/1/1936 s Harry Albert Weiler & Bertha Florence. BD Reformed Epis Sem 1961; BA U of Pennsylvania 1961; Cert PDS 1962; PhD Hebr Un Coll 1971. D 6/9/1962 Bp Oliver J Hart P 12/1/1962 Bp Joseph Gillespie Armstrong. m 9/10/1960 Carol Ruth Arnold c 3. Assoc R S Mich's Epis Ch Arlington VA 1998-2000; Luth Theo Sthrn Sem Columbia SC 1993-1996; Ch Of The Gd Shpd Lexington KY 1992-1993; Dir of Dvlpmt Nash Nashotah WI 1989-1991; S Ptr's Epis Ch Arlington VA 1989; Epis Ch Cntr New York NY 1979-1989; S Geo's Epis Ch Arlington VA 1979-1981; Natl Coun Of Ch New York NY 1974-1979; R Ch Of S Jn The Evang Essington PA 1964-1967; Cur H Apos And Medtr Philadelphia PA 1962-1963. AAR. Fell ECF 1967. wweiler@vts.edu

WEINER, Margaret (Ia) 2525 Patricia Dr, Urbandale IA 50322 **Asst to Bp (Vol) Dio Iowa Des Moines IA 2008-; supply Cler S Paul Epis Ch Des Moines IA 2003-** B Washington DC 11/14/1940 d Samuel Levi Yoder & Jete Barbara. BA Duke 1963; MA Penn 1968; PhD Penn 1975; MDiv SWTS 1987. D 6/13/1987 P 12/19/1987 Bp Walter Cameron Righter. m 9/22/2002 Jerry Stanley Weiner. Vic S Jas Epis Ch Oskaloosa IA 1990-2002; Dio Iowa Des Moines IA 1987-2002; Trin Ch Ottumwa IA 1987-2002. Whipple Schlr SWTS 1987; Anderson Schlr SWTS 1986. meyweiner@q.com

WEINER, Mary Lou (Ida) 4933 W View Dr, Meridian ID 83642 **D S Mich's Cathd Boise ID 1991-** B Deer Lodge MT 10/27/1941 d Ralph James Beck & Marjorie Mildred. BS U of Washington 1965; Rad 1969; MS U of Washington 1978; MA NW Nazarere U 2007. D 10/4/1991 Bp John Stuart Thornton. m 8/20/1989 Morton Alan Weiner. "Response to a Call," *Love Among Us*, 2009; "Demons Amongst Us/Sermon," *Prchr's mag*, Nazarere Pub Hse, 2007. Diac Mnstry In Tradition Of S Steph Naad 2001.

WEINER TOMPKINS, Rebecca (NY) 145 W 46th St, New York NY 10036 **CGS Catechist Ch Of S Mary The Vrgn New York NY 2010-; D Ch Of S Mary The Vrgn New York NY 2009-** B Cleveland OH d Jack Bernard Weiner & Gloria Bernice. D Formation Prog; ABD- Engl Grad Cntr - CUNY; BA in Lit UCSB 1974; MFA in Writing Goddard Coll 1981. D 5/2/2009 Bp Mark Sean Sisk. m 4/18/1997 Ptolemy Tompkins c 2. redboat@erols.com

WEINREICH, Gabriel (Mich) 2116 Silver Maples Drive, Chelsea MI 48118 B Vilna PL 2/12/1928 s Max Weinreich & Regina. BA Col 1948; MA Col 1949; PhD Col 1954. D 6/29/1985 P 1/1/1986 Bp H Coleman McGehee Jr. m 10/23/1971 Gerane Siemering Benamou. R S Steph's Ch Hamburg MI 1993-1996; Adj Min S Clare Of Assisi Epis Ch Ann Arbor MI 1985-1990. weinreic@umich.edu

WEIR, Daniel Sargent (WNY) 139 Locust St, Danvers MA 01923 B Ithaca NY 11/2/1946 s Charles Ignatius Weir & Gertrude. BA U of Massachusetts 1969; MDiv EDS 1972; Oxf 1973; Cert Hartford Sem 1991. D 9/17/1972 P 10/21/1973 Bp Alexander Doig Stewart. m 5/20/1972 Janette MacLean c 2. R S Mths Epis Ch E Aurora NY 2001-2010; Int Ch Of The H Comm Lakeview NY 2000-2001; Trin Epis Ch Buffalo NY 1993-1999; Int Calv Epis Ch Williamsville NY 1991-1993; Convenor Cler Assn Dio Wstrn New York Tonawanda NY 1991-1993; Cmsn on Racism Dio Wstrn New York Tonawanda NY 1989-1991; BEC Dio Wstrn New York Tonawanda NY 1988-1992; Dep for Outreach Mnstrs Dio Wstrn New York Tonawanda NY 1988-1991; BEC Dio Wstrn Massachusetts Springfield MA 1986-1988; Dep GC Dio Wstrn Massachusetts Springfield MA 1982-1988; R H Trin Epis Ch Southbridge MA 1979-1988; H Trin Ch Chesapeake VA 1979-1986; R Trin Epis Ch Ware MA 1976-1979; P-in-c S Mart's Ch Pittsfield MA 1974-1976; Dio Wstrn Massachusetts Springfield MA 1973-1988; Asst S Steph's Ch Pittsfield MA 1973-1976. EPF 1972. Hon Cn S Paul's Cathd Buffalo NY 1988. dsweir@alumni.umass.edu

WEIR, Silas Michael (Colo) 4009 Histead Way, Evergreen CO 80439 B Chicago IL 4/1/1939 s Homer Faquier Weir & Mildred Elizabeth. BS NWU 1961; MA U MI 1969; MA Iliff TS 1997; MDiv Iliff TS 2000. D 11/9/2002 Bp William Jerry Winterrowd. m 9/27/1959 Eunice Elizabeth Black c 3. Par of St Paul's Ch Norwalk Norwalk CT 2005-2008; D Ch Of The Trsfg Evergreen CO 2003-2005.

WEISE, John Winfred Thorburn (WVa) Po Box 1642, Parkersburg WV 26102 B Philadelphia PA 3/7/1931 s George Albert Weise & Georgia Carol. BS Salisbury St U 1959; MDiv Nash 1962; DD Epis TS In Kentucky 1983; DMin GTF 1992. D 6/9/1962 Bp Oliver J Hart P 12/1/1962 Bp Joseph Gillespie Armstrong. S Steph's Epis Ch Beckley WV 2002-2003; Chr Ch Clarksburg WV 2001-2002; Int Zion Epis Ch Chas Town WV 1999-2001; Int S Mary's Epis Ch Pocomoke City MD 1998-1999; S Ptr's Ch Huntington WV 1997; Trin Ch Parkersburg WV 1994-1997; S Mk's Epis Ch S Albans WV 1993-1994; Calv Epis Ch Ashland KY 1974-1992; P-in-c Chr Ch Ironton OH 1974-1982; R S Steph's Epis Ch Cincinnati OH 1968-1974; Cn To Bp Dio Eau Claire Eau Claire WI 1965-1968; Cur S Paul's Ch Albany GA 1964-1965; Cur S Clements Ch Philadelphia PA 1962-1964. Auth, "arts Ch Pub".

WEISER, Samuel Ivan (RG) 848 Camino De Levante, Santa Fe NM 87501 B New York NY 4/1/1935 BA U Chi 1957; MA U Tor 1960; MA Oxf 1967. D 10/12/1962 Bp James Winchester Montgomery P 4/20/1963 Bp The Bishop Of Quebec. m 1/18/1967 Antoinette Graham c 3. Ch of the H Faith Santa Fe NM 1995-1996; Hon Asst S Thos Ch New York NY 1989-1994; R Ch Of The Epiph Tempe AZ 1966-1973; Vic S Tim's Ch Fairfield CT 1965-1966; Asst S Paul's Ch Fairfield CT 1964-1966; Cur Chr Ch Winnetka IL 1962-1964. Phi Beta Kappa. SUPERDAD3@Q.COM

WEISS, Charles Sumner (Pgh) 732 Dorseyville Rd, Pittsburgh PA 15238 **S Thos' Epis Ch Canonsburg PA 2007-** B Pittsburgh PA 5/16/1961 s Charles Weiss & Mary Augusta. BA Witt 1983; MS Drexel U 1986; MDiv VTS 1997. D 6/21/1997 Bp Alden Moinet Hathaway P 1/17/1998 Bp Robert William Duncan. m 3/5/1988 Martha Anne Hill c 2. Asst Chr Ch Greenville Wilmington DE 1997-2002. revcsw@aol.com

WEISS, Edward Allen (CFla) 200 Nw 3rd St, Okeechobee FL 34972 **R Ch Of Our Sav Okeechobee FL 2000-** B Paterson NJ 10/5/1935 s George Harry Weiss & Florence. BA Drew U 1955; MCP U of Nuevo Leon Monterey MX 1967; MD U NC 1972; Cert Inst for Chr Stds Florida 1991; DMin Drew U 1996. Rec from Roman Catholic 5/30/1973 Bp (George) Paul Reeves. m 7/6/1974 JoAnne Fite c 2. P-in-c Emm Ch Orlando FL 1998-2000; Asst S Marg's Ch Inverness FL 1996-1998. Acad of Par Cler 2001; All Mltry & Med Societies 1966; Ord St. Ben (O) 1985. coos@okeechobee.com

WEISS, James Michael Egan (Mass) Dept of Theology, Boston College, Chestnut Hill MA 02467 **Asst Emm Ch Boston MA 2001-** B Chicago IL 12/2/1946 s Walter Stephen Weiss & Mary Virginia. BA Loyola U 1967; MA U Chi 1970; PhD U Chi 1979; Pre-Ord Stds EDS 1996; Doctoral Study Ludwig-Maximilian U, Munich 1997. D 6/7/1997 P 5/30/1998 Bp M(arvil) Thomas Shaw III. Assoc S Mary's Epis Ch Dorchester MA 1997-2006; Chair, Forum for Faith & the Future Dio Massachusetts Boston MA 1983-1986. Auth, "Humanist Biography in Renaissance Italy & Reformation Germany," Ashgate, 2010; Auth, "Humanism Renaissance, Oxford Encyclopedia Of The Reformation," 1996; Auth, "Var Scholarly arts Renaissance & Reformation Hist," 1979. Soc For The Study Of Chr Sprtlty 2001; Sprtl Dir Intl 2002. Waldron Tchg Awd Boston Coll Undergraduate Govt. 2007. james.weiss@bc.edu

WEISS, Louise Lindecamp (RG) 3900 Trinity Dr, Los Alamos NM 87544 **Asstg P Trin On The Hill Epis Ch Los Alamos NM 2008-** B Sandusky OH 11/4/1949 d Charles Lindecamp & Margery C. BA Thos Edison St Coll 2005; DCS Trin Sch for Mnstry 2008. D 6/7/2008 P 12/13/2008 Bp William Carl Frey. m 7/24/1969 Douglas Weiss c 1. llweiss@mesatop.com

WEISSERT, Richard H (U) 147 S 800 E, Orem UT 84097 B Horbury Wakefield UK 10/20/1923 s William S Weissert & Gertrude. BS USMMA 1944; BD Utah St U 1952. D 5/20/1976 Bp Otis Charles P 5/1/1990 Bp George Edmonds Bates. m 9/15/1947 Anna L Schleef. Loc P S Mary's Ch Provo UT 1990-1998; D Dio Utah Salt Lake City UT 1976-1982.

WEISSMAN, Stephen Edward (Mo) 434 Gorman Bridge Rd, Asheville NC 28806 **P Assoc S Mary's Ch Asheville NC 2007-** B Cincinnati OH 4/14/1940 s Frederick Burchard Weissman & Margot Isabel. BA Ken 1962; Kelham Theol Coll 1964; MDiv EDS 1965; BS OH SU 1968. D 6/26/1965 P 1/8/1966 Bp Roger W Blanchard. m 6/22/2006 Gary George Reynolds c 5. No Convoc Hannibal MO 1995-2000; Vic S Steph's Ch S Louis MO 1991-1995; Vic S Paul's Ch Windham CT 1990-1991; Jub Min Dio Springfield Springfield IL 1985-1990; R S Andr's Epis Ch Edwardsville IL 1975-1990; Cur S Phil's Ch Columbus OH 1966-1968. Auth, *Word & Wit*. sweissma@earthlink.net

WEITZEL, Mark Augustin (Los) 1020 N. Brand Blvd., Glendale CA 91202 **R S Mk's Par Glendale CA 1993-; Assoc S Mk's Par Glendale CA 1991-** B Los Angeles CA 6/1/1962 s Harlan Irving Weitzel & Jane. BA U CA 1984; U of Kansas 1986; MDiv GTS 1989. D 9/16/1989 Bp Oliver Bailey Garver Jr P 3/24/1990 Bp Frederick Houk Borsch. m 6/20/1992 Shelley Leanne Filip c 2. Asst S Mart-In-The-Fields Par Winnetka CA 1990-1991; Chapl Dio Los Angeles Los Angeles CA 1989-1990. frweitzel@stmarksglendale.org

WELCH, Elizabeth Jean (Cal) Sojourn Chaplain, San Fransico General Hospital, San Fransico CA 94110 **Assoc All SS' Ch San Francisco CA 2008-; Sojourn Multifaith Chapl San Francisco CA 2008-** B Colorado Springs CO 3/14/1978 d Rock Elliott Welch & Jean Casey. BA S Olaf Coll 2000; MDiv CDSP 2004. D 6/13/2008 P 12/6/2008 Bp Marc Handley Andrus. Sojourn Multifaith Chapl San Francisco CA 2006-2008. welche_00@yahoo.com

WELCH, George Truman (Mass) 1692 Beacon St, Waban MA 02468 **Chair Com Dio Massachusetts Boston MA 1994-; R Ch Of The Gd Shpd Waban**

MA 1991- B Montgomery AL 8/26/1946 s George Truman Welch & Jean. BA U of Alabama 1968; MDiv GTS 1974. D 6/17/1974 P 10/5/1974 Bp Furman Stough. H Trin Epis Ch Hot Sprg Vill AR 1985; Assoc S Mk's Epis Ch Little Rock AR 1982-1991; Asst S Mart's Epis Ch Metairie LA 1979-1982; Asst All SS Epis Ch Birmingham AL 1974-1979. Auth, "Var arts". gtwelchjr@comcast.net

WELCH, Lauren Marie (Md) 1925 Ewald Ave, Baltimore MD 21222 **Archd for Formation Dio Maryland Baltimore MD 2006-** B Fairmont WV 8/16/1947 d Leo Jr Kullman & Martha Louise. AA Potomac St Coll 1967; BS W Virginia U 1969. D 6/17/1989 Bp A(lbert) Theodore Eastman. m 8/19/1978 Clifford Welch c 1. Liaison for Justice and Peace Dio Maryland Baltimore MD 1996-2006; Serv The Ch Of The Nativ Cedarcroft Baltimore MD 1992-1996; Serv Ch Of The Guardian Ang Baltimore MD 1989-1992. Assn for Epis Deacons 1996. lmwelch16@verizon.net

WELCH, Robert Eugene (Colo) 15126 West Camino Estrella Drive, Surprise AZ 85374 B Hays KS 10/3/1931 s Harry Earl Welch & Anna Violet. BA U of Nthrn Colorado 1957; Med Wayne 1975; MDiv 1988; CTh 1989. D 6/8/1989 P 12/1/1989 Bp William Carl Frey. c 3. Asstg S Steph's Ch Longmont CO 1992-1998; Emmaus Ch Longmont CO 1992; Dio Colorado Denver CO 1990-1992; Vic Emmaus Ch Longmont CO 1990-1992; Asst S Barth's Ch Estes Pk CO 1989-1990. frbobwel@cox.net

WELD II, George Francis (SC) 15 Old English Dr, Charleston SC 29407 B Salem MA 4/21/1946 s Sumner Appleton Weld & Margaret Elizabeth. Cert Bryant and Stratton Coll 1966; LTh VTS 1976. D 10/28/1976 Bp Alexander Doig Stewart P 6/1/1977 Bp Albert William Hillestad. c 2. Assoc R S Phil's Ch Charleston SC 1995-1997; S Jn's Epis Par Johns Island SC 1987-1996; R Ascen Epis Ch Amherst VA 1980-1987; R S Mk's Ch Clifford VA 1980-1987; Com Dio Springfield Springfield IL 1979-1980; Assoc Chr Ch Springfield IL 1976-1980. Efac. CASAUMILE@GMAIL.COM

WELD, Louise (SC) 136 Oyster Point Row, Charleston SC 29412 **Pstr S Jas Ch Charleston SC 2006-** B Wilmington NC 9/8/1944 d Richard Gwathmey & Louise. M.Div. TESM 2005. D 2/8/2006 P 9/10/2006 Bp Edward Lloyd Salmon Jr. c 4. lweld@saint-james.org

WELDON, Ariel Kennth (SC) 1419 Church Street, Charleston SC 29407 **R S Jn's Ch Florence SC 2008-** B Sumter SC 11/18/1967 s William Edward Sumter & Eliose Travis. BA Coll of Charleston 1991; MDiv STUSo 2001. D 6/5/2001 P 12/8/2001 Bp Edward Lloyd Salmon Jr. m 5/22/1993 Mary Daland Lovejoy c 2. Porter-Gaud Sch Charleston SC 2001-2008; Cur S Phil's Ch Charleston SC 2001-2008. KENWELDON@STJOHNSFLORENCE.ORG

WELDON JR, James A (Ga) 802 Broadway, New York NY 10003 **S Patricks Ch Albany GA 2009-** B Griffin GA 1/28/1978 s James Adams Weldon & Marilyn Watson. BBA U GA 2000; MDiv Merc 2007; STM The GTS 2009. D 7/2/2008 P 2/11/2009 Bp Henry Irving Louttit. m 9/23/2006 Alison S Alison Michelle Sarrat c 1. Asst Gr Epis Ch New York NY 2008-2009; Lay Cur King Of Peace Kingsland GA 2007-2008. jayxvi@aol.com

WELDON, Jonathon (Oly) Episcopal Diocese Of Oregon, 11800 S.W. Military Ln., Portland OR 97219 **Cn Mssnr S Paul Epis Ch Bellingham WA 2008-** B Portland OR 10/20/1954 s Herbert Weldon Butt & Olive. BA U of Oregon 1980; MDiv GTS 1989. D 6/18/1989 P 2/1/1990 Bp Robert Louis Ladehoff. m 5/31/1980 Sharon Lee Lowe c 2. Cn to the Ordnry Dio Oregon Portland OR 2004-2008; Dio Oregon Portland OR 1991-2008; R Ch Of The Resurr Eugene OR 1991-2004; Asst S Mk's Epis Par Medford OR 1989-1991. jnweldon@q.com

WELIN, Amy Doyle (Ct) 58 Brookfield Rd, Seymour CT 06483 **Int Trin Ch Torrington CT 2011-** B Hackensack NJ 8/17/1957 d Francis Doyle & AnnMarie. BA Chestnut Hill Coll Philadelphia PA 1979; MA Ford 1981; MDiv Ya Berk 2004. D 6/12/2004 Bp Andrew Donnan Smith P 1/15/2005 Bp Wilfrido Ramos-Orench. m 10/11/2003 Gregory William Welin c 4. P-in-c Chr Ch Ansonia CT 2006-2011; Cur S Paul's Ch Riverside CT 2004-2006. ADWELIN@GMAIL.COM

WELIN, Gregory William (Ct) Po Box 1214, New Britain CT 06050 **Stndg Com Dio Connecticut Hartford CT 2010-; P-in-c S Jn's Ch New Milford CT 2009-** B New Haven CT 3/24/1961 s Leonard Helge Welin & Mary Lou. BA Gordon Coll 1983; MDiv Gordon-Conwell TS 1989; STM Ya Berk 1991; CAS Ya Berk 1991; DMin Hartford Sem 2012. D 6/13/1992 Bp Arthur Edward Walmsley P 1/15/1994 Bp Clarence Nicholas Coleridge. m 10/11/2003 Amy Doyle. Int Trin Ch Seymour CT 2008-2009; Vic Trin-S Mich's Ch Fairfield CT 2004-2008; Asst R S Mk's Ch New Britain CT 1996-2003; Cur S Jas Ch New London CT 1993-1996. gwwelin@gmail.com

WELLER, Edith Beardall (Oly) 8216 14th Ave Ne, Seattle WA 98115 **Ch Of The Resurr Bellevue WA 2008-** B Winchester VA 11/11/1953 BS U of Wisconsin. D 6/28/2003 P 1/17/2004 Bp Vincent Waydell Warner. m 12/29/1973 Albert John Weller c 2. Cur Trin Epis Ch Everett WA 2003-2006. ebweller53@q.com

WELLER, Gordon Frederick (Mich) 218 W Ottawa St, Lansing MI 48933 **R S Paul's Epis Ch Lansing MI 1999-** B Utica NY 2/11/1947 s Grant Lynford Weller & Mary Kennedy. MDiv Bex; DMin Drew U; AA Hudson Vlly Cmnty Coll; BA Johnson St Coll. D 6/9/1973 P 12/15/1973 Bp Charles Bowen Persell Jr. m 6/18/1970 Linda Jo Gallup. R S Jn's Ch Mt Pleasant MI 1987-1999; Asst S Jas Epis Ch Birmingham MI 1976-1986; Cur S Jn's Ch Massena NY 1973-1976; P S Paul's Ch Waddington NY 1973-1976. gordonweller@stpaulslansing.org

WELLER, Gretchen Kay (WMich) 435 SOM Center Road, Mayfield Village OH 44143 **Emm Ch Hastings MI 2009-** B Springfield OH 8/25/1944 d Harry Robert Weller & Gretchen Weller. BS OH SU 1988; MDiv Ya Berk 1993. D 6/24/1996 P 2/21/1997 Bp Edward Witker Jones. c 1. S Barth's Ch Mayfield Vill OH 2002-2009; R S Alb's Ch Sussex WI 2000-2002; Assoc S Jn's Ch Lynchburg VA 1998-2000; S Steph's Ch Ridgefield CT 1997-1998; Chr Ch Cathd Indianapolis IN 1996-1997. DOK 2000. gretchen@revmom.com

WELLER JR, Thomas Carroll (CGC) 2300 W Beach Dr, Panama City FL 32401 **Assoc H Nativ Epis Ch Panama City FL 2009-** B Panama City FL 9/14/1935 s Thomas Carroll Weller & Louise. BA/BS U of Florida 1957; MBA U MI 1963; U.S. Naval War Coll Newport RI 1969; Cert Luth TS at Gettysburg 1984. D 6/10/1983 P 3/1/1984 Bp Charlie Fuller McNutt Jr. m 6/29/1957 Linda Noble Peters c 4. Vic S Thos By The Sea Panama City Bch FL 2004-2009; Assoc H Nativ Epis Ch Panama City FL 2003-2004; Int Gr Epis Ch Panama City Bch FL 2000-2001; Assoc H Nativ Epis Ch Panama City FL 1999-2000; Vic Trin Ch Apalachicola FL 1984-1998; Cur Mt Calv Camp Hill PA 1983-1984. twellerpc@knology.net

WELLES JR, Donald Roderick (Del) 2303 Ridgeway Rd, Wilmington DE 19805 **Assoc Ch of St Andrews & St Matthews Wilmington DE 2002-** B Wilmington DE 4/17/1935 s Donald Roderick Welles & Elinor Scott. BA Ya 1959; MDiv EDS 1962. D 9/15/1962 Bp John Brooke Mosley P 4/16/1963 Bp Charles F Hall. m 10/6/1973 Susan Gale Weck c 2. Arlington Sch Fairburn GA 1982-1986; The TS at The U So Sewanee TN 1977-1982; Cur Chr Ch Exeter NH 1962-1964. rwelles475@verizon.net

WELLES JR, George H(ayward) (Mass) 550 Main St, West Dennis MA 02670 **R Ch Of Our Sav Milton MA 1999-** B Norwood MA 10/18/1935 s George Hayward Welles & Flora Lydia. BA Wms 1957; MDiv VTS 1964. D 6/20/1964 Bp Anson Phelps Stokes Jr P 1/1/1965 Bp William Foreman Creighton. m 6/8/1958 Annie M Murphy c 4. The Ch Of S Mary Of The Harbor Provincetown MA 1989-1997; S Mary's Epis Ch Barnstable MA 1986-1989; Convenor Dist 1916 Dio Massachusetts Boston MA 1985-1986; Asst Min S Dav's Epis Ch So Yarmouth MA 1983-1986; Asst Min The Ch Of The Epiph Washington DC 1964-1966.

WELLFORD, Eleanor L (Va) 510 S Gaskins Rd, Richmond VA 23238 **Assoc R S Mary's Ch Richmond VA 2007-** B Richmond VA 9/18/1953 d Maynard Smith & Mary Young. BA Hollins U 1975; MBA Virginia Commonwealth U 1977; MDiv UTS Richmond VA 2005. D 6/24/2006 P 2/3/2007 Bp Peter James Lee. m 6/24/1978 Ten Eyck T Wellford c 3. ewellford@aol.com

WELLNER, robert harry (Ct) 4750 Welby Drive, P.O. Box 142, Schnecksville PA 18078 **Supply P Trin And S Phil's Epis Ch Lansford PA 1991-** B Brooklyn NY 4/22/1928 s Robert John Wellner & Harriet Hanna. BA Leh 1952; MDiv Ya Berk 1955. D 4/16/1955 P 11/5/1955 Bp James P De Wolfe. m 12/27/2003 Ruth S Wellner c 1. R S Jn's Epis Ch Vernon Rock Vernon CT 1969-1988; R S Jas Ch Hartford CT 1961-1969; R Chr Ch Towanda PA 1957-1961, Asst Trin Ch Ft Wayne IN 1956-1957; Vic S Alb's Ch Brooklyn NY 1955-1956. Educ Awd Rockville ChmbrCom 1981. bobwell@ptd.net

WELLS, Ben Reid (At) 228 Pine Grove Church Rd, Culloden GA 31016 **Asst S Fran Ch Macon GA 2011-** B Frenchburg KY 3/30/1959 s William Earl Wells & Edith Marie. BS U of Kentucky 1981; MS U of Kentucky 1982; MDiv CDSP 2011. D 12/18/2010 P 8/27/2011 Bp J(ohn) Neil Alexander. benrwells@gmail.com

WELLS, Charlotte E (Ore) 11265 SW Cabot St, Beaverton OR 97005 **Asst to the R/Yth Min S Barth's Ch Beaverton OR 2008-** B Plainfield NJ 12/22/1957 d Charles Edward Risberg & Margaret Edythe. BS Kean U 1995; MDiv The GTS 2008. D 6/7/2008 Bp George Edward Councell P 12/10/2008 Bp Sanford Zangwill Kaye Hampton. m 7/11/1998 Donald Wells. charlotteewells@gmail.com

WELLS, Edgar Fisher (NY) 400 W 43rd St Apt V V, New York NY 10036 B New York NY 3/26/1930 s Edgar F Wells & Isabelle Eliza. BA Br 1954; MDiv Nash 1960; Marq 1969. D 1/28/1960 P 8/9/1960 Bp William Hampton Brady. Evang Com Dio New York New York City NY 1980-1985; Sprtl Dir, Curs Dio New York New York City NY 1980-1982; R Ch Of S Mary The Vrgn New York NY 1979-1998; Alum Wrdn Nash Nashotah WI 1974-1979; The Annunc Of Our Lady Gurnee IL 1965-1979; Asst S Ptr's Ch Bronx NY 1963-1965; Vic S Paul's Ch Plymouth WI 1961-1963; S Bon Plymouth WI 1960-1963. Affirming Catholicism 1990; Pres, CCU, Dio New York 1983-1984. Hon DD GTS New York NY 1998. edgarcito30@verizon.net

WELLS, Fletcher Marshall (Va) St George's Episcopal Church, 905 Princess Anne St, Fredericksburg VA 22401 **S Jas Par Wilmington NC 2009-** B Albuquerque NM 8/31/1980 s Peter Crawford Wells & Jane Marshall. BS Jas Madison U VA; MDiv VTS 2007. D 6/16/2007 P 12/18/2007 Bp Peter James

Lee. m Lori A Wells. Assitant To The R S Geo's Ch Fredericksburg VA 2007-2009. FLETCHERMWELLS@GMAIL.COM

WELLS, Jane Ely (O) 105 S Cedar St, Oberlin OH 44074 B Lexington KY 2/15/1939 d Fordyce Ely & Dikka. BA Ob 1961; MA U IL 1962; Med Kent St U 1980. D 11/13/2004 Bp Mark Hollingsworth Jr. m 12/28/1962 Charles F Wells c 2. jwells@oberlin.net

WELLS, Jason Aubrey (NH) 30 Cherry Street, Apartment 109, Concord NH 03104 **Vic Gr Epis Ch Concord NH 2007-** B Dallas TX 8/23/1979 s John Andrew Wells & Diane Patricia. BS SMU 2001; BS SMU 2001; MDiv PrTS 2004. D 9/18/2004 P 4/9/2005 Bp V Gene Robinson. Cur Gr Ch Manchester NH 2004-2007. fr.jawells@gmail.com

WELLS SR, John T (Tex) 14043 Horseshoe Cir, Woodway TX 76712 **R Epis Ch Of The H Sprt Waco TX 2003-** B Harmony KY 5/31/1941 s Jack Dale Wells & Eila Shirley. BS E Kentucky U Richmond KY 1964; MS Shippensburg U Shippensburg PA 1984; MDiv Epis TS of The SW 1998. D 11/7/1998 Bp Leopoldo Jesus Alard P 8/8/1999 Bp Claude Edward Payne. m 10/24/1981 Su T Han c 2. Vic S Paul's Epis Ch Woodville TX 2000-2003; R Trin Epis Ch Jasper TX 1998-2003. coljtw@yahoo.com

WELLS JR, Llewellyn Wallace (Colo) 8705 N Pinewood Ct, Castle Rock CO 80108 **Died 10/2/2009** B Ben Run WV 3/1/1923 s Llewellyn W Wells & Martha Jane. BA Bethany Coll 1948; MDiv VTS 1956. D 6/11/1956 P 12/1/1956 Bp Wilburn Camrock Campbell. c 3.

WELLS, Lloyd Francis (At) 291 Fayette Dr, Winder GA 30680 B Woodstock VA 11/4/1942 s Lloyd Francis Wells & Rose Ann. BA U Of Delaware Newark 1965; BD EDS 1968; MS Atlanta U Atlanta GA 1974. D 9/21/1968 Bp John Brooke Mosley P 3/1/1969 Bp William Henry Mead. m 2/17/1979 Patricia Joan Peterson c 2. S Mary And S Martha Ch Buford GA 2001-2003; Vic S Anth's Epis Ch Winder GA 1990-1997; S Julian's Epis Ch Douglasville GA 1989-1990; Cathd Of S Phil Atlanta GA 1984-1988; Vic S Martha's Epis Ch Bethany Bch DE 1968-1971; Vic S Martins-In-The-Fields Selbyville DE 1968-1971. lfw1104@yahoo.com

WELLS, Lynwood Daves (SwVa) Po Box 4103, Martinsville VA 24115 B Danville VA 10/23/1926 s Jabe Peter Wells & Claudine. BS VPI 1951; MDiv VTS 1986. D 5/14/1987 P 11/14/1987 Bp William Franklin Carr. m 6/11/1977 Anna Bowe Lester c 3. Int S Thos Epis Ch White Sulphur Sprg WV 1994-1995; Int S Jas' Epis Ch Lewisburg WV 1990-1991; Vic All SS Ch Un WV 1987-1996; Vic Ch Of The Incarn Ronceverte WV 1987-1994. lwells@kimbanet.com

WELLS, Mary Beth (SeFla) 231 Spring Hill Dr, Gordonsville VA 22942 **D Chr Epis Ch Gordonsville VA 2010-; Mssnr, Mnstry w Aging Dio Virginia Richmond VA 2008-; Mssnr, Mnstry w Aging Dio Virginia Richmond VA 2008-** B Dallas TX 10/9/1936 d Owen Perry Thompson & Ruth Marie. BA Syr 1958; MA Tufts U 1964; Med Tufts U 1975; MA St. Vinc De Paul Reg Sem Boynton Bch FL 2005. D 5/4/2002 Bp John Lewis Said. c 2. S Paul's Ch Delray Bch FL 2002-2007. Auth, "Parents And Creativity In Young Chld," *Journ Of Mar And Fam Living*, 1966. Acpe 1999; Apa 1973; Apc 1999; SDI 2000. mbtwells@aol.com

WELLS, Robert Louis (Tex) 9302 Sunlake Dr, Pearland TX 77584 **Pstr Care Assoc S Fran Ch Houston TX 2011-** B Alexandria LA 3/18/1939 s Charles Alexander Wells & Marie Elouise. BA LSU 1961; BD Golden Gate Bapt TS 1965; MDiv Golden Gate Bapt TS 1971. D 11/19/1990 P 6/4/1991 Bp Sam Byron Hulsey. m 4/3/1983 Carol Hunter c 3. Asstg P for Pstr Care S Dunst's Epis Ch Houston TX 2009-2011; Dir, The Cmnty of Hope St Lk's Epis Hosp Houston TX 2002-2009; Asstg P Trin Ch Galveston TX 1996-2002; Exec Dir Wm Temple Epis Ctr Galveston TX 1995-2002; Asst R S Paul's Ch Waco TX 1991-1995; Cbury Chapl S Paul's Ch Waco TX 1991-1995. AAPC 1981-1993; Assn of Psychol Type 1988-2001; Lambda Chi Alpha Fraternity 1958; Masons: Jas H. Lockwood Lodge #1343, Waco, TX 1993; Masons: Oliver Lodge #084, Alexandria, La 1961; Natl Assn of Eagle Scouts; Scottish Rite of Freemasonry, Waco, TX 1993; York Rite Masonic Bodies, Alexandria, La 1961. Par Min's Fell The Fund for Theol Educ, Inc. 1975. bobwells4383@att.net

WELLS JR, Roy Draydon (Ala) 800 Conroy Rd, Birmingham AL 35222 B Tuskegee AL 12/22/1935 s Roy Draydon Wells & Pollie Jane. BA Birmingham-Sthrn Coll 1957; BD Van 1960; PhD Van 1969. D 5/26/1999 P 5/23/2000 Bp Henry Nutt Parsley Jr. m 2/15/1957 Laura Elizabeth Stephenson. R S Andrews's Epis Ch Birmingham AL 2011. Auth, "Var arts," 2003. Aabs; SBL. rwells@bsc.edu

WELLS, William Edward (Los) 202 Avenida Aragon, San Clemente CA 92672 **Chapl in Res S Clem's-By-The-Sea Par San Clemente CA 2009-** B Santa Ana CA 5/8/1963 s Richard Wells & Nancy Nason. BMus Biola U 1987; MDiv Claremont TS 2007; Dplma ETS 2007. D 6/6/2009 Bp Sergio Carranza-Gomez P 1/9/2010 Bp Chester Lovelle Talton. bill3180@aol.com

WELLS JR, William Smith (Va) 4819 Monument Ave, Richmond VA 23230 B Durham NC 9/20/1941 s William Smith Wells & Margaret Virginia. BA U NC 1963; M. Div. EDS 1968. D 6/28/1968 P 6/1/1969 Bp Thomas Augustus Fraser Jr. m 8/8/1964 Marion Wells c 4. S Cathr's Sch Richmond VA 2000-2007; P-in-c S Mart's Ch Doswell VA 1996-2002; R Ch Of The H Comf Richmond VA 1987-1994; S Anne's Ch Winston Salem NC 1978-1987; Assoc S Jn's Ch Roanoke VA 1975-1978. pozos1941@yahoo.com

WELSAND, Randy Arthur (Minn) PO Box 344, Little Falls MN 56345 **P Ch Of Our Sav Little Falls MN 2002-** B Duluth, MN 4/28/1953 s Arthur Welsand & Joyce. Bachelor U MN Duluth 1991. D 4/6/2002 Bp Frederick Warren Putnam P 10/6/2002 Bp Daniel Lee Swenson. m 7/8/1978 Maren Kay Peterson c 1. ramkw78@gmail.com

WELSH, Clement William (WA) 16 N. Cherry Grove Ave., Annapolis MD 21401 B Oakmont PA 5/21/1913 s James Winfield Welsh & Ada Page. BA Harv 1934; UTS 1935; BD EDS 1937; PhD Harv 1958; STD Ken 1960. D 2/15/1939 P 10/31/1939 Bp Henry Knox Sherrill. c 3. Int S Jas Epis Ch Firenze IA IT 1982-1983; Bec Dio Washington Washington DC 1964-1971; Cathd of St Ptr & St Paul Washington DC 1963-1981; Asst. Prof Bex Columbus OH 1949-1952; R S Jas Ch Groveland Groveland MA 1939-1942; Serv S Jn's Epis Par Waterbury CT 1937-1939. Auth, "Preaching In A New Key," Pilgrim Press, 1974.

WELSH, Harlan Eugene (Az) 12642 N 66th St, Scottsdale AZ 85254 **Died 11/24/2010** B Topeka KS 10/23/1930 s Gilbert Francis Welsh & Sabra May. BS U of Puget Sound 1958; LTh SWTS 1965; MA U of Nthrn Colorado 1978; BD Arizona St U 1987. D 6/24/1965 Bp Philip Frederick McNairy P 3/1/1966 Bp Hamilton Hyde Kellogg. c 3. KI7EF@cox.net

WELTSEK JR, Gustave John (Fla) 7504 Holiday Rd S, Jacksonville FL 32216 B New York NY 4/23/1935 s Gustave Weltsek & Teresa. BA CUNY 1958; MDiv PDS 1961. D 4/1/1961 P 10/1/1961 Bp James P De Wolfe. m 6/28/1958 Gail Russell c 4. Dep GC Dio Florida Jacksonville FL 1988-1997; Chair Cler Compstn Com Dio Florida Jacksonville FL 1987-1990; ExCoun Dio Florida Jacksonville FL 1986-1988; S Jn's Cathd Jacksonville FL 1985-2000; Cler Coordntrv VIM Dio Florida Jacksonville FL 1980-1985; R S Jas Epis Ch Birmingham MI 1978-1985; R Ch Of The Mssh Lower Gwynedd PA 1967-1978; R Ch Of The Redemp Southampton PA 1963-1967; Cur Ch Of The Mssh Lower Gwynedd PA 1961-1963. Dn Emer St. Jn's Cathd, Jacksonville FL 2011. gweltsek@att.net

WELTY IV, Terrence Anthony (Dal) 11122 Midway Rd, Dallas TX 75229 **R Ch Of The Gd Shpd Dallas TX 2010-** B 4/17/1969 s Terrence Anthony Welty & Elizabeth. BBA U of Mississippi 1992; MDiv TESM 2001. D 12/8/2001 P 6/9/2002 Bp Robert William Duncan. m 8/18/1989 Carol C Carol Cherie Suares c 4. S Geo's Ch Nashville TN 2006-2010; Asst S Mk's Ch Geneva IL 2003-2006; Asst Chr Ch Greensburg PA 2001-2003. tonyw@goodshepherddallas.org

WELTY III, Terrence Anthony (Tex) 267 S. Bay Dr., Bullard TX 75757 B Charleston WV 11/13/1941 s Terrence Anthony Welty & Martha Regina. MA Cntrl Michigan U; BA Texas Luth U 1972; MLITT U of St. Andrews 2005. D 12/1/2005 P 6/10/2006 Bp Daniel William Herzog. m 8/31/1968 Elizabeth Fish c 3. Asst Chr Epis Ch Tyler TX 2007-2008; Nash Nashotah WI 2005-2007. twelty4235@aol.com

WELTY, Winston Wayne (Pa) Santa Clara #613, Riberas del Pilar, Chapala Jalisco 45900 Mexico B Dallas TX 8/30/1942 s Daniel John Welty & Erlene. BA CUNY 1963; MDiv PDS 1966. D 6/4/1966 P 12/17/1966 Bp Horace W B Donegan. m 11/22/1975 Mary Jean Gustafson c 4. Int Chr Epis Ch Pottstown PA 2004-2007; Int Incarn H Sacr Epis Ch Drexel Hill PA 2003-2005; Int S Jn The Evang Ch Lansdowne PA 2001-2003; R S Alb's Ch Newtown Sq PA 1982-2000; Assoc S Dav's Ch Wayne PA 1978-1982; Asst S Dav's Ch Wayne PA 1975-1978; R Trin Ch Gulph Mills King Of Prussia PA 1970-1974; R H Cross Epis Ch Wilkes Barre PA 1967-1969; Cur Trin S Paul's Epis New Rochelle NY 1966-1967. wwwelty@yahoo.com

WENDEL JR, David Deaderick (Ala) 210 Oak Ct, New Braunfels TX 78132 B Montgomery AL 7/20/1930 s David Deaderick Wendel & Elizabeth. BA U So 1951; MDiv VTS 1959; MA Lon 1970. D 6/8/1959 Bp George Mosley Murray P 6/1/1960 Bp Samuel B Chilton. m 9/7/1957 Ruth Clark. Asst S Mary's-On-The-Highlands Epis Ch Birmingham AL 1991-1995; R Trin Epis Ch Bessemer AL 1987-1991; R S Fran Epis Ch Victoria TX 1978-1986; R S Jn's Ch New Braunfels TX 1972-1977; Asst Ch Of The Gd Shpd Corpus Christi TX 1970-1972; Asst S Jn's Epis Ch McLean VA 1959-1960. randdwendel@sbcglobal.net

WENDEL, Richard Joseph Bosley (Chi) 536 W Fullerton Pkwy, Chicago IL 60614 B Pittsburgh PA 9/20/1951 s Robert Joseph Wendel & Virginia Lee. BA Penn 1973; MDiv PrTS 1976; DMin McCormick TS 1985; PhD Loyola U Chicago 2010. D 4/26/1985 P 8/28/1985 Bp O'Kelley Whitaker. m 12/30/1998 Mina Dulcan c 1. Assoc Ch Of Our Sav Chicago IL 1999; Assoc P S Matt's Ch Evanston IL 1993-1998; Advoc Hlth Care Oak Brook IL 1992-1998; R Calv Ch Homer NY 1985-1987; R S Matt's Ch Moravia NY 1985-1987. AAPC; Clincl Mem AAMFT, Supvsr; Mem KON. r-wendel@northwestern.edu

WENDELL, Christopher Scott (Mass) St Andrew's Church, 79 Denton Rd, Wellesley MA 02482 **R S Paul's Epis Ch Bedford MA 2011-** B Chicago IL 9/3/1981 s Peter Charles Wendell & Lynn Mellen. AB Pr 2003; MDiv EDS 2007. D 6/9/2007 Bp George Edward Councell P 1/12/2008 Bp M(arvil)

W

Thomas Shaw III. m 8/11/2007 Kristen Bethke c 1. Asst R S Andr's Ch Wellesley MA 2007-2011. subject, "Blessed are the Poor in Sprt: Chris's Story," *Claiming the Beatitudes: Nine Stories from a New Generation)*, Alb, 2009. chriswendell@gmail.com

WENDELL, Martin Paul (Alb) 405 Master St, Valley Falls NY 12185 **P-in-c Trin Ch Watervliet NY 1998-** B Ticonderoga NY 4/3/1945 s Walton Francis Wendell & Mary Elizabeth. BA S Piux X Sem, Graymoor, Garrison NY 1967; Ford, Bronx, NY 1968; CUA, Washington,DC 1969; MA St. Bern's Inst, Rochester NY 1992. D 5/31/1988 Bp David Standish Ball P 9/5/1998 Bp Daniel William Herzog. m 9/6/1981 Judy Margaret Spink. D S Paul's Epis Ch Greenwich NY 1988-1998. wendell217@gmail.com

WENDFELDT, Stephen Hoff (SanD) 2728 Sixth Avenue, San Diego CA 92103 **P-in-c Dio San Diego San Diego CA 2011-; Plnng and Dvlpmt S Jas By The Sea La Jolla CA 2011-** B Duluth MN 9/18/1947 s Ole A Wendfedt & Erlene Raynette. USAF Acad 1966; BA U MN 1969; MDiv CDSP 1982. D 6/20/1982 P 6/29/1983 Bp Victor Manuel Rivera. m 1/28/2011 Linda Ardell Smith c 2. P-in-c Dio San Diego San Diego CA 2010; R S Ptr's Epis Ch Del Mar CA 2001-2007; Dir New Cong Dvlpmt Dio No Carolina Raleigh NC 1998-2001; R S Steph's Epis Ch Longview WA 1994-1998; R S Paul's Epis Ch Bremerton WA 1988-1994; Int S Jos And S Jn Ch Steilacoom WA 1987-1988; Vic S Antony Of Egypt Silverdale WA 1985-1986; Asst S Barn Epis Ch Bainbridge Island WA 1984-1985; Vic S Jas Ch Lindsay CA 1983-1984; Cur S Jn The Bapt Lodi CA 1982-1983. steve@ardellwendfeldt.com

WENGROVIUS, John H. (Colo) 1320 Arapahoe St, Golden CO 80401 **Sr Pstr Calv Ch Golden CO 1988-** B Colorado Springs CO 5/5/1950 s John Erwin Wengrovius & Stella Mae. Pr 1970; BA Colorado St U 1973; MDiv Nash 1977; DMin SWTS 2007. D 12/21/1976 P 3/5/1978 Bp William Carl Frey. m 5/29/1976 Ruth Etherington c 3. Cur/Assoc The Epis Par of S Greg Littleton CO 1984-1988; Vic S Aug's Ch Creede CO 1983-1984; Vic S Pat's Epis Ch Pagosa Sprg CO 1983-1984; Vic S Steph The Mtyr Epis Ch Monte Vista CO 1983-1984; Dio Colorado Denver CO 1980-1983; Cur S Paul's Epis Ch Lakewood CO 1978-1980; Ast to Bp Dio Colorado Denver CO 1977-1978. Auth, "From Pstr to Prog in the Epis Ch: The Pilgrimage through the Transitional Swamp," *DMin Thesis*, SWTS, 2007; Auth, "Adult Track II, Epiph Year B: Evangelization," *Living the Gd News*, 1988; Auth, "Adult Track II, Lent Year A, Epiph Year B: Pryr," *Lectionary Curric*, 1987. Cn of St. Paul's Cathd; Blantyre, Malawi The Dio Sthrn Malawi 2004. fr.john@calvarygolden.net

WENGROVIUS, Stephen A (Colo) 3712 W 99th Ave, Westminster CO 80031 **R S Martha's Epis Ch Westminster CO 2003-** B Colorado Springs CO 9/21/1948 s John Erwin Wengrovius & Stella Mae. BS Colorado St U 1971; BS U of Utah 1972; MDiv Nash 1979. D 6/29/1979 P 3/1/1980 Bp William Carl Frey. m 8/27/1978 Christine Lynne Focht c 2. Int All SS Luth Ch Cory CO 1997-2003; P-in- Charge S Lk's Epis Ch Delta CO 1995; Asst Dio Colorado Denver CO 1992-1995; Vic S Jn's Epis Ch Ouray CO 1985-1992; R Trin Ch Arkansas City KS 1982-1985; Cur S Aid's Epis Ch Boulder CO 1979-1982. swengrovius@yahoo.com

WENNER, Peter Woodring (Mass) 137 Auburndale Ave, West Newton MA 02465 B Baltimore MD 3/21/1944 s Herbert Allan Wenner & Ruth Ingeborg. BA Carleton Coll 1966; BD SWTS 1970. D 6/21/1970 Bp Edward Clark Turner P 1/25/1971 Bp James Walmsley Frederic Carman. m 11/11/1995 Barbara Williamson c 2. Int Ch Of S Jn The Evang Hingham MA 2007-2009; Int S Paul's Ch Newburyport MA 2005-2007; P-in-c Chr Ch Waltham MA 2000-2005; Int S Jas' Epis Ch Cambridge MA 1998-2000; R S Mk's Ch Milwaukee WI 1984-1998; R H Trin Epis Ch Manistee MI 1976-1984; Asst S Mk's Ch Grand Rapids MI 1972-1976; Chapl Oregon Epis Sch Portland OR 1970-1972. co-Auth, "Welcome to the Bible," Morehouse Pub, 2007. peternbarb@verizon.net

WENNER, Rachel Elizabeth (SwVa) 117 Autumn Circle, Boones Mill VA 24065 **Mem, COM Dio SW Virginia Roanoke VA 2007-; Co-R Trin Epis Ch Rocky Mt VA 2006-** B Grand Rapids MI 6/3/1974 d Peter Woodring Wenner & Wendy June. BA Kalamazoo Coll 1996; MDiv VTS 2002. D 4/6/2002 P 10/17/2002 Bp Roger John White. m 2/8/2003 John Burke Gardner c 3. Mem, Higher Educ Com Dio SW Virginia Roanoke VA 2008-2011; Mem, COM Dio SW Virginia Roanoke VA 2007-2011; Mem, Cmsn on Minsitry Dio Milwaukee Milwaukee WI 2003-2006; Asst Trin Ch Wauwatosa WI 2002-2006. rwennergardner@gmail.com

WENRICK, Heather Marie (Ore) 1444 Liberty St SE, Salem OR 97302 **S Paul's Epis Ch Salem OR 2011-** B Corvallis OR 9/22/1978 d John Michael Chilcote & Mary Kathryn. BA Gonzaga U 2000; MDiv Ya Berk 2011. D 6/18/2011 Bp Michael J Hanley. m 10/6/2001 Michael Wenrick. heather.wenrick@gmail.com

WENTT, Allan Rudolphus (Va) 7503 Noble Avenue, Richmond VA 23227 **S Jas Chuch Warfield VA 2006-** B Kingston JM 9/30/1931 s Walter Edwards Wentt & Janetta Emerson. BA Juilliard Sch 1967; STB Ya Berk 1968; MS Juilliard Sch 1968; MDiv Ya Berk 1971; NYU 1979; Virginia Commonwealth U 1995. D 6/14/1956 Bp Duncan Montgomery Gray P 12/1/1956 Bp Reginald Heber Gooden. m 10/15/1983 Karen Buster Brown c 4. S Phil's Ch Richmond VA 1979-1996; Cn to the Ordnry Dio Sthrn Ohio Cincinnati OH 1973-1979; Cn to the Ordnry Dio Sthrn Ohio Cincinnati OH 1973-1979; R S Phil's Ch Columbus OH 1972-1979; R Ch Of Our Merc Sav Louisville KY 1970-1972; R S Lk's Epis Ch Bronx NY 1960-1970; Asst S Lk's Epis Ch New Haven CT 1959-1960. kwentt7897@msn.com

WENTZ, Herbert Stephenson (At) Po Box 3190, Sewanee TN 37375 B Salisbury NC 10/22/1934 s Charles Herbert Wentz & Carolyn. AB U NC 1956; STB GTS 1960; MA Oxf 1963; PhD U of Exeter GB 1971. D 6/29/1960 Bp Richard Henry Baker P 12/31/1960 Bp Thomas Augustus Fraser Jr. m 7/9/1980 Sofia Lilijencrants. Prof The U So (Sewanee) Sewanee TN 1965-1997; Cur S Lk's Epis Ch Atlanta GA 1962-1965; Vic S Chris's Epis Ch Garner NC 1960-1962. hwentz@bellsouth.net

WERDAL, Evelyn Paige (NY) 522 Walnut St, Mamaroneck NY 10543 **D S Thos Ch Mamaroneck NY 1994-** B Mount Vernon NY 6/18/1934 d Philip Abram Paige & Christine Lauer. RN Mt Vernon Hosp Sch of Nrsng Mt Vernon NY 1956; BS Mercy Coll 1975; MS LIU 1978. D 6/4/1994 Bp Richard Frank Grein. m 8/3/1957 George Norman Werdal c 2. Auth, "Through the Patient's Eyes," *Hlth Care Forum*, 1995. deacon@saintthomasmmrk.org

WERNER, Frederick John Emil (Mich) 13070 Independence Ave, Utica MI 48315 B Brooklyn NY 11/8/1928 s Frederick Werner & Anna. Edgewood Coll 1949; LIU 1950. D 12/6/1975 Bp H Coleman McGehee Jr. m 6/20/1959 Marilyn Rose Barrett c 4. Ord S Paul Tentmaker.

WERNER, George Louis William (Pgh) 106 Sewickley Heights Dr., Sewickley PA 15143 B New York NY 2/3/1938 s Louis Reynolds Werner & Alvine Bertha. BA Laf 1959; MDiv/STB Ya Berk 1962. D 6/23/1962 Bp Walter H Gray P 3/9/1963 Bp John Henry Esquirol. m 6/18/1960 Audrey Diane Volker c 4. Dn Trin Cathd Pittsburgh PA 1979-1999; Asst to Bp Dio New Hampshire Concord NH 1970-1979; R Gr Ch Manchester NH 1968-1979; R S Lk's/S Paul's Ch Bridgeport CT 1964-1968; Cur S Ptr's Epis Ch Milford CT 1962-1964. Auth, *Prolonging Life*, Forw Mvmt Press, 1993; Auth, "Chapt: A Word From the Other Players," *Reaping the Harvest*, Humana, 1988. Natl Ntwk of Cler Assns. 1970. DD (Hon) Nash 2003; DD (Hon) Berkeley at Yale 1979. glww17@gmail.com

WERNER, Mark (USC) 2 N Hill Ct, Columbia SC 29223 B Ridgewood NJ 11/12/1952 d Herbert Blake Werner & Margaret May. BA Coll of Wooster 1975; DMin UTS Richmond VA 1979; MS U GA 1997. D 6/5/1991 Bp Richard Lester Shimpfky P 12/21/1991 Bp David Charles Bowman. m 3/23/1974 Barbara Ann Tinley. Off Of Bsh For ArmdF New York NY 1991-1997. Auth, "Alcosm Resrch & Educ Wrld". AEHC; OHC. marktwerner@cornwalladvisors.com

WERNICK, Mike (WMich) 1800 Bloomfield Dr. SE, Kentwood MI 49508 **R Ch Of The H Cross Kentwood MI 2011-** B Brooklyn NY 10/8/1953 s Eli Wernick & Joan Gladys. BA U of Florida 1977; M.Div. Bex 2010. D 6/13/2009 P 6/19/2010 Bp Thomas Edward Breidenthal. m 7/21/2009 Joel Flint c 2. P-in-c Dio Pittsburgh Monroeville PA 2011; Asstg P S Steph's Epis Ch And U Columbus OH 2011; Asstg P S Steph's Epis Ch And U Columbus OH 2010-2011. mkwrnck@comcast.net

WERNTZ, Pamela Louise (Mass) 120 Marshall St, Watertown MA 02472 **R Emm Ch Boston MA 2000-** B Lancaster PA 2/7/1960 d William Garner Werntz & Marcia Louise. AB Franklin & Marshall Coll 1981; MDiv EDS 2000. D 6/15/2002 P 5/31/2003 Bp M(arvil) Thomas Shaw III. m 2/15/1999 Audrey Joy Howard c 4. Assoc R S Paul's Ch Brookline MA 2002-2008. werntz.emmanuel@gmail.com

WERTS, Eric Hilary (Oly) 426 E Fourth Plain Blvd, Vancouver WA 98663 **Died 2/14/2011** B Los Angeles CA 3/20/1944 s Charles F Werts & Virginia V. U of Santa Clara 1965; BPh Gonzaga U 1967; MDiv Jesuit TS 1978. Rec from Roman Catholic 4/15/2010 as Priest Bp Gregory Harold Rickel. c 1. ericwerts@comcast.net

WESCH, Kate (Oly) 3631 46th Ave SW, Seattle WA 98116 **Assoc Ch Of The Epiph Seattle WA 2009-** B Ponca City Oklahoma 1/8/1981 d James Emig & Caroline. BA U of Oklahoma 2002; MDiv Epis TS of The SW 2006. D 7/1/2006 Bp Robert Manning Moody P 1/6/2007 Bp Bavi Rivera. m 8/27/2005 Joel Wesch c 1. P-in-c Ch Of The H Sprt Vashon WA 2008-2009; S Jn The Bapt Epis Ch Seattle WA 2007-2008; Dio Olympia Seattle WA 2006. kwesch@epiphanyseattle.org

WESEN, Vicki Jane Smaby (Oly) 1500A E College Way # 447, Mount Vernon WA 98273 B Mount Vernon WA 10/11/1945 d Lloyd George Smaby & Betty Jane. BS WA SU 1971; MEd No Carolina St U 1983; MDiv Duke 1988; VTS 1988. D 6/5/1988 P 6/16/1989 Bp Robert Whitridge Estill. c 2. Komo Kulshan Cluster Mt Vernon WA 2000-2009; Asst S Paul's Epis Ch Mt Vernon WA 2000-2004; Cn Cong Spprt/Deploy Dio No Carolina Raleigh NC 1995-2000; Vic All SS Ch Warrenton NC 1989-1994; Vic Chap Of The Gd Shpd Ridgeway NC 1989-1994; Emm Ch Warrenton NC 1988-1994; Prog Dir S Tim's Ch Wilson NC 1984-1985. vwesen@verizon.net

WESLEY, Carol Ann (Mo) 5519 Alaska Ave, Saint Louis MO 63111 **P-in-c St Johns & St Jas Ch Sullivan MO 2003-** B Springfield IL 7/13/1952 d John

Lewis Wesley & Johanna Lindsay. AA Lincoln Land Cmnty Coll 1972; BA U IL-Springfield 1973; MSW St. Louis U 1975; PhD St. Louis U 1987; MDiv Aquinas Inst of Theol 1995. D 3/28/2003 P 10/3/2003 Bp George Wayne Smith. cwesley@siue.edu

WESLEY JR, John William (NwPa) 407 E King St, Smethport PA 16749 B Columbus OH 1/16/1944 s John William Wesley & Esther Janet. OH SU 1963; BA U Cinc 1966; MDiv VTS 1970; Med U of No Florida 1990. D 6/20/1970 P 5/23/1971 Bp Philip Alan Smith. m 2/8/1986 Sandra L Pollard c 2. R S Lk's Epis Ch Smethport PA 2008-2009; Bi-Cnty Epis Cmnty Mnstry Smethport PA 2006-2007; Ch Of Our Sav Palm Bay FL 1998-2006; R S Thos Epis Ch Reidsville NC 1993-1998; R Trin Epis Ch Bessemer AL 1991-1993; Vic St Pat's Epis Ch S Johns Fl 1984-1986; All Souls Epis Ch Jacksonville FL 1981-1985; Asst Trin Cathd Columbia SC 1975-1977; Cur The Epis Ch Of The Medtr Allentown PA 1972-1975; Cur S Mich's Epis Ch Arlington VA 1970-1972. jwesley1644@charter.net

WESSELL, David E (FdL) 2805 Elgin St, Durham NC 27704 B Wilmington NC 2/8/1938 s William Edward Wessell & Mary Doris. BA Rhodes Coll 1960; Nash 1963; S Vladimir's TS 1976; AOS New Engl Culinary Inst 1994. D 4/1/1966 Bp John Melville Burgess P 1/1/1967 Bp The Bishop Of Damaraland. Dio Fond du Lac Appleton WI 1984-1992; Vic St Ambr Epis Ch Antigo WI 1984-1992; S Barn Epis Ch Tomahawk WI 1984-1987; Serv Dio Colorado Denver CO 1975-1976; Cur Ch Of The Gd Samar Gunnison CO 1970-1973; Cur Epis Ch Of S Ptr And S Mary Denver CO 1969-1970; Cur Imm Ch Bellows Falls VT 1968-1969. dewessell@verizon.net

WEST, Anne (SwVa) Christchurch School, Christchurch VA 23031 **S Cathr's Sch Richmond VA 2009-; Chr Ch Pearisburg VA 2008-** B Clarksburg WV 9/30/1959 d Eugene Richard Kersting & MaryAnne. BS W Virginia U 1981; MDiv VTS 1989. D 8/24/1989 P 6/16/1990 Bp John H(enry) Smith. m 5/25/1991 Scott West c 1. S Paul's Epis Ch Alexandria VA 2006-2007; Chr Epis Ch Saluda VA 2004-2005; Christchurch Sch Christchurch VA 1998-2004; Olde S Jn's Ch Colliers WV 1997-2004; Brooke-Hancock Cluster Wellsburg WV 1997-1998; Yth Mnstrs Coordntr Dio W Virginia Charleston WV 1994-1996; Tchr Cathd Of St Jn The Div New York NY 1992-1994; The Cathd Sch New York NY 1992-1994; The Cathd Sch New York NY 1992; Yth Mnstrs Coordntr Dio Newark Newark NJ 1990-1992; Dio Newark Newark NJ 1990-1991; D S Jn's Ch Huntington WV 1989-1990. westsinbburg@gmail.com

WEST, Barbara Field (Ct) 7 Hillcrest Rd, Manchester CT 06040 B Manchester CT 6/6/1936 d William John Field & Florence W. SMU; BA Colby Coll 1958; SMU 1975. D 6/20/1975 Bp A Donald Davies P 12/1/1980 Bp Morgan Porteus. Grtr Hartford Reg Mnstry E Hartford CT 1991-1999; Int Calv Ch Enfield CT 1991; Supply P Dio Connecticut Hartford CT 1988-1990; Asst S Jas Ch Glastonbury CT 1979-1987; Asst S Mary's Epis Ch Manchester CT 1977-1978; E D Farmer Fndt Dallas TX 1976.

WEST, Carolyn H (USC) 120 Glenbrooke Way, Greenville SC 29615 **Died 10/2/2011** B San Antonio TX 3/30/1937 d John Campbell Kern & Vivien Gould. BA Bryn 1959; MDiv VTS 1993. D 6/5/1993 Bp O'Kelley Whitaker P 12/5/1993 Bp Frank Harris Vest Jr. c 2. carjoe@bellsouth.net

WEST, Clark Russell (CNY) G3 Anabel Taylor Hall, Ithaca NY 14853 **Epis Ch At Cornell Ithaca NY 2009-** B Rochester NY 1/9/1967 s George Russell West & Judith. MDiv U Chi 1997; BA Wms 1997. D 6/24/1997 Bp Edward Witker Jones P 2/1/1998 Bp Catherine Elizabeth Maples Waynick. m 9/13/1997 Sarah Nell Chenoweth. R Trin Ch Geneva NY 2000-2006; Asst R Gr Epis Ch Hinsdale IL 1997-2000.

WEST, Craig Alan (SD) Po Box 532, Martin SD 57551 **Vic Dio So Dakota Sioux Falls SD 2007-; Pine Ridge Mssn Mart SD 2007-** B Seattle WA 7/4/1950 s George Bennett West & Joan Evelyn. BA U of Washington 1979; MDiv VTS 1994. D 7/9/1994 P 1/20/1995 Bp Vincent Waydell Warner. m 7/1/1975 Miriam Kathleen Durland c 3. Dio Olympia Seattle WA 2003-2004; Emm Ch Orcas Island Eastsound WA 1996-2003; The Epis Ch Of The Cross Ticonderoga NY 1995-1996; D-in-c S Germains Epis Ch Hoodsport WA 1994-1995. stlhdcaw@gmail.com

WEST, Geoffrey George (NJ) No address on file. B Plainfield NJ 10/16/1944 s Gerald B West & C Kathleen. MDiv PDS; BA Rutgers-The St U. D 4/27/1974 P 10/1/1974 Bp Albert Wiencke Van Duzer. Chr Ch Middletown NJ 1974-1976.

WEST, Hilary Morgan (EC) No address on file. B Lancaster PA 7/2/1946 d Morgan Lincoln West & Mary-Louise. BA Lebanon Vlly Coll 1968; MS + doctoral Wk Ohio U 1971; Cert Shalem Inst Washington DC 1986; MDiv VTS 1990. D 6/16/1990 Bp John H(enry) Smith P 2/23/1991 Bp Brice Sidney Sanders. Dio E Carolina Kinston NC 2001-2008; Washington-Tyrrell Epis Mnstry Roper NC 1999-2001; S Geo Epis Ch Engelhard NC 1995-1996; S Andr's By The Sea Nags Hd NC 1990-1993. hilaryw@hotmail.com

WEST, Hillary T (Va) 4212 Kingcrest Pkwy, Richmond VA 23221 **Assoc S Thos' Ch Whitemarsh Ft Washington PA 2011-** B Detroit MI 1/26/1951 d Bernard Dale Davis & Mary Patricia. BS Virginia Commonwealth U 2002; MDiv Un Theol Seminaunion TS & Presbyt 2004. D 6/26/2004 P 1/18/2005 Bp Peter James Lee. m 6/19/1971 Frederic Kemp West c 2. Asst R Chr Ch Glen Allen VA 2004-2011; S Jas' Ch Richmond VA 1987-1996. kyleswest@aol.com

WEST JR OSB, Irvin D (Ark) 401 E 10th St, Little Rock AR 72202 B Russellville AR 11/15/1945 s Irvin D West & Dora J. BA Arkansas Tech U 1968; MDiv STUSo 1974. D 11/7/1974 Bp Christoph Keller Jr. Cur S Paul's Ch Fayetteville AR 1974-1986.

WEST, Jan Hickman (Cal) 171 Prospect Ave, San Anselmo CA 94960 **Int Assoc R St Johns Epis Ch Ross CA 2001-** B Santa Monica CA 10/25/1935 d Howard Wallace Hickman & Margarette Ann. BA U CA 1957; MDiv CDSP 1989. D 6/3/1989 P 6/1/1990 Bp William Edwin Swing. m 9/14/1957 Herbert West c 2. San Rafael Canal Mnstry San Rafael CA 1991-1997; St Johns Epis Ch Ross CA 1989-1990. revjansky@pacbell.net

WEST, Jennifer K (SO) 233 S. State St., Westerville OH 43081 **Dioc Coun Dio Sthrn Ohio Cincinnati OH 2009-; R S Matt's Ch Westerville OH 2009-** B Providence RI 7/26/1952 d Mitchell Kezirian & Arleen. BA Wheaton Coll at Norton 1974; MS Loyola Coll 1992; MDiv EDS 1997; Cert Int Mnstry 2003. D 6/7/1997 P 12/13/1997 Bp Robert Wilkes Ihloff. m 5/16/1993 Benjamin H West. Natl & Wrld Mssn Cmsn Dio Sthrn Ohio Cincinnati OH 2009-2011; Pres Stndg Com Dio Rhode Island Providence RI 2007-2008; Assoc S Jn's Ch Barrington RI 2006-2008; Stndg Com Dio Rhode Island Providence RI 2005-2008; P-in-c S Mk's Epis Ch Riverside RI 2005-2006; Int S Paul's Ch No Kingstown RI 2002-2004; R S Barth's Ch Baltimore MD 1999-2002; Asst Chr Ch Columbia MD 1997-1999. benjenden@msn.com

WEST JR, John Richard (Ga) 4227 Columbia Rd, Martinez GA 30907 **R Ch Of Our Sav Martinez GA 2011-** B Augusta GA 8/17/1962 s John Richard West & Martha. BFA U GA 1986; BA U GA 1988; MDiv VTS 2000. D 2/5/2000 P 9/5/2000 Bp Henry Irving Louttit. m 4/26/1997 Sallie S Shuford c 4. R Emm Ch At Brook Hill Richmond VA 2004-2011; R S Eliz's Epis Ch Richmond Hill GA 2001-2004; Cur Chr Ch Frederica St Simons Island GA 2000-2001. fr.johnwest@knology.net

WEST, John Timothy (SO) 600 Dorothy Moore Avenue, Unit 10, Urbana OH 43078 B Los Angeles CA 7/26/1945 s Clifton Eugene West & Georgia. BA U CA at Santa Barbara 1967; BD CDSP 1970; MA U of San Francisco 1980; DMin Fuller TS 1992; LPCC U of Dayton 1994. D 9/12/1970 Bp Francis E I Bloy P 3/1/1971 Bp Edward McNair. m 6/15/1996 Rebecca Pooler c 1. Mssnr Ch Of The H Trin Epis Bellefontaine OH 1999-2011; Nthrn Miami Vlly Cluster Urbana OH 1999-2011; Mssnr Ch Of The Epiph Urbana OH 1998-2011; Mssnr Our Sav Ch Mechanicsburg OH 1998-2011; R The Epis Ch Of The Ascen Middletown OH 1985-1990; R St Johns Epis Ch Petaluma CA 1973-1985; Cur Ch Of The Ascen Vallejo CA 1970-1973. Auth, "Workbook for the Decade of Evang," Dio Sthrn Ohio, 1987. Amer Counslg Assn 2001. Chi Sigma Iota Natl Counslg hon Soc. 1998. jwest012@woh.rr.com

WEST, Kathleen Farson (EpisSanJ) 2857 N 175 E, Provo UT 84604 **Asst S Paul's Epis Ch Modesto CA 2010-** B Los Angeles CA 2/14/1955 d Kenneth Arthur Farson & Helen Elizabeth. BA Westmont Coll 1977; MA Occ 1978; MDiv ETSBH 1999. D 6/12/1999 Bp Chester Lovelle Talton P 1/8/2000 Bp Frederick Houk Borsch. m 12/29/1979 Ira West c 1. Dio Utah Salt Lake City UT 2008-2009; R S Mary's Ch Provo UT 2006-2008; Asst S Mths' Par Whittier CA 2006; Asstg P S Paul's Pomona Pomona CA 2003-2005; Asst S Geo's Par La Can CA 2003; Asstg P S Barn' Epis Ch Los Angeles CA 2001-2002; Asst R Trin Epis Par Los Angeles CA 1999-2001. kathleenfwest@att.net

WEST, Philip (RG) 2243 Henry Rd Sw, Albuquerque NM 87105 B Santa Fe NM 10/17/1939 s Harold E West & Mildred J. CPE Epis TS of The SW 1975. D 9/10/1974 P 4/1/1975 Bp Richard Mitchell Trelease Jr. m 9/7/1965 Elizabeth Tertia c 1. S Matt's Mssn Los Lunas NM 1999-2001; S Phil's Ch Belen NM 1994-1999; Ch Of The H Sprt Gallup NM 1990-1992; S Mk's Epis Ch Pecos TX 1978-1979; Trans Pecos Team Mnstry Pecos TX 1977; All SS Farmington NM 1975-1976; Dio The Rio Grande Albuquerque NM 1974-1976.

WEST, R(andolph) Harrison (Ct) 11 Park St, Guilford CT 06437 **Chr Ch Guilford CT 2010-; Dio Washington Washington DC 2004-; Weca Bd Dio Washington Washington DC 2004-** B Portland OR 2/15/1952 s Harry Jorgensen West & Sarah Pauline. BA Carleton Coll 1974; U of Oregon 1976; MDiv STUSo 1990. D 5/14/1991 P 1/28/1992 Bp Robert Louis Ladehoff. Bp'S Mssn Strtgy Advsry Grp Dio Washington Washington DC 1999-2000; Assoc R S Jn's Ch Chevy Chase MD 1995-2010; Com Dio E Tennessee Knoxville TN 1994-1995; Yth Team Dio E Tennessee Knoxville TN 1993-1995; Gr Ch Chattanooga TN 1992-1995; Par Intern Gr Memi Portland OR 1991-1992. Shettle (Litug) Prize In Litug STUSo Sewanee TN 1990; Woods Ldrshp Awd STUSo Sewanee TN 1987. harrisoncec@snet.net

WEST, Scott (SwVa) 120 Church St NE, P.O. Box 164, Blacksburg VA 24063 **R Chr Ch Blacksburg VA 2007-** B Weirton WV 7/13/1964 s John Francis West & Freda Mae. BBA Marshall U 1986; MDiv GTS 1994; MA Marshall U 1994. D 6/11/1994 P 6/10/1995 Bp John H(enry) Smith. m 5/25/1991 Anne Kersting c 1. Asst S Paul's Epis Ch Alexandria VA 2006-2007; S Mary's Whitechapel Epis Lancaster VA 1998-2005; P-in-c Trin Epis Ch Lancaster VA 1998-2000; Brooke-Hancock Cluster Wellsburg WV 1997-1998; Chr Ch

Wellsburg WV 1995-1997; D S Steph's Epis Ch Beckley WV 1994-1995. Auth, "Last Obstacle to Wheeling: The Bd Tree Tunnel," *The Sentinel*, Baltimore & Ohio Railroad Hist Soc, 2007. saw764@yahoo.com

WESTBERG, Daniel Arnold (Mil) 2777 Mission Rd, Nashotah WI 53058 **Nash Nashotah WI 2000-** B Chicago IL 8/24/1949 s Harry Edwin Westberg & Gladys Jean. Trans from Anglican Church of Canada 6/5/2001 Bp Roger John White. m 8/31/1985 Lisa Westberg c 4. S Paul's Ch Ashippun Oconomowoc WI 2000-2002.

WESTBURY JR, Richard Smith (Fla) 15 N Wilderness Trl, Ponte Vedra Beach FL 32082 **R Chr Epis Ch Ponte Vedra Bch FL 2001-** B Palatka FL 10/9/1959 s Richard Smith Westbury & Doris Ann. AA S Jn River Cmnty 1979; BA U Of Florida 1981; MDiv SWTS 1989. D 6/11/1989 P 12/1/1989 Bp Frank Stanley Cerveny. m 6/25/1983 Carole Doreen Conlee c 2. S Paul's Epis Ch Jacksonville FL 1992-2001; S Paul's By-The-Sea Epis Ch Jacksonville Bch FL 1989-1992. rickwestbury@bellsouth.net

WEST-DOOHAN, Sue (Be) HC 75 Box 32, Strange Creek WV 25063 B Bethlehem PA 1/31/1949 d Frank Windish & Betty. BA Moravian TS 1982; MDiv Nash 1990. D 11/19/1991 P 8/28/1992 Bp James Michael Mark Dyer. m 4/17/1999 William Doohan c 1. S Mich's Epis Ch Bethlehem PA 1998-2003; R All SS Epis Ch Williamsport PA 1994-1997; Dio Bethlehem Bethlehem PA 1991-1993; D S Gabr's Ch Douglassville PA 1991-1992.

WESTERBERG, George Arthur (Mass) 212 North Lower Bay Road, Lovell ME 04051 B Bellefonte PA 1/11/1933 s Arnold George Westerberg & Gladys. BA Bow 1959; UTS 1960; STB GTS 1962. D 6/9/1962 P 12/1/1962 Bp Horace W B Donegan. m 8/3/1963 Joan Weigl c 3. R S Mich's Ch Marblehead MA 1968-1998; Vic S Dav's Epis Ch Kennebunk ME 1964-1968; Vic S Geo's Epis Ch York Harbor ME 1964-1968; Cur S Mk's Ch Mt Kisco NY 1962-1964. Chapl Soc Comp H Cross. gwest@fairpoint.net

WESTERHOFF III, John Henry (At) 49 Old Ivy Sq Ne, Atlanta GA 30342 **S Anne's Epis Ch Atlanta GA 2000-** B Paterson NJ 6/28/1933 s John Henry Westerhoff & Nona Cecelia. STB Harvard DS 1958; EdD Col 1973; BS Ursinus Coll 1990. D 5/21/1978 P 9/23/1978 Bp William Augustus Jones Jr. m 10/27/1991 Caroline A Askew. Assoc and Dir Inst Pstr Stds S Lk's Epis Ch Atlanta GA 1994-2005; Int S Barth's Epis Ch Atlanta GA 1993-1994. Auth, *Will Our Chld Have Faith?*, Morehouse Pub, 2000; Auth, *The Sprtl Life: Fndt of Preaching & Tchg*, Knox, 1998. Assn of Professors & Researchers in Rel Educ 1974; Rel Educ Assn 1984; Soc of S Jn the Evang 1974. Hon DD Ursinus 1990. johnwest33@bellsouth.net

WESTFALL, Doris Ann (Mo) 28 Whinhill Ct, Saint Peters MO 63304 B NJ 1/21/1959 d Denziel Ellsworth Colby & Marie Georgette. BA Valparaiso U 1981; MS St. Louis U 1993; MDiv STUSo 2005. D 12/22/2004 P 6/24/2005 Bp George Wayne Smith. m 8/21/1982 David Allen Westfall c 3. S Matt's Epis Ch Warson Warson Woods MO 2007; Dio Missouri S Louis MO 2006. dcwestfall@sbcglobal.net

WESTHORP, Peter Henry Glen (RI) 2574 Creve Coeur Mill Rd, Maryland Heights MO 63043 B Montreal QC CA 12/12/1942 s Clifford Sidney Westhorp & Harriet Dorothy. BA Leh 1965; MDiv Ya Berk 1968. D 6/24/1968 P 3/1/1969 Bp John S Higgins. m 11/13/1999 Beverly J Westhorp. R S Paul's Ch Portsmouth RI 1969-1972. Realtor of Year 81 No Suburban Bd Realtors 1981. pwesthorp@earthlink.net

WESTLING JR, Lester Leon (NCal) 573 Royal Oaks Dr, Redding CA 96001 **Died 8/1/2011** B Oakland CA 10/19/1930 s Lester Leon Westling & June Minerva. Stan 1948; USMMA 1949; Tul 1950; MDiv CDSP 1955; MA SFTS 1973; DMin SFTS 1974. D 6/13/1955 Bp Sumner Walters P 1/7/1956 Bp Karl M Block. c 3. Auth, "When Johnny/Joanie cames marching Hm:," *When Johnny/Joanie cames marching Hm:*, Praxis Press, INC, 2006; Auth, "All that Glitter...Memoirs of a Min," *All that Glitter...Memoirs of a Min*, Hillwood Pub Co., 2003; Auth, "Mnstry to POW Returnees & Their Fam," *Doctoral Dissertation*, 1974. PBp Jubilee Mnstry Awd TEC 1985. inasmuch@digitalpath.net

WESTMAN, Paul Allen (NJ) Po Box 882, Narberth PA 19072 **Died 9/24/2009** B Los Angeles,CA 6/14/1930 D 11/28/1959 P 6/1/1960 Bp Alfred L Banyard.

WESTON, English Hopkins (USC) 1017 Elm Savannah Rd, Hopkins SC 29061 B Hopkins SC 12/12/1920 s Christian Tucker Weston & Mary Postell. BA Cit 1941; BD VTS 1943. D 9/16/1943 P 12/1/1944 Bp John J Gravatt. c 4. R Ch Of The Nativ Un SC 1978-1987; Calv Ch Pauline SC 1978-1980; P-in-c Epis Ch Of The H Trin Ridgeland SC 1976-1978; The Ch Of The Cross Bluffton SC 1976-1978; S Alb's Ch Blackville SC 1972-1976; P-in-c Ch Of The H Apos Barnwell SC 1971-1976; P-in-c S Alb's Ch Kingstree SC 1962-1971; Asst to R S Paul's Epis Ch Chattanooga TN 1960-1962; R Ch Of The Gd Shpd York SC 1952-1956; P-in-c Ch Of The Epiph Laurens SC 1948-1951; P-in-c Ch Of The Gd Shpd Greer SC 1945-1952; R S Andr's Epis Ch Greenville SC 1945-1952; Cur Trin Cathd Columbia SC 1943-1945.

WESTON, Myrtle Marguerite (NMich) 107 Forest Ridge Dr, Marquette MI 49855 B Marquette MI 6/13/1926 d Carl Carlson Kiel & Blanche Marguerite. Nthrn Michigan U. D 4/1/1999 P 3/5/2000 Bp James Arthur Kelsey. myweston@mailstation.com

WESTON, Stephen Richard (Colo) 432 N Whiting, Mesa AZ 85213 B New London CT 2/10/1941 s William Borge Weston & Ruth Catherine. BA Colorado St Coll 1966; MDiv VTS 1969. D 7/12/1969 P 5/23/1970 Bp J(ohn) Joseph Meakins Harte. m 7/1/2011 Peggy Joanne Harrison c 2. R S Mk's Epis Ch Mesa AZ 1998-2005; R S Matt's Ch Edinburg TX 1995-1998; R Chr Epis Ch Pulaski VA 1991-1994; Ed for Crossroads Dioc Nwspr Dio Dallas Dallas TX 1985-1991; Assoc R S Alb's Epis Ch Arlington TX 1981-1985; Vic S Phil Amarillo TX 1976-1981; Yth Dir Dio NW Texas Lubbock TX 1973-1981; Vic S Mk's Epis Ch Coleman TX 1973-1976; Vic Trin Ch Albany TX 1973-1976; Cur Ch Of The H Trin Midland TX 1972-1973; Cur S Mk's Epis Ch Mesa AZ 1970-1972. Ed/Writer/Producer, "Our Hisp Mnstry II," 1991; Ed/Writer/Producer, "Our Hisp Mnstry," 1989. Polly Bond Awd 1988. longs14259@gmail.com

WESTPFAHL, Carol Elizabeth (ETenn) 110 Sugarwood Dr, Knoxville TN 37934 **R S Eliz's Epis Ch Knoxville TN 2011-** B Burien WA 8/22/1958 d Charles Lewis Westpfahl & Dona Fae. BA U of Washington 1981; MBA U of Washington 1983; MA Grad Theol Un 2001; MDiv CDSP 2002. D 6/24/2000 Bp Vincent Waydell Warner P 1/13/2001 Bp Sanford Zangwill Kaye Hampton. Assoc R for Adult Formation & Sprtl Developme Trin Ch Newtown CT 2003-2009. NAECED 2005. cew4@uw.edu

WESTPHAL, Stacey Elizabeth (CFla) 522 Summerset Ct, Indian Harbour Beach FL 32937 **D H Trin Epis Ch Melbourne FL 2007-** B Orleans France 9/15/1954 d William George Stacey & Maria Joanne. MS St Fran U 1995; MS St Fran U 2004. D 12/9/2006 Bp John Wadsworth Howe. m 11/1/1983 Frank Westphal. staceywestphal@hotmail.com

WETHERED, Stephanie Keith (Nwk) 224 Cornelia St, Boonton NJ 07005 **S Ptr's Ch Essex Fells NJ 2005-** B Burlington VT 10/10/1958 d Richard Leonard Keith & Jeane. BS U Of Bridgeport 1982; MDiv Ya Berk 1993. D 6/5/1993 Bp Jack Marston McKelvey P 12/4/1993 Bp John Shelby Spong. m 6/10/1995 Simon Wethered. R S Jn's Epis Ch Boonton NJ 1996-2005; Assoc S Ptr's Ch Morristown NJ 1993-1996. Auth, "Ch Of The Year 2000 In Dio Newark". Phi Kappa Phi U Of Bridgeport; Dana Schlr U Of Bridgeport; Mercer Preaching Prize Yale DS. revmothers@gmail.com

WETHERILL, Benjamin Wade (Me) P.O. Box 156, Rangeley ME 04970 B 9/10/1962 s Benjamin Alfred Wetherill & Mary Jane. US Mltry Acad; BS Arizona St U 1987; MDiv Asbury TS 2008. D 9/26/2009 Bp Stephen Taylor Lane. m 1/9/1988 Ana Kristan Rhinehart-Wetherill c 3. bjammin45@myfairpoint.net

WETHERINGTON, Robert William (Miss) PO Box 366, Sumner MS 38957 B Kinston, NC 10/28/1980 s Robert Lee Wetherington & Carolyn Warren. BA Kennesaw St U 2003; M. Div VTS 2009. D 12/20/2008 P 6/28/2009 Bp J(ohn) Neil Alexander. m 4/19/2008 Betsy Ann Baumgarten. Delta Mssnr Dio Mississippi Jackson MS 2009-2011. rwwether@gmail.com

WETHERN, James Douglas (Ga) PO Box 20327, Saint Simons Island GA 31522 **D Chr Ch Frederica St Simons Island GA 1991-** B Minneapolis MN 7/12/1926 s Rudolph Jesse Wethern & Ida Olivia. MS Lawr 1949; PhD Lawr 1952; BChE U of Wisconsin 2047. D 11/1/1991 Bp Harry Woolston Shipps. m 9/11/1948 Yvonne Marie Zuehlke c 4.

WETTSTEIN, David William (Ida) 6925 Copper Dr, Boise ID 83704 **R S Steph's Boise ID 1992** B San Diego CA 11/11/1955 s William Dewel Wettstein & Diane Hillis. BA Sacramento St U 1979; MDiv SFTS 1983; CAS CDSP 1992. D 4/25/1992 Bp George Edmonds Bates P 11/1/1992 Bp John Stuart Thornton. m 2/26/2000 Belinda Suzanne Wheelock.

WETZEL, Edward Albert (Wyo) PO Box 846, Powell WY 82435 **Died 1/2/2010** B New York NY 6/11/1933 s Edward Wetzel & Gertrude. BA H Cross Coll 1955. D 7/19/2007 P 1/30/2008 Bp Bruce Edward Caldwell. c 4.

WETZEL, Mary A (At) P.O. Box 490, Clarkesville GA 30523 **The Ch of the Common Ground Atlanta GA 2010-; Chr Ch Cathd S Louis MO 2009-** B Benton Harbor MI 11/16/1945 d Kenneth Lester Wetzel & Helen Stephanie. BS Jn Br 1969; MS Minnesota St U 1978; MEd Georgia St U 1981; MDiv EDS 2006. D 10/12/2008 P 6/28/2009 Bp J(ohn) Neil Alexander. Gr-Calv Epis Ch Clarkesville GA 2009-2010. marywetz@gmail.com

WETZEL, Todd Harold (Dal) Po Box 429, Cedar Hill TX 75106 **Anglicans Untd & Latimer Press Dallas TX 2005-; R Ch Of The Gd Shpd Cedar Hill TX 2002-** B Warren OH 7/7/1946 s Harold Craver Wetzel & June Rae. BA Ohio U 1968; MDiv Bex 1971. D 6/26/1971 P 5/1/1972 Bp John Harris Burt. m 4/20/1968 Cheryl M Meyer c 2. Anglicans Untd & Latimer Press Dallas TX 1989-2002; R S Geo Ch San Antonio TX 1987-1989; R Adv Epis Ch Westlake OH 1972-1987; Asst S Paul's Epis Ch Of E Cleveland Cleveland OH 1971-1972. Auth, "Steadfast Faith," Latimer Press, 1994; Auth, "H Euch Sacr Of Love," self, 1974. scl Ohio U 1968; Phi Beta Kappa 1967; Omicron Delta Kappa 1966. frwetzel@yahoo.com

WEYMOUTH, Richard Channing (NH) RR3 Box 18, Plymouth NH 03264 B Norwalk CT 5/18/1952 s Tyler Weymouth & Francis Virginia. U of New Hampshire 1975; MDiv Ya Berk 1980. D 6/21/1980 P 6/1/1981 Bp Philip Alan Smith. m 8/21/1976 Katherine Lovett c 2. Cur Chr Ch Exeter NH 1980-1984.

WEYRICH, Charles David (O) 615 Matterhorn Dr, Park City UT 84098 **Int R S Lk's Ch Pk City UT 2002-; Adv Epis Ch Westlake OH 1996-** B Dayton OH 2/26/1935 s Charles John Weyrich & Marion Virginia. BA Muskingum Coll 1967; BD Bex 1970; MA Ashland TS 1984. D 6/21/1970 P 1/10/1971 Bp Roger W Blanchard. m 7/3/1959 Kay L Wyer c 3. S Andr's Epis Ch Elyria OH 1989-1995; R Ch Of S Paul The Apos Baltimore MD 1989; S Jn's Ch Worthington OH 1985-1988; S Jn's Ch Columbus OH 1970-1985. AAPC.

WHALEN, Donald (Eas) 2929 SE Ocean Blvd O-5, Stuart FL 34996 B Bay Shore NY 7/2/1934 s Harold Whalen & Evelyn. BS SUNY 1958; MS SUNY 1959; Med Col 1973; Mercer TS 1989; Cert Gerontological Mnstry 1991; CPE 1992. D 6/17/1989 Bp Orris George Walker Jr. m 9/25/1981 Constance Kneisel. D S Lk's Epis Ch Port Salerno FL 2000-2002; D-in-c S Mths Epis Ch No Bellmore NY 1995-2000; Asst S Lk's Epis Ch Port Salerno FL 1992-1993; D / Asst S Ann's Ch Sayville NY 1990-1992; D / Asst The Ch Of The Ascen Rockville Cntr NY 1989-1990. deacdonw@dmv.com

WHALEN, Peter James (Tenn) 105 Audubon Rd, Shelbyville TN 37160 **R Ch Of The Redeem Shelbyville TN 2007-** B Hartford CT 7/24/1939 s John Joseph Whalen & Sophie Anne. Assumption Sem 1967; Epis TS of The SW 1983. Rec from Roman Catholic 12/19/1983 as Deacon Bp Scott Field Bailey. m 7/21/1984 Barabara Anne Brown c 2. R S Phil's Ch Nashville TN 1989-2006; S Annes Ch Can TX 1987-1989; Asst R S Barth's Ch Corpus Christi TX 1983-1987. pjwhalen@charter.net

WHALEY, Stephen Foster (Tex) 605 Dulles Avenue, Stafford TX 77477 **R All SS Epis Ch Stafford TX 2009-** B Houston TX 1/8/1973 BEd Texas A&M U 1996; MDiv STUSo 2003. D 6/21/2003 P 12/21/2003 Bp Don Adger Wimberly. m 11/1/1997 Kathryn Gray Robson c 2. Asst Chr Ch Nacogdoches TX 2005-2009; Asst Ch Of The Gd Shpd Kingwood TX 2003-2005. fr.stephen@allsaintsstafford.org

WHALLON, Diane (Fla) 1640 NE 40th Ave Apt 106, Ocala FL 34470 **D Ch Of The Medtr Micanopy FL 2010-** B Shelbyville IN 5/13/1949 d Daniel O Whallon & Carolyn. BA/BS U of Missouri 1977; MBA U of Missouri 1978; PhD U of Missouri 1983; EFM STUSo 1985. D 10/24/1986 Bp Richard Frank Grein. D S Pat's Ch Ocala FL 1998-1999; D S Aid's Ch Olathe KS 1991-1995; Pstr Admin S Thos The Apos Ch Overland Pk KS 1988-1991; Dioc Admin Dio Kansas Topeka KS 1985-1988. Auth, "Gifts Identification Ldr'S Manual," Dio Kansas, 1988; Auth, "Decision Maker Uncertainty Effects Of Environ-Tech &," U of Missouri, 1983; Auth, "Contemporary Wrshp Serv Workbook For Chapl," Untd St AF, 1972. Beta Gamma Sigma 1977; Natl Hospice Orgnztn 1987; NAAD 1984; Zeta Tau Alpha 1967. Outstanding Paper by a Stdt Am Inst for Decision Sciences 1980; Outstanding Mgmt Stdt of the Year U of MIssouri 1977; AF Commendation Medal USAF 1974; AF Commendation Medal USAF 1971; Maud Ainslie Schlrshp Maud Ainslie Trust 1967. dianehwa@embarqmail.com

✠ WHALON, Rt Rev Pierre W (Eur) 23 Avenue George V, Paris 75008 France **Bp Suffr of Convoc of Ch in Europe Convoc of Amer Ch in Europe Paris FR 2001-** B Newport RI 11/12/1952 s Raymond Davenport Whalon & Marthe Welté. BA Bos 1974; Schola Cantorum 1977; MA Duquesne U 1981; MDiv VTS 1985. D 6/8/1985 P 12/21/1985 Bp Alden Moinet Hathaway Con 11/18/2001 for Eur. m 11/15/1980 Melinda Jane McCulloch c 1. Epis Ch Cntr New York NY 2001-2004; Chair COM Dio Cntrl Florida Orlando FL 2000-2001; Chair Inst of Chr Stds Dio Cntrl Florida Orlando FL 1997-1999; Econ Justice Off Dio Cntrl Florida Orlando FL 1994-1996; R S Andr's Epis Ch Ft Pierce FL 1993-2001; Chair Advocacy Serv & Justice Cmsn Dio Pennsylvania Philadelphia PA 1992-1993; R S Paul's Ch Elkins Pk PA 1991-1993; Econ Justice Off Dio Pittsburgh Monroeville PA 1989-1991; BEC Dio Pittsburgh Monroeville PA 1988-1991; All Souls Ch No Versailles PA 1985-1991; Co-chair Wrshp & Mus Cmsn Dio Pittsburgh Monroeville PA 1985-1988. "The Future of the PB Tradition," *Oxford Guide to BCP*, Oxf, 2006; Auth, "Toward an Adequate Moral Evaltn of Homosexuality," *ATR*, 1997; Auth, "Angl Comprehensiveness & the Thought of Dav Tracy," *Journ of Ecum Stds*, 1991; Auth, "A Critique of Sedwick's Revising Angl Moral Theol," *S Lk's Journ of Theol*, 1989. DD VTS 2003. bishop@tec-europe.org

WHARTON III, George Franklin (Ia) 502 W Broadway St, Decorah IA 52101 **P-in-c Gr Ch Decorah IA 1979-** B Lake Charles LA 12/20/1929 s George Franklin Wharton & Fleda Garfield. BS U So 1951; GTS 1954; BA Oxf 1956; MA Oxf 1961. D 7/2/1954 P 8/1/1956 Bp Girault M Jones. m 6/11/1967 Marjorie R Running. S Andr's Epis Ch Waverly IA 1991-1993; Gr Ch Decorah IA 1980-1993; Vic S Ptr's Ch Bettendorf IA 1977-1979; S Peters Ch Fairfield IA 1976-1979; Serv S Andr's Paradis Luling LA 1969-2002; R Ch Of The Epiph Opelousas LA 1959-1965; Asst S Mk's Cathd Shreveport LA 1956-1959; M-in-c S Jn's Epis Ch Thibodaux LA 1954-1955.

WHARTON, Roger E (ECR) 1404 Arnold Ave, San Jose CA 95110 B Mansfield OH 3/21/1947 s Kenneth Eugene Wharton & Marie May. BS Otterbein Coll 1969; MA except thesis Nthrn Illinois U 1971; MDiv Nash 1976; Ldrshp Acad for New Directions 1979; MA Loyola U 1982; DMin PSR 1995. D 1/10/1976 P 7/10/1976 Bp William Hampton Brady. m 9/29/2008 Marc Fuentes. Assoc S Phil's Ch San Jose CA 1992-2002; R The Ch Of The H Trin Juneau AK 1985-1991; R S Brendan's Epis Ch Juneau AK 1985-1989; Yth Chapl Dio New York New York City NY 1982-1985; Epis Dio Of Ny Mid Hudson Regio Boiceville NY 1982-1985; P-in-c S Andr's Ch Walden NY 1982-1985; P-in-c St Fran of Assisi Montgomery NY 1982-1985; Vic Ch Of S Mary Of The Snows Eagle River WI 1976-1981; Dio Fond du Lac Appleton WI 1976-1981; S Mths Minocqua WI 1976-1981. Auth, "The Sprtl Roots of Chr Environmentalism," *Desert Call*, Nova Nada, 2009; Auth, "Palm Sunday," *Upper Room*, Upper Room, 1997; Auth, "Bethlehem as Sacr Place," *The Power of Sacr Places*, Quest, 1992; Auth, "H Week Devotions," *Disciplines*, Upper Room, 1990; Auth, "Connections," *Cries from the Heart: Alaskan Respond to the Exxon Valdez Oil Spill*, Wizard Works, 1989; Ed, *Christians In Comm w Creation*, EcoSpirit; Ed, *Ch In Comm w Creation*, EcoSpirit. Amer Teilhard Soc; Sis of the H Nativ; Soc Of S Jn The Evang. roger@ecospirit.org

WHEATCROFT, George Richard (Tex) 8707 Valley Ranch Pkwy W Apt 339, Irving TX 75063 **Died 11/12/2009** B Quincy IL 8/8/1918 s George Frederick Wheatcroft & Margaret Elizabeth. BA Washington U 1940; MDiv VTS 1943; MA Truman U MO 1949; DD VTS 1980. D 5/1/1942 P 2/27/1943 Bp William Scarlett. c 3. Auth, *Who Was Jesus*, Brockton Pub Co., 1997. grwheat@tx.rr.com

WHEATLEY, Gail (Oly) St Andrew's Episcopal Church, 510 E. Park Ave, Port Angeles WA 98362 **R S Andrews Epis Ch Port Angeles WA 2008-** B Springfield OH 8/2/1953 d Robert Thomas Fortin & Fay Lurose. BS Ithaca Coll 1976; MDiv STUSo 2005. D 9/18/2005 P 3/25/2006 Bp Charles Franklin Brookhart Jr. m 5/24/1975 Douglas G Wheatley c 2. R S Mk's Ch Havre MT 2005-2008. gail.wheatley@gmail.com

WHEATLEY-JONES, Elizabeth (Miss) P.O. Box 345, Grenada MS 38902 **P-in-c All SS Epis Ch Grenada MS 2010-** B Greenwood MS 9/23/1968 d Dudley Seth Wheatley & Mary Melinda. BS U So 1990; MDiv Epis TS of The SW 1999. D 6/11/1999 P 3/4/2000 Bp Alfred Clark Marble Jr. m 11/26/2006 Robert J Jones. R S Jos's On-The-Mtn Mentone AL 2008-2009; Cn-Mssnr/R Chr Ch Bay St Louis MS 2007-2008; Cn for Yth and YA Trin Cathd Little Rock AR 2003-2005; Chapl/Asst R Ch Of The Resurr Starkville MS 1999-2003. ehwj68@gmail.com

WHEATON, Philip Eugene (Roch) 7211 Spruce Ave, Takoma Park MD 20912 B Minneapolis MN 5/21/1925 s Grier Franklin Wheaton & Claudia. BA U MN 1948; MDiv VTS 1952; Amer U 1972. D 6/21/1952 Bp Stephen E Keeler P 12/1/1952 Bp Charles Alfred Voegeli. m 7/8/2009 Phyllis Porter c 6. Exec Coun Appointees New York NY 1989-1990; Dio Washington Washington DC 1968-1988; R S Lk's Ch Brockport NY 1964-1968; Min In Charge Iglesia Epis San Andres Santo Domingo DO 1955-1964; Min in charge Iglesia Epis San Marcos Haitiana 1955-1964; Min in charge Iglesia Epis Epifania Santo Domingo Di DO 1952-1954. Auth, "Flowering of the Prophetic Wk in Latin Amer"; Co-Auth, "Puerto Rico: People Challenging Colonialism"; Co-Auth, "Nicaragua: People'S Revolution"; Co-Auth, "Empire & The Word"; Co-Auth, "Guatemala: Path To Liberation"; Co-Auth, "Triufando Sobre Las Tragedias," *Centennial Hist Of The Epis Ch In The Dominican Republic*. Hon Theol Cn Epis Ch In The Dominican Republic 1997. phil.wheaton@juno.com

WHEELER, Charles Ralph (WNY) 161 E Main St, Westfield NY 14787 B Olean NY 12/31/1946 s Kenneth Eugene Wheeler & Mary. BA SUNY 1969. D 11/13/1994 Bp David Charles Bowman. m 8/5/1972 Christine Frances Nash c 2. S Mich And All Ang Buffalo NY 2004-2008; Dio Wstrn New York Tonawanda NY 2000-2003.

WHEELER, Diana Roberta (Cal) 573 Dolores st., San Francisco CA 94110 **St. Ambr Sea Breeze Epis Sch San Mateo CA 1995-** B San Francisco CA 8/30/1954 AA City Coll of San Francisco; BTS Epis Sch for Deacons 2000. D 12/6/2003 Bp William Edwin Swing. m 11/16/1996 Richard Brandon c 3. D S Edm's Epis Ch Pacifica CA 2005-2007; S Aid's Ch San Francisco CA 2003-2009. dianarwheeler@gmail.com

WHEELER, Elisa Desportes (Va) 638 Burton Point Rd, Mathews VA 23068 B Columbia SC 5/22/1946 d Fay Wheeler & Margaret. BA Converse Coll 1968; MDiv VTS 1981. D 6/22/1981 Bp Orris George Walker Jr P 1/3/1982 Bp John Thomas Walker. m 10/25/2011 Maurice Levis. P-in-c Ch Of The Sprt Alexandria VA 1999-2007; Kingston Par Epis Ch Mathews VA 1999-2005; Asst S Jn's Ch Hampton VA 1997-1999; Ch Of The Gd Shpd Norfolk VA 1997; S Fran Ch Virginia Bch VA 1995-1996; Int S Chris's Epis Ch Portsmouth VA 1994-1995; S Nich Epis Ch Germantown MD 1991-1992; S Martins-In-The-Field Columbia SC 1987-1988; S Jas Ch Potomac MD 1985-1989; Asst S Columba's Ch Washington DC 1981-1984. Auth, "Congregations In Change". elisadwheeler@gmail.com

WHEELER, Evelyn (Va) 19 Spencer Ave, Guiliford CT 06437 **D Middlesex Area Cluster Mnstry Higganum CT 2011-** B Meidelberg Germany 1/17/1953 d David B Wheeler & Janet Brooks. BS U of Vermont 1976; JD Gonzaga U Sch of Law 1979; MS JHU 1997; MDiv Ya Berk 2011. D 6/4/2011 Bp Shannon Sherwood Johnston. ekwhlr64@gmail.com

WHEELER, Fran (Kan) 14301 S Blackbob Rd, Olathe KS 66062 B Corpus Christi TX 8/11/1966 d Amos Robert Salinas & Elvira. BS Marymount Coll

W

Tarrytown NY 1990; Kansas Sch for Mnstry 2010. D 1/8/2011 Bp Dean Elliott Wolfe. m 11/1/1986 Raymond Wheeler c 2. frances.wheeler11@gmail.com

WHEELER, Gloria Elizabeth (CFla) 4016 Maguire Blvd., Apt 3110, Orlando FL 32803 B Washington DC 2/9/1930 d Dewey Clyde Morris & Sophia Elizabeth. Dio Cntrl Florida Inst for Chr Stds 1977. D 9/21/1983 Bp William Hopkins Folwell. m 11/21/1964 Robert Raymond Wheeler. D Cathd Ch Of S Lk Orlando FL 1992-2007; D S Jas Epis Ch Ormond Bch FL 1988-1991; D Cathd Ch Of S Lk Orlando FL 1983-1987. Chapl Ord of S Lk 1986; NAAD 1983. Presidents Awd NAAD 1995. gewheeler@cfl.rr.com

WHEELER, James R (Ct) Po Box 10, Woodbury CT 06798 **R S Jn's Ch Stamford CT 2008-** B Chicago IL 12/28/1953 s Charles Wakefield Wheeler & Margaret Ann. BA Coll of Wooster 1976; MDiv CRDS 1979; DMin VTS 2004. D 6/23/1979 Bp John Harris Burt P 1/13/1980 Bp David Keller Leighton Sr. m 6/19/1976 Carol Mead c 3. R S Paul's Ch Woodbury CT 1987-2007; R S Ptr's Epis Ch Eggertsville NY 1981-1987; Asst Ch Of The Mssh Baltimore MD 1979-1981. jwheeler@stjohns-stamford.org

WHEELER, John Bevan (Md) 2795 Topmast Ct, Annapolis MD 21401 B Baltimore MD 12/5/1931 s Clarence Eldred Wheeler & Carolyn Taylor. BA W&L 1953; LTh GTS 1956; STB GTS 1959; MAE GW 1977. D 9/29/1956 Bp Harry Lee Doll P 7/13/1957 Bp Noble C Powell. m 10/5/1957 Helen Chase Ward c 2. Vic All SS Ch Annapolis Jct MD 1995-1999; Asst S Anne's Par Annapolis MD 1989-1995; S Barth's Ch Baltimore MD 1987-1988; Int Epiph Epis Ch Odenton MD 1985-1986; Int All Hallows Par So River Davidsonville MD 1982; Asst S Anne's Par Annapolis MD 1979-1981; Int S Lk's Ch Annapolis MD 1978-1979; R S Jas The Apos Epis Ch Conroe TX 1959-1961; Vic S Andr's Ch Clear Sprg MD 1956-1958.

WHEELER, J(ohn) Michael (Mo) 6316 Wydown Blvd, Saint Louis MO 63105 **S Mich & S Geo Clayton MO 2005-** B Beaumont TX 9/20/1953 s J R Wheeler & Linda Jean. BA Dallas Bapt Coll Dallas TX 1978; MDiv SW Bapt TS 1981; CTh Epis TS of The SW 1990. D 6/16/1990 Bp Maurice Manuel Benitez P 1/1/1991 Bp Anselmo Carral-Solar. m 11/1/1996 Robin S Saville c 4. R S Chris's Ch Houston TX 1994-2005; Asst to R S Mart's Epis Ch Houston TX 1990-1994. robinswheeler@gmail.com

WHEELER, Kathryn Brown (CGC) 2002 W Lakeridge Dr, Albany GA 31707 **D S Steph's Lee Cnty Leesburg GA 1999-** B SC 12/25/1934 d Stanley Brown & Catherine. BS Albany St U 1984. D 6/17/1999 Bp Henry Irving Louttit. m 11/20/1994 Daniel Gustavson Wheeler.

WHEELER JR, Louis (Md) 20204 Yankee Harbor Pl, Montgomery Village MD 20886 **S Mich And All Ang Ch Baltimore MD 2010-; Asst R S Jn's Epis Ch Columbia SC 2005-** B Homestead PA 10/15/1965 s Louis Wheeler & Lillie Mary. BA Edinboro U 1987; MS Natl-Louis U 1998; MDiv How 2003. D 6/12/2005 P 1/21/2006 Bp John Chane. m 9/9/1989 Tracy Douglas c 2. S Mary's Epis Ch Foggy Bottom Washington DC 2007-2010; Asst S Alb's Par Washington DC 2005-2006; Ch Of The Ascen Gaithersburg MD 2000-2005. LBAC99@AOL.COM

WHEELER, Rhonda Estes (SVa) St. Andrew's Episcopal Church, 45 Main Street, Newport News VA 23601 **Living a H Life T/F Dio Sthrn Virginia Norfolk VA 2011-; Virginia Interfaith Plcy Ntwk Dio Sthrn Virginia Norfolk VA 2010-; Ecum Cmsn Dio Sthrn Virginia Norfolk VA 2008-; CE-Net Dio Sthrn Virginia Norfolk VA 2007-; Asst R S Andr's Epis Ch Newport News VA 2007-** B Waynesboro, VA 6/14/1962 d Vernon Lonzy Estes & Joyce Marie. BA Carson-Newman Coll, Jefferson City, TW 1984; MDiv SE Bapt TS 1987; Post-Grad in Angl Stds VTS 2007. D 5/26/2007 P 12/6/2007 Bp Frank Neff Powell. c 1. Sem Intern S Barn' Ch Leeland Upper Marlboro MD 2006-2007; Educ Consortium Dio SW Virginia Roanoke VA 2002-2006; R E Lee Memi Ch (Epis) Lexington VA 2002-2006. saec.rhonda11@verizon.net

WHEELER CSL, William Ramsey (Alb) Po Box 354, Boonville NY 13309 **P/Vic Dio Albany Albany NY 2007-; Moliawk Correctional Fac kairos Mnstry Dio Albany Albany NY 2002-; Moliawk Correctional Fac kairos Mnstry Dio Albany Albany NY 2002-; Sprtl Dir Kairos #1 Dio Albany Albany NY 2002-** B Utica NY 3/29/1932 s Everett Jesse Wheeler & Marjorie Elizabeth. BA Syr 1955; BAS TESM 2009. D 11/1/1986 Bp Donald James Parsons P 12/23/2007 Bp William Howard Love. m 11/23/1957 Darlene Joyce Benson c 2. D Gr Ch Mohawk NY 2003-2007; D Gr Ch Mohawk NY 2003-2007; Sprtl Advsry Happ #38 & #39 Dio Cntrl New York Syracuse NY 2002-2004; Dep Sprtl Dir for Curs Dio Cntrl New York Syracuse NY 1998-1999; Dep Sprtl Dir, Curs Dio Cntrl New York Syracuse NY 1998-1999; D Trin Ch Boonville NY 1993-2003; D S Mk's Ch Sidney OH 1989-1993; D Chr Ch (Limestone) Peoria IL 1986-1989; D S Andr's Ch Peoria IL 1986-1989. NAAD 1986. wheelsram@aol.com

WHEELOCK, Janet (Minn) 90 Seymour Ave SE, Minneapolis MN 55414 **S Tim's Epis Ch Mtn View CA 2010-; Chr Formation Com Dio Minnesota Minneapolis MN 1993-** B Minneapolis MN 3/16/1957 d Robert Edward Wheelock & Jean. BA U MN 1982; CAS CDSP 1993; MDiv Luther TS 1993. D 6/24/1993 Bp Robert Marshall Anderson P 1/1/1994 Bp James Louis Jelinek. Ch Of The Ascen Stillwater MN 2009-2010; P-in-c S Edw The Confessor Wayzata MN 2004-2007; Cn Cathd Ch Of S Mk Minneapolis MN 2002-2004; Com Dio Minnesota Minneapolis MN 1998-2001; U Epis Cntr Minneapolis MN 1996-1998; Assoc R Adv Ch Farmington MN 1995-1996; Cmsn On Mus And Liturg Dio Minnesota Minneapolis MN 1993-1999; Int Yth Coordntr Dio Minnesota Minneapolis MN 1993-1995; S Jn The Bapt Epis Ch Minneapolis MN 1993-1994. Auth, "Luth Wmn Today". ESMHE, Mneca, Neca. janubojou@gmail.com

WHEELOCK, L(eslie) Gail (RI) 8 Neptune St, Jamestown RI 02835 B New York NY 11/2/1939 d Roy Smith Penner & Ruth. BA St. Lawr Canton NY 1960; MA U of Rhode Island 1970; A.D.N/RN Rhode Island Cmnty Coll 1977; Sch for Deacons 1988. D 2/4/1989 Bp George Nelson Hunt III. m 5/6/2000 Richard J Ayen c 5. D Ch Of The Ascen Wakefield RI 2000-2003; D S Matt's Par Of Jamestown Jamestown RI 1995-1999; D S Ptr's By The Sea Narragansett RI 1990-1994; D S Aug's Ch Kingston RI 1989-1990. Phi Beta Kappa 1960. lgailwheelock@aol.com

WHELAN, Edgar Joseph (WMo) 13500 Rinehart Ln, Parkville MO 64152 B Detroit MI 5/27/1936 s Henry J Whelan & Theresa M. CG Jung Inst; H Cross Coll; BA U of Notre Dame 1960. Rec from Roman Catholic. m 3/21/1981 Janet Kay Gabbert. R Ch Of The Redeem Kansas City MO 1988-2003; Vic S Nich Ch Noel MO 1986-1988; Dio W Missouri Kansas City MO 1985-1988; P-in-c S Jn's Ch Neosho MO 1985-1986. priest.deacon@yahoo.com

WHELAN, Janet Kay (WMo) 13500 Rinehart Ln, Parkville MO 64152 B Oak Park IL 11/8/1935 d John Paul Gabbert & Fern A. BA/BS No Pk U 1977; MS Cntrl Bapt TS 1997. D 2/5/2000 Bp Barry Robert Howe. m 3/21/1981 Edgar Joseph Whelan. D Ch Of The Redeem Kansas City MO 2000-2003. priest.deacon@yahoo.com

WHELAN, Peter Hainsworth (Ky) 1207 Meadowridge Trl, Goshen KY 40026 **P-in-c S Jas Ch Shelbyville KY 2009-** B Pawtucket RI 6/24/1941 s Kenneth Elsworth Whelan & Muriel. BA Providence Coll 1963; Ya Berk 1966. D 6/18/1966 P 3/18/1967 Bp John S Higgins. m 2/28/1987 Janice Gostling. R S Mary's Ch Madisonville KY 1996-2004; R S Jn In-The-Wilderness Copake Falls NY 1989-1996; Ch Of The Mssh Foster RI 1986-1989; Dio Rhode Island Providence RI 1984; R Ch Of The Ascen Cranston RI 1970-1984; Asst R The Epis Ch Of S Andr And S Phil Coventry RI 1967-1970; Cur Chr Ch Westerly RI 1966-1967. pwhelan1064@bellsouth.net

WHELCHEL, Judith Hester (WNC) 67 Windsor Rd, Asheville NC 28804 B Atlanta GA 12/5/1966 d Thomas Rod Hester & Judith Appleton. BA U So 1989; MS U GA 1991; MDiv SWTS 1996. D 6/8/1996 Bp Frank Kellogg Allan P 12/7/1996 Bp Robert Hodges Johnson. m 8/3/1991 David Michael Whelchel c 1. Ch Of The Gd Shpd Lookout Mtn TN 2006-2009; Assoc The Cathd Of All Souls Asheville NC 1998-2001; Asst Trin Epis Ch Asheville NC 1996-1997. mjwhelchel@aol.com

WHENAL, Barry (FdL) 6535 Oriole Road, Lake Tomahawk WI 54539 B Exeter NH 1/23/1947 s John William Whenal & Hazel Lovett. BA MI SU 1969; MDiv EDS 1972. D 6/10/1972 Bp Charles F Hall P 12/9/1972 Bp Francis W Lickfield. m 8/8/1987 Barbara Esther Groth. R Ch Of The Intsn Stevens Point WI 1996-2004; R S Anskar's Epis Ch Hartland WI 1989-1996; Vic S Mths Minocqua WI 1984-1989; Assoc Adirondack Missions Brant Lake NY 1980-1984; Vic S Jn's Epis Ch Oxford WI 1974-1980; Vic S Mary's Epis Ch Tomah WI 1974-1980; Cur Trin Epis Ch Peoria IL 1972-1974. cheersbw@frontiernet.net

WHEPLEY, Earl Allen (WMass) 5837 Brockton Drive, Indianapolis IN 46220 **Died 4/8/2010** B Visalia CA 8/3/1934 s Earl Allen Whepley & Norca Elizabeth. BS OR SU 1957; MDiv EDS 1965. D 6/24/1965 P 2/1/1966 Bp Robert McConnell Hatch. c 2. OHC 1966. earlandcolleen@sbcglobal.net

WHISENHUNT, William Allen (WNC) Trinity Episcopal Church, 60 Church St, Asheville NC 28801 B Waynesville NC 9/18/1949 s Harry Eugene Whisenhunt & Louise. BA Lenoir-Rhyne Coll 1971; MDiv STUSo 1985. D 6/15/1985 P 1/1/1986 Bp William Gillette Weinhauer. m 1/9/1971 Nancy Cook c 1. R Trin Epis Ch Asheville NC 1999-2010; Cn Dio Wstrn No Carolina Asheville NC 1991-1999; P-in-c Ch Of S Mths Asheville NC 1991-1992; R Ch Of The Epiph Newton NC 1985-1991. billwnc@aol.com

WHISTLER, Tamsen Elizabeth (Mo) 1020 N Duchesne Dr, Saint Charles MO 63301 **R Trin Ch St Chas MO 1995-** B San Francisco CO 1/3/1953 d Donald Frederick Whistler & Elizabeth Lawrence. BS U of Missouri 1973; MA U of Missouri 1975; MDiv SWTS 1984. D 6/15/1984 P 2/1/1985 Bp William Augustus Jones Jr. m 11/25/1983 Robert F Brown c 1. Assoc Calv Ch Columbia MO 1986-1995; Asst Gr Ch Jefferson City MO 1984-1986. trinity318@msn.com

WHITACRE, Rodney Alan (Pgh) 107 Colonial Dr, Sewickley PA 15143 B Des Moines IA 12/28/1949 s Charles Edwin Whitacre & Leah. U of Cambridge; BA Gordon Coll 1973; MA Gordon-Conwell TS 1976. D 6/1/1986 P 2/1/1987 Bp James Michael Mark Dyer. m 6/26/1972 Margaret Ann Kerr c 2. TESM Ambridge PA 1986-1999. Auth, "Johannine Polemic". SBL, Ibr.

WHITAKER, Ann Latham (Miss) 806 Prairie View Road, Oxford MS 38655 **S Ptr's Ch Oxford MS 2011-** B New Orleans LA 1/11/1953 d Wilbur Darrell Latham & Alice May. BS Mississippi St U 1978; MDiv STUSo 2001. D 6/23/2001 P 1/16/2002 Bp Alfred Clark Marble Jr. m 3/5/1977 Jerry A Whitaker c

1. R Ch Of The Creator Clinton MS 2007-2011; S Alb's Epis Ch Vicksburg MS 2003-2007; Cur The Epis Ch Of The Medtr Meridian MS 2001-2003. Soc of S Fran, Third Ord 1997. jandawhitaker@bellsouth.net

WHITAKER III, Howard Wilson (Eas) PO Box 596, Scottsboro AL 35768 **Supply Cler Dio Alabama Birmingham AL 2011-; Supply Cler Dio Newark Newark NJ 2004-** B Jackson MS 4/30/1953 s Howard Wilson Whitaker & Margaret Hannah. BS Amer U 1974; MDiv Epis TS In Kentucky 1988; DMin Wesley TS 1994. D 6/18/1988 P 12/21/1988 Bp Don Adger Wimberly. m 12/21/2007 Kay Elaine Hamrick c 2. Int Thankful Memi Ch Chattanooga TN 1998-2000; Int S Lk's Ch Scottsboro AL 1997-1998; R S Steph's Ch Earleville MD 1990-1994; Asst to Cn for Mssn Dio Lexington Lexington KY 1988-1990. Auth, "A Pstr Commentary on Dissociative Disorders," Morris / CPS, 1994; Auth, "arts, Revs, sermons," *Multiple Profsnl Pub*. AEHC 1990; Assn of Mntl Hlth Cler (Bd Cert) 1994; Assn of Profsnl Chapl (Bd Cert) 1994; Columbia Mltry Acad Alum Assn; Ldrshp Acad for New Directions 1987; Religous Cltn for Reproductive Choice 2006. Polly Bond- Photography ECom 1988. hwhitaker@howardwhitaker.net

WHITAKER, James Stewart (Mass) 44 Newport Dr, Westford MA 01886 B Boston MA 7/15/1931 s James Norman Whitaker & Esther. BS NEU 1954; BD EDS 1957; MD 1972. D 6/22/1957 Bp Anson Phelps Stokes Jr P 5/1/1958 Bp Frederic Cunningham Lawrence. m 1/19/1957 Janice Lee Granncll c 4. Off Of Bsh For ArmdF New York NY 1981-1996; R S Paul's Epis Ch Bedford MA 1960-1981; Cur Trin Epis Ch Portland ME 1957-1960.

✠ **WHITAKER, Rt Rev O'Kelley** (CNY) 3800 Shamrock Dr, Charlotte NC 28215 B Durham NC 12/26/1926 s Faison Young Whitaker & Margaret Louise. BA Duke 1949; MDiv SWTS 1952; DD SWTS 1981. D 5/22/1952 P 12/19/1952 Bp Edwin A Penick Con 5/16/1981 for CNY. m 8/16/1955 Betty A Abernethy c 3. Asst Dio Sthrn Virginia Norfolk VA 1992-1997; Bp Dio Cntrl New York Syracuse NY 1981-1991; Dn Cathd Ch Of S Lk Orlando FL 1973-1981; R Emm Ch Orlando FL 1969-1973; R S Lk's Ch Salisbury NC 1957-1969; Min in charge S Andr's Epis Ch Charlotte NC 1952-1955. Auth, "Sis Death," Morehouse-Barlow, 1974. Phi Beta Kappa Duke 1949. okwhitl@carolina.rr.com

WHITAKER, Robert H (Mich) 10501 Lagrima De Oro Rd NE, Apt 714, Albuquerque NM 87111 **Died 4/24/2010** B Malden MA 12/17/1918 s Harold Alden Whitaker & Beulah Maud. BA Gordon Coll 1940; MA Bos 1941; BD EDS 1943; PhD U of Edinburgh GB 1948; MA U of Windsor 1969. D 9/15/1943 Bp Raymond A Heron P 3/22/1944 Bp Henry Knox Sherrill. c 3. Auth, *Theo of Tarsus: Archbp of Cbury AD 668-690*, 1948; Auth, *Timaeus as a Basis for Platos Ethics*, 1941.

WHITBECK, Bailey Ogden (Mass) 29 Princess Rd, West Newton MA 02465 **Int All SS Epis Ch Attleboro MA 2008-** B Rochester NY 10/19/1941 d Kenneth Charles Ogden & Jean Olney. Vas 1964; BS U of Wisconsin 1965; MDiv EDS 1979. D 12/19/1980 Bp Morris Fairchild Arnold P 10/4/1981 Bp George Leslie Cadigan. m 6/16/1962 Philip Fletcher Whitbeck c 2. Dioc Coun Dio Massachusetts Boston MA 2010-2011; Int Trin Ch Newton Cntr MA 2005-2006; Int Trin Epis Ch Wrentham MA 2002-2005; Int Epis Ch Of S Thos Taunton MA 1998-2002; Int S Jn's Epis Ch Franklin MA 1995-1997; Int S Jn's Ch Newtonville MA 1993-1995; Int S Mk's Epis Ch Burlington MA 1991-1992; Int Emm Ch Boston MA 1989-1990; Int S Mk's Ch Westford MA 1987-1989; Int S Paul's Ch Lynnfield MA 1986-1987; Int All SS Ch W Newbury MA 1984-1986; Int Emm Epis Ch Wakefield MA 1983-1984; Asst Gr Ch Newton MA 1981-1983. bpwhitbeck@rcn.com

WHITE, Andrew D'Angio (Ct) 3601 Russell Rd, Alexandria 22305 **Gr Epis Ch Alexandria VA 2011-** B Hartford CT 5/22/1984 s Robert Allen White & Mary Ellen Malone. BA Hav 2006; MDiv VTS 2011. D 6/11/2011 Bp Laura Ahrens. m 7/19/2008 Sara D'Angio Sara Jean D'Angio. andrew.dangio.white@gmail.com

WHITE JR, Arthur Bain (Colo) St Paul Episcopal Church, PO Box 770722, Steamboat Springs CO 80477 **D S Paul's Epis Ch Steamboat Sprg CO 2007-** B Ft Benning GA 4/23/1949 s Arthur Bain White & Sally Mewshaw. BGS Chaminade U of Honolulu 1976. D 11/17/2007 Bp Robert John O'Neill. m 10/5/1968 Christine Draves c 2. haydenin1@mindspring.com

WHITE, Bruce Alan (Az) 4880 Sabino Canyon Rd, Tucson AZ 85750 **R S Alb's Epis Ch Tucson AZ 2011-** B Washington IA 10/3/1952 s Max Maurice White & Dorthy Lee. Kirkwood Cmnty Coll 1972; AA Muscatine Cmnty Coll Muscatine IA 1977; BA Grand View Coll Des Moines IA 1993; MDiv STUSo 1998. D 4/25/1998 Bp Carl Christopher Epting P 1/9/1999 Bp Edwin Funsten Gulick Jr. m 11/9/1974 Pamela J Rathburn c 2. R S Mich And All Ang Anniston AL 2001-2011; Chr Epis Ch Bowling Green KY 1998-2001. revbaw103@yahoo.com

WHITE, Carolyn Constance (ECR) 13723 Monte Bello, Castroville CA 95012 B Birmingham AL 2/8/1934 d Tracy Cornell Cowan & Alma Kathleen. BA Stan 1955; MDiv CDSP 1988. D 6/24/1988 P 5/31/1989 Bp Charles Shannon Mallory. m 12/25/1955 Marvin Lee White c 3. S Fran Cmnty Serv Inc. Salina KS 2001-2006; R S Geo's Ch Salinas CA 1994-2001; Asst Ch Of S Jude The Apos Cupertino CA 1993; Asst S Paul's Epis Ch Salinas CA 1991-1993; Dio El Camino Real Monterey CA 1988-1993. cwhite@st-francis.org

WHITE SR, Cyril Edward (SeFla) 15001 Polk St, Miami FL 33176 B Miami FL 8/24/1935 s Simeon White & Rose Elizabeth. BS Florida A&M U 1959; BS Florida Intl U 1978; MDiv VTS 1995. D 9/11/1983 P 8/26/1995 Bp Calvin Onderdonk Schofield Jr. m 7/3/1960 Christine W Williams c 4. R S Kevin's Epis Ch Opa Locka FL 1995-2001. Epis Curs 1975. cy1ch2003@yahoo.com

WHITE, George DH (Mass) 423 Lund Farm Way, Brewster MA 02631 **Died 11/4/2009** B Palmer MA 7/18/1927 s George Herbert White & Sydna Frances. BA Amer Intl Coll 1950; MDiv Bex 1953. D 5/23/1953 Bp William A Lawrence P 11/30/1953 Bp William Crittenden. c 2. Cape Cod Conservatory of Mus 1967-1993; Coll of Preachers - Fell 1969.

WHITE, Hank (Pa) 408 Valley Ave, Atglen PA 19310 **Int The Free Ch Of S Jn Philadelphia PA 2011-; Int The Free Ch Of S Jn Philadelphia PA 2011-** B Bayside NY 12/31/1944 s Harry Nixon White & Jane. BA Hob 1968; MDiv SWTS 1971; Cert Mar & Fam Ther 1990. D 6/19/1971 Bp Gerald Francis Burrill P 12/18/1971 Bp James Winchester Montgomery. m 4/13/1984 Jacqueline Villas c 2. P-in-c Ch Of The Ascen Parkesburg PA 2000-2011; Int Calv And S Paul Philadelphia PA 2000; Asst Trin Ch Swarthmore PA 1997-1998; Int Ch Of Our Sav Jenkintown PA 1995-1998; Int S Andr's Epis Ch Glenmoore PA 1994-1995; Int H Trin Ch Lansdale PA 1993-1994; Int Trin Epis Ch Ambler PA 1991-1993; Int S Ptr's Ch Phoenixville PA 1990-1991; Int S Jas Epis Ch Prospect Pk PA 1988-1990; R Chr Ch Sidney NE 1979-1981; Asst Trin Ch Easton PA 1974-1976. hwhitewolf2@gmail.com

WHITE, Harold Naylor (Va) Po Box 326, Wicomico Church VA 22579 B Charlottesville VA 3/12/1937 s Beverley Tucker White & Elizabeth Steelman. BA Randolph-Macon Coll 1960; VTS 1961; MA W Virginia Coll Of Grad Stds 1975; Inst Pstr Psych 1981; DMin Wesley TS 1992. D 6/29/1965 Bp Beverley D Tucker P 6/1/1966 Bp George P Gunn. m 8/20/1960 Sally Butler Brock c 3. S Jn's Epis Ch Tappahannock VA 1999-2000; Ch Of The Gd Shpd Burke VA 1997-1999; VTS Alexandria VA 1987-1990; Dio Virginia Richmond VA 1986-1991; R S Aid's Ch Alexandria VA 1977-1997; R S Mk's Epis Ch S Albans WV 1969-1977; R Trin Epis Ch So Boston VA 1966-1969; M-in-c Chr Ch Glen Allen VA 1965-1966; Cur Ch Of The Epiph Danville VA 1965-1966. AAPC, Amer Aassociat 1984; Lic Profsnl Counslr, St Of Virginia 1991.

WHITE, Helen S (Ga) 15 Willow Rd, Savannah GA 31419 **All SS Ch Tybee Island GA 2010-** B Dothan AL 5/22/1971 d Betts Simmons Slingluff & Margaret. BA Furman U 1993; MEd Georgia Sthrn U 1997; MDiv VTS 2008. D 2/9/2008 P 8/23/2008 Bp Henry Irving Louttit. m 7/22/1995 Michael S White c 2. Dio Georgia Savannah GA 2011; Asst S Geo's Epis Ch Savannah GA 2008-2010. helenslingluffwhite@mac.com

WHITE, Herman Joseph (Az) Grace St. Paul's Church, 2331 E. Adams St., Tucson AZ 85719 **Died 12/9/2010** B Hastings MN 10/7/1925 s George Thomas White & Marie Margaret. D Formation Prog 1981; EFM STUSo 1982. D 1/25/1982 Bp Robert Marshall Anderson. c 4.

WHITE JR, Howard Willard (CPa) 4016 Lincoln Dr, Bedford PA 15522 **P-in-c S Jas Bedford PA 2006-** B Clarksburg WV 6/8/1941 s Howard Willard White & Pauline Mallory. BA W Virginia U 1963; SWTS 1964; MDiv VTS 1966; EdD W Virginia U 1977. D 6/3/1966 P 12/21/1966 Bp Wilburn Camrock Campbell. R Gr Ch In The Mountains Waynesville NC 1984-2006; Chatham Hall Chatham VA 1978-1982; Assoc S Geo's Ch Portsmouth RI 1971-1974; Mstr S Paul's Ch Concord NH 1967-1971; Cur Trin Epis Ch Martinsburg WV 1966-1967. cl Soc 1978; PhI Kappa Psi 1960; Phi Delta Kappa 1976. cl Soc 1978; Phi Delta Kappa 1976. howdyww@hotmail.com

WHITE III, Hugh Couch (Va) 664 Dungeons Thicket Rd, White Stone VA 22578 B Nashville TN 5/4/1938 s Hugh Couch White & Martha. BS VPI 1961; MDiv VTS 1966. D 6/29/1966 P 6/1/1967 Bp William Henry Marmion. m 11/24/1979 Laurie B Winchester c 3. R Gr Ch Kilmarnock VA 1996-2004; Stndg Com Dio Sthrn Virginia Norfolk VA 1990-1992; Exec Bd Dio Sthrn Virginia Norfolk VA 1985-1988; Chair Dio Sthrn Virginia Norfolk VA 1983-1989; R S Paul's Ch Norfolk VA 1982-1996; Chair Dio Sthrn Virginia Norfolk VA 1976-1978; Dep Gc Dio SW Virginia Roanoke VA 1973-1979; R Emm Ch Staunton VA 1971-1982; R Chr Epis Ch Pulaski VA 1968-1971; Chair- Liturg Com. Dio SW Virginia Roanoke VA 1968-1970; Vic Emm Ch Covington VA 1966-1968; Vic S Mk's Ch Fincastle VA 1966-1968; Vic Trin Ch Buchanan VA 1966-1968. Auth, "Archit & Wrshp, Pulaski," *Va Times (Swva Dioc Nwspr)*; Auth, "Dawn Of Correction, Pulaski," *Va Times (Swva Dioc Nwspr)*. Boys Hm 1983-1989; Disciples Of Chr In Cmnty 1982-1996; Epis Conf Of The Deaf Of The Epis Ch In The 1971-1978; Meals On Wheels & Half-Way Hsng, Staunton Va 1973-1978; Plumbline Mnstrs, Norfolk Va 1988-1998; Rappahanock Westminster Cbury 1991; Tidewater Goodwill Industry 1984-1989. Dsa Staunton VA StauntonVA 1978; Mha Outstanding Serv Awd Staunton VA 1976. madamelww@gmail.com

WHITE, James Lee (Del) 39 Gainsborough Dr, Lewes DE 19958 **Chr Ch Milford DE 2003-; Int/Supply Dio Delaware Wilmington DE 1999-** B Litchfield IL 11/27/1946 s Forrest Lee White & Lucille Francis. LTh Epis TS In Kentucky 1973; BS Amer Inst of Holistic Theol 1994; MS Amer Inst of

Holistic Theol 1995; PhD Amer Inst of Holistic Theol 1996; MDiv Epis TS In Kentucky 1996. D 5/26/1973 P 6/8/1974 Bp Addison Hosea. m 9/11/1982 Gale Ganaway c 2. R Hope - S Jn's Epis Ch Oscoda MI 1978-1980; P-in-c S Jas Epis Ch Independence IA 1976-1978; P-in-c S Mary's Ch Oelwein IA 1976-1978; P-in-c Gr Ch Albia IA 1974-1976; P-in-c Ch Of The Epiph Centerville IA 1974; Dio Iowa Des Moines IA 1974; Locten & P In Charge S Steph's Epis Ch Covington KY 1973-1974. "Healings Are Happ In Delaware," Sharing mag, 2004. Ord Of S Lk - Chapl 1972. drjim39@comcast.net

WHITE, James Tracy (Va) 2609 E Kalispell Ave, Sierra Vista AZ 85650 B Arkansas City KS 10/15/1932 s James Arthur White & Theresa Ina. BA Wichita St U 1953; MDiv STUSo 1963. D 6/24/1963 P 6/1/1964 Bp William Henry Marmion. m 8/31/1957 Patricia Alice Loper. Pohick Epis Ch Lorton VA 1993-1997; Off Of Bsh For ArmdF New York NY 1977-1992; R Ch Of The Gd Shpd Little Rock AR 1967-1970; Cur S Mk's Epis Ch Little Rock AR 1965-1967.

WHITE, K Alon (NY) 124 N Broadway, Nyack NY 10960 **Vic Gr Epis Ch Monroe NY 2008-** B Berkeley CA 10/25/1952 d Geoffrey Warner White & Dorothy. BA San Francisco St U 1976; MA U of San Francisco 1984; MDiv GTS 1991. D 6/8/1991 P 1/19/1992 Bp Arthur Edward Walmsley. Dioc Trng Cntr New York NY 2008; Int S Alb's Ch Simsbury CT 2007; S Jn's Ch Pleasantville NY 2004-2006; Chapl and DDO The GTS New York NY 1999-2004; All SS Epis Ch Meriden CT 1998-1999; Asst S Mk's Ch New Britain CT 1991-1993.

WHITE, Karin Kay (ECR) 40938 Griffin Drive, Oakhurst CA 93644 **Supply P Epis Dio San Joaquin Modesto CA 2011-** B Boise ID 9/13/1945 d Fred Edward Johnson & Marie J. BA Seattle Pacific Coll 1967; Candler TS Emory U 1983; MA SMU 1985; MPA Seattle U 1986; CAS CDSP 1998. D 12/5/1998 P 6/5/1999 Bp William Edwin Swing. m 3/27/1971 Stephen White c 2. P-in-c Ch Of S Jos Milpitas CA 2006-2009; Supply P Dio El Camino Real Monterey CA 2004-2005; Assoc S Jn's Ch Asheville NC 2002; Int Epis Ch Of The H Sprt Mars Hill NC 2001; Supply P Dio Wstrn No Carolina Asheville NC 2000-2004; Assistiing P S Thos Epis Ch Sunnyvale CA 1999-2000; Pstr Care Asst Ch Of The Epiph San Carlos CA 1998-1999. revkarinwhite@yahoo.com

WHITE, Kathryn L (Chi) 3052 Jeffrey Dr, Joliet IL 60435 **R S Edw The Mtyr and Chr Epis Ch Joliet IL 2002-** B Columbus OH 4/15/1951 d George C Wolfe & Marjorie Lou. Kent St U 1970; AA/RN Riverside City Coll 1977; MDiv SWTS 1997. D 12/18/2001 P 6/18/2002 Bp William Dailey Persell. m 6/7/1970 Jeffrey A White c 3. kwhite@secec.net

WHITE, Kathryn Sawyer (WMass) 129 Roseland Park Road, Woodstock CT 06281 B Boston MA 9/2/1945 d Motley Sawyer & Betty. BA Wells Coll 1967; MDiv Bex 1992. D 6/6/1992 P 1/16/1993 Bp David Charles Bowman. m 8/26/1967 Ewart John White c 2. Asst S Jn's Epis Ch Sutton MA 2009-2011; R Trin Epis Ch Ware MA 1998-2005; Assoc R Chr Ch Dearborn MI 1996-1998; Bd The Record Dio Michigan Detroit MI 1996-1998; Int Chr Ch Cranbrook Bloomfield Hills MI 1993-1995; Assoc Trin Epis Ch Hamburg NY 1992-1993. kswhite45@gmail.com

WHITE, Kenneth Gordon (Mass) 11 Anita St, Sabattus ME 04280 B Boston MA 2/22/1941 s Kenneth Golder White & Jesuina. BS Bos 1963; STB PDS 1968. D 6/22/1968 Bp Anson Phelps Stokes Jr P 5/24/1969 Bp John Melville Burgess. Mass Comm On Chr Unity Fall River MA 1984-2004, All SS Ch Chelmsford MA 1981-1982; Supplement Accounts Boston MA 1975-1977; R S Jn's Epis Ch Lowell MA 1972-2004; Asst S Anne's Ch Lowell MA 1968-1972. Ed, "Baptismal Pract in an Ecum Context," 2008; "Baptism Today: Understanding, Practicing, Ecum Implications"; "Faith and Ord Paper No. 207," *WCC Pub*, Pueblo Bk, Liturg Press. Ord of S Lk 1974; Ord of S Lk, Reg Wrdn 1980-1984. Harvest of Hope Awd Houre of Hope, Lowell, MA 1993; Forrest L Knapp Awd Massachusetts Coun of Ch 1993; Bp Morris Arnold Annual Awd Epis City Mssn 1991. kgordonwhite@msn.com

WHITE, Kenneth Orgill (WLa) 13118 Feather Sound Dr Apt 212, Fort Myers FL 33919 B Philadelphia MS 10/13/1954 s Kenneth Orgill & Nancy. BA Rhodes Coll 1977; MDiv VTS 1981. D 6/28/1981 Bp William F Gates Jr P 4/11/1982 Bp William Evan Sanders. m 5/10/1991 Laura Marie Coleman. Asst S Alb's Par Washington DC 1994-2000; S Paul's Epis Ch Shreveport LA 1990; Samar Counceling Cntr Amarillo TX 1988-1989; Asst S Mk's Cathd Shreveport LA 1984-1985; Vic S Fran' Ch Norris TN 1982-1983; D-In-T Gr Ch Chattanooga TN 1981-1982. Auth, "Between Us: Bk Revs". orgillko6760@aol.com

WHITE, Konrad Shepard (Los) 524 E Duffy St, Savannah GA 31401 B Savannah GA 1/10/1942 s Julius Shepard White & Ethel Brannen. Dade Jr Coll Miami FL 1962; BA Belhaven Coll 1965; STUSo 1970; MDiv Nash 1972. D 5/21/1972 P 5/31/1973 Bp John M Allin. m 6/8/1974 Elizabeth McGlothlin c 2. R S Mk's Epis Ch Upland CA 2001-2008; R S Barth's Epis Ch Florence AL 1989-2001; R S Mary's Epis Ch Milton FL 1984-1989; R Par Of The Medtr-Redeem McComb MS 1977-1984; R Chap Of The Cross ROLLING FORK MS 1974-1977; Cur S Jas Ch Jackson MS 1972-1974. R Emer St. Mk's Epis Ch 2010. kswret@aol.com

WHITE, Kristin Lee Uffelman (Chi) 400 E Westminster, Lake Forest IL 60045 **Assoc R The Ch Of The H Sprt Lake Forest IL 2009-** B Anchorage AK 10/15/1971 d Stephen Paul Uffelman & Janet Marie. BS Wstrn Oregon U 1995; MA Willamette U 1997; MDiv SWTS 2009. D 5/30/2009 Bp Sanford Zangwill Kaye Hampton. m 11/12/1994 John David White c 1. kristinuwhite@gmail.com

WHITE, Laura Dale (USC) 522 NW 8th St, Pendleton MI 97801 B United Kingdom 1/27/1971 d Edward Craig MacBean & Mary Elizabeth. BA Colg 1993; BA Colg 1993; MDiv VTS 2001. D 2/23/2001 P 10/22/2001 Bp Frank Neff Powell. m 5/23/1998 Alexander F White c 4. Long-term Supply Trin Epis Ch Farmington Hills MI 2007-2009; H Trin Par Epis Clemson SC 2001-2002. lwhite9263@sbcglobal.net

WHITE, Lynn Scott (Chi) 1546 Bobolink Cir, Woodstock IL 60098 B Chicago IL 3/23/1942 d Kingsley Dale Scott & Nancy Warner. BA Barat Coll 1977; MDiv SWTS 1983; DMin SWTS 1996. D 12/15/1983 Bp James Winchester Montgomery P 9/1/1984 Bp Quintin Ebenezer Primo Jr. m 8/26/1961 Michael White c 3. S Andr Ch Grayslake IL 2003; Int R S Andr Ch Grayslake IL 2002-2003; Int Chr Ch Winnetka IL 2000-2002; Int S Mich's Cathd Boise ID 1997-1998; Assoc R The Ch Of The H Sprt Lake Forest IL 1985-1997; Pstr Assoc Chr Ch Winnetka IL 1984-1985. revwhit@ix.netcom.com

WHITE, M(ary) (Md) 2125 Beach Village Court, Annapolis MD 21403 **Sherwood Epis Ch Cockeysville MD 2004-** B Lackawanna NY 1/6/1945 d Raymond Cleary & Ruth. AD Wesley Coll 1969; BS Mercy Coll 1977; MS LIU 1986; MDiv Ya Berk 1989; MA Loyola Coll 2003. D 6/10/1989 Bp Paul Moore Jr P 5/19/1990 Bp Walter Cameron Righter. m 3/1/1967 Francis White c 3. Assoc R S Barn Epis Ch Sykesville MD 2001-2003; S Paul's Epis Ch Prince Frederick MD 2000-2001; R S Andr's Epis Ch Staten Island NY 1995-1999; Assoc R S Jn's Epis Ch Lancaster PA 1991-1995; Vic S Barn Ch Newark NJ 1990-1991; Dio Newark Newark NJ 1990; Cur S Paul's Epis Ch Morris Plains NJ 1989-1990. joannawhite@comcast.net

WHITE, Mary Margaret Robinson (Alb) 10 N Main Ave, Albany NY 12203 **R S Andr's Epis Ch Albany NY 2002-** B Tucson AZ 6/13/1956 d William Dorrah Robinson & Mary. BA U of Arizona 1979; MRE U of San Diego 1984; MDiv CDSP 1994. D 6/4/1994 P 6/3/1995 Bp William Edwin Swing. m 5/17/1980 John L White c 3. S Barth's Epis Ch Poway CA 1997-2002; P Ch Of The Epiph Flagstaff AZ 1995-1996; P Epis Cbury Fllshp - Northen Arizona U Flagstaff AZ 1995-1996; D H Cross Epis Ch Castro Vlly CA 1994-1995. mcswegan@nycap.rr.com

WHITE, Michael S (Ga) 621 E 50th St, Savannah GA 31405 **R Chr Ch Epis Savannah GA 2008-** B Valdosta GA 5/23/1969 s James Earnest White & Shirley Annette. BA Valdosta St U 1992; MDiv VTS 1995; Cert Duke 2005. D 5/28/1995 P 1/5/1996 Bp Henry Irving Louttit. m 7/22/1995 Helen S Helen Margaret Slingluff c 2. Chr Ch Georgetown Washington DC 2006-2008; Ecum Off Dio No Carolina Raleigh NC 2003-2005; R S Lk's Epis Ch Durham NC 2000-2005; Vic S Eliz's Epis Ch Richmond Hill GA 1997-2000; Dio Georgia Savannah GA 1995-1997; Trin Ch Statesboro GA 1995-1997. "You Is Plural," *Sermons that Wk*, Morehouse Pub, 2003. michaelswhite@mac.com

WHITE, Michelle Denise (Nwk) 707 Washington St, Hoboken NJ 07030 B New York City NY 1/3/1951 d Gloria Elaine. BS SUNY@Stony Brook 1974; MS Ford 1981; PhD Ford 1992; MDiv UTS 2002. D 12/21/2009 Bp Paul Victor Marshall P 6/21/2010 Bp Mark M Beckwith. c 1. All SS Epis Par Hoboken NJ 2009-2011. carbon153@yahoo.com

WHITE, Nancy Anne (Md) 3267 Stepney St, Edgewater MD 21037 B Washington D.C. 11/25/1936 d James Garfield Stevens & Mini Ethel. Gallaudet U; U of Maryland; BA U of Maryland 1958; MA Gallaudet U 1970; EFM STUSo 2000. D 6/2/2001 Bp Robert Wilkes Ihloff. m 7/9/1974 Thomas White c 2. S Marg's Ch Annapolis MD 2004-2007; Yth Min + D S Jas' Par Lothian MD 2001-2004. Auth, "Pub Var chapters," *arts and Revs in Spec Educ/deaf Educ Pub; contributed Nwsltr (Loc and Dioc) arts*, AGBell Assoc.for the Deaf et al, 1978. Advsry Coun for HI Infants 1991; No Amer Assn for the Deaconate 1998. JB Mason Awd - Outstanding Spec Educ Ldrshp Coun for Exceptional Chld - PFCO 1999; Resolution of Recognition Maryland St Senate 1999. muffwhite@comcast.net

WHITE, Nicholson Barney (O) 1109 Hollyheath Ln, Charlotte NC 28209 B Washington DC 5/18/1941 s E B White & Elizabeth. BA Trin 1963; MDiv VTS 1973. D 6/9/1973 Bp Joseph Warren Hutchens P 1/1/1974 Bp Charles Gresham Marmion. m 8/26/1961 Diana Watkins c 2. Int Chr Ch Charlotte NC 2005-2006; S Paul's Epis Ch Cleveland Heights OH 1983-2003; R Emm Par Epis Ch And Day Sch Sthrn Pines NC 1979-1983; Assoc Chr Ch Charlotte NC 1974-1979; Assoc S Fran In The Fields Harrods Creek KY 1973-1974. Soc Of S Marg 1981. nukadede@sprynet.com

WHITE JR, Paul Donald (WTenn) 3553 Windgarden Cv, Memphis TN 38125 B Camp Chaffee AR 11/28/1952 s Paul Donald White & Lillian Joanne. BS LSU 1973; JD Loyola U 1976; MDiv CDSP 1991; DMin SWTS 1999. D 6/8/1991 Bp Robert Jefferson Hargrove Jr P 12/1/1991 Bp John Lester Thompson III. m 5/27/1972 Kathryn Aitkens c 2. R S Geo's Ch Germantown TN 2002-2005; R

S Lk's Epis Ch No Little Rock AR 1992-2002; Cn-In-Res Trin Cathd Sacramento CA 1991-1992. pdwhitejr@aol.com

WHITE, R(ita) Ellen (Va) 805 Savoy Rd, Cheshire MA 01225 **S Anne's Par Scottsville VA 2009-; S Mk's Ch Adams MA 2006-** B Galax VA 6/27/1955 d Ernest Linwood White & Violet Marie. BA Berea Coll 1977; MDiv Sthrn Bapt TS Louisville KY 1984; DAS VTS 2002. D 6/22/2002 P 1/25/2003 Bp Frank Neff Powell. Dio Wstrn Massachusetts Springfield MA 2006-2009; Hanover w Brunswick Par - S Jn King Geo VA 2005-2006; Cople Par Hague VA 2004; Asst R S Andr's Epis Ch Arlington VA 2002-2004. rellenwhiteva@aol.com

WHITE, Roger Bradley (Ct) Po Box 309, Kent CT 06757 **R S Andr's Ch Kent CT 1985-** B Chicago IL 2/13/1952 s Alfred Harry White & Mildred Alfrida. MA Ya 1976; MPhil Ya 1977; MA Yale DS 1979. D 6/12/1982 P 1/6/1983 Bp Arthur Edward Walmsley. Chair Exam Chapl Com Dio Connecticut Hartford CT 1992-1997; Secy Bd Secy Ya Berk New Haven CT 1991-1999; The Ch Of The H Sprt Lake Forest IL 1982-1985; Asst Ya Berk New Haven CT 1981-1982. Contrib, *Forw Day by Day*, 1999; Auth, *Var arts & Revs*. Amer Soc of Ch Historians 1979; HSEC 1978; Soc of S Jn the Evang 1979. Jarvis Fllshp Berk 1979. CANTUAR@SNET.NET

✠ WHITE, Rt Rev Roger John (Mil) 700 Waters Edge Rd Apt 25, Racine WI 53402 B Leeds Yorkshire UK 1/31/1941 s John William White & Ettie. BD Eden TS 1965; WCC 1965; Kelham Theol Coll 1966; DCL SWTS 1988. Trans from Church Of England 10/1/1969 Con 9/8/1984 for Mil. m 8/11/1966 Prudence Anne Paine. Pres Prov V Dio Milwaukee Milwaukee WI 1991-1997; Bp Of Mil Dio Milwaukee Milwaukee WI 1984-2003; Bp Coadj Of Mil Dio Milwaukee Milwaukee WI 1984-1985; R Trin Ch Indianapolis IN 1980-1984; R S Paul's/Trin Chap Alton IL 1971-1980; Vic S Alb's Epis Ch Olney IL 1969-1981. Auth, "Toward 2015 - The Ch'S Odyssey," 1997; Auth, "New Millennium - New Ch," Cowley Press, 1992; Auth, "Of Being A Bp," Ch Hymnal, 1992; Contrib, "Baptismal Mystery & Catecumenate," Ch Hymnal, 1990; Auth, "Reshaping Mnstry," Jethro, 1990; Auth, "Realities & Visions," Seabury Press, 1976. Natl Pres Dok 1994-2000. rjwhite787@aol.com

WHITE, Rowena Ruth (WLa) 8212 Argosy Ct, Baton Rouge LA 70809 **S Mk's Cathd Shreveport LA 2011-; Supply P S Andr's Ch Clinton LA 2001-** B Napa CA 3/5/1944 d Lloyd Hilton White & Nancy Vivian. BS Mississippi Coll 1966; MD U of Mississippi 1970; Med U of Arkansas 1985; MDiv Epis TS of The SW 1995. D 6/3/1995 P 12/9/1995 Bp Robert Jefferson Hargrove Jr. Amer Psych Assn, La Psych Assn; Bd Cert Mem Coll Of Chapl. rowenawhite@earthlink.net

WHITE, R Scott (NC) 231 N Church Street, Rocky Mount NC 27804 **Fair Share Appeals Bd, Chair Dio No Carolina Raleigh NC 2010-; R Ch Of The Gd Shpd Rocky Mt NC 2004-; Alum Exec Com The GTS New York NY 2004-; Pstr Response Team Dio No Carolina Raleigh NC 2000-; Property Mgmt Dio No Carolina Raleigh NC 2000-** B Newport RI 7/30/1966 s Robert Paul White & Patricia Hickson. BA Rhode Island Coll 1989; MDiv GTS 1996; Cert Duke 2001. D 6/15/1996 P 1/25/1997 Bp Geralyn Wolf. m 1/6/2001 Michele E Sherburne c 2. Dioc Coun Mem Dio No Carolina Raleigh NC 2000-2003; Pstr Response Team Dio No Carolina Raleigh NC 2000-2003; Assoc Chr Epis Ch Raleigh NC 1998-2004; Asstg P S Mart's Epis Ch Charlotte NC 1996-1998. Fac Hist Prize GTS 1996; Sutton Prize For Best Grad Thesis GTS 1996. rswgsrmt@gmail.com

WHITE, Stanley James (Ga) 101 E Central Ave Fl 3, Valdosta GA 31601 **Vic Ch Of Chr The King Valdosta GA 1990-** B Dothan,AL 5/9/1962 s James E White & S Anne. Valdosta St U; Berean U 1987. D 10/21/1990 P 6/1/1991 Bp Harry Woolston Shipps. m 8/27/1982 Deidra A White c 4. EFM. ctksw@bellsouth.net

WHITE, Stephen J (Me) 49 Mills Road, Newcastle ME 04553 B Portland OR 8/9/1945 s Earle Victor White & Phyllis Marjorie. BA U of Redlands 1967; MDiv EDS 1971; DMin EDS 1987. D 6/5/1971 P 12/18/1971 Bp Horace W B Donegan. m 6/20/1969 Charlotte A Turgeon c 3. Int Gr Ch Norwood MA 2009-2010; Int S Andr's Ch Edgartown MA 2008-2009; Chair, COM Dio Maine Portland ME 2003-2008; R S Andr's Ch Newcastle ME 1997-2008; Int S Mk's Ch Foxborough MA 1995-1996; Chair, Recently Ord Cler Dio Massachusetts Boston MA 1991-1996; R Ch Of The Redeem Chestnut Hill MA 1989-1995; Ecum Off Dio Dallas Dallas TX 1987-1989; R Ch Of The Epiph Richardson TX 1985-1989; R S Anne's In The Fields Epis Ch Lincoln MA 1978-1985; R S Steph's Ch Middlebury VT 1974-1978; Asst S Mary's Epis Ch Manchester CT 1972-1974. Auth, "Intercessions for Sundays, H Days, and Spec Occasions - Year B," Ch Pub, Inc., 2008. sjwhite45@gmail.com

WHITE, Stephen Lawrence (NJ) 2325 Hancock Road, Williamstown MA 01267 **Assoc P Trin Ch Princeton NJ 2000-** B Leominster MA 6/2/1949 s Lawrence Albert White & Marie Claire. BA Sthrn Connecticut St U 1971; MS Smith 1974; MPA Golden Gate U 1980; PhD Brandeis U 1985; MDiv GTS 2000; LHD Cuttington U Coll 2001. D 5/20/2000 P 12/2/2000 Bp David B(ruce) Joslin. m 7/26/1996 Andrea Louise Saville c 2. Asst S Steph's Ch Pittsfield MA 2008-2010; Chapl Epis Ch at Pr Princeton NJ 2000-2008. "The Coll Chapl: A Practical Guide to Campus Mnstry," Pilgrim Press, 2005; "Calling YP to Ord Mnstry," *Living Ch*, 2004; "Eulogy for Christen," *Angl Dig*, 2003; "BCP and the Standardization of the Engl Lang: Avenues for Future Resrch," *The Angl*, 2003; Auth, "Two Bishops of Liberia: Race and Mssn ...," *Angl and Epis Hist*, 2001; Auth, "Parishes and Campus Mnstrs: It's a Two-Way St," *Living Ch*, 2001; Auth, "Colonial Era Missionaries' Understanding of the Afr...," *Angl and Epis Hist*, 1999; Auth, "The Ang of the LORD: Mssngr or Euphemism?," *Tyndale Bulletin*, 1999. Angl Soc 2002-2004; Colleges & Universities of the Angl Comm 1994-2002; HSEC 2000-2005. Sam Portaro Awd for Creative Expression and Intellectual Enqu Prov Coordinators for MHE of the 2006; Nelson Burr Prize HSEC 2002; Clem Whipple Prize GTS 2000; Clem Whipple Prize GTS 1999. jerichovalley@gmail.com

✠ **WHITE, Rt Rev Terry Allen** (Ky) 7302 Arrowwood Rd, Louisville KY 40222 **Bp of Kentucky Dio Kentucky Louisville KY 2010-** B Mount Pleasant IA 9/26/1959 s Dennis Edmond White & Carolyn Kay. BA Iowa Wesleyan Coll 1982; MDiv SWTS 1985; DD SWTS 2010. D 5/6/1985 Bp Lawrence Edward Luscombe P 4/25/1986 Bp James Winchester Montgomery Con 9/25/2010 for Ky. m 7/19/1986 Linda Johnston c 2. Dn And R Gr And H Trin Cathd Kansas City MO 2004-2010; Dio Chicago Chicago IL 2003-2004; Com Dio Chicago Chicago IL 1997-2001; R Trin Ch Highland Pk IL 1995-2004; Assoc R Chr Ch Winnetka IL 1991-1995; Dio Fond du Lac Appleton WI 1987-1991; P-in-c S Bon Plymouth WI 1987-1991; Vic S Paul's Ch Plymouth WI 1987-1991; Cur Chr Ch Winnetka IL 1985-1987. bishopwhite@episcopalky.org

WHITE, Thomas Harrington (Colo) 1215 Union Ave, North Platte NE 69101 **Vic All SS Epis Ch Battlement Mesa CO 1998-; Vic S Jn's Epis Ch New Castle CO 1998-** B Fort Worth TX 11/11/1931 s Harrington H White & Lida G. BS U Of Houston 1954; LTh STUSo 1964; MS Our Lady Of The Lake U San Antonio TX 1973; DMin GTF 1991. D 6/28/1964 Bp Everett H Jones P 1/1/1965 Bp Richard Earl Dicus. m 10/18/1958 Patsy La Rue LaRue c 2. Int S Andr's Ch Montevallo AL 1997-1998; R S Mich's Epis Ch Birmingham AL 1994-1996; S Martins-In-The-Pines Ret Comm Birmingham AL 1990-1995; Epis Black Belt Mnstry Demopolis AL 1990; Dio Alabama Birmingham AL 1989; R S Steph's Ch Eutaw AL 1988-1989; R S Jn's Ch Birmingham AL 1987-1988; H Comf Ch Gadsden AL 1986-1987; S Jas The Fisherman Kodiak AK 1983-1985; S Helena's Epis Ch Boerne TX 1976-1984; Assoc S Lk's Epis Ch San Antonio TX 1974-1976; P-in-c S Tim's Ch Cotulla TX 1972-1974; Asst S Mk's Epis Ch San Antonio TX 1971-1972; Vic S Mk's Ch Austin TX 1968-1971; Asst R S Mk's Epis Ch San Antonio TX 1964-1966. frthomas1@gmail.com

WHITE, Thomas Rees (Ct) 109 Sand Hill Rd, South Windsor CT 06074 **R S Ptr's Ch So Windsor CT 1992-** B Pittsburgh PA 6/3/1952 s John Joseph White & Margaret Evelyn. Edinboro U 1971; BS Penn 1974; BA Trin Theol Coll Bristol GB 1978; MDiv GTS 1979. D 6/9/1979 Bp Robert Bracewell Appleyard P 12/10/1979 Bp Morris Fairchild Arnold. m 4/16/1983 Christina Lewis c 2. R All SS Ch Whitman MA 1984-1992; Asst All SS Epis Ch Attleboro MA 1979-1984. Efac-Usa, Acts 29, Curs. tom.white@juno.com

WHITE, Warner Clock (WMich) 12 Harbor Watch Rd., Burlington VT 05401 B Hampton IA 10/25/1926 s Russell Peregrine White & Evelyn Laura. MA U Chi 1950; MDiv SWTS 1954; DMin Chicago TS 1976. D 6/1/1953 P 12/6/1953 Bp Charles L Street. m 5/24/2008 Roberta Baker c 5. R Trin Epis Ch Marshall MI 1979-1991; S Paul's By The Lake Chicago IL 1968-1978; Ch Of S Paul And The Redeem Chicago IL 1962-1978; P-in-c S Dunst's Epis Ch Westchester IL 1954-1957; P-in-c St Cyprians Ch Chicago IL 1953-1954. Auth, "Should I Lv?, Conflict Mgmt In Congregations," *Chap. 6*, ATR, 2001. warnercwhite@yahoo.com

WHITE, William DeAlton (Me) 21 Bodwell St, Brunswick ME 04011 B Seaford DE 5/2/1924 s Raymond Thomas White & Amelia Ann. BA Daniel Baker Coll 1951; STB GTS 1954. D 6/25/1954 P 3/1/1955 Bp Noble C Powell. c 5. R S Ptr's Ch Rockland ME 1981-1986; R S Andr's Ch Millinocket ME 1977-1981; Ex Coun Dio Rochester Rochester NY 1975-1977; P-in-c S Jn's Ch Mt Morris NY 1974-1977; R S Mich's Ch Geneseo NY 1974-1977; Chair Dio Maine Portland ME 1969-1974; R S Paul's Ch Brunswick ME 1969-1974; R S Alb's Epis Ch Wickenburg AZ 1966-1969; R Ch Of The Ascen Westminster MD 1958-1966. mbsgrs@gwi.net

WHITE, William Robert (Miss) 6730 Alewa Pl, Diamondhead MS 39525 **R S Thos Epis Ch Diamondhead MS 2006-** B Dayton OH 3/26/1941 s Elmer David White & Ruth Louise. BS OH SU Columbus OH 1964; JD OH SU Columbus OH 1967; MDiv VTS 2006. D 6/24/2006 Bp Peter James Lee P 1/7/2007 Bp Duncan Montgomery Gray III. m 11/19/1995 Susan Drake Susan Drake Long c 5. frbill@stthomasdiamondhead.org

WHITEFORD, Cecily (WNY) 85 Manchester Pl, Buffalo NY 14213 B Albany NY 10/5/1936 d Grant Melville Selch & Jean. Cor. D 6/20/1982 Bp Harold B Robinson. c 6. D S Jn's Gr Ch Buffalo NY 2002-2010; Asst S Jn's Gr Ch Buffalo NY 1982-1984.

WHITE-HASSLER, M(argaret) Jane (Ct) 130 Vincent Dr, Newington CT 06111 **R Gr Ch Newington CT 2004-** B Charleston WV 7/30/1944 d Ralph Albert White & Margaret Randolph. BS W Virginia Wesleyan Coll 1966; MDiv Ya Berk 1996. D 9/4/1999 P 3/10/2000 Bp Andrew Donnan Smith. m

10/4/1997 Thomas Jackson Hassler c 3. Asst S Andr's Ch Meriden CT 1999-2004. mjwhassler@aol.com

WHITEHEAD, Danny Ray (ND) 808 4th Ave NE, Devils Lake ND 58301 **Chapl Ch Of The Adv Devils Lake ND 2010-; Chapl S Thos Ch Ft Totten ND 2010-** B Winfield AL 10/4/1956 s Rayburn Whitehead & Mary Florence. BSW U of Alabama 1981; MS U of Alabama 1989. D 7/24/2003 P 2/14/2004 Bp Charles Edward Jenkins III. dannyrw@peoplepc.com

WHITEHEAD, Philip Hoyle (USC) 6026 Crabtree Rd, Columbia SC 29206 B Columbus OH 2/20/1935 s Harry Whitehead & Mildred Cecile. BA U So 1957; MDiv STUSo 1960; STM UTS 1962; DMin UTS Richmond VA 1974. D 6/6/1960 P 6/1/1961 Bp Edward Hamilton West. m 12/30/1960 Eleanor Kessler c 2. Dep Gc Dio Upper So Carolina Columbia SC 1985-1997; Stndg Com Dio Upper So Carolina Columbia SC 1984-1987; Liturg Cmsn Dio Upper So Carolina Columbia SC 1983-1995; Ecum Cmsn Epis Ch Cntr New York NY 1978-2004; R S Mich And All Ang' Columbia SC 1978-2004; Vic S Mart's Epis Ch Henrico VA 1977-1978; Vic Epis Ch of Our Sav Richmond KY 1973-1977; S Cathr's Sch Richmond VA 1965-1978. phw@sc.rr.com

WHITE HORSE-CARDA, Patricia Ann (SD) 500 S Main Ave, Sioux Falls SD 57104 **Vic of the Yankton Dio So Dakota Sioux Falls SD 2010-** B Wagner SD 10/24/1951 d Louis White Horse & Ruby. BS U of So Dakota 1983; MEd Penn 1988. D 12/4/2010 P 6/19/2011 Bp John Thomas Tarrant. m 1/9/2006 Dean J Carda. PWHCARDA@GMAIL.COM

WHITEHOUSE, Rempfer Lees (Chi) 3246 Geronimo Ave, San Diego CA 92117 B Indianapolis IA 12/10/1922 s Horace Whitehouse & Emma. BS NWU 1949; LTh SWTS 1952. D 5/29/1952 P 12/1/1952 Bp Wallace E Conkling. m 11/29/1947 Frances Irene Duncan c 4. Ch Of The Epiph Chicago IL 1963-1987. mcw95@san.rr.com

WHITEHURST, Joseph Stewart (USC) 173 Kendallwood Ct, Aiken SC 29803 **Asst S Thad Epis Ch Aiken SC 2007-** B Charlotte NC 11/19/1978 s J Daniel Whitehurst & Trudy Hoover. BS U Of So Carolina Columbia SC 2001; MA U Of So Carolina Columbia SC 2004; MDiv SWTS 2007. D 5/26/2007 Bp Dorsey Felix Henderson. joseph.whitehurst@gmail.com

WHITELAW, Eleanor Drake (Ala) 1242 Felder Ave, Montgomery AL 36106 **R Ch Of The H Comf Montgomery AL 2011-** B Mobile AL 8/26/1947 d G Mills Whitelaw & Eleanor Rose. BA Auburn U 1969; MA U of So Alabama 1972; MDiv VTS 1998. D 6/6/1998 Bp Frank Kellogg Allan P 12/11/1998 Bp Clifton Daniel III. c 2. Asst S Jas Par Wilmington NC 1998-2001. ewhitelaw1@gmail.com

WHITELEY, Raewynne Jean (LI) 15 Highland Ave, Saint James NY 11780 **R S Jas Epis Ch S Jas NY 2007-** B Camden NSW AU 7/23/1966 d Andrew Laughlin Whiteley & Susan Gwyneth. BA U of Melbourne 1989; MA U of Melbourne 1992; BTh Australian Coll of Theol 1995; BMin Australian Coll of Theol 1995; PhD PrTS 2003. Trans from Anglican Church Of Australia 3/24/1999 Bp Joe Morris Doss. Vic Trin Epis Old Swedes Ch Swedesboro NJ 2002-2006; Assoc P Trin Cathd Trenton NJ 2001-2002; Pstr Assoc Trin Ch Princeton NJ 1998-2001. Auth, "Steeped in the H: Preaching as Sprtl Pract," Cowley, 2008; Auth, "Homiletical Perspectives," *Feasting on the Word*, Westminster Jn Knox Press, 2008; CoEditor, "Get Up Off Your Knees: Preaching the U2 Catalog," Cowley, 2003; Auth, "Geography And Gr: Preaching The Gospel w An Australian Accent," *St Mk's Revs*, 2001; Auth, "Sermons And Wrshp Resources," *The Abingdon Wmn Preaching Annual, Series 2, Year A*, Abingdon, 2001; Auth, "Pryr For Bronte," *Wmn Uncommon Prayers*, Morehouse, 2000; Auth, "Var arts," *NRSV Wmn Study Bible*, Marshall Pickering, 1995. Acad Of Homil 1998. rjwhiteley@rjwhiteley.net

WHITESEL, Ann Brier (CPa) 12 Strawberry Dr, Carlisle PA 17013 B Honolulu HI 12/2/1928 d William Wallace Brier & Vera Hall. AA Stratford Coll Woodbridge VA 1950; Meredith Coll 1951; Sch Of Chr Stds 1982. D 6/10/1983 Bp Charlie Fuller McNutt Jr. m 6/17/1950 William Monitor Whitesel c 3. Dir S Jn's Epis Ch Carlisle PA 1979-1985. Cntr Diac. whitesel@aol.com

WHITESELL, Hugh A (NC) 756 Apple Ct. Apt A, Lebanon OH 45036 B Dayton OH 10/24/1925 s Carl Everett Whitesell & Jeannette Fitch. ThD Bex 1964; DMin Untd TS Dayton OH 2000. D 12/11/1959 P 6/13/1964 Bp Roger W Blanchard. m 4/29/1950 Ruth Osterman c 1. Vic S Mary's Ch Waynesville OH 1989-1999; Ecum Off Dio No Carolina Raleigh NC 1982-1989; R S Steph's Epis Ch Erwin NC 1976-1989; Liturg Cmsn Dio Virginia Richmond VA 1970-1973; Vic S Barth's Ch Richmond VA 1968-1976; Liturg Cmsn Dio Sthrn Ohio Cincinnati OH 1966-1968; Asst S Geo's Epis Ch Dayton OH 1964-1968; Asst S Paul's Epis Ch Dayton OH 1959-1964. Auth, "Identity, Loss, and Change," Bell & Howell, 2000; Auth, *Liturg & Life*, St. Geo's Epis Ch, 1965. frhugh@embarqmail.com

WHITESIDE, Henry Burton (EC) 7 Masonic Ave, Shelburne Falls MA 01370 **Barrier Free Living New York NY 2009-; Plainfield Congrl Ch Plainfield MA 2009-** B Burgaw NC 7/14/1952 s Heustis Pennington Whiteside & Beulah Gibbons. BA U NC 1974; MDiv UTS Richmond VA 1982; Cert GTS 1983. D 6/11/1983 Bp Robert Bruce Hall P 1/1/1984 Bp Brice Sidney Sanders. m 8/21/1976 Susan Shelby Horsley c 1. Dio Wstrn Massachusetts Springfield MA 2005-2008; Ch Of The Gd Shpd Wilmington NC 1986-1995; Asst R Chr Ch New Bern NC 1983-1986. hbwhiteside@juno.com

WHITFIELD, Ann Adams (Oly) 10810 NE Sherwood Dr., Vancouver WA 98686 B New York NY 6/22/1943 d Walter Edmund Loebmann & Janet Ann. AS Lasell Coll 1963; Pharmd Wstrn Career Coll 1986; Dioc TS, W. Kansas 1988; St. Mary's on the Plains 1990; Epis TS of The SW 1994. D 6/7/1992 P 12/22/1994 Bp John Forsythe Ashby. m 5/13/2006 James Whitfield c 2. Asst Ch Of The Gd Shpd Vancouver WA 2009; Vic All SS' Epis Ch Vancouver WA 1998-2006; P-in-c Ch Of The Nativ Rosedale LA 1995-1998; Epis HS Baton Rouge LA 1995-1998; Dio Wstrn Kansas Hutchinson KS 1993-1995; Vic S Eliz's Ch Russell KS 1993-1995; Vic Ch Of The Epiph Concordia KS 1992-1994. revannwhitfield@gmail.com

WHITFIELD, Deirdre (Pa) 126 Westminster Dr, Wallingford PA 19086 **D S Mary Epis Ch Chester PA 2001-** B Baltimore MD 12/23/1961 d John Allen Rouse & Betty Ann. BS Indiana U of Pennsylvania 1983; MS Bryn 2001. D 6/23/2001 Bp Charles Ellsworth Bennison Jr P 6/6/2009 Bp Edward Lewis Lee Jr. m 6/30/1984 George C Whitfield c 2. H Apos And Medtr Philadelphia PA 2009-2010. revdwhitfield@comcast.net

WHITFIELD, Mary Dean (NwT) Rr 2 Box 460, Quanah TX 79252 B Hardeman County TX 9/2/1935 d Hoye Lemuel Walser & Kathleen. D 8/25/1997 Bp Sam Byron Hulsey P 10/6/2001 Bp C(harles) Wallis Ohl. m 6/1/1952 Chester Leroy Whitfield.

WHITFIELD, Raymond Palmer (Tex) 531 Rock Bluff Dr, Lakeway TX 78734 B San Antonio TX 1/17/1925 s Raymond Palmer Whitfield & Mary Bennet. BS USMA at W Point 1946; MS OH SU 1954; MDiv Epis TS of The SW 1979; DMin GTF 1996. D 6/10/1979 Bp A Donald Davies P 5/1/1980 Bp Robert Elwin Terwilliger. m 5/8/1982 Roberta Raithel c 3. Assoc S Mk's Epis Ch San Antonio TX 1995-2001; Assoc R The Ch of the Gd Shpd Austin TX 1986-1989; P The Ch of the Gd Shpd Austin TX 1979-1985. Auth, "Freedom to Love," Sailors Pub. Fllshp S Alb & S Sergius Friends Angl Cntr Rome. raywhitfield@worldnet.att.net

WHITFIELD, Stephen Ray (Tex) 2301 Lauren Loop, Leander TX 78641 B Fort Worth TX 5/21/1949 s Raymond Palmer Whitfield & Ila Mae. BA U of Texas 1971; MDiv VTS 1975. D 6/15/1975 P 12/1/1975 Bp A Donald Davies. m 10/19/2002 Rosalba Munoz. R Chr Ch Eagle Lake TX 1999-2009; R Ch Of The Gd Shpd Kingwood TX 1985-1992; Assoc S Dav's Ch Austin TX 1980-1985; R S Mary's Epis Ch Inc Lampasas TX 1977-1979; Cur Ch Of The Incarn Dallas TX 1975-1977. Comt. whitfieldsteve@gmail.com

WHITFORD, Michele E (FdL) 1220 N 7th St, Sheboygan WI 53081 **Gr Epis Ch Sheboygan WI 2009-; D All SS Elkhart Lake Sheboygan WI 2005-** B Janesville WI 2/8/1963 d Michael John Burg & Valerie Jean. D 8/27/2005 Bp Russell Edward Jacobus. m 6/10/1983 Jon P Whitford c 2. mwhitford@charter.net

WHITING, William Richard (WMich) 2165 Chesapeake Dr Ne, Grand Rapids MI 49505 **Int S Tim Ch Richland MI 2010-** B Phillipsburg PA 8/1/1949 s Francis Emory Whiting & Luella Grace. BS MI SU 1975; MDiv GTS 1982. D 6/7/1982 Bp Robert Campbell Witcher Sr P 12/4/1982 Bp Henry Boyd Hucles III. c 3. Epis Ch Of The Gd Shpd Allegan MI 2005-2010; P-in-c S Paul's Ch Boston MA 2003-2005; Supply P S Alb's Ch Lynn MA 1999-2002; S Mich's Epis Ch Holliston MA 1986-1997; Cur Trin Ch Northport NY 1983-1986; Cur S Jn's Epis Ch Southampton NY 1982-1983. williamrwhiting@comcast.net

WHITLEY, Harry Brearley (Nwk) 143 Day Ct, Mahwah NJ 07430 **P Assoc Chr Ch Ridgewood NJ 1991-** B Detroit MI 7/11/1921 s George Herbert Whitley & Eileen. MDiv GTS; LTh GTS; STB GTS; BA MI SU 1942. D 5/25/1945 Bp Frank W Creighton P 11/1/1945 Bp Charles B Colmore. m 6/24/1972 Jane Logie c 6. Chair, Bd Trst The GTS New York NY 1989-1994; Ch Pension Fund New York NY 1981-1988; R S Paul's Epis Ch Paterson NJ 1971-1981; R S Ptr's Ch Essex Fells NJ 1966-1970; Stndg Com Dio Connecticut Hartford CT 1963-1966; R S Jn's Ch Bridgeport CT 1962-1966; Gnrl Secy, Dept of CE & BEC Dio Connecticut Hartford CT 1960-1966; R S Jas Epis Ch Farmington CT 1954-1960; Asst Min S Jn's Ch Royal Oak MI 1952-1954; R S Andr's Epis Ch Algonac MI 1950-1952; R S Paul's Epis Ch Harsens Island MI 1950-1952. JLW1206@AOL.COM

WHITLEY, Ryan Randolph (Pa) 1 W Ardmore Ave, Ardmore PA 19003 **R Nevil Memi Ch Of S Geo Ardmore PA 2010-** B Ft Myers FL 5/22/1981 s Steven Ruskin Whitley & Melissa Peterman. BA Wake Forest U 2003; MDiv SWTS 2006. D 6/10/2006 Bp John Bailey Lipscomb P 12/16/2006 Bp William Jones Skilton. Asst S Mk's Epis Ch Of Tampa Tampa FL 2006-2010. whitleyrr@gmail.com

WHITLOCK III, Robin (SwFla) 949 41st Ave N, Saint Petersburg FL 33703 **Dioc Coun Dio SW Florida Sarasota FL 2011-; P-in-c S Aug's Epis Ch St Petersburg FL 2005-** B Rockford IL 12/9/1946 s Robert Alfred Whitlock & Mary Elizabeth. BA MacMurray Coll 1968; Cert Lon 1971; MDiv CDSP 1972; MS (ABT) U of Wisconsin, LaCrosse 1976; Post Grad Loyola U 1992. D 5/20/1972 Bp Albert A Chambers P 11/30/1972 Bp Stanley Hamilton Atkins. m 11/25/1989 Ann L Clark c 4. Assoc S Jas Epis Ch Baton Rouge LA 1999-2001; Chapl/Prof Dio Louisiana Baton Rouge LA 1995-1999; Higher

Educ Chapl Revs Appointee Ch Of Engl London 1985; Chair, Yth and YA Com Dio Maryland Baltimore MD 1982-1987; Natl Higher Educ Rep. Prov IV 1976-1982; Assitant/Higher Ed Chapl S Jn's Epis Ch Johnson City TN 1976-1979; Cur Chr Ch Par La Crosse WI 1972-1974. Auth, "The Clincl Symptoms of Sprtl Deterioration, Churchwork," *Diocesean Nwspr*, Dio Louisiana, 1999; Auth, "Stwdshp is...," *LivCh*, Living Ch Fndt, 1995; Auth, "Ethical Issues and the Nurse, Sprtl Dimensions of Nrsng Pract," *Sprtl Dimensions of Nrsng*, Saunders, 1989; Auth, "Gandi: Reflecting on Freedom and Nonviolence," *Plumbline*, ESMHE, 1983; Ed, "Profsnl Ethics," *The Profsnl Ethics Forum*, Epis Chapl, Baltimore, MD, 1983. AAR 2000-2004; ESMHE 1974-1992; Kappa Delti Pi: Hon Educators Soc 1974; Soc for Hlth and Human Values 1981-1999. Polly Bond Awd ECom 1999. revrobin@tampabay.rr.com

WHITMAN, Allen (NwT) 2001 W Missouri Ave, Midland TX 79701 **Died 7/16/2011** B Saint Paul MN 2/16/1925 s Frank Emerson Whitman & Edith Randal. Cert Shalem Inst Washington DC; BD U MN 1948; BD U Chi 1952; STM NW Luth Sem 1965; DD Nash 1973. D 9/30/1952 Bp Stephen E Keeler P 6/1/1953 Bp Hamilton Hyde Kellogg. Auth, "Parson Mcfright"; Auth, "Fairytale & Kingdom Of God"; Auth, "Gospel Comes Alive"; Auth, "Pray For Life"; Auth, "A Witness To Chr Healing"; Auth, "The Death Of The Min'S Wife".

WHITMAN, Robert Shaw Sturgis (WMass) 56 Union St, Guilford CT 06437 **Died 2/9/2010** B New York NY 7/27/1915 s Armitage Whitman & Mary Lyman. Harv 1933; GW 1938; DuBose Memi Ch Trng Sch 1940; GTh Ya Berk 1943; STB Ya Berk 1955; S Aug's Coll Cbury GB 1960. D 9/26/1943 P 3/25/1944 Bp William A Lawrence. Auth, "Var arts," *Living Ch*; Auth, "Var arts," *The Angl*. Angl Soc; Episcopalians Untd; Evang Cath Mssn; SPBCP. Hon Cn Chr Ch Cathd Springfield MA 1982.

WHITMER, Marlin Lee (Ia) 2602 250th St, De Witt IA 52742 B Muscatine IA 6/1/1930 s Lee Albert Whitmer & Leora Augusta. BA Hamline U 1952; BD VTS 1955; Cert Coll Chapl Amer Prot Hosp Assn 1965. D 6/22/1955 P 5/1/1956 Bp Gordon V Smith. c 3. St Lukes Hosp Davenport IA 1964-1992; Asst Trin Cathd Davenport IA 1961-1964; P-in-c Gr Ch Boone IA 1959-1961; Cur S Thos' Epis Ch Sioux City IA 1955-1959; D S Geo's Epis Ch Le Mars IA 1955-1956. Auth, "Healing Power of Story Listening," 2009; Auth, "Befrienders: A Model For Trng Lay People For Caring," 1978; Auth, "An Experiment Trng Lay People In Pstr Tasks," 1973. Assn of Profsnl Chapl 1965; Wayne Oates Inst 2003. Hon Cn Trin Cathd, Dio Iowa 1980. mwhitmer80@gmail.com

WHITMER, Ronald Delane (La) 1617 Tallwood Dr, Baton Rouge LA 70816 **Supply P S Andr's Ch Clinton LA 2000-** B Muscatine IA 7/31/1936 s Lee Albert Whitmer & Leora Augusta. BA Gri 1959; BD EDS 1965. D 6/24/1965 P 1/1/1966 Bp Gordon V Smith. m 8/1/1964 Martha Connolly. Pulse Of Louisiana Baton Rouge LA 1991-1993; S Marg's Epis Ch Baton Rouge LA 1987-1991; Par Of Ames Ames IA 1970-1987; Vic S Jas Epis Ch Independence IA 1965-1970. Auth, "Casebook For Iowa'S Future: Visions From The Heartland Proj". rdwhitmer7@msn.com

WHITMIRE JR, Norman (Los) 43600 Russell Branch Pkwy, Ashburn VA 20147 **S Dav's Ch Ashburn VA 2011-** B Las Vegas NV 11/6/1968 s Norman Whitmire & Dorothy Deon. AB Harv 1990; MD Yale Sch of Med 1995; MDiv VTS 2011. D 6/11/2011 Bp Mary Douglas Glasspool. normmd2@gmail.com

WHITMIRE JR, Roland Jackson (NC) 165 Marlborough Rd, Asheville NC 28804 **Died 9/24/2009** B Asheville NC 7/20/1924 s Roland Jackson Whitmire & Margaret Louise. BS Clemson U 1950; MDiv STUSo 1953. D 5/27/1953 P 5/26/1954 Bp Matthew G Henry. c 2.

WHITMORE, Bruce Gregory (Tex) 1401 Avenue O #F, Huntsville TX 77340 B 11/23/1954 s Page Gregory Whitmore & Arvella Dorothy. BA Bemidji St U 1977; MDiv STUSo 1980. D 9/13/1980 Bp Robert Marshall Anderson P 3/19/1981 Bp C(hristopher) FitzSimons Allison. m 9/17/2006 Darleen Whitmore c 2. R S Steph's Ch Huntsville TX 1986-1993; Asst S Mart's Epis Ch Houston TX 1985-1986; R Ch Of S Ben Bolingbrook IL 1982-1985; S Matt's Ch Bogalusa LA 1982-1985; Asst S Phil's Ch Charleston SC 1980-1982. BRUCESFERALPATH@HOTMAIL.COM

WHITMORE, Charles William (WNY) 6595 E Quaker St, Orchard Park NY 14127 **Asst S Paul Epis Ch Bellingham WA 2006-** B Lockport NY 1/13/1945 s Charles Francis Whitmore & Muriel Joy. BS Cor 1967; MDiv PDS 1973. D 6/16/1973 P 12/16/1973 Bp Harold B Robinson. m 8/26/1972 Linda J Newell. Dio Wstrn New York Tonawanda NY 1997-2007; Chair Dioc Evang Com Dio Wstrn New York Tonawanda NY 1989-1992; R S Mk's Ch Orchard Pk NY 1988-2007; Dep Gc Dio Wstrn New York Tonawanda NY 1988-2000; Pres Stndg Com Dio Wstrn New York Tonawanda NY 1985-1986; Team Mnstry S Paul's Epis Ch Springville NY 1983-1988; Trin Epis Ch Hamburg NY 1983-1988; Rurd Chaut Dnry Dio Wstrn New York Tonawanda NY 1980-1983; R S Paul's Epis Ch Mayville NY 1978-1982; Asst Calv Epis Ch Williamsville NY 1973-1978. Vietnam Veteran Of The Year. cww8@cornell.edu

WHITMORE, Elizabeth Needham (NCal) 2227 32nd Ave, San Francisco CA 94116 B New York NY 7/22/1946 d David Whitmore & Eileen. RN Helene Fuld Sch Nrsng 1973; BA Sch for Deacons 1991. D 6/6/1992 Bp William Edwin Swing. D Ch Of The Incarn San Francisco CA 1992-1997.

✠ WHITMORE, Rt Rev Keith Bernard (Eau) 3496 Paces Pl NW, Atlanta GA 30327 **Asstg Bp of Atlanta Dio Atlanta Atlanta GA 2008-** B Fond du Lac WI 11/28/1945 s Bernard George Whitmore & Winifred Cecilia. U of Wisconsin 1974; MDiv Nash 1977; BS Marian Coll of Fond Du Lac 1983. D 1/15/1977 P 7/23/1977 Bp William Hampton Brady Con 4/10/1999 for Eau. m 11/19/1966 Suzanne J Capelle c 2. Bp of Eau Dio Eau Claire Eau Claire WI 1999-2008; Dn Chr Cathd Salina KS 1994-1999; S Phil's Ch Joplin MO 1984-1994; S Paul's Cathd Fond du Lac WI 1982-1984; R S Jn The Bapt Portage WI 1980-1982; Dio Fond du Lac Appleton WI 1977-1980; Vic S Barn Epis Ch Tomahawk WI 1977-1980; Vic St Ambr Epis Ch Antigo WI 1977-1980. Affirming Catholicism 1986; SHN 1977. DD Nash 2000. bishopkeith@dioceseofeauclaire.org

WHITMORE, Paula Michele (Spok) 602 Nw 10th St, Pendleton OR 97801 **Vic Trin Ch Gonzales CA 1997-** B Yakima WA 8/12/1950 d Paul E M Whitmore & Dorothy Louise. BA Chapman U 1973; MDiv Claremont TS 1981; DMin Claremont TS 1982; CAS CDSP 1990. D 12/6/1992 P 10/9/1993 Bp Richard Lester Shimpfky. S Paul's Ch Walla Walla WA 2006-2009; Ch Of The Redeem Pendleton OR 2003-2006; Trin Ch Gonzales CA 1995-2003; Asstg P Ch Of S Jude The Apos Cupertino CA 1993-1997; Trin Cathd San Jose CA 1992-1994. pmwhitmore@netzero.net

WHITNAH JR, John (Ct) 400 Humphrey St., New Haven CT 06511 **P-in-c S Jn's Ch New Haven CT 2009-** B Newark NJ 11/6/1952 s John Carey Whitnah & Elizabeth. BA Gordon Coll 1974; MA Gordon-Conwell TS 1978; MDiv VTS 1989. D 6/10/1989 Bp Peter James Lee P 3/29/1990 Bp Robert Poland Atkinson. m 7/13/1980 Nina R Rynd c 3. R Chr Ch Avon CT 1999-2008; Asst Truro Epis Ch Fairfax VA 1989-1999. jnwhitnah5@aol.com

WHITNEY, Ann Carolyn (Ak) 4530 S. Teton Cir., Wasilla AK 99654 **Int S Dav's Ch Wasilla AK 2010-** B Montpelier VT 8/27/1949 d Clifton Eugene Whitney & Mary Elizabeth. BS Plymouth St Coll 1971. D 5/12/1997 Bp A(lbert) Theodore Eastman P 10/8/2009 Bp Rustin Ray Kimsey. OHC 1993; SocMary 1993. revannw@gmail.com

WHITNEY, Gladys Kee (Ct) 194 Homeside Ave, West Haven CT 06516 **D Gr And S Ptr's Epis Ch Hamden CT 1996-** B Montclair NJ 2/2/1924 d William Garland Kee & Gladys Grantlin. BA Fisk U 1947; MS Sthrn Connecticut St U 1975; Sthrn Connecticut St U 1982; EFM STUSo 1992; Mnstry Educ & Exploration Prog Dio Connecti 1996. D 6/8/1996 Bp Clarence Nicholas Coleridge.

WHITNEY, Marilla Jane (Minn) 1305 - 4th Ave., Windom MN 56101 **Supply Dio Minnesota Minneapolis MN 2005-** B Berkeley CA 11/16/1944 d Robert Lester Whitney & Lorraine. BA U CA 1966; MEd Ft Wright Coll of H Names 1981; MA U of Montana 1985; MDiv VTS 1987. D 6/20/1987 Bp Leigh Wallace Jr P 12/21/1987 Bp Robert Poland Atkinson. m 2/18/1966 Thomas W Hasseries c 1. Assoc R Ch Of S Nich Paradise CA 1998-2001; Dio Nthrn California Sacramento CA 1996-2004; Int/Supply S Jn's Epis Ch Lakeport CA 1994-1996; Vic S Paul's Mssn Cres City CA 1993-1994; S Jn's Ch Harpers Ferry WV 1987-1992. Cistercian Lay Contemplatives of Gethsemani 2002. marillaw@juno.com

WHITNEY-WISE, Stephen D (Ore) 4033 SE Woodstock Blvd., Portland OR 97202 B Peoria IL 12/1/1947 s Roy Wise & Mary. BA S Jos 1972; MDiv Sacr Heart TS Hales Corners WI 1976. Rec from Roman Catholic 3/20/1988 Bp John Lester Thompson III. m 12/18/1983 Patricia Whitney c 2. Dio Oregon Portland OR 2007-2010; R All SS Ch Portland OR 1996-2007; Trin Ch Folsom CA 1990-1996; Asst P Trin Cathd Sacramento CA 1988-1990. Natl Ntwk of Epis Cler Assn 1996. Cmnty Serv Awd Salvation Army 1988; Awd of Merit City of San Francisco 1984. stephenwhitneywise@comcast.net

WHITSITT, Helen Bonita (WMo) PO Box 57, Fayette MO 65248 **S Mary's Ch Fayette MO 2010-** B Council Grove KS 6/3/1943 d William Andrew Thowe & Dorothy Faye Smith. BS Cntrl Missouri St U 1983; Completed W Missouri Sch for Mnstry 2008. D 2/7/2010 Bp Barry Robert Howe. m 12/21/1985 James Lloyd Whitsitt c 6. hwhitsit@hotmail.com

WHITTAKER, Brendan Joseph (NH) 1788 Vt Route 102, Guildhall VT 05905 B Boston MA 6/6/1934 s Brendan Joseph Whittaker & Julia Marie. BS U of Massachusetts 1957; MDiv EDS 1966. D 6/4/1966 Bp Leland Stark P 12/17/1966 Bp Harvey D Butterfield. m 5/26/1956 Dorothy A Alden c 3. S Mk's Ch Groveton NH 1985-1994; R S Paul's Ch Lancaster NH 1985-1992; Cn Mssnr Dio Vermont Burlington VT 1973-1978; R S Thos' Epis Ch Brandon VT 1968-1973. Auth, "P/Conservationist," *Mod Tentmakers*. Forest Stewards Gld (Founding Mem); Soc Of S Jn The Evang. Epa Reg I DSA Environ Protection Agcy 1984; Distinguished Alumnini U Of Massachusetts Sch Of Forestry 1981.

WHITTAKER JR, Richard Russell (U) 1784 Aaron Dr., Tooele UT 84074 **P-in-c S Barn EpiscopalChurch Tooele UT 2009-** B Los Angeles CA 11/29/1953 s Richard Russell Whittaker & Anna B. BS U CA 1975; BA U CA 1977; MRP Syr 1979; MDiv The ETS At Claremont 2008. D 6/7/2008 P 1/10/2009 Bp

Joseph Jon Bruno. m 6/21/1997 Sandra Kay Leininger c 1. whittakerfamily@wirelessbeehive.com

WHITTAKER - NAVEZ, Christine Ruth (Mass) 223 Pond St, Hopkinton MA 01748 **R S Mich's Epis Ch Holliston MA 2001-; Dio Wstrn Massachusetts Springfield MA 1997-** B Walton-On-Thames Surrey UK 2/20/1947 d James Douglas Whittaker & Ruth Mary Elizabeth. BA Oxf 1967; MA Smith 1968; MA Ya 1972; JD Geo 1977; MDiv VTS 1990. D 6/9/1990 P 1/5/1991 Bp Ronald Hayward Haines. m 9/23/1995 Andre Navez c 2. P-in-c S Mich's Epis Ch Holliston MA 1998-2000; Assoc Trin Ch In The City Of Boston Boston MA 1996-1997; Stndg Com Dio Washington Washington DC 1994-1995; S Jn's Ch Georgetown Par Washington DC 1992-1995; Adj Prof Cn Law VTS Alexandria VA 1992; Econ Justice Cmsn Dio Washington Washington DC 1991-1993; Asst Ch Of The Ascen Silver Sprg MD 1990-1991. cnavez@aol.com

WHITTED, Warren Rohde (Neb) 8141 Farnam Dr Apt 328, Omaha NE 68114 B Omaha NE 7/19/1920 s Ira Oscar Whitted & Emily. BA U of Nebraska 1941; JD Creighton U 1947. D 11/8/1985 Bp James Daniel Warner. m 3/14/1942 Marjorie Clair Disbrow c 4. D Trin Cathd Omaha NE 1985-1992.

WHITTEMORE JR, H(enry) Lawrence (Be) 49 Maple St Apt 207, Manchester Center VT 05255 **Died 1/30/2011** B Ardmore PA 1/8/1918 s Henry Lawrence Whittemore & Caroline Doremus. BA Wms 1939; MDiv EDS 1948. D 5/28/1948 P 12/16/1948 Bp Frederick G Budlong. c 2. hlweew@comcast.net

WHITTEMORE, James R (Me) PO Box 933, Castine ME 04421 **Trin Ch Castine ME 2000-** B Detroit MI 1/13/1925 s Lewis Bliss Whittemore & Helen Marie. BA Ya 1947; BD EDS 1951; Fllshp Harv 1965; STM NYTS 1976; DMin NYTS 1985. D 6/8/1951 P 12/10/1951 Bp Lewis B Whittemore. m 12/4/1982 Mary Bolling Fooks c 5. Dir of Maritime Mnstry Dio So Carolina Charleston SC 2001-2003; Hon Assoc Gr Ch Charleston SC 2001-2003; EDS Cambridge MA 1996; Trin Ch Castine ME 1994-1999; EDS Cambridge MA 1989; Pres Alum/ae Assn EDS Cambridge MA 1983-1985; Seamens Ch Inst Income New York NY 1977-1992; Cn Trin Cathd Trenton NJ 1967-1977; R Trin Ch Princeton NJ 1967-1977; EDS Cambridge MA 1964-1967; Chr Ch So Hamilton MA 1956-1967; R S Jas Ch Of Sault S Marie Sault Ste Marie MI 1953-1956; Cur Chr Ch Grosse Pointe Grosse Pointe Farms MI 1951-1953. jmbwhittemore@yahoo.com

WHITTEN, W Roy (ECR) 11197 Via Vis, Nevada City CA 95959 B Bellingham WA 10/17/1947 s Jesse Ross Whitten & Mary Miller. BA San Jose St U 1969; MDiv VTS 1973; PhD California Inst of Integral Stds 2004. D 6/22/1973 P 2/20/1974 Bp C Kilmer Myers. m 6/28/1969 Jeanne Browning c 2. Vic S Steph's In-The-Field Epis Ch San Jose CA 1975-1981; Asst Chr Epis Ch Los Altos CA 1974-1975; Intern Asst Ch Of The Ascen Silver Sprg MD 1971-1972. Auth, "Awake and Aware," CIIS, San Francisco, 2004; Auth, "I Think My Mind Is Tricking Me," Lifetimes Press, London, 1989; Auth, "Simply Being Happy," Lifetimes Press, London, 1988. cl VTS 1973. wroywhitten@mac.com

WHITTINGTON, Nancy Susan (WNC) 140 Chestnut Cir, Blowing Rock NC 28605 B Statesville NC 4/26/1950 d Odell Whittington & Grace Rhodes. BA U NC 1972; MBA Wake Forest U 1984. D 1/22/2011 Bp Granville Porter Taylor. ridinhabit@gmail.com

WHITTINGTON, Richard Culbertson (Tex) No address on file. B Oklahoma City OK 9/27/1921 s Eugene Whittington & Florence Fonshill. BBA U of Texas 1947. D 12/17/1954 Bp Clinton Simon Quin. m 3/13/1948 Lettalou Garth. Asst S Jn The Div Houston TX 1954-1958.

WHITTLE, Natalie Wang (Ga) 102 S Jackson Rd, Statesboro GA 30461 B Beijing China 8/10/1945 d M J Wang & Yi Zen. BA Natl Taiwan U; MA/DA U of Oregon. D 6/29/2006 Bp Henry Irving Louttit. m 7/18/1972 Amberys Whittle c 2. nwwhittle@yahoo.com

WHITWORTH, Julia E (NY) 19 Walden St, West Hartford CT 06107 **Asst S Jas's Ch W Hartford CT 2010-** B Richmond VA 7/3/1971 d Frank Dixon Whitworth & Kay Sutton. AB Dart 1993; MA NYU 1998; MPhil NYU 2002; MDiv UTS 2010. D 3/13/2010 P 9/25/2010 Bp Mark Sean Sisk. m 8/22/1998 Raymond John Neufeld c 3. assistant@stjameswh.org

WHYTE, Horace Maxwell (NY) 170 W End Ave Apt 30-H, New York NY 10023 B Darliston JM 7/20/1941 s Roland Samuel Whyte & Estella Bernice. D 4/26/1997 Bp Richard Frank Grein. The Ch of S Matt And S Tim New York NY 1997-2007. NAAD 1996; The Fund for the Diac in the USA 1998-2007. h.whyte@att.net

WIBLE, Christina Karen Kirchner (NJ) 10 N Slope, Clinton NJ 08809 B Plainfield NJ 12/14/1946 d William Walter Kirchner & Ruth Walborg. BA Rutgers-The St U 1969; MDiv GTS 1999. D 10/23/1999 Bp Herbert Alcorn Donovan Jr. m 8/23/1971 Barry R Wible. D Calv Epis Ch Flemington NJ 2001-2002; D S Thos Ch Alexandria Pittstown NJ 1999-2000. ckwible@gmail.com

WIBLE, Terrence Linn (CPa) 57 Piper Dr, New Oxford PA 17350 **R S Lk's Ch Lebanon PA 2003-** B Chambersburg PA 5/28/1949 s Charles Norbitt Wible & Catherine Gelwicks. MA Lebanon Vlly Coll 1971; MDiv Evang TS 1974; VTS 1993. D 6/11/1993 P 12/10/1993 Bp Charlie Fuller McNutt Jr. m 1/15/1977 Lenoir Young. R All SS Ch Hanover PA 1994-2003; D Intern All SS' Epis Ch Hershey PA 1993-1994. wibles1@verizon.net

WICHAEL, Karen (Kan) 5648 W 92nd Pl, Overland Park KS 66207 B New York NY 9/13/1947 d Arthur Stephenson & Doris. BA Wm Penn U 1969. D 10/20/2000 Bp William Edward Smalley. m 5/24/1969 Robert Lester Wichael c 3. D Gd Shpd Epis Ch Wichita KS 2000-2011. karen.wichael@att.net

WICHELNS, Anne Brett (CNY) Shared Episcopal Ministry of North, 314 Clay St, Watertown NY 13601 **Vic S Andr's Ch Watertown NY 2009-; Shared Mnstry Of Nny Watertown NY 2009-** B Tarrytown NY 6/5/1950 d George P Ludlam & Beatrice Kieffer. BA SUNY Empire St Coll 1981; MST SUNY Potsdam 1991. D 10/7/2006 P 6/16/2007 Bp Gladstone Bailey Adams III. m 7/6/1974 Jerome Bailey Wichelns c 4. awichelns@twcny.rr.com

WICHELNS, Jerome Bailey (CNY) 10751 Limburg Forks Rd, Carthage NY 13619 B Newark NJ 10/25/1937 s Walter Henry Wichelns & Ethelyn Eunice. BA Rutgers-The St U 1959; MA Col 1990; DMin STUSo 1998. D 12/12/1998 P 6/12/1999 Bp David B(ruce) Joslin. m 7/6/1974 Anne Brett Wichelns c 4. Dio Cntrl New York Syracuse NY 2005; R S Paul's Ch Brownville NY 2003-2009; Shared Mnstry Of Nny Watertown NY 1999-2008; Assoc Pstr S Paul's Ch Watertown NY 1999-2002. Auth, "The New Physics: An Intro," *Fractals And Ferns- The New Physics: Uniting The Sciences And Arts*, Suny Press, 1998; Auth, "China And The W: A Study In (Bus) Culture Clash," *Whose Values? Ethics In The Intl Bus Environ*, Coll Consortium For Intl Stds, 1996; Auth, "Poem," *Sunlight Fails November Wood*, 1993; Auth, "Hunger On The Lifeboat," Natl Wrld Food Day Com, 1991; Auth, "In Defense Of The Coll Taking A Leading Role In The Cmnty In Confronting Issues In Soc Reform: A Contractarian Approach In Critical Thinkin," Inst For Critical Thinking, 1989; Auth, "Ethics In Bus," Cntr For Bus Ethics, 1989. Amer Philos Assn 1993; Intl Symposium On Ethics 1996; People To People 1993. "Who'S Who In Amer Colleges And Universities". wichelns@westelcom.com

WICHMAN, James Henry (O) 2314 Oak Glen Ct, Akron OH 44333 **D Gr Ch Ravenna OH 1999-** B Sandusky OH 11/14/1929 s Paul Gerhardt Wichman & Osie Jeanette. U of Wisconsin. D 11/13/1992 Bp James Russell Moodey. m 5/26/1951 Charlene H Cockrell c 2. D S Jn's Epis Ch Cuyahoga Falls OH 1998-1999; D S Lk's Epis Ch Niles OH 1995-1998. NAAD.

WICK, Calhoun Warren (Del) Po Box 3719, Wilmington DE 19807 **Spec Asst To The Bp Of Delaware Dio Delaware Wilmington DE 1985-** B Cleveland OH 5/21/1944 s Warren Corning Wick & Mildred Washington. BA TESM 1967; MDiv VTS 1970; MS MIT 1975. D 6/27/1970 Bp John Harris Burt P 4/1/1971 Bp Nelson Marigold Burroughs. m 6/8/1980 Ann D Laird. R S Michaels In The Hills Toledo OH 1975-1978. Auth, "Mgmt Side Of Mnstry"; Auth, "The Lrng Edge: How Smart Mgrs & Smart Cos Stay Ahead". Alfred P Sloan Fell; Rockefeller Fell. johnwick@forthillcompany.com

WICKHAM, Jonathan William (WTex) 14222 Cougar Crk, San Antonio TX 78230 **Asst S Mk's Epis Ch San Antonio TX 2007-** B Oneonta NY 3/31/1969 s J Thomas Wickham & Diane Davison. AS No Country Cmnty Coll Saranac Lake NY 1989; BA SUNY 1992; MDiv STUSo 2002. D 6/13/2002 Bp Robert Boyd Hibbs P 2/28/2003 Bp James Edward Folts. m 10/20/1990 Jennifer Tyndall c 2. Dio W Texas San Antonio TX 2004-2006; Asst S Geo Ch San Antonio TX 2002-2004. The ABS CE Prize The U So TS Sewanee TN 2002. jwwickham@sbcglobal.net

WICKHAM III, William Hunt (Del) 205 Chad Pl, Millville DE 19970 B NorwichNY 4/3/1940 s William Hunt Wickham & Barbara. BA RPI 1962; MDiv VTS 1968. D 6/11/1968 Bp Walter M Higley P 5/28/1969 Bp Ned Cole. m 1/1/1990 Joyce Murphy c 5. R S Martha's Epis Ch Bethany Bch DE 2004-2010; Dn Convoc VII Dio Sthrn Virginia Norfolk VA 1996-1998; Chair Richmond Epis Cler Dio Sthrn Virginia Norfolk VA 1991-1992; R S Mich's Ch Bon Air VA 1990-2004; Stndg Com Dio Cntrl New York Syracuse NY 1975-1986; Ch of the Gd Shpd Syracuse NY 1974-1985; R S Jas' Ch Clinton NY 1973-1989; Cur Trin Epis Ch Watertown NY 1968-1973. whwickham@mchsi.com

WICKIZER, Bob (Okla) 218 N 6th St, Muskogee OK 74401 **R Gr Ch Muskogee OK 2010-** B Springfield MO 12/9/1951 s Wilbur Francis Wickizer & Catherine Edith. BS U of Missouri 1972; MA Washington U 1975; MDiv EDS 1998. D 6/27/1998 P 2/23/1999 Bp Richard Lester Shimpfky. m 5/17/1980 Joan Theresa Speckhals c 2. Actg R S Anne's Par Annapolis MD 2006-2008; Int S Alb's Epis Ch Glen Burnie MD 2005-2006; R S Phil's Epis Ch Laurel MD 2001-2004; H Trin Epis Ch Greensboro NC 2001; Asst S Mary's Epis Ch High Point NC 1998-2001. Auth, "Creation & Revelation," *Journ of Faith & Sci Exch*, 1997. Inst of Electrical & Electronic Engr (Mem) 1977. 2nd Prize - Faith & Sci Essay Templeton Fndt 1997. bob.wickizer@verizon.net

WICKMAN, Charles Robert (Minn) 4620 Gaywood Dr, Minnetonka MN 55345 **Asst The Epis Par Of S Dav Minnetonka MN 2000-** B Escanaba MI 1/3/1933 s Carl Rudolph Wickman & Ruth Aurelia. BD U MI 1955; MS U MI 1958. D 1/24/1984 Bp Robert Marshall Anderson. m 11/22/1956 Mary Jane Larson c 2. Asst The Epis Par Of S Dav Minnetonka MN 1995-1998; Asst S Edw The Confessor Wayzata MN 1992-1995; Asst Trin Ch Excelsior MN

1989-1992; D The Epis Par Of S Dav Minnetonka MN 1984-1989. charlesrwickman@earthlink.net

WICKMAN, Christine Rosamund (Alb) 171d Hague Blvd, Glenmont NY 12077 B London UK 4/5/1939 d Roger Francis Henry & Dorothea Eva. Langham Secretarial Coll. D 6/10/2006 Bp Daniel William Herzog. m 8/18/1979 Thomas Wickman c 5. christinewickman@nycap.rr.com

WICKS, John Walker (Eau) Po Box 117, Cornucopia WI 54827 **Died 1/1/2010** B Ashland WI 3/30/1927 s Wilbur James Wicks & Margaret Elizabeth Beebe. BA Northland Coll Ashland WI 1952. D 11/6/1976 Bp Charles Thomas Gaskell. c 2.

WIDDOWS, John Herbert (Me) 340 Promenade #125, Portland ME 04101 B Yonkers NY 2/20/1932 s Arthur Widdows & Maud. BA Col 1954; STB Ya Berk 1958; M.S.Ed Iona Coll 1974. D 5/11/1958 P 12/11/1958 Bp Horace W B Donegan. m 10/3/1992 Cynthia Widdows c 2. Asstg Cathd Ch Of S Lk Portland ME 1993-2000; Asst S Ptr's Ch Bronx NY 1967-1968; Cur Par Of Chr The Redeem Pelham NY 1958-1962. jwiddows@maine.rr.com

WIDING, C(arl) Jon (Ct) 47 Fox Holw, Avon CT 06001 B Philadelphia PA 12/22/1937 s Theodore Widing & Esther. BA Trin Hartford CT 1959; MDiv EDS 1966; MSW U of Pennsylvania 1972. D 9/21/1966 P 4/12/1967 Bp Robert Lionne DeWitt. m 7/2/1966 Carol S Widing c 1. Asst Gr Ch Newington CT 2001-2003; Asst S Monica's Ch Hartford CT 2000-2001; P-in-c S Thos of Cbury New Fairfield CT 1998-2000; R Chr Ch Avon CT 1983-1997; R St Annes Epis Ch Middletown DE 1972-1983; Asst Chr Ch Philadelphia Philadelphia PA 1966-1970. Tertiary of the Soc of S Fran. jon_widing@yahoo.com

WIECKING III, Frederick August (Ind) 4 Sunnyside Rd, Silver Spring MD 20910 B Milwaukee WI 12/8/1947 s Frederick Wiecking & Catherine Louise. BA Wesl 1969; MDiv Yale DS 1972. D 2/8/1972 P 10/1/1972 Bp John P Craine. m 9/6/1969 Debra Lynn Ness. Auth, "The New Puritans: Achievement & Power Motive Of New Left Radicals"; Auth, "Reversing Tax Shift: Opportunity To Make Mn'S Taxes Progressive"; Auth, "Organizing For Just Econ".

✠ **WIEDRICH, Rt Rev William Walter** (Chi) 15269 Hofma Drive, Grand Haven MI 49417 B Stambaugh MI 8/19/1931 s William Walter Wiedrich & Muriel Jesse. BA U MI 1953; MDiv Bex 1956; DD Bex 2003. D 6/29/1956 P 3/1/1957 Bp Herman R Page Con 2/23/1991 for Chi. m 6/18/1955 Theresa Ann Eccel c 2. Bp Suffr of Chicago Dio Chicago Chicago IL 1991-1996; R Gr Ch Madison WI 1981-1991; R S Jas Ch Of Sault S Marie Sault Ste Marie MI 1971-1981; R Trin Epis Ch Houghton MI 1963-1971; Archd Dio Nthrn Michigan Marquette MI 1961-1963; Vic All SS Ch Newberry MI 1956-1963; Vic S Jn's Ch Munising MI 1956-1963. Auth, "Not Simply Simon". DD, Honoris CAUSA Bex Sem 2003.

WIEHE, Philip Freeman (NC) 102 N. Second Street, Memphis TN 38103 **Int R Calv Ch Memphis TN 2010-** B Cincinnati OH 10/1/1949 s Theodore Baird Wiehe & Mary House. BA Jn Hopkins U 1971; MDiv Yale DS 1975; STM Yale DS 1976. D 5/24/1975 P 1/31/1976 Bp John Mc Gill Krumm. m 2/16/1985 Linda W Woofter c 2. Int R S Geo's Epis Ch Arlington VA 2009-2010; Int R Emm Ch Harrisonburg VA 2008-2009; Int R All SS Ch Frederick MD 2006-2008; Consult S Mk's Epis Ch Raleigh NC 1996-1997; Chapl N. C. St Dio No Carolina Raleigh NC 1993-2003; Chapl Stanford Cbury Fndt Standford CA 1980-1984; Exec Dir The Epis Fndt For Drama Palo Alto CA 1979-1984; Chapl Harvard-Westlake Sch N Hollywood CA 1976-1979; Asst Trin Ch On The Green New Haven CT 1975-1976. Co-Auth, "More Dumb Things Ch Do," Morehouse, 2009; Auth, "Ten Dumb Things Ch Do," Morehouse, 2001. pfwiehe@mac.com

WIELAND, William David (Ind) 520 E Seminary St, Greencastle IN 46135 B New Brunswick NJ 7/4/1942 s Willard William Wieland & Naomi Ruth. BA Wesl 1964; MA Indiana U 1966; MDiv STUSo 1981. D 6/24/1981 P 3/19/1982 Bp Edward Witker Jones. m 6/15/1975 Lucille Bird c 2. Dio Indianapolis Indianapolis IN 2010-2011; R S Andr's Epis Ch Greencastle IN 1987-2011; Asst S Paul's Epis Ch Indianapolis IN 1981-1983. wieland@ccrtc.com

WIENK, Dennis L (Roch) 274 Rosedale St, Rochester NY 14620 B Gowanda NY 3/4/1942 s Leslie Carl Wienk & Gladys Victoria. BA SUNY 1964; BD Nash 1970. D 6/13/1970 P 12/19/1970 Bp Allen Webster Brown. m 6/16/1962 Marilyn Rose Dowd c 2. Dio Rochester Rochester NY 2003-2010; Chapl & Dir of Pstr Care, Epis Sr Life The Chap of the Gd Shpd Rochester NY 2003-2010; Ch Of The Gd Shpd Savona NY 1996-2003; S Thos' Ch Bath NY 1984-2003; P-in-c Ch Of The Gd Shpd Savona NY 1981-1984; Sum LocTen S Jn's Ch Massena NY 1977-1979; R Gr And H Innoc Albany NY 1975-1977; Cur S Geo's Epis Ch Schenectady NY 1970-1973. wienk@episcopalseniorlife.org

WIENS, Dolores Flaming (NI) 315 W Harrison Ave, Wheaton IL 60187 B Enid OK 7/22/1942 d Menno Flama & Emma Corace. BA Bethel Coll 1965; Wheaton Coll 1987; MDiv Bethany TS 1990; CAS SWTS 1993. D 6/18/1994 P 12/1/1994 Bp Frank Tracy Griswold III. m 5/30/1964 Paul Wiens c 2. S Barn-In-The-Dunes Gary IN 2008-2011; Calv Ch Lombard IL 2001; Ch Of The Resurr W Chicago IL 1995-1996. revdfw@gmail.com

WIESNER, A(ugust) Donald (NJ) 208 Live Oak Ln, Washington NC 27889 **Regular Supply S Jas Epis Ch Belhaven NC 2004-** B Englewood NJ 12/11/1935 s August Joseph Wiesner & Tilda Elmita. AB Pr 1957; MDiv GTS 1960; STM NYTS 1970; Cert Post Grad Cntrl Mntl Hlth for Pstr Counslg 1970; Cert Int Mnstry Prog 1996. D 6/11/1960 Bp Leland Stark P 1/7/1961 Bp William Francis Moses. m 1/4/1975 Judy Henriksen c 3. P Assoc S Ptr's Epis Ch Washington NC 2001-2009; Int H Trin Epis Ch Hertford NC 1999-2001; Int S Mary's Ch Kinston NC 1998-1999; Int Ch Of The Gd Shpd Pitman NJ 1997-1998; Int S Mary's Epis Ch Stone Harbor NJ 1996-1997; Vic Trin Epis Ch Stratford NJ 1982-1996; Int Ch Of The H Comm Norwood NJ 1981-1982; Int S Andr's Ch Harrington Pk NJ 1981-1982; R S Andr's Epis Ch Lincoln Pk NJ 1974-1980; R S Lk's Ch Katonah NY 1964-1972; Cur Ch Of The Resurr Biscayne Pk FL 1963-1964; Vic S Steph's Ch New Port Richey FL 1962-1963; Cur Gr Epis Ch Of Ocala Ocala FL 1960-1962. wiesner@centurylink.net

WIESNER, Elizabeth Phenix (Mass) 21 Ellsworth Ave # 2, Cambridge MA 02139 **P Assoc S Ptr's Epis Ch Cambridge MA 1992-** B New York NY 5/3/1917 d Evelyn Bolles. VTS; Wells Coll 1936; BA Stan 1938. D 5/30/1973 Bp Harold B Robinson P 1/1/1977 Bp William Foreman Creighton. m 6/3/1950 Louis A Wiesner. Int S Ptr's Epis Ch Cambridge MA 1989-1991; Int S Matt And The Redeem Epis Ch So Boston MA 1987-1988; Int Chr Ch No Conway NH 1984-1985; Asst R All Souls Memi Epis Ch Washington DC 1982-1984; Asst S Marg's Ch Washington DC 1973-1976. Auth, "Between The Lines: Ovrs w The Red Cross And Oss," Posterity Press, 1998; Auth, "Pilgrim & Pioneer A Journey w God," Churchman Pub, Ltd, 1989. Assn Soc Of S Jn The Evang; Natl Assn For The Self- Supporting Active Mnstry.

WIESNER, Kurt Christopher (NH) 29 School St., Littleton NH 03561 **R All SS Epis Ch Littleton NH 2008-** B Hinsdale IL 3/18/1972 s Kurt Salerno Wiesner & Mary Ann. BA Indiana U 1995; MDiv Epis TS of The SW 1998. D 12/15/2002 Bp Arthur Benjamin Williams Jr P 6/16/2003 Bp J Clark Grew II. m 1/26/2002 Darlene P Perez. Cur Trin Cathd Cleveland OH 2003-2008; The Ch of the Gd Shpd Austin TX 1998-2001. kcwiesner@hotmail.com

WIGGERS, John Mark (ETenn) 1101 N Broadway St, Knoxville TN 37917 **R St Jas Epis Ch at Knoxville Knoxville TN 2009-** B Pensacola FL 1/20/1971 s Bert Edward Wiggers & Dean Ray. BA Baylor U 1993; MDiv GTS 1999. D 6/5/1999 P 2/19/2000 Bp Charles Farmer Duvall. m 4/20/1996 Elizabeth Dees c 2. Cn Cathd Of S Phil Atlanta GA 2002-2009; Cur The Epis Ch Of The Nativ Dothan AL 1999-2002. jwiggers@stjamesknox.org

WIGGINS JR, Eschol Vernon (Ga) 1009 Hillcrest Dr, Cochran GA 31014 **P Trin Ch Cochran GA 2005-** B Garfield GA 11/21/1936 s Eschol Vernon Wiggins & Hilda. BS Georgia Coll Milledgeville GA 1982. D 2/5/2005 P 8/7/2005 Bp Henry Irving Louttit. m Joan Myers c 2. eschol@communicomm.com

WIGGINS, Reese H (La) 17764 Jefferson Ridge Dr, Baton Rouge LA 70817 **S Lk's Ch Baton Rouge LA 2007-** B Beaumont TX 4/27/1949 s Leo Wiggins & Fay. Rec from Roman Catholic 9/13/2003 Bp Charles Edward Jenkins III. c 2. reese@stlukesbr.org

WIGG-MAXWELL, Elizabeth Parker (Nwk) 44 Pittsford Way, New Providence NJ 07974 **R S Ptr's Epis Ch Livingston NJ 2009-** B Minneapolis MN 11/27/1956 d Norman Parker Wigg & Joan Marilyn. BA Coe Coll 1978; MA U of Wisconsin 1981; MDiv GTS 1986. D 6/28/1986 Bp Henry Irving Mayson P 2/2/1987 Bp H Coleman McGehee Jr. m 5/18/1985 Paul Douglas Maxwell c 2. Chr Ch Short Hills NJ 2004-2009; Vic S Fran Ch Dunellen NJ 2000-2002; Int St Jn the Bapt Epis Ch Linden NJ 1998-2000; Int S Jas' Epis Ch Hackettstown NJ 1994; Int Ch Of The Mssh Chester NJ 1993-1994; Ch of S Jn on the Mtn Bernardsville NJ 1992-1993; Int The Ch Of The Sav Denville NJ 1991-1992; Asst R S Paul's Epis Ch Chatham NJ 1986-1990. wiggmax27@verizon.net

WIGHT, Andrea Lee (Chi) 7398 Bell Vista Terrace, Rockford IL 61107 **S Anskar's Ch Rockford IL 2005-; D S Matt's Ch Las Vegas NV 2003-** B Montclair NJ 7/25/1952 d Andrew LeRoy Harland & Merle Lillace. BS U of Wyoming 1975; MDiv CDSP 2003. D 2/22/2003 P 10/25/2003 Bp Katharine Jefferts Schori. c 2. S Mary Epis Ch Crystal Lake IL 2003-2005. andreawight@sbcglobal.net

WIGHT, Susan Moore (USC) 5 Blackhawk Ct, Blythewood SC 29016 **S Ptr's Ch Great Falls SC 2004-** B Columbia SC 8/10/1949 d Jean Heyward Moore & Catherine Helen. BA U of So Carolina 1971; Med U of So Carolina 1977; BA Cath U of Leuven 1996; Spec Stds Luth Theol Sthrn Sem 1998; MDiv VTS 2001. D 6/16/2001 P 4/25/2002 Bp Dorsey Felix Henderson. m 7/30/1983 William Wallace Wight. S Mich And All Ang' Columbia SC 2001-2003. wwwight@earthlink.net

WIGHT, William Wallace (USC) 5 Blackhawk Ct, Blythewood SC 29016 **S Jn's Epis Ch Columbia SC 1969-** B Enid OK 7/16/1942 s Philip Franklin Wight & Luella Marie. BA Phillips U 1964; Spec Stds Cath U of Louvain 1968; STB GTS 1969. D 6/7/1969 Bp Horace W B Donegan P 4/18/1970 Bp John Brooke Mosley. m 7/30/1983 Susan Moore. Int Gr Epis Ch And Kindergarten Camden SC 2003-2004; Asst To The R S Martins-In-The-Field Columbia SC 2001-2003; Dio Upper So Carolina Columbia SC 2001; Off Of

Bsh For ArmdF New York NY 1982-2001; Chair Of The Armed Forced Cmsn Epis Dio San Joaquin Modesto CA 1980-1982; CE Cmsn Epis Dio San Joaquin Modesto CA 1979-1982; Vic S Andr's Ch Taft CA 1979-1981; Cmsn On Ecum Rel Dio Oklahoma Oklahoma City OK 1977-1979; S Jn's Ch Oklahoma City OK 1977-1979; Asst S Jas Epis Ch Danbury CT 1973-1977; R Ch Of The Redeem Okmulgee OK 1970-1973. Legion Of Merit Us Army 2001. fatherwight@earthlink.net

WIGHT-HOLBY, Patricia Ann Page (NJ) 76920 Oklahoma Ave, Palm Desert CA 92211 **Asst S Marg's Epis Ch Palm Desert CA 2001-** B Albany NY 6/24/1929 d William Meloon Page & Frances Elizabeth. BA Westminster Choir Coll of Rider U 1951; MS UTS 1953; MDiv PrTS 1983; CAS GTS 1984. D 6/7/1987 Bp Vincent King Pettit P 6/25/1990 Bp George Phelps Mellick Belshaw. m Kenneth Raymond Wight. Assoc Trin Cathd Trenton NJ 1995-1999; Assoc Gr-S Paul's Ch Mercerville NJ 1990-1994. Assn of Profsnl Chapl 1990; DOK 1976-1980; Epis Cleric Assn 1987-1988; Intl Ord of S Lk 1976. Music4clergy@aol.com

WIGLE, John Whitcombe (O) 814 Westport Dr, Youngstown OH 44511 **Assoc S Jas Epis Ch Boardman OH 2008-** B Windsor ON CA 5/10/1927 s John Harold Wigle & Camilla Marie. BA U of Wstrn Ontario 1950; MDiv VTS 1956. D 6/21/1956 Bp Archie H Crowley P 1/12/1957 Bp Richard S M Emrich. m 5/5/1951 Barbara A Bevington c 3. Int Gr Epis Ch Mansfield OH 1999-2000; Extended Supply S Lk's Epis Ch Niles OH 1998-2007; Our Sav Ch Mechanicsburg OH 1992-1998; Metro Counslg Serv Youngstown OH 1987; S Jn's Ch Youngstown OH 1968-1979; R The Epis Ch Of The Adv W Bloomfield MI 1956-1968. Chi Sigma Iota Kent St, Kent Ohio 1980; Kappa Delta Pi Kent St, Kent Ohio 1980. babswigle@zoominternet.net

WIGMORE, William Joseph (Tex) 1701 Rock Creek Dr, Round Rock TX 78681 B New York NY 11/14/1945 s James Wigmore & Dorothy. Iona Sch for Mnstry; BA U Of Dayton OH 1967. D 6/24/2006 Bp Don Adger Wimberly P 1/26/2007 Bp Dena Arnall Harrison. m 1/1/1976 Geraldine Ann List c 3. billw@austinrecovery.org

WIGNER JR, J(ohn) (SwVa) 104 Yorkshire Circle, Lynchburg VA 24502 **Trst VTS Alexandria VA 1999-** B Baltimore MD 9/6/1943 s John Douglas Wigner & Bernice Josephine. BS VPI 1965; MDiv VTS 1972; Cert GTS 1997; DMin VTS 2007. D 5/27/1972 P 5/13/1973 Bp Robert Bruce Hall. m 11/28/1987 Nancy Hein c 2. Pres - Stndg Com Dio SW Virginia Roanoke VA 2008-2009; Chair - Long Range Plnng Com Dio SW Virginia Roanoke VA 2007-2008; Exam Chapl Dio SW Virginia Roanoke VA 2006-2011; Stndg Com Dio SW Virginia Roanoke VA 2006-2009; COM Dio SW Virginia Roanoke VA 2005-2011; Dn, Lynchburg Convoc Dio SW Virginia Roanoke VA 2005-2010; Alt Dep to GC Dio SW Virginia Roanoke VA 2005-2007; Chair - ad hoc Com Dio SW Virginia Roanoke VA 2005-2006; Pres - Stndg Com Dio SW Virginia Roanoke VA 2003-2004; Stndg Com Dio SW Virginia Roanoke VA 2001-2004; Chair, Resolutns Com Dio SW Virginia Roanoke VA 2000-2008; Dn, Lynchburg Convoc Dio SW Virginia Roanoke VA 1999-2002; Exec Bd Dio SW Virginia Roanoke VA 1998-2001; R S Paul's Epis Ch Lynchburg VA 1997-2009; Com on Ch Revitalization Dio Virginia Richmond VA 1994-1997; R S Ptr's Par Ch New Kent VA 1990-1997; Int Assoc S Jn's Ch Stamford CT 1986-1989; Dn - Waterbury Dnry Dio Connecticut Hartford CT 1981-1984; R S Paul's Ch Woodbury CT 1977-1986; Assoc S Chris's Ch Springfield VA 1974-1977; Cur Ch Of The H Comf Vienna VA 1972-1974. Ch Dvlpmt Inst 1997; HSEC 2003. stpauldoug@yahoo.com

WIGODSKY, Andrea Lynn (NC) Saint Mary's School, 900 Hillsborough St., Raleigh NC 27603 B Winston-Salem NC 7/23/1977 d John David Wigodsky & Mary Lynn. BA Duke 2000; CAS Ya Berk 2005; MDiv Yale DS 2005. D 6/26/2005 P 2/12/2006 Bp Michael Bruce Curry. m 10/18/2003 John D Rohrs. S Mary's Sch Raleigh NC 2007; Dio No Carolina Raleigh NC 2005-2006. Jn A. Wade Preaching Awd Yale DS 2005. andiewigodsky@aya.yale.edu

WIKE, Antoinette Ray (NC) 221 Union St, Cary NC 27511 **P Assoc S Paul's Epis Ch Cary NC 1983-** B Lenoir NC 2/6/1945 d Carl Edwin Wike & Gertrude Antoinette. BA Guilford Coll 1968; JD U NC 1974; MDiv Duke DS 1981; Cert VTS 1982. D 4/25/1983 P 4/30/1984 Bp Robert Whitridge Estill.

WILBANKS SR, James Luther (ETenn) 297 Alexian Way Apt 417, Signal Mountain TN 37377 **Died 10/5/2010** B Rome GA 8/18/1918 s John Luther Wilbanks & Emma Mae. Baylor Sch; MDiv STUSo 1961. D 6/27/1962 Bp John Vander Horst P 3/18/1972 Bp William F Gates Jr. c 6. Chapl Alexian Vill-Signal Mt. TN 1999-2005; Chapl CADAS(AA) Half-Century Club DVA. Who's Who in Rel 1982. goal18@comcast.net

WILBERT, Brian Kurt (O) 162 S Main St, Oberlin OH 44074 **Secy of Dio Conv Dio Ohio Cleveland OH 2005-; R Chr Ch Oberlin OH 1996-** B Elyria OH 5/2/1960 s Richard Paul Wilbert & Linda Lee. BA Ken 1982; MDiv Bex 1985; DMin SWTS 2002. D 6/15/1985 P 4/12/1986 Bp James Russell Moodey. Dep to GC Dio Ohio Cleveland OH 2008-2010; Stndg Com Dio Ohio Cleveland OH 2004-2008; Epis Transition Dio Ohio Cleveland OH 2003-2004; R Gr Ch Ravenna OH 1988-1996; Cur S Michaels In The Hills Toledo OH 1985-1988. EPF 1985; Integrity U.S.A. 1986. Alum Hall Of Fame Elyria Publ Schools 2001. bwilbert@oberlin.net

WILBUR, John Eldredge (Md) 111 Delight Road, Reisterstown MD 21136 **Died 8/10/2009** B Baltimore,MD 1/9/1942 s A Jackson Wilbur & Marjorie Creighton. BA Moravian TS 1965; MDiv PDS 1968; MA U of Pennsylvania 1968. D 4/20/1968 P 10/1/1968 Bp Alfred L Banyard. c 2. Ord Of S Lk, Chapl 1972-1997; OHC 1963. Men Of Achievement 1971; Who'S Who Rel 1971; Outstanding Young Men Of Amer 1970. fr.john_e.wilbur@comcast.net

WILBURN, J Mark (Tex) 24 McFaddan LN, Temple TX 76502 **Asstg P Chr Epis Ch Temple TX 2006-** B Philadelphia,PA 4/16/1946 s James Russell Wilburn & Evelyn Ada. BS Belhaven Coll 1969; MDiv Columbia TS 1973; Columbia TS 1983; STUSo 2009. D 12/16/1982 Bp Roger Howard Cilley P 6/1/1983 Bp Maurice Manuel Benitez. c 1. Assoc R S Fran Ch Houston TX 2000-2003; Asst R S Paul's Ch Waco TX 1995-2000; R S Tim's Epis Ch Lake Jackson TX 1991-1995; R S Paul's Ch Kilgore TX 1989-1991; Assoc R Trin Ch Longview TX 1987-1989. Bro of S Andr - Life Mem 1992; Cmnty of S Mary - Assoc 1985; ESMHE 1982-2000; Vocare - Dio Texas 1983-2000; Vocare - Natl 1983-1988. markofthewildboar@att.net

WILBURN, Merry Ilene (Tex) 16830 Blairstone, Houston TX 77084 B Marshall TX 12/16/1954 d Thomas Roche Rideout & Enid Orris. BS Texas A&M U 1976; MS Texas A&M U 1979; MDiv Epis TS of The SW 1991. D 6/22/1991 Bp Maurice Manuel Benitez P 2/1/1992 Bp Anselmo Carral-Solar. c 1. S Fran Par Temple TX 2003-2007; S Fran Ch Houston TX 2002-2003; Vic Chr Epis Ch Mexia Mexia TX 1995-2000; Dio Texas Houston TX 1994; S Paul's Ch Waco TX 1991-1994. merrywilburn@sbcglobal.net

WILCOX, Glen Miley (Ak) Po Box 72934, Fairbanks AK 99707 B Biddeford ME 2/27/1928 s Thomas Raymond Wilcox & Leah Dell. BA Hamline U 1950; MDiv Ya Berk 1953. D 6/15/1953 Bp Stephen E Keeler P 12/1/1953 Bp William J Gordon Jr. m 9/1/1951 Joan Louise Wilcox c 2. P-in-c Ch Of The Epiph - Luth Valdez AK 1964-1967; P-in-c S Geo's Ch Cordova AK 1961-1968; P-in-c Chr Ch Anvik AK 1953-1961. Auth, "Nthrn Cross".

WILCOX JR, Jack Franklyn (Okla) 101 Great Oaks Dr, Norman OK 73071 B Kansas City MO 3/10/1952 s Jack Franklyn Wilcox & Jane Louise. BA SW Bapt U 1974; MRE MidWestern Bapt TS 1979; MDiv MidWestern Bapt TS 1984; S Thos TS Denver CO 1992. D 3/18/1992 Bp William Harvey Wolfrum P 9/23/1992 Bp William Jerry Winterrowd. m 1/6/1990 Gail Patricia Waters c 4. R S Mich's Epis Ch Norman OK 2005-2008; R S Jas Epis Ch of Greeneville Greeneville TN 2002-2005; Chapl Chr Ch Blacksburg VA 1996-2001; S Phil In-The-Field Sedalia CO 1992-1993. OSL 2005. revjwilcox@earthlink.net

WILCOX, John Milton (EpisSanJ) 3909 Noel Pl, Bakersfield CA 93306 B Macon MO 10/2/1927 s Ray Milton Wilcox & Julia Fairfield. BA U of Kansas 1949; MDiv GTS 1952. D 6/8/1952 Bp Horace W B Donegan P 12/12/1952 Bp Sumner Walters. m 7/23/1949 Jewell Mishler c 2. Hstgr Epis Dio San Joaquin Modesto CA 1989-1993; R Ch Of The Gd Shpd Reedley CA 1985-1989; Stndg Com Epis Dio San Joaquin Modesto CA 1985-1988; Vic S Dunstans Epis Ch Modesto CA 1981-1985; R S Lk's Ch Bakersfield CA 1970-1981; Dep GC Epis Dio San Joaquin Modesto CA 1969-1973; Chair Liturg Cmsn Epis Dio San Joaquin Modesto CA 1969-1972; Chair Div Coll Wk Epis Dio San Joaquin Modesto CA 1964-1971; Assoc S Paul's Epis Ch Visalia CA 1961-1965; Vic S Mary's Ch Manteca CA 1959-1961; Asst S Andr's Par Fullerton CA 1958-1959; Fndr Ch Of The Epiph Corcoran CA 1957-1958; Vic S Jn's Epis Ch Tulare CA 1952-1958. Intl Ord of S Lk 1959. wilcoxjohn2judy@cs.com

WILCOX, Melissa Quincy (Mil) 313 S Orange St, Media PA 19063 **Asst Ch Of The Redeem Bryn Mawr PA 2010-** B Willimantic CT 3/15/1972 d Michael Wilcox & Dephne. BA Colby Coll 1994; MDiv VTS 2001. D 6/9/2001 P 2/23/2002 Bp Andrew Donnan Smith. m 7/28/2001 Adam P Kradel c 2. S Fran Hse U Epis Ctr Madison WI 2003-2006; Gr Ch Madison WI 2003; Cur Ch Of The H Comf Kenilworth IL 2001-2003. "Body Members," *Preaching As Pstr Caring*, Sermons that Wk, 2005; "Remembering In Abundance," *Preaching Through H Days And Holidays*, Sermons that Wk, 2003. mwilcox@theredeemer.org

WILCOXSON, Frederick Dean (CFla) 14531 Wishing Wind Way, Clermont FL 34711 **D Ch Of The Mssh Winter Garden FL 2006-** B Hominy OK 10/8/1947 s William J Wilcoxson & [illegible] BS Florida [illegible] Coll 1980; MA U Of Cntrl Florida 1995; PhD Intl Sem 2004. D 12/9/2006 Bp John Wadsworth Howe. m 10/8/1986 JoAnn Vanessa Wilcoxson. Assn of Chr Counselors 2006; Florida Bioethics Ntwk 2006; Intl Conf of Police Chapl 2004; The Coll of Pstr Supervision and Psych 2009. Bd Cert Clincl Chapl Coll of Pstr Supervision and Psych 2009; Bd Cert Pstr Counslr Coll of Pstr Supervision and Psych 2009. fred.wilcoxson@healthcentral.org

WILCOXSON, JoAnn Vanessa (CFla) 260 N Woodland St, Winter Garden FL 34787 B Panama City FL 6/13/1954 d William Charles Kane & Glory Ann. MCC Int'l Sem; BA U of Cntrl Florida; AA/AS Valencia Cmnty. D 12/13/2008 Bp John Wadsworth Howe. m 10/8/1986 Frederick Dean Wilcoxson c 2. josnothome@msn.com

WILD, Geoffrey Mileham (NwPa) PO Box 287, Grove City PA 16127 **Vic Ch Of The Epiph Grove City PA 2008-** B 10/24/1951 s Russell Mileham Wild &

Molly Irene. BA Malquarie U - Australia 1999. D 1/27/2008 P 11/15/2008 Bp Sean Walter Rowe. m 9/11/1999 Cheryl Wild c 2. pax@zoominternet.net

WILD III, Philip Charles (La) 120 S New Hampshire St, Covington LA 70433 B Algiers LA 11/29/1946 s Philip C Wild & Anna Mae Rosalee. Assoc MET Delgado Jr Coll 1969. D 10/23/2005 Bp Charles Edward Jenkins III. m 7/4/1974 Phyllis Eileen Wild c 3. pwild3@hotmail.com

WILDE, Gary A (SwFla) 28030 Dovewood Ct Apt 303, Bonita Springs FL 34135 **Assoc S Mary's Epis Ch Bonita Sprg FL 2009-** B Holyoke MA 11/7/1952 s Harry Wilde & Joann. BA Moody Bible Inst 1978; MDiv Bethany TS Oakbrook IL 1985; Cert Nash 2006. D 5/27/2006 Bp John Wadsworth Howe P 12/9/2006 Bp Henry Irving Louttit. m 7/3/1973 Carol A McLean c 3. R S Jn's Ch Moultrie GA 2006-2009. gwilde@stmarysbonita.org

WILDE, Gregory Dean (At) PO Box 1146, Columbus GA 31902 **Assoc R Trin Epis Ch Columbus GA 2010-** B Minneapolis, MN 1/7/1958 s Stewart Arthur Wilde & Janet Darlene. MA U of Notre Dame 1992; DWS RE Webber Inst. for WS 2009; MDiv The U So (Sewanee) 2010. D 12/20/2009 P 8/20/2010 Bp Edward Stuart Little II. m 9/6/1980 Janice A Strand c 2. m3sterium@gmail.com

WILDER, Marilyn Mae (Spok) 617 10th St, Oroville WA 98844 **Vic Trin Ch Oroville WA 2007-** B Tonasket WA 1/19/1940 d Joseph Tunis Hardenburgh & Doris Allender. D 6/11/2005 P 9/17/2006 Bp James Edward Waggoner. m 3/28/1960 Dennis W Wilder c 2. mdwilder2@yahoo.com

WILDER III, Tracy Hartwell (SwFla) St. John the Divine Church, P.O. Box 87, Ruskin FL 33575 **R S Jn The Div Epis Ch Sun City Cntr FL 2001-** B Syracuse NY 4/17/1945 s Tracy Hartwell Wilder & Barbara. BA Randolph-Macon Coll 1967; MDiv Yale DS 1970; VTS 1972. D 6/17/1972 P 12/16/1972 Bp Leland Stark. m 10/17/1998 Susan Louise Hawkinson c 2. R S Matt's Epis Ch Horseheads NY 1996-2001; Chr Ch Prince Geo's Par Rockville MD 1985-1997; R Chr Ch Short Hills NJ 1985-1996; R H Trin Epis Ch Dickinson TX 1979-1985; Asst S Dav's Ch Austin TX 1977-1979; Cur Chr Ch Short Hills NJ 1972-1976. Auth, *Angl Dig*. sandtwilder@yahoo.com

WILDGOOSE, Angelo Stanley (Tenn) 2008 Meharry Blvd, Nashville TN 37208 **Vic S Anselm's Epis Ch Nashville TN 2010-** B Bahamas 8/3/1976 s Stanley Wildgoose & Charlsetta. Dplma Pstr Stds Codrington Coll 1999; BA Codrington Coll TS 2000; BA U of the W Indies 2000; Dplma ED Coll of the Bahamas 2002. Trans from Church of Bermuda 11/17/2010 Bp John Crawford Bauerschmidt. m 12/1/2001 Tonya Elaine Wildgoose c 2. angelo.wildgoose@gmail.com

WILDSMITH, Joseph Ned (NJ) 808 S Delhi St, Philadelphia PA 19147 B Danville PA 10/29/1941 s Charles DeHart Wildsmith & Mabel Eilene. BA Lycoming Coll 1964; MDiv PDS 1968; U of Pennsylvania 1969. D 12/21/1968 P 3/1/1970 Bp Dean T Stevenson. Cur H Trin Ch Collingswood NJ 1970-1971.

WILE, Mary Lee Hanford (Me) 45 Baker St, Yarmouth ME 04096 **Archd Dio Maine Portland ME 2010-; D S Paul's Ch Brunswick ME 2001-** B Boston MA 3/10/1947 d George H Hanford & Elaine. Rad 1968; BA Colorado St U 1969; MA Colorado St U 1971; MA Bangor TS 1999. D 12/1/2001 Bp Chilton Abbie Richardson Knudsen. m 6/24/1986 Richard L Wile c 2. Auth, "Chr's Own Forever," *Living the Gd News*, 2003; Auth, "I Will w God's Help," *Living the Gd News*, 2000; Auth, "Monastic Life in the Epis Ch," *Forw Mvmt*, FMP, 1999; Auth, "The Stones Hold the Heat," *The Other Side*, 1999; Auth, "Books or Shoes?," *Educ Week*, 1997; Auth, "From Concept to Bookshelf," *Maine in Print*, 1996; Auth, "Serene Light, Unspoken Word," *Daughters of Sarah*, 1995; Auth, "Ancient Rage," *Larson Pub*, Larson Pub, 1995. Assn for Epis Deacons 2001; Maine Educ Assn 1986. Profsnl Pub Awd Maine Coun of Engl Lang Arts 1993. wiles2@gwi.net

WILEMON, Zane Howard (Kan) 81 N 2nd St, San Jose CA 95113 B Arlington TX 8/12/1977 s Stan Wilemon & Cindy. Ba U of Kansas 2000; MDiv Epis TS of the SW 2007. D 6/9/2007 P 1/26/2008 Bp Dean Elliott Wolfe. m 9/7/2004 Natalie Wilemon. Assoc Trin Cathd San Jose CA 2007-2009; Yth Dir Trin Ch Lawr KS 2002-2004. zane@trinitysj.org

WILES, Charles Preston (Dal) 7023 Northwood Rd, Dallas TX 75225 **Died 9/3/2011** B New Market MD 8/5/1918 s Charles Wesley Wiles & Nellie Lillian. BA Washington Coll 1939; U of Virginia 1940; MA Duke 1945; MDiv VTS 1947; Fllshp Duke 1951; PhD Duke 1951. D 11/24/1947 Bp Noble C Powell P 12/22/1948 Bp Edwin A Penick. c 3. Auth, "Troubadours Of God," 1998; Auth, "Centennial Hist Of Dio Dallas," 1996; Auth, "The Gate Of Heaven," 1994; Auth, "Sacr & Sacrifice"; Auth, "The Windows Of S Matthews Cathd". CHS 1978; CBS 1983; Ovrs Mssn Soc. Dn Emer Dio And S Mattius Cathd 1989; Distinguished Citizen City Of Brunswick, Md 1986; Intl "P Of Year" Awd Dsa Kiwanis Dio Dal 1969; Pres Burlington Coll, Nj 1956; Troubadours Of God 98. drcpwiles@dallastexas.com

WILEY, George Bell (Kan) Po Box 432, Baldwin City KS 66006 B Jackson TN 11/26/1946 s Bell Irvin Wiley & Mary Frances. BA U NC 1968; MDiv Candler TS Emory U 1971; PhD Emory U 1978. D 12/10/1975 P 7/10/1977 Bp Bennett Jones Sims. m 11/13/1993 Kathleen Ruth Bradt c 1. Ed, "A Hist of Baldwin City Rel Institutions," *Fac Web Site*, Baker U, 2005; Ed, "Wrld Rel in NE Kansas," *Profiles of Rel Centers*, The Pluralism Proj, Harv, 2002. AAR 1980-2008. Meth Ch Exemplary Tchr Baker U 2011; Distinguished Fac Awd Baker U 1989; Osborne Chair Of Rel Baker U 1980; Phi Beta Kappa U NC 1968; Morehead Schlr U NC 1964. george.wiley@bakeru.edu

WILEY, Judi A (SO) 234 N. High St., Hillsboro OH 45133 **R S Mary's Epis Ch Hillsboro OH 2009-** B Cumberland MD 2/14/1948 d Herbert Lester Leydig & Dorothy Jeanne. MA Amer St U Honolulu HI 1998; PhD Amer St U Honolulu HI 1998. D 1/23/2005 Bp Daniel Lee Swenson P 9/10/2005 Bp James Louis Jelinek. m 2/15/1992 Larry Wiley c 3. S Andr's Ch Omaha NE 1991-1994. jawiley2002@yahoo.com

WILEY, Ronald Lee (Neb) 102 Lakeview Rd, Fremont NE 68025 B Chadron NE 11/22/1938 s Clyde Morrel Wiley & Irene Mardell. BA Chadron St Coll 1960; BD SWTS 1963; MA U of Nebraska 1973. D 6/8/1963 P 12/17/1963 Bp Russell T Rauscher. m 6/1/1984 Linda Lane c 1. S Jas' Epis Ch Fremont NE 1986-1998; Cn To Ord Dio Nebraska Omaha NE 1978-1987; Dio Nebraska Omaha NE 1978-1986; Dep Gc Dio Nebraska Omaha NE 1976; Vic S Mk's On The Campus Lincoln NE 1967-1978; Vic S Jn's Ch Valentine NE 1963-1967. rwiley@neb.rr.com

WILHELM, Joseph Franklin (Los) 404 W Santa Ana St., Ojai CA 93023 **R S Andr's Epis Ch Ojai CA 2010-** B Noblesville IN 12/17/1946 s Lowell Eugene Wilhelm & Eleanor Louise. BA DePauw U 1969; MDiv SWTS 2005; U of Notre Dame 2005. D 4/15/2005 P 10/31/2005 Bp Edward Stuart Little II. m 1/31/1970 Barbara Brown c 2. R S Steph's Par Beaumont CA 2005-2010. jrev58@yahoo.com

WILHITE JR, MacDonald (WTenn) 6 S Mclean Blvd Apt 204, Memphis TN 38104 B Memphis TN 3/19/1947 s MacDonald Wilhite & Mary Louise. BBA U of Memphis 1971; MDiv SWTS 1974. D 6/23/1974 Bp William F Gates Jr P 6/15/1975 Bp John Vander Horst. m 8/15/1981 Dixie Josephine Wilhite. Dio Fond du Lac Appleton WI 1995; St Ambr Epis Ch Antigo WI 1993-1997; Dn Wisconsin River Vlly Dnry Dio Fond du Lac Appleton WI 1987-1991; Stndg Com Dio Fond du Lac Appleton WI 1985-1994; Chair Of Mar & Fam Life Cmsn Dio Fond du Lac Appleton WI 1983-1984; R Ch Of S Jn The Bapt Wausau WI 1982-1993; Asst S Jas By The Sea La Jolla CA 1977-1982; Vic S Andr's Epis Ch New Johnsonville TN 1975-1977; D S Tim's Ch Signal Mtn TN 1974-1975.

WILKE, Carl Edward (WMo) 3 Pursuit, #323, Aliso Viejo CA 92656 B Milwaukee WI 4/1/1920 s Carl August Wilke & Edith. BBA Marq 1941; MDiv GTS 1944; STM Nash 1956. D 4/12/1944 P 10/12/1944 Bp Benjamin F P Ivins. c 4. Asst S Jn's Ch Springfield MO 1989-1996; R Chr Epis Ch Springfield MO 1970-1985; R All SS Epis Ch Appleton WI 1957-1970; Cur Trin Ch Wauwatosa WI 1953-1957; San Mateo Epis Ch Bellaire TX 1951-1953; R Calv Epis Ch Richmond TX 1947-1951; S Mk's Ch So Milwaukee WI 1944-1946. Hon Cn Cathd H Cross, Gaborone, Botswana Gabarone Botswana 1984.

WILKERSON, Charles Edward (Md) St Luke's Episcopal Church, 1101 Bay Ridge Ave, Annapolis MD 21403 B New Church VA 6/1/1939 s Woodrow Marion Wilkerson & Ruth Hope. BS Salisbury St U 1964; MLA JHU 1975. D 6/4/2005 Bp Robert Wilkes Ihloff. RevDnWilkerson@verizon.net

WILKES, Hugh (Alb) No address on file. **D S Eliz's Epis Ch Zephyrhills FL 2008-; D Trin Ch Lansingburgh Troy NY 2001-; Asst Cathd Of All SS Albany NY 1987-; Asst Chr & S Barn Troy NY 1972-; Asst Ch Of Beth Saratoga Sprg NY 1972-** B Troy NY 9/19/1927 s Winfield Wilkes & Maude Evelyn. D 12/21/1972 Bp Allen Webster Brown. OHC. hewilkes@hotmail.com

WILKES III, Joe (Mass) 186 Upham St, Melrose MA 02176 **S Andr's Ch Methuen MA 2007-** B Soneham MA 12/31/1953 s Joseph Warren Wilkes & Margaret. BS Tufts U 1975; DMD Harv 1979; MD Harv 1981; MDiv EDS 2006. D 6/3/2006 Bp M(arvil) Thomas Shaw III P 1/6/2007 Bp Gayle Elizabeth Harris. m 6/20/1981 Karen Barbara Karen B Harvey c 2. josephwilkes1@verizon.net

WILKES, Larry Glynn (WLa) 1265 Meche Rd, Arnaudville LA 70512 **Stndg Com Dio Wstrn Louisiana Alexandria LA 2010-; R The Epis Ch Of The Epiph New Iberia LA 2010-** B Dublin GA 9/11/1950 s David Baum Wilkes & Martha Adel. AS U of the St of New York 1989; BS U of the St of New York 1989; MDiv VTS 1992. Trans 1/21/2004 Bp Stephen Hays Jecko. m 8/13/1981 Deborah M Smith c 3. Cn to the Ordnry Dio Wstrn Louisiana Alexandria LA 2007-2010; R Ch Of The Ascen Lafayette LA 2003-2007; Assoc San Jose Epis Ch Jacksonville FL 2001-2003; LT CHC USNR Off Of Bsh For ArmdF New York NY 1996-2001; R The Epis Cluster Of Southside Kenbridge VA 1992-1996. lgwilkes@centurytel.net

WILKING, Spencer Van Bokkelen (NY) 35 Robin Wood Rd, Concord MA 01742 B New York NY 8/24/1948 s Leo Franciscus Johannes Wilking & Virginia. BA Col 1970; MDiv CDSP 1973; BS/MB Lon 1982; MPH Bos 1987. D 6/9/1973 Bp Paul Moore Jr P 7/25/1974 Bp James Stuart Wetmore. m 9/16/1972 Louisa Dennis c 3. Asst Trin Ch Concord MA 1985-2001; Asst Min S Andr's Ch Longmeadow MA 1983-1985. Auth, "Multiple arts on Geriatric Med". Hosp Chapl Fllshp 1973; Soc of the Resurr, Mirfield, Engl (Cler Assoc.

1978. Fell Amer Coll of Physicians 1996; Fell Amer Geriatric Soc 1996; Fell Royal Soc of Med 1991. swilking@partners.org

WILKINS JR, Aaron Ellis (CGC) 6604 Carolina Ct, Mobile AL 36695 B Columbus MS 1/5/1929 s Aaron Ellis Wilkins & Lucy May. Auburn U; STUSo; Sprg Hill Coll; U of So Alabama. D 6/28/1981 P 5/1/1982 Bp Charles Farmer Duvall. m 12/5/1987 Virginia Ann Bell c 2. Chr Ch Cathd Mobile Mobile AL 2000; Ch Of S Marys-By-The-Sea Coden AL 1988-1991; Vic S Fran Ch Dauphin Island AL 1982-2000; Cur Trin Epis Ch Mobile AL 1981-1982. VIRLIS@BELLSOUTH.NET

WILKINS, Ann Purkeypile (NwT) 808 Stone Mountain Dr, Conroe TX 77302 B Newport RI 9/26/1932 d Jackson Bankhead Williams & Louria Boon. D 10/25/1985 Bp Sam Byron Hulsey. m 4/14/1987 James Roland Wilkins c 6.

WILKINS, Christopher Ian (WA) PO Box 207, St Marys City MD 20686 **Chr Ch Chaptico MD 2011-** B New Brighton PA 6/1/1969 s Dennis Sinclair Wilkins & Theresa Alma. BA Hav 1991; MTS Harvard DS 1993; PhD Bos 2000. D 6/13/2009 P 1/16/2010 Bp John Chane. m 10/9/1993 Hilary Laskey c 2. St Marys Par St Marys City MD 2009-2011. ciwilkins@juno.com

WILKINS, Leon Ray (Colo) Po 881809, Box 719, Steamboat Spgs CO 80488 B Keokuk IA 11/17/1925 s Albert Ray Wilkins & Minnie Rosalie. BA U of Iowa 1949. D 6/29/1961 P 1/6/1962 Bp Joseph Summerville Minnis. m 11/8/1962 Mary Calhoun. S Paul's Epis Ch Steamboat Sprg CO 1982-1987; Vic S Mk's Ch Craig CO 1971-1975; Vic S Tim's Epis Ch Rangely CO 1961-1971.

WILKINS, Palmer Oliver (Cal) 58 Robinhood Dr, Novato CA 94945 **D Ch Of The H Innoc Corte Madera CA 1994-** B Saint Louis MO 12/2/1934 s Oliver Jerome Wilkins & Dorothy Jane. BA Antioch Coll 1970; Cert California TS 1977; ThB Amer Bible Coll 1980; ThM Amer Bible Coll 1982; MS Wstrn St U 1983; PhD Wstrn St U 1993. D 11/23/1977 Bp C Kilmer Myers. m 6/2/1956 Joyce Ann Mudd. Assoc S Paul's Epis Ch San Rafael CA 1982-1987; Asst S Fran Of Assisi Ch Novato CA 1977-1982. Chapl Ord S Jn Jerusalem 1990. revrobinhood@aol.com

WILKINSON, Donald Charles (Mo) 17210 Fawn Cloud Ln, San Antonio TX 78248 B Detroit MI 8/21/1934 s Laurel Charles Wilkinson & Phyllis Viola. BA U of Massachusetts 1964; MDiv Bex 1967; Cov Sem S Louis MO 1981. D 6/17/1967 P 12/24/1967 Bp Roger W Blanchard. m 8/25/1968 Kathleen Carol Peach c 2. Ch Of The Annunc Luling TX 1994-1996; P-in-c Ch Of The Ascen S Louis MO 1989-1992; P-in-c All SS Epis Ch Farmington MO 1987-1988; P-in-c S Pauls Epis Ch Ironton MO 1987-1988; Ch Of The Epiph Kirkwood S Louis MO 1971-1986; Assoc Trin Ch Columbus OH 1967-1971. dwilkin@swbell.net

WILKINSON, Ernest Benjamin (NwT) 12245 State Highway 273, Pampa TX 79065 B Maimi TX 2/27/1937 D 10/29/2000 Bp C(harles) Wallis Ohl. m 7/23/1960 Mary Suzanne Murphy c 2. scna@cableone.net

WILKINSON, Hazel Livingston (SC) 3521 Ashwycke St, Mount Pleasant SC 29466 **P Assoc Ch Of The H Cross Sullivans Island SC 2004-** B Birmingham AL 8/4/1941 d Joseph Edgar Wilkinson & Alida Van Rensselaer. BS U GA 1963; MS U GA 1965; PhD U GA 1972; MDiv TESM 2002. D 6/15/2002 P 1/5/2003 Bp Robert William Duncan. Asst All SS Ch Of Winter Pk Winter Pk FL 2003-2004. Amer Angl Coun; The Evang Fllshp In The Angl Comm.

WILKINSON, James Royse (Ky) 1804 Leawood Ct, Louisville KY 40222 **Hstgr Dio Kentucky Louisville KY 2010-** B Saint Louis MO 12/14/1943 s Oliver Wightmann Wilkinson & Thelma Opal. BS U of Missouri 1965; MDiv VTS 1968; MA LIU 1977; U Of Basel Basel Ch 1983. D 6/22/1968 Bp George Leslie Cadigan P 6/16/1969 Bp Charles Gresham Marmion. m 7/11/1987 Mary Kay Shields. Temporary P S Paul's Jeffersonville IN 2010-2011; Mssn and Vision T/F Dio Kentucky Louisville KY 2004-2005; Mnstry on the River Seamens Ch Inst Income New York NY 1998-2010; Int S Mary's Ch Madisonville KY 1995-1996; Chapl Off Of Bsh For ArmdF New York NY 1974-1995; Vic S Paul's Ch Hickman KY 1970-1974; Vic Trin Epis Ch Fulton KY 1970-1974; Dept of Human Relatns Dio Kentucky Louisville KY 1968-1970; Asst S Jas Ch Pewee Vlly KY 1968-1970; Asst S Lk's Ch Anchorage KY 1968-1970. Hymn Soc of the Untd States and Can. Hon Assoc R Pohick Epis Ch, Fairfax, Va 1974. jamesrwilkinson@msn.com

WILKINSON, John Preston (SwVa) 1207 Middlebrook Rd, Staunton VA 24401 **R Trin Ch Staunton VA 2003-** B Milwaukee WI 9/28/1937 s John Henry Wilkinson & Mary Francis. BS GW; MA Pepperdine U. D 2/14/2003 Bp Frank Neff Powell. m 7/18/1998 Donna Fa Heener c 3.

WILKINSON, Joyce Ann (WVa) D 5/11/2002 P 11/16/2002 Bp Larry Earl Maze.

WILKINSON, Julia Sierra (Ga) 611 E Bay St, Savannah GA 31401 **Asst Chr Ch Epis Savannah GA 2011-** B Atlanta GA 7/19/1986 d Remi A Wilkinson & Julia U. BA Agnes Scott Coll 2008; MDiv Harvard DS 2011. D 2/11/2011 Bp Scott Anson Benhase. sierra.wilkinson@ccesavannah.org

WILKINSON, Kirsteen (Ind) 7834 Grand Gulch Dr, Indianapolis IN 46239 **P-in-c S Mk's Ch Plainfield IN 2011-; Coun on the Diac - Mem Dio Indianapolis Indianapolis IN 2010-; Assoc S Alb's Ch Indianapolis IN 2010-; Commision on Mnstry - Mem Dio Indianapolis Indianapolis IN 2009-; Facilitar of Dioc Wmn Week Prog Dio Indianapolis Indianapolis IN 2006-; Camp Chapl Dio Indianapolis Indianapolis IN 2000-** B Famagusta Cyprus 7/21/1961 d Richard Donnelly & Anne. BS Pur 1984; MS Butler U 1990; MDiv SWTS 2006. D 6/24/2006 P 2/18/2007 Bp Catherine Elizabeth Maples Waynick. c 3. Coun on the Diac - Mem Dio Indianapolis Indianapolis IN 2010-2011; Vic S Tim's Ch Indianapolis IN 2008-2011. kawilkinson@att.net

WILKINSON, Marcia Campbell (Ala) 6634 31st Pl NW, Washington DC 20015 B New London CT 2/17/1944 d William Neal Campbell & Margaret Kent. VTS; RN New Engl Bapt Hosp 1965; BA Hood Coll 1990; MDiv Luth TS at Gettysburg 1996. D 6/9/1995 Bp Charlie Fuller McNutt Jr P 3/2/1996 Bp Michael Whittington Creighton. m 4/23/1965 Rowland Wilkinson c 2. Assoc R All SS' Epis Ch Chevy Chase MD 2005-2009; Cn Mssnr The Cathd Ch Of The Adv Birmingham AL 2000-2005; S Jn's Epis Ch Carlisle PA 1995-2000. rnw51@yahoo.com

WILKINSON, Mark David (SVa) St. Aidan's Episc Church, 3201 Edinburgh Dr., Virginia Beach VA 23452 **R S Aid's Ch Virginia Bch VA 2007-** B Lakewood OH 8/21/1955 BA Kent St U 1976; BA Kent St U 1983; MDiv VTS 2004. D 6/12/2004 Bp Mark Hollingsworth Jr P 1/8/2005 Bp Gayle Elizabeth Harris. m 9/7/1974 Wendy Johns c 2. Cur The Ch Of The H Sprt Orleans MA 2004-2007. markwilk@verizon.net

WILLARD, Neil Alan (Minn) Church of St. Stephen the Martyr, 4439 West 50th Street, Edina MN 55424 **R S Steph The Mtyr Ch Minneapolis MN 2007-** B High Point NC 6/7/1970 s Clyde Cornelius Willard & Shirley Ann. BA Wake Forest U 1992; MDiv Yale DS 1995. D 6/29/1996 Bp Robert Carroll Johnson Jr P 6/29/1997 Bp Edward Lloyd Salmon Jr. m 10/11/2003 Carrie Danielle Klitzke c 2. Assoc Bruton Par Williamsburg VA 2001-2007; Cur All SS Ch Hilton Hd Island SC 1998-2001; The Epis Ch Of The Resurr Surfside Bch SC 1996-1998; Bp's Clerk Dio Virginia Richmond VA 1995-1996. Phi Beta Kappa. britishpoundsterling@yahoo.com

WILLARD JR, Wilson Howard (SO) 3827 Paxton Ave Apt 531, Cincinnati OH 45209 B Lochgelly WV 3/27/1937 s Wilson Howard Willard & Jessie Rosetta. BA Berea Coll 1959; STB GTS 1963. D 6/5/1963 P 12/18/1963 Bp Wilburn Camrock Campbell. m 6/16/2007 Geri Johnson Lewis c 3. Cn Dio Sthrn Ohio Cincinnati OH 1991-1998. Hon Cn Chr Ch Cathd Cincinnati OH 1993. wwillard@fuse.net

WILLARD-WILLIFORD, Joyce Ann (CFla) 5625 Holy Trinity Dr, Melbourne FL 32940 **H Trin Epis Acad Melbourne FL 2009-** B Memphis TN 3/2/1953 d Herald Glen Willard & Mary Earick. BA U of Florida 1974; BSN U of Florida 1976; MPA U of Cntrl Florida 1990; MDiv The TS at The U So 2009. D 5/30/2009 P 12/5/2009 Bp John Wadsworth Howe. m 12/28/1974 Mark Williford c 2. joy.williford@gmail.com

WILLCOX, Halley Luddy (At) 805 Mount Vernon Hwy Nw, Atlanta GA 30327 B Camden NJ 12/3/1952 d Edward Noel Luddy & Mary Ellen. BS U of Maryland 1975; MDiv Wesley TS 1980; DMin Andover-Newton TS 1984; Cert Boston Inst of Psych 1984. D 8/15/1981 Bp Morris Fairchild Arnold P 3/5/1982 Bp William Benjamin Spofford. m 7/3/2004 Robert Hamilton Strotz c 2. Ch Of Our Sav Charlottesville VA 2001-2003; Upper Sch Chapl H Innoc Ch Atlanta GA 1997-2000; H Innoc' Epis Sch Atlanta GA 1997-2000; Chapl Belmont Chap at S Mk's Sch Southborough MA 1989-1995; Assoc R S Mk's Ch Southborough MA 1989-1994; R S Paul's Epis Ch Hopkinton MA 1984-1989; Educ Assoc S Paul's Ch Natick MA 1981-1984. AAPC 1984. Halley1203@yahoo.com

WILLE, Elizabeth Suzanne (Chi) 50 South St, Warwick NY 10990 **Int Pstr Chr Ch Warwick NY 2011-; Advsry Bd, Epis New Yorker Dio New York New York City NY 2011-** B Pittsburgh PA 1/19/1970 d Richard Alan Wille & Elizabeth Marsh. AB Randolph-Macon Wmn's Coll 1992; MA Indiana U 1996; MDiv Ya Berk 2009. D 6/6/2009 Bp Jeffrey Dean Lee P 12/9/2009 Bp Catherine Scimeca Roskam. m Tracey E Lemon. Assoc R Chr Ch Warwick NY 2011; Asst P Chr Ch Warwick NY 2009-2011. Writer, "Sometimes Only the Flesh Will Do: Musing on the Faithful Use of Tech," *The Epis New Yorker*, Epis Dio New York, 2011; Writer, "Water is a Chr Issue," *The Epis New Yorker*, Epis Dio New York, 2011. E. Wm Muehl Prize in Preaching Ya Berk 2009; scl Randolph-Macon Wmn's Coll 1992. ESWILLE@HOTMAIL.COM

WILLEMS, James Rutherford (Los) 404 Franklin Dr, Ojai CA 93023 B Colorado CA 10/11/1944 s Everleigh Darward Willems & Miriam May. BA San Diego St U 1966; MDiv EDS 1984; MA Bos 1988. D 6/9/1984 P 4/17/1985 Bp William Edwin Swing. m 10/6/2002 Christina Fernandez. Cn To Ordnry Dio Rhode Island Providence RI 1988-1990; Dio Rhode Island Providence RI 1987-1988; Asst Calv Ch Providence RI 1986-1995; Assoc S Andr's Epis Ch Ojai CA 1985-2000; Dio California San Francisco CA 1984-1985; Asst S Jn's Epis Ch Westwood MA 1984-1985. Auth, "Meditation And Physical Pain," *Ariadnes Web*, 1998; Auth, "Mystery Of The Self," *Theosophist*, 1998; Auth, "The Harlequin Poems," Isthmus Press, 1976; Auth, "Opening The Cube (Poetry)," Tree Books, 1975. Mem Of Pen. Mem Pen Poets, Essayists, Novelists 1992. wzerocmf@earthlink.net

WILLERER, Rhonda Louise (Fla) Church of Our Saviour, 12236 Mandarin Road, Jacksonville FL 32223 **Assoc R Ch Of Our Sav Jacksonville FL 2008-** B Houston TX 3/6/1957 d James A Frost & Adella A. BSBA U of N. Florida

2001; MDiv STUSo 2007. D 5/27/2007 P 12/9/2007 Bp Samuel Johnson Howard. m 6/10/1978 Max Willerer c 2. Cur All SS Epis Ch Jacksonville FL 2007-2008. rwillerer.coos@bellsouth.net

WILLETS, John Walker (Chi) 120 Springbrook Rd, Jacksonville IL 62650 **D Dio Los Angeles Los Angeles CA 1992-** B Blue Mound IL 7/6/1941 s Carl Austin Willets & Norma Ann. BA Illinois Coll 1963; Med U IL 1976; PhD U IL 1978. D 6/27/1992 Bp Chester Lovelle Talton. Auth, "Change: A Theol Perspective," AED Monograph, 2009; Auth, "Lifelong Lrng is a Moral Imperative," AED Monograph, 2009; Auth, "D As Learner And Mentor For Today'S Ch," AED Monograph, 2005; Co-Auth, "Lifelong Lrng and Mnstry," AED Monograph, 2005. Assn of Epis Deacone 1992. Phi Delta Kappa U IL [Urbana-Champaign] 1978. john@willets.us

WILLETT, Patty (Dal) 4132 Southwestern Blvd., Dallas TX 75225 **Assoc for Pstr Care S Mich And All Ang Ch Dallas TX 2008-** B Charlotte NC 3/1/1954 d William Patterson & Betty Jane. BA Brenau U 1976; MDiv TS 2006. D 6/24/2006 P 1/24/2007 Bp Dorsey Felix Henderson. m 12/3/1977 Joseph Francis Willett c 3. Assoc Chr Ch Greenville SC 2006-2008. pwillett@saintmichael.org

WILLEY, Seaver Alston (SeFla) 4 Church St # 48, Saint Johnsbury VT 05819 B Minneapolis MN 1/23/1916 s Alston Jesse Willey & Lena. MDiv Ya Berk 1965. D 6/11/1964 Bp Harvey D Butterfield P 12/1/1964 Bp Walter H Gray. Dept Of Missions Dio NW Pennsylvania Erie PA 1970-1971; Yth Advsr Sum Conferences Dio NW Pennsylvania Erie PA 1968-1970; R S Clem's Epis Ch Hermitage PA 1967-1974; Dept Of Coll Wk Dio NW Pennsylvania Erie PA 1967-1970; Cur S Ptr's Epis Ch Milford CT 1965-1967; Asst S Mich's Ch Naugatuck CT 1964-1965.

WILLIAMS JR, A Lenwood (Miss) 9378 Harroway Rd, Summerville SC 29485 B Charleston SC 11/8/1940 s Arthur Lenwood Williams & Belva Marcella. BA Wofford Coll 1963; MDiv Epis TS In Kentucky 1982. D 6/5/1982 Bp Charles Gresham Marmion P 12/1/1982 Bp Duncan Montgomery Gray Jr. c 3. Vic S Timothys Epis Ch Southaven MS 1986-2002; Vic S Mary's Ch Lexington MS 1982-1986. frlenw@aol.com

WILLIAMS, Alfredo Ricardo (Dal) 1516 N Leland Ave, Indianapolis IN 46219 **Assoc S Barn Ch Garland TX 2011-** B 5/24/1944 s Alfredo R Williams & Servia Maria. LTh U Of Santo Domingo Santo Domingo Do 1981. Trans from La Iglesia Anglicana de Mex 1/1/2000. m 7/14/1995 Maria Williams c 3. Dio Dallas Dallas TX 2007-2010; P Chr Ch Cathd Indianapolis IN 2000-2007; Dio Cuernavaca 1997-2000; Iglesia Epis Del Ecuador Ecuador 1996-1997; Dio The Dominican Republic (Iglesia Epis Dominicana) Santo Domingo DO 1981-1995. alfredow_44@yahoo.com

WILLIAMS, Alton Paul (CPa) 5 Greenway Dr, Mechanicsburg PA 17055 **D Cathd Ch Of S Steph Harrisburg PA 1994-** B Leonard TX 11/24/1919 s George Silas Williams & Maude. D 6/7/1974 Bp Dean T Stevenson. m 7/24/1948 Frances A Scott c 2. Asst S Lk's Epis Ch Mechanicsburg PA 1974-1992.

WILLIAMS, Andrew Dodge (WMass) PO Box 447, Ware MA 01082 **S Mary's Epis Ch Thorndike MA 2007-; Trin Epis Ch Ware MA 2007-** B Fairfax VA 6/5/1980 s Harrison Williams & Priscilla Dodge. BA VMI 2003; MDiv VTS 2006. D 6/3/2006 Bp Peter James Lee P 1/20/2007 Bp Gordon Paul Scruton. m 5/5/2007 Jill Barton Williams c 1. Trin Ch Manassas VA 2006-2007. awilliams@trinityware.org

✠ **WILLIAMS JR, Rt Rev Arthur Benjamin** (O) 25530 Edgecliff Dr, Euclid OH 44132 **Dio Ohio Cleveland OH 2005-; Asstg Bp of Ohio Dio Ohio Cleveland OH 2005-; Ret Bp Suffr Of Ohio Dio Ohio Cleveland OH 2003-** B Providence RI 6/25/1935 s Arthur Benjamin Williams & Eleanor Enid. BA Br 1957; MDiv GTS 1964; MA U MI 1974. D 6/20/1964 P 3/27/1965 Bp John S Higgins Con 10/11/1986 for O. m 7/27/1985 Lynette R Rhodes. Bp Suffr of Ohio Dio Ohio Cleveland OH 1986-2002; Trst The GTS New York NY 1979-1988; Dep Gc Dio Ohio Cleveland OH 1979-1985; Archd Dio Ohio Cleveland OH 1977-1986; Archd Dio Ohio Cleveland OH 1977-1986; Asst To Bp, Mnstry Deploy & Urban Affrs Dio Michigan Detroit MI 1970-1977; Assoc Gr Ch Detroit MI 1968-1969; Dn Cathd Of S Jn Providence RI 1967-1968; Asst S Mk's Epis Ch Riverside RI 1965-1967; Clarence Horner Fell Gr Ch In Providence Providence RI 1964-1965. Chrmn Ed Com, "Lift Every Voice & Sing, II," Ch Hymnal Corp., 1993. EPF 1977; UBE 1967. DD GTS 1987. bishsuffret@aol.com

WILLIAMS, Arthur Glenn (NwPa) St Andrew's Episcopal Church, 102 E Cherry St, Clearfield PA 16830 **R S Andr's Ch Clearfield PA 2004-** B Curwensville PA 11/14/1940 s James Glenn Williams & Dorothy Jane. DC Palmer Coll of Chiropractic 1963. D 11/26/2005 P 6/7/2006 Bp Robert Deane Rowley Jr. kiva@pennswoods.net

WILLIAMS, Arthur Wordsworth Lonfellow (NY) 3412 103rd St, Corona NY 11368 B 8/20/1928 s Cyril Hudson Luice Williams & Hilda Juliana. SWTS 1975; MDiv The Interdenominational Theol Cntr 1978. D 6/10/1989 Bp Paul Moore Jr. c 1. S Phil's Ch New York NY 1991-1994.

WILLIAMS JR, Brevard Springs (RG) 157 Hillcrest Dr, Florence MA 01062 **Died 7/1/2010** B Atlanta GA 4/28/1931 s Brevard Springs Williams & Lucille. BA U So 1953; BD STUSo 1958. D 6/21/1958 Bp Robert E Gribbin P 12/1/1958 Bp Randolph R Claiborne. c 2. brevard@aol.com

WILLIAMS, Bruce McKennie (RG) 7201 San Benito St Nw, Albuquerque NM 87120 B Pittsfield MA 5/28/1930 s Lester Alvin Williams & Ethel May. Mus B Peabody Conservatory Of Mus 1953; GO AGO 1956; MM Peabody Conservatory Of Mus 1956; STB GTS 1960; LIU 1970; PhD Pacific Wstrn U Long Bch 1983. D 6/22/1960 Bp Robert McConnell Hatch P 12/17/1960 Bp Horace W B Donegan. m 9/24/1955 Charlotte Ellen Lee c 2. Ecum Off Dio The Rio Grande Albuquerque NM 1990-1996; Cn S Jn's Cathd Albuquerque NM 1990-1993; Asst To Dn S Jn's Cathd Albuquerque NM 1986-1990; R S Phil's Ch Brooklyn NY 1980-1986; Asst Cathd Of St Jn The Div New York NY 1960-1962. Auth, "Adv;Christmas;Lent;Passion;Easter(Three);Pentecost;Patriotic Occasions;Healing;The Ch Year," *The Ix Lessons (Printed Separately)*, 2000; Auth, "Pstr Care Of Drug Abusers," Priv Printing, 1983. AGO 1946; AAM 1988; Assn Of Dioc Liturgies And Musicians Com 1981-2001; Bd Dir, The Sprtl Renwl Cntr:Albuquerque 2007; EDEO 1996-2000; Exec Bd,AGO; Albuquerque 1987-2005. Fifty Year Cert AGO 1993; Assoc AGO 1956.

WILLIAMS, Carla Jean (NwPa) St Andrew's Episcopal Church, 102 E Cherry St, Clearfield PA 16830 **Died 10/12/2010** B Curwensville PA 10/5/1941 d William H Rishel & Edith Irene. RN Indiana Hosp Sch of Nrsng 1962. D 11/26/2005 P 6/7/2006 Bp Robert Deane Rowley Jr. kiva@pennswoods.net

WILLIAMS, Carolynne Juanita Grant (At) 2088 Cloverdale Dr Se, Atlanta GA 30316 **Cn Asst. - Pstr Care Cathd Of S Phil Atlanta GA 1999-** B Albany GA 8/31/1948 d Edward James Grant & Rubye. BA Spelman Coll 1969; MDiv The Interdenominational Theol Cntr 1995. D 7/31/1999 P 2/5/2000 Bp Frank Kellogg Allan. m 11/24/1971 Perry Edwin Williams c 2.

WILLIAMS, C(ecil) David (Nwk) 515 Parker St, Newark NJ 07104 B Valhalla NY 5/3/1942 s Cecil Lee Williams & Colithia Elizabeth. Cntrl Coll; DD Chr TS; BA SUNY 1991; GTF 1994; DMin GTF 1998. D 12/14/1974 Bp James Stuart Wetmore P 12/20/1975 Bp Harold Louis Wright. Trin And S Phil's Cathd Newark NJ 2000-2008; R S Geo's Ch Brooklyn NY 1984-2000; Epis Mssn Soc New York NY 1981-1984; Epis Mssn Soc New York NY 1981-1984; The Ch of S Matt And S Tim New York NY 1975-1979. Auth, "Adversary," 1986.

WILLIAMS, Charles James (Md) P.O. Box 327, Frostburg MD 21532 B Mt Savage MD 3/16/1932 s Charles Walter Robinson & Pauline. BSEd Frostburg St U 1954; MEd Frostburg St U 1963. D 7/6/2008 P 2/14/2009 Bp John Leslie Rabb. c 3. cjwms@atlanticbb.net

WILLIAMS, Colin Harrington (CNY) 2850 SW Scenic Drive, Portland OR 97225 **Assoc Epis Par Of S Jn The Bapt Portland OR 2005-** B Fayetteville NC 3/23/1970 s William Edward Williams & Angeline. Ya Berk; BA Cor 1992; MDiv Yale DS 1995; MBA UNC Chap Hill 2004. D 11/11/1995 P 10/26/1996 Bp David B(ruce) Joslin. m 9/5/2004 Lindsey Woodley c 1. Cur Calv Ch Pittsburgh PA 1997-2001; Cur Ch Of The Resurr Oswego NY 1996-1997; Asst Chr Ch Clayton NY 1995; Asst St Jn's Ch Clayton NY 1995. colinoregon@yahoo.com

WILLIAMS, Courtlyn G (Ore) 1465 Coburg Rd, Eugene OR 97401 **S Thos' Epis Ch Eugene OR 2009-** B Bellingham WA 3/16/1963 s Maurice C Williams & Virginia M. BSGS NWU 2005; MDiv SWTS 2008. D 6/7/2008 P 12/6/2008 Bp Jeffrey Dean Lee. m 8/6/1988 Julie DeGraff c 3. Assoc The Epis Ch Of S Jas The Less Northfield IL 2008-2009. court@stjamestheless.org

WILLIAMS, David Alexander (EC) 115 NE 66th Street, Oak Island NC 28645 B Indianapolis IN 11/3/1936 s Wayne Veron Williams & Sarah Lucretia. AA Prince Geo Cmnty Coll 1976; BS Appalachian St U 1980; MDiv VTS 1984. D 12/18/1982 P 4/30/1985 Bp William Gillette Weinhauer. m 10/7/1961 Henrietta Rhodes Smith c 2. S Jas Epis Ch Lenoir NC 1999-2000; Vic S Jas Ch New Castle IN 1989-1998; Vic & P-in-c The Sav Epis Ch Newland NC 1989-1998; R S Eliz's Ch Roanoke VA 1986-1987; D Ch Of The H Cross Valle Crucis NC 1982-1985. vicarhaven@yahoo.com

WILLIAMS, David Anthony (SC) St. Stephen's Episcopal Church, 67 Anson St, Charleston SC 29401 **S Steph's Epis Ch Charleston SC 2004-** B Philadelphia PA 7/13/1945 s Percy Williams & Clementine. BA Desales U Allentown PA 1969; MDiv EDS 1972; DMin Andover Newton TS 1973. D 7/24/1972 P 1/13/1973 Bp Robert Lionne DeWitt. m 10/24/1970 Linda Williams. Assoc R S Jn's Ch Georgetown Par Washington DC 1999-2004; S Jn's Ch Georgetown Par Washington DC 1973-1978; Sr. Asst Min S Jn's Ch Lafayette Sq Washington DC 1973-1978. "Proper Reaction To Epis Ch Changes Is Real Challenge," Post & Courier Of So Carolina, 2005; "Assorted arts," Jubilate Deo (Dio So Carolina), 2004. Dplma AAPC. david9612@aol.com

WILLIAMS, David R (NC) 1406 Victoria Ct, Elon NC 27244 B Wilmington DE 11/13/1945 s John Randolph Williams & Frances Stubblefield. BA Roa 1968; MDiv VTS 1972. D 6/5/1972 P 4/15/1973 Bp Wilburn Camrock Campbell. m 2/4/1977 Sarah Williams c 4. R Ch Of The H Comf Burlington NC 1985-2010; Imm Ch-On-The-Hill Alexandria VA 1982-1985; Ch Of The Epiph Cape Coral FL 1981-1982; Chr Epis Ch Winchester VA 1974-1978; Vic Chr Memi Ch Williamstown WV 1972-1974. davidwilliams@triad.rr.com

WILLIAMS, Donald B (Kan) 9165 West 102nd Terrace, Overland Park KS 66212 B Oakland CA 10/25/1934 s Alan Baird Williams & Martha Virginia. BS Cntrl Missouri St U 1974; MS Cntrl Missouri St U 1975; EDS Cntrl Missouri St U 1977. D 1/18/2003 Bp William Edward Smalley. m 6/9/1958 Patricia Ann Markham c 2. D Ch Of The Gd Shpd Kansas City MO 2003-2006. dbw@kc.rr.com

WILLIAMS, Douglas Elliott (ECR) 1718 Crater Lake Ave, Milpitas CA 95035 B San Bernardino CA 10/9/1938 s Keith Sydney Williams & Elizabeth Donly. BA U CA 1960; GOE Ripon Coll Cuddesdon 1962; GTS 1963; U of Redlands 1967. D 9/5/1963 P 3/1/1964 Bp Francis E I Bloy. m 10/25/1963 Helen Margaret Grayston c 2. Trin Cathd San Jose CA 1995-2000; Asst Trin Cathd San Jose CA 1982-1993; Asst Ch Of S Jos Milpitas CA 1980-1981; LocTen S Lk's Ch Jolon CA 1973-1974; LocTen S Mk's Ch KING CITY CA 1973-1974; LocTen S Matt's Ch San Ardo CA 1973-1974; Asst S Lk's Ch Los Gatos CA 1971-1980; Asst S Edw The Confessor Epis Ch San Jose CA 1970-1971; Asst Ch Of S Jos Milpitas CA 1969-1970; Asst S Phil's Ch San Jose CA 1968-1969; Cur Trin Epis Ch Redlands CA 1966-1967; Vic S Andr's By The Lake Temecula CA 1963-1964. canonwms@ix.netcom.com

WILLIAMS, Douglas Maclin (Colo) 28 Cunningham Pond Rd, Peterborough NH 03458 B Springfield MA 9/14/1934 s Ralph Coplestone Williams & Corilla Green. BA Amh 1956; MDiv VTS 1960; CG Jung Inst 1981. D 6/25/1960 P 1/1/1961 Bp Robert McConnell Hatch. m 9/20/1987 Joy Jacobs c 2. Logos Colorado Sprg CO 1967-1977; Cur S Steph's Ch Pittsfield MA 1960-1964. dwilliam@worldpath.net

WILLIAMS, Edward Earl (NY) No address on file. B 6/19/1943 D 5/26/1973 P 5/18/1975 Bp Addison Hosea. All Souls Ch New York NY 1975-1976.

WILLIAMS, Edward S (Ga) 353 Midway Circ, Brunswick GA 31523 **D S Mk's Ch Brunswick GA 2000-** B Wilmington DE 5/28/1932 s Edward Satterfield Williams & Kathleen. Washington Coll 1953; EFM STUSo 1999. D 1/14/2000 Bp Henry Irving Louttit. m 11/23/1980 Barbara S Harrell c 1.

WILLIAMS, Eric Matthew (WNY) 410 North Main Street, Jamestown NY 14701 **R S Lk's Epis Ch Jamestown NY 2000-** B Los Angeles CA 1/24/1965 s Kenneth Owen Williams & Sally. BA Wms 1986; MDiv GTS 1992. D 6/13/1992 P 12/19/1992 Bp Andrew Frederick Wissemann. m 10/8/1994 Susan Anslow Williams c 2. Vic Ch Of The H Comm Lakeview NY 1994-1999; P-t Asst S Paul's Cathd Buffalo NY 1994-1995; Cur S Steph's Ch Pittsfield MA 1992-1994. revemw@gmail.com

WILLIAMS JR, Ernest Franklin (Los) 1438 Coronado Ter, Los Angeles CA 90026 **The Gooden Cntr Pasadena CA 1992-; Exec Dir Of The Bp Gooden Hm Dio Los Angeles Los Angeles CA 1991-** B Pelham GA 1/10/1948 s Ernest Franklin Williams & Irene. BBA Georgia St U 1971; MDiv GTS 1988; MBA Amer Jewish U 2004. D 6/25/1988 P 6/1/1989 Bp Frederick Houk Borsch. Assoc S Fran' Par Palos Verdes Estates CA 1989-1991; Bp's Chapl Dio Los Angeles Los Angeles CA 1988-1989; Chapl To Bp Of Los Angeles Dio Los Angeles Los Angeles CA 1988-1989. Soc Of S Paul. soberbud@gmail.com

WILLIAMS, Forrest James (Az) 1851 E Morten Ave Apt 153, Phoenix AZ 85020 **Died 2/17/2011** B Lima OH 5/19/1928 s Forrest O Williams & Mary Evelyn. BA Ohio Nthrn U 1953; MDiv Epis TS In Kentucky 1964; MA S Fran Coll Loretto PA 1968. D 5/30/1964 Bp William R Moody P 3/1/1965 Bp John Henry Esquirol. c 4. Auth, "Journey To Awareness & Meditation - The Wrld Within ,"; Auth, "Yoga Jyoti (Light Of Yoga) Quarterly".

WILLIAMS, Francis Edward (RG) 3714 N Highway 28 Trlr 33, Las Cruces NM 88005 **Asst S Jas' Epis Ch Mesilla Pk NM 2006-** B Omaha NE 11/29/1926 s Leslie Frasier Williams & Lucy. BA Harv 1947; BD Nash 1951; BA Hebr Un Coll 1953; STM Nash 1954; PhD Oxf 1954; PhD Oxf 1961. D 4/10/1951 P 10/12/1951 Bp Benjamin F P Ivins. m 9/18/1954 Charlotte Condia c 3. Assoc S Lk's Epis Ch Anth NM 1992-1998; Asst All SS Epis Ch El Paso TX 1988-1990; Chapl Dio The Rio Grande Albuquerque NM 1976-1986; Sch Hdmstr S Paul's Epis Ch Visalia CA 1971-1974; R Epis Ch Of S Anne Stockton CA 1969-1971; P S Andr's Ch Milwaukee WI 1955-1956. Auth, "Panarion of Epiphanius of Salamis," *Bk 1 Revised and Expanded*, Brill, 2008; Auth, *Mntl Perception: A Commentary on NHC VI*, Brill, 2001; Auth, "Panarion of Epiphanius of Salamis," *Bk II and III*, Brill, 1994; Auth, "Panarion of Epiphanius of Salamis," *Bk I*, Brill, 1988. Inst For Antiquity and Chrsnty 1963; SBL 1953. fwilliams2@aol.com

WILLIAMS, Gary Wayne (Okla) 3804 Cobble Cir, Norman OK 73072 B Norman OK 3/4/1933 s Wayne W Williams & Willie Jo. BBA U of Oklahoma 1958. D 6/17/1966 Bp Chilton Powell. m 6/14/1957 Deborah L Robinson c 2. Asst S Jn's Ch Norman OK 1989-2000; Asst S Mich's Epis Ch Norman OK 1979-1983; Asst S Jn's Ch Norman OK 1968-1974; Asst All Souls Epis Ch Oklahoma City OK 1967-1968.

WILLIAMS, Glenn Thomas (ND) 3613 River Dr S, Fargo ND 58104 **Asst Geth Cathd Fargo ND 2003-** B Minneapolis MN 12/17/1948 s Milton T Williams & Judy N. BS U of No Dakota 1970. D 5/10/2002 P 5/9/2003 Bp Andrew Hedtler Fairfield. m 3/13/1971 Jane Arman c 3. duffywilliams@cableone.net

WILLIAMS, Glen Parker (WMich) 3975 Blue Heights Dr, Traverse City MI 49686 B Woodbridge NJ 4/24/1925 s Carl Stuart Williams & Emilie Judd. BA Hob 1949; MA U of Pennsylvania 1950; ThM PDS 1953; MA Wstrn Michigan U 1971. D 4/25/1953 P 10/1/1953 Bp Wallace J Gardner. m 9/11/1948 Dorothy Mary Tongue c 4. R Ch Of Our Merc Sav Penns Grove NJ 1955-1959; R S Mk's Ch Hammonton NJ 1953-1955; Asst S Ptr's Ch Medford NJ 1953-1955. glenwilliams08@charter.net

WILLIAMS, Henrietta Rhodes Smith (Ind) 115 Ne 66th St, Oak Island NC 28465 **D S Phil's Ch Southport NC 2006-; D Dio E Carolina Kinston NC 2004-; D S Mary Of The Hills Epis Par Blowing Rock NC 1999-; D Dio Indianapolis Indianapolis IN 1993-** B Windsor NC 5/25/1940 d William Speller Smith & Margaret Elizabeth. AA Prince Geo Cmnty Coll 1974; BA Bowie St U 1976; MA VTS 1978. D 6/24/1993 Bp Edward Witker Jones. m 10/7/1961 David Alexander Williams. D S Jas Ch New Castle IN 1993-1999. evew99@yahoo.com

WILLIAMS, Henry Neil (Pa) 1029 Fox Hollow Rd, Shermans Dale PA 17090 B Palmerton PA 7/22/1936 s Henry Grey Williams & Myrtle Elizabeth. Cert PDS; BA Muhlenberg Coll 1958; BD Luth TS 1961; ThM PrTS 1970. D 6/24/1962 P 12/21/1962 Bp Oliver J Hart. m 8/13/1960 Belva Anne Elliston c 2. Vic All SS Epis Ch Fallsington PA 1965-1968; Cur S Paul's Ch Philadelphia PA 1962-1965. fritz@pa.net

WILLIAMS JR, Hollis R (Oly) 2600 2nd Ave Apt 707, Seattle WA 98121 B Fort Worth TX 11/13/1938 s Hollis R Williams & Hildreth Helen. BA Hendrix Coll 1961; MDiv Duke 1964; CAS STUSo 1966. D 6/29/1966 P 4/17/1967 Bp Robert Raymond Brown. m 2/3/1968 Katherine B Brown c 2. Int S Paul Epis Ch Bellingham WA 2001-2002; Int S Steph's Epis Ch Longview WA 1999-2000; Bd Dir Dio Olympia Seattle WA 1994-1998; Stnd Com Dio Olympia Seattle WA 1988-1991; Trin Epis Ch Everett WA 1985-1999; ExCoun Dio Louisiana Baton Rouge LA 1981-1985; Assoc Epis Ch Of The Gd Shpd Lake Chas LA 1980-1985; R S Phil's Ch Jackson MS 1974-1980; Chair Liturg Com Dio Mississippi Jackson MS 1972-1980; R Trin Ch Yazoo City MS 1970-1974; Vic S Steph's Epis Ch Jacksonville AR 1966-1970. Auth, *A Partnership of Trust*, Alb, 1999; Auth, "Cler and Laity in Parntership for Mutual Mnstry," *Congregations*, Alb, 1998; Auth, "Leading a Cong Today," *Congregations*, Alb, 1995. hollis707@msn.com

WILLIAMS, Howard Kently (LI) 1102 E 73rd St Apt C, Brooklyn NY 11234 **Int S Aug's Epis Ch Brooklyn NY 1999-** B Kingston JM 2/23/1951 s Clement Roy Williams & Florence May. Cert Untd Theol Coll of the W Indies Kingston JM 1974; LTh U of The W Indies 1974; MA PrTS 1983; DMin GTF 2007. Trans from Church in the Province Of The West Indies 10/28/1984 as Priest Bp C(hristopher) FitzSimons Allison. c 2. Coordntr Epis Ch Cntr New York NY 1988-1996; R S Lk's Epis Ch Columbia SC 1986-1988; Voorhees Coll Denmark SC 1984-1985. Co-Ed, "Fashion Me A People"; Co-Auth, "Blood Thicker Than Water". Rel Educational Assn of the Untd States of Ameri; UBE. hkentlyw@me.com

WILLIAMS III, Hugh Elton (CFla) Po Box 91777, Lakeland FL 33804 **S Alb's Epis Ch Auburndale FL 2008-** B Tallahassee FL 9/2/1946 s Hugh Williams & E Marie. BS Florida St U 1970; MDiv VTS 1977. D 6/12/1977 P 12/1/1977 Bp Frank Stanley Cerveny. m 1/12/1974 Frances Elizabeth Harrison c 2. Epis Ch Of The Ascen Orlando FL 2002-2003; S Alb's Epis Ch Auburndale FL 2001-2002; Bud Williams Mnstrs Lakeland FL 1995; R Chr The King Ch Lakeland FL 1991-1994; Vic Chr The King Ch Lakeland FL 1984-1990; All SS Epis Ch Lakeland FL 1981-1985; Asst S Mk's Epis Ch Jacksonville FL 1977-1981. Auth, "Fire In The Wax Museum," Destiny Image, 1999. joelsplace@aol.com

✠ WILLIAMS JR, Rt Rev Huntington (NC) 2410 Roswell Ave Apt 104, Charlotte NC 28209 **Ret Bp Suffr of No Carolina Dio No Carolina Raleigh NC 1996-** B Albany NY 10/27/1925 s Huntington Williams & Mary Camilla. BA Harv 1949; MDiv VTS 1952. D 1/1/1953 P 6/1/1953 Bp Noble C Powell Con 4/28/1990 for NC. m 6/18/1949 Mary Britton c 4. Bp Dio No Carolina Raleigh NC 1990-1995; Stndg Com Dio No Carolina Raleigh NC 1986-1989; Com on Const and Cn Dio No Carolina Raleigh NC 1974-1990; Stndg Com Dio No Carolina Raleigh NC 1969-1977; Com on Const and Cn Dio No Carolina Raleigh NC 1967-1968; R S Ptr's Epis Ch Charlotte NC 1963-1990; Dioc Coun Dio No Carolina Raleigh NC 1963-1967; Chair, Dept of Institutions Dio No Carolina Raleigh NC 1963-1965; R S Tim's Epis Ch Winston Salem NC 1956-1963; Asst Calv and St Geo New York NY 1954-1956; Cur S Thos' Ch Garrison Forest Owings Mills MD 1952-1954. DD VTS 1991; Fllshp Coll of Preachers 1962. mbrit27@bellsouth.net

WILLIAMS, Jacqueline Miller (SO) 6461 Tylersville Rd, West Chester OH 45069 B Lancaster OH 3/24/1943 d Clarence Ellsworth Miller & Helen Marie. Cert Ord Acad for the Diac 2008. D 6/14/2008 Bp Thomas Edward Breidenthal. m 2/1/1964 Thomas Howard Williams c 2. jackiewilliams@fuse.net

WILLIAMS, James Armstrong (Tex) 11403 Madrid Dr, Austin TX 78759 B Port Arthur TX 1/12/1935 s Theodore Roger Williams & Bolena. BA Lamar U 1957; BD CRDS 1964; MS U of Texas 1975; Epis TS of The SW 1988. D 3/14/1988 Bp Anselmo Carral-Solar P 8/28/1988 Bp Gordon Taliaferro

Charlton. m 2/9/1957 Barbara Ellen Dalton c 3. Vic S Ptr's Epis Ch Lago Vista TX 1996-2003; Int All SS Epis Ch Austin TX 1995-1996; Asst S Matt's Ch Austin TX 1990-1995; Int S Mich's Ch Austin TX 1989-1990; Asst R S Geo's Ch Austin TX 1988-1989. Lifetime Achievement Awd Nasw-Austin/Travis Co. Ch. 1996. bewilliams@mail.utexas.edu

WILLIAMS II, James Edward (Los) 580 Hilgard Ave, Los Angeles CA 90024 B Saint Louis MO 3/29/1945 s Joseph V Journeay & Marguerite E. BA U CA 1968; MDiv CDSP 1971; Journalism Stds/Grad Stds On Educ Admin 1975. D 6/24/1972 P 2/1/1973 Bp C Kilmer Myers. R S Jn's Memi Ch Ramsey NJ 2001-2005; S Martha's Epis Ch W Covina CA 1996-2001; S Alb's Epis Ch Los Angeles CA 1989-1995; Assoc R S Mk's Par Glendale CA 1987-1989; Dio California San Francisco CA 1978-2005; Asst R S Clem's Ch Berkeley CA 1976-1987; Cur S Paul's Ch Oakland CA 1972-1975. Sigma Delta Chi 1968; Mem Usn Inst 68; Mem 68 San Francisco Press Club. USPOLO@MSN.COM

WILLIAMS, James Wallace (Ala) 2130 Enon Mill Dr Sw, Atlanta GA 30331 B Huntington NY 4/1/1948 s David J Williams & Marguerite. BA Lynchburg Coll; MDiv S Lk Sem. D 6/3/1974 P 12/1/1974 Bp Furman Stough. Gr Ch Birmingham AL 2004-2006; R Ch Of The Incarn Atlanta GA 1999-2004; Asst Emm Epis Ch Athens GA 1995-1998; R Ch Of The Mssh Heflin AL 1992-1995; Vic S Lk's Ch Remington VA 1987-1992; Dio Alabama Birmingham AL 1976-1977; Assoc Min Trin Epis Ch Florence AL 1974-1976. Auth, "Meeting Him To Find Me"; Auth, "How To Cut Medicare Cost"; Auth, "Money," *Priests & The Bed Of Academe*; Auth, "Recruit Or Retreat," *Pub Or Perish*.

WILLIAMS, Jeremiah Tilghman (Ind) 1060 Amsterdam Ave., Apt. 924, New York NY 10025 B Bedford IN 7/24/1935 s Perry Howard Williams & Bonnie Evelyn. BA DePauw U 1957; M.Div. Epis TS of The SW 1961. D 6/24/1961 P 3/1/1962 Bp John P Craine. c 2. Asst S Paul's Ch Morrisania Bronx NY 1992-2007; Chair On The Yth Div Dio Indianapolis Indianapolis IN 1961-1964; Cur S Paul's Epis Ch Indianapolis IN 1961-1964. EPF 1964-1975; OHC (Assoc) 1969-1971; Third OSF 1971-1998.

WILLIAMS JR, (Jerre) Stockton (WTex) 320 Saint Peter St, Kerrville TX 78028 **R S Ptr's Epis Ch Kerrville TX 2002-** B Austin TX 9/9/1951 s Jerre Stockton Williams & Mary Pearl. BA, cl Amh 1973; JD U of Texas 1976; MDiv, w hon VTS 1986. D 6/24/1986 Bp Maurice Manuel Benitez P 2/24/1987 Bp Anselmo Carral-Solar. m 12/30/1978 Leslie Miller c 2. R Ch Of The H Trin Midland TX 1994-2001; S Mary's Epis Ch Cypress TX 1989-1994; Asst S Paul's Ch Waco TX 1986-1989. Auth, "The Tractarian Deviation on the Episcopacy," *Ch Div 86*. OSL the Physcn 2003. accounting@stpeterskerrville.com

WILLIAMS, Jeryln Ann (Me) 431 Sweden St, Caribou ME 04736 **D Aroostook Epis Cluster Caribou ME 2006-** B Erie PA 7/25/1945 d William E Talkington & Ella Ruth. No Cntrl Coll; BS Indiana U 1983. D 8/5/2006 Bp Chilton Abbie Richardson Knudsen. m 2/7/1968 Gary Williams c 4. jeriwilliams431@yahoo.com

WILLIAMS, Jill Barton (WMass) St Francis, 70 Highland St, Holden MA 01520 **Assoc S Fran Ch Holden MA 2008-; Dio Wstrn Massachusetts Springfield MA 2007-** B Worcester MA 4/4/1981 d Bruce Barton & Holly. BA Florida Sthrn Coll 2003; MDiv VTS 2007. D 6/2/2007 P 1/26/2008 Bp Gordon Paul Scruton. m 5/5/2007 Andrew Dodge Williams. jwilliams@diocesewma.org

WILLIAMS II, John F (U) 9997 Aplomado Cir, Sandy UT 84092 **Coun Cong Funding Com Dio Utah Salt Lake City UT 2010-; Dioc Coun Dio Utah Salt Lake City UT 2009-; Dioc Coun Exec Com Dio Utah Salt Lake City UT 2009-; R S Jas Epis Ch Midvale UT 2008-** B Champaign IL 8/1/1961 s Thomas Joseph Williams & Marlene C. AAS Cmnty Coll of the AF Macomb GA 1989; BA Wstrn Illinois U 1999; MDiv CDSP 2002. D 6/22/2002 Bp Richard Lester Shimpfky P 1/8/2003 Bp David Conner Bane Jr. m 8/1/1998 Margie B Sapp c 1. Fin and Bdgt Com Dio Utah Salt Lake City UT 2009-2011; Sum Yth Camp Dir Dio Pennsylvania Philadelphia PA 2008; Assoc P Philadelphia Cathd Philadelphia PA 2008; Bdgt Com Dio Pennsylvania Philadelphia PA 2006-2008; Dioc Coun Exec Com Dio Pennsylvania Philadelphia PA 2006-2008; Dioc Coun Dio Pennsylvania Philadelphia PA 2005-2008; Fin Com Dio Pennsylvania Philadelphia PA 2005-2008; R S Steph's Epis Ch Clifton Heights PA 2003-2008; Exec Com Dio Sthrn Virginia Norfolk VA 2002-2003; Assoc R Old Donation Ch Virginia Bch VA 2002-2003; Yth Min All SS Ch Carmel CA 1996-1999. OHC 2009. revjohnwilliams@q.com

WILLIAMS, John Gerald (Tex) 1101 Rock Prairie Rd, College Station TX 77845 **R S Fran Epis Ch Coll Sta TX 2005-** B Texas City TX 8/16/1949 s John B Williams & Juanita Georgia. BA U of No Texas 1971; MA U of No Texas 1973; Texas A&M U 1978; MDiv Epis TS of The SW 1990. D 6/16/1990 Bp Maurice Manuel Benitez P 1/7/1991 Bp William Elwood Sterling. m 5/24/1975 Rita Ragsdale c 2. R S Mich's Ch La Marque TX 1999-2004; Chapl St Lk's Epis Hosp Houston TX 1997-1999; R S Jas The Apos Epis Ch Conroe TX 1995-1997; R S Jn's Epis Ch Silsbee TX 1990-1995. frjohn.williams@gmail.com

WILLIAMS, Joseph Anthony (CNY) 11 Gillette Ln, Cazenovia NY 13035 B Rome NY 5/11/1930 s Leonard Guglielmo & Beatrice Marie. MDiv PDS; BS SUNY. D 5/21/1968 Bp Ned Cole P 1/1/1969 Bp Walter M Higley. m 6/3/1957 Ruth Joyce Roberts. R S Paul's Ch Chittenango NY 1984-1997; Gr Epis Ch Waterville NY 1975-1982.

WILLIAMS, Joseph David (NwT) 1105 1/2 Madison St, Borger TX 79007 B Galena Park TX 12/3/1947 s Melvin Williams & Ann. AA Frank Phillips Jr Coll 2002. D 9/30/2006 P 3/1/2007 Bp C(harles) Wallis Ohl. m 6/23/1984 Rinica N Williams c 1. rhyno@cableone.net

WILLIAMS, Josie Marie (Miss) 5930 Warriors Trl, Vicksburg MS 39180 B Vicksburg MS 9/7/1954 d William Washington & Malinda. BS U of Sthrn Mississippi 1972; MS U of Sthrn Mississippi 1976; AAA Mississippi Dept of Educ 1980. D 1/15/2011 Bp Duncan Montgomery Gray III. m 7/9/1977 Theo Williams c 1. josiew48@yahoo.com

WILLIAMS, Larry C (At) Po Box 1117, Hot Springs AR 71902 **S Teresa Acworth GA 2009-** B Inyokern CA 5/27/1950 s Clarence Wilbert Williams & Mary Helen. BA U So 1972; MDiv Nash 1975; Grad Ldrshp 1980. D 1/25/1975 P 10/1/1975 Bp (George) Paul Reeves. m 1/22/1983 Deborah Price c 3. R S Lk's Ch Hot Sprg AR 1998-2006; R S Lk's Ch Hot Sprg AR 1998; Cn S Mk's Cathd Shreveport LA 1990-1998; R The Epis Ch Of The Medtr Meridian MS 1984-1990; R S Thos Ch Greenville AL 1981-1984; Cur S Lk's Epis Ch Mobile AL 1978-1981; Asst S Paul's Ch Augusta GA 1975-1978. Soc Of S Jn The Evang. Outstanding Young Men Amer 1982. lcw527@aol.com

WILLIAMS, Laurens Ray (FtW) 736 Bluebonnet Dr, Hurst TX 76053 **Died 8/21/2009** B Dallas,TX 8/7/1930 s Ray Williams & Leola. U Of Dallas Dallas 1958; Ya Berk 1961. D 6/1/1961 Bp Charles A Mason P 12/31/1967 Bp J(ohn) Joseph Meakins Harte. CBS; Iccm; Ord Of S Ben; Our Lady Of Walsingham; Pa; SSC. Outstanding Young Men Amer 1982. laurenswilliams@charter.net

WILLIAMS, Lloyd Clyde (Ind) 3163 Homestead Commons Dr, Ann Arbor MI 48108 B Tuskegee Inst AL 7/6/1947 s Theodore S Williams & Charlotte C. BA Earlham Coll 1969; MS Sthrn Connecticut St U 1971; MDiv Yale DS 1971; DMin Chr TS 1974. D 6/11/1971 P 12/1/1971 Bp John P Craine. m 12/27/1968 Gloria Jean Vaughn c 1. S Phil's Ch Indianapolis IN 1974-1976.

WILLIAMS, Lorna Hyacinth (Mich) 1224 West Chester Pike, Apt C11, West Chester PA 19382 **The Ch Of The H Trin W Chester PA 2011-** B Kingston 8/10/1969 d Linville Williams & Hazel Hyacinth. BS SUNY 1992; PrTS 1994; MDiv SWTS 1997. D 6/20/1998 Bp Chilton Abbie Richardson Knudsen P 1/1/1999 Bp David Charles Bowman. Cn S Jn's Cathd Jacksonville FL 2010-2011; Asst Trin Ch In The City Of Boston Boston MA 2009-2010; Sr Assoc S Andr's Ch Ann Arbor MI 2000-2008; Chapl Dio Wstrn New York Tonawanda NY 1999-2000; Cn S Paul's Cathd Buffalo NY 1998-2000. "Liturg Prayers," *Race and Pryr*, Morehouse, 2003; Auth, "Commemorative Collects," *Wmn Uncommon Prayers*, Morehouse, 2000; Auth, "A Pryr for Healing," *Wmn Uncommon Prayers*, Morehouse, 2000; Auth, "A Safe Place," *Angl Dig*, 1999; Auth, "The Power of Personal Witness," *Journ of Wmn Mnstrs*, 1999. CHS 1995. lw1997@yahoo.com

WILLIAMS, Margaret Mary Oetjen (Tex) 18319 Otter Creek Trl, Humble TX 77346 B Beacon NY 6/16/1942 d Robert Adrian Oetjen & Dorothy Mae. BS U of Maryland 1969; STUSo 1986; MS Neumann Coll Aston PA 1987; Cert Luth TS at Gettysburg 1992; CAS GTS 1994. D 6/20/1987 P 10/22/1994 Bp Allen Lyman Bartlett Jr. m 6/26/1966 William Kinsey Williams c 3. R Chr The King Epis Ch Humble TX 2005-2009; Memi Ch Of S Lk Philadelphia PA 1998-2003; Asst Ch Of The Mssh Lower Gwynedd PA 1994-1997; DCE/Pstr Asst The Epis Ch Of The Adv Kennett Sq PA 1987-1992. mwilliams616@comcast.net

WILLIAMS, Marianne Rockett (Ala) 1152 Fairmont Ln, Auburn AL 36830 **D H Trin Epis Ch Auburn AL 2002-** B Tulsa OK 3/12/1930 d Carson Horace Rockett & Lucille. MDiv STUSo; BA U of Memphis. D 10/28/2000 Bp James Malone Coleman. c 3. D Calv Ch Memphis TN 2001-2002; D Chr Ch Brownsville TN 2000-2001. mwilli1334@aol.com

WILLIAMS, Mary Grace (Ct) 36 New Canaan Road, Wilton CT 06897 **R S Matt's Epis Ch Wilton CT 2002-** B Kansas City MO 5/1/1954 d Ewing Francis Williams & Dona. BA Rutgers-The St U 1976; MA Ford 1980; MDiv Ya Berk 1988. D 10/9/1988 Bp Paul Moore Jr P 4/9/1989 Bp Arthur Anton Vogel. c 2. R The Ch Of S Jn The Evang Flossmoor IL 1995-2002; Assoc R S Ptr's Epis Ch Kansas City MO 1991-1995. magrwi@aol.com

WILLIAMS, Melody Sue (SO) 60 S. Dorset Road, Troy OH 45373 B Louisville KY 1/23/1953 d Besfred Rufus Williams & Catherine Madeline. BA U of Louisville 1975; BA Bellarmine U 1977; MA Duquesne U 1979; Cert./Angl Studi TS 1989; Cert STUSo 1989. D 6/3/1989 Bp Alden Moinet Hathaway P 12/1/1989 Bp William Davidson. R Trin Epis Ch Troy OH 2005-2011; Asst R S Paul's Epis Ch Dayton OH 1998-2005; Columbus Comm Mnstrs Columbus OH 1996-1998; Vic Ch Of S Edw Columbus OH 1995-1998; Vic S Paul's Ch Columbus OH 1995-1998; Assoc R S Mk's Epis Ch Columbus OH

1991-1995; Cn Trin Cathd Pittsburgh PA 1989-1991. mwilliams87@woh.rr.com

WILLIAMS, Michael Robert (ND) 10315 Ross Lake Dr, Peyton CO 80831 **Off Of Bsh For ArmdF New York NY 1995-** B Fairfield IA 12/15/1954 s Roger Daryl Williams & Doris Jeanne. BA Iowa St U 1977; MDiv TESM 1986. D 8/5/1989 P 9/1/1990 Bp George Clinton Harris. m 6/19/1976 Rebecca Ann Shook. R S Paul's Epis Ch Grand Forks ND 1991-1995; Assoc S Jude's Epis Ch No Pole AK 1989-1991. Bro Of S Andr. michael.r.williams@iraq.centco

WILLIAMS, Mildred (Alb) Po Box 415, Morris NY 13808 **D S Mary's Epis Ch Inc Lampasas TX 2002-; D Zion Ch Morris NY 1988-; D Dio Albany Albany NY 1986-** B Norfolk VA 4/29/1933 d Joseph Martin & Bessie. D 1/6/1986 Bp David Standish Ball. m 12/16/1951 Phillip Williams c 2. NAAD.

WILLIAMS JR, Milton (WA) 222 8th St NE, Washington DC 20002 **P-in-c Par of St Monica & St Jas Washington DC 2008-** B Suffolk VA 6/12/1961 s Milton Williams & Goldie. BS Virginia St U 1983; MDiv Sthrn Bapt TS Louisville KY 1987; DAS VTS 1995. D 6/8/1996 Bp William Jerry Winterrowd P 2/16/1997 Bp Peter James Lee. S Tim's Epis Ch Washington DC 2006-2008; Assoc Trin Par New York NY 1999-2006; Asst Pohick Epis Ch Lorton VA 1996-1999. mwmsjr@verizon.net

WILLIAMS, Mollie A. (Ind) 11335 Winding Wood Ct, Indianapolis IN 46235 B Baltimore MD 11/5/1939 d Harold Dungan Alexander & Effie May. BA U Roch 1961; MDiv EDS 1964; MA U Chi 1978; Cert Cntr For Fam Consult 1989. D 6/17/1989 P 12/16/1989 Bp Frank Tracy Griswold III. m 6/12/1964 F. Peter Williams c 2. Int S Paul's Ch Richmond IN 2004-2008; Int The Cathd Ch Of S Paul Des Moines IA 2002-2003; Vic Ch Of The H Fam Lake Villa IL 1995-2001; Int Trin Ch Highland Pk IL 1993-1995; Int S Aug's Epis Ch Wilmette IL 1992-1993; Int S Andr's and Pentecostal Epis Ch Evanston IL 1991-1992; Int All SS Ch Wstrn Sprg IL 1989-1991; S Mk's Ch Evanston IL 1989; Dio Chicago Chicago IL 1987-1994. OHC 1987-1991; SSJE 1993. mollie.williams88@gmail.com

WILLIAMS, Monrelle (Cal) 1075 Santa Maria Ct, Oakland CA 94601 **R S Aug's Ch Oakland CA 2006-** B Barbados 1/1/1954 s Theolphilus Taylor & Una. BA Codrington Coll St. Jn 1979; Mphil Trin 1984; PhD Dur 1991. Trans from Church in the Province Of The West Indies 4/3/2007 Bp Marc Handley Andrus. c 3. monrellewilliams@comcast.net

WILLIAMS, Patricia S. (Mo) 336 N Lorimier St, Cape Girardeau MO 63701 B Williston ND 5/9/1932 d John Shemorry & Juanita. BA Carleton Coll 1954; MA SWTS 1990. D 5/5/1990 P 11/30/1990 Bp William Augustus Jones Jr. m 6/22/1957 Charles Edwin Williams c 2. S Fran Epis Ch Eureka MO 1994-1995; Dep for Mnstry and Pstr Care Dio Missouri S Louis MO 1993-2001; Dio Missouri S Louis MO 1990-2001; Bps Asst Dio Missouri S Louis MO 1990-1993. pswrev59@sbcglobal.net

WILLIAMS, Paul Brazell (SO) 5857 Vandeleur Place, Dublin OH 43016 **Bex Columbus OH 2008-; Vic S Andr's Ch Pickerington OH 2008-** B High Point NC 7/6/1957 s Benjamin Jackson Williams & Mary. U NC; BA U NC 1981; MDiv GTS 1996. D 6/8/1996 Bp Frank Kellogg Allan P 12/7/1996 Bp Richard Frank Grein. m 10/28/1994 Larry D Hayes. Chr Ch Glen Ridge NJ 2001-2006; Cur Ch Of The H Trin New York NY 1996-2001. H Cross 1994. frpauloh@aol.com

WILLIAMS, Persis Preston (Alb) Po Box 1662, Blue HIll ME 04614 B Troy NY 4/24/1942 d Carl Burton Williams & Claire Margaret. BS U of Connecticut 1974; MDiv GTS 1987. D 6/6/1987 Bp Edward Cole Chalfant P 12/19/1987 Bp Clarence Nicholas Coleridge. c 2. Gr Ch Cherry Vlly NY 1996-2008; R S Mary's Ch Springfield Cntr NY 1996-2008; R The Ch Of The Redeem Rochester NH 1992-1996; Int St Mich & Gr Ch Rumford RI 1991-1992; P-in-c S Aug's Ch Kingston RI 1990-1991; Asst Vic S Aug's Ch Kingston RI 1988-1989. Fllshp of Way of The Cross 1997. daisydog.williams0@gmail.com

WILLIAMS, Peter A (CNY) 310 Montgomery St., Syracuse NY 13202 **Gr Ch Cortland NY 2010-; Dio Cntrl New York Syracuse NY 2009-; Ephphatha Epis Par Of The Deaf Syracuse NY 2009-** B Syracuse NY 6/12/1956 s Edward Myron Williams & Mary Agnes. BA SUNY 1978; STM St Mary's Sem and U 1982. Rec from Roman Catholic 10/18/2008 Bp Gladstone Bailey Adams III. peterawill@juno.com

WILLIAMS, Priscilla Mudge (Ct) 80 Lyme Rd., Apt. 212, Hanover NH 03755 B New York NY 6/9/1933 d Louis Goldtwaite Mudge & Priscilla. BS Skidmore Coll 1955; MDiv Yale DS 1981. D 6/13/1981 P 1/28/1982 Bp Arthur Edward Walmsley. m 3/9/1957 Whitney Williams c 3. P-in-c S Jn's Ch Stamford CT 1981-1987.

WILLIAMS, Richard Alan (EpisSanJ) 28052 Foxfire St, Sun City CA 92586 B Berkeley CA 2/15/1930 s Charles Everett Williams & Wilma Florence. CDSP; BA U of Redlands 1953; MDiv Amer Bapt Sem of The W 1956. D 6/10/1982 Bp Robert Munro Wolterstorff P 10/17/1982 Bp Charles Brinkley Morton. m 8/26/1951 Barbara Ruark c 3. Int S Judes In The Mountains Ch Tehachapi CA 2001-2002; Asstg R All SS Epis Ch Riverside CA 1996-2000; Int S Andr's Ch Taft CA 1994-1996; Assoc S Steph's Ch Stockton CA 1993-1994; Vic S Mary's Ch Manteca CA 1990-1993; Vic S Andr's By The Lake Temecula CA 1984-1990; Vic S Steph's Mssn Menifee CA 1984-1986; Cur S Andr's Ch La Mesa CA 1982-1983; Min S Anne's Epis Ch Oceanside CA 1978-1981. rawill21530@verizon.net

WILLIAMS, Richard Alex (NC) PO Box 1852, Salisbury NC 28145 **Vic S Paul's Ch Salisbury NC 2010-** B Newport News VA 12/18/1946 s Cecil Harold Williams & Hester. BS Tennessee Tech U 1969; MDiv Candler TS Emory U 1977. D 6/11/1977 P 2/24/1978 Bp Bennett Jones Sims. m 11/27/2002 Judith Berneice Williams c 1. US Navy Pension Fund Mltry New York NY 2002-2004; Non-Dioc 1993-2002; Assoc Trin Epis Ch Columbus GA 1988-1992; R Ch Of The Incarn Atlanta GA 1986-1988; Yth Cmsn Dio Atlanta Atlanta GA 1986-1988; Assoc S Edw's Epis Ch Lawrenceville GA 1985-1986; Assoc S Barth's Epis Ch Atlanta GA 1984-1985; Vic Chr Epis Ch Kennesaw GA 1982-1984; Assoc S Edw's Epis Ch Lawrenceville GA 1977-1978. Alpha Kappa Psi 1969; Sigma Chi 1973. Who's Who Worldwide Who's Who Bus Leaders 1994; Gd Samar Awd Amer Police Hall Of Fame 1981. rickwttu69@hotmail.com

WILLIAMS, R(ichard) Rhys (NY) 338 Scribner Hill Rd, Otisfield ME 04270 **Died 7/5/2010** B Bethlehem PA 4/21/1923 s Loren Edward Williams & Margaret Eleanor. BA Leh 1944; MDiv GTS 1947; MA Col 1950; ThD GTS 1960. D 5/24/1947 Bp Frank W Sterrett P 11/30/1947 Bp Wallace E Conkling. c 4. Auth, *Let Each Gospel Speak for Itself*, 1987; Auth, *PB Psalter Revised*, 1976. Prof Emer Marist Coll. PIXIEGEMW@GWI.NET

WILLIAMS, Robert Bruce (Az) 2242 E 8th St, Tucson AZ 85719 B Welch WV 2/12/1942 s William Otis Williams & Cecilia Elvine. BA U of Arizona 1964; MDiv VTS 1967. D 6/21/1967 P 12/1/1967 Bp J(ohn) Joseph Meakins Harte. Asst S Andr's Epis Ch Tucson AZ 1994-2006; S Andr's Epis Ch Tucson AZ 1993-2006; COM Dio Arizona Phoenix AZ 1980-2008; Secy Of Dio Dio Arizona Phoenix AZ 1977-1979; Epis Ch of the H Sprt Phoenix AZ 1975-1980; Chair Dio Arizona Phoenix AZ 1973-1978; Dept Of Mssn Dio Arizona Phoenix AZ 1973-1975; Dioc Coun Dio Arizona Phoenix AZ 1972-1975; Vic S Raphael In The Vlly Mssn Benson AZ 1970-1975; Vic S Steph's Ch Sierra Vista AZ 1970-1975; BEC Dio Arizona Phoenix AZ 1970-1972; Dept Of CE Dio Arizona Phoenix AZ 1968-1970; Cur S Mk's Epis Ch Mesa AZ 1967-1970. thevicar@cox.net

WILLIAMS, Robert Carson (ETenn) 217 Castle Heights Ave N, Lebanon TN 37087 **Chair CE Taskforce Dio Tennessee Nashville TN 1974-** B Kingston TN 4/11/1930 s James Otha Williams & Hazel Lee. BA Scarritt Coll 1952; BD STUSo 1956. D 7/7/1956 Bp John Vander Horst P 1/1/1957 Bp Theodore N Barth. Dio E Tennessee Knoxville TN 1985-1992; Dio Tennessee Nashville TN 1981-1984; S Paul's Epis Ch Chattanooga TN 1965-1981; In-Charge Chr Ch Brownsville TN 1956-1958.

WILLIAMS, Robert Ernest (ECR) 231 Sunset Ave, Sunnyvale CA 94086 **D S Thos Epis Ch Sunnyvale CA 1969-** B Danville VA 5/29/1928 s Edgar Ernest Williams & Mary Stuart. BS Georgia Inst of Tech 1951; MS Georgia Inst of Tech 1960; CDSP 1975. D 12/17/1969 Bp George Richard Millard. c 4. bob_williams1@comcast.net

WILLIAMS, Robert Harry (Oly) 1805 38th Ave, Seattle WA 98122 B Kansas City MO 6/26/1940 s Payton Howard Williams & Mary Elizabeth. BS U of Missouri 1964; MDiv Nash 1971; DMin McCormick TS 1976; EdD Tem 1979. D 12/6/1970 P 6/11/1971 Bp Edward Randolph Welles II. c 1. Ch Of The Epiph Seattle WA 1997-2005; Off Of Bsh For ArmdF New York NY 1974-1997; Vic All SS Ch W Plains MO 1971-1974. Legion Of Merit; Meritorious Serv Medal; Commendation Medal USN. parishepiphany@worldnet.att.net

WILLIAMS JR, Robert Lewis (SwFla) 2903 Diamond A Dr, Roswell NM 88201 B Concord NC 3/24/1942 s Robert Lewis Williams & Louise. BA U NC 1964; MDiv GTS 1967. D 6/24/1967 P 6/29/1968 Bp Thomas Augustus Fraser Jr. m 8/20/1989 Gwendolyn R Hoover. R Ch Of The Gd Shpd Dunedin FL 2003-2010; R S Andr's Ch Roswell NM 1990-2003; R S Fran Of Assisi Gulf Breeze FL 1982-1990; R S Dav's Ch Cheraw SC 1977-1982; Assoc Par Ch of St. Helena Beaufort SC 1975-1977; Assoc S Lk's Epis Ch Birmingham AL 1972-1975; Cur S Jn's Epis Ch Charlotte NC 1969-1972; D Ch Of The Mssh Mayodan NC 1967-1969. Auth, "arts," *Living Ch*, 1990; Auth, "arts," [illegible] 1982; Auth, "arts," *[illegible] Day By Day*, [illegible]. Ord Of S Helena. Ord Of S Helena. frbob@tampabay.rr.com

WILLIAMS, Robert Lewis (Oly) 3300 Carpenter Rd SE, Electra 109, Lacey WA 98503 **Vic S Nich Ch Tahuya WA 1998-** B Findlay OH 6/30/1936 s Vern Dixon Williams & Eva Mae. CTh Other Other 1977; BA Evergreen St Coll 1987; CAS CDSP 1992; Cert Cler Ldrshp Inst 2004. Rec from Roman Catholic 6/27/1992 as Deacon Bp Vincent Waydell Warner. m 12/7/1957 Daphne Beryl Grint c 5. Asst S Jn's Epis Ch Gig Harbor WA 1996-2006; P-in-c S Germains Epis Ch Hoodsport WA 1995-1997; Pstr's Asst Ch Of The Resurr Bellevue WA 1992-1994. dnrwi@msn.com

WILLIAMS, Robert Roy (WMass) PO Box 395, Millville MA 01529 **Vic S Jn's Ch Millville MA 2011-** B Walla Walla WA 1/31/1946 s Roy Earl Williams & Melva Aliza. BA Whitman Coll 1969; MS OR SU 1972; PhD OR SU 1982; EFM Cert The TS at The U So 2006. D 6/11/2011 Bp Gordon Paul Scruton. m 12/29/1984 Sharon Bailey c 2. robertrw46@hotmail.com

WILLIAMS, R(obert) Samuel (Neb) 509 W 1st St, Mccook NE 69001 B Cape Girardeau MO 7/27/1940 s Murlin Coleman Williams & Maryan. No Carolina St U; BA Methodist Coll 1973; MA Pepperdine U 1978; MDiv STUSo 1984. D 6/24/1984 Bp C(laude) Charles Vache P 1/24/1985 Bp Brice Sidney Sanders. m 7/28/1962 Sally Jean Williams. R S Alb's Epis Ch McCook NE 1999-2007; R S Jn's Ch Franklin PA 1987-1999; Asst to R S Andr's Ch Morehead City NC 1984-1987. alban@ocsmccook.com

WILLIAMS, Roger Sherfey (Ore) 1064 Se Creekside Dr, College Place WA 99324 B Pomeroy WA 10/13/1939 s Roy Eugene Williams & Marguerite Sherfey. BA Whitman Coll 1962; STB ATC 1965; ABS/MA Whitworth U 1983; CSD Sch for Sprtl Dir Pecos Benedictine Abbey 1996. D 6/30/1965 P 2/20/1966 Bp Russell S Hubbard. m 11/18/1984 Jane Zak c 2. R Calv Ch Seaside OR 1989-1997; R S Matt's Epis Ch Fairbanks AK 1984-1989; Coordntr Chr Nurture Dio Spokane Spokane WA 1982-1984; Asst H Trin Epis Ch Spokane WA 1982-1984; Exec Coun Appointees New York NY 1978-1982; R H Trin Epis Ch Sunnyside WA 1971-1978; Asst S Paul's Ch Walla Walla WA 1967-1971. rwilliams0109@charter.net

WILLIAMS, Roger Verne (EO) St. Paul's Episcopal Church, 505 Bower Ave., Nyssa OR 97913 B San Francisco CA 2/15/1936 D 3/9/1995 P 11/19/1995 Bp Rustin Ray Kimsey. m 9/22/1972 Elva Duncan c 3. renewil@fmtc.com

WILLIAMS, Russell Thayer (NwPa) 867 Smithson Ave, Erie PA 16511 B Pittsburgh PA 11/17/1931 s Alonzo Ellsworth Williams & Ruth Eliza. BA U Pgh 1953; MDiv PDS 1958. D 6/14/1958 Bp William S Thomas P 12/20/1958 Bp Austin Pardue. m 6/6/1959 Kittie E Eldridge c 2. Chapl S Vinc Hlth Cntr Dio NW Pennsylvania Erie PA 1976-1997; Dn NW Deanry Dio NW Pennsylvania Erie PA 1975-1976; ExCoun Dio NW Pennsylvania Erie PA 1974-1976; BEC Dio NW Pennsylvania Erie PA 1965-1974; ExCoun Dio NW Pennsylvania Erie PA 1964-1969; Yth Advsr Dio NW Pennsylvania Erie PA 1963-1967; Vic S Mary's Ch Erie PA 1961-1976.

WILLIAMS, R(uth) Jane (Be) 4601 Normandy Ave, Memphis TN 38117 **Prof Moravian TS Bethlehem PA 2010-** B Fillmore NY 1/17/1949 d Kenneth Edgar Dearstyne & Ruth Marian. BA W Virginia U 1971; MDiv Drew U 1985; PhD Leh 1994. D 6/14/1997 P 12/19/1997 Bp Paul Victor Marshall. m 5/19/1989 William Treible c 1. Chapl S Mary's Epis Sch Memphis TN 2005-2010; Assoc Chr Ch Reading PA 1997-2005. Auth, "Silent Casusualties: Partnr, Fam and Spouses of Persons w AIDS," *Journ of Counslg & Dvlpmt*, 1992. Phi Beta Kappa W Virginia U 1971. jane.williams.phd@gmail.com

WILLIAMS, Ruth Theresa Prudeaux (Chi) 1031 E Hyde Park Blvd, Chicago IL 60615 **Died 6/6/2011** B New Orleans LA 10/4/1927 d George Ernest Prudeaux & Louise Elizabeth Cassimere. BA Xavier U 1948; MS S Louis U 1950; MDiv Chicago TS 1982; DMin Chicago TS 1983; Cert SWTS 1986; DD Chicago TS 1995; Ph. D. Chicago TS 2007. D 6/1/1987 Bp James Winchester Montgomery P 12/1/1987 Bp Frank Tracy Griswold III. c 1. Auth, "Grief Following The Loss Of An Adult Chld," Sem, 1987; Auth, "Rel Dimensions Of The Funeral Direcotr'S Role". Soc For The Comp Of The H Cross 1990.

WILLIAMS, Sam Farrar (SVa) P O Box 62184, Virginia Beach VA 23466 B Newport News VA 11/20/1945 d William Nelson Farrar & Florence Lee. Diac Sch-Duke Durham NC. D 6/4/2005 Bp David Conner Bane Jr. m 12/15/2007 Ronald Charles Williams c 2. S Steph's Ch Newport News VA 2006-2008. samfarrarwilliams@cox.net

WILLIAMS, Sandra Kaye (SD) 509 Jackson St, Belle Fourche SD 57717 **P S Jas Epis Ch Belle Fourche SD 2005-** B Platte SD 2/21/1956 d George A Kuipers & Joann Ilene. BS Dakota St U 1978. D 6/11/2005 P 2/12/2006 Bp Creighton Leland Robertson. m 6/10/1978 George Williams c 2. ydnaswil@yahoo.com

WILLIAMS, Sandy (Mass) 173 Georgetown Rd, Boxford MA 01921 B Columbus OH 6/18/1955 d Robert Charles Williams & Faye. BA U MI 1977; MDiv EDS 1981. D 10/18/1981 Bp Henry Irving Mayson P 1/1/1983 Bp H Coleman McGehee Jr. m 6/30/1984 Brian Lawrence c 1. Vic S Andr's Ch Of The Deaf Natick MA 1989-1999; Dio Massachusetts Boston MA 1989-1997; Dio Michigan Detroit MI 1981-1982. Epis Conf Deaf.

WILLIAMS, Scott Eugene (Miss) 1909 15th St, Gulfport MS 39501 B Williamsport PA 10/7/1953 s Robert E Williams & Robertha M. D 1/9/2010 Bp Duncan Montgomery Gray III. m 12/11/1993 Tracy Skinner c 2. scott_e_wms@yahoo.com

WILLIAMS, Shawn Mcnown (LI) 64 Mount Misery Dr, Sag Harbor NY 11963 **P-in-c Chr Ch Sag Harbor NY 1999-; Com Dio Long Island Garden City NY 1993-** B Lincoln NE 2/4/1966 s John Stanley Williams & Kathleen Diane. BA U of Nebraska 1989; MDiv GTS 1993. D 6/13/1992 P 1/1/1993 Bp Orris George Walker Jr. S Elis's Epis Ch Floral Pk NY 1994-1999; Fin Cmsn Dio Long Island Garden City NY 1994-1996; S Thos' Epis Ch Bellerose Vill NY 1994; Cur S Gabr's Ch Brooklyn NY 1992-1994; Cmsn On Racism Dio Long Island Garden City NY 1991-1995. swms@optonline.net

WILLIAMS, Shearon (Va) 2500 Cameron Mills Rd, Alexandria VA 22302 **S Geo's Epis Ch Arlington VA 2010-; Asst Gr Ch Washington DC 2003-** B Newport News VA 8/19/1960 BA U of Virginia. D 6/7/2003 Bp Gethin Benwil Hughes P 12/14/2003 Bp Allen Lyman Bartlett Jr. m 2/7/1987 Robbie Williams c 1. S Gabr's Epis Ch Leesburg VA 2010; S Mk's Ch Washington DC 2004-2007. shearon.williams@comcast.net

WILLIAMS, Stephen Junior Cherrington (RG) 49 ½ Draper Avenue, Pittsfield MA 01201 B East Liverpool OH 3/22/1932 s Louis Howard Williams & Alberta Grace. BA Syr 1957; MDiv Ya Berk 1960; Tchg cert California St U 1964. D 6/22/1960 P 6/24/1961 Bp Walter M Higley. c 3. Dioc Coun Dio The Rio Grande Albuquerque NM 1990-1994; R S Chris's Epis Ch Hobbs NM 1986-1994; R S Pat's Epis Ch Lebanon OH 1977-1986; Chr Epis Ch Warren OH 1977-1982; Ch Of Gd Shpd Cincinnati OH 1976-1977; Vic Ch Of The H Comm Gardena CA 1964-1966; Mssy Gr Epis Ch Whitney Point NY 1960-1963; Mssy S Jn's Ch Marathon NY 1960-1963. Auth, *Enroute and Other Poems*, Morris Pub, 1997. OHC. stephen.j.c.williams@gmail.com

WILLIAMS, Stephen Lee (Los) St. Gregory's Episcopal Church, 6201 East Willow Street, Long Beach CA 90815 **R S Greg's Par Long Bch CA 2000-** B Memphis TN 11/27/1945 s Harry Leon Williams & Nellie Elizabeth. BSc U of Memphis 1971; MDiv Trin, U Tor 1976. D 6/20/1976 Bp William Evan Sanders P 1/23/1977 Bp The Bishop Of Toronto. m 11/8/2011 Rachel H Stacey c 1. R S Lk's Ch Racine WI 1998-2000; Asst Chr Ch Greenville SC 1987-1998; Assoc Ch Of The Ascen Lafayette LA 1983-1987. Soc of Cath Priests 2010; The Sovereign Mltry Ord of the Temple of Jerusalem 2000. slw5312@aol.com

WILLIAMS, Susan Anslow (WNY) 311 Crossman St, Jamestown NY 14701 **Assoc R S Lk's Epis Ch Jamestown NY 2000-; Dioc Liturg Cmsn Dio Wstrn New York Tonawanda NY 1994-** B Detroit MI 5/17/1965 d Richard Davies Anslow & Katherine Margaret. BA Ya 1987; MDiv GTS 1992. D 6/27/1992 Bp Henry Irving Mayson P 1/30/1993 Bp R(aymond) Stewart Wood Jr. m 10/8/1994 Eric Matthew Williams. Dep Gc Dio Wstrn New York Tonawanda NY 2000-2003; Int S Pat's Ch Cheektowaga NY 1998-1999; Cn S Paul's Cathd Buffalo NY 1992-1998. momsusan@madbbs.com

WILLIAMS, Susanna Elizabeth (NY) 100 Underhill St, Yonkers NY 10710 B Waterbury CT 12/5/1953 CUNY 1975; BA SUNY 1985; MDiv GTS 1988. D 6/17/1988 Bp Paul Moore Jr P 12/17/1988 Bp George Phelps Mellick Belshaw. m 11/8/1979 Alan Slater c 2. R S Jn's Ch Tuckahoe Yonkers NY 1991-2011; Asst Chr Ch New Brunswick NJ 1988-1991. mosusanna@yahoo.com

WILLIAMS, Thomas (Ia) 9404 Oak Meadow Ct, Tampa FL 33647 **Asst S Mk's Epis Ch Of Tampa Tampa FL 2008-** B Memphis TN 5/11/1967 s Wayne Thomas Williams & Frankie Davis. BA Van 1988; PhD U of Notre Dame 1994. D 6/4/2008 P 12/13/2008 Bp Alan Scarfe. Auth, "Early Hobartian Reaction to the Oxford Mvmt," *Angl and Epis Hist*, 2012; Auth, "Human Freedom and Agcy," *The Oxford Handbook of Aquinas*, Oxf Press, 2012; Auth, "The Fransciscans," *The Oxford Handbook of the Hist of Ethics*, Oxf Press, 2012; Auth, "Duns Scotus," *A Comp to the Philos of Action*, Wiley-Blackwell, 2010; Auth, "Anselm," *Hist of Wstrn Philos of Rel*, Oxf Press, 2009; Auth, "Describing God," *The Cambridge Hist of Medieval Philos*, Camb Press, 2009; Auth, "God Who Sows the Seed and Gives the Growth: Anselm's Theol of the H Sprt," *ATR*, 2007; Auth, "The Doctrine of Univocity is True and Salutary," *Mod Theol*, 2005; co-Auth, "Anselm on Truth," *The Cambridge Comp to Anselm*, Camb Press, 2005; co-Auth, "Anselm's Account of Freedom," *The Cambridge Comp to Anselm*, Camb Press, 2005; Auth, "Sin, Gr, and Redemp," *The Cambridge Comp to Abelard*, Camb Press, 2004; Auth, "Moral Vice, Cognitive Virtue: Jane Austen on Jealousy and Envy," *Philos and Lit*, 2003; Auth, "Transmission and Translation," *The Cambridge Comp to Medieval Philos*, Camb Press, 2003; Auth, "Two Aspects of Platonic Recollection," *Apeiron*, 2002; Auth, "Aug vs Plotinus: The Uniqueness of the Vision at Ostia," *Medieval Philos and the Classical Tradition*, Curzon Press, 2002; Auth, "Biblic Interp," *The Cambridge Comp to Aug*, Camb Press, 2001; Auth, "Lying, Deception, and the Virtue of Truthfulness," *Faith and Philos*, 2000; Auth, "A Most Methodical Lover? On Scotus's Arbitrary Creator," *Journ of the Hist of Philos*, 2000; Auth, "The Unmitigated Scotus," *Archiv fuer Geschichte der Philosophie*, 1998; Auth, "The Libertarian Foundations of Scotus's Moral Philos," *The Thomist*, 1998; Auth, "A Reply to the Ramsey Colloquium," *Same Sex: Debating the Ethics, Sci, and Culture of Homosexuality*, Rowman & Littlefield, 1997; Auth, "Reason, Morality, and Voluntarism in Duns Scotus: A Pseudo-Problem Dissolved," *The Mod Schoolman*, 1997; Auth, "How Scotus Separates Morality from Happiness," *Amer Cath Philos Quarterly*, 1995. profthomaswilliams@gmail.com

WILLIAMS, Thomas Donald (CFla) 3015 Indian River Drive, Palm Bay FL 32905 **D Ch Of Our Sav Palm Bay FL 2009-** B Rochester NY 12/9/1946 s Donald Charles Williams & Mary Josephine. AAS Monroe Cmnty Coll 1969; BA Morehead St U 1971; MA St. Bern's Inst Rochester NY 1988. D 12/13/1986 Bp William George Burrill. m 5/24/1969 Sandra Marie Moran c 2. NAAD 2007. tdw12946@msn.com

WILLIAMS, Tracey Mark (LI) 8545 96th St, Woodhaven NY 11421 B Brooklyn NY 7/11/1961 s Alonzo Williams & Geraldine. BA Cathd Coll of the Immac Concep 1983; MDiv SWTS 1995. D 6/23/1995 P 3/25/1996 Bp Orris George Walker Jr. S Matt's Ch Woodhaven NY 1997-2011.

WILLIAMS, Wendy Ann (SeFla) 400 Seabrook Rd, Tequesta FL 33469 B Mount Kisco NY 6/29/1944 d Lyle Kim Williams & Marie Helen. BA Ge 1966; Duke 1976; MDiv STUSo 1980. D 6/28/1981 P 1/30/1982 Bp William Grant Black. Dio Oklahoma Oklahoma City OK 1994-1997; Assoc The Epis Ch Of The Gd Shpd Tequesta FL 1990-2006; Asst S Paul's Ch Rochester NY 1982-1990; Chr Ch - Glendale Cincinnati OH 1981-1982. NECA 1982. wendywilliams3@mac.com

WILLIAMS JR, Wesley Samuel (VI) 6501 Red Hook Plz Ste 201, St Thomas VI 00802 Virgin Islands (U.S.) B Philadelphia PA 11/13/1942 s Wesley Samuel Willliams & Bathrus Bailey. BA Harv 1963; MA Fletcher Sch 1964; JD Harv 1967; LLM Col 1969; LLD Virginia Un U 2002; VTS 2012. D 6/28/2008 Bp Gayle Elizabeth Harris P 3/6/2010 Bp Edward Ambrose Gumbs. m 8/17/1968 Karen Hastie c 3. wesley-williams@lockhart.com

WILLIAMS-DUNCAN, Stacy (WA) 372 El Camino Real, Atherton CA 94027 **Cathd of St Ptr & St Paul Washington DC 2008-** B Pauls Valley OK 12/6/1971 d Larry Williams & Frances. D 6/26/1999 P 1/18/2000 Bp Barry Robert Howe. m 12/28/1996 Joel Richard Duncan. S Matt's Epis Day Sch San Mateo CA 2006-2008; S Matt's Epis Ch San Mateo CA 2005-2006; Assoc S Jas Ch Fremont CA 2002-2004; Cur Trin Par Menlo Pk CA 2000-2002; Ch Of The Ascen Vallejo CA 1999-2000. swilliamsduncan@cathedral.org

WILLIAMSON, Barbara (Mass) 451 Concord Rd, Sudbury MA 01776 **R S Eliz's Ch Sudbury MA 1998-** B Orlando FL 1/5/1953 d Franklyn Lee Williamson & Barbara. BA Bos 1977; MDiv VTS 1992. D 5/30/1992 Bp David Elliot Johnson P 5/14/1993 Bp Roger John White. m 11/11/1995 Peter Woodring Wenner. Assoc For Educ Chr Ch Whitefish Bay WI 1992-1998. barbara_williamson@st-elizabeths.org

WILLIAMSON, Daniel (NCal) 1090 Main St, Roseville CA 95678 B Birmingham AL 10/21/1943 BA U of Alabama 1965; MA U of Alabama 1966; MDiv TESM 1986. D 6/11/1986 P 1/17/1987 Bp Oliver Bailey Garver Jr. m 8/3/1968 Diane Williamson c 3. R St Johns Epis Ch Roseville CA 1994-2008; Vic S Jn's Mssn La Verne CA 1989-1993; Cur All SS Par Los Angeles CA 1986-1989. Auth, "Feature Writing For Nwspr". drwdmw1@quiknet.com

WILLIAMSON, Emmanuel Richard (Pa) 1101 2nd Street Pike, Southampton PA 18966 **Ch Of The Redemp Southampton PA 2010-** B Maha MT 2/22/1966 s Richard G Williamson & Kathleen S. Mt Ang Abbey; Vancouver TS. D 6/13/2004 Bp Mark Lawrence Mac Donald. Assoc S Ptr's Ch Seward AK 2004-2008. myunclemonk@gmail.com

WILLIAMSON, James Edward (Mass) 201 Oakwood Lane, Columbus NC 28722 **Died 7/10/2010** B Newark NJ 7/22/1926 s George Williamson & Edith. BS New Jersey St Teachers Coll 1949; MA Col 1953; VTS 1960; Cert U of Massachusetts 1983; MS U of Massachusetts 1992. D 6/24/1965 P 5/15/1966 Bp Edward Hamilton West. c 2. Auth, "How to Help the Hearing Impaired in Your Classroom," *The Massachusettes*, 1975. The Epis Conf of the Deaf 1961-1970; The SSM 1977-2008. holycrosstryon@msn.com

WILLIAMSON JR, James Gray (SwFla) 7313 Merchant Ct, Sarasota FL 34240 **Cn for Chr Formation Dio SW Florida Sarasota FL 2010-; Vic S Edm's Epis Ch Arcadia FL 2007-** B Birmingham AL 2/26/1954 s James Gray Williamson & June Carolyn. BS Louisiana Coll 1976; MDiv SW Sem Dallas TX 1979; CTh Epis TS of The SW 1985; PhD Baylor U 1988. D 8/25/1985 Bp Anselmo Carral-Solar P 3/17/1986 Bp [illegible] Manuel Benitez. c 1. Int Emm Epis Ch Chestertown MD 2005-2006; Vic S Mary Magd Lakewood Ranch FL 1999-2005; R Gd Samar Epis Ch Clearwater FL 1993-1998; R Ch Of The Gd Shpd Tomball TX 1988-1993; Assoc R Trin Ch Longview TX 1985-1987. Auth, "Discovering Tim, Tit, & Philemon," *Guideposts Bible Study Series*, Guideposts. jgwmson@gmail.com

WILLIAMSON, Jeremiah D (O) 3154 Goddard Rd, Toledo OH 43606 **GC Dep Dio Ohio Cleveland OH 2010-; R S Andr's Epis Ch Toledo OH 2009-** B Wheeling WV 7/15/1980 s Robert David Williamson & Connie. BS Greenville Coll 2002; MDiv Drew U 2005; Angl Stds GTS 2006. D 9/19/2006 Bp John Palmer Croneberger P 4/17/2007 Bp Mark Hollingsworth Jr. m 11/21/2009 Jennifer Smith c 1. Cur S Jn's Ch Youngstown OH 2006-2009. 40 Under 40 Mahoning Vlly Young Profsnl's Club 2008. fatherj@standrewsepiscopal.net

WILLIAMSON, Randolph Lewis (Pa) 343 Michigan Ave, Swarthmore PA 19081 B Morgantown WV 3/4/1948 s Robert Burwell Williamson & Norma Jean. BS U NC 1970; MDiv EDS 1975. D 6/14/1975 Bp Lyman Cunningham Ogilby P 6/1/1976 Bp John Brooke Mosley. m 8/21/1976 Carol Stevick c 2. R Trin Ch Swarthmore PA 1986-2005; R Ch Of The Adv Hatboro PA 1979-1986; Asst Ch Of S Mart-In-The-Fields Philadelphia PA 1977-1979; Asst S Ptr's Ch Glenside PA 1975-1977. randywilliamson@rcn.com

WILLIAMSON, Rebecca Ann (Az) 1735 S College Ave, Tempe AZ 85281 B Laramie WY 10/28/1951 d Clarence Elwood Williamson & Virginia Drake. BA U of Nthrn Colorado 1975; MS Texas A&M U-Corpus Christi 1980; D Formation Acad 2011. D 1/29/2011 Bp Kirk Stevan Smith. 1beckyw@earthlink.net

WILLIAMSON III, Stephen Girard (SO) 1058 Vernon Rd, Bexley OH 43209 B Williamsport PA 7/31/1938 s Stephen Girard Williamson & Eleanor. BA Ge 1962; MDiv VTS 1965; MBA Wilkes Coll 1976. D 6/19/1965 P 2/12/1966 Bp John S Higgins. m 8/8/1964 Anita Jarbeau c 4. P-in-c Ch Of S Edw Columbus OH 1999-2001; S Phil's Ch Circleville OH 1998-1999; P-in-c S Phil's Ch Circleville OH 1994-1996; Midwest Career Dvlpmt Serv Columbus OH 1992-1998; Vic S Andr's Ch Pickerington OH 1992-1994; Dio Sthrn Ohio Cincinnati OH 1989-1991; Dio Sthrn Ohio Cincinnati OH 1982-1988; Cn Cathd Of All SS Albany NY 1978-1982; Dio Albany Albany NY 1977-1982; R The Epis Ch Of S Clem And S Ptr Wilkes Barre PA 1970-1977; Vic S Jas-S Geo Epis Ch Jermyn PA 1966-1970; Cur S Mich's Ch Bristol RI 1965-1966. Amos Seven 1982. SWILLIAMSON@COLUMBUS.RR.COM

WILLIAMSON JR, Wayne Bert (EpisSanJ) 13373 N Plaza Del Rio Blvd, Peoria AZ 85381 B Casper WY 9/7/1918 s Wayne Bert Williamson & Agnes. CDSP 1952; Oxf 1953; BA USC 1954; ThM Fuller TS 1978. D 6/1/1953 Bp Francis E I Bloy P 2/18/1954 Bp Donald J Campbell. c 2. Epis Dio San Joaquin Modesto CA 1982-1987; Exec Asst to Ord Epis Dio San Joaquin Modesto CA 1982-1984; R S Mk's Par Glendale CA 1971-1980; R S Mary's Ch Lakewood WA 1964-1971; R Trin Epis Ch Reno NV 1962-1964; ExCoun Dio Nevada Las Vegas NV 1960-1963; R S Paul's Epis Ch Elko NV 1959-1962; Vic S Clem's-By-The-Sea Par San Clemente CA 1957-1959. Auth, *Growth & Decline in the Epis Ch*, 1979. wwilliamson12@cox.net

WILLIS, Anisa Cottrell (Lex) 11 Beechwood Road, Fort Mitchell KY 41017 **Assoc S Jas Epis Ch Cincinnati OH 2011-** B Pikeville KY 12/1/1969 d Kenneth Wayne Cottrell & Marigrace. BA Rhodes Coll 1992; DAS Ya Berk 1995; MDiv Yale DS 1995; CPE Residency UK Med Cntr 1996; MS U of Kentucky 1998. D 12/9/1998 P 6/24/1999 Bp Don Adger Wimberly. m 10/16/1999 John Kevin Willis c 2. R Adv Ch Cynthiana KY 2001-2004; Asst Ch Of The H Trin Georgetown KY 1999-2001; S Jas Epis Ch Prestonsburg KY 1999. anisacottrellwillis@aya.yale.edu

WILLIS, Arthur Douglas (NJ) 319 S 7th St, Darby PA 19023 B Bakersville NC 12/31/1929 s Charles Edgar Willis & Pauline Mollie. BA Berea Coll 1951; MDiv Epis TS In Kentucky 1956. D 6/1/1955 P 6/14/1956 Bp William R Moody. R S Geo's Ch Pennsville NJ 1983-1993; P Ch Of S Andr The Apos Camden NJ 1973-1979; R S Wilfrid's Ch Camden NJ 1971-1983; Cur S Lk's Ch Philadelphia PA 1969-1971; Vic Gr Epis Ch Florence KY 1957-1967. serge.adw@earthlink.net

WILLIS, Barbara Creighton (Va) 1905 Wildflower Terrace, Richmond VA 23238 **P-in-c S Asaph's Par Ch Bowling Green VA 2010-** B Cleveland OH 5/29/1951 d George Wishart Creighton & Barbara. BA MWC 1973; MA VTS 1997; MS Virginia Commonwealth U 2002; MDiv VTS 2005. D 6/18/2005 P 12/19/2005 Bp Peter James Lee. m 6/3/1972 Addison Willis c 3. Asst. R S Barth's Ch Richmond VA 2005-2010. "Processing w Pooh," *Journ of Pstr Care*, Journ of Pstr Care Pub, 2001. bcwillis@aol.com

WILLIS JR, Frederick Webber (SwVa) 5119 Blake Point Rd, Chincoteague Island VA 23336 B Bogalusa LA 8/1/1940 s Frederick Webber Willis & Mary Bankston. BA U Of Delaware Newark 1962; MDiv VTS 1965. D 9/26/1965 P 5/1/1966 Bp John Brooke Mosley. m 6/16/1962 Laura Ellis c 1. Int S Dav's Epis Ch Richmond VA 2008-2010; Vic Emm Ch Oak Hall VA 2001-2007; Assoc S Paul's Ch Richmond VA 1972-1977; Assoc S Barth's Ch Richmond VA 1969-1971; Vic All SS Epis Ch Delmar DE 1965-1968. [illegible]@charter.net

WILLIS OHC, Jean Elainie (Ia) 3526 Grand Ave, 3524 Grand Ave, Des Moines IA 50312 B Menominee MI 1/11/1923 d David Hardie & Irene Mary. MDiv GTS 1983; BA U of Iowa 2045; MA U of Iowa 2047. D 6/13/1983 P 12/1/1983 Bp Walter Cameron Righter. m 7/16/1944 Ned Willis c 4. Asst S Tim's Epis Ch W Des Moines IA 1999-2002; Cn Pstr The Cathd Ch Of S Paul Des Moines IA 1990-2000; Vic All SS Epis Ch Storm Lake IA 1983-1989. Ord of S Helena 1983. Mortar Bd U of Iowa 2045; Phi Beta Kappa U of Iowa 2045. ELIZAWILLIS@EARTHLINK.NET

WILLIS, Laurie Joy (Chi) 7916 Earl St, Oakland CA 94605 **Assoc P S Cuth's Epis Ch Oakland CA 2005-** B Cook County IL 4/15/1957 d Walter Siebenmann & Jeanne. BA Blackburn Coll 1978; MLS U IL 1979; MA Loyola U 1990; MDiv CDSP 1995. D 6/17/1995 Bp Frank Tracy Griswold III P 12/6/1995 Bp William Edwin Swing. Asst P S Alb's Ch Albany CA 1995-2003. Auth, "Wrld Rel Fact Cards," Toucan Vlly Pub, 2000. goinpeace1@yahoo.com

WILLIS, Nancy Appleby (RI) 86 Dendron Rd, Wakefield RI 02879 B Baltimore MD 7/31/1942 d Joseph Lamb Appleby & Mary. BA Wilson Coll 1964; MAT Harv 1965; MDiv Ya Berk 1996. D 6/15/1996 P 4/5/1997 Bp Geralyn Wolf. m 7/9/1966 George H Willis c 2. Co-Int R Ch Of The Ascen Wakefield RI 2009-2010; R S Dav's On The Hill Epis Ch Cranston RI 2002-2008; Asst / Assoc R Chr Ch Westerly RI 1997-2001; Asst Ch Of The Ascen Wakefield RI 1996-1997; Dir. Sch for Mnstrs Dio Rhode Island Providence RI 1996-1997. Auth, "The Trsfg as a Model of Rel Experience," *Preaching Through the Year of Mk: Sermons that Wk VIII*, Morehouse Pub, 1999. nawlls@yahoo.com

WILLIS, Ronnie Walker (Cal) 137 Caselli Ave, San Francisco CA 94114 B Richmond CA 12/30/1958 s Ronnie Lee Willis & Mourna Lyvonne. BA Dominican TS Berkeley CA 1999; MDiv VTS 2002. D 6/1/2002 P 12/7/2002

Bp William Edwin Swing. Vic S Aid's Mssn Bolinas CA 2003-2009; S Steph's Par Belvedere CA 2002-2003. rwillis@raptindustries.com

WILLKE, Herbert Alexander (Tex) 11110 Tom Adams Drive, Austin TX 78753 B Houston TX 12/13/1920 s Herbert Herman Willke & Nettie. Texas Mltry Inst 1940; BS U Of Houston 1954; MDiv VTS 1954. D 7/1/1954 P 7/1/1955 Bp Clinton Simon Quin. c 3. Chr Ch Matagorda TX 1985-1991; S Jn's Epis Ch Palacios TX 1985-1991; Vic Gr Epis Ch Houston TX 1970-1985; Vic S Chris's Ch Houston TX 1954-1956.

WILLMANN JR, Robert Everett (SO) 155 N 6th St, Zanesville OH 43701 **R S Jas Epis Ch Zanesville OH 2010-** B Newark OH 5/24/1965 s Robert Willmann & Joyce. Angl Cert Bex; STB Theol Coll 1992; JCD No Amer Coll 1997. Rec from Roman Catholic 11/3/2009 as Priest Bp Thomas Edward Breidenthal. m 6/30/2007 Maria S Jamiolkonski c 1. EXURGENS@YAHOO.COM

WILLMS, Ann Bagley (Va) 1700 University Ave., Charlottesville VA 22903 **Assoc R S Paul's Meml Charlottesville VA 2009-** B St Paul MN 10/2/1961 d Parker Keenan Bagley & Suzanne Elizabeth. AB Br 1982; MD Jefferson Med Coll 1987; MDiv VTS 2009. D 6/13/2009 Bp Clifton Daniel III P 1/9/2010 Bp David Colin Jones. m 10/15/1994 Christopher Willms c 2. abwillms@gmail.com

WILLMS, John Karl Peter (Minn) 801 E 2nd St Apt 102, Duluth MN 55805 **Supply S Jn's Ch Aitkin MN 1994-** B Gretna MT CA 3/29/1927 s Peter Jacob Willms & Anna Theodora. CTh S Chad's Coll 1959; LTh S Chad's Coll 1974; BA U MN 1974; MDiv The Coll of Emm and St. Chad 1986. Trans from Anglican Church of Canada 10/1/1964 as Priest Bp Philip Frederick McNairy. c 2. Supply P S Andr's Ch Moose Lake MN 2004-2011; Duluth Congrl Ch Duluth MN 1974-1976; Cur S Paul's Epis Ch Duluth MN 1972-1974; Vic S Lk's Ch Detroit Lakes MN 1968-1972; P-in-c S Helen's Ch Wadena MN 1964-1968; P-in-c Trin Epis Ch Pk Rapids MN 1964-1968. Bd Mem, Lake Superior Life Care Ctr (Duluth, Minn) 1981; EvangES; Harvest Ntwk Intl -Assoc. of Evang & Charismat 1990; Intl Ord of S Lk 1999. Prince of Oeace Fellowowship AECM Chrsmtc Ch Duluth Minn 1992.

WILLOUGHBY, Robert Geddes (Mich) 16256 Terra Bella St., Clinton Township MI 48038 B Northville MI 12/30/1935 s Robert Dwight Willoughby & Maxine Elizabeth. Estrn Michigan U; Wayne, Detroit; BA Estrn Michigan U 1958; BD Bex 1961; MA U Of Detroit 1969; MSW Wayne 1985. D 6/29/1961 Bp Robert Lionne DeWitt P 1/5/1962 Bp Richard S M Emrich. m 4/16/1983 Saundra J Garden c 5. Emm Ch Detroit MI 1996-1999; R Emm Ch Detroit MI 1986-1991; Dio Michigan Detroit MI 1985-1986; Chair Spec Mnstrs Com Exec Coun Dio Michigan Detroit MI 1981-1982; S Matt's Epis Ch Saginaw MI 1979-1982; Chair Spec Mnstrs Com Exec Coun Dio Michigan Detroit MI 1972-1975; R Trin Ch S Clair Shores MI 1969-1979; R All SS Ch Brooklyn MI 1963-1969; Cur S Phil's Epis Ch Rochester MI 1961-1963. Auth, "Theol Of Anger," *Sharing*, Michigan Cancer Fndt, 1978; Auth, "Sprtl Pain," *Sharing*, Michigan Cancer Fndt, 1978. ACPE; Clincl Mem AAPC. rwilloughby23@comcast.net

WILLOUGHBY III, William (Ga) The Ibert, 224 E 34th Street, Savannah GA 31401 **Dn, Savannah Convoc Dio Georgia Savannah GA 2005-; Mem of Dioc Coun Dio Georgia Savannah GA 2005-; Dep to GC Dio Georgia Savannah GA 2003-; Vic S Barth's Ch Burro Savannah GA 2000-; Dn/R S Paul's Ch Savannah GA 1987-** B Anniston AL 10/19/1955 s William Willoughby & Doris. BA U Chi 1977; CTh Oxf 1981; MDiv Nash 1982; EdD GTF 2005. D 6/19/1982 Bp Quintin Ebenezer Primo Jr P 1/27/1983 Bp James Winchester Montgomery. m 8/14/1982 Mary C Crane c 3. VP, Dioc Coun Dio Georgia Savannah GA 2007-2009; Mem of Dioc Coun Dio Georgia Savannah GA 2005-2009; Pres of Stndg Com Dio Georgia Savannah GA 1995-1996; Mem of Stndg Com Dio Georgia Savannah GA 1992-1996; Mem of Mssn Dvlpmt Cmsn Dio Georgia Savannah GA 1989-1997; Asst Ch Of S Mary The Vrgn New York NY 1984-1987; Chapl/Asst. Hd S Hilda's And S Hugh's Sch New York NY 1984-1987; Cur Par of St Paul's Ch Norwalk Norwalk CT 1982-1984. Auth, "Singing God's Song of Love," GTF, 2005; Auth, "A Short Hist of S Paul's," St Paul's, Savannah, 2003; Auth, "A Pilgrimage of Pryr through the W of Ireland," GTF, 2002; Auth, "Theol Considerations in Writing an Icon," GTF, 2001; Auth, "A Jerusalem Pilgrim: A Guest of the Oriental Orth," GTF, 2000. Bd Mem, Amer Friends of the Angl Cntr in Rome 2010; Comp of the OGS 2002; Conf Assoc of the CHS 1982; GAS 1987; P Assoc of the SocOLW 1983; Secy Gnrl, CBS 1997; Soc of Chas, King and Mtyr 1995; Ward Superior, CBS 1987. Serving Bro Ord of St. Jn of Jerusalem 2010; Chapl Sovereign Mltry Ord of the Temple in Jerusalem 2004; Chapl Sovereign Mltry Ord of the Temple of Jerusalem 2004; Chapl Sovereign Mltry Ord of the Temple in Jerusalem 2000; Maroon Key U Chi 1976. frwwiii@aol.com

WILLOW, Mary Margaret Gregory (SwFla) 127 Gesner St, Linden NJ 07036 B Okmulgee OK 11/24/1926 d Fountain Leverne Gregory & Ivy Ione. BA Jersey City St Coll 1965; MS Rutgers-The St U 1975. D 10/26/1986 Bp Emerson Paul Haynes. m 9/6/1947 James Mark Willow c 1. D S Andr's Epis Ch Sprg Hill FL 1986-2006. Ord Of S Lk 1973. mwillow@msn.com

WILLS, Clark Edward (Oly) 308 - 14th Avenue East #111, Seattle WA 98112 B Cincinnati OH 12/7/1942 s Edward Joseph Wills & Anna Cost. S Meinrad's TS; BA The Athenaeum of Ohio 1965; MDiv Nash 1974. D 12/14/1973 P 6/15/1974 Bp James Winchester Montgomery. Asst S Paul's Ch Seattle WA 2000; Ch Of The Annunc Bridgeview IL 1996-1997; Asst All SS Epis Ch Chicago IL 1985-1999; Assoc S Andr's Ch Chicago IL 1977-1985; R S Marg's Ch Chicago IL 1975-1977; Cur S Phil's Epis Palatine IL 1974-1975. chisag99@yahoo.com

WILLS JR, Edwin Francis (Ark) 321 Crystal Ct, Little Rock AR 72205 **S Mich's Epis Ch Little Rock AR 2004-** B Memphis TN 10/5/1955 s Edwin Francis Wills & Carolyn Joy. BBA U of Memphis 1978. D 8/31/2002 P 3/1/2003 Bp Larry Earl Maze. m 10/13/1979 Andrea Newsom c 3. Trin Cathd Little Rock AR 2002-2004; Asst For Formation S Andr's Cathd Jackson MS 1992-1995; Asst For Yth & Educ All SS Epis Ch Memphis TN 1977-1981. ewills@stmichaels-church.net

WILLS, Henry Dale (WMo) 11970 4th St, Yucaipa CA 92399 **S Alb's Epis Ch Yucaipa CA 2005-** B Wichita KS 1/21/1944 s Henry G Wills & Julia Cristy. BA California St U 1968; MDiv CDSP 1972. D 9/9/1972 P 3/1/1973 Bp Francis E I Bloy. m 4/26/1974 Mary Lee Steward. R S Aug's Ch Kansas City MO 1990-1999; Asst Epis Ch Of The H Sprt Kansas City KS 1981-1990; Asst Ch Of The H Trin and S Ben Alhambra CA 1980-2004; Asst S Mary's Epis Ch Kansas City MO 1978-1980; Asst S Cyp's Ch San Francisco CA 1976-1977; Dio Los Angeles Los Angeles CA 1975-1976; Asst Ch Of The H Trin and S Ben Alhambra CA 1974-1976; Cur Chr The Gd Shpd Par Los Angeles CA 1973-1974.

WILLS, Robert Murlin (Mich) 1506 Eagle Crest Dr, Prescott AZ 86301 B Port Huron MI 4/11/1941 s William Murlin Wills & Margaret Fay. BA U of Wstrn Ontario 1963; M.Div EDS 1966; MS Wayne 1972. D 6/29/1966 Bp C Kilmer Myers P 2/1/1968 Bp Richard S M Emrich. c 3. S Geo's Epis Ch Warren MI 2003-2007; Chr Ch Cranbrook Bloomfield Hills MI 1995-1996; Asst Min S Mart Ch Detroit MI 1967-1972. Auth, *Var arts*. willsrm@gmail.com

WILLSON, William George (WLa) 328 Ann Ave, Sulphur LA 70663 **Died 10/25/2010** B Trinidad CO 9/13/1929 s James William Clarence Willson & Wildagene. AA Trinidad St Jr Coll Trinidad CO 1949; BA SW LSU 1954; ThM Iliff TS 1958; U of Pennsylvania 1967; Col 1968. D 3/1/1987 P 7/1/1987 Bp Willis Ryan Henton. Bp'S Cross Bp Winterwood 2002. wmwillson@hotmail.com

WILMER, Amelie Allen (WA) 12291 River Rd, Richmond VA 23238 B Los Angeles 11/21/1959 d John Lemuel Wilmer & Pauline Rejane. BA Ya 1981; MDiv UTS 2010; Post Grad Degree in Angl Stds VTS 2011. D 6/4/2011 Bp Shannon Sherwood Johnston. c 3. amelie.allen@comcast.net

WILMINGTON, Richard Newton (Cal) 2 Columbia Dr, Rancho Mirage CA 92270 **Non Stipendiary S Marg's Epis Ch Palm Desert CA 2008-; Gr Cathd San Francisco CA 1999-** B New York NY 5/30/1939 s Edward Newton Wilmington & Muriel E. BA Hob 1961; M.Div GTS 1965. D 6/16/1965 P 12/1/1965 Bp Horace W B Donegan. m 9/10/2008 Robert V Lilley c 3. Pstr Gr Cathd San Francisco CA 1970-1979; Cur St Johns Epis Ch Ross CA 1965-1967. Auth, "NT Roots of AntiSemitism," *Epis Life*; Auth, "Meditation On Magic," *LivCh*.

WILMOT, Susan Elizabeth (Az) 5147 Show Low Lake Road, Lakeside AZ 85929 **Dioc Coun Dio Arizona Phoenix AZ 2010-; R Ch Of Our Sav Lakeside AZ 2008-** B Halifax England 1/22/1961 d Stanley Rowell Hinley & Rosemary Lilian. BSc(HONS) Sheffield City Polytechnic 1983; MDiv Epis TS of the SW 2008. D 10/20/2007 P 6/14/2008 Bp Kirk Stevan Smith. m 9/8/1984 Stephen Anthony Wilmot. wilmot1322@gmail.com

WILNER, Janice Marilyn (Warner) (Az) 14228 N Yerba Buena Way, Fountain Hills AZ 85268 **Died 5/24/2010** B Springfield MA 9/22/1935 d Elmer John Warner & Genevieve Lenore. BS U MI 1958. D 10/14/2000 Bp Robert Reed Shahan.

WILS, Duane Michael (NMich) 6971 Days River 24.5 Rd, Gladstone MI 49837 B 7/2/1959 D 5/20/2001 Bp James Arthur Kelsey P 9/21/2010 Bp Thomas Kreider Ray. m 9/18/1982 Wendy Elya c 2.

WILSON, Amanda J (CFla) 942 Cobbler Ct, Longwood FL 32750 **Corpus Christi Epis Ch Okahumpka FL 2010-** B 10/17/1959 d Ronald Lewis Slee & Joyce Carr. BA Regis U Colorado Sprg CO 2001; MDiv Asbury TS Orlando FL 2008. D 5/30/2009 P 12/12/2009 Bp John Wadsworth Howe. m 6/28/2007 Barclay DeVane Wilson c 4. amandajwilson61@gmail.com

WILSON, Anne Warrington (SO) 7730 Tecumseh Trl, Cincinnati OH 45243 **P-in-c S Mary Magd Ch Maineville OH 2011-** B Cincinnati OH 12/10/1952 d John Wesley Warrington & Suzanne. BA Trin Hartford CT 1975; MDiv EDS 1979. D 6/4/1983 P 9/16/1984 Bp William Grant Black. m 5/9/1986 Gene Merrill Wilson c 2. P-in-c The Ch Of Ascen And H Trin Cincinnati OH 2009-2010; Int R All SS Ch Cincinnati OH 2007-2009; P-in-c Ch Of S Mich And All Ang Cincinnati OH 1998-2005; Asst S Thos Epis Ch Terrace Pk OH 1994-1996; Int S Tim's Epis Ch Cincinnati OH 1991-1993; Int Gr Ch Cincinnati OH 1989-1990; Int All SS Ch Cincinnati OH 1988-1989; Asst Chr Ch -

Glendale Cincinnati OH 1986-1988; Int Dio Sthrn Ohio Cincinnati OH 1985-1986; Vic Chap Of The Nativ Cincinnati OH 1983-1985. aww@eos.net

WILSON, Barbara A(nn) T(heresa) (WMich) 9713 Oakview Dr, Portage MI 49024 **S Fran Ch Orangeville Shelbyville MI 2000-** B Wyandotte MI 8/19/1951 d John Schofield Wilson & Joyce Ann. BA U Of Detroit 1980; MDiv Ya Berk 1984; CSD Colombiere Cntr For Sprtlty Clarkston MI 1991; MA Wstrn Michigan U 1998. D 6/30/1984 Bp Henry Irving Mayson P 7/29/1985 Bp H Coleman McGehee Jr. m 12/5/1997 Lynne Jacobson. S Steph's Epis Ch Plainwell MI 1997-1999; R Ch Of The Medtr Harbert MI 1994-1996; R S Aug Of Cbury Epis Ch Benton Harbor MI 1994-1996; S Barn Epis Ch Portage MI 1994; S Lk's Par Kalamazoo MI 1991-1993; Dio Michigan Detroit MI 1987-1988. Apc (Assn Of Profsnl Chapl) 2000. bwilson@memorialsb.org

WILSON, Barclay DeVane (CFla) Po Box 0103, Zellwood FL 32798 B Washington DC 11/8/1936 s Duane Barclay Wilson & Ruth Elizabeth. BS Florida St U; LTh STUSo; MS U of Tennessee 1972. D 6/22/1965 P 3/1/1966 Bp Edward Hamilton West. m 6/28/2007 Amanda J Wilson c 2. Epis Counslg Cntr Orlando FL 1988-1989; All SS Ch Of Winter Pk Winter Pk FL 1975-1979; R S Jas Epis Ch Un City TN 1969-1975; Asst S Mk's Epis Ch Jacksonville FL 1968-1969; M-in-c Bethany Ch Hilliard FL 1965-1968; M-in-c S Jas Ch Macclenny FL 1965-1968. Cfla Sprtl Dvlpmt T/F. Past Pres Rotary Club Un City TN. bdwfsu@netzero.com

WILSON, Barrie Andrew (CFla) 331 Lake Avenue #308, Maitland FL 32751 B 11/19/1940 Trans from Anglican Church of Canada 2/2/1972 Bp George Leslie Cadigan.

WILSON JR, Charles Alexander (NwT) 1524 S. Alabama St., Amarilo TX 79102 B Kalispell MT 7/25/1933 s Charles A Wilson & Edith S. BA U of Montana 1957; MDiv CDSP 1962; U of New Mex 1973. D 7/2/1962 P 1/2/1963 Bp Chandler W Sterling. m 4/23/1989 Emily Meredith Neece c 2. S Thos Epis Ch Hereford TX 1992-1998; Asst to R S Andr's Epis Ch Amarillo TX 1987-1991; R S Paul's Ch Artesia NM 1986-1987; Locten S Jas' Epis Ch Dalhart TX 1985-1986; R S Chris's Epis Ch El Paso TX 1981-1984; R S Jn's Ch Farmington NM 1973-1981; R All SS Ch Minot ND 1969-1972; Vic S Jn's Epis Ch Clayton CA 1964-1969; Cur S Jn's Ch Butte MT 1962-1964. Intl Bonhoeffer Soc. cawilson3@suddenlink.net

WILSON, C(harles) Bradley (Pgh) 3 Suntrace Ct, Columbia SC 29229 B Wichita KS 12/20/1951 s Robert George Wilson & Janice Beverly. BA U of Kansas 1974; Trin Bristol Gb 1977; MDiv SWTS 1980. D 6/11/1980 Bp Edward Clark Turner P 5/1/1981 Bp Matthew Paul Bigliardi. m 10/7/1983 Carol Lynn Wilson c 2. Int Chr Epis Ch Mt Pleasant SC 2011; R Fox Chap Epis Ch Pittsburgh PA 1996-2008; R S Ptr's Epis Ch Uniontown PA 1992-1996; Asst Ch Of The Ascen Montgomery AL 1984-1991; Min S Paul's Epis Ch Salem OR 1980-1984. Soc For Promoting Chr Knowledge; SAMS. Polly Bond Awd For Humor In Ch Pub; Alum Awd SWTS. revbwilson@aol.com

WILSON JR, Charles Edward (SO) 77 Sherman Ave, Columbus OH 43205 **Transitional D S Paul's Ch Dekalb IL 2005-** B Holyoke MA 7/23/1965 s Charles E Wilson & Anne M. AA Holyoke Cmnty Coll 1986; BS Franklin U 2002; MDiv Bex 2005. D 5/22/2004 P 6/25/2005 Bp Herbert Thompson Jr. m 7/6/1996 Julie Barry c 2. S Mary's Epis Ch Hillsboro OH 2005-2007; S Ptr's Epis Ch Delaware OH 2005-2007. chasebwilson@yahoo.com

WILSON, Charles Ralph (Wyo) 14971 SE 107th Ave, Summerfield FL 34491 B Sharon PA 6/13/1927 s Ralph Warender Wilson & Helen. DIT ATC 1960. D 7/18/1960 P 1/25/1961 Bp Norman L Foote. c 4. Intsn Epis Ch Thornton CO 1987-1999; Ch Of S Jn Chrys Golden CO 1984-1985; S Aid's Epis Ch Boulder CO 1984; Satff Dio Idaho Boise ID 1965-1966; Vic S Paul's Ch Blackfoot ID 1960-1965. Auth, *Sustaining the NEW Sm Ch (Fall)*, ATR, 1996; Auth, *Fixing the Microwave (A Primer on Ch Structuring)*, Jethro, 1994; Auth, *Search*, Jethro, 1993; Auth, *Par Admin*, Jethro, 1990; Auth, *Under Auth*, Jethro, 1989. Living Stones; Sindicators. wilson161327@comcast.net

WILSON, Claudia Marie (NY) 1085 Warburton Ave Apt 326, Yonkers NY 10701 **P-in-c Ch Of The H Comm Mahopac NY 2006-; Cn for Cong. Dev. Dio New York New York City NY 2006-** B New York NY 7/12/1944 d George Henry Wilson & Lilly Mae. BA Harpur Coll, SUNY 1965; MA U Tor 1968; MTS SWTS 2006. D 5/30/1992 Bp Richard Frank Grein P 9/23/2006 Bp Mark Sean Sisk. D S Jn's Ch Getty Sq Yonkers NY 1994-2006; Asst Dio New York New York City NY 1992-2004; D The Ch of S Ign of Antioch New York NY 1992-1994. dcmw367@aol.com

WILSON, Conrad Bruce (WTex) 10 Tanglewood St, San Marcos TX 78666 **The Ch Of The Recon Corpus Christi TX 2011-** B Midland TX 5/7/1954 s James Henry Wilson & Sophie Jean. BS Agape Sem of Jesus Chr 1975; MA U of Texas 1980; MDiv VTS 1986. D 6/15/1986 Bp John Herbert MacNaughton P 1/1/1987 Bp Stanley Fillmore Hauser. m 9/2/1978 Sandra Wilson c 2. S Mk's Ch San Marcos TX 1996-2011; Asst to R Ch Of The Gd Shpd Corpus Christi TX 1994-1996; Gr Ch Cuero TX 1989-1994; Asst to R S Jn's Ch McAllen TX 1986-1989. bruce.wilson@grandecom.net

WILSON JR, Dallas Henry (SC) 21 Aiken St, Charleston SC 29403 **Ch Of The H Cross Sullivans Island SC 2008-** B Hillsborough SC 6/12/1942 s Dallas Henry Wilson & Mary Magdeline. BS Coastal Carolina U 1980; MTh Gulf Coast Sem Panama City FL 1988; ThD Gulf Coast Sem Panama City FL 1991. D 6/15/2005 P 1/14/2006 Bp Edward Lloyd Salmon Jr. m 11/24/1996 Janie Ruth Dingle c 2. vicarstjohns@bellsouth.net

WILSON, Dana Jane Gant (FtW) 124 Oakmont Dr, Weatherford TX 76088 B Clovis NM 9/6/1951 d George Abraham Gant & Neta Nell. BS Estrn New Mex U 1974. D 7/1/1989 Bp Robert Manning Moody. m 12/30/1972 Gary Dan Wilson c 3. Co-Mentor D Formation Prog Archd Dio NW Texas Lubbock TX 1997-2006; D Ch Of The H Trin Midland TX 1997-2004; Dio NW Texas Lubbock TX 1997-2004; D H Comf Epis Ch Sprg TX 1994-1997; S Mths Epis Ch Tuscaloosa AL 1990-1991. dana9651@sbcglobal.net

WILSON, Donald Grant (WMo) 232 S State Fair Blvd, Sedalia MO 65301 B Kalamazoo MI 8/4/1934 s Donald Henry Wilson & Florence A. Wstrn Michigan U 1959; BS Cntrl Michigan U 1966; Bex 1969. D 6/28/1969 Bp Archie H Crowley P 1/5/1970 Bp Richard S M Emrich. m 12/28/1956 Gwendolyn S Tolhurst c 4. R Calv Epis Ch Sedalia MO 1983-1990; R Chr Ch Epis Hudson OH 1978-1983; R S Matt's Ch Westerville OH 1972-1978; Vic Gr Epis Ch Standish MI 1969-1972; Vic Ch Of S Mary And Our Blessed Redeem Flandreau SD 1961-1964; Vic H Cross Epis Ch Mart SD 1956-1961. Auth, "No Pat Answers". Ord Of S Lk 1975-1988. dwilson@iland.net

WILSON, Donald Rexford (Ore) 7065 S.W. Molalla Bend Rd., Wilsonville OR 97070 **Asst S Tim's Epis Ch Salem OR 2003-** B Portland OR 7/15/1926 s Harry Rexford Wilson & Hazel. DipTh ATC 1964. D 6/29/1964 P 1/25/1965 Bp James Walmsley Frederic Carman. m 3/29/2008 Marilyn Louise Craghead. Asst S Jas Epis Ch Tigard OR 2001-2003; P S Paul's Par Oregon City OR 1992-1993; P S Mary's Ch Woodburn OR 1991-1993; R S Mart's Ch Lebanon OR 1985-1989; S Matt's Epis Ch Eugene OR 1983-1984; S Thos' Epis Ch Eugene OR 1982-1983; Vic S Mich's/San Miguel Newberg OR 1970-1979; Vic S Bede's Ch Forest Grove OR 1970-1975; Dio Oregon Portland OR 1969-1979; Vic S Steph's Ch Newport OR 1964-1970. fr.dwilson@comcast.net

WILSON, Donald Robert (Mass) 76 Old Pine Hill Rd N, Berwick ME 03901 B Boston MA 1/9/1931 s Clark Wentworth Wilson & Helen Nelson. BA Estrn Nazarene Coll 1953; BD Bex 1956. D 6/9/1956 Bp Norman B Nash P 12/18/1956 Bp Conrad Gesner. m 6/4/1961 Linda Koelin c 4. S Paul's Ch Peabody MA 1983-1996; Chr Epis Ch Yankton SD 1977-1983; All SS Epis Ch Wolfeboro NH 1964-1977. LAND76@COMCAST.NET

WILSON, Edward Adrian (ECR) 90 Cashew Blossom Drive, San Jose CA 95123 **Epis Sr Communities Walnut Creek CA 2002-** B Northampton UK 10/11/1949 s James Philip Wilson & Annie Elizabeth. BA U of Scranton 1976; MA Ya 1978; MDiv CDSP 1983; DMin SFTS 2000. D 6/25/1983 P 7/1/1984 Bp William Edwin Swing. m 6/22/1980 Dorothy S Sibley c 2. Assoc S Thos Epis Ch Sunnyvale CA 2002-2003; Supply P Dio Oregon Portland OR 1995-2000; Ch Of The Epiph Lake Oswego OR 1987-1994; Asst P Trin Epis Ch Ashland Ashland OR 1983-1987. Alpha Sigma Nu Natl Jesuit hon Soc 1976; Delta Tau Kappa Natl Soc Sci hon Soc 1976. shalomed@live.com

WILSON, Edward John (Ala) 1019 Woodmere Creek Trl, Birmingham AL 35226 **Died 4/1/2010** B Mobile AL 7/31/1932 s Edward Wilson & Sally. Cert Our Lady of Lake Sem 1955; Cert Crosier Hse of Stds 1962; BA Hastings Coll of Law, Nebraska 1963; MA LIU, NY 1978. Rec from Roman Catholic 9/1/1975 as Priest Bp Jonathan Goodhue Sherman. c 3. ejwicc@aol.com

WILSON, Eugenia Theresa (NY) 5030 Henry Hudson Pkwy E, Bronx NY 10471 **D Chr Ch Riverdale Bronx NY 2007-** B New York NY 8/1/1949 d Eugenie. BS CUNY 1975. D 5/5/2007 Bp Mark Sean Sisk. c 1. ugena101@verizon.net

WILSON JR, Frank E (Minn) 16376 7th Street Lane S, Lakeland MN 55043 B Big Sprg TX 1/20/1949 s Frank E Wilson & Carolyn. BUS U of New Mex 1971; MDiv Epis TS of The SW 1974. D 9/10/1974 P 5/1/1975 Bp Richard Mitchell Trelease Jr. m 4/14/1973 Alys Gilcrease c 3. R S Jn The Evang S Paul MN 2000-2010; R S Lk's Ch Minneapolis MN 1993-2000; Cn S Mk's Cathd Shreveport LA 1988-1993; Assoc Epis Ch Of The Gd Shpd Lake Chas LA 1986-1988; Cur Ch Of The H Cross Shreveport LA 1983-1985; Vic H Trin Epis Ch - Mssn Raton NM 1976; Vic S Paul's/Peace Ch Las Vegas NM 1975-1976. FRANKWILSONL@AOL.COM

WILSON, Frank F(enn) (At) 803 Wilkins Dr, Monroe GA 30655 **R S Clare's Epis Ch Blairsville GA 2010-** B Brunswick GA 12/1/1947 s Clyde Augustus Wilson & Melba Kathryn. Georgia Sthrn U 1966; Brunswick Jr Coll 1968; BA W Georgia Coll 1970; Med W Georgia Coll 1971; MDiv STUSo 1988. D 6/6/1998 P 2/20/1999 Bp Frank Kellogg Allan. m 11/25/1979 Pamela Kaye Souther c 3. R S Alb's Ch Monroe GA 2004-2006; Assoc Epis Ch Of The H Fam Jasper GA 1998-2004. (Bldg Named After) The Ext 1999. rector@brmemc.net

WILSON, Frank K (RG) 12 Indian Maid Ln, Alamogordo NM 88310 **COM Dio The Rio Grande Albuquerque NM 2008-2012** B Sharon PA 1/17/1948 s Walter Wilson & Dolores B. BA Ken 1969; JD U of New Mex 1976; Rio Grande Sch for Mnstry TESM 2004. D 6/19/2004 P 3/5/2005 Bp Terence Kelshaw. m 6/28/1988 Carolyn J Taylor c 2. P-in-c S Andr's Ch Roswell NM 2010-2011; R S Jn's Epis Ch Alamogordo NM 2005-2009. fkwilson01@beyondbb.com

WILSON, George Ira (Mich) 7903 Mesa Trails Cir, Austin TX 78731 **Asstg Cler S Matt's Ch Austin TX 1990-** B 1/12/1930 s George Ira Wilson & Elizabeth. BA U Chi 1950; GTS 1953; MBA U Of Detroit 1959; Cert Michigan TS 1971. D 3/28/1971 Bp Archie H Crowley P 3/1/1972 Bp Richard S M Emrich. m 4/6/1953 Cynthia Gurstell. Locten Trin Ch S Clair Shores MI 1979-1980; Asst Ch Of The H Cross Novi MI 1976-1979; Asst S Anne's Epis Ch Walled Lake MI 1976-1979; Asst S Steph's Ch Troy MI 1971-1975. Bsp; Ord Of S Lk.

WILSON, George Steil (Oly) 3607 214th Street Southwest, Brier WA 98036 B Seattle WA 5/17/1939 s William Charles Eade Wilson & Naomi Clara. BA U of Washington 1963; STB ATC 1966. D 6/8/1966 P 2/23/1967 Bp Ivol I Curtis. m 2/3/1996 Claire Louise McClenny c 2. Int Ch Of The Gd Shpd Fed Way WA 1996-1997; Int S Dav's Ch Spokane WA 1995-1996; Int Emm Ch Coos Bay OR 1993-1994; R S Alb's Ch Edmonds WA 1976-1993; R S Jn's Ch Hermiston OR 1970-1976; Cur S Lk's Ch Tacoma WA 1966-1967. georgeswilson@frontier.com

WILSON, Gregory (Pa) 246 Fox Rd, Media PA 19063 **P-in-c S Jas Ch Greenridge Aston PA 2010-** B Lower Merion PA 2/27/1976 s Thomas R Wilson & Sally W. BA U of Delaware Newark 1999; MDiv EDS 2002. D 6/22/2002 Bp Charles Bennison P 5/31/2003 Bp Charles Ellsworth Bennison Jr. m 5/21/2010 Brenda Stewart c 1. Dio Pennsylvania Philadelphia PA 2004-2010; Cur Ch Of The Redeem Bryn Mawr PA 2002-2004. revgregwilson@gmail.com

WILSON, Harold David (CFla) 1629 Championship Blvd, Franklin TN 37064 B Raton NM 10/25/1939 s Brownlow Villiers Wilson & Joyce Mearns. BS USNA 1962; MA U Denv 1969; MDiv Nash 1972. D 12/29/1971 P 6/29/1972 Bp Edwin B Thayer. m 6/7/1962 Katrina Cakste c 1. Stndg Com Dio Cntrl Florida Orlando FL 1997-2000; Dep GC Dio Cntrl Florida Orlando FL 1994-1997; Dioc Bd Dio Cntrl Florida Orlando FL 1993-2000; Dn Cntrl Deanry Dio Cntrl Florida Orlando FL 1993-1996; Bd TESM Ambridge PA 1992-2002; Chair Structure Cmsn Dio Cntrl Florida Orlando FL 1992-1996; COM Dio Cntrl Florida Orlando FL 1985-1988; R All SS Ch Of Winter Pk Winter Pk FL 1984-2005; Bp Admin Cbnt Dio Colorado Denver CO 1980-1984; COM Dio Colorado Denver CO 1975-1979; R Chr Epis Ch Denver CO 1974-1984; ExCoun Dio Colorado Denver CO 1974-1979; Cur Chr Epis Ch Denver CO 1972-1973. AAC 1999; AFP 1988-1990; BRF 1987-1990; ERM. father_dave@comcast.net

WILSON, Harold J(ames). (Pa) 9 Avery Court, Hernes Road, Oxford UK OX2 7QU Great Britain (UK) **Died 5/21/2011** B New York NY 5/14/1934 s Harold David Wilson & Sarah Elizabeth. BA Wms 1956; U NC 1957; STB GTS 1961; MA U of Pennsylvania 1970. D 6/11/1961 P 12/1/1961 Bp Wilburn Camrock Campbell. c 2. Auth, "Translation," *Duino Elegies - R.M. Rilke*, Harper & Rowe, 1974. haroldjaywilson@btinternet.com

WILSON, Henry Haddon (Eur) Stautland, Finnas N-5437 Norway B Wichita KS 2/24/1931 s Orlando Winfield Wilson & Vernis. BA U CA 1960; BD CDSP 1963. D 12/1/1963 P 11/1/1964 Bp Stephen F Bayne Jr. m 8/24/1952 Florence Ann Swan c 1. Ch Of The Ascen New York NY 1976-1992; The Angl/Epis Ch Of Chr The King Frankfurt am Main 60323 DE 1973-1976. ComT. flohenry@c2i.net

WILSON, Howard Lee (Okla) 1017 Kiheka St, Grove OK 74344 B Canton IL 11/1/1925 s Adolph Howard Wilson & Ruth Lucille. BA U of Wyoming 1950; BD CDSP 1953. D 6/11/1953 P 12/15/1953 Bp James W Hunter. m 6/11/1952 Ruth Saathoff c 3. Vic S Andr's Ch Grove OK 1983-1990; Vic S Jn's Epis Ch Vinita OK 1983-1990; Dn S Matt's Epis Cathd Laramie WY 1967-1980; Vic S Steph's Ch Casper WY 1963-1967; Archd Dio Wyoming Casper WY 1958-1963; Vic S Helen's Epis Ch Laramie WY 1956-1958; Vic S Thos Ch Dubois WY 1955-1958; Cur S Mk's Epis Ch Casper WY 1953-1955. Hon DD CDSP 1976; Phi Beta Kappa U of Wyoming 1950. wyokie@att.net

WILSON, Jack Fowler (EC) 4910 Crosswinds Dr., Apt. 210, Huntsville AL 35816 B Fairfield AL 8/13/1945 s John William Wilson & Olive Crooks. BA U of Alabama 1971; MDiv CDSP 1977. D 4/2/1977 P 10/13/1977 Bp Furman Stough. S Fran by the Sea Bogue Banks Salter Path NC 2004-2007; Ch Of The Nativ Epis Huntsville AL 1997-2004. presterjack1@aol.com

WILSON, James Barrett (Ky) 7619 Beech Spring Ct, Louisville KY 40241 **Eccl Trial Crt Dio Kentucky Louisville KY 2005-** B Denver CO 1/13/1941 s Joseph Friend Wilson & Jane Elizabeth. BA U CO 1962; BD SWTS 1965. D 6/14/1965 Bp Edwin B Thayer P 12/21/1965 Bp Joseph Summerville Minnis. m 8/8/1964 Beverly C Auther c 2. Dio Kentucky Louisville KY 2000-2006; Exec Coun Dio Kentucky Louisville KY 2000-2003; Vic H Trin Ch Brandenburg KY 1998-2006; Dir, Colo. Epis Fndt Dio Colorado Denver CO 1990-1995; Assoc S Steph's Epis Ch Aurora CO 1990-1995; Exec Coun Dio Colorado Denver CO 1969-1970; Vic S Paul's Epis Ch Lamar CO 1966-1975; Ch Of The Mssh Las Animas CO 1966-1973; Asst S Paul's Epis Ch Lakewood CO 1965-1966. Int Mnstry Ntwk 1997. jbw7619@aol.com

WILSON, James G. (Ct) 54 Harbour View Place, Stratford CT 06615 B Brooklyn NY 7/8/1940 s William Wallace Wilson & Jane Johnston. RPI 1960; BA Adel 1963; MDiv Ya Berk 1967. D 6/17/1967 P 12/23/1967 Bp Jonathan Goodhue Sherman. m 2/9/1963 Regina Ann Riley c 2. Epis Ch Cntr New York NY 1992-2004; Assoc Dir, CDO Epis Ch Cntr New York NY 1988-1991; Pres Natl Ntwk Of Epis Cler Assn Lynnwood WA 1981-1984; Exec Bd Natl Ntwk Of Epis Cler Assn Lynnwood WA 1979-1987; R S Jn's Epis Par Waterbury CT 1979-1987; Vic/Yoked Congregations S Jn's Epis Ch Oakdale NY 1970-1979; Vic S Lukes Ch Bohemia NY 1968-1979; Cur S Geo's Ch Hempstead NY 1967-1968. Co-Auth, "More Than Fine Gold," CDO, 1978; Auth, *Var Deploy Booklets & Resources*, CDO. CT Cler Assn 1980-1984; LI Cler Assn 1967-1979; NNECA 1971. reggiejim@att.net

WILSON II, James N (Minn) 5700 73rd Ave N Apt 204, Brooklyn Park MN 55429 **St Phil & St Thos Epis Ch S Paul MN 2009-** B LR 2/23/1960 s Ben W Wilson & Sophia T. BTh Cuttington U Coll 1988; ThM VTS 1999. D 4/8/1989 P 5/8/1990 Bp George Daniel Browne. m 8/31/1991 Eliza Wilson. S Thos Ch Minneapolis MN 2007-2008; S Andr's Epis Ch Minneapolis MN 2004-2007; P-in-c S Phil's Ch S Paul MN 2002-2003; Dio Liberia 1000 Monrovia 10 Liberia 1989-2001. JNWILSONII@EARTHLINK.NET

WILSON, Jane Rogers (Lex) St Mark's Episcopal Church, 317 Walnut St, Hazard KY 41701 **Chr Ch Cathd Lexington KY 2010-; Asst S Aug's Chap Lexington KY 2010-** B Davenport, IA 6/8/1959 d William Butterworth & Jane Rogers. BA Youngstown St U 1989; MA Youngstown St U 1991; MLS Clarion U of PA 1992; CATS SWTS 2006; MDiv Lexington TS 2007. D 6/9/2007 P 12/16/2007 Bp Stacy F Sauls. m 7/10/1993 Shannon Hunt Wilson c 3. Dio Lexington Lexington KY 2007-2010. janey.wilson@gmail.com

WILSON JR, John Dorr (Chi) 57 Partridge Dr, Chatham IL 62629 **D The Cathd Ch Of S Paul Springfield IL 2000-** B Hinsdale IL 8/20/1924 s John Wilson & Helen. D 12/26/1987 Bp Frank Tracy Griswold III. m 9/30/1950 Alverda Gyneth Olson c 4. D Dio Chicago Chicago IL 1987-2000; D Gr Ch Pontiac IL 1987-2000.

WILSON, John Morris (ETenn) 118 Dupont Smith Ln, Kingston TN 37763 **D (non-stipendiary) S Steph's Epis Ch Oak Ridge TN 2009-** B Nashville TN 5/27/1939 s Charles William Wilson & Barbara. BA Van 1961; MS Van 1969; U of Tennessee 1976. Rec from Roman Catholic 10/17/1993 Bp Robert Gould Tharp. m 6/28/1987 Delores Faye Brewer. D S Steph's Epis Ch Oak Ridge TN 1993-2000.

WILSON, Kate Wilson (ECR) 2614 Glenn Ave, Evansville IN 47711 **Assoc S Paul's Epis Ch Evansville IN 2010-** B Pittsburgh PA 7/25/1948 d John Paul Wilson & Mary Virginia. BA Coll of Mt S Vinc 1970; MS Ed Ford 1979; MDiv CDSP 2006. D 6/24/2006 P 8/4/2007 Bp Sylvestre Donato Romero. m 3/26/1994 Arlene Dutro. Assoc S Mk's Epis Ch Santa Clara CA 2006-2010. Assn of Profsnl Chapl 2011. katewilson725@yahoo.com

WILSON, Kenneth Wayne (CNY) 7863 Russell Ln, Manlius NY 13104 B Atlantic City NJ 12/3/1935 s Kenneth Wilson & Ruth. BS Indiana St U 1958; MDiv GTS 1961; Cert Inst Of Rel & Hlth 1969. D 4/8/1961 P 10/28/1961 Bp James P De Wolfe. m 7/29/1961 Nancy Louise Gasson c 3. Com Dio Cntrl New York Syracuse NY 1973-1974; Vic S Pat's Ch Deer Pk NY 1963-1968; Cur Chr Ch Babylon NY 1961-1963. Aamft; AAPC. wwilson2@twcny.rr.com

WILSON, Linda Latham (Alb) PO Box 154, 627 Roses Brook Rd, South Kortright NY 13842 B Norfolk VA 2/9/1942 d Jesse Brown Latham & Ruth O'Connor. BA Old Dominion U 1971; MTh St Jos's Coll-Maine 2006. D P 10/23/2005 Bp David John Bena. m 5/5/1973 Howard Lee Wilson. S Paul's Ch Bloomville NY 2003-2006. littlegidding@hughes.net

WILSON, Linda R (Wyo) 2012 Mcduffie St, Houston TX 77019 B Atoka OK 7/4/1947 d David Scarlett Wilson & Peggy June. BD McNeese St U 1972; MS U of Texas 1986; MDiv Epis TS of The SW 1993. D 7/28/1993 Bp William Jackson Cox P 5/1/1994 Bp Maurice Manuel Benitez. m 9/26/2007 Carl Means. Dio Wyoming Casper WY 2007-2010; S Jas Ch Riverton WY 2004-2006; S Jn's Ch La Porte TX 2004-2006; St Lk's Epis Hosp Houston TX 2004; Assoc R Trin Ch Houston TX 2001-2004; S Mk's Ch Houston TX 1999-2001; S Mart's Epis Ch Houston TX 1997-1999; All SS Epis Ch Austin TX 1994-1997. pr.lindawilson@mac.com

WILSON, Linda Tardy (Pgh) 215 Canterbury Ln, North Versailles PA 15137 B Pittsburgh PA 10/2/1949 d Harold Paul Tardy. BA U MI 1971. D 10/17/2009 Bp Robert Hodges Johnson. m 8/12/1972 James M Wilson c 2. deaconlindawilson@gmail.com

WILSON, Louis James (Eau) 2611 Mont Claire Rd, Eau Claire WI 54703 **D Chr Ch Cathd Eau Claire WI 1982-** B Minneapolis MN 4/19/1923 s Rolland Harvey Wilson & Hildred Rosamund. BA U MN; MA U MN; BS U MN. D 3/1/1959 Bp Philip Frederick McNairy. m 4/7/1945 Rita Victoria Tarras c 4. Archd Dio Eau Claire Eau Claire WI 1992-2000; Com Dio Eau Claire Eau Claire WI 1990-2000; Exec Coun Dio Eau Claire Eau Claire WI 1990-2000; Exec Coun Dio Eau Claire Eau Claire WI 1984-1986; Asst S Paul's Ch Winona MN 1970-1977; Asst Emm Ch Rushford MN 1961-1965; Asst S Paul's Ch Winona MN 1959-1965.

WILSON, Mark Howard (CGC) 860 N Section St, Fairhope AL 36532 **R S Jas Ch Fairhope AL 2000-** B Montgomery AL 3/23/1951 s L Dan Wilson & Elizabeth. BA Huntingdon Coll 1974; MDiv VTS 1993. D 5/29/1993 P 1/25/1994 Bp Charles Farmer Duvall. m 6/26/1976 Elizabeth Wiley c 2. Pres, Stndg Com Dio Cntrl Gulf Coast Pensacola FL 1998-1999; Dep, GC Dio Cntrl Gulf

Coast Pensacola FL 1997-2003; R S Jn's Ch Pensacola FL 1995-2000; Cur S Chris's Ch Pensacola FL 1993-1995. markhwil@bellsouth.net

WILSON, Mary Elizabeth (Tex) 717 Sage Road, Houston TX 77056 **Sr Assoc R for CE and Sprtl Formation S Mart's Epis Ch Houston TX 2010-** B Luling TX 11/5/1951 d Thomas Wilson & Nell. Austin Cmnty Coll 1988; BBA U of Texas 1990; MDiv VTS 1997. D 6/21/1997 Bp Claude Edward Payne P 4/25/1998 Bp Leopoldo Jesus Alard. c 2. R S Richard's Of Round Rock Round Rock TX 2006-2010; R S Jn's Epis Ch Silsbee TX 2000-2006; Asst P Chr Epis Ch Tyler TX 1997-2000. mwilson@stmartinsepiscopal.org

WILSON JR, Mason (Mass) 105 Stuyvesant Rd, Asheville NC 28803 B Kansas City MO 8/31/1924 s Mason Wilson & Eula Jane. BA U of Texas 1948; BD EDS 1951. D 6/1/1951 P 12/16/1951 Bp Norman B Nash. m 1/2/1960 Barbara Sherrill c 2. S Andr's Ch Framingham MA 1961-1992; R Ch Of The Mssh Woods Hole MA 1951-1961. masonprue@mindspring.com

WILSON, Mauricio Jose (Cal) 114 Montecito Ave, Oakland CA 94610 **R S Paul's Ch Oakland CA 2009-** B Costa Rica 4/24/1966 BBA Universidad De Costa Rica 1992; CPA Universidad De Costa Rica 1994; MDiv GTS 2000; STM GTS 2001. Trans from Iglesia Anglicana de la Region Central de America 8/13/2003 Bp Orris George Walker Jr. m 9/9/2002 Karla Vanessa Morris c 2. R All SS Ch Great Neck NY 2003-2009. mauricio_wilson@hotmail.com

WILSON, Michael H. (SwFla) 5108 Plainfield Street, Midland MI 48642 **S Jn's Epis Ch Midland MI 2006-** B Greenwich CT 10/6/1937 s Clyde Daniel Wilson & Dorothy Mildred. BA U So 1961; BD Ya Berk 1964. D 6/14/1964 Bp Charles L Street P 6/29/1965 Bp Ned Cole. c 3. Vacancy Consult Dio SW Florida Sarasota FL 1993-1998; R S Jas Epis Ch Port Charlotte FL 1983-2002; Dn Sw Dist Dio Rochester Rochester NY 1981-1983; R Zion Ch Avon NY 1975-1983; R Chr Epis Ch Jordan NY 1967-1975; Cur S Jn's Ch Ithaca NY 1964-1967. retiredpadre@charter.net

WILSON III, Morris Karl (Tenn) 3002 Westmoreland Dr, Nashville TN 37212 B Evanston IL 9/14/1947 s Morris Karl Wilson & Monterey. BA Ya 1969; MDiv Van 1973. D 6/24/1973 Bp William F Gates Jr P 6/2/1974 Bp John Vander Horst. m 4/25/1981 Deborah Butler c 1. Sr Assoc S Geo's Ch Nashville TN 1995-2005; Dio Florida Jacksonville FL 1992-1994; Assoc S Jn's Epis Ch Tallahassee FL 1986-1995; Asst S Geo's Ch Germantown TN 1984-1986; Dio W Tennessee Memphis TN 1983-1984; R S Matt's Ch Covington TN 1974-1984; S Thos Ch Elizabethton TN 1973-1974. No Amer Assn for Catechumenate 1995. MK3Wilson@comcast.net

WILSON, Phillip Dana (Nwk) 36 South St, Morristown NJ 07960 B Wilmington DE 7/25/1942 s William Sellers Wilson & Isabelle. BA U of Delaware Newark 1965; MDiv EDS 1969; Med U of Delaware Newark 1974. D 6/19/1969 P 1/1/1970 Bp William Henry Mead. m 7/20/1968 Susan Henckel c 2. COM Dio Newark Newark NJ 1992-2009; Ch Of The Redeem Morristown NJ 1987-2009; Dio Delaware Wilmington DE 1986-1987; Int Gr Epis Ch Wilmington DE 1986-1987; Asst Nevil Memi Ch Of S Geo Ardmore PA 1984-1986; Asst S Mary's Ch Hamilton Vill Philadelphia PA 1976-1979; Asst Pstr Cathd Ch Of S Jn Wilmington DE 1971-1973; Cur Ch of St Andrews & St Matthews Wilmington DE 1969-1971. Auth, *Tchg Exceptional Chld.* 2005 Distinguished Hm Alumnal Epis Div 2005. phillip@svcable.net

WILSON, Ray E(ugene) (Tex) Po Box 1943, Lenox MA 01240 **P-in-c S Jas Ch Great Barrington MA 1999-** B Little Rock AR 8/11/1943 s Leonard Frank Wilson & Reseda Marie. BA Amer J 1965; MDiv EDS 1971. D 6/26/1971 P 3/1/1972 Bp William Foreman Creighton. Dio Wstrn Massachusetts Springfield MA 1988-2002; Cn Chr Ch Cathd Houston TX 1978-1981; Vic S Jas Epis Ch Bowie MD 1975-1978; Asst S Jn's Ch Georgetown Par Washington DC 1973-1975; Cur Chr Ch Georgetown Washington DC 1971-1973.

WILSON, Raymond G (LI) 133 N Ocean Ave, Freeport NY 11520 **Ch Of The Trsfg Freeport NY 1992-** B Georgetown GY 11/16/1954 s Alan Wilson & Stella. Cert Coll Educ For Secondary Teachers Educ 1978; DIT Codrington Coll 1983; BA U of The W Indies 1983; MA CUNY 1992. Trans 4/20/1993 Bp Orris George Walker Jr. m 4/9/1983 Carol Bacchus c 4. rwilson5458@yahoo.com

WILSON, Richard (Az) 4267 N Limberlost Pl, Tucson AZ 85705 **R Ch Of S Matt Tucson AZ 2009-** B Peoria IL 2/26/1955 s Glenn Willard Wilson & Della Mae. BA Trin 1977; MDiv St Mary of the Lake 1984. Rec from Roman Catholic 12/21/2007 Bp Kirk Stevan Smith. rickaw@cox.net

WILSON, Richard Wadsworth (La) 2820 Burdette St Apt 310, New Orleans LA 70125 **Died 1/25/2010** B New Orleans LA 7/8/1928 s John Alexander M Wilson & Rena. BA Tul 1950; MDiv GTS 1954. D 6/30/1954 Bp Girault M Jones P 6/1/1955 Bp Iveson Batchelor Noland. c 2. Auth, *The Ch News*.

WILSON, Robert George (RG) 8001 Carter St Apt 2707, Overland Park KS 66204 **S Lk's Epis Ch Port Salerno FL 1996-** B Albuquerque NM 5/21/1923 s Clarence Robert Wilson & Eunice Verda. BS Hardin-Simmons U 1950; U CA 1952; Michigan TS 1968; U of Alabama 1979. D 4/5/1968 Bp Archie H Crowley P 2/28/1987 Bp Howard Samuel Meeks. m 2/12/1961 Patricia Ann Shay c 3. Asst S Andr's Epis Ch Las Cruces NM 1996-2003; Secy; Dioc Stndg Com Dio Wstrn Michigan Kalamazoo MI 1990-1992; Stndg Com Dio Wstrn Michigan Kalamazoo MI 1989-1992; Vic S Christophers Ch Northport MI 1989-1992; Epis Search Com Dio Wstrn Michigan Kalamazoo MI 1988-1989; V-Dn Traverse Dnry Dio Wstrn Michigan Kalamazoo MI 1985-1990; Asst Gr Epis Ch Traverse City MI 1970-1992; Asst S Ptr's Epis Ch Hillsdale MI 1968-1970. bob-pat@kc.rr.com

WILSON, Roy Dennis (Miss) 1954 Spillway Rd, Brandon MS 39047 **D S Ptr's By The Lake Brandon MS 2010-** B San Antonio TX 3/8/1961 s Roy Wilson & Edna Yvonne. AA Hinds Cmnty Coll 1985; BSN U of Texas 1987. D 1/9/2010 Bp Duncan Montgomery Gray III. m 5/25/1985 Rebecca Blackwell c 2. d_wilsonm@conmcast.net

WILSON, Sandra Antoinette (Nwk) 116 Turrell Ave, South Orange NJ 07079 **Collegial Cn Trin And S Phil's Cathd Newark NJ 2008-; R S Andr And H Comm Ch So Orange NJ 2004-** B 10/10/1952 d William Llewellyn Wilson & Anne Cooke. BA Vas 1975; MDiv UTS 1981; MBA GTF 1990; DMin GTF 1991. D 6/7/1980 Bp Paul Moore Jr P 1/23/1981 Bp Walter Decoster Dennis Jr. R Geth Ch Minneapolis MN 1998-2004; S Thos Epis Ch Denver CO 1989-1999; S Aug's Epis Ch Asbury Pk NJ 1986-1989; S Dav's Epis Ch Topeka KS 1982-1986; S Mk's Ch Bridgeport CT 1982-1986; Gr Ch White Plains NY 1980-1981. Auth, "Toward A Black Theol Of Liberation For The Ch Of Engl In The 80'S,'" *Anglicans & Racism*, 1985; Auth, "Living The Gd News CE Curric"; Auth, "Just Which Me Will Survive All These Liberations," *Ten Who Tithe*. Ch & City; Epgm; ESMHE; EUC; EWC; Impact; Rewim; UBE. sandyea@aol.com

WILSON, Stephen Thomas (Ky) 1530 Cherry St, Denver CO 80220 **Ch Of The H Redeem Denver CO 2008-** B Denver CO 4/18/1966 s James Barrett Wilson & Beverly Colleen. BS The London Sch of Econ and Political Sci 1989; MDiv SWTS 1995. D 6/10/1995 P 12/16/1995 Bp William Jerry Winterrowd. m 3/14/1998 Maria Wilson. All SS Epis Ch Denver CO 2005-2006; R S Andr's Ch Louisville KY 2001-2004; Cn Evang S Jn's Cathd Denver CO 1997-2001; Cmsn Mnsry Ya Berk New Haven CT 1995-1996; Cur S Lk's Ch Denver CO 1995-1996. swilson07@law.du.edu

WILSON, Steven Clark (WMo) 1213 Grand Ave, Carthage MO 64836 **R Gr Ch Carthage MO 1999-** B Lebanon MO 7/2/1965 s Clark Lee Wilson & Marie W. BA Drury U 1987; Kz - Lizenz U of Heidelberg DE 1989; MA Missouri St U 1991; MDiv Ya Berk 1994. D 6/4/1994 Bp John Clark Buchanan P 12/14/1994 Bp Peter James Lee. m 10/29/2001 Melinda Ann Dunaway c 2. Asst R Chr Ch Alexandria VA 1994-1999. gracechcar@sbcglobal.net

WILSON, Thomas Andrew (SanD) 339 Brightwood Ave, Chula Vista CA 91910 **Dioc Coun Dio San Diego San Diego CA 2011-; Pstr Assoc S Dav's Epis Ch San Diego CA 2011-** B Bucyrus OH 9/15/1948 s Robert Clinton Wilson & Leona Mary. BMe Baldwin-Wallace Coll 1971; M Div S Mich's Coll 1980; CAS CDSP 2008. D 6/7/2008 Bp James Robert Mathes. m 9/20/2008 John Joseph Will. Asstg Cler All Souls' Epis Ch San Diego CA 2009-2011; D (Non-stip) All Souls' Epis Ch San Diego CA 2008-2009. twilssdca@gmail.com

WILSON, Thomas Everitt (EC) 101 Bear Track Ln, Kitty Hawk NC 27949 **R All SS' Ch Sthrn Shores NC 2003-** B Saint Louis MO 12/20/1946 s William Everitt Wilson & Marian Peoples. BA U NC 1968; MSW U NC 1975; MDiv STUSo 1984. D 6/23/1984 P 1/24/1985 Bp William Gillette Weinhauer. m 9/3/1989 Patricia Leuck c 1. R S Paul's Ch Macon GA 1995-2003; R Gr Memi Ch Lynchburg VA 1986-1995; Cur Chr Ch Blacksburg VA 1984-1986. Auth, "A Pax On Both Your Houses," *Sewanee Theol Revs*, 1996. fathertom21@hotmail.com

WILSON, Thomas Lynn (Kan) 1308 Broadmoor St, Derby KS 67037 **R S Andr's Ch Derby KS 2008-** B Wichita KS 10/3/1952 s James Arthur Wilson & Marjorie Louise. Allen Cmnty Coll 1971; Baker U 1973; BA Washburn U 1974; JD U of Kansas 1977. D 1/20/1994 P 7/1/1994 Bp William Edward Smalley. m 8/8/1981 Ruth Weber c 2. rector@standrewsderby.org

WILSON, Thomas Stuart (Tenn) 1000 Sunnyside Dr, Columbia TN 38401 B Detroit MI 12/3/1941 s John Henry Wilson & Edith Emilie. BA Wayne 1965; STB Ya Berk 1968. D 6/29/1968 Bp Archie H Crowley P 1/4/1969 Bp Richard S M Emrich. m 1/31/1976 Jean Wilson c 4. R S Ptr's Ch Columbia TN 1988-2007; R S Jn's Ch Westland MI 1972-1988; Asst S Cyp's Epis Ch Detroit MI 1968-1972. twilson@cpws.net

WILSON, Tom Stacey (Nev) 324 Dayton St, Yerington NV 89447 B 12/3/1929 D 7/21/1960 Bp Lane W Barton P 6/27/1961 Bp William G Wright. m 2/2/1952 Eileen Teachout. S Paul Epis Ch Des Moines IA 1974-1979. teeuu12329@webtv.net

WILSON, William Henry (Ala) 800 Lake Colony Cir, Birmingham AL 35242 B Philadelphia PA 8/16/1937 s William Holmes Wilson & Elizabeth Rose. MDiv New Melleray Abbey 1968; DMin Drew U 1999. Rec from Roman Catholic 9/1/1990 Bp Robert Oran Miller. m 3/23/1989 Susan Winchester c 2. S Lk's Epis Ch Birmingham AL 1998-2003; Chr Ch Fairfield AL 1995-1996; Dio Alabama Birmingham AL 1994-1995. Auth, "Looking Deeper," *Fllshp In Pryr*. Hon Citizen (Soc Serv Awd) Cochabamba Bolivia. wsws@bellsouth.net

WILSON, William Jackson (Az) 1246 W Caida Del Sol Dr, Pueblo West CO 81007 B Kansas City MO 7/12/1927 s George Campbell Wilson & Marjorie Mckay. BA Wm Jewell Coll 1947; MA U of Missouri 1954; Redd Cntrl Bapt

TS 1956; Dplma in Angl Stds STUSo 1967; Cert Meharry Med Coll 1974; Audit Van 1975; Audit Med Coll of Georgia 1976; Cert Harv 1977. D 6/25/1967 Bp John Vander Horst P 12/21/1967 Bp William F Gates Jr. m 3/4/1947 Bettie Phillips c 3. Vic S Paul's Ch Payson AZ 1989-1996; Dio Arizona Phoenix AZ 1989-1992; Chair - Dept. Of Missions Dio Arizona Phoenix AZ 1983-1985; R S Ptr's Ch Litchfield Pk AZ 1979-1989; R Chr Ch Epis So Pittsburg TN 1967-1979. Auth, "Views of a Vill Idiot," *Bk*, GOPress, 2006; Auth, "Var," *Profsnl & Popular Pub*, Woodfin Press, 1978; Auth, "The First 100 Years," *Bk*, Woodfin, 1976; Auth, "10 Commandments For 20th Century Christians," *Bk*, Whitaker, 1963. AAMFC 1962-1979; Natl Assn Of Scholars 1988; Natl Assn Of Theol Professors 1956-1960. Best Rel Nwspr column So. Colorado Press Club 2008; Hon Prof Of Med Ukranian Natl Med Acad 1997; Outstanding Young Man Of The Year Mo Jaycees 1962. wjw@jwco.us

WILSON-BARNARD, M Letha (Minn) Holy Apostles, 2200 Minnehaha Ave E, Saint Paul MN 55119 **Ch Of The H Apos S Paul MN 2008-** B Minneapolis MN 1/5/1957 d LeRoy W Wilson & Ardis Masine. Cert. in Angl Stds VTS; BA Bethel U 1979; MDiv Luther TS 2007. D 6/14/2007 P 12/20/2007 Bp James Louis Jelinek. m 10/13/1981 Scott Wilson-Barnard c 1. lethawbmn@yahoo.com

WILT, David Ruhl (SeFla) 415 Duval St, Key West FL 33040 **R H Trin Epis Ch W Palm Bch FL 2008-** B Cumberland MD 3/17/1950 s Henry Wilt & R(hoda) Maxine. BBA Wstrn Michigan U 1972; JD Stetson U 1975; MDiv VTS 1996. D 6/16/1996 P 12/8/1996 Bp Stephen Hays Jecko. m 3/17/1979 Sandra J Wilt c 3. S Paul's Ch Key W FL 2004-2008; St Fran in the Field Ponte Vedra FL 2001-2004; Par Mssnr Chr Epis Ch Ponte Vedra Bch FL 1996-2000. davidkw@aol.com

WILTON, (Glenn) (Warner) Paul (Oly) 10 Lichfield Avenue, CANTERBURY CT1 3YA Great Britain (UK) B Cincinnati OH 3/24/1933 s Frank Starr Wilton & Virginia. BS Mia 1955; Beda Col. Rome Italy 1966; CUA 1969; MSW U of Washington 1976; CDSP 1977. Rec from Roman Catholic 12/1/1977 as Deacon Bp Robert Hume Cochrane. m 3/22/1975 Daniele Marie Christiane Ligneau c 3. P S Andr's Ch Seattle WA 1979-1980; P S Jn The Bapt Epis Ch Seattle WA 1978-1979; D & P Ch Of The Epiph Seattle WA 1977-1978. gwpaulwilton@yahoo.co.uk

WILTSE, Roderic Duncan (Mo) 209 S Woods Mill Rd Apt. 3311, Chesterfield MO 63017 B Catskill NY 12/10/1934 s Alexander Wiltse & Helena May. Int Mnstry Prog; BA Syr 1957; STB GTS 1960. D 5/28/1960 Bp Frederick Lehrle Barry P 12/10/1960 Bp Allen Webster Brown. m 8/5/1961 Patricia Bordley c 3. Int Chr Ch Covington LA 1996-1997; Int S Wlfd's Epis Ch Sarasota FL 1994-1996; Int Trin Epis Ch Kirksville MO 1993-1994; Chair of Stweardship Com Dio Missouri S Louis MO 1983-1998; R Ch Of The H Comm U City MO 1983-1993; R S Mk's Ch Coldwater MI 1973-1983; R H Trin Epis Ch Wyoming MI 1967-1973; R Trin Ch Gouverneur NY 1963-1967; Cur Chr Ch Cooperstown NY 1960-1963. Auth, *Comm for Unconfirmed Chld*; Auth, *Contrib Bible Workbench*; Auth, *Journeying w S Paul*. Soc of S Jn the Evang 1978. wiltse@charter.net

WILTSEE JR, Leon Lamont (ECR) 13083 Middle Canyon Rd, Carmel Valley CA 93924 B Minot ND 1/20/1947 s Leon Lamont Wiltse & Dorothy. BA NWU 1968; BA TS at Claremont 1971; MDiv TS at Claremont 1978; DMin Claremont TS 2006. D 7/14/1974 P 6/14/1975 Bp Robert C Rusack. m 3/26/2001 Edith Freeman White. Int S Jn's Chap Monterey CA 2000; Int S Mk's Ch KING CITY CA 1997-1998; Int S Mths Ch Seaside CA 1995-1996; Robert Louis Stevenson Sch Pebble Bch CA 1987-1993; S Patricks Ch And Day Sch Thousand Oaks CA 1981-1984; Asst All SS-By-The-Sea Par Santa Barbara CA 1978-1980; S Andr's Epis Ch Irvine CA 1975-1977; D Dio Los Angeles Los Angeles CA 1974-1975. elwiltsee@sbcglobal.net

WILTSEY SMITH, Susan (U) 450 Shinava Dr, Ivins UT 84738 **Dio Utah Salt Lake City UT 2007-; Vic S Jude's Ch Cedar City UT 2007-; Gr Epis Ch St Geo UT 2001-** B Richmond VA 7/16/1945 d John Martin Allman & Marjorie Emma. AB Randolph-Macon Wmn's Coll 1967; MA U CA 1975. D 1/18/2001 P 8/4/2001 Bp Carolyn Tanner Irish. m 6/30/2007 Michael Smith c 3. Dio Utah Salt Lake City UT 2005-2006; Assoc H Trin Epis Ch Inwood New York NY 2005. wiltseysmith@gmail.com

✠ WIMBERLY, Rt Rev Don Adger (Tex) 3515 Plumb St, Houston TX 77005 **Ret Bp of Texas Dio Texas Houston TX 2009-** B Baton Rouge LA 6/10/1937 s Herbert Wright Wimberly & Mary Elizabeth. BS LSU 1959; MDiv VTS 1971; DD STUSo 1988; DD VTS 1988. D 6/21/1971 Bp Iveson Batchelor Noland P 12/21/1971 Bp Harold B Robinson Con 9/22/1984 for Lex. m 4/16/1966 Edwina Jones c 2. Dio Texas Houston TX 1999-2009; Bd Rgnts, Chncllr The TS at The U So Sewanee TN 1991-2003; Bp of Lex Dio Lexington Lexington KY 1985-1999; Dio Lexington Lexington KY 1984-1999; Bp Coadj of Lex Dio Lexington Lexington KY 1984-1985; Dn S Jn's Cathd Jacksonville FL 1978-1984; Chr Ch Overland Pk KS 1974-1978; Dio Wstrn Kansas Hutchinson KS 1974-1978; Assoc S Jas Epis Ch Baton Rouge LA 1972-1974; Asst Calv Epis Ch Williamsville NY 1971-1972. DD TS U So 1988; DD VTS Alexandria VA 1988. dawimberly@att.net

WIMBUSH, Claire S (SVa) 1333 Jamestown Rd, Williamsburg VA 23185 B Oxford England 3/19/1983 d Samuel Enders Wimbush & Jane Ann D. BA W&M 2005; MDiv Duke DS 2009. D 1/9/2010 Bp Herman Hollerith IV P 4/10/2011 Bp Michael Bruce Curry. D S Mart's Epis Ch Williamsburg VA 2010. education@stthomasrochester.org

WINBORN JR, James Henderson (SVa) 8880 Colonnades Ct W Apt 412, Bonita Springs FL 34135 B Detroit MI 5/31/1942 s James Henderson Winborn & Esther Lee. BA U Of Dallas Dallas 1971; MDiv Epis TS In Kentucky 1979; Coll of Preachers 1983. D 5/18/1980 P 12/13/1980 Bp Addison Hosea. m 11/12/1999 Barbara Jucius c 1. R Emm Epis Ch Chatham VA 2005-2007; R Ch Of The Nativ Maysville KY 2002-2005; R S Jas Epis Ch Belle Fourche SD 1999-2001; P-in-c S Andr's Ch Lexington KY 1995-1999; P-in-c S Alb's Ch Morehead KY 1992-1995; P-in-c S Andr's Ch Lexington KY 1986-1992; Vic S Phil's Ch Harrodsburg KY 1982-1984; Asst Trin Ch Wauwatosa WI 1980-1982. jimwinborn@yahoo.com

WINCHELL, Ronald (Va) 128 Eagle Ct, Locust Grove VA 22508 B Baltimore MD 6/2/1943 s Lawrence Lee Winchell & Jane Evelyn. BS U Of Florida 1964; MDiv EDS 1982; DMin McCormick TS 1992. D 6/19/1982 Bp Wilbur Emory Hogg Jr P 12/19/1982 Bp A(rthur) Heath Light. m 2/6/1965 Judith C Clements c 2. Int The Fork Ch Doswell VA 2002-2003; Int Hanover w Brunswick Par - S Jn King Geo VA 1998-2000; R All SS Ch Alexandria VA 1992-1996; Gr Epis Ch St Geo UT 1990-1992; Dio Utah Salt Lake City UT 1988-1990; Vic H Sprt Roanoke VA 1986-1988; Int S Eliz's Ch Roanoke VA 1985; Asst S Jn's Ch Roanoke VA 1982-1985. rxgator64@charter.net

WINDAL, Claudia L (Minn) 1532 Randolph Ave, Apt. 8, St. Paul, MN 55105 B Chicago IL 9/18/1949 d Joseph S Windal & Evelyn M. RN Franciscan Sch Nrsng 1973; BA St. Ambr U Davenport IA 1975; MDiv SWTS 1981; MA Norwich U 1983; DMin Luther TS 1993; BS U MN 2003. D 6/18/1982 Bp James Winchester Montgomery P 12/1/1982 Bp Quintin Ebenezer Primo Jr. m 4/23/1990 Susan M Severud. Dio Minnesota Minneapolis MN 2000-2001; Emm Epis Ch Alexandria MN 1985-1986; Asst Ch Of Our Sav Chicago IL 1984-1985; Assoc S Andr's Ch Chicago IL 1983-1984; CE Supvsr S Clem's Ch Harvey IL 1979-1982. Auth, "Stations Of The Cross For Persons w Aids"; Auth, "Stations Of The Cross For The Lesbian & Gay Cmnty"; Auth, "Bk Chapt Cultural & Societal Impediments To Aids Educ In"; Auth, "Native Amer Cmnty". Integrity 1987. cwindal@aol.com

WINDEL, Marian Kathleen (Va) 1782 Yanceyville Road, 7182 Yanceyville Road, Louisa VA 23093 **Vic Ch of the Incarn Mineral VA 2006-; Peace In The Vlly Ch Afton VA 1992-** B Washington DC 5/21/1946 d Glenn McInturff Windel & Rosalie Eugenia. BA Ohio U 1968; MS Amer U 1972; MDiv VTS 1979; DMin U of Wexford 1998. D 6/23/1979 P 12/23/1979 Bp John Thomas Walker. R Westover Epis Ch Chas City VA 1982-1990; Asst S Jn's Ch Chevy Chase MD 1979-1982. marian_1782@cvakink.com

WINDER, Francis (U) 4546 Jupiter Dr, Salt Lake City UT 84124 B Fallon NV 6/9/1932 s William Lee Winder & Greta Mildred. BS U of Utah 1954; BD CDSP 1957. D P 12/21/1957 Bp Richard S Watson. m 6/18/1965 Bonnie Jean E Oss c 2. Archd & Exec Off Dio Utah Salt Lake City UT 1989-1997; Dio Utah Salt Lake City UT 1988-1997; Pres Stndg Com Dio Utah Salt Lake City UT 1979-1980; Pres Stndg Com Dio Utah Salt Lake City UT 1974-1975; Ch Of The Gd Shpd Ogden UT 1971-1988; Cn Mssnr Dio Utah Salt Lake City UT 1960-1969; Asst Cathd Ch Of S Mk Salt Lake City UT 1957-1960. Paul Harris Fell Rotary 1983. goshepherd@msn.com

WINDOM, Barbara Sewell (At) 432 Forest Hill Rd, Macon GA 31210 B Ft Bragg NC 2/9/1955 d Bobby Rex Sewell & Martha Leona. BA Merc 2012. D 8/6/2011 Bp J(ohn) Neil Alexander. m 10/23/1976 Michael Young Windom c 1. barbara.window@gmail.com

WINDSOR, Janice Priebe (Colo) 33741 State Highway 257, Windsor CO 80550 **D Assoc S Alb's Ch Windsor CO 2002-** B Kansas City MO 8/26/1934 d Elden Paul Priebe & Jeanette Frances. CSD S Thos Sem Denver CO; BS Colorado St U 1956. D 7/31/2002 Bp William Jerry Winterrowd. m 6/9/1956 John Clark Windsor. jwindsor@iglide.net

WINDSOR, Robert Grover (Mass) 1132 Highland Ave, Needham MA 02494 **R Chr Ch Needham MA 2002-** B San Diego CA 7/31/1947 s Robert Wilks Windsor & Elizabeth. BA Dickinson Coll 1969; MBA Cor 1975; MA EDS 1979; MDiv Harvard DS 1987. D 6/11/1988 P 6/10/1989 Bp David Elliot Johnson. m 8/8/1970 Kathryn W Windsor c 3. R S Jn's Ch Newtonville MA 1995-2002; Int Gr Ch Newton MA 1995; Int S Mich's Ch Milton MA 1992-1994; Int S Ptr's Ch Weston MA 1991-1992; Cox Fell The Cathd Ch Of S Paul Boston MA 1988-1990. Ord Of St Jn Of Jerusalem 2007. tuckernuck@comcast.net

WINDSOR, Walter Van Zandt (Ark) Po Box 8069, Pine Bluff AR 71611 **R Trin Ch Pine Bluff AR 2002-** B Gallipolis OH 10/4/1958 s Walter Mills Windsor & Caroline. B.A.R. Transylvania 1981; MA 1986; Cert. CDSP 1988; M.T.S. 1997; DMin EDS 2000; Cert. Loyola U 2007. D 2/22/1994 P 6/29/1994 Bp Alfred Clark Marble Jr. m 11/4/1996 Harra Dickson Shortle c 2. R S Jn's Ch Monroeville AL 2000-2002; S Paul's Ch Woodville MS 1997-2000; Int Trin Ch Natchez MS 1996; Vic S Matt's Epis Ch Forest MS 1994-1996.

Auth, "Establishing and Maintaining an Anti-Racism Prison Mnstry in Mississippi," *Thesis*, EDS, 2000. The GAS 2000. waltwindsor@aol.com

WINELAND, Richard Kevin (NI) 64669 Orchard Dr, Goshen IN 46526 B Altoona PA 9/13/1959 s John Merle Wineland & Bettyl Louise. Luth TS at Chicago; BA Goshen Coll 1991; MDiv Mennonite Brethren Biblic Sem 1996. Rec 7/24/2006 as Priest Bp Edward Stuart Little II. m 7/19/1986 Machelle Stump c 3. S Jn Of The Cross Bristol IN 2006-2008. wineland5@verizon.net

WING III, Arthur Kyle (NY) 7 Van Alstine Ave, Suffern NY 10901 B Newark NJ 4/4/1934 s Arthur Kyle Wing & Phebe. BA Leh 1956; MDiv VTS 1961. D 6/10/1961 Bp Leland Stark P 12/1/1961 Bp Donald MacAdie. m 6/29/1957 Alice Joan Finney c 3. S Jas Ch Upper Montclair NJ 1977-1982. twing3@verizon.net

WINGER, Nordon W. (Az) Good Shepherd Episcopal Church, P.O. Box 110, Cave Creek AZ 85327 **R Gd Shpd Of The Hills Cave Creek AZ 2010-; Dioc Total Mnstry Assessment Team Dio Nthrn California Sacramento CA 2009-** B Shreveport LA 2/19/1953 s Donald Martin Winger & Norma Lola. Sthrn Mssy Coll 1972; Newbold Coll, Great Britain 1973; BA Pacific Un Coll 1975; MDiv Andrews U 1981; CAS CDSP 1996. D 3/17/1996 P 9/28/1996 Bp Jerry Alban Lamb. m 12/31/1978 Christine A Mulroney c 3. Acad Com Dio Nthrn California Sacramento CA 2007-2010; COM Dio Nthrn California Sacramento CA 2007-2010; Chair of Liturg & Mus Cmsn Dio Nthrn California Sacramento CA 2003-2007; Vic S Aug Of Cbury Rocklin CA 2000-2010; Cmsn on Liturg & Mus Dio Nthrn California Sacramento CA 1999-2008; Int All SS Memi Sacramento CA 1998-2000; Cur S Fran On The Hill El Paso TX 1997-1998; Int S Jn The Evang Ch Chico CA 1996. No Ca Cleric Assn 1996. nordonwinger@gmail.com

WINGERT, Anita LaVonne (NMich) 550 N Ravine St, Sault Sainte Marie MI 49783 B Walla Walla WA 7/29/1948 d Frank Saint Clair Wingert & Viola Maxine. BA NEU 1971; MA U of Iowa 1975; MDiv CDSP 2001. D 6/24/2000 P 2/17/2001 Bp Chilton Abbie Richardson Knudsen. m 2/20/2004 Harold Martin c 2. S Jas Ch Of Sault S Marie Sault Ste Marie MI 2007-2008; S Jude's Ch Edina MN 2002-2008. Epis Womens Caucus 2000; Living Stones 2002; Mnstry Developers Collaborative 2000; Sindicators 2001. demagda2@gmail.com

WINGERT JR, John Alton (CNY) 1244 Great Pond Road, Box 116, Great Pond ME 04408 **Int Trin Epis Ch Fayetteville NY 1995-** B Waynesboro PA 6/21/1943 s John Alton Wingert & Elizabeth Ellen. BA Ham 1965; STB GTS 1969. D 3/12/1970 Bp Harry Lee Doll P 12/1/1970 Bp David Keller Leighton Sr. m 5/25/1968 Jacqueline Rueff. Int S Paul's Epis Ch Albany NY 2007-2009; Int S Jn's Ch Bangor ME 2005-2007; Asst Dio Cntrl New York Syracuse NY 2004-2005; Int S Thos' Epis Ch Syracuse NY 2004-2005; Int S Thos Ch Hamilton NY 2002-2004; Int Chr Ch Binghamton NY 2001-2002; Vic Ch Of The Sav Syracuse NY 1996-2001; R Ch Of St Jn The Evang Shady Side MD 1971-1977; D Epiph Epis Ch Odenton MD 1970-1971. wingertjj@aol.com

WINGFIELD, Vest Garrett (Tex) PO Box 540742, Houston TX 77254 B Washington DC 5/22/1935 s Burnley Magruder Wingfield & Carrie Jones. BA U of Houston 1958; MDiv CDSP 1966. D 6/24/1966 Bp J Milton Richardson P 6/1/1967 Bp Frederick P Goddard. m 5/7/1983 Mary C Borg c 7. Founding Vic Lord Of The St Epis Mssn Ch Houston TX 1993-1999; Asst R Trin Ch Houston TX 1987-1993; Vic S Jn's Epis Ch Silsbee TX 1966-1969; Vic S Paul's Epis Ch Woodville TX 1966-1969.

WINGO, Patrick James (Ala) 3608 Dabney Dr, Birmingham AL 35243 **Dio Alabama Birmingham AL 2077-; Dep to Bp/Deploy Dio Alabama Birmingham AL 2008-; Stndg Com Dio Alabama Birmingham AL 2001-** B Birmingham AL 4/2/1960 s James Pope Wingo & Nancy Belle. Auburn U; BA/BS U of Alabama 1982; MDiv Epis TS of The SW 1992. D 6/13/1992 P 12/19/1992 Bp Robert Oran Miller. m 5/2/1987 Sara Scott Nelson Wingo c 3. R S Thos Epis Ch Birmingham AL 1996-2008; Ch Of The Resurr Rainbow City AL 1992-1996. PATWINGO@CHARTER.NET

WINGO, Sara Scott Nelson (Ala) 2813 Godfrey Ave Ne, Fort Payne AL 35967 **S Mk's Ch Birmingham AL 2009-** B Nashville TN 11/13/1961 d Innes Armisted Nelson & Sara Scott. BA U So 1984; MDiv Epis TS of The SW 1991. D 6/11/1991 P 6/1/1992 Bp Robert Oran Miller. m 5/2/1987 Patrick James Wingo. S Lk's Epis Ch Birmingham AL 2003-2008; Dio Alabama Birmingham AL 1997-1998; S Phil's Ch Ft Payne AL 1994-1997; Asst S Lk's Epis Ch Jacksonville AL 1992-1994; Chld'S Mnstrs S Dav's Ch Austin TX 1991-1992.

WINKLER, Anne Louise (Ind) 10482 Muirfield Trce, Fishers IN 46037 B Indianapolis IN 7/9/1961 d Earl Hunt Johnson & Anita Sue. BS Duke 1983; Duke 1987; MDiv GTS 1989. D 6/23/1989 Bp Edward Witker Jones. m 7/11/1987 Steven William Dougherty. Ch Of The Nativ Indianapolis IN 1989-1990.

WINKLER, Barbara Jo (NMich) 852 E D St, Iron Mountain MI 49801 B Saint Paul MN 4/25/1939 d Rudolph Miresse & Alice. D 3/1/1998 Bp Thomas Kreider Ray. m 2/4/1961 James Winkler c 2.

WINKLER JR, Richard Edward (Haw) 202 Pin Oak Dr, Harker Heights TX 76548 B Chicago IL 9/11/1944 s Richard E Winkler & Dorothy. MD U of Hawaii; BA U IL; MDiv CDSP 1971. D 6/12/1971 P 12/12/1971 Bp Edwin Lani Hanchett. m 4/19/1983 Judy Winkler c 2. S Jn's Ch Eleele HI 1976; Asst The Par Of S Clem Honolulu HI 1971-1974. judy@centraltx.net

WINKLER, Thomas E. (Minn) 39259 K-C Dr, Winona MN 55987 **Assoc Chr Ch Par La Crosse WI 2004-** B Milwaukee WI 8/2/1943 s Earl H Winkler & Margaret Adele. BA U of Wisconsin 1965; BD EDS 1969. D 11/16/1969 P 7/19/1970 Bp William Benjamin Spofford. P-in-c Gr Memi Ch Wabasha MN 1997-1999; R S Paul's Ch Winona MN 1991-1996; Dn The Epis Cathd Of Our Merc Sav Faribault MN 1979-1991; R S Paul's Epis Ch Owatonna MN 1972-1979; Gnrl Mssnr Dio Estrn Oregon The Dalles OR 1970-1972; Vic H Trin Vale OR 1969-1970; Vic S Paul's Epis Ch Nyssa OR 1969-1970. Hon Cn Cathd of Our Merc Sav, Faribault MN 2002. thomas_e_winkler@yahoo.com

WINKLER JR, William Edward (NY) 7 Lyons Dr, Poughkeepsie NY 12601 B New York NY 9/26/1942 s William E Winkler & Dorithy. Norwalk Cmnty Coll Norwalk CT; AA Rca Inst 1967; Dio New York Diac Trng NY 1994. D 6/4/1994 Bp Richard Frank Grein. m 4/30/1987 Kathleen DePasquale c 4.

WINN, John Barrington (Oly) Po Box 1961, Silverdale WA 98383 B Chicago IL 10/20/1931 s John George Winn & Evelyn Clara. BA U So 1954; LTh SWTS 1957. D 6/13/1957 Bp Charles L Street P 12/21/1957 Bp Gerald Francis Burrill. c 2. P-in-c S Mich And All Ang Ch Issaquah WA 1992-1995; Vic S Antony Of Egypt Silverdale WA 1986-1992; Dio Olympia Seattle WA 1977-1992; Vic All SS Ch Tacoma WA 1974-1986; Ch Of The H Comm Seattle WA 1974-1976; R S Paul Epis Ch Bellingham WA 1965-1974; Cur Gr Ch Oak Pk IL 1957-1959.

WINSETT, Stephen Metcalfe (Chi) 1024 24th Ave W, Palmetto FL 34221 **P-in-c S Mary's Epis Ch Palmetto FL 2011-** B Dallas TX 8/22/1939 s Milo Asa Winsett & Louise Love. BA U of Texas 1961; MDiv SWTS 1964. D 6/18/1964 P 12/18/1964 Bp Theodore H McCrea. m 6/29/1979 Veronica Helman c 4. Vic H Trin Ch Brandenburg KY 2007-2011; Int Emm Epis Ch Rockford IL 2002-2004; Int Ch of the Gd Shpd Rahway NJ 2001-2002; Int Gr Ch Van Vorst Jersey City NJ 2001-2002; Int S Paul's Epis Ch Paterson NJ 2000-2001; Int S Dav's Ch Southfield MI 1998-2000; R S Chas Ch S Chas IL 1993-1998; R The Par Of S Clem Honolulu HI 1991-1993; R S Paul's Epis Ch New Albany IN 1980-1991; Asst S Lk's Par Kalamazoo MI 1974-1980; Vic S Phil's Ch Beulah MI 1969-1972; Cur S Aug's Epis Ch Wilmette IL 1966-1968; Vic S Laurence Epis Ch Grapevine TX 1965-1966; Cur Ch Of The Annunc Lewisville TX 1964-1965; Cur S Lk's Epis Ch Dallas TX 1964-1965. Dir of RACA 1989-1994; Off, RACA 1995. stevewinsett@gmail.com

WINSLETT JR, Hoyt (Ala) 1224 - 37th Avenue East, Tuscaloosa AL 35404 B Tuscaloosa AL 10/28/1934 s Hoyt Candler Winslett & Louise. BA U of Alabama 1956; STB GTS 1961; STUSo 1969; Fllshp Coll of Preachers 1979. D 6/19/1961 Bp George Mosley Murray P 5/1/1962 Bp Charles C J Carpenter. c 2. Chr Ch Tuscaloosa AL 1996-1999; COM Dio Alabama Birmingham AL 1981-1993; R S Paul's Ch Greensboro AL 1978-1989; Admin Dio Georgia Savannah GA 1974-1978; Dio Alabama Birmingham AL 1971-1974; Assoc Ch Of The Nativ Epis Huntsville AL 1970-1973; R Ch Of The Epiph Guntersville AL 1963-1970; Cur All SS Epis Ch Mobile AL 1961-1963. Phi Beta Kappa 1955. hwinslett1@comcast.net

WINSLOW, Gail George (NwPa) Trinity Memorial, 444 Pennsylvania Ave W, Warren PA 16365 B Warren PA 5/29/1945 s George Dewey Winslow & Evelyn Mary. D 11/11/2002 Bp Robert Deane Rowley Jr. m 9/6/1980 Barbara A Winslow c 3. ggwinslow@yahoo.com

WINSLOW, K Dennis (NY) 380 Mountain Rd Apt 304, Union City NJ 07087 B Worcester MA 12/20/1949 s Kenneth Dennis Winslow & Ada Jeanette. AA Worcester Jr Coll 1969; BA Emerson Coll 1971; MDiv Nash 1974. D 9/15/1974 P 6/15/1975 Bp Alexander Doig Stewart. m 8/3/2011 Mark Alan Lewis. R S Ptr's Ch New York NY 1998-2010; Dio New York New York City NY 1997-1998; Ch Of The Atone Bronx NY 1995-1996; Cn S Paul's Cathd Syracuse NY 1979-1985; Asst Ch Of Beth Saratoga Sprg NY 1976-1979; Cur S Jn's Ch Northampton MA 1974-1976. Cmnty of S Mary 1986-2000. rville2012@gmail.com

WINSLOW, Thomas Frank (Mil) N12 W29810, Southampton Drive, Waukesha WI 53188 **Chapl to the Bp Dio Milwaukee Milwaukee WI 2006-** B Milwaukee WI 5/24/1944 s Carl Andrew Winslow & Marion Ina. AAS Milwaukee Area Tech Coll 1979; Cert Dio Milwaukee Inst WI 1983; Cert Univ. of Virginia / FBI Natl Acad 1984; BS Cardinal Stritch U 1988; MTS Nash 2007. D 11/26/1983 Bp Charles Thomas Gaskell P 1/6/2006 Bp Steven Andrew Miller. m 6/27/1964 Margaret Anna Warner c 2. Archd Dio Milwaukee Milwaukee WI 2001-2006; Dio Milwaukee Milwaukee WI 2000-2003; D S Alb's Ch Sussex WI 1996-2002; D S Dav Of Wales Ch New Berlin WI 1983-1995; D St Philips Epis Ch Waukesha WI 1983-1985. Curs 1978; Intl Conf of Police Chapl (ICPC) 1993; No Amer Assn Diac 1983-2006; RACA 1981. Bp's Shield Awd Dio Milwaukee 2009; 911 hon Bar Intl Conf of Police Chapl 2002; Cler Person of Year Dio Milwaukee 1987. twinslow@wi.rr.com

WINSOR, Ann Roberts (NY) P O Box 129, East Chatham NY 12060 B Chelsea MA 8/4/1943 d Frank Jones Roberts & Marie MacDonnell. BA Smith 1964; Cert U CA 1967; MDiv CDSP 1982; PhD Grad Theol Un 1996. D 1/9/

1983 P 3/19/1984 Bp Charles Shannon Mallory. m 11/26/1966 Robert George Winsor c 5. Grants Off Trin Par New York NY 2002-2008; Assoc for Educ and Sprtlty Ch Of The H Trin New York NY 2001-2003; Int Dn and R Trin Cathd San Jose CA 1998-1999; Adj Fac CDSP Berkeley CA 1997-1998; Asstg P Gr Cathd San Francisco CA 1989-1997; Asstg P S Mk's Epis Ch Palo Alto CA 1987-1989; S Mk's Epis Ch Santa Clara CA 1984. Auth, *A King Is Bound in the Tresses: Allusions to the Song of Songs in the 4th Gospel*, Ptr Lang, 1998. AAR 1986; Angl Assn of Biblic Scholars 1995; Cath Biblic Assn 1988; Soc for Study of Chr Sprtlty 1990; SBL 1986; Sprtl Dir Intl 1995. annrobertswinsor@gmail.com

WINSOR, Edward Stiness (RI) 28 Mcallister St, Newport RI 02840 B Providence RI 8/28/1929 s Edward Winsor & Mary M. BA Dart 1951; MIA Col 1954; STB Ya Berk 1958. D 6/7/1958 P 3/7/1959 Bp John S Higgins. m 8/15/1952 Jean Sherwood Fowler c 4. Asst S Columba Epis Ch Marathon FL 2002-2003; S Ptr's Epis Ch Key W FL 1996-1998; P-in-c S Fran-In-The-Keys Episcop Big Pine Key FL 1993-1995; R S Columba's Chap Middletown RI 1964-1989; In-c S Paul's Ch Portsmouth RI 1958-1961. Ord of S Lk 1974; OHC 1955. e.winsor@yahoo.com

WINSOR, J(ames) Michael (NY) 3824 Cedar Springs Road, Box 203, Dallas TX 75219 B Dallas TX 10/10/1947 s James Kenneth Winsor & Elsie Madolin. BA Lake Forest Coll 1969; MDiv (equivalent) Cuddesdon Coll, Oxford 1972; Assoc. El Centro Coll 2004. Trans from Church Of England 6/1/1976 Bp A Donald Davies. Ch Of The Gd Samar Dallas TX 1997-2002; R S Jas Ch Hyde Pk NY 1986-1995; R Chr The King Epis Ch Ft Worth TX 1981-1986; S Pat's Ch Bowie TX 1979-1981; Vic S Mk's Ch Bridgeport CT 1977-1981; Asst To Dn S Matt's Cathd Dallas TX 1976-1977. OHC, Assoc 1989. mwinsor@sbcglobal.net

WINSTON, William Scott (FtW) 3313 Minot Ave, Fort Worth TX 76133 B Temple TX 5/27/1946 s Maurice Long Winston & Thelma Ruth. BA Oklahoma U 1969; STB GTS 1972. D 7/1/1972 P 12/17/1972 Bp Chilton Powell. m 6/7/1969 Charlotte Rather. R Gr Ch Lockport NY 2008-2011; Vic S Lk's Epis Ch Rincon GA 2007-2008; R Zion Epis Ch Washington NC 2003-2007; R S Anne's Ch Ft Worth TX 1995-2003; R S Jn's Ch Bangor ME 1988-1995; Vic S Basil's Epis Ch Tahlequah OK 1977-1988; Cur Trin Epis Ch Ft Worth TX 1975-1977; Vic S Ptr's Ch Coalgate OK 1972-1974. Soc of S Jn the Evang 1978. williamswinston@yahoo.com

WINTER, Brian William (RG) 12408 Prospect Ave. NE, Albuquerque NM 87112 **R S Chad's Epis Ch Albuquerque NM 2005-** B Saint Louis MO 7/24/1965 s Fred Willard Winter & Inez. BS Nthrn Arizona U 1988; MDiv VTS 2002. D 7/11/2002 P 1/18/2003 Bp Carolyn Tanner Irish. m 4/28/1990 Cheryl K Petty c 2. Stndg Com Dio The Rio Grande Albuquerque NM 2008-2010; Assoc for Yth and Young Families Trin On The Hill Epis Ch Los Alamos NM 2004-2005; Vic S Mich's Ch Brigham City UT 2002-2004. tightlinebri@hotmail.com

WINTER, Cheryl Ann (WVa) Po Box 424, Hurricane WV 25526 **R S Tim's In The Vlly Hurricane WV 1993-; Bd Trst VTS Alexandria VA 1992-** B Providence RI 3/29/1957 d Lewis J Winter & Helen B. BS Marshall U 1980; MDiv VTS 1987. D 6/1/1988 Bp Robert Poland Atkinson P 6/10/1989 Bp William Franklin Carr. Dioc Deploy Off Dio W Virginia Charleston WV 2000-2006; Vic S Mths Grafton WV 1989-1993; Vic S Paul Avondale WV 1989-1993; Cres Par Philippi WV 1988-1990. cwinter@wvdiocese.org

WINTER, James L (Miss) 105 N. Montgomery St, Starkville MS 39759 **Ch Of The Resurr Starkville MS 2007-** B Anderson SC 6/19/1948 s William Edward Winter & Adalee. BS U of Alabama 1971; MA Louisiana Tech U 1977; MSW U of Alabama 1980; MDiv STUSo 1983. D 5/31/1983 P 12/7/1983 Bp Furman Stough. m 8/17/1969 Ruth S Stewart c 1. Trin Ch New Orleans LA 2004-2007; R Chr Ch Slidell LA 2001-2004; Dio Mississippi Jackson MS 1997-2004; R Calv Epis Ch Cleveland MS 1995-2001; Gr Ch Rosedale MS 1995-2001; Vic Ch Of The Ascen Hattiesburg MS 1987-1995; R Emm Epis Ch Opelika AL 1983-1987. jlwinter531@gmail.com

WINTER, Laren Royce (RG) Po Box 2963, Ruidoso NM 88355 B Garden City KS 12/24/1947 s Harold Robert Winter & Neoma Mae. DEd U of Nthrn Colorado 1977; MDiv STUSo 1984. D 6/16/1984 Bp William Carl Frey P 12/1/1984 Bp William Harvey Wolfrum. m 2/18/1978 ML Hewitt. Epis Ch In Lincoln Cnty Ruidoso NM 2004; Assoc S Matt's Ch Austin TX 1988-1990; Epis Ch Of S Jn The Bapt Breckenridge CO 1986-1988; Ch Of Our Sav Colorado Sprg CO 1984-1986. Auth, "An Expository Analysis Of 6 Selected Naturalists' Life Styles"; Auth, "Environ Beliefs & Contributions To Environ Educ". lrwinter@skybeam.com

WINTER JR, Lloyd Henry (Pa) 429 New Rd, Churchville PA 18966 B Philadelphia PA 8/18/1938 s Lloyd Henry Winter & Anne. BA U of Pennsylvania 1960; MDiv GTS 1966. D 6/11/1966 Bp Robert Lionne DeWitt P 12/18/1966 Bp Albert Ervine Swift. m 6/18/1966 Nancy G Guillet c 2. R S Jas Ch Langhorne PA 1974-2004; R Chr And S Ambr Ch Philadelphia PA 1968-1974; Cur Ch Of The Advoc Philadelphia PA 1966-1968. Assoc OHC 1976. lhwinterjr@earthlink.net

WINTERMUTE, Albert Earl (EO) 2311 Se Maphet Rd, Prineville OR 97754 **D S Andr's Epis Ch Prineville OR 1999-** B Gaston OR 4/28/1927 s Albert Crooker Wintermute & Charlotte Venita. EFM. D 5/23/1999 Bp Rustin Ray Kimsey. m 11/15/1947 Dorothy Marie Goss.

✠ WINTERROWD, Rt Rev William Jerry (Colo) 10955 E Crestline Pl, Englewood CO 80111 **Ret Bp Dio Colorado Denver CO 2003-** B Shreveport LA 7/24/1938 s William Perry Winterrowd & Ruth. BA Centenary Coll 1959; STB GTS 1963; DD GTS 1991. D 6/15/1963 Bp Iveson Batchelor Noland P 4/1/1964 Bp Girault M Jones Con 1/19/1991 for Colo. m 8/25/1964 Ann LaBarre. Bp of Colo Dio Colorado Denver CO 1991-2003; R Ch Of S Jas The Less Scarsdale NY 1985-1990; Assoc S Steph The Mtyr Ch Minneapolis MN 1983-1984; P-in-c Geth Ch Minneapolis MN 1981-1983; Epis Cmnty Serv Philadelphia PA 1976-1980; Asst S Phil's Ch Garrison NY 1972-1976; S Peters Day Care Cntr Peekskill NY 1970-1976; Exec Dir S Ptr's Epis Ch Peekskill NY 1970-1976; Asst S Mary's Ch Mohegan Lake NY 1969-1971; Asst Gr Ch Brooklyn NY 1965-1969; Cur S Jas Epis Ch Alexandria LA 1963-1965. Auth, *Natl Cmsn on the Fam*; Auth, *Rel & Dependent Chld*; Auth, *The Ch & Fam Systems*. DD GTS 1991. bishopjerry@comcast.net

WINTERS JR, Charles Layfaette (WNC) 6 Timson Road, Apt B4, Asheville NC 28803 B Norfolk VA 12/30/1924 s Charles Layfaette Winters & Gladys Irene. Leh 1943; Swarthmore Coll 1944; BA Br 1945; BD VTS 1949; STM UTS 1950; ThD GTS 1956. D 5/20/1949 P 5/28/1950 Bp Granville G Bennett. c 2. Prof SWTS Evanston IL 1988-1994; Int Gr Epis Ch Gainesville GA 1987-1988; Dep GC Dio Tennessee Nashville TN 1969-1979; Prof The TS at The U So Sewanee TN 1966-1980; The U So (Sewanee) Sewanee TN 1954-1981; Instr The TS at The U So Sewanee TN 1954-1957; Vic S Jn The Div Ch Saunderstown RI 1950-1952; D S Paul's Ch Englewood NJ 1949-1950. Auth, "Ch," *Mnstry & Sacraments*, Loyola U, 1983; Auth, *Method in Mnstry*, Loyola U, 1982; Auth, *EFM*; Auth, "Textbooks," *Journ Arts*, U So; Auth, *Lk Journ*, U So. Fell/Tutor GTS New York NY 1952. ross_win@charter.net

WINTERS JR, Rhett Youmans (USC) 236 Border Dr, Belvedere SC 29841 **Hon P S Barth's Ch No Augusta SC 2000-** B Raleigh NC 11/30/1922 s Rhett Y Winters & Elizabeth Washington. BA U NC 1946; MDiv VTS 1949. D 9/8/1949 P 4/1/1950 Bp Matthew G Henry. m 4/25/1951 Mary Turner c 5. Chapl To Ret Cler Dio Upper So Carolina Columbia SC 1996-1998; Vic S Jn's Ch No Augusta SC 1987-1992; P-in-c S Mk's Ch Chester SC 1976-1987; P-in-c S Ptr's Ch Great Falls SC 1976-1987; S Thad Epis Ch Aiken SC 1972-1976; R S Jn's Ch No Augusta SC 1965-1967; Dn of Aiken Dnry S Paul's Ch Graniteville SC 1964-1966; P-in-c Ch Of The H Cross Valle Crucis NC 1955-1963; P-in-c Ch Of The Mssh Murphy NC 1951-1955; D & P in Charge Ch Of The Trsfg Bat Cave NC 1949-1951. "Lk Journ," U So, 2003; "EFM," 2003; "Ch Mnstry & Sacraments," Loyola U, 1983; "Method In Mnstry," Loyola U, 1982. Fell/Tutor GTS 1952. w_rhett@bellsouth.net

WINTERS, William Michael (Ala) PO Box 116, Guntersville AL 35976 **R Ch Of The Epiph Guntersville AL 2000-** B Chicago IL 5/5/1950 s Robert C Winters & Shirley M. BA No Pk U 1972; BA NE Illinois U 1977; MDiv STUSo 1988. D 6/4/1988 P 5/20/1989 Bp Charles Farmer Duvall. m 8/4/1973 Wauria Wylantha Moore c 2. Dn Calv Cathd Sioux Falls SD 1995-2000; R S Mk's Epis Ch Aberdeen SD 1990-1995; S Jn's Epis Ch Mobile AL 1988-1990. "Hosp Changes Everything," Samford U Press, 2006. brwinters@bellsouth.net

WINTON, Paul Steve (At) 1015 Old Roswell Rd, Roswell GA 30076 **S Jn's Epis Ch Charlotte NC 2010-** B Albany NY 10/22/1954 s James Roger Winton & Jeanne Downes. BS Missouri Sthrn St U 1976; MDiv STUSo 1996. D 6/3/1996 P 12/11/1996 Bp Edward Lloyd Salmon Jr. m 6/12/1981 Nancy Ruth Schuman c 1. R S Dav's Ch Roswell GA 2001-2010; Assoc Gr Ch Charleston SC 1996-2001. psw@stdavidchurch.org

WINWARD, Mark Scott (Spr) 206 Jenkins Rd, Saco ME 04072 **Co-Chair Ecusa Sci Dio Maine Portland ME 1998-** B Hartford CT 9/28/1960 s Douglas Joseph Winward & Virginia Carol. BA Gordon Coll 1983; MDiv VTS 1997. Trans 2/23/2004 Bp Chilton Abbie Richardson Knudsen. m 8/8/1987 Kathleen Noelle Collopy c 2. R Trin Ch Saco ME 1999-2002; Asst S Andr's Epis Ch Newport News VA 1997-1999. mwinward@vts.edu

WIPFLER, William Louis (WNY) 121 Carla Ln, West Seneca NY 14224 **Vol Assoc P S Mths Epis Ch E Aurora NY 1996-** B Astoria NY 5/19/1931 s William Edward Wipfler & Eleonora Marguerite. BA Adams St Coll 1952; STB GTS 1955; STM UTS 1965; MA UTS 1975; PhD UTS 1978. D 4/16/1955 Bp James P De Wolfe P 11/20/1955 Bp Charles Alfred Voegeli. c 4. Asst Ch Of The Trsfg Freeport NY 1994-1996; Epis Ch Cntr New York NY 1989-1991; Asst H Trin Epis Ch Vlly Stream NY 1987-1994; Asst P Ch Of The Trsfg Freeport NY 1973-1987; Natl Coun Of Ch New York NY 1967-1988; Asst Chr Epis Ch Lynbrook NY 1967-1973. Co-Auth, "Triunfando Sobre Las Tragedias," Editora Educativa Dominicana, 1997; Auth, "Poder, Influencia E Impotencia," Ediciones CEPAE, 1980; Co-Auth, "Mbarete: The Higher Law of Paraguay," Int League for Human Rts, 1980; Ed, *Human Rts Perspectives*, 1977; Ed, *Latin Amer News Letter*, 1967; Auth, "Dominican Ch in the Light of Hist," CIDOC, 1966; Auth, "Jas Theo Holly of Haiti," *Builders for Chr Series*,

Epis Nat Counc, 1956. Restoration of Democracy Awd Govt of Chile 2003; Hon Cn Theol Dominican Epis Ch 1997; Democracy Awd The Brazilians Journ 1986; Letelier-Moffitt Human Rts Awd Inst for Plcy Stds 1980; Acad of Sci Dominican Republic 1976; Who's Who in Rel 1975. revwif@aol.com

WIRES, John William (At) 4900 English Dr, Annandale VA 22003 B Macon GA 9/16/1944 s William M Wires & Irene. BA Merc 1966; MA Jn Hopkins U 1969; MDiv VTS 1972; MA Geo Mason U 1985; PhD Geo Mason U 1988. D 6/24/1972 Bp R(aymond) Stewart Wood Jr P 8/1/1973 Bp Bennett Jones Sims. m 3/1/1980 Karen Rae Navratil c 1. Epis HS Alexandria VA 1972-1987. Auth, *S Lk Journ Theol*; Auth, *Var Bk Revs*. APA, Natl Acad Neuropsych; Intl Neuropsychological Soc; Natl Acad of Neuropsychology.

WIRTH, Bradley S (Mont) All Saints' Church, PO Box 1923, Whitefish MT 59937 **Int R All SS Epis Ch Whitefish MT 2004-** B Great Falls MT 5/2/1955 s Raymond Lucas Wirth & Nina Delaine. BA U of Washington 1977; MA U of Washington 1978; MDiv EDS 1980. D 7/25/1980 Bp Robert Hume Cochrane P 2/1/1981 Bp Otis Charles. m 6/17/1978 Jeannine Urback c 2. Int H Trin Epis Ch Troy MT 2002-2004; R All SS Ch Salt Lake City UT 1993-2000; Dep Gc Dio Utah Salt Lake City UT 1991-1994; Cn To Ordnry Dio Utah Salt Lake City UT 1988-1993; VP Dio Utah Salt Lake City UT 1984-1985; Stndg Com Dio Utah Salt Lake City UT 1982-1985; Cathd Ch Of S Mk Salt Lake City UT 1980-1987. Auth, "A Gr Observed-Sermons By The Reverend Cn Albert J Colton". bwirth@bresnan.net

WISBAUER JR, Edward August (LI) 31 Ridgeway Ave, Setauket NY 11733 **Supply P S Andr's Ch Yaphank NY 2008-** B Brooklyn NY 8/13/1929 s Edward August Wisbauer & Helen Ida. BA W&M 1952; MDiv GTS 1958; MS S Jn's U 1972. D 4/12/1958 P 10/25/1958 Bp James P De Wolfe. c 5. Cn Pstr S Jn's Ch Huntington NY 1997-2002; S Mary's Ch Lake Ronkonkoma NY 1959-1996; Asst Cathd Of The Incarn Garden City NY 1958-1959. New Directions 1972-1980.

WISCHMEYER, Kara Leslie (NwT) 226 Chuck Wagon Rd., Lubbock TX 79404 B Charleston SC 7/15/1968 AA Emory U 1988; BA Emory U 1990; Med Texas Tech U 1994; MDiv Candler TS Emory U 1998. D 6/4/2005 P 4/1/2006 Bp James Monte Stanton. m 2/14/2004 Jason B Wischmeyer. S Steph's Ch Lubbock TX 2009-2010; D S Matt's Cathd Dallas TX 2005-2007. karawisch@swbell.net

WISE, Christopher Matthew (WTex) 8900 Starcrest Dr, San Antonio TX 78217 **Asst R Ch Of Recon San Antonio TX 2008-** B Conroe TX 11/2/1979 s Ted William Wise & Andrea Jeanne. BA Texas A&M U-Coll Sta 2002; MDiv STUSo 2008. D 6/4/2008 Bp Gary Richard Lillibridge. Dir of Yth Mnstrs S Thos Epis Ch And Sch San Antonio TX 2002-2005. Mwise@churchofreconciliation.org

WISE JR, Eugene Field (Tenn) Po Box 261, Murfreesboro TN 37133 B Orlando FL 10/2/1937 s Eugene Wise & Lillian. BS Florida St U 1961; MDiv VTS 1984. D 6/11/1984 P 12/22/1984 Bp Calvin Onderdonk Schofield Jr. m 8/12/1961 Janelee Jewell c 1. Stndg Com Dio Tennessee Nashville TN 2004-2007; Pres Dio Tennessee Nashville TN 2001-2002; Stndg Com Dio Tennessee Nashville TN 1999-2002; Dep Gc Dio Tennessee Nashville TN 1997-2003; Pres Dio Tennessee Nashville TN 1995-1996; Stndg Com Dio Tennessee Nashville TN 1994-1997; Sprtl Dir Curs Dio Tennessee Nashville TN 1992-2007; R S Paul's Epis Ch Murfreesboro TN 1991-2006; Com Dio SE Florida Miami FL 1989-1991; Sprtl Dir Curs Dio SE Florida Miami FL 1988-1990; H Sprt Epis Ch W Palm Bch FL 1986-1991; Cur S Andr's Ch Lake Worth FL 1984-1986. wisegene@bellsouth.net

WISE, Roger Francis (Haw) 712 E Serena Ave, Fresno CA 93720 B Reno NV 5/18/1938 s Francis Harry Wise & Martha Pearl. BS Cntrl Michigan U 1978; Cert D Formation Prog 1985; MDiv CDSP 1991; Cert Napa Cnty CA Soc Serv 1997; Cert Int Mnstry Prog 2000. D 12/18/1985 Bp Edmond Lee Browning P 6/4/1991 Bp William Edwin Swing. m 1/8/1978 Mary Sherroll May c 3. Rev Roger Fran Wise Incline Vill NV 1994-1998; S Andr's In The Redwoods Monte Rio CA 1993-1998; Assoc S Steph's Epis Ch Sebastopol CA 1993-1994; D S Tim's Ch Aiea HI 1985-1988. Excellence in Preaching Epis Preaching Prog 1990. rfwpoet@yahoo.com

WISELEY, Jerry Lee (SC) 1746 Summit Rd, Hot Springs SD 57747 B Okmulgee OK 12/19/1935 s Jess Porter Wiseley & Gussie. BS U of Tulsa 1963; MDiv TESM 1986. D 6/14/1986 P 7/1/1987 Bp Donis Dean Patterson. c 4. R S Geo's Epis Ch Summerville SC 1989-1998; Asst Chr Epis Ch Plano TX 1986-1989. Ord Of S Lk.

WISEMAN, Grant Buchanan (USC) 125 Pendleton St. S.W., Aiken SC 29801 **R S Thad Epis Ch Aiken SC 2009-** B Saint Louis MO 3/2/1966 s Philip Marshall Wiseman & Heather Buchanan. BA Bethel Coll 1995; MDiv SWTS 2001. D 10/28/2000 P 6/23/2001 Bp Herbert Thompson Jr. m 7/22/1995 Heather K Klitzke c 2. R S Andr's Ch Omaha NE 2003-2009; S Pat's Epis Ch Dublin OH 2001-2003. atwinfather@gmail.com

WISEMAN, Heather Buchanan (SO) 2489 Walnutview Ct, Cincinnati OH 45230 **S Tim's Epis Ch Cincinnati OH 2003-** B Cincinnati OH 1/7/1944 d Gordon John Buchanan & Virginia. Lindenwood U 1965; Angl Acad 1992; MDiv Bex 2003. D 12/3/1993 P 6/21/2003 Bp Herbert Thompson Jr. c 2. D Calv Ch Cincinnati OH 2000-2002; D Gr Ch Cincinnati OH 1993-2000; D S Andr's Epis Ch Cincinnati OH 1993-2000. Comt. heatherbwiseman@yahoo.com

WISEMAN, Philip Marshall (SO) 2489 Walnutview Ct, Cincinnati OH 45230 B Morgan City LA 8/29/1946 s Arl Lafayette Wiseman & Ethel Lee. BS Georgia Inst of Tech 1968. D 10/25/1997 Bp Herbert Thompson Jr. c 4. D Ch Of S Mich And All Ang Cincinnati OH 2000-2004; D All SS Ch Cincinnati OH 1997-1999. marshallwiseman@yahoo.com

WISHART, Raymond Douglas (CGC) 925 E Pierson Dr, Lynn Haven FL 32444 **D Gr Epis Ch Panama City Bch FL 2011-** B Fort Campbell KY 6/19/1953 s David E Wishart & Beatrice H. BS U of W Florida 1976; MEd U of W Florida 1979; DOCGC Sch for Deacons 2010. D 2/10/2011 Bp Philip Menzie Duncan II. m 4/29/1977 Diane P Wishart c 2. revraymondw@gmail.com

WISMER III, Frank E (WMass) 445 Chapel St, Stratford CT 06614 **Vic Chr Ch Norwalk CT 2008-; Pension Fund Mltry New York NY 2003-** B Philadelphia PA 1/1/1948 s Frank Wismer & Nancy. Command and Gnrl Stff Coll; BA SE Massachusetts U Dartmouth MA 1970; MDiv Ya Berk 1973. D 6/23/1973 P 1/20/1974 Bp Robert Lionne DeWitt. m 8/8/2009 Patricia Marie McClaren c 2. Ch Pension Fund New York NY 2001-2003; R S Mich's-On-The-Heights Worcester MA 1998-2003; Dio Wstrn Massachusetts Springfield MA 1997-2003; R S Ptr's Ch Smyrna DE 1989-1997; R S Alb's Epis Ch Reading PA 1983-1989; R S Mary's Epis Par Northfield VT 1978-1982; Asst Chr Ch Reading PA 1975-1978; Cur S Matt's Epis Ch Wilton CT 1974-1975. Auth, "War in the Garden of Eden," *A Chapl's Memoir from Baghdad*, Seabury, 2008; Auth, "The Gospel of Mk," *The Gospel of Mk: A Guide for Apostolic Living*, 2002; Auth, "Daily Mediation Guide," *Daily Meditation Guide*, 1997. rf300@hotmail.com

WISMER, Robert David (Tex) 11310 Meadow Lake Dr, Houston TX 77077 **S Fran Epis Day Sch Houston TX 2007-; Day Sch Chapl/Asst Pstr S Fran Ch Houston TX 2002-** B Toronto Ontario CA 9/1/1954 s Edwin Jacob Wismer & Gladys May. BA McMaster U 1976; MDiv Regent Coll Vancouver Bc CA 1984; MA McGill U 1991. Trans from Anglican Church of Canada 10/24/2002 Bp Claude Edward Payne. m 10/21/1989 Jennifer L Thomson c 4. bwismer@sfedshouston.org

WISNER, Stephen Forster (NJ) 3402 Woodfield Ave, Wall Township NJ 07719 **R Ch Of S Mich The Archangel Wall Township NJ 1996-; Dio New Jersey Trenton NJ 1971-** B Philadelphia PA 4/11/1946 s Stephen Harry Wisner & Eva Doris. BA Glassboro St Coll 1968; MDiv PDS 1971; Cert. Estrn Bapt Sem 1990. D 4/24/1971 P 10/23/1971 Bp Alfred L Banyard. m 12/19/1970 Theresa Ann Farkas c 3. P-in-c S Lk's Ch Woodstown NJ 1994-1996; Assoc S Andr's Epis Ch Bridgeton NJ 1990-1997; R Trin Epis Ch Vineland NJ 1976-1990; R H Sprt Bellmawr NJ 1973-1976; Vic S Alb's Epis Ch New Brunswick NJ 1971-1973. revsfw@aol.com

WISNEWSKI JR, Robert Carew (Ala) 113 Madison Ave, Montgomery AL 36104 **R S Jn's Ch Montgomery AL 1995-** B Augusta GA 9/1/1955 s Robert Carew Wisnewski & Barbara Allison. BA Wofford Coll 1977; MDiv VTS 1983. D 6/11/1983 P 5/12/1984 Bp William Arthur Beckham. m 9/8/1978 MaryWard T Wisnewski c 2. Stwdshp Dio Upper So Carolina Columbia SC 1998-2001; Trst Dio Alabama Birmingham AL 1996-1999; Ecum Cmsn Dio Upper So Carolina Columbia SC 1990-1995; R S Mary's Ch Columbia SC 1987-1995; Stndg Com Dio Upper So Carolina Columbia SC 1987-1992; Cmsn MHE Dio Upper So Carolina Columbia SC 1985-1989; COM Dio Upper So Carolina Columbia SC 1984-1995; Asst to R S Jas Epis Ch Greenville SC 1983-1987. robert@stjohnsmontgomery.org

WISNIEWSKI, Richard Joseph (NJ) St. David's Episcopal Church, 90 S. Main St., Cranbury NJ 08512 **D S Dav's Ch Cranbury NJ 2007-** B Irvington NJ 3/13/1947 s Casimir Raymond Wisniewski & Eleanore. B.S. Monmouth U 1969. D 6/9/2007 Bp George Edward Councell. m 11/3/1990 Sarah Ruth Wisniewski c 2. richnewski@hotmail.com

✠ WISSEMANN, Rt Rev Andrew Frederick (WMass) 9 Ridgeway Cir, Springfield MA 01118 B Bronx NY 6/9/1928 s Frederick Conrad Wissemann & Helen Anna. BA Wesl 1950; UTS 1951; STB GTS 1953; Fllshp Coll of Preachers 1967. D 5/31/1953 Bp Horace W B Donegan P 12/1/1953 Bp Lewis B Whittemore Con 4/7/1984 for WMass. m 7/16/1953 Nancy Whittemore c 4. Trst The GTS New York NY 1992-1995; Bp Dio Wstrn Massachusetts Springfield MA 1984-1992; COM Dio Wstrn Massachusetts Springfield MA 1979-1984; Dep GC Dio Wstrn Massachusetts Springfield MA 1976-1982; Stndg Com Dio Wstrn Massachusetts Springfield MA 1974-1982; R S Steph's Ch Pittsfield MA 1968-1984; Dept of Admin & Fin Dio Wstrn Massachusetts Springfield MA 1968-1974; Exec Coun Dio Wstrn Massachusetts Springfield MA 1962-1968; R S Jas' Ch Greenfield MA 1960-1968; Asst Chr Ch Greenwich CT 1953-1956. Hon DD GTS 1984.

WISSINK, Charles Jay (Pa) 54 Sugarplum Rd, Levittown PA 19056 B Orange City IA 5/23/1930 s Charles Bernard Wissink & Geraldine Winifred. BA Hope Coll 1952; BD PrTS 1955; STM UTS 1965; PhD Wstrn TS 1975. D 10/7/1984 P 2/1/1985 Bp John Shelby Spong. m 8/30/1952 Barbara Wierenga c 5. Memi

Ch Of S Lk Philadelphia PA 1985-1995; Int S Lk's Ch Philadelphia PA 1985-1987. EDEO, Phila Cler. wissinkcj@aol.com

WISSLER, Kenneth John (Pa) 1112 Wilson Ave, Roslyn PA 19001 B Wilmington DE 4/6/1946 s Lloyd Kenneth Wissler & Doris. BA U of Delaware Newark 1968; MDiv U of King's Coll Halifax NS CA 1971; DMin Fuller TS 1983. Trans from Anglican Church of Canada 9/30/1985 Bp Lyman Cunningham Ogilby. m 9/2/1967 Bernice Miles c 2. P-in-c S Alb's Ch Roxborough Philadelphia PA 2009-2010; S Jn The Evang Ch Lansdowne PA 2002-2009; Dio Pennsylvania Philadelphia PA 2000-2002; Int Gr Epis Ch Hulmeville PA 2000-2002; Int S Jas Epis Ch Bristol PA 1998-2000; Memi Ch Of S Lk Philadelphia PA 1996-1997; Int S Lk's Ch Philadelphia PA 1996-1997; Ch Of Our Sav Jenkintown PA 1985-1996. Archeol Inst of Amer 2000; Epis Cler Assn Pennsylvania 1986; Int Mnstry Ntwk 1996. kjwissler@comcast

✠ WITCHER SR, Rt Rev Robert Campbell (LI) 1934 Steele Blvd, Baton Rouge LA 70808 **Ret Bp of Long Island S Jas Epis Ch Baton Rouge LA 1991-** B New Orleans LA 10/5/1926 s Charles Swanson Witcher & Lily Sebastiam. BA Tul 1949; MDiv SWTS 1952; MA LSU 1960; PhD LSU 1968; DD SWTS 1974; DCL Nash 1989. D 7/6/1952 Bp Girault M Jones P 6/1/1953 Bp Iveson Batchelor Noland Con 4/1/1975 for LI. m 6/4/1957 Elisabeth Alice Cole c 2. Epis Ch Cntr New York NY 1989-1990; Exec & Secy Off New York NY 1989; Dio Long Island Garden City NY 1975-1990; Trst The CPG New York NY 1975-1989; Bp Coadj Dio Long Island Garden City NY 1975-1977; Chair of ArmdF Cmsn Dio Louisiana Baton Rouge LA 1963-1975; R S Jas Epis Ch Baton Rouge LA 1962-1975; Bd Examing Chapl Dio Louisiana Baton Rouge LA 1960-1975; R S Aug's Ch Baton Rouge LA 1953-1961; P-in-c S Andr's Ch Clinton LA 1953-1956; P-in-c S Pat's Ch Zachary LA 1953-1956. Auth, *Founding of Epis Ch in LA 1805-1838*, 1969. Angl Soc 1976; MOWW 1970; Mltry & Hospitaller Ord of S Lazarus of Jerusalem 1995; Mltry Ord of Frgn Wars 1998; SAR 1963; Soc of Colonial Wars 1990. Epsilon Sigma Phi; Phi Alpha Theta; Phi Kappa Phi. cusnr@aol.com

WITH, David Fergus (WMo) 160 Terrace Trl W, Lake Quivira KS 66217 B Milwaukee WI 5/1/1938 s Arthur Fergus With & Beatrice Milicent. BS U of Wisconsin 1960; MDiv Nash 1963. D 3/1/1963 P 9/21/1963 Bp Donald H V Hallock. m 3/31/1964 Nancy Shaw c 3. Int Trin Ch Independence MO 2002-2004; Int S Paul's Epis Ch Lees Summit MO 2000-2002; Int S Paul's Ch Leavenworth KS 1999-2000; S Marg's Ch Lawr KS 1996-1997; S Aid's Ch Olathe KS 1996; R S Mich And All Ang Ch Mssn KS 1981-1995; Asst S Andr's Ch Madison WI 1972-1975; Vic H Cross Epis Ch Wisconsin Dells WI 1970-1972; R S Jas Ch Marshall MN 1966-1970; Cur Geth Ch Minneapolis MN 1963-1966. dfwith@kc.rr.com

WITHROCK JR, John William (CGC) 401 W College St, Troy AL 36081 B Trinidad CO 9/21/1948 s John William Withrock. BA U of So Carolina 1970; MDiv Luth Theo Sthrn Sem 1975. D 6/7/2008 P 6/13/2009 Bp Philip Menzie Duncan II. m 7/5/1969 Elaine Bush Withrock c 3. jwwithrock@comcast.net

WITKE, E(dward) Charles (Mich) 3000 Glazier Way, Ann Arbor MI 48105 **P S Andr's Ch Ann Arbor MI 1995-** B Los Angeles CA 9/22/1931 s Emil Ernst Witke & Ethel Ann. BA U CA Los Angeles 1953; MA Harv 1957; PhD Harv 1960. D 6/25/1988 Bp Henry Irving Mayson P 1/10/1989 Bp R(aymond) Stewart Wood Jr. m 10/10/1975 Aileen Patricia Gatten. Asst H Faith Ch Saline MI 1993-1995; Exam Dio Michigan Detroit MI 1991-1996; Asst S Lk's Epis Ch Ypsilanti MI 1989-1991; D S Jas' Epis Ch Dexter MI 1988-1989. Auth, "Horace's Roman Odes: A Critical Approach," Mnemosyne, 1978; Auth, "Numen Litterarum: Chr Latin Poetry from Greg the Great to Constantine," Mittellateinische Studien, 1971. CBS 1949; Ord of S Ben Confrater 1988; SocMary 1988. Fell Amer Acad in Rome Rome Italy 1960. frchas@umich.edu

WITT, Anne Lane (Va) PO Box 1059, Kilmarnock VA 22482 **Gr Ch Kilmarnock VA 2010-** B Richmond VA 4/30/1974 d Thomas Foster Witt & Ann Lane Crittenden. BA The U of Virginia 1997; MDiv The GTS 2010. D 6/5/2010 P 12/11/2010 Bp Shannon Sherwood Johnston. annelanewitt@msn.com

WITT JR, Richard Cyril (NY) 16 Lawrence Rd, Accord NY 12404 **Mid Hudson Catskill Rural and Migrant Min Poughkeepsie NY 1991-** B Pittsburgh PA 8/29/1959 s Richard Cyril Witt & Cynthia Anne. The London Sch of Econ and Political Sci 1981; BA Bos 1982; MDiv EDS 1986. D 6/11/1988 Bp David Elliot Johnson P 5/1/1989 Bp Barbara Clementine Harris. m 8/31/1990 Tracy Leavitt c 2. Assoc R Chr Ch Poughkeepsie NY 1988-1991; Asst to R Par Of The Epiph Winchester MA 1986-1988. taleavitt@aol.com

WITT JR, Robert Edward (Alb) P.O. Box 123, Morris NY 13808 **R All SS' Chap Morris NY 2003-; R Zion Ch Morris NY 2003-; R Zion Ch Morris NY 1981-** B Plainfield NJ 9/15/1946 s Robert Edward Witt & Nicolina. BA Alfred U 1968; MDiv GTS 1978; STM GTS 1989. D 6/3/1978 Bp Frederick Barton Wolf P 12/15/1978 Bp Harvey D Butterfield. m 12/27/1967 Marion B Burdick c 3. Dioc Coun Dio Albany Albany NY 1999-2003; Chapl, Profile & Search Com Dio Albany Albany NY 1996-1997; Chair, Dioc Stwdshp Com Dio Albany Albany NY 1990-1998; S Paul's Ch Utica NY 1989-1994; P-in-c Gr Ch Mohawk NY 1987-2003; S Margarets Hse New Hartford NY 1987-2003; R Chr Ch Gilbertsville NY 1981-1987; Dioc Coun Dio Albany Albany NY 1981-1985; Ch Of St Jn Bapt Sebec ME 1978-1981; S Johns Epis Ch Brownville ME 1978-1981; St Josephs Ch Sebec ME 1978-1981. Bro of S Andr 1980; Soc of S Marg 1988. Who's Who in Rel 1981. zionrector@frontiernet.net

WITTE JR, Walter William (Nwk) Po Box 4781, Vineyard Haven MA 02568 B North Tonawanda NY 9/11/1927 s Walter William Witte & Pauline Rose. BA Hob 1949; MDiv Ya Berk 1952; STM UTS 1970. D 6/9/1952 P 9/29/1954 Bp Lauriston L Scaife. m 6/5/1954 Patricia Griffin c 1. S Andr's Ch Edgartown MA 1992; S Mk's Ch Dorchester MA 1990-1991; Par Of S Paul Newton Highlands MA 1987-1988; Cn Trin And S Phil's Cathd Newark NJ 1969-1971; R S Steph's Ch S Louis MO 1963-1969; Vic Ch Of The Epiph Kirkwood S Louis MO 1956-1963; Asst Gr Ch Kirkwood MO 1955-1958; Cur Gr Ch Lockport NY 1953-1955; D-In-C S Paul's Epis Ch Springville NY 1952-1953. Auth, "arts," *Living Ch*; Auth, "arts," *Wit*. wittewalter@cs.com

WITTENBURG, Edwin Philip (Minn) 2150 Scheffer Ave, Saint Paul MN 55116 B Mukwonago WI 5/3/1922 s Robert Klaus Wittenburg & Mathilda Caroline. BA Carroll Coll 1949; BD Garrett Evang TS 1951; Nash 1958; Advncd CPE 1976. D 11/30/1957 P 5/31/1958 Bp Donald H V Hallock. m 11/29/1952 Diane Jennings c 4. R Mssh Epis Ch S Paul MN 1977-1981; Untd Hospitals Inc S Paul MN 1964-1987; Vic S Lk's Ch Madison WI 1960-1963; Asst S Matt's Ch Kenosha WI 1958-1960; Vic S Barth's Ch Pewaukee WI 1957-1958. Amer Prot Hosp Chapl Assn; OHC, Ord Of S Lk, Epis Chapl & Counslrs, ACPE, Fell Coll Chapl, AEHC.

WITTIG, Nancy Constantine Hatch (Pa) 21801 Elizabeth Ave, Fairview Park OH 44126 **Ret S Ptr's Epis Ch Lakewood OH 2006-** B Takoma Park MD 8/23/1945 d William Nagel Hatch & Nancy Constantine. BA U NC 1969; MDiv VTS 1972; DMin Estrn Bapt TS 2005. D 9/8/1973 Bp George E Rath P 7/29/1974 Bp Edward Randolph Welles II. c 2. Dn Of Pennypack Dnry Dio Pennsylvania Philadelphia PA 1992-1998; R S Andr's In The Field Ch Philadelphia PA 1988-2006; Adjucnt Fac Of Pstr Theol The GTS New York NY 1988-1990; R Ch Of S Jn The Div Hasbrouck Heights NJ 1983-1988; Int R Ch Of S Jn The Div Hasbrouck Heights NJ 1982-1983; Cur S Ptr's Ch Morristown NJ 1974; D All SS Ch Millington NJ 1973-1974. Co-Fndr Pa Wmn'S Cleric Assn 1990-2006; Ord Of S Helena 1992. Fell Etssw 1997; Fell Coll Of Preachers 1992; Hon Cn Trin Cathd Newark NJ 1981. n.wittig@att.net

WITTMAYER, Kevin Edward (Tex) 906 Padon St, Longview TX 75601 **R Trin Ch Longview TX 2003-** B Cedar Falls IA 8/14/1955 s Edward Wittmayer & Annetta Mae. BS Oral Roberts U 1978; MBA Oral Roberts U 1980; MDiv VTS 1991. D 6/22/1991 P 1/11/1992 Bp Robert Manning Moody. m 8/13/1977 Pamela E MacDonald c 2. Mssnr Ch Of The Sav Yukon OK 1994-2003; Asst R Epis Ch Of The Resurr Oklahoma City OK 1991-1994. frkevin@trinityparish.org

WIZOREK, Julie C (Md) 249 Double Oak Rd N, Prince Frederick MD 20678 **R S Paul's Epis Ch Prince Frederick MD 2004-** B Los Angeles CA 11/7/1950 d Marshall William Craw & Virginia Edith. BA USC 1972; MA U of Arizona 1974; MDiv CDSP 2001. D 6/23/2001 P 2/9/2002 Bp Richard Lester Shimpfky. m 1/6/1973 Martin William Wizorek c 2. Asst to the R S Patricks Ch Kenwood CA 2001-2003. jwizorek@ix.netcom.com

WLOSINSKI, Stephen Stanley Peterson (Minn) 1121 W Morgan St, Duluth MN 55811 B Hazelton PA 8/8/1942 s Stephen Stanley Wlosinski & Helen Marion. BA Macalester Coll 1964; MDiv Nash 1967; MS U of Wisconsin 1995. Rec from Polish National Catholic Church 10/1/1983 as Priest Bp Robert Marshall Anderson. m 12/28/1983 Cynthia M E Peterson-Wlosinski c 1. Asst S Andr's By The Lake Duluth MN 1988-2004; Calv Ch Rochester MN 1986; Dio Minnesota Minneapolis MN 1984-1986; P S Edw The Confessor Wayzata MN 1984-1986. swlosinski@slhduluth.com

WOEHLER, Charles George (WTex) 1416 North Loop 1604 East, San Antonio TX 78232 **R S Thos Epis Ch And Sch San Antonio TX 1990-** B Minneapolis MN 4/21/1950 s Charles George Woehler & Dorothy I. BA U of the Incarnate Word 1973; MDiv Epis TS of The SW 1977. D 6/21/1977 P 4/1/1978 Bp Scott Field Bailey. m 5/24/1975 Kathryn Paulette Stanley c 2. Asst S Mk's Epis Ch San Antonio TX 1988-1990; R Epis Ch Of The Mssh Gonzales TX 1984-1988; R H Trin Carrizo Sprg TX 1980-1984; Asst S Mk's Ch San Marcos TX 1977-1980. cwoehler@tom1604.org

WOGGON, Harry Arthur (WNC) 118 Macon Ave, Asheville NC 28801 **P Assoc S Mary's Ch Asheville NC 2000-** B New York NY 5/26/1932 s Arthur Carl Woggon & Mary Jane. BA Ham 1954; MA U of Oregon 1959; STB GTS 1963. D 6/29/1963 P 6/1/1964 Bp Richard Henry Baker. m 7/4/1959 Genelda Kepley c 4. P-in-c St Georges Epis Ch Asheville NC 1998-2004; Int Old Trin Ch Ch Creek MD 1993-1997; Dio Easton Easton MD 1993-1995; Int S Andr's Epis Ch Newport News VA 1992-1993; Int S Tim's Epis Ch W Des Moines IA 1991-1992; Int Trin Ch Iowa City IA 1990-1991; Int Chr Epis Ch Smithfield VA 1988-1989; Int S Jas Epis Ch Greenville SC 1988; Int S Jn's Ch Ithaca NY 1986-1987; Int S Jn's Epis Ch Columbia SC 1986; Int Gr Epis Ch And Kindergarten Camden SC 1985; Int Ch Of The H Comf Burlington NC 1984; Dio Wstrn No Carolina Asheville NC 1981-1983; S Jas Ch Mooresville NC 1963-1968; Asst to R Ch Of The H Comf Burlington NC 1963-1965. Co-Auth, "Journey to the Cntr," Polus/Prayers, 2005; Auth, *Trsfg into Wholeness*,

1988. Assoc of OHC 1964; Natl Assn for the Self- Supporting Active Mnstry 1971-1977. hawandgkw@charter.net

WOGGON, Karla M (WA) 1048 15th Ave. N.W., Hickory NC 28601 **R Ch Of The Ascen Hickory NC 2007-** B Kannapolis NC 5/9/1966 d Harry Arthur Woggon & Genelda. BA Appalachian St U 1989; MA LSU 1991; MDiv SWTS 1995. D 5/20/1995 P 12/1/1995 Bp James Barrow Brown. m 6/23/2007 John Walker. R S Andr's Epis Ch Coll Pk MD 1999-2007; Assoc R Ch Of The Ascen Gaithersburg MD 1996-1999; Assoc R Chr Ch Covington LA 1995-1996. kmwoggon@gmail.com

WOHLEVER, Russell John (CFla) All Saints Church, 338 E Lyman Ave, Winter Park FL 32789 **Asst All SS Ch Of Winter Pk Winter Pk FL 2007-** B Danbury CT 8/25/1967 s James Wohlever & Mary Ann. BA Pennsylvani St U St Coll PA 1990; MDiv Nash 2007. D 6/2/2007 P 12/2/2007 Bp John Wadsworth Howe. m 8/13/2004 Amaryllis S Wohlever c 3. frrussellw@allsaintswp.com

WOJAHN, Karen Ann (Dix) (Los) 1012 East Van Owen Avenue, Orange CA 92867 B Fargo ND 9/29/1947 d Orion Lysle Dix & Helen Sophia. AA Fullerton Coll 1992; BA California St Polytechnic U 1994; MDiv Claremont TS 2000. D 6/17/2000 Bp Chester Lovelle Talton P 1/6/2001 Bp Frederick Houk Borsch. m 4/1/1968 Roy Edward Wojahn c 3. S Jn Chrys Ch And Sch Rancho Santa Margarita CA 2005-2008; Dir of Chld's & Fam Mnstrs S Wilfrid Of York Epis Ch Huntington Bch CA 2000-2004. Auth, "numerous arts," *The Epis News*, 1989; Auth, *Growing Up w Roy and Dale*, Regal Books, 1986; Auth, *Var mag and Nwspr arts*, 1972. Golden Key hon Soc 1994; Sigma Tau Delta 1992. Outstanding Grad, Coll Arts California Polytechnical U 1994; Pacesetter Awd Biola U writer's Inst 1988. preachwoj@yahoo.com

WOJCIEHOWSKI, Arthur Anthony (Minn) 1500 Prospect Ave, Cloquet MN 55720 B Saint Cloud MN 10/24/1940 s Anthony Joseph Wojciehowski & Sophia Catherine. Dioces of Mn Theol Sch 1994; AAS Lake Superior Coll 1996. D 11/22/1993 P 6/1/1994 Bp Sanford Zangwill Kaye Hampton. c 2. S Andr's Ch Le Sueur MN 1993-2002; Trin Epis Ch Hermantown MN 1993-2002. wojosr@hotmail.com

WOLCOTT, Sarah Elizabeth (Neb) 1926 N Rodgers Ave, Alton IL 62002 B Oswego NY 11/13/1947 d Alan Phelps Wolcott & Sally Elizabeth. BS Illinois St U 1969; MS Loyola U 1994. D 2/14/1998 Bp John Clark Buchanan. NAAD.

WOLF, David B (Nwk) 451 Van Houten St, Paterson NJ 07501 **R S Paul's Epis Ch Paterson NJ 2001-** B Springfield MA 8/16/1961 s Paul D Wolf & Katherine M. BA Bates Coll 1983; JD GW 1989; MDiv VTS 1996. D 6/15/1996 P 1/7/1997 Bp Peter James Lee. m 5/23/1998 Martha E Wolf c 1. Asst R S Alb's Par Washington DC 1996-2001. Auth, "A Critical Examination of Stanley Hauerwas' Ethical Ideal," VTS Libr Collection, 1996; Auth, "Pardon for No Would be Unconstitutional," *Manhattan Lawyer*, Legal Times, 1988; Auth, "Imm Kants' Theory of Moral Value," Bates Coll Libr Collection, 1983. Phil Beta Kappa 1983; The Connecticut Bar 1989. Chas A. Dana Schlr Bates Coll 1980. mdwolf@verizon.net

WOLF, Donn Loren (HB) 23826 Barfield St, Farmington Hills MI 48336 B Detroit MI 4/18/1935 s Carl William Wolf & Lorene Kathryn. BA U MI 1958; ThM EDS 1961. D 6/29/1961 Bp Robert Lionne DeWitt P 2/1/1962 Bp Archie H Crowley. m 5/1/1954 Shirley Ann Spence. Cur Gr Epis Ch Port Huron MI 1961-1964. Auth, "Action Politics Working Politics".

✠ WOLF, Rt Rev Geralyn (RI) 275 N Main St, Providence RI 02903 **Bp of Rhode Island Dio Rhode Island Providence RI 1996-** B New York NY 4/30/1947 d Joseph David Wolf & Harriet. BS W Chester U 1968; MA Trenton St Coll 1971; MDiv EDS 1977. D 6/11/1977 P 5/25/1978 Bp Lyman Cunningham Ogilby Con 2/17/1996 for RI. m 4/21/2007 Thomas C Bair c 2. Dn Chr Ch Cathd Louisville KY 1987-1995; Vic S Mary's Epis Ch Philadelphia PA 1981-1987; Asst Ch Of S Mart-In-The-Fields Philadelphia PA 1979-1981; Asst S Mary's Epis Ch Ardmore PA 1977-1979. Auth, "Down and Out in Providence," Crossroads, 2004; Auth, "Ldrshp:Being A Holding Container," *S Mk's Revs*, 2002; Auth, "Sewanee Theol Revs". SSM, Assoc 1974. LLD U of Rhode Island 2004; Dhl Roger Williams U 1999. beeplepeople@cox.net

WOLF, Max Joseph (Del) 20 Olive Ave, Rehoboth Beach DE 19971 **R All SS Ch Rehoboth Bch DE 2001-; R S Geo's Chap Rehoboth Bch DE 2001-** B Providence RI 5/24/1955 s Joseph Francis Wolf & Jacquin Joanne. MDiv EDS 1996; BA U of Rhode Island 1996. D 6/15/1996 P 2/16/1997 Bp Geralyn Wolf. m 12/5/1987 Audre Alissa Olly Parker. Bp and Coun Mem Dio Delaware Wilmington DE 2002-2005; Cn Mssnr Yth Dio Pennsylvania Philadelphia PA 1999-2001; COM Dio Rhode Island Providence RI 1998-1999; Evang & Cmncatn Dio Rhode Island Providence RI 1998-1999; Cler Conf Com Dio Rhode Island Providence RI 1997-1999; S Andr's Ch New London NH 1997-1999; Cur S Paul's Ch No Kingstown RI 1997-1999; Assoc S Phil's In The Hills Tucson AZ 1996-1997; Bd for Theol Educ Epis Ch Cntr New York NY 1994-1997. Fllshp of SSJE 1991. wolfsanddogs@verizon.net

WOLFE, Alexander (ND) No address on file. B Grenfell SK CA 4/30/1927 s Charles Wolfe & Harriet. D 6/11/1970 Bp George Theodore Masuda. m 9/2/1952 Elizabeth Johnson.

WOLFE, Connie (Tex) 306 Boys Home Rd, Covington VA 24426 **Dio Texas Houston TX 2011-; Chapl/Asst. Dir. of Prog All SS Chap Covington VA 2001-** B Radford VA 10/25/1944 d Claude C Wolfe & Ruth Odell. MS Old Dominion U 1981; MDiv VTS 2001. D 6/9/2001 Bp David Conner Bane Jr P 12/15/2001 Bp Frank Neff Powell. c 1. Boys Hm Covington VA 2002-2009; Emm Ch Covington VA 2001-2002. cwolfe1@live.com

✠ **WOLFE, Rt Rev Dean Elliott** (Kan) 835 SW Polk St, Topeka KS 66612 **Bp of Kansas Dio Kansas Topeka KS 2003-** B Dayton OH 6/4/1956 s William Virgil Wolfe & Mildred Eileen. Bethany TS 1983; BA Mia of Ohio 1987; Cert Washington Hosp Cntr, Washington, DC 1990; Cert S Geo's Coll, Jerusalem 1991; MDiv VTS 1992; S Deiniol's Libr, Hawarden, Wales 1996. D 6/6/1992 P 6/5/1993 Bp William Edwin Swing Con 11/8/2003 for Kan. m 12/27/1980 Ellen Marie Frantz c 1. Convenor Dio Dallas Dallas TX 1999-2003; Vice R S Mich And All Ang Ch Dallas TX 1998-2003; Assoc R Trin Ch In The City Of Boston Boston MA 1994-1998; COM Dio California San Francisco CA 1992-1994; Asst R S Clem's Ch Berkeley CA 1992-1994; Sr Wrdn Ch Of The Epiph San Carlos CA 1987-1988. Ord of the Hosp of S Jn of Jerusalem - Asst Ch 2000; The Soc of S Jn the Evang - Assoc 2002. DD Virginia Theol Serminary 2004. dwolfe@episcopal-ks.org

WOLFE, Dorothy Annabell (Neb) 603 3rd Ave, Bayard NE 69334 B Burlington CO 6/3/1929 d John Auterson & Sarah. D 6/2/2002 Bp James Edward Krotz. m 8/8/1954 Elmer Wolfe c 1.

WOLFE, James Edward (HB) No address on file. B Cleveland OH 11/26/1933 s Joseph Richard Wolfe & Anna. BS Baldwin-Wallace Coll 1956; BD EDS 1960. D 12/17/1960 Bp Frederic Cunningham Lawrence P 6/1/1961 Bp Malcolm E Peabody. R S Lk's Epis Ch Malden MA 1962-1966.

WOLFE, John McRae (SwFla) 501 Erie Ave, Tampa FL 33606 **D S Mary's Par Tampa FL 2004-** B Indianapolis IN 5/18/1943 s Arthor Wolfe & Elizabeth Katherine. BA U of Tampa 1972; MBA U of So Florida 1988. D 6/12/2004 Bp John Bailey Lipscomb. m 10/21/1972 Patricia Ann Rosedahl Wolfe c 2. wolfejohn@aol.com

WOLFE JR, Kenneth A (WMass) 13589 N Heritage Canyon Dr, Marana AZ 85658 **R Chr Ch Fitchburg MA 2006-** B Philadelphia PA 6/14/1944 s Kenneth Andrew Wolfe & Dorothy Emma. BA U of Pennsylvania 1967; MDiv EDS 1970; JD Boston Coll 1973; Coll of Preachers 1986; DMin Estrn Sem Philadelphia PA 1988. D 6/19/1971 Bp Robert Lionne DeWitt P 10/16/1979 Bp James Barrow Brown. m 1/23/1999 Shelley L Stone c 4. S Mk's Ch Southborough MA 2009-2011; Dio Wstrn Massachusetts Springfield MA 2006-2009; P Assoc S Mk's Ch Southborough MA 2003-2006; Supply P Dio Massachusetts Boston MA 1991-2002; R Chr Epis Ch Villanova PA 1981-1991; S Mk's Ch New Canaan CT 1980-1981; D Chr Ch Slidell LA 1976-1979. Auth, *Journ for Hlthcare Quality*, 1994; Ed, *Annual Survey of MA Law*, 1973; Auth, *Expansion of the Const Privlege to Defame*; Co-Auth, *The Quality Profsnl's Expanding Role as Intl Consult*. Ch Hist Prize EDS 1970. wolfek1@comcast.net

WOLFE, V Eugene (Oly) 53565 W Ferndale Rd, Milton Freewater OR 97862 B Baker OR 3/25/1925 s Vernon Eldred Wolfe & Ruby Ellen. MDiv CDSP 1967; Seattle Pacific Coll 1970; BA U of Puget Sound 1970; Med Seattle U 1971. D 5/20/1967 Bp George Richard Millard P 11/21/1967 Bp John Raymond Wyatt. m 8/3/1980 Nancy Huff c 2. Mssn to Seafarers Seattle WA 1986-1990; S Clem's Epis Ch Seattle WA 1979-1990; Dio Olympia Seattle WA 1972-1985; Asst S Lk's Epis Ch Renton WA 1970-1971; Cur S Lk's Epis Ch Wenatchee WA 1967-1969. emwolfe@msn.com

WOLFENBARGER, Mary Suzanne (Mo) 55 Magnolia Dr, Belleville IL 62221 B Knoxville TN 6/24/1958 d David McWhirter & Mary. MS U of Tennessee 1983. D 6/11/2000 Bp Peter Hess Beckwith P 6/24/2011 Bp George Wayne Smith. m 3/17/1979 William C Wolfenbarger c 1. D S Geo's Ch Belleville IL 2001-2006. suzannewolfenbarger@sbcglobal.net

WOLFF, John Ludwig (Alb) 103 Bundy Rd., Ithaca NY 14850 B Oakland CA 8/9/1923 s John Ludwig Wolff & Elizabeth Cathryn. USMMA 1944; Untd States Maritime Serv Off Sch New London CT 1946; Col 1949; GTS 1959. D 1/10/1959 P 7/11/1959 Bp Charles Francis Boynton. m 11/26/1949 Emmylou Schemmer c 3. Dio Albany Albany NY 1982-1988; The Missions To Seamen Coll Hill LONDON 1982-1988; Secy Dio Albany Albany NY 1974-1981; R Trin Ch Watervliet NY 1967-1981; R Gr Ch Mohawk NY 1960-1967; Vic La Misión Epis Santiago Apóstol [La MESA] Dover Plains NY 1959-1960. Ord Of S Lk 1958; OHC 1960. abigailnyc@aol.com

WOLFF, Pierre Maurice (Ct) 108 C North Turnpike Road, Wallingford CT 06492 B Marseille FR 11/2/1929 s Leopold Wolff & Marguerite. Trng In Soc Of Jesus Fr 1963. Rec from Roman Catholic 11/10/1989 Bp Arthur Edward Walmsley. m 9/10/1988 Mary Morgan. Auth, "Sprtl Exercises S Ignatus," 1997; Auth, "May I Hate God".

WOLFF, William George (Kan) 306 W. Euclid St., Pittsburg KS 66762 **Coun of Trst/Stndg Com Dio Kansas Topeka KS 2008-; COM Dio Kansas Topeka KS 2006-; Kansas Sch For Mnstry/Advsry Com Dio Kansas Topeka KS 2006-; R S Ptr's Ch Pittsburg KS 2005-** B Schaller IA 10/7/1943 s Leo T Wolff & Marccella. PhD Sthrn Illinois U 1974; Cert of Wk

Completed VTS 2005. D 9/9/2000 Bp William Edward Smalley. m 12/27/1964 Luella Mae Wohlers. D Gr Cathd Topeka KS 2000-2004. WWOLFF3@COX.NET

WOLFORD, Arthur C (NI) Po Box 152, Corona CA 92878 **D S Jn The Bapt Par Corona CA 1997-** B South Bend IN 4/3/1920 D 10/9/1991 Bp Francis Campbell Gray. m Ruth Wolford. D Dio The Rio Grande Albuquerque NM 1994-1996; D S Mich And All Ang Ch So Bend IN 1991-1994.

WOLFORD, (Mary) Rachael Rossiter (Oly) PO Box 522, Cathlamet WA 98612 **D S Jas Epis Ch Cathlamet WA 1998-** B Bournemouth Hampshire UK 5/11/1937 d Edward Janes Rossiter & Mary Knox. Gd Samar Hosp Oregon Radiological Tech Port 1961. D 10/3/1998 Bp Vincent Waydell Warner. m 6/3/1961 John Leroy Wolford. NAAD.

WOLLARD, Robert Foster (Mich) 4505 Westlawn Pkwy, Waterford MI 48328 B Detroit MI 4/29/1938 s Wilbur Benton Wollard & Margaret Priscilla. BA Alma Coll 1960; MDiv VTS 1963; Wayne 1970. D 6/29/1963 Bp Robert Lionne DeWitt P 1/25/1964 Bp Richard S M Emrich. m 5/17/1975 Carole A Abrams c 3. Assoc R S Andr's Ch Waterford MI 1999-2011; Cbury on the Lake Waterford MI 1996-1998; Int Chr Ch Cranbrook Bloomfield Hills MI 1994-1996; Epis Tri-Par Cluster Standish MI 1991-1994; R S Gabr's Epis Ch Eastpointe MI 1977-1985; Dio Michigan Detroit MI 1969-1977; Asst Cathd Ch Of S Paul Detroit MI 1966-1969; Asst Min S Columba Ch Detroit MI 1963-1966. carobertw@comcast.net

WOLSONCROFT III, Arthur Mathew (NY) 414 E 52nd St, New York NY 10022 B Philadelphia PA 2/12/1933 s Arthur Mathew Wolsoncroft & Anna. BA Tem 1955; MA NYU 1975; MDiv Nash 1987. D 6/13/1987 P 1/1/1988 Bp Paul Moore Jr. Asst Ch Of S Mary The Vrgn New York NY 1988-2004; Dpt Of Missions Ny Income New York NY 1987-1991; S Lk's-Roosevelt Hosp Cntr New York NY 1987-1991. Tertiary Of The Soc Of S Fran.

WOLTER, Allan Richard (ECR) Po Box 2352, Carmel CA 93921 B Sioux Falls SD 4/19/1924 s Richard Wolter & Emily Mavilla. BA Chapman U; USC 1948; CDSP 1951; MDiv CDSP 1961; Inst of Advncd Pstr Stds 1964; Coll of Preachers 1965. D 6/18/1951 P 2/28/1952 Bp Francis E I Bloy. c 2. Asst S Jn's Chap Monterey CA 1988-2001; Int S Lk's Ch Jolon CA 1984-1986; Int S Matt's Ch San Ardo CA 1984-1986; Asst All SS Ch Carmel CA 1973-1988; Bd Trsts CDSP Berkeley CA 1970-1974; R Ch of S Mary's by the Sea Pacific Grove CA 1968-1972; R Trin Epis Ch Orange CA 1957-1968; Vic All SS Ch Vista CA 1951-1957. stjohnschapel@redshift.com

WOLTER, Jack M (WNY) 668 Shadow Mountain Dr, Prescott AZ 86301 **Supply P/ Numerous Parishes Dio Arizona Phoenix AZ 2002-** B Mason City IA 9/12/1934 s Marvin Edwin Wolter & Irene Annette. BS Iowa St U 1956; MDiv GTS 1961. D 6/9/1961 P 12/18/1961 Bp Gordon V Smith. m 4/27/1957 Mary Elizabeth Dickerson c 5. Int S Lk's Ch Prescott AZ 2006-2007; Calling Consult Dio Wstrn New York Tonawanda NY 1997-2001; Trst Dio Wstrn New York Tonawanda NY 1995-2001; Plan and Vision Com Dio Wstrn New York Tonawanda NY 1994-1997; Hlth Ins Com Dio Wstrn New York Tonawanda NY 1992-2001; GC/Alt Dep Dio Wstrn New York Tonawanda NY 1988-1994; Resolutns Com/Chair Dio Wstrn New York Tonawanda NY 1988-1990; Genesee Reg Dn Dio Wstrn New York Tonawanda NY 1987-2001; Dept of Congrl Spprt Dio Wstrn New York Tonawanda NY 1984-1987; FA/ Natl Bd Dio Wstrn New York Tonawanda NY 1982-1986; Dioc Coun Dio Wstrn New York Tonawanda NY 1980-1983; Lay Mnstry Com Dio Wstrn New York Tonawanda NY 1979-1992; Stndg Com/Pres Dio Wstrn New York Tonawanda NY 1979-1983; R S Jas' Ch Batavia NY 1978-2001; Bd Trst The GTS New York NY 1977-1980; COM Dio Fond du Lac Appleton WI 1976-1978; Dioc Coun Dio Fond du Lac Appleton WI 1975-1978; Ecum Cmsn Dio Fond du Lac Appleton WI 1975-1978; Prov V Alum Rep The GTS New York NY 1972-1975; R S Anne's Ch De Pere WI 1971-1978; Dioc Coun Dio Iowa Des Moines IA 1970-1971; Stndg Com Dio Iowa Des Moines IA 1968-1971; Soc Concerns Cmsn Dio Iowa Des Moines IA 1967-1971; Prov VI Alum Rep The GTS New York NY 1967-1971; R S Alb's Ch Davenport IA 1963-1971; Yth Div Dio Iowa Des Moines IA 1962-1967; Camp Morrison, Asst. Dir Dio Iowa Des Moines IA 1958. OHC, P Assoc 1963. frjackwolter@juno.com

WOLTERSTORFF, Claire Kingma (WMich) 58 Sunnybrook Ave Se, Grand Rapids MI 49506 B Marshalltown IA 5/29/1934 d Jan Willem Kingma & Gezina. BA Calvin Coll 1955; MDiv SWTS 1985. D 6/8/1985 P 11/16/1996 Bp Howard Samuel Meeks. m 6/25/1955 Nicholas Paul Wolterstorff c 5. Sprtl Dir Annand Cntr Ya Berk New Haven CT 1989-1995. Auth, "Birth, Death, Hunger and Love"; Auth, *Garland for a Faint Soirit: A Bk of Prayers for Ian and India*; Auth, *Hemmed in by Darkness (a PB for the ill)*; Auth, *In The Shadow of Your Wings (a PB for the dying)*. nicholas.woltersorff@yale.edu

WOLTZ, Charles M (Okla) 924 N Robinson Ave, Oklahoma City OK 73102 B Oklahoma City OK 12/19/1936 s Elzo Morris Woltz & Audrey Fay. U of Oklahoma; BA U of Cntrl Oklahoma 1961. D 8/31/1985 Bp Gerald Nicholas McAllister. m 11/21/1962 Kathryn Jan Harris c 2. Dio Oklahoma Oklahoma City OK 1985-2008. cmwoltz@gmail.com

WOLVERTON JR, Wallace Irving (EC) 3200 Ridge Mill Run, Apt. 101, Raleigh NC 27612 **Died 11/9/2009** B Smithfield NC 9/18/1931 s Wallace Irving Wolverton & Elizabeth Lucille. BA E Carolina U 1956; MDiv CDSP 1959; VTS 1974. D 6/27/1959 P 2/1/1960 Bp Thomas H Wright. c 3.

WOMACK JR, Egbert Morton (Colo) 7500 E Dartmouth Ave Unit 31, Denver CO 80231 B Houston TX 7/11/1931 s Egbert Morton Womack & Kitty Ruth. BS U of Houston 1963; BD Epis TS of The SW 1968; MDiv Epis TS of The SW 1971. D 6/27/1968 Bp J Milton Richardson P 5/15/1969 Bp Scott Field Bailey. m 7/6/1957 Joanne Nuhn c 2. S Jn's Cathd Denver CO 2000-2002; S Fran Cntr Denver CO 1993; Bp's Exec Stff Dio Colorado Denver CO 1992-2000; P-in-c S Fran Chap Denver CO 1983-1994; Cn to the Ordnry Dio Colorado Denver CO 1982-2000; Vic S Martha's Epis Ch Westminster CO 1977-1979; Vic S Andr's Ch Manitou Sprg CO 1975-1977; Cn Mssnr Chr Ch Cathd Houston TX 1974-1975; Asst to the Dn Chr Ch Cathd Houston TX 1971-1972; P-in-c All SS Epis Ch Hitchcock TX 1969-1971; Asst The Ch of the Gd Shpd Austin TX 1968-1969. Cn To The Ordnry Emer Bp of Colorado 2002; The 2002 Hal Brook Perry Awd Epis Sem of The SW Austin TX 2002; Bp's Cross Bp of Colorado 1993. canonbert@comcast.net

WOMACK, Lawrence Melvin (NC) 8725 Sedgeburn Drive, Charlotte NC 28278 **S Anne's Ch Winston Salem NC 2011-** B Indianapolis IN 4/8/1972 s Johnella. BA Wabash Coll 1994; MA Jn Hopkins U 1996; MDiv Bex 2003. D 6/14/2003 Bp Robert Wilkes Ihloff P 1/10/2004 Bp John Leslie Rabb. m 4/12/1997 Sharita D Womack c 3. S Mart's Epis Ch Charlotte NC 2006-2011; S Lk's Ch Baltimore MD 2003-2006. frlmw1@aol.com

WOMBLE JR, Carey Clayton (Az) 6653 E Carondelet Dr Apt 234, Tucson AZ 85710 **Died 10/12/2010** B Oneco FL 7/21/1916 s Carey Clayton Womble & Edyth Maud. BA LSU 1939; MD Tul 1943; BD EDS 1968. D 12/14/1967 P 6/1/1968 Bp Francisco Reus-Froylan. c 4. ESMHE 1969-1986; UMHE 1972-1986.

WOMELSDORF, Charles Stowers (CGC) 327 Honeysuckle Hill, Tallassee AL 36078 B Wilmington OH 9/17/1943 s William Norvell Womelsdorf & Helen. BA Auburn U 1965; MDiv Nash 1968. D 6/5/1968 P 1/1/1969 Bp Albert R Stuart. m 6/12/1967 Sarah Bell c 3. R S Mk's Epis Ch Troy AL 1991-1998; R S Mich And All Ang Lake Chas LA 1988-1991; Chr Ch Napoleonville LA 1977-1988; R S Jn's Epis Ch Thibodaux LA 1977-1988; R S Jn's Epis Ch Bainbridge GA 1970-1977; Vic S Lk's Epis Hawkinsville GA 1968-1970.

WON, Ho Gil Hilary (Nwk) 403 79th St, North Bergen NJ 07047 **Vic S Ptr's Korean Ch No Bergen NJ 2006-** B South Korea 10/23/1961 s Duk Won & Ki. BA Sung Kong Hoe U Kr 1989; MDiv Sung Kong Hoe TS Kr 1994. Trans from Anglican Church Of Korea 6/14/2006 Bp John Palmer Croneberger. m 11/11/1989 Hye Kyung Jang c 1. hogilwon@gmail.com

WON, S. (Nwk) 16423 Maidstone Avenue, Norwalk CA 90650 B Pochon Kyunggi Do KR 8/25/1938 s Soon Kyung Won & Jae Eun. Becon Yonsei U 1962; MDiv EDS 1970; ThM S Mich's Sem Kr 1982; Concordia U 1998. Rec 12/31/1981 Bp John Shelby Spong. m 2/26/1972 Gemma Yong Ja Kim c 2. S Ptr's Korean Ch No Bergen NJ 2000-2006; Vic S Fran Mssn Norwalk CA 1989-2000; Ch Of The Annunc Los Angeles CA 1987-1989; S Peters Ch Bogota NJ 1981-1987. Auth, *Ch & Sacr*. Cn The Dio Los Angeles 1998.

WONDRA, Ellen K (Chi) 2122 Sheridan Rd, Evanston IL 60201 B Santa Monica CA 9/3/1950 d Gerald Wondra & Elizabeth. BA Pomona Coll 1972; ETSBH 1973; MDiv CDSP 1976; PhD U Chi 1991. D 6/26/1976 Bp C Kilmer Myers P 10/22/1977 Bp Philip Frederick McNairy. Bex Columbus OH 2003-2004; SWTS Evanston IL 2000-2003; Adj P S Lk And S Simon Cyrene Rochester NY 1991-2004; Assoc Chpl U Epis Cntr Minneapolis MN 1976-1978. Ed, *Common Witness to the Gospel*; Auth, *Humanity Has Been a H Thing*; Co-Auth, *Intro to Theol*; Ed, *Reconstructing Chr Ethics*; Auth, *Var essays*. AAR; Angl-RC Consult; Bd, ATR; Epis Womens Caucus; GBEC; SALT; SCER 1997-2003. Fell Cntr of Theol Inquiry; Fell Coll of Preachers; Fell ECF. ewondra@comcast.net

WONG, Diane C K (Mass) 14-A Fair St, Nantucket MA 02554 **P-in-c S Jn's Epis Ch Holbrook MA 2011-** B Hong Kong 11/16/1953 d Y B Wong & So-Yuet. BS U Of Alberta Edmonton Ab CA 1982; MDiv Weston Jesuit TS (Boston Coll) 1997; Atc EDS 1999; MA Simmons Coll 2013. D 6/15/2002 P 5/31/2003 Bp M(arvil) Thomas Shaw III. Mssy P-in-c Exec Coun Appointees New York NY 2006-2011; Assoc S Paul's Ch In Nantucket Nantucket MA 2003-2006; D Ch Of Our Sav Arlington MA 2002-2003; Dioc Stff Dio Massachusetts Boston MA 2002-2003. "In The Footsteps Of The Foremothers: The Mnstrs Of Asian And Asian Amer Lay Wmn Deeper Joy," Ch Pub, 2005. dianeckwong@gmail.com

WONG, Gloria Violet Lee (Mass) Po Box 825, Oak Bluffs MA 02557 **D Gr Ch Vineyard Haven MA 1999-** B Victoria BC CA 2/24/1928 d Clarence LT Lee & Edith Lois. BA U CA 1949; MS Smith Sch for Soc Wk 1953; Rhode Island Sch for Deacons 1993. D 6/23/1993 Bp George Nelson Hunt III. m 7/3/1954 Backman Wong c 5. S Jas Ch The Par Of N Providence RI 1993-1996. Intl Ord of S Lk the Physcn; NASW; NAAD.

WONG, Philip Yau-Ming (Oly) 62 Pine St., Rockville Centre NY 11570 B Hong Kong CN 12/4/1946 s Sai-Kung Wong & King. Hong Kong Biblic Inst

HK 1967; BA Houng Kong Coll HK 1971; MDiv Taiwan Theol Coll TW 1987. D 6/10/1988 P 9/30/1989 Bp John Chih-Tsung Chien. m 3/24/1973 Sylvia SL Liu c 2. Vic Ch Of The H Apos Bellevue WA 2000-2010; Staten Island Chinese Chr Ch Staten Island NY 1998-2000; Dio New Jersey Trenton NJ 1995; Chinese Mssn, Vic and Jubilee Mnstry, Dir S Lk And All SS' Ch Un NJ 1994-1998; Chinese Mnstry Of Dio Of Newark Nutley NJ 1992-1994; Assoc, Chinese Mssn, Vic Gr Ch Nutley NJ 1992-1994; Cur S Paul's Ch No Arlington NJ 1989-1991. Seaman's Ch of the Seafarers, Newark, NJ 1997-1999. philipwong46@msn.com

WONG, Salying (Cal) 77 Cielito Dr, San Francisco CA 94134 **Asst S Mk's Epis Ch Palo Alto CA 2011-** B China 9/15/1972 d Sher Chup Wong & Ling Tu. D 6/11/2005 Bp Robert John O'Neill P 12/3/2005 Bp William Edwin Swing. m 1/5/2002 Shannon M Preto. S Matt's Epis Day Sch San Mateo CA 2011; Asst R S Clem's Ch Berkeley CA 2005-2011. salying@gmail.com

WOOD, Ann Patricia (WMass) 13 Kelleher Dr, South Deerfield MA 01373 B Stoke-on-Trent England 5/19/1937 D 6/19/2004 Bp Gordon Paul Scruton. m 9/8/1962 John Stanley Wood c 2. ann_wood@cooley-dickinson.org

WOOD, Camille Carpenter (La) 3552 Morning Glory Ave, Baton Rouge LA 70808 B Evanston IL 6/29/1944 d Nathaniel Leslie Carpenter & Ethel Strong. D 12/4/2010 Bp Morris King Thompson Jr. m 2/7/1994 Fernie Wood c 2. camwood@cox.net

WOOD JR, Charles Amos (La) 532 Stanford Ave, Baton Rouge LA 70808 B Syracuse NY 8/21/1932 s Charles Amos Wood & Florence. BA Cor 1954; MDiv VTS 1966; STM Nash 1973. D 6/28/1966 Bp J Milton Richardson P 6/2/1967 Bp Scott Field Bailey. m 11/4/1955 Gay Worrall c 3. Chapl S Alb's Chap & Epis U Cntr Baton Rouge LA 1970-1997; Vic All SS Epis Ch Hitchcock TX 1966-1967. Auth, "Premarital Counslg: A Working Model," *Journ of Pstr Care*. AAMFT 1976-2007; AAPC 1974-1985; ESMHE 1971-1997. howmuchwood@att.net

WOOD JR, Charles Edwards (Spok) 426 Lilly Road NE Apt 248, Olympia WA 98506 **Dio Spokane Spokane WA 1983-** B Carneys Pt NJ 4/18/1919 s Charles Edwards Wood & Maria Antonia. U Cinc 1938; BS USNA 1941; MDiv SWTS 1965. D 6/20/1965 P 3/6/1966 Bp Russell S Hubbard. m 8/22/1942 Ann Rayner c 4. Chair ArmdF Com Dio Spokane Spokane WA 1984-1989; Chair Const & Cas Dio Spokane Spokane WA 1983-2005; Const & Cns Mem Dio Spokane Spokane WA 1978-2006; Const & Cns Mem Dio Spokane Spokane WA 1978-2006; Dep GC Dio Spokane Spokane WA 1976-1979; Dep GC Dio Spokane Spokane WA 1976-1979; Secy of Conv Dio Spokane Spokane WA 1973-1988; Admin Asst to Bp Dio Spokane Spokane WA 1969-1980; Dio Coun Dio Spokane Spokane WA 1968-1988; Dioc Coun Dio Spokane Spokane WA 1968-1987; Chair ArmdF Com Dio Spokane Spokane WA 1966-1972; Vic Epis Ch Of The Redeem Republic WA 1965-1969; Vic S Jn's Epis Ch Colville WA 1965-1969. Cler Advsry Com, Planned Parenthood of Spokane & Wh 1995; Integrity 1985-2009; Parents, Fam and Friends Of Lesbian and Gays 1984-2009. Hon Cn Cathd of S Jn the Evang Spokane WA 1980. chaannwood@gmail.com

WOOD, Charles Leon (Mich) PO Box 2001, Southern Pines NC 28388 B Rahway NJ 11/10/1927 s Charles Leon Wood & Helen. GTS 1954; ThB PDS 1955; Doctor of Educ/Rutgers 1964; STB GTS 1965; Air War Coll 1968; Indstrl Coll of the ArmdF Ft McNair DC 1972; DHum Great Lakes Reg Chapl Stff Coll 1987; Middle E Reg Chapl Stff Coll 1992. D 7/3/1954 Bp Wallace J Gardner P 1/22/1955 Bp Alfred L Banyard. m 6/23/1956 Nancy Phillips c 2. Vic S Lk's Epis Ch Yanceyville NC 1991-2007; COM Dio Michigan Detroit MI 1983-1988; R Trsfg Epis Ch Indn River MI 1981-1990; Advsr of Yth Cmsn Dio New Jersey Trenton NJ 1970-1980; R H Trin Epis Ch Ocean City NJ 1967-1980; R St Jn the Bapt Epis Ch Linden NJ 1958-1967; Vic The Epis Ch Of The H Comm Fair Haven NJ 1955-1958; Cur H Trin Ch Collingswood NJ 1954-1955. Auth, *Nine collections of Prayers*; Auth, *Two Hospice Books*, Grand Chapl RAM NJ 1980; DSM CAP 1973; Geo Wash hon Medal Freedoms Fndt Vlly Forge 1972. SKYPILOTCHAP@YAHOO.COM

WOOD, David Romaine (Colo) 1233 24th Ave. Ct., Greeley CO 80634 B Poplar Bluff MO 9/1/1938 s Romaine D Wood & Alice Jean. BS U CO 1969. D 3/17/1983 P 10/15/1983 Bp William Harvey Wolfrum. m 10/15/1957 Donna Jean Linville c 4. S Alb's Ch Windsor CO 1990-2003; S Steph's Ch Longmont CO 1990-2003. davidwood1233@comcast.net

WOOD, Erica Brown (CPa) 15-A Saint Johns Rd, Cambridge MA 02138 **Died 5/10/2011** B Hartford CT 2/17/1946 d Winston Booth Brown & Edith Frances. BA Bard Coll 1968; MA CUNY 1973; PhD Syr 1983; MDiv CRDS 1987. D 6/20/1987 P 4/12/1988 Bp O'Kelley Whitaker. c 2. Coll Of Preachers, AAR, Bvd, Bd EvangES. EBWCAMBRIDGE@AOL.COM

WOOD, Grace Marie (EC) 198 Dogwood Trl, Elizabeth City NC 27909 B Montreal Canada 6/5/1947 d Saboits Serpico & Grace. BA Wag 1969; MS Gordham Grad Sch Of Soc Sciences NY 1984; D Formation Prog 2004. D 6/25/2005 Bp Clifton Daniel III. m 8/3/1985 Allen Wood c 3.

WOOD, Gregg Douglas (NY) Po Box 62, Wawarsing NY 12489 B Stoneham MA 2/1/1941 s Harry Lee Wood & Edna. BA Harv 1962; Harvard DS 1963; MDiv EDS 1967. D 6/24/1967 Bp Anson Phelps Stokes Jr P 6/29/1968 Bp Frederic Cunningham Lawrence. m 10/15/1977 Jane S Strunsky c 2. S Jn's Memi Ch Ellenville NY 1995-1996; Team Monticello NY 1992-1995; S Jn's Ch Huntington NY 1991-1992; S Steph's Ch Port Washington NY 1989-1991; Chr Ch Brentwood NY 1984-1985; S Johns Epis Hosp Far Rockaway NY 1979-1992; R The Ch Of The Epiph And S Simon Brooklyn NY 1970-1977; S Ann's Ch Sayville NY 1969-1970; P-in-c S Jn's Epis Ch Oakdale NY 1969-1970; Cur All SS Epis Ch Attleboro MA 1967-1969. AAPC 1978-1983; Fell Coll Chapl (inactive) 1982-1992. Robbins Fellowlowship EDS 1976; JA Mueller Hist Prize Epis TS 1967. greggwd@yahoo.com

WOOD, Gretchen A (SO) 24 High Ridge Loop Apt 605, Pawleys Island SC 29585 B Upland PA 4/11/1944 d James H Wood & Barbara L. BA Ob 1966; PhD U Chi 1970. D 6/11/1983 P 6/1/1984 Bp Lyman Cunningham Ogilby. Int S Mary Epis Ch Crystal Lake IL 2007-2008; Int S Anne Epis Ch W Chester OH 2005; Int The Epis Ch Of The Ascen Middletown OH 2005; Dir of the Sch for the Diac Dio Sthrn Ohio Cincinnati OH 1998-2002; Stndg Com Dio Sthrn Ohio Cincinnati OH 1992-2000; R S Jas Epis Ch Cincinnati OH 1990-2005; Assoc The Ch of the Redeem Cincinnati OH 1986-1990; P Ch Of S Jn The Evang Essington PA 1985-1986; D S Mary's Ch Hamilton Vill Philadelphia PA 1983-1984. Tertiary Of The Soc Of S Fran, Caso. retgret1@gmail.com

WOOD, Howard Fitler (Pa) 526 Washington Ave, Hulmeville PA 19047 B Philadelphia PA 7/14/1937 s William Meredith Wood & Margaret Louise. BA U of Pennsylvania 1959; M Ed Nazareth Coll 1978; M Div STUSo 1979; D Min STUSo/Vanderbilt Unive 1981. D 6/14/1986 P 6/1/1987 Bp Charles Brinkley Morton. S Paul Ch Levittown PA 1989-2003; Day Sch Headmaster Chr Ch Coronado CA 1987-1988; Vol Assoc Chr Ch Toms River Toms River NJ 1986-1989. Natl Epis Aids Cltn; Ord S Mary. hfwretyred@aol.com

WOOD, H Palmer (CFla) 720 S Lakeshore Blvd, Lake Wales FL 33853 B Jacksonville FL 4/29/1936 s Julien G Wood & Harriet A. Ics Orlando FL; BS Rol 1971. D 12/18/2004 Bp John Wadsworth Howe. m 1/17/1970 Ronali Anderson c 2. palmer.wood@verizon.net

WOOD JR, Hubert Stanley (CNY) 1706 Dahlgren Rd, Middletown MD 21769 **Dn Binghamton Dist Dio Cntrl New York Syracuse NY 1970-; Dn, Finger Lakes Dist Dio Cntrl New York Syracuse NY 1960-** B Utica NY 2/15/1923 s Hubert Stanley Wood & Marion Winifred. BA Ya 1944; STB GTS 1947; MDiv PDS 1951. D 4/19/1947 Bp James P De Wolfe P 11/30/1947 Bp Richard Ainslie Kirchhoffer. m 8/15/1998 Constance Hurney c 2. R All SS Epis Ch Johnson City NY 1970-1987; Dn Binghamton Dist Dio Cntrl New York Syracuse NY 1970-1982; R S Paul's Ch Waterloo NY 1955-1970; P-in-c Gr Ch Willowdale Geneva NY 1955-1956; Cur S Paul's Ch Philadelphia PA 1948-1951; Assoc S Steph's Ch Terre Haute IN 1947-1948. stapletonwood@aol.com

WOOD, Hunter Holmes (Va) 901 Fendall Ter, Charlottesville VA 22903 B Charlottesville VA 7/6/1938 s William Hoge Wood & Anne Cary. BA Pr 1960; MDiv VTS 1965; PhD Amer U 1978. D 6/12/1965 Bp Robert Fisher Gibson Jr P 6/1/1966 Bp Samuel B Chilton. m 1/1/1990 Christian Roberts c 2. Asst Imm Ch-On-The-Hill Alexandria VA 1965-1970. Auth, "Journ Of Rel & Hlth"; Auth, "Wood Test Of Life Position". hhwood@ntelos.net

WOOD, Jan Smith (ECR) Grace Episcopal Church, 315 Wayne Street, Sandusky OH 44870 **P-in-c Gr Epis Ch Sandusky OH 2011-** B Los Angeles CA 6/13/1954 d Tom Earl Smith & Leona Dolores. BA U CA 1976; MDiv CDSP 1986. D 6/24/2000 P 2/10/2001 Bp Richard Lester Shimpfky. m 6/30/1979 Philip Wood c 2. Dn of Students CDSP Berkeley CA 2005-2011; Cn Eductr Dio El Camino Real Monterey CA 1990-2005. jansmithwood@gmail.com

WOOD, Kathrine Ringold (Ore) 437 Franklin St, Denver CO 80218 B Denver CO 10/5/1943 d Frederick Hunt Wood & Mary Katherine. MA S Thos Sem Denver CO; BA U Denv. D 10/4/1988 Bp William Carl Frey P 4/14/2007 Bp Johncy Itty. S Matt's Epis Ch Gold Bch OR 2001-2004; Dio Colorado Denver CO 1992-1999; D Epis Ch Of S Ptr And S Mary Denver CO 1989-2001; Dio Colorado Denver CO 1989-1991; Dir Bp's for Dcnal Formation Dio Colorado Denver CO 1989-1991; D The Ch Of The Ascen Denver CO 1988-1989. jubiloso@charter.net

WOOD, Linda Anne (Cal) 3080 Birdsall Ave, Oakland CA 94619 B Chelsea MA 3/3/1948 d Franklin Edward Lahr & Virginia Ruth. BS H Name U 1979; MDiv CDSP 1992. D 6/6/1992 P 6/5/1993 Bp William Edwin Swing. c 2. Assoc All SS Epis Ch San Leandro CA 2003-2008; Dn Of Students CDSP Berkeley CA 2002-2004; S Andr's Ch Ben Lomond CA 1997-2001; Asst R S Paul's Epis Ch Burlingame CA 1994-1996; All Souls' Epis Ch San Diego CA 1993-1994; Asst To P S Mich And All Ang Concord CA 1992-1993. revlawood@att.net

WOOD, Mark Raymond (Ct) 180 W 20th Street, 10N, New York NY 10011 B Beaumont TX 2/1/1958 s William Raymond Wood & Patsy Lambert. BA TCU 1980; MDiv Epis TS of the SW 1985; MPA Harv 2000; ThM Harvard DS 2002; JD NYU 2006. D 6/16/1985 Bp A Donald Davies P 5/31/1986 Bp Clarence Cullam Pope Jr. Int Ch Of The Ascen Staten Island NY 2008-2010; Cn The Amer Cathd of the H Trin Paris 75008 FR 1996-1999; Int Emm Epis Ch Geneva 1201 CH 1995-1996; Asst to R S Paul's Ch Riverside CT 1987-1993; Cur S Alb's Epis Ch Arlington TX 1985-1987. wood@post.harvard.edu

✠ WOOD, Rt Rev Milton LeGrand (At) Po Box 820, Elberta AL 36530 B Selma AL 8/21/1922 s Milton LeGrand Wood & Roberta Owen. BA U So 1943; MDiv STUSo 1945. D 11/18/1945 P 8/24/1946 Bp Charles C J Carpenter Con 6/29/1967 for At. m 5/3/1949 Ann Scott. Epis Ch Cntr New York NY 1974-1983; Bp Dio Atlanta Atlanta GA 1967-1974; Cn to the Bp Dio Atlanta Atlanta GA 1963-1967; Dep, GC Dio Atlanta Atlanta GA 1961-1964; Archd Dio Atlanta Atlanta GA 1960-1963; R All SS Epis Ch Atlanta GA 1952-1960; R S Paul's Ch Mobile AL 1946-1952. DD U So TS 1967.

WOOD, Nancy Currey (SVa) 1524 Southwick Rd, Virginia Beach VA 23451 **Chapl Dio Sthrn Virginia Norfolk VA 1999-** B Chattanooga TN 11/9/1941 d Doyle Eason Currey & Mary Ruth. BA Wellesley Coll 1964; BS U of Nebraska 1987. D 11/8/1985 Bp James Daniel Warner. m 6/27/1964 William Drane Wood c 2. D Trin Ch Portsmouth VA 1997-1998; D Gd Samar Epis Ch Virginia Bch VA 1992-1996; D Old Donation Ch Virginia Bch VA 1987-1992; D All SS Epis Ch Omaha NE 1985-1987.

WOOD, Priscilla Peacock (Mass) 1 Hickey Dr, Framingham MA 01701 B Jacksonville FL 2/11/1944 d Chester Harvey Peacock & Lavinnia Lois. BA San Francisco St Coll 1966; MDiv GTS 1979. D 6/9/1979 P 12/11/1979 Bp John Shelby Spong. m 6/27/1976 Stewart Wood c 2. Chr Ch Medway MA 2004-2007; R S Andr's Ch Framingham MA 1995-2004; Dep Gc Dio Sthrn Ohio Cincinnati OH 1991-1994; R S Jas Ch Piqua OH 1985-1994; Treas Assoc Alum The GTS New York NY 1985-1991; Cur Chr Ch Bronxville NY 1982-1985; Assoc S Paul's Epis Ch Morris Plains NJ 1979-1982. SCHC 1985. Bp Of Newark Preaching Prize GTS 1979; Geo Cabot Ward Prize GTS 1979. priscillawood@gmail.com

✠ **WOOD JR, Rt Rev R(aymond) Stewart** (Mich) P. O. Box 968, 255 Robert Frost Lane, Quechee VT 05059 B Detroit MI 6/25/1934 s Raymond Stewart Wood & Marjorie Campbell. BA Dart 1956; MDiv VTS 1959; MA Ball St U 1973. D 6/11/1959 P 12/18/1959 Bp John P Craine Con 10/15/1988 for Mich. m 6/25/1955 Kristin Lie Miller c 3. Dio Michigan Detroit MI 1988-2000; R S Jn's Epis Ch Memphis TN 1984-1988; R Chr Ch - Glendale Cincinnati OH 1976-1984; All SS Ch Indianapolis IN 1974-1976; Episc Cmnty Serv Indianapolis IN 1970-1976; R Gr Ch Muncie IN 1966-1970; Vic All SS Ch Seymour IN 1960-1963; Vic S Dav's Ch Beanblossom Nashville IN 1960-1963; Assoc S Paul's Ch Columbus IN 1959-1960. Auth, *Seabury Selected Sermons*, Seabury Press. DD VTS 1960. stewwood@aol.com

WOOD, Robert Bradford (At) 3995 Schooner Rdg, Alpharetta GA 30005 **R S Aid's Epis Ch Milton GA 2004-** B Athens GA 12/14/1966 s Robert Manning Wood & Susan Lynne. BA U So 1989; MDiv GTS 1996. D 6/8/1996 P 12/14/1996 Bp Frank Kellogg Allan. m 3/19/2009 Linda Wood c 2. R S Paul's Ch Columbus MS 2000-2004; Asst R H Innoc Ch Atlanta GA 1997-2000; Assoc Gr-Calv Epis Ch Clarkesville GA 1996-1997. fr.wood@earthlink.net

WOOD, Robert Earl (WMo) 1009 W 57th St, Kansas City MO 64113 **Pres Dio Tennessee Nashville TN 1992-** B Nashville TN 2/27/1937 s William Justus Wood & Mildred Elizabeth. BS Tennessee Tech U 1960; MDiv Candler TS Emory U 1964; U So 1971. D 2/27/1971 Bp William F Gates Jr P 7/4/1971 Bp John Vander Horst. m 7/18/1984 Sheridan Y Yates c 4. R S Paul's Ch Kansas City MO 1993-2005; Stndg Com Dio Tennessee Nashville TN 1990-2006; Trin Ch Clarksville TN 1983-1993; Chair - COM Dio Tennessee Nashville TN 1973-1989; Ch Of The Gd Shpd Lookout Mtn TN 1971-1983. sageing@kc.rr.com

WOOD, Rodgers T(aylor) (WVa) 5301 Morning Dove Ln., Cross Lanes WV 25313 B Pittsburgh PA 12/16/1933 s Robert Elliott Wood & Margaret. BS U Pgh 1972; MDiv VTS 1975. D 6/27/1975 P 12/13/1975 Bp Robert Bracewell Appleyard. m 8/6/1955 Roselind D Davis c 3. Int S Mk's Epis Ch S Albans WV 2007-2008; Assoc S Matt's Ch Charleston WV 2005-2006; P-in-c S Jas Ch Charleston WV 2003-2005; P-in-c S Andr's Ch Oak Hill WV 2001-2003; Chr Epis Ch No Hills Pittsburgh PA 1981-1999; S Phil's Ch Coraopolis PA 1975-1981. rodgewood@aol.com

WOOD, Roger Hoffman (Los) 38 E Grandview Ave, Sierra Madre CA 91024 B Pasadena CA 11/9/1923 s Henry Randolph Wood & Janet. BA Stan 1948; LLB Stan 1952; BD CDSP 1957. D 6/29/1957 P 12/21/1957 Bp Richard S Watson. Asst The Ch Of The Ascen Sierra Madre CA 1995-2003; Epis Hm For The Aged Camp Hill PA 1988-1994; The Epis Hm Communities Pasadena CA 1988-1994; Ch Of The Epiph Los Angeles CA 1978-1982; Dio Los Angeles Los Angeles CA 1966-1977; R S Mary's Ch Provo UT 1961-1966; Vic S Fran Ch Moab UT 1957-1960. Cn of the Cathd St. Paul, Los Angeles 2007.

WOOD, Roger Lee (EMich) 106 S Kennefic St, Yale MI 48097 **D Gr Epis Ch Port Huron MI 1996-** B Lansing MI 4/9/1939 s Raymond Wood & Roma June. BA Olivet Coll 1961; MA MI SU 1970; Cert. Whitaker TS 1996. D 10/19/1996 Bp Edwin Max Leidel Jr. m 6/18/1963 Gwendolyn Jane Fett. NAAD. rogerw@greatlakes.net

WOOD, Sammy (Mass) 30 Brimmer St, Boston MA 02108 **The Ch Of The Adv Boston MA 2009-** B New Orleans, LA 10/3/1967 s Samuel Webb Wood & Madeline Cain. JD U of Mississippi Sch of Law 1994; MDiv Gordon-Conwell TS 2003; Angl Stds VTS 2006. D 6/2/2007 Bp M(arvil) Thomas Shaw III P 12/8/2007 Bp James Winchester Montgomery. m 10/30/1999 Renee C Caston c 3. Ch Of The Ascen And S Agnes Washington DC 2007-2009. cubswn@gmail.com

WOOD, Sarah Anne (Va) 209 14th St., NE, Apartment 102, Atlanta GA 30309 **Gr Ch Sch New York New York NY 2011-; H Innoc' Epis Sch Atlanta GA 2008-** B Washington DC 2/2/1973 d Edward Manning Wood & Deborah Wood. BA W&M 1995; MDiv VTS 2004. D 11/22/2004 P 5/25/2005 Bp Peter James Lee. Upper Sch Chapl H Innoc Ch Atlanta GA 2007-2011; Christchurch Sch Christchurch VA 2004-2007. "Sophie Scholl," *CSEE*, CSEE, 2008. sarah_anne_wood@hotmail.com

WOOD, Stuart Clary (Va) 7120 Ore Bank Rd, Port Republic VA 24471 **R Gr Ch Port Republic VA 1990-; R Lynnwood Par Port Republic VA 1990-; R S Steph And The Gd Shpd Elkton Port Republic VA 1990-** B Richmond VA 1/10/1959 s Jordan Edward Wood & Mary Clary. AA Ferrum Coll 1978; BA Geo Mason U 1980; MDiv VTS 1988. D 6/18/1988 Bp Peter James Lee P 3/18/1989 Bp Robert Manning Moody. Cur Dio Oklahoma Oklahoma City OK 1988-1990. stucwood@comcast.net

WOOD III, William Hoge (Pa) 226 Righters Mill Rd, Gladwyne PA 19035 **Stndg Com Dio Pennsylvania Philadelphia PA 1991-; R S Chris's Ch Gladwyne PA 1991-; Chair On New Mssn Com Dio Pennsylvania Philadelphia PA 1990-; Dioc Coun Dio Pennsylvania Philadelphia PA 1986-** B Charlottesville VA 3/2/1940 s William Hoge Wood & Anne Cary. BA U of Virginia 1962; BD VTS 1970. D 6/20/1970 Bp Philip Alan Smith P 12/1/1970 Bp William Henry Marmion. m 6/15/1974 Kristine Alma Carlson. Mssn Strtgy Cmsn Dio Pennsylvania Philadelphia PA 1988-1991; R Trin Ch Solebury PA 1978-1991; Assoc R S Dav's Ch Wayne PA 1972-1978; Asst to R S Jn's Ch Roanoke VA 1970-1972. Auth, "Abm & The Arms Race". Pa Fndt Pstr Counselors. billwood@saintchristophers.org

WOOD, William James (Kan) 30 Spofford Lane, Trevett ME 04571 **Mssn Dvlpmt Com Dio Maine Portland ME 2007-; Intl Dvlpmt Com Dio Maine Portland ME 2006-; Intl Dvlpmt Com Dio Maine Portland ME 2006-** B Suffern NY 8/29/1942 s Alfred George Wood & Flora E. BA Leh 1964; MDiv EDS 1967; DMin EDS 2007. D 6/10/1967 P 12/11/1967 Bp Leland Stark. m 11/25/1967 Susan P Pettingill c 2. Trst Dio Kansas Topeka KS 1998-2006; Cmsn On Wrld Mssn Dio Kansas Topeka KS 1996-2006; R S Jn's Ch Wichita KS 1996-2006; R Trin Ch S Clair Shores MI 1987-1995; P-in-c St Andrews Memi Ch Detroit MI 1974-1987; Asst S Paul's Epis Ch Paterson NJ 1970. Auth, "Whence Cometh Our Cmnty?," *Plumbline*, ESMHE, 1974. ESMHE 1971-1987; Global Epis Mssn Ntwk 1995; Integrity 2000-2008. williamjwood@hotmail.com

WOOD JR, William Reed (WVa) 107 Elma Dr, Williamstown WV 26187 B Galveston TX 9/8/1941 s William Reed Wood & Georgia. BA Guilford Coll 1967; MDiv VTS 1970. Trans 9/8/2003 Bp Creighton Leland Robertson. m 5/1/1985 Jett Groves c 1. S Andr's in the Vill Ch Barboursville WV 2004-2006; Dio So Dakota Sioux Falls SD 1998-1999; Chr Memi Ch Williamstown WV 1994-2000; Ohio Vlly Epis Cluster Williamstown WV 1994-1998; S Paul's Ch Hamilton MT 1991-1992; S Steph's Epis Ch Stevensville MT 1989-2006; Dio Montana Helena MT 1989-1994; R S Matt's Ch Glasgow MT 1985-1989; S Mk's Ch St Paul VA 1980-1985.

WOODALL JR, P J (At) 3663 SE Cambridge Drive, Stuart FL 34997 B Roxboro NC 5/25/1942 s Percy Jerome Woodall & Vena Hawkins. BS U NC 1971; MDiv STUSo 1983. D 6/18/1983 Bp Hunley Agee Elebash P 12/1/1983 Bp Brice Sidney Sanders. m 2/19/1972 Loraine McIlwain. Int R S Thos Epis Par Coral Gables FL 2010-2011; Int Dn S Jn's Cathd Jacksonville FL 2009; Int R Chr Ch Norcross GA 2007-2009; Int R The Epis Ch Of The Nativ Fayetteville GA 2006-2007; Int R S Greg The Great Athens GA 2004-2006; Int R S Dunst's Epis Ch Atlanta GA 2003-2004; Mssnr Dio Virginia Richmond VA 2002-2003; Mssnr Dio Haiti Ft Lauderdale FL 1998-2004; Appointed Mssnr Exec Coun Appointees New York NY 1998-2003; R S Paul's Ch Natick MA 1988-1998; R S Paul's Epis Ch Clinton NC 1983-1988. christwood@earthlink.net

WOODARD JR, George H Jack (Va) 7450 Spring Village Dr, Apt. 406, Springfield VA 22150 B Tampa FL 8/16/1926 s George Henry Woodard & Bess. Fllshp Coll of Preachers; BS U of Texas 1946; MDiv Epis TS of the SW 1961. D 5/27/1961 Bp Frederick P Goddard P 5/26/1962 Bp John E Hines. m 3/7/1970 Lucilia Sophia George c 4. Adj Prof Urban Mnstry VTS Alexandria VA 1988-1997; R Meade Memi Epis Ch Alexandria VA 1986-1991; Stndg Com Metro Areas Dio Washington Washington DC 1980-1985; Ch Of S Steph And The Incarn Washington DC 1979-1986; Dep Gc Dio Washington Washington DC 1979-1985; R Iglesia Epis Epifania Santo Domingo Di DO 1977-1979; Dio The Dominican Republic (Iglesia Epis Dominicana) 100 Airport AvVenice FL 1977; Excoun Dio New York New York City NY 1976-1977; Com Fin Structure Dio New York New York City NY 1973-1977; Dep R Trin Par New York NY 1970-1977. Auth, "Challenge Of Future For Trin Par Nyc"; Auth, "A Time For Planting"; Auth, "Ch In Metropolis". DD Epis TS of the SW 1985. lwjackluci@gmail.com

WOODARD, Sarah Wilson (NC) 400 Moline St., Durham NC 27707 B Raleigh NC 1/25/1955 d Walter Howard Wilson & Eleanor Eunice Pope. AA Mt Vernon 1975; BA U of NC 1977. D 6/20/2009 Bp Michael Bruce Curry. m 6/20/1989 James Michael Woodard. sarah.woodard@duke.edu

WOODBURY, Robert Lane (Mil) 5558 N Berkeley Blvd, Whitefish Bay WI 53217 B Chicago IL 12/11/1940 s Arthur Sennott Woodbury & Mary Lucile. BA Elmhurst Coll 1962; MDiv Garrett Evang TS 1965; Cert SWTS 1968. D 6/15/1968 Bp James Winchester Montgomery P 12/21/1968 Bp Gerald Francis Burrill. c 2. S Johns Communities INC Milwaukee WI 1996-2004; Asst Trin Ch Wauwatosa WI 1990-1995; Asst S Bon Ch Mequon WI 1987-1990; Asst All SS' Cathd Milwaukee WI 1982-1987; Chr Ch Whitefish Bay WI 1975-1981; S Dunst's Epis Ch Westchester IL 1970-1975; Cur S Mich's Ch Barrington IL 1968-1970. rwoodbury@wi.rr.com

WOODCOCK, Bruce W (SeFla) 106 Castle Heights Ave, Nyack NY 10960 **Vic S Matt's Ch Paramus NJ 2005-; Mgr, Int'l Relatns Ch Pension Fund New York NY 2004-** B New York City NY 12/3/1953 s Wilson Wiley Woodcock & Edith Christensen. BA Hob 1976; MA Sch for Intl Trng/EIL 1985; NTL 1986; NTL 1987; Cert Natl Trng Labs (NTL) 1988; MDiv GTS 2002; STM GTS 2003. D 7/26/2003 Bp Leopold Frade P 2/18/2004 Bp Michael Bruce Curry. m 5/28/1984 Thayer Evelyn Preece c 2. Sigma Phi 1973. Hon Cn Epis Ch of Liberia/Trin Cathd 2008; Cbury Chr Ldrshp Awd Hob 1976; Pres's Awd Sigma Phi Soc - Hob 1975. bwoodcock@cpg.org

WOODEN, Lorentho (SO) 550 E 4th St, Cincinnati OH 45202 B Dayton Bch FL 6/25/1927 s Lorentha Wallace Wooden & Leila. BA Morehouse Coll 1949; U Chi 1952; EDS 1960. D 10/9/1960 Bp Donald MacAdie P 6/1/1961 Bp Henry I Louttit. c 4. Vic Ch Of S Simon The Cyrenian New Rochelle NY 1989-1995; All SS Ch Pasadena CA 1986-1989; Dio Sthrn Ohio Cincinnati OH 1975-1986; R Ch Of S Simon The Cyrenian New Rochelle NY 1965-1971; Vic Ch Of The H Comf Richmond VA 1960-1962; Vic S Andr's Epis Ch Of Hollywood Dania Bch FL 1960-1962. Hon Cn Chr Ch Cathd Cincinnati OH 1989.

WOODHOUSE, Marjorie Michelle (Los) 4125 Creciente Dr, Santa Barbara CA 93110 B San Mateo CA 5/17/1934 d Charles Douglas Woodhouse & Muriel. BA Mt Holyoke Coll 1956; MA Luth TS Philadelphia 1984; STM Luth TS Philadelphia 1987; DMin Claremont TS 1997. D 6/1/1985 P 6/21/1986 Bp John Bowen Coburn. c 2. All SS-By-The-Sea Par Santa Barbara CA 1992-2006; Int Chr The King Epis Ch Santa Barbara CA 1991-1992; Pstr Assoc Chr The King Epis Ch Santa Barbara CA 1989-1991; Pstr Assoc S Matt's Ch Maple Glen PA 1986-1989. Auth, "A Meditation On The Status Of The Cross," 1974; Auth, "Crisis In Faith: The Challenge Of Pvrty," 1968. Coll Of Chapl, Assn Mntl Hlth Cleric, Amer 1991; SCHC 1969. 4th Annual Awd Clincl Schlrshp Horsham Clnc 1988. revmmw@cox.net

WOOD-HULL, L. D. (Ore) 5616 SW 18th Dr, Portland OR 97239 **R S Barn Par Portland OR 2007-** B Cooperstown NY 4/22/1965 s Larry Dale Hull & Aarlie Jean. AB Harv 1988; DAS Ya Berk 1995; MDiv Yale DS 1995; JD Ya 1995; MA Ya 1998. D 6/10/2000 Bp Andrew Donnan Smith P 1/12/2001 Bp Wilfrido Ramos-Orench. m 11/9/2009 Elizabeth N Wood c 2. Asstg P All SS Ch Portland OR 2006-2007; Assoc for Adult Faith Formation S Jn's Epis Ch Olympia WA 2004-2006; Vic S Edw's Ch Silverton OR 2002-2004; Cur Trin Ch Branford CT 2000-2001. EPF 2002; Integrity 2005. Grad Fell ECF 1995.

WOODLE JR, Tom Frederick (SC) PO Box 16056, Mytle Beach SC 29587 **The Well by the Sea Ch Myrtle Bch SC 2010-; The Well by the Sea Myrtle Bch SC 2010-; P Assoc The Epis Ch Of The Resurr Surfside Bch SC 2003-** B Bennettsville SC 12/15/1952 s Thomas Jr Frederick Woodle & Gladys Mae. BA S Andr's Presb Coll Laurinburg NC 1976; M.Ed U of So Carolina 1983; PhD Columbia Pacific U 1993; M.A. TESM 2000. D 6/3/2000 P 12/12/2000 Bp Edward Lloyd Salmon Jr. m 9/14/2003 Janet Ballou c 5. Trin Ch Myrtle Bch SC 2000-2001. tomwoodle1@aol.com

WOODLEY, Claire (NY) 2 Glendale Rd, Ossining NY 10562 **R S Mary's Ch Mohegan Lake NY 2001-** B Minneapolis PA 12/16/1955 d Norman Elbert Woodley & Mary Walleena. BA U MN 1979; MDiv UTS 1988. D 6/10/1989 Bp Paul Moore Jr P 12/1/1989 Bp Richard Frank Grein. m 9/10/1983 Michael John Aitchison c 1. Int S Andr's Ch Beacon NY 1999-2001; S Ptr's Epis Ch Peekskill NY 1996-1999; Ch Of S Mary The Vrgn Chappaqua NY 1995-1996; H Innoc Highland Falls NY 1992-1994; Int The Ch Of S Jos Of Arimathea White Plains NY 1992; S Barn Ch Irvington on Hudson NY 1989-1992. Auth, "No No Or So," Pecusa, 1993; Auth, "Stories From The Cir ," Moorhouse/Barlow, 1991; Auth, "Out Of Nairobi: A New Era For Wmn In The Ch"; Auth, "Ordnry Wmn". cwoodley@usa.net

WOODLIEF, Vern Andrews (Az) 1069 N Paseo Iris, Green Valley AZ 85614 **D Epis Ch Of S Fran-In-The-Vlly Green Vlly AZ 2004-** B Gainesville FL 9/10/1936 d Edwin Haymond Andrews & Ellen Collins. BA Lake Erie Coll 1958; Fuller TS 2001; Death & Grief Stds Cert Cntr for Loss and Life Transition 2002; Certification as Sprtl Dir Cntr for Sprtl Direction 2002. D 11/1/1995 Bp Chester Lovelle Talton. c 2. vwdeacon@aol.com

WOODLIFF III, George Franklin (Miss) 712 S Montgomery St, Starkville MS 39759 **R Trin Ch Yazoo City MS 1998-** B Jackson MS 6/16/1948 s George Franklin Woodliff & Ann. BBA U of Mississippi 1970; JD U of Virginia 1973; BTh Oxf 1995. D 8/19/1995 P 3/1/1996 Bp Alfred Clark Marble Jr. m 11/24/1976 Jill M McLaurin c 3. Dio Mississippi Jackson MS 1995-2003; Ch Of The Resurr Starkville MS 1995-1998.

WOODLIFF, Kirk Alan (Nev) 3035 Segre Ct, Sparks NV 89436 **R S Paul's Epis Ch Sparks NV 2008-** B Henryetta OK 12/11/1970 s Duane Alan Woodliff & F(lorence) Eloise. AS Conners St Coll Warner OK 1991; BS SE Oklahoma St U 1994; MDiv Epis TS of The SW 2001. D 6/23/2001 P 1/5/2002 Bp Robert Manning Moody. m 5/20/1995 Tricia Ann Nelson c 3. R Gr Ch Muskogee OK 2003-2008; Cur S Pat's Epis Ch Broken Arrow OK 2001-2002. frkirk@hotmail.com

WOODLIFF-STANLEY, Ruth Morse (Colo) 1945 Ivanhoe St, Denver CO 80220 **Dio Colorado Denver CO 2010-; P-in-c S Thos Epis Ch Denver CO 2007-** B Jackson MS 8/9/1962 d George Franklin Woodliff & Ann Sullivan. BA Swarthmore Coll 1985; MDiv Ya Berk 1991; MS Col 1991. D 6/13/1990 P 6/1/1991 Bp Duncan Montgomery Gray Jr. m 7/4/1987 Nathan David Stanley. Asst S Jas Ch Jackson MS 2000-2002; S Phil's Ch Jackson MS 1991-1995; Asst Trin Ch Branford CT 1990-1991.

WOODLING, Edith Walker (At) 25 Battle Ridge Pl Ne, Atlanta GA 30342 **S Mart's Epis Sch Atlanta GA 2005-** B Chattanooga TN 11/30/1950 d Walter Walker & Mattie. BA Emory U 1972; MA U Pgh 1976; EFM STUSo 1995. D 10/28/1995 Bp Frank Kellogg Allan. m 10/6/2001 James Royall Dillon c 4. S Mart In The Fields Ch Atlanta GA 2003-2005; Chr Ch Norcross GA 1999-2003; D S Anne's Epis Ch Atlanta GA 1995-1999. NAAD. ewoodling@stmartinschool.org

WOODRIDGE, Douglas Earl (SanD) 16017 Oakridge Ct, Lake Oswego OR 97035 B Dansville NY 2/17/1931 s Earl Woodridge & Doris. BBA Loyola U 1955; MDiv SWTS 1968. D 9/7/1968 P 3/8/1969 Bp Francis E I Bloy. m 9/5/1954 Clara B Litchfield c 1. R S Michaels By-The-Sea Ch Carlsbad CA 1979-1996; Asst All SS Ch San Diego CA 1968-1979. FIF; SSC. woodridge9554@comcast.net

WOODROFFE, Eleanor Thurston (Cal) 5421 Germantown Ave, Philadelphia PA 19144 **Assoc S Lk's Ch Philadelphia PA 1994-** B Philadelphia PA 12/7/1919 d George Henry Woodroffe & Eleanor Haupt. BA Smith 1941; S Petersburg Jr Coll 1972; PDS 1974; MDiv Luth TS at Gettysburg 1976. D 4/30/1973 Bp William Loftin Hargrave P 6/29/1981 Bp Lyman Cunningham Ogilby. Cur S Mary's Epis Ch Ardmore PA 1989-1993; Asst Gr Cathd San Francisco CA 1985-1989; Asst Iglesia Epis Del Buen Samaritano San Francisco CA 1985-1986; Cur S Mary's Epis Ch Ardmore PA 1980-1984; Asst S Steph's Ch Philadelphia PA 1979-1980; Asst S Geo S Barn Ch Philadelphia PA 1978-1979; Asst S Geo S Barn Ch Philadelphia PA 1974-1977. Associated Parishes; Tertiary Of The Soc Of S Fran.

WOODROOFE III, Robert William (Ct) 42 Christian Street, New Preston CT 06777 B New York NY 8/19/1941 s Robert William Woodroofe & Lindsay. BA Ya 1963; MDiv EDS 1968; DMin Pittsburgh TS 1990. D 6/24/1968 Bp Hamilton Hyde Kellogg P 12/21/1968 Bp Robert Bracewell Appleyard. m 4/12/1969 Sarah Waterman c 2. R S Gabr's Epis Ch Marion MA 1994-2007; R S Ptr's Epis Ch Butler PA 1981-1994; Old S Lk's Pittsburgh PA 1978-1981; Epis Residences Inc Pittsburgh PA 1977-1981; Dio Pittsburgh Monroeville PA 1976-1981; Asst Min Calv Ch Pittsburgh PA 1968-1976. Sydney Adams Awd Inter-Ch Coun of Grtr New Bedford 2007. robert.woodroofe@gmail.com

WOODRUFF, Karen B (Va) Po Box 367, Lively VA 22507 B Findlay OH 5/4/1943 d Joy V Bishop & Nedra E. BS Witt 1965; MDiv Ya Berk 1989. D 6/11/1994 P 12/14/1994 Bp Peter James Lee. c 2. P-in-c S Ptr's Port Royal Port Royal VA 1994-2003; P-in-c Vauters Ch Champlain VA 1994-2001. WOODRUFFKAREN@HOTMAIL.COM

WOODRUFF, William David (SwVa) 2151 Blue Jay Lane, Blacksburg VA 24060 B Hayes NC 9/27/1930 s William David Woodruff & Elizabeth. BA U NC 1952; MDiv VTS 1955; MA Wake Forest U 1976. D 6/30/1955 Bp Richard Henry Baker P 1/1/1956 Bp Edwin A Penick. m 8/28/1988 Elizabeth Griffin. S Paul's Epis Ch Salem VA 1986-1989; R S Eliz's Ch Roanoke VA 1976-1985; Galloway Memi Chap Elkin NC 1975-1976; R S Andr's Epis Ch Charlotte NC 1963-1974; R The Epis Ch Of Gd Shpd Asheboro NC 1957-1963. bmwhokie@yahoo.com

WOODRUM, Donald Lee (Fla) Po Box 1238, Live Oak FL 32064 **Cn Santa Fe Reg Dio Florida Jacksonville FL 1996-; Dioc Coun Dio Florida Jacksonville FL 1996-; R S Lk's Epis Ch Live Oak FL 1980-** B Sarasota FL 9/1/1949 s Donald Dewitt Woodrum & Dorothy Rachel. BA U of So Florida 1971; MDiv GTS 1975. D 8/15/1975 P 2/24/1976 Bp Emerson Paul Haynes. m 8/26/1972 Melissa Jane Grabe c 4. Dio Florida Jacksonville FL 1997-2001; Dio Florida Jacksonville FL 1984-1987; Cur Chr Ch Bradenton FL 1975-1980. don@stlukesliveoak.org

WOODRUM, Lawrence Paul (Nwk) 651 East 102nd St, Brooklyn NY 11236 B Bradford PA 7/11/1940 s Robert Andrew Woodrum & Jean Elizabeth. BA Ohio Wesl 1962; STB GTS 1965. D 6/12/1965 P 6/11/1966 Bp William Crittenden. m 11/6/2011 Victor A Philipse-Challenor. Int S Marg's Ch Plainview NY 2009-2011; Asst Ch Of S Alb The Mtyr S Albans NY 1993-2005; Assoc

W

Ch Of The Intsn New York NY 1981-1983; Vic Ch Of Our Sav Secaucus NJ 1976-1980; Vic Gr Epis Ch Rutherford NJ 1976-1979; Vic S Gabr's Ch Oak Ridge NJ 1969-1976; Vic Ch Of Our Fr Foxburg PA 1966-1969; Asst S Jn's Ch Franklin PA 1965-1966. ECVA 2000; Integrity, Inc. 1975. challwood@optonline.net

WOODS, Harold Dean (Vt) 233 South Street, South Hero VT 05486 B Henryetta OK 8/10/1939 s Elmer W Woods & Edith May. BA NWU 1961; BD Drew U 1965; MEd U of Vermont 1971. D 6/11/1966 P 10/13/1966 Bp Leland Stark. m 7/12/1986 Stephanie A Cordner c 4. R All SS' Epis Ch S Burlington VT 1990-2000; Assoc Gr Ch Madison NJ 1966-1969. halwoods99@gmail.com

WOODS, James Christopher (Mass) 121 Freeport Boulevard, Toms River NJ 08757 B Murrysville PA 8/22/1939 s Stewart Hugh Ingles & Dorothy. BA U Roch 1960; STB EDS 1964; Syr 1972. D 6/16/1964 P 12/1/1964 Bp George West Barrett. m 6/2/1962 Nancy Ryan c 4. All SS Epis Ch Attleboro MA 2000-2001; R Trin Par Melrose MA 1982-1999; S Jn's Ch Clifton Sprg NY 1964-1967. kayakrguy@yahoo.com

WOODS, James Edward (Oly) 22226 6th Ave S Apt 201, Des Moines WA 98198 **Dioc Coun Dio Massachusetts Boston MA 1986-** B Seattle WA 7/21/1920 s Harvey Edgar Woods & Ruth Frances. Olympia TS. D 6/27/1990 Bp Vincent Waydell Warner. m 8/25/1962 Ann Woods. D Dio Olympia Seattle WA 1990-1992; D S Lk's Epis Ch Seattle WA 1990-1992; R Trin Par Melrose MA 1982-1999; R All SS' Epis Ch Belmont MA 1978-1982; Asst Prof Dio Rochester Rochester NY 1972-1976; Asst Chr Epis Ch Hornell NY 1967-1969; P-in-c Dio New York New York City NY 1967-1969.

WOODS JR, JC (Mass) 62 Las Casas St, Malden MA 02148 **Trin Epis Ch Weymouth MA 2009-** B Memphis TN 1/15/1954 s J C Woods & Elnora. BA Gri 1975; MDiv EDS 1979. D 6/17/1979 P 5/18/1980 Bp William Evan Sanders. m 1/6/1983 Elise Woods. S Jas Ch Preston CT 2008-2009; The Ch Of The H Name Swampscott MA 2005-2006; S Paul's Ch Malden MA 2001-2004; Int All SS Epis Ch Attleboro MA 2000-2001; Int Epiph Par Walpole MA 1998-1999; Int The Ch Of The Gd Shpd Acton MA 1996-1998; Int Par Of S Paul Newton Highlands MA 1995-1996; Int S Jn The Evang Taunton MA 1993-1994; Assoc S Jn's S Jas Epis Ch Roxbury MA 1992-1993; S Aug And S Mart Ch Boston MA 1988-1992; Assoc S Aug And S Mart Ch Boston MA 1983-1987; S Paul's Epis Ch Chattanooga TN 1979-1980. silvannus@verizon.net

WOODS, John Michael (Dal) Rr 1 Box 253-A, Mount Vernon TX 75457 B Atlanta TX 7/25/1942 s John Wesley Woods & Helen. MA U of Arkansas 1973; MDiv Nash 1975. D 6/16/1975 P 12/1/1975 Bp A Donald Davies. m 12/19/1970 Dianna M McKinley. S Paul's Epis Ch Greenville TX 2001-2002; Par Asst Ch Of The Epiph Richardson TX 2000-2002; S Wm Laud Epis Ch Pittsburg TX 1989-1996; Dept Of Missions Dallas TX 1984-1989; All SS Ch Atlanta TX 1979-1983; S Mart Epis Ch New Boston TX 1979-1983; Cur S Jas Epis Ch Texarkana TX 1977-1978; Cur S Jn's Epis Ch Corsicana TX 1975-1977. RWF. mikendee@peoplescom.net

WOODS, Joshua Blake (Okla) 5635 E 71st St, Tulsa OK 74136 **P S Dunst's Ch Tulsa OK 2011-** B Muskogee OK 8/12/1984 s James Aaron Woods & Cheryl Diane. BA U of Oklahoma 2007; MDiv VTS 2011. D 1/22/2011 P 7/30/2011 Bp Edward Joseph Konieczny. m 1/7/2008 Laura Beth Stafford c 1. JOSHUA.BLAKE.WOODS@GMAIL.COM

WOODS SSP, Robert D (EpisSanJ) Po Box 1837, Kernville CA 93238 **Vic St Sherrian Epis Ch Kernville CA 2008-** B Wimbledon Surrey UK 7/31/1946 s Eric Robert Woods & Dorothy Elizabeth. BA U of San Diego 1968; JD U of San Diego 1973; ETSBH 1986; Cert Geo 1988. D 6/14/1986 Bp Charles Brinkley Morton P 5/11/1988 Bp Victor Manuel Rivera. m 5/23/1975 Alexis Jean Perry. Vic S Ptr's Epis Ch Kernville CA 1998-2008; Asst S Lk's Ch Bakersfield CA 1988-2000; Supply Epis Dio San Joaquin Modesto CA 1986-1988. Auth, "Obligation to Provide Abortion Serv: What Happens When Physicians Refuse," *Journ of Med Ethics*, Royal Med Soc, 1996. Soc of S Paul, Assoc 1981. Fell Kegley Inst of Ethics California St U - Bakersfield CA 1990; Assoc Kennedy Sch of Ethics Geo 1980. bobsacerdo@aol.com

WOODS, Stephen I (NY) Po Box 1221, Kingston NY 12402 B Nevada MO 2/22/1944 s Hammond C Woods & Virginia Elizabeth. BA Armstrong Atlantic St Coll 1970; MSW Brandeis U 1974; PhD Brandeis U 1978; MA Nash 1987. D 6/6/1987 P 12/1/1987 Bp Edward Cole Chalfant. m 11/1/2000 Roberta Ervine c 2. S Jn's Epis Ch Kingston NY 2003-2004; Chr Ch Manhasset NY 2002-2003; Int Chr Ch Babylon NY 2001-2002; Dir Of Pilgrimage Mnstrs And Cler Wellness Dio Florida Jacksonville FL 1995-2000; Fresh Mnstrs Jacksonville FL 1995-1999; R S Jn's Epis Ch Gloucester MA 1991-1995; Assoc R S Barn Ch Falmouth MA 1988-1991; R S Giles Ch Jefferson ME 1987-1988. stephenwds@gmail.com

WOODS, Thomas Craighead (Tex) 306 College Ave, Henderson TX 75654 B Houston TX 12/25/1928 s David Flavel Woods & Marie Shields. BBA U of Houston 1953; MDiv VTS 1969. D 7/1/1969 Bp J Milton Richardson P 6/1/1970 Bp Scott Field Bailey. m 11/3/2000 Roberta Ervine c 4. S Jn's Epis Ch Kingston NY 2000-2003; R S Matt's Ch Henderson TX 1992; Vic S Matt's Ch Henderson TX 1978-1992; Trin Ch Houston TX 1973-1977; Min in charge S Mk's Epis Ch Cleveland TX 1970-1973. ibwoods@worldnet.att.net

WOODSON JR, James Pettigrew (Ala) 313 Riverdale Dr # 35406-, Tuscaloosa AL 35406 B Birmingham AL 10/22/1923 s James Pettigrew Woodson & Anna Huger. BD Auburn U 1948; MDiv VTS 1953. D 6/20/1953 P 9/18/1953 Bp Charles C J Carpenter. m 9/8/1951 Abbie Wendel c 3. R H Trin Epis Ch Auburn AL 1957-1973; Vic S Mary's Epis Ch Andalusia AL 1955-1957; Vic S Steph's Ch Brewton AL 1955-1957; R S Mich's Ch Faunsdale AL 1953-1955.

WOODSUM, Mark (Me) PO Box 1576, Fallbrook CA 92088 B Portland, ME 7/15/1958 s Kenneth Woodsum York & Martha Elizabeth. BA Bow 1980; MA Dartmoth Coll 1997; MDiv Bangor TS 2010. D 6/19/2010 Bp Stephen Taylor Lane P 12/18/2010 Bp James Robert Mathes. m 1/3/1987 Claire Haffey c 4. S Jn's Ch Fallbrook CA 2010-2011. markwoodsum@roadrunner.com

WOODWARD JR, Brinton Webb (NH) RR3 Box 18, Plymouth NH 03264 B Topeka KS 1/16/1940 s Brinton Webb Woodward & Agnes. BA U of Kansas 1962; MDiv GTS 1965. D 6/9/1965 P 12/21/1965 Bp Edward Clark Turner. m 7/5/1985 Kathleen Crothers c 1. The Holderness Sch Plymouth NH 1977-2001; Kent Sch Kent CT 1967-1977; Cur S Dav's Epis Ch Topeka KS 1965-1967. bwwjr@worldpath.net

WOODWARD, Deborah Marshall (Mass) 1080 Hillside St, Milton MA 02186 B Glen Ridge NJ 10/3/1944 d John Hart Marshall & Constance Edmonds. BA Br 1966; MDiv Gordon-Conwell TS 1987. D 6/13/1987 Bp David Elliot Johnson P 4/1/1988 Bp George E Rath. m 12/27/1965 James Woodward c 3. P-in-c Ch Of The Gd Shpd Reading MA 2007-2010; EDS Cambridge MA 2002-2003; EDS Cambridge MA 2001-2002; Trin Ch Randolph MA 1999-2007; EDS Cambridge MA 1993-1995; Chr Ch Somerville MA 1988-1995. Phillips Brooks Cleric Club of Boston. Phi Alpha Chi Gordon-Conwell TS 1987. dmwoodward@mvfintry.com

WOODWARD III, George Frederick (Los) 1294 Westlyn Pl, Pasadena CA 91104 **R S Edm's Par San Marino CA 1995-** B Greensburg PA 6/24/1955 s George Frederick Woodward & Louise Adele. BA Ohio U 1978; MA Ashland TS 1981; MDiv SWTS 1983. D 6/25/1983 Bp John Harris Burt P 1/21/1984 Bp Robert C Rusack. Dn Estrn Deanry Dio Los Angeles Los Angeles CA 1993-1995; R S Tim's Epis Ch Apple Vlly CA 1991-1995; Assoc All SS-By-The-Sea Par Santa Barbara CA 1983-1988. Co-Auth, "Introducing the Lessons of the Ch Year," 2009. Fndt Cristosal, El Salvador 2005; Global Epis Mssn Ntwk 2008-2011; Hillsides Hm for Chld; Bd Dir 1997-2008. gfwtres@aol.com

WOODWARD, Lynn Christophersen (Okla) P.O. Box 23, Shattuck OK 73858 B Lincoln NE 6/29/1948 d Donald Neil Bykerk & Sonja. AA Seminole Jr Coll 1983; STUSo 1990; Oklahoma Diac Trng Sch 1991. D 6/29/1991 Bp Robert Manning Moody. m 12/13/2001 E Davis Woodward c 2. D S Jas Epis Ch Oklahoma City OK 2006-2009; D S Mich's Epis Ch Norman OK 1991-2006. "Living Bibles," *Preaching as Prophetic Calling: Sermons That Wk XII*, Morehouse Pub, 2004. marmeelynn@gmail.com

WOODWARD, Matthew Thomas (Cal) 3900 Alameda De Las Pulgas, San Mateo CA 94403 **Trsfg Epis Ch San Mateo CA 2011-** B London UK 4/9/1975 s Eric Charles Woodward & Jean Claire. BA London TS 1998; MA Kings Coll of London 1999; MA Westcott Hse 2001. Trans from Church Of England 4/19/2011 Bp Marc Handley Andrus. rector@trnsfig-sm.org

WOODWARD, Thomas Bullene (RG) 13 Calle Loma, Santa Fe NM 87507 B Topeka KS 12/24/1937 s Brinton Webb Woodward & Agnes Bessie. BA, cl Harv 1960; Ecumencial Inst 1962; STB GTS 1963; U of Kansas 1967. D 6/23/1963 P 12/21/1963 Bp Edward Clark Turner. m 5/22/1988 Marianne H Cunningham c 5. Com on the Status of Wmn Exec Coun Appointees New York NY 2006-2009; T/F on Comm Dio The Rio Grande Albuquerque NM 2006-2007; Dioc. Corp Dio El Camino Real Monterey CA 1991-1995; R S Paul's Epis Ch Salinas CA 1988-2005; Chapl S Fran Hse U Epis Ctr Madison WI 1977-1988; Chapl Chap Of The Cross Chap Hill NC 1974-1977; Natl Advsry Com Higher Ed Exec Coun Appointees New York NY 1974-1977; Prot Chapl U Roch Med Cntr - Strong Meml Hosp Rochester NY 1971-1974; R Chr Ch Warrensburg MO 1968-1971; Chapl Cbury At Kansas U Lawr KS 1963-1968. Librettist, "And the Winner Is . .," Var, 2010; Playwright, "Var Plays," Var, 2008; Auth, "The Undermining of the Epis Ch," The Epis Majority, 2007; Auth, "The Parables of Jesus from the Inside," *Sewanee Theol Revs*, TS, Sewanee, 2003; Co-Auth, "Liturg Pryr," Pueblo Press, 1977; Auth, "Turning Things Upside Down: A Theol Workbook," Seabury Press, 1975; Auth, "To Celebrate," Seabury Press, 1971. Pres ESMHE 1975-1976. Ben Heller Awd for Courage and Ldrshp w the Farmworker Cntr for Cmnty Advocacy 2004; The Bp's Cross Dio El Camino Real 2004. tbwsalinas@aol.com

WOODWORTH, Laura T(ufts) (NMich) 2500 South Hill Road, Gladstone MI 49837 **P S Steph's Ch Escanaba MI 1997-** B Worcester MA 10/2/1946 d Donald Irving Tufts & Joanne Elizabeth. BS NWU 1968; MS Illinois Inst of Tech 1976; BS U IL 1982; Michigan TS 1997. D 11/6/1996 P 5/18/1997 Bp Thomas Kreider Ray. m 6/14/1968 David Arthur Woodworth c 2. lauraw@chartermi.net

W

WOODY, Robert James (WTex) 13638 Liberty Oak, San Antonio TX 78232 **Co-Chair Recon Cmsn Dio W Texas San Antonio TX 2008-; Coordntr Cler Lenten Retreat Dio W Texas San Antonio TX 2005-; Exam Chapl Dio W Texas San Antonio TX 2004-; R Ch Of Recon San Antonio TX 2002-** B Midland TX 1/16/1953 s Alvin Howard Woody & Joanna. BA Baylor U 1975; JD Baylor U 1978; MDiv Epis TS of The SW 1999. D 6/19/1999 Bp Claude Edward Payne P 6/19/2000 Bp Leopoldo Jesus Alard. m 10/17/1987 Julie P Plantes c 2. Asst to R Ch Of The Gd Shpd Tomball TX 1999-2002. rwoody@churchofreconciliation.org

WOOLARD, Lynn Phillip (CFla) PO Box 541025, Merritt Island FL 32954 B Meeker CO 3/23/1942 s Harold Ira Woolard & L Doris Hinkson. BA U of Arkansas 1965; MA Embry-Riddle Aeronaut U 1985; Graduated Inst of Chr Stds 2010. D 12/11/2010 Bp John Wadsworth Howe. m 8/16/1964 Pamela June Phifer c 2. lwoolard@cfl.rr.com

WOOLEY, Sandra Carroll Long (Tenn) 1417 N Mack Smith Rd Apt 200, Chattanooga TN 37412 **Died 10/8/2010** B Maryville TN 4/24/1944 d James Leonard Long & Rubye Eleanor. BA Wesleyan Coll 1975; MS Augusta St U 1978; MDiv STUSo 1983. D 6/25/1983 P 5/2/1984 Bp William Gillette Weinhauer. c 4. mamawooley@highstream.net

WOOLIVER, Tammy S (Md) 264 Woodbriar, Noble OK 73068 **Vic S Dav's Ch Oklahoma City OK 2011-; Vic S Dav's Ch Oklahoma City OK 2011-** B Oklahoma City OK 3/1/1959 d Paul Lloyd Lewis & Frances Lee. BA Phillips U 1996; MDiv VTS 2001. D 6/23/2001 P 1/6/2002 Bp Robert Manning Moody. c 1. R Chr Ch Delaware City DE 2010-2011; Chapl Dio Maryland Baltimore MD 2002-2007; Asst R S Dav's Par Washington DC 2001-2002; Chapl Washington Epis Sch Beth MD 2001-2002. tammywooliver@gmail.com

WOOLLEN, Nancy Sewell (Ind) No address on file. B 11/26/1927 D.

WOOLLETT JR, Donald Mathew (WLa) 2023 Marye St, Alexandria LA 71301 B San Antonio TX 1/14/1952 s Donald M Woollett & Patricia. Mechanized Agriculture Texas A & M U 1974; MDiv Notre Dame Sem 1982. Rec from Roman Catholic 3/5/2011 Bp D(avid) Bruce Mac Pherson. m 11/23/2002 Harriet Walker c 2. dmataruski@aol.com

WOOLLEY JR, Arthur Everett (Md) 13 Basswood Ct, Catonsville MD 21228 B Bronxville,NY 7/27/1931 s Arthur Everett Woolley & Hazel Adel. BA CUNY 1953; Nash 1954; MDiv PDS 1957; GTS 1960; Nash 1960; MLS Drexel U 1963. D 4/27/1957 Bp James P De Wolfe P 11/23/1957 Bp Jonathan Goodhue Sherman. Int Mt Calv Ch Baltimore MD 2000-2001; R S Lk's Par Bladensburg MD 1986-1996; Yth Co Coordntr Dio Quincy Peoria IL 1983-1986; St Christophers Ch Princeton IL 1981-1986; Yth Advsr Dio Quincy Peoria IL 1979-1981; S Simeon's By The Sea No Wildwood NJ 1969-1981. *Var Bk Revs & arts*, 2003. CBS Life Mem 1950; Forw in Faith No Amer 1989; GAS Life Mem 1990. awooll@aol.com

WOOLLEY JR, Stanley Marsh (WMass) 590 W 9th St, Winner SD 57580 **P-in-c Ch Of The H Sprt Winner SD 2009-; R Trin Epis Ch Winner SD 2009-** B Fulton NY 10/12/1937 s Stanley Marsh Woolley & Irene. BA MI SU 1960; MDiv PDS 1963. D 4/27/1963 P 11/2/1963 Bp Alfred L Banyard. m 11/19/2000 Patricia E Godfroy c 3. Int Ch of the H Sprt Wagner SD 2010; Int S Lk's Ch Catskill NY 1997; Int The Epis Ch Of S Andr And S Phil Coventry RI 1996-1997; Int S Lk's Ch Mechanicville NY 1994-1996; Int S Bon Ch Guilderland NY 1993-1994; Vic S Helena's Epis Ch Lenox MA 1975-1993; Dio Wstrn Massachusetts Springfield MA 1975-1992; Vic S Andr's Ch Turners Falls MA 1968-1975; Assoc S Jas' Ch Greenfield MA 1968-1975; Asst S Mich's-On-The-Heights Worcester MA 1967-1968; Vic S Jas Memi Ch Eatontown NJ 1963-1967. stanwoolley@me.com

WOOLLEY, Steven Eugene (Spok) 1803 Crestline Dr, Walla Walla WA 99362 B Amarillo TX 2/24/1943 s Eugene Woolley & Frances. BA U MN 1965; MDiv GTS 1996. D 6/8/1996 Bp Clarence Nicholas Coleridge P 1/5/1997 Bp Andrew Donnan Smith. m 4/26/1985 Dianna Stevens. R S Paul's Ch Walla Walla WA 2000-2008; Assoc Ch Of The Heav Rest New York NY 1996-2000. sewoolley@mac.com

WOOLSEY, Deborah J (Mil) St Alban's Episcopal Church, W239N6440 Maple Ave, Sussex WI 53089 **R S Alb's Ch Sussex WI 2007-** B Stevens Point, WI 3/10/1973 d Roy William Woolsey & Karen Jean. BA Northland Coll 1995; MDiv Nash 2007. D 12/16/2006 P 6/30/2007 Bp Russell Edward Jacobus. revdeb@stalbans-sussex.org

WOOLVERTON, John Frederick (Me) Po Box 230, Center Sandwich NH 03227 B New York NY 7/14/1926 s William Henderson Woolverton & Frances. AB Harv 1950; MDiv VTS 1953; PhD UTS 1963. D 6/1/1953 Bp Robert Fisher Gibson Jr P 5/17/1954 Bp John E Hines. m 7/1/1950 Margaret Richardson c 4. R Trin Epis Ch Portland ME 1983-1989; Prof VTS Alexandria VA 1958-1983; P H Trin Epis Ch Austin TX 1953-1956. Auth, "Robert H. Gardiner and the Reunification of Worldwide Chrnty in the Progressive Era," U of Missouri Press, 2005; "Hope Dismantled?," *ATR*, 2000; "The Sceptical Vestryman: Geo Whitney Mart," Colophon Press, 1997; Auth, "The Educ of Phillips Brooks," U IL Press, 1997; "Hans W. Frei in Context: A Theol and Hist Memoir," *ATR*, 1997; Auth, "Colonial Anglicanism in No Amer," Wayne Press, 1985; "Whither Episcopalianism?: A Century of Apologetic Interpretations of the Epis Ch," *ATR*, 1973; "Huntington's Quadrilateral -- A Critical Study," *Ch Hist*, 1970. Boston Athenaeum 1992; HSEC 1963; OAH 1963. Hon DD VTS Alexandria VA 1984. johnwoolvertou@aol.com

WOOTEN JR, William Russell (WA) 40 Black Hickory Way, Ormond Beach FL 32174 **Ret Assoc S Jas Epis Ch Ormond Bch FL 1999-** B Richmond VA 5/12/1933 s William Russell Wooten & Dorothy Louise. BA U Rich 1954; MDiv VTS 1957; DMin VTS 1987. D 6/7/1957 P 6/8/1958 Bp Frederick D Goodwin. m 6/20/1964 Sara L Mellon c 2. Ret Assoc S Thos Flagler Cnty Palm Coast FL 1996-1999; Personl Com Dio Washington Washington DC 1984-1986; Stndg Com Dio Washington Washington DC 1981-1986; Fin Com Dio Washington Washington DC 1980-1984; R Gr Epis Ch Silver Sprg MD 1974-1996; Sem Supvsr VTS Alexandria VA 1963-1995; Asst Gr Epis Ch Silver Sprg MD 1963-1966; Asst S Andr's Ch Richmond VA 1957-1963. Auth, *The Supervision of Lay Pstr Ministers*, Steph Ministers, 1986. billwoot33@gmail.com

WOOTTEN, Jo Ann H (Ark) 346 Rock Springs Rd., Wake Forest NC 27587 B Wilmington NC 3/25/1941 d Richard Charlie Hardison & Bessie. BA Duke 1963; MLS U NC 1966; MBA E Carolina U 1976; PhD U NC 1980; Dio E Carolina Diac Sch 1990. D 6/22/1991 Bp Brice Sidney Sanders. m 6/26/1997 Middleton Lane Wootten. D S Paul's Epis Ch Batesville AR 1998-2008; D S Jos Of Arimathaea Ch Hendersonville TN 1997-1998; D S Paul's Epis Ch Greenville NC 1992-1997; D Emm Ch Farmville NC 1991-1992. Fell Med Libr Assn 1997. jomidwoo@cei.net

WOOTTEN III, Middleton Lane (Ark) 346 N Rock Springs Rd, Wake Forest NC 27587 B Hot Sprgs AR 6/25/1943 s Middleton Lane Wootten & Emily Frances. BA U of Mississippi 1966; MDiv VTS 1969. D 6/26/1969 P 5/1/1970 Bp John M Allin. m 6/26/1997 Jo Ann H Hardison c 3. R S Paul's Epis Ch Batesville AR 1998-2008; R S Jos Of Arimathaea Ch Hendersonville TN 1992-1998; Assoc R S Paul's Epis Ch Greenville NC 1984-1992; R S Paul's Epis Ch Clinton NC 1981-1982; R S Thos' Ch Windsor NC 1974-1981; Asst S Jn's Epis Ch Fayetteville NC 1971-1974; Vic H Trin Ch Crystal Sprg MS 1969-1971; Vic S Steph's Ch Hazlehurst MS 1969-1971. jomidwoo2@gmaiil.com

WOOTTON, Roger William (Mass) 24 Otis St, Malden MA 02148 B Cleveland OH 10/19/1925 s George Stanley Wootton & Bertha Matilda. BS OH SU 1949; MDiv EDS 1952. D 6/29/1952 P 12/29/1952 Bp Henry W Hobson. m 6/28/1986 Jane E Passant c 4. Asst Chr Ch So Hamilton MA 1998-2004; Asst The Ch Of The Adv Boston MA 1994-1997; Int All SS Ch W Newbury MA 1992-1993; Dioc Counc Dio Massachusetts Boston MA 1985-1988; Asst S Paul's Ch Malden MA 1982-1991; Dio Massachusetts Boston MA 1976-1985; Correspondent GC Dio Massachusetts Boston MA 1969-1970; Secy Epis Nomin Com Dio Massachusetts Boston MA 1965-1975; Chair Com Alco Dio Massachusetts Boston MA 1965-1967; R The Ch Of The Gd Shpd Acton MA 1960-1982; R S Jn's Epis Ch Cambridge OH 1952-1960. Compiler / Ed, *Fifty Years of Chr Mnstry: 50th Year Report*, Class of 1952, ETS, 2002; Contrib, *Chr Healing Today*. Massachusetts Cler Assn 1960. zorbaw@verizon.net

WORKMAN, James K. (USC) 1200 Powdersville Rd., Easley SC 29642 B Little Rock AR 8/26/1948 s Charles Douglas Workman & Hazel Gweniveve. Columbia Bible Coll 1968; BA Cov Coll Lookout Mtn GA 1970; MDiv Reformed TS 1974; Cert Steph Mnstry 1991; DAS VTS 1993. D 6/18/1993 Bp John Wadsworth Howe P 12/1/1993 Bp A(rthur) Heath Light. c 3. R S Mich's Epis Ch Easley SC 2004-2010; Assoc All SS Of The Desert Epis Ch Sun City AZ 1999-2004; R Gr Ch Radford VA 1996-1999; R S Mk's Ch Fincastle VA 1993-1996. lucky14661@gmail.com

WORLEY, James Paul (WTex) 389 Valley View Dr, Cibolo TX 78108 B Houston TX 3/19/1947 s Carlos Byrl Worley & Viola Virginia. BS Texas A&M U 1969; MA Webster U 1977; MDiv Epis TS of The SW 1981. D 6/23/1981 Bp Stanley Fillmore Hauser P 1/10/1982 Bp Scott Field Bailey. m 2/17/1968 Mary R Meador c 3. R Ch Of The Resurr San Antonio TX 1987-2007; Dio W Texas San Antonio TX 1987; Evang Dept, Chairman Dio W Texas San Antonio TX 1986-1989; R Ch Of The Redeem Eagle Pass TX 1982-1987; Asst R Ch Of The Adv Brownsville TX 1981-1982. "Basic Tools for a Gd Mar: Pre-Marital Counslg," Brazos Vlly Bride/WTAW, 2001. raven44@hughes.net

WORRELL JR, John Durant (Tex) 3514 Grennoch Ln, Houston TX 77025 **Died 7/24/2010** B Eagle Pass TX 5/24/1924 s John Durant Worrell & Dorothy. BA U So 1944; STB Ya Berk 1950. D 6/24/1950 P 1/1/1951 Bp Everett H Jones. c 2. ESMHE, Ch Soc For Col Wk, Soc For Hlth & Human Values. jdworrell4@yahoo.com

WORTH, Elsa (Ct) 8 Glencrest Ave, Dover NH 03820 **P-in-c Gr Epis Ch Trumbull CT 2009-** B Norwood MA 1/12/1961 d Richard Hagberg & Elsie. BA Sarah Lawr Coll 1982; MDiv Andover Newton TS 1996. D 12/20/2006 P 6/25/2007 Bp V Gene Robinson. c 3. Chr And H Trin Ch Westport CT 2007-2009. elsa@gracetrumbull.org

WORTHINGTON, Cynthia Muirhead (RG) 6043 Royal Crk, San Antonio TX 78239 B Saint Louis MO 10/18/1933 d Robert Mowatt Muirhead & Cynthia Ethel. Cert Prchr Lewis Sch Of Mnstry. D 8/5/1987 Bp Richard Mitchell

Trelease Jr P 2/1/1988 Bp William Davidson. D Ch Of The H Sprt Gallup NM 1987-2000.

WORTHINGTON JR, Daniel Owen (Va) P O Box 83, Gloucester VA 23061 **R Ware Epis Ch Gloucester VA 1985-** B University VA 2/22/1947 s Daniel O Worthington & Estelle B. Randolph-Macon Coll 1969; BA Virginia Commonwealth U 1973; MDiv VTS 1976; DMin SWTS 2004. D 5/22/1976 P 5/14/1977 Bp John Alfred Baden. m 6/17/1978 Jane Davenport Rixey c 2. R S Jas Ch Montross VA 1979-1985; R S Ptr's Ch Oak Grove Montross VA 1979-1985; Vic Piedmont Ch Madison VA 1976-1979. *Land Purchasing for New Congregations*, 2004. jrwdow@cox.net

WORTHINGTON, William Ray (Ga) 207 Hermitage Way, Saint Simons Island GA 31522 B Oxford MS 8/21/1941 s John Adams Worthington & Grayson Marye. BA Mississippi St U 1963; MDiv EDS 1966; STM STUSo 1975; Med Virginia Commonwealth U 1982. D 6/24/1966 P 5/1/1967 Bp John M Allin. m 1/28/1966 Ann Haliday Chase c 3. Vic S Richard's Of Chichester Ch Jekyll Island GA 1999-2006; Frederica Acad St Simons Island GA 1992-1997; Trin Epis Day Sch Natchez MS 1988-1992; Asst S Barn On The Desert Scottsdale AZ 1987-1988; All SS Ch Phoenix AZ 1982-1986; Chapl S Chris's Sch Richmond VA 1974-1982; Asst To Dn Chr Ch Cathd Houston TX 1971-1974; Vic S Patricks Epis Ch Long Bch MS 1967-1969; Cur Chr Ch Bay St Louis MS 1966-1967. rawor@bellsouth.net

WORTHLEY, Christopher Thomas (Los) 2114 De La Vina St Unit 1, Santa Barbara CA 93105 B Lowell MA 2/5/1968 D 6/19/2004 P 1/22/2005 Bp Joseph Jon Bruno. christopher.worthley@aya.yale.edu

WOSIKOWSKI, Thomas J (Mil) 4901 Hob St, Madison WI 53716 B Chicago IL 3/17/1930 s Felix Chester Wosikowski & Agnes Barbara. BA Elmhurst Coll 1952; MDiv Nash 1955. Rec from Polish National Catholic Church 12/1/1979 as Priest Bp Charles Thomas Gaskell. c 3. S Chad's Ch Sun Prairie WI 1980-1987; P-in-c S Andr's Epis Ch Monroe WI 1972-1973. OHC 1952.

WRAMPELMEIER, Christopher Kent (NwT) 2602 Parker St, Amarillo TX 79109 B Amman Jordan 1/7/1964 s Brooks Wrampelmeier & Ann. BA Pr 1986; JD U of Texas 1993. D 11/9/2003 Bp C(harles) Wallis Ohl. m 10/7/1995 Hortencia Q Quinonez c 3. D S Andr's Epis Ch Amarillo TX 2003-2006. ckw@uwlaw.com

WRATHALL, Susan L (RI) 70 Moore St., Warwick RI 02889 **R S Mk's Ch Warwick RI 2009-** B Newport RI 10/19/1952 d Robert Wrathall & Carol Ann. BS Rhode Island Coll 1974; MEd Rhode Island Coll 1978; MDiv GTS 2006. D 5/25/2006 Bp David B(ruce) Joslin P 12/16/2006 Bp Geralyn Wolf. c 3. Assoc R S Paul's Ch Pawtucket RI 2006-2009. slwrathall@gmail.com

WRATTEN, Kenneth Bruce (ECR) 8640 Solera Drive, San Jose CA 95135 **R S Steph's In-The-Field Epis Ch San Jose CA 2002-** B Watertown NY 9/9/1946 s Algernon Eston Wratten & Lois Ann. BS Syr 1968; M. Div. CDSP 2003. D 6/22/2002 P 1/4/2003 Bp Richard Lester Shimpfky. m 8/6/1966 Ruth K Kirch c 2. ken@kwratten.com

WREDE, Anne McRae (NJ) 37 Northfield Rd, Millington NJ 07946 **Trin Epis Old Swedes Ch Swedesboro NJ 2009-** B Cincinnati OH 4/24/1952 d John Grauer McRae & Jule Ann. BA Amer U 1974; MDiv VTS 1989. D 3/31/1990 Bp Clarence Nicholas Coleridge P 10/6/1990 Bp Arthur Edward Walmsley. m 5/20/1989 Richard Charles Wrede c 1. Gr Ch Merchantville NJ 2008-2009; Trin Epis Ch Vineland NJ 2006-2008; S Steph's Ch Whiting NJ 2004-2006; S Jas Ch Bradley Bch NJ 2003-2004; Dn Trin Cathd Trenton NJ 2000; All SS Ch Millington NJ 1997-2000; Int S Mk's Ch Mendham NJ 1995-1996; Assoc R All SS Ch Millington NJ 1994-2000; Int S Andr's Ch Harrington Pk NJ 1993-1994; Int S Geo's Epis Ch Maplewood NJ 1992-1993; Int S Mary's Ch Haledon NJ 1990-1991; Asst S Barn' Ch Leeland Upper Marlboro MD 1989-1990. Cnvnt Soc S Jn Bapt 1992; GSA 1959. arkwrede@juno.com

WREDE, Richard Charles (NJ) 500 Fourth St, Riverton NJ 08077 **R Chr Ch Riverton NJ 2005-** B Englewood NJ 7/22/1956 s Howard Wrede & Eloise Elise. BA FD 1978; MS Col 1979; MDiv VTS 1990. D 6/2/1990 P 12/6/1990 Bp John Shelby Spong. m 5/20/1989 Anne McRae c 1. R All SS Epis Ch Lakewood NJ 2000-2005; R All SS Ch Millington NJ 1994-2000; R S Ptr's Ch Newark NJ 1990-1994. Bp'S Cert Of Merit 1998; Outstanding Young Men Of Amer 1978. rwrede@juno.com

WREN, Dane Clark (CFla) 302 Bent Way Ln, 700 Rinehart Rd, Lake Mary FL 32746 B Reading PA 5/20/1947 s Russell R Wren & Ruth R. BS Pennsylvania Mltry Coll 1969. D 12/1/2007 Bp John Wadsworth Howe. m 11/28/1987 Laurie Wren c 3. Angilcans for Life 2002; BroSA 2006. dwren47@aol.com

WRENN, William Charles (O) 17 Sandy Neck Rd, East Sandwich MA 02537 B Milford MA 8/23/1929 s Linwood Richard Wrenn & Ada Marion. BA Tufts U 1952; STM Ya Berk 1955; EDS 1970. D 5/21/1955 P 11/1/1955 Bp William A Lawrence. m 7/4/1991 Barbara Ann Ellis c 3. Vic S Matt's Epis Ch Brecksville OH 1960-1968; R Ch Of The Gd Shpd Fitchburg MA 1955-1960. wcwrenn@aol.com

WRIDER, Annc Johnson (SO) 6000 Drake Rd., Cincinnati OH 45243 **Int R Indn Hill Ch Cincinnati OH 2008-** B Concord MA 2/5/1948 d Franklin R Johnson & Hope Grey. BA Simmons Coll 1971; MSW U of Iowa 1977; MDiv SWTS 1984. D 6/2/1984 Bp Walter Cameron Righter P 4/1/1986 Bp William Bradford Hastings. c 1. Epis Soc Of Chr Ch Cincinnati OH 2000-2008; Cn Pstr and Precentor Epis Soc of Chr Ch Cincinnati OH 2000-2008; Vic S Ambr Ch Chicago Heights IL 1995-2000; Vic Chr The King Ch Lansing IL 1995-1997; Middlesex Area Cluster Mnstry Higganum CT 1994-1995; S Jn's Ch Guilford CT 1989-1991; Asst S Mary's Epis Ch Manchester CT 1986-1989; Asst S Geo/S Mths Ch Chicago IL 1984-1985. Auth, "Looking For The Perfect Ch," Forw Mvmt, 1998; Auth, "WaterFire & Blood Defilement & Purification from a Ricoeurian Perspective," *ATR*, 1985. Polly Bond Awd ECom 1999. revajw@live.com

WRIGHT, Allan McLean (WMass) No address on file. B 8/21/1932 s John William Wright & Catherine Mclean. BS U of Rhode Island 1955; BD EDS 1960. D 6/25/1960 P 2/1/1961 Bp Robert McConnell Hatch. m 6/20/1959 Joan Fay Wuerker. Vic S Mk's Epis Ch E Longmeadow MA 1962-1970; Asst Ch Of The Atone Westfield MA 1960-1962.

WRIGHT, Andrew Ray (Dal) 1700 N. Westmoreland Rd., Desoto TX 75115 **R S Anne's Epis Ch Desoto TX 2009-; Liturg and Mus Com Dio Maryland Baltimore MD 2008-; Supply P Dio Maryland Baltimore MD 2008-** B Borger TX 1/12/1969 s Kenneth Welsh Wright & Marcia Marie. BA TCU 1991; MDiv STUSo 1995; STM GTS 2003. D 6/4/1995 Bp Sam Byron Hulsey P 4/21/1996 Bp Bertram Nelson Herlong. m 6/1/1991 Melanie B Barnett c 3. R S Jas' Epis Ch Fremont NE 1999-2002; Asst to the R S Paul's Epis Ch Murfreesboro TN 1995-1999; Happ Strng Com Dio Tennessee Nashville TN 1995-1998. Angl Colloquium of No Amer Acad of Liturg 2008; ESMHE 1996-2000; The Jn Henry Hobart Soc (at GTS) 2002. arw247@gmail.com

WRIGHT, Benjamin R(ush) (RG) 3709 Sam Snead Place, P.O. Box 883, Clovis NM 88102 B Alpine TX 7/25/1946 s Joel Ellis Wright & Onie Elizabeth May. BBA Texas Pan Amer U 1968; LSU 1969; MDiv TESM 1994; Fuller TS 2000. D 6/29/1994 P 1/6/1995 Bp Bob Gordon Jones. m 5/28/2000 Beryl Pretty c 4. R Ch Of S Jas The Apos Clovis NM 2006-2010; Team Mnstry Ldr S Jn's Ch Ft Sumner NM 2006-2010; Cn Mssnr Vic All SS Epis Ch Pleasanton TX 2001-2006; Cn Mssnr Vic Epis Ch Of The Gd Shepard Geo W TX 2001-2006; Cn Mssnr Vic S Mich's Ch Sandia TX 2001-2006; Cn Mssnr Sthrn Partnr In Mnstry Geo W TX 2001-2006; Vic Chr Ch - Epis Newcastle WY 1996-2001; Vic Ch Of The Gd Shpd Sundance WY 1996-2001; Asst R S Mk's Epis Ch Casper WY 1994-1996. ben_wright1@verizon.net

WRIGHT, Brian Theodore (Oly) 4228 Factoria Blvd SE, Bellevue WA 98006 B Philadelphia PA 12/17/1944 s Theodore William Wright & Ruth Dorothea Klein. BS Auburn U 1966; MS Naval Post Grad Sch 1971. D 10/17/2009 Bp Gregory Harold Rickel. m 3/16/1966 Julene Capps c 1. btwright@verizon.net

WRIGHT, Carl Walter (NCal) Apo Ae 0962, PSC2 Box 9808, Ramstein Germany **Off Of Bsh For ArmdF New York NY 1993-** B Baltimore MD 8/12/1959 s Monaelmer Wright & Eva Lavania. Coppin St Coll 1978; Cert Peabody Inst of Mus (Prep Dept.) 1978; BA Loyola U 1985; MDiv VTS 1990; Brooke Army Med Cntr, San Antonio 2005. D 6/16/1990 P 5/1/1991 Bp A(lbert) Theodore Eastman. S Mk's Epis Ch Charleston SC 1992-1993; Cur Emm Ch Cumberland MD 1990-1992. Auth, "Var arts," *Dioc Dialogue Nwsltr of Dio Utah*, 2008; Auth, "Var arts," *LivCh*, 2008; Auth, "Var arts," *Mssy Nwsltr of Dio Nthrn California*, 2007; Auth, "Var arts," *Linkage*, 1990. OHC; UBE. carl.wright@hill.af.mil

WRIGHT, Catherine Louise (O) St Andrew's Episcopal Church, 300 Third St., Elyria OH 44035 **R S Andr's Epis Ch Elyria OH 2009-** B Phoeniz AZ 12/12/1967 d Karl Augustine Leuba & Diane Lydia. BA Claremont McKenna U 1989; MDiv Perkins TS 2005. D 11/1/2007 Bp Victor Alfonso Scantlebury P 6/4/2008 Bp Jeffrey Dean Lee. m 6/29/1996 James D Wright c 3. Assoc P S Mk's Epis Ch Glen Ellyn IL 2007-2009; Yth Dir Epis Ch Of The Ascen Dallas TX 2005-2007; Dir. Chld's Min The Epis Ch Of The Trsfg Dallas TX 2003-2004. catherine_wright@alumni.cmc.edu

WRIGHT, David Hendren (NC) 1341 Abingdon Way, Winston Salem NC 27106 B North Caldwell NJ 12/5/1922 s Chester Arthur Wright & Grace Elizabeth. D 6/22/1974 P 6/14/1975 Bp Thomas Augustus Fraser Jr. m 10/3/1942 Mary Stager Wright. Vic S Clem's Epis Ch Clemmons NC 1986-1989; Cler Assn Bd Dir Dio No Carolina Raleigh NC 1986-1988; Dioc Sm Ch Cmsn Dio No Carolina Raleigh NC 1985-1989; P-in-c S Matt's Epis Ch Kernersville NC 1979-1986; Assoc R Ch Of The Redeem Morristown NJ 1977-1979; P-in-c Chr Ch Walnut Cove NC 1975-1977; Asst Ch Of The H Comf Burlington NC 1974-1975.

WRIGHT, Elizabeth Louise (RI) 10 Eustis Ave, Newport RI 02840 **D S Columba's Chap Middletown RI 2000-** B New Haven CT 6/26/1937 d Richmond Carter Nyman & Jennie Lynn. BA Colby Coll 1959; MA Col 1960; Rhode Island Sch For Deacons 1989. D 2/4/1989 Bp George Nelson Hunt III. m 8/19/1961 Peter Gwin Patton Wright c 2. D Emm Ch Newport RI 1989-2000. lizzielou@cox.net

WRIGHT, Elton Stanley (Colo) 342 Old Cahaba Trail, Helena AL 35080 **P-in-c Trin Epis Ch Bessemer AL 2011-** B Ogden UT 8/4/1931 s Lawrence Wright & Vera May. Bp's TS Dio Colorado; U CO; BA Metropltn St Coll of Denver 1990. D 11/30/1979 P 6/30/1980 Bp William Carl Frey. m 4/1/1956 Roxene Roi Weichel c 4. R S Matt's Ch Grand Jct CO 1992-2001; R S Mart In

The Fields Aurora CO 1982-1992; Vic S Martha's Epis Ch Westminster CO 1980-1982; D Dio Colorado Denver CO 1979-1980. mp2panda@bellsouth.net

WRIGHT, Gwynne Ann (Chi) 804 Kent Cir, Bartlett IL 60103 **Int R The Epis Ch Of S Jas The Less Northfield IL 2010-** B New York NY 4/22/1949 d George Jerus & Margaret. BA Marymount Coll 1971; MBA St. Johns U 1980; MA Keller Grad Sch of Mgmt 1998; MDiv SWTS 2004; DMin GTF 2010. D 6/19/2004 P 12/18/2004 Bp William Dailey Persell. Int S Paul's Ch Dekalb IL 2008-2010; P-in-c S Jas Ch W Dundee IL 2006-2008; Asst R S Simons Ch Arlington Heights IL 2004-2006. gwynne.wright@sbcglobal.net

WRIGHT, Hollis E (Colo) 92-1010 Kanehoa Loop, Kapolei HI 96707 **S Matt's Ch Grand Jct CO 2009-** B Glendale CA 5/12/1951 d William Pyle Wright & Leone Marianne. BA U of Hawaii 1973; MBA U of Hawaii 1975; MDiv CDSP 1996. D 6/22/1996 Bp George Nelson Hunt III P 1/17/1997 Bp Richard Sui On Chang. m 5/8/1976 Christopher Parsons c 2. S Nich Epis Ch Kapolei HI 2002-2009; R S Jas Epis Ch Kamuela HI 1998-2002; Assoc R Ch Of The H Nativ Honolulu HI 1996-1998. pastorhollis@bresnan.net

WRIGHT, Hugh Maxwell (ECR) 205 Casitas Bulevar, Los Gatos CA 95032 B Middletown OH 2/26/1929 s Hugh Webster Wright & Jeane. BA Alleg 1955; BA Sch for Deacons 1994. D 9/6/1995 Bp Richard Lester Shimpfky. m 2/25/1986 Ann C Clark c 3.

WRIGHT, James Dale (Fla) 3231 Nw 47th Pl, Gainesville FL 32605 **Vic Chr Ch Cedar Key FL 2007-** B Richmond VA 7/15/1955 s James Wesley Wright & Barbara Ann. BS U IL 1977; JD Florida St U 1980; MDiv Bex 1989. D 6/11/1989 P 12/1/1989 Bp Frank Stanley Cerveny. m 12/30/1978 Nancy Ericksen c 3. Asst H Trin Ch Gainesville FL 1989-2007. JIM.WRIGHT123@GMAIL.COM

WRIGHT, James O. Pete (Los) 1505 Monticello Ct, Redlands CA 92373 **Supply P Dio Los Angeles Los Angeles CA 2005-** B Hanford CA 12/18/1942 s James Orland Wright & Caroline Rita. St. Lawr Sem 1960; BA S Anth Coll Hudson NH 1966; Bos 1970; ThM Capuchin TS 1970; MA Maryknoll Ossining NY 1971; Pasadena City Coll 1971. Rec from Roman Catholic 11/4/2005 Bp Sergio Carranza-Gomez. m 10/22/1988 Penelope Irene White c 5. fatherpetewright@yahoo.com

WRIGHT, Janice Bracken (At) 101 East Fourth Avenue, Rome GA 30161 **Dn of NW Georgia Convoc Dio Atlanta Atlanta GA 2010-; Dep to GC Dio Atlanta Atlanta GA 2010-; Assoc R S Ptr's Ch Rome GA 2003-** B Richmond VA 5/17/1957 d Lawrence Wade Bracken & Kathleen Fitzgerald. BA U of Virginia 1978; MDiv Candler TS Emory U 1981. D 7/18/1981 P 6/26/1982 Bp Robert Bruce Hall. m 6/30/1990 Cecil Baker Wright. Exec Bd Dio Atlanta Atlanta GA 2006-2010; Asst R S Ptr's Ch Rome GA 1983-1987; Asst Ch Of The H Comf Richmond VA 1981-1982. Auth, *Wmn of the Word: Comtemporary Sermons by Wmn Cler*. Theta Phi; Phi Beta Kappa. jbwright@bellsouth.net

WRIGHT, Jean Ann Frances (At) 5228 Stone Village Cir Nw, Kennesaw GA 30152 **D S Mk's Ch Palm Bch Gardens FL 1987-** B Flint MI 11/22/1941 d Max Henry Wright & Ernestine Elaine. Dio SE Florida Sch Mnstry FL; Palm Bch Jr Coll. D 11/27/1987 Bp Calvin Onderdonk Schofield Jr. m 3/5/1971 Fredrick Eitel. Auth, "Creative Quiltmaking In The Mandala Tradition"; Auth, "Quilt". jafwright59@bellsouth.net

WRIGHT, Jeannene Fee (DR) Eps G 2517, Box 02-5540, Miami FL 33102 **D Centro Buen Pstr San Pedro de Macoris DO 1984-** B Columbus OH 8/8/1934 d John Elmer Wright & Evelyne Belle. BA OH SU 1956; BS OH SU 1957; MA SWTS 1964; STM GTS 1980. D 6/18/1964 Bp Francis E I Bloy. D S Ptr's Ch McKinney TX 1971-1973; DRE Ch Of The Gd Shpd Ft Defiance AZ 1964-1965. Auth, "Forw Mvmt". GAS; Natl Conf Of Wmn Deacons. ct. sisters@codetel.net.do

WRIGHT, Jo Anne (Okla) 821 N Foreman St Apt 118, Vinita OK 74301 B Wichita KS 5/31/1935 d Everett Joseph Steinheimer & Agnes Josephine. BA Ob 1955; MDiv CDSP 1987. D 6/11/1987 P 12/21/1987 Bp Richard Frank Grein. c 4. R S Jn's Epis Ch Vinita OK 1999-2004; Coun on Missn Ch Dio Oklahoma Oklahoma City OK 1999-2002; Coun Trst Dio Kansas Topeka KS 1997-1999; R S Lk's Ch Wamego KS 1987-1998. Associated Parishes 1987; EWC; Integrity. Who's Who in Amer Marquis Who's Who 2000; Phi Beta Kappa Ob 1955. jowright@junct.com

WRIGHT, John Hamil Spedden (Del) 54 Ridge Ave, Edgewater MD 21037 **R S Steph's Ch Harrington DE 2008-** B Cambridge MD 6/9/1934 s John A Wright & Louise S. MDiv VTS 1974. D 5/18/1974 P 11/1/1974 Bp E(gbert) Don Taylor. m 1/5/2002 Mary Ann Holmes c 4. Dio Delaware Wilmington DE 2000-2003; R The Ch Of The H Sprt Ocean City MD 1985-1987; All Faith Chap Miles River Par Easton MD 1982-1984; P-in-c S Paul's Epis Ch Hebron MD 1980-1982; Chesapeake Rehab Cntr Easton MD 1977-1983; P-in-c S Phil's Ch Laurel DE 1977-1978; R Chr Ch Denton MD 1974-1977. jhswright@yahoo.com

WRIGHT, J(ohn) Robert (NY) General Theological Seminary, 175 9th Ave, New York NY 10011 B Carbondale IL 10/20/1936 s John Wright & Ruth Agnes. BA U So 1958; MA Emory U 1959; MDiv GTS 1963; DPhil Oxf 1967. D 6/11/1963 Bp John P Craine P 6/29/1964 Bp Mervyn Stockwood. The GTS New York NY 1968-2007. Auth, "A Comp to Bede," Eerdmans, 2006; Auth/Ed, "Ancient Chr Commentaries on Scripture," Inter-Varsity Press, 2005; Ed and Auth, "Russo-Gk Papers 1863-1874," Norman Ross Pub, 2001; Auth, "S Thos Ch Fifth Av," Eerdmans, 2001; Ed and Auth, "On Being a Bp," Ch Pub, 1993; Ed & Auth, "They Still Speak: Readings For The Lesser Feasts & Fasts," Ch Pub, 1993; "The Angl Tradition," SPCK, 1991; Ed & Auth, "Readings For The Daily Off From The Early Ch," Ch Pub, 1991; Auth, "PB Sprtlty," Ch Pub, 1989; Ed & Auth, "Quadrilateral at One Hundred," Forw Mvmt, 1988; Auth, "Called to Full Unity," US Cath Conf, 1986; Ed & Co-Auth, "Lift High the Cross," Forw Mvmt, 1984; Auth, "Ch Engl Crown 1305-1334," Pacific Inst. Medieval Stds (Toronto), 1980; Ed & Co-Auth, "A Comm of Communions," Seabury, 1979. Amer Cath Hist Soc Hist Soc Of The 1989-1991; Angl Theol Conf, Conf Of Angl Ch; Pres Angl Soc 1994. Festschrift, One Lord, One Faith, One Baptism Eerdmans 2006; Hon ThD U of Bern, Switzerland 2000; Hon D. Cu. L., Cn Law STUSo 1996; Patriarchal Cross Of The Ecum Patriarch Of Constantinople 1994; Patriarchal Cross Of The Ecum Patriarch Of Moscow And All Russi 1993; Patriarchal Cross Of The Armenian Patriarch Of Jerusalem 1992; Hon DD Trin Luth Sem 1991; Patriarchal Cross Of The Syrian Patriarch Of Antioch 1990; Hon DD Epis TS of the SW 1983. wright@gts.edu

WRIGHT, Jonathan Michael Andrew (SC) 1295 Abercorn Trce, Mount Pleasant SC 29466 **R Gr Ch Charleston SC 2006-** B Canada 12/4/1960 s Robert Wright & Dorothy. BA Queens U 1981; MDiv Trin U of Toronto 1984. Trans from Anglican Church of Canada 7/27/2006 Bp Edward Lloyd Salmon Jr. m 6/25/1988 Margriet Wright c 2. mwright@gracesc.org

WRIGHT, Lonell (La) 7696 Stevenson Way, San Diego CA 92120 **Dio Louisiana Baton Rouge LA 2009-** B Bernice LA 9/12/1939 s Douglas Wright & LaRue C. BS Sthrn U Baton Rouge LA 1961; MPA U CA Riverside 1976; MDiv Nash 2007. D 5/31/2008 P 1/31/2009 Bp Charles Edward Jenkins III. m 4/26/1964 Dessie B Blount c 4. lonell@cox.net

WRIGHT, Lynn Cochran (Wyo) 93 Whitlock Square SW, Marietta GA 30064 **Asst Ch Of The Atone Sandy Sprg GA 2010-** B Athens GA 1/11/1939 s David Cady Wright & Mildred Cochran. BA Birmingham-Sthrn Coll 1962; MDiv VTS 1982. D 6/26/1982 Bp Clarence Edward Hobgood P 3/1/1983 Bp C(laude) Charles Vache. c 2. Asst S Jn's Epis Ch Jackson WY 1990-2000; Vic S Helen's Epis Ch Laramie WY 1985-1990; R S Thos Ch Dubois WY 1985-1990; Asst S Andr's Epis Ch Newport News VA 1982-1985. Auth, "Textbook - Mus Improvisation," *Elements of Informal Mus*, Canyon Press, Cincinatti, OH, 1975. lynncwright70@gmail.com

WRIGHT, Mark R (Dal) 2019 Highland Forest Dr, Highland Village TX 75077 **S Nich Ch Flower Mound TX 1995-** B Fort Eustis VA 4/1/1959 s Richard Edwin Wright & Barbara. BA Duquesne U 1981; MDiv TESM 1984. D 9/20/1984 P 3/1/1985 Bp Alden Moinet Hathaway. m 8/21/1982 Laurel C Crompton c 2. S Dav's Epis Ch Venetia PA 1995-2008; R S Paul's Epis Ch Shreveport LA 1991-1995; R Trin Epis Ch Jasper TX 1989-1991; Asst Ch Of The Ascen Houston TX 1986-1989; Assoc S Mk's Epis Ch Riverside RI 1985-1986; D/P-In-C Ch Of The Trsfg Clairton PA 1984-1985. revmarkwright@verizon.net

WRIGHT III, Martin Luther (Pgh) Rr 8 Box 1240, Latrobe PA 15650 B Leavenworth KS 10/6/1959 s Martin Luther Wright & Mary Elizabeth. BS U of Kansas 1983; MDiv TESM 2002. D 6/15/2002 P 1/8/2003 Bp Robert William Duncan. m 7/11/1987 Dawn Holbrook c 4. S Fran In The Fields Somerset PA 2004-2006; Asst S Michaels Of The Vlly Epis Ch Ligonier PA 2002-2004. REVMWRIGHT3@GMAIL.COM

WRIGHT, Melanie B (FtW) 12700 Hall Shop Rd, Highland MD 20777 **S Alb's Epis Ch Arlington TX 2010-** B Dayton TX 2/6/1969 d Gordan Barnett & Andrea. BS TCU Ft Worth TX 1991; MDiv GTS 2006. D 6/1/2006 Bp Joe Goodwin Burnett P 12/15/2006 Bp Robert Wilkes Ihloff. m 6/1/1991 Andrew Ray Wright c 3. Cur S Mk's Ch Highland MD 2006-2009. melaniebwright@gmail.com

WRIGHT, Milton King (Minn) 707 Saint Olaf Ave, Northfield MN 55057 B Hampton VA 12/27/1936 s Ray Herbert Wright & Elsie Ray. BA W&M 1959; Ya 1962; BD STUSo 1964; MBA U NC 1978. D 6/19/1964 Bp George P Gunn P 6/1/1965 Bp John B Bentley. m 8/6/1994 Bonnie Susanne Sherman c 2. R S Jn's And S Mk's Grifton NC 1972-1974; Vic All SS Epis Ch Norton VA 1971-1972; Vic Chr Epis Ch Big Stone Gap VA 1971-1972; S Jas Ch Boydton VA 1965-1971; Cur Chr and S Lk's Epis Ch Norfolk VA 1964-1965. Auth, "An Index Of Hymns Of The Proposed Calendar".

WRIGHT, Priscilla Jean (SO) 495 Albion Ave, Glendale OH 45246 B 8/8/1934

WRIGHT, Rick Lynn (At) 707 Woodson St SE, Atlanta GA 30315 B Oneonta AL 1/5/1964 s Eldon Wright & Ida Mae Bailey. BS Lee U 1987; MA Ch of God TS 1991; MLS U of Alabama 1994. D 8/6/2011 Bp J(ohn) Neil Alexander. rickwright13@yahoo.com

WRIGHT, Robert Christopher (At) 306 Peyton Rd Sw, Atlanta GA 30311 **R S Paul's Epis Ch Atlanta GA 2002-** B Pittsburgh PA 2/3/1964 s Earl Chester Wright & Charlene C. BA How 1992; MDiv VTS 1998. D 6/13/1998 Bp Ronald Hayward Haines P 2/13/1999 Bp Jane Hart Holmes Dixon. m 7/4/1998 Beth-Sarah Panton c 4. Vic/Cn Cong Of S Sav New York NY 2000-2002;

Cathd Of St Jn The Div New York NY 1998-2002. Bro Of S Andr. STPAULS696@AOL.COM

WRIGHT, Ross McGowan (SVa) 1547 Cedar Ln, Norfolk VA 23508 **R Ch Of The Gd Shpd Richmond VA 2006-** B Orangeburg SC 7/16/1954 s Samuel E Wright & Ellen. BA Davidson Coll 1976; MDiv TESM 1981; GTS 1982. D 6/12/1982 Bp William Arthur Beckham P 4/20/1983 Bp Paul Moore Jr. m 11/30/1985 Lynda Wornom c 3. R Ch Of The Gd Shpd Norfolk VA 1987-2002. Cmnty Of S Mary. Ldrshp Hampton Roads 1994. rossmwright@gmail.com

WRIGHT, Ryan A (SwFla) Saint Paul's, 3901 Davis Blvd, Naples FL 34104 **Ch Of The Epiph Cape Coral FL 2009-** B Baltimore MD 2/19/1977 s Donald B zumFelde & Ruth Ann. BA Stetson U 1999; MDiv The GTS 2006. D 5/27/2006 Bp John Wadsworth Howe P 11/3/2007 Bp Dabney Tyler Smith. Asst. R S Paul's Ch Naples FL 2007-2009. fatherwright@gmail.com

WRIGHT, Scot R (Oly) 650 12th Ave, Kirkland WA 98033 **S Jn's Ch Kirkland WA 1999-** B Denver CO 3/14/1957 s Elton Stanley Wright & Roxene Roi. BA SE Coll 1980; MDiv Gordon-Conwell TS 1987. D 10/28/1987 P 5/22/1988 Bp Donald Purple Hart. m 7/9/1977 Chitra Watumull c 3. St Steph's Epis Ch Oak Harbor WA 1992-1998; All SS Ch Bakersfield CA 1989-1992; Assoc R Calv Epis Ch Kaneohe HI 1987-1989. scotrwright@msn.com

WRIGHT, Stanalee (Spok) P.O. Box D, Mallot WA 98829 **Vic S Anne's Ch Omak WA 2004-** B Colville WA 1/30/1956 BS WA SU 1978. D 11/20/2004 P 6/11/2005 Bp James Edward Waggoner. m 9/7/1996 Michael Wright. stanaleew@televar.com

WRIGHT, Stuart Wayne (Md) 4 E. University Pkwy., Baltimore MD 21218 **Dir for HR Dio Maryland Baltimore MD 2009-** B Apple Valley CA 3/11/1959 s Bobby Lee Wright & Gladys Christene. BBA U of No Texas 1981; MDiv Luth TS 1989. Rec from Evangelical Lutheran Church in America 6/26/2009 Bp John Leslie Rabb. m 8/9/1989 Melvin F Wright. swright@episcopalmaryland.org

✠ **WRIGHT, Rt Rev Wayne Parker** (Del) 2020 N Tatnall St, Wilmington DE 19802 **Bp Of Delaware Dio Delaware Wilmington DE 1998-** B Richmond VA 5/4/1951 s George Wright & Margaret Louise. BA W&M 1975; MDiv STUSo 1980. D 6/14/1980 P 5/9/1981 Bp C(laude) Charles Vache Con 6/20/1998 for Del. m 8/17/1985 Holly B Wright c 1. Joint Stndg Com On Nomin Dio Louisiana Baton Rouge LA 1995-1996; Pres - Nneca Dio Louisiana Baton Rouge LA 1993-1994; Dep Gc Dio Louisiana Baton Rouge LA 1991-1994; Exec Bd Dio Louisiana Baton Rouge LA 1991-1993; Pres La Cler Assn Dio Louisiana Baton Rouge LA 1989-1990; R Gr Ch New Orleans LA 1987-1998; Exec Bd Dio Sthrn Virginia Norfolk VA 1982-1984; S Jn's Ch Suffolk VA 1980-1987; D-in-c Glebe Ch Suffolk VA 1980-1981. Hon DD U So Sewanee TN. wright2106@verizon.net

WRIGHT, William Baskin (NwT) 3549 Clearview Dr, San Angelo TX 76904 **Int Trin Epis Ch Ft Worth TX 2011-; Int Ch Of The Heav Rest Abilene TX 2009-** B Tuscaloosa AL 3/26/1943 s Ernest Baskin Wright & Martha Euginia. BA Birmingham-Sthrn Coll 1964; MDiv STUSo 1970; DMin VTS 1984. D 6/24/1970 Bp George Mosley Murray P 5/18/1971 Bp Furman Stough. m 10/30/1964 Patricia Lyles c 2. R S Jn's Epis Ch Ft Smith AR 1998-2004; R S Paul's On The Plains Epis Ch Lubbock TX 1992-1998; Dioc Exec Counsel Dio NW Texas Lubbock TX 1992-1995; R Ch Of The Resurr Austin TX 1987-1992; R S Mich's Ch La Marque TX 1982-1986; P-in-c S Mich's Ch Faunsdale AL 1981-1982; R S Mich's (Faunsdale) Faunsdale AL 1975-1982; R Trin Ch Demopolis AL 1975-1982; Assoc Chr Epis Ch San Antonio TX 1973-1975; Vic Emm Epis Ch Opelika AL 1970-1973; Vic S Matthews In The Pines Seale AL 1970-1973. OHC 1973. bwright8@juno.com

WRIGHT, Winston Antony (SeFla) 1466 39th St, West Palm Beach FL 33407 **R Gr Ch W Palm Bch FL 2000-** B Rock Spring Trelawny JM 8/18/1963 s Leolyn Mae. GTF; DIT Untd Theol Coll Of The W Indies Kingston Jm 1991; BA U of The W Indies 1991. Trans from Anglican Church of Canada 10/12/2000 Bp Leopold Frade. m 4/30/1994 Gillian Wright c 1. gec_mail@bellsouth.net

WUBBENHORST, Wesley (Md) 4 East University Pkwy, Baltimore MD 21218 **Yth Mssnr Dio Maryland Baltimore MD 2004-** B Minneola NY 5/5/1953 s William Henry Wubbenhorst & Arvilla. BA Laf 1976; MS Ford 1982; MDiv VTS 1989. D 6/9/1990 Bp Arthur Edward Walmsley P 3/1/1991 Bp Clarence Nicholas Coleridge. m 10/16/1982 Vivienne F Thompson c 5. Assoc S Marg's Ch Annapolis MD 1997-2004; Gr Ch Madison NJ 1994-1997. wwubbenhorst@ang-md.org

WURM, Laurie Jean (Nwk) 224 Cornelia St, Boonton NJ 07005 **S Jn's Epis Ch Boonton NJ 2007-** B Woodbury NY 2/14/1969 d Jesse Wurm & Heather. BA Bard Coll 1991; MDiv UTS 1995. D 9/11/2004 P 4/2/2005 Bp John Palmer Croneberger. c 1. All SS Epis Par Hoboken NJ 1996-2004; All SS Cmnty Serv and Dvlpmt Corp Hoboken NJ 1995-2007. revlwurm@optonline.net

WYATT II, Robert Odell (Chi) 3526 Maple Ave, Berwyn IL 60402 **Epis Chars Trst Dio Chicago Chicago IL 2007-; R S Helena's Ch Willowbrook IL 2006-** B Jackson TN 2/7/1946 BA U So 1968; MA NWU 1970; PhD NWU 1973; MS U of Tennessee 1976; Cert SWTS 2002; MTS Van 2003; Cert Loyola U Chicago 2008. D 6/19/2004 P 12/18/2004 Bp William Dailey Persell. m 5/16/1997 Terri Anne Lackey. Cur Ch Of The Trsfg Palos Pk IL 2004-2006; Trst SWTS Evanston IL 1996-2001. Co-Auth, "Free Expression In Five Democratic Publics," Hampton Press, 2004; Auth, "Free Expression And The Ameican Publ," Amer Soc Of Nwspr Editors, 1991. Fndr's Medal Van Divnity Sch 2004; Worcester Prize For Best Article Wrld Assn. For Publ Opinion Resrch 1996; DSA Soc Of Profsnl Journalists 1991. robertowyatt@gmail.com

WYCKOFF, Michael Hirsch (Tex) 2857 Grimes Ranch Rd, Austin TX 78732 **R S Lk's On The Lake Epis Ch Austin TX 2004-** B Ithaca NY 4/18/1959 s Wendell James Wyckoff & Fredericka. BA Wesl 1981; MDiv VTS 1987. D 6/29/1987 Bp Gordon Taliaferro Charlton P 4/13/1988 Bp Maurice Manuel Benitez. m 6/11/1988 Martha Conley Talbot c 2. R Chr Ch Tuscaloosa AL 1998-2004; R Chr Epis Ch Temple TX 1991-1998; Assoc The Ch of the Gd Shpd Austin TX 1987-1990. mwyckoff1@att.net

WYER, George William (Va) Po Box 638, Ivy VA 22945 B Bucyrus OH 1/6/1931 s John Philip Wyer & Hazel. BA Ob 1952; MLitt U Pgh 1953; MDiv Bex 1967. D 6/17/1967 Bp Nelson Marigold Burroughs P 12/17/1967 Bp Beverley D Tucker. m 10/3/1954 Nancy Vogt c 4. S Paul's Ch Ivy VA 1974-1993; Ch Of S Jn The Bapt Ivy VA 1974-1987; Assoc The Epis Ch Of Beth-By-The-Sea Palm Bch FL 1969-1974. gwhobbit@aol.com

WYES, Gregory Walter (Az) 6960 N Alvernon Way, Tucson AZ 85718 B Duesseldorf Germany 3/14/1940 s Emil Wyes & Henny. BA S Albert's 1963; MDiv Oxf 1967; DMin GTF 1990. Rec from Roman Catholic 1/1/1977 as Priest Bp J(ohn) Joseph Meakins Harte. m 9/27/1975 Lotti Mottscheller. Chr The King Ch Tucson AZ 1976-2002. wyes@comcast.net

WYLAND, Richard Rees (Roch) 41 Great Oak Ln, Redding CT 06896 **Trin Ch Litchfield MN 2007-; Trin Epis Ch Litchfield CT 2007-** B Hartford CT 4/21/1948 s Richard Gilbert Wyland & Helen. BA Trin Hartford CT 1970; MA Trin Hartford CT 1970; MDiv GTS 1973; Cert Sacr Heart U Fairfield CT 1993. D 2/24/1973 P 4/22/1974 Bp Robert Rae Spears Jr. m 6/10/1989 Jeanne Wyland c 1. Trin Epis Ch Trumbull CT 2006; Chr Ch Redding Ridge CT 2005; Trin-S Mich's Ch Fairfield CT 2003-2004; Int S Ptr's Epis Ch Monroe CT 2002; Int Chr Ch Clayton NY 1998-1999; Int St Jn's Ch Clayton NY 1998-1999; St. Mk's Sch of Southborough Inc. Southborough MA 1980-1981. Auth, *Ch of the Dio Massachusetts*, 1983. wyland@optonline.net

WYLD, Kevin Andrew (CFla) No address on file. B Bishop Auckland Durham UK 5/22/1958 s Albert Wyld & Margaret. MA Oxf; BA Oxf 1979; MS U Of Durham Durham Gb 1981; BD U Of Edinburgh Edinburgh Gb 1985. Trans from Church Of England 7/24/2000 Bp John Wadsworth Howe. R S Richard's Ch Winter Pk FL 2000-2004. kevinwyld@earthlink.net

WYLIE, Craig Robert (SwVa) 170 Crestview Dr, Abingdon VA 24210 B East Grand Rapids MI 7/24/1948 s Robert Milton Wylie & Peggy Ann Dorothy. BA Shimer Coll 1970; MDiv SWTS 1974; MEdAdmin U of Texas at El Paso 1983; DMin SWTS 2009. D 6/22/1974 Bp Charles Bennison P 5/14/1975 Bp Iveson Batchelor Noland. m 8/22/1970 Judith Swanson c 2. R S Thos' Epis Ch Abingdon VA 2002-2011; Dio New Jersey Trenton NJ 1999-2002; R Trin Epis Ch Cranford NJ 1995-2002; Int S Jas Hse Of Pryr Tampa FL 1994-1995; Headmaster S Mary's Par Tampa FL 1991-1994; P-in-c Bethany Ch Hilliard FL 1990-1991; Dio Florida Jacksonville FL 1989-1991; Headmaster S Paul's By-The-Sea Epis Ch Jacksonville Bch FL 1988-1991; Dio Louisiana Baton Rouge LA 1984-1988; Assoc R Chr Ch Covington LA 1983-1988; Int Ch Of The Gd Shpd Forrest City AR 1982-1983; Headmaster Ch Of The H Cross W Memphis AR 1982-1983; H Cross Epis Sch W Memphis AR 1982-1983; Int Pro Cathd Epis Ch Of S Clem El Paso TX 1980-1981; S Clem's Epis Par Sch El Paso TX 1978-1982; Asst Chapl S Mart's Epis Ch Metairie LA 1974-1978; S Mart's Epis Sch Metairie LA 1974-1978. crwylie@comcast.net

WYMAN, Deborah W (Me) 986 Memorial Dr, Cambridge MA 02138 B Miami FL 4/18/1945 d Thomas Wolcott Little & Helen. BA Chatham Coll 1967; MA Bos 1979; MDiv GTS 1994; DMin EDS 2000. D 6/4/1994 Bp David Elliot Johnson P 10/14/1995 Bp Barbara Clementine Harris. Ecclesia Mnstrs Boston MA 2004-2011; The Cathd Ch Of S Paul Boston MA 1995-2003; Trin Epis Ch So Boston VA 1995-1996. "Theol of the Poor," *Handbook on U.S. Theologies of Liberation*, Chalice Press, 2004; Auth, "Hm Care for the Dying," Dial/Doubleday, 1985. deblitwym1@myfairpoint.net

WYMAN, Irma Marian (Minn) 1840 University Ave W Apt 411, Saint Paul MN 55104 B Detroit MI 1/31/1928 d Max Carroll Wyman & Marie Matilda. BSE U MI 2049. D 6/28/1990 Bp Sanford Zangwill Kaye Hampton. Archd Dio Minnesota Minneapolis MN 1998-2009; D Geth Ch Minneapolis MN 1995-2002; Dio Dn Coun Dio Minnesota Minneapolis MN 1992-1994; D S Mary's Ch St Paul MN 1990-1992. SCHC 1979. irmawy11@gmail.com

WYNDHAM, Beth Ann (Dal) 4101 Sigma Rd, Dallas TX 75244 **The Par Epis Sch Dallas TX 2010-** B Ankara Turkey 1/22/1970 d Richard Hendricks & Dorothy. BAS Dallas Bapt U 2007; MDiv Epis TS Of The SW 2010. D 6/5/2010 P 4/14/2011 Bp James Monte Stanton. m 8/15/1993 Jeremy J Wyndham c 2. beth@wyndhamfamily.org

WYNEN, Nancy Hartmeyer (SeFla) 1399 Sw 17th St, Boca Raton FL 33486 **P-in-c S Mary's Epis Ch Of Deerfiel Deerfield Bch FL 2010-; Bd Mem Jas L Duncan Conf Cntr Delray Bch FL 2008-** B Teaneck NJ 6/30/1946 d

W

Walter Andrew Hartmeyer & Marjorie Isabel. BA U of Massachusetts 1968; MLS Rutgers-The St U 1973; MA Florida Atlantic U 1991; MDiv GTS 2005. D 4/17/2005 P 12/10/2005 Bp Leopold Frade. m 12/6/1969 Alfons C Wynen c 1. Cler Asst H Trin Epis Ch W Palm Bch FL 2006-2009. Auth, "Journey Through Adv," *Skiturgies*, Ch Pub Grp, 2011. nancy.wynen@gmail.com

WYNN, James E (Pa) 520 S 61st St, Philadelphia PA 19143 **Vic S Geo S Barn Ch Philadelphia PA 1996-** B Wilkes-Barre PA 8/24/1945 s Melvin Samuel Wynn & Ella Merit. BA Wilkes Coll 1969; MDiv PDS 1973. D 6/7/1973 P 6/27/1974 Bp Lloyd Edward Gressle. m 9/24/1977 Jacqueline Hyman c 2. Dio Pennsylvania Philadelphia PA 1996-2009; S Aug's Epis Ch Asbury Pk NJ 1995-1996; Trin Cathd Trenton NJ 1984-1995; R S Aug's Ch Camden NJ 1976-1981; Asst S Lk's Epis Ch Bronx NY 1974-1975. Hon Cn Trin Cathd Trenton NJ 1982.

WYNN, Ronald Lloyd (Ore) 355 Stadium Dr S, Monmouth OR 97361 **D S Hilda's Ch Monmouth OR 2003-** B Farmington NM 11/4/1928 BA Highland U Las Vegas NM 1950; MA U CO 1956; PhD U CO 1969. D 10/4/2003 Bp Johncy Itty. m 9/9/1950 Marilyn Jean Staley c 7.

WYPER, Susan Cavanagh (Ct) St Matthew's Episcopal Church, 382 Cantitoe st, Bedford NY 10506 **Asst Min S Matt's Ch Bedford NY 2007-** B New Haven, CT 4/26/1962 d Robert Fick Cavanagh & Patricia McLaughlan. BA Ya 1984; MA Dioc Study Prog For Lay People Middlebury VT 1989; MDiv Ya Berk 2007. D 6/9/2007 P 12/15/2007 Bp Andrew Donnan Smith. m 11/24/1984 George Urban Wyper c 3. susan.wyper@yale.edu

WYSOCK, Christine Phillips (Spok) 535 Shelokum Dr, Silverton OR 97381 B Yakima WA 5/12/1948 d Roy Lewis Phillips & Margaret Helen. Heritage Coll Toppenish WA; A.D.N Yakima Vlly Coll 1990. D 4/14/1999 Bp Cabell Tennis P 10/16/1999 Bp John Stuart Thornton. m 12/3/1994 John Rodney Wysock c 3.

WYSONG, Terry Marie (Ct) PO Box 606, Marion CT 06444 B Galveston TX 1/15/1945 d George Thompson & Jeanette. BS U IL 1967; MDiv Ya Berk 1994. D 6/10/1995 P 1/12/1996 Bp Clarence Nicholas Coleridge. m 9/6/1969 Bryan Wysong c 4. R S Paul's Ch Southington CT 2002-2007; Int All SS Epis Ch Oakville CT 2001-2002; Grtr Waterbury Mnstry Middlebury CT 2000-2001; Asst S Jas's Ch W Hartford CT 1995-1999. revtw@cox.net

X

XIE, Songling (LI) 13532 38th Ave, Flushing NY 11354 **Cur S Geo's Par Flushing NY 2006-** B Shanghai China 2/23/1951 s Jiliang Xie & Jinxia. MB Nantong Med Coll CN 1978; MA Ashland TS 2002; MA GTS 2004. D 1/24/2006 Bp Rodney Rae Michel P 10/28/2006 Bp Orris George Walker Jr. m 7/23/1979 Aner Wu c 1. "Yin-Yang and Five Elements and Chinese Med," Xinhua, 1992; "A Hist of Yin-Yang and Five Elements Theory," Shandong, 1989; "Disabil and Sxlty," Huaxia, 1986. paulslx@yahoo.com

Y

YABROFF, Martin I(rving) (Oly) 3914 136th Street Ct NW, Gig Harbor WA 98332 **Dioc Coun Dio Olympia Seattle WA 2007-; R S Andr's Epis Ch Tacoma WA 2007-** B San Mateo CA 8/31/1956 s Irving Wollin Yabroff & Esther Lou. BA U CA 1978; MDiv Bos 1982. D 12/9/1984 P 10/6/1985 Bp Charles Shannon Mallory. m 6/14/1980 Eve Merriman Armitage c 6. Dep Gc Dio Nthrn Indiana So Bend IN 2006-2007; Stndg Com Dio Nthrn Indiana So Bend IN 2005-2006; Dn The Cathd Ch Of S Jas So Bend IN 2004-2007; Dep Gc Dio El Camino Real Monterey CA 1991-1997; Vic S Phil The Apos Scotts Vlly CA 1987-2004; Assoc Ch of S Mary's by the Sea Pacific Grove CA 1982-1987. Auth, "Regular Contrib To Loc Newspapers". yabroff@net-venture.com

YAGERMAN, Steven Jay (NY) 234 E 60th St, New York NY 10022 **R All SS Ch New York NY 1993-; Trst Cathd Of St Jn The Div New York NY 1990-** B Miami FL 4/25/1954 s George Samuel Yagerman & Betty Gay. GTS; BA U Of Florida 1975; MDiv Gordon-Conwell TS 1979; CAS GTS 1981; DMin Hebr Un Coll 1997. D 5/31/1981 P 11/1/1981 Bp Calvin Onderdonk Schofield Jr. c 4. R All SS' Epis Ch Briarcliff Manor NY 1984-1993; Asst S Greg's Ch Boca Raton FL 1981-1983. syagerman@earthlink.net

YAKUBU-MADUS, Fatima Emitsela (Ind) 5625 W 30th St, Speedway IN 46224 B Auchi Nigeria 1/21/1956 d Yakubu Makhu & Aja. BSC Kentucky St U 1982; MSC U of Mississippi 1985. D 10/23/2010 Bp Catherine Elizabeth Maples Waynick. c 2. fmadus@gmail.com

YALE, Richard Arthur (Pa) 712 Taranto Ct, Virginia Beach VA 23454 B Walnutport PA 2/14/1924 s Charles Oliver Yale & Laura Mae. BS Illinois Inst of Tech 1947; MDiv SWTS 1954; MA SWTS 1969. D 6/6/1953 P 12/11/1953 Bp Charles L Street. m 7/1/1950 Theresa Marie Taylor c 2. St Leonards Hse Chicago IL 1983-1986; Cathd Shltr Chicago IL 1975-1983; Cathd Shltr Of Chicago Dio Chicago Chicago IL 1975-1983; Bp Advsry Cmsn Alcosm Dio Chicago Chicago IL 1970-1986; R S Tim's Ch Milwaukee WI 1955-1958; Cur S Matt's Ch Evanston IL 1953-1955.

YALE, Richard Barrington (NCal) 4 Quista Dr., Chico CA 95926 **R S Jn The Evang Ch Chico CA 1997-** B Otsu Japan 9/16/1957 s Theodore Humphrey Yale & Elizabeth Anne. DMin Fuller TS; Pasadena City Coll; BA Westmont Coll 1979; MDiv CDSP 1985. D 6/15/1985 Bp Robert C Rusack P 1/1/1986 Bp Oliver Bailey Garver Jr. m 8/28/1982 Linda J Fortine c 3. Chair, Open Comm T/F Dio Nthrn California Sacramento CA 2004-2006; Dn, Superior California Dnry Dio Nthrn California Sacramento CA 2003-2007; Cmsn on Liturg and Mus Dio Nthrn California Sacramento CA 1997-2009; Dio Nthrn California Sacramento CA 1997; Vic S Paul's Mssn Cres City CA 1994-1996; Int S Lk's Par Monrovia CA 1993-1994; Assoc Ch Of Our Sav Par San Gabr CA 1987-1994; Ecum Cmsn Dio Los Angeles Los Angeles CA 1987-1994; Cur S Geo's Epis Ch Laguna Hills CA 1985-1987. rbyale@att.net

YAMAMOTO, Keith Akio (Los) 330 E. 16th Street, Upland CA 91784 **R S Mk's Epis Ch Upland CA 2009-** B Los Angeles CA 12/27/1967 s Clarence Akiyoshi Yamamoto & Maxine Hayami. BA U CA Santa Cruz 1990; MDiv GTS 1997. D 6/7/1997 Bp Artemio M Zabala P 1/17/1998 Bp Frederick Houk Borsch. m 5/30/1998 Patricia Susanne McCaughan. Assoc S Marg Of Scotland Par San Juan Capistrano CA 2001-2009; Asst S Mk's Epis Ch Upland CA 1997-2001. patmkeithy@aol.com

YANCEY, David Warren (Tenn) 1390 Jones Creek Rd, Dickson TN 37055 **P-in-c S Andr's Epis Ch New Johnsonville TN 1999-** B Lubbock TX 7/13/1951 s Warren Hadden Yancey & Betty. BA Shimer Coll 1973; MDiv Nash 1980; MS Van 1992. D 6/11/1980 Bp William Cockburn Russell Sheridan P 12/17/1980 Bp Duncan Montgomery Gray Jr. m 10/17/1992 Ellen M Lloyd. Hon Assoc S Barth's Ch Bristol TN 1991-1997; Ecum Off Dio Wstrn Massachusetts Springfield MA 1986-1990; Dio Wstrn Massachusetts Springfield MA 1982-1990; R Gr Ch Dalton MA 1982-1990; S Mich's Campus Picayune MS 1980-1982. Sigma Theta Tau. mcewenclinic@bellsouth.net

YANCEY, Nancy Rollins (At) 5480 Clinchfield Trl, Norcross GA 30092 **CEO Rainbow Vill Inc Duluth GA 2009-** B Atlanta GA 9/27/1952 d Royston Rollins & Geneva. D 10/18/1998 Bp Onell Asiselo Soto. m 11/19/1971 Charles J Yancey c 3. D Chr Ch Norcross GA 1998-2009. nyancey@comcast.net

YANCY, Stephanie Pauline (Md) 1510 Rising Ridge Rd, Mount Airy MD 21771 **S Geo Ch Hampstead MD 2011-** B Nassau Bahamas 1/9/1951 d John Edward Taylor & Coral Louise. BA Cor 1972; MDiv GTS 2006. D 6/24/2006 Bp John Leslie Rabb P 1/20/2007 Bp Robert Wilkes Ihloff. m 6/3/1972 Joseph Yancy c 2. Trin Ch Towson MD 2010-2011; Int S Jn's Par Hagerstown MD 2006-2010. rev.yancy@gmail.com

YANDELL, George Shaw (At) Church of the Holy Family, 202 Griffith Rd, Jasper GA 30143 **Epis Ch Of The H Fam Jasper GA 2010-** B Mobile AL 2/17/1953 s William Francis Yandell & Winifred. BA Emory U 1975; MDiv VTS 1979. D 7/1/1979 Bp William Evan Sanders P 5/1/1980 Bp William F Gates Jr. m 10/9/1999 Susan Burnett Rowland c 2. Assoc to the R Calv Ch Memphis TN 2002-2010; R Ch Of The Gd Shpd Dallas TX 1992-1997; Assoc to the R Ch Of The H Comm Memphis TN 1985-1992; R S Jas The Less Madison TN 1980-1985; D Ch Of The H Comm Memphis TN 1979-1980. Auth, "150 Days- Engaging Students in Epis Campus Mnstrs," Dio W Tennessee, 2007; Auth, "Comm of the Absent," *Angl Dig*, Calv Epis Ch, 2007; Auth, "Ch Builds Hse, Hse Builds Ch," *Dallas Morning News*, Dallas Morning News, 1996; Auth, "SCI Comes of Age," *Sthrn Communities Journ*, Sthrn Communities Journ, 1990. gyandell@etcmail.com

YANG CHOU, Chou (June) Yun Kuang (Tai) St. Mark, 120-11 Chung Hsiao Road, Ping Tung 900 Taiwan **Dio Taiwan Taipei TW TW 2008-** B Fukien TW 3/8/1940 BD H Light Sem Kaihsiung Cn 1993. D 1/25/2002 Bp Jung-Hsin Lai. m 6/7/1964 Jun-shen Yang c 4.

YAO, Ting Chang (Cal) 1111 Larch Ave, Moraga CA 94556 **Assoc S Anselm's Epis Ch Lafayette CA 1990-; Asst P Epis Ch Of Our Sav Oakland CA 1973-** B 2/12/1923 s K S Yao & Mildred. BS S Jn U CN 1946; MS Utah St U 1949. D 6/19/1966 Bp James Albert Pike P 1/1/1970 Bp C Kilmer Myers. m 4/17/1984 Joan Lok c 5. Vic S Giles Ch Moraga CA 1970-1976; S Steph's Epis Ch Orinda CA 1966-1970. tcyao@comcast.net

YARBOROUGH, Clare McJimsey (Az) 5671 E. Copper Street, Tucson AZ 85712 **P Epis Par Of S Mich And All Ang Tucson AZ 2011-** B Austin TX 6/18/1957 d Richard Warren Yarborough & Ann Graham. BA Ob 1979; MA U of Arizona 1983; PhD U of Arizona 1993; MDiv EDS 1996. D 6/15/1996 Bp Robert Reed Shahan P 1/4/1997 Bp William George Burrill. m 9/8/2007 Laurie Louise Chase. Assoc S Phil's In The Hills Tucson AZ 2009-2011; R Trin Epis Ch Weymouth MA 2004-2009; P-in-c Ch Of Our Sav Somerset MA 2000-2004; Cur S Paul's Ch Rochester NY 1996-2000. clarev@aol.com

YARBOROUGH, Jesse H (Buzz) (WTex) 121 Peppertree Crossing Ave, Brunswick GA 31525 **Int Chr Ch Monticello FL 2010-** B Miami FL 9/8/1939 s

Jesse Harden Yarborough & Louise. BS Clemson U 1963; MDiv STUSo 1978. D 6/24/1978 P 1/21/1979 Bp William Gillette Weinhauer. m 11/30/1963 Kathryne Manheim. Assoc Chr Ch Frederica St Simons Island GA 2006-2010; R Epis Ch Of The Mssh Gonzales TX 1999-2005; R Chr Epis Ch Little Rock AR 1989-1999; R S Mk's Ch Brunswick GA 1981-1989; Asst S Ptr's by-the-Sea Epis Ch Bay Shore NY 1978-1981. bkyarb@bellsouth.net

YARBROUGH, C(laire) Denise (Roch) St. Mark's Episcopal Church, 179 Main St., Penn Yan NY 14527 B Tulsa OK 5/23/1956 d John Floyd Yarbrough & Eileen Denise. BA Barnard Coll of Col 1978; JD U MI 1982; MDiv PrTS 1997; DMin PrTS 2006. Trans 9/16/2003 Bp John Palmer Croneberger. c 2. Ch Of The Ascen Rochester NY 2010-2011; Dio Rochester Rochester NY 2008-2010; S Mk's Epis Ch Penn Yan NY 2003-2008; R Ch Of The Trsfg Towaco NJ 1999-2003; Asst Trin Ch Toledo OH 1997-1999. "Many Faces of God," *Interfaith Educ Resource*, LeaderResources, 2006; "Apocalyptic Living," *Sermons That Wk*, Morehouse Pub, 2006; Auth, "Giving Birth to God," *Sermons That Wk*, Morehouse Pub, 2001; Auth, "Toil for Joy," *Sermons That Wk*, Morehouse Pub, 2000; Auth, "Fragments of Our Lives," *Sermons That Wk*, Morehouse Pub, 1999. OHC 1998. Phi Beta Kappa. dyarbrough1024@gmail.com

YARBROUGH, Douglas Wayne (Ida) 1312 W Elmore Ave, Nampa ID 83651 B Denver CO 10/2/1952 s Donald Yarbrough & Rowena L. MA Acadia U; MA Rockmont Coll; EdD Texas Tech U 1986; MA Iliff TS 1998. D 6/17/1995 P 12/14/1995 Bp John Stuart Thornton. m 6/24/1995 Eileen Yarbrough c 2. R Gr Epis Ch Nampa ID 1997-2004; Mtn Rivers Epis Cmnty Idaho Falls ID 1995-1997. Auth, "Educ & Educational Psychol". Atty Gnrl'S Victim Assistance Awd. grace@dmi.net

YARBROUGH, Eileen (Ida) 1312 W Elmore Ave, Nampa ID 83651 **D Gr Epis Ch Nampa ID 1997-** B Cardston AB CA 10/22/1955 d Thomas Arthur Close & Elsie Eileen. BS Idaho St U 1980; Med Idaho St U 1982. D 12/16/1995 Bp John Stuart Thornton. m 6/24/1995 Douglas Wayne Yarbrough c 1. Dok.

YARBROUGH, Oliver Larry (Vt) 24 Oak Dr, Middlebury VT 05753 B Tuscaloosa AL 12/19/1949 s Farris Eugene Yarbrough & Maudelle. BA Birmingham-Sthrn Coll 1972; MA U of Cambridge 1974; MDiv Candler TS Emory U 1975; PhD Ya 1984. D 8/13/2000 Bp Mary Adelia Rosamond McLeod P 3/25/2001 Bp Craig Barry Anderson. m 7/17/1976 Amy Hastings c 2. Auth, "Early Chr Jerusalem: The City of the Cross," *Jerusalem: Idea and Reality*, Routledge, 2008; Auth, "Mar and Divorce," *Paul in the Greco-Roman Wrld*, Trin Press Intl , 2003; Co-Ed, "The Soc Wrld of Paul," Fortress, 1995; Auth, "Parents and Chld in the Jewish Fam of Antiquity," *The Jewish Fam in Antiquity*, Scholars Press, 1993; Auth, "Not Like the Gentiles: Mar Rules in the Letters of Paul," Scholars Press, 1985. yarbrough@middlebury.edu

YARBROUGH, Rebecca Ricketts (NC) P.O. Box 970, Davidson NC 28036 B Charlotte NC 2/2/1953 d Edgar Ricketts & Hilde Barwig. BA Queens Coll 1975. D 6/14/2008 Bp Michael Bruce Curry. m 9/20/1975 David Yarbrough c 2. ryarbrough@centralina.org

YARDLEY, Theodore (NH) 410 Davisville Rd, East Falmouth MA 02536 **Died 7/26/2009** B Pittsfield MA 2/3/1920 s Jonathan C Yardley & Ethel May. BA Harv 1942; STB GTS 1945. D 3/31/1945 P 10/1/1945 Bp Wallace J Gardner. c 3.

YARSIAH, James T (SC) 1324 Marvin Ave, Charleston SC 29407 **S Andr's Mssn Charleston SC 2004-** B Liberia 10/9/1965 s John Yarsiah & Sobondo. TS Sewanee; BA Cuttingham U Coll Liberia 1999. Trans from Church of the Province of West Africa 5/7/2006 Bp Edward Lloyd Salmon Jr. m 5/9/2000 Ophelia Yarsiah c 3. Old S Andr's Par Ch Charleston SC 2009; Liberia Monrovia 1998-2004. jyarsiah@yahoo.com

YATES, Adam Benjamin (Ct) 60 East Ave, Norwalk CT 06851 **Assoc. for Mem Incorporation Par of St Paul's Ch Norwalk Norwalk CT 2010-** B Bethesda MD 3/24/1985 s Benjamin S Yates & Lisa Eleanor. BA,BS Northland Coll 2007; MDiv Chicago TS 2010. D 6/5/2010 Bp Jeffrey Dean Lee P 1/6/2011 Bp Ian Theodore Douglas. YATESA01@GMAIL.COM

YATES, Robert Gordon (SwFla) 37505 Moore Dr, Dade City FL 33525 B Louisville KY 9/14/1939 s Robert Lee Yates & Emma Cecilia. BA California St U 1968; Cert D Formation Prog 1995. D 6/24/1995 Bp Telesforo A Isaac. m 12/4/1964 Linda Kay Hays c 4.

YATES, William Jeffrey (CFla) 3400 Wingmann Rd., Avon Park FL 33825 **Camp Wingmann Avon Pk FL 1998-** B Chickasha OK 4/7/1951 s George Yates & Helen Parkin. BA Florida Sthrn Coll 1974; MDiv STUSo 1984. D 6/29/1984 Bp William Hopkins Folwell P 1/6/1985 Bp Frank Stanley Cerveny. m 5/6/1972 Joan G Gast c 2. P-in-c The Epis Ch Of The Redeem Avon Pk FL 2000-2001; Cn to Ordnry Dio Florida Jacksonville FL 1995-1998; R Chr Ch Monticello FL 1988-1994; Asst Ch Of The Adv Tallahassee FL 1984-1988. wingmann@strato.net

YAW, Chris (Mich) St David's Episcopal Church, 16200 W 12 Mile Rd, Southfield MI 48076 **R S Dav's Ch Southfield MI 2007-** B Detroit MI 4/9/1962 s James John Yaw & Nancy. BS JCU 1984; MDiv Fuller TS 1997; ThM Fuller TS 2000. D 6/16/2001 Bp Chester Lovelle Talton P 1/12/2002 Bp Frederick Houk Borsch. m 8/23/2003 Natlie Lynn Priest. Asst S Thos Epis Ch Battle Creek MI 2001-2007. Fndr, "Grow My Ch!," *www.growmychurch.com*, Grow My Ch!, 2011; Auth, "Through a Mirror Dimly," *www.chrisyaw.com*, Personal Blog, 2009; Co-Auth, "The Epis Handbook," *Bk*, Ch Pub, 2008; Auth, "Jesus Was an Epis (and you can be one too!)," *Bk*, LeaderResources, 2007; Auth, "Epis Ch Names," *The Chr Century*, The Chr Century, 2004; Auth, "Clearing Your Thanksgiving Plate," *LivCh*, LivCh Fndt, 2002; Auth, "Holidays and Holiness," *LivCh*, LivCh Fndt, 2001. BroSA 2002-2003. therevchrisyaw@gmail.com

YAW, David Dixon (Ak) 3195 Jackson Heights St, Ketchikan AK 99901 **R S Jn's Ch Ketchikan AK 2010-** B Logan OH 11/4/1947 s Owen Foley Yaw & Margaret Elizabeth. BS Ohio U 1969; MDiv EDS 1978; New Engl Dss Hosp 1987. D 12/3/1978 P 6/30/1979 Bp John Mc Gill Krumm. m 10/7/1967 Marily Hadley c 1. Chapl Howe Mltry Sch Howe IN 2000-2010; R/Chapl S Mk's Par Howe IN 2000-2010; Chapl S Jn's Mltry Acad Delafield WI 1993-1997; R Trin Ch Moundsville WV 1991-1993; Dio Sthrn Ohio Cincinnati OH 1989-1990; Int S Jn's Epis Ch Lancaster OH 1988-1989; H Trin Epis Ch In Countryside Clearwater FL 1985-1986; H Trin Epis Ch W Palm Bch FL 1985-1986; Cur Ch Of The Ascen Clearwater FL 1982-1984; P-in-c Ch Of The Ascen Donaldsonville LA 1980-1982; Chapl Epis HS Baton Rouge LA 1979-1982; Epis Soc Of Chr Ch Cincinnati OH 1979; D Epis Soc of Chr Ch Cincinnati OH 1978-1979. david.yaw1947@yahoo.com

YAWN, Justin Sidney (Ga) 4401 Country Club Rd, Statesboro GA 30458 **Assoc R Trin Ch Statesboro GA 2010-** B Atlanta GA 4/3/1985 s Gary Wayne Yawn. BBA The U GA 2007; MDiv Candler TS Emory U 2010. D 2/6/2010 P 8/21/2010 Bp Scott Anson Benhase. therevjustinyawn@gmail.com

YEAGER, Alice Elizabeth (ND) 301 Main St S, Minot ND 58701 B Davenport IA 2/13/1945 d Carl T Kurtz & Elizabeth. D 7/23/2010 Bp Michael Gene Smith. c 2. shylow13@medco.net

YEAGER, Linda (WMo) 11534 Knox St, Overland Park KS 66210 **Assoc Bp Spencer Place Inc Kansas City MO 2006-** B Kansas City MO 5/1/1941 d Russell Clarence Swanson & Martha Grace. BA Truman St U Kirksville MO 1980; MA Truman St U Kirksville MO 1984. D 2/4/1995 Bp John Clark Buchanan. m 6/10/1961 Jon Gordon Yeager c 3. lyeager@everestkc.net

YEAGER, Robert Timothy (Chi) 924 Lake Street, Oak Park IL 60301 B Charles City IA 8/24/1950 s Robert Benjamin Yeager & Bernadine Ann. BA U of Iowa 1972; JD U of Iowa 1977. D 12/22/2010 P 8/26/2011 Bp Jeffrey Dean Lee. m 6/19/1999 Sarah Moores c 1. EPF 2001. Hugh White "Trumpet of Justice" Awd Epis Ntwk for Econ Justice 2011; Hugh White Trumpet of Justice Awd Epis Ntwk for Econ Justice 2011. rtyeager@gmail.com

YEARWOOD, Kirtley (Oly) Saint John's University, PO Box 7066, Collegeville MN 56321 B BB 10/12/1961 s Herman DaCosta Yearwood & Joyce Dulcina. BS Tuskegee Inst 1983; MPH U of Oklahoma Hlth Sciences Cntr 1988; MD U of Arkansas for Med Sciences 1993; MDiv GTS 1998; STM GTS 1999. Trans from Church in the Province Of The West Indies 5/31/1998 Bp Herbert Alcorn Donovan Jr. m 12/12/2008 Stacey Murray Yearwood. S Andr's Epis Ch Lawton OK 2010-2011; Cmsn on Ch Archit Dio Olympia Seattle WA 2009-2011; S Clem's Epis Ch Seattle WA 2009-2010; Bd Mem, Dominican Dvlpmt Grp Dio The Dominican Republic (Iglesia Epis Dominicana) Santo Domingo DO 2008-2011; Gr Ch Charleston SC 2007-2008; Com on Ch Archit Dio Washington Washington DC 2001-2003; Com on Liturg and Mus Dio Washington Washington DC 2001-2003; Consecration Com for VIIIth Bp of Washington Dio Washington Washington DC 2001-2002; Dioc Coun Dio Washington Washington DC 2001-2002; S Mary's Epis Ch Foggy Bottom Washington DC 2000-2003; Cur Trin Cathd Little Rock AR 1998-1999; D Ch Of The Trsfg New York NY 1997-1998; Chapl Asst The GTS New York NY 1997-1998. The Alcuin Club 2011. kady.doulos@gmail.com

YEARY, James Knox (At) 242 Maplecrest Ln SE, Rome GA 30161 B Elberton GA 1/1/1942 s Charles Joseph Yeary & Katherine. BA U So 1965; MDiv STUSo 1969; DMin STUSo 1989. D 6/29/1969 Bp Milton LeGrand Wood P 6/29/1970 Bp Randolph R Claiborne. m 9/4/1965 Frieda Chandler c 1. Trin Epis Ch Columbus GA 2004-2005; S Ptr's Ch Rome GA 2003-2004; Gr-Calv Epis Ch Clarkesville GA 2002; S Ptr's Ch Rome GA 2000-2001; Cn Cathd Of S Phil Atlanta GA 1994-2000; R Emm Epis Ch Athens GA 1989-1994; Dep Gc Dio Atlanta Atlanta GA 1988-1997; S Mk's Epis Ch Lagrange GA 1979-1989; Stwdshp Dept Dio Atlanta Atlanta GA 1979; R S Mths Epis Ch Toccoa GA 1974-1979; Cur Ch Of The Ascen Lafayette LA 1972-1974; Asst S Ptr's Ch Rome GA 1969-1972. Auth, "Sprtl Direction & Its Place Within The Regular Life Of The Par," U So Press, 1989. jkyeary@bellsouth.net

YEATES, Judith Ann (Neb) 4003 County Road P41, Fort Calhoun NE 68023 **GC Dep Dio Nebraska Omaha NE 2006-; Secy to Exec Cmsn Dio Nebraska Omaha NE 2005-** B Oklahoma City OK 8/30/1950 d Russell Grandell Adcock & Mary. BS Dana Coll 1995; MA Creighton U 1998; MDiv Nash 1999. D 4/29/1998 P 11/1/1998 Bp James Edward Krotz. m 7/18/1987 James Burnet Yeates c 1. GC Dep Dio Nebraska Omaha NE 2006-2007; Stndg Com Pres Dio Nebraska Omaha NE 2004-2007; R Ch Of The Resurr Omaha NE 2002-2008; Asst All SS Epis Ch Omaha NE 1998-2002; All SS Epis Ch

Omaha NE 1995-1998. Doctorate of Div Providence Theol Schoo 2009. jyeates@episcopal-ne.org

YEOMAN III, Eric Burdett (Cal) 1633 Argonne Dr, Stockton CA 95203 B Martinez CA 7/21/1926 s Eric Burdett Yeoman & Florence. CDSP; CDSP; Dominican Coll; New Mex St U. 1960; BA U CA 1961; MS U of Oregon 1964; Sonoma St Coll Rohnert Pk 1977. D 12/24/1961 Bp James Albert Pike P 6/1/1975 Bp C Kilmer Myers. m 6/27/1948 Norma Evelyn Wagner. Vol P Epis Ch Of S Anne Stockton CA 1983-2008; Asst S Jn's Epis Ch Stockton CA 1978-1989; Asst S Jn's Epis Ch Clayton CA 1962-1977; Asst Ch Of The Resurr Pleasant Hill CA 1961-1977. OHC.

YEPES LOPEZ, Alvaro Nelson (DR) Iglesia Episcopal Dominicana, Calle Santiago No 114, Santo Domingo 764 Dominican Republic **Dio The Dominican Republic (Iglesia Epis Dominicana) Santo Domingo DO 2007-** B 10/6/1966 D 2/12/2006 Bp Julio Cesar Holguin-Khoury. m 1/21/2006 Angela Maria Maria Pulido Pulido-Giraldo. alvarin08@hotmail.com

YERKES, Kenneth Bickford (Mo) 1 Macarthur Blvd Apt S503, Haddon Township NJ 08108 B Philadelphia PA 8/18/1934 s Horace Dilwyn Yerkes & Esther Chesley. BA Tem 1956; MDiv PrTS 1960; Cert GTS 1985. D 6/15/1985 Bp Lyman Cunningham Ogilby P 10/18/1985 Bp William Augustus Jones Jr. Int S Paul's Epis Ch Sikeston MO 1999-2001; Int H Cross Epis Ch Poplar Bluff MO 1998-1999; Int S Paul's Ch Kankakee IL 1997-1998; Int Chr Ch Rolla MO 1996-1997; Int S Lk's Epis Ch Manchester MO 1994-1996; Vic Trin Epis Ch Kirksville MO 1985-1993. ACPE 1993-2001. keneyerkes@comcast.net

YETTER, Joan M (Mont) 932 Avenue F, Billings MT 59102 **R Calv Epis Ch Red Lodge MT 2010-** B Billings MT 11/18/1947 d Clyde Raymond Mitchell & Nina Mae. U Denv 1967; BS Montana St U 1971; Claremont TS 1996; MDiv CDSP 1998. D 6/20/1998 Bp Robert Marshall Anderson P 1/3/1999 Bp Leigh Wallace Jr. m 6/29/1969 Benjamin A Yetter c 3. Int R All SS Ch Richland WA 2009-2010; Int Rectro St. Mich & All Ang Dio Oregon Portland OR 2007-2009; Int R Gr Ch Jefferson City MO 2005-2007; Int R Yellowstone Epis Mnstry Dio Montana Helena MT 2003-2005; Dioc Coun Dio Montana Helena MT 2000-2002; Asst R Ch Of The H Sprt Missoula MT 1998-2003. jmyetter@yahoo.com

YODER, John Henry (Nev) 1151 Carlton Ct Apt202, Fort Pierce FL 34949 B Birdsboro PA 2/25/1936 s Stanley Sunday Yoder & Beatrice Elva. BA California St U 1973; MDiv CDSP 1976. D 6/19/1976 P 1/15/1977 Bp Robert C Rusack. R All SS Epis Ch Las Vegas NV 1981-1999; Asst S Cross By-The-Sea Ch Hermosa Bch CA 1980-1981; Asst S Lk's Par Monrovia CA 1976-1979. johnyoder@bellsouth.net

YON, William A(bbott) (Ala) 140 Whisenhunt Rd, Chelsea AL 35043 B Knoxville TN 3/17/1931 s Terrell Higdan Yon & Catherine. BA Emory U 1952; MDiv VTS 1955; DD VTS 1995. D 6/20/1955 Bp George Mosley Murray P 12/21/1955 Bp Randolph R Claiborne. c 4. Admin Asst Dio Alabama Birmingham AL 1990-1997; Assoc The Epis Ch Of S Fran Of Assisi Indn Sprg Vill AL 1988-1990; Exec Coun Appointees New York NY 1986-1990; Ch Of The Trsfg Chelsea AL 1975-1983; DCE Dio Alabama Birmingham AL 1963-1972; Assoc DCE Dio No Carolina Raleigh NC 1960-1963; Chair Of The Yth Div Dio Atlanta Atlanta GA 1957-1960; Vic S Alb's Ch Elberton GA 1955-1960; Vic S Andr's Ch Hartwell GA 1955-1960. "No Trumpets-No Drums," *Postnet*, 2004; Auth, "On The Battle Lines"; Auth, "Prime Time For Renwl-Ptp"; Auth, "Lks Journ"; Auth, "To Build The City: Too Long A Dream Alb Inst/EUC". Apos in Stwdshp The Epis Ntwk for Stwdshp (TENS) 2003. Nandjedi@aol.com

YONKERS, Michael Allan (Chi) 920 S Aldine Ave, Park Ridge IL 60068 B Chicago IL 4/22/1950 s Joseph Allan Yonkers & Rita. BA St. Johns U 1968; MA Loyola U 1976. D 12/7/1991 Bp Frank Tracy Griswold III. m 6/2/1973 Dianne Illiano c 2.

YOON, Paul Hwan (Los) Box 22, Taejon 300 Korea (South) B Choong Joo KR 2/28/1938 s Chi Duk Yoon & Ok Ei. BA Soong Jun U 1962; ThD S Mich's Sem 1965. D 6/1/1966 P 7/1/1967 Bp The Bishop Of Taejon. m 1/11/1964 Susanna Eun Sook Kim. Ch Of The Annunc Los Angeles CA 1982-1987.

YORK, Susan Spence (WMich) 2490 Basswood St, Jenison MI 49428 **Ch Of The H Sprt Livonia MI 2007-** B Akron OH 12/18/1943 d Lewis Meek Oattey & Julianne. BA Detroit Mercy Coll Detroit MI; AA Grand Rapids Cmnty Coll; MDiv SWTS. D 6/22/1996 P 1/1/1997 Bp Edward Lewis Lee Jr. m 8/22/1967 Roger York c 4. Vic Ch of the H Sprt Belmont MI 2006-2008; Dio Wstrn Michigan Kalamazoo MI 2003-2006; S Andr's Ch Grand Rapids MI 1996-2003. susanyork@protogy.net

YORK-SIMMONS, Noelle Marie (At) 634 W Peachtree St Nw, Atlanta GA 30308 **Assoc R All SS Epis Ch Atlanta GA 2004-** B Atlanta GA 12/24/1976 BA Emory U 1999; DAS Ya Berk 2003; MDiv Yale DS 2003. D 12/6/2003 P 8/1/2004 Bp J(ohn) Neil Alexander. m 8/2/2003 Kevin N York-Simmons c 2. noelleys@gmail.com

YOSHIDA, Thomas Kunio (Haw) 1410 Makiki St, Honolulu HI 96814 **Assoc P S Lk's Epis Ch Honolulu HI 2003-** B Honolulu HI 1/23/1936 s Masao Yoshida & Mitsuko. BS Marq 1959; MDiv CDSP 1962; Cert Amer Acad Of Bereavement Tucson AZ 1997; Cert Amer Acad Of Bereavement Mesa AZ 2001. D 6/9/1962 Bp George Richard Millard P 12/16/1962 Bp Harry S Kennedy. m 8/8/1964 Winona Katsue Tasaka. S Alb's Chap Honolulu HI 1979-1995; Vic S Jn's Ch Eleele HI 1966-1969; S Steph's Ch Wahiawa HI 1962-1979; Assoc All SS Ch Kapaa HI 1962-1966; Vic Chr Memi Ch Kilauea HI 1962-1966; Vic St Thos Ch Hanalei HI 1962-1966. Auth, "Dioc Hospice/Bereavement & Palliative Care Resource Packet," 2000. Amer Acad Of Bereavement 1997-2001; AFP 1963-1972; Hospice Ntwk Hawaii 2000. Bp'S DSA Epis Ch In Hawaii 1969. wky@aol.com

YOST, Martin Clark (Dal) 401 S. Crockett St, Sherman TX 75090 **Nthrn Convoc Chairman Dio Dallas Dallas TX 2009-; R S Steph's Epis Ch Sherman TX 2006-** B Arlington MA 2/10/1964 s Paul Wesley Yost & Eunice Joan. BA Tufts U 1997; MDiv Nash 2002. D 12/6/2001 P 9/4/2002 Bp Keith Lynn Ackerman. m 9/12/1999 Katherine P Philp c 6. Cur & Chapl to the Sch S Jn's Epis Ch Dallas TX 2002-2006; Trin Ch Wauwatosa WI 2002; S Jn's Epis Ch Dallas TX 2001-2002. Auth, "The Paschal Lamb," *Forw in Chr*, FIFNA, 2011; Auth, "Why Mary Matters," *Forw in Chr*, FIFNA, 2010. CCU 2002; CBS 1999; GAS 2003; Soc of King Chas the Mtyr 1993; SocMary 1999; SSC 2006. rector@saintstephenssherman.org

YOUNG JR, A LeRoy (Los) 1215 Del Mar Dr, Los Osos CA 93402 B Torrance CA 6/29/1930 s Albert Le Roy Young & Rose Ann. BA Sthrn California Bible Coll 1952; BA U of Redlands 1955; ThM Claremont TS 1958; CDSP 1960. D 12/14/1960 P 7/1/1961 Bp Ivol I Curtis. m 8/11/1951 Janice B Brooks c 2. The Par Ch Of S Lk Long Bch CA 1967-1990; Asst Min S Mths' Par Whittier CA 1961-1967. jyoung1550@aol.com

YOUNG JR, A(rchibald) Patterson (Dal) 617 Church St., Sulphur Springs TX 75482 B Bryan TX 10/2/1937 s Archibald Patterson Young & Pauline. U of Texas at Arlington, Tx; STL Angl TS 1978. D 6/24/1977 Bp Robert Elwin Terwilliger P 3/18/1979 Bp A Donald Davies. m 12/21/1958 Janet Anne Dotson c 2. P-in-c S Fran Ch Winnsboro TX 2002-2006; P-in-c S Phil's Epis Ch Sulphur Sprg TX 1996-2006; Vic Ch Of The Epiph Commerce TX 1996-1998; S Fran + S Clare 1992-1995; Int Dio Dallas Dallas TX 1983-1989; P-in-c Ascen And S Mk Bridgeport TX 1981-1982; Ch of the Ascen Decatur TX 1981-1982; S Andr's Ch Farmers Branch TX 1979-1981; Asst S Jn's Epis Ch Dallas TX 1978-1979; The Epis Ch Of The Trsfg Dallas TX 1978-1979. patterson491@verizon.net

YOUNG, Bernard Orson Dwight (LI) 18917 Turin Dr, Saint Albans NY 11412 **R Ch Of S Alb The Mtyr S Albans NY 1977-** B Georgetown GY 1/19/1947 s Richard Linton Young & Ethel Dorothy. Codrington Coll 1970. Rec 5/9/1975 Bp Jonathan Goodhue Sherman. m 8/22/1981 Deborah Corley c 1. Cur S Phil's Ch Brooklyn NY 1975-1977. bodyoung@aol.com

YOUNG, Bruce Alan (Mass) 46 Laurel St., Gloucester MA 01930 B Danvers MA 7/12/1937 s Charles B Young & Marjorie F. BA Trin 1959; STB Ya Berk 1962. D 6/23/1962 Bp Anson Phelps Stokes Jr P 6/1/1963 Bp Frederic Cunningham Lawrence. c 2. R Trin Ch Woburn MA 1966-1999; Asst Min All SS Epis Ch Attleboro MA 1962-1966. Ml King Jr Awd. beamepond@comcast.net

YOUNG, Christopher Breese (CFla) Po Box 1089, Sanford FL 32772 **Died 6/25/2011** B Syracuse NY 10/12/1929 s Robert Theodore Young & Roma Schermerhorn. Palm Bch Jr Coll 1948; BA Florida St U 1954; MDiv STUSo 1957; Pepperdine U 1975; USN Newport RI 1976. D 6/24/1957 Bp Henry I Louttit P 12/30/1957 Bp William Francis Moses. Ed/Cartoonist, *White Elephant News*; Ed Cartoonist, *White Elephant News USN Vietnam 67-69*. Fleet Reserve Assn; Life Mem: Mltry Chapl Assn. Meritorious Serv Medal 1986; Commendation Medal USN USCG 1968; 1st Angl P to Celebrate H Comm So Pole Antartica 1962; Bronze Star w Combat "V" for "Valor". cbyoung@webtv.net

YOUNG, Christopher Richard (Q) 1717 8th Ave, Moline IL 61265 B Fullerton CA 9/13/1960 s Leo Emmet Young & Helen Louise. BS California St Polytechnic U 1984; U of Arizona 1988; MDiv Nash 1998. D 6/13/1998 P 1/9/1999 Bp John-David Mercer Schofield. m 12/29/1984 Amy Jo Jennison c 3. Chr Ch Peoria IL 2004-2005; R Trin Ch Baraboo WI 2000-2004; Asst R S Paul's Epis Ch Visalia CA 1998-2000. young5@charter.net

YOUNG, Estelle Pope (Fla) 4811 Nw 17th Pl, Gainesville FL 32605 **D H Trin Ch Gainesville FL 1997-** B Vidalia GA 1/6/1924 d Estel Alexander Pope & Ruth. AA Young Harris Coll 1942; BA Merc 1946. D 10/6/1991 Bp Frank Stanley Cerveny. m 6/23/1946 James Joseph Young c 2. D-In-Res S Barth's Ch High Sprg FL 1991-1997. NAAD; Oreder Of S Lk. repyoung@aol.com

YOUNG, Francene (Tex) 3530 Wheeler St, Houston TX 77004 B Augusta GA 1/26/1953 d James Young & Ollie Elkins. BA Cleveland St U 1975; MPH U Pgh 1978; Bi-Vocational Mnstry Iona Sch of Mnstry 2011. D 6/18/2011 Bp C(harles) Andrew Doyle. m 4/29/2000 Kenneth Randolph Jones. francene.young@att.net

YOUNG, Franklin Woodrow (NC) 4 Carolina Meadows #103, Chapel Hill NC 27517 **Died 9/25/2010** B Lima OH 3/16/1915 s Oscar N Young & Evalette. BA Dart 1937; BD Crozer TS 1942; PhD Duke 1946. D 8/13/1950 Bp Edwin A Penick P 6/1/1951 Bp Duncan Montgomery Gray. c 2. Auth, *Understanding the NT*, Prentice Hall, 1957. Phi Beta Kappa Duke 1946.

YOUNG, Frank Whitman (Ala) 8 W Walnut St, Sylacauga AL 35150 **R S Andr's Epis Ch Sylacauga AL 1998-; R S Mary's Epis Ch Childersburg AL 1998-; R Trin Epis Ch Alpine AL 1998-** B Grand Rapids MI 8/5/1948 s James M Young & Sara. BA U CA 1970; MDiv VTS 1974. D 5/24/1974 Bp John Alfred Baden P 5/25/1975 Bp Robert Bruce Hall. m 11/24/2009 Elizabeth J Jefferson c 2. So Talladega Cnty Epis Mnstry Sylacacga AL 1998-2009; Gr Ch Cullman AL 1995-1998; Dep, GC Dio Michigan Detroit MI 1991-1994; Asst S Paul's Epis Ch Flint MI 1991-1994; R S Dunst's Epis Ch Davison MI 1985-1991; Vic Nativ Cmnty Epis Ch Holly MI 1977-1985; Vic Gr Ch Bremo Bluff VA 1974-1977. Ord of S Lk the Physcn - St Chapl 1994-2005. Best Article Associated Ch Press 1974. frfrank@earthlink.net

YOUNG, Gary John (EO) 665 Parsons Road, Hood River OR 97031 B Roslyn WA 7/23/1942 s Lena. MDiv CDSP 1975; BA Assn of Profsnl Chapl 2006. D 5/25/1975 Bp John Raymond Wyatt P 5/29/1976 Bp George Richard Millard. m 6/28/1980 Barbara Barnett c 5. R The Par Of S Mk The Evang Hood River OR 1986-1994; Vic S Matt's Ch Prosser WA 1978-1986; S Geo's Epis Ch Antioch CA 1977; Dio California San Francisco CA 1975-1976. garyyoung.hoodriver@gmail.com

YOUNG, Gary Reid (Neb) 17 Brentwood Ct, Scottsbluff NE 69361 B Scottsbluff NE 9/13/1932 s Elmer Reid Young & Katherine Irene. Cert Nash 1968; MDiv Nash 1988; BS SUNY 1988. D 12/21/1967 P 6/1/1968 Bp Russell T Rauscher. m 6/12/1952 Neta Smith c 2. Dn Trin Cathd Omaha NE 1991-1994; Int S Steph's Ch Grand Island NE 1990-1991; Cn to Ordnry Dio Nebraska Omaha NE 1987-1991; Dio Nebraska Omaha NE 1987-1990; R Ch Of The H Apos Mitchell NE 1981-1987; R S Mk's Ch Havre MT 1969-1972; P-in-c S Mary's Epis Ch Bassett NE 1968-1969; P-in-c S Ptr's Ch Neligh NE 1968-1969. Ord of S Lk.

✠ **YOUNG III, Rt Rev George D** (ETenn) 814 Episcopal School Way, Knoxville TN 37932 **Bp of E Tennessee Dio E Tennessee Knoxville TN 2011-** B Jacksonville FL 9/28/1955 s George Dibrell Young & Margaret Miller. Wesley Coll 1974; BS Florida St U 1978; MDiv SWTS 1990. D 6/10/1990 P 12/9/1990 Bp Frank Stanley Cerveny Con 6/25/2011 for ETenn. m 8/22/1981 Kathryn M Young c 2. R S Ptr's Ch Fernandina Bch FL 1997-2011; R S Eliz's Epis Ch Jacksonville FL 1992-1997; DRE S Giles' Ch Northbrook IL 1990-1992. gyoung@etdiocese.net

YOUNG JR, George Dibrell (Fla) 2727 San Lucas Rd, Jacksonville FL 32217 **Chair - BEC Dio Florida Jacksonville FL 1984-; COM Dio Florida Jacksonville FL 1980-** B Saint Augustine FL 2/26/1925 s George Dibrell Young & Ellen Eunice. BA U So 1949; STB GTS 1952; Chr Ch Coll 1981. D 6/2/1952 P 12/19/1952 Bp Frank A Juhan. m 6/28/1952 Margaret Miller c 4. Asst All SS Epis Ch Jacksonville FL 1980-1990; Jacksonville Epis HS Jacksonville FL 1973-1990; COM Dio Florida Jacksonville FL 1971-1976; Del Prov IV Syn Dio Florida Jacksonville FL 1960-1965; Adult Div DeptCE Dio Florida Jacksonville FL 1959-1968; R Ch Of Our Sav Jacksonville FL 1955-1973; Vic S Mary's Epis Ch Madison FL 1953-1955; Vic S Jas Epis Ch Perry FL 1952-1955. Omicron Delta Kappa 1949; Blue Key 1948; Phi Beta Kappa 1948. gyoung2727@aol.com

YOUNG, James Joseph (Los) 12868 Hacienda Dr., Studio City CA 91604 **Harvard-Westlake Sch N Hollywood CA 1997-** B Dearborn MI 12/29/1954 s James Willard Young & Patricia Louise. BA Rice U 1977; MDiv Epis TS of The SW 1988. D 6/14/1988 P 12/21/1988 Bp Gordon Taliaferro Charlton. m 3/10/1978 Cynthia Beth Kennedy. Holland Hall Sch Tulsa OK 1991-1997; Asst Ch Of The Gd Shpd Kingwood TX 1988-1991. jyoung@hw.com

YOUNG, James Oliver (Okla) 2207 Ridgeway St, Ardmore OK 73401 B Parris Island SC 4/19/1945 s William Oliver Young & Ruth Cherokee. BS SE St Coll Durant OK 1967; DDS Baylor U 1972. D 6/16/2001 Bp Robert Manning Moody. m 5/27/1967 Virginia Evelyn Koontz. D St Phil's Epis Ch Ardmore OK 2001-2003. jameso@starband.net

YOUNG, James Robert (Minn) 101 Plum St S, Northfield MN 55057 **S Jas On The Pkwy Minneapolis MN 2011-; Chair of Dioc Exam Chapl Dio Minnesota Minneapolis MN 2006-** B Wadsworth OH 8/28/1950 s Benjamin Robert Young & Anne King. STUSo; BS Bowling Green St U 1972; MA U of Iowa 1978; MDiv Untd TS Of The Twin Cities 1994. D 6/10/1984 Bp Robert Marshall Anderson P 8/18/1994 Bp Sanford Zangwill Kaye Hampton. m 6/16/1973 Lynne Marie Weins c 2. Chr Ch Albert Lea MN 2004-2011; Assoc P The Epis Cathd Of Our Merc Sav Faribault MN 1999-2001; P-in-c Ch Of The Redeem Cannon Falls MN 1995-2001. revjryoung@gmail.com

YOUNG, James Robert (NCal) Po Box 2334, Avila Beach CA 93424 **Assoc S Mich Ch Alturas CA 1991-** B Athol MA 8/7/1922 s James Robert Young & Mabel Lottie. BS Babson Coll 1949; Cert ETSBH 1975; MA Claremont TS 1984. D 6/21/1975 P 8/1/1994 Bp Sanford Zangwill Kaye Hampton. Assoc Ch Of S Nich Paradise CA 1991-1993; Vic S Ptr's Ch Casa Grande AZ 1990-1991; Vic S Fran In The Redwoods Mssn Willits CA 1988-1990; Assoc R S Jn The Div Epis Ch Costa Mesa CA 1985-1988; Asst S Andr's Epis Ch Irvine CA 1983-1984; Asst S Paul's Epis Ch Tustin CA 1976-1982.

YOUNG, James Robert (Ore) 5260 Triad Court SE, Salem OR 97306 **S Paul's Epis Ch Salem OR 2009-** B Chattanooga TN 2/2/1961 s Marshall Young & Jackie. BS U of Tennessee 1984; MDiv Ya Berk 1996. D 6/15/1996 P 12/20/1996 Bp James Barrow Brown. m 8/10/1991 Niki Vee Lilienthal c 3. Assoc S Paul's Epis Ch Salem OR 2005-2009; Stanford Cbury Fndt Standford CA 2003-2005; Asst S Paul's Epis Ch Modesto CA 2000-2003; R S Lk's Ch Denison TX 1998-2000; R Ch Of The H Comm Plaquemine LA 1996-1998. fatherjimyoung@yahoo.com

YOUNG, Kathryn (Tenn) 704 Park Blvd, Austin TX 78751 B Terrell TX 10/31/1948 d Dehart Earl McMillan & Patricia. BA Van 1970; MS Van 1972; MDiv Epis TS of The SW 1990; MA SW Texas St U San Marcos 1999. D 7/14/1990 Bp George Lazenby Reynolds Jr P 7/26/1991 Bp Anselmo Carral-Solar. c 2. Colloquy Ldr Epis TS Of The SW Austin TX 1995-2002. Alb Inst 1990-1994; Amer Counslg Assn 1999-2011. kmyoung@austin.rr.com

YOUNG, Kathryn M (Fla) 204 S 6th St, Fernandina Beach FL 32034 **Chr Epis Ch Ponte Vedra Bch FL 2009-** B Munchwieller DE 8/19/1962 d Paul M Beich & Kathleen Oehler. Florida St U; SWTS; U So. D 6/14/1992 P 12/1/1992 Bp Frank Stanley Cerveny. m 8/22/1981 George D Young c 2. S Geo's Epis Ch Jacksonville FL 1999-2009; Asst R S Mk's Epis Ch Jacksonville FL 1992-1997. Phi Beta Kappa. kammyyoung1@gmail.com

YOUNG, Linda M (SO) 10345 Montgomery Rd, Cincinnati OH 45242 B Cleveland OH 10/5/1956 d Raymond David Petti & Marie Rose. BS Coll of Mt St Jos 1978; MEd U Cinc 1989; MDiv Bex 2010. D 6/13/2009 P 6/19/2010 Bp Thomas Edward Breidenthal. m 9/7/1991 Christopher H Young c 2. Cur S Barn Epis Ch Montgomery OH 2010-2011. youngmlinda@gmail.com

YOUNG, Malcolm Clemens (Cal) 2674 St. Giles Lane, Mt. View CA 94040 **R Chr Epis Ch Los Altos CA 2001-** B Cambridge MA 5/5/1967 s Stephen Pomeroy Young & Clarc. BA U CA 1989; MDiv Harvard DS 1994; ThD Harv 2004. D 8/20/1994 P 2/27/1995 Bp Jerry Alban Lamb. m 8/29/1992 Heidi Ho c 2. Asstg Cler S Anne's In The Fields Epis Ch Lincoln MA 1998-2000; Int S Clem's Ch Berkeley CA 1994-1997. Auth, "The Sprtl Journ of Henry Dav Thoreau," *The Sprtl Journ of Henry Dav Thoreau*, Merc Press, 2009. AAR 1993. Fell ECF 1999. malcolm@ccla.us

YOUNG, Mary Catherine (USC) Canterbury Downtown, 12 W. 11th Street, New York NY 10011 **Epis Campus Min for NYU and Surrounding campuses Dio New York New York City NY 2011-** B Little Rock AR 7/8/1978 d Donald Enockson & Dorothy. AA Cottey Coll 1998; BA Morningside Coll 2000; MDiv EDS 2006. D 6/8/2006 Bp James Louis Jelinek P 1/20/2007 Bp Dorsey Felix Henderson. m 4/19/2009 Chad Robert Young. P Asst for Faith Formation Ch Of Our Sav Rock Hill SC 2006-2011. rev.marycat@gmail.com

YOUNG, Robert Lee (Dal) 105 Morningside Dr, Grand Prairie TX 75052 B Smith Center KS 7/29/1950 s Orval Alfred Young & Carrie Aldena. BS U of Oregon 1972; MDiv Epis TS of The SW 1980. D 9/19/1980 P 6/23/1981 Bp Matthew Paul Bigliardi. m 2/4/1978 Elizabeth Bilodeau c 1. Spec Mobilization Spprt Plan Washington DC 2008-2011; Pension Fund Mltry New York NY 2008-2009; R S Clem Epis Ch Tampa FL 1986-1996; Cur S Barth's Ch Beaverton OR 1981-1986; Legacy Gd Samar Hosp Portland OR 1980-1981. Assn Epis Chapl; SSC. lizyoung44@hotmail.com

YOUNG, Shari Maruska (Cal) 3 Bayview Ave., Belvedere CA 94920 **Assoc R S Steph's Par Belvedere CA 2010-** B Santa Monica CA 3/13/1949 d Marvin Young & (dec). U CA 1972; BA Pacific Oaks Coll 1973; MDiv CDSP 1988. D 6/25/1988 Bp Frederick Houk Borsch P 4/7/1989 Bp William Edwin Swing. m 2/14/1992 Robert J Hartnett c 1. Int S Aid's Mssn Bolinas CA 2009-2010; Assoc R S Jas Epis Ch San Francisco CA 1998-2009; P-in-c S Aid's Mssn Bolinas CA 1993-1996; Adj P Gr Cathd San Francisco CA 1988-2000; Chapl Cathd Sch For Boys San Francisco CA 1988-1993. Epis Peace Fell. revshari@earthlink.net

YOUNG, Sherry Lawry (EMich) 5584 Lapeer Rd Apt 1D, Kimball MI 48074 B Lansing MI 5/15/1949 d William Ambrose Lawry & Clarice Virginia. Kendall Coll 1970; Diac Whitaker TS 1983; Wayne BIS Detroit MI 1992; Natl Bd Cert Coun 1997; MA Oakland U 1997. D 11/19/1983 Bp William J Gordon Jr. D All SS Epis Ch Fair Haven MI 2000-2002; D S Paul's Epis Ch Port Huron MI 1998-2006; Coordntr Epis Relief and Dvlpmt Dio Estrn Michigan Saginaw MI 1998-2002; D S Mk's Epis Ch Marine City MI 1998-2000; Asst Gr Epis Ch Port Huron MI 1984-1998; D S Mich's Epis Ch Lansing MI 1983-1984. Auth, "Chapt: From the Ther Room," *Chld and Stress: Understanding and Helping*, Assn of Childhood Educ Intl , 2001.

YOUNG, Stephen Matthew (Lex) 7 Court Pl, Newport KY 41071 **Gr Epis Ch Florence KY 2011-; S Paul's Ch Newport KY 2011-** B Covington KY 7/23/1970 s Robert Joseph Young & Lee Ellen C. BA Witt 1994; MDiv Trin Luth Sem 1998. Rec from Evangelical Lutheran Church in America 8/24/2011 as Priest Bp Stacy F Sauls. MATTEWYOUNG@FUSE.NET

YOUNG, Todd (Ore) 11800 SW Military Lane, Portland OR 97219 **S Lk's Ch Grants Pass OR 2010-; Congrl Dvlpmt Com Dio Montana Helena MT 2005-; Vic Chr Ch Sheridan MT 2004-** B Seattle WA 8/21/1964 s Gary John Young & Betty Jane. BA Whitworth U 2000; MDiv SWTS 2004. D 6/12/2004 Bp James Edward Waggoner P 12/18/2004 Bp Charles Franklin Brookhart Jr. m 9/8/1990 Joelene K Warner c 1. S Paul's Ch Virginia City MT 2010; Dio Montana Helena MT 2004-2009. revtoddyoung@gmail.com

YOUNG, William King (Az) 12440 W Firebird Dr, Sun City West AZ 85375 **Assoc All SS Ch Phoenix AZ 2010-** B El Paso TX 6/21/1938 s King William Young & Sue Fellers. BA U of Texas 1962; SMM UTS 1969; MDiv CDSP 1978. D 9/15/1978 P 5/1/1979 Bp Richard Mitchell Trelease Jr. m 4/1/1978 Katharine Lenore Wright c 2. R Ch Of The Adv Sun City W AZ 1997-2004; Stndg Com Dio Arizona Phoenix AZ 1993-1997; Dep To Gc Dio El Camino Real Monterey CA 1988-1994; Dioc Coun Dio Arizona Phoenix AZ 1985-1987; Dio Arizona Phoenix AZ 1982-2004; R All SS Epis Ch Watsonville CA 1980-1997; Epis Ch In Lincoln Cnty Ruidoso NM 1979-1980; Com Dio The Rio Grande Albuquerque NM 1978-1979. Auth, "If The Householder Had Known - Adv Meditation," *LivCh*, 1989. wmkayyoung@earthlink.net

YOUNGBLOOD, Susan Russell (Az) Saint Matthew's, 901 W Erie St, Chandler AZ 85225 **D S Matt's Ch Chandler AZ 2008-** B Lucas OH 6/20/1945 d Ross Russell & Virginia. BA Coll of Wooster 1963; MS Suny Geneseo 1973. D 1/26/2008 Bp Kirk Stevan Smith. m 12/27/2003 Harlie Youngblood c 2. youngblood@wbhsi.net

YOUNGE, Richard Gibbs (Oly) 4832 52nd Ave S, Seattle WA 98118 B Brooklyn NY 6/28/1925 s Richard Younge & Ethel. BA Cor 1946; MA Col 1950; STB GTS 1959; PhD Grad Theol Un 1979. D 7/4/1959 Bp James P De Wolfe P 1/1/1960 Bp Jonathan Goodhue Sherman. m 7/3/1949 Edith Adele Trice c 4. P-in-c Chr Epis Ch Puyallup WA 1991-2007; Aids Taskforce Dio Wstrn Louisiana Alexandria LA 1987-1990; Dept Of Chr Serv Dio Wstrn Louisiana Alexandria LA 1987-1990; Dio Wstrn Louisiana Alexandria LA 1986-1990; S Dav Emm Epis Ch Shoreline WA 1984-1985; BEC Dio Olympia Seattle WA 1982-1985; S Columba's Epis Ch And Chilren's Sch Kent WA 1982-1983; P-in-c S Andr's Ch Seattle WA 1981-1982; Dio Olympia Seattle WA 1980-1986; Asst The Epis Ch In Almaden San Jose CA 1978-1980; Asst S Eliz's Epis Ch So San Francisco CA 1977-1980; P-in-c S Cyp's Ch San Francisco CA 1971-1975; Cler Senate Dio El Camino Real Monterey CA 1969-1970; Div Vol Ministers Dio El Camino Real Monterey CA 1966-1973; BEC Dio El Camino Real Monterey CA 1966-1970; Div Vol Ministers Dio California San Francisco CA 1962-1966; R S Aug's Ch Oakland CA 1961-1966; Cur S Geo's Ch Brooklyn NY 1959-1961. EUC, ESMHE, UBE, Integrity, NEAC. youngerg3@comcast.net

YOUNGER, Leighton Keith (Tex) 2727 Nasa Pkwy Apt 901, Seabrook TX 77586 B Brookshire TX 8/13/1932 s Lovic Pierce Younger & Velma Jean. BS U of Texas 1955; LLB U of Texas 1958; MDiv Epis TS of The SW 1964. D 6/1/1964 Bp Frederick P Goddard P 6/1/1965 Bp Scott Field Bailey. m 1/11/1993 Sarah M Younger. R S Jn's Ch La Porte TX 1972-1997; Assoc H Sprt Epis Ch Houston TX 1967-1972. erealm@hughes.net

YOUNGSON, Charles Mitchell (Ala) 315 Devon Dr., Birmingham AL 35209 **R S Thos Epis Ch Birmingham AL 2009-** B Tuscaloosa AL 5/11/1975 s George Mitchell Youngson & Leslie Woollen. BA Trin U San Antonio TX 1997; M.Div TS 2003. D 6/24/2003 Bp Robert Boyd Hibbs P 1/6/2004 Bp James Edward Folts. m 6/19/1999 Susan C Youngson c 2. Assoc All SS Epis Ch Birmingham AL 2005-2009; Asst S Steph's Epis Ch Wimberley TX 2003-2005. cyoungson@bellsouth.net

YOUNKIN, Randy John (Pgh) 431 Alameda Ave, Youngstown OH 44504 B Johnstown PA 8/20/1949 s Warren D Younkin & Olive J. BS Robert Morris Coll 1972; MDiv EDS 1975. D 5/30/1976 Bp Robert Bracewell Appleyard. m 5/27/1974 Candace M Mihalic. D Ch Of Our Sav Glenshaw PA 1976-2004; No Hills Yth Mnstry Pittsburgh PA 1976-1977; Asst All SS Epis Ch Brighton Heights Pittsburgh PA 1975-1976.

YOUNKIN, Ronald Willingham (Pgh) D 6/18/1969 P 12/1/1969 Bp Charles A Mason.

YOUNT, Amy Clark (WA) 3801 Newark St Nw Apt E431, Washington DC 20016 **S Pat's Ch Washington DC 2011-** B Washington DC 12/23/1964 d Frank Wilfong Yount & Jean. BA Bow 1987; MDiv Ya Berk 1992. D 9/1/1992 Bp Edward Cole Chalfant P 10/1/1993 Bp Charles Lindsay Longest. m 8/20/1994 Nathan Hemenway Price. S Pat's Epis Day Sch Washington DC 2005-2011; Cathd of St Ptr & St Paul Washington DC 1994-2001; Pstr Assoc S Anne's Par Annapolis MD 1992-1994. amy-yount@cathedral.org

YOUSE JR, Don C (Pgh) 955 West North Avenue, Pittsburgh PA 15233 **Vic Emm Ch Pittsburgh PA 1994-** B Warsaw IN 4/20/1958 s Don C Youse & Helene Person. BS U NC 1980; MD U of Florida 1984; MDiv TESM 1994. D 6/11/1994 Bp Peter James Lee P 12/17/1994 Bp Alden Moinet Hathaway. dyouse@aol.com

YSKAMP, Janis (CPa) 813 Valley Rd, Mansfield PA 16933 **R All SS Ch Coudersport PA 2010-; R Chr Ch Coudersport PA 2010-** B Chester PA 2/14/1956 d James William Ross & Janet Austin. D 10/26/2008 P 6/12/2010 Bp Nathan Dwight Baxter. m 9/12/1977 Wayne A Yskamp c 3. S Paul's Ch Wellsboro PA 2008-2010. jyskamp@gmail.com

YULE, Marilynn Fritz (Spok) PO Box 6318, Kennewick WA 99336 **D S Paul's Epis Ch Kennewick WA 2003-** B Buffalo NY 7/12/1934 d Carl Edwin Fritz & Ravenna Hannah. BD U Roch 1957. D 11/22/2003 Bp James Edward Waggoner. m 7/7/1957 William David Yule c 3. wyule3066@charter.net

Z

✠ **ZABALA, Rt Rev Artemio M** (Los) 5048 Brunswick Dr, Fontana CA 92336 B Bontoc Philippines 3/22/1938 s Pedro Pablo Zabala & Patricia. BTh St. Andr's TS Philippines 1963; BA U of The Philippines 1964; ThM Trin Toronto Can 1974; ThD U of Heidelbery Germany 1980. Trans from Episcopal Church in the Philippines 2/11/1999 Bp Frederick Houk Borsch Con 10/28/1989 for Episcopal Church in the Philippines. m 11/28/1963 Mary Capuyan c 3. Dio No Cntrl Philippines 1991-1993; Dio Cntrl Philippines 1964-1990. "The Enigma of Jn 19:13 Reconsidered," *SE Asia Journ of Theol, Vol. 23*, 1982; "The Enigma of Jn 19:13 Reconsidered," *SE Asia Journ of Theol, Vol. 22*, 1981. amzabala@roadrunner.com

ZABRISKIE JR, Alexander Clinton (Be) 119 Northshore Dr, Burlington VT 05408 B Alexandria VA 1/27/1930 s Alexander Clinton Zabriskie & Mary E. BA Pr 1952; U of Edinburgh GB 1953; MDiv VTS 1956; DMin PrTS 1985. D 6/1/1956 Bp Frederick D Goodwin P 12/16/1956 Bp William J Gordon Jr. m 1/21/1958 Marguerite M Lane c 5. Exec Coun Appointees New York NY 1987-1995; Int S Clem's Ch Hawthorne NJ 1986-1987; Int Chr Ch Teaneck NJ 1985-1986; R Trin Ch Bethlehem PA 1969-1984; R S Mary's Ch Anchorage AK 1958-1969; Asst S Matt's Epis Ch Fairbanks AK 1956-1958. amzab2@myfairpoint.net

ZABRISKIE II, George (Mont) 4283 Monroe St Apt D, Bozeman MT 59718 B Chestnut Hill PA 3/30/1926 s Alexander Clinton Zabriskie & Mary. BA Pr 1950; MDiv VTS 1954; EDS 1972. Trans 11/19/2003 Bp Mark Sean Sisk. m 6/20/1959 Thyrza Day c 3. Supply P Dio Vermont Burlington VT 1992-1998; Trst, Cathd Sch Cathd Of St Jn The Div New York NY 1987-1992; Stndg Com Dio New York New York City NY 1983-1986; R S Jn's Ch Larchmont NY 1977-1992; Chair, Com on Cont Ed. Dio Missouri S Louis MO 1975-1977; Stndg Com Dio Missouri S Louis MO 1975-1977; COM Dio Missouri S Louis MO 1973-1977; Chr Ch Cathd S Louis MO 1972-1977; Asst S Thos Ch New York NY 1956-1959. Auth, *Seed & Harvest*, 1988; "Misc. Letters to the Ed," *LivCh*. Integrity 2004; Trst - Cathd Sch, Cathd of S Jn the Div 1987-1992. Bp's Awd Dio New York 1992; Rotary Pres's Awd Rotary Club, Larchmont, NY 1980; Dn's Awd St Andr's Epis. Sem, Manila, Philippines 1970. gtzab@in-tch.com

ZABRISKIE, Marek P (Pa) 212 Washington Ln, Fort Washington PA 19034 **R S Thos' Ch Whitemarsh Ft Washington PA 1995-** B Detroit MI 7/13/1960 s Charles Zabriskie & Catherine. Institut Catholique De Paris; BA Emory U 1982; MDiv Ya Berk 1989. D 6/24/1989 P 6/23/1990 Bp George Lazenby Reynolds Jr. m 1/15/1994 Isabel Mims Maynard. Assoc R S Jas' Ch Richmond VA 1991-1995; Asst to R S Geo's Ch Nashville TN 1989-1991. Auth, "Living Ch".

ZACHRITZ, John Louis (RG) 13 County Road 126, Espanola NM 87532 B Tulsa OK 2/10/1942 s John Louis Zachritz & Nancy Denoon. BA U of Tulsa 1966; MDiv EDS 1977. D 6/18/1977 P 5/21/1978 Bp Gerald Nicholas McAllister. m 9/7/1968 Helenmarie Gauchat c 3. S Fran Cmnty Serv Inc. Salina KS 2000-2005; Asst S Paul's Epis Ch Salinas CA 1999-2000; S Lk's Epis Ch Anth NM 1994-1999; Vic S Matt's Ch Sand Sprg OK 1983-1994; Asst Trin Ch Tulsa OK 1978-1983. helenmariez@gmail.com

ZACKER, John Garner Worrell (NY) 64 Weir Ln, Locust Valley NY 11560 **P Assoc Chr Ch Oyster Bay NY 2005-; P Assoc Par Of Chr The Redeem Pelham NY 1988-** B Brooklyn NY 3/24/1947 s John Lewis Zacker & Gwendolyn Rose. BA Wag 1969; GTS 1970; MDiv Drew U 1972; UTS 1975; JD Ford 1978. D 6/3/1972 P 12/1/1972 Bp Paul Moore Jr. m 4/11/1986 Joan Giordano. Assoc S Edm's Par San Marino CA 1982-1984; Assoc S Mary's Epis Ch Los Angeles CA 1980-1982; Vic Epis Ch Of SS Jn Paul And S Clem Mt Vernon NY 1977-1980; R S Jn's Epis Ch Mt Vernon NY 1977-1980; Ch Of The Atone Bronx NY 1976-1977; S Martha's Ch Bronx NY 1976-1977; Asst Chr Ch Bronxville NY 1973-1975; Asst S Jn's Ch Larchmont NY 1972-1973. Auth, *Legacy Plan Protection: Preserve Your Estate*. jgz64@hotmail.com

ZADIG SR, Alfred Thomas Kurt (WMass) Grace Church Rectory, 270 Main Street, Oxford MA 01540 **P-in-c Gr Ch Oxford MA 2009-** B New Rochelle NY 11/2/1931 s Alfred Erwin Zadig & Rose Violet. BA Brandeis U 1953; Long Island Dioc TS 1961; MA Bos 1973; PhD Columbia Pacific U 1989. D 4/8/1961 P 10/28/1961 Bp James P De Wolfe. c 1. Int P S Paul's Epis Ch Morganton NC 2005-2008; Int S Mary's Ch Asheville NC 2003-2004; Int Ch Of Our Sav Johns Island SC 2001-2002; P-in-c S Ptr's Ch Springfield MA 1997-2001; Ch Of The Atone Westfield MA 1995-1996; Int S Andr's Ch Longmeadow MA 1993-1995; Chr Ch Portsmouth NH 1989-1990; S Mary's Epis Ch Rockport MA 1987-1991; R Ch Of The Gd Shpd Waban MA 1975-1983; Ecum Counslg Serv Melrose MA 1972-1983; Assoc Trin-S Mich's Ch Fairfield CT 1966-1968. Confrater, Ord of S Ben 1962; CBS 1958; GAS 1958; P Assoc, Shrine of Our Lady of Walsingham 1962. azadigsr@yahoo.com

ZADIG JR, Alfred Thomas Kurt (SC) St Michael's Church, 76 Meeting St, Charleston SC 29401 **R S Mich's Epis Ch Charleston SC 2007-** B

Bridgeport CT 1/2/1968 s Alfred Thomas Kurt Zadig & Ina. BA U of Massachusetts 1990; MDiv STUSo 1997. D 6/21/1997 P 1/3/1998 Bp Edward Lloyd Salmon Jr. m 5/13/1995 Elizabeth Wimberly Lesto. R All SS' Epis Ch Chevy Chase MD 2002-2007; Chair Evang Dept Dio So Carolina Charleston SC 1999-2003; Asst S Mich's Epis Ch Charleston SC 1997-2002. al@stmichaelschurch.net

ZAHL, John Arthur (SC) 193 Fishburne St, Charleston SC 29403 **Ch Of The H Cross Sullivans Island SC 2008-** B New York NY 6/20/1977 s Paul Francis Matthew Zahl & Mary Mclaine. BA Ken Gambier OH 2000; BD Wycliffe Hall Oxford Uk 2008. D 6/6/2007 P 12/16/2007 Bp Edward Lloyd Salmon Jr. m Deirdre H Zahl. deirdrezahl@gmail.com

ZAHL, Paul Francis Matthew (WA) All Saints' Episcopal Church, 3 Chevy Chase Cir, Chevy Chase MD 20815 B New York NY 5/24/1951 s Paul Arthur Zahl & Eda Seasongood. BA Harv 1972; MPhil U of Nottingham 1974; DPS St. Jn's Theol Coll Nottingham GB 1975; ThD Tubingen U Tubingen DE 1994. D 9/28/1975 Bp William Foreman Creighton P 6/3/1976 Bp Richard Beamon Martin. m 12/29/1973 Mary Mclean Cappleman c 3. R All SS' Epis Ch Chevy Chase MD 2008-2009; Dn TESM Ambridge PA 2004-2006; Dn The Cathd Ch Of The Adv Birmingham AL 1995-2004; R S Jas Ch Charleston SC 1988-1992; R S Mary's Ch Of Scarborough Scarborough NY 1982-1988; Tutor The GTS New York NY 1979-1982; Cur Gr Epis Ch New York NY 1976-1982; D-in-Trng Gd Shpd Epis Ch Silver Sprg MD 1975-1976. "2000 Years of Amazing Gr," Rowman & Littlefield, 2007; "Gr in Pract," Eerdmans, 2007; Auth, *The Collects of S of Thos Crammer*, 1999; Auth, *The Prot Face of Anglicanism*, 1998; Auth, *Die Rechtfertigungslehre Ernst Kasemanns*, 1996; Auth, *ATR*, 1995; Auth, "Theses from Our Cathd Door," *Angl Dig*, 1994; Auth, "A View from Abroad and Tracts for These Times," *Angl Dig*, 1988; Auth, *Message of the Bible*, 1988; Auth, *Who Will Deliver Us?*, 1983. Evang ES/PECUSA Schlrshp 1993; Fllshp ECF 1993. paulfmzahl@gmail.com

ZAISS, John Deforest (Nev) No address on file. B Los Angeles CA 9/10/1953 s Sam Richards Zaiss & Virginia. BA/BS Creighton U 1974. D 2/6/1994 P 10/1/1994 Bp Stewart Clark Zabriskie. m 11/2/1985 Anne Aileen VandenDries.

ZALESAK, Richard Joseph (Tenn) 311 W 7th St, Columbia TN 38401 **R S Ptr's Ch Columbia TN 2009-** B San Antonio TX 3/22/1962 s Joseph Bernard Zalesak & Marie Rosalie. BA U of St. Thos 1984; MDiv VTS 1989; MA U of St. Thos 1994; DMin Gordon-Conwell TS 1999. Trans 9/19/2003 Bp James Monte Stanton. m 5/26/1990 Meredith Uher c 2. Dio Virginia Richmond VA 2003-2009; Vic S Fran Epis Ch Manakin Sabot VA 2003-2009; Ch Of The Incarn Dallas TX 2003; Chr Epis Ch Plano TX 2001-2003; Assoc H Cross Epis Ch Sugar Land TX 1998-2001; R S Paul's Ch Katy TX 1994-1998; Trin Ch Houston TX 1992-1994; Assoc Trin Ch Galveston TX 1989-1992. St. Geo Awd ECUSA 2005. rjzalesak@gmail.com

ZALNERAITIS JR, Herbert Benedict (Mass) 93 Main St Apt 3, Brattleboro VT 05301 B Worcester MA 11/7/1946 s Herbert Zalneraitis & Rosemary. BA H Cross Coll 1968; MDiv Ya Berk 1971; M.Ed Walden U 2006. D 6/20/1971 P 4/7/1972 Bp Alexander Doig Stewart. m 6/24/2004 Jan Marie Zalneraitis. Trin Epis Ch Haverhill MA 1977-1980; Vic S Clem's Epis Ch Hermitage PA 1974-1975; Chr Ch Ansonia CT 1972-1974.

ZAMBONI, John V (NJ) 400 New Market Road, Dunellen NJ 08812 **Vic S Fran Ch Dunellen NJ 2008-; Dep to GC Dio New Jersey Trenton NJ 2003-2012** B Suffern NY 2/16/1954 s Frank Joseph Zamboni & Janet Edwards. BA Ya 1976; MDiv GTS 1983. D 6/4/1983 Bp George Phelps Mellick Belshaw P 12/10/1983 Bp Philip Edward Randolph Elder. m 7/29/2006 Judith Yannariello c 1. Chapl to Dioc Coun Dio New Jersey Trenton NJ 1997-1998; Exam Chapl Dio New Jersey Trenton NJ 1991-1994; R Gr-S Paul's Ch Mercerville NJ 1990-2008; Asst Chr Ch Toms River Toms River NJ 1985-1990; Int Chr Ch Toms River Toms River NJ 1984-1985; Cur Chr Ch Toms River Toms River NJ 1983-1984. Fllshp of St. Jn 1978. jzamboni@juno.com

ZANETTI, Diane P (Be) 4484 Heron Dr, Reading PA 19606 B Monticello NY 12/1/1947 BA Syr; MDiv Drew U 1985; MS Walden U 2006. D 5/31/2003 P 12/19/2003 Bp Paul Victor Marshall. S Alb's Epis Ch Reading PA 2004-2007.

ZANGER, Francis Charles (SC) 665 Fair Spring Dr, Charleston SC 29414 B Columbus OH 4/9/1955 s Jules Nmn Zanger & Mary Evelyn. Truman Coll Chicago IL 1978; BA Sch of Intl Trng Brattleboro VT 1983; MDiv GTS 1988; DMin GTF 2000. D 6/15/1988 P 12/16/1989 Bp Daniel Lee Swenson. m 8/25/1991 Virginia Elaine Zanger c 1. Assoc Ch Of The H Comm Charleston SC 2002-2005; Off Of Bsh For ArmdF New York NY 1993-2004; Evang Cmsn Dio Spokane Spokane WA 1991-1993; R S Mart's Ch Moses Lake WA 1990-1993; Int S Jas Epis Ch Arlington VT 1989-1990; Vic Cathd Of All SS Albany NY 1988-1989. Auth, "Collect for a Nation Under Attack," *Healing Mnstry*, 2002; Auth, "Mrs. Smith? I have bad news: Chapl & Death Notifications," *Healing Mnstry*, 2001; Auth, "CISM at Sea; Preventing Traumatic Stress," *Journ of Trauma Response*, 1999; Auth, "Combating Combat Stress: The Chapl' Role U.S. Navy," *Journ of the Amer Assn of Experts in Trauma Stress*, 1999; Auth, "Cross-Cultural Problems of St. Columban's Mssn to Burgundy," *Ch Div*, 1988; Auth, *Var arts & Pub*. Disabled Amer Veterans 2002; Intl Conf of Police Chapl 1990; Intl Critical Incident Stress Fndt 1992; Soc of King Chas the Mtyr 2000; SocMary 1990; SocOLW 2002. Thanatologist Assn of Death Educ and Counslg 2004; Meritorious Serv Medal U.S. Navy 2002; "Subject Matter Expert" in Combat Stress U.S. Navy 1999; Diplomate, Bd Certification Amer Acad of Experts in Traumatic Stress 1998. fatherz@gmail.com

ZAPATA-GARCIA, Carlos Alberto (EcuC) Calle Hernando Sarmiento, N 39-54 Y Portete Ecuador **Ecuador New York NY 2009-; Iglesia Epis Del Ecuador Ecuador 2009-** B 2/11/1971 s Guillermo Raymundo Zapata & Teresa Palacios. D 11/7/2009 P 10/2/2010 Bp Luis Fernando Ruiz Restrepo. m 5/24/2008 Yenny del Pilar Garcia-Juarez.

ZEESE, Dolores Anita (WNC) Po Box 978, Columbus NC 28722 **D Ch Of The H Cross Tryon NC 1996-** B Middletown NY 3/12/1932 d Charles Misner & Evelyn Mae. D 12/21/1996 Bp Robert Hodges Johnson. m 10/15/1978 Paul Willie Zeese. NAAD. deacond@alltel.net

ZEIGLER, Luther (WA) 12 Devon Ter, Newton MA 02459 **Epis Chapl At Harvard & Radcliffe Cambridge MA 2011-; Brandon Ch Hopewell VA 2007-; Washington Epis Sch Beth MD 2007-** B Aurora CO 4/23/1958 BA Ob 1980; MA Stan 1982; MDiv VTS 2007. D 6/9/2007 P 1/19/2008 Bp John Chane. m 6/7/1980 Patricia Rose c 2. luther.zeigler@gmail.com

ZEILFELDER, Eugene Walter (NJ) Psc 3 Box 3251, Apo AP 96266 B Bronx NY 10/9/1942 s Eugene Jacob Zeilfelder & Walli Ella. BA U of Maryland 1973; MDiv VTS 1976. D 6/5/1976 P 12/11/1976 Bp Albert Wiencke Van Duzer. m 2/6/1984 Eunsook Lee c 4. Off Of Bsh For ArmdF New York NY 1980-1987; R Chr Ch Collingswood NJ 1976-1980. Auth, "Snow Flower Songs - Claudia Hae In Lee's Lyrics of Nature] w Kim Jin Sup," Yolimwon, 2005; Auth, "On A Journey (An anthology of selected poems by Hae In Lee) (w Kim Jin Sup)," Parkwoosa, 2003; Auth, "Heaven, Wind, Stars and Poems (Selected poems by Jun Dong-Ju) (w Kim Jin Sup)]," Parkwoosa, 2001; Auth, "At The Sea Again (An anthology of selected poems by Hae In Lee) (w Kim Jin Sup)," Parkwoosa, 1998; Auth, "They Are Never Lonely (An anthology of poems by Kim Yang-shik) (w Kim Jin Sup)," Parkwoosa, 1998. ezeilf@kornet.net

ZELLER, Margaret King (ETenn) 1108 Meadow Ln, Kingsport TN 37663 **P-in-c S Chris's Ch Kingsport TN 2007-; R S Chris's Ch Kingsport TN 2007-** B Wilmington DE 4/19/1948 d J Robert King & Beryl. BA Florida St U 1970; MLS SUNY 1978; MDiv STUSo 2002. D 12/27/2001 Bp Charles Edward Jenkins III P 9/14/2002 Bp Charles Glenn VonRosenberg. c 2. Int S Jn's Epis Ch Johnson City TN 2004-2007; Assoc S Jn's Epis Ch Johnson City TN 2002-2004. altomom@gmail.com

ZELLERMAYER, Charles Clayton (Mil) 400 Garland Ct, Waukesha WI 53188 **D S Mary's Epis Ch Dousman WI 2007-; Archd Dio Milwaukee Milwaukee WI 2005-** B Plainview TX 10/30/1949 s Robert Zellermayer & Laverne Elizabeth. Dade Cmnty Coll Miami FL; UW Waukesha. D 12/2/1995 Bp Roger John White. m 12/16/1972 Janet Susan Miller c 3. D S Anskar's Epis Ch Hartland WI 2004-2006; D St Mths Epis Ch Waukesha WI 1995-2004. czellermayer@ultracom.com

ZELLEY III, Edmund W (NJ) 11 North Monroe Ave, Wenonah NJ 08090 **Vic H Trin Epis Ch Wenonah NJ 1995-** B Plainfield NJ 12/12/1965 s E(dmund) Walton Zelley & Susan Milbrey. BA Gri 1988; MDiv EDS 1993. D 6/12/1993 Bp George Phelps Mellick Belshaw P 1/15/1994 Bp Joe Morris Doss. m 8/18/1990 Gail K Kolombatovich c 2. Asst Gr Ch In Haddonfield Haddonfield NJ 1993-1995. frzell@verizon.net

ZELLEY JR, E(dmund) Walton (NJ) P.O. Box 2, Copake Falls NY 12517 B Philadelphia PA 10/10/1938 s Edmund Walton Zelley & Ruth Bradbury. BA Trin Hartford CT 1961; MDiv PDS 1964; STM NYTS 1974; MSW Rutgers-The St U 1991. D 4/25/1964 P 10/31/1964 Bp Alfred L Banyard. m 8/27/1960 Milbrey Turner c 2. Dioc Coun Pres Dio New Jersey Trenton NJ 1996-1997; Liturg Comm. Dio New Jersey Trenton NJ 1971-1994; R S Lk's Epis Ch Metuchen NJ 1970-1998; Vic S Aid's Ch Olathe KS 1966-1969; Cur S Lk's Epis Ch Metuchen NJ 1964-1966. Auth, "Is the Underclass a Class?," *Journ of Soc & Soc Welf*, 1995. AP 1970-1998; Assn of Dioc Liturg & Mus Commissions 1970-1998; NNECA 1974. Edgar Awd (Citizen of the Year) Metuchen YMCA Metuchen NJ 1991. waltzell@fairpoint.net

ZELLNER, John Clement (WNC) 230 Depot St, Tryon NC 28782 **Vic S Phil's Epis Ch Greenville SC 2011-** B Hazleton PA 11/30/1952 s Clement Zellner & Rita Louise. BA Bloomsburg U 1974; MS Shippensburg U 1978; MDiv VTS 1979; DMin Estrn Bapt TS 1990. D 7/8/1979 Bp James Loughlin Duncan P 1/1/1980 Bp Calvin Onderdonk Schofield Jr. m 2/8/1981 Christine Halligan c 2. Exec Coun Dio Wstrn No Carolina Asheville NC 2008-2009; R Ch Of The H Cross Valle Crucis NC 2001-2009; R Ch Of The H Cross Tryon NC 1992-2001; R Dio Easton Easton MD 1991-1992; R Ch Of S Paul's By The Sea Ocean City MD 1986-1992; R S Mary's Fleeton Reedville VA 1982-1986; Cur S Jn's Epis Ch Homestead FL 1979-1982. Amer Assn For Mar And Fam Therapists. jcz427@gmail.com

ZEMAN, Andrew Howard (Ct) 135 Ball Farm Rd, Oakville CT 06779 B Hartford CT 5/7/1946 s William Saxe Zeman & Evelyn. BA Mar 1968; MDiv Ya Berk 1971. D 6/12/1971 Bp Joseph Warren Hutchens P 12/18/1971 Bp

Morgan Porteus. m 5/29/2010 Joyce Lanham c 1. Exec Coun Dio Connecticut Hartford CT 2004-2010; Archv Com Dio Connecticut Hartford CT 2002-2011; R All SS Epis Ch Oakville CT 2002-2010; R H Trin Prot Epis Ch Onancock VA 1990-2002; Angl - RC Dialogue Chairman Dio Connecticut Hartford CT 1988-1990; R Chr Ch Easton CT 1981-1990; Soc Concerns Coordntr Dio Connecticut Hartford CT 1977-1981; Vic Chr Ch Bethlehem CT 1975-1981; Cur Chr Ch Cathd Hartford CT 1971-1975. azeman07@gmail.com

ZEPEDA PADILLA, Jorge Alberto (Hond) 002, 2da, Barrio San Juan Honduras **Dio Honduras Miami FL 2006-; Iglesia Epis Hondurena San Pedro Sula 2006-** B San Pedro Sula 6/4/1957 s Miguel Zepeda & Elia. DIT Programa Diocesono Educacion Teologica. D 10/28/2005 Bp Lloyd Emmanuel Allen. m 9/9/2001 Maria Antoni Lemus c 4.

ZETTINGER, William Harry (SanD) 1920 Hamilton Ln, Escondido CA 92029 **D S Barth's Epis Ch Poway CA 2007-** B Brooklyn NY 12/24/1943 s Carl Zettinger & Mildred. MS Harvard Bus Sch Long Island Campus; BS New York Inst Tech Long Island NY 1966; CTh ETSBH 2007. D 6/9/2007 Bp James Robert Mathes. m 1/25/1969 Antonina Zettinger. wzettinger@cox.net

ZIEGENFUSS, Charles William (La) 2919 Saint Charles Ave, New Orleans LA 70115 **Org/Chrmstr S Andr's Epis Ch New Orleans LA 2007-** B Easton PA 2/16/1933 s Charles Luther Ziegenfuss & Myra Lapp. BS Susquahanna U 1955; MDiv Nash 1966. D 6/1/1966 Bp Henry I Louttit P 6/30/1966 Bp James Loughlin Duncan. Mus Instr S Andr's Epis Ch New Orleans LA 1976-1985; Org/Chrmstr Chr Ch Cathd New Orleans LA 1968-2006; Cur S Jas Epis Ch Ormond Bch FL 1966-1968. ziegenfussc@bellsouth.net

ZIEGENHINE, Kathleen Roach (NwPa) 458 E 23rd St, Erie PA 16503 B Dallas TX 10/1/1953 d Robert E Roach & Sherry. D 10/25/2003 P 12/18/2004 Bp Robert Deane Rowley Jr. m 6/24/1978 James Patrick Ziegenhine c 3.

ZIEGLER, Sally McIntosh (Colo) 2205 Paseo Del Oro, Colorado Springs CO 80904 **D Gr And S Steph's Epis Ch Colorado Sprg CO 1997-** B Savannah GA 12/16/1935 d Olin Tally McIntosh & Sally. BA Duke 1957. D 6/4/1994 Bp Richard Frank Grein. m 6/15/1957 Edward William Ziegler c 3. D All SS' Epis Ch Briarcliff Manor NY 1994-1997. sallyzee@aol.com

ZIELINSKI, Frances Gertrude (Chi) 710 S Paulina St # 904, Chicago IL 60612 B Detroit MI 4/5/1930 d George Zielinski & D Gertrude. Walsh Inst Acctg 1952. D 10/1/1963 Bp Richard S M Emrich. Asst S Martha's Ch Detroit MI 1963-1967. franzie@catlover.com

ZIEMANN, Judith Jon (NCal) 111 N. West St., Yreka CA 96097 B Marinette WI 5/28/1943 d Roy McLean Ziemann & Elizabeth Fitch. BS U CO 1965; MS U of Wisconsin 1970; MA U of Wisconsin 1972; MDiv CDSP 1989. D 7/16/1989 P 7/1/1990 Bp Carl Christopher Epting. Ch Of S Nich Paradise CA 2004-2005; S Mk's Ch Yreka CA 2001-2004; Trin Epis Ch Houghton MI 2000-2001; Ch Of Our Sav DuBois PA 1997-1999; Pstr For Lasalle Cnty Epis Mnstry Dio Chicago Chicago IL 1993-2005; Chr Ch Streator IL 1990-1996; Int S Paul's Ch Coun Bluffs IA 1990. RWF, EWC, Land. JZIEMANN@NCTV.COM

ZIFCAK, Patricia (Mass) 2100 County St Apt 31, South Attleboro MA 02703 **Chr Ch Cambridge Cambridge MA 2005-** B Providence RI 12/10/1945 d Edward George McMahon & Dorothy Bingham. BS Bridgewater Coll 1967; Med Bridgewater Coll 1978; MDiv Andover Newton TS 1998. D 6/8/2002 Bp M(arvil) Thomas Shaw III. patzifcak@cccambridge.org

ZILE, ERic Neil (Md) 4500 C Dunton Terrace, Perry Hall MD 21128 **Chair, Rt to Seats and Votes Dio Maryland Baltimore MD 2011-; Cont Edducation Grants Dio Maryland Baltimore MD 2006-; Resolutns Com Dio Maryland Baltimore MD 2006-; R H Trin Epis Ch Baltimore MD 2000-** B Baltimore MD 12/5/1959 s James Earl Lavene Zile & Theresa Rae. S Fran Coll Loretto PA 1977; AA Catonsville Cmnty Coll 1988; Johns Hopkins 1999; Proctor Schlr EDS 2010. D 6/14/1997 Bp Charles Lindsay Longest P 1/15/2000 Bp Robert Wilkes Ihloff. m 1/10/2009 Cynthia Tipton c 2. Compstn and Benefits Dio Maryland Baltimore MD 1998-2011; D S Lk's Ch Baltimore MD 1998-2000; D The Ch Of The Nativ Cedarcroft Baltimore MD 1997-1998. vicar.zile@verizon.net

ZIMMER, Layton Parkhurst (Haw) 3740 Glen Canyon Rd Ne, Albuquerque NM 87111 **Died 5/4/2011** B Honolulu HI 9/11/1931 s Layton Allen Zimmer & Katharine [illegible]. BA W&M 1932; STB EDS 1955; Fllshp Coll of Preachers 1966. D 6/4/1955 P 6/1/1956 Bp John Brooke Mosley. c 3. Auth, "arts In Var mag". EPF, Associated Parishes, Neca.

ZIMMERMAN, Bryce Dennis (WK) 1817 Fairway Dr Apt A, Dodge City KS 67801 **P-in-c Ch Of The H Nativ Kinsley KS 2011-; Mem of the Dioc Coun Dio Wstrn Kansas Hutchinson KS 2011-; Chair of Deputies to the 2009 GC Dio Wstrn Kansas Hutchinson KS 2007-; P-in-c S Aug's Ch Meade KS 1999-; R S Corn Epis Ch Dodge City KS 1999-** B Greensburg KS 7/18/1952 s Bryce D Zimmerman & Ellen L. BA Ft Hays St U 1974; Universtiy of Kansas 1976; Read for H Ord Dio Wstrn Kansas 1996. D 4/12/1996 P 5/10/1997 Bp Vernon Edward Strickland. m 10/26/1974 Karen Lynn Van Meter c 2. Chair of the COM Dio Wstrn Kansas Hutchinson KS 2010-2011; Chair of the Dioc Stndg Com Dio Wstrn Kansas Hutchinson KS 2010-2011; P S Jn's Ch Ulysses KS 1996-1999. dzimmerman70@cox.net

ZIMMERMAN, Curtis Roy (Oly) 11410 NE 124 St, #624, Kirkland WA 98034 B Santa Monica CA 12/22/1942 s Thomas Henry Zimmerman & Verna Ruth. BMus U of Redlands 1966; MDiv CDSP 1974; Cert Int Mnstry Prog 1999. D 6/10/1974 P 12/21/1974 Bp Edwin Lani Hanchett. Cn Gd Samar Epis Ch Sammamish WA 2008-2009; Int S Fran Epis Ch Mill Creek WA 2006-2008; P-in-c S Barn Epis Ch Bainbridge Island WA 2004-2006; S Pat's Ch Incline Vill NV 2003-2004; Int Trin Epis Ch Wheaton IL 2001-2003; Int S Matt's Epis Ch Wilton CT 2000-2001; Int S Dav's Ch Gales Ferry CT 1999-2000; S Jn's Ch Chehalis WA 1997-1999; Chr Ch Tacoma WA 1991-1998; Instr of Liturg in TS Dio Olympia Seattle WA 1980-1982; R Chr Epis Ch Puyallup WA 1979-1991; Chair of Liturg Cmsn Dio Hawaii Honolulu HI 1976-1979; Cn S Andr's Cathd Honolulu HI 1974-1979. Auth, *arts*. Acad of Par Cler 1981; AGO 1960; Assoc, OHC 1971; Int Mnstry Ntwk 1999; Trng and Consulting Serv 1985. Kaleleonalani Cn S Andr Cathd, Honolulu, HI Honolulu HI 1975. canonscottage@mac.com

ZIMMERMAN, Douglas L (SwFla) 4033 Lancaster Dr, Sarasota FL 34241 **R S Wlfd's Epis Ch Sarasota FL 2009-; Stndg Com Dio SW Florida Sarasota FL 2006-** B Boynton Beach FL 2/18/1969 s Lee Tyrell Zimmerman & Mary Beth. BA Rhodes Coll 1991; MDiv VTS 1998. D 6/20/1998 Bp Calvin Onderdonk Schofield Jr P 1/1/1999 Bp John Lewis Said. m 10/14/1998 Tamara G Clewett c 4. R S Mary's Ch Dade City FL 2004-2008; S Wlfd's Epis Ch Sarasota FL 2004-2008; Asst H Trin Epis Ch In Countryside Clearwater FL 2000-2004; Yth Min S Thos Epis Par Coral Gables FL 1998-2000. frdougz@comcast.net

ZIMMERMAN, Gretchen Densmore (NJ) 410 S Atlantic Ave, Beach Haven NJ 08008 **Chair, Bd Missions Dio New Jersey Trenton NJ 2010-; R S Raphael The Archangel Brick NJ 2007-** B Boston MA 4/24/1949 d Bruce Densmore Zimmerman & Judith WhittierSawyer. BA U of Washington 1980; MDiv GTS 1983. D 6/4/1983 P 3/25/1984 Bp Paul Moore Jr. m 8/11/1984 Frank B Crumbaugh c 2. P-in-c S Raphael The Archangel Brick NJ 2002-2007; Int S Raphael The Archangel Brick NJ 1999-2001; Int S Steph's Ch Whiting NJ 1998; Int S Andr's Ch Carbondale IL 1996-1997; Int S Mich's Epis Ch O Fallon IL 1994-1996; R S Mary's Ch Belvidere NJ 1987-1992; R S Ptr's Ch Washington NJ 1987-1992; Asst S Jn's Memi Ch Ramsey NJ 1985-1987; Pstr Assoc Ch Of The Ascen New York NY 1983-1984; Fac Secy The GTS New York NY 1983-1984. zcatthebeach@msn.com

ZIMMERMAN, Janet Lynn Whaley (Tex) 209 W 27th St, Austin TX 78705 **S Pat's Ch Washington DC 2011-; S Pat's Epis Day Sch Washington DC 2011-** B Corpus Christi, TX 11/25/1952 d Frank Bernard Whaley & Golda Batson. BS The U of Texas at Austin 1974; PhD The U Texas at Austin 1981; MDiv VTS 2009. D 6/20/2009 Bp C(harles) Andrew Doyle P 1/29/2010 Bp Dena Arnall Harrison. m 8/9/1975 Louis Seymour Zimmerman c 3. All SS Epis Ch Austin TX 2009-2011. JANETZIMM@GMAIL.COM

ZIMMERMAN, Jervis Sharp (Ct) 400 Seabury Dr Apt 1106, Bloomfield CT 06002 **Supply P Dio Connecticut Hartford CT 1994-** B Harvey IL 8/29/1922 s Jacob Fredrich Zimmerman & India Ethelyn. BA U IL 1942; MDiv McCormick TS 1945; MA U Chi 1950; Ya Berk 1953; S Aug's Coll Cbury GB 1963; Cert S Geo's Coll Jerusalem IL 1982. D 3/14/1953 P 10/8/1953 Bp Walter H Gray. c 3. Asst Ch Of The Gd Shpd Hartford CT 1987-1994; Stndg Com Dio Connecticut Hartford CT 1984-1989; Chr Ch Cathd Hartford CT 1983; Chair, Cmsn on Mininstry Dio Connecticut Hartford CT 1971-1983; Dio Connecticut Hartford CT 1970-1983; Stff Dio Connecticut Hartford CT 1967-1983; Chr Epis Ch Norwich CT 1953-1967. The Trsfg Cmnty 1993. Supvsr Emer ACPE 1983; Hon Cn Chr Ch Cathd Hartford CT 1983. canonjz@yahoo.com

ZIMMERMAN, John Paul (Alb) 6459 Vosburgh Rd, Altamont NY 12009 B Rochester NY 1/25/1946 s Robert J Zimmerman & Lorene K. BA S Andrews/S Bern Coll Rochester NY 1967; BD St. Bern's Sem Rochester NY 1970; ThM St. Bern's Sem Rochester NY 1971; MDiv St. Bern's Sem Rochester NY 1974. Rec from Roman Catholic 10/20/1990 as Priest Bp William George Burrill. m 3/4/1989 Katherine E Jankowiak. R S Bon Ch Guilderland NY 1994-2008; Asst S Ptr's Memi Geneva NY 1990-1994. Auth, "The [illegible] In S Paul," *The Shell*). jz246@yahoo.com

ZIMMERMAN, Stephen Francis (SeFla) Grace and Saint Stephen's Church, 601 North Tejon St, Colorado Springs CO 80903 **P-in-c Gr And S Steph's Epis Ch Colorado Sprg CO 2009-** B Sanford FL 2/25/1949 s H Lyttleton Zimmerman & Mary Amice. BA U So 1971; MDiv VTS 1978. D 6/4/1978 P 12/1/1978 Bp James Loughlin Duncan. m 8/29/1970 Kathryn D Dix c 1. R Chap Of S Andr Boca Raton FL 1986-2009; R All SS Epis Ch Grenada MS 1981-1986; Cur S Mk's Ch Palm Bch Gardens FL 1978-1981. father.steve@gracestephensepiscopal.org

ZIMMERMAN, Whitney Bland (Va) St Jame's Episcopal, 1205 W Franklin St, Richmond VA 23220 B Richmond VA 6/27/1976 d Eric Bland Zimmerman & Karen Thorne. BA U of Pennsylvania 1998; MDiv Ya Berk 2007. D 6/16/2007 P 12/18/2007 Bp Peter James Lee. S Jas' Ch Richmond VA 2007-2011. wzimmerman@yahoo.com

ZIMMERMANN, Matthew Shelby (Kan) 214 Laura Ln, Bastrop TX 78602 **S Marg's Ch Lawr KS 2009-** B Kansas City MO 5/22/1955 s Matthew H Zimmermann & Barbara. BD U of Kansas 1986; MDiv Epis TS of The SW 1996. D 6/18/1996 Bp William Edward Smalley P 12/1/1996 Bp John Clark Buchanan. m 12/11/1976 Catherine A Montgomery c 2. R Calv Epis Ch Bastrop TX 2001-2009; R Calv Epis Ch Sedalia MO 1996-2001. Outstanding Undergraduate Classics Stdt U Of Kansas 1986. fathermatt@sbcglobal.net

ZIMMERSCHIED, Jill Whitney (Wyo) 202 12th St, Wheatland WY 82201 **D All SS Ch Wheatland WY 2002-; D Ch Of The Redeem Kenmore WA 2002-** B Laramie WY 1/14/1954 d William Warren Whitney & Gertrude Jeanne. AAS U of Wyoming. D 9/21/2002 Bp Bruce Edward Caldwell.

ZITO, Robert John Amadeus (NY) 95 Reade St, New York NY 10013 **Cn IV Ch Atty Dio New York New York City NY 2009-** B New York NY 9/11/1956 s Joseph J Zito & Phyllis Ann. BA Tul 1978; JD New York Law Sch 1981. D 5/19/2001 Bp Richard Frank Grein. m 7/4/1992 Dana Sabin Cole. Dir Of Evang And Outreach Mnstrs Ch Of The Incarn New York NY 2001-2010. Auth, "Andrea Yates And Capital Punishment," Epis New Yorker, 2002. St. Geo's Soc 2007. Cmdr Bro, Chair of New York Com The Venerable Ord Of St. Jn 2007; Knight Ord of Merit of Savoy 2004. deaconzito@msn.com

ZITTLE, Twyla Jeanne (Colo) 2902 Airport Rd Apt 123, Colorado Springs CO 80910 **Asst S Raphael Epis Ch Colorado Sprg CO 2010-** B Colorado Springs CO 12/12/1948 d Thomas Williams & L Mae. BS Sthrn Colorado St Coll Pueblo 1971; MA Adams St Coll 1977; MDiv SWTS 2006. D 6/10/2006 P 12/9/2006 Bp Robert John O'Neill. tjzittle@comcast.net

ZIVANOV, Elizabeth Ann (Haw) 1515 Wilder Ave, Honolulu HI 96822 **Trst CDSP Berkeley CA 2008-; R The Par Of S Clem Honolulu HI 2001-** B Detroit MI 6/4/1949 d Michael Zivanov & Mary. BA Oakland U 1971; MEd Penn 1973; MDiv Bex 1991. D 4/30/1993 P 12/4/1993 Bp William George Burrill. R In Res S Andr's Ch Edgartown MA 2000; Int S Mich's Ch Geneseo NY 1997-1999; S Geo's Ch Hilton NY 1997; Int S Jn's Epis Ch Honeoye Falls NY 1996; Int Zion Ch Avon NY 1995-1996; Int The Ch Of The Epiph Rochester NY 1994-1995; Asst R S Ptr's Epis Ch Henrietta NY 1993-1994. Soc of St Marg 1998. cranmer49@gmail.com

ZLATIC, Martin William (SeFla) 6321 Lansdowne Cir, Boynton Beach FL 33472 **S Jos's Epis Ch Boynton Bch FL 2001-** B Saint Louis MO 8/19/1956 s Frank George Zlatic & Mary. BA Cardinal Glennon Coll 1978; STB St. Thos U Rome (Angelicum) 1981; Gregorian U 1982. Rec from Roman Catholic 4/1/1998 as Priest Bp Calvin Onderdonk Schofield Jr. m 4/17/1993 Dorothy Z Zahra c 1. Assoc S Andr's Ch Lake Worth FL 1998-2001. frmarty@stjoesweb.org

ZOGG, Jennifer Gaye (Roch) 25 Westminster Rd., Rochester NY 14607 **Cur S Paul's Ch Rochester NY 2008-** B Albany NY 6/21/1983 d Jeffrey J Zogg & Marie. BA U Roch 2005; Angl Dplma Ya Berk 2008; M.Div. Yale DS 2008. D 6/14/2008 P 1/6/2009 Bp Prince Grenville Singh. jennifer.zogg@gmail.com

ZOLLER, Joan Duncan (WMo) Po Box 967, Blue Springs MO 64013 **D S Paul's Epis Ch Lees Summit MO 2007-** B Elkhart IN 11/25/1936 d John Matthias Duncan & Jenny Maude. Johnson Cnty Cmnty Coll; BS U of Missouri 1989. D 2/4/1995 Bp John Clark Buchanan. m 10/12/1957 David Debois Zoller. zolrsys@discoverynet.com

ZOOK-JONES, Jill (Tenn) 1209 Countryside Rd, Nolensville TN 37135 **P-in-c The Ch Of The Epiph Lebanon TN 2011-** B Minot ND 3/16/1951 d Lester Alvin Zook & Elsie Mae. BA NWU 1974; PrTS 1978; MDiv STUSo 2000. D 6/25/2000 P 4/22/2001 Bp Bertram Nelson Herlong. m 5/27/1978 Timothy Kent Jones c 3. Int S Jos Of Arimathaea Ch Hendersonville TN 2007-2009; Cn Dio Tennessee Nashville TN 2005-2007; Int S Barth's Ch Bristol TN 2004-2005; Yth Dir Dio Tennessee Nashville TN 2000-2007; Vic S Jn's Epis Ch Mt Juliet TN 2000-2001. "arts," *The Pryr Bible*, Zondervan, 2004; "Pryr," Harold Shaw, 1994; "Brethren Bulletin Series," Brethren Press, 1987; "Adult Curric," Brethren Press, 1984. CODE 2005; Int Mnstry Ntwk 2007. jzojo@comcast.net

ZORAWICK, Joseph Marion (NY) 40 W 67th St, New York NY 10023 **P Assoc The Ch Of The Epiph New York NY 1998-** B New York NY 8/22/1931 s Michael M Zorawick & Mary. BA Col 1953; STB GTS 1966. D 6/4/1966 P 12/1/1966 Bp Horace W B Donegan. m 1/28/1968 Lois Ellen Atha c 1. Chair Assessment Adjust Bd Dio New York New York City NY 1977-1996; Pres Alum Assoc The GTS New York NY 1975-1981; Chr And S Steph's Ch New York NY 1970-1996; Cur Chr And S Steph's Ch New York NY 1966-1968. lojozor@aol.com

ZOSEL, James Raymond (Minn) 2304 Fremont Ave S, Minneapolis MN 55405 B Wadena MN 3/29/1929 s Raymond Zosel & Myrabelle. BS U MN 1954; MDiv Nash 1963. D 6/29/1963 Bp Hamilton Hyde Kellogg P 3/25/1964 Bp Philip Frederick McNairy. m 9/20/1952 Carolyn Ann Raymond c 5. Vic Ch Of The Nativ Burnsville MN 1967-1971; Vic Geth Ch Appleton MN 1964-1967. zosel@mead.edu

ZOTALIS, James C (Minn) 1663 Buckingham Path, Faribault MN 55021 **Dn The Epis Cathd Of Our Merc Sav Faribault MN 2001-** B Mankato MN 8/7/1951 s Cly Chris Zotalis & Mary Emigean. BS Minnesota St U Mankato 1973; MA Minnesota St U Mankato 1978; MDiv Nash 1987. D 6/24/1987 P 1/9/1988 Bp Robert Marshall Anderson. m 11/2/1973 Paula Marie Nelson c 4. R S Jas' Epis Ch Fergus Falls MN 1989-2001. comsl@q.com

ZSCHEILE, Dwight J (Minn) 4883 Churchill St, Shoreview MN 55126 B Johnson City NY 1/9/1973 s Richard E Zscheile & Judith C. BA Stan 1995; MDiv Yale DS 1998; PhD Luther Sem 2008. D 12/5/2005 Bp Peter James Lee P 6/8/2006 Bp James Louis Jelinek. m 5/27/2000 Blair A Pogue c 1. S Dav's Ch Ashburn VA 2001-2005. Ed, "Cultivating Sent Communities: Missional Sprtl Formation," Eerdmans, 2012; Co-Auth, "The Missional Ch in Perspective: Mapping Trends and Shaping the Conversation," Baker Acad, 2011; Auth, "Soc Networking and Ch Systems," *Word and Wrld, 30/3*, 2010; Auth, "The Trin, Ldrshp and Power," *Journ of Rel Ldrshp, Vol 6 No 2 Fall 2007*, 2007; Auth, "A More True 'Dom and Frgn Mssy Soc': Toward a Missional Polity for the Epis Ch," *Journ of Rel Ldrshp, Vol 5 No. 1&2*, 2006. dzscheile001@luthersem.edu

ZUBIETA, Agustin Theodore (Pgh) 5660 Lonesome Dove Ct, Clifton VA 20124 B La Paz BO 3/18/1941 s Agustin Zubieta Iriarte & Teodora Gutierrez. Cert VTS 1995. Trans from Iglesia Anglicana del Cono Sur de America 3/31/2001 Bp Robert William Duncan. m 1/15/1966 Amanda Cristina Fajardo Alvarez. SAMS Ambridge PA 2001-2007; SAMS Ambridge PA 1996-2001. pepezubieta@hotmail.com

ZUBIZARRETA, Dorenda C (WTex) PO Box 6885, San Antonio TX 78209 **Dio W Texas San Antonio TX 2010-** B Kansas City MO 4/19/1950 Trans from Province IX 1/1/2001 Bp Leopold Frade. m 1/23/2002 Pedro Zubizarreta. Vic S Bon Ch Comfort TX 2008-2010; All SS Epis Ch San Benito TX 2003-2008; Exec Coun Appointees New York NY 2001-2003. doriolr@aol.com

ZUBLER, Eric J (EC) PO Box 257, Bath NC 27808 **S Thos' Epis Ch Bath NC 2010-** B Michigan City IN 7/18/1963 s Chester Edwin Zubler & Cecilia Anne. U of Texas; BS Pur 1987; MDiv TS 2007. D 6/9/2007 Bp Robert John O'Neill P 12/10/2007 Bp Rayford Baines High Jr. m 7/31/1993 Connie Ann Zubler c 2. Asst S Mary's Epis Ch Cypress TX 2009-2010; Cur Trin Ch Longview TX 2007-2009. eric_zubler@yahoo.com

ZUG, Albert Edward Roussel (Pa) 2 E Spring Oak Cir, Media PA 19063 **The Epis Acad Newtown Sq PA 1999-** B Merion PA 12/2/1959 s Thomas Veasey Zug & Lenore. BA Trin 1982; MDiv TESM 1990. D 6/16/1990 P 6/1/1991 Bp Allen Lyman Bartlett Jr. m 11/12/1994 Suzanne Verner. S Alb's Ch Newtown Sq PA 1990-1999.

ZULL, Aaron Beatty (Mich) 250 E Harbortown Dr, Detroit MI 48207 B Eaton Rapids MI 9/12/1944 s Harley Duwayne Zull & Eileen Leslie. BA Westmont Coll 1967; MA U Tor 1974; MDiv U Tor 1976. Trans from Anglican Church of Canada 5/1/1980. m 3/17/1979 Sandra Flanigan c 1. Trin Epis Ch Farmington Hills MI 2007-2009; P-in-c Trin Ch S Clair Shores MI 2002-2006; S Andr's Epis Ch Livonia MI 2000-2002; All SS' Epis Ch Hershey PA 1998; Vic S Edw's Epis Ch Lancaster PA 1990-1998; Ch Of Our Sav Glenshaw PA 1981-1990; Chr The Redeem Ch Montgomery AL 1981. sandyfz@aol.com

ZUMBRUNNEN, Richard Irvin (Md) 2611 Palmyra Dr, Churchville MD 21028 B Salisbury NC 9/4/1928 s Thomas Park ZumBrunnen & Veda Mae. BA U So 1959; MDiv STUSo 1963. D 7/19/1963 Bp Noble C Powell P 6/29/1964 Bp Harry Lee Doll. c 2. P Ascen Ch St MD 2001-2004; Assoc S Mary's Ch Abingdon MD 1991-1998; R S Lk's Ch Baltimore MD 1983-1991; R S Geo's Ch Perryman MD 1975-1983; R H Trin Ch Churchville MD 1964-1966; Cur Ch Of The H Nativ Baltimore MD 1963-1964. Auth, "Thoomistic Concep of Essence & Existence," *S Lk's Journ of Theol*, 1959. bettrick1@aol.com

ZUMPF, Michael James (NC) 600 Morgan Rd, Eden NC 27288 **R S Lk's Ch Eden NC 1998-** B Fargo ND 8/16/1946 s Harold Lewis Zumpf & Mai Rita. BA Palm Bch Atlantic Coll 1989; MDiv VTS 1992. D 6/29/1992 Bp Calvin Onderdonk Schofield Jr P 12/20/1992 Bp A(rthur) Heath Light. m 11/10/2009 Carol N Noe c 3. Vic S Mary's Ch Eden NC 1998-2006; R Chr Epis Ch Marion VA 1992-1998. mzumpf@centurylink.net

ZUNES, John Athas (NC) Heartfields at Cary, Room 5, 1050 Crescent Green Drive, Cary NC 27518 B Norfolk VA 9/2/1927 Duke DS; VTS. D 6/16/1955 Bp Edwin A Penick P 12/1/1955 Bp Richard Henry Baker. m 6/16/1955 Sarah Helen Karnes c 1. zw@coho.org

ZUNKEL, Alvin Paul (NI) 24670 Aric Way, Elkhart IN 46517 B Chicago IL 1/14/1930 s John William Zunkel & Leah. BA McPherson Coll 1953; BD Bethany TS 1956; STM PSR 1968. D 7/1/1991 Bp Francis Campbell Gray. m 2/11/1984 Sharon Eileen Zunkel c 4. D S Jn Of The Cross Bristol IN 1991-2007. AAPC, Aamft. apz147@juno.com

ZUST, Vicki (WNY) 4289 Harris Hill Rd, Buffalo NY 14221 **Chair, Dispatch of Bus Dio Wstrn New York Tonawanda NY 2010-; Exam Chapl Dio Wstrn New York Tonawanda NY 2010-; R S Paul's Epis Ch Harris Hill Williamsville NY 2009-** B Columbus OH 2/6/1968 d Robert Francis Zust & Geraldine. MA Ohio Wesl 1990; MDiv SWTS 1997. D 6/21/1997 P 1/31/1998 Bp Herbert Thompson Jr. Dio Sthrn Ohio Cincinnati OH 2004-2009; R Trin Ch Newark OH 1998-2004; Asst S Alb's Epis Ch Of Bexley Columbus OH 1997-1998. vzust@aol.com

ZWICK, Patricia Diane (Lex) 1337 Winchester Ave, Ashland KY 41101 B Chicago 9/15/1941 d Frederick V Lacock & Patricia N. BA U Cinc 1963; MA U MN 1969; PhD Ohio U 1992. D 8/22/2009 Bp Stacy F Sauls. m 10/24/1992 David Zwick c 4. dianezwick@windstream.net

ZWIFKA, David Alan (CPa) 21 S Main St, Lewistown PA 17044 **Dio Cntrl Pennsylvania Harrisburg PA 2011-; S Mk's Epis Ch Lewistown PA 2010-** B Rochester NY 12/11/1955 s David Leo Zwifka & Eleanor. BA Houghton Coll 1977; MA Chr the King Sem 1980; JCL CUA 1987; JCD CUA 1998. Rec from Roman Catholic 11/26/2006 Bp J Michael Garrison. m 10/11/2003 Kenneth Suter. P-in-c S Mich And All Ang Ch Middletown PA 2008-2010. dazwifka@comcast.net